PHILIP'S

ATLAS
OF THE
WORLD

COMPREHENSIVE EDITION

IN ASSOCIATION WITH
THE ROYAL GEOGRAPHICAL SOCIETY
WITH THE INSTITUTE OF BRITISH GEOGRAPHERS

ACKNOWLEDGEMENTS

IMAGES OF EARTH (PAGES IX–XXIV)
All satellite images in this section courtesy
of NPA Group Limited, Edenbridge, Kent
(www.satmaps.com)

THE GAZETTEER OF NATIONS
TEXT Keith Lye

INTRODUCTION TO WORLD GEOGRAPHY
PICTURE ACKNOWLEDGEMENTS
Courtesy of NPA Group, Edenbridge,
  UK 9, 48
Science Photo Library /Earth Satellite
  Corporation 20, /NOAA 22 bottom left
  and bottom right

ILLUSTRATIONS
Stefan Chabluk, William Donohoe,
Bernard Thornton Artists /Steve Seymour

STAR CHARTS
John Cox and Richard Monkhouse

CARTOGRAPHY BY PHILIP'S

CITY MAPS
PAGE 11, DUBLIN: The town plan of Dublin
is based on Ordnance Survey Ireland by
permission of the Government Permit
Number 7516. © Ordnance Survey Ireland
and Government of Ireland.

 PAGE 11, EDINBURGH,
and PAGE 15, LONDON:
This product includes mapping data licensed
from Ordnance Survey® with the permission
of the Controller of Her Majesty's Stationery
Office. © Crown copyright 2002. All rights
reserved. Licence number 100011710.

VECTOR DATA: Courtesy of Gräfe and Unser
Verlag GmbH, München, Germany (city
centre maps of Bangkok, Beijing, Cape Town,
Jerusalem, Mexico City, Moscow, Singapore,
Sydney, Tokyo and Washington D.C.)

Published in Great Britain in 2002
by Philip's, a division of
Octopus Publishing Group Ltd,
2–4 Heron Quays, London E14 4JP

Copyright © 2002 Philip's

ISBN 0–540–08218–X

A CIP catalogue record for this book is
available from the British Library.

Printed in Spain

Details of other Philip's titles and services
can be found on our website at:
www.philips-maps.co.uk

FOREWORD

PHILIP'S HAVE BEEN MAPPING the world since 1834. The *Atlas of the World* is the flagship of the Philip's range, an authoritative and serious reference work and one of the finest atlases available anywhere in the world. The atlas incorporates computer-derived maps that have been produced using the very latest in digital cartographic techniques.

Philip's Atlas of the World has been revised and updated with the help of a panel of specialist geography consultants from the United Kingdom and the United States, whose specialities range from the history of cartography, urban and social geography, epidemiology and the European Union to biogeography and applied geomorphology. The result of their valuable input can be seen in the wealth of up-to-date maps and data contained in the 'Introduction to World Geography' section of this atlas.

Country names are shown in conventional English form and are those that are in common usage. They are the forms used by publications such as *Newsweek* and *The Washington Post,* and by the BBC and the British Foreign Office. Alternative country names appear in brackets on the maps where space permits – for example, Burma (Myanmar) – and are cross-referenced in the index, for example, Côte d'Ivoire = Ivory Coast.

SPECIALIST GEOGRAPHY CONSULTANTS

PHILIP'S are grateful to the following people for acting as specialist geography consultants on the 'Introduction to World Geography' front section:
Professor D. Brunsden Kings College, University of London, UK
Dr C. Clarke Oxford University, UK
Professor P. Haggett University of Bristol, UK
Professor M-L. Hsu University of Minnesota, Minnesota, USA
Professor K. McLachlan Geopolitical and International Boundaries Research Centre, School of Oriental and African Studies, University of London, UK

Professor M. Monmonier Syracuse University, New York, USA
Professor M. J. Tooley University of St Andrews, UK
Dr T. Unwin Royal Holloway, University of London, UK

PHILIP'S would also like to thank
Keith Lye
Robin Scagell
Dr I. S. Evans Durham University, UK
Dr Andrew Tatham The Royal Geographical Society

PHILIP'S World Atlases are published in association with THE ROYAL GEOGRAPHICAL SOCIETY (with THE INSTITUTE OF BRITISH GEOGRAPHERS).

The Society was founded in 1830 and given a Royal Charter in 1859 for 'the advancement of geographical science'. It holds historical collections of national and international importance, many of which relate to the Society's association with and support for scientific exploration and research from the 19th century onwards. It was pivotal in establishing geography as a teaching and research discipline in British universities close to the turn of the century, and has played a key role in geographical and environmental education ever since.

Today the Society is a leading world centre for geographical learning – supporting education, teaching, research and expeditions, and promoting public understanding of the subject. The Society welcomes those interested in geography as members. For further information, please visit the website at: www.rgs.org

PHILIP'S WORLD MAPS

The reference maps which form the main body of this atlas have been prepared in accordance with the highest standards of international cartography to provide an accurate and detailed representation of the Earth. The scales and projections used have been carefully chosen to give balanced coverage of the world, while emphasizing the most densely populated and economically significant regions. A hallmark of Philip's mapping is the use of hill shading and relief colouring to create a graphic impression of landforms: this makes the maps exceptionally easy to read. However, knowledge of the key features employed in the construction and presentation of the maps will enable the reader to derive the fullest benefit from the atlas.

MAP SEQUENCE

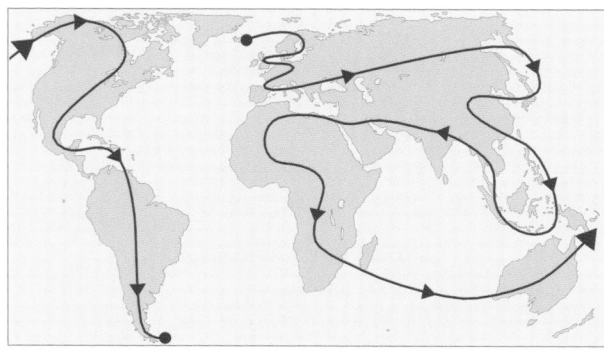

The atlas covers the Earth continent by continent: first Europe; then its land neighbour Asia (mapped north before south, in a clockwise sequence), then Africa, Australia and Oceania, North America and South America. This is the classic arrangement adopted by most cartographers since the 16th century. For each continent, there are maps at a variety of scales. First, physical relief and political maps of the whole continent; then a series of larger-scale maps of the regions within the continent, each followed, where required, by still larger-scale maps of the most important and densely populated areas. The governing principle is that by turning the pages of the atlas, the reader moves steadily from north to south through each continent, with each map overlapping its neighbours.

MAP PRESENTATION

With very few exceptions (for example, for the Arctic and Antarctic), the maps are drawn with north at the top, regardless of whether they are presented upright or sideways on the page. In the borders will be found the map title; a locator diagram showing the area covered; continuation arrows showing the page numbers for maps of adjacent areas; the scale; the projection used; the degrees of latitude and longitude; and the letters and figures used in the index for locating place names and geographical features. Physical relief maps also have a height reference panel identifying the colours used for each layer of contouring.

MAP SYMBOLS

Each map contains a vast amount of detail which can only be conveyed clearly and accurately by the use of symbols. Points and circles of varying sizes locate and identify the relative importance of towns and cities; different styles of type are employed for administrative, geographical and regional place names to aid identification. A variety of pictorial symbols denote landforms such as glaciers, marshes and coral reefs, and man-made structures including roads, railways, airports and canals. International borders are shown by red lines. Where neighbouring countries are in dispute, for example in parts of the Middle East, the maps show the *de facto* boundary between nations, regardless of the legal or historical situation. The

symbols are explained on the first page of the World Maps section of the atlas.

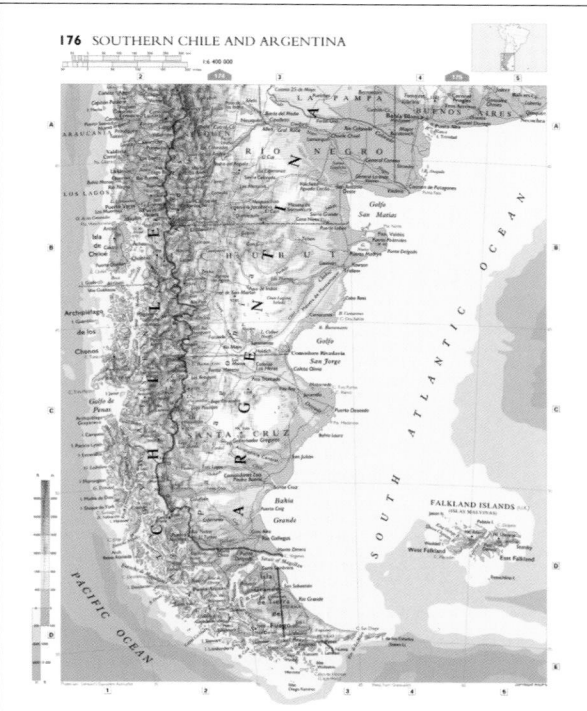

MAP SCALES

1:16 000 000
1 inch = 252 statute miles

The scale of each map is given in the numerical form known as the 'representative fraction'. The first figure is always one, signifying one unit of distance on the map; the second figure, usually in millions, is the number by which the map unit must be multiplied to give the equivalent distance on the Earth's surface. Calculations can easily be made in centimetres and kilometres, by dividing the Earth units figure by 100 000 (i.e. deleting the last five 0s). Thus 1:1 000 000 means 1 cm = 10 km. The calculation for inches and miles is more laborious, but 1 000 000 divided by 63 360 (the number of inches in a mile) shows that 1:1 000 000 means approximately 1 inch = 16 miles. The table below provides distance equivalents for scales down to 1:50 000 000.

LARGE SCALE		
1:1 000 000	1 cm = 10 km	1 inch = 16 miles
1:2 500 000	1 cm = 25 km	1 inch = 39.5 miles
1:5 000 000	1 cm = 50 km	1 inch = 79 miles
1:6 000 000	1 cm = 60 km	1 inch = 95 miles
1:8 000 000	1 cm = 80 km	1 inch = 126 miles
1:10 000 000	1 cm = 100 km	1 inch = 158 miles
1:15 000 000	1 cm = 150 km	1 inch = 237 miles
1:20 000 000	1 cm = 200 km	1 inch = 316 miles
1:50 000 000	1 cm = 500 km	1 inch = 790 miles
SMALL SCALE		

MEASURING DISTANCES

Although each map is accompanied by a scale bar, distances cannot always be measured with confidence because of the distortions involved in portraying the curved surface of the Earth on a flat page. As a general rule, the larger the map scale, the more accurate and reliable will be the distance measured. On small-scale maps such as those of the world and of entire continents, measurement may only be accurate along the 'standard parallels', or central axes, and should not be attempted without considering the map projection.

MAP PROJECTIONS

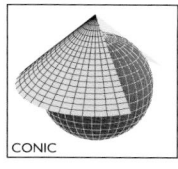  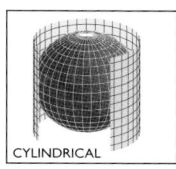

Unlike a globe, no flat map can give a true scale representation of the world in terms of area, shape and position of every region. Each of the numerous systems that have been devised for projecting the curved surface of the Earth on to a flat page involves the sacrifice of accuracy in one or more of these elements. The variations in shape and position of landmasses such as Alaska, Greenland and Australia, for example, can be quite dramatic when different projections are compared.

For this atlas, the guiding principle has been to select projections that involve the least distortion of size and distance. The projection used for each map is noted in the border. Most fall into one of three categories – conic, azimuthal or cylindrical – whose basic concepts are shown above. Each involves plotting the forms of the Earth's surface on a grid of latitude and longitude lines, which may be shown as parallels, curves or radiating spokes.

LATITUDE AND LONGITUDE

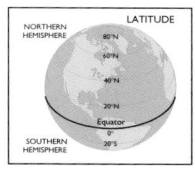 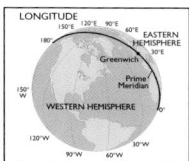 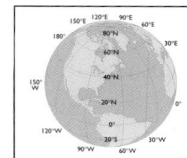

Accurate positioning of individual points on the Earth's surface is made possible by reference to the geometrical system of latitude and longitude. Latitude parallels are drawn west–east around the Earth and numbered by degrees north and south of the Equator, which is designated 0° of latitude. Longitude meridians are drawn north–south and numbered by degrees east and west of the prime meridian, 0° of longitude, which passes through Greenwich in England. By referring to these co-ordinates and their subdivisions of minutes (1/60th of a degree) and seconds (1/60th of a minute), any place on Earth can be located to within a few hundred metres. Latitude and longitude are indicated by blue lines on the maps; they are straight or curved according to the projection employed. Reference to these lines is the easiest way of determining the relative positions of places on different maps, and for plotting compass directions.

NAME FORMS

For ease of reference, both English and local name forms appear in the atlas. Oceans, seas and countries are shown in English throughout the atlas; country names may be abbreviated to their commonly accepted form (e.g. Germany, not The Federal Republic of Germany). Conventional English forms are also used for place names on the smaller-scale maps of the continents. However, local name forms are used on all large-scale and regional maps, with the English form given in brackets only for important cities – the large-scale map of Russia and Central Asia thus shows Moskva (Moscow). For countries which do not use a Roman script, place names have been transcribed according to the systems adopted by the British and US Geographic Names Authorities. For China, the Pin Yin system has been used, with some more widely known forms appearing in brackets, as with Beijing (Peking). Both English and local names appear in the index, the English form being cross-referenced to the local form.

Contents

World Statistics

Countries	VI
Physical Dimensions	VII
Regions in the News	VIII

Images of Earth

Vancouver, Canada	IX
Los Angeles, USA	X
New York, USA	XI
River Amazon, Brazil	XII
Santiago, Chile	XIII
London, UK	XIV
IJsselmeer, Netherlands	XV
Naples, Italy	XVI
Strait of Gibraltar	XVII
Cairo, Egypt	XVIII
Western Cape, South Africa	XIX
Tehran, Iran	XX
Karachi, Pakistan	XXI
Tokyo, Japan	XXII
Sydney, Australia	XXIII
Christchurch, New Zealand	XXIV

The Gazetteer of Nations

An A–Z Gazetteer of Countries	1–32

Introduction to World Geography

The Universe	2–3
The Solar System	4–5
Time and Motion	6–7
Oceans	8–9
Geology	10–11
Landforms	12–13
Atmosphere and Weather	14–15
Climate	16–17
Water and Vegetation	18–19
The Natural Environment	20–21
People and the Environment	22–23
Population	24–25
Cities	26–27
The Human Family	28–29
Conflict and Co-operation	30–31
Agriculture	32–33
Energy	34–35
Minerals	36–37
Manufacturing	38–39
Trade	40–41
Health	42–43
Wealth	44–45
Standards of Living	46–47

City Maps

Amsterdam	2
Athens	2
Atlanta	3
Baghdad	3
Bangkok	3
Barcelona	4
Beijing	4
Berlin	5
Boston	6
Brussels	6
Budapest	7
Buenos Aires	7
Cairo	7
Calcutta (Kolkata)	8
Canton	8
Cape Town	8
Chicago	9
Copenhagen	10
Delhi	10
Dublin	11
Edinburgh	11
Helsinki	12
Hong Kong	12
Istanbul	12
Jakarta	13
Jerusalem	13
Johannesburg	13
Karachi	14
Lagos	14
Lisbon	14
London	15
Los Angeles	16
Lima	16
Madrid	17
Manila	17
Melbourne	17
Mexico City	18
Miami	18
Milan	18
Montreal	19
Moscow	19
Mumbai	20
Munich	20
New York	21
Osaka	22
Oslo	22
Paris	23
Prague	24
Rio de Janeiro	24
Rome	25
San Francisco	25
St Petersburg	26
Santiago	26
São Paulo	26
Seoul	26
Shanghai	27
Singapore	27
Stockholm	28
Sydney	28
Tokyo	29
Tehran	30
Tianjin	30
Toronto	30
Vienna	31
Warsaw	31
Washington	32
Wellington	32

Index to City Maps

	33–39

World Maps

The World

Map Symbols	1
The World: Physical 1:76 000 000	2–3
The World: Political 1:76 000 000	4–5
Arctic Ocean 1:28 000 000	6
Antarctica 1:28 000 000	7
Atlantic Ocean 1:41 000 000	8
Islands of the Atlantic	9
Bermuda 1:400 000	
New Providence Island 1:400 000	
Madeira 1:800 000	
Azores 1:1 600 000	
Canary Islands 1:1 600 000	
Falkland Islands 1:6 400 000	
Ascension Island 1:400 000	
St Helena 1:400 000	
Cape Verde Islands 1:8 000 000	
Greenland 1:10 000 000	10
Iceland 1:2 000 000	11

Europe

Europe: Physical 1:16 000 000	12
Europe: Political 1:16 000 000	13
Scandinavia 1:4 000 000	14–15
Iceland 1:4 000 000	
Denmark and Southern Sweden 1:2 000 000	16–17
Southern Norway 1:2 000 000	18
British Isles 1:4 000 000	19
England and Wales 1:1 600 000	20–21
Scotland 1:1 600 000	22
Ireland 1:1 600 000	23
Netherlands, Belgium and Luxembourg 1:2 000 000	24
France 1:4 000 000	25
Northern France 1:2 000 000	26–27
Southern France 1:2 000 000	28–29
Germany 1:2 000 000	30–31
Switzerland 1:800 000	32–33
Austria, Czech Republic and Slovak Republic 1:2 000 000	34–35
Central Europe 1:4 000 000	36–37
Mediterranean Islands	38–39
Ibiza, Majorca, Minorca 1:800 000	
Malta 1:400 000	
Corfu 1:800 000	
Rhodes 1:800 000	
Levkas, Zante, Cephalonia 1:800 000	
Crete 1:1 000 000	
Cyprus 1:1 000 000	
Eastern Spain 1:2 000 000	40–41
Western Spain and Portugal 1:2 000 000	42–43
Northern Italy, Slovenia and Croatia 1:2 000 000	44–45
Southern Italy 1:2 000 000	46–47
Southern Greece and South-east Turkey 1:2 000 000	48–49
Northern Greece, Bulgaria and Yugoslavia 1:2 000 000	50–51
Hungary, Romania and the Lower Danube 1:2 000 000	52–53
Poland and the Southern Baltic 1:2 000 000	54–55
Eastern Europe and Turkey 1:8 000 000	56–57
Baltic States, Belarus and Ukraine 1:4 000 000	58–59
Volga Basin and the Caucasus 1:4 000 000	60–61

Asia

Asia: Physical   62
1:40 000 000

Asia: Political   63
1:40 000 000

Southern Urals   64
1:4 000 000

Central Asia   65
1:4 000 000

Russia and Central Asia   66–67
1:16 000 000

China and the Far East   68–69
1:12 000 000
Hong Kong and Macau 1:800 000

Japan   70–71
1:4 000 000
Ryukyu Islands 1:4 000 000

Southern Japan   72–73
1:2 000 000

Northern China and Korea   74–75
1:4 800 000

Southern China   76–77
1:4 800 000

Indonesia and the Philippines   78–79
1:10 000 000
Java and Madura 1:6 000 000
Bali 1:1 600 000

Philippines   80–81
1:3 200 000

Eastern Indonesia   82–83
1:5 600 000

Western Indonesia   84–85
1:5 600 000

Mainland South-east Asia   86–87
1:4 800 000
Ko Phuket 1:800 000
Ko Samui 1:800 000
Pinang 1:800 000
Singapore 1:800 000

Southern Asia and the Middle East   88–89
1:14 000 000

Bangladesh, North-eastern India and Burma   90
1:4 800 000

Afghanistan and Pakistan   91
1:5 600 000

Northern India and Nepal   92–93
1:4 800 000

Southern India and Sri Lanka   94–95
1:4 800 000

Lakshadweep Islands 1:4 800 000
Andaman and Nicobar Islands 1:4 800 000

The Middle East   96–97
1:5 600 000

Southern Arabian Peninsula   98–99
1:5 600 000

Turkey and Transcaucasia   100–101
1:4 000 000

Arabia and the Horn of Africa   102
1:12 000 000

The Near East   103
1:2 000 000

Africa

Africa: Physical   104
1:33 600 000

Africa: Political   105
1:33 600 000

The Nile Valley   106–107
1:6 400 000
The Nile Delta 1:3 200 000

Central North Africa   108–109
1:6 400 000

North-west Africa   110–111
1:6 400 000

West Africa   112–113
1:6 400 000

Central Africa   114–115
1:6 400 000

Southern Africa   116–117
1:6 400 000

East Africa   118–119
1:6 400 000

Horn of Africa   120
1:6 400 000

Indian Ocean   121
1:40 000 000
Comoros 1:6 400 000
Seychelles 1:2 000 000
Réunion 1:2 000 000
Mauritius 1:2 000 000

Australia and Oceania

Australia and the South-west Pacific: Physical and Political   122–123
1:16 000 000

Western Australia   124–125
1:6 400 000

Eastern Australia   126–127
1:6 400 000
Whitsunday Group 1:2 000 000
Tasmania 1:6 400 000

South-east Australia   128–129
1:3 200 000

New Zealand – North Island   130
1:2 800 000

New Zealand – South Island   131
1:2 800 000

Papua New Guinea   132
1:5 200 000

Islands of the South-west Pacific   133
1:4 000 000
Fiji 1:4 000 000
Vanuatu 1:4 000 000
Solomon Islands 1:4 000 000
Tonga 1:4 000 000
Guam 1:4 000 000
Tahiti and Moorea 1:4 000 000
Samoan Islands 1:4 000 000
New Caledonia and Loyalty Islands 1:4 000 000

Pacific Ocean   134–135
1:43 200 000

North America

North America: Physical   136
1:28 000 000

North America: Political   137
1:28 000 000

Canada   138–139
1:12 000 000
Alaska 1:24 000 000

Eastern Canada   140–141
1:5 600 000

Western Canada   142–143
1:5 600 000

Alaska   144
1:8 000 000

Hawaii   145
1:2 000 000
Oahu 1:500 000

United States   146–147
1:9 600 000
Hawaii 1:8 000 000

Eastern United States   148–149
1:4 800 000

North-eastern United States   150–151
1:2 000 000

South-eastern United States   152–153
1:2 000 000

Middle United States   154–155
1:4 800 000

Chicago and the Midwest   156–157
1:2 000 000

Western United States   158–159
1:4 800 000

Central and Southern California and Western Washington   160–161
1:2 000 000

Mexico   162–163
1:6 400 000

Central America and the West Indies   164–165
1:6 400 000
Jamaica 1:2 400 000
Guadeloupe 1:1 600 000
Martinique 1:1 600 000
Puerto Rico 1:2 400 000
Virgin Islands 1:1 600 000
St Lucia 1:800 000
Barbados 1:800 000

South America

South America: Physical   166
1:28 000 000

South America: Political   167
1:28 000 000

South America – North-west   168–169
1:6 400 000
Trinidad and Tobago 1:2 000 000

Eastern Brazil   170–171
1:6 400 000

South America – West   172–173
1:6 400 000
Galapagos Islands 1:3 200 000
Easter Island 1:400 000

Central South America   174–175
1:6 400 000

Southern Chile and Argentina   176
1:6 400 000

Index to World Maps
177–304

WORLD STATISTICS: COUNTRIES

This alphabetical list includes all the countries and territories of the world. If a territory is not completely independent, the country it is associated with is named. The area figures give the total area of land, inland water and ice.

The population figures are 2001 estimates. The annual income is the Gross Domestic Product per capita[†] in US dollars. The figures are the latest available, usually 2000 estimates.

Country/Territory	Area km² Thousands	Area miles² Thousands	Population Thousands	Capital	Annual Income US $
Afghanistan	652	252	26,813	Kabul	800
Albania	28.8	11.1	3,510	Tirana	3,000
Algeria	2,382	920	31,736	Algiers	5,500
American Samoa (US)	0.2	0.08	67	Pago Pago	8,000
Andorra	0.45	0.17	68	Andorra La Vella	18,000
Angola	1,247	481	10,366	Luanda	1,000
Anguilla (UK)	0.1	0.04	12	The Valley	8,200
Antigua & Barbuda	0.44	0.17	67	St John's	8,200
Argentina	2,767	1,068	37,385	Buenos Aires	12,900
Armenia	29.8	11.5	3,336	Yerevan	3,000
Aruba (Netherlands)	0.19	0.07	70	Oranjestad	28,000
Australia	7,687	2,968	19,358	Canberra	23,200
Austria	83.9	32.4	8,151	Vienna	25,000
Azerbaijan	86.6	33.4	7,771	Baku	3,000
Azores (Portugal)	2.2	0.87	243	Ponta Delgada	11,040
Bahamas	13.9	5.4	298	Nassau	15,000
Bahrain	0.68	0.26	645	Manama	15,900
Bangladesh	144	56	131,270	Dhaka	1,570
Barbados	0.43	0.17	275	Bridgetown	14,500
Belarus	207.6	80.1	10,350	Minsk	7,500
Belgium	30.5	11.8	10,259	Brussels	25,300
Belize	23	8.9	256	Belmopan	3,200
Benin	113	43	6,591	Porto-Novo	1,030
Bermuda (UK)	0.05	0.02	64	Hamilton	33,000
Bhutan	47	18.1	2,049	Thimphu	1,100
Bolivia	1,099	424	8,300	La Paz/Sucre	2,600
Bosnia-Herzegovina	51	20	3,922	Sarajevo	1,700
Botswana	582	225	1,586	Gaborone	6,600
Brazil	8,512	3,286	174,469	Brasília	6,500
Brunei	5.8	2.2	344	Bandar Seri Begawan	17,600
Bulgaria	111	43	7,707	Sofia	6,200
Burkina Faso	274	106	12,272	Ouagadougou	1,000
Burma (= Myanmar)	677	261	41,995	Rangoon	1,500
Burundi	27.8	10.7	6,224	Bujumbura	720
Cambodia	181	70	12,492	Phnom Penh	1,300
Cameroon	475	184	15,803	Yaoundé	1,700
Canada	9,976	3,852	31,593	Ottawa	24,800
Canary Is. (Spain)	7.3	2.8	1,577	Las Palmas/Santa Cruz	17,100
Cape Verde Is.	4	1.6	405	Praia	1,700
Cayman Is. (UK)	0.26	0.1	36	George Town	24,500
Central African Republic	623	241	3,577	Bangui	1,700
Chad	1,284	496	8,707	Ndjaména	1,000
Chile	757	292	15,328	Santiago	10,100
China	9,597	3,705	1,273,111	Beijing	3,600
Colombia	1,139	440	40,349	Bogotá	6,200
Comoros	2.2	0.86	596	Moroni	720
Congo	342	132	2,894	Brazzaville	1,100
Congo (Dem. Rep. of the)	2,345	905	53,625	Kinshasa	600
Cook Is. (NZ)	0.24	0.09	21	Avarua	5,000
Costa Rica	51.1	19.7	3,773	San José	6,700
Croatia	56.5	21.8	4,334	Zagreb	5,800
Cuba	111	43	11,184	Havana	1,700
Cyprus	9.3	3.6	763	Nicosia	13,800
Czech Republic	78.9	30.4	10,264	Prague	12,900
Denmark	43.1	16.6	5,353	Copenhagen	25,500
Djibouti	23.2	9	461	Djibouti	1,300
Dominica	0.75	0.29	71	Roseau	4,000
Dominican Republic	48.7	18.8	8,581	Santo Domingo	5,700
East Timor	14.9	5.7	737	Dili	N/A
Ecuador	284	109	13,184	Quito	2,900
Egypt	1,001	387	69,537	Cairo	3,600
El Salvador	21	8.1	6,238	San Salvador	4,000
Equatorial Guinea	28.1	10.8	486	Malabo	2,000
Eritrea	94	36	4,298	Asmara	710
Estonia	44.7	17.3	1,423	Tallinn	10,000
Ethiopia	1,128	436	65,892	Addis Ababa	600
Faroe Is. (Denmark)	1.4	0.54	46	Tórshavn	20,000
Fiji	18.3	7.1	844	Suva	7,300
Finland	338	131	5,176	Helsinki	22,900
France	552	213	59,551	Paris	24,400
French Guiana (France)	90	34.7	178	Cayenne	6,000
French Polynesia (France)	4	1.5	254	Papeete	10,800
Gabon	268	103	1,221	Libreville	6,300
Gambia, The	11.3	4.4	1,411	Banjul	1,100
Gaza Strip (OPT)*	0.36	0.14	1,178	–	1,000
Georgia	69.7	26.9	4,989	Tbilisi	4,600
Germany	357	138	83,030	Berlin	23,400
Ghana	239	92	19,894	Accra	1,900
Gibraltar (UK)	0.007	0.003	28	Gibraltar Town	17,500
Greece	132	51	10,624	Athens	17,200
Greenland (Denmark)	2,176	840	56	Nuuk (Godthåb)	20,000
Grenada	0.34	0.13	89	St George's	4,400
Guadeloupe (France)	1.7	0.66	431	Basse-Terre	9,000
Guam (US)	0.55	0.21	158	Agana	21,000
Guatemala	109	42	12,974	Guatemala City	3,700
Guinea	246	95	7,614	Conakry	1,300
Guinea-Bissau	36.1	13.9	1,316	Bissau	850
Guyana	215	83	697	Georgetown	4,800
Haiti	27.8	10.7	6,965	Port-au-Prince	1,800
Honduras	112	43	6,406	Tegucigalpa	2,700
Hong Kong (China)	1.1	0.4	7,211	–	25,400
Hungary	93	35.9	10,106	Budapest	11,200
Iceland	103	40	278	Reykjavik	24,800
India	3,288	1,269	1,029,991	New Delhi	2,200
Indonesia	1,890	730	227,701	Jakarta	2,900
Iran	1,648	636	66,129	Tehran	6,300
Iraq	438	169	23,332	Baghdad	2,500
Ireland	70.3	27.1	3,841	Dublin	21,600
Israel	20.6	7.96	5,938	Jerusalem	18,900
Italy	301	116	57,680	Rome	22,100
Ivory Coast (= Côte d'Ivoire)	322	125	16,393	Yamoussoukro	1,600
Jamaica	11	4.2	2,666	Kingston	3,700
Japan	378	146	126,772	Tokyo	24,900
Jordan	89.2	34.4	5,153	Amman	3,500
Kazakhstan	2,717	1,049	16,731	Astana	5,000
Kenya	580	224	30,766	Nairobi	1,500
Kiribati	0.72	0.28	94	Tarawa	850
Korea, North	121	47	21,968	Pyŏngyang	1,000
Korea, South	99	38.2	47,904	Seoul	16,100
Kuwait	17.8	6.9	2,042	Kuwait City	15,000
Kyrgyzstan	198.5	76.6	4,753	Bishkek	2,700
Laos	237	91	5,636	Vientiane	1,700
Latvia	65	25	2,385	Riga	7,200
Lebanon	10.4	4	3,628	Beirut	5,000
Lesotho	30.4	11.7	2,177	Maseru	2,400
Liberia	111	43	3,226	Monrovia	1,100
Libya	1,760	679	5,241	Tripoli	8,900
Liechtenstein	0.16	0.06	33	Vaduz	23,000
Lithuania	65.2	25.2	3,611	Vilnius	7,300
Luxembourg	2.6	1	443	Luxembourg	36,400
Macau (China)	0.02	0.006	454	–	17,500
Macedonia (FYROM)	25.7	9.9	2,046	Skopje	4,400
Madagascar	587	227	15,983	Antananarivo	800
Madeira (Portugal)	0.81	0.31	259	Funchal	12,120
Malawi	118	46	10,548	Lilongwe	900
Malaysia	330	127	22,229	Kuala Lumpur	10,300
Maldives	0.3	0.12	311	Malé	2,000
Mali	1,240	479	11,009	Bamako	850
Malta	0.32	0.12	395	Valletta	14,300
Marshall Is.	0.18	0.07	71	Dalap-Uliga-Darrit	1,670
Martinique (France)	1.1	0.42	418	Fort-de-France	11,000
Mauritania	1,030	398	2,747	Nouakchott	2,000
Mauritius	2	0.72	1,190	Port Louis	10,400
Mayotte (France)	0.37	0.14	163	Mamoundzou	600
Mexico	1,958	756	101,879	Mexico City	9,100
Micronesia, Fed. States of	0.7	0.27	135	Palikir	2,000
Moldova	33.7	13	4,432	Chişinău	2,500
Monaco	0.002	0.001	32	Monaco	27,000
Mongolia	1,567	605	2,655	Ulan Bator	1,780
Montserrat (UK)	0.1	0.04	8	Plymouth	5,000
Morocco	447	172	30,645	Rabat	3,500
Mozambique	802	309	19,371	Maputo	1,000
Namibia	825	318	1,798	Windhoek	4,300
Nauru	0.02	0.008	12	Yaren District	5,000
Nepal	141	54	25,284	Katmandu	1,360
Netherlands	41.5	16	15,981	Amsterdam/The Hague	24,400
Netherlands Antilles (Neths)	0.99	0.38	212	Willemstad	11,400
New Caledonia (France)	18.6	7.2	205	Nouméa	15,000
New Zealand	269	104	3,864	Wellington	17,700
Nicaragua	130	50	4,918	Managua	2,700
Niger	1,267	489	10,355	Niamey	1,000
Nigeria	924	357	126,636	Abuja	950
Northern Mariana Is. (US)	0.48	0.18	75	Saipan	12,500
Norway	324	125	4,503	Oslo	27,700
Oman	212	82	2,622	Muscat	7,700
Pakistan	796	307	144,617	Islamabad	2,000
Palau	0.46	0.18	19	Koror	7,100
Panama	77.1	29.8	2,846	Panamá	6,000
Papua New Guinea	463	179	5,049	Port Moresby	2,500
Paraguay	407	157	5,734	Asunción	4,750
Peru	1,285	496	27,484	Lima	4,550
Philippines	300	116	82,842	Manila	3,800
Poland	313	121	38,634	Warsaw	8,500
Portugal	92.4	35.7	9,444	Lisbon	15,800
Puerto Rico (US)	9	3.5	3,939	San Juan	10,000
Qatar	11	4.2	769	Doha	20,300
Réunion (France)	2.5	0.97	733	St-Denis	4,800
Romania	238	92	22,364	Bucharest	5,900
Russia	17,075	6,592	145,470	Moscow	7,700
Rwanda	26.3	10.2	7,313	Kigali	900
St Kitts & Nevis	0.36	0.14	39	Basseterre	7,000
St Lucia	0.62	0.24	158	Castries	4,500
St Vincent & Grenadines	0.39	0.15	116	Kingstown	2,800
Samoa	2.8	1.1	179	Apia	3,200
San Marino	0.06	0.02	27	San Marino	32,000
São Tomé & Príncipe	0.96	0.37	165	São Tomé	1,100
Saudi Arabia	2,150	830	22,757	Riyadh	10,500
Senegal	197	76	10,285	Dakar	1,600
Seychelles	0.46	0.18	80	Victoria	7,700
Sierra Leone	71.7	27.7	5,427	Freetown	510
Singapore	0.62	0.24	4,300	Singapore	26,500
Slovak Republic	49	18.9	5,415	Bratislava	10,200
Slovenia	20.3	7.8	1,930	Ljubljana	12,000
Solomon Is.	28.9	11.2	480	Honiara	2,000
Somalia	638	246	7,489	Mogadishu	600
South Africa	1,220	471	43,586	C. Town/Pretoria/Bloem.	8,500
Spain	505	195	38,432	Madrid	18,000
Sri Lanka	65.6	25.3	19,409	Colombo	3,250
Sudan	2,506	967	36,080	Khartoum	1,000
Suriname	163	63	434	Paramaribo	3,400
Swaziland	17.4	6.7	1,104	Mbabane	4,000
Sweden	450	174	8,875	Stockholm	22,200
Switzerland	41.3	15.9	7,283	Bern	28,600
Syria	185	71	16,729	Damascus	3,100
Taiwan	36	13.9	22,370	Taipei	17,400
Tajikistan	143.1	55.2	6,579	Dushanbe	1,140
Tanzania	945	365	36,232	Dodoma	710
Thailand	513	198	61,798	Bangkok	6,700
Togo	56.8	21.9	5,153	Lomé	1,500
Tonga	0.75	0.29	104	Nuku'alofa	2,200
Trinidad & Tobago	5.1	2	1,170	Port of Spain	9,500
Tunisia	164	63	9,705	Tunis	6,500
Turkey	779	301	66,494	Ankara	6,800
Turkmenistan	488.1	188.5	4,603	Ashkhabad	4,300
Turks & Caicos Is. (UK)	0.43	0.17	18	Cockburn Town	7,300
Tuvalu	0.03	0.01	11	Fongafale	1,100
Uganda	236	91	23,986	Kampala	1,100
Ukraine	603.7	233.1	48,760	Kiev	3,850
United Arab Emirates	83.6	32.3	2,407	Abu Dhabi	22,800
United Kingdom	243.3	94	59,648	London	22,800
United States of America	9,373	3,619	278,059	Washington, DC	36,200
Uruguay	177	68	3,360	Montevideo	9,300
Uzbekistan	447.4	172.7	25,155	Tashkent	2,400
Vanuatu	12.2	4.7	193	Port-Vila	1,300
Vatican City	0.0004	0.0002	0.89	Vatican City	N/A
Venezuela	912	352	23,917	Caracas	6,200
Vietnam	332	127	79,939	Hanoi	1,950
Virgin Is. (UK)	0.15	0.06	21	Road Town	16,000
Virgin Is. (US)	0.34	0.13	122	Charlotte Amalie	15,000
Wallis & Futuna Is. (France)	0.2	0.08	15	Mata-Utu	2,000
West Bank (OPT)*	5.86	2.26	2,091	–	1,500
Western Sahara	266	103	251	El Aaiún	N/A
Yemen	528	204	18,078	Sana	820
Yugoslavia (Serbia & Montenegro)	102.3	39.5	10,677	Belgrade	2,300
Zambia	753	291	9,770	Lusaka	880
Zimbabwe	391	151	11,365	Harare	2,500

*OPT = Occupied Palestinian Territory   N/A = Not Available

[†] Gross Domestic Product per capita has been measured using the purchasing power parity method. This enables comparisons to be made between countries through their purchasing power (in US dollars), showing real price levels of goods and services rather than using currency exchange rates.

World Statistics: Physical Dimensions

Each topic list is divided into continents and within a continent the items are listed in order of size. The bottom part of many of the lists is selective in order to give examples from as many different countries as possible. The order of the continents is the same as in the atlas, beginning with Europe and ending with South America. The figures are rounded as appropriate.

World, Continents, Oceans

	km²	miles²	%
The World	509,450,000	196,672,000	–
Land	149,450,000	57,688,000	29.3
Water	360,000,000	138,984,000	70.7
Asia	44,500,000	17,177,000	29.8
Africa	30,302,000	11,697,000	20.3
North America	24,241,000	9,357,000	16.2
South America	17,793,000	6,868,000	11.9
Antarctica	14,100,000	5,443,000	9.4
Europe	9,957,000	3,843,000	6.7
Australia & Oceania	8,557,000	3,303,000	5.7
Pacific Ocean	179,679,000	69,356,000	49.9
Atlantic Ocean	92,373,000	35,657,000	25.7
Indian Ocean	73,917,000	28,532,000	20.5
Arctic Ocean	14,090,000	5,439,000	3.9

Ocean Depths

Atlantic Ocean	m	ft
Puerto Rico (Milwaukee) Deep	9,220	30,249
Cayman Trench	7,680	25,197
Gulf of Mexico	5,203	17,070
Mediterranean Sea	5,121	16,801
Black Sea	2,211	7,254
North Sea	660	2,165
Indian Ocean	m	ft
Java Trench	7,450	24,442
Red Sea	2,635	8,454
Pacific Ocean	m	ft
Mariana Trench	11,022	36,161
Tonga Trench	10,882	35,702
Japan Trench	10,554	34,626
Kuril Trench	10,542	34,587
Arctic Ocean	m	ft
Molloy Deep	5,608	18,399

Mountains

Europe		m	ft
Elbrus	*Russia*	5,642	18,510
Mont Blanc	*France/Italy*	4,807	15,771
Monte Rosa	*Italy/Switzerland*	4,634	15,203
Dom	*Switzerland*	4,545	14,911
Liskamm	*Switzerland*	4,527	14,852
Weisshorn	*Switzerland*	4,505	14,780
Taschorn	*Switzerland*	4,490	14,730
Matterhorn/Cervino	*Italy/Switzerland*	4,478	14,691
Mont Maudit	*France/Italy*	4,465	14,649
Dent Blanche	*Switzerland*	4,356	14,291
Nadelhorn	*Switzerland*	4,327	14,196
Grandes Jorasses	*France/Italy*	4,208	13,806
Jungfrau	*Switzerland*	4,158	13,642
Grossglockner	*Austria*	3,797	12,457
Mulhacén	*Spain*	3,478	11,411
Zugspitze	*Germany*	2,962	9,718
Olympus	*Greece*	2,917	9,570
Triglav	*Slovenia*	2,863	9,393
Gerlachovka	*Slovak Republic*	2,655	8,711
Galdhöpiggen	*Norway*	2,468	8,100
Kebnekaise	*Sweden*	2,117	6,946
Ben Nevis	*UK*	1,343	4,406
Asia		m	ft
Everest	*China/Nepal*	8,850	29,035
K2 (Godwin Austen)	*China/Kashmir*	8,611	28,251
Kanchenjunga	*India/Nepal*	8,598	28,208
Lhotse	*China/Nepal*	8,516	27,939
Makalu	*China/Nepal*	8,481	27,824
Cho Oyu	*China/Nepal*	8,201	26,906
Dhaulagiri	*Nepal*	8,172	26,811
Manaslu	*Nepal*	8,156	26,758
Nanga Parbat	*Kashmir*	8,126	26,660
Annapurna	*Nepal*	8,078	26,502
Gasherbrum	*China/Kashmir*	8,068	26,469
Broad Peak	*China/Kashmir*	8,051	26,414
Xixabangma	*China*	8,012	26,286
Kangbachen	*India/Nepal*	7,902	25,925
Trivor	*Pakistan*	7,720	25,328
Pik Kommunizma	*Tajikistan*	7,495	24,590
Demavend	*Iran*	5,604	18,386
Ararat	*Turkey*	5,165	16,945
Gunong Kinabalu	*Malaysia (Borneo)*	4,101	13,455
Fuji-San	*Japan*	3,776	12,388
Africa		m	ft
Kilimanjaro	*Tanzania*	5,895	19,340
Mt Kenya	*Kenya*	5,199	17,057
Ruwenzori (Margherita)	*Ug./Congo (D.R.)*	5,109	16,762
Ras Dashan	*Ethiopia*	4,620	15,157
Meru	*Tanzania*	4,565	14,977
Karisimbi	*Rwanda/Congo (D.R.)*	4,507	14,787
Mt Elgon	*Kenya/Uganda*	4,321	14,176
Batu	*Ethiopia*	4,307	14,130
Toubkal	*Morocco*	4,165	13,665
Mt Cameroon	*Cameroon*	4,070	13,353
Oceania		m	ft
Puncak Jaya	*Indonesia*	5,029	16,499
Puncak Trikora	*Indonesia*	4,750	15,584
Puncak Mandala	*Indonesia*	4,702	15,427
Mt Wilhelm	*Papua New Guinea*	4,508	14,790
Mauna Kea	*USA (Hawaii)*	4,205	13,796
Mauna Loa	*USA (Hawaii)*	4,169	13,681
Mt Cook (Aoraki)	*New Zealand*	3,753	12,313
Mt Kosciuszko	*Australia*	2,237	7,339
North America		m	ft
Mt McKinley (Denali)	*USA (Alaska)*	6,194	20,321
Mt Logan	*Canada*	5,959	19,551
Citlaltepetl	*Mexico*	5,700	18,701
Mt St Elias	*USA/Canada*	5,489	18,008
Popocatepetl	*Mexico*	5,452	17,887
Mt Foraker	*USA (Alaska)*	5,304	17,401
Ixtaccihuatl	*Mexico*	5,286	17,342
Lucania	*Canada*	5,227	17,149
Mt Steele	*Canada*	5,073	16,644
Mt Bona	*USA (Alaska)*	5,005	16,420
Mt Whitney	*USA*	4,418	14,495
Tajumulco	*Guatemala*	4,220	13,845
Chirripó Grande	*Costa Rica*	3,837	12,589
Pico Duarte	*Dominican Rep.*	3,175	10,417
South America		m	ft
Aconcagua	*Argentina*	6,960	22,834
Bonete	*Argentina*	6,872	22,546
Ojos del Salado	*Argentina/Chile*	6,863	22,516
Pissis	*Argentina*	6,779	22,241
Mercedario	*Argentina/Chile*	6,770	22,211
Huascaran	*Peru*	6,768	22,204
Llullaillaco	*Argentina/Chile*	6,723	22,057
Nudo de Cachi	*Argentina*	6,720	22,047
Yerupaja	*Peru*	6,632	21,758
Sajama	*Bolivia*	6,542	21,463
Chimborazo	*Ecuador*	6,267	20,561
Pico Colon	*Colombia*	5,800	19,029
Pico Bolivar	*Venezuela*	5,007	16,427
Antarctica		m	ft
Vinson Massif		4,897	16,066
Mt Kirkpatrick		4,528	14,855

Rivers

Europe		km	miles
Volga	*Caspian Sea*	3,700	2,300
Danube	*Black Sea*	2,850	1,770
Ural	*Caspian Sea*	2,535	1,575
Dnepr (Dnipro)	*Black Sea*	2,285	1,420
Kama	*Volga*	2,030	1,260
Don	*Black Sea*	1,990	1,240
Petchora	*Arctic Ocean*	1,790	1,110
Oka	*Volga*	1,480	920
Dnister (Dniester)	*Black Sea*	1,400	870
Vyatka	*Kama*	1,370	850
Rhine	*North Sea*	1,320	820
N. Dvina	*Arctic Ocean*	1,290	800
Elbe	*North Sea*	1,145	710
Asia		km	miles
Yangtze	*Pacific Ocean*	6,380	3,960
Yenisey–Angara	*Arctic Ocean*	5,550	3,445
Huang He	*Pacific Ocean*	5,464	3,395
Ob–Irtysh	*Arctic Ocean*	5,410	3,360
Mekong	*Pacific Ocean*	4,500	2,795
Amur	*Pacific Ocean*	4,400	2,730
Lena	*Arctic Ocean*	4,400	2,730
Irtysh	*Ob*	4,250	2,640
Yenisey	*Arctic Ocean*	4,090	2,540
Ob	*Arctic Ocean*	3,680	2,285
Indus	*Indian Ocean*	3,100	1,925
Brahmaputra	*Indian Ocean*	2,900	1,800
Syrdarya	*Aral Sea*	2,860	1,775
Salween	*Indian Ocean*	2,800	1,740
Euphrates	*Indian Ocean*	2,700	1,675
Amudarya	*Aral Sea*	2,540	1,575
Africa		km	miles
Nile	*Mediterranean*	6,670	4,140
Congo	*Atlantic Ocean*	4,670	2,900
Niger	*Atlantic Ocean*	4,180	2,595
Zambezi	*Indian Ocean*	3,540	2,200
Oubangi/Uele	*Congo (D.R.)*	2,250	1,400
Kasai	*Congo (D.R.)*	1,950	1,210
Shaballe	*Indian Ocean*	1,930	1,200
Orange	*Atlantic Ocean*	1,860	1,155
Cubango	*Okavango Swamps*	1,800	1,120
Limpopo	*Indian Ocean*	1,600	995
Senegal	*Atlantic Ocean*	1,600	995
Australia		km	miles
Murray–Darling	*Indian Ocean*	3,750	2,330
Darling	*Murray*	3,070	1,905
Murray	*Indian Ocean*	2,575	1,600
Murrumbidgee	*Murray*	1,690	1,050
North America		km	miles
Mississippi–Missouri	*Gulf of Mexico*	6,020	3,740
Mackenzie	*Arctic Ocean*	4,240	2,630
Mississippi	*Gulf of Mexico*	3,780	2,350
Missouri	*Mississippi*	3,780	2,350
Yukon	*Pacific Ocean*	3,185	1,980
Rio Grande	*Gulf of Mexico*	3,030	1,880
Arkansas	*Mississippi*	2,340	1,450
Colorado	*Pacific Ocean*	2,330	1,445
Red	*Mississippi*	2,040	1,270
Columbia	*Pacific Ocean*	1,950	1,210
Saskatchewan	*Lake Winnipeg*	1,940	1,205
South America		km	miles
Amazon	*Atlantic Ocean*	6,450	4,010
Paraná–Plate	*Atlantic Ocean*	4,500	2,800
Purus	*Amazon*	3,350	2,080
Madeira	*Amazon*	3,200	1,990
São Francisco	*Atlantic Ocean*	2,900	1,800
Paraná	*Plate*	2,800	1,740
Tocantins	*Atlantic Ocean*	2,750	1,710
Paraguay	*Paraná*	2,550	1,580
Orinoco	*Atlantic Ocean*	2,500	1,550
Pilcomayo	*Paraná*	2,500	1,550
Araguaia	*Tocantins*	2,250	1,400

Lakes

Europe		km²	miles²
Lake Ladoga	*Russia*	17,700	6,800
Lake Onega	*Russia*	9,700	3,700
Saimaa system	*Finland*	8,000	3,100
Vänern	*Sweden*	5,500	2,100
Asia		km²	miles²
Caspian Sea	*Asia*	371,800	143,550
Lake Baykal	*Russia*	30,500	11,780
Aral Sea	*Kazakhstan/Uzbekistan*	28,687	11,086
Tonlé Sap	*Cambodia*	20,000	7,700
Lake Balqash	*Kazakhstan*	18,500	7,100
Africa		km²	miles²
Lake Victoria	*East Africa*	68,000	26,000
Lake Tanganyika	*Central Africa*	33,000	13,000
Lake Malawi/Nyasa	*East Africa*	29,600	11,430
Lake Chad	*Central Africa*	25,000	9,700
Lake Turkana	*Ethiopia/Kenya*	8,500	3,300
Lake Volta	*Ghana*	8,500	3,300
Australia		km²	miles²
Lake Eyre	*Australia*	8,900	3,400
Lake Torrens	*Australia*	5,800	2,200
Lake Gairdner	*Australia*	4,800	1,900
North America		km²	miles²
Lake Superior	*Canada/USA*	82,350	31,800
Lake Huron	*Canada/USA*	59,600	23,010
Lake Michigan	*USA*	58,000	22,400
Great Bear Lake	*Canada*	31,800	12,280
Great Slave Lake	*Canada*	28,500	11,000
Lake Erie	*Canada/USA*	25,700	9,900
Lake Winnipeg	*Canada*	24,400	9,400
Lake Ontario	*Canada/USA*	19,500	7,500
Lake Nicaragua	*Nicaragua*	8,200	3,200
South America		km²	miles²
Lake Titicaca	*Bolivia/Peru*	8,300	3,200
Lake Poopo	*Bolivia*	2,800	1,100

Islands

Europe		km²	miles²
Great Britain	*UK*	229,880	88,700
Iceland	*Atlantic Ocean*	103,000	39,800
Ireland	*Ireland/UK*	84,400	32,600
Novaya Zemlya (N.)	*Russia*	48,200	18,600
Sicily	*Italy*	25,500	9,800
Corsica	*France*	8,700	3,400
Asia		km²	miles²
Borneo	*South-east Asia*	744,360	287,400
Sumatra	*Indonesia*	473,600	182,860
Honshu	*Japan*	230,500	88,980
Sulawesi (Celebes)	*Indonesia*	189,000	73,000
Java	*Indonesia*	126,700	48,900
Luzon	*Philippines*	104,700	40,400
Hokkaido	*Japan*	78,400	30,300
Africa		km²	miles²
Madagascar	*Indian Ocean*	587,040	226,660
Socotra	*Indian Ocean*	3,600	1,400
Réunion	*Indian Ocean*	2,500	965
Oceania		km²	miles²
New Guinea	*Indonesia/Papua NG*	821,030	317,000
New Zealand (S.)	*Pacific Ocean*	150,500	58,100
New Zealand (N.)	*Pacific Ocean*	114,700	44,300
Tasmania	*Australia*	67,800	26,200
Hawaii	*Pacific Ocean*	10,450	4,000
North America		km²	miles²
Greenland	*Atlantic Ocean*	2,175,600	839,800
Baffin Is.	*Canada*	508,000	196,100
Victoria Is.	*Canada*	212,200	81,900
Ellesmere Is.	*Canada*	212,000	81,800
Cuba	*Caribbean Sea*	110,860	42,800
Hispaniola	*Dominican Rep./Haiti*	76,200	29,400
Jamaica	*Caribbean Sea*	11,400	4,400
Puerto Rico	*Atlantic Ocean*	8,900	3,400
South America		km²	miles²
Tierra del Fuego	*Argentina/Chile*	47,000	18,100
Falkland Is. (E.)	*Atlantic Ocean*	6,800	2,600

World: Regions in the News

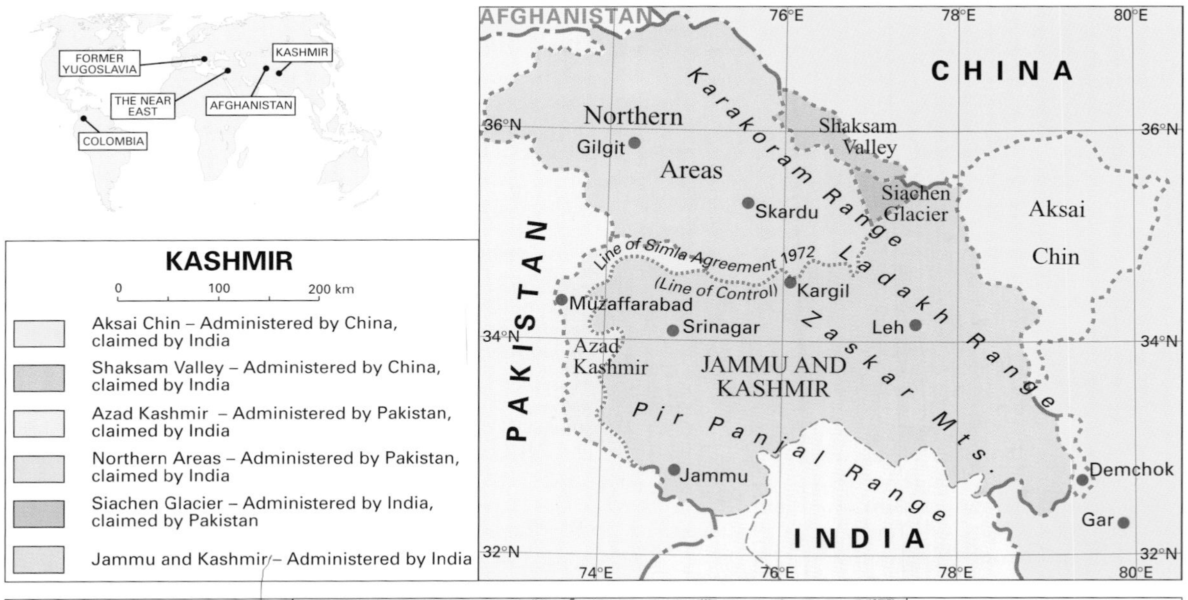
FORMER YUGOSLAVIA
KASHMIR
THE NEAR EAST
AFGHANISTAN
COLOMBIA
KASHMIR
0 100 200 km
Aksai Chin – Administered by China, claimed by India
Shaksam Valley – Administered by China, claimed by India
Azad Kashmir – Administered by Pakistan, claimed by India
Northern Areas – Administered by Pakistan, claimed by India
Siachen Glacier – Administered by India, claimed by Pakistan
Jammu and Kashmir – Administered by India
AFGHANISTAN
CHINA
PAKISTAN
INDIA
Northern Areas
Gilgit
Shaksam Valley
Siachen Glacier
Aksai Chin
Skardu
Karakoram Range
Ladakh Range
Zaskar Mts.
Pir Panjal Range
Line of Simla Agreement 1972 (Line of Control)
Muzaffarabad
Kargil
Azad Kashmir
Srinagar
Leh
JAMMU AND KASHMIR
Jammu
Demchok
Gar
74°E 76°E 78°E 80°E
32°N 34°N 36°N

YUGOSLAVIA

POPULATION: 10,677,000 (Serb 62.6%, Albanian 16.5%, Montenegrin 5%, Hungarian 3.3%, Muslim 3.2%)

Serbia **POPULATION:** 5,799,800 (Serb 87.7%, excluding the provinces of Kosovo and Vojvodina)

Kosovo **POPULATION:** 2,084,4000 (Albanian 81.6%, Serb 9.9%)

Vojvodena **POPULATION:** 1,980,800 (Serb 56.8%, Hungarian 16.9%)

Montenegro **POPULATION:** 635,000 (Montenegrin 61.9%, Muslim 14.6%, Albanian 7%)

CROATIA

POPULATION: 4,334,000 (Croat 78.1%, Serb 12.2%)

SLOVENIA

POPULATION: 1,930,000 (Slovene 88%, Croat 3%, Serb 2%)

MACEDONIA (FYROM)

POPULATION: 2,046,000 (Macedonian 64%, Albanian 21.7%, Turkish 5%, Romanian 3%, Serb 2%)

BOSNIA-HERZEGOVINA

POPULATION: 3,922,000 (Muslim 49%, Serb 31.2%, Croat 17.2%)

FORMER YUGOSLAVIA
AUSTRIA
HUNGARY
ROMANIA
SLOVENIA
CROATIA
BOSNIA-HERZEGOVINA
YUGOSLAVIA
SERBIA
Vojvodina
Kosovo
MONTENEGRO
MACEDONIA
ALBANIA
BULGARIA
GREECE
ITALY
ADRIATIC SEA
Ljubljana
Zagreb
Rijeka
Maribor
Osijek
Vukovar
Subotica
Novi Sad
Zrenjanin
Timişoara
Beograd (Belgrade)
Smederevo
Kragujevac
Banja Luka
Bihać
Tuzla
Zenica
Srebrenica
Sarajevo
Goražde
Kraljevo
Split
Mostar
Nikšić
Novi Pazar
Niš
Leskovac
Dubrovnik
Podgorica
Priština
Vranje
Đakovica
Prizren
Skopje
Shkodër
Kukës
Tetovo
Durrës
Tirana
Prilep
Bitola
Krajina
Drava
Danube
Tisa
Morava
Ibar
0 100 200 km
International boundaries
Republic boundaries
Province boundaries
Capital cities
Dayton Peace Agreement Boundary
Muslim–Croat Federation
Bosnian Serb Republic
14°E 16°E 18°E 20°E
42°N 44°N 46°N

COLOMBIA

0 200 400 km

- International boundaries
- Province boundaries
- FARC Demilitarized Zone
- Land over 3,000 m
- Capital cities
- Main towns

POPULATION: 40,349,388 (Mestizo 58%, White 20%, Mulatto 14%, Black 4%, Mixed Black-Amerindian 3%, Amerindian 1%)
RELIGIONS: Roman Catholic 90%
FARC MEMBERS: 18,000 (Revolutionary Armed Forces of Colombia)
CIVILIANS IN FARC ZONE: 90,000
AID RECEIVED (US) 2000: US $1.3 billion
AID RECEIVED (US) 2002: US $0.3 billion

CARIBBEAN SEA
PACIFIC OCEAN
PANAMA
Panamá
VENEZUELA
COLOMBIA
ECUADOR
PERU
BRAZIL
Barranquilla
Cartagena
Caracas
Medellín
Bogotá
Cali
Uribe
San Vicente del Caguán
Quito
FARC Demilitarized Zone
GUAJIRA
ATLANTICO
MAGDALENA
CÉSAR
CÓRDOBA
SUCRE
BOLÍVAR
NORTE DE SANTANDER
SANTANDER
ANTIOQUIA
ARAUCA
CHOCÓ
BOYACÁ
CASANARE
VICHADA
TOLIMA
VALLE DEL CAUCA
HUILA
META
CAUCA
GUAINÍA
GUAVIARE
NARIÑO
PUTUMAYO
CAQUETÁ
VAUPÉS
AMAZONAS
Equator
Amazon
80°W 75°W 70°W
10°N 5°N 0°

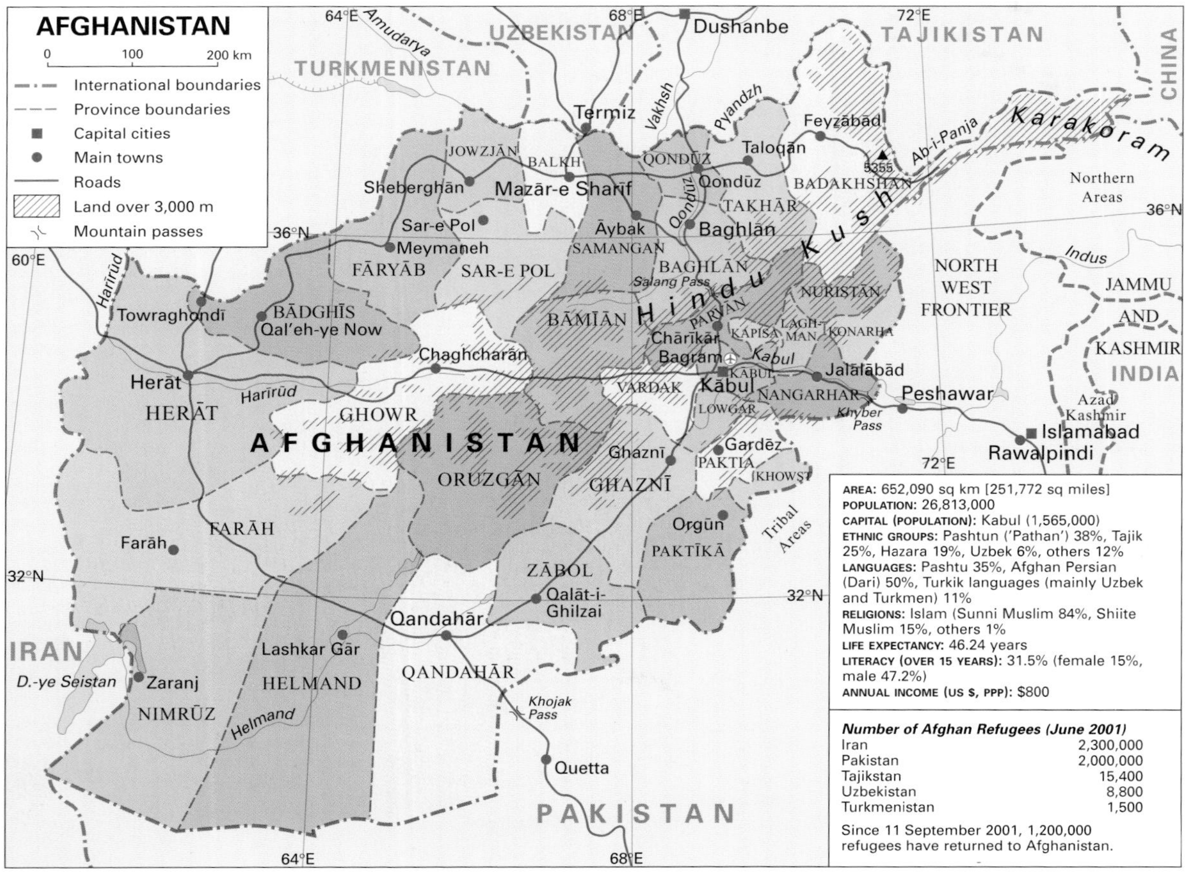
AFGHANISTAN
0 100 200 km
International boundaries
Province boundaries
Capital cities
Main towns
Roads
Land over 3,000 m
Mountain passes
UZBEKISTAN
TURKMENISTAN
TAJIKISTAN
CHINA
IRAN
PAKISTAN
INDIA
AFGHANISTAN
Dushanbe
Termiz
Mazār-e Sharīf
Sheberghān
Qondūz
Feyzābād
Tāloqān
Baghlān
Sar-e Pol
Meymaneh
Aybak
Chārīkār
Bagrām
Kābul
Jalālābād
Peshawar
Islamabad
Rawalpindi
Herāt
Qal'eh-ye Now
Towraghondī
Chaghcharān
Ghaznī
Gardēz
Orgūn
Qalāt-i-Ghilzai
Qandahār
Quetta
Lashkar Gāh
Zaranj
Farāh
Hindu Kush
Karakoram
Amudarya
Harīrūd
Helmand
Indus
Khyber Pass
Khojak Pass
Salang Pass
NORTH WEST FRONTIER
JAMMU AND KASHMIR
Azad Kashmir
Northern Areas
Tribal Areas
JOWZJĀN
BALKH
QONDŪZ
TAKHĀR
BADAKHSHĀN
SAMANGĀN
FĀRYĀB
SAR-E POL
BAGHLĀN
BĀMĪĀN
PARVĀN
NŪRISTĀN
KAPISA
LAGHMĀN
KONARHA
BĀDGHĪS
HERĀT
GHOWR
VARDAK
KĀBUL
LOWGAR
NANGARHĀR
PAKTĪA
KHOWST
ORUZGĀN
GHAZNĪ
PAKTĪKĀ
FARĀH
ZĀBOL
HELMAND
NIMRŪZ
QANDAHĀR
D.-ye Seistan
60°E 64°E 68°E 72°E
32°N 36°N

AREA: 652,090 sq km [251,772 sq miles]
POPULATION: 26,813,000
CAPITAL (POPULATION): Kabul (1,565,000)
ETHNIC GROUPS: Pashtun ('Pathan') 38%, Tajik 25%, Hazara 19%, Uzbek 6%, others 12%
LANGUAGES: Pashtu 35%, Afghan Persian (Dari) 50%, Turkik languages (mainly Uzbek and Turkmen) 11%
RELIGIONS: Islam (Sunni Muslim 84%, Shiite Muslim 15%, others 1%
LIFE EXPECTANCY: 46.24 years
LITERACY (OVER 15 YEARS): 31.5% (female 15%, male 47.2%)
ANNUAL INCOME (US $, PPP): $800

Number of Afghan Refugees (June 2001)	
Iran	2,300,000
Pakistan	2,000,000
Tajikstan	15,400
Uzbekistan	8,800
Turkmenistan	1,500

Since 11 September 2001, 1,200,000 refugees have returned to Afghanistan.

THE NEAR EAST
0 25 50 km
1949 Armistice Line
1974 Cease-fire Line
Palestinian control
Joint Israeli/ Palestinian control
Efrata
Main Jewish settlements in the West Bank and Gaza Strip
Halhul
Main Palestinian Arab towns in the West Bank and Gaza Strip
Road corridor linking Gaza and West Bank
LEBANON
SYRIA
Golan Heights
ISRAEL
West Bank
JORDAN
EGYPT
MEDITERRANEAN SEA
Dead Sea
Gaza Strip
Saydā
Beqaa Valley
Litani
Şūr (Tyre)
Qiryat Shemona
Nahariyya
Zefat
Akko
Yam Kinneret
Hefa
Terverya
Nazerat
Irbid
Jordan
Jenin
Hadera
Ţūlkarm
Shavel Shomron
Tūbās
Netanya
Kedumim
Elon More
Qalqīlya
Nabulus
Karne Shomron
Emanuel
Kfar Tapuah
Elkana
Ariel
Shiloh
Tel Aviv-Yafo
As Salt
Rām Allāh
Beit El
Al Birah
Rehovot
Beit Horon
'Ammān
Al Arīhā (Jericho)
Ashdod
Jerusalem
Maale Adumim
Bayt Lahm (Bethlehem)
Ashqelon
Efrata
Tkoa
Halhul
Alei Sinai
Gaza
Nisanit
Al Khalīl (Hebron)
Qiryat Arba
Netzarin
Kfar Darom
Gadid
Khān Yūnis
Be'er Sheva
35°E
32°N 33°N

ISRAEL
POPULATION: 5,938,000 (inc. East Jerusalem and Jewish settlers in the areas under Israeli administration. Jewish 82%, Arab Muslim 13.8%, Arab Christian 2.5%, Druze 1.7%)

West Bank
POPULATION: 2,091,000 (Palestinian Arab 97% [of whom Arab Muslim 85%, Jewish 7%, Christian 8%])

Gaza Strip
POPULATION: 1,178,000 (Arab 98%)

JORDAN
POPULATION: 5,153,000 (Arab 99% [of whom about 50% are Palestinian Arab])

LEBANON
POPULATION: 3,628,000 (Arab 93% [of whom 83% are Lebanese Arab and 10% Palestinian Arab])

IMAGES OF EARTH

– VANCOUVER, CANADA –

The city of Vancouver grew up around its fine, natural harbour on the north side of the Fraser River delta, developing as the western railhead of the Canadian Pacific Railroad. Just to the south of the delta runs the 49th parallel, the boundary between Canada and the USA. To the north of the city lie the Coast Mountains, and to the west, across the Strait of Georgia, is Vancouver Island with the town of Victoria visible at the bottom left of the image.

– LOS ANGELES, USA –

The sprawling urban area of Greater LA covers most of the area to the south of the San Gabriel Mountains, which run across the top of the image. The population of the whole area is over 14 million people. Jutting into the left-hand side of the image, just below centre, the darker colours of the eastern end of the Santa Monica range can be seen; the centre of the city proper is just to the south-east of the end of the range. On its southern slopes lie Beverly Hills and Hollywood, with the San Fernando Valley to the north.

– NEW YORK, USA –
This image covers most of the largest urban area in
the USA, which has a population of over 20 million people.
Flowing from the north, the Hudson River divides the two
cities of New York (to the east) and New Jersey (to the west).
Towards its mouth on the east bank lies Manhattan Island,
with Central Park clearly visible. Below this is the end
of Long Island, which is connected by bridge to
Staten Island, to the west.

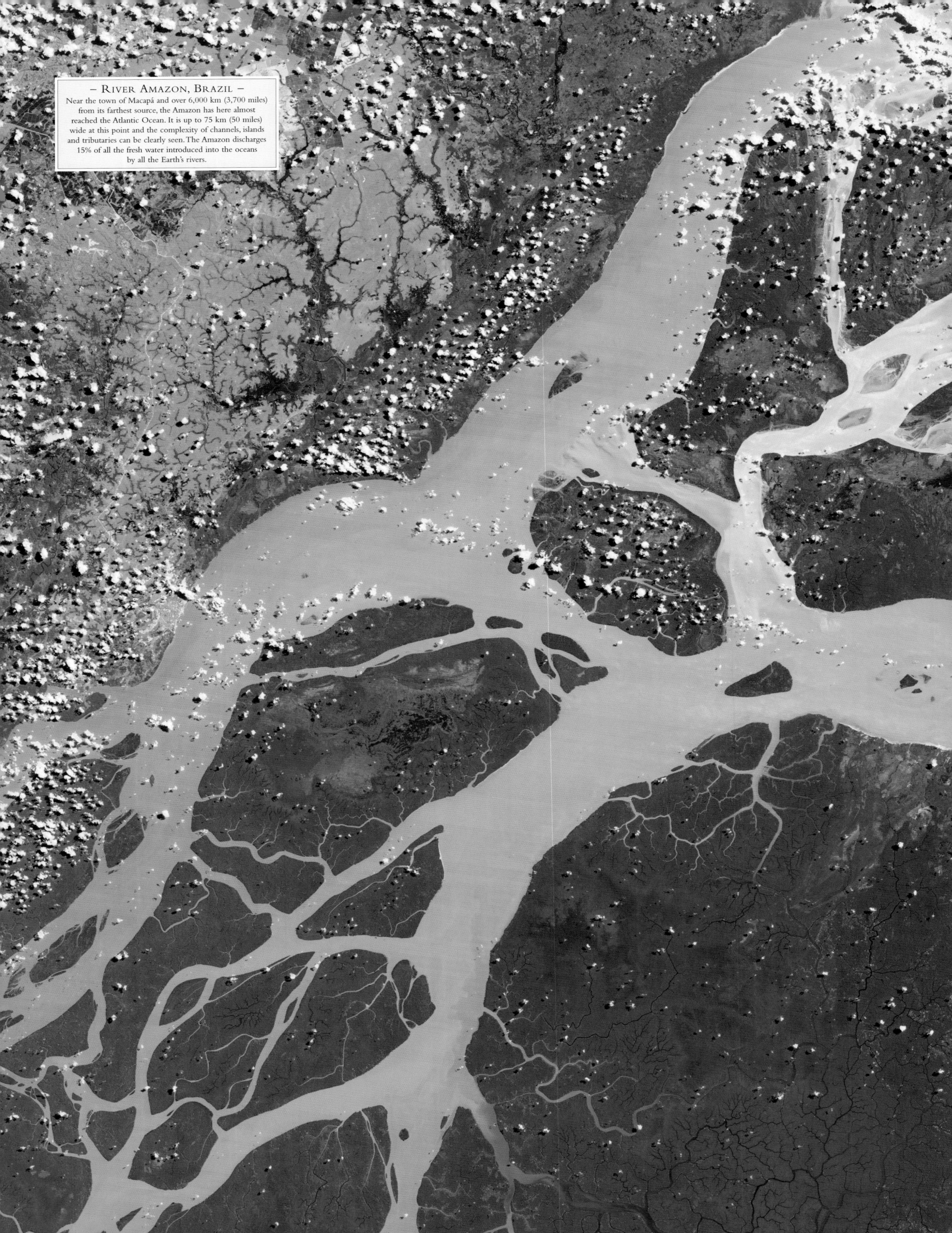

— RIVER AMAZON, BRAZIL —
Near the town of Macapá and over 6,000 km (3,700 miles)
from its farthest source, the Amazon has here almost
reached the Atlantic Ocean. It is up to 75 km (50 miles)
wide at this point and the complexity of channels, islands
and tributaries can be clearly seen. The Amazon discharges
15% of all the fresh water introduced into the oceans
by all the Earth's rivers.

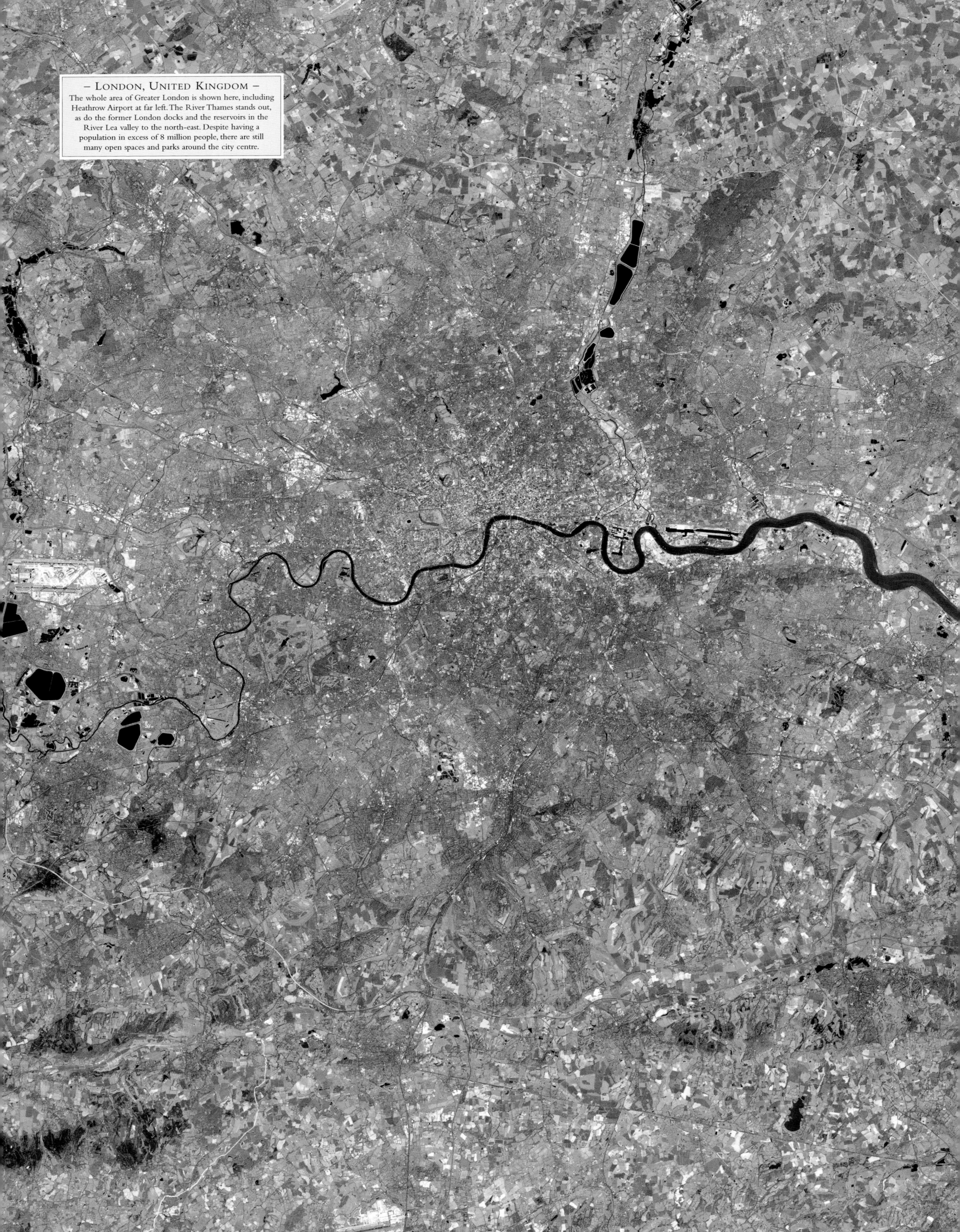

– LONDON, UNITED KINGDOM –
The whole area of Greater London is shown here, including
Heathrow Airport at far left. The River Thames stands out,
as do the former London docks and the reservoirs in the
River Lea valley to the north-east. Despite having a
population in excess of 8 million people, there are still
many open spaces and parks around the city centre.

— WESTERN CAPE, SOUTH AFRICA —
Cape Town sits to the bottom left of this image, with
the Cape Peninsula running south-east to the Cape of
Good Hope. Inland from the fertile coastal plain, where
most of South Africa's wine is produced, is the rugged
interior of the Great Karoo where parallel mountain
ranges are dissected by river valleys.

— KARACHI, PAKISTAN —

The largest city in Pakistan with over 9 million inhabitants,
Karachi is the administrative headquarters of Sind province
and is also the commercial and industrial capital of the whole
country. To its south lie the mangrove swamps of the vast
delta of the River Indus, 210 km (130 miles) wide where it
flows into the Arabian Sea. To the north and east of the city
are the dry, hot Sind plains, which are subject to a mean
annual rainfall of only 125–250 mm (5–10 inches).

— SYDNEY, AUSTRALIA —

Sydney, the largest city in Australia, was founded at the
end of the 18th century on the north shore of Botany Bay,
the southern of the two enclosed bays shown here. The
runways of the international airport project into this, and
to the north, on the south shore of Sydney Harbour, the
shadows of the skyscrapers in the central business district
can be seen, with the Sydney Harbour Bridge beyond.

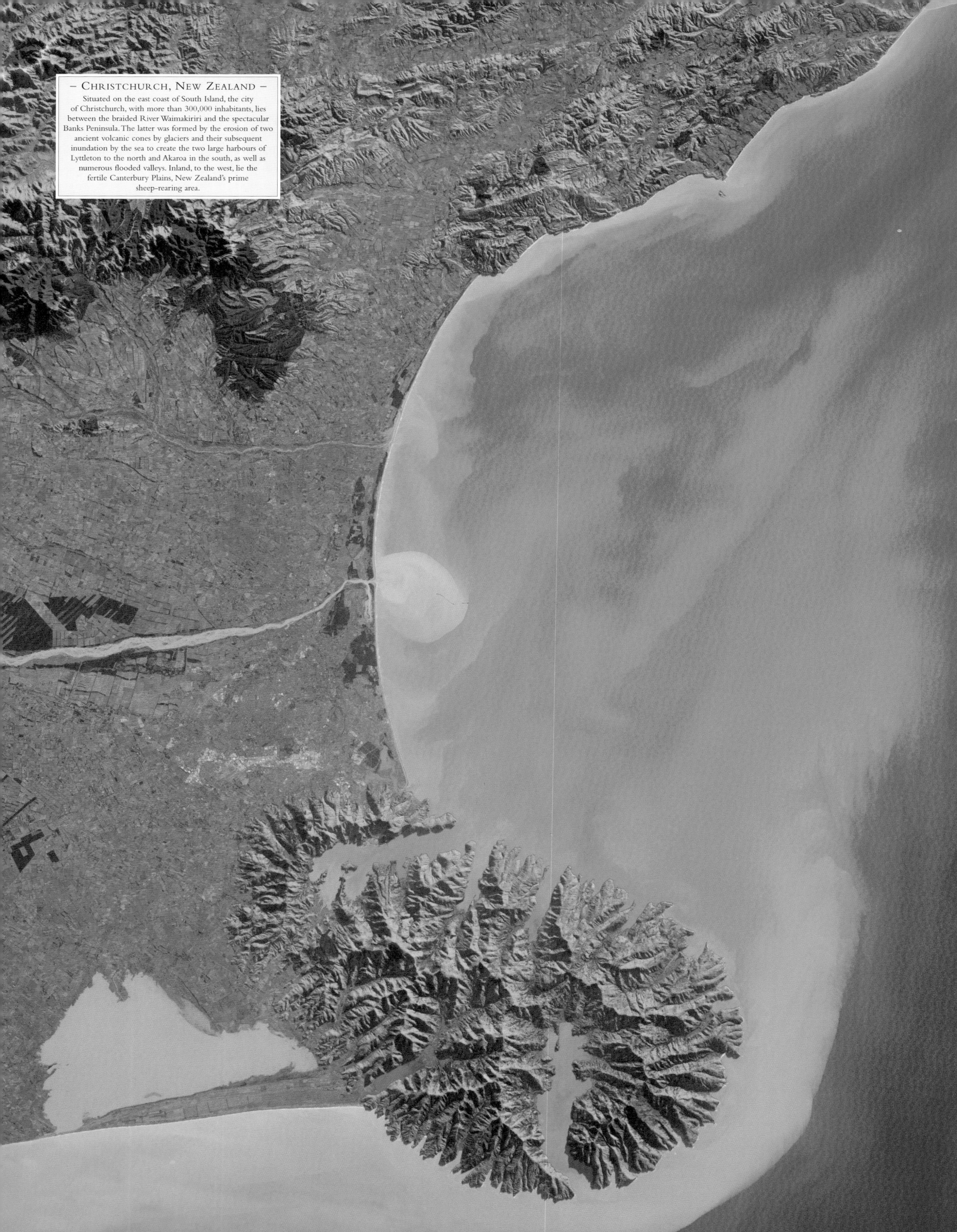

The Gazetteer of Nations

AFGHANISTAN

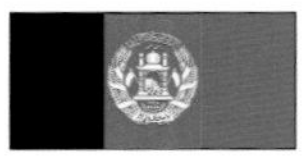

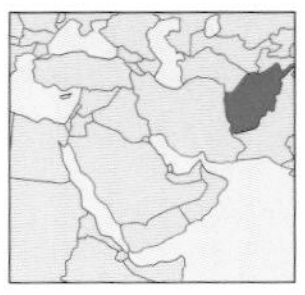

GEOGRAPHY The Republic of Afghanistan is a landlocked, mountainous country in southern Asia. The central highlands reach a height of more than 7,000 m [22,966 ft] in the east and make up nearly three-quarters of Afghanistan. The main range is the Hindu Kush, which is cut by deep, fertile valleys.

In winter, northerly winds bring cold, snowy weather to the mountains, but summers are hot and dry.

POLITICS & ECONOMY The modern history of Afghanistan began in 1747, when the various tribes in the area united for the first time. In the 19th century, Russia and Britain struggled for control of the country. Following Britain's withdrawal in 1919, Afghanistan became fully independent. Soviet troops invaded Afghanistan in 1979 to support a socialist regime in Kabul, but they withdrew in 1989. By the early 21st century, a group called the Taliban ('Islamic students') controlled 90% of the country. In 2001, following the refusal of the Taliban government to hand over the terrorist leader Osama bin Laden, an international force overthrew the Taliban regime and a coalition government was set up.

Afghanistan is one of the world's poorest countries. About 60% of the people live by farming. Many people are semi-nomadic herders. Natural gas is produced, together with some coal, copper, gold, precious stones and salt.

AREA 652,090 sq km [251,772 sq mi] **POPULATION** 26,813,000
CAPITAL (POPULATION) Kabul (1,565,000)
GOVERNMENT Islamic state **ETHNIC GROUPS** Pashtun ('Pathan') 38%, Tajik 25%, Hazara 19%, Uzbek 6%, others 12%
LANGUAGES Pashtu, Dari/Persian (both official), Uzbek
RELIGIONS Islam (Sunni Muslim 84%, Shiite Muslim 15%)
CURRENCY Afghani = 100 puls

ALBANIA

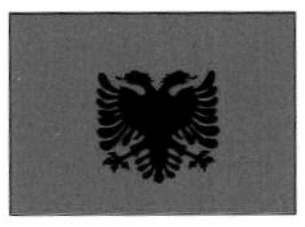

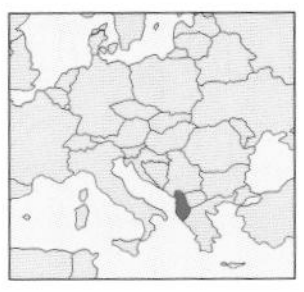

GEOGRAPHY The Republic of Albania lies in the Balkan peninsula, facing the Adriatic Sea. About 70% of the land is mountainous, but most Albanians live in the west on the coastal lowlands.

The coastal areas of Albania experience a typical Mediterranean climate, with fairly dry, sunny summers and cool, moist winters. The mountains have a severe climate, with heavy winter snowfalls.

POLITICS & ECONOMY Albania is Europe's poorest country. Formerly a Communist regime, Albania introduced a multiparty system in the early 1990s. The change proved difficult. But, following elections in 1997, a socialist government committed to a market system took office. In 2001, the stability of the region was threatened when Albanian-speaking Kosovars and Macedonians, many of whom favoured the creation of a Greater Macedonia, fought with government forces in north-western Macedonia.

In the early 1990s, agriculture employed 56% of the people. The land was divided into large collective and state farms, but private ownership has been encouraged since 1991. Albania has some minerals and chromite, copper and nickel are exported.

AREA 28,750 sq km [11,100 sq mi] **POPULATION** 3,510,000
CAPITAL (POPULATION) Tirana (251,000) **GOVERNMENT** Multiparty republic **ETHNIC GROUPS** Albanian 95%, Greek 3%, Macedonian, Vlachs, Gypsy **LANGUAGES** Albanian (official) **RELIGIONS** Many people say they are non-believers; of the believers, 65% follow Islam and 33% follow Christianity (Orthodox 20%, Roman Catholic 13%)
CURRENCY Lek = 100 qindars

ALGERIA

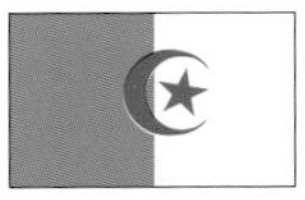

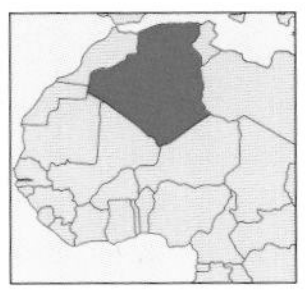

GEOGRAPHY The People's Democratic Republic of Algeria is Africa's second largest country after Sudan. Most Algerians live in the north, on the fertile coastal plains and hill country bordering the Mediterranean Sea. Four-fifths of Algeria is in the Sahara. The coast has a Mediterranean climate, but the arid Sahara is hot by day and cool at night.

POLITICS & ECONOMY France ruled Algeria from 1830 until 1962, when the socialist FLN (National Liberation Front) formed a one-party government. Following the recognition of opposition parties in 1989, a Muslim group, the FIS (Islamic Salvation Front), won an election in 1991. The FLN cancelled the elections and civil conflict broke out. About 100,000 people were killed in the 1990s. In 1999, following the withdrawal of the other candidates who alleged fraud, Abdelaziz Bouteflika, who was assumed to be favoured by the army, was elected president. Bouteflika's peace offensive reduced the violence, but sporadic killings continued into 2001.

Algeria is a developing country, whose chief resources are oil and natural gas, which were discovered in the Sahara in 1956. The natural gas reserves are among the world's largest, and gas and oil account for 90% of Algeria's exports. Cement, iron and steel, textiles and vehicles are manufactured. Barley, citrus fruits, dates, potatoes and wheat are the major crops.

AREA 2,381,740 sq km [919,590 sq mi] **POPULATION** 31,736,000
CAPITAL (POPULATION) Algiers (1,722,000)
GOVERNMENT Socialist republic **ETHNIC GROUPS** Arab-Berber 99%
LANGUAGES Arabic (official), Berber, French **RELIGIONS** Sunni Muslim 99% **CURRENCY** Algerian dinar = 100 centimes

AMERICAN SAMOA

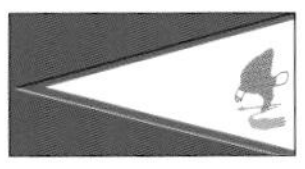

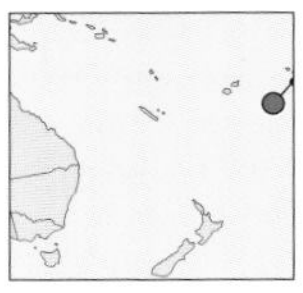

An 'unincorporated territory' of the United States, American Samoa lies in the south-central Pacific Ocean.

AREA 200 sq km [77 sq mi]
POPULATION 67,000 **CAPITAL** Pago Pago

ANDORRA

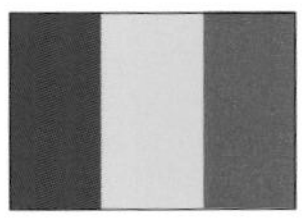

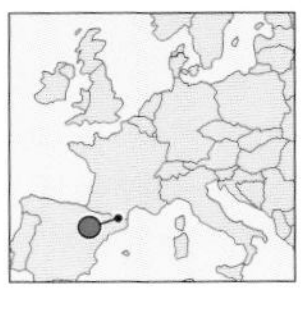

A mini-state situated in the Pyrenees Mountains, Andorra is a co-principality whose main activity is tourism. Most Andorrans live in the six valleys (the Valls) that drain into the River Valira.

AREA 453 sq km [175 sq mi]
POPULATION 68,000 **CAPITAL** Andorra La Vella

ANGOLA

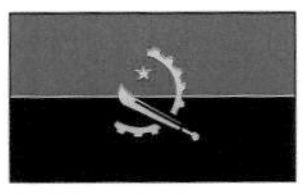

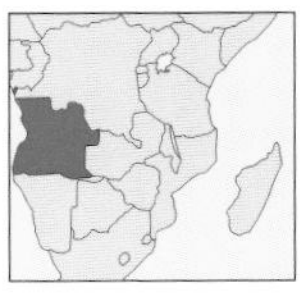

GEOGRAPHY The Republic of Angola is a large country in south-western Africa. Much of the country is part of the plateau that forms most of southern Africa, with a narrow coastal plain in the west.

Angola has a tropical climate, with temperatures of over 20°C [68°F] throughout the year, though the highest areas are cooler. The coastal regions are dry, but the rainfall increases to the north and east.

POLITICS & ECONOMY A former Portuguese colony, Angola gained its independence in 1975, after which rival nationalist forces began a struggle for power. A long-running civil war developed which, despite a cease-fire in the mid-1990s, continued until 2002, when the rebel leader, Jonas Savimbi, was killed in action and his successors negotiated peace.

Angola is a developing country, where 70% of the people are poor farmers. The main food crops are cassava and maize. Coffee is exported. Angola has much economic potential. It has oil reserves near Luanda and in the Cabinda enclave, which is separated from Angola by a strip of land belonging to Congo (Dem. Rep.). Oil is the leading export. Angola also produces diamonds and has reserves of copper, manganese and phosphates.

AREA 1,246,700 sq km [481,351 sq mi] **POPULATION** 10,366,000
CAPITAL (POPULATION) Luanda (2,250,000)
GOVERNMENT Multiparty republic
ETHNIC GROUPS Ovimbundu 37%, Kimbundu 25%, Bakongo 13%, others 25% **LANGUAGES** Portuguese (official), many others
RELIGIONS Traditional beliefs 47%, Roman Catholic 38%, Protestant 15%
CURRENCY Kwanza = 100 lwei

ANGUILLA

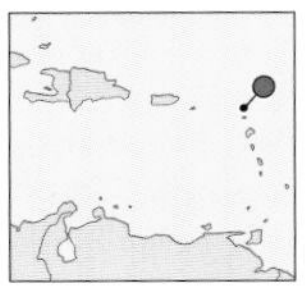

Formerly part of St Kitts and Nevis, Anguilla, the most northerly of the Leeward Islands, became a British dependency (now a British overseas territory) in 1980. The main source of revenue is now tourism, although lobster still accounts for half the island's exports.

AREA 96 sq km [37 sq mi] **POPULATION** 12,000
CAPITAL The Valley

ANTIGUA & BARBUDA

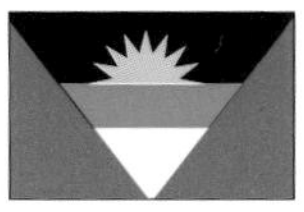

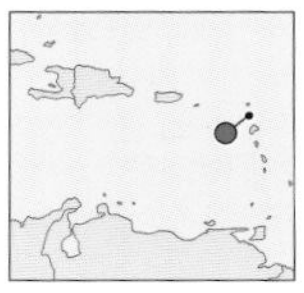

A former British dependency in the Caribbean, Antigua and Barbuda became independent in 1981. Tourism is the main industry, though sugar is an important product.

AREA 442 sq km [170 sq mi]
POPULATION 67,000 **CAPITAL** St John's

ARGENTINA

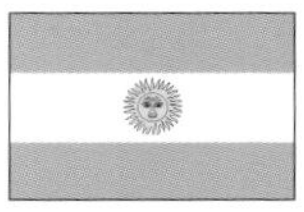

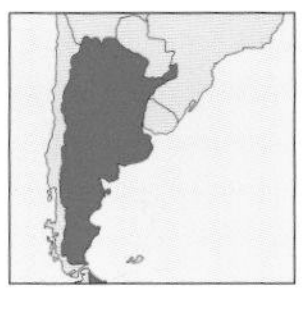

GEOGRAPHY The Argentine Republic is South America's second largest and the world's eighth largest country. The high Andes range in the west contains Mount Aconcagua, the highest peak in the Americas. In southern Argentina, the Andes Mountains overlook Patagonia, a plateau region. In east-central Argentina lies a fertile plain called the pampas.

The climate varies from subtropical in the north to temperate in the south. Rainfall is abundant in the north-east, but is lower to the west and south. Patagonia is a dry region, crossed by rivers that rise in the Andes.

POLITICS & ECONOMY Argentina became independent from Spain in the early 19th century, but it later suffered from instability and periods of military rule. In 1982, Argentina invaded the Falkland (Malvinas) Islands, but Britain regained the islands later in the year. Elections were held in 1983 and a new constitution was adopted in 1994.

According to the World Bank, Argentina is an 'upper-middle-income' developing country. Large areas are fertile and the main agricultural products are beef, maize and wheat. But about 87% of the people live in cities and towns. Industries include food processing and the manufacture of cars, electrical equipment and textiles. Oil is the chief natural resource. Major exports include meat, wheat, maize, vegetable oils, hides and skins, and wool. In 1991, Argentina. Brazil, Paraguay and Uruguay set up Mercosur, an alliance aimed to create a common market. However, in late 2001, a severe economic crisis forced the government to devalue the peso.

AREA 2,766,890 sq km [1,068,296 sq mi] **POPULATION** 37,385,000
CAPITAL (POPULATION) Buenos Aires (10,990,000)
GOVERNMENT Federal republic **ETHNIC GROUPS** European 97%, Mestizo, Amerindian **LANGUAGES** Spanish (official)
RELIGIONS Roman Catholic 92%, Protestant 2%, Jewish 2%
CURRENCY Peso = 10,000 australs

ARMENIA

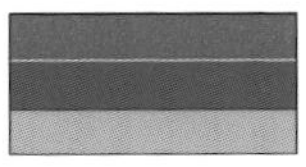

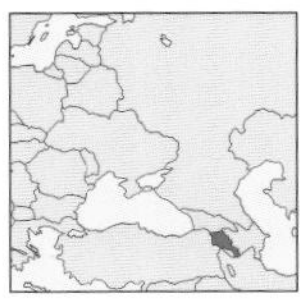

GEOGRAPHY The Republic of Armenia is a landlocked country in south-western Asia. Most of Armenia consists of a rugged plateau, criss-crossed by long faults (cracks). Movements along the faults cause earthquakes. The highest point is Mount Aragats, at 4,090 m [13,419 ft] above sea level.

The height of the land, which averages 1,500 m [4,920 ft] above sea level gives rise to severe winters and cool summers. The highest peaks are snow-capped, but the total yearly rainfall is generally low.

POLITICS & ECONOMY In 1920, Armenia became a Communist republic and, in 1922, it became, with Azerbaijan and Georgia, part of the Transcaucasian Republic within the Soviet Union. But the three territories became separate Soviet Socialist Republics in 1936. After the break-up of the Soviet Union in 1991, Armenia became an independent republic. Fighting broke out over Nagorno-Karabakh, an area enclosed by Azerbaijan where the majority of the people are Armenians. In 1992, Armenia occupied the territory between it and Nagorno-Karabakh. A cease-fire agreed in 1994 left Armenia in control of about 20% of Azerbaijan's land area. Talks aimed at settling the dispute failed in 2001.

The World Bank classifies Armenia as a 'lower-middle-income' economy. The conflict has badly damaged the economy, but the government has encouraged free enterprise, selling farmland and government-owned businesses.

AREA 29,800 sq km [11,506 sq mi] **POPULATION** 3,336,000
CAPITAL (POPULATION) Yerevan (1,256,000)
GOVERNMENT Multiparty republic
ETHNIC GROUPS Armenian 93%, Azerbaijani 3%, Russian, Kurd
LANGUAGES Armenian (official) **RELIGIONS** Armenian Orthodox
CURRENCY Dram = 100 couma

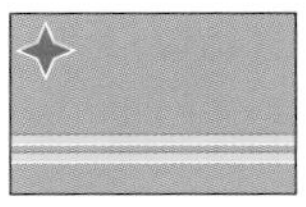
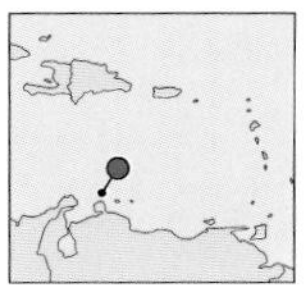

ARUBA

Formerly part of the Netherlands Antilles, Aruba (the most western of the Lesser Antilles) became a separate self-governing Dutch territory in 1986.

AREA 193 SQ KM [75 SQ MI]
POPULATION 70,000 **CAPITAL** ORANJESTAD

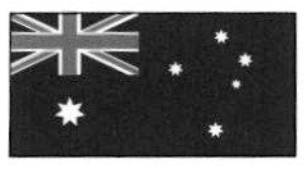
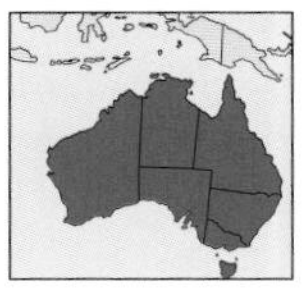

AUSTRALIA

GEOGRAPHY The Commonwealth of Australia, the world's sixth largest country, is also a continent. Australia is the flattest of the continents and the main highland area is in the east. Here the Great Dividing Range separates the eastern coastal plains from the Central Plains. This range extends from the Cape York Peninsula to Victoria in the far south. The longest rivers, the Murray and Darling, drain the south-eastern part of the Central Plains. The Western Plateau makes up two-thirds of Australia. A few mountain ranges break the monotony of the generally flat landscape.

Only 10% of Australia has an average yearly rainfall of more than 1,000 mm [39 in]. These areas include the tropical north, where Darwin is situated, the north-east coast, and the south-east, where Sydney is located. The interior is dry, and water is quickly evaporated in the heat.

POLITICS & ECONOMY The Aboriginal people of Australia entered the continent from South-east Asia more than 50,000 years ago. The first European explorers were Dutch in the 17th century, but they did not settle. In 1770, the British Captain Cook explored the east coast and, in 1788, the first British settlement was established for convicts on the site of what is now Sydney. Australia has strong ties with the British Isles. But in the last 50 years, people from other parts of Europe and, most recently, from Asia have settled in Australia. Ties with Britain were also weakened by Britain's membership of the European Union. Many Australians believe that they should become more involved with the nations of eastern Asia and the Americas rather than with Europe. In 1999, Australia held a referendum on whether the country should become a republic or remain a constitutional monarchy. By a majority of about 55 to 45, the country retained its status as a monarchy.

Australia is a prosperous country. Crops can be grown on only 6% of the land, but dry pasture covers another 58%. Yet the country remains a major producer and exporter of farm products, particularly cattle, wheat and wool. Grapes grown for winemaking are also important. The country is a major producer of minerals, including bauxite, coal, copper, diamonds, gold, iron ore, manganese, nickel, silver, tin, tungsten and zinc. Australia also produces oil and natural gas. Metals, minerals and farm products account for the bulk of exports. Australia's imports are mostly manufactured products, although the country makes many factory products, especially consumer goods, such as foods and household articles. Major imports include machinery.

AREA 7,686,850 SQ KM [2,967,893 SQ MI] **POPULATION** 19,358,000 **CAPITAL (POPULATION)** CANBERRA (325,000) **GOVERNMENT** FEDERAL CONSTITUTIONAL MONARCHY **ETHNIC GROUPS** CAUCASIAN 92%, ASIAN 7.5%, ABORIGINAL 1.5% **LANGUAGES** ENGLISH (OFFICIAL) **RELIGIONS** ROMAN CATHOLIC 26%, ANGLICAN 26%, OTHER CHRISTIAN 24%, NON-CHRISTIAN 24% **CURRENCY** AUSTRALIAN DOLLAR = 100 CENTS

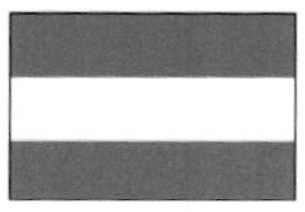
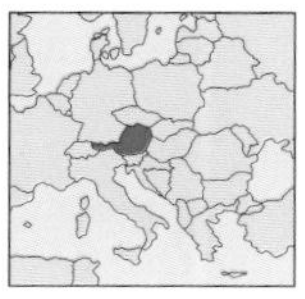

AUSTRIA

GEOGRAPHY Austria is a landlocked country in Europe. Northern Austria contains the valley of the River Danube, which flows from Germany to the Black Sea, and the Vienna basin. Southern Austria contains ranges of the Alps, their highest point at Grossglockner, 3,797 m [12,457 ft] above sea level.

The climate is influenced by westerly and easterly winds. Moist westerly winds bring rain and snow, and moderate temperatures. Dry easterly winds bring cold weather in winter and hot weather in summer.

POLITICS & ECONOMY Formerly part of the monarchy of Austria-Hungary, which collapsed in 1918, Austria was annexed by Germany in 1938. After World War II, the Allies partitioned and occupied the country. In 1955, Austria became a neutral federal republic. It joined the European Union on 1 January 1995, but was a focus of controversy when, in 2000, a coalition government was formed by the right-wing People's Party and the extreme right-wing Freedom Party.

Austria is a prosperous country. It has plenty of hydroelectric power, as well as some oil, gas and coal reserves. The country's leading economic activity is manufacturing metals and metal products. Crops are grown on 18% of the land, and another 24% is pasture. Dairy and livestock farming are the leading activities. Major crops include barley, potatoes, rye, sugar beet and wheat. Tourism is a major activity in this scenic country.

AREA 83,850 SQ KM [32,374 SQ MI] **POPULATION** 8,151,000 **CAPITAL (POPULATION)** VIENNA (1,560,000) **GOVERNMENT** FEDERAL REPUBLIC **ETHNIC GROUPS** AUSTRIAN 93%, CROATIAN, SLOVENE, OTHER **LANGUAGES** GERMAN (OFFICIAL) **RELIGIONS** ROMAN CATHOLIC 78%, PROTESTANT 5%, ISLAM **CURRENCY** EURO; SCHILLING = 100 GROSCHEN

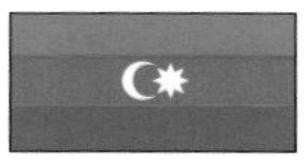
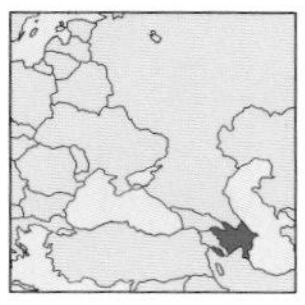

AZERBAIJAN

GEOGRAPHY The Azerbaijani Republic is a country in the south-west of Asia, facing the Caspian Sea to the east. It includes an area called the Naxçivan Autonomous Republic, which is completely cut off from the rest of Azerbaijan by Armenian territory. The Caucasus Mountains border Russia in the north.

Azerbaijan has hot summers and cool winters. The plains are fairly dry, but the mountains are rainy.

POLITICS & ECONOMY After the Russian Revolution of 1917, attempts were made to form a Transcaucasian Federation made up of Armenia, Azerbaijan and Georgia. When this failed, Azerbaijanis set up an independent state. But Russian forces occupied the area in 1920. In 1922, the Communists set up a Transcaucasian Republic consisting of Armenia, Azerbaijan and Georgia under Russian control. In 1936, the three areas became separate Soviet Socialist Republics within the Soviet Union. In 1991, following the break-up of the Soviet Union, Azerbaijan became an independent nation. After independence, the country's economic progress was slow, partly because of the conflict with Armenia over the enclave of Nagorno-Karabakh, a region in Azerbaijan where the majority of people are Armenians. A cease-fire in 1994 left Armenia in control of about 20% of Azerbaijan's area, including Nagorno-Karabakh. Attempts to resolve the problem failed in 2001.

In the mid-1990s, the World Bank classified Azerbaijan as a 'lower-middle-income' economy. Yet by the late 1990s, the enormous oil reserves in the Baku area, on the Caspian Sea and in the sea itself, held out great promise for the future. Oil extraction and manufacturing, including oil refining and the production of chemicals, machinery and textiles, are now the most valuable activities.

AREA 86,600 SQ KM [33,436 SQ MI] **POPULATION** 7,771,000 **CAPITAL (POPULATION)** BAKU (1,713,000) **GOVERNMENT** FEDERAL MULTIPARTY REPUBLIC **ETHNIC GROUPS** AZERI 90%, DAGESTANI 3%, RUSSIAN, ARMENIAN, OTHER **LANGUAGES** AZERBAIJANI (OFFICIAL) **RELIGIONS** ISLAM 93%, RUSSIAN ORTHODOX 2%, ARMENIAN ORTHODOX 2% **CURRENCY** MANAT = 100 GOPIK

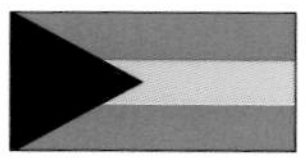
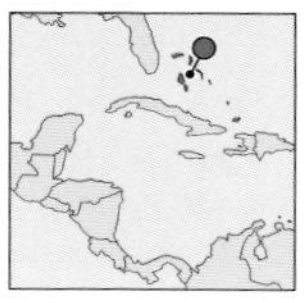

BAHAMAS

A coral-limestone archipelago off the coast of Florida, the Bahamas became independent from Britain in 1973, and has since developed strong ties with the United States. Tourism and banking are major activities.

AREA 13,940 SQ KM [5,380 SQ MI]
POPULATION 298,000 **CAPITAL** NASSAU

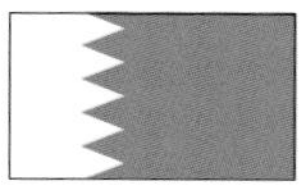
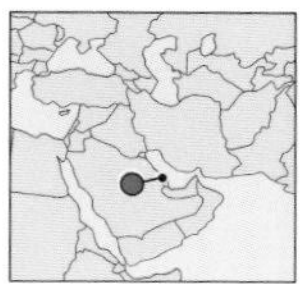

BAHRAIN

The Emirate of Bahrain, an island nation in the Gulf, became independent from the UK in 1971. Oil accounts for 80% of the country's exports.

AREA 678 SQ KM [262 SQ MI]
POPULATION 645,000 **CAPITAL** MANAMA

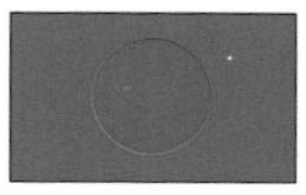
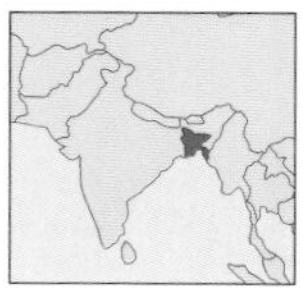

BANGLADESH

GEOGRAPHY The People's Republic of Bangladesh is one of the world's most densely populated countries. Apart from hilly regions in the far north-east and south-east, most of the land is flat and covered by fertile alluvium spread over the land by the Ganges, Brahmaputra and Meghna rivers. These rivers overflow when they are swollen by the annual monsoon rains. Floods also occur along the coast, 575 km [357 mi] long, when cyclones (hurricanes) drive seawater inland. Bangladesh has a tropical monsoon climate. Dry northerly winds blow in winter, but, in summer, moist winds from the south bring monsoon rains. Heavy monsoon rains cause floods. In 1998, about two-thirds of the entire country was submerged, causing great suffering.

POLITICS & ECONOMY In 1947, British India was partitioned between the mainly Hindu India and the Muslim Pakistan. Pakistan consisted of two parts, West and East Pakistan, which were separated by about 1,600 km [1,000 mi] of Indian territory. Differences developed between West and East Pakistan. In 1971, the East Pakistanis rebelled. After a nine-month civil war, they declared East Pakistan to be a separate nation named Bangladesh.

Bangladesh is one of the world's poorest countries. Its economy depends mainly on agriculture, which employs over half the population. Bangladesh is the world's fourth largest producer of rice.

AREA 144,000 SQ KM [55,598 SQ MI] **POPULATION** 131,270,000 **CAPITAL (POPULATION)** DHAKA (7,832,000) **GOVERNMENT** MULTIPARTY REPUBLIC **ETHNIC GROUPS** BENGALI 98%, TRIBAL GROUPS **LANGUAGES** BENGALI, ENGLISH (BOTH OFFICIAL) **RELIGIONS** ISLAM 83%, HINDUISM 16% **CURRENCY** TAKA = 100 PAISAS

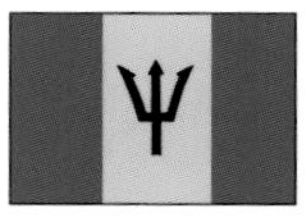
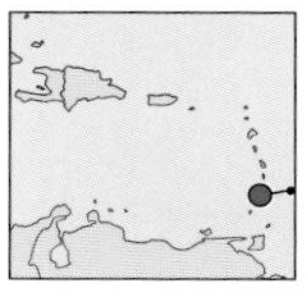

BARBADOS

The most easterly Caribbean country, Barbados became independent from the UK in 1960. A densely populated island, Barbados is prosperous by comparison with most Caribbean countries.

AREA 430 SQ KM [166 SQ MI]
POPULATION 275,000 **CAPITAL** BRIDGETOWN

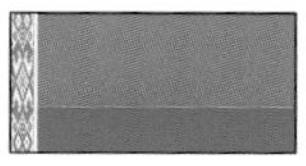
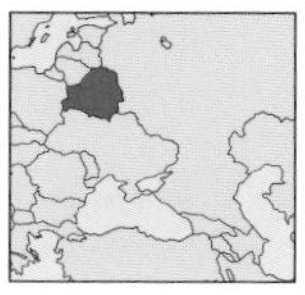

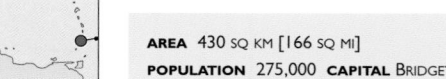

BELARUS

GEOGRAPHY The Republic of Belarus is a landlocked country in Eastern Europe. The land is low-lying and mostly flat. In the south, much of the land is marshy and this area contains Europe's largest marsh and peat bog, the Pripet Marshes.

The climate of Belarus is affected by both the moderating influence of the Baltic Sea and continental conditions to the east. The winters are cold and the summers warm.

POLITICS & ECONOMY In 1918, Belarus (White Russia) became an independent republic, but Russia invaded the country and, in 1919, a Communist state was set up. In 1922, Belarus became a founder republic of the Soviet Union. In 1991, Belarus again became an independent republic, though Belarus continued to support reunification with Russia. In 1998, Belarus and Russia set up a 'union state', with plans to have a common currency, a customs union, and common foreign and defence policies. But any surrender of sovereignty was not anticipated. A union treaty aimed at a merger of the two countries, but in reality largely symbolic, was signed in 1999.

The World Bank classifies Belarus as an 'upper-middle-income' economy. Like other former republics of the Soviet Union, it faces many problems in turning from Communism to a free-market economy.

AREA 207,600 SQ KM [80,154 SQ MI] **POPULATION** 10,350,000 **CAPITAL (POPULATION)** MINSK (1,717,000) **GOVERNMENT** MULTIPARTY REPUBLIC **ETHNIC GROUPS** BELARUSSIAN 81%, RUSSIAN 11%, POLISH, UKRAINIAN **LANGUAGES** BELARUSSIAN, RUSSIAN (BOTH OFFICIAL) **RELIGIONS** EASTERN ORTHODOX 80%, OTHER 20% **CURRENCY** BELARUSSIAN ROUBLE = 100 KOPECKS

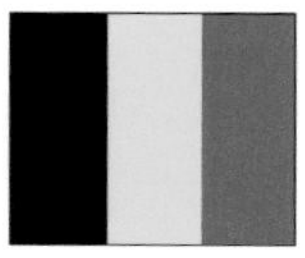
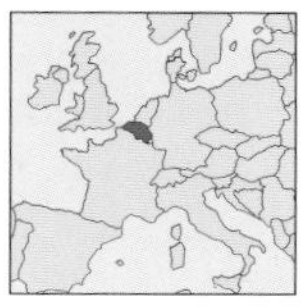

BELGIUM

GEOGRAPHY The Kingdom of Belgium is a densely populated country in western Europe. Behind the coastline on the North Sea, which is 63 km [39 mi] long, lie its coastal plains. Central Belgium consists of low plateaux and the only highland region is the Ardennes in the south-east.

Belgium has a cool, temperate climate. Moist winds from the Atlantic Ocean bring fairly heavy rain, especially in the Ardennes. In January and February much snow falls on the Ardennes.

POLITICS & ECONOMY In 1815, Belgium and the Netherlands united as the 'low countries', but Belgium became independent in 1830. Belgium's economy was weakened by the two World

Wars, but, from 1945, the country recovered quickly, first through collaboration with the Netherlands and Luxembourg, which formed a customs union called Benelux, and later through its membership of the European Union.

A central political problem in Belgium has been the tension between the Dutch-speaking Flemings and the French-speaking Walloons. In the 1970s, the government divided the country into three economic regions: Dutch-speaking Flanders, French-speaking Wallonia and bilingual Brussels. In 1993, Belgium adopted a federal system of government. Each of the regions now has its own parliament, which is responsible for local matters. Elections under this system were held in 1995 and 1999.

Belgium is a major trading nation, with a highly developed economy. Most of the materials needed for manufacturing are imported. Its main products include chemicals, processed food and steel. The textile industry is also important and has existed since medieval times in the Belgian province of Flanders.

Agriculture employs only 3% of the people, but Belgian farmers produce most of the food needed by the people. Barley and wheat are the chief crops, followed by flax, hops, potatoes and sugar beet, but the most valuable activities are dairy farming and livestock rearing.

AREA 30,510 sq km [11,780 sq mi]
POPULATION 10,259,000
CAPITAL (POPULATION) Brussels (948,000)
GOVERNMENT Federal constitutional monarchy
ETHNIC GROUPS Belgian 91% (Fleming 58%, Walloon 31%), other 11% **LANGUAGES** Dutch, French, German (all official)
RELIGIONS Roman Catholic 75%, other 25%
CURRENCY Euro = 100 cents

BELIZE

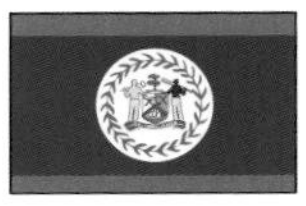

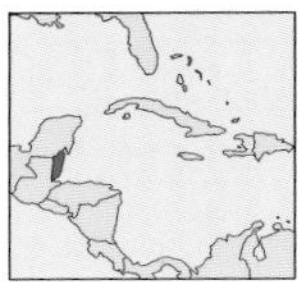

GEOGRAPHY Behind the swampy coastal plain in the south, the land rises to the low Maya Mountains, which reach a height of 1,120 m [3,674 ft] at Victoria Peak. The north is mostly low-lying and swampy.

Belize has a tropical, humid climate. Temperatures are high throughout the year and the average yearly rainfall ranges from 1,300 mm [51 in] in the north to over 3,800 mm [150 in] in the south.

POLITICS & ECONOMY From 1862, Belize (then called British Honduras) was a British colony. Full independence was achieved in 1981, but Guatemala, which had claimed the area since the early 19th century, opposed Belize's independence and British troops remained to prevent a possible invasion. In 1983, Guatemala reduced its claim to the southern fifth of Belize. Improved relations in the early 1990s led Guatemala to recognize Belize's independence and, in 1992, Britain agreed to withdraw its troops from the country.

The World Bank classifies Belize as a 'lower-middle-income' developing country. Its economy is based on agriculture and sugar cane is the chief commercial crop and export. Other crops include bananas, beans, citrus fruits, maize and rice. Forestry, fishing and tourism are other important activities.

AREA 22,960 sq km [8,865 sq mi] **POPULATION** 256,000
CAPITAL (POPULATION) Belmopan (4,000)
GOVERNMENT Constitutional monarchy **ETHNIC GROUPS** Mestizo (Spanish-Indian) 44%, Creole (mainly African American) 30%, Mayan Indian 11%, Garifuna (Black-Carib Indian) 7%, other 8%
LANGUAGES English (official), Creole, Spanish **RELIGIONS** Roman Catholic 62%, Protestant 30% **CURRENCY** Belize dollar = 100 cents

BENIN

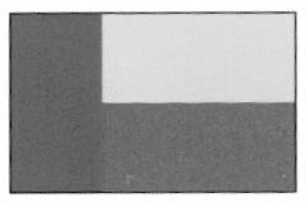

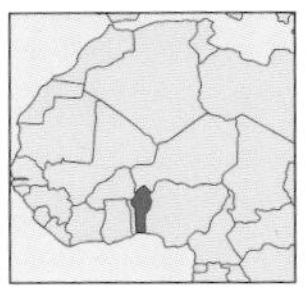

GEOGRAPHY The Republic of Benin is one of Africa's smallest countries. It extends north–south for about 620 km [390 mi]. Lagoons line the short coastline, and the country has no natural harbours.

Benin has a hot, wet climate. The average annual temperature on the coast is about 25°C [77°F], and the average rainfall is about 1,330 mm [52 in]. The inland plains are wetter than the coast.

POLITICS & ECONOMY After slavery was ended in the 19th century, the French began to gain influence in the area. Benin became self-governing in 1958 and fully independent in 1960. After much instability and many changes of government, a military group took over in 1972. The country, renamed Benin in 1975, became a one-party socialist state. Socialism was abandoned in 1989, and multiparty elections were held in 1991, 1996, 1999 and 2001.

Benin is a poor developing country. About 70% of the people earn their living by farming, though many remain at subsistence level. The chief exports include cotton, petroleum and palm products. Cocoa, coffee, groundnuts (peanuts), tobacco and shea nuts are also grown for export.

AREA 112,620 sq km [43,483 sq mi] **POPULATION** 6,591,000
CAPITAL (POPULATION) Porto-Novo (179,000)
GOVERNMENT Multiparty republic **ETHNIC GROUPS** Fon, Adja, Bariba, Yoruba, Fulani **LANGUAGES** French (official), Fon, Adja, Yoruba
RELIGIONS Traditional beliefs 50%, Christianity 30%, Islam 20%
CURRENCY CFA franc = 100 centimes

BERMUDA

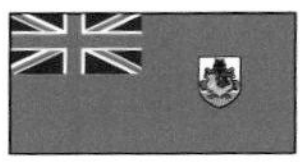

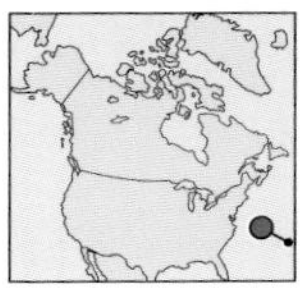

A group of about 150 small islands situated 920 km [570 mi] east of the USA. Bermuda remains Britain's oldest overseas territory, but it has a long tradition of self-government.

AREA 53 sq km [20 sq mi] **POPULATION** 64,000
CAPITAL Hamilton

BHUTAN

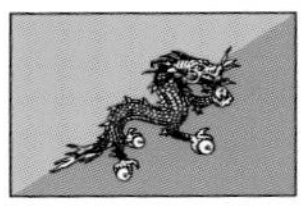

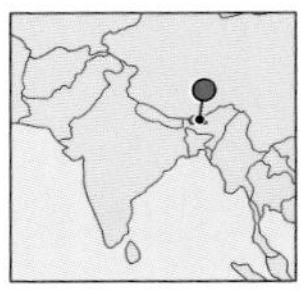

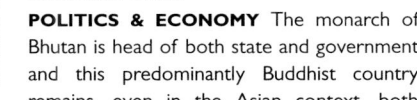

GEOGRAPHY A mountainous, isolated Himalayan country located between India and Tibet. The climate is similar to that of Nepal, being dependent on altitude and affected by monsoonal winds.

POLITICS & ECONOMY The monarch of Bhutan is head of both state and government and this predominantly Buddhist country remains, even in the Asian context, both conservative and poor. Bhutan is the world's most 'rural' country, with about 87% of the population dependent on agriculture and only 7% living in towns.

AREA 47,000 sq km [18,147 sq mi] **POPULATION** 2,049,000
CAPITAL (POPULATION) Thimphu (30,000)
GOVERNMENT Constitutional monarchy **ETHNIC GROUPS** Bhutanese 50%, Nepali 35% **LANGUAGES** Dzongkha (official) **RELIGIONS** Buddhism 75%, Hindu 25% **CURRENCY** Ngultrum = 100 chetrum

BOLIVIA

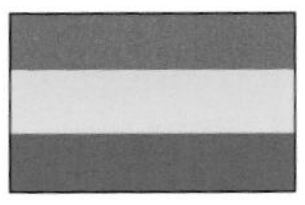

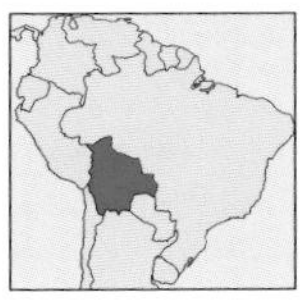

GEOGRAPHY The Republic of Bolivia is a landlocked country which straddles the Andes Mountains in central South America. The Andes rise to a height of 6,542 m [21,464 ft] at Nevado Sajama in the west.

About 40% of Bolivians live on a high plateau called the Altiplano in the Andean region, while the sparsely populated east is essentially a vast lowland plain.

The Bolivian climate is greatly affected by altitude, with the Andean peaks permanently snow-covered, and the eastern plains remaining hot and humid.

POLITICS & ECONOMY American Indians have lived in Bolivia for at least 10,000 years. The main groups today are the Aymara and Quechua people.

In the last 50 years, Bolivia, an independent country since 1825, has been ruled by a succession of civilian and military governments, which violated human rights. Constitutional government was restored in 1982. From the 1980s, Bolivia has pursued economic reforms and free-market policies.

Bolivia is one of the poorest countries in South America. It has several natural resources, including tin, silver and natural gas, but the chief activity is agriculture, which employs 47% of the people. Coca, which is used to make cocaine, is exported illegally. In the early 2000s, the government was trying to stamp out the coca trade, while experts estimated that oil and gas were beginning to replace coca as the chief export.

AREA 1,098,580 sq km [424,162 sq mi] **POPULATION** 8,300,000
CAPITAL (POPULATION) La Paz (1,126,000)
GOVERNMENT Multiparty republic **ETHNIC GROUPS** Mestizo 30%, Quechua 30%, Aymara 25%, White 15%
LANGUAGES Spanish, Aymara, Quechua (all official)
RELIGIONS Roman Catholic 95%
CURRENCY Boliviano = 100 centavos

BOSNIA-HERZEGOVINA

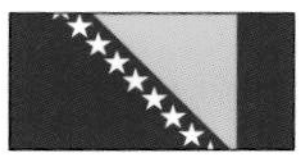

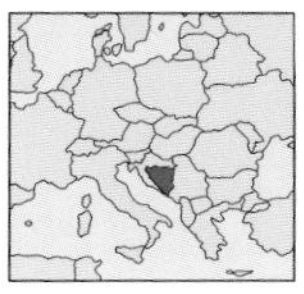

GEOGRAPHY The Republic of Bosnia-Herzegovina is one of the five republics to emerge from the former Federal People's Republic of Yugoslavia. Much of the country is mountainous or hilly, with an arid limestone plateau in the south-west. The River Sava, which forms most of the northern border with Croatia, is a tributary of the River Danube. Because of the country's odd shape, the coastline is limited to a short stretch of 20 km [13 mi] on the Adriatic coast.

A Mediterranean climate, with dry, sunny summers and moist, mild winters, prevails only near the coast. Inland, the weather is more severe, with hot, dry summers and bitterly cold, snowy winters.

POLITICS & ECONOMY In 1918, Bosnia-Herzegovina became part of the Kingdom of the Serbs, Croats and Slovenes, which was renamed Yugoslavia in 1929. Germany occupied the area during World War II (1939–45). From 1945, Communist governments ruled Yugoslavia as a federation containing six republics, one of which was Bosnia-Herzegovina. In the 1980s, the country faced problems as Communist policies proved unsuccessful and differences arose between ethnic groups.

In 1990, free elections were held in Bosnia-Herzegovina and the non-Communists won a majority. A Muslim, Alija Izetbegovic, was elected president. In 1991, Croatia and Slovenia, other parts of the former Yugoslavia, declared themselves independent. In 1992, Bosnia-Herzegovina held a vote on independence. Most Bosnian Serbs boycotted the vote, while the Muslims and Bosnian Croats voted in favour. Many Bosnian Serbs, opposed to independence, started a war against the non-Serbs. They soon occupied more than two-thirds of the land. The Bosnian Serbs were accused of 'ethnic cleansing' – that is, the killing or expulsion of other ethnic groups from Serb-occupied areas. The war was later extended when Croat forces seized other parts of the country.

In 1995, the warring parties agreed to a solution to the conflict. This involved keeping the present boundaries of Bosnia-Herzegovina, but dividing it into two self-governing provinces, one Bosnian Serb and the other Muslim-Croat, under a central, unified, multi-ethnic government. Elections were held in 1996 and 1998 under this new arrangement.

The economy of Bosnia-Herzegovina, the least developed of the six republics of the former Yugoslavia apart from Macedonia, was shattered by the war in the early 1990s. Before the war, manufactures were the main exports, including electrical, machinery and transport equipment, and textiles. Farm products include fruits, maize, tobacco, vegetables and wheat, but food has to be imported.

AREA 51,129 sq km [19,745 sq mi] **POPULATION** 3,922,000
CAPITAL (POPULATION) Sarajevo (526,000)
GOVERNMENT Federal republic **ETHNIC GROUPS** Bosnian 49%, Serb 31%, Croat 17% **LANGUAGES** Serbo-Croatian **RELIGIONS** Islam 40%, Serbian Orthodox 31%, Roman Catholic 15%, Protestant 4%
CURRENCY Convertible mark = 100 paras

BOTSWANA

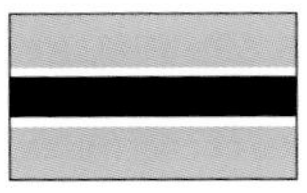

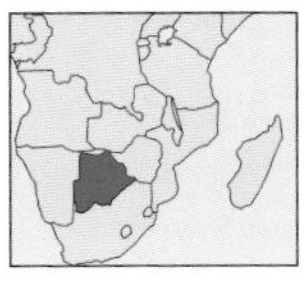

GEOGRAPHY The Republic of Botswana is a landlocked country in southern Africa. The Kalahari, a semi-desert area covered mostly by grasses and thorn scrub, covers much of the country. Most of the south has no permanent streams. But large depressions in the north are inland drainage basins. In one of them, the Okavango River, which rises in Angola, forms a large, swampy delta.

Temperatures are high in the summer months (October to April), but the winter months are much cooler. In winter, night-time temperatures sometimes drop below freezing point. The average annual rainfall ranges from over 400 mm [16 in] in the east to less than 200 mm [8 in] in the south-west.

POLITICS & ECONOMY The earliest inhabitants of the region were the San, who are also called Bushmen. They had a nomadic way of life, hunting wild animals and collecting wild plant foods.

Britain ruled the area as the Bechuanaland Protectorate between 1885 and 1966. When the country became independent, it was renamed Botswana. Since then, the country has been a stable, multiparty democracy. However, a major setback occurred in the early 21st century, when health officials announced that around 25% of the people were infected with HIV/AIDS. In 1966, Botswana was extremely poor, depending on meat and live cattle for its exports. But the discovery of minerals, including coal, cobalt, copper, diamonds and nickel, has boosted the economy. About 22% of the people now depend on agriculture, raising cattle and growing crops. Industries include the processing of farm products.

AREA 581,730 sq km [224,606 sq mi] **POPULATION** 1,586,000
CAPITAL (POPULATION) Gaborone (133,000)
GOVERNMENT Multiparty republic **ETHNIC GROUPS** Tswana 75%, Shona 12%, San (Bushmen) 3% **LANGUAGES** English (official), Setswana **RELIGIONS** Traditional beliefs 50%, Christianity 50%
CURRENCY Pula = 100 thebe

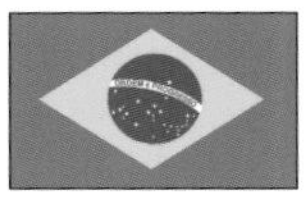
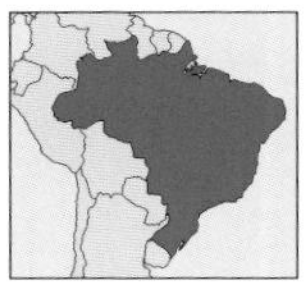

BRAZIL

GEOGRAPHY The Federative Republic of Brazil is the world's fifth largest country. It contains three main regions. The Amazon basin in the north covers more than half of Brazil. The Amazon, the world's second longest river, has a far greater volume than any other river. The second region, the north-east, consists of a coastal plain and the *sertão*, which is the name for the inland plateaux and hill country. The main river in this region is the São Francisco.

The third region is made up of the plateaux in the south-east. This region, which covers about a quarter of the country, is the most developed and densely populated part of Brazil. Its main river is the Paraná, which flows south through Argentina.

Manaus has high temperatures all through the year. The rainfall is heavy, though the period from June to September is drier than the rest of the year. The capital, Brasília, and the city Rio de Janeiro also have tropical climates, with much more marked dry seasons than Manaus. The far south has a temperate climate. The north-eastern interior is the driest region, with an average annual rainfall of only 250 mm [10 in] in places. The rainfall is also unreliable and severe droughts are common in this region.

POLITICS & ECONOMY The Portuguese explorer Pedro Alvarez Cabral claimed Brazil for Portugal in 1500. With Spain occupied in western South America, the Portuguese began to develop their colony, which was more than 90 times as big as Portugal. To do this, they enslaved many local Amerindian people and introduced about 4 million African slaves. Brazil declared itself an independent empire in 1822 and a republic in 1889. From the 1930s, Brazil faced periods of military rule and widespread corruption. Civilian rule was restored in 1985. Brazil adopted a new constitution in 1988, though it was amended in 1997 to allow presidents to serve for two four-year terms.

The United Nations has described Brazil as a 'Rapidly Industrializing Country', or RIC. Its total volume of production is one of the largest in the world. But many people, including poor farmers and residents of the *favelas* (city slums), do not share in the country's fast economic growth. Widespread poverty, together with high inflation and unemployment, cause political problems.

By the early 1990s, industry was the most valuable activity, employing 25% of the people. Brazil is among the world's top producers of bauxite, chrome, diamonds, gold, iron ore, manganese and tin. It is also a major manufacturing country. Its products include aircraft, cars, chemicals, processed food, including raw sugar, iron and steel, paper and textiles.

Brazil is one of the world's leading farming countries and agriculture employs 22% of the people. Coffee is a major export. Other leading products include bananas, citrus fruits, cocoa, maize, rice, soya beans and sugar cane. Brazil is also the top producer of eggs, meat and milk in South America.

Forestry is a major industry, though many people fear that the exploitation of the rainforests, with 1.5% to 4% of Brazil's forest being destroyed every year, is a disaster for the entire world.

AREA 8,511,970 sq km [3,286,472 sq mi] **POPULATION** 174,469,000
CAPITAL (POPULATION) Brasília (2,051,000)
GOVERNMENT Federal republic **ETHNIC GROUPS** White 55%, Mulatto 38%, African American 6%, other 1%
LANGUAGES Portuguese (official)
RELIGIONS Roman Catholic 80%
CURRENCY Real = 100 centavos

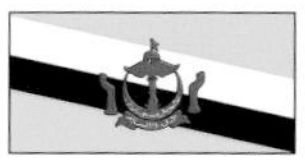
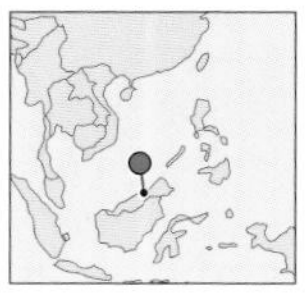

BRUNEI

The Islamic Sultanate of Brunei, a British protectorate until 1984, lies on the north coast of Borneo. The climate is tropical and rainforests cover large areas. Brunei is a prosperous country because of its oil and natural gas production, and the Sultan is said to be among the world's richest men.

AREA 5,770 sq km [2,228 sq mi] **POPULATION** 344,000
CAPITAL Bandar Seri Begawan

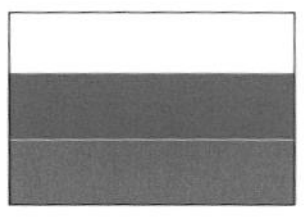
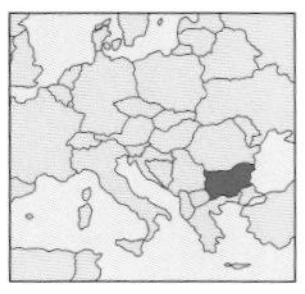

BULGARIA

GEOGRAPHY The Republic of Bulgaria is a country in the Balkan peninsula, facing the Black Sea in the east. The heart of Bulgaria is mountainous. The main ranges are the Balkan Mountains in the centre and the Rhodope (or Rhodopi) Mountains in the south.

Summers are hot and winters are cold, though seldom severe. The rainfall is moderate.

POLITICS & ECONOMY Ottoman Turks ruled Bulgaria from 1396 and ethnic Turks still form a sizeable minority in the country. In 1879, Bulgaria became a monarchy, and in 1908 it became fully independent. Bulgaria was an ally of Germany in World War I (1914–18) and again in World War II (1939–45). In 1944, Soviet troops invaded Bulgaria and, after the war, the monarchy was abolished and the country became a Communist ally of the Soviet Union. In the late 1980s, reforms in the Soviet Union led Bulgaria's government to introduce a multiparty system in 1990. A non-Communist government was elected in 1991, the first free elections in 44 years. Throughout the 1990s, Bulgaria faced many problems. In 2001, a coalition led by the former King Siméon, who had left Bulgaria in 1948, won the elections. Siméon became prime minister.

According to the World Bank, Bulgaria in the 1990s was a 'lower-middle-income' developing country. Bulgaria has some deposits of minerals, including brown coal, manganese and iron ore. But manufacturing is the leading economic activity, though problems arose in the early 1990s, because much industrial technology is outdated. The main products are chemicals, processed foods, metal products, machinery and textiles. Manufactures are the leading exports. Bulgaria trades mainly with countries in Eastern Europe.

AREA 110,910 sq km [42,822 sq mi] **POPULATION** 7,707,000
CAPITAL (POPULATION) Sofia (1,139,000) **GOVERNMENT** Multiparty republic **ETHNIC GROUPS** Bulgarian 83%, Turkish 8%, Gypsy 3%, Macedonian, Armenian, other **LANGUAGES** Bulgarian (official), Turkish **RELIGIONS** Christianity (Eastern Orthodox 87%), Islam 13%
CURRENCY Lev = 100 stotinki

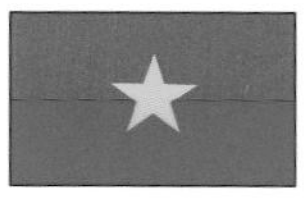
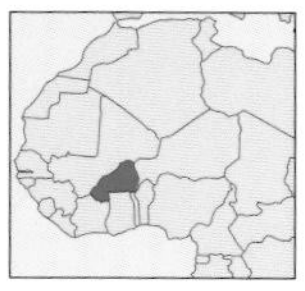

BURKINA FASO

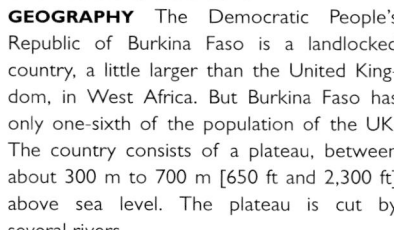

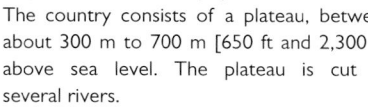

GEOGRAPHY The Democratic People's Republic of Burkina Faso is a landlocked country, a little larger than the United Kingdom, in West Africa. But Burkina Faso has only one-sixth of the population of the UK. The country consists of a plateau, between about 300 m to 700 m [650 ft and 2,300 ft] above sea level. The plateau is cut by several rivers.

The capital city, Ouagadougou, in central Burkina Faso, has high temperatures throughout the year. Most of the rain falls between May and September, but the rainfall is erratic and droughts are common.

POLITICS & ECONOMY The people of Burkina Faso are divided into two main groups. The Voltaic group includes the Mossi, who form the largest single group, and the Bobo. The French conquered the Mossi capital of Ouagadougou in 1897 and they made the area a protectorate. In 1919, the area became a French colony called Upper Volta. After independence in 1960, Upper Volta became a one-party state. But it was unstable – military groups seized power several times and political killings took place. In 1984, the country's name was changed to Burkina Faso. In 1991 and 1998, the former military leader, Captain Blaise Compaoré, was elected president, but the military continued to play an important part in the government.

Burkina Faso is one of the world's 20 poorest countries and has become very dependent on foreign aid. Most of Burkina Faso is dry with thin soils. The country's main food crops are beans, maize, millet, rice and sorghum. Cotton, groundnuts and shea nuts, whose seeds produce a fat used to make cooking oil and soap, are grown for sale abroad. Livestock are also an important export.

The country has few resources and manufacturing is on a small scale. There are some deposits of manganese, zinc, lead and nickel in the north of the country, but there is not yet a good enough transport system there. Many young men seek jobs abroad in Ghana and Ivory Coast. The money they send home to their families is important to the country's economy.

AREA 274,200 sq km [105,869 sq mi] **POPULATION** 12,272,000
CAPITAL (POPULATION) Ouagadougou (690,000)
GOVERNMENT Multiparty republic **ETHNIC GROUPS** Mossi 48%, Gurunsi, Senufo, Lobi, Bobo, Mande, Fulani **LANGUAGES** French (official), Mossi, Fulani **RELIGIONS** Islam 50%, traditional beliefs 40%, Christianity 10% **CURRENCY** CFA franc = 100 centimes

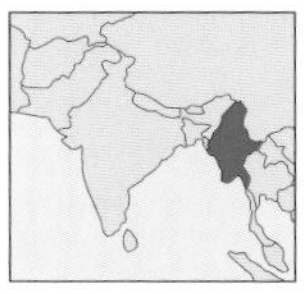

BURMA (MYANMAR)

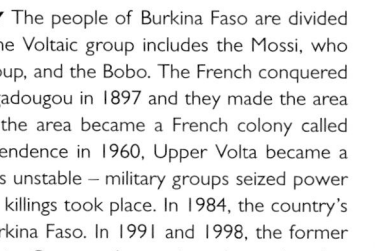

GEOGRAPHY The Union of Burma is now officially known as the Union of Myanmar; its name was changed in 1989. Mountains border the country in the east and west, with the highest mountains in the north. Burma's highest mountain is Hkakabo Razi, which is 5,881 m [19,294 ft] high. Between these ranges is central Burma, which contains the fertile valleys of the Irrawaddy and Sittang rivers. The Irrawaddy delta on the Bay of Bengal is one of the world's leading rice-growing areas. Burma also includes the long Tenasserim coast in the south-east.

Burma has a tropical monsoon climate. There are three seasons. The rainy season runs from late May to mid-October. A cool, dry season follows, between late October and the middle part of February. The hot season lasts from late February to mid-May, though temperatures remain high during the humid rainy season.

POLITICS & ECONOMY Many groups settled in Burma in ancient times. Some, called the hill peoples, live in remote mountain areas where they have retained their own cultures. The ancestors of the country's main ethnic group today, the Burmese, arrived in the 9th century AD.

Britain conquered Burma in the 19th century and made it a province of British India. But, in 1937, the British granted Burma limited self-government. Japan conquered Burma in 1942, but the Japanese were driven out in 1945. Burma became a fully independent country in 1948.

Revolts by Communists and various hill people led to instability in the 1950s. In 1962, Burma became a military dictatorship and, in 1974, a one-party state. Attempts to control minority liberation movements and the opium trade led to repressive rule. The National League for Democracy led by Aung San Suu Kyi won the elections in 1990, but the military continued their repressive rule throughout the 1990s, earning Burma the reputation for having one of the world's worst human rights records. Burma's internal political problems have helped to make it one of the world's poorest countries. Its admission to ASEAN (Association of South-east Asian Nations) in 1997 may have implied regional recognition of the regime, but the European Union continues to voice its concern over human rights abuses.

Agriculture is the main activity, employing 64% of the people. The chief crop is rice. Maize, pulses, oilseeds and sugar-cane are other major products. Forestry is important. Teak and rice together make up about two-thirds of the total value of the exports. Burma has many mineral resources, though they are mostly undeveloped, but the country is famous for its precious stones, especially rubies. Manufacturing is mostly on a small scale.

AREA 676,577 sq km [261,228 sq mi] **POPULATION** 41,995,000
CAPITAL (POPULATION) Rangoon (2,513,000) **GOVERNMENT** Military regime **ETHNIC GROUPS** Burman 69%, Shan 9%, Karen 6%, Rakhine 5%, Mon 2%, Kachin 1% **LANGUAGES** Burmese (official), Shan, Karen, Rakhine, Mon, Kachin, English, Chin **RELIGIONS** Buddhism 89%, Christianity, Islam **CURRENCY** Kyat = 100 pyas

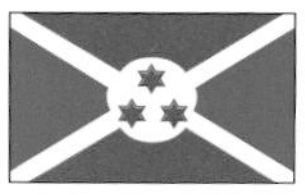
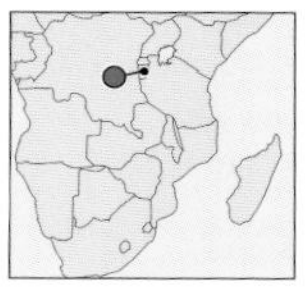

BURUNDI

GEOGRAPHY The Republic of Burundi is the fifth smallest country in mainland Africa. It is also the second most densely populated after its northern neighbour, Rwanda. Part of the Great African Rift Valley, which runs throughout eastern Africa into south-western Asia, lies in western Burundi. It includes part of Lake Tanganyika.

Bujumbura, the capital city, lies on the shore of Lake Tanganyika. It has a warm climate. A dry season occurs from June to September, but the other months are fairly rainy. The mountains and plateaux to the east are cooler and wetter, but the rainfall generally decreases to the east.

POLITICS & ECONOMY The Twa, a pygmy people, were the first known inhabitants of Burundi. About 1,000 years ago, the Hutu, a people who speak a Bantu language, gradually began to settle the area, pushing the Twa into remote areas.

From the 15th century, the Tutsi, a cattle-owning people from the north-east, gradually took over the country. The Hutu, though greatly outnumbering the Tutsi, were forced to serve the Tutsi overlords.

Germany conquered the area that is now Burundi and Rwanda in the late 1890s. The area, called Ruanda-Urundi, was taken by Belgium during World War I (1914–18). In 1961, the people of Urundi voted to become a monarchy, while the people of Ruanda voted to become a republic. The two territories became fully independent as Burundi and Rwanda in 1962. After 1962, the rivalries between the Hutu and Tutsi led to periodic outbreaks of

fighting. The Tutsi monarchy was ended in 1966 and Burundi became a republic. Instability continued with frequent coups and massacres of thousands of people as Tutsis and Hutus fought for power. In 2001, leaders signed a power-sharing agreement.

Burundi is one of the world's ten poorest countries. About 92% of the people are farmers, who mostly grow little more than they need to feed their own families. The main food crops are beans, cassava, maize and sweet potatoes. Cattle, goats and sheep are raised, while fish are an important supplement to people's diets. However, Burundi has to import food.

AREA 27,830 sq km [10,745 sq mi] **POPULATION** 6,224,000
CAPITAL (POPULATION) Bujumbura (300,000) **GOVERNMENT** Republic
ETHNIC GROUPS Hutu 85%, Tutsi 14%, Twa (pygmy) 1%
LANGUAGES French and Kirundi (both official)
RELIGIONS Roman Catholic 62%, traditional beliefs 23%, Islam 10%, Protestant 5% **CURRENCY** Burundi franc = 100 centimes

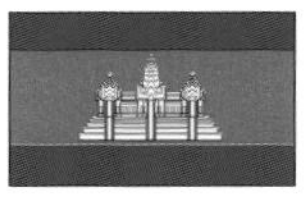
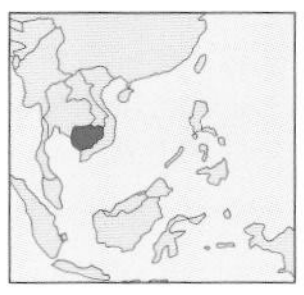

CAMBODIA

GEOGRAPHY The Kingdom of Cambodia is a country in South-east Asia. Low mountains border the country except in the south-east. But most of Cambodia consists of plains drained by the River Mekong, which enters Cambodia from Laos in the north and exits through Vietnam in the south-east. The north-west contains Tonlé Sap (or Great Lake). In the dry season, this lake drains into the River Mekong. But in the wet season, the level of the Mekong rises and water flows in the opposite direction from the river into Tonlé Sap – the lake then becomes the largest freshwater lake in Asia.

Cambodia has a tropical monsoon climate, with high temperatures throughout the year. The dry season, when winds blow from the north or north-east, runs from November to April. During the rainy season (May to October), moist winds blow from the south or south-east. The high humidity and heat often make conditions unpleasant. Rainfall is heaviest near the coast, and rather lower inland.

POLITICS & ECONOMY From 802 to 1432, the Khmer people ruled a great empire, which reached its peak in the 12th century. The Khmer capital was at Angkor. The Hindu stone temples built there and at nearby Angkor Wat form the world's largest group of religious buildings. France ruled the country between 1863 and 1954, when the country became an independent monarchy. But the monarchy was abolished in 1970 and Cambodia became a republic.

In 1970, US and South Vietnamese troops entered Cambodia but left after destroying North Vietnamese Communist camps in the east. The country became involved in the Vietnamese War, and then in a civil war as Cambodian Communists of the Khmer Rouge organization fought for power. The Khmer Rouge took over Cambodia in 1975 and launched a reign of terror in which between 1 million and 2.5 million people were killed. In 1979, Vietnamese and Cambodian troops overthrew the Khmer Rouge government. But fighting continued between factions. Vietnam withdrew in 1989, and in 1991 Prince Sihanouk was recognized as head of state. Elections were held in May 1993, and in September 1993 the monarchy was restored. Sihanouk again became king. In 1997, the prime minister, Prince Norodom Ranariddh, was deposed, so ending four years of democratic rule. Further elections were held in 1998 and, in 2001, the government set up courts to try leaders of the Khmer Rouge.

Cambodia is a poor country whose economy has been wrecked by war. Until the 1970s, the country's farmers produced most of the food needed by the people. But by 1986, it was only able to supply 80% of its needs. Farming is the main activity and rice, rubber and maize are major products. Manufacturing is almost non-existent, apart from rubber processing and a few factories producing items for sale in Cambodia.

AREA 181,040 sq km [69,900 sq mi] **POPULATION** 12,492,000
CAPITAL (POPULATION) Phnom Penh (570,000)
GOVERNMENT Constitutional monarchy **ETHNIC GROUPS** Khmer 90%, Vietnamese 5%, Chinese 1%, other 5% **LANGUAGES** Khmer (official)
RELIGIONS Buddhism 95%, other 5% **CURRENCY** Riel = 100 sen

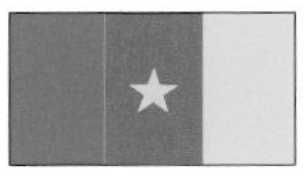
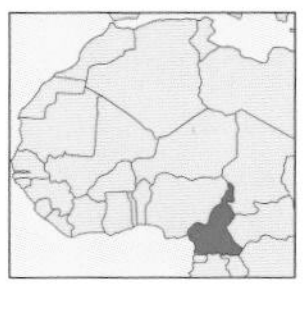

CAMEROON

GEOGRAPHY The Republic of Cameroon in West Africa got its name from the Portuguese word *camarões*, or prawns. This name was used by Portuguese explorers who fished for prawns along the coast. Behind the narrow coastal plains on the Gulf of Guinea, the land rises to a series of plateaux, with a mountainous region in the south-west where the volcano Mount Cameroon is situated. In the north, the land slopes down towards the Lake Chad basin.

The rainfall is heavy, especially in the highlands. The rainiest months near the coast are June to September. The rainfall decreases to the north and the far north has a hot, dry climate. Temperatures are high on the coast, whereas the inland plateaux are cooler.

POLITICS & ECONOMY Germany lost Cameroon during World War I (1914–18). The country was then divided into two parts, one ruled by Britain and the other by France. In 1960, French Cameroon became the independent Cameroon Republic. In 1961, after a vote in British Cameroon, part of the territory joined the Cameroon Republic to become the Federal Republic of Cameroon. The other part joined Nigeria. In 1972, Cameroon became a unitary state called the United Republic of Cameroon. It adopted the name Republic of Cameroon in 1984, but the country had two official languages. In 1995, partly to placate English-speaking people, Cameroon became the 52nd member of the Commonwealth.

Like most countries in tropical Africa, Cameroon's economy is based on agriculture, which employs 73% of the people. The chief food crops include cassava, maize, millet, sweet potatoes and yams. The country also has plantations to produce such crops as cocoa and coffee for export.

Cameroon is fortunate in having some oil, the country's chief export, and bauxite. Although Cameroon has few manufacturing and processing industries, its mineral exports and its self-sufficiency in food production make it one of the better-off countries in tropical Africa.

AREA 475,440 sq km [183,567 sq mi] **POPULATION** 15,803,000
CAPITAL (POPULATION) Yaoundé (800,000) **GOVERNMENT** Multiparty republic **ETHNIC GROUPS** Fang 20%, Bamileke and Bamum 19%, Duala, Luanda and Basa 15%, Fulani 10% **LANGUAGES** French and English (both official), many others **RELIGIONS** Christianity 40%, traditional beliefs 40%, Islam 20% **CURRENCY** CFA franc = 100 centimes

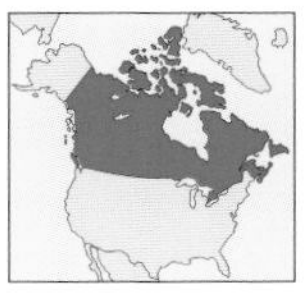

CANADA

GEOGRAPHY Canada is the world's second largest country after Russia. It is thinly populated, however, with much of the land too cold or too mountainous for human settlement. Most Canadians live within 300 km [186 mi] of the southern border.

Western Canada is rugged. It includes the Pacific ranges and the mighty Rocky Mountains. East of the Rockies are the interior plains. In the north lie the bleak Arctic islands, while to the south lie the densely populated lowlands around lakes Erie and Ontario and in the St Lawrence River valley.

Canada has a cold climate. In winter, temperatures fall below freezing point throughout most of Canada. But the south-western coast has a relatively mild climate. Along the Arctic Circle, mean temperatures are below freezing for seven months a year.

Western and south-eastern Canada experience high rainfall, but the prairies are dry with 250 mm to 500 mm [10 in to 20 in] of rain every year.

POLITICS & ECONOMY Canada's first people, the ancestors of the Native Americans, or Indians, arrived in North America from Asia around 40,000 years ago. Later arrivals were the Inuit (Eskimos), who also came from Asia. Europeans reached the Canadian coast in 1497 and a race began between Britain and France for control of the territory.

France gained an initial advantage, and the French founded Québec in 1608. But the British later occupied eastern Canada. In 1867, Britain passed the British North America Act, which set up the Dominion of Canada, which was made up of Québec, Ontario, Nova Scotia and New Brunswick. Other areas were added, the last being Newfoundland in 1949. Canada fought alongside Britain in both World Wars and many Canadians feel close ties with Britain. Canada is a constitutional monarchy, and the British monarch is Canada's head of state.

Rivalries between French- and English-speaking Canadians continue. In 1995, Québeckers voted against a move to make Québec a sovereign state. The majority was less than 1% and this issue seems unlikely to disappear. Another problem concerns the rights of the Aboriginal minorities, who would like to have more say in the running of their own affairs. To this end, in 1999, Canada created a new territory called Nunavut for the Inuit population in the north. Nunavut covers approximately 64% of what was formerly the eastern part of Northwest Territories.

Canada is a highly developed and prosperous country. Although farmland covers only 8% of the country, Canadian farms are highly productive. Canada is one of the world's leading producers of barley, wheat, meat and milk. Forestry and fishing are other important industries. It is rich in natural resources, especially oil and natural gas, and is a major exporter of minerals. The country also produces copper, gold, iron ore, uranium and zinc. Manufacturing is highly developed, especially in the cities where 78% of the people live. Canada has many factories that process farm and mineral products. It also produces cars, chemicals, electronic goods, machinery, paper and timber products.

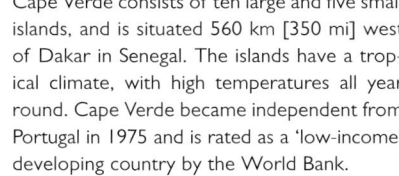

AREA 9,976,140 sq km [3,851,788 sq mi] **POPULATION** 31,593,000
CAPITAL (POPULATION) Ottawa (1,107,000)
GOVERNMENT Federal multiparty constitutional monarchy
ETHNIC GROUPS British 28%, French 23%, other European 15%, Native American (Amerindian/Inuit) 2%, other 32%
LANGUAGES English and French (both official)
RELIGIONS Roman Catholic 42%, Protestant 40%, Judaism, Islam, Hinduism **CURRENCY** Canadian dollar = 100 cents

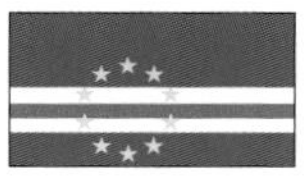
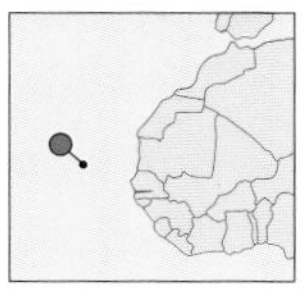

CAPE VERDE

Cape Verde consists of ten large and five small islands, and is situated 560 km [350 mi] west of Dakar in Senegal. The islands have a tropical climate, with high temperatures all year round. Cape Verde became independent from Portugal in 1975 and is rated as a 'low-income' developing country by the World Bank.

AREA 4,030 sq km [1,556 sq mi]
POPULATION 405,000 **CAPITAL** Praia

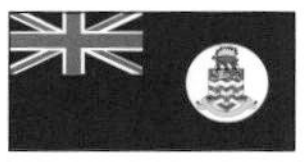
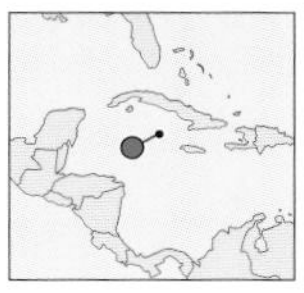

CAYMAN ISLANDS

The Cayman Islands are an overseas territory of the UK, consisting of three low-lying islands. Financial services are the main economic activity and the islands offer a secret tax haven to many companies and banks.

AREA 259 sq km [100 sq mi]
POPULATION 36,000 **CAPITAL** George Town

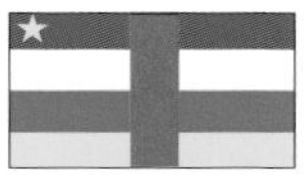
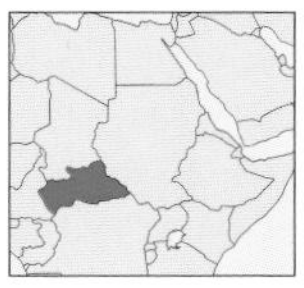

CENTRAL AFRICAN REPUBLIC

GEOGRAPHY The Central African Republic is a remote, landlocked country in the heart of Africa. It consists mostly of a plateau lying between 600 m to 800 m [1,970 ft and 2,620 ft] above sea level. The Ubangi drains the south, while the Chari (or Shari) River flows from the north to the Lake Chad basin.

Bangui, the capital, lies in the south-west of the country on the Ubangi River. The climate is warm throughout the year, with average yearly rainfall totalling 1,574 mm [62 in]. The north is drier, with an average yearly rainfall of about 800 mm [31 in].

POLITICS & ECONOMY France set up an outpost at Bangui in 1899 and ruled the country as a colony from 1894. Known as Ubangi-Shari, the country was ruled by France as part of French Equatorial Africa until it gained independence in 1960.

Central African Republic became a one-party state in 1962, but army officers seized power in 1966. The head of the army, Jean-Bedel Bokassa, made himself emperor in 1976. The country was renamed the Central African Empire, but after a brutal reign, the tyrannical Bokassa was overthrown in a military coup in 1979. The country again became a republic.

The country adopted a new, multiparty constitution in 1991. Multiparty elections were held in 1993 and 1998. An army rebellion in 1996 was put down in 1977 with French help. Another unsuccessful coup, put down with Libyan help, occurred in 2001.

The World Bank classifies Central African Republic as a 'low-income' developing country. Over 80% of the people are farmers, and most of them produce little more than they need to feed their families. The main crops are bananas, maize, manioc, millet and yams. Coffee, cotton, timber and tobacco are produced for export, mainly on commercial plantations. The country's development has been impeded by its remote position, its poor transport system and its untrained workforce. The country depends heavily on aid, especially from France.

AREA 622,980 sq km [240,533 sq mi] **POPULATION** 3,577,000
CAPITAL (POPULATION) Bangui (553,000) **GOVERNMENT** Multiparty republic **ETHNIC GROUPS** Baya 34%, Banda 27%, Mandjia 21%, Sara 10%, Mbaka 4%, Mboum 4% **LANGUAGES** French (official), Sangho
RELIGIONS Traditional beliefs 57%, Christianity 35%, Islam 8%
CURRENCY CFA franc = 100 centimes

CHAD

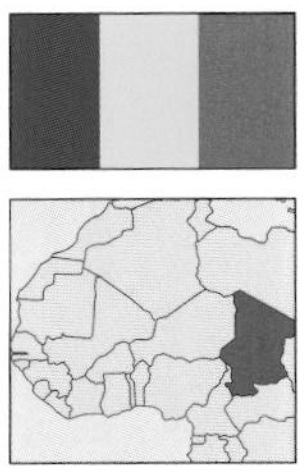

GEOGRAPHY The Republic of Chad is a landlocked country in north-central Africa. It is Africa's fifth largest country and is over twice the size of France, the country which once ruled it as a colony.

Ndjamena in central Chad has a hot, tropical climate, with a marked dry season from November to April. The south of the country is wetter, with an average yearly rainfall of around 1,000 mm [39 in]. The burning-hot desert in the north has an average yearly rainfall of less than 130 mm [5 in].

POLITICS & ECONOMY Chad straddles two worlds. The north is populated by Muslim Arab and Berber peoples, while black Africans, who follow traditional beliefs or who have converted to Christianity, live in the south.

French explorers were active in the area in the late 19th century. France finally made Chad a colony in 1902. After becoming independent in 1960, Chad has been hit by ethnic conflict. The 1970s were marked by civil war and coups. Chad and Libya agreed a truce in 1987 and, in 1994, the International Court of Justice ruled against Libya's claim on the Aozou Strip. Chad enjoyed more stability in the 1990s. A new constitution was adopted in 1997.

Hit by drought and civil war, Chad is one of the world's poorest countries. Farming, fishing and livestock raising employ 83% of the people. Groundnuts, millet, rice and sorghum are major food crops in the wetter south, but the most valuable crop in export terms is cotton. The country has few natural resources and very few manufacturing industries.

AREA 1,284,000 sq km [495,752 sq mi] **POPULATION** 8,707,000
CAPITAL (POPULATION) Ndjamena (530,000)
GOVERNMENT Multiparty republic **ETHNIC GROUPS** Bagirmi, Kreish and Sara 31%, Sudanic Arab 26%, Teda 7%, Mbum 6%
LANGUAGES French and Arabic (both official), many others
RELIGIONS Islam 50%, Christianity 25%, traditional beliefs 25%
CURRENCY CFA franc = 100 centimes

CHILE

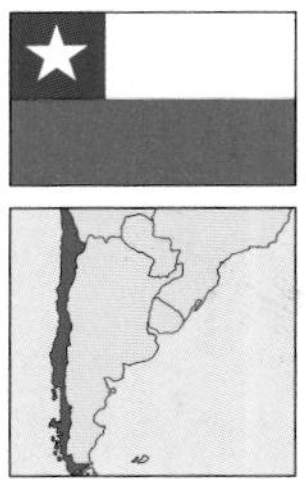

GEOGRAPHY The Republic of Chile stretches about 4,260 km [2,650 mi] from north to south, although the maximum east–west distance is only about 430 km [267 mi]. The high Andes Mountains form Chile's eastern borders with Argentina and Bolivia. To the west are basins and valleys, with coastal uplands overlooking the shore. Most people live in the central valley, where Santiago is situated.

Santiago has a Mediterranean climate, with hot, dry summers from November to March and mild, moist winters from April to October. The Atacama Desert in the north is one of the world's driest places, while southern Chile is cold and stormy.

POLITICS & ECONOMY Amerindian people reached the southern tip of South America 8,000 years ago. In 1520, Portuguese navigator Ferdinand Magellan was the first European to sight Chile. The country became a Spanish colony in the 1540s. Chile became independent in 1818. During a war (1879–83), it gained mineral-rich areas from Peru and Bolivia.

In 1970, Salvador Allende became the first Communist leader to be elected democratically. He was overthrown in 1973 by army officers, who were supported by the CIA. General Augusto Pinochet then ruled as a dictator. A new constitution was introduced in 1981 and elections were held in 1989. In 2000, a socialist, Ricardo Lagos, was elected president. Pinochet, who had been charged with presiding over acts of torture, was found to be too ill to stand trial in 2001.

The World Bank classifies Chile as a 'lower-middle-income' developing country. Mining is important, especially copper production. Minerals dominate exports. The most valuable activity is manufacturing; products include processed foods, metals, iron and steel, transport equipment and textiles. The chief crop is wheat, while beans, fruits, maize and livestock products are also important. Chile's fishing industry is one of the world's largest.

AREA 756,950 sq km [292,258 sq mi] **POPULATION** 15,328,000
CAPITAL (POPULATION) Santiago (4,691,000)
GOVERNMENT Multiparty republic **ETHNIC GROUPS** Mestizo 95%, Amerindian 3% **LANGUAGES** Spanish (official)
RELIGIONS Roman Catholic 89%, Protestant 11%
CURRENCY Peso = 100 centavos

CHINA

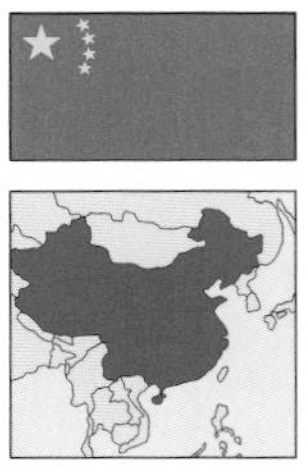

GEOGRAPHY The People's Republic of China is the world's third largest country. Most people live in the east – on the coastal plains or in the fertile valleys of the Huang He (Hwang Ho or Yellow River), the Chang Jiang (Yangtze Kiang), which is Asia's longest river at 6,380 km [3,960 mi], and the Xi Jiang (Si Kiang). Western China is thinly populated. It includes the bleak Tibetan plateau which is bounded by the Himalaya, the world's highest mountain range. Other ranges include the Kunlun Shan, the Altun Shan and the Tian Shan. Deserts include the Gobi Desert along the Mongolian border and the Taklimakan Desert in the far west.

Beijing in north-eastern China has cold winters and warm summers, with a moderate rainfall. Shanghai, in the east-central region of China, has milder winters and more rain. The south-east has a wet, subtropical climate. In the west, the climate is severe. Lhasa has very cold winters and a low rainfall.

POLITICS & ECONOMY China is one of the world's oldest civilizations, going back 3,500 years. Under the Han dynasty (202 BC to AD 220), the Chinese empire was as large as the Roman empire. Mongols conquered China in the 13th century, but Chinese rule was restored in 1368. The Manchu people of Mongolia ruled the country from 1644 to 1912, when the country became a republic.

War with Japan (1937–45) was followed by civil war between the nationalists and the Communists. The Communists triumphed in 1949, setting up the People's Republic of China. In the 1980s, following the death of the revolutionary leader Mao Zedong (Mao Tse-tung) in 1976, China encouraged formerly forbidden policies, namely private enterprise and foreign investment. But the Communist leaders have not permitted political freedom. Opponents are still harshly treated, while attempts to negotiate some degree of autonomy for Tibet were rejected in 1998.

China's economy, which is one of the world's largest, has expanded rapidly since the late 1970s. This is partly the result of the gradual abandonment of some fundamental Communist policies, including the setting up of many private manufacturing industries in the east. China's sheer size, combined with its rapid economic growth, led to predictions in the 1990s that China would become the world's biggest economy 'within a generation'. This was made more likely by the return of Hong Kong in 1997 and the admission of China into the World Trade Organization (WTO) in 2001. China would like to regain the prosperous island of Taiwan, which was admitted to the WTO on 1 January 2002, but this seemed unlikely in the early 21st century.

In the early 1990s, agriculture employed about 70% of the people, although only 10% of the land is used for crops. Major products include rice, sweet potatoes, tea and wheat, together with many fruits and vegetables. Livestock farming is also important. Pork is a popular meat and China has more than a third of the world's pigs.

China's resources include coal, oil, iron ore and various other metals. China has huge steel industries and manufactures include cement, chemicals, fertilizers, machinery, telecommunications and recording equipment, and textiles. Consumer goods, such as bicycles and radios, are becoming increasingly important.

AREA 9,596,960 sq km [3,705,386 sq mi]
POPULATION 1,273,111,000 **CAPITAL (POPULATION)** Beijing (12,362,000) **GOVERNMENT** Single-party Communist republic
ETHNIC GROUPS Han Chinese 92%, 55 minority groups
LANGUAGES Mandarin Chinese (official) **RELIGIONS** Atheist (official)
CURRENCY Renminbi yuan = 10 jiao = 100 fen

COLOMBIA

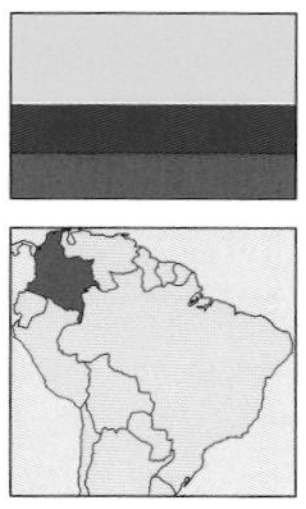

GEOGRAPHY The Republic of Colombia, in north-eastern South America, is the only country in the continent to have coastlines on both the Pacific and the Caribbean Sea. Colombia also contains the northernmost ranges of the Andes Mountains.

There is a tropical climate in the lowlands. But the altitude greatly affects the climate of the Andes. The capital, Bogotá, which stands on a plateau in the eastern Andes at about 2,800 m [9,200 ft] above sea level, has mild temperatures throughout the year. The rainfall is heavy, especially on the Pacific coast

POLITICS & ECONOMY Amerindian people have lived in Colombia for thousands of years. But today, only a small proportion of the people are of unmixed Amerindian ancestry. Mestizos (people of mixed white and Amerindian ancestry) form the largest group, followed by whites and mulattos (people of mixed European and African ancestry).

Spaniards opened up the area in the early 16th century. They set up a territory known as the Vice-royalty of the New Kingdom of Granada, including Colombia, Ecuador, Panama and Venezuela. In 1819, the area became independent, but Ecuador and Venezuela soon split away, followed by Panama in 1903. Recent history has been unstable. Rivalries between main political parties led to civil wars in 1899–1902 and 1949–57, when the parties agreed to form a coalition. The coalition government ended in 1986 when the Liberal Party was elected. Colombia faces economic problems, as well as the difficulty of controlling a large illicit drug industry run by violent dealers. In 2000, the United States began to provide military aid to help Colombia fight drug-trafficking. Colombia exports oil, coffee and chemicals.

AREA 1,138,910 sq km [439,733 sq mi] **POPULATION** 40,349,000
CAPITAL (POPULATION) Bogotá (6,005,000)
GOVERNMENT Multiparty republic **ETHNIC GROUPS** Mestizo 58%, White 20%, Mulatto 14%, Black 4% **LANGUAGES** Spanish (official)
RELIGIONS Roman Catholic 90% **CURRENCY** Peso = 100 centavos

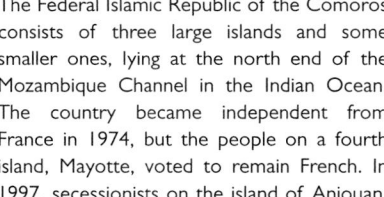

COMOROS

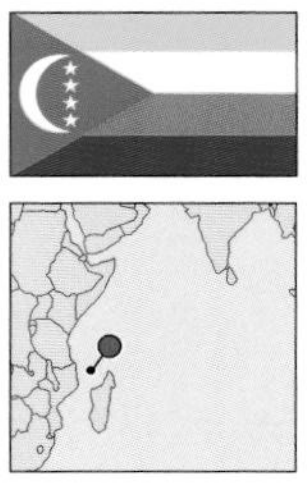

The Federal Islamic Republic of the Comoros consists of three large islands and some smaller ones, lying at the north end of the Mozambique Channel in the Indian Ocean. The country became independent from France in 1974, but the people on a fourth island, Mayotte, voted to remain French. In 1997, secessionists on the island of Anjouan, who favoured a return to French rule, defeated forces from Grand Comore and, in 1998, they voted overwhelmingly to break away from the Comoros. Most people are subsistence farmers, although cash crops such as coconuts, coffee, cocoa and spices are also produced. The main exports are cloves, perfume oils and vanilla.

AREA 2,230 sq km [861 sq mi] **POPULATION** 596,000 **CAPITAL** Moroni

CONGO

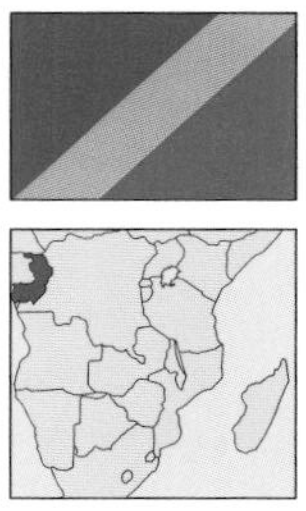

GEOGRAPHY The Republic of Congo is a country on the River Congo in west-central Africa. The Equator runs through the centre of the country. Congo has a narrow coastal plain on which its main port, Pointe Noire, stands. Behind the plain are uplands through which the River Niari has carved a fertile valley. Central Congo consists of high plains. The north contains large swampy areas in the valleys of the tributaries of the River Congo.

Congo has a hot, wet equatorial climate. Brazzaville has a dry season between June and September. The coast is drier and cooler than the rest of Congo, because of the cold offshore Benguela ocean current.

POLITICS & ECONOMY Part of the huge Kongo kingdom between the 15th and 18th centuries, the coast of the Congo later became a centre of the European slave trade. The area came under French protection in 1880. It was later governed as part of a larger region called French Equatorial Africa. The country remained under French control until 1960.

Congo became a one-party state in 1964 and a military group took over the government in 1968. In 1970, Congo declared itself a Communist country, though it continued to seek aid from Western countries. The government officially abandoned its Communist policies in 1990. Multiparty elections were held in 1992, but the elected president, Pascal Lissouba, was overthrown in 1997 by former president Denis Sassou-Nguesso. Civil war again occurred in January 1999, but peace was restored. In 2002, Sassou-Nguesso was elected president.

The World Bank classifies Congo as a 'lower-middle-income' developing country. Agriculture is the most important activity, employing more than 60% of the people. But many farmers produce little more than they need to feed their families. Major food crops include bananas, cassava, maize and rice, while the leading cash crops are coffee and cocoa. Congo's main exports are oil (which makes up 70% of the total) and timber. Manufacturing is relatively unimportant at the moment, still hampered by poor transport links, but it is gradually being developed.

AREA 342,000 sq km [132,046 sq mi] **POPULATION** 2,894,000
CAPITAL (POPULATION) Brazzaville (938,000)
GOVERNMENT Military regime **ETHNIC GROUPS** Kongo 48%, Sangha 20%, Teke 17%, M'bochi 12% **LANGUAGES** French (official), many others **RELIGIONS** Christianity 50%, Animist 48%, Islam 2%
CURRENCY CFA franc = 100 centimes

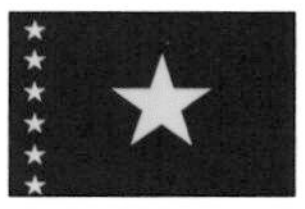
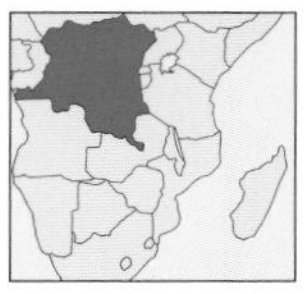

CONGO (DEM. REP. OF THE)

GEOGRAPHY The Democratic Republic of the Congo, formerly known as Zaïre, is the world's 12th largest country. Much of the country lies within the drainage basin of the huge River Congo. The river reaches the sea along the country's coastline, which is 40 km [25 mi] long. Mountains rise in the east, where the country's borders run through lakes Tanganyika, Kivu, Edward and Albert.

The equatorial region has high temperatures and heavy rainfall throughout the year.

POLITICS & ECONOMY Pygmies were the first inhabitants of the region, with Portuguese navigators not reaching the coast until 1482, but the interior was not explored until the late 19th century. In 1885, the country, called Congo Free State, became the personal property of King Léopold II of Belgium. In 1908, the country became a Belgian colony.

The Belgian Congo became independent in 1960 and was renamed Zaïre in 1971. Ethnic rivalries caused instability until 1965, when the country became a one-party state, ruled by President Mobutu. The government allowed the formation of political parties in 1990, but elections were repeatedly postponed. In 1996, fighting broke out in eastern Zaïre, as the Tutsi–Hutu conflict in Burundi and Rwanda spilled over. The rebel leader Laurent Kabila took power in 1997, ousting Mobutu and renaming the country. A rebellion against Kabila broke out in 1998. Rwanda and Uganda supported the rebels, while Angola, Chad, Namibia and Zimbabwe assisted Kabila. A peace treaty was signed in 1999, but the fighting continued. However, hopes for peace were rekindled when Kabila was assassinated in 2001 and succeeded by his son, Major-General Joseph Kabila.

The World Bank classifies the Democratic Republic of the Congo as a 'low-income' developing country, despite its reserves of copper, the main export, and other minerals. Agriculture, mainly at subsistence level, employs 71% of the people.

AREA 2,344,885 sq km [905,365 sq mi] **POPULATION** 53,625,000
CAPITAL (POPULATION) Kinshasa (2,664,000)
GOVERNMENT Single-party republic
ETHNIC GROUPS Over 200; the largest are Mongo, Luba, Kongo, Mangbetu-Azande
LANGUAGES French (official), tribal languages
RELIGIONS Roman Catholic 50%, Protestant 20%, Islam 10%, others 20%
CURRENCY Congolese franc

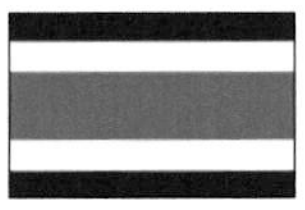
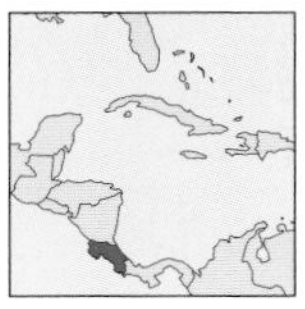

COSTA RICA

GEOGRAPHY The Republic of Costa Rica in Central America has coastlines on both the Pacific Ocean and also on the Caribbean Sea. Central Costa Rica consists of mountain ranges and plateaux with many volcanoes.

The coolest months are December and January. The north-east trade winds bring heavy rain to the Caribbean coast. There is less rainfall in the highlands and on the Pacific coastlands.

POLITICS & ECONOMY Christopher Columbus reached the Caribbean coast in 1502 and rumours of treasure soon attracted many Spaniards to settle in the country. Spain ruled the country until 1821, when Spain's Central American colonies broke away to join Mexico in 1822. In 1823, the Central American states broke with Mexico and set up the Central American Federation. Later, this large union broke up and Costa Rica became fully independent in 1838.

From the late 19th century, Costa Rica experienced a number of revolutions, with periods of dictatorship and periods of democracy. In 1948, following a revolt, the armed forces were abolished. Since 1948, Costa Rica has enjoyed a long period of stable democracy, which many in Latin America admire and envy.

Costa Rica is classified by the World Bank as a 'lower-middle-income' developing country and one of the most prosperous countries in Central America. There are high educational standards and a high life expectancy (to an average of 73.5 years). Agriculture employs 20% of the people.

The country's resources include its forests, but it lacks minerals apart from some bauxite and manganese. Manufacturing is increasing. The United States is Costa Rica's chief trading partner. Tourism is a fast-growing industry.

AREA 51,100 sq km [19,730 sq mi] **POPULATION** 3,773,000
CAPITAL (POPULATION) San José (1,220,000)
GOVERNMENT Multiparty republic **ETHNIC GROUPS** White 85%, Mestizo 8%, Black and Mulatto 3%, East Asian (mostly Chinese) 1%
LANGUAGES Spanish (official) **RELIGIONS** Roman Catholic 76%, Evangelical 14% **CURRENCY** Colón = 100 céntimos

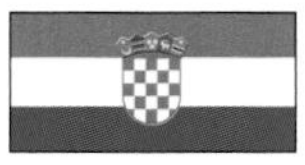
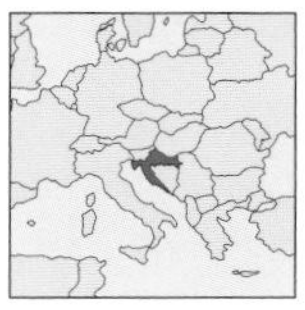

CROATIA

GEOGRAPHY The Republic of Croatia was one of the six republics that made up the former Communist country of Yugoslavia until it became independent in 1991. The region bordering the Adriatic Sea is called Dalmatia. It includes the coastal ranges, which contain large areas of bare limestone. Most of the rest of the country consists of the fertile Pannonian plains.

The coastal area has a typical Mediterranean climate, with hot, dry summers and mild, moist winters. Inland, the climate becomes more continental. Winters are cold, while temperatures often soar to 38°C [100°F] in the summer months.

POLITICS & ECONOMY Slav people settled in the area around 1,400 years ago. In 803, Croatia became part of the Holy Roman empire and the Croats soon adopted Christianity. Croatia was an independent kingdom in the 10th and 11th centuries. In 1102, the king of Hungary also became king of Croatia, creating a union that lasted 800 years. In 1526, part of Croatia came under the Turkish Ottoman empire, while the rest came under the Austrian Habsburgs.

After Austria–Hungary was defeated in World War I (1914–18), Croatia became part of the new Kingdom of the Serbs, Croats and Slovenes. This kingdom was renamed Yugoslavia in 1929. Germany occupied Yugoslavia during World War II (1939–45). Croatia was proclaimed independent, but it was really ruled by the invaders.

After the war, Communists took power with Josip Broz Tito as the country's leader. Despite ethnic differences between the people, Tito held Yugoslavia together until his death in 1980. In the 1980s, economic and ethnic problems, including a deterioration in relations with Serbia, threatened stability. In the 1990s, Yugoslavia split into five nations, one of which was Croatia, which declared itself independent in 1991.

After Serbia supplied arms to Serbs living in Croatia, war broke out between the two republics, causing great damage. Croatia lost more than 30% of its territory. But in 1992, the United Nations sent a peacekeeping force to Croatia, which effectively ended the war with Serbia.

In 1992, when war broke out in Bosnia-Herzegovina, Bosnian Croats occupied parts of the country. But in 1994, Croatia helped to end Croat–Muslim conflict in Bosnia-Herzegovina and, in 1995, after retaking some areas occupied by Serbs, it helped to draw up the Dayton Peace Accord which ended the civil war there.

The wars of the early 1990s disrupted Croatia's economy, though the election of a pro-democratic coalition government in 2000 held out hope for the future, including a revival of the valuable tourist industry. The country has many manufacturing industries and manufactures are the main exports.

AREA 56,538 sq km [21,824 sq mi] **POPULATION** 4,334,000
CAPITAL (POPULATION) Zagreb (868,000)
GOVERNMENT Multiparty republic **ETHNIC GROUPS** Croat 78%, Serb 12% **LANGUAGES** Serbo-Croatian **RELIGIONS** Roman Catholic 77%, Eastern Orthodox 11%, Islam 1% **CURRENCY** Kuna = 100 lipas

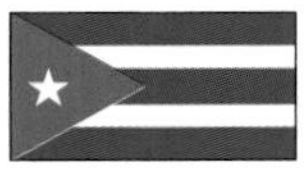
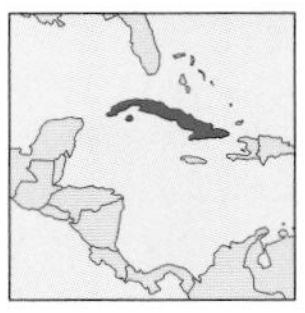

CUBA

GEOGRAPHY The Republic of Cuba is the largest island country in the Caribbean Sea. It consists of one large island, Cuba, the Isle of Youth (Isla de la Juventud) and about 1,600 small islets. Mountains and hills cover about a quarter of Cuba. The highest mountain range, the Sierra Maestra in the south-east, reaches 2,000 m [6,562 ft] above sea level. The rest of the land consists of gently rolling country or coastal plains, crossed by fertile valleys carved by the short, mostly shallow and narrow rivers.

Cuba lies in the tropics. But sea breezes moderate the temperature, warming the land in winter and cooling it in summer.

POLITICS & ECONOMY Christopher Columbus discovered the island in 1492 and Spaniards began to settle there from 1511. Spanish rule ended in 1898, when the United States defeated Spain in the Spanish–American War. American influence in Cuba remained strong until 1959, when revolutionary forces under Fidel Castro overthrew the dictatorial government of Fulgencio Batista.

The United States opposed Castro's policies, when he turned to the Soviet Union for assistance. In 1961, Cuban exiles attempting an invasion were defeated. In 1962, the US learned that nuclear missile bases armed by the Soviet Union had been established in Cuba. The US ordered the Soviet Union to remove the missiles and bases and, after a few days, when many people feared that a world war might break out, the Soviet Union agreed to the American demands.

Cuba's relations with the Soviet Union remained strong until 1991, when the Soviet Union was broken up. The loss of Soviet aid greatly damaged Cuba's economy, but Castro continued the country's left-wing policies. In 2000, the United States lifted its food embargo on Cuba. The ban on travel was also liberalized, though the ban on tourists remained.

The government runs Cuba's economy and owns 70% of the farmland. Agriculture is important and sugar is the chief export, followed by refined nickel ore. Other exports include cigars, citrus fruits, fish, medical products and rum.

Before 1959, US companies owned most of Cuba's manufacturing industries. But under Fidel Castro, they became government property. After the collapse of Communist governments in the Soviet Union and its allies, Cuba worked to increase its trade with Latin America and China.

AREA 110,860 sq km [42,803 sq mi] **POPULATION** 11,184,000
CAPITAL (POPULATION) Havana (2,204,000)
GOVERNMENT Socialist republic **ETHNIC GROUPS** White 37%, Mulatto 51%, Black 11% **LANGUAGES** Spanish (official)
RELIGIONS Roman Catholic 40%, Protestant 3%
CURRENCY Cuban peso = 100 centavos

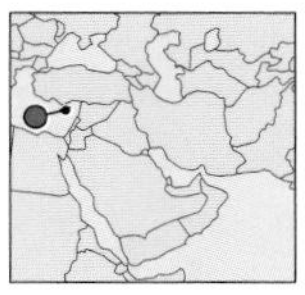

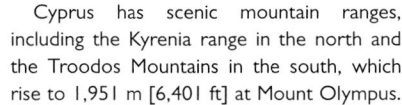

CYPRUS

GEOGRAPHY The Republic of Cyprus is an island nation in the north-eastern Mediterranean Sea. Geographers regard it as part of Asia, but it resembles southern Europe in many ways.

Cyprus has scenic mountain ranges, including the Kyrenia range in the north and the Troodos Mountains in the south, which rise to 1,951 m [6,401 ft] at Mount Olympus. The island also contains several fertile lowlands, including the broad Mesaoria plain between the Kyrenia and Troodos mountains.

Cyprus has a Mediterranean climate, with hot, dry summers and mild, moist winters. But the summers are hotter than in the western Mediterranean lands; this is because Cyprus lies close to the hot mainland of south-western Asia.

POLITICS & ECONOMY Greeks settled on Cyprus around 3,200 years ago. From AD 330, the island was part of the Byzantine empire. In the 1570s, Cyprus became part of the Turkish Ottoman empire. Turkish rule continued until 1878 when Cyprus was leased to Britain. Britain annexed the island in 1914 and proclaimed it a colony in 1925.

In the 1950s, Greek Cypriots, who made up four-fifths of the population, began a campaign for *enosis* (union) with Greece. Their leader was the Greek Orthodox Archbishop Makarios. A secret guerrilla force called EOKA attacked the British, who exiled Makarios. Cyprus became an independent country in 1960, although Britain retained two military bases. Independent Cyprus had a constitution which provided for power-sharing between the Greek and Turkish Cypriots. But the constitution proved unworkable and fighting broke out between the two communities. In 1964, the United Nations sent in a peacekeeping force, but communal clashes recurred in 1967.

In 1974, Cypriot forces led by Greek officers overthrew Makarios. This led Turkey to invade northern Cyprus, a territory occupying about 40% of the island. Many Greek Cypriots fled from the north which, in 1979, was proclaimed an independent state called the Turkish Republic of Northern Cyprus. But the United Nations still regarded Cyprus as a single nation under the Greek-Cypriot government in the south. In 2002, new talks were opened to resolve the conflict as negotiations for Cyprus's entry to the European Union reached an advanced stage.

Cyprus got its name from the Greek word *kypros*, meaning copper. But little copper remains and the chief minerals today are asbestos and chromium. However, the most valuable activity in Cyprus is tourism. Manufactures include cement, clothes, footwear, tiles and wine.

In the early 1990s, the United Nations reclassified Cyprus as a developed rather than a developing country. But the economy of the Turkish-Cypriot north lags behind that of the more prosperous Greek-Cypriot south.

AREA 9,250 SQ KM [3,571 SQ MI] **POPULATION** 763,000
CAPITAL (POPULATION) NICOSIA (189,000)
GOVERNMENT MULTIPARTY REPUBLIC **ETHNIC GROUPS** GREEK CYPRIOT 78%, TURKISH CYPRIOT 18% **LANGUAGES** GREEK AND TURKISH (BOTH OFFICIAL), ENGLISH **RELIGIONS** GREEK ORTHODOX 78%, ISLAM 18%
CURRENCY CYPRUS POUND = 100 CENTS

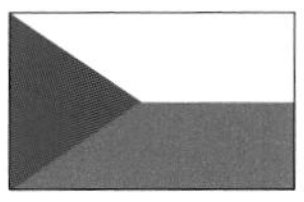

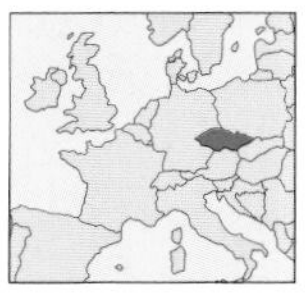

CZECH REPUBLIC

GEOGRAPHY The Czech Republic is the western three-fifths of the former country of Czechoslovakia. It contains two regions: Bohemia in the west and Moravia in the east. Mountains border much of the country in the west. The Bohemian basin in the north-centre is a fertile lowland region, with Prague, the capital city, as its main centre. Highlands cover much of the centre of the country, with lowlands in the south-east.

The climate is influenced by its landlocked position in east-central Europe. Prague has warm, sunny summers and cold winters. The average rainfall is moderate, with 500 mm to 750 mm [20 in to 30 in] every year in lowland areas.

POLITICS & ECONOMY After World War I (1914–18), Czechoslovakia was created. Germany seized the country in World War II (1939–45). In 1948, Communist leaders took power and Czechoslovakia was allied to the Soviet Union. When democratic reforms were introduced in the Soviet Union in the late 1980s, the Czechs also demanded reforms. Free elections were held in 1990, but differences between the Czechs and Slovaks and a resurgence of Slovak nationalism led the government to agree in 1992 to the partitioning of the country on 1 January 1993. The break was peaceful. In 1999, the Czech Republic became a member of NATO.

Under Communist rule the Czech Republic became one of the most industrialized parts of Eastern Europe. The country has deposits of coal, uranium, iron ore, magnesite, tin and zinc. Manufacturing employs about 40% of the Czech Republic's entire workforce. Farming is also important. Under Communism, the government owned the land, but private ownership is now being restored. The country was admitted into the OECD in 1995.

AREA 78,864 SQ KM [30,449 SQ MI] **POPULATION** 10,264,000
CAPITAL (POPULATION) PRAGUE (1,203,000) **GOVERNMENT** MULTIPARTY REPUBLIC **ETHNIC GROUPS** CZECH 81%, MORAVIAN 13%, SLOVAK 3%, POLISH, GERMAN, SILESIAN, GYPSY, HUNGARIAN, UKRAINIAN
LANGUAGES CZECH (OFFICIAL)
RELIGIONS ATHEIST 40%, ROMAN CATHOLIC 39%, PROTESTANT 4%
CURRENCY CZECH KORUNA = 100 HALER

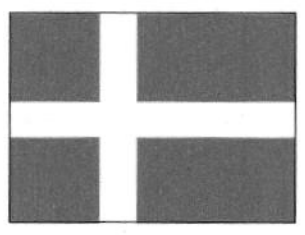

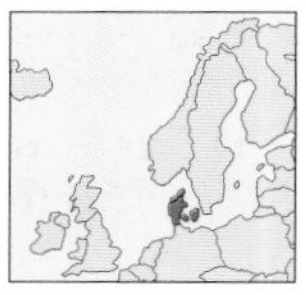

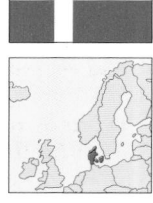

DENMARK

GEOGRAPHY The Kingdom of Denmark is the smallest country in Scandinavia. It consists of a peninsula, called Jutland (or Jylland), which is joined to Germany, and more than 400 islands, 89 of which are inhabited.

The land is flat and mostly covered by rocks dropped there by huge ice sheets during the last Ice Age. The highest point in Denmark is on Jutland. It is only 173 m [568 ft] above sea level.

Denmark has a cool but pleasant climate, except during cold spells in the winter when The Sound between Sjælland and Sweden may freeze over. Summers are warm. Rainfall occurs all through the year.

POLITICS & ECONOMY Danish Vikings terrorized much of Western Europe for about 300 years after AD 800. Danish kings ruled England in the 11th century. In the late 14th century, Denmark formed a union with Norway and Sweden (which included Finland). Sweden broke away in 1523, while Denmark lost Norway to Sweden in 1814.

After 1945, Denmark played an important part in European affairs, becoming a member of the North Atlantic Treaty Organization (NATO). In 1973, Denmark joined the European Union, although it rejected the adoption of the euro in 2000. The Danes now enjoy some of the world's highest living standards, although the extensive social welfare provisions exert a considerable cost.

Denmark has few natural resources apart from some oil and gas from wells deep under the North Sea. But the economy is highly developed. Manufacturing industries, which employ about 17% of all workers, produce a wide variety of products, including furniture, processed food, machinery, television sets and textiles. Farms cover about three-quarters of the land. Farming employs only 4% of the workers, but it is highly scientific and productive. Meat and dairy farming are the chief activities.

AREA 43,070 SQ KM [16,629 SQ MI] **POPULATION** 5,353,000
CAPITAL (POPULATION) COPENHAGEN (1,362,000)
GOVERNMENT PARLIAMENTARY MONARCHY **ETHNIC GROUPS** DANISH 97%
LANGUAGES DANISH (OFFICIAL) **RELIGIONS** LUTHERAN 95%, ROMAN CATHOLIC 1% **CURRENCY** KRONE = 100 ØRE

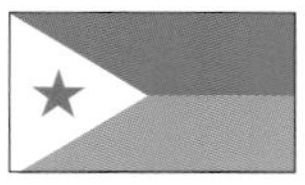

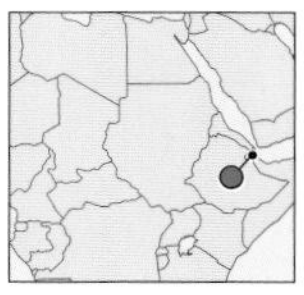

DJIBOUTI

GEOGRAPHY The Republic of Djibouti in eastern Africa occupies a strategic position where the Red Sea meets the Gulf of Aden. Djibouti has one of the world's hottest and driest climates.

POLITICS & ECONOMY France set up a territory called French Somaliland in 1888. Its capital, Djibouti, became important when a railway was built to Addis Ababa and Djibouti became the main outlet for Ethiopian trade. In 1967, France renamed the dependency the French Territory of the Afars and Issas, but it was renamed Djibouti on independence in 1977. It became a one-party state in 1981, but a new constitution (1992) permitted four parties which had to maintain a balance between the country's ethnic groups. Conflict between the Afars and Issas flared up in 1992 and 1993, but a peace agreement was signed in 1994. Djibouti is a poor country. Its economy is based largely on the revenue it gets from its port and the railway to Addis Ababa.

AREA 23,200 SQ KM [8,958 SQ MI] **POPULATION** 461,000
CAPITAL (POPULATION) DJIBOUTI (383,000) **GOVERNMENT** MULTIPARTY REPUBLIC **ETHNIC GROUPS** SOMALI 60%, AFAR 35% **LANGUAGES** ARABIC AND FRENCH (BOTH OFFICIAL) **RELIGIONS** ISLAM 94%, CHRISTIANITY 6%
CURRENCY DJIBOUTI FRANC = 100 CENTIMES

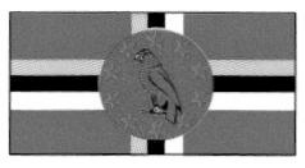

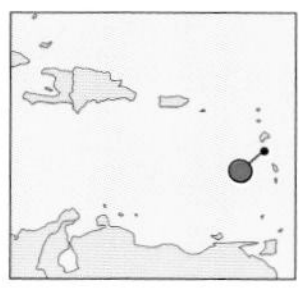

DOMINICA

The Commonwealth of Dominica, a former British colony, became independent in 1978. The island has a mountainous spine and less than 10% of the land is cultivated. Yet agriculture employs more than 60% of the people. The manufacturing of coconut-based soap is important, while mining and tourism are other minor activities.

AREA 751 SQ KM [290 SQ MI] **POPULATION** 71,000 **CAPITAL** ROSEAU

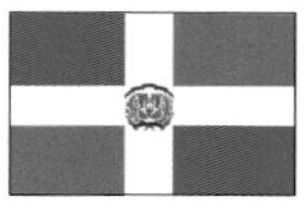

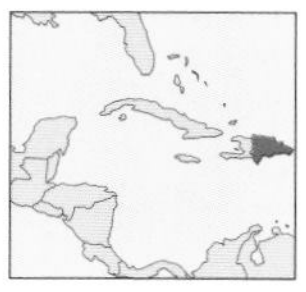

DOMINICAN REPUBLIC

GEOGRAPHY Second largest of the Caribbean nations in both area and population, the Dominican Republic shares the island of Hispaniola with Haiti, with the Dominican Republic occupying the eastern two-thirds. The country is mountainous, and the generally hot and humid climate eases with altitude.

POLITICS & ECONOMY The Dominican Republic has chaotic origins, having been held by Spain, France, Haiti and the USA at various times. Civil war broke out in 1966 but soon ended after US intervention. Joaquín Balaguer, elected president in 1966 under a new constitution, stood down in 1996 and was replaced by Leonel Fernández Reyna.

AREA 48,730 SQ KM [18,815 SQ MI] **POPULATION** 8,581,000
CAPITAL (POPULATION) SANTO DOMINGO (2,135,000)
GOVERNMENT MULTIPARTY REPUBLIC **ETHNIC GROUPS** MULATTO 73%, WHITE 16%, BLACK 11% **LANGUAGES** SPANISH (OFFICIAL)
RELIGIONS ROMAN CATHOLIC 95% **CURRENCY** PESO = 100 CENTAVOS

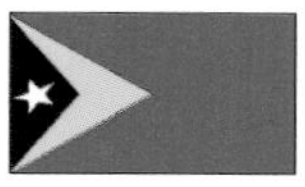

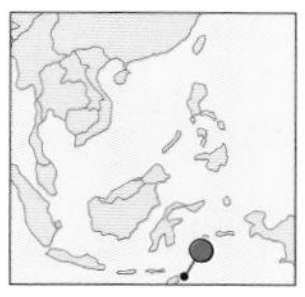

EAST TIMOR

The Republic of East Timor became fully independent and the world's newest country on 20 May 2002. The land is mainly rugged. Temperatures are generally high and the rainfall is moderate. Portugal ruled the area from the late 19th century, when it was called Portuguese Timor. Portugal withdrew in 1975 and Indonesia seized the area. Guerrilla activity mounted under Indonesian rule and, in 1999, the people voted for independence. Agriculture is the main activity. East Timor is heavily dependent on foreign aid, but its offshore deposits of oil and natural gas are due to come on line in 2004.

AREA 14,870 SQ KM [5,731 SQ MI] **POPULATION** 737,000 **CAPITAL** DILI

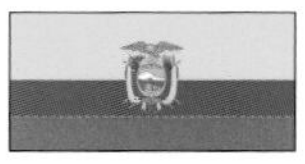

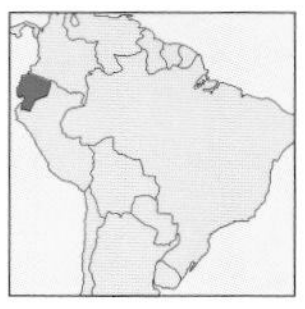

ECUADOR

GEOGRAPHY The Republic of Ecuador straddles the Equator on the west coast of South America. Three ranges of the high Andes Mountains form the backbone of the country. Between the towering, snow-capped peaks of the mountains, some of which are volcanoes, lie a series of high plateaux, or basins. Nearly half of Ecuador's population lives on these plateaux.

The climate in Ecuador depends on the height above sea level. Though the coastline is cooled by the cold Peruvian Current, temperatures are between 23°C to 25°C [73°F and 77°F] all through the year. In Quito, at 2,500 m [8,200 ft] above sea level, temperatures are 14°C to 15°C [57°F to 59°F], though the city is just south of the Equator.

POLITICS & ECONOMY The Inca people of Peru conquered much of what is now Ecuador in the late 15th century. They introduced their language, Quechua, which is widely spoken today. Spanish forces defeated the Incas in 1533 and took control of Ecuador. The country became independent in 1822, following the defeat of a Spanish force in a battle near Quito.

In the 19th and 20th centuries, Ecuador suffered from political instability, while successive governments failed to tackle the country's social and economic problems. A war with Peru in 1941 led to a loss of territory. Disputes continued until 1995, but a border agreement was signed in January 1998. Economic crises in the early 21st century led the government to abolish the sucre, its official currency, and replace it with the US dollar.

The World Bank classifies Ecuador as a 'lower-middle-income' developing country. Agriculture employs 30% of the people and bananas, cocoa and coffee are all important crops. Fishing, forestry, mining and manufacturing are other activities.

AREA 283,560 SQ KM [109,483 SQ MI] **POPULATION** 13,184,000
CAPITAL (POPULATION) QUITO (1,574,000)
GOVERNMENT MULTIPARTY REPUBLIC
ETHNIC GROUPS MESTIZO (MIXED WHITE AND AMERINDIAN) 40%, AMERINDIAN 40%, WHITE 15%, BLACK 5%
LANGUAGES SPANISH (OFFICIAL), QUECHUA
RELIGIONS ROMAN CATHOLIC 92%
CURRENCY US DOLLAR = 100 CENTS

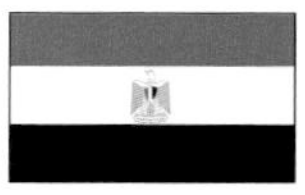

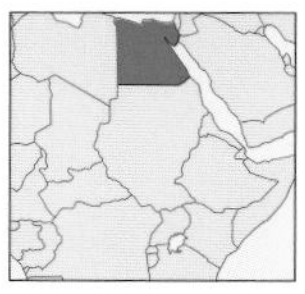

EGYPT

GEOGRAPHY The Arab Republic of Egypt is Africa's second largest country by population after Nigeria, though it ranks 13th in area. Most of Egypt is desert. Almost all the people live either in the Nile Valley and its fertile delta or along the Suez Canal, the artificial waterway between the Mediterranean and Red seas. This canal shortens the sea journey between the United Kingdom and India by 9,700 km [6,027 mi]. Recent attempts have been made to irrigate parts of the western desert and thus redistribute the rapidly growing Egyptian population into previously uninhabited regions.

Apart from the Nile Valley, Egypt has three other main regions. The Western and Eastern deserts are parts of the Sahara. The Sinai peninsula (Es Sina), to the east of the Suez Canal, is a mountainous desert region, geographically within Asia. It contains Egypt's highest peak, Gebel Katherina (2,637 m [8,650 ft]); few people live in this area.

Egypt is a dry country. The low rainfall occurs, if at all, in winter and the country is one of the sunniest places on Earth.

POLITICS & ECONOMY Ancient Egypt, which was founded about 5,000 years ago, was one of the great early civilizations. Throughout the country, pyramids, temples and richly decorated tombs are memorials to its great achievements.

After Ancient Egypt declined, the country came under successive foreign rulers. Arabs occupied Egypt in AD 639–42. They introduced the Arabic language and Islam. Their influence was so great that most Egyptians now regard themselves as Arabs.

Egypt came under British rule in 1882, but it gained partial independence in 1922, becoming a monarchy. The monarchy was abolished in 1952, when Egypt became a republic. The creation of Israel in 1948 led Egypt into a series of wars in 1948–9, 1956, 1967 and 1973. Since the late 1970s, Egypt has sought for peace. In 1979, Egypt signed a peace treaty with Israel and regained the Sinai region which it had lost in a war in 1967. Extremists opposed contacts with Israel and, in 1981, President Sadat, who had signed the treaty, was assassinated.

While Egypt plays a major part in Arab affairs, most of its people are poor. Some Islamic fundamentalists, who dislike Western

influences on their way of life, have resorted to violence. In the 1990s, attacks on foreign visitors caused a decline in the valuable tourist industry. In 1999, Hosni Mubarak, president since 1981, was himself attacked by extremists, but he was re-elected to a fourth term in office.

Egypt is Africa's second most industrialized country after South Africa, but it remains a developing country and income levels remain low for the vast majority of Egyptian people. Oil and textiles are the chief exports.

AREA 1,001,450 sq km [386,660 sq mi] **POPULATION** 69,537,000
CAPITAL (POPULATION) Cairo (6,800,000)
GOVERNMENT Republic
ETHNIC GROUPS Egyptian 99%
LANGUAGES Arabic (official), French, English
RELIGIONS Islam (Sunni Muslim 94%), Christianity (mainly Coptic Christian 6%)
CURRENCY Pound = 100 piastres

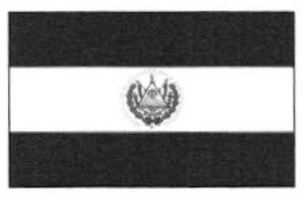
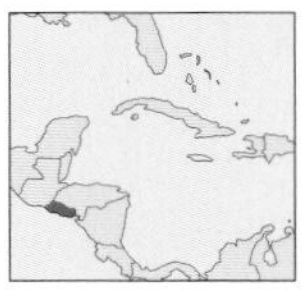

EL SALVADOR

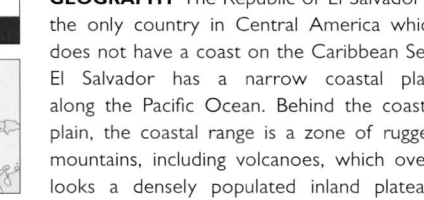

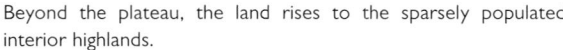

GEOGRAPHY The Republic of El Salvador is the only country in Central America which does not have a coast on the Caribbean Sea. El Salvador has a narrow coastal plain along the Pacific Ocean. Behind the coastal plain, the coastal range is a zone of rugged mountains, including volcanoes, which overlooks a densely populated inland plateau. Beyond the plateau, the land rises to the sparsely populated interior highlands.

The coast has a hot, tropical climate. Inland, the climate is moderated by the altitude. Rain falls on practically every afternoon between May and October.

POLITICS & ECONOMY Amerindians have lived in El Salvador for thousands of years. The ruins of Mayan pyramids built between AD 100 and 1000 are still found in the western part of the country. Spanish soldiers conquered the area in 1524 and 1525, and Spain ruled until 1821. In 1823, all the Central American countries, except for Panama, set up a Central American Federation. But El Salvador withdrew in 1840 and declared its independence in 1841. El Salvador suffered from instability throughout the 19th century. The 20th century saw a more stable government, but from 1931 military dictatorships alternated with elected governments and the country remained poor.

In the 1970s, El Salvador was plagued by conflict as protesters demanded that the government introduce reforms to help the poor. Kidnappings and murders committed by left- and right-wing groups caused instability. A civil war broke out in 1979 between the US-backed, right-wing government forces and left-wing guerrillas in the FMLN (Farabundo Marti National Liberation Front). In 12 years, more than 750,000 people died and hundreds of thousands were made homeless. A cease-fire was agreed on 1 February 1992, and elections were held in 1993 and 1999.

With its economy shattered by war, El Salvador remains a 'lower-middle-income' economy, according to the World Bank. Farmland and pasture cover about three-quarters of the country. Coffee, grown in the highlands, is the main export, followed by sugar and cotton, which grow on the coastal lowlands. Fishing for lobsters and shrimps is important, but manufacturing is on a small scale.

AREA 21,040 sq km [8,124 sq mi] **POPULATION** 6,238,000
CAPITAL (POPULATION) San Salvador (1,522,000)
GOVERNMENT Republic **ETHNIC GROUPS** Mestizo (mixed White and Amerindian) 89%, White 10%, Amerindian 1%
LANGUAGES Spanish (official) **RELIGIONS** Roman Catholic 86%
CURRENCY US dollar; Colón = 100 centavos

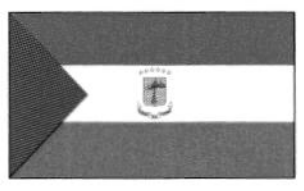
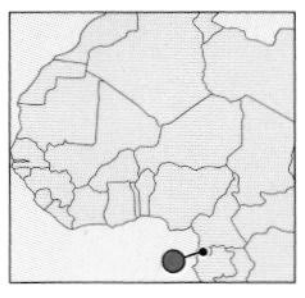

EQUATORIAL GUINEA

GEOGRAPHY The Republic of Equatorial Guinea is a small republic in west-central Africa. It consists of a mainland territory which makes up 90% of the land area, called Mbini (or Rio Muni), between Cameroon and Gabon, and five offshore islands in the Bight of Bonny, the largest of which is Bioko. The island of Annobon lies 560 km [350 mi] south-west of Mbini. Mbini consists mainly of hills and plateaux behind the coastal plains.

The climate is hot and humid. Bioko is mountainous, with the land rising to 3,008 m [9,869 ft], and hence it is particularly rainy. However, there is a marked dry season between the months of December and February. Mainland Mbini has a similar climate, though the rainfall diminishes inland.

POLITICS & ECONOMY Portuguese navigators reached the area in 1471. In 1778, Portugal granted Bioko, together with rights over Mbini, to Spain.

In 1959, Spain made Bioko and Mbini provinces of overseas Spain and, in 1963, it gave the provinces a degree of self-government. Equatorial Guinea became independent in 1968.

The first president of Equatorial Guinea, Francisco Macias Nguema, proved to be a tyrant. He was overthrown in 1979 and a group of officers, led by Lt-Col. Teodoro Obiang Nguema Mbasogo, set up a Supreme Military Council to rule the country. In 1991, the people voted to set up a multiparty democracy. Elections were held in the 1990s, but accusations of human rights abuses continued.

Equatorial Guinea is a poor country. Agriculture employs up to 66% of the people. The main food crops are bananas, cassava and sweet potatoes, but the most valuable crop is cocoa, grown on Bioko.

AREA 28,050 sq km [10,830 sq mi] **POPULATION** 486,000
CAPITAL (POPULATION) Malabo (35,000) **GOVERNMENT** Multiparty republic (transitional) **ETHNIC GROUPS** Fang 83%, Bubi 10%, Ndowe 4% **LANGUAGES** Spanish and French (both official) **RELIGIONS** Roman Catholic 89% **CURRENCY** CFA franc = 100 centimes

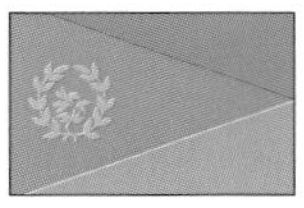
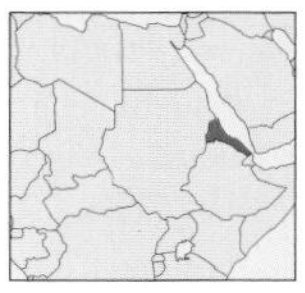

ERITREA

GEOGRAPHY The State of Eritrea consists of a hot, dry coastal plain facing the Red Sea, with a fairly mountainous area in the centre. Most people live in the cooler highland area.

POLITICS & ECONOMY Eritrea, which was an Italian colony from the 1880s, was part of Ethiopia from 1952 until 1993, when it became a fully independent nation. National reconstruction was hampered by conflict with Yemen over three islands in the Red Sea, while in 1998–9, border clashes with Ethiopia caused loss of life. However, a peace agreement was signed in 2000. Farming and livestock rearing are the main activities in this war-ravaged territory. Eritrea has few manufacturing industries, based mainly in Asmara.

AREA 94,000 sq km [36,293 sq mi] **POPULATION** 4,298,000
CAPITAL (POPULATION) Asmara (367,500)
GOVERNMENT Transitional government **ETHNIC GROUPS** Tigrinya 49%, Tigre 32%, Afar 4%, Beja 3%, Saho 3%, Kunama 3%, Nara 2%
LANGUAGES Afar, Amharic, Arabic, Tigrinya **RELIGIONS** Coptic Christian 50%, Islam 50% **CURRENCY** Nakfa

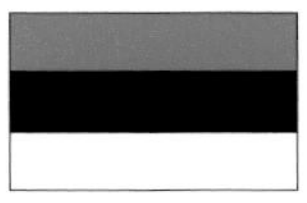
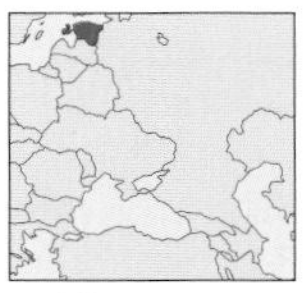

ESTONIA

GEOGRAPHY The Republic of Estonia is the smallest of the three states on the Baltic Sea, which were formerly part of the Soviet Union, but which became independent in the early 1990s. Estonia consists of a generally flat plain which was covered by ice sheets during the Ice Age. The land is strewn with moraine (rocks deposited by the ice).

The country is dotted with more than 1,500 small lakes, and water, including the large Lake Peipus (Chudskoye Ozero) and the River Narva makes up much of Estonia's eastern border with Russia. Estonia has more than 800 islands, which together make up about a tenth of the country. The largest island is Saaremaa (Sarema).

Despite its northerly position, Estonia has a fairly mild climate because of its nearness to the sea. This is because sea winds tend to warm the land in winter and cool it in summer.

POLITICS & ECONOMY The ancestors of the Estonians, who are related to the Finns, settled in the area several thousand years ago. German crusaders, known as the Teutonic Knights, introduced Christianity in the early 13th century. By the 16th century, German noblemen owned much of the land in Estonia. In 1561, Sweden took the northern part of the country and Poland the south. From 1625, Sweden controlled the entire country until Sweden handed it over to Russia in 1721.

Estonian nationalists campaigned for their independence from around the mid-19th century. Finally, Estonia was proclaimed independent in 1918. In 1919, the government began to break up the large estates and distribute land among the peasants.

In 1939, Germany and the Soviet Union agreed to take over parts of Eastern Europe. In 1940, Soviet forces occupied Estonia, but they were driven out by the Germans in 1941. Soviet troops returned in 1944 and Estonia became one of the 15 Soviet Socialist Republics of the Soviet Union. The Estonians strongly opposed Soviet rule. Many of them were deported to Siberia.

Political changes in the Soviet Union in the late 1980s led to renewed demands for freedom. In 1990, the Estonian government declared the country independent and, finally, the Soviet Union recognized this act in September 1991, shortly before the Soviet Union was dissolved. Estonia adopted a new constitution in 1992, when multiparty elections were held for a new national assembly. In 1993, Estonia negotiated an agreement with Russia to withdraw its troops.

Under Soviet rule, Estonia was the most prosperous of the three Baltic states. Since 1988, Estonia has begun to change its government-dominated economy to one based on private enterprise, and the country has started to strengthen its links with the rest of Europe. Estonia's resources include oil shale and its forests. Industries produce fertilizers, machinery, petrochemical products, processed food, wood products and textiles. Agriculture and fishing are also important.

AREA 44,700 sq km [17,300 sq mi] **POPULATION** 1,423,000
CAPITAL (POPULATION) Tallinn (435,000) **GOVERNMENT** Multiparty republic **ETHNIC GROUPS** Estonian 65%, Russian 28%, Ukrainian 3%, Belarussian 2%, Finnish 1% **LANGUAGES** Estonian (official), Russian **RELIGIONS** Lutheran, Russian and Estonian Orthodox, Methodist, Baptist, Roman Catholic **CURRENCY** Kroon = 100 sents

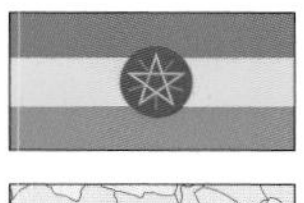
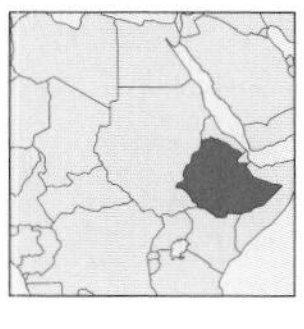

ETHIOPIA

GEOGRAPHY Ethiopia is a landlocked country in north-eastern Africa. The land is mainly mountainous, though there are extensive plains in the east, bordering southern Eritrea, and in the south, bordering Somalia. The highlands are divided into two blocks by an arm of the Great Rift Valley which runs throughout eastern Africa. North of the Rift Valley, the land is especially rugged, rising to 4,620 m [15,157 ft] at Ras Dashen. South-east of Ras Dashen is Lake Tana, source of the River Abay (Blue Nile).

The climate in Ethiopia is greatly affected by the altitude. Addis Ababa, at 2,450 m [8,000 ft], has an average yearly temperature of 20°C [68°F]. The rainfall is generally more than 1,000 mm [39 in]. But the lowlands bordering the Eritrean coast are hot.

POLITICS & ECONOMY Ethiopia was the home of an ancient monarchy, which became Christian in the 4th century. In the 7th century, Muslims gained control of the lowlands, but Christianity survived in the highlands. In the 19th century, Ethiopia resisted attempts to colonize it. Italy invaded Ethiopia in 1935, but Ethiopian and British troops defeated the Italians in 1941.

In 1952, Eritrea, on the Red Sea coast, was federated with Ethiopia. But in 1961, Eritrean nationalists demanded their freedom and began a struggle that ended in their independence in 1993. Clashes along the border with Eritrea occurred in 1998 and 1999, but a peace agreement was signed in 2000. Ethnic diversity in Ethiopia has led to demands by some minorities for self-government. As a result, the government divided Ethiopia into nine provinces in 1995. Each province has its own regional assembly.

Ethiopia is one of the world's poorest countries, particularly in the 1970s and 1980s when it was plagued by civil war and famine caused partly by long droughts. Many richer countries have sent aid (money and food) to help the Ethiopian people. Agriculture remains the leading activity.

AREA 1,128,000 sq km [435,521 sq mi] **POPULATION** 65,892,000
CAPITAL (POPULATION) Addis Ababa (2,316,000)
GOVERNMENT Federation of nine provinces
ETHNIC GROUPS Oromo 40%, Amharic 32%, Sidamo 9%, Shankella 6%, Somali 6% **LANGUAGES** Amharic (official), 280 others
RELIGIONS Islam 47%, Ethiopian Orthodox 40%, traditional beliefs 11% **CURRENCY** Birr = 100 cents

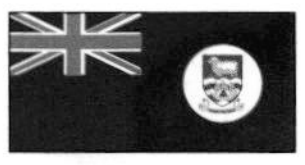
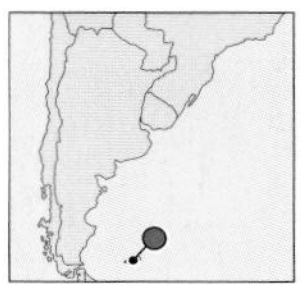

FALKLAND ISLANDS

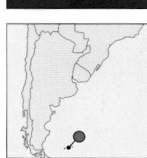

Comprising two main islands and over 200 small islands, the Falkland Islands (or the Islas Malvinas, as they are called in Argentina) lie 480 km [300 mi] from South America. Sheep farming is the main activity, though the search for oil and diamonds holds out hope for the future of this harsh and virtually treeless environment.

AREA 12,170 sq km [4,699 sq mi] **POPULATION** 2,895
CAPITAL Stanley

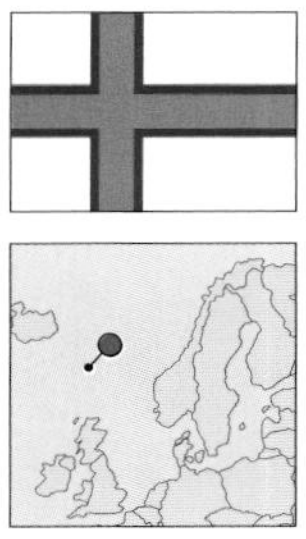

FAROE ISLANDS

The Faroe Islands are a group of 18 volcanic islands and some reefs in the North Atlantic Ocean. The islands have been Danish since the 1380s, but they became largely self-governing in 1948. In 1998, the government of the Faroes announced its intention to become independent of Denmark.

AREA 1,400 SQ KM [541 SQ MI]
POPULATION 46,000 **CAPITAL** TORSHÁVN

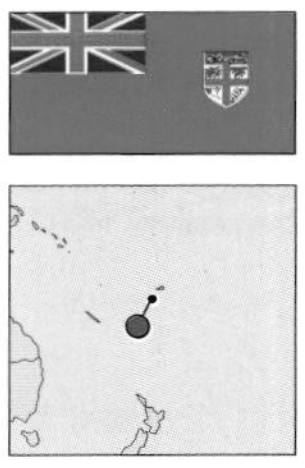

FIJI

The Republic of Fiji comprises more than 800 Melanesian islands, the biggest being Viti Levu and Vanua Levu. The climate is tropical, with south-east trade winds blowing throughout the year. A former British colony, Fiji became independent in 1970. Its recent history has been marred by efforts by ethnic Fijians to impose their rule, stopping members of the ethnic Indian community from holding senior cabinet posts. Their actions have provoked international criticism.

AREA 18,270 SQ KM [7,054 SQ MI] **POPULATION** 844,000 **CAPITAL** SUVA

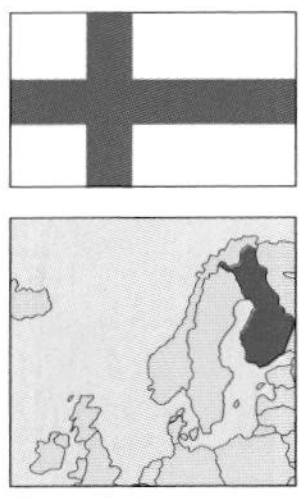

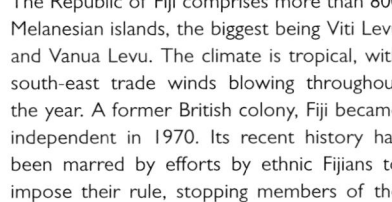

FINLAND

GEOGRAPHY The Republic of Finland is a beautiful country in northern Europe. In the south, behind the coastal lowlands where most Finns live, lies a region of sparkling lakes worn out by ice sheets in the Ice Age. The thinly populated northern uplands cover about two-fifths of the country.

Helsinki, the capital city, has warm summers, but the average temperatures between the months of December and March are below freezing point. Snow covers the land in winter. The north has less precipitation than the south, but it is much colder.

POLITICS & ECONOMY Between 1150 and 1809, Finland was under Swedish rule. The close links between the countries continue today. Swedish remains an official language in Finland and many towns have Swedish as well as Finnish names.

In 1809, Finland became a grand duchy of the Russian empire. It finally declared itself independent in 1917, after the Russian Revolution and the collapse of the Russian empire. But during World War II (1939–45), the Soviet Union declared war on Finland and took part of Finland's territory. Finland allied itself with Germany, but it lost more land to the Soviet Union at the end of the war.

After World War II, Finland became a neutral country and negotiated peace treaties with the Soviet Union. Finland also strengthened its relations with other northern European countries and became an associate member of the European Free Trade Association (EFTA) in 1961. Finland became a full member of EFTA in 1986, but in 1992, along with most of its fellow EFTA members, it applied for membership of the European Union, which it finally achieved on 1 January 1995. On 1 January 2002, the euro became Finland's sole official unit of currency.

Forests are Finland's most valuable resource, and forestry accounts for about 35% of the country's exports. The chief manufactures are wood products, pulp and paper. Since World War II, Finland has set up many other industries, producing such things as machinery and transport equipment. Its economy has expanded rapidly, but there has been a large increase in the number of unemployed people.

AREA 338,130 SQ KM [130,552 SQ MI] **POPULATION** 5,176,000
CAPITAL (POPULATION) HELSINKI (532,000)
GOVERNMENT MULTIPARTY REPUBLIC **ETHNIC GROUPS** FINNISH 93%, SWEDISH 6% **LANGUAGES** FINNISH AND SWEDISH (BOTH OFFICIAL)
RELIGIONS EVANGELICAL LUTHERAN 88% **CURRENCY** EURO = 100 CENTS

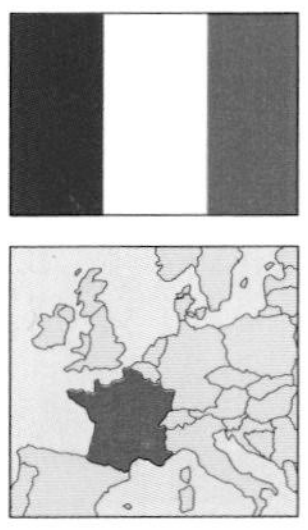

FRANCE

GEOGRAPHY The Republic of France is the largest country in Western Europe. The scenery is extremely varied. The Vosges Mountains overlook the Rhine valley in the north-east, the Jura Mountains and the Alps form the borders with Switzerland and Italy in the south-east, while the Pyrenees straddle France's border with Spain. The only large highland area entirely within France is the Massif Central between the Rhône-Saône valley and the basin of Aquitaine in southern France.

Brittany (Bretagne) and Normandy (Normande) form a scenic hill region. Fertile lowlands cover most of northern France, including the densely populated Paris basin. Another major lowland area, the Aquitanian basin, is in the south-west, while the Rhône-Saône valley and the Mediterranean lowlands are in the south-east.

The climate of France varies from west to east and from north to south. The west comes under the moderating influence of the Atlantic Ocean, giving generally mild weather. To the east, summers are warmer and winters colder. The climate also becomes warmer as one travels from north to south. The Mediterranean Sea coast has hot, dry summers and mild, moist winters. The Alps, Jura and Pyrenees mountains have snowy winters. Winter sports centres are found in all three areas. Large glaciers occupy high valleys in the Alps.

POLITICS & ECONOMY The Romans conquered France (then called Gaul) in the 50s BC. Roman rule began to decline in the fifth century AD and, in 486, the Frankish realm (as France was called) became independent under a Christian king, Clovis. In 800, Charlemagne, who had been king since 768, became emperor of the Romans. He extended France's boundaries, but, in 843, his empire was divided into three parts and the area of France contracted. After the Norman invasion of England in 1066, large areas of France came under English rule, but this was finally ended in 1453.

France later became a powerful monarchy. But the French Revolution (1789–99) ended absolute rule by French kings. In 1799, Napoleon Bonaparte took power and fought a series of brilliant military campaigns before his final defeat in 1815. The monarchy was restored until 1848, when the Second Republic was founded. In 1852, Napoleon's nephew became Napoleon III, but the Third Republic was established in 1875. France was the scene of much fighting during World War I (1914–18) and World War II (1939–45), causing great loss of life and much damage to the economy.

In 1946, France adopted a new constitution, establishing the Fourth Republic. But political instability and costly colonial wars slowed France's post-war recovery. In 1958, Charles de Gaulle was elected president and he introduced a new constitution, giving the president extra powers and inaugurating the Fifth Republic.

Since the 1960s, France has made rapid economic progress, becoming one of the most prosperous nations in the European Union. But France's government faced a number of problems, including unemployment, pollution and the growing number of elderly people, who find it difficult to live when inflation rates are high. One social problem concerns the presence in France of large numbers of immigrants from Africa and southern Europe, many of whom live in poor areas.

A socialist government under Lionel Jospin was elected in 1997. Under Jospin, France adopted the euro, the single European currency, and shortened the working week. The French system of high social security taxes seemed likely to continue, although the economy continued to thrive. In the early 21st century, French politicians were plagued by allegations of corruption and illegal party funding.

France is one of the world's most developed countries. Its natural resources include its fertile soil, together with deposits of bauxite, coal, iron ore, oil and natural gas, and potash. France is also one of the world's top manufacturing nations, and it has often innovated in bold and imaginative ways. The TGV and hypermarkets are typical examples. Paris is a world centre of fashion industries, but France has many other industrial towns and cities. Major manufactures include aircraft, cars, chemicals, electronic and metal products, machinery, processed food, steel and textiles.

Agriculture employs about 7% of the people, but France is the largest producer of farm products in Western Europe, producing most of the food it needs. Wheat is the leading crop and livestock farming is of major importance. Fishing and forestry are leading industries, while tourism is a major activity.

AREA 551,500 SQ KM [212,934 SQ MI] **POPULATION** 59,551,000
CAPITAL (POPULATION) PARIS (11,175,000) **GOVERNMENT** MULTIPARTY REPUBLIC **ETHNIC GROUPS** CELTIC, LATIN, ARAB, TEUTONIC, SLAVIC
LANGUAGES FRENCH (OFFICIAL), BRETON, OCCITAN **RELIGIONS** ROMAN CATHOLIC 90%, ISLAM 3% **CURRENCY** EURO = 100 CENTS

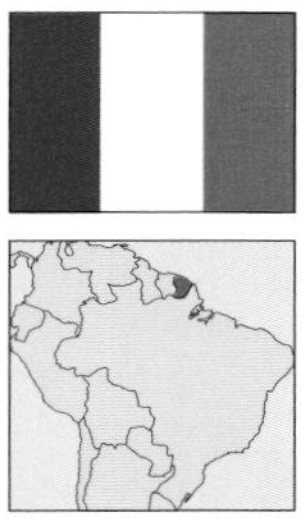

FRENCH GUIANA

GEOGRAPHY French Guiana is the smallest country in mainland South America. The coastal plain is swampy in places, but some dry areas are cultivated. Inland lies a plateau, with the low Tumachumac Mountains in the south. Most of the rivers run north towards the Atlantic Ocean.

French Guiana has a hot, equatorial climate, with high temperatures throughout the year. The rainfall is heavy, especially between December and June, but it is dry between August and October. The north-east trade winds blow constantly across the country.

POLITICS & ECONOMY The first people to live in what is now French Guiana were Amerindians. Today, only a few of them survive in the interior. The first Europeans to explore the coast arrived in 1500, and they were followed by adventurers seeking El Dorado, the mythical city of gold. Cayenne was founded in 1637 by a group of French merchants. The area became a French colony in the late 17th century.

France used the colony as a penal settlement for political prisoners from the times of the French Revolution in the 1790s. From the 1850s to 1945, the country became notorious as a place where prisoners were harshly treated. Many of them died, unable to survive in the tropical conditions.

In 1946, French Guiana became an overseas department of France, and in 1974 it also became an administrative region. An independence movement developed in the 1980s, but most people want to retain their links with France and continue to obtain financial aid to develop their territory.

Although it has rich forest and mineral resources, such as bauxite (aluminium ore), French Guiana is a developing country. It depends greatly on France for money to run its services and the government is the country's biggest employer. Since 1968, Kourou in French Guiana, the European Space Agency's rocket-launching site, has earned money for France by sending communications satellites into space.

AREA 90,000 SQ KM [34,749 SQ MI] **POPULATION** 178,000
CAPITAL (POPULATION) CAYENNE (42,000) **GOVERNMENT** OVERSEAS DEPARTMENT OF FRANCE **ETHNIC GROUPS** MULATTO 66%, CHINESE AND AMERINDIAN 12%, WHITE 10% **LANGUAGES** FRENCH (OFFICIAL)
RELIGIONS CHRISTIANITY (ROMAN CATHOLIC 80%, PROTESTANT 4%)
CURRENCY FRENCH FRANC = 100 CENTIMES

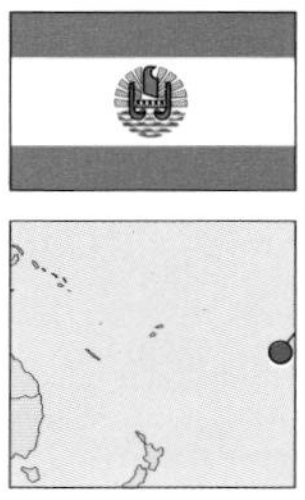

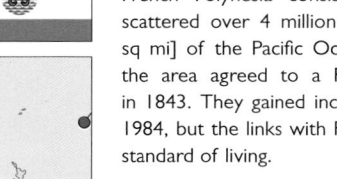

FRENCH POLYNESIA

French Polynesia consists of 130 islands, scattered over 4 million sq km [1.5 million sq mi] of the Pacific Ocean. Tribal chiefs in the area agreed to a French protectorate in 1843. They gained increased autonomy in 1984, but the links with France ensure a high standard of living.

AREA 3,941 SQ KM [1,520 SQ MI]
POPULATION 254,000 **CAPITAL** PAPEETE

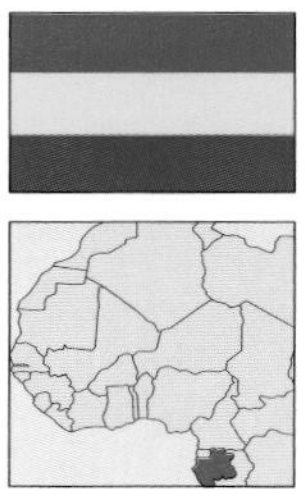

GABON

GEOGRAPHY The Gabonese Republic lies on the Equator in west-central Africa. In area, it is a little larger than the United Kingdom, with a coastline 800 km [500 mi] long. Behind the narrow, partly lagoon-lined coastal plain, the land rises to hills, plateaux and mountains divided by deep valleys carved by the River Ogooué and its tributaries.

Most of Gabon has an equatorial climate, with high temperatures and humidity throughout the year. The rainfall is heavy and the skies are often cloudy.

POLITICS & ECONOMY Gabon became a French colony in the 1880s, but it achieved full independence in 1960. In 1964, an attempted coup was put down when French troops intervened and crushed the revolt. In 1967, Bernard-Albert Bongo, who later renamed himself El Hadj Omar Bongo, became president. He declared Gabon a one-party state in 1968. Opposition parties were legalized in 1991, but Bongo was re-elected president in 1993 and 1998.

Gabon's abundant natural resources include its forests, oil and gas deposits near Port Gentil, together with manganese and uranium. These mineral deposits make Gabon one of Africa's better-off countries. But agriculture still employs about 75% of the population and many farmers produce little more than they need to support their families.

AREA 267,670 SQ KM [103,347 SQ MI] **POPULATION** 1,221,000
CAPITAL (POPULATION) LIBREVILLE (418,000)
GOVERNMENT MULTIPARTY REPUBLIC
ETHNIC GROUPS FOUR MAJOR BANTU TRIBES: FANG, ESHIRA, BAPOUNOU AND BATEKE **LANGUAGES** FRENCH (OFFICIAL), BANTU LANGUAGES **RELIGIONS** ROMAN CATHOLIC 65%, PROTESTANT 19%, AFRICAN CHURCHES 12%, TRADITIONAL BELIEFS 3%, ISLAM 2%
CURRENCY CFA FRANC = 100 CENTIMES

GAMBIA, THE

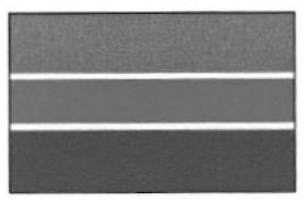

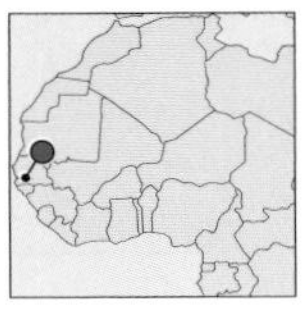

GEOGRAPHY The Republic of The Gambia is the smallest country in mainland Africa. It consists of a narrow strip of land bordering the River Gambia. The Gambia is almost entirely enclosed by Senegal, except along the short Atlantic coastline.

The Gambia has hot and humid summers, but the winter temperatures (November to May) drop to around 16°C [61°F]. In the summer, moist south-westerlies bring rain, which is heaviest on the coast.

POLITICS & ECONOMY English traders bought rights to trade on the River Gambia in 1588, and in 1664 the English established a settlement on an island in the river estuary. In 1765, the British founded a colony called Senegambia, which included parts of The Gambia and Senegal. In 1783, Britain handed this colony over to France.

In the 1860s and 1870s, Britain and France discussed the exchange of The Gambia for some other French territory. But no agreement was reached and Britain made The Gambia a British colony in 1888. It remained under British rule until it achieved full independence in 1965. In 1970, The Gambia became a republic. Relations between the English-speaking Gambians and the French-speaking Senegalese form a major political issue. In 1981, an attempted coup in The Gambia was put down with the help of Senegalese troops. In 1982, The Gambia and Senegal set up a defence alliance, called the Confederation of Senegambia. But this alliance was dissolved in 1989. In July 1994, a military group overthrew the president, Sir Dawda Jawara, who fled into exile. Captain Yahya Jammeh, who took power, was elected president in 1996.

Agriculture employs more than 80% of the people. The main food crops include cassava, millet and sorghum, but groundnuts and groundnut products are the chief exports. Tourism is a growing industry.

AREA 11,300 SQ KM [4,363 SQ MI] **POPULATION** 1,411,000
CAPITAL (POPULATION) BANJUL (171,000)
GOVERNMENT MILITARY REGIME
ETHNIC GROUPS MANDINKA 42%, FULA 18%, WOLOF 16%, JOLA 10%, SERAHULI 9%
LANGUAGES ENGLISH (OFFICIAL), MANDINKA, WOLOF, FULA
RELIGIONS ISLAM 90%, CHRISTIANITY 9%, TRADITIONAL BELIEFS 1%
CURRENCY DALASI = 100 BUTUT

GEORGIA

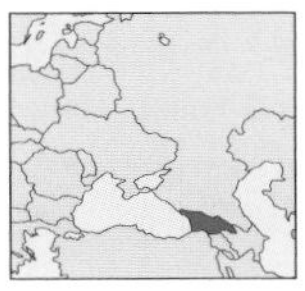

GEOGRAPHY Georgia is a country on the borders of Europe and Asia, facing the Black Sea. The land is rugged with the Caucasus Mountains forming its northern border. The highest mountain in this range, Mount Elbrus (5,633 m [18,481 ft]), lies over the border with Russia.border in Russia.

The Black Sea plains have hot summers and mild winters, when the temperatures seldom drop below freezing point. The rainfall is heavy, but inland Tbilisi has moderate rainfall, with the heaviest rains in the spring and early summer.

POLITICS & ECONOMY The first Georgian state was set up nearly 2,500 years ago. But for much of its history, the area was ruled by various conquerors. Christianity was introduced in AD 330. Georgia freed itself of foreign rule in the 11th and 12th centuries, but Mongol armies attacked in the 13th century. From the 16th to the 18th centuries, Iran and the Turkish Ottoman empire struggled for control of the area, and in the late 18th century Georgia sought the protection of Russia and, by the early 19th century, Georgia was part of the Russian empire. After the Russian Revolution of 1917, Georgia declared its independence, but Russia invaded, making the country part of the Soviet regime. Georgia declared itself independent in 1991. It became a separate country when the Soviet Union was dissolved in December 1991.

Georgia contains three regions containing minority peoples: Abkhazia in the north-west, South Ossetia in north-central Georgia, and Adjaria (also spelled Adzharia) in the south-west. Civil war broke out in South Ossetia in the early 1990s, while fierce fighting continued in Abkhazia until the late 1990s. In 2000, Georgia agreed to recognize Adjaria's autonomy in the country's constitution. In 2002, Russia stated that Chechen rebels were taking refuge in eastern Georgia, while the US alleged that terrorists from Afghanistan and elsewhere were moving into the area.

Georgia is a developing country. Agriculture is important. Major products include barley, citrus fruits, grapes for winemaking, maize, tea, tobacco and vegetables. Food processing and silk and perfume-making are other important activities. Sheep and cattle are reared.

AREA 69,700 SQ KM [26,910 SQ MI] **POPULATION** 4,989,000
CAPITAL (POPULATION) TBILISI (1,253,000)
GOVERNMENT MULTIPARTY REPUBLIC **ETHNIC GROUPS** GEORGIAN 70%, ARMENIAN 8%, RUSSIAN 6%, AZERI 6%, OSSETIAN 3%, GREEK 2%, ABKHAZ 2%, OTHERS 3% **LANGUAGES** GEORGIAN (OFFICIAL), RUSSIAN
RELIGIONS GEORGIAN ORTHODOX 65%, ISLAM 11%, RUSSIAN ORTHODOX 10%, ARMENIAN APOSTOLIC 8%
CURRENCY LARI = 100 TETRI

GERMANY

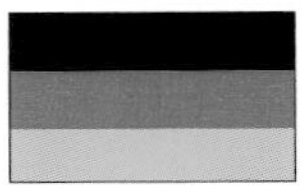

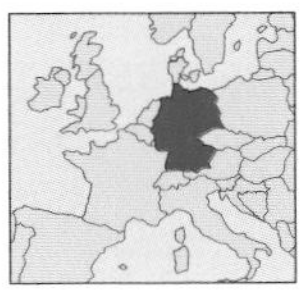

GEOGRAPHY The Federal Republic of Germany is the fourth largest country in Western Europe, after France, Spain and Sweden. The North German plain borders the North Sea in the north-west and the Baltic Sea in the north-east. Major rivers draining the plain include the Weser, Elbe and Oder.

The central highlands contain plateaux and highlands, including the Harz Mountains, the Thuringian Forest (Thüringer Wald), the Ore Mountains (Erzgebirge), and the Bohemian Forest (Böhmerwald) on the Czech border. South Germany is largely hilly, but the land rises in the south to the Bavarian Alps, which contain Germany's highest peak, Zugspitze, at 2,963 m [9,721 ft] above sea level. The scenic Black Forest (Scharzwald) overlooks the River Rhine, which flows through a rift valley in the south-west. The Black Forest contains the source of the River Danube.

North-western Germany has a mild climate, but the Baltic coastlands are cooler. To the south, the climate becomes more continental, especially in the highlands. The precipitation is greatest on the uplands, many of which are snow-capped in winter.

POLITICS & ECONOMY Germany and its allies were defeated in World War I (1914–18) and the country became a republic. Adolf Hitler came to power in 1933 and ruled as a dictator. His order to invade Poland led to the start of World War II (1939–45), which ended with Germany in ruins.

In 1945, Germany was divided into four military zones. In 1949, the American, British and French zones were amalgamated to form the Federal Republic of Germany (West Germany), while the Soviet zone became the German Democratic Republic (East Germany), a Communist state. Berlin, which had also been partitioned, became a divided city. West Berlin was part of West Germany, while East Berlin became the capital of East Germany. Bonn was the capital of West Germany.

Tension between East and West mounted during the Cold War, but West Germany rebuilt its economy quickly. In East Germany, the recovery was less rapid. In the late 1980s, reforms in the Soviet Union led to unrest in East Germany. Free elections were held in East Germany in 1990 and, on 3 October 1990, Germany was reunited.

The united Germany adopted West Germany's official name, the Federal Republic of Germany. Elections in December 1990 returned Helmut Kohl, West Germany's Chancellor (head of government) since 1982, to power. His government faced many problems, especially the restructuring of the economy of the former East Germany. Kohl was defeated in elections in 1998 and was succeeded as Chancellor by Social Democrat Gerhard Schröder. In 1999, Germany's parliament moved from Bonn to the reconstructed Reichstag building in Berlin.

West Germany's 'economic miracle' after the destruction of World War II was greatly helped by foreign aid. Today, despite all the problems caused by reunification, Germany is one of the world's greatest economic and trading nations.

Manufacturing is the most valuable part of Germany's economy and manufactured goods make up the bulk of the country's exports. Cars and other vehicles, cement, chemicals, computers, electrical equipment, processed food, machinery, scientific instruments, ships, steel, textiles and tools are among the leading manufactures. Germany has some coal, lignite, potash and rock salt deposits. But it imports many of the raw materials needed by its industries.

Germany also imports food. Major agricultural products include fruits, grapes for winemaking, potatoes, sugar beet and vegetables. Beef and dairy cattle are raised, together with many other livestock.

AREA 356,910 SQ KM [137,803 SQ MI] **POPULATION** 83,030,000
CAPITAL (POPULATION) BERLIN (3,426,000)
GOVERNMENT FEDERAL MULTIPARTY REPUBLIC **ETHNIC GROUPS** GERMAN 93%, TURKISH 2%, SERBO-CROAT 1%, ITALIAN 1%, GREEK, POLISH, SPANISH
LANGUAGES GERMAN (OFFICIAL) **RELIGIONS** PROTESTANT (MAINLY LUTHERAN) 38%, ROMAN CATHOLIC 34%, ISLAM 2%
CURRENCY EURO = 100 CENTS

GHANA

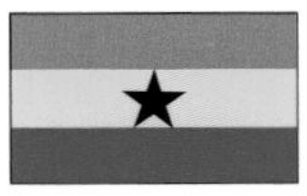

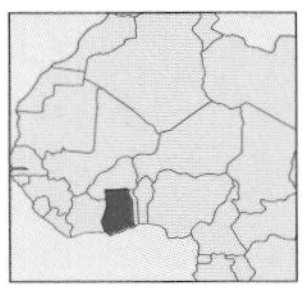

GEOGRAPHY The Republic of Ghana faces the Gulf of Guinea in West Africa. This hot country, just north of the Equator, was formerly called the Gold Coast. Behind the thickly populated southern coastal plains, which are lined with lagoons, lies a plateau region in the south-west.

Accra has a hot, tropical climate. Rain occurs all through the year, though Accra is drier than areas inland.

POLITICS & ECONOMY Portuguese explorers reached the area in 1471 and named it the Gold Coast. The area became a centre of the slave trade in the 17th century. The slave trade was ended in the 1860s and, gradually, the British took control of the area. After independence in 1957, attempts were made to develop the economy by creating large state-owned manufacturing industries. But debt and corruption, together with falls in the price of cocoa, the chief export, caused economic problems. This led to instability and frequent coups. In 1981, power was invested in a Provisional National Defence Council, led by Flight-Lieutenant Jerry Rawlings.

The government steadied the economy and introduced several new policies, including the relaxation of government controls. In 1992, the government introduced a new constitution, which allowed for multiparty elections. Rawlings was elected president in 1992 and 1996, but he retired in 2002.

The World Bank classifies Ghana as a 'low-income' developing country. Most people are poor and farming employs 59% of the population.

AREA 238,540 SQ KM [92,100 SQ MI] **POPULATION** 19,894,000
CAPITAL (POPULATION) ACCRA (1,781,000) **GOVERNMENT** REPUBLIC
ETHNIC GROUPS AKAN 44%, MOSHI-DAGOMBE 16%, EWE 12%, GA 8%
LANGUAGES ENGLISH (OFFICIAL), AKAN, MOSHI-DAGOMBE
RELIGIONS TRADITIONAL BELIEFS 38%, ISLAM 30%, CHRISTIANITY 24%
CURRENCY CEDI = 100 PESEWAS

GIBRALTAR

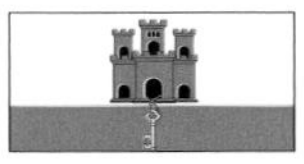

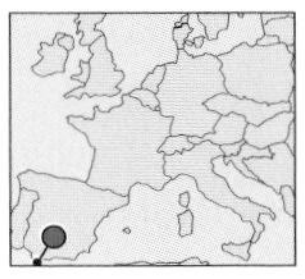

Gibraltar occupies a strategic position on the south coast of Spain where the Mediterranean meets the Atlantic. It was recognized as a British possession in 1713 and, despite Spanish claims, its population has consistently voted to retain its contacts with Britain.

AREA 6.5 SQ KM [2.5 SQ MI] **POPULATION** 28,000
CAPITAL GIBRALTAR TOWN

GREECE

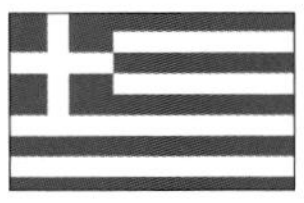

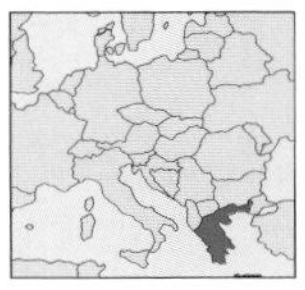

GEOGRAPHY The Hellenic Republic, as Greece is officially called, is a rugged country situated at the southern end of the Balkan peninsula. Olympus, at 2,917 m [9,570 ft] is the highest peak. Islands make up about a fifth of the land.

Low-lying areas in Greece have mild, moist winters and hot, dry summers. The east coast has more than 2,700 hours of sunshine a year and only about half of the rainfall of the west. The mountains have a much more severe climate, with snow on the higher slopes in winter.

POLITICS & ECONOMY After World War II (1939–45), when Germany had occupied Greece, a civil war broke out between Communist and nationalist forces. This war ended in 1949. A military dictatorship took power in 1967. The monarchy was abolished in 1973 and democratic government was restored in 1974. Greece joined the European Community (now the EU) in 1981. Despite efforts to develop the economy, Greece remains one of the EU's poorest nations. On 1 January 2002, the euro became Greece's sole official unit of currency.

Manufacturing is important. Products include processed food, cement, chemicals, metal products, textiles and tobacco. Greece also mines lignite (brown coal), bauxite and chromite.

Farmland covers about a third of the country, and grazing land another 40%. Major crops include barley, grapes for winemaking, dried fruits, olives, potatoes, sugar beet and wheat. Poultry, sheep, goats, pigs and cattle are raised. Greece's beaches and ancient ruins make it a major tourist destination.

AREA 131,990 SQ KM [50,961 SQ MI] **POPULATION** 10,624,000
CAPITAL (POPULATION) ATHENS (3,097,000)
GOVERNMENT MULTIPARTY REPUBLIC **ETHNIC GROUPS** GREEK 98%
LANGUAGES GREEK (OFFICIAL) **RELIGIONS** GREEK ORTHODOX 98%
CURRENCY EURO = 100 CENTS

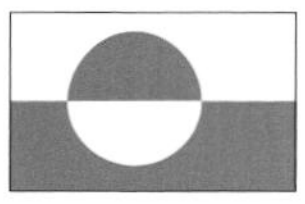
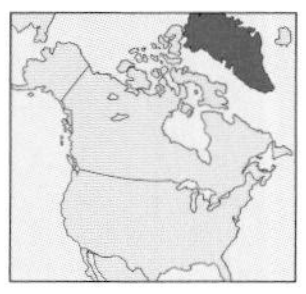

GREENLAND

Greenland is the world's largest island. Settlements are confined to the coast, because an ice sheet covers four-fifths of the land. Greenland became a Danish possession in 1380. Full internal self-government was granted in 1981 and, in 1997, Danish place names were superseded by Inuit forms. However, Greenland remains heavily dependent on Danish subsidies.

AREA 2,175,600 SQ KM [838,999 SQ MI] **POPULATION** 56,000
CAPITAL NUUK (GODTHAAB)

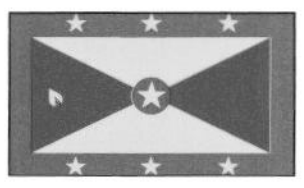
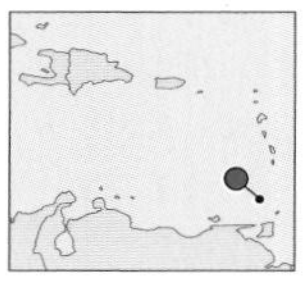

GRENADA

The most southerly of the Windward Islands in the Caribbean Sea, Grenada became independent from the UK in 1974. A military group seized power in 1983, when the prime minister was killed. US troops intervened and restored order and constitutional government.

AREA 340 SQ KM [131 SQ MI]
POPULATION 89,000 **CAPITAL** ST GEORGE'S

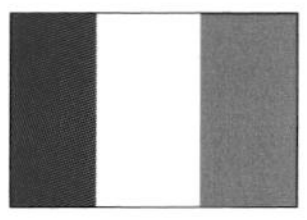
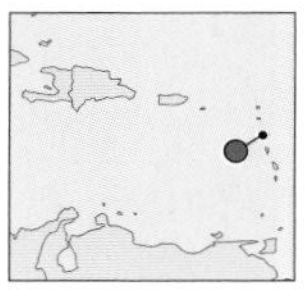

GUADELOUPE

Guadeloupe is a French overseas department which includes seven Caribbean islands, the largest of which is Basse-Terre. French aid has helped to mantain a reasonable standard of living for the people.

AREA 1,706 SQ KM [658 SQ MI]
POPULATION 431,000 **CAPITAL** BASSE-TERRE

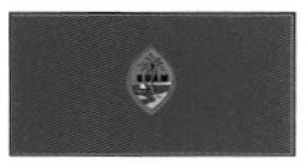
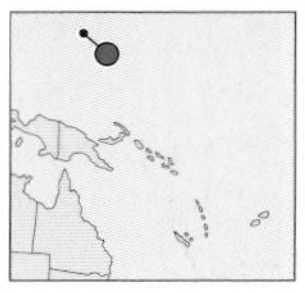

GUAM

Guam, a strategically important 'unincorporated territory' of the USA, is the largest of the Mariana Islands in the Pacific Ocean. It is composed of a coralline limestone plateau.

AREA 549 SQ KM [212 SQ MI]
POPULATION 158,000 **CAPITAL** AGANA

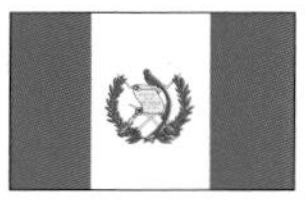
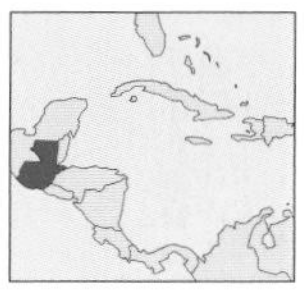

GUATEMALA

GEOGRAPHY The Republic of Guatemala in Central America contains a thickly populated mountain region, with fertile soils. The mountains, which run in an east–west direction, contain many volcanoes, some of which are active. Volcanic eruptions and earthquakes are common in the highlands. South of the mountains lie the thinly populated Pacific coastlands, while a large inland plain occupies the north.

Guatemala lies in the tropics. The lowlands are hot and rainy, but the central mountain region is cooler and drier. Guatemala City, at about 1,500 m [5,000 ft] above sea level, has a pleasant, warm climate, with a marked dry season between November and April.

POLITICS & ECONOMY In 1823, Guatemala joined the Central American Federation. But it became fully independent in 1839. Since independence, Guatemala has been plagued by instability and periodic violence.

Guatemala has a long-standing claim over Belize, but this was reduced in 1983 to the southern fifth of the country. Violence became widespread in Guatemala from the early 1960s, because of the conflict between left-wing groups, including many Amerindians, and government forces. A peace accord was signed in 1996, ending a war that had lasted 36 years and claimed perhaps 200,000 lives.

The World Bank classifies Guatemala as a 'lower-middle-income' developing country. Agriculture employs nearly half of the population and coffee, sugar, bananas and beef are the leading exports. Other important crops include the spice cardamom and cotton, while maize is the chief food crop.

AREA 108,890 SQ KM [42,042 SQ MI] **POPULATION** 12,974,000
CAPITAL (POPULATION) GUATEMALA CITY (1,167,000)
GOVERNMENT REPUBLIC **ETHNIC GROUPS** LADINO (MIXED HISPANIC AND AMERINDIAN) 55%, AMERINDIAN 43%, OTHER 2%
LANGUAGES SPANISH (OFFICIAL), AMERINDIAN LANGUAGES
RELIGIONS ROMAN CATHOLIC 75%, PROTESTANT 25%
CURRENCY US DOLLAR; QUETZAL = 100 CENTAVOS

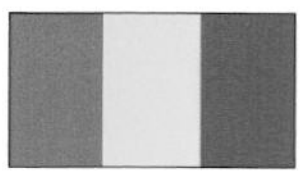
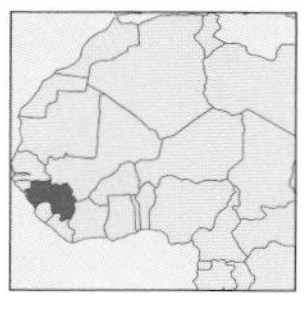

GUINEA

GEOGRAPHY The Republic of Guinea faces the Atlantic Ocean in West Africa. A flat, swampy plain borders the coast. Behind this plain, the land rises to a plateau region called Fouta Djalon. The Upper Niger plains, named after one of Africa's longest rivers, the Niger, which rises there, are in the north-east.

Guinea has a tropical climate and Conakry, on the coast, has heavy rains between May and November. This is also the coolest period in the year. During the dry season, hot, dry harmattan winds blow south-westwards from the Sahara Desert.

POLITICS & ECONOMY Guinea became independent in 1958. Its president, Sékou Touré, pursued socialist policies, though he had to resort to repressive policies to hold on to power. After his death in 1984, a military government, under President Lansana Conté, introduced free enterprise policies. In the late 1990s and early 2000s, Guinea was drawn into the civil conflicts which were taking place in neighbouring Liberia and Sierra Leone.

The World Bank classifies Guinea as a 'low-income' developing country. It has several natural resources, including bauxite (aluminium ore), diamonds, gold, iron ore and uranium. Bauxite and alumina (processed bauxite) account for 90% of the value of the exports. Agriculture, however, employs 78% of the people, many of whom produce little more than they need for their own families. Guinea has some manufacturing industries. Products include alumina, processed food and textiles.

AREA 245,860 SQ KM [94,927 SQ MI] **POPULATION** 7,614,000
CAPITAL (POPULATION) CONAKRY (1,508,000)
GOVERNMENT MULTIPARTY REPUBLIC
ETHNIC GROUPS PEUML 40%, MALINKE 30%, SOUSSOU 20%, OTHER 10%
LANGUAGES FRENCH (OFFICIAL)
RELIGIONS ISLAM 85%, CHRISTIANITY 8%, TRADITIONAL BELIEFS 7%
CURRENCY GUINEAN FRANC = 100 CAURIS

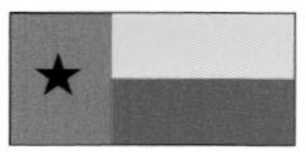
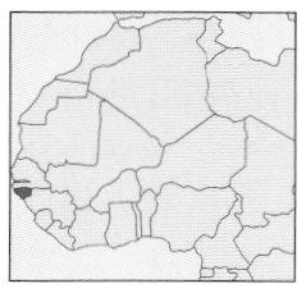

GUINEA-BISSAU

GEOGRAPHY The Republic of Guinea-Bissau, formerly known as Portuguese Guinea, is a small country in West Africa. The land is mostly low-lying, with a broad, swampy coastal plain and many flat offshore islands, including the Bijagós Archipelago.

The country has a tropical climate, with one dry season (December to May) and a rainy season from June to November.

POLITICS & ECONOMY Portugal appointed a governor to administer Guinea-Bissau and the Cape Verde Islands in 1836, but in 1879 the two territories were separated and Guinea-Bissau became a colony, then called Portuguese Guinea. But development was slow, partly because the territory did not attract settlers on the same scale as Portugal's much healthier African colonies of Angola and Mozambique.

In 1956, African nationalists in Portuguese Guinea and Cape Verde founded the African Party for the Independence of Guinea and Cape Verde (PAIGC). Because Portugal seemed determined to hang on to its overseas territories, the PAIGC began a guerrilla war in 1963. By 1968, it held two-thirds of the country. In 1972, a rebel National Assembly, elected by the people in the PAIGC-controlled area, voted to make the country independent as Guinea-Bissau.

In 1974, newly independent Guinea-Bissau faced many problems arising from its under-developed economy and its lack of trained people to work in the administration. One objective of the leaders of Guinea-Bissau was to unite their country with Cape Verde. But, in 1980, army leaders overthrew Guinea-Bissau's government. The Revolutionary Council, which took over, opposed unification with Cape Verde. Guinea-Bissau ceased to be a one-party state in 1991 and multiparty elections were held in 1994. Civil war broke out in 1998 and a military coup occurred in May 1999. In elections in 1999 and 2000, Kumba Ialá was elected president.

Guinea-Bissau is a poor country. Agriculture employs more than 80% of the people, but most farming is at subsistence level. Major crops include beans, coconuts, groundnuts, maize and rice.

AREA 36,120 SQ KM [13,946 SQ MI] **POPULATION** 1,316,000
CAPITAL (POPULATION) BISSAU (145,000)
GOVERNMENT 'INTERIM' GOVERNMENT
ETHNIC GROUPS BALANTA 30%, FULA 20%, MANJACA 14%, MANDINGA 13%, PAPEL 7% **LANGUAGES** PORTUGUESE (OFFICIAL), CRIOULO
RELIGIONS TRADITIONAL BELIEFS 50%, ISLAM 45%, CHRISTIANITY 5%
CURRENCY CFA FRANC = 100 CENTIMES

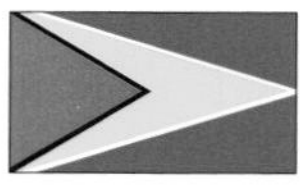
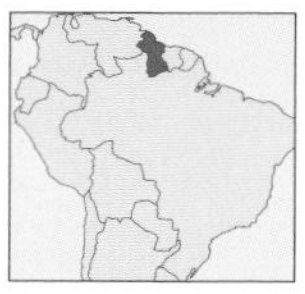

GUYANA

GEOGRAPHY The Co-operative Republic of Guyana is a country facing the Atlantic Ocean in north-eastern South America. The coastal plain is flat and much of it is below sea level.

The climate is hot and humid, though the interior highlands are cooler than the coast. The rainfall is heavy, occurring on more than 200 days a year.

POLITICS & ECONOMY British Guiana became independent in 1966. A black lawyer, Forbes Burnham, became the first prime minister. Under a new constitution adopted in 1980, the president's powers were increased. Burnham became president until his death in 1985. He was succeeded by Hugh Desmond Hoyte. Hoyte was defeated in elections in 1993 by an ethnic Indian, Cheddi Jagan. Jagan died in 1997 and was succeeded by his wife, Janet. In 1999, Bharrat Jagdeo was elected president.

Guyana is a poor country. Its resources include gold, bauxite (aluminium ore) and other minerals, forests and fertile soils. sugar cane and rice are leading crops. Electric power is in short supply, although the country has great potential for producing hydroelectricity from its many rivers.

AREA 214,970 SQ KM [83,000 SQ MI] **POPULATION** 697,000
CAPITAL (POPULATION) GEORGETOWN (200,000)
GOVERNMENT MULTIPARTY REPUBLIC **ETHNIC GROUPS** EAST INDIAN 49%, BLACK 32%, MIXED 12%, AMERINDIAN 6%, PORTUGUESE, CHINESE
LANGUAGES ENGLISH (OFFICIAL), CREOLE, HINDI, URDU
RELIGIONS PROTESTANT 34%, ROMAN CATHOLIC 18%, HINDUISM 34%, ISLAM 9% **CURRENCY** GUYANA DOLLAR = 100 CENTS

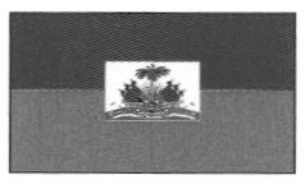
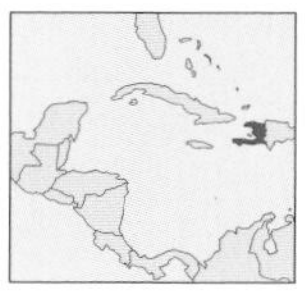

HAITI

GEOGRAPHY The Republic of Haiti occupies the western third of Hispaniola in the Caribbean. The land is mainly mountainous. The climate is hot and humid, though the northern highlands, with about 200 mm [79 in], have more than twice as much rainfall as the southern coast.

POLITICS & ECONOMY Visited by Christopher Columbus in 1492, Haiti was later developed by the French. The African slaves revolted in 1791 and the country became independent in 1804.

Since independence, Haiti has suffered from instability, violence and dictatorial rule. Elections in 1990 returned Jean-Bertrand Aristide as president, but he was overthrown in 1991. Following US intervention, he returned in 1994. In 1995, René Préval was elected president, but Aristide was again elected president in 2000 amid accusations of vote-rigging.

AREA 27,750 SQ KM [10,714 SQ MI] **POPULATION** 6,965,000
CAPITAL (POPULATION) PORT-AU-PRINCE (885,000)
GOVERNMENT MULTIPARTY REPUBLIC **ETHNIC GROUPS** BLACK 95%, MULATTO 5% **LANGUAGES** FRENCH AND CREOLE (BOTH OFFICIAL)
RELIGIONS ROMAN CATHOLIC 80%, VOODOO
CURRENCY GOURDE = 100 CENTIMES

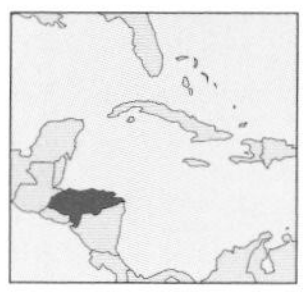

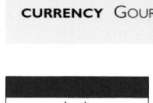

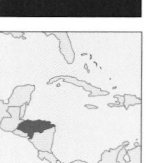

HONDURAS

GEOGRAPHY The Republic of Honduras is the second largest country in Central America. The northern coast on the Caribbean Sea extends more than 600 km [373 mi], but the Pacific coast in the south-east is only about 80 km [50 mi] long.

Honduras has a tropical climate, but the highlands, where the capital Tegucigalpa is situated, have a cooler climate than the hot coastal plains. The months between May and November are the rainiest. The north coast is often hit by hurricanes. In 1998, Hurricane Mitch caused the worst destruction in the area in modern times.

POLITICS & ECONOMY In the 1890s, American companies developed plantations in Honduras to grow bananas, which soon became the country's chief source of income. The companies exerted great political influence in Honduras and the country became known as a 'banana republic', a name that was later applied to several other Latin American nations. Instability has continued to mar the country's progress. In 1969, Honduras fought the short 'Soccer War' with El Salvador. The war was sparked off by the treatment of fans during a World Cup soccer series. But the real reason was that Honduras had forced Salvadoreans in Honduras to give up land. A peace agreement was signed in 1980.

Honduras is a developing country – one of the poorest in the Americas. It has few resources besides some silver, lead and zinc, and agriculture dominates the economy. Bananas and coffee are the leading exports, and maize is the main food crop.

Honduras is the least industrialized country in Central America. Manufactures include processed food, textiles, and a wide variety of wood products.

AREA 112,090 sq km [43,278 sq mi] **POPULATION** 6,406,000
CAPITAL (POPULATION) Tegucigalpa (813,000)
GOVERNMENT Republic **ETHNIC GROUPS** Mestizo 90%, Amerindian 7%, Black (including Black Carib) 2%, White 1%
LANGUAGES Spanish (official) **RELIGIONS** Roman Catholic 85%
CURRENCY Honduran lempira = 100 centavos

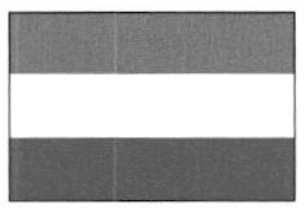
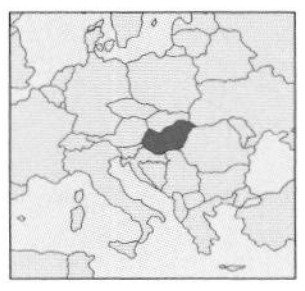

HUNGARY

GEOGRAPHY The Hungarian Republic is a landlocked country in central Europe. The land is mostly low-lying and drained by the Danube (Duna) and its tributary, the Tisza. Most of the land east of the Danube belongs to a region called the Great Plain (Nagyalföld), which covers about half of Hungary.

Hungary lies far from the moderating influence of the sea. As a result, summers are warmer and sunnier, and the winters colder than in Western Europe.

POLITICS & ECONOMY Hungary entered World War II (1939–45) in 1941, as an ally of Germany, but the Germans occupied the country in 1944. The Soviet Union invaded Hungary in 1944 and, in 1946, the country became a republic. The Communists gradually took over the government, taking complete control in 1949. From 1949, Hungary was an ally of the Soviet Union. In 1956, Soviet troops crushed an anti-Communist revolt. But in the 1980s, reforms in the Soviet Union led to the growth of anti-Communist groups in Hungary.

In 1989, Hungary adopted a new constitution making it a multiparty state. Elections held in 1990 led to a victory for the non-Communist Democratic Forum. However, in 2002, the Hungarian Socialist Party, in alliance with the liberal Free Democrats, won a majority in parliament, defeating the Fidesz-Hungarian Civic Party.

Before World War II, Hungary's economy was based mainly on agriculture. But the Communists set up many manufacturing industries. The new factories were owned by the government, as also was most of the land. However, from the late 1980s, the government has worked to increase private ownership. This change of policy caused many problems, including inflation and high rates of unemployment. Manufacturing is the chief activity. Major products include aluminium, chemicals, and electrical and electronic goods.

AREA 93,030 sq km [35,919 sq mi] **POPULATION** 10,106,000
CAPITAL (POPULATION) Budapest (1,885,000)
GOVERNMENT Multiparty republic **ETHNIC GROUPS** Magyar 90%, Gypsy, German, Croat, Romanian, Slovak **LANGUAGES** Hungarian (official) **RELIGIONS** Roman Catholic 64%, Protestant 23%, Orthodox 1%, Judaism 1%
CURRENCY Forint = 100 fillér

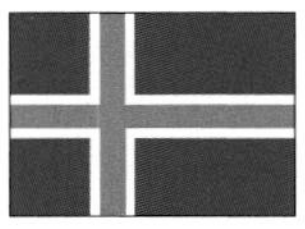
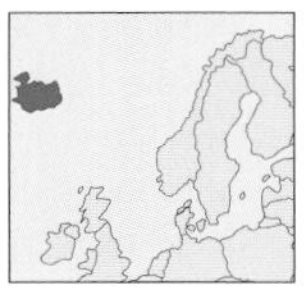

ICELAND

GEOGRAPHY The Republic of Iceland, in the North Atlantic Ocean, is closer to Greenland than Scotland. Iceland sits astride the Mid-Atlantic Ridge. It is slowly getting wider as the ocean is being stretched apart by continental drift.

Iceland has around 200 volcanoes, and eruptions are frequent. An eruption under the Vatnajökull ice cap in 1996 created a subglacial lake which subsequently burst, causing severe flooding. Geysers and hot springs are other common volcanic features. Ice caps and glaciers cover about an eighth of the land. The only habitable regions are the coastal lowlands.

Although it lies far to the north, Iceland's climate is moderated by the warm waters of the Gulf Stream. The port of Reykjavik is ice-free all the year round.

POLITICS & ECONOMY Norwegian Vikings colonized Iceland in AD 874, and in 930 the settlers founded the world's oldest parliament, the Althing.

Iceland united with Norway in 1262. But when Norway united with Denmark in 1380, Iceland came under Danish rule. Iceland became a self-governing kingdom, united with Denmark, in 1918. It became a fully independent republic in 1944, following a referendum in which 97% of the people voted to break their country's ties with Denmark.

Iceland has played an important part in European affairs and is a member of the North Atlantic Treaty Organization. Conflict with Britain over fishing rights have occurred since Iceland extended its territorial waters in the 1970s. Other fishing disputes with Norway, Russia and others continued in the 1990s.

Iceland has few resources besides the fishing grounds which surround it. Fishing and fish processing are major industries which dominate Iceland's overseas trade. Barely 1% of the land is used to grow crops, mainly root vegetables and fodder for livestock, but 23% of the country is used for grazing sheep and cattle. Vegetables and fruits are grown in greenhouses heated by water from hot springs.

AREA 103,000 sq km [39,768 sq mi] **POPULATION** 278,000
CAPITAL (POPULATION) Reykjavik (103,000)
GOVERNMENT Multiparty republic **ETHNIC GROUPS** Icelandic 97%, Danish 1% **LANGUAGES** Icelandic (official)
RELIGIONS Evangelical Lutheran 92%, other Lutheran 3%, Roman Catholic 1%
CURRENCY Króna = 100 aurar

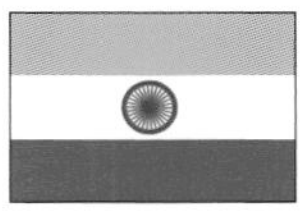
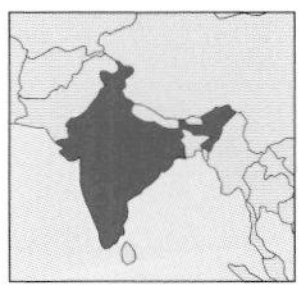

INDIA

GEOGRAPHY The Republic of India is the world's seventh largest country. In population, it ranks second only to China. The north is mountainous, with mountains and foothills of the Himalayan range. Rivers, such as the Brahmaputra and Ganges (Ganga), rise in the Himalaya and flow across the fertile northern plains. Southern India consists of a large plateau, called the Deccan. The Deccan is bordered by two mountain ranges, the Western Ghats and the Eastern Ghats.

India has three main seasons. The cool season runs from October to February. The hot season runs from March to June. The rainy monsoon season starts in the middle of June and continues into September. Delhi has a moderate rainfall, with about 640 mm [25 in] a year. The south-western coast and the north-east have far more rain. Darjeeling in the north-east has an average annual rainfall of 3,040 mm [120 in]. But parts of the Thar Desert in the north-west have only 50 mm [2 in] of rain per year.

POLITICS & ECONOMY In southern India, most of the people are descendants of the dark-skinned Dravidians, who were among India's earliest people. Most northerners are descendants of lighter-skinned Aryans who arrived around 3,500 years ago.

India was the birthplace of several major religions, including Hinduism, Buddhism and Sikhism. Islam was introduced from about AD 1000. The Muslim Mughal empire was founded in 1526. From the 17th century, Britain began to gain influence. From 1858 to 1947, India was ruled as part of the British empire. An independence movement began after the Sepoy Rebellion (1857–9) and, in 1885, the Indian National Congress was formed. In 1920, Mohandas K. Gandhi became its leader and it soon became a mass movement. When independence was finally achieved in 1947, British India was divided into modern India and Muslim Pakistan. Partition was marred by mass slaughter as Hindus and Sikhs fled from Pakistan, and Indian Muslims poured into Pakistan. In the ensuing disputes, some 1 million people were killed.

Although India has 15 major languages and hundreds of minor ones, together with many religions, the country remains the world's largest democracy. It has faced many problems, especially with Pakistan, over the disputed territory of Jammu and Kashmir. Two wars in 1965 and 1972 failed to alter greatly the 1948 cease-fire lines. In the late 1980s, Kashmiri nationalists in the Indian-controlled area waged a campaign, demanding either integration into Pakistan or independence. India sent in troops and accused Pakistan of intervention. In the 1990s, Pakistani-backed guerrillas fought to break India's hold on the Srinigar valley, Kashmir's most populous region. The tense situation was further aggravated by the testing of nuclear devices by both India and Pakistan in 1998. Between 2000 and 2002, attempts were made to achieve a lasting cease-fire in the region, but the negotiations were unsuccessful.

Economic development has been a major problem and, according to the World Bank, India is a 'low-income' developing country. After socialist policies failed to raise the living standards of the poor, the government introduced private enterprise. Farming employs 64% of the people. The main crops are rice, wheat, millet, sorghum, peas and beans. India has more cattle than any other country. Milk is produced but Hindus do not eat beef. India has reserves of coal, iron ore and oil, and manufacturing has expanded greatly since 1947. Iron and steel, machinery, refined petroleum, textiles and transport equipment are major products. India also imports rough diamonds and exports jewellery.

AREA 3,287,590 sq km [1,269,338 sq mi] **POPULATION** 1,029,991,000
CAPITAL (POPULATION) New Delhi (7,207,000)
GOVERNMENT Multiparty federal republic
ETHNIC GROUPS Indo-Aryan (Caucasoid) 72%, Dravidian (Aboriginal) 25%, other (mainly Mongoloid) 3%
LANGUAGES Hindi, English, Telugu, Bengali, Marati, Urdu, Gujarati, Malayalam, Kannada, Oriya, Punjabi, Assamese, Kashmiri, Sindhi and Sanskrit are all official languages **RELIGIONS** Hinduism 83%, Islam (Sunni Muslim) 11%, Christianity 2%, Sikhism 2%, Buddhism 1%
CURRENCY Rupee = 100 paisa

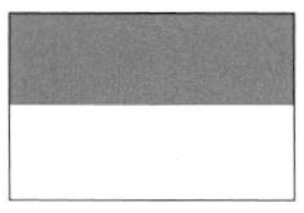
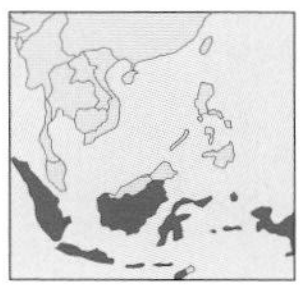

INDONESIA

GEOGRAPHY The Republic of Indonesia is an island nation in South-east Asia. In all, Indonesia contains about 13,600 islands, less than 6,000 of which are inhabited. Three-quarters of the country is made up of five main areas: the islands of Sumatra, Java and Sulawesi (Celebes), together with Kalimantan (southern Borneo) and Irian Jaya (western New Guinea). The islands are generally mountainous, with many volcanoes. The larger islands have extensive coastal lowlands. Indonesia has a hot and humid equatorial climate, with a high rainfall. Only Java and the Sunda Islands have a relatively dry season.

POLITICS & ECONOMY Indonesia is the world's most populous Muslim nation, though Islam was introduced as recently as the 15th century. The Dutch became active in the area in the early 17th century and Indonesia became a Dutch colony in 1799. After a long struggle, the Netherlands recognized Indonesia's independence in 1949. The economy has expanded, but ethnic and religious conflict have slowed down economic progress. In the early 21st century, Indonesia was facing many problems, arising from widespread corruption in the government and the army. Separatists were operating in Aceh province in northern Sumatra and in West Papua (formerly Irian Jaya), Christian-Muslim clashes led to loss of life in the Moluccas, and East (formerly Portuguese) Timor seceded from Indonesia, becoming an independent country, in May 2002.

Indonesia is a developing country. Its resources include oil, natural gas, tin and other minerals, its fertile volcanic soils and its forests. Oil and gas are major exports. Timber, textiles, rubber, coffee and tea are also exported. The principal food crop is rice. Manufacturing is increasing, particularly on Java.

AREA 1,889,700 sq km [729,613 sq mi] **POPULATION** 227,701,000
CAPITAL (POPULATION) Jakarta (11,500,000)
GOVERNMENT Multiparty republic
ETHNIC GROUPS Javanese 45%, Sundanese 14%, Madurese 7%, Coastal Malays 7%, more than 300 others
LANGUAGES Bahasa Indonesian (official), others
RELIGIONS Islam 88%, Roman Catholic 3%, Hinduism 2%, Buddhism 1%
CURRENCY Indonesian rupiah = 100 sen

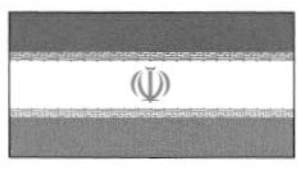
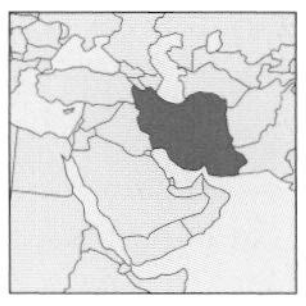

IRAN

GEOGRAPHY The Republic of Iran contains a barren central plateau which covers about half of the country. It includes the Dasht-e-Kavir (Great Salt Desert) and the Dasht-e-Lut (Great Sand Desert). The Elburz Mountains north of the plateau contain Iran's highest peak, Damavand, while narrow lowlands lie between the mountains and the Caspian Sea. West of the plateau are the Zagros Mountains, beyond which the land descends to the plains bordering the Gulf.

Much of Iran has a severe, dry climate, with hot summers and cold winters. In Tehran, rain falls on only about 30 days in the year and the annual temperature range is more than 25°C [45°F]. The climate in the lowlands, however, is generally milder.

POLITICS & ECONOMY Iran was called Persia until 1935. The empire of Ancient Persia flourished between 550 and 350 BC, when it fell to Alexander the Great. Islam was introduced in AD 641.

Britain and Russia competed for influence in the area in the 19th century, and in the early 20th century the British began to develop the country's oil resources. In 1925, the Pahlavi family took power.

Reza Khan became shah (king) and worked to modernize the country. The Pahlavi dynasty was ended in 1979 when a religious leader, Ayatollah Ruhollah Khomeini, made Iran an Islamic republic. In 1980–8, Iran and Iraq fought a war over disputed borders. Khomeini died in 1989, but his fundamentalist views and anti-Western attitudes continued to dominate politics. In 1997, Mohammad Khatami, a liberal, was elected president. His reform policies won support in elections in 2000, but the conservative clerics made actual reform difficult.

Iran's prosperity is based on its oil production and oil accounts for 95% of the country's exports. However, the economy was severely damaged by the Iran–Iraq war in the 1980s. Oil revenues have been used to develop a growing manufacturing sector. Agriculture is important even though farms cover only a tenth of the land. The main crops are wheat and barley. Livestock farming and fishing are other important activities, although Iran has to import much of the food it needs.

AREA 1,648,000 sq km [636,293 sq mi] **POPULATION** 66,129,000
CAPITAL (POPULATION) Tehran (6,759,000)
GOVERNMENT Islamic republic
ETHNIC GROUPS Persian 51%, Azeri 24%, Gilaki and Mazandarani 8%, Kurd 7%, Arab 3%, Lur 2%, Baluchi 2%, Turkmen 2% **LANGUAGES** Persian 58%, Turkic 26%, Kurdish
RELIGIONS Islam 99% **CURRENCY** Rial = 100 dinars

IRAQ

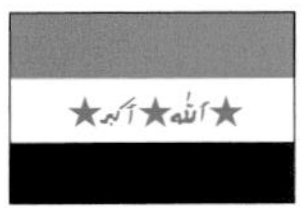

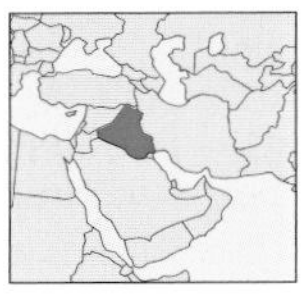

GEOGRAPHY The Republic of Iraq is a south-west Asian country at the head of the Gulf. Rolling deserts cover western and south-western Iraq, with part of the Zagros Mountains in the north-east, where farming can be practised without irrigation. The northern plains, across which flow the rivers Euphrates (Nahr al Furat) and Tigris (Nahr Dijlah), are dry. But the southern plains, including Mesopotamia, and the delta of the Shatt al Arab, the river formed south of Al Qurnah by the combined Euphrates and Tigris, contain irrigated farmland, together with marshes.

The climate of Iraq ranges from temperate in the north to subtropical in the south. Baghdad, in central Iraq, has cool winters, with occasional frosts, and hot summers. The rainfall is generally low.

POLITICS & ECONOMY Mesopotamia was the home of several great civilizations, including Sumer, Babylon and Assyria. It later became part of the Persian empire. Islam was introduced in AD 637 and Baghdad became the brilliant capital of the powerful Arab empire. But Mesopotamia declined after the Mongols invaded it in 1258. From 1534, Mesopotamia became part of the Turkish Ottoman empire. Britain invaded the area in 1916. In 1921, Britain renamed the country Iraq and set up an Arab monarchy. Iraq finally became independent in 1932.

By the 1950s, oil dominated Iraq's economy. In 1952, Iraq agreed to take 50% of the profits of the foreign oil companies. This revenue enabled the government to pay for welfare services and development projects. But many Iraqis felt that they should benefit more from their oil.

Since 1958, when army officers killed the king and made Iraq a republic, the country has undergone turbulent times. In the 1960s, the Kurds, who live in northern Iraq and also in Iran, Turkey, Syria and Armenia, asked for self-rule. The government rejected their demands and war broke out. A peace treaty was signed in 1975, but conflict has continued.

In 1979, Saddam Hussein became Iraq's president. Under his leadership, Iraq invaded Iran in 1980, starting an eight-year war. During this war, Iraqi Kurds supported Iran and the Iraqi government attacked Kurdish villages with poison gas.

In 1990, Iraqi troops occupied Kuwait but an international force drove them out in 1991. Since 1991, Iraqi troops have attacked Shiite Marsh Arabs and Kurds. In 1998, Iraq's failure to permit UNSCOM, the United Nations body charged with disposing of Iraq's deadliest weapons, access to all suspect sites, led to Western bombardment of military sites in Iraq. Another major Western offensive against strategic sites was launched in February 2001, while threats of war again mounted following the terrorist attacks on the United States on 11 September 2001.

Civil war, war damage, UN sanctions and economic mismanagement have all contributed to economic chaos in the 1990s. Oil remains Iraq's main resource, but a UN trade embargo in 1990 halted oil exports. Farmland, including pasture, covers about a fifth of the land. Products include barley, cotton, dates, fruit, livestock, wheat and wool, but Iraq still has to import food. Industries include oil refining and the manufacture of petrochemicals and consumer goods.

AREA 438,320 sq km [169,235 sq mi] **POPULATION** 23,332,000
CAPITAL (POPULATION) Baghdad (3,841,000)
GOVERNMENT Republic **ETHNIC GROUPS** Arab 77%, Kurdish 19%, Turkmen, Persian, Assyrian **LANGUAGES** Arabic (official), Kurdish (official in Kurdish areas) **RELIGIONS** Islam 96%, Christianity 4%
CURRENCY Iraqi dinar = 20 dirhams = 1,000 fils

IRELAND

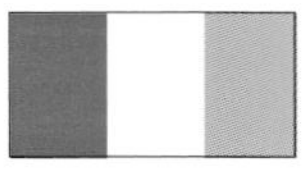

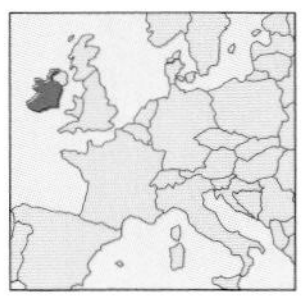

GEOGRAPHY The Republic of Ireland occupies five-sixths of the island of Ireland. The country consists of a large lowland region surrounded by a broken rim of low mountains. The uplands include the Mountains of Kerry where Carrauntoohill, Ireland's highest peak at 1,041 m [3,415 ft], is situated. The River Shannon is the longest in the British Isles. It flows through three large lakes, loughs Allen, Ree and Derg.

Ireland has a mild, damp climate greatly influenced by the warm Gulf Stream current that washes its shores. The effects of the Gulf Stream are greatest in the west. Dublin in the east is cooler than places on the west coast. Rain occurs throughout the year.

POLITICS & ECONOMY In 1801, the Act of Union created the United Kingdom of Great Britain and Ireland. But Irish discontent intensified in the 1840s when a potato blight caused a famine in which a million people died and nearly a million emigrated. Britain was blamed for not having done enough to help. In 1916, an uprising in Dublin was crushed, but between 1919 and 1922 civil war occurred. In 1922, the Irish Free State was created as a Dominion in the British Commonwealth. But Northern Ireland remained part of the UK.

Ireland became a republic in 1949. Since then, Irish governments have sought to develop the economy, and it was for this reason that Ireland joined the European Community in 1973. In 1998, Ireland took part in the negotiations to produce a constitutional settlement in Northern Ireland. As part of the agreement, Ireland agreed to give up its constitutional claim on Northern Ireland.

Major farm products in Ireland include barley, cattle and dairy products, pigs, potatoes, poultry, sheep, sugar beet and wheat, while fishing provides another valuable source of food. Farming is now profitable, aided by European Union grants, but manufacturing is the leading economic sector. Many factories produce food and beverages. Chemicals and pharmaceuticals, electronic equipment, machinery, paper and textiles are also important.

AREA 70,280 sq km [27,135 sq mi] **POPULATION** 3,841,000
CAPITAL (POPULATION) Dublin (1,024,000)
GOVERNMENT Multiparty republic **ETHNIC GROUPS** Irish 94%
LANGUAGES Irish and English (both official)
RELIGIONS Roman Catholic 93%, Protestant 3%
CURRENCY Euro = 100 cents

ISRAEL

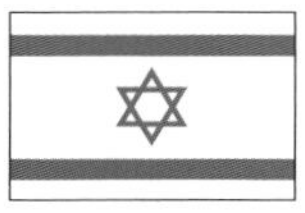

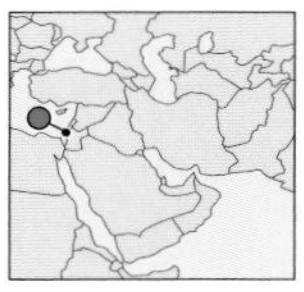

GEOGRAPHY The State of Israel is a small country in the eastern Mediterranean. It includes a fertile coastal plain, where Israel's main industrial cities, Haifa (Hefa) and Tel Aviv-Jaffa are situated. Inland lie the Judaeo-Galilean highlands, which run from northern Israel to the northern tip of the Negev Desert. To the east lies part of the Great Rift Valley which contains the River Jordan, the Sea of Galilee and the Dead Sea. Summers are hot and dry. Winters on the coast are mild and moist, but the rainfall decreases from west to east and from north to south.

POLITICS & ECONOMY Israel is part of a region called Palestine. Some Jews have always lived in the area, though most modern Israelis are descendants of immigrants who began to settle there from the 1880s. Britain ruled Palestine from 1917. Large numbers of Jews escaping Nazi persecution arrived in the 1930s, provoking an Arab uprising against British rule. In 1947, the UN agreed to partition Palestine into an Arab and a Jewish state. Fighting broke out after Arabs rejected the plan. The State of Israel came into being in May 1948, but fighting continued into 1949. Other Arab-Israeli wars in 1956, 1967 and 1973 led to land gains for Israel.

In 1978, Israel signed a treaty with Egypt which led to the return of the occupied Sinai peninsula to Egypt in 1979. But conflict continued between Israel and the PLO (Palestine Liberation Organization). In 1993, the PLO and Israel agreed to establish Palestinian self-rule in two areas: the occupied Gaza Strip, and in the town of Jericho in the occupied West Bank. The agreement was extended in 1995 to include more than 30% of the West Bank. Israel's prime minister, Yitzhak Rabin, was assassinated in 1995. In 1996, his successor, Simon Peres, was defeated by the right-wing Benjamin Netanyahu, under whom the peace process stalled. In 1999, the left-wing Ehud Barak defeated Netanyahu and revived the peace process. But, following violence between the Palestinians and Israeli forces, Barak resigned. In 2001, Barak was defeated by the right-wing Ariel Sharon, who adopted a hardline policy against the Palestinians. In early 2002, the violence mounted and the killing of Israelis by Arab suicide bombers brought the region close to war.

Israel's most valuable activity is manufacturing and the country's products include chemicals, electronic equipment, fertilizers, military equipment, plastics, processed food, scientific instruments and textiles. Fruits and vegetables are leading exports.

AREA 20,600 sq km [7,960 sq mi] **POPULATION** 5,938,000
CAPITAL (POPULATION) Jerusalem (591,000)
GOVERNMENT Multiparty republic **ETHNIC GROUPS** Jewish 82%, Arab and others 18% **LANGUAGES** Hebrew and Arabic (both official)
RELIGIONS Judaism 80%, Islam (mostly Sunni) 14%, Christianity 2%, Druze and others 2% **CURRENCY** New Israeli sheqel = 100 agorat

ITALY

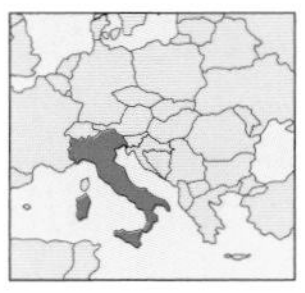

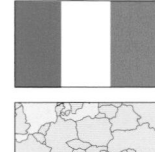

GEOGRAPHY The Republic of Italy is famous for its history and traditions, its art and culture, and its beautiful scenery. Northern Italy is bordered in the north by the high Alps, with their many climbing and skiing resorts. The Alps overlook the northern plains – Italy's most fertile and densely populated region – drained by the River Po. The rugged Apennines form the backbone of southern Italy. Bordering the range are scenic hilly areas and coastal plains. Southern Italy contains a string of volcanoes, stretching from Vesuvius, through the Lipari Islands, to Etna on Sicily, the largest Mediterranean island. Northern Italy has cold, often snowy, winters, but the summer months are warm and sunny, with brief summer thunderstorms. Rainfall is abundant. The south has mild, moist winters and warm, dry summers.

POLITICS & ECONOMY Magnificent ruins throughout Italy testify to the glories of the ancient Roman Empire, which was founded, according to legend, in 753 BC. It reached its peak in the AD 100s. It finally collapsed in the 400s, although the Eastern Roman empire, also called the Byzantine empire, survived for another 1,000 years.

In the Middle Ages, Italy was split into many tiny states. These states made a great contribution to the revival of art and learning, called the Renaissance, in the 14th to 16th centuries. Beautiful cities, such as Florence (Firenze) and Venice (Venézia), testify to the artistic achievements of this period.

Italy finally became a united kingdom in 1861, although the Papal Territories (a large area ruled by the Roman Catholic Church) was not added until 1870. The Pope and his successors disputed the takeover of the Papal Territories. The dispute was finally resolved in 1929, when the Vatican City was set up in Rome as a fully independent state.

Italy fought in World War I (1914–18) alongside the Allies – Britain, France and Russia. In 1922, the dictator Benito Mussolini, leader of the Fascist party, took power. Under Mussolini, Italy conquered Ethiopia. During World War II (1939–45), Italy at first fought on Germany's side against the Allies. But in late 1943, Italy declared war on Germany. Italy became a republic in 1946. It has played an important part in European affairs. It was a founder member of the North Atlantic Treaty Organization (NATO) in 1949 and also of what has now become the European Union in 1958.

After the setting up of the European Union, Italy's economy developed quickly. But the country faced many problems. For example, much of the economic development was in the north. This forced many people to leave the poor south to find jobs in the north or abroad. Social problems, corruption at high levels of society, and a succession of weak coalition governments all contributed to instability. Elections in 1996 were won by the left-wing Olive Tree alliance led by Romano Prodi, who was replaced in 1998 by an ex-Communist, Massimo d'Alema, who tried but failed to introduce a two-party system. In 2001, a centre-right coalition won a substantial majority in parliament and its leader, media tycoon Silvio Berlusconi, became prime minister.

Only 50 years ago, Italy was a mainly agricultural society. But today it is a leading industrial power. It lacks mineral resources, and imports most of the raw materials used in industry. Manufactures include textiles and clothing, processed food, machinery, cars and chemicals. The chief industrial region is in the north-west.

Farmland covers around 42% of the land, pasture 17%, and forest and woodland 22%. Major crops include citrus fruits, grapes which are used to make wine, olive oil, sugar beet and vegetables. Livestock farming is important, though meat is imported.

AREA 301,270 sq km [116,320 sq mi] **POPULATION** 57,680,000
CAPITAL (POPULATION) Rome (2,654,000) **GOVERNMENT** Multiparty republic **ETHNIC GROUPS** Italian 94%, German, French, Albanian, Ladino, Slovene, Greek **LANGUAGES** Italian 94% (official), German, French, Slovene **RELIGIONS** Roman Catholic 83%
CURRENCY Euro = 100 cents

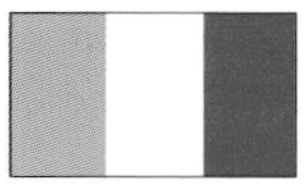

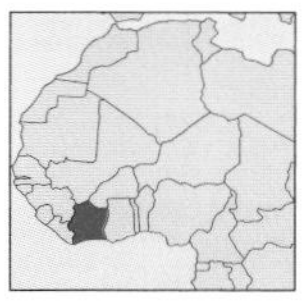

IVORY COAST

GEOGRAPHY The Republic of the Ivory Coast, in West Africa, is officially known as Côte d'Ivoire. The south-east coast is bordered by sand bars that enclose lagoons. The south-west coast is lined by rocky cliffs.

Ivory Coast has a hot and humid tropical climate, with high temperatures all year. The south has two rainy seasons: between May and July, and from October to November. Inland, the rainfall decreases and the north has one dry and one rainy season.

POLITICS & ECONOMY From 1895, Ivory Coast was governed as part of French West Africa, a massive union which also included what are now Benin, Burkina Faso, Guinea, Mali, Mauritania, Niger and Senegal. In 1946, Ivory Coast became a territory in the French Union.

Ivory Coast became fully independent in 1960. Its first president, Félix Houphouët-Boigny, became the longest serving head of state in Africa with an uninterrupted period in office which ended with his death in 1993. Houphouët-Boigny was a paternalistic, pro-Western leader, who made his country a one-party state. In 1983, the National Assembly agreed to make Yamoussoukro, the president's birthplace, the new capital. In 1993, Henri Konan Bédié became president. In 1999, he was overthrown by a military coup led by General Robert Guei. However, in presidential elections in 2000, Guei was defeated by a veteran politician, Laurent Gbagbo.

Agriculture employs about two-thirds of the people, and farm products make up nearly half the value of the exports. Manufacturing has grown in importance since 1960; products include fertilizers, processed food, refined oil, textiles and timber.

AREA 322,460 sq km [124,502 sq mi] **POPULATION** 16,393,000
CAPITAL (POPULATION) Yamoussoukro (120,000)
GOVERNMENT Multiparty republic **ETHNIC GROUPS** Akan 42%, Voltaic 18%, Northern Mande 16%, Kru 11%, Southern Mande 10%
LANGUAGES French (official), Akan, Voltaic
RELIGIONS Christianity 34%, Islam 27%, traditional beliefs 17%
CURRENCY CFA franc = 100 centimes

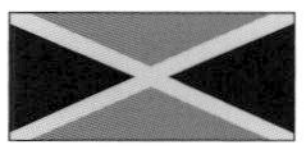

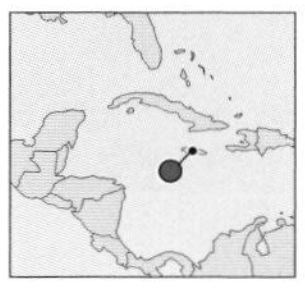

JAMAICA

GEOGRAPHY Third largest of the Caribbean islands, half of Jamaica lies above 300 m [1,000 ft] and moist south-east trade winds bring rain to the central mountain range.

The 'cockpit country' in the north-west of the island is an inaccessible limestone area of steep broken ridges and isolated basins.

POLITICS & ECONOMY Britain took Jamaica from Spain in the 17th century, and the island did not gain its independence until 1962. Some economic progress was made by the socialist government in the 1980s, but migration and unemployment remain high. Farming is the leading activity and sugar cane is the main crop, though bauxite production provides much of the country's income. Jamaica has some industries and tourism is a major industry.

AREA 10,990 sq km [4,243 sq mi] **POPULATION** 2,666,000
CAPITAL (POPULATION) Kingston (644,000)
GOVERNMENT Constitutional monarchy
ETHNIC GROUPS Black 91%, Mixed 7%, East Indian 1%
LANGUAGES English (official), Creole
RELIGIONS Protestant 61%, Roman Catholic 4%
CURRENCY Dollar = 100 cents

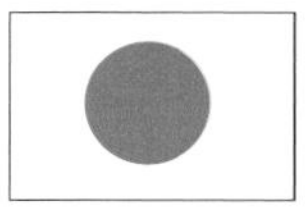

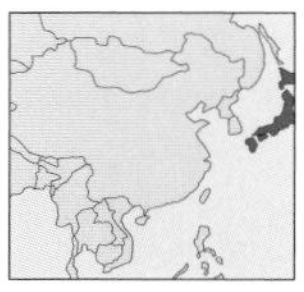

JAPAN

GEOGRAPHY Japan's four largest islands – Honshu, Hokkaido, Kyushu and Shikoku – make up 98% of the country. But Japan contains thousands of small islands. The four largest islands are mainly mountainous, while many of the small islands are the tips of volcanoes. Japan has more than 150 volcanoes, about 60 of which are active. Volcanic eruptions, earthquakes and tsunamis (destructive sea waves triggered by underwater earthquakes and eruptions) are common because the islands lie in an unstable part of our planet, where continental plates are always on the move. One powerful recent earthquake killed more than 5,000 people in Kobe in 1995.

The climate of Japan varies greatly from north to south. Hokkaido in the north has cold, snowy winters. At Sapporo, temperatures below –20°C [4°F] have been recorded between December and March. But summers are warm, with temperatures sometimes exceeding 30°C [86°F]. Rain falls throughout the year, though Hokkaido is one of the driest parts of Japan.

Tokyo has higher rainfall and temperatures, though frosts may occur as late as April when north-westerly winds are blowing. The southern islands of Shikoku and Kyushu have warm temperate climates. Summers are long and hot. Winters are mild.

POLITICS & ECONOMY In the late 19th century, Japan began a programme of modernization. Under its new imperial leaders, it began to look for lands to conquer. In 1894–5, it fought a war with China and, in 1904–5, it defeated Russia. Soon its overseas empire included Korea and Taiwan. In 1930, Japan invaded Manchuria (north-east China) and, in 1937, it began a war against China. In 1941, Japan launched an attack on the US base at Pearl Harbor in Hawaii. This drew both Japan and the United States into World War II.

Japan surrendered in 1945 when the Americans dropped atomic bombs on two cities, Hiroshima and Nagasaki. The United States occupied Japan until 1952. During this period, Japan adopted a democratic constitution. The emperor, who had previously been regarded as a god, became a constitutional monarch. Power was vested in the prime minister and cabinet, who are chosen from the Diet (elected parliament).

From the 1960s, Japan experienced many changes as the country rapidly built up new industries. By the early 1990s, Japan had become the world's second richest economic power after the US. But economic success has brought problems. For example, the rapid growth of cities has led to housing shortages and pollution. Another problem is that the proportion of people over 65 years of age is steadily increasing.

Japan has the world's second highest gross domestic product (GDP) after the United States. [The GDP is the total value of all goods and services produced in a country in one year.] The most important sector of the economy is industry. Yet Japan has to import most of the raw materials and fuels it needs for its industries. Its success is based on its use of the latest technology, its skilled and hard-working labour force, its vigorous export policies and its comparatively small government spending on defence. Manufactures dominate its exports, which include machinery, electrical and electronic equipment, vehicles and transport equipment, iron and steel, chemicals, textiles and ships.

Japan is one of the world's top fishing nations and fish is an important source of protein. Because the land is so rugged, only 15% of the country can be farmed. Yet Japan produces about 70% of the food it needs. Rice is the chief crop, taking up about half of the total farmland. Other major products include fruits, sugar beet, tea and vegetables. Livestock farming has increased since the 1950s.

AREA 377,800 sq km [145,869 sq mi] **POPULATION** 126,772,000
CAPITAL (POPULATION) Tokyo (17,950,000)
GOVERNMENT Constitutional monarchy
ETHNIC GROUPS Japanese 99%, Chinese, Korean, Ainu
LANGUAGES Japanese (official) **RELIGIONS** Shintoism and Buddhism 84% (most Japanese consider themselves to be both Shinto and Buddhist) **CURRENCY** Yen = 100 sen

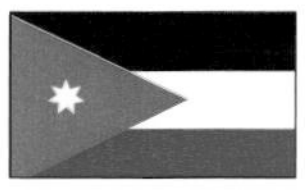

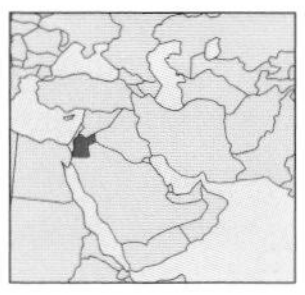

JORDAN

GEOGRAPHY The Hashemite Kingdom of Jordan is an Arab country in south-western Asia. The Great Rift Valley in the west contains the River Jordan and the Dead Sea, which Jordan shares with Israel. East of the Rift Valley is the Transjordan plateau, where most Jordanians live. To the east and south lie vast areas of desert.

Amman has a much lower rainfall and longer dry season than the Mediterranean lands to the west. The Transjordan plateau, on which Amman stands, is a transition zone between the Mediterranean climate zone to the west and the desert climate to the east.

POLITICS & ECONOMY In 1921, Britain created a territory called Transjordan east of the River Jordan. In 1923, Transjordan became self-governing, but Britain retained control of its defences, finances and foreign affairs. This territory became fully independent as Jordan in 1946.

Jordan has suffered from instability arising from the Arab–Israeli conflict since the creation of the State of Israel in 1948. After the first Arab–Israeli War in 1948–9, Jordan acquired East Jerusalem and a fertile area called the West Bank. In 1967, Israel occupied this area. In Jordan, the presence of Palestinian refugees led to civil war in 1970–1.

In 1974, Arab leaders declared that the PLO (Palestine Liberation Organization) was the sole representative of the Palestinian people. In 1988, King Hussein of Jordan renounced Jordan's claims to the West Bank and passed responsibility for it to the PLO. Opposition parties were legalized in 1991 and elections were held in 1993. In October 1994, Jordan and Israel signed a peace treaty, ending a state of war that had lasted more than 40 years. Jordan's King Hussein commanded respect for his role in Middle Eastern affairs until his death in 1999. He was succeeded by his eldest son who became Abdullah II.

Jordan lacks natural resources, apart from phosphates and potash, and the economy depends substantially on aid. The World Bank classifies Jordan as a 'lower-middle-income' developing country. Because of the dry climate, less than 6% of the land is farmed or used as pasture. Jordan has an oil refinery and manufactures include cement, pharmaceuticals, processed food, fertilizers and textiles.

AREA 89,210 sq km [34,444 sq mi] **POPULATION** 5,153,000
CAPITAL (POPULATION) Amman (1,752,000)
GOVERNMENT Constitutional monarchy **ETHNIC GROUPS** Arab 99%, of which Palestinians make up roughly half **LANGUAGES** Arabic (official) **RELIGIONS** Islam (mostly Sunni) 93%, Christianity (mostly Greek Orthodox) 5% **CURRENCY** Jordan dinar = 1,000 fils

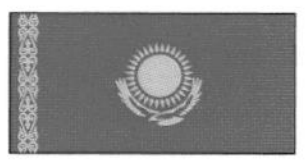

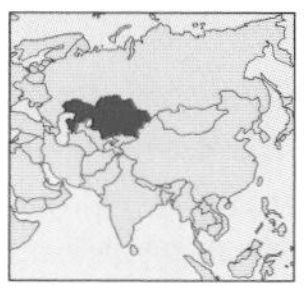

KAZAKHSTAN

GEOGRAPHY Kazakhstan is a large country in west-central Asia. In the west, the Caspian Sea lowlands include the Karagiye depression, which reaches 132 m [433 ft] below sea level. The lowlands extend eastwards through the Aral Sea area. The north contains high plains, but the highest land is along the eastern and southern borders. These areas include parts of the Altai and Tian Shan mountain ranges.

Eastern Kazakhstan contains several freshwater lakes, the largest of which is Lake Balkhash. The water in the rivers has been used for irrigation, causing ecological problems. For example, the Aral Sea, deprived of water, shrank from 66,900 sq km [25,830 sq mi] in 1960 to 33,642 sq km [12,989 sq mi] in 1993. Areas which once provided fish have dried up and are now barren desert.

The climate reflects Kazakhstan's position in the heart of Asia, far from the moderating influence of the oceans. Winters are cold and snow covers the land for about 100 days, on average, at Almaty. The rainfall is generally low.

POLITICS & ECONOMY After the Russian Revolution of 1917, many Kazakhs wanted to make their country independent. But the Communists prevailed and in 1936 Kazakhstan became a republic of the Soviet Union, called the Kazakh Soviet Socialist Republic. During World War II and also after the war, the Soviet government moved many people from the west into Kazakhstan. From the 1950s, people were encouraged to work on a 'Virgin Lands' project, which involved bringing large areas of grassland under cultivation.

Reforms in the Soviet Union in the 1980s led to its break-up in December 1991. Kazakhstan kept contacts with Russia and most of the other republics in the former Soviet Union by joining the Commonwealth of Independent States (CIS), and in 1995 Kazakhstan announced that its army would unite with that of Russia. In 1997, the government moved the capital from Almaty to Aqmola (later renamed Astana), a town in the Russian-dominated north. It was hoped that this move would bring some Kazakh identity to the area.

The World Bank classifies Kazakhstan as a 'lower-middle-income' developing country. Livestock farming, especially sheep and cattle, is an important activity, and major crops include barley, cotton, rice and wheat. The country is rich in mineral resources, including coal and oil reserves, together with bauxite, copper, lead, tungsten and zinc. Manufactures include chemicals, food products, machinery and textiles. Oil is exported via a pipeline through Russia; however, to reduce dependence on Russia, Kazakhstan signed an agreement in 1997 to build a new pipeline to China. Other exports include metals, chemicals, grain, wool and meat.

AREA 2,717,300 sq km [1,049,150 sq mi] **POPULATION** 16,731,000
CAPITAL (POPULATION) Astana (280,000) **GOVERNMENT** Multiparty republic **ETHNIC GROUPS** Kazakh 53%, Russian 30%, Ukrainian 4%, German 2%, Uzbek 2% **LANGUAGES** Kazakh (official); Russian, the former official language, is widely spoken **RELIGIONS** Islam 47%, Russian Orthodox 44% **CURRENCY** Tenge

KENYA

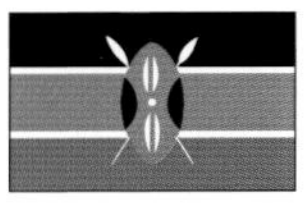
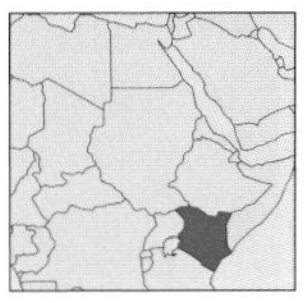

GEOGRAPHY The Republic of Kenya is a country in East Africa which straddles the Equator. Behind the narrow coastal plain on the Indian Ocean, the land rises to high plains and highlands, broken by volcanic mountains, including Mount Kenya, the country's highest peak at 5,199 m [17,057 ft]. Crossing the country is an arm of the Great Rift Valley, on the floor of which are several lakes, including Baringo, Magadi, Naivasha, Nakuru and, on the northern frontier, Lake Turkana (formerly Lake Rudolf).

Mombasa on the coast is hot and humid. But inland, the climate is moderated by the height of the land. As a result, Nairobi, in the thickly populated south-western highlands, has summer temperatures which are 10°C [18°F] lower than Mombasa. Nights can be cool, but temperatures do not fall below freezing. Nairobi's main rainy season is from April to May, with 'little rains' in November and December. However, only about 15% of the country has a reliable rainfall of 800 mm [31 in].

POLITICS & ECONOMY The Kenyan coast has been a trading centre for more than 2,000 years. Britain took over the coast in 1895 and soon extended its influence inland. In the 1950s, a secret movement, called Mau Mau, launched an armed struggle against British rule. Although Mau Mau was eventually defeated, Kenya became independent in 1963.

Many Kenyans felt that Kenya should have a strong central government, and Kenya was a one-party state for much of the time since 1963. But democracy was restored in the early 1990s and elections were held in 1992 and 1997. In 1999, Kenya, with Tanzania and Uganda, set up an East African Community, which aimed to create a customs union, a common market, a monetary union, and, ultimately a political union.

According to the United Nations, Kenya is a 'low-income' developing country. Agriculture employs about 80% of the people, but many Kenyans are subsistence farmers, growing little more than they need to support their families. The chief food crop is maize. The main cash crops and leading exports are coffee and tea. Manufactures include chemicals, leather and footwear, processed food, petroleum products and textiles.

AREA 580,370 sq km [224,081 sq mi] **POPULATION** 30,766,000
CAPITAL (POPULATION) Nairobi (2,000,000)
GOVERNMENT Multiparty republic **ETHNIC GROUPS** Kikuyu 21%, Luhya 14%, Luo 13%, Kalenjin 12%, Kamba 11% **LANGUAGES** Kiswahili and English (both official) **RELIGIONS** Protestant 38%, Roman Catholic 28%, other Christian 27%, traditional beliefs 26%, Islam 7% **CURRENCY** Kenya shilling = 100 cents

KIRIBATI

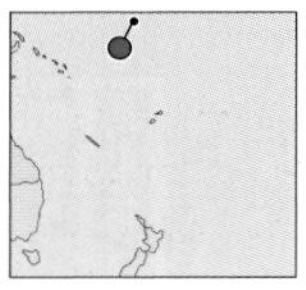

The Republic of Kiribati comprises three groups of corall atolls scattered over about 5 million sq km [2 million sq mi]. Kiribati straddles the equator and temperatures are high and the rainfall is abundant.

Formerly part of the British Gilbert and Ellice Islands, Kiribati became independent in 1979. The main export is copra and the country depends heavily on foreign aid.

AREA 728 sq km [281 sq mi] **POPULATION** 94,000 **CAPITAL** Tarawa

KOREA, NORTH

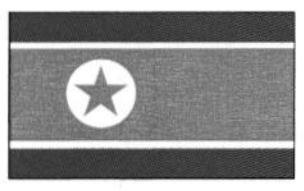
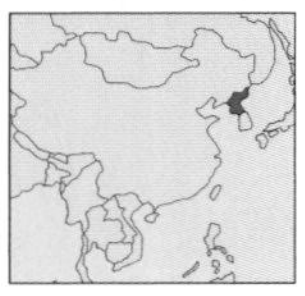

GEOGRAPHY The Democratic People's Republic of Korea occupies the northern part of the Korean peninsula which extends south from north-eastern China. Mountains form the heart of the country, with the highest peak, Paektu-san, reaching 2,744 m [9,003 ft] on the northern border.

North Korea has a fairly severe climate, with bitterly cold winters when winds blow from across central Asia, bringing snow and freezing conditions. In summer, moist winds from the oceans bring rain.

POLITICS & ECONOMY North Korea was created in 1945, when the peninsula, which had been a Japanese colony since 1910, was divided into two parts. Soviet forces occupied the north, with US forces in the south. Soviet occupation led to a Communist government being established in 1948 under the leadership of Kim Il Sung. He initiated a Stalinist regime in which he assumed the role of dictator, and a personality cult developed around him. He was to become the world's most durable Communist leader.

The Korean War began in June 1950 when North Korean troops invaded the south. North Korea, aided by China and the Soviet Union, fought with South Korea, which was supported by troops from the United States and other UN members. The war ended in July 1953. An armistice was signed but no permanent peace treaty was agreed. After the war, North Korea adopted a hostile policy towards South Korea in pursuit of its policy of reunification.

The ending of the Cold War in the late 1980s eased the situation and both North and South Korea joined the United Nations in 1991. The two countries made several agreements, including one in which they agreed not to use force against each other. However, North Korea remained as isolated as ever.

In 1993, North Korea began a new international crisis by announcing that it was withdrawing from the Nuclear Non-Proliferation Treaty. This led to suspicions that North Korea, which had signed the Treaty in 1985, was developing its own nuclear weapons. Kim Il Sung, who had ruled as a virtual dictator from 1948 until his death in 1994, was succeeded by his son, Kim Jong Il. In the early 2000s, attempts were made to reconcile the two Koreas, though the prospect of reunification seemed remote, especially after the United States accused North Korea of supporting international terrorism in 2002.

North Korea has considerable resources, including coal, copper, iron ore, lead, tin, tungsten and zinc. Under Communism, North Korea has concentrated on developing heavy, state-owned industries. Manufactures include chemicals, iron and steel, machinery, processed food and textiles. Agriculture employs about a third of the people of North Korea and rice is the leading crop. Economic decline and mismanagement, aggravated by three successive crop failures caused by floods in 1995 and 1996 and a drought in 1997, led to famine on a large scale.

AREA 120,540 sq km [46,540 sq mi] **POPULATION** 21,968,000
CAPITAL (POPULATION) Pyŏngyang (2,741,000)
GOVERNMENT Single-party people's republic
ETHNIC GROUPS Korean 99%
LANGUAGES Korean (official)
RELIGIONS Buddhism and Confucianism
CURRENCY North Korean won = 100 chon

KOREA, SOUTH

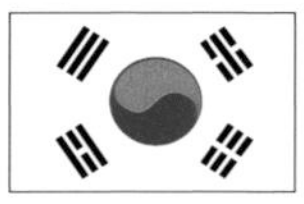
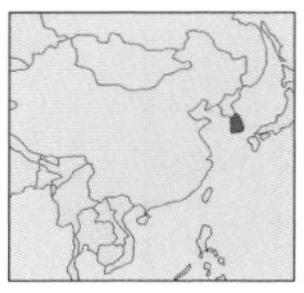

GEOGRAPHY The Republic of Korea, as South Korea is officially known, occupies the southern part of the Korean peninsula. Mountains cover much of the country. The southern and western coasts are major farming regions. Many islands are found along the west and south coasts. The largest of these is Cheju-do, which contains South Korea's highest peak, Halla-San, which rises to 1,950 m [6,398 ft].

Like North Korea, South Korea is chilled in winter by cold, dry winds blowing from central Asia. Snow often covers the mountains in the east. The summers are hot and wet, especially in July and August.

POLITICS & ECONOMY After Japan's defeat in World War II (1939–45), North Korea was occupied by troops from the Soviet Union, while South Korea was occupied by United States forces. Attempts to reunify Korea failed and, in 1948, a National Assembly was elected in South Korea. This Assembly created the Republic of Korea, while North Korea became a Communist state. North Korean troops invaded the South in June 1950, sparking off the Korean War (1950–3).

In the 1950s, South Korea had a weak economy, which had been further damaged by the destruction caused by the Korean War. From the 1960s to the 1980s, South Korean governments worked to industrialize the economy. The governments were dominated by military leaders, who often used authoritarian methods and flouted human rights. In 1987, a new constitution was approved, enabling presidential elections to be held every five years. In 1991, South and North Korea became members of the United Nations and they signed agreements, including one in which they agreed not to use force against each other. Tensions continued, though hopes were raised when negotiations between the two countries took place in the early 21st century.

The World Bank classifies South Korea as an 'upper-middle-income' developing country. It is also one of the world's fastest growing industrial economies. The country's resources include coal and tungsten, and its main manufactures are processed food and textiles. Since partition, heavy industries have been built up, making chemicals, fertilizers, iron and steel, and ships. South Korea has also developed the production of such things as computers, cars and television sets. In late 1997, however, the dramatic expansion of the economy was halted by a market crash which affected many of the booming economies of Asia. In an effort to negate the economic and social turmoil that resulted, tough reforms were demanded by the International Monetary Fund and an agreement was reached to restructure much of the short-term debt faced by the government.

Farming remains important in South Korea. Rice is the chief crop, together with fruits, grains and vegetables, while fishing provides a major source of protein.

AREA 99,020 sq km [38,232 sq mi] **POPULATION** 47,904,000
CAPITAL (POPULATION) Seoul (10,231,000)
GOVERNMENT Multiparty republic
ETHNIC GROUPS Korean 99% **LANGUAGES** Korean (official)
RELIGIONS Christianity 49%, Buddhism 47%, Confucianism 3%
CURRENCY South Korean won = 100 chon

KUWAIT

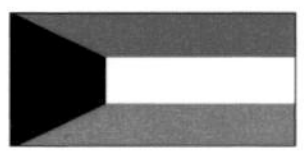
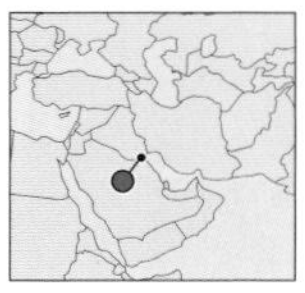

The State of Kuwait at the north end of the Gulf is largely made up of desert. Temperatures are high and the rainfall low. Kuwait became independent from Britain in 1961 and revenues from its oil wells have made it highly prosperous. Iraq invaded Kuwait in 1990 and much damage was inflicted in the ensuing conflict in 1991 when Kuwait was liberated.

AREA 17,820 sq km [6,880 sq mi] **POPULATION** 2,042,000
CAPITAL Kuwait City

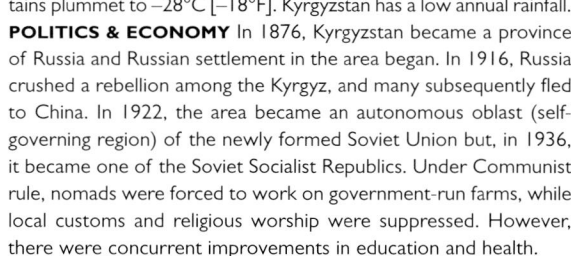

KYRGYZSTAN

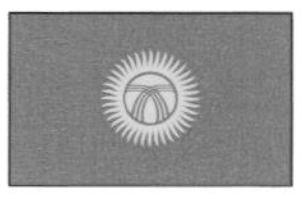
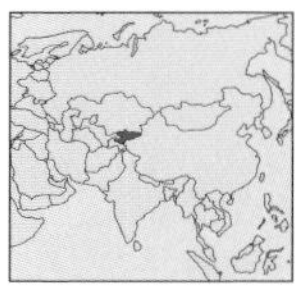

GEOGRAPHY The Republic of Kyrgyzstan is a landlocked country between China, Tajikistan, Uzbekistan and Kazakhstan. The country is mountainous, with spectacular scenery. The highest mountain, Pik Pobedy in the Tian Shan range, reaches 7,439 m [24,406 ft] in the east. The lowlands have warm summers and cold winters. But January temperatures in the mountains plummet to –28°C [–18°F]. Kyrgyzstan has a low annual rainfall.

POLITICS & ECONOMY In 1876, Kyrgyzstan became a province of Russia and Russian settlement in the area began. In 1916, Russia crushed a rebellion among the Kyrgyz, and many subsequently fled to China. In 1922, the area became an autonomous oblast (self-governing region) of the newly formed Soviet Union but, in 1936, it became one of the Soviet Socialist Republics. Under Communist rule, nomads were forced to work on government-run farms, while local customs and religious worship were suppressed. However, there were concurrent improvements in education and health.

In 1991, Kyrgyzstan became an independent country following the break-up of the Soviet Union. The Communist party was dissolved, but the country maintained ties with Russia through an organization called the Commonwealth of Independent States. Kyrgyzstan adopted a new constitution in 1994 and parliamentary elections were held in 1995. However, in the late 1990s, the government increased presidential powers and curbed press freedoms.

In the early 1990s, when Kyrgyzstan was working to reform its economy, the World Bank classified it as a 'lower-middle-income' developing country. Agriculture, especially livestock rearing, is the chief activity. The chief products include cotton, eggs, fruits, grain, tobacco, vegetables and wool. But food must be imported. Industries are mainly concentrated around the capital Bishkek.

AREA 198,500 sq km [76,640 sq mi] **POPULATION** 4,753,000
CAPITAL (POPULATION) Bishkek (589,000) **GOVERNMENT** Multiparty republic **ETHNIC GROUPS** Kyrgyz 52%, Russian 18%, Uzbek 13%, Ukrainian 3%, German, Tatar **LANGUAGES** Kyrgyz and Russian (both official), Uzbek **RELIGIONS** Islam **CURRENCY** Som = 100 tyiyn

LAOS

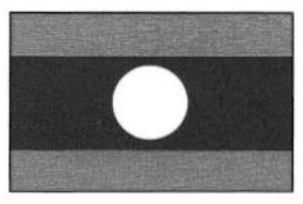
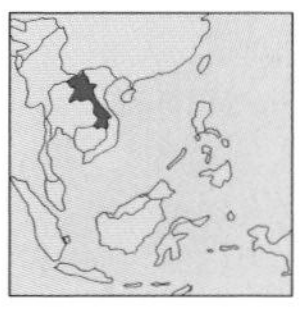

GEOGRAPHY The Lao People's Democratic Republic is a landlocked country in South-east Asia. Mountains and plateaux cover much of the country. Most people live on the plains bordering the River Mekong and its tributaries. This river, one of Asia's longest, forms much of the country's north-western and south-western borders.

Laos has a tropical monsoon climate.

Winters are dry and sunny, with winds blowing in from the north-east. The temperatures rise until April, when the wind directions are reversed and moist south-westerly winds reach Laos, heralding the start of the wet monsoon season.

POLITICS & ECONOMY France made Laos a protectorate in the late 19th century and ruled it as part of French Indo-China, a region which also included Cambodia and Vietnam. Laos became a member of the French Union in 1948 and an independent kingdom in 1954.

After independence, Laos suffered from instability caused by a long power struggle between royalist government forces and a pro-Communist group called the Pathet Lao. A civil war broke out in 1960 and continued into the 1970s. The Pathet Lao took control in 1975 and the king abdicated. Laos then came under the influence of Communist Vietnam, which had used Laos as a supply base during the Vietnam War (1957–75). From the early 1980s, the economy deteriorated and opposition appeared when bombings occurred in Vientiane in 2000. They were attributed to rebels in the minority Hmong tribe or to politicians who wanted faster economic reforms.

Laos is one of the world's poorest countries. Agriculture employs about 76% of the people, compared with 7% in industry and 17% in services. Rice is the main crop, and timber and coffee are both exported. But the most valuable export is electricity, which is produced at hydroelectric power stations on the River Mekong and is exported to Thailand. Laos also produces opium.

AREA 236,800 SQ KM [91,428 SQ MI] **POPULATION** 5,636,000
CAPITAL (POPULATION) VIENTIANE (532,000)
GOVERNMENT SINGLE-PARTY REPUBLIC **ETHNIC GROUPS** LAO LOUM 68%, LAO THEUNG 22%, LAO SOUNG 9% **LANGUAGES** LAO (OFFICIAL), KHMER, TAI, MIAO **RELIGIONS** BUDDHISM 58%, TRADITIONAL BELIEFS 34%, CHRISTIANITY 2%, ISLAM 1% **CURRENCY** KIP = 100 AT

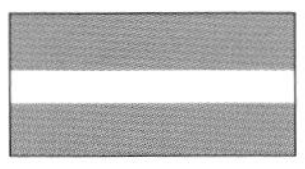
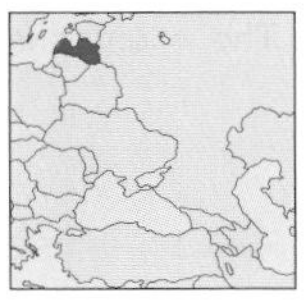

LATVIA

GEOGRAPHY The Republic of Latvia is one of three states on the south-eastern corner of the Baltic Sea which were ruled as parts of the Soviet Union between 1940 and 1991. Latvia consists mainly of flat plains separated by low hills, composed of moraine (ice-worn rocks).

Riga has warm summers, but the winter months (from December to March) are subzero. In the winter, the sea often freezes over. The rainfall is moderate and it occurs throughout the year, with light snow in winter.

POLITICS & ECONOMY In 1800, Russia was in control of Latvia, but Latvians declared their independence after World War I. In 1940, under a German-Soviet pact, Soviet troops occupied Latvia, but they were driven out by the Germans in 1941. Soviet troops returned in 1944 and Latvia became part of the Soviet Union. Under Soviet rule, many Russian immigrants settled in Latvia and many Latvians feared that the Russians would become the dominant ethnic group.

In the late 1980s, when reforms were being introduced in the Soviet Union, Latvia's government ended absolute Communist rule and made Latvian the official language. In 1990, it declared the country to be independent, an act which was finally recognized by the Soviet Union in September 1991.

Latvia held its first free elections to its parliament (the Saeima) in 1993. Voting was limited only to citizens of Latvia on 17 June 1940 and their descendants. This meant that about 34% of Latvian residents were unable to vote. In 1994, Latvia restricted the naturalization of non-Latvians, including many Russian settlers, who were not allowed to vote or own land. However, in 1998, the government agreed that all children born since independence should have automatic citizenship regardless of the status of their parents.

The World Bank classifies Latvia as a 'lower-middle-income' country and, in the 1990s, it faced many problems in turning its economy into a free-market system. Products include electronic goods, farm machinery, fertilizers, processed food, plastics, radios and vehicles. Latvia produces only about a tenth of the electricity it needs. It imports the rest from Belarus, Russia and Ukraine.

AREA 64,589 SQ KM [24,938 SQ MI] **POPULATION** 2,385,000
CAPITAL (POPULATION) RIGA (811,000)
GOVERNMENT MULTIPARTY REPUBLIC **ETHNIC GROUPS** LATVIAN 56%, RUSSIAN 30%, BELARUSSIAN 4%, UKRAINIAN 3%, POLISH 2%, LITHUANIAN, JEWISH **LANGUAGES** LATVIAN (OFFICIAL), RUSSIAN
RELIGIONS LUTHERAN, RUSSIAN ORTHODOX AND ROMAN CATHOLIC
CURRENCY LATS = 10 SANTIMI

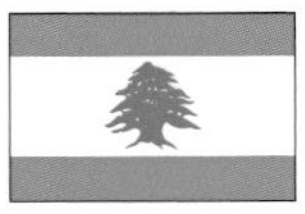
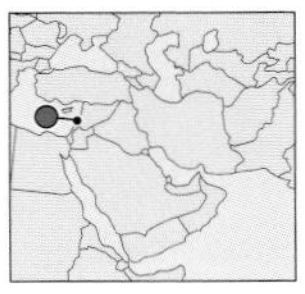

LEBANON

GEOGRAPHY The Republic of Lebanon is a country on the eastern shores of the Mediterranean Sea. Behind the coastal plain are the rugged Lebanon Mountains (Jabal Lubnan), which rise to 3,088 m [10,131 ft]. Another range, the Anti-Lebanon Mountains (Al Jabal Ash Sharqi), form the eastern border with Syria. Between the two ranges is the Bekaa (Beqaa) Valley, a fertile farming region.

The Lebanese coast has the hot, dry summers and mild, wet winters that are typical of many Mediterranean lands. Inland, onshore winds bring heavy rain to the western slopes of the mountains in the winter months, with snow at the higher altitudes.

POLITICS & ECONOMY Lebanon was ruled by Turkey from 1516 until World War I. France ruled the country from 1923, but Lebanon became independent in 1946. After independence, the Muslims and Christians agreed to share power, and Lebanon made rapid economic progress. But from the late 1950s, development was slowed by periodic conflict between Sunni and Shia Muslims, Druze and Christians. The situation was further complicated by the presence of Palestinian refugees who used bases in Lebanon to attack Israel.

In 1975, civil war broke out as private armies representing the many factions struggled for power. This led to intervention by Israel in the south and Syria in the north. UN peacekeeping forces arrived in 1978, but bombings, assassinations and kidnappings became almost everyday events in the 1980s. From 1991, Lebanon enjoyed an uneasy peace. But, Israel continued to occupy an area in the south. In the 1990s, Israel launched several attacks on pro-Iranian Hezbollah guerrillas in Lebanon, but all Israeli troops were withdrawn in May 2000.

Lebanon's civil war almost destroyed valuable trade and financial services that had been Lebanon's chief source of income, together with tourism. Manufacturing, formerly a major activity, was badly hit.

AREA 10,400 SQ KM [4,015 SQ MI] **POPULATION** 3,628,000
CAPITAL (POPULATION) BEIRUT (1,500,000)
GOVERNMENT MULTIPARTY REPUBLIC
ETHNIC GROUPS LEBANESE 80%, PALESTINIAN 12%, ARMENIAN 5%, SYRIAN, KURDISH **LANGUAGES** ARABIC (OFFICIAL) **RELIGIONS** ISLAM 70%, CHRISTIANITY 30% **CURRENCY** LEBANESE POUND = 100 PIASTRES

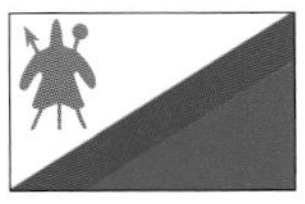
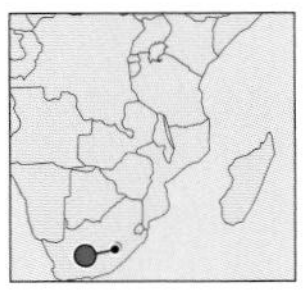

LESOTHO

GEOGRAPHY The Kingdom of Lesotho is a landlocked country, completely enclosed by South Africa. The land is mountainous, rising to 3,482 m [11,424 ft] on the north-eastern border. The Drakensberg range covers most of the country.

The climate of Lesotho is greatly affected by the altitude, because most of the country lies above 1,500 m [4,921 ft]. Maseru has warm summers, but the temperatures fall below freezing in the winter. The mountains are colder. The rainfall varies, averaging around 700 mm [28 in].

POLITICS & ECONOMY The Basotho nation was founded in the 1820s by King Moshoeshoe I, who united various groups fleeing from tribal wars in southern Africa. Britain made the area a protectorate in 1868 and, in 1971, placed it under the British Cape Colony in South Africa. But in 1884, Basutoland, as the area was called, was reconstituted as a British protectorate, where whites were not allowed to own land.

The country finally became independent in 1966 as the Kingdom of Lesotho, with Moshoeshoe II, great-grandson of Moshoeshoe I, as its king. Since independence, Lesotho has suffered instability. The military seized power in 1986 and stripped Moshoeshoe II of his powers in 1990, installing his son, Letsie III, as monarch. After elections in 1993, Moshoeshoe II was restored to office in 1995. But after his death in a car crash in 1996, Letsie III again became king. In 1998, an army revolt, following an election in which the ruling party won 79 out of the 80 seats, caused much damage to the economy, despite the intervention of a South African force intended to maintain order.

Lesotho is a 'low-income' developing country. It lacks natural resources. Agriculture, mainly at subsistence level, light manufacturing and money sent home by Basotho working abroad are the main sources of income.

AREA 30,350 SQ KM [11,718 SQ MI] **POPULATION** 2,177,000
CAPITAL (POPULATION) MASERU (130,000)
GOVERNMENT CONSTITUTIONAL MONARCHY
ETHNIC GROUPS SOTHO 99% **LANGUAGES** SESOTHO AND ENGLISH (BOTH OFFICIAL) **RELIGIONS** CHRISTIANITY 80%, TRADITIONAL BELIEFS 20%
CURRENCY LOTI = 100 LISENTE

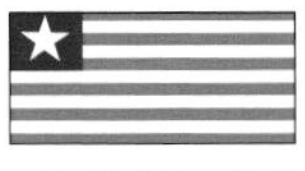
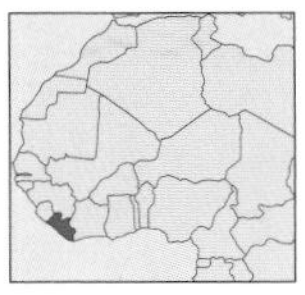

LIBERIA

GEOGRAPHY The Republic of Liberia is a country in West Africa. Behind the coastline, 500 km [311 mi] long, lies a narrow coastal plain. Beyond, the land rises to a plateau region, with the highest land along the border with Guinea. Liberia has a tropical climate with high temperatures and high humidity all through the year. The rainfall is abundant all year round, but there is a particularly wet period from June to November. The rainfall generally increases from east to west.

POLITICS & ECONOMY In the late 18th century, some white Americans in the United States wanted to help freed black slaves to return to Africa. In 1816, they set up the American Colonization Society, which bought land in what is now Liberia.

In 1822, the Society landed former slaves at a settlement on the coast which they named Monrovia. In 1847, Liberia became a fully independent republic with a constitution much like that of the United States. For many years, the Americo-Liberians controlled the country's government. US influence remained strong and the American Firestone Company, which ran Liberia's rubber plantations, was especially influential. Foreign companies were also involved in exploiting Liberia's mineral resources, including its huge iron-ore deposits.

In 1980, a military group composed of people from the local population killed the Americo-Liberian president, William R. Tolbert. An army sergeant, Samuel K. Doe, was made president of Liberia. Elections held in 1985 resulted in victory for Doe. From 1989, the country was plunged into civil war between various ethnic groups. Doe was assassinated in 1990 and the struggle with rebel groups continued. West African peacekeeping forces arrived in Liberia and, in 1995, a cease-fire was agreed. A council of state, composed of former warlords, was set up and, in 1997, one of the warlords, Charles Taylor, was elected president. A cease-fire in 1998 led to the withdrawal of the peacekeeping forces. But unrest continued and, in 2002, a state of emergency was declared.

Liberia's civil war devastated its economy. Three out of every four people depend on agriculture, though many of them grow little more than they need to feed their families. Major food crops include cassava, rice and sugar cane, while rubber, cocoa and coffee are exported. But the most valuable export is iron ore.

Liberia also obtains revenue from its 'flag of convenience', which is used by about one-sixth of the world's commercial shipping, exploiting low taxes.

AREA 111,370 SQ KM [43,000 SQ MI] **POPULATION** 3,226,000
CAPITAL (POPULATION) MONROVIA (962,000)
GOVERNMENT MULTIPARTY REPUBLIC **ETHNIC GROUPS** KPELLE 19%, BASSA 14%, GREBO 9%, GIO 8%, KRU 7%, MANO 7%
LANGUAGES ENGLISH (OFFICIAL), MANDE, MEL, KWA
RELIGIONS CHRISTIANITY 40%, ISLAM 20%, TRADITIONAL BELIEFS AND OTHERS 40% **CURRENCY** LIBERIAN DOLLAR = 100 CENTS

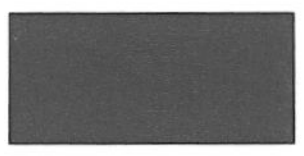
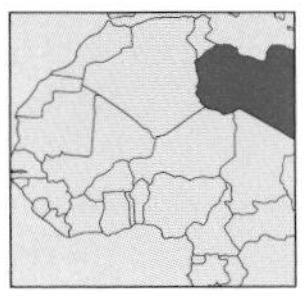

LIBYA

GEOGRAPHY The Socialist People's Libyan Arab Jamahiriya, as Libya is officially called, is a large country in North Africa. Most people live on the coastal plains in the north-east and north-west. The Sahara, the world's largest desert which occupies 95% of Libya, reaches the Mediterranean coast along the Gulf of Sidra (Khalij Surt).

The coastal plains in the north-east and north-west have Mediterranean climates, with hot, dry summers and mild, sometimes wet winters. Inland, the average yearly rainfall drops to 100 mm [4 in] or less.

POLITICS & ECONOMY Italy took over Libya in 1911, but lost it during World War II. Britain and France then jointly ruled Libya until 1951, when the country became an independent kingdom.

In 1969, a military group headed by Colonel Muammar Gaddafi deposed the king and set up a military government. Under Gaddafi, the government took control of the economy and used money from oil exports to finance welfare services and development projects. Gaddafi was criticized for supporting terrorist groups around the world, and Libya became isolated from the mid-1980s. In 1998, he tried to restore Libya's reputation by surrendering for trial two Libyans suspected of planting a bomb on a PanAm plane which exploded over the Scottish town of Lockerbie in 1988. In 2001, one of the Libyans was found guilty and the other acquitted of the bombing. Gaddafi also compensated the family of a British policewoman killed in 1984 in London. However, in 2002, Libya remained on the US blacklist for its alleged support for international terrorism.

The discovery of oil and natural gas in 1959 led to the transformation of Libya's economy. Once one of the world's poorest countries, it has become Africa's richest in terms of its per capita income. It remains a developing country because of its dependence on oil, which accounts for nearly all of its export revenues.

Agriculture is important, although Libya has to import food. Crops include barley, citrus fruits, dates, olives, potatoes and wheat. Cattle, sheep and poultry are raised. Libya has oil refineries and petrochemical plants. Other manufactures include cement and steel.

AREA 1,759,540 sq km [679,358 sq mi] **POPULATION** 5,241,000
CAPITAL (POPULATION) Tripoli (960,000)
GOVERNMENT Single-party socialist state **ETHNIC GROUPS** Libyan Arab and Berber 97% **LANGUAGES** Arabic (official), Berber
RELIGIONS Islam (Sunni) **CURRENCY** Libyan dinar = 1,000 dirhams

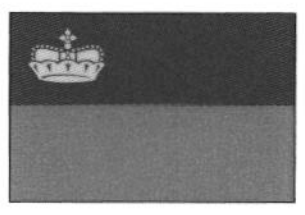

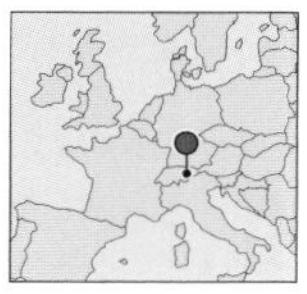

LIECHTENSTEIN

The tiny Principality of Liechtenstein is sandwiched between Switzerland and Austria. The River Rhine flows along its western border, while Alpine peaks rise in the east and south. The climate is relatively mild. Since 1924, Liechtenstein has been in a customs union with Switzerland and, like its neighbour, it is extremely prosperous. Taxation is low and, as a result, the country has become a haven for international companies.

AREA 157 sq km [61 sq mi] **POPULATION** 33,000 **CAPITAL** Vaduz

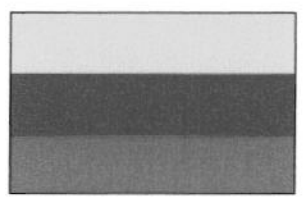

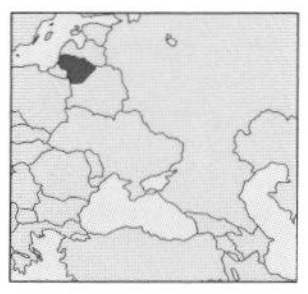

LITHUANIA

GEOGRAPHY The Republic of Lithuania is the southernmost of the three Baltic states which were ruled as part of the Soviet Union between 1940 and 1991. Much of the land is flat or gently rolling, with the highest land in the south-east.

Winters are cold. January's temperatures average –3°C [27°F] in the west and –6°C [21°F] in the east. Summers are warm, with average temperatures in July of 17°C [63°F]. The average rainfall in the west is about 630 mm [25 in]. Inland areas are drier.

POLITICS & ECONOMY The Lithuanian people were united into a single nation in the 12th century, and later joined a union with Poland. In 1795, Lithuania came under Russian rule. After World War I (1914–18), Lithuania declared itself independent, and in 1920 it signed a peace treaty with the Russians, though Poland held Vilnius until 1939. In 1940, the Soviet Union occupied Lithuania, but the Germans invaded in 1941. Soviet forces returned in 1944, and Lithuania was integrated into the Soviet Union. In 1988, when the Soviet Union was introducing reforms, the Lithuanians demanded independence. Their language is one of the oldest in the world, and the country was always the most homogenous of the Baltic states, staunchly Catholic and resistant of attempts to suppress their culture. Pro-independence groups won the national elections in 1990 and, in 1991, the Soviet Union recognized Lithuania's independence.

After independence, Lithuania faced many problems as it sought to reform its economy and introduce a private enterprise system. In 1998, Valdas Adamkus, a Lithuanian-American who had fled the country in 1944, was elected president.

The World Bank classifies Lithuania as a 'lower-middle-income' developing country. Lithuania lacks natural resources, but manufacturing, based on imported materials, is the most valuable activity.

AREA 65,200 sq km [25,200 sq mi] **POPULATION** 3,611,000
CAPITAL (POPULATION) Vilnius (580,000)
GOVERNMENT Multiparty republic
ETHNIC GROUPS Lithuanian 80%, Russian 9%, Polish 7%, Belarussian 2% **LANGUAGES** Lithuanian (official), Russian, Polish
RELIGIONS Mainly Roman Catholic **CURRENCY** Litas = 100 centai

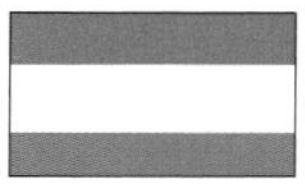

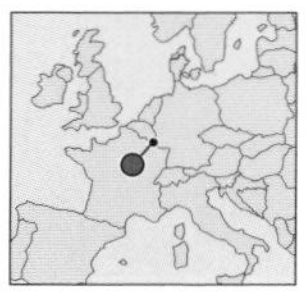

LUXEMBOURG

GEOGRAPHY The Grand Duchy of Luxembourg is one of the smallest and oldest countries in Europe. The north belongs to an upland region which includes the Ardenne in Belgium and Luxembourg, and the Eifel highlands in Germany.

Luxembourg has a temperate climate. The south has warm summers and autumns, when grapes ripen in sheltered south-eastern valleys. Winters are sometimes severe, especially in upland areas.

POLITICS & ECONOMY Germany occupied Luxembourg in World Wars I and II. In 1944–5, northern Luxembourg was the scene of the famous Battle of the Bulge. In 1948, Luxembourg joined Belgium and the Netherlands in a union called Benelux and, in the 1950s, it was one of the six founders of what is now the European Union. Luxembourg has played a major role in Europe. Its capital contains the headquarters of several international agencies, including the European Coal and Steel Community and the European Court of Justice. The city is also a major financial centre.

Luxembourg has iron-ore reserves and is a major steel producer. It also has many high-technology industries, producing electronic goods and computers. Steel and other manufactures, including chemicals, rubber products, glass and aluminium, dominate the country's exports. Other major activities include tourism and financial services.

AREA 2,590 sq km [1,000 sq mi] **POPULATION** 443,000
CAPITAL (POPULATION) Luxembourg (76,000)
GOVERNMENT Constitutional monarchy (Grand Duchy)
ETHNIC GROUPS Luxembourger 71%, Portuguese 10%, Italian 5%, French 3%, Belgian 3% **LANGUAGES** Luxembourgish (official), French, German **RELIGIONS** Roman Catholic 95%
CURRENCY Euro = 100 cents

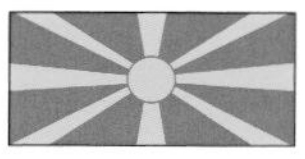

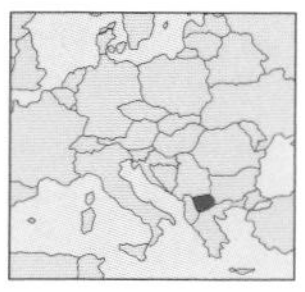

MACEDONIA (FYROM)

GEOGRAPHY The Republic of Macedonia is a country in south-eastern Europe, which was once one of the six republics that made up the former Federal People's Republic of Yugoslavia. This landlocked country is largely mountainous or hilly. Macedonia has hot summers, though highland areas are cooler. Winters are cold and snowfalls are often heavy. The climate is fairly continental in character and rain occurs throughout the year.

POLITICS & ECONOMY Until the 20th century, Macedonia's history was closely tied to a larger area, also called Macedonia, which included parts of northern Greece and south-western Bulgaria. This region reached its peak in power at the time of Philip II (382–336 BC) and his son Alexander the Great (336–323 BC). After Alexander's death, his empire was split up and it gradually declined. The area became a Roman province in the 140s BC and part of the Byzantine Empire from AD 395. In the 6th century, Slavs from eastern Europe settled in the area, followed by the Bulgars from central Asia in the 9th century. The Byzantine Empire regained control in 1018, but Serbia took Macedonia in the early 14th century. In 1371, the Ottoman Turks conquered the area and ruled it for more than 500 years. In 1913, at the end of the Balkan Wars, the area was divided between Serbia, Bulgaria and Greece. At the end of World War I, Serbian Macedonia became part of the Kingdom of the Serbs, Croats and Slovenes, which was renamed Yugoslavia in 1929. After World War II, Yugoslavia became a Communist country under ex-partisan leader Josip Broz Tito.

Tito died in 1980 and, in the early 1990s, the country broke up into five separate republics. Macedonia declared its independence in September 1991. Greece objected to this territory using the name Macedonia, which it considered to be a Greek name. It also objected to a symbol on Macedonia's flag and a reference in the constitution to the desire to reunite the three parts of the old Macedonia.

Macedonia adopted a new clause in its constitution rejecting any Macedonian claims on Greek territory and, in 1993, the United Nations accepted the new republic as a member under the name of The Former Yugoslav Republic of Macedonia (FYROM).

By the end of 1993, all the countries of the EU, except Greece, were establishing diplomatic relations with the FYROM. In 1995, Greece lifted its trade ban, when Macedonia agreed to redesign its flag and remove territorial claims from its constitution. In 2001, fighting along the Kosovo border spilled over into north-western Macedonia. It was attributed to nationalists who want to create a Great Albania, including part of Macedonia. The uprising ended when the Macedonian government gave its Albanian-speakers increased rights.

The World Bank describes Macedonia as a 'lower-middle-income' developing country. Manufactures dominate the country's exports. Macedonia mines coal, but imports all its oil and natural gas. The country is self-sufficient in its basic food needs.

AREA 25,710 sq km [9,927 sq mi] **POPULATION** 2,046,000
CAPITAL (POPULATION) Skopje (541,000) **GOVERNMENT** Multiparty republic **ETHNIC GROUPS** Macedonian 67%, Albanian 23%, Turkish 4%, Romanian 2%, Serb 2% **LANGUAGES** Macedonian (official), Albanian **RELIGIONS** Macedonian Orthodox, Islam
CURRENCY Dinar = 100 paras

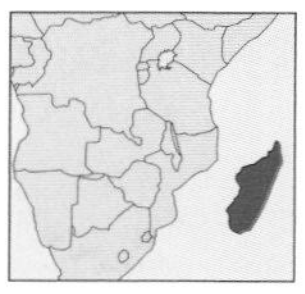

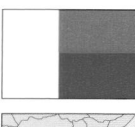

MADAGASCAR

GEOGRAPHY The Democratic Republic of Madagascar, in south-eastern Africa, is an island nation, which has a larger area than France. Behind the narrow coastal plains in the east lies a highland zone, mostly between 610 m to 1,220 m [2,000 ft and 4,000 ft] above sea level. Broad plains border the Mozambique Channel in the west.

Temperatures in the highlands are moderated by the altitude. The winters (from April to September) are dry, but heavy rains occur in summer. The eastern coastlands are warm and humid. The west is drier and the south and south-west are hot and dry.

POLITICS & ECONOMY People from South-east Asia began to settle on Madagascar around 2,000 years ago. Subsequent influxes from Africa and Arabia added to the island's diverse heritage, culture and language.

French troops defeated a Malagasy army in 1895 and Madagascar became a French colony. In 1960, it achieved full independence as the Malagasy Republic. In 1972, army officers seized control and, in 1975, under the leadership of Lt-Commander Didier Ratsiraka, the country was renamed Madagascar. Parliamentary elections were held in 1977, but Ratsiraka remained president of a one-party socialist state. The government resigned in 1991, following huge demonstrations. In 2002, the country came close to civil war when Ratsiraka and his opponent, Marc Ravalomanana, both claimed victory in presidential elections.

Madagascar is one of the world's poorest countries. The land has been badly eroded because of the cutting down of the forests and overgrazing of the grasslands. Farming, fishing and forestry employ about 80% of the people. The country's food crops include bananas, cassava, rice and sweet potatoes. Coffee is the leading export.

AREA 587,040 sq km [226,656 sq mi] **POPULATION** 15,983,000
CAPITAL (POPULATION) Antananarivo (1,053,000)
GOVERNMENT Republic **ETHNIC GROUPS** Merina 27%, Betsimisaraka 15%, Betsileo 11%, Tsimihety 7%, Sakalava 6%
LANGUAGES Malagasy and French (both official)
RELIGIONS Traditional beliefs 52%, Christianity 41%, Islam 7%
CURRENCY Malagasy franc = 100 centimes

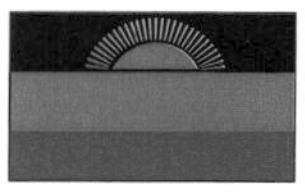

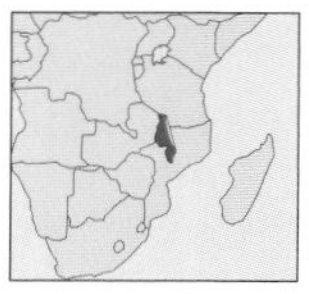

MALAWI

GEOGRAPHY The Republic of Malawi includes part of Lake Malawi, which is drained by the River Shire, a tributary of the River Zambezi. The land is mostly mountainous. The highest peak, Mulanje, reaches 3,000 m [9,843 ft] in the south-east.

While the low-lying areas of Malawi are hot and humid all year round, the uplands have a pleasant climate. Lilongwe, at about 1,100 m [3,609 ft] above sea level, has a warm and sunny climate. Frosts sometimes occur in July and August, in the middle of the long dry season.

POLITICS & ECONOMY Malawi, then called Nyasaland, became a British protectorate in 1891. In 1953, Britain established the Federation of Rhodesia and Nyasaland, which also included what are now Zambia and Zimbabwe. Black African opposition, led in Nyasaland by Dr Hastings Kamuzu Banda, led to the dissolution of the federation in 1963. In 1964, Nyasaland became independent as Malawi, with Banda as prime minister. Banda became president when the country became a republic in 1966 and, in 1971, he was made president for life. Banda ruled autocratically through the only party, the Malawi Congress Party. A multiparty system was restored in 1993. Banda and his party were defeated in elections in 1993. Bakili Muluzi became president and was re-elected in 1999. Banda died in 1997.

Malawi is one of the world's poorest countries. More than 80% of the people are farmers, but many grow little more than they need to feed their families.

AREA 118,480 sq km [45,745 sq mi] **POPULATION** 10,548,000
CAPITAL (POPULATION) Lilongwe (395,000)
GOVERNMENT Multiparty republic
ETHNIC GROUPS Maravi (Chewa, Nyanja, Tonga, Tumbuka) 58%, Lomwe 18%, Yao 13%, Ngoni 7%
LANGUAGES Chichewa and English (both official)
RELIGIONS Protestant 55%, Roman Catholic 20%, Islam 20%
CURRENCY Kwacha = 100 tambala

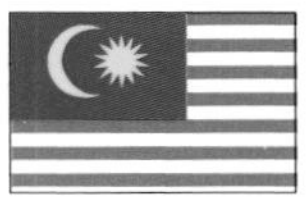

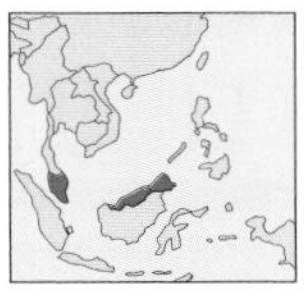

MALAYSIA

GEOGRAPHY The Federation of Malaysia consists of two main parts. Peninsular Malaysia, which is joined to mainland Asia, contains about 80% of the population. The other main regions, Sabah and Sarawak, are in northern Borneo, an island which Malaysia shares with Indonesia. Much of the land is mountainous, with coastal lowlands bordering the rugged interior. The highest peak, Kinabalu, reaches 4,101 m [13,455 ft] in Sabah.

Malaysia has a hot equatorial climate. The temperatures are high all through the year, though the mountains are much cooler than the lowland areas. The rainfall is heavy throughout the year.

POLITICS & ECONOMY Japan occupied what is now Malaysia during World War II, but British rule was re-established in 1945. In the 1940s and 1950s, British troops fought a war against Communist guerrillas, but Peninsular Malaysia (then called Malaya) became independent in 1957. Malaysia was created in 1963, when Malaya, Singapore, Sabah and Sarawak agreed to unite, but Singapore withdrew in 1965.

From the 1970s, Malaysia achieved rapid economic progress and, by the mid-1990s, it was playing a major part in regional affairs, especially through its membership of ASEAN (Association of South-east Asian Nations). However, together with several other countries in eastern Asia, Malaysia was hit by economic recession in 1997, including a major fall in stock market values. In response to the crisis, the government ordered the repatriation of many temporary foreign workers and initiated a series of austerity measures aimed at restoring confidence and avoiding the chronic debt problems affecting some other Asian countries.

The World Bank classifies Malaysia as an 'upper-middle-income' developing country. Malaysia is a leading producer of palm oil, rubber and tin.

Manufacturing now plays a major part in the economy. Manufactures are diverse, including cars, chemicals, a wide range of electronic goods, plastics, textiles, rubber and wood products.

AREA 329,750 sq km [127,316 sq mi] **POPULATION** 22,229,000
CAPITAL (POPULATION) Kuala Lumpur (1,145,000)
GOVERNMENT Federal constitutional monarchy
ETHNIC GROUPS Malay and other indigenous groups 58%, Chinese 27%, Indian 8% **LANGUAGES** Malay (official), Chinese, English **RELIGIONS** Islam 53%, Buddhism 17%, Chinese folk religionist 12%, Hinduism 7%, Christianity 6%
CURRENCY Ringgit (Malaysian dollar) = 100 cents

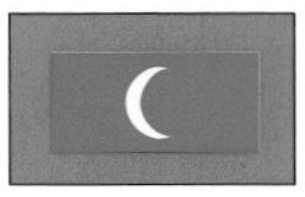

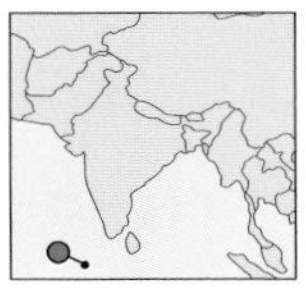

MALDIVES

The Republic of the Maldives consists of about 1,200 low-lying coral islands, south of India. The highest point is 24 m [79 ft], but most of the land is only 1.8 m [6 ft] above sea level. The islands became a British territory in 1887 and independence was achieved in 1965. Tourism and fishing are the main industries.

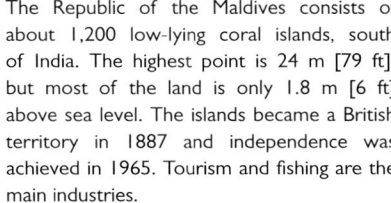

AREA 298 sq km [115 sq mi] **POPULATION** 311,000 **CAPITAL** Malé

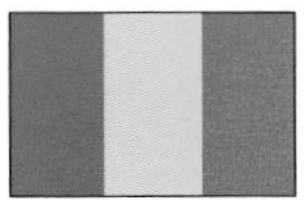

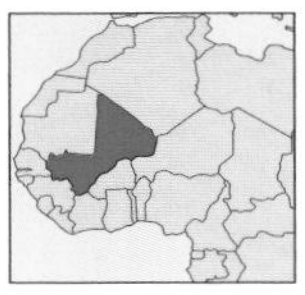

MALI

GEOGRAPHY The Republic of Mali is a landlocked country in northern Africa. The land is generally flat, with the highest land in the Adrar des Iforhas on the border with Algeria.

Northern Mali is part of the Sahara, with a hot, practically rainless climate. But the south has enough rain for farming.

POLITICS & ECONOMY France ruled the area, then known as French Sudan, from 1893 until the country became independent as Mali in 1960.

The first socialist government was overthrown in 1968 by an army group led by Moussa Traoré, but he was ousted in 1991. Multiparty democracy was restored in 1992 and Alpha Oumar Konaré was elected president. The new government agreed a pact providing for a special administration for the Tuareg minority in the north.

Mali is one of the world's poorest countries and 70% of the land is desert or semi-desert. Only about 2% of the land is used for growing crops, while 25% is used for grazing animals. Despite this, agriculture employs more than 80% of the people, many of whom still subsist by nomadic livestock rearing.

AREA 1,240,190 sq km [478,837 sq mi] **POPULATION** 11,009,000
CAPITAL (POPULATION) Bamako (810,000) **GOVERNMENT** Multiparty republic **ETHNIC GROUPS** Bambara 32%, Fulani (or Peul) 14%, Senufo 12%, Soninke 9%, Tuareg 7%, Songhai 7%, Malinke (Mandingo or Mandinke) 7% **LANGUAGES** French (official), Voltaic languages
RELIGIONS Islam 90%, traditional beliefs 9%, Christianity 1%
CURRENCY CFA franc = 100 centimes

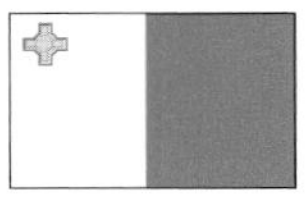

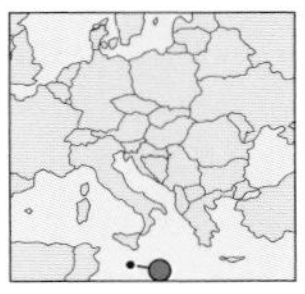

MALTA

GEOGRAPHY The Republic of Malta consists of two main islands, Malta and Gozo, a third, much smaller island called Comino lying between the two large islands, and two tiny islets.

Malta's climate is typically Mediterranean, with hot and dry summers and mild and wet winters. The sirocco, a hot wind that blows from North Africa, may raise temperatures considerably during the spring.

POLITICS & ECONOMY During World War I (1914–18) Malta was an important naval base. In World War II (1939–45), Italian and German aircraft bombed the islands. In recognition of the bravery of the Maltese, the British King George VI awarded the George Cross to Malta in 1942. In 1953, Malta became a base for NATO (North Atlantic Treaty Organization). Malta became independent in 1964, and in 1974 it became a republic. In 1979, Britain's military agreement with Malta expired, and Malta ceased to be a military base when all the British forces withdrew. In the 1980s, the people declared Malta a neutral country. In the 1990s, Malta applied to join the European Union. The application was scrapped when the Labour Party won the elections in 1996, but, in 2000, after the Labour Party's defeat in 1998, Malta formally reopened negotiations for its entry into the EU.

The World Bank classifies Malta as an 'upper-middle-income' developing country. It lacks natural resources, and most people work in the former naval dockyards, which are now used for commercial shipbuilding and repair, in manufacturing industries and in the tourist industry.

Manufactures include chemicals, processed food and chemicals. Farming is difficult, because of the rocky soils. Crops include barley, fruits, potatoes and wheat. Malta also has a small fishing industry.

AREA 316 sq km [122 sq mi] **POPULATION** 395,000
CAPITAL (POPULATION) Valletta (102,000)
GOVERNMENT Multiparty republic **ETHNIC GROUPS** Maltese 96%, British 2% **LANGUAGES** Maltese and English (both official)
RELIGIONS Roman Catholic 91%
CURRENCY Maltese lira = 100 cents

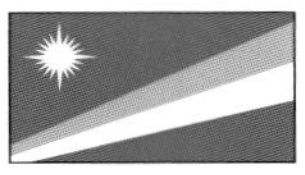

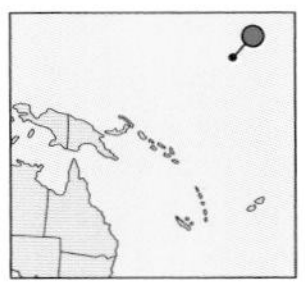

MARSHALL ISLANDS

The Republic of the Marshall Islands, a former US territory, became fully independent in 1991. This island nation, lying north of Kiribati in a region known as Micronesia, is heavily dependent on US aid. The main activities are agriculture and tourism.

AREA 181 sq km [70 sq mi] **POPULATION** 71,000
CAPITAL Dalap-Uliga-Darrit, on Majuro island

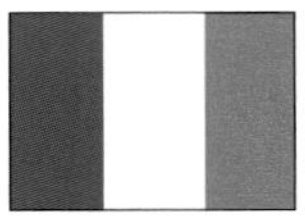

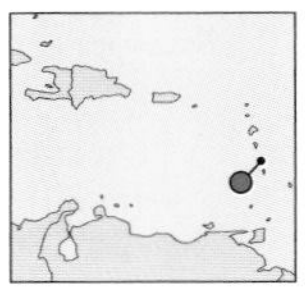

MARTINIQUE

Martinique, a volcanic island nation in the Caribbean, was colonized by France in 1635. It became a French overseas department in 1946. Tourism and agriculture are major activities. About 70% of Martinique's gross domestic product is provided by the French government, allowing for a good standard of living.

AREA 1,100 sq km [425 sq mi]
POPULATION 418,000 **CAPITAL** Fort-de-France

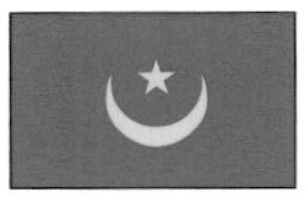

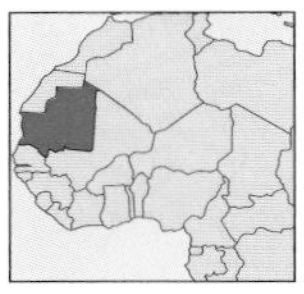

MAURITANIA

GEOGRAPHY The Islamic Republic of Mauritania in north-western Africa is nearly twice the size of France. But France has more than 28 times as many people. Part of the world's largest desert, the Sahara, covers northern Mauritania and most Mauritanians live in the south-west.

The amount of rainfall and the length of the rainy season increase from north to south. Much of the land is desert, with dry north-east and easterly winds throughout the year. But south-westerly winds bring summer rain to the south.

POLITICS & ECONOMY Originally part of the great African empires of Ghana and Mali, France set up a protectorate in Mauritania in 1903, attempting to exploit the trade in gum arabic. The country became a territory of French West Africa and a French colony in 1920. French West Africa was a huge territory, which included present-day Benin, Burkina Faso, Guinea, Ivory Coast, Mali, Niger and Senegal, as well as Mauritania. In 1958, Mauritania became a self-governing territory in the French Union and it became fully independent in 1960.

In 1976, Spain withdrew from Spanish (now Western) Sahara, a territory bordering Mauritania to the north. Morocco occupied the northern two-thirds of this territory, while Mauritania took the rest. But Saharan guerrillas belonging to POLISARIO (the Popular Front for the Liberation of Saharan Territories) began an armed struggle for independence. In 1979, Mauritania withdrew from the southern part of Western Sahara, which was then occupied by Morocco. In 1991, the country adopted a new constitution when the people voted to create a multiparty government. Multiparty elections were held in 1992 and 1996–7.

The World Bank classifies Mauritania as a 'low-income' developing country. Agriculture employs 40% of the people. Some are herders who move around with herds of cattle and sheep, though recent droughts forced many farmers to seek aid in the cities.

AREA 1,030,700 sq km [397,953 sq mi] **POPULATION** 2,747,000
CAPITAL (POPULATION) Nouakchott (735,000)
GOVERNMENT Multiparty Islamic republic
ETHNIC GROUPS Moor (Arab-Berber) 70%, Wolof 7%, Tukulor 5%, Soninke 3%, Fulani 1%
LANGUAGES Arabic and Wolof (both official), French
RELIGIONS Islam 99% **CURRENCY** Ouguiya = 5 khoums

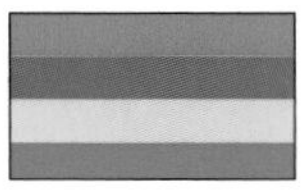

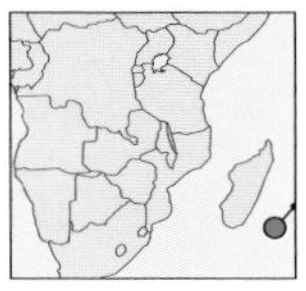

MAURITIUS

The Republic of Mauritius, an Indian Ocean nation lying east of Madagascar, was previously ruled by France and Britain until it achieved independence in 1968. It became a republic in 1992. Sugar production is in decline but tourism is vital to the economy.

AREA 1,860 sq km [718 sq mi]
POPULATION 1,190,000 **CAPITAL** Port Louis

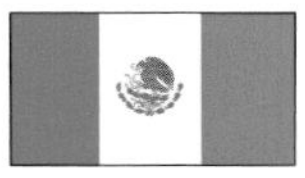

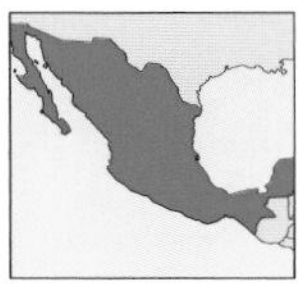

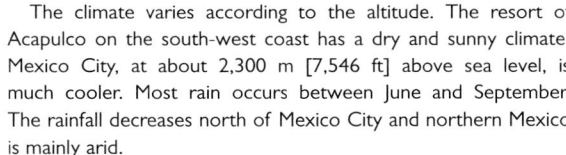

MEXICO

GEOGRAPHY The United Mexican States, as Mexico is officially named, is the world's most populous Spanish-speaking country. Much of the land is mountainous, although most people live on the central plateau. Mexico contains two large peninsulas, Lower (or Baja) California in the north-west and the flat Yucatán peninsula in the south-east.

The climate varies according to the altitude. The resort of Acapulco on the south-west coast has a dry and sunny climate. Mexico City, at about 2,300 m [7,546 ft] above sea level, is much cooler. Most rain occurs between June and September. The rainfall decreases north of Mexico City and northern Mexico is mainly arid.

POLITICS & ECONOMY In the mid-19th century, Mexico lost land to the United States, and between 1910 and 1921 violent revolutions created chaos.

Reforms were introduced in the 1920s and, in 1929, the Institutional Revolutionary Party (PRI) was formed. The PRI ruled Mexico effectively as a one-party state until it was finally defeated in 2001. The new president, Vicente Fox, faced many problems, including unemployment and rapid urbanization especially around Mexico City, demands for indigenous rights by Amerindian groups, and illegal emigration to the United States.

The World Bank classifies Mexico as an 'upper-middle-income' developing country. Agriculture is important. Food crops include beans, maize, rice and wheat, while cash crops include coffee, cotton, fruits and vegetables. Beef cattle, dairy cattle and other livestock are raised and fishing is also important.

But oil and oil products are the chief exports, while manufacturing is the most valuable activity. Mexico is the world's leading silver producer, and it also mines copper, gold, lead, zinc and other minerals. Many factories near the northern border assemble goods, such as car parts and electrical products, for US companies. These factories are called *maquiladoras*. Hope for the future lies in increasing economic co-operation with the USA and Canada

through NAFTA (North American Free Trade Association), which came into being on 1 January 1994.

AREA 1,958,200 sq km [756,061 sq mi] **POPULATION** 101,879,000
CAPITAL (POPULATION) Mexico City (15,643,000)
GOVERNMENT Federal republic
ETHNIC GROUPS Mestizo 60%, Amerindian 30%, White 9%
LANGUAGES Spanish (official)
RELIGIONS Roman Catholic 90%, Protestant 5%
CURRENCY New peso = 100 centavos

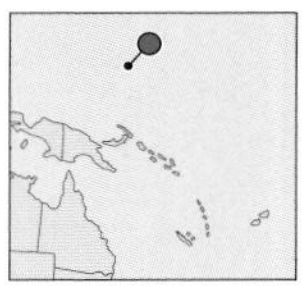

MICRONESIA

The Federated States of Micronesia, a former US territory covering a vast area in the western Pacific Ocean, became fully independent in 1991. The main export is copra. Fishing and tourism are also important.

AREA 705 sq km [272 sq mi]
POPULATION 135,000 **CAPITAL** Palikir

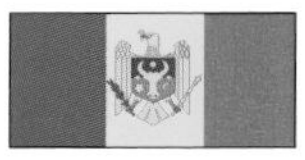

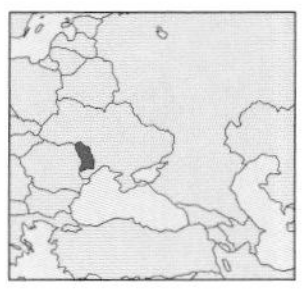

MOLDOVA

GEOGRAPHY The Republic of Moldova is a small country sandwiched between Ukraine and Romania. It was formerly one of the 15 republics that made up the Soviet Union. Much of the land is hilly and the highest areas are near the centre of the country.

Moldova has a moderately continental climate, with warm summers and fairly cold winters when temperatures dip below freezing point. Most of the rain comes in the warmer months.

POLITICS & ECONOMY In the 14th century, the Moldavians formed a state called Moldavia. It included part of Romania and Bessarabia (now the modern country of Moldova). The Ottoman Turks took the area in the 16th century, but in 1812 Russia took over Bessarabia. In 1861, Moldavia and Walachia united to form Romania. Russia retook southern Bessarabia in 1878.

After World War I (1914–18), all of Bessarabia was returned to Romania, but the Soviet Union did not recognize this act. From 1944, the Moldovan Soviet Socialist Republic was part of the Soviet Union.

In 1989, the Moldovans asserted their independence and ethnicity by making Romanian the official language and, at the end of 1991, Moldova became an independent country. In 1992, fighting occurred between Moldovans and Russians in Trans-Dniester, a mainly Russian-speaking area east of the River Dniester. The first multiparty elections were held in 1994, when a proposal to unite with Romania was rejected. Economic problems made the government unpopular and, in 2001, Moldova became the first former Soviet state to return the Communist party to power in a general election.

Moldova is a fertile country in which agriculture remains central to the economy. Major products include fruits, maize, tobacco and wine. Moldova has few natural resources and the country imports materials and fuels for its industries. Light industries, such as food processing and the manufacturing of household appliances, are gradually expanding.

AREA 33,700 sq km [13,010 sq mi] **POPULATION** 4,432,000
CAPITAL (POPULATION) Chişinău (658,000)
GOVERNMENT Multiparty republic
ETHNIC GROUPS Moldovan 65%, Ukrainian 14%, Russian 13%, Gagauz 4%, Jewish 2%, Bulgarian
LANGUAGES Moldovan/Romanian (official)
RELIGIONS Eastern Orthodox
CURRENCY Leu = 100 bani

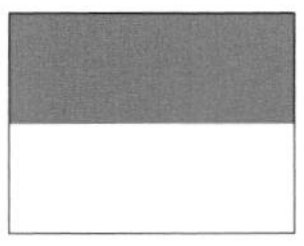

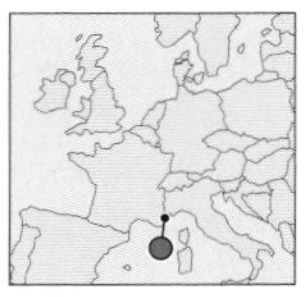

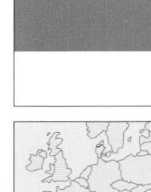

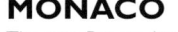

MONACO

The tiny Principality of Monaco consists of a narrow strip of coastline and a rocky peninsula on the French Riviera. Its considerable wealth is derived largely from banking, finance, gambling and tourism. Monaco's citizens do not pay any state tax. Its attractions include the Monte Carlo casino and such sporting events as the Monte Carlo Rally and the Monaco Grand Prix.

AREA 1.5 sq km [0.6 sq mi] **POPULATION** 32,000 **CAPITAL** Monaco

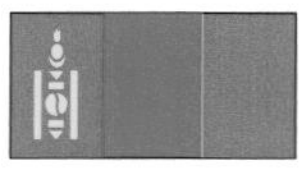

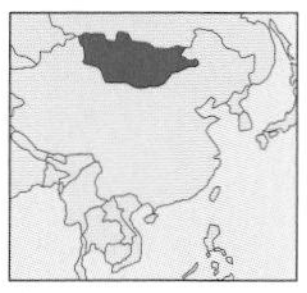

MONGOLIA

GEOGRAPHY The State of Mongolia is the world's largest landlocked country. It consists mainly of high plateaux, with the Gobi Desert in the south-east.

Ulan Bator lies on the northern edge of a desert plateau. It has bitterly cold winters. Summer temperatures are moderated by the altitude.

POLITICS & ECONOMY In the 13th century, Genghis Khan united the Mongolian peoples and built up a great empire. Under his grandson, Kublai Khan, the Mongol empire extended from Korea and China to eastern Europe and present-day Iraq.

The Mongol empire broke up in the late 14th century. In the early 17th century, Inner Mongolia came under Chinese control, and by the late 17th century Outer Mongolia had become a Chinese province. In 1911, the Mongolians drove the Chinese out of Outer Mongolia and made the area a Buddhist kingdom. But in 1924, under Russian influence, the Communist Mongolian People's Republic was set up. From the 1950s, Mongolia supported the Soviet Union in its disputes with China. In 1990, the people demonstrated for more freedom, and free elections in June 1990 resulted in victory for the Mongolian People's Revolutionary Party, which was composed of Communists. Communist rule ended in 1996, when the Democratic Union coalition won power. But the Communists regained power in 2000, though they were expected to continue free-market policies.

The World Bank classifies Mongolia as a 'lower-middle-income' developing country. Most people were once nomads, who moved around with their herds of sheep, cattle, goats and horses. Under Communist rule, most people were moved into permanent homes on government-owned farms. But livestock and animal products remain leading exports. The Communists also developed industry, especially the mining of coal, copper, gold, molybdenum, tin and tungsten, and manufacturing. Minerals and fuels now account for around half of Mongolia's exports.

AREA 1,566,500 sq km [604,826 sq mi] **POPULATION** 2,655,000
CAPITAL (POPULATION) Ulan Bator (673,000)
GOVERNMENT Multiparty republic **ETHNIC GROUPS** Khalkha Mongol 85%, Kazakh 6% **LANGUAGES** Khalkha Mongolian (official), Turkic, Russian **RELIGIONS** Tibetan Buddhist (Lamaist)
CURRENCY Tugrik = 100 möngös

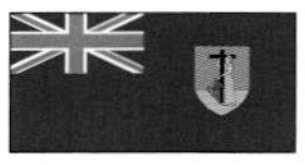

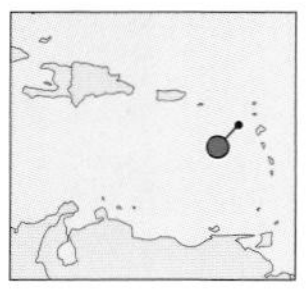

MONTSERRAT

Monserrat is a British overseas territory in the Caribbean Sea. The climate is tropical and hurricanes often cause much damage. Intermittent eruptions of the Soufrière Hills volcano between 1995 and 1998 led to the emigration of many of the inhabitants and the virtual destruction of Plymouth, the capital, in the southern part of the island.

AREA 1,100 sq km [39 sq mi] **POPULATION** (prior to the volcanic activity) 8,000 **CAPITAL** Plymouth

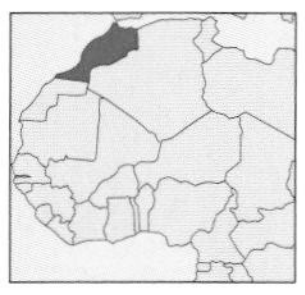

MOROCCO

GEOGRAPHY The Kingdom of Morocco lies in north-western Africa. Its name comes from the Arabic Maghreb-el-Aksa, meaning 'the farthest west'. Behind the western coastal plain the land rises to a broad plateau and ranges of the Atlas Mountains. The High (Haut) Atlas contains the highest peak, Djebel Toubkal, at 4,165 m [13,665 ft]. East of the mountains, the land descends to the arid Sahara.

The Atlantic coast of Morocco is cooled by the Canaries Current. Inland, summers are hot and dry. The winters are mild. In winter, between October and April, south-westerly winds from the Atlantic Ocean bring moderate rainfall, and snow often falls on the High Atlas Mountains.

POLITICS & ECONOMY The original people of Morocco were the Berbers. But in the 680s, Arab invaders introduced Islam and the Arabic language. By the early 20th century, France and Spain controlled Morocco, which became an independent kingdom in 1956. Although Morocco is a constitutional monarchy, King Hassan II ruled the country in a generally authoritarian way since his accession to the throne in 1961 to his death in 1999. His son and successor Mohamed VI faced several problems, including the future of Western Sahara which Hassan II had vigorously claimed for Morocco.

Morocco is classified as a 'lower-middle-income' developing country. It is the world's third largest producer of phosphate rock, which is used to make fertilizer. One of the reasons why Morocco wants to keep Western Sahara is that it, too, has large phosphate reserves. Farming employs 44% of Moroccans. Chief crops include barley, beans, citrus fruits, maize, olives, sugar beet and wheat. Processed phosphates are exported, but most of Morocco's manufactures are for home consumption. Fishing and tourism are also important.

AREA 446,550 sq km [172,413 sq mi] **POPULATION** 30,645,000
CAPITAL (POPULATION) Rabat (1,220,000)
GOVERNMENT Constitutional monarchy **ETHNIC GROUPS** Arab 70%, Berber 30% **LANGUAGES** Arabic (official), Berber, French
RELIGIONS Islam 99%, Christianity 1%
CURRENCY Moroccan dirham = 100 centimes

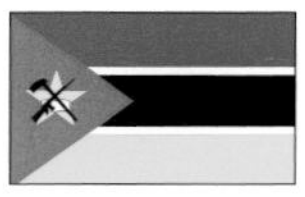

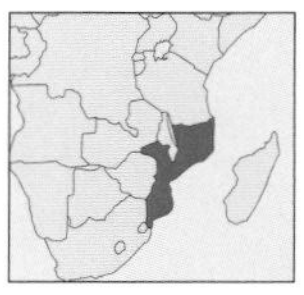

MOZAMBIQUE

GEOGRAPHY The Republic of Mozambique borders the Indian Ocean in south-eastern Africa. The coastal plains are narrow in the north but broaden in the south. Inland lie plateaux and hills, which make up another two-fifths of Mozambique.

Mozambique has a mostly tropical climate. The capital Maputo, which lies outside the tropics, has hot and humid summers, though the winters are mild and fairly dry.

POLITICS & ECONOMY In 1885, when the European powers divided Africa, Mozambique was recognized as a Portuguese colony. But black African opposition to European rule gradually increased. In 1961, the Front for the Liberation of Mozambique (FRELIMO) was founded to oppose Portuguese rule. In 1964, FRELIMO launched a guerrilla war, which continued for ten years. Mozambique became independent in 1975.

After independence, Mozambique became a one-party state. Its government aided African nationalists in Rhodesia (now Zimbabwe) and South Africa. But the white governments of these countries helped an opposition group, the Mozambique National Resistance Movement (RENAMO) to lead an armed struggle against Mozambique's government. Civil war, combined with droughts, caused much suffering in the 1980s. In 1989, FRELIMO declared that it had dropped its Communist policies and ended one-party rule. The war ended in 1992 and multiparty elections in 1994 heralded more stable conditions. In 1995 Mozambique became the 53rd member of the Commonwealth.

In the early 1990s, the UN rated Mozambique as one of the world's poorest countries. The second half of the 1990s saw a surge in economic growth, but huge floods in 2000 and 2001 proved to be a major setback. About 80% of the people are poor and agriculture is the main activity. Crops include cassava, cotton, maize, rice and tea.

AREA 801,590 sq km [309,494 sq mi] **POPULATION** 19,371,000
CAPITAL (POPULATION) Maputo (2,000,000)
GOVERNMENT Multiparty republic **ETHNIC GROUPS** Indigenous tribal groups (Shangaan, Chokwe, Manyika, Sena, Makua, others) 99%
LANGUAGES Portuguese (official), many others
RELIGIONS Traditional beliefs 48%, Roman Catholic 31%, Islam 20%
CURRENCY Metical = 100 centavos

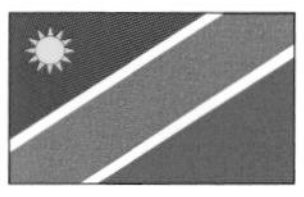

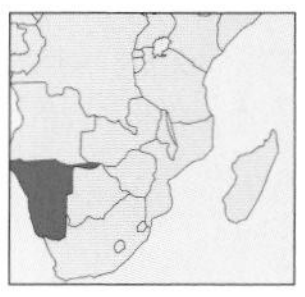

NAMIBIA

GEOGRAPHY The Republic of Namibia was formerly ruled by South Africa, which called it South West Africa. The country became independent in 1990. The coastal region contains the arid Namib Desert, which is virtually uninhabited. Inland is a central plateau, bordered by a rugged spine of mountains stretching north–south. Eastern Namibia contains part of the Kalahari Desert, a semi-desert area which extends into Botswana.

Namibia is a warm and arid country. Lying at 1,700 m [5,500 ft] above sea level, Windhoek has an average annual rainfall of about 370 mm [15 in], often occurring during thunderstorms in the hot summer months.

POLITICS & ECONOMY During World War I, South African troops defeated the Germans who ruled what is now Namibia. After World War II, many people challenged South Africa's right to govern the territory and a civil war began in the 1960s between African guerrillas and South African troops. A cease-fire was agreed in 1989 and Namibia became independent in 1990. In the 1990s, the government pursued a policy of 'national reconciliation'. An enclave on the coast, called Walvis Bay (Walvisbaai), remained part of South Africa until 1994, when it

was transferred to Namibia. In 1999, a secessionist group staged an unsuccessful uprising in the Caprivi Strip.

Namibia is rich in mineral reserves, including diamonds, uranium, zinc and copper. Minerals make up 90% of the exports. But farming employs about two out of every five Namibians. Sea fishing is also important, though overfishing has reduced the yields of the country's fishing fleet. The country has few industries, but tourism is increasing.

AREA 825,414 SQ KM [318,434 SQ MI] **POPULATION** 1,798,000
CAPITAL (POPULATION) WINDHOEK (126,000)
GOVERNMENT MULTIPARTY REPUBLIC **ETHNIC GROUPS** OVAMBO 50%, KAVANGO 9%, HERERO 7%, DAMARA 7%, WHITE 6%, NAMA 5%
LANGUAGES ENGLISH (OFFICIAL), OVAMBO, AFRIKAANS, GERMAN
RELIGIONS CHRISTIANITY 90% (LUTHERAN 51%)
CURRENCY NAMIBIAN DOLLAR = 100 CENTS

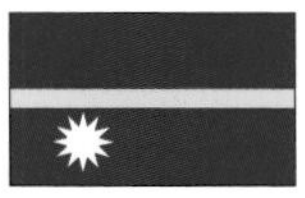
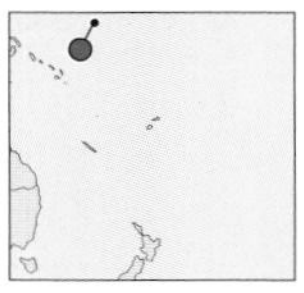

NAURU

Nauru is the world's smallest republic, located in the western Pacific Ocean, close to the equator. Independent since 1968, Nauru's prosperity is based on phosphate mining, but the reserves are running out.

AREA 21 SQ KM [8 SQ MI] **POPULATION** 12,000
CAPITAL YAREN

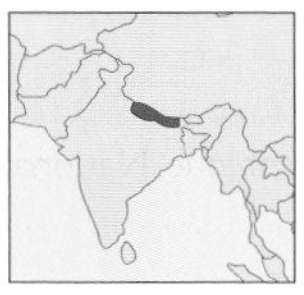

NEPAL

GEOGRAPHY Over three-quarters of Nepal lies in the Himalayan region, culminating in the world's highest peak (Mount Everest, or Chomolongma in Nepali) at 8,850 m [29,035 ft]. As a result, climatic conditions vary widely according to the altitude.

POLITICS & ECONOMY Nepal was united in the late 18th century, although its complex topography has ensured that it remains a diverse patchwork of peoples. From the mid-19th century to 1951, power was held by the royal Rana family. Attempts to introduce a democratic system in the 1950s failed. The first democratic elections in 32 years were held in 1991, but, by the early 21st century, Nepal faced many problems, including the activities of Maoist guerrillas and corruption. In 2001, King Birendra and other members of the royal family were shot dead by his heir, Crown Prince Dipendra, who was upset that his mother refused to accept his choice of a bride.

Agriculture remains the chief activity in this overwhelmingly rural country and the government is heavily dependent on aid. Tourism, centred around the high Himalaya, grows in importance each year, although Nepal was closed to foreigners until 1951. There are also ambitious plans to exploit the hydroelectric potential offered by the ferocious Himalayan rivers.

AREA 140,800 SQ KM [54,363 SQ MI] **POPULATION** 25,284,000
CAPITAL (POPULATION) KATMANDU (535,000)
GOVERNMENT CONSTITUTIONAL MONARCHY **ETHNIC GROUPS** NEPALESE 53%, BIHARI 18%, THARU 5%, TAMANG 5%, NEWAR 3%
LANGUAGES NEPALI (OFFICIAL), LOCAL LANGUAGES
RELIGIONS HINDU 86%, BUDDHIST 8%, ISLAM 4%
CURRENCY NEPALESE RUPEE = 100 PAISA

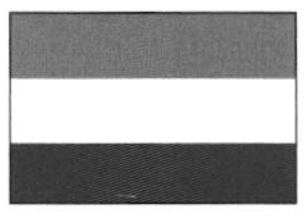
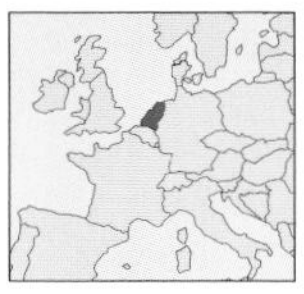

NETHERLANDS

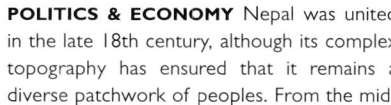

GEOGRAPHY The Netherlands lies at the western end of the North European Plain, which extends to the Ural Mountains in Russia. Except for the far south-eastern corner, the Netherlands is flat and about 40% lies below sea level at high tide. To prevent flooding, the Dutch have built dykes (sea walls) to hold back the waves. Large areas which were once under the sea, but which have been reclaimed, are called polders.

Because of its position on the North Sea, the Netherlands has a temperate climate. The winters are mild, with rain coming from the Atlantic depressions which pass over the country. North Sea storms often batter the coasts.

POLITICS & ECONOMY Before the 16th century, the area that is now the Netherlands was under a succession of foreign rulers, including the Romans, the Germanic Franks, the French and the Spanish. The Dutch declared their independence from Spain in 1581 and their status was finally recognized by Spain in 1648. In the 17th century, the Dutch built up a great overseas empire, especially in South-east Asia. But in the early 18th century, the Dutch lost control of the seas to England.

France controlled the Netherlands from 1795 to 1813. In 1815, the Netherlands, then containing Belgium and Luxembourg, became an independent kingdom. Belgium broke away in 1830 and Luxembourg followed in 1890.

The Netherlands was neutral in World War I (1914–18), but was occupied by Germany in World War II (1939–45). After the war, the Netherlands Indies became independent as Indonesia. The Netherlands became active in West European affairs. With Belgium and Luxembourg, it formed a customs union called Benelux in 1948. In 1949, it joined NATO (the North Atlantic Treaty Organization), and the European Coal and Steel Community (ECSC) in 1953. In 1957, it became a founder member of the European Economic Community (now the European Union), and its economy prospered. On 1 January 2002, the Netherlands became one of the 12 EU countries to adopt the euro as its sole official unit of currency.

The Netherlands is a highly industrialized country and industry and commerce are the most valuable activities. Its resources include natural gas, some oil, salt and china clay. But the Netherlands imports many of the materials needed by its industries and it is, therefore, a major trading country. Industrial products are wide-ranging, including aircraft, chemicals, electronic equipment, machinery, textiles and vehicles. Agriculture employs only 5% of the people, but scientific methods are used and yields are high. Dairy farming is the leading farming activity. Major products include barley, flowers and bulbs, potatoes, sugar beet and wheat.

AREA 41,526 SQ KM [16,033 SQ MI] **POPULATION** 15,981,000
CAPITAL (POPULATION) AMSTERDAM (1,115,000); THE HAGUE (SEAT OF GOVERNMENT, 700,000)
GOVERNMENT CONSTITUTIONAL MONARCHY
ETHNIC GROUPS DUTCH 95%, INDONESIAN, TURKISH, MOROCCAN
LANGUAGES DUTCH (OFFICIAL), FRISIAN
RELIGIONS ROMAN CATHOLIC 34%, PROTESTANT 21%, ISLAM 4%
CURRENCY EURO = 100 CENTS

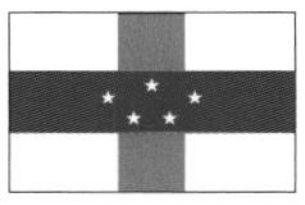
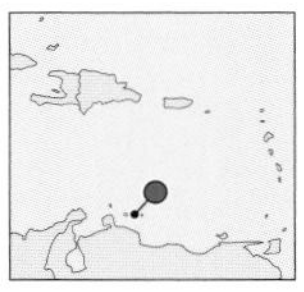

NETHERLANDS ANTILLES

The Netherlands Antilles consists of two different island groups; one off the coast of Venezuela, and the other at the northern end of the Leeward Islands, some 800 km [500 mi] away. They remain a self-governing Dutch territory. The island of Aruba was once part of the territory, but it broke away in 1986. Oil refining and tourism are important activities.

AREA 993 SQ KM [383 SQ MI] **POPULATION** 212,000 **CAPITAL** WILLEMSTAD

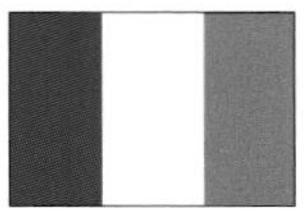
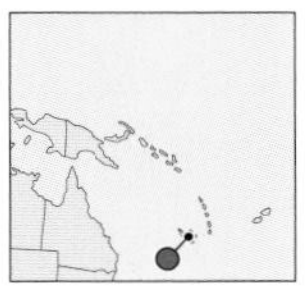

NEW CALEDONIA

New Caledonia is the most southerly of the Melanesian countries in the Pacific. A French possession since 1853 and an Overseas Territory since 1958. In 1998, France announced an agreement with local Melanesians that a vote on independence would be postponed until 2014. The country is rich in mineral resources, especially nickel.

AREA 18,580 SQ KM [7,174 SQ MI] **POPULATION** 205,000 **CAPITAL** NOUMÉA

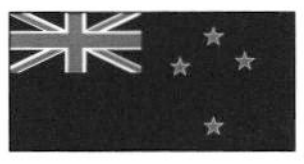
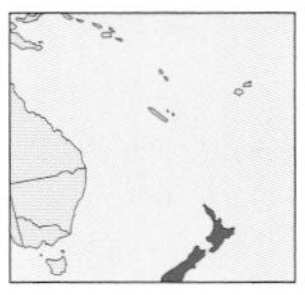

NEW ZEALAND

GEOGRAPHY New Zealand lies about 1,600 km [994 mi] south-east of Australia. It consists of two main islands and several other small ones. Much of North Island is volcanic. Active volcanoes include Ngauruhoe and Ruapehu. Hot springs and geysers are common, and steam from the ground is used to produce electricity. The Southern Alps, which contain the country's highest peak Mount Cook (Aoraki), at 3,753 m [12,313 ft] form the backbone of South Island. The island also has some large, fertile plains.

Auckland in the north has a warm, humid climate throughout the year. Wellington has cooler summers, while in Dunedin, in the south-east, temperatures sometimes dip below freezing in winter. The rainfall is heaviest on the western highlands.

POLITICS & ECONOMY Evidence suggests that early Maori settlers arrived in New Zealand more than 1,000 years ago. The Dutch navigator Abel Tasman reached New Zealand in 1642, but his discovery was not followed up. In 1769, the British Captain James Cook rediscovered the islands. In the early 19th century, British settlers arrived and, in 1840, under the Treaty of Waitangi, Britain took possession of the islands. Clashes occurred with the Maoris in the 1860s but, from the 1870s, the Maoris were gradually integrated into society.

In 1907, New Zealand became a self-governing dominion in the British Commonwealth. The country's economy developed quickly and the people became increasingly prosperous. However, after Britain joined the European Economic Community in 1973, New Zealand's exports to Britain shrank and the country had to reassess its economic and defence strategies and seek new markets. The world economic recession also led the government to cut back on its spending on welfare services in the 1990s. Maori rights and the preservation of Maori culture are other major political issues.

New Zealand's economy has traditionally depended on agriculture, but manufacturing now employs twice as many people as agriculture. Meat and dairy products are the most valuable agricultural products. The country has more than 44 million sheep, 4 million dairy cattle and 4 million beef cattle. Major crops include barley, fruits, potatoes and other vegetables, and wheat. Fishing is also important.

AREA 268,680 SQ KM [103,737 SQ MI] **POPULATION** 3,864,000
CAPITAL (POPULATION) WELLINGTON (329,000)
GOVERNMENT CONSTITUTIONAL MONARCHY
ETHNIC GROUPS NEW ZEALAND EUROPEAN 74%, NEW ZEALAND MAORI 10%, POLYNESIAN 4% **LANGUAGES** ENGLISH AND MAORI (BOTH OFFICIAL) **RELIGIONS** ANGLICAN 24%, PRESBYTERIAN 18%, ROMAN CATHOLIC 15%
CURRENCY NEW ZEALAND DOLLAR = 100 CENTS

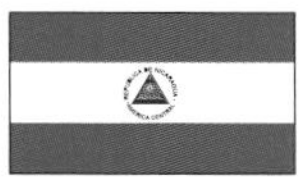
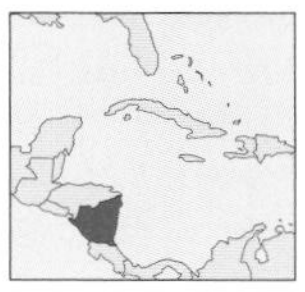

NICARAGUA

GEOGRAPHY The Republic of Nicaragua is a large country in Central America. In the east is a broad plain bordering the Caribbean Sea. The plain is drained by rivers that flow from the Central Highlands. The fertile western Pacific region contains about 40 volcanoes, many of which are active, and earthquakes are common.

Nicaragua has a tropical climate. Managua is hot throughout the year and there is a marked rainy season from May to October. In October 1998, Hurricane Mitch caused great devastation in Nicaragua. The Central Highlands and Caribbean region are cooler and wetter. The wettest region is the humid Caribbean plain.

POLITICS & ECONOMY In 1502, Christopher Columbus claimed the area for Spain, which ruled Nicaragua until 1821. By the early 20th century, the United States had considerable influence in the country and, in 1912, US forces entered Nicaragua to protect US interests. From 1927 to 1933, rebels under General Augusto César Sandino, tried to drive US forces out of the country. In 1933, US marines set up a Nicaraguan army, the National Guard, to help to defeat the rebels. Its leader, Anastasio Somoza Garcia, had Sandino murdered in 1934 and, from 1937, Somoza ruled as a dictator.

In the mid-1970s, many people began to protest against Somoza's rule. Many joined a guerrilla force, called the Sandinista National Liberation Front, named after General Sandino. The rebels defeated the Somoza regime in 1979. In the 1980s, the US-supported forces, called the 'Contras', launched a campaign against the Sandinista government. The US government opposed the Sandinista regime, under Daniel José Ortega Saavedra, claiming that it was a Communist dictatorship. A coalition, the National Opposition Union, defeated the Sandinistas in elections in 1990. In 1996 and again in 2001, the Sandinista candidate Daniel Ortega was defeated in presidential elections.

In the early 1990s, Nicaragua faced many problems in rebuilding its shattered economy. Agriculture is the main activity, employing nearly half of the people. Coffee, cotton, sugar and bananas are grown for export, while rice is the main food crop.

AREA 130,000 SQ KM [50,193 SQ MI] **POPULATION** 4,918,000
CAPITAL (POPULATION) MANAGUA (864,000)
GOVERNMENT MULTIPARTY REPUBLIC
ETHNIC GROUPS MESTIZO 69%, WHITE 17%, BLACK 9%, AMERINDIAN 5%
LANGUAGES SPANISH (OFFICIAL), MISUMALPAN
RELIGIONS ROMAN CATHOLIC 85%
CURRENCY CÓRDOBA ORO (GOLD CÓRDOBA) = 100 CENTAVOS

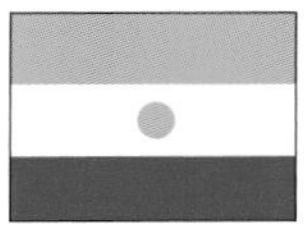
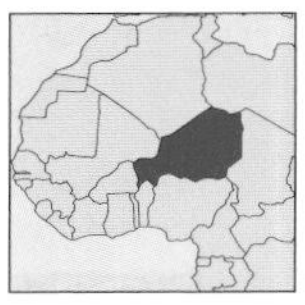

NIGER

GEOGRAPHY The Republic of Niger is a landlocked nation in north-central Africa. The northern plateaux lie in the Sahara Desert, while Central Niger contains the rugged Aïr Mountains. The most fertile, densely populated region is the Niger valley in the south-west.

Niger has a tropical climate and the south has a rainy season between June and September. The north is practically rainless.

POLITICS & ECONOMY Since independence in 1960, Niger, a French territory from 1900, has suffered severe droughts. Food shortages and the collapse of the traditional nomadic way of life of some of Niger's people have caused political instability. After a period of military rule, a multiparty constitution was adopted in 1992, but the military again seized power in 1996. Later that year, the coup leader, Col. Ibrahim Barre Mainassara, was elected president. He was assassinated in 1999, but parliamentary rule was rapidly restored and Tandja Mamadou was elected president in November.

Niger's chief resource is uranium and it is the fourth largest producer in the world. Some tin and tungsten are also mined, although other mineral resources are largely untouched.

Despite its resources, Niger is one of the world's poorest countries. Farming employs 85% of the population, but only 3% of the land can be used for crops and 7% for grazing.

AREA 1,267,000 sq km [489,189 sq mi] **POPULATION** 10,355,000
CAPITAL (POPULATION) Niamey (398,000)
GOVERNMENT Multiparty republic
ETHNIC GROUPS Hausa 56%, Djerma 22%, Tuareg 8%, Fula 8%
LANGUAGES French (official), Hausa, Djerma
RELIGIONS Islam 98% **CURRENCY** CFA franc = 100 centimes

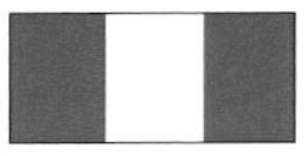
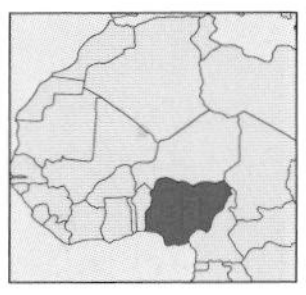

NIGERIA

GEOGRAPHY The Federal Republic of Nigeria is the most populous nation in Africa. The country's main rivers are the Niger and Benue, which meet in central Nigeria. North of the two river valleys are high plains and plateaux. The Lake Chad basin is in the north-east, with the Sokoto plains in the north-west. The south contains hilly uplands and coastal plains.

The south has high temperatures and rain throughout the year. The north is drier and often hotter than the south.

POLITICS & ECONOMY Nigeria has a long artistic tradition. Major cultures include the Nok (500 BC to AD 200), the Ife, a major Yoruba culture which developed about 1,000 years ago, and the Benin, which flourished between the 15th and 17th centuries. Britain gradually extended its influence over the area in the second half of the 19th century.

Nigeria became independent in 1960 and a federal republic in 1963. A federal constitution dividing the country into regions was necessary because Nigeria contains more than 250 ethnic and linguistic groups, as well as several religious ones. Local rivalries have long been a threat to national unity, and six new states were created in 1996 in an attempt to overcome this. Civil war occurred between 1967 and 1970, when the people of the south-east attempted unsuccessfully to secede during the Biafran War. Between 1960 and 1998, Nigeria had only nine years of civilian government. However, in 1988–9, Nigeria held elections restoring civilian rule. A former general, Olusegun Obasanjo, was elected president. The new regime faced many problems. In 2000, Muslim–Christian clashes occurred in the north when several states adopted *sharia* (Islamic law).

Nigeria is a developing country with great potential. Its chief natural resource is oil, which accounts for most of its exports. Agriculture employs 43% of the people and the country is a major producer of cocoa, palm oil and palm kernels, groundnuts (peanuts) and rubber. Industry is increasing and manufactures include cement, chemicals, fertilizers, textiles and timber.

AREA 923,770 sq km [356,668 sq mi] **POPULATION** 126,636,000
CAPITAL (POPULATION) Abuja (339,000)
GOVERNMENT Federal multiparty republic
ETHNIC GROUPS Hausa and Fulani 29%, Yoruba 21%, Ibo (or Igbo) 18%, Ijaw 10%, Kanuri 4%
LANGUAGES English (official), Hausa, Yoruba, Ibo
RELIGIONS Islam 50%, Christianity 40%, traditional religions 10%
CURRENCY Naira = 100 kobo

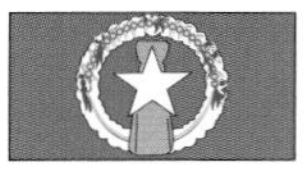
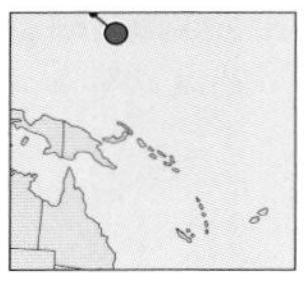

NORTHERN MARIANA ISLANDS

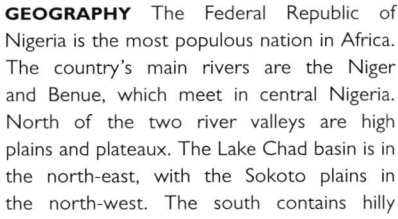

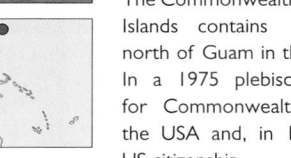

The Commonwealth of the Northern Mariana Islands contains 16 mountainous islands north of Guam in the western Pacific Ocean. In a 1975 plebiscite, the islanders voted for Commonwealth status in union with the USA and, in 1986, they were granted US citizenship.

AREA 477 sq km [184 sq mi] **POPULATION** 75,000 **CAPITAL** Saipan

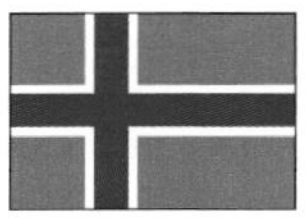
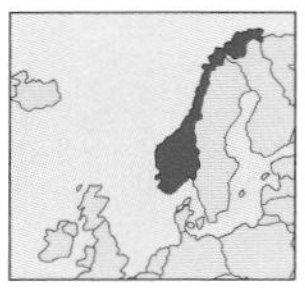

NORWAY

GEOGRAPHY The Kingdom of Norway forms the western part of the rugged Scandinavian peninsula. The deep inlets along the highly indented coastline were worn out by glaciers during the Ice Age.

The warm North Atlantic Drift off the coast of Norway moderates the climate, with mild winters and cool summers. Nearly all the ports are ice-free throughout the year. Inland, winters are colder and snow cover lasts for at least three months a year.

POLITICS & ECONOMY Under a treaty in 1814, Denmark handed Norway over to Sweden, but it kept Norway's colonies – Greenland, Iceland and the Faroe Islands. Norway briefly became independent, but Swedish forces defeated the Norwegians and Norway had to accept Sweden's king as its ruler.

The union between Norway and Sweden ended in 1903. During World War II (1939–45), Germany occupied Norway. Norway's economy developed quickly after the war and the country now enjoys one of the world's highest standards of living. In 1960, Norway, together with six other countries, formed the European Free Trade Association (EFTA). In 1994, the Norwegians voted against joining the EU.

Norway's chief resources and exports are oil and natural gas which come from wells under the North Sea. Farmland covers only 3% of the land. Dairy farming and meat production are important, but Norway has to import food. Norway has many industries powered by cheap hydroelectricity.

AREA 323,900 sq km [125,050 sq mi] **POPULATION** 4,503,000
CAPITAL (POPULATION) Oslo (502,000)
GOVERNMENT Constitutional monarchy
ETHNIC GROUPS Norwegian 97%
LANGUAGES Norwegian (official)
RELIGIONS Lutheran 88%
CURRENCY Krone = 100 ore

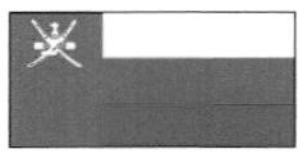
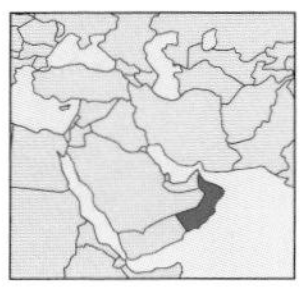

OMAN

GEOGRAPHY The Sultanate of Oman occupies the south-eastern corner of the Arabian peninsula. It also includes the tip of the Musandam peninsula, overlooking the strategic Strait of Hormuz.

Oman has a hot tropical climate. In Muscat, temperatures may reach 47°C [117°F] in summer.

POLITICS & ECONOMY British influence in Oman dates back to the end of the 18th century, but the country became fully independent in 1971. Since then, using revenue from oil, which was discovered in 1964, the absolute ruler, Qaboos ibn Said, and his government have sought to modernize the country. In 2000, Oman held its first direct elections to its consultative parliament. Unusually for the Gulf region, two women were returned.

The World Bank classifies Oman as an 'upper-middle-income' country. Oil accounts for the bulk of the exports, while huge natural gas deposits were discovered in 1991. However, agriculture remains important. Major crops include alfalfa, bananas, coconuts, dates, limes, tobacco, vegetables and wheat. Some cattle are raised and fishing, especially for sardines, is important. But Oman still has to import food.

AREA 212,460 sq km [82,031 sq mi] **POPULATION** 2,622,000
CAPITAL (POPULATION) Muscat (350,000)
GOVERNMENT Monarchy with consultative council
ETHNIC GROUPS Omani Arab 74%, Pakistani 21%
LANGUAGES Arabic (official), Baluchi, English
RELIGIONS Islam (Ibadiyah), Hinduism
CURRENCY Omani rial = 100 baizas

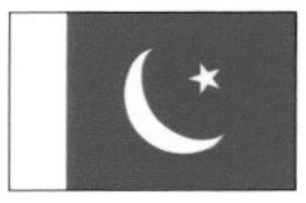
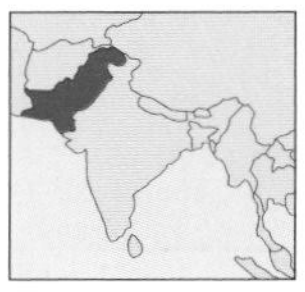

PAKISTAN

GEOGRAPHY The Islamic Republic of Pakistan contains high mountains, fertile plains and rocky deserts. The Karakoram range, which contains K2, the world's second highest peak, lies in the northern part of Jammu and Kashmir, which is occupied by Pakistan but claimed by India. Other mountains rise in the west. Plains, drained by the River Indus and its tributaries, occupy much of eastern Pakistan. Arid areas include the Thar Desert and the Baluchistan plateau.

Most of Pakistan has hot summers and mild winters, though the mountains have cold winters. The rainfall is generally sparse. Most of it occurs between July and September.

POLITICS & ECONOMY Pakistan was the site of the Indus Valley civilization which developed about 4,500 years ago. But Pakistan's modern history dates from 1947, when British India was divided into India and Pakistan. Muslim Pakistan was divided into two parts: East and West Pakistan, but East Pakistan broke away in 1971 to become Bangladesh. In 1948–9, 1965 and 1971, Pakistan and India clashed over the disputed territory of Kashmir. In 1998, Pakistan responded in kind to a series of Indian nuclear weapon tests, provoking global controversy.

Pakistan has been subject to several periods of military rule, but elections in 1988 led to Benazir Bhutto becoming prime minister. She was removed from office in 1990, but she returned as prime minister between 1993 and 1996. In 1997, Narwaz Sharif was elected prime minister, but he was overthrown in 1999 by a military coup led by General Pervez Musharraf. In 2001, Pakistan supported the Western attacks on the Taliban forces in Afghanistan. The United States responded by lifting sanctions on Pakistan and promising more aid.

According to the World Bank, Pakistan is a 'low-income' developing country. The economy is based on farming or rearing goats and sheep. Agriculture employs nearly half the people. Major crops include cotton, fruits, rice, sugar cane and wheat.

AREA 796,100 sq km [307,374 sq mi] **POPULATION** 144,617,000
CAPITAL (POPULATION) Islamabad (525,000)
GOVERNMENT Military regime **ETHNIC GROUPS** Punjabi 60%, Sindhi 12%, Pashtun 13%, Baluch, Muhajir
LANGUAGES Urdu (official), many others
RELIGIONS Islam 97%, Christianity, Hinduism
CURRENCY Pakistan rupee = 100 paisa

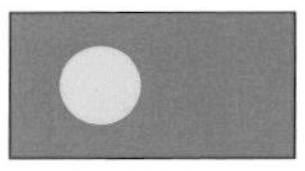
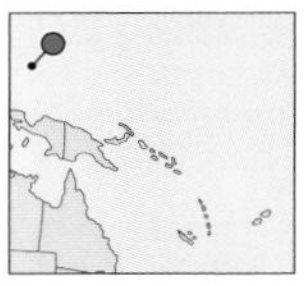

PALAU

The Republic of Palau became fully independent in 1994, after the USA refused to accede to a 1979 referendum that declared this island nation a nuclear-free zone. In December 1994 Palau joined the United Nations. The economy relies heavily on US aid, tourism, fishing and subsistence agriculture. The main crops include cassava, coconuts and copra.

AREA 458 sq km [177 sq mi] **POPULATION** 19,000 **CAPITAL** Koror

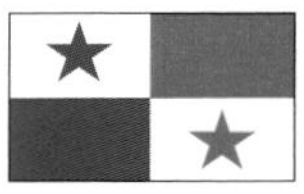
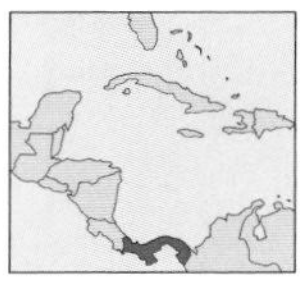

PANAMA

GEOGRAPHY The Republic of Panama forms an isthmus linking Central America to South America. The Panama Canal, which is 81.6 km [50.7 mi] long, cuts across the isthmus. It has made the country a major transport centre.

Panama has a tropical climate. Temperatures are high, though the mountains are much cooler than the coastal plains. The main rainy season is between May and December.

POLITICS & ECONOMY Christopher Columbus landed in Panama in 1502 and Spain soon took control of the area. In 1821, Panama became independent from Spain and a province of Colombia.

In 1903, Colombia refused a request by the United States to build a canal. Panama then revolted against Colombia, and became independent. The United States then began to build the canal, which was opened in 1914. The United States administered the Panama Canal Zone, a strip of land along the canal. But many Panamanians resented US influence and, in 1979, the Canal Zone was returned to Panama. Control of the canal itself was handed over by the USA to Panama on 31 December 1999.

Panama's government has changed many times since independence, and there have been periods of military dictatorships. In 1983, General Manuel Antonio Noriega became

Panama's leader. In 1988, two US grand juries in Florida indicted Noriega on charges of drug trafficking. In 1989, Noriega was apparently defeated in a presidential election, but the government declared the election invalid. After the killing of a US marine, US troops entered Panama and arrested Noriega, who was convicted by a Miami court of drug offences in 1992. However, Panama held national elections in 1994. In 1999, Mireya Moscoso became Panama's first woman president.

The World Bank classifies Panama as a 'lower-middle-income' developing country. The Panama Canal is an important source of revenue and it generates many jobs in commerce, trade, manufacturing and transport. Away from the Canal, the main activity is agriculture, which employs 27% of the people.

AREA 77,080 sq km [29,761 sq mi] **POPULATION** 2,846,000
CAPITAL (POPULATION) Panama City (452,000)
GOVERNMENT Multiparty republic **ETHNIC GROUPS** Mestizo 70%, Black and Mulatto 14%, White 10%, Amerindian 6%
LANGUAGES Spanish (official) **RELIGIONS** Roman Catholic 84%, Protestant 5% **CURRENCY** US dollar; Balboa = 100 centésimos

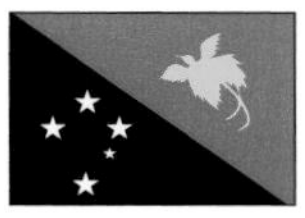
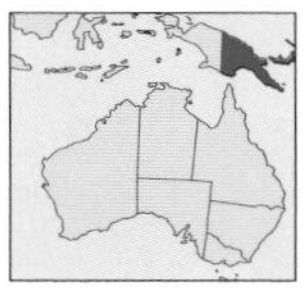

PAPUA NEW GUINEA

GEOGRAPHY Papua New Guinea is an independent country in the Pacific Ocean, north of Australia. It is part of a Pacific island region called Melanesia. Papua New Guinea includes the eastern part of New Guinea, the Bismarck Archipelago, the northern Solomon Islands, the D'Entrecasteaux Islands and the Louisiade Archipelago. The land is largely mountainous.

Papua New Guinea has a tropical climate, with high temperatures throughout the year. Most of the rain occurs during the monsoon season (from December to April), when the north-westerly winds blow. Winds blow from the south-east during the dry season.

POLITICS & ECONOMY The Dutch took western New Guinea (now part of Indonesia) in 1828, but it was not until 1884 that Germany took north-eastern New Guinea and Britain took the south-east. In 1906, Britain handed the south-east over to Australia. It then became known as the Territory of Papua. When World War I broke out in 1914, Australia took German New Guinea and, in 1921, the League of Nations gave Australia a mandate to rule the area, which was named the Territory of New Guinea.

Japan invaded New Guinea in 1942, but the Allies reconquered the area in 1944. In 1949, Papua and New Guinea were combined into the Territory of Papua and New Guinea. Papua New Guinea became fully independent in 1975.

Since independence, the government has worked to develop its mineral reserves. One of the most valuable mines was on Bougainville, in the northern Solomon Islands. But the people of Bougainville demanded a larger share in the profits of the mine. Conflict broke out, the mine was closed and the Bougainville Revolutionary Army proclaimed the island independent. But their attempted secession was not recognized internationally. An agreement to end the conflict was signed in 1998 and the island was granted local autonomy in 2000.

The World Bank classifies Papua New Guinea as a 'lower-middle-income' developing country. Agriculture employs three out of every four people, many of whom produce little more than they need to feed their families. Minerals, notably copper and gold, are the most valuable exports.

AREA 462,840 sq km [178,703 sq mi] **POPULATION** 5,049,000
CAPITAL (POPULATION) Port Moresby (174,000)
GOVERNMENT Constitutional monarchy **ETHNIC GROUPS** Papuan, Melanesian **LANGUAGES** English (official), Pidgin English, about 800 others **RELIGIONS** Traditional beliefs 34%, Roman Catholic 22%, Lutheran 16% **CURRENCY** Kina = 100 toea

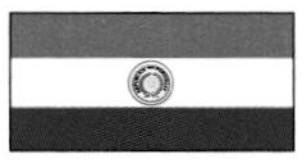
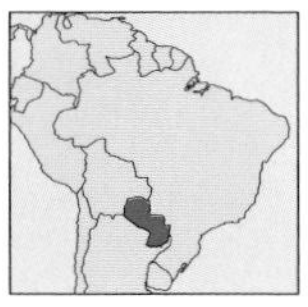

PARAGUAY

GEOGRAPHY The Republic of Paraguay is a landlocked country and rivers, notably the Paraná, Pilcomayo (Brazo Sur) and Paraguay, form most of its borders. A flat region called the Gran Chaco lies in the north-west, while the south-east contains plains, hills and plateaux.

Northern Paraguay lies in the tropics, while the south is subtropical. Most of the country has a warm, humid climate.

POLITICS & ECONOMY In 1776, Paraguay became part of a large colony called the Vice-royalty of La Plata, with Buenos Aires as the capital. Paraguayans opposed this move and the country declared its independence in 1811.

For many years, Paraguay was torn by internal strife and conflict with its neighbours. A war against Brazil, Argentina and Uruguay (1865–70) led to the deaths of more than half of Paraguay's population, and a great loss of territory.

General Alfredo Stroessner took power in 1954 and ruled as a dictator. His government imprisoned many opponents. Stroessner was overthrown in 1989. Free multiparty elections were held in 1993 and 1998. However, the return of democracy frequently seemed precarious because of rivalries between politicians and army leaders.

The World Bank classifies Paraguay as a 'lower-middle-income' developing country. Agriculture and forestry are the leading activities, employing 48% of the population. The country has abundant hydroelectricity and it exports power to Argentina and Brazil.

AREA 406,750 sq km [157,046 sq mi] **POPULATION** 5,734,000
CAPITAL (POPULATION) Asunción (945,000)
GOVERNMENT Multiparty republic **ETHNIC GROUPS** Mestizo 90%, Amerindian 3% **LANGUAGES** Spanish and Guaraní (both official)
RELIGIONS Roman Catholic 96%, Protestant 2%
CURRENCY Guaraní = 100 céntimos

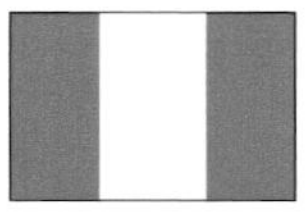
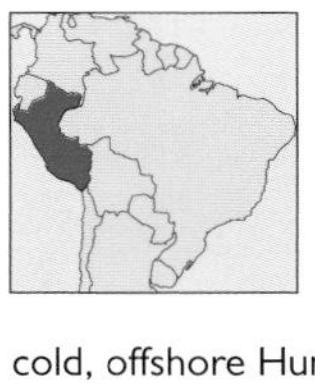

PERU

GEOGRAPHY The Republic of Peru lies in the tropics in western South America. A narrow coastal plain borders the Pacific Ocean in the west. Inland are ranges of the Andes Mountains, which rise to 6,768 m [22,205 ft] at Mount Huascarán, an extinct volcano. East of the Andes lies the Amazon basin.

Lima, on the coastal plain, has an arid climate. The coastal region is chilled by the cold, offshore Humboldt Current. The rainfall increases inland and many mountains in the high Andes are snow-capped.

POLITICS & ECONOMY Spanish conquistadors conquered Peru in the 1530s. In 1820, an Argentinian, José de San Martín, led an army into Peru and declared it independent. But Spain still held large areas. In 1823, the Venezuelan Simon Bolívar led another army into Peru and, in 1824, one of his generals defeated the Spaniards at Ayacucho. The Spaniards surrendered in 1826. Peru suffered much instability throughout the 19th century.

Instability continued in the 20th century. In 1980, when civilian rule was restored, a left-wing group called the Sendero Luminoso, or the 'Shining Path', began guerrilla warfare against the government. In 1990, Alberto Fujimori, son of Japanese immigrants, became president. In 1992, he suspended the constitution and dismissed the legislature. The guerrilla leader, Abimael Guzmán, was arrested in 1992, but instability continued. Following his victory in disputed presidential elections in 2000, Fujimori resigned and sought sanctuary in Japan. In 2001, Alejandro Toledo became the first Peruvian of Amerindian descent to be elected president.

The World Bank classifies Peru as a 'lower-middle-income' developing country. Agriculture employs 35% of the people and major food crops include beans, maize, potatoes and rice. Fish products are exported, but the most valuable export is copper. Peru also produces lead, silver, zinc and iron ore.

AREA 1,285,220 sq km [496,223 sq mi] **POPULATION** 27,484,000
CAPITAL (POPULATION) Lima (Lima-Callao, 6,601,000)
GOVERNMENT Transitional republic **ETHNIC GROUPS** Quechua 45%, Mestizo 37%, White 15% **LANGUAGES** Spanish and Quechua (both official), Aymara **RELIGIONS** Roman Catholic 90%
CURRENCY New sol = 100 centavos

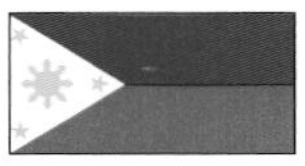
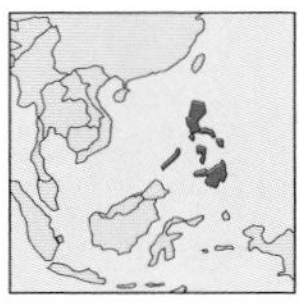

PHILIPPINES

GEOGRAPHY The Republic of the Philippines is an island country in south-eastern Asia. It includes about 7,100 islands, of which 2,770 are named and about 1,000 are inhabited. Luzon and Mindanao, the two largest islands, make up more than two-thirds of the country. The land is mainly mountainous.

The country has a tropical climate, with high temperatures all through the year. The dry season runs from December to April. The rest of the year is wet. The high rainfall is associated with typhoons which periodically strike the east coast.

POLITICS & ECONOMY The first European to reach the Philippines was the Portuguese navigator Ferdinand Magellan in 1521. Spanish explorers claimed the region in 1565 when they established a settlement on Cebu. The Spaniards ruled the country until 1898, when the United States took over at the end of the Spanish–American War. Japan invaded the Philippines in 1941, but US forces returned in 1944. The country became fully independent as the Republic of the Philippines in 1946.

Since independence, the country's problems have included armed uprisings by left-wing guerrillas demanding land reform, and Muslim separatist groups, crime, corruption and unemployment. The dominant figure in recent times was Ferdinand Marcos, who ruled in a dictatorial manner from 1965 to 1986. His successors were Corazon Aquino (1986–92), Fidel Ramos (1992–8), and Joseph Estrada, who resigned after massive public protests against his alleged corruption in 2001. He was succeeded by the vice-president, Gloria Macapagal Arroyo.

The Philippines is a developing country which has a 'lower-middle-income' economy. Agriculture employs 45% of the people. The main foods are rice and maize, while such crops as bananas, cocoa, coconuts, coffee, sugar cane and tobacco are all grown commercially. Manufacturing now plays an increasingly important role in the economy.

AREA 300,000 sq km [115,300 sq mi] **POPULATION** 82,842,000
CAPITAL (POPULATION) Manila (8,594,000)
GOVERNMENT Multiparty republic **ETHNIC GROUPS** Tagalog 30%, Cebuano 24%, Ilocano 10%, Hiligaynon Ilongo 9%, Bicol 6%
LANGUAGES Pilipino (Tagalog) and English (both official), Spanish, many others
RELIGIONS Roman Catholic 83%, Protestant 9%, Islam 5%
CURRENCY Philippine peso = 100 centavos

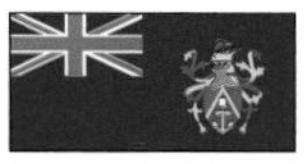
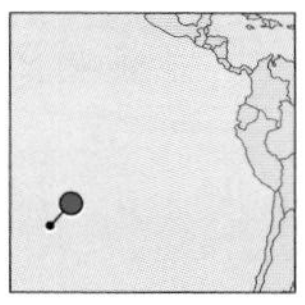

PITCAIRN ISLANDS

Pitcairn Island is a British overseas territory in the Pacific Ocean. Its inhabitants are descendants of the original settlers – nine mutineers from HMS *Bounty* and 18 Tahitians who arrived in 1790.

AREA 48 sq km [19 sq mi] **POPULATION** 47
CAPITAL Adamstown

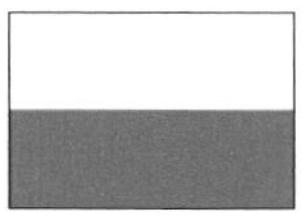
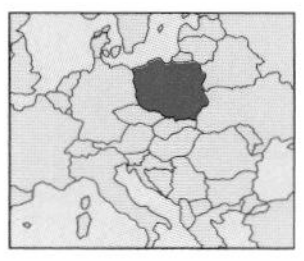

POLAND

GEOGRAPHY The Republic of Poland faces the Baltic Sea and, behind its lagoon-fringed coast, lies a broad plain. A plateau lies in the south-east, while the Sudeten Highlands straddle part of the border with the Czech Republic. Part of the Carpathian Range (the Tatra) lies in the south-east.

Poland's climate is influenced by its position in Europe. Warm, moist air masses come from the west, while cold air masses come from the north and east. Summers are warm, but winters are cold and snowy.

POLITICS & ECONOMY Poland's boundaries have changed several times in the last 200 years, partly as a result of its geographical location between the powers of Germany and Russia. It disappeared from the map in the late 18th century, when a Polish state called the Grand Duchy of Warsaw was set up. But in 1815, the country was partitioned, between Austria, Prussia and Russia. Poland became independent in 1918, but in 1939 it was divided between Germany and the Soviet Union. The country again became independent in 1945, when it lost land to Russia but gained some from Germany. Communists took power in 1948, but opposition mounted and eventually became focused through an organization called Solidarity.

Solidarity was led by a trade unionist, Lech Walesa. A coalition government was formed between Solidarity and the Communists in 1989. In 1990, the Communist party was dissolved and Walesa became president. But Walesa faced many problems in turning Poland towards a market economy. In presidential elections in 1995, Walesa was defeated by ex-Communist Aleksander Kwasniewski. However, Kwasniewski continued to follow westwards-looking policies and he was re-elected president in 2000. Poland joined NATO in 1999 and seemed likely to be among the first eastern European countries to join an expanded European Union.

Poland has large reserves of coal and deposits of various minerals which are used in its factories. Manufactures include chemicals, processed food, machinery, ships, steel and textiles.

AREA 312,680 sq km [120,726 sq mi] **POPULATION** 38,634,000
CAPITAL (POPULATION) Warsaw (1,626,000)
GOVERNMENT Multiparty republic **ETHNIC GROUPS** Polish 98%, Ukrainian 1%, German 1% **LANGUAGES** Polish (official)
RELIGIONS Roman Catholic 94%, Orthodox 2%
CURRENCY Zloty = 100 groszy

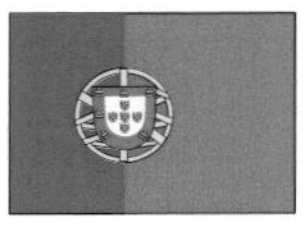

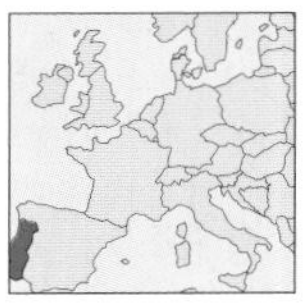

PORTUGAL

GEOGRAPHY The Republic of Portugal is the most westerly of Europe's mainland countries. The land rises from the coastal plains on the Atlantic Ocean to the western edge of the huge plateau, or Meseta, which occupies most of the Iberian peninsula. Portugal also contains two autonomous regions, the Azores and Madeira island groups.

The climate is moderated by winds blowing from the Atlantic Ocean. Summers are cooler and winters are milder than in other Mediterranean lands.

POLITICS & ECONOMY Portugal became a separate country, independent of Spain, in 1143. In the 15th century, Portugal led the 'Age of European Exploration'. This led to the growth of a large Portuguese empire, with colonies in Africa, Asia and, most valuable of all, Brazil in South America. Portuguese power began to decline in the 16th century and, between 1580 and 1640, Portugal was ruled by Spain. Portugal lost Brazil in 1822 and, in 1910, Portugal became a republic. Instability hampered progress and army officers seized power in 1926. In 1928, they chose Antonio de Salazar to be minister of finance. He became prime minister in 1932 and ruled as a dictator from 1933.

Salazar ruled until 1968, but his successor, Marcello Caetano, was overthrown in 1974 by a group of army officers. The new government made most of Portugal's remaining colonies independent. Free elections were held in 1978. Portugal joined the European Community (now the European Union) in 1986 and, on 1 January 2002, the euro replaced the escudo as Portugal's sole official unit of currency.

Agriculture and fishing were the mainstays of the economy until the mid-20th century. However, manufacturing is now the most valuable sector.

AREA 92,390 SQ KM [35,670 SQ MI] **POPULATION** 9,444,000
CAPITAL (POPULATION) LISBON (2,561,000)
GOVERNMENT MULTIPARTY REPUBLIC
ETHNIC GROUPS PORTUGUESE 99%
LANGUAGES PORTUGUESE (OFFICIAL)
RELIGIONS ROMAN CATHOLIC 95%, OTHER CHRISTIANS 2%
CURRENCY EURO = 100 CENTS

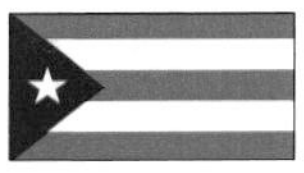

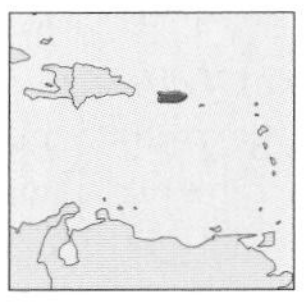

PUERTO RICO

The Commonwealth of Puerto Rico, a mainly mountainous island, is the easternmost of the Greater Antilles chain. The climate is hot and wet. Puerto Rico is a dependent territory of the USA and the people are US citizens. In 1998, 50.2% of the population voted in a referendum on possible statehood to maintain the status quo. Puerto Rico is the most industrialized country in the Caribbean. Tax exemptions attract US companies to the island and manufacturing is expanding. The chief exports are chemicals and chemical products, machinery and food.

AREA 8,900 SQ KM [3,436 SQ MI] **POPULATION** 3,939,000
CAPITAL SAN JUAN

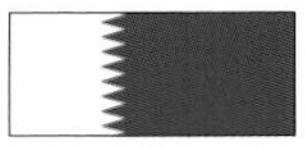

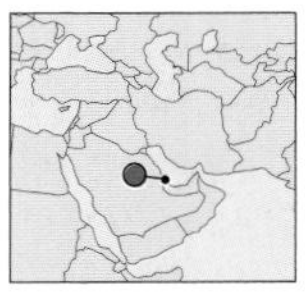

QATAR

The State of Qatar occupies a low, barren peninsula that extends northwards from the Arabian peninsula into the Gulf. The climate is hot and dry. Qatar became a British protectorate in 1916, but it became fully independent in 1971. Oil, first discovered in 1939, is the mainstay of the economy of this prosperous nation.

AREA 11,000 SQ KM [4,247 SQ MI] **POPULATION** 769,000 **CAPITAL** DOHA

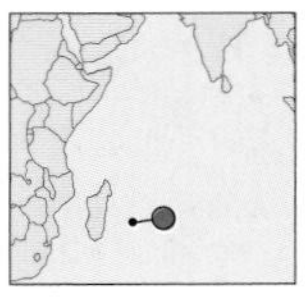

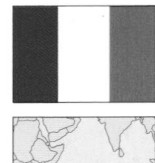

RÉUNION

Réunion is a French overseas department in the Indian Ocean. The land is mainly mountainous, though the lowlands are intensely cultivated. Sugar and sugar products are the main exports, but French aid, given to the island in return for its use as a military base, is important to the economy.

AREA 2,510 SQ KM [969 SQ MI]
POPULATION 733,00 **CAPITAL** SAINT-DENIS

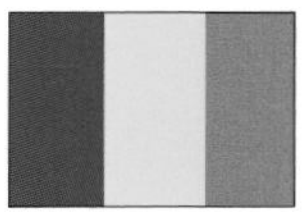

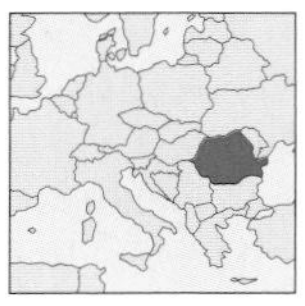

ROMANIA

GEOGRAPHY Romania is a country on the Black Sea in eastern Europe. Eastern and southern Romania form part of the Danube river basin. The delta region, near the mouths of the Danube, where the river flows into the Black Sea, is one of Europe's finest wetlands. The southern part of the coast contains several resorts. The heart of the country is called Transylvania. It is ringed in the east, south and west by scenic mountains which are part of the Carpathian mountain system.

Romania has hot summers and cold winters. The rainfall is heaviest in spring and early summer, when thundery showers are common.

POLITICS & ECONOMY From the late 18th century, the Turkish empire began to break up. The modern history of Romania began in 1861 when Walachia and Moldavia united. After World War I (1914–18), Romania, which had fought on the side of the victorious Allies, obtained large areas, including Transylvania, where most people were Romanians. This almost doubled the country's size and population. In 1939, Romania lost territory to Bulgaria, Hungary and the Soviet Union. Romania fought alongside Germany in World War II, and Soviet troops occupied the country in 1944. Hungary returned northern Transylvania to Romania in 1945, but Bulgaria and the Soviet Union kept former Romanian territory. In 1947, Romania officially became a Communist country.

In 1990, Romania held its first free elections since the end of World War II. The National Salvation Front, led by Ion Iliescu and containing many former Communist leaders, won a large majority. A new constitution, approved in 1991, made the country a democratic republic. Elections held under this constitution in 1992 again resulted in victory for Ion Iliescu, whose party was renamed the Party of Social Democracy (PDSR) in 1993. But the government faced many problems. In 1996, the centre-right Democratic Convention defeated the PDSR, led by Emil Constantinescu, who became president. But Iliescu was re-elected president in 2000.

According to the World Bank, Romania is a 'lower-middle-income' economy. Under Communist rule, industry, including mining and manufacturing, became more important than agriculture.

AREA 237,500 SQ KM [91,699 SQ MI] **POPULATION** 22,364,000
CAPITAL (POPULATION) BUCHAREST (2,028,000)
GOVERNMENT MULTIPARTY REPUBLIC **ETHNIC GROUPS** ROMANIAN 89%, HUNGARIAN 7%, ROMA 2% **LANGUAGES** ROMANIAN (OFFICIAL), HUNGARIAN, GERMAN **RELIGIONS** ROMANIAN ORTHODOX 70%, PROTESTANT 6%, ROMAN CATHOLIC 3%
CURRENCY ROMANIAN LEU = 100 BANI

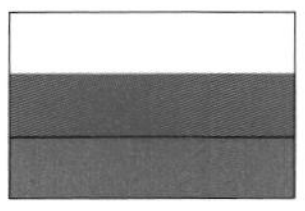

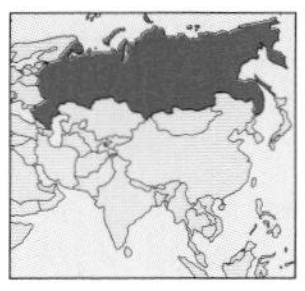

RUSSIA

GEOGRAPHY Russia is the world's largest country. About 25% lies west of the Ural Mountains in European Russia, where 80% of the population lives. It is mostly flat or undulating, but the land rises to the Caucasus Mountains in the south, where Russia's highest peak, Elbrus, at 5,633 m [18,481 ft], is found. Asian Russia, or Siberia, contains vast plains and plateaux, with mountains in the east and south. The Kamchatka peninsula in the far east has many active volcanoes. Russia contains many of the world's longest rivers, including the Yenisey-Angara and the Ob-Irtysh. It also includes part of the world's largest inland body of water, the Caspian Sea, and Lake Baikal, the world's deepest lake.

Moscow has a continental climate with cold and snowy winters and warm summers. Krasnoyarsk in south-central Siberia has a harsher, drier climate, but it is not as severe as parts of northern Siberia.

POLITICS & ECONOMY In the 9th century AD, a state called Kievan Rus was formed by a group of people called the East Slavs. Kiev, now capital of Ukraine, became a major trading centre, but, in 1237, Mongol armies conquered Russia and destroyed Kiev. Russia was part of the Mongol empire until the late 15th century. Under Mongol rule, Moscow became the leading Russian city.

In the 16th century, Moscow's grand prince was retitled 'tsar'. The first tsar, Ivan the Terrible, expanded Russian territory. In 1613, after a period of civil war, Michael Romanov became tsar, founding a dynasty which ruled until 1917. In the early 18th century, Tsar Peter the Great began to westernize Russia and, by 1812, when Napoleon failed to conquer the country, Russia was a major European power. But during the 19th century, many Russians demanded reforms and discontent was widespread.

In World War I (1914–18), the Russian people suffered great hardships and, in 1917, Tsar Nicholas II was forced to abdicate. In November 1917, the Bolsheviks seized power under Vladimir Lenin. In 1922, the Bolsheviks set up a new nation, the Union of Soviet Socialist Republics (also called the USSR or the Soviet Union).

From 1924, Joseph Stalin introduced a socialist economic programme, suppressing all opposition. In 1939, the Soviet Union and Germany signed a non-aggression pact, but Germany invaded the Soviet Union in 1941. Soviet forces pushed the Germans back, occupying eastern Europe. They reached Berlin in May 1945. From the late 1940s, tension between the Soviet Union and its allies and Western nations developed into a 'Cold War'. This continued until 1991, when the Soviet Union was dissolved.

The Soviet Union collapsed because of the failure of its economic policies. From 1991, President Boris Yeltsin introduced democratic and economic reforms. Yeltsin retired in 1999 and, in 2000, was succeeded by Vladimir Putin. Russia maintains contacts with 11 of the republics in the former Soviet Union through the Commonwealth of Independent States. However, fighting in Chechenia in the 1990s and early 21st century showed that Russia's sheer size and diverse population makes national unity difficult to achieve.

Russia's economy was thrown into disarray after the collapse of the Soviet Union, and in the early 1990s the World Bank described Russia as a 'lower-middle-income' economy. Russia was admitted to the Council of Europe in 1997, essentially to discourage instability in the Caucasus. More significantly still, Boris Yeltsin was invited to attend the G7 summit in Denver in 1997. The summit became known as 'the Summit of the Eight' and it appeared that Russia will now be included in future meetings of the world's most powerful economies. Industry is the most valuable activity, though, under Communist rule, manufacturing was less efficient than in the West, and the emphasis was on heavy industry. Today, light industries producing consumer goods are becoming important. Russia's adundant resources include oil and natural gas, coal, timber, metal ores and hydroelectric power.

Most farmland is still government-owned or run as collectives. Russia is a major producer of farm products, though it imports grains. Major crops include barley, flax, fruits, oats, rye, potatoes, sugar beet, sunflower seeds, vegetables and wheat.

AREA 17,075,000 SQ KM [6,592,800 SQ MI] **POPULATION** 145,470,000
CAPITAL (POPULATION) MOSCOW (8,405,000) **GOVERNMENT** FEDERAL MULTIPARTY REPUBLIC **ETHNIC GROUPS** RUSSIAN 82%, TATAR 4%, UKRAINIAN 3%, CHUVASH 1%, MORE THAN 100 OTHER NATIONALITIES
LANGUAGES RUSSIAN (OFFICIAL), MANY OTHERS
RELIGIONS MAINLY RUSSIAN ORTHODOX, ISLAM, JUDAISM
CURRENCY RUSSIAN ROUBLE = 100 KOPEKS

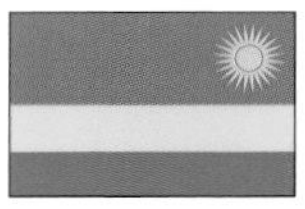

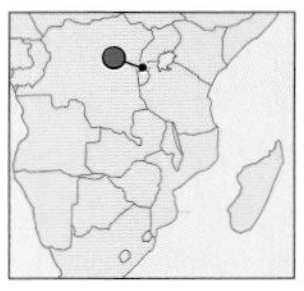

RWANDA

GEOGRAPHY The Republic of Rwanda is a small, landlocked country in east-central Africa. Lake Kivu and the River Ruzizi in the Great African Rift Valley form the country's western border.

Kigali stands on the central plateau of Rwanda. Here, temperatures are moderated by the altitude. The rainfall is abundant, but much heavier rain falls on the western mountains.

POLITICS & ECONOMY Germany conquered the area, called Ruanda-Urundi, in the 1890s. However, Belgium occupied the region during World War I (1914–18) and ruled it until 1961, when the people of Ruanda voted for their country to become a republic, called Rwanda. This decision followed a rebellion by the majority Hutu people against the Tutsi monarchy. About 150,000 deaths resulted from this conflict. Many Tutsis fled to Uganda, where they formed a rebel army. Burundi became independent as a monarchy, though it became a republic in 1966. Relations between Hutus and Tutsis continued to cause friction. Civil war broke out in 1994 and in 1996 the conflict spilled over into Congo (then Zaïre), where Zaïrean Tutsis staged a rebellion. This led to political instability.

According to the World Bank, Rwanda is a 'low-income' developing country. Most people are poor farmers. Food crops include bananas, beans, cassava and sorghum. Some cattle are raised.

AREA 26,340 SQ KM [10,170 SQ MI] **POPULATION** 7,313,000
CAPITAL (POPULATION) KIGALI (235,000) **GOVERNMENT** REPUBLIC
ETHNIC GROUPS HUTU 84%, TUTSI 15%, TWA 1%
LANGUAGES FRENCH, ENGLISH AND KINYARWANDA (ALL OFFICIAL)
RELIGIONS ROMAN CATHOLIC 53%, PROTESTANT 24%, ADVENTIST 10%
CURRENCY RWANDA FRANC = 100 CENTIMES

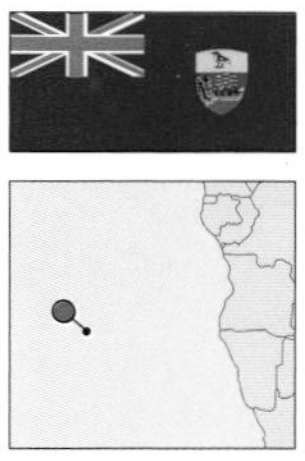

ST HELENA

St Helena, which became a British colony in 1834, is an isolated volcanic island in the south Atlantic Ocean. Now a British overseas territory, it is also the administrative centre of Ascension and Tristan da Cunha.

AREA 122 sq km [47 sq mi]
POPULATION 7,266 **CAPITAL** Jamestown

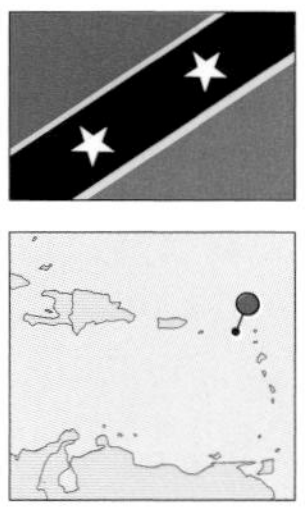

ST KITTS AND NEVIS

The Federation of St Kitts and Nevis became independent from Britain in 1983. In 1998, a vote for the secession of Nevis fell short of the two-thirds required.

AREA 360 sq km [139 sq mi]
POPULATION 39,000 **CAPITAL** Basseterre

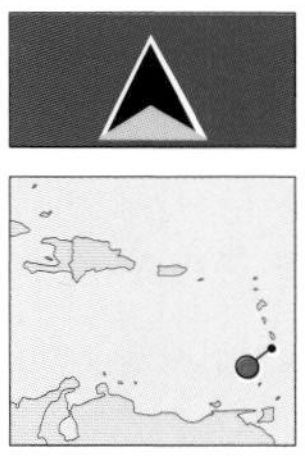

ST LUCIA

St Lucia, which became independent from Britain in 1979, is a mountainous, forested island of extinct volcanoes. It exports bananas and coconuts, and now attracts many tourists.

AREA 610 sq km [236 sq mi]
POPULATION 158,000 **CAPITAL** Castries

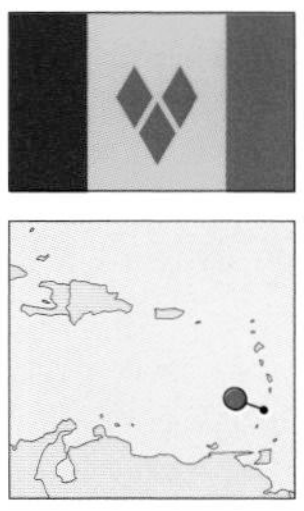

ST VINCENT AND THE GRENADINES

St Vincent and the Grenadines achieved its independence from Britain in 1979. Tourism is growing, but the territory is less prosperous than its neighbours.

AREA 388 sq km [150 sq mi]
POPULATION 116,000 **CAPITAL** Kingstown

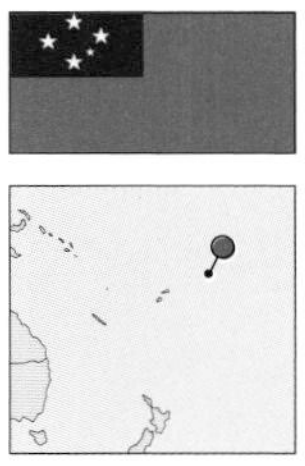

SAMOA

The Independent State of Samoa (formerly Western Samoa) comprises two islands in the South Pacific Ocean. Governed by New Zealand from 1920, the territory became independent in 1962. Exports include coconut cream and beer.

AREA 2,840 sq km [1,097 sq mi]
POPULATION 179,000 **CAPITAL** Apia

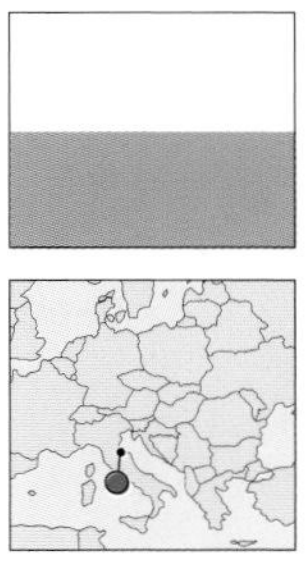

SAN MARINO

San Marino in northern Italy has been independent since 885 and a republic since the 14th century. It is the world's oldest republic.

AREA 61 sq km [24 sq mi] **POPULATION** 27,000
CAPITAL San Marino

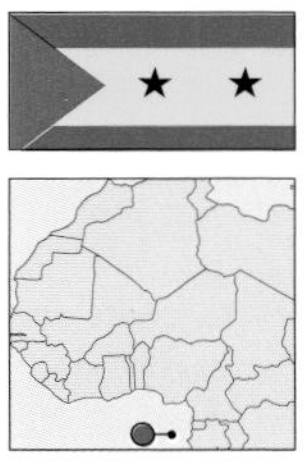

SÃO TOMÉ AND PRÍNCIPE

The Democratic Republic of São Tomé and Príncipe, a mountainous island territory west of Gabon, became a Portuguese colony in 1522. Following independence in 1975, the islands became a one-party Marxist state, but multiparty elections were held in 1991.

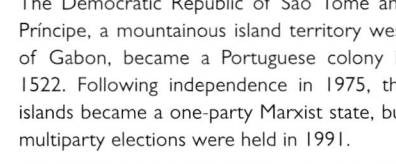

AREA 964 sq km [372 sq mi] **POPULATION** 165,000 **CAPITAL** São Tomé

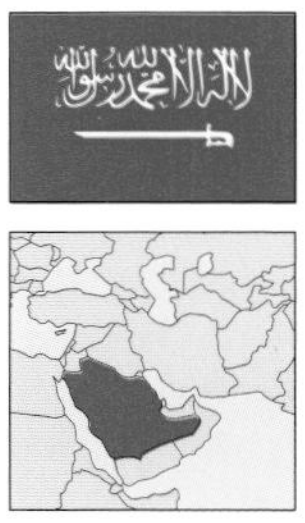

SAUDI ARABIA

GEOGRAPHY The Kingdom of Saudi Arabia occupies about three-quarters of the Arabian peninsula in south-west Asia. Deserts cover most of the land. Mountains border the Red Sea plains in the west. In the north is the sandy Nafud Desert (An Nafud). In the south is the Rub' al Khali (the 'Empty Quarter'), one of the world's bleakest deserts.

Saudi Arabia has a hot, dry climate. In the summer months, the temperatures in Riyadh often exceed 40°C [104°F], though the nights are cool.

POLITICS & ECONOMY Saudi Arabia contains the two holiest places in Islam – Mecca (or Makka), the birthplace of the Prophet Muhammad in AD 570, and Medina (Al Madinah) where Muhammad went in 622. These places are visited by many pilgrims.

Saudi Arabia was poor until the oil industry began to operate on the eastern plains in 1933. Oil revenues have been used to develop the country and Saudi Arabia has given aid to poorer Arab nations. The monarch has supreme authority and Saudi Arabia has no formal constitution. In the first Gulf War (1980–8), Saudi Arabia supported Iraq against Iran. But when Iraq invaded Kuwait in 1990, it joined the international alliance to drive Iraq's forces out of Kuwait in 1991. In 2001, relations with the US became strained after the terrorist attacks on 11 September 2001, partly because many alleged terrorists were Saudi nationals. However, Saudi Arabia denounced the attacks.

Saudi Arabia has about 25% of the world's known oil reserves, and oil and oil products make up 85% of its exports. But agriculture still employs 48% of the people. Irrigation and desalination schemes have increased crop production, while the government continues to diversify the country's economy.

AREA 2,149,690 sq km [829,995 sq mi] **POPULATION** 22,757,000
CAPITAL (POPULATION) Riyadh (1,800,000)
GOVERNMENT Absolute monarchy with consultative assembly
ETHNIC GROUPS Arab 90%, Afro-Asian 10%
LANGUAGES Arabic (official) **RELIGIONS** Islam 100%
CURRENCY Saudi riyal = 100 halalas

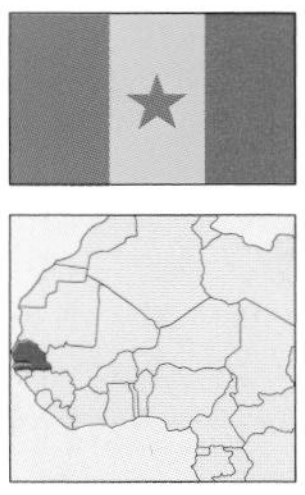

SENEGAL

GEOGRAPHY The Republic of Senegal is on the north-west coast of Africa. The volcanic Cape Verde (Cap Vert), on which Dakar stands, is the most westerly point in Africa. Plains cover most of Senegal, though the land rises gently in the south-east.

Dakar has a tropical climate, with a short rainy season between July and October.

POLITICS & ECONOMY In 1882, Senegal became a French colony, and from 1895 it was ruled as part of French West Africa, the capital of which, Dakar, developed as a major port and city.

In 1959, Senegal joined French Sudan (now Mali) to form the Federation of Mali. But Senegal withdrew in 1960 and became the separate Republic of Senegal. Its first president, Léopold Sédar Senghor, served until 1981, when he was succeeded by Abdou Diouf, who was later made 'president for life'. However, in 2000, Diouf was defeated in presidential elections by Abdoulaye Wade.

Senegal and The Gambia have always enjoyed close relations despite their differing French and British traditions. In 1981, Senegalese troops put down an attempted coup in The Gambia and, in 1982, the two countries set up a defence alliance, called the Confederation of Senegambia. But this confederation was dissolved in 1989.

According to the World Bank, Senegal is a 'lower-middle-income' developing country. It was badly hit in the 1960s and 1970s by droughts, which caused starvation. Agriculture still employs 81% of the population though many farmers produce little more than they need to feed their families. Food crops include groundnuts, millet and rice. Phosphates are the country's chief resource, but Senegal also refines oil which it imports from Gabon and Nigeria. Dakar is a busy port and has many industries.

AREA 196,720 sq km [75,954 sq mi] **POPULATION** 10,285,000
CAPITAL (POPULATION) Dakar (1,905,000)
GOVERNMENT Multiparty republic
ETHNIC GROUPS Wolof 44%, Pular 24%, Serer 15%
LANGUAGES French (official), tribal languages
RELIGIONS Islam 92%, traditional beliefs and others 6%, Christianity (mainly Roman Catholic) 2%
CURRENCY CFA franc = 100 centimes

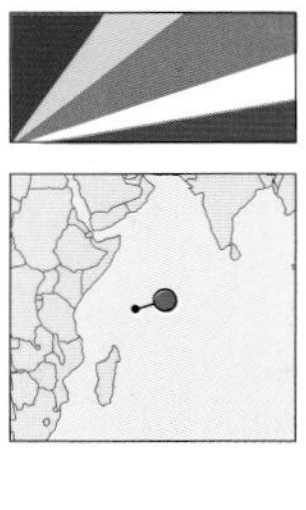

SEYCHELLES

The Republic of Seychelles in the western Indian Ocean achieved independence from Britain in 1976. Coconuts are the main cash crop and fishing and tourism are important.

AREA 455 sq km [176 sq mi]
POPULATION 80,000 **CAPITAL** Victoria

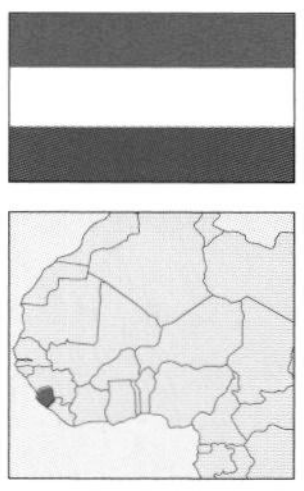

SIERRA LEONE

GEOGRAPHY The Republic of Sierra Leone in West Africa is about the same size as the Republic of Ireland. The coast contains several deep estuaries in the north, with lagoons in the south. The most prominent feature is the mountainous Freetown (or Sierra Leone) peninsula.

Sierra Leone has a tropical climate, with heavy rainfall between April and November.

POLITICS & ECONOMY A former British territory, Sierra Leone became independent in 1961 and a republic in 1971. It became a one-party state in 1978, but, in 1991, the people voted for the restoration of democracy. The military seized power in 1992 and a civil war caused much destruction in 1994–5. Elections in 1996 were followed by another military coup. In 1998, the West African Peace Force restored the deposed President Ahmed Tejan Kabbah. In 1999, a peace agreement followed further conflict. As part of this agreement, Foday Sankoh, one of the rebel leaders, became vice-president. However, he was arrested in 2000 and charged with war crimes. Conflict resumed, but another cease-fire was agreed. Disarmament continued through 2001 and, in 2002, the war seemed to be over.

The World Bank classifies Sierra Leone among the 'low-income' economies. Agriculture provides a living for 70% of the people, though farming is mainly at subsistence level. The most valuable exports are minerals, including diamonds, bauxite and rutile (titanium ore). The country has few manufacturing industries.

AREA 71,740 sq km [27,699 sq mi] **POPULATION** 5,427,000
CAPITAL (POPULATION) Freetown (505,000) **GOVERNMENT** Single-party republic **ETHNIC GROUPS** Mende 35%, Temne 30%, Creole
LANGUAGES English (official), Mende, Temne, Krio **RELIGIONS** Islam 60%, traditional beliefs 30%, Christianity 10% **CURRENCY** Leone = 100 cents

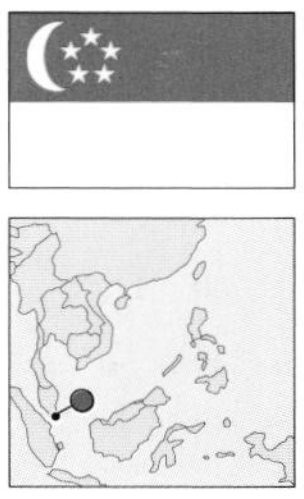

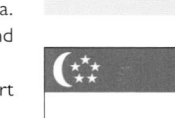

SINGAPORE

GEOGRAPHY The Republic of Singapore is an island country at the southern tip of the Malay peninsula. It consists of the large Singapore Island and 58 small islands, 20 of which are inhabited.

Singapore has a hot, humid climate. Temperatures are high and rainfall is heavy throughout the year.

POLITICS & ECONOMY In 1819, Sir Thomas Stamford Raffles (1781–1826), agent of the British East India Company, made a treaty with the Sultan of Johor allowing the British to build a settlement on Singapore Island. Singapore soon became the leading British trading centre in South-east Asia and it later became a naval base. Japanese forces seized the island in 1942, but British rule was restored in 1945.

In 1963, Singapore became part of the Federation of Malaysia, which also included Malaya and the territories of Sabah and Sarawak on Borneo. In 1965, Singapore broke away and became independent.

The People's Action Party (PAP) has ruled Singapore since 1959. Its leader, Lee Kuan Yew, served as prime minister from 1959 until 1990, when he resigned and was succeeded by Goh Chok Tong. Under the PAP, the economy has expanded rapidly though some consider its rule rather dictatorial.

The World Bank classifies Singapore as a 'high-income' economy. A skilled workforce has created a fast growing economy, but the recession in 1997–8 was a setback. Trade and finance are leading activities. Manufactures include electronic products, machinery, scientific instruments, textiles and ships. Singapore has a large oil refinery. Petroleum products and manufactures are the main exports.

AREA 618 sq km [239 sq mi] **POPULATION** 4,300,000
CAPITAL (POPULATION) Singapore City (3,866,000)
GOVERNMENT Multiparty republic **ETHNIC GROUPS** Chinese 77%, Malay 14%, Indian 8%
LANGUAGES Chinese, Malay, Tamil and English (all official)
RELIGIONS Buddhism, Islam, Christianity, Hinduism
CURRENCY Singapore dollar = 100 cents

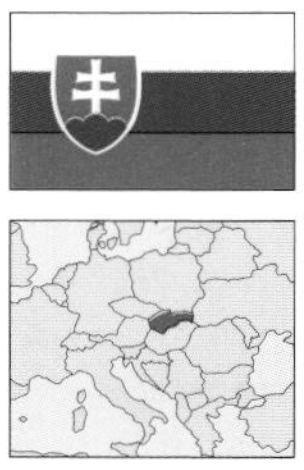

SLOVAK REPUBLIC

GEOGRAPHY The Slovak Republic is a predominantly mountainous country, consisting of part of the Carpathian range. The highest peak is Gerlachovka in the Tatra Mountains, which reaches 2,655 m [8,711 ft]. The south is a fertile lowland.

The Slovak Republic has cold winters and

warm summers. Kosice, in the east, has average temperatures ranging from –3°C [27°F] in January to 20°C [68°F] in July. The highland areas are much colder. Snow or rain falls throughout the year. Kosice has an average annual rainfall of 600 mm [24 in], the wettest months being July and August.

POLITICS & ECONOMY Slavic peoples settled in the region in the 5th century AD. They were subsequently conquered by Hungary, beginning a millennium of Hungarian rule and suppression of Slovak culture.

In 1867, Hungary and Austria united to form Austria–Hungary, of which the present-day Slovak Republic was a part. Austria–Hungary collapsed at the end of World War I (1914–18). The Czech and Slovak people then united to form a new nation, Czechoslovakia. But Czech domination led to resentment by many Slovaks. In 1939, the Slovak Republic declared itself independent, but Germany occupied the country. At the end of World War II, the Slovak Republic again became part of Czechoslovakia.

The Communist party took control in 1948. In the 1960s, many people sought reform, but they were crushed by the Russians. In the late 1980s, demands for democracy mounted and a non-Communist government took office in 1990. Elections in 1992 led to victory for the Movement for a Democratic Slovakia headed by a former Communist and nationalist, Vladimir Meciar, and the independent Slovak Republic came into existence on 1 January 1993.

Independence raised national aspirations among Slovakia's Magyar-speaking community, but relations with Hungary deteriorated when the Magyars felt that administrative changes under-represented them politically. The government also made Slovak the only official language. The government's autocratic rule and human rights record provoked international criticism. In 1998, Meciar's party was defeated and Mikulas Dzurinda replaced Meciar as prime minister. In 2001, the parliament approved changes to the constitution that would enable Slovakia to become a member of NATO and the European Union.

Before 1948, the Slovak Republic's economy was based on farming, but Communist governments developed manufacturing industries, producing such things as chemicals, machinery, steel and weapons. Since the late 1980s, many state-run businesses have been handed over to private owners.

AREA 49,035 SQ KM [18,932 SQ MI] **POPULATION** 5,415,000
CAPITAL (POPULATION) BRATISLAVA (451,000)
GOVERNMENT MULTIPARTY REPUBLIC
ETHNIC GROUPS SLOVAK 86%, HUNGARIAN 11%, ROMA 2%
LANGUAGES SLOVAK (OFFICIAL), HUNGARIAN
RELIGIONS ROMAN CATHOLIC 60%, PROTESTANT 8%, ORTHODOX 4%
CURRENCY KORUNA = 100 HALIEROV

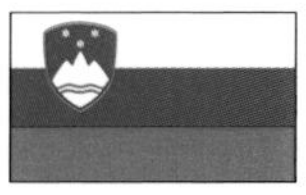
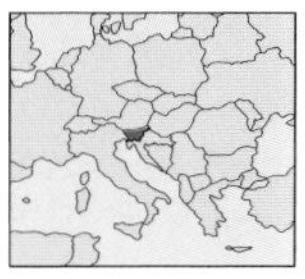

SLOVENIA

GEOGRAPHY The Republic of Slovenia was one of the six republics which made up the former Yugoslavia. Much of the land is mountainous, rising to 2,863 m [9,393 ft] at Mount Triglav in the Julian Alps (Julijske Alpe) in the north-west. Central Slovenia contains the limestone Karst region. The Postojna caves near Ljubljana are among the largest in Europe.

The coast has a mild Mediterranean climate, but inland the climate is more continental. The mountains are snow-capped in winter.

POLITICS & ECONOMY In the last 2,000 years, the Slovene people have been independent as a nation for less than 50 years. The Austrian Habsburgs ruled over the region from the 13th century until World War I. Slovenia became part of the Kingdom of the Serbs, Croats and Slovenes (later called Yugoslavia) in 1918. During World War II, Slovenia was invaded and partitioned between Italy, Germany and Hungary but, after the war, Slovenia again became part of Yugoslavia.

From the late 1960s, some Slovenes demanded independence, but the central government opposed the break-up of the country. In 1990, when Communist governments had collapsed throughout Eastern Europe, elections were held and a non-Communist coalition government was set up. Slovenia then declared itself independent. This led to fighting between Slovenes and the federal army, but Slovenia did not become a battlefield like other parts of the former Yugoslavia. The European Community recognized Slovenia's independence in 1992. The electors returned a coalition led by the Liberal Democrats in 1992, 1996 and again in 2000.

The reform of the economy, formerly run by the government, and the fighting in areas to the south have caused problems for Slovenia, although it remains one of the fastest growing economies in Europe. In 1992, the World Bank classified Slovenia as an 'upper-middle-income' developing country, and it is expected to be among the first countries to join an expanded European Union.

Manufacturing is the leading activity and manufactures are the main exports. Manufactures include chemicals, machinery and transport equipment, metal goods and textiles. Slovenia mines some iron ore, lead, lignite and mercury. Agriculture employs 8% of the people. Fruits, maize, potatoes and wheat are major crops, and many farmers raise animals.

AREA 20,251 SQ KM [7,817 SQ MI] **POPULATION** 1,930,000
CAPITAL (POPULATION) LJUBLJANA (280,000)
GOVERNMENT MULTIPARTY REPUBLIC
ETHNIC GROUPS SLOVENE 88%, CROAT 3%, SERB 2%, BOSNIAN 1%
LANGUAGES SLOVENE (OFFICIAL), SERBO-CROAT
RELIGIONS MAINLY ROMAN CATHOLIC
CURRENCY TOLAR = 100 STOTIN

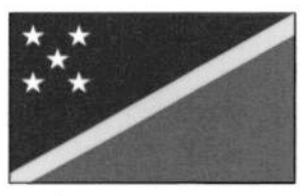
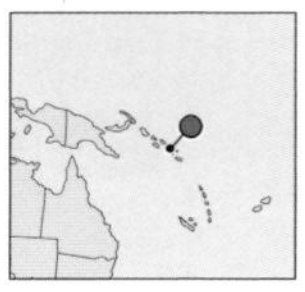

SOLOMON ISLANDS

The Solomon Islands, a chain of mainly volcanic islands in the Pacific Ocean, were a British territory between 1893 and 1978. The chain extends for some 2,250 km [1,400 mi]. They were the scene of fierce fighting during World War II. Most people are Melanesians, and the islands have a young population profile, with half the people aged under 20. Fish, coconuts and cocoa are leading products, though development is hampered by mountainous, forested terrain.

AREA 28,370 SQ KM [10,954 SQ MI] **POPULATION** 480,000
CAPITAL HONIARA

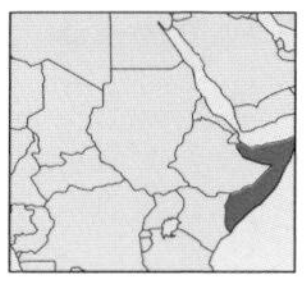

SOMALIA

GEOGRAPHY The Somali Democratic Republic, or Somalia, is in a region known as the 'Horn of Africa'. It is more than twice the size of Italy, the country which once ruled the southern part of Somalia. The most mountainous part of the country is in the north, behind the narrow coastal plains that border the Gulf of Aden.

Rainfall is light throughout Somalia. The wettest regions are the south and the northern mountains, but droughts often occur. Temperatures are high on the low plateaux and plains.

POLITICS & ECONOMY European powers became interested in the Horn of Africa in the 19th century. In 1884, Britain made the northern part of what is now Somalia a protectorate, while Italy took the south in 1905. The new boundaries divided the Somalis into five areas: the two Somalilands, Djibouti (which was taken by France in the 1880s), Ethiopia and Kenya. Since then, many Somalis have longed for reunification in a Greater Somalia.

Italy entered World War II in 1940 and invaded British Somaliland. But British forces conquered the region in 1941 and ruled both Somalilands until 1950, when the United Nations asked Italy to take over the former Italian Somaliland for ten years. In 1960, both Somalilands became independent and united to become Somalia.

Somalia has faced many problems since independence. Economic problems led a military group to seize power in 1969. In the 1970s, Somalia supported an uprising of Somali-speaking people in the Ogaden region of Ethiopia. But Ethiopian forces prevailed and, in 1988, Somalia signed a peace treaty with Ethiopia. The cost of the fighting weakened Somalia's economy. In the 1990s, Somalia gradually broke apart. In 1991, the people in what was formerly British Somaliland set up the 'Somaliland Republic', although it never received international recognition. The north-east, which was called Puntland, also seceded from Somalia, while civil war, based on clan rivalry, raged in the south. US troops sent into the south by the UN in 1993 were forced to withdraw in 1994 and the clan warfare continued. However, hopes of reunification were raised in 2000, when a three-year transitional Assembly was set up in the south, following a peace conference held in Djibouti.

Somalia is a developing country, whose economy has been shattered by drought and war. Catastrophic flooding in late 1997 displaced tens of thousands of people, further damaging the country's infrastructure and destroying hopes of economic recovery.

Many Somalis are nomads who raise livestock. Live animals, meat and hides and skins are major exports, followed by bananas grown in the wetter south. Other crops include citrus fruits, cotton, maize and sugar cane. Mining and manufacturing remain relatively unimportant in the economy.

AREA 637,660 SQ KM [246,201 SQ MI] **POPULATION** 7,489,000 **CAPITAL (POPULATION)** MOGADISHU (997,000) **GOVERNMENT** SINGLE-PARTY REPUBLIC, MILITARY DOMINATED **ETHNIC GROUPS** SOMALI 85%, ARAB 1% **LANGUAGES** SOMALI AND ARABIC (BOTH OFFICIAL), ENGLISH, ITALIAN **RELIGIONS** ISLAM 99% **CURRENCY** SOMALI SHILLING = 100 CENTS

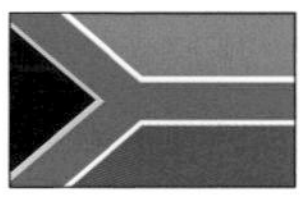
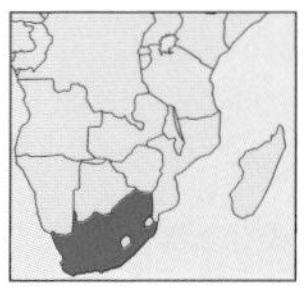

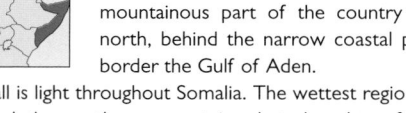

SOUTH AFRICA

GEOGRAPHY The Republic of South Africa is made up largely of the southern part of the huge plateau which makes up most of southern Africa. The highest peaks are in the Drakensberg range, which is formed by the uplifted rim of the plateau. The coastal plains include part of the Namib Desert in the north-west. Most of South Africa has a mild, sunny climate. Much of the coastal strip, including Cape Town, has warm, dry summers and mild, rainy winters. Inland, large areas are arid.

POLITICS & ECONOMY Early inhabitants in South Africa were the Khoisan. In the last 2,000 years, Bantu-speaking people moved into the area. Their descendants include the Zulu, Xhosa, Sotho and Tswana. The Dutch founded a settlement at the Cape in 1652, but Britain took over in the early 19th century, making the area a colony. The Dutch, called Boers or Afrikaners, resented British rule and moved inland. Rivalry between the groups led to Anglo-Boer Wars in 1880–1 and 1899–1902.

In 1910, the country was united as the Union of South Africa. In 1948, the National Party won power and introduced a policy known as apartheid, under which non-whites had no votes and their human rights were strictly limited. In 1990, Nelson Mandela, leader of the African National Congress (ANC), was released from prison. Multi-racial elections were held in 1994 and Mandela became president. After Mandela's retirement in 1999, his successor, Thabo Mbeki, led the ANC to victory in the elections. Mbeki faces many problems, including a health crisis arising from a government estimate in the early 21st century that one in five South Africans is infected with the HIV virus.

South Africa is Africa's most developed country. However, most of the black people are poor, with low standards of living. Natural resources include diamonds, gold and many other metals. Mining and manufacturing are the most valuable activities.

AREA 1,219,916 SQ KM [470,566 SQ MI] **POPULATION** 43,586,000 **CAPITAL (POPULATION)** CAPE TOWN (LEGISLATIVE, 2,350,000); PRETORIA (ADMINISTRATIVE, 1,080,000); BLOEMFONTEIN (JUDICIARY, 300,000) **GOVERNMENT** MULTIPARTY REPUBLIC **ETHNIC GROUPS** BLACK 76%, WHITE 13%, COLORED 9%, ASIAN 2% **LANGUAGES** AFRIKAANS, ENGLISH, NDEBELE, NORTH SOTHO, SOUTH SOTHO, SWAZI, TSONGA, TSWANA, VENDA, XHOSA, ZULU (ALL OFFICIAL) **RELIGIONS** CHRISTIANITY 68%, ISLAM 2%, HINDUISM 1% **CURRENCY** RAND = 100 CENTS

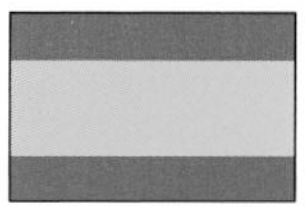
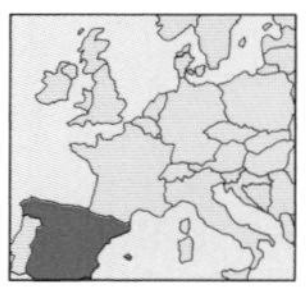

SPAIN

GEOGRAPHY The Kingdom of Spain is the second largest country in Western Europe after France. It shares the Iberian peninsula with Portugal. A large plateau, called the Meseta, covers most of Spain. Much of the Meseta is flat, but it is crossed by several mountain ranges, called sierras.

The northern highlands include the Cantabrian Mountains (Cordillera Cantabrica) and the high Pyrenees, which form Spain's border with France. But Mulhacén, the highest peak on the Spanish mainland, is in the Sierra Nevada in the south-east. Spain also contains fertile coastal plains. Other major lowlands are the Ebro river basin in the north-east and the Guadalquivir river basin in the south-west. Spain also includes the Balearic Islands in the Mediterranean Sea and the Canary Islands off the north-west coast of Africa.

The Meseta has a continental climate, with hot summers and cold winters, when temperatures often fall below freezing point. Snow frequently covers the mountain ranges on the Meseta. The Mediterranean coastal regions also have hot, dry summers, but the winters are mild.

POLITICS & ECONOMY In the 16th century, Spain became a world power. At its peak, it controlled much of Central and South America, parts of Africa and the Philippines in Asia. Spain began to decline in the late 16th century. Its sea power was destroyed by a British fleet in the Battle of Trafalgar (1805). By the 20th century, it was a poor country.

Spain became a republic in 1931, but the republicans were defeated in the Spanish Civil War (1936–9). General Francisco Franco (1892–1975) became the country's dictator, though, technically, it was a monarchy. When Franco died, the monarchy was restored. Prince Juan Carlos became king.

Spain has several groups with their own languages and cultures. Some of these people want to run their own regional affairs. In the northern Basque region, some nationalists have waged a terrorist campaign. A truce in 1998 was ended in 1999 when talks failed to produce results.

Since the late 1970s, a regional parliament with a considerable degree of autonomy has been set up in the Basque Country (called Euskadi in the indigenous tongue and Pais Vasco in Spanish). Similar parliaments have been initiated in Catalonia in the north-east and Galicia in the north-west. All these regions have their own languages.

The revival of Spain's economy, which was shattered by the Civil War, began in the 1950s and 1960s, especially through the growth of tourism and manufacturing. Since the 1950s, Spain has changed from a poor country, dependent on agriculture, to a fairly prosperous industrial nation.

By the early 1990s, agriculture employed 10% of the people, as compared with industry 35% and services, including tourism, 55%. Farmland, including pasture, makes up about two-thirds of the land, with forest making up most of the rest. Major crops include barley, citrus fruits, grapes for winemaking, olives, potatoes and wheat.

Spain has some high-grade iron ore in the north, though otherwise it lacks natural resources. But it has many manufacturing industries. Manufactures include cars, chemicals, clothing, electronics, processed food, metal goods, steel and textiles. The leading manufacturing centres are Barcelona, Bilbao and Madrid.

AREA 504,780 sq km [194,896 sq mi] **POPULATION** 38,432,000
CAPITAL (POPULATION) Madrid (3,030,000)
GOVERNMENT Constitutional monarchy
ETHNIC GROUPS Castilian Spanish 72%, Catalan 16%, Galician 8%, Basque 2% **LANGUAGES** Castilian Spanish (official) 74%, Catalan 17%, Galician 7%, Basque 2%
RELIGIONS Roman Catholic 99%
CURRENCY Euro = 100 cents

SRI LANKA

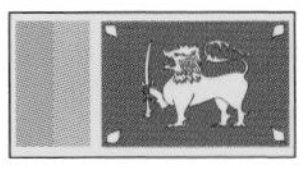
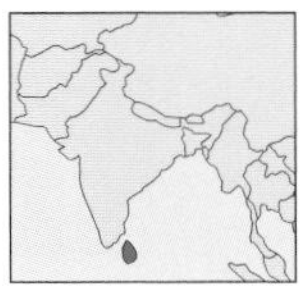

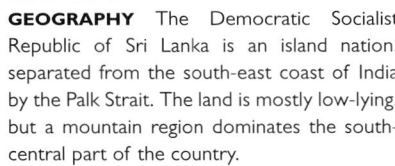

GEOGRAPHY The Democratic Socialist Republic of Sri Lanka is an island nation, separated from the south-east coast of India by the Palk Strait. The land is mostly low-lying, but a mountain region dominates the south-central part of the country.

The western part of Sri Lanka has a wet equatorial climate. Temperatures are high and the rainfall is heavy. Eastern Sri Lanka is drier than the west.

POLITICS & ECONOMY From the early 16th century, Ceylon (as Sri Lanka was then known) was ruled successively by the Portuguese, Dutch and British. Independence was achieved in 1948 and the country was renamed Sri Lanka in 1972.

After independence, rivalries between the two main ethnic groups, the Sinhalese and Tamils, marred progress. In the 1950s, the government made Sinhala the official language. Following protests, the prime minister made provisions for Tamil to be used in some areas. In 1959, the prime minister was assassinated by a Sinhalese extremist and he was succeeded by Sirimavo Bandanaraike, who became the world's first woman prime minister.

Conflict between Tamils and Sinhalese continued in the 1970s and 1980s. In 1987, India helped to engineer a cease-fire. Indian troops arrived to enforce the agreement, but withdrew in 1990 after failing to subdue the main guerrilla group, the Tamil Tigers, who wanted to set up an independent Tamil homeland in northern Sri Lanka. In 1993, the country's president was assassinated by a suspected Tamil separatist. Offensives against the Tamil Tigers continued until hopes of peace were raised in 2002, with the signing of a long-term cease-fire.

The World Bank classifies Sri Lanka as a 'low-income' developing country. Agriculture employs half of the workforce, and coconuts, rubber and tea are exported. Rice is the chief food crop. Manufacturing is concerned mainly with processing agricultural products and producing textiles.

AREA 65,610 sq km [25,332 sq mi] **POPULATION** 19,409,000
CAPITAL (POPULATION) Colombo (1,863,000)
GOVERNMENT Multiparty republic
ETHNIC GROUPS Sinhalese 74%, Tamil 18%, Sri Lankan Moor 7% **LANGUAGES** Sinhala and Tamil (both official)
RELIGIONS Buddhism 69%, Hinduism 16%, Christianity 8%, Islam 7%
CURRENCY Sri Lankan rupee = 100 cents

SUDAN

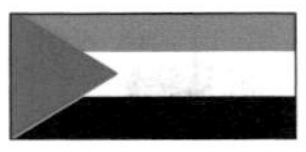
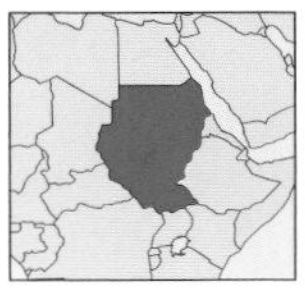

GEOGRAPHY The Republic of Sudan is the largest country in Africa. From north to south, it spans a vast area extending from the arid Sahara in the north to the wet equatorial region in the south. The land is mostly flat, with the highest mountains in the far south. The main physical feature is the River Nile.

The climate of Khartoum represents a transition between the virtually rainless northern deserts and the equatorial lands in the south. Some rain falls in Khartoum in summer.

POLITICS & ECONOMY In the 19th century, Egypt gradually took over Sudan. In 1881, a Muslim religious teacher, the Mahdi ('divinely appointed guide'), led an uprising. Britain and Egypt put the rebellion down in 1898. In 1899, they agreed to rule Sudan jointly as a condominium.

After independence in 1952, the black Africans in the south, who were either Christians or followers of traditional beliefs, feared domination by the Muslim northerners. For example, they objected to the government declaring that Arabic was the only official language. In 1964, civil war broke out and continued until 1972, when the south was given regional self-government, though executive power was still vested in the military government in Khartoum.

In 1983, the government established Islamic law throughout the country. This sparked off further conflict when the Sudan People's Liberation Army in the south launched attacks on government installations. Despite attempts to restore order, the fighting continued into the 21st century. In 1998, the government announced that it accepted the idea of a referendum on the secession of the south, though definitions of the 'south' varied. Widespread famine in southern Sudan in 1998 attracted global attention and humanitarian aid.

AREA 2,505,810 sq km [967,493 sq mi] **POPULATION** 36,080,000
CAPITAL (POPULATION) Khartoum (925,000) **GOVERNMENT** Military regime **ETHNIC GROUPS** Sudanese Arab 49%, Dinka 12%, Nuba 8%, Beja 6%, Nuer 5%, Azande 3% **LANGUAGES** Arabic (official), Nubian, Dinka **RELIGIONS** Islam (mainly Sunni) 70%, traditional beliefs 25%, Christianity 5% **CURRENCY** Dinar = 10 Sudanese pounds

SURINAME

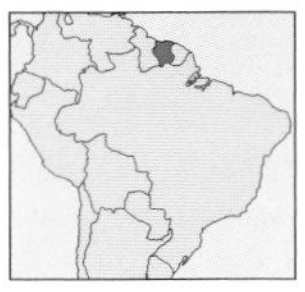

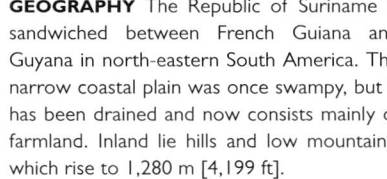

GEOGRAPHY The Republic of Suriname is sandwiched between French Guiana and Guyana in north-eastern South America. The narrow coastal plain was once swampy, but it has been drained and now consists mainly of farmland. Inland lie hills and low mountains, which rise to 1,280 m [4,199 ft].

Suriname has a hot, wet and humid climate. Temperatures are high throughout the year.

POLITICS & ECONOMY In 1667, the British handed Suriname to the Dutch in return for New Amsterdam, an area that is now the state of New York. Slave revolts and Dutch neglect hampered development. In the early 19th century, Britain and the Netherlands disputed the ownership of the area. The British gave up their claims in 1813. Slavery was abolished in 1863 and, soon afterwards, Indian and Indonesian labourers were introduced to work on the plantations. Suriname became fully independent in 1975, but the economy was weakened when thousands of skilled people emigrated from Suriname to the Netherlands. Following a coup in 1980, Suriname was ruled by a military dictator, Dési Bouterse. The adoption of a new constitution led to the restoration of democracy in 1988, though another military coup occurred in 1990. Elections were held in 1996, but instability, deteriorating relations with the Netherlands and economic problems continued. In 1999, Bouterse was convicted in absentia in the Netherlands of having led a cocaine-trafficking ring during and after his tenure in office.

The World Bank classifies Suriname as an 'upper-middle-income' developing country. Its economy is based on mining and metal processing. Suriname is a leading producer of bauxite, from which the metal aluminium is made.

AREA 163,270 sq km [63,039 sq mi] **POPULATION** 434,000
CAPITAL (POPULATION) Paramaribo (201,000)
GOVERNMENT Multiparty republic **ETHNIC GROUPS** Asian Indian 37%, Creole (mixed White and Black) 31%, Indonesian 14%, Black 9%, Amerindian 3%, Chinese 3%, Dutch 1% **LANGUAGES** Dutch (official), Sranantonga **RELIGIONS** Hinduism 27%, Roman Catholic 23%, Islam 20%, Protestant 19%
CURRENCY Suriname guilder = 100 cents

SWAZILAND

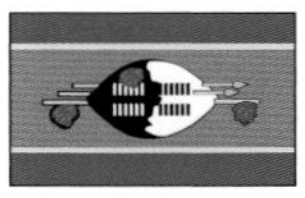
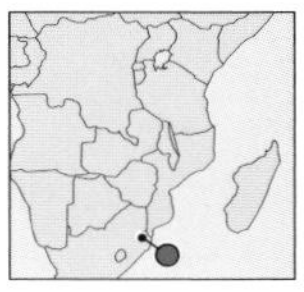

GEOGRAPHY The Kingdom of Swaziland is a small, landlocked country in southern Africa. The country has four regions which run north–south. In the west, the Highveld, with an average height of 1,200 m [3,937 ft], makes up 30% of Swaziland. The Middleveld, between 350 m to 1,000 m [1,148 ft and 3,281 ft], covers 28% of the country. The Lowveld, with an average height of 270 m [886 ft], covers another 33%. Finally, the Lebombo Mountains reach 800 m [2,600 ft] along the eastern border.

The Lowveld is almost tropical, with an average temperature of 22°C [72°F] and low rainfall. The altitude moderates the climate in the west.

POLITICS & ECONOMY In 1894, Britain and the Boers of South Africa agreed to put Swaziland under the control of the South African Republic (the Transvaal). But at the end of the Anglo–Boer War (1899–1902), Britain took control of the country. In 1968, when Swaziland became fully independent as a constitutional monarchy, the head of state was King Sobhuza II. Sobhuza died in 1982 and was succeeded by one of his sons, Prince Makhosetive, who, in 1986, was installed as King Mswati III. Elections in 1993 and 1998, in which political parties were banned, failed to satisfy protesters who opposed the absolute monarchy. But Mswati continued to rule by decree and freedom of speech was severely restricted.

The World Bank classifies Swaziland as a 'lower-middle-income' developing country. Agriculture employs 74% of the people, and farm products and processed foods, including soft drink concentrates, sugar, wood pulp, citrus fruits and canned fruit, are the leading exports. Many farmers live at subsistence level, producing little more than they need to feed their own families. Swaziland is heavily dependent on South Africa and the two countries are linked through a customs union.

AREA 17,360 sq km [6,703 sq mi] **POPULATION** 1,104,000
CAPITAL (POPULATION) Mbabane (42,000)
GOVERNMENT Monarchy **ETHNIC GROUPS** Swazi 84%, Zulu 10%, Tsonga **LANGUAGES** Siswati and English (both official)
RELIGIONS Protestant 55%, Islam 10%, Roman Catholic 5%
CURRENCY Lilangeni = 100 cents

SWEDEN

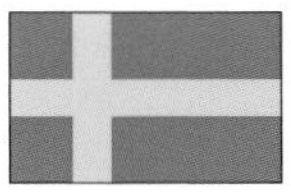
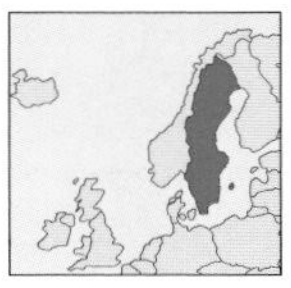

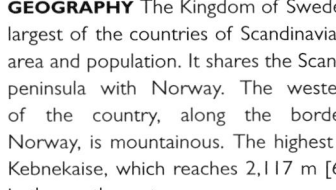

GEOGRAPHY The Kingdom of Sweden is the largest of the countries of Scandinavia in both area and population. It shares the Scandinavian peninsula with Norway. The western part of the country, along the border with Norway, is mountainous. The highest point is Kebnekaise, which reaches 2,117 m [6,946 ft] in the north-west.

The climate of Sweden becomes more severe from south to north. Stockholm has cold winters and cool summers. The far south is much milder.

POLITICS & ECONOMY Swedish Vikings plundered areas to the south and east between the 9th and 11th centuries. Sweden, Denmark and Norway were united in 1397, but Sweden regained its independence in 1523. In 1809, Sweden lost Finland to Russia, but, in 1814, it gained Norway from Denmark. The union between Sweden and Norway was dissolved in 1905. Sweden was neutral in World Wars I and II. Since 1945, Sweden has become a prosperous country. In 1995, it joined the European Union. However, many people were sceptical about the advantages of EU membership and Sweden did not adopt the euro, the single EU currency, in 1999.

Sweden has wide-ranging welfare services. But many people are concerned about the high cost of these services and the high taxes they must pay. In 1991, the Social Democrats, who had built up the welfare state, were defeated. They were re-elected in 1994 and 1998, but they tried to control public spending and expand the economy.

Sweden is a highly developed industrial country. Major products include steel and steel goods. Steel is used in the engineering industry to manufacture aircraft, cars, machinery and ships. Sweden has some of the world's richest iron ore deposits. They are located near Kiruna in the far north. But most of this ore is exported, and Sweden imports most of the materials needed by its industries. Sweden also has a major forestry industry.

Development of hydroelectricity has made up for the lack of oil and coal. In 1996, a decision was taken to decommission all of Sweden's nuclear power stations. This is said to be one of the boldest and most expensive environmental pledges ever made by a government.

AREA 449,960 SQ KM [173,730 SQ MI] **POPULATION** 8,875,000
CAPITAL (POPULATION) STOCKHOLM (727,000)
GOVERNMENT CONSTITUTIONAL MONARCHY
ETHNIC GROUPS SWEDISH 91%, FINNISH 3% **LANGUAGES** SWEDISH (OFFICIAL), FINNISH **RELIGIONS** LUTHERAN 89%, ROMAN CATHOLIC 2%
CURRENCY SWEDISH KRONA = 100 ÖRE

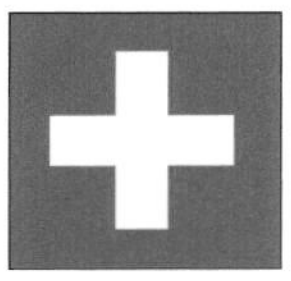
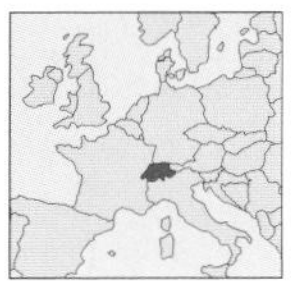

SWITZERLAND

GEOGRAPHY The Swiss Confederation is a landlocked country in Western Europe. Much of the land is mountainous. The Jura Mountains lie along Switzerland's western border with France, while the Swiss Alps make up about 60% of the country in the south and east. Four-fifths of the people of Switzerland live on the fertile Swiss plateau, which contains most of Switzerland's large cities.

The climate of Switzerland varies greatly according to the height of the land. The plateau region has a central European climate with warm summers, but cold and snowy winters. Rain occurs all through the year. The rainiest months are in summer.

POLITICS & ECONOMY In 1291, three small cantons (states) united to defend their freedom against the Habsburg rulers of the Holy Roman Empire. They were Schwyz, Uri and Unterwalden, and they called the confederation they formed 'Switzerland'. Switzerland expanded and, in the 14th century, defeated Austria in three wars of independence. After a defeat by the French in 1515, the Swiss adopted a policy of neutrality, which they still follow. In 1815, the Congress of Vienna expanded Switzerland to 22 cantons and guaranteed its neutrality. Switzerland's 23rd canton, Jura, was created in 1979 from part of Bern. Neutrality combined with the vigour and independence of its people have made Switzerland prosperous. In 1993 and again in 2001, the Swiss people voted against starting negotiations to join the European Union. However, in 2002, the Swiss voted by a narrow majority to join the United Nations.

Although lacking in natural resources, Switzerland is a wealthy, industrialized country. Many workers are highly skilled. Major products include chemicals, electrical equipment, machinery and machine tools, precision instruments, processed food, watches and textiles. Farmers produce about three-fifths of the country's food – the rest is imported. Livestock raising, especially dairy farming, is the chief agricultural activity. Crops include fruits, potatoes and wheat. Tourism and banking are also important. Swiss banks attract investors from all over the world.

AREA 41,290 SQ KM [15,942 SQ MI] **POPULATION** 7,283,000
CAPITAL (POPULATION) BERN (942,000) **GOVERNMENT** FEDERAL REPUBLIC **ETHNIC GROUPS** GERMAN 64%, FRENCH 19%, ITALIAN 10%, YUGOSLAV 3%, SPANISH 2%, ROMANSCH 1% **LANGUAGES** FRENCH, GERMAN, ITALIAN, ROMANSCH (ALL OFFICIAL) **RELIGIONS** ROMAN CATHOLIC 46%, PROTESTANT 40% **CURRENCY** SWISS FRANC = 100 CENTIMES

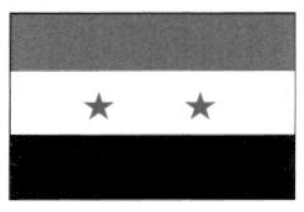
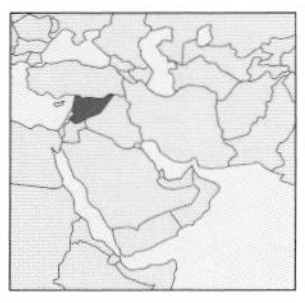

SYRIA

GEOGRAPHY The Syrian Arab Republic is a country in south-western Asia. The narrow coastal plain is overlooked by a low mountain range which runs north–south. Another range, the Jabal ash Sharqi, runs along the border with Lebanon. South of this range is the Golan Heights, which Israel has occupied since 1967.

The coast has a Mediterranean climate, with dry, warm summers and wet, mild winters. The low mountains cut off Damascus from the sea. It has less rainfall than the coastal areas. To the east, the land becomes drier.

POLITICS & ECONOMY After the collapse of the Turkish Ottoman empire in World War I, Syria was ruled by France. Since independence in 1946, Syria has been involved in the Arab–Israeli wars and, in 1967, it lost a strategic border area, the Golan Heights, to Israel. In 1970, Lieutenant-General Hafez al-Assad took power, establishing a stable but repressive regime. In 1999, Syria had talks with Israel concerning the future of the Golan Heights. These talks formed part of an attempt to establish a peace settlement for the entire east Mediterranean region. Following the death of Assad in 2000, his son, Bashar Assad, succeeded him.

The World Bank classifies Syria as a 'lower-middle-income' developing country. But it has great potential for development. Its main resources are oil, hydroelectricity from the dam at Lake Assad, and fertile land. Oil is the main export; farm products, textiles and phosphates are also important. Agriculture employs about 26% of the workforce.

AREA 185,180 SQ KM [71,498 SQ MI] **POPULATION** 16,729,000
CAPITAL (POPULATION) DAMASCUS (1,394,000)
GOVERNMENT MULTIPARTY REPUBLIC
ETHNIC GROUPS ARAB 90%, KURDISH, ARMENIAN, OTHERS
LANGUAGES ARABIC (OFFICIAL) **RELIGIONS** ISLAM 90%, CHRISTIANITY 9% **CURRENCY** SYRIAN POUND = 100 PIASTRES

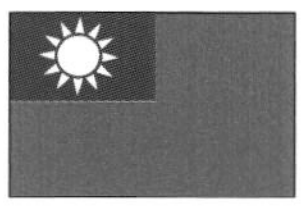
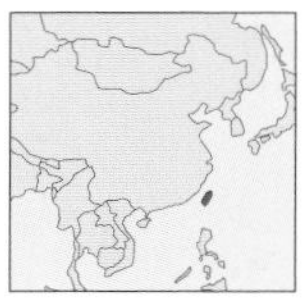

TAIWAN

GEOGRAPHY High mountain ranges run down the length of the island, with dense forest in many areas.

The climate is warm, moist and suitable for agriculture.

POLITICS & ECONOMY Chinese settlers occupied Taiwan from the 7th century. In 1895, Japan seized the territory from the Portuguese, who had named it Isla Formosa, or 'beautiful island'. China regained the island after World War II. In 1949, it became the refuge of the Nationalists who had been driven out of China by the Communists. They set up the Republic of China, which, with US help, launched an ambitious programme of economic development. Today, it produces a wide range of manufactured goods. Mainland China regards Taiwan as one of its provinces, though reunification seems unlikely in the foreseeable future.

AREA 36,000 SQ KM [13,900 SQ MI] **POPULATION** 22,370,000
CAPITAL (POPULATION) TAIPEI (2,596,000)
GOVERNMENT UNITARY MULTIPARTY REPUBLIC
ETHNIC GROUPS TAIWANESE (HAN CHINESE) 84%, MAINLAND CHINESE 14% **LANGUAGES** MANDARIN (OFFICIAL), MIN, HAKKA **RELIGIONS** BUDDHISM 43%, TAOISM AND CONFUCIANISM 49%
CURRENCY NEW TAIWAN DOLLAR = 100 CENTS

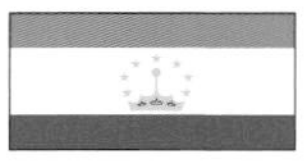
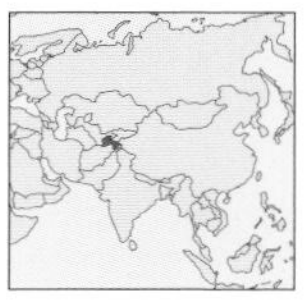

TAJIKISTAN

GEOGRAPHY The Republic of Tajikistan is one of the five central Asian republics that formed part of the former Soviet Union. Only 7% of the land is below 1,000 m [3,280 ft], while almost all of eastern Tajikistan is above 3,000 m [9,840 ft]. The highest point is Communism Peak (Pik Kommunizma), which reaches 7,495 m [24,590 ft]. The main ranges are the westwards extension of the Tian Shan Range in the north and the snow-capped Pamirs in the south-east. Earthquakes are common throughout the country.

Tajikistan has a severe continental climate. Summers are hot and dry in the lower valleys, and winters are long and bitterly cold in the mountains.

POLITICS & ECONOMY Russia conquered parts of Tajikistan in the late 19th century and, by 1920, Russia took complete control. In 1924, Tajikistan became part of the Uzbek Soviet Socialist Republic, but, in 1929, it was expanded, taking in some areas populated by Uzbeks, becoming the Tajik Soviet Socialist Republic.

While the Soviet Union began to introduce reforms during the 1980s, many Tajiks demanded freedom. In 1989, the Tajik government made Tajik the official language instead of Russian and, in 1990, it stated that its local laws overruled Soviet laws. Tajikistan became fully independent in 1991, following the break-up of the Soviet Union. As the poorest of the ex-Soviet republics, Tajikistan faced many problems in trying to introduce a free-market system.

In 1992, civil war broke out between the government, which was run by former Communists, and an alliance of democrats and Islamic forces. A cease-fire was agreed in 1996, and in 1997 representatives of the opposition were brought into the government. Presidential elections were held in 1999, followed by parliamentary elections in 2000.

The World Bank classifies Tajikistan as a 'low-income' developing country. Agriculture, mainly on irrigated land, is the main activity and cotton is the chief product. Other crops include fruits, grains and vegetables. The country has large hydroelectric power resources and it produces aluminium.

AREA 143,100 SQ KM [55,520 SQ MI] **POPULATION** 6,579,000
CAPITAL (POPULATION) DUSHANBE (524,000)
GOVERNMENT TRANSITIONAL DEMOCRACY
ETHNIC GROUPS TAJIK 65%, UZBEK 25%, RUSSIAN 3%, TATAR, KYRGYZ, UKRAINIAN, GERMAN **LANGUAGES** TAJIK (OFFICIAL), UZBEK, RUSSIAN
RELIGIONS ISLAM (MAINLY SUNNI) 80%
CURRENCY SOMONI = 100 DIRAMS

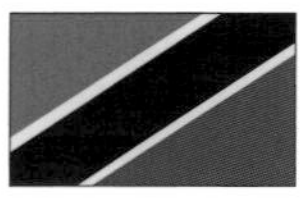
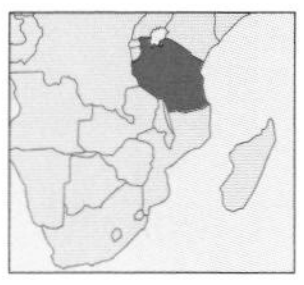

TANZANIA

GEOGRAPHY The United Republic of Tanzania consists of the former mainland country of Tanganyika and the island nation of Zanzibar, which also includes the island of Pemba. Behind a narrow coastal plain, most of Tanzania is a plateau, which is broken by arms of the Great African Rift Valley. In the west, this valley contains lakes Nyasa and Tanganyika. The highest peak is Kilimanjaro, Africa's tallest mountain.

The coast has a hot and humid climate, with the greatest rainfall in April and May. The inland plateaux and mountains are cooler and less humid.

POLITICS & ECONOMY Mainland Tanganyika became a German territory in the 1880s, while Zanzibar and Pemba became a British protectorate in 1890. Following Germany's defeat in World War I, Britain took over Tanganyika, which remained a British territory until its independence in 1961. In 1964, Tanganyika and Zanzibar united to form the United Republic of Tanzania. The country's president, Julius Nyerere, pursued socialist policies of self-help (*ujamaa*) and egalitarianism. Many of its social reforms were successful, though the country failed to make economic progress. Nyerere resigned as president in 1985, although he retained much influence until his death in 1999. His successors, Ali Hassan Mwinyi and, from 1995, Benjamin Mkapa, introduced more liberal economic policies.

Tanzania is one of the world's poorest countries. Crops are grown on only 5% of the land, yet agriculture employs 85% of the people. Food crops include bananas, cassava, maize, millet and rice.

AREA 945,090 SQ KM [364,899 SQ MI] **POPULATION** 36,232,000
CAPITAL (POPULATION) DODOMA (204,000)
GOVERNMENT MULTIPARTY REPUBLIC
ETHNIC GROUPS NYAMWEZI AND SUKUMA 21%, SWAHILI 9%, HEHET AND BENA 7%, MAKONDE 6%, HAYA 6%
LANGUAGES SWAHILI AND ENGLISH (BOTH OFFICIAL)
RELIGIONS CHRISTIANITY (MOSTLY ROMAN CATHOLIC) 45%, ISLAM 35% (99% IN ZANZIBAR), TRADITIONAL BELIEFS AND OTHERS 20%
CURRENCY TANZANIAN SHILLING = 100 CENTS

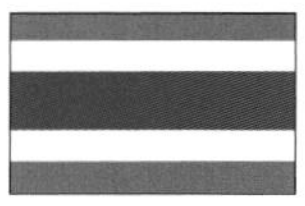
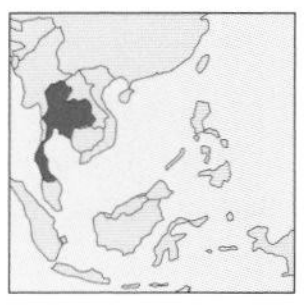

THAILAND

GEOGRAPHY The Kingdom of Thailand is one of the ten countries in South-east Asia. The highest land is in the north, where Doi Inthanon, the highest peak, reaches 2,595 m [8,514 ft]. The Khorat plateau, in the north-east, makes up about 30% of the country and is the most heavily populated part of Thailand. In the south, Thailand shares the finger-like Malay peninsula with Burma and Malaysia.

Thailand has a tropical climate. Monsoon winds from the south-west bring heavy rains between the months of May and October. The rainfall in Bangkok is lower than in many other parts of South-east Asia, because mountains shelter the central plains from the rain-bearing winds.

POLITICS & ECONOMY The first Thai state was set up in the 13th century. By 1350, it included most of what is now Thailand. European contact began in the early 16th century. But, in the late 17th century, the Thais, fearing interference in their affairs, forced all Europeans to leave. This policy continued for 150 years. In 1782, a Thai General, Chao Phraya Chakkri, became king, founding a dynasty which continues today. The country became known as Siam, and Bangkok became its capital. From the mid-19th century, contacts with the West were restored. In World War I, Siam supported the Allies against Germany and Austria-Hungary. But in 1941, the country was conquered by Japan and became its ally. However, after the end of World War II, it became an ally of the United States.

Since 1967, when Thailand became a member of ASEAN (the Association of South-east Asian Nations), its economy has grown, especially its manufacturing and service industries. However, in 1997, it suffered recession along with other fast-developing countries in eastern Asia, and its economic policies had to be modified.

The economy still depends on agriculture, which employs more than two-fifths of the people. Rice is the chief crop. Cassava, cotton, maize, rubber, sugar cane and tobacco are also grown. Thailand also mines tin and other minerals. However, the chief exports are manufactures, including food products, machinery, timber products and textiles. Tourism is another major source of income.

AREA 513,120 sq km [198,116 sq mi] **POPULATION** 61,798,000
CAPITAL (POPULATION) Bangkok (7,507,000)
GOVERNMENT Constitutional monarchy
ETHNIC GROUPS Thai 75%, Chinese 14%, Malay 4%, Khmer 3%
LANGUAGES Thai (official), Chinese, Malay, English
RELIGIONS Buddhism 94%, Islam 4%, Christianity 1%
CURRENCY Thai baht = 100 satang

TOGO

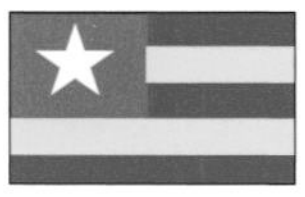

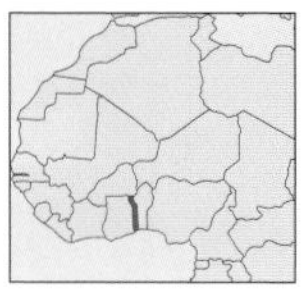

GEOGRAPHY The Republic of Togo is a long, narrow country in West Africa. From north to south, it extends about 500 km [311 mi]. Its coastline on the Gulf of Guinea is only 64 km [40 mi] long and it is only 145 km [90 mi] at its widest point.

Togo has high temperatures all through the year. The main wet season is from March to July, with a minor wet season in October and November.

POLITICS & ECONOMY Togo became a German protectorate in 1884 but, in 1919, Britain took over the western third of the territory, while France took over the eastern two-thirds. In 1956, the people of British Togoland voted to join Ghana, while French Togoland became an independent republic in 1960.

A military regime took power in 1963. In 1967, General Gnassingbe Eyadema became head of state and suspended the constitution. Under a new constitution adopted in 1992, multiparty elections were held in 1994. However, in 1998, paramilitary policies stopped the count in the presidential elections when it became clear that Eyadema had been defeated. As a result, the leading opposition parties boycotted the general elections in 1999.

Togo is a poor, developing country. Farming employs 65% of the people and major food crops include cassava, maize, millet and yams. The leading export is phosphate rock, which is used to make fertilizers.

AREA 56,790 sq km [21,927 sq mi] **POPULATION** 5,153,000
CAPITAL (POPULATION) Lomé (590,000)
GOVERNMENT Multiparty republic **ETHNIC GROUPS** Ewe-Adja 43%, Tem-Kabre 26%, Gurma 16% **LANGUAGES** French (official), Ewe, Kabiye
RELIGIONS Traditional beliefs 50%, Christianity 35%, Islam 15%
CURRENCY CFA franc = 100 centimes

TONGA

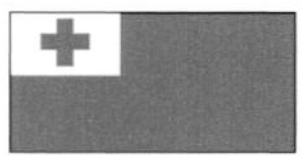

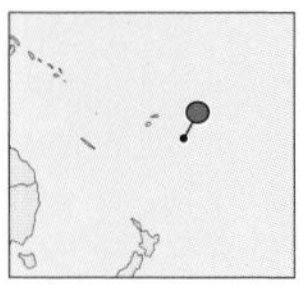

The Kingdom of Tonga, a former British protectorate, became independent in 1970. Situated in the South Pacific Ocean, it contains more than 170 islands, 36 of which are inhabited. Agriculture is the main activity; coconuts, copra, fruits and fish are leading products.

AREA 750 sq km [290 sq mi] **POPULATION** 104,000 **CAPITAL** Nuku'alofa

TRINIDAD AND TOBAGO

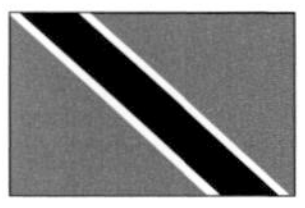

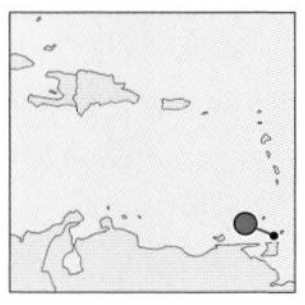

The Republic of Trinidad and Tobago became independent from Britain in 1962. These tropical islands, populated by people of African, Asian (mainly Indian) and European origin, are hilly and forested, though there are some fertile plains. Oil production is the mainstay of the economy.

AREA 5,130 sq km [1,981 sq mi]
POPULATION 1,170,000 **CAPITAL** Port-of-Spain

TUNISIA

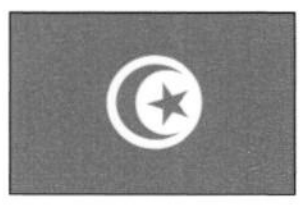

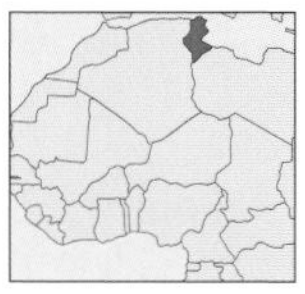

GEOGRAPHY The Republic of Tunisia is the smallest country in North Africa. The mountains in the north are an eastwards and comparatively low extension of the Atlas Mountains. To the north and east of the mountains lie fertile plains, especially between Sfax, Tunis and Bizerte. In the south, low-lying regions contain a vast salt pan, called the Chott Djerid, and part of the Sahara Desert.

Northern Tunisia has a Mediterranean climate, with dry, sunny summers, and mild winters with a moderate rainfall. The average yearly rainfall decreases towards the south.

POLITICS & ECONOMY In 1881, France established a protectorate over Tunisia and ruled the country until 1956. The new parliament abolished the monarchy and declared Tunisia to be a republic in 1957, with the nationalist leader, Habib Bourguiba, as president. His government introduced many reforms, including votes for women, but various problems arose, including unemployment among the middle class and fears that Western values introduced by tourists might undermine Muslim values. In 1987, the prime minister Zine el Abidine Ben Ali removed Bourguiba from office and succeeded him as president. He was elected in 1989 and re-elected in 1994 and 1999.

The World Bank classifies Tunisia as a 'middle-income' developing country. The main resources and chief exports are phosphates and oil. Most industries are concerned with food processing. Agriculture employs 22% of the people; major crops being barley, dates, grapes, olives and wheat. Fishing is important, as is tourism.

AREA 163,610 sq km [63,170 sq mi] **POPULATION** 9,705,000
CAPITAL (POPULATION) Tunis (1,827,000)
GOVERNMENT Multiparty republic **ETHNIC GROUPS** Arab 98%, Berber 1%, French **LANGUAGES** Arabic (official), French
RELIGIONS Islam 99% **CURRENCY** Dinar = 1,000 millimes

TURKEY

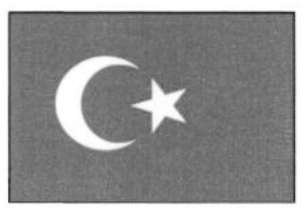

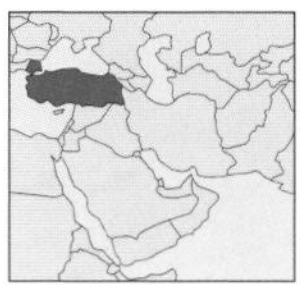

GEOGRAPHY The Republic of Turkey lies in two continents. European Turkey, also called Thrace, lies west of a waterway linking the Mediterranean and Black seas. Most of Asian Turkey consists of plateaux and mountains, which rise to 5,165 m [16,945 ft] at Mount Ararat (Agri Dagi) near the border with Armenia. Earthquakes are common.

Central Turkey has a dry climate, with hot, sunny summers and cold winters. The driest part of the central plateau lies south of the city of Ankara, around Lake Tuz. The west has a Mediterranean climate, but the Black Sea coast has cooler summers.

POLITICS & ECONOMY In AD 330, the Roman empire moved its capital to Byzantium, which it renamed Constantinople. Constantinople became capital of the East Roman (or Byzantine) empire in 395. Muslim Seljuk Turks from central Asia invaded Anatolia in the 11th century. In the 14th century, another group of Turks, the Ottomans, conquered the area. In 1435, the Ottoman Turks took Constantinople, which they called Istanbul.

The Ottoman Turks built up a large empire which finally collapsed during World War I (1914–18). In 1923, Turkey became a republic. Its leader Mustafa Kemal, or Atatürk ('father of the Turks'), launched policies to modernize and secularize the country.

Since the 1940s, Turkey has sought to strengthen its ties with Western powers. It joined NATO (North Atlantic Treaty Organization) in 1951 and it applied to join the European Economic Community in 1987. But Turkey's conflict with Greece, together with its invasion of northern Cyprus in 1974, have led many Europeans to treat Turkey's aspirations with caution. Political instability, military coups, conflict with Kurdish nationalists in eastern Turkey and concern about the country's record on human rights are other problems. Turkey has enjoyed democracy since 1983, though, in 1998, the government banned the Islamist Welfare Party, which it accused of violating secular principles. In 1999, the Muslim Virtue Party (successor to Islamist Welfare Party) lost ground. The largest numbers of parliamentary seats were won by the ruling Democratic Left Party and the far-right National Action Party. In 2001, the government introduced a package of reforms, including one that recognized men and women as equals. The reforms were apparently intended to ease Turkey's entry into the European Union.

The World Bank classifies Turkey as a 'lower-middle-income' developing country. Agriculture employs 37% of the people, and barley, cotton, fruits, maize, tobacco and wheat are major crops. Livestock farming is important and wool is a leading product.

Turkey produces chromium, but manufacturing is the chief activity. Manufactures include processed farm products and textiles, cars, fertilizers, iron and steel, machinery, metal products and paper products. Over 9 million tourists visited Turkey in 1998.

AREA 779,450 sq km [300,946 sq mi] **POPULATION** 66,494,000
CAPITAL (POPULATION) Ankara (3,294,000)
GOVERNMENT Multiparty republic
ETHNIC GROUPS Turkish 80%, Kurdish 20%
LANGUAGES Turkish (official), Kurdish
RELIGIONS Islam 99% **CURRENCY** Turkish lira = 100 kurus

TURKMENISTAN

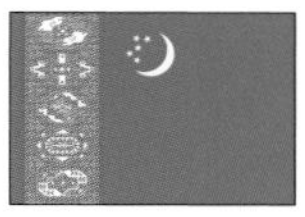

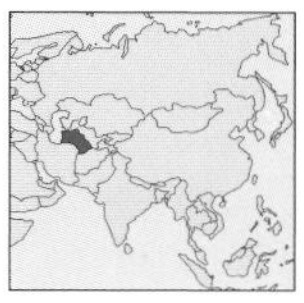

GEOGRAPHY The Republic of Turkmenistan is one of the five central Asian republics which once formed part of the former Soviet Union. Most of the land is low-lying, with mountains lying on the southern and south-western borders. In the west lies the salty Caspian Sea. Most of Turkmenistan is arid and the Garagum, Asia's largest sand desert, covers about 80% of the country. Turkmenistan has a continental climate, with average annual rainfall varying from 80 mm [3 in] in the desert to 300 mm [12 in] in the mountains. Summer months are hot but winter temperatures drop well below freezing point.

POLITICS & ECONOMY Just over 1,000 years ago, Turkic people settled in the lands east of the Caspian Sea and the name 'Turkmen' comes from this time. Mongol armies conquered the area in the 13th century and Islam was introduced in the 14th century. Russia took over the area in the 1870s and 1880s. After the Russian Revolution of 1917, the area came under Communist rule and, in 1924, it became the Turkmen Soviet Socialist Republic. The Communists strictly controlled all aspects of life and discouraged religion. But they improved such services as education, health, housing and transport.

In the 1980s, when the Soviet Union began to introduce reforms, the Turkmen began to demand more freedom. In 1990, the Turkmen government stated that its laws overruled Soviet laws. In 1991, Turkmenistan became fully independent after the break-up of the Soviet Union. But the country kept ties with Russia through the Commonwealth of Independent States (CIS).

In 1992, Turkmenistan adopted a new constitution, allowing for the setting up of political parties, providing that they were not ethnic or religious in character. But, effectively, Turkmenistan remained a one-party state and, in 1992, Saparmurad Niyazov, the former Communist and now Democratic Party leader, was the only candidate. In 1994, a referendum prolonged Niyazov's term of office to 2002, while, in 1999, the parliament declared him president for life, though he later said that he would retire before 2010.

Faced with many economic problems, Turkmenistan began to look south rather than to the CIS for support. As part of this policy, it joined the Economic Co-operation Organization which had been set up in 1985 by Iran, Pakistan and Turkey. In 1996, the completion of a rail link from Turkmenistan to the Iranian coast was seen as a highly significant step for the future economic development of Central Asia.

Turkmenistan's chief resources are oil and natural gas, but the main activity is agriculture, with cotton, grown on irrigated land, as the main crop. Grain and vegetables are also important. Manufactures include cement, glass, petrochemicals and textiles.

AREA 488,100 sq km [188,450 sq mi] **POPULATION** 4,603,000
CAPITAL (POPULATION) Ashkhabad (536,000) **GOVERNMENT** Single-party republic **ETHNIC GROUPS** Turkmen 77%, Russian 17%, Uzbek 9%, Kazakh 2%, Tatar **LANGUAGES** Turkmen (official), Russian, Uzbek, Kazakh **RELIGIONS** Islam **CURRENCY** Manat = 100 tenesi

TURKS AND CAICOS ISLANDS

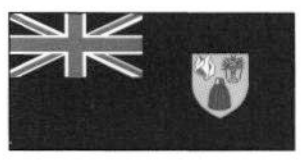

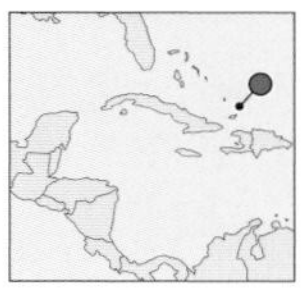

The Turks and Caicos Islands, a British territory in the Caribbean since 1776, are a group of about 30 islands. Fishing and tourism are major activities.

AREA 430 sq km [166 sq mi]
POPULATION 18,000 **CAPITAL** Cockburn Town

TUVALU

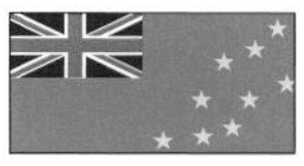

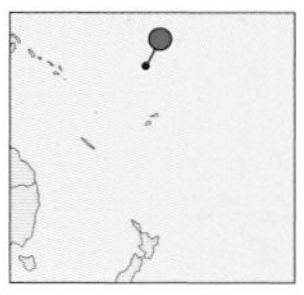

Tuvalu, formerly called the Ellice Islands, was a British territory from the 1890s until it became independent in 1978. It consists of nine low-lying coral atolls in the southern Pacific Ocean. Copra is the chief export.

AREA 24 sq km [9 sq mi] **POPULATION** 11,000
CAPITAL Fongafale

UGANDA

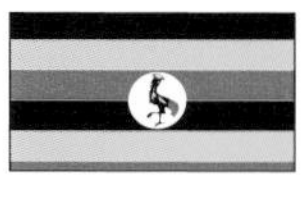

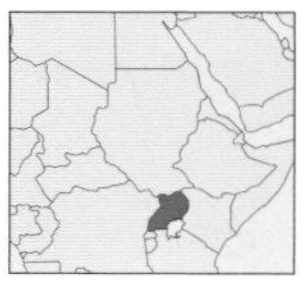

GEOGRAPHY The Republic of Uganda is a landlocked country on the East African plateau. It contains part of Lake Victoria, Africa's largest lake and a source of the River Nile, which occupies a shallow depression in the plateau.

The equator runs through Uganda and the country is warm throughout the year, though

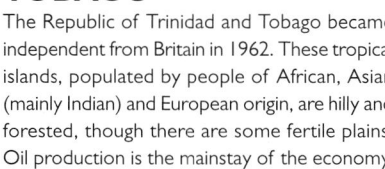

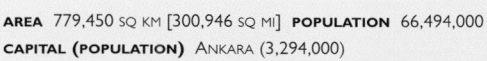

the high altitude moderates the temperature. The wettest regions are the lands to the north of Lake Victoria, where Kampala is situated, and the western mountains, especially the high Ruwenzori range.

POLITICS & ECONOMY Little is known of the early history of Uganda. When Europeans first reached the area in the 19th century, many of the people were organized in kingdoms, the most powerful of which was Buganda, the home of the Baganda people. Britain took over the country between 1894 and 1914, and ruled it until independence in 1962.

In 1967, Uganda became a republic and Buganda's Kabaka (king), Sir Edward Mutesa II, was made president. But tensions between the Kabaka and the prime minister, Apollo Milton Obote, led to the dismissal of the Kabaka in 1966. Obote also abolished the traditional kingdoms, including Buganda. Obote was overthrown in 1971 by an army group led by General Idi Amin Dada. Amin ruled as a dictator. He forced most of the Asians who lived in Uganda to leave the country and had many of his opponents killed.

In 1978, a border dispute between Uganda and Tanzania led Tanzanian troops to enter Uganda. With help from Ugandan opponents of Amin, they overthrew Amin's government. In 1980, Obote led his party to victory in national elections. But after charges of fraud, Obote's opponents began guerrilla warfare. A military group overthrew Obote in 1985, though strife continued until 1986, when Yoweri Museveni's National Resistance Movement seized power. In 1993, Museveni restored the traditional kingdoms, including Buganda where a new Kabaka was crowned. Museveni also held elections in 1994 but political parties were not permitted. Museveni was elected president in 1996 and re-elected in 2001.

The strife since the 1960s has greatly damaged the economy, but the economy grew during a period of stability in the 1990s. The situation worsened when Uganda intervened militarily in Congo (then Zaïre) in 1998. Agriculture dominates the economy, employing 86% of the people. The chief export is coffee.

AREA 235,880 SQ KM [91,073 SQ MI] **POPULATION** 23,986,000
CAPITAL (POPULATION) KAMPALA (954,000)
GOVERNMENT REPUBLIC IN TRANSITION
ETHNIC GROUPS BAGANDA 17%, KARAMOJONG 12%, BASOGO 8%, ITESO 8%, LANGI 6%, RWANDA 6%, BAGISU 5%, ACHOLI 4%, LUGBARA 4%
LANGUAGES ENGLISH AND SWAHILI (BOTH OFFICIAL), GANDA
RELIGIONS ROMAN CATHOLIC 33%, PROTESTANT 33%, TRADITIONAL BELIEFS 18%, ISLAM 16%
CURRENCY UGANDA SHILLING = 100 CENTS

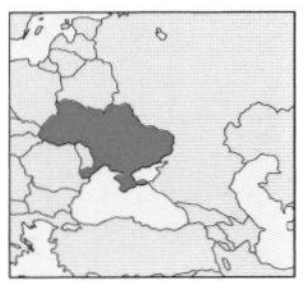

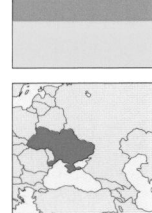

UKRAINE

GEOGRAPHY Ukraine is the second largest country in Europe after Russia. It was formerly part of the Soviet Union, which split apart in 1991. This mostly flat country faces the Black Sea in the south. The Crimean peninsula includes a highland region overlooking Yalta.

Ukraine has warm summers, but the winters are cold, becoming more severe from west to east. In the summer, the east of the country is often warmer than the west. The heaviest rainfall occurs in the summer.

POLITICS & ECONOMY Kiev was the original capital of the early Slavic civilization known as Kievan Rus. In the 17th and 18th centuries, parts of Ukraine came under Polish and Russian rule. But Russia gained most of Ukraine in the late 18th century. In 1918, Ukraine became independent, but in 1922 it became part of the Soviet Union. Millions of people died in the 1930s as a result of Soviet policies, while millions more died during the Nazi occupation (1941–4).

In the 1980s, Ukrainian people demanded more say over their affairs. The country finally became independent when the Soviet Union broke up in 1991. Ukraine continued to work with Russia through the Commonwealth of Independent States. But Ukraine differed with Russia on some issues, including control over Crimea. In 1999, a treaty ratifying Ukraine's present boundaries failed to get the approval of Russia's upper house.

The World Bank classifies Ukraine as a 'lower-middle-income' economy. Agriculture is important. Crops include wheat and sugar beet, which are the major exports, together with barley, maize, potatoes, sunflowers and tobacco. Livestock rearing and fishing are also important industries.

Manufacturing is the chief economic activity. Major manufactures include iron and steel, machinery and vehicles. Ukraine has large coalfields. The country imports oil and natural gas, but it has hydroelectric and nuclear power stations. In 1986, an accident at the Chernobyl (Chornobyl) nuclear power plant caused widespread nuclear radiation. The plant was finally closed in 2001.

AREA 603,700 SQ KM [233,100 SQ MI] **POPULATION** 48,760,000
CAPITAL (POPULATION) KIEV (2,621,000)
GOVERNMENT MULTIPARTY REPUBLIC
ETHNIC GROUPS UKRAINIAN 73%, RUSSIAN 22%, JEWISH 1%, BELARUSSIAN 1%, MOLDOVAN, BULGARIAN, POLISH
LANGUAGES UKRAINIAN (OFFICIAL), RUSSIAN
RELIGIONS MOSTLY UKRAINIAN ORTHODOX)
CURRENCY HRYVNIA = 100 KOPIYKAS

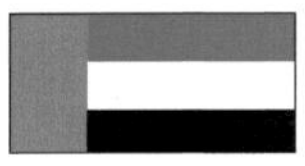

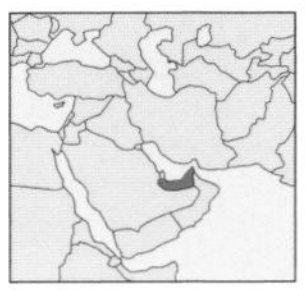

UNITED ARAB EMIRATES

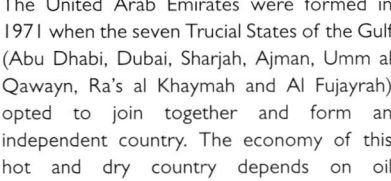

The United Arab Emirates were formed in 1971 when the seven Trucial States of the Gulf (Abu Dhabi, Dubai, Sharjah, Ajman, Umm al Qawayn, Ra's al Khaymah and Al Fujayrah) opted to join together and form an independent country. The economy of this hot and dry country depends on oil production, and oil revenues give the United Arab Emirates one of the highest per capita GNPs in Asia.

AREA 83,600 SQ KM [32,278 SQ MI] **POPULATION** 2,407,000
CAPITAL ABU DHABI

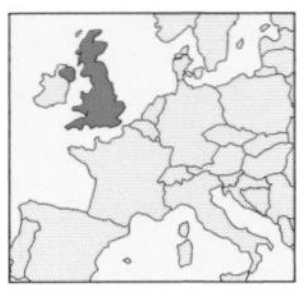

UNITED KINGDOM

GEOGRAPHY The United Kingdom (or UK) is a union of four countries. Three of them – England, Scotland and Wales – make up Great Britain. The fourth country is Northern Ireland. The Isle of Man and the Channel Islands, including Jersey and Guernsey, are not part of the UK. They are self-governing British dependencies.

The land is highly varied. Much of Scotland and Wales is mountainous, and the highest peak is Scotland's Ben Nevis at 1,343 m [4,406 ft]. England has some highland areas, including the Cumbrian Mountains (or Lake District) and the Pennine range in the north. But England also has large areas of fertile lowland. Northern Ireland is also a mixture of lowlands and uplands. It contains the UK's largest lake, Lough Neagh.

The UK has a mild climate, influenced by the warm Gulf Stream which flows across the Atlantic from the Gulf of Mexico, then past the British Isles. Moist winds from the south-west bring rain, but the rainfall decreases from west to east. Winds from the east and north bring cold weather in winter.

POLITICS & ECONOMY In ancient times, Britain was invaded by many peoples, including Iberians, Celts, Romans, Angles, Saxons, Jutes, Norsemen, Danes, and Normans, who arrived in 1066. The evolution of the United Kingdom spanned hundreds of years. The Normans finally overcame Welsh resistance in 1282, when King Edward I annexed Wales and united it with England. Union with Scotland was achieved by the Act of Union of 1707. This created a country known as the United Kingdom of Great Britain.

Ireland came under Norman rule in the 11th century, and much of its later history was concerned with a struggle against English domination. In 1801, Ireland became part of the United Kingdom of Great Britain and Ireland. But in 1921, southern Ireland broke away to become the Irish Free State. Most of the people in the Irish Free State were Roman Catholics. In Northern Ireland, where the majority of the people were Protestants, most people wanted to remain citizens of the United Kingdom. As a result, the country's official name changed to the United Kingdom of Great Britain and Northern Ireland.

The modern history of the UK began in the 18th century when the British empire began to develop, despite the loss in 1783 of its 13 North American colonies which became the core of the modern United States. The other major event occurred in the late 18th century, when the UK became the first country to industrialize its economy.

The British empire broke up after World War II (1939–45), though the UK still administers many small, mainly island, territories around the world. The empire was transformed into the Commonwealth of Nations, a free association of independent countries which numbered 54 in 2001.

The UK retained an important world role through the Commonwealth and the United Nations, both diplomatically and militarily. For example, in 2001, it played a prominent role in creating the broad alliance to counter international terrorism following the attacks on the United States. However, it recognized that its economic future lay within Europe. As a result, it became a member of the European Economic Community (now the European Union) in 1973. In the early 2000s, most people accepted the importance of the EU to the UK's economic future. But some feared a loss of British identity should the EU ever evolve into a political federation.

The UK is a major industrial and trading nation. It lacks natural resources apart from coal, iron ore, oil and natural gas, and has to import most of the materials it needs for its industries. The UK also has to import food, because it produces only about two-thirds of the food it needs. In the first half of the 20th century, Britain was a major exporter of cars, ships, steel and textiles. But many industries have suffered from competition from other countries, with lower labour costs. Today, industries have to use high-technology in order to compete on the world market.

The UK is one of the world's most urbanized countries, and agriculture employs only 1% of the people. Production is high because of the use of scientific methods and modern machinery. However, in the early 21st century, especially following the outbreak of foot-and-mouth disease in 2001, questions were raised about the future of rural industries. Major crops include barley, potatoes, sugar beet and wheat. Sheep are the leading livestock, but beef and dairy cattle, pigs and poultry are also important. Fishing is another major activity and the UK is one of the largest fishing countries in the EU. Important catches include cod, haddock, plaice and mackerel.

Service industries play a major part in the UK's economy. Financial and insurance services bring in much-needed foreign exchange, while tourism has become a major earner.

AREA 243,368 SQ KM [94,202 SQ MI] **POPULATION** 59,648,000
CAPITAL (POPULATION) LONDON (8,089,000)
GOVERNMENT CONSTITUTIONAL MONARCHY
ETHNIC GROUPS WHITE 94%, ASIAN INDIAN 1%, PAKISTANI 1%, WEST INDIAN 1%
LANGUAGES ENGLISH (OFFICIAL), WELSH, GAELIC
RELIGIONS ANGLICAN 57%, ROMAN CATHOLIC 13%, PRESBYTERIAN 7%, METHODIST 4%, BAPTIST 1%, ISLAM 1%, JUDAISM, HINDUISM, SIKHISM
CURRENCY POUND STERLING = 100 PENCE

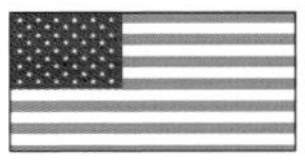

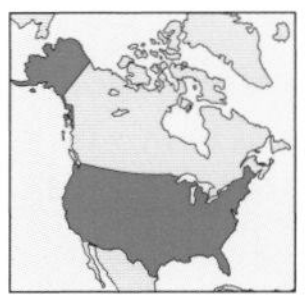

UNITED STATES OF AMERICA

GEOGRAPHY The United States of America is the world's fourth largest country in area and the third largest in population. It contains 50 states, 48 of which lie between Canada and Mexico, plus Alaska in north-western North America, and Hawaii, a group of volcanic islands in the North Pacific Ocean. Densely populated coastal plains lie to the east and south of the Appalachian Mountains. The central lowlands drained by the Mississippi–Missouri rivers stretch from the Appalachians to the Rocky Mountains in the west. The Pacific region contains fertile valleys, separated by mountain ranges.

The climate varies greatly, ranging from the Arctic cold of Alaska to the intense heat of Death Valley, a bleak desert in California. Of the 48 states between Canada and Mexico, winters are cold and snowy in the north, but mild in the south, a region which is often called the 'Sun Belt'.

POLITICS & ECONOMY The first people in North America, the ancestors of the Native Americans (or American Indians) arrived perhaps 40,000 years ago from Asia. Although Vikings probably reached North America 1,000 years ago, European exploration proper did not begin until the late 15th century.

The first Europeans to settle in large numbers were the British, who founded settlements on the eastern coast in the early 17th century. British rule ended in the War of ndependence (1775–83). The country expanded in 1803 when a vast territory in the south and west was acquired through the Louisiana Purchase, while the border with Mexico was fixed in the mid-19th century. The Civil War (1861–5) ended slavery and the serious threat that the nation might split into two parts. In the late 19th century, the West was opened up, while immigrants flooded in from Europe and elsewhere.

During the late 19th and early 20th centuries, industrialization led to the United States becoming the world's leading economic superpower and a pioneer in science and technology. Because of its economic strength, it took on the mantle of the champion of Western democracy. The fall of Communism and the break-up of the Soviet Union left the US as the world's only real

superpower. But the attacks on New York City and Washington, D.C., on 11 September 2001, demonstrated the vulnerability of the country to the threat of terrorists or rogue states. The response of the government was vigorous, in creating an international alliance to combat terrorism and any nation that aids terrorists.

The United States has the world's largest economy in terms of the total value of its production. Although agriculture employs only 2% of the people, farming is highly mechanized and scientific, and the United States leads the world in farm production. Major products include beef and dairy cattle, together with such crops as cotton, fruits, groundnuts, maize, potatoes, soya beans, tobacco and wheat.

The country's natural resources include oil, natural gas and coal. There are also a wide range of metal ores which are used in manufacturing industries, together with timber, especially from the forests of the Pacific north-west. Manufacturing is the single most important activity, employing about 17% of the population. Major products include vehicles, food products, chemicals, machinery, printed goods, metal products and scientific instruments. California is now the leading manufacturing state. Many southern states, petroleum rich and climatically favoured, have also become highly prosperous in recent years.

AREA 9,372,610 sq km [3,618,765 sq mi] **POPULATION** 278,059,000
CAPITAL (POPULATION) Washington, D.C. (4,466,000)
GOVERNMENT Federal republic
ETHNIC GROUPS White 83%, African American 12%, Asian 3%, other races 2%
LANGUAGES English (official), Spanish, more than 30 others
RELIGIONS Protestant 56%, Roman Catholic 28%, Islam 2%, Judaism 2% **CURRENCY** US dollar = 100 cents

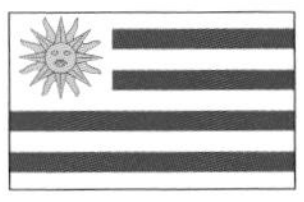

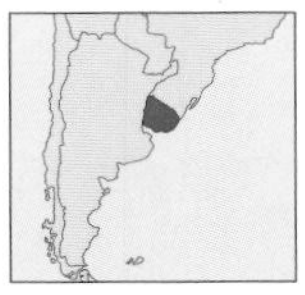

URUGUAY

GEOGRAPHY Uruguay is South America's second smallest independent country after Suriname. The land consists mainly of flat plains and hills. The River Uruguay, which forms the country's western border, flows into the Río de la Plata, a large estuary which leads into the South Atlantic Ocean.

Uruguay has a mild climate, with rain in every month, though droughts sometimes occur. Summers are pleasantly warm, especially near the coast. The weather remains relatively mild throughout the winter.

POLITICS & ECONOMY In 1726, Spanish settlers founded Montevideo in order to halt the Portuguese gaining influence in the area. By the late 18th century, Spaniards had settled in most of the country. Uruguay became part of a colony called the Viceroyalty of La Plata, which also included Argentina, Paraguay, and parts of Bolivia, Brazil and Chile. In 1820 Brazil annexed Uruguay, ending Spanish rule. In 1825, Uruguayans, supported by Argentina, began a struggle for independence. Finally, in 1828, Brazil and Argentina recognized Uruguay as an independent republic. Social and economic developments were slow in the 19th century, but, from 1903, Uruguay became stable and democratic.

From the 1950s, economic problems caused unrest. Terrorist groups, notably the Tupumaros, carried out murders and kidnappings. The army crushed the Tupumaros in 1972, but the army took over the government in 1973. Military rule continued until 1984 when elections were held. Julio Maria Sanguinetti, who led Uruguay back to civilian rule, was re-elected president in 1994. He was succeeded in 2000 by Jorge Batlle of the incumbent Colorado Party.

The World Bank classifies Uruguay as an 'upper-middle-income' developing country. Agriculture employs only 5% of the people, but farm products, notably hides and leather goods, beef and wool, are the leading exports, while the leading manufacturing industries process farm products. The main crops include maize, potatoes, wheat and sugar beet. Uruguay depends largely on hydro-electric power for energy and exports electricity to Argentina.

AREA 177,410 sq km [68,498 sq mi] **POPULATION** 3,360,000
CAPITAL (POPULATION) Montevideo (1,379,000)
GOVERNMENT Multiparty republic
ETHNIC GROUPS White 88%, Mestizo 8%, Mulatto or Black 4%
LANGUAGES Spanish (official)
RELIGIONS Roman Catholic 66%, Protestant 2%, Judaism 1%
CURRENCY Uruguay peso = 100 centésimos

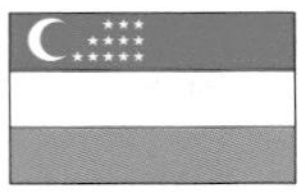

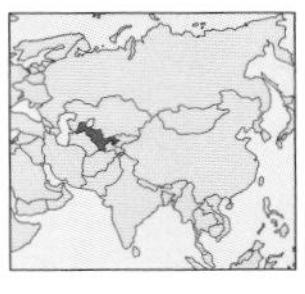

UZBEKISTAN

GEOGRAPHY The Republic of Uzbekistan is one of the five republics in Central Asia which were once part of the Soviet Union. Plains cover most of western Uzbekistan, with highlands in the east. The main rivers, the Amu (or Amu Darya) and Syr (or Syr Darya), drain into the Aral Sea. So much water has been taken from these rivers to irrigate the land that the Aral Sea shrank from 66,900 sq km [25,830 sq mi] in 1960 to 33,642 sq km [12,989 sq mi] in 1993. The dried-up lake area has become desert, like much of the rest of the country.

Uzbekistan has a continental climate. The winters are cold, but the temperatures soar in the summer months. The west is extremely arid, with an average annual rainfall of about 200 mm [8 in].

POLITICS & ECONOMY Russia took the area in the 19th century. After the Russian Revolution of 1917, the Communists took over and, in 1924, they set up the Uzbek Soviet Socialist Republic. Under Communism, all aspects of Uzbek life were controlled and religious worship was discouraged. But education, health, housing and transport were improved. In the late 1980s, the people demanded more freedom and, in 1990, the government stated that its laws overruled those of the Soviet Union. Uzbekistan became independent in 1991 when the Soviet Union broke up, but it retained links with Russia through the Commonwealth of Independent States. Islam Karimov, leader of the People's Democratic Party (formerly the Communist Party), was elected president in December 1991. In 1992–3, many opposition leaders were arrested because the government said that they threatened national stability. In 1994–5, the PDP was victorious in national elections and, in 1995, a referendum extended Karimov's term in office until 2000, when he was again re-elected. In 2001, Karimov declared his support for the United States in its campaign against terrorist bases in Afghanistan.

The World Bank classifies Uzbekistan as a 'lower-middle-income' developing country and the government still controls most economic activity. The country produces coal, copper, gold, oil and natural gas.

AREA 447,400 sq km [172,740 sq mi] **POPULATION** 25,155,000
CAPITAL (POPULATION) Tashkent (2,118,000)
GOVERNMENT Socialist republic **ETHNIC GROUPS** Uzbek 80%, Russian 5%, Tajik 5%, Kazakh 3%, Tatar 2%, Kara-Kalpak 2%
LANGUAGES Uzbek (official), Russian **RELIGIONS** Islam 88%, Eastern Orthodox 9% **CURRENCY** Som = 100 tyiyn

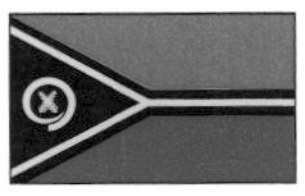

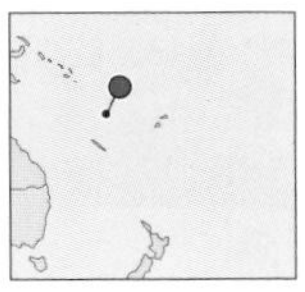

VANUATU

The Republic of Vanuatu, formerly the Anglo-French Condominium of the New Hebrides, became independent in 1980. It consists of a chain of 80 islands in the South Pacific Ocean. Its economy is based on agriculture and it exports copra, beef and veal, timber and cocoa.

AREA 447,400 sq km [4,707 sq mi]
POPULATION 193,000 **CAPITAL** Port-Vila

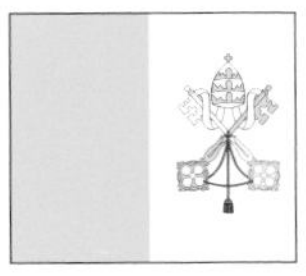

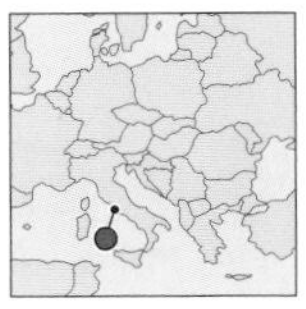

VATICAN CITY

Vatican City State, the world's smallest independent nation, is an enclave on the west bank of the River Tiber in Rome. It forms an independent base for the Holy See, the governing body of the Roman Catholic Church.

AREA 0.44 sq km [0.17 sq mi]
POPULATION 890

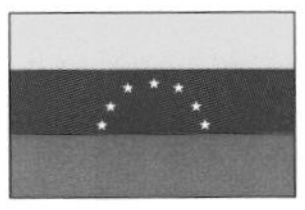

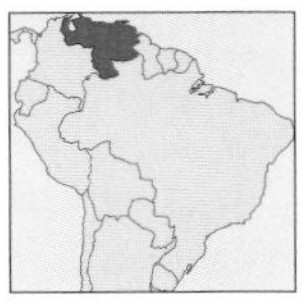

VENEZUELA

GEOGRAPHY The Bolivarian Republic of Venezuela, in northern South America, contains the Maracaibo lowlands around the oil-rich Lake Maracaibo in the west. Andean ranges enclose the lowlands and extend across most of northern Venezuela. The Orinoco river basin, containing tropical grasslands called *llanos*, lies between the northern highlands and the Guiana Highlands in the south-east. The Orinoco is Venezuela's longest river.

Venezuela has a tropical climate. Temperatures are high throughout the year on the lowlands, though the mountains are much cooler. The rainfall is heaviest in the mountains. But much of the country has a marked dry season between December and April.

POLITICS & ECONOMY In the early 19th century, Venezuelans, such as Simón Bolívar and Francisco de Miranda, began a struggle against Spanish rule. Venezuela declared its independence in 1811. But it only became truly independent in 1821, when the Spanish were defeated in a battle near Valencia.

The development of Venezuela in the 19th and the first half of the 20th centuries was marred by instability, violence and periods of harsh dictatorial rule. But Venezuela has had elected governments since 1958. The country has greatly benefited from its oil resources which were first exploited in 1917. In 1960, Venezuela helped to form OPEC (the Organization of Petroleum Exporting Countries) and, in 1976, the government of Venezuela took control of the entire oil industry. In 1999, Hugo Chavez, who had staged an unsuccessful coup in 1992, was elected president and a new constitution, giving the president considerably more power, was adopted. In April 2002, Chavez survived an attempted coup.

The World Bank classifies Venezuela as an 'upper-middle-income' developing country. Oil accounts for 80% of the exports. Other exports include bauxite and aluminium, iron ore and farm products. Agriculture employs 13% of people and cattle ranching is important; dairy cattle and poultry are also raised. Major crops include bananas, cassava, citrus fruits, coffee and rice. The chief industry is petroleum refining. Other manufactures include aluminium, cement, processed food, steel and textiles.

AREA 912,050 sq km [352,143 sq mi] **POPULATION** 23,917,000
CAPITAL (POPULATION) Caracas (1,975,000)
GOVERNMENT Federal republic **ETHNIC GROUPS** Mestizo 67%, White 21%, Black 10%, Amerindian 2% **LANGUAGES** Spanish (official), Goajiro **RELIGIONS** Roman Catholic 96%
CURRENCY Bolívar = 100 céntimos

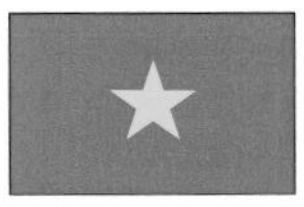

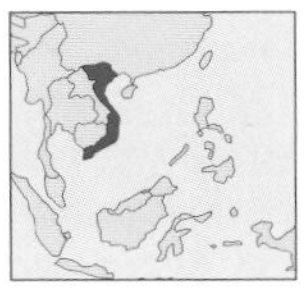

VIETNAM

GEOGRAPHY The Socialist Republic of Vietnam occupies an S-shaped strip of land facing the South China Sea in South-east Asia. The coastal plains include two densely populated, fertile delta regions: the Red (Hong) delta facing the Gulf of Tonkin in the north, and the Mekong delta in the south.

Vietnam has a tropical climate, though the driest months of January to March are a little cooler than the wet, hot summer months, when monsoon winds blow from the south-west. Typhoons (cyclones) sometimes hit the coast, causing much damage.

POLITICS & ECONOMY China dominated Vietnam for a thousand years before AD 939, when a Vietnamese state was founded. The French took over the area between the 1850s and 1880s. They ruled Vietnam as part of French Indo-China, which also included Cambodia and Laos.

Japan conquered Vietnam during World War II (1939–45). In 1946, war broke out between a nationalist group, called the Vietminh, and the French colonial government. France withdrew in 1954 and Vietnam was divided into a Communist North Vietnam, led by the Vietminh leader, Ho Chi Minh, and a non-Communist South.

A force called the Viet Cong rebelled against South Vietnam's government in 1957 and a war began, which gradually increased in intensity. The United States aided the South, but after it withdrew in 1975, South Vietnam surrendered. In 1976, the united Vietnam became a Socialist Republic.

Vietnamese troops intervened in Cambodia in 1978 to defeat the Communist Khmer Rouge government, but it withdrew its troops in 1989. In the 1990s, Vietnam began to introduce reforms. In 1995, the United States opened an embassy in Hanoi and, in 2000, a major trade pact was agreed by the countries.

The World Bank classifies Vietnam as a 'low-income' developing country and agriculture employs 67% of the population. The main food crop is rice. The country also produces chromium, oil (which was discovered off the south coast in 1986), phosphates and tin.

AREA 331,689 sq km [128,065 sq mi] **POPULATION** 79,939,000
CAPITAL (POPULATION) Hanoi (3,056,000)
GOVERNMENT Socialist republic **ETHNIC GROUPS** Vietnamese 87%, Tho (Tay), Chinese (Hoa), Tai, Khmer, Muong, Nung
LANGUAGES Vietnamese (official), Chinese
RELIGIONS Buddhism 55%, Roman Catholic 7%
CURRENCY Dong = 10 hao = 100 xu

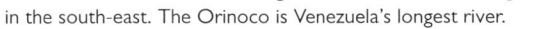

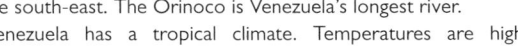

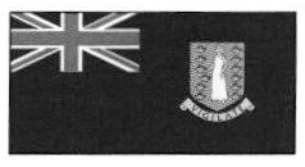
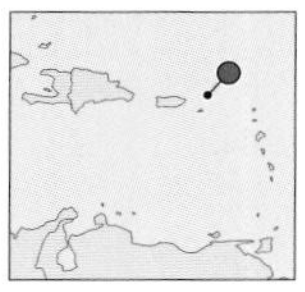

VIRGIN ISLANDS, BRITISH

The British Virgin Islands, the most northerly of the Lesser Antilles, are a British overseas territory, with a substantial measure of self-government.

AREA 153 sq km [59 sq mi]
POPULATION 21,000 **CAPITAL** Road Town

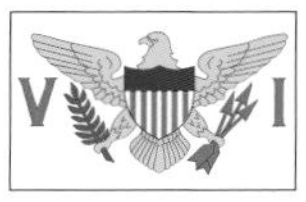
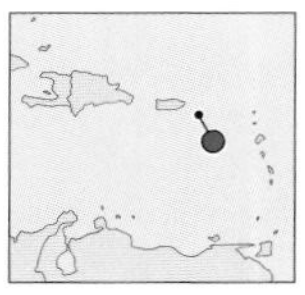

VIRGIN ISLANDS, US

The Virgin Islands of the United States, a group of three islands and 65 small islets, are a self-governing US territory. Purchased from Denmark in 1917, its residents are US citizens and they elect a non-voting delegate to the US House of Representatives.

AREA 340 sq km [130 sq mi]
POPULATION 122,000 **CAPITAL** Charlotte Amalie

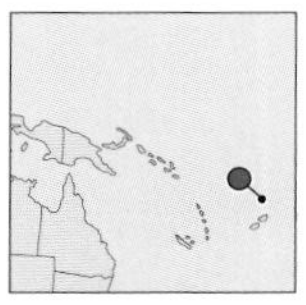

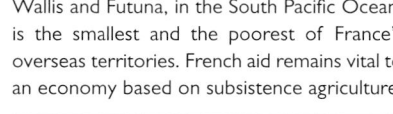

WALLIS AND FUTUNA

Wallis and Futuna, in the South Pacific Ocean, is the smallest and the poorest of France's overseas territories. French aid remains vital to an economy based on subsistence agriculture.

AREA 200 sq km [77 sq mi]
POPULATION 15,000 **CAPITAL** Mata-Utu

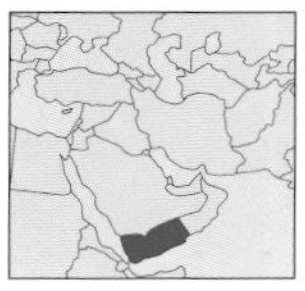

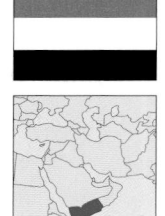

YEMEN

GEOGRAPHY The Republic of Yemen faces the Red Sea and the Gulf of Aden in the south-western corner of the Arabian peninsula. Behind the narrow coastal plain along the Red Sea, the land rises to a mountain region called High Yemen. The climate ranges from hot and often humid conditions on the coast to the cooler highlands. Most of the country is arid. The south coasts are particularly hot and humid, especially from June to September.

POLITICS & ECONOMY After World War I, northern Yemen, which had been ruled by Turkey, began to evolve into a separate state from the south, where Britain was in control. Britain withdrew in 1967 and a left-wing government took power in the south. In North Yemen, the monarchy was abolished in 1962 and the country became a republic.

Clashes occurred between the traditionalist Yemen Arab Republic in the north and the formerly British Marxist People's Democratic Republic of Yemen but, in 1990, the two Yemens merged to form a single country. Further conflict occurred in 1994, when southern secessionist forces were defeated. In 1998 and 1999, militants in the Aden-Abyan Islamic army sought to destabilize the country. In 2000, suicide bombers, thought to be part of the al Qaida network, steered a craft into a US destroyer in Aden harbour, killing 17 sailors.

The World Bank classifies Yemen as a 'low-income' developing country. Agriculture employs up to 63% of the people. Herders raise sheep and other animals, while farmers grow such crops as barley, fruits, wheat and vegetables in highland valleys and around oases. Cash crops include coffee and cotton.

Imported oil is refined at Aden and petroleum extraction began in the north-west in the 1980s. Handicrafts, leather goods and textiles are manufactured. Remittances from Yemenis abroad are a major source of revenue.

AREA 527,970 sq km [203,849 sq mi] **POPULATION** 18,078,000 **CAPITAL (POPULATION)** Sana' (972,000) **GOVERNMENT** Multiparty republic **ETHNIC GROUPS** Arab 96%, Somali 1% **LANGUAGES** Arabic (official) **RELIGIONS** Islam **CURRENCY** Rial = 100 fils

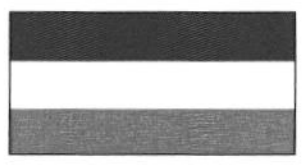
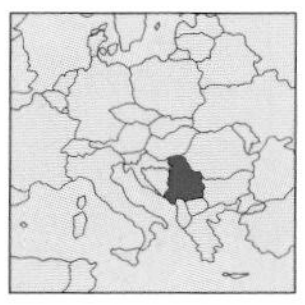

YUGOSLAVIA

GEOGRAPHY The Federal Republic of Yugoslavia consists of Serbia and Montenegro, two of the six republics which made up the former country of Yugoslavia until it broke up in the early 1990s. In 2002, the government announced plans to give both republics semi-independence under the name of the Union of Serbia and Montenegro.

Behind the coastline on the Adriatic Sea lies an upland region, including the Dinaric Alps and part of the Balkan Mountains. The Pannonian plains, which are drained by the River Danube, are in the north.

The coast has a Mediterranean climate. The interior highlands have bitterly cold winters and cool summers. The wettest season is the summer, but there is also plenty of sunshine.

POLITICS & ECONOMY People who became known as the South Slavs began to move into the region around 1,500 years ago. Each group, including the Serbs and Croats, founded its own state. But, by the 15th century, foreign countries controlled the region. Serbia and Montenegro were under the Turkish Ottoman empire.

In the 19th century, many Slavs worked for independence and Slavic unity. In 1914, Austria-Hungary declared war on Serbia, blaming it for the assassination of Archduke Francis Ferdinand of Austria–Hungary. This led to World War I and the defeat of Austria–Hungary. In 1918, the South Slavs united in the Kingdom of the Serbs, Croats and Slovenes, which consisted of Bosnia-Herzegovina, Croatia, Dalmatia, Montenegro, Serbia and Slovenia. The country was renamed Yugoslavia in 1929. Germany occupied Yugoslavia during World War II, but partisans, including a Communist force led by Josip Broz Tito, fought the invaders.

From 1945, the Communists controlled the country, which was called the Federal People's Republic of Yugoslavia. But after Tito's death in 1980, the country faced many problems. In 1990, non-Communist parties were permitted and non-Communists won majorities in elections in all but Serbia and Montenegro, where Socialists (former Communists) won control. Yugoslavia split apart in 1991–2 with Bosnia-Herzegovina, Croatia, Macedonia and Slovenia proclaiming their independence. The two remaining republics of Serbia and Montenegro became the new Yugoslavia.

Fighting broke out in Croatia and Bosnia-Herzegovina as rival groups struggled for power. In 1992, the United Nations withdrew recognition of Yugoslavia because of its failure to halt atrocities committed by Serbs living in Croatia and Bosnia. In 1995, Yugoslavia was involved in the talks that led to the Dayton Peace Accord, which brought peace to Bosnia-Herzegovina. But the issue of Yugoslav repression of minorities flared up again in 1998 in Kosovo, a province where the majority are ethnic Albanians. In response to Serb ethnic cleansing, NATO forces began an offensive against Yugoslavia. A Serb withdrawal was agreed in June 1999. Elections in 2000 resulted in defeat for Slobodan Milosevic, who was succeeded by Vojislav Kostunica. In 2002, Milosevic, whom many regarded as responsible for much of the conflict in the 1990s, faced charges of crimes against humanity at the UN War Crimes Tribunal in The Hague.

Under Communist rule, manufacturing became increasingly important in Yugoslavia. But in the early 1990s, the World Bank classified Yugoslavia as a 'lower-middle-income' economy. Its resources include bauxite, coal, copper and other metals, together with oil and natural gas. Manufactures include aluminium, machinery, plastics, steel, textiles and vehicles. Chief exports are manufactures, but agriculture remains important. Crops include fruits, maize, potatoes, tobacco and wheat. Cattle, pigs and sheep are reared.

AREA 102,170 sq km [39,449 sq mi] **POPULATION** 10,677,000
CAPITAL (POPULATION) Belgrade (1,598,000)
GOVERNMENT Federal republic
ETHNIC GROUPS Serb 62%, Albanian 17%, Montenegrin 5%, Hungarian, Muslim, Croat
LANGUAGES Serbo-Croat (official), Albanian
RELIGIONS Christianity (mainly Serbian Orthodox), Islam
CURRENCY Yugoslav new dinar = 100 paras

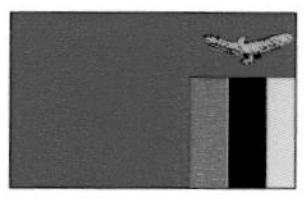
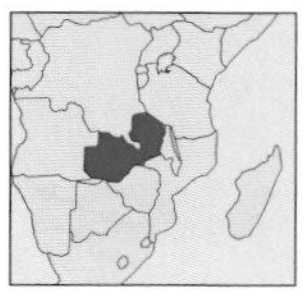

ZAMBIA

GEOGRAPHY The Republic of Zambia is a landlocked country in southern Africa. Zambia lies on the plateau that makes up most of southern Africa. Much of the land is between 900 m to 1,500 m [2,950 ft and 4,920 ft] above sea level. The Muchinga Mountains in the north-east rise above this flat land. Lakes include Bangweulu, which is entirely within Zambia, together with parts of lakes Mweru and Tanganyika in the north.

Zambia lies in the tropics, but temperatures are moderated by the altitude. The rainy season runs from November to March.

POLITICS & ECONOMY European contact with Zambia began in the 19th century, when the explorer David Livingstone crossed the River Zambezi. In the 1890s, the British South Africa Company, set up by Cecil Rhodes (1853–1902), the British financier and statesman, made treaties with local chiefs and gradually took over the area. In 1911, the Company named the area Northern Rhodesia. In 1924, Britain took over the government of the country.

In 1953, Britain formed a federation of Northern Rhodesia, Southern Rhodesia (now Zimbabwe) and Nyasaland (now Malawi). Because of African opposition, the federation was dissolved in 1963 and Northern Rhodesia became independent as Zambia in 1964. Kenneth Kaunda became president and one-party rule was introduced in 1972. However, a new constitution was adopted in 1990 and, in 1991, Kaunda's party was defeated and Frederick Chiluba became president. Chiluba was re-elected in 1996. Chiluba stood down in 2001 and his party's candidate, Levy Mwanawasa, was elected president.

Copper is the main resource, accounting for 80% of Zambia's exports in 1997. Zambia also produces cobalt, lead, zinc and gemstones. Agriculture employs 69% of workers, as compared with 4% in industry and mining. Major food crops include cassava, fruits and vegetables, maize, millet and sorghum, while cash crops include coffee, sugar cane and tobacco. The production of copper products in the leading industrial activity.

AREA 752,614 sq km [290,586 sq mi] **POPULATION** 9,770,000
CAPITAL (POPULATION) Lusaka (982,000)
GOVERNMENT Multiparty republic
ETHNIC GROUPS Bemba 36%, Maravi (Nyanja) 18%, Tonga 15%
LANGUAGES English (official), Bemba, Nyanja, and about 70 others
RELIGIONS Christianity 68%, Islam, Hinduism
CURRENCY Kwacha = 100 ngwee

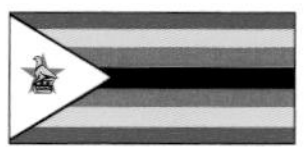
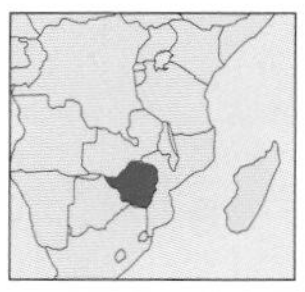

ZIMBABWE

GEOGRAPHY The Republic of Zimbabwe is a landlocked country in southern Africa. Most of the country lies on a high plateau between the Zambezi and Limpopo rivers between 900 m to 1,500 m [2,950 ft and 4,920 ft] above sea level.

From October to March, the weather is hot and wet. But in the winter, daily temperatures can vary greatly. Frosts have been recorded between June and August. The climate varies according to the altitude.

POLITICS & ECONOMY The Shona people became dominant in the region about 1,000 years ago. The British South Africa Company, under the statesman Cecil Rhodes (1853–1902), occupied the area in the 1890s, after obtaining mineral rights from local chiefs. The area was named Rhodesia and later Southern Rhodesia. It became a self-governing British colony in 1923. Between 1953 and 1963, Southern and Northern Rhodesia (now Zambia) were joined to Nyasaland (Malawi) in the Central African Federation.

In 1965, the European government of Southern Rhodesia (then called Rhodesia) declared their country independent but Britain refused to accept this. Finally, after a civil war, the country became legally independent in 1980, though rivalries between the Shona and Ndebele people threatened stability. Order was restored when the Shona prime minister, Robert Mugabe, brought his Ndebele rivals into his government. In 1987, Mugabe became the country's executive president and, in 1991, the government renounced its Marxist ideology. Mugabe was re-elected president in 1990 and 1996. During the late 1990s, Mugabe threatened to seize white-owned farms without paying compensation to the owners. Despite international pressure, landless 'war veterans' began to occupy white farms. The situation worsened in the early 2000s, resulting in violence and murder. In 2002, Mugabe was re-elected president amid accusations of electoral irregularities. As a result, the Commonwealth suspended Zimbabwe's membership for 12 months.

The World Bank classifies Zimbabwe as a 'low-income' developing country. The country has valuable mineral resources and mining accounts for a fifth of the country's exports. Agriculture employs 27% of working people. Maize is the chief food crop, while cash crops include cotton, sugar and tobacco. Cattle ranching is another important activity.

AREA 390,579 sq km [150,873 sq mi] **POPULATION** 11,365,000
CAPITAL (POPULATION) Harare (1,189,000)
GOVERNMENT Multiparty republic
ETHNIC GROUPS Shona 71%, Ndebele 16%, other Bantu-speaking Africans 11%, White 1%, Asian 1%
LANGUAGES English (official), Shona, Ndebele
RELIGIONS Christianity 45%, traditional beliefs 40%
CURRENCY Zimbabwe dollar = 100 cents

INTRODUCTION TO WORLD GEOGRAPHY

THE UNIVERSE	2	WATER AND VEGETATION	18	AGRICULTURE	32
THE SOLAR SYSTEM	4	THE NATURAL ENVIRONMENT	20	ENERGY	34
TIME AND MOTION	6	PEOPLE AND THE ENVIRONMENT	22	MINERALS	36
OCEANS	8			MANUFACTURING	38
GEOLOGY	10	POPULATION	24	TRADE	40
LANDFORMS	12	CITIES	26	HEALTH	42
ATMOSPHERE AND WEATHER	14	THE HUMAN FAMILY	28	WEALTH	44
CLIMATE	16	CONFLICT AND CO-OPERATION	30	STANDARDS OF LIVING	46

THE UNIVERSE

For more information:
4 Orbits of the planets
  Planetary data

About 15 billion years ago, time and space began with the most colossal explosion in cosmic history: the so-called 'Big Bang' that is believed to have initiated the universe. According to current theory, in the first millionth of a second of its existence it expanded from a dimensionless point of infinite mass and density into a fireball about 30 billion kilometres across; and it has been expanding ever since.

It took almost a million years for the primal fireball to cool enough for atoms to form. They were mostly hydrogen, still the most abundant material in the universe. But the new matter was not evenly distributed around the young universe, and a few billion years later atoms in relatively dense regions began to cling together under the influence of gravity, forming distinct masses of gas separated by vast expanses of empty space. To begin with, these first proto-galaxies were dark places: the universe had cooled. But gravitational attraction continued, condensing matter into coherent lumps inside the galactic gas clouds. About 3 billion years later, some of these masses had contracted so much that internal pressure produced the high temperatures necessary to bring about nuclear fusion: the first stars were born.

There were several generations of stars, each feeding on the wreckage of its extinct predecessors as well as the original galactic gas swirls. With each new generation, progressively larger atoms were forged in stellar furnaces and the galaxy's range of elements, once restricted to hydrogen, grew larger. About 10 billion years after the Big Bang, a star formed on the outskirts of our galaxy with enough matter left over to create a retinue of planets. Nearly 5 billion years after that human beings evolved.

The Sun is one of more than 100 billion stars in the home galaxy alone. Our galaxy, in turn, forms part of a local group of approximately 30 similar structures, some much larger than our own; there are at least 100 billion other galaxies in the universe as a whole. The most distant ever observed, a highly energetic galactic core known only as quasar PC 1247 +3406, lies about 12 billion light-years away.

Life of a Star

For most of its existence, a star produces energy by the nuclear fusion of hydrogen into helium at its core. The duration of this hydrogen-burning period – known as the main sequence – depends on the star's mass; the greater the mass, the higher the core temperatures and the sooner the star's supply of hydrogen is exhausted. Dim, dwarf stars consume their hydrogen slowly, eking it out over 1,000 billion years or more. The Sun, like other stars of its mass, should spend about 10 billion years on the main sequence; since it was formed less than 5 billion years ago, it still has half its life left.

Once all a star's core hydrogen has been fused into helium, nuclear activity moves outwards into layers of unconsumed hydrogen. For a time, energy production sharply increases: the star grows hotter and expands enormously, turning into a so-called red giant. Its energy output will increase a thousandfold, and it will swell to a hundred times its present diameter.

After a few hundred million years, helium in the core will become sufficiently compressed to initiate a new cycle of nuclear fusion: from helium to carbon. The star will contract somewhat, before beginning its last expansion, in the Sun's case engulfing the Earth and perhaps Mars. In this bloated condition, the Sun's outer layers will break off into space, leaving a tiny inner core, mainly of carbon, that shrinks progressively under the force of its own gravity: dwarf stars can attain a density more than 10,000 times that of normal matter, with crushing surface gravities to match. Gradually, the nuclear fires will die down, and the Sun will reach its terminal stage: a black dwarf, emitting insignificant amounts of energy.

However, stars more massive than the Sun may undergo another transformation. The additional mass allows gravitational collapse to continue indefinitely: eventually, all the star's remaining matter shrinks to a point, and its density approaches infinity – a state that will not permit even subatomic structures to survive.

The star has become a black hole: an anomalous 'singularity' in the fabric of space and time. Although vast coruscations of radiation will be emitted by any matter falling into its grasp, the singularity itself has an escape velocity that exceeds the speed of light, and nothing can ever be released from it. Within the boundaries of the black hole, the laws of physics are suspended, but no physicist can ever observe the extraordinary events that may occur.

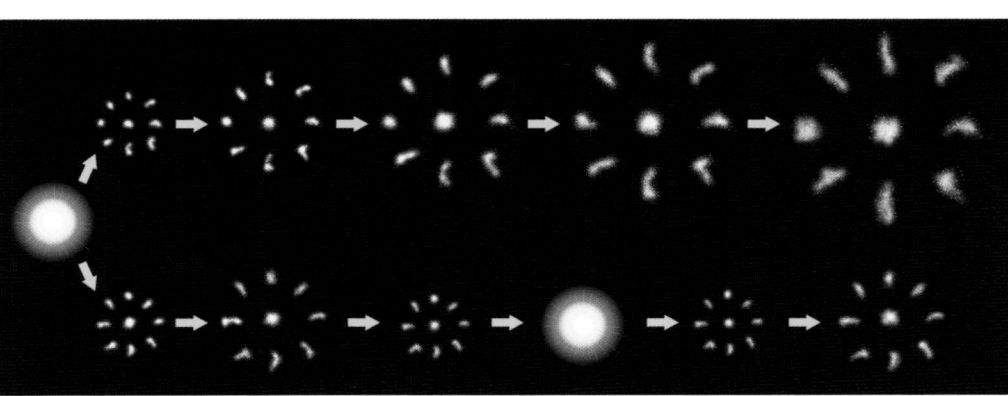

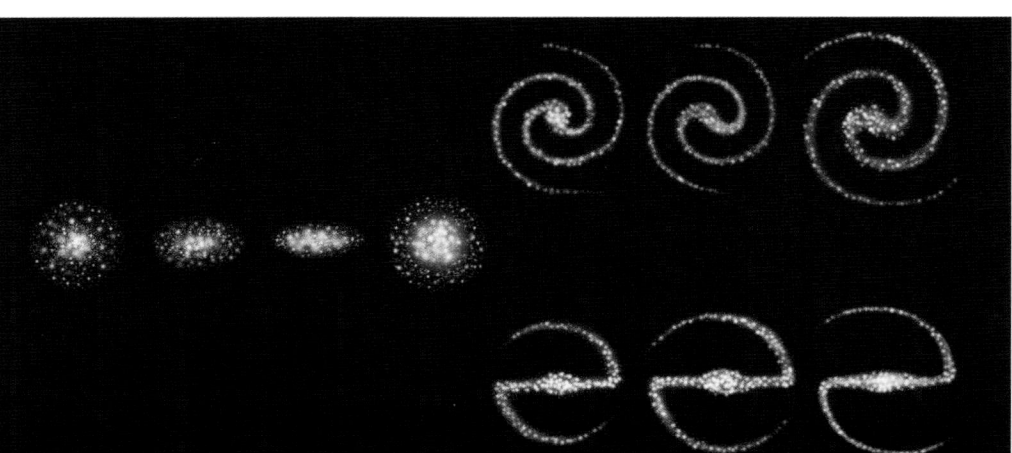

The End of the Universe

The likely fate of the universe is disputed. One theory (*top left*) dictates that the expansion begun at the time of the Big Bang will continue 'indefinitely', with ageing galaxies moving further and further apart in an immense, dark graveyard. Alternatively, gravity may overcome the expansion (*bottom left*). Galaxies will fall back together until everything is again concentrated at a single point, followed by a new Big Bang and a new expansion, in an endlessly repeated cycle.

The first theory is supported by the amount of visible matter in the universe; the second assumes there is enough dark material to bring about the gravitational collapse.

Galactic Structures

Many of the universe's 100 billion galaxies show clear structural patterns, originally classified by the American astronomer Edwin Hubble in 1925. Spiral galaxies like our own (*top row*) have a central, almost spherical bulge and a surrounding disk composed of spiral arms. Barred spirals (*bottom row*) have a central bar of stars across the nucleus, with spiral arms trailing from the ends of the bar. Elliptical galaxies (*far left*) have a uniform appearance, ranging from a flattened disk to a near sphere. So-called SO galaxies (*left row, right*) have a central bulge, but no spiral arms. Most galaxies, however, have no obvious structure at all.

Galaxies also vary enormously in size, from dwarfs only 2,000 light-years across to great assemblies of stars 80 or more times larger.

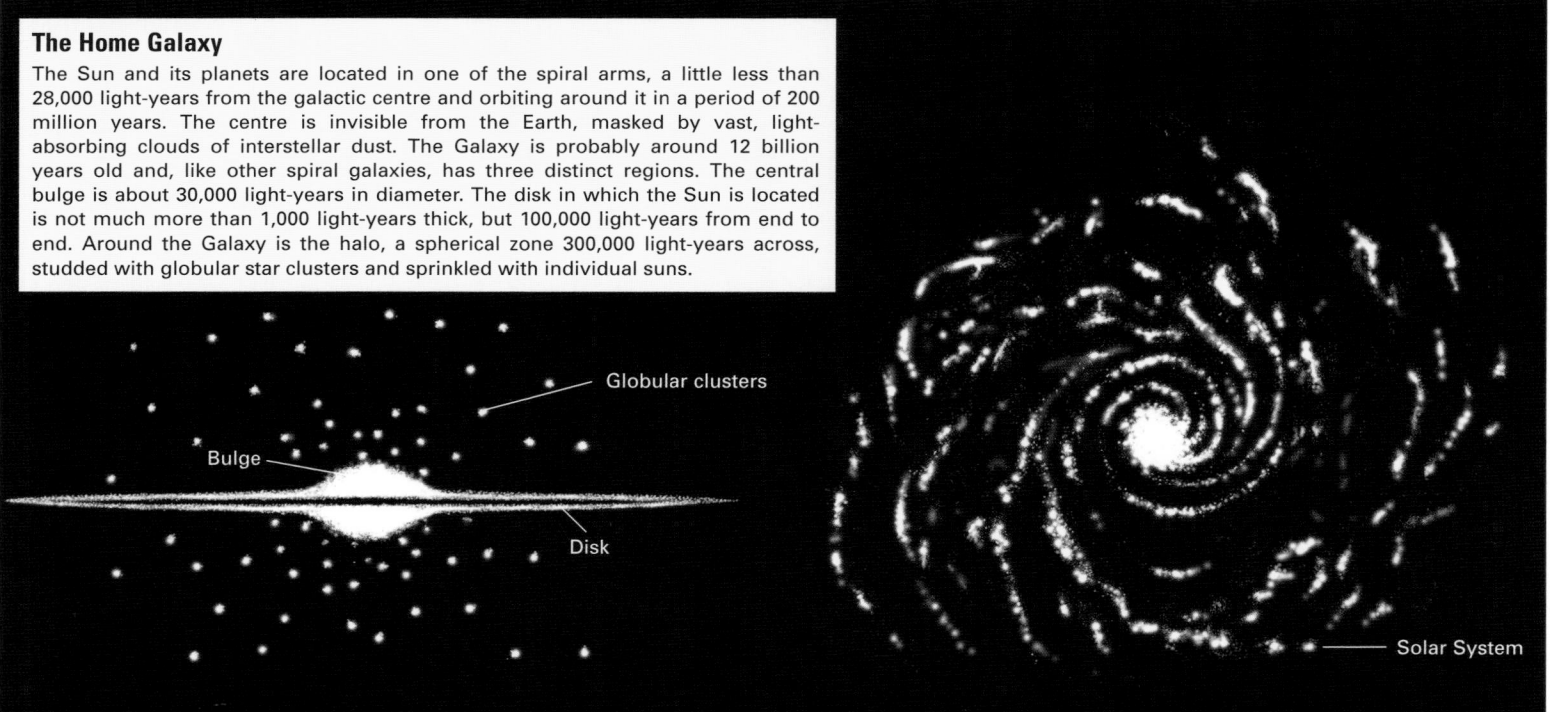

The Home Galaxy

The Sun and its planets are located in one of the spiral arms, a little less than 28,000 light-years from the galactic centre and orbiting around it in a period of 200 million years. The centre is invisible from the Earth, masked by vast, light-absorbing clouds of interstellar dust. The Galaxy is probably around 12 billion years old and, like other spiral galaxies, has three distinct regions. The central bulge is about 30,000 light-years in diameter. The disk in which the Sun is located is not much more than 1,000 light-years thick, but 100,000 light-years from end to end. Around the Galaxy is the halo, a spherical zone 300,000 light-years across, studded with globular star clusters and sprinkled with individual suns.

Globular clusters

Bulge

Disk

Solar System

Star Charts

Star charts are drawn as projections of a vast, hollow sphere with the observer in the middle. Each circle below represents slightly more than one hemisphere, centred on the north and south celestial poles respectively – projections of the Earth's poles in the heavens. At the present era, the north pole is marked by the star Polaris; the south pole has no such convenient reference point.

Astronomical co-ordinates are normally given in terms of 'Right Ascension' for longitude and 'Declination' for latitude or altitude. Since the stars appear to rotate around the Earth once every 24 hours, Right Ascension is measured eastwards – anticlockwise – in hours and minutes and is marked around the edge of the map. One hour is equivalent to 15 angular degrees; zero on the scale is the point at which the Sun crosses the celestial equator at the spring equinox, known to astronomers as the First Point in Aries. Unlike the Sun, stars always rise and set at the same point on the horizon. Declination measures (in degrees) a star's angular distance above or below the celestial equator and is marked on the vertical line.

To use the maps, first choose the one for your hemisphere and hold it with the month at the bottom. The stars in the lower part of the map are then due south (or north, in the southern hemisphere) at about 1 AM local time, not allowing for summer or daylight saving time. Their exact position above the horizon depends on your latitude. The closer to the Equator you live, the higher in the sky these stars will appear. Some additional stars from the map for the other hemisphere will be visible in the lower sky.

Stars near the top of the map will be below the opposite horizon at this date and time but will be visible at other times of the night and year. The sky appears to move anticlockwise around the celestial pole during the course of the day (clockwise in the southern hemisphere), so the same stars will be visible at 11 PM a month earlier.

NORTHERN HEAVENS

SOUTHERN HEAVENS

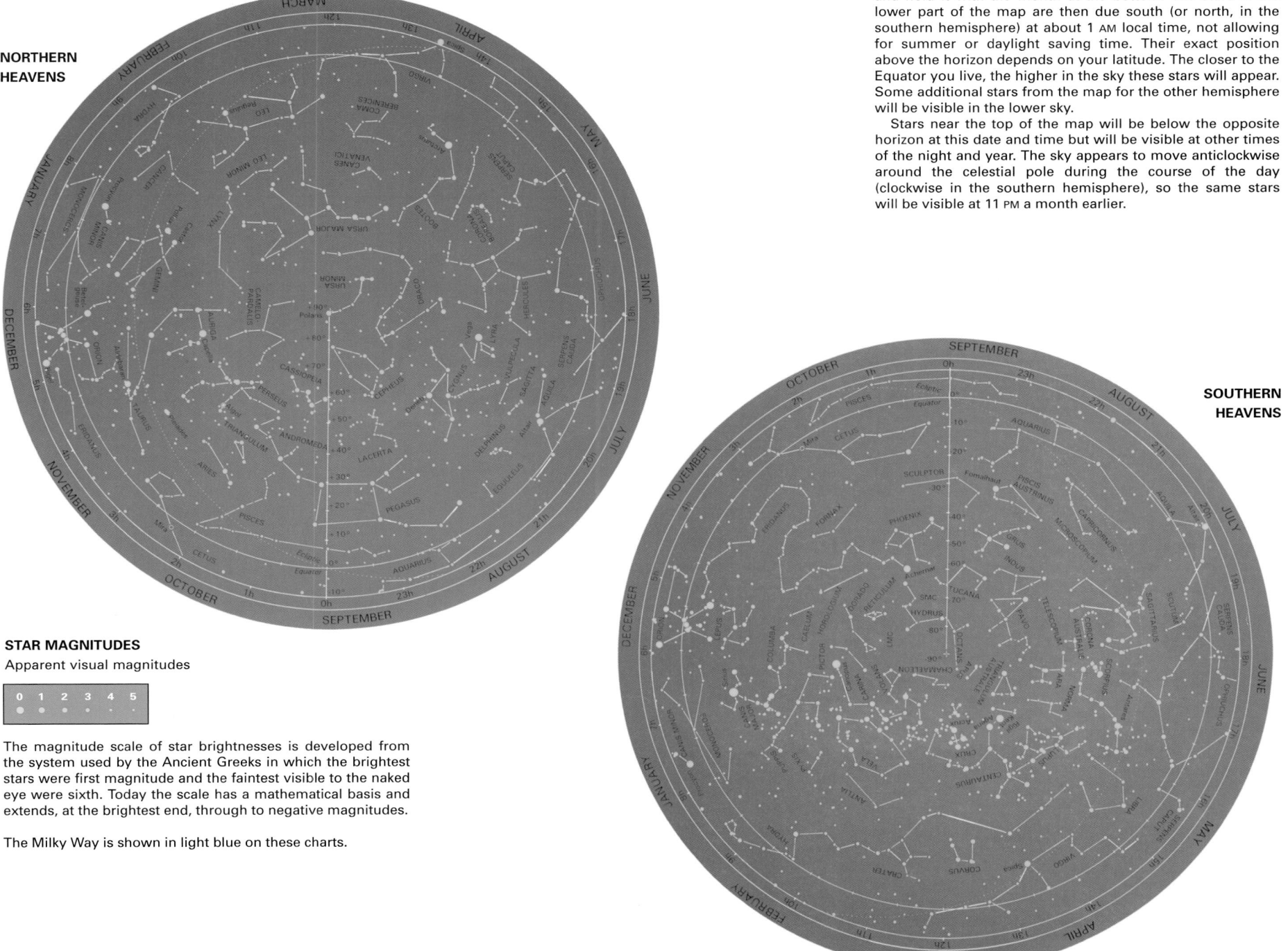

STAR MAGNITUDES
Apparent visual magnitudes

| 0 | 1 | 2 | 3 | 4 | 5 |

The magnitude scale of star brightnesses is developed from the system used by the Ancient Greeks in which the brightest stars were first magnitude and the faintest visible to the naked eye were sixth. Today the scale has a mathematical basis and extends, at the brightest end, through to negative magnitudes.

The Milky Way is shown in light blue on these charts.

THE NEAREST STARS

The 20 nearest stars, excluding the Sun, with their distance from Earth in light-years*

Proxima Centauri	4.25	Many of the nearest stars, like
Alpha Centauri A	4.3	Alpha Centauri A and B, are
Alpha Centauri B	4.3	doubles, orbiting about the
Barnard's Star	6.0	common centre of gravity
Wolf 359	7.8	and to all intents and
Lalande 21185	8.3	purposes equidistant from
Sirius A	8.7	Earth. Many of them are dim
Sirius B	8.7	objects, with no name other
UV Ceti A	8.7	than the designation given
UV Ceti B	8.7	by the astronomers who
Ross 154	9.4	investigated them. However,
Ross 248	10.3	they include Sirius, the
Epsilon Eridani	10.7	brightest star in the sky,
Ross 128	10.9	and Procyon, the seventh
61 Cygni A	11.1	brightest. Both are far larger
61 Cygni B	11.1	than the Sun; of the nearest
Epsilon Indi	11.2	stars, only Epsilon Eridani is
Groombridge 34A	11.2	similar in size and luminosity.
Groombridge 34B	11.2	
L789-6	11.2	* A light-year equals approx.
Procyon A	11.4	9,500,000,000,000 kilometres
Procyon B	11.4	

THE CONSTELLATIONS

The constellations and their English names

Andromeda	Andromeda	Circinus	Compasses	Lacerta	Lizard	Piscis Austrinus	Southern Fish
Antlia	Air Pump	Columba	Dove	Leo	Lion	Puppis	Ship's Stern
Apus	Bird of Paradise	Coma Berenices	Berenice's Hair	Leo Minor	Little Lion	Pyxis	Mariner's Compass
Aquarius	Water Carrier	Corona Australis	Southern Crown	Lepus	Hare	Reticulum	Net
Aquila	Eagle	Corona Borealis	Northern Crown	Libra	Scales	Sagitta	Arrow
Ara	Altar	Corvus	Crow	Lupus	Wolf	Sagittarius	Archer
Aries	Ram	Crater	Cup	Lynx	Lynx	Scorpius	Scorpion
Auriga	Charioteer	Crux	Southern Cross	Lyra	Lyre	Sculptor	Sculptor
Boötes	Herdsman	Cygnus	Swan	Mensa	Table	Scutum	Shield
Caelum	Chisel	Delphinus	Dolphin	Microscopium	Microscope	Serpens	Serpent
Camelopardalis	Giraffe	Dorado	Swordfish	Monoceros	Unicorn	Sextans	Sextant
Cancer	Crab	Draco	Dragon	Musca	Fly	Taurus	Bull
Canes Venatici	Hunting Dogs	Equuleus	Little Horse	Norma	Level	Telescopium	Telescope
Canis Major	Great Dog	Eridanus	Eridanus	Octans	Octant	Triangulum	Triangle
Canis Minor	Little Dog	Fornax	Furnace	Ophiuchus	Serpent Bearer	Triangulum Australe	Southern Triangle
Capricornus	Goat	Gemini	Twins	Orion	Orion	Tucana	Toucan
Carina	Keel	Grus	Crane	Pavo	Peacock	Ursa Major	Great Bear
Cassiopeia	Cassiopeia	Hercules	Hercules	Pegasus	Winged Horse	Ursa Minor	Little Bear
Centaurus	Centaur	Horologium	Clock	Perseus	Perseus	Vela	Sails
Cepheus	Cepheus	Hydra	Water Snake	Phoenix	Phoenix	Virgo	Virgin
Cetus	Whale	Hydrus	Sea Serpent	Pictor	Easel	Volans	Flying Fish
Chamaeleon	Chamaeleon	Indus	Indian	Pisces	Fishes	Vulpecula	Fox

THE SOLAR SYSTEM

For more information:
2 The home Galaxy
6 The seasons
  Day and night
7 The Moon

Lying 28,000 light-years from the centre of one of billions of galaxies that comprise the observable universe, our Solar System contains nine planets and their moons, innumerable asteroids and comets, and a miscellany of dust and gas, all tethered by the immense gravitational field of the Sun, the middling-sized star whose thermonuclear furnaces provide them all with heat and light. The Solar System was formed about 4,600 million years ago, when a spinning cloud of gas, mostly hydrogen but seeded with other, heavier elements, condensed enough to ignite a nuclear reaction and create a star. The Sun still accounts for almost 99.9% of the system's total mass; one planet, Jupiter, contains most of the remainder.

By composition as well as distance, the planetary array divides quite neatly in two: an inner system of four small, solid planets, including the Earth, and an outer system, from Jupiter to Neptune, of four much larger planets composed of lighter materials, such as gas, liquid and ice. Between the two groups lies a scattering of rocky asteroids, perhaps as many as 400,000. They may be debris left over from the inner Solar System's formation. The outermost planet, Pluto, may simply be the largest of a number of bodies composed of rock and ice orbiting beyond Neptune, similarly left over from the formation of the outer Solar System.

By the 1990s, however, the Solar System also included some newer anomalies: several thousand spacecraft. Most were in orbit around the Earth, but some had probed far and wide around the system. The valuable information beamed back by these robotic investigators has transformed our knowledge of our celestial environment.

Much of the early history of science is the story of people trying to make sense of the errant points of light that were all they knew of the planets. Now, men have themselves stood on the Earth's Moon; probes have landed on Mars and Venus, and orbiting radars have mapped far distant landscapes with astonishing accuracy. In the 1980s, the US Voyager probes skimmed all four major planets of the outer system, bringing new revelations with each close approach. Only Pluto, inscrutably distant in an orbit that takes it 50 times the Earth's distance from the Sun, remains unvisited by our messengers.

Orbits of the Planets

The planets of the Solar System and their orbits, showing the relative position of each planet at the vernal equinox of 1992.

Orbits are drawn to exact scale, but with the Sun and planets greatly enlarged for clarity. The Solar System is shown from the viewpoint of an observer a few light-hours distant in the direction of the constellation Hercules. Seen from such a position, above the plane of the ecliptic, all the planets revolve about the Sun in an anticlockwise direction. The perspective view exaggerates the elliptical form of all the planetary orbits: only Pluto and Mercury follow paths that deviate noticeably from circularity. Near perihelion – its closest approach to the Sun – Pluto actually passes inside the orbit of Neptune, an event that last occurred in 1983. Pluto did not regain its station as the Sun's outermost planet until February 1999.

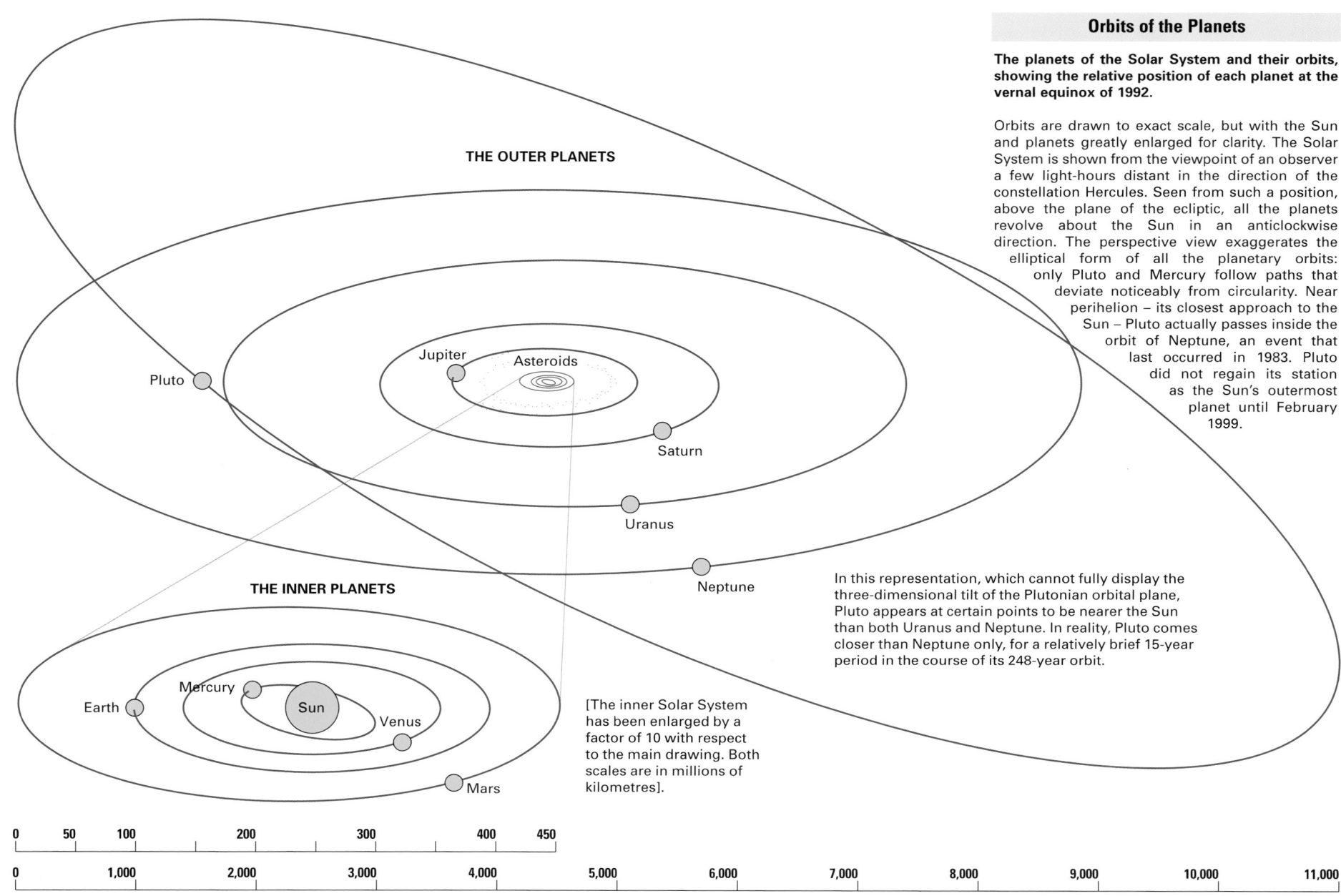

THE OUTER PLANETS

THE INNER PLANETS

In this representation, which cannot fully display the three-dimensional tilt of the Plutonian orbital plane, Pluto appears at certain points to be nearer the Sun than both Uranus and Neptune. In reality, Pluto comes closer than Neptune only, for a relatively brief 15-year period in the course of its 248-year orbit.

[The inner Solar System has been enlarged by a factor of 10 with respect to the main drawing. Both scales are in millions of kilometres].

Planetary Data

	Mean distance from Sun (million km)	Mass (Earth = 1)	Period of orbit (Earth years)	Period of rotation (Earth days)	Equatorial diameter (km)	Average density (water = 1)	Surface gravity (Earth = 1)	Escape velocity (km/sec)	Number of known satellites
Sun	–	*332,946*	–	*25.38*	*1,392,000*	*1.41*	*27.9*	*617.5*	–
Mercury	57.9	0.06	0.241	58.67	4,878	5.43	0.38	4.25	0
Venus	108.2	0.8	0.615	243.00	12,100	5.24	0.90	10.36	0
Earth	149.6	1.0	1.00	1.00	12,756	5.52	1.00	11.18	1
Mars	227.9	0.1	1.88	1.02	6,794	3.93	0.38	5.03	2
Jupiter	778.3	317.8	11.86	0.41	142,800	1.33	2.69	59.60	27
Saturn	1,426.8	95.2	29.46	0.42	120,000	0.706	1.16	35.60	30
Uranus	2,869.4	14.5	84.01	0.45	52,400	1.25	0.93	21.10	21
Neptune	4,496.3	17.1	164.79	0.71	48,400	1.77	1.21	24.60	8
Pluto	5,900.1	0.002	247.7	6.39	2,445	1.40	0.05	1.20	1

Planetary days are given in sidereal time – that is, with respect to the stars rather than the Sun. Most of the information in the table was confirmed by spacecraft and often obtained from photographs and other data transmitted back to the Earth. In the case of Pluto, however, only Earthbound observations have been made, and no spacecraft will encounter it until well into the 21st century. Given the planet's small size and great distance, figures for its diameter and rotation period have only recently been confirmed.

Pluto is not massive enough to account for the perturbations in the orbits of Uranus and Neptune that led to its discovery in 1930, but it is now widely believed that these perturbations can be explained away as observational errors made by the earlier observers.

The Planets

Mercury is the closest planet to the Sun and hence the fastest-moving. It is very hot, with a cratered, wrinkled surface very similar to that of Earth's Moon. It is small and has no gravity, hence there is no significant atmosphere.

Venus has much the same physical dimensions as Earth. Its dense atmosphere is composed of 97% CO_2 resulting in a runaway greenhouse effect that makes the Venusian surface, at 477°C, the hottest of all the planets in the Solar System. Radar mapping shows the land to be relatively level, with volcanic regions whose sulphurous discharges explain the sulphuric-acid rains reported by soft-landing space probes before they succumbed to Venus' fierce climate.

Earth seen from space is easily the most beautiful of the inner planets; it is also, and more objectively, the largest, as well as the only home of known life. Living things are the main reason why the Earth is able to retain a substantial proportion of corrosive and highly reactive oxygen in its atmosphere, a state of affairs that contradicts the laws of chemical equilibrium; the oxygen in turn supports the life that constantly regenerates it.

Mars, smaller and cooler than the Earth, is nevertheless the most likely planet other than Earth where life may have formed. Vast water channels show that it was once warmer and wetter; there may still be traces of former simple life forms, though whether life could thrive in its current cold, dry and thin atmosphere is doubtful. The ice caps are mainly frozen carbon dioxide, and whatever oxygen the planet once possessed is now locked up in the iron-bearing rock that covers its cratered surface and gives it its characteristic red hue. Mars is a dustbowl with occasional storms whirling the dust high into the atmosphere.

Jupiter masses almost three times as much as all the other planets combined; had it scooped up rather more matter during its formation, it might have evolved into a small companion star for the Sun. The planet is mostly gas, under intense pressure in the lower atmosphere above a core of fiercely compressed hydrogen and helium. The upper layers form strikingly-coloured rotating belts, the outward sign of the intense storms created by Jupiter's rapid diurnal rotation. Close approaches by spacecraft have shown an orbiting ring system and discovered several previously unknown moons: Jupiter has at least 27 moons.

Saturn is structurally similar to Jupiter, rotating fast enough to produce an obvious bulge at its equator. It is composed of 89% hydrogen and 11% helium, and has wind velocities in the outer atmosphere of 500 metres per second. Ever since the invention of the telescope, however, Saturn's rings have been the feature that has attracted most observers. Voyager probes in 1980 and 1981 sent back detailed pictures that showed them to be composed of thousands of separate ringlets, each in turn made up of tiny icy particles.

Uranus was unknown to the ancients. Although it is faintly visible to the naked eye, it was not discovered until 1781. Its interior is largely water, with an atmosphere of hydrogen, helium and some methane, which gives the planet its blue-green colour. Observations in 1977 suggested the presence of a faint ring system, amply confirmed when Voyager 2 swung past the planet in 1986.

Neptune is always more than 4,000 million km from Earth, and despite its diameter of almost 50,000 km, it can only be seen by telescope. Its 1846 discovery was the result of mathematical predictions by astronomers seeking to explain irregularities in the orbit of Uranus, but until Voyager 2 closed with the planet in 1989, very little was known of it. Like Uranus, it has a ring system; Voyager's photographs revealed a total of eight moons.

Pluto is the most mysterious of the solar planets, if only because even the most powerful telescopes can scarcely resolve it from a point of light to a disk. It was discovered as recently as 1930, as the result (like Neptune) of perturbations in the orbits of the two then outermost planets. Its small size, as well as its eccentric and highly tilted orbit, has led to suggestions that it is a former satellite of Neptune, somehow liberated from its primary. In 1978 Pluto was found to have a moon of its own, Charon, apparently half the size of Pluto itself.

Mean distance from the
Sun in million kilometres
(not to scale)

57.9	Mercury
108.2	Venus
149.6	Earth
227.9	Mars
778.3	Jupiter
1,426.8	Saturn
2,869.4	Uranus
4,496.3	Neptune
5,900.1	Pluto

Diagram not drawn to scale

TIME AND MOTION

For more information:

4 Orbits of the planets

9 Ocean currents

14 Circulation of the air

16 Climate

The basic unit of time measurement is the day, that is, one rotation of the Earth on its axis. Our present calendar is based on the solar year of 365.24 days, the time taken by the Earth to orbit the Sun.

Calendars based on the movements of the Sun and Moon have been used since ancient times. The average length of the year, according to the Julian Calendar introduced by Julius Caesar, was about 11 minutes too long. The cumulative error was rectified in 1582 by the Gregorian Calendar, when Pope Gregory XIII decreed that the day following 4 October was 15 October, and in that century years did not count as leap years unless they were divisible by 400. England finally adopted the reformed calendar in 1752, when it was 11 days behind the European mainland.

The rotation of the Earth on its axis causes day and night. Because the Earth rotates through 360° every 24 hours, the world is divided into 24 time zones centred on lines of longitude at 15° longitude.

The tilt of the Earth's axis, also called the obliquity of the ecliptic, accounts for the seasons which are so familiar in the middle latitudes. But geological evidence shows that, over long periods of time, climates change, and the advances and retreats of the ice during the Pleistocene Ice Age may have been caused by regular variations in the Earth's tilt, its orbit around the Sun, and changes in the season when it is closest to the Sun (perihelion).

Earth Data

Aphelion (maximum distance from Sun): 152,007,016 km

Perihelion (minimum distance from Sun): 147,000,830 km

Angle of tilt (obliquity of the ecliptic): 23° 27' 08"

Length of year – solar tropical (equinox to equinox): 365.24 days

Length of year: 365 days, 5 hours, 48 minutes, 46 seconds of mean solar time

Superficial area: 510,000,000 sq km

Land surface: 149,000,000 sq km (29.2%)

Water surface: 361,000,000 sq km (70.8%)

Equatorial circumference: 40,077 km

Polar circumference: 40,009 km

Equatorial diameter: 12,756.8 km

Polar diameter: 12,713.8 km

Equatorial radius: 6,378.4 km

Polar radius: 6,356.9 km

Volume of the Earth: $1,083,230 \times 10^6$ cu km

Mass of the Earth: 5.9×10^{21} tonnes

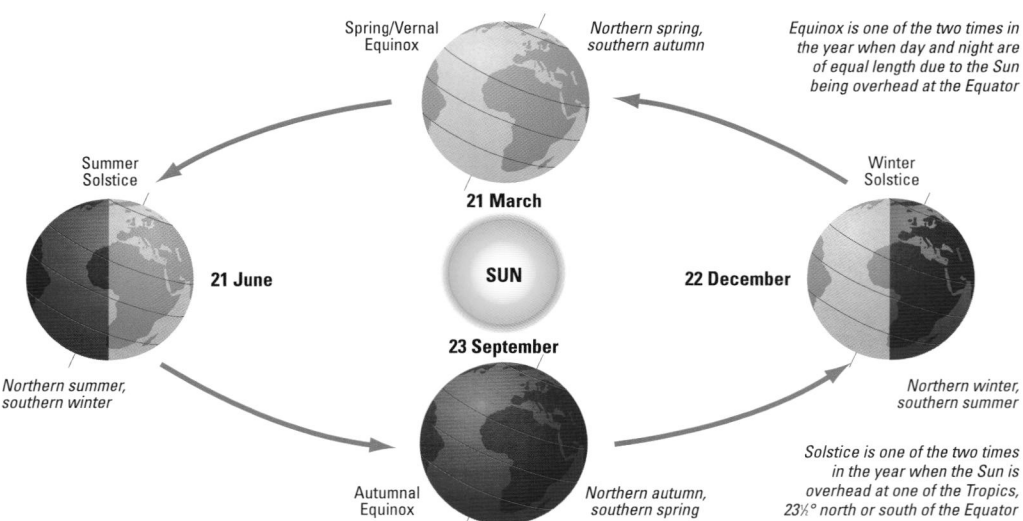

The Seasons

Seasons occur because the Earth's axis is tilted at a constant angle of 23½°. When the northern hemisphere is tilted to a maximum extent towards the Sun, on 21 June, the Sun is overhead at the Tropic of Cancer (latitude 23½° North). This is midsummer, or the summer solstice, in the northern hemisphere.

On 22 or 23 September, the Sun is overhead at the Equator, and day and night are of equal length throughout the world. This is the autumn equinox in the northern hemisphere. On 21 or 22 December, the Sun is overhead at the Tropic of Capricorn (23½° South), the winter solstice in the northern hemisphere. The overhead Sun then tracks north until, on 21 March, it is overhead at the Equator. This is the spring (vernal) equinox in the northern hemisphere.

In the southern hemisphere, the seasons are the reverse of those in the north.

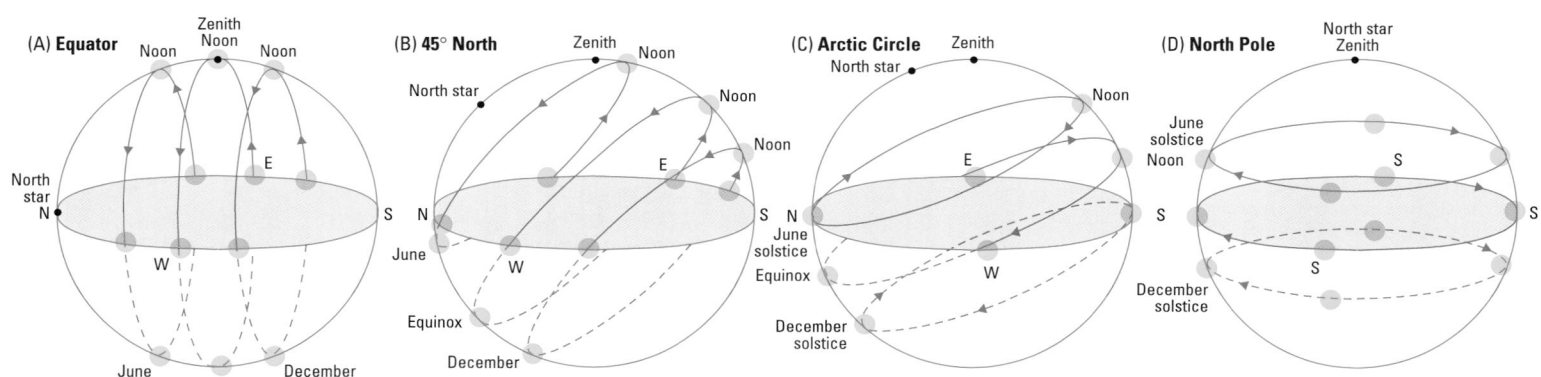

Day and Night

The Sun appears to rise in the east, reach its highest point at noon, and then set in the west, to be followed by night. In reality, it is not the Sun that is moving but the Earth rotating from west to east. The moment when the Sun's upper limb first appears above the horizon is termed sunrise; the moment when the Sun's upper limb disappears below the horizon is sunset.

At the summer solstice in the northern hemisphere (21 June), the Arctic has total daylight and the Antarctic total darkness. The opposite occurs at the winter solstice (21 or 22 December). At the Equator, the length of day and night are almost equal all year.

The Sun's Path

The diagrams on the right illustrate the apparent path of the Sun at (A) the Equator, (B) in mid-latitude (45°), (C) at the Arctic Circle (66½°), and (D) at the North Pole, where there are six months of continuous daylight and six months of continuous night.

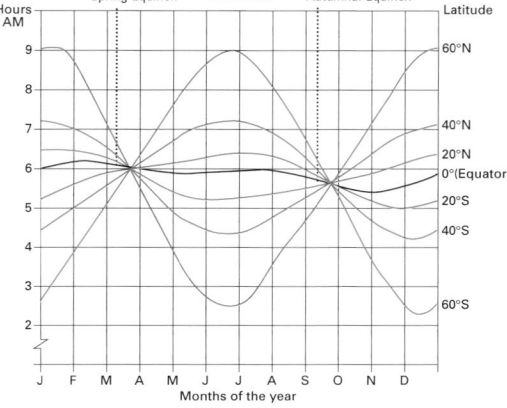 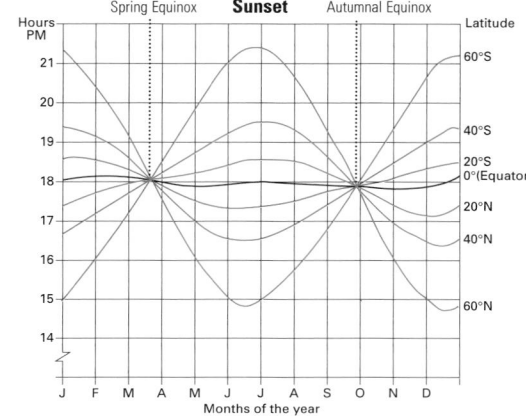

Sunrise and Sunset

The term equinox comes from two Latin words meaning 'equal night'. At the spring and autumn equinoxes, the Sun is vertically overhead at the Equator and all places on Earth have 12 hours of darkness and 12 hours of daylight. The graphs showing sunrise and sunset show that these occasions occur on 21 March and on 22 or 23 September. The graphs also show that, because the Sun remains high in the sky throughout the year, the length of the day and night at the Equator remain roughly the same throughout the year, with sunrise occurring around 6 AM and sunset at around 6 PM. The further north or south one travels, the greater the difference between the number of hours of daylight and darkness. For example, the graph (right) shows that at latitude 60°N sunrise varies from just after 9 AM in midwinter (on 22 or 23 December) to about 2.30 AM in midsummer (around the summer solstice on 21 June). By contrast, the second graph (far right) shows that sunset at latitude 60°N occurs at about 2.45 PM in midwinter and 9.20 PM in midsummer.

The Moon

The Moon rotates more slowly than the Earth, making one complete turn on its axis in just over 27 days. Since this corresponds to its period of revolution around the Earth, the Moon always presents the same hemisphere or face to us, and we never see 'the dark side'. The interval between one full Moon and the next (and between new Moons) is about 29½ days – a lunar month. The apparent changes in the shape of the Moon are caused by its changing position in relation to the Earth; like the planets, it produces no light of its own and shines only by reflecting the rays of the Sun.

Phases of the Moon

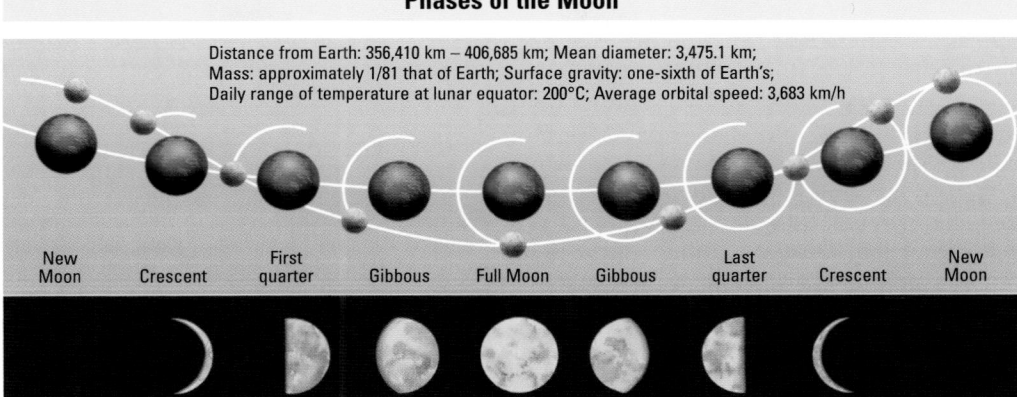

Distance from Earth: 356,410 km – 406,685 km; Mean diameter: 3,475.1 km; Mass: approximately 1/81 that of Earth; Surface gravity: one-sixth of Earth's; Daily range of temperature at lunar equator: 200°C; Average orbital speed: 3,683 km/h

New Moon · Crescent · First quarter · Gibbous · Full Moon · Gibbous · Last quarter · Crescent · New Moon

Moon Data

Distance from Earth

The Moon orbits at a mean distance of 384,199.1 km, at an average speed of 3,683 km/h in relation to the Earth.

Size and mass

The average diameter of the Moon is 3,475.1 km. It is 400 times smaller than the Sun but is about 400 times closer to the Earth, so we see them as the same size. The Moon has a mass of $7,348 \times 10^{19}$ tonnes, with a density 3.344 times that of water.

Visibility

Only 59% of the Moon's surface is directly visible from Earth. Reflected light takes 1.25 seconds to reach Earth – compared to 8 minutes 27.3 seconds for light to reach us from the Sun.

Temperature

With the Sun overhead, the temperature on the lunar equator can reach 117.2°C [243°F]. At night it can sink to −162.7°C [−261°F].

Eclipses

When the Moon passes between the Sun and the Earth it causes a partial eclipse of the Sun (1) if the Earth passes through the Moon's outer shadow (P), or a total eclipse (2) if the inner cone shadow crosses the Earth's surface. In a lunar eclipse, the Earth's shadow crosses the Moon and, again, provides either a partial or total eclipse.

Eclipses of the Sun and the Moon do not occur every month because of the 5° difference between the plane of the Moon's orbit and the plane in which the Earth moves. In the 1990s only 14 lunar eclipses were possible, for example, seven partial and seven total; each was visible only from certain, and variable, parts of the world. The same period witnessed 13 solar eclipses – six partial (or annular) and seven total.

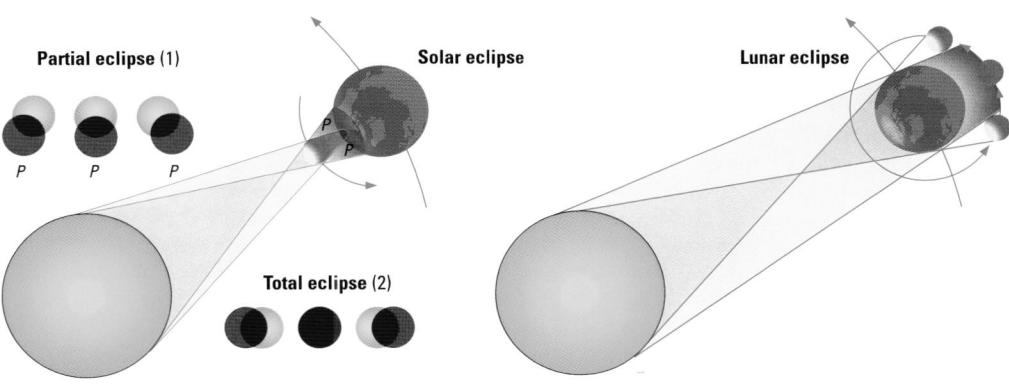

Partial eclipse (1)

Solar eclipse

Lunar eclipse

Total eclipse (2)

Tides

The daily rise and fall of the ocean's tides are the result of the gravitational pull of the Moon and that of the Sun, though the effect of the latter is only 46.6% as strong as that of the Moon. This effect is greatest on the hemisphere facing the Moon and causes a tidal 'bulge'. When the Sun, Earth and Moon are in line, tide-raising forces are at a maximum and Spring tides occur: high tide reaches the highest values, and low tide falls to low levels. When lunar and solar forces are least coincidental with the Sun and Moon at an angle (near the Moon's first and third quarters), Neap tides occur, which have a small tidal range.

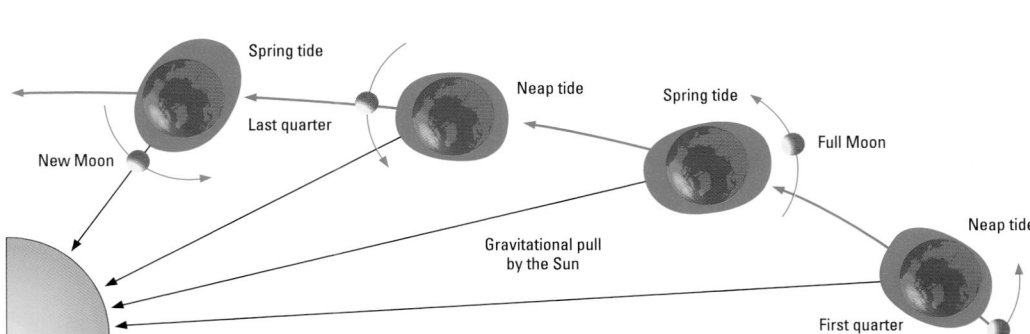

Spring tide

Neap tide

Spring tide

Last quarter

Full Moon

New Moon

Neap tide

Gravitational pull by the Sun

First quarter

Time Zones

The Earth rotates through 360° in 24 hours, and so moves 15° every hour. The world is divided into 24 standard time zones, each centred on lines of longitude at 15° intervals. At the centre of the first zone is the Prime meridian or Greenwich meridian. All places to the west of Greenwich are one hour behind for every 15° of longitude; places to the east are ahead by one hour for every 15°. When it is 12 noon at the Greenwich meridian, 180° east it is midnight of the same day – while 180° west the day is just beginning. To overcome this, the International Date Line was established, approximately following the 180° meridian. Thus, if you travelled eastwards from Japan (140°E) to Samoa (170°W), you would pass from Sunday night into Sunday morning.

10 Hours slow or fast of UT or Co-ordinated Universal Time

Zones using UT (GMT)

Zones slow of UT (GMT)

International boundaries

Zones fast of UT (GMT)

Half-hour zones

Time zone boundaries

International Date Line

Actual Solar Time when time at Greenwich is 12:00 (noon)

Note: Certain of the above time zones are affected by the incidence of 'Summer Time' in countries where it is adopted.

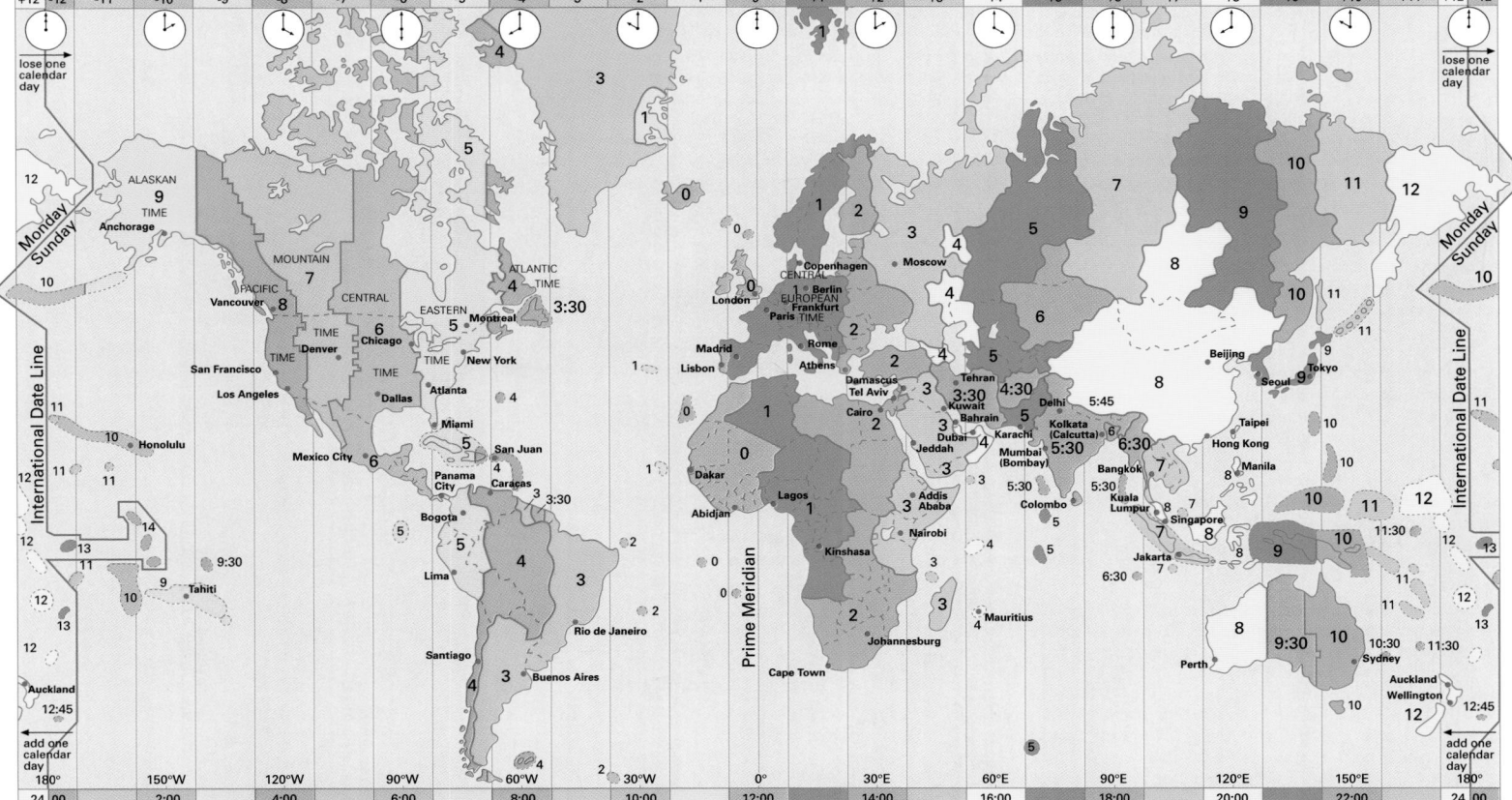

Projection: Mercator

OCEANS

For more information:

7 Tides
10 The spreading Earth
14 Atmosphere
18 Hydrological cycle
   Water distribution
19 Watersheds
23 Water pollution
41 Shipping

The last 40 years have been described as the 'Space Age', but another exciting and perhaps even more important area of discovery, proceeding at the same time, has been the exploration of 'inner space', namely the oceans which cover more than 70% of our planet. The study of the ocean floor and oceanic islands has revealed features that help to explain how continents move, and how the movements are related to earthquakes and volcanic activity.

Manned submersibles have established that life exists even in the deepest trenches, where the pressure reaches 1,000 atmospheres, the equivalent of the force of one tonne bearing down on every square centimetre. Further exploration in the pitch-black environment of the ocean ridges has revealed strange forms of marine life around scalding hot vents. The creatures include giant tubeworms, blind shrimps, and bacteria, some of which are genetically very different from any other known life forms. In 1996, an analysis of one microorganism revealed that at least half of its 1,700 or so genes were hitherto unknown. This environment, which is based on chemicals, not sunlight, may resemble the places where life on Earth first began.

Another vital area of contemporary research concerns the interactions between the oceans and the atmosphere, as exemplified in the El Niño–Southern Oscillation (ENSO), and the bearing that these have on climatic change.

Most geographers divide the world's ocean waters into four areas: the Pacific, Atlantic, Indian and Arctic oceans. The most active zone in the oceans is the sunlit upper layer, where the water is moved around by wind-blown currents. It is the home of most sea life and acts as a membrane through which the ocean breathes,

Seawater

The chemical composition of the sea, by percentage, excluding the elements of water itself

Chloride (Cl)	55.04%
Sodium (Na)	30.61%
Sulphate (SO₄)	7.69%
Magnesium (Mg)	3.69%
Calcium (Ca)	1.16%
Potassium (K)	1.10%
Bicarbonate (HCO₃)	0.41%
Bromide (Br)	0.19%
Boric Acid (H₃BO₃)	0.07%
Strontium (Sr)	0.04%
Fluoride (Fl)	0.003%
Lithium (Li)	trace
Rubidium (Rb)	trace
Phosphorus (P)	trace
Iodine (I)	trace
Barium (Ba)	trace
Arsenic (As)	trace
Caesium (Cs)	trace

Eleven constituents account for over 99% of the salt content of seawater, but seawater also contains virtually every other element. In natural conditions, its composition is broadly consistent across the world's seas and oceans; but in coastal areas, especially, variations are sometimes substantial. The oceans are about 35 parts water to one part salt.

Atoll Building

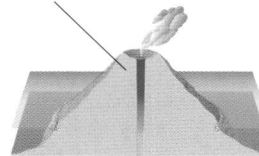

Volcano rises from ocean floor

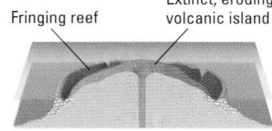

Extinct, eroding volcanic island

Fringing reef

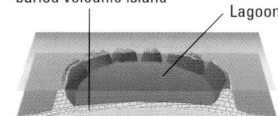

After subsidence, reef covers buried volcanic island

Lagoon

A coral atoll usually begins existence as a bare volcanic peak, thrusting above the surface of the ocean. A colony of coral – organisms with calcium carbonate skeletons – forms itself in the shallow water around the peak. The volcano is eroded and slowly sinks, leaving the coral forming a ring of hard limestone around its remnant. In time, the barrier reef of an atoll is all that remains.

Life in the Oceans

An imaginary profile of the typical coastal and oceanic zones is shown, with a selection of the life forms that might occur in the water off the Pacific Coast of Central America. The animals illustrated are not drawn to scale as the range of sizes is too great. Most marine life is confined to the first 200 metres, the upper sunlit (photic) zone, where sunlight can still penetrate. Plant and animal plankton, the basis of life in the ocean, occur in great quantities in all zones.

In the pelagic environment (open sea), vertical gradients, including those of light, temperature and salinity, determine the distribution of organisms. From the tidal zone at the coastline, the continental shelf, geologically still part of the continental landmass, drops gently to about 200 metres – the sunlit zone. At the end of the shelf, the seabed falls away in the steeper angle of the continental slope. The subsequent descent to the deep ocean floor, known as the continental rise, is more gentle, with gradients between 1 in 100 and 1 in 700 until the abyssal plains and hills between 2,500 and 6,000 metres below the surface.

The deep sea floor contains seamounts, some of which are capped by coral reefs, ocean ridges, the longest mountain chains on Earth, and deep ocean trenches, especially in the Pacific Ocean where six trenches reach depths of more than 10,000 metres, including the 11,022-metre deep Mariana Trench.

Each of these zones contains a distinctive community of species adapted to the different conditions of salinity, temperature and light intensity. Indeed, a few organisms have been found even in the abyssal darkness of the great ocean trenches.

absorbing great quantities of carbon dioxide and partly exchanging it for oxygen.

As the depth increases, so light fades and temperatures fall until just before 1,000 metres where there is a marked temperature change at the thermocline, the boundary between the warm surface zone and the cold deep zone. Below the thermocline, slow currents are caused by density differences between bodies of water with varying temperatures and salinity.

The El Niño Phenomenon

The importance of the ocean–atmosphere interaction is nowhere more dramatically demonstrated than in the El Niño phenomenon of the southern Pacific Ocean.

Under normal conditions, shown in the diagram (right, top), surface water flows eastwards from South America under the influence of trade winds while, near the coast, cold, nutrient-rich water (dark blue) rises to the surface and spreads westwards. In the western Pacific, sea surface temperatures reach 28°C or more and warm air rises, creating a low-pressure air system and causing heavy rains. The rising warm air spreads out and some of it descends over South America and the eastern Pacific, creating a high-pressure air system from which winds blow westwards. This rotating system is called a Walker Circulation Cell.

An El Niño event, also called an El Niño–Southern Oscillation cycle, or ENSO cycle, is characterized by a reversal of currents, whereby the eastwards-moving South Equatorial Current extends much further to the east and the trade winds weaken. The upwelling of cold water off South America is greatly reduced and surface water temperatures rise, causing a drastic reduction in fish life. The heaviest rainfall is over the eastern Pacific, while South-east Asia is much drier than usual. Warm air rises in the east and spreads out, descending in the western Pacific, which then becomes a high-pressure area, as shown on the second diagram (below right).

During an intense El Niño, such as in 1982–3 when sea temperatures in the eastern Pacific rose by 6°C, the effects of the current and wind reversals affect the weather around the world. In Australia and South-east Asia, the monsoon rainfall is reduced, while, in 1983–4, a severe drought occurred in the Sahel, south of the Sahara, and also in southern Africa. The south-east coast of the United States also suffered storms and heavy rainfall, and even Europe experienced changes in weather patterns, possibly as a result of consequent changes in the course of the jet stream.

Scientists have found evidence that the frequency of the El Niño event, which normally occurs every two to seven years, may have increased in recent years with warm conditions persisting in the eastern Pacific from 1990 until mid-1995, an unprecedented length of time during the 114 years for which data exist. Another intense El Niño occurred in 1997–8, with resultant freak weather conditions across the entire Pacific region. Scientists do not know the causes of the El Niño event, though some researchers are investigating possible connections between major volcanic eruptions in the tropical Pacific region, the ENSO cycle and atmospheric circulation.

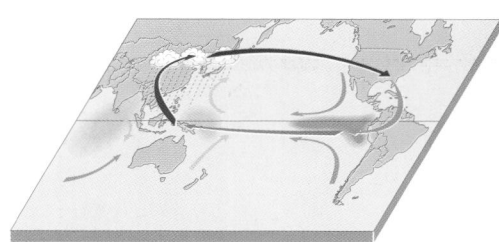

Normal year – Walker Circulation Cell

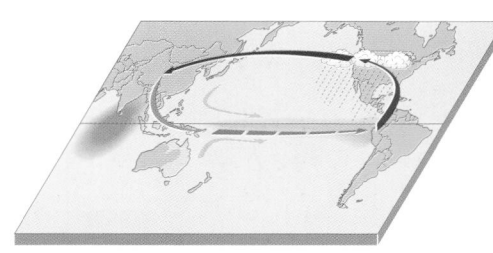

El Niño event

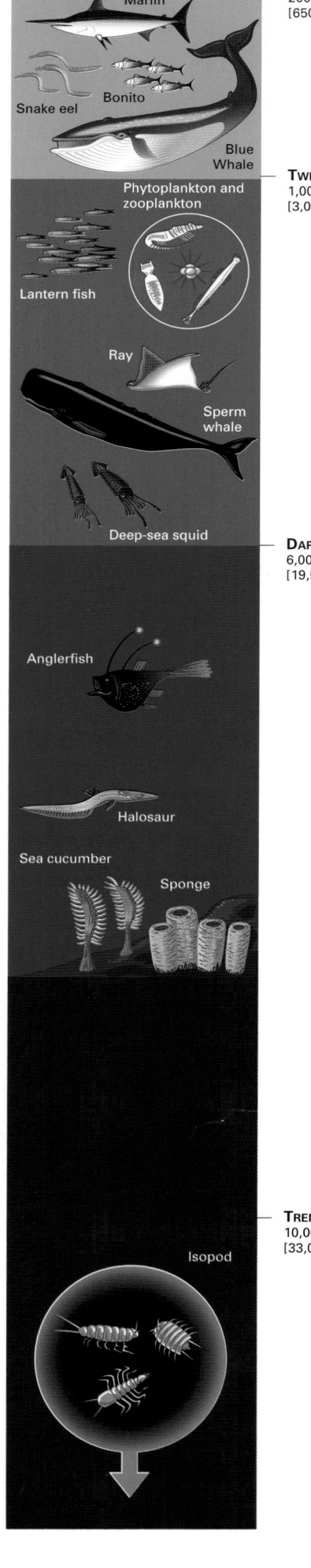

Crab
Seaweed
Jellyfish
Anchovy
Green turtle
Dolphin

SEA LEVEL

Marlin
Bonito
Snake eel
Blue Whale

SUNLIT ZONE
200 metres
[650 feet]

Phytoplankton and zooplankton
Lantern fish

TWILIGHT ZONE
1,000 metres
[3,000 feet]

Ray
Sperm whale

Deep-sea squid

DARK ZONE
6,000 metres
[19,500 feet]

Anglerfish

Halosaur

Sea cucumber
Sponge

Isopod

TRENCH ZONE
10,000 metres
[33,000 feet]

Ocean Currents

JANUARY CURRENTS AND TEMPERATURES

(Northern Hemisphere: winter)

ACTUAL SURFACE
TEMPERATURE

°C
30
20
10
0
−10
−20
−30
−40

OCEAN CURRENTS

Cold Warm Speed (knots)
Less than 0.5
0.5 – 1.0
Over 1.0

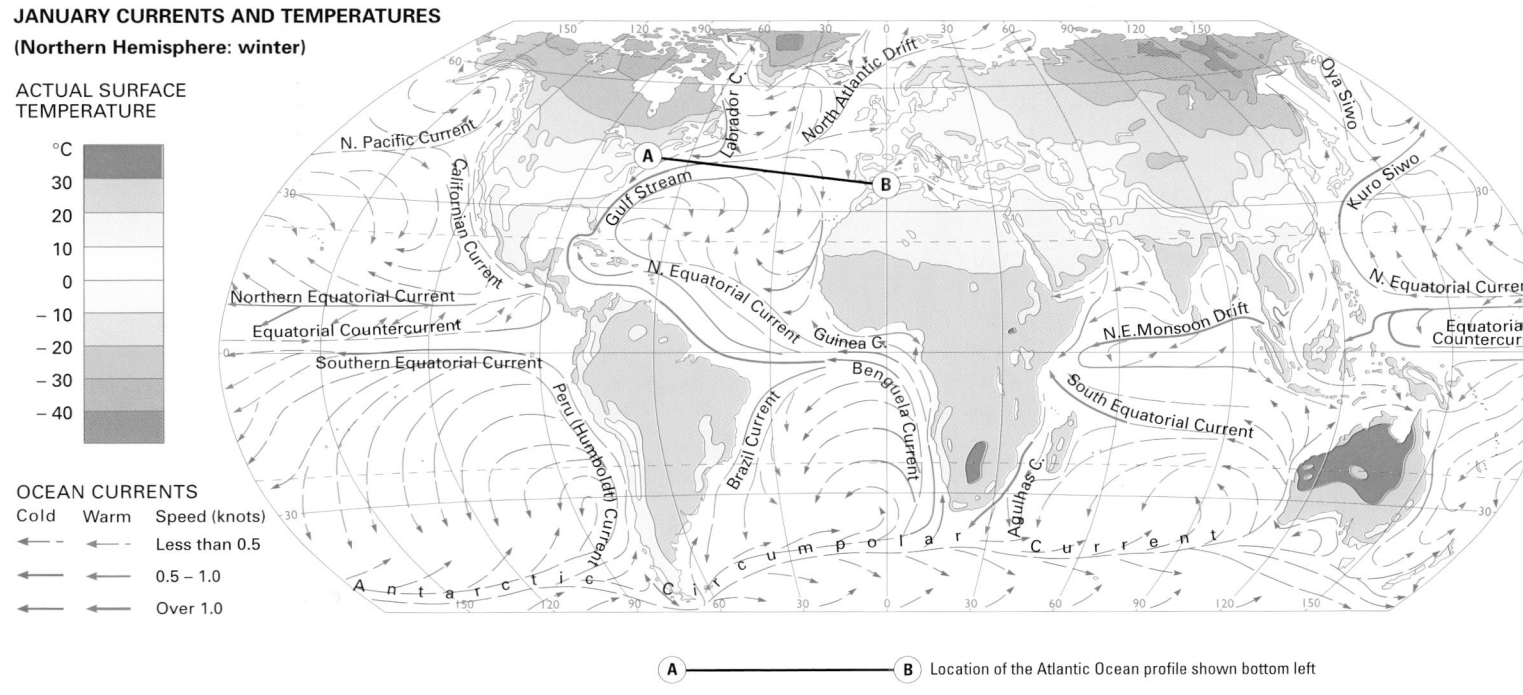

A ———————————— B Location of the Atlantic Ocean profile shown bottom left

JULY CURRENTS AND TEMPERATURES

(Northern Hemisphere: summer)

ACTUAL SURFACE
TEMPERATURE

°C
30
20
10
0
−10

OCEAN CURRENTS

Cold Warm Speed (knots)
Less than 0.5
0.5 – 1.0
Over 1.0

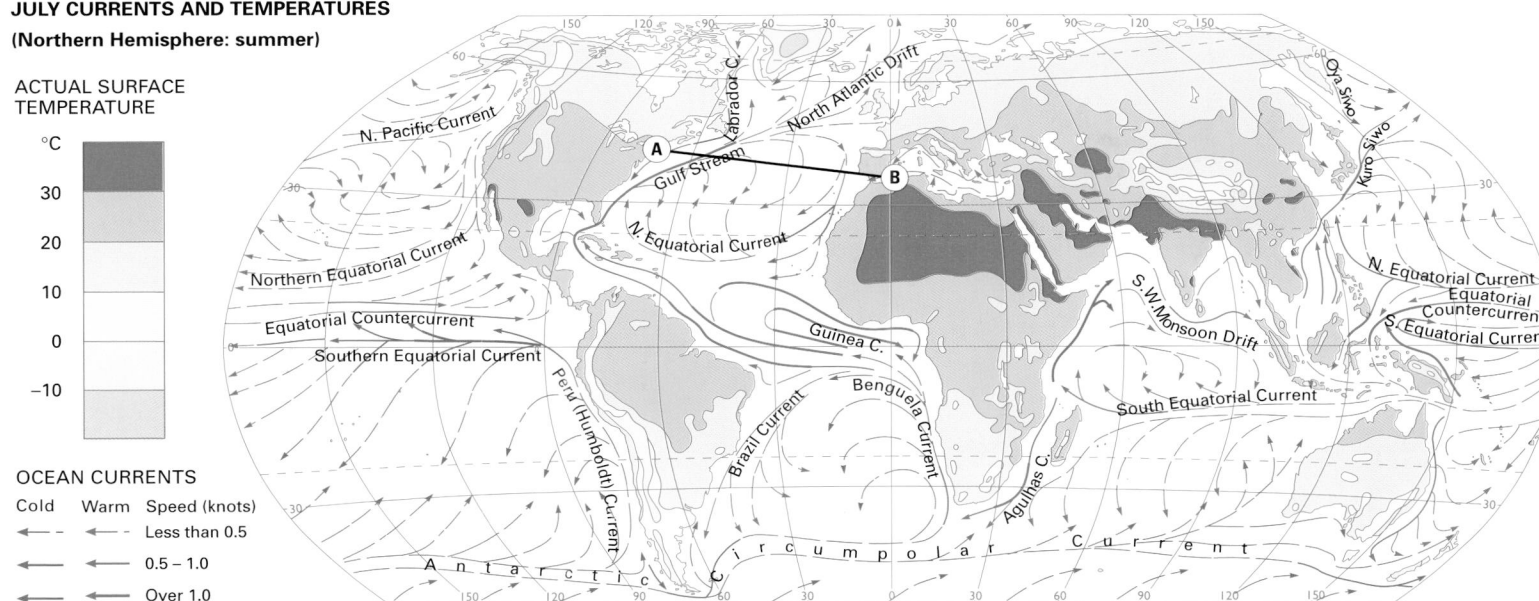

Moving immense quantities of energy as well as billions of tonnes of water every hour, the ocean currents are a vital part of the great heat engine that drives the Earth's climate. They themselves are produced by a twofold mechanism. At the surface, winds push huge masses of water before them; in the deep ocean, below an abrupt temperature gradient that separates the churning surface waters from the still depths, density variations cause slow vertical movements.

The pattern of circulation of the great surface currents is determined by the displacement known as the Coriolis effect. As the Earth turns beneath a moving object – whether it is a tennis ball or a vast mass of water – it appears to be deflected to one side. The deflection is most obvious near the Equator, where the Earth's surface is spinning eastwards at 1,700 km/h; currents moving polewards are curved clockwise in the northern hemisphere and anti-clockwise in the southern.

The result is a system of spinning circles known as gyres. Warm currents move constantly from the Equator towards the poles, while cold water moves in the reverse direction. In this way, ocean currents act like a thermostat, helping to regulate temperatures around the world.

Depending on the annual movements of the prevailing wind belts, some currents on or near the Equator may reverse their direction in the course of the year, a variation on which Asia's monsoon rains depend and whose occasional failure has brought disaster to millions of people.

Topography of the Ocean Floor

Profile of the Atlantic Ocean

The deep ocean floor was once believed to be flat, but maps compiled from readings made by sonar equipment show that it is no more uniform than the surface of the continents. The profile (*below*) shows some of the features on the Atlantic Ocean floor between Massachusetts in North America and Gibraltar (*for location of profile, see maps above*). Around the continents are shallow continental shelves composed of rocks which are less dense than the underlying oceanic crust. The continents end at the top of the steep continental slope, which descends to the abyss via the continental rise, made up of sediments washed down from the continental shelves. The abyss contains large plains overlain by oozes, but the plains are broken by volcanic seamounts and guyots (flat-topped seamounts), a few of which reach the surface as islands. The other main feature is the Mid-Atlantic Ridge, through which runs a rift valley where new crustal rock is being formed as the plates on either side move apart.

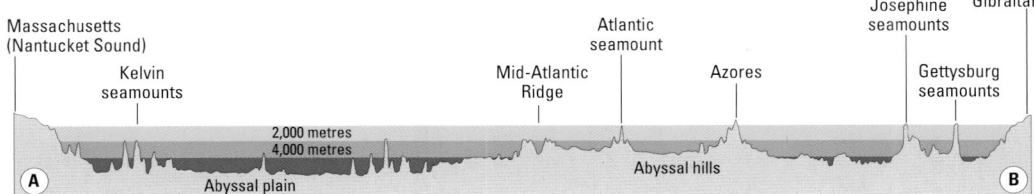

Topography of the ocean floor around Australia

In the image on the right, land areas are shown in grey, with shaded relief. The colours represent sea depth, with red representing the shallowest areas, through yellow and green to dark blue (the deepest). The data for the sea topography are from the Seasat radar satellite. The deep blue area in the upper left is the Java Trench which forms the boundary between the Indo-Australian plate and the Eurasian plate. In the top right, the New Guinea trench, which has a maximum depth of 9,103 metres, forms the border of the Indo-Australian and Pacific plates. Alongside the trenches are volcanic islands formed from magma, created as the edge of the Indo-Australian plate is subducted and melted.

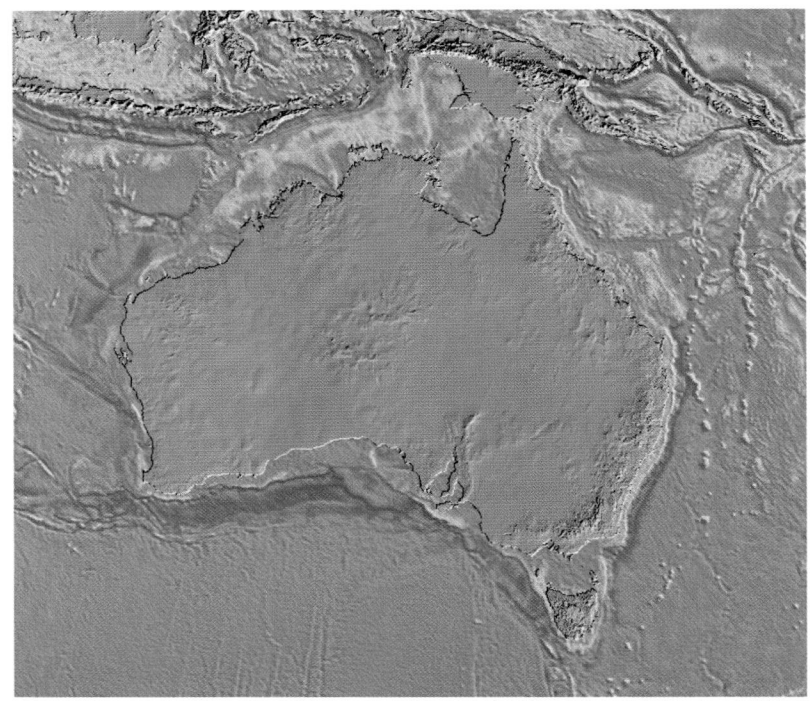

GEOLOGY OF THE EARTH

For more information:

12 Types of rock
   Mountain building
13 Surface processes
21 The carbon cycle
36 Minerals

Every year, earthquakes and volcanic eruptions cause much destruction throughout the world. Such phenomena were once thought to be unconnected, but since the late 1960s, scientists have understood that these events are surface manifestations of the tremendous forces operating in the Earth's interior that are slowly but constantly changing the face of our planet.

The Earth is divided into three zones. The crust, a brittle, low-density zone, overlies the dense mantle. Separating the crust from the mantle is a distinct boundary called the Mohorovičić (or Moho) discontinuity. Enclosed by the mantle is the Earth's core, which consists mainly of iron and nickel.

Temperatures inside the Earth range from about 870°C in the upper mantle to perhaps 5,000°C in the core. Heat creates convection currents in a semi-molten part of the mantle called the asthenosphere. Above the asthenosphere is the lithosphere, a solid layer about 70 km thick, consisting of the crust and part of the mantle. The lithosphere is divided into rigid plates, moved around by the currents in the asthenosphere, a process named plate tectonics.

The Earth was formed around 4.6 billion years ago. Lighter elements floated towards the surface, where they formed crustal rocks. The oldest rocks so far discovered are nearly 4 billion years old, while the oldest fossils occur in rocks formed around 3.5 billion years ago. An explosion of life occurred at the start of the Cambrian period, 570 million years ago. The fossil record since the start of the Cambrian has enabled scientists to piece together the story of life on Earth.

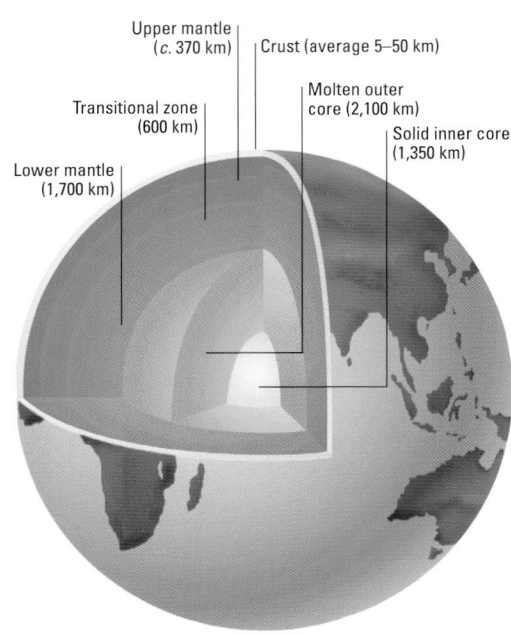

Upper mantle (c. 370 km) | Crust (average 5–50 km)
Transitional zone (600 km)
Molten outer core (2,100 km)
Solid inner core (1,350 km)
Lower mantle (1,700 km)

Plate Tectonics

In the early 20th century, the German scientist Alfred Wegener and others noticed similarities between the shapes of the continents. From a study of rocks and fossils in widely separated continents, they suggested that the continents had once been joined together and that somehow they had drifted apart. But no one knew of a mechanism that might cause continents to drift. However, in the 1950s and 1960s, evidence from studies of the ocean floor suggested that the low-density continents rest on huge slow-moving plates.

Sea-floor spreading in the Indian Ocean and continental plate collision

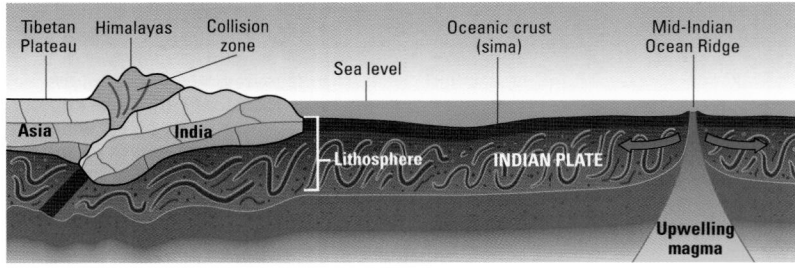

Tibetan Plateau | Himalayas | Collision zone | Oceanic crust (sima) | Mid-Indian Ocean Ridge | Sea level | Asia | India | Lithosphere | INDIAN PLATE | Upwelling magma

Sea-floor spreading in the Atlantic Ocean and plate collision

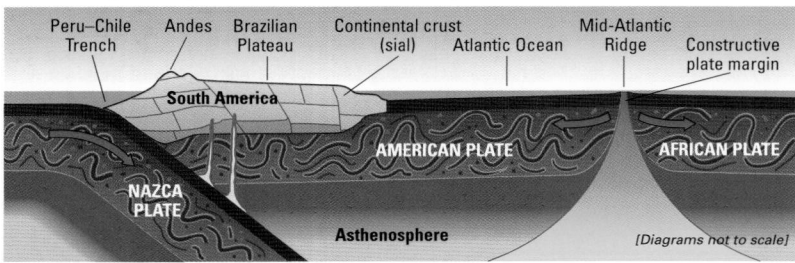

Peru–Chile Trench | Andes | Brazilian Plateau | Continental crust (sial) | Atlantic Ocean | Mid-Atlantic Ridge | Constructive plate margin | South America | AMERICAN PLATE | AFRICAN PLATE | NAZCA PLATE | Asthenosphere | [Diagrams not to scale]

The huge ridges that run through the oceans represent boundaries between plates. Here plates are diverging at rates of 20–41 mm a year. Molten magma from the mantle rises along a central rift valley to form new crustal rock. These ocean ridges, which are active zones where earthquakes and volcanic eruptions are common, are called constructive plate margins. Destructive plate margins, which occur when two plates converge, are marked by deep ocean trenches as one plate is forced under the other. The descending plate is melted to produce the magma that fuels volcanoes alongside the trenches. Movements of descending plates are often sudden and violent, triggering earthquakes in overlying continental areas. Where two continents collide, their margins are buckled up to form fold mountain ranges. A third type of plate margin, the transform fault, is not illustrated above. Along these plate margins, such as California's San Andreas fault, plates are moving parallel to each other.

The debate about plate tectonics is not over. Questions still arise as to why some active volcanoes lie far from plate margins, and why major earthquakes occur in mid-plate areas.

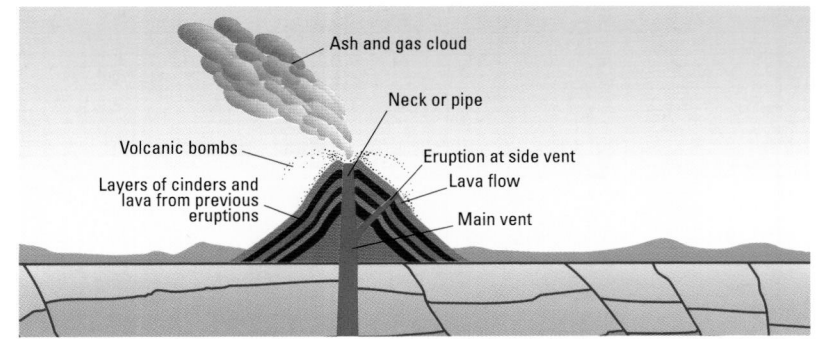

Ash and gas cloud | Neck or pipe | Volcanic bombs | Eruption at side vent | Lava flow | Layers of cinders and lava from previous eruptions | Main vent

Continental Drift

In 1915, Alfred Wegener produced a series of world maps proposing that, around 200 million years ago, the continents had been joined together in a supercontinent which he called Pangaea. This landmass started to break up about 180 million years ago and the parts drifted to their present positions. The arrows on the present-day world map shows that the continents are still on the move.

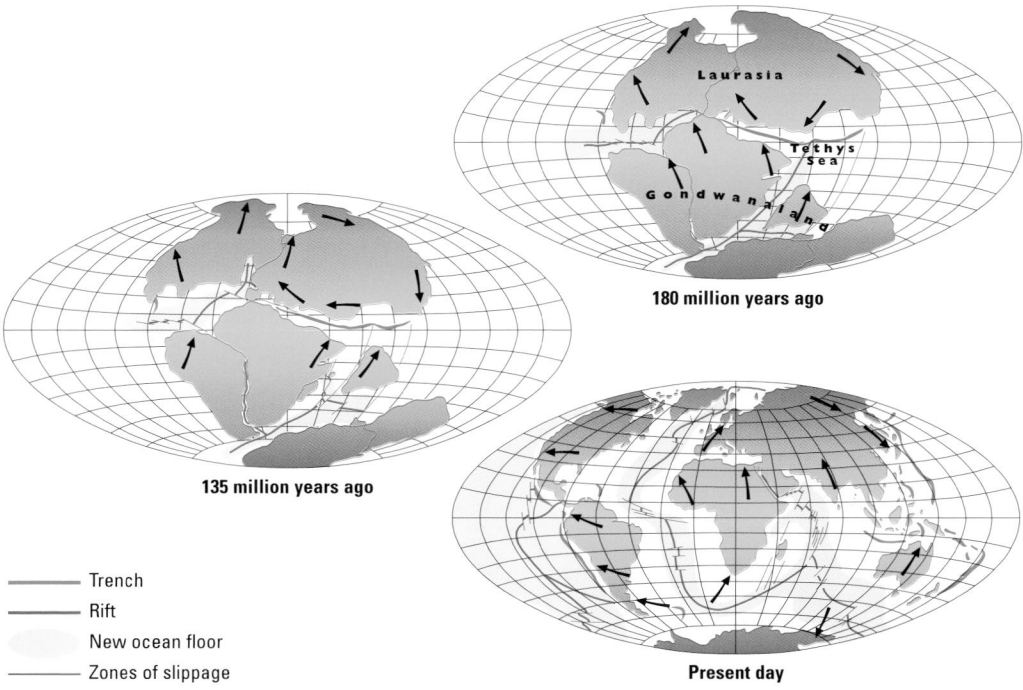

180 million years ago
Laurasia | Tethys Sea | Gondwanaland

135 million years ago

Trench
Rift
New ocean floor
Zones of slippage

Present day

Distribution of Volcanoes

Volcanoes occur when hot liquefied rock beneath the Earth's crust is pushed up by pressure to the surface as molten lava. There are some 550 known active volcanoes, around 20 of which are erupting at any one time.

▲ Land volcanoes active since 1700
5.5 Direction of movement (cm/year)
~ Boundaries of tectonic plates
• Submarine volcanoes
♦ Geysers

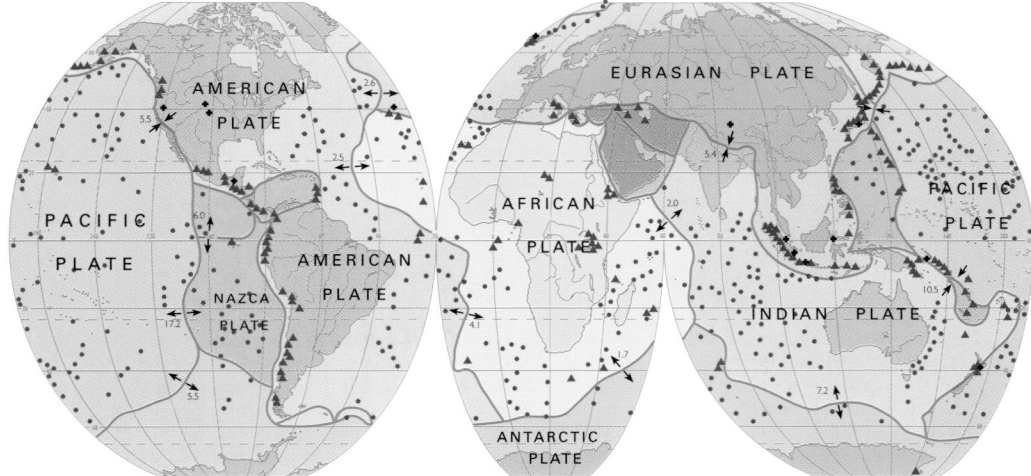

AMERICAN PLATE | PACIFIC PLATE | AMERICAN PLATE | NAZCA PLATE | EURASIAN PLATE | AFRICAN PLATE | PACIFIC PLATE | INDIAN PLATE | ANTARCTIC PLATE

Geological Time

Time, in millions of years before the present, is shown on a sliding scale, greatly compressed in the distant past.

ERA	PERIOD	EPOCH
PRE-CAMBRIAN (4600–570)		
PALEOZOIC	Cambrian (570–500)	
	Ordovician (500–430)	
	Silurian (430–395)	
	Devonian (395–345)	
	Carboniferous (345–280)	
	Permian (280–225)	
MESOZOIC	Triassic (225–190)	
	Jurassic (190–135)	
	Cretaceous (135–65)	
CENOZOIC	Tertiary	Paleocene (65–53)
		Eocene (53–37)
		Oligocene (37–26)
		Miocene (26–12)
		Pliocene (12–2)
	Quaternary	Pleistocene (2–)
		Holocene 10,000 BP to present

Geologists devised their timescale on the basis of relative, not calendar, ages. Accurate dating was impossible and estimates were often bitterly disputed, but the order in which the rocks were formed could be deduced from careful observation. The advent of radioactive dating – culminating in the 1950s with the development of a mass spectrometer capable of accurately measuring tiny quantities of isotopes – appears to have settled the arguments. The Earth is far older than geologists first imagined, but their painstakingly-created structure of geological time has withstood the advent of high technology.

The 4.6 billion (4,600 million) years since the formation of the Earth are divided into four great eras, further split into periods and, in the case of the most recent era, epochs. The present era is the Cenozoic ('new life'), extending backwards through 'middle life' and 'ancient life' to the Pre-Cambrian, named after the Latin word for Wales, the location of some of the earliest known fossils. Most of the Earth's geological history is encompassed by the Pre-Cambrian: though traces of ancient life have since been found, it was largely the proliferation of fossils from the beginning of the Paleozoic era onwards, some 570 million years ago, which first allowed precise subdivisions to be made.

Like the Cambrian, most are named after regions exemplifying a period's geology. Others – such as the Carboniferous ('coal-bearing') or the Cretaceous ('chalk-bearing') – are more directly descriptive.

- Pre-Cambrian shields
- Sedimentary cover on Pre-Cambrian shields
- Paleozoic (Caledonian and Hercynian) folding
- Sedimentary cover on Paleozoic folding
- Mesozoic folding
- Sedimentary cover on Mesozoic folding
- Cenozoic (Alpine) folding
- Sedimentary cover on Cenozoic folding
- Intensive Mesozoic and Cenozoic vulcanism
- Principal faults
- Oceanic marginal troughs
- Mid-oceanic ridges
- Overthrust faults

Earthquakes

Earthquake magnitude is usually rated according to either the Richter or the Modified Mercalli scale, both devised by seismologists in the 1930s. The Richter scale measures absolute earthquake power with mathematical precision: each step upwards represents a tenfold increase in the amplitude of the shockwave. Theoretically, there is no upper limit, but the largest earthquakes measured have been rated at between 8.8 and 8.9. The 12-point Mercalli scale, based on observed effects, is often more meaningful, ranging from I (earthquakes noticed only by seismographs) to XII (total destruction); intermediate points include V (people awakened at night; unstable objects overturned), VII (collapse of ordinary buildings; chimneys and monuments fall) and IX (conspicuous cracks in ground; serious damage to reservoirs).

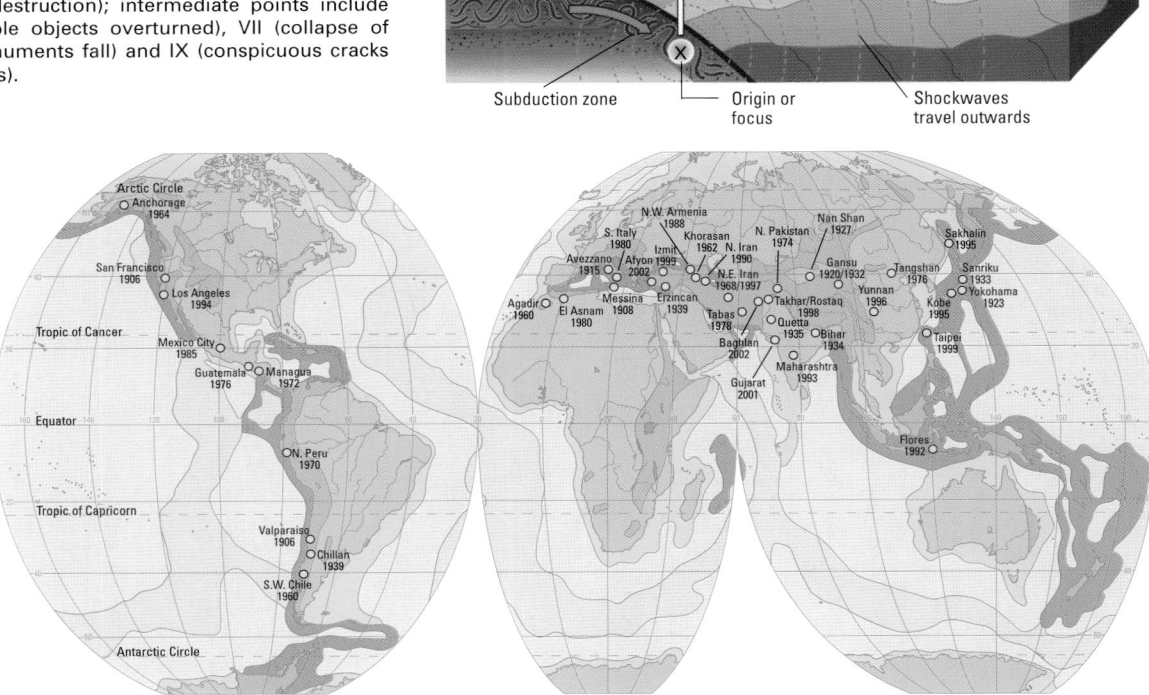

Epicentre – point on the surface directly above the origin

Shockwaves reach the surface

Subduction zone

Origin or focus

Shockwaves travel outwards

- Mobile land areas
- Submarine zones of mobile land areas
- Stable land platforms
- Submarine extensions of land platforms
- Mid-oceanic volcanic ridges
- Oceanic platforms

1976 — Principal earthquakes and dates (since 1900)

Earthquakes are a series of rapid vibrations originating from the slipping or faulting of parts of the Earth's crust when stresses within build up to breaking point. They usually happen at depths varying from 8 km to 30 km. Severe earthquakes cause extensive damage when they take place in populated areas, destroying structures and severing communications. Most initial loss of life occurs due to secondary causes such as falling masonry, fires and flooding.

Notable Earthquakes Since 1900

Year	Location	Mag.	Deaths
1906	San Francisco, USA	7.7	3,000
1906	Valparaiso, Chile	8.6	22,000
1908	Messina, Italy	7.5	83,000
1915	Avezzano, Italy	7.5	30,000
1920	Gansu (Kansu), China	8.6	180,000
1923	Yokohama, Japan	8.3	143,000
1927	Nan Shan, China	8.3	200,000
1932	Gansu (Kansu), China	7.6	70,000
1933	Sanriku, Japan	8.9	2,990
1934	Bihar, India/Nepal	8.4	10,700
1935	Quetta, India*	7.5	60,000
1939	Chillan, Chile	8.3	28,000
1939	Erzincan, Turkey	7.9	30,000
1960	S. W. Chile	9.5	2,200
1960	Agadir, Morocco	5.8	12,000
1962	Khorasan, Iran	7.1	12,230
1964	Anchorage, USA	9.2	125
1968	N. E. Iran	7.4	12,000
1970	N. Peru	7.7	66,794
1972	Managua, Nicaragua	6.2	5,000
1974	N. Pakistan	6.3	5,200
1976	Guatemala	7.5	22,778
1976	Tangshan, China	8.2	255,000
1978	Tabas, Iran	7.7	25,000
1980	El Asnam, Algeria	7.3	20,000
1980	S. Italy	7.2	4,800
1985	Mexico City, Mexico	8.1	4,200
1988	N.W. Armenia	6.8	55,000
1990	N. Iran	7.7	36,000
1992	Flores, Indonesia	6.8	1,895
1993	Maharashtra, India	6.4	30,000
1994	Los Angeles, USA	6.6	51
1995	Kobe, Japan	7.2	5,000
1995	Sakhalin Is., Russia	7.5	2,000
1996	Yunnan, China	7.0	240
1997	N. E. Iran	7.1	2,400
1998	Takhar, Afghanistan	6.1	4,200
1998	Rostaq, Afghanistan	7.0	5,000
1999	Izmit, Turkey	7.4	15,000
1999	Taipei, Taiwan	7.6	1,700
2001	Gujarat, India	7.7	14,000
2002	Afyon, Turkey	6.5	44
2002	Baghlan, Afghanistan	6.1	1,000

The most devastating quake ever was at Shaanxi (Shenshi) province, central China, on 3 January 1556, when an estimated 830,000 people were killed.

* now Pakistan

Landforms

For more information:
8 Oceans
10 The Earth's structure
   Plate tectonics
   Volcanoes
11 Geological time
18 Hydrological cycle
37 Structural regions

The theory of plate tectonics has offered new insights as to how the Earth works, elucidating mysteries concerning continental drift, volcanic eruptions and earthquakes. It has also contributed to our understanding of how plate collisions can squeeze up layers of sediments on seabeds into fold mountain ranges, such as the Himalayas.

Yet even as mountains rise, natural forces are wearing them away. In hot, dry climates, mechanical weathering, a result of rapid temperature changes, causes the outer layers of rocks to peel away, while, in cold mountain regions, boulders are prised apart when water freezes in cracks in rocks. Chemical weathering is responsible for hollowing out limestone caves and decomposing granites.

Climatic conditions have a great bearing on the principal agent of erosion in any particular area. Running water is most important in moist temperate regions. In cold regions, ice is the major agent of erosion, and in many mountain ranges, U-shaped valleys are evidence of the erosive power of valley glaciers. Ice sheets moulded much of the Earth's surface during the Ice Ages, the most recent of which, in the northern hemisphere, ended only 10,000 years ago. Polar climates also shape the scenery of the periglacial areas that border bodies of ice. Such areas are subject to constant freeze-thaw action, which creates such features as pingos (domed mounds).

Climatic change has also affected many of the landforms in hot deserts, which were shaped by running water at a time when the deserts enjoyed much wetter climates. However, the major agent of erosion in deserts today is wind-blown sand, which erodes rock strata to form mushroom-shaped rocks and caves.

The surface of the Earth is under constant assault from tectonic processes and the agents of erosion. The products of erosion, fragments of rock such as sand, are deposited to form sedimentary rocks. Metamorphic rocks are created when igneous or sedimentary rocks are buried and metamorphosed by heat and pressure. Eventually the rocks are recycled to form magma, which rises upwards to start the rock cycle all over again.

The Rock Cycle

James Hutton first proposed the rock cycle in the late 1700s after he observed the slow but steady effects of erosion.

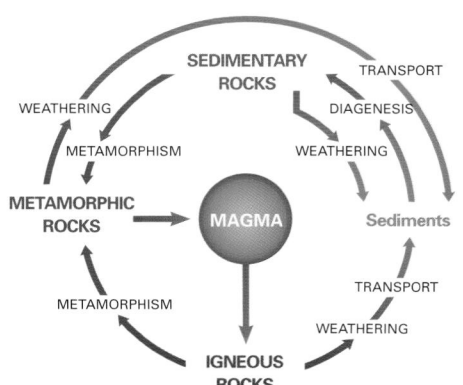

Rocks are divided into three types, according to the way in which they are formed:

Igneous rocks, including granite and basalt, are formed by the cooling of magma from within the Earth's crust.

Metamorphic rocks, such as slate, marble and quartzite, are formed below the Earth's surface by the compression or baking of existing rocks.

Sedimentary rocks, like sandstone and limestone, are formed on the surface of the Earth from the remains of living organisms and eroded fragments of older rocks.

Mountain Building

Mountains are formed when pressures on the Earth's crust caused by continental drift become so intense that the surface buckles or cracks. This happens where oceanic crust is subducted by continental crust or, more dramatically, where two tectonic plates collide: the Rockies, Andes, Alps, Urals and Himalayas resulted from such impacts. These are all known as fold mountains because they were formed by the compression of the rocks, forcing the surface to bend and fold like a crumpled rug. The Himalayas are formed from the folded former sediments of the Tethys Sea, which was trapped in the collision zone between the Indian and Eurasian plates.

The other main mountain-building process occurs when the crust fractures to create faults, allowing rock to be forced upwards in large blocks; or when the pressure of magma within the crust forces the surface to bulge into a dome, or erupts to form a volcano. Large mountain ranges may reveal a combination of these features; the Alps, for example, have been compressed so violently that the folds are fragmented by numerous faults and intrusions of molten igneous rock.

Over millions of years, even the greatest mountain ranges can be reduced by the agents of erosion (especially rivers) to a low, rugged landscape known as a peneplain.

Types of faults: Faults occur where the crust is being stretched or compressed so violently that the rock strata break in a horizontal or vertical movement. They are classified by the direction in which the blocks of rock have moved. A normal fault results when a vertical movement causes the surface to break apart; compression causes a reverse fault. Horizontal movement causes shearing, known as a strike-slip fault. When the rock breaks in two places, the central block may be pushed up in a horst fault, or sink (creating a rift valley) in a graben fault.

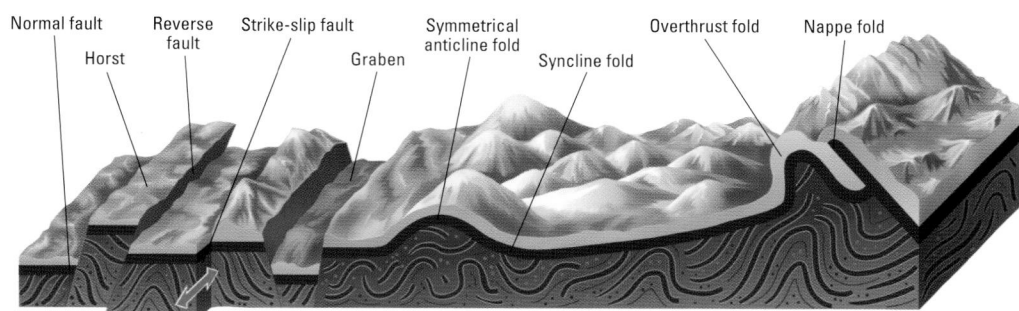

Normal fault · Horst · Reverse fault · Strike-slip fault · Symmetrical anticline fold · Graben · Syncline fold · Overthrust fold · Nappe fold

Types of fold: Folds occur when rock strata are squeezed and compressed. They are common, therefore, at destructive plate margins and where plates have collided, forcing the rocks to buckle into mountain ranges. Geographers give different names to the degrees of fold that result from continuing pressure on the rock. A simple fold may be symmetric, with even slopes on either side, but as the pressure builds up, one slope becomes steeper and the fold becomes asymmetric. Later, the ridge or 'anticline' at the top of the fold may slide over the lower ground or 'syncline' to form a recumbent fold. Eventually, the rock strata may break under the pressure to form an overthrust and finally a nappe fold.

Continental Glaciation

Annual Fluctuations for Selected Glaciers

Glacier name and location	Change in mass balance 1970–90
Wolverine, USA	+2,320
Storglaciaren, Sweden	−120
Djankuat, Russia	−1,890
Grasubreen, Norway	−2,530
Ürümqi, China	−3,828
Golubin, Kyrgyzstan	−7,105
Gries, Switzerland	−10,600
Careser, Italy	−11,610
Abramov, Tajikistan	−13,700
Sarennes, France	−15,020
Place, Canada	−15,175

The mass balance is defined as the difference between glacier accumulation and ablation (melting), and is expressed as water equivalent in millimetres. A minus indicates a reduction in the depth or length of a glacier. As can be seen from this geographically diverse selection, glaciers are retreating in many areas worldwide. The most dramatic and serious example of this phenomenon is the continuing distintegration of several large Antarctic ice-shelves.

The extent to which glacial retreat is due to global warming, or to longer term climatic fluctuations, remains a matter for debate.

Many landforms in the northern hemisphere were shaped by ice sheets and meltwater during the Pleistocene Ice Age, which began about 2 million years ago. During the Ice Age, the ice sheets periodically advanced and retreated. The first map (*below left*) shows the ice cover at its greatest extent about 200,000 years BP (before the present), when it covered about 30% of the land surface, as compared with 10% today. About 18,000 years BP, the ice covered most of Canada and extended as far south as the Bristol Channel in England. Around the ice sheets, land areas experienced periglacial conditions.

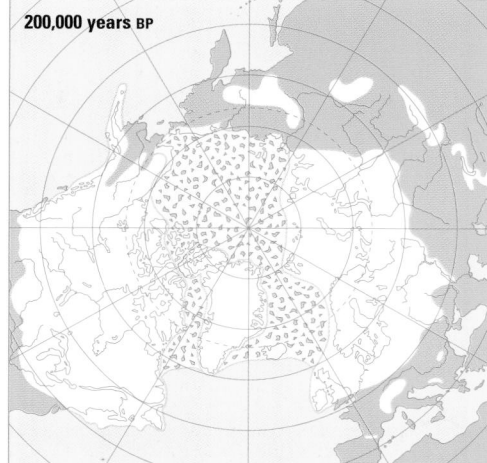

200,000 years BP

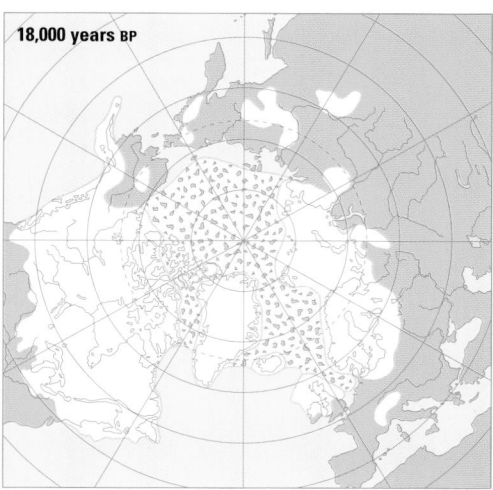

18,000 years BP

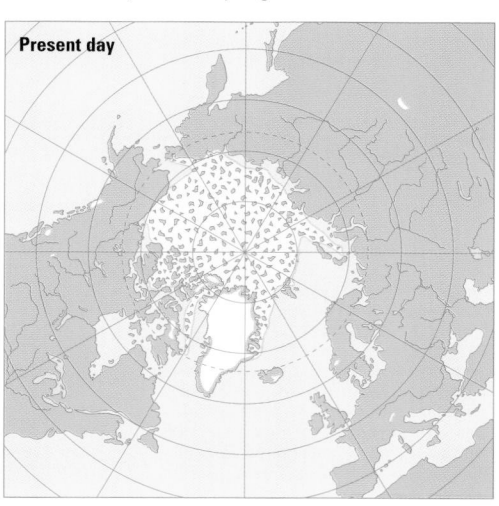

Present day

Natural Landforms

Natural landforms reflect the influence of plate tectonics through mountain-building and the generation of new rocks from the interior, together with the agents of erosion: running water, ice, winds and coastal waves. Over millions of years, mountains are gradually eroded, producing landforms that reflect the major forces that have been at work, as well as the underlying geology, the climatic conditions, which often vary over time, and the vegetation cover. The stylized diagram (*below*) shows some major natural landforms found in the mid-latitudes.

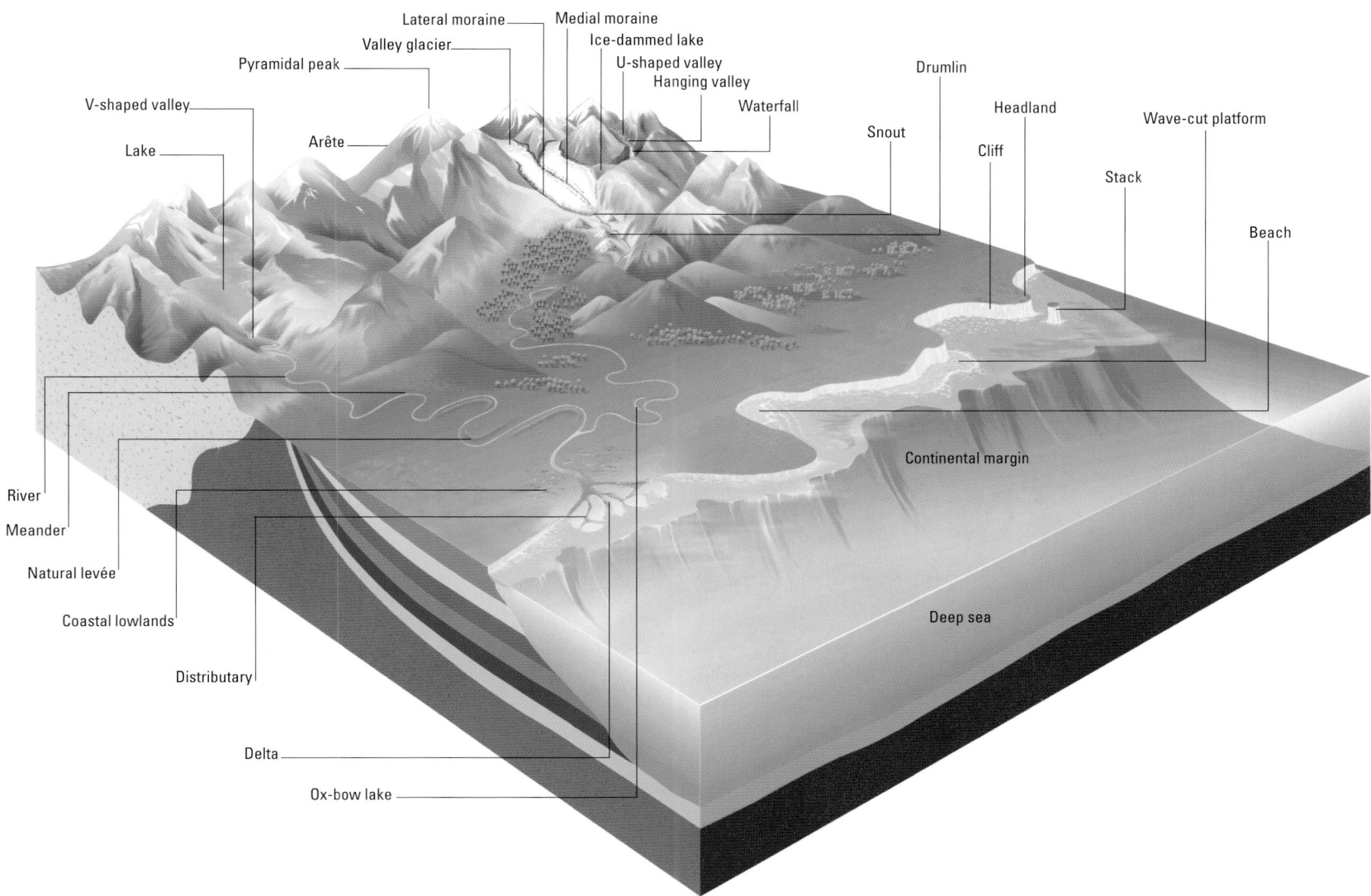

Desert Landforms

Deserts are defined as places with an average annual precipitation of 250 mm per year, though places with a higher rainfall and a high evaporation rate may also qualify as deserts. The three types of desert landforms are known by their Arabic names, a reflection of the fact that the Sahara in North Africa is the world's largest desert. Sand desert, called erg, covers about one-fifth of the world's deserts. The rest is divided between hammada (areas of bare rock) and reg (broad plains covered by loose gravel or pebbles).

The shapes of dunes in sand deserts reflect the character of local winds. Where winds are constant in direction, the sand often piles up in crescent-shaped dunes, called barchans. Barchans are constantly on the move and their forward march, unless halted by vegetation, may overwhelm settlements at oases. Seif dunes, named after the Arabic word for 'sword', are long ridges of sand that lie parallel to the direction of the wind, but where winds are variable, the sand sheets are often featureless.

Wind-blown sand is an effective agent of erosion, but because of the weight of sand grains, this type of erosion is confined to within 2 metres of the land surface, creating caves and mushroom-shaped rocks.

In assessing desert landforms, it is important to remember that other processes were at work in the past when the climate was very different from today. For example, cave paintings suggest that the Sahara had a much wetter climate after the end of the Ice Age and only began to dry up after about 5000 BC. However, human action, including overgrazing and the cutting down of trees for firewood, can turn a grassland region into desert – a process known as desertification.

Erg

Hammada

Reg

Surface Processes

Catastrophic changes to landforms are periodically caused by such phenomena as avalanches, landslides and volcanic eruptions, but most of the processes that shape the Earth's surface operate extremely slowly in human terms. One estimate, based on a study of landforms in the United States, suggests that, on average, 1 metre of land is removed from the entire surface of the country every 29,500 years. However, the terrain and the climate have a great effect on the erosion rate. For example, on cold plains, such as the Hudson Bay lowlands, the rate drops to around 1 metre for every 154,200 years, while in wet, tropical mountain areas, the rate may reach 1 metre for every 1,300 years.

Chemical weathering is at its greatest in warm, humid regions, while mechanical weathering, or the physical break-up of rocks, predominates in cold mountain or hot desert regions. The most familiar type of chemical weathering is caused by the reaction of rainwater containing dissolved carbon dioxide on limestone. This leads to the creation of labyrinthine cave networks dissolved by groundwater. Mechanical weathering includes frost action, while in hot deserts, rapid temperature changes cause the outer layers of rocks to expand and contract until they crack and peel away, a process called exfoliation.

The most important product of weathering is soil, which consists of rock fragments and humus, the decayed remains of plants and animals, together with living organisms, including vast numbers of micro-organisms. Soils vary in character according to the climate, ranging from the heavily leached, red laterite soils of wet tropical areas to the fertile, brown soils of dry grasslands. Soils are important because they support plants, which in turn anchor the soil and act as a protection against erosion. Soil erosion is greatest on sloping land because the steeper the slope, the greater the tendency for the soil to creep or flow downhill. The degree of movement of soil and rock downhill under the influence of gravity, called mass wasting, depends on a slope's stability. The stability may be disturbed by earthquakes or by heavy rain (water acts as a lubricant and increases the weight of the overlying material), which may trigger flows, slides or large falls of rock.

Running water is probably the world's leading agent of erosion and transportation. The energy of a river depends on several factors, including its velocity and volume, and its erosive power is at its peak when it is in full flood, sweeping soil, pebbles and even boulders along its course, cutting downwards into the bedrock or widening its valley. Sea waves also exert tremendous erosive power during storms, when they hurl pebbles and large rocks against the shore, undercutting cliffs and hollowing out caves. Headlands are often attacked on both sides, forming caves, then a natural arch and eventually an isolated stack.

Glacier ice forms in mountain hollows, called cirques, and spills out to form valley glaciers, which transport rocks shattered by frost action. As a glacier moves, rocks embedded in the base and sides scrape away bedrock, eroding steep-sided, flat-bottomed, U-shaped valleys. Evidence of past glaciation in mountain regions includes cirques, knife-edged ridges, or arêtes, and pyramidal peaks, or horns.

Geologists once considered that landforms evolved from 'young', newly uplifted mountainous areas, through a 'mature' hilly stage, to an 'old age' stage when the land was reduced to an almost flat plain, or peneplain. This theory, called the 'cycle of erosion', fell into disuse when it became evident that so many factors, including the effects of plate tectonics and climatic change, constantly interrupt the cycle, which takes no account of the highly complex interactions that shape the surface of our planet.

THE ATMOSPHERE

For more information:
9 Ocean currents
17 Beaufort wind scale
Climate change
Monsoon
21 Solar energy
Greenhouse effect
22 Greenhouse power
23 Acid rain

The atmosphere is a meteor shield, a radiation deflector, a thermal blanket and a source of chemical energy for the Earth's diverse life forms. Five-sixths of its mass is in the lowest layer, the troposphere, which ranges in thickness from 18 to 10 km between the Equator and the poles. Powered by the Sun, the air is always on the move, flowing generally from high- to low-pressure areas. The troposphere is the layer where virtually all weather phenomena, including clouds, precipitation and winds, occur. Above the troposphere is the stratosphere, which contains the important ozone layer and extends to about 50 km above the Earth's surface. Beyond 100 km, atmospheric density is lower than most laboratory vacuums.

Circulation of the Air

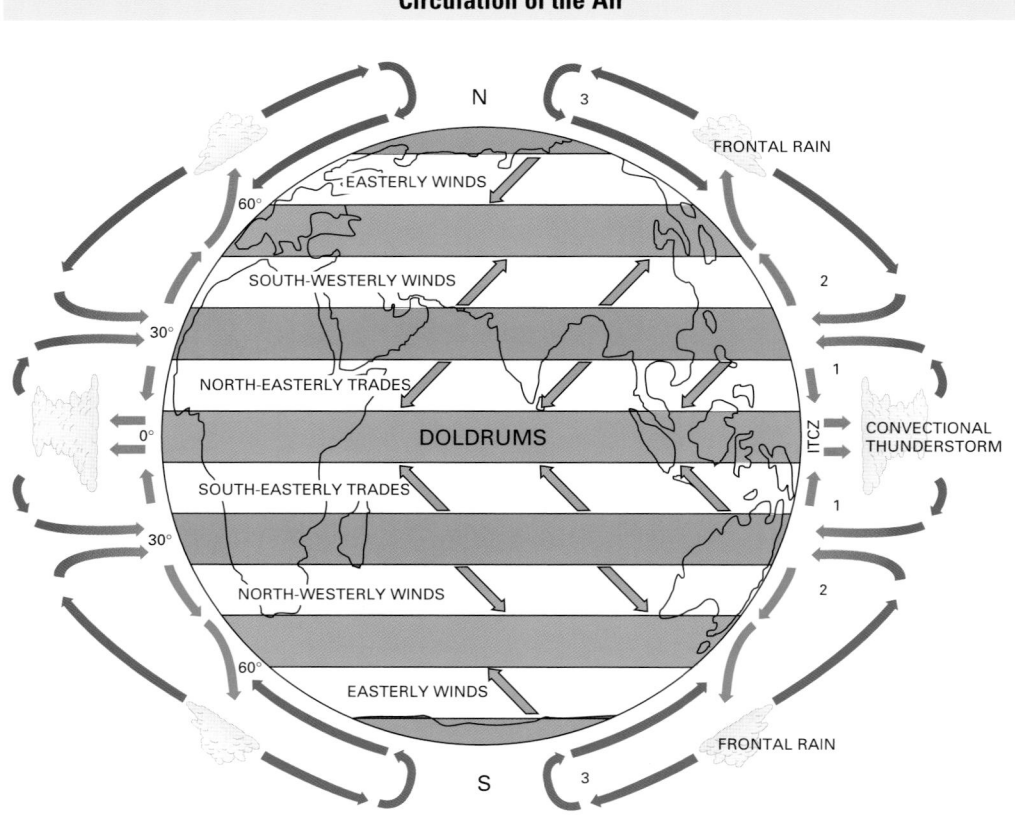

High pressure
Low pressure
Warm air
Cold air
Surface winds
Clouds

1 Hadley Cell
2 Ferrel Cell
3 Polar Cell

ITCZ Intertropical convergence zone

Structure of the Atmosphere

600 km — Hubble Space Telescope — pressure 10^{-20}mb

exosphere
400 km — International Space Station — 10^{-12}mb
350 km

300 km — Space Shuttle — 10^{-10}mb

250 km

thermosphere
200 km — 10^{-10}mb

aurorae
150 km

mesosphere
100 km — meteor trails — 10^{-3}mb

50 km — ozone layer
stratosphere

10 km — Concorde — 10^{3}mb
troposphere
Mount Everest 8,850 m

Chemical Composition

Gaseous composition of the principal atmospheric layers

50–100% hydrogen — 25–50% helium
Exosphere
Helium vanishes with increasing altitude. Above 2,400 km the exosphere is almost entirely composed of hydrogen.

70% nitrogen — 15% oxygen — 15% helium
Mesosphere
The high energy of mesospheric gas gives it a notional temperature of more than 2,000°C, although its density is negligible.

80% nitrogen — 18% oxygen — 1% argon — 1% ozone
Stratosphere
Stratospheric air contains enough ozone to make it poisonous, although it is in any case too rarified to breathe.

78% nitrogen — 21% oxygen — 1% argon
Troposphere
The narrowest of all the layers, this thin region contains about 85% of the atmosphere's total mass and almost all of its water vapour. It is also the realm of the Earth's weather.

Frontal Systems

Depressions, or cyclones, form along the polar front where dense polar easterlies meet warm subtropical westerlies. Depressions occur when warm air flows into waves in the polar front, while cold air flows in behind it, creating rotating air systems that bring changeable weather. Along the warm front (the boundary on the ground between the warm and cold air), the warm air flows upwards over the cold air, producing a sequence of clouds which help forecasters to predict a depression's advance. Along the cold front, the advancing cold air forces warm air to rise steeply. Towering cumulonimbus clouds form in the rising air. When the cold front overtakes the warm front, the warm air is pushed above ground level to form an occluded front. Cloud and rain persist along occlusions until temperatures equalize, the air mixes, and the depression dies out.

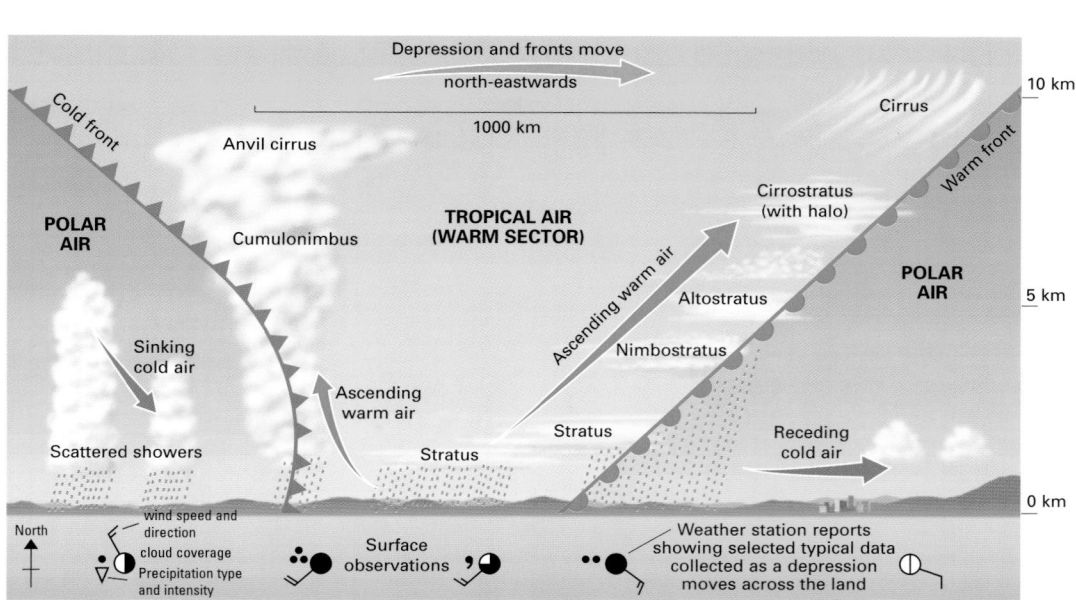

Air Masses

Air masses are bodies of air whose characteristics are broadly the same over a large area. Around the Equator, where the Sun's heat creates relatively high surface temperatures, warm air rises to create a zone of low pressure called the doldrums. The air cools and finally spreads out towards the poles. Around latitudes 30° north and south, the air sinks back to the surface, becoming warmer as it descends and creating zones of high pressure called the horse latitudes.

The high- and low-pressure zones are both areas of comparative calm, but between them lie the prevailing trade wind belts. Air also flows north and south from the high-pressure horse latitudes and these air flows meet up with cold, dense air flowing from the poles along the polar front. This basic circulatory system is complicated by the Coriolis effect, brought about by the spinning Earth. Because of the Coriolis effect, the prevailing winds do not flow directly north–south but are deflected to the right in the northern hemisphere and to the left in the southern. Along the polar front, depressions form where the polar easterlies meet the westerlies.

The first classification of clouds was developed by a London chemist, Luke Howard, in 1803, and it was later modified by the World Meteorological Organization. The main types are divided into three groups according to their altitude, and into subgroups according to their shape, which vary from hairlike filaments (cirrus), heaps or piles (cumulus), and layers (stratus). Each cloud carries some kind of message, though not always a clear one, to weather forecasters.

Classification of Clouds

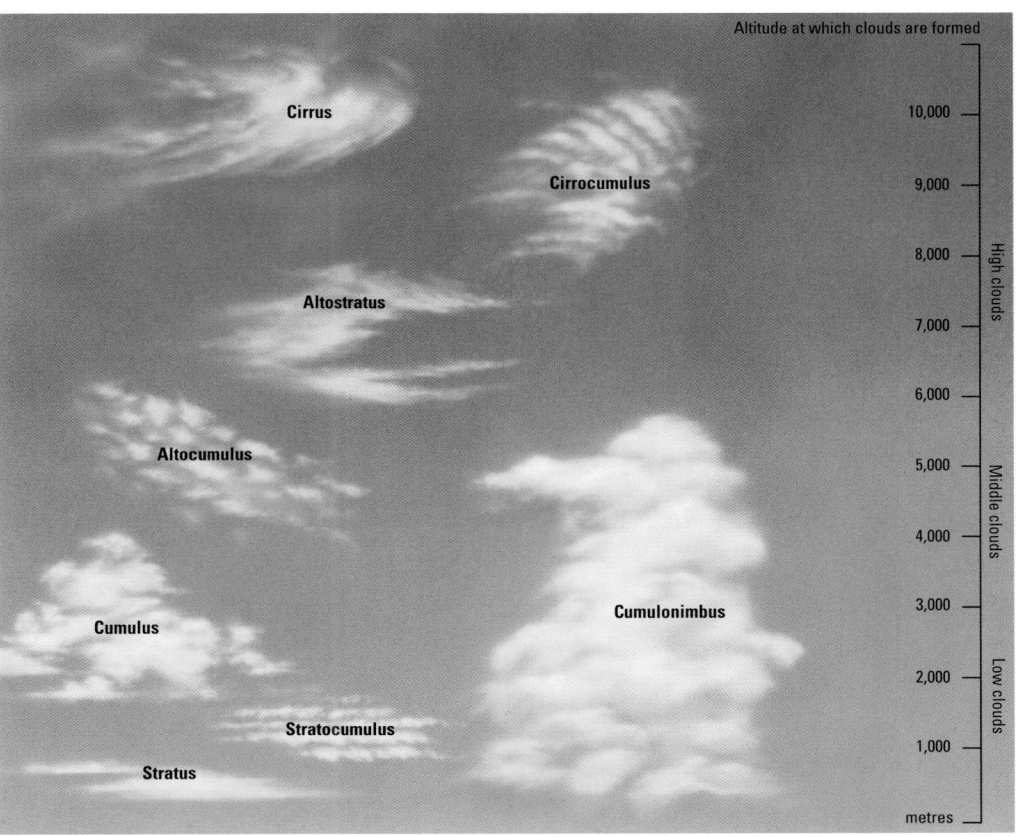

Altitude at which clouds are formed

Clouds form when damp, usually rising, air is cooled. Thus they form when a wind rises to cross hills or mountains; when a mass of air rises over, or is pushed up by, another mass of denser air; or when local heating of the ground causes convection currents.

The types of clouds are classified according to altitude as high, middle or low. The high ones, composed of ice crystals, are cirrus, cirrostratus and cirrocumulus. The middle clouds are altostratus, a grey or bluish striated, fibrous or uniform sheet producing light drizzle, and altocumulus, a thicker and fluffier version of cirrocumulus.

Low clouds include nimbo-stratus, a dark grey layer that brings rain or snow; cumulus, a detached heap, dark at the base; stratus, which forms dull, overcast skies at low levels; and stratocumulus, which consists of fluffy greyish-white layers.

Cumulonimbus, associated with storms and rains, heavy and dense with a flat base and a high, fluffy outline, can be tall enough to occupy middle as well as low altitudes.

Pressure and Surface Winds

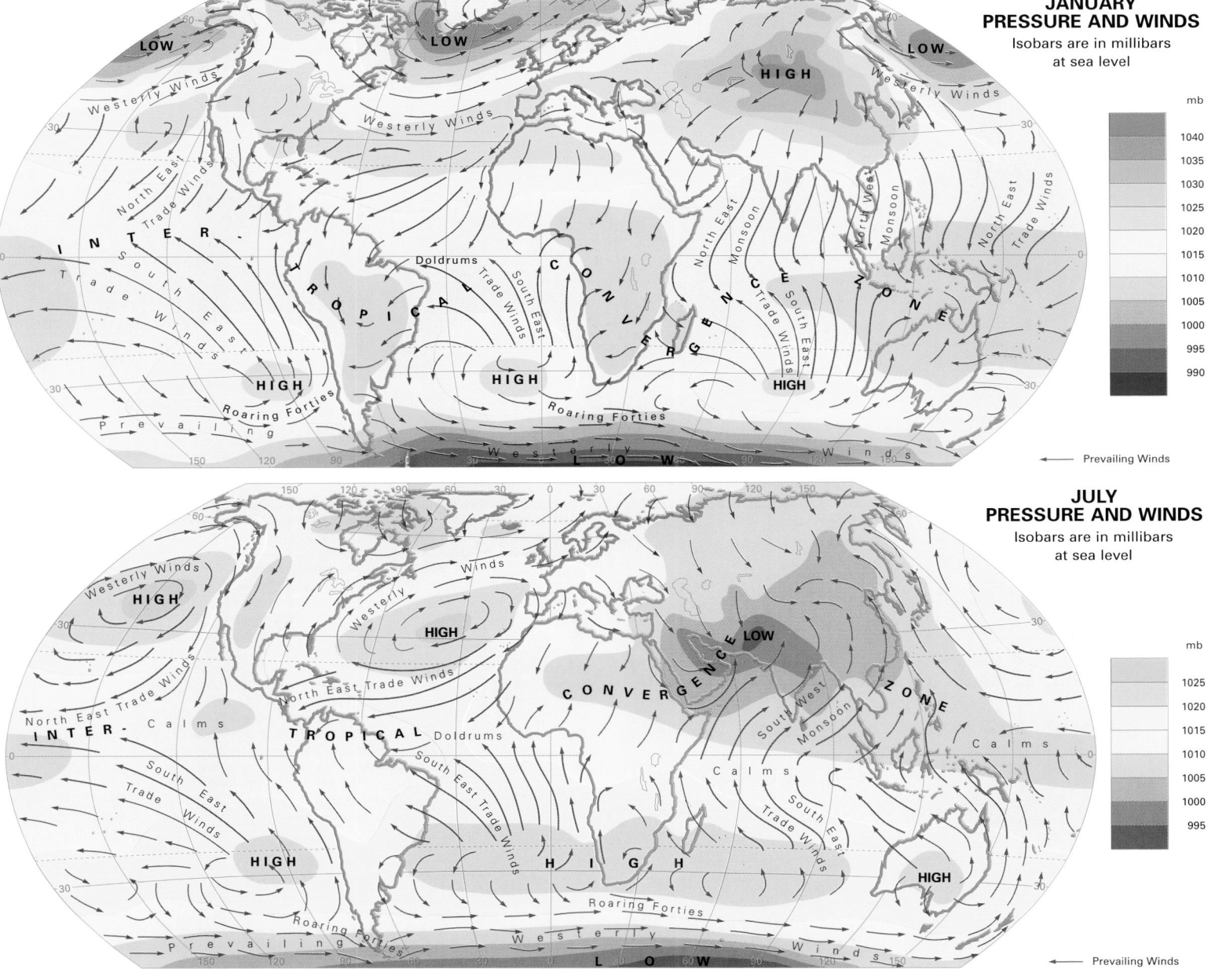

JANUARY PRESSURE AND WINDS
Isobars are in millibars at sea level

JULY PRESSURE AND WINDS
Isobars are in millibars at sea level

← Prevailing Winds

Climate Records

Pressure and winds

Highest barometric pressure: Agata, Siberia, 1,083.8 mb at altitude 262 m [862 ft], 31 December 1968.

Lowest barometric pressure: Typhoon Tip, 480 km [300 mi] west of Guam, Pacific Ocean, 870 mb, 12 October 1979.

Highest recorded wind speed: Mt Washington, New Hampshire, USA, 371 km/h [231 mph], 12 April 1934. This is three times as strong as hurricane force on the Beaufort Scale.

Windiest place: Commonwealth Bay, George V Coast, Antarctica, where gales frequently reach over 320 km/h [200 mph].

Worst recorded storm: Bangladesh (then East Pakistan) cyclone*, 13 November 1970 – over 300,000 dead or missing. The 1991 cyclone, Bangladesh's and the world's second worst in terms of loss of life, killed an estimated 138,000 people.

Worst recorded tornado: Missouri/Illinois/Indiana, USA, 18 March 1925 – 792 deaths. The tornado was only 275 m [300 yds] wide.

* Tropical cyclones are known as hurricanes in Central and North America, as typhoons in the Far East, and as willy-willies in northern Australia.

CLIMATE

For more information:

9 Ocean currents
14 Circulation of the air
15 Classification of clouds
   Pressure and winds
18 Hydrological cycle
19 Natural vegetation
21 Greenhouse effect
22 Global warming

Weather is the day-to-day or hour-to-hour condition of the air, while climate is weather in the long term, the seasonal pattern of hot and cold, wet and dry, averaged over a long period. Most classifications of climate are based on a system developed by a Russian meteorologist, Vladimir Köppen, in the early 19th century. Using a code based on letters and a classification centred on two main features, temperature and precipitation, he identified five main climatic types: tropical (A), dry (B), warm temperate (C), cold temperate (D), and polar (E). A highland mountain climate (H), was added later to account for the variety of altitudinal climatic zones on high mountains. Each of these

main regions was then further subdivided.

Latitude is a major factor in determining climate, but other factors add to the complexity. They include the differential heating of land and sea, the distance from the sea, the effect of mountains on winds, and the influence of ocean currents. For example, New York City, Naples and the Gobi Desert share almost the same latitude, but their climates are very different.

Climates are not indefinitely stable. During the last Ice Age, the Earth underwent alternating cold periods, called glacials, separated by warm interglacials. The Milankovich theory suggests such cycles may be caused by variations in the Earth's path around the Sun, changing

from almost circular to elliptical every 95,000 years, and variations in the Earth's tilt from 21.5° to 24.5° every 42,000 years. Another factor is that the Earth is now closest to the Sun in the middle of winter in the northern hemisphere and furthest away in summer. But 12,000 years ago, at the height of the last glacial period, the northern winter fell with the Sun at its most distant.

Studies of these cycles suggest that we are now in an interglacial with a new glacial period on the way. However, many scientists believe that global warming, largely a result of burning fossil fuels and deforestation, may be occurring much faster than the great, slow cycles of the Solar System.

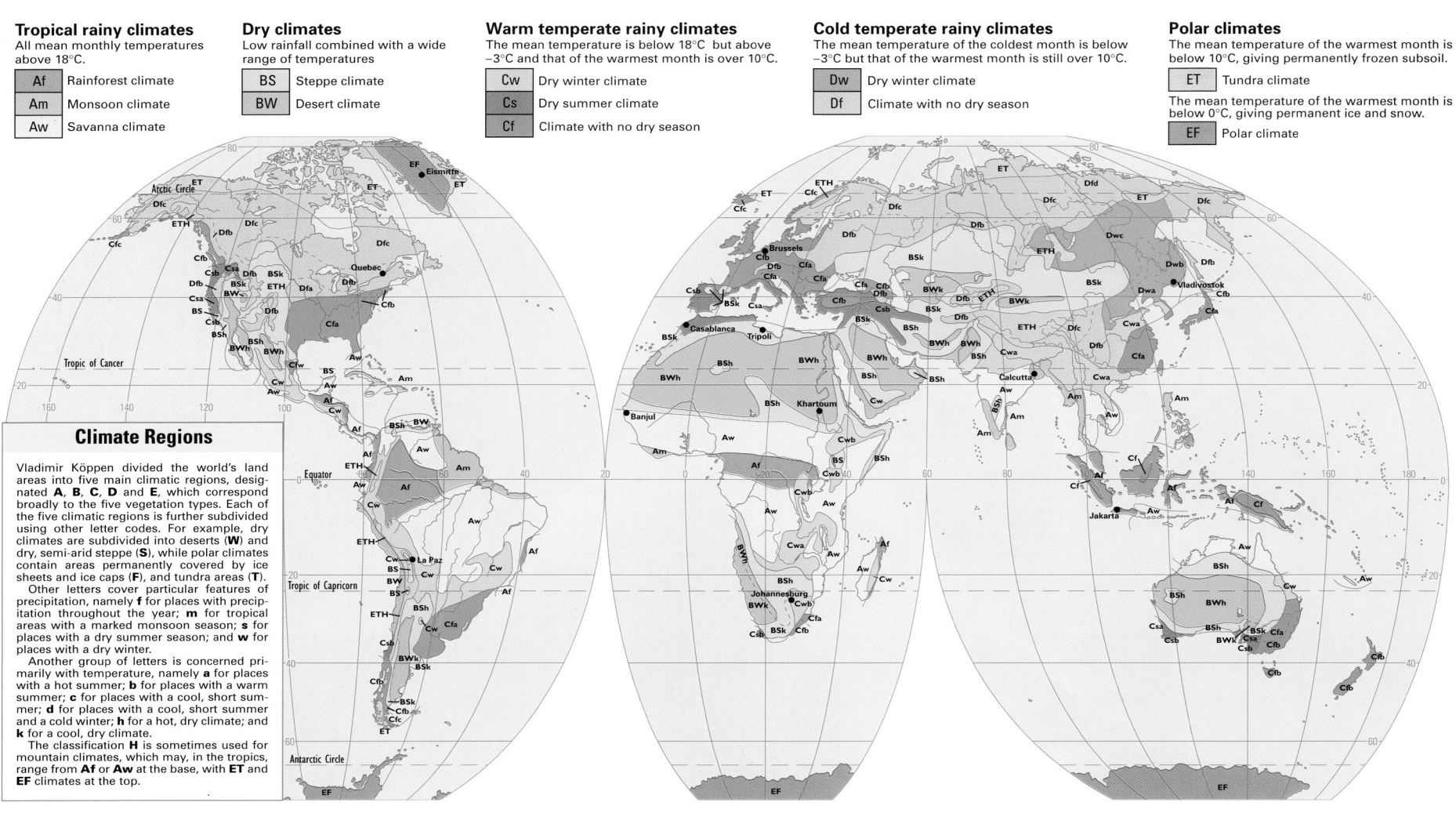

Tropical rainy climates
All mean monthly temperatures above 18°C.

Af	Rainforest climate
Am	Monsoon climate
Aw	Savanna climate

Dry climates
Low rainfall combined with a wide range of temperatures

| BS | Steppe climate |
| BW | Desert climate |

Warm temperate rainy climates
The mean temperature is below 18°C but above −3°C and that of the warmest month is over 10°C.

Cw	Dry winter climate
Cs	Dry summer climate
Cf	Climate with no dry season

Cold temperate rainy climates
The mean temperature of the coldest month is below −3°C but that of the warmest month is still over 10°C.

| Dw | Dry winter climate |
| Df | Climate with no dry season |

Polar climates
The mean temperature of the warmest month is below 10°C, giving permanently frozen subsoil.

| ET | Tundra climate |

The mean temperature of the warmest month is below 0°C, giving permanent ice and snow.

| EF | Polar climate |

Climate Regions

Vladimir Köppen divided the world's land areas into five main climatic regions, designated **A, B, C, D** and **E**, which correspond broadly to the five vegetation types. Each of the five climatic regions is further subdivided using other letter codes. For example, dry climates are subdivided into deserts (**W**) and dry, semi-arid steppe (**S**), while polar climates contain areas permanently covered by ice sheets and ice caps (**F**), and tundra areas (**T**).

Other letters cover particular features of precipitation, namely **f** for places with precipitation throughout the year; **m** for tropical areas with a marked monsoon season; **s** for places with a dry summer season; and **w** for places with a dry winter.

Another group of letters is concerned primarily with temperature, namely **a** for places with a hot summer; **b** for places with a warm summer; **c** for places with a cool, short summer; **d** for places with a cool, short summer and a cold winter; **h** for a hot, dry climate; and **k** for a cool, dry climate.

The classification **H** is sometimes used for mountain climates, which may, in the tropics, range from **Af** or **Aw** at the base, with **ET** and **EF** climates at the top.

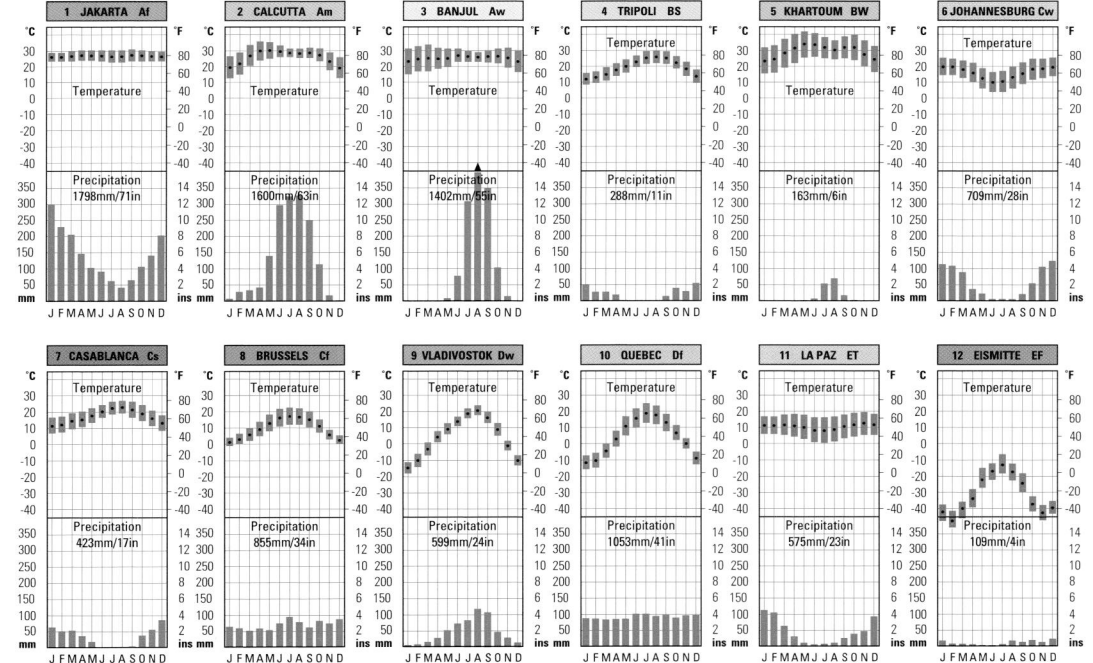

Climate and Weather Terms

Anticyclone: area of high pressure with light winds and generally quiet weather.
Absolute humidity: amount of water vapour contained in a given volume of air.
Cloud cover: amount of cloud in the sky; measured in oktas (from 1 – 8), with 0 clear, and 8 total cover.
Condensation: the conversion of water vapour, or moisture in the air, into liquid.
Cyclone: violent storm resulting from anticlockwise rotation of winds in the northern hemisphere and clockwise in the southern: called hurricane in N. America, typhoon in the Far East.
Depression: area of low pressure. The pressure gradient is towards the centre.
Dew: water droplets condensed out of the air after the ground has cooled at night.
Dew point: temperature at which air becomes saturated (reaches a relative humidity of 100%) at a constant pressure.
Drizzle: precipitation where drops are less than 0.5 mm [0.02 in] in diameter.
Evaporation: conversion of water from liquid into vapour, or moisture in the air.
Front: the dividing line between two air masses.
Frost: dew that has frozen when the air temperature falls below freezing point.
Hail: frozen rain; small balls of ice, often falling during thunderstorms.
Hoar frost: formed on objects when the dew point is below freezing point.
Humidity: amount of moisture in the air.
Isobar: cartographic line connecting places of equal atmospheric pressure.
Isotherm: cartographic line connecting places of equal temperature.
Lightning: massive electrical discharge released in thunderstorm from cloud to cloud or cloud to ground, the result of the top becoming positively charged and the bottom negatively charged.
Precipitation: measurable rain, snow, sleet or hail.
Prevailing wind: most common direction of wind at a given location.
Rain: precipitation of liquid particles with diameter larger than 0.5 mm [0.02 in].
Relative humidity: amount of water vapour contained in a given volume of air at a given temperature.
Snow: formed when water vapour condenses below freezing point.
Thunder: sound produced by the rapid expansion of air heated by lightning.
Tornado: severe funnel-shaped storm that twists as hot air spins vertically (waterspout at sea).
Whirlwind: rapidly rotating column of air, only a few metres across, made visible by dust.

Climate Change

Human factors, such as the emission of greenhouse gases through the burning of fossil fuels and deforestation, have contributed to global warming. The histogram (*below*) shows in blue the average global temperatures from 1860 (when sufficient observations became available for global averages to be calculated) to 1996. The red line is a 10-year running average. Overall, there is an upwards trend, particularly so since the 1970s, when global warming became a matter of concern in scientific circles. The large year-to-year changes indicate the Earth's natural climatic variability and the influence of such factors as major volcanic eruptions.

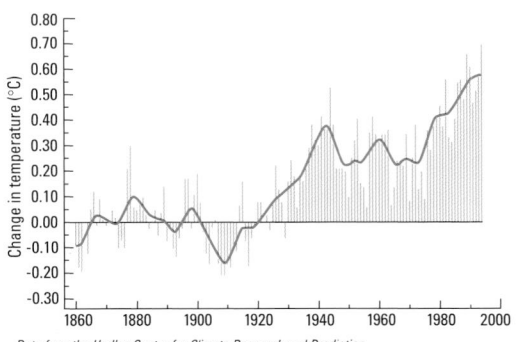

Data from the Hadley Centre for Climate Research and Prediction

Beaufort Wind Scale

Named after the 19th-century British naval officer who devised it, Admiral Beaufort, the Beaufort Scale assesses wind speed according to its effects. It was originally designed as an aid for sailors, but has since been adapted for use on the land. It is used internationally.

Scale	Wind speed km/h	mph	Effect
0	0–1	0–1	**Calm** Smoke rises vertically
1	1–5	1–3	**Light air** Wind direction shown only by smoke drift
2	6–11	4–7	**Light breeze** Wind felt on face; leaves rustle; vanes moved by wind
3	12–19	8–12	**Gentle breeze** Leaves and small twigs in constant motion; wind extends small flag
4	20–28	13–18	**Moderate** Raises dust and loose paper; small branches move
5	29–38	19–24	**Fresh** Small trees in leaf sway; crested wavelets on inland waters
6	39–49	25–31	**Strong** Large branches move; difficult to use umbrellas; overhead wires whistle
7	50–61	32–38	**Near gale** Whole trees in motion; difficult to walk against wind
8	62–74	39–46	**Gale** Twigs break from trees; walking very difficult
9	75–88	47–54	**Strong gale** Slight structural damage
10	89–102	55–63	**Storm** Trees uprooted; serious structural damage
11	103–117	64–72	**Violent storm** Widespread damage
12	118+	73+	**Hurricane**

The Monsoon

Monsoon is the term given to the seasonal reversal of wind direction, most noticeably in South-east Asia. It results from a combination of factors: the extreme heating and cooling of large landmasses in relation to the less marked changes in temperature of the adjacent seas; the northwards movement of the Intertropical Convergence Zone (ITCZ); and the effect of the Himalayas on the circulation of the air.

In early March, which normally marks the end of the subcontinent's cool season and the start of the hot season, winds blow outwards from the mainland. But as the overhead Sun and the ITCZ move northwards, the land is intensely heated, and a low-pressure system develops. The south-east trade winds, which are drawn across the Equator, change direction and are sucked into the interior to become south-westerly winds, bringing heavy rain. By November, the overhead Sun and the ITCZ have again moved southwards and the wind directions are again reversed. Cool winds blow from the Asian interior to the sea, losing any moisture on the Himalayas before descending to the coast.

Temperature

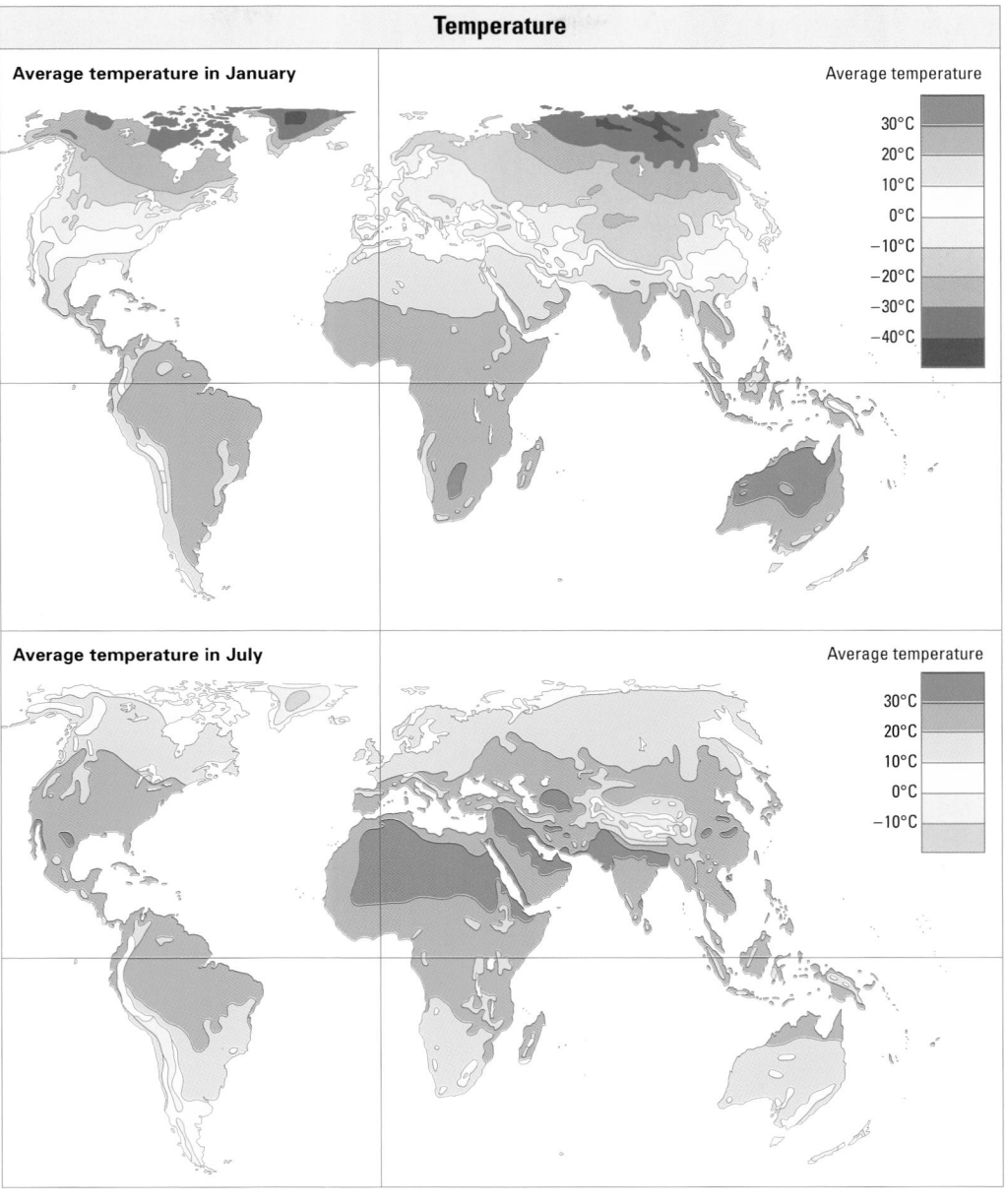

Average temperature in January

Average temperature
- 30°C
- 20°C
- 10°C
- 0°C
- −10°C
- −20°C
- −30°C
- −40°C

Average temperature in July

Average temperature
- 30°C
- 20°C
- 10°C
- 0°C
- −10°C

Precipitation

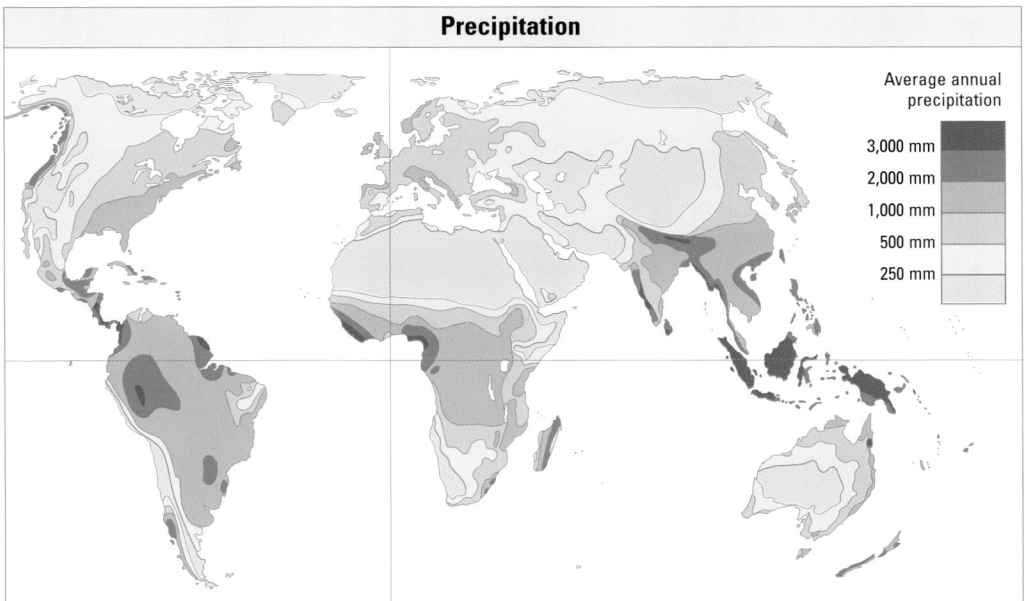

Average annual precipitation
- 3,000 mm
- 2,000 mm
- 1,000 mm
- 500 mm
- 250 mm

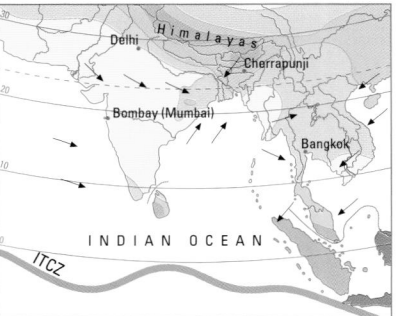

March – Start of the hot, dry season. The ITCZ is over the southern Indian Ocean.

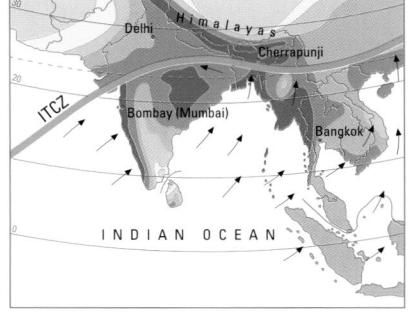

July – The rainy season. The ITCZ has migrated northwards; winds blow onshore.

November – The ITCZ has returned south. The offshore winds are cool and dry.

Monthly rainfall (mm)
- >400
- 200–400
- 100–200
- 50–100
- 25–50
- <25

→ wind direction
- - - ITCZ

Climate Records

Temperature

Highest recorded temperature: Al Aziziyah, Libya, 58°C [136.4°F], 13 September 1922.

Highest mean annual temperature: Dallol, Ethiopia, 34.4°C [94°F], 1960–6.

Longest heatwave: Marble Bar, W. Australia, 162 days over 38°C [100°F], 23 October 1923 to 7 April 1924.

Lowest recorded temperature (outside poles): Verkhoyansk, Siberia, −68°C [−90°F], 6 February 1933. Verkhoyansk also registered the greatest annual range of temperature: −70°C to 37°C [−94°F to 98°F].

Lowest mean annual temperature: Polus Nedostupnosti, Pole of Cold, Antarctica, −57.8°C [−72°F].

Precipitation

Driest place: Calama, N. Chile: no recorded rainfall in 400 years to 1971.

Wettest place (average): Tututendo, Colombia: mean annual rainfall 11,770 mm [463.4 in].

Wettest place (12 months): Cherrapunji, Meghalaya, N.E. India, 26,470 mm [1,040 in], August 1860 to August 1861. Cherrapunji also holds the record for rainfall in one month: 2,930 mm [115 in], July 1861. (*See maps below.*)

Wettest place (24 hours): Cilaos, Réunion, Indian Ocean, 1,870 mm [73.6 in], 15–16 March 1952.

Heaviest hailstones: Gopalganj, Bangladesh, up to 1.02 kg [2.25 lb], 14 April 1986 (killed 92 people).

Heaviest snowfall (continuous): Bessans, Savoie, France, 1,730 mm [68 in] in 19 hours, 5–6 April 1969.

Heaviest snowfall (season/year): Paradise Ranger Station, Mt Rainier, Washington, USA, 31,102 mm [1,224.5 in], 19 February 1971 to 18 February 1972.

WATER AND VEGETATION

For more information:

12 Rivers and glaciers
14 Types of precipitation
20 Biodiversity

Without the hydrological cycle, whereby water is constantly recycled between the oceans, the atmosphere and the land, the continents would be barren. Precipitation enables plants to grow and soils to form, creating the world's natural vegetation regions and the ecosystems that support animal life. Running water also plays a major role in shaping landforms. Yet in many parts of the world, people do not have safe water to drink and suffer from diseases caused by water-borne organisms or pollution. In addition, the limited water supplies have to be shared with agriculture and industry.

In 1996, UN experts argued that the demand for water is increasing at about twice the rate of population growth. It is predicted that, by 2025, two-thirds of the world's population will face water shortages. This could lead to conflict and even boundary wars, especially because 300 major rivers cross national frontiers and access to their water is likely to be disputed.

The Hydrological Cycle

The world's water balance is regulated by the constant recycling of water between the oceans, atmosphere and land. The movement of water between these three reservoirs is known as the hydrological cycle. The oceans play a vital role in the hydrological cycle: 74% of the total precipitation falls over the oceans and 84% of the total evaporation comes from the oceans. Water vapour in the atmosphere circulates around the planet, transporting energy as well as the water itself. When the vapour cools, it falls as rain or snow. The whole cycle is driven by the Sun.

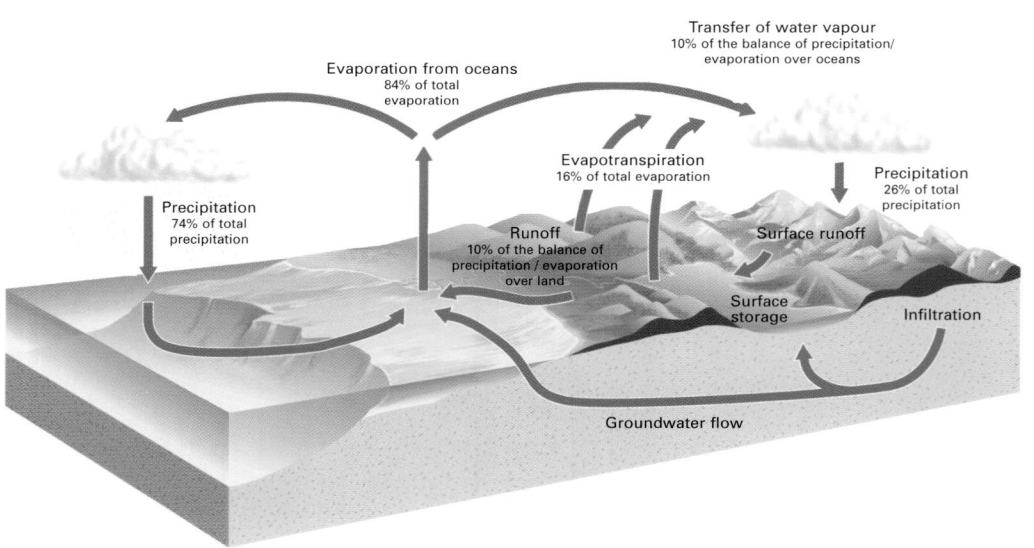

Water Distribution

The distribution of planetary water, by percentage. Oceans and ice caps together account for more than 99% of the total; the breakdown of the remainder is estimated.

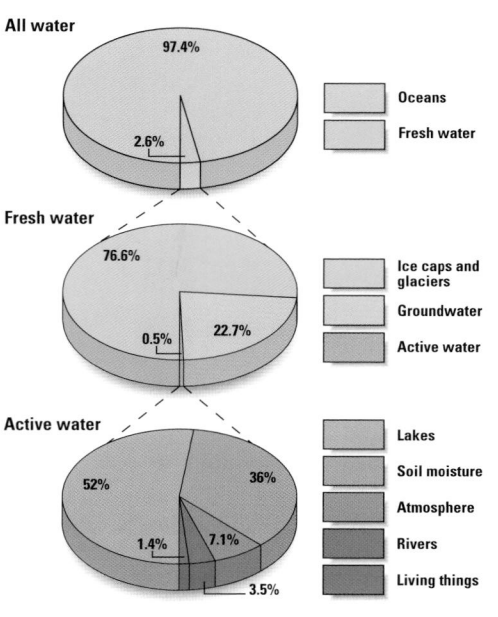

Almost all the world's water is 3,000 million years old, and all of it cycles endlessly through the hydrosphere, though at different rates. Water vapour circulates over days, even hours; deep ocean water circulates over millennia; and ice-cap water remains solid for millions of years.

Water Utilization

The percentage breakdown of water usage by sector, selected countries (1996)

Domestic
Industrial
Agriculture

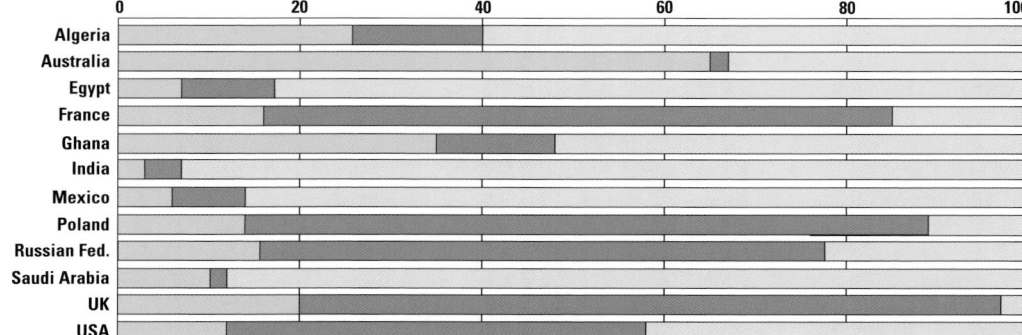

Water Runoff

Annual freshwater runoff by continent in cubic kilometres

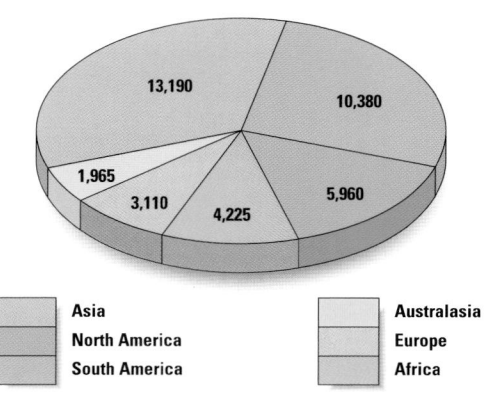

Asia
North America
South America
Australasia
Europe
Africa

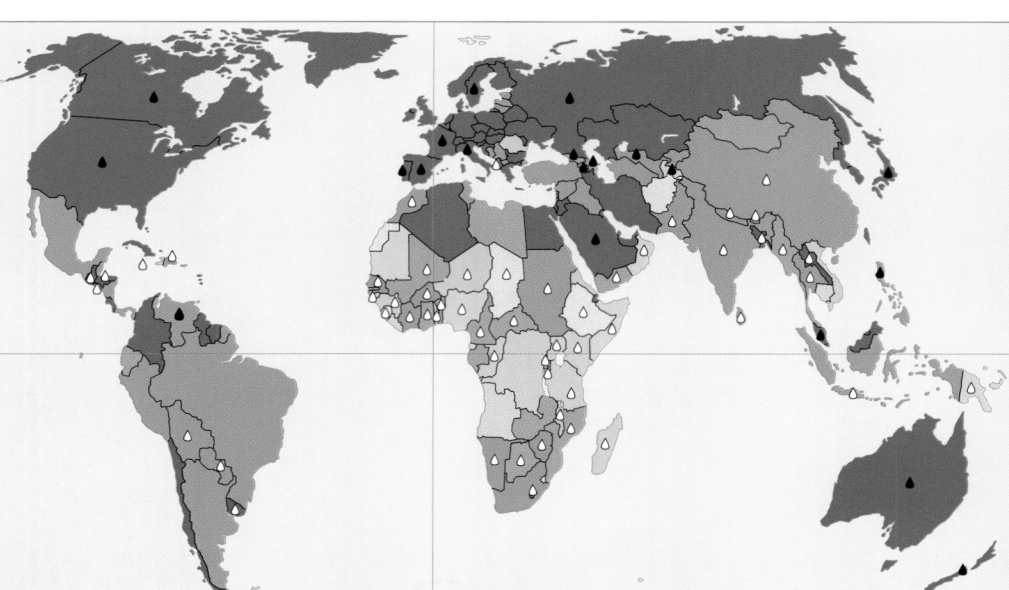

Water Supply

Percentage of total population with access to safe drinking water (2000)

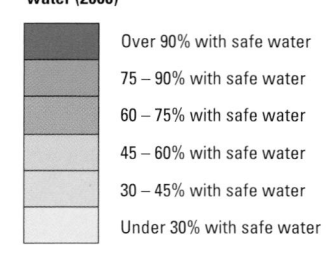

Over 90% with safe water
75 – 90% with safe water
60 – 75% with safe water
45 – 60% with safe water
30 – 45% with safe water
Under 30% with safe water

△ Under 80 litres average per capita daily water consumption

▲ Over 320 litres average per capita daily water consumption

80 litres of water a day is considered necessary for a reasonable quality of life

Least well-provided countries

Afghanistan	13%	Cambodia	30%
Ethiopia	24%	Mauritania	37%
Chad	27%	Angola	38%
Sierra Leone	28%	Oman	39%

18

Watersheds

The world's major rivers; the rank of the world's 20 longest is shown in square brackets, led by the Nile and the Amazon.

Where the rivers run

- Pacific Ocean
- Indian Ocean
- Arctic Ocean
- Atlantic Ocean
- Caribbean Sea–Gulf of Mexico
- Mediterranean Sea
- Inland basins, ice caps and deserts

The map shows the direction of freshwater flow on a continental scale; the water runoff chart on the facing page indicates the quantities involved. The rate of runoff varies seasonally and is affected by the surface vegetation. Most of the world's major rivers discharge into the Atlantic Ocean.

Annual Sediment Yield

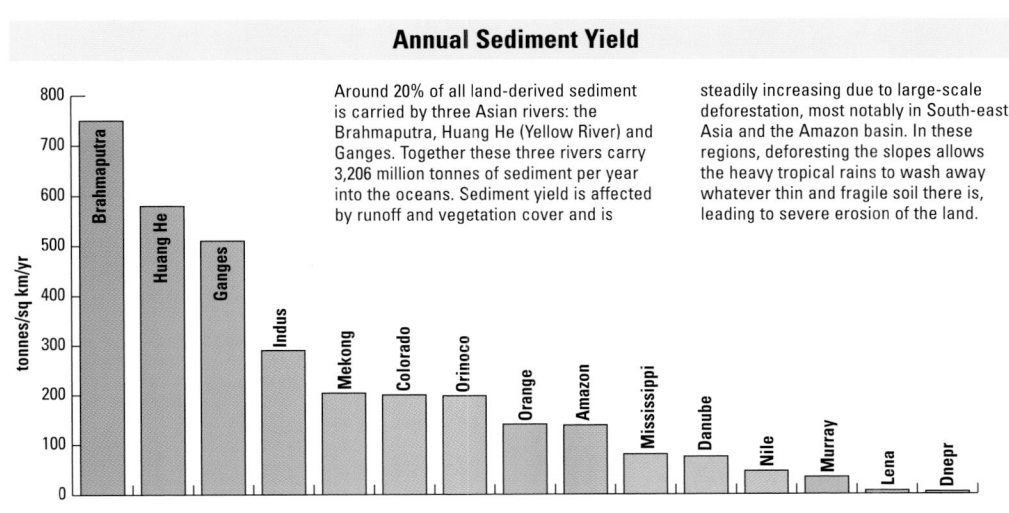

Around 20% of all land-derived sediment is carried by three Asian rivers: the Brahmaputra, Huang He (Yellow River) and Ganges. Together these three rivers carry 3,206 million tonnes of sediment per year into the oceans. Sediment yield is affected by runoff and vegetation cover and is steadily increasing due to large-scale deforestation, most notably in South-east Asia and the Amazon basin. In these regions, deforesting the slopes allows the heavy tropical rains to wash away whatever thin and fragile soil there is, leading to severe erosion of the land.

Land Use by Continent

The proportion of productive land has reached its upper limit in Europe, and in Asia more than 80% of potential cropland is already under cultivation.

- Forest
- Permanent pasture and rough grazing
- Permanent crops and plantations
- Arable
- Non-productive

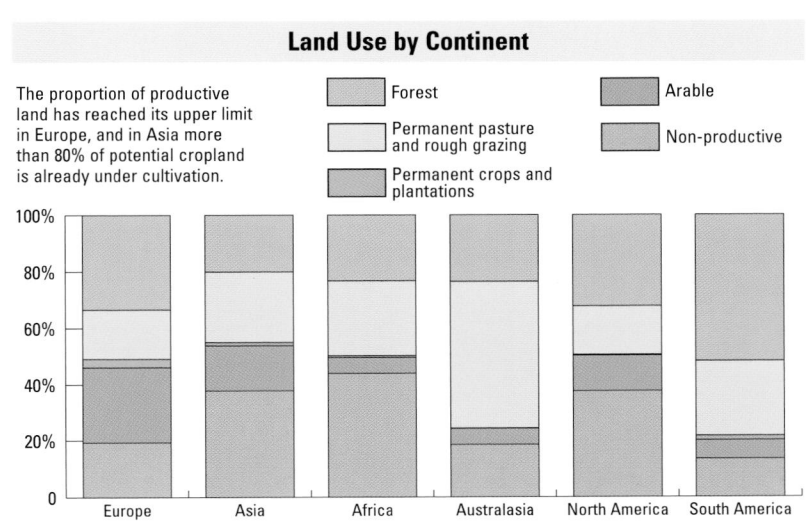

Natural Vegetation

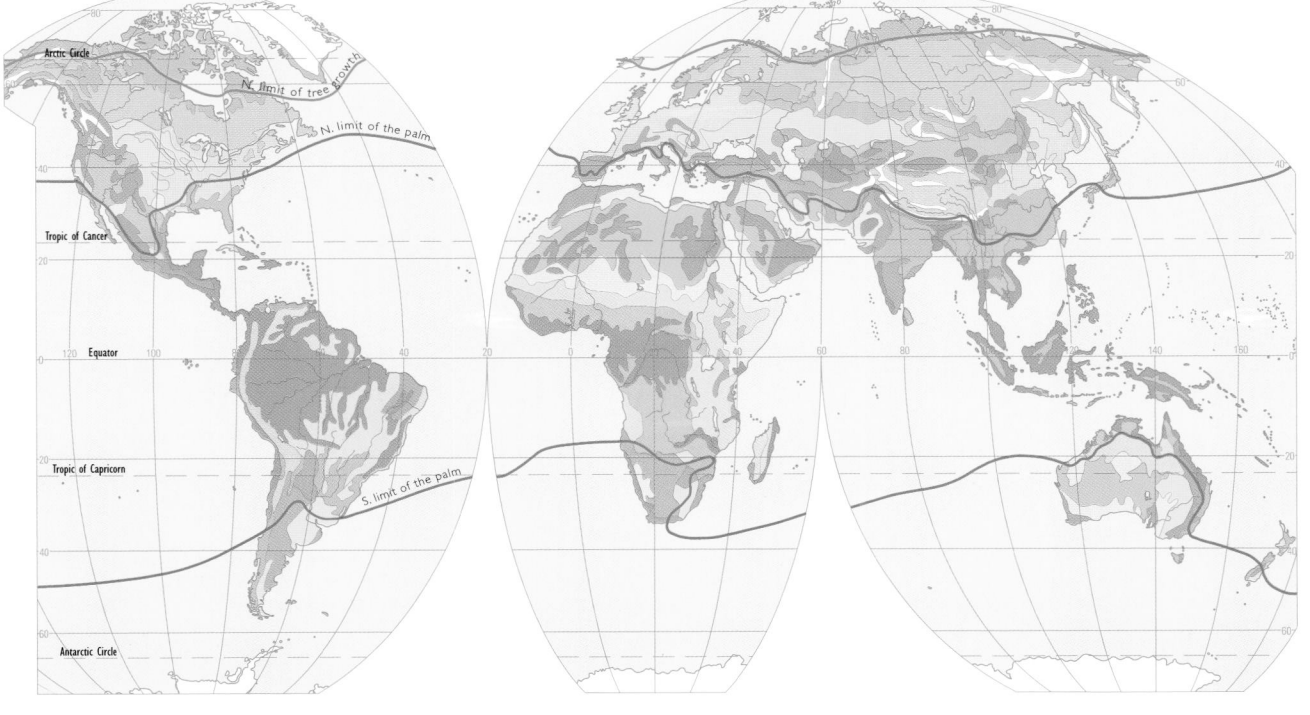

- Tropical rainforest
- Subtropical and temperate rainforest
- Monsoon woodland and open jungle
- Subtropical and temperate woodland, scrub and bush
- Tropical savanna, with low trees and bush
- Tropical savanna and grasslands
- Dry semi-desert, with shrub and grass
- Desert shrub
- Desert
- Dry steppe and shrub
- Temperate grasslands, prairie and steppe
- Mediterranean hardwood forest and scrub
- Temperate deciduous forest and meadow
- Temperate deciduous and coniferous forest
- Northern coniferous forest (taïga)
- Mountainous forest, mainly coniferous
- High plateau steppe and tundra
- Arctic tundra
- Polar and mountainous ice desert

The map illustrates the natural 'climax vegetation' of a region, as dictated by its climate and topography. In most cases, human agricultural activity has drastically altered the vegetation pattern. Western Europe, for example, lost most of its broadleaf forest many centuries ago, while elsewhere irrigation has turned some natural semi-desert into productive land. The various vegetation regions support different kinds of animals and, in an undisturbed state, they are highly developed biological communities, or biomes.

The blue line on the map represents the northern limit of tree growth, and the red lines indicate the northern and southern limits of palm growth.

THE NATURAL ENVIRONMENT

For more information:
8 Oceans
14 Atmosphere
19 Natural vegetation
22 Carbon dioxide
   Greenhouse power
   Global warming
23 Acid rain
   Desertification
   Deforestation
   Water pollution

Recent discoveries of life forms in some of the world's most hostile environments, such as around the black smokers along the ocean ridges, prepared the way for the announcement by NASA scientists in 1996 that they had found microfossils in a Martian meteorite. But other scientists were sceptical, believing them to be natural mineral structures and not evidence of extraterrestrial life.

Until further evidence is available, the Earth remains the only planet where we know for sure that life exists. According to the fossil record, life on Earth appeared at least 3,500 million years ago. Since then, it has evolved from its primitive beginnings to its modern biodiversity, including millions of plants, animals and micro-organisms. Living organisms have not only adapted to the environ-

ment but they have also changed their environment to suit themselves. For example, the Earth's early atmosphere contained little oxygen but the emergence of multi-celled, oxygen-producing algae, around 2,000 million years ago, led to the creation of an oxygen-rich atmosphere. This enabled land animals to populate the ancient continents.

The amount of the greenhouse gas carbon dioxide in the atmosphere would steadily increase from its present 0.03% were it not for plants. Without them, the Earth's atmosphere would, in a few million years, be similar to that of Venus, where surface temperatures reach 477°C. The Earth has evolved into a complex control system, sensing and reacting to changes and tending always to maintain the balance it has achieved.

Much discussion has centred on how that balance changes. Only recently, scientists were suggesting that we may be living in an interglacial stage of the Pleistocene Ice Age. From the 1980s, however, predictions of future climates have concentrated more on global warming, caused by pollution which has led to an increase in greenhouse gases in the atmosphere. Interference in the natural cycles that control the environment may have consequences that are hard to predict.

Furthermore, we are currently experiencing a period of mass extinction of species, causing a rapid reduction in our planet's biodiversity. A report by the World Conservation Union in 1996 stated that, of the 4,327 known mammal species, 1,096 were at risk and 169 'critically endangered'.

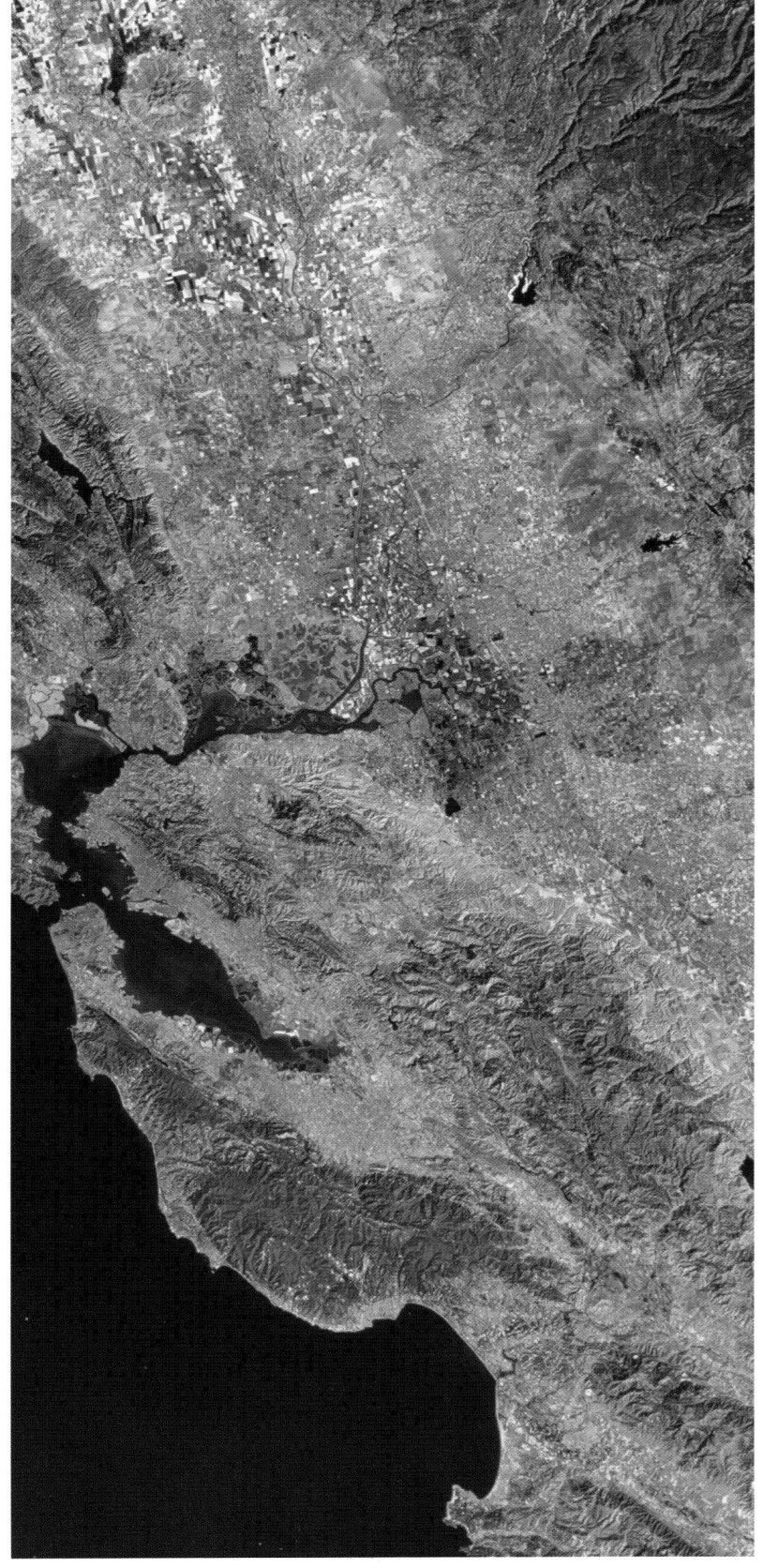

Biodiversity in California

The photograph (*left*) is a false-colour satellite image of central California in the south-western United States. The large inlet of the Pacific Ocean is San Francisco Bay. San Francisco lies just below the entrance to the bay, with Oakland on the far side and San Jose to the south-east. California, nicknamed the Golden State, is the third largest state in the United States and the most populous.

Because of its varied terrain and climate, California has a wide range of diverse habitats within a relatively small area. East of the forested Coast Ranges (the grey and red areas just inland from the bay) lies the fertile Central Valley, which appears as a red and blue chequerboard. The Sierra Nevada is the red area in the top right-hand corner. In the north-west and south-west of the state (*not shown here*) lie parts of the Basin and Range region, much of which is desert. It includes Death Valley, which contains the country's lowest point on land at 86 m below sea level.

Forests cover about 40% of California and they include bristlecone pines, thought to be the oldest living things on Earth, together with coastal redwoods, the world's tallest trees. Wildlife is still abundant, though some species, such as the rare California condor, are on the endangered list.

The state has achieved much to protect its biodiversity. It contains eight of the 54 national parks in the United States. Two of them, Death Valley and Joshua Tree, were designated national parks as recently as 1994, as part of a conservation measure, including the protection of large areas of wilderness in the deserts.

California has vast resources and, were it a separate nation, it would rank among the world's ten most productive in terms of the total value of its goods and services. This means that, like the United States as a whole, it has resources, which many developing countries lack, to finance conservation measures. For example, the World Conservation Union reported in 1996 that 8% of mammals were threatened in the United States, as compared with 32% in the Philippines and 44% in Madagascar, two countries where habitat destruction has been on a large scale.

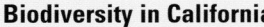
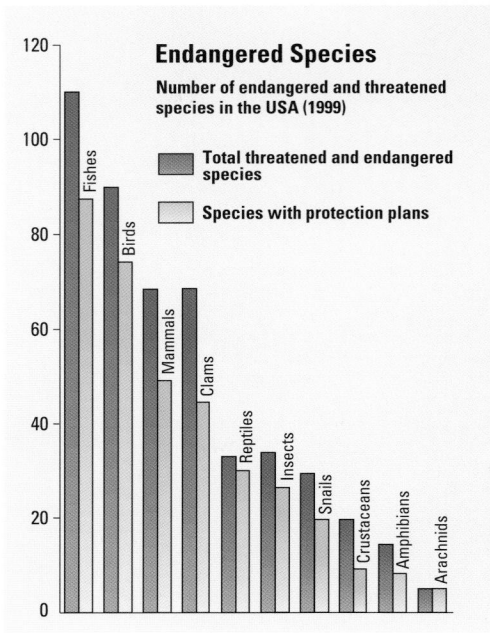

Endangered Species

Number of endangered and threatened species in the USA (1999)

- ■ Total threatened and endangered species
- □ Species with protection plans

(bar chart categories: Fishes, Birds, Mammals, Clams, Reptiles, Insects, Snails, Crustaceans, Amphibians, Arachnids)

Threatened Mammals

Percentage of mammal species classified as threatened (1996)
Many scientists believe we are currently experiencing a period of mass extinction of species rivalling five other periods in the past half a billion years. Among the most threatened mammals are elephants, primates and rhinoceroses.

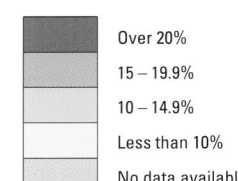

- Over 20%
- 15 – 19.9%
- 10 – 14.9%
- Less than 10%
- No data available

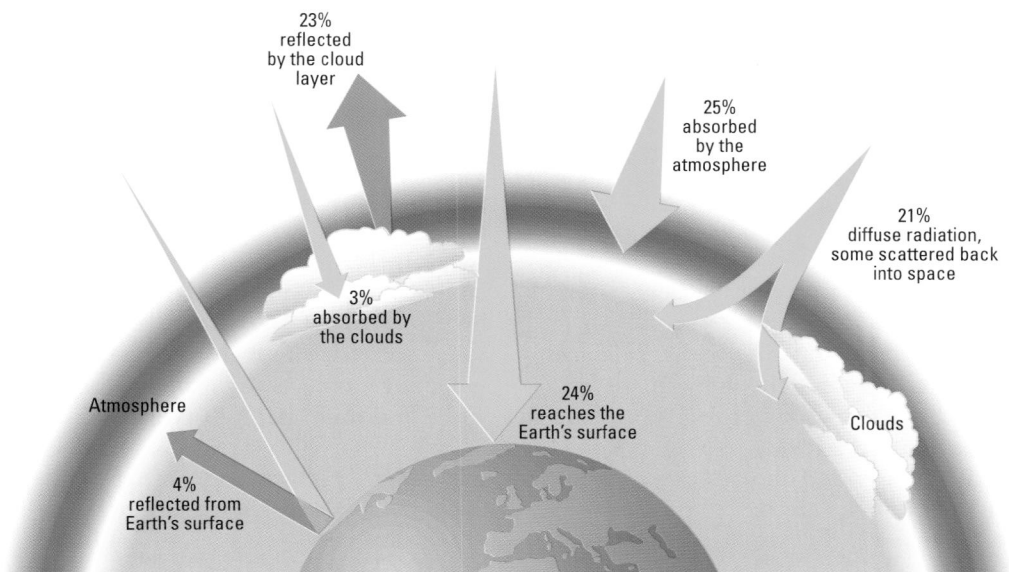

23%
reflected
by the cloud
layer

25%
absorbed
by the
atmosphere

21%
diffuse radiation,
some scattered back
into space

3%
absorbed by
the clouds

Atmosphere

24%
reaches the
Earth's surface

Clouds

4%
reflected from
Earth's surface

The Earth's Energy Balance

Apart from a modest quantity of internal heat from its molten core, the Earth receives all of its energy from the Sun. If the planet is to remain at a constant temperature, it must reradiate exactly as much energy as it receives. Even a minute surplus would lead to a warmer Earth, a deficit to a cooler one. The temperature at which thermal equilibrium is reached depends on a multitude of interconnected factors. Two of the most important are the relative brightness of the Earth – its index of reflectivity, called the 'albedo' – and the heat-trapping capacity of the atmosphere – the celebrated 'greenhouse effect' (*see below*).

Because the Sun is very hot, most of its energy arrives in the form of relatively short-wave radiation: the shorter the waves, the more energy they carry. Some of the incoming energy is reflected straight back into space, exactly as it arrived; some is absorbed by the atmosphere on its way towards the surface; some is absorbed by the Earth itself. Absorbed energy heats the Earth and its atmosphere alike. But since its temperature is very much lower than that of the Sun, the outgoing energy is emitted at much longer infrared wavelengths. Some of the outgoing radiation escapes directly into outer space; some of it is reabsorbed by the atmosphere. Atmospheric energy eventually finds its way back into space, too, after a complex series of interactions. These include the air movements we call the weather and, almost incidentally, the maintenance of life on Earth.

This diagram (*left*) does not attempt to illustrate the actual mechanisms of heat exchange, but gives a reasonable account (in percentages) of what happens to 100 energy 'units'. Short-wave radiation is shown in yellow, long-wave in orange.

The Carbon Cycle

Most of the constituents of the atmosphere are kept in constant balance by complex cycles in which life plays an essential and indeed a dominant part. The control of carbon dioxide, which if left to its own devices would be the dominant atmospheric gas, is possibly the most important, although since all the Earth's biological and geophysical cycles interact and interlock, it is hard to separate them even in theory and quite impossible in practice.

The Earth has a huge supply of carbon, only a small quantity of which is in the form of carbon dioxide. Of that, around 98% is dissolved in the sea; the fraction circulating in the air amounts to only 340 parts per million of the atmosphere, where its capacity as a greenhouse gas is the key regulator of the planetary temperature. In turn, life regulates the regulator, keeping carbon dioxide concentrations below danger level.

If all life were to vanish from the Earth tomorrow, the atmosphere would begin the process of change immediately, although it might take several million years to achieve a new, inorganic stability. First, the oxygen content would begin to fall away; with no more assistance than a little solar radiation, a few electrical storms and its own high chemical potential, oxygen would steadily combine with atmospheric nitrogen and volcanic outgassing. In doing so, it would yield sufficient acid to react with carbonaceous rocks such as limestone, releasing carbon dioxide. Once carbon dioxide levels exceeded about 1%, its greenhouse power would increase disproportionately. Rising temperatures – well above the boiling point of water – would speed chemical reactions; in time, the Earth's atmosphere would consist of little more than carbon dioxide and superheated water vapour.

Living things, however, circulate carbon. They do so first by simply existing: after all, the carbon atom is the basic building block of living matter.

During life, plants absorb carbon dioxide from the atmosphere and, along with various chemicals, as soluble salts from the soil, incorporating the carbon into their structure – leaves and trunks in the case of land plants, shells in the case of plankton and the tiny creatures that feed on it. The oxygen thereby freed is added to the atmosphere, at least for a time. The carbon is returned to circulation when the plants die or is passed up the food chain to the herbivores, and then to the carnivores that feed on them. As organisms at each of these trophic levels die, they decay, releasing the carbon, which then combines once more with the oxygen released during life. However, a small proportion of carbon, about one part in 1,000, is removed almost permanently, buried beneath mud on land or at sea, sinking as dead matter to the ocean floor. In time, it is slowly compressed into sedimentary rocks such as limestone and chalk.

But in the evolution of the Earth, nothing is quite permanent. On an even longer timescale, the planet's crustal movements force new rock upwards in mid-ocean ridges. Limestone deposits are moved, and sea levels change; ancient carboniferous rocks are exposed to weathering, and a little of their carbon is released to be fixed in turn by the current generation of plants.

The carbon cycle has continued quietly for an immensely long time, and without gross disturbance there is no reason why it would not continue almost indefinitely in the future. However, human beings have found a way to release fixed carbon at a rate far faster than existing global systems can re-circulate it. The fossil fuels – coal, oil, gas and peat deposits – represent the work of millions of years of carbon accumulation; but it has taken only a few human generations of high-energy scavenging to endanger the entire complex regulatory cycle.

pool of CO$_2$
in atmosphere

combustion   photosynthesis

respiration   respiration   respiration

CO$_2$

CO$_2$

decay
organisms

respiration

death

carbonification,
gradual production
of fossil fuels

death

decay
organisms

peat

coal

oil and gas

N.B. The thickness of the Earth's atmosphere is proportionately much thinner than the peel of an apple.

The Greenhouse Effect

Constituting less than 1% of the atmosphere, the natural greenhouse gases (water vapour, carbon dioxide, methane, nitrous oxide and ozone) have a hugely disproportionate effect on the Earth's climate, and even its habitability. Like the glass panes in a greenhouse, the gases are transparent to most incoming short-wave radiation, which passes freely to heat the planet beneath. But when the warmed Earth retransmits that energy, in the form of longer-wave infrared radiation, the gases function as an opaque shield preventing some of it from escaping, so that the planetary surface (like the interior of a greenhouse) stays relatively hot.

Over the last 150 years, there has been a gradual increase in the levels of greenhouse gases (with the exception of water vapour, which remains a constant in the system). These increases are causing alarm – global warming associated with a runaway greenhouse effect could bring disaster – and, what is more, predictions suggest that there could be a further rise of 1.5–4.5°C by the year 2100. A serious reduction in the greenhouse gases would be just as damaging; a total absence of CO$_2$, for example, would leave the planet with a temperature roughly 33°C colder than at present.

Sun

Less heat escapes
into space

Outgoing long-
wave radiation
(infared) is radiated
back into space

Increased greenhouse
gases means that more long-
wave radiation is reflected
back to Earth

Atmosphere

The atmosphere of the
Earth gets hotter as
more heat is trapped

Increased
greenhouse
gases act as a shield
to long-wave radiation

Incoming short-wave
radiation (ultraviolet)
reaches the surface
of the Earth

PEOPLE AND THE ENVIRONMENT

For more information:
8 Oceans
14 Atmosphere
16 Climate
21 Greenhouse effect
27 Urban pollution

In 1996, the Intergovernmental Panel on Climate Change issued a report stating that 'The balance of evidence suggests a discernible human influence on global climate through emissions of carbon dioxide and other greenhouse gases.' The report acknowledged that average global temperatures have risen by about 0.5°C since the mid-19th century, but there were still reasons for caution, such as discrepancies between measurements of temperatures around the world. Furthermore, our knowledge about how climates change of their own accord is incomplete, as is our understanding of human interference, how this varies in different parts of the world and how it differs from natural climatic variability.

Human interference with nature is nothing new, at least since people turned from hunting and gathering to agriculture more than 10,000 years ago. At first, human actions seemed to have no ill effects because the systems that regulate the global environment were able to absorb damage. But from the late 18th century, the Industrial Revolution and the population explosion have caused pollution on a scale that threatens to overwhelm the Earth's ability to cope.

The 20th century experienced many disasters, including the dumping of industrial wastes in rivers and seas, accidents at nuclear power stations, and the creation of acid rain through the release of sulphur dioxides and nitrous oxides by the burning of fossil fuels. The release of greenhouse gases are held to be the main reason for global warming, while CFCs (chlorofluoro-carbons) have damaged the ozone layer in the stratosphere, the planet's screen against ultraviolet radiation.

Global warming will lead to melting ice sheets and the flooding of fertile coastal plains. Computer models suggest that it might affect ocean currents so that north-western Europe, which owes its mild climate to the Gulf Stream, could expect bitterly cold winters. Some models have suggested that cloud cover could increase, reflecting more solar energy back into space and thus start a new Ice Age.

In many tropical areas, deforestation is making productive land barren, while in the dry grasslands bordering deserts, the removal of plant cover is causing desertification. But human ingenuity can respond to this crisis in planet management.

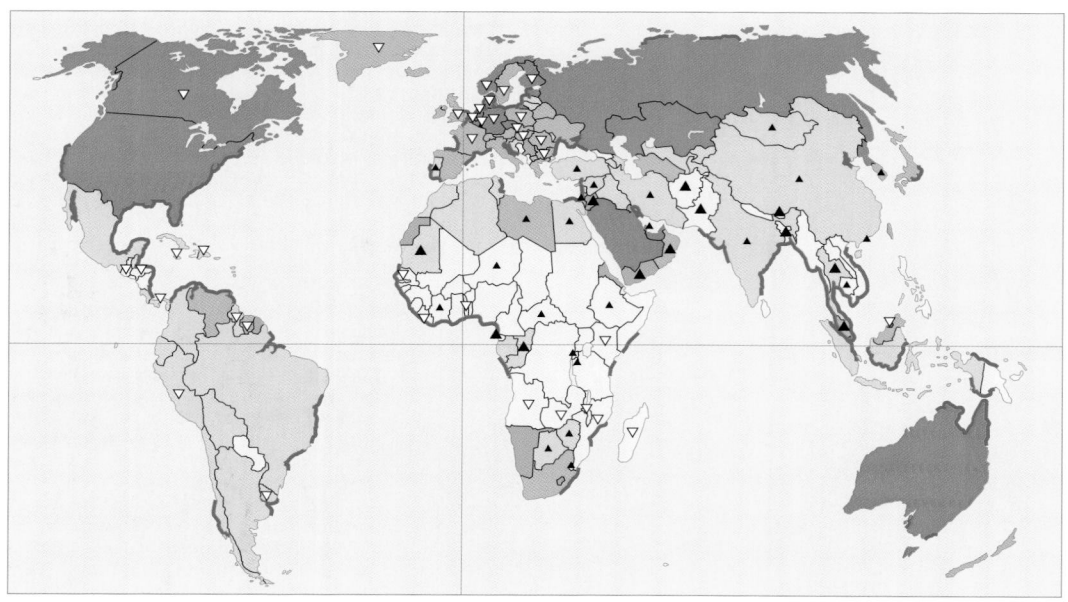

Global Warming

Carbon dioxide emissions in tonnes per person per year (latest available year)

- Over 10 tonnes of CO_2
- 5 – 10 tonnes of CO_2
- 1 – 5 tonnes of CO_2
- Under 1 tonne of CO_2
- No data available

Changes in CO_2 emissions 1980–90

- ▲ Over 100% increase
- ▲ 50–100% increase
- ▽ Reduction
- — Coasts in danger of flooding from rising sea levels

High atmospheric concentrations of heat-absorbing gases appear to be causing a rise in average temperatures worldwide – up to 1.5°C (3°F) by the year 2020, according to some estimates. Global warming is likely to bring about a rise in sea levels that may flood some of the world's densely populated coastal areas.

Evidence of global warming is attributed mainly to the Greenhouse Effect, caused by the emission of certain gases, notably carbon dioxide (CO_2), into the atmosphere since the start of the Industrial Revolution. At first, much of the CO_2 was absorbed by the oceans. However, the vast increase in fuel combustion since 1950 has led CO_2 content in the atmosphere to increase gradually from 280 parts per million to more than 350 parts per million. Despite international action to control the emissions of some greenhouse gases, CO_2 levels are still rising.

Greenhouse Power

Relative contributions to the Greenhouse Effect by the major heat-absorbing gases in the atmosphere

The chart combines greenhouse potency and volume. Carbon dioxide has a greenhouse potential of only 1, but its concentration of 350 parts per million makes it predominate. CFC 12, with 25,000 times the absorption capacity of CO_2, is present only as 0.00044 ppm.

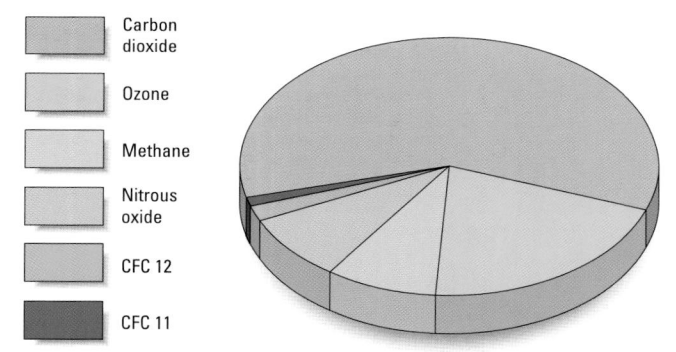

- Carbon dioxide
- Ozone
- Methane
- Nitrous oxide
- CFC 12
- CFC 11

Carbon Dioxide

Cumulative carbon emissions, million tonnes of carbon (1950–96)

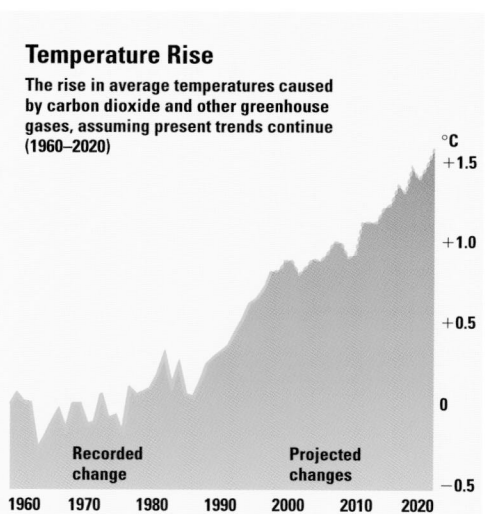

USA 50,795, China, Germany, Japan, UK, India, Canada, South Africa, Mexico, Brazil, Poland, Australia

Temperature Rise

The rise in average temperatures caused by carbon dioxide and other greenhouse gases, assuming present trends continue (1960–2020)

Recorded change / Projected changes

°C +1.5 +1.0 +0.5 0 −0.5
1960 1970 1980 1990 2000 2010 2020

The Thinning Ozone Layer

Total atmospheric ozone concentration in the southern and northern hemispheres (Dobson units, 1995)

In 1985, scientists working in Antarctica discovered a thinning of the ozone layer, commonly known as an 'ozone violet'. This caused immediate alarm because the ozone layer absorbs most of the Sun's dangerous ultraviolet radiation, which is believed to cause an increase in skin cancer, cataracts and damage to the immune system. Since 1985, ozone depletion has increased and, by 1996, the ozone hole over the South Pole was estimated to be as large as North America. The false-colour images (*right*) show the total atmospheric ozone concentration in the southern hemisphere (in October 1995) and the northern hemisphere (in March 1995), with the ozone hole clearly identifiable at the centre. The data are from the Tiros Ozone Vertical Sounder, an instrument on the American TIROS weather satellite. The colours represent the ozone concentration in Dobson Units (DU). Normal healthy values are around 280 DU but the lowest value in the northern hemisphere reached 98 DU. Scientists agree that ozone depletion is caused by CFCs, a group of manufactured chemicals used in air-conditioning systems and refrigerators. In a 1987 treaty most industrial nations agreed to phase out CFCs, and a complete ban on most CFCs was agreed after the end of 1995. However, scientists believe that the chemicals will remain in the atmosphere for 50 to 100 years. As a result, ozone depletion will continue for many years.

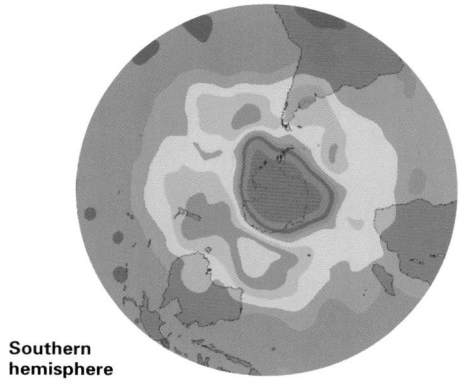

Southern hemisphere

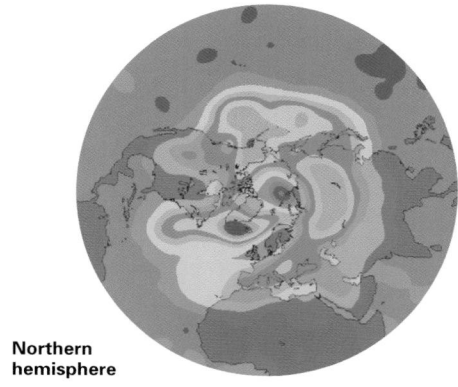

Northern hemisphere

World Pollution

Acid rain and sources of acidic emissions (latest available year)

Acid rain is caused by high levels of sulphur and nitrogen in the atmosphere. They combine with water vapour and oxygen to form acids (H_2SO_4 and HNO_3) which fall as precipitation.

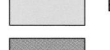 Regions where sulphur and nitrogen oxides are released in high concentrations, mainly from fossil fuel combustion

 Major cities with high levels of air pollution (including nitrogen and sulphur emissions)

Areas of heavy acid deposition

pH numbers indicate acidity, decreasing from a neutral 7. Normal rain, slightly acid from dissolved carbon dioxide, never exceeds a pH of 5.6.

 pH less than 4.0 (most acidic)

pH 4.0 to 4.5

pH 4.5 to 5.0

 Areas where acid rain is a potential problem

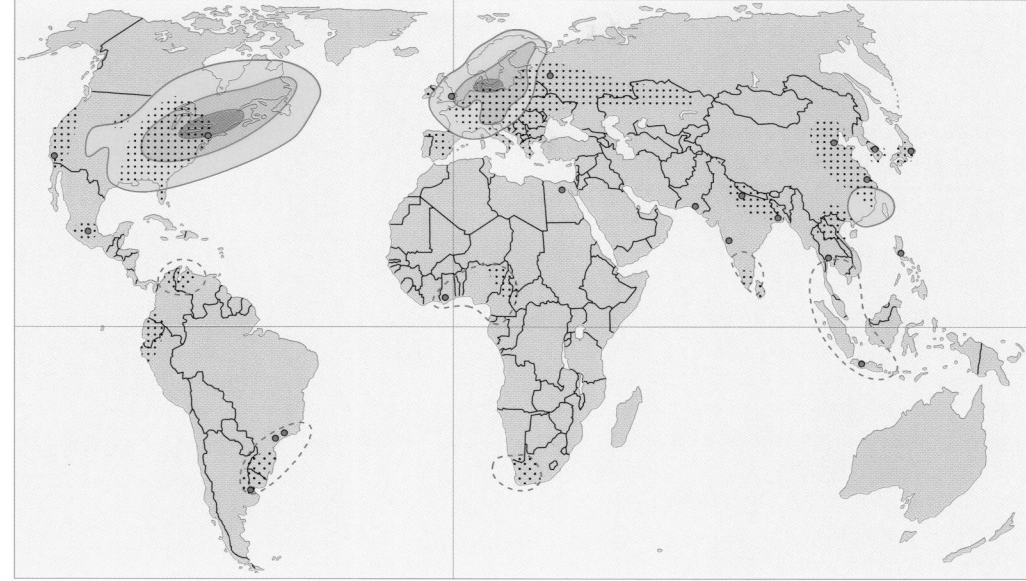

Desertification

Existing deserts

Areas with a high risk of desertification

Areas with a moderate risk of desertification

Former areas of rainforest

Existing rainforest

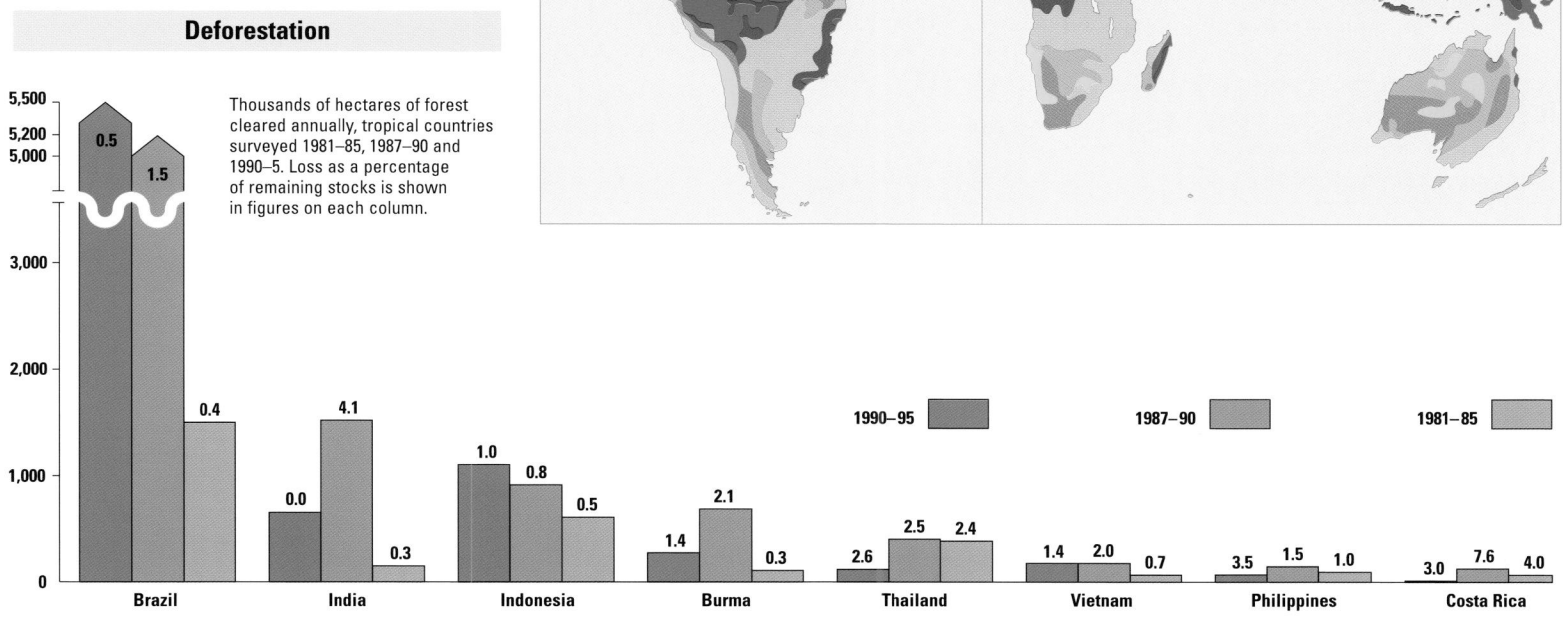

Deforestation

Thousands of hectares of forest cleared annually, tropical countries surveyed 1981–85, 1987–90 and 1990–5. Loss as a percentage of remaining stocks is shown in figures on each column.

1990–95   1987–90   1981–85

	Brazil	India	Indonesia	Burma	Thailand	Vietnam	Philippines	Costa Rica
1990–95	0.5	0.0	1.0	1.4	2.6	1.4	3.5	3.0
1987–90	1.5	4.1	0.8	2.1	2.5	2.0	1.5	7.6
1981–85	0.4	0.3	0.5	0.3	2.4	0.7	1.0	4.0

Water Pollution

Severely polluted sea areas and lakes

Polluted sea areas and lakes

Areas of frequent oil pollution by shipping

 Major oil tanker spills

 Major oil rig blow-outs

 Offshore dumpsites for industrial and municipal waste

 Severely polluted rivers and estuaries

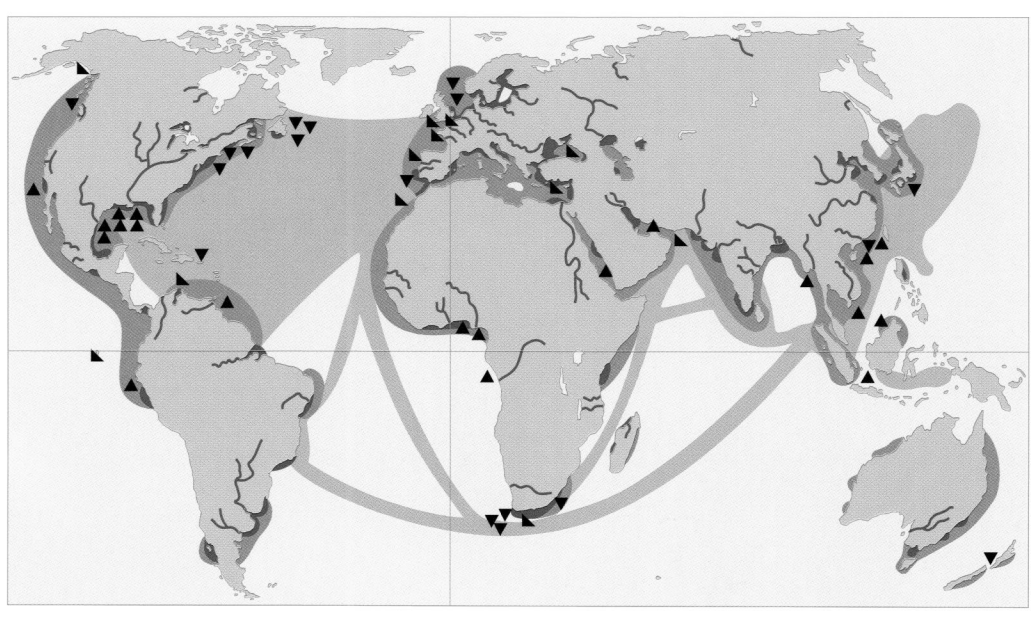

Antarctica

The vast Antarctic ice sheet, containing some 70% of the Earth's fresh water, plays a crucial role in the circulation of the atmosphere and oceans, and hence in determining the planetary climate. The frozen southern continent is also the last remaining wilderness – the largest area to remain free from human colonization.

Ever since Amundsen and Scott raced for the South Pole in 1911, various countries have pressed territorial claims over sections of Antarctica, spurred in recent years by its known and suspected mineral wealth: enough iron ore to supply the world at present levels for 200 years, large oil reserves and, probably, the biggest coal deposits on Earth.

However, the 1961 Antarctic Treaty set aside the area for peaceful uses only, guaranteeing freedom of scientific investigation, banning waste disposal and nuclear testing, and suspending the issue of territorial rights. By 1990, the original 12 signatories had grown to 25, with a further 15 nations granted observer status in subsequent deliberations. However, the Treaty itself was threatened by wrangles between different countries, government agencies and international pressure groups.

Finally, in July 1991, the belated agreement of the UK and the USA assured unanimity on a new accord to ban all mineral exploration for a further 50 years. The ban can only be rescinded if all the present signatories, plus a majority of any future adherents, agree. While the treaty has always lacked a formal mechanism for enforcement, it is firmly underwritten by public concern generated by the efforts of environmental pressure groups such as Greenpeace, which has been foremost in the campaign to have Antarctica declared a 'World Park'.

However, from the mid-1990s, the continent appeared to be under threat from global warming, which some scientists believe was the cause of the break-up of ice shelves along the Antarctic peninsula. Rising temperatures have also disturbed the breeding patterns of Adelie penguins.

Poisoned rivers, domestic sewage and oil spillage have combined in recent years to reduce the world's oceans to a sorry state of contamination, notably near the crowded coasts of industrialized nations. Shipping routes, too, are constantly affected by tanker discharges. Oil spills of all kinds, however, declined significantly during the 1980s, from a peak of 750,000 tonnes in 1979 to under 50,000 tonnes in 1990. The most notorious tanker spill of that period – when the *Exxon Valdez* (94,999 grt) ran aground in Prince William Sound, Alaska, in March 1989 – released only 267,000 barrels, a relatively small amount compared to the results of blow-outs and war damage. Over 2,500,000 barrels were spilled during the Gulf War of 1991. The worst tanker accident in history occurred in July 1979, when the *Atlantic Empress* and the *Aegean Captain* collided off Trinidad, polluting the Caribbean with 1,890,000 barrels of crude oil.

POPULATION

For more information:

26 Urbanization of the Earth

Urban population

27 Largest cities

33 Food and population

44 Wealth and population

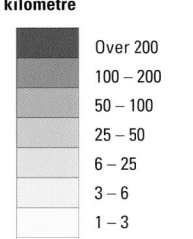

In 8000 BC, following the development of agriculture, the world had an estimated population of 8 million and by AD 1000 it was about 300 million. The onset of the Industrial Revolution in the late 18th century led to a population explosion. The 1,000 million mark was passed by 1850, it doubled by the 1920s, and doubled again to 4,000 million by 1975.

Most demographers agree that the world's population, which passed the 6 billion mark in 1999, will reach 8.9 billion by 2050. It is not expected to level out until 2200, when it will peak at around 11 billion. After 2200, it is expected to level out or even decline a little. Rapid population growth is concentrated in the developing world; the populations of some developed countries are static or have even started to decline.

The developing world includes what the World Bank (2001) describes as low-income economies (average per capita GNP of US $420), lower-middle-income economies (average per capita GNP of US $1,200) and upper-middle-income economies (average per capita GNP of US $4,870). Most developing countries are in Africa, Asia and Latin America. The developed world, made up of high-income, industrialized economies (average per capita GNP of US $26,440), contains Australasia, most of Europe and North America, and Japan.

In the poorer developing countries, a high proportion of the population is young, and they face high levels of expenditure on education and health until population growth rates start to decline. In developed countries, where the population pyramids are becoming increasingly top-heavy, expenditure on pensions and healthcare for the elderly is becoming a major social problem.

Most Crowded Nations

Population per square kilometre (2001 est.)

1.	Monaco	16,000
2.	Singapore	6,935
3.	Vatican City	2,225
4.	Malta	1,234
5.	Maldives	1,037
6.	Bahrain	949
7.	Bangladesh	912
8.	Barbados	640
9.	Taiwan	621
10.	Nauru	600

Least Crowded Nations

Population per square kilometre (2001 est.)

1.	Mongolia	1.7
2.	Namibia	2.2
3.	Australia	2.5
4.	Suriname	2.7
5.	Mauritania	2.7
6.	Iceland	2.7
7.	Botswana	2.7
8.	Libya	3.0
9.	Canada	3.2
10.	Guyana	3.2

Largest Nations

The world's most populous nations, in millions (2001 est.)

1.	China	1,273
2.	India	1,030
3.	USA	278
4.	Indonesia	228
5.	Brazil	174
6.	Russia	145
7.	Pakistan	145
8.	Bangladesh	131
9.	Japan	127
10.	Nigeria	127
11.	Mexico	102
12.	Germany	83
13.	Philippines	83
14.	Vietnam	80
15.	Egypt	70
16.	Turkey	66
17.	Iran	66
18.	Ethiopia	66
19.	Thailand	62
20.	UK	60
21.	France	60
22.	Italy	58
23.	Congo (Dem.Rep.)	54
24.	Ukaine	49
25.	South Korea	48

Population Density

Inhabitants per square kilometre

- Over 200
- 100 – 200
- 50 – 100
- 25 – 50
- 6 – 25
- 3 – 6
- 1 – 3
- Under 1

Urban population

- ■ Over 10,000,000
- ● 5,000,000 – 10,000,000
- • 1,000,000 – 5,000,000

Places marked are conurbations, not city limits; San Francisco itself, for example, has an official population of less than a million.

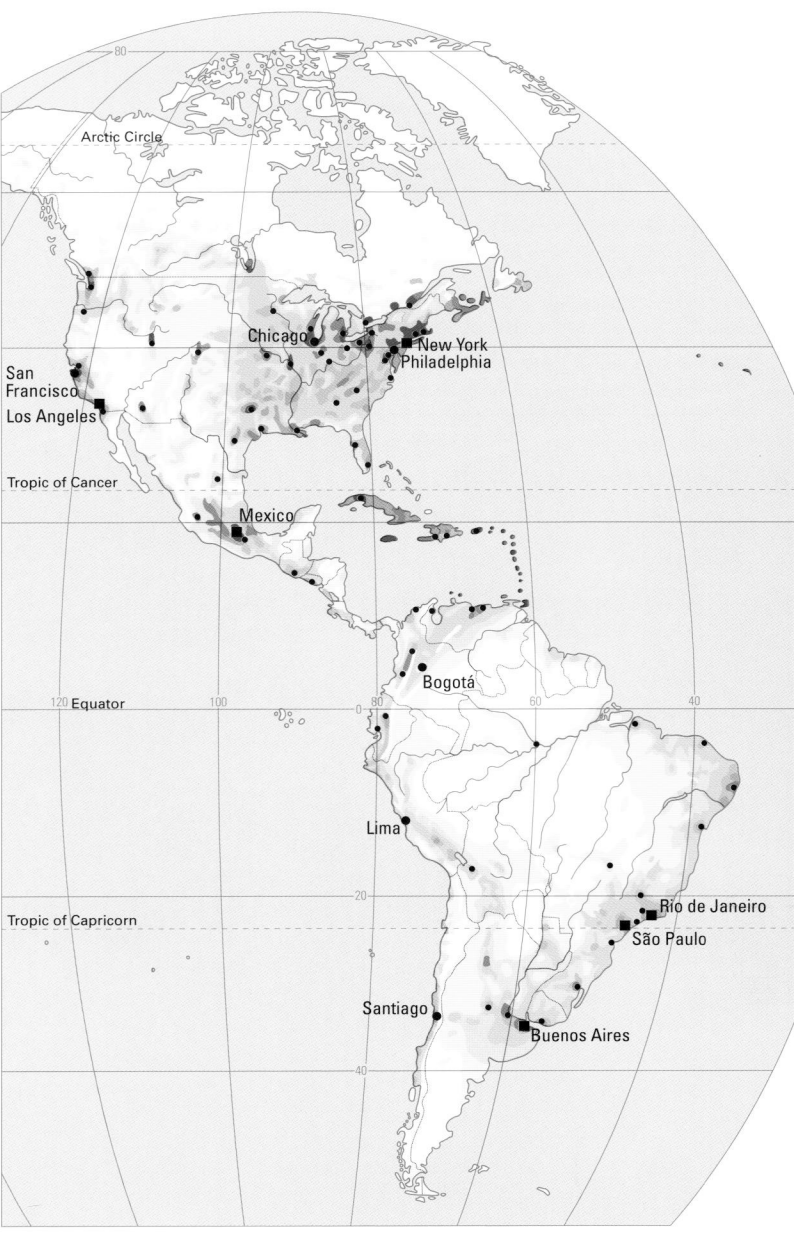

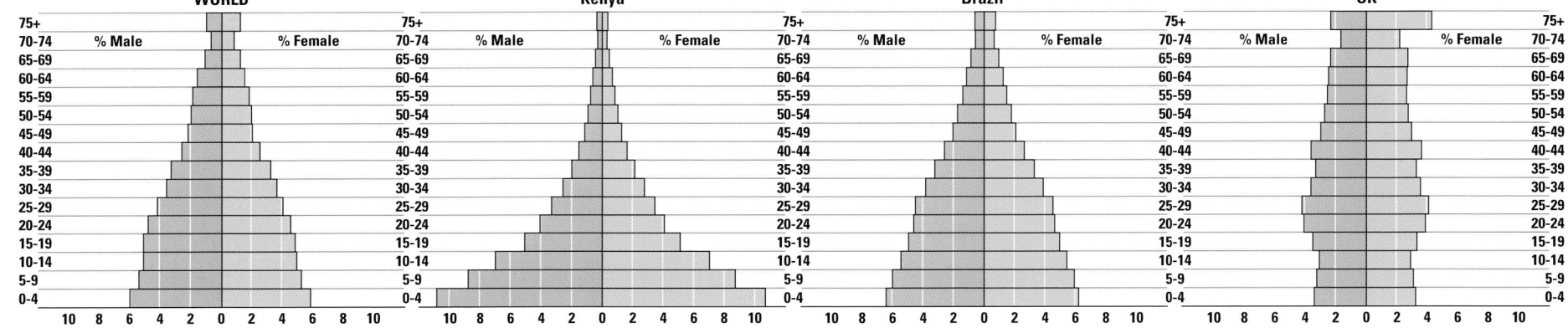

Rates of Growth

The world population doubled between 1950 and 1990. Small rates of population growth led to dramatic increases over two or three generations. The table below translates annual percentage growth into the number of years required to double a population.

% change	Doubling time
0.5	139.0
1.0	69.7
1.5	46.6
2.0	35.0
2.5	28.1
3.0	23.4
3.5	20.1
4.0	17.7

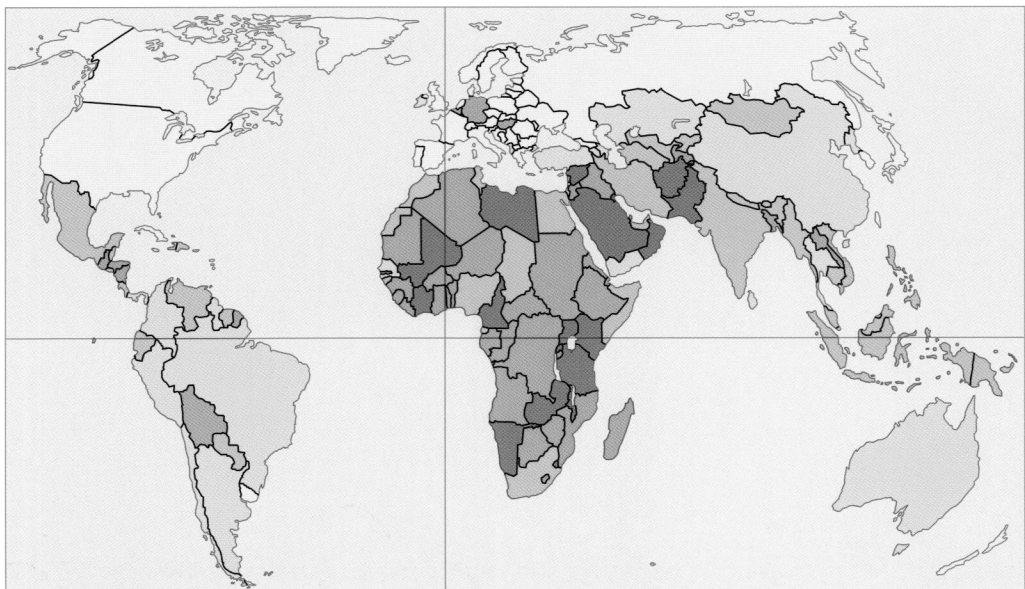

Population Change 1990–2000

The population change for the years 1990–2000

- Over 40% population gain
- 30 – 40% population gain
- 20 – 30% population gain
- 10 – 20% population gain
- 0 – 10% population gain
- No change or population loss

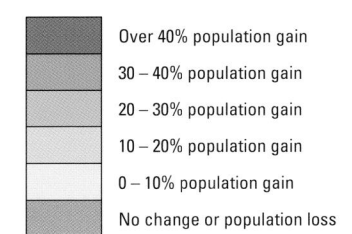

Top 5 countries		Bottom 5 countries	
Kuwait	+75.9%	Belgium	−0.1%
Namibia	+62.5%	Hungary	−0.2%
Afghanistan	+60.1%	Grenada	−2.4%
Mali	+55.5%	Germany	−3.2%
Tanzania	+54.6%	Tonga	−3.2%

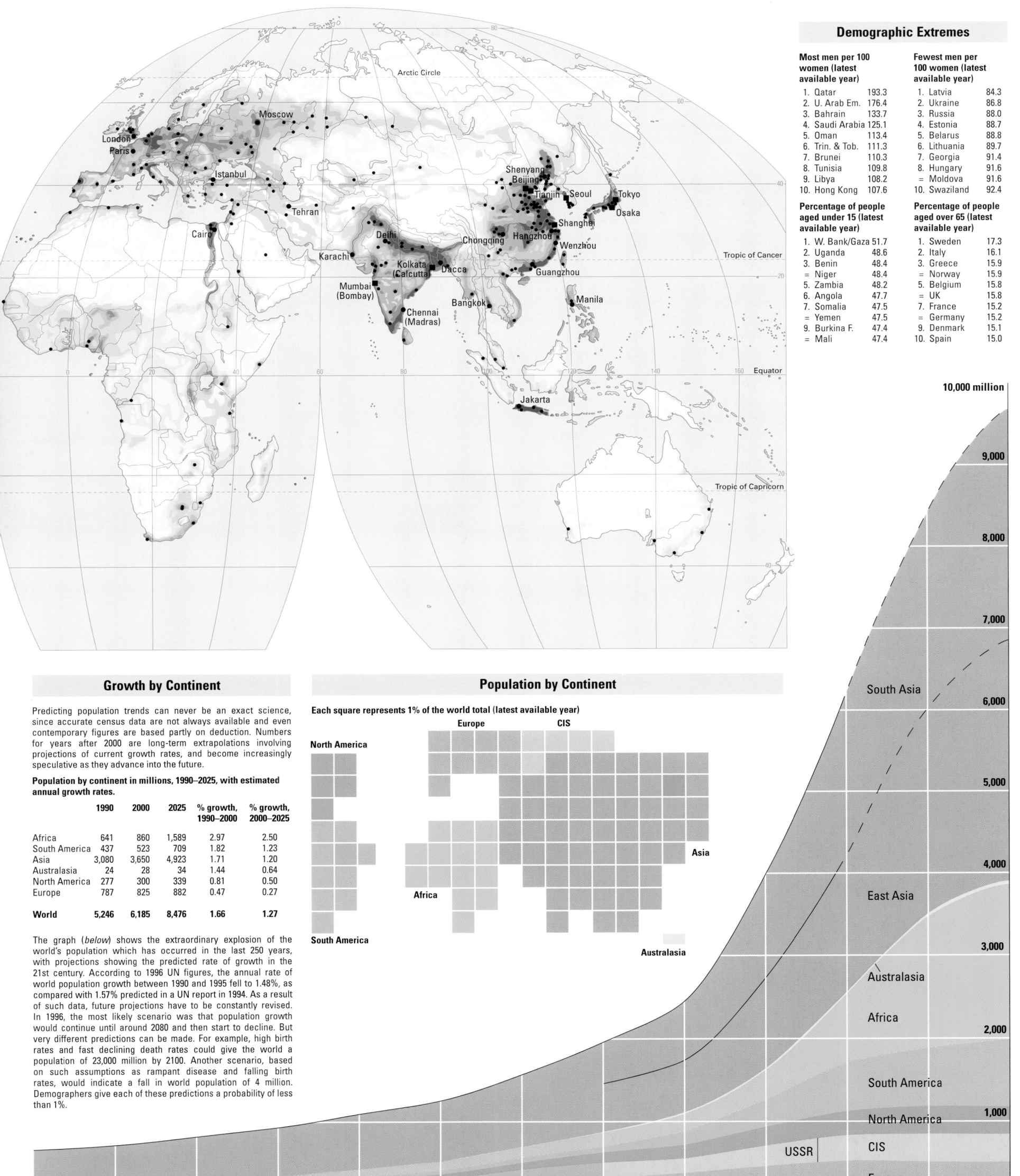

Demographic Extremes

Most men per 100 women (latest available year)		Fewest men per 100 women (latest available year)	
1. Qatar	193.3	1. Latvia	84.3
2. U. Arab Em.	176.4	2. Ukraine	86.8
3. Bahrain	133.7	3. Russia	88.0
4. Saudi Arabia	125.1	4. Estonia	88.7
5. Oman	113.4	5. Belarus	88.8
6. Trin. & Tob.	111.3	6. Lithuania	89.7
7. Brunei	110.3	7. Georgia	91.4
8. Tunisia	109.8	8. Hungary	91.6
9. Libya	108.2	= Moldova	91.6
10. Hong Kong	107.6	10. Swaziland	92.4

Percentage of people aged under 15 (latest available year)		Percentage of people aged over 65 (latest available year)	
1. W. Bank/Gaza	51.7	1. Sweden	17.3
2. Uganda	48.6	2. Italy	16.1
3. Benin	48.4	3. Greece	15.9
= Niger	48.4	= Norway	15.9
5. Zambia	48.2	5. Belgium	15.8
6. Angola	47.7	= UK	15.8
7. Somalia	47.5	7. France	15.2
= Yemen	47.5	= Germany	15.2
9. Burkina F.	47.4	9. Denmark	15.1
= Mali	47.4	10. Spain	15.0

Growth by Continent

Predicting population trends can never be an exact science, since accurate census data are not always available and even contemporary figures are based partly on deduction. Numbers for years after 2000 are long-term extrapolations involving projections of current growth rates, and become increasingly speculative as they advance into the future.

Population by continent in millions, 1990–2025, with estimated annual growth rates.

	1990	2000	2025	% growth, 1990–2000	% growth, 2000–2025
Africa	641	860	1,589	2.97	2.50
South America	437	523	709	1.82	1.23
Asia	3,080	3,650	4,923	1.71	1.20
Australasia	24	28	34	1.44	0.64
North America	277	300	339	0.81	0.50
Europe	787	825	882	0.47	0.27
World	**5,246**	**6,185**	**8,476**	**1.66**	**1.27**

The graph (*below*) shows the extraordinary explosion of the world's population which has occurred in the last 250 years, with projections showing the predicted rate of growth in the 21st century. According to 1996 UN figures, the annual rate of world population growth between 1990 and 1995 fell to 1.48%, as compared with 1.57% predicted in a UN report in 1994. As a result of such data, future projections have to be constantly revised. In 1996, the most likely scenario was that population growth would continue until around 2080 and then start to decline. But very different predictions can be made. For example, high birth rates and fast declining death rates could give the world a population of 23,000 million by 2100. Another scenario, based on such assumptions as rampant disease and falling birth rates, would indicate a fall in world population of 4 million. Demographers give each of these predictions a probability of less than 1%.

Population by Continent

Each square represents 1% of the world total (latest available year)

North America
Europe
CIS
Asia
Africa
South America
Australasia

10,000 million
9,000
8,000
7,000
South Asia
6,000
5,000
East Asia
4,000
Australasia
Africa
3,000
South America
2,000
North America
1,000
USSR
CIS
Europe

1750 1775 1800 1825 1850 1875 1900 1925 1950 1975 2000 2025 2050

25

CITIES

For more information:

18 Water supply

24 Population density

41 The great ports

Following the development of agriculture more than 10,000 years ago, people began to live in farming villages. Around 5,500 years ago, the world's first cities appeared in the lower Tigris and Euphrates valleys in Mesopotamia. Cities were founded in Ancient Egypt around 5,000 years ago and in China around 3,600 years ago. By contrast with the villages, most people in the early cities were not engaged in farming. Instead, they worked in craft industries, in government services, in religion and in trade. The cities became centres of early civilizations and, through trade, their influence spread far and wide. However, they were dependent on the surrounding farming communities for their food and other materials.

In 1750, prior to the start of the Industrial Revolution, barely 3% of the world's population lived in urban areas. By 1850, London and Paris had more than a million people, and, by 1900, 14% of the world's population lived in cities. By 1950, the world had 83 cities with more than a million people, and

by 1996, there were 280. By 2015, experts predict that there will be more than 500. New York City was the only city with a population in excess of 10 million in 1950; by 2015 the experts predict 27 such cities worldwide, the majority located in the developing world.

By the end of the 20th century, more than half of the world's population was living in urban areas. Despite the rapid growth of cities in developing countries, urbanization is highest in industrialized countries. For example, 78% of the people in the United States live in urban areas, with the European Union not far behind with 77%. But in countries with low-income economies, which contained nearly 60% of the world's total population by the late 1990s, only 28% lived in urban areas.

The rapid rate of urbanization has created problems, especially in cities which have not been able to provide enough jobs and services for the expanding population. Most new city dwellers are people from rural areas, and because many of them are young there is a consequent acceleration in the rate of city

population growth. In developed countries, with highly mechanized agriculture, it is population pressure that drives many people into urban areas. In developing countries, the grinding poverty of rural life and the lack of services leads to migration to urban areas.

A typical city in a developing country contains millions of people living, often illegally, in shanty towns (or 'informal settlements' in politically-correct parlance), while thousands live on the streets. Yet many of these shanty towns are healthier than the industrial cities of 19th-century Europe and North America. Indeed, surveys have shown that the migrants to the cities in developing countries are less likely to face poverty than they are in rural areas, while benefiting from greater access to healthcare services and education.

Modern cities face many problems, including pollution, crime and unemployment. Yet, given competent central and local government, they are capable of generating the wealth they need to solve them, as well as making a major contribution to the economy.

The Urbanization of the Earth

City-building, 1850–2000; each white spot represents a city of at least 1 million inhabitants.

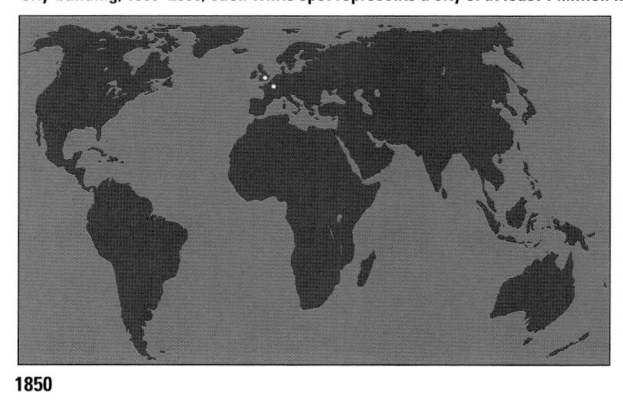

1850

1900

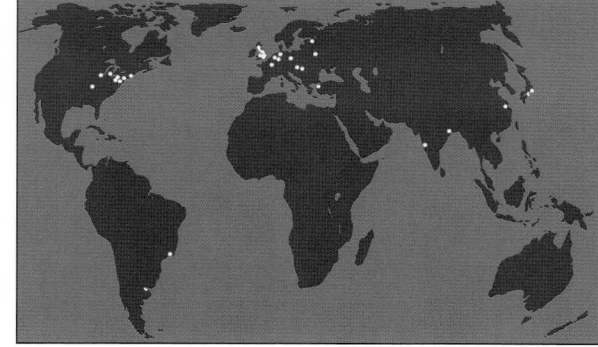

1925

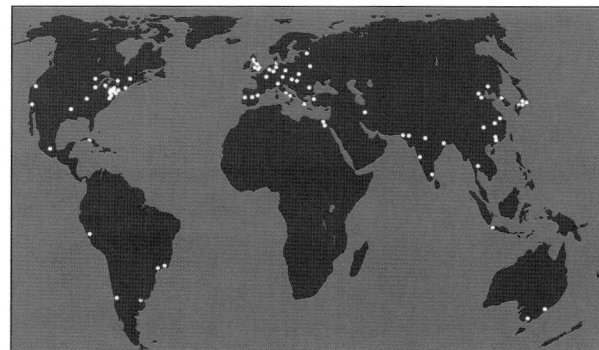

1950

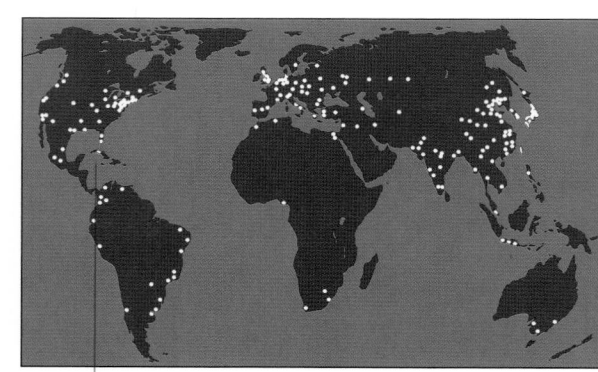

1975

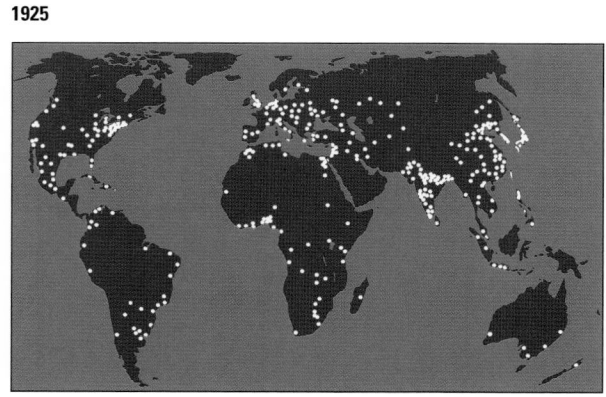

2000

Urban Population

Percentage of total population living in towns and cities (2000)

Most urbanized

Belgium	97%	Over 80%
W. Sahara	96%	60 – 80%
Singapore	93%	40 – 60%
UAE	93%	20 – 40%
Iceland	93%	Under 20%
[UK 89%]		

Least urbanized

Rwanda	6%
Bhutan	7%
East Timor	7%
Burundi	9%
Nepal	11%

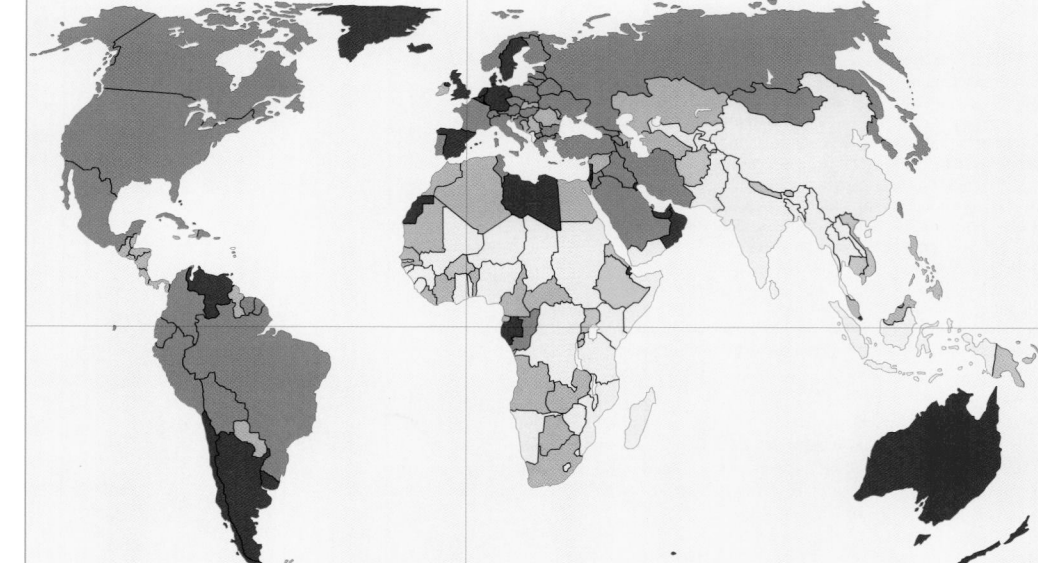

Expanding Cities

The growth of some of the world's largest cities in millions, 1950–2015.
Comparisons of city populations over time are problematic due to changes in the definition of the city limits.
These figures attempt to take such changes into consideration. The figure for London is the metropolitan region.

| ■ 1950 | ■ 2015 |

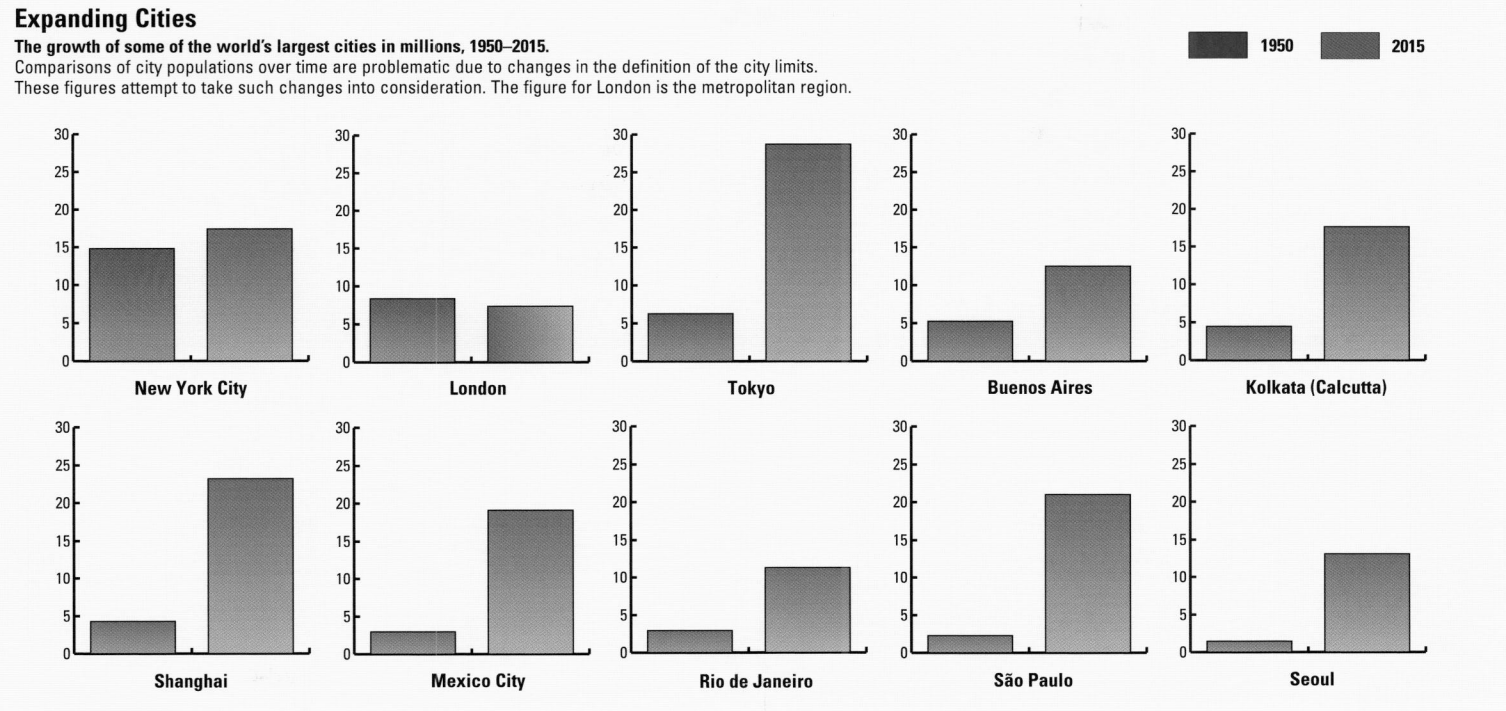

New York City · London · Tokyo · Buenos Aires · Kolkata (Calcutta)

Shanghai · Mexico City · Rio de Janeiro · São Paulo · Seoul

The graphs show the projected growth of megacities between 1950 and 2015. New York City, the world's largest city in 1950, reached a peak in 1970, but it has experienced periods of negative growth. London's population also declined between 1970 and 1985, before resuming a modest rate of increase. In both cases, the divergence from world trends is explained in part by counting methods. Each lies at the centre of a great agglomeration, and definitions of the 'city limits' may vary over time. Also, in developing countries, many areas around the megacities, which are counted as urban, are rural in character. The rates of city population growth in developing countries have also often been over-estimated. For example, it was once predicted that Kolkata (Calcutta) would have a population of 40 million by the late 1990s. The reason why many estimates have proven incorrect is partly explained by a new trend, namely that rapid urban growth is now greatest, in some regions, in the smaller cities. For example, the main expansion in West Bengal is no longer in Kolkata (Calcutta), but in a rash of small cities across the state.

Cities in Danger

As the decade of the 1980s advanced, most industrial countries, alarmed by acid rain and urban smog, took significant steps to limit air pollution. Well into the 1990s, however, these controls proved expensive to install and difficult to enforce, and clean air remains a luxury most developed, as well as developing, cities must live without.

Those taking part in the United Nations' Global Environment Monitoring System (*see right*) frequently show dangerous levels of pollutants ranging from soot to sulphur dioxide and photo-chemical smog; air in the majority of cities without such sampling equipment is likely to be at least as bad. Traffic, a major source of air pollution worldwide, loses Thailand's workforce 44 working days each year.

Urban Air Pollution

The world's most polluted cities: number of days each year when sulphur dioxide levels exceeded the WHO threshold of 150 micrograms per cubic metre (averaged over 4 to 15 years, 1970s – 1980s)

Sulphur dioxide is the main pollutant associated with industrial cities. According to the World Health Organization, more than seven days in a year above 150 µg per cubic metre bring a serious risk of respiratory disease: at least 600 million people live in urban areas where SO_2 concentrations regularly reach damaging levels.

Manila, Philippines
Kolkata (Calcutta), India
Milan, Italy
Zagreb, Croatia
Guangzhou, China
Madrid, Spain
Beijing, China
Xian, China
Seoul, South Korea
Tehran, Iran
Shenyang, China

120   90   60   30

Urban Housing Needs

Proportion of the population living in squatter settlements and the number of homeless per thousand, for selected cities.

Urbanization in most developing countries has been proceeding so rapidly that local governments have been unable to provide the necessary services and housing. In some cities, many people find their homes in squatter settlements, frequently without power, water and sanitation. Yet these communities are often a dynamic part of the city's economy, while their inhabitants sometimes take all kinds of initiatives, including the setting up of their own local government and self-help associations. Some of the world's richest cities also have a homeless underclass, although calculating the numbers of people involved is problematic. Yet it is the case that homelessness and unemployment are currently affecting an increasing number of people in the developed world.

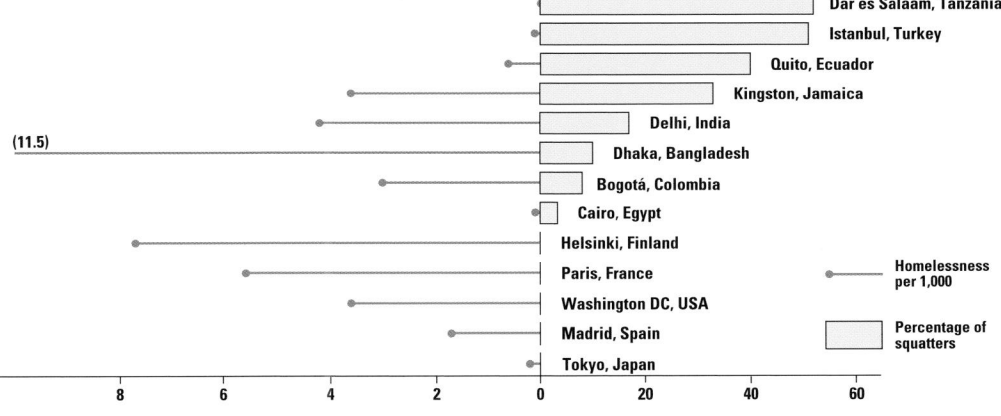

Dar es Salaam, Tanzania
Istanbul, Turkey
Quito, Ecuador
Kingston, Jamaica
Delhi, India
(11.5) Dhaka, Bangladesh
Bogotá, Colombia
Cairo, Egypt
Helsinki, Finland
Paris, France — Homelessness per 1,000
Washington DC, USA
Madrid, Spain — Percentage of squatters
Tokyo, Japan

8   6   4   2   0   20   40   60

Largest Cities

Early in the 21st century for the first time in history, the majority of the world's population will live in cities. Below is a list of all the cities with more than 10 million inhabitants, based on estimates for the year 2015.

1. Tokyo–Yokohama 28.7
2. Mumbai (Bombay) 27.4
3. Lagos 24.1
4. Shanghai 23.2
5. Jakarta 21.5
6. São Paulo 21.0
7. Karachi 20.6
8. Beijing 19.6
9. Dhaka 19.2
10. Mexico City 19.1
11. Kolkata (Calcutta) 17.6
12. Delhi 17.5
13. New York City 17.4
14. Tianjin 17.1
15. Manila 14.9
16. Cairo 14.7
17. Los Angeles 14.5
18. Seoul 13.1
19. Buenos Aires 12.5
20. Istanbul 12.1
21. Rio de Janeiro 11.3
22. Lahore 10.9
23. Hyderabad 10.6
24. Bangkok 10.4
25. Osaka 10.2
26. Lima 10.1
27. Tehran 10.0

City populations are based on urban agglomerations rather than legal city limits. In some cases where two adjacent cities have merged into one concentration, such as Tokyo–Yokohama, they have been regarded as a single unit.

Urban Advantages

Despite overcrowding and poor housing, living standards in the developing world's cities are almost invariably better than in the surrounding countryside. Resources – financial, material and administrative – are concentrated in the towns, which are usually also the centres of political activity and pressure. Governments – frequently unstable, and rarely established on a solid democratic base – are usually more responsive to urban discontent than rural misery.

In many countries, especially in Africa, food prices are kept artificially low, appeasing the underemployed urban masses at the expense of agricultural development. The imbalance encourages further citywards migration, helping to account for the astonishing rate of post-1950 urbanization and putting great strain on the ability of many nations to provide even modest improvements for their people.

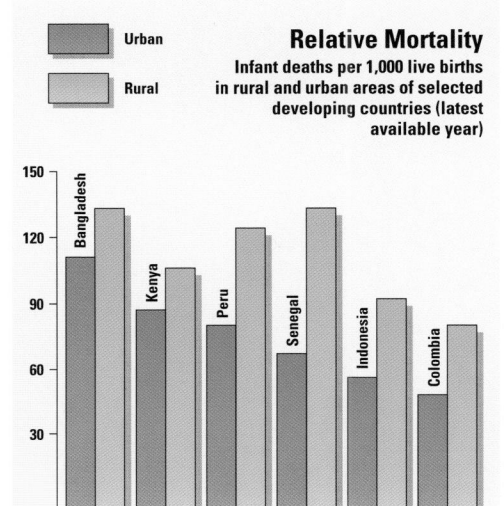

Relative Mortality
■ Urban ■ Rural
Infant deaths per 1,000 live births in rural and urban areas of selected developing countries (latest available year)

Bangladesh · Kenya · Peru · Senegal · Indonesia · Colombia

150 · 120 · 90 · 60 · 30

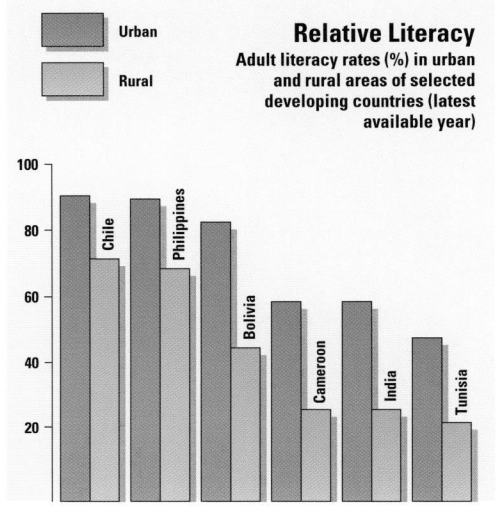

Relative Literacy
■ Urban ■ Rural
Adult literacy rates (%) in urban and rural areas of selected developing countries (latest available year)

Chile · Philippines · Bolivia · Cameroon · India · Tunisia

100 · 80 · 60 · 40 · 20

THE HUMAN FAMILY

For more information:
24 Population density
30 The world's refugees
   War since 1945
31 United Nations
   International
   organizations

Racial, language and religious differences have led to appalling acts of inhumanity throughout history. Yet strictly speaking, all human beings belong to one species, *Homo sapiens*, which has no subspecies. The differences between the three racial types which most people identify – namely Caucasoid, Mongoloid and Negroid – reflect not so much evolutionary differences as long periods of separation.

Migration has recently mingled the various groups to an unprecedented extent, and most nations now have some degree of racial mixing. For example, the United States has often been called a melting pot, because of the large numbers of people from various geographical locations which make up the population. The country has

no official language but, until recently, English was spoken by the vast majority of the people. But in recent years, some of the immigrants from Mexico, Cuba and other parts of Latin America have not learned English and speak only Spanish. This development disturbs those Americans who believe that the use of English binds the nation together, and several states have passed laws stating that English is their only official language.

Language is fundamental to human culture and any particular language is almost the definition of that particular culture. Because definitions of languages vary, estimates of the total number range from 3,000 to 6,000, although most are spoken by only a few people. The world's languages

are grouped into families, the largest of which are the Indo-European and Sino-Tibetan. Chinese, a Sino-Tibetan language, is spoken by more people as a first language than any other. English, an Indo-European tongue, ranks second, but it is the leading international language, because so many people speak it as their second tongue.

Like language, religion encourages cohesion in single human groups and it satisfies a deep human need by assigning people a place in a divinely ordered world. Religion is a way in which a culture can express its individuality. For example, the rise of Islamic fundamentalism in the late 20th century was partly an expression of resentment that secular Western values were being imposed on Muslims.

World Migration

The greatest voluntary migration was the colonization of North America by 30–35 million European settlers during the 19th century. The greatest forced migration involved 9–11 million Africans taken as slaves to America between 1550 and 1860. The migrations shown on the map below are mostly international, as population movements within borders are not usually recorded. Many of the statistics are necessarily estimates as so many refugees and migrant workers enter countries illegally and unrecorded. Emigrants may have a variety of motives for leaving, thus making it difficult to distinguish between voluntary and involuntary migrations.

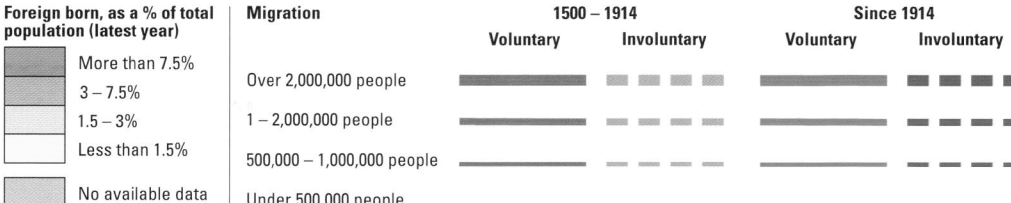

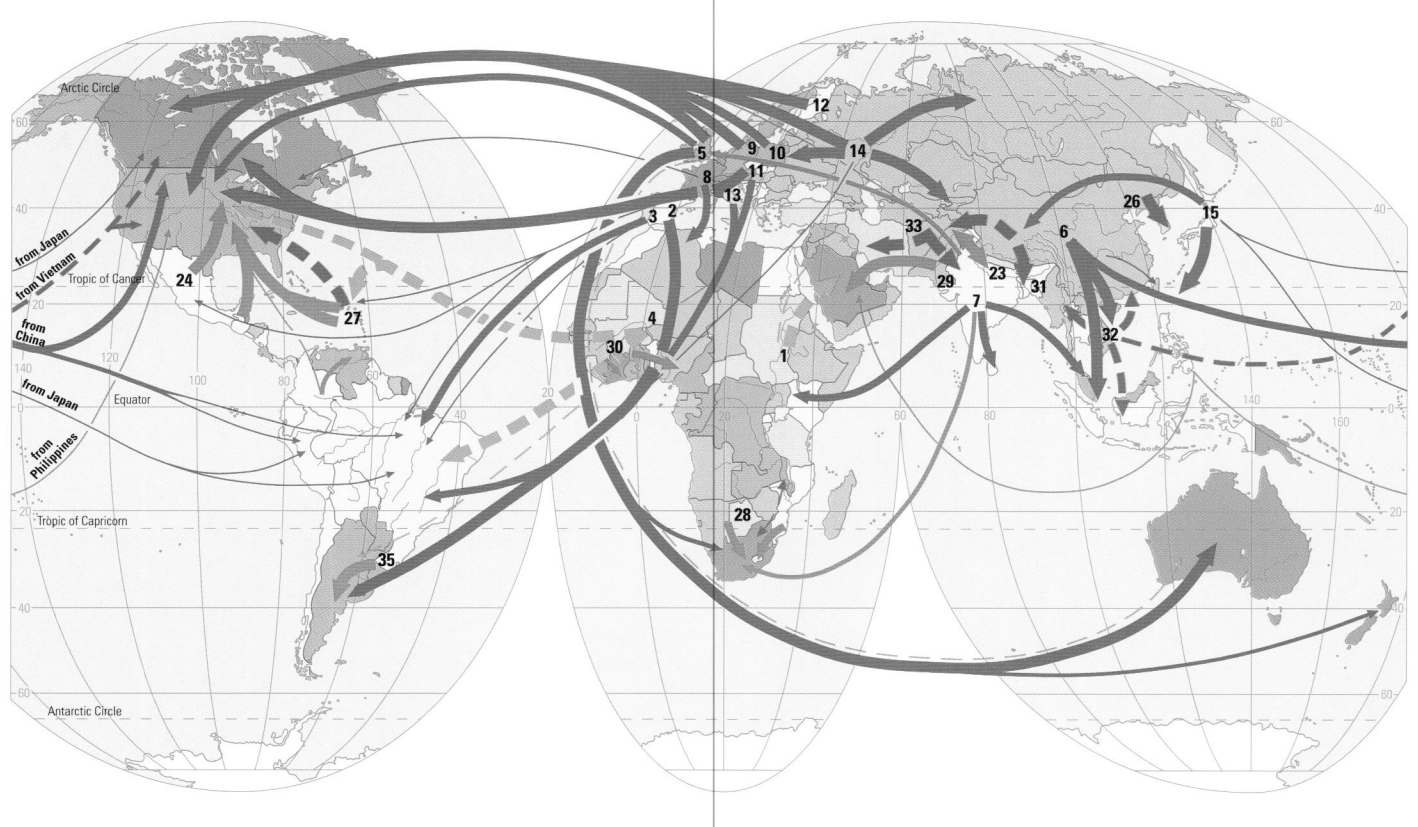

Building the USA

US Immigration 1820–1990

'Give me your tired, your poor / Your huddled masses yearning to breathe free....'

So starts Emma Lazarus's poem 'The New Colossus', inscribed on the Statue of Liberty. For decades the USA was the magnet that attracted millions of immigrants, notably from Central and Eastern Europe, the flow peaking in the early years of the 20th century. By the mid-1990s the proportion of immigrants had increased again to pre-World War II rates. In 1993–4, net immigration accounted for 30% of US population growth. Of the 904,000 immigrants, 40% were from Asia and 31% from Central America and the Caribbean.

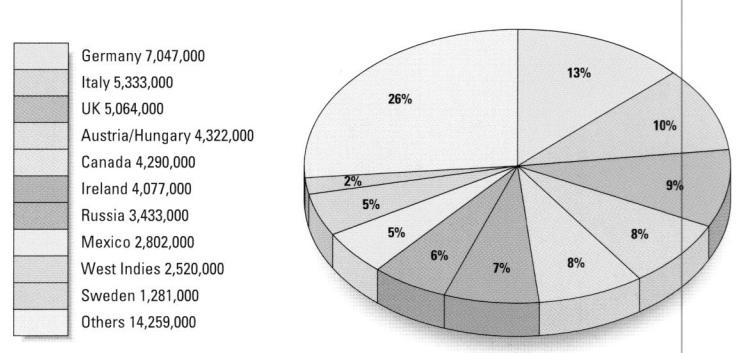

Germany 7,047,000
Italy 5,333,000
UK 5,064,000
Austria/Hungary 4,322,000
Canada 4,290,000
Ireland 4,077,000
Russia 3,433,000
Mexico 2,802,000
West Indies 2,520,000
Sweden 1,281,000
Others 14,259,000

Major world migrations since 1500 (over 1,000,000 people)

1. North and East African slaves to Arabia (4.3m)..........1500–1900
2. Spanish to South and Central America (2.3m) 1530–1914
3. Portuguese to Brazil (1.4m) 1530–1914
4. West African slaves to South America (4.6m)...........1550–1860
   to Caribbean (4m).......................1580–1860
   to North/Central America (1m) ...1650–1820
5. British and Irish to North America (13.5m) 1620–1914
   to Australasia and
   South Africa (3m)...............................1790–1914
6. Chinese to South-east Asia (22m).............................1820–1914
   to North America (1m) 1880–1914
7. Indian migrant workers (3m)..1850–1914
8. French to North Africa (1.5m) 1850–1914
9. Germans to North America (5m)..................................1850–1914
10. Poles to North America (3.6m).....................................1850–1914
11. Austro-Hungarians to North America (3.2m)............1850–1914
   to Western Europe (3.4m)...........1850–1914
   to South America (1.8m).............1850–1914
12. Scandinavians to North America (2.7m) 1850–1914
13. Italians to North America (5m).....................................1860–1914
   to South America (3.7m)..................1860–1914
14. Russians to North America (2.2m) 1880–1914
   to Western Europe (2.2m)...............1880–1914
   to Siberia (6m)..................................1880–1914
   to Central Asia (4m).........................1880–1914

15. Japanese to Eastern Asia, South-east Asia
   and America (8m)...1900–1914
16. Poles to Western Europe (1m) 1920–1940
17. Greeks and Armenians from Turkey (1.6m) 1922–1923
18. European Jews to extermination camps (5m)............1940–1944
19. Turks to Western Europe (1.9m) 1940–
20. Yugoslavs to Western Europe (2m) 1940–
21. Germans to Western Europe (9.8m) 1945–1947
22. Palestinian refugees (2m)..1947–
23. Indian and Pakistani refugees (15m)..................................1947
24. Mexicans to North America (9m).......................................1950–
25. North Africans to Western Europe (1.1m) 1950–
26. Korean refugees (5m)...1950–1954
27. Latin Americans and West Indians to
   North America (4.7m) 1960–
28. Migrant workers to South Africa (1.5m) 1960–
29. Indians and Pakistanis to The Gulf (2.4m).......................1970–
30. Migrant workers to Nigeria and Ivory Coast (3m)......1970–
31. Bangladeshi and Pakistani refugees (2m)..........................1972
32. Vietnamese and Cambodian refugees (1.5m) 1975–
33. Afghan refugees (6.1m)..1979–
34. Egyptians to The Gulf and Libya (2.9m) 1980–
35. Migrant workers to Argentina (2m) 1980–
36. Mozambique refugees (1.7m)...1985–
37. Yugoslav/Balkan refugees (1.7m).....................................1992–
38. Rwanda/Burundi refugees (2.6m)......................................1994–

Predominant Languages

INDO-EUROPEAN FAMILY
1. Balto-Slavic group (incl. Russian, Ukrainian)
2. Germanic group (incl. English, German)
3. Celtic group
4. Greek
5. Albanian
6. Iranian group
7. Armenian
8. Romance group (incl. Spanish, Portuguese, French, Italian)
9. Indo-Aryan group (incl. Hindi, Bengali, Urdu, Punjabi, Marathi)
10. **CAUCASIAN FAMILY**

AFRO-ASIATIC FAMILY
11. Semitic group (incl. Arabic)
12. Kushitic group
13. Berber group

14. **KHOISAN FAMILY**

15. **NIGER-CONGO FAMILY**

16. **NILO-SAHARAN FAMILY**

17. **URALIC FAMILY**

ALTAIC FAMILY
18. Turkic group (incl. Turkish)
19. Mongolian group
20. Tungus-Manchu group
21. Japanese and Korean

SINO-TIBETAN FAMILY
22. Sinitic (Chinese) languages (incl. Mandarin, Wu, Yue)
23. Tibetic-Burmic languages

24. **TAI FAMILY**

AUSTRO-ASIATIC FAMILY
25. Mon-Khmer group
26. Munda group
27. Vietnamese

28. **DRAVIDIAN FAMILY** (incl. Telugu, Tamil)

29. **AUSTRONESIAN FAMILY** (incl. Malay-Indonesian, Javanese)

30. **OTHER LANGUAGES**

First-language speakers, in millions (1999)	
Mandarin Chinese	885m
Spanish	332m
English	322m
Bengali	189m
Hindi	182m
Portuguese	170m
Russian	170m
Japanese	125m
German	98m
Wu Chinese	77m
Javanese	76m
Korean	75m
French	72m
Vietnamese	68m
Yue Chinese	66m
Marathi	65m
Tamil	63m
Turkish	59m
Urdu	58m

Languages form a kind of tree of development, splitting from a few ancient proto-tongues into branches that have grown apart and further divided with the passage of time. English and Hindi, for example, both belong to the great Indo-European family, although the relationship is only apparent after much analysis and comparison with non-Indo-European languages such as Chinese or Arabic; Hindi is part of the Indo-Aryan subgroup, whereas English is a member of Indo-European's Germanic branch; French, another Indo-European tongue, traces its descent through the Latin, or Romance, branch. A few languages – Basque is one example – have no apparent links with any other, living or dead. Most modern languages, of course, have acquired enormous quantities of vocabulary from each other.

Distribution of Living Languages

The figures refer to the number of languages currently in use in the regions shown.

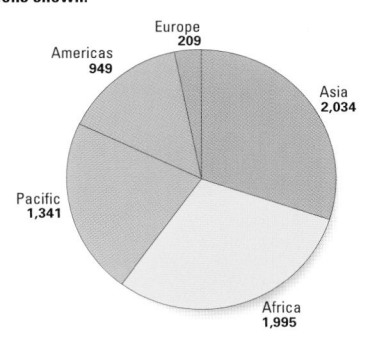

- Europe 209
- Americas 949
- Asia 2,034
- Pacific 1,341
- Africa 1,995

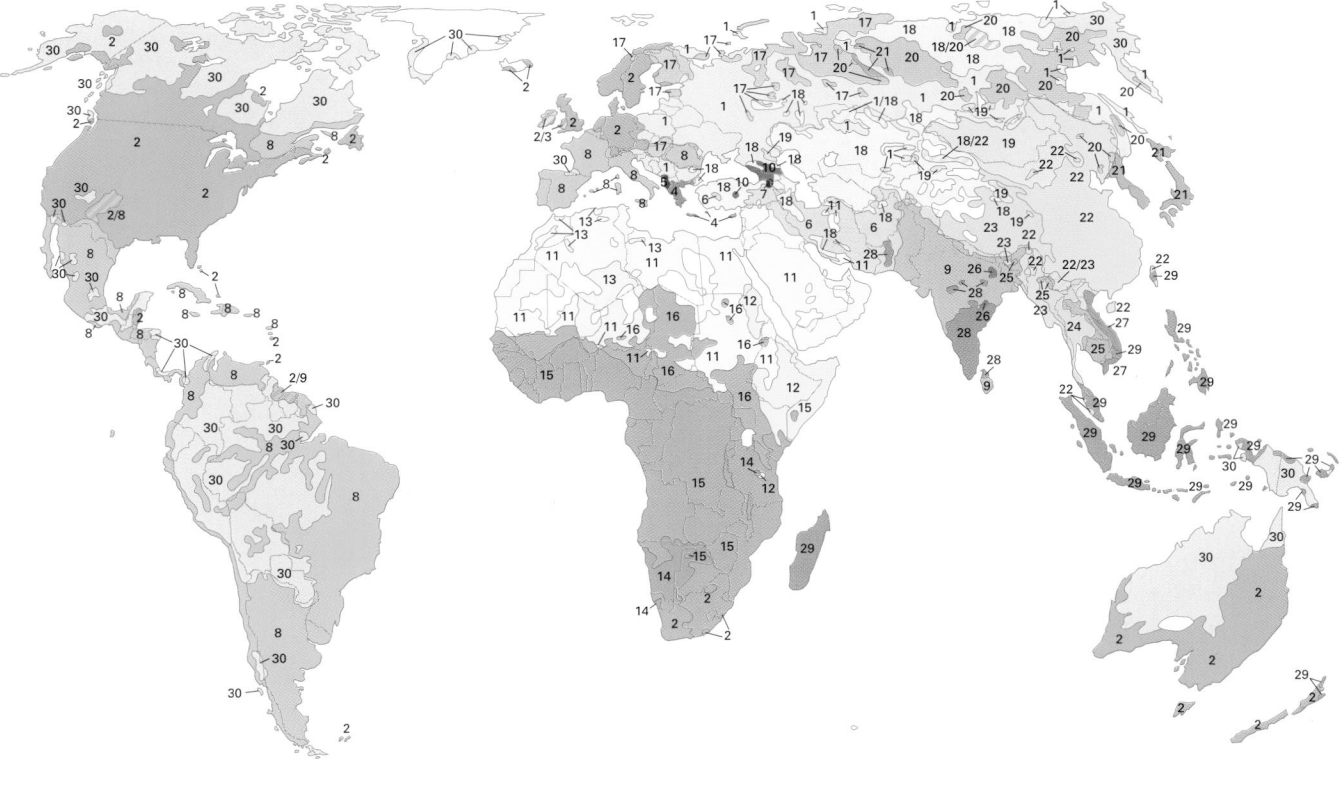

Predominant Religions

- ▲ Roman Catholicism
- Orthodox and other Eastern Churches
- • Protestantism
- Sunni Islam
- Shia Islam
- Buddhism
- Hinduism
- Confucianism
- ✳ Judaism
- Shintoism
- Tribal Religions

Religions are not as easily mapped as the physical contours of the land. Divisions are often blurred and frequently overlapping: most nations include people of many different faiths – or no faith at all. Some religions, like Islam and Christianity, have proselytes worldwide; others, like Hinduism and Confucianism, are restricted to a particular area, though modern migrations have taken some Indians and Chinese very far from their cultural origins. It is also difficult to show the degree to which religion controls daily life: Christian Western Europe, for example, is now far less dominated by its religion than are the Islamic nations of the Middle East. Similarly, figures for the major faiths' adherents make no distinction between nominal believers enrolled at birth and those for whom religion is a vital part of existence.

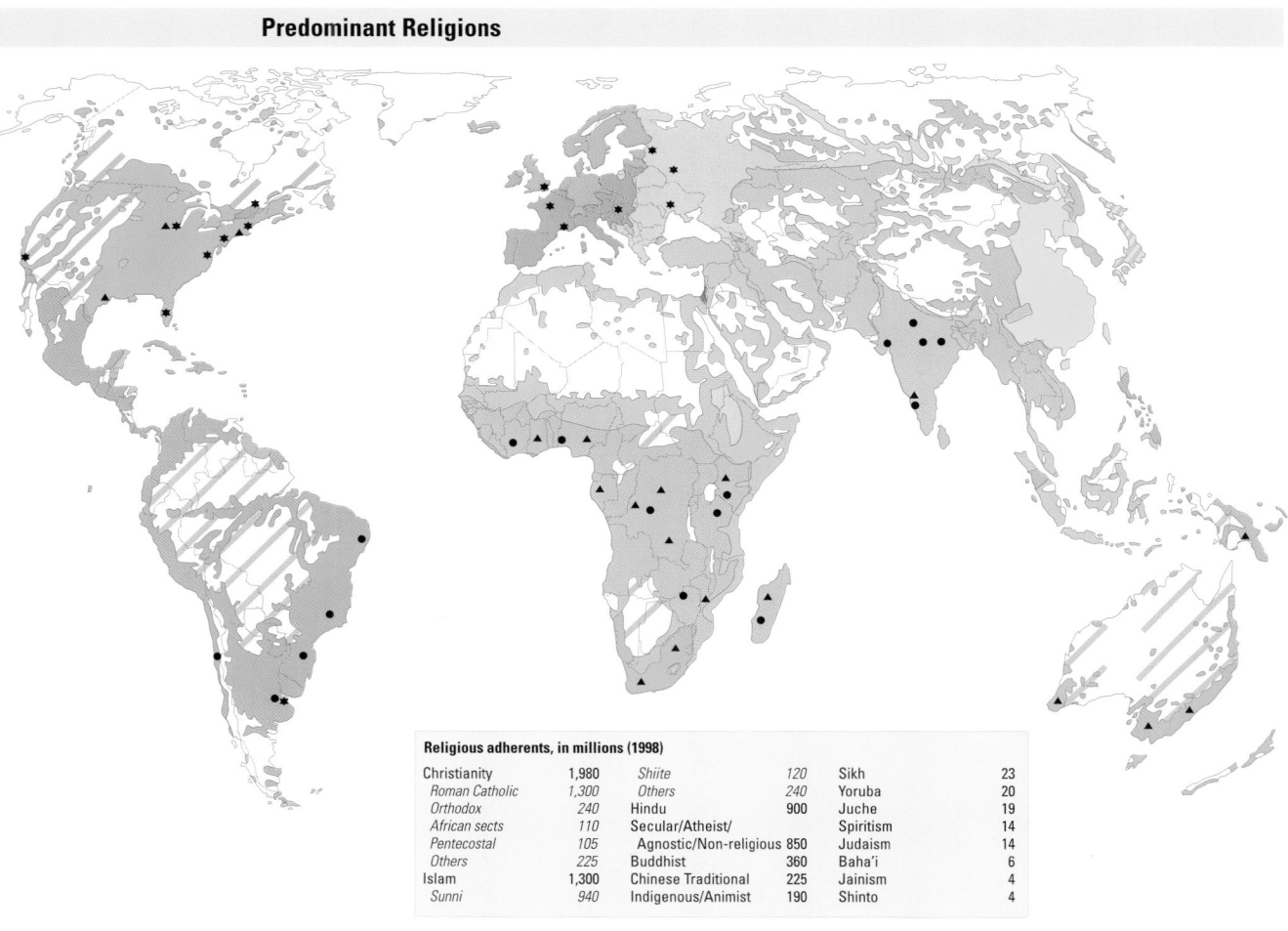

Religious adherents, in millions (1998)					
Christianity	1,980	*Shiite*	120	Sikh	23
Roman Catholic	*1,300*	*Others*	240	Yoruba	20
Orthodox	*240*	Hindu	900	Juche	19
African sects	*110*	Secular/Atheist/		Spiritism	14
Pentecostal	*105*	Agnostic/Non-religious	850	Judaism	14
Others	*225*	Buddhist	360	Baha'i	6
Islam	1,300	Chinese Traditional	225	Jainism	4
Sunni	*940*	Indigenous/Animist	190	Shinto	4

CONFLICT AND CO-OPERATION

For more information:
28 Migration
29 Religion

The 20th century witnessed two world wars, followed by a Cold War which several times threatened to erupt into a third world war, fought with nuclear weapons. The Cold War was marked by a great number of conflicts. Some were colonial wars, as the empires of the first half of the century fell apart, some were border wars, and some were civil wars. All the wars have caused great suffering among civilians, many of whom were forced to join the ranks of the world's refugees.

In the late 1980s, many people hoped that the end of the Cold War, following the collapse of Communist regimes in the former Soviet Union and Eastern Europe, would herald a new era of international stability. Instead, old ethnic and religious antagonisms surfaced in many areas, leading to civil war in such places as Chechenia, in Russia, and the former Yugoslavia. Nationalist rivalries, suppressed under Communist rule, replaced ideological factors as the major cause of conflict.

War is a very human activity, with no real equivalent in any other species. Yet humans also function well when they co-operate. Evolution has made this so. Hunter-gatherers in co-operative bands were far more effective than animals that prowled. Agriculture, urbanization and industrialization all depend on the ability of humans to co-operate.

The creation of the United Nations in 1945 held out hope that the world's nations, tired of war, would have the means to control humanity's aggressive instincts. Although the UN lacks the power to halt conflicts, it has often helped to achieve negotiation. Economic pressures have led to another kind of co-operation, the creation of common markets and economic unions, such as ASEAN in South-east Asia, the European Union and NAFTA in North America.

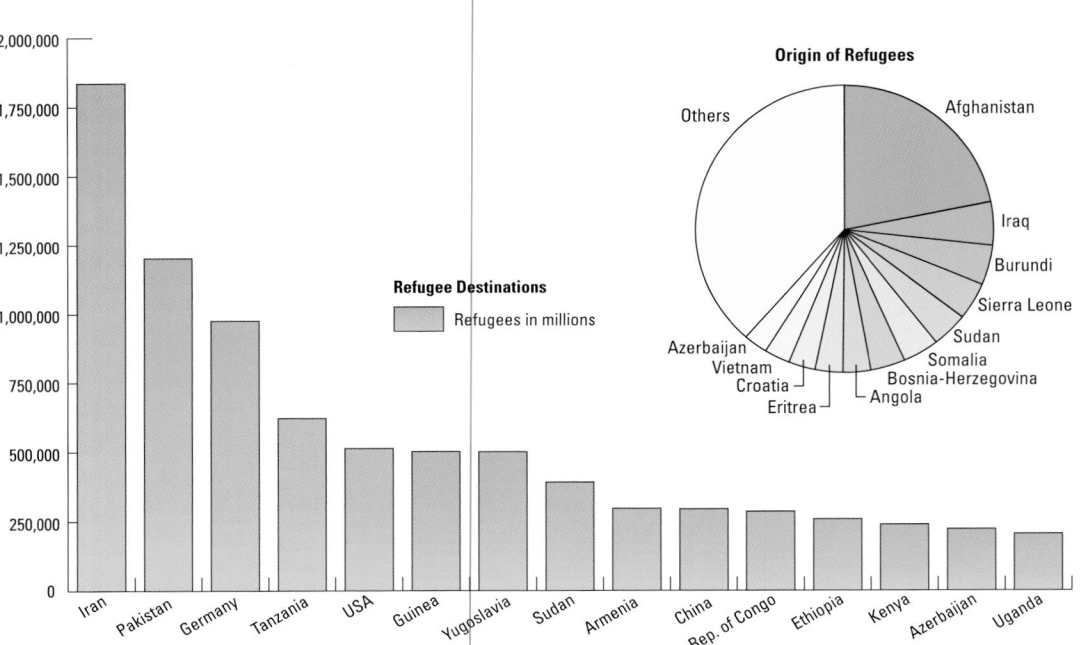

Refugee Destinations
◻ Refugees in millions

Origin of Refugees

The World's Refugees

Refugees by host nation (bar-chart, left) and by nation of origin (pie-chart, left) (2000). The source is the United Nations High Commission for Refugees (UNHCR). The 3.2 million Palestinian refugees living in Jordan, Syria, Lebanon, Gaza and the West Bank fall under the mandate of United Nations Relief and Works Agency (UNRWA) and are not included on the graphs.

The pie-chart shows the origins of the world's refugees, while the bar-chart below shows their destinations. According to the United Nations High Commission for Refugees (UNHCR) in 2000 there were 12.1 million refugees. However, the UNHCR definition of a refugee, 'a person who has left or remains outside their own country because they have a well-founded fear of persecution, or because their safety is threatened by events seriously disturbing public order', does not include people who are in a refugee-like situation but who have not been formally recognized. In 2000, there were a further 5.3 million people who were internally displaced, and a total 'population of concern' 21.1 million people, worldwide.

All but a few who cross international boundaries seek asylum in neighbouring countries, which are often the least equipped to deal with them. Lacking any rights or power, they frequently become an unwelcome burden to their hosts. Usually, the best any refugee can hope for is rudimentary food and shelter in temporary camps. Many Palestinians have been forced to live in camps since 1948.

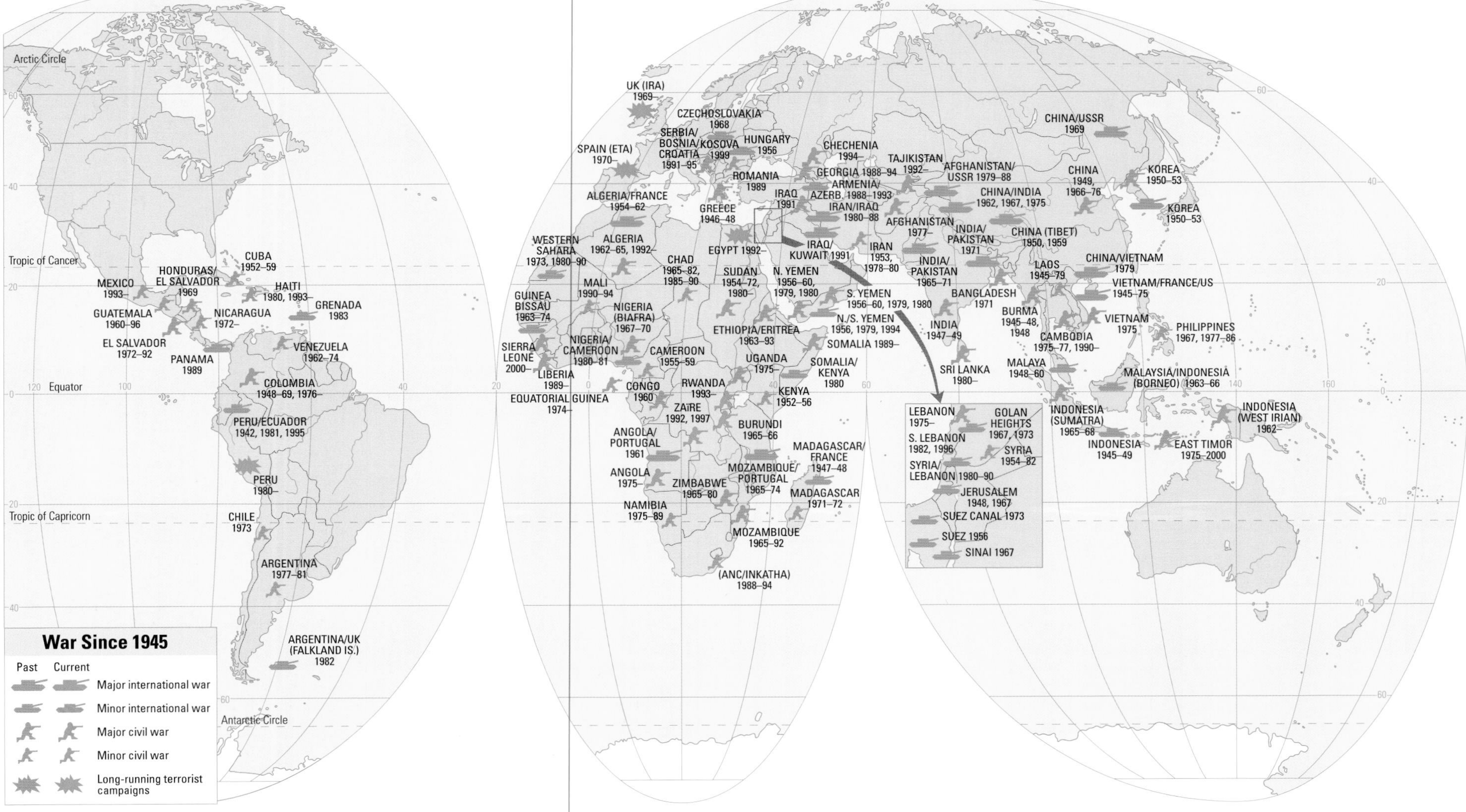

War Since 1945

Past	Current	
		Major international war
		Minor international war
		Major civil war
		Minor civil war
		Long-running terrorist campaigns

CARTOGRAPHY BY PHILIP'S. COPYRIGHT PHILIP'S

United Nations

The United Nations Organization was born as World War II drew to its conclusion. Six years of strife had strengthened the world's desire for peace, but an effective international organization was needed to help achieve it. That body would replace the League of Nations which, since its inception in 1920, had failed to curb the aggression of at least some of its member nations. At the United Nations Conference on International Organization held in San Francisco, the United Nations Charter was drawn up. Ratified by the Security Council and signed by the 51 original members, it came into effect on 24 October 1945.

The Charter set out the aims of the organization: to maintain peace and security, and develop friendly relations between nations; to achieve international co-operation in solving economic, social, cultural and humanitarian problems; to promote respect for human rights and fundamental freedoms; and to harmonize the activities of nations in order to achieve these common goals.

The United Nations has five principal organs :

The General Assembly
The forum at which member nations discuss moral and political issues affecting world development, peace and security meets annually in September, under a newly-elected President whose tenure lasts one year. Any member can bring business to the agenda, and each member nation has one vote.

The Security Council
A legislative and executive body, the Security Council is the primary instrument for establishing and maintaining international peace by attempting to settle disputes between nations. It has the power to dispatch UN forces, and member nations undertake to provide armed forces, assistance and facilities. The Security Council has ten temporary members elected by the General Assembly for two-year terms, and five permanent members – China, France, Russia, UK and USA.

The Economic and Social Council
By far the largest United Nations executive, the Council operates as a conduit between the General Assembly and the many United Nations agencies it instructs to implement Assembly decisions, and whose work it co-ordinates. The Council also commissions studies on economic conditions, collects data and makes recommendations to the Assembly.

The Secretariat
This is the staff of the United Nations, and its task is to administer the policies and programmes of the UN and its organs, and assist and advise the Head of the Secretariat, the Secretary-General – a full-time, non-political appointment made by the General Assembly.

The Trusteeship Council
This no longer administers any of the original 11 trust territories as they are all now independent.

The International Court of Justice (the World Court)
The World Court is the judicial organ of the United Nations. It deals only with United Nations disputes and all members are subject to its jurisdiction. There are 15 judges, elected for nine-year terms by the General Assembly and the Security Council.

The social and humanitarian operations of the UN include:
United Nations Development Programme (UNDP) Plans and funds projects to help developing countries make better use of their resources.
United Nations International Childrens' Fund (UNICEF) Created at the General Assembly's first session in 1945 to help children in the aftermath of World War II, it now provides basic health care and aid worldwide.
Food and Agriculture Organization (FAO) Aims to raise living standards and nutrition levels in rural areas by improving food production and distribution.
United Nations Educational, Scientific and Cultural Organization (UNESCO) Promotes international co-operation through broader and better education.
World Health Organization (WHO) Promotes and provides for better health care, public and environmental health and medical research.

United Nations agencies are involved in many aspects of international trade, safety and security:
International Maritime Organization (IMO) Promotes unity amongst merchant shipping, especially in regard to safety, marine pollution and standardization.
International Labour Organization (ILO) Seeks to improve labour conditions and promote productive employment to raise living standards.
World Meteorological Organization (WMO) Promotes co-operation in weather observation, reporting and forecasting.
World Trade Organization (WTO) On 1 January 1995 the WTO replaced GATT. It advocates a common code of conduct and its aim is the liberalization of world trade.
Disarmament Commission Considers and makes recommendations to the General Assembly on disarmament issues.
International Atomic Energy Agency (IAEA) Fosters development of peaceful uses for nuclear energy and establishes safety standards.

The World Bank comprises three United Nations agencies:
International Monetary Fund (IMF) Cultivates international monetary co-operation and expansion of trade.
International Bank for Reconstruction and Development (IBRD) Provides funds and technical assistance to developing countries.
International Finance Corporation (IFC) Encourages the growth of productive private enterprise in less developed countries.

Membership There are three independent states which are not members of the UN – Switzerland, Taiwan and Vatican City. Official languages are Chinese, English, French, Russian, Spanish and Arabic.
Funding The UN regular budget for 2002 is US $1.3 billion. Contributions are assessed by the members' ability to pay, with the maximum 22% of the total (USA's share), the minimum 0.01%. The 15-country EU pays over 37% of the budget.
Peacekeeping The UN has been involved in 54 peacekeeping operations worldwide since 1948.

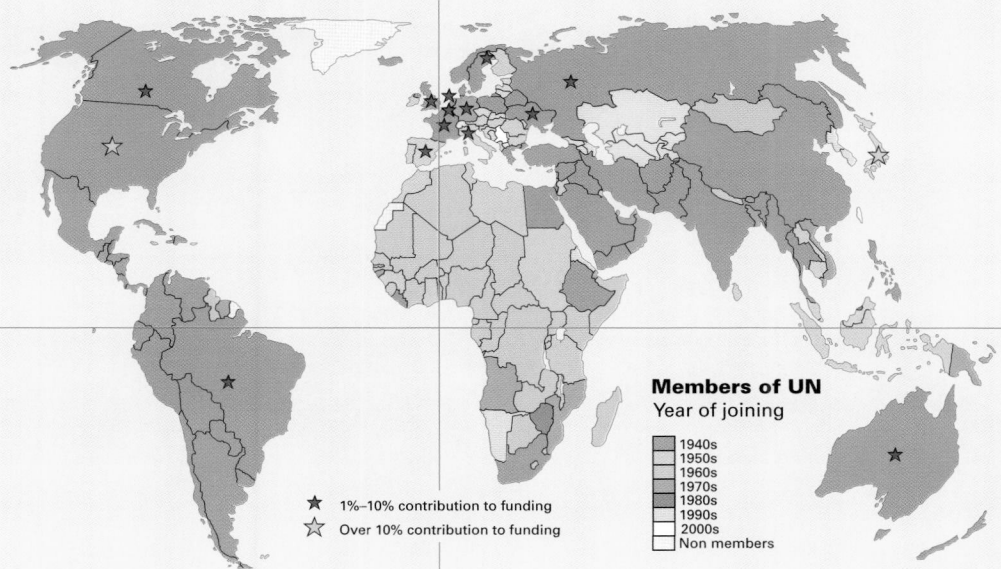

Members of UN
Year of joining

- 1940s
- 1950s
- 1960s
- 1970s
- 1980s
- 1990s
- 2000s
- Non members

★ 1%–10% contribution to funding
☆ Over 10% contribution to funding

International Organizations

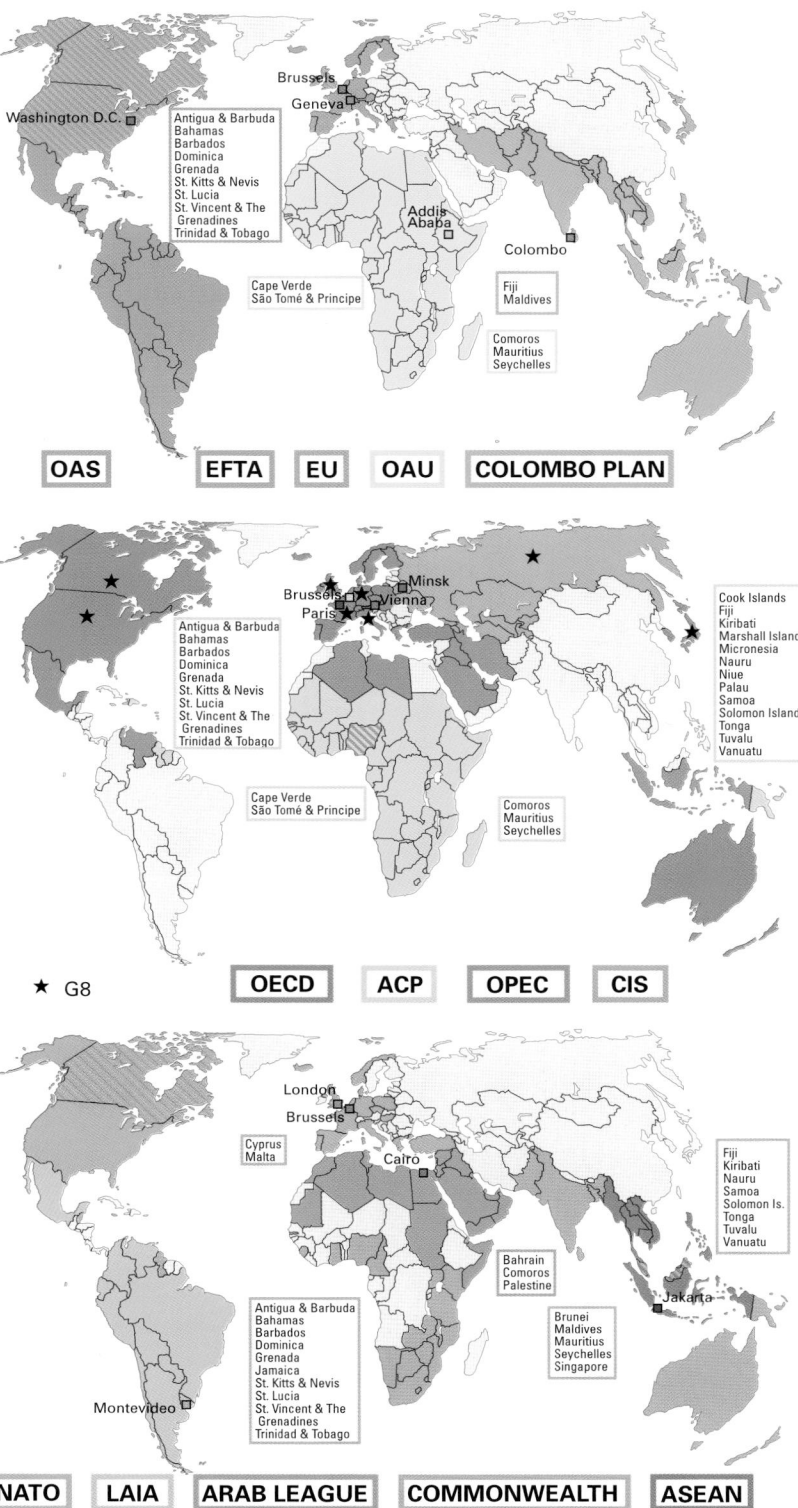

OAS | **EFTA** | **EU** | **OAU** | **COLOMBO PLAN**

★ G8

OECD | **ACP** | **OPEC** | **CIS**

NATO | **LAIA** | **ARAB LEAGUE** | **COMMONWEALTH** | **ASEAN**

ACP African-Caribbean-Pacific (formed in 1963). Members enjoy economic ties with the EU.
ARAB LEAGUE (1945) Aims to promote economic, social, political and military co-operation.
ASEAN Association of South-east Asian Nations (formed in 1967). Cambodia joined in 1999.
CIS The Commonwealth of Independent States (formed in 1991) comprises the countries of the former Soviet Union except for Estonia, Latvia and Lithuania.
COLOMBO PLAN (formed in 1951) Its 25 members aim to promote economic and social development in Asia and the Pacific.
COMMONWEALTH The Commonwealth of Nations evolved from the British Empire; it comprises 16 nations recognizing the British monarch as head of state, 32 republics and 5 indigenous monarchies, giving a total of 53. Nigeria was suspended in 1995, but reinstated in 1999.
EFTA European Free Trade Association (formed in 1960). Portugal left the original 'Seven' in 1989 to join what was then the EC, followed by Austria, Finland and Sweden in 1995. There are now only four members: Iceland, Liechtenstein, Norway and Switzerland.
EU The European Union evolved from the European Community (EC) in 1993. The original body, the European Coal and Steel Community (ECSC), was created in 1951 following the signing of the Treaty of Paris. The 15 members of the EU – Austria, Belgium, Denmark, Finland, France, Germany, Greece, Ireland, Italy, Luxembourg, Netherlands, Portugal, Spain, Sweden and the UK – aim to integrate economies, co-ordinate social developments and bring about political union. These members, of what is now the world's biggest market, share agricultural and industrial policies and tariffs on trade.
LAIA The Latin American Integration Association (formed in 1980) superceded the Latin American Free Trade Association formed in 1961. Its aim is to promote freer regional trade.
NATO North Atlantic Treaty Organization (formed in 1949). It continues despite the winding up of the Warsaw Pact in 1991. The Czech Rep., Hungary and Poland were the latest to join in 1999.
OAS Organization of American States (formed in 1948). It aims to promote social and economic co-operation between countries in the developed North America and developing Latin America.
OAU Organization of African Unity (1963). Its 53 members represent over 94% of Africa's population. Arabic, English, French and Portuguese are recognized as working languages.
OECD Organization for Economic Co-operation and Development (formed in 1961). It comprises 29 major free-market economies. The 'G8' is its 'inner group' of leading industrial nations, comprising Canada, France, Germany, Italy, Japan, Russia, UK and the USA.
OPEC Organization of Petroleum Exporting Countries (formed in 1960). It controls about three-quarters of the world's oil supply. Gabon formally withdrew from OPEC in August 1996.

Military Spending

Military expenditure as a % of GNP or GDP (1998–9)

1. North Korea	29%	14. Cyprus	5.5%
2. Eritrea	28.6%	15. Malta	5.5%
3. Angola	20%	16. Bahrain	5.2%
4. Saudi Arabia	12%	17. Brunei	5.1%
5. Oman	11.1%	18. Botswana	5%
6. Israel	9.7%	19. Croatia	5%
7. Egypt	8.2%	20. Iraq	4.9%
8. Qatar	8.1%	21. Singapore	4.9%
9. Jordan	7.8%	22. UAE	4.8%
10. Yemen	7.6%	23. Congo (Dem. Rep.)	4.6%
11. Yugoslavia	6.5%	24. Sri Lanka	4.2%
12. Burundi	6%	25. Armenia	4%
13. Syria	5.9%		

It is worth noting that the total amount of expenditure varies considerably depending on the size of the economy, so that although the percentages show the importance given to military spending within each country, they give no idea as to the total expenditure. In 1997, for example, the USA spent a total of US $271 billion, Russia US $70 billion, and the UK US $36 billion. In 1993, the USA also provided the most military assistance worldwide, providing US $3.4 billion, compared to a total of US $0.9 billion from Western Europe.

The period 1987–94 saw a decline in global military spending which generated what the United Nations Development Programme term a 'peace dividend' of US $935 billion. Unfortunately, there is no clear link between reduced military spending and enhanced expenditure on human development. Moreover, the poorest regions of the world (notably sub-Saharan Africa) failed to contain their military spending and, in some cases, it increased.

AGRICULTURE

For more information:

16 Climate regions
17 Temperature and
   precipitation
18 Water utilization
19 Natural vegetation
   Land use by
   continent
38 Division of
   employment

Bad harvests in 1995 caused a drop in world grain reserves to a 20-year low. This revived the ongoing debate as to whether the population explosion will cause major food crises in the 21st century.

Experts estimate that 3 billion tonnes of cereals will be needed to feed the world's population in 25 years' time, as compared with 1.9 billion tonnes at present. To expand food production to this extent, some argue, will place great strain on the environment. One suggestion to alleviate the situation is that people in developed countries should eat less meat. This would release more grain, which is used as cattle fodder, to feed people.

Other experts argue that there should be no food crises. World grain production tripled between 1950 and 1990, largely as a result of the Green Revolution, during which genetically improved, high-yield varieties of maize, rice and wheat, the world's three leading staple crops, were developed. These new varieties have helped many developing countries to achieve food surpluses and prevent widespread starvation.

The only region of the world which seems likely to suffer food shortages in the 21st century is sub-Saharan Africa, where in the late 1990s the average daily calorie intake was 6% less than what was needed and where the population is expected to double in 20 years. Improved land management and a huge increase in global trade, especially in food distribution, is necessary if sub-Saharan Africans are not to go hungry.

The development of agriculture more than 10,000 years ago transformed human existence more than any other major advance. By supporting larger populations, it led to the growth of early civilizations and later it sustained people in the industrial cities which sprang up in the 19th century.

Today, agricultural production varies a great deal between the developed world, where it is highly mechanized and employs few people, such as 3% of the workforce in the United States, and the developing world, such as sub-Saharan Africa, where it employs 66% of the workforce. Many Africans are engaged in subsistence farming, providing the basic needs of their families but not contributing to the national economy. Much of Africa also suffers from economic mismanagement, as well as civil war and banditry.

Political problems have also affected food production in other parts of the world. The former USSR had much excellent farmland, but the failure of the collectives and state farms to maintain sufficiently high levels of production helped to bring about the collapse of Communism.

Farmers are under great pressure not only to maintain high levels of production but to increase them. However, the cultivation of marginal areas is one of the prime causes of soil erosion and desertification.

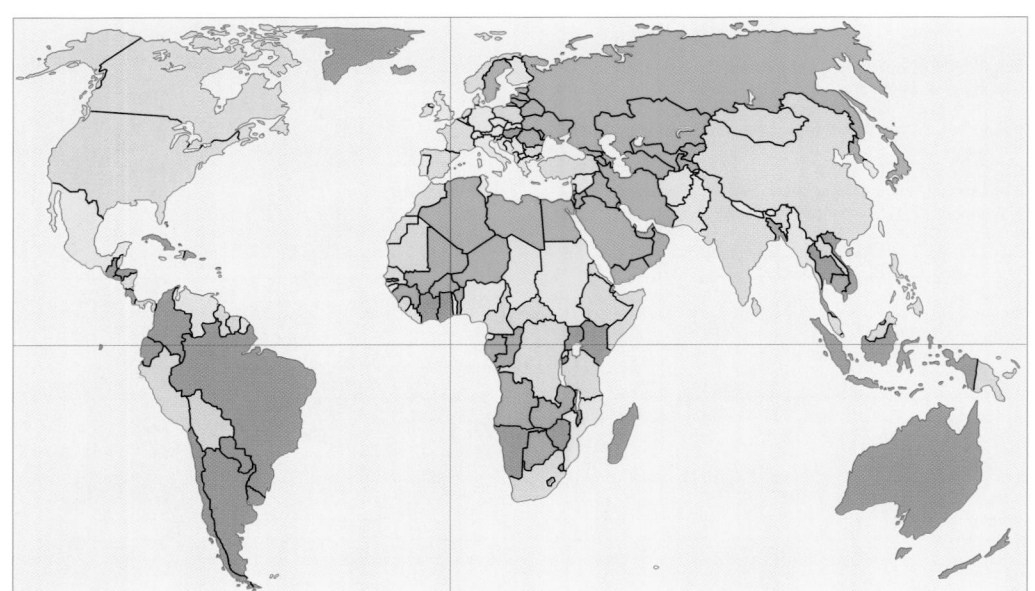

Self-sufficiency in Food

Balance of trade in food products as a percentage of total trade in food products – S.I.T.C. Classes 0, 1 and 4 (latest available year)

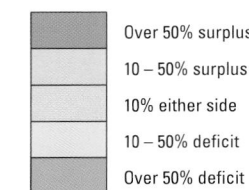

- Over 50% surplus
- 10 – 50% surplus
- 10% either side
- 10 – 50% deficit
- Over 50% deficit

Most self-sufficient		Least self-sufficient	
Argentina	95%	Algeria	−98%
Zimbabwe	87%	Djibouti	−97%
Honduras	81%	Yemen	−95%
Malawi	81%	Zambia	−95%
Costa Rica	79%	Japan	−91%
Iceland	78%	Gabon	−90%
Chile	75%	Kuwait	−90%
Uruguay	75%	Brunei	−89%
Ecuador	74%	Burkina Faso	−82%

Land Use

- Arable
- Arable and pasture
- Market gardening
- Woods and forests
- Rough grazing
- Non-productive
- Pasture
- Savanna
- Fishing
- Industrial areas

Staple Crops

Wheat: Grown in a range of climates, with most varieties – including the highest-quality bread wheats – requiring temperate conditions. Mainly used in baking, it is also used for pasta and breakfast cereals.

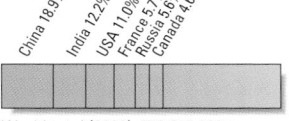

World total (2000): 576,317,000 tonnes

Maize: Originating in the New World and still an important human food in Africa and Latin America, in the developed world it is processed into breakfast cereals, oil, starches and adhesives. It is also used for animal feed.

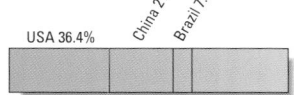

World total (2000): 590,791,000 tonnes

Oats: Most widely used to feed livestock, but eaten by humans as oatmeal or porridge. Oats have a beneficial effect on the cardiovascular system, and human consumption is likely to increase.

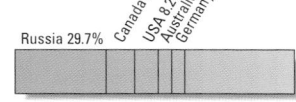

World total (2000): 25,953,000 tonnes

Millet: The name covers a number of small-grained cereals, members of the grass family with a short growing season. Used to produce flour, meal and animal feed, and fermented to make beer, especially in Africa.

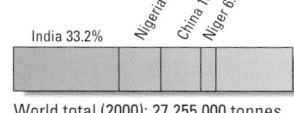

World total (2000): 27,255,000 tonnes

Rice: Thrives on the high humidity and temperatures of the Far East, where it is the traditional staple food of half the human race. Usually grown standing in water, rice responds well to continuous cultivation, with three or four crops annually.

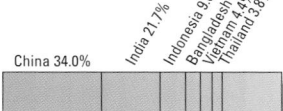

World total (2000): 598,852,000 tonnes

Potatoes: The most important of the edible tubers, potatoes grow in well-watered, temperate areas. Weight for weight less nutritious than grain, they are a human staple as well as an important animal feed.

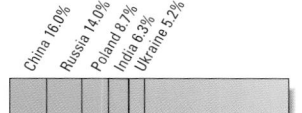

World total (2000): 311,288,000 tonnes

Soya: Beans from soya bushes are very high (30–40%) in protein. Most are processed into oil and proprietary protein foods. Consumption since 1950 has tripled, mainly due to the health-conscious developed world.

World total (2000): 161,993,000 tonnes

Cassava: A tropical shrub that needs high rainfall (over 1,000 mm annually) and a 10–30 month growing season to produce its large, edible tubers. Used as flour by humans, as cattle feed and in industrial starches.

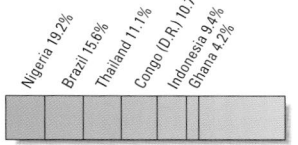

World total (2000): 172,737,000 tonnes

Sugars

Sugar cane: Confined to tropical regions, cane sugar accounts for the bulk of international trade in sugar. Most is produced as a foodstuff, but some countries, notably Brazil and South Africa, distil sugar cane to make motor fuels.

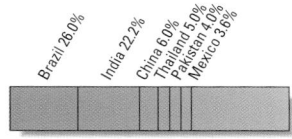

World total (2000): 1,278,093,000 tonnes

Sugar beet: Closely related to the beetroot, sugar beet's yield after processing is indistinguishable from cane sugar. It is replacing sugar-cane imports in Europe, to the detriment of the developing countries that rely on it as a major cash crop.

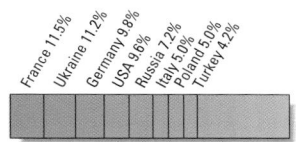

World total (2000): 244,780,000 tonnes

Cereals are grasses with starchy, edible seeds; every important civilization has depended on them as a source of food. The major cereal grains contain about 10% protein and 75% carbohydrate. Grain contributes more than any other group of foods to the energy and protein content of the human diet. Starchy tuber crops or root crops are second in importance after cereals as staple foods; easily cultivated, they provide high yields for little effort.

Food and Population

Comparison of food production and population by continent
The left column indicates the % of world food production and the right shows population in proportion.

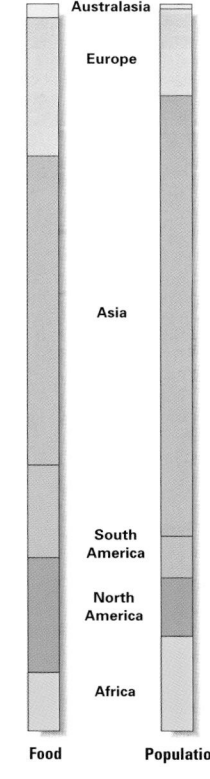

Food   Population

Agricultural Population

Percentage of the total population dependent on agriculture for their livelihood (2000)

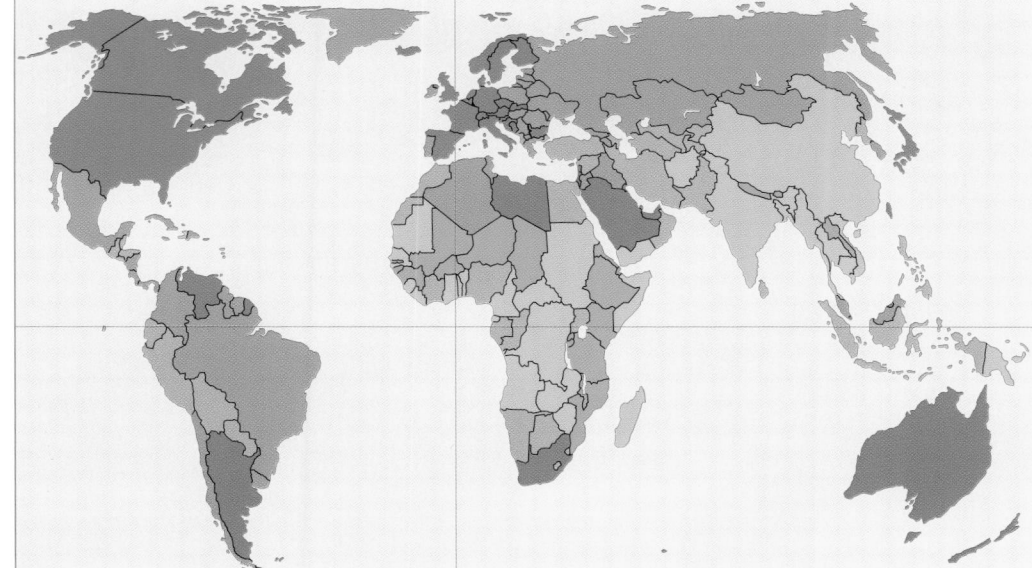

- Over 75% dependent
- 50 – 75% dependent
- 25 – 50% dependent
- 10 – 25% dependent
- Under 10% dependent

Top 5 countries		Bottom 5 countries	
Bhutan	93.7%	Singapore	0.1%
Nepal	93.0%	Brunei	0.7%
Burkina Faso	92.3%	Bahrain	1.0%
Burundi	90.4%	Kuwait	1.1%
Rwanda	90.3%	Qatar	1.3%

Animal Products

Traditionally, food animals subsisted on land unsuitable for cultivation, supporting agricultural production with their fertilizing dung. But free-ranging animals grow slowly and yield less meat than those more intensively reared; the demands of urban markets in the developed world have encouraged the growth of factory-like production methods. A large proportion of staple crops, especially cereals, are fed to animals, an inefficient way to produce protein but one likely to continue as long as people value meat and dairy products in their diet.

Cheese: Least perishable of all dairy products, cheese is milk fermented with selected bacterial strains to produce a foodstuff with a potentially immense range of flavours and textures. The vast majority of cheeses are made from cow's milk, although sheep and goat cheeses are highly prized.

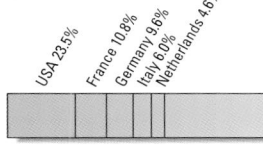

World total (2000): 16,045,000 tonnes

Beef and Veal: Most beef and veal is reared for home markets, and the top five producers are also the biggest consumers. The USA produces nearly a quarter of the world's beef and eats even more.

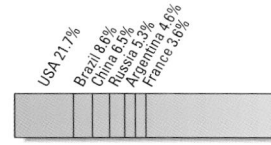

World total (2000): 57,170,000 tonnes

Milk: Many human groups, including most Asians, find raw milk indigestible after infancy, and it is often only the starting point for other dairy products such as butter, cheese and yoghurt. Most world milk production comes from cows, but sheep's milk and goats' milk are also important.

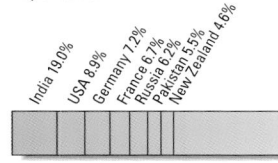

World total (2000): 2,504,000 tonnes

Butter: A traditional source of vitamin A as well as calories, butter has lost much popularity in the developed world for health reasons, although it remains a valuable food. Most butter from India, the world's largest producer, is clarified into ghee, which has religious as well as nutritional importance.

World total (2000): 7,049,000 tonnes

Pork: Although pork is forbidden to many millions, notably Muslims, on religious grounds, more is produced than any other meat in the world, mainly because it is the cheapest. It accounts for about 90% of China's meat output, although per capita meat consumption is relatively low.

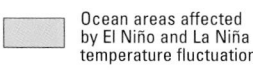

World total (2000): 90,909,000 tonnes

Crop Failure

- Areas liable to periodic crop failure
- Areas where crop failures are rare
- Desert

Crisis in Africa

Each year 40 million people, almost half of whom are children, die from starvation and related diseases. In 2000, 600 million people worldwide were estimated to be suffering from malnutrition. Africa suffers from more natural disasters than any other continent; pests such as locusts destroy crops, and tropical storms and floods ruin harvests. Famines periodically affect parts of Africa causing widespread hardship, even though enough food is produced worldwide to feed everyone. There are two major phenomena contributing to these famines. One is called El Niño (the unusual warming of the Pacific Ocean's surface water) and the reverse is called La Niña (the unusual cooling of the Pacific's surface water).The higher or lower the temperature of each event, the more extreme the weather or drought. El Niño peak years were 1973–4, 1982–3, 1986–7, 1992 and 1997. La Niña peak years were 1972, 1974, 1976 and 1988.

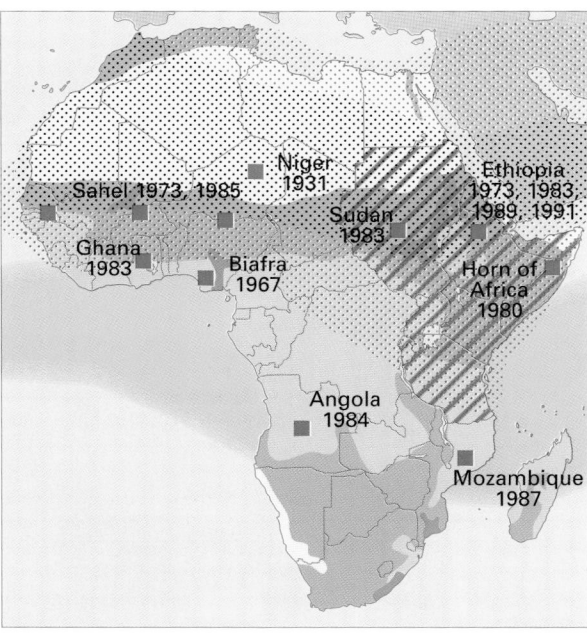

- Ocean areas affected by El Niño and La Niña temperature fluctuations

Desert Locusts

- Areas liable to invasions by desert locusts
- Areas affected by 1993 swarm of desert locusts
- Countries affected by four years of continuous drought 1996–2000
- Areas liable to flood
- Major famines since 1900 (with dates)

ENERGY

For more information:
22 Carbon dioxide
   Greenhouse power
   CO₂ producers
   Global warming
23 Water pollution
41 World shipping

Every year, the world's energy consumption is about the equivalent of what would come from burning 8,000 million tonnes of oil (8,000 MtOe) – a 20-fold increase since 1850. Two-fifths of this total actually comes from burning oil and most of the rest comes from coal and natural gas.

The oil crises in the 1970s precipitated concern over dependence on finite fossil fuels as the primary source of energy, and growing environmental awareness has added impetus to the search for alternative energy resources.

Fossil fuel combustion damages the environment through the release of gases and particulate matter, but two other major sources of energy, hydroelectricity and nuclear power, are also controversial. For example, hydroelectricity production involves flooding large areas to create reservoirs, while nuclear power stations, which are costly to build, generate dangerous radioactive wastes, and can lead to disasters on an international scale.

Alternative energy resources may soon provide a much larger proportion of the world's energy consumption, especially in developing countries where millions of people currently have no access to electricity. Experts have predicted that solar and wind energy may have an important future in such countries as China and India, while other areas under development, such as tidal, wave and geothermal power, all have potential in appropriate areas. World Bank experts have calculated that solar power could, in theory, supply between five and ten times the present electricity supply of developing countries.

Conversions

For historical reasons, oil is still traded in barrels. The weight and volume equivalents shown below are all based on average density 'Arabian light' crude oil, and should be considered approximate.

The energy equivalents given for a tonne of oil are also somewhat imprecise: oil and coal of different qualities will have varying energy contents, a fact usually reflected in their price on world markets.

1 barrel:
0.136 tonnes
159 litres
35 Imperial gallons
42 US gallons

1 tonne:
7.33 barrels
1185 litres
256 Imperial gallons
261 US gallons

1 tonne oil:
1.5 tonnes hard coal
3.0 tonnes lignite
12,000 kWh

1 gallon (Imperial):
227,42 cubic inches
1.201 US gallons
4,546 litres

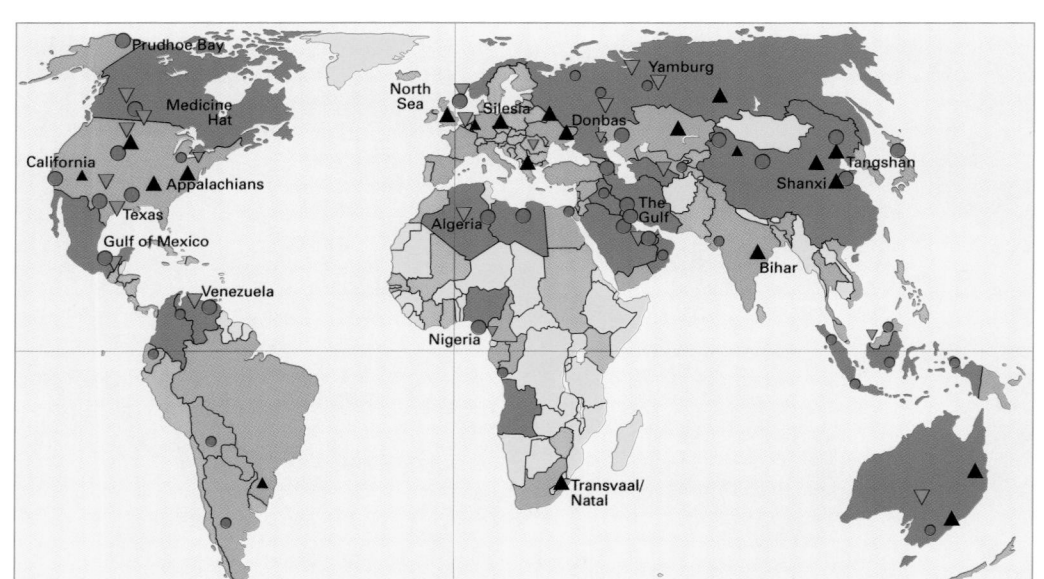

Energy Balance

Difference between energy production and consumption in millions of tonnes of oil equivalent (MtOe) (1997)

Energy deficit ↑

- Over 35 MtOe
- 1 – 35 MtOe
- Approx. balance
- 1 – 35 MtOe
- Over 35 MtOe

Energy surplus ↓

- ● Principal oilfields   ● Secondary oilfields
- ▽ Principal gasfields   ▽ Secondary gasfields
- ▲ Principal coalfields   ▲ Secondary coalfields

World Energy Consumption

Energy consumed by world regions, measured in million tonnes of oil equivalent in 1997. Total world consumption was 8,509 MtOe. Only energy from oil, gas, coal, nuclear and hydroelectric sources are included. Excluded are fuels such as wood, peat, animal waste, wind, solar and geothermal which, though important in some countries, are unreliably documented in terms of consumption statistics.

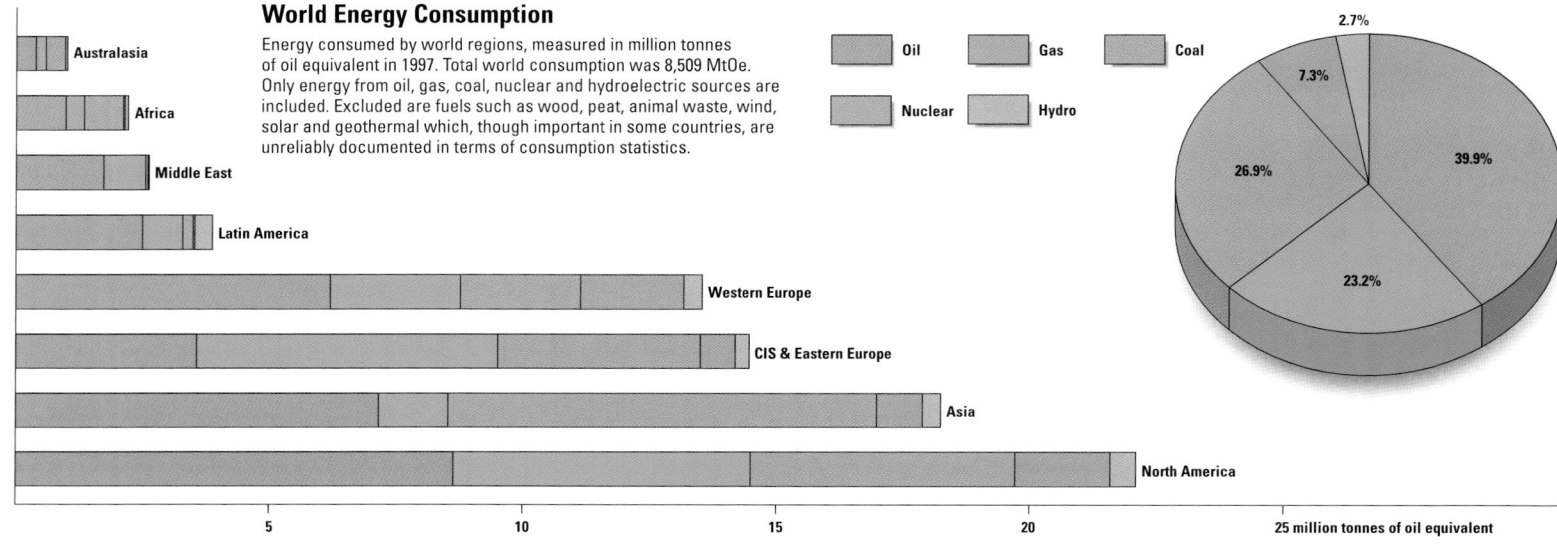

Oil | Gas | Coal | Nuclear | Hydro

Australasia
Africa
Middle East
Latin America
Western Europe
CIS & Eastern Europe
Asia
North America

5   10   15   20   25 million tonnes of oil equivalent

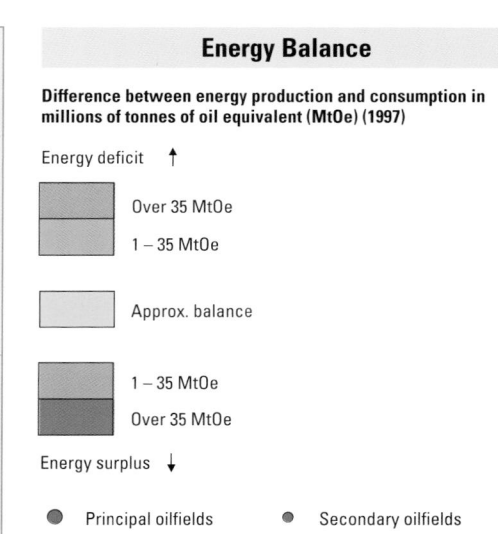

2.7%
7.3%
26.9%   39.9%
23.2%

Energy Production

Commercial energy production expressed in kilograms of oil equivalent per person (1998)

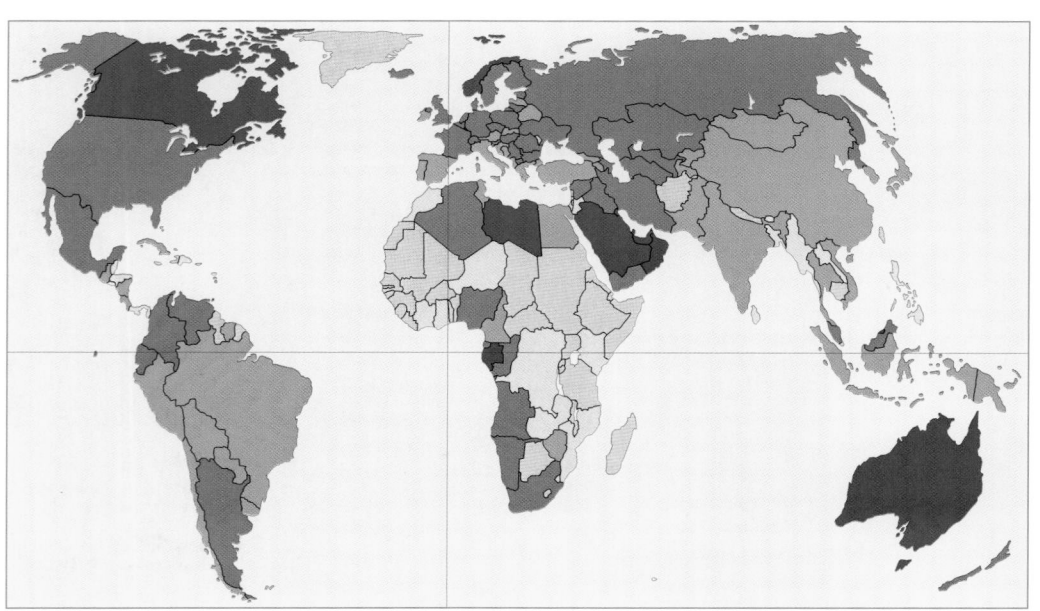

- Over 10,000 kg per person
- 1,000 – 10,000 kg per person
- 100 – 1,000 kg per person
- 10 – 100 kg per person
- Under 10 kg per person

In developing countries traditional fuels are still very important. These so-called biomass fuels include wood, charcoal and dried dung. The pie-chart (*right*) highlights the importance of biomass in terms of energy consumption in Nigeria. Collecting fuelwood can be a time-consuming task, sometimes taking all day.

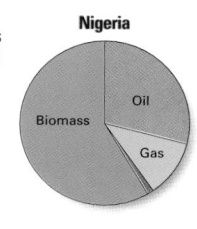

Nigeria

Oil
Gas
Biomass

Oil Movements

Major world movements of oil in millions of tonnes (1999)

Middle East to Asia (not Japan)	292.0
Middle East to Japan	207.4
Middle East to Western Europe	188.8
South and Central America to USA	128.5
Middle East to USA	120.7
Former Soviet Union to Western Europe	111.7
North Africa to Western Europe	96.0
Canada to USA	74.4
Mexico to USA	64.6
West Africa to USA	59.7
Western Europe to USA	39.1
Former Soviet Union to Eastern Europe	34.9
Middle East to Africa	34.7
West Africa to Western Europe	30.1
Western Europe to Canada	22.7
Middle East to South and Central America	20.3
Total world imports	**2,025,700,000 tonnes**

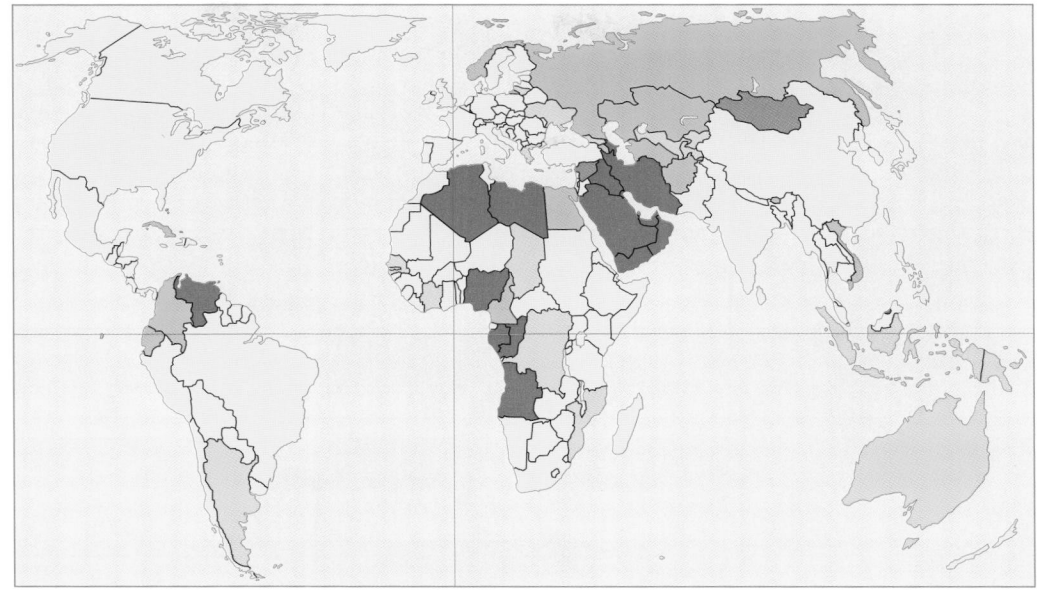

Fuel Exports

Fuels as a percentage of total value of exports (1999)

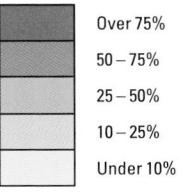

	Over 75%
	50 – 75%
	25 – 50%
	10 – 25%
	Under 10%

In the 1970s, oil exports became a political issue when OPEC sought to increase the influence of developing countries in world affairs by raising oil prices and restricting production. But its power was short-lived, following a fall in demand for oil in the 1980s, due to an increase in energy efficiency and development of alternative resources.

World Coal Reserves

Proved coal reserves in place by region and country, thousand million tonnes (1999)

World Total = 984,211 million tonnes

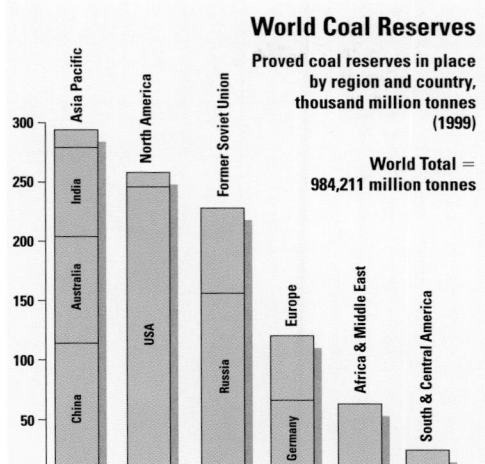

World Gas Reserves

Proved recoverable natural gas reserves by region and country, trillion cubic metres (1999)

World Total = 146 trillion cubic metres

World Oil Reserves

Crude oil reserves by region and country, thousand million tonnes (1999)

World Total = 140,400 million tonnes

Nuclear Power

Major producers by percentage of world total and by percentage of domestic electricity generation (1998)

Country	% of world total production	Country	% of nuclear as proportion of domestic electricity
1. USA	29.2%	1. France	77%
2. France	15.9%	2. Sweden	47%
3. Japan	13.6%	3. Ukraine	44%
4. Germany	6.6%	4. South Korea	38%
5. Russia	4.3%	5. Japan	32%
6. UK	4.1%	6. Germany	29%
7. South Korea	3.7%	7. UK	28%
8. Ukraine	3.1%	8. USA	19%
9. Sweden	3.0%	9. Canada	13%
10. Canada	2.9%	10. Russia	13%

Although the 1980s were a bad time for the nuclear power industry (major projects ran over budget and fears of long-term environmental damage were heavily reinforced by the 1986 disaster at Chernobyl), the industry picked up in the early 1990s. Whilst the number of reactors is still increasing, however, orders for new plants have shrunk. In 1997, the Swedish government began to decommission the country's 12 nuclear power plants.

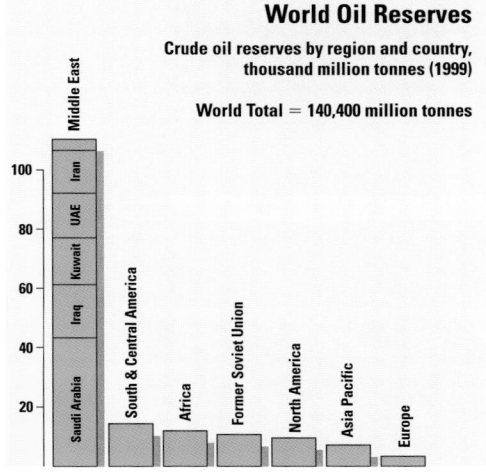

Renewable Energy

Average annual solar irradiance in kWh/m², with selected major hydroelectric and geothermal power stations

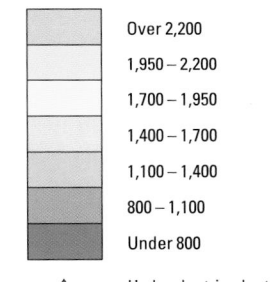

	Over 2,200
	1,950 – 2,200
	1,700 – 1,950
	1,400 – 1,700
	1,100 – 1,400
	800 – 1,100
	Under 800
△	Hydroelectric plants
●	Geothermal plants

Hydroelectricity

Major producers by percentage of world total and by percentage of domestic electricity generation (1998)

Country	% of world total production	Country	% of hydroelectric as proportion of domestic electricity
1. Canada	12.6%	1. Norway	99.4%
2. USA	12.2%	2. Brazil	90.6%
3. Brazil	11.0%	3. Canada	59.1%
4. China	7.9%	4. Sweden	47.0%
5. Russia	6.0%	5. Russia	19.3%
6. Norway	4.4%	6. China	17.4%
7. Japan	3.9%	7. India	16.8%
8. India	3.1%	8. France	12.9%
9. Sweden	2.8%	9. Japan	9.8%
10. France	2.5%	10. USA	8.4%

Countries heavily reliant on hydroelectricity are usually small and non-industrial: a high proportion of hydroelectric power more often reflects a modest energy budget than vast hydroelectric resources. The USA, for instance, produces only 8% of power requirements from hydroelectricity; yet that 8% amounts to more than three times the hydropower generated by the whole of Africa.

Alternative Energy Resources

Solar: Each year the Sun bestows upon the Earth almost a million times as much energy as is locked up in all the planet's oil reserves, but only an insignificant fraction is trapped and used commercially. In a few installations around the world, mirrors focus the Sun's rays on to boilers, whose steam generates electricity by spinning turbines.

Wind: Caused by uneven heating of the Earth, winds are themselves a form of solar energy. Windmills have been used for centuries to turn wind power into mechanical work; recent models, often arranged in banks on wind-swept high ground, usually generate electricity. Figures for wind power worldwide are given in the table (*right*). It is the world's fastest growing energy source.

Tidal: The energy from tides is potentially enormous, although only a few installations have so far been built to exploit it. In theory at least, waves and currents could also provide almost unimaginable power, and the thermal differences in the ocean depths are another huge well of potential energy. But work on extracting it is still at the experimental stage.

Geothermal: The Earth's temperature rises by 1°C for every 30 metres descent, with much steeper temperature gradients in geologically active areas. El Salvador, for example, produces 39% of its electricity from geothermal power stations, whilst the USA is the world's leading producer. Some of the oldest and most successful applications are in Iceland, where 86% of all households are heated by geothermal energy.

Biomass: The oldest of human fuels ranges from animal dung, still burned in cooking fires in much of North Africa and elsewhere, to sugar-cane plantations feeding high-technology distilleries to produce ethanol for motor-vehicle engines. In Brazil and South Africa, plant ethanol provides up to 25% of motor fuel. Throughout the developing world, most biomass energy comes from firewood: although accurate figures are impossible to obtain, it may yield as much as 10% of the world's total energy consumption.

Wind Power

World wind energy generating capacity, in megawatts

1980	10
1982	90
1984	600
1986	1,270
1988	1,580
1989	1,730
1990	1,930
1991	2,170
1992	2,510
1993	3,050
1994	3,710
1995	4,820
1996	6,115
1997	7,630
1998	9,600

Wind power is the fastest growing source of energy worldwide but still provides only 1% of the world's energy. Output grew by 35% in 1998.

MINERALS

For more information:
10 Geology
39 Patterns of production
41 World shipping

The use of metals played a vital part in the evolving technologies of early peoples. Copper first came into use around 10,000 years ago, bronze about 5,000 years ago, and iron 3,300 years ago. In the early stages of the Industrial Revolution, the location of coal, iron ore and water power usually determined the location of new industries. But due to continuing improvements in transport, including oil pipelines, industries can now be located almost anywhere.

Minerals are distributed unevenly and some industrial countries, lacking their own mineral resources, import most of the raw materials they need. Some imports come from mineral-rich countries, such as Australia, but others come from developing countries, especially in Africa and South America.

Most of the developing countries export unprocessed ores, losing out on the much higher revenues gained from exporting metals.

Most minerals come from land deposits, because undersea deposits, with the exception of oil reserves under the continental shelves, have been regarded as inaccessible. But shortages of terrestrial minerals may one day encourage exploitation of the ocean floor.

Mineral Exports

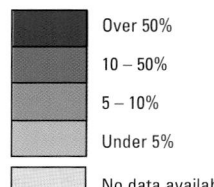

Minerals and metals as a percentage of total exports (latest available year)

- Over 50%
- 10 – 50%
- 5 – 10%
- Under 5%
- No data available

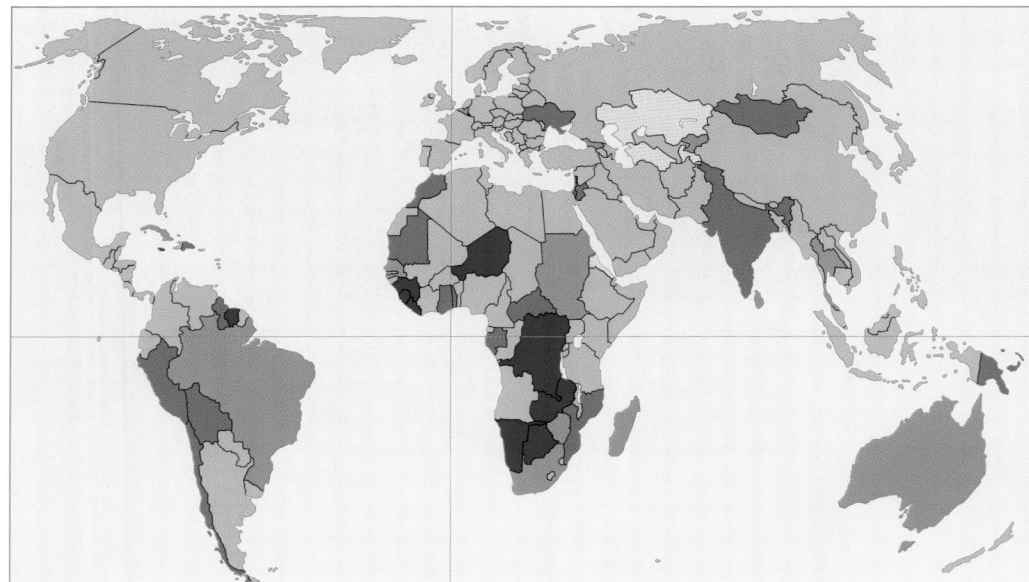

Uranium

In its pure state, uranium is an immensely heavy, white metal; but although spent uranium is employed as projectiles in anti-missile cannons, where its mass ensures a lethal punch, its main use is as a fuel in nuclear reactors, and in nuclear weaponry. Uranium is very scarce: the main source is the rare ore pitchblende, which itself contains only 0.2% uranium oxide. Only a minute fraction of that is the radioactive U^{235} isotope, though so-called breeder reactors can transmute the more common U^{238} into highly radioactive plutonium.

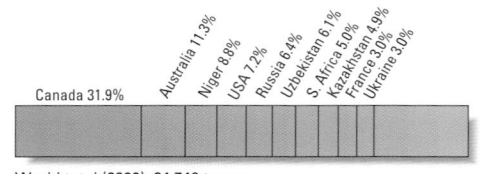

Canada 31.9% | Australia 11.3% | Niger 8.8% | USA 7.2% | Russia 6.4% | Uzbekistan 6.1% | S. Africa 5.0% | Kazakhstan 4.9% | France 3.0% | Ukraine 3.0%

World total (2000): 34,746 tonnes

Metals

* Figures for aluminium are for refined metal; all other figures refer to ore production.

The world's leading producers of aluminium ore (bauxite) in 2000 were as follows:

1. Australia 38.6%
2. Guinea 11.8%
3. Brazil 10.4%
4. Jamaica 8.8%
5. China 6.3%
6. India 4.9%
7. Venezuela 3.5%
8. Suriname 3.1%
9. Russia 3.1%
10. Guyana 2.6%

The figures shown above are in stark contrast to the figures showing aluminium production on the right. Australia, for example, produces 38.6% of the world's bauxite but only 5.9% of the aluminium metal. Guinea and Jamaica account for over 20% of the bauxite mined but have no smelters and export virtually all of it to countries like the USA and Canada.

Diamond

Most of the world's diamond is found in kimberlite, or 'blue ground', a basic peridotite rock; erosion may wash the diamond from its kimberlite matrix and deposit it with sand or gravel on river beds. Only a small proportion of the world's diamond, the most flawless, is cut into gemstones – 'diamonds'; most is used in industry, where the material's remarkable hardness and abrasion resistance finds a use in cutting tools, drills and dies. Australia produced 31.6% of the world's total in 2000. The other main producers are the Democratic Republic of the Congo (24.7%), Russia (20%), South Africa (10.5%) and Botswana (8.5%). Natural diamonds now account for less than 10% of all industrial diamond output. Synthetic diamond production in centres such as Ireland, Japan, Russia and the USA far exceeds it.

Aluminium: Produced mainly from its oxide, bauxite, which yields 25% of its weight in aluminium. The cost of refining and production is often too high for producer-countries to bear, so bauxite is largely exported. Lightweight and corrosion resistant, aluminium alloys are widely used in aircraft, vehicles, cans and packaging.

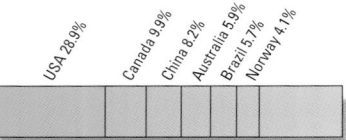

USA 28.9% | Canada 9.9% | China 8.2% | Australia 5.9% | Brazil 5.7% | Norway 4.1%

World total (2000): 23,900,000 tonnes *

Lead: A soft metal, obtained mainly from galena (lead sulphide), which occurs in veins associated with iron, zinc and silver sulphides. Its use in vehicle batteries accounts for the USA's prime consumer status; lead is also made into sheeting and piping. Its use as an additive to paints and petrol is decreasing.

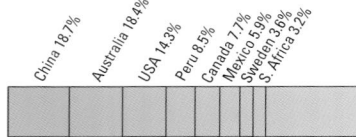

China 18.7% | Australia 18.4% | USA 14.3% | Peru 8.5% | Canada 7.7% | Mexico 3.6% | Sweden 3.6% | S. Africa 3.2%

World total (2000): 2,980,000 tonnes *

Tin: Soft, pliable and non-toxic, used to coat 'tin' (tin-plated steel) cans, in the manufacture of foils and in alloys. The principal tin-bearing mineral is cassiterite (SnO_2), found in ore formed from molten rock. Producers and refiners were hit by a price collapse in 1991.

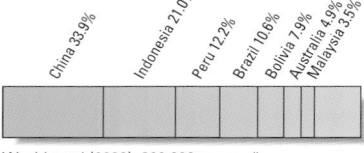

China 33.9% | Indonesia 21.0% | Peru 12.2% | Brazil 10.6% | Bolivia 7.9% | Australia 4.9% | Malaysia 3.5%

World total (2000): 200,000 tonnes *

Gold: Regarded for centuries as the most valuable metal in the world and used to make coins, gold is still recognized as the monetary standard. A soft metal, it is alloyed to make jewellery; the electronics industry values its corrosion resistance and conductivity.

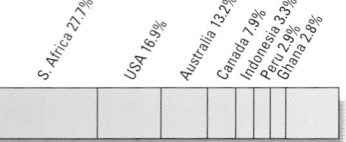

S. Africa 27.7% | USA 16.9% | Australia 13.2% | Canada 7.9% | Indonesia 3.9% | Peru 2.9% | Ghana 2.8%

World total (2000): 2,445 tonnes *

Copper: Derived from low-yielding sulphide ores, copper is an important export for several developing countries. An excellent conductor of heat and electricity, it forms part of most electrical items, and is used in the manufacture of brass and bronze. Major importers include Japan and Germany.

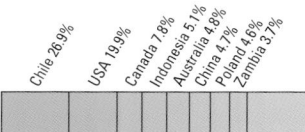

Chile 26.9% | USA 19.9% | Canada 7.8% | Indonesia 5.1% | Australia 4.8% | China 4.7% | Poland 4.6% | Zambia 3.7%

World total (2000): 12,900,000 tonnes *

Mercury: The only metal that is liquid at normal temperatures, most is derived from its sulphide, cinnabar, found only in small quantities in volcanic areas. Apart from its value in thermometers and other instruments, most mercury production is used in anti-fungal and anti-fouling preparations, and to make detonators.

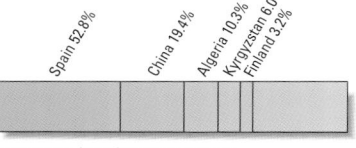

Spain 52.8% | China 19.4% | Algeria 10.3% | Kyrgyzstan 6.0% | Finland 3.2%

World total (2000): 1,800 tonnes *

Zinc: Often found in association with lead ores, zinc is highly resistant to corrosion, and about 40% of the refined metal is used to plate sheet steel, particularly vehicle bodies – a process known as galvanizing. Zinc is also used in dry batteries, paints and dyes.

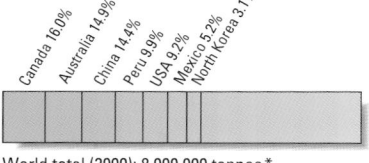

Canada 16.0% | Australia 14.9% | China 14.4% | Peru 9.9% | USA 9.2% | Mexico 5.2% | North Korea 3.1%

World total (2000): 8,000,000 tonnes *

Silver: Most silver comes from ores mined and processed for other metals (including lead and copper). Pure or alloyed with harder metals, it is used for jewellery and ornaments. Industrial use includes dentistry, electronics, photography and as a chemical catalyst.

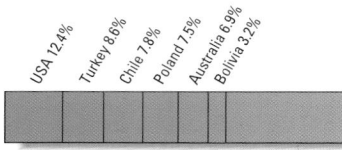

USA 12.4% | Turkey 8.8% | Chile 7.8% | Poland 7.5% | Australia 6.9% | Bolivia 3.2%

World total (2000): 17,900 tonnes *

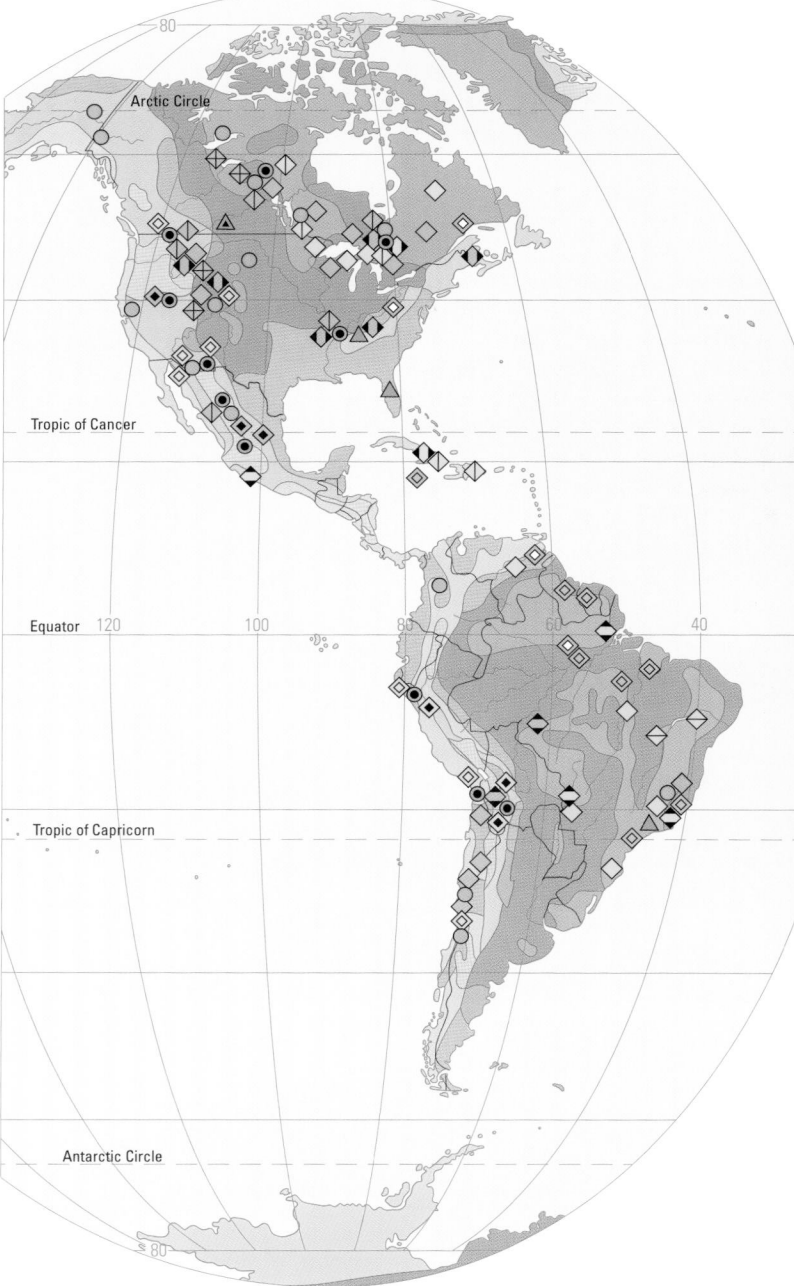

Strategic Minerals

Ever since the art of high-temperature smelting was discovered, some time in the second millennium BC, iron has been by far the most important metal known to man. The earliest iron ploughs transformed primitive agriculture and led to the first human population explosion, while iron weapons – or the lack of them – ensured the rise or fall of entire cultures.

Widely distributed around the world, iron ores usually contain 25–60% iron; blast furnaces process the raw product into pig-iron, which is then alloyed with carbon and other minerals to produce steels of various qualities. From the time of the Industrial Revolution, steel has been almost literally the backbone of modern civilization, the prime structural material on which all else is built.

Iron smelting usually developed close to the sources of ore and, later, to the coalfields that fuelled the furnaces. Today, most ore comes from a few richly-endowed locations where large-scale mining is possible. Iron and steel plants are generally built at coastal sites so that giant ore carriers, which account for a sizeable proportion of the world's merchant fleet, can easily discharge their cargoes.

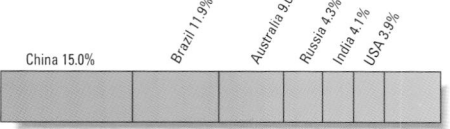

China 15.0%   Brazil 11.9%   Australia 9.0%   Russia 4.3%   India 4.1%   USA 3.9%

World total production of iron ore (2000): 1,010,000,000 tonnes

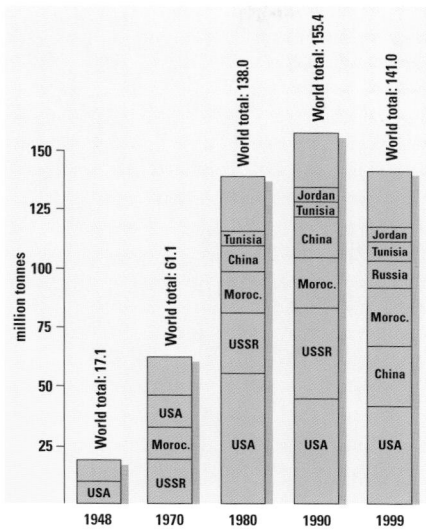

World production of phosphates in millions of tonnes (1999): Phosphate production is vital to the economies of several small countries. Nauru, for example, is heavily dependent on phosphate exports – the island has one of the world's richest deposits. In 1999, 500,000 tonnes were mined, employing 1,000 people. In Togo, earnings from phosphate exports have superseded all agricultural exports.

Percentage of total world phosphate production (1999)

1. USA	28.8%	7. Brazil	2.9%
2. China	17.8%	8. Israel	2.9%
3. Morocco	17.0%	9. South Africa	2.1%
4. Russia	7.9%	10. Syria	1.5%
5. Tunisia	5.7%	11. Senegal	1.3%
6. Jordan	4.3%	12. India	1.2%

World production of pig-iron (2000): All countries with an annual output of more than 1 million tonnes are shown

Total world production: 571 million tonnes

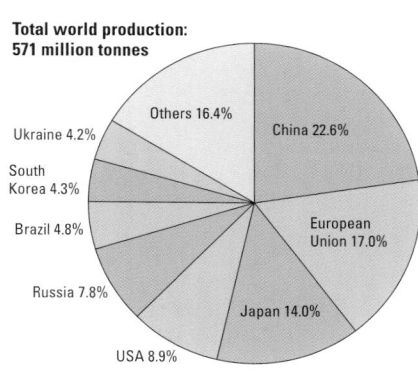

China 22.6%
European Union 17.0%
Japan 14.0%
USA 8.9%
Russia 7.8%
Brazil 4.8%
South Korea 4.3%
Ukraine 4.2%
Others 16.4%

Manganese: In its pure state, manganese is a hard, brittle metal. Alloyed with chrome, iron and nickel, it produces abrasion-resistant steels; manganese-aluminium alloys are light but tough. Found in batteries and inks, manganese is also used in glass production. Manganese ores are frequently found in the same location as sedimentary iron ores. Pyrolusite (MnO_2) and psilomelane are the main economically-exploitable sources.

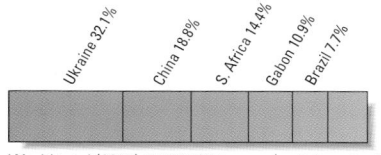

Ukraine 32.1%   China 18.8%   S. Africa 14.4%   Gabon 10.9%   Brazil 7.7%

World total (2000): 7,450,000 tonnes (metal content)

Chromium: Most of the world's chromium production is alloyed with iron and other metals to produce steels with various different properties. Combined with iron, nickel, cobalt and tungsten, chromium produces an exceptionally hard steel, resistant to heat; chrome steels are used for many household items where utility must be matched with appearance – cutlery, for example. Chromium is also used in the production of refractory bricks, and its salts for tanning and dyeing leather and cloth.

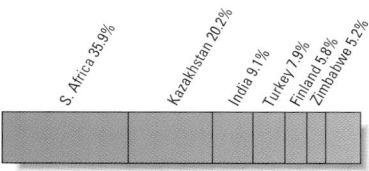

S. Africa 35.9%   Kazakhstan 20.2%   India 9.1%   Turkey 7.9%   Finland 5.8%   Zimbabwe 5.2%

World total (2000): 13,700,000 tonnes

Nickel: Combined with chrome and iron, nickel produces stainless and high-strength steels; similar alloys go to make magnets and electrical heating elements. Nickel combined with copper is widely used to make coins; cupro-nickel alloy is very resistant to corrosion. Its ores yield only modest quantities of nickel – 0.5% to 3.0% – but also contain copper, iron and small amounts of precious metals. Japan, USA, UK, Germany and France are the principal importers.

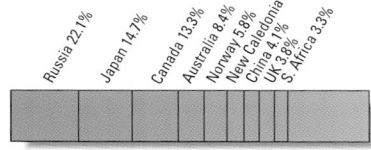

Russia 22.1%   Japan 14.7%   Canada 13.3%   Australia 8.4%   Norway 5.3%   New Caledonia 4.6%   China 4.1%   UK 3.8%   S. Africa 3.3%

World total (2000): 1,230,000 tonnes

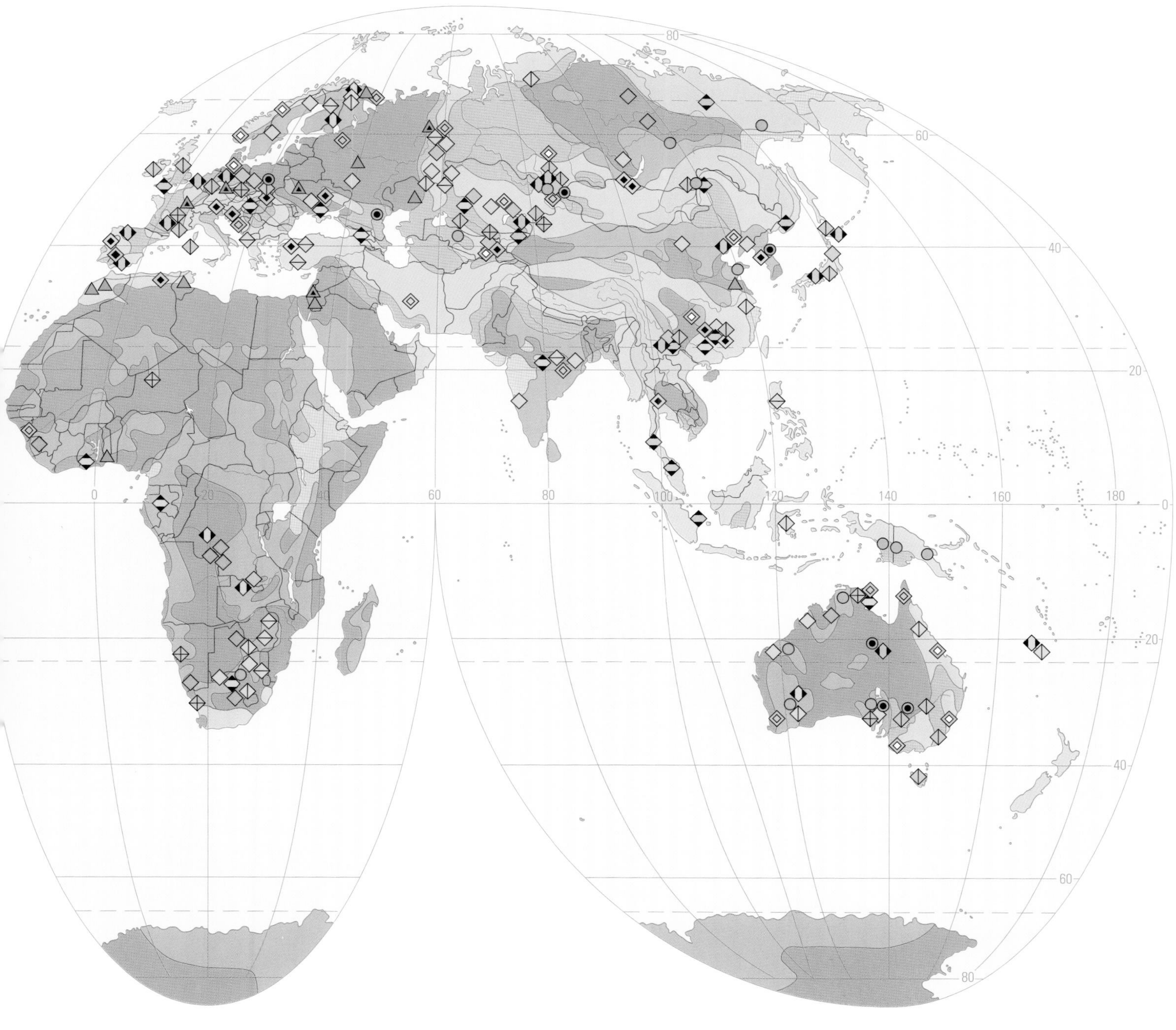

World production of pig-iron bar chart
million tonnes

- 1948 – World total: 17.1 (USA)
- 1970 – World total: 61.1 (USSR, Moroc., USA)
- 1980 – World total: 138.0 (USSR, Moroc., Tunisia, China, USA)
- 1990 – World total: 155.4 (USSR, Moroc., China, Jordan, Tunisia, USA)
- 1999 – World total: 141.0 (Moroc., China, Russia, Jordan, Tunisia, USA)

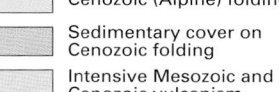

Distribution of Minerals

Structural Regions

- Pre-Cambrian shields
- Sedimentary cover on Pre-Cambrian shields
- Paleozoic (Caledonian and Hercynian) folding
- Sedimentary cover on Paleozoic folding
- Mesozoic folding
- Sedimentary cover on Mesozoic folding
- Cenozoic (Alpine) folding
- Sedimentary cover on Cenozoic folding
- Intensive Mesozoic and Cenozoic vulcanism

Distribution
Iron and ferro-alloys

- Chrome
- Cobalt
- Iron Ore
- Manganese
- Molybdenum
- Nickel Ore
- Tungsten

Non-ferrous metals

- Bauxite (Aluminium)
- Copper
- Lead
- Mercury
- Tin
- Zinc
- Uranium

Precious metals and stones

- Diamonds
- Gold
- Silver

Fertilizers

- Phosphates
- Potash

MANUFACTURING

For more information:
18 Water utilization
32 Land use and economy
36 Mineral production
37 Iron and ferro-alloys
40 Trading nations
    Major exports
    Traded products

The Industrial Revolution which began in Britain in the late 18th century, represented a major technological advance in the evolution of human society. It enabled a group of countries to become prosperous by replacing expensive human labour with increasingly sophisticated machinery. In economic terms, manufacturing is the transformation of raw materials, energy, labour and machines into finished goods, which have a higher value than the various elements used in production.

The economies of countries can be compared by reference to their per capita Gross National Products (or per capita GNPs), namely, the total value of goods and services produced in a country in a year, divided by the population.

The industrialized, or developed, countries accounted for 16% of the world's population in 1997 with an average per capita GNP of US $25,700. On the other hand, developing countries, with comparatively small industrial sectors and low-income economies, accounted for 35% of the world's population, with an average per capita GNP of just $350.

Kenya, with its low-income economy, had a per capita GNP in 1998 of $330. Agriculture employs 77% of the people, industry 8% and services 15%. The major industries are the processing of agricultural products and import substitution (the manufacture of such necessities as cement, footwear and textiles). Heavy industry plays a comparatively small part in the economy. By contrast, Germany, a major industrialized nation, had a per capita GNP in 1998 of $25,850. Agriculture employs only 1% of the population, with 32% in industry, and 67% in services. Germany's industrial sector differs greatly from Kenya's, with an emphasis on the manufacture of vehicles, machinery and chemicals.

Since the 1970s, some former developing countries in Asia have been transformed by rapid industrialization. These 'economic tigers', including China, Malaysia, South Korea, Singapore, Taiwan and Thailand, owe their success to low labour costs and substantial investment in education, together with advances in telecommunications, transport and computers, which have made technology more readily transferable around the world than ever before. They have also benefited from economic freedom and trade liberalization.

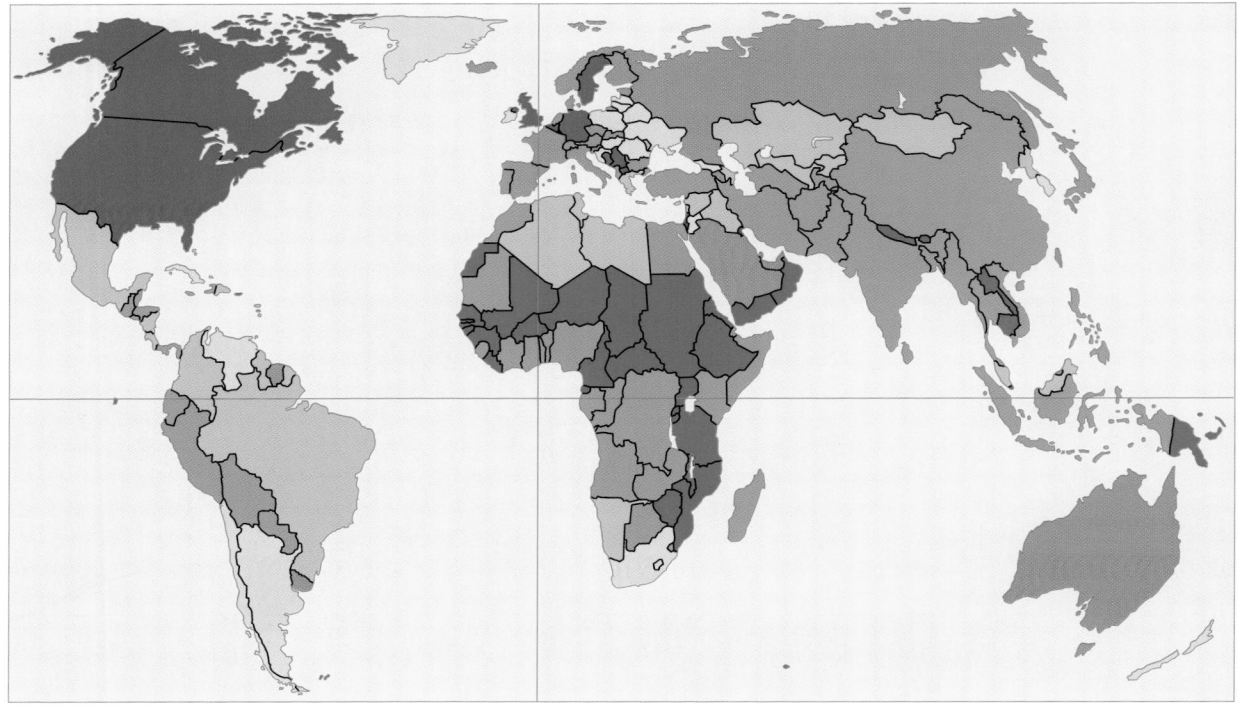

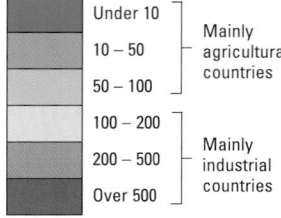

Employment

The number of workers employed in manufacturing for every 100 workers engaged in agriculture (latest available year)

Under 10	Mainly
10 – 50	agricultural
50 – 100	countries
100 – 200	Mainly
200 – 500	industrial
Over 500	countries

Selected countries (latest available year)

Singapore	8,860
UK	1,270
Belgium	820
Germany	800
Kuwait	767
Bahrain	660
USA	657
Israel	633

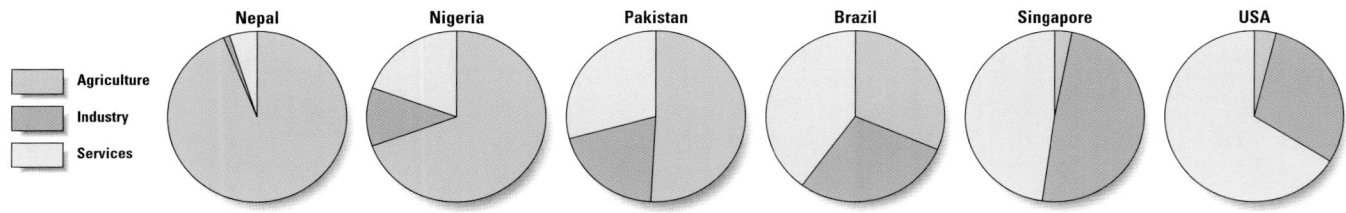

Nepal Nigeria Pakistan Brazil Singapore USA

- Agriculture
- Industry
- Services

Division of Employment

Distribution of workers between agriculture, industry and services, selected countries (latest available year)

The six countries selected illustrate the usual stages of economic development, from dependence on agriculture through industrial growth to the expansion of the service sector.

The Workforce

Percentages of men and women between 15 and 64 in employment, selected countries (latest available year)

The figures include employees and the self-employed, who in developing countries are often subsistence farmers. People in full-time education are excluded. Because of the population age structure in developing countries, the employed population has to support a far larger number of non-workers than its industrial equivalent. For example, more than 52% of Kenya's people are under 15, an age group that makes up less than a tenth of the UK population.

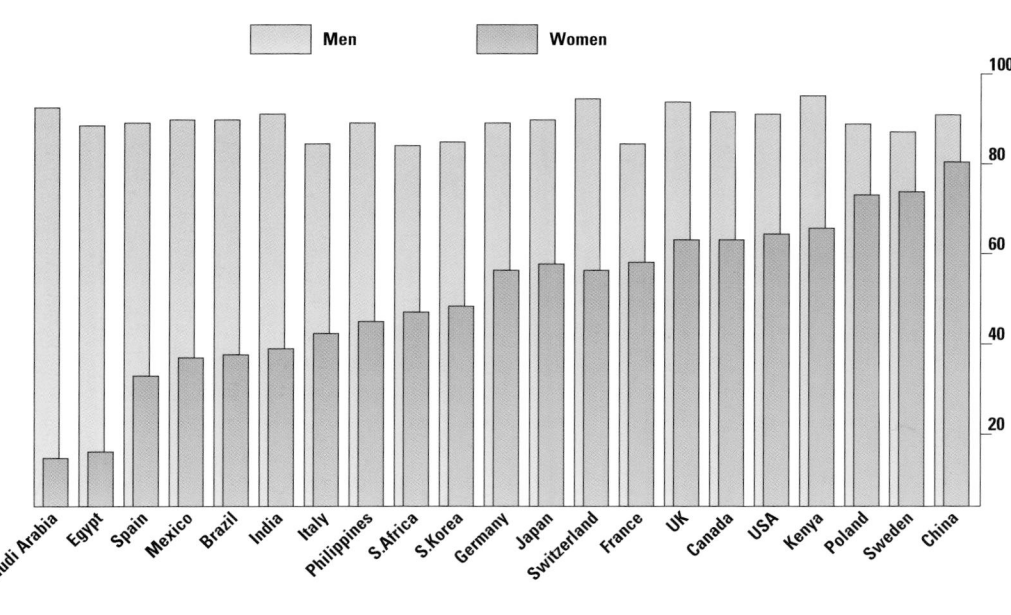

Men   Women

Saudi Arabia, Egypt, Spain, Mexico, Brazil, India, Italy, Philippines, S.Africa, S.Korea, Germany, Japan, Switzerland, France, UK, Canada, USA, Kenya, Poland, Sweden, China

Wealth Creation

The Gross National Product (GNP) of the world's largest economies, US $ million (1998)

1.	USA	7,922,651	21.	Austria	217,163
2.	Japan	4,089,910	22.	Turkey	200,505
3.	Germany	2,122,673	23.	Saudi Arabia	186,000
4.	Italy	1,666,178	24.	Denmark	176,374
5.	France	1,466,014	25.	Hong Kong	158,286
6.	UK	1,263,777	26.	Norway	152,082
7.	China	928,950	27.	Poland	150,798
8.	Brazil	758,043	28.	Indonesia	138,501
9.	Canada	612,332	29.	Thailand	134,433
10.	Spain	553,690	30.	Finland	124,293
11.	India	421,259	31.	Greece	122,880
12.	Netherlands	388,682	32.	South Africa	119,001
13.	Mexico	380,917	33.	Iran	109,645
14.	Australia	380,625	34.	Portugal	106,376
15.	South Korea	369,890	35.	Colombia	106,090
16.	Russia	337,914	36.	Israel	95,179
17.	Argentina	324,084	37.	Singapore	95,095
18.	Switzerland	284,808	38.	Venezuela	81,347
19.	Belgium	259,045	39.	Malaysia	79,848
20.	Sweden	226,861	40.	Egypt	79,208

Patterns of Production

Breakdown of industrial output by value, selected countries (latest available year)

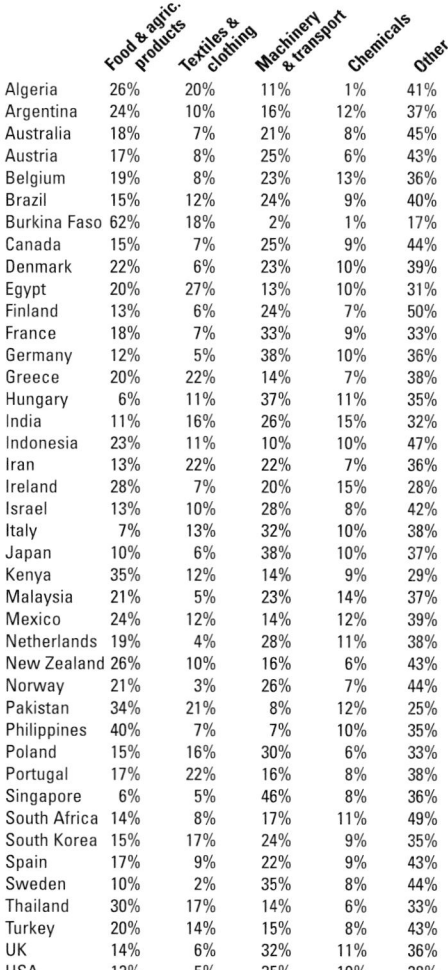

	Food & agric. products	Textiles & clothing	Machinery & transport	Chemicals	Other
Algeria	26%	20%	11%	1%	41%
Argentina	24%	10%	16%	12%	37%
Australia	18%	7%	21%	8%	45%
Austria	17%	8%	25%	6%	43%
Belgium	19%	8%	23%	13%	36%
Brazil	15%	12%	24%	9%	40%
Burkina Faso	62%	18%	2%	1%	17%
Canada	15%	7%	25%	9%	44%
Denmark	22%	6%	23%	10%	39%
Egypt	20%	27%	13%	10%	31%
Finland	13%	6%	24%	7%	50%
France	18%	7%	33%	9%	33%
Germany	12%	5%	38%	10%	36%
Greece	20%	22%	14%	7%	38%
Hungary	6%	11%	37%	11%	35%
India	11%	16%	26%	15%	32%
Indonesia	23%	11%	10%	10%	47%
Iran	13%	22%	22%	7%	36%
Ireland	28%	7%	20%	15%	28%
Israel	13%	10%	28%	8%	42%
Italy	7%	13%	32%	10%	38%
Japan	10%	6%	38%	10%	37%
Kenya	35%	12%	14%	9%	29%
Malaysia	21%	5%	23%	14%	37%
Mexico	24%	12%	14%	12%	39%
Netherlands	19%	4%	28%	11%	38%
New Zealand	26%	10%	16%	6%	43%
Norway	21%	3%	26%	7%	44%
Pakistan	34%	21%	8%	12%	25%
Philippines	40%	7%	7%	10%	35%
Poland	15%	16%	30%	6%	33%
Portugal	17%	22%	16%	8%	38%
Singapore	6%	5%	46%	8%	36%
South Africa	14%	8%	17%	11%	49%
South Korea	15%	17%	24%	9%	35%
Spain	17%	9%	22%	9%	43%
Sweden	10%	2%	35%	8%	44%
Thailand	30%	17%	14%	6%	33%
Turkey	20%	14%	15%	8%	43%
UK	14%	6%	32%	11%	36%
USA	12%	5%	35%	10%	38%
Venezuela	23%	8%	9%	11%	49%

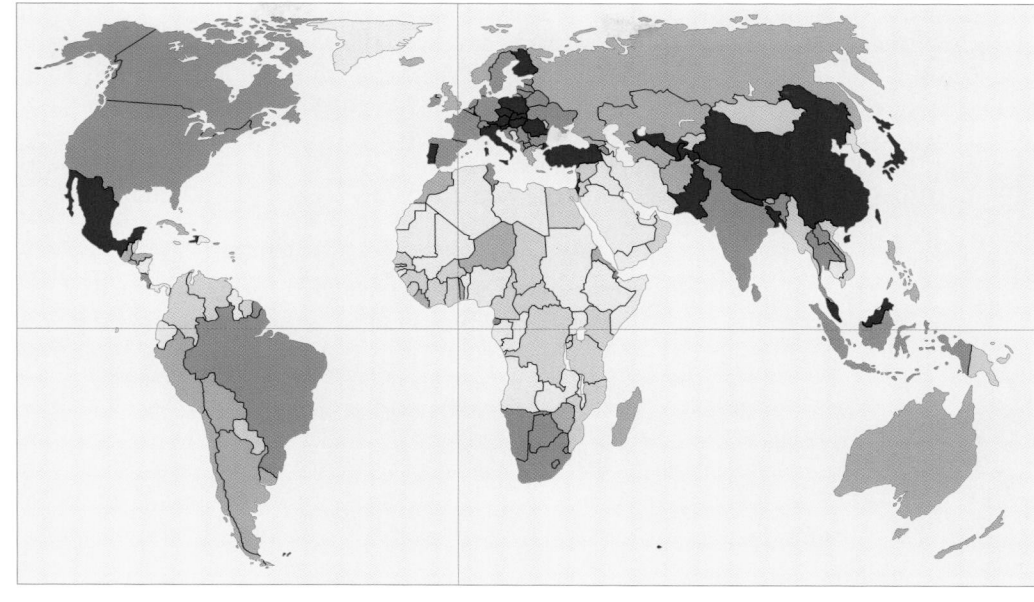

Industry and Trade

Manufactured goods (including machinery and transport) as a percentage of total exports (1999)

- Over 75%
- 50 – 75%
- 25 – 50%
- 10 – 25%
- Under 10%

Countries most dependent on the export of manufactured goods

Macau (China)	97%
Malta	91%
Hong Kong (China)	90%
Bangladesh	90%
China	90%
Japan	88%
South Korea	83%
Luxembourg	83%
Pakistan	83%

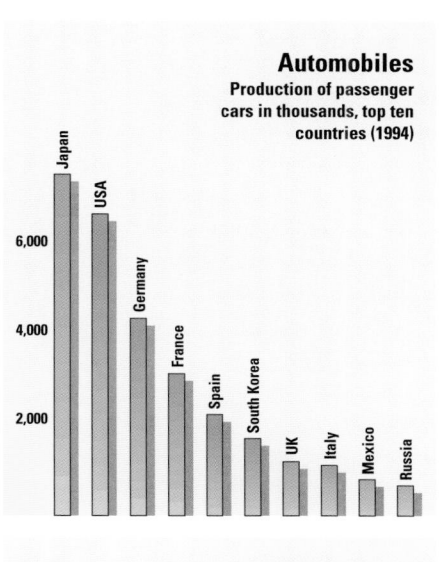

Automobiles
Production of passenger cars in thousands, top ten countries (1994)

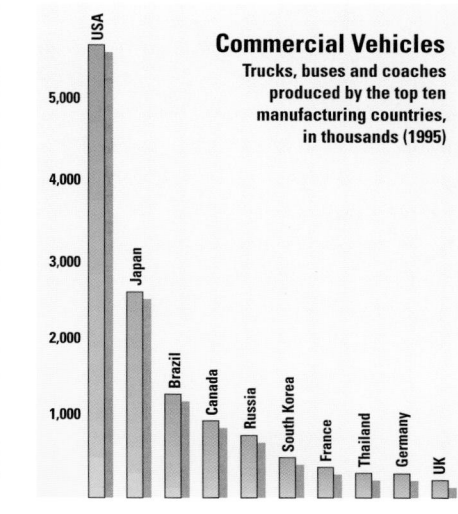

Commercial Vehicles
Trucks, buses and coaches produced by the top ten manufacturing countries, in thousands (1995)

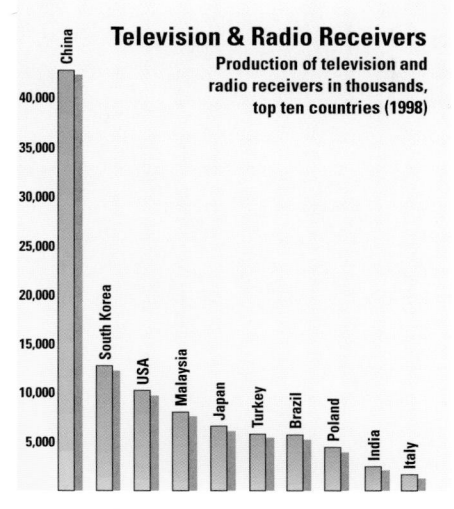

Television & Radio Receivers
Production of television and radio receivers in thousands, top ten countries (1998)

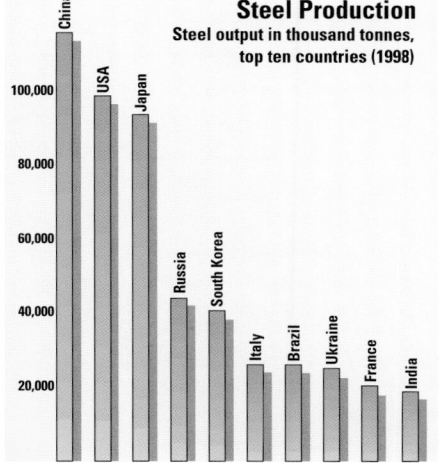

Steel Production
Steel output in thousand tonnes, top ten countries (1998)

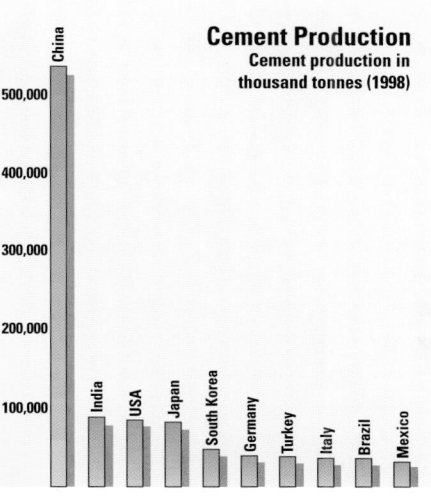

Cement Production
Cement production in thousand tonnes (1998)

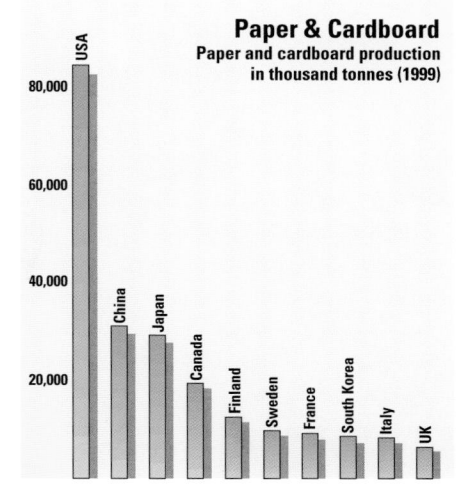

Paper & Cardboard
Paper and cardboard production in thousand tonnes (1999)

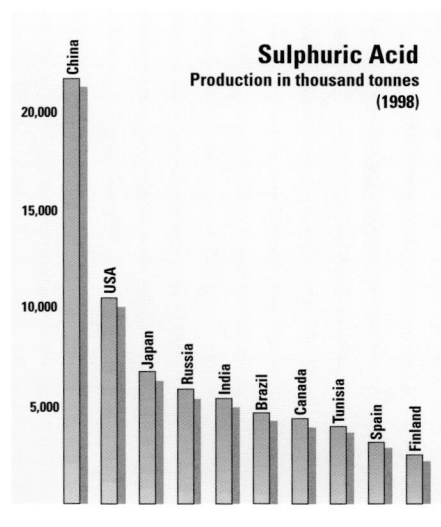

Sulphuric Acid
Production in thousand tonnes (1998)

Industrial Output

Industrial output (mining, manufacturing, construction, energy and water production), US $ billion (latest available year)

1.	Japan	1,941	21.	Sweden	73
2.	USA	1,808	22.	Saudi Arabia	67
3.	Germany	780	=	Thailand	67
4.	France	415	24.	Mexico	65
5.	UK	354	25.	Turkey	51
6.	Italy	337	26.	Denmark	50
7.	China	335	27.	Finland	46
8.	Brazil	255	=	Poland	46
9.	South Korea	196	29.	Norway	44
10.	Spain	187	30.	Malaysia	37
11.	Canada	174	=	Portugal	37
12.	Russia	131	32.	Ukraine	34
13.	Netherlands	107	33.	Greece	33
14.	Australia	98	34.	Singapore	30
15.	Switzerland	96	35.	Venezuela	29
16.	India	94	=	Israel	29
17.	Argentina	87	37.	Chile	24
18.	Belgium	83	=	Colombia	24
=	Indonesia	83	=	Hong Kong	24
20.	Austria	79	=	Philippines	24

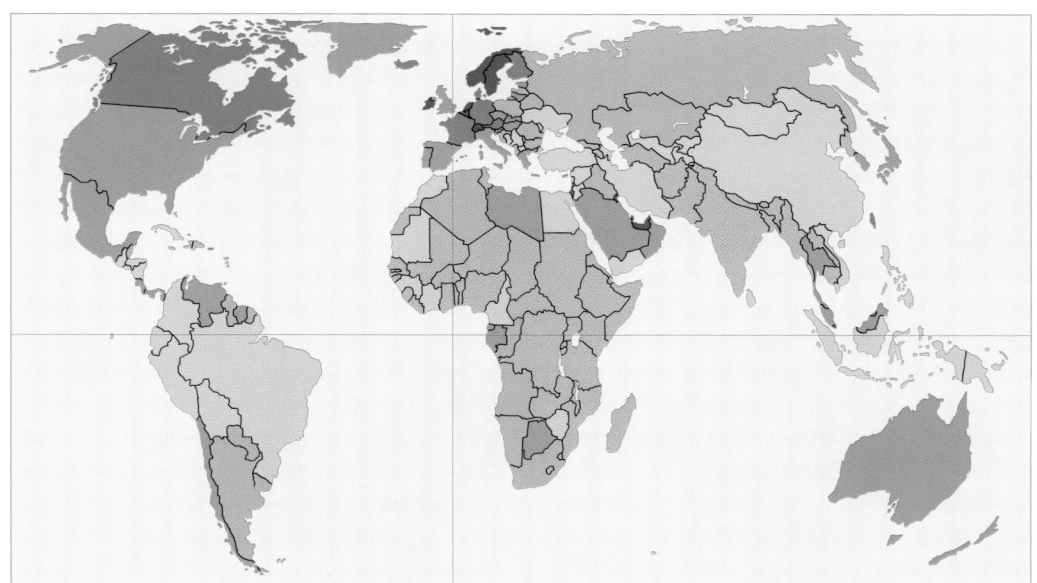

Exports Per Capita

Value of exports in US $, divided by total population (2000)

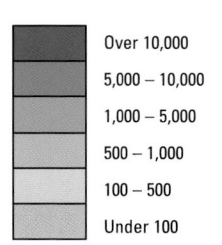

- Over 10,000
- 5,000 – 10,000
- 1,000 – 5,000
- 500 – 1,000
- 100 – 500
- Under 100

[UK 4,728]   [USA 2,791]

Highest per capita

Kuwait	113,614
Liechtenstein	78,848
Singapore	31,860
Aruba (Neths)	31,429
Hong Kong (China)	28,290
Ireland	19,136

TRADE

For more information:

31 International organizations
35 Fuel exports
   Movements of oil
36 Mineral exports
39 Industry and trade
   Exports per capita
45 Tourism

Trade played a vital role in the growth of early civilizations and it was later a spur to European exploration and colonization. The colonial powers grew rich by exporting cheap manufactures, such as clothing and footwear, while obtaining primary products from their colonies.

From the late 19th century to the early 1950s, as transport technology improved, primary products, especially oil in the later stages of this period, dominated world trade. However, since that time, manufactures have become the chief commodities in world trade, which is dominated by the industrialized countries. Nearly half of all world trade flows between the developed market economies of the European Union, the United States and Japan, although a number of Asian economies, notably Singapore, South Korea, Taiwan, Malaysia and Thailand, increased their share in the 1990s. Recent predictions suggest that the next 'tiger economies' might include Chile and Argentina in South America, Vietnam, Indonesia and the Philippines in Asia, and the Czech Republic and Poland in Europe.

There is little trade between developing countries, although some mineral- and oil-rich nations obtain a high proportion of their GNP from export sales. Growth in world trade is regarded as a sign of economic health, as is a favourable balance of trade (or trade surplus) in any country.

World Trade

Percentage share of total world exports by value (1999)

- Over 10% of world trade
- 5 – 10% of world trade
- 1 – 5% of world trade
- 0.5 – 1% of world trade
- 0.1 – 0.5% of world trade
- Under 0.1% of world trade

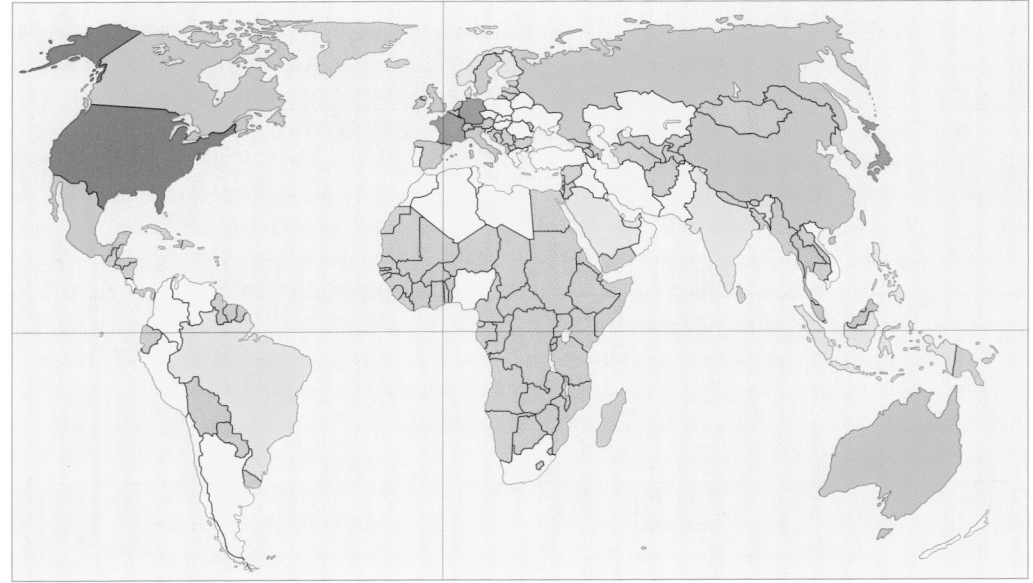

The Main Trading Nations

The imports and exports of the top ten trading nations as a percentage of world trade (1999). Each country's trade in manufactured goods is shown in dark blue.

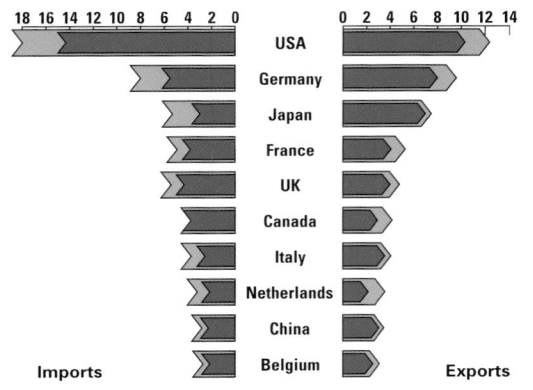

USA
Germany
Japan
France
UK
Canada
Italy
Netherlands
China
Belgium

Imports   Exports

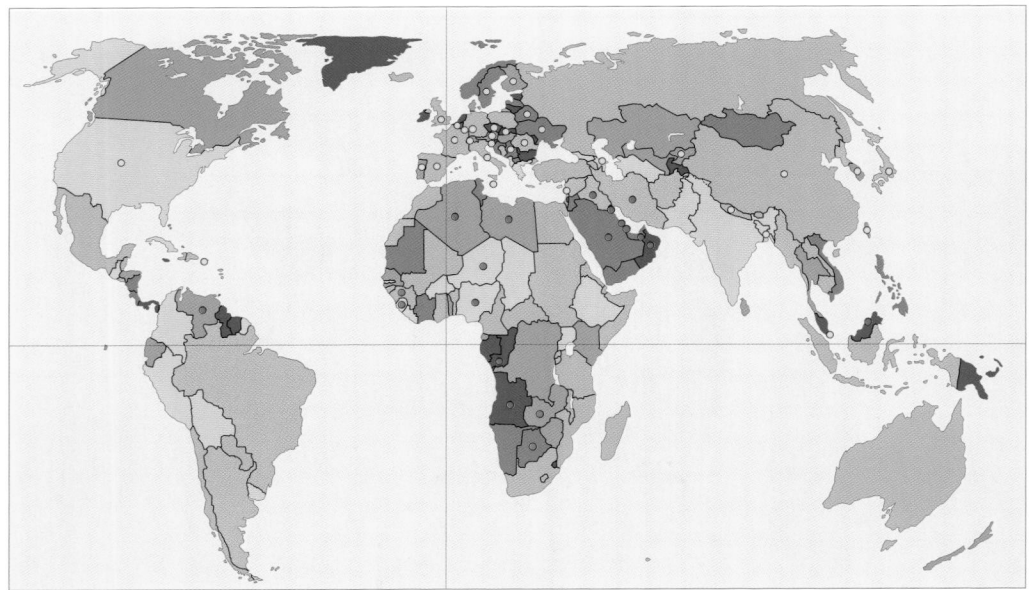

Dependence on Trade

Value of exports as a percentage of Gross Domestic Product (1997)

- Over 50% GDP from exports
- 40 – 50% GDP from exports
- 30 – 40% GDP from exports
- 20 – 30% GDP from exports
- 10 – 20% GDP from exports
- Under 10% GDP from exports

○ Most dependent on industrial exports (over 75% of total exports)
● Most dependent on fuel exports (over 75% of total exports)
● Most dependent on metal and mineral exports (over 75% of total exports)

Major Exports

Leading manufactured items and their exporters, by percentage of world total in US $ (latest available year)

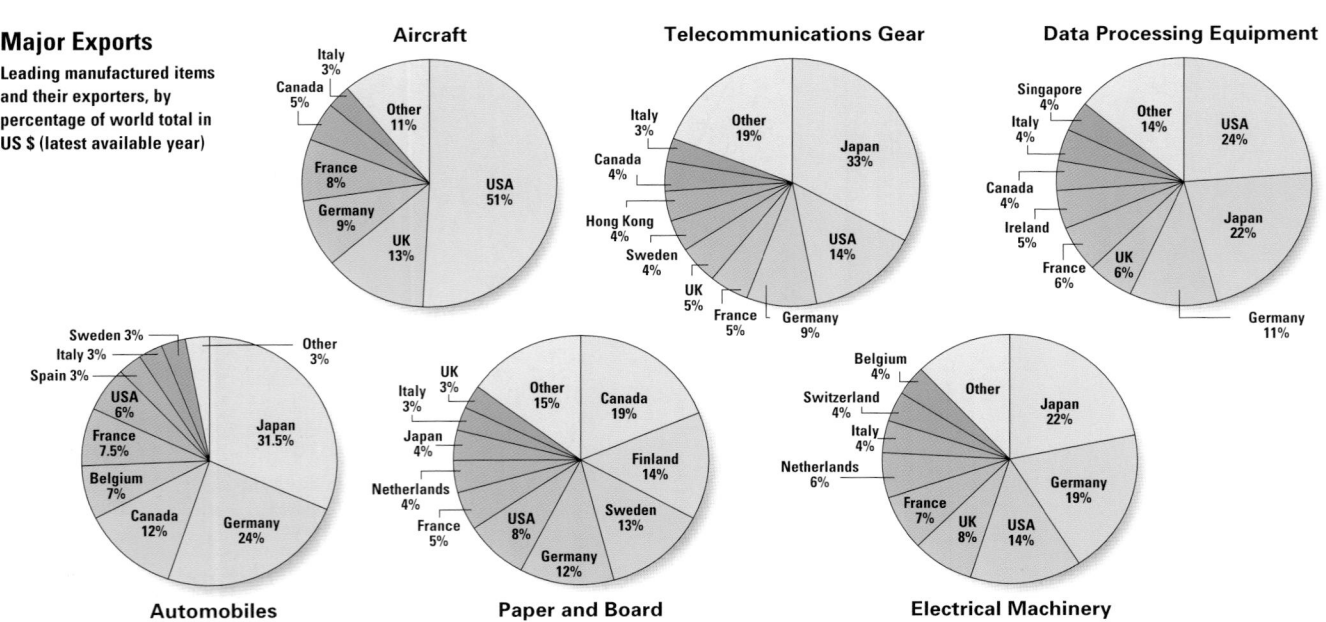

Aircraft
USA 51%, UK 13%, Germany 9%, France 8%, Other 11%, Canada 5%, Italy 3%

Telecommunications Gear
Japan 33%, USA 14%, Germany 9%, France 5%, UK 5%, Sweden 4%, Hong Kong 4%, Canada 4%, Italy 3%, Other 19%

Data Processing Equipment
USA 24%, Japan 22%, Germany 11%, France 6%, UK 6%, Ireland 5%, Canada 4%, Italy 4%, Singapore 4%, Other 14%

Automobiles
Japan 31.5%, Germany 24%, Canada 12%, Belgium 7%, France 7.5%, USA 6%, Spain 3%, Italy 3%, Sweden 3%, Other 3%

Paper and Board
Canada 19%, Finland 14%, Sweden 13%, Germany 12%, USA 8%, France 5%, Netherlands 4%, Japan 4%, Italy 3%, UK 3%, Other 15%

Electrical Machinery
Japan 22%, Germany 19%, USA 14%, UK 8%, France 7%, Netherlands 6%, Switzerland 4%, Italy 4%, Belgium 4%, Other

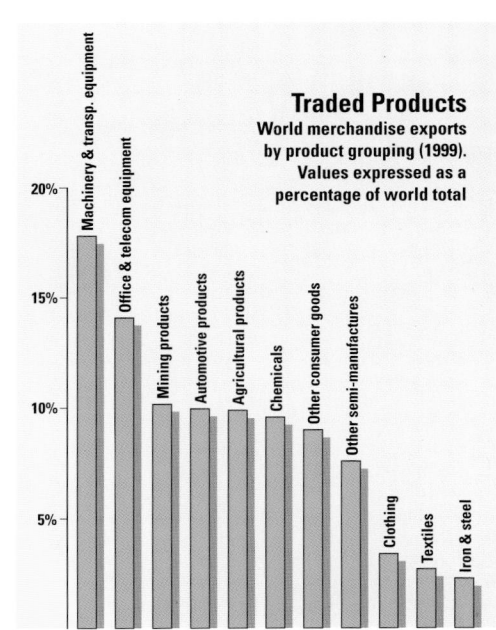

Traded Products

World merchandise exports by product grouping (1999). Values expressed as a percentage of world total

- Machinery & transp. equipment
- Office & telecom equipment
- Mining products
- Automotive products
- Agricultural products
- Chemicals
- Other consumer goods
- Other semi-manufactures
- Clothing
- Textiles
- Iron & steel

World Shipping

While ocean passenger traffic is nowadays relatively modest, sea transport still carries most of the world's trade. Oil and bulk carriers make up the majority of the world fleet, although the general cargo category is the fastest growing. Two innovations have revolutionized sea transport. The first is the development of the roll-on/roll-off (Ro-Ro) method where lorries or even trains loaded with freight are driven straight on to the ship, thus saving time. The second is containerization in which goods are packed into containers (the dimensions of which are fixed) at the factory, driven to the port and loaded on board by specialist machinery.

Almost 30% of world shipping sails under a 'flag of convenience', whereby owners take advantage of low taxes by registering their vessels in a foreign country the ships will never see, notably Panama and Liberia.

Merchant Fleets

Merchant fleets in thousand gross tonnage (1999). A large number of vessels are registered in Liberia and Panama but they are not part of the national fleet.

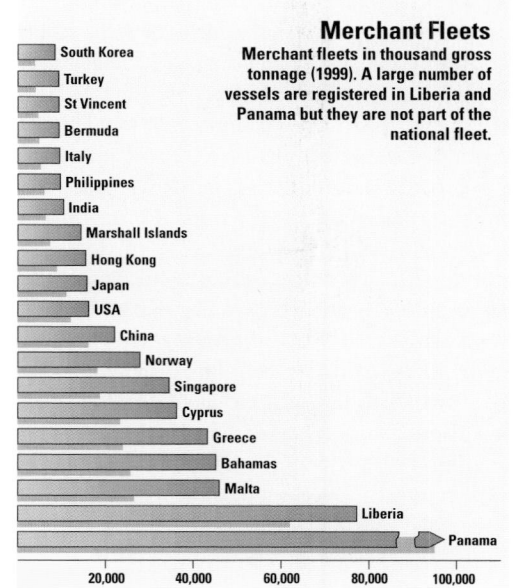

South Korea, Turkey, St Vincent, Bermuda, Italy, Philippines, India, Marshall Islands, Hong Kong, Japan, USA, China, Norway, Singapore, Cyprus, Greece, Bahamas, Malta, Liberia, Panama

20,000 — 40,000 — 60,000 — 80,000 — 100,000

Trade in Primary Products

Primary products (excluding fuels, metals and minerals) as a percentage of total export value (latest available year)

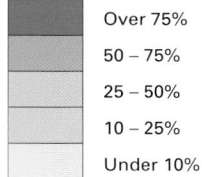

- Over 75%
- 50 – 75%
- 25 – 50%
- 10 – 25%
- Under 10%

Primary products are raw materials or partly processed products which form the basis for manufacturing. They are the necessary requirements of industries and include agricultural products, minerals and timber, as well as many semi-manufactured goods such as cotton, which has been spun but not woven, wood pulp or flour. Many developed countries have few natural resources and rely on imports for the majority of their primary products. The countries of South-east Asia export hardwoods to the rest of the world, whilst many South American countries are heavily dependent on coffee exports.

Balance of Trade

Value of exports in proportion to the value of imports (1999)

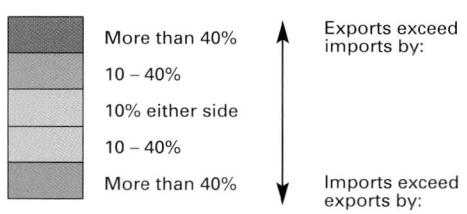

- More than 40%
- 10 – 40%
- 10% either side
- 10 – 40%
- More than 40%

Exports exceed imports by:

Imports exceed exports by:

The total world trade balance should amount to zero, since exports must equal imports on a global scale. In practice, at least $100 billion in exports go unrecorded, leaving the world with an apparent deficit and many countries in a better position than public accounting reveals. However, a favourable trade balance is not necessarily a sign of prosperity: many poorer countries must maintain a high surplus in order to service debts, and do so by restricting imports below the levels needed to sustain successful economies.

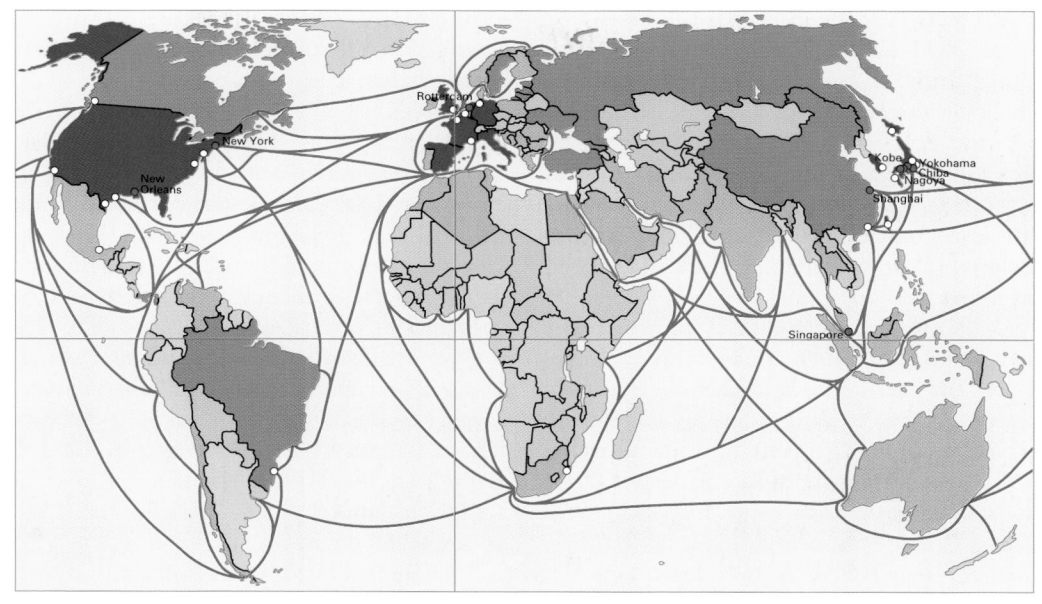

Types of Vessels

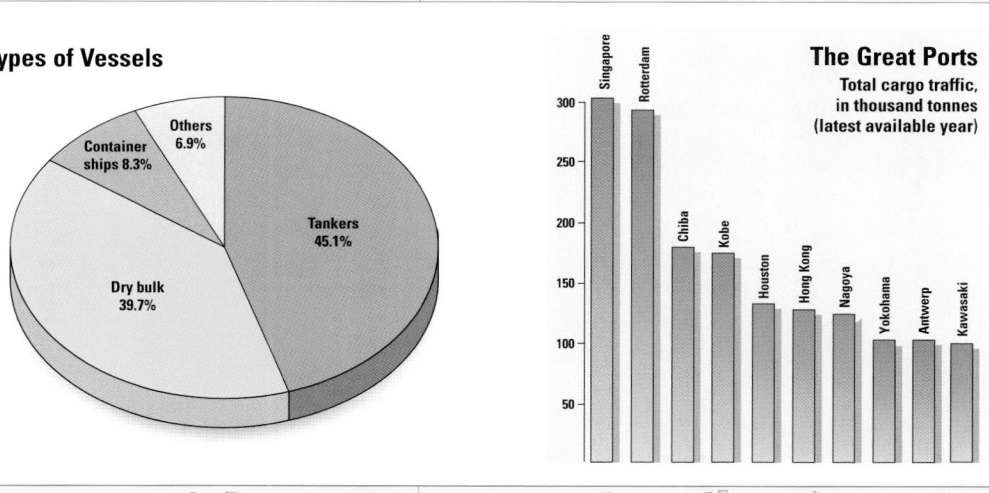

- Others 6.9%
- Container ships 8.3%
- Tankers 45.1%
- Dry bulk 39.7%

The Great Ports

Total cargo traffic, in thousand tonnes (latest available year)

Singapore, Rotterdam, Chiba, Kobe, Houston, Hong Kong, Nagoya, Yokohama, Antwerp, Kawasaki

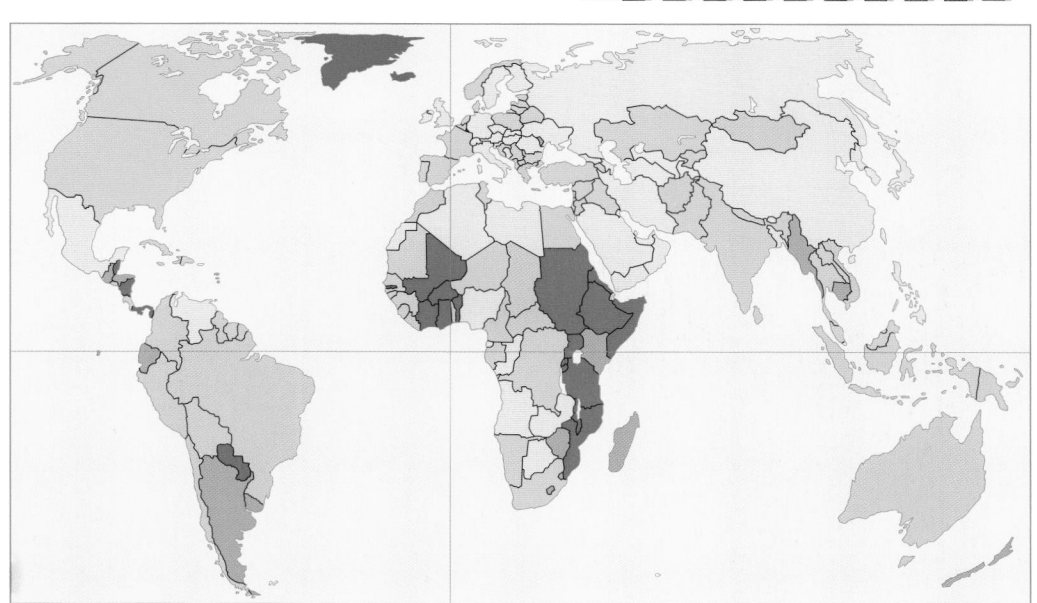

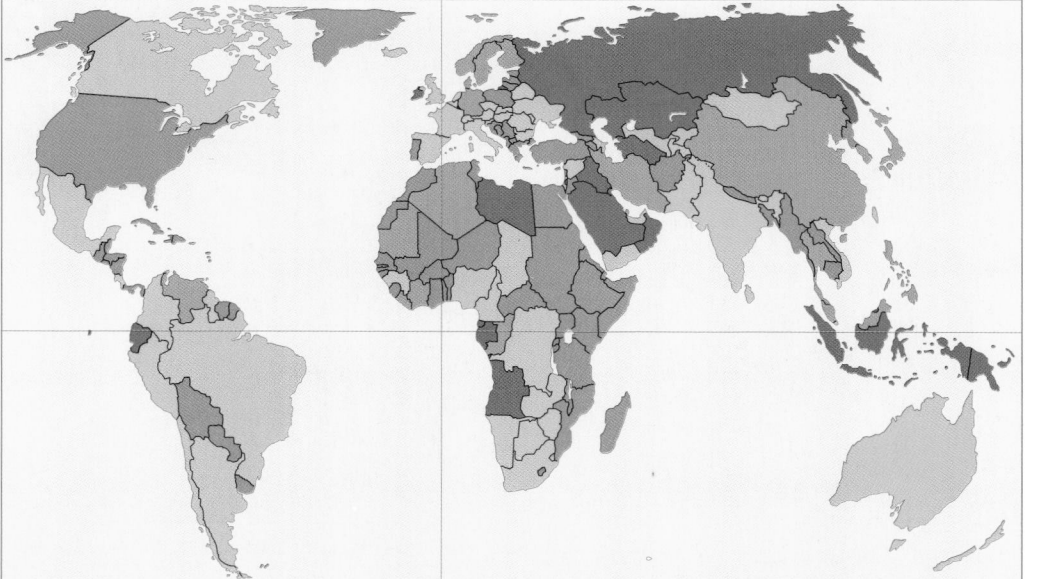

Freight

Freight unloaded in millions of tonnes (latest available year)

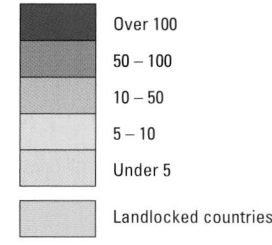

- Over 100
- 50 – 100
- 10 – 50
- 5 – 10
- Under 5
- Landlocked countries

Major seaports

- ● Over 100 million tonnes per year
- ○ 50 – 100 million tonnes per year
- —— Major shipping routes

Air Freight

Trends in air freight in million tonne-km*, selected countries (1995–9)

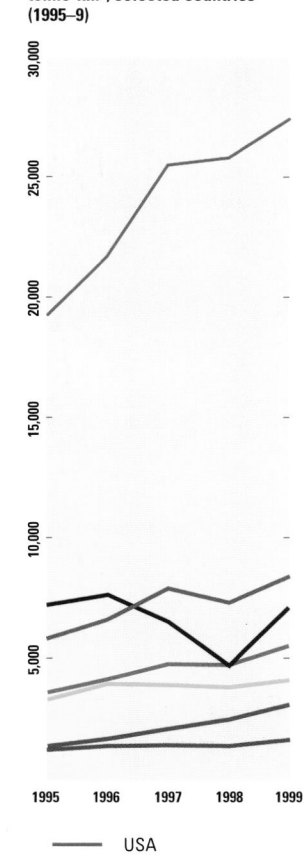

30,000
25,000
20,000
15,000
10,000
5,000

1995 1996 1997 1998 1999

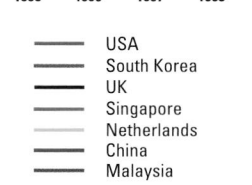

- USA
- South Korea
- UK
- Singapore
- Netherlands
- China
- Malaysia

* Equivalent to million tonnes of air freight flown over 1 million kilometres per year.

Air transport is important to countries of considerable size; where ground terrain is difficult; when crossing short stretches of sea; and where goods are of high value, light in weight or perishable. The deregulation of airlines (in the USA since 1978 and the EU in 1993) has led to increased competition and lower fares.

41

HEALTH

For more information:
18 Water supply
27 Urban pollution
   Urban advantages
33 Crisis in Africa
   Food and population
47 Distribution of
   spending

Average life expectancies all over the world have never been higher. They range from an average of 77 years in high-income economies, to 67 years in middle-income economies and 63 in low-income economies. Even in poverty-stricken and strife-torn Burundi and Ethiopia, average life expectancies are around 50 years, as compared with less than 30 years for a citizen of Berlin in 1880.

In global terms, the radical improvements in health have much to do with improvements in agriculture and, hence, nutrition, as well as health education, an increase in sanitation and the quality of drinking water, together with advances in medicine. These radical changes have been responsible for falling death rates and rapid population growth, together with the expectation by most people that improvements in health will continue.

Health standards, life expectancies and causes of death vary considerably between the developed and developing world. The map on this page shows that in most of Africa, Asia and Latin America, the average daily calorie supply per person is so low as to cause malnutrition. (The daily requirement rated adequate by the World Health Organization is between 2,300 and 2,500 calories per person per day.) Malnutrition is a serious condition.

For example, among pregnant women it causes high rates of child mortality.

Deficiency diseases occur when people do not have a balanced diet. Protein deficiency causes stunting and kwashiorkor, which can be fatal, especially among young children, while vitamin deficiencies cause such illnesses as beri beri, pellagra, scurvy and rickets. Iron deficiency causes anaemia, while a lack of iodine causes mental retardation. A UN report in the early 1990s reported that iodine deficiency affected 458 million women world-wide, as compared with 238 million men. Women's nutritional problems are especially acute in southern Asia. For example, the UN report stated that 88% of pregnant women in India were anaemic, as compared with 15% in developed countries.

Infectious diseases in association, directly or indirectly, with deficient diets, continue to affect people in developing countries, especially the 48 countries in the low human development category, where only 32% of the people have access to sanitation and 68% to safe water supplies.

A World Health report in 1999 stated that infectious diseases cause over 16 million deaths per year. Most of the victims are young and otherwise fit people in developing countries. The major killers in 1999 were respiratory infections, including pneumonia

(which caused 3.5 million deaths), AIDS (2.8 million), cholera, typhoid, dysentery (2.2 million together), tuberculosis (1.5 million), malaria (1.1 million) and measles (0.9 million). Many of these diseases are preventable and, according to the United Nations Children's Fund, an investment of US $25,000 million per year, about half the money spent annually on cigarettes in Europe alone, would save the lives of all the children who currently die from avoidable diseases.

Infectious diseases are much less important as causes of death in developed countries, where cancer and circulatory diseases, such as atherosclerosis and hypertension, which cause strokes and heart attacks, are the most common causes of fatality. Because these diseases tend to kill older people, they are relatively less important in developing countries where people have shorter lifespans.

Harmful habits are also generally practised more by the rich than the poor. For example, smoking is an important cause of death in developed countries, though, curiously, the Japanese, with an average life expectancy of 80 years in 2000, are among the highest tobacco consumers. Similarly, high alcohol consumption, although it has bad effects on health, does not seem to affect longevity. The leading consumers, the French, had a life expectancy of 79 in 2000.

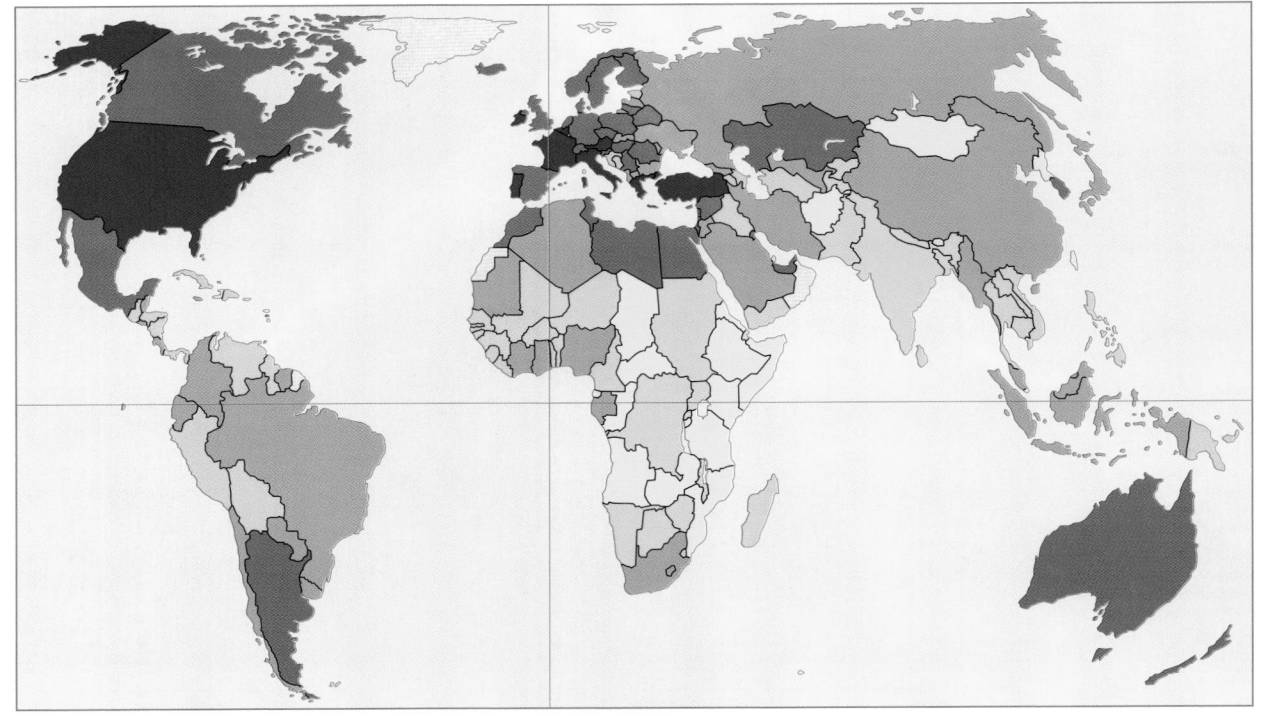

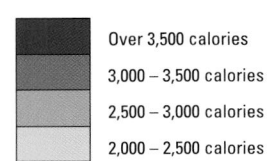

Food Consumption

Average daily food intake in calories per person (1997)

- Over 3,500 calories
- 3,000 – 3,500 calories
- 2,500 – 3,000 calories
- 2,000 – 2,500 calories
- Under 2,000 calories
- No available data

Top 5 countries

Portugal . . . . 3,654 calories
Greece . . . . 3,617 calories
Belgium . . . . 3,602 calories
Ireland . . . . 3,557 calories
Austria . . . . 3,555 calories

Bottom 5 countries

Somalia . . . . 1,573 calories
Eritrea . . . . 1,627 calories
Burundi . . . . 1,687 calories
Afghanistan . . . . 1,732 calories
Mozambique . . . . 1,782 calories

[UK 3,211 calories]

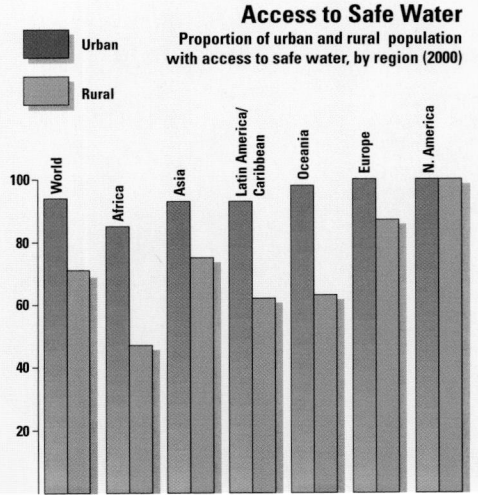

Access to Safe Water
Proportion of urban and rural population with access to safe water, by region (2000)

Urban / Rural

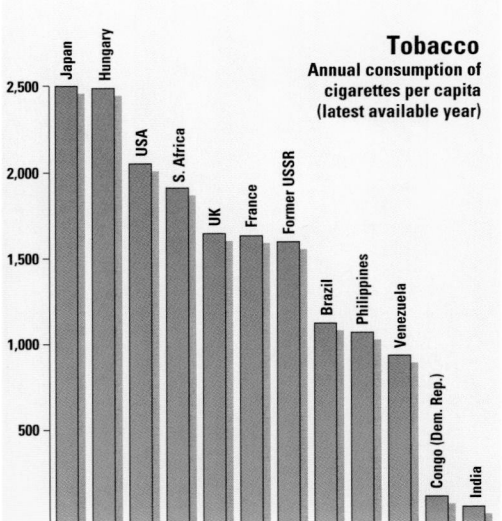

Tobacco
Annual consumption of cigarettes per capita (latest available year)

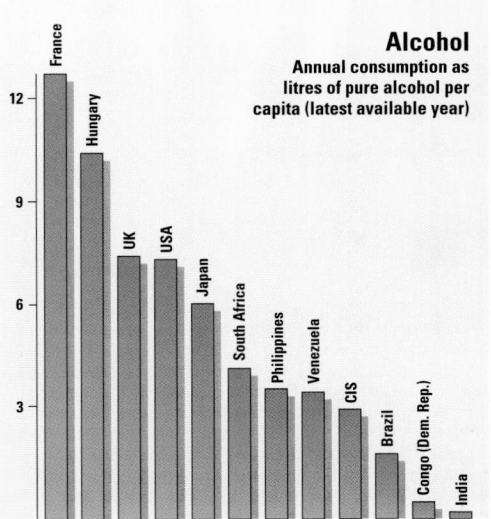

Alcohol
Annual consumption as litres of pure alcohol per capita (latest available year)

Life Expectancy

Years of life expectancy at birth, selected countries (1997)

The chart shows combined data for both sexes. On average, women live longer than men worldwide, even in developing countries with high maternal mortality rates. Overall, life expectancy is steadily rising, though the difference between rich and poor nations remains dramatic.

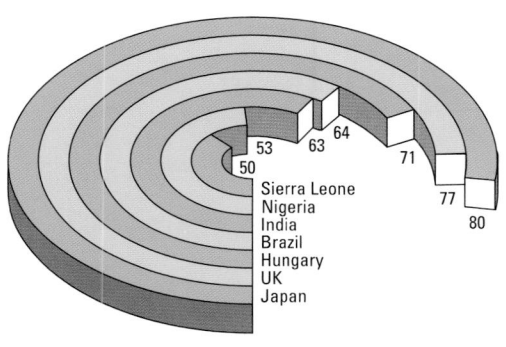

50 53 63 64 71 77 80

Sierra Leone
Nigeria
India
Brazil
Hungary
UK
Japan

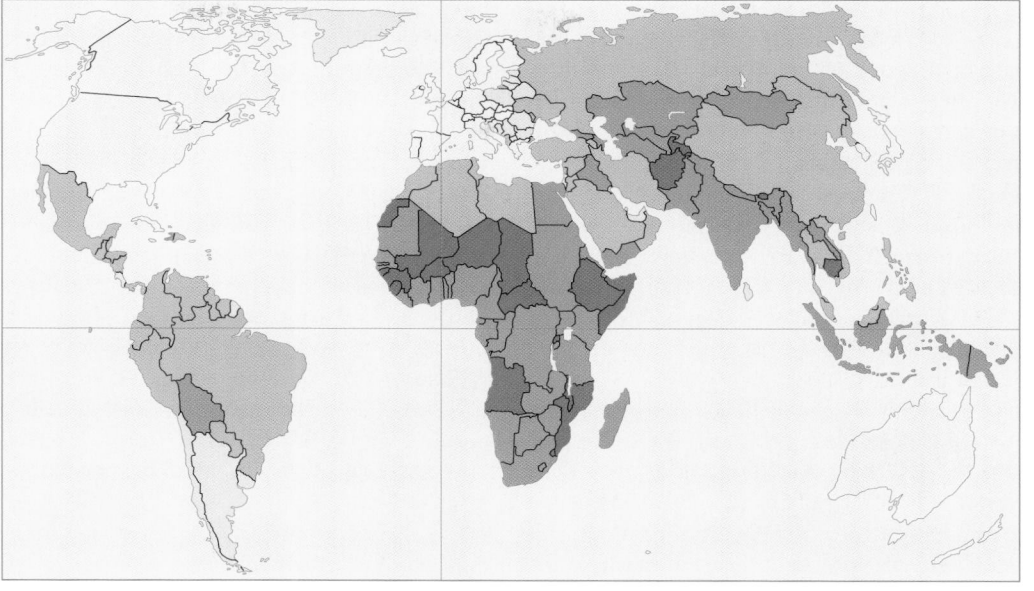
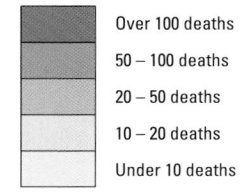

Infant Mortality

Number of babies who died under the age of one, per 1,000 births (2000)

Over 100 deaths

50 – 100 deaths

20 – 50 deaths

10 – 20 deaths

Under 10 deaths

Highest infant mortality

Afghanistan .... 137 deaths
Western Sahara .... 134 deaths
Malawi .... 131 deaths

Lowest infant mortality

Iceland .... 5 deaths
Finland .... 4 deaths
Japan .... 4 deaths

[UK 6 deaths]

Expenditure on Health

Public expenditure on health as a percentage of GDP (1997)

Countries with the highest spending		Countries with the lowest spending	
USA	13.7	Somalia	1.5
Germany.............................	10.5	Indonesia	1.7
Switzerland........................	10.1	Guatemala	2.4
Lebanon..............................	10.1	Malaysia	2.4
Uruguay..............................	10.0	Syria......................................	2.5
Kiribati	9.9	Burma (Myanmar)...............	2.6
France..................................	9.8	China.....................................	2.7
Slovenia..............................	9.4	Cape Verde..........................	2.8
Austria	9.0	Djibouti	2.8
Netherlands........................	8.8	Togo	2.8

The allocation of limited funds for health care in developing countries is rarely evenly spread – the quality of treatment can vary enormously from place to place within the same country. Urban dwellers tend to have much better access to health provisions than those living in rural areas.

Medical Provision

Doctors per 100,000 population, selected countries (2000)

Although the ratio of people to doctors gives a good approximation of a country's health provision, it is not an absolute indicator. Raw numbers may mask inefficiency and other weaknesses: the high proportion of physicians in Hungary, for example, has not prevented infant mortality rates more than twice as high as in the United Kingdom.

The definition of a doctor also varies from nation to nation. As well as registered medical practitioners, it may include trained medical assistants – an especially important category in developing countries, where they provide many of the same services as fully qualified physicians, including simple operations.

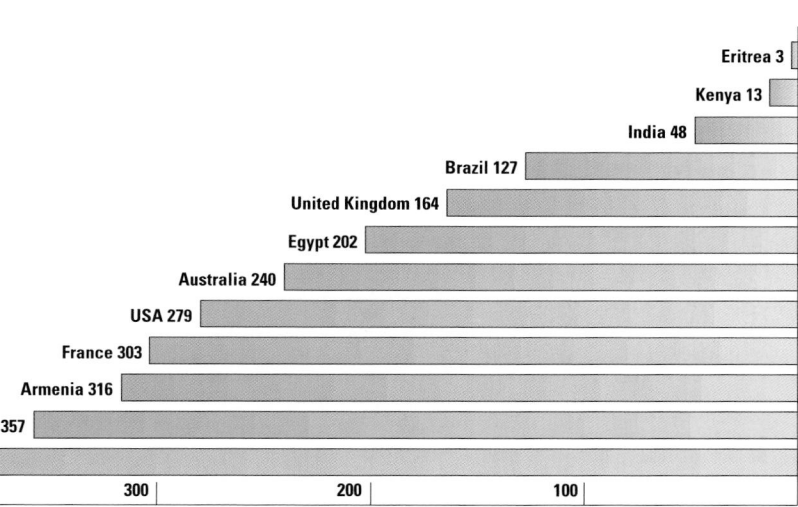

Eritrea 3
Kenya 13
India 48
Brazil 127
United Kingdom 164
Egypt 202
Australia 240
USA 279
France 303
Armenia 316
Hungary 357
Italy 554

600   500   400   300   200   100

The Aids Crisis

The Acquired Immune Deficiency Syndrome (AIDS) was first identified in 1981 when American doctors found otherwise healthy young men succumbing to rare infections. By 1984 the cause had been traced to the Human Immunodeficiency Virus (HIV) which can remain dormant for many years and perhaps indefinitely: only half of those known to carry the virus in 1981 had developed AIDS ten years later.

In Western countries in the 1990s, most AIDS deaths were among male homosexuals or needle-sharing drug-users. However, the disease is spreading fastest among heterosexual men and women, which is its usual vector in the developing world where most of its victims live.

The World Health Organization estimated that 2.8 million people died of AIDS in 1999 and that by the end of the same year 34 million people were HIV-positive. Over 24 million of these were in sub-Saharan Africa. South Africa had the largest number of HIV infections, totalling over 4 million, of which 95,000 were children. In Africa, over 12 million children have been orphaned as a direct result of AIDS-related deaths.

By 2015, the UN Population Fund estimates that life expectancy in the worst affected countries will be 60, five years lower than it would be in the absence of AIDS.

Causes of Death

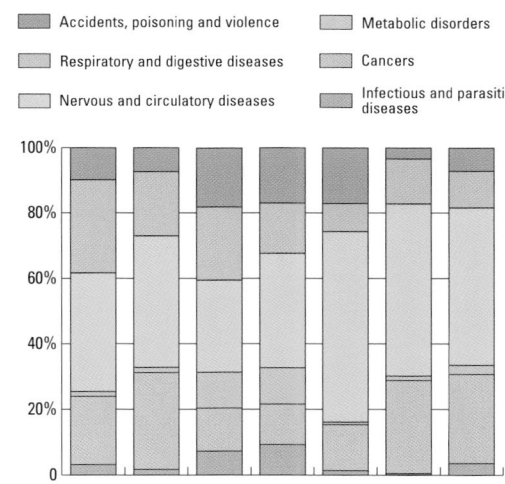

Accidents, poisoning and violence

Respiratory and digestive diseases

Nervous and circulatory diseases

Metabolic disorders

Cancers

Infectious and parasitic diseases

100%

80%

60%

40%

20%

0

China Japan Mexico Morocco Russia UK USA

Circulatory Disease in Europe

Diseases of the circulatory system per 100,000 people (latest available year)

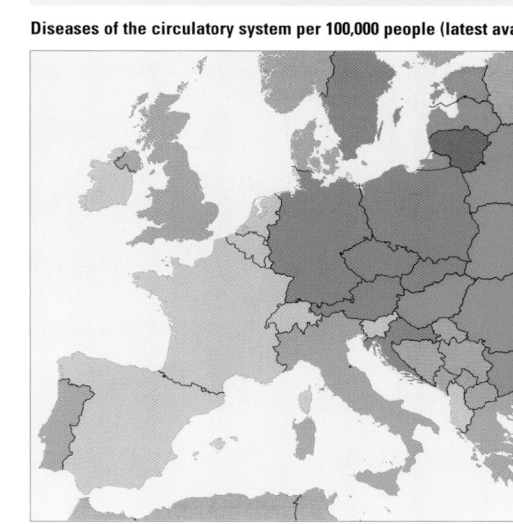

>700 per 100,000

600 – 699 per 100,000

500 – 599 per 100,000

400 – 499 per 100,000

<400 per 100,000

No data available

By comparison, over 354 people per 100,000 living in the USA die of heart disease.

AIDS

Cases reported in 1999

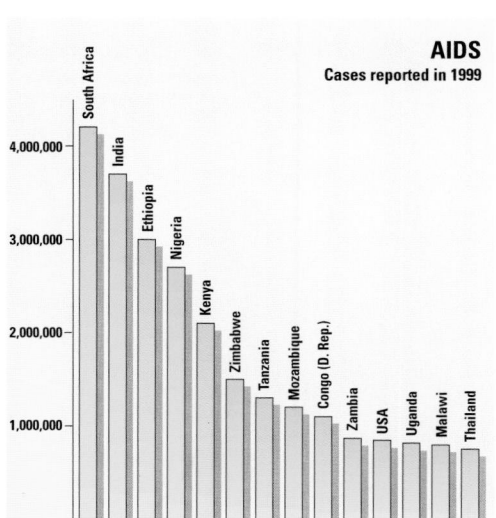

4,000,000

3,000,000

2,000,000

1,000,000

South Africa
India
Ethiopia
Nigeria
Kenya
Zimbabwe
Tanzania
Mozambique
Congo (D. Rep.)
Zambia
USA
Uganda
Malawi
Thailand

Sanitation

Percentage of the population with access to sanitation services, selected countries (latest available year)

Urban
Rural

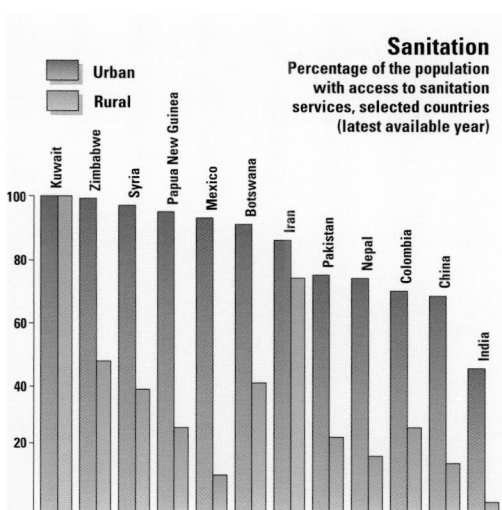

100

80

60

40

20

Kuwait
Zimbabwe
Syria
Papua New Guinea
Mexico
Botswana
Iran
Pakistan
Nepal
Colombia
China
India

Malaria

Cases of malaria per 100,000 people exposed to malaria-infected environments, selected countries* (latest available year)

* data are not available for Africa where 80% of malaria cases occur

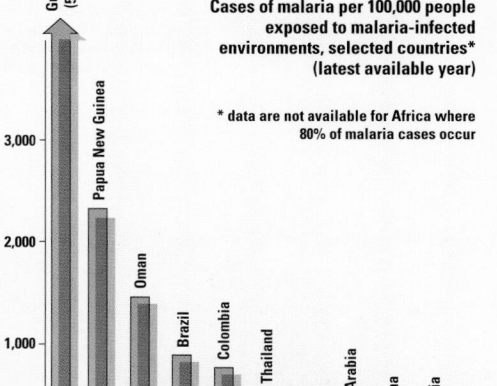

Guyana (5,280)

3,000

2,000

1,000

Papua New Guinea
Oman
Brazil
Colombia
Thailand
Iran
Saudi Arabia
Argentina
Indonesia
China

Infectious and parasitic diseases, such as malaria, which claimed 1.1 million lives in 1999, remain a scourge in the developing countries. Respiratory infections and injury also claim more lives in developing countries, which lack the drugs and the medical personnel to deal with them. Developing countries lack the basic services taken for granted in developed nations. For example, in rural Africa in 2000, only 49% of the population had access to sanitation and 44% to safe water, with the situation being worse in rural areas. By contrast, circulatory diseases and cancer are the main causes of death in the rich, industrialized countries. For example, in the UK in the 1990s, circulatory diseases, which cause heart attacks and strokes, accounted for nearly half the deaths, with cancer accounting for nearly a quarter.

WEALTH

For more information:
38 Wealth creation
39 Industrial power
   Exports per capita
40 World trade
   Major exports
41 Balance of trade
47 Distribution of spending
   Distribution of income

Perhaps the most glaring differences in the world today are those between the rich and the poor. The World Bank divides countries into three main groups based on average economic production expressed in terms of per capita GNP (Gross National Product). They are the low-income economies, including most African countries and much of Asia; the middle-income economies, including most of Latin America and most of the former USSR; and the high-income economies of Canada, the United States, Western Europe, Japan and Australia.

Per capita GNPs are a measure of the total goods and services produced by a country divided by the population, and then converted into US dollars at official exchange rates. They are useful indicators of a country's prosperity, though, like all statistics, they must be treated with care. For example, the prices for goods and services in China are far cheaper than they are in the United States. China's per capita GNP in 1998 was $750 (as compared with $29,340 in the USA), but the PPP (Purchasing-Power Parity) estimate of China's per capita GNP was considerably higher at $3,570. Another problem with per capita GNPs is that they are averages, which often conceal wide internal variations.

The pattern of poverty varies from region to region. In Latin America, much progress has been made through industrialization, though startling inequalities still exist between rich and poor. In Asia, the 'tiger economies' of the late 1990s have followed Japan's example in pursuing export-led industrial policies, while the success of China's Special Economic Zones, where foreign investment is encouraged, has led to a huge rise in China's per capita GNP, as shown on the map on page 45, bottom right.

Solutions to poverty in Africa are much harder to find because of its high population growth, civil wars, natural disasters and high inflation rates. Although Africa receives more aid than any other continent, aid is only a partial solution. Much aid has been wasted on overambitious projects, in the servicing of huge national debts, or lost by inexperienced or corrupt governments. One initiative in some African countries has been to improve the infrastructure and develop tourism, creating employment and providing much-needed foreign currency. But tourism alone cannot solve the problems of under-development.

The International Monetary Fund and the World Bank argue that real economic progress in Africa will be achieved only when African countries create market-friendly economies that encourage trade through export-led manufacturing, while at the same time strictly controlling public spending on welfare, the civil service and other areas.

Continental Shares

Shares of population and of wealth (GNP) by continent

These generalized continental figures show the startling difference between rich and poor but mask the successes or failures of individual countries. Japan, for example, with less than 4% of Asia's population, produces almost 70% of the continent's output. Within countries, the difference between rich and poor can also be startling. In Brazil, for example, the richest 20% of the population own 60% of the wealth.

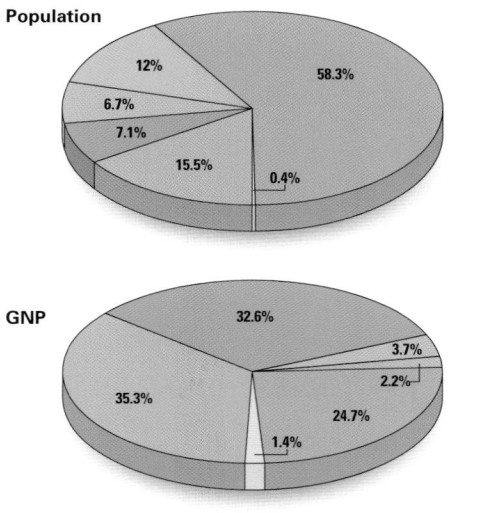

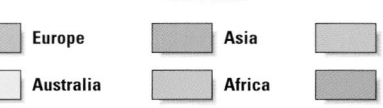

Europe | Asia | South America
Australia | Africa | North America

Currencies

Currency units of the world's most powerful economies

1. USA: US dollar ($, US $) = 100 cents
2. Japan: Yen (Y, ¥) = 100 sen
3. EU: euro = 100 cent
4. UK: Pound sterling (£) = 100 pence
5. Canada: Canadian dollar (C$, Can$) = 100 cents
6. China: Renminbi yuan (RMBY, $, Y) = 10 jiao = 100 fen
7. Brazil: Cruzeiro real (BRC) = 100 centavos
8. India: Indian rupee (Re, Rs) = 100 paisa
9. Australia: Australian dollar ($A) = 100 cents
10. Switzerland: Swiss franc (SFr, SwF) = 100 centimes
11. South Korea: Won (W) = 100 chon
12. Sweden: Swedish krona (SKr) = 100 ore
13. Mexico: Mexican peso (Mex$) = 100 centavos
14. Denmark: Danish krone (DKr) = 100 øre
15. Norway: Norwegian krone (NKr) = 100 øre
16. Saudi Arabia: Riyal (SAR, SRI$) = 100 halalah
17. Indonesia: Rupiah (Rp) = 100 sen
18. South Africa: Rand (R) = 100 cents

On 1 January 2002, three years after the launch of Europe's single currency, euro banknotes and coins were brought into circulation in the 12 member states of the European Union that had adopted the euro. Their former national currencies remained in dual circulation with the euro until the end of February 2002.
The 12 countries in the euro area are: Austria, Belgium, Germany, Greece, Finland, France, Ireland, Italy, Luxembourg, the Netherlands, Portugal and Spain.

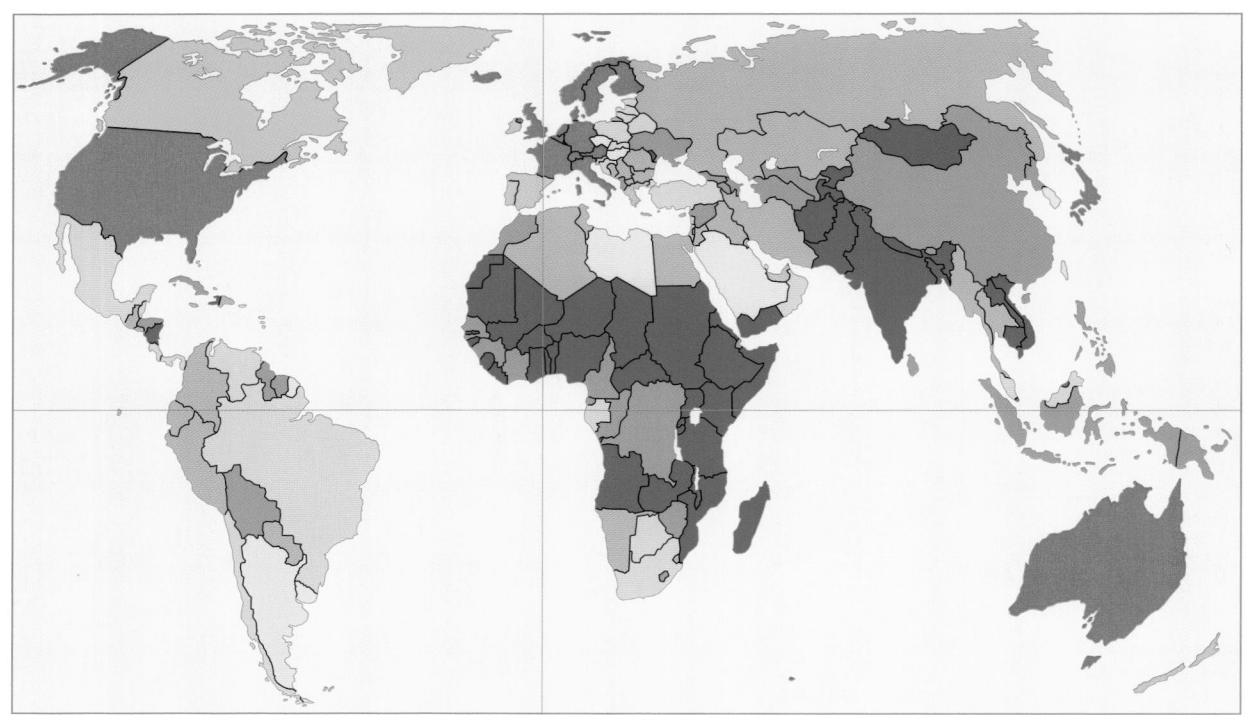

Levels of Income

Gross National Product per capita: the value of total production divided by the population (1999)

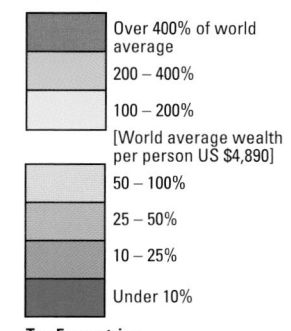

Over 400% of world average
200 – 400%
100 – 200%
[World average wealth per person US $4,890]
50 – 100%
25 – 50%
10 – 25%
Under 10%

Top 5 countries
Luxembourg $44,640
Switzerland $38,350
Bermuda $35,590
Norway $32,880
Japan $32,230

Bottom 5 countries
Ethiopia $100
Burundi $120
Sierra Leone $130
Guinea-Bissau $160
Niger $190

Indicators

The gap between the world's rich and poor is now so great that it is difficult to illustrate on a single graph. Within each income group (as defined by the World Bank), however, comparisons have some meaning; the Chinese, perhaps because of propaganda value, have more TV sets than Indians, whereas Nigerians prefer to spend their money on radios. However, the wealth gap in many developing countries is wide, with a small, rich class and a large, impoverished majority, while many high-income countries contain an underclass of unemployed and homeless people.

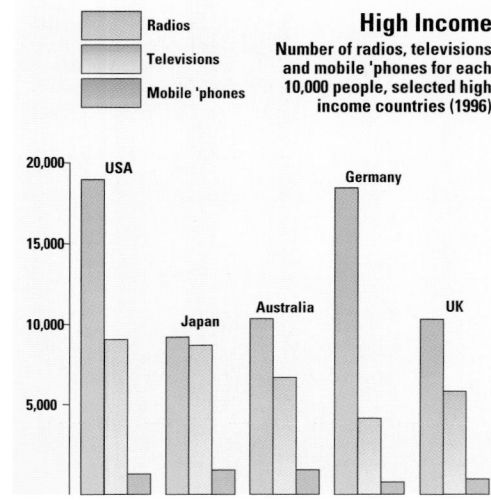

Radios
Televisions
Mobile 'phones

High Income
Number of radios, televisions and mobile 'phones for each 10,000 people, selected high income countries (1996)

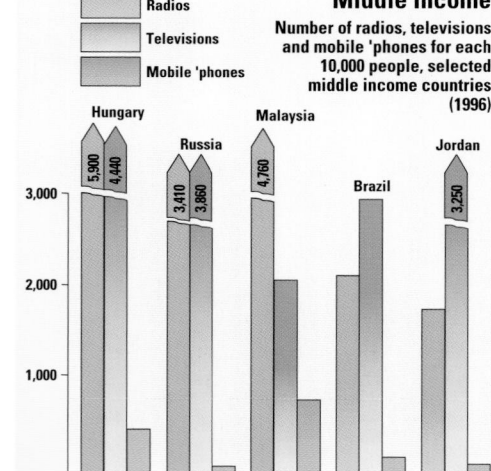

Radios
Televisions
Mobile 'phones

Middle Income
Number of radios, televisions and mobile 'phones for each 10,000 people, selected middle income countries (1996)

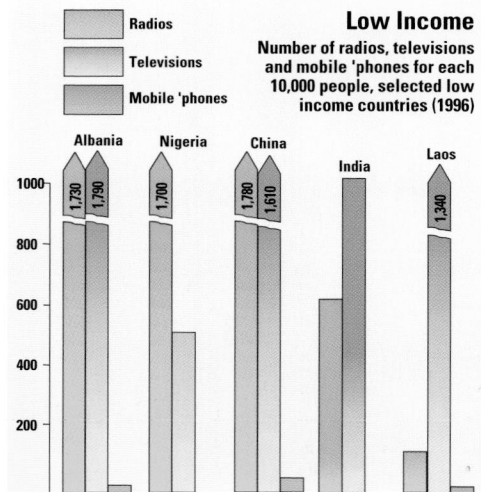

Radios
Televisions
Mobile 'phones

Low Income
Number of radios, televisions and mobile 'phones for each 10,000 people, selected low income countries (1996)

World Tourism

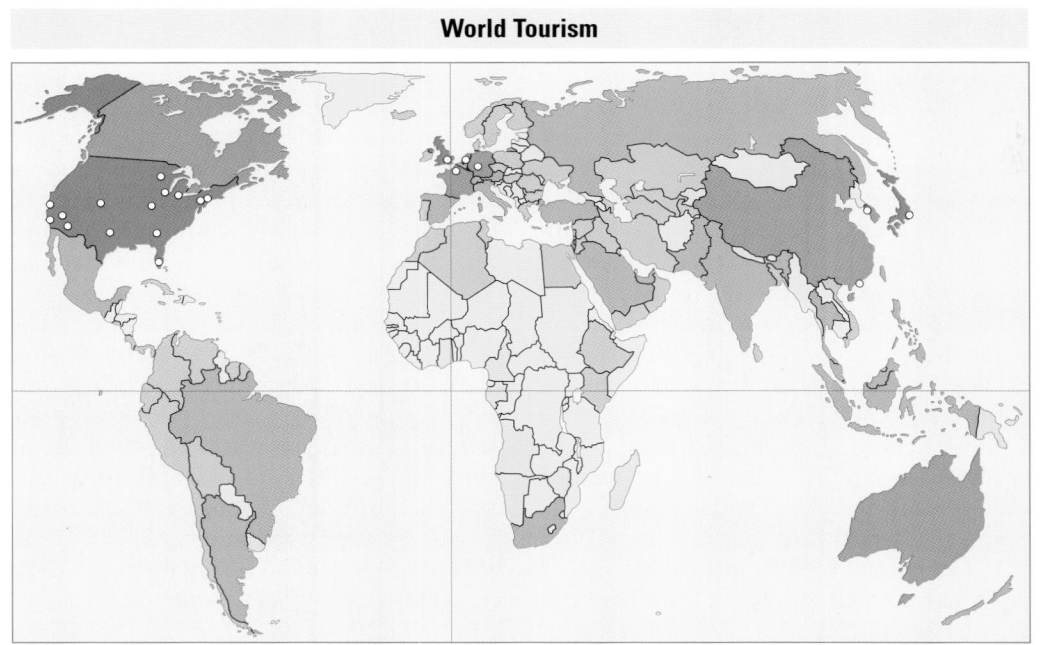

Passenger km flown (the number of passengers multiplied by the distance flown by each passenger from the airport of origin) (1997)

- Over 100,000 million
- 50,000 – 100,000 million
- 10,000 – 50,000 million
- 1,000 – 10,000 million
- 500 – 1,000 million
- Under 500 million

○ Major airports (handling over 25 million passengers in 2000)

Leisure and tourism is the world's second largest industry in terms of revenue generated. Small economies in attractive areas are often completely dominated by tourism: in some Caribbean islands, tourist spending provides over 90% of the total income and is the biggest foreign exchange earner. In cash terms the USA is the world leader: its 1999 earnings exceeded US $74 billion, though that sum amounted to approximately 0.9% of its total GDP. Of the 48 million visitors to the USA, 34% came from Canada and 25% from Mexico. Germany spends the most on overseas tourism; this amounts to over US $50,000 million. The next biggest spenders are the USA, Japan and the UK.

The world's busiest airport in terms of total number of passengers is Atlanta (78.1 million passengers in 1999); the busiest international airport is London's Heathrow.

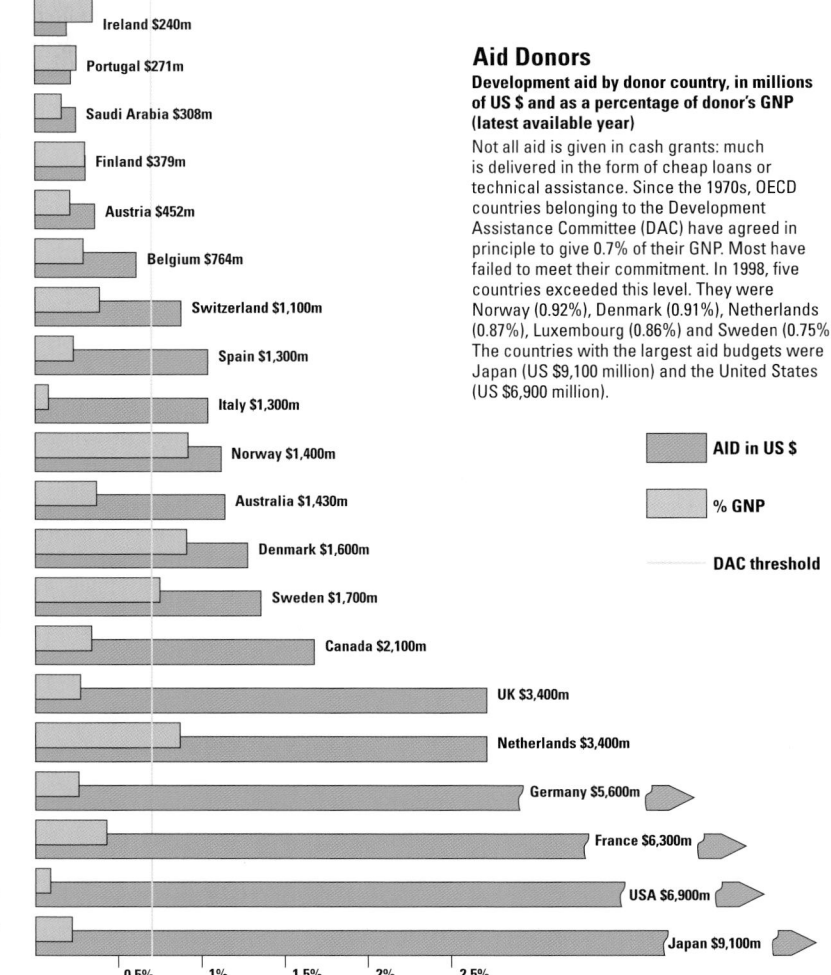

Aid Donors

Development aid by donor country, in millions of US $ and as a percentage of donor's GNP (latest available year)

Not all aid is given in cash grants: much is delivered in the form of cheap loans or technical assistance. Since the 1970s, OECD countries belonging to the Development Assistance Committee (DAC) have agreed in principle to give 0.7% of their GNP. Most have failed to meet their commitment. In 1998, five countries exceeded this level. They were Norway (0.92%), Denmark (0.91%), Netherlands (0.87%), Luxembourg (0.86%) and Sweden (0.75%). The countries with the largest aid budgets were Japan (US $9,100 million) and the United States (US $6,900 million).

- AID in US $
- % GNP
- DAC threshold

Bar chart labels:
Ireland $240m, Portugal $271m, Saudi Arabia $308m, Finland $379m, Austria $452m, Belgium $764m, Switzerland $1,100m, Spain $1,300m, Italy $1,300m, Norway $1,400m, Australia $1,430m, Denmark $1,600m, Sweden $1,700m, Canada $2,100m, UK $3,400m, Netherlands $3,400m, Germany $5,600m, France $6,300m, USA $6,900m, Japan $9,100m

Axis: 0.5%, 1%, 1.5%, 2%, 2.5%

State Finance

Inflation rates, shown on the map (*right*) are an index of a country's financial stability and usually of its prosperity. Annual inflation rates above 20% are usually marked by slow or even negative growth of the GNP. Above 50%, it becomes hyperinflation and an economy is reeling. In the late 1980s and early 1990s, many high-income countries had to contend with annual inflation rates of 10% or more, while Japan, the growth leader, had an average inflation rate of 1.3% between 1985 and 1994.

The per capita GNP figures listed below are useful indicators of economic success or failure, but they do not account for living costs. Nor do they reveal the gaps between the rich and poor within countries.

Market-friendly policies, including low taxes and state spending, liberal trade policies and a welcome for foreign investors, are major factors in countries that have enjoyed rapid economic growth since 1980. For example, the setting up of Special Economic Zones in eastern China has led to a spectacular rise in the per capita GNP. Other successful countries included the 'tiger economies' of South Korea, Thailand and Singapore, although an Asian market crash in 1997 halted the dramatic economic expansion in these countries.

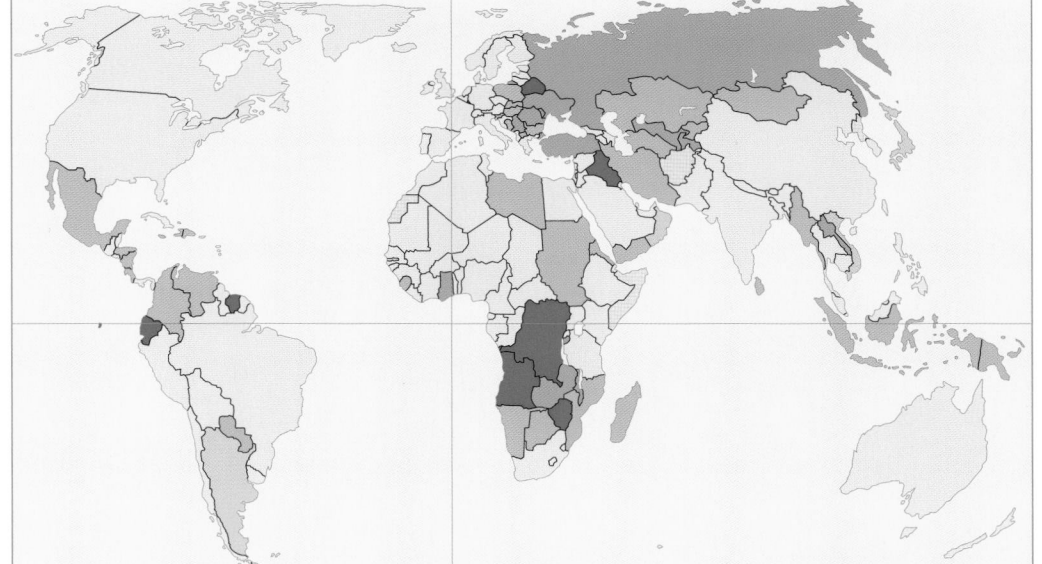

Inflation

Average annual rate of inflation (2000 est.)

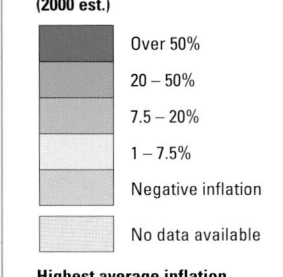

- Over 50%
- 20 – 50%
- 7.5 – 20%
- 1 – 7.5%
- Negative inflation
- No data available

Highest average inflation
Congo (Dem. Rep.)	540%
Angola	325%
Belarus	200%

Lowest average inflation
Nauru	–3.6%
Macau (China)	–1.8%
Argentina*	–0.9%

* During 2002, Argentina experienced a sharp rise in inflation which is not reflected on this map.

The Wealth Gap

The world's richest and poorest countries, by Gross National Product per capita in US $ (1999 estimates)

1.	Liechtenstein	50,000	1.	Ethiopia	100
2.	Luxembourg	44,640	2.	Congo (D. Rep.)	110
3.	Switzerland	38,350	3.	Burundi	120
4.	Bermuda	35,590	4.	Sierra Leone	130
5.	Norway	32,880	5.	Guinea-Bissau	160
6.	Japan	32,230	6.	Niger	190
7.	Denmark	32,030	7.	Malawi	190
8.	USA	30,600	8.	Eritrea	200
9.	Singapore	29,610	9.	Chad	200
10.	Iceland	29,280	10.	Nepal	220
11.	Austria	25,970	11.	Angola	220
12.	Germany	25,350	12.	Mozambique	230
13.	Sweden	25,040	13.	Tanzania	240
14.	Monaco	25,000	14.	Burkina Faso	240
15.	Belgium	24,510	15.	Mali	240
16.	Brunei	24,630	16.	Rwanda	250
17.	Netherlands	24,320	17.	Madagascar	250
18.	Finland	23,780	18.	Cambodia	260
19.	Hong Kong	23,520	19.	São Tomé & Príncipe	270
20.	France	23,480	20.	Laos	280

GNP per capita is calculated by dividing a country's Gross National Product by its total population.

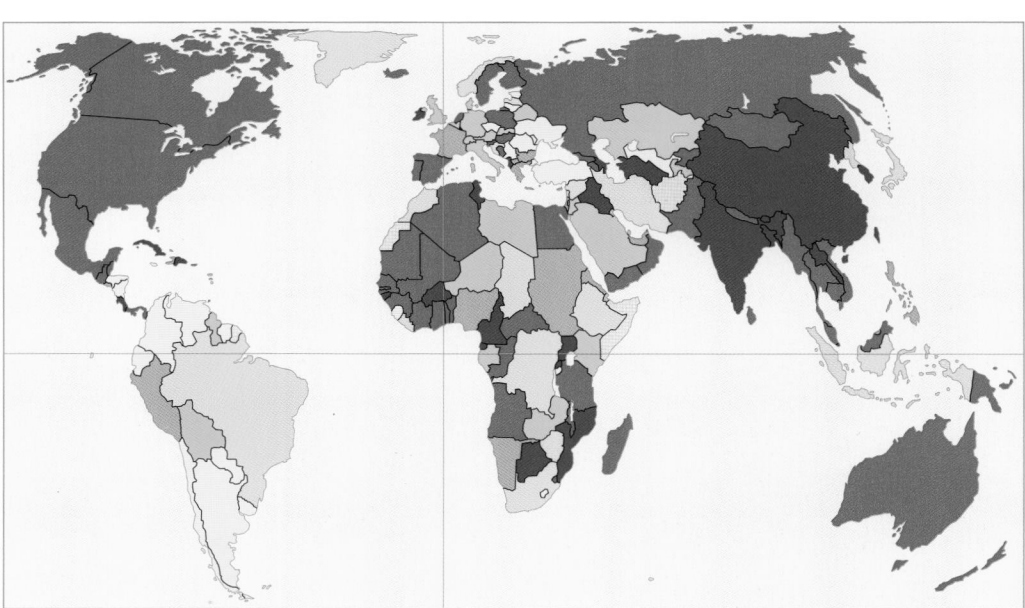

Growth in GNP

GNP per capita annual growth rate (1998–9)

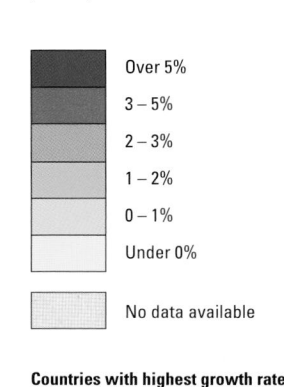

- Over 5%
- 3 – 5%
- 2 – 3%
- 1 – 2%
- 0 – 1%
- Under 0%
- No data available

Countries with highest growth rates
Equatorial Guinea	15.0%
Mozambique	10.0%
Palau	10.0%
South Korea	10.0%
Guinea-Bissau	9.5%

STANDARDS OF LIVING

For more information:
18 Water supply
24 Population density
27 Urban pollution
    Squatter settlements
    Urban advantages
30 World's refugees
    War since 1945
38 Employment
    The workforce
43 Life expectancy
    Infant mortality
45 The wealth gap
    Aid donors

Wealth is a basic factor in determining standards of living. Everywhere, the rich have more of everything, including higher average life expectancies, while the poor have to spend most of their income on basic human needs, such as food and clothing. Yet poverty and wealth are relative terms. Slum dwellers living on social security in an industrial society feel their poverty acutely, but they have far more resources than an average African living in a rural area.

In 1990 the United Nations Development Programme published its first Human Development Index (HDI), an attempt to construct a comparative scale by which a simplified form of well-being might be measured. The HDI, expressed as a value between 0 and 0.999, combines figures for life expectancy and literacy with a wealth scale, based on Purchasing-Power Parity. The world's countries are divided into three groups, those with a high HDI (0.800 and above); those with a medium HDI (0.500 to 0.799); and those with a low HDI (below 0.500).

In 1999, Canada was top in the world rankings and Sierra Leone was bottom. In fact, of the 48 countries with a low HDI, 37 were from Africa, 10 from Asia, plus Haiti from the Caribbean. Besides having low per capita GNPs, the average life expectancy in these countries was 56 years, while the adult literacy rate was 49%. By comparison, the average life expectancy at birth in countries in the high HDI group was 74 years, while the literacy rate was 97%.

Comparisons between countries with similar per capita GNPs reveal the effects of government actions. For example, the World Bank classifies both India and China as low-income economies, but India's HDI at 0.436 is much lower than that of China, at 0.609. This reflects not only China's economic progress in the 1980s and 1990s, but also differences in average life expectancies (63 years in India and 70 years in China), and adult literacy rates (51% in India and 80% in China).

Disparities in standards of living exist not only between countries but also between individuals, groups and regions within countries. For example, income distribution figures for 1995 show that, in the United States, the poorest 20% of households received less than 4% of the income.

Other contrasts exist in developing countries between rural communities, where incomes are low and basic services are often in short supply, and urban areas, where even those living in slums are generally better off than their rural neighbours. Other striking differences exist between men and women. For example, while adult literacy rates for men and women living in developed countries are more or less the same, large differences exist in many developing countries. In 1995, in countries in the lowest HDI category, only 37% of women were literate, as compared with 62% of men.

Female education is a factor in population control, especially as women's fertility rates appear to fall in direct proportion to the amount of secondary education they receive. This point was acknowledged in 1994 by the UN Population Fund, which defined four main objectives relating to women and population control. They were: the reduction of maternal, infant and child mortality; better education, especially for girls; universal access to reproductive health services; and gender equality.

Statistical analysis presents many problems of interpretation, especially when trying to define such intangible factors as a sense of well-being. For example, education helps create wealth; but are rich countries wealthy because their people are well educated, or are they well educated because they are rich?

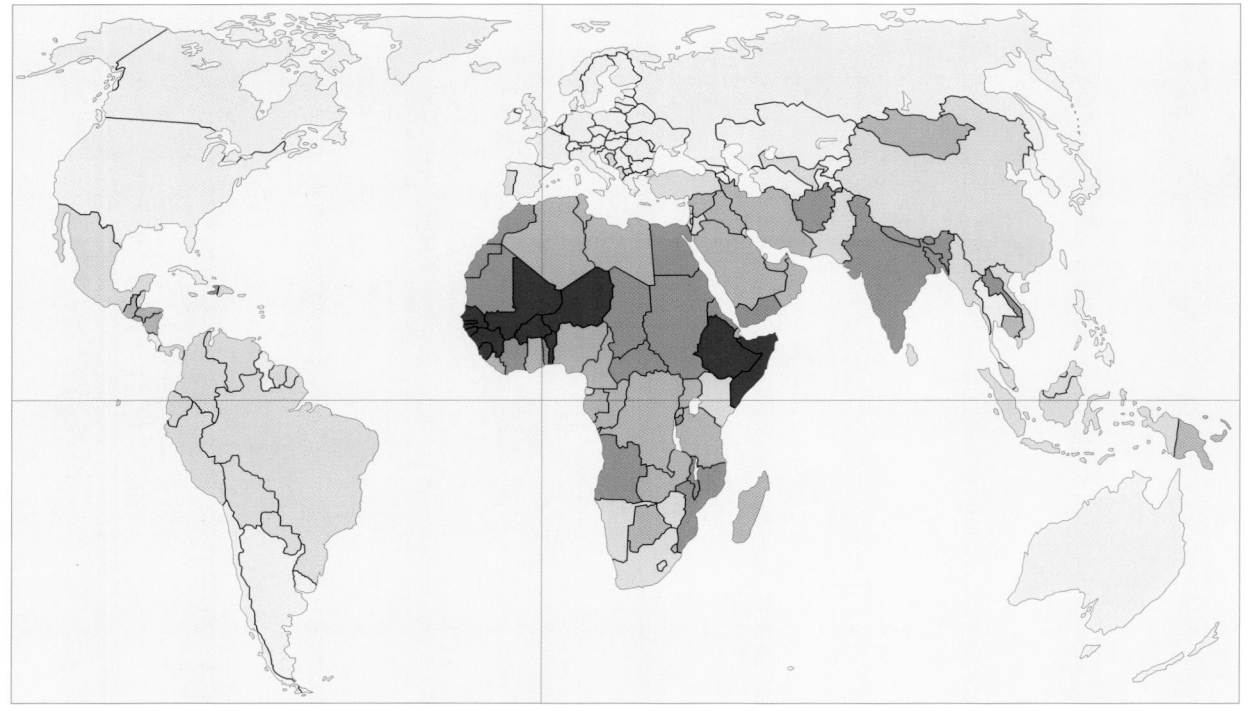

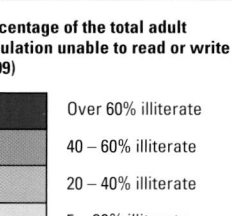

Illiteracy

Percentage of the total adult population unable to read or write (1999)

- Over 60% illiterate
- 40 – 60% illiterate
- 20 – 40% illiterate
- 5 – 20% illiterate
- Under 5% illiterate

Educational expenditure per person (latest available year)

Top 5 countries
Sweden	$997
Qatar	$989
Canada	$983
Norway	$971
Switzerland	$796

Bottom 5 countries
Chad	$2
Bangladesh	$3
Ethiopia	$3
Nepal	$4
Somalia	$4

[UK $447]

Education

The developing countries made great efforts in the 1970s and 1980s to bring at least a basic education to their people. Primary school enrolments rose above 60% in all but the poorest nations. Figures often include teenagers or young adults, however, and there are still an estimated 300 million children worldwide who receive no schooling at all. A lack of resources has restricted the development of secondary and higher education. Most primary school education is free in the poorer countries, but fees are often paid for secondary and higher education, thus heightening the differences between rich and poor.

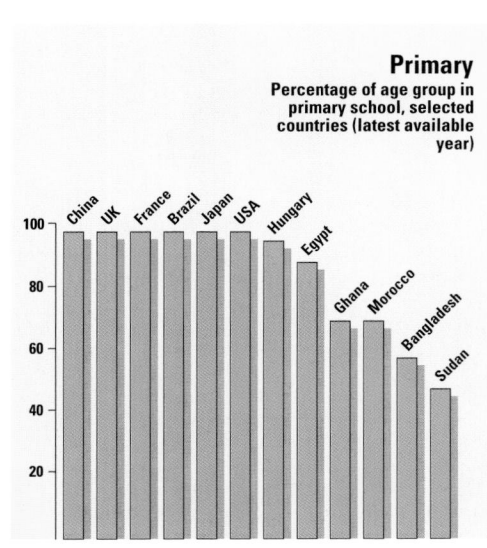

Primary Percentage of age group in primary school, selected countries (latest available year)

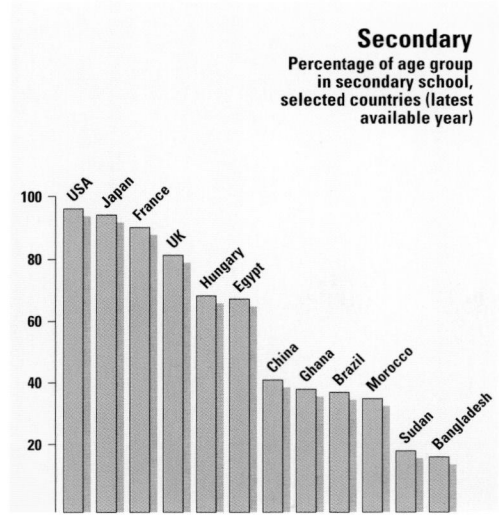

Secondary Percentage of age group in secondary school, selected countries (latest available year)

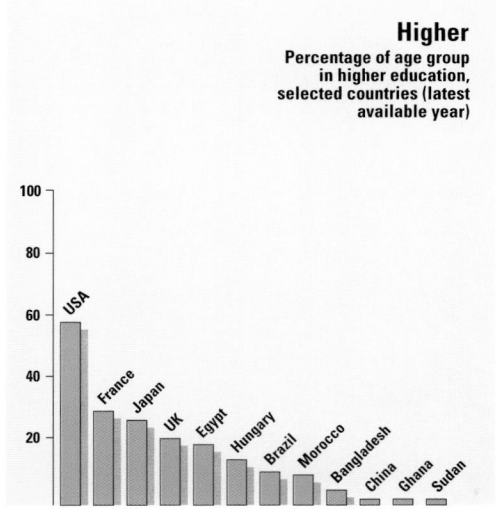

Higher Percentage of age group in higher education, selected countries (latest available year)

Distribution of Spending

Percentage share of household spending (latest available year)

A high proportion of the average income of households in developing nations is spent on basic needs such as food and clothing. In most Western countries food and clothing account for less than 25% of expenditure.

Food
Medicine & Education
Clothing
Transport
Energy & Housing
Other

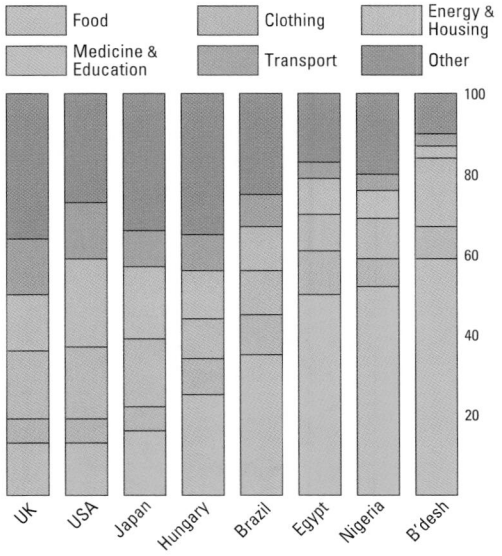

Distribution of Income

Percentage share of household income from poorest fifth to richest fifth, selected countries (latest available year)

The graph (*below*) shows that wealth is not distributed evenly throughout the population of the six countries. In every country worldwide the richest 20% of the population have a disproportionately high percentage of the income. This disparity between rich and poor is nowhere more pronounced than in Brazil, where the richest 20% of the population have over 60% of the income. The poorest 20%, on the other hand, have less than 5%.

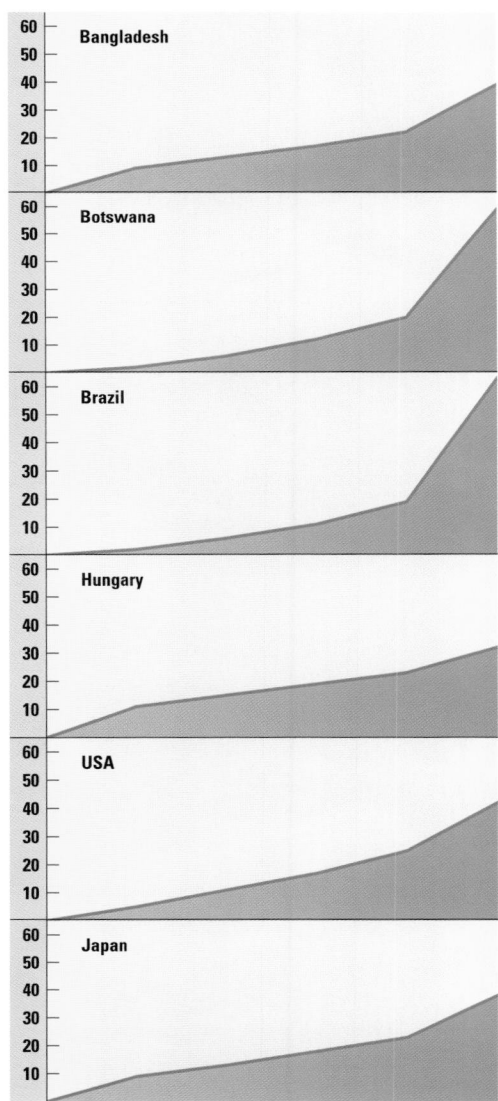

Fertility and Education

Fertility rates compared with female education, selected countries (1992–95)

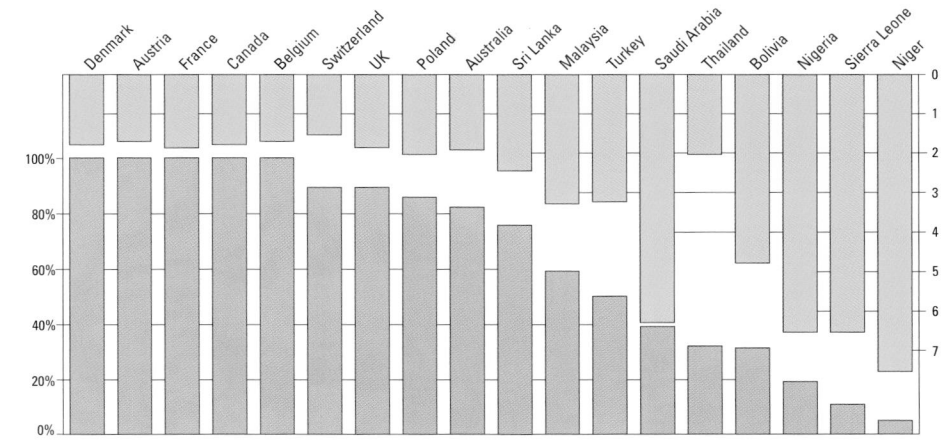

Percentage of females aged 12–17 in secondary education

Fertility rate: average number of children borne per woman

Access to secondary education is closely linked to low fertility rates in developed countries. By contrast, in many developing countries, women's lives are dominated by agriculture, or they lack access to secondary and higher education for cultural reasons, as in Muslim countries. Such disparities are reflected in women's parliamentary representation which is only one-seventh that of men, despite the emergence of such figures as Mrs Indira Gandhi, India's former prime minister. Female wages are also, on average, only two-thirds of those of men.

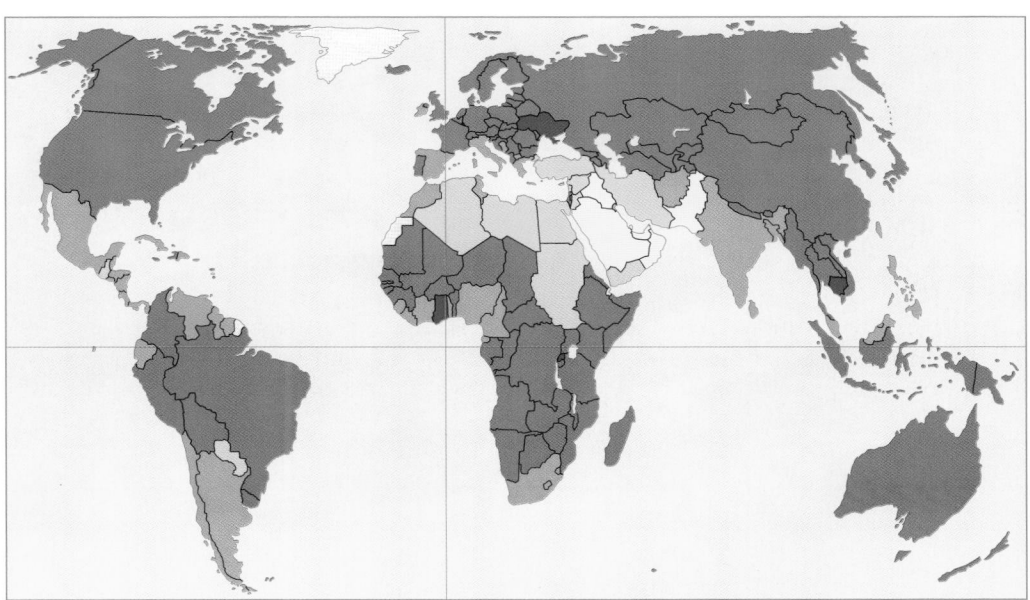

Women at Work

Women in paid employment as a percentage of the total workforce (1997)

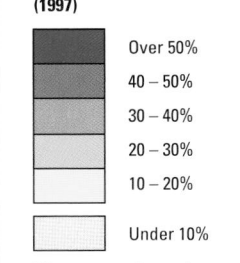

Over 50%
40 – 50%
30 – 40%
20 – 30%
10 – 20%
Under 10%

Most women in work
Rwanda 56%
Cambodia 53%
Ghana 51%
Ukraine 50%

Fewest women in work
Oman 14%
Saudi Arabia............................. 13%
UAE 13%
Qatar 13%

Car Ownership

Proportion of the world's vehicles, by region (1996)

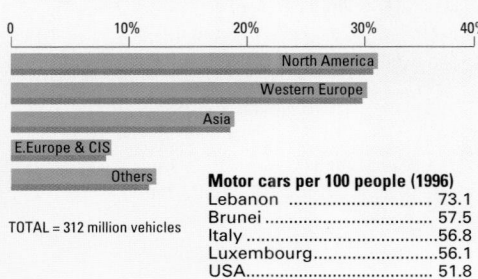

North America
Western Europe
Asia
E.Europe & CIS
Others

TOTAL = 312 million vehicles

Motor cars per 100 people (1996)
Lebanon 73.1
Brunei 57.5
Italy 56.8
Luxembourg.........................56.1
USA......................................51.8

Standards of Living in the USA by Race, Age and Region

A comparison of measures of income and education, by selected characteristics (1999)

Median income per household (US $), by age and region

15–24 years 23,564
25–34 years 40,069
35–44 years 48,451
45–54 years 54,148
55–64 years 43,167
65 years and over.............. 21,729

North-east.......................... 40,634
Mid-west 40,609
South 35,797
West 40,983

Per capita income (US $), by race and Hispanic origin of householder

ALL RACES	21,181
White	22,375
Black	14,397
Asian & Pacific Is.	21,134
Hispanic (any race)............	11,621

The poorest 20% of households received just 3.6% of the income, whereas the richest 20% received 48.2%.

Percentage of persons aged 25 and over who have completed High School, by race or origin

ALL RACES	1975	62.5
	1999	83.4
White	1975	64.5
	1999	84.3
Black	1975	42.5
	1999	77.0
Hispanic	1975	37.9
	1999	56.1

Regional Inequality in Italy

Gross Domestic Product (GDP) per capita in Italy, by region (1999)

Over US $20,000
$16,000 – $19,999
$12,000 – $15,999
$8,000 – $11,999
Under $8,000

The average GNI (Gross National Income) per capita for Italy was US $20,170. By comparison, the GNI for the UK was $23,590; for the USA $31,910; and for the EU $22,250.

The number of inhabitants per doctor, another social indicator, varies from less than 500 in the north-west of Italy to over 800 in the far south (the *Mezzogiorno*), with a national average of 607.

The southern part of Italy, known as the *Mezzogiorno* (or 'Land of the midday sun'), has been described as the poorest part of the European Union. It is identifiable on the map (*left*) as all the regions with a GDP per capita of less than US $12,000 (including the two islands of Sicily and Sardinia), plus Abruzzi whose capital is L'Aquila.

The *Mezzogiorno* region suffers from a lack of mineral and energy resources, industry, commerce, services and skilled labour. As a result, standards of living in the region are well below the rest of Italy and Europe. Employment is predominantly agricultural and small-scale.

The north of Italy accounts for 60% of the population but 80% of the GDP, whereas the *Mezzogiorno* accounts for 40% of the population and only 20% of the GDP. Manpower surpluses in the south led to emigration to other parts of Europe and the Americas. It has also led, especially in the last 50 years, to inter-regional migration from the islands and the southern mainland to the north. The main regions attracting migrants were the north-west – the prosperous Liguria–Piedmont–Lombardy triangle with its great industrial cities of Genoa, Milan and Turin – and the Venetia region in the north-east. As a result, the north has experienced much higher population growth rates than the rest of Italy.

In 1996 the Northern League, one of Italy's political parties, exploited the regional differences by declaring the north to be the independent 'Republic of Padania'. However, only a small minority of northerners supports secession.

— MT EVEREST, CHINA/NEPAL —
Part of the Himalaya range, Mt Everest – the highest
mountain in the world at 8,850 m (29,035 ft) – lies just
north of centre in this image. The two arms of the Rongbuk
glacier flow away from the triangular shaded north wall, with
the Kangshung glacier due east. The international boundary
between China and Nepal bisects the peak, which was
first climbed on 28 May 1953.

CITY MAPS

AMSTERDAM	2	COPENHAGEN	10	MANILA	17	ST PETERSBURG	26
ATHENS	2	DELHI	10	MELBOURNE	17	SANTIAGO	26
ATLANTA	3	DUBLIN	11	MEXICO CITY	18	SÃO PAULO	26
BAGHDAD	3	EDINBURGH	11	MIAMI	18	SEOUL	26
BANGKOK	3	HELSINKI	12	MILAN	18	SHANGHAI	27
BARCELONA	4	HONG KONG	12	MONTREAL	19	SINGAPORE	27
BEIJING	4	ISTANBUL	12	MOSCOW	19	STOCKHOLM	28
BERLIN	5	JAKARTA	13	MUMBAI	20	SYDNEY	28
BOSTON	6	JERUSALEM	13	MUNICH	20	TOKYO	29
BRUSSELS	6	JOHANNESBURG	13	NEW YORK	21	TEHRAN	30
BUDAPEST	7	KARACHI	14	OSAKA	22	TIANJIN	30
BUENOS AIRES	7	LAGOS	14	OSLO	22	TORONTO	30
CAIRO	7	LISBON	14	PARIS	23	VIENNA	31
CALCUTTA (KOLKATA)	8	LONDON	15	PRAGUE	24	WARSAW	31
CANTON	8	LOS ANGELES	16	RIO DE JANEIRO	24	WASHINGTON	32
CAPE TOWN	8	LIMA	16	ROME	25	WELLINGTON	32
CHICAGO	9	MADRID	17	SAN FRANCISCO	25	INDEX	33–39

CITY MAPS

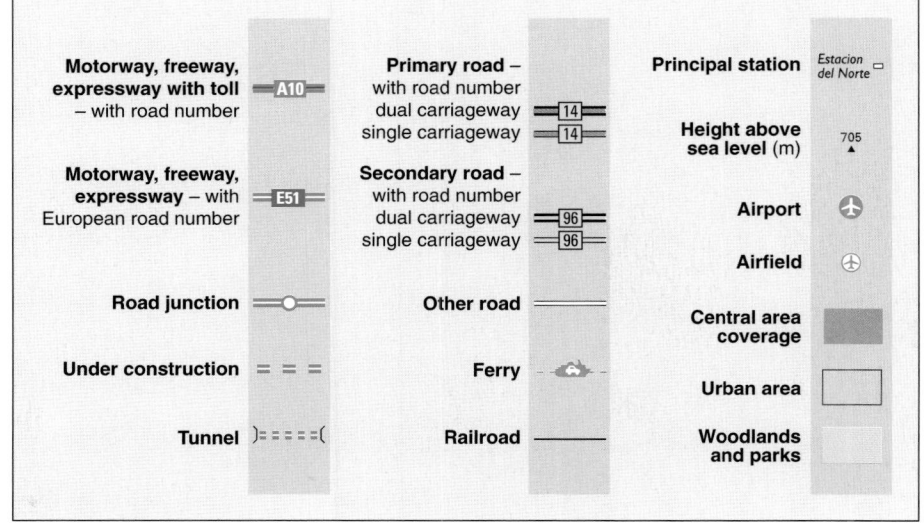

CENTRAL AREA MAPS

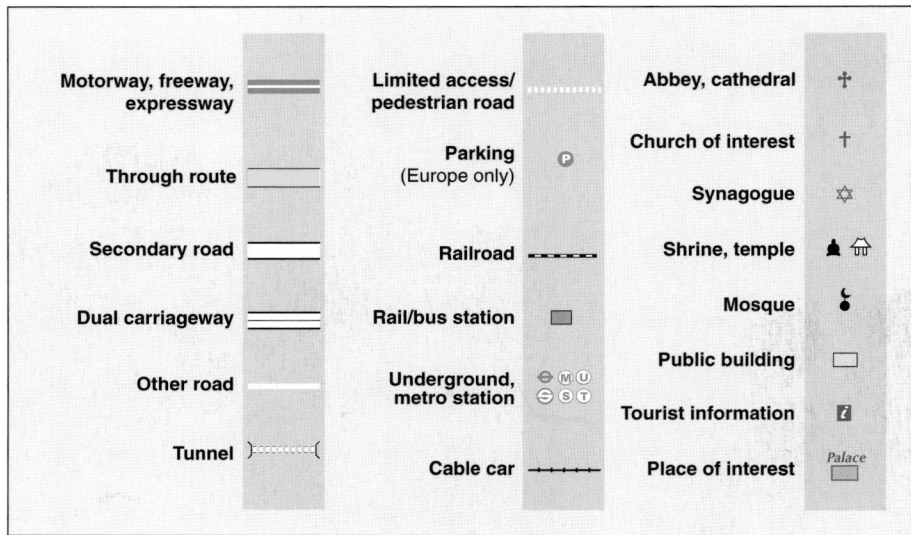

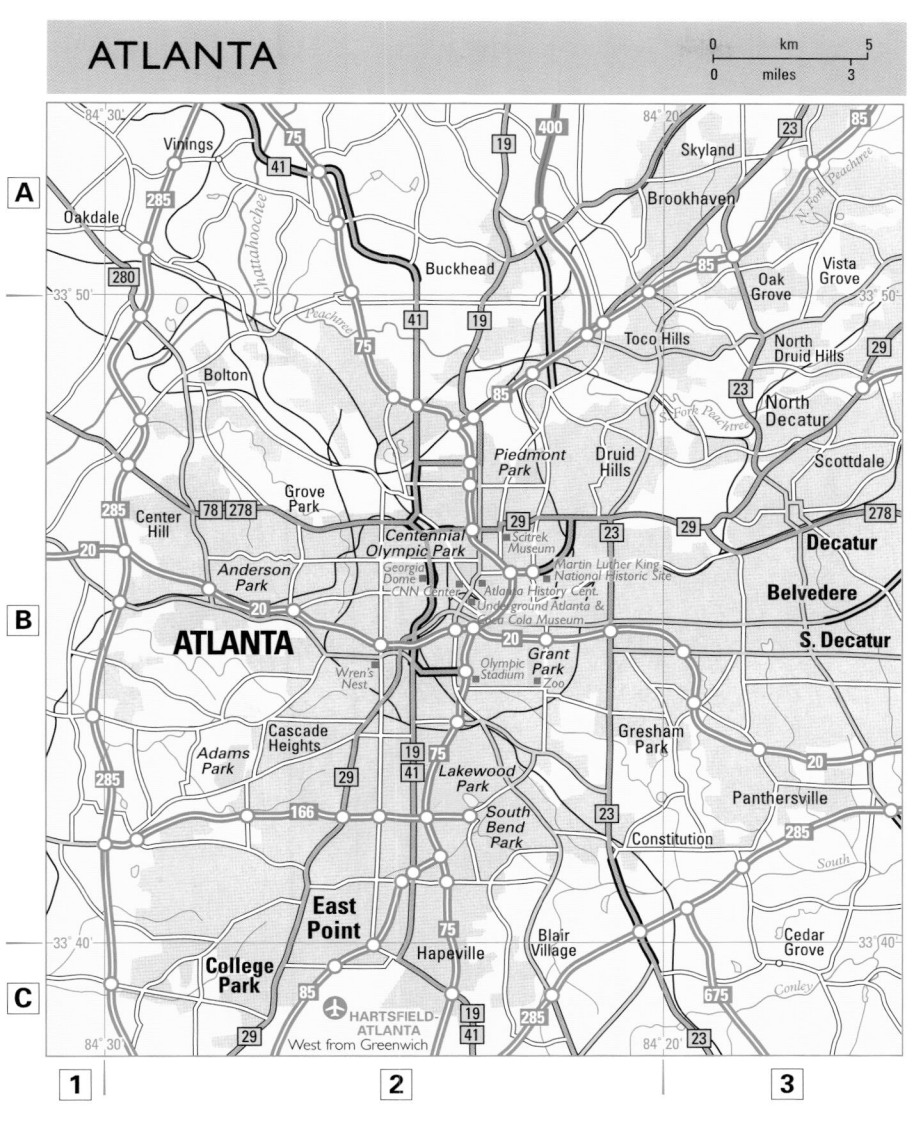

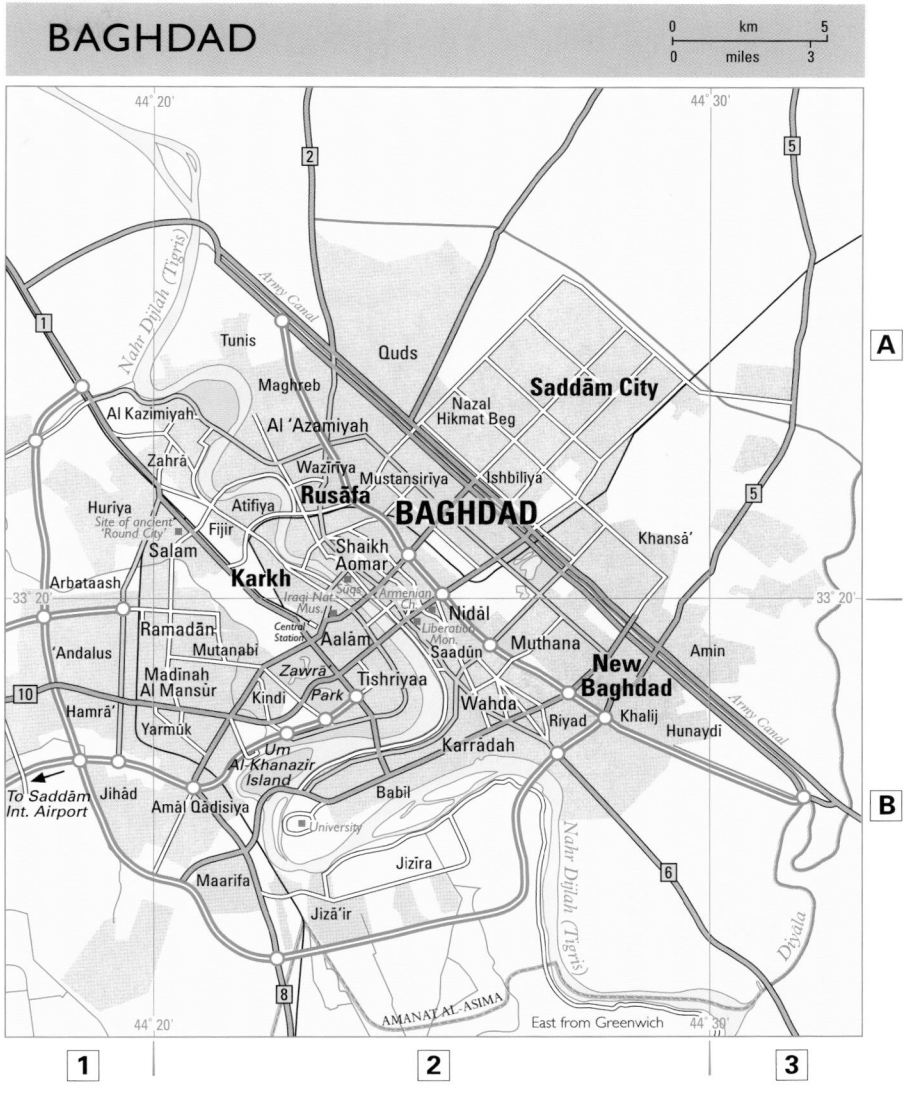

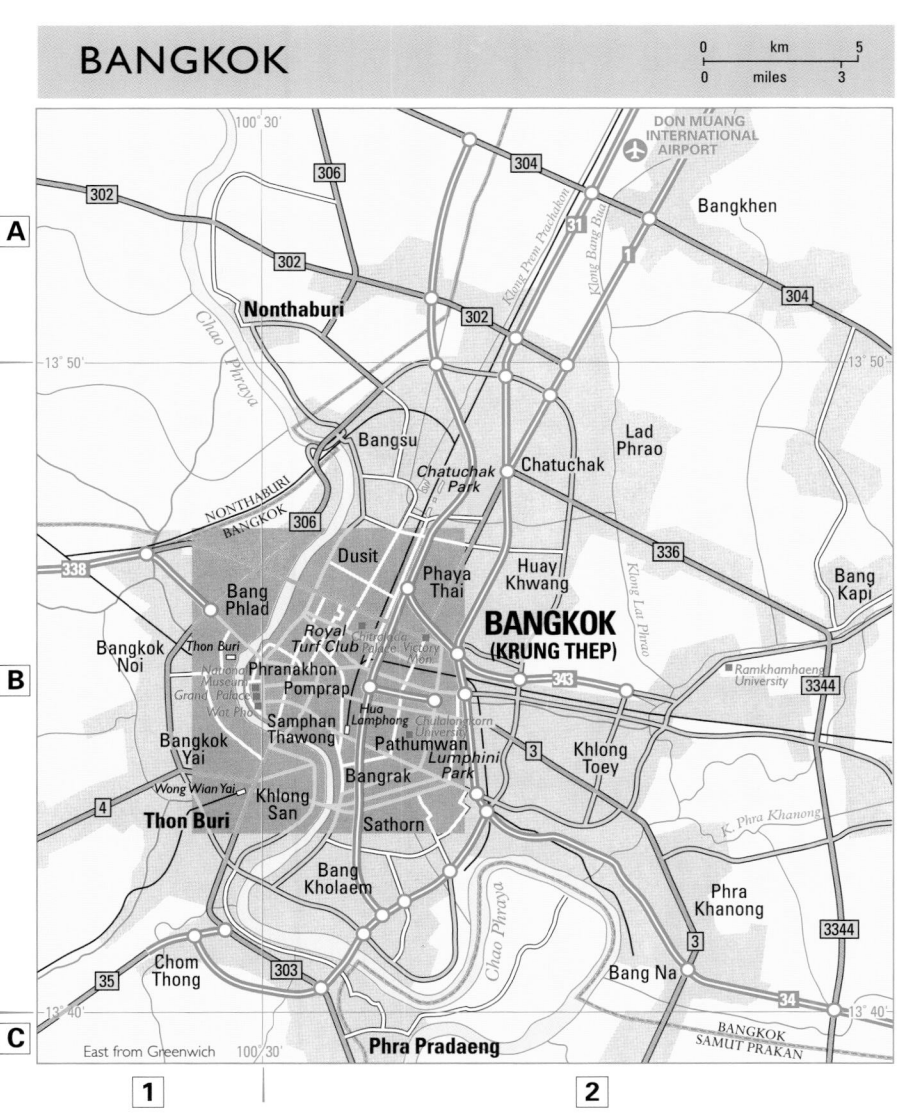

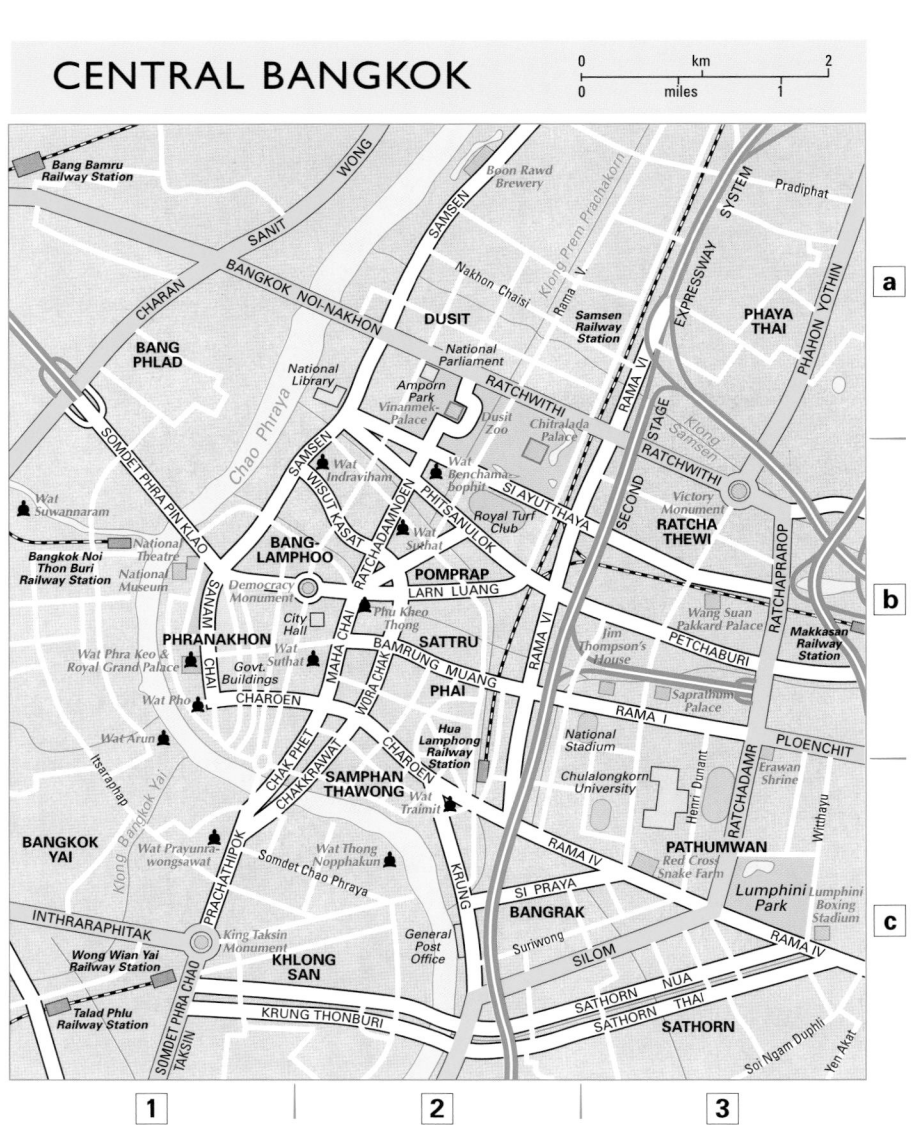

BARCELONA

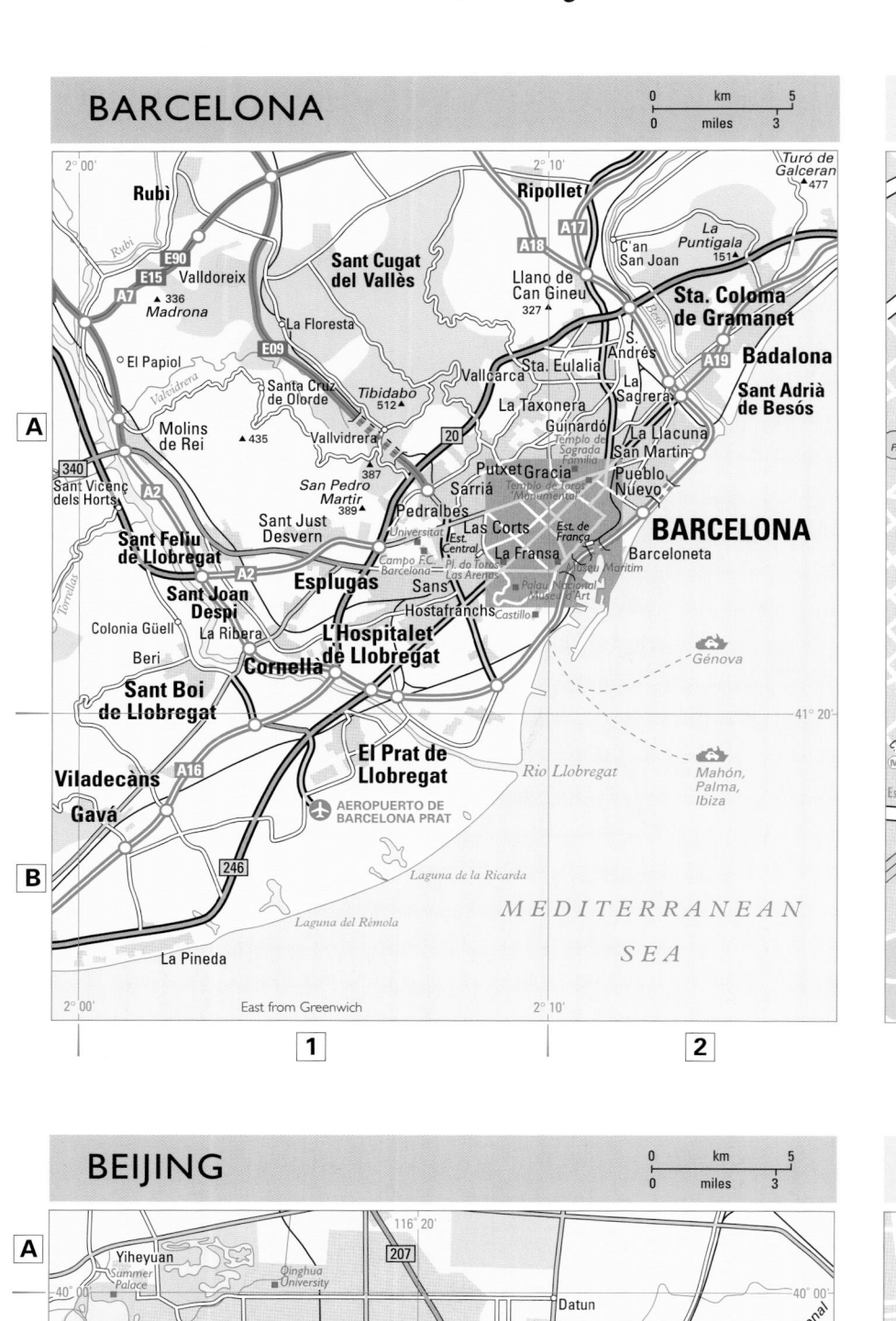

CENTRAL BARCELONA

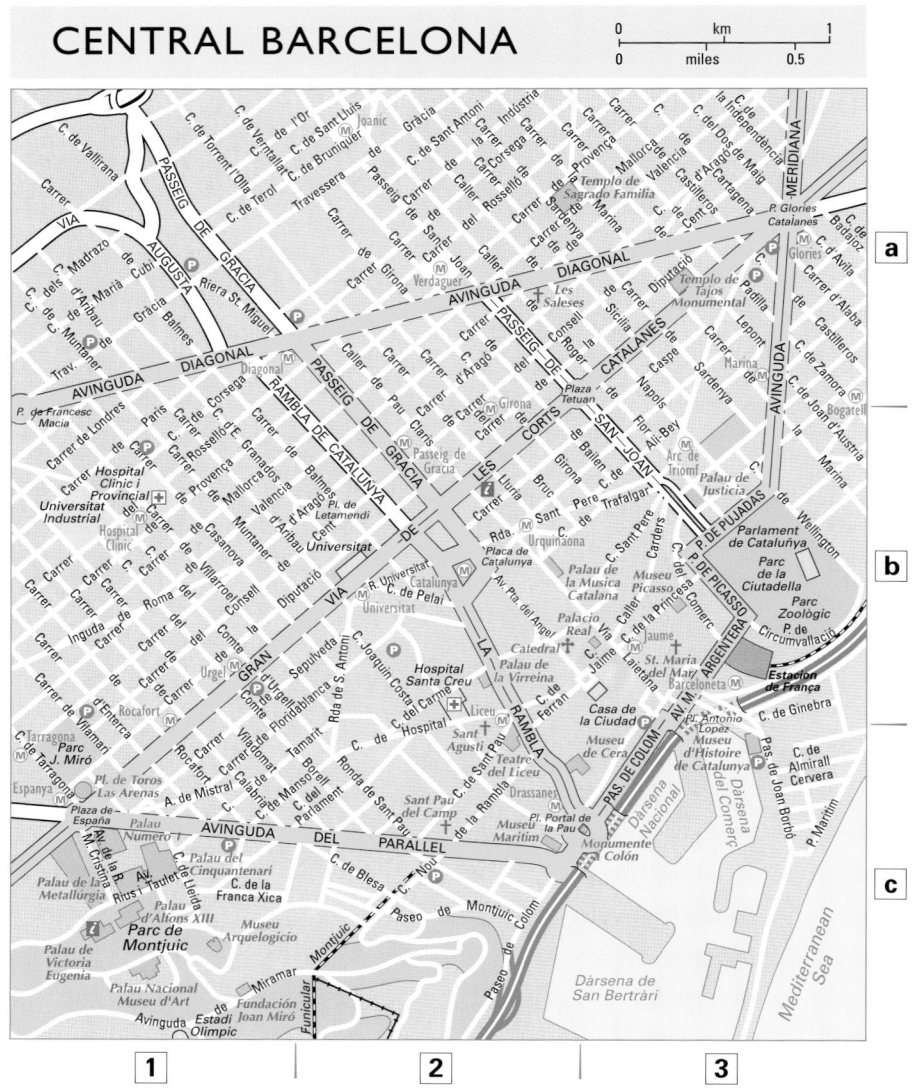

BEIJING

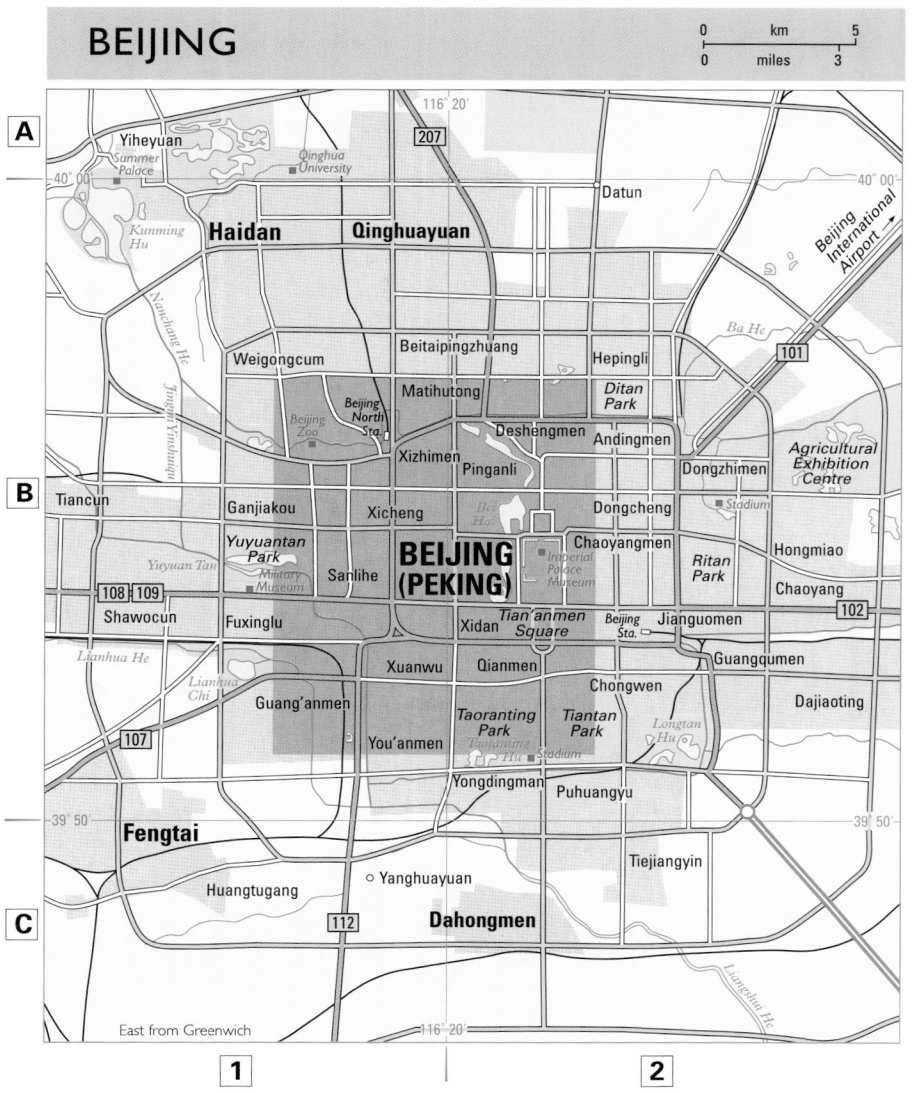

CENTRAL BEIJING

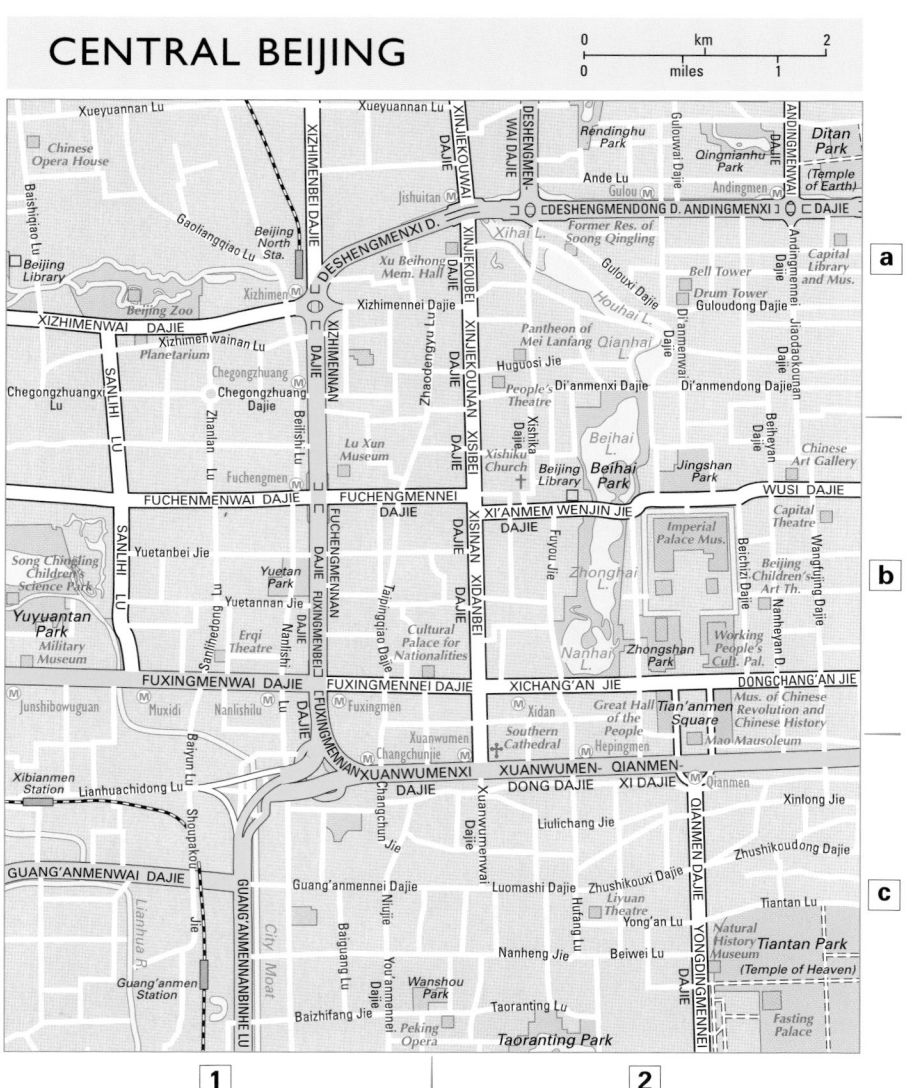

BERLIN

km 5 / miles 3

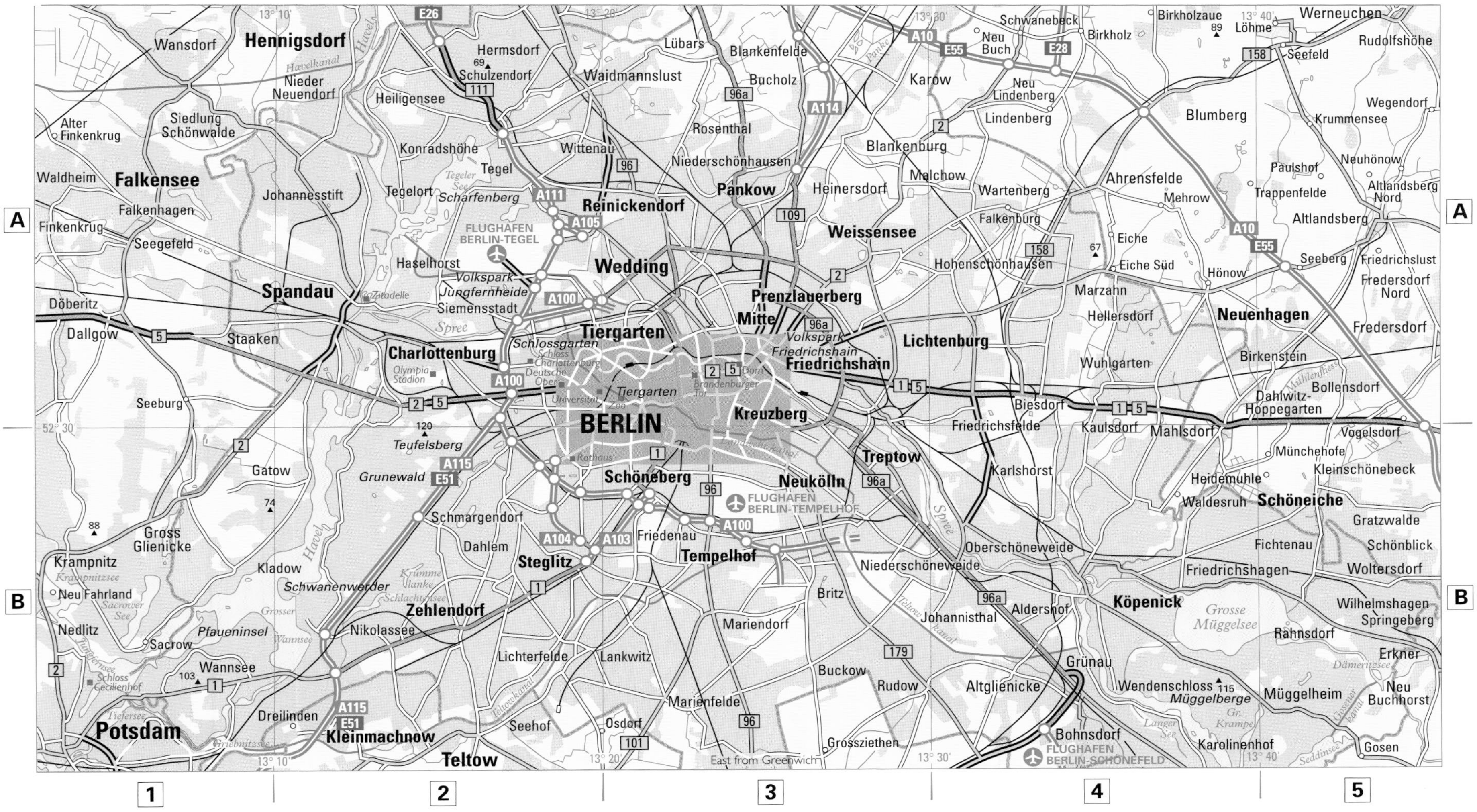

Wansdorf • Hennigsdorf • Hermsdorf • Schulzendorf • Lübars • Blankenfelde • Schwanebeck • Birkholzaue • Werneuchen • Rudolfshöhe
Niederneuendorf • Heiligensee • Waidmannslust • Bucholz • Neu Buch • Birkholz • Löhme • Seefeld
Alter Finkenkrug • Siedlung Schönwalde • Johannesstift • Tegel • Tegelort • Scharfenberg • Wittenau • Niederschönhausen • Rosenthal • Karow • Neu Lindenberg • Lindenberg • Blumberg • Krummensee • Wegendorf
Waldheim • **Falkensee** • Falkenhagen • Konradshöhe • Haselhorst • **Reinickendorf** • **Pankow** • Blankenburg • Heinersdorf • Melchow • Wartenberg • Ahrensfelde • Mehrow • Trappenfelde • Altlandsberg Nord • Neuhönow • Paulshof
Finkenkrug • Seegefeld • FLUGHAFEN BERLIN-TEGEL • Volkspark Jungfernheide • **Wedding** • **Weissensee** • Falkenberg • Hohenschönhausen • Eiche • Eiche Süd • Seeberg • Friedrichslust • Altlandsberg
Spandau • Staaken • Siemensstadt • **Tiergarten** • **Mitte** • **Prenzlauerberg** • Marzahn • Hellersdorf • **Neuenhagen** • Fredersdorf
Dallgow • Zitadelle • **Charlottenburg** • Schlossgarten • **Friedrichshain** • **Lichtenburg** • Wuhlgarten • Birkenstein • Bollensdorf
Döberitz • Olympia Stadion • Deutsche Oper • **BERLIN** • **Kreuzberg** • Biesdorf • Dahlwitz-Hoppegarten
Seeburg • Teufelsberg • Rathaus • Friedrichsfelde • Kaulsdorf • Mahlsdorf • Vogelsdorf
Krampnitz • Gatow • Grunewald • **Schöneberg** • **Neukölln** • **Treptow** • Karlshorst • Münchehofe • Kleinschönebeck
Gross Glienicke • Schmargendorf • Dahlem • Friedenau • FLUGHAFEN BERLIN-TEMPELHOF • Heidemühle • Waldesruh • **Schöneiche** • Gratzwalde
Neu Fahrland • Kladow • Schwanenwerder • **Steglitz** • **Tempelhof** • Niederschöneweide • Oberschöneweide • Fichtenau • Schönblick
Nedlitz • Sacrow • Nikolassee • **Zehlendorf** • Lichterfelde • Britz • Johannisthal • Aldershof • **Köpenick** • Grosse Müggelsee • Wilhelmshagen Springeberg
Sacrow • Wannsee • Lankwitz • Mariendorf • Buckow • Grünau • Wendenschloss • Müggelberge • Rahnsdorf • Erkner
Potsdam • Dreilinden • **Kleinmachnow** • Seehof • Osdorf • Marienfelde • Rudow • Altglienicke • Bohnsdorf • Müggelheim • Neu Buchhorst
Teltow • Grossziethen • FLUGHAFEN BERLIN-SCHÖNEFELD • Karolinenhof • Gosen

CENTRAL BERLIN

km 1 / miles 0.5

CHARLOTTENBURG • **TIERGARTEN** • **MITTE** • Hansatheater • Moabit • Bellevue • Schloss Bellevue • Reichstag • Brandenburger Tor • UNTER DEN LINDEN • Alexanderplatz • **KREUZBERG** • **WILMERSDORF** • Zoologischer Garten • Kaiser Wilhelm Kirche • KURFÜRSTENDAMM • TAUENTZIEN STR • Potsdamer Pl. • Anhalter Bf. • YORCKSTRASSE • GNEISENAU STRASSE • HASEN HEIDE

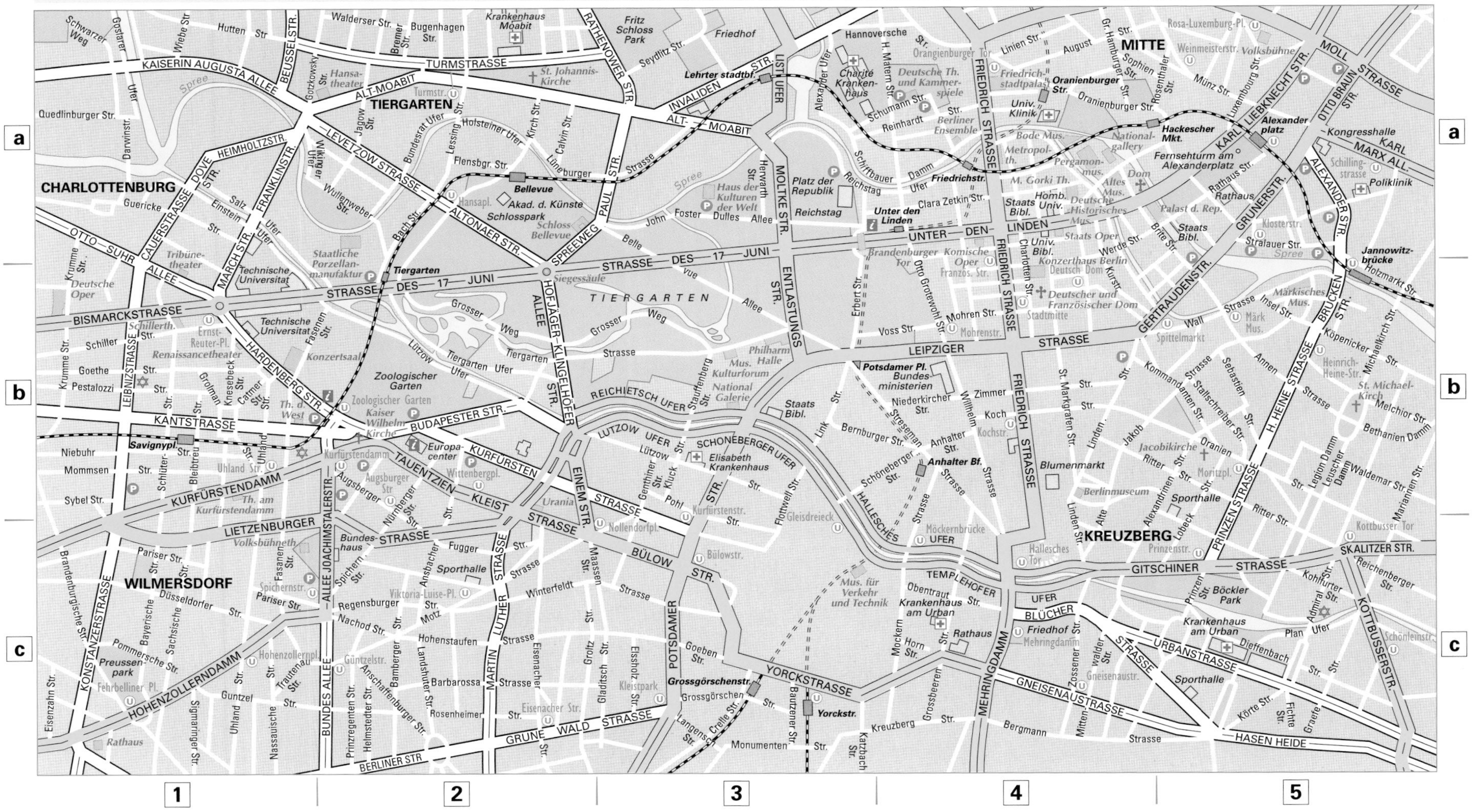

COPYRIGHT PHILIP'S

BOSTON

km 0 — 5
miles 0 — 3

Great Meadows Nat. Wildlife Refuge
Bedford
Burlington
Wakefield
Marblehead
East Acton
West Bedford
North Saugus
Breakheart Reservation
Greenwood
Clifton
Woburn
Stoneham
LAURENCE G. HANSCOM FIELD
Concord
North Lexington
Walter D. Stone Mem. Zoo
Lynn
Swampscott
West Concord
Fairhaven Hill
Minute Man Natural History Park
Winchester
Saugus
West Lynn
Lincoln
North Lexington
Middlesex Fells Reservation
Melrose
Cliftondale
Lynn Harbor
ATLANTIC OCEAN
Fairhaven Bay
Sandy Pond
Lexington
East Lexington
114
Arlington Heights
West Medford
Mt. Hood Mem. Park
Malden
Nahant
Nahant Bay
North Sudbury
South Lincoln
Cambridge Reservoir
Arlington
East Arlington
Medford
Revere
East Point
Sudbury
Silver Hill
Prospect Hill Park
Belmont
Waverley
Tufts Univ.
Wellington
Everett
Beachmont
Nahant Harbor
Goodman Hill
Kendall Green
Waltham
Fresh Pond
Harvard University
Charlestown
Chelsea
Orient Heights
Broad Sound
ESSEX SUFFOLK
Wayland
Weston
Watertown
Radcliffe Coll.
Somerville
East Boston
Winthrop
Reeves Hill
Weston Reservoir
Auburndale
Brandeis Univ.
Charles R.
Cambridge
Mass. Inst. of Tech.
Bunker Hill
Massachusetts Bay
South Sudbury
Heard Pond
Norumbega Reservoir
Newtonville
Allston
BOSTON
LOGAN INTERNATIONAL AIRPORT
Deer Island
Cochituate
Newton
Brighton
Northeastern Univ.
John F. Kennedy Nat. Hist. Site
Museum of Fine Arts
South Boston
Boston Harbor
Spectacle Island
Saxonville
MIDDLESEX NORFOLK
Chestnut Hill
Brookline
Roxbury
Blake House
Dorchester Hts. Nat. Hist. Site
Old Harbor
Dorchester Bay
Thompson Island
Long Island
Georges Island
Point Allerton
Framingham
Wellesley Falls
Wellesley Hills
Jamaica Plain
Franklin Park
Grove Hall
Fields Corner
Squantum
Quincy Bay
PLYMOUTH NORFOLK
Hingham Bay
Hull
Peddocks Island
Nantasket Beach
Wellesley
Needham Heights
Oak Hill
MIDDLESEX
Roslindale
Dorchester
North Quincy
Grape Island
Natick
Needham
W. Roxbury
Mattapan
Adams Shore
Houghs Neck
North Cohasset
Brush Hill 121
West from Greenwich
Dedham
Stony Brook Res.
Hyde Park
Milton
Quincy
Wollaston
Hingham
Hingham Hark.

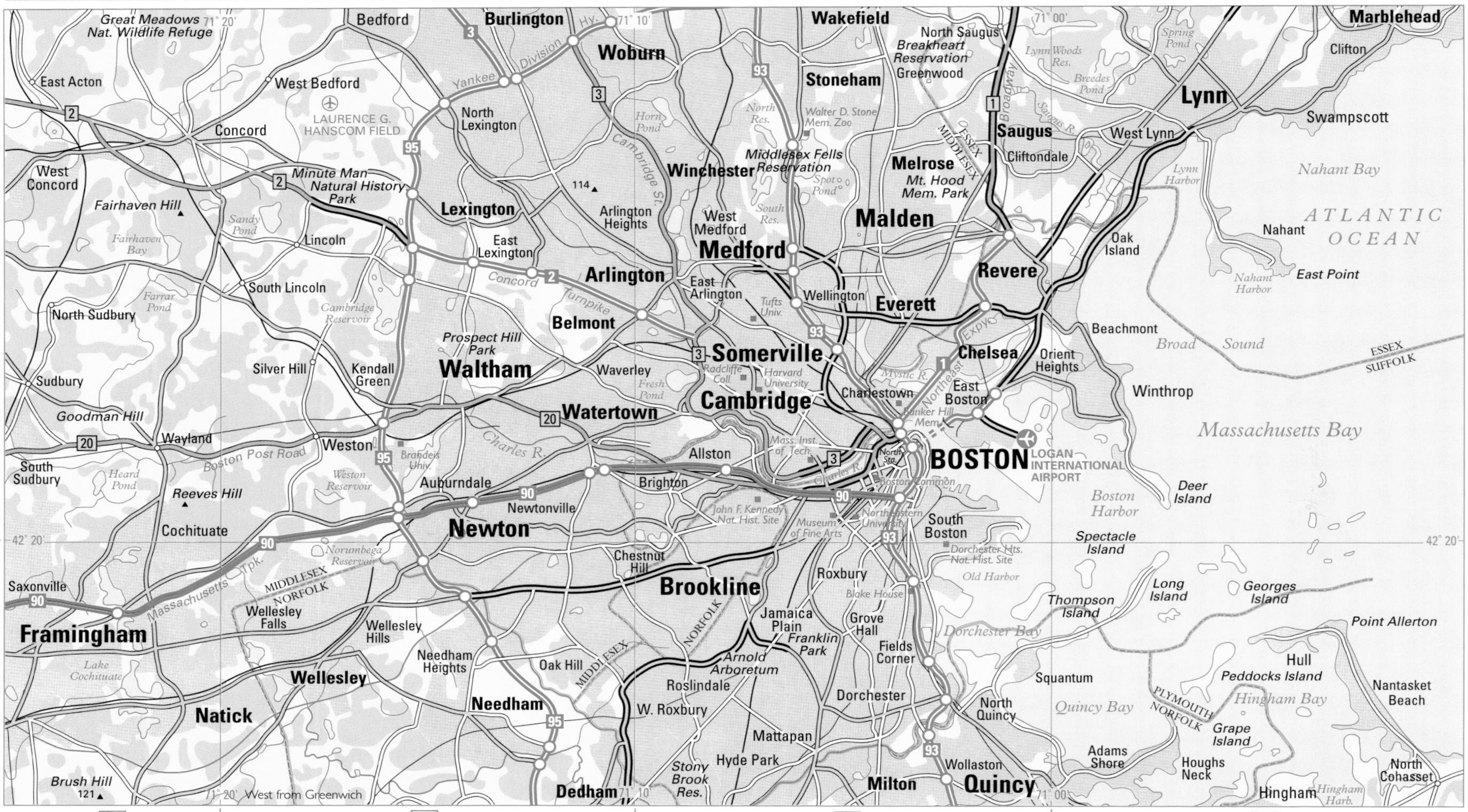

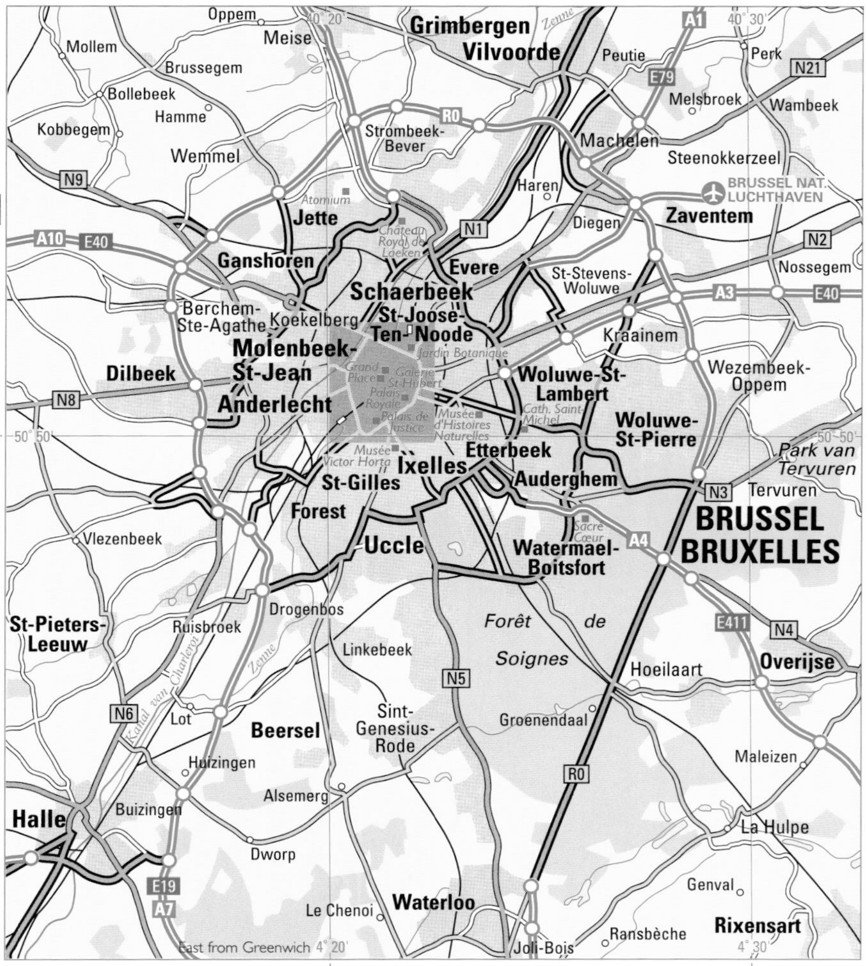

BRUSSELS

km 0 — 5
miles 0 — 3

Oppem
Mollem
Meise
Grimbergen
Vilvoorde
Peutie
Perk
N21
Brussegem
Bollebeek
Hamme
Wemmel
Strombeek-Bever
Machelen
Steenokkerzeel
Kobbegem
N9
Atomium
Haren
BRUSSEL NAT. LUCHTHAVEN
Jette
N1
Diegem
Zaventem
N2
Ganshoren
Evere
St-Stevens-Woluwe
Nossegem
E40
Berchem-Ste-Agathe
Koekelberg
Schaerbeek
St-Joose-Ten-Noode
Jardin Botanique
Kraainem
Molenbeek-St-Jean
Woluwe-St-Lambert
Wezembeek-Oppem
Dilbeek
N8
Anderlecht
Woluwe-St-Pierre
Park van Tervuren
Ixelles
Etterbeek
Auderghem
BRUSSEL BRUXELLES
St-Pieters-Leeuw
St-Gilles
Forest
Tervuren
N3
Uccle
Watermael-Boitsfort
A4
Vlezenbeek
Drogenbos
Forêt de Soignes
E411
N4
Ruisbroek
Linkebeek
Hoeilaart
Overijse
N6
Lot
Huizingen
Sint-Genesius-Rode
Groenendaal
R0
Beersel
Alsemberg
Maleizen
Halle
Buizingen
Dworp
La Hulpe
E19 A7
Waterloo
Genval
Rixensart
East from Greenwich
Le Chenoi
Joli-Bois
Ransbèche

CENTRAL BRUSSELS

km 0 — 1
miles 0 — 0.5

Gare du Nord
Parc Maximilian
Ste-Marie
Jardin Botanique
CH. DE GAND GENTSE
NIEUPORT STEENWEG
ANTOINE DANSAERT
Place Ste-Catherine
Poste Centrale
Cité Administrative
Place Quetelet
Bourse
ANSPACH
Théâtre de la Monnaie
Colonne du Congrès
Cirque Royale
CHAUSSÉE DE NINOVE
Grand Place
Galerie St. Hubert
Banque Nationale
Croix de Fer
CHAUSSÉE
Institut des Arts et Métiers
Rue de Fabriques
Parlement Flamand
Palais de la Nation Arts-Loi
Hôtel de Ville
Musée Communale
Gare Centrale
Palais des Beaux-Arts
AVENUE DES ARTS
RUE DE LA LOI
CHAUSSÉE DE MONS
Manneken-Pis
Académie des Beaux-Arts
Théâtre du Parc
Parc de Bruxelles
BELLIARD
Notre-Dame du Midi
Palais Albert I d'Art
Notre-Dame du Sablon
Palais Royale
Trône
BOULEVARD DU MIDI
Palais de Justice
Jardin d'Egmont
Porte de Namur
Luxembourg
Gare du Midi (Eurostar)
Hôpital St-Pierre
Hotel des Monnaies
AVENUE DE LA TOISON D'OR
LOUISE
Musée Ixelles
AVENUE DE LA PORTE DE HAL
ST-GILLES
IXELLES
Pl. Fernand Cocq

COPYRIGHT PHILIP'S

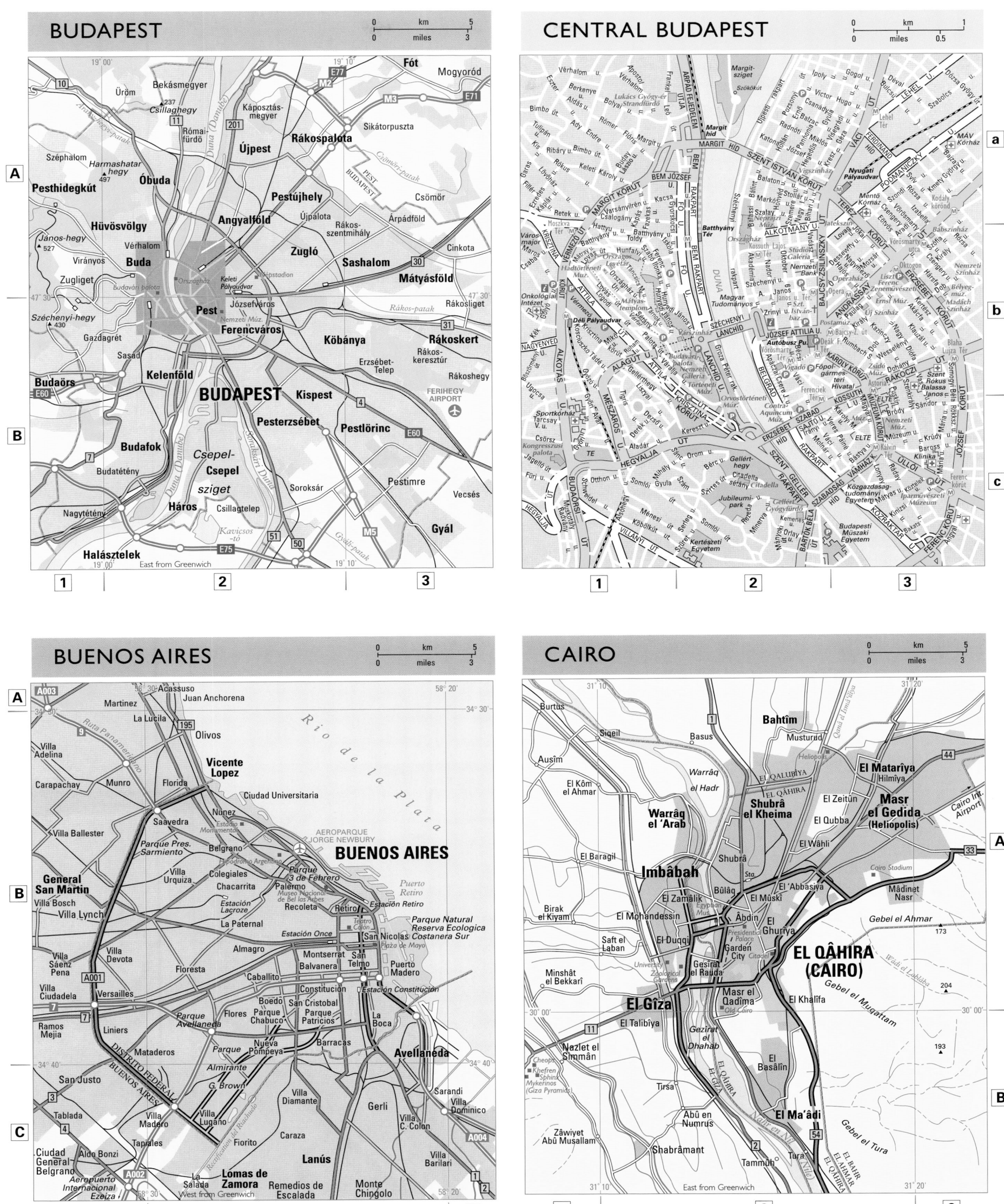

BUDAPEST

km 0 — 5
miles 0 — 3

10
Üröm
Békásmegyer
237
Csillaghegy
11
Fót
Mogyoród
M2
E77
Káposztás-
megyer
201
Rómaifürdő
Sikátorpuszta
M3
E71
Rákospalota
Széphalom
Harmashatár-
hegy 497
Újpest
Pesthidegkút
Óbuda
Pestújhely
Angyalföld
Úipalota
Rákos-
szentmihály
Árpádföld
Csömör
Hüvösvölgy
János-hegy 527
Vérhalom
Zugló
Sashalom
Cinkota
Virányos
Buda
Rákos-patak
Mátyásföld
Zugliget
Budavári palota
Orszagház
Keleti
Pályaudvar
Népstadion
Széchenyi-hegy 430
Pest
Józsefváros
Rákos-patak
Rákosliget
Gazdagrét
Nemzeti Múz.
Ferencváros
30
Budaörs
Sasad
Kelenföld
Köbánya
Erzsébet-
Telep
Rákoskert
Rákos-
keresztúr
Rákoshegy
E60
BUDAPEST
Kispest
4
FERIHEGY
AIRPORT
Budafok
Pesterzsébet
Pestlörinc
E60
Budatétény
Csepel-
Csepel
sziget
Soroksár
Pestimre
Vecsés
7
Nagytétény
Háros
Csillagtelep
M5
Gyál
Halásztelek
51
50
E75
East from Greenwich

CENTRAL BUDAPEST

km 0 — 1
miles 0 — 0.5

BUENOS AIRES

km 0 — 5
miles 0 — 3

A003
Acassuso
Juan Anchorena
Martinez
58° 30'
58° 20'
La Lucila
34° 30'
9
195
Olivos
Villa
Adelina
Vicente
Lopez
Carapachay
Munro
Florida
Ciudad Universitaria
Río de la Plata
Villa
Ballester
Saavedra
Núñez
Parque Pres.
Sarmiento
Belgrano
Estadio
Monumental
Aeroparque
2 Jorge Newbury
General
San Martin
Villa
Urquiza
Colegiales
Hipódromo Argentino
BUENOS AIRES
Villa Bosch
Villa Lynch
Chacarrita
Palermo
Parque
3 de Febrero
Museo Nacional
de Bel las Artes
Puerto
Retiro
Villa
Sáenz
Peña
Villa
Devota
Estación
Lacroze
La Paternal
Recoleta
Retiro
Estación Retiro
Parque Natural
Reserva Ecológica
Villa
Ciudadela
A001
Almagro
Estación Once
Teatro
Colón
Plaza de Mayo
Puerto
Madero
Versailles
Caballito
Montserrat
Balvanera
San Nicolas
San Telmo
7
Parque
Avellaneda
Flores
Boedo
Parque
Chacabuco
Parque
Patricios
La Boca
Ramos
Mejia
Liniers
Constitución
Estación Constitución
San Cristobal
Matadeiros
DISTRITO FEDERAL
BUENOS AIRES
Nuéva
Pompeya
Barracas
Avellaneda
34° 40'
34° 40'
San Justo
3
Almirante
G. Brown
Parque
Villa
Lugáno
Villa
Diamante
Gerli
Sarandi
Villa
Dominico
4
Tablada
Villa
Madero
Fiorito
Caraza
Villa
C. Colon
Villa
Barilari
1
Ciudad
General
Belgrano
Aldo Bonzi
Tapiales
Lanús
Monte
Chingolo
2
Aeropuerto
Internacional
Ezeiza
A002
La
Salada
Lomas de
Zamora
Remedios de
Escalada
58° 20'
West from Greenwich
58° 30'

CAIRO

km 0 — 5
miles 0 — 3

Burtus
31° 10'
1
Bahtîm
Musturud
31° 20'
Siqeil
Basus
Heliopolis
Ausîm
Warrâq
el Hadr
EL QALUBIYA
44
El Kôm
el Ahmar
EL QÂHIRA
El Zeitûn
El Matarîya
Hilmîya
Cairo Int.
Airport
Warrâq
el 'Arab
Shubrâ
el Kheima
El Qubba
Masr
el Gedida
(Heliópolis)
El Baragil
Shubrâ
El Wâhli
33
A
Imbâbah
Bûlâq
El 'Abbasîya
Cairo Stadium
Mâdinet
Nasr
Birak
el Kiyam
El Zamâlik
Egyptian Mus.
El Mûski
Gebel el Ahmar
173
Saft el
Laban
El Mohandessin
El Duqqi
Âbdin
El
Ghurîya
Presidential
Palace
EL QÂHIRA
(CAIRO)
Gebel el Muqattam
Minshât
el Bekkarî
University
Gesira
el Rauda
Garden
City
Citadel
Masr el
Qadîma
204
El Gîza
El Talibîya
Old Cairo
El Khalîfa
Gezîrat
el Dhahab
Masr el
Qadîma
193
30° 00'
11
Nazlet el
Simmân
El
Basâlîn
B
Cheops
Khefren
Sphinx
Mykerinos
(Giza Pyramids)
Tirsa
Zâwiyet
Abû Musallam
Abû en
Numrus
El Ma'âdi
Gebel el Tura
Shabrâmant
Tammûh
54
Tura
31° 10'
East from Greenwich
31° 20'

COPYRIGHT PHILIP'S

CALCUTTA (KOLKATA)

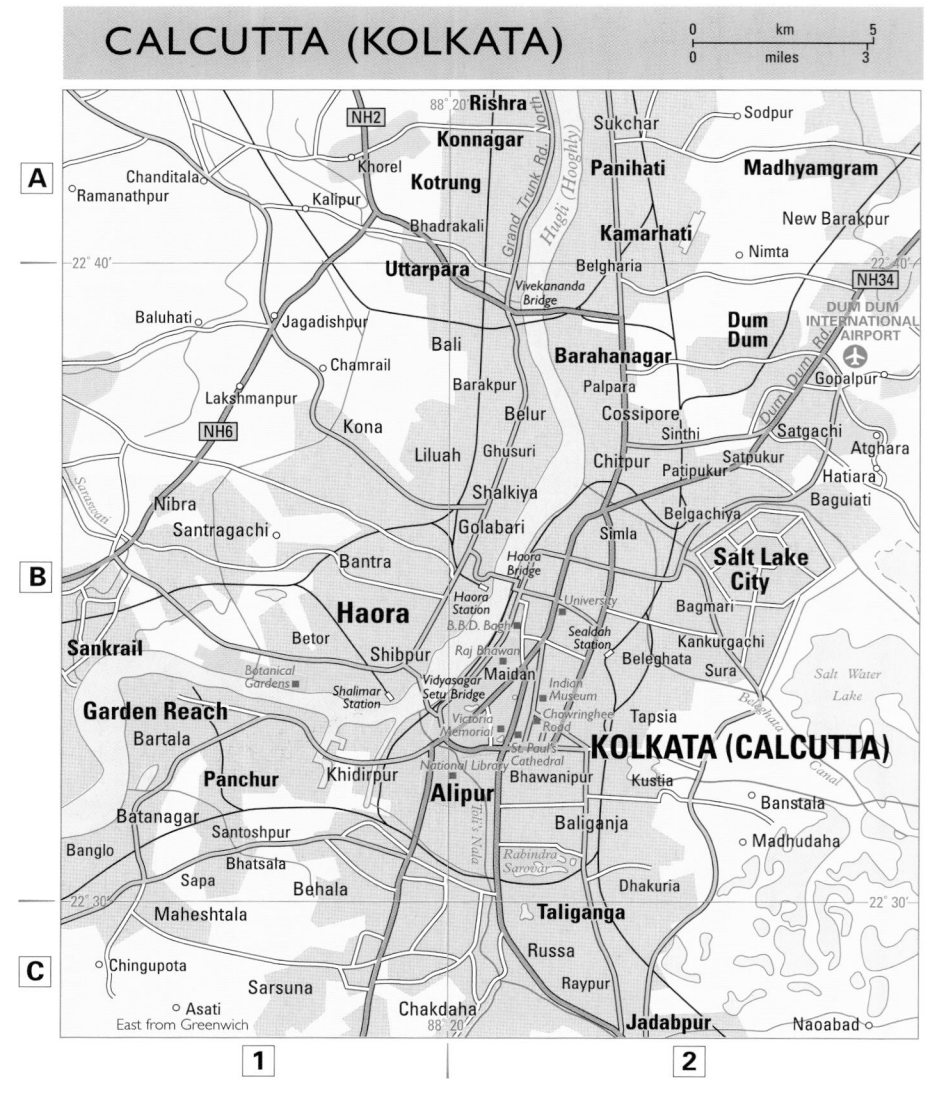

CANTON

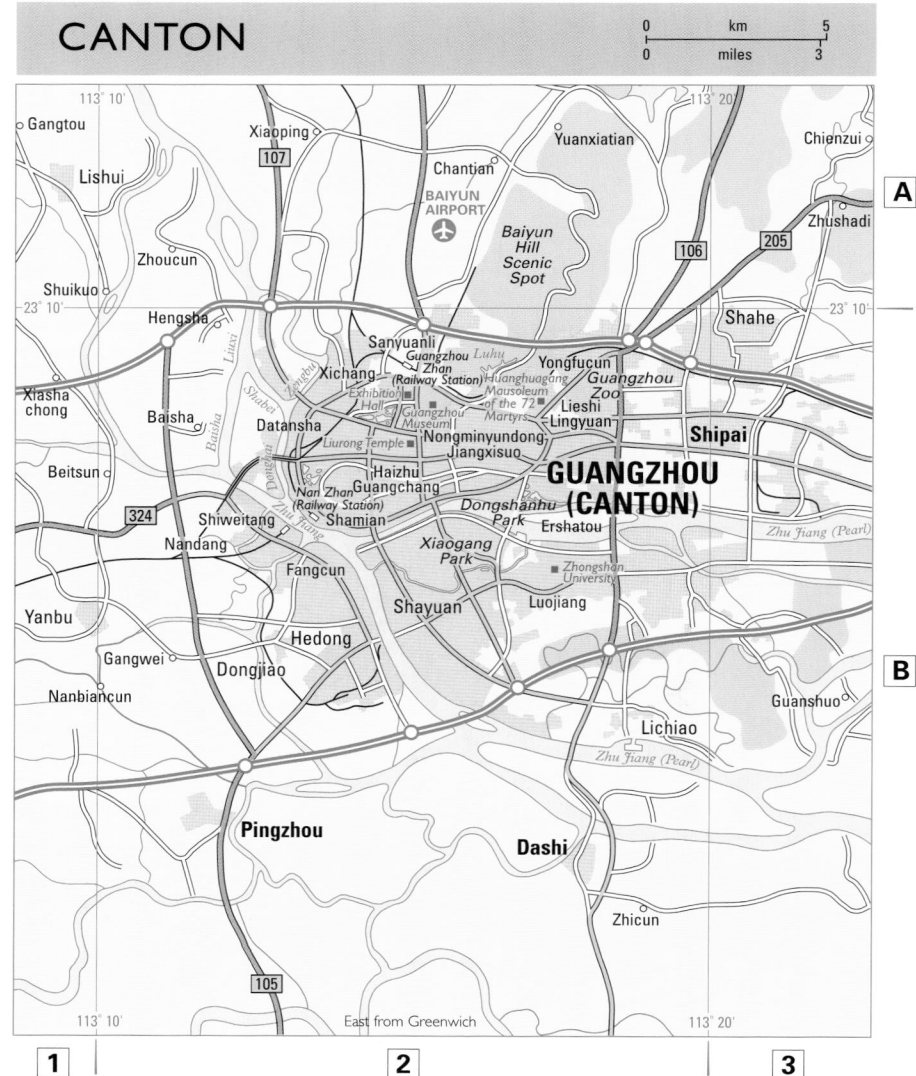

CAPE TOWN

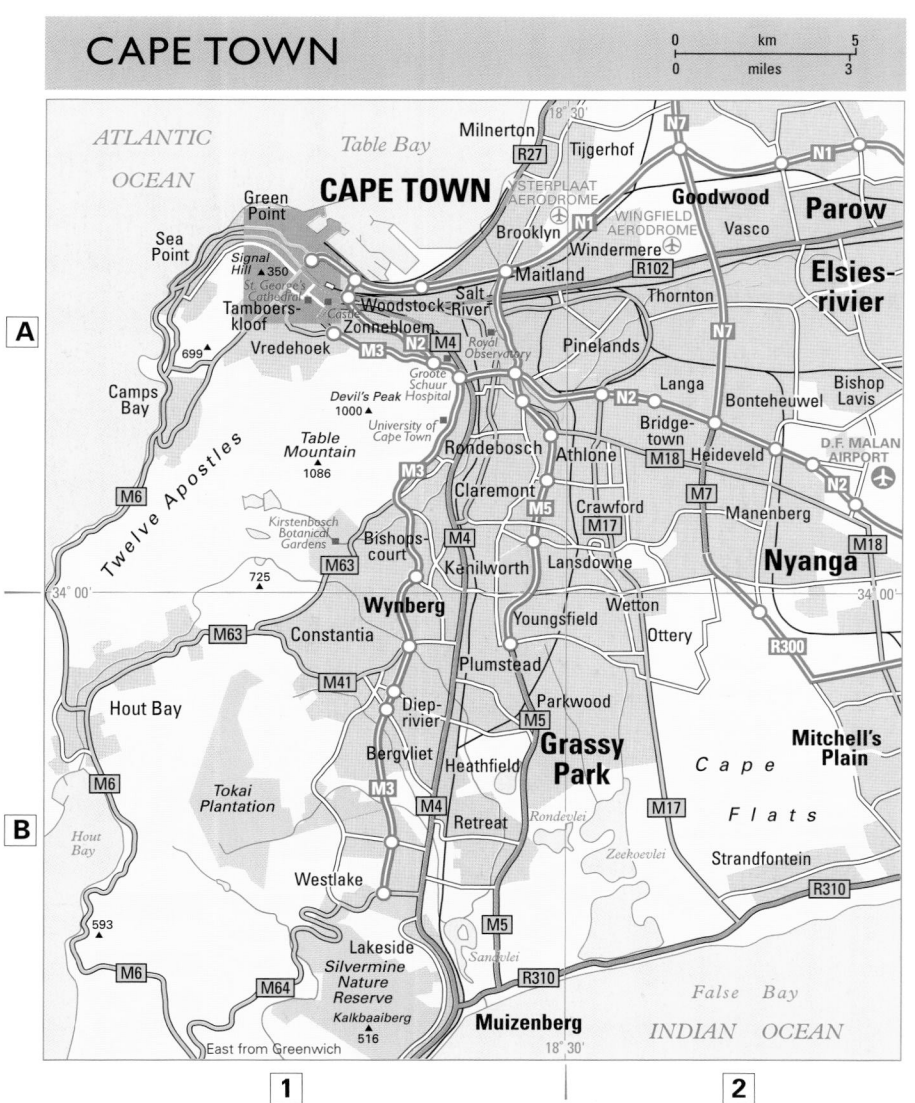

CENTRAL CAPE TOWN

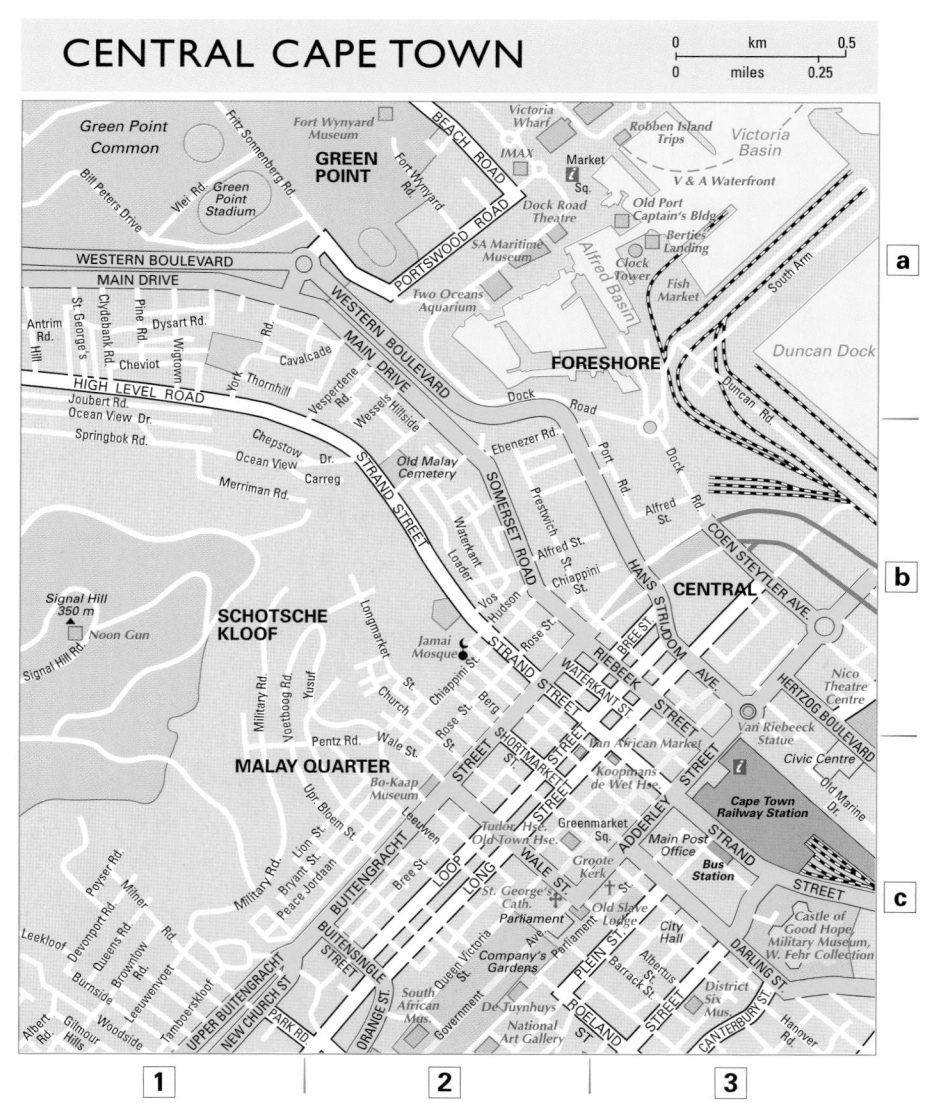

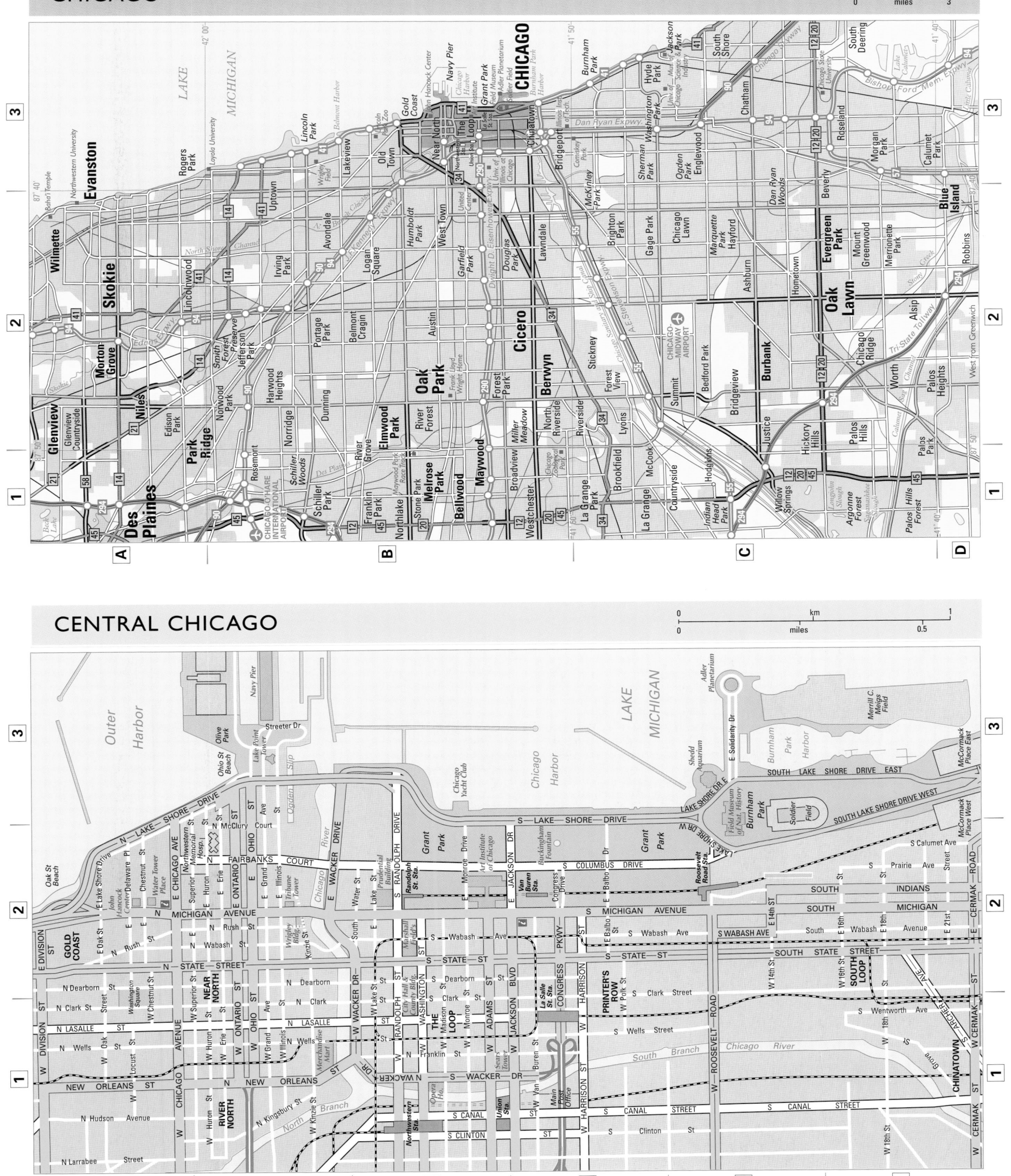

CHICAGO

km 0 — 5
miles 0 — 3

CENTRAL CHICAGO

km 0 — 1
miles 0 — 0.5

COPYRIGHT PHILIP'S

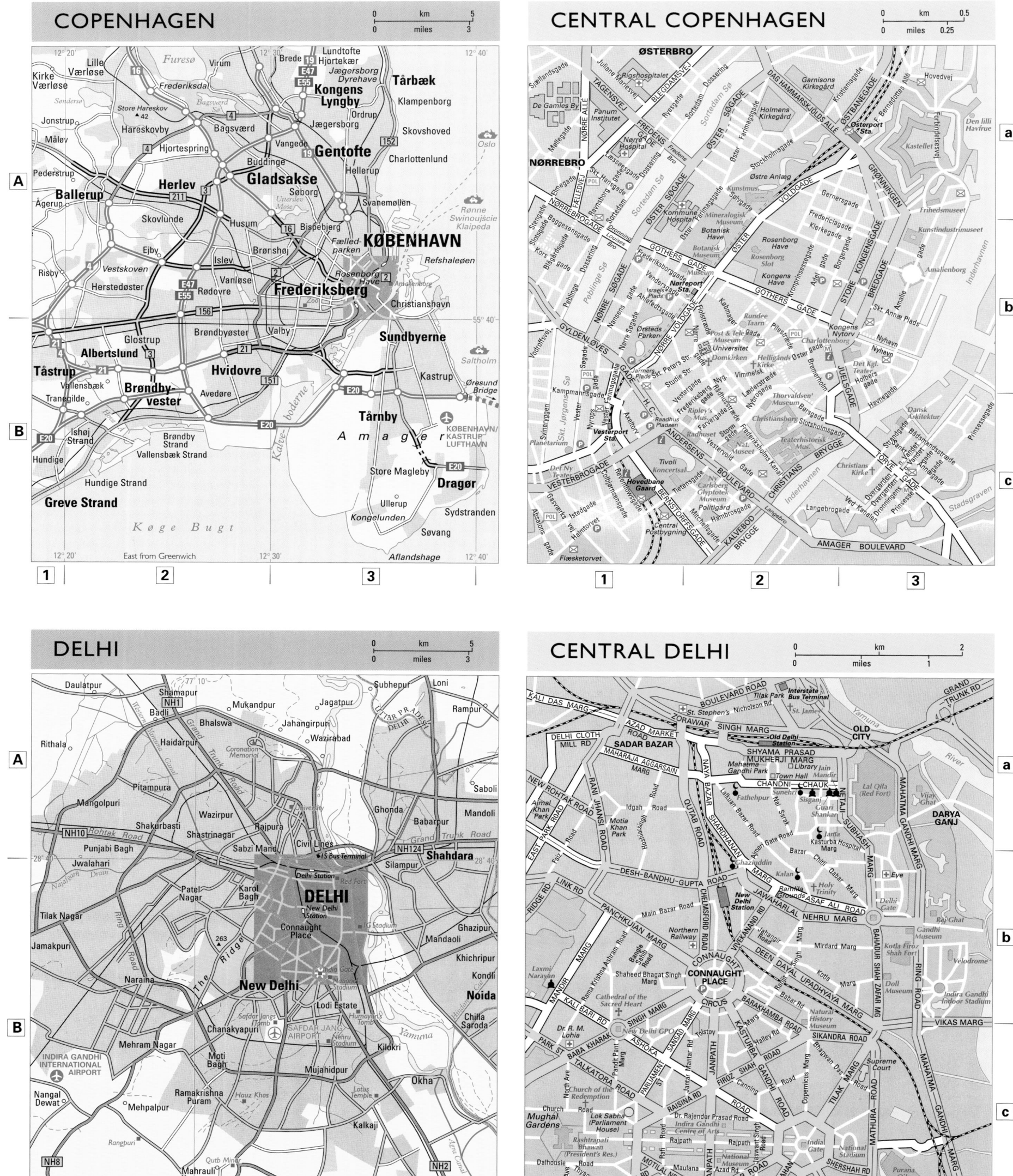

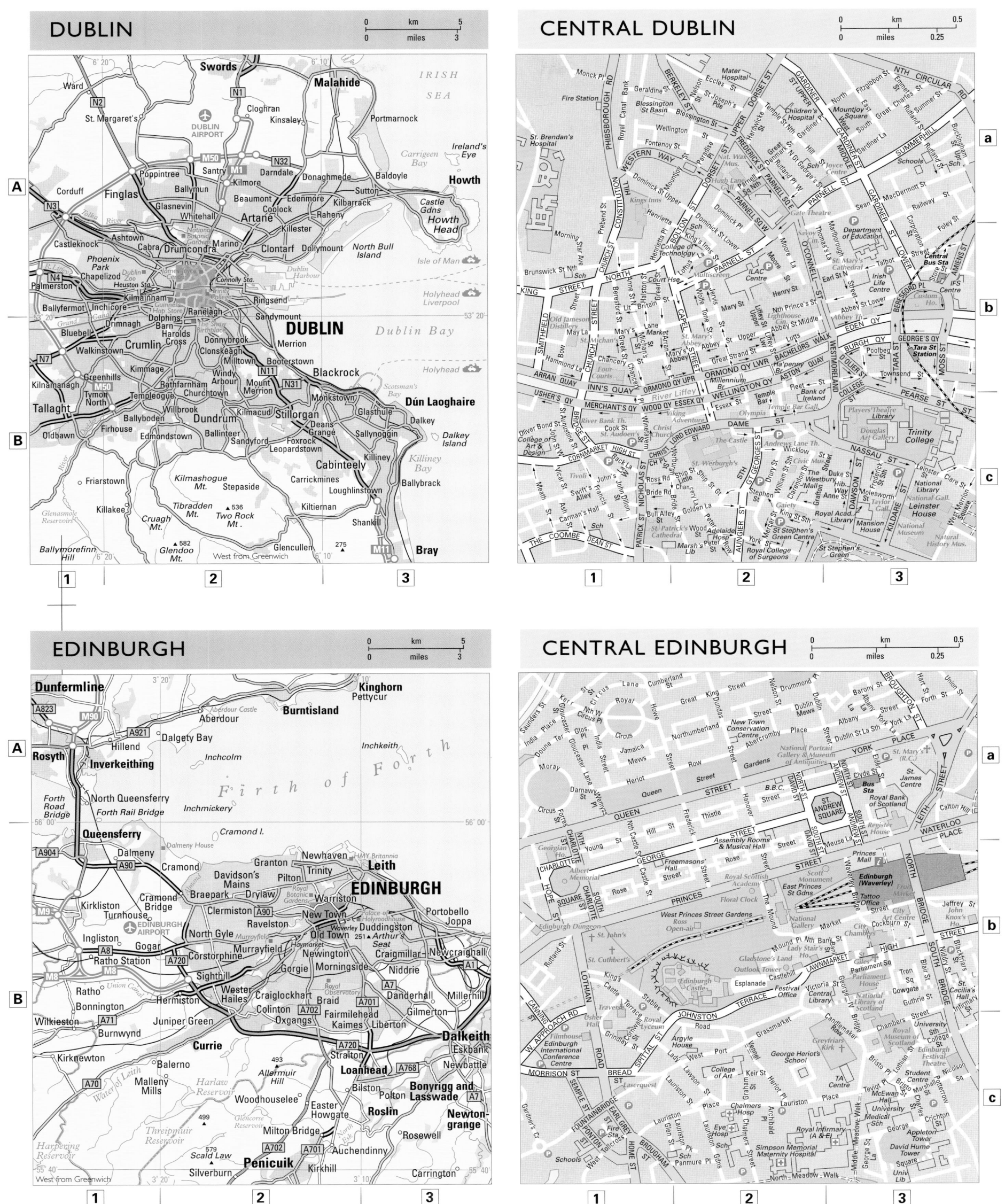

HELSINKI

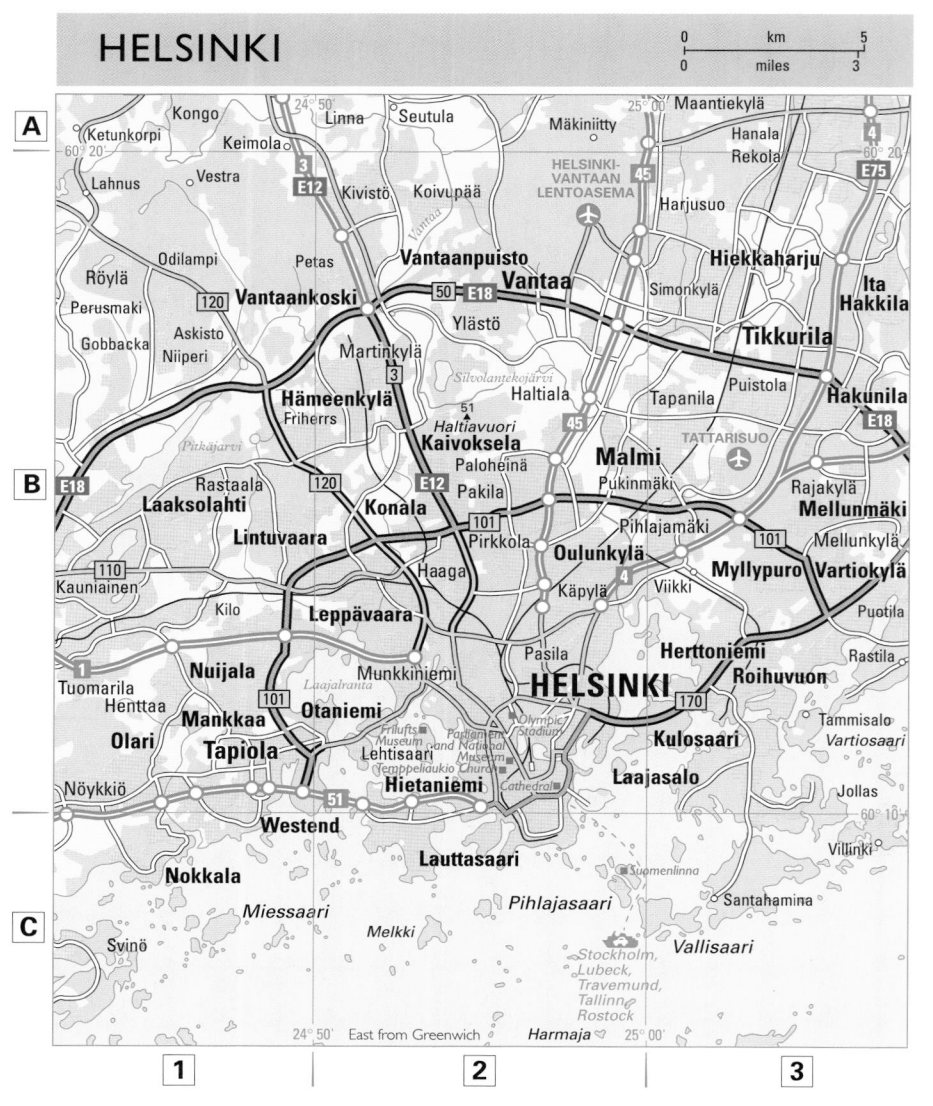

ISTANBUL

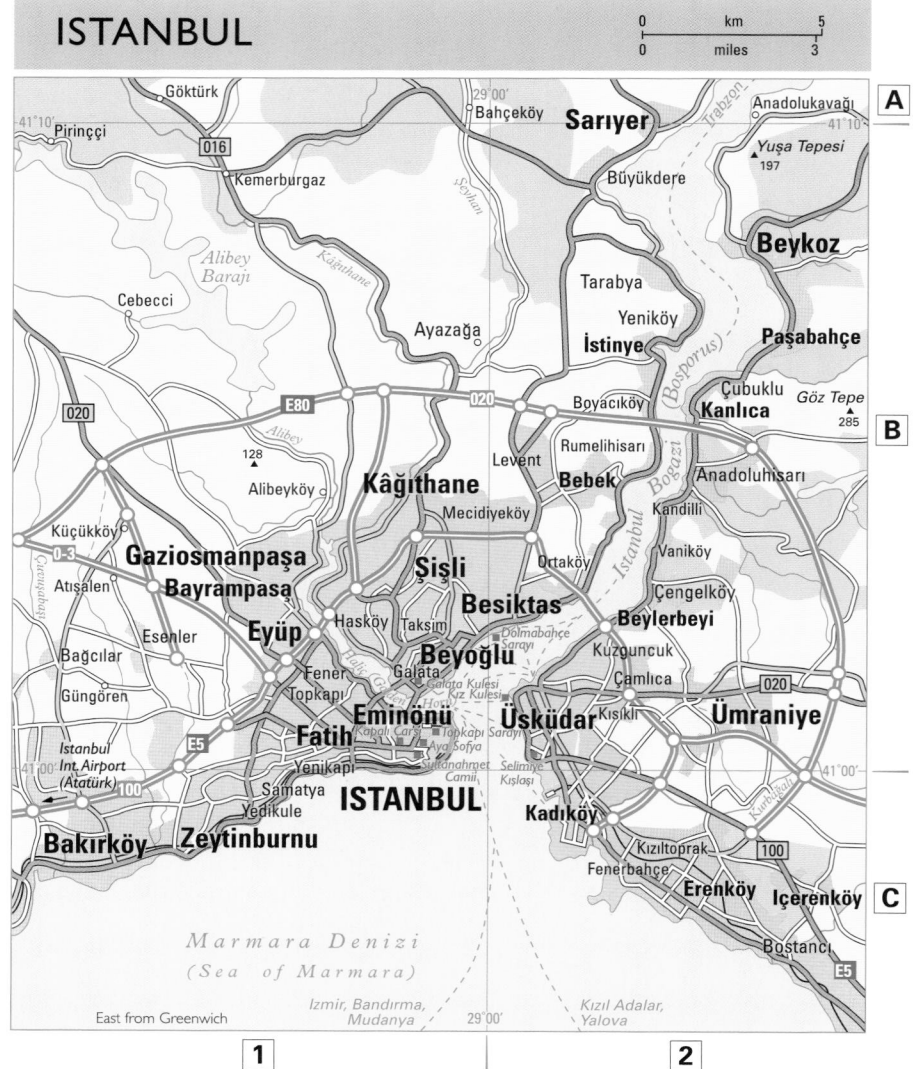

HONG KONG

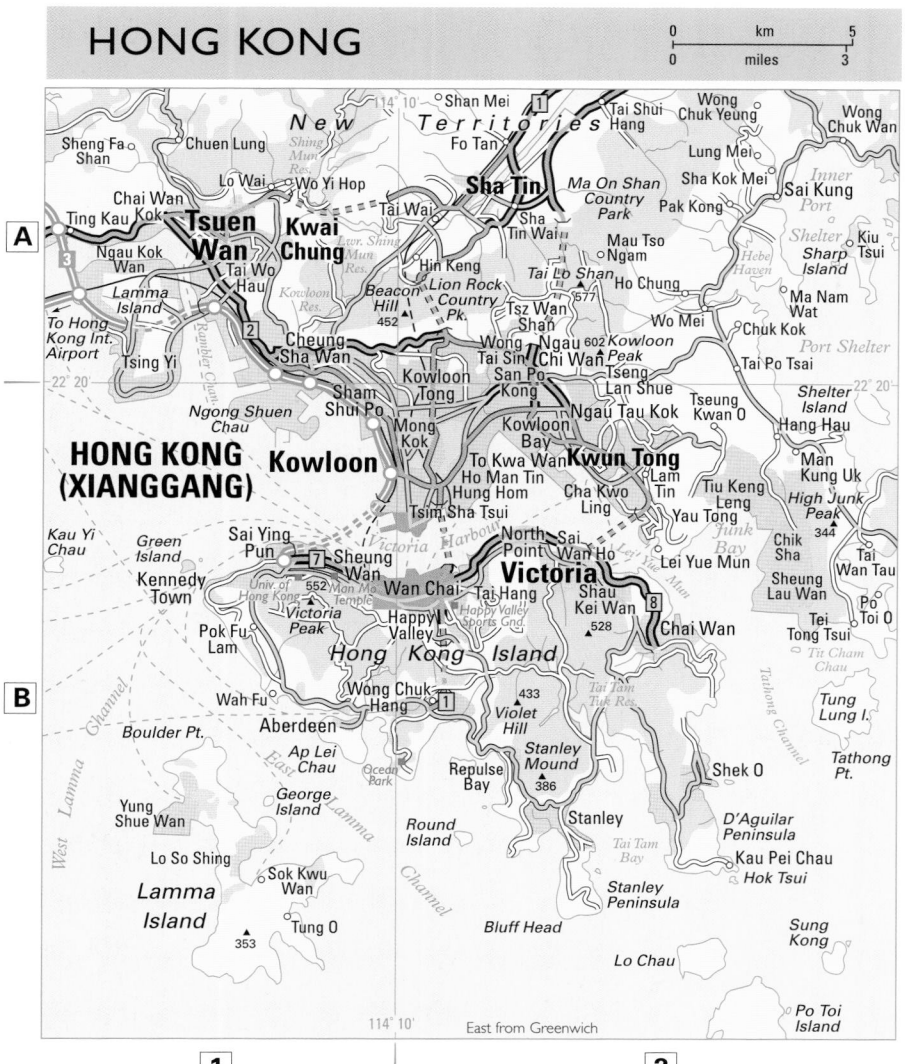

CENTRAL HONG KONG

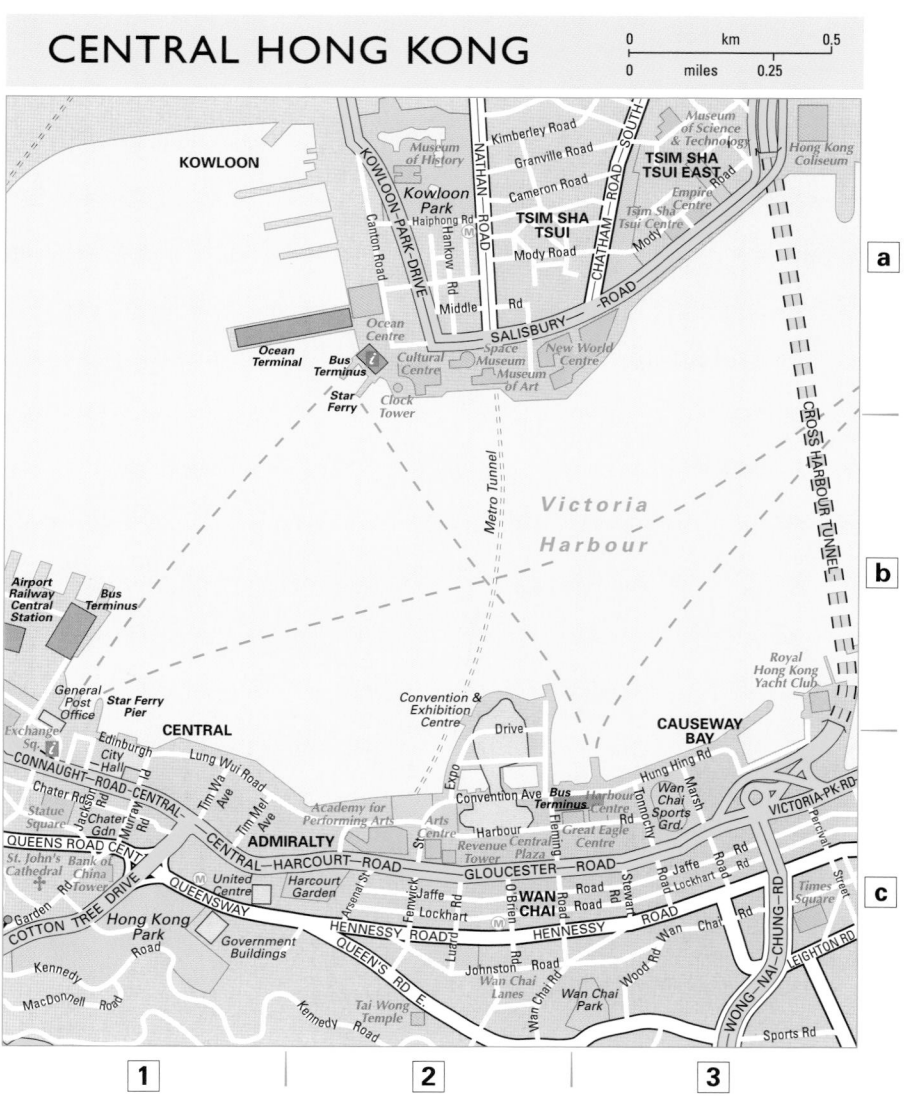

JERUSALEM

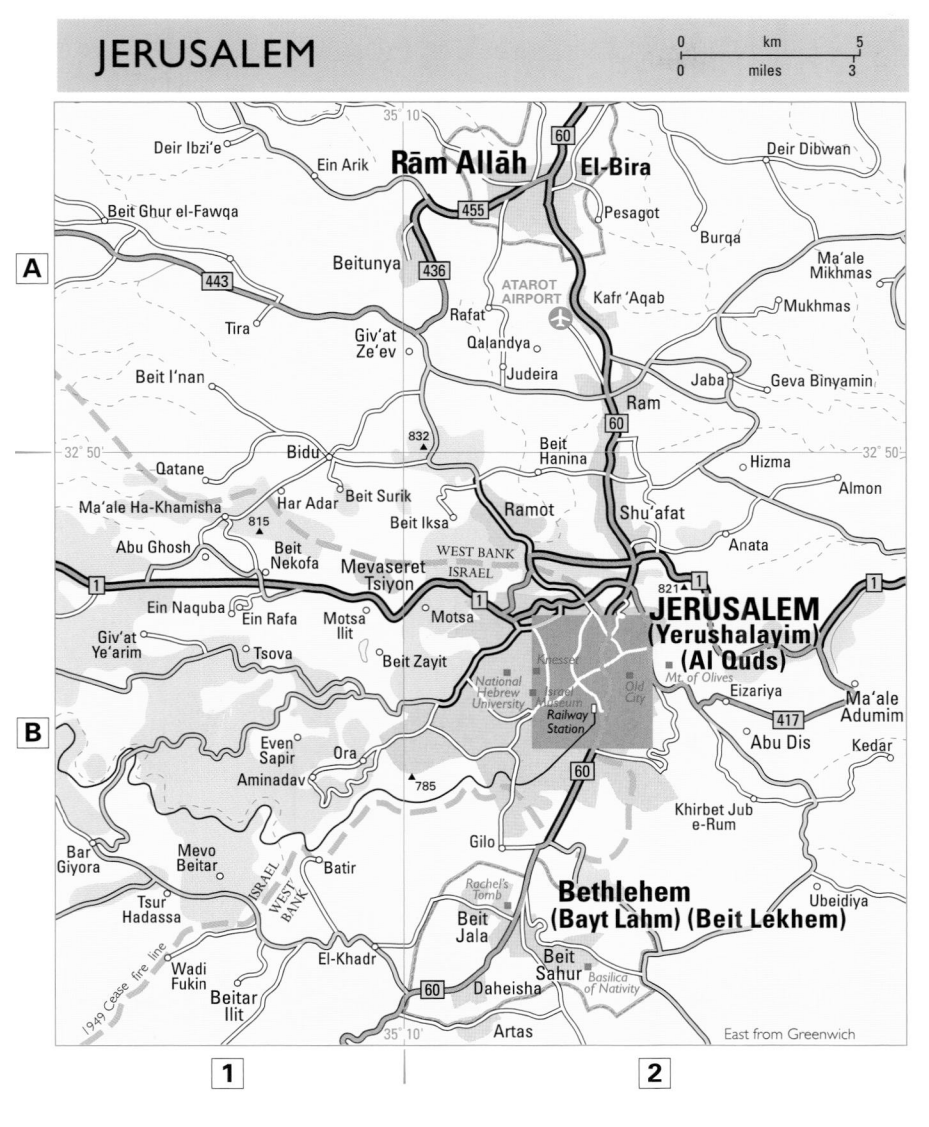

CENTRAL JERUSALEM

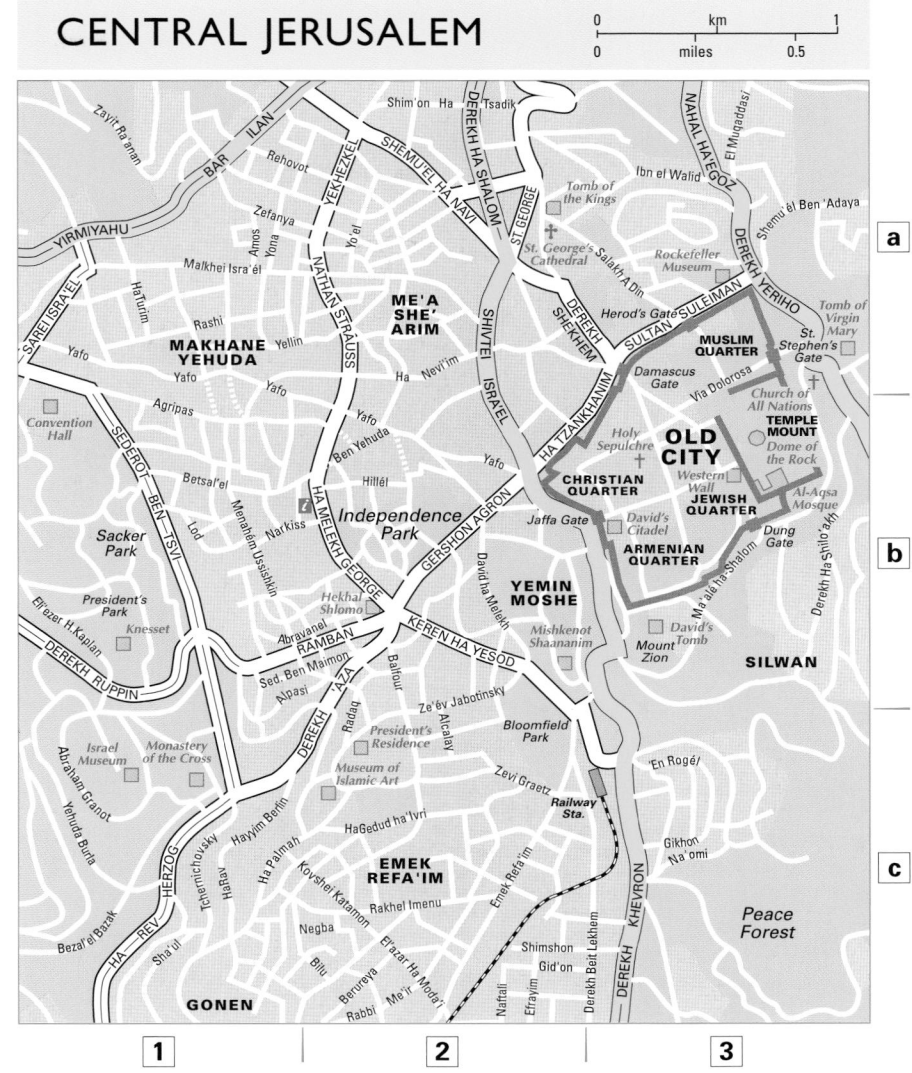

JAKARTA

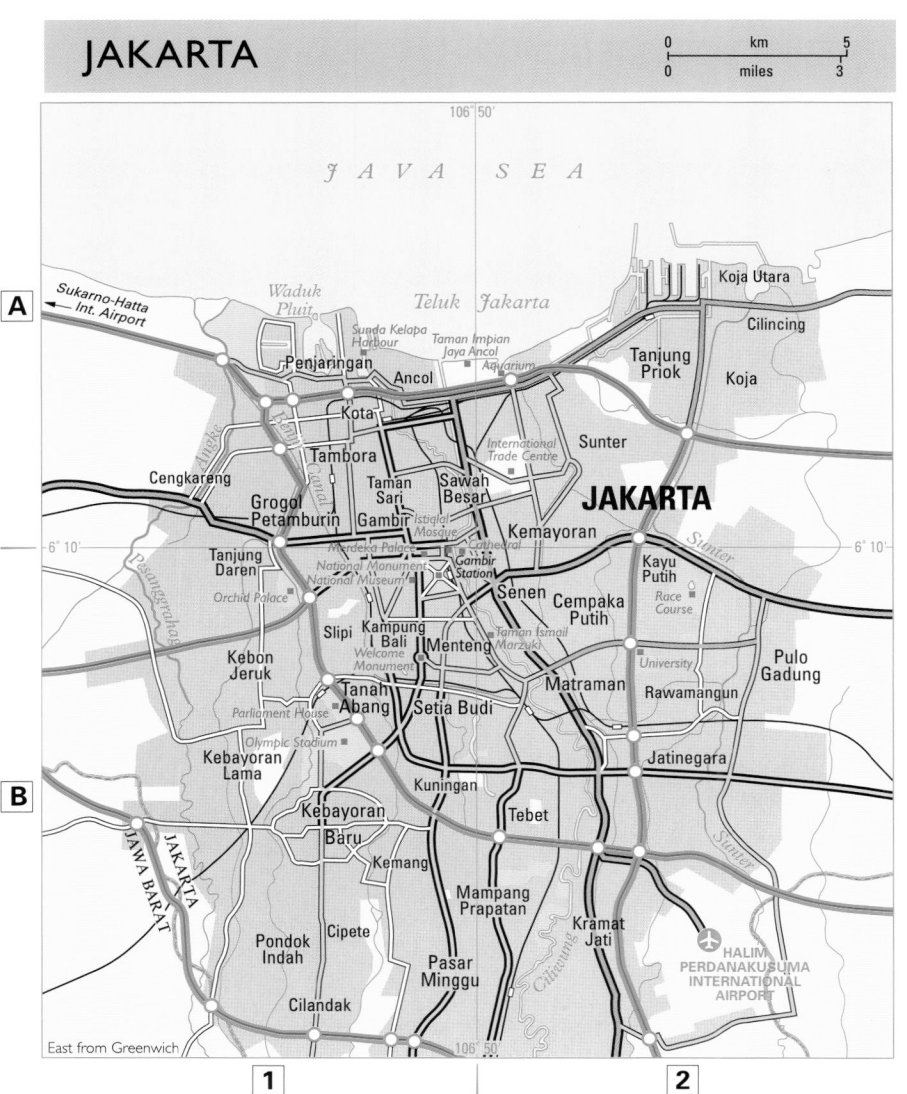

JOHANNESBURG

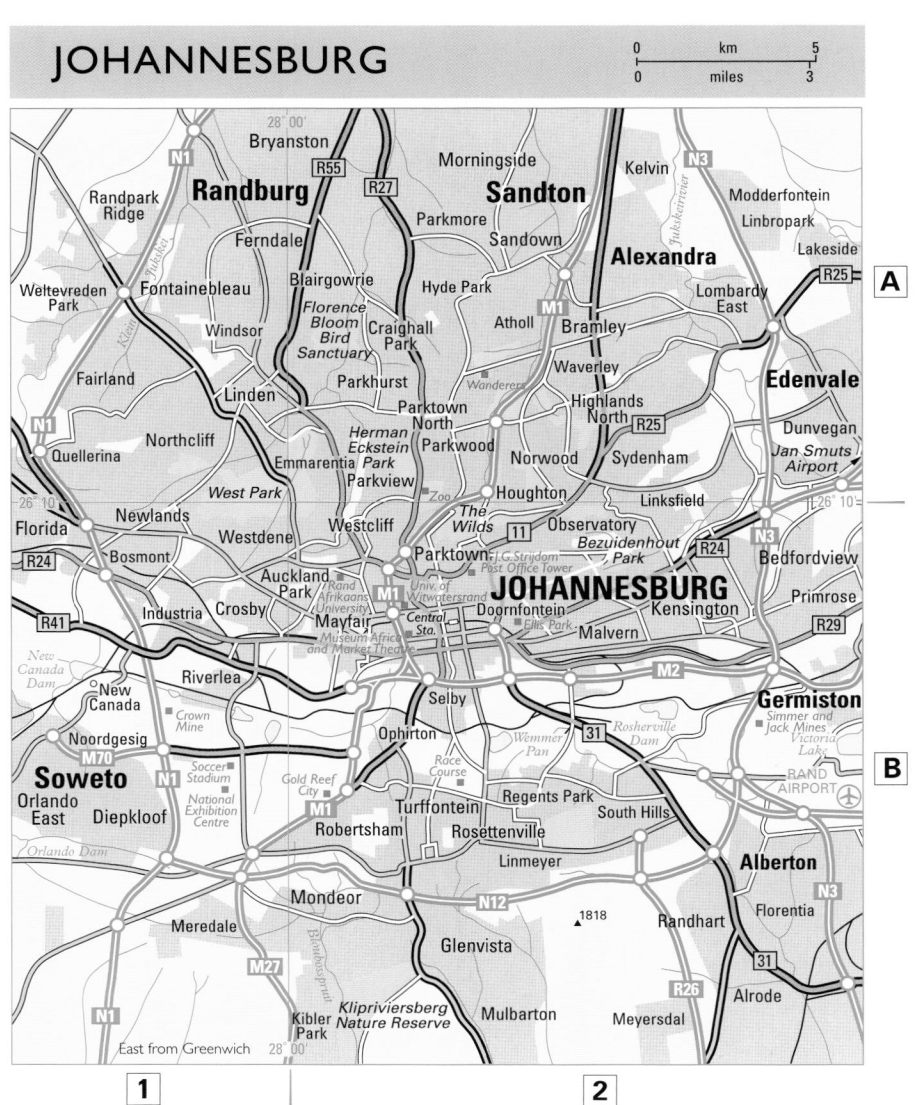

KARACHI

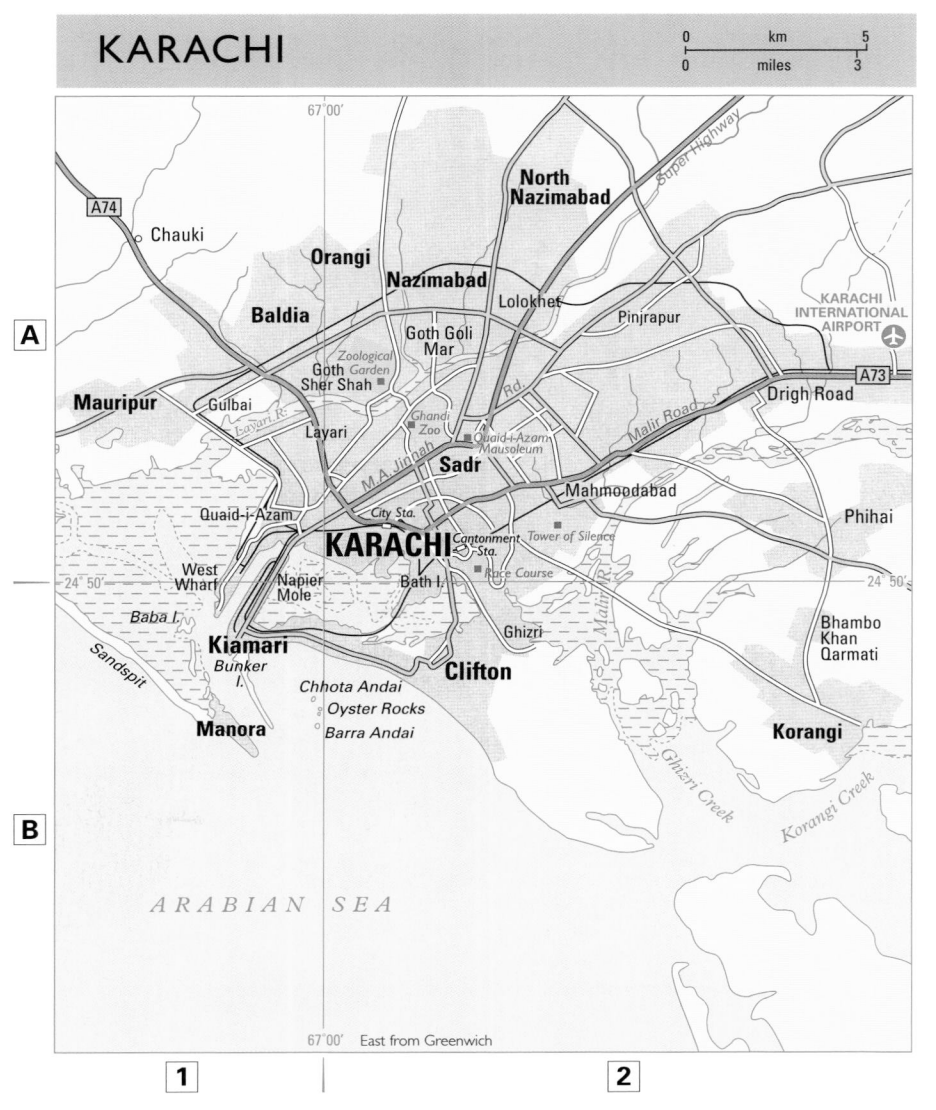

LAGOS

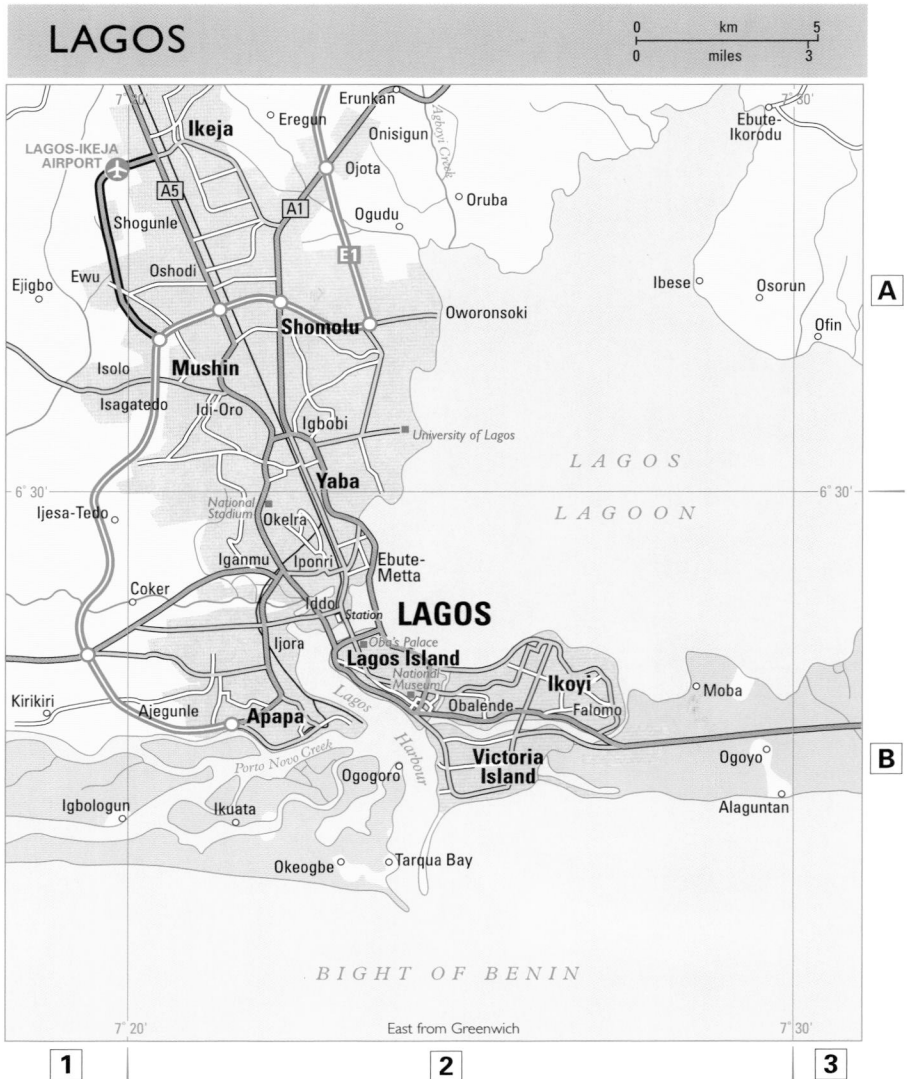

LISBON

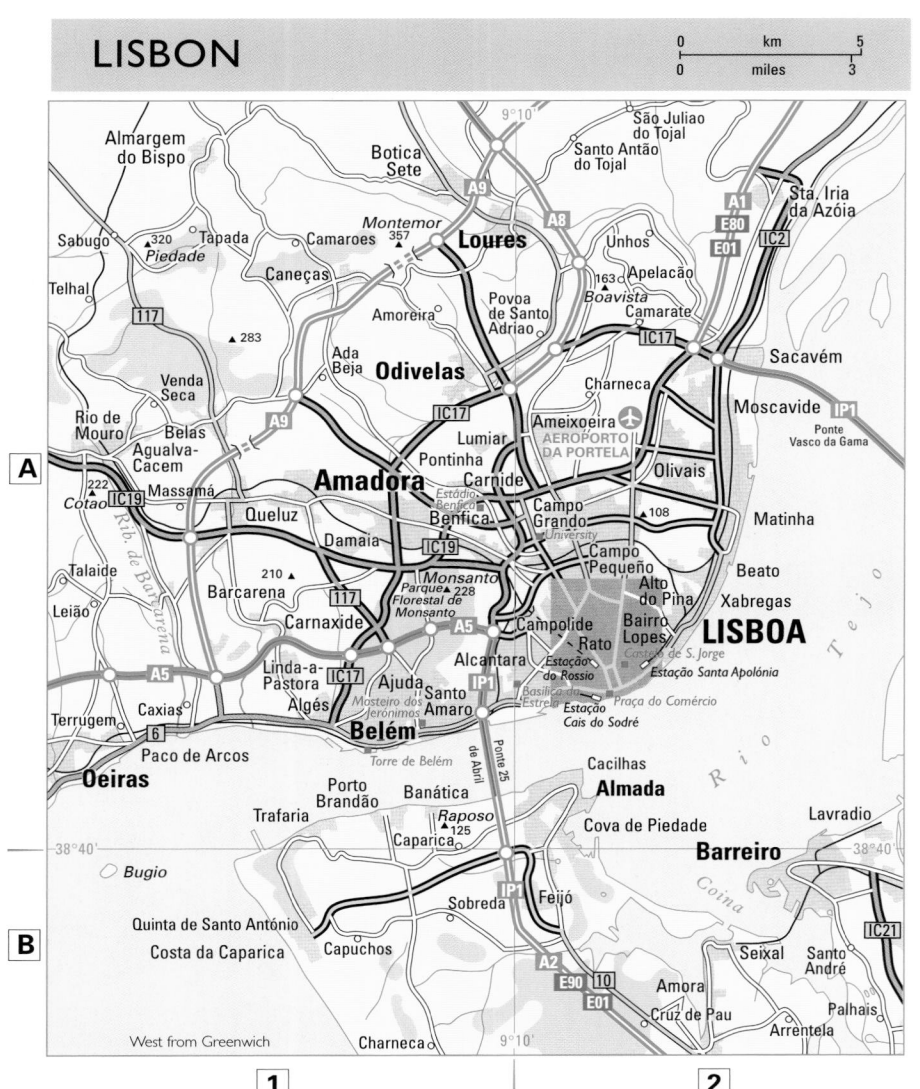

CENTRAL LISBON

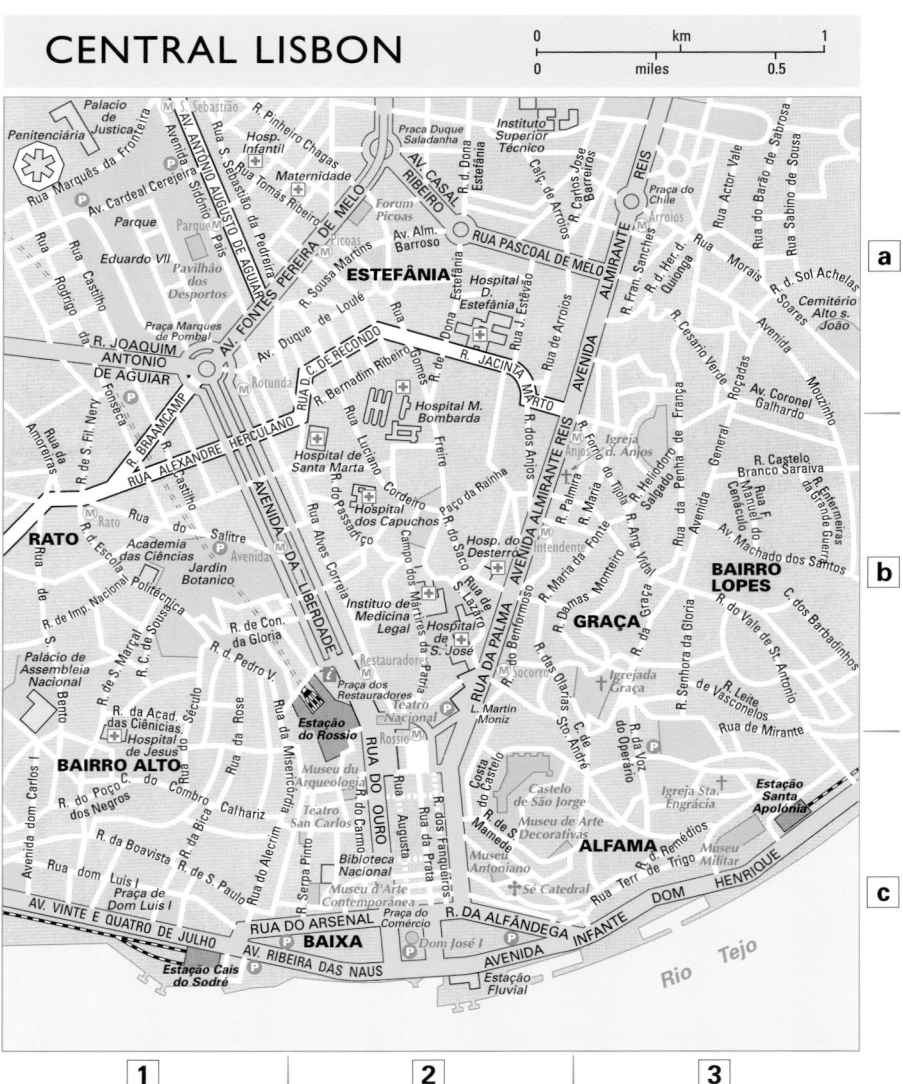

LONDON

km 5
miles 3

A | A
B | B

1 2 3 4 5

Northwood · Stanmore · Mill Hill · Barnet · Finchley · Colney Hatch · Wood Green · Waltham Forest · Woodford · To Stansted Airport · Woodford Bridge · GREATER LONDON · Hainault · Havering-atte-Bower · Harold Hill
Pinner Green · Belmont · Burnt Oak · Hendon · Church End · Muswell Hill · Tottenham · Clayhall · Barkingside · Collier Row · Gidea Park · Harold Wood
Harrow Weald · Queensbury · Coldindale · East Finchley · Hornsey · Haringey · Walthamstow · Wanstead · Newbury Park · Chadwell Heath · Romford
Harrow · Wealdstone · Kingsbury · Hampstead Garden Suburb · Golders Green · Highgate · Crouch End · Leyton · Leytonstone · Redbridge · Ilford · Seven Kings · Goodmayes · Becontree · Rush Green · Hornchurch · Havering
Pinner · West Harrow · Greenhill · Kenton · Crouch End · Tufnell Park · Finsbury Park · Clapton · Stoke Newington · Forest Gate · Manor Park · Becontree · Elm Park
Ickenham · South Ruislip · Roxeth · Harrow on the Hill · Hampstead Heath · Hampstead · Kentish Town · Highbury · Hackney Wick · Stratford · West Ham · East Ham · Barking · Dagenham · South Hornchurch
Ruislip Common · Eastcote · Rayners Lane · Wembley · Sudbury · Willesden Green · Brondesbury · Camden · Islington · Dalston · Hackney · Bethnal Green · Bow · Upton · A406 · A13 · Rainham
Hillingdon · Brent · Acton · Paddington · Westminster · City · Tower Hamlets · Newham · Creekmouth
Cowley · Yeading · Perivale · Stonebridge · Harlesden · Maida Vale · Regents Park · Holborn · Finsbury · Shoreditch · Whitechapel · Stepney · Poplar · Canning Town · North Woolwich · Thamesmead · Wennington
Ealing · Southall · Hanwell · Shepherd's Bush · Notting Hill · Hyde Park · Southwark · Bermondsey · Rotherhithe · Isle of Dogs · Millennium Dome · Woolwich · Plumstead · Belvedere · Erith
West Drayton · Heston · Cranford · Gunnersbury · Turnham Green · Hammersmith · Kensington · Chelsea · LONDON · Deptford · Greenwich · Charlton · East Wickham · Northumberland Heath
HEATHROW · Brentford · Chiswick · Barnes · Kew · Fulham · Battersea · Vauxhall · Camberwell · Peckham · New Cross · Blackheath · Kidbrooke · Welling · Slade Green · Crayford
Hounslow · Isleworth · Syon Park · Mortlake · Putney · Lambeth · Clapham · Brixton · Herne Hill · Nunhead · Lewisham · Hither Green · Bexleyheath · Bexley · Dartford
Feltham · Richmond upon Thames · East Sheen · Roehampton · Wandsworth · Balham · Dulwich · Forest Hill · Brockley · Catford · Eltham · New Eltham · A2
Ashford · SURREY · Hanworth · Twickenham · Richmond Park · Wimbledon Common · Southfields · Earlsfield · Streatham · Tulse Hill · Circular Road · Bellingham · Grove Park · Mottingham · Sidcup · North Cray · Coldblow · Wilmington
Queen Mary Res. · Teddington · Ham · Kingston Vale · Wimbledon · Streatham Vale · West Norwood · Crystal Palace · Sydenham · Penge · Southend · Chislehurst · Foots Cray · St.Paul's Cray · Hextable · Swanley Village · Hawley
Sunbury-on-Thames · Bushy Park · Hampton Wick · Raynes Park · Merton · Mitcham · Thornton Heath · South Norwood · Beckenham · Elmstead · Bickley · Swanley · Farningham
Shepperton · West Molesey · East Molesey · Hampton Court Palace · New Malden · Morden · Mitcham Common · Upper Norwood · Bromley · Shortlands · Southborough · Petts Wood · Orpington
Walton on Thames · Surbiton · Malden · Motspur Park · Worcester Park · St. Helier · Beddington Corner · To Gatwick Airport · Hackbridge · Elmers End · Eden Park · Hayes · Bromley Common · Crockenhill
Weybridge · Esher · Hook · Sutton · Croydon · Addiscombe · Woodside · West from Greenwich · East from Greenwich · GREATER LONDON KENT · M20

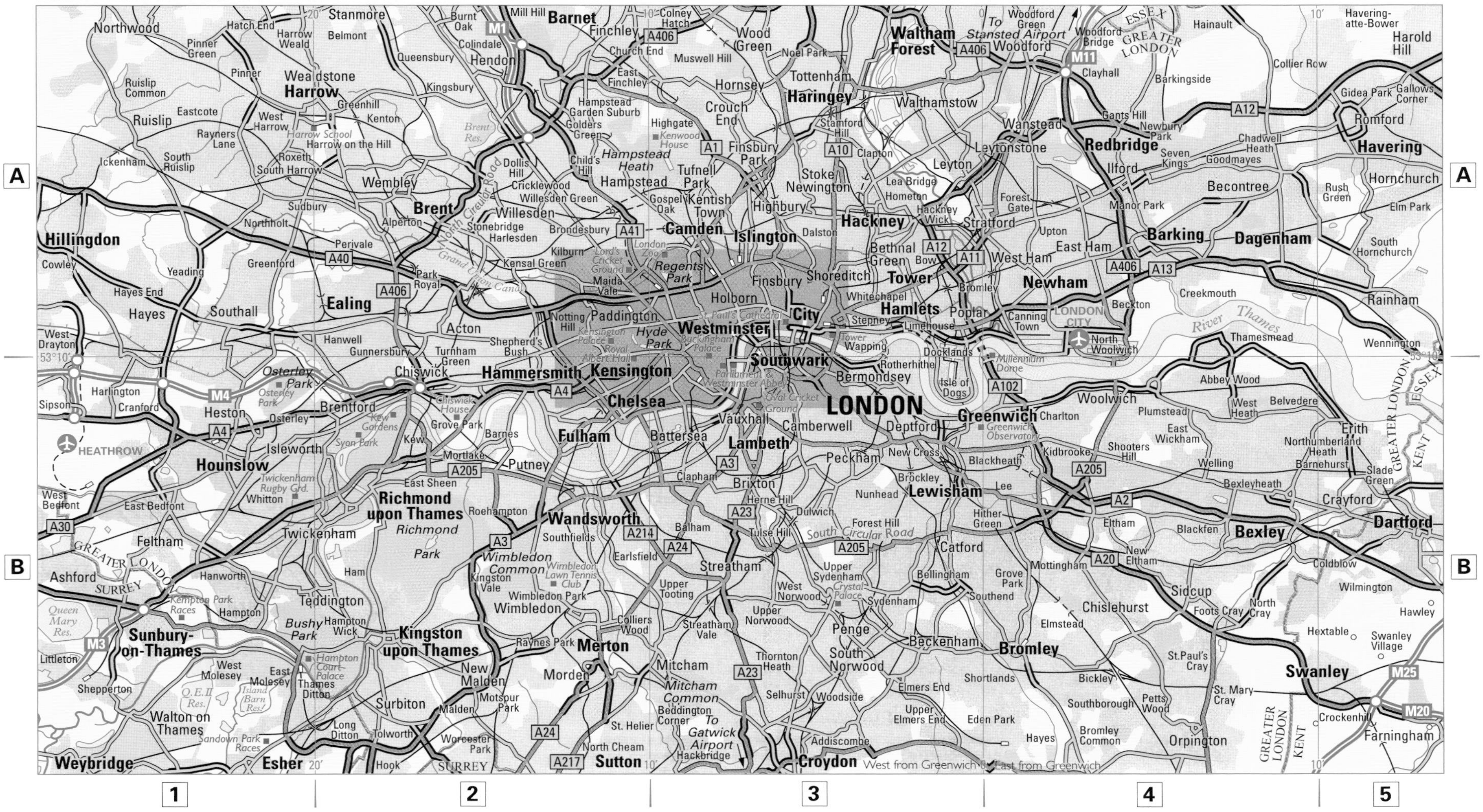

CENTRAL LONDON

km 2
miles 1

a | a
b | b
c | c

1 2 3 4 5

KENSAL RISE · ST. JOHN'S WOOD · King's Cross · HOXTON
WEST KILBURN · Queen's Park · Lord's Cricket Ground · London Zoo · REGENT'S PARK · Euston · St. Pancras · King's Cross Thameslink · SHOREDITCH
MAIDA VALE · Regent's Park · Madame Tussaud's · BLOOMSBURY · CLERKENWELL · Old Street · Wesley's Chapel
WESTBOURNE GREEN · Marylebone · British Museum · HOLBORN · Barbican · Moorgate · Liverpool St. · Whitechapel Art Gall.
PADDINGTON · BAYSWATER · SOHO · Farringdon · CITY · St. Paul's · Leadenhall · Fenchurch St.
NOTTING HILL · HYDE PARK · KENSINGTON GARDENS · MAYFAIR · PICCADILLY CIRCUS · Covent Garden · Temple · Blackfriars · Tate Modern · The Monument · Tower Gateway (DLR) · Tower of London
Holland Park · KENSINGTON · ST. JAMES'S · Charing Cross · National Gallery · Embankment · SOUTHWARK · HMS Belfast · River Thames
Olympia · Kensington Palace · Serpentine Gallery · Apsley House & Wellington Mus. · Buckingham Palace · St. James's Park · Downing Street · Waterloo East · London Bridge · The Design Museum
WEST KENSINGTON · Royal Albert Hall · KNIGHTSBRIDGE · BELGRAVIA · Green Park · Whitehall · London Eye · Waterloo International · BOROUGH · Bermondsey
Earl's Court Exhibition Hall · Nat. History Mus. · Science Mus. · BROMPTON · Victoria · Houses of Parliament · Westminster Abbey · Lambeth · NEWINGTON · NEW KENT ROAD
Hammersmith Cemetery · SOUTH KENSINGTON · SLOANE SQ. · PIMLICO · Tate Britain · Elephant & Castle · KENNINGTON · WALWORTH
CHELSEA · CHELSEA EMBANKMENT · River Thames · The Oval · Burgess Park

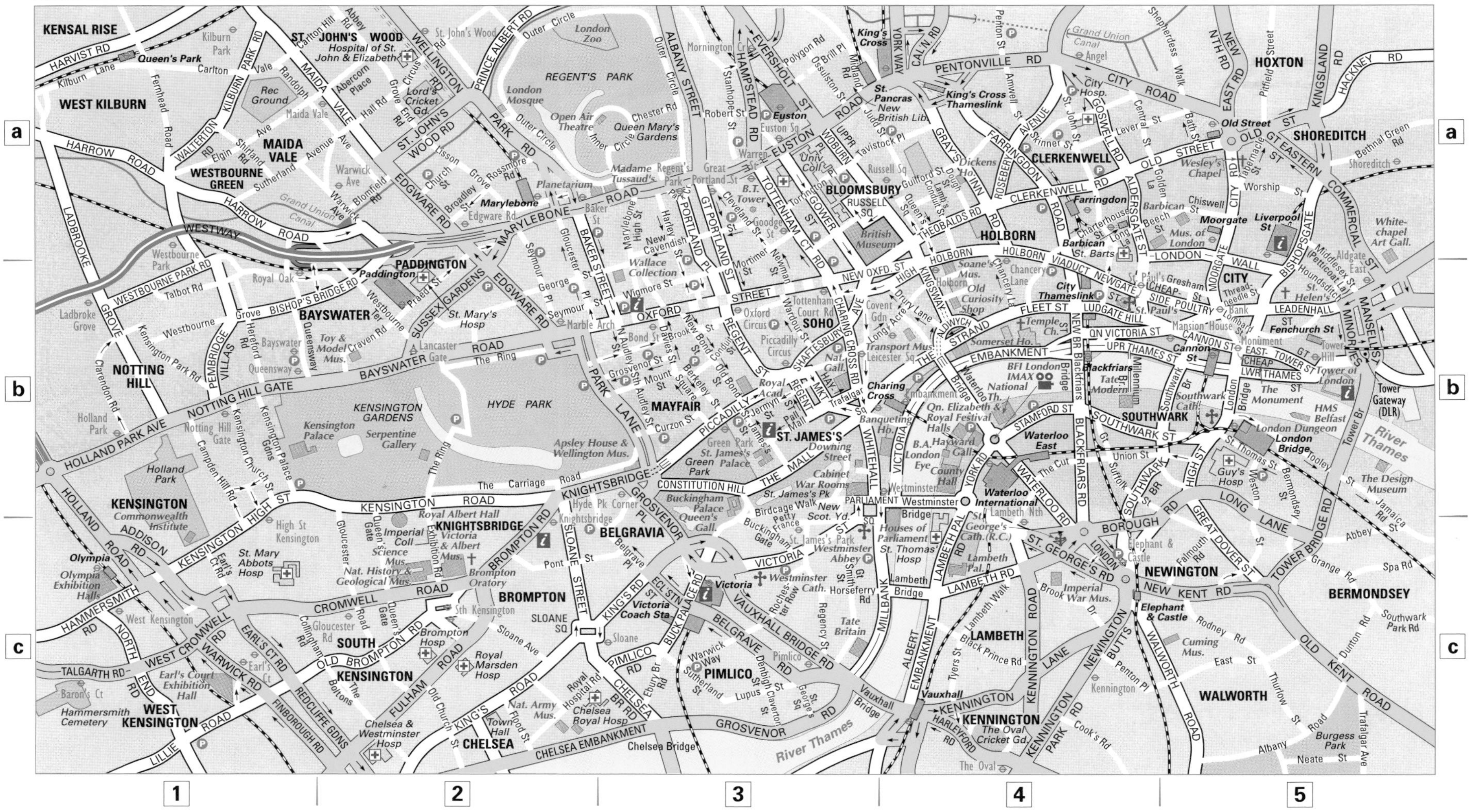

COPYRIGHT PHILIP'S

LOS ANGELES

km 5
miles 3

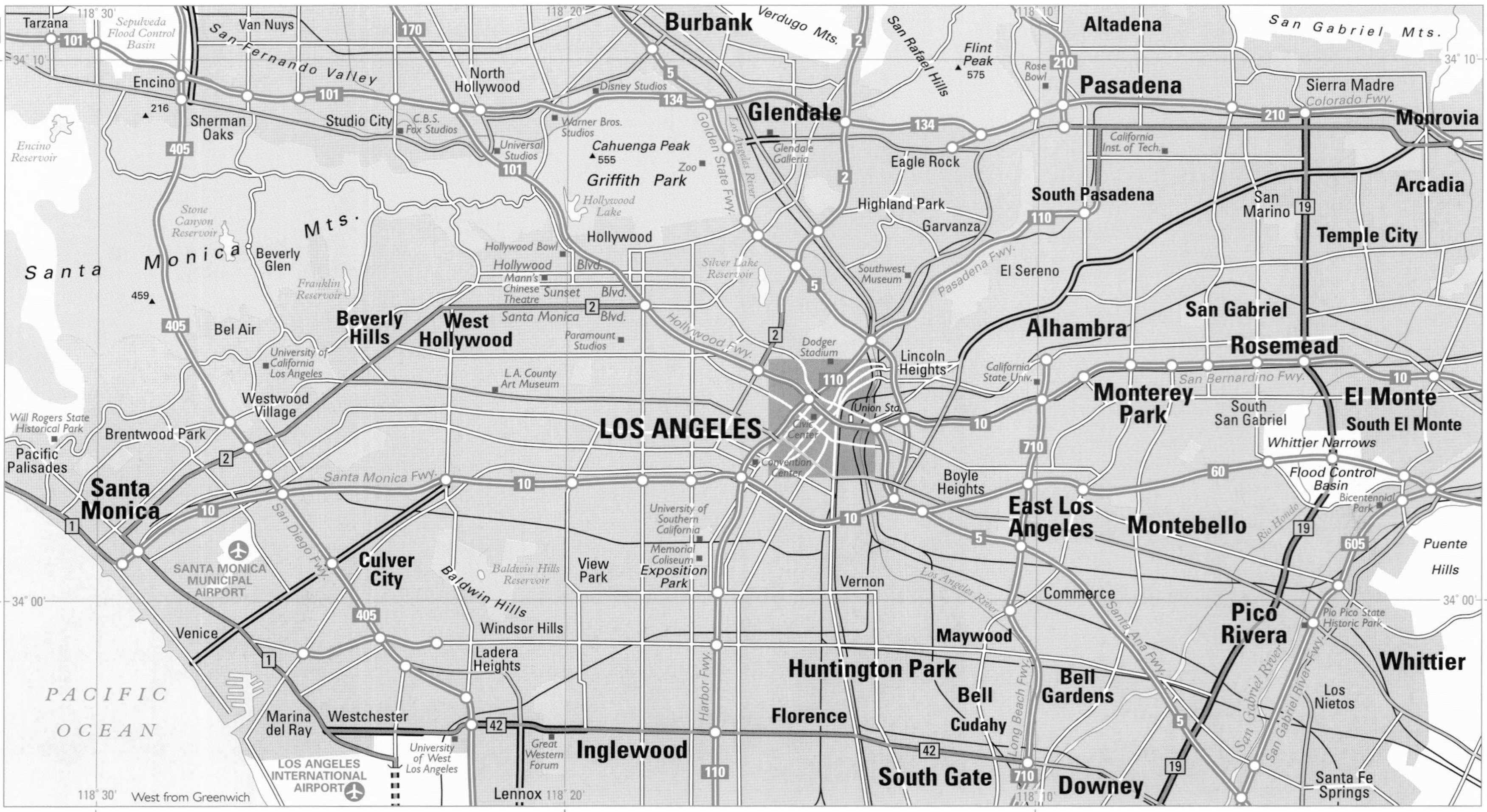

A Tarzana · 118° 30′ · Sepulveda Flood Control Basin · Van Nuys · San Fernando Valley · 118° 20′ · Burbank · Verdugo Mts. · San Rafael Hills · Flint Peak 575 · Altadena · San Gabriel Mts. · 118° 10′ · A 34° 10′

Encino · 216 · 101 · 170 · North Hollywood · C.B.S. Fox Studios · Disney Studios · 134 · 5 · Glendale · Rose Bowl · 210 · Pasadena · Sierra Madre · Colorado Fwy. · Monrovia

Sherman Oaks · 405 · Studio City · Universal Studios · Warner Bros. Studios · Cahuenga Peak 555 · Griffith Park · Hollywood Lake · Zoo · Glendale Galleria · 134 · 2 · Eagle Rock · California Inst. of Tech. · Arcadia

Encino Reservoir · Stone Canyon Reservoir · Santa · Monica · Mts. · 459 · Beverly Glen · Hollywood Bowl · Mann's Chinese Theatre · Hollywood · Sunset Blvd. · 2 · Highland Park · Garvanza · 110 · South Pasadena · San Marino · 19 · Temple City

405 · Bel Air · Beverly Hills · West Hollywood · Franklin Reservoir · Santa Monica Blvd. · Paramount Studios · L.A. County Art Museum · Hollywood Fwy. · 2 · Dodger Stadium · Lincoln Heights · 110 · California State Univ. · El Sereno · Alhambra · San Gabriel · Rosemead · 10

B Will Rogers State Historical Park · University of California Los Angeles · Westwood Village · 2 · Union Sta. · San Bernardino Fwy. · Monterey Park · South San Gabriel · El Monte · South El Monte · B 34° 10′

Pacific Palisades · Brentwood Park · 2 · Santa Monica Fwy. · Convention Center · Boyle Heights · 10 · 710 · Whittier Narrows · Flood Control Basin · 60 · 19 · Bicentennial Park

Santa Monica · 10 · 1 · San Diego Fwy. · University of Southern California · Memorial Coliseum · Exposition Park · 10 · East Los Angeles · Montebello · Rio Hondo · Puente Hills

Santa Monica Municipal Airport · Culver City · Baldwin Hills Reservoir · View Park · Vernon · Commerce · Pio Pico State Historic Park · Pico Rivera · 34° 00′

Venice · 405 · Windsor Hills · Baldwin Hills · Maywood · Bell Gardens · Santa Ana Fwy. · 605 · Whittier

C Pacific Ocean · Marina del Ray · Westchester · Ladera Heights · 42 · Great Western Forum · Huntington Park · Bell · Cudahy · San Gabriel River · Los Nietos · C

Los Angeles International Airport · University of West Los Angeles · Inglewood · 110 · Florence · South Gate · Downey · 19 · Santa Fe Springs

Lennox · 118° 20′ · 710 · 42

118° 30′ West from Greenwich

1 · 2 · 3 · 4

LIMA

km 5
miles 3

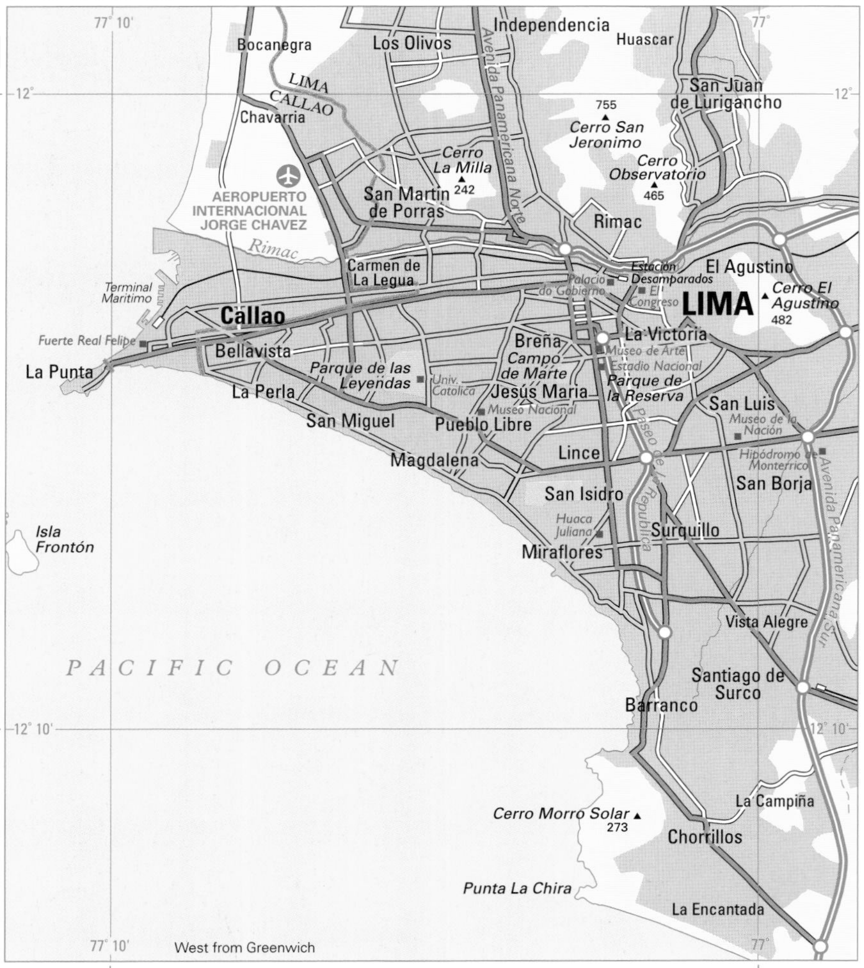

A 77° 10′ · Bocanegra · Los Olivos · Independencia · Huascar · 77° · A 12°

LIMA CALLAO · Chavarria · 755 · San Juan de Lurigancho · 12°

Aeropuerto Internacional Jorge Chavez · San Martin de Porras · Cerro La Milla · 242 · Cerro San Jeronimo · Cerro Observatorio 465

Terminal Maritimo · Carmen de La Legua · Rimac · Rimac · El Agustino · Cerro El Agustino 482

Callao · Palacio do Gobierno · Estación Desamparados · El Congreso · LIMA

B La Punta · Fuerte Real Felipe · Bellavista · La Perla · Parque de las Leyendas · Breña · Campo de Marte · Estadio Nacional · La Victoria · Museo de Arte · Parque de la Reserva · San Luis · Museo de la Nación · B

San Miguel · Pueblo Libre · Jesús Maria · Museo Nacional · Univ. Católica · San Borja

Magdalena · Lince · Hipódromo Monterrico · Huaca Juliana · San Isidro · Surquillo

Isla Fronton · Miraflores · Vista Alegre

PACIFIC OCEAN · Santiago de Surco

12° 10′ · Barranco · 12° 10′

Cerro Morro Solar 273 · La Campiña · Chorrillos · La Encantada

Punta La Chira

77° 10′ West from Greenwich · 77°

1 · 2 · 3

CENTRAL LOS ANGELES

km 1
miles 0.5

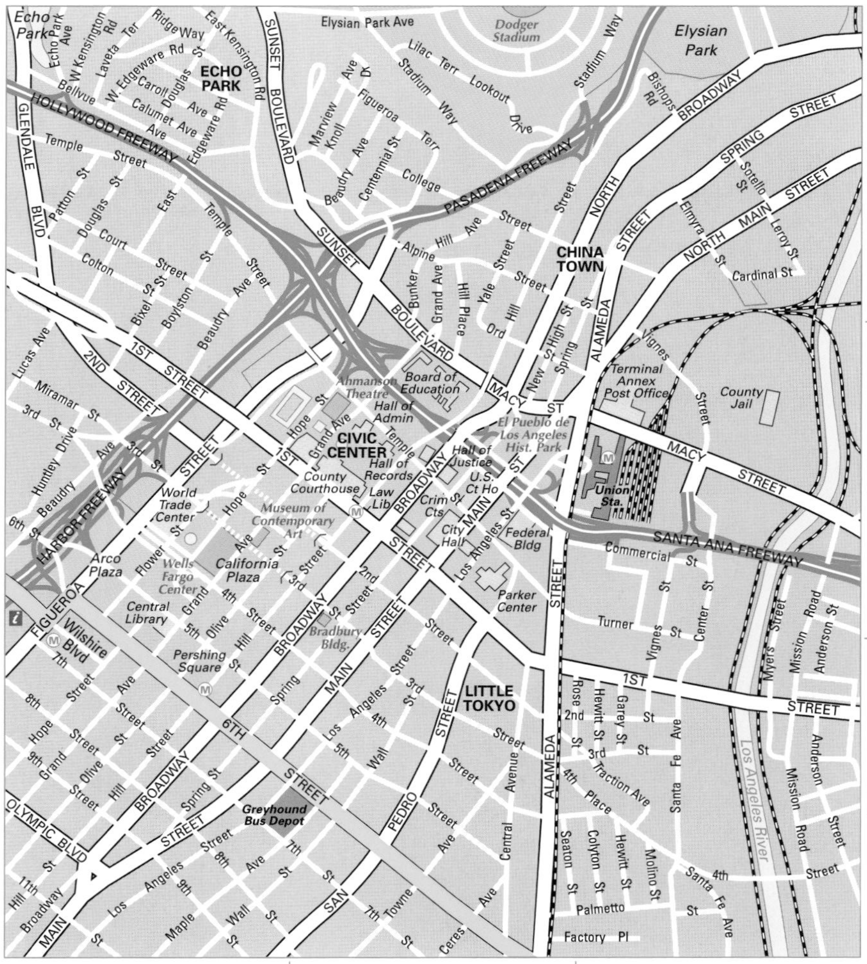

Echo Park · Elysian Park Ave · Dodger Stadium · Elysian Park

ECHO PARK · SUNSET BOULEVARD · PASADENA FREEWAY · BROADWAY · SPRING STREET · a

GLENDALE BLVD · HOLLYWOOD FREEWAY · Temple Street · CHINA TOWN · NORTH SPRING ST · NORTH MAIN STREET · Cardinal St · ALAMEDA · Terminal Annex Post Office · County Jail

SUNSET BOULEVARD · Board of Education · Hall of Admin · El Pueblo de Los Angeles Hist. Park · MACY · b

HARBOR FREEWAY · 2ND STREET · 1ST STREET · CIVIC CENTER · County Courthouse · Hall of Records · U.S. Ct Ho · Union Sta. · SANTA ANA FREEWAY

World Trade Center · Museum of Contemporary Art · Law Lib · City Hall · Hall of Justice · Federal Bldg · Commercial St · Turner

Arco Plaza · California Plaza · Crim Cts · Los Angeles · Parker Center · 1ST STREET

FIGUEROA · Wilshire Blvd · Flower · Wells Fargo Center · Bradbury Bldg · LITTLE TOKYO · Mission Road · Los Angeles River

Central Library · Pershing Square · BROADWAY · SPRING · MAIN · SAN PEDRO · ALAMEDA · Santa Fe Ave

Hope · Grand · Olive · 6th · 7th · Hill · Broadway

OLYMPIC BLVD · Greyhound Bus Depot · Factory Pl · c

1 · 2 · 3

MADRID

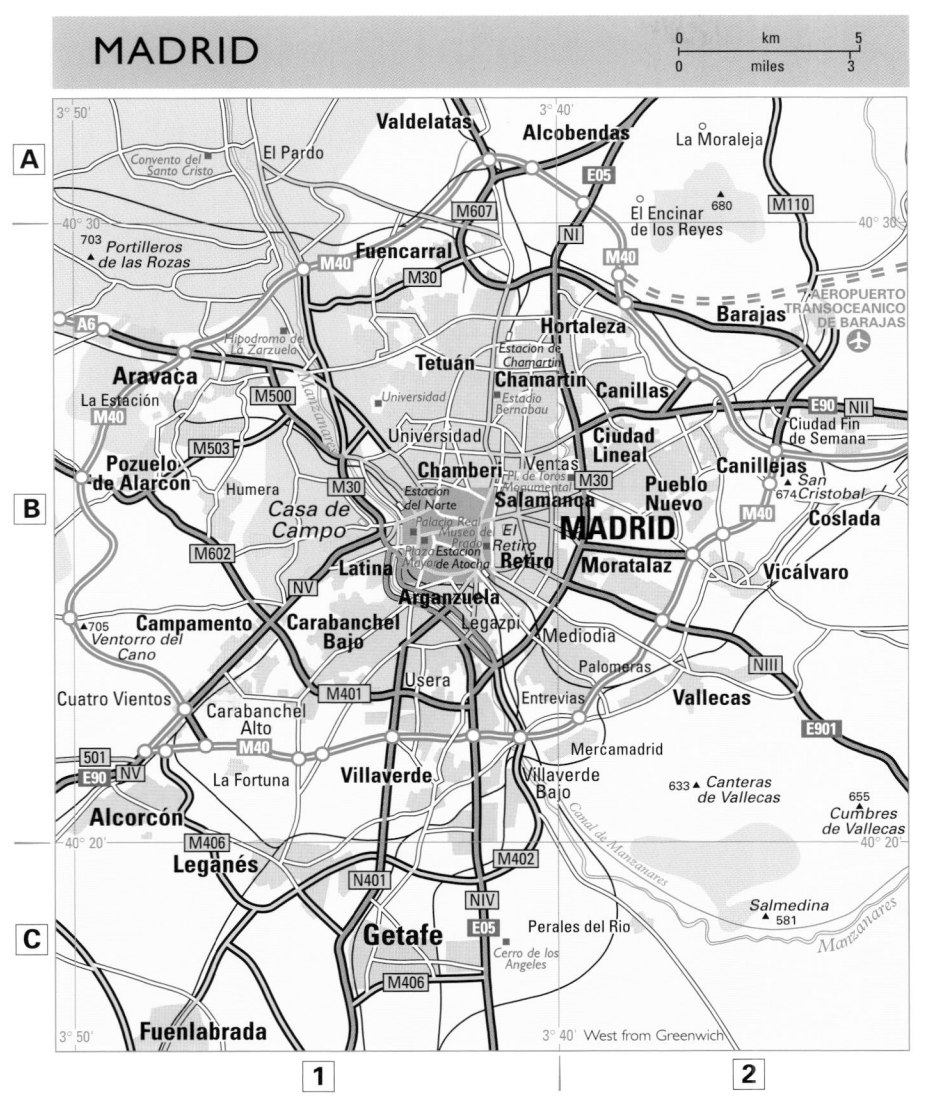

CENTRAL MADRID

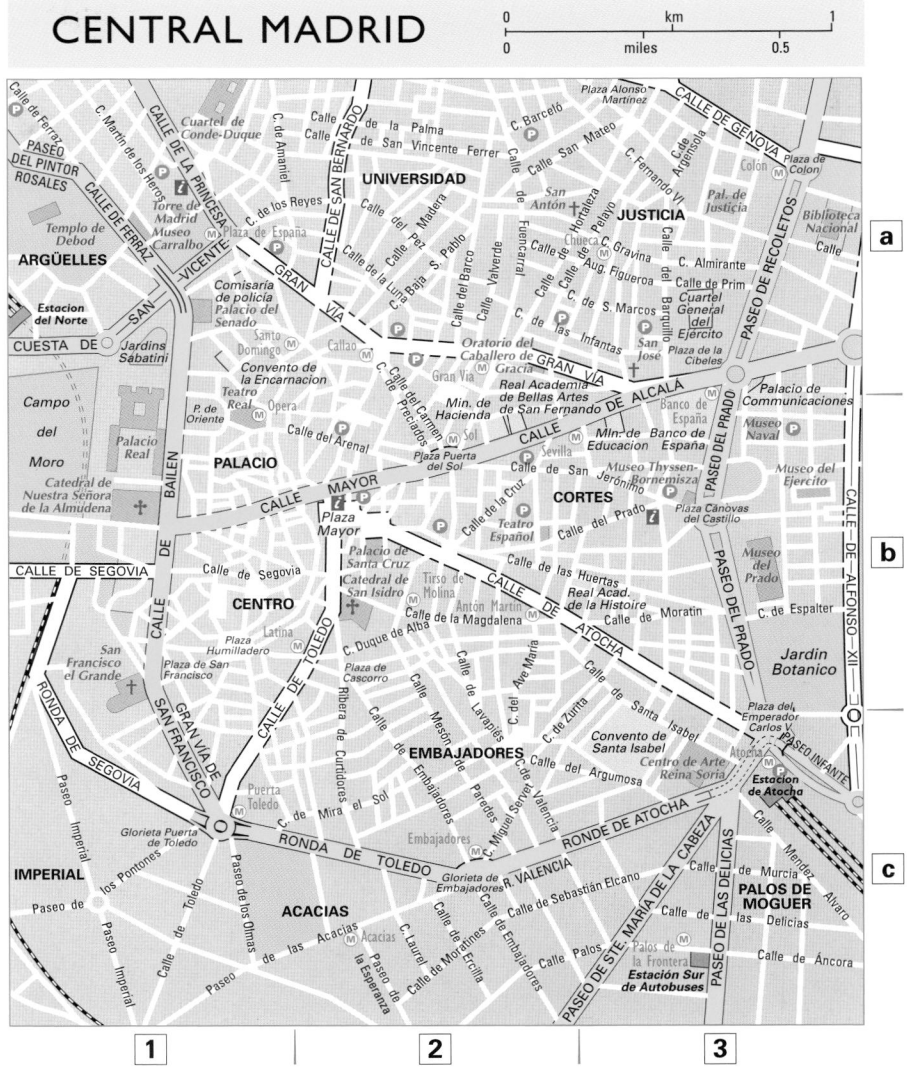

MANILA

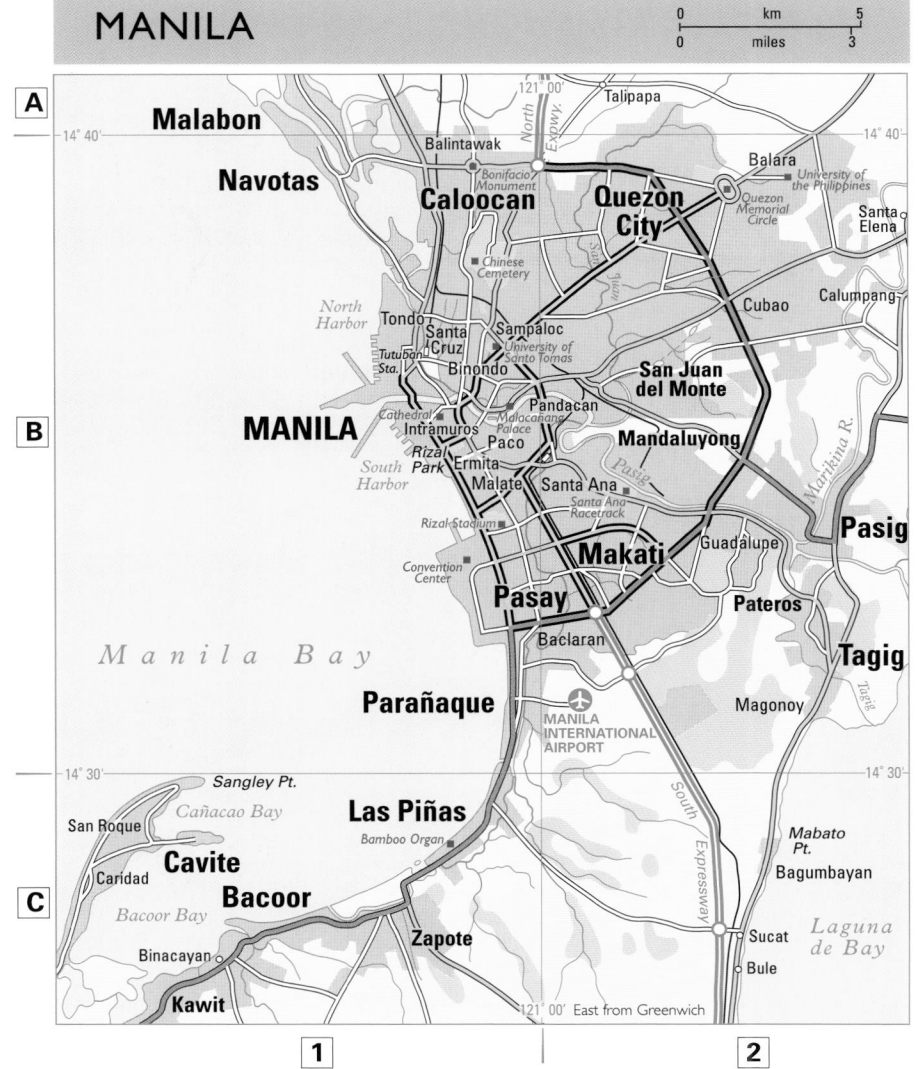

MELBOURNE

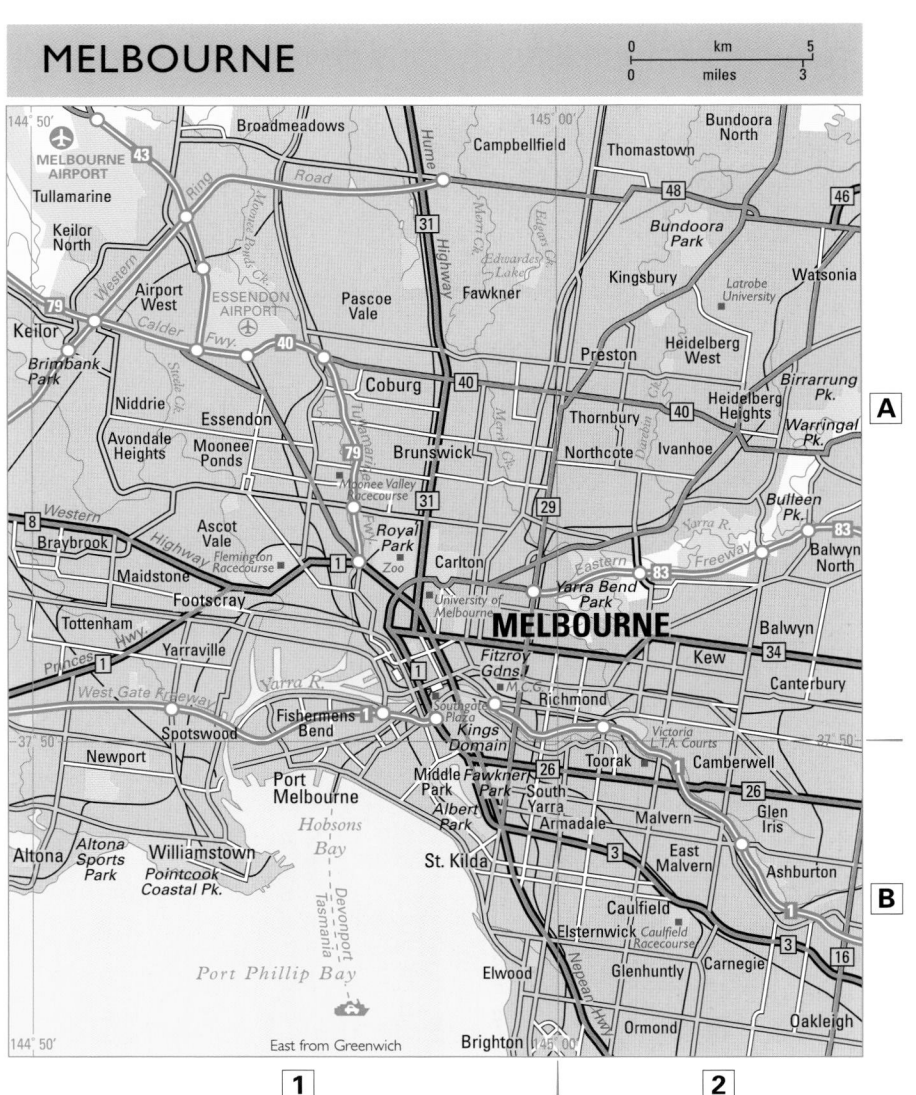

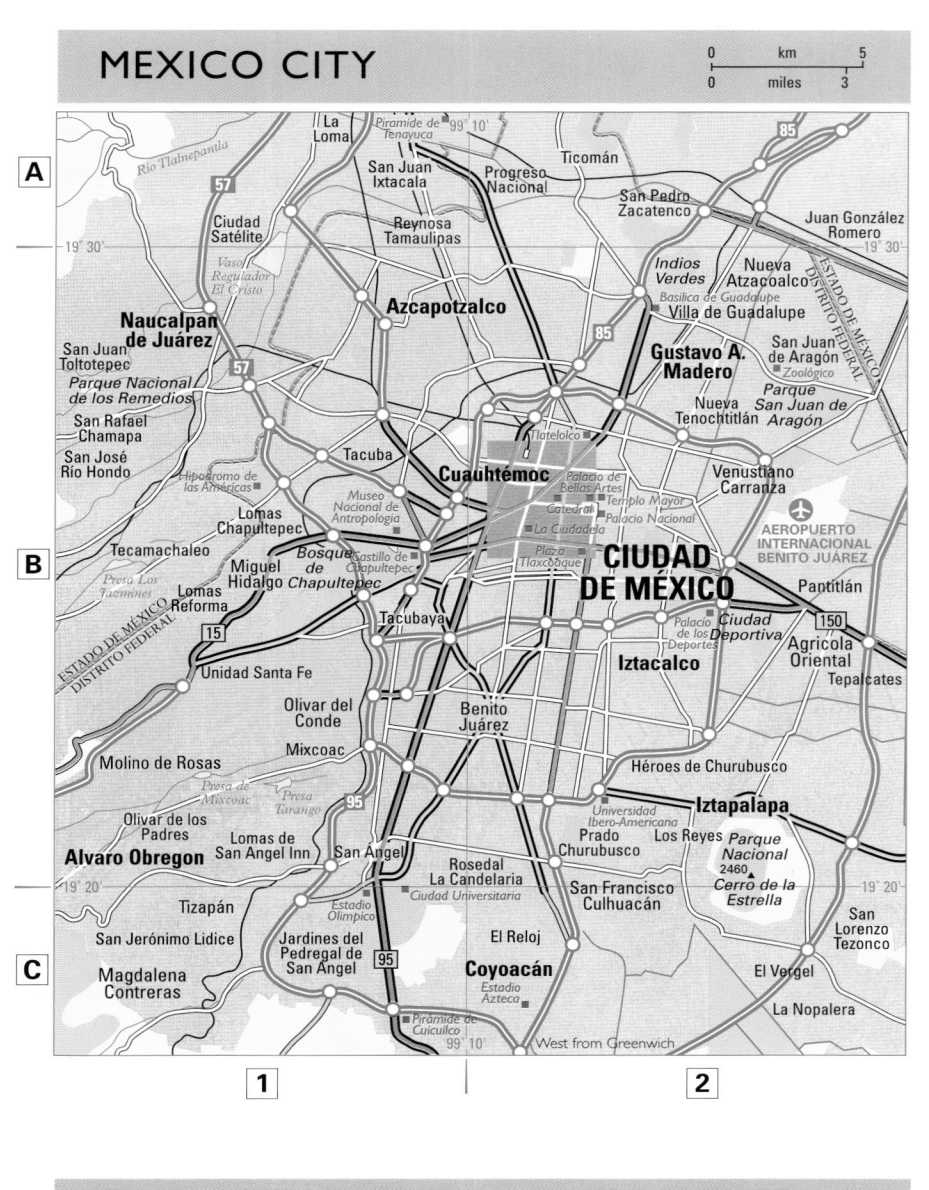

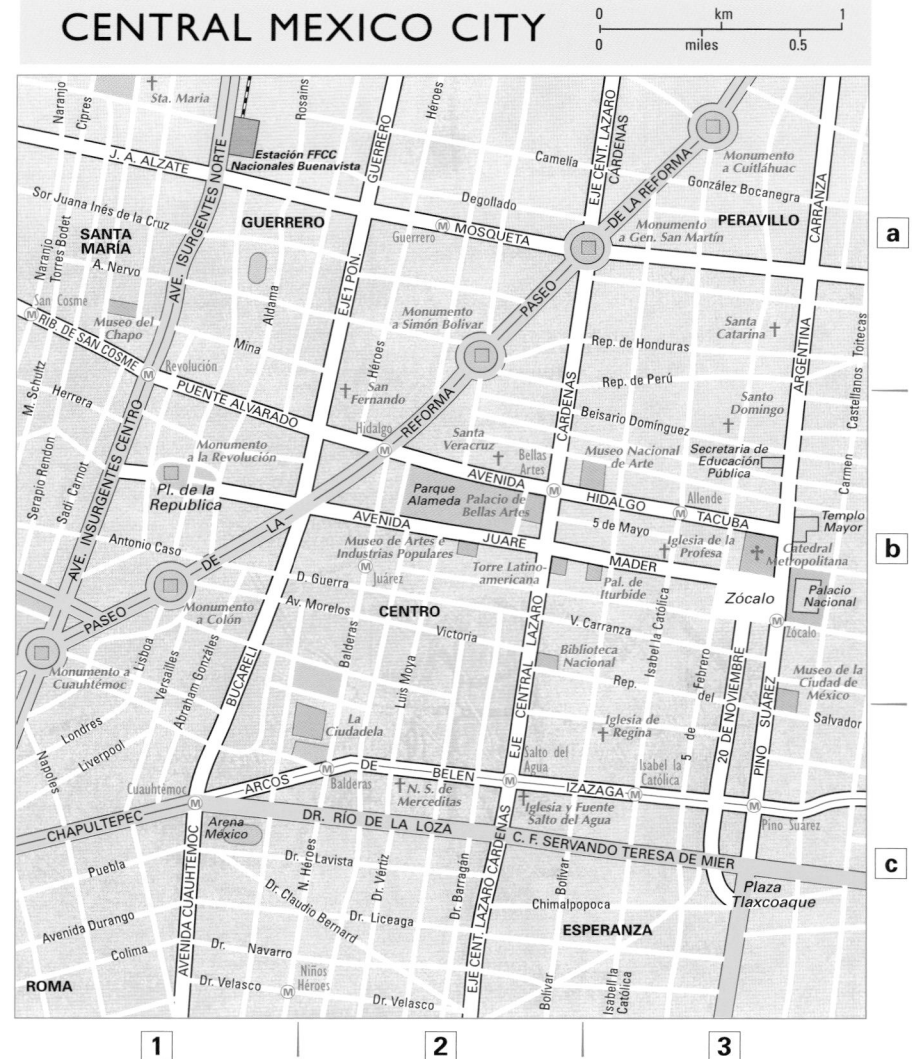

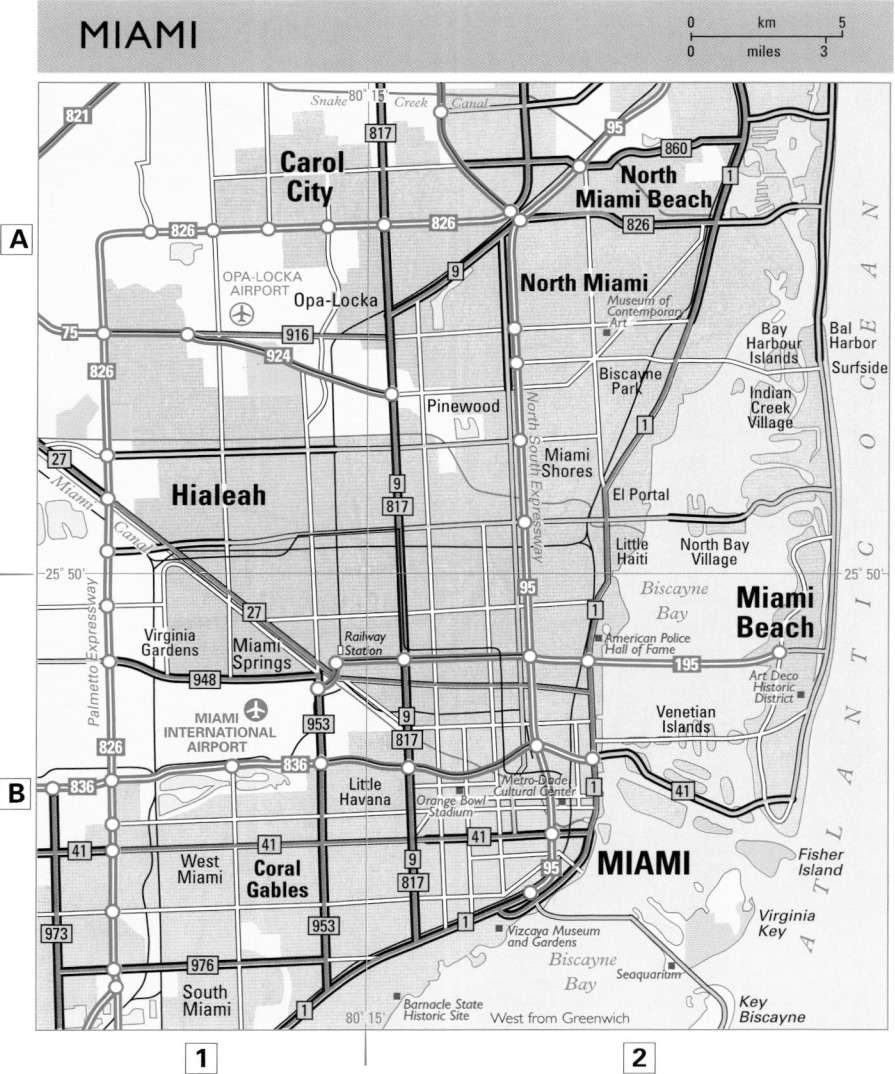

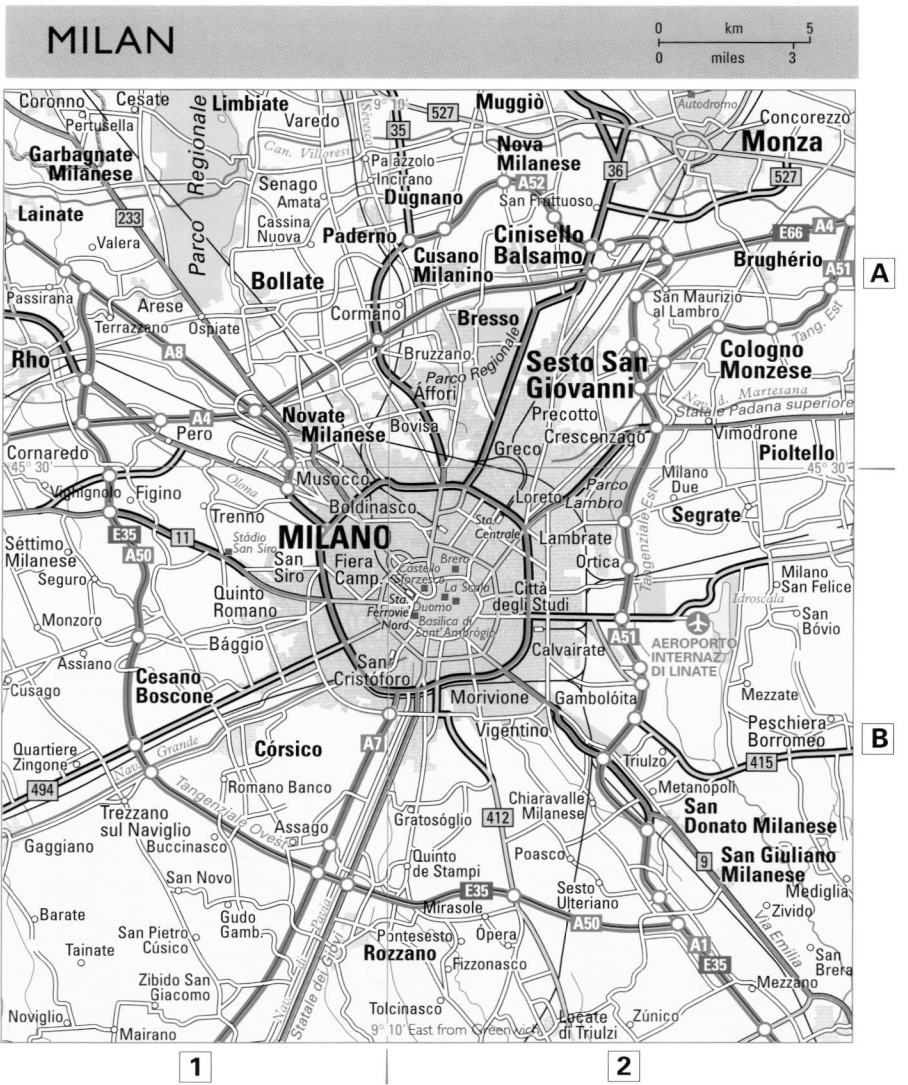

MOSCOW

0 km 5
0 miles 3

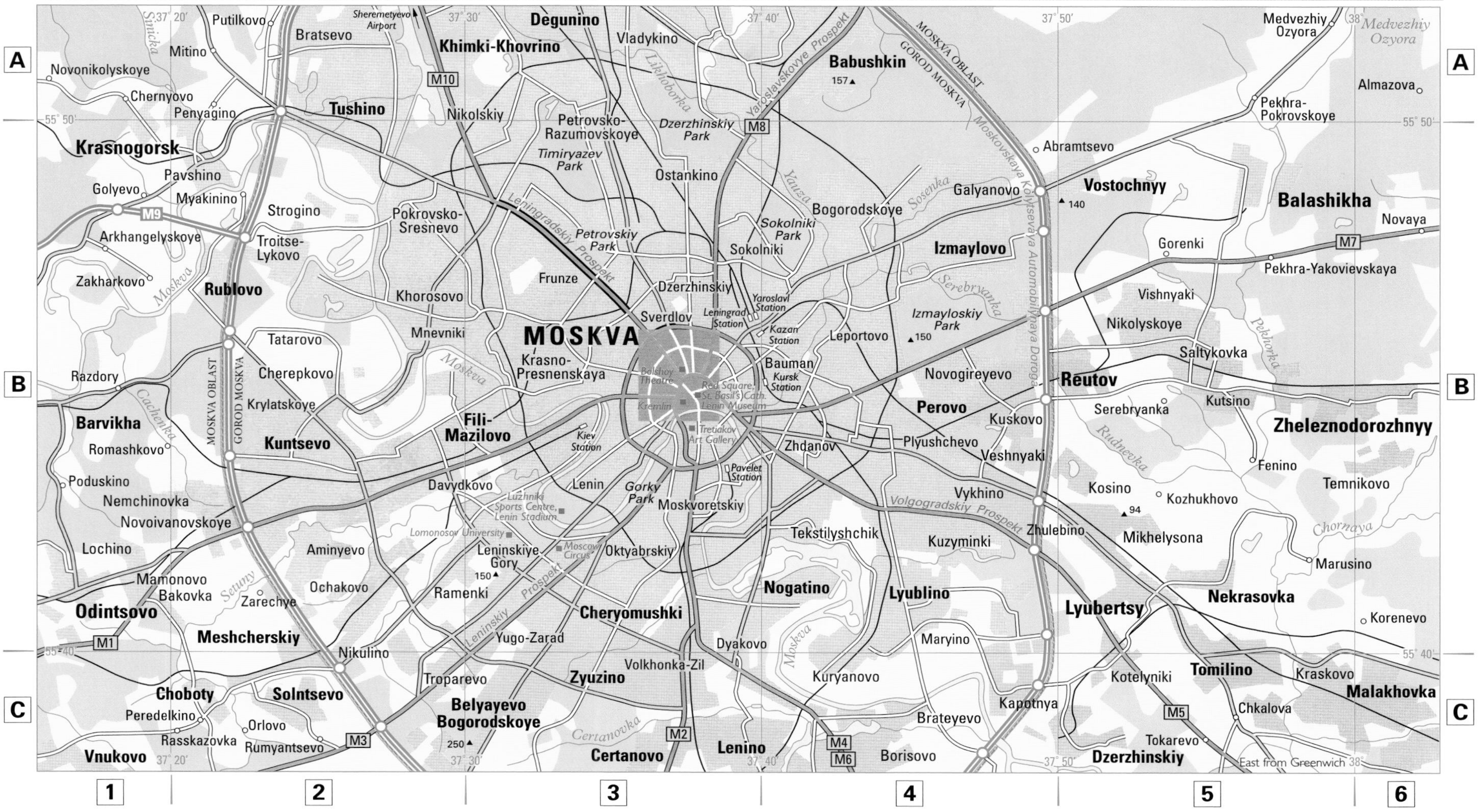
A
B
C
1
2
3
4
5
6
37° 20'
37° 30'
37° 40'
37° 50'
38°
55° 50'
55° 40'
Putilkovo
Sheremetyevo Airport
Degunino
Medvezhiy Ozyora
Mitino
Bratsevo
Khimki-Khovrino
Vladykino
Babushkin
MOSKVA OBLAST
GOROD MOSKVA
Novonikolyskoye
M10
157
Almazova
Chernyovo
Penyagino
Tushino
Nikolskiy
Petrovsko-Razumovskoye
Dzerzhinskiy Park
M8
Pekhra-Pokrovskoye
Krasnogorsk
Timiryazev Park
Abramtsevo
Pavshino
Ostankino
Golyevo
Myakinino
Galyanovo
Vostochnyy
Strogino
Pokrovsko-Sresnevo
Bogorodskoye
140
Balashikha
M9
Novaya
Arkhangelyskoye
Troitse-Lykovo
Petrovskiy Park
Sokolniki Park
Izmaylovo
Gorenki
M7
Zakharkovo
Rublovo
Frunze
Sokolniki
Pekhra-Yakovievskaya
Khorosovo
Dzerzhinskiy
Vishnyaki
Yaroslavl Station
Izmayloskiy Park
Leningrad Station
Sverdlov
Nikolyskoye
Tatarovo
Mnevniki
MOSKVA
Kazan Station
Leportovo
150
Saltykovka
Razdory
Cherepkovo
Krasno-Presnenskaya
Bauman
Kursk Station
Novogireyevo
Reutov
Bolshoy Theatre
Red Square, St. Basil's Cath. Lenin Museum
Kutsino
Krylatskoye
Kremlin
Serebryanka
Barvikha
Fili-Mazilovo
Perovo
Zheleznodorozhnyy
Kuntsevo
Tretyakov Art Gallery
Kuskovo
Romashkovo
Kiev Station
Plyushchevo
Zhdanov
Veshnyaki
Fenino
Poduskino
Pavelet Station
Davydkovo
Lenin
Kosino
Temnikovo
Nemchinovka
Luzhniki Sports Centre, Lenin Stadium
Gorky Park
Vykhino
Kozhukhovo
Moskvoretskiy
94
Novoivanovskoye
Volgogradskiy Prospekt
Zhulebino
Lomonosov University
Lochino
Aminyevo
Leninskiye Gory
Moscow Circus
Oktyabrskiy
Tekstilyshchik
Kuzyminki
Mikhelysona
Mamonovo
Marusino
Bakovka
Ochakovo
Nogatino
Lyublino
Zarechye
Ramenki
Nekrasovka
Odintsovo
Cheryomushki
Lyubertsy
Korenevo
Meshcherskiy
Yugo-Zarad
Dyakovo
Maryino
M1
Nikulino
Tomilino
Volkhonka-Zil
Kraskovo
Chоboty
Solntsevo
Troparevo
Zyuzino
Kuryanovo
Kotelyniki
Malakhovka
Peredelkino
Belyayevo Bogorodskoye
Kapotnya
Chkalova
Orlovo
M5
Brateyevo
Rasskazovka
M2
250
Tokarevo
Rumyantsevo
M3
Lenino
M4
Vnukovo
Certanovo
M6
Borisovo
Dzerzhinskiy
East from Greenwich
Moskva
Yauza
Leningradskiy Prospekt
Yaroslavskoye Prospekt
Moskovskaya Koltsevaya Avtomobilnaya Doroga
Leninskiy Prospekt
Setuny
Gertanovka
Chornaya

MONTRÉAL

0 km 5
0 miles 3

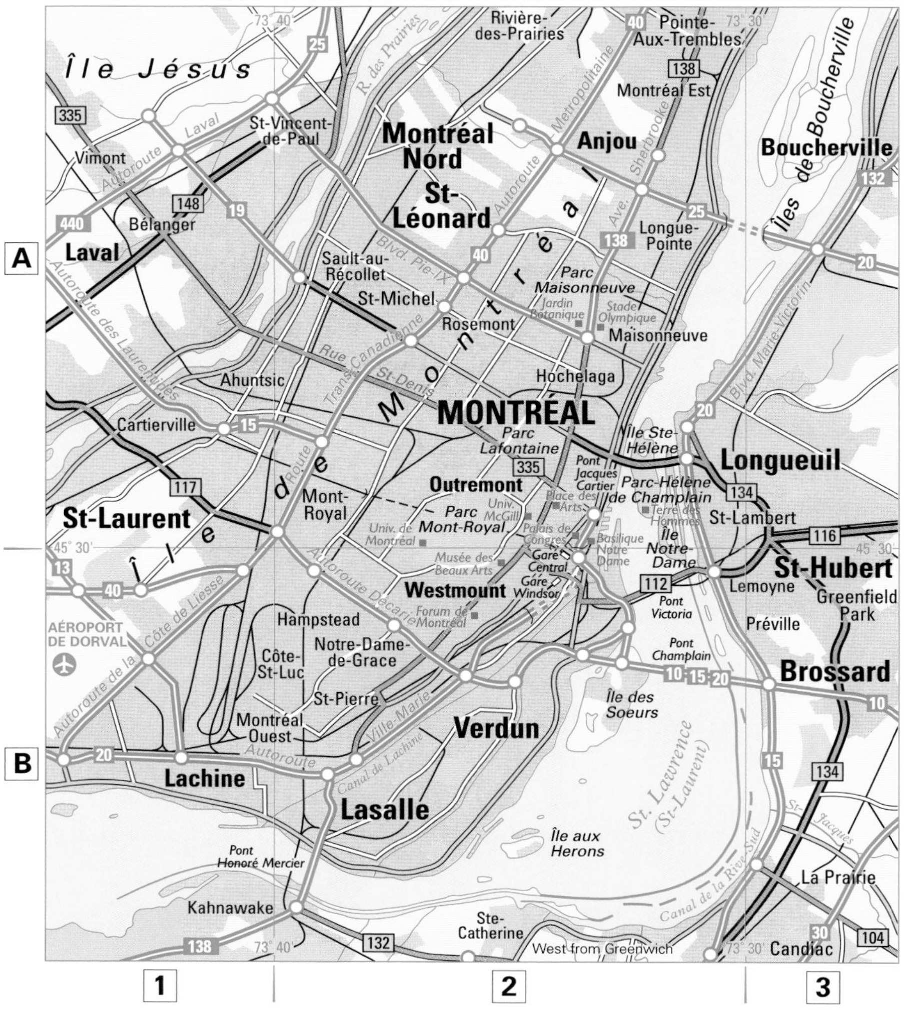
A
B
1
2
3
73° 40'
73° 30'
45° 30'
Rivière-des-Prairies
Pointe-Aux-Trembles
25
40
138
Île Jésus
Montréal Est
Boucherville
335
St-Vincent-de-Paul
Montréal Nord
Anjou
Vimont
Laval
148
19
St-Léonard
Îles de Boucherville
132
440
Bélanger
Laval
Longue-Pointe
Sault-au-Récollet
Parc Maisonneuve
Jardin Botanique
Stade Olympique
St-Michel
Rosemont
Maisonneuve
20
Ahuntsic
Hochelaga
Montréal
MONTRÉAL
Cartierville
15
Parc Lafontaine
Île Ste-Hélène
Longueuil
117
Outremont
Pont Jacques Cartier
Parc-Hélène de Champlain
Mont-Royal
Parc Mont-Royal
134
St-Lambert
St-Laurent
Univ. McGill
Place des Arts
Terre des Hommes
116
Univ. de Montréal
Musée des Beaux Arts
Palais des Congrès
Basilique Notre Dame
St-Hubert
Île de Montréal
13
Gare Centrale
Île Notre-Dame
112
Lemoyne
Greenfield Park
40
Westmount
Gare Windsor
Pont Victoria
AÉROPORT DE DORVAL
Forum de Montréal
Préville
Hampstead
Côte-St-Luc
Notre-Dame-de-Grace
Pont Champlain
Brossard
St-Pierre
10
Île des Soeurs
Montréal Ouest
Verdun
20
Lachine
Lasalle
Canal de Lachine
15
134
St. Lawrence (St-Laurent)
Île aux Herons
Pont Honoré Mercier
La Prairie
Kahnawake
Canal de la Rive Sud
Ste-Catherine
138
132
30
104
Candiac
West from Greenwich
Autoroute des Laurentides
Autoroute Métropolitaine
Trans Canadienne
Autoroute Décarie
Autoroute de la Côte de Liesse
Blvd. Pie-IX
Rue St-Denis
Ave. Sherbrooke
Blvd. Marie Victorin
Ville-Marie
Autoroute Laval
R. des Prairies

CENTRAL MOSCOW

0 km 1
0 miles 0.5

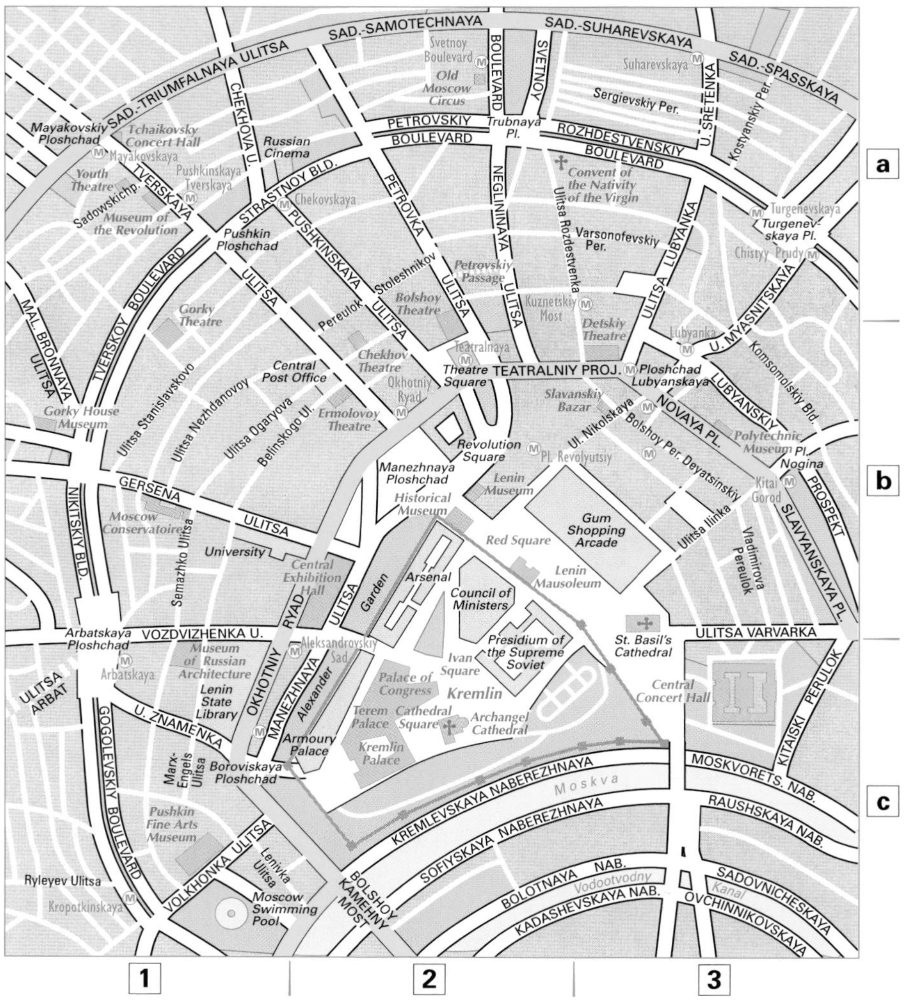
a
b
c
1
2
3
SAD. SAMOTECHNAYA
SAD. SUHAREVSKAYA
SAD. SPASSKAYA
SAD. TRIUMFALNAYA ULITSA
Svetnoy Boulevard
Old Moscow Circus
BOULEVARD
SVETNOY
Suharevskaya
U. SRETENKA
Mayakovskiy Ploshchad
Tchaikovsky Concert Hall
Mayakovskaya
CHEKHOVA U.
Russian Cinema
PETROVSKIY BOULEVARD
Trubnaya Pl.
ROZHDESTVENSKIY BOULEVARD
Sergievskiy Per.
Kostyanskiy Per.
Youth Theatre
Pushkinskaya
Tverskaya
STRASTNOY BLD.
Chekovskaya
Convent of the Nativity of the Virgin
Turgenevskaya
Turgenevskaya Pl.
Chistye Prudy
Sadovskichip
Museum of the Revolution
TVERSKAYA
Pushkin Ploshchad
PUSHKINSKAYA
PETROVKA
NEGLINNAYA ULITSA
Ulitsa Rozhdestvenka
Varsonofevskiy Per.
ULITSA LUBYANKA
Stoleshnikov
Petrovskiy Passage
TVERSKOY BOULEVARD
ULITSA
Bolshoy Theatre
Kuznetskiy Most
Detskiy Theatre
MAL. BRONNAYA ULITSA
Gorky Theatre
Pereulok
Lubyanka
U. MYASNITSKAYA
Komsomolskiy Bld.
Teatralnaya
Chekhov Theatre
Theatre Square
TEATRALNIY PROJ.
Ploshchad Lubyanskaya
LUBYANSKIY
Central Post Office
Okhotniy Ryad
Slavyanskiy Bazar
Gorky House Museum
Ulitsa Stanislavskogo
Ulitsa Nezhdanovoy
Ulitsa Ogaryova
Belinskogo Ul.
Ermolovoy Theatre
Revolution Square
Pl. Revolyutsii
U. Nikolskaya
Bolshoy Per. Deyatsinskiy
NOVAYA PL.
Polytechnic Museum
Nogina
PROSPEKT
NIKITSKIY BLD.
GERSENA
Manezhnaya Ploshchad
Historical Museum
Lenin Museum
Kitai Gorod
Moscow Conservatoire
ULITSA
Gum Shopping Arcade
Ulitsa Ilinka
Vladimirova Pereulok
SLAVYANSKAYA
Semazhko Ulitsa
University
Central Exhibition Hall
Red Square
Lenin Mausoleum
Arsenal
Council of Ministers
Garden
RYAD
ULITSA
Arbatskaya Ploshchad
VOZDVIZHENKA U.
Presidium of the Supreme Soviet
St. Basil's Cathedral
ULITSA VARVARKA
Arbatskaya
Museum of Russian Architecture
Aleksandrovskiy Sad
Ivan Square
Kremlin
Central Concert Hall
ULITSA ARBAT
Lenin State Library
OKHOTNIY
MANEZHNAYA
Alexander
Palace of Congress
Terem Palace
Cathedral Square
Archangel Cathedral
KITAISKI PERULOK
U. ZNAMENKA
Armoury Palace
Kremlin Palace
MOSKVORETS. NAB.
GOGOLEVSKIY BOULEVARD
Marx-Engels Ulitsa
Borovitskaya Ploshchad
KREMLEVSKAYA NABEREZHNAYA
Moskva
RAUSHSKAYA NAB.
Pushkin Fine Arts Museum
SOFIYSKAYA NABEREZHNAYA
Vodootvodny
Ryleyev Ulitsa
VOLKHONKA ULITSA
Lenivka Ulitsa
BOLSHOY KAMENNY MOST
BOLOTNAYA NAB.
Kanal
SADOVNICHESKAYA
Kropotkinskaya
Moscow Swimming Pool
KADASHEVSKAYA NAB.
OVCHINNIKOVSKAYA

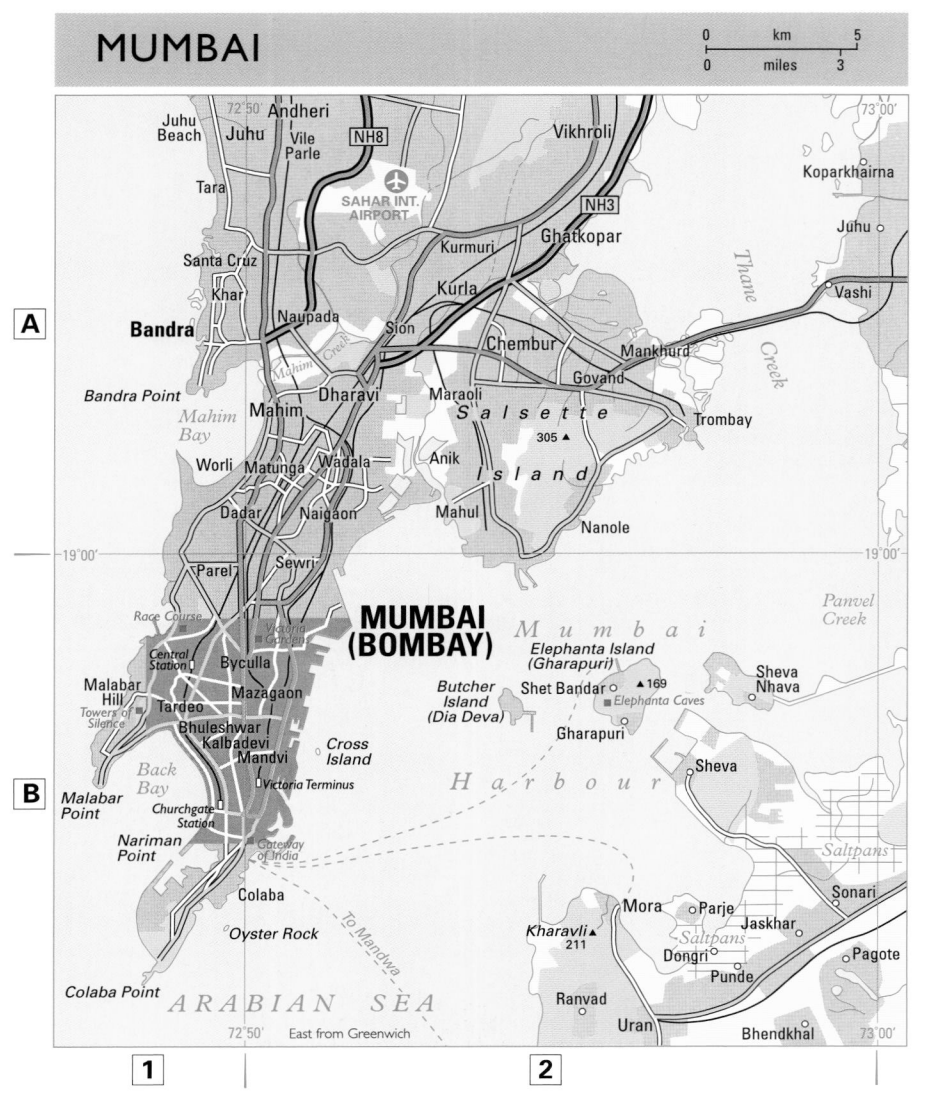

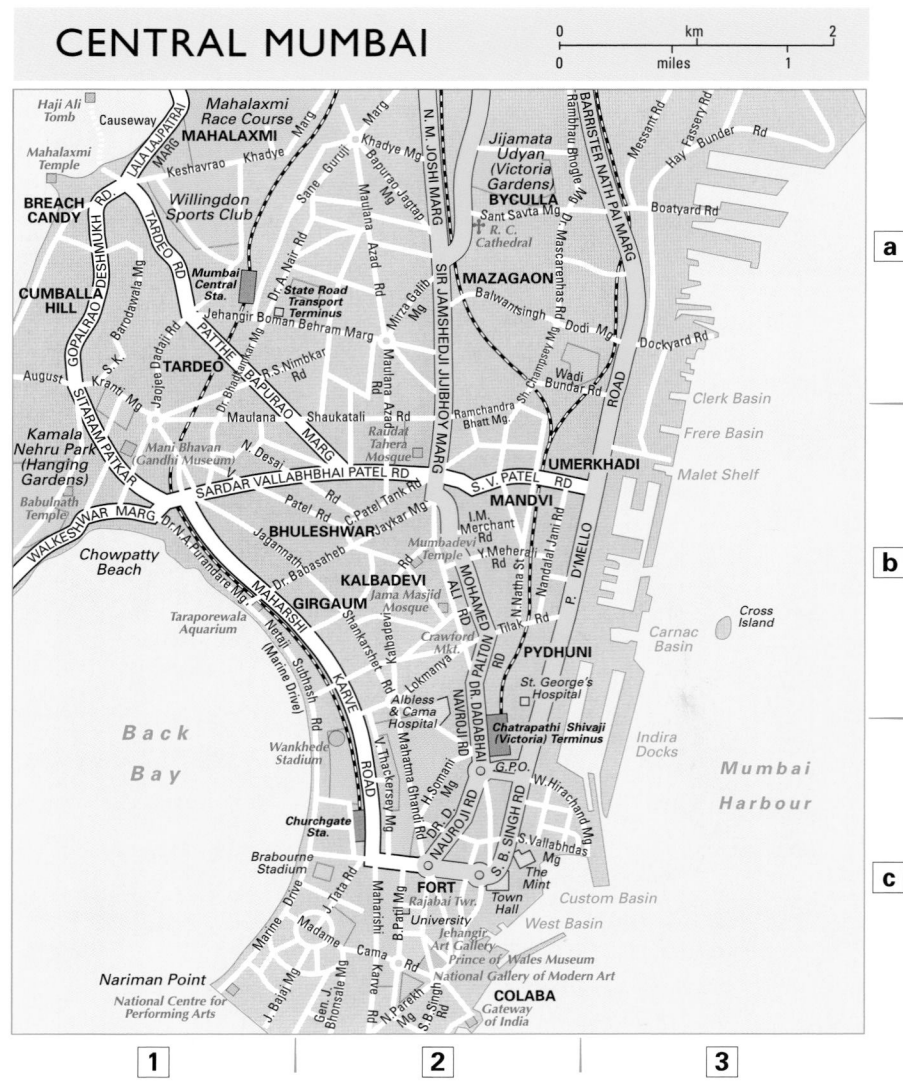

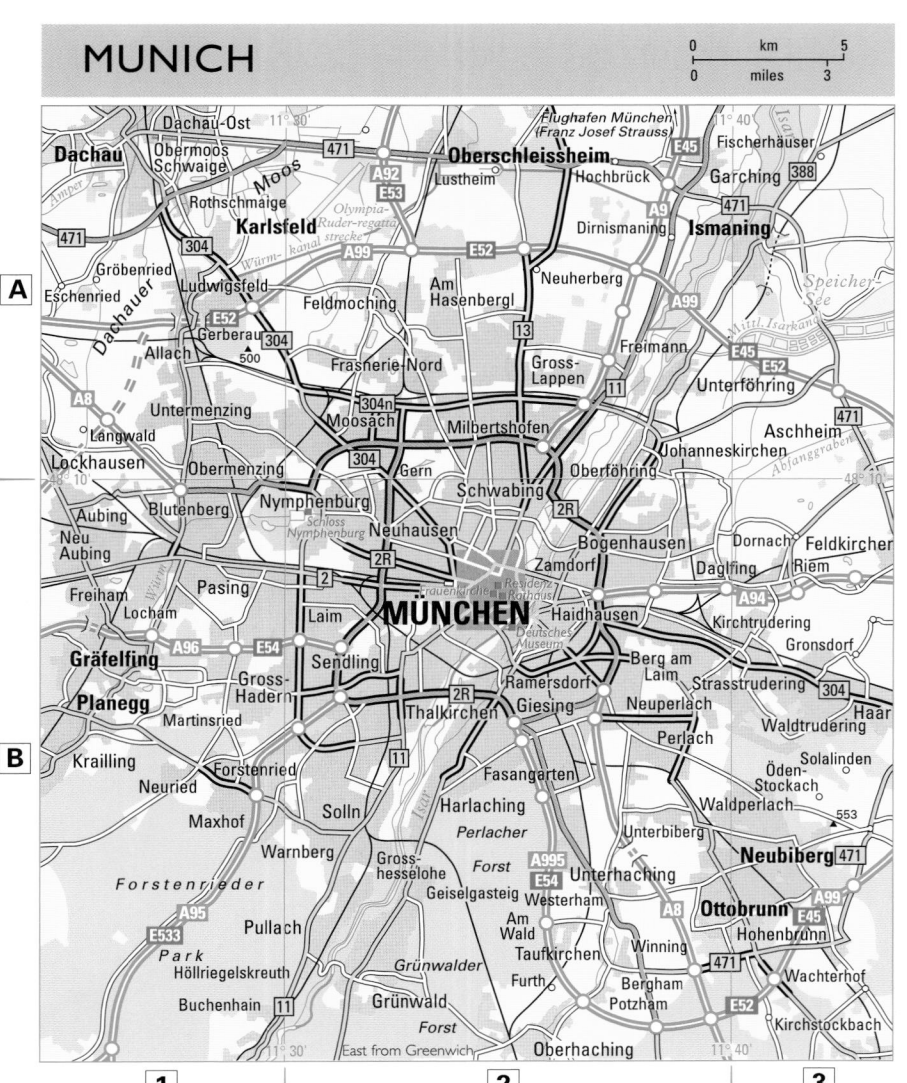

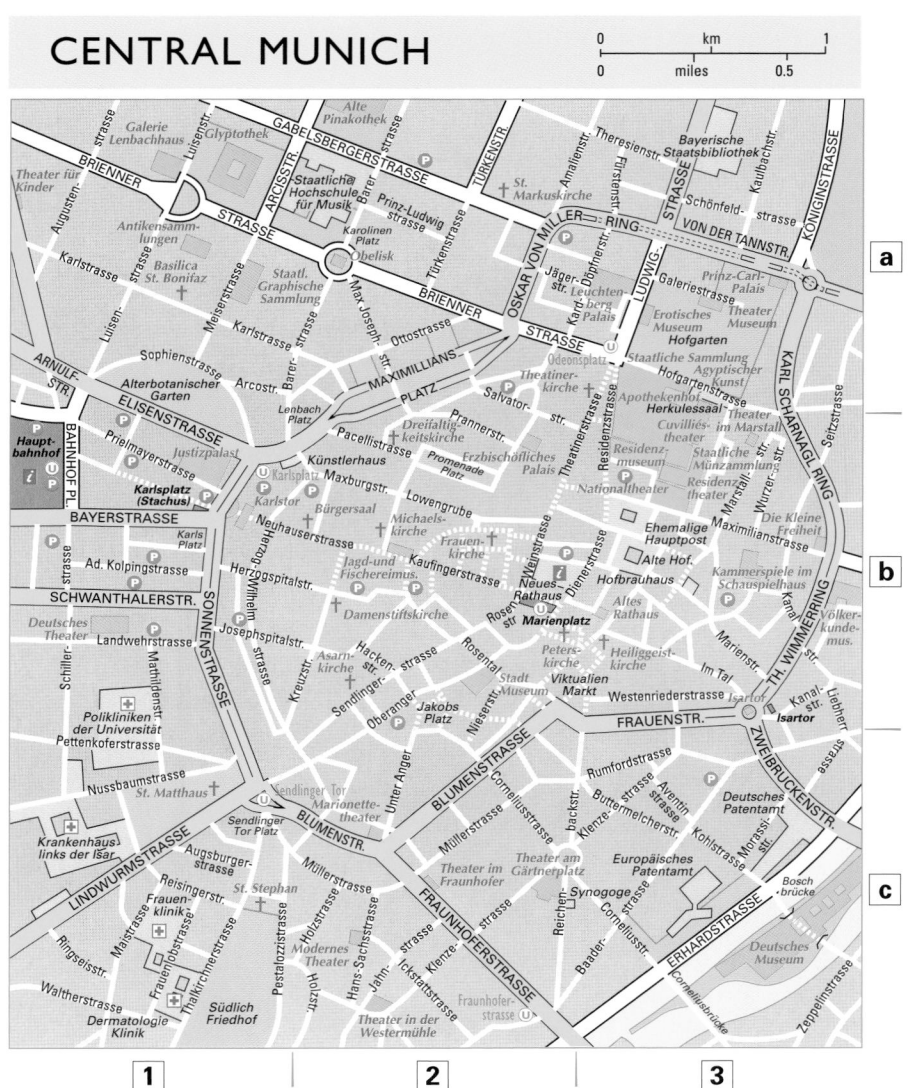

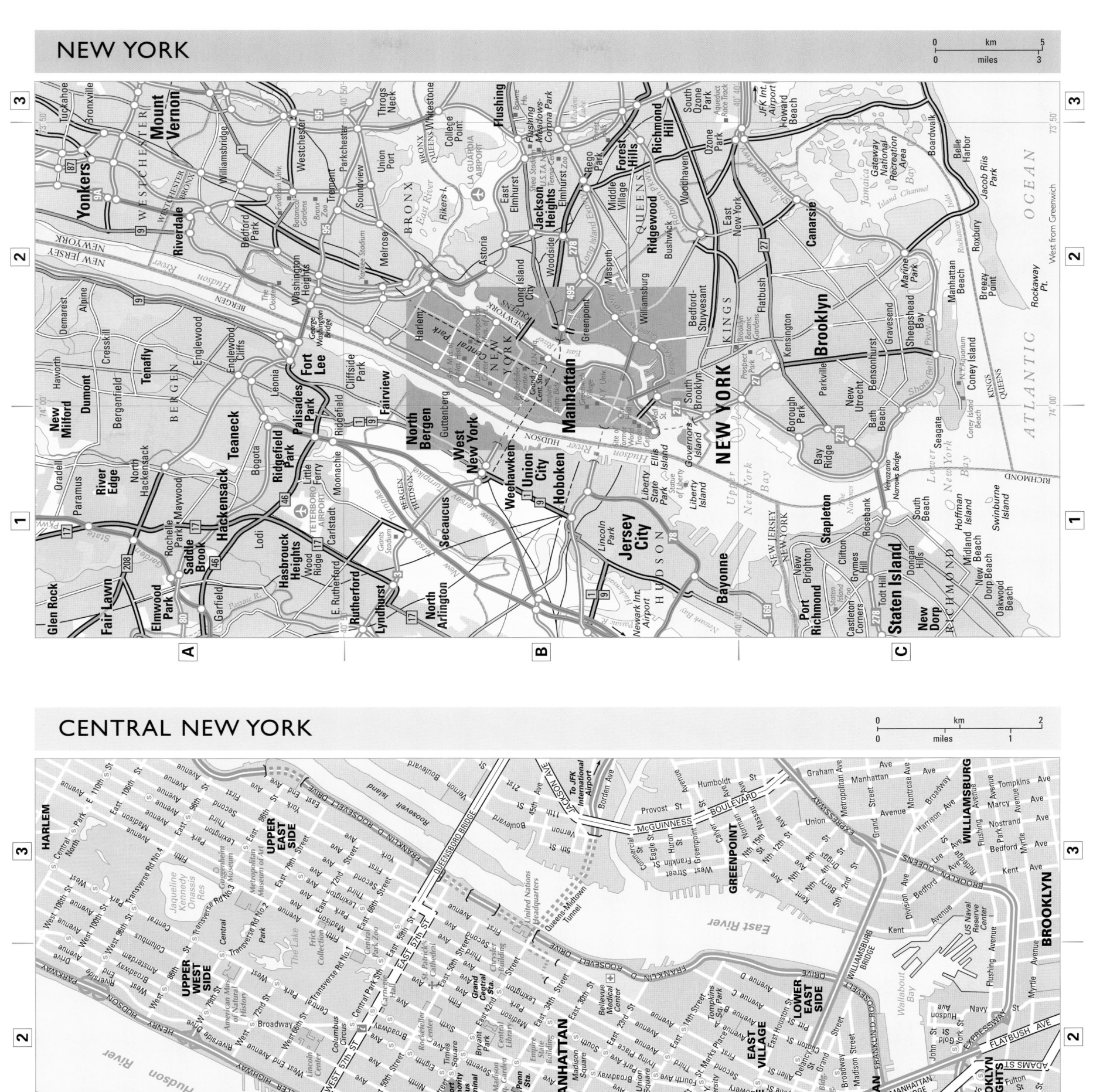

NEW YORK

km 0 — 5
miles 0 — 3

Mount Vernon
Bronxville
Tuckahoe
Yonkers
WESTCHESTER
Williamsbridge
Westchester
Parkchester
Throgs Neck
Whitestone
Flushing
College Point
South Ozone Park
JFK Int. Airport
Howard Beach
ATLANTIC OCEAN
West from Greenwich

Riverdale
Bedford Park
BRONX
Fordham
Tremont
Union Port
Soundview
BRONX
Flushing
Meadows-Corona Park
Richmond Hill
Aqueduct Race Track
Boardwalk
Belle Harbor
Jacob Riis Park

NEW JERSEY
NEW YORK
Hudson River
Washington Heights
Astoria
Long Island City
Jackson Heights
Woodside
QUEENS
Middle Village
Elmhurst
Forest Hills
Rego Park
Ridgewood
Woodhaven
East New York
Ozone Park
Canarsie
Manhattan Beach
Marine Park
Breezy Point
Rockaway Pt.
Rockaway Beach

Englewood
Fort Lee
Cliffside Park
Fairview
Harlem
Central Park
NEW YORK
Greenpoint
Williamsburg
Bedford-Stuyvesant
KINGS
Brooklyn
Kensington
Flatbush
Gravesend
Sheepshead Bay
Coney Island

New Milford
Demarest
Alpine
Cresskill
Haworth
Tenafly
Leonia
Palisades Park
Ridgefield Park
Teaneck
Ridgefield
North Bergen
West New York
Guttenberg
Union City
Weehawken
Hoboken
Manhattan
South Brooklyn
Prospect Park
Borough Park
New Utrecht
Bath Beach
Bay Ridge
Bensonhurst
Verrazano Narrows Bridge
New York

Oradell
River Edge
Paramus
Hackensack
BERGEN
Bogota
Maywood
Lodi
Little Ferry
Moonachie
Secaucus
HUDSON
Liberty State Park
Liberty Island
Ellis Island
Governors Island
Upper New York Bay
RICHMOND
Stapleton
Rosebank
South Beach
Midland Beach

Glen Rock
Fair Lawn
Elmwood Park
Saddle Brook
Rochelle Park
Garfield
Hasbrouck Heights
Wood Ridge
Carlstadt
TETERBORO AIRPORT
E. Rutherford
Rutherford
Lyndhurst
North Arlington
Secaucus
Lincoln Park
Jersey City
Bayonne
NEW JERSEY
Newark Int. Airport
Port Richmond
New Brighton
Clifton
Grymes Hill
Dongan Hills
Staten Island
New Dorp
Oakwood Beach
Todt Hill
Castleton Corners
RICHMOND

A   B   C

CENTRAL NEW YORK

km 0 — 2
miles 0 — 1

HARLEM
UPPER EAST SIDE
UPPER WEST SIDE
Roosevelt Island
To JFK International Airport
WILLIAMSBURG
BROOKLYN
GREENPOINT
East River

Central Park
Jacqueline Kennedy Onassis Res.
The Lake
Metropolitan Museum of Art
Guggenheim Museum
Frick Collection
Central Park Zoo
Queensboro Bridge
United Nations Headquarters
MANHATTAN
American Mus. of Natural History
Lincoln Center
Columbus Circle
Rockefeller Center
Grand Central Sta.
St. Patrick's Cathedral
Chrysler Building
Bellevue Medical Center
Times Square
Bryant Park
N.Y. Public Library
Empire State Building
Madison Square
EAST VILLAGE
LOWER EAST SIDE
Williamsburg Bridge

Hudson River
GUTTENBERG
WEST NEW YORK
Port Authority Bus Terminal
Penn Sta.
G.P.O.
CHELSEA
GREENWICH VILLAGE
Washington Square
LITTLE ITALY
CHINA TOWN
Manhattan Bridge
BROOKLYN HEIGHTS

WEEHAWKEN
Passenger Ship Terminal
Intrepid Air & Space Museum
Lincoln Tunnel
SOHO
LOWER MANHATTAN
Brooklyn Bridge
Fulton Fish Market

UNION CITY
HOBOKEN
Holland Tunnel to Newark
Hudson River
World Financial Center
Site of former World Trade Center
Battery Park
Ellis I. & Statue of Liberty Ferry
Staten Island Ferry
Brooklyn-Battery Tunnel
Governors Island

a   b   c   d   e   f

COPYRIGHT PHILIP'S

OSAKA

km 5
miles 3

135° 10' 135° 20' 135° 30'
East from Greenwich

▲509 Funasaka **Takarazuka** Ina Ōsaka-fido-sha Expressway Senriyama Yamada **Hirakata** 171
Arima ▲462 171 **Itami** Yamada Kori 1
Karato ▲722 **Settsu** Meishin Kosoku Expressway
▲598 Rokkō-Zan ▲932 OSAKA INTERNATIONAL AIRPORT **Toyonaka** **Neyagawa**
Tanigami Yamada Kwansei Gakuin University 173 **Suita** Yodo
Iwazono Hirota Higashiyodogawa **Kadoma** **Moriguchi** **Shijonawate**
428 Rokkō Tunnel Asahi 1 170
Obu-tōge ▲365 Maya-Zan ▲699 Kōbe University **Nishinomiya** 43 Naruo **Amagasaki** Jūsō Oyodo Miyakojima Jōtō **Daitō**
▲403 Okamoto **Ashiya** 2 Umeda Kita Higashi Kōnoike
Fukiai Nada Higashinada Fukushima Ōsaka Castle Higashinari Ishikiri
Ikuta Aji Nishiyodogawa Minami 308
KŌBE Rokkō Island Konohana Nishi Ikuno Higashinari
Nagata Kōbe Port Island Minato Naniwa **ŌSAKA** Kizuri **Higashiōsaka**
Suma Harbour Tennōji Abeno Kyūhōji Yamamoto
34° 40' Ōsaka Museum Suntory Museum Zoo Ōsaka Museum
Taishō Shitennō Temple **Yao**
Ōsaka Harbour Nishinari Sumiyoshi Shrine Sumiyoshi 25
Kisa Higashisumiyoshi Tainaka Onchi
O s a k a   B a y Sakai Harbour Ikeuchi YAO AIRPORT
Yamato 26 **Kashiwara**
Matsubara Fujidera
Sakai

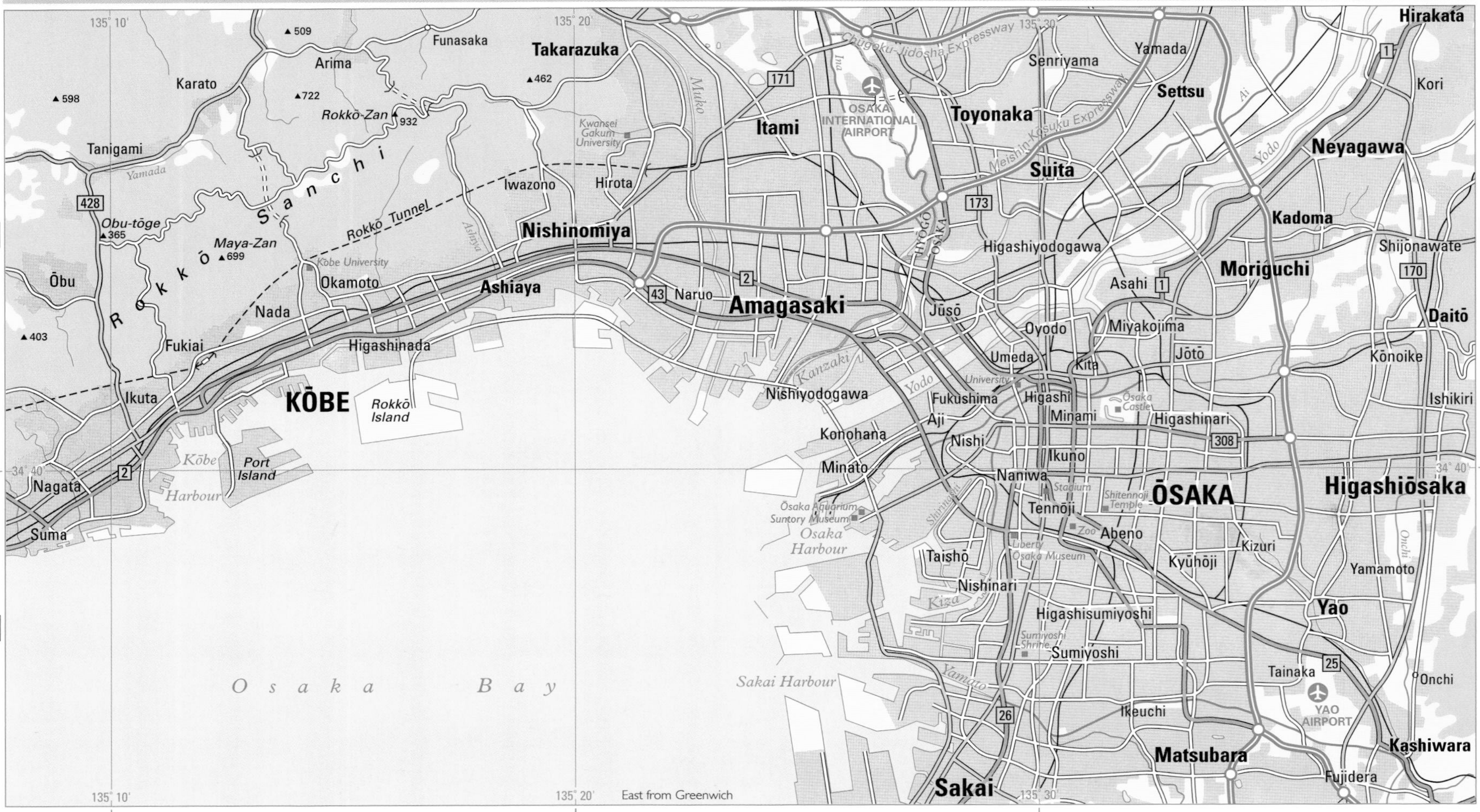

1 2 3 4

OSLO

km 5
miles 3

60° 00' 10° 30' 10° 40' 10° 50' 60° 00'
By OSLO AKERSHUS **Tryvannshøgda** ▲531 **Maridalen**
Bogstadvann Maridalsvatnet Alnsjøen
Burudvatn ▲418 Sognsvann
Ila **Holmenkollen** Kjelsås **Gorud**
Røa Ris Ullevål Rødtvet
Bærums Verk 168 RING 3 Sinsen 163 4
Lijordet **Ullern** **OSLO** RING 2 Alna E6
Bryn ▲379 Haslum Skøyen 4 **Tøyen**
Kolsås Vestbane sta. Sentralsta. Bryn
164 160 Stabekk Norsk Folke Museum Akershus Slott Ryen E6
E16 **Bærum** Høvik 166 Bygdøy Hovedøya Oppsal Bøler
Tanum E18 Lindøya
Sandvika Snarøya Fornebu Ormøya **Bekkelaget**
Slependen Frederikshavn Helsingborg København Hirtshals, Kiel Lambertseter Østmark-kapellet
Hvalstad Nesøya Østøya **Nesoddtangen** Nordstrand
Nesbru Brønnøya Oksval Malmøya Ljabru
Asker 165 Flaskebekk Skoklefall 155 Hauketo
E18 Konglungen Ingierstrand Klemetsrud
167 Vollen 157 ▲215 Torvvik **Kolbotn** E6
59° 50' Blakstad Nesodden 155 **Oppegård** E6
Slemmestad Fjellstrand 156 Hasle
Svestad Oppegård 152 Myrvoll
Garder Blylaget E18 **Oppegård**
59° 30' Nærsnes ▲134 10° 50'
10° 40' East from Greenwich

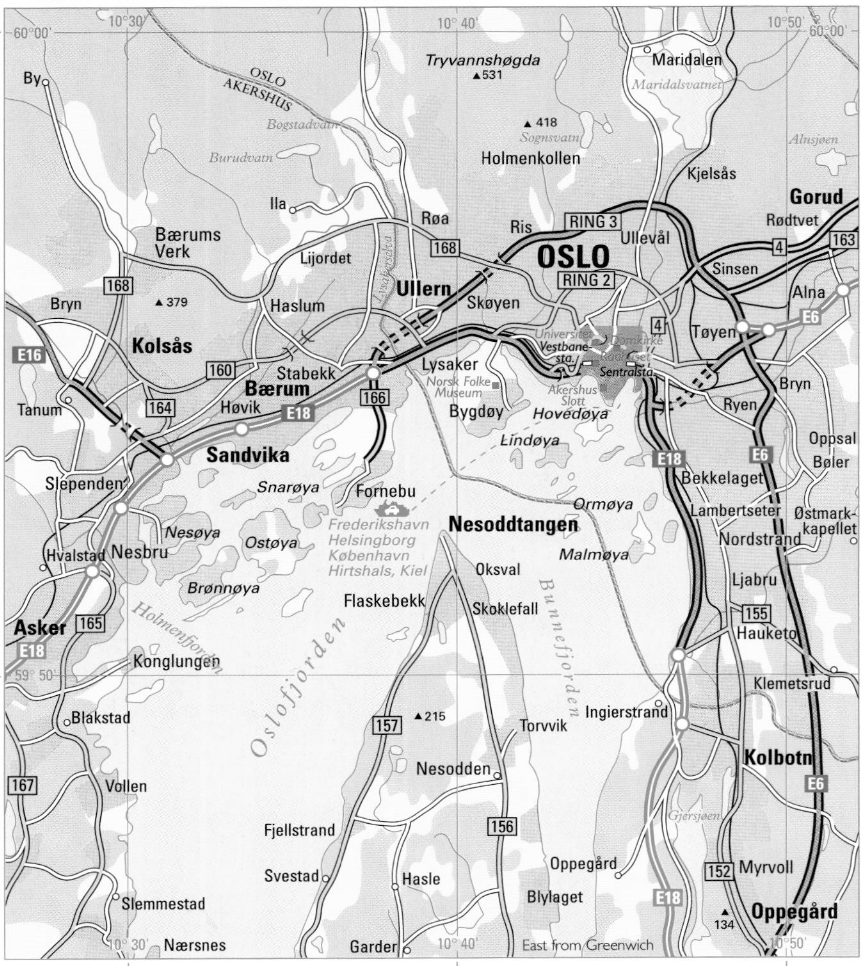

1 2 3 4

CENTRAL OSLO

km 0,5
miles 0.25

Stens bergg. Rikshospitalet Vår Frelsers Gravlund Westye Egebergs gate Nordre gate Korsgata Markveien Torvald Meyers gate
Welhavens gate PARKVEIEN Hegdehaugsveien PILESTREDET Vor Frue kirke Brenneriveien
WERGELANDSVEIEN Hofsvens Langes Damstredet veien Rostedsgt. Hausmans gate Akerselva
Slotts parken Wessels gate Bruns gate Vulkan Deichmansgate Osterhaus gate
Nordahl Kunstindustri mus. St. Olavs gate Fredens gate Maribos gate Torggata Mariboes gate
Det Kongelige Slottet ST. OLAVS GATE PILESTREDET St. Olavs gate Thor Olsens gate HAMMERSBORG TUNNELEN Henrik Ibsens gate Calmeyers gate Storgata
KRISTIAN GATE Keysers Deichmanske bibliotek Youngs-Torget Bern Anker's gate Christian Krohgs gate
Dronningparken Historisk museum Fredensborgveien Grubbegata MØLLERGATA
DRAMMENSVEIEN IV GATE Nasjonal galleriet Karl Johans gate MØLLERGATA Hausmanns gate
Universitet Det Norske Teater GRENSEN Brugata
Ibsen-museet National-museet National theatret Stortinget Operaen VATERLANDS TUNNELEN STENERSGATA
MUNKEDAMSVEIEN Stenersens museum Klingenberggata Stortingsgata Biskop Gunnerus' gate Oslo Spektrum
Konserthuset Oslo Nansens plass Kronpr. Marthas plass Karl Johans Jernbane-torget Buss-terminalen
Vestbane stasjonen Rådhuset Rosenkrantz Prinsens Kongens Domkirke Jernbane Torget Grønland
Dokkveien Nedre Vollgata Øvre Slotts gate Skippergata NYLANDSVEIEN **Sentralstasjon**
OSLOTUNNELEN Akersgata Prinsens gate Hovedpost-kontor Strandgata Havnegata
Christiania torv Rådhusgata Tollbugata Dronningens gate Fred Olsens gate Børsen Skippergata
Teater-museet Kongens Arkitektur museet Myntgata BISPEGATA
Museet for samtidskunst Akershus Slott og festning Astrup Fearnley museet Kongens
Pipervika Hjemmefront-museet **Bjørvika** **Bispevika**
Forsvars-museet Kongens Havneveien
Festningsplass **Frederikshavn, Helsingborg, København**

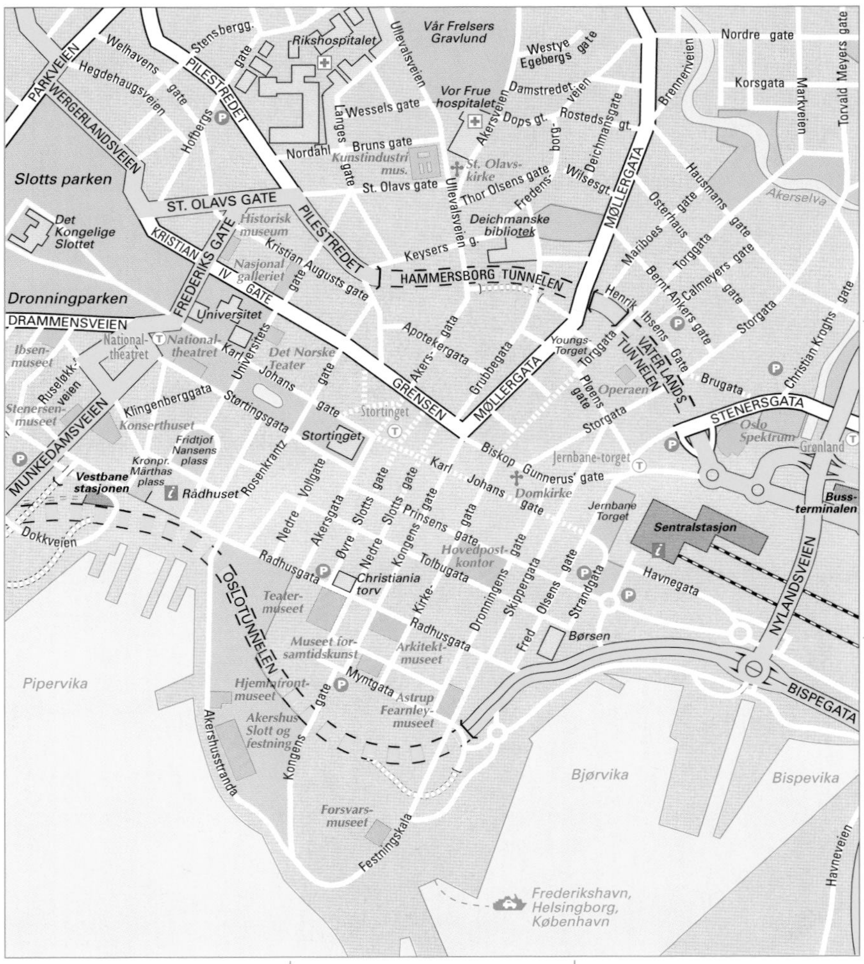

1 2 3

PARIS

km 5
miles 3

Carrières- Achères St.-Germain de Forêt de Maisons-Laffitte Argenteuil Sartrouville Gennevilliers Stains St.-Denis Parc de la Courneuve Le Blanc Mesnil Aulnay-sous-Bois Sevran Tremblay-en-France Villeparisis
Poissy Chambourcy St.-Germain-en-Laye Aigremont Mesnil-le-Roi Houilles Bezons Bois-Colombes La Courneuve Le Bourget Drancy Livry-Gargan Coubron Le Pin Courtry Villevaudé
Le Pecq Montesson Carrières-sur-Seine La Garenne-Colombes Colombes Asnières Clichy St.-Ouen Aubervilliers Bobigny Les Pavillons-sous-Bois Clichy-sous-Bois Montfermeil Chantereine Brou-sur-Chantereine Montjay-la-Tour
Chatou Croissy-sur-Seine Courbevoie Puteaux Levallois-Perret Pantin Le Pré-St.-Gervais Les Lilas Noisy-le-Sec Romainville Rosny-sous-Bois Gagny Chelles
Le Port-Marly Nanterre Suresnes Neuilly-sur-Seine Gare St.-Lazare Gare du Nord Gare de l'Est Bagnolet Villemomble Neuilly-sur-Marne Vaires-sur-Marne
Mareil-Marly Rueil-Malmaison Bois de Boulogne Arc de Triomphe PARIS Notre Dame Montreuil Fontenay-sous-Bois Vincennes Neuilly-Plaisance Gournay-sur-Marne Noisiel Torcy
La Celle-St.-Cloud Garches St.-Cloud Vaucresson Tour Eiffel Invalides Gare d'Austerlitz Gare de Lyon St.-Mandé Nogent-sur-Marne Le Perreux-sur-Marne Villiers-sur-Marne Noisy-le-Grand Champs-sur-Marne Marne-la-Vallée
Rennemoulin Le Chesnay Versailles Ville-d'Avray Boulogne-Billancourt Vanves Gare Montparnasse Charenton-le-P. St.-Maurice Joinville-le-Pont Champigny-sur-Marne Cœuilly Le Plessis-Trévise Émerainville
Fontenay-le-Fleury Meudon Issy-les-Moulineaux Malakoff Montrouge Gentilly Le Kremlin-Bicêtre Ivry-sur-Seine Maisons-Alfort St.-Maur-des-Fossés Chennevières-sur-Marne La Queue-en-Brie Combault Roissy-en-Brie
Bois d'Arcy Chaville Clamart Châtillon Bagneux Arcueil Cachan Alfortville Créteil Ormesson-sur-Marne Pontault-Combault
St.-Cyr-l'École Vélizy-Villacoublay Le Plessis-Robinson Fontenay-aux-Roses Villejuif Vitry-sur-Seine Bonneuil-sur-Marne Sucy-en-Brie Ozoir-la-Ferrière
Montigny-le-Bretonneux Guyancourt Buc Viroflay Châtenay-Malabry Sceaux Bourg-la-Reine L'Haÿ-les-Roses Chevilly-Larue Thiais Choisy-le-Roi Noiseau Notre-Dame Forêt de
Magny-les-Hameaux St.-Lambert Châteaufort Les Loges-en-Josas Jouy-en-Josas Bièvres Verrières-le-Buisson Antony Fresnes Rungis Orly Valenton Limeil-Brévannes Boissy-St.-Léger Lésigny
Milon-la-Chapelle Cresserly Toussus-le-Noble Igny Vauhallan Saclay Massy Wissous Aéroport de Paris-Orly Villeneuve-le-Roi Ablon-sur-Seine Villeneuve-St.-Georges Marolles-en-Brie Grosbois Santeny Férolles-Attilly
Rhodon St.-Aubin Palaiseau Chilly-Mazarin Paray-Vieille Poste Athis-Mons Crosne Yerres Villecresnes Chevry-Cossigny

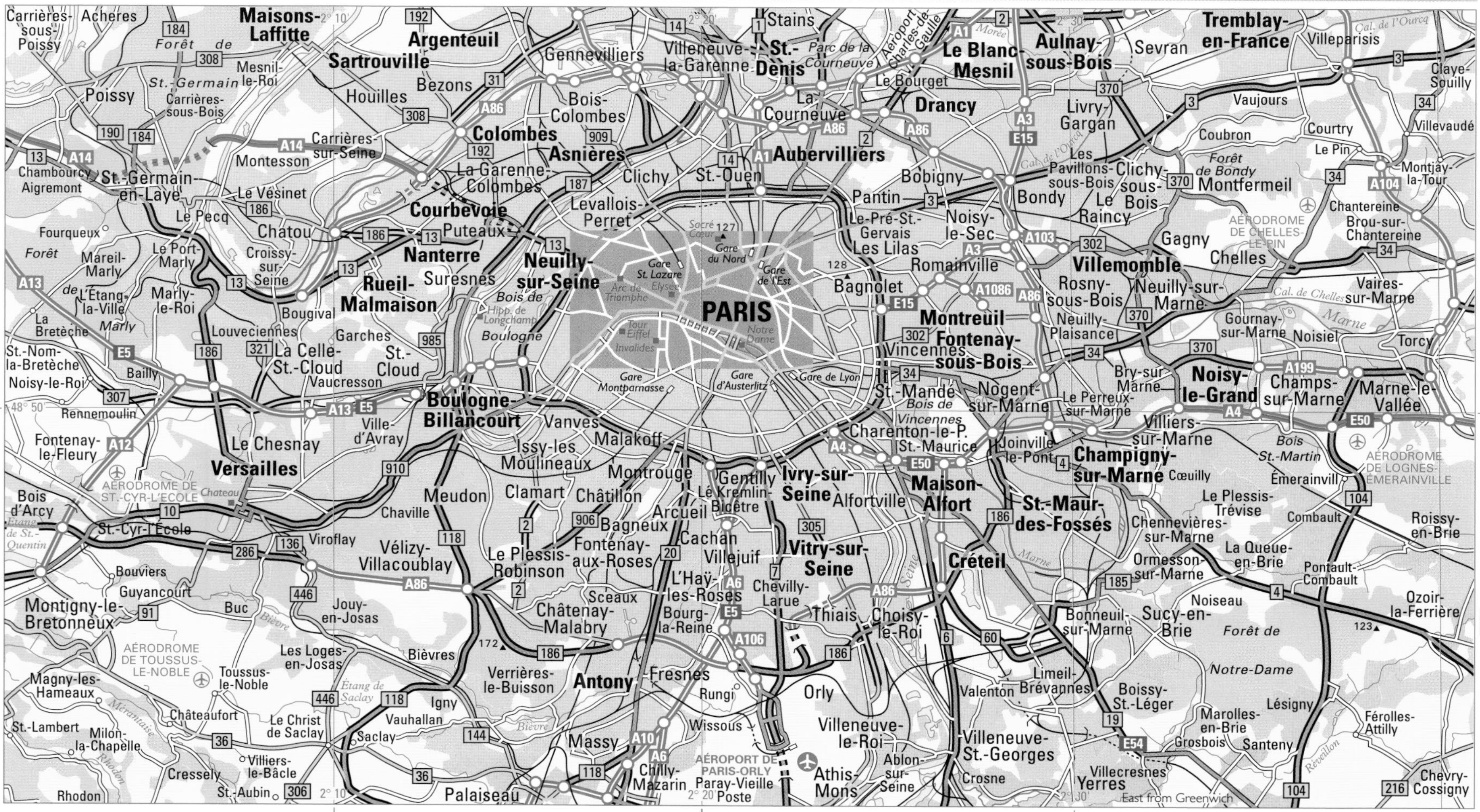

East from Greenwich

1 2 3 4

CENTRAL PARIS

km 1
miles 0.5

Av. de la Pte. de Champerret Porte de Champerret Pte. de Champerret Sacré Cœur Moulin Rouge Abbesses La Chapelle Stalingrad
Clinique Henri Hartman Péreire R. des Batignolles Pl. de Clichy Barbès Rochechouart Av. de Flandre
Porte Maillot Palais des Congrès Parc Monceau St.-Augustin Gare St.-Lazare Gare du Nord Hôpital Fernand Widal Av. Jean Jaurès
Arc de Triomphe Avenue Foch Pl. Charles de Gaulle Étoile Av. des Champs Élysées Opéra Madeleine Gare de l'Est Bd. de la Villette
Bois de Boulogne Porte Dauphine Trocadéro Palais de Chaillot Grand Palais Petit Palais Place de la Concorde Jardin des Tuileries Louvre Forum Les Halles Centre Pompidou Musée Picasso
Tour Eiffel Champ de Mars Hôtel des Invalides Musée d'Orsay Musée du Louvre Palais de Justice Île de la Cité Notre Dame Hôtel de Ville Place de la Bastille
U.N.E.S.C.O. École Militaire Palais du Luxembourg Panthéon Sorbonne Île St. Louis Gare de Lyon

1 2 3 4 5

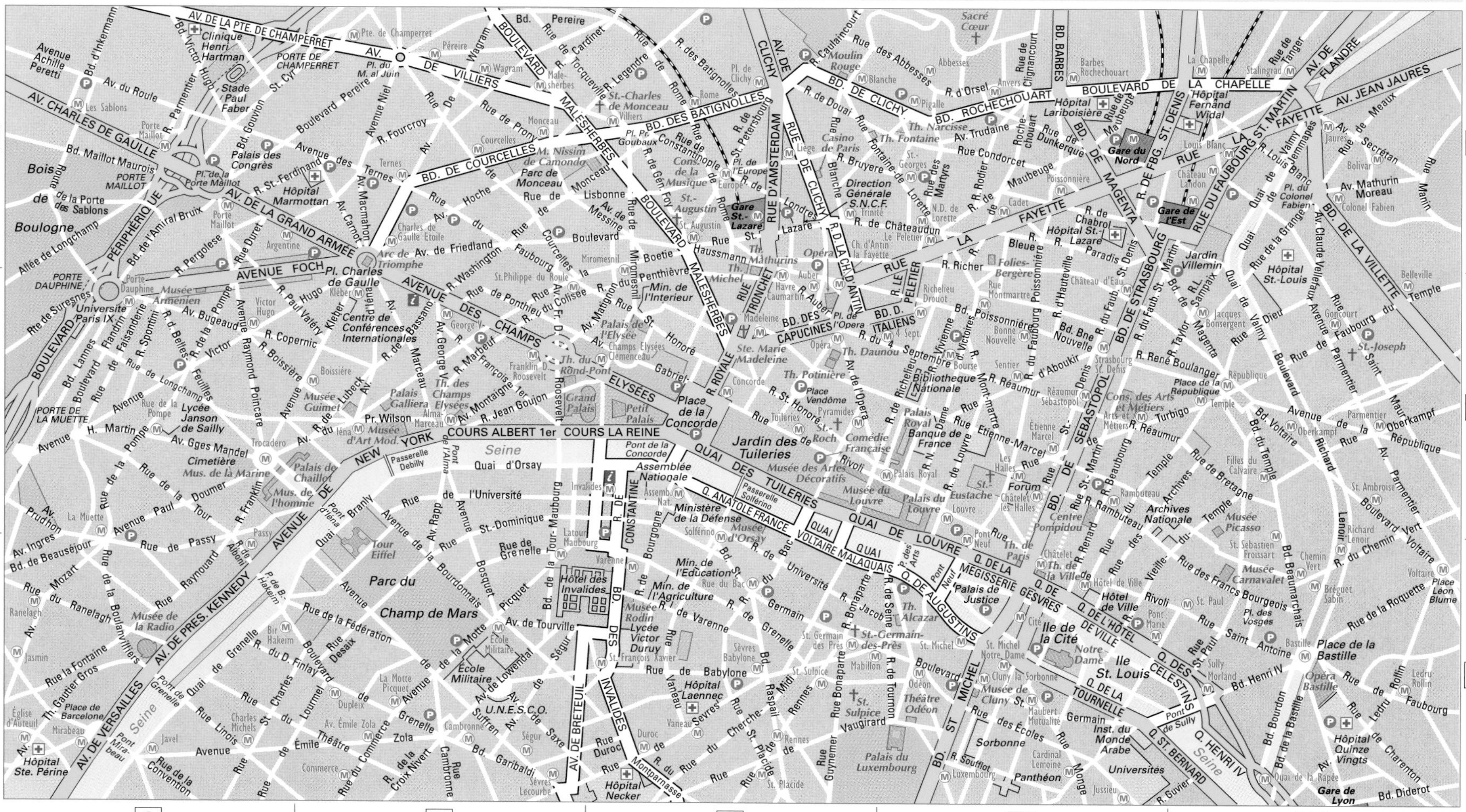

COPYRIGHT PHILIP'S

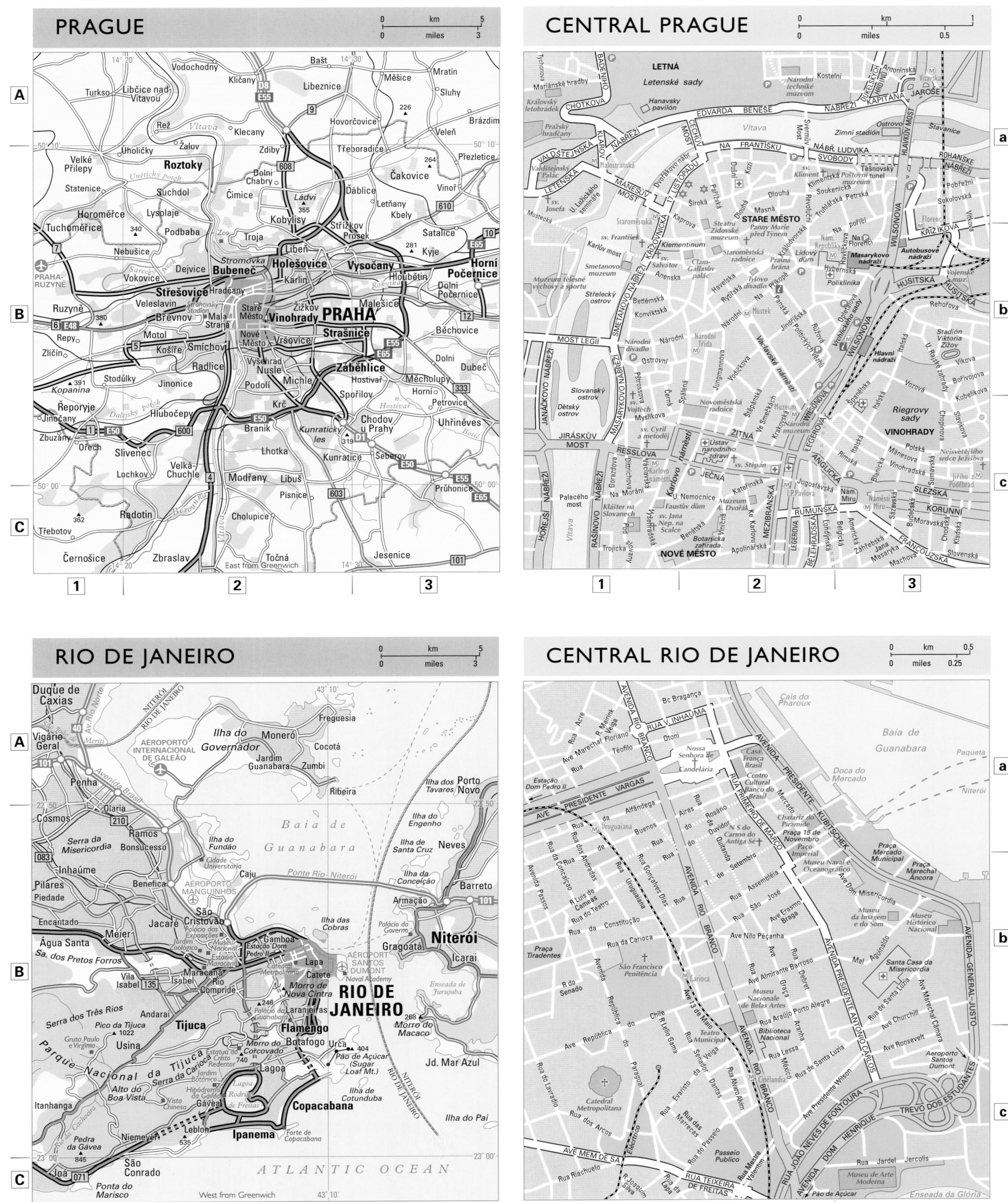

PRAGUE

km 0 5
miles 0 3

CENTRAL PRAGUE

km 0 1
miles 0 0.5

RIO DE JANEIRO

km 0 5
miles 0 3

CENTRAL RIO DE JANEIRO

km 0 0.5
miles 0 0.25

ROME

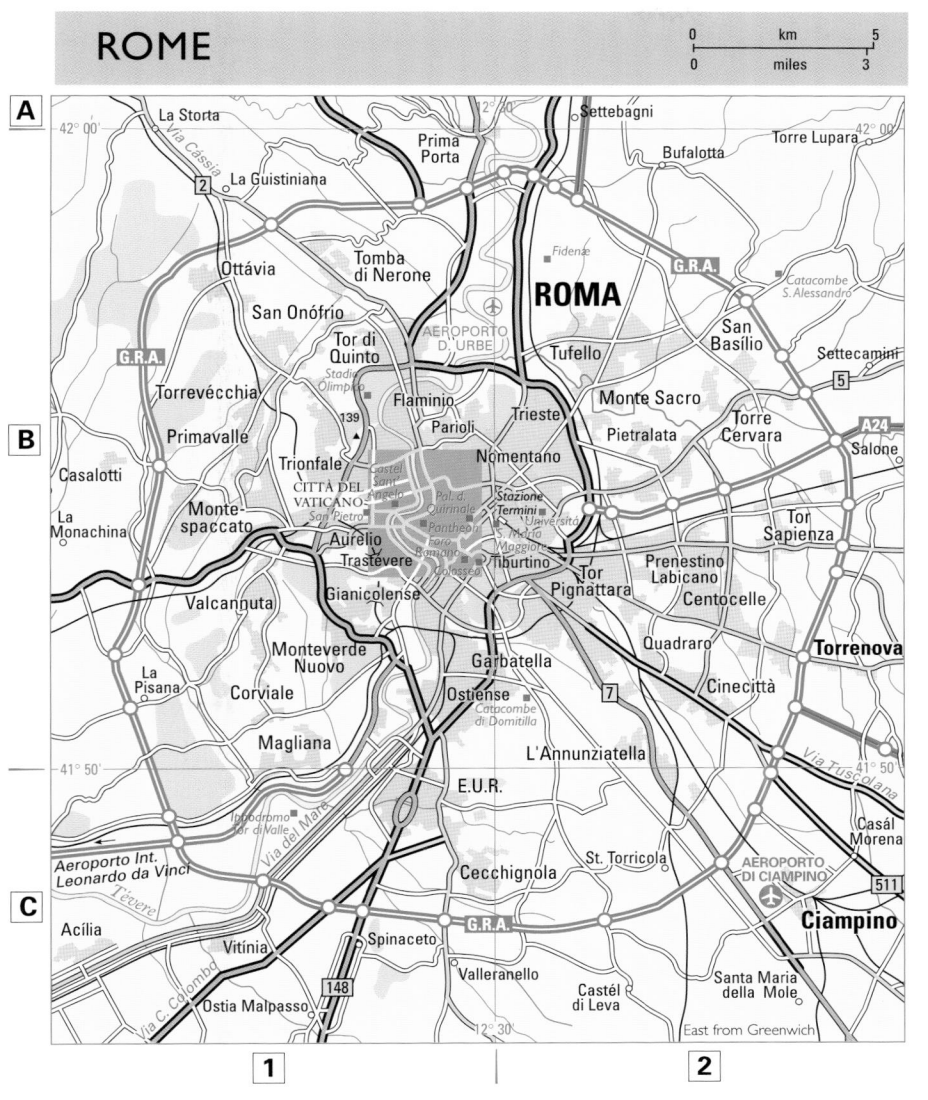

CENTRAL ROME

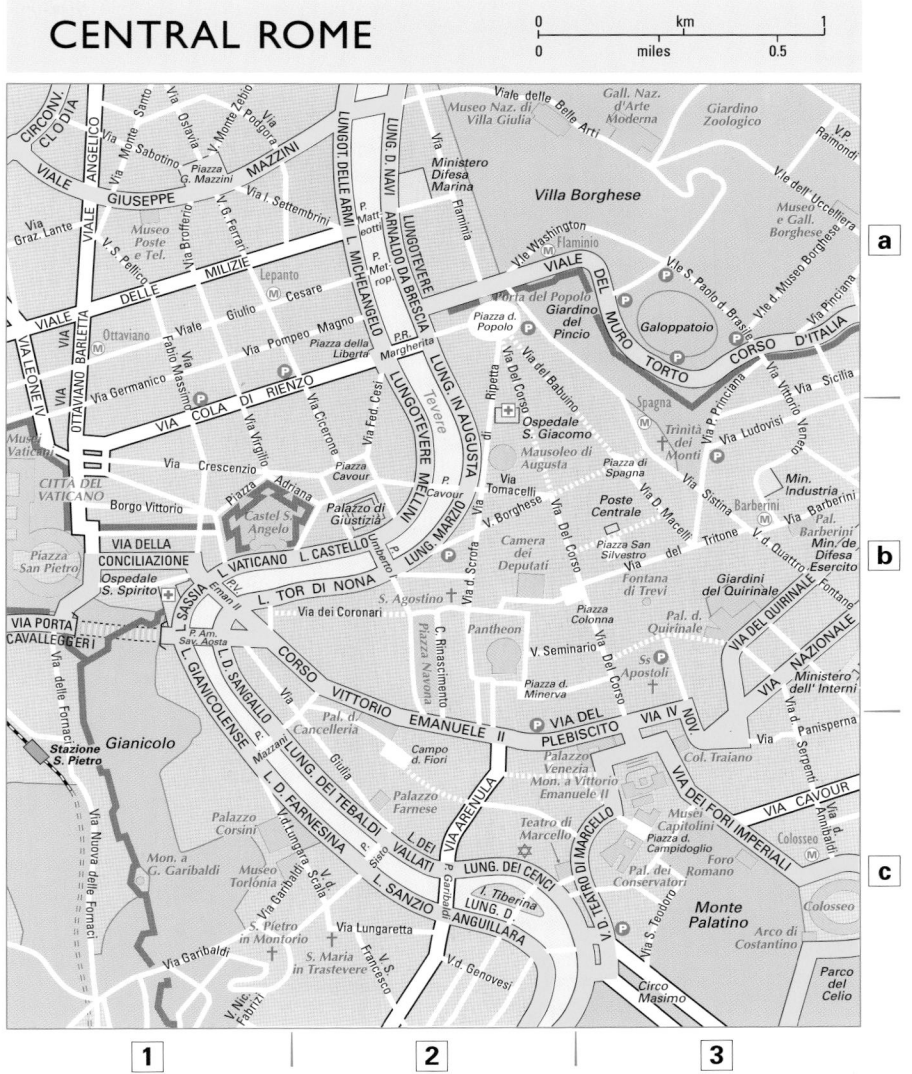

SAN FRANCISCO

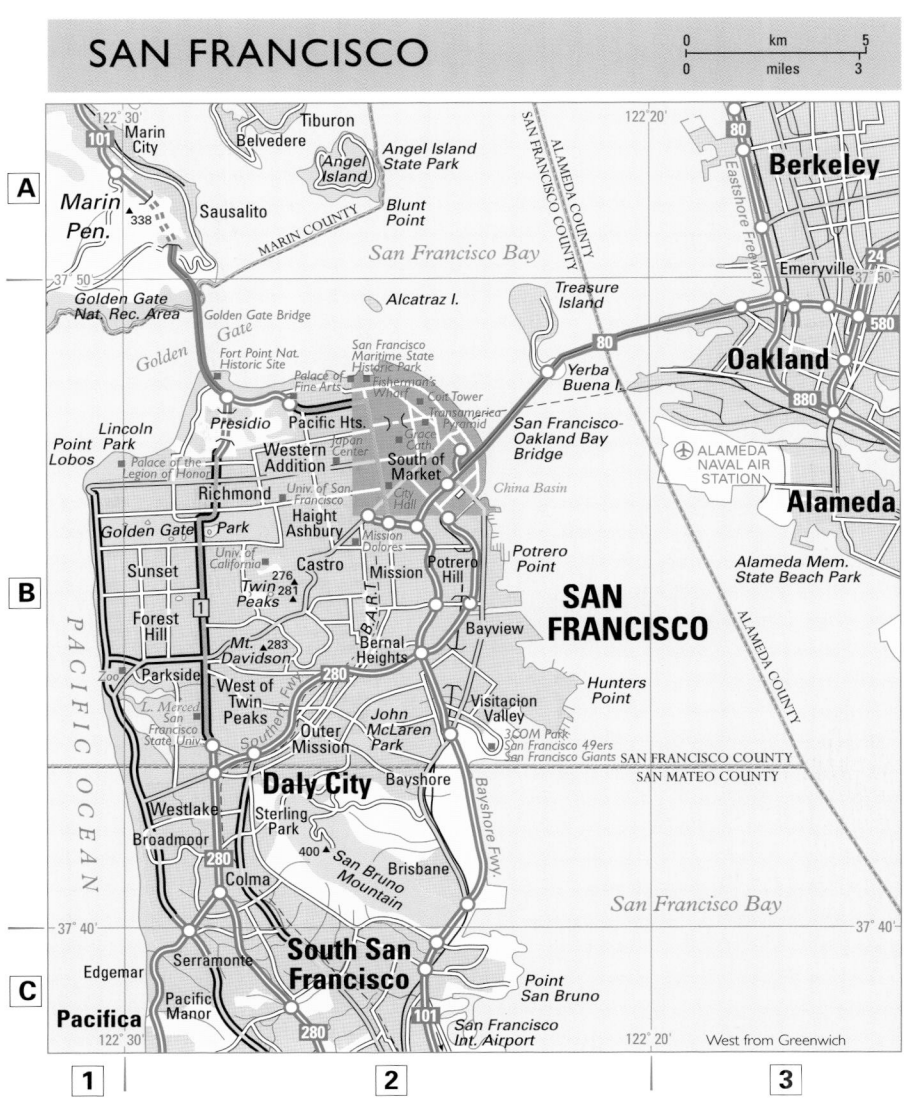

CENTRAL SAN FRANCISCO

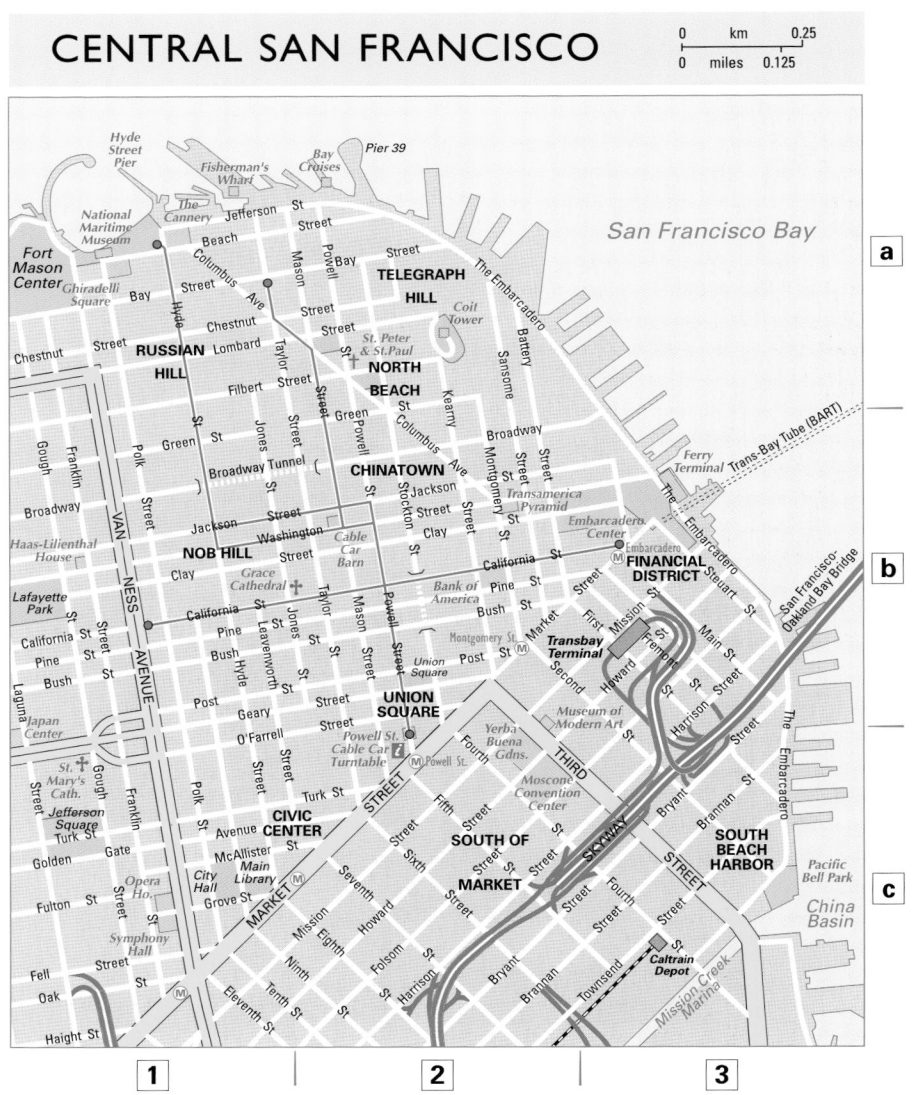

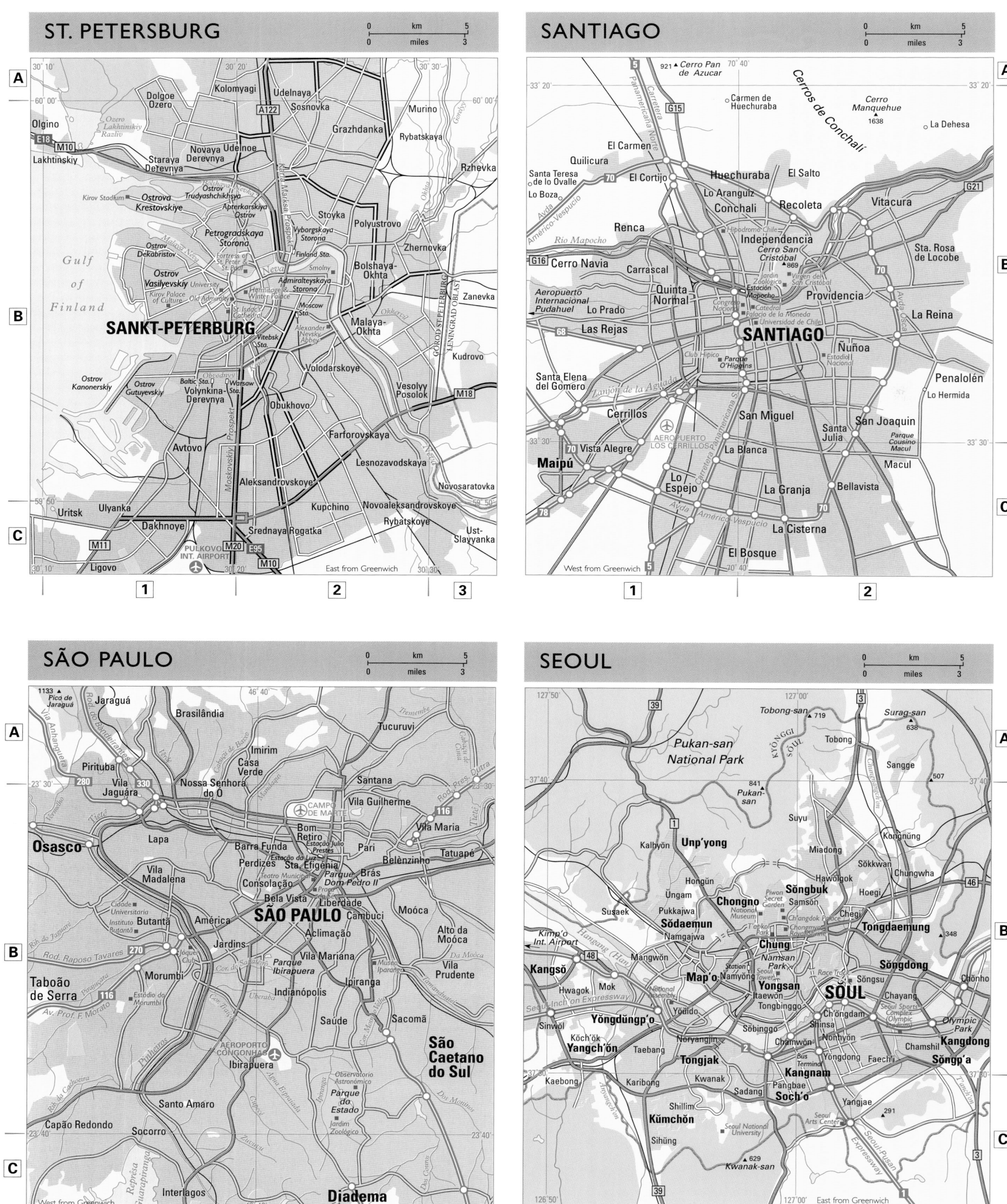

ST. PETERSBURG

km | miles

ST. PETERSBURG map labels

30° 10' · 30° 20' · 30° 30'
60° 00'

Olgino
Dolgoe Ozero
Kolomyagi
Udelnaya
Sosnovka
Murino
A122
Lakhtinskiy
Ostrov Lakhtinskiy Razliv
Grazhdanka
Rybatskaya
Staraya Derevnya
Novaya Udelnoe Derevnya
Rzhevka
Kirov Stadium
Ostrova Krestovskiye
Ostrov Trudyashchikhsya
Apterkarskiy Ostrov
Stoyka
Polyustrovo
Viborgskaya Storona
Petrogradskaya Storona
Finland Sta.
Zhernovka
Ostrov Dekabristov
University
Fortress of St. Peter & St. Paul
Smolny
Bolshaya-Okhta
Ostrov Vasilyevskiy
Nevka
Hermitage & Winter Palace
Moscow Sta.
Zanevka
SANKT-PETERBURG
Admiralteyskaya
Old Admiralty
St. Isaac's Cathedral
Vitebsk Sta.
Alexander Nevsky Abbey
Malaya-Okhta
Kudrovo
Gulf of Finland
Ostrov Kanonerskiy
Ostrov Gutuyevskiy
Baltic Sta.
Warsaw Sta.
Volynkina-Derevnya
Volodarskoye
Vesolyy Posolok
M18
Obukhovo
Farforovskaya
Avtovo
Lesnozavodskaya
Aleksandrovskoye
Novosaratovka
Uritsk
Ulyanka
Kupchino
Novoaleksandrovskoye
Dakhnoye
Srednyaya Rogatka
Rybatskoye
Ust-Slavyanka
M11
PULKOVO INT. AIRPORT
M20
E95
M10
Ligovo

East from Greenwich

SANTIAGO

km | miles

SANTIAGO map labels

921 ▲ Cerro Pan de Azucar
70° 40'
33° 20'
Cerros de Conchali
Cerro Manquehue 1638
Carmen de Huechuraba
La Dehesa
El Carmen
G15
Quilicura
Santa Teresa de lo Ovalle
Lo Boza
El Cortijo
Huechuraba
El Salto
Lo Aranguiz
Recoleta
Vitacura
G21
Renca
Conchali
Hipodromo Chile
Independencia
Sta. Rosa de Locobe
Río Mapocho
Cerro San Cristóbal 869
Jardin Zoológico
Parque Metropolitano San Cristóbal
70
G16
Cerro Navia
Carrascal
Estación Mapocho
Providencia
Aeropuerto Internacional Pudahuel
Quinta Normal
Lo Prado
Congreso Nacional
Catedral
Palacio de la Moneda
Universidad de Chile
La Reina
68
Las Rejas
SANTIAGO
Ñuñoa
Club Hípico
Parque O'Higgins
Estadio Nacional
Santa Elena del Gomero
Zanjón de la Aguada
Penalolén
Lo Hermida
Cerrillos
AEROPUERTO LOS CERRILLOS
San Miguel
Santa Julia
San Joaquin
Parque Cousino Macul
33° 30'
70
Vista Alegre
La Blanca
Macul
Maipú
Lo Espejo
La Granja
Bellavista
78
Avda. Américo Vespucio
70
La Cisterna
El Bosque
5

West from Greenwich · 70° 40'

SÃO PAULO

km | miles

SÃO PAULO map labels

1133 ▲ Pico de Jaraguá
Jaraguá
46° 40'
Brasilândia
Tucuruvi
Tremembé
Via Anhanguera
Rodovia Bandeirantes
Imirim
Casa Verde
Santana
Pirituba
280
330
Nossa Senhora do Ó
Vila Jaguára
23° 30'
Santana
Rod. Pres. Dutra
Osasco
Lapa
Vila Guilherme
116
Vila Maria
Bom Retiro
Pari
Tatuapé
Vila Madalena
Barra Funda
Estação Julio Prestes
Belènzinho
Perdizes
Sta. Efigênia
Estação da Luz
Brás
Cidade Universitária
Consolação
Teatro Municipal
Parque Dom Pedro II
América
Butantã
Bela Vista
Liberdade
Moóca
Instituto Butantã
SÃO PAULO
Cambuci
Aclimação
Alto da Moóca
270
Jóquei Clube
Jardins
Vila Mariana
Museu Iparanga
Vila Prudente
Taboão de Serra
Morumbi
Parque Ibirapuera
Ipiranga
116
Estádio do Morumbi
Indianópolis
Av. Prof. F. Morato
Saúde
Sacomã
AEROPORTO CONGONHAS
São Caetano do Sul
Ibirapuera
Observatorio Astronómico
Santo Amaro
Parque do Estado
Jardim Zoológico
Capão Redondo
Socorro
23° 40'
Represa Guarapiranga
Interlagos
Diadema

West from Greenwich · 46° 40'

SEOUL

km | miles

SEOUL map labels

127° 50'
39
Tobong-san 719
3
Surag-san 638
KYÕNGGI-DO
Pukan-san National Park
Tobong
Sangge
507
37° 40'
841 Pukan-san
Suyu
Kalbyõn
Unp'yong
Miadong
Kongnûng
1
Hongûn
Hawõlgok
Sõkkwan
Chungwha
Ungam
Pukkajwa
Samsõn
Hoegi
Chegi
46
Susaek
Chongno
Piwon Secret Garden
National Museum
Ch'angdok Palace
Tongdaemung
348
Sõdaemun
Kimp'o Int. Airport
Namgajwa
Chung
Changgyong Royal Palace
Songsu
Sõngdong
48
Mangwõn
Namsan Park
T'apkol Park
Station
Seoul Tower
Chõngdong
Chayang
Ch'õnho
Kangsõ
Hwagok
Mok
Mangwõn
Map'o
Namyõng
Yongsan
SÕUL
Seoul Sports Complex
Olympic Park
Sinwõl
Yõido
Itaewon
Tongbinggo
Shinsa
Nonhyon
Yõngdûngp'o
Sõbinggo
Kangdong
Köch'ök
Noryangjin
Chamwõn
Yõngdong
Faech'i
Chamshil
Yangch'ön
2
Taebang
Bus Terminal
Songp'a
Kaebong
Karibong
Kwanak
Sadang
Pangbae
Kangnam
Tongjak
Yangjae
291
Soch'o
Kümch'ön
Seoul National University
Seoul Arts Center
Sihûng
3
126° 50'
39
629 ▲ Kwanak-san
127° 00'

East from Greenwich · 127° 00'

SHANGHAI

km 5
miles 3

A
Liuhang · Yangjiazhuang · Wusong
Tangqiao · Baoshan
Gaoqiao
Yinhangzhen
31° 20'
31°20'
DACHANG AIRFIELD
Jiangwan
Wujiaochang
Zhenru · Dachang · Beijing
Hongkou Stadium · Yangpu Park · Donggou
Heping Park · Yangpu · Fuxing Dao
Hongkou · Zhabei · Hongkou · Qingningsi
Zhenru · Hongqiao Stadium · Tomb of Lu Xun · Yangpu Bridge · Zhoujiazhen
312
Jade Buddha Temple · Pudong Dadao · Yangjing
B
Putuo · Jingan · Jade Buddha Temple · Huangpu Park · Yangjing
Beixing Jing Park · Shanghai University · Huangpu
Changfeng Park · Zhongshan Park · People's Park · People's Square · Huangpu · Huangpu
Changning · Xi Zhan · Yan'an Lu · Shanghai Museum · SHANGHAI
Fuxing Park · Old City · Pudong New Area
Shanghai Zoo · Xujiahui Zhan · Luwan · Puxi · Nanshi
318
Xuhui · Nampu Bridge
Hongqiao · Hongqiao Airport · Zhoujiadu · Beicai
Gymnasium · Nanshi
Longhua Park · Chuanyang
Caoheijing · Longhua Pagoda · Sanlintang
31° 10' · LONGHUA AIRFIELD · 31°10'
C
Botanical Gardens · East from Greenwich 121° 30'
320
Gangkou

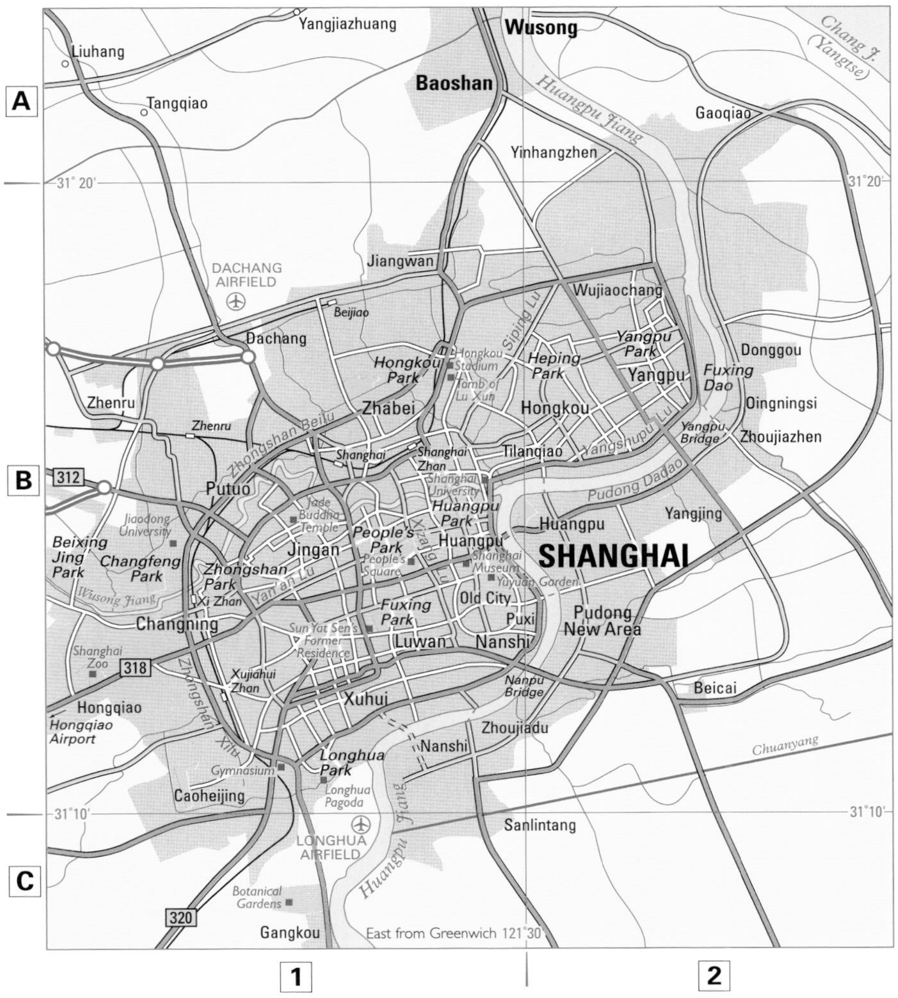

1   2

CENTRAL SINGAPORE

km 1
miles 0.5

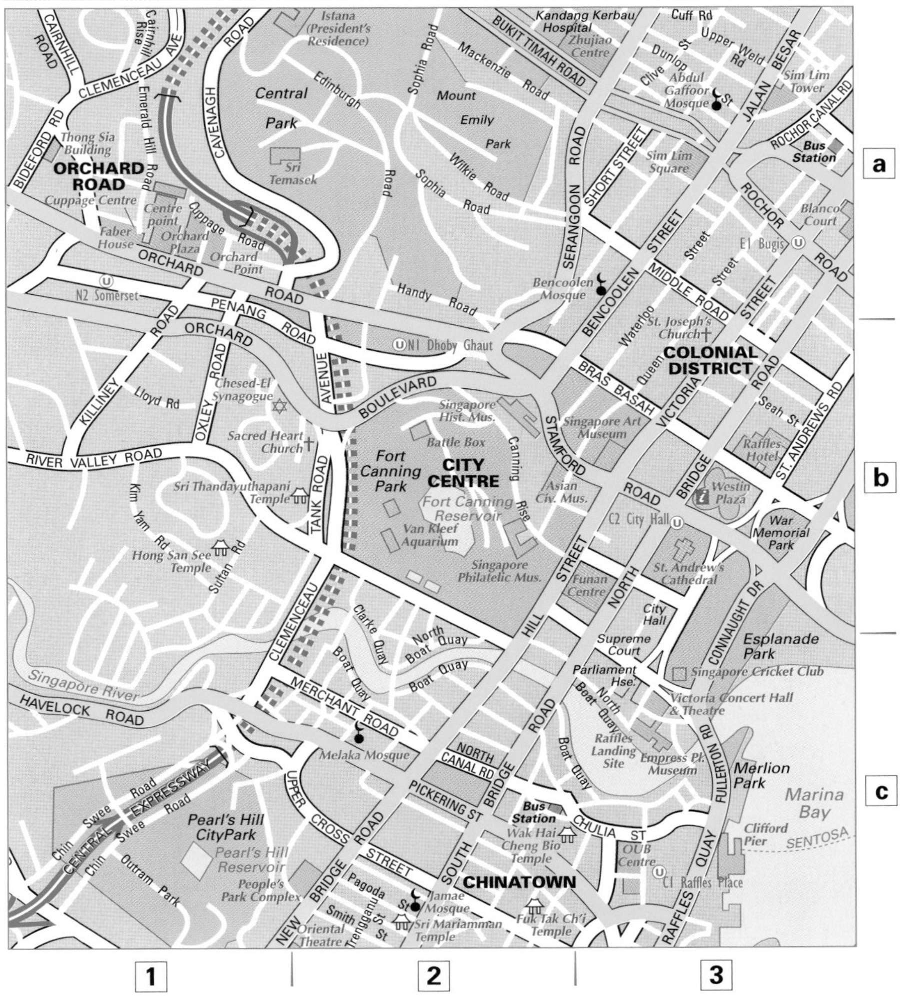

CAIRNHILL ROAD · CLEMENCEAU · ROAD · Istana (President's Residence) · Kandang Kerbau Hospital · Cuff Rd
Cairnhill Rise · BUKIT TIMAH ROAD · Upper Weld Rd
BIDEFORD RD · Emerald Hill · Central Park · Edinburgh · Sophia Road · Mackenzie Road · Dunlop · Jalan Besar · Sim Lim Tower
Thong Sia Building · CAVENAGH · Sri Temasek · Mount Emily Park · Wilkie Road · Sophia Road · Abdul Gaffoor Mosque
ORCHARD ROAD · Cuppage Centre · Centre point · Orchard Plaza · Orchard Point · Handy Road · Bencoolen Mosque · SERANGOON · SHORT STREET · Sim Lim Square · El Bogis · ROCHOR · Blanco Court
Faber House · ORCHARD · N2 Somerset · PENANG ROAD · U N1 Dhoby Ghaut · Waterloo · BRAS BASAH · St Joseph's Church · MIDDLE ROAD · ROAD · a
KILLINEY · ORCHARD · Chesed-El Synagogue · BOULEVARD · COLONIAL DISTRICT
Lloyd Rd · AVENUE · Singapore Hist. Mus. · Singapore Art Museum · VICTORIA · Raffles Hotel
RIVER VALLEY ROAD · OXLEY · Sacred Heart Church · Fort Canning Park · Battle Box · STAMFORD · Strah St · ST ANDREW'S RD
Sri Thandayuthapani Temple · CITY CENTRE · Singapore · b
Km · Yam · Fort Canning Reservoir · Camp · Chinese Meth. Mus. · C2 City Hall · Westin Plaza
Hong San See Temple · Van Kleef Aquarium · STREET · NORTH · St Andrew's Cathedral · War Memorial Park
CLEMENCEAU · TANK · Singapore Philatelic Mus. · Funan Centre · City Hall · BRIDGE · ROAD · Esplanade Park
Sultan Rd · Clarke Quay · North Quay · Supreme Court · CONNAUGHT DR · Singapore Cricket Club
MERCHANT ROAD · North Boat Quay · Parliament Hse · Victoria Concert Hall & Theatre · c
HAVELOCK ROAD · Singapore River · South Boat Quay · Raffles Landing Site · FULLERTON RD · Empress Pl. Museum · Merlion Park
Swee · EXPRESSWAY · Melaka Mosque · NORTH · Raffles · Marina Bay
Pearl's Hill City Park · UPPER CROSS · CANAL · PICKERING ST · SOUTH · Place · OUB Centre · Clifford Pier · SENTOSA
Pearl's Hill Reservoir · Bus Station · Wak Hai Cheng Bio Temple · C1 Raffles Place
CENTRAL · Pagoda · Fuk Tak Ch'i Temple
People's Park Complex · BRIDGE · Jamae Mosque · CHINATOWN
NEW · Smith · ROAD · RAFFLES · QUAY
Oriental Theatre · Sri Mariamman Temple

1   2   3

SINGAPORE

km 10
miles 6

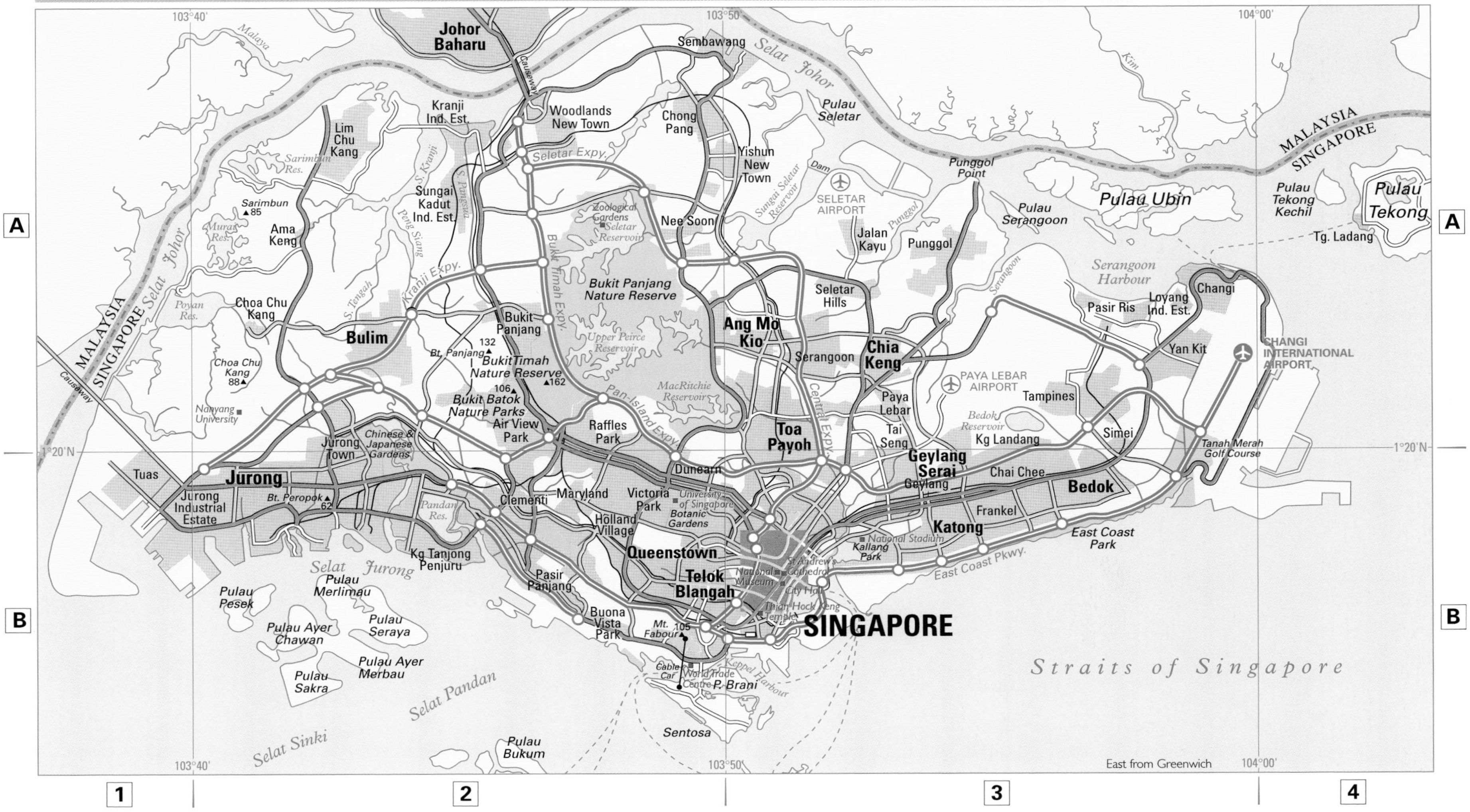

103° 40' · Johor Baharu · 103° 50' · Sembawang · Selat Johor · 104° 00'
Kranji Ind. Est. · Woodlands New Town · Chong Pang · Pulau Seletar · MALAYSIA SINGAPORE
Lim Chu Kang · Yishun New Town · Punggol Point · Pulau Tekong Kechil · Pulau Tekong
A · Sarimbun Res. · Sarimbun · SELETAR AIRPORT · Pulau Ubin · Tg. Ladang · A
Ama Keng · Sungai Kadut Ind. Est. · Zoological Gardens Seletar Reservoir · Nee Soon · Jalan Kayu · Pulau Serangoon · Serangoon Harbour · Loyang Ind. Est. · Changi
Choa Chu Kang · Bukit Panjang Nature Reserve · Seletar Hills · Punggol · Pasir Ris · CHANGI INTERNATIONAL AIRPORT
Bulim · Bukit Panjang · 132 · Upper Peirce Reservoir · Ang Mo Kio · Serangoon · PAYA LEBAR AIRPORT · Tampines · Yan Kit
Choa Chu Kang · Bukit Timah Nature Reserve · MacRitchie Reservoir · Chia Keng · Paya Lebar · Bedok Reservoir · Simei · Tanah Merah Golf Course
88 · 162 · Bukit Batok Nature Parks · Air View Park · Raffles Park · Toa Payoh · Tai Seng · 1° 20'N
Nanyang University · Jurong Town · Dunearn · Geylang Serai · Chai Chee · Bedok
Jurong · Bt. Peropok · 62 · Chinese & Japanese Gardens · Maryland · Victoria Park · University of Singapore Botanic Gardens · Geylang · Frankel · Katong · East Coast Park
Tuas · Jurong Industrial Estate · Clementi · Holland Village · National Stadium · Kallang Park · East Coast Pkwy
Pulau Pesek · Pandan Res. · Pasir Panjang · Queenstown · Kg Tanjong Penjuru · Telok Blangah · SINGAPORE
B · Pulau Merlimau · Selat Jurong · Buona Vista Park · Mt Faber 105 · B
Pulau Ayer Chawan · Pulau Seraya · Cable Car · World Trade Centre · P. Brani · Straits of Singapore
Pulau Ayer Merbau · Pulau Sakra · Selat Pandan · Sentosa
Selat Sinki · Pulau Bukum · 103° 50' · East from Greenwich 104° 00'

1   2   3   4

STOCKHOLM

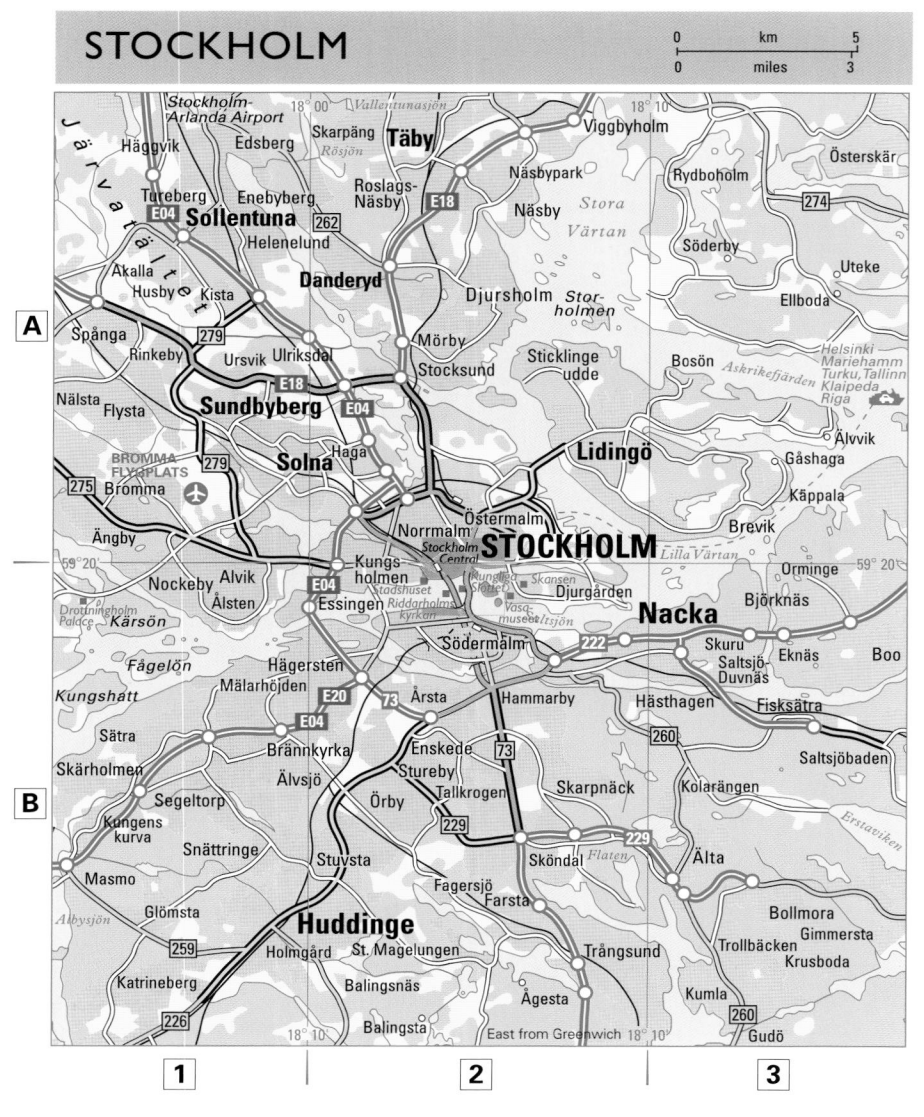

CENTRAL STOCKHOLM

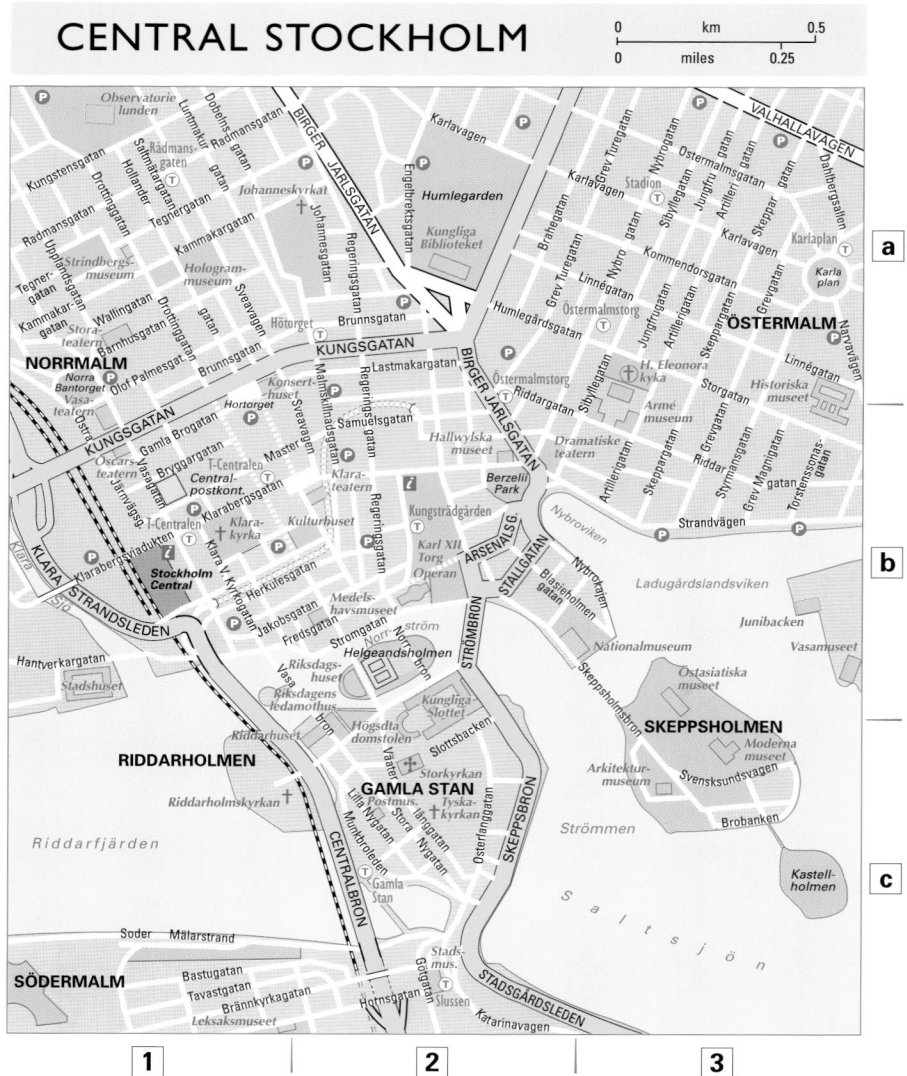

SYDNEY

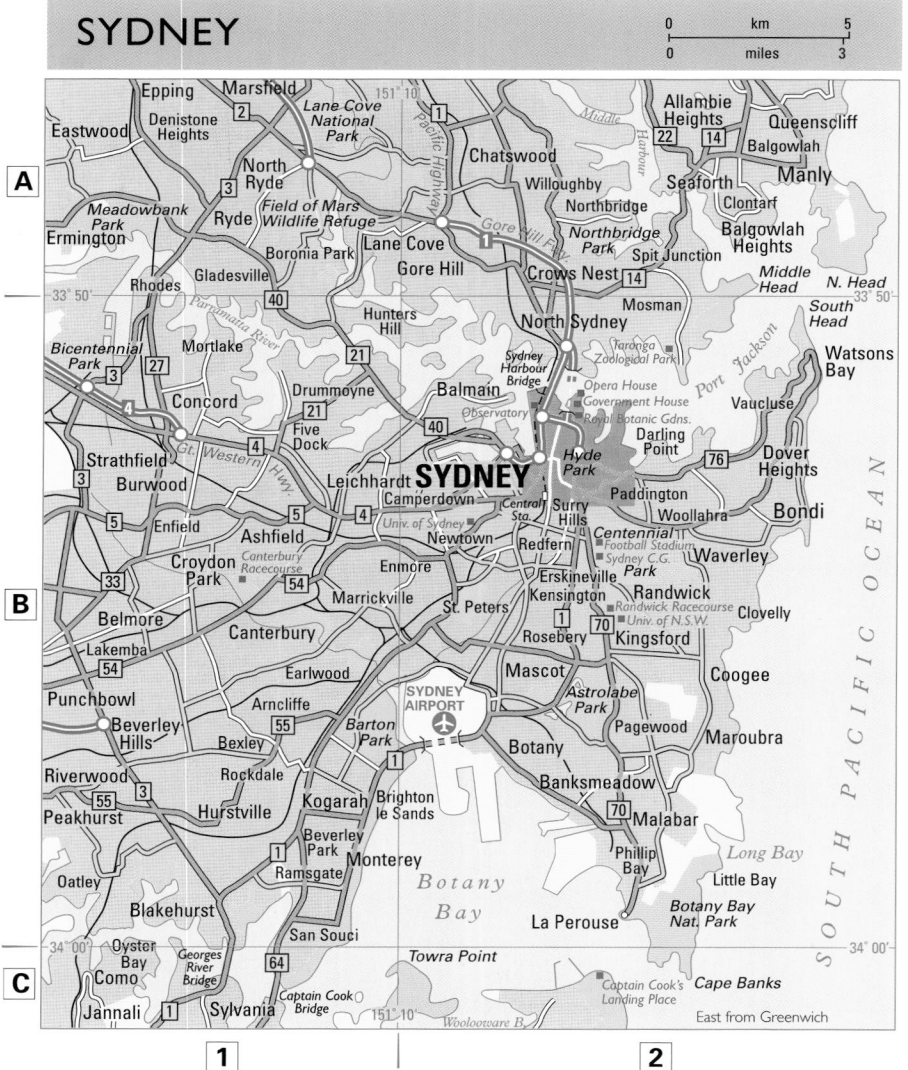

CENTRAL SYDNEY

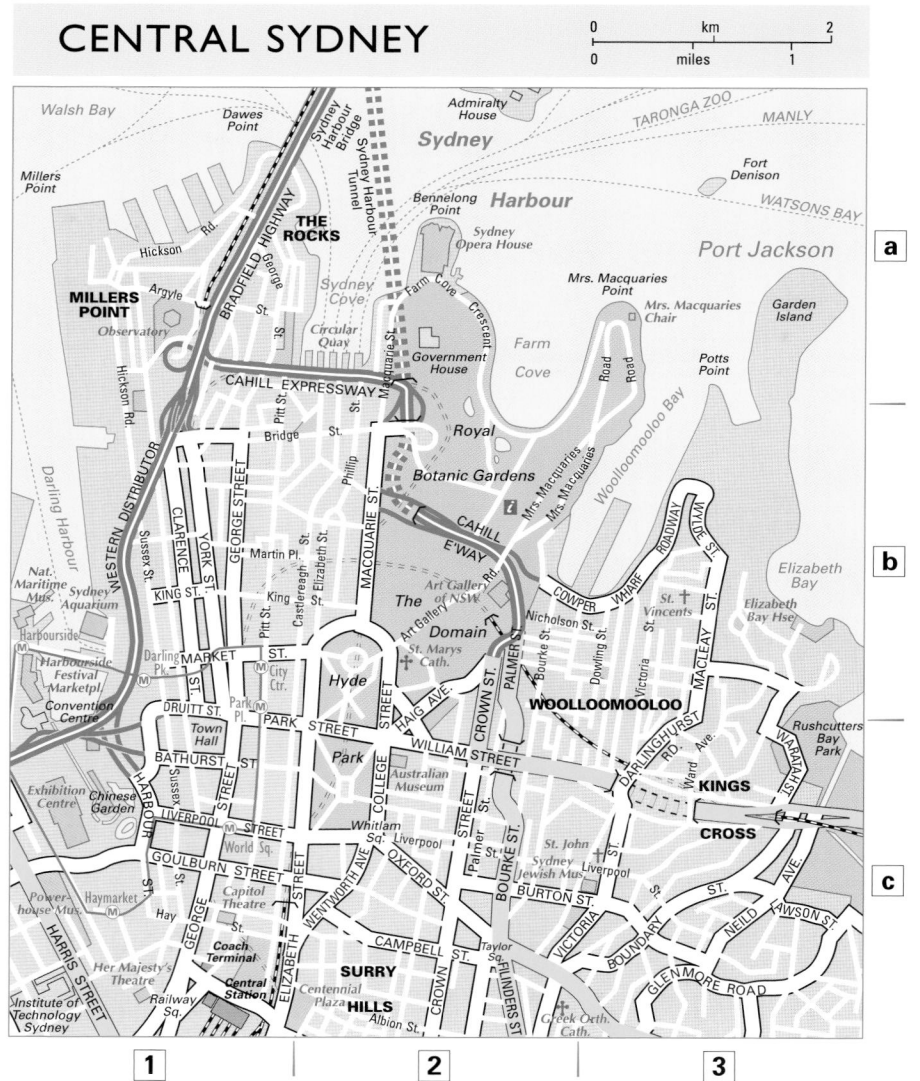

TOKYO

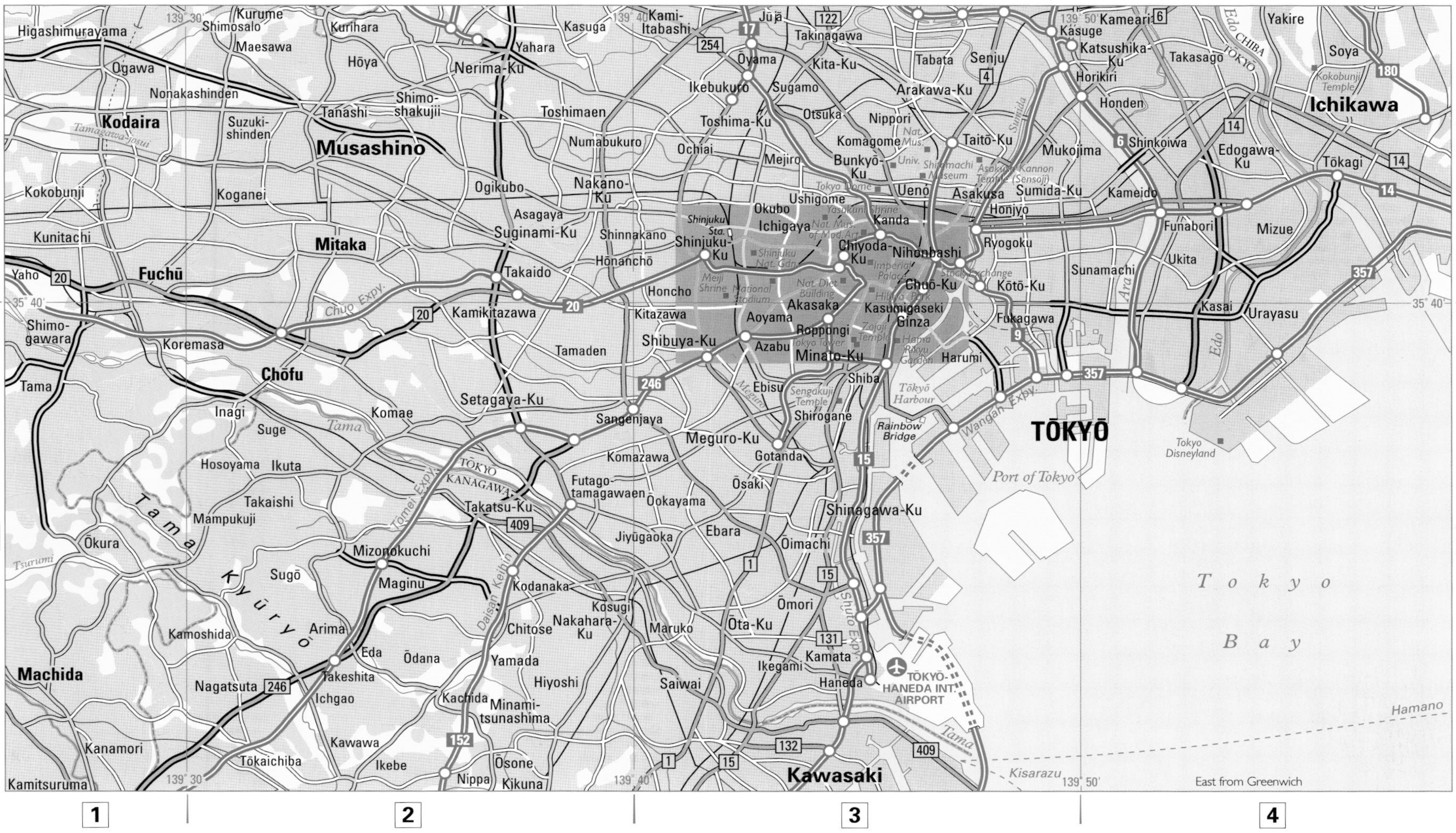

0 km 5
0 miles 3

Higashimurayama · Kurume · Shimosalo · Kami-Itabashi · Jūjō · Takinagawa · Kameari · Yakire · Soya
Kurihara · Kasuga · 122 · 17 · Kita-Ku · Senju · Kasuge · Katsushika-Ku · Takasago · Kokubunji Temple
Ogawa · Maesawa · 254 · Ōyama · Sugamo · Nippori · Horikiri · Honden · 180
Higashimurayama · Shimosakujii · Ikebukuro · Toshima-Ku · Otsuka · Komagome · Mukojima · Shinkoiwa · Ichikawa
Kodaira · Suzuki-shinden · Tanashi · Toshimaen · Numabukuro · Ochiai · Bunkyō-Ku · Ueno · Asakusa · Taitō-Ku · Sumida-Ku · Kameido · Edogawa-Ku · Tōkagi · 14
Musashino · Nakano-Ku · Okubo · Ichigaya · Kanda · Nihonbashi · Honjyo · Funabori · Mizue
Mitaka · Suginami-Ku · Shinnakano · Shinjuku-Ku · Chiyoda-Ku · Chūō-Ku · Kōtō-Ku · Sunamachi · Ukita · 357
Fuchū · Takaido · Honcho · Akasaka · Kasumigaseki Ginza · Fukagawa · Kasai · Urayasu
Kamikitazawa · Kitazawa · Aoyama · Roppongi · 9 · 357
Koremasa · Tamaden · Shibuya-Ku · Azabu · Minato-Ku · Harumi
Chōfu · Setagaya-Ku · Ebisu · Shiba · Tōkyō Harbour · Rainbow Bridge · **TŌKYŌ** · Tokyo Disneyland
Inagi · Komae · Sangenjaya · Meguro-Ku · Shirogane · Gotanda · Port of Tokyo
Suge · Futago-tamagawaen · Komazawa · 15 · Shinagawa-Ku
Takaishi · Takatsu-Ku · Ookayama · Ōsaki
Machida · Mizonokuchi · Jiyūgaoka · Ebara · Ōimachi · T o k y o · B a y
Nagatsuta · Ichgao · Chitose · Kodanaka · 1 · 15 · Ōmori
Maginu · Nakahara-Ku · Maruko · Ōta-Ku · Kamata · Haneda · **TŌKYŌ HANEDA INT'L AIRPORT**
Takeshita · 246 · 152 · Minami-tsunashima · Hiyoshi · Ikegami · 131
Kanamori · Tōkaichiba · Ōsone · 132 · 409 · Hamano
Kamitsuruma · Nippa · Kikuna · **Kawasaki** · Kisarazu · East from Greenwich

CENTRAL TOKYO

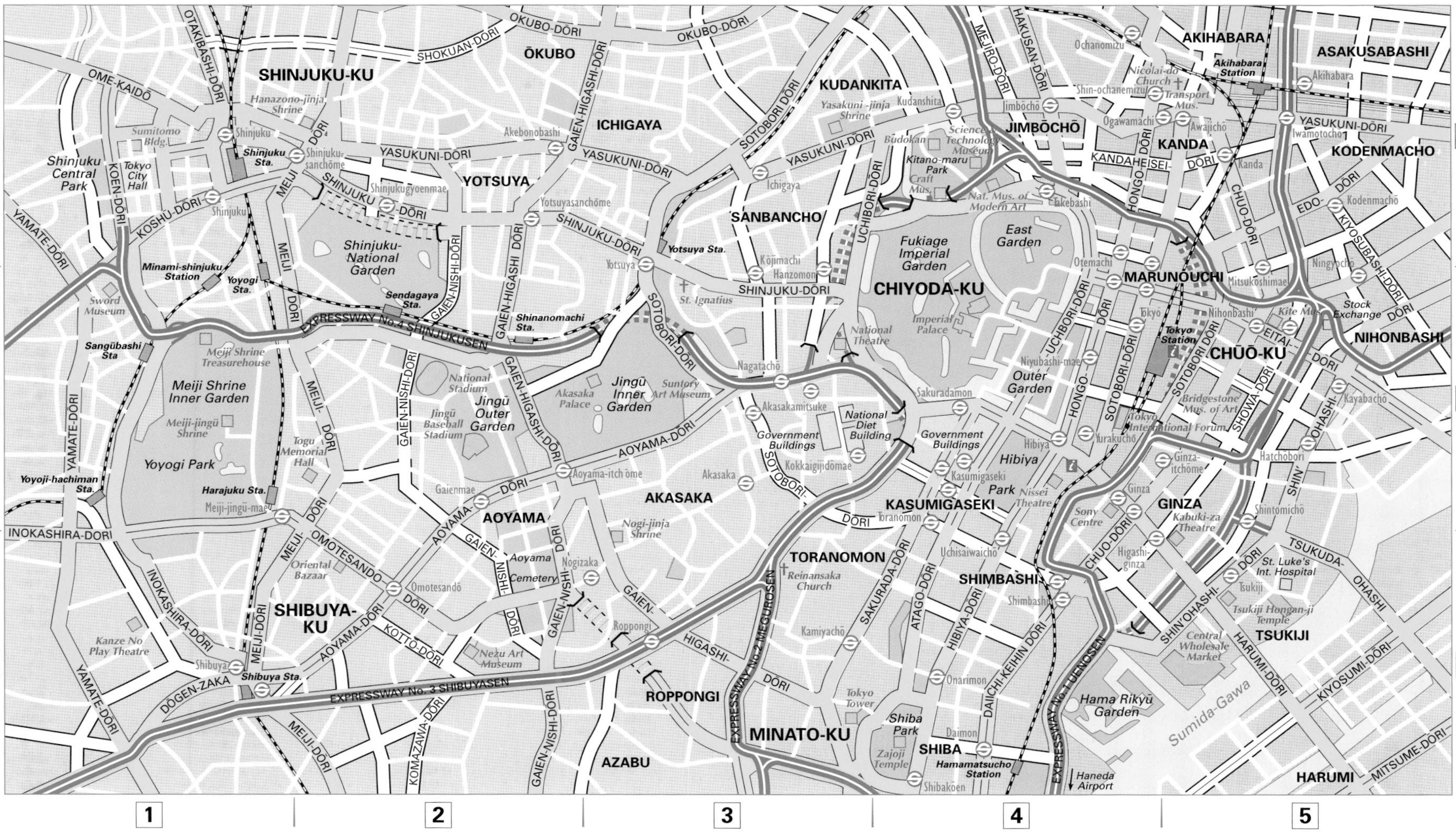

0 km 1
0 miles 0.5

(street map with labels: SHINJUKU-KU, ŌKUBO, ICHIGAYA, YOTSUYA, SANBANCHO, KUDANKITA, JIMBŌCHŌ, KANDA, AKIHABARA, ASAKUSABASHI, KODENMACHO, CHIYODA-KU, MARUNOUCHI, CHŪŌ-KU, NIHONBASHI, Meiji Shrine Inner Garden, Yoyogi Park, Jingū Inner Garden, AOYAMA, AKASAKA, KASUMIGASEKI, TORANOMON, SHIMBASHI, GINZA, TSUKIJI, SHIBUYA-KU, ROPPONGI, AZABU, MINATO-KU, SHIBA, HARUMI, Imperial Palace, Fukiage Imperial Garden, East Garden, National Diet Building, Hibiya Park, Hama Rikyū Garden, Sumida-Gawa)

COPYRIGHT PHILIP'S

TEHRAN

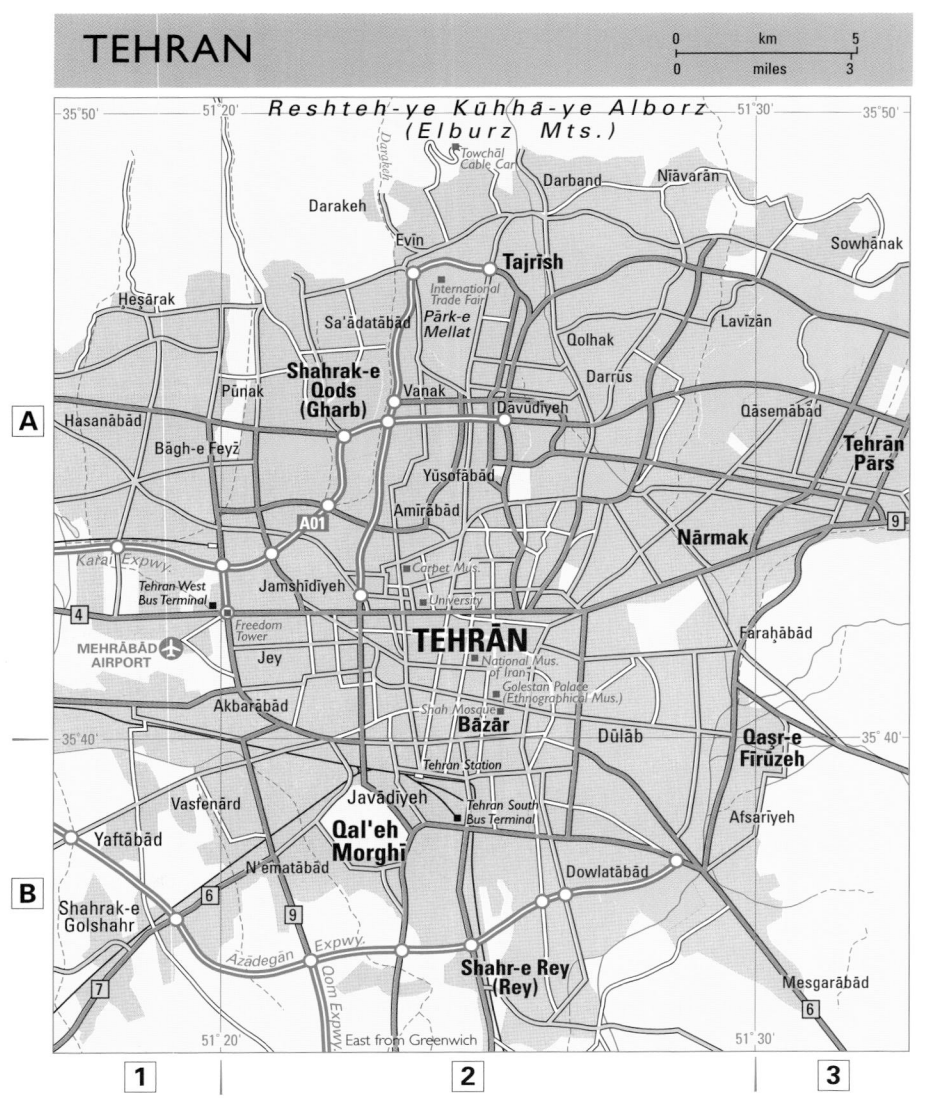

TIANJIN

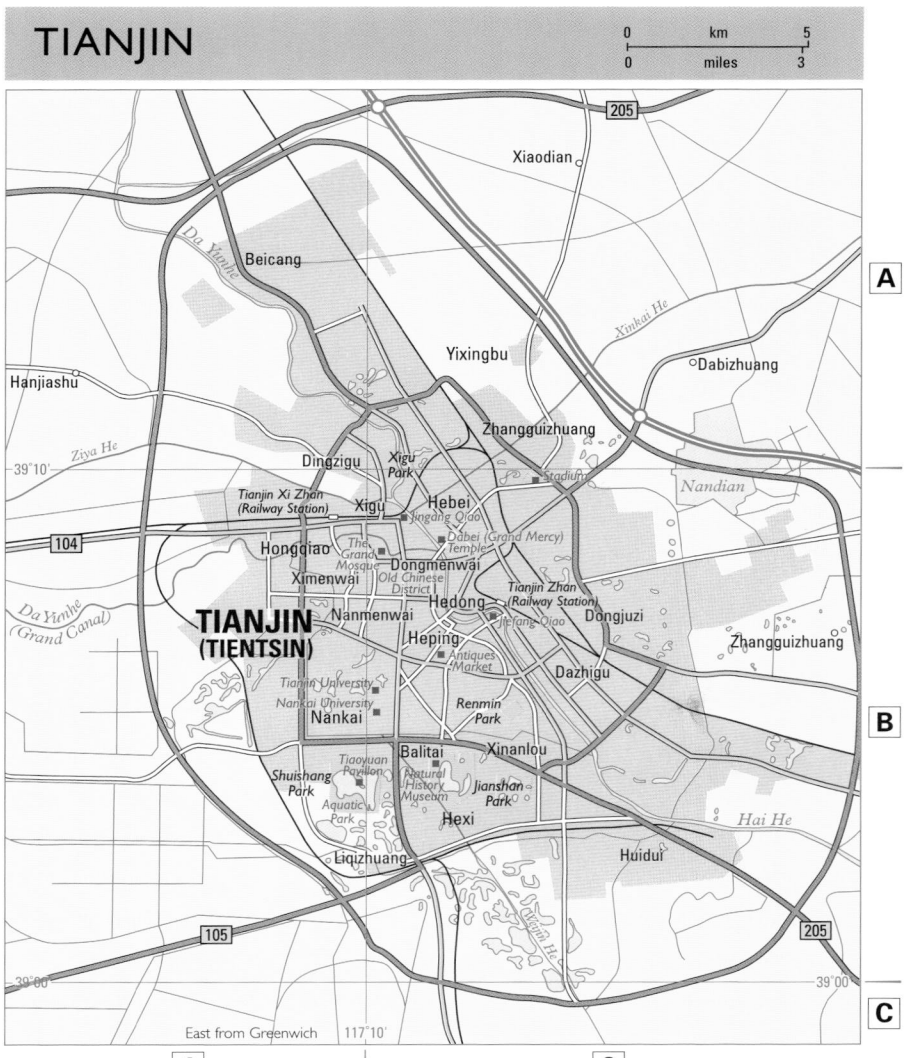

TORONTO

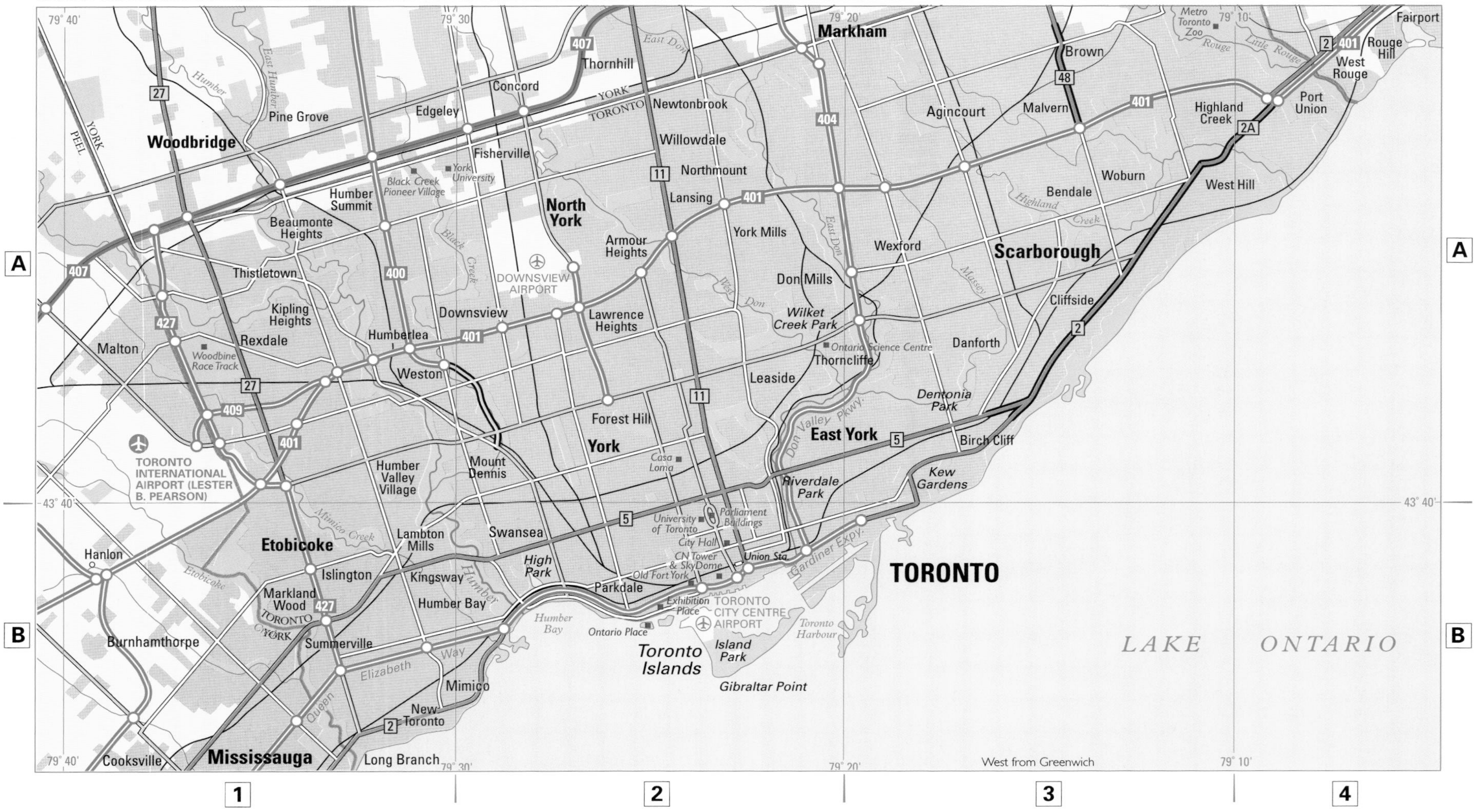

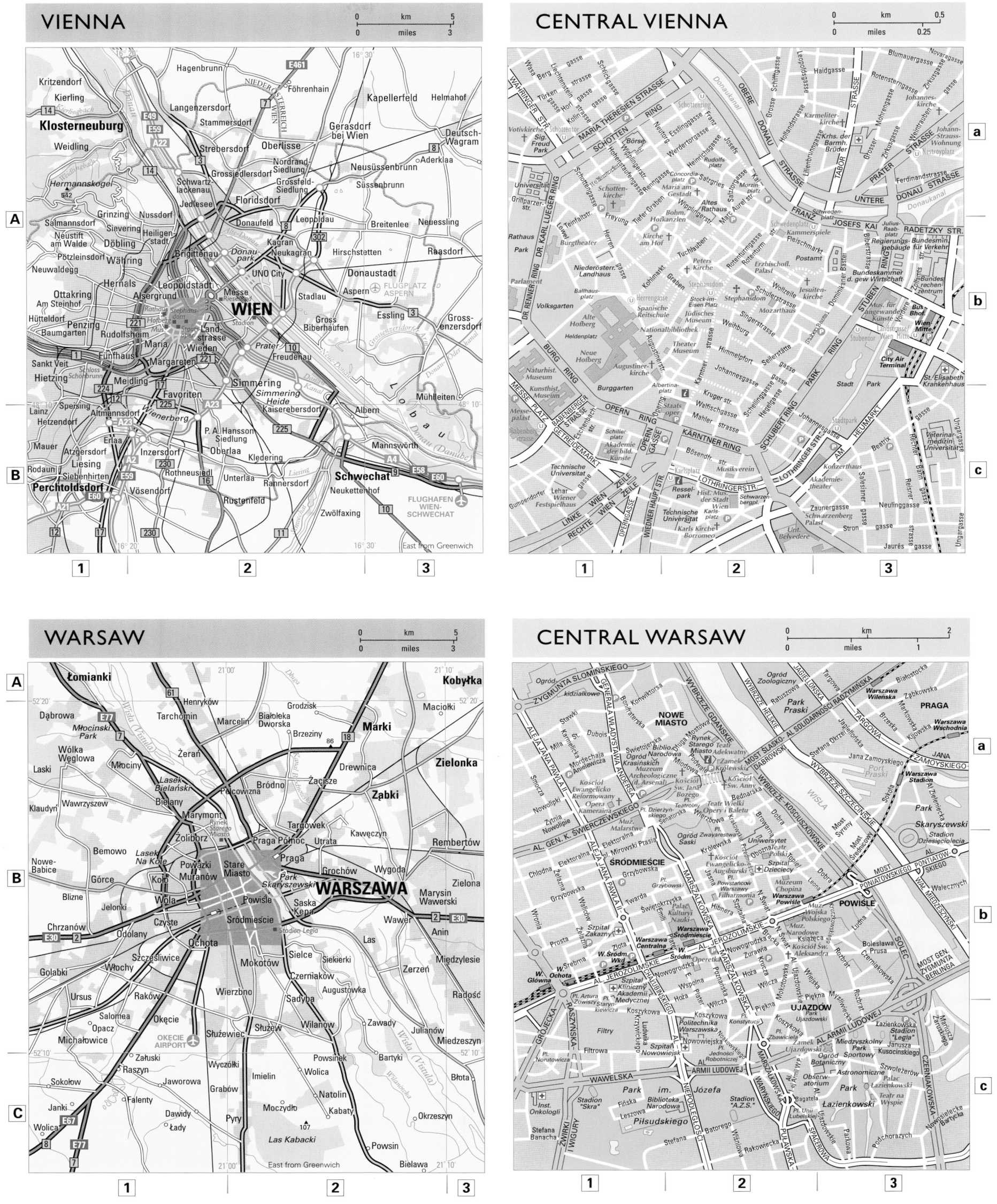

VIENNA

km 5 / miles 3

A

B

1 2 3

Kritzendorf · Kierling · 14 · Hagenbrunn · Föhrenhain · E461 · Kapellerfeld · Helmahof · 16° 30′
Klosterneuburg · E49 · E59 · A22 · Langenzersdorf · 7 · Gerasdorf bei Wien · Deutsch-Wagram
Weidling · Stammersdorf · Oberlisse · 8 · Aderklaa
Hermannskogel 542 · 14 · Schwartz-lackenau · Nordrand-Siedlung · Grossfeld-Siedlung · Neusüssenbrunn · Süssenbrunn
Salmannsdorf · Grinzing · Nussdorf · Floridsdorf · Leopoldau · Breitenlee · Neuessling
Neustift am Walde · Sievering · Heiligen-stadt · Kagran · Neukagran · Hirschstetten · Raasdorf
Pötzleinsdorf · Döbling · Wätring · Brigittenau · Donau-park · UNO City · Stadlau · Donaustadt
Neuwaldegg · Hernals · Alsergrund · WIEN · Messe · Aspern · FLUGPLATZ ASPERN · Gross-enzersdorf
Ottakring · Am Steinhof · Rudolfsheim · Land-strasse · Prater · Essling · 3
Hütteldorf · Penzing · Baumgarten · Maria · Wieden · Freudenau · 10 · Gross Biberhaufen
Sankt Veit · Hietzing · Fünfhaus · Margareten · 221 · Simmering · Simmering Heide · Kaiserebersdorf · Albern
Spersing · Meidling · Favoriten · 225 · A23 · Mühlleiten · Lobau
Lainz · Hetzendorf · Altmannsdorf · A23 · Wienerberg · Donau (Danube)
Mauer · Erlaa · P. A. Hansson Siedlung · Oberlaa · Kledering · A4 · Mannswörth · E58 · E60
Rodaun · Atzgersdorf · Liesing · Inzersdorf · 230 · Rothneusiedl · Unterlaa · Rannersdorf · Schwechat · Neukettenhof
Perchtoldsdorf · E59 · Vösendorf · 16 · Rustenfeld · Zwölfaxing · FLUGHAFEN WIEN-SCHWECHAT
A21 · E60 · 12 · 17 · 230 · 11 · 10 · 16° 30′ · East from Greenwich

CENTRAL VIENNA

km 0.5 / miles 0.25

a

b

c

1 2 3

WARSAW

km 5 / miles 3

A

B

C

1 2 3

Łomianki · 61 · Kobyłka · 21° 00′ · 52° 20′ · 21° 10′
Dąbrowa · Henryków · Grodzisk · Maciołki · E77
Młociński Park · 7 · Tarchomin · Marcelin · Białołeka Dworska · Brzeziny · 18 · Marki
Wólka Węglowa · Żerań · Żeń · Zielonka
Laski · Młociny · Drewnica · Ząbki
Klaudyn · Wawrzyszew · Lasek Bielański · Bielany · Bródno · Zacisze
Nowe-Babice · Marymont · Żoliborz · Targówek · Rembertów
Bemowo · Lasek Na Kole · Powązki · Praga Północ · Utrata · Kawęczyn
Górce · Koło · Muranów · Stare Miasto · Praga · Wygoda
Blizne · Jelonki · Wola · WARSZAWA · Marysin Wawerski
Chrzanów · Czyste · Powiśle · Park Skaryszewski · Saska Kępa · Zielona
E30 · 2 · Odolany · Śródmieście · Wawer · Anin · 2 · E30
Szczęśliwice · Ochota · Stadion Legia · Las
Gołąbki · Włochy · Raków · Mokotów · Sielce · Siekierki · Międzylesie
Ursus · Salomea · Wierzbno · Czerniaków · Sadyba · Zerzeń
Opacz · Okęcie · Służewiec · Wilanów · Augustówka · Radość
Michałowice · OKĘCIE AIRPORT · Służew · Zawady · Julianów · Miedzeszyn
Załuski · Powsinek · Wolica · 52° 10′ · Bartyki
Sokołów · Wyczółki · Imielin · Błota
Janki · E67 · Raszyn · Jaworowa · Grabów · Natolin · Miedzeszyn
Wolica · Falenty · Dawidy · Moczydło · Kabaty · Okrzeszyn
8 · E77 · Łady · Pyry · 107 · Powsin
7 · Las Kabacki · Bielawa · 21° 00′ · 21° 10′ · East from Greenwich

CENTRAL WARSAW

km 2 / miles 1

a

b

c

1 2 3

WASHINGTON

0 km 5
0 miles 3

CENTRAL WASHINGTON

0 km 1
0 miles 0.5

WELLINGTON

0 km 5
0 miles 3

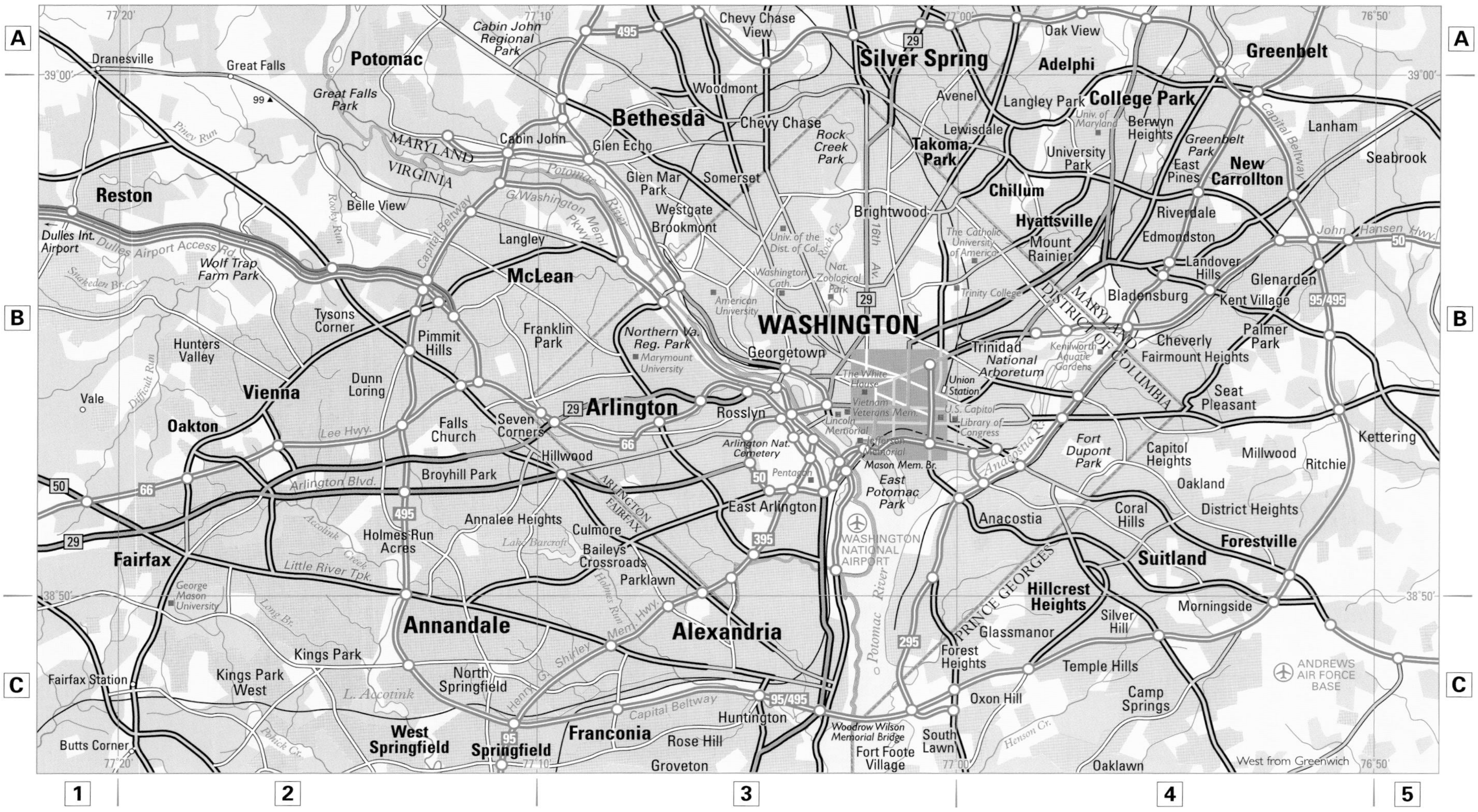

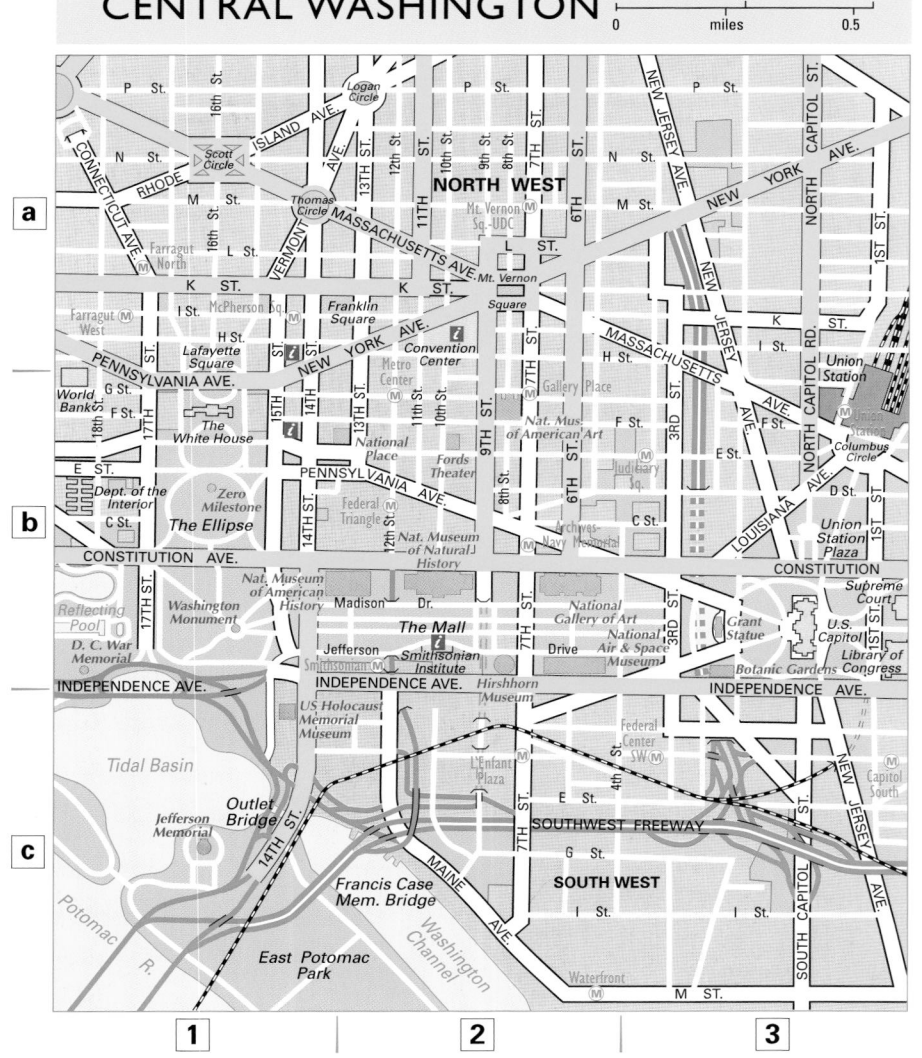

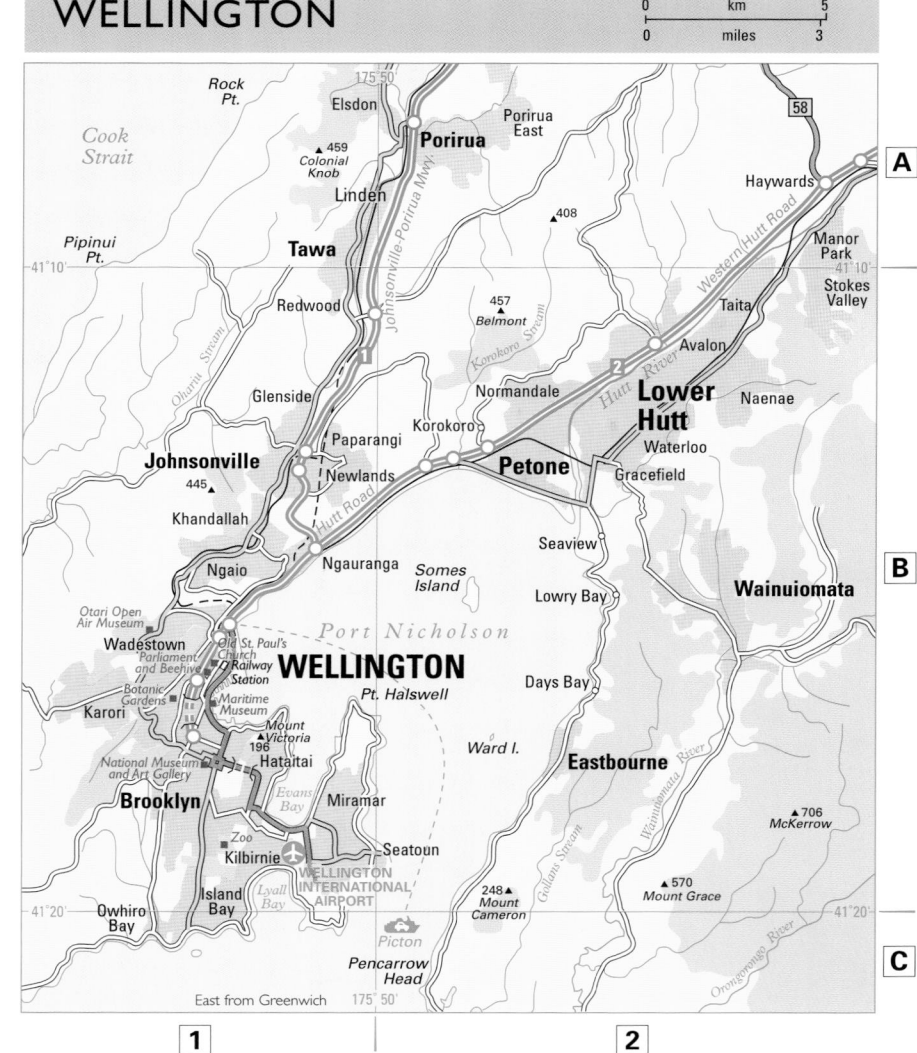

INDEX TO CITY MAPS

The index contains the names of all the principal places and features shown on the City Maps. Each name is followed by an additional entry in italics giving the name of the City Map within which it is located.

The number in bold type which follows each name refers to the number of the City Map page where that feature or place will be found.

The letter and figure which are immediately after the page number give the grid square on the map within which the feature or place is situated. The letter represents the latitude and the figure the longitude. Upper case letters refer to the City Maps, lower case letters to the Central Area Maps. The full geographic reference is provided in the border of the City Maps.

The location given is the centre of the city, suburb or feature and is not necessarily the name. Rivers, canals and roads are indexed to their name. Rivers carry the symbol ➤ after their name.

An explanation of the alphabetical order rules and a list of the abbreviations used are to be found at the beginning of the World Map Index.

A

Aalām, *Baghdad* **3** B2
Aalsmeer, *Amsterdam* **2** B1
Abbey Wood, *London* **15** B4
Abcoude, *Amsterdam* **2** B2
Âbdin, *Cairo* **7** A2
Abeno, *Osaka* **22** B4
Aberdeen, *Hong Kong* **12** B2
Aberdour, *Edinburgh* **11** A2
Aberdour Castle, *Edinburgh* **11** A2
Abfanggraben ➤, *Munich* **20** A3
Ablon-sur-Seine, *Paris* **23** B3
Abramtsevo, *Moscow* **19** B4
Abu Dis, *Jerusalem* **13** B2
Abū en Numrus, *Cairo* **7** B2
Abu Ghosh, *Jerusalem* **13** B1
Acacias, *Madrid* **17** c2
Acassuso, *Buenos Aires* **7** A1
Accotink Cr. ➤, *Washington* **32** B2
Acheres, *Paris* **23** A1
Acília, *Rome* **25** C1
Aclimação, *São Paulo* **26** B2
Acton, *London* **15** A2
Açúcar, Pão de, *Rio de Janeiro* **24** B2
Ada Beja, *Lisbon* **14** A1
Adams Park, *Atlanta* **3** B2
Adams Shore, *Boston* **6** B4
Addiscombe, *London* **15** B3
Adelphi, *Washington* **32** A4
Aderklaa, *Vienna* **31** A3
Admiralteyskaya Storona, *St. Petersburg* **26** B2
Âfiori, *Milan* **18** A2
Aflandshage, *Copenhagen* **10** B3
Afsarîyeh, *Tehran* **30** B2
Agboyi Cr. ➤, *Lagos* **14** A2
Agerup, *Copenhagen* **10** A1
Ägesta, *Stockholm* **28** B2
Agincourt, *Toronto* **30** A3
Agora, Arhéa, *Athens* **2** c1
Agra Canal, *Delhi* **10** B2
Agricola Oriental, *Mexico City* **18** B2
Agua Espraiada ➤, *São Paulo* **26** B2
Agualva-Cacem, *Lisbon* **14** A1
Agustino, Cerro El, *Lima* **16** B2
Ahrensfelde, *Berlin* **5** A4
Ahuntsic, *Montreal* **19** A1
Ai ➤, *Osaka* **22** A4
Aigremont, *Paris* **23** A1
Air View Park, *Singapore* **27** A2
Airport West, *Melbourne* **17** A1
Aiyaleo, *Athens* **2** B1
Aiyáleos, Óros, *Athens* **2** B1
Ajegunle, *Lagos* **14** B2
Aji, *Osaka* **22** A3
Ajuda, *Lisbon* **14** A1
Akalla, *Stockholm* **28** A1
Akasaka, *Tokyo* **29** b3
Akbarābād, *Tehran* **30** A2
Akershus Slott, *Oslo* **22** A3
Akihabara, *Tokyo* **29** a5
Akrópolis, *Athens* **2** c2
Al 'Azamiyah, *Baghdad* **3** A2
Al Quds = Jerusalem, *Jerusalem* **13** B2
Alaguntan, *Lagos* **14** B2
Alameda, *San Francisco* **25** B3
Alameda, Parque, *Mexico City* **18** b2
Alameda Memorial State Beach Park, *San Francisco* **25** B3
Albern, *Vienna* **31** B2
Albert Park, *Melbourne* **17** B1
Alberton, *Johannesburg* **13** B2
Albertslund, *Copenhagen* **10** B2
Albysjön, *Stockholm* **28** B1
Alcantara, *Lisbon* **14** A1
Alcatraz I., *San Francisco* **25** B2
Alcobendas, *Madrid* **17** A2
Alcorcón, *Madrid* **17** B1
Aldershof, *Berlin* **5** B4
Aldo Bonzi, *Buenos Aires* **7** C1
Aleksandrovskoye, *St. Petersburg* **26** B2
Alexander Nevsky Abbey, *St. Petersburg* **26** B2
Alexander Soutzos Moussio, *Athens* **2** b3
Alexandra, *Johannesburg* **13** A2
Alexandra, *Singapore* **27** B2
Alexandria, *Washington* **32** C3
Alfama, *Lisbon* **14** c3
Alfortville, *Paris* **23** B3
Algés, *Lisbon* **14** A1
Alhambra, *Los Angeles* **16** B4
Alibey ➤, *Istanbul* **12** B1
Alibey Baraji, *Istanbul* **12** B1
Alibeyköy, *Istanbul* **12** B1
Alimos, *Athens* **2** B2
Alipur, *Calcutta* **8** B1
Allach, *Munich* **20** A1
Allambie Heights, *Sydney* **28** A2
Allard Pierson Museum, *Amsterdam* **2** b1
Allermuir Hill, *Edinburgh* **11** B2
Allerton, Pt., *Boston* **6** B4
Allston, *Boston* **6** A3
Almada, *Lisbon* **14** A2

Almagro, *Buenos Aires* **7** B2
Almargem do Bispo, *Lisbon* **14** A1
Almazovo, *Moscow* **19** A6
Almirante G. Brown, Parque, *Buenos Aires* **7** C2
Almon, *Jerusalem* **13** B2
Almond ➤, *Edinburgh* **11** B2
Alnabru, *Oslo* **22** A4
Alnsjøen, *Oslo* **22** A4
Alperton, *London* **15** A2
Alpine, *New York* **21** A2
Alrode, *Johannesburg* **13** B2
Alsemerg, *Brussels* **6** B1
Alsergrund, *Vienna* **31** A2
Alsip, *Chicago* **9** C2
Älsten, *Stockholm* **28** B1
Alta, *Stockholm* **28** B3
Altadena, *Los Angeles* **16** A4
Alte-Donau ➤, *Vienna* **31** A2
Alte Hofburg, *Vienna* **31** b1
Alter Finkenkrug, *Berlin* **5** A1
Altes Rathaus, *Munich* **20** b3
Altglienicke, *Berlin* **5** B4
Altlandsberg, *Berlin* **5** A5
Altlandsberg Nord, *Berlin* **5** A5
Altmannsdorf, *Vienna* **31** B1
Alto da Moóca, *São Paulo* **26** B2
Alto do Pina, *Lisbon* **14** A2
Altona, *Melbourne* **17** B1
Alvaro Obregon, *Mexico City* **18** B1
Alvik, *Stockholm* **28** B1
Alvsjo, *Stockholm* **28** B2
Alvvik, *Stockholm* **28** A3
Am Hasenbergl, *Munich* **20** A2
Am Steinhof, *Vienna* **31** A1
Am Wald, *Munich* **20** B2
Ama Keng, *Singapore* **27** A2
Amadora, *Lisbon* **14** A1
Amagasaki, *Osaka* **22** A3
Amager, *Copenhagen* **10** B3
Amâl Qâdisiya, *Baghdad* **3** B2
Amalienborg, *Copenhagen* **10** b3
Amata, *Milan* **18** A1
Ameixoeira, *Lisbon* **14** A2
América, *São Paulo* **26** B1
Amin, *Baghdad* **3** B2
Aminadov, *Jerusalem* **13** B1
Aminyevo, *Moscow* **19** B2
Amirâbâd, *Tehran* **30** A2
Amora, *Lisbon* **14** B2
Amoreira, *Lisbon* **14** A1
Ampelokipi, *Athens* **2** B2
Amper ➤, *Munich* **20** A1
Amstel, *Amsterdam* **2** b2
Amstel ➤, *Amsterdam* **2** c2
Amstel-Drecht-Kanaal, *Amsterdam* **2** B2
Amstel Station, *Amsterdam* **2** c3
Amstelhof, *Amsterdam* **2** b2
Amstelveen, *Amsterdam* **2** B2
Amsterdam, *Amsterdam* **2** A2
Amsterdam-Rijnkanaal, *Amsterdam* **2** B3
Amsterdam Zoo, *Amsterdam* **2** b3
Amsterdam Zuidoost, *Amsterdam* **2** B2
Amsterdamse Bos, *Amsterdam* **2** B1
Anacostia, *Washington* **32** B4
Anadoluhisarı, *Istanbul* **12** B2
Anadolukavağı, *Istanbul* **12** A2
Anata, *Jerusalem* **13** A1
Ancol, *Jakarta* **13** A1
'Andalus, *Baghdad* **3** B2
Andarai, *Rio de Janeiro* **24** B1
Anderlecht, *Brussels* **6** A1
Anderson Park, *Atlanta* **3** B2
Andingmen, *Beijing* **4** B2
Andrews Air Force Base, *Washington* **32** C4
Ang Mo Kio, *Singapore* **27** A3
Angby, *Stockholm* **28** A1
Angel I., *San Francisco* **25** A2
Angel Island State Park, *San Francisco* **25** A2
Angke, Kali ➤, *Jakarta* **13** A1
Angyalföld, *Budapest* **7** A2
Anik, *Mumbai* **20** A2
Anin, *Warsaw* **31** B2
Anjou, *Montreal* **19** A2
Annalee Heights, *Washington* **32** B2
Annandale, *Washington* **32** C2
Anne Frankhuis, *Amsterdam* **2** a1
Antony, *Paris* **23** B2
Anyangch'on, *Seoul* **26** C1
Aoyama, *Tokyo* **29** b2
Ap Lei Chau, *Hong Kong* **12** B1
Apapa, *Lagos* **14** B2
Apelacão, *Lisbon* **14** A2
Apterkarskiy Ostrov, *St. Petersburg* **26** B2
Ar Kazimiyah, *Baghdad* **3** B1
Ara ➤, *Tokyo* **29** A4
Arakawa-Ku, *Tokyo* **29** A3
Arany-hegyi-patak ➤, *Budapest* **7** A2
Aravaca, *Madrid* **17** B1
Arbataash, *Baghdad* **3** A1
Arc de Triomphe, *Paris* **23** a2
Arcadia, *Los Angeles* **16** B4
Arceuil, *Paris* **23** B2
Arco Plaza, *Los Angeles* **16** b1
Arese, *Milan* **18** A1
Arganzuela, *Madrid* **17** B1

Argenteuil, *Paris* **23** A2
Argonne Forest, *Chicago* **9** C1
Argüelles, *Madrid* **17** a1
Arima, *Osaka* **22** A2
Arima, *Tokyo* **29** B2
Arios Págos, *Athens* **2** c1
Arkhangelskoye, *Moscow* **19** B1
Arlington, *Boston* **6** A3
Arlington, *Washington* **32** B3
Arlington Heights, *Boston* **6** A2
Arlington Nat. Cemetery, *Washington* **32** B3
Armação, *Rio de Janeiro* **24** B2
Armadale, *Melbourne* **17** B2
Armenian Quarter, *Jerusalem* **13** b3
Armour Heights, *Toronto* **30** A2
Arncliffe, *Sydney* **28** B1
Arnold Arboretum, *Boston* **6** B3
Árpádföld, *Budapest* **7** A3
Arrentela, *Lisbon* **14** B2
Ârsta, *Stockholm* **28** B2
Art Institute, *Chicago* **9** c2
Artane, *Dublin* **11** A2
Artas, *Jerusalem* **13** B2
Arthur's Seat, *Edinburgh* **11** B3
Aryiroúpolis, *Athens* **2** B2
Asagaya, *Tokyo* **29** A2
Asahi, *Osaka* **22** A4
Asakusa, *Tokyo* **29** A3
Asakusabashi, *Tokyo* **29** a5
Asati, *Calcutta* **8** C1
Aschheim, *Munich* **20** A3
Ascot Vale, *Melbourne* **17** A1
Ashburn, *Chicago* **9** C2
Ashburton, *Melbourne* **17** B2
Ashfield, *Sydney* **28** B1
Ashford, *London* **15** B1
Ashiya, *Osaka* **22** A2
Ashiya ➤, *Osaka* **22** A2
Ashtown, *Dublin* **11** A2
Asisto, *Helsinki* **12** B1
Askrikefjärden, *Stockholm* **28** A3
Asnières, *Paris* **23** A2
Aspern, *Vienna* **31** A3
Aspern, Flugplatz, *Vienna* **31** A3
Assago, *Milan* **18** B1
Assemblée Nationale, *Paris* **23** b3
Assendelft, *Amsterdam* **2** A1
Assiano, *Milan* **18** B1
Astoria, *New York* **21** B2
Astrolabe Park, *Sydney* **28** B2
Atarot Airport, *Jerusalem* **13** A2
Atghara, *Calcutta* **8** B2
Athens = Athínai, *Athens* **2** B2
Athínai, *Athens* **2** B2
Athinai-Ellinikón Airport, *Athens* **2** B2
Athis-Mons, *Paris* **23** B3
Athlone, *Cape Town* **8** A2
Atholl, *Johannesburg* **13** A2
Atifiya, *Baghdad* **3** A2
Atisalen, *Istanbul* **12** B1
Atlanta, *Atlanta* **3** B2
Atlanta History Center, *Atlanta* **3** B2
Atomium, *Brussels* **6** A2
Attiki, *Athens* **2** A2
Atzgersdorf, *Vienna* **31** B1
Aubervilliers, *Paris* **23** A2
Aubing, *Munich* **20** B1
Auburndale, *Boston* **6** A2
Aucherdinny, *Edinburgh* **11** B2
Auckland Park, *Johannesburg* **13** B2
Auderghem, *Brussels* **6** B2
Augusta, Mausoleo di, *Rome* **25** b2
Augustówka, *Warsaw* **31** B2
Aulnay-sous-Bois, *Paris* **23** A3
Aurelio, *Rome* **25** B1
Ausim, *Cairo* **7** A1
Austerlitz, Gare d', *Paris* **23** A3
Austin, *Chicago* **9** B2
Avalon, *Wellington* **32** B2
Avedøre, *Copenhagen* **10** B2
Avellaneda, *Buenos Aires* **7** C2
Avenel, *Washington* **32** B4
Avondale, *Chicago* **9** B2
Avondale Heights, *Melbourne* **17** A1
Avtovo, *St. Petersburg* **26** B1
Ayazağa, *Istanbul* **12** B1
Ayer Chawan, P., *Singapore* **27** B2
Ayer Merbau, P., *Singapore* **27** B2
Ayía Marina, *Athens* **2** B2
Ayía Paraskevi, *Athens* **2** A2
Ayios Dhimitrios, *Athens* **2** B2
Ayios Ioánnis Rendis, *Athens* **2** B1
Azabu, *Tokyo* **29** c3
Azcapotzalco, *Mexico City* **18** B1
Azteca, Estadia, *Mexico City* **18** C2
Azucar, Cerro Pan de, *Santiago* **26** A1

B

Baambrugge, *Amsterdam* **2** B2
Baba I., *Karachi* **14** B1
Babarpur, *Delhi* **10** A2
Babushkin, *Moscow* **19** A4
Back B., *Mumbai* **20** B1
Baclaran, *Manila* **17** B2

Bacoor, *Manila* **17** C1
Bacoor B., *Manila* **17** C1
Badalona, *Barcelona* **4** A2
Badhoevedorp, *Amsterdam* **2** A1
Badli, *Delhi* **10** A1
Bærum, *Oslo* **22** A2
Bâğcılar, *Istanbul* **12** B1
Bâğgio, *Milan* **18** B1
Bâğh-e-Feyz, *Tehran* **30** A1
Baghdâd, *Baghdad* **3** A2
Bagmari, *Calcutta* **8** B2
Bagneux, *Paris* **23** B2
Bagnolet, *Paris* **23** A3
Bagsværd, *Copenhagen* **10** A2
Bagsværd Sø, *Copenhagen* **10** A2
Baguiati, *Calcutta* **8** B2
Bagumbayan, *Manila* **17** C2
Bahçeköy, *Istanbul* **12** A1
Bahtîm, *Cairo* **7** A2
Baileys Crossroads, *Washington* **32** B3
Bailly, *Paris* **23** A1
Bairro Alto, *Lisbon* **14** c1
Bairro Lopes, *Lisbon* **14** b3
Baisha, *Canton* **8** B2
Baisha ➤, *Canton* **8** B2
Baixa, *Lisbon* **14** c2
Baiyun Airport, *Canton* **8** A2
Baiyun Hill Scenic Spot, *Canton* **8** B2
Bakırköy, *Istanbul* **12** C1
Bakovka, *Moscow* **19** B2
Bal Harbor, *Miami* **18** A2
Balara, *Manila* **17** B2
Balashikha, *Moscow* **19** B5
Baldia, *Karachi* **14** A1
Baldoyle, *Dublin* **11** A3
Baldwin Hills, *Los Angeles* **16** B2
Baldwin Hills Res., *Los Angeles* **16** B2
Balgowlah, *Sydney* **28** A2
Balgowlah Heights, *Sydney* **28** A2
Balham, *London* **15** B3
Bali, *Calcutta* **8** B1
Baliganja, *Calcutta* **8** B1
Balingsnäs, *Stockholm* **28** B2
Balingsta, *Stockholm* **28** B2
Balintawak, *Manila* **17** B1
Balitai, *Tianjin* **30** B2
Ballerup, *Copenhagen* **10** A2
Ballinteer, *Dublin* **11** B2
Ballyboden, *Dublin* **11** B2
Ballybrack, *Dublin* **11** B3
Ballyfermot, *Dublin* **11** A1
Ballymorefinn Hill, *Dublin* **11** B1
Ballymun, *Dublin* **11** A2
Balmain, *Sydney* **28** B2
Balmhati, *Calcutta* **8** A2
Balvanera, *Buenos Aires* **7** B2
Balwyn, *Melbourne* **17** A2
Balwyn North, *Melbourne* **17** A2
Banática, *Lisbon* **14** A1
Banco do Brasil, Centro Cultural, *Rio de Janeiro* **24** a2
Bandra, *Mumbai* **20** A1
Bandra Pt., *Mumbai* **20** A1
Bang Kapi, *Bangkok* **3** B2
Bang Kholaem, *Bangkok* **3** B2
Bang Na, *Bangkok* **3** B2
Bang Phlad, *Bangkok* **3** a1
Bangkhen, *Bangkok* **3** A2
Bangkok = Krung Thep, *Bangkok* **3** B2
Bangkok Noi, *Bangkok* **3** B1
Bangkok Yai, *Bangkok* **3** B1
Banglamphoo, *Bangkok* **3** b2
Banglo, *Calcutta* **8** B1
Bangrak, *Bangkok* **3** B2
Bangsu, *Bangkok* **3** B2
Bank, *London* **15** b5
Bank of America, *San Francisco* **25** b2
Bank of China Tower, *Hong Kong* **12** c1
Banks, C., *Sydney* **28** C2
Banksmeadow, *Sydney* **28** B2
Banstala, *Calcutta* **8** B2
Bantra, *Calcutta* **8** B1
Baoshan, *Shanghai* **27** A1
Bar Giyora, *Jerusalem* **13** B1
Barahanagar, *Calcutta* **8** A2
Barajas, *Madrid* **17** B2
Barajas, Aeropuerto Transoceanico de, *Madrid* **17** B2
Barakpur, *Calcutta* **8** A2
Barberini, Palazzo, *Rome* **25** b3
Barbican, *London* **15** a4
Barcarena, *Lisbon* **14** A1
Barcarena, Rib. de ➤, *Lisbon* **14** A1
Barcelona, *Barcelona* **4** A1
Barcelona-Prat, Aeropuerta de, *Barcelona* **4** B1
Barceloneta, *Barcelona* **4** c3
Barking, *London* **15** A4
Barkingside, *London* **15** A4
Barnes, *London* **15** B2
Barnet, *London* **15** A2
Barra Arial, *Karachi* **14** B2
Barra Funda, *São Paulo* **26** B2
Barracas, *Buenos Aires* **7** B2
Barranco, *Lima* **16** B2
Barreiro, *Lisbon* **14** B2
Barreto, *Rio de Janeiro* **24** B2
Bartala, *Calcutta* **8** B1

Barton Park, *Sydney* **28** B1
Bartyki, *Warsaw* **31** C2
Barvikha, *Moscow* **19** B1
Bastille, Place de la, *Paris* **23** c5
Basus, *Cairo* **7** A2
Batanagar, *Calcutta* **8** B1
Bath Beach, *New York* **21** C1
Bath I., *Karachi* **14** B2
Batir, *Jerusalem* **13** B1
Batok, Bukit, *Singapore* **27** A2
Battersea, *London* **15** B3
Battery Park, *New York* **21** f1
Bauman, *Moscow* **19** B4
Baumgarten, *Vienna* **31** A1
Bay Harbour Islands, *Miami* **18** A2
Bay Ridge, *New York* **21** C1
Bayonne, *New York* **21** B1
Bayshore, *San Francisco* **25** B3
Bayswater, *London* **15** b2
Bayt Lahm = Bethlehem, *Jerusalem* **13** B2
Bayview, *San Francisco* **25** B2
Bāzâr, *Tehran* **30** A2
Beachmont, *Boston* **6** A4
Beacon Hill, *Hong Kong* **12** A2
Beato, *Lisbon* **14** A2
Beaumont, *Dublin* **11** A2
Beaumonte Heights, *Toronto* **30** A1
Bebek, *Istanbul* **12** B2
Bèchovice, *Prague* **24** B3
Beck L., *Chicago* **9** A1
Beckenham, *London* **15** B3
Beckton, *London* **15** A4
Becontree, *London* **15** A4
Beddington Corner, *London* **15** B3
Bedford, *Boston* **6** A2
Bedford Park, *Chicago* **9** C2
Bedford Park, *New York* **21** A2
Bedford Stuyvesant, *New York* **21** B2
Bedford View, *Johannesburg* **13** B2
Bedok, *Singapore* **27** B3
Bedok, Res., *Singapore* **27** A3
Beersel, *Brussels* **6** B1
Behala, *Calcutta* **8** B1
Bei Hai, *Beijing* **4** B2
Beicai, *Shanghai* **27** B2
Beicang, *Tianjin* **30** A1
Beihai Park, *Beijing* **4** b2
Beijing, *Beijing* **4** B1
Beit Ghur el-Fawqa, *Jerusalem* **13** A1
Beit Hanina, *Jerusalem* **13** B2
Beit Iksa, *Jerusalem* **13** B1
Beit I'nan, *Jerusalem* **13** A1
Beit Jala, *Jerusalem* **13** B1
Beit Lekhem = Bethlehem, *Jerusalem* **13** B2
Beit Nekofa, *Jerusalem* **13** B1
Beit Sahur, *Jerusalem* **13** B2
Beit Surik, *Jerusalem* **13** B1
Beit Zayit, *Jerusalem* **13** B1
Beitaipingzhuan, *Beijing* **4** B1
Beitar Ilit, *Jerusalem* **13** B1
Beitsun, *Canton* **8** B2
Beitunya, *Jerusalem* **13** A2
Beixing Dajie, *Shanghai* **27** B1
Békásmegyer, *Budapest* **7** A2
Bekkelaget, *Oslo* **22** A3
Bel Air, *Los Angeles* **16** B2
Bela Vista, *São Paulo* **26** B2
Bélanger, *Montreal* **19** A1
Belas, *Lisbon* **14** A1
Belas Artes, Museu Nacionale de, *Rio de Janeiro* **24** b2
Beleghata, *Calcutta* **8** B2
Belém, *Lisbon* **14** A1
Belém, Torre de, *Lisbon* **14** A1
Belénzinho, *São Paulo* **26** B2
Belgachiya, *Calcutta* **8** B2
Belgharia, *Calcutta* **8** A2
Belgrano, *Buenos Aires* **7** B2
Belgravia, *London* **15** c3
Bell Gardens, *Los Angeles* **16** C4
Bell Tower, *Beijing* **4** a2
Bellavista, *Lima* **16** B2
Bellavista, *Santiago* **26** C2
Belle Harbor, *New York* **21** C2
Belle View, *Washington* **32** B2
Bellevue, Schloss, *Berlin* **5** a2
Bellingham, *London* **15** B3
Bellwood, *Chicago* **9** B1
Belmont, *Boston* **6** A3
Belmont, *London* **15** B2
Belmont, *Wellington* **32** B2
Belmont Harbor, *Chicago* **9** B3
Belmore, *Sydney* **28** B1
Belur, *Calcutta* **8** B1
Belvedere, *Atlanta* **3** B3
Belvedere, *London* **15** B4
Belvedere, *San Francisco* **25** A2
Belyayevo Bogorodskoye, *Moscow* **19** C3
Bemowo, *Warsaw* **31** B1
Benaki, Moussío, *Athens* **2** b3
Bendale, *Toronto* **30** A3
Bendkhal, *Mumbai* **20** B2
Benfica, *Rio de Janeiro* **24** B1
Benfica, *Lisbon* **14** A1
Benito Juárez, *Mexico City* **18** B2
Benito Juárez, Aeropuerto Int., *Mexico City* **18** B2
Bensonhurst, *New York* **21** C2

Berchem-Sainte-Agathe, *Brussels* **6** A1
Berg am Laim, *Munich* **20** B2
Bergenfield, *New York* **21** A2
Bergham, *Munich* **20** B2
Bergvliet, *Cape Town* **8** A1
Beri, *Barcelona* **4** A1
Berkeley, *San Francisco* **25** A3
Berlin, *Berlin* **5** A3
Bermondsey, *London* **15** B3
Bernabeu, Estadio, *Madrid* **17** B1
Bernal Heights, *San Francisco* **25** B2
Berwyn, *Chicago* **9** B2
Berwyn Heights, *Washington* **32** B4
Besiktas, *Istanbul* **12** B2
Besòs ➤, *Barcelona* **4** A2
Bethesda, *Washington* **32** B3
Bethlehem, *Jerusalem* **13** B2
Bethnal Green, *London* **15** A3
Betor, *Calcutta* **8** B1
Beurs, *Amsterdam* **2** b2
Beverley Hills, *Sydney* **28** B1
Beverley Park, *Sydney* **28** B2
Beverly, *Chicago* **9** C3
Beverly Glen, *Los Angeles* **16** B2
Beverly Hills, *Los Angeles* **16** B2
Bexley, *London* **15** B4
Bexley, *Sydney* **28** B1
Bexleyheath, *London* **15** A4
Beykoz, *Istanbul* **12** B2
Beylerbeyi, *Istanbul* **12** B2
Beyoğlu, *Istanbul* **12** B1
Bezons, *Paris* **23** A2
Bezuidenhout Park, *Johannesburg* **13** B2
Bhadrakali, *Calcutta* **8** A2
Bhalswa, *Delhi* **10** A2
Bhambo Khan Qarmati, *Karachi* **14** B2
Bhatsala, *Calcutta* **8** B1
Bhawanipur, *Calcutta* **8** B2
Bhuleshwar, *Mumbai* **20** b2
Białoleka Dworska, *Warsaw* **31** B2
Biblioteca Nacional, *Rio de Janeiro* **24** c2
Bicentennial Park, *Sydney* **28** B1
Bickley, *London* **15** B4
Bidu, *Jerusalem* **13** B1
Bielany, *Warsaw* **31** B1
Bielawa, *Warsaw* **31** C2
Biesdorf, *Berlin* **5** A4
Bièvre ➤, *Paris* **23** B1
Bièvres, *Paris* **23** B2
Bilston, *Edinburgh* **11** B3
Binacayan, *Manila* **17** C1
Binondo, *Manila* **17** B1
Birak el Kiyam, *Cairo* **7** A1
Birch Cliff, *Toronto* **30** A3
Birkenstein, *Berlin* **5** A5
Birkholz, *Berlin* **5** A4
Birkholzaue, *Berlin* **5** A4
Birrarrung Park, *Melbourne* **17** A2
Biscayne Bay, *Miami* **18** B2
Biscayne Park, *Miami* **18** A2
Bishop Lavis, *Cape Town* **8** A2
Bishopscourt, *Cape Town* **8** A1
Bispebjerg, *Copenhagen* **10** A3
Biwon Secret Garden, *Seoul* **26** B1
Björknas, *Stockholm* **28** B3
Black Cr. ➤, *Toronto* **30** A2
Blackfen, *London* **15** B4
Blackheath, *London* **15** B3
Blackrock, *Dublin* **11** B2
Bladensburg, *Washington* **32** B4
Blair Village, *Atlanta* **3** C2
Blairgowrie, *Johannesburg* **13** A2
Blakehurst, *Sydney* **28** B1
Blakstad, *Oslo* **22** B1
Blankenburg, *Berlin* **5** A3
Blankenfelde, *Berlin* **5** A3
Blizne, *Warsaw* **31** B1
Bloomsbury, *London* **15** a3
Blota, *Warsaw* **31** C3
Blue Island, *Chicago* **9** C2
Bluebell, *Dublin* **11** B1
Bluff Hd., *Hong Kong* **12** B2
Blumberg, *Berlin* **5** A4
Blunt Pt., *San Francisco* **25** A2
Blutenburg, *Munich* **20** B1
Blylaget, *Oslo* **22** B3
Bo-Kaap Museum, *Cape Town* **8** c2
Boa Vista, Alto do, *Rio de Janeiro* **24** B1
Boardwalk, *New York* **21** C3
Boavista, *Lisbon* **14** A2
Bobigny, *Paris* **23** A3
Bocanegra, *Lima* **16** A2
Boedo, *Buenos Aires* **7** B2
Bogenhausen, *Munich* **20** B2
Bogorodskoye, *Moscow* **19** B4
Bogota, *New York* **21** A1
Bogstadvatnet, *Oslo* **22** A2
Bohnsdorf, *Berlin* **5** B4
Bois-Colombes, *Paris* **23** A2
Bois-d'Arcy, *Paris* **23** B1
Boissy-St.-Léger, *Paris* **23** B3
Boldinasco, *Milan* **18** B1
Bollate, *Milan* **18** A1
Bollebeek, *Brussels* **6** A1
Bollmora, *Stockholm* **28** B3
Bolshaya-Okhta, *St. Petersburg* **26** B2

Bolton, *Atlanta* **3** B2
Bom Retiro, *São Paulo* **26** B2
Bombay = Mumbai, *Mumbai* **20** B2
Bondi, *Sydney* **28** B2
Bondy, *Paris* **23** A3
Bondy, Forêt de, *Paris* **23** A4
Bonifacio Monument, *Manila* **17** B1
Bonneuil-sur-Marne, *Paris* **23** B4
Bonnington, *Edinburgh* **11** B1
Bonnyrig and Lasswade, *Edinburgh* **11** B3
Bonsuccesso, *Rio de Janeiro* **24** B1
Bonteheuwel, *Cape Town* **8** A2
Boo, *Stockholm* **28** A3
Booterstown, *Dublin* **11** B2
Borle, *Mumbai* **20** A2
Boronia Park, *Sydney* **28** A1
Borough Park, *New York* **21** C2
Bosmont, *Johannesburg* **13** B1
Bosön, *Stockholm* **28** A3
Bosporus = Istanbul Boğazi, *Istanbul* **12** C2
Bostancı, *Istanbul* **12** C2
Boston Harbor, *Boston* **6** A4
Botafogo, *Rio de Janeiro* **24** B1
Botanisk Have, *Copenhagen* **10** b2
Botany, *Sydney* **28** B2
Botany B., *Sydney* **28** B2
Botany Bay Nat. Park, *Sydney* **28** B2
Botič ➤, *Prague* **24** B3
Botica Sete, *Lisbon* **14** A1
Boucherville, *Montreal* **19** A3
Boucherville, Îs. de, *Montreal* **19** A3
Bougival, *Paris* **23** A1
Boulder Pt., *Hong Kong* **12** B1
Boulogne, Bois de, *Paris* **23** A2
Boulogne-Billancourt, *Paris* **23** B2
Bourg-la-Reine, *Paris* **23** B2
Bouviers, *Paris* **23** B1
Bovenkerk, *Amsterdam* **2** B2
Bovenkerker Polder, *Amsterdam* **2** B2
Bovisa, *Milan* **18** A2
Bow, *London* **15** A3
Bowery, *New York* **21** e2
Boyacıköy, *Istanbul* **12** B2
Boyle Heights, *Los Angeles* **16** B3
Bradbury Building, *Los Angeles* **16** b2
Braepark, *Edinburgh* **11** B2
Braid, *Edinburgh* **11** B2
Bramley, *Johannesburg* **13** A2
Brandenburger Tor, *Berlin* **5** A3
Brani, P., *Singapore* **27** B3
Branik, *Prague* **24** B2
Brānnkyrka, *Stockholm* **28** B2
Brás, *São Paulo* **26** B2
Brasilândia, *São Paulo* **26** A1
Brateyevo, *Moscow* **19** C4
Bratsevo, *Moscow* **19** A2
Bray, *Dublin* **11** B3
Braybrook, *Melbourne* **17** A1
Brázdim, *Prague* **24** A3
Breach Candy, *Mumbai* **20** a1
Breakheart Reservation, *Boston* **6** A3
Brede, *Copenhagen* **10** A3
Breeds Pond, *Boston* **6** A4
Breezy Point, *New York* **21** C2
Breitenlee, *Vienna* **31** A3
Breña, *Lima* **16** B2
Brent, *London* **15** A2
Brent Res., *London* **15** A2
Brentford, *London* **15** B2
Brentwood Park, *Los Angeles* **16** B2
Brera, *Milan* **18** B2
Bresso, *Milan* **18** A2
Brevik, *Stockholm* **28** A3
Břevnov, *Prague* **24** B2
Bridgeport, *Chicago* **9** B3
Bridgetown, *Cape Town* **8** A2
Bridgeview, *Chicago* **9** C2
Brighton, *Boston* **6** A3
Brighton, *Melbourne* **17** B1
Brighton le Sands, *Sydney* **28** B1
Brighton Park, *Chicago* **9** C2
Brightwood, *Washington* **32** B3
Brigittenau, *Vienna* **31** A2
Brimbank Park, *Melbourne* **17** A1
Brisbane, *San Francisco* **25** B2
British Museum, *London* **15** a3
Britz, *Berlin* **5** B3
Brixton, *London* **15** B3
Broad Sd., *Boston* **6** A4
Broadmeadows, *Melbourne* **17** A1
Broadmoor, *San Francisco* **25** B2
Broadway, *Chicago* **9** B1
Broadway, *New York* **21** e1
Brockley, *London* **15** B3
Brodno, *Warsaw* **31** B2
Bródnowski, Kanal, *Warsaw* **31** B2
Broek in Waterland, *Amsterdam* **2** A2
Bromley, *London* **15** B4
Bromley Common, *London* **15** B4
Bromma, *Stockholm* **28** A1
Bromma flygplats, *Stockholm* **28** A1
Brompton, *London* **15** c2
Brøndby Strand, *Copenhagen* **10** B2
Brøndbyøster, *Copenhagen* **10** B2
Brøndbyvester, *Copenhagen* **10** B2
Brondesbury, *London* **15** A2

Brønnøya, Oslo 22 A2
Brønshøj, Copenhagen 10 A2
Bronxville, New York 21 A3
Brookfield, Chicago 9 C1
Brookhaven, Atlanta 3 B2
Brookline, Boston 6 A3
Brooklyn, Cape Town 8 A1
Brooklyn, New York 21 C2
Brooklyn, Wellington 32 B1
Brooklyn Bridge, New York . . 21 f2
Brookmont, Washington 32 B3
Brossard, Montreal 19 B3
Brou-sur-Chantereine, Paris . . 23 A4
Brown, Toronto 30 A3
Broyhill Park, Washington . . . 32 B2
Brughério, Milan 18 A2
Brunswick, Melbourne 17 A1
Brush Hill, Boston 6 B1
Brussegem, Brussels 6 A1
Brussel Nat. Luchthaven, Brussels 6 A2
Brussels = Bruxelles, Brussels . 6 A2
Bruxelles, Brussels 6 A2
Bruzzano, Milan 18 A2
Bry-sur-Marne, Paris 23 A4
Bryanston, Johannesburg . . . 13 A1
Bryn, Oslo 22 A1
Brzeziny, Warsaw 31 B2
Bubeneč, Prague 24 B2
Buc, Paris 23 B1
Buchenhain, Munich 20 B1
Buchholz, Berlin 5 A3
Buckhead, Atlanta 3 A2
Buckingham Palace, London . 15 b3
Buckow, Berlin 5 B3
Buda, Budapest 7 B2
Budafok, Budapest 7 B2
Budaörs, Budapest 7 B1
Budapest, Budapest 7 B2
Budatétény, Budapest 7 B2
Budavaripalota, Budapest . . . 7 B2
Buddinge, Copenhagen 10 A3
Budokan, Tokyo 29 a4
Buena Vista, San Francisco . . 25 B2
Buenos Aires, Buenos Aires . . 7 B2
Bufalotta, Rome 25 B2
Bugio, Lisbon 14 B1
Buiksloot, Amsterdam 2 A2
Buitenveldert, Amsterdam . . . 2 B2
Buizingen, Brussels 6 B1
Bukit Panjang Nature Reserve, Singapore 27 A2
Bukit Timah Nature Reserve, Singapore 27 A2
Bukum, P., Singapore 27 B2
Bûlâq, Cairo 7 A2
Bule, Manila 17 C2
Bulim, Singapore 27 A1
Bullen Park, Melbourne 17 A2
Bundoora North, Melbourne . 17 A2
Bundoora Park, Melbourne . . 17 A2
Bunker I., Karachi 14 B1
Bunkyo-Ku, Tokyo 29 A3
Bunnefjorden, Oslo 22 A3
Buona Vista Park, Singapore . 27 B2
Burbank, Chicago 9 C2
Burbank, Los Angeles 16 A3
Burlington, Boston 6 A3
Burnham Park, Chicago 9 c2
Burnham Park Harbor, Chicago 9 B3
Burnhamthorpe, Toronto . . . 30 B1
Burnt Oak, London 15 A2
Burntisland, Edinburgh 11 A2
Burnwynd, Edinburgh 11 B1
Burqa, Jerusalem 13 A2
Burtus, Cairo 7 A1
Burudvatn, Oslo 22 A2
Burwood, Sydney 28 B1
Bushwick, New York 21 B2
Bushy Park, London 15 B1
Butantã, São Paulo 26 B1
Butcher I., Mumbai 20 B2
Butts Corner, Washington . . . 32 C2
Büyükdere, Istanbul 12 B2
Byculla, Mumbai 20 B2
Bygdøy, Oslo 22 A3

C

C.N. Tower, Toronto 30 B2
Cabaçu de Cima ➤, São Paulo 26 A2
Caballito, Buenos Aires 7 B2
Cabin John, Washington 32 B2
Cabin John Regional Park, Washington 32 A2
Cabinteely, Dublin 11 B3
Cabra, Dublin 11 A2
Cabuçu de Baixo ➤, São Paulo 26 A1
Cachan, Paris 23 B2
Cachenka ➤, Moscow 19 B1
Cachoeira, Rib. da ➤, São Paulo 26 B1
Cacilhas, Lisbon 14 A2
Cahuenga Pk., Los Angeles . . 16 B3
Cairo = El Qâhira, Cairo . . . 7 A2
Caju, Rio de Janeiro 24 B1
Čakovice, Prague 24 B3
Calcutta = Kolkata, Calcutta . 8 B2
California Inst. of Tech., Los Angeles 16 B4
California Plaza, Los Angeles . 16 b1
California State Univ., Los Angeles 16 B3
Callao, Lima 16 B2
Caloocan, Manila 17 B1
Calumet Park, Chicago 9 C3
Calumet Sag Channel ➤, Chicago 9 C2
Calumpang, Manila 17 B2
Calvairate, Milan 18 B2
Camarate, Lisbon 14 A2
Camaroes, Lisbon 14 A1
Camberwell, London 15 B3
Camberwell, Melbourne 17 B2
Cambridge, Boston 6 A3
Cambridge Res., Boston 6 A2
Cambuci, São Paulo 26 B2
Camden, London 15 A3
Cameron, Mt., Wellington . . . 32 B2
Çamlıca, Istanbul 12 B2
Camp Springs, Washington . . 32 C4
Campamento, Madrid 17 B1
Campbellfield, Melbourne . . . 17 A1
Camperdown, Sydney 28 B2
Campidoglio, Rome 25 c3
Campo, Casa de, Madrid . . . 17 B1
Campo F.C. Barcelona, Barcelona 4 A1
Campo Grando, Lisbon 14 A2
Campo Pequeño, Lisbon . . . 14 A2
Campolide, Lisbon 14 A2
Camps Bay, Cape Town 8 A1
C'an San Joan, Barcelona . . . 4 A2

Cañacao B., Manila 17 C1
Canarsie, New York 21 C2
Cancelleria, Palazzo dei, Rome 25 c2
Candiac, Montreal 19 B3
Caneças, Lisbon 14 A1
Canillas, Madrid 17 B2
Canillejas, Madrid 17 B2
Canning Town, London 15 A4
Canterbury, Melbourne 17 A2
Canterbury, Sydney 28 B1
Canton = Guangzhou, Canton 8 B2
Caohejing, Shanghai 27 B1
Capão Redondo, São Paulo . . 26 B1
Caparica, Lisbon 14 A2
Caparica, Costa da, Lisbon . . 14 B1
Cape Flats, Cape Town 8 B2
Cape Town, Cape Town 8 A1
Capitol Heights, Washington . 32 B4
Capitol Hill, Washington . . . 32 B4
Capitolini, Musei, Rome 25 c3
Captain Cook Bridge, Sydney 28 C1
Captain Cook Landing Place Park, Sydney 28 C2
Capuchos, Lisbon 14 B1
Carabanchel Alto, Madrid . . . 17 B1
Carabanchel Bajo, Madrid . . 17 B1
Carapachay, Buenos Aires . . . 7 B2
Caraza, Buenos Aires 7 C2
Caridad, Manila 17 C1
Carioca, Sa. da, Rio de Janeiro 24 B1
Carlstadt, New York 21 A1
Carlton, Melbourne 17 A1
Carmen de Huechuraba, Santiago 26 B1
Carmen de la Legua, Lima . . 16 B2
Carnaxide, Lisbon 14 A1
Carnegie, Melbourne 17 B2
Carnegie Hall, New York . . . 21 c2
Carnide, Lisbon 14 A1
Carol City, Miami 18 A1
Carrascal, Santiago 26 B1
Carrickmines, Dublin 11 B3
Carrières-sous-Bois, Paris . . . 23 A1
Carrières-sous-Poissy, Paris . . 23 A1
Carrières-sur-Seine, Paris . . . 23 A2
Carrigeen Bay, Dublin 11 A3
Cartierville, Montreal 19 A1
Casa Verde, São Paulo 26 A1
Casál Morena, Rome 25 C2
Casalotti, Rome 25 B1
Cascade Heights, Atlanta . . . 3 B2
Castél di Leva, Rome 25 C2
Castel Sant'Angelo, Rome . . . 25 B1
Castle, Dublin 11 c2
Castle, Edinburgh 11 b2
Castle of Good Hope, Cape Town 8 a3
Castleknock, Dublin 11 A1
Castleton Corners, New York . 21 C1
Catedral Metropolitana, Mexico City 18 b3
Catedral Metropolitana, Rio de Janeiro 24 c1
Catete, Rio de Janeiro 24 B1
Catford, London 15 B3
Caulfield, Melbourne 17 B2
Causeway Bay, Hong Kong . . 12 c3
Cavite, Manila 17 C1
Caxias, Lisbon 14 A1
Cebecci, Istanbul 12 B1
Cechingnola, Rome 25 C2
Cecilienhof, Schloss, Berlin . . 5 B1
Cedar Grove, Atlanta 3 C3
Cempaka Putih, Jakarta 13 B2
Çengelköy, Istanbul 12 B2
Cengkareng, Jakarta 13 A1
Centennial Park, Sydney . . . 28 B2
Center Hill, Atlanta 3 B2
Centocelle, Rome 25 B2
Centraal Station, Amsterdam . 2 a2
Central Park, New York 21 B2
Cerillos, Santiago 26 B1
Cerro de la Estrella, Mexico City 18 B2
Cerro de los Angeles, Madrid . 17 C1
Cerro Navia, Santiago 26 B1
Certanovka ➤, Moscow 19 C3
Certanovo, Moscow 19 C3
Cesano Boscone, Milan 18 B1
Cesate, Milan 18 A1
Cha Kwo Ling, Hong Kong . . 12 B2
Chacarita, Buenos Aires 7 B2
Chadwell Heath, London . . . 15 A4
Chai Chee, Singapore 27 B3
Chai Wan, Hong Kong 12 B2
Chai Wan Kok, Hong Kong . . 12 A1
Chaillot, Palais de, Paris . . . 23 b1
Chakdaha, Calcutta 8 C1
Chamartin, Madrid 17 B1
Chamberi, Madrid 17 B1
Chambourcy, Paris 23 A1
Champ de Mars, Parc du, Paris 23 c2
Champigny-sur-Marne, Paris . 23 B4
Champlain, Pont, Montreal . . 19 B2
Champs Elysées, Avenue des, Paris 23 b2
Champs-sur-Marne, Paris . . . 23 A4
Chamrail, Calcutta 8 B1
Chamshil, Seoul 26 B2
Chamwón, Seoul 26 B2
Chanakyapuri, Delhi 10 B2
Chanditala, Calcutta 8 A1
Changfeng Park, Shanghai . . 27 B1
Changi, Singapore 27 A3
Changi Int. Airport, Singapore 27 A3
Changning, Shanghai 27 B1
Chantereine, Paris 23 A4
Chantian, Canton 8 A2
Chao Phraya ➤, Bangkok . . . 3 B2
Chaoyang, Beijing 4 B2
Chaoyangmen, Beijing 4 B2
Chapelizod, Dublin 11 A1
Chapultepec, Bosque de, Mexico City 18 B1
Chapultepec, Castillo de, Mexico City 18 B1
Charenton-le-Pont, Paris . . . 23 B3
Charing Cross, London 15 b4
Charleroi, Kanal de ➤, Brussels 6 B1
Charles Bridge, Prague 24 b1
Charles Square, Prague 24 c2
Charlestown, Boston 6 A3
Charlottenburg, Berlin 5 A2
Charlottenburg, Schloss, Berlin 5 A2
Charlottenlund, Copenhagen . 10 A3
Charlton, London 15 B4
Charneca, Lisbon 14 A2
Charneca, Lisbon 14 B1
Châtenay-Malabry, Paris . . . 23 B2
Chatham, Chicago 9 C3

Châtillon, Paris 23 B2
Chatou, Paris 23 A1
Chatpur, Calcutta 8 B2
Chatswood, Sydney 28 A2
Chatuchak, Bangkok 3 B2
Chatuchak Park, Bangkok . . 3 B2
Chauki, Karachi 14 A1
Chavarria, Lima 16 B2
Chaville, Paris 23 B2
Chayang, Seoul 26 B2
Chegi, Seoul 26 B2
Chelles, Paris 23 A4
Chelles, Canal de, Paris 23 A4
Chells-le-Pin, Aerodrome, Paris 23 A4
Chelsea, Boston 6 A3
Chelsea, London 15 B2
Chelsea, New York 21 c1
Chembur, Mumbai 20 A2
Chennevières-sur-Marne, Paris 23 B4
Cheops, Cairo 7 B1
Cherepkovo, Moscow 19 B2
Chernyovo, Moscow 19 A1
Cheryomushki, Moscow 19 B3
Chestnut Hill, Boston 6 B2
Cheung Sha Wan, Hong Kong 12 A1
Cheverly, Washington 32 B4
Chevilly-Larue, Paris 23 B3
Chevry-Cossigny, Paris 23 B4
Chevy Chase, Washington . . . 32 B3
Chevy Chase View, Washington 32 A3
Chia Keng, Singapore 27 A3
Chiaravalle Milanese, Milan . 18 B2
Chicago, Chicago 9 B3
Chicago Harbor, Chicago . . . 9 B3
Chicago Lawn, Chicago 9 C2
Chicago-Midway Airport, Chicago 9 C2
Chicago-O'Hare Int. Airport, Chicago 9 B1
Chicago Ridge, Chicago 9 C2
Chicago Sanitary and Ship Canal, Chicago 9 C2
Chienzui, Canton 8 A2
Chik Sha, Hong Kong 12 B2
Child's Hill, London 15 A2
Chilla Saroda, Delhi 10 B2
Chillum, Washington 32 B4
Chilly-Mazarin, Paris 23 B2
Chinatown, Los Angeles 16 a3
Chinatown, New York 21 e2
Chinatown, San Francisco . . . 25 b2
Chinatown, Singapore 27 c2
Chinguota, Calcutta 8 C1
Chislehurst, London 15 B4
Chiswick, London 15 B2
Chiswick House, London . . . 15 B2
Chitose, Tokyo 29 B2
Chitralada Palace, Bangkok . . 3 B2
Chiyoda-Ku, Tokyo 29 b4
Chkalova, Moscow 19 B5
Choboty, Moscow 19 C2
Chodov u Prahy, Prague 24 B3
Chōfu, Tokyo 29 B2
Choisy-le-Roi, Paris 23 B3
Cholupice, Prague 24 C2
Chom Thong, Bangkok 3 B1
Chong Pang, Singapore 27 A2
Ch'ŏngdam, Seoul 26 B2
Chongmyo Royal Shrine, Seoul 26 B1
Chongno, Seoul 26 B1
Chongwen, Beijing 4 B2
Chŏnho, Seoul 26 B2
Chopin, Muzeum, Warsaw . . 31 b2
Chornaya ➤, Moscow 19 B6
Chorrillos, Lima 16 C2
Chowpatty Beach, Mumbai . . 20 b1
Christian Quarter, Jerusalem . 13 b3
Christiansborg, Copenhagen . 10 c2
Christianshavn, Copenhagen . 10 A3
Chrzanów, Warsaw 31 B1
Chuen Lung, Hong Kong . . . 12 A1
Chuk Kok, Hong Kong 12 A2
Chulalongkom Univ., Bangkok 3 B2
Chung, Seoul 26 B1
Chunghwa, Seoul 26 B2
Chungnangch'on ➤, Seoul . . 26 B1
Chūō-Ku, Tokyo 29 b5
Church End, London 15 A2
Churchtown, Dublin 11 B2
Ciampino, Rome 25 C2
Ciampino, Aeroporto di, Rome 25 C2
Cicero, Chicago 9 B2
Cilandak, Jakarta 13 B1
Cilincing, Jakarta 13 A2
Ciliwung ➤, Jakarta 13 B2
Čimice, Prague 24 B2
Cinecittà, Rome 25 B2
Cinisello Bálsamo, Milan . . . 18 A2
Cinkota, Budapest 7 A3
Cipete, Jakarta 13 B1
Citadella, Budapest 7 c2
Città del Vaticano, Rome . . . 25 B1
Città degli Studi, Milan 18 B2
City, London 15 A3
City Hall, New York 21 e1
Ciudad Deportiva, Mexico City 18 B2
Ciudad Fin de Semana, Madrid 17 B2
Ciudad General Belgrano, Buenos Aires 7 C1
Ciudad Lineál, Madrid 17 B1
Ciudad Satélite, Mexico City . 18 A1
Ciudad Universitaria, Buenos Aires 7 B2
Ciudad Universitaria, Mexico City 18 C1
Ciutadella, Parc de la, Barcelona 4 A2
Civic Center, Los Angeles . . . 16 b2
Clamart, Paris 23 B2
Clapham, London 15 B3
Clapton, London 15 A3
Claremont, Cape Town 8 A1
Clayhall, London 15 A4
Clerkenwell, London 15 a4
Clermiston, Edinburgh 11 B2
Clichy, Paris 23 A2
Clichy-sous-Bois, Paris 23 A4
Cliffside, Toronto 30 A3
Cliffside Park, New York . . . 21 B2
Clifton, Boston 6 A4
Clifton, Karachi 14 B2
Cliftondale, Boston 6 A3
Cloghran, Dublin 11 A2
Clondalkin, Dublin 11 A1
Clonkeagh, Dublin 11 B2
Clonsilla, Dublin 11 A1
Clontarf, Dublin 11 A2
Clontarf, Sydney 28 A2
Clovelly, Sydney 28 B2

Cobras, I. das, Rio de Janeiro 24 B2
Coburg, Melbourne 17 A1
Cochituate, Boston 6 A1
Cochituate, L., Boston 6 B1
Cocotá, Rio de Janeiro 24 A1
Cœuilly, Paris 23 B4
Coina, Lisbon 14 B2
Coit Tower, San Francisco . . . 25 a2
Coker, Lagos 14 B2
Colaba, Mumbai 20 B1
Colaba Pt., Mumbai 20 B1
Colégiales, Buenos Aires 7 B2
Colindale, London 15 A2
Colinton, Edinburgh 11 B2
College Park, Atlanta 3 C2
College Park, Washington . . . 32 B4
College Point, New York 21 B2
Collégien, Paris 23 A4
Collier Row, London 15 A4
Colliers Wood, London 15 B2
Colma, San Francisco 25 B2
Colney Hatch, London 15 A3
Cologno Monzese, Milan . . . 18 A2
Colombes, Paris 23 A2
Colón, Monumente, Barcelona 4 A3
Colon, Plaza de, Madrid 17 a3
Colonia Güell, Barcelona . . . 4 A1
Colonial Knob, Wellington . . 32 A1
Colosseo, Rome 25 c3
Columbus Circus, New York . 21 b2
Combault, Paris 23 B4
Comércio, Praça do, Lisbon . . 14 A2
Commerce, Los Angeles 16 B4
Como, Sydney 28 C1
Company's Gardens, Cape Town 8 c2
Conceição, I. da, Rio de Janeiro 24 B2
Concertgebouw, Amsterdam . 2 c1
Conchali, Santiago 26 B2
Concord, Boston 6 A1
Concord, Sydney 28 B1
Concord, Toronto 30 A2
Concorde, Place de la, Paris . 23 b3
Concorezzo, Milan 18 A2
Coney Island, New York 21 C2
Congonhas, Aéroporto, São Paulo 26 B2
Connaught Place, Delhi 10 B2
Conservatori, Palazzo dei, Rome 25 c3
Consolação, São Paulo 26 B2
Constantia, Cape Town 8 B1
Constitución, Buenos Aires . . 7 B2
Constitution, Atlanta 3 B2
Convention and Exhibition Centre, Hong Kong 12 b2
Coogee, Sydney 28 B2
Cook Str., Wellington 32 A1
Cooksville, Toronto 30 B1
Coolock, Dublin 11 A2
Copacabana, Rio de Janeiro . 24 B2
Copenhagen = København, Copenhagen 10 A2
Coral Gables, Miami 18 B2
Coral Hills, Washington 32 B4
Corcovado, Morro do, Rio de Janeiro 24 B1
Corduff, Dublin 11 A1
Cormano, Milan 18 A2
Cornaredo, Milan 18 A1
Córsico, Milan 18 B1
Corsini, Palazzo, Rome 25 c1
Corviale, Rome 25 B1
Coslada, Madrid 17 B2
Cossipy, Paris 23 A4
Cossipore, Calcutta 8 B2
Costantino, Arco di, Rome . . 25 c3
Costorphine, Edinburgh 11 B2
Cotao, Lisbon 14 A1
Côte St.-Luc, Montreal 19 B2
Cotunduba, I. de, Rio de Janeiro 24 B2
Covent Garden, London 15 b4
Cowgate, Edinburgh 11 b3
Cowley, London 15 A1
Coyoacán, Mexico City 18 B2
Cragin, Chicago 9 B2
Craighall Park, Johannesburg 13 A2
Craiglockhart, Edinburgh . . . 11 B2
Craigmillar, Edinburgh 11 B3
Cramond, Edinburgh 11 B2
Cramond Bridge, Edinburgh . 11 B1
Cramond I., Edinburgh 11 B2
Cranford, London 15 B1
Crawford, Cape Town 8 A2
Crayford, London 15 B5
Creekmouth, London 15 A4
Crescenzago, Milan 18 A2
Cressely, Paris 23 B1
Cresskill, New York 21 A2
Creteil, Paris 23 B3
Cricklewood, London 15 A2
Cristo Redentor, Estatua do, Rio de Janeiro 24 B1
Crockenhill, London 15 B5
Croissy-Beaubourg, Paris . . . 23 B4
Croissy-sur-Seine, Paris 23 A1
Crosne, Paris 23 B3
Cross I., Mumbai 20 B2
Crouch End, London 15 A3
Crown Mine, Johannesburg . 13 B1
Crows Nest, Sydney 28 A2
Croydon, London 15 B3
Croydon Park, Sydney 28 B1
Cruagh Mt., Dublin 11 B2
Crumlin, Dublin 11 B2
Cruz de Pau, Lisbon 14 B2
Crystal Palace, London 15 B3
Csepel, Budapest 7 B2
Csepelsziget, Budapest 7 B2
Csillaghegy, Budapest 7 A2
Csillagtelep, Budapest 7 B2
Csömör, Budapest 7 A3
Csömöri-patak ➤, Budapest . 7 A3
Cuatro Vientos, Madrid 17 B1
Cuauhtémoc, Mexico City . . 18 B2
Cubao, Manila 17 B2
Čubuklu, Istanbul 12 B2
Cudahy, Los Angeles 16 C3
Cuicuilco, Pirámido de, Mexico City 18 C1
Culver City, Los Angeles . . . 16 B2
Cumballa Hill, Mumbai 20 b1
Cumbres de Vallecas, Madrid 17 B2
Cupecé, São Paulo 26 B1
Currie, Edinburgh 11 B2
Cusago, Milan 18 B1
Cusano Milanino, Milan . . . 18 A2
Custom House, Dublin 11 b3
Čuvuşabaşı ➤, Istanbul 12 B1
Czerniaków, Warsaw 31 B2
Cyste, Warsaw 31 B1

D

D.F. Malan Airport, Cape Town 8 A2
Da Mooca ➤, São Paulo 26 B2
Da Yunhe ➤, Tianjin 30 A1
Dabizhuang, Tianjin 30 A1
Dablice, Prague 24 B2
Dabrowa, Warsaw 31 B1
Dachang, Shanghai 27 B1
Dachang Airfield, Shanghai . . 27 B1
Dachau-Ost, Munich 20 A1
Dachauer Moos, Munich . . . 20 A1
Dadar, Mumbai 20 A2
Dagenham, London 15 A4
Daglfing, Munich 20 A2
Dahisha, Jerusalem 13 B2
Dahlem, Berlin 5 B2
Dahlwitz-Hoppegarten, Berlin 5 A5
Dahongmen, Beijing 4 C2
Daitō, Osaka 22 A4
Dajiaoting, Beijing 4 B2
Dakhnoye, St. Petersburg . . . 26 C1
Dalejsky potok ➤, Prague . . . 24 B2
Dalgety Bay, Edinburgh 11 A1
Dalkeith, Edinburgh 11 B3
Dalkey, Dublin 11 B3
Dalkey Island, Dublin 11 B3
Dallgow, Berlin 5 A1
Dalmeny, Edinburgh 11 B1
Dalston, London 15 A3
Daly City, San Francisco 25 B2
Dam, Amsterdam 2 b2
Dam Rak, Amsterdam 2 a2
Damaia, Lisbon 14 A1
Damenstrasse, Berlin 5 B5
Dan Ryan Woods, Chicago . . 9 C2
Danderhall, Edinburgh 11 B3
Danderyd, Stockholm 28 A2
Danforth, Toronto 30 A2
Darakeh, Tehran 30 A2
Darband, Tehran 30 A2
Darling Harbour, Sydney . . . 28 b1
Darling Point, Sydney 28 B2
Darndale, Dublin 11 A2
Darrûs, Tehran 30 A2
Dartford, London 15 B5
Darya Ganj, Delhi 1 a3
Dashi, Canton 8 B2
Datansha, Canton 8 B2
Datun, Beijing 4 B2
Daulatpur, Delhi 10 A1
David's Citadel, Jerusalem . . . 13 b3
David's Tomb, Jerusalem . . . 13 b3
Davidson, Mt., San Francisco 25 B2
Davidson's Mains, Edinburgh 11 B2
Davûdiyeh, Tehran 30 A2
Davydkovo, Moscow 19 B2
Dawidy, Warsaw 31 C1
Days Bay, Wellington 32 B2
Dazhigu, Tianjin 30 B2
De Waag, Amsterdam 2 b2
Decatur, Atlanta 3 B3
Dedham, Boston 6 B2
Deer I., Boston 6 A4
Deginnos, Moscow 19 A3
Deir Dibwan, Jerusalem 13 A2
Deir Ibzi'e, Jerusalem 13 A1
Dejvice, Prague 24 B2
Dekabristov, Ostrov, St. Petersburg 26 B1
Delhi, Delhi 10 B2
Delhi Gate, Delhi 1 b3
Demarest, New York 21 A2
Den Ilp, Amsterdam 2 A2
Denistone Heights, Sydney . . 28 A1
Dentona Park, Toronto 30 A3
Deptford, London 15 B3
Deputati, Camera dei, Rome . 25 b2
Des Plaines, Chicago 9 A1
Des Plaines ➤, Chicago 9 B1
Deshengmen, Beijing 4 B2
Deutsch-Wagram, Vienna . . . 31 A3
Deutsche Oper, Berlin 5 A2
Deutscher Museum, Munich . 20 B2
Devil's Peak, Cape Town . . . 8 A1
Dhafni, Athens 2 B2
Dhakuria, Calcutta 8 B2
Dhamarakia, Athens 2 A2
Dharavi, Mumbai 20 A2
Dhrapersón, Athens 2 A2
Diadema, São Paulo 26 C2
Diegen, Brussels 6 A2
Diemen, Amsterdam 2 A2
Diepkloof, Johannesburg . . . 13 B1
Dieprivier, Cape Town 8 B1
Difficult Run ➤, Washington . 32 B2
Dilbeek, Brussels 6 A1
Dinzigu, Tianjin 30 A1
Dirnismaning, Munich 20 A2
District Heights, Washington . 32 B4
Ditan Park, Beijing 4 a2
Diyālā ➤, Baghdad 3 B2
Djursholm, Stockholm 28 A2
Dobřejovice, Prague 24 C3
Döberitz, Berlin 5 A1
Döbling, Vienna 31 A2
Docklands, London 15 A3
Dodder, R. ➤, Dublin 11 B1
Dodger Stadium, Los Angeles 16 B3
Dolgoe Ozero, St. Petersburg 26 B1
Doll Museum, Delhi 1 b3
Dollis Hill, London 15 A2
Dollymount, Dublin 11 A2
Dolni, Prague 24 B3
Dolni Chabry, Prague 24 B2
Dolni Počernice, Prague 24 B3
Dolphins Barn, Dublin 11 B2
Dom Pedro II, Parque, São Paulo 26 B2
Domain, The, Sydney 28 b2
Dome of the Rock, Jerusalem 13 b3
Don Mills, Toronto 30 A2
Don Muang Int. Airport, Bangkok 3 A2
Donaghmede, Dublin 11 A3
Donau-Oder Kanal, Vienna . . 31 A3
Donaufeld, Vienna 31 A2
Donaupark, Vienna 31 A2
Donaustadt, Vienna 31 A2
Dongan Hills, New York 21 C1
Dongcheng, Beijing 4 B2
Dongguzi, Tianjin 30 A2
Dongjiao, Canton 8 B2
Dongjimen, Beijing 4 B2
Dongmenwai, Tianjin 30 B2
Dongri, Mumbai 20 b2
Dongshanhu Park, Canton . . 8 B2
Dongzhimen, Beijing 4 B2
Donnybrook, Dublin 11 B2
Doornfontein, Johannesburg . 13 B2
Dorchester, Boston 6 A3
Dorchester B., Boston 6 A3
Dornach, Munich 20 B3
Dorval, Aéroport de, Montreal 19 B1

Dos Couros ➤, São Paulo . . . 26 C2
Dos Moninos ➤, São Paulo . . 26 C2
Douglas Park, Chicago 9 B2
Dover Heights, Sydney 28 B2
Dowlatābād, Tehran 30 B2
Downey, Los Angeles 16 C4
Downsview, Toronto 30 A1
Dragør, Copenhagen 10 B3
Drancy, Paris 23 A3
Dranesville, Washington 32 A1
Dreilinden, Berlin 5 B2
Drewnica, Warsaw 31 B2
Drigh Road, Karachi 14 A2
Drimnagh, Dublin 11 B2
Drogenbos, Brussels 6 B1
Druid Hills, Atlanta 3 B2
Drum Towwer, Beijing 4 A2
Drumcondra, Dublin 11 A2
Drummoyne, Sydney 28 B1
Drylaw, Edinburgh 11 B2
Dubeč, Prague 24 B3
Dublin, Dublin 11 A2
Dublin Airport, Dublin 11 A2
Dublin Bay, Dublin 11 B3
Dublin Harbour, Dublin 11 A2
Duddingston, Edinburgh . . . 11 B3
Dugnano, Milan 18 A2
Dūlāb, Tehran 30 B2
Dulwich, London 15 B3
Dum Dum, Calcutta 8 B2
Dum Dum Int. Airport, Calcutta 8 B2
Dumont, New York 21 A2
Dún Laoghaire, Dublin 11 B3
Duna ➤, Budapest 7 A2
Duncan Dock, Cape Town . . 8 a3
Dundrum, Dublin 11 B2
Dunearn, Singapore 27 B2
Dunfermline, Edinburgh . . . 11 A1
Dunn Loring, Washington . . . 32 B2
Dunning, Chicago 9 B2
Dunvegan, Johannesburg . . . 13 A2
Duomo, Milan 18 c2
Duque de Caxias, Rio de Janeiro 24 A1
Dusit, Bangkok 3 B2
Dusit Zoo, Bangkok 3 a2
Dworp, Brussels 6 B1
Dyakovo, Moscow 19 B3
Dzerzhinsky, Moscow 19 C5
Dzerzhinskiy, Moscow 19 B3
Dzerzhinskiy Park, Moscow . 19 B3

E

Eagle Rock, Los Angeles 16 B3
Ealing, London 15 A2
Earl's Court, London 15 c1
Earlsfield, London 15 B2
Earlwood, Sydney 28 B1
East Acton, London 15 A2
East Arlington, Boston 6 A3
East Arlington, Washington . . 32 B3
East Bedfont, London 15 B1
East Boston, Boston 6 A3
East Don ➤, Toronto 30 A2
East Elmhurst, New York . . . 21 B2
East Finchley, London 15 A2
East Ham, London 15 A4
East Humber ➤, Toronto . . . 30 A1
East Lamma Channel, Hong Kong 12 B1
East Lexington, Boston 6 A2
East Los Angeles, Los Angeles 16 B3
East Molesey, London 15 B1
East New York, New York . . . 21 B2
East Pines, Washington 32 B4
East Point, Atlanta 3 C2
East Potomac Park, Washington 32 B3
East Pt., Boston 6 A4
East River ➤, New York 21 B2
East Rutherford, New York . . 21 B1
East Sheen, London 15 B2
East Village, New York 21 e2
East Wickham, London 15 B4
East York, Toronto 30 A2
Eastbourne, Wellington 32 B2
Eastcote, London 15 A1
Easter Howgate, Edinburgh . . 11 B2
Eastwood, Sydney 28 A1
Ebara, Tokyo 29 B3
Ebisu, Tokyo 29 c2
Ebute-Ikorodu, Lagos 14 A2
Ebute-Metta, Lagos 14 B2
Eda, Tokyo 29 B2
Edendale, Johannesburg 13 A2
Edenmore, Dublin 11 A2
Edgars Cr. ➤, Melbourne . . . 17 A1
Edgeley, Toronto 30 A1
Edgemar, San Francisco 25 C2
Edinburgh, Edinburgh 11 B2
Edison Park, Chicago 9 B2
Edmondson, Washington . . . 32 B3
Edmondstown, Dublin 11 B2
Edo ➤, Tokyo 29 A4
Edogawa-Ku, Tokyo 29 A4
Edsberg, Stockholm 28 A1
Edwards L., Melbourne 17 A1
Egebjerg, Copenhagen 10 A3
Eiche Sud, Berlin 5 A4
Eiffel, Tour, Paris 23 c2
Ein Arik, Jerusalem 13 A1
Ein Naquba, Jerusalem 13 B1
Ein Rafa, Jerusalem 13 B1
Eizariya, Jerusalem 13 B2
Ejby, Copenhagen 10 A2
Ejigbo, Lagos 14 A2
Ekeberg, Oslo 22 A3
Eknäs, Stockholm 28 B3
El 'Abbasiya, Cairo 7 A2
El Agustino, Lima 16 B2
El Baragil, Cairo 7 A1
El Basâlin, Cairo 7 A2
El Bosque, Santiago 26 B1
El Carmen, Santiago 26 B1
El Duqqi, Cairo 7 A2
El Encinar de los Reyes, Madrid 17 A2
El Ghuriya, Cairo 7 A2
El Giza, Cairo 7 A1
El Khadr, Jerusalem 13 B1
El Khalifa, Cairo 7 A2
El Kôm el Ahmar, Cairo 7 A2
El Ma'âdi, Cairo 7 A2
El Matarîya, Cairo 7 A2
El Mohandesin, Cairo 7 A2
El Monte, Los Angeles 16 B4
El Mûski, Cairo 7 A2
El Pardo, Madrid 17 A1
El Portal, Miami 18 A2

El Prat de Llobregat, Barcelona 4 B1
El Pueblo de L.A. Historic Park, Los Angeles 16 b2
El Qâhira, Cairo 7 A2
El Qubba, Cairo 7 A2
El Reloj, Mexico City 18 C2
El Retiro, Madrid 17 B1
El Salto, Santiago 26 B2
El Sereno, Los Angeles 16 B3
El Talibîya, Cairo 7 B2
El Vergel, Mexico City 18 C2
El Wâhli, Cairo 7 A2
El Zamâlik, Cairo 7 A2
El Zeitûn, Cairo 7 A2
Elephanta Caves, Mumbai . . 20 B2
Elephanta I., Mumbai 20 B2
Ellboda, Stockholm 28 A3
Ellinikón, Athens 2 B2
Ellis I., New York 21 B1
Elm Park, London 15 A5
Elmers End, London 15 B3
Elmhurst, New York 21 B2
Elmstead, London 15 B4
Elmwood Park, Chicago 9 B2
Elmwood Park, New York . . . 21 A1
Elsdon, Wellington 32 A1
Elsiesrivier, Cape Town 8 A2
Elsternwick, Melbourne 17 B2
Eltham, London 15 B4
Elwood, Melbourne 17 B1
Elysée, Paris 23 b2
Elysian Park, Los Angeles . . . 16 a3
Embajadores, Madrid 17 c3
Embarcadero Center, San Francisco 25 b3
Emek Refa'im, Jerusalem . . . 13 c2
Emerainville, Paris 23 B4
Emeryville, San Francisco . . . 25 A3
Eminönü, Istanbul 12 B1
Emmarentia, Johannesburg . . 13 A2
Empire State Building, New York 21 c2
Encantado, Rio de Janeiro . . 24 B1
Encino, Los Angeles 16 B2
Encino Res., Los Angeles . . . 16 B1
Eneybyerg, Stockholm 28 A1
Enfield, Sydney 28 B1
Engenho, I. do, Rio de Janeiro 24 B2
Englewood, Chicago 9 C3
Englewood, New York 21 A2
Englewood Cliffs, New York . 21 A2
Enmore, Sydney 28 B2
Enskede, Stockholm 28 B2
Entrevias, Madrid 17 B1
Epping, Sydney 28 A1
Erawan Shrine, Bangkok . . . 3 c3
Eregun, Lagos 14 A2
Erenköy, Istanbul 12 C2
Erith, London 15 B5
Erlaa, Vienna 31 B1
Ermington, Sydney 28 A1
Ermita, Manila 17 B1
Erstarov, Canton 8 B2
Erskineville, Sydney 28 B2
Erunkan, Lagos 14 A2
Erzsébet-Telep, Budapest . . . 7 B3
Eschenried, Munich 20 A1
Esenler, Istanbul 12 B1
Esher, London 15 B1
Eskbank, Edinburgh 11 B3
Esperanza, Mexico City 18 c3
Esplanade Park, Singapore . . 27 c3
Esplugas, Barcelona 4 A1
Esposizione Univ. di Roma (E.U.R.), Rome 25 C1
Essendon, Melbourne 17 A1
Essendon Airport, Melbourne 17 A1
Essingen, Stockholm 28 B1
Essling, Vienna 31 A3
Est, Gare de l', Paris 23 a5
Estadio Maracanã, Rio de Janeiro 24 B1
Estado, Parque do, São Paulo 26 B2
Estefânia, Lisbon 14 a2
Estrela, Basilica da, Lisbon . . 14 A2
Ethnikó Arheologiko Moussio, Athens 2 A2
Etobicoke, Toronto 30 B1
Etobicoke Cr. ➤, Toronto . . . 30 B1
Etterbeek, Brussels 6 A2
Euston, London 15 a3
Evanston, Chicago 9 A2
Even Sapir, Jerusalem 13 B1
Evere, Brussels 6 A2
Everett, Boston 6 A3
Evergreen Park, Chicago 9 C2
Evin, Tehran 30 A2
Evínos, Athens 2 B2
Ewu, Lagos 14 A1
Exchange Square, Hong Kong 12 c1
Exposições, Palácio das, Rio de Janeiro 24 B1
Eyüp, Istanbul 12 B1

F

Fabour, Mt., Singapore 27 B2
Facchi, Seoul 26 B2
Falledparken, Copenhagen . . 10 A3
Fågelön, Stockholm 28 B1
Fagersjö, Stockholm 28 B2
Fair Lawn, New York 21 A1
Fairfax, Washington 32 C2
Fairfax Station, Washington . . 32 C2
Fairhaven Bay, Boston 6 A1
Fairhaven Hill, Boston 6 A1
Fairland, Johannesburg 13 A1
Fairmilehead, Edinburgh . . . 11 B2
Fairmount Heights, Washington 32 B4
Fairport, Toronto 30 A4
Fairview, New York 21 A1
Falenty, Warsaw 31 C1
Fálirou, Órmos, Athens 2 B2
Falkenberg, Berlin 5 A4
Falkenhagen, Berlin 5 A1
Falkensee, Berlin 5 A1
Falls Church, Washington . . . 32 B2
False Bay, Cape Town 8 B2
Farahâbâd, Tehran 30 B2
Farforovskaya, St. Petersburg 26 B5
Farningham, London 15 B5
Farrar Pond, Boston 6 A1
Farsta, Stockholm 28 B2
Fasanerie-Nord, Munich . . . 20 A2
Fasting Palace, Beijing 4 c2
Fatih, Istanbul 12 B1
Favoriten, Vienna 31 B2

Fawkner, *Melbourne* ... 17 A1
Fawkner Park, *Melbourne* ... 17 B1
Feijó, *Lisbon* ... 14 B2
Feldkirchen, *Munich* ... 20 A2
Feltham, *London* ... 15 B1
Fener, *Istanbul* ... 12 B1
Fenerbahçe, *Istanbul* ... 12 C2
Fengtai, *Beijing* ... 4 C1
Fenino, *Moscow* ... 19 B5
Ferencváros, *Budapest* ... 7 B2
Ferihegy Airport, *Budapest* ... 7 B3
Ferndale, *Johannesburg* ... 13 A2
Férolles-Attilly, *Paris* ... 23 B4
Fichtenau, *Berlin* ... 5 B5
Fields Corner, *Boston* ... 6 B3
Fierra Camp, *Milan* ... 18 B1
Fifth Avenue, *New York* ... 21 b3
Figino, *Milan* ... 18 B1
Fijir, *Baghdad* ... 3 A2
Filadélfia, *Athens* ... 2 A1
Fili-Mazilovo, *Moscow* ... 19 B2
Filothei, *Athens* ... 2 A2
Finchley, *London* ... 15 A2
Finglas, *Dublin* ... 11 A2
Finsbury, *London* ... 15 A3
Finsbury Park, *London* ... 15 A3
Fiorito, *Buenos Aires* ... 7 C2
Fishouse, *Dublin* ... 11 B2
Fischerhäuser, *Munich* ... 20 A3
Fisher Island, *Miami* ... 18 B2
Fishermans Bend, *Melbourne* ... 17 A1
Fisherman's Wharf, *San Francisco* ... 25 a1
Fisherville, *Toronto* ... 30 A2
Fisksätra, *Stockholm* ... 28 B3
Fitzroy Gardens, *Melbourne* ... 17 A1
Five Dock, *Sydney* ... 28 B1
Fjellstrand, *Oslo* ... 22 B2
Flamengo, *Rio de Janeiro* ... 24 B1
Flaminio, *Rome* ... 25 B1
Flaskebekk, *Oslo* ... 22 A3
Flatbush, *New York* ... 21 C2
Flaten, *Stockholm* ... 28 B2
Flemington Racecourse, *Melbourne* ... 17 A1
Flint Pk., *Los Angeles* ... 16 B3
Florence, *Los Angeles* ... 16 C3
Florence Bloom Bird Sanctuary, *Johannesburg* ... 13 A2
Florentia, *Johannesburg* ... 13 B2
Flores, *Buenos Aires* ... 7 B2
Floresta, *Buenos Aires* ... 7 B2
Florida, *Buenos Aires* ... 7 B2
Florida, *Johannesburg* ... 13 A1
Floridsdorf, *Vienna* ... 31 A2
Flushing, *New York* ... 21 B3
Flushing Meadows Corona Park, *New York* ... 21 B2
Flysta, *Stockholm* ... 28 A1
Fo Tan, *Hong Kong* ... 12 A2
Föhrenhain, *Vienna* ... 31 A2
Fontainebleau, *Johannesburg* ... 13 A1
Fontenay-aux-Roses, *Paris* ... 23 B2
Fontenay-le-Fleury, *Paris* ... 23 A1
Fontenay-sous-Bois, *Paris* ... 23 A3
Foots Cray, *London* ... 15 B4
Footscray, *Melbourne* ... 17 A1
Foreshore, *Cape Town* ... 8 a3
Forest, *Brussels* ... 6 B1
Forest Gate, *London* ... 15 A4
Forest Heights, *Washington* ... 32 C3
Forest Hill, *London* ... 15 B3
Forest Hill, *Toronto* ... 30 A2
Forest Hills, *New York* ... 21 B2
Forest Park, *Chicago* ... 9 B2
Forest View, *Chicago* ... 9 C2
Forestville, *Washington* ... 32 B4
Fornebu, *Oslo* ... 22 A2
Fornebu Airport, *Oslo* ... 22 A2
Foro Romano, *Rome* ... 25 c3
Forstenried, *Munich* ... 20 c2
Forstenrieder Park, *Munich* ... 20 B1
Fort, *Mumbai* ... 20 c2
Fort Canning Park, *Singapore* ... 27 b2
Fort Dupont Park, *Washington* ... 32 B4
Fort Foote Village, *Washington* ... 32 C3
Fort Lee, *New York* ... 21 A2
Fort Mason Center, *San Francisco* ... 25 a1
Forth, Firth of, *Edinburgh* ... 11 A2
Forth Rail Bridge, *Edinburgh* ... 11 A1
Forth Road Bridge, *Edinburgh* ... 11 A1
Fót, *Budapest* ... 7 A3
Fourqueux, *Paris* ... 23 A1
Foxrock, *Dublin* ... 11 B2
Framingham, *Boston* ... 6 B1
Franconia, *Washington* ... 32 C3
Frankel, *Singapore* ... 27 B3
Franklin Park, *Boston* ... 6 B3
Franklin Park, *Chicago* ... 9 B1
Franklin Park, *Washington* ... 32 B3
Franklin Res., *Los Angeles* ... 16 B2
Frauenkirche, *Munich* ... 20 B2
Frederiksberg, *Copenhagen* ... 10 A3
Frederiksdal, *Copenhagen* ... 10 A2
Fredersdorf, *Berlin* ... 5 A5
Freguesia, *Rio de Janeiro* ... 24 A1
Freidrichshain, Volkspark, *Berlin* ... 5 A3
Freiham, *Munich* ... 20 B1
Freimann, *Munich* ... 20 A2
Fresh Pond, *Boston* ... 6 A3
Fresnes, *Paris* ... 23 B2
Freudenau, *Vienna* ... 31 A2
Friarstown, *Dublin* ... 11 B1
Frick Collection, *New York* ... 21 b3
Friedenau, *Berlin* ... 5 B3
Friedrichsfelde, *Berlin* ... 5 B4
Friedrichshagen, *Berlin* ... 5 B5
Friedrichshain, *Berlin* ... 5 A3
Friedrichslust, *Berlin* ... 5 A5
Friherrs, *Helsinki* ... 12 B1
Frontón, I., *Lima* ... 16 B1
Frunze, *Moscow* ... 19 B3
Fuchū, *Tokyo* ... 29 A1
Fuencarral, *Madrid* ... 17 B1
Fuenlabrada, *Madrid* ... 17 C1
Fujidera, *Osaka* ... 22 B4
Fukagawa, *Tokyo* ... 29 B3
Fukiage Imperial Garden, *Tokyo* ... 29 a4
Fukiai, *Osaka* ... 22 A2
Fukushima, *Osaka* ... 22 A3
Fulham, *London* ... 15 B2
Funabori, *Tokyo* ... 29 A4
Funasaka, *Osaka* ... 22 A3
Fundão, I. do, *Rio de Janeiro* ... 24 B1
Fünfhaus, *Vienna* ... 31 A2
Furcsø, *Copenhagen* ... 10 A2
Furth, *Munich* ... 20 B2
Futago-tamagawaen, *Tokyo* ... 29 B2
Fuxing Dao, *Shanghai* ... 27 B2
Fuxing Park, *Shanghai* ... 27 B1
Fuxinglu, *Beijing* ... 4 B1

G

Gage Park, *Chicago* ... 9 C2
Gagny, *Paris* ... 23 A4
Galata, *Istanbul* ... 12 B1
Galátsion, *Athens* ... 2 A2
Galeão, Aéroporto Int. de, *Rio de Janeiro* ... 24 A1
Galyanovo, *Moscow* ... 19 B4
Gambir, *Jakarta* ... 13 A1
Gamboa, *Rio de Janeiro* ... 24 B1
Gambôlta, *Milan* ... 18 B2
Gamla Stan, *Stockholm* ... 28 c2
Gamlebyen, *Oslo* ... 22 A3
Gangtou, *Canton* ... 8 A1
Gangwei, *Canton* ... 8 B2
Ganjiakou, *Beijing* ... 4 B1
Ganshoren, *Brussels* ... 6 A1
Gants Hill, *London* ... 15 A4
Gaoqiao, *Shanghai* ... 27 A2
Garbagnate Milanese, *Milan* ... 18 A1
Garbatella, *Rome* ... 25 B2
Garches, *Paris* ... 23 A2
Garching, *Munich* ... 20 A3
Garden City, *Cairo* ... 7 A2
Garden Reach, *Calcutta* ... 8 B1
Garder, *Oslo* ... 22 B2
Garfield, *New York* ... 21 A1
Garfield Park, *Chicago* ... 9 B2
Gargareta, *Athens* ... 2 B2
Garvanza, *Los Angeles* ... 16 B3
Gåshaga, *Stockholm* ... 28 A3
Gateway National Recreation Area, *New York* ... 21 C2
Gateway of India, *Mumbai* ... 20 B2
Gatow, *Berlin* ... 5 B1
Gávea, *Rio de Janeiro* ... 24 B1
Gávea, Pedra da, *Rio de Janeiro* ... 24 B1
Gazdagrét, *Budapest* ... 7 B1
Gebel el Ahmar, *Cairo* ... 7 A2
Gebel el Mugattam, *Cairo* ... 7 A2
Gebel el Tura, *Cairo* ... 7 B2
Geiselgasteig, *Munich* ... 20 B2
General San Martin, *Buenos Aires* ... 7 B1
Gennevilliers, *Paris* ... 23 A2
Gentilly, *Paris* ... 23 B3
Gentofte, *Copenhagen* ... 10 A3
Genval, *Brussels* ... 6 B2
George I., *Hong Kong* ... 12 A1
Georges I., *Boston* ... 6 B4
Georges River Bridge, *Sydney* ... 28 C1
Georgetown, *Washington* ... 32 B3
Georgia Dome, *Atlanta* ... 3 B2
Gerasdorf bei Wien, *Vienna* ... 31 A2
Gerberau, *Munich* ... 20 A2
Gerli, *Buenos Aires* ... 7 C2
Germiston, *Johannesburg* ... 13 B2
Gern, *Munich* ... 20 B2
Gesirat el Rauda, *Cairo* ... 7 A2
Getafe, *Madrid* ... 17 C1
Geva Binyamin, *Jerusalem* ... 13 A2
Geylang Serai, *Singapore* ... 27 B3
Gezīrat el Dhahab, *Cairo* ... 7 B2
Gharapuri, *Mumbai* ... 20 B2
Ghatkopar, *Mumbai* ... 20 A2
Ghazipur, *Delhi* ... 10 B2
Ghizri, *Karachi* ... 14 B2
Ghizri Cr. →, *Karachi* ... 14 B2
Ghonda, *Delhi* ... 10 A2
Ghusuri, *Calcutta* ... 8 B2
Gianicolense, *Rome* ... 25 B1
Gianicolo, *Rome* ... 25 c1
Gibraltar Pt., *Toronto* ... 30 B2
Gidea Park, *London* ... 15 A5
Giesing, *Munich* ... 20 B2
Gilmerton, *Edinburgh* ... 11 B2
Gilo, *Jerusalem* ... 13 B2
Gimmersta, *Stockholm* ... 28 B3
Ginza, *Tokyo* ... 29 b5
Girgaum, *Mumbai* ... 20 b2
Giv'at Ye'arim, *Jerusalem* ... 13 B1
Giv'at Ze'ev, *Jerusalem* ... 13 A2
Giza Pyramids = Pyramids, *Cairo* ... 7 B1
Gjersjøen, *Oslo* ... 22 B3
Gladesville, *Sydney* ... 28 B1
Gladsakse, *Copenhagen* ... 10 A2
Glasnevin, *Dublin* ... 11 A2
Glassmanor, *Washington* ... 32 C3
Glasthule, *Dublin* ... 11 B3
Glen Iris, *Melbourne* ... 17 B2
Glen Mar Park, *Washington* ... 32 B3
Glen Rock, *New York* ... 21 A1
Glenarden, *Washington* ... 32 B4
Glenasmole Reservoirs, *Dublin* ... 11 B1
Glenvista, *Johannesburg* ... 13 B2
Glifádha, *Athens* ... 2 B2
Glömsta, *Stockholm* ... 28 B1
Glostrup, *Copenhagen* ... 10 B2
Gogar, *Edinburgh* ... 11 B2
Göktürk, *Istanbul* ... 12 B1
Golabari, *Calcutta* ... 8 B2
Golabki, *Warsaw* ... 31 B1
Gold Coast, *Chicago* ... 9 a2
Golden Gate, *San Francisco* ... 25 B2
Golden Gate Bridge, *San Francisco* ... 25 B2
Golden Gate Park, *San Francisco* ... 25 B2
Golden Horn, *Istanbul* ... 12 B1
Golders Green, *London* ... 15 A2
Gollans Stream →, *Wellington* ... 32 B2
Golyevo, *Moscow* ... 19 B1
Goodman Hill, *Boston* ... 6 A1
Goodmayes, *London* ... 15 A4
Goodwood, *Cape Town* ... 8 A2
Górce, *Warsaw* ... 31 B1
Gore Hill, *Sydney* ... 28 A2
Gorelyy →, *St. Petersburg* ... 26 A3
Gorenki, *Moscow* ... 19 B5
Gorgie, *Edinburgh* ... 11 B2
Gorky Park, *Moscow* ... 19 B3
Gosen, *Berlin* ... 5 B5
Gosener kanal, *Berlin* ... 5 B5
Gospel Oak, *London* ... 15 A2
Gotanda, *Tokyo* ... 29 B3
Goth Goli Mar, *Karachi* ... 14 A2
Goth Sher Shah, *Karachi* ... 14 A1
Gournay-sur-Marne, *Paris* ... 23 A4
Governor, I. do, *Rio de Janeiro* ... 24 A1

Governor's I., *New York* ... 21 B1
Graben, *Vienna* ... 31 b2
Grabów, *Warsaw* ... 31 C1
Graça, *Lisbon* ... 14 b3
Grace, Mt., *Wellington* ... 32 B2
Grace Cathedral, *San Francisco* ... 25 b1
Gracefield, *Wellington* ... 32 B2
Gracia, *Barcelona* ... 4 A1
Gräfelfing, *Munich* ... 20 B1
Gragoatá, *Rio de Janeiro* ... 24 B2
Grand Cemtral Station, *New York* ... 21 c2
Grand Union Canal, *London* ... 15 A2
Grande Place, *Brussels* ... 6 b2
Grant Park, *Atlanta* ... 3 B2
Grant Park, *Chicago* ... 9 c2
Granton, *Edinburgh* ... 11 B2
Grape I., *Boston* ... 6 B4
Grassy Park, *Cape Town* ... 8 B2
Gratosóglio, *Milan* ... 18 B2
Gratzwalde, *Berlin* ... 5 B5
Gravesend, *New York* ... 21 C2
Grazhdanka, *St. Petersburg* ... 26 B2
Great Falls, *Washington* ... 32 B2
Great Falls Park, *Washington* ... 32 B2
Great Hall of the People, *Beijing* ... 4 b2
Great Meadows National Wildlife Refuge, *Boston* ... 6 A1
Greco, *Milan* ... 18 A2
Green I., *Hong Kong* ... 12 B1
Green Point, *Cape Town* ... 8 A1
Greenbelt, *Washington* ... 32 A4
Greenbelt Park, *Washington* ... 32 A4
Greenfield Park, *Montreal* ... 19 B3
Greenford, *London* ... 15 A1
Greenhill, *London* ... 15 A2
Greenhills, *Dublin* ... 11 B1
Greenmarket Square, *Cape Town* ... 8 c2
Greenpoint, *New York* ... 21 B2
Greenwich, *London* ... 15 B3
Greenwich Observatory, *London* ... 15 B3
Greenwich Village, *New York* ... 21 c1
Greenwood, *Boston* ... 6 A3
Grefsen, *Oslo* ... 22 A3
Gresham Park, *Atlanta* ... 3 B2
Greve Strand, *Copenhagen* ... 10 B1
Greyfriars Kirk, *Edinburgh* ... 11 c2
Griebnitzsee, *Berlin* ... 5 B2
Griffen Park, *Los Angeles* ... 16 B3
Grimbergen, *Brussels* ... 6 A2
Grinzing, *Vienna* ... 31 A2
Grobbenried, *Munich* ... 20 A1
Grochów, *Warsaw* ... 31 B2
Grodzisk, *Warsaw* ... 31 B2
Groenendaal, *Brussels* ... 6 B2
Grogol Petamburin, *Jakarta* ... 13 A1
Gronsdorf, *Munich* ... 20 B3
Grorud, *Oslo* ... 22 A4
Gross Glienicke, *Berlin* ... 5 A1
Gross-Hadern, *Munich* ... 20 B1
Gross-Lappen, *Munich* ... 20 A2
Grosse Krampe, *Berlin* ... 5 B5
Grosse Müggelsee, *Berlin* ... 5 B4
Grossenzersdorf, *Vienna* ... 31 A3
Grossenzersdorfer Arm →, *Vienna* ... 31 A3
Grosser Biberhaufen, *Vienna* ... 31 A2
Grosser Wannsee, *Berlin* ... 5 B2
Grossfeld-Siedlung, *Vienna* ... 31 A2
Grosshesselohe, *Munich* ... 20 B2
Grossziethen, *Berlin* ... 5 B3
Grove Hall, *Boston* ... 6 B3
Grove Park, *Atlanta* ... 3 B2
Grove Park, *London* ... 15 A1
Grove Park, *London* ... 15 B4
Groveton, *Washington* ... 32 C3
Grünau, *Berlin* ... 5 B4
Grunewald, *Berlin* ... 5 B2
Grünwald, *Munich* ... 20 B2
Grünwalder Forst, *Munich* ... 20 B2
Grymes Hill, *New York* ... 21 C1
Guadalupe, *Manila* ... 17 B2
Guadalupe, Basilica de, *Mexico City* ... 18 B2
Guanabara, B. de, *Rio de Janeiro* ... 24 B1
Guanabara, Jardim, *Rio de Janeiro* ... 24 A1
Guanabara, Palácio da, *Rio de Janeiro* ... 24 B1
Guang'anmen, *Beijing* ... 4 B1
Guangqumen, *Beijing* ... 4 B2
Guangzhou, *Canton* ... 8 B2
Guanshuo, *Canton* ... 8 B2
Gudö, *Stockholm* ... 28 B3
Güell, Parque de, *Barcelona* ... 4 A2
Guerrero, *Mexico City* ... 18 a1
Guggenheim Museum, *New York* ... 21 b3
Guinardó, *Barcelona* ... 4 A2
Gulbai, *Karachi* ... 14 A1
Güngören, *Istanbul* ... 12 B1
Gunnersbury, *London* ... 15 B2
Gustavo A. Madero, *Mexico City* ... 18 B2
Guttenberg, *New York* ... 21 B1
Gutuyevskiy, Ostrov, *St. Petersburg* ... 26 B1
Guyancourt, *Paris* ... 23 B1
Gyál, *Budapest* ... 7 B3
Gyáli-patak →, *Budapest* ... 7 B2

H

Haaga, *Helsinki* ... 12 B2
Haar, *Munich* ... 20 B3
Hackbridge, *London* ... 15 B3
Hackensack, *New York* ... 21 A1
Hackensack →, *New York* ... 21 B1
Hackney, *London* ... 15 A3
Hackney Wick, *London* ... 15 A3
Haga, *Stockholm* ... 28 A2
Hagenbrunn, *Vienna* ... 31 A2
Hägersten, *Stockholm* ... 28 A1
Hai Ho →, *Tianjin* ... 30 B2
Haidan, *Beijing* ... 4 B1
Haidarpur, *Delhi* ... 10 A1
Haidhausen, *Munich* ... 20 B2
Haight-Ashbury, *San Francisco* ... 25 B2
Hainault, *London* ... 15 A4
Haizhu Guangchang, *Canton* ... 8 B2
Hakunila, *Helsinki* ... 12 B3
Halásztelek, *Budapest* ... 7 B1
Haliç = Golden Horn, *Istanbul* ... 12 B1
Halim Perdanakusuma International Airport, *Jakarta* ... 13 B2

Halle, *Brussels* ... 6 B1
Hallia, *Helsinki* ... 12 B2
Haltiavuori, *Helsinki* ... 12 B2
Ham, *London* ... 15 B2
Hameenkylä, *Helsinki* ... 12 B1
Hammarby, *Stockholm* ... 28 B2
Hamme, *Brussels* ... 6 A1
Hammersmith, *London* ... 15 B2
Hampstead, *London* ... 15 A2
Hampstead, *Montreal* ... 19 B2
Hampstead Garden Suburb, *London* ... 15 A2
Hampstead Heath, *London* ... 15 A2
Hampton, *London* ... 15 B1
Hampton Court Palace, *London* ... 15 B1
Hampton Wick, *London* ... 15 B2
Hamra', *Baghdad* ... 3 B1
Hanala, *Helsinki* ... 12 A3
Haneda, *Tokyo* ... 29 B3
Hang Hau, *Hong Kong* ... 12 B2
Hanging Gardens, *Mumbai* ... 20 b1
Hanjiashu, *Tianjin* ... 30 A1
Hanlon, *Toronto* ... 30 B1
Hanwell, *London* ... 15 B1
Hanworth, *London* ... 15 B1
Haora, *Calcutta* ... 8 B2
Hapeville, *Atlanta* ... 3 C2
Happy Valley, *Hong Kong* ... 12 B2
Har Adar, *Jerusalem* ... 13 B1
Haren, *Brussels* ... 6 A2
Hareskovby, *Copenhagen* ... 10 A2
Haringey, *London* ... 15 A3
Harjusuo, *Helsinki* ... 12 B3
Harlem, *New York* ... 21 B2
Harlesden, *London* ... 15 A2
Harlington, *London* ... 15 B1
Harmaja, *Helsinki* ... 12 C2
Harmashatar hegy, *Budapest* ... 7 A2
Harolds Cross, *Dublin* ... 11 B2
Háros, *Budapest* ... 7 B2
Harperrig Reservoir, *Edinburgh* ... 11 B1
Harrow, *London* ... 15 A1
Harrow on the Hill, *London* ... 15 A1
Harrow School, *London* ... 15 A1
Harrow Weald, *London* ... 15 A1
Hartsfield-Atlanta International Airport, *Atlanta* ... 3 C2
Harumi, *Tokyo* ... 29 c5
Harvard Univ., *Boston* ... 6 A3
Harwood Heights, *Chicago* ... 9 B2
Hasanābād, *Tehran* ... 30 A1
Hasbrouck Heights, *New York* ... 21 A1
Haselhorst, *Berlin* ... 5 A2
Hasköy, *Istanbul* ... 12 B1
Hasle, *Oslo* ... 22 A3
Haslum, *Oslo* ... 22 A2
Hästhagen, *Stockholm* ... 28 B2
Hatch End, *London* ... 15 A1
Hatiara, *Calcutta* ... 8 B2
Hauketo, *Oslo* ... 22 A3
Havel →, *Berlin* ... 5 A2
Havelkanal, *Berlin* ... 5 A1
Havering, *London* ... 15 A5
Havering-atte-Bower, *London* ... 15 A5
Hawölgok, *Seoul* ... 26 B2
Haworth, *New York* ... 21 A2
Hawthorne, *Chicago* ... 9 C2
Hayes, *London* ... 15 A5
Hayes, *London* ... 15 B1
Hayes End, *London* ... 15 A1
Hayford, *Chicago* ... 9 C2
Haywards, *Wellington* ... 32 A2
Heard Pond, *Boston* ... 6 A1
Heathfield, *Cape Town* ... 8 B1
Heathrow Airport, *London* ... 15 B1
Hebe Haven, *Hong Kong* ... 12 A2
Hebei, *Tianjin* ... 30 B2
Hedong, *Canton* ... 8 B2
Hedong, *Tianjin* ... 30 B2
Heidelberg Heights, *Melbourne* ... 17 A2
Heidelberg West, *Melbourne* ... 17 A2
Heidemühle, *Berlin* ... 5 B5
Heideveld, *Cape Town* ... 8 A2
Heiligensee, *Berlin* ... 5 A2
Heiligenstadt, *Vienna* ... 31 A2
Heinersdorf, *Berlin* ... 5 A3
Heldenplatz, *Vienna* ... 31 b1
Hélène Champlain, Parc, *Montreal* ... 19 A2
Helenelund, *Stockholm* ... 28 A1
Heliopolis = Masr el Gedida, *Cairo* ... 7 A2
Hellersdorf, *Berlin* ... 5 A4
Hellerup, *Copenhagen* ... 10 A3
Helmahof, *Vienna* ... 31 A3
Helsingfors = Helsinki, *Helsinki* ... 12 B2
Helsinki, *Helsinki* ... 12 B2
Helsinki Airport, *Helsinki* ... 12 B2
Hendon, *London* ... 15 A2
Hengsha, *Canton* ... 8 B2
Hennigsdorf, *Berlin* ... 5 A2
Henryków, *Warsaw* ... 31 B1
Henson Cr. →, *Washington* ... 32 C4
Hentiaa, *Helsinki* ... 12 B2
Heping, *Tianjin* ... 30 B2
Heping Park, *Shanghai* ... 27 B2
Hepingli, *Beijing* ... 4 B2
Herman Eckstein Park, *Johannesburg* ... 13 A2
Hermannskogel, *Vienna* ... 31 A1
Hermiston, *Edinburgh* ... 11 B2
Hermsdorf, *Berlin* ... 5 A3
Hernals, *Vienna* ... 31 A2
Herne Hill, *London* ... 15 B3
Herons, Î. aux, *Montreal* ... 19 B2
Herstedøster, *Copenhagen* ... 10 A2
Hertfoniemi, *Helsinki* ... 12 B3
Heşārak, *Tehran* ... 30 A1
Heston, *London* ... 15 B1
Hetzendorf, *Vienna* ... 31 B1
Hextable, *London* ... 15 B4
Hialeah, *Miami* ... 18 A1
Hickory Hills, *Chicago* ... 9 C2
Hiekkaharju, *Helsinki* ... 12 B3
Hietaniemi, *Helsinki* ... 12 B2
Hietzing, *Vienna* ... 31 A1
Higashi, *Osaka* ... 22 A4
Higashimurayama, *Tokyo* ... 29 A1
Higashinada, *Osaka* ... 22 A2
Higashiōsaka, *Osaka* ... 22 B4
Higashisumiyoshi, *Osaka* ... 22 B4
Higashiyodogawa, *Osaka* ... 22 A3
High Park, *Toronto* ... 30 B2
Highbury, *London* ... 15 A3

Highgate, *London* ... 15 A3
Highland Cr. →, *Toronto* ... 30 A3
Highland Creek, *Toronto* ... 30 A3
Highland Park, *Los Angeles* ... 16 B3
Highlands North, *Johannesburg* ... 13 A2
Hillcrest Heights, *Washington* ... 32 C4
Hillend, *Edinburgh* ... 11 A1
Hillingdon, *London* ... 15 A1
Hillwood, *Washington* ... 32 B3
Hilmîya, *Cairo* ... 7 A2
Hin Keng, *Hong Kong* ... 12 A2
Hingham, *Boston* ... 6 B4
Hingham B., *Boston* ... 6 B4
Hingham Harbor, *Boston* ... 6 B4
Hirakata, *Osaka* ... 22 A4
Hirota, *Osaka* ... 22 A3
Hirschstetten, *Vienna* ... 31 A2
Histórico Nacional, Museu, *Rio de Janeiro* ... 24 b3
Hither Green, *London* ... 15 B3
Hiyoshi, *Tokyo* ... 29 B2
Hizma, *Jerusalem* ... 13 B2
Hjortekær, *Copenhagen* ... 10 A3
Hjortspring, *Copenhagen* ... 10 A2
Hlubočepy, *Prague* ... 24 B2
Ho Chung, *Hong Kong* ... 12 A2
Ho Man Tin, *Hong Kong* ... 12 B2
Hoboken, *New York* ... 21 B1
Hobsons B., *Melbourne* ... 17 B1
Hochbrück, *Munich* ... 20 A2
Hochelaga, *Montreal* ... 19 A2
Hodgkins, *Chicago* ... 9 C1
Hoegi, *Seoul* ... 26 B2
Hoeilaart, *Brussels* ... 6 B2
Hofberg, *Vienna* ... 31 A2
Hoffman I., *New York* ... 21 C1
Hofgarten, *Munich* ... 20 a3
Högsdtadomstolen, *Stockholm* ... 28 c2
Hohenbrunn, *Munich* ... 20 B3
Hohenschönhausen, *Berlin* ... 5 A4
Holborn, *London* ... 15 a4
Holešovice, *Prague* ... 24 B2
Holland Village, *Singapore* ... 27 B2
Höllriegelskreuth, *Munich* ... 20 B2
Hollywood, *Los Angeles* ... 16 B3
Holmenkollen, *Oslo* ... 22 A3
Holmes Run Acres, *Washington* ... 32 B2
Holmgård, *Stockholm* ... 28 B1
Holysloot, *Amsterdam* ... 2 A3
Homerton, *London* ... 15 A3
Hometown, *Chicago* ... 9 C2
Hōmanchō, *Tokyo* ... 29 A3
Honchō, *Tokyo* ... 29 A3
Honden, *Tokyo* ... 29 A4
Hondo, Rio →, *Los Angeles* ... 16 B4
Hong Kong, *Hong Kong* ... 12 B1
Hong Kong, Univ. of, *Hong Kong* ... 12 B1
Hong Kong I., *Hong Kong* ... 12 B2
Hong Kong Park, *Hong Kong* ... 12 c1
Hongkou, *Shanghai* ... 27 B1
Hongkou Park, *Shanghai* ... 27 B1
Hongmiao, *Beijing* ... 4 B2
Hongqiao, *Shanghai* ... 27 B1
Hongqiao, *Tianjin* ... 30 B1
Hongqiao Airport, *Shanghai* ... 27 B1
Hongün, *Seoul* ... 26 B1
Honjyo, *Tokyo* ... 29 A3
Honoré Mercier, Pont, *Montreal* ... 19 B1
Hönow, *Berlin* ... 5 A4
Hooghly = Hugli →, *Calcutta* ... 8 B2
Hook, *London* ... 15 B2
Horikiri, *Tokyo* ... 29 A4
Horn Pond, *Boston* ... 6 A3
Hornchurch, *London* ... 15 A5
Horni, *Prague* ... 24 B3
Horni Počernice, *Prague* ... 24 B3
Horničměřice, *Prague* ... 24 B2
Horoměřice, *Prague* ... 24 B1
Hortaleza, *Madrid* ... 17 B2
Hosoyama, *Tokyo* ... 29 B2
Hostafranchs, *Barcelona* ... 4 A1
Hostivař, *Prague* ... 24 B3
Hôtel des Invalides, *Paris* ... 23 c2
Houbětín, *Prague* ... 24 B3
Houghs Neck, *Boston* ... 6 B4
Houston, *Johannesburg* ... 13 B2
Houilles, *Paris* ... 23 A2
Hounslow, *London* ... 15 B1
Houses of Parliament, *London* ... 15 c3
Hout Bay, *Cape Town* ... 8 B1
Hove A →, *Copenhagen* ... 10 A1
Hovedøya, *Oslo* ... 22 A3
Høvik, *Oslo* ... 22 A2
Hovorčovice, *Prague* ... 24 A3
Howard Beach, *New York* ... 21 C2
Howth, *Dublin* ... 11 A3
Howth Head, *Dublin* ... 11 A3
Hoxton, *London* ... 15 a5
Hōya, *Tokyo* ... 29 A2
Hradčany, *Prague* ... 24 B2
Huanghuagang Mausoleum of the 72 Martyrs, *Canton* ... 8 B2
Huangpu, *Shanghai* ... 27 B1
Huangpu Jiang →, *Shanghai* ... 27 B1
Huangpu Park, *Shanghai* ... 27 B1
Huangtang, *Beijing* ... 4 C1
Huascar, *Lima* ... 16 B2
Huay Khwang, *Bangkok* ... 3 B2
Huddinge, *Stockholm* ... 28 B2
Hudson →, *New York* ... 21 A2
Huechuraba, *Santiago* ... 26 B1
Huertas de San Beltran, *Barcelona* ... 4 A1
Hugli →, *Calcutta* ... 8 B2
Huidui, *Tianjin* ... 30 B2
Huizingen, *Brussels* ... 6 B1
Hull, *Boston* ... 6 B4
Humber →, *Toronto* ... 30 A1
Humber B., *Toronto* ... 30 B2
Humber Bay, *Toronto* ... 30 B2
Humber Summit, *Toronto* ... 30 A1
Humber Valley Village, *Toronto* ... 30 A1
Humberlea, *Toronto* ... 30 A1
Humboldt Park, *Chicago* ... 9 B2
Humera, *Madrid* ... 17 B1
Hurīya, *Baghdad* ... 3 A2
Hurstville, *Sydney* ... 28 B1
Husby, *Stockholm* ... 28 A1
Husum, *Copenhagen* ... 10 A2
Hutt →, *Wellington* ... 32 A2
Hütteldorf, *Vienna* ... 31 A1

Hüvösvölgy, *Budapest* ... 7 A2
Hvalstad, *Oslo* ... 22 A1
Hvalstrand, *Oslo* ... 22 A2
Hvidovre, *Copenhagen* ... 10 B3
Hwagok, *Seoul* ... 26 B1
Hyattsville, *Washington* ... 32 B4
Hyde Park, *Boston* ... 6 B3
Hyde Park, *Chicago* ... 9 C3
Hyde Park, *Johannesburg* ... 13 A2
Hyde Park, *London* ... 15 A2
Hyde Park, *Sydney* ... 28 B2

I

Ibese, *Lagos* ... 14 A2
Ibirapuera, *São Paulo* ... 26 B1
Ibirapuera, Parque, *São Paulo* ... 26 B2
Icaraí, *Rio de Janeiro* ... 24 B2
Içerenköy, *Istanbul* ... 12 C2
Ichgao, *Tokyo* ... 29 B2
Ichigaya, *Tokyo* ... 29 A3
Ichikawa, *Tokyo* ... 29 A4
Ickenham, *London* ... 15 A1
Iddo, *Lagos* ... 14 B2
Idi-Oro, *Lagos* ... 14 A2
Iganmu, *Lagos* ... 14 B2
Igbobi, *Lagos* ... 14 A2
Igbologun, *Lagos* ... 14 B1
Igny, *Paris* ... 23 B2
IJ, Het →, *Amsterdam* ... 2 A2
IJ-meer, *Amsterdam* ... 2 A3
Ijesa-Tedo, *Lagos* ... 14 B1
Ijora, *Lagos* ... 14 B2
Ikebukuro, *Tokyo* ... 29 A3
Ikegami, *Tokyo* ... 29 B3
Ikeja, *Lagos* ... 14 A2
Ikeuchi, *Osaka* ... 22 B4
Ikoyi, *Lagos* ... 14 B2
Ikuata, *Lagos* ... 14 A2
Ikuno, *Osaka* ... 22 A4
Ikuta, *Tokyo* ... 29 B2
Ila, *Oslo* ... 22 A2
Ilford, *London* ... 15 A4
Ilioúpolis, *Athens* ... 2 B2
Ilpendam, *Amsterdam* ... 2 A2
Ilsōs →, *Athens* ... 2 B2
Imagem e do Som, Museu da, *Rio de Janeiro* ... 24 b3
Imbābah, *Cairo* ... 7 A2
Imielin, *Warsaw* ... 31 C2
Imittós, *Athens* ... 2 B2
Imittós, Óros, *Athens* ... 2 B2
Imperial Palace Museum, *Beijing* ... 4 b2
Inagi, *Tokyo* ... 29 B1
Incheon, *Edinburgh* ... 11 A2
Inchicore, *Dublin* ... 11 A1
Inchkeith, *Edinburgh* ... 11 A3
Inchmickery, *Edinburgh* ... 11 A2
Inchmore, *Edinburgh* ... 11 A2
Incirano, *Milan* ... 18 A1
Inhaúme, *Rio de Janeiro* ... 24 B1
Inner Port Shelter, *Hong Kong* ... 12 A2
Interlagos, *São Paulo* ... 26 C1
Intramuros, *Manila* ... 17 B1
Invalides, *Paris* ... 23 B2
Inverkeithing, *Edinburgh* ... 11 A1
Inzersdorf, *Vienna* ... 31 B2
Ipanema, *Rio de Janeiro* ... 24 B1
Ipiranga, *São Paulo* ... 26 B2
Ipiranga →, *São Paulo* ... 26 B2
Iponri, *Lagos* ... 14 B2
Ireland's Eye, *Dublin* ... 11 A3
Irving Park, *Chicago* ... 9 B2
Isabel, *Rio de Janeiro* ... 24 B1
Isar →, *Munich* ... 20 A2
Isagatedo, *Lagos* ... 14 A1
Isbíliya, *Baghdad* ... 3 A2
Ishikiri, *Osaka* ... 22 A4
Ishøj Strand, *Copenhagen* ... 10 B2
Island Bay, *Wellington* ... 32 B1
Island Park, *Toronto* ... 30 B2
Islev, *Copenhagen* ... 10 A2
Isleworth, *London* ... 15 B2
Islington, *London* ... 15 A3
Islington, *Toronto* ... 30 B1
Ismaning, *Munich* ... 20 A3
Ismaylovskiy Park, *Moscow* ... 19 B4
Isolo, *Lagos* ... 14 A1
Issy-les-Moulineaux, *Paris* ... 23 B2
Istanbul, *Istanbul* ... 12 C1
Istanbul Boğazi, *Istanbul* ... 12 B2
Istinye, *Istanbul* ... 12 B2
Itä Hakkila, *Helsinki* ... 12 B3
Itaewŏn, *Seoul* ... 26 B1
Itahanga, *Rio de Janeiro* ... 24 B1
Itami, *Osaka* ... 22 A3
Ivanhoe, *Melbourne* ... 17 A2
Ivry-sur-Seine, *Paris* ... 23 B3
Iwazono, *Osaka* ... 22 A2
Ixelles, *Brussels* ... 6 B2
Izmaylovo, *Moscow* ... 19 B4
Iztacalco, *Mexico City* ... 18 B2
Iztapalapa, *Mexico City* ... 18 B2

J

Jaba, *Jerusalem* ... 13 A2
Jababpur, *Calcutta* ... 8 C2
Jacaré, *Rio de Janeiro* ... 24 B1
Jackson Heights, *New York* ... 21 B2
Jackson Park, *Chicago* ... 9 C3
Jacques Cartier, *Montreal* ... 19 A3
Jacques Cartier, Pont, *Montreal* ... 19 A2
Jade Buddha Temple, *Shanghai* ... 27 B1
Jægersborg, *Copenhagen* ... 10 A3
Jægersborg Dyrehave, *Copenhagen* ... 10 A3
Jagadishpur, *Calcutta* ... 8 B1
Jagatpur, *Delhi* ... 10 A2

Jaguaré, Rib. do →, *São Paulo* ... 26 B1
Jahangirpur, *Delhi* ... 10 A2
Jakarta, *Jakarta* ... 13 A1
Jakarta, Teluk, *Jakarta* ... 13 A1
Jalan Kayu, *Singapore* ... 27 A3
Jamaica B., *New York* ... 21 C3
Jamaica Plain, *Boston* ... 6 B3
Jamakpuri, *Delhi* ... 10 B1
Jamshīdīyeh, *Tehran* ... 30 A2
Janki, *Warsaw* ... 31 C1
Jannali, *Sydney* ... 28 C1
Japan Center, *San Francisco* ... 25 c1
Jaraguá, *São Paulo* ... 26 A1
Jaraguá, Pico de, *São Paulo* ... 26 A1
Jardim Paulista, *São Paulo* ... 26 B2
Jardin Botanique, *Brussels* ... 6 a3
Järvafältet, *Stockholm* ... 28 A1
Jaskhar, *Mumbai* ... 20 B2
Jatinegara, *Jakarta* ... 13 B2
Javādīyeh, *Tehran* ... 30 B2
Jaworowa, *Warsaw* ... 31 C1
Jedlesee, *Vienna* ... 31 A2
Jefferson Memorial, *Washington* ... 32 c1
Jefferson Park, *Chicago* ... 9 B2
Jelonki, *Warsaw* ... 31 B1
Jerónimos, Mosteiro dos, *Lisbon* ... 14 A1
Jersey City, *New York* ... 21 B1
Jerusalem, *Jerusalem* ... 13 B2
Jésus, I., *Montreal* ... 19 A1
Jesús Maria, *Lima* ... 16 B2
Jette, *Brussels* ... 6 A1
Jewish Quarter, *Jerusalem* ... 13 b3
Jey, *Tehran* ... 30 B2
Jiangsumen, *Beijing* ... 4 B2
Jiangwan, *Shanghai* ... 27 B1
Jianshan Park, *Tianjin* ... 30 B2
Jīnočany, *Prague* ... 24 B1
Jihād, *Baghdad* ... 3 B1
Jīzira, *Baghdad* ... 3 B2
Jim Thompson's House, *Bangkok* ... 3 b3
Jimbōchō, *Tokyo* ... 29 a4
Jingan, *Shanghai* ... 27 B1
Jinga Outer Garden, *Tokyo* ... 29 b2
Jīnočany, *Prague* ... 24 B1
Jinonice, *Prague* ... 24 B2
Jiyūgaoka, *Tokyo* ... 29 B3
Jizā'ir, *Baghdad* ... 3 B2
Jizira, *Baghdad* ... 3 B2
Johannesburg, *Johannesburg* ... 13 B2
Johanneskirchen, *Munich* ... 20 A2
Johannesstift, *Berlin* ... 5 A2
Johannisthal, *Berlin* ... 5 B4
John Hancock Center, *Chicago* ... 9 a2
John McLaren Park, *San Francisco* ... 25 B2
Johnsonville, *Wellington* ... 32 B1
Joinville-le-Pont, *Paris* ... 23 B3
Joli-Bois, *Brussels* ... 6 B2
Jollas, *Helsinki* ... 12 C3
Jonstrup, *Copenhagen* ... 10 A2
Joppa, *Edinburgh* ... 11 B3
Jorge Chavez, Aeropuerto Int., *Lima* ... 16 B2
Jorge Newbury, Aeroparque, *Buenos Aires* ... 7 B2
Jósefa Pilsudskiego Park, *Warsaw* ... 31 B1
Jōtō, *Osaka* ... 22 A4
Jouy-en-Josas, *Paris* ... 23 B2
Juan Anchorena, *Buenos Aires* ... 7 A2
Juan González Romero, *Mexico City* ... 18 A2
Judeira, *Jerusalem* ... 13 A2
Juhu, *Mumbai* ... 20 A2
Jūjā, *Tokyo* ... 29 A3
Jukskeirivier →, *Johannesburg* ... 13 A2
Julianów, *Warsaw* ... 31 B2
Jungfernheide, Volkspark, *Berlin* ... 5 A2
Jungfernsee, *Berlin* ... 5 B1
Juniper Green, *Edinburgh* ... 11 B2
Junk B., *Hong Kong* ... 12 B2
Jurong, *Singapore* ... 27 B2
Jurong, Selat, *Singapore* ... 27 B2
Jurong Industrial Estate, *Singapore* ... 27 B1
Jurujuba, Enseada de, *Rio de Janeiro* ... 24 B2
Jūsō, *Osaka* ... 22 A3
Justice, *Chicago* ... 9 C2
Justicia, *Madrid* ... 10 a3
Jwalahari, *Delhi* ... 10 B1

K

Kabaty, *Warsaw* ... 31 C2
Kadıköy, *Istanbul* ... 12 C2
Kadoma, *Osaka* ... 22 A4
Kaebong, *Seoul* ... 26 C1
Kafr 'Aqab, *Jerusalem* ... 13 A2
Kâğıthane, *Istanbul* ... 12 B1
Kâğıthane →, *Istanbul* ... 12 B1
Kagran, *Vienna* ... 31 A2
Kahnawake, *Montreal* ... 19 B1
Kaimes, *Edinburgh* ... 11 B2
Kaisariani, *Athens* ... 2 B2
Kaiser Wilhelm Kirche, *Berlin* ... 5 b2
Kaiserebersdorf, *Vienna* ... 31 A2
Kaivoksela, *Helsinki* ... 12 B2
Kalamákion, *Athens* ... 2 B2
Kalbadevi, *Mumbai* ... 20 b2
Kalhyŏn, *Seoul* ... 26 B1
Kalipur, *Calcutta* ... 8 A1
Kallithéa, *Athens* ... 2 B2
Kalveboderne, *Copenhagen* ... 10 B3
Kamarhati, *Calcutta* ... 8 A2
Kamata, *Tokyo* ... 29 B3
Kameari, *Tokyo* ... 29 A4
Kameido, *Tokyo* ... 29 A4
Kami-Itabashi, *Tokyo* ... 29 A3
Kamikitazawa, *Tokyo* ... 29 B2
Kamisuruma, *Tokyo* ... 29 B1
Kamoshida, *Tokyo* ... 29 B2
Kampong Landang, *Singapore* ... 27 A3
Kampong Tanjong Penjuru, *Singapore* ... 27 B1
Kampung Bali, *Jakarta* ... 13 B1
Kanda, *Tokyo* ... 29 a5
Kandilli, *Istanbul* ... 12 B2
Kangdong, *Seoul* ... 26 B2
Kangnam, *Seoul* ... 26 B1
Kangsŏ, *Seoul* ... 8 B2
Kankali, *Calcutta* ... 8 B2
Kanlıca, *Istanbul* ... 12 B2
Kanonerskiy, Ostrov, *St. Petersburg* ... 26 B1
Kanzaki →, *Osaka* ... 22 A3

Kapellerfeld, *Vienna* **31 A2**
Káposztásmegyer, *Budapest* .. **7 A2**
Kapotnya, *Moscow* **19 C4**
Käppala, *Stockholm* **28 A3**
Käpylä, *Helsinki* **12 B2**
Karachi, *Karachi* **14 A2**
Karachi Int. Airport, *Karachi* **14 A2**
Karato, *Osaka* **22 A2**
Karibong, *Seoul* **26 C1**
Karkh, *Baghdad* **3 A2**
Karlin, *Prague* **24 B2**
Karlsfeld, *Munich* **20 A1**
Karlshorst, *Berlin* **5 B4**
Karlsfeld, *Berlin* **5 B4**
Karntner Strasse, *Vienna* ... **31 b2**
Karol Bagh, *Delhi* **10 B2**
Karolinenhof, *Berlin* **5 B4**
Karori, *Wellington* **32 B1**
Karow, *Berlin* **5 A3**
Karrädah, *Baghdad* **3 A2**
Kärsön, *Stockholm* **28 B1**
Kasai, *Tokyo* **29 B4**
Kashiwara, *Osaka* **22 B4**
Kastellet, *Copenhagen* **10 a3**
Kastrup, *Copenhagen* **10 B3**
Kastrup Lufthavn,
Copenhagen **10 B3**
Kasuga, *Tokyo* **29 A2**
Kasuge, *Tokyo* **29 A2**
Kasumigaseki, *Tokyo* **29 b4**
Katsushika-Ku, *Tokyo* **29 A4**
Katong, *Singapore* **27 B3**
Katrineberg, *Stockholm* **28 B1**
Kau Pei Chau, *Hong Kong* . **12 B2**
Kau Yi Chau, *Hong Kong* ... **12 B1**
Kaulsdorf, *Berlin* **5 B4**
Kauniainen, *Helsinki* **12 B1**
Kawasaki, *Tokyo* **29 B3**
Kawawa, *Tokyo* **29 B2**
Kawęczyn, *Warsaw* **31 B2**
Kayu Putih, *Jakarta* **13 B2**
Kbely, *Prague* **24 B3**
Kebayoran Baru, *Jakarta* **13 B1**
Kebayoran Lama, *Jakarta* ... **13 B1**
Kebon Jeruk, *Jakarta* **13 B1**
Kedar, *Jerusalem* **13 B2**
Keilor, *Melbourne* **17 A1**
Keilor North, *Melbourne* **17 A1**
Keimola, *Helsinki* **12 A1**
Kelenföld, *Budapest* **7 B2**
Kelvin, *Johannesburg* **13 A2**
Kemang, *Jakarta* **13 B2**
Kemayoran, *Jakarta* **13 B2**
Kemerburgaz, *Istanbul* **12 B1**
Kempton Park Races,
London **15 B1**
Kendall Green, *Boston* **6 A2**
Kenilworth, *Cape Town* **8 A1**
Kennedy Town, *Hong Kong* . **12 B1**
Kennington, *London* **15 c4**
Kensal Green, *London* **15 A2**
Kensal Rise, *London* **15 a1**
Kensington, *Johannesburg* ... **13 B2**
Kensington, *London* **15 A2**
Kensington, *New York* **21 C2**
Kensington, *Sydney* **28 B1**
Kensington Palace, *London* . **15 b2**
Kent Village, *Washington* ... **32 B4**
Kentish Town, *London* **15 A3**
Kenton, *London* **15 A2**
Kenwood House, *London* **15 A2**
Kepa, *Warsaw* **31 B2**
Keppel Harbour, *Singapore* . **27 B2**
Keramíkos, *Athens* **2 b1**
Kettering, *Washington* **32 B5**
Kew, *London* **15 A2**
Kew, *Melbourne* **17 A2**
Kew Gardens, *London* **15 A2**
Kew Gardens, *Toronto* **30 B3**
Key Biscayne, *Miami* **18 B2**
Khaidhárion, *Athens* **2 A1**
Khalándrion, *Athens* **2 A2**
Khalji, *Baghdad* **3 B2**
Khandallah, *Wellington* **32 B1**
Khansá', *Baghdad* **3 A2**
Kharavli, *Mumbai* **20 A2**
Khefren, *Cairo* **7 A2**
Khichripur, *Delhi* **10 B2**
Khidirpur, *Calcutta* **8 B1**
Khimki-Khovrino, *Moscow* . **19 A3**
Khirbet Jub e-Rum,
Jerusalem **13 B2**
Khlong San, *Bangkok* **3 B2**
Khlong Toey, *Bangkok* **3 B2**
Kholargós, *Athens* **2 A2**
Khorel, *Calcutta* **8 A1**
Khorosovo, *Moscow* **19 B2**
Kiamari, *Karachi* **14 B1**
Kierling, *Vienna* **31 A1**
Kierlingbach →, *Vienna* **31 A1**
Kifisós →, *Athens* **2 B2**
Kikuna, *Tokyo* **29 B2**
Kilbarrack, *Dublin* **11 A3**
Kilbirnie, *Wellington* **32 B2**
Kilburn, *London* **15 A2**
Killakee, *Dublin* **11 B2**
Killester, *Dublin* **11 A2**
Killiney, *Dublin* **11 B3**
Killiney Bay, *Dublin* **11 B3**
Kilmacud, *Dublin* **11 B2**
Kilmainham, *Dublin* **11 A2**
Kilmashogue Mt., *Dublin* ... **11 B2**
Kilmore, *Dublin* **11 A2**
Kilnamanagh, *Dublin* **11 A1**
Kilo, *Helsinki* **12 B1**
Kilokri, *Delhi* **10 B2**
Kiltiernan, *Dublin* **11 B2**
Kimmage, *Dublin* **11 B2**
Kindi, *Baghdad* **3 B2**
Kinghorn, *Edinburgh* **11 A2**
King's Cross, *London* **15 a4**
Kings Cross, *Sydney* **28 c3**
Kings Domain, *Melbourne* .. **17 A1**
Kings Park, *Washington* **32 C2**
Kings Park West, *Washington* **32 C2**
Kingsbury, *London* **15 A2**
Kingsland, *Sydney* **28 A2**
Kingston upon Thames,
London **15 B2**
Kingston Vale, *London* **15 B2**
Kingsway, *Toronto* **30 B1**
Kinsaley, *Dublin* **11 A2**
Kipling Heights, *Toronto* **30 A1**
Kipséli, *Athens* **2 B2**
Kirchstockbach, *Munich* **20 B3**
Kirchtrudering, *Munich* **20 B3**
Kirkiri, *Lagos* **14 B1**
Kirke Værløse, *Copenhagen* . **10 A1**
Kirkhill, *Edinburgh* **11 B3**
Kirkliston, *Edinburgh* **11 B1**
Kirknewton, *Edinburgh* **11 B1**
Kirov Palace of Culture,
St. Petersburg **26 B1**
Kısıklı, *Istanbul* **12 B2**
Kispest, *Budapest* **7 B2**
Kista, *Stockholm* **28 A1**
Kita, *Osaka* **22 A3**
Kita-Ku, *Tokyo* **29 A3**
Kitazawa, *Tokyo* **29 B3**

Kiu Tsiu, *Hong Kong* **12 A2**
Kivistö, *Helsinki* **12 B2**
Kızıltoprak, *Istanbul* **12 C2**
Kizu →, *Osaka* **22 B3**
Kizuri, *Osaka* **22 A3**
Kjelsås, *Oslo* **22 A4**
Kladow, *Berlin* **5 B1**
Klampenborg, *Copenhagen* .. **10 A3**
Klaudyń, *Warsaw* **31 B1**
Klecany, *Prague* **24 A2**
Kledering, *Vienna* **31 B2**
Klein Jukskei →,
Johannesburg **13 A1**
Kleinmachnow, *Berlin* **5 B2**
Kleinschönebeck, *Berlin* **5 B5**
Klemetsrud, *Oslo* **22 A4**
Klipriviersberg Nature
Reserve, *Johannesburg* **13 B2**
Klosterneuburg, *Vienna* **31 A1**
Knesset, *Jerusalem* **13 b1**
Knightsbridge, *London* **15 c2**
Kőbánya, *Budapest* **7 B2**
Kobbegem, *Brussels* **6 A1**
Kōbe, *Osaka* **22 A2**
Kōbe Harbour, *Osaka* **22 A2**
Kobenhavn, *Copenhagen* **10 A2**
Kobylisy, *Prague* **24 B2**
Kobyłka, *Warsaw* **31 A3**
Kōch'ŏk, *Seoul* **26 B1**
Kodaira, *Tokyo* **29 A2**
Kodanaka, *Tokyo* **29 B2**
Kodenmacho, *Tokyo* **29 a5**
Koekelberg, *Brussels* **6 A1**
Koganei, *Tokyo* **29 A2**
Kogarah, *Sydney* **28 B1**
Køge Bugt, *Copenhagen* **10 B2**
Koivupää, *Helsinki* **12 B1**
Koja, *Jakarta* **13 A2**
Koja Utara, *Jakarta* **13 A2**
Kokobunji, *Tokyo* **29 A1**
Kokobunji-Temple, *Tokyo* ... **29 A1**
Kolarängen, *Stockholm* **28 B3**
Kolbotn, *Oslo* **22 B3**
Kolkata, *Calcutta* **8 B2**
Kolo, *Warsaw* **31 B1**
Kolokinthóu, *Athens* **2 B1**
Kolomyagi, *St. Petersburg* ... **26 A1**
Kolónos, *Athens* **2 B2**
Kolsås, *Oslo* **22 A2**
Komae, *Tokyo* **29 B2**
Komagome, *Tokyo* **29 A3**
Komazawa, *Tokyo* **29 B3**
Kona, *Calcutta* **8 B1**
Konala, *Helsinki* **12 B2**
Kondli, *Delhi* **10 B2**
Kongelige Slottet, *Oslo* **22 a1**
Kongelunden, *Copenhagen* .. **10 B3**
Kongens Lyngby,
Copenhagen **10 A3**
Kongnŭng, *Seoul* **26 B2**
Kongo, *Helsinki* **12 B1**
Koninklijk Paleis,
Amsterdam **2 b2**
Konnagar, *Calcutta* **8 A2**
Kōnohana, *Osaka* **22 A3**
Kōnoike, *Osaka* **22 A4**
Konradshöhe, *Berlin* **5 A2**
Kopanina, *Prague* **24 B1**
Koparkhairna, *Mumbai* **20 A2**
Köpenick, *Berlin* **5 B4**
Korangi, *Karachi* **14 B2**
Koremasa, *Tokyo* **29 B1**
Korenevo, *Moscow* **19 B6**
Kori, *Osaka* **22 A4**
Koridhallós, *Athens* **2 B1**
Korokoro, *Wellington* **32 B2**
Korokoro Stream →,
Wellington **32 B2**
Kosino, *Moscow* **19 B5**
Kosugi, *Tokyo* **29 B2**
Kota, *Jakarta* **13 A1**
Kotelniki, *Moscow* **19 C5**
Kōtō-Ku, *Tokyo* **29 A3**
Kotrung, *Calcutta* **8 A2**
Kouponia, *Athens* **2 B1**
Kowloon, *Hong Kong* **12 A2**
Kowloon Park, *Hong Kong* . **12 a2**
Kowloon Peak, *Hong Kong* . **12 A2**
Kowloon Res., *Hong Kong* .. **12 A1**
Kowloon Tong, *Hong Kong* . **12 A2**
Kozhukhovo, *Moscow* **19 B5**
Kraainem, *Brussels* **6 A2**
Krailling, *Munich* **20 B1**
Krampnitz, *Berlin* **5 B1**
Krampnitzsee, *Berlin* **5 B1**
Kranji, Sungei →, *Singapore* **27 A2**
Kranji Industrial Estate,
Singapore **27 A2**
Kraskovo, *Moscow* **19 C5**
Krasno-Presnenskaya,
Moscow **19 B3**
Krasnogorsk, *Moscow* **19 B1**
Krč, *Prague* **24 B2**
Krestovskiye, Ostrov,
St. Petersburg **26 B1**
Kreuzberg, *Berlin* **5 A3**
Kritzendorf, *Vienna* **31 A1**
Krumme Lanke, *Berlin* **5 B2**
Krummensee, *Berlin* **5 A5**
Krung Thep, *Bangkok* **3 B2**
Krusboda, *Stockholm* **28 B3**
Krylatskoye, *Moscow* **19 B2**
Küçükköy, *Istanbul* **12 B1**
Kudankita, *Tokyo* **29 a3**
Kudrovo, *St. Petersburg* **26 B3**
Kudosaari, *Helsinki* **12 B3**
Kulturforum, *Berlin* **5 b3**
Kultury i Nauki, Palac,
Warsaw **31 b2**
Kümch'ŏn, *Seoul* **26 C1**
Kumla, *Stockholm* **28 B3**
Kungens kurva, *Stockholm* .. **28 B1**
Kungliga Slottet, *Stockholm* **28 b2**
Kungshatt, *Stockholm* **28 B1**
Kungsholmen, *Stockholm* **28 A2**
Kuningan, *Jakarta* **13 B1**
Kunitachi, *Tokyo* **29 A1**
Kunming Hu, *Beijing* **4 B1**
Kunratice, *Prague* **24 B2**
Kunsthistorischesmuseum,
Vienna **31 b1**
Kuntsevo, *Moscow* **19 B2**
Kupchino, *St. Petersburg* **26 B2**
Kurbağalı →, *Istanbul* **12 C2**
Kurihara, *Tokyo* **29 A2**
Kurla, *Mumbai* **20 A2**
Kurmuri, *Mumbai* **20 A2**
Kurume, *Tokyo* **29 A2**
Kuryanovo, *Moscow* **19 C3**
Kuskovo, *Moscow* **19 B4**
Kustia, *Calcutta* **8 B2**
Kutsino, *Moscow* **19 B5**
Kuzguncuk, *Istanbul* **12 B2**
Kuzyminki, *Moscow* **19 B4**
Kwai Chung, *Hong Kong* ... **12 A1**
Kwanak, *Seoul* **26 C1**
Kwanak-san, *Seoul* **26 C1**
Kyje, *Prague* **24 B3**
Kyūhōji, *Osaka* **22 B4**

L

La Blanca, *Santiago* **26 C2**
La Boca, *Buenos Aires* **7 B2**
La Bretèche, *Paris* **23 A1**
La Campiña, *Lima* **16 C2**
La Celle-St.-Cloud, *Paris* **23 A1**
La Ciudadela, *Mexico City* . **18 c2**
La Courneuve, *Paris* **23 A3**
La Dehesa, *Santiago* **26 B2**
La Encantada, *Lima* **16 C2**
La Estación, *Madrid* **17 B1**
La Floresta, *Barcelona* **4 A1**
La Fortuna, *Madrid* **17 B1**
La Fransa, *Barcelona* **4 A1**
La Garenne-Colombes, *Paris* **23 A2**
La Giustiniana, *Rome* **25 B1**
La Grange, *Chicago* **9 C1**
La Grange Park, *Chicago* ... **9 C1**
La Granja, *Santiago* **26 C2**
La Guardia Airport,
New York **21 B2**
La Hulpe, *Brussels* **6 B2**
La Llacuna, *Barcelona* **4 A2**
La Loma, *Mexico City* **18 A1**
La Lucila, *Buenos Aires* **7 B2**
La Maladrerie, *Paris* **23 A1**
La Milla, Cerro, *Lima* **16 B2**
La Monachina, *Rome* **25 B1**
La Moraleja, *Madrid* **17 A2**
La Nopalera, *Mexico City* ... **18 C2**
La Paternal, *Buenos Aires* .. **7 B2**
La Perla, *Lima* **16 B2**
La Perouse, *Sydney* **28 B2**
La Pineda, *Barcelona* **4 B1**
La Pisana, *Rome* **25 B1**
La Prairie, *Montreal* **19 B3**
La Punta, *Lima* **16 B1**
La Puntigala, *Barcelona* **4 A2**
La Queue-en-Brie, *Paris* **23 B4**
La Reina, *Santiago* **26 B2**
La Ribera, *Barcelona* **4 A1**
La Sagrera, *Barcelona* **4 A2**
La Salada, *Buenos Aires* **7 C2**
La Scala, *Milan* **18 B2**
La Storta, *Rome* **25 A1**
La Taxonera, *Barcelona* **4 A2**
La Victoria, *Lima* **16 B2**
Laajalahti, *Helsinki* **12 B1**
Laajasalo, *Helsinki* **12 B3**
Laaksolahti, *Helsinki* **12 B1**
Lablåba, W. el →, *Cairo* **7 A2**
Lac Cisterna, *Santiago* **26 C2**
Lachine, *Montreal* **19 B1**
Lad Phrao, *Bangkok* **3 B2**
Ladera Heights, *Los Angeles* **16 C2**
Ládví, *Prague* **24 B2**
Łady, *Warsaw* **31 C1**
Lafontaine, Parc, *Montreal* .. **19 A2**
Lagoa, *Rio de Janeiro* **24 B1**
Lagos, *Lagos* **14 B2**
Lagos Harbour, *Lagos* **14 B2**
Lagos-Ikeja Airport, *Lagos* .. **14 A1**
Lagos Island, *Lagos* **14 B2**
Lagos Lagoon, *Lagos* **14 B2**
Laguna de B., *Manila* **17 C2**
Laim, *Munich* **20 B2**
Lainate, *Milan* **18 A1**
Lainz, *Vienna* **31 B1**
Lakemba, *Sydney* **28 B1**
Lakeside, *Cape Town* **8 B2**
Lakeside, *Johannesburg* **13 B2**
Lakeview, *Chicago* **9 B3**
Lakewood Park, *Atlanta* **3 B2**
Lakhtinskiy, *St. Petersburg* . **26 B1**
Lakhtinskiy Razliv, Oz.,
St. Petersburg **26 B1**
Lakshmanpur, *Calcutta* **8 B1**
Lal Qila, *Delhi* **1 a3**
Lam Tin, *Hong Kong* **12 B2**
Lambert, *Oslo* **22 A3**
Lambeth, *London* **15 B3**
Lambrate, *Milan* **18 B2**
Lambro, Parco, *Milan* **18 B1**
Lambton Mills, *Toronto* **30 B1**
Lamma I., *Hong Kong* **12 B1**
Landover Hills, *Washington* . **32 B4**
Landsmeer, *Amsterdam* **2 A2**
Landstrasse, *Vienna* **31 A2**
Landwehr kanal, *Berlin* **5 B3**
Lane Cove, *Sydney* **28 A1**
Lane Cove National Park,
Sydney **28 A1**
Langa, *Cape Town* **8 A2**
Langenzersdorf, *Vienna* **31 A2**
Langer See, *Berlin* **5 B4**
Langley, *Washington* **32 B2**
Langley Park, *Washington* ... **32 B4**
Langwald, *Munich* **20 B3**
Lanham, *Washington* **32 B4**
Lankwitz, *Berlin* **5 B3**
L'Annunziatella, *Rome* **25 C2**
Lansdowne, *Cape Town* **8 A2**
Lansing, *Toronto* **30 A2**
Lanús, *Buenos Aires* **7 C2**
Lapa, *Rio de Janeiro* **24 B1**
Laranjeiras, *Rio de Janeiro* . **24 B1**
Larísa Sta., *Athens* **2 a1**
Las, *Warsaw* **31 B2**
Las Corts, *Barcelona* **4 A1**
Las Kabacki, *Warsaw* **31 C2**
Las Pinas, *Manila* **17 C1**
Las Rejas, *Santiago* **26 B1**
Lasalle, *Montreal* **19 B2**
Lasek Bielański, *Warsaw* **31 B1**
Lasek Na Kole, *Warsaw* **31 B1**
Laski, *Warsaw* **31 B1**
Latina, *Madrid* **17 B1**
Laurence G. Hanscom Field,
Boston **6 A2**
Lauttasaari, *Helsinki* **12 C2**
Laval, *Montreal* **19 A1**
Lavizán, *Tehran* **30 A2**
Lavradio, *Lisbon* **14 A2**
Lawndale, *Chicago* **9 B2**
Lawrence Heights, *Toronto* .. **30 A2**
Layari, *Karachi* **14 A1**
Layari →, *Karachi* **14 A1**
Lazare, Gare St., *Paris* **23 a3**
Łazienkowski, Palac, *Warsaw* **31 c2**
Łazienkowski Park, *Warsaw* **31 B2**
Le Blanc-Mesnil, *Paris* **23 A3**
Le Bourget, *Paris* **23 A3**
Le Chenoi, *Brussels* **6 B2**
Le Chesnay, *Paris* **23 B1**
Le Christ de Saclay, *Paris* ... **23 B2**
Le Kremlin-Bicêtre, *Paris* ... **23 A3**
Le Mesnil-le-Roi, *Paris* **23 A1**
Le Pecq, *Paris* **23 A1**
Le Perreux, *Paris* **23 A3**
Le Pin, *Paris* **23 A4**
Le Plessis-Robinson, *Paris* .. **23 B2**
Le Plessis-Trévise, *Paris* **23 B4**
Le Port-Marly, *Paris* **23 A1**
Le Pré-St.-Gervais, *Paris* **23 A3**
Le Raincy, *Paris* **23 A4**
Le Vésinet, *Paris* **23 A1**

Lea Bridge, *London* **15 A3**
Leaside, *Toronto* **30 A2**
Leblon, *Rio de Janeiro* **24 B1**
Lee, *London* **15 B4**
Leganés, *Madrid* **17 C1**
Legazpi, *Madrid* **17 B1**
Lehtisaari, *Helsinki* **12 B2**
Lei Yue Mun, *Hong Kong* .. **12 B2**
Leião, *Lisbon* **14 A1**
Leicester Square, *London* **15 b3**
Leichhardt, *Sydney* **28 B1**
Leith, *Edinburgh* **11 B3**
Lemoyne, *Montreal* **19 B3**
Lenin, *Moscow* **19 B3**
Lenina, *Moscow* **19 C3**
Leninskiye Gory, *Moscow* ... **19 B3**
Lennox, *Los Angeles* **16 C2**
Leonia, *New York* **21 A2**
Leopardstown, *Dublin* **11 B2**
Leopoldau, *Vienna* **31 A2**
Leopoldstadt, *Vienna* **31 A2**
Leportovo, *Moscow* **19 B4**
Leppävaara, *Helsinki* **12 B1**
Les Lilas, *Paris* **23 A3**
Les Loges-en-Josas, *Paris* ... **23 B1**
Les Pavillons-sous-Bois,
Paris **23 A4**
Lésigny, *Paris* **23 B4**
Lesnozavodskaya,
St. Petersburg **26 B2**
L'Étang-la-Ville, *Paris* **23 A1**
Letná, *Prague* **24 a1**
Letňany, *Prague* **24 B3**
Levallois-Perret, *Paris* **23 A2**
Levent, *Istanbul* **12 B2**
Lewisdale, *Washington* **32 B4**
Lewisham, *London* **15 B3**
Lexington, *Boston* **6 A2**
Leyton, *London* **15 A3**
Leytonstone, *London* **15 A4**
L'Hay-les-Roses, *Paris* **23 B3**
L'Hospitalet de Llobregat,
Barcelona **4 A1**
Lhotka, *Prague* **24 B2**
Liangshui He →, *Beijing* **4 C2**
Lianhua Chi, *Beijing* **4 B1**
Lianhua He →, *Beijing* **4 B1**
Libčice nad Vltavou, *Prague* **24 A1**
Libeň, *Prague* **24 B2**
Liberdade, *São Paulo* **26 B2**
Liberdade, Ave da, *Lisbon* .. **14 b1**
Liberton, *Edinburgh* **11 B3**
Liberty I., *New York* **21 B1**
Liberty State Park, *New York* **21 B1**
Libeznice, *Prague* **24 A2**
Library of Congress,
Washington **32 c3**
Libuš, *Prague* **24 B2**
Lichiao, *Canton* **8 B2**
Lichtenburg, *Berlin* **5 A4**
Lichterfelde, *Berlin* **5 B3**
Lidingö, *Stockholm* **28 A2**
Lieshi Lingyuan, *Canton* **8 B2**
Liesing, *Vienna* **31 B1**
Liesing →, *Vienna* **31 B2**
Liffey, R. →, *Dublin* **11 A1**
Ligovo, *St. Petersburg* **26 C1**
Lijordet, *Oslo* **22 A2**
Likavitos, *Athens* **2 b3**
Likhoborka →, *Moscow* **19 A3**
Lilla Värtan, *Stockholm* **28 A3**
Lille Værløse, *Copenhagen* .. **10 A2**
Liluah, *Calcutta* **8 B1**
Lim Chu Kang, *Singapore* .. **27 A2**
Lima, *Lima* **16 B2**
Limbiate, *Milan* **18 A1**
Limehouse, *London* **15 A3**
Limeil-Brévannes, *Paris* **23 B3**
Linate, Aeroporto
Internazionale di, *Milan* .. **18 B2**
Linbropark, *Johannesburg* ... **13 A2**
Lincoln, *Boston* **6 A1**
Lincoln Center, *New York* ... **21 b2**
Lincoln Heights, *Los Angeles* **16 B3**
Lincoln Park, *Chicago* **9 B3**
Lincoln Park, *New York* **21 B1**
Lincoln Park, *San Francisco* **25 B1**
Lincolnwood, *Chicago* **9 A2**
Linda-a-Pastora, *Lisbon* **14 A1**
Linden, *Johannesburg* **13 A2**
Linden, *Wellington* **32 B2**
Lindenberg, *Berlin* **5 A4**
Lindøya, *Oslo* **22 A3**
Liniers, *Buenos Aires* **7 B1**
Linkebeek, *Brussels* **6 B2**
Linksfield, *Johannesburg* **13 A2**
Linmeyer, *Johannesburg* **13 B2**
Linna, *Helsinki* **12 B3**
Lintuvaara, *Helsinki* **12 B1**
Lion Rock Country Park,
Hong Kong **12 A2**
Lioúmi, *Athens* **2 A2**
Liqizhuang, *Tianjin* **30 B2**
Lisboa, *Lisbon* **14 A2**
Lisbon = Lisboa, *Lisbon* **14 A2**
Lishui, *Canton* **8 A1**
Little B., *Sydney* **28 B2**
Little Calumet →, *Chicago* .. **9 D3**
Little Ferry, *New York* **21 A2**
Little Italy, *New York* **21 e2**
Little Mermaid, *Copenhagen* **10 a3**
Little Rouge →, *Toronto* **30 A4**
Little Tokyo, *Los Angeles* ... **16 c2**
Liuhang, *Shanghai* **27 A1**
Liurong Temple, *Canton* **8 B2**
Liuxi →, *Canton* **8 B2**
Liverpool Street, *London* **15 a5**
Livry-Gargan, *Paris* **23 A4**
Ljan, *Oslo* **22 A3**
Llano de Can Gineu,
Barcelona **4 A2**
Llobregat →, *Barcelona* **4 B1**
Lo Aranguiz, *Santiago* **26 B2**
Lo Boza, *Santiago* **26 B1**
Lo Chau, *Hong Kong* **12 B2**
Lo Espejo, *Santiago* **26 C1**
Lo Hermida, *Santiago* **26 B2**
Lo Prado, *Santiago* **26 B1**
Lo So Shing, *Hong Kong* **12 B1**
Lo Wai, *Hong Kong* **12 A1**
Loanhead, *Edinburgh* **11 B3**
Lobau, *Vienna* **31 A3**
Lobos, Pt., *San Francisco* **25 B1**
Locham, *Munich* **20 B1**
Lochino, *Moscow* **19 B1**
Lochkov, *Prague* **24 B2**
Lockhausen, *Munich* **20 A1**
Lodi, *New York* **21 A1**
Lodi Estate, *Delhi* **10 B2**
Logan Int. Airport, *Boston* .. **6 A4**
Logan Square, *Chicago* **9 B2**
Lognes-Émerainville,
Aérodrome de, Paris **23 B4**
Lõhme, *Berlin* **5 A5**
Lolokhet, *Karachi* **14 A2**
Lomas Chapultepec,
Mexico City **18 B1**
Lomas de San Angel Inn,
Mexico City **18 B1**

Lomas de Zamora,
Buenos Aires **7 C2**
Lombardy East,
Johannesburg **13 A2**
Łomianki, *Warsaw* **31 A1**
Lomus Reforma, *Mexico City* **18 B1**
London, *London* **15 A3**
London City Airport,
London **15 A4**
London Bridge, *London* **15 b5**
London Zoo, *London* **15 A3**
Long B., *Sydney* **28 B2**
Long Branch, *Toronto* **30 B1**
Long Brook →, *Washington* . **32 C2**
Long Ditton, *London* **15 B2**
Long I., *Boston* **6 A4**
Long Island City, *New York* **21 B2**
Long Street, *Cape Town* **8 c2**
Longchamp, Hippodrome de,
Paris **23 A2**
Longhua Pagoda, *Shanghai* .. **27 B1**
Longhua Park, *Shanghai* **27 B1**
Longjohn Slough, *Chicago* .. **9 C1**
Longtan Hu →, *Beijing* **4 B2**
Longue-Pointe, *Montreal* **19 A3**
Longueuil, *Montreal* **19 A3**
Loni, *Delhi* **10 A2**
Loop, The, *Chicago* **9 c1**
Lord's Cricket Ground,
London **15 A2**
Loreto, *Milan* **18 B2**
Los Angeles Int. Airport,
Los Angeles **16 C2**
Los Cerrillos, Aeropuerto,
Santiago **26 B1**
Los Nietos, *Los Angeles* **16 C4**
Los Olivos, *Lima* **16 B2**
Los Reyes, *Mexico City* **18 B2**
Lot, *Brussels* **6 B1**
Loughlinstown, *Dublin* **11 B3**
Loures, *Lisbon* **14 A1**
Louveciennes, *Paris* **23 A1**
Louvre, Musée du, *Paris* **23 b4**
Louvre, Palais du, *Paris* **23 b4**
Lower East Side, *New York* . **21 e2**
Lower Hutt, *Wellington* **32 B2**
Lower Manhattan, *New York* **21 e1**
Lower New York B.,
New York **21 C1**
Lower Shing Mun Res.,
Hong Kong **12 A2**
Lowry Bay, *Wellington* **32 B2**
Lu Xun Museum, *Beijing* ... **4 b1**
Lübars, *Berlin* **5 A3**
Ludwigsfeld, *Munich* **20 A1**
Luhu, *Canton* **8 B2**
Lumiar, *Lisbon* **14 A2**
Lumphini Park, *Bangkok* **3 B2**
Lundtofte, *Copenhagen* **10 A3**
Lung Mei, *Hong Kong* **12 A2**
Luojiang, *Canton* **8 B2**
Lustheim, *Munich* **20 A2**
Luwan, *Shanghai* **27 B1**
Luxembourg, Palais du, *Paris* **23 c4**
Luzhniki Sports Centre,
Moscow **19 B3**
Lyndhurst, *New York* **21 B1**
Lynn, *Boston* **6 A4**
Lynn Harbor, *Boston* **6 A4**
Lynn Woods Res., *Boston* ... **6 A3**
Lyon, Gare de, *Paris* **23 c5**
Lyons, *Chicago* **9 C2**
Lysaker, *Oslo* **22 A2**
Lysakerselva →, *Oslo* **22 A2**
Lysolaje, *Prague* **24 B2**
Lyubertsy, *Moscow* **19 B5**
Lyublino, *Moscow* **19 B4**

M

Ma Nam Wat, *Hong Kong* .. **12 A2**
Ma On Shan Country Park,
Hong Kong **12 A2**
Ma'ale Adumim, *Jerusalem* . **13 B2**
Ma'ale Ha Khamisha,
Jerusalem **13 B1**
Ma'ale Mikhmas, *Jerusalem* **13 A2**
Maantiekylä, *Helsinki* **12 A3**
Maarifa, *Baghdad* **3 B1**
Mabato Pt., *Manila* **17 C2**
Macaco, Morro do,
Rio de Janeiro **24 B2**
McCook, *Chicago* **9 C2**
Machelen, *Brussels* **6 A2**
Machida, *Tokyo* **29 B1**
Maciołki, *Warsaw* **31 B2**
McKerrow, *Wellington* **32 B2**
McKinley Park, *Chicago* **9 C2**
Mclean, *Washington* **32 B2**
Macopocho, R. →, *Santiago* **26 B1**
MacRitchie Res., *Singapore* . **27 A2**
Macul, *Santiago* **26 C2**
Madame Tussaud's, *London* . **15 a3**
Madhudaha, *Calcutta* **8 B2**
Madhyamgram, *Calcutta* **8 A2**
Madīnah Al Mansūr,
Baghdad **3 B2**
Mādinet Nasr, *Cairo* **7 A2**
Madison Avenue, *New York* . **21 c2**
Madison Square, *New York* . **21 d2**
Madrona, *Barcelona* **4 A1**
Maesawa, *Tokyo* **29 A2**
Mafeking, *Lima* **16 B2**
Magdalena Contreras,
Mexico City **18 C1**
Maghreb, *Baghdad* **3 B2**
Maginu, *Tokyo* **29 B2**
Magliana, *Rome* **25 B1**
Magny-les-Hameaux, *Paris* .. **23 B1**
Magonoy, *Manila* **17 B2**
Mahalaxmi, *Mumbai* **20 a1**
Mahesthala, *Calcutta* **8 C1**
Mahim, *Mumbai* **20 A2**
Mahim B., *Mumbai* **20 A2**
Mahlsdorf, *Berlin* **5 A4**
Mahmoodabad, *Karachi* **14 A2**
Mahrauli, *Delhi* **10 B1**
Mahul, *Mumbai* **20 A2**
Maida Vale, *London* **15 a1**
Maidstone, *Melbourne* **17 A1**
Maipú, *Santiago* **26 C1**
Maisons-Alfort, *Paris* **23 B3**
Maisons-Laffitte, *Paris* **23 A1**
Maisonneuve, *Montreal* **19 A2**
Maitland, *Cape Town* **8 A1**
Makati, *Manila* **17 B2**
Mākiniitty, *Helsinki* **12 B2**
Malabar, *Mumbai* **20 B1**
Malabar, *Sydney* **28 B2**
Malabar Hill, *Mumbai* **20 B1**
Malabar Pt., *Mumbai* **20 B1**
Malabon, *Manila* **17 B1**
Malacañang Palace, *Manila* . **17 B1**

Malahide, *Dublin* **11 A3**
Malakhovka, *Moscow* **19 C6**
Malakoff, *Paris* **23 B2**
Malärhöjaen, *Stockholm* **31 A1**
Malate, *Manila* **17 B1**
Malay Quarter, *Cape Town* . **8 c2**
Malaya Neva, *St. Petersburg* **26 B1**
Malaya-Okhta, *St. Petersburg* **26 B2**
Malchow, *Berlin* **5 A3**
Malden, *Boston* **6 A3**
Malden, *London* **15 B2**
Maleizen, *Brussels* **6 B3**
Malešice, *Prague* **24 B2**
Malir →, *Karachi* **14 B2**
Mall, The, *Washington* **32 c3**
Malleny Mills, *Edinburgh* ... **11 B2**
Malmi, *Helsinki* **12 B2**
Malmöya, *Oslo* **22 A3**
Mãløv, *Copenhagen* **10 A2**
Malpasso, Ost., *Rome* **25 C1**
Malton, *Toronto* **30 A1**
Malvern, *Johannesburg* **13 B2**
Malvern, *Melbourne* **17 B2**
Malvern, *Toronto* **30 A3**
Mamonovo, *Moscow* **19 B2**
Mampang Prapatan, *Jakarta* **13 B1**
Mampukuji, *Tokyo* **29 B2**
Man Budrukh, *Mumbai* **20 A2**
Man Khurd, *Mumbai* **20 A2**
Mandaluyong, *Manila* **17 B2**
Mandaoli, *Delhi* **10 B2**
Mandaqui →, *São Paulo* **26 A2**
Mandoli, *Delhi* **10 A2**
Mandvi, *Mumbai* **20 B1**
Manenberg, *Cape Town* **8 A2**
Mang Kung Uk, *Hong Kong* **12 B2**
Mangolpuri, *Delhi* **10 A1**
Manguinhos, Aéroporto,
Rio de Janeiro **24 B1**
Mangwŏn, *Seoul* **26 B1**
Manhattan, *New York* **21 B2**
Manhattan Beach, *New York* **21 C2**
Manila, *Manila* **17 B1**
Manila B., *Manila* **17 B1**
Manila Int. Airport, *Manila* **17 B1**
Mankkaa, *Helsinki* **12 B1**
Manly, *Sydney* **28 A2**
Mannswörth, *Vienna* **31 B3**
Manor Park, *London* **15 A4**
Manor Park, *Wellington* **32 A2**
Manora, *Karachi* **14 B1**
Manquehue, Cerro, *Santiago* **26 B2**
Manzanares, Canal de,
Madrid **17 C2**
Mao Mausoleum, *Beijing* **4 b2**
Map'o, *Seoul* **26 B1**
Maracanã, *Rio de Janeiro* ... **24 B1**
Maraoli, *Mumbai* **20 A2**
Marblehead, *Boston* **6 A4**
Marcelin, *Warsaw* **31 B1**
Mareil-Marly, *Paris* **23 A1**
Margareten, *Vienna* **31 B2**
Maria, *Vienna* **31 A2**
Maridalen, *Oslo* **22 A3**
Maridalsvatnet, *Oslo* **22 A3**
Mariendorf, *Berlin* **5 B3**
Marienfelde, *Berlin* **5 B3**
Marienplatz, *Munich* **20 b2**
Marikina →, *Manila* **17 B2**
Marin City, *San Francisco* ... **25 A1**
Marin Headlands State Park,
San Francisco **25 A2**
Marin Pen., *San Francisco* ... **25 A1**
Marina del Rey, *Los Angeles* **16 C2**
Marine Drive, *Mumbai* **20 b1**
Marino, *Dublin* **11 A2**
Maritim, Museu, *Barcelona* . **4 c2**
Markham, *Toronto* **30 A3**
Marki, *Warsaw* **31 B2**
Markland Wood, *Toronto* **30 B1**
Marly, Forêt de, *Paris* **23 A1**
Marly-le-Roi, *Paris* **23 A1**
Marne →, *Paris* **23 A3**
Marne-la-Vallée, *Paris* **23 A4**
Marolles-en-Brie, *Paris* **23 B4**
Maroubra, *Sydney* **28 B2**
Marquette Park, *Chicago* **9 C2**
Marrickville, *Sydney* **28 B1**
Marsfield, *Sydney* **28 A1**
Marshall Field's, *Chicago* **9 c2**
Marte, Campo de, *São Paulo* **26 B2**
Martesana, Navíglio della,
Milan **18 A2**
Martin Luther King National
Historic Site, *Atlanta* **3 B2**
Martinez, *Buenos Aires* **7 A1**
Martinkylä, *Helsinki* **12 B2**
Martinsried, *Munich* **20 B1**
Maruko, *Tokyo* **29 B3**
Marunouchi, *Tokyo* **29 b4**
Marusino, *Moscow* **19 B5**
Maryino, *Moscow* **19 B4**
Maryland, *Singapore* **27 B2**
Marylebone, *London* **15 A3**
Marymont, *Warsaw* **31 B1**
Marysin Wawerski, *Warsaw* **31 B2**
Marzahn, *Berlin* **5 A4**
Mascot, *Sydney* **28 B1**
Masmo, *Stockholm* **28 B1**
Maspeth, *New York* **21 B2**
Masr el Gedida, *Cairo* **7 A2**
Masr el Qadīma, *Cairo* **7 A2**
Massachusetts B., *Boston* **6 A4**
Massachusett's Inst. of Tech.,
Boston **6 A3**
Massamá, *Lisbon* **14 A1**
Massey →, *Toronto* **30 B4**
Massy, *Paris* **23 B2**
Matihutong, *Beijing* **4 B1**
Matinha, *Lisbon* **14 A2**
Matramam, *Jakarta* **13 B2**
Matsubara, *Osaka* **22 B4**
Mattapan, *Boston* **6 A3**
Mátyásföld, *Budapest* **7 A3**
Mattenheiligtempelem, *Budapest* **7 b1**
Mau Tso Ngam, *Hong Kong* **12 A2**
Mauer, *Vienna* **31 B1**
Mauripur, *Karachi* **14 A1**
Maxhof, *Munich* **20 B2**
Maya-Zan, *Osaka* **22 A2**
Mayfair, *Johannesburg* **13 B2**
Mayfair, *London* **15 b3**
Mayor, Plaza, *Madrid* **17 b2**
Maywood, *Chicago* **9 B1**
Maywood, *Los Angeles* **16 C3**
Maywood, *New York* **21 A1**
Mazagaon, *Mumbai* **20 B2**
Me'a She'arim, *Jerusalem* **13 a2**
Meadowbank Park, *Sydney* . **28 A1**
Mêcice, *Prague* **24 A2**
Mecidiyeköy, *Istanbul* **12 B2**
Medford, *Boston* **6 A3**
Mediodia, *Madrid* **17 B1**
Medvezhiy Ozyora, *Moscow* **19 A5**
Meguro →, *Tokyo* **29 B3**
Meguro-Ku, *Tokyo* **29 B3**
Mehpalpur, *Delhi* **10 B1**
Mehrābād Airport, *Tehran* ... **30 A1**
Mehram Nagar, *Delhi* **10 B1**

Mehrow, *Berlin* **5 A4**
Mei Lanfang, *Beijing* **4 a2**
Meidling, *Vienna* **31 B2**
Méier, *Rio de Janeiro* **24 B1**
Meiji Shrine, *Tokyo* **29 b1**
Meise, *Brussels* **6 A1**
Mejiro, *Tokyo* **29 A3**
Melbourne, *Melbourne* **17 A1**
Melbourne Airport,
Melbourne **17 A1**
Melkki, *Helsinki* **12 C2**
Mellunkylä, *Helsinki* **12 B3**
Mellunmäki, *Helsinki* **12 B3**
Melrose, *Boston* **6 A3**
Melrose, *New York* **21 B2**
Melrose Park, *Chicago* **9 B1**
Melsbroek, *Brussels* **6 A2**
Menteng, *Jakarta* **13 B2**
Mérantaise →, *Paris* **23 B1**
Mercamadrid, *Madrid* **17 B2**
Merced, L., *San Francisco* ... **25 B2**
Meredale, *Johannesburg* **13 B2**
Merlimau, P., *Singapore* **27 B2**
Merri Cr. →, *Melbourne* **17 A2**
Merrion, *Dublin* **11 B2**
Merrionette Park, *Chicago* .. **9 C2**
Merton, *London* **15 B2**
Mesgarábád, *Tehran* **30 B3**
Meschcherskiy, *Moscow* **19 B2**
Messe, *Vienna* **31 A2**
Messe-palast, *Vienna* **31 c1**
Metanópoli, *Milan* **18 B2**
Metropolitan Museum of
Art, *New York* **21 b3**
Meudon, *Paris* **23 B2**
Mevaseret Tsiyon, *Jerusalem* **13 B1**
Mevo Beitar, *Jerusalem* **13 B1**
México, Ciudad de,
Mexico City **18 B1**
Meyersdal, *Johannesburg* **13 B2**
Mezzano, *Milan* **18 A2**
Mezzate, *Milan* **18 B2**
Miadong, *Seoul* **26 B2**
Miami, *Miami* **18 B2**
Miami Beach, *Miami* **18 B2**
Miami Canal →, *Miami* **18 A1**
Miami Int. Airport, *Miami* .. **18 B2**
Miami Shores, *Miami* **18 A2**
Miami Springs, *Miami* **18 B1**
Miasto, *Warsaw* **31 B2**
Michałowice, *Warsaw* **31 B1**
Michigan Avenue, *Chicago* .. **9 b2**
Michle, *Prague* **24 B2**
Middle Harbour, *Sydney* **28 A2**
Middle Hd., *Sydney* **28 A2**
Middle Park, *Melbourne* **17 B1**
Middle Village, *New York* ... **21 B2**
Middlesex Fells Reservation,
Boston **6 A3**
Midi, Gare du, *Brussels* **6 b1**
Midland Beach, *New York* .. **21 C1**
Miedzeszyn, *Warsaw* **31 B3**
Międzylesie, *Warsaw* **31 B3**
Miessaari, *Helsinki* **12 C1**
Miguel Hidalgo, *Mexico City* **18 B1**
Mikhelysona, *Moscow* **19 B5**
Milano, *Milan* **18 B1**
Milano Due, *Milan* **18 B2**
Milano San Felice, *Milan* ... **18 B2**
Milbertshofen, *Munich* **20 A2**
Mill Hill, *London* **15 A2**
Millennium Dome, *London* . **15 A4**
Miller Meadow, *Chicago* **9 B1**
Millerhill, *Edinburgh* **11 B3**
Millers Point, *Sydney* **28 a1**
Milltown, *Dublin* **11 B2**
Millwood, *Washington* **32 B4**
Milnerton, *Cape Town* **8 A1**
Milon-la-Chapelle, *Paris* **23 B1**
Milton, *Boston* **6 A3**
Milton Bridge, *Edinburgh* ... **11 B2**
Mimico, *Toronto* **30 B2**
Minami, *Osaka* **22 A4**
Minamitsunashima, *Tokyo* .. **29 B2**
Minato, *Osaka* **22 A3**
Minato-Ku, *Tokyo* **29 c3**
Minshāt el Bekkarî, *Cairo* ... **7 A1**
Minute Man Nat. Hist. Park,
Boston **6 A2**
Miraflores, *Lima* **16 B2**
Miramar, *Wellington* **32 B2**
Misericordia, Sa. da,
Rio de Janeiro **24 B1**
Mission, *San Francisco* **25 B2**
Mississauga, *Toronto* **30 B1**
Mitaka, *Tokyo* **29 A2**
Mitcham, *London* **15 B3**
Mitcham Common, *London* . **15 B3**
Mitchell's Plain, *Cape Town* **8 B2**
Mitino, *Moscow* **19 A2**
Mitte, *Berlin* **5 A3**
Mittel Isarkanal →, *Munich* **20 A3**
Mixcoac, *Mexico City* **18 B1**
Mixcoac, Presa de,
Mexico City **18 C1**
Miyakojima, *Osaka* **22 A4**
Mizonokuchi, *Tokyo* **29 B2**
Mizue, *Tokyo* **29 A4**
Mlocinski Park, *Warsaw* **31 B1**
Mlociny, *Warsaw* **31 B1**
Mnevniki, *Moscow* **19 B2**
Moba, *Lagos* **14 B2**
Moczydło, *Warsaw* **31 C2**
Modderfontein,
Johannesburg **13 A2**
Modřany, *Prague* **24 B2**
Mogyoród, *Budapest* **7 A3**
Moinho Velho, Cor. →,
São Paulo **26 B2**
Mok, *Seoul* **26 B1**
Mokotów, *Warsaw* **31 B2**
Molenbeek-Saint-Jean,
Brussels **6 A1**
Molino de Rosas,
Mexico City **18 B1**
Mollem, *Brussels* **6 A1**
Mollins de Rey, *Barcelona* ... **4 A1**
Mondeor, *Johannesburg* **13 B2**
Moneda, Palacio de la,
Santiago **26 B2**
Moneró, *Rio de Janeiro* **24 A1**
Mong Kok, *Hong Kong* **12 A2**
Monkstown, *Dublin* **11 B3**
Monnickendam, *Amsterdam* **2 A3**
Monrovia, *Los Angeles* **16 B4**
Monsanto, *Lisbon* **14 A1**
Monsanto, Parque Florestal
de, *Lisbon* **14 A1**
Mont Royal, *Montreal* **19 A2**
Mont-Royal, Parc du, *Montreal* **19 A2**
Montana de Montjuich,
Barcelona **4 c1**
Monte Chingolo,
Buenos Aires **7 C2**
Monte Palatino, *Rome* **25 c3**
Montemor, *Lisbon* **14 A1**
Monterey Park, *Los Angeles* **16 B4**
Montespaccato, *Rome* **25 B1**
Montessori, *Delhi* **10 A1**

Monteverde Nuovo, Rome . 25 B1
Montfermeil, Paris 23 A4
Montigny-le-Bretonneux, Paris . . . 23 A4
Montjay-la-Tour, Paris . . 23 A4
Montjuic, Parc de, Barcelona . 4 c1
Montparnasse, Gare, Paris . 23 A2
Montréal, Montreal 19 A2
Montréal, Î. de, Montreal . 19 A2
Montréal Est, Montreal . . 19 B2
Montréal Est, Montreal . . 19 A2
Montréal Nord, Montreal . 19 A2
Montréal Ouest, Montreal . 19 B1
Montreuil, Paris 23 A3
Montrouge, Paris 23 A2
Montserrat, Buenos Aires . 7 B2
Monza, Milan 18 A2
Monzoro, Milan 18 B1
Mooca, São Paulo 26 B2
Moonachie, New York . . . 21 B1
Moonee Ponds, Melbourne . 17 A1
Moonee Valley Racecourse, Melbourne . 17 A1
Moosach, Munich 20 A2
Mora, Mumbai 20 B2
Moratalaz, Madrid 17 B1
Mörby, Stockholm 28 A2
Morden, London 15 B2
Moróe →, Paris 23 A2
Morgan Park, Chicago . . . 9 C3
Moriguchi, Osaka 22 A4
Morivione, Milan 18 B2
Morningside, Edinburgh . . 11 B2
Morningside, Johannesburg . 13 A2
Morningside, Washington . 32 C4
Morro Solar, Cerro, Lima . 16 C2
Mortlake, London 15 B2
Mortlake, Sydney 28 B1
Morton Grove, Chicago . . 9 A2
Morumbi, São Paulo 26 B1
Moscavide, Lisbon 14 A2
Moscow = Moskva, Moscow 19 B3
Moskhaton, Athens 2 B2
Moskva, Moscow 19 B2
Moskva →, Moscow 19 B2
Moskvoretskiy, Moscow . . 19 B2
Mosman, Sydney 28 A2
Móstoles, Madrid 17 C1
Moti Bagh, Delhi 10 B2
Motol, Prague 24 B1
Motsa, Jerusalem 13 B2
Motsa Ilit, Jerusalem . . . 13 B1
Motspur Park, London . . 15 B2
Mottingham, London . . . 15 B4
Moulin Rouge, Paris 23 a3
Mount Dennis, Toronto . . 30 A2
Mount Greenwood, Chicago 9 C2
Mount Hood Memorial Park, Boston . 6 A3
Mount Merrion, Dublin . . 11 B2
Mount Rainier, Washington 32 B4
Mount Vernon, New York . 21 A3
Mount Vernon Square, Washington . 32 a2
Mount Zion, Jerusalem . . 13 b3
Mozarthaus, Vienna 31 b2
Müggelberge, Berlin 5 B4
Müggelheim, Berlin 5 B5
Muggiò, Milan 18 A2
Mughal Gardens, Delhi . . 1 c1
Mühleiten, Vienna 31 A3
Mühlenfliess →, Berlin . . . 5 A5
Muiden, Amsterdam 2 A3
Muiderpoort Station, Amsterdam . 2 b3
Muizenberg, Cape Town . . 8 B1
Mujahidpur, Delhi 10 B2
Mukandpur, Delhi 10 A2
Mukhmas, Jerusalem . . . 13 A2
Muko →, Osaka 22 A3
Mukojima, Tokyo 29 A3
Mulbarton, Johannesburg . 13 B2
Mumbai, Mumbai 20 A2
Mumbai Harbour, Mumbai . 20 B2
Münchehofe, Berlin 5 B5
München, Munich 20 B2
Munich = München, Munich 20 B2
Munkkiniemi, Helsinki . . 12 B2
Munro, Buenos Aires . . . 7 B1
Murai Res., Singapore . . . 27 A2
Muranów, Warsaw 31 B1
Murino, St. Petersburg . . 26 B2
Murrayfield, Edinburgh . . 11 B2
Musashino, Tokyo 29 A2
Museu Nacional, Rio de Janeiro . 24 B1
Muslax, Lagos 14 A2
Musictheater, Amsterdam . 2 b2
Muslim Quarter, Jerusalem . 13 a3
Musocco, Milan 18 B1
Mustansiriya, Baghdad . . 3 A2
Musturud, Cairo 7 A2
Muswell Hill, London . . . 15 A3
Mutanabi, Baghdad 3 B2
Muthana, Baghdad 3 B2
Myakinino, Moscow 19 B2
Mykerinos, Cairo 7 B1
Myllypuro, Helsinki 12 B3

N

Nacka, Stockholm 28 B3
Nada, Osaka 22 A4
Naenae, Wellington 32 A2
Nærsnes, Oslo 22 B1
Nagata, Osaka 22 B1
Nagatsuta, Tokyo 29 B2
Nagytétény, Budapest . . . 7 B1
Nahant, Boston 6 A4
Nahant B., Boston 6 A4
Nahant Harbor, Boston . . 6 A4
Nahr Dijlah →, Baghdad . . 3 B2
Najafgarh Drain →, Delhi . 10 B1
Nakahara-Ku, Tokyo . . . 29 B2
Nakano-Ku, Tokyo 29 A2
Namgaiwa, Seoul 26 B1
Namsan Park, Seoul 26 B1
Namyông, Seoul 26 B1
Nanbiancun, Canton 8 B1
Nanchang He →, Beijing . . 4 B1
Nandang, Canton 8 B2
Nandian, Tianjin 30 A2
Nangal Dewat, Delhi . . . 10 B1
Naniwa, Osaka 22 B3
Nankai, Tianjin 30 B2
Nanmenwai, Tianjin 30 B2
Nanole, Mumbai 20 A2
Nanpu Bridge, Shanghai . . 27 B2
Nanshi, Shanghai 27 B2
Nantasket Beach, Boston . . 6 B4
Nanterre, Paris 23 A2
Naoabad, Calcutta 8 C2
Napier Mole, Karachi . . . 14 B1
Naraina, Delhi 10 B1
Nariman Point, Mumbai . . 20 c1
Nariman Pt., Mumbai . . . 20 B1

Närmak, Tehran 30 A2
Naruo, Osaka 22 A3
Näsby, Stockholm 28 A2
Näsbypark, Stockholm . . . 28 A2
Nathan Road, Hong Kong . 12 a2
Natick, Boston 6 B2
National Maritime Museum, San Francisco . 25 a1
National Museum, Bangkok . 3 b1
National Museum, Stockholm 28 b2
Natolin, Warsaw 31 C2
Naturhistorischesmuseum, Vienna . 31 b1
Naucalpan de Juárez, Mexico City . 18 A2
Naupada, Mumbai 20 A2
Navíglio di Pavia, Milan . . 18 B1
Navíglio Grande, Milan . . 18 B1
Navona, Piazza, Rome . . . 25 b2
Navotas, Manila 17 B1
Navy Pier, Chicago 9 b3
Nazal Hikmat Beg, Baghdad 3 A2
Nazimabad, Karachi 14 A2
Nazlet el Simmân, Cairo . . 7 B1
Néa Alexandhria, Athens . 2 B2
Néa Faliron, Athens 2 B1
Néa Ionía, Athens 2 A2
Néa Liósia, Athens 2 A1
Néa Smírni, Athens 2 B2
Neapolis, Athens 2 B2
Near North, Chicago 9 b2
Nebušice, Prague 24 B1
Nederhorst, Amsterdam . . 2 B3
Nedlitz, Berlin 5 B1
Nee Soon, Singapore . . . 27 A2
Needham Heights, Boston . 6 B2
Nekrasovka, Moscow . . . 19 B5
N'ematâbâd, Tehran 30 B1
Nemchinovka, Moscow . . 19 B1
Nemzeti Muz, Budapest . . 7 c2
Neponset, New York 21 C2
Nerima-Ku, Tokyo 29 A3
Nesodden, Oslo 22 B3
Nesoddtangen, Oslo 22 B3
Nesøya, Oslo 22 A2
Neu Aubing, Munich 20 B1
Neu Buch, Berlin 5 A4
Neu Buchhorst, Berlin . . 5 B5
Neu Fahrland, Berlin . . . 5 B1
Neu Lindenberg, Berlin . . 5 A4
Neubiberg, Munich 20 B3
Neue Hofburg, Vienna . . . 31 b1
Neuenhagen, Berlin 5 A4
Neuessling, Vienna 31 A3
Neuhausen, Munich 20 B2
Neuherberg, Munich 20 A2
Neuhönow, Berlin 5 A5
Neuilly-Plaisance, Paris . . 23 A4
Neuilly-sur-Marne, Paris . 23 A4
Neuilly-sur-Seine, Paris . . 23 A2
Neukagran, Vienna 31 A2
Neukettenhof, Vienna . . . 31 B2
Neukölln, Berlin 5 B3
Neuperlach, Munich 20 B3
Neuried, Munich 20 B1
Neustift am Walde, Vienna . 31 A1
Neusüssenbrunn, Vienna . 31 A3
Neva →, St. Petersburg . . 26 B2
Neves, Rio de Janeiro . . . 24 B2
New Baghdad, Baghdad . . 3 B2
New Barakpur, Calcutta . . 8 A2
New Brighton, New York . 21 C1
New Canada, Johannesburg 13 B1
New Canada Dam, Johannesburg . 13 B1
New Carrollton, Washington 32 B4
New Cross, London 15 B3
New Delhi, Delhi 10 B2
New Dorp, New York . . . 21 C1
New Dorp Beach, New York 21 C1
New Malden, London . . . 15 B2
New Milford, New York . . 21 A1
New Territories, Hong Kong 12 B1
New Toronto, Toronto . . . 30 B1
New Town, Edinburgh . . . 11 B2
New Utrecht, New York . . 21 C2
Newark B., New York . . . 21 B2
Newbattle, Edinburgh . . . 11 B3
Newbury Park, London . . 15 A4
Newcraighall, Edinburgh . 11 B3
Newham, London 15 A4
Newhaven, Edinburgh . . . 11 B2
Newington, Edinburgh . . . 11 B2
Newington, London 15 c5
Newlands, Johannesburg . 13 B1
Newlands, Wellington . . . 32 B2
Newport, Melbourne . . . 17 B1
Newton, Boston 6 B2
Newtonbrook, Toronto . . 30 A2
Newtongrange, Edinburgh . 11 B3
Newtonville, Boston 6 B2
Newtown, Sydney 28 B2
Neyagawa, Osaka 22 A4
Ngaio, Wellington 32 B1
Ngau Chi Wan, Hong Kong 12 A2
Ngau Tau Kok, Hong Kong 12 B2
Ngauranga, Wellington . . 32 B2
Ngong Shuen Chau, Hong Kong . 12 B1
Ngua Kok Wan, Hong Kong 12 B1
Niävärän, Tehran 30 A2
Nibra, Calcutta 8 B1
Nidâl, Baghdad 3 B2
Niddrie, Edinburgh 11 B3
Niddrie, Melbourne 17 A1
Nieder Neuendorf, Berlin . 5 A2
Niederschöneweide, Berlin . 5 B3
Niederschönhausen, Berlin 5 A3
Niemczer, Rio de Janeiro . 24 B1
Nieuw Zuid, Amsterdam . 2 c2
Nieuwe Kerk, Amsterdam . 2 b2
Nieuwendam, Amsterdam . 2 A2
Nihonbashi, Tokyo 29 b5
Nijpperi, Helsinki 12 B1
Nîkaia, Athens 2 B1
Nikolassee, Berlin 5 B2
Nikolskiy, Moscow 19 B3
Nikolyskoye, Moscow . . . 19 B5
Nikulino, Moscow 19 B2
Nil, Nahr en →, Cairo . . . 7 B2
Nile = Nil, Nahr en →, Cairo 7 B2
Niles, Chicago 9 A2
Nimta, Calcutta 8 A2
Ningyuan, Tianjin 30 B2
Nippa, Tokyo 29 B2
Nippori, Tokyo 29 A3
Nishi, Osaka 22 A3
Nishinari, Osaka 22 B3
Nishiyodogawa, Osaka . . 22 A3
Niterói, Rio de Janeiro . . 24 B2
Nob Hill, San Francisco . . 25 b2
Nockeby, Stockholm 28 B1
Nogatino, Moscow 19 B4
Nogent-sur-Marne, Paris . 23 A3
Noida, Delhi 10 B2
Noiseau, Paris 23 A4
Noisiel, Paris 23 A4
Noisy-le-Grand, Paris . . . 23 A4

Noisy-le-Roi, Paris 23 A1
Noisy-le-Sec, Paris 23 A3
Nokkala, Helsinki 12 C1
Nomentano, Rome 25 B2
Nonakashinden, Tokyo . . 29 A2
Nongminyundong Jiangxisuo, Canton . 8 B2
Nonhyôn, Seoul 26 B2
Nonthaburi, Bangkok . . . 3 A1
Noon Gun, Cape Town . . 8 b1
Noorder Kerk, Amsterdam . 2 a1
Noordgesig, Johannesburg . 13 B1
Noordzeekanaal, Amsterdam 2 A1
Nord, Gare du, Paris . . . 23 a4
Nordrand-Siedlung, Vienna . 31 A2
Nordstrand, Oslo 22 A3
Normandale, Wellington . . 32 B2
Nørrebro, Copenhagen . . 10 a1
Norridge, Chicago 9 B2
Norrmalm, Stockholm . . . 28 a2
North Arlington, New York 21 B1
North Bay Village, Miami . 18 A2
North Bergen, New York . 21 B1
North Branch Chicago River →, Chicago . 9 B2
North Bull Island, Dublin . 11 A3
North Cambridge, Boston . 6 A3
North Cheam, London . . 15 B2
North Cohasset, Boston . . 6 B4
North Cray, London 15 B4
North Decatur, Atlanta . . 3 B3
North Druid Hills, Atlanta . 3 B3
North Esk →, Edinburgh . . 11 B3
North Gyle, Edinburgh . . 11 B2
North Hackensack, New York . 21 A1
North Harbor, Manila . . . 17 B1
North Hd., Sydney 28 A2
North Hollywood, Los Angeles . 16 B2
North Lexington, Boston . 6 A2
North Miami, Miami 18 A2
North Miami Beach, Miami 18 A2
North Nazimabad, Karachi 14 A2
North Pt., Hong Kong . . . 12 B2
North Queensferry, Edinburgh . 11 A1
North Quincy, Boston . . . 6 B3
North Res., Boston 6 A3
North Riverside, Chicago . 9 B2
North Saugus, Boston . . . 6 A3
North Shore Channel →, Chicago . 9 B2
North Springfield, Washington . 32 C2
North Sudbury, Boston . . 6 A1
North Sydney, Sydney . . . 28 B2
North Woolwich, London . 15 A4
North York, Toronto . . . 30 A2
Northbridge, Sydney . . . 28 A2
Northbridge Park, Sydney . 28 A2
Northcliff, Johannesburg . 13 A1
Northcote, Melbourne . . . 17 A2
Northlake, Chicago 9 B1
Northmount, Toronto . . . 30 A2
Northolt, London 15 A2
Northumberland Heath, London . 15 B5
Northwood, London 15 A1
Norumbega Res., Boston . 6 B2
Norwood, Johannesburg . 13 A2
Norwood Park, Chicago . . 9 B2
Noryangjin, Seoul 26 B1
Nossa Senhora de Candelária, Rio de Janeiro 24 a2
Nossa Senhora do Ó, São Paulo . 26 B1
Nossegem, Brussels 6 A3
Notre-Dame, Paris 23 c4
Notre-Dame, Bois, Paris . 23 B4
Notre-Dame-de-Grace, Montreal . 19 B2
Notting Hill, London . . . 15 b1
Nova Milanese, Milan . . . 18 A1
Novate Milanese, Milan . . 18 A1
Novaya Derevnya, St. Petersburg . 26 A1
Nové Město, Prague 24 B2
Novoaleksandrovskoye, St. Petersburg . 26 B2
Novogireyevo, Moscow . . 19 B4
Novoivanovskoye, Moscow . 19 B1
Novonikolyskoye, Moscow . 19 A1
Novosaratovka, St. Petersburg . 26 B2
Nowe-Babice, Warsaw . . 31 B1
Nöykkiö, Helsinki 12 B1
Nueva Atracoaico, Mexico City . 18 B2
Nueva Pompeya, Buenos Aires . 7 C2
Nueva Tenochtitlán, Mexico City . 18 B2
Nuijala, Helsinki 12 B1
Numabukuro, Tokyo . . . 29 A2
Nunez, Buenos Aires . . . 7 B2
Nunhead, London 15 B3
Nuñoa, Santiago 26 B2
Nusle, Prague 24 B2
Nussdorf, Vienna 31 A2
Nyanga, Cape Town 8 A2
Nymphenburg, Munich . . 20 B2
Nymphenburg, Schloss, Munich . 20 B2

O

Oak Grove, Atlanta 3 A3
Oak Island, Boston 6 A4
Oak Lawn, Chicago 9 C2
Oak Park, Chicago 9 B2
Oak View, Washington . . 32 A4
Oakdale, Atlanta 3 A2
Oakland, San Francisco . . 25 B3
Oakland, Washington . . . 32 C4
Oaklawn, Washington . . . 32 C4
Oakleigh, Melbourne . . . 17 B2
Oakton, Washington 32 B2
Oakwood Beach, New York 21 C1
Oatley, Sydney 28 B1
Obalende, Lagos 14 B2
Oba's Palace, Lagos 14 B2
Oberföhring, Munich . . . 20 B2
Oberhaching, Munich . . . 20 B2
Oberlaa, Vienna 31 B2
Oberlisse, Vienna 31 A2
Obermenzing, Munich . . . 20 B1
Obermoos Schwaige, Munich 20 A1
Oberschleissheim, Munich . 20 A2
Oberschöneweide, Berlin . 5 B4
Observatory, Johannesburg 13 B2
Observatory, Sydney . . . 28 a1
Ôbu, Osaka 22 A1
Obu-Ube, Osaka 22 A1
Óbuda, Budapest 7 A2
Obukhovo, St. Petersburg . 26 B2

Obvodnyy Kanal, St. Petersburg . 26 B1
Ocean Park, Hong Kong . . 12 B2
Ochakovo, Moscow 19 B2
Ochota, Warsaw 31 B1
O'Connell Street, Dublin . 11 b2
Ôdana, Tokyo 29 B2
Öden-Stockach, Munich . . 20 B3
Odilampi, Helsinki 12 B1
Odintsovo, Moscow 19 B1
Odivelas, Lisbon 14 A1
Odolany, Warsaw 31 B1
Oeiras, Lisbon 14 A1
Ofin, Lagos 14 A3
Ogawa, Tokyo 29 A1
Ogden Park, Chicago . . . 9 C2
Ogikubo, Tokyo 29 A2
Ogogoro, Lagos 14 B2
Ogridge, Chicago 9 B2
Ogudu, Lagos 14 A2
Ohariu Stream →, Wellington . 32 B1
O'Higgins, Parque, Santiago 26 B2
Oimachi, Tokyo 29 B3
Ojota, Lagos 14 A2
Okamoto, Osaka 22 A2
Okęcie, Warsaw 31 B1
Okęcie Airport, Warsaw . . 31 B1
Okęra, Lagos 14 B2
Okeogbe, Lagos 14 B2
Okha, Delhi 10 B2
Okhta →, St. Petersburg . . 26 B2
Okkervil →, St. Petersburg . 26 B2
Okrzeszyn, Warsaw 31 C2
Oksval, Oslo 22 A3
Oktyabrskiy, Moscow . . . 19 B3
Ôkubo, Tokyo 29 a2
Ôkura, Tokyo 29 B2
Olari, Helsinki 12 B1
Olaria, Rio de Janeiro . . . 24 B1
Old Admiralty, St. Petersburg 26 B1
Old City, Delhi 1 a3
Old City, Jerusalem 13 b3
Old City, Shanghai 27 B2
Old Fort = Purana Qila, Delhi . 1 c3
Old Harbor, Boston 6 B3
Old Town, Chicago 9 B3
Old Town, Edinburgh . . . 11 b2
Oldham, Dublin 11 B1
Olgino, St. Petersburg . . 26 A1
Olímpico, Estadio, Mexico City . 18 C1
Olivais, Lisbon 14 A2
Olivar de los Padres, Mexico City . 18 B1
Olivar del Conde, Mexico City . 18 B1
Olivos, Buenos Aires . . . 7 B2
Olona →, Milan 18 B1
Olympia, London 15 c1
Olympic Stadium, Munich . 20 B2
Olympique, Stade, Montreal 19 A2
Omonias, Pl., Athens . . . 2 b1
Omori, Osaka 22 B4
Onchi, Osaka 22 A2
Onchi →, Osaka 22 B4
Onisigun, Lagos 14 A2
Óokayama, Tokyo 29 B3
Oosterpark, Amsterdam . . 2 b3
Oostzaan, Amsterdam . . . 2 A2
Opa-Locka, Miami 18 A1
Opa-Locka Airport, Miami . 18 A1
Opacz, Warsaw 31 B1
Opera House, Sydney . . . 28 a2
Ophirton, Johannesburg . 13 B2
Oppegård, Oslo 22 B3
Oppem, Brussels 6 A1
Opwijk, Brussels 6 A1
Ora, Jerusalem 13 B1
Oradell, New York 21 A1
Orange Bowl Stadium, Miami . 18 B2
Orangi, Karachi 14 A1
Orchard Road, Singapore . 27 a1
Ordrup, Copenhagen . . . 10 A3
Orech, Prague 24 B1
Øresund, Copenhagen . . 10 A3
Orient Heights, Boston . . 6 A4
Orlando Dam, Johannesburg 13 B1
Orlando East, Johannesburg 13 B1
Orlovo, Moscow 19 C2
Orly, Paris 23 B3
Ormesson-sur-Marne, Paris 23 B4
Ormond, Melbourne 17 B2
Ormøya, Oslo 22 A3
Orpington, London 15 B4
Orsay, Musée d', Paris . . 23 b3
Orszâghâz, Budapest . . . 7 b2
Országos Levéltár, Budapest 7 b1
Ortaköy, Istanbul 12 B2
Ortica, Milan 18 B2
Oruba, Lagos 14 A2
Orvostörteneti Múz., Budapest . 7 c2
Osaka, Osaka 22 B4
Osaka B., Osaka 22 B4
Osaka Castle, Osaka 22 A4
Osaka Harbour, Osaka . . 22 B3
Osaka International Airport, Osaka . 22 A3
Ôsaki, Tokyo 29 B3
Osasco, São Paulo 26 B1
Osdorf, Berlin 5 B3
Osdorp, Amsterdam 2 A1
Oshodi, Lagos 14 A2
Oslo, Oslo 22 A3
Oslofjorden, Oslo 22 B2
Ôsone, Tokyo 29 B2
Osorun, Lagos 14 A2
Ospiate, Milan 18 A1
Ostankino, Moscow 19 B3
Østasiatiskamuséet, Stockholm . 28 a3
Osteralm, Stockholm . . . 28 a3
Österbro, Copenhagen . . 10 a1
Osterley, London 15 B1
Osterley Park, London . . 15 B1
Östermalm, Stockholm . . 28 a3
Ostiense, Rome 25 B1
Østmarkkapellet, Oslo . . 22 A4
Ostøya, Oslo 22 A2
Østre Aker, Oslo 22 A3
Ôta-Ku, Tokyo 29 B3
Otaniemi, Helsinki 12 B1
Otari Open Air Museum, Wellington . 32 B1
Otsuka, Tokyo 29 A3
Ottakring, Vienna 31 A1
Ottávia, Rome 25 B1
Ottery, Cape Town 8 A2
Ottobrunn, Munich 20 B3
Oud Zuid, Amsterdam . . . 2 b1
Ouderkerk, Amsterdam . . 2 B2
Oude Kerk, Amsterdam . . 2 a2
Oulunkylä, Helsinki 12 B2
Ourcq, Canal de l', Paris . 23 A3
Outer Mission, San Francisco 25 B2
Outremont, Montreal . . . 19 A2

Overijse, Brussels 6 B3
Owhiro Bay, Wellington . . 32 C1
Oworonsoki, Lagos 14 A2
Oxford Street, London . . 15 b3
Oxgangs, Edinburgh . . . 11 B2
Oxon Hill, Washington . . 32 C4
Oyodo, Osaka 22 A3
Oyster B., Sydney 28 C1
Oyster Rocks, Mumbai . . 20 B1
Oyster Rocks, Karachi . . 14 B2
Ozoir-la-Ferrière, Paris . . 23 B4
Ozone Park, New York . . 21 B2

P

Pacific Heights, San Francisco . 25 B2
Pacific Manor, San Francisco 25 C2
Pacific Palisades, Los Angeles 16 B1
Pacifica, San Francisco . . 25 C2
Paco, Manila 17 B1
Paco de Arcos, Lisbon . . 14 A1
Paco Imperial, Rio de Janeiro 24 a2
Paddington, London . . . 15 b2
Paddington, Sydney 28 B2
Paderno, Milan 18 A1
Pagewood, Sydney 28 B2
Pagote, Mumbai 20 B2
Pai, I. do, Rio de Janeiro . 24 B2
Pak Kong, Hong Kong . . 12 A2
Pakila, Helsinki 12 B2
Palacio de Bellas Artes, Mexico City . 18 b2
Palacio de Communicaciones, Madrid 17 a3
Palacio Nacional, Mexico City . 18 b3
Palacio Real, Barcelona . . 4 b3
Palacio Real, Madrid . . . 17 b1
Palaión Fáliron, Athens . . 2 B2
Palais de Justice, Brussels . 6 c2
Palais Royal, Paris 23 b4
Palais Royale, Brussels . . 6 c2
Palaiseau, Paris 23 B2
Palau Nacional Museu d'Art, Barcelona . 4 c1
Palazzolo, Milan 18 A1
Palermo, Buenos Aires . . 7 B2
Palhais, Lisbon 14 B2
Palisades Park, New York . 21 A1
Palmer Park, Washington . 32 B4
Palmerston, Dublin 11 A1
Paloheinä, Helsinki 12 B2
Palomeras, Madrid 17 B2
Palos Heights, Chicago . . 9 C2
Palos Hills, Chicago . . . 9 C1
Palos Hills Forest, Chicago 9 C1
Palos Park, Chicago 9 C1
Palpara, Calcutta 8 B2
Panchur, Calcutta 8 B1
Pandacan, Manila 17 B2
Pandan, Selat, Singapore . 27 B2
Pandan Res., Singapore . . 27 B2
Pandebistnio, Athens . . . 2 b2
Pangbae, Seoul 26 C1
Pangrati, Athens 2 b2
Pangsua, Sungei →, Singapore . 27 A2
Panihati, Calcutta 8 A2
Panjang, Bukit, Singapore . 27 A2
Panje, Mumbai 20 B2
Panke →, Berlin 5 A3
Pankow, Berlin 5 A3
Panthéon, Paris 23 c4
Panthéon, Paris 23 B3
Pantin, Paris 23 A3
Pantitlán, Mexico City . . 18 B2
Panvel →, Mumbai 20 B2
Paparangi, Wellington . . 32 B1
Papiol, Barcelona 4 A1
Paramus, New York 21 A1
Paranaque, Manila 17 B1
Paray-Vieille-Poste, Paris . 23 B3
Parco Regionale, Milan . . 18 A1
Parel, Mumbai 20 B2
Pari, São Paulo 26 B2
Parioli, Rome 25 B1
Paris, Paris 23 A3
Paris-Orly, Aéroport de, Paris . 23 B3
Pârk-e Mellat, Tehran . . 30 A2
Park Ridge, Chicago . . . 9 A1
Park Royal, London 15 A2
Parkchester, New York . . 21 B2
Parkdale, Toronto 30 B2
Parkhurst, Johannesburg . 13 A2
Parklawn, Washington . . 32 B3
Parkmore, Johannesburg . 13 A2
Parkside, San Francisco . . 25 B2
Parktown, Johannesburg . 13 B2
Parktown North, Johannesburg . 13 A2
Parkview, Johannesburg . 13 A1
Parkville, New York 21 C2
Parkwood, Cape Town . . 8 A2
Parkwood, Johannesburg . 13 A2
Parow, Cape Town 8 A2
Parque Chabuco, Buenos Aires . 7 B2
Parque Patricios, Buenos Aires . 7 B2
Parramatta →, Sydney . . 28 A1
Parthenon, Athens 2 c2
Paşabahçe, Istanbul 12 B2
Pasadena, Los Angeles . . 16 B4
Pasar Minggu, Jakarta . . 13 B2
Pasay, Manila 17 B1
Pascoe Vale, Melbourne . 17 A1
Paseo de la Reforma, Mexico City . 18 b2
Pasig, Manila 17 b2
Pasig →, Manila 17 B2
Pasila, Helsinki 12 B2
Pasing, Munich 20 B1
Pasir Panjang, Singapore . 27 B2
Pasir Ris, Singapore . . . 27 A3
Passaic →, New York . . . 21 B1
Passirana, Milan 18 A1
Patel Nagar, Delhi 10 B2
Pateros, Manila 17 B2
Pathersville, Atlanta . . . 3 B3
Pathumwan, Bangkok . . . 3 B2
Patipukur, Calcutta 8 B2
Patisia, Athens 2 A2
Paulo E. Virginia, Gruta, Rio de Janeiro . 24 B1
Paulshof, Berlin 5 A5
Pavshino, Moscow 19 B2
Paya Lebar, Singapore . . 27 A3
Peachtree →, Atlanta . . . 3 A2
Peakhurst, Sydney 28 B1
Peania, Athens 2 B2
Peckham, London 15 B3
Peddocks I., Boston 6 B4
Pederstrup, Copenhagen . 10 A2
Pedralbes, Barcelona . . . 4 A1

Pedregal de San Angel, Jardines del, Mexico City 18 C1
Pekhorka →, Moscow . . . 19 C6
Pekhra-Pokrovskoye, Moscow . 19 A5
Pekhra-Yakovievskaya, Moscow . 19 B5
Peking = Beijing, Beijing . 4 B1
Pelcowizna, Warsaw . . . 31 B2
Pelopónnisos Sta., Athens . 2 a1
Penalolén, Santiago 26 B2
Pencarrow Hd., Wellington 32 C2
Peng Siang →, Singapore . 27 A2
Penge, London 15 B3
Penha, Rio de Janeiro . . . 24 B1
Penicuik, Edinburgh . . . 11 B2
Penjaringan, Jakarta . . . 13 A1
Penn Station, New York . . 21 c2
Pennsylvania Avenue, Washington . 32 b1
Pentland Hills, Edinburgh . 11 B1
Penyagino, Moscow 19 A3
Penzing, Vienna 31 A1
People's Park, Shanghai . . 27 B1
People's Square, Shanghai . 27 B1
Perales del Rio, Madrid . . 17 C2
Peravillo, Mexico City . . 18 a3
Perchtoldsdorf, Vienna . . 31 B1
Perdizes, São Paulo 26 B1
Peredelkino, Moscow . . . 19 C2
Pergamon Museum, Berlin . 5 a4
Peristérion, Athens 2 A1
Perivale, London 15 A2
Perk, Brussels 6 A2
Perlach, Munich 20 B2
Perlacher Forst, Munich . . 20 B2
Perovo, Moscow 19 B4
Pershing Square, Los Angeles 16 c1
Pertusella, Milan 18 A1
Pesagot, Jerusalem 13 A2
Pesanggrahan, Kali →, Jakarta . 13 B1
Peschiera Borromeo, Milan 18 B2
Pesek, P., Singapore . . . 27 B2
Pest, Budapest 7 B2
Pesterzsébet, Budapest . . 7 B2
Pesthidegkút, Budapest . . 7 A1
Pestimre, Budapest 7 B3
Pestlörinc, Budapest . . . 7 B3
Pestújhely, Budapest . . . 7 A2
Petas, Helsinki 12 B2
Petone, Wellington 32 B2
Petrogradskaya Storona, St. Petersburg . 26 B2
Petroúpolis, Athens 2 A2
Petrovice, Prague 24 B3
Petrovskiy Park, Moscow . 19 B3
Petrovsko-Razumovskoye, Moscow . 19 B3
Pettycur, Edinburgh . . . 11 A2
Peutie, Brussels 6 A2
Pfaueninsel, Berlin 5 B1
Phaya Thai, Bangkok . . . 3 B2
Phihai, Karachi 14 B1
Phillip B., Sydney 28 B2
Phoenix Park, Dublin . . . 11 A1
Phra Khanong, Bangkok . 3 B2
Phra Pradeng, Bangkok . . 3 C2
Phranakhon, Bangkok . . . 3 B1
Picasso, Museu, Barcelona . 4 c2
Piccadilly, London 15 b3
Pico Rivera, Los Angeles . 16 C4
Piedade, Lisbon 14 A1
Piedade, Rio de Janeiro . . 24 B1
Piedade, Cova da, Lisbon . 14 A2
Piedmont Park, Atlanta . . 3 B2
Pietralata, Rome 25 B2
Pihlajamäki, Helsinki . . . 12 B2
Pihlajasaari, Helsinki . . . 12 C2
Pilares, Rio de Janeiro . . 24 B1
Pilton, Edinburgh 11 B2
Pimlico, London 15 c3
Pimmit Hills, Washington . 32 B2
Pine Grove, Toronto . . . 30 A1
Pinewood, Miami 18 A2
Piney Run →, Washington . 32 B2
Pinganli, Beijing 4 B2
Pingzhou, Canton 8 B2
Pinheiros →, São Paulo . . 26 B1
Pinjrapur, Karachi 14 A2
Pinner, London 15 A1
Pinner Green, London . . 15 A1
Pioltello, Milan 18 B2
Pipinui Pt., Wellington . . 32 A1
Piraévs, Athens 2 B1
Pirajuçara →, São Paulo . 26 B1
Pirinçci, Istanbul 12 B1
Pirituba, São Paulo 26 A1
Pirkkola, Helsinki 12 B2
Písnice, Prague 24 B2
Pitampura, Delhi 10 A1
Pitkäjärvi, Helsinki 12 B1
Planegg, Munich 20 B1
Plumstead, Cape Town . . 8 A1
Plumstead, London 15 B4
Plyushchevo, Moscow . . 19 B4
Pnika, Athens 2 c1
Po Toi I., Hong Kong . . . 12 B2
Po Toi O, Hong Kong . . . 12 B2
Poasco, Milan 18 B2
Podaba, Prague 24 B2
Podoli, Prague 24 B2
Poduskino, Moscow 19 B1
Pointe-Aux-Trembles, Montreal . 19 A2
Poissy, Paris 23 A1
Pok Fu Lam, Hong Kong . 12 B1
Pokrovsko-Stresnevo, Moscow . 19 B2
Polton, Edinburgh 11 B3
Polyustrovo, St. Petersburg 26 B2
Pompidou, Centre, Paris . 23 b4
Pomprap, Bangkok 3 B2
Pondok Indah, Jakarta . . 13 B1
Ponta do Marisco, Rio de Janeiro . 24 C1
Pontault-Combault, Paris . 23 B4
Pontinha, Lisbon 14 A1
Poplar, London 15 A3
Popolo, Porta del, Rome . 25 a2
Poppintree, Dublin 11 A2
Porirua, Wellington 32 A2
Porirua East, Wellington . 32 A2
Port I., Osaka 22 B3
Port Melbourne, Melbourne 17 B1
Port Nicholson, Wellington 32 B1
Port Philip Bay, Melbourne 17 B1
Port Richmond, New York 21 C1
Port Shelter, Hong Kong . 12 A2
Port Union, Toronto . . . 30 A4
Portage Park, Chicago . . 9 B2
Portal de la Pau, Pl., Barcelona . 4 c2
Portela, Aeroporto da, Lisbon . 14 A2
Portmarnock, Dublin . . . 11 A3
Porto Brandão, Lisbon . . 14 A1
Porto Novo, Rio de Janeiro 24 A2

Porto Novo Cr. →, Lagos . 14 B2
Portobello, Edinburgh . . 11 B3
Portrero, San Francisco . . 25 B3
Potomac, Washington . . . 32 B2
Potomac →, Washington . 32 B3
Potrero Pt., San Francisco . 25 B2
Potsdam, Berlin 5 B1
Potsdamer Platz, Berlin . . 5 b3
Potzham, Munich 20 B3
Pötzleinsdorf, Vienna . . . 31 A1
Povoa de Santo Adriao, Lisbon . 14 A2
Powązki, Warsaw 31 B1
Powiśle, Warsaw 31 B2
Powsin, Warsaw 31 C2
Powsinek, Warsaw 31 C2
Poyan Res., Singapore . . 27 A2
Pozuelo de Alarcon, Madrid 17 B1
Prado, Museo del, Madrid . 17 b3
Prado Churubusco, Mexico City . 18 B2
Praga, Warsaw 31 B2
Prague = Praha, Prague . . 24 B2
Praha, Prague 24 B2
Praha-Ruzyně Airport, Prague . 24 B1
Praires, R. des →, Montreal 19 A2
Prater, Vienna 31 A2
Precotto, Milan 18 A2
Prenestino Labicano, Rome 25 B2
Prenžlauerberg, Berlin . . 5 A3
Preston, Melbourne 17 A1
Pretos Forros, Sa. dos, Rio de Janeiro . 24 B1
Préville, Montreal 19 B3
Přezletice, Prague 24 B2
Prima Porta, Rome 25 B1
Primavalle, Rome 25 B1
Primrose, Johannesburg . 13 B2
Princes Street, Edinburgh . 11 b2
Printer's Row, Chicago . . 9 d2
Progreso Nacional, Mexico City . 18 A2
Prosek, Prague 24 B2
Prospect Hill Park, Boston . 6 A2
Providencia, Santiago . . . 26 B2
Prudential Building, Chicago 9 c2
Průhonice, Prague 24 C3
Psikhikón, Athens 2 A2
Pudong New Area, Shanghai 27 B2
Pueblo Libre, Lima 16 B2
Pueblo Nuevo, Barcelona . 4 A2
Pueblo Nuevo, Madrid . . 17 B2
Puerta del Sol, Plaza, Madrid 17 b2
Puerto Madero, Buenos Aires 7 B2
Puerto Retiro, Buenos Aires 7 B2
Puhuangyu, Beijing 4 B2
Puistola, Helsinki 12 B3
Pukan-san, Seoul 26 B1
Pukinmäki, Helsinki . . . 12 B2
Pukkajwa, Seoul 26 B1
Pulkovo Int. Airport, St. Petersburg . 26 C1
Pullach, Munich 20 B2
Pulo Gadung, Jakarta . . . 13 B2
Pünak, Tehran 30 A2
Punchbowl, Sydney 28 B1
Punde, Mumbai 20 B2
Punggol, Singapore 27 A3
Punggol, Sungei →, Singapore . 27 A3
Punggol Pt., Singapore . . 27 A3
Punjabi Bagh, Delhi . . . 10 A1
Puotila, Helsinki 12 B3
Purana Qila, Delhi 1 c3
Puteaux, Paris 23 A2
Putilkovo, Moscow 19 A2
Putney, London 15 B2
Putuo, Shanghai 27 B1
Putxet, Barcelona 4 A1
Puxi, Shanghai 27 B1
Pydhuni, Mumbai 20 b2
Pyramids, Cairo 7 B1
Pyry, Warsaw 31 C1

Q

Qalandya, Jerusalem . . . 13 A2
Qal'eh Morghi, Tehran . . 30 B2
Qamâ el Ismâ'iliya, Cairo . 7 A2
Qâsemâbâd, Tehran 30 A3
Qasr-e Firûzeh, Tehran . . 30 B3
Qatane, Jerusalem 13 B1
Qianmen, Beijing 4 B2
Qinghuayuan, Beijing . . . 4 B1
Qingningsi, Shanghai . . . 27 B2
Qolhak, Tehran 30 A2
Quadraro, Rome 25 B2
Quaid-i-Azam, Karachi . . 14 B2
Quartiere Zingone, Milan . 18 B1
Ouds, Baghdad 3 A2
Queen Mary Res., London . 15 B1
Queen Street, Edinburgh . 11 a1
Queensbury, London . . . 15 A2
Queenscliffe, Sydney . . . 28 A2
Queensferry, Edinburgh . 11 B1
Queenstown, Singapore . . 27 B2
Quellerina, Johannesburg . 13 A1
Queluz, Lisbon 14 A1
Quezon City, Manila . . . 17 B2
Quezon Memorial Circle, Manila . 17 B2
Quilicura, Santiago 26 B1
Quincy, Boston 6 B3
Quincy B., Boston 6 B4
Quinta Normal, Santiago . 26 B1
Quinto de Stampi, Milan . 18 B2
Quinto Romano, Milan . . 18 B1
Quirinale, Rome 25 B1
Quirinale, Palazzo dei, Rome 25 b3

R

Raasdorf, Vienna 31 A3
Rådhuset, Oslo 22 A3
Radlice, Prague 24 B2
Radosé, Warsaw 31 B3
Radotin, Prague 24 C2
Rafat, Jerusalem 13 A2
Raffles Hotel, Singapore . 27 b3
Raffles Park, Singapore . . 27 B2
Rahnsdorf, Berlin 5 B5
Rainham, London 15 A5
Raj Ghat, Delhi 1 b3
Rajakylä, Helsinki 12 B3
Rajpath, Delhi 1 c2
Rajpura, Delhi 10 A2
Rákos-patak →, Budapest . 7 A3
Rákoshegy, Budapest . . . 7 B3
Rákoskeresztúr, Budapest . 7 B3

38 Rákoskert

INDEX TO CITY MAPS

Rákoskert, *Budapest* 7 B3
Rákosliget, *Budapest* 7 B3
Rákospalota, *Budapest* 7 A2
Rákosszentmihály, *Budapest* 7 A2
Raków, *Warsaw* 31 B1
Ram, *Jerusalem* 13 A2
Rām Allāh, *Jerusalem* 13 A2
Ramadān, *Baghdad* 3 B2
Ramakrishna Puram, *Delhi* 10 B1
Ramanathpur, *Calcutta* 8 A1
Rambla, La, *Barcelona* 4 b2
Rambler Channel, *Hong Kong* 12 A1
Ramenki, *Moscow* 19 B2
Ramersdorf, *Munich* 20 B2
Ramos, *Rio de Janeiro* 24 B1
Ramos Mejia, *Buenos Aires* 7 B1
Ramot, *Jerusalem* 13 B2
Rampur, *Delhi* 10 A2
Ramsgate, *Sydney* 28 B1
Rand Afrikaans Univ., *Johannesburg* 13 B2
Rand Airport, *Johannesburg* 13 B2
Randburg, *Johannesburg* 13 A1
Randhart, *Johannesburg* 13 B2
Randpark Ridge, *Johannesburg* 13 A1
Randwick, *Sydney* 28 B2
Ranelagh, *Dublin* 11 A2
Rannersdorf, *Vienna* 31 B2
Ransbèche, *Brussels* 6 B2
Ransdorp, *Amsterdam* 2 A2
Ranvad, *Mumbai* 20 B2
Raposo, *Lisbon* 14 A1
Rashtrapati Bhawan, *Delhi* 1 c1
Rasskazovka, *Moscow* 19 C2
Rastaala, *Helsinki* 12 B1
Rastila, *Helsinki* 12 B3
Raszyn, *Warsaw* 31 C1
Ratcha Thewi, *Bangkok* 3 b3
Rathfarnham, *Dublin* 11 B2
Ratho, *Edinburgh* 11 B1
Ratho Station, *Edinburgh* 11 B1
Rato, *Lisbon* 14 A2
Ravelston, *Edinburgh* 11 B2
Rawamangun, *Jakarta* 13 B2
Rayners Lane, *London* 15 A1
Raynes Park, *London* 15 B2
Raypur, *Calcutta* 8 C2
Razdory, *Moscow* 19 B1
Real Felipe, Fuerte, *Lima* 16 B2
Recoleta, *Buenos Aires* 7 B2
Recoleta, *Santiago* 26 B2
Red Fort = Lal Qila, *Delhi* 1 a3
Redbridge, *London* 15 A4
Redfern, *Sydney* 28 B2
Redwood, *Wellington* 32 B1
Reeves Hill, *Boston* 6 A1
Refshaleøen, *Copenhagen* 10 A3
Regents Park, *Johannesburg* 13 B2
Regent's Park, *London* 15 a2
Rego Park, *New York* 21 B2
Reichstag, *Berlin* 5 a3
Reina Sofia, Centro de Arte, *Madrid* 17 c3
Reinickendorf, *Berlin* 5 A3
Rekola, *Helsinki* 12 B3
Rembertów, *Warsaw* 31 B2
Rembrandthuis, *Amsterdam* 2 b2
Rembrandtpark, *Amsterdam* 2 A2
Rembrandtsplein, *Amsterdam* 2 b2
Remedios, Parque Nacional de los, *Mexico City* 18 B1
Remedios de Escalada, *Buenos Aires* 7 C2
Rémola, Laguna del, *Barcelona* 4 B1
Renca, *Santiago* 26 B1
Renmin Park, *Tianjin* 30 B2
Rennemoulin, *Paris* 23 A1
Řeporyje, *Prague* 24 B1
Republica, Plaza de la, *Mexico City* 18 b1
République, Place de la, *Paris* 23 b5
Repulse Bay, *Hong Kong* 12 B2
Repy, *Prague* 24 B1
Residenz, *Munich* 20 B2
Residenzmuseum, *Munich* 20 b3
Reston, *Washington* 32 B2
Retiro, *Buenos Aires* 7 B2
Retiro, *Madrid* 17 B1
Retreat, *Cape Town* 8 B1
Reutov, *Moscow* 19 B5
Réveillon →, *Paris* 23 B4
Revere, *Boston* 6 A3
Rexdale, *Toronto* 30 A1
Reynosa Tamaulipas, *Mexico City* 18 A1
Rho, *Milan* 18 A1
Rhodes, *Sydney* 28 A1
Rhodon, *Paris* 23 B1
Rhodon →, *Paris* 23 B1
Ribeira, *Rio de Janeiro* 24 A1
Ricarda, Laguna de la, *Barcelona* 4 B1
Richmond, *Melbourne* 17 A2
Richmond, *San Francisco* 25 B2
Richmond Hill, *New York* 21 B2
Richmond Park, *London* 15 B2
Richmond upon Thames, *London* 15 B2
Riddarholmen, *Stockholm* 28 c1
Riddarhuset, *Stockholm* 28 c2
Ridgefield, *New York* 21 B1
Ridgefield Park, *New York* 21 A1
Ridgewood, *New York* 21 B2
Riem, *Munich* 20 B3
Rijksmuseum, *Amsterdam* 2 b1
Rikers I., *New York* 21 B2
Riksdagensledamothus, *Stockholm* 28 b2
Riksdagshuset, *Stockholm* 28 b2
Rimac, *Lima* 16 B2
Ringsend, *Dublin* 11 A2
Rinkeby, *Stockholm* 28 A1
Rio Compride, *Rio de Janeiro* 24 B1
Rio de Janeiro, *Rio de Janeiro* 24 B1
Rio de la Plata, *Buenos Aires* 7 B2
Rio de Mouro, *Lisbon* 14 A1
Ripollet, *Barcelona* 4 A1
Ris, *Oslo* 22 A3
Risby, *Copenhagen* 10 A1
Rishra, *Calcutta* 8 A2
Ritchie, *Washington* 32 B4
Rithala, *Delhi* 10 A1
Rive Sud, Canal de la, *Montreal* 19 B2
River Edge, *New York* 21 A1
River Forest, *Chicago* 9 B2
River Grove, *Chicago* 9 B1
Riverdale, *New York* 21 A2
Riverdale, *Washington* 32 B4
Riverdale Park, *Toronto* 30 A2
Riverlea, *Johannesburg* 13 B1
Riverside, *Chicago* 9 C2
Riverwood, *Sydney* 28 B1
Rivière-des-Praires, *Montreal* 19 A2
Rixensart, *Brussels* 6 B3
Riyad, *Baghdad* 3 B2
Rizal Park, *Manila* 17 B1
Rizal Stadium, *Manila* 17 B1
Røa, *Oslo* 22 A2
Robbins, *Chicago* 9 D2
Robertsham, *Johannesburg* 13 B2
Rochelle Park, *New York* 21 A1
Rock Cr. →, *Washington* 32 B3
Rock Creek Park, *Washington* 32 B3
Rock Pt., *Wellington* 32 A1
Rockaway Pt., *New York* 21 C2
Rockdale, *Sydney* 28 B1
Rockefeller Center, *New York* 21 c2
Rodaon, *Vienna* 31 B1
Rødovre, *Copenhagen* 10 A2
Rodrigo de Freitas, L., *Rio de Janeiro* 24 B1
Roehampton, *London* 15 B2
Rogers Park, *Chicago* 9 A2
Roihuvuori, *Helsinki* 12 B3
Roissy-en-Brie, *Paris* 23 B4
Rokin, *Amsterdam* 2 b2
Rokkō I., *Osaka* 22 A2
Rokkō Sanchi, *Osaka* 22 A2
Rokkō-Zan, *Osaka* 22 A2
Rokytka →, *Prague* 24 B3
Roma, *Rome* 25 B1
Római-Fürdö, *Budapest* 7 A2
Romainville, *Paris* 23 A3
Romano Banco, *Milan* 18 B1
Romashkovo, *Moscow* 19 B1
Rome = Roma, *Rome* 25 B1
Romford, *London* 15 A5
Rondebosch, *Cape Town* 8 A1
Roppongi, *Tokyo* 29 c3
Rose Hill, *Washington* 32 C3
Rosebank, *New York* 21 C1
Rosebery, *Sydney* 28 B2
Rosedal La Candelaria, *Mexico City* 18 B2
Roseland, *Chicago* 9 C3
Rosemead, *Los Angeles* 16 B4
Rosemont, *Montreal* 19 A2
Rosenborg Have, *Copenhagen* 10 A3
Rosenthal, *Berlin* 5 A3
Rosettenville, *Johannesburg* 13 B2
Rosewell, *Edinburgh* 11 B3
Rosherville Dam, *Johannesburg* 13 B2
Rösjön, *Stockholm* 28 A2
Roslags-Näsby, *Stockholm* 28 A2
Roslin, *Edinburgh* 11 B3
Roslindale, *Boston* 6 B3
Rosny-sous-Bois, *Paris* 23 A4
Rosslyn, *Washington* 32 B3
Rosyth, *Edinburgh* 11 A1
Rotherhithe, *London* 15 B3
Rothneusiedl, *Vienna* 31 B2
Rothschmaige, *Munich* 20 A1
Rouge Hill, *Toronto* 30 A4
Round I., *Hong Kong* 12 B2
Roxbury, *Boston* 6 B3
Roxeth, *London* 15 A1
Royal Botanic Garden, *Edinburgh* 11 B2
Royal Botanic Gardens, *Sydney* 28 b2
Royal Grand Palace, *Bangkok* 3 b1
Royal Observatory, *Edinburgh* 11 B2
Royal Park, *Melbourne* 17 A1
Royal Turf Club, *Bangkok* 3 b2
Röylä, *Helsinki* 12 B1
Rozas, Portilleros de las, *Madrid* 17 B1
Roztoky, *Prague* 24 B2
Rozzano, *Milan* 18 B1
Rubi →, *Barcelona* 4 A1
Rublovo, *Moscow* 19 B2
Rudnevka →, *Moscow* 19 B5
Rudolfsheim, *Vienna* 31 A2
Rudolfshöhe, *Berlin* 5 A5
Rudow, *Berlin* 5 B3
Rueil-Malmaison, *Paris* 23 A2
Ruisbroek, *Brussels* 6 B1
Ruislip, *London* 15 A1
Rumelihisarı, *Istanbul* 12 B2
Rumyantsevo, *Moscow* 19 C2
Rungis, *Paris* 23 B3
Rusāfa, *Baghdad* 3 A2
Rush Green, *London* 15 A5
Russa, *Calcutta* 8 C2
Russian Hill, *San Francisco* 25 a1
Rustenfeld, *Vienna* 31 B2
Rutherford, *New York* 21 B1
Ruzyně, *Prague* 24 B1
Rybatskaya, *St. Petersburg* 26 B2
Rydboholm, *Stockholm* 28 A3
Ryde, *Sydney* 28 A1
Rynek, *Warsaw* 31 a2
Ryogoku, *Tokyo* 29 A3
Rzhevka, *St. Petersburg* 26 B3

S

Sa'ādatābād, *Tehran* 30 A2
Saadūn, *Baghdad* 3 B2
Saavedra, *Buenos Aires* 7 B2
Saboli, *Delhi* 10 A2
Sabugo, *Lisbon* 14 A1
Sabzi Mand, *Delhi* 10 A2
Sacavém, *Lisbon* 14 A2
Saclay, *Paris* 23 B2
Saclay, Étang de, *Paris* 23 B1
Sacomã, *São Paulo* 26 B2
Sacré Cœur, *Paris* 23 a4
Sacrow, *Berlin* 5 B1
Sacrower See, *Berlin* 5 B1
Sadang, *Seoul* 26 C1
Sadar Bazar, *Delhi* 1 a1
Saddām City, *Baghdad* 3 A2
Saddle Brook, *New York* 21 A1
Sadr, *Karachi* 14 A2
Sadyba, *Warsaw* 31 B2
Saft el Laban, *Cairo* 7 A2
Saganashkee Slough, *Chicago* 9 C1
Sagene, *Oslo* 22 A3
Sagrada Família, Templo de, *Barcelona* 4 A2
Sagrado Familia, Templo de, *Barcelona* 4 a2
Sahar Int. Airport, *Mumbai* 20 A2
Sai Kung, *Hong Kong* 12 A2
Sai Wan Ho, *Hong Kong* 12 B2
Sai Ying Pun, *Hong Kong* 12 B1
St.-Aubin, *Paris* 23 B1
St.-Cloud, *Paris* 23 A2
St.-Cyr-l'École, *Paris* 23 B1
St.-Cyr-l'École, Aérodrome de, *Paris* 23 B1
St.-Denis, *Paris* 23 A3
St.-Germain, Forêt de, *Paris* 23 A1
St.-Germain-en-Laye, *Paris* 23 A1
St. Giles Cathedral, *Edinburgh* 11 b2
St. Helier, *London* 15 B2
St.-Hubert, *Montreal* 19 B3
St. Hubert, Galerie, *Brussels* 6 b2
St. Isaac's Cathedral, *St. Petersburg* 26 B1
St. Jacques →, *Montreal* 19 B3
St. James's, *London* 15 b3
St. John's Cathedral, *Hong Kong* 12 c1
St. Kilda, *Melbourne* 17 B1
St. Lambert, *Montreal* 19 A3
St.-Lambert, *Paris* 23 B1
St.-Laurent, *Montreal* 19 A1
St. Lawrence →, *Montreal* 19 B2
St.-Lazare, Gare, *Paris* 23 A2
St.-Léonard, *Montreal* 19 A2
St. Magelungen, *Stockholm* 28 B2
St.-Mandé, *Paris* 23 A3
St. Margaret's, *Dublin* 11 A2
St.-Martin, Bois, *Paris* 23 B4
St. Mary Cray, *London* 15 B4
St.-Maur-des-Fossés, *Paris* 23 B3
St.-Maurice, *Paris* 23 B3
St.-Michel, *Montreal* 19 A2
St. Nikolaus-Kirken, *Prague* 24 B2
St.-Ouen, *Paris* 23 A3
St. Patrick's Cathedral, *Dublin* 11 c1
St. Patrick's Cathedral, *New York* 21 c2
St. Paul's Cathedral, *London* 15 b4
St. Paul's Cray, *London* 15 B4
St. Peters, *Sydney* 28 B2
St. Petersburg = Sankt Peterburg, *St. Petersburg* 26 B1
St.-Pierre, *Montreal* 19 B2
St.-Quentin, Étang de, *Paris* 23 B1
St. Stephen's Green, *Dublin* 11 c3
St.-Vincent-de-Paul, *Montreal* 19 A2
Ste.-Catherine, *Montreal* 19 B2
Ste.-Hélène, Î., *Montreal* 19 A2
Saiwai, *Tokyo* 29 B3
Sakai, *Osaka* 22 B3
Sakai Harbour, *Osaka* 22 B3
Sakra, P., *Singapore* 27 B2
Salam, *Baghdad* 3 A2
Salamanca, *Madrid* 17 B1
Sâllynoggin, *Dublin* 11 B3
Salmannsdorf, *Vienna* 31 A1
Salmedina, *Madrid* 17 C2
Salomea, *Warsaw* 31 B1
Salsette I., *Mumbai* 20 A2
Salt Lake City, *Calcutta* 8 B2
Salt River, *Cape Town* 8 A1
Salt Water L., *Calcutta* 8 B2
Saltsjö-Duvnäs, *Stockholm* 28 B3
Saltykovka, *Moscow* 19 B5
Samatya, *Istanbul* 12 C1
Sampaloc, *Manila* 17 B1
Samphan Thawong, *Bangkok* 3 B2
Samsŏn, *Seoul* 26 B2
San Andrés, *Barcelona* 4 A2
San Angel, *Mexico City* 18 B1
San Angelo, Castel, *Rome* 25 b1
San Basilio, *Rome* 25 B2
San Borja, *Lima* 16 B3
San Bóvio, *Milan* 18 B2
San Bruno, Pt., *San Francisco* 25 C2
San Bruno Mt., *San Francisco* 25 B2
San Cristobal, *Buenos Aires* 7 B2
San Cristobal, *Madrid* 17 B2
San Cristóbal, Cerro, *Santiago* 26 B2
San Cristoforo, *Milan* 18 B1
San Donato Milanese, *Milan* 18 B2
San Francisco, *San Francisco* 25 B2
San Francisco B., *San Francisco* 25 B3
San Francisco Culhuacán, *Mexico City* 18 C2
San Fruttuoso, *Milan* 18 A2
San Gabriel, *Los Angeles* 16 B4
San Giuliano Milanese, *Milan* 18 B2
San Isidro, *Lima* 16 B2
San Jerónimo Lidice, *Mexico City* 18 C1
San Joaquin, *Santiago* 26 B2
San José Rio Hondo, *Mexico City* 18 B1
San Juan →, *Manila* 17 B2
San Juan de Aragón, *Mexico City* 18 B2
San Juan de Aragón, Parque, *Mexico City* 18 B2
San Juan de Lurigancho, *Lima* 16 A2
San Juan del Monte, *Manila* 17 B2
San Juan Ixtacala, *Mexico City* 18 A1
San Juan Toltotepec, *Mexico City* 18 B1
San Just Desvern, *Barcelona* 4 A1
San Justo, *Buenos Aires* 7 C1
San Lorenzo Tezonco, *Mexico City* 18 C2
San Luis, *Lima* 16 B2
San Marino, *Los Angeles* 16 B4
San Martin, *Barcelona* 4 A2
San Martin de Porras, *Lima* 16 B2
San Miguel, *Lima* 16 B2
San Miguel, *Santiago* 26 B2
San Nicolas, *Buenos Aires* 7 B2
San Onófrio, *Rome* 25 B1
San Pedro Martir, *Barcelona* 4 A1
San Pedro Zacatenco, *Mexico City* 18 A2
San Pietro, Piazza, *Rome* 25 b1
San Po Kong, *Hong Kong* 12 A2
San Rafael Chamapa, *Mexico City* 18 B1
San Rafael Hills, *Los Angeles* 16 A3
San Roque, *Manila* 17 B2
San Siro, *Milan* 18 B1
San Souci, *Sydney* 28 B1
San Telmo, *Buenos Aires* 7 B2
San Vicenc dels Horts, *Barcelona* 4 A1
Sanbancho, *Tokyo* 29 a3
Sandown, *Johannesburg* 13 A2
Sandown Park Races, *London* 15 B1
Sandton, *Johannesburg* 13 A2
Sandvika, *Oslo* 22 A2
Sandy Pond, *Boston* 6 A2
Sandyford, *Dublin* 11 B2
Sandymount, *Dublin* 11 B2
Sangenjaya, *Tokyo* 29 B2
Sangge, *Seoul* 26 B2
Sangley Pt., *Manila* 17 C1
Sankrail, *Calcutta* 8 B1
Sankt Peterburg, *St. Petersburg* 26 B1
Sankt Veit, *Vienna* 31 A1
Sanlihe, *Beijing* 4 B1
Sanlintang, *Shanghai* 27 C1
Sans, *Barcelona* 4 A1
Sant Agusti, *Barcelona* 4 c2
Sant Ambrogio, Basilica di, *Milan* 18 B2
Sant Boi de Llobregat, *Barcelona* 4 A1
Sant Cugat, *Barcelona* 4 A1
Sant Feliu de Llobregat, *Barcelona* 4 A1
Sant Joan Despi, *Barcelona* 4 A1
Sant Maria del Mar, *Barcelona* 4 b3
Sant Pau del Camp, *Barcelona* 4 c2
Santa Ana, *Manila* 17 B2
Santa Coloma de Gramanet, *Barcelona* 4 A2
Santa Cruz, *Manila* 17 B1
Santa Cruz, *Mumbai* 20 A1
Santa Cruz, I. de, *Rio de Janeiro* 24 B2
Santa Cruz de Olorde, *Barcelona* 4 A1
Santa Efigénia, *São Paulo* 26 B2
Santa Elena, *Manila* 17 B2
Santa Elena del Gomero, *Santiago* 26 B1
Santa Eulalia, *Barcelona* 4 A2
Santa Fe Springs, *Los Angeles* 16 C4
Santa Iria da Azóia, *Lisbon* 14 A2
Santa Julia, *Santiago* 26 C2
Santa Maria, *Mexico City* 18 a1
Santa Monica, *Los Angeles* 16 B2
Santa Monica Mts., *Los Angeles* 16 B2
Santa Rosa De Locobe, *Santiago* 26 B2
Santa Teresa de la Ovalle, *Santiago* 26 B1
Santahamina, *Helsinki* 12 C3
Santana, *São Paulo* 26 A2
Santeny, *Paris* 23 B4
Santiago, *Santiago* 26 B2
Santiago de Surco, *Lima* 16 B2
Santo Amaro, *Lisbon* 14 A1
Santo Amaro, *São Paulo* 26 B1
Santo Andre, *Lisbon* 14 B2
Santo Antão do Tojal, *Lisbon* 14 A2
Santo António, Qta. de, *Lisbon* 14 B1
Santo Tomas, Univ. of, *Manila* 17 B1
Santos Dumont, Aéroport, *Rio de Janeiro* 24 B2
Santoshpur, *Calcutta* 8 B1
Santragachi, *Calcutta* 8 B1
Santry, *Dublin* 11 A2
Sanyuanli, *Canton* 8 B2
São Caetano do Sul, *São Paulo* 26 B2
São Conrado, *Rio de Janeiro* 24 C1
São Cristovão, *Rio de Janeiro* 24 B1
São Francisco Penitência, *Rio de Janeiro* 24 b1
São Jorge, Castelo de, *Lisbon* 14 A2
São Juliao do Tojal, *Lisbon* 14 A2
São Paulo, *São Paulo* 26 B2
Sapa, *Calcutta* 8 B1
Sapateiro, Cor. do →, *São Paulo* 26 B1
Sarandi, *Buenos Aires* 7 C2
Saraswati →, *Calcutta* 8 A1
Sarecky potok →, *Prague* 24 B2
Sarimbun, *Singapore* 27 A2
Sarimbun Res., *Singapore* 27 A2
Sarıyer, *Istanbul* 12 A2
Saronikós Kólpos, *Athens* 2 B1
Sarriá, *Barcelona* 4 A1
Sarsuna, *Calcutta* 8 C1
Sartrouville, *Paris* 23 A2
Sasad, *Budapest* 7 B2
Sashalom, *Budapest* 7 A3
Saska, *Warsaw* 31 B2
Satalice, *Prague* 24 B3
Satgachi, *Calcutta* 8 B2
Sathorn, *Bangkok* 3 B2
Satpukur, *Calcutta* 8 B2
Sätra, *Stockholm* 28 B1
Sattru Pha, *Bangkok* 3 b2
Saúde, *São Paulo* 26 B2
Saugus, *Boston* 6 A3
Saugus →, *Boston* 6 A3
Sault-au-Récollet, *Montreal* 19 A2
Sausalito, *San Francisco* 25 A2
Sawah Besar, *Jakarta* 13 A1
Saxonville, *Boston* 6 B1
Scald Law, *Edinburgh* 11 B2
Scarborough, *Toronto* 30 A3
Sceaux, *Paris* 23 B2
Schaerbeek, *Brussels* 6 A2
Scharfenberg, *Berlin* 5 A2
Scheepvartmuseum, *Amsterdam* 2 b3
Schiller Park, *Chicago* 9 B1
Schiller Woods, *Chicago* 9 B1
Schiphol, Luchthaven, *Amsterdam* 2 B1
Schlachtensee, *Berlin* 5 B2
Schlossgarten, *Berlin* 5 A2
Schmargendorf, *Berlin* 5 B2
Schönblick, *Berlin* 5 B5
Schönbrunn, Schloss, *Vienna* 31 A1
Schöneberg, *Berlin* 5 B3
Schöneiche, *Berlin* 5 B5
Schönwalde, *Berlin* 5 A1
Schotschekloof, *Cape Town* 8 b1
Schulzendorf, *Berlin* 5 A2
Schwabing, *Munich* 20 B2
Schwanebeck, *Berlin* 5 A4
Schwanenwerder, *Berlin* 5 B2
Schwarzlackenau, *Vienna* 31 A2
Schwechat, *Vienna* 31 B2
Scitrek Museum, *Atlanta* 3 B2
Scott Monument, *Edinburgh* 11 b2
Scottdale, *Atlanta* 3 B3
Sea Point, *Cape Town* 8 A1
Seabrook, *Washington* 32 B5
Seacliff, *San Francisco* 25 B2
Seaforth, *Sydney* 28 A2
Seagate, *New York* 21 C1
Sears Tower, *Chicago* 9 c1
Seat Pleasant, *Washington* 32 B4
Seaview, *Wellington* 32 B2
Šeberov, *Prague* 24 B3
Secaucus, *New York* 21 B1
Seddinsee, *Berlin* 5 B5
Seeberg, *Berlin* 5 A5
Seeburg, *Berlin* 5 A1
Seefeld, *Berlin* 5 A5
Seegefeld, *Berlin* 5 A1
Seehof, *Berlin* 5 B2
Segeltorp, *Stockholm* 28 B1
Segrate, *Milan* 18 B2
Seguro, *Milan* 18 B1
Seine →, *Paris* 23 B3
Seixal, *Lisbon* 14 B2
Selby, *Johannesburg* 13 B2
Seletar, P., *Singapore* 27 A3
Seletar Hills, *Singapore* 27 A3
Seletar Res., *Singapore* 27 A2
Selhurst, *London* 15 B3
Sembawang, *Singapore* 27 A2
Senago, *Milan* 18 A1
Sendinger Tor Platz, *Munich* 20 c1
Sendling, *Munich* 20 B2
Senju, *Tokyo* 29 A3
Senriyama, *Osaka* 22 A4
Sentosa, P., *Singapore* 27 B2
Seoul = Sŏul, *Seoul* 26 B2
Seoul National Univ., *Seoul* 26 C1
Seoul Tower, *Seoul* 26 B1
Sepolia, *Athens* 2 A2
Sepulveda Flood Control Basin, *Los Angeles* 16 A2
Serangoon, *Singapore* 27 A3
Serangoon, P., *Singapore* 27 A3
Serangoon, Sungei →, *Singapore* 27 A3
Serangoon Harbour, *Singapore* 27 A3
Seraya, P., *Singapore* 27 B2
Serebryanka, *Moscow* 19 B5
Serebryanka →, *Moscow* 19 B4
Serramonte, *San Francisco* 25 C2
Sesto San Giovanni, *Milan* 18 A2
Sesto Ulteriano, *Milan* 18 B2
Setagaya-Ku, *Tokyo* 29 B2
Seter, *Oslo* 22 A3
Setia Budi, *Jakarta* 13 B1
Settebagni, *Rome* 25 A2
Settecamini, *Rome* 25 B2
Séttimo Milanese, *Milan* 18 B1
Settsu, *Osaka* 22 A4
Setuny →, *Moscow* 19 B2
Seutula, *Helsinki* 12 A2
Seven Corners, *Washington* 32 B3
Seven Kings, *London* 15 A4
Sévesco →, *Milan* 18 A1
Sevran, *Paris* 23 A4
Sewri, *Mumbai* 20 B2
Sforzesso, Castello, *Milan* 18 B2
Sha Kok Mei, *Hong Kong* 12 A2
Sha Tin, *Hong Kong* 12 A2
Sha Tin Wai, *Hong Kong* 12 A2
Shabrâmant, *Cairo* 7 B2
Shahdara, *Delhi* 10 A2
Shahe, *Canton* 8 B2
Shahr-e Rey, *Tehran* 30 B2
Shahrak-e Golshahr, *Tehran* 30 B1
Shahrak-e Qods, *Tehran* 30 A2
Shaikh Aomar, *Baghdad* 3 A2
Shakurbasti, *Delhi* 10 A1
Shalkiya, *Calcutta* 8 B2
Sham Shui Po, *Hong Kong* 12 B1
Shamapur, *Delhi* 10 A1
Shamian, *Canton* 8 B2
Shan Mei, *Hong Kong* 12 A2
Shanghai, *Shanghai* 27 B2
Shankill, *Dublin* 11 B3
Sharp I., *Hong Kong* 12 A2
Shastrinagar, *Delhi* 10 A2
Shau Kei Wan, *Hong Kong* 12 B2
Shawocun, *Beijing* 4 B1
Shayuan, *Canton* 8 B2
Sheepshead Bay, *New York* 21 C2
Shek O, *Hong Kong* 12 B2
Shelter I., *Hong Kong* 12 B2
Sheng Fa Shan, *Hong Kong* 12 A1
Shepherds Bush, *London* 15 A2
Shepperton, *London* 15 B1
Sherman Oaks, *Los Angeles* 16 B2
Sherman Park, *Chicago* 9 C2
Shet Bandar, *Mumbai* 20 B2
Sheung Lau Wan, *Hong Kong* 12 B2
Sheung Wan, *Hong Kong* 12 B1
Sheva, *Mumbai* 20 B2
Sheva Nhava, *Mumbai* 20 B2
Shiba, *Tokyo* 29 c4
Shibpur, *Calcutta* 8 B1
Shibuya-Ku, *Tokyo* 29 c1
Shijōnawate, *Osaka* 22 A4
Shillim, *Seoul* 26 C1
Shimogawara, *Tokyo* 29 B1
Shimosalo, *Tokyo* 29 A2
Shimoshakujii, *Tokyo* 29 A2
Shinagawa-Ku, *Tokyo* 29 B3
Shing Mun Res., *Hong Kong* 12 A1
Shinjuku-Ku, *Tokyo* 29 a1
Shinjuku National Garden, *Tokyo* 29 a2
Shinkoiwa, *Tokyo* 29 A4
Shinnakano, *Tokyo* 29 A3
Shinsa, *Seoul* 26 B2
Shipai, *Canton* 8 B3
Shirinashi →, *Osaka* 22 B3
Shirogane, *Tokyo* 29 B3
Shiweitang, *Canton* 8 B2
Shogunle, *Lagos* 14 A2
Shomolu, *Lagos* 14 A2
Shooters Hill, *London* 15 B4
Shoreditch, *London* 15 a5
Shortlands, *London* 15 B4
Shu' afat, *Jerusalem* 13 B2
Shubrâ, *Cairo* 7 A2
Shubrâ el Kheima, *Cairo* 7 A2
Shuikuo, *Canton* 8 A2
Shuishang Park, *Tianjin* 30 B1
Sidcup, *London* 15 B4
Siebenhirten, *Vienna* 31 B1
Siedlung, *Berlin* 5 A1
Siekierki, *Warsaw* 31 B2
Sielce, *Warsaw* 31 B2
Siemensstadt, *Berlin* 5 A2
Sierra Madre, *Los Angeles* 16 B4
Sievering, *Vienna* 31 A2
Sighthill, *Edinburgh* 11 B2
Signal Hill, *Cape Town* 8 A1
Sihŭng, *Seoul* 26 C1
Sikátorpuszta, *Budapest* 7 A3
Silampur, *Delhi* 10 B2
Silver Hill, *Boston* 6 A2
Silver Hill, *Washington* 32 C4
Silver Spring, *Washington* 32 A3
Silvermine Nature Reserve, *Cape Town* 8 B1
Silvolantekojärvi, *Helsinki* 12 B2
Simei, *Singapore* 27 A3
Simla, *Calcutta* 8 B2
Simmering, *Vienna* 31 A2
Simmering Heide, *Vienna* 31 A2
Simonkylä, *Helsinki* 12 B3
Singapore, *Singapore* 27 B3
Singapore, Univ. of, *Singapore* 27 B2
Sinicka →, *Moscow* 19 A1
Sinki, Selat, *Singapore* 27 B2
Sint-Genesius-Rode, *Brussels* 6 B2
Sinwŏl, *Seoul* 26 B1
Sion, *Mumbai* 20 A2
Sipson, *London* 15 B1
Siqeil, *Cairo* 7 A1
Şişli, *Istanbul* 12 B1
Skansen, *Stockholm* 28 B2
Skärholmen, *Stockholm* 28 B1
Skarpäng, *Stockholm* 28 A2
Skarpnäck, *Stockholm* 28 B2
Skaryszewski Park, *Warsaw* 31 B2
Skeppsholmen, *Stockholm* 28 c3
Skokie, *Chicago* 9 A2
Skokie →, *Chicago* 9 A2
Skoklefall, *Oslo* 22 A3
Sköndal, *Stockholm* 28 B2
Skovlunde, *Copenhagen* 10 A2
Skovshoved, *Copenhagen* 10 A3
Skuru, *Stockholm* 28 B3
Skyland, *Atlanta* 3 A3
Slade Green, *London* 15 B5
Slemmestad, *Oslo* 22 B1
Slependen, *Oslo* 22 A2
Slipi, *Jakarta* 13 B1
Slivenec, *Prague* 24 B2
Sloten, *Amsterdam* 2 A1
Sloterpark, *Amsterdam* 2 A1
Sluhy, *Prague* 24 A3
Służew, *Warsaw* 31 B2
Służewiec, *Warsaw* 31 B2
Smíchov, *Prague* 24 B2
Smith Forest Preserve, *Chicago* 9 B2
Smithsonian Institute, *Washington* 32 b2
Smolny, *St. Petersburg* 26 B2
Snake Creek Canal →, *Miami* 18 A2
Snarøya, *Oslo* 22 A2
Snättringe, *Stockholm* 28 B1
Sŏbinggo, *Seoul* 26 B1
Søborg, *Copenhagen* 10 A2
Sobreda, *Lisbon* 14 B1
Soch'o, *Seoul* 26 C1
Sŏdaemun, *Seoul* 26 B1
Söderby, *Stockholm* 28 A3
Södermalm, *Stockholm* 28 B2
Sodpur, *Calcutta* 8 A2
Soeurs, Î. des, *Montreal* 19 B2
Sognsvatn, *Oslo* 22 A3
Soho, *London* 15 b3
Soho, *New York* 21 e1
Soignes, Forêt de, *Brussels* 6 B2
Sok Kwu Wan, *Hong Kong* 12 B1
Sŏkkwan, *Seoul* 26 B2
Sokolniki, *Moscow* 19 B4
Sokolniki Park, *Moscow* 19 B4
Sokołów, *Warsaw* 31 C1
Solalinden, *Munich* 20 B3
Soldier Field, *Chicago* 9 e3
Sollentuna, *Stockholm* 28 A1
Solln, *Munich* 20 B2
Solna, *Stockholm* 28 A1
Solntsevo, *Moscow* 19 C2
Somerset, *Washington* 32 B3
Somerville, *Boston* 6 A3
Somes Is., *Wellington* 32 B2
Sonari, *Mumbai* 20 B2
Søndersø, *Copenhagen* 10 A2
Sŏngbuk, *Seoul* 26 B2
Sŏngdong, *Seoul* 26 B2
Sŏngp'a, *Seoul* 26 B2
Sŏngsu, *Seoul* 26 B2
Soong Qingling, Former Res. of, *Beijing* 4 a2
Soroksár, *Budapest* 7 B2
Soroksari Duna →, *Budapest* 7 B2
Sosenka →, *Moscow* 19 B4
Sosnovka, *St. Petersburg* 26 B2
Sŏul, *Seoul* 26 B2
Soundview, *New York* 21 B2
South Beach, *New York* 21 C1
South Beach Harbor, *San Francisco* 25 c3
South Bend Park, *Atlanta* 3 B2
South Boston, *Boston* 6 A3
South Brooklyn, *New York* 21 B2
South Decatur, *Atlanta* 3 B3
South Deering, *Chicago* 9 C3
South El Monte, *Los Angeles* 16 B4
South Gate, *Los Angeles* 16 C3
South Harbor, *Manila* 17 B1
South Harrow, *London* 15 A1
South Hd., *Sydney* 28 B2
South Hills, *Johannesburg* 13 B2
South Hornchurch, *London* 15 A5
South Kensington, *London* 15 c2
South Lawn, *Washington* 32 C3
South Lincoln, *Boston* 6 A2
South Miami, *Miami* 18 B1
South Norwood, *London* 15 B3
South of Market, *San Francisco* 25 B2
South Ozone Park, *New York* 21 B3
South Pasadena, *Los Angeles* 16 B4
South Res., *Boston* 6 A3
South Ruislip, *London* 15 A1
South San Francisco, *San Francisco* 25 C2
South San Gabriel, *Los Angeles* 16 B4
South Shore, *Chicago* 9 C3
South Sudbury, *Boston* 6 A1
Southall, *London* 15 A1
Southborough, *London* 15 B4
Southend, *London* 15 B3
Southfields, *London* 15 B2
Southwark, *London* 15 B3
Søvang, *Copenhagen* 10 B3
Soweto, *Johannesburg* 13 B1
Sowhānak, *Tehran* 30 A3
Soya, *Tokyo* 29 A4
Spandau, *Berlin* 5 A1
Spånga, *Stockholm* 28 A1
Spanische Reitschule, *Vienna* 31 b1
Spectacle I., *Boston* 6 A4
Speicher-See, *Munich* 20 A3
Speising, *Vienna* 31 B1
Sphinx, *Cairo* 7 B1
Spinaceto, *Rome* 25 C1
Spit Junction, *Sydney* 28 A2
Spořilov, *Prague* 24 B3
Spot Pond, *Boston* 6 A3
Spotswood, *Melbourne* 17 B1
Spree →, *Berlin* 5 A2
Spring Pond, *Boston* 6 A4
Springeberg, *Berlin* 5 B5
Springfield, *Washington* 32 C2
Squantum, *Boston* 6 B3
Srednaya Rogatka, *St. Petersburg* 26 C2
Sródmieście, *Warsaw* 31 B2
Saint-Gilles, *Brussels* 6 B2
Saint-Joose-Ten-Noode, *Brussels* 6 A2
Saint-Pieters-Leeuw, *Brussels* 6 B1
Saint-Stevens-Woluwe, *Brussels* 6 A2
Staaken, *Berlin* 5 A1
Stabekk, *Oslo* 22 A2
Stadhion, *Athens* 2 c3
Stadhuis, *Amsterdam* 2 b2
Stadlau, *Vienna* 31 A2
Stadshuset, *Stockholm* 28 b1
Stains, *Paris* 23 A3
Stamford Hill, *London* 15 A3
Stammersdorf, *Vienna* 31 A2
Stanley, *Hong Kong* 12 B2
Stanley Mound, *Hong Kong* 12 B2
Stanley Pen., *Hong Kong* 12 B2
Stanmore, *London* 15 A2
Stapleton, *New York* 21 C1
Star Ferry, *Hong Kong* 12 a2
Staraya Derevnya, *St. Petersburg* 26 B1
Stare, *Warsaw* 31 B2
Staré Město, *Prague* 24 B2
Starego Miasto, *Warsaw* 31 a2
Staten Island Zoo, *New York* 21 C1
Statenice, *Prague* 24 B1
Statue Square, *Hong Kong* 12 c1
Stedelijk Museum, *Amsterdam* 2 c1
Steele Creek, *Melbourne* 17 A1
Steenokkerzeel, *Brussels* 6 A2
Steglitz, *Berlin* 5 B2
Stepaside, *Dublin* 11 B2
Stephansdom, *Vienna* 31 b2
Stepney, *London* 15 A3
Sterling Park, *San Francisco* 25 B2
Sticklinge udde, *Stockholm* 28 A2
Stickney, *Chicago* 9 C2
Stillorgan, *Dublin* 11 B2
Stockholm, *Stockholm* 28 B2
Stocksund, *Stockholm* 28 A2
Stodůlky, *Prague* 24 B1
Stoke Newington, *London* 15 A3
Stokes Valley, *Wellington* 32 B2
Stone Canyon Res., *Los Angeles* 16 B2
Stone Park, *Chicago* 9 B1
Stonebridge, *London* 15 A2
Stoneham, *Boston* 6 A3
Stony Brook Res., *Boston* 6 B3
Stora Värtan, *Stockholm* 28 A2
Store Hareskov, *Copenhagen* 10 A2
Store Magleby, *Copenhagen* 10 B3
Storholmen, *Stockholm* 28 A2
Stoyka, *St. Petersburg* 26 B2
Straiton, *Edinburgh* 11 B3
Strand, *London* 15 b4
Strandfontein, *Cape Town* 8 B2
Strašnice, *Prague* 24 B2
Strasstrudering, *Munich* 20 B3
Stratford, *London* 15 A4
Strathfield, *Sydney* 28 B1
Streatham, *London* 15 B3
Streatham Vale, *London* 15 B3
Strebersdorf, *Vienna* 31 A2
Střešovice, *Prague* 24 B2
Střížkov, *Prague* 24 B2
Strogino, *Moscow* 19 B2
Strombeek-Bever, *Brussels* 6 A2
Stromovka, *Prague* 24 B2
Studio City, *Los Angeles* 16 B2
Stureby, *Stockholm* 28 B2
Stuvsta, *Stockholm* 28 B2
Subhepur, *Delhi* 10 A2
Sucat, *Manila* 17 C2
Suchdol, *Prague* 24 B2
Sucy-en-Brie, *Paris* 23 B4
Sudbury, *Boston* 6 A1
Sugamo, *Tokyo* 29 A3
Sugar Loaf Mt. = Açúcar, Pão de, *Rio de Janeiro* 24 B2
Suge, *Tokyo* 29 B2
Suginami-Ku, *Tokyo* 29 A2
Sugō, *Tokyo* 29 B2
Suita, *Osaka* 22 A4
Suitland, *Washington* 32 B4
Sukchar, *Calcutta* 8 A2
Suma, *Osaka* 22 B1
Sumida →, *Tokyo* 29 A3
Sumida-Ku, *Tokyo* 29 A3
Sumiyoshi, *Osaka* 22 B4
Summerville, *Toronto* 30 B1
Summit, *Chicago* 9 C2
Sunamachi, *Tokyo* 29 A4
Sunbury-on-Thames, *London* 15 B1
Sundbyberg, *Stockholm* 28 A1
Sundbyerne, *Copenhagen* 10 B3
Sung Kong, *Hong Kong* 12 B2
Sungei Kadut Industrial Estate, *Singapore* 27 A2
Sungei Selatar Res., *Singapore* 27 A3
Sunter, *Jakarta* 13 A2
Sunter, Kali →, *Jakarta* 13 B2
Suomenlinna, *Helsinki* 12 C2
Supreme Court, *Washington* 32 b3
Sura, *Calcutta* 8 B2
Surag-san, *Seoul* 26 A2
Surbiton, *London* 15 B2
Suresnes, *Paris* 23 A2
Surfside, *Miami* 18 A2
Surquillo, *Lima* 16 B2
Surrey Hills, *Sydney* 28 B2
Susaek, *Seoul* 26 B1
Süssenbrunn, *Vienna* 31 A2
Sutton, *Dublin* 11 A3
Sutton, *London* 15 B2
Suyu, *Seoul* 26 B2
Suzukishinden, *Tokyo* 29 A2
Svanemøllen, *Copenhagen* 10 A3
Sverdlov, *Moscow* 19 B3
Svestad, *Oslo* 22 B2
Svinö, *Helsinki* 12 C1
Swampscott, *Boston* 6 A4
Swanley, *London* 15 B4
Swansea, *Toronto* 30 B2
Swinburne I., *New York* 21 C1
Swords, *Dublin* 11 A2
Sydenham, *Johannesburg* 13 A2
Sydney, *Sydney* 28 B2
Sydney, Univ. of, *Sydney* 28 B2
Sydney Airport, *Sydney* 28 B2
Sydney Harbour Bridge, *Sydney* 28 B2
Sydstranden, *Copenhagen* 10 B3
Sylvania, *Sydney* 28 C1
Syntagma, Pl., *Athens* 2 b3
Syon Park, *London* 15 B2
Szczęśliwice, *Warsaw* 31 B1
Széchnenyi-hegy, *Budapest* 7 B1
Szent Istvánbaz, *Budapest* 7 b2
Széphalom, *Budapest* 7 A1

T

Tabata, *Tokyo* 29 A3
Tablada, *Buenos Aires* 7 C1
Table Bay, *Cape Town* 8 A1
Table Mountain, *Cape Town* 8 A1
Taboão da Serra, *São Paulo* 26 B1
Täby, *Stockholm* 28 A2
Tacuba, *Mexico City* 18 B1
Tacubaya, *Mexico City* 18 B1
Taebang, *Seoul* 26 B1
Tagig, *Manila* 17 B2
Tagig →, *Manila* 17 B2
Tai Hang, *Hong Kong* 12 B2
Tai Lo Shan, *Hong Kong* 12 A2

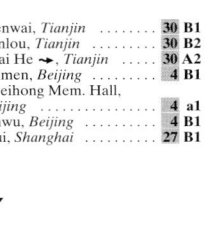
Tai Po Tsai, *Hong Kong* — 12 A2
Tai Seng, *Singapore* — 27 A3
Tai Shui Hang, *Hong Kong* — 12 A2
Tai Tam B., *Hong Kong* — 12 B2
Tai Tam Tuk Res., *Hong Kong* — 12 B2
Tai Wai, *Hong Kong* — 12 A1
Tai Wan Tau, *Hong Kong* — 12 A1
Tai Wo Hau, *Hong Kong* — 12 A1
Tainaka, *Osaka* — 22 B4
Taishō, *Osaka* — 22 A4
Taita, *Wellington* — 32 B2
Tajrīsh, *Tehran* — 30 A2
Takaido, *Tokyo* — 29 A2
Takaishi, *Tokyo* — 29 B2
Takarazuka, *Osaka* — 22 A2
Takasago, *Tokyo* — 29 A4
Takasu-Ku, *Tokyo* — 29 B2
Takeshita, *Tokyo* — 29 B2
Takinegawa, *Tokyo* — 29 A2
Takoma Park, *Washington* — 32 B3
Taksim, *Istanbul* — 12 B2
Talaide, *Lisbon* — 14 A1
Taliganga, *Calcutta* — 8 B2
Talipapa, *Manila* — 17 A2
Tallaght, *Dublin* — 11 B1
Tallkrogen, *Stockholm* — 28 B2
Tama, *Tokyo* — 29 B2
Tama ➡, *Tokyo* — 29 B2
Tama Kyūryō, *Tokyo* — 29 B2
Tamaden, *Tokyo* — 29 B2
Tamagawa-josui ➡, *Tokyo* — 29 A1
Taman Sari, *Jakarta* — 13 A1
Tamanduateí ➡, *São Paulo* — 26 B2
Tamboerskloof, *Cape Town* — 8 A1
Tambora, *Jakarta* — 13 A1
Tammisalo, *Helsinki* — 12 B3
Tammūh, *Cairo* — 7 B2
Tampines, *Singapore* — 27 A3
Tanah Abang, *Jakarta* — 13 B1
Tanigami, *Osaka* — 22 A2
Tanjung Duren, *Jakarta* — 13 B1
Tanjung Priok, *Jakarta* — 13 A2
Tanum, *Oslo* — 22 A1
Taoranting Park, *Beijing* — 4 c2
Tapada, *Lisbon* — 14 A1
Tapanila, *Helsinki* — 12 B3
Tapiales, *Buenos Aires* — 7 C1
Tapiola, *Helsinki* — 12 A1
Tapsia, *Calcutta* — 8 B2
Tara, *Mumbai* — 20 A1
Tarabya, *Istanbul* — 12 B2
Tarango, Presa, *Mexico City* — 18 B1
Tårbæk, *Copenhagen* — 10 A3
Tarchomin, *Warsaw* — 31 B1
Tardeo, *Mumbai* — 20 B1
Targówek, *Warsaw* — 31 B2
Tårnby, *Copenhagen* — 10 B3
Tarqua Bay, *Lagos* — 14 B2
Tåstrup, *Copenhagen* — 10 B1
Tatarovo, *Moscow* — 19 B2
Tathong Channel, *Hong Kong* — 12 B2
Tathong Pt., *Hong Kong* — 12 B2
Tatuapé, *São Paulo* — 26 B2
Taufkirchen, *Munich* — 20 B2
Tavares, I. dos, *Rio de Janeiro* — 24 A2
Távros, *Athens* — 2 B1
Tawa, *Wellington* — 32 A1
Teaneck, *New York* — 21 A1
Teatro Municipal, *Rio de Janeiro* — 24 c2
Tebet, *Jakarta* — 13 B2
Tecamachaleo, *Mexico City* — 18 B1
Teddington, *London* — 15 B1
Tegel, *Berlin* — 5 A2
Tegel, Flughafen, *Berlin* — 5 A2
Tegeler See, *Berlin* — 5 A2
Tegelort, *Berlin* — 5 A2
Tehrān, *Tehran* — 30 A2
Tehrān Pārs, *Tehran* — 30 A3
Tei Tong Tsui, *Hong Kong* — 12 B2
Tejo, Rio ➡, *Lisbon* — 14 A2
Tekstilyshchik, *Moscow* — 19 B4
Telegraph hill, *San Francisco* — 25 a2
Telhal, *Lisbon* — 14 A1
Telok Blangah, *Singapore* — 27 B2
Teltow, *Berlin* — 5 B2
Telow kanal, *Berlin* — 5 B2
Temnikovo, *Moscow* — 19 B6
Tempelhof, *Berlin* — 5 B3
Tempelhof, Flughafen, *Berlin* — 5 B3
Temple City, *Los Angeles* — 16 B4
Temple Hills Park, *Washington* — 32 C4
Temple Mount, *Jerusalem* — 13 b3
Templeogue, *Dublin* — 11 B2
Templo Mayor, *Mexico City* — 18 B2
Tenafly, *New York* — 21 A2
Tenayuca, Piramide de, *Mexico City* — 18 A1
Tengah ➡, *Singapore* — 27 A2
Tennoji, *Osaka* — 22 B4
Tepalcates, *Mexico City* — 18 B2
Terrazzano, *Milan* — 18 A1
Terrugem, *Lisbon* — 14 A1
Tervuren, *Brussels* — 6 B3
Tervuren, Park van, *Brussels* — 6 B3
Tetuán, *Madrid* — 17 B1
Teufelsberg, *Berlin* — 5 B2
Tévere ➡, *Rome* — 25 B2
Thalkirchen, *Munich* — 20 B2
Thames ➡, *London* — 15 A4
Thames Ditton, *London* — 15 B1
Thamesmead, *London* — 15 A4
Thana Cr. ➡, *Mumbai* — 20 A2
The Loop, *Chicago* — 9 B3
The Ridge, *Delhi* — 10 B2
The Wilds, *Johannesburg* — 13 B2
Theater Carré, *Amsterdam* — 2 b2
Théatro Dionissou, *Athens* — 2 c1
Thiais, *Paris* — 23 B3
Thissio, *Athens* — 2 c1
Thistletown, *Toronto* — 30 A1
Thomastown, *Melbourne* — 17 A2
Thompson I., *Boston* — 6 B4
Thon Buri, *Bangkok* — 3 B1
Thornbury, *Melbourne* — 17 A2
Thorncliffe, *Toronto* — 30 A2
Thornhill, *Toronto* — 30 A2
Thornton, *Cape Town* — 8 A2
Thornton Heath, *London* — 15 B3
Threipmuir Res., *Edinburgh* — 11 B2
Throgs Neck, *New York* — 21 B3
Thyssen Bornemisza, Museo, *Madrid* — 17 b3
Tian'anmen Square, *Beijing* — 4 B2
Tiancun, *Beijing* — 4 B1
Tianjin, *Tianjin* — 30 B1
Tiantan Park, *Beijing* — 4 c3
Tibidabo, *Barcelona* — 4 A1
Tibradden Mt., *Dublin* — 11 B2
Tiburon, *San Francisco* — 25 A2
Tiburtino, *Rome* — 25 B2
Ticomán, *Mexico City* — 18 A2
Tiefersee, *Berlin* — 5 B1
Tiejiangyin, *Beijing* — 4 C2
Tientsin = Tianjin, *Tianjin* — 30 B1

Tiergarten, *Berlin* — 5 A3
Tietê ➡, *São Paulo* — 26 B2
Tigerhof, *Cape Town* — 8 A2
Tigris = Nahr Dijlah ➡, *Baghdad* — 3 B2
Tijuca, *Rio de Janeiro* — 24 B1
Tijuca, Parque Nacional da, *Rio de Janeiro* — 24 B1
Tijuca, Pico da, *Rio de Janeiro* — 24 B1
Tikkurila, *Helsinki* — 12 B3
Tilak Nagar, *Delhi* — 10 B1
Tilanqiao, *Shanghai* — 27 B1
Timah, Bukit, *Singapore* — 27 A2
Times Square, *New York* — 21 c2
Timiryazev Park, *Moscow* — 19 B3
Ting Kau, *Hong Kong* — 12 A1
Tira, *Jerusalem* — 13 A1
Tirsa, *Cairo* — 7 B2
Tishriyaa, *Baghdad* — 3 A2
Tiu Keng Leng, *Hong Kong* — 12 B2
Tivoli, *Copenhagen* — 10 a3
Tizapán, *Mexico City* — 18 C1
Tlalnepantla ➡, *Mexico City* — 18 A1
To Kwai Wan, *Hong Kong* — 12 B2
Toa Payoh, *Singapore* — 27 A3
Tobong, *Seoul* — 26 A2
Tobong-san, *Seoul* — 26 A2
Tocná, *Prague* — 24 C2
Toco Hills, *Atlanta* — 3 B2
Todt Hill, *New York* — 21 C1
Tōkagi, *Tokyo* — 29 A4
Tokai Plantation, *Cape Town* — 8 B1
Tōkaichiba, *Tokyo* — 29 B2
Tokarevo, *Moscow* — 19 C5
Tōkyō, *Tokyo* — 29 A3
Tokyo B., *Tokyo* — 29 B4
Tokyo-Haneda Int. Airport, *Tokyo* — 29 B3
Tokyo Harbour, *Tokyo* — 29 B3
Tolka R. ➡, *Dublin* — 11 A1
Tolworth, *London* — 15 B2
Tomb of Lu Xun, *Shanghai* — 27 B1
Tomb of the Kings, *Jerusalem* — 13 a2
Tomba di Nerone, *Rome* — 25 B1
Tomelino, *Moscow* — 19 C5
Tondo, *Manila* — 17 B1
Tongbingao, *Seoul* — 26 B1
Tongjak, *Seoul* — 26 B1
Tongmaemung, *Seoul* — 26 B2
Tongqiao, *Shanghai* — 27 A1
Toorak, *Melbourne* — 17 B2
Topkapı, *Istanbul* — 12 B1
Tor di Quinto, *Rome* — 25 B1
Tor Pignattara, *Rome* — 25 B2
Tor Sapienza, *Rome* — 25 B2
Toranomon, *Tokyo* — 29 c3
Torcy, *Paris* — 23 B4
Toronto, *Toronto* — 30 B3
Toronto, Univ. of, *Toronto* — 30 B2
Toronto Harbour, *Toronto* — 30 B2
Toronto I., *Toronto* — 30 B2
Toronto Int. Airport, *Toronto* — 30 A1
Toros Las Arenas, Pl. de, *Barcelona* — 4 c1
Toros Monumental, Templo de, *Barcelona* — 4 a3
Torre Latino-americana, *Mexico City* — 18 b2
Torre Lupara, *Rome* — 25 B2
Torre Nova, *Rome* — 25 B2
Torrelles ➡, *Barcelona* — 4 A1
Torrevécchia, *Rome* — 25 B1
Toshima-Ku, *Tokyo* — 29 A3
Toshimaen, *Tokyo* — 29 A2
Tottenham, *London* — 15 A3
Tottenham, *Melbourne* — 17 A1
Tour Eiffel, *Paris* — 23 b2
Toussus-le-Noble, *Paris* — 23 B1
Toussus-le-Noble, Aérodrome de, *Paris* — 23 B1
Tower Bridge, *London* — 15 b5
Tower Hamlets, *London* — 15 A3
Tower of London, *London* — 15 A3
Towra Pt., *Sydney* — 28 C2
Tøyen, *Oslo* — 22 A3
Toyonaka, *Osaka* — 22 A3
Trafalgar Square, *London* — 15 b3
Trafaria, *Lisbon* — 14 A1
Traição, Cor. ➡, *São Paulo* — 26 B2
Traneplade, *Copenhagen* — 10 B2
Trångsund, *Stockholm* — 28 B2
Transamerica Pyramid, *San Francisco* — 25 b2
Transbay Terminal, *San Francisco* — 25 b3
Trappenfelde, *Berlin* — 5 A4
Trastévere, *Rome* — 25 B1
Treasure I., *San Francisco* — 25 B2
Treboradice, *Prague* — 24 A3
Trebotov, *Prague* — 24 C1
Tremblay-en-France, *Paris* — 23 A4
Tremembe ➡, *São Paulo* — 26 A2
Tremont, *New York* — 21 A2
Trenno, *Milan* — 18 B1
Treptow, *Berlin* — 5 B3
Trés Rios, Sa. dos, *Rio de Janeiro* — 24 B1
Trevi, Fontana di, *Rome* — 25 b3
Trezzano sul Navíglio, *Milan* — 18 B1
Tribune Tower, *Chicago* — 9 b2
Trieste, *Rome* — 25 B2
Trinidad, *Washington* — 32 B4
Trinity, *Edinburgh* — 11 B2
Trinity College, *Dublin* — 11 c3
Trionfale, *Rome* — 25 B1
Triulzo, *Milan* — 18 B2
Trocadero, *Paris* — 23 b1
Troitse-Lykovo, *Moscow* — 19 B2
Troja, *Prague* — 24 B2
Trollbäcken, *Stockholm* — 28 B2
Trombay, *Mumbai* — 20 A2
Troparevo, *Moscow* — 19 C2
Tropenmuseum, *Amsterdam* — 2 b3
Trudyashchikhsya, Ostrov, *St. Petersburg* — 26 B1
Tryvasshøgda, *Oslo* — 22 A3
Tseng Lan Shue, *Hong Kong* — 12 A2
Tsim Sha Tsui, *Hong Kong* — 12 a2
Tsing Yi, *Hong Kong* — 12 A1
Tsova, *Jerusalem* — 13 B1
Tsuen Wan, *Hong Kong* — 12 A1
Tsukiji, *Tokyo* — 29 c5
Tsur Hadassa, *Jerusalem* — 13 B1
Tsurumi ➡, *Tokyo* — 29 B3
Tsz Wan Shan, *Hong Kong* — 12 A2
Tuas, *Singapore* — 27 B1
Tuchoměřice, *Prague* — 24 B1
Tuckahoe, *New York* — 21 A3
Tucuruví, *São Paulo* — 26 A2
Tufello, *Rome* — 25 B2
Tufnell Park, *London* — 15 A3
Tughlakabad, *Delhi* — 10 B2
Tuileries, Jardin des, *Paris* — 23 b3
Tuindorp Oostzaan, *Amsterdam* — 2 A2
Tullamarine, *Melbourne* — 17 A1
Tulse Hill, *London* — 15 B3

Tung Lung I., *Hong Kong* — 12 B2
Tung O, *Hong Kong* — 12 B1
Tunis, *Baghdad* — 3 A2
Tuomarila, *Helsinki* — 12 B1
Tureberg, *Stockholm* — 28 A1
Turffontein, *Johannesburg* — 13 B2
Turkso, *Prague* — 24 A1
Turnham Green, *London* — 15 B2
Turnhouse, *Edinburgh* — 11 B1
Tuscolana, Via, *Rome* — 25 B2
Tushino, *Moscow* — 19 B3
Twelve Apostles, *Cape Town* — 8 A1
Twickenham, *London* — 15 B1
Twickenham Rugby Ground, *London* — 15 B1
Twin Peaks, *San Francisco* — 25 B2
Two Rock Mt., *Dublin* — 11 B2
Tymon North, *Dublin* — 11 B1
Tysons Corner, *Washington* — 32 B2

U

U.S. Capitol, *Washington* — 32 b3
Ubeidiya, *Jerusalem* — 13 B2
Uberaba ➡, *São Paulo* — 26 B2
Ubin, P., *Singapore* — 27 A3
Uccle, *Brussels* — 6 B2
Udelnaya, *St. Petersburg* — 26 B2
Udelnoe, *St. Petersburg* — 26 B3
Udling, *Munich* — 20 A1
Ueno, *Tokyo* — 29 A3
Ūholičky, *Prague* — 24 B1
Uhříněves, *Prague* — 24 B3
Uithoorn, *Amsterdam* — 2 B1
Ujpalota, *Budapest* — 7 A2
Újpest, *Budapest* — 7 A2
Ukita, *Tokyo* — 29 A4
Ullerup, *Copenhagen* — 10 B3
Ullevål, *Oslo* — 22 A3
Ulriksdal, *Stockholm* — 28 A1
Ulyanka, *St. Petersburg* — 26 B1
Um Al-Khanazir Island, *Baghdad* — 3 B2
Umeda, *Osaka* — 22 A3
Umerkhadi, *Mumbai* — 20 B2
Umraniye, *Istanbul* — 12 B2
Underground Atlanta, *Atlanta* — 3 B2
Uněticky potok ➡, *Prague* — 24 B1
Ŭngam, *Seoul* — 26 B1
Unhos, *Lisbon* — 14 A2
Unidad Santa Fe, *Mexico City* — 18 B1
Union City, *New York* — 21 B1
Union Port, *New York* — 21 B2
Union Square, *New York* — 21 d2
Union Square, *San Francisco* — 25 b2
Union Station, *Washington* — 32 b3
United Nations H.Q., *New York* — 21 c3
Universidad, *Madrid* — 17 B1
Universidad de Chile, *Santiago* — 26 B2
University Park, *Washington* — 32 B4
Un'p'yong, *Seoul* — 26 a1
Unter den Linden, *Berlin* — 5 a4
Unterberg, *Munich* — 20 B2
Unterföhring, *Munich* — 20 A3
Unterhaching, *Munich* — 20 B2
Unterlaa, *Vienna* — 31 B2
Untermenzing, *Munich* — 20 A1
Upper East Side, *New York* — 21 b3
Upper Elmers End, *London* — 15 B3
Upper New York B., *New York* — 21 C1
Upper Norwood, *London* — 15 B3
Upper Peirce Res., *Singapore* — 27 A2
Upper Sydenham, *London* — 15 B3
Upper Tooting, *London* — 15 B3
Upper West Side, *New York* — 21 a2
Upton, *London* — 15 A4
Uptown, *Chicago* — 9 B2
Uran, *Mumbai* — 20 B2
Urayasu, *Tokyo* — 29 B4
Urbe, Aeroporto d', *Rome* — 25 B2
Uritsk, *St. Petersburg* — 26 C1
Ŭroŭm, *Budapest* — 7 A2
Ursus, *Warsaw* — 31 B1
Ursvik, *Stockholm* — 28 A1
Usera, *Madrid* — 17 B1
Ushigome, *Tokyo* — 29 A3
Usina, *Rio de Janeiro* — 24 B1
Ŭsküdar, *Istanbul* — 12 B2
Ust-Slavyanka, *St. Petersburg* — 26 C3
Uteke, *Stockholm* — 28 A3
Utrata, *Warsaw* — 31 B2
Uttarpara, *Calcutta* — 8 A1
Utterslev Mose, *Copenhagen* — 10 A2

V

Vadaul, *Mumbai* — 20 A2
Vaires-sur-Marne, *Paris* — 23 A4
Valby, *Copenhagen* — 10 B2
Valcannuta, *Rome* — 25 B1
Valdelatas, *Madrid* — 17 A1
Vale, *Washington* — 32 B2
Valenton, *Paris* — 23 B3
Valera, *Milan* — 18 A1
Vallcarca, *Barcelona* — 4 A1
Valldoreix, *Barcelona* — 4 A1
Vallecas, *Madrid* — 17 B2
Vallensbæk, *Copenhagen* — 10 B2
Vallensbæk Strand, *Copenhagen* — 10 B2
Vallentunasjön, *Stockholm* — 28 A2
Valleranello, *Rome* — 25 C2
Vallisaari, *Helsinki* — 12 C3
Vallvidrera, *Barcelona* — 4 A1
Vallvidrera ➡, *Barcelona* — 4 A1
Van Goghmuseum, *Amsterdam* — 2 c1
Vanak, *Tehran* — 30 A2
Vangede, *Copenhagen* — 10 A3
Vanikøy, *Istanbul* — 12 B2
Vankøse, *Copenhagen* — 10 A2
Vantaa, *Helsinki* — 12 B2
Vantaa ➡, *Helsinki* — 12 B2
Vantaankoski, *Helsinki* — 12 B2
Vantaanpuisto, *Helsinki* — 12 B2
Vanves, *Paris* — 23 B2
Varedo, *Milan* — 18 A1
Varkiza, *Athens* — 2 C2
Varsinnház, *Budapest* — 7 B2
Vartiokylä, *Helsinki* — 12 B3
Vartiosaari, *Helsinki* — 12 B3
Vasamuseet, *Stockholm* — 28 a3
Vasco, *Cape Town* — 8 A2
Vasfanārd, *Tehran* — 30 A2
Vashi, *Mumbai* — 20 A2

Vasilyevskiy, Ostrov, *St. Petersburg* — 26 B1
Vaso Regulador El Cristo, *Mexico City* — 18 B1
Vaucluse, *Sydney* — 28 B2
Vaucresson, *Paris* — 23 A1
Vauhallan, *Paris* — 23 B2
Vaujours, *Paris* — 23 A4
Vauxhall, *London* — 15 c4
Vecsés, *Budapest* — 7 B3
Veikkola, *Prague* — 24 A3
Veleslavin, *Prague* — 24 B2
Vélizy-Villacoublay, *Paris* — 23 B2
Velka-Chuchle, *Prague* — 24 B2
Velké Přílepy, *Prague* — 24 B1
Venda Seca, *Lisbon* — 14 A1
Venetian Islands, *Miami* — 18 B2
Venezia, Palazzo, *Rome* — 25 c2
Venice, *Los Angeles* — 16 C2
Ventas, *Madrid* — 17 B1
Ventorro del Cano, *Madrid* — 17 B1
Venustiano Carranza, *Mexico City* — 18 B2
Verde ➡, *São Paulo* — 26 A1
Verdi, *Athens* — 2 A2
Vérnheim, *Budapest* — 7 A2
Vermelho ➡, *São Paulo* — 26 B1
Vernon, *Los Angeles* — 16 B3
Verrières-le-Buisson, *Paris* — 23 B2
Versailles, *Buenos Aires* — 7 B1
Versailles, *Paris* — 23 B1
Veshnyaki, *Moscow* — 19 B4
Vesolyy Posolok, *St. Petersburg* — 26 B2
Vestra, *Helsinki* — 12 B2
Vestskoven, *Copenhagen* — 10 A2
Vicálvaro, *Madrid* — 17 B2
Vicente Lopez, *Buenos Aires* — 7 B2
Victoria, *Hong Kong* — 12 B2
Victoria, *London* — 15 c3
Victoria, Mt., *Wellington* — 32 B1
Victoria, Pont, *Montreal* — 19 B2
Victoria and Albert Waterfront, *Cape Town* — 8 a1
Victoria Gardens, *Mumbai* — 20 B2
Victoria Harbour, *Hong Kong* — 12 B1
Victoria Island, *Lagos* — 14 B2
Victoria L., *Johannesburg* — 13 B2
Victoria Lawn Tennis Courts, *Melbourne* — 17 B2
Victoria Park, *Singapore* — 27 B2
Victoria Peak, *Hong Kong* — 12 B1
Victoria Wharf, *Cape Town* — 8 a1
Vienna = Wien, *Vienna* — 31 A2
Vienna, *Washington* — 32 B2
View Park, *Los Angeles* — 16 C3
Vigário Geral, *Rio de Janeiro* — 24 A1
Vigentino, *Milan* — 18 B2
Viggbyholm, *Stockholm* — 28 A2
Vighignolo, *Milan* — 18 B1
Viikki, *Helsinki* — 12 B3
Vikhroli, *Mumbai* — 20 A2
Vila Guilherme, *São Paulo* — 26 B2
Vila Isabel, *Rio de Janeiro* — 24 B1
Vila Jaguara, *São Paulo* — 26 B1
Vila Madalena, *São Paulo* — 26 B1
Vila Maria, *São Paulo* — 26 B2
Vila Mariana, *São Paulo* — 26 B2
Vila Prudente, *São Paulo* — 26 B2
Viladecans, *Barcelona* — 4 B1
Vile Parle, *Mumbai* — 20 A2
Villa Adelina, *Buenos Aires* — 7 B1
Villa Ballester, *Buenos Aires* — 7 B1
Villa Barilari, *Buenos Aires* — 7 C2
Villa Borghese, *Rome* — 25 a3
Villa Bosch, *Buenos Aires* — 7 B1
Villa C. Colon, *Buenos Aires* — 7 C2
Villa Ciudadela, *Buenos Aires* — 7 B1
Villa de Guadalupe, *Mexico City* — 18 B2
Villa Devoto, *Buenos Aires* — 7 B1
Villa Diamante, *Buenos Aires* — 7 C2
Villa Dominico, *Buenos Aires* — 7 C3
Villa Lugano, *Buenos Aires* — 7 C2
Villa Lynch, *Buenos Aires* — 7 B1
Villa Madero, *Buenos Aires* — 7 C1
Villa Sáenz Pena, *Buenos Aires* — 7 B1
Villa Urquiza, *Buenos Aires* — 7 B1
Villaverde, *Madrid* — 17 B1
Villaverde Bajo, *Madrid* — 17 B1
Ville-d'Avray, *Paris* — 23 B1
Villecresnes, *Paris* — 23 B4
Villejuif, *Paris* — 23 B3
Villemomble, *Paris* — 23 A4
Villeneuve-la-Garenne, *Paris* — 23 A3
Villeneuve-le-Roi, *Paris* — 23 B3
Villeneuve-St.-Georges, *Paris* — 23 B4
Villeparisis, *Paris* — 23 A4
Villevaudé, *Paris* — 23 A4
Villiers-le-Bâcle, *Paris* — 23 B1
Villiers-sur-Marne, *Paris* — 23 B4
Villnki, *Helsinki* — 12 C3
Villoresi, Canale, *Milan* — 18 A1
Vilvoorde, *Brussels* — 6 A2
Vimodrone, *Milan* — 18 A2
Vimont, *Montreal* — 19 A1
Vinanmek Palace, *Bangkok* — 3 a2
Vincennes, *Paris* — 23 A3
Vincennes, Bois de, *Paris* — 23 A3
Vinings, *Atlanta* — 3 A2
Vinohrady, *Prague* — 24 B2
Vinoř, *Prague* — 24 B3
Violet Hill, *Hong Kong* — 12 B2
Irányos, *Budapest* — 7 A1
Virgen del San Cristóbal, *Santiago* — 26 B2
Virginia Gardens, *Miami* — 18 B1
Virginia Key, *Miami* — 18 B2
Viroflay, *Paris* — 23 B1
Víron, *Athens* — 2 B2
Virum, *Copenhagen* — 10 A2
Visão, *Moscow* — 19 B5
Visitacion Valley, *San Francisco* — 25 B2
Vista Alegre, *Lima* — 16 B3
Vista Alegre, *Santiago* — 26 C1
Vista Grove, *Atlanta* — 3 A3
Vitacura, *Santiago* — 26 B2
Vitinia, *Rome* — 25 C1
Vitry-sur-Seine, *Paris* — 23 B3
Vizandinó, Mussió, *Athens* — 2 A3
Vladykino, *Moscow* — 19 A3
Vlezenbeek, *Brussels* — 6 B1
Vltava ➡, *Prague* — 24 B2
Vnukovo, *Moscow* — 19 C1
Vösendorf, *Vienna* — 31 B2
Volgelsdorf, *Berlin* — 5 B5
Volhonka-Zil, *Moscow* — 19 C3
Vollen, *Oslo* — 22 B1
Volodarskoye, *St. Petersburg* — 26 B3
Volynkina-Derevnya, *St. Petersburg* — 26 B1
Voula, *Athens* — 2 C2

Vouliagmeni, *Athens* — 2 C2
Vredehoek, *Cape Town* — 8 A1
Vršovice, *Prague* — 24 B2
Vyborgskaya Storona, *St. Petersburg* — 26 B2
Vykhino, *Moscow* — 19 B4
Vyšehrad, *Prague* — 24 B2

W

Wachterhof, *Munich* — 20 B3
Wadala, *Mumbai* — 20 A2
Wadestown, *Wellington* — 32 B1
Wadi Fukin, *Jerusalem* — 13 B1
Wah Fu, *Hong Kong* — 12 B1
Wahda, *Baghdad* — 3 B2
Währing, *Vienna* — 31 A2
Waidmannslust, *Berlin* — 5 A3
Wainuiomata, *Wellington* — 32 B2
Wainuiomata R. ➡, *Wellington* — 32 B2
Wakefield, *Boston* — 6 A3
Waldesruh, *Berlin* — 5 B4
Waldperlach, *Munich* — 20 B3
Waldtrudering, *Munich* — 20 B3
Walkinstown, *Dublin* — 11 B1
Wall Street, *New York* — 21 f1
Waltham, *Boston* — 6 A2
Waltham Forest, *London* — 15 A3
Walthamstow, *London* — 15 A3
Walton on Thames, *London* — 15 B1
Wambeck, *Brussels* — 6 A1
Wan Chai, *Hong Kong* — 12 B2
Wan Chai Lanes, *Hong Kong* — 12 c2
Wandsworth, *London* — 15 B2
Wankhede Stadium, *Mumbai* — 20 a2
Wannsee, *Berlin* — 5 B1
Wansdorf, *Berlin* — 5 A1
Wanstead, *London* — 15 A4
Wapping, *London* — 15 A3
Ward, *Dublin* — 11 A1
Ward I., *Wellington* — 32 B2
Warmberg, *Munich* — 20 B2
Warrāq el 'Arab, *Cairo* — 7 A2
Warrāq el Hadr, *Cairo* — 7 A2
Warringen Park, *Melbourne* — 17 A2
Warriston, *Edinburgh* — 11 B2
Warsaw = Warszawa, *Warsaw* — 31 B2
Warszawa, *Warsaw* — 31 B2
Wartenberg, *Berlin* — 5 A4
Washington, *Washington* — 32 B3
Washington Heights, *New York* — 21 A2
Washington Monument, *Washington* — 32 b1
Washington Nat. Airport, *Washington* — 32 B3
Washington Park, *Chicago* — 9 C3
Wat Arun, *Bangkok* — 3 b1
Wat Pho, *Bangkok* — 3 b1
Wat Phra Keo, *Bangkok* — 3 b1
Wat Traimit, *Bangkok* — 3 b2
Water of Leith, *Edinburgh* — 11 B1
Water Tower Place, *Chicago* — 9 a2
Watergraafsmeer, *Amsterdam* — 2 A2
Waterland, *Amsterdam* — 2 A2
Waterloo, *Brussels* — 6 B2
Waterloo, *Wellington* — 32 B2
Waterloo International, *London* — 15 b4
Watermael-Boitsfort, *Brussels* — 6 B2
Watertown, *Boston* — 6 A3
Watsonia, *Melbourne* — 17 A2
Waverley, *Boston* — 6 A2
Waverley, *Johannesburg* — 13 A2
Waverley, *Sydney* — 28 B2
Waverley Station, *Edinburgh* — 11 b3
Wawer, *Warsaw* — 31 B2
Wawrzyszew, *Warsaw* — 31 B1
Wayland, *Boston* — 6 A1
Wazirabad, *Delhi* — 10 A2
Wazīrīya, *Baghdad* — 3 A2
Wazirpur, *Delhi* — 10 A2
Wealdstone, *London* — 15 A1
Wedding, *Berlin* — 5 A3
Weehawken, *New York* — 21 B1
Weesp, *Amsterdam* — 2 B3
Weidling, *Vienna* — 31 A1
Weidlingbach, *Vienna* — 31 A1
Weigongcun, *Beijing* — 4 B1
Weijin He ➡, *Tianjin* — 30 B2
Weissensee, *Berlin* — 5 A3
Wellesley, *Boston* — 6 B2
Wellesley Falls, *Boston* — 6 B2
Wellesley Hills, *Boston* — 6 B2
Welling, *London* — 15 B4
Wellington, *Wellington* — 32 B1
Wells Fargo Center, *Los Angeles* — 16 b1
Weltevreden Park, *Johannesburg* — 13 A1
Wembley, *London* — 15 A2
Wemmel, *Brussels* — 6 A1
Wemmer Pan, *Johannesburg* — 13 B2
Wenceslas Square, *Prague* — 24 b2
Wendenschloss, *Berlin* — 5 B4
Wenhuagong, *Tianjin* — 30 B2
Wennington, *London* — 15 A5
Werneuchen, *Berlin* — 5 A5
West Bedford, *Boston* — 6 A1
West Don ➡, *Toronto* — 30 A2
West Drayton, *London* — 15 A1
West Ham, *London* — 15 A4
West Harrow, *London* — 15 A1
West Heath, *London* — 15 B4
West Hill, *Toronto* — 30 A3
West Hollywood, *Los Angeles* — 16 B2
West Kensington, *London* — 15 c1
West Kilburn, *London* — 15 a1
West Lamma Channel, *Hong Kong* — 12 B1
West Lynn, *Boston* — 6 A4
West Medford, *Boston* — 6 A3
West Miami, *Miami* — 18 B1
West Molesey, *London* — 15 B1
West New York, *New York* — 21 B1
West of Twin Peaks, *San Francisco* — 25 B2
West Park, *Johannesburg* — 13 A1
West Rouge, *Toronto* — 30 A4
West Roxbury, *Boston* — 6 B3
West Springfield, *Washington* — 32 C2
West Wharf, *Karachi* — 20 B1
Westbourne Green, *London* — 15 a1
Westchester, *Chicago* — 9 B1
Westchester, *Los Angeles* — 16 C2
Westcliff, *Johannesburg* — 13 B2
Westdene, *Johannesburg* — 13 B1

Westend, *Helsinki* — 12 C1
Wester Hailes, *Edinburgh* — 11 B2
Westerham, *Munich* — 20 B2
Western Addition, *San Francisco* — 25 B2
Western Wall, *Jerusalem* — 13 b3
Westgate, *Washington* — 32 B3
Westlake, *Cape Town* — 8 B1
Westlake, *San Francisco* — 25 B2
Westminster, *London* — 15 A3
Westmount, *Montreal* — 19 B2
Weston, *Boston* — 6 A2
Weston, *Toronto* — 30 A2
Weston Res., *Boston* — 6 A2
Westwood Village, *Los Angeles* — 16 B2
Westzaan, *Amsterdam* — 2 A1
Wetton, *Cape Town* — 8 B2
Wexford, *Toronto* — 30 A3
Weybridge, *London* — 15 B1
Wezembeek-Oppem, *Brussels* — 6 A2
White House, The, *Washington* — 32 b1
Whitechapel, *London* — 15 A3
Whitehall, *Dublin* — 11 A2
Whitehall, *London* — 15 b3
Whittier, *Los Angeles* — 16 C4
Whitton, *London* — 15 B1
Wieden, *Vienna* — 31 A2
Wien, *Vienna* — 31 A2
Wien-Schwechat, Flughafen, *Vienna* — 31 B3
Wienerberg, *Vienna* — 31 B2
Wierzbno, *Warsaw* — 31 B2
Wijde Wormer, *Amsterdam* — 2 A2
Wilanów, *Warsaw* — 31 B2
Wilanówka ➡, *Warsaw* — 31 C2
Wilhelmshagen, *Berlin* — 5 B5
Wilket Creek Park, *Toronto* — 30 A2
Wilkieston, *Edinburgh* — 11 B1
Willbrook, *Dublin* — 11 B2
Willesden, *London* — 15 A2
Willesden Green, *London* — 15 A2
Williamsbridge, *New York* — 21 B2
Williamstown, *Melbourne* — 17 B1
Willoughby, *Sydney* — 28 A2
Willow Springs, *Chicago* — 9 C1
Willowdale, *Toronto* — 30 A2
Wilmersdorf, *Berlin* — 5 c1
Wilmette, *Chicago* — 9 A2
Wilmington, *London* — 15 B5
Wilshire Boulevard, *Los Angeles* — 16 c1
Wimbledon, *London* — 15 B2
Wimbledon Common, *London* — 15 B2
Wimbledon Park, *London* — 15 B2
Wimbledon Tennis Ground, *London* — 15 B2
Winchester, *Boston* — 6 A3
Windermere, *Cape Town* — 8 A2
Windsor, *Johannesburg* — 13 A1
Windsor Hills, *Los Angeles* — 16 C2
Windy Arbour, *Dublin* — 11 B2
Winning, *Munich* — 20 B2
Winthrop, *Boston* — 6 A4
Wissous, *Paris* — 23 B2
Wittenau, *Berlin* — 5 A2
Witwatersrand, Univ. of, *Johannesburg* — 13 B2
Wlochy, *Warsaw* — 31 B1
Wo Mei, *Hong Kong* — 12 A2
Wo Yi Hop, *Hong Kong* — 12 A1
Woburn, *Boston* — 6 A3
Woburn, *Toronto* — 30 A3
Woduk Pluit, *Jakarta* — 13 A1
Wola, *Warsaw* — 31 B1
Wolf Trap Farm Park, *Washington* — 32 B2
Wolica, *Warsaw* — 31 C2
Wolica, *Warsaw* — 31 C1
Wólka Węglowa, *Warsaw* — 31 B1
Wollaston, *Boston* — 6 B3
Woltersdorf, *Berlin* — 5 B5
Woluwe-Saint-Lambert, *Brussels* — 6 A2
Woluwe-Saint-Pierre, *Brussels* — 6 A2
Wong Chuk Hang, *Hong Kong* — 12 B2
Wong Chuk Wan, *Hong Kong* — 12 A2
Wong Tai Sin, *Hong Kong* — 12 A2
Wood Green, *London* — 15 A3
Wood Ridge, *New York* — 21 A1
Woodbridge, *Toronto* — 30 A1
Woodford, *London* — 15 A4
Woodford Bridge, *London* — 15 A4
Woodford Green, *London* — 15 A4
Woodhouselee, *Edinburgh* — 11 B2
Woodlands New Town, *Singapore* — 27 A2
Woodmont, *Washington* — 32 B3
Woodside, *London* — 15 B3
Woodside, *New York* — 21 B2
Woodstock, *Cape Town* — 8 A1
Woollahra, *Sydney* — 28 B2
Woolloomooloo, *Sydney* — 28 B2
Woolooware B., *Sydney* — 28 C1
Woolwich, *London* — 15 A4
Woolworth Building, *New York* — 21 e1
World Trade Center, site of former, *New York* — 21 B1
Worli, *Mumbai* — 20 A1
Worth, *Chicago* — 9 C2
Wren's Nest, *Atlanta* — 3 B2
Wrigley Building, *Chicago* — 9 b2
Wuhlgarten, *Berlin* — 5 A5
Wujiaochang, *Shanghai* — 27 B1
Würm ➡, *Munich* — 20 A1
Würm-kanal, *Munich* — 20 A1
Wusong, *Shanghai* — 27 A2
Wyczółki, *Warsaw* — 31 C1
Wygoda, *Warsaw* — 31 B2
Wynberg, *Cape Town* — 8 B1

X

Xabregas, *Lisbon* — 14 A2
Xianggang = Hong Kong, *Hong Kong* — 12 B1
Xiaodian, *Tianjin* — 30 B2
Xiaogang Park, *Canton* — 8 B2
Xiaoping, *Canton* — 8 B1
Xiasha chong, *Canton* — 8 B1
Xichang, *Canton* — 8 B1
Xicheng, *Beijing* — 4 B1
Xidan, *Beijing* — 4 B2
Xigu Park, *Tianjin* — 30 A1
Xigucun, *Tianjin* — 30 A1

Ximenwai, *Tianjin* — 30 B1
Xinanlou, *Tianjin* — 30 B2
Xinkai He ➡, *Tianjin* — 30 A2
Xinjiekou, *Beijing* — 4 B1
Xu Beihong Mem. Hall, *Beijing* — 4 a1
Xuanwu, *Beijing* — 4 B1
Xuhui, *Shanghai* — 27 B1

Y

Yaba, *Lagos* — 14 A2
Yaftābād, *Tehran* — 30 B1
Yahara, *Tokyo* — 29 A2
Yaho, *Tokyo* — 29 A1
Yakire, *Tokyo* — 29 B2
Yamada, *Osaka* — 22 A4
Yamada, *Tokyo* — 29 B2
Yamamoto, *Osaka* — 22 B4
Yamato ➡, *Osaka* — 22 B4
Yamuna ➡, *Delhi* — 10 B2
Yan Kit, *Singapore* — 27 A3
Yanbu, *Canton* — 8 B2
Yangch'ŏn, *Seoul* — 26 B1
Yanghuayuan, *Beijing* — 4 C1
Yangjae, *Seoul* — 26 C2
Yangjiazhuang, *Shanghai* — 27 A1
Yangpu, *Shanghai* — 27 B2
Yangpu Park, *Shanghai* — 27 B2
Yao, *Osaka* — 22 B4
Yao Airport, *Osaka* — 22 B4
Yarmūk, *Baghdad* — 3 B1
Yarra ➡, *Melbourne* — 17 A1
Yarra Bend Park, *Melbourne* — 17 A1
Yarraville, *Melbourne* — 17 A1
Yau Tong, *Hong Kong* — 12 B2
Yauza ➡, *Moscow* — 19 A4
Yeading, *London* — 15 A1
Yedikule, *Istanbul* — 12 C1
Yemin Moshe, *Jerusalem* — 13 b2
Yenikapı, *Istanbul* — 12 C1
Yeniköy, *Istanbul* — 12 B2
Yerba Buena Gardens, *San Francisco* — 25 c2
Yerba Buena I., *San Francisco* — 25 B2
Yerres, *Paris* — 23 B4
Yerushalayim = Jerusalem, *Jerusalem* — 13 B2
Yiheyuan, *Beijing* — 4 A1
Yinhangzhen, *Shanghai* — 27 A2
Yishun New Town, *Singapore* — 27 A3
Yixingbu, *Tianjin* — 30 A2
Ylästö, *Helsinki* — 12 B2
Yodo ➡, *Osaka* — 22 A3
Yongdingmen, *Beijing* — 4 B2
Yōngdong, *Seoul* — 26 B2
Yŏngdŭngp'o, *Seoul* — 26 B1
Yongfucun, *Canton* — 8 B2
Yongjing, *Shanghai* — 27 B2
Yongsan, *Seoul* — 26 B1
Yonkers, *New York* — 21 A2
York, *Toronto* — 30 A2
York Mills, *Toronto* — 30 A2
Yotsuya, *Tokyo* — 29 a2
You'anmen, *Beijing* — 4 B1
Yōodo, *Seoul* — 26 B1
Youndsfield, *Cape Town* — 8 B1
Yuanxiatian, *Canton* — 8 B2
Yugo-Zarad, *Moscow* — 19 B3
Yung Shue Wan, *Hong Kong* — 12 B1
Yūsofābād, *Tehran* — 30 A2
Yuyuantan Park, *Beijing* — 4 b2

Z

Zaandam, *Amsterdam* — 2 A1
Zaandijk, *Amsterdam* — 2 A1
Zaanstad, *Amsterdam* — 2 A1
Zábĕhlice, *Prague* — 24 B2
Ząbki, *Warsaw* — 31 B2
Zacisze, *Warsaw* — 31 B2
Zahrā, *Baghdad* — 3 B2
Zalarkovo, *Moscow* — 19 B1
Zalov, *Prague* — 24 A2
Zaluski, *Warsaw* — 31 C1
Zamdorf, *Munich* — 20 B2
Zamek Królewski, *Warsaw* — 31 a2
Zamek Ujazdowski, *Warsaw* — 31 c3
Zanevka, *St. Petersburg* — 26 B3
Zapote, *Manila* — 17 C1
Záppeio, *Athens* — 2 B2
Zaventem, *Brussels* — 6 A2
Zawady, *Warsaw* — 31 B2
Zâwiyet Abū Musallam, *Cairo* — 7 B1
Zawrā' Park, *Baghdad* — 3 B2
Zbraslav, *Prague* — 24 C2
Zbuzany, *Prague* — 24 B1
Zdiby, *Prague* — 24 B2
Zeekoevlei, *Cape Town* — 8 B2
Zehlendorf, *Berlin* — 5 B2
Zenne ➡, *Brussels* — 6 A1
Zerań, *Warsaw* — 31 B1
Zerzeń, *Warsaw* — 31 B2
Zeytinburnu, *Istanbul* — 12 C1
Zhabei, *Shanghai* — 27 B1
Zhangguizhuang, *Tianjin* — 30 B3
Zhdanov, *Moscow* — 19 B4
Zheleznodorozhnyy, *Moscow* — 19 B6
Zhenru, *Shanghai* — 27 B1
Zhernovka, *St. Petersburg* — 26 B2
Zhicun, *Canton* — 8 B1
Zhongshan Park, *Beijing* — 4 b2
Zhongshan Park, *Shanghai* — 27 B1
Zhoucun, *Canton* — 8 A2
Zhoujiadu, *Shanghai* — 27 B2
Zhoujiazhen, *Shanghai* — 27 A1
Zhu Jiang ➡, *Canton* — 8 B2
Zhulebino, *Moscow* — 19 B5
Zhushadi, *Canton* — 8 A3
Zielona, *Warsaw* — 31 B2
Zielonka, *Warsaw* — 31 B2
Ziya He ➡, *Tianjin* — 30 B2
Žižkov, *Prague* — 24 B2
Zličin, *Prague* — 24 B1
Zografos, *Athens* — 2 B2
Zoliborz, *Warsaw* — 31 B1
Zonnebloem, *Cape Town* — 8 a2
Zoo, *Beijing* — 4 a1
Zugliget, *Budapest* — 7 A2
Zugló, *Budapest* — 7 A2
Zuiderwoude, *Amsterdam* — 2 A2
Zumbi, *Rio de Janeiro* — 24 A3
Zunderdorp, *Amsterdam* — 2 A2
Zuvuvu ➡, *São Paulo* — 26 C1
Zwaanshoek, *Amsterdam* — 2 A1
Zwölfaxing, *Vienna* — 31 B2
Zyuzino, *Moscow* — 19 C3

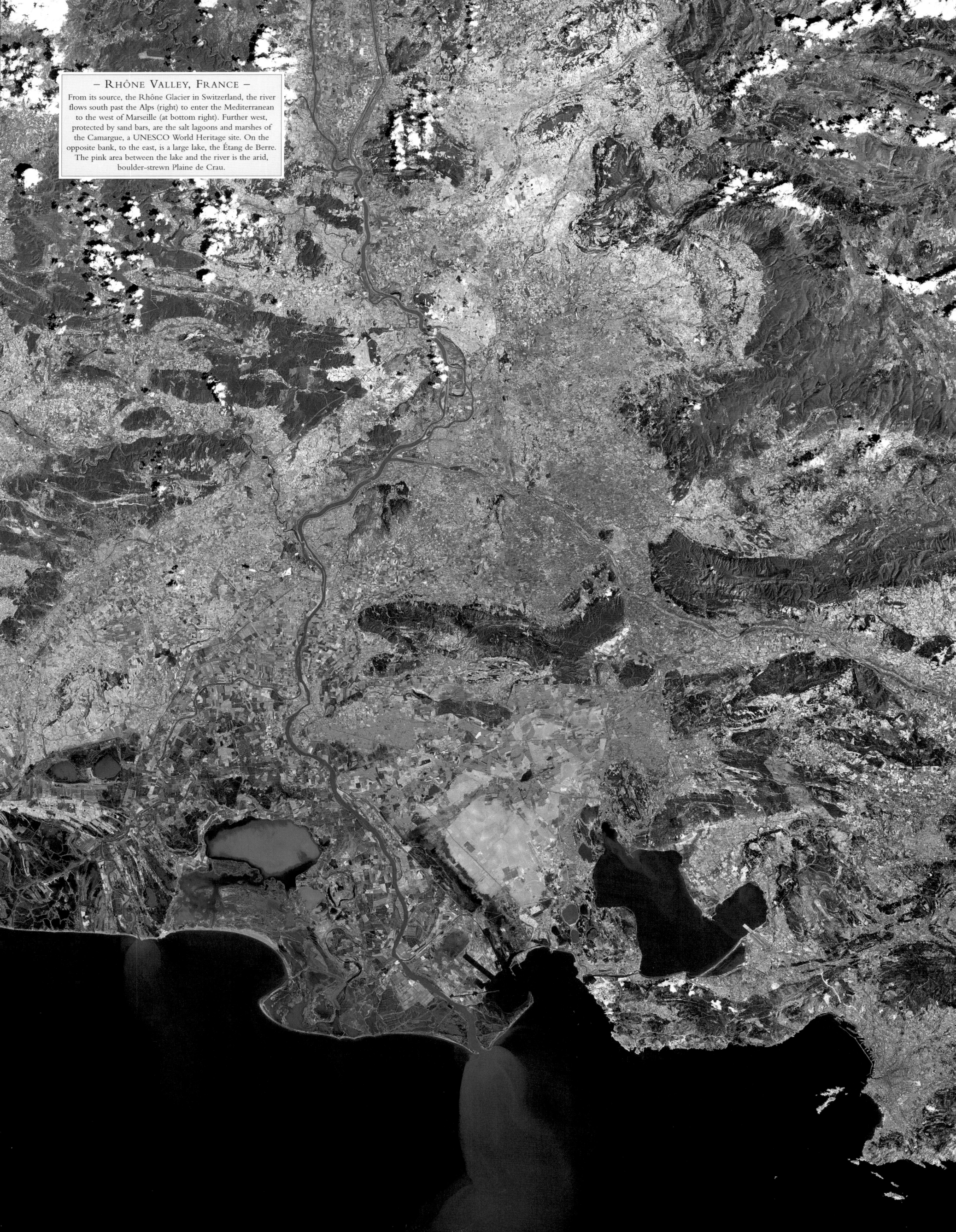

– RHÔNE VALLEY, FRANCE –

From its source, the Rhône Glacier in Switzerland, the river
flows south past the Alps (right) to enter the Mediterranean
to the west of Marseille (at bottom right). Further west,
protected by sand bars, are the salt lagoons and marshes of
the Camargue, a UNESCO World Heritage site. On the
opposite bank, to the east, is a large lake, the Étang de Berre.
The pink area between the lake and the river is the arid,
boulder-strewn Plaine de Crau.

WORLD MAPS

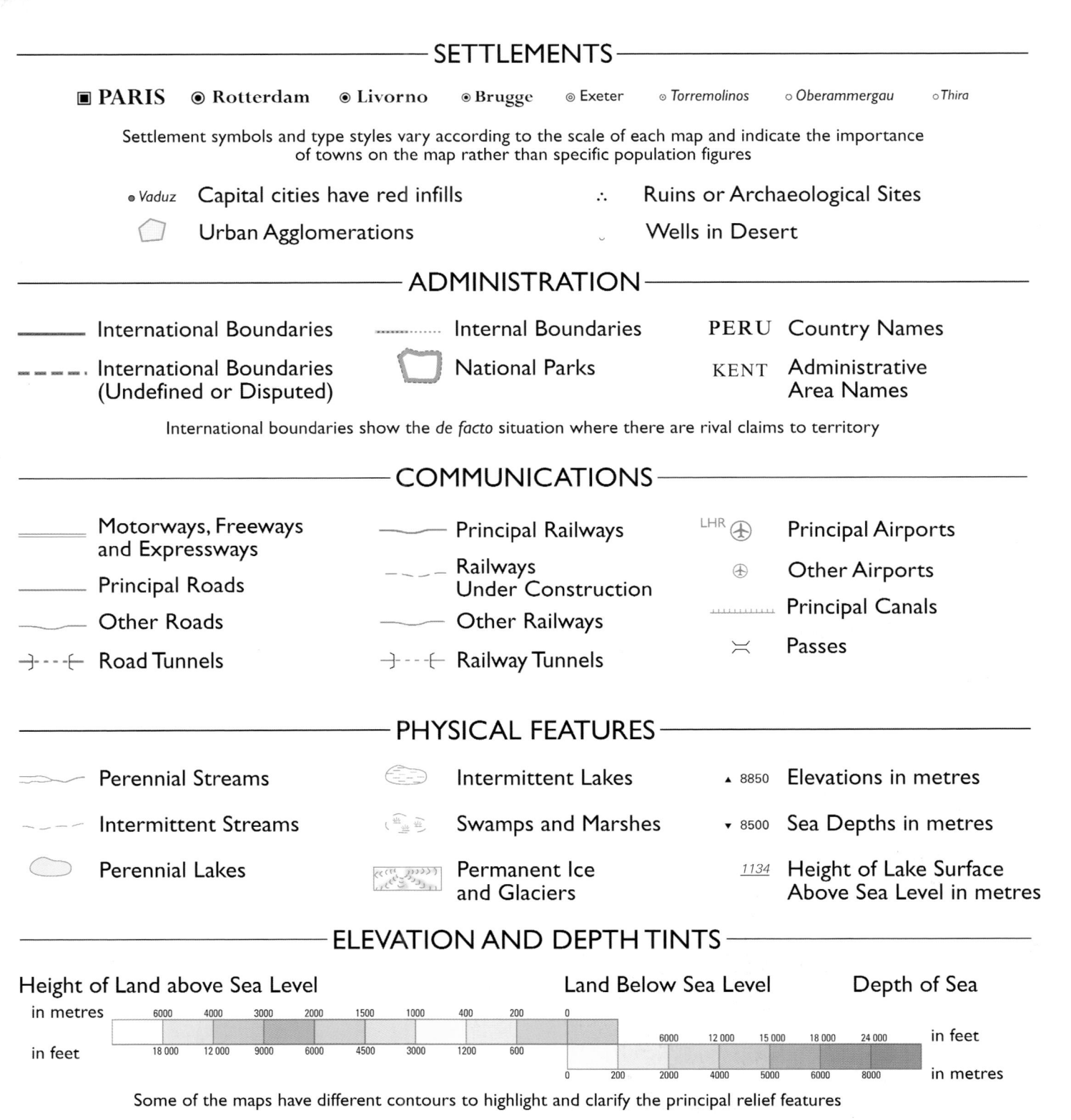

SETTLEMENTS

■ **PARIS** ◉ Rotterdam ⊙ **Livorno** ◎ **Brugge** ◎ Exeter ⊙ *Torremolinos* ○ *Oberammergau* ○ *Thira*

Settlement symbols and type styles vary according to the scale of each map and indicate the importance
of towns on the map rather than specific population figures

• *Vaduz* Capital cities have red infills
⬠ Urban Agglomerations

∴ Ruins or Archaeological Sites
⌣ Wells in Desert

ADMINISTRATION

——— International Boundaries
– – – – International Boundaries (Undefined or Disputed)

········ Internal Boundaries
National Parks

PERU Country Names
KENT Administrative Area Names

International boundaries show the *de facto* situation where there are rival claims to territory

COMMUNICATIONS

——— Motorways, Freeways and Expressways
——— Principal Roads
——— Other Roads
+---← Road Tunnels

——— Principal Railways
– – – Railways Under Construction
——— Other Railways
+---← Railway Tunnels

LHR ✈ Principal Airports
⊕ Other Airports
············ Principal Canals
⤫ Passes

PHYSICAL FEATURES

~~~ Perennial Streams
– – – Intermittent Streams
⬭ Perennial Lakes

◌ Intermittent Lakes
Swamps and Marshes
Permanent Ice and Glaciers

▲ 8850 Elevations in metres
▼ 8500 Sea Depths in metres
1134 Height of Lake Surface Above Sea Level in metres

ELEVATION AND DEPTH TINTS

Height of Land above Sea Level

in metres | 6000 4000 3000 2000 1500 1000 400 200 0

in feet | 18 000 12 000 9000 6000 4500 3000 1200 600

Land Below Sea Level

6000 12 000 15 000 18 000 24 000 in feet

0 200 2000 4000 5000 6000 8000 in metres

Depth of Sea

Some of the maps have different contours to highlight and clarify the principal relief features

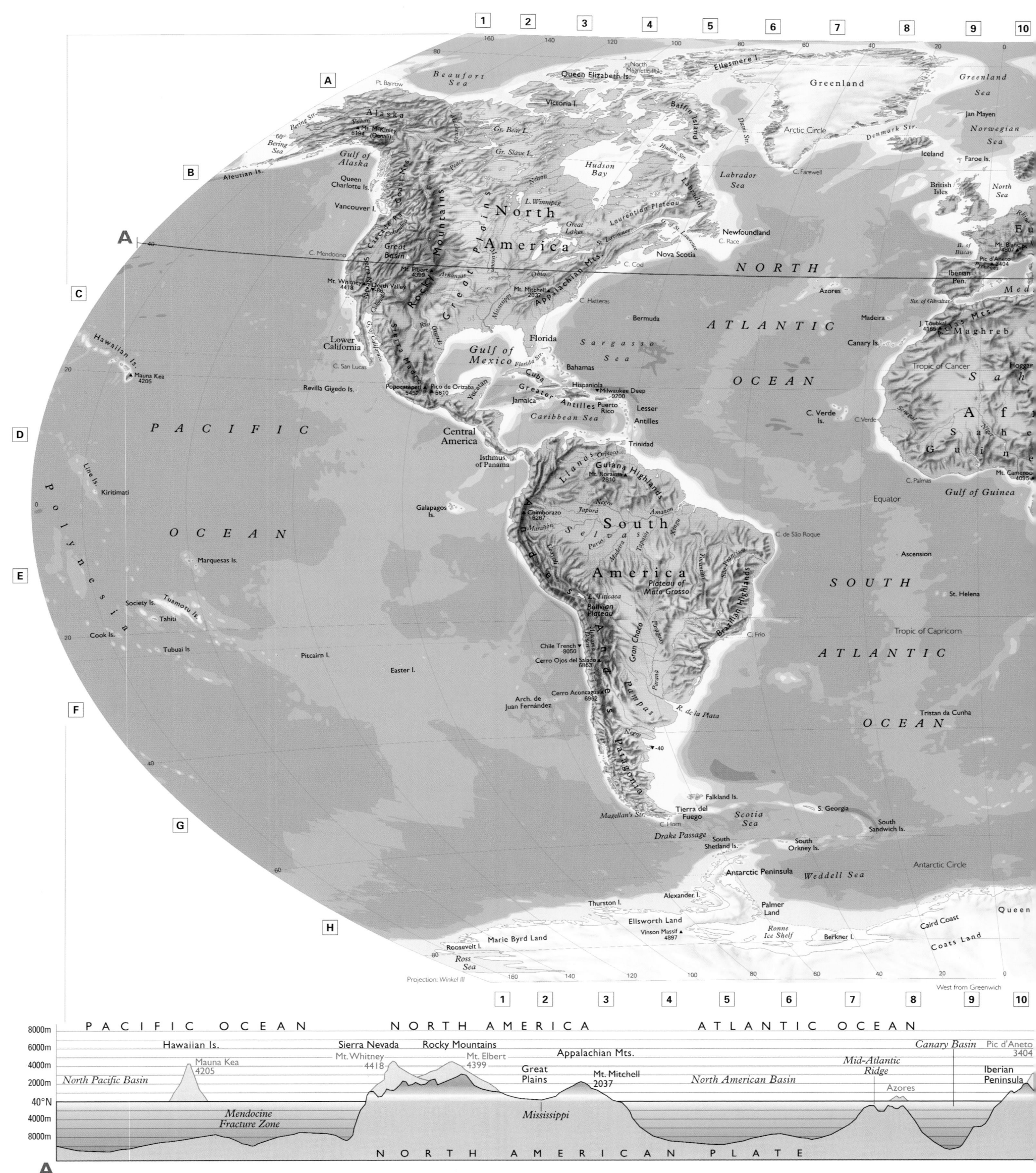

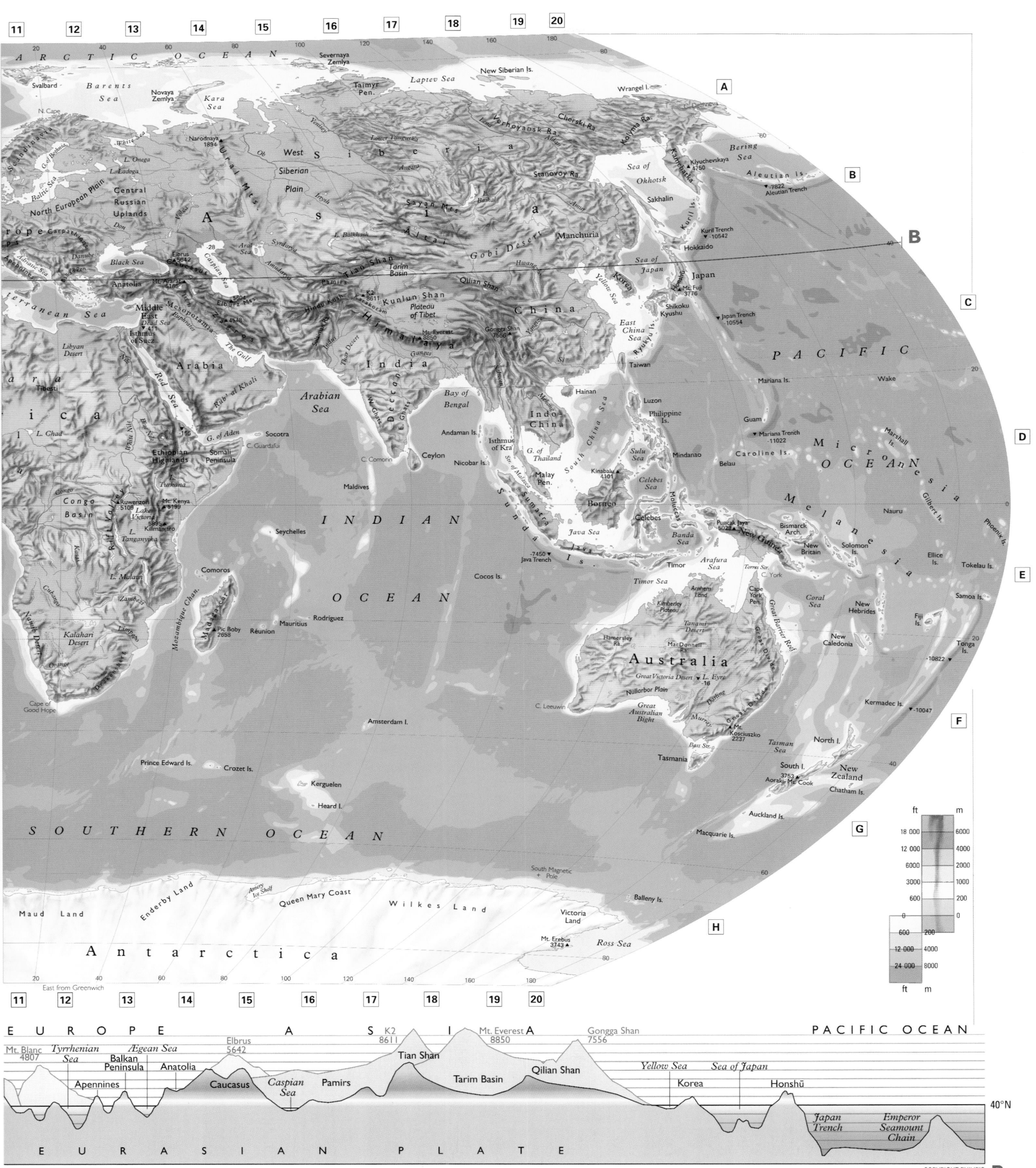

11 12 13 14 15 16 17 18 19 20

ARCTIC OCEAN
Svalbard
Barents Sea
N. Cape
Novaya Zemlya
Kara Sea
Severnaya Zemlya
Taimyr Pen.
Laptev Sea
New Siberian Is.
Wrangel I.
Dezhneva
A
Narodnaya 1894
Ural Mts.
West Siberian Plain
Yenisey
Lower Tunguska
Verhoyansk Ra.
Cherski Ra.
Kolyma Ra.
Kamchatka
Klyuchevskaya 4750
Bering Sea
Aleutian Is.
B
7822 Aleutian Trench
White Sea
L. Onega
L. Ladoga
Central Russian Uplands
Ob
Angara
S I B E R I A
Stanovoy Ra.
Sea of Okhotsk
Sakhalin
Kuril Is.
Kuril Trench 10542
Hokkaido
B
North European Plain
Don
Volga
Balkhash
A L T A I
Sayan Mts.
Baikal
Altai
Manchuria
Amur
Japan
Mt Fuji 3776
Japan Trench 10554
Carpathians
Danube
Black Sea
Aral Sea
Caspian Sea
Syrdarya
Amudarya
Tian Shan
Tarim Basin
Gobi Desert
Hwang
Sea of Japan
Korea
Shikoku Kyushu
C
Europe
Adriatic Sea
Anatolia
Elbrus 5642
Mt Ararat 5165
Elburz Mts. 5604
Pamirs
8611 Kunlun Shan
Plateau of Tibet
CHINA
Yellow Sea
Gongga Shan 7556
Yangtze
East China Sea
Ryukyu Is.
P A C I F I C
Mediterranean Sea
Middle East Dead Sea
Mesopotamia
Euphrates
Hindu Kush 4538
Himalaya
Mt Everest 8850
Si
Taiwan
Mariana Is.
Wake
Libyan Desert
Isthmus of Suez
The Gulf
Arabia
Indus
Thar Desert
India
Ganges
Mekong
Hainan
Luzon
Philippine Is.
Guam
Mariana Trench 11022
M i c r o n e s i a
O C E A N
D
Red Sea
G. of Aden
Socotra
C. Guardafui
Indo-China
G. of Thailand
South China Sea
Mindanao
Caroline Is.
Belau
Tibesti
L. Chad
Blue Nile
Ethiopian Highlands
Somali Peninsula
Andaman Is.
Isthmus of Kra
Sulu Sea
Kinabalu 4101
Celebes Sea
a
C. Comorin
Ceylon
Nicobar Is.
Malay Pen.
Borneo
Celebes
Molucca
Nauru
Gilbert Is.
Congo Basin
Ruwenzori 5109
L. Victoria
Mt Kenya 5199
Kilimanjaro 5895
Turkana
Maldives
Seychelles
Sumatra
Java Sea
Banda Sea
Puncak Jaya 5028
New Guinea
Bismarck Arch.
New Britain
Solomon Is.
M e l a n e s i a
Ellice Is.
Tokelau Is.
E
Kasai
Tanganyika
L. Malawi
Zambezi
Comoros
Madagascar
I N D I A N
Sunda Is.
Java
7450 Java Trench
Timor
Arafura Sea
Torres Str.
C. York
Coral Sea
New Hebrides
Fiji Is.
Samoa Is.
North Desert
Okavango
Limpopo
Pic Boby 2658
Réunion
Mauritius
Rodriguez
O C E A N
Cocos Is.
Timor Sea
Arnhem Land
Kimberley Plateau
Tanami Desert
Cape York Pen.
Great Dividing Range
New Caledonia
Tonga Is.
10822
Kalahari Desert
Orange
Mozambique Chan.
Hamersley Ra.
MacDonnell Ra.
Murray
Mt Kosciuszko 2237
Kermadec Is.
10047
F
Cape of Good Hope
Drakensberg
Amsterdam I.
A U S T R A L I A
Great Victoria Desert
L. Eyre 16
Nullarbor Plain
Great Australian Bight
C. Leeuwin
C. York
Darling
Bass Str.
Tasman Sea
North I.
G
Prince Edward Is.
Crozet Is.
Kerguelen
Heard I.
Tasmania
South I. 3753 Aoraki Mt Cook
New Zealand
Chatham Is.
Auckland Is.
S O U T H E R N   O C E A N
South Magnetic Pole
Macquarie Is.
Maud Land
Enderby Land
Amery Ice Shelf
Queen Mary Coast
Wilkes Land
Victoria Land
Balleny Is.
H
A n t a r c t i c a
Mt Erebus 3743
Ross Sea
East from Greenwich

ft   m
18 000   6000
12 000   4000
6000   2000
3000   1000
600   200
0
600   200
12 000   4000
24 000   8000
ft   m

E U R O P E   A   S   I   A   PACIFIC OCEAN
Mt Blanc 4807
Tyrrhenian Sea
Apennines
Balkan Peninsula
Ægean Sea
Anatolia
Elbrus 5642
Caucasus
Caspian Sea
Pamirs
K2 8611
Tian Shan
Tarim Basin
Mt Everest 8850
Qilian Shan
Gongga Shan 7556
Yellow Sea
Sea of Japan
Korea
Honshū
40°N
Japan Trench
Emperor Seamount Chain
E U R A S I A N   P L A T E

COPYRIGHT PHILIP'S   **B**

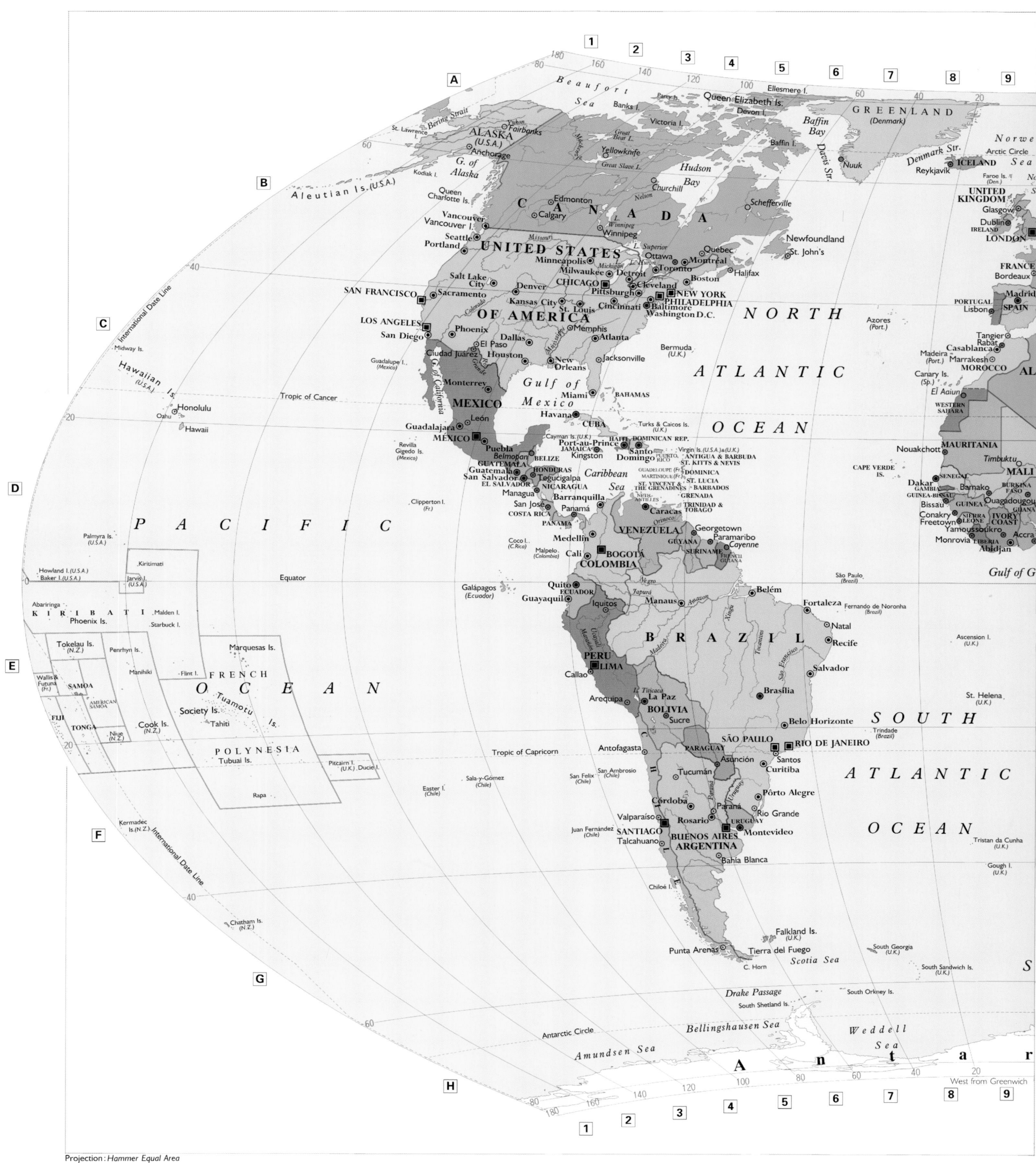

Projection: *Hammer Equal Area*

Hanoi ● Capital Cities

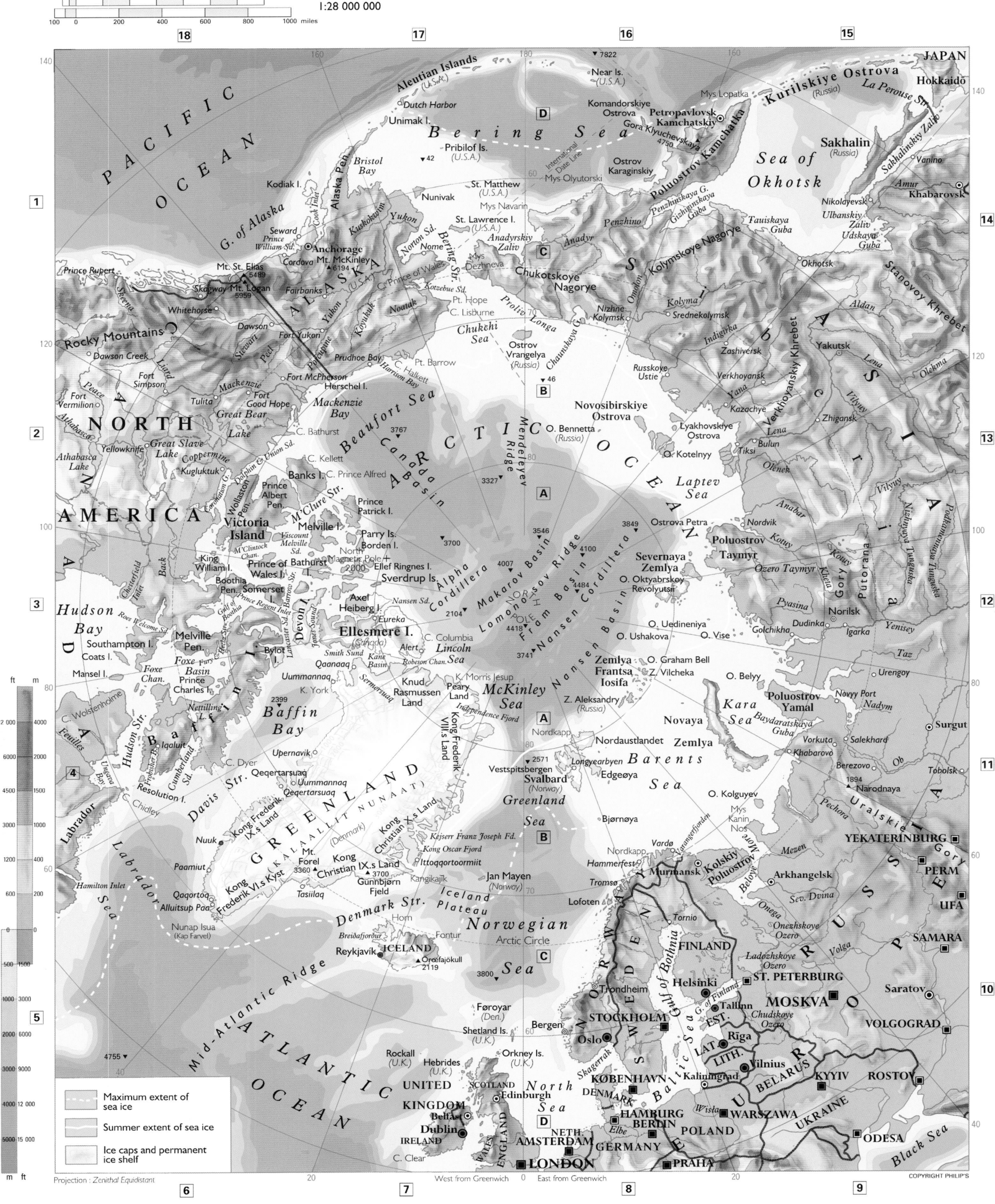

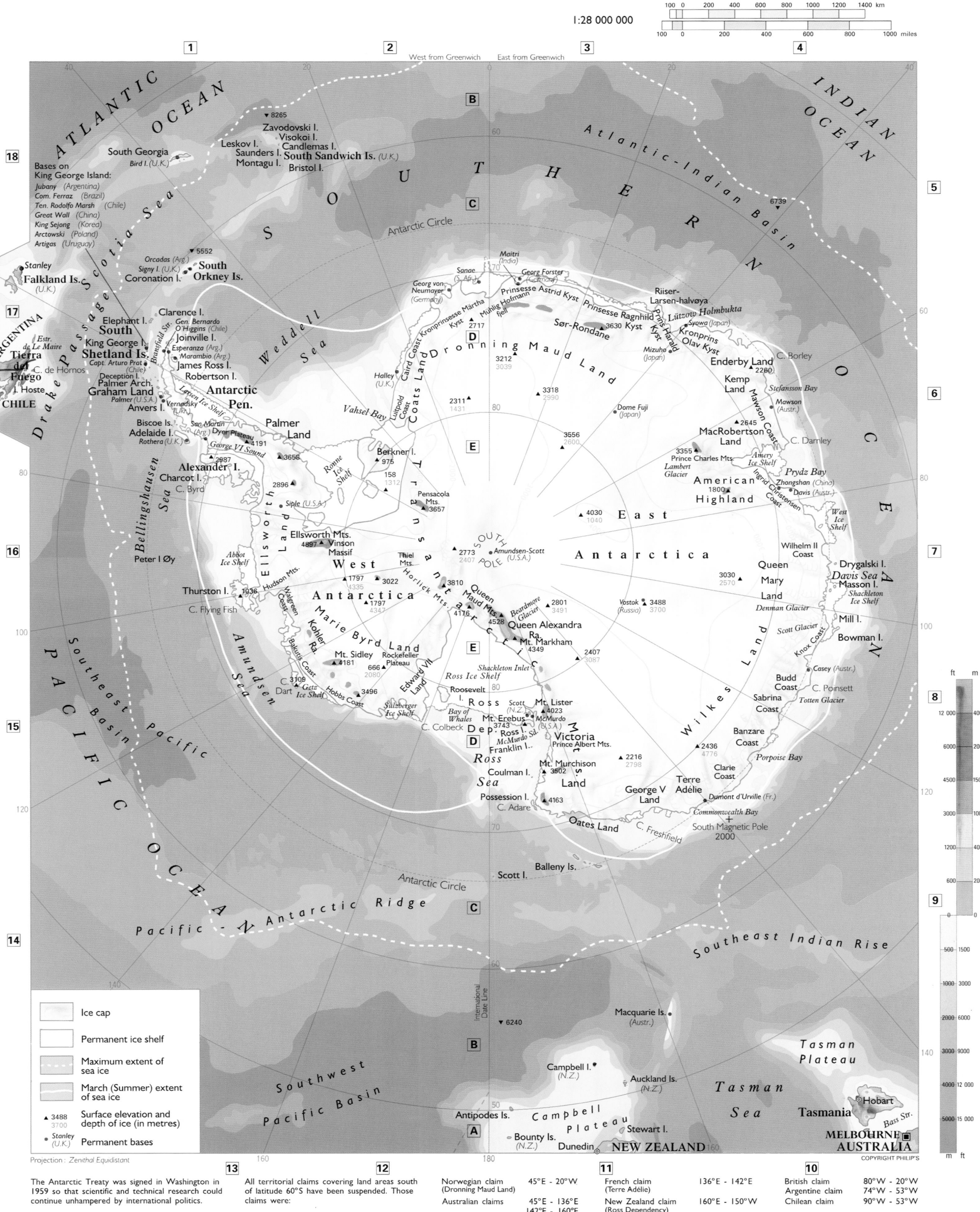

1:28 000 000

West from Greenwich   East from Greenwich

ATLANTIC   OCEAN

INDIAN OCEAN

South Georgia
Bird I. (U.K.)

Bases on
King George Island:
Jubany (Argentina)
Com. Ferraz (Brazil)
Ten. Rodolfo Marsh (Chile)
Great Wall (China)
King Sejong (Korea)
Arctowski (Poland)
Artigas (Uruguay)

Zavodovski I.
Visokoi I.
Leskov I.   Candlemas I.
Saunders I.   **South Sandwich Is.** (U.K.)
Montagu I.   Bristol I.

▼ 8265

S O U T H E R N

Atlantic-Indian Basin

6739

Antarctic Circle

S C O T I A   S E A

Orcadas (Arg) ▼ 5552
Signy I. (U.K.)   **South**
Coronation I.   **Orkney Is.**

Stanley
Falkland Is.
(U.K.)

ARGENTINA

Maitri (India)
Sanae (S. Afr.)   Georg Forster (Germany)

Georg von
Neumayer
(Germany)

Prinsesse Astrid Kyst
Prinsesse Ragnhild Kyst

Riiser-
Larsen-halvøya

Lützow Holmbukta

Elephant I.
Clarence I.
Gen. Bernardo
O'Higgins (Chile)
South   Joinville I.
Shetland Is.   Esperanza (Arg.)
King George I.   Marambio (Arg.)
Deception I.   James Ross I.
Capt. Arturo Prat   Robertson I.
(Chile)

Tierra
del
Fuego
C. de Hornos
I. Hoste
CHILE

Kronprinsesse Märtha
Kyst

Mühlig Hofmann
fjell

Prins Harald
Kyst   Prins Olav Kyst

Syowa (Japan)
Kronprins
Olav Kyst

Enderby Land
C. Borley

W E D D E L L   S E A

Halley
(U.K.)

2717

D r o n n i n g   M a u d   L a n d

3212
3039

Mizuho
(Japan)

3630

Kemp
Land

2280

Stefansson Bay

Mawson
(Austr.)

Palmer
Arch.
Graham Land
Palmer (U.S.A.)
Anvers I.   *Vernadsky* (U.K.)

**Antarctic
Pen.**

Larsen Ice Shelf

Vahsel Bay

Caird Coast

Coats Land

Luitpold Coast

3318
2990

3556
2600

Dome Fuji
(Japan)

3355

2645

**MacRobertson
Land**

C. Darnley

**Palmer
Land**

Berkner I.

American

1800

Prince Charles Mts

Lambert
Glacier

Amery
Ice Shelf

Prydz Bay

Zhongshan (China)
Davis (Austr.)

Biscoe Is.
Adelaide I.
Rothera (U.K.)

4191

3658

Ronne
Ice
Shelf

975
158
1312

Pensacola
Mts.
3657

4030
1040

Highland

Ingrid Christensen
Coast

East

West
Ice
Shelf

Alexander I.
Charcot I.
C. Byrd

2896

Siple (U.S.A.)

Vostok
(Russia)

3488
3700

Peter I Øy

Bellingshausen
Sea

San Martin
(Arg.)

Dyer Plateau

George VI Sound

2987

Ellsworth Mts.
4897 Vinson
Massif

Thiel
Mts.

2773

**South
Pole**

Amundsen-Scott
(U.S.A.)
2407

A n t a r c t i c a

3030
2570

**Queen
Mary
Land**

Davis Sea
Masson I.

Drygalski I.

Shackleton
Ice Shelf

Abbot
Ice Shelf

Hudson Mts.

West

Horlick Mts.

1797
4335

3022

3810

Mill I.

Thurston I.   1036

C. Flying Fish

Walgreen
Coast

Antarctica

1797
4347

Queen
Maud Mts

4176

Beardmore
Glacier
4528

2801

Queen Alexandra
Ra.

2407
3087

Denman Glacier

Scott Glacier

Knox Coast

Bowman I.

Ellsworth Land

Marie Byrd Land

Kohler
Ra.

Mt. Sidley
4181

Rockefeller
Plateau

666
2080

Mt. Markham
4349

Wilkes   Land

2436
4776

**Budd
Coast**

Casey (Austr.)

C. Poinsett

Totten Glacier

Bakutis Coast

3109
Dart

Getz
Ice Shelf

3496

Hobbs Coast

Salzberger
Ice Shelf

Edward VII
Land

Shackleton Inlet

Ross Ice Shelf

Bay of
Whales
C. Colbeck

Roosevelt
I.

**Ross
Dep.**

Ross

Sea

Scott (N.Z.)
Mt. Lister
4023
Ross I.   McMurdo (U.S.A.)
Mt. Erebus
3743
McMurdo Sd.

Franklin I.

Victoria

Mt. Murchison
3502

Prince Albert Mts.

2216
2798

Clarie
Coast

Sabrina
Coast

Banzare
Coast

Porpoise Bay

**Terre
Adélie**

Dumont d'Urville (Fr.)

**George V
Land**

Commonwealth Bay
+
South Magnetic Pole
2000

Coulman I.

Land

Possession I.

4163

C. Adare

Oates Land

C. Freshfield

P A C I F I C   O C E A N

Southeast   Pacific

Amundsen
Sea

Southeast Indian Rise

Pacific - Antarctic   Ridge

Antarctic Circle

Scott I.

Balleny Is.

6240

Macquarie Is.
(Austr.)

Southwest
Pacific Basin

Campbell I.
(N.Z.)

Auckland Is.
(N.Z.)

**Tasman
Plateau**

Tasman

Sea

Tasmania

Hobart

Bass Str.

**MELBOURNE
AUSTRALIA**

COPYRIGHT PHILIP'S

Antipodes Is.

Campbell
Plateau

Stewart I.

Bounty Is.
(N.Z.)

Dunedin   **NEW ZEALAND**

Legend

	Ice cap
	Permanent ice shelf
	Maximum extent of sea ice
	March (Summer) extent of sea ice
▲ 3488 / 3700	Surface elevation and depth of ice (in metres)
• Stanley (U.K.)	Permanent bases

Projection : Zenithal Equidistant

All territorial claims covering land areas south of latitude 60°S have been suspended. Those claims were:

Norwegian claim (Dronning Maud Land)	45°E - 20°W	
Australian claims	45°E - 136°E / 142°E - 160°E	
French claim (Terre Adélie)	136°E - 142°E	
New Zealand claim (Ross Dependency)	160°E - 150°W	
British claim	80°W - 20°W	
Argentine claim	74°W - 53°W	
Chilean claim	90°W - 53°W	

ft   m

12 000   4000

6000   2000

4500   1500

3000   1000

1200   600

0   0

500   1500

1000   3000

2000   6000

3000   9000

4000   12 000

5000   15 000

m   ft

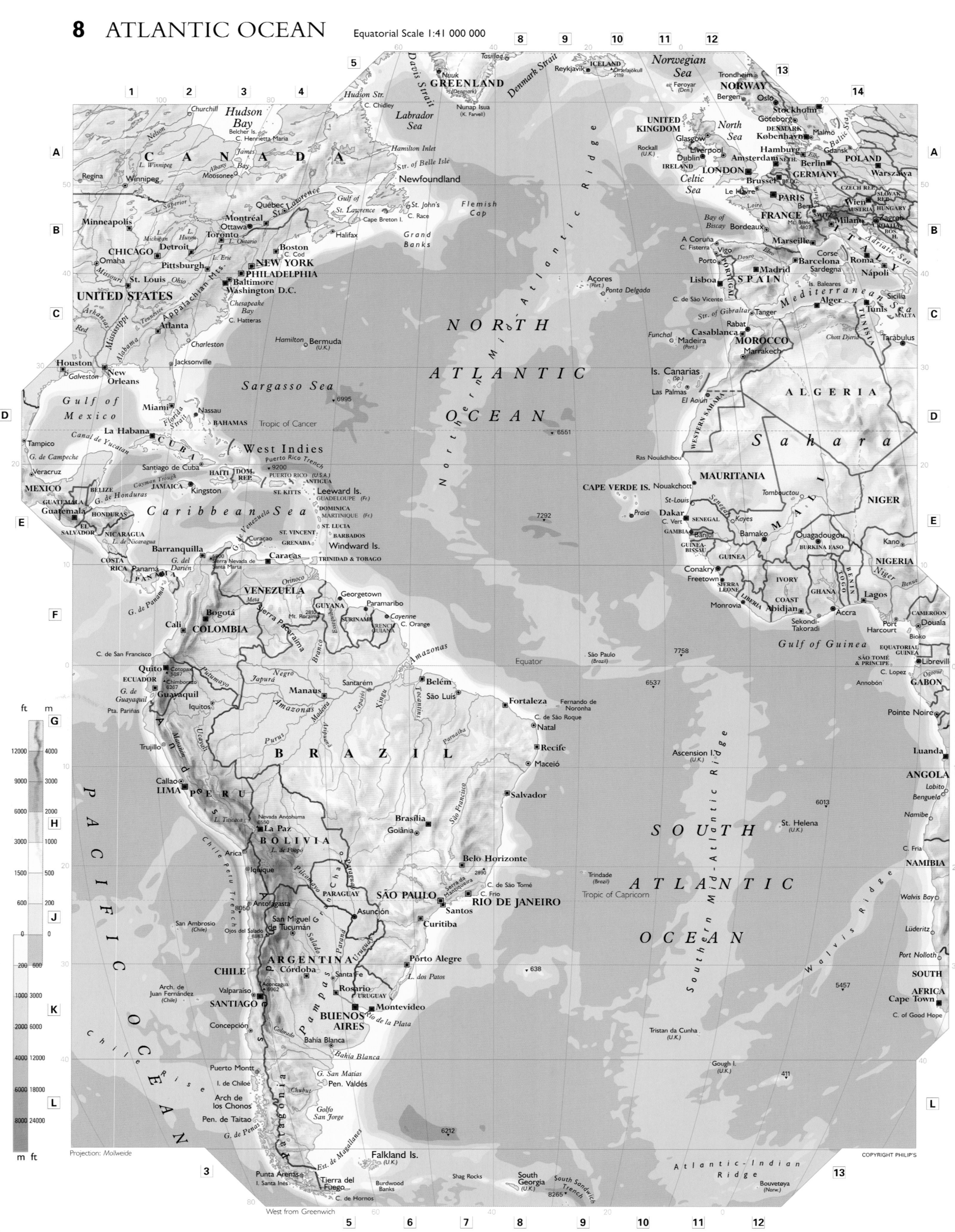

Projection: Mollweide

West from Greenwich

COPYRIGHT PHILIP'S

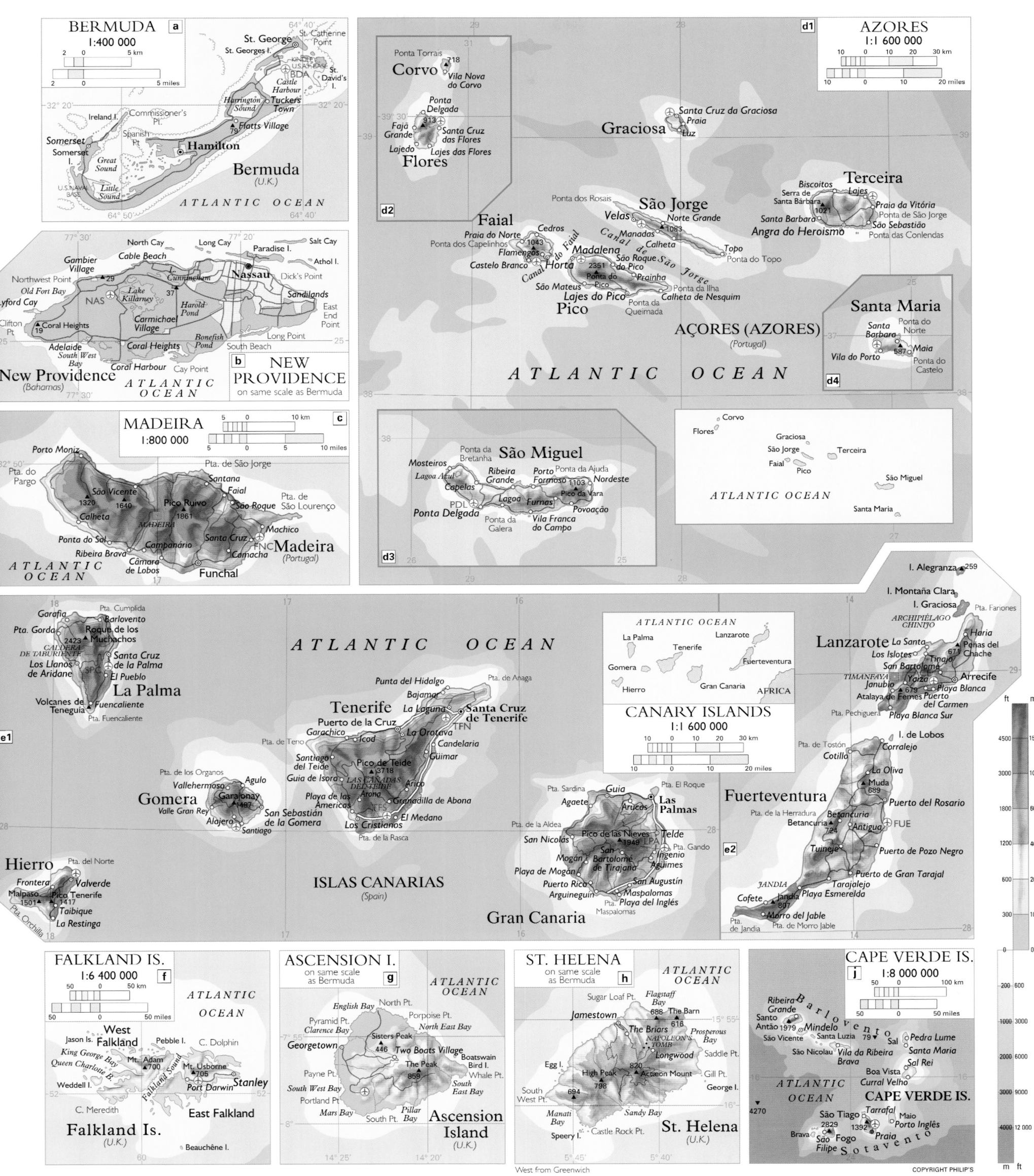

1:10 000 000

ARCTIC OCEAN

CANADA

Axel Heiberg I.

Ellesmere Island

Cape Columbia

ELLESMERE ISLAND

Alert

Lincoln Sea

Robeson Chan.

Nyeboe Land

Nansen Land

J. P. Koch Fjord

Jørgen Brønlund Fjord

Peary Land

Frederick E. Hyde Fjord

1920

McKinley Sea

Kap Morris Jesup

Nordkapp

Olgastredet

Nordaust-landet

Spitsbergen

Longyearbyen

Edgeøya

Storfjorden

Svalbard (Norway)

Sørkapp

Barentsburg

Newtontoppen 1717

Hall Land

Washington Land

Nares Str. Kennedy Kanal

Warming Land

Wulff Land

Mylius Erichsen Land

Hellprin Land

Kronprins Christian Land

Independence Fjord

Station Nord

Nordostrundingen

Denmark Fjord

Ingolf Fjord

Mallemukfjeld

Hovgaard Ø

Nioghalvfjerdsfjorden

GREENLAND SEA

Kane Basin

Inglefield Land

Smith Sd. Storapoluk

Qeqertarssuaq (Thule)

Qaanaaq (Thule)

Jones Sd.

Devon Island

Kap Atholl

Pituffik (Thule Air Base)

Dundas

Kap York

Knud Rasmussen Land

Kronprins Frederik Land

Lauge Koch Kyst

Sermersuaq

2170

AVANNAARSUA) (NORDGRØNLAND)

Kong Frederik VIII.s Land

Lambert Land

Norske Øer

Franske Øer

Germania Land

Danmarkshavn

Store Koldewey

Dove Bugt

Hochstetter Forland

Shannon

Melville Bugt

Steenstrup Gletscher

Nuussuaq (Kraulshavn)

Baffin Bay

Clyde River

Upernavik

Kangersuatsiaq

Upernavik Kujalleq

Nunavik

Illorsuit

Uummannaq

2092

Ikerasak

Saqqaq

Maarmorilik

KITAA (VESTGRØNLAND)

TUNU (ØSTGRØNLAND)

NATIONALPARKEN I NORD-OG ØSTGRØNLAND

2935

3220

Dronning Margrethe II Land

Zackenberg

Wollaston Forland

Clavering Ø

Ole Rømer Land

Andrée Land

Kejser Franz Joseph Fd.

Traill Ø

Petermann Bjerg 2940

Mestersvig

Kong Oscar Fjord

Stauning Alper

Renland

Jameson Land

Ittoqqortoormiut (Scoresbysund)

Ittaajimmiut

Milne Land

Scoresby Sund

Uunarteq

Kangikajik (Kap Brewster)

Jan Mayen (Norway)

Baffin I.

Davis Strait

Qeqertarsuaq (Disko)

Qeqertarsuaq (Godhavn)

Kangerluk

Disko Bugt

Aasiaat (Egedesminde)

Ilulissat (Jakobshavn)

Ikamut

Qasigiannguit (Christianshåb)

Kangaatsiaq

Nordre Strømfjord

Sisimiut (Holsteinsborg)

Hilleø

Kong Frederik IX.s Land

Kangerlussuaq (Søndre Strømfjord)

Søndre Strømfjord

Kangaamiut

Maniitsoq (Sukkertoppen)

GREENLAND (KALAALLIT NUNAAT)

(Denmark)

Gunnbjørn Fjeld 3760

Kong Christian IX.s Land

Kap Dalton

Kangerdlugssuaq

Blosseville Kyst

Mt. Forel 3360

Kap Gustav Holm

Arctic Circle

Ísafjörður

Húnaflói

Horn

Breiðafjörður

Snæfellsnes

Eyjafjörður

Akureyri

Neskaupstaður

ICELAND

Vatnajökull 2119

Öræfajökull

Dronning Ingrid Land

Nuuk (Godthåb)

Kapisillit

Ikkattoq

Kuummiut

Isortoq

Kulusuk

Tasiilaq (Ammassalik)

Dohrne Banke

Denmark Strait

Faxaflói

Reykjavík

Vestmannaeyjar

Heimaey

Surtsey

Kong Frederik VI.s Kyst

2850

Kangerluarsoruseq (Færingehavn)

Qeqertarsuatsiaat (Fiskenæsset)

Paamiut (Frederikshåb)

Narsalik

Arsuk

Ivittuut

Kangilinnguit (Grønnedal)

Narsaq

Qaqortoq (Julianehåb)

Narsarsuaq

Alluitsup Paa (Sydprøven)

Gyldenløve Fjord

Kap Møsting

Kap Moltke

Kap Skjold

Timmiarmiut

Mogens Heinesen Fjord

ATLANTIC OCEAN

Labrador Sea

Nanortalik

Nunap Isua (Kap Farvel)

Lindenow Fjord

Prins Christian Sund

Projection: Conic

COPYRIGHT PHILIP'S

Underlined towns give their name to the administrative area in which they stand.

139

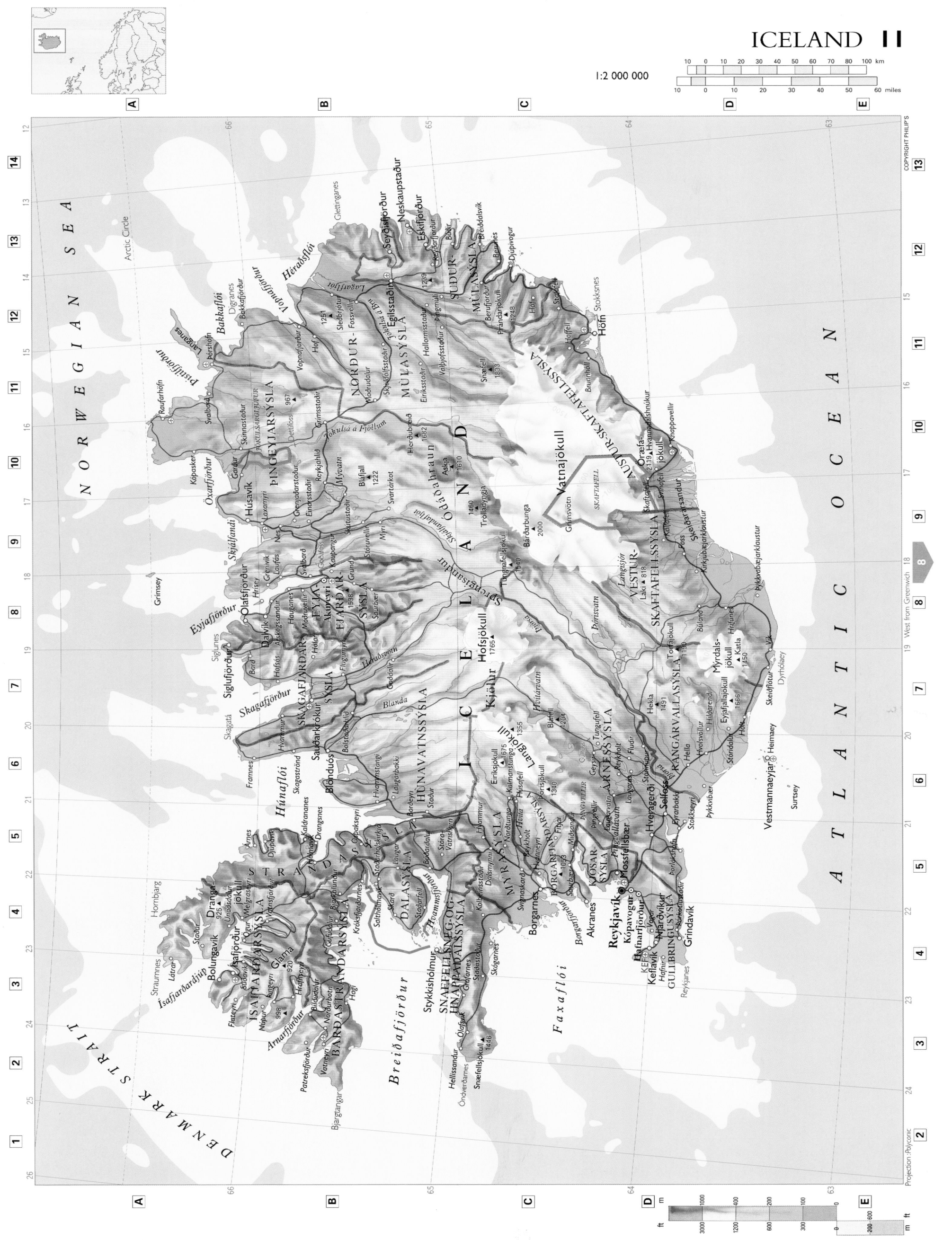

1:2 000 000

Projection : Polyconic

1:16 000 000

1:16 000 000

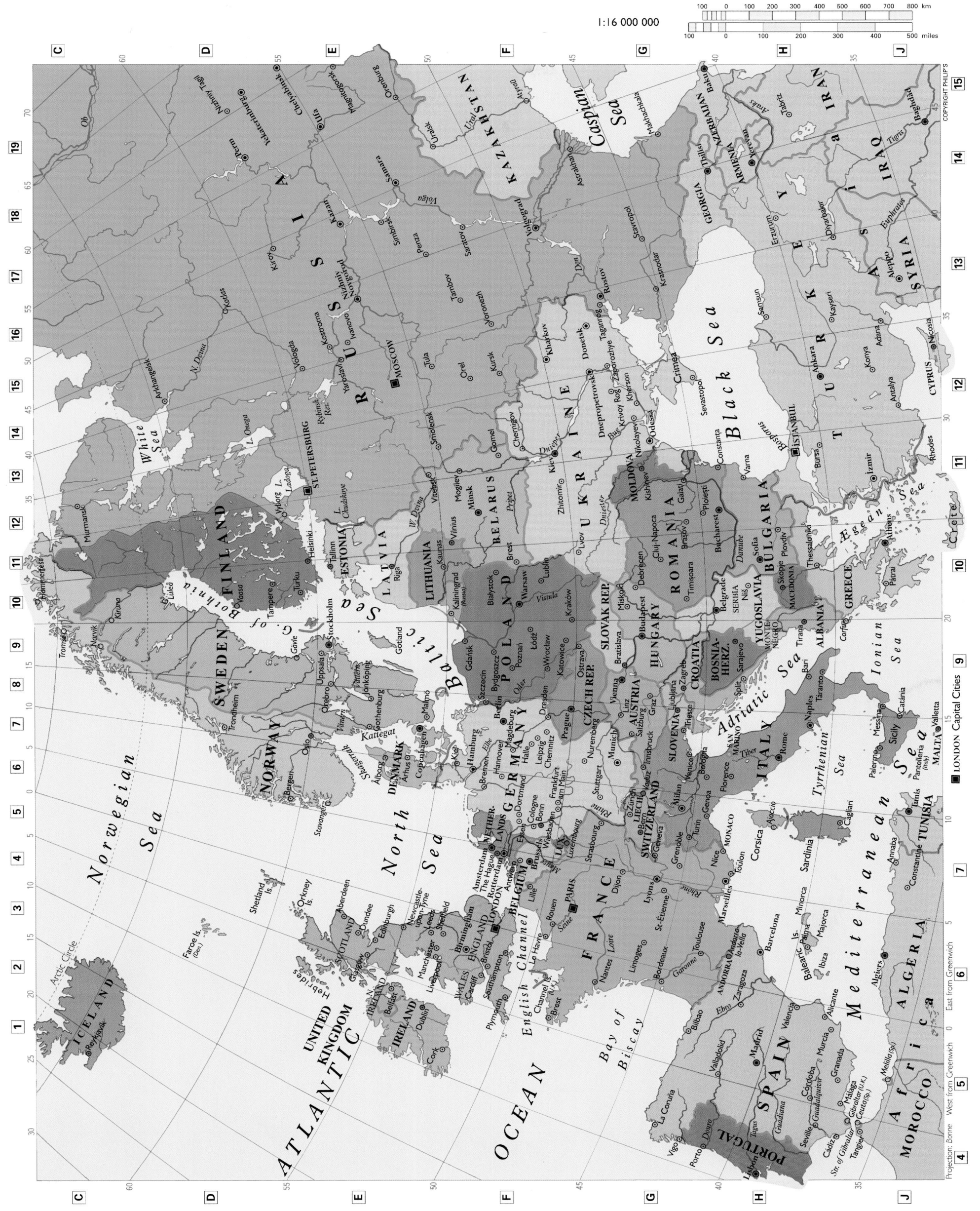

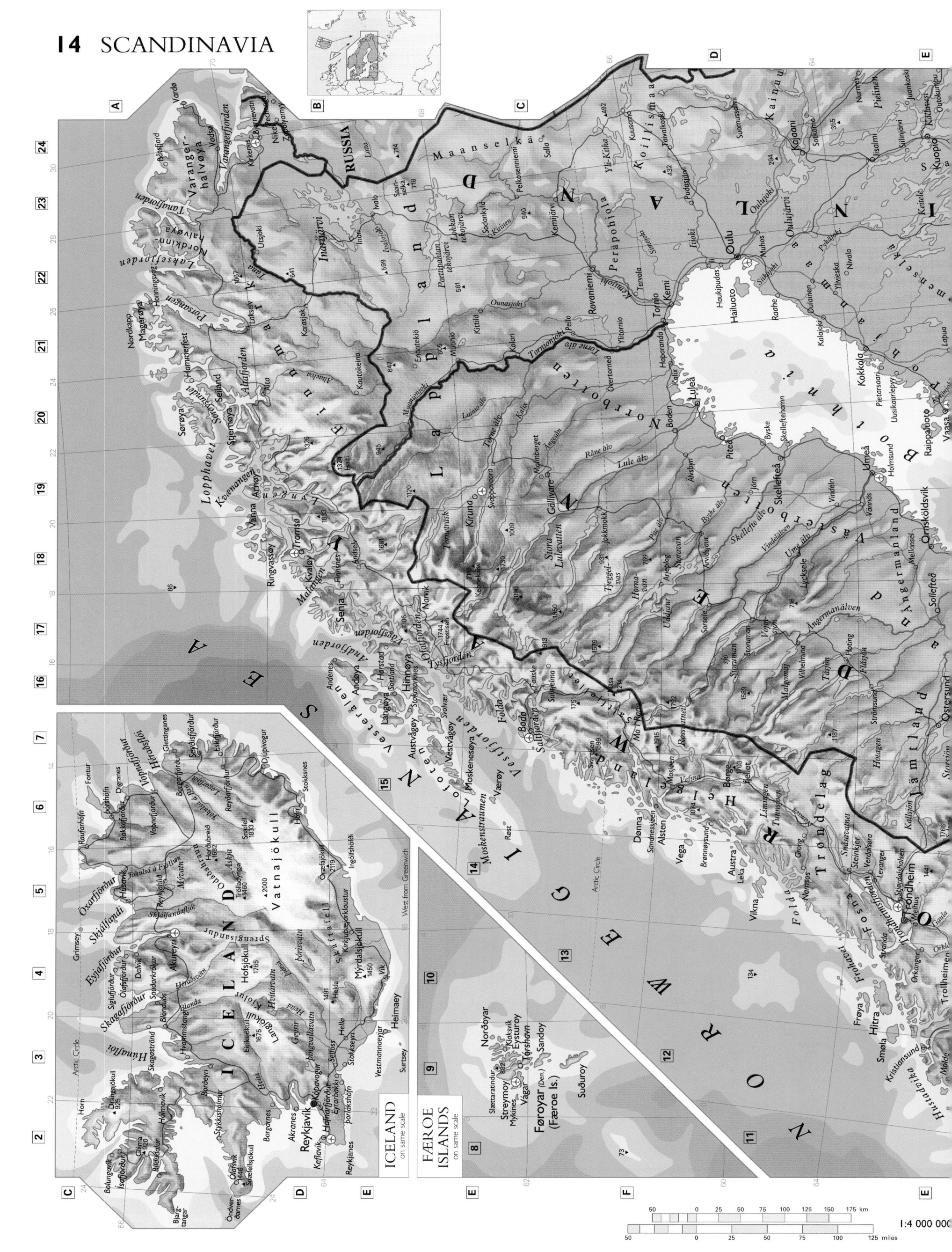

RUSSIA

ICELAND
on same scale

FÆROE
ISLANDS
on same scale

Føroyar (Den)
(Faeroe Is.)

1:4 000 000

50   0   25   50   75   100 125 150 175 km

50   0   25   50   75   100   125 miles

F G H J

56 58

K

21 20 19 54 18 17 16 15 14 30 13 12

COPYRIGHT PHILIP'S

East from Greenwich

Projection: Conic with two standard parallels

Countries and regions:
FINLAND
ESTONIA
LATVIA
LITHUANIA
RUSSIA
BALTIC SEA
SWEDEN
NORWAY
DENMARK
GERMANY
POLAND

Gulf of Finland
Gulf of Riga
Ålands hav
Skagerrak
Kattegat

Major cities / places:
Helsinki (Helsingfors), Espoo, Vantaa, Turku (Åbo), Tampere, Mikkeli, Jyväskylä, Kotka, Lahti, Pori, Rauma, Vaasa, Seinäjoki

Tallinn, Pärnu, Tartu, Narva, Haapsalu, Hiiumaa (Dagö), Saaremaa (Ösel), Kuressaare

Riga, Jūrmala, Jelgava, Ventspils, Liepāja, Valmiera, Daugavpils, Rēzekne

Vilnius, Kaunas, Klaipėda, Panevėžys, Šiauliai, Marijampolė

Kaliningrad (Russia), Chernyakhovsk, Sovetsk

Stockholm, Uppsala, Norrtälje, Västerås, Eskilstuna, Södertälje, Örebro, Gävle, Falun, Karlstad, Linköping, Norrköping, Jönköping, Växjö, Kalmar, Karlskrona, Kristianstad, Halmstad, Göteborg (Gothenburg), Borås, Helsingborg, Malmö, Lund, Trelleborg, Ystad, Visby, Gotland, Öland, Bornholm

Oslo, Fredrikstad, Sarpsborg, Moss, Drammen, Tønsberg, Sandefjord, Larvik, Kristiansand, Arendal, Stavanger, Haugesund, Bergen, Ålesund

København (Copenhagen), Helsingør, Roskilde, Odense, Ålborg, Århus, Esbjerg, Randers, Kolding, Vejle, Horsens, Viborg, Sjælland, Fyn, Lolland, Falster, Møn

Rostock, Lübeck, Kiel, Flensburg, Cuxhaven, Greifswald, Stralsund, Rügen, Usedom

Gdańsk, Gdynia, Sopot, Słupsk, Koszalin, Kołobrzeg, Elbląg, Malbork

Mountain heights / spot values (Norway):
2469, 2286, 2405, 1721, 1374

1:2 000 000

BALTIC SEA

POLAND

GERMANY

DENMARK

Gotland (Sweden)

GOTLANDS LÄN

Öland (Sweden)

KALMAR LÄN

Småland

JÖNKÖPINGS LÄN

KRONOBERGS LÄN

BLEKINGE LÄN

SKÅNE LÄN

SÖDERMANLANDS LÄN

ÖSTERGÖTLANDS LÄN

VÄSTRA GÖTALANDS LÄN

HALLANDS LÄN

Bohuslän

Dalsland

Västergötland

BORNHOLMS AMT.

Bornholm (Denmark)

NORDJYLLANDS AMT.

VIBORG AMT.

RINGKØBING AMT.

VEJLE AMT.

SØNDERJYLLANDS AMT.

FYNS AMT.

VESTSJÆLLANDS AMT.

ROSKILDE AMT.

FREDERIKSBORG AMT.

KØBENHAVNS AMT.

STORSTRØMS AMT.

København

Malmö

Göteborg

Helsingborg

Helsingør

Odense

Århus

Ålborg

Esbjerg

Kolding

Visby

Kalmar

Karlskrona

Växjö

Nykøbing

Norrköping

Linköping

Jönköping

Borås

Varberg

Halmstad

Lund

Landskrona

Kristianstad

National Parks

SOUTHERN NORWAY

1:2 000 000

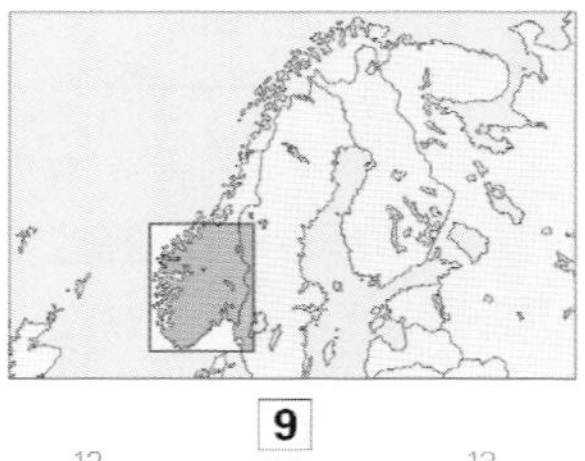

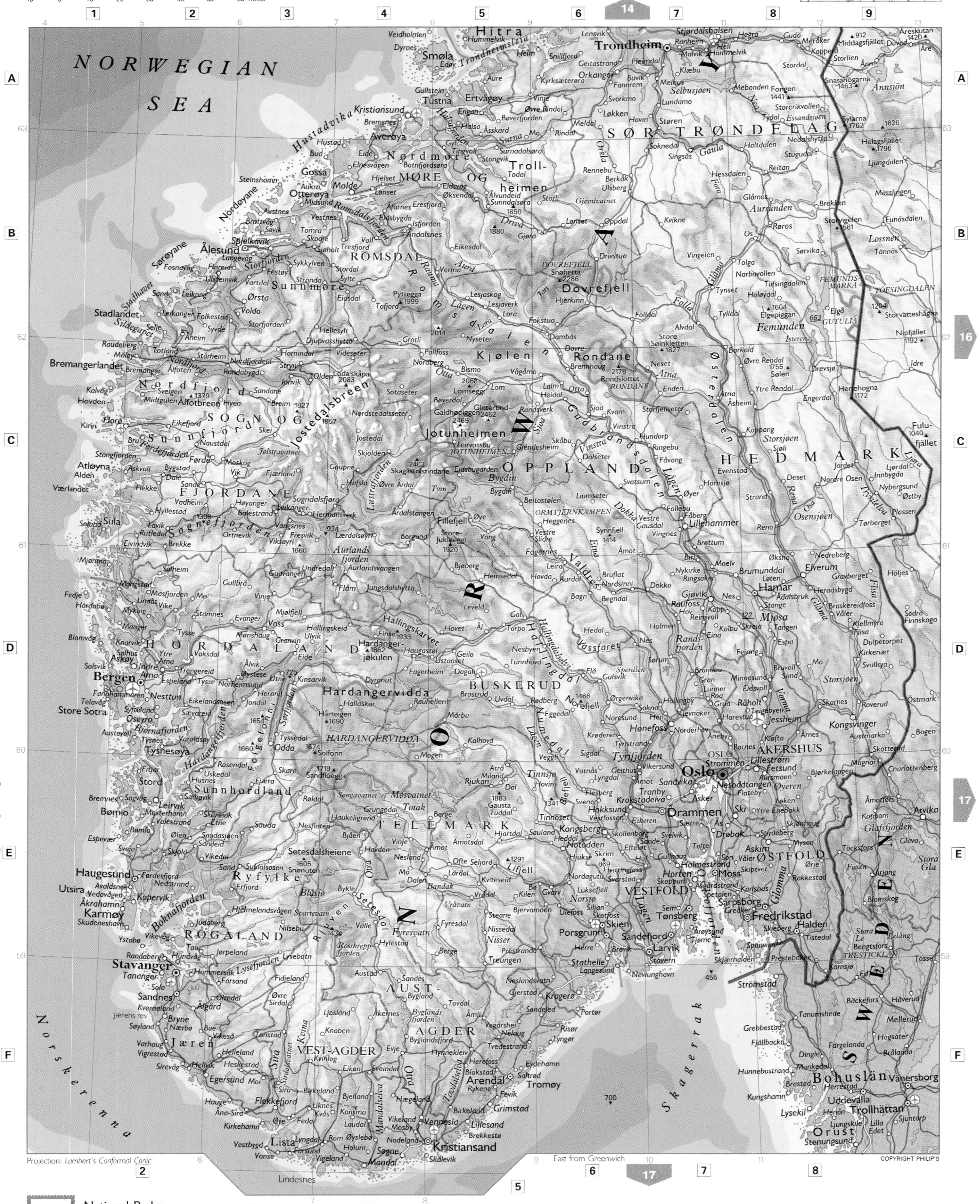

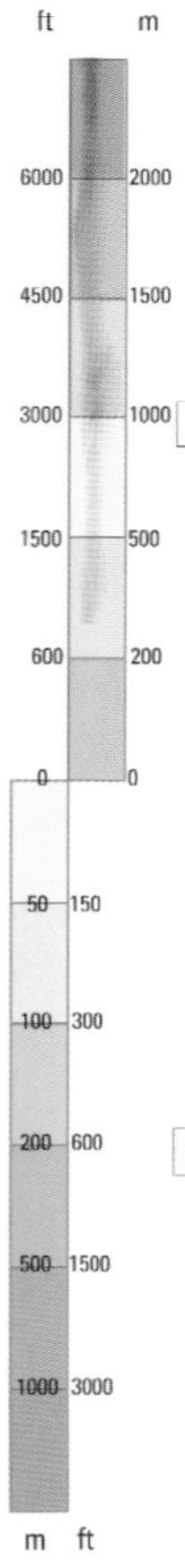

National Parks

1:4 000 000

50   0   25   50   75   100   125   150   175 km
50   0   25   50   75   100   125 miles

Projection: Conical with two standard parallels

East from Greenwich
COPYRIGHT PHILIP'S

West from Greenwich

10 0 10 20 30 40 50 60 70 80 km

10 0 10 20 30 40 50 miles

1:1 600 000

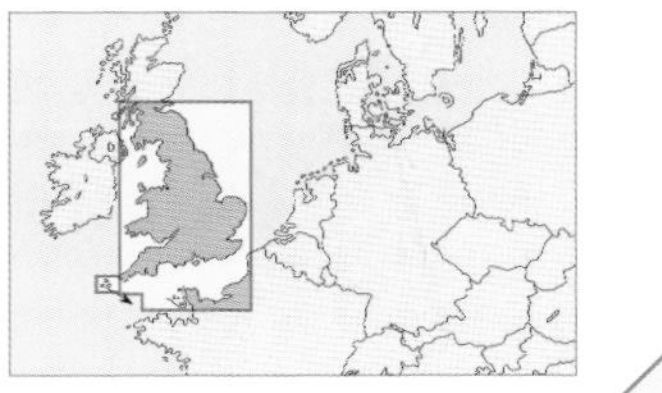

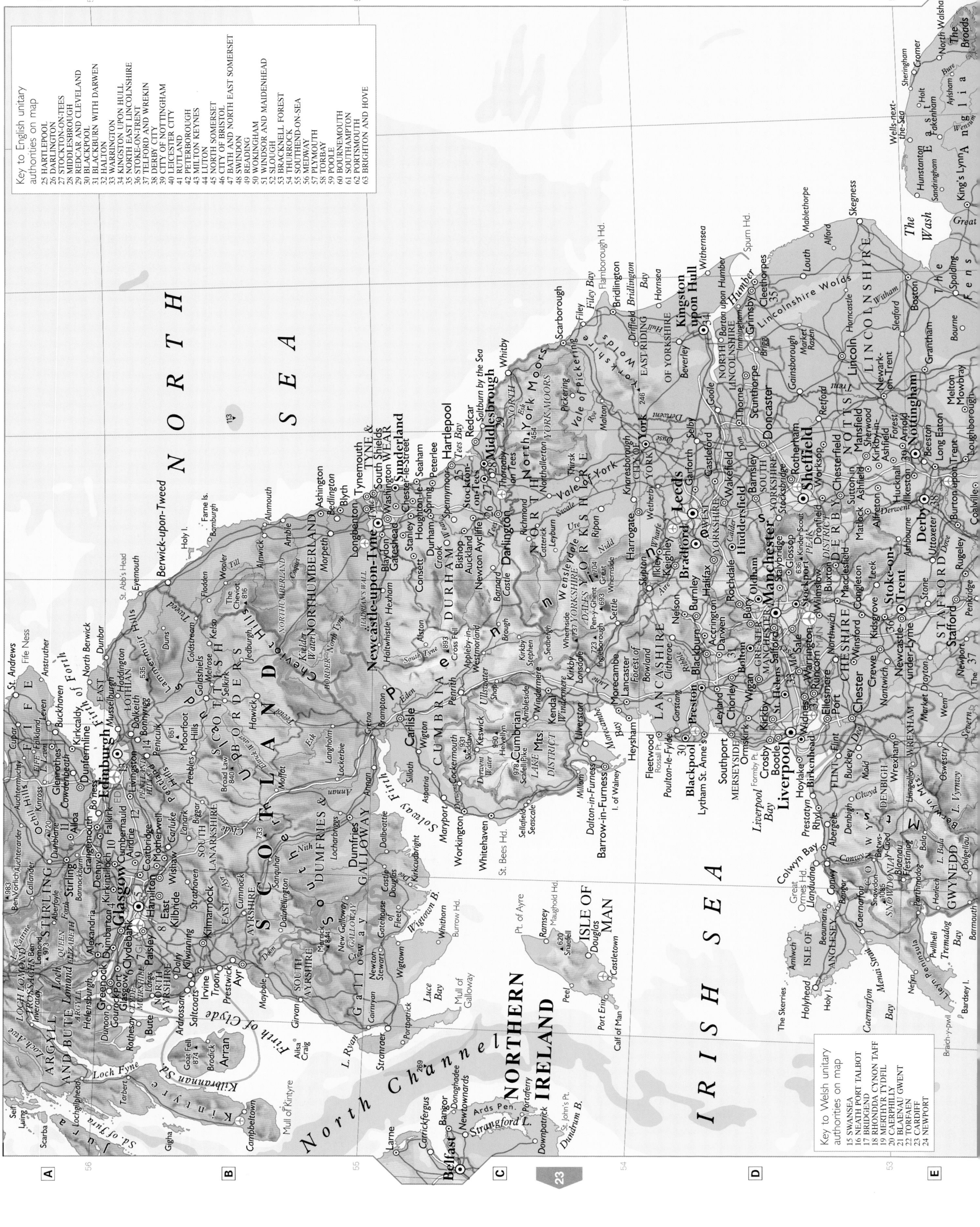
Key to English unitary authorities on map
25 HARTLEPOOL
26 DARLINGTON
27 STOCKTON-ON-TEES
28 MIDDLESBROUGH
29 REDCAR AND CLEVELAND
30 BLACKPOOL
31 BLACKBURN WITH DARWEN
32 HALTON
33 WARRINGTON
34 KINGSTON UPON HULL
35 NORTH EAST LINCOLNSHIRE
36 STOKE-ON-TRENT
37 TELFORD AND WREKIN
38 DERBY CITY
39 CITY OF NOTTINGHAM
40 LEICESTER CITY
41 RUTLAND
42 PETERBOROUGH
43 MILTON KEYNES
44 LUTON
45 NORTH SOMERSET
46 CITY OF BRISTOL
47 BATH AND NORTH EAST SOMERSET
48 SWINDON
49 READING
50 WOKINGHAM
51 WINDSOR AND MAIDENHEAD
52 SLOUGH
53 BRACKNELL FOREST
54 THURROCK
55 SOUTHEND-ON-SEA
56 MEDWAY
57 PLYMOUTH
58 TORBAY
59 POOLE
60 BOURNEMOUTH
61 SOUTHAMPTON
62 PORTSMOUTH
63 BRIGHTON AND HOVE
Key to Welsh unitary authorities on map
15 SWANSEA
16 NEATH PORT TALBOT
17 BRIDGEND
18 RHONDDA CYNON TAFF
19 MERTHYR TYDFIL
20 CAERPHILLY
21 BLAENAU GWENT
22 TORFAEN
23 CARDIFF
24 NEWPORT
NORTH SEA
IRISH SEA
North Channel
NORTHERN IRELAND
ISLE OF MAN
SCOTLAND
22
23

FRANCE

HAUTE NORMANDIE

SEINE MARITIME

CALVADOS

MANCHE

COTENTIN

CHANNEL ISLANDS (U.K.)

Alderney
Guernsey
St. Peter Port
Herm
Sark
Jersey
St. Helier

ENGLISH CHANNEL

Baie de la Seine

Le Havre
Rouen
Dieppe
Évreux
Cherbourg
Caen

ENGLAND

WALES

LONDON
GREATER LONDON

Birmingham
Coventry
Cardiff
Bristol
Bath
Plymouth
Portsmouth
Southampton
Bournemouth
Brighton
Hove
Norwich
Ipswich
Cambridge
Peterborough
Leicester
Oxford
Reading
Swindon
Gloucester
Exeter
Torquay

Cornwall
Devon
Dorset
Somerset
Wiltshire
Hampshire
Berkshire
Surrey
West Sussex
East Sussex
Kent
Essex
Suffolk
Norfolk
Cambridgeshire
Bedford
Hertfordshire
Bucks
Northampton
Warwickshire
Worcester
Hereford
Shropshire
Staffs
Powys
Ceredigion
Carmarthenshire
Pembrokeshire
Vale of Glamorgan

Cardigan Bay
Bristol Channel
Lyme Bay
Strait of Dover

ISLE OF WIGHT

ISLES OF SCILLY
on same scale

Land's End
Lizard Pt.
St. Mary's
Isles of Scilly

National Parks in England and Wales
Forest Parks in Scotland

Projection: Lambert's Conformal Conic

COPYRIGHT PHILIP'S

10 0 10 20 30 40 50 60 70 80 km
1:1 600 000
10 0 10 20 30 40 50 miles

Key to Scottish unitary authorities on map
1 CITY OF ABERDEEN
2 DUNDEE CITY
3 WEST DUNBARTONSHIRE
4 EAST DUNBARTONSHIRE
5 CITY OF GLASGOW
6 INVERCLYDE
7 RENFREWSHIRE
8 EAST RENFREWSHIRE
9 NORTH LANARKSHIRE
10 FALKIRK
11 CLACKMANNANSHIRE
12 WEST LOTHIAN
13 CITY OF EDINBURGH
14 MIDLOTHIAN

ORKNEY IS. on same scale
North Ronaldsay
Papa Westray
Westray
Eday
Sanday
Rousay
Shapinsay
Stronsay
Stromness
Mainland
Kirkwall
Brough Hd.
481
Scapa Flow
St. Mary's
Burray
Hoy
Burwick
South Ronaldsay
Dunnet Hd.
Stroma
Duncansby Head
John o' Groats
Pentland Firth
Sinclair's Bay
Thurso

SHETLAND IS. on same scale
Muckle Flugga
Unst
Haroldswick
Yell
Fetlar
Yell Sound
Ulsta
Esha Ness
453
Sullom Voe
Out Skerries
Whalsay
St. Magnus Bay
Mainland
Voe
Papa Stour
Walls
Foula
Scalloway
Bressay
Lerwick
West Burra
Boddam
Sumburgh Hd.

WESTERN ISLES / OUTER HEBRIDES
Flannan Is.
Butt of Lewis
Broad Bay
Gallan Hd.
Stornoway
Eye Peninsula
Lewis
Scarp
799
Clisham
Taransay
Harris
Tarbert
Toe Hd.
Pabbay
Berneray
North Uist
Baleshare
Lochmaddy
Grimsay
Wiay
Benbecula
Ardivachar Pt.
South Uist
Ben Mhor 620
Lochboisdale
Eriskay
Barra
Castlebay
Vatersay
Sandray
Barra Hd. 268

HIGHLANDS / mainland north
C. Wrath
Durness
L. Eriboll
Strathy Pt.
Dunnet Hd.
Dounreay
Thurso
Stroma
Scapa Flow
Hoy
481
Burwick
Pentland Firth
John o' Groats
Reay Forest
Tongue
Ben Hope 927
Halkirk
Wick
Sinclair's Bay
Noss Hd.
Caithness
L. Laxford
Eddrachillis B.
Pt. of Stoer
L. Assynt
Lochinver
Ben More Assynt 998
961
Sutherland
Naver
Helmsdale
705
Lybster
Rubha Coigeach
Enard B.
L. Shin
Lairg
Brora
Ord of Caithness
L. Broom
Oykel
Golspie
Ullapool
Gruinard B.
Greenstone Pt.
L. Ewe
1081 Ben Dearg
Bonar Bridge
Dornoch
Dornoch Firth
Tarbat Ness
Gairloch
1109
Ben Wyvis 1045
Alness
Invergordon
Cromarty
Lossiemouth
Portknockie
Portsoy
L. Maree 1053
Strathpeffer
Dingwall
Nairn
Forres
Elgin
Buckie
Cullen
Banff
Macduff
Fraserburgh
Kinnairds Hd.
Rattray Hd.
Fortrose
Muir of Ord
MORAY
Rothes
Fochabers
Keith
Aberchirder
Turriff
Peterhead
Buchan Ness
L. Fannich
Beauly
Inverness
Burghead
Charlestown of Aberlour
Dufftown
Huntly
Oldmeldrum
Cruden Bay
Ellon

WEST HIGHLANDS / SKYE
North Minch
Little Minch
Sea of the Hebrides
Inner Hebrides
Rubha Hunish
Uig
Rona
Raasay
Scalpay
Portree
Sound of Raasay
Dunvegan
Skye
Cuillin Hills 992
Cuillin Sound
Sd. of Sleat
Kyle of Lochalsh
Kyleakin
Dornie
Glenelg
Mallaig
Arisaig
L. Torridon
L. Carron
Strome ferry
Carn Eige 1182
Glen Affric
1068
Glen Moriston
Fort Augustus
Loch Ness
Drumnadrochit
Beauly
Carn Ban
Newtonmore
941
Monadhliath Mts.
Kingussie
Aviemore
Grantown-on-Spey
Strath Spey
Tomintoul
Cairngorm 1245
Cairn Gorm
Ben Macdhui 1309
Braemar
Ballater
Banchory
Aberdeen
Peterculter
Westhill
Girdle Ness
ABERDEENSHIRE
Alford
Kintore
Inverurie
Dyce
Don
Deveron
Ythan
Buchan

FORT WILLIAM / LOCHABER area
L. Arkaig
L. Lochy 1128
Glen Spean
L. Morar
L. Eil
Fort William
Ben Nevis 1342
Kinlochleven
Glen Coe 1148
Ballachulish
Lochaber
Spean Bridge
Glen Garry
L. Ericht
1148
Rannoch Moor
L. Rannoch
Forest of Atholl
Blair Atholl
1121
Garry
Pitlochry
Kirriemuir
Brechin
Laurencekirk
Montrose
1154 Lochnagar
ANGUS
Forfar
Arbroath
Carnoustie
Monifieth
N. Esk
S. Esk
Strathmore
455
Sidlaw Hills
Stonehaven
Inverbervie
Grampian Mountains

ARGYLL / west coast islands
Pt. of Ardnamurchan
Coll
Tiree
Tobermory
Morvern
Sound of Mull
Staffa
Ulva
Mull
Ben More 966
Iona
Kerrera
Lismore
Oban
Lorn
ARGYLL
Passage of Tiree
Colonsay
Oronsay
Scarba
Luing
Seil
Firth of Lorn
L. Awe
L. Etive
Crianlarich
Ben Cruachan 1126
Inveraray
Lochgilphead
Jura
Sd. of Jura
Rubh' a' Mhail
Ardnave Pt.
Islay
Bowmore
Port Ellen
Rhinns Pt.
Gigha
Kintyre
Tarbert
L. Fyne
ARGYLL AND BUTE
Rhum (Rùm)
Eigg
Muck
Canna
Rhum
Sanday
Mull of Oa
Campbeltown
Mull of Kintyre

CENTRAL / Loch Lomond
Glen Lyon
Ben Lawers 1214
Aberfeldy
Dunkeld
Loch Tay
Kenmore
983
Crieff
Ben Vorlich
Comrie
Auchterarder
Ben More 1174
Killin
L. Earn
L. Lomond
Loch Katrine
Ben Lomond 973
Callander
PERTH AND KINROSS
Perth
Scone
KINROSS
Dundee
Broughty Ferry
Firth of Tay
Tayport
Newport
Taybolt
TROSSACHS
Aberfoyle
QUEEN ELIZABETH
STIRLING
Dunblane
Doune
Stirling
Bannockburn
Denny
Alloa
CLACKMANNANSHIRE
Dollar
Ochil Hills
Auchtermuchty
Cupar
FIFE
Fife Ness
St. Andrews
Leuchars
Falkland
Glenrothes
Kinross
L. Leven
Leven
Buckhaven
Anstruther

GLASGOW / EDINBURGH belt
Helensburgh
Alexandria
Dumbarton
Kirkintilloch
Cumbernauld
Falkirk
Bo'ness
Grangemouth
Musselburgh
Haddington
EAST LOTHIAN
North Berwick
Dunbar
St. Abb's Head
Eyemouth
Greenock
Gourock
Port Glasgow
Clydebank
Glasgow
Airdrie
Coatbridge
Motherwell
Livingston
Dalkeith
Bonnyrigg
Penicuik
Edinburgh
EDIN.
Dunoon
Rothesay
Bute
NORTH AYRSHIRE
Largs
Paisley
Hamilton
East Kilbride
Wishaw
Carluke
Lanark
Carlops
Peebles
Moorfoot Hills
Biggar
651
Galashiels
Melrose
SCOTTISH BORDERS
Selkirk
Jedburgh
Kelso
Coldstream
Duns
Lammermuir Hills
Pentland Hills
MEIKLE
Strathaven
SOUTH LANARKSHIRE
Kilmarnock
Dalry
Kilwinning
Ardrossan
Saltcoats
Irvine
Troon
Prestwick
Ayr
Broad Law 840

ARRAN
Goat Fell 874
Brodick
Arran
Kilbrannan Sd.
Firth of Clyde
Ailsa Craig

SOUTHERN Scotland
EAST AYRSHIRE
Cumnock
Sanquhar
733
Maybole
Girvan
SOUTH AYRSHIRE
Dalmellington
New Galloway
Moffat
Hawick
The Cheviot 816
Cheviot Hills
Alnwick
Almouth
Amble
Morpeth
NORTHUMBERLAND
Kielder Water
Bamburgh
Wooler
Holy I.
Farne Is.
Berwick-upon-Tweed
Flodden
Tweed
DUMFRIES & GALLOWAY
Lochmaben
Lockerbie
Langholm
Merrick 844
GALLOWAY
Dumfries
Annan
Gretna
ENGLAND
Newcastle-upon-Tyne
Blaydon
Gateshead
Stanley
Consett
DURHAM
Bishop Auckland
Crook
Barnard Castle
931 Skiddaw
CUMBRIA
Carlisle
Brampton
Haltwhistle
Hexham
Alston
Penrith
Appleby-in-Westmorland
950 Helvellyn
Ullswater
Keswick
Derwent Water
Cockermouth
Workington
Maryport
Whitehaven
St. Bees Hd.
Silloth
Aspatria
Wigton
893
Cross Fell
Eden
North Tyne
South Tyne
Derwent
Weir
Tees
Stranraer
Cairnryan
Newton Stewart
Gatehouse of Fleet
Castle Douglas
Dalbeattie
Kirkcudbright
L. Ryan
Wigtown
Whithorn
Wigtown B.
Burrow Hd.
Mull of Galloway
Luce Bay
Portpatrick
Solway Firth
Galloway Forest

NORTHERN IRELAND
Larne
Carrickfergus
Belfast L.
Bangor
Donaghadee
Newtownards
Belfast
269
Garron Pt.

SEAS
NORTH SEA
ATLANTIC OCEAN
North Channel
Firth of Forth
Moray Firth
Pentland Firth

SCOTLAND

ft m (elevation scale)
3000 / 1000
1500 / 500
600 / 200
300 / 100
100 / 300
200 / 600
500 / 1500
1000 / 3000
0 / 0

115

58
57
56
60

West from Greenwich

Projection: Lambert's Conformal Conic

COPYRIGHT PHILIP'S

☐ Forest Parks in Scotland

1:1 600 000

10 0 10 20 30 40 50 60 70 80 km
10 0 10 20 30 40 50 miles

SCOTLAND
Mull of Oa
Kintyre
Brodick
Arran
Firth of Clyde
Campbeltown
Mull of Kintyre
Ailsa Craig

Inishtrahull
Malin Hd.
Lough Swilly
Fanad Hd.
Malin Pen.
Carndonagh
Moville
Inishowen Pen.
Buncrana
Giants Causeway
Rathlin I.
Fair Hd.
Ballycastle

Tory I.
Sheep Haven
Mulroy B.
Horn Hd.
Portstewart
Portrush
Coleraine
L. Foyle
Limavady
Ballymoney
Garron Pt.
554 Trostan
GLENARIFF
269

Bloody Foreland
Gweedore
Errigal 752
The Rosses
Rathmelton
GLENVEAGH
Londonderry
LONDONDERRY
Ballymena
Randalstown Ballyclare
Larne

Inishfree B.
Aran I.
683
Letterkenny
DONEGAL
Lifford
Strabane
Sawel Mt. 683
Sion Mills
Newtownstewart
Mts. of Antrim
Roe
Magherafelt
Moneymore
Moneymore
ANTRIM
Antrim
Lough Neagh
Newtownabbey
Belfast L.
Bangor
Donaghadee
Newtownards

Crohy Hd.
Gweebarra B.
Dawros Hd.
Glenties
Lavagh More 676
Finn
Castlederg
TYRONE
Omagh
Cookstown
Coalisland
Dungannon
Belfast
Lisburn
Comber
Ards Pen.
Strangford L.
Portaferry
Portavogie
Ballyquintin Pt.

Loughros More B.
Rossan Pt.
601
Slieve League
Killybegs
Donegal
Dromore
Irvinestown
Enniskillen
Blackwater
Aughnacloy
Craigavon
Lurgan
Portadown
Banbridge
Lagan
DOWN
Ballynahinch
Downpatrick

St. John's Pt.
Donegal Bay
Ballyshannon
Bundoran
Erne
Lower L. Erne
FERMANAGH
Upper Erne
Clones
MONAGHAN
Monaghan
Keady
ARMAGH
Armagh
Middletown
Tandragee
Newry
Dundrum
Newcastle
852 Slieve Donard
Dundrum B.

Broad Haven
Erris Hd.
Downpatrick Hd.
Killala B.
Sligo Bay
Sligo
380
Killala
Dromore West
544
SLIGO
Colooney
L. Allen
LEITRIM
Leitrim
Belturbet
Annalee
Cootehill
Castleblaney
Carrickmacross
Slieve Gullion 577
Warrenpoint
Mourne Mts.
Kilkeel
Greenore
Carlingford L.
Dundalk

Mullet Pen.
Inishkea North
Inishkea South
Blacksod Bay
Belmullet
Ballina
Ballymote
L. Arrow
Boyle
Carrick-on-Shannon
CAVAN
L. Gowna
Cavan
Kingscourt
Ardee
LOUTH
Louth
Dundalk Bay

Achill I.
672
Corraun Pen.
L. Conn
806
Nephin
Swinford
Charlestown
Ballaghaderreen
ROSCOMMON
L. Sheelin
Oldcastle
Ceanannus Mor (Kells)
Blackwater
Dunleer
Clogher Hd.
Drogheda

Clare I.
Clew Bay
Newport
Castlebar
Westport
Knock
Ballyhaunis
Castlerea
Granard
LONGFORD
Longford
Castlepollard
An Uaimh (Navan)
Balbriggan

Inishturk
765 Croagh Patrick
Killary Harbour
Mweelrea 819
C o n n a c h t
Claremorris
Roscommon
Boyne
MEATH
Trim
Rush
Lambay I.

Inishbofin
Inishshark
CONNEMARA
Ballinrobe
Lough Mask
Glennamaddy
Tuam
Lough Ree
Athlone
WESTMEATH
Mullingar
Royal Canal
Swords
Malahide
Howth Hd.

Slyne Hd.
Clifden
Oughterard
Lough Corrib
I R E L A N D
Moate
Bofin
Edenderry
Grand Canal
Maynooth
DUB
DUBLIN
Dublin
Dun Laoghaire

G A L W A Y
Galway
Athenry
Ballinasloe
Clara
Tullamore
Daingean
Bog of Allen
KILDARE
Naas
Clondalkin

Galway Bay
Black Hd.
Inishmore
Aran Is.
Inishmaan
Inisheer
Loughrea
Suck
OFFALY
Portlaoise
Portarlington
Kildare
Monasterevin
Droichead Nua
L e i n s t e r
Kippure 754
Bray
Greystones

Cliffs of Moher
Hags Hd.
BURREN
368 Slieve Aughty
Gort
Portumna
Shannon
Birr
Mountmellick
Port Laoise
Poulaphouca Res.
WICKLOW
Wicklow Mts.
123

Liscannor Bay
Ennistimon
Tulla
Lough Derg
Roscrea
Slieve Bloom 528
Arderin
Mountrath
LAOIS
Athy
Lugnaquilla 926
Wicklow
Wicklow Hd.

Mal Bay
Mutton I.
Ennis
CLARE
Sixmilebridge
Nenagh
Templemore
Durrow
Carlow
Tullow
Arklow
Avoca
Rathdrum

Kilkee
Kilrush
Shannon Airport
Killaloe
Keeper Hill 694
Thurles
CARLOW
Muine Bheag
Slaney
Shillelagh
Mizen Hd.

Loop Hd.
Foynes
Limerick
TIPPERARY
Kilkenny
KILKENNY
Callan
796 Mt. Leinster
Bunclody
Gorey

Mouth of the Shannon
Ballybunion
LIMERICK
Rathkeale
Golden Vale
Tipperary
Cashel
Nore
WEXFORD
Cahore Pt.

Kerry Hd.
Listowel
Newcastle West
M u n s t e r
Kilfinnane
Galtymore 920
Galty Mts.
Caher
Slievenamon 722
Carrick-on-Suir
Clonmel
New Ross
Enniscorthy
Wexford

Brandon B.
Smerwick Harbour
953 Brandon Mt.
Tralee B.
Tralee
Slieve Mish 853
Maine
Newmarket
Kanturk
Buttevant
Mitchelstown
Fermoy
Knockmealdown Mts. 796 792
Comeragh Mts.
WATERFORD
Waterford
Tramore
Waterford Harbour
Rosslare
Rosslare Harbour
Greenore Pt.
Carnsore Pt.

Great Blasket I.
Dunmore Hd.
Dingle
Dingle Bay
KERRY
Killorglin
Laune
Killarney
L. Leane
Mallow
Blackwater
Lismore
Dungarvan
Dungarvan Harbour
Tramore B.
Hook Hd.
Saltee Is.

Inishvickillane
Carrauntoohil 1041
Macgillycuddy's Reeks
KILLARNEY
646
Boggeragh Mts.
Macroom
Lee
Blarney
CORK
Cork
Midleton
Youghal
Youghal B.

Valencia I.
Puffin I.
Cahersiveen
Kenmare
707
Caha Mts.
Glengarriff
586
Dunmanway
Bandon
Passage West
Cobh
Crosshaven
Cork Harbour
115
St. David's Hd.
St. David's

Great Skellig
Ballinskelligs B.
Scariff I.
Kenmare River
Bantry
Clonakilty
Kinsale
St. Brides Bay
WALES

Dursey I.
Castletown Bearhaven
Bear I.
Bantry Bay
Dunmanus B.
Skull
Clonakilty B.
Old Head of Kinsale

Crow Hd.
Mizen Hd.
Long I.
Baltimore
Sherkin I.
Skibbereen
Galley Hd.
C. Clear
Clear I.
Fastnet Rock

A T L A N T I C   O C E A N

NORTH CHANNEL

IRISH SEA

St. George's Channel

C E L T I C   S E A

Projection: Lambert's Conformal Conic
West from Greenwich
COPYRIGHT PHILIP'S

National Parks

ft m
1500 500
600 200
300 100
0 0
50 150
100 300
200 600
500 1500
1000 3000
2000 6000
m ft

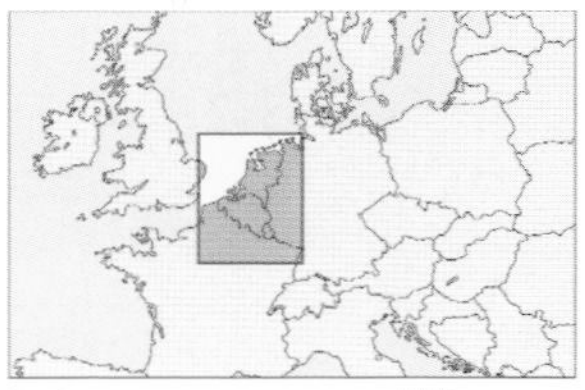

10 0 10 20 30 40 50 60 70 80 90 km

1:2 000 000

10 0 10 20 30 40 50 60 miles

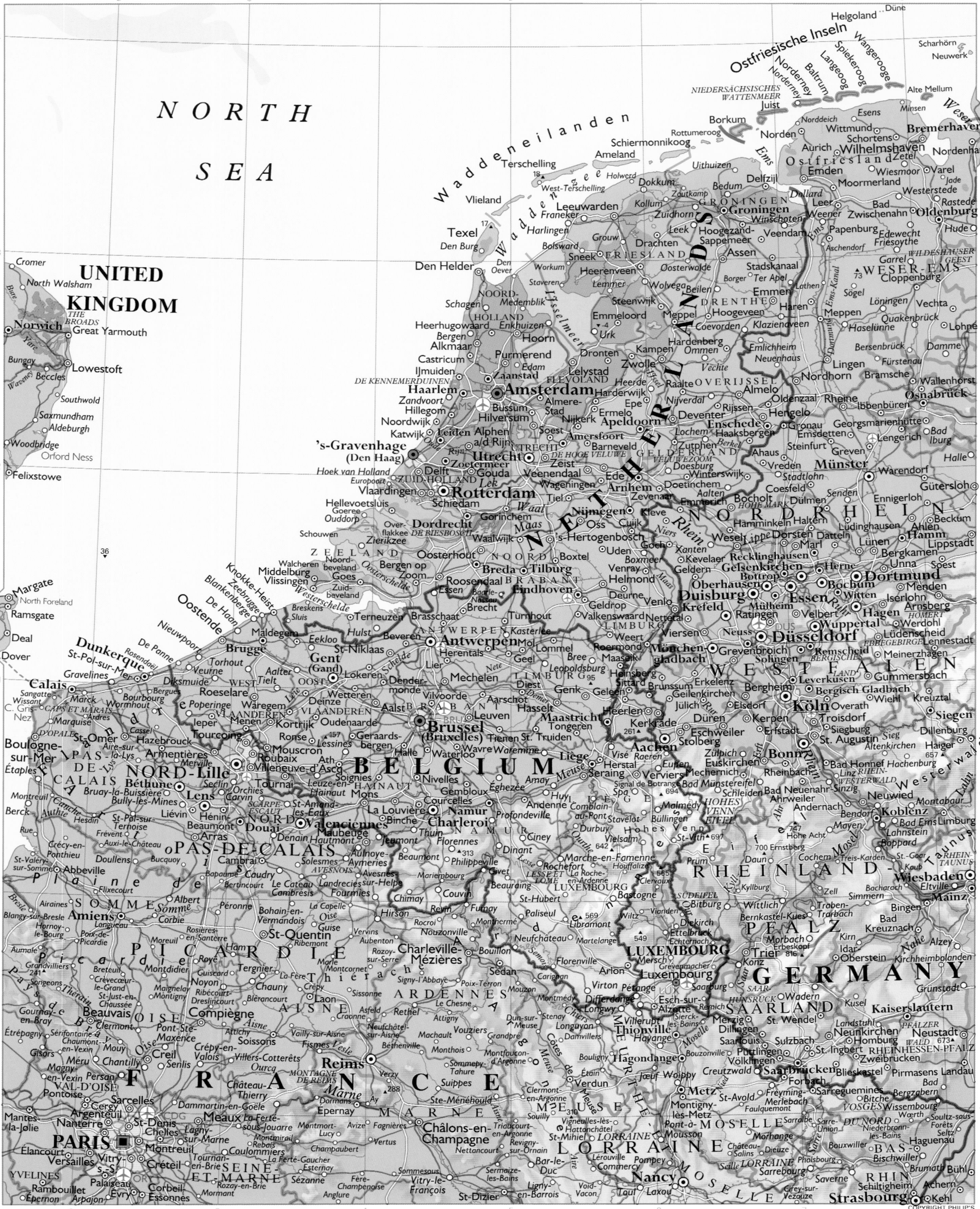

NORTH SEA

UNITED KINGDOM

NETHERLANDS

BELGIUM

GERMANY

FRANCE

LUXEMBOURG

Amsterdam · 's-Gravenhage (Den Haag) · Rotterdam · Utrecht · Haarlem · Groningen · Leeuwarden · Arnhem · Nijmegen · Eindhoven · Tilburg · Breda · Dordrecht · Enschede · Apeldoorn · Zwolle

Antwerpen · Brussel (Bruxelles) · Gent (Gand) · Brugge · Namur · Charleroi · Liège · Mons · Hasselt · Maastricht · Aachen · Leuven

Köln · Düsseldorf · Duisburg · Essen · Dortmund · Bonn · Koblenz · Münster · Wiesbaden · Mainz · Saarbrücken · Trier · Kaiserslautern

Nord-Lille · Calais · Dunkerque · Boulogne-sur-Mer · Amiens · Reims · Metz · Nancy · Strasbourg · Paris · Versailles

ZEELAND · HOLLAND · FRIESLAND · DRENTHE · OVERIJSSEL · FLEVOLAND · NOORD BRABANT · LIMBURG · GELDERLAND

NORDRHEIN-WESTFALEN · RHEINLAND-PFALZ · SAARLAND

PAS-DE-CALAIS · PICARDIE · NORD · SOMME · OISE · AISNE · ARDENNES · LORRAINE · MOSELLE · MARNE · VOSGES

Waddeneilanden · Ostfriesische Inseln · Texel · Terschelling · Vlieland · Ameland · Schiermonnikoog · Borkum

Rhein · Maas · Mosel · Moselle · Meuse · Waal · Lek · IJsselmeer

National Parks

Underlined towns give their name to the administrative area in which they stand.

ft m / m ft

COPYRIGHT PHILIP'S

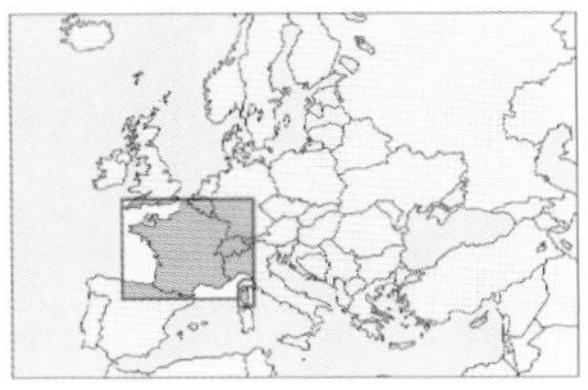

1:4 000 000

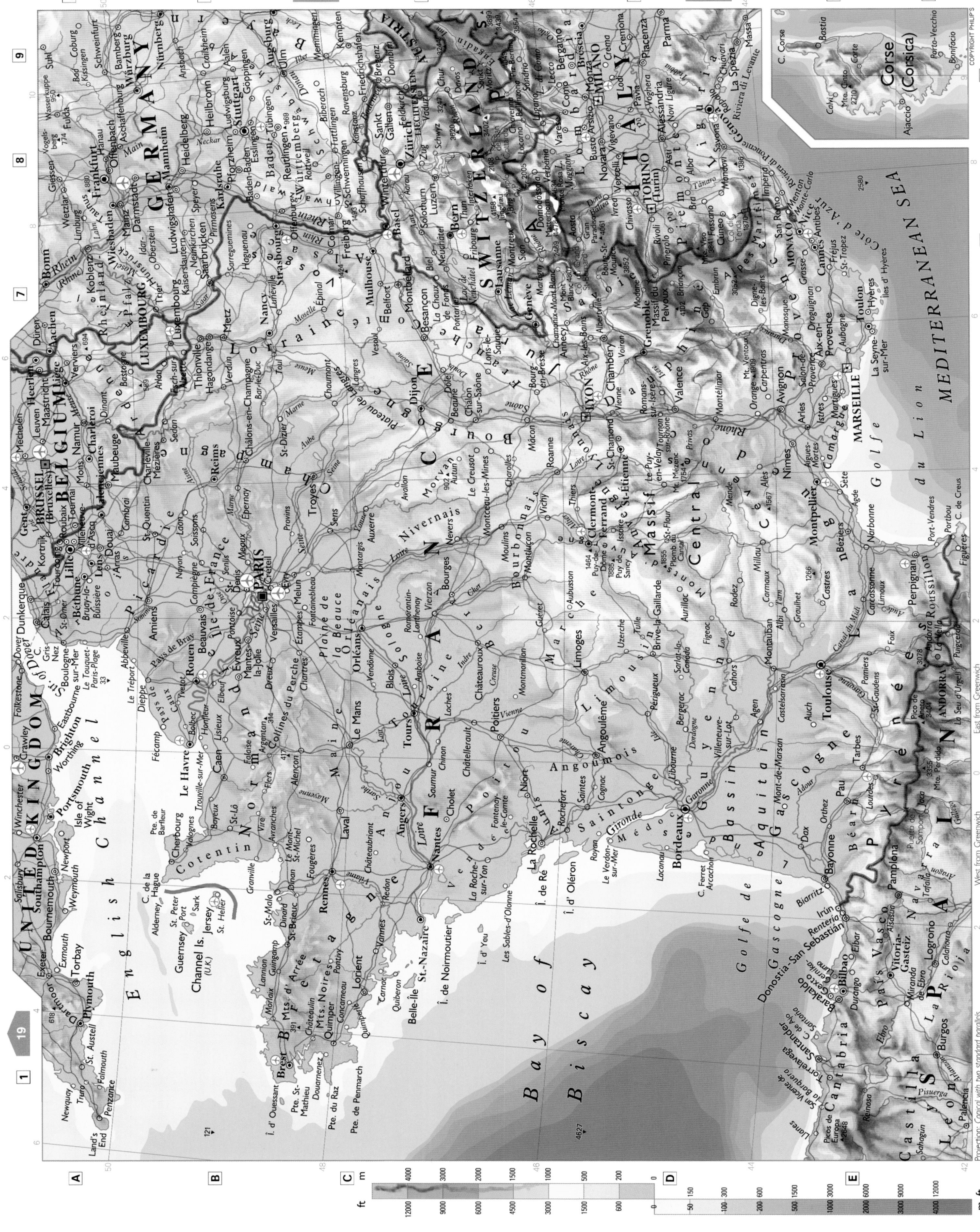

Projection: Conical with two standard parallels

COPYRIGHT PHILIP'S

Corse (Corsica)

UNITED KINGDOM

GERMANY

BELGIUM

LUXEMBOURG

SWITZERLAND

ITALY

FRANCE

ANDORRA

English Channel

Bay of Biscay

MEDITERRANEAN SEA

Golfe du Lion

Golfe de Gascogne

PARIS

MARSEILLE

LYON

Bordeaux

Toulouse

MONACO

Normandie

Bretagne

Bourgogne

Massif Central

Pyrénées

Provence

Aquitaine

ft m
12000 4000
9000 3000
6000 2000
4500 1500
3000 1000
1500 500
600 200
0 0

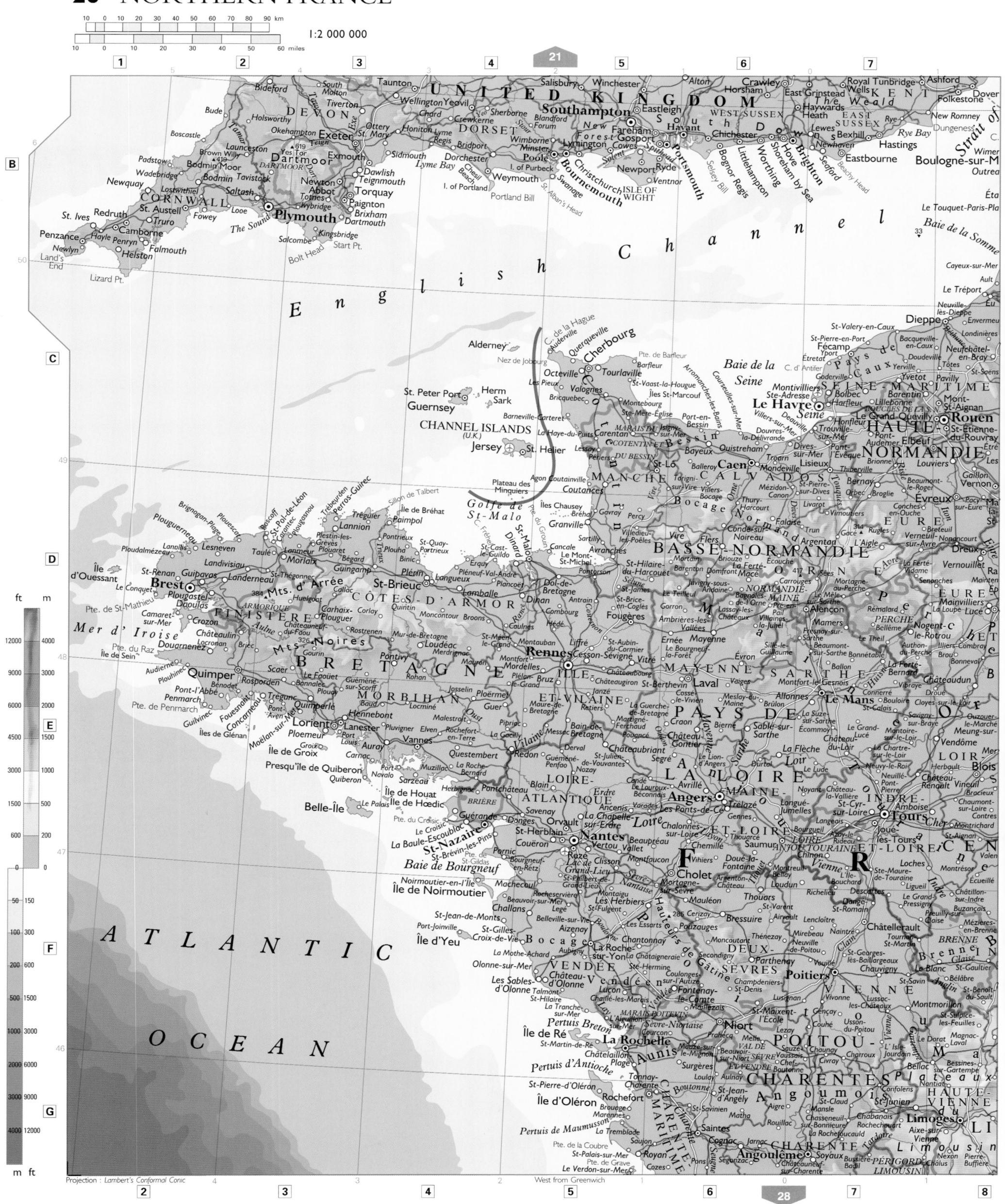

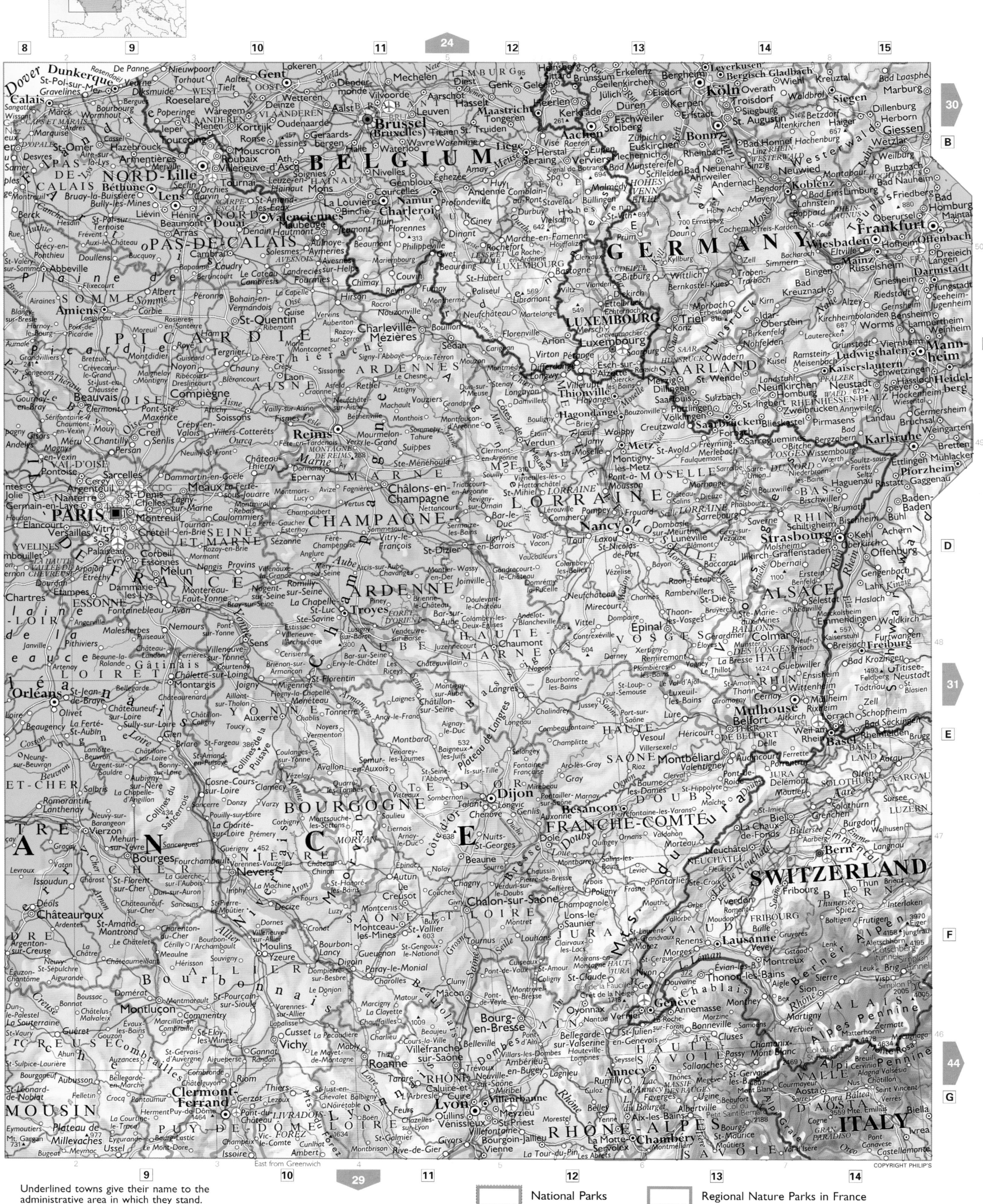

Underlined towns give their name to the
administrative area in which they stand.

National Parks

Regional Nature Parks in France

East from Greenwich

COPYRIGHT PHILIP'S

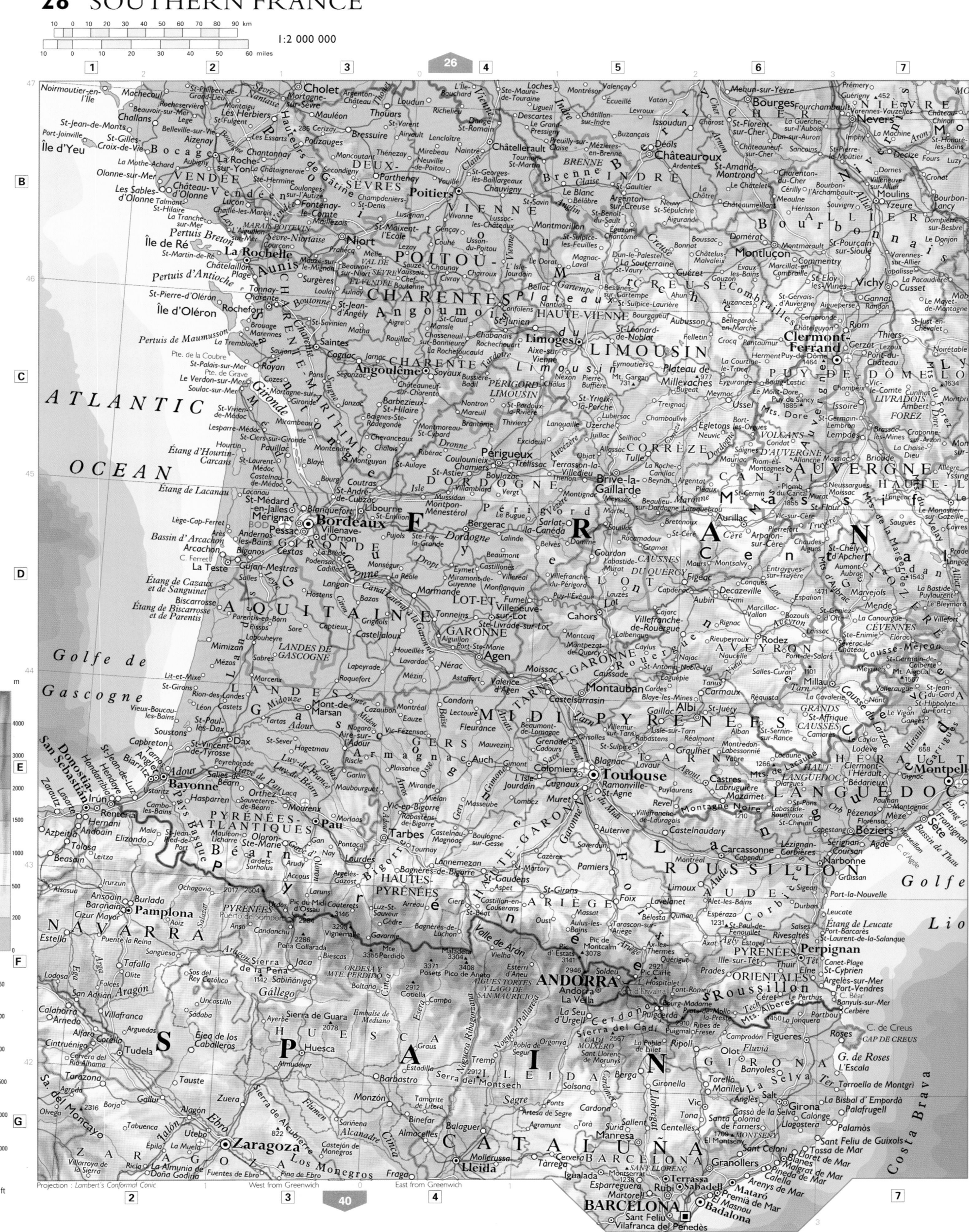

SWITZERLAND

GRAUBÜNDEN

Bern

NEUCHÂTEL

FRIBOURG

VAUD

Lausanne

Genève

VALAIS

TICINO

HAUTE-SAVOIE

Annecy

RHÔNE-ALPES

SAVOIE

Lyon

St-Étienne

ISÈRE

Grenoble

DRÔME

ARDÈCHE

VERCORS

HAUTES-ALPES

ÉCRINS

PROVENCE

ALPES-DE-HAUTE-PROVENCE

VAUCLUSE

LUBERON

Avignon

Nîmes

BOUCHES-DU-RHÔNE

CAMARGUE

Marseille

Toulon

CÔTE D'AZUR

MERCANTOUR

ALPES-MARITIMES

VAR

VERDON

Nice

MONACO

Cannes

LOMBARDIA

MILANO

PIEMONTE

Torino

Génova

ITALY

LIGURIAN SEA

Riviera di Ponente

Riviera di Levante

Golfo di Génova

La Spezia

Livorno

Elba

ARCIPELAGO TOSCANO

CORSE

HAUTE-CORSE

Bastia

CORSE-DU-SUD

Ajaccio

Bonifacio

ARCIPELAGO DE LA MADDALENA

M E D I T E R R A N E A N   S E A

National Parks

Regional Nature Parks in France

COPYRIGHT PHILIP'S

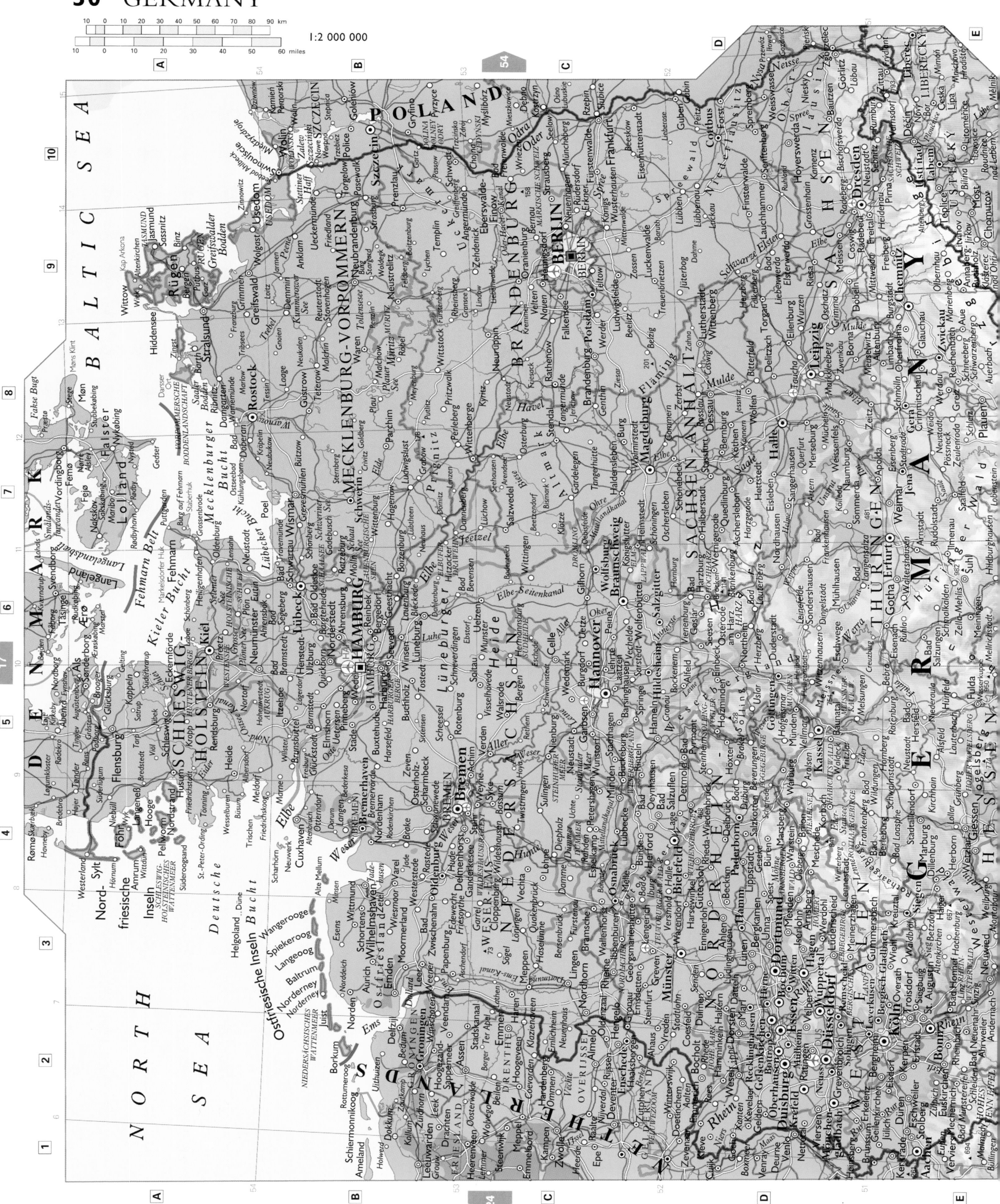

1:2 000 000

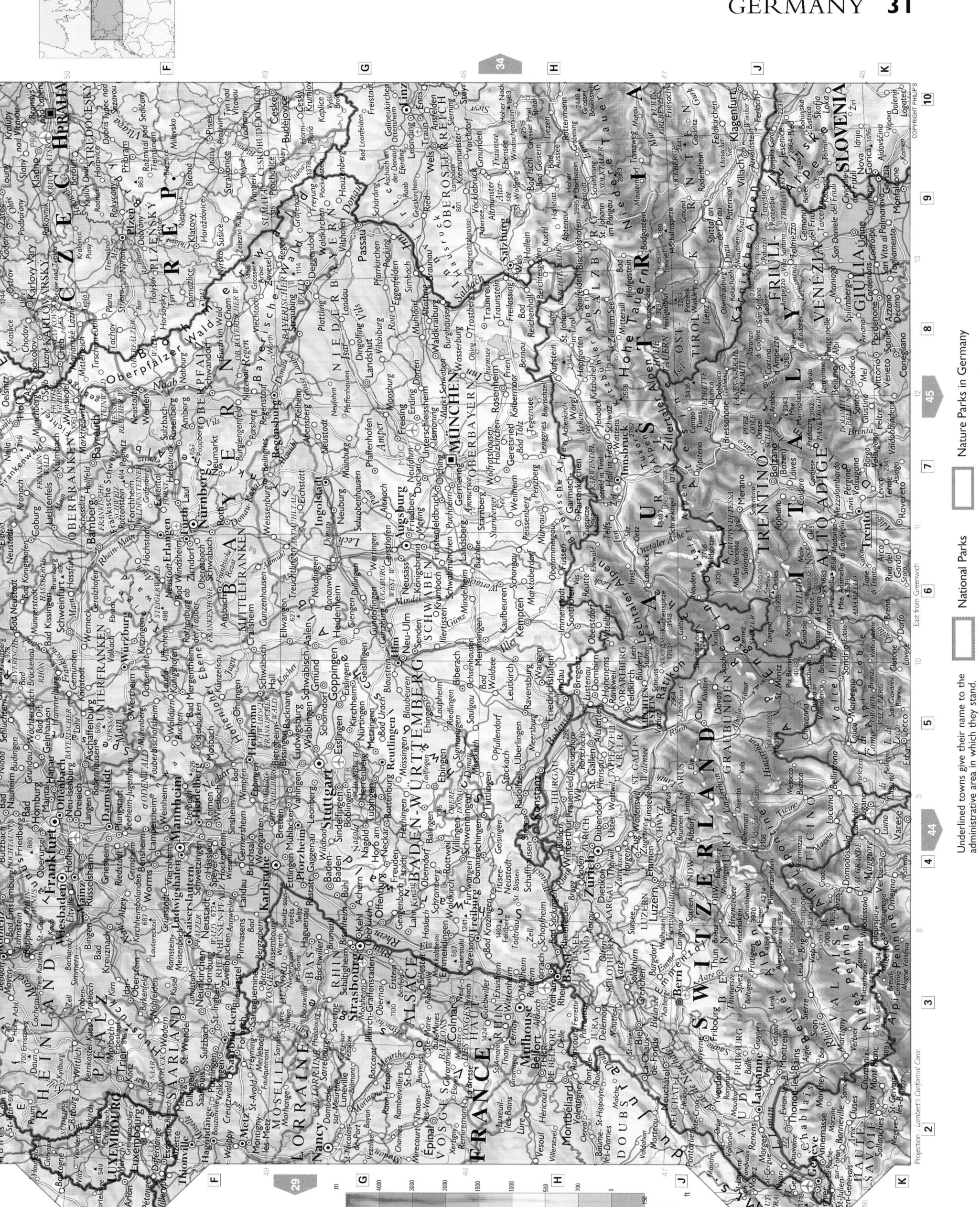

Projection : Lambert's Conformal Conic

East from Greenwich

Nature Parks in Germany

National Parks

Underlined towns give their name to the
administrative area in which they stand.

1:800 000

Projection: Conical with two standard parallels

7
8
31
9
10
11
A
B
34
C
D
E
6
7
44
8
9
10
11
8 30'
9 30'
9
10
10 30'
East from Greenwich
47 30'
47
46 30'
46
BADEN WÜRTTEMBERG
GERMANY
BAYERN
AUSTRIA
TIROL
VORARLBERG
LIECHTENSTEIN
SWITZERLAND
ITALY
PIEMONTE
LOMBARDIA
TRENTINO-ALTO ÁDIGE
SCHAFFHAUSEN
THURGAU
ZÜRICH
SANKT GALLEN
APPENZELL A. R.
APPENZELL I. R.
ZUG
SCHWYZ
GLARUS
NIDWALDEN
OBWALDEN
URI
GRAUBÜNDEN
TICINO
STELVIO
Bonndorf
Blumberg
Engen
Stockach
Sipplingen
Heiligenberg
Baienfurt
Wolfegg
Leutkirch
Obergünzburg
Schongau
Weingarten
Kisslegg
Altusried
Wildpoldsried
Unterthingau
Marktoberdorf
Hilzingen
Singen
Überlingen
Ravensburg
Stühlingen
Thayngen
Radolfzell
Markdorf
Isny
Kempten
Durach
Steingaden
Schaffhausen
Allensbach
Meckenbeuren
Buchenberg
Neunkirch
Diessenhofen
Konstanz
Meersburg
Tettnang
Wangen
Rosshaupten
Neuhausen
Feuerthalen
Stein am Rhein
Steckborn
Friedrichshafen
Sulzberg
Mittelberg
Tiengen
Rheinfall
Kreuzlingen
Langenargen
Kressbronn
Lindenberg
Weitnau
Nesselwang
Forggensee
Zurzach
Andelfingen
Weiler-Simmerberg
1243
Rettenberg
Wertach
Schwangau
Rhein
Eglisau
Thur
Weinfelden
Pfronten
Füssen
Döttingen (Rhine)
Glattfelden
Neftenbach
Seuzach
Frauenfeld
Romanshorn
Lindau
Scheidegg
Oberstaufen
Immenstadt
1738
Blaichach
Vils
Würenlingen
Bülach
Sulgen
Amriswil
Arbon
Sonthofen
Hindelang
Reutte
Obersiggenthal
Embrach
Winterthur
Wängi
Bischofszell
Rorschach
Hard
Bregenz
Baden
Wettingen
Kloten
Elgg
Aadorf
Wil
Rheineck
Wolfurt
Hittisau
Fischen
Weissenbach
Regensdorf
Wallisellen
Effretikon
Sirnach
Uzwil
Sankt Gallen
Sankt Margrethen
Lustenau
Egg
Oberstdorf
Ehrwald
Neuenhof
Limmat
Dübendorf
Turbenthal
Kirchberg
Gossau
Trogen
Widnau
Dornbirn
Bezau
Allgäuer Alpen
2594
Dietikon
Zürich
Pfäffikon
Flawil
Teufen
Diepoldsau
Bregenzer Wald
Schlieren
Bremgarten
Fällanden
Uster
Bauma
Degersheim
Herisau
Altstätten
Hohenems
Nassereith
Wohlen
Reuss
Zollikon
Wetzikon
Bütschwil
Gais
Götzis
Hoher Freschen
2004
Au
Mittelberg
Mädelegabel
2645
Häselgehr
Kilchberg
Küsnacht
Hinwil
Wattwil
Urnäsch
Oberriet
Lech
Muri
Adliswil
Meilen
Wald
Wasserauen
Rankweil
Damüls
Schröcken
Bach
2777
Silz
Thalwil
Männedorf
Ebnat-Kappel
Säntis
2501
Feldkirch
Warth
Imst
Affoltern
Horgen
Rüti
Zürichsee
Toggenburg
Lechtaler Alpen
Inn
Wädenswil
Stäfa
Jona
Nesslau
Unterwasser
Gams
Rote Wand
2704
Parseier-Sp.
3036
Oetz
Sins
Baar
Richterswil
Rapperswil
Kaltbrunn
Speer
1950
Grabs
Nenzing
Bludenz
Lech
Stuben
St. Anton
Zams
2974
Cham
Pfäffikon
Lachen
Schänis
Churfirsten
Buchs
Schaan
Langen
Flirsch
Landeck
Hochdorf
Egg
Walensee
Sevelen
Vaduz
Arlbergpass
1793
Rothenburg
Root
Unterägeri
Sihlsee
Walenstadt
Dalaas
Prutz
Ebikon
Zugersee
Einsiedeln
Näfels
Murg
Schruns
Kuchenspitze
3148
St. Leonhard
Küssnacht
Trisanna
Emmenbrücke
Arth
Netstal
Linth
Glarus
Mels
Sargans
Rätikon
Montafon
Ill
Luzern
Rigi
Mythen
1899
Schesaplana
2964
Feuchten
Kriens
Weggis
Goldau
Schwyz
Glärnisch
2914
Bad Ragaz
2817
Ischgl
Vesulspitze
3089
3533
Horw
Vitznau
Brunnen
Muotathal
Schwanden
St-Gallenkirch
Gaschurn
Mittelberg
Vierwaldstättersee
434
Glarner Alpen
Pizol
2844
Schiers
Galtür
Samnaun
Alpnach
Stans
Landquart
Prättigau
Küblis
2853
3294
Martina
Dorf
Nidwaldner
Bauen
Linthal
Elm
Vättis
Silvretta Gruppe
3399
Nauders
Kerns
Altdorf
2794
3247
Klosters
Wildspitze
3768
Sachseln
Alpen
Urirotstock
2928
Bürglen
Hausstock
3158
Chur
Langwies
3312
Piz Buin
Unter-engadin
Resia
Weisskugel
3736
Ötztaler Alpen
Engelberg
Erstfeld
Tödi
3614
Flims
Domat Ems
Davos
Titlis
3239
Urner Alpen
Oberalpstock
3328
Trun
Ilanz
Bonaduz
Arosa
2383
3085
Ardez
Scuol (Schuls)
San Valentino alla Muta
3602
Gadmen
Disentis (Muster)
Vorderrhein
Oberland
Churwalden
Flüelapass
Susch
Málles Venosta
Wassen
Oberalppass
2044
Lenzerheide
Thusis
Wiesen
3063
Piz Vadret
3229
Zernez
Piz Sesvenna
3205
Sluderno
Silandro (Schlanders)
Guttannen
Göschenen
Sedrun
Filisur
3165
Val Venosta
Dammastock
3630
Tiefencastel
Albula
Piz Kesch
3418
Santa Maria
Láces
3283
Hospental
Andermatt
Piz Medel
3210
Vals
Thalkirch
Savognin
3339
La Punt
Engadin
Prato allo Stelvio
Adige
Furkapass
2431
Realp
Hinterrhein
3000
Andeer
Grimselpass
2165
2108
St. Gotthard
3149
3199
Lepontine Alpen
Splügen
Piz d'Err
3378
Samedan
Livigno
Passo dello Stelvio
2757
Ortles
3905
Martello
Gletsch
Airolo
Olivone
Adula-Gruppe
Splügenpass
2113
Mulegns
Sankt Moritz
Pontresina
Bórmio
Ulrichen
Bedretto
Rheinwaldhorn
3402
2065
Passo del San Bernardino
Piz Platta
3392
Julierpass
2284
Silvaplana
Passo del Bernina
2323
Münster
Faido
San Bernardino
3209
Fusio
Campo Tencia
3072
Malvaglia
Ticino
3063
Maloja
Malojapass
1815
Piz Bernina
4049
3302
Blinnenhorn
3374
Basodino
3273
Sonogno
Bodio
Campodolcino
3025
3163
Pizzo Stella
3131
Alpi Retiche
Formazza
Bignasco
Biasca
Mesocco
Rossa
Vicosoprano
Poschiavo
Sóndalo
3006
Vermiglio
Dimaro
Cevio
Chiavenna
Castasegna
Grosio
Grosotto
Ponte di Legno
Passo del Tonale
Prémia
Toce
2792
Maggia
Moesa
Mera
Monte Disgrazia
3678
Chiesa in Valmalenco
Brusio
Vezza d'Oglio
La Presanella
3558
Madonna di Campiglio
2322
Maggia
Vogorno
Novate Mezzola
Tirano
Crodo
2237
Arbedo
Sóndrio
Chiuro
Téglio
Edolo
Varzo
Intragna
Locarno
Minusio
Bellinzona
Verceia
Aprica
Mte. Adamello
3554
Crevoladossola
Losone
Ascona
Giubiasco
Gravedona
Morbegno
Talamona
Albosaggia
Adda
Malonno
Pinzolo
Masera
Brissago
Vira
Cadenazzo
Pzo. di Gino
2245
Dongo
Cólico
Delébio
Valtellina
Val Camónica
Domodóssola
Santa Maria Maggiore
Lago di Como
Monte Legnone
2609
Pizzo di Coca
3052
Cedégolo
Villadóssola
Cannóbio
Maccagno
Porlezza
Bellano
Gerola Alta
Valbondione
Capo di Ponte
Tione di Trento
Cannero Riviera
Agno
Lugano
Menággio
Varenna
Branzi
Orobie
Schilpario
Vogogna
VALGRANDE
Lago Maggiore
193
Luino
Lago di Lugano
Tremezzo
199
Bellágio
Intróbio
Alpi
Valli Giudicárie
Ornavasso
Ghiffa
Ponte Tresa
Melide
Mte. Generoso
1701
Argegno
Monte San Primo
1685
Mandello del Lário
Piazza Brembano
Borno
Breno
Bienno
Pieve di Bono
Riva del Garda
Gravellona Toce
Pallanza
Verbánia
Laveno
Mendrisio
Nesso
Valle Seriana
Clusone
Condino
Omegna
Stresa
Balerna
Moltrásio
Canzo
Lecco
San Giovanni Bianco
Brembo
Darfo
Monte Colombine
2215
Bagolino
Storo
Gavirate
Chiasso
Gandino
Lóvere
Limone sul Garda
Varallo
L. d'Orta
Varese
Malnate
Como
Pisogne
Cóllio
Malcesine
Erba
Oggiono
Calolziocorte
Zogno
Gazzaniga
L. d'Idro
Méina
Lago di Varese
Olgiate Comasco
Brianza
Albino
Marone
Gardone Val Trómpia
Vestone
Arona
Sesto Calende
Cantù
Ponte San Pietro
Bérgamo
Casazza
L. d'Iseo
Idro
Borgosésia
Borgomanero
Tradate
Carate Brianza
Trescore Balneário
Gargnano
L. di Garda
Serravalle Sésia
Somma Lombardo
Cassano Magnago
Meda
Merate
Seriate
Sárnico
Sarezzo
Chiese
Vobarno
Gallarate
Saronno
Séveso
Seregno
Dálmine
Stezzano
Iseo
Sabbio Chiese
Gardone Riviera
396
252
1125

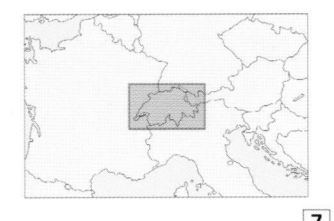

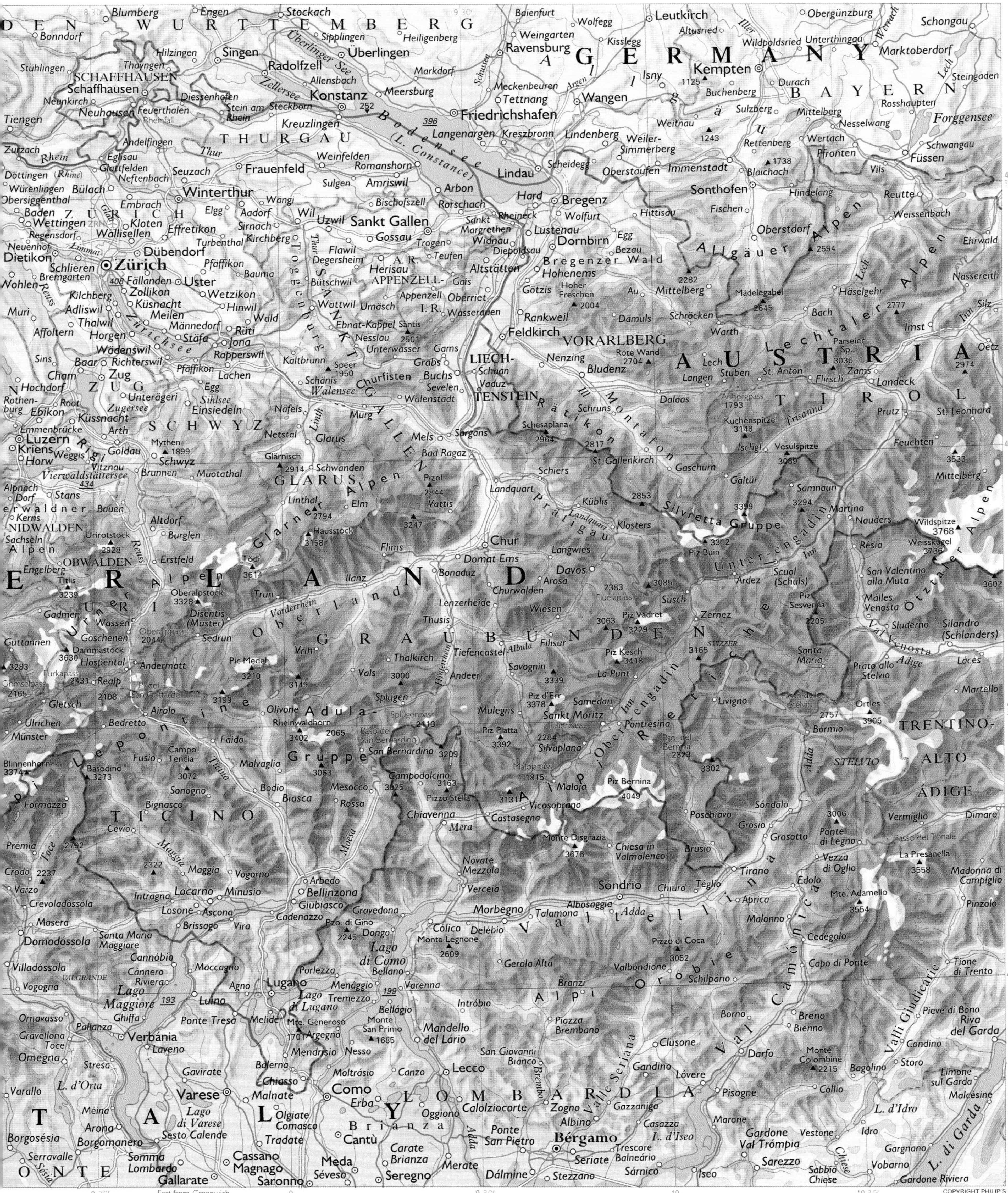

1:2 000 000

National Parks

Underlined towns give their name to the
administrative area in which they stand.

COPYRIGHT PHILIP'S

East from Greenwich

50 0 25 50 75 100 125 150 175 km
50   25   75   100   125 miles

1 : 4 000 000

NORTH SEA

BALTIC SEA

DENMARK

UNITED KINGDOM

NETHERLANDS

BELGIUM

LUXEMBOURG

GERMANY

FRANCE

SWITZERLAND

LIECHTENSTEIN

AUSTRIA

CZECH R

SLOVENIA

ITALY

ADRIATIC SEA

CRO

Major cities and towns include:
Sylt, Åbenrå, Flensburg, Schleswig, Kiel, Rostock, Stralsund, Rügen, Lübeck, HAMBURG, Bremen, Bremerhaven, Cuxhaven, Groningen, AMSTERDAM, ROTTERDAM, Utrecht, Hannover, BERLIN, Potsdam, Magdeburg, Leipzig, Dresden, Szczecin, BRUSSEL (Bruxelles), Antwerpen, Köln (Cologne), Bonn, Dortmund, Essen, Düsseldorf, Frankfurt, Mainz, Wiesbaden, Mannheim, Nürnberg, Stuttgart, München (Munich), Augsburg, PRAHA (Prague), Plzeň, České Budějovice, PARIS, Reims, Metz, Nancy, Strasbourg, Dijon, Mulhouse, Basel, Zürich, Bern, Genève, Lausanne, Innsbruck, Salzburg, Linz, Graz, Klagenfurt, Ljubljana, Zagreb, MILANO, TORINO (Turin), Genova, Verona, Venézia (Venice), Bologna, LYON, MARSEILLE, Nice, MONACO

Projection: Conical with two standard parallels

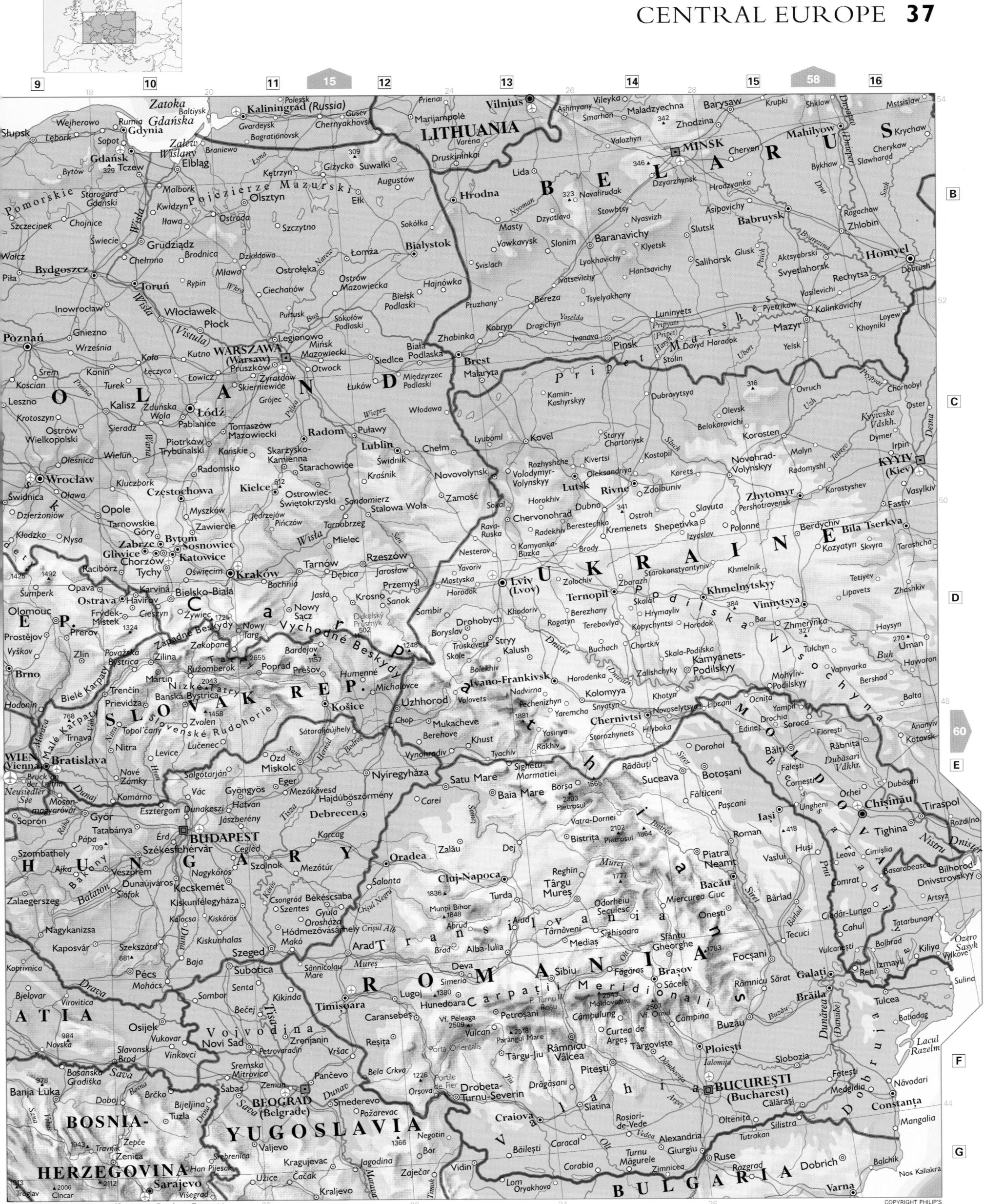

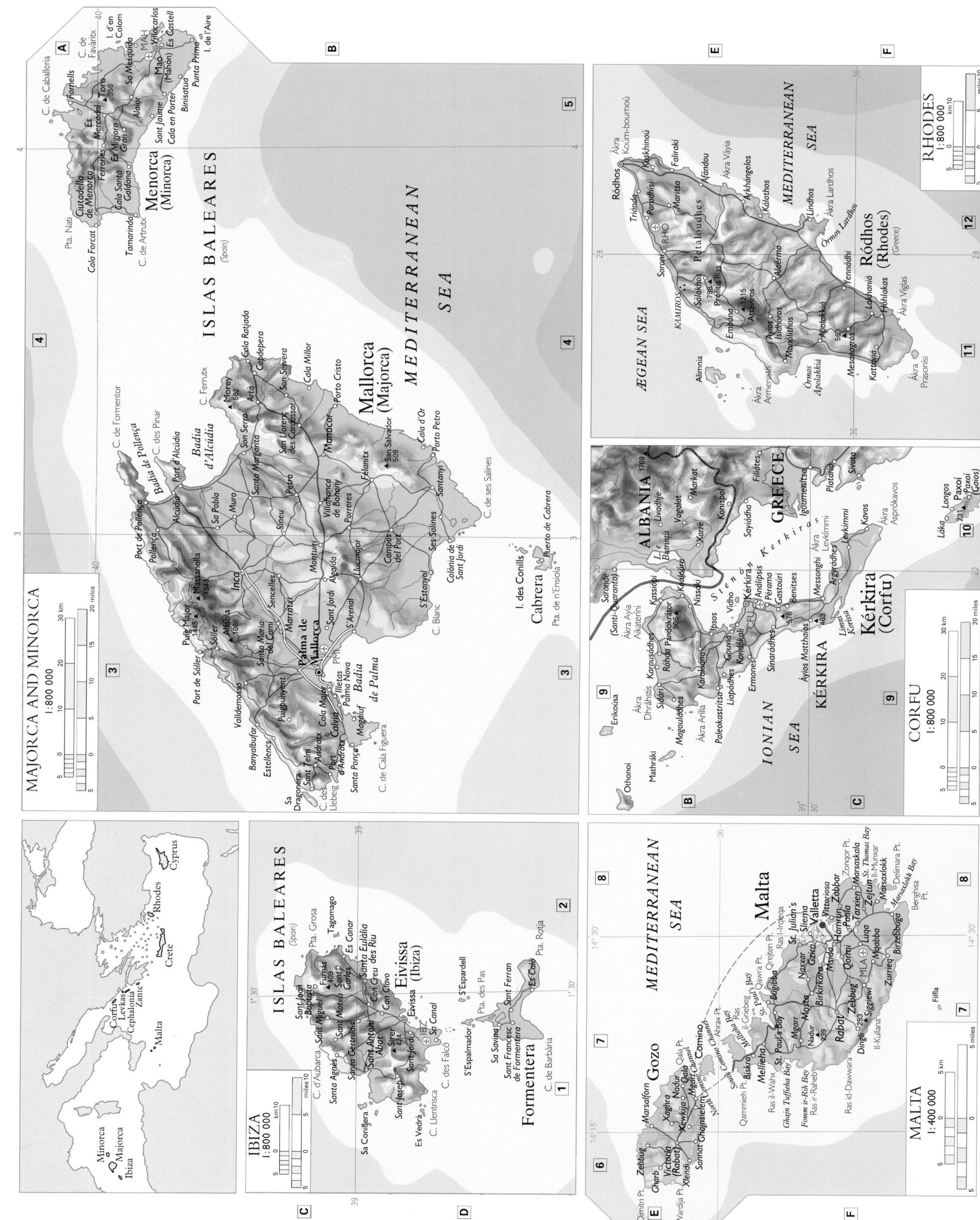

MENORCA (Minorca)

C. de Caballería · Fornells · Pta. Nati · Cala Forcat · C. de Arrutx · Tamarinda · Cutadella de Menorca · Ferreríes · Es Mercadal · Toro 358 · Alaior · Cala Santa Galdána · Sant Jaume (Mao) · Cala en Porter · Binisafua · Sant Lluís · Mao (Mahón) · MAH · Villacarlos · Es Castell · Punta Prima · I. de l'Aire · I. d'en Colom · C. de Favàritx · Sa Mesquida · I. des Conills

ISLAS BALEARES (Spain)

MAJORCA AND MINORCA
1:800 000

MALLORCA (Majorca)

C. de Formentor · Port de Pollença · Pollença · C. de Pollença · Badia de Pollença · Port d'Alcúdia · C. des Pinar · Cala Ratjada · Capdepera · Artà · Alcúdia · Badia d'Alcúdia · Son Serra · Santa Margarita · Morey 562 · Maracot · Cala Millor · San Servera · Sa Pobla · Muro · Sant Llorenç des Cardassar · Porto Cristo · Valldemossa · Banyalbufar · Estellencs · Sa Dragonera · C. des Llebeig · Sant Telm · Andratx · Port d'Andratx · Sóller · Port de Sóller · Puig Major 1445 · Massanella 1340 · Alfàbia 1068 · Inca · Santa Maria del Camí · Sencelles · Sineu · Petra · Santany · Villafranca de Bonany · Porreres · Felanitx · San Salvador 509 · Cala d'Or · Porto Petro · Santany · C. de ses Salines · Montuïri · Algaida · Marràtxi · Sant Jordi · Palma de Mallorca · PM · Badia de Palma · Puigpunyent · Calvià · Andratx · Port · Santa Ponça · Magaluf · Palma Nova · Illetas · Cala Major · S'Arenal · Llucmajor · Campos del Port · Ses Salines · S'Estanyol · S'Estanyol · C. Blanc · Colónia de Sant Jordi · Pta. de n'Ensiola · Puerto de Cabrera · C. de Cala Figuera · C. des Falcó · Santa Ponça · C. de Cala Figuera

Cabrera

I. des Conills · Puerto de Cabrera · Pta. de n'Ensiola

MEDITERRANEAN SEA

ISLAS BALEARES (Spain)

IBIZA
1:800 000

Pta. Grosa · Sant Joan Baptista · Santa Eulària des Riu · Tagomago · Es Canar · Es Canar · Furnàs 409 · Santa Gertrudis · Santa Eulària · Sant Miguel · Sant Mateu · Sant Antoni · Sant Rafel · Can Clavo · Can Creu des Riu · IBZ · Eivissa · Sant Agnès · Sant Josep · Sant Jordi · Sa Talaia 424 · Sant Francesc de Formentera · Ses Salines · Sa Conillera · Es Vedrà · C. d'Aubarca · C. Llentrisca · S'Espalmador · Sa Savina · Sa Canal · Pta. des Pas · S'Espardell · Sant Ferran · Es Caló · Pta. Rotja

EIVISSA (Ibiza)

Formentera

C. de Barbària

MEDITERRANEAN SEA

RHODES
1:800 000

Ákra Koúm-bournoú · Ródhos · RHO · Triánda · Kalithiés · Koskinoú · Faliráki · Paradhísi · Maritsa · Afándou · Ákra Vávia · Arkhángelos · Kálathos · Ákra Lárdhos · Sálakhos · Sóroni · KÁMIROS · Petaloúdhes · Profítis Ilías 798 · Líndhos · Ládhos · Ákra Lárdhos · Embóna · Atáviros 1215 · Áyios Isídhoros · Apóllona · Monólithos · Arkhípolis · Ákra Armenistís · Ródhos (Rhodes) (Greece) · Láerma · Asklipió · Yennádhi · Ákra Fourní · Lákhaniá · Kattaviá · Mesanagrós 563 · Hóhlakas · Ákra Prasonísi · Órmos Apolakkiá · Ákra Lárdhos · Órmos Lárdhou · Alimniá

AEGEAN SEA · *MEDITERRANEAN SEA*

CORFU
1:800 000

ALBANIA 1769 · **GREECE**

Sarandë · (Santi-Quaranta) · Ákra Ayía Aikateríni · Ákra Dhrástis · Sidhári · Karousádhes · Róda · Kassiópi · Nissáki · Ipsos · Vidho · Kérkira · Perama · CFU · Andípsis · Gastoúri · Benítses · Messonghi · Argyrádhes · Levkimmi · Kávos · Ákra Asprókavos · Mogoulídhes · Ákra Arílla · Paleokastrítsa · Liapádhes · Ermones · Glyfáda · Áyios Matthéos 463 · Áyios Góurdin · Ákra Lefkímmi · Lefkímmi · Sinarádhes · Pélekas · Kondókali · Kontokáli · Vátos · Gouviá · Káto Korakiána · Kérkira (Corfu) · Stení · Stenó · Filiátes · Konispol · Markat · Igoumenítsa · Sívota · Platariá · Plataría

KÉRKIRA (Corfu)

Erikoúsa · Mathráki · Othonoí

Láka · Longós · Paxoí (Gáios) 231 · Antípaxi

IONIAN SEA · *KÉRKIRA*

MALTA
1:400 000

Gozo · San Dimitri Pt. · Żebbuġ · Marsalforn · Xagħra · Nadur · Victoria (Rabat) · Qala Pt. · Xewkija · Xlendi · Għarb · Charb · Sannat · Għajnsielem · Mġarr · Comino · South Comino Channel · North Comino Channel

Malta · Qammieh Pt. · Marfa Ridge · Mellieħa · Mellieħa Bay · Ras il-Wahx · Ghajn Tuffieha Bay · Fomm ir-Rih Bay · Ras ir-Raħeb · St. Paul's Bay · St. Paul's Islands · Għargħur · Mġarr · Mosta · Naxxar · Birkirkara · Msida · Valletta · MLA · Luqa · Qormi · Żebbuġ · Żurrieq · Rabat · Dingli · Dingli Cliffs · 239 · Siġġiewi · Mdina · Hamrun · Gżira · Sliema · St. Julian's · Tarxien · Żabbar · Paola · Żejtun · Vittoriosa · Marsaskala · Marsaxlokk · Birżebbuġa · St. Thomas Bay · Delimara Pt. · Benghsa Pt. · Marsaxlokk Bay · Żonqor Pt. · Il-Munxar · Qrendi · Ħal Qawra Pt. · Il-Kullana · Ras id-Dawwara · Filfla · Grieba Pt. · Abrax Pt. · Ras il-Ħamrija

MEDITERRANEAN SEA

Minorca · Majorca · Ibiza
Corfu · Levkás · Cephalonia · Zante · Rhodes · Crete · Cyprus · Malta

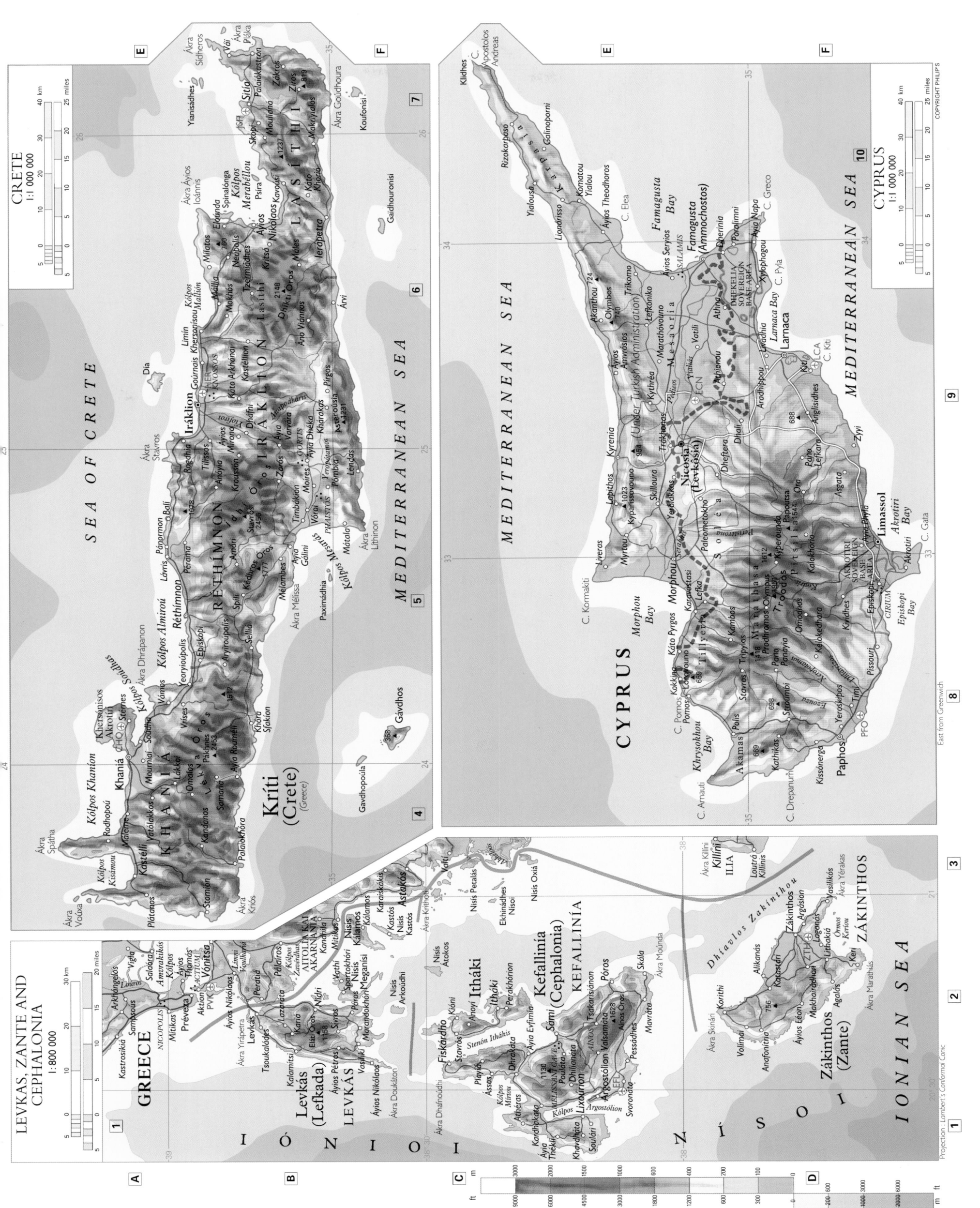

CRETE
1:1 000 000

CRETE

SEA OF CRETE

KHANIÁ

RÉTHIMNON

IRÁKLION

LASÍTHI

Kríti (Crete)
(Greece)

MEDITERRANEAN SEA

LEVKAS, ZANTE AND CEPHALONIA
1:800 000

GREECE

AITOLÍA KAÍ
AKARNANÍA

Levkás
(Lefkada)

LEVKÁS

Kefallinía
(Cephalonia)

KEFALLINÍA

Zákinthos
(Zante)

ZÁKINTHOS

I Ó N I O I   N Í S O I

IONIAN SEA

CYPRUS
1:1 000 000

CYPRUS

MEDITERRANEAN SEA

Tróodos

Mesaoría

(Under Turkish Administration)

DHEKELIA
SOVEREIGN
BASE AREA

AKROTIRI
SOVEREIGN
BASE AREA

MEDITERRANEAN SEA

Projection: Lambert's Conformal Conic

East from Greenwich

COPYRIGHT PHILIP'S

1:2 000 000

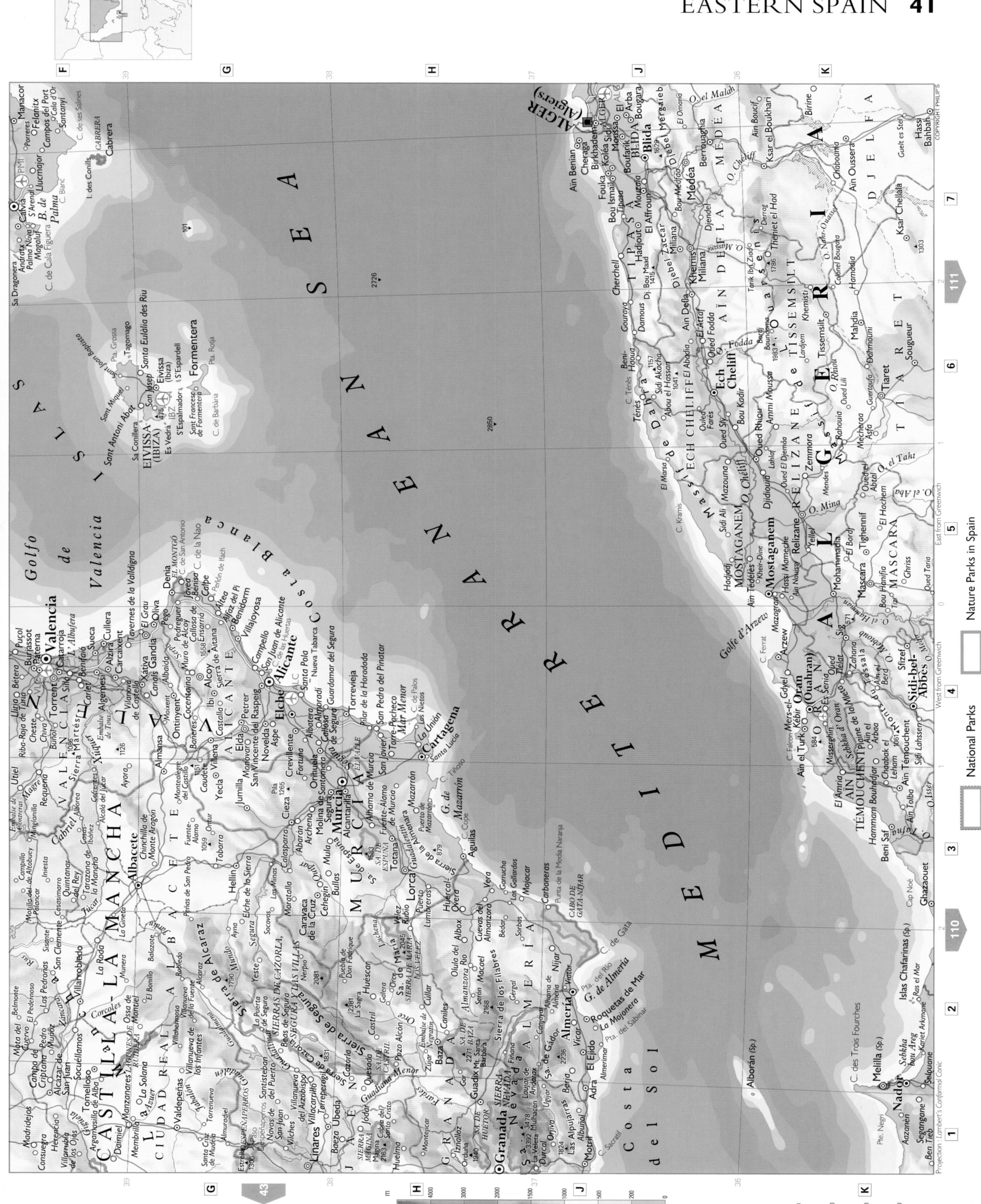

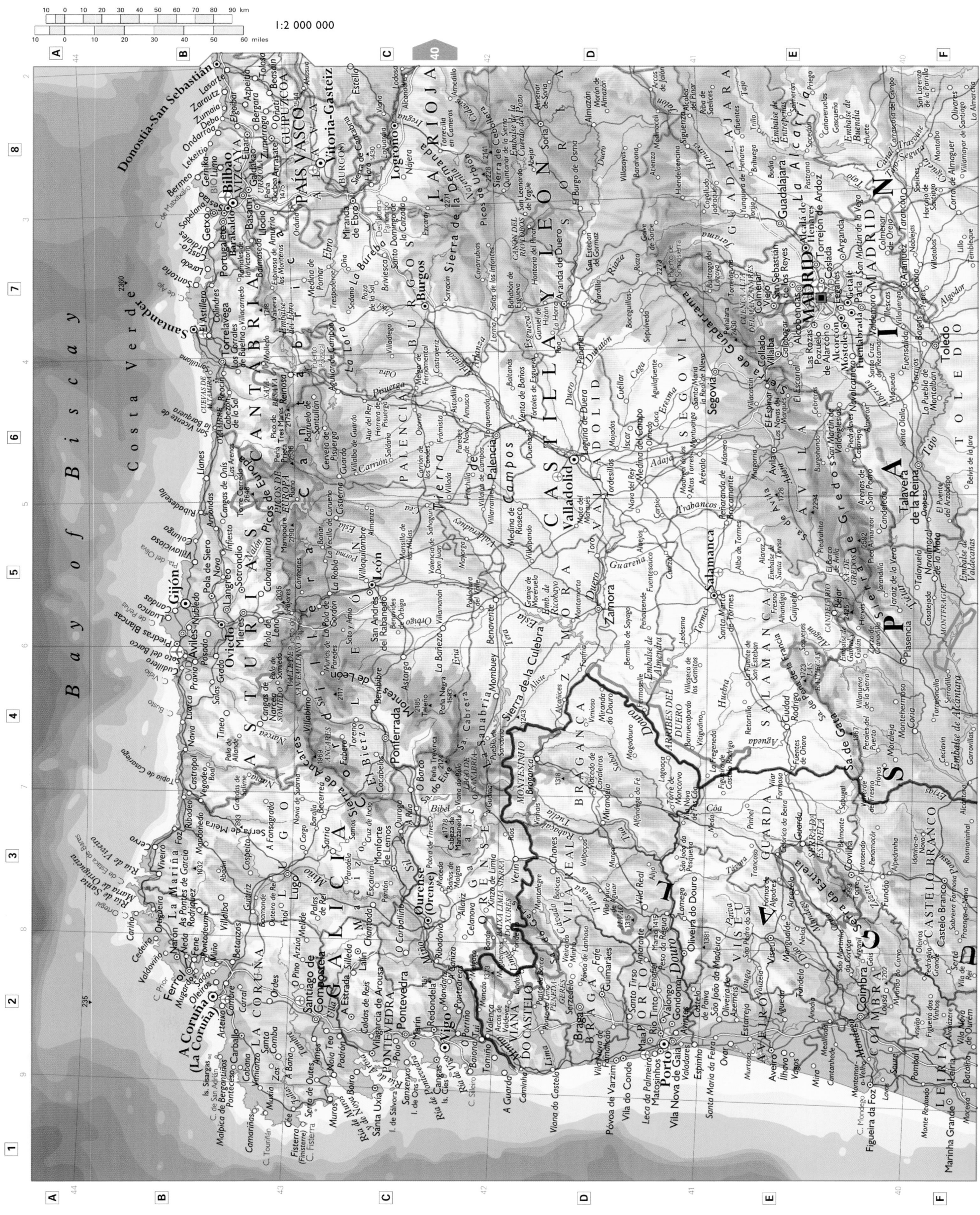

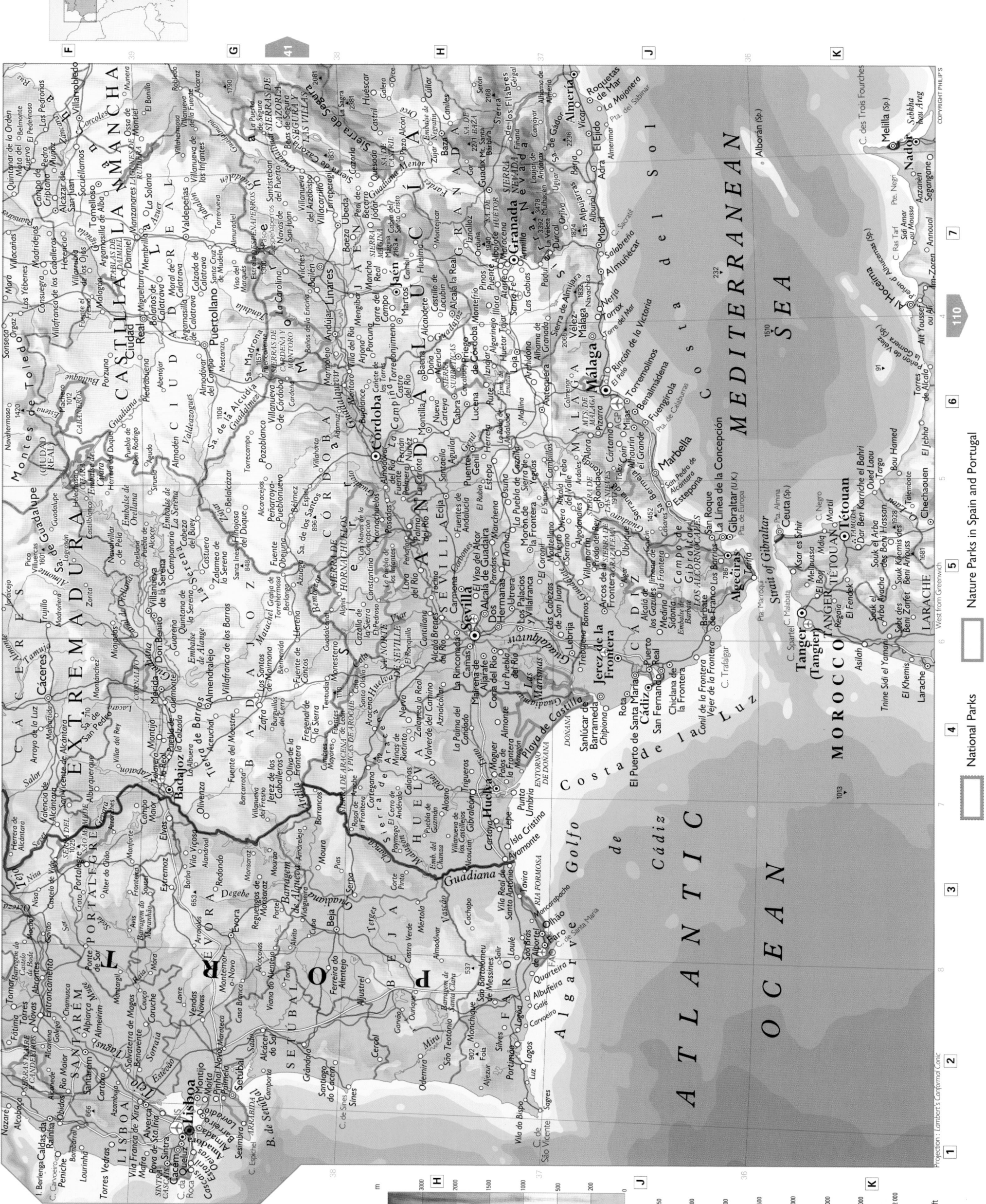

Projection : Lambert's Conformal Conic

Nature Parks in Spain and Portugal

National Parks

West from Greenwich

MEDITERRANEAN SEA

ATLANTIC OCEAN

CASTILLA-LA MANCHA

ANDALUCÍA

EXTREMADURA

PORTUGAL

ALGARVE

MOROCCO

Strait of Gibraltar

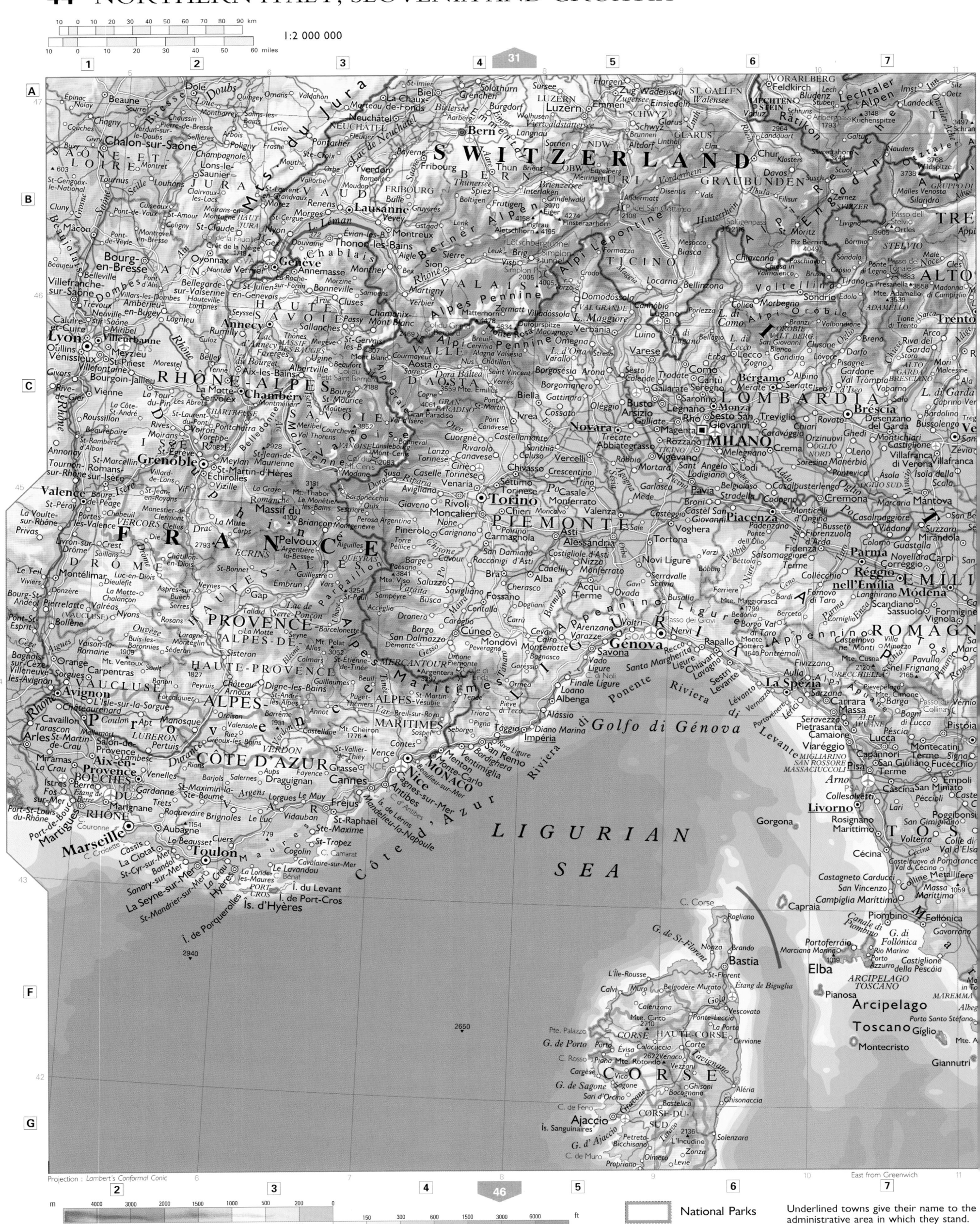

1:2 000 000

Projection : Lambert's Conformal Conic

National Parks

Underlined towns give their name to the administrative area in which they stand.

Administrative divisions in Croatia:

1 Brodsko-Posavska	4 Medimurska	8 Virovitičko-Podravska
2 Koprivničko-Križevačka	6 Požeško-Slavonska	10 Zagreba čka
3 Krapinsko-Zagorska	7 Varaždinska	

☐ Nature Parks in Italy

- - - Inter-entity boundaries as agreed
at the 1995 Dayton Peace Agreement

COPYRIGHT PHILIP'S

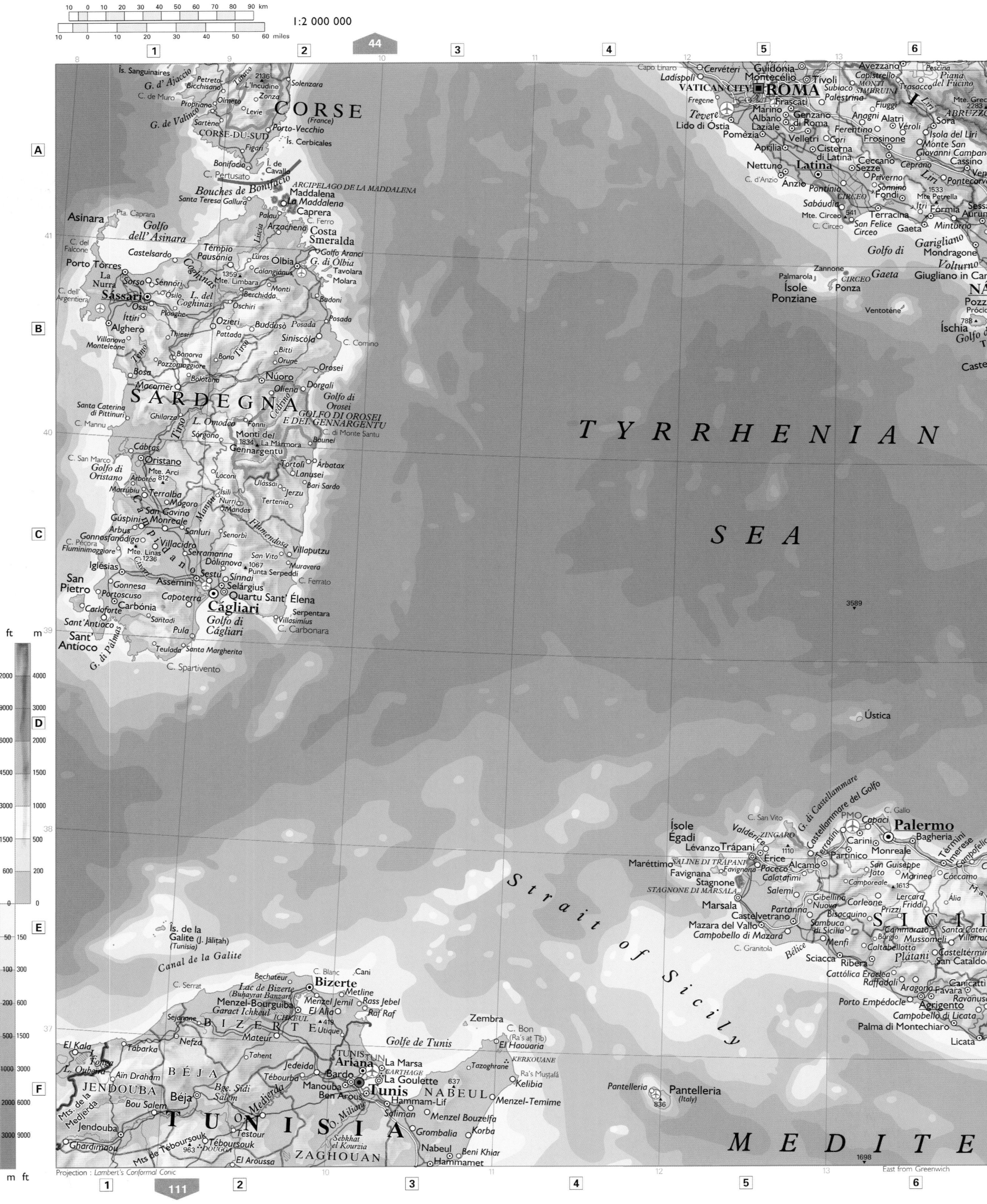

1:2 000 000

TYRRHENIAN

SEA

CORSE
(France)

SARDEGNA

TUNISIA

Strait of Sicily

SICIL

Palermo

ROMA

Nature Parks in Italy

National Parks

Underlined towns give their name to the administrative area in which they stand.

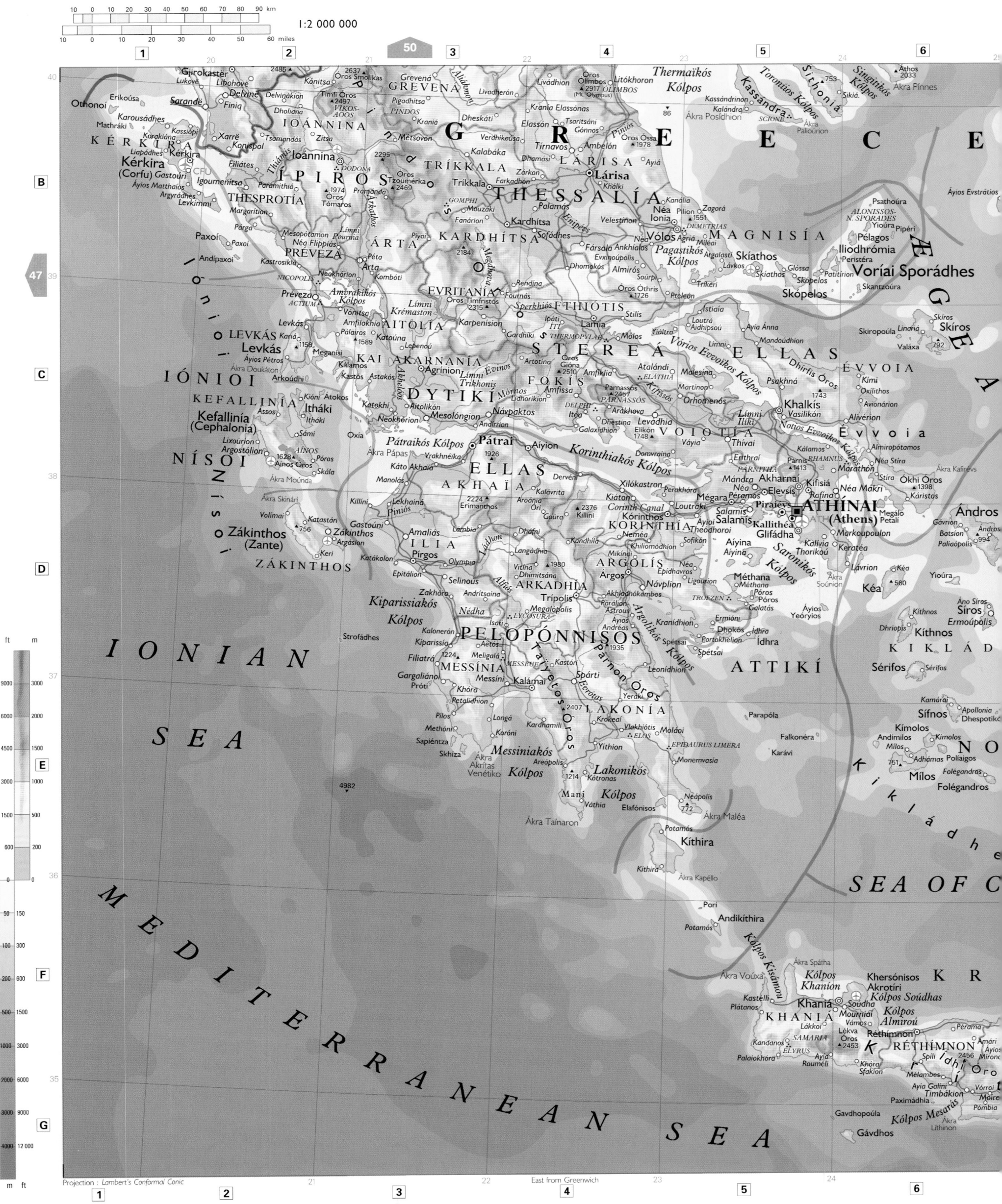

10 0 10 20 30 40 50 60 70 80 90 km

1:2 000 000

10 0 10 20 30 40 50 60 miles

IONIAN SEA

MEDITERRANEAN SEA

GREECE

ÍPIROS
IOÁNNINA
THESSALÍA
LÁRISA
MAGNISÍA
TRÍKKALA
KARDHÍTSA
EVRITANÍA
AITOLÍA
KAI AKARNANÍA
STEREÁ ELLAS
FOKÍS
FTHIÓTIS
DYTIKÍ ELLAS
AKHAΪA
VOIOTÍA
ÉVVOIA
ÉVVOIA
ATTIKÍ
ARGOLÍS
ARKADHÍA
ILÍA
MESSINÍA
LAKONÍA
PELOPÓNNISOS
ATHÍNAI (Athens)

KÉRKIRA
KEFALLINÍA
NÍSOI
ZÁKINTHOS
IÓNIOI

Voríai Sporádhes

KIKLÁD

SEA OF C

Projection : Lambert's Conformal Conic

East from Greenwich

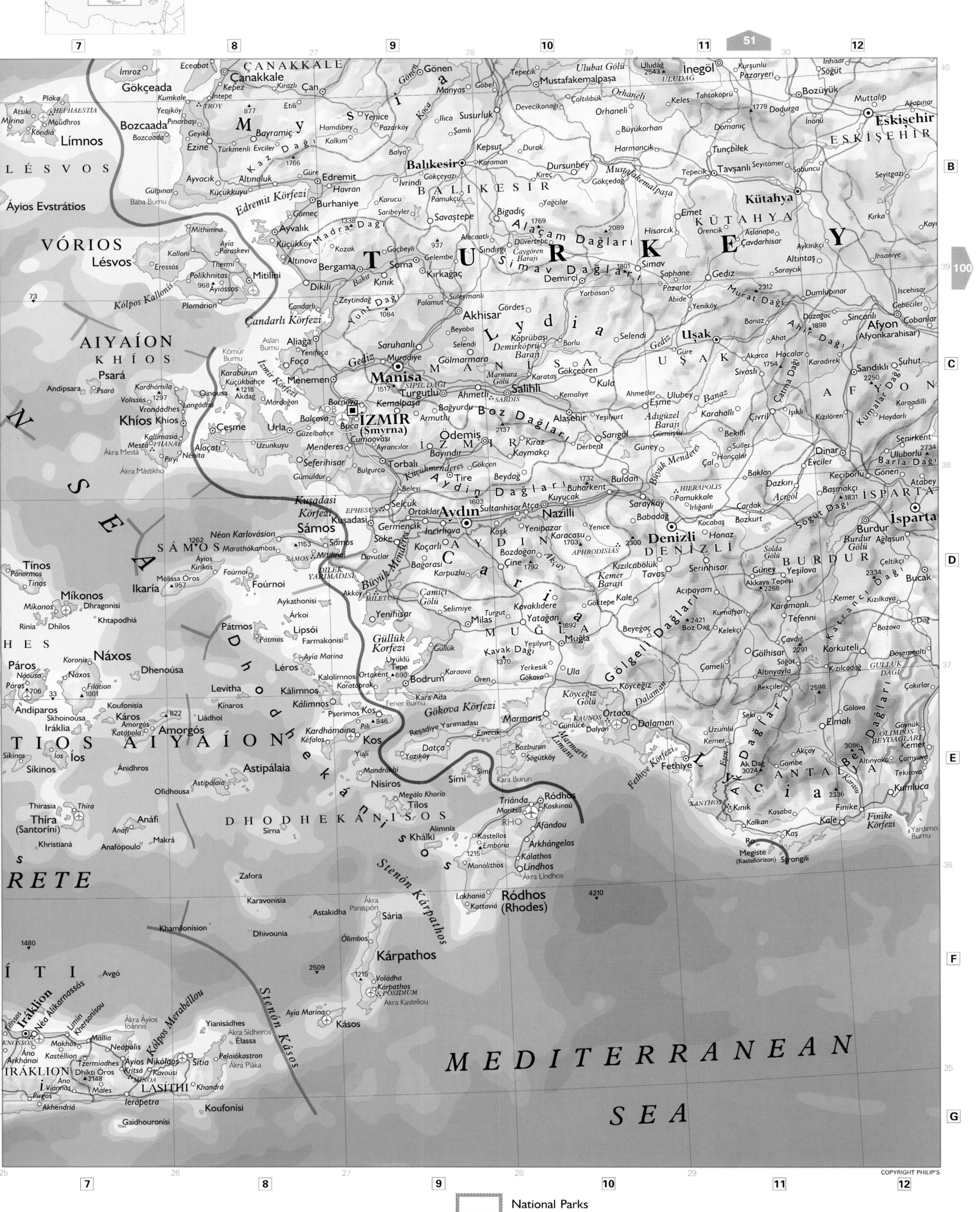

National Parks

1:2 000 000

Projection : Lambert's Conformal Conic

East from Greenwich

Inter-entity boundaries as agreed
at the 1995 Dayton Peace Agreement

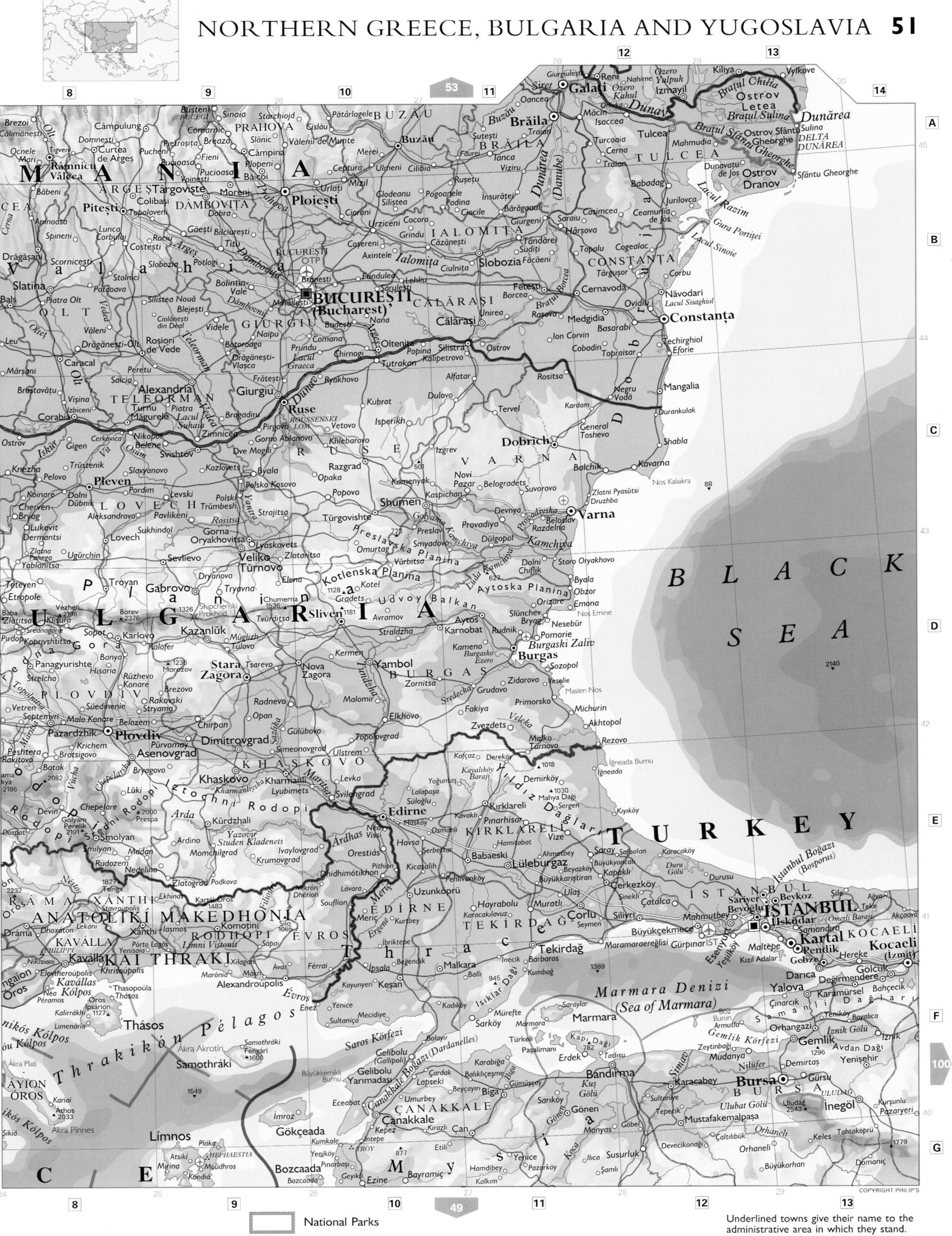

National Parks

Underlined towns give their name to the
administrative area in which they stand.

1:2 000 000

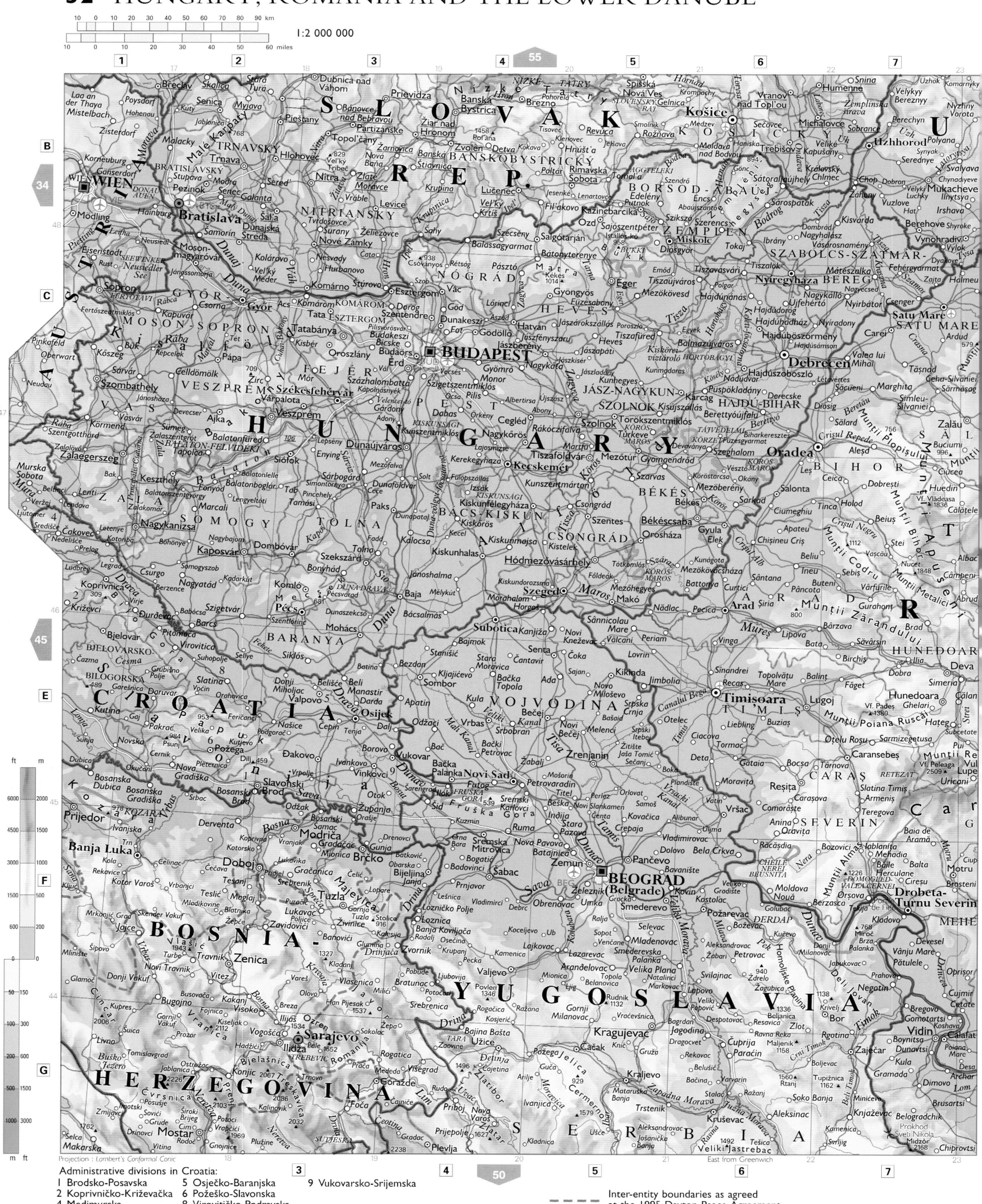

Administrative divisions in Croatia:
1 Brodsko-Posavska   5 Osječko-Baranjska   9 Vukovarsko-Srijemska
2 Koprivničko-Križevačka   6 Požeško-Slavonska
4 Medimurska   8 Virovitičko-Podravska

East from Greenwich

- - - - Inter-entity boundaries as agreed
at the 1995 Dayton Peace Agreement

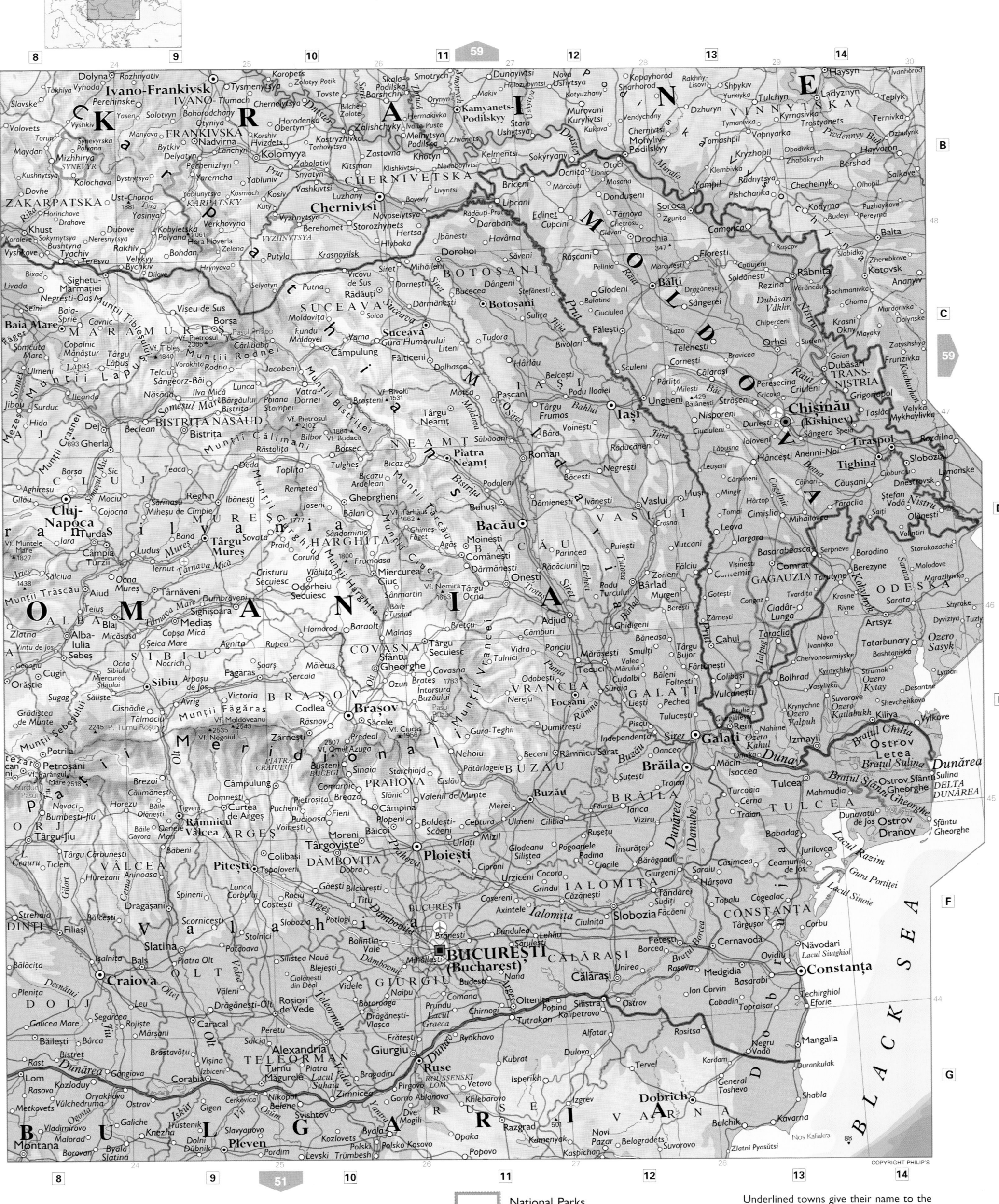

National Parks

Underlined towns give their name to the
administrative area in which they stand.

COPYRIGHT PHILIP'S

10 0 10 20 30 40 50 60 70 80 90 km

10 0 10 20 30 40 50 60 miles

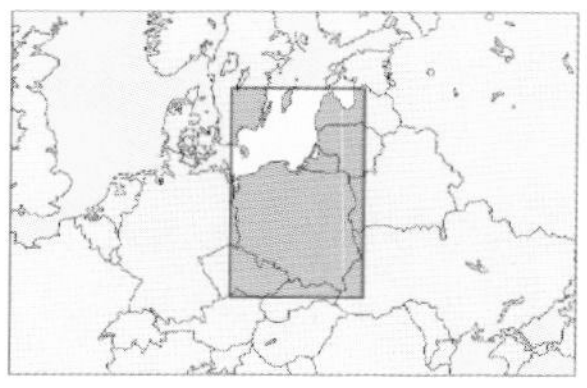

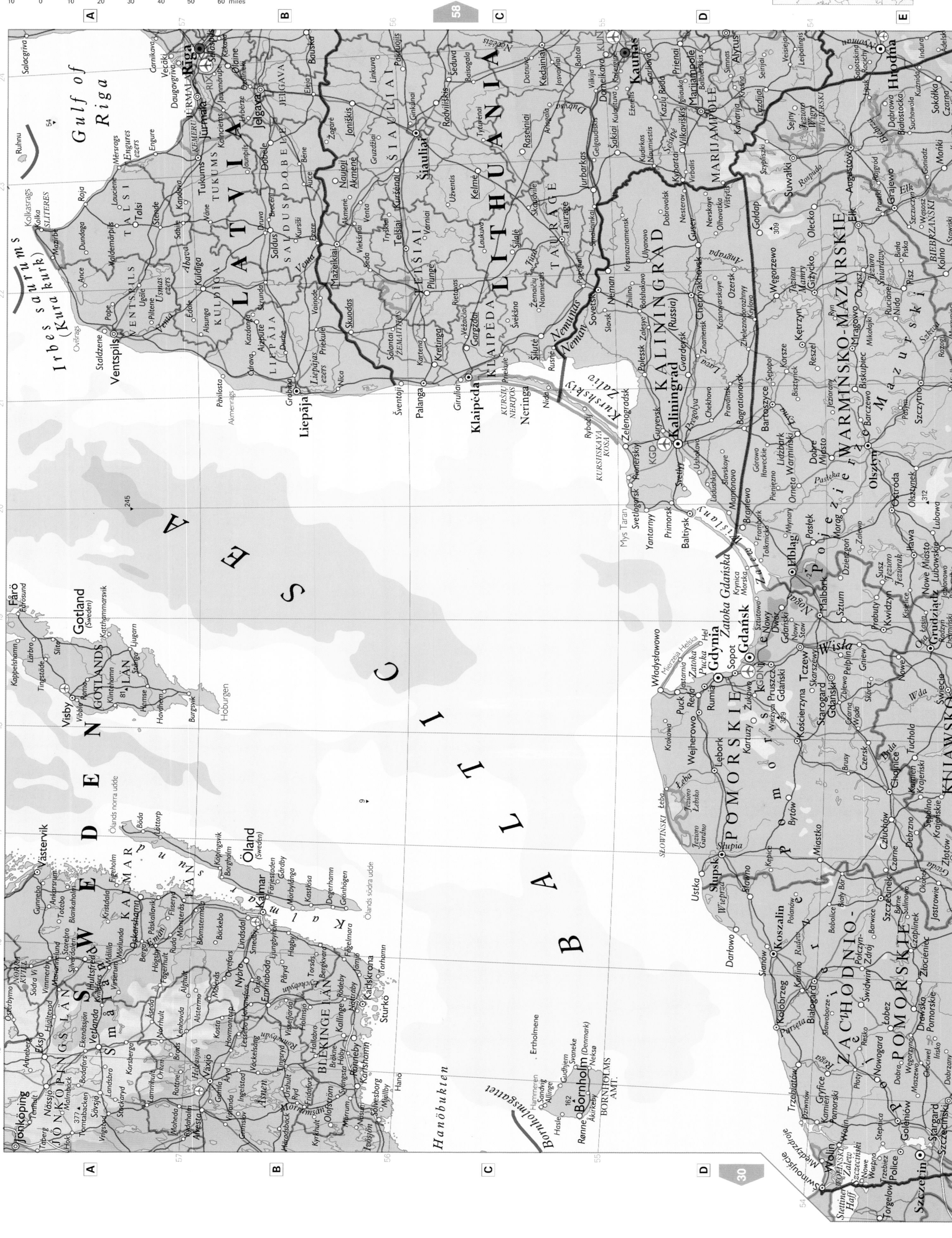

1:2 000 000

Gulf of Riga

LATVIA

LITHUANIA

KALININGRAD (Russia)

SWEDEN

Gotland (Sweden)

Öland (Sweden)

BALTIC SEA

Bornholm (Denmark)

Riga

Jūrmala

Ventspils

Liepāja

Klaipėda

Palanga

Šiauliai

Mažeikiai

Kaunas

MARIJAMPOLE

Kaliningrad

Gdynia

Sopot

Gdańsk

Gdańsk

Zatoka Gdańska

Elbląg

Malbork

Grudziądz

WARMIŃSKO-MAZURSKIE

POMORSKIE

ZACHODNIO-POMORSKIE

KUJAWSKO-

Koszalin

Słupsk

Ustka

Kołobrzeg

Szczecin

Wisła

Hrodna

Jönköping

Kalmar

Karlskrona

Visby

Hanöbukten

Irbes šaurums (Kura kurk)

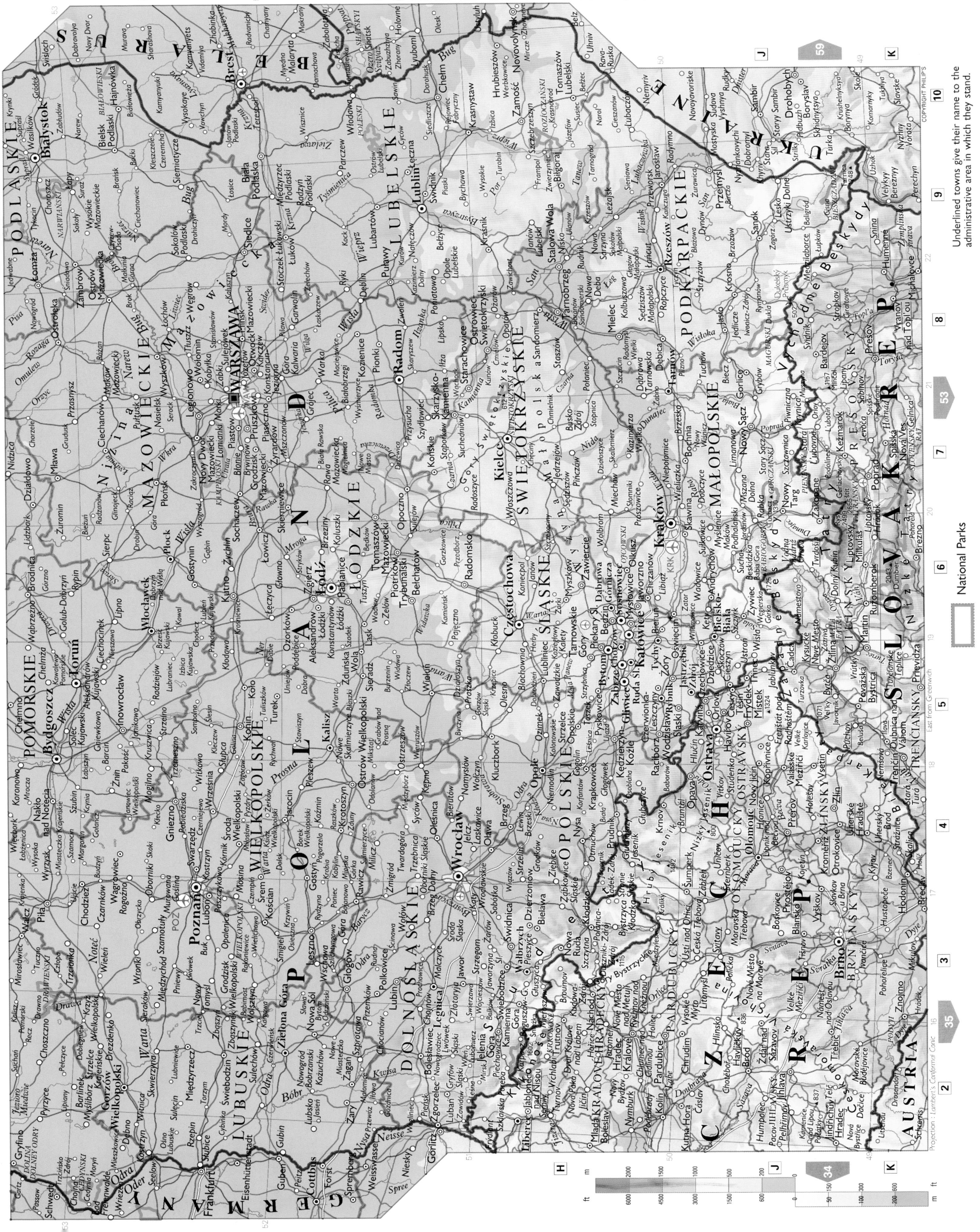

Underlined towns give their name to the
administrative area in which they stand.

National Parks

Projection: Lambert's Conformal Conic

COPYRIGHT PHILIP'S

East from Greenwich

1:8 000 000

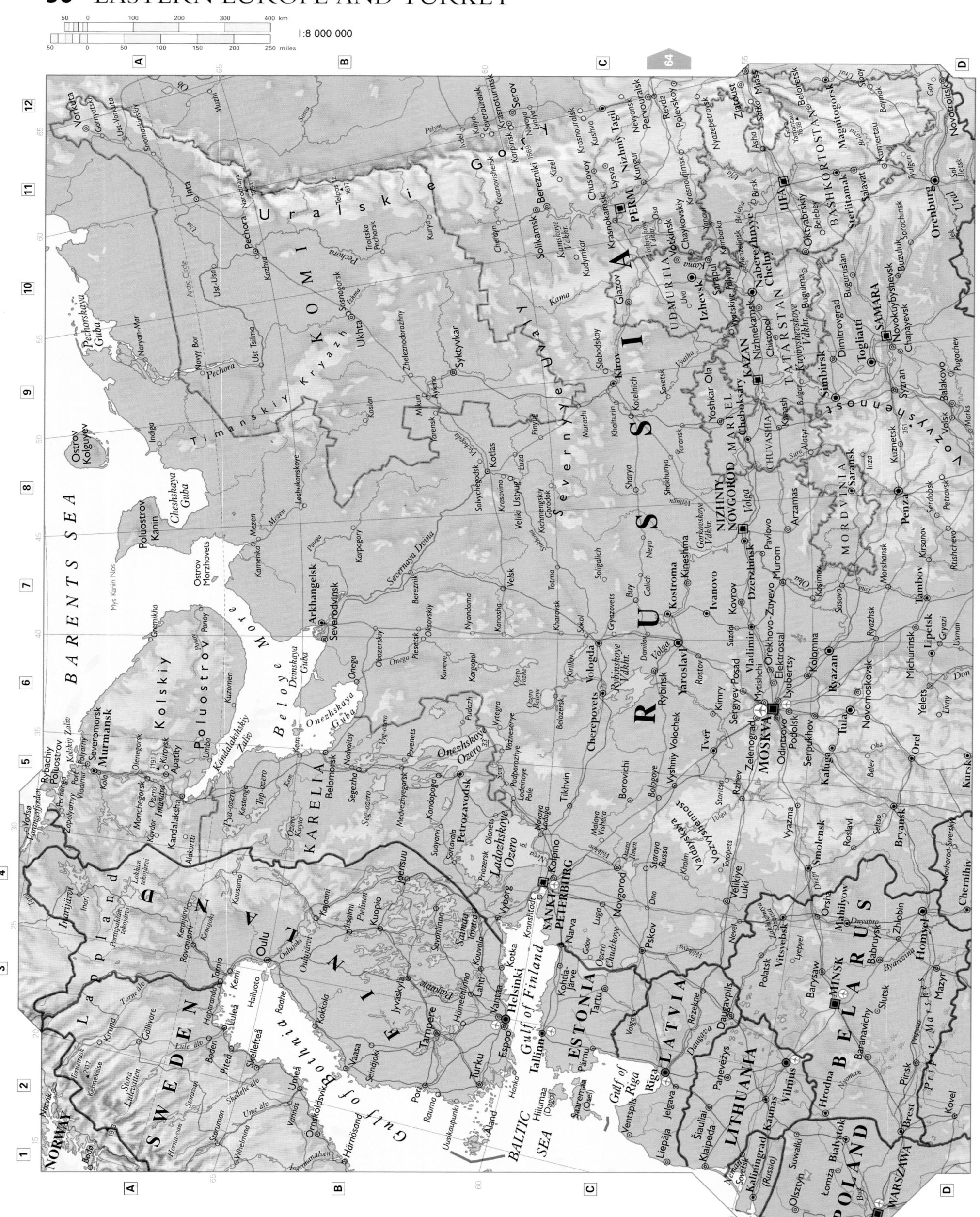

BLACK SEA
CASPIAN SEA
MEDITERRANEAN SEA
Sea of Azov
UKRAINE
KAZAKHSTAN
TURKMENISTAN
GEORGIA
ARMENIA
AZERBAIJAN
TURKEY
SYRIA
IRAQ
IRAN
ROMANIA
MOLDOVA
BULGARIA
CYPRUS
LEBANON
CRIMEA
KYYIV
KHARKIV
ODESA
DONETSK
DNIPROPETROVSK
VOLGOGRAD
ROSTOV
TBILISI
YEREVAN
BAKI
TEHRĀN
TABRĪZ
ANKARA
İSTANBUL
İZMIR
BURSA
KONYA
ADANA
HALAB
DIMASHQ
BAYRŪT
BUCUREŞTI
CHIŞINĂU
Caucasus Mountains
Kuzey Anadolu Dağları
Toros Dağları
Anadolu
Projection: Conical with two standard parallels
East from Greenwich
COPYRIGHT PHILIP'S

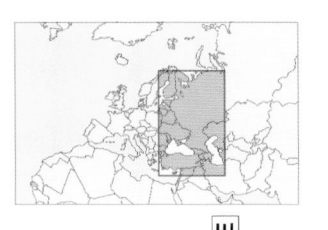

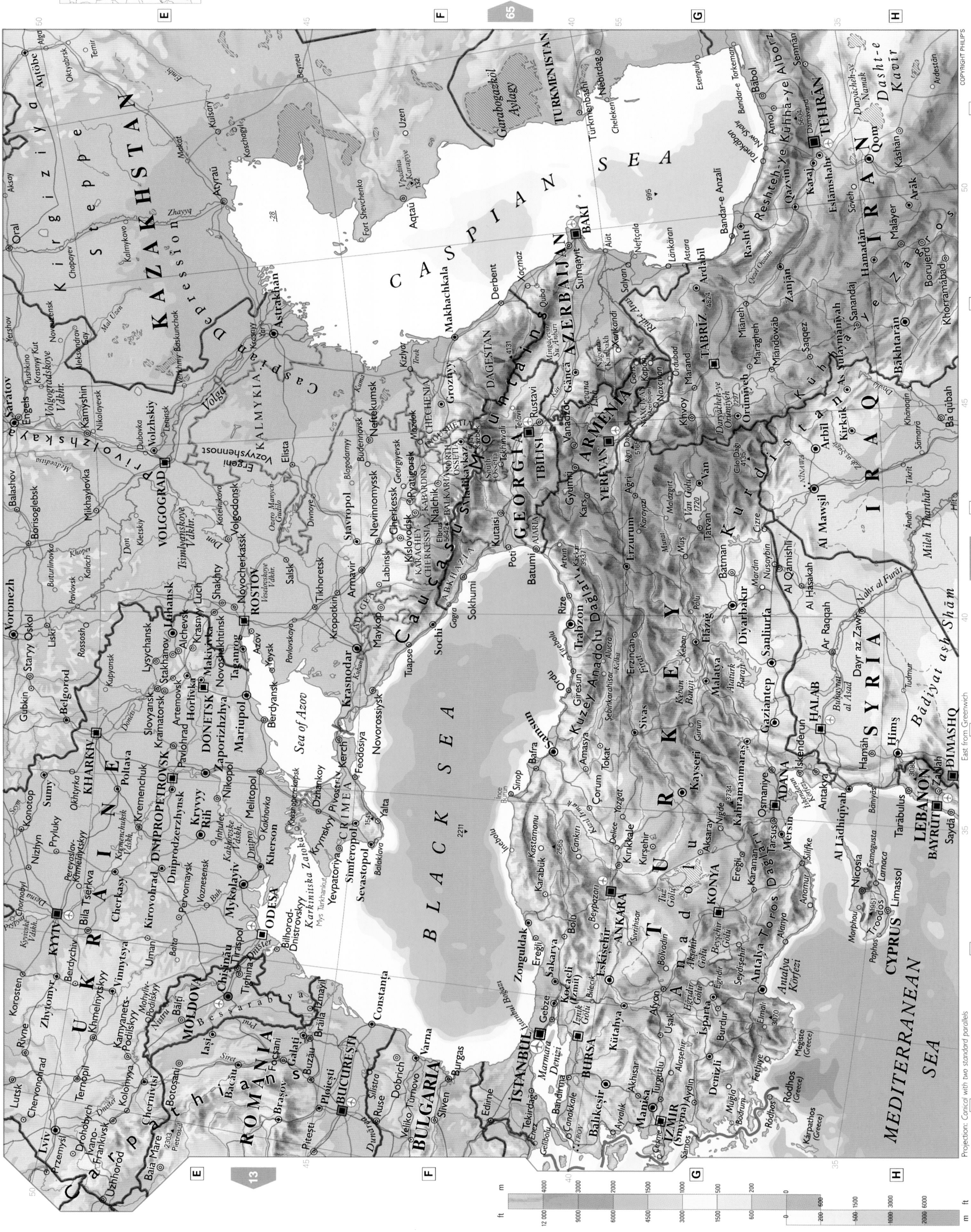

1:4 000 000

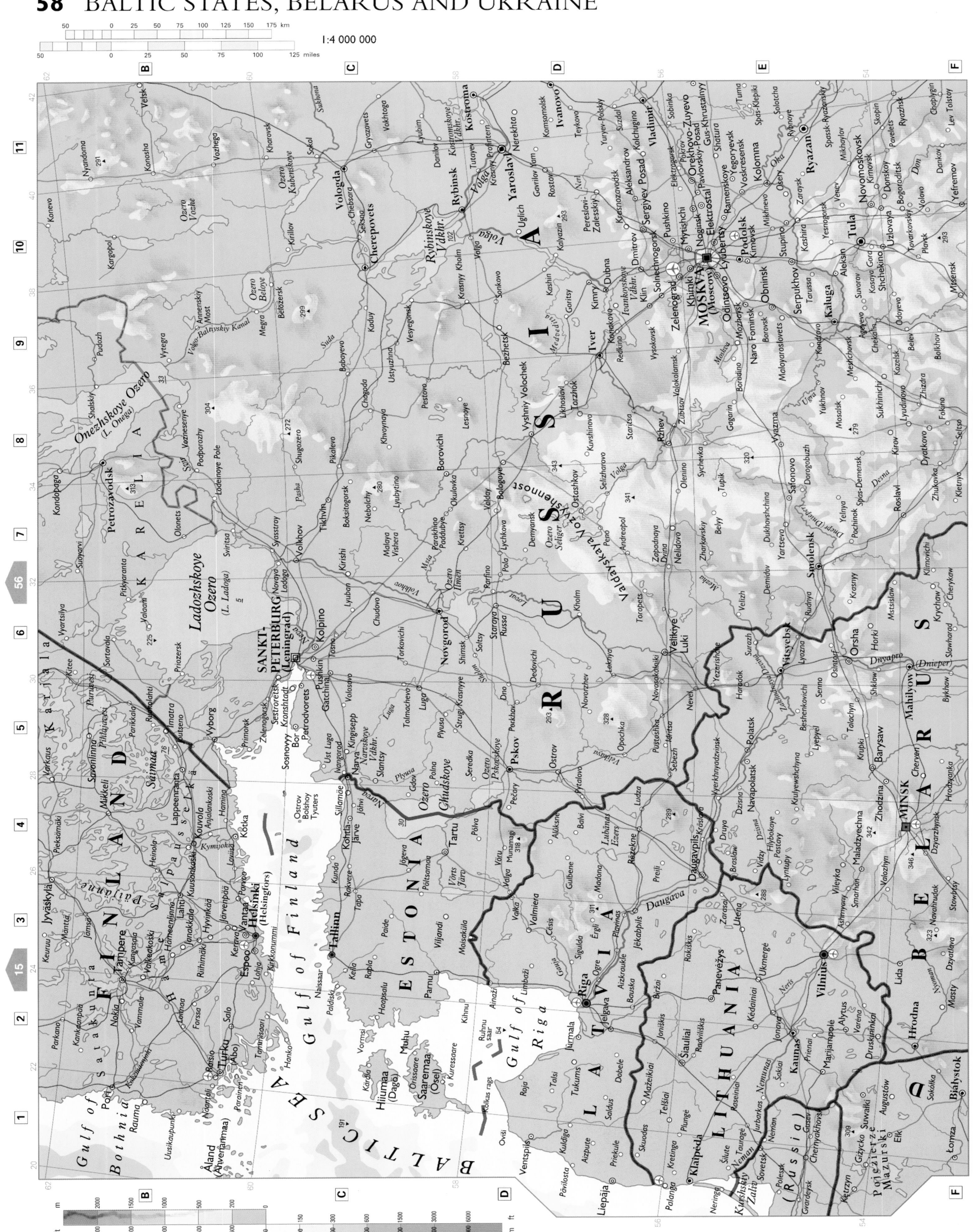

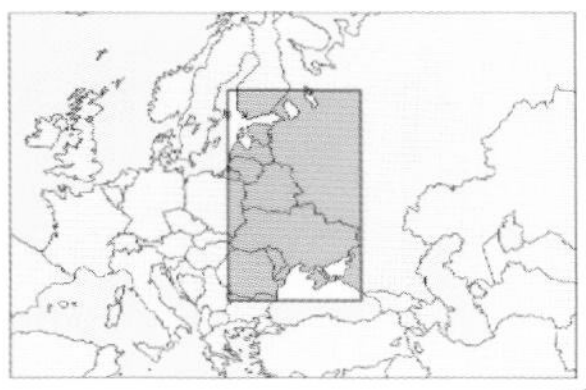

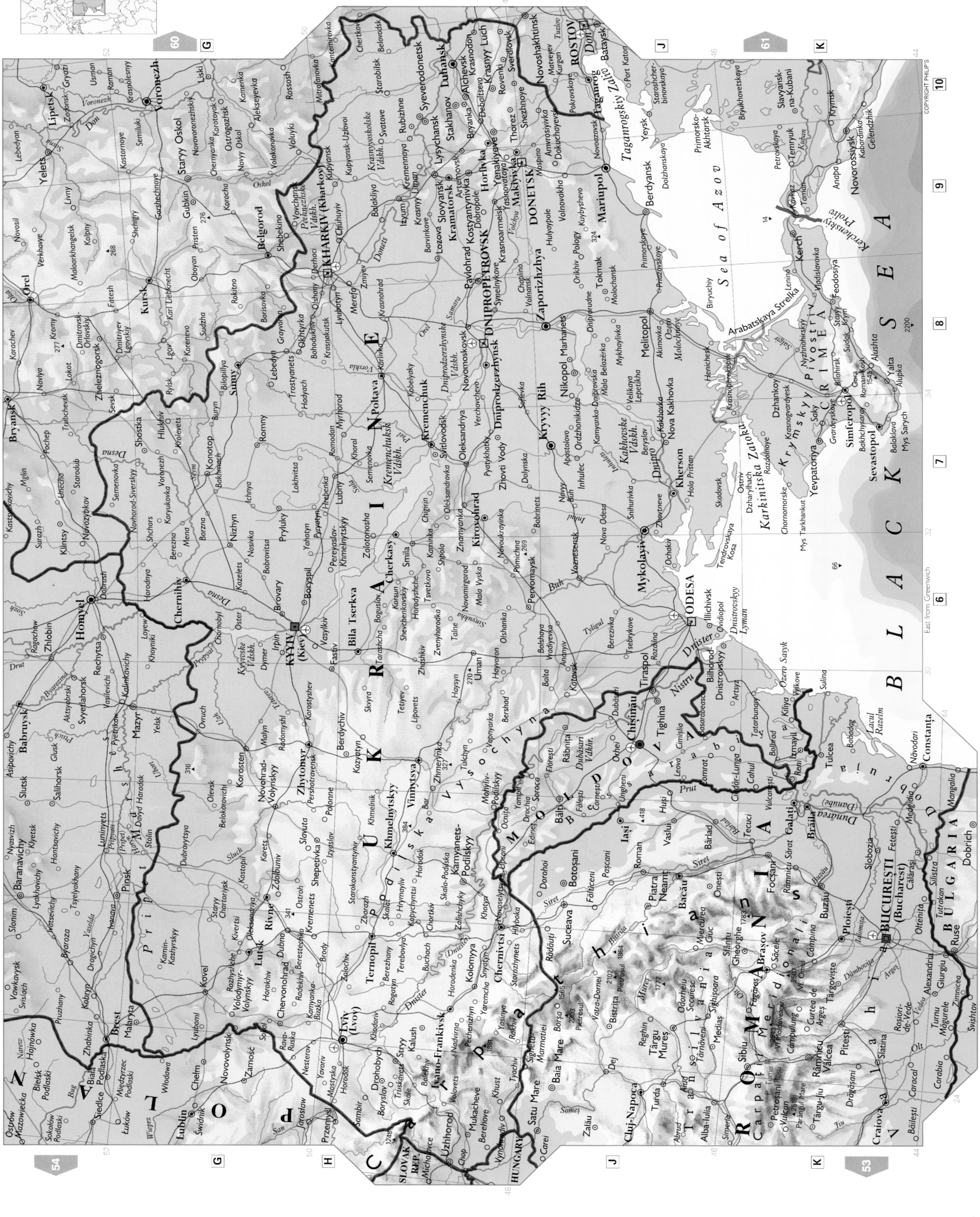
UKRAINE
MOLDOVA
ROMANIA
BULGARIA
BLACK SEA
Sea of Azov
CRIMEA
KYYIV (Kiev)
ODESA
KHARKIV (Kharkov)
DNIPROPETROVSK
DONETSK
ROSTOV
Projection: Conical with two standard parallels
COPYRIGHT PHILIP'S

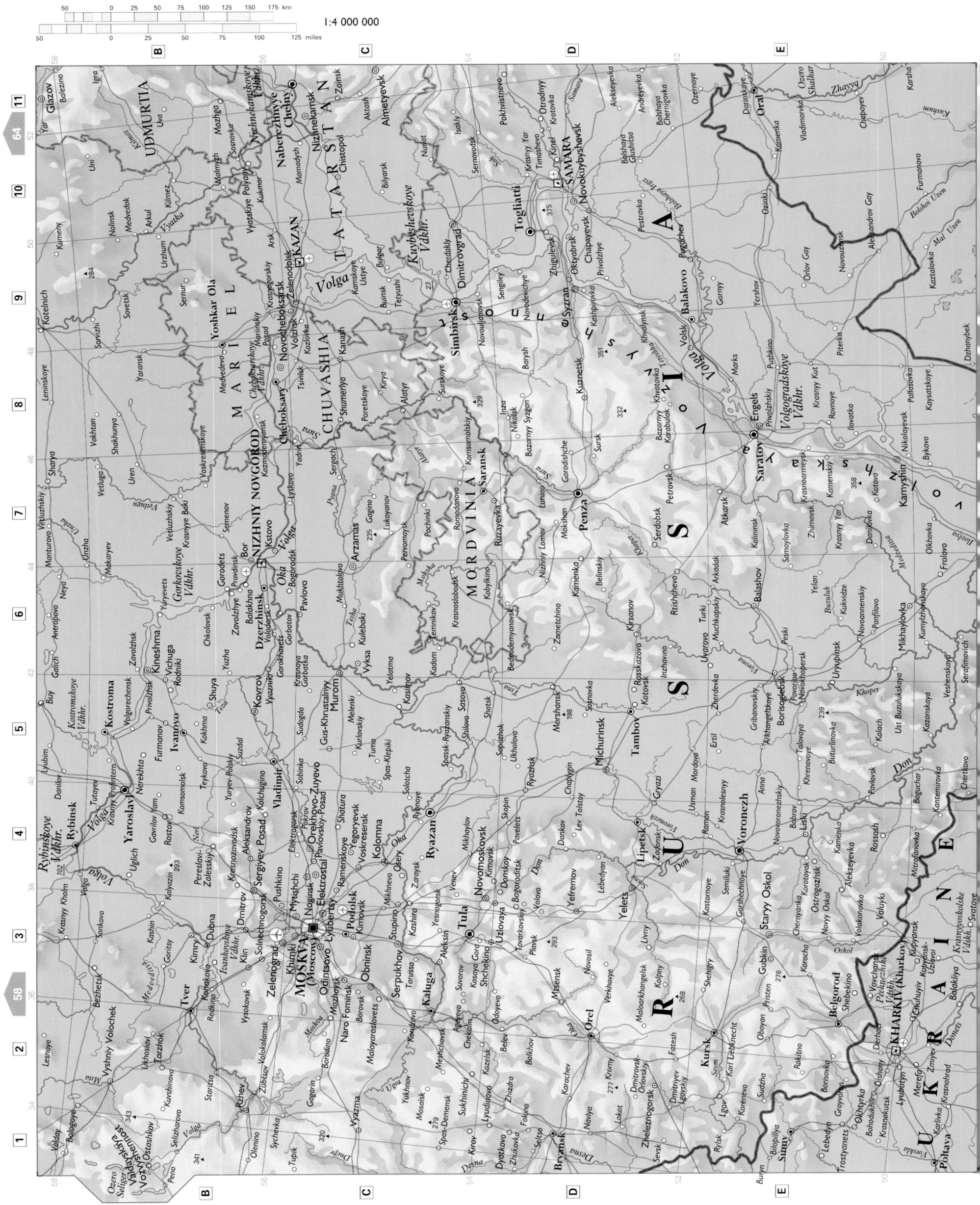

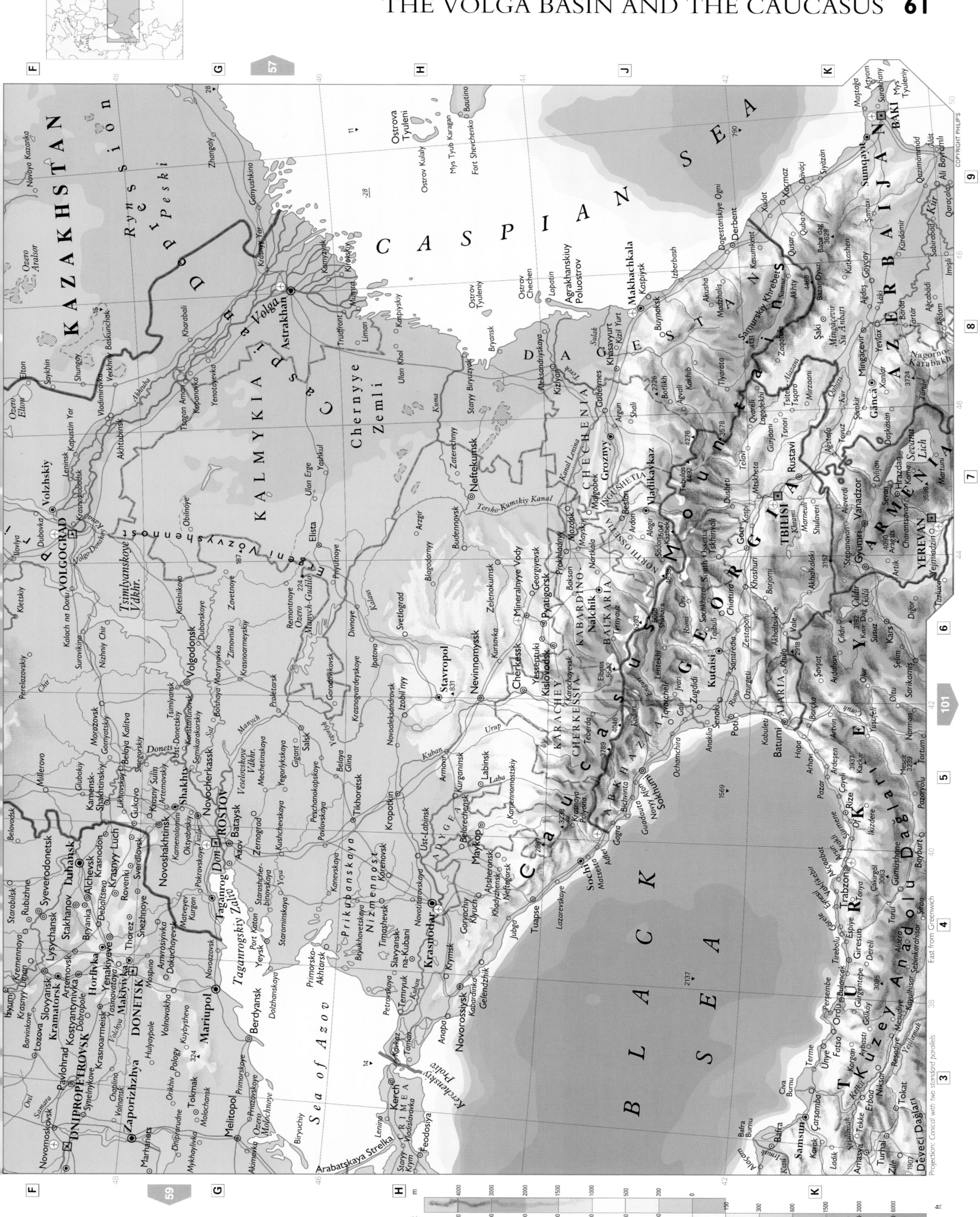

KAZAKHSTAN

Ozero Kazanka
Novaya Kazanka
Ozero Aralsor

Ryn s Peski

 R Volga Astrakhan

VOLGOGRAD
Volzhskiy

KALMYKIA

Chernyye Zemli

C A S P I A N   S E A

Ostrova Tyuleni
Mys Tyub Karagan
Ostrov Kulaly
Fort Shechenko

Ostrov Chechen
Ostrov Tyuleniy
Agrakhanskiuy Poluostrov

Makhachkala
Kaspiysk
Buynaksk
Izberbash
Derbent

D A G E S T A N

C H E C H E N I A
Grozny
INGUSHETIA
Vladikavkaz.
NORTH OSSETIA
Elbrus 5642

KABARDINO-BALKARIA
Nalchik
CHERKESSIA
KARACHEY-

Stavropol

Mineralnye Vody
Pyatigorsk
Kislovodsk
Cherkessk

BAKI
SUMQAYIT

A Z E R B A I J A N

Nagorno-Karabakh

ARMENIA
YEREVAN

GEORGIA
TBILISI
Kutaisi

Caucasus

A B K H A Z I A
Sokhumi

Sochi

ROSTOV
DONETSK

Sea of Azov

Krasnodar

B L A C K   S E A

T U R K E Y
K u z e y   A n a d o l u   D a ğ l a r ı

Samsun
Trabzon

Devici Dağları

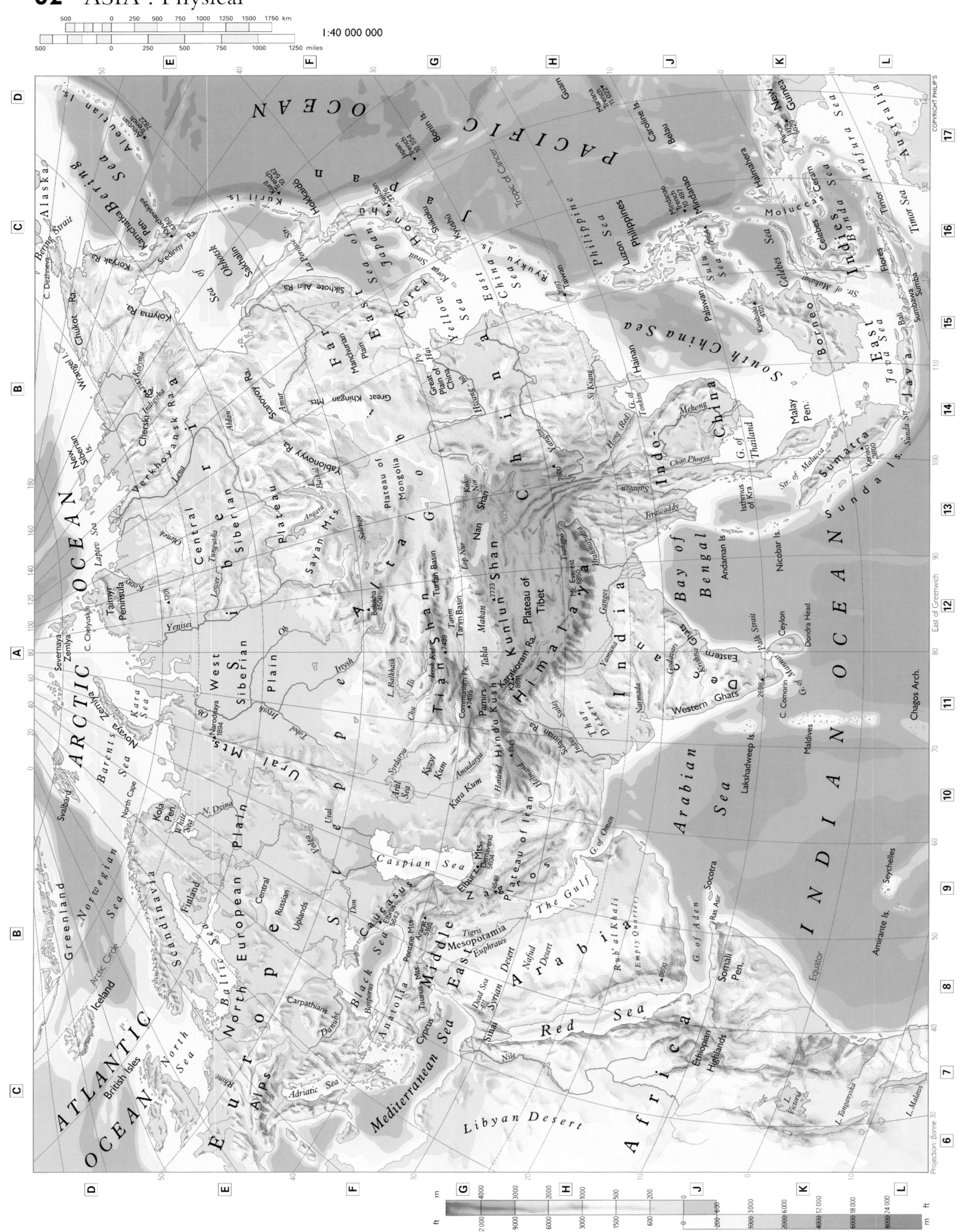

1:40 000 000

COPYRIGHT PHILIP'S

Projection: Bonne

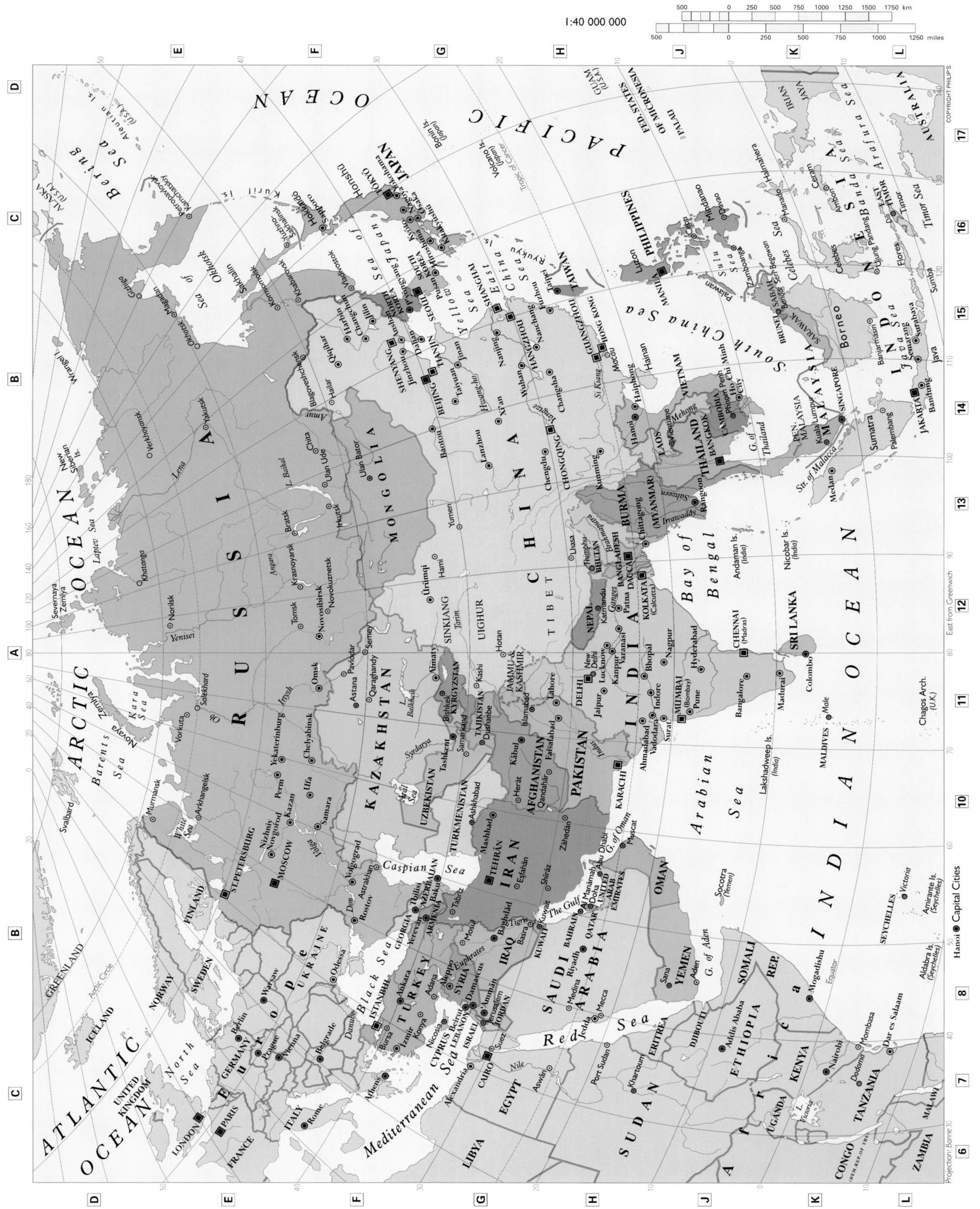

1:40 000 000

50   0 25 50 75 100 125 150 175 km
50   0   25   50   75   100 125 miles

1:4 000 000

Projection: Conical with two standard parallels

East from Greenwich

COPYRIGHT PHILIP'S

Countries / Regions

KOMI
Severnyye Uvaly
RUSSIA
UDMURTIA
MARI EL
TATARSTAN
BASHKORTOSTAN
KAZAKHSTAN
Kirgiziya Steppe
Obshchi Syrt
Ural'skiy
Mugodzhary
Turgayskaya Stolovaya Strana

Place names

Pinyug, Kazhim, Veslyana, Gayny, Kama, Cherdyn, Vishera, Krasnovishersk, Gora Denezhkin Kamen 1493, Kalya, Lozva, Pelym
Murashi, Krasnoye, Moloma, Nagorsk, Kay, Kosa, 1065, Pokrovsk-Uralskiy, Severouralsk, Volchansk, Krasnoturinsk, Serov, Pelym
Kirs, Kosa 255, Yuria, Borovsk, Solikamsk, Gora Konzhakovskiy Kamen 1569, Karpinsk, 937, Gari
Yurya, Vyatka, Belaya Kholunitsa, Chernaya Kholunitsa, Peskovka, Kamu, Kudymkar, Pozhva, Kamskoye Vdkhr., Berezniki, Usolye, Aleksandrovsk, Kizel, Kytlym, Lobva, Sosva, Sosva
Khalturin, Slobodskoy, Omutninsk, Zalazna, Chermoz, Ugleuralskiy, Gubakha 993, Gremyachinsk, Usva, Kachkanar, Novaya Lyalya, Verkhoturye, Tura
Kirov, Novovyatsk, Chapetsk, Zuyevka, 337, Dobryanka, Pashiya, Verkhnyaya Tura, Krasnouralsk, Bolotovskoye
Kotelnich, Kirovo-Chepetsk, Falenki, Yar, Glazov, Vereshchagino, Krasnokamsk, Chusovoy, Lysva, Kushva, Nizhnyaya Salda, Turinsk
Sorvizhi, 284, Nolinsk, Kumeny, Balezino, Kez, Nytva, Ocher, PERM, Kungur, 482, Nizhniy Tagil, Verkhnyaya Salda, Alapayevsk, Irbit, Nitsa
Yaransk, Sovetsk, Medvedok, Arkul, Uni, Igra, Zura, Sylva, 452, 746, Verkhniy Tagil, Nevyansk, Rezh, Artemovskiy, Troitskiy
Kilmez, Yakshur Bodya, Osa, Krasnoufimsk, Achit, Kuzino, Revda, Pervouralsk, YEKATERINBURG, Beloyarskiy, Bogdanovich, Kamyshlov, Talitsa
MARI EL, Yoshkar Ola, Urzhum, Kilmez, Izhevsk, Votkinsk, Votkinskoye Vdkhr., Chernushka, Oktyabrskiy, Mikhaylovski, Nizhniye Sergi, Polevskoy, 678, Sysert, Kamensk Uralskiy, Dalmatovo
Medvedevo, Malmyzh, Mozhga, Chaykovskiy, Krasnoufimsk, Nyazepetrovsk, Verkhniy Ufaley, Kasli, Kataysk, Shadrinsk
Mariinskiy Posad, Krasnogorskiy, Sosnovka, Sarapul, Kambarka, Yanaul, 517, Verkhniye Kigi, Kyshtym, Argayash, Techa
Volzhsk, Zelenodolsk, Arsk, Kukmor, Vyatskiye Polyany, Neftekamsk, Belaya, Ufa, Karabash, Kusa, Zlatoust, Shchuchye, Shumikha
Kozlovka, KAZAN, Mamadysh, Nizhnekamskoye Vdkhr., Menzelinsk, Birsk, Ulya, Krasnyy Klyuch, Asha, Yuryuzan, Satka, Bakal, Miass, CHELYABINSK, Kopeysk, Miass
Kamskoye Ustye, Yelabuga, Naberezhnyye Chelny, Dyartyuli, Blagoveshchensk, Minyar, Katav Ivanovsk, 1406, Chebarkul, Novosineglazovskiy, Korkino
Buinsk, Bulgar, Chistopol, Zainsk, Kushnarenkovo, Asha, Berdyaush, Gora Iremel 1582, Yuzhnouralsk, Yemanzhelinsk
Tetyushi, Bilyarsk, Aktash, Almetyevsk, UFA, Iglino, Inzer, Uchaly, Plast, Uvelskiy, Oktyabrskoye
Kuybyshevskoye Vdkhr., 23, Leninogorsk, Tuymazy, Chishmy, Gora Yamantau 1639, Tirlyanskiy, Stepnoye, Troitsk, Uy
Simbirsk, Novoulyanovsk, Nurlat, Bugulma, Oktyabrskiy, Belebey, 420, Davlekanovo, Krasnousolskiy, Beloretsk, Verkhneuralsk, Buskul, Togusak, Komsomolets
Sengiley, Dimitrovgrad, Isakly, 383, Rayevskiy, Priyutovo, BASHKORTOSTAN, Verkhniy Avzyan 1118, Magnitogorsk, Varna, Kartaly, Rudnyy
Novodevichye, Togliatti, Krasnyy Yar, Timashevo, Bugulslan, Abdulino, Sterlitamak, Petrovskoye, 1039, 452, Tobol
Zhigulevsk, 375, Pokhvistnevo, Otradnyy, Krotovka, Ponomarevka, Salavat, Ishimbay, 659, Sibay, Baymak 758, Kizilskoye, Ordzhonikidze, Lisakovsk
Oktyabrsk, Syzran, Kinel, SAMARA, Novokuybyshevsk, Buzuluk, Grachevka, Sorochinsk, Meleuz, Kumertau, Bredy, Zhetiqara
Kashpirovka, Chapayevsk, Samara, Alekseyevka, Totskoye, Bulanovo, Tyulgan, Iriklinskoye Vdkhr., Krasnoyarskiy, Aydyrlinskiy, 414, Zhailma
Privolzhye, Pestravka, Bolshaya Glushitsa, Andreyevka, 405, Novo-Sergiyevskiy, Chernyy Otrog, Energetik, Adamovka, Ozërnyy
Pugachev, Bolshaya Chernigovka, Ozernoye, Perevolotskiy, Orenburg, Saraktash, Iriklinskiy, Gay, Novoorsk, 418, Kumak
Bolshaya Irgiz, Ozinki, Darinskoye, Ilek, Krasnyy Kholm, Ural, Pervomayskiy, Kuvandyk, Novoorsk, Orsk, Yasnyy, Svetlyy
Oral, Zhayyq, Burli, Aksay, Ilek, Sol Iletsk, Mednogorsk, Novotroitsk, Orsk, Dombarovskiy, Aktasty, Tolybay
Kamenka, Vladimirovka, Chingirlau, Akbulak, Martuk, Leninskoye 509, Khromtau, Ozërnyy, Zhabasak
Ozero Shalkar, Shalkar, Utva, Martuk, Aqtöbe, Khromtau, Novorossiyskoye, Qarabutaq
Chapayev, Dzhambeyty, Novoalekseyevka, Alga, Furmanov, Karsha, Karatobe, Oktyabrsk

Rivers / Water
Volga, Kama, Belaya, Ural, Ik, Ay, Sakmara, Zhayyq, Ilek, Bolshoy Uzen, Bolshoy Kushum, Irgiz

Elevation scale
ft — m
3000 — 1000
1500 — 500
600 — 200
0 — 0

1:4 000 000

50 0 25 50 75 100 125 150 175 km
50 0 25 50 75 100 125 miles

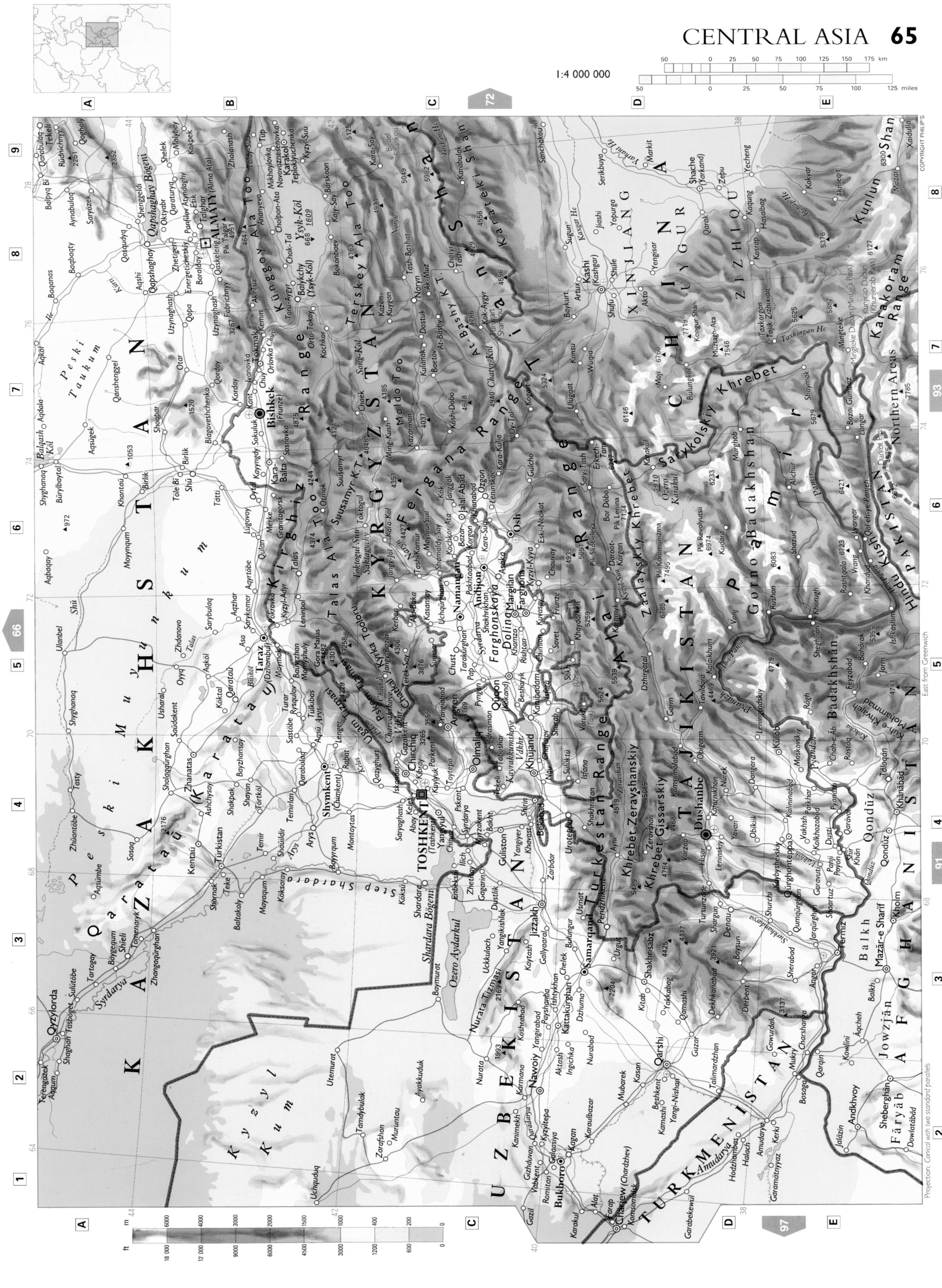

COPYRIGHT PHILIP'S

East from Greenwich

Projection: Conical with two standard parallels

KAZAKHSTAN

UZBEKISTAN

KYRGYZSTAN

TAJIKISTAN

TURKMENISTAN

AFGHANISTAN

CHINA

XINJIANG UYGUR ZIZHIQU

Peski Taukum

Peski Karakumy

Kyzyl Kum

Tian Shan

Kunlun Shan

Karakoram Range

Hindu Kush

Pamir

Gorno-Badakhshan

Badakhshan

Fergana Range

Talas Ala-Too

Terskey Ala-Too

Küngöy Ala-Too

Kirghiz Range

Moldo-Too

Kara-Too

Zaalayskiy Khrebet

Turkestan Range

Zeravshanskiy

Khrebet Gissarskiy

Satykölskiy Khrebet

Ysyk-Köl

Balqash Köl

ALMATY (Alma Ata)

Bishkek (Frunze)

TOSHKENT (Tashkent)

Shymkent (Chimkent)

Taraz (Dzhambul)

Qyzylorda

Dushanbe

Samarqand

Bukhoro

Qarshi

Nawoiy

Khujand

Namangan

Andijon

Farghona

Margilan

Osh

Jalal-Abad

Turkistan

Kashi (Kashgar)

Shache (Yarkand)

Qonduz

Mazâr-e Sharif

Balkh

Syrdarya

Amudarya

Shū

Northern Areas PAKISTAN

m
ft
18 000 6000
12 000 4000
9000 3000
6000 2000
4500 1500
3000 1000
600 200
0 0

A
B
C
D
E
F
8
9
10
11
12
13
14
15
16
17
18
19
Mys Dezhneva (East C.)
Chukchi Sea
St. Lawrence I. (U.S.A.)
Provideniya
Anadyrskiy Zaliv
Beringovskiy
Uelen
Vankarem
Egvekinot
Chukotskoye Nagorye
Pevek
Ust Chaun
Bilibino
Ostrov Vrangelya
East Siberian Sea
Ostrova Medvezhi
Ostrov Ayon
Ambarchik
Cherskiy
Nizhne Kolymsk
Bolshoy Anyuy
Oloy
Yeropol
Markovo
Anadyr
Koryakskoye Nagorye
Khatyrka
Penzhino
Kamenskoye
Omolon
Tilichiki
Korf
Bering Sea
Ostrov Karaginskiy
Ossora
Komandorskiye Ostrova
Nikolskoye
Ust-Kamchatsk
Klyuchevskaya
Poluostrov Kamchatka
Sredinnyy Khrebet
Kamchatka Khrebet
Petropavlovsk-Kamchatskiy
Ust-Bolsheretsk
Kirovskiy
Ust Khayryuzovo
Tigil
Palana
Paren
Gizhiga
Penzhinskaya Guba
Gizhiginskaya Guba
Zaliv Shelikhova
Evensk
Novakhan
Kolymskoye Nagorye
Kolyma
Seymchan
Srednekolymsk
Zyryanka
Pobeda 3147
Taskan
Omsukchan
Orotukan
Yagodnoye
Palatka
Magadan
Atka
Susuman
Ust-Nera
Khrebet Cherskogo
Gora Chen 2682
Oymyakon
Ust-Omchug
Okhotsk
Ulya
Arka
Sea of Okhotsk
Ostrov Novaya Sibir
Ostrov Zhokhova
Ostrova Delonga
Ostrov Zhannetty
Ostrov Genrietty
Ostrov Bennetta
Novosibirskiye Ostrova
Ostrov Faddeyevskiy
Ostrov Kotelnyy
Ostrov Belkovskiy
Ostrov Stolbovoy
Lyakhovskiye Ostrova
Proliv Dmitriya Lapteva
Laptev Sea
OCEAN
Mys Arkticheskiy
Ostrov Shmidta
Ostrov Komsomolets
Ostrov Oktyabrskoy Revolyutsii
Ostrov Pioner
Ostrov Bolshevik
Severnaya Zemlya
Proliv Vilkitskogo
Mys Chelyuskin
Poluostrov Taymyr
Gory Byrranga
Oz. Taymyr
Nordvik
Ostrov Bolshoy Begichev
Ust Olenek
Saskylakh
Novorybnoye
Khatanga
Volochanka
Kheta
Chernaya
Dudinka
Norilsk
Gory Putorana 1701
Yessey
Zhilinda
Olenek
Tiksi
Mys Buorkhaya
Kazachye
Ust Kuyga
Chokurdakh
Indigirka
Deputatskiy
Druzhina
Khonau
Bulun
Kyusyur
Tit-Ary
Verkhoyansk
Batagai
Verkhoyanskiy Khrebet
Kystatyam
Zhigansk
Arctic Circle
Sangar
Batamay
Borogontsy
Khandyga
Okhotskiy Perevoz
Lena
Vilyuy
Vilyuysk
Verkhnevilyuysk
Nyurba
Namtsy
Yakutsk
Mayya
Pokrovsk
Amga
Ust Maya
Suntar
Mirnyy
Sinsk
Ust-Mil
Aim
Maya
Nelkan
Chernyshevskiy
Olekminsk
Lensk
Aldan
Tommot
Chogda
Ayan
Khrebet Dzhugdzhur
Neryungri
Nagornyy
Chumikan
Tugur
Stanovoy Khrebet
Tynda
Skovorodino
Zeya
Dzhalinda
Ushumun
Turukhansk
Noginsk
Nizhnyaya Tunguska
Tura
Yukta
Yerbogachen
Kuyumba
Mutoray
Vanavara
Podkamennaya Tunguska
Yartsevo
Severo-Yeniseyskiy
Kezhma
Yeniseysk
Strelka
Angara
Boguchany
Ust-Ilimsk
Korshunovo
Kirensk
Mama
Vitim
Bodaybo
Chara
Kalakan
Ust-Nyukzha
Makarovo
Ust-Kut
Kondratyevo
Zheleznogorsk-Ilimskiy
Magistralnyy
Nizhneangarsk
Bagdarin
Achinsk
Krasnoyarsk
Kansk
Ilanskiy
Tayshet
Bratsk
Nizhneudinsk
Tulun
Zima
Artemovsk
Chernogorsk
Minusinsk
Abakan
Vostochnyy Sayan
Zapadnyy Sayan
Cheremkhovo
Usolye Sibirskoye
Angarsk
Irkutsk
Munku-Sardyk 3491
Ulan Ude
Barguzin
Oz. Baykal
Yablonovyy Khrebet
Chita
Shilka
Nerchinsk
Sretensk
Mogocha
Aginskoye
Olovyannaya
Borzya
Zabaykalsk
Petrovsk-Zabaykalskiy
Khilok
Slyudyanka
Gusinoozersk
Kyakhta
Zakamensk
Kyzyl
Turan
Chadan
TUVA
Tannu Ola
Samagaltay
Erzin
Uvs Nuur
Hövsgöl Nuur
Hatgal
Darhan
Hentiyn Nuruu
Choybalsan
Ulaanbaatar
Hangayn Nuruu
Har Us Nuur
Hyargas Nuur
Hovd
Uliastay
Tsetserleg
Lün
Öndörhaan
Tamsagbulag
Altay
MONGOLIA
Gobi
Saynshand
Dalandzadgad
Erenhot
Hami
Gaxun Nur
Manzhouli
Hailar
Hulun Nur
Da Hinggan Ling
Nenjiang
Qiqihar
Amur
Gulian
Shimanovsk
Svobodnyy
Belogorsk
Blagoveshchensk
Poyarkovo
Chegdomyn
Zavitinsk
Obluchye
Birobidzhan
Raychikhinsk
Komsomolsk
Amursk
Khabarovsk
Smidovich
Bikin
Vyazemskiy
Sikhote Alin
Hegang
Jiamusi
Harbin
Mudanjiang
Lesozavodsk
Spassk Dalniy
Ussuriysk
Artem
Vladivostok
Nakhodka
Kraskino
Dalnegorsk
Terney
Olga
Amgu
Vanino
Sakhalin
Okha
Nikolayevsk-na-Amure
Ostrov Bolshoy Shantar
Sakhalinskiy Zaliv
Aleksandrovsk-Sakhalinskiy
Gora Lopatina
Poronaysk
Uglegorsk
Yuzhno-Sakhalinsk
Kholmsk
Korsakov
Kurilskiye Ostrova
Ostrov Paramushir
Severo-Kurilsk
Ostrov Onekotan
Ostrov Simushir
Ostrov Urup
Ostrov Iturup
Kurilsk
Ostrov Kunashir
Wakkanai
Abashiri
Kushiro
Asahikawa
Obihiro
Rumoi
Otaru
Sapporo
Hokkaidō
Hakodate
Aomori
Hachinohe
Akita
Honshū
Niigata
Sea of Japan (East Sea)
Kanazawa
Fuji-San 3776
JAPAN
Osaka
Taonan
Ang'angxi
Nen Jiang
Dongbei
Jilin
Changchun
Siping
Yanji
Chongjin
Fushun
Tonghua
Shenyang
Anshan
Dandong
NORTH KOREA
Wonsan
Kansong
Nampo
P'yongyang
Dalian
Yingkou
Chifeng
Linxi
Xilinhot
Chengde
Beijing
Zhangjiakou
Hohhot
Baotou
CHINA
Soul (Seoul)
Inch'on
SOUTH KOREA
Taejon
Taegu
Pusan
COPYRIGHT PHILIP'S

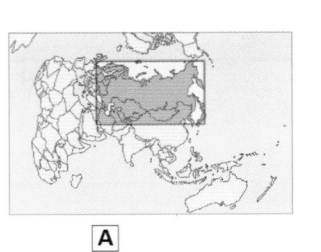

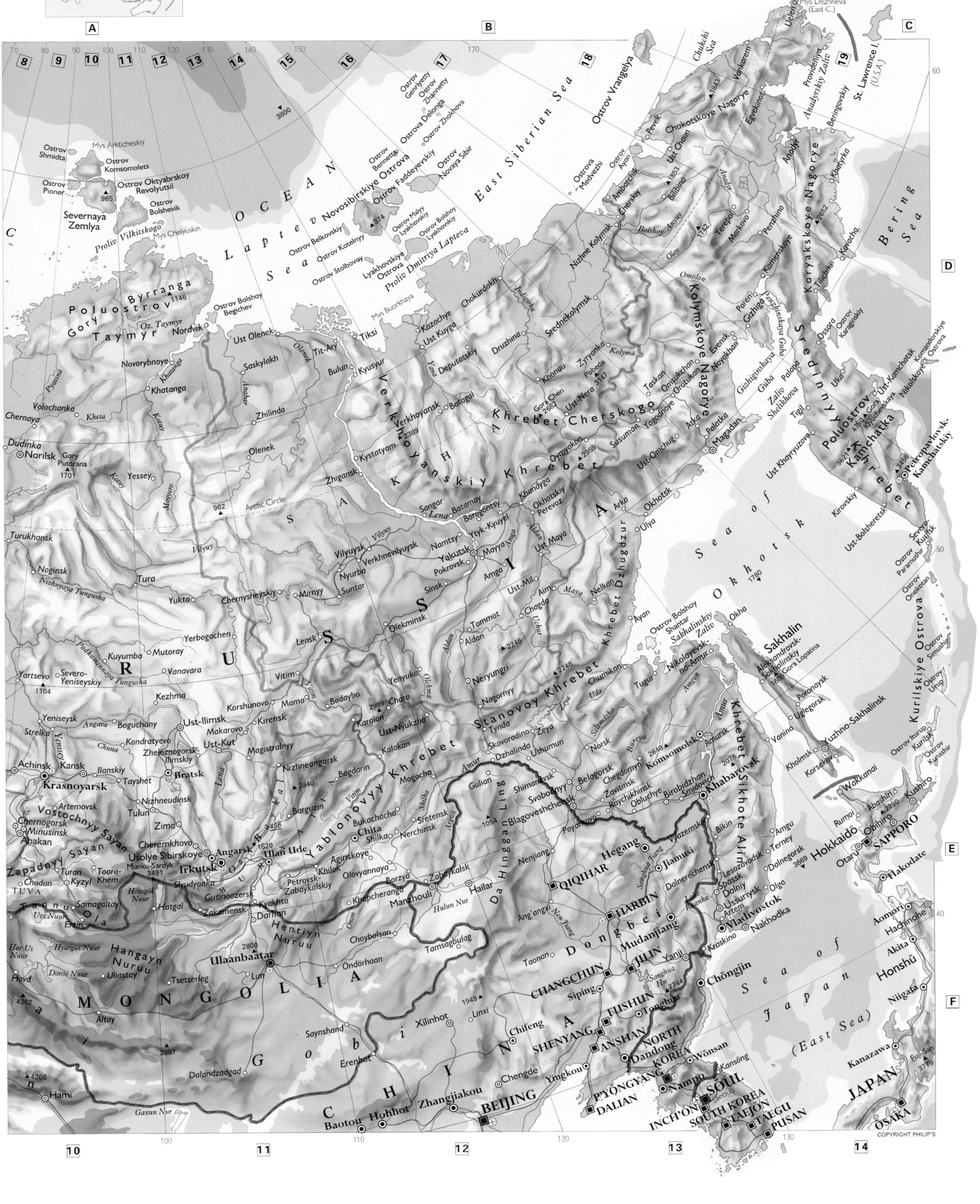

1:12 000 000

Projection: Bonne

East from Greenwich

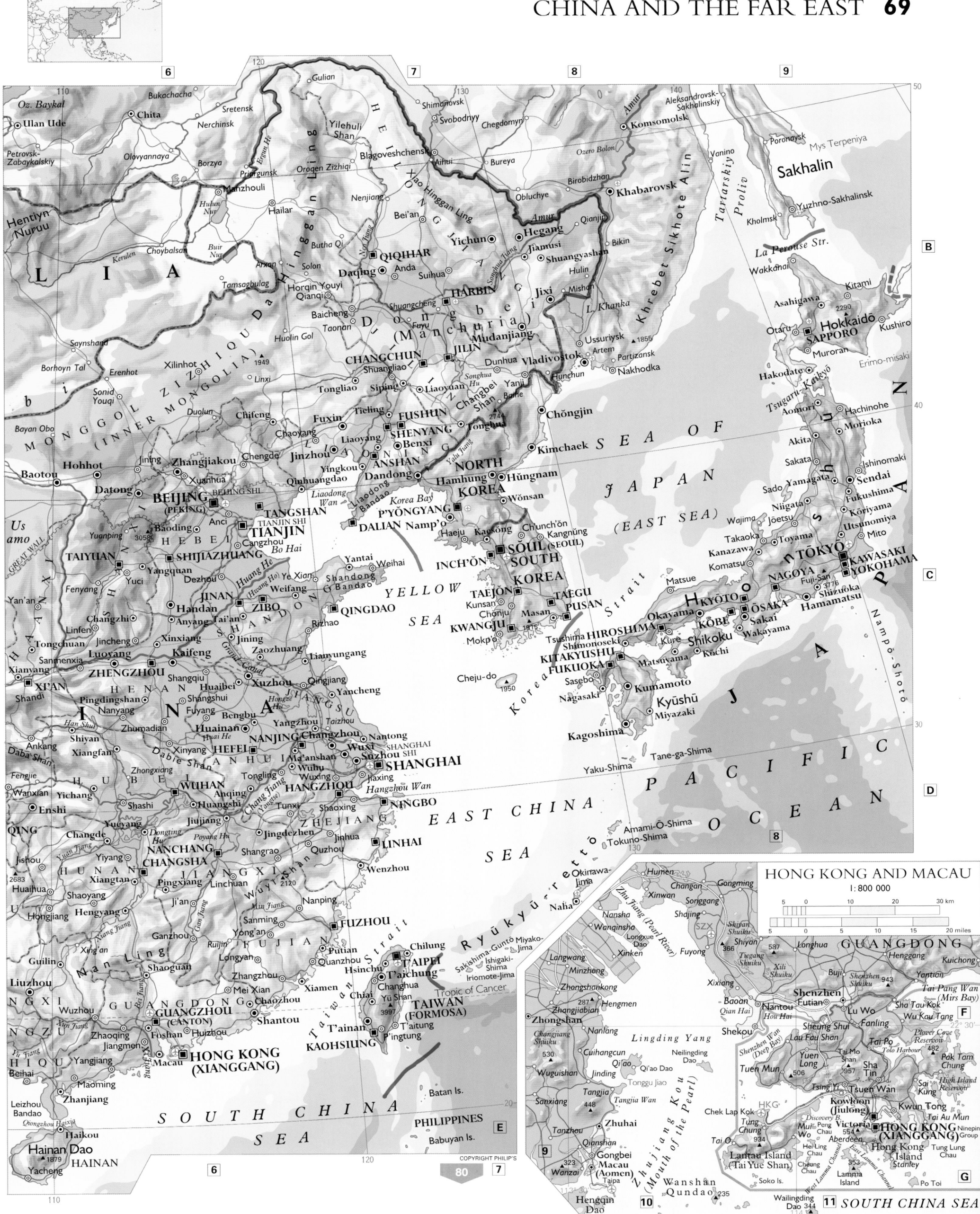

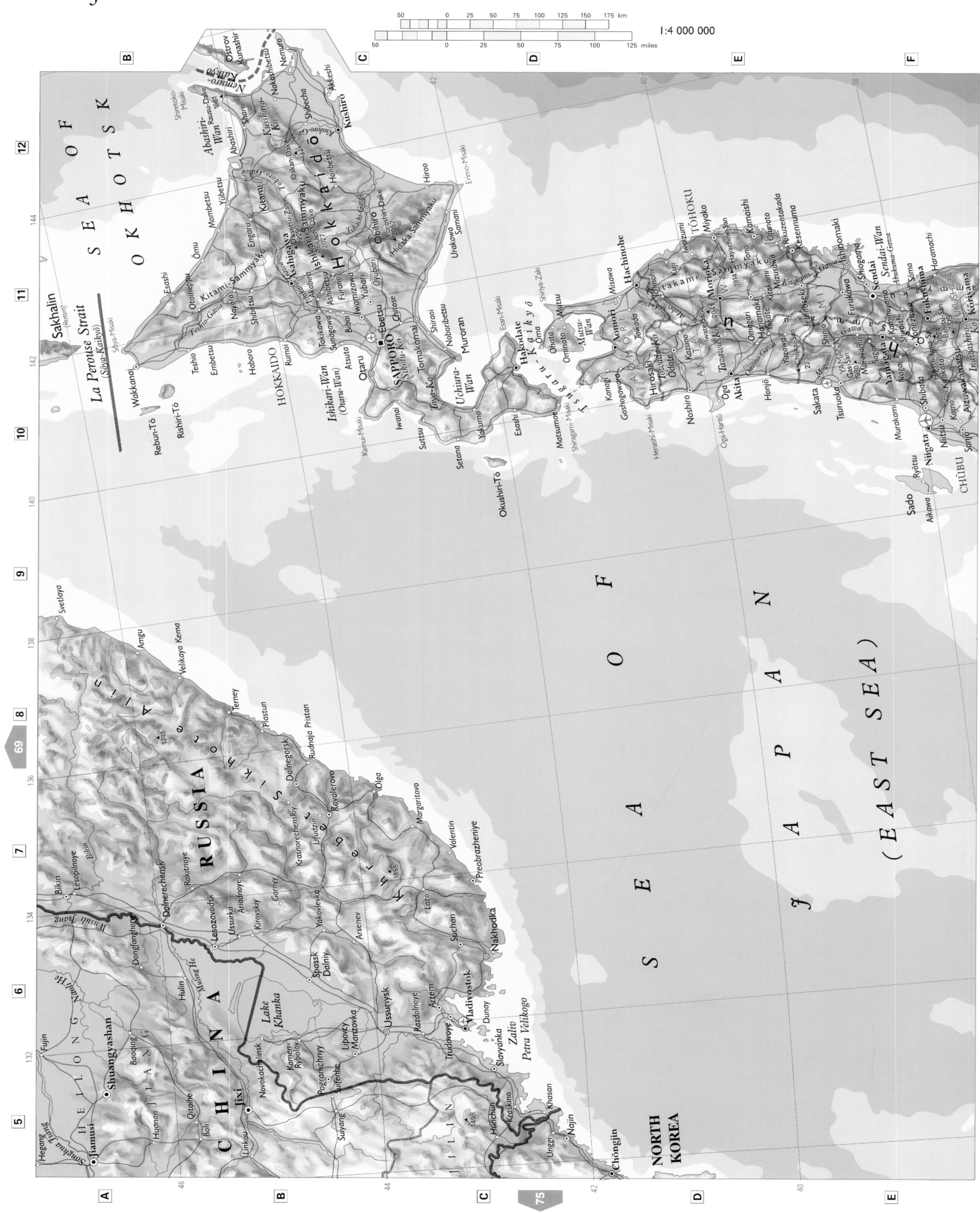

50 0 25 50 75 100 125 150 175 km

50 0 25 50 75 100 125 miles

1:4 000 000

SEA OF OKHOTSK

Sakhalin
(Rossy)

La Perouse Strait
(Sōya-Kaikyō)

HOKKAIDO

Ostrov Kunashir

Nemuro-Kaikyō

Kitami-Sammyaku

Hokkaidō

SAPPORO

Tsugaru-Kaikyō

TŌHOKU

Sammyaku

CHŪBU

SEA OF JAPAN

(EAST SEA)

RUSSIA

Sikhote Alin

Lake Khanka

Zaliv Petra Velikogo

Vladivostok

Nakhodka

CHINA

HEILONGJIANG

JILIN

NORTH KOREA

Chŏngjin

Wusuli Jiang

Nen Jiang

Sado

Niigata

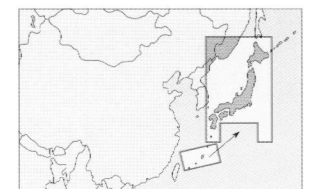

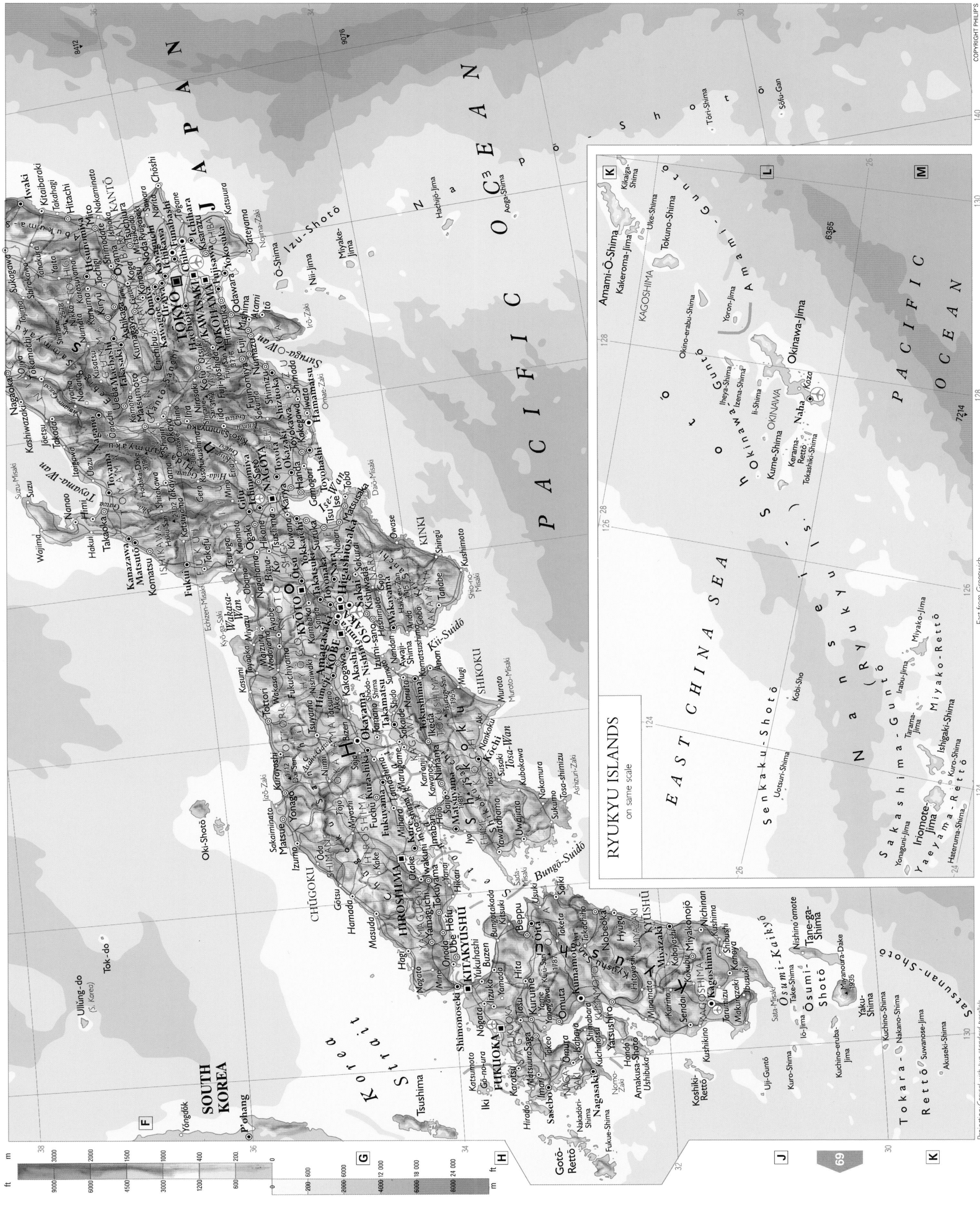

RYUKYU ISLANDS
on same scale

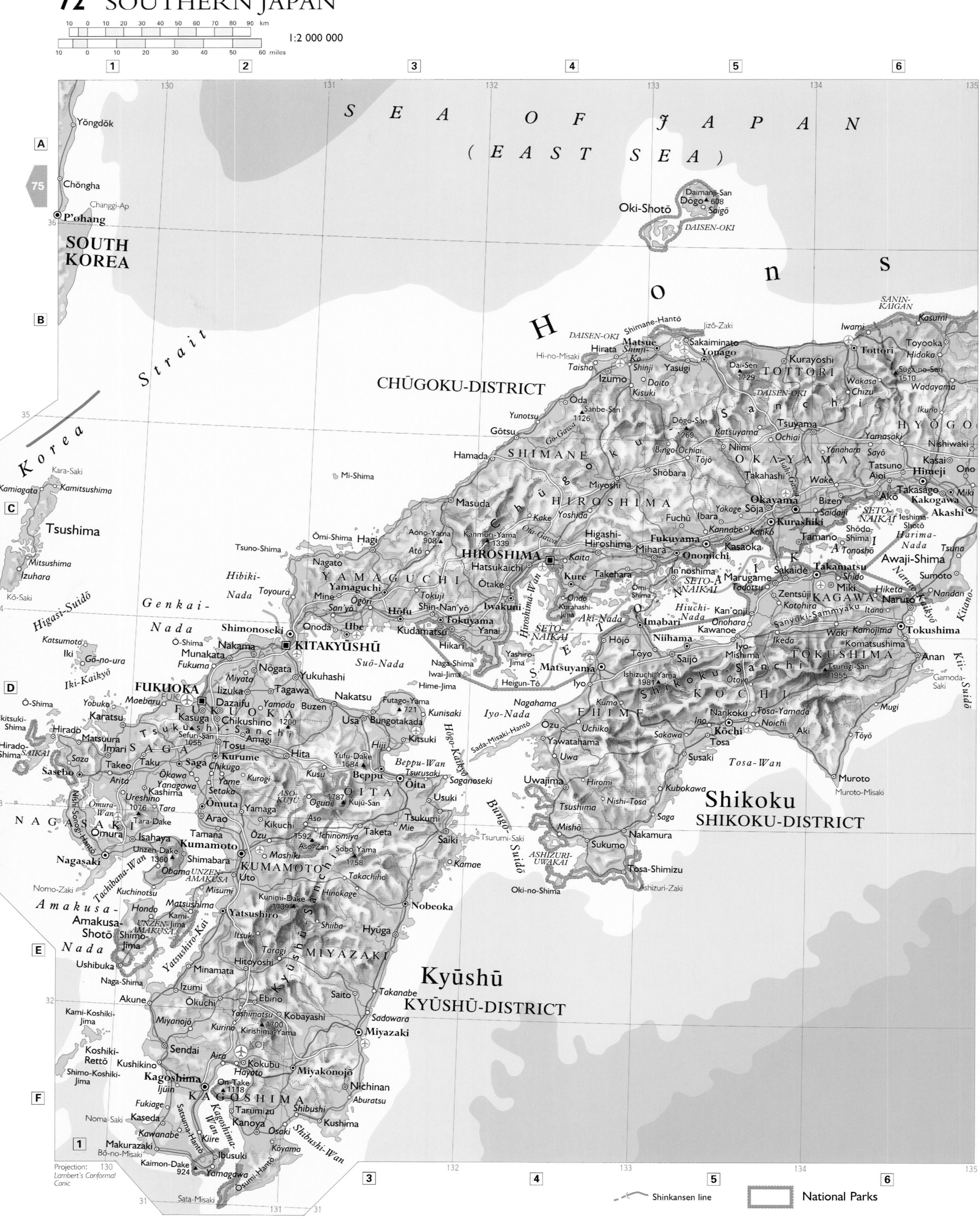

10 0 10 20 30 40 50 60 70 80 90 km
1:2 000 000
10 0 10 20 30 40 50 60 miles

1 **2** **3** **4** **5** **6**

130 131 132 133 134 135

A

SEA   OF   JAPAN

(E A S T   S E A)

Yŏngdŏk
75
Chŏngha
Changgi-Ap
P'ohang
36
SOUTH
KOREA

Oki-Shotō
Daimanji-San
Dōgo ▲608
Saigō
DAISEN-OKI

B

HONSHU

CHŪGOKU-DISTRICT

Korea

Strait

35

C

Tsushima

Kamiagata
Kara-Saki
Kamitsushima
Mitsushima
Izuhara
Kō-Saki

Daisen-Oki
Shimane-Hantō
Jizō-Zaki
Iwami
Kasumi
Hi-no-Misaki
Hirata
Matsue
Shinji-Ko
Sakaiminato
Yonago
Tottori
Toyooka
Hidaka
Izumo
Shinji
Yasugi
Dai-Sen ▲1729
TOTTORI
Kurayoshi
Wakasa
Chizu
Suga-no-Sen 1510
Wadayama
Taisha
Daito
Kisuki
Dōgo-San 1269
Katsuyama
Tsuyama
Yanahara
Yamasaki
Ikuno
Yunotsu
Oda
Sanbe-San 1126
Miyoshi
Ochiai
Tōjō
Niimi
Ochiai
OKAYAMA
Sayō
HYŌGO
Nishiwaki
Hamada
SHIMANE
Shōbara
Takahashi
Wake
Tatsuno
Aioi
Himeji

Mi-Shima
Go-Gawa
Bingo-Ochiai
Kasai
Ono

34

Ōmi-Shima
Hagi
Tsuno-Shima
Aono-Yama 908 ▲
Kanmuri-Yama ▲1339
HIROSHIMA
Higashi-Hiroshima
Fukuyama
Onomichi
Kurashiki
OKAYAMA
Bizen
Saidaiji
Tamano
Shōdo-Shima
Ieshima-Shotō
Harima-Nada
Akashi
Nagato
Masuda
Kake
Yoshida
Ōta-Gawa
Mihara
Kasaoka
A Tonoshō
Tsuna
Yamaguchi
YAMAGUCHI
Atō
HIROSHIMA
Kaita
In'noshima
SETO-NAIKAI
Takamatsu

N A G A S A K I

Nagasaki

E

Amakusa-Shotō
Ushibuka
Naga-Shima

Kyūshū
KYŪSHŪ-DISTRICT

F

Kagoshima
KAGOSHIMA

Shinkansen line   National Parks

Projection:
Lambert's Conformal
Conic

CHŪBU-DISTRICT

h ū

h

KANTŌ-DISTRICT

KINKI-DISTRICT

Kumano-Nada

Enshū-Nada

PACIFIC OCEAN

Zampo-Shoto

ft   m

9000   3000

6000   2000

4500   1500

3000   1000

1200   400

600   200

0   0

200   600

2000   6000

4000   12 000

m   ft

1:4 800 000

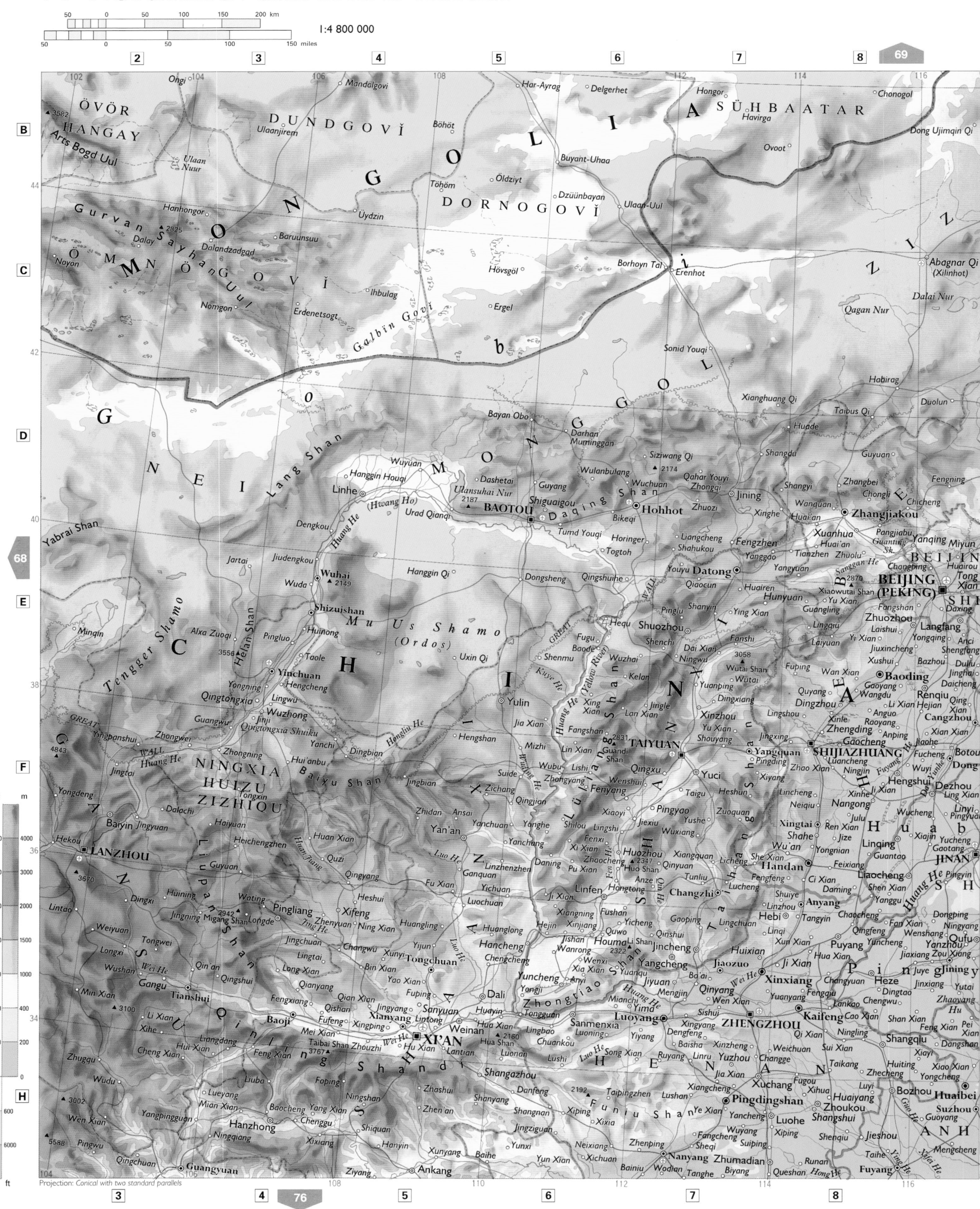

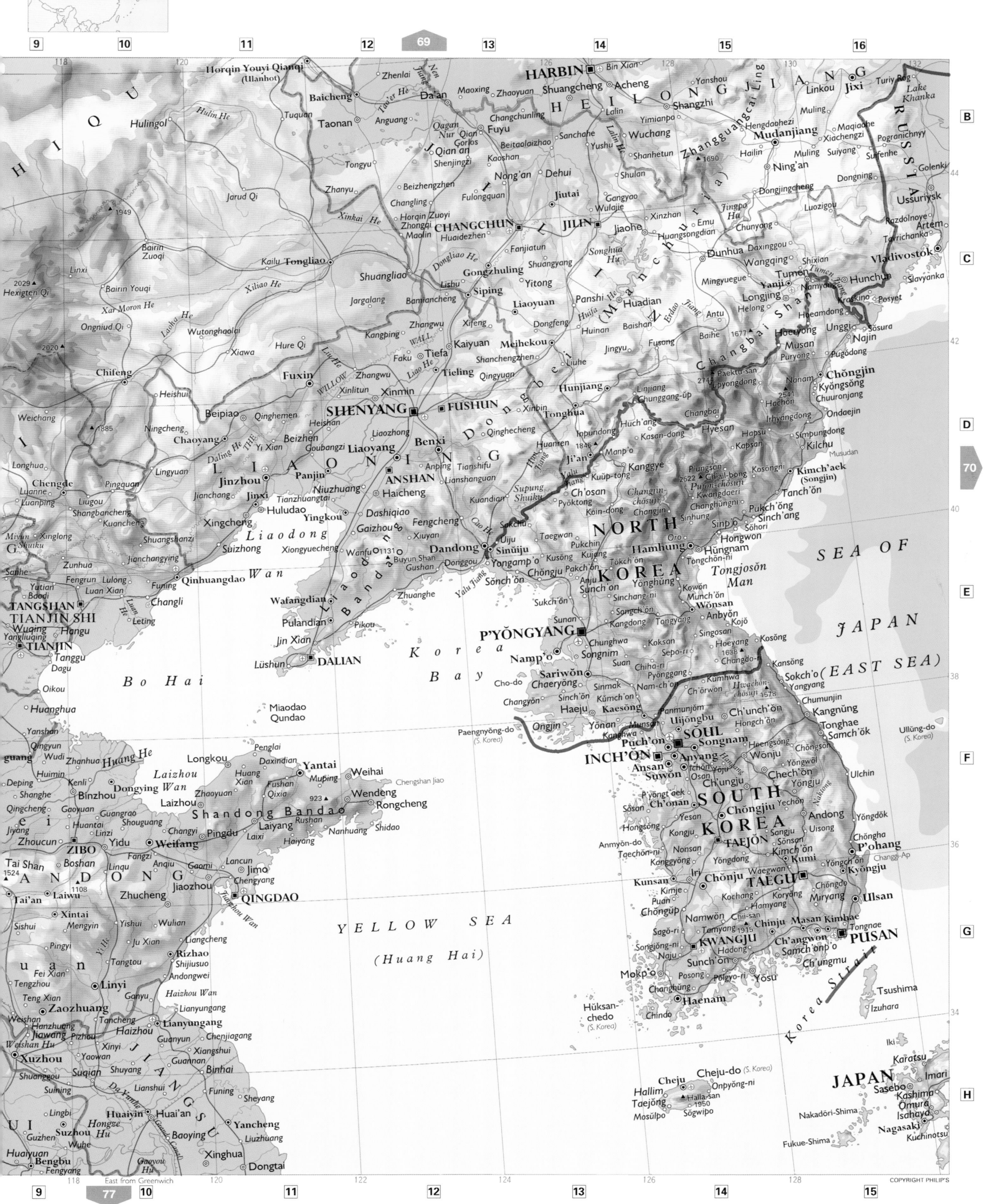

1:4 800 000

Projection: Conical with two standard parallels

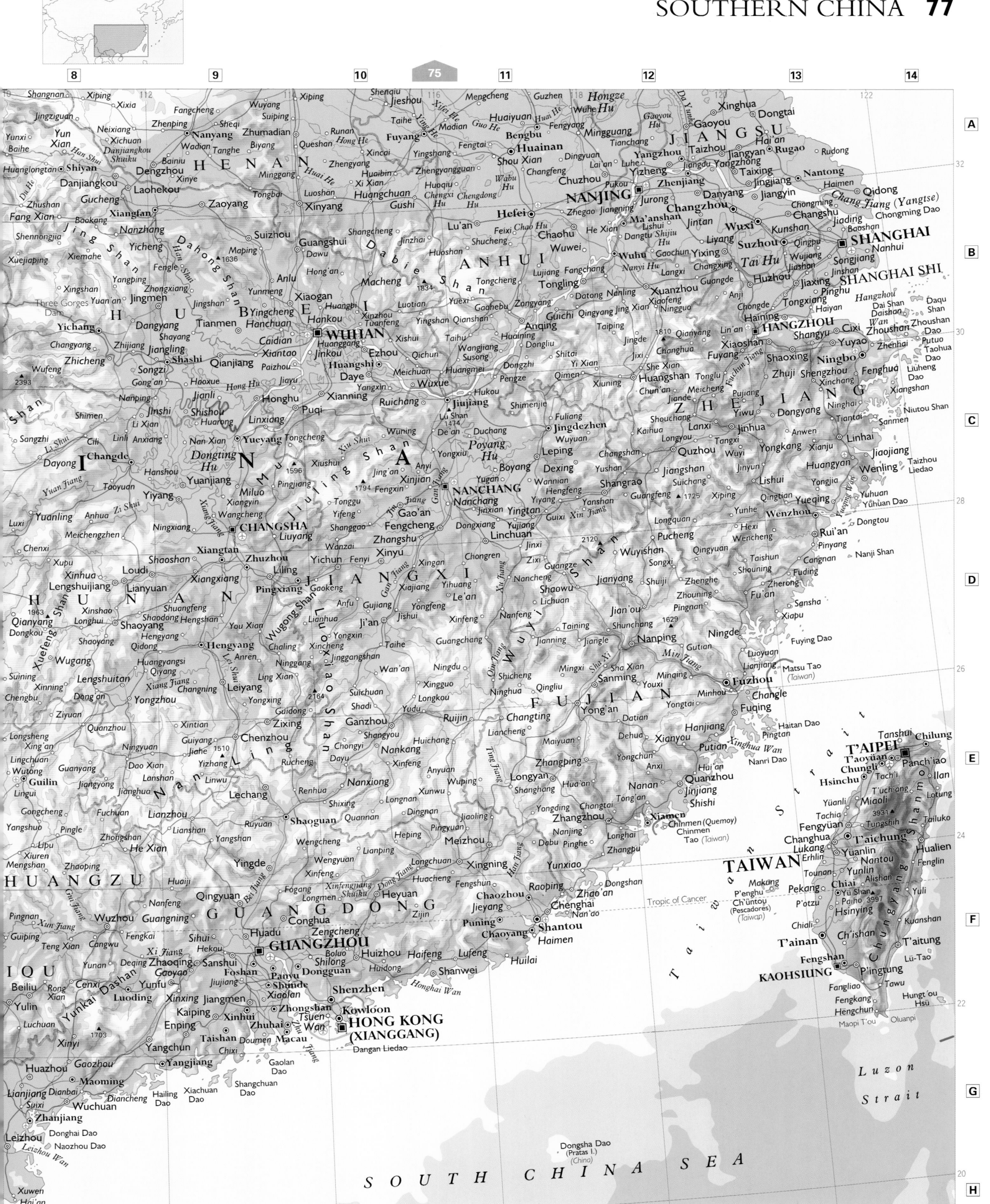

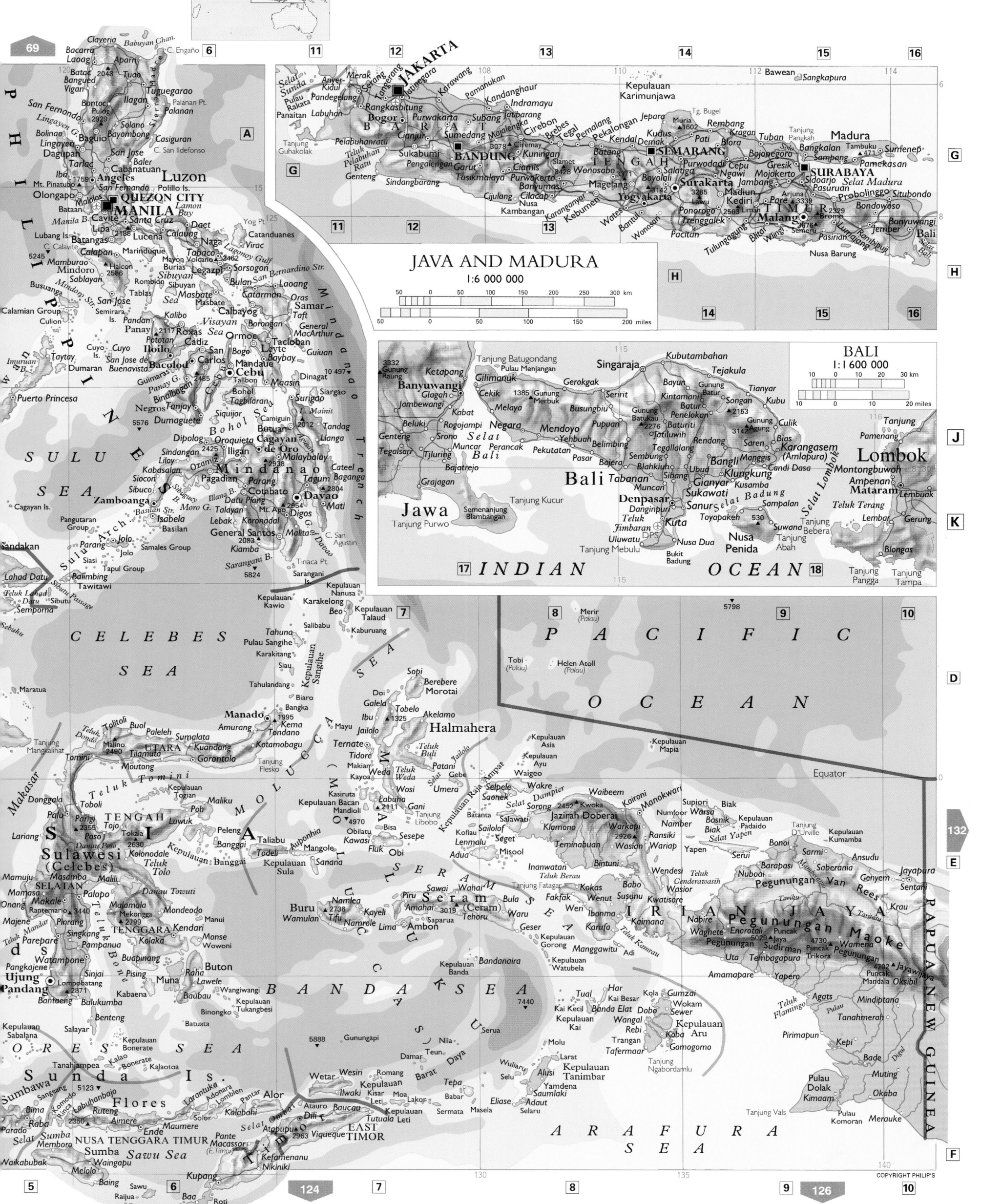

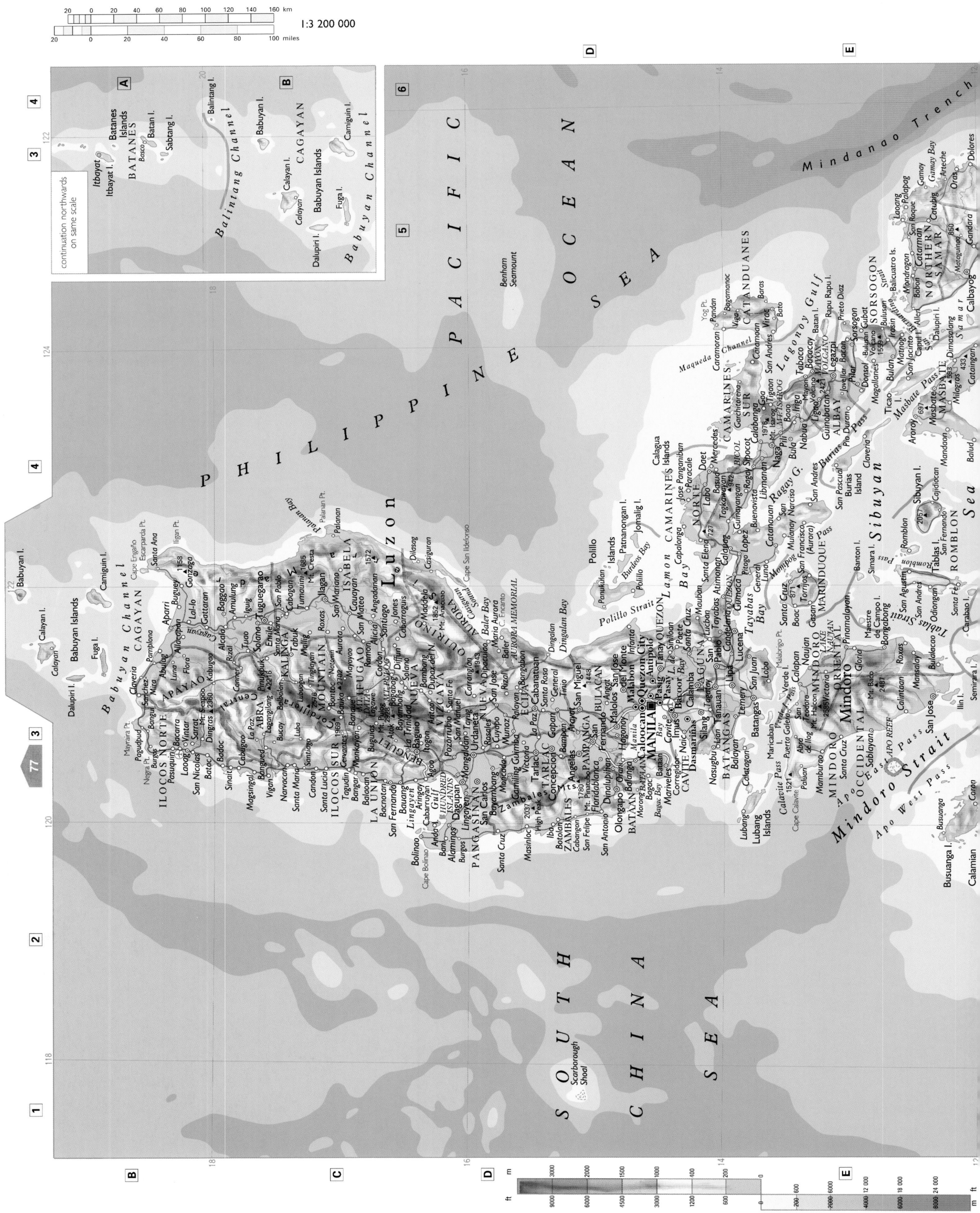

1:3 200 000

continuation northwards on same scale

East from Greenwich

Projection: Lambert Conformal Conic

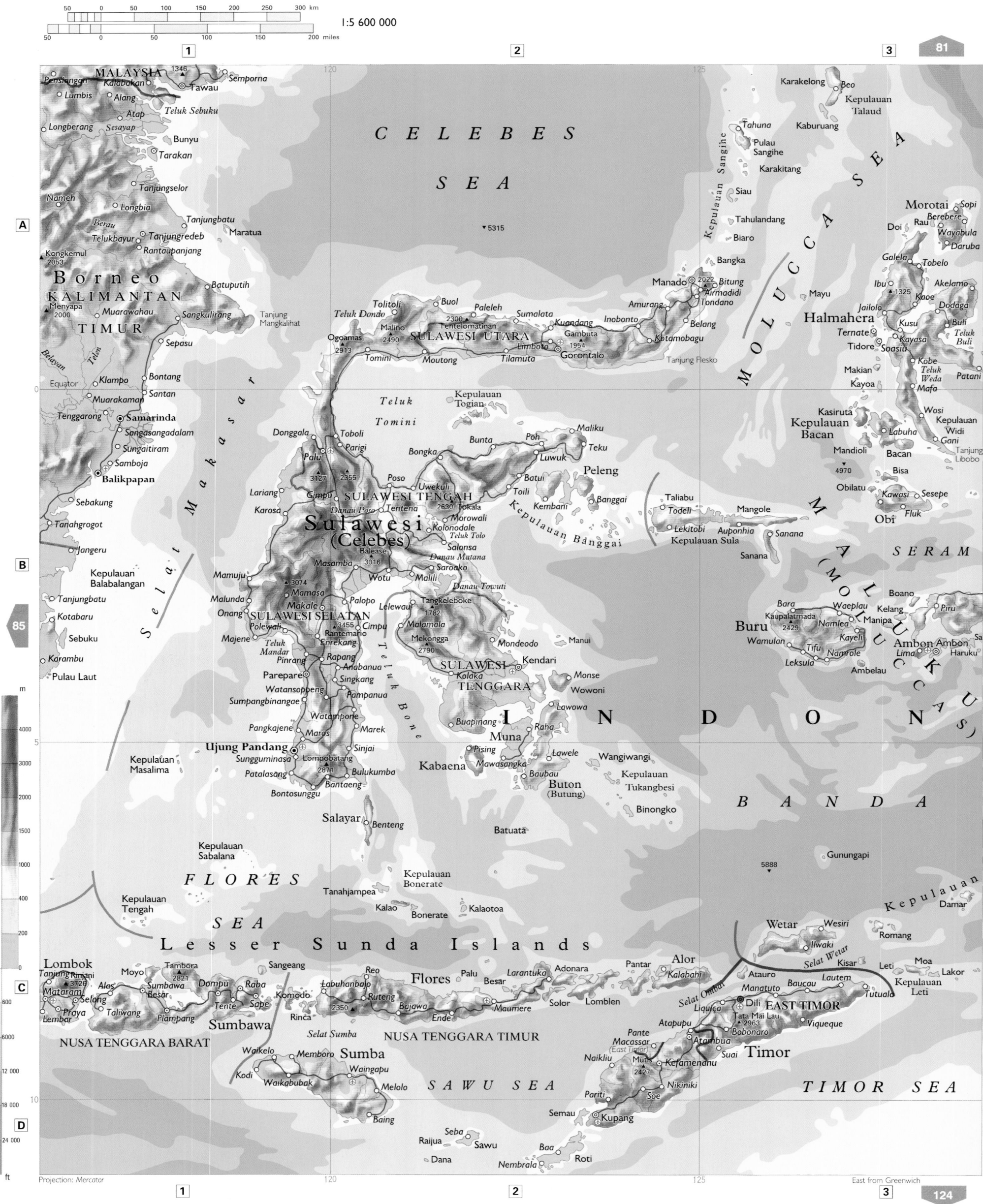

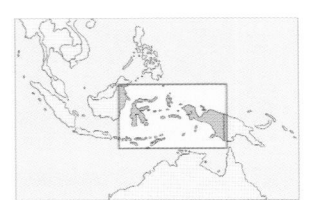

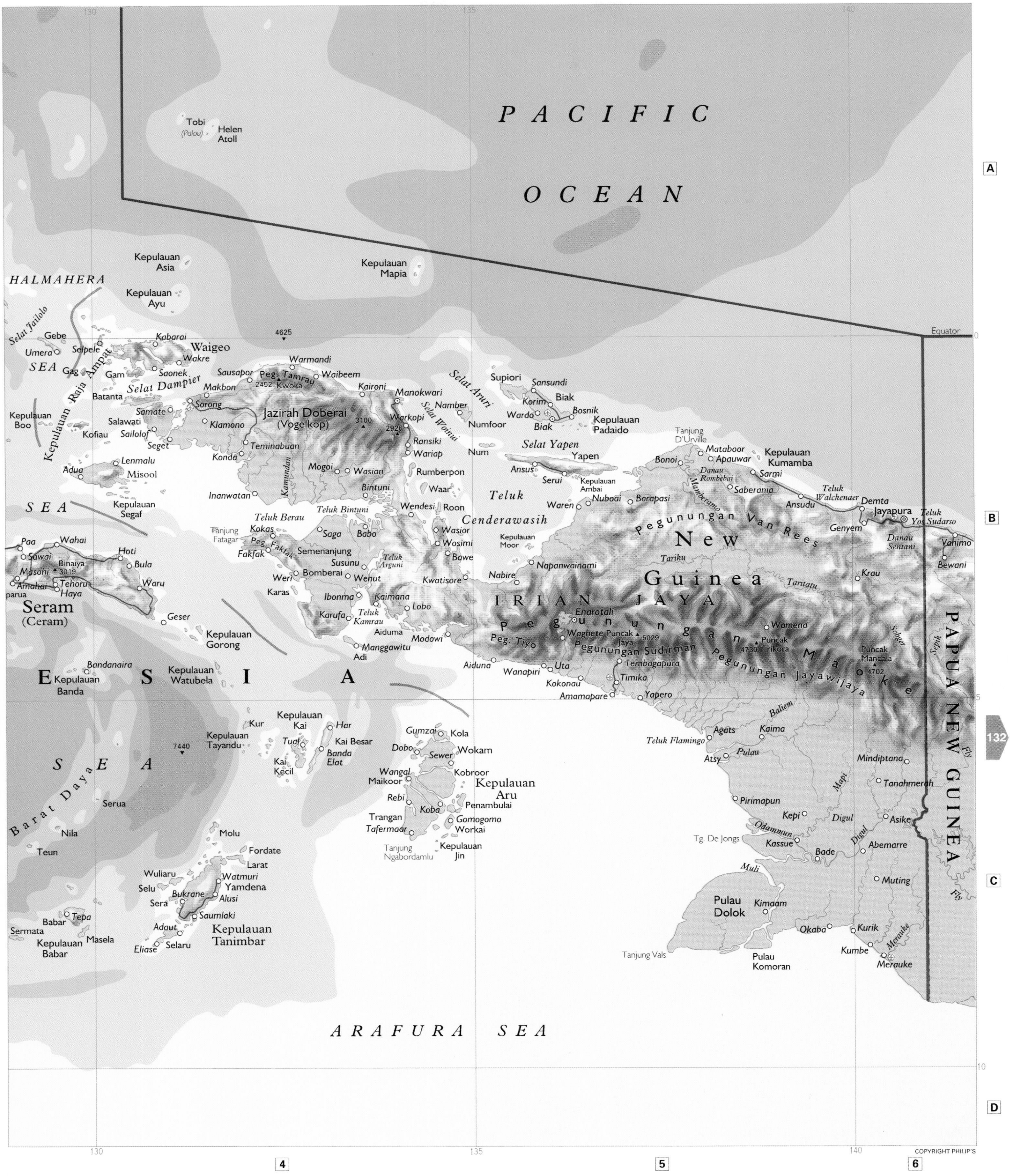

P A C I F I C

O C E A N

A

Tobi
(Palau)   Helen
Atoll

Kepulauan
Asia

Kepulauan
Mapia

HALMAHERA

Kepulauan
Ayu

Selat Jailolo
Gebe
Umera   Selpele   Kabarai   Wakre   Waigeo   Warmandi   4625
SEA   Gag   Saonek   Sausapor   Peg. Tamrau   Waibeem   Supiori   Sansundi
Kepulauan Raja Ampat   Gam   Samate   Makbon   2452   Kwoka   Kaironi   Korim   Biak
Kepulauan   Batanta   Sorong   *Jazirah Doberai*   Warkopi   Manokwari   Number   Warda   Bosnik   Kepulauan
Boo   Salawati   Klamono   *(Vogelkop)*   3100   2928   Ransiki   Num   Numfoor   Biak   Padaido
Kofiau   Sailolof   Seget   Konda   Teminabuan   Wariap   *Selat Yapen*   Tanjung
Adua   Lenmalu   Mogoi   Wasian   Rumberpon   Ansus   Yapen   D'Urville
Misool   Inanwatan   Bintuni   Waar   Serui   Kepulauan   Bonoi   Mataboor   Kepulauan
SEA   Kepulauan   *Teluk Berau*   Saga   Babo   Wendesi   Roon   *Teluk*   Ambai   Apauwar   Kumamba
Segaf   Tanjung   Kokas   Semenanjung   Susunu   Waren   Nuboai   Barapasi   Sarmi
Paa   Wahai   Fatagar   Peg. Fakfak   Wasior   *Cenderawasih*   Saberania   Teluk
Sawai   Hoti   Fakfak   Bomberai   Wenut   Wosimi   Kepulauan   *New*   Walckenaer
Masohi   Binaiya   Bula   Weri   Bawe   Moor   Bewani   Ansudu   Demta   Jayapura
SEA   3019   Tehoru   Karas   Ibonma   Kaimana   Napanwainami   *Guinea*   Genyem   Yos Sudarso
Amahai   Haya   Karufa   *Teluk*   Lobo   Nabire   *Pegunungan Van Rees*   B
parua   *Kamrau*   Tariku   Krau   Vahimo
Seram   Kwatisore   *IRIAN*   *JAYA*   Taritatu
(Ceram)   Geser   Aiduma   Modowi   Enarotali   Tembagapura   Wamena
Kepulauan   Manggawitu   Waghete   Puncak   Puncak   Puncak
Gorong   Adi   Aiduna   Uta   *Peg. Tiyo*   Jaya   5029   4730   Trikora   Mandala
Bandanaira   Wanapiri   *Pegunungan Sudirman*   4702
E   Kepulauan   Kokonau   *Pegunungan Jayawijaya*
Banda   Kepulauan   Timika
S   Watubela   *I*   *A*   Amamapare   Yapero
Kepulauan   Baliem
Kur   Kai   Har   Agats   Kaima
Kepulauan   Tual   Kai Besar   Gumzai   Kola   *Teluk Flamingo*
S   Tayandu   Banda   Dobo   Wokam   Atsy   Pulau   Mindiptana
7440   Kai   Elat   Sewer   Kobroor   Kepulauan   Pirimapun   Tanahmerah
E   Kecil   Wangal   *Aru*   Kepi
Barat Daya   Maikoor   Rebi   Penambulai   Odammun   Digul   Asike
Serua   Koba   Gomogomo   Kassue   Bade   Abemarre
Nila   Trangan   Workai   Tg. De Jongs
Teun   Tafermaar   Kepulauan   Muli
Molu   Tanjung   Jin   Muting
Fordate   Ngabordamlu   Kurik
Wuliaru   Larat   Pulau   Okaba   Merauke
Babar   Selu   Watmuri   Yamdena   *Dolok*   Kimaam   Kumbe
Tepa   Bukrane   Alusi   Pulau   Merauke
Sermata   Sera   Saumlaki   Komoran
Kepulauan   Adaut   Kepulauan   Tanjung Vals
Babar   Masela   Eliase   Selaru   *Tanimbar*

PAPUA NEW GUINEA

132

C

A R A F U R A   S E A

10

D

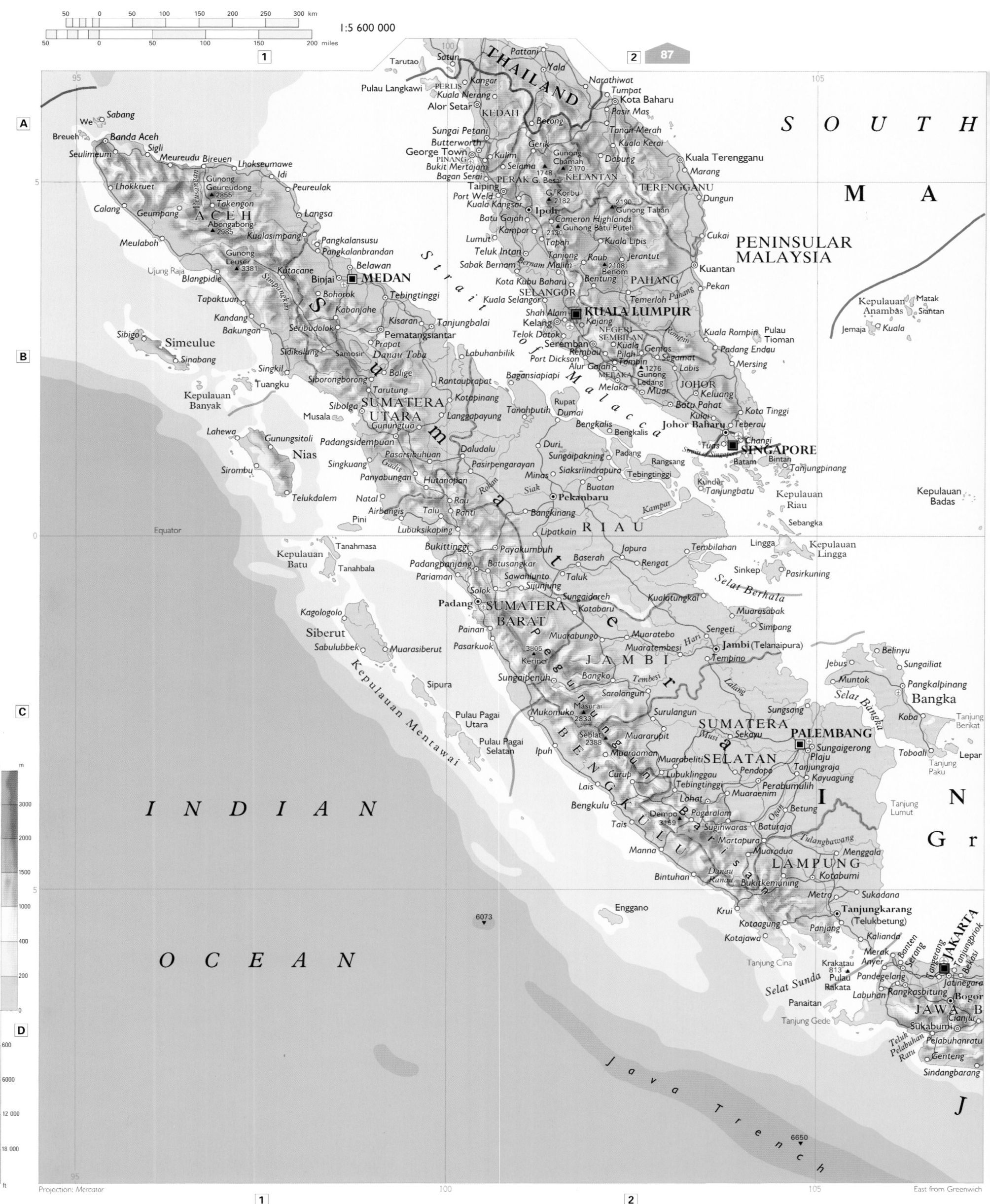

50 0 50 100 150 200 250 300 km
50 0 50 100 150 200 miles
1:5 600 000
1

2 87

THAILAND

Pattani
Yala
Satun
Tarutao
Pulau Langkawi
Narathiwat
PERLIS
Kangar
Kuala Nerang
Tumpat
Kota Baharu
Alor Setar
Pasir Mas
KEDAH
Betong
Tanah Merah
Kuala Kerai
S O U T H

A
We Sabang
Breueh Banda Aceh
Seulimeum Sigli
Meureudu Bireuen
Lhokseumawe
Idi

M
Sungai Petani
Butterworth
George Town
Bukit Mertajam
Bagan Serai
PINANG
Kulim
Selama
Gunong
Chamah
Gerik
Dabung
Kuala Terengganu
Marang

Lhokkruet
Gunong
Geureudong
2855
Takengon
Abongabong
2985
Langsa
Peureulak
Kualasimpang
Pangkalansusu
Pangkalanbrandan

Taiping
Port Weld
Kuala Kangsar
PERAK G. Besar
1748
G. Korbu
2182
TERENGGANU
2170
Gunong Tahan
Dungun
Cukai

PENINSULAR
MALAYSIA

Calang
Geumpang
ACEH
Meulaboh
Gunong
Leuser
3381
Kutacane

Ipoh
Batu Gajah
Kampar
Lumut
Teluk Intan
Sabak Bernam
Kota Kubu Baharu
Cameron Highlands
2130
Gunong Batu Puteh
2108
Tapah
Tanjong Malim
Bernam
Kuala Lipis
Jerantut
Raub
Bentong Benom
2190
Gunong Tahan
Kuantan
Pekan
Temerloh Pahang

Ujung Raja
Blangpidie
Tapaktuan
Kandang
Bakungan
S
U
M
Binjai
Bohorok
MEDAN
Belawan
Tebingtinggi
Kabanjahe
PAHANG
Kepulauan
Anambas
Matak
Siantan
Jemaja Kuala

B
Sibigo
Simeulue
Sinabang
Seribudolok
Sidikalang
Samosir
Prapat
Danau Toba
Balige
Kisaran
Pematangsiantar
Tanjungbalai
Labuhanbilik
SELANGOR
Shah Alam
KUALA LUMPUR
Kelang
Kajang
Seremban
NEGERI
SEMBILAN
Kuala
Pilah
Tampin
Gentas
Segamat
Labis
Kuala Rompin
Pulau
Tioman
Padang Endau
Mersing

Kepulauan
Banyak
Singkil
Tuangku
SUMATERA
UTARA
Siborongborong
Tarutung
Sibolga
Musala
Gunungtua
Rantauprapat
Kotapinang
Langgapayung
Tanahputih
Bagansiapiapi
Telok Datok
Port Dickson
Alur Gajah
1276
Gunong
Ledang
Muar
MELAKA
Meleka
JOHOR
Keluang
Batu Pahat
Kulai

Lahewa
Gunungsitoli
Nias
Sirombu
Padangsidempuan
Pasarsiandapura
Panyabungan
Natal
Hutanopan
Rau
Pahti
Talu
Daludalu
Pasirpengarayan
Duri
Sungaipakning
Minas
Siaksriindrapura
Padang
Dumai
Bengkalis
Bengkalis
Rangsang
Rupat
Johor Baharu
Tuas
Changi
SINGAPORE
Teberau
Kota Tinggi
Bintan
Tanjungpinang
Batam
Kundur
Tanjungbatu
Kepulauan
Riau
Sebangka
Kepulauan
Badas

0
Sinabang
Singkuang
Siak
Rokan
Pekanbaru
Bangkinang
Lipatkain
RIAU

Equator
Kepulauan
Batu
Tanahmasa
Bukittinggi
Payakumbuh
Batusangkar
Baserah
Japura
Rengat
Tembilahan
Lingga
Kepulauan
Lingga

Tanahbala
Padangpanjang
Pariaman
Sawahlunto
Sijunjung
Taluk
Sinkep
Pasirkuning

Kagologolo
Siberut
Sabulubbek
Muarasiberut
Padang
SUMATERA
BARAT
Painan
Pasarkuok
Solok
Kotabaru
Sungaidareh
Kualatungkal
Selat Berhala

3805
Kerinci
Sungaipenuh
Muarabungo
Muaratebo
Muaratembesi
Sengeti
Simpang
Muarasabak

C
Sipura
Kepulauan Mentawai
Pulau Pagai
Utara
Pulau Pagai
Selatan
Ipuh
Masurai
2833
Bangko
Tembesi
JAMBI
Sarolangun
Jambi (Telanaipura)
Tempino
Jebus
Muntok
Belinyu
Sungailiat
Pangkalpinang
Bangka
Selat Bangka

I N D I A N

Seblat
2388
Mukomuko
Muararupit
Surulangun
Lubuklinggau
Muarabeliti
Musi
Sekayu
Sungsang
SUMATERA
SELATAN
Plaju
Sungaigerong
PALEMBANG
Koba
Tanjung
Berikat
Toboali
Tanjung
Paku

Muaraaman
Curup
Pendopo
Tanjungraja
Kayuagung
Lepar
N

I

6073

O C E A N

Lais
Bengkulu
BENGKULU
Tais
Dempo
3159
Pagaralam
Sugihwaras
Batukaja
Lahat
Muaraenim
Perabumulih
Betung
Ogan
Martapura
Tulangbawang
Muaradua
Menggala
Tanjung
Lumut

Gr

Manna
Bintuhan
Danau
Ranau
LAMPUNG
Kotabumi
Bukitkemuning
Metro
Sukadana

5

Enggano
Krui
Kotaagung
Kotajawa
Panjang
Tanjung Cina
Kalianda
Tanjungkarang
(Telukbetung)
JAKARTA
Tangerang
Tanjungpriok
Bekasi

Merak
Anyer
Serang
Banten
813
Krakatau
Pulau
Rakata
Pandegelang
Labuhan
Rangkasbitung
Jatinegara
Bogor
JAWA B

Selat Sunda
Panaitan
Sukabumi
Cianjur

Tanjung Gede
Teluk
Pelabuhan
Ratu
Pelabuhanratu
Genteng
Sindangbarang

J a v a   T r e n c h
6650

Projection: Mercator
95 100 105 East from Greenwich
1 2

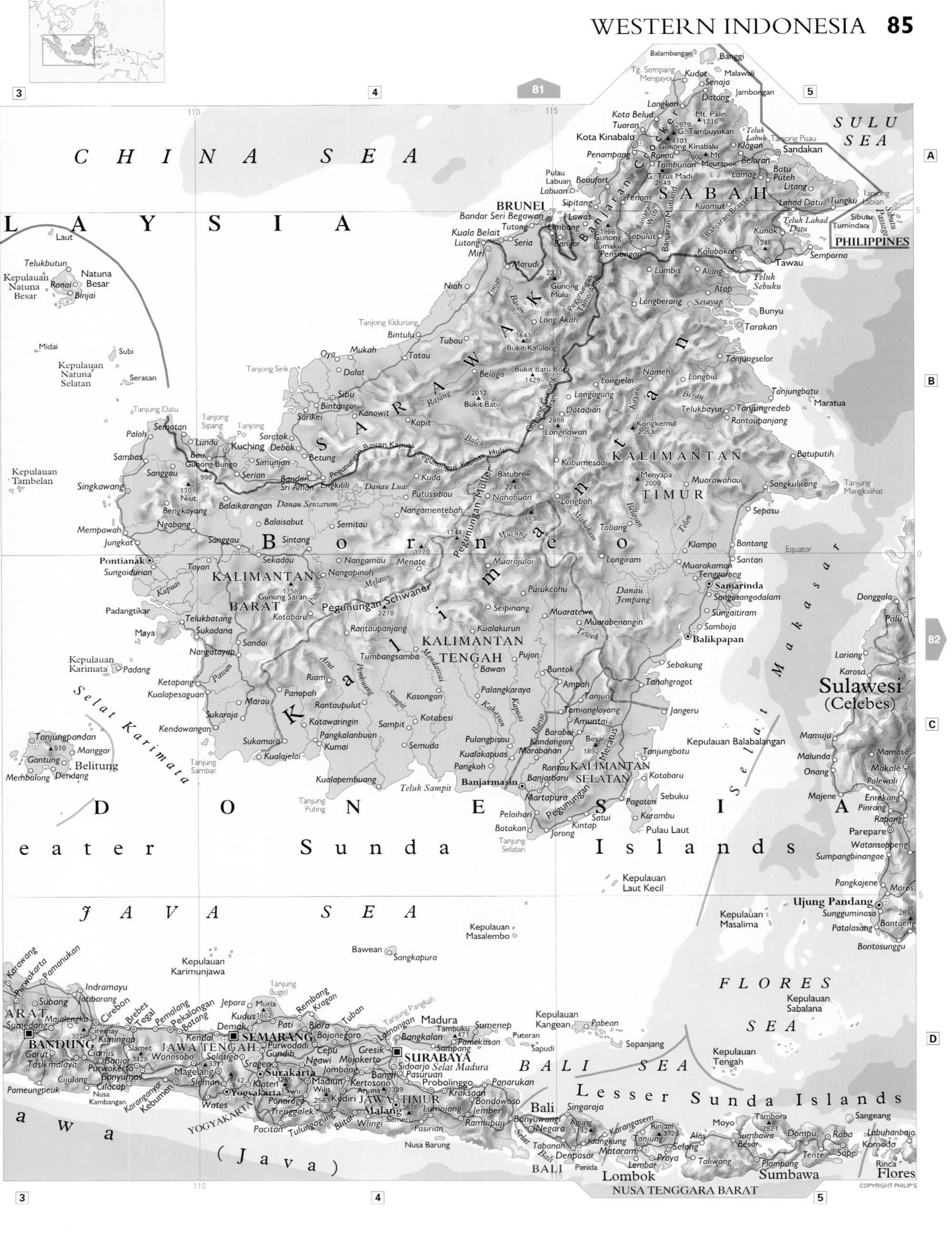

1:4 800 000

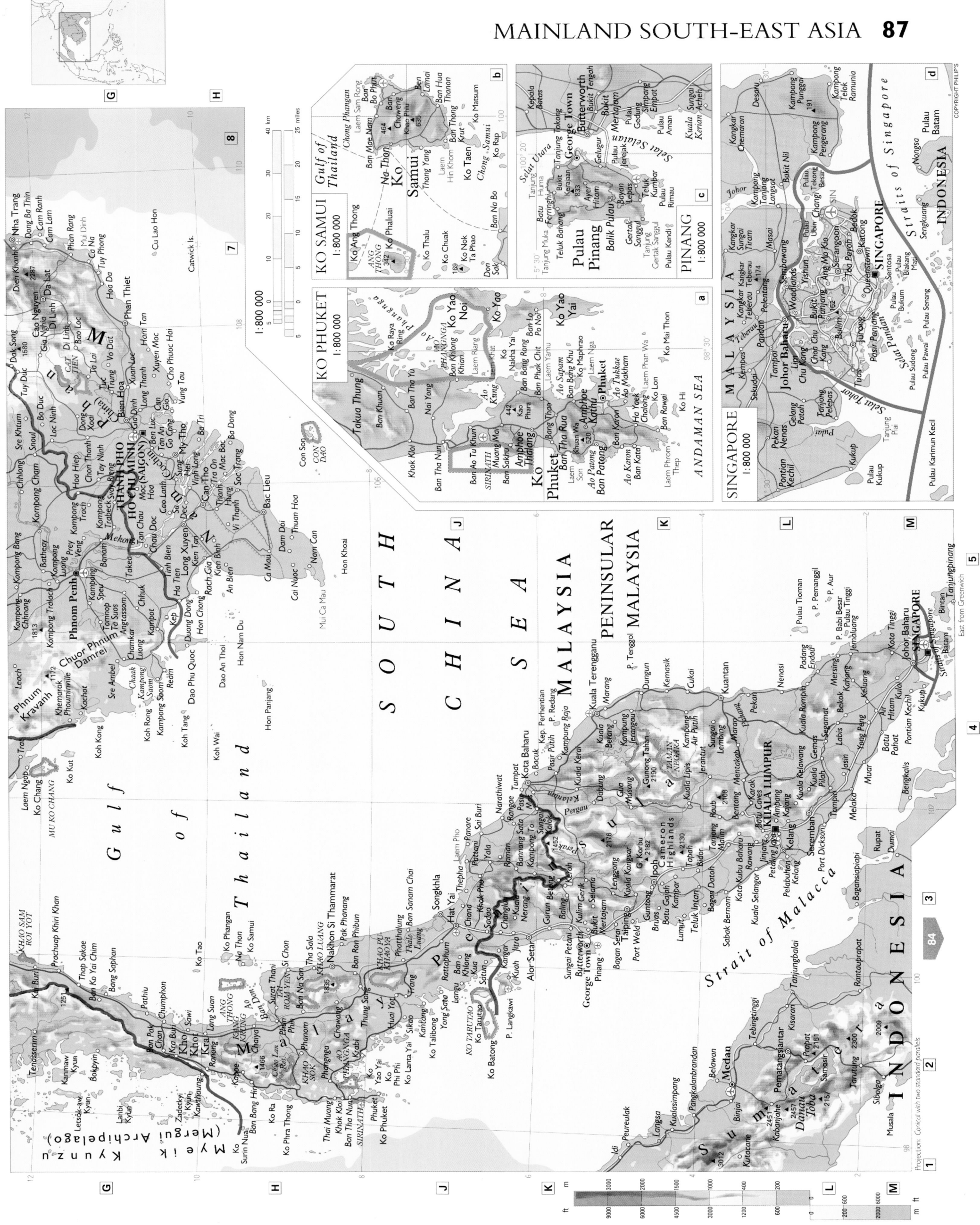

KO SAMUI 1:800 000

Gulf of Thailand

KO PHUKET 1:800 000

PINANG 1:800 000

Pulau Pinang

George Town

Butterworth

SINGAPORE 1:800 000

Singapore

MALAYSIA

INDONESIA

Straits of Singapore

ANDAMAN SEA

SOUTH CHINA SEA

Gulf of Thailand

PENINSULAR MALAYSIA

MALAYSIA

INDONESIA

Strait of Malacca

Myeik (Mergui Archipelago)

Kyunzu

Ho Chi Minh (Saigon)

Phnom Penh

Phuket

Kuala Lumpur

Medan

Singapore

Projection: Conical with two standard parallels

East from Greenwich

50 0 100 200 300 400 500 600 km
1:14 000 000
50 100 200 300 400 miles

1   2   57   3   4   5   66

B

Mediterranean Sea
Ródhos
Antalya
Toros Dağları
Konya
TURKEY
Gyumri
Ganca
YEREVAN
ARMENIA
AZERBAIJAN
BAKI
KAZAKHSTAN
Garabogazköl Aylagy
Nukus
KAZAKH
Türkistan
Adana
Mersin
Gaziantep
Diyarbakır
Van Gölü
Erzurum
Elazığ
Muş
Bitlis
Aras
TABRIZ
Ardabīl
Lankaran
Türkmenbashi
Urganch
UZBEKISTAN
Samarqand
CYPRUS
Nicosia
HALAB (ALEPPO)
Al Lādhiqīyah
Al Mawşil
Orūmīyeh
Daryācheh-ye Orūmīyeh
Rasht
Caspian Sea
Babōl
Gorgān
TURKMENISTAN
Kara Kum
Chärjew
Bukhoro
Qarshi

ELISKANDARÎYA (ALEXANDRIA)
Damanhûr
El Mansûra
Tarābulus
LEBANON
BAYRŪT (BEIRUT)
Hamâh
SYRIA
Hims
DIMASHQ (DAMASCUS)
Nahr al Furāt
Al Qā'im
Dayr az Zawr
Arbīl
Kirkūk
Zanjān
Qazvīn
TEHRĀN
Hamadān
5601 Damāvand
Emāmrūd
Ashgabat
Kopet Dagh
Mary
Bayramaly
Kerki
Termiz
Sheberghān
MASHHAD
Meymaneh
Mazār-e Sharīf

30

106

El Qâhira (CAIRO)
Tanta
Qanâ es Suweis
ISRAEL
Tel Aviv-Yafo
Jerusalem
AMMĀN
JORDAN
Bādiyat ash Shām
Ar Ramādī
Karbalā
BAGHDAD
Al Hillah
An Najaf
Al Kut
Nahr Dijlah
Bākhtarān
Arāk
Qom
Kāshān
Dasht-e Kavīr
Gonābād
Ţabas
Bīrjand
Herāt
Farāh
Ghaznī
Chaghcharān
AFGHANISTAN

El Faiyûm
Es Sinâ'
El Suweis (Suez)
263
Bûr Sa'îd
Ismâ'îlîya
Ma'ân
Al 'Aqabah
Tabuk
Al Jawf
An Nāṣirīyah
Dezful
4548
ESFAHĀN
Yazd
Dasht-e Lūt
Gereshk
Qandahār
PAKIS

C

Qena
El Uqsur
El Sharqîya
An Nafūd
Hā'il
Ahvāz
Khorramshahr
Bandar-e Emām Khomeynī
Abādān
KUWAIT
Al Kuwayt
Shatt al Arab
Shīrāz
Kāzerūn
4075
Būshehr
Jahrom
Kermān
Sīrjān
Bam
Zāhedān
Mirjāveh
Dasht-i Tahlab
Nushki
Sibi
Quetta

Ras Bânâs
Yanbu al Baḥr
Buraydah
SAUDI
Al Madīnah
AR RIYĀD
Ad Dammām
Al Mubarraz
BAHRAIN
Al Manāmah
QATAR
Ad Dawḥah
Ra's al Khaymah
Ash Shāriqah
Dubayy
Qeshm
Ra's al Hadd
Bandar-e Abbās
Jāsk
Gābrīk
Chāh Bahār
Dasht
Central Makran Ra.
Pasni
Ormara
Gwādar
Hyderabad
KARACHI
Baluchistan

20

Halaib
Râbigh
ARABIA
JIDDAH (JEDDA)
Makkah (Mecca)
Aţ Ţā'if
Layla
As Sulayyil
Al Hufūf
Al Qaţīf
Abū Zaby
Al Ḥajar al Gharbī
3019
Masqaṭ
Sūḥār
UNITED ARAB EMIRATES
Gulf of Oman
Tropic of Cancer
Indus Delta
G. of

2269
Bûr Sûdân
Suakin
SUDAN
RED
'Asīr
Rub' al Khālī
OMAN
Maşīrah
Ra's al Madrakah

107

D

Mitsiwa
Jazā'ir Farasān
Dahlak Kebir
Abha
Zُfār
Salālah
J. Khurīyā Murīyā
Mirbāṭ

Asmera
ERITREA
Al Hudaydah
SEA
Sana'
3350
Shibām
Ḥaḍramawt
Sayḥūt
Ras Fartak

Adwa
Mekele
Ţa'izz
YEMEN
Al Mukallā
Ras Fartak

E

Dese
-116
Al Mukhā
Shaqrā
Madīnat ash Sha'b
Al 'Adan (Aden)
Gulf of Aden
Socotra (Yemen)
ARABIAN

Dire Dawa
DJIBOUTI
Djibouti
Bab el Mandeb
Bosaso
Ras Asir (C. Guardafui)

ETHIOPIA
Harer
Berbera
Erigavo
SEA

Hargeisa
Burao
Kebri Dehar
Bender Beila

Ogaden
SOMALI REP.

Garoe
Eil

Obbia

Giuba
Wabi Scebeli
MUQDISHO (MOGADISHO)

INDIA

ft m
18 000 6000
12 000 4000
9000 3000
6000 2000
3000 1000
1200 400
600 200
0 0
200 600
2000 6000
4000 12 000
m ft

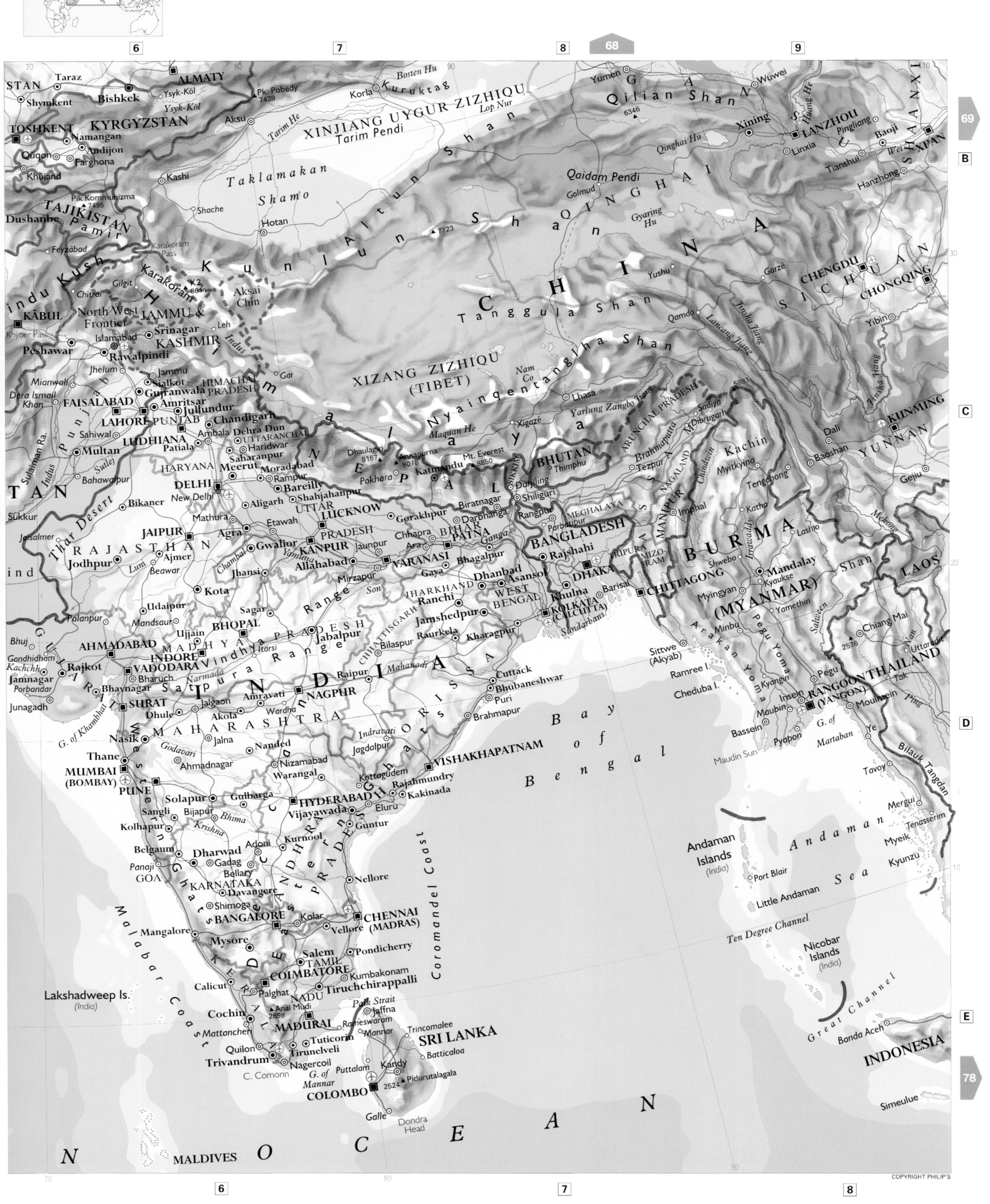

STAN
Taraz
Shymkent
ALMATY
Ysyk-Köl
Bosten Hu
Yumen
Wuwei
TOSHKENT
Bishkek
Korla
Kuruktag
Qilian Shan
KYRGYZSTAN
Namangan
Andijon
Aksu
Tarim He
XINJIANG UYGUR ZIZHIQU
Lop Nur
6346
Xining
LANZHOU
Pingliang
Baoji
Quqon
Farghona
Tarim Pendi
Qinghai Hu
Linxia
Tianshui
Wei
XI'AN
Khujand
Kashi
Shamo
Golmud
Hanzhong
SHANXI
TAJIKISTAN
Shache
Taklamakan
QINGHAI
Qaidam Pendi
CHENGDU
SICHUAN
CHONGQING
Dushanbe
Pamir
Hotan
7723
Garzê
Yushu
Qamdo
Yibin
Feyzabad
Kun
lun
Shan
CHINA
Dali
KUNMING
K2
Aksai
Tanggula Shan
Lhasa
Brahmaputra
Baoshan
YUNNAN
KABUL
North West
Frontier
JAMMU &
KASHMIR
Leh
XIZANG ZIZHIQU
(TIBET)
Nyaingentanglha Shan
Xigazê
Yarlung Zangbo Jiang
ARUNACHAL PRADESH
Dibrugarh
Kachin
Myitkyina
Tengchong
Geju
Peshawar
Khyber Pass
Islamabad
Srinagar
Jammu
HIMACHAL
PRADESH
Gar
Dhaulagiri
Annapurna
Mt. Everest
Katmandu
BHUTAN
Thimphu
NAGALAND
MANIPUR
Imphal
BURMA
Lashio
Mandalay
Chiang Mai
FAISALABAD
LAHORE
Amritsar
Jullundur
Chandigarh
Dehra Dun
N
E
P
A
L
Pokhara
Darjiling
Shiliguri
MEGHALAYA
BANGLADESH
Rajshahi
TRIPURA
DHAKA
MIZORAM
CHITTAGONG
(MYANMAR)
LAOS
Shan
THAILAND
LUDHIANA
Patiala
Haridwar
UTTARANCHAL
Bareilly
Moradabad
Rampur
Gorakhpur
Darbhanga
BIHAR
PATNA
Khulna
Barisal
Mandalay
DELHI
New Delhi
Meerut
LUCKNOW
UTTAR
PRADESH
Chhapra
Ganga
RANGOON
(YANGON)
JAIPUR
Agra
Gwalior
KANPUR
Jaunpur
VARANASI
Bhagalpur
Asansol
WEST
BENGAL
KOLKATA
(CALCUTTA)
INDIA

MALDIVES

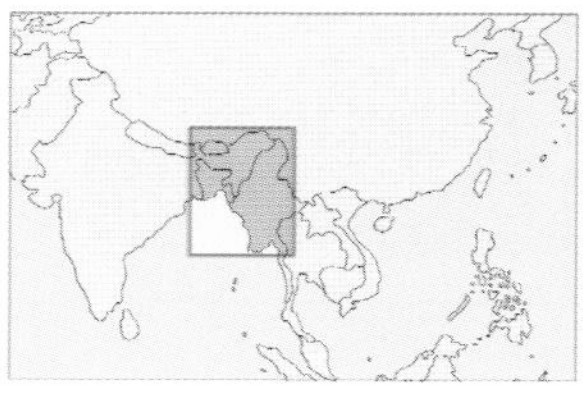

1:4 800 000

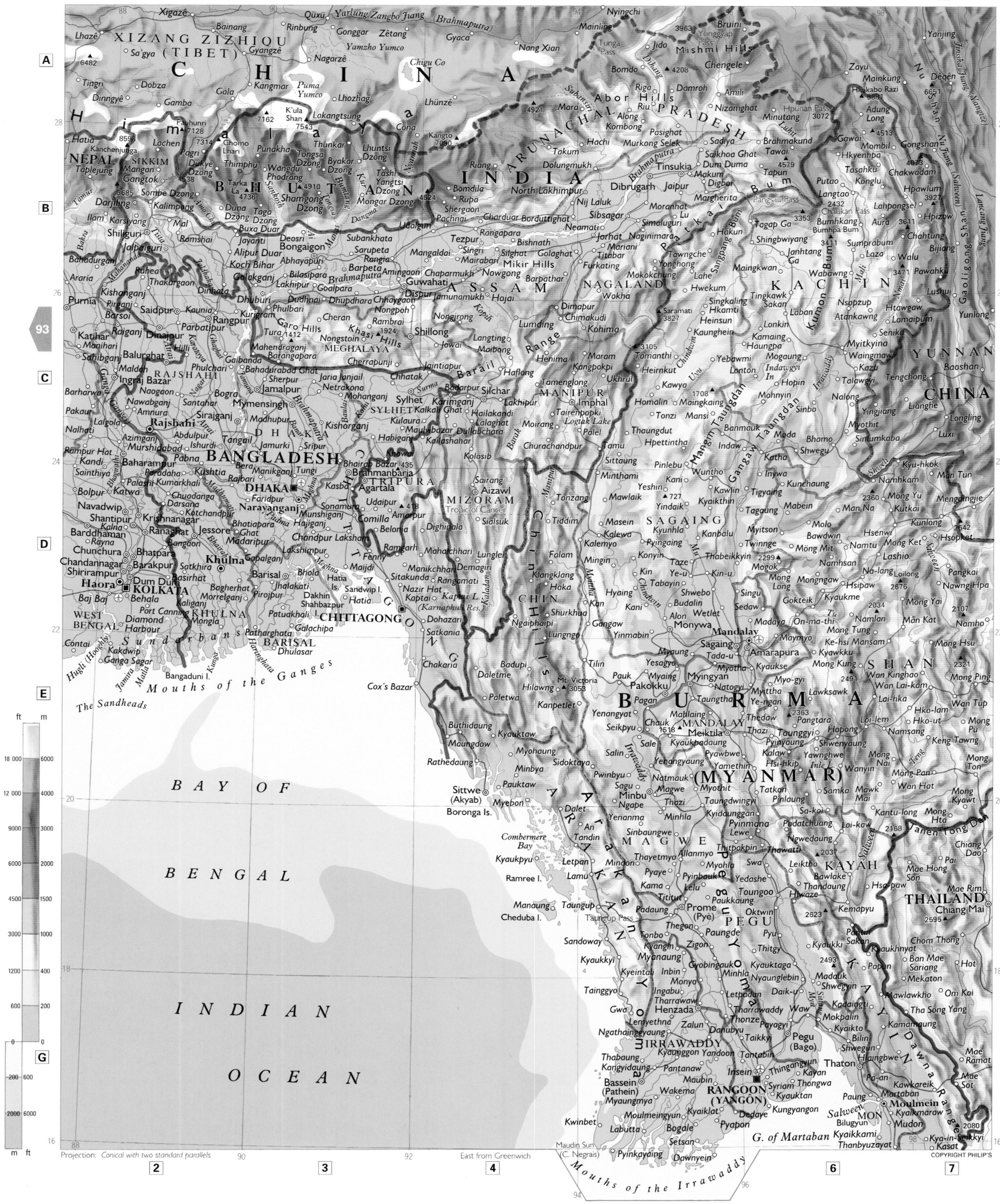

50 0 50 100 150 200 km
50 0 50 100 150 miles

CHINA

XIZANG ZIZHIQU (TIBET)

Himalaya

NEPAL

SIKKIM

BHUTAN

ARUNACHAL PRADESH

INDIA

ASSAM

NAGALAND

KACHIN

YUNNAN

MEGHALAYA

Garo Hills

Khasi Hills

Barail Range

MANIPUR

CHINA

BANGLADESH

DHAKA

RAJSHAHI

KHULNA

WEST BENGAL

KOLKATA

TRIPURA

MIZORAM

Tropic of Cancer

Chittagong

SYLHET

SAGAING

SHAN

CHIN Hills

BURMA (MYANMAR)

Mandalay

Arakan Yoma

Pegu Yoma

MAGWE

PEGU

KAYAH

THAILAND

Chiang Mai

Sunderbans

Mouths of the Ganges

The Sandheads

BAY

OF

BENGAL

INDIAN

OCEAN

Sittwe (Akyab)

RANGOON (YANGON)

IRRAWADDY

MON

Moulmein

G. of Martaban

Mouths of the Irrawaddy

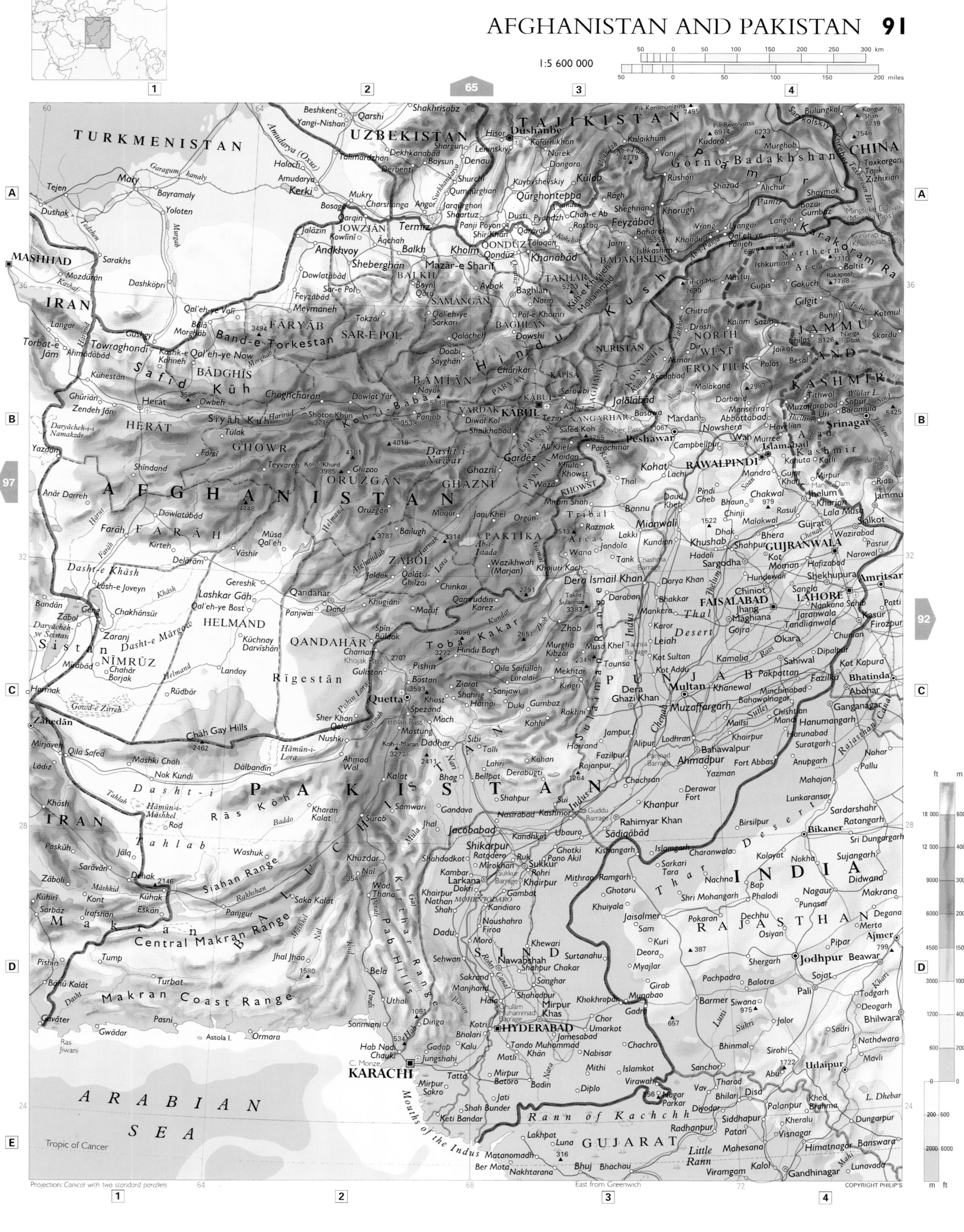

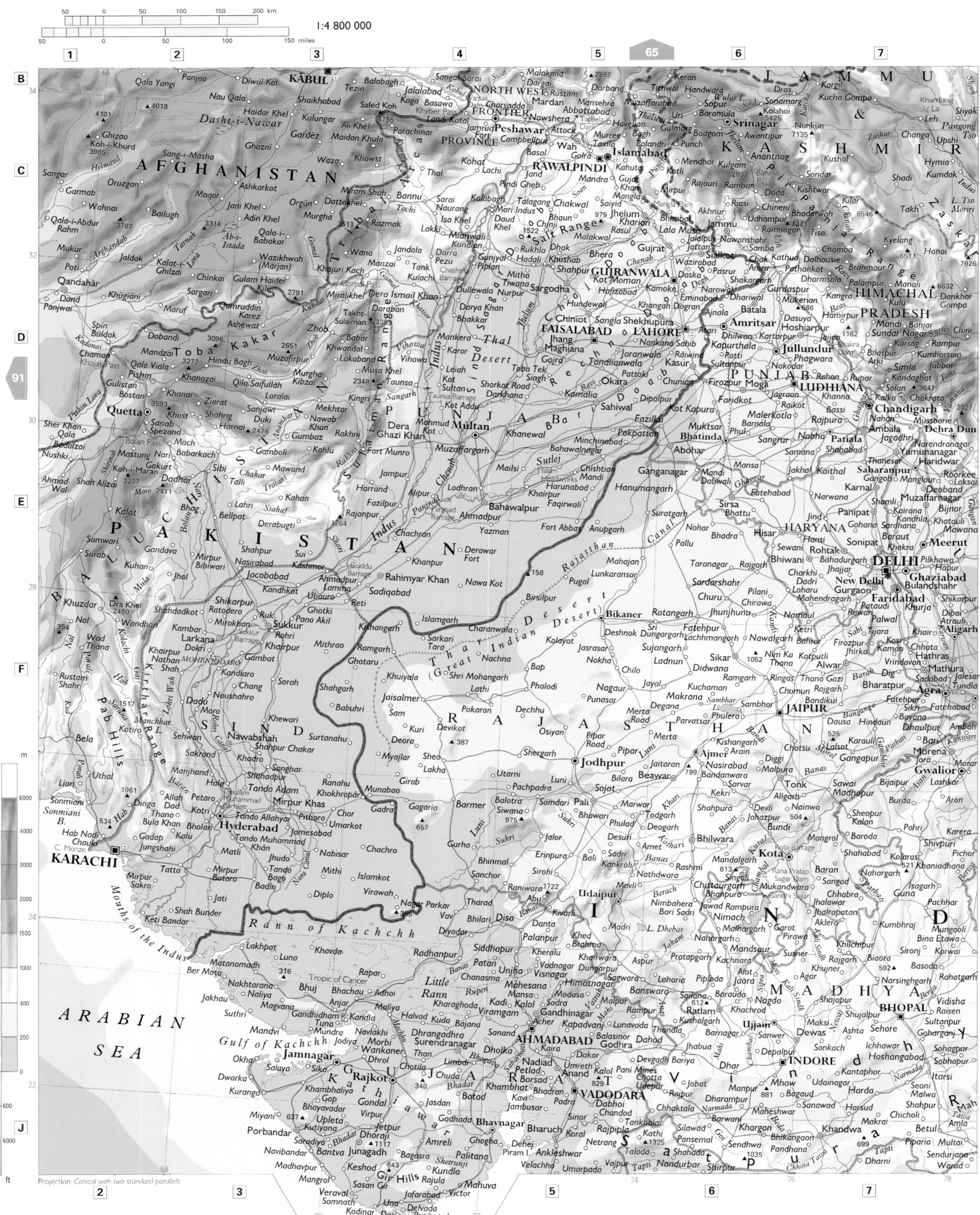

1:4 800 000

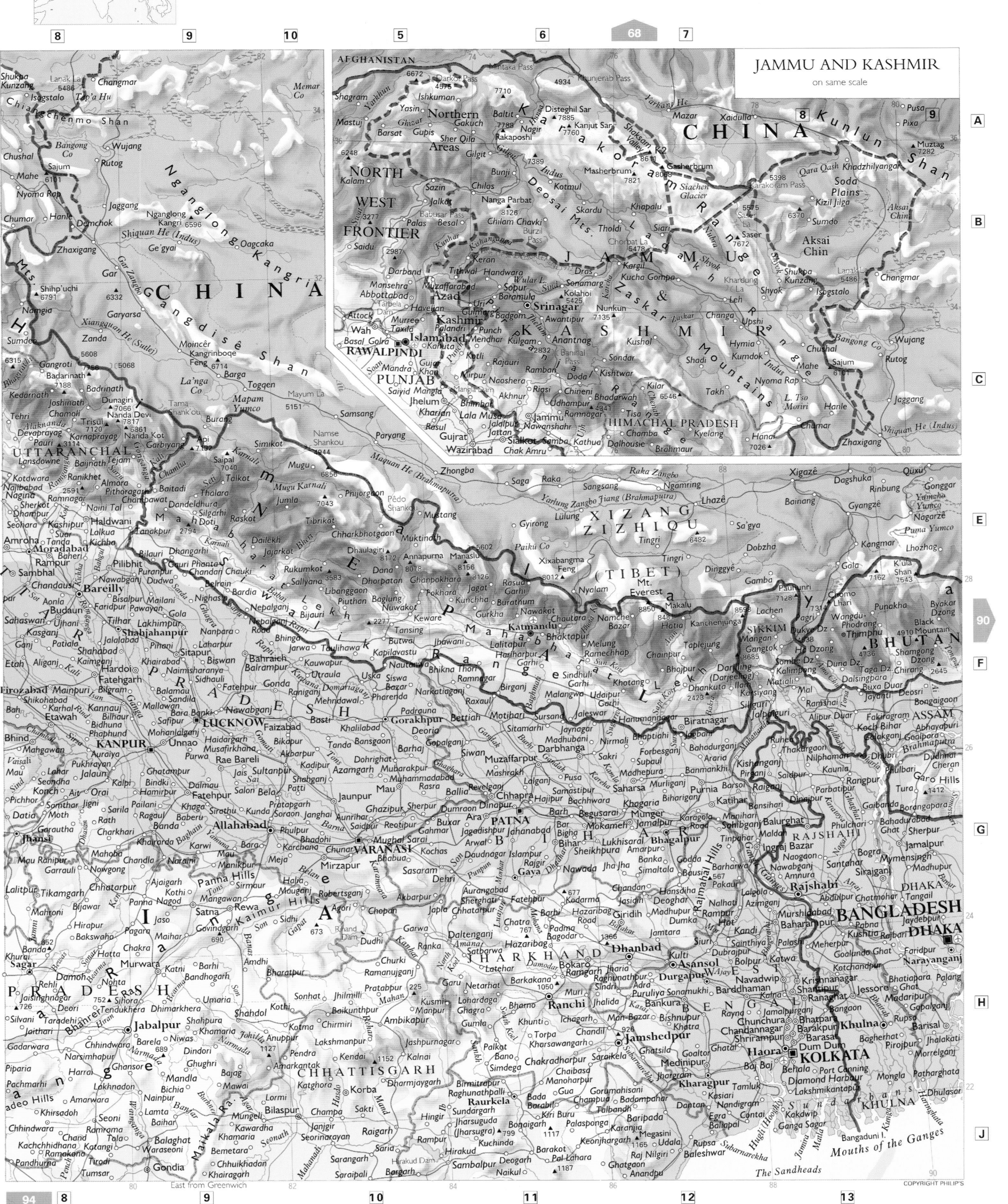

JAMMU AND KASHMIR
on same scale

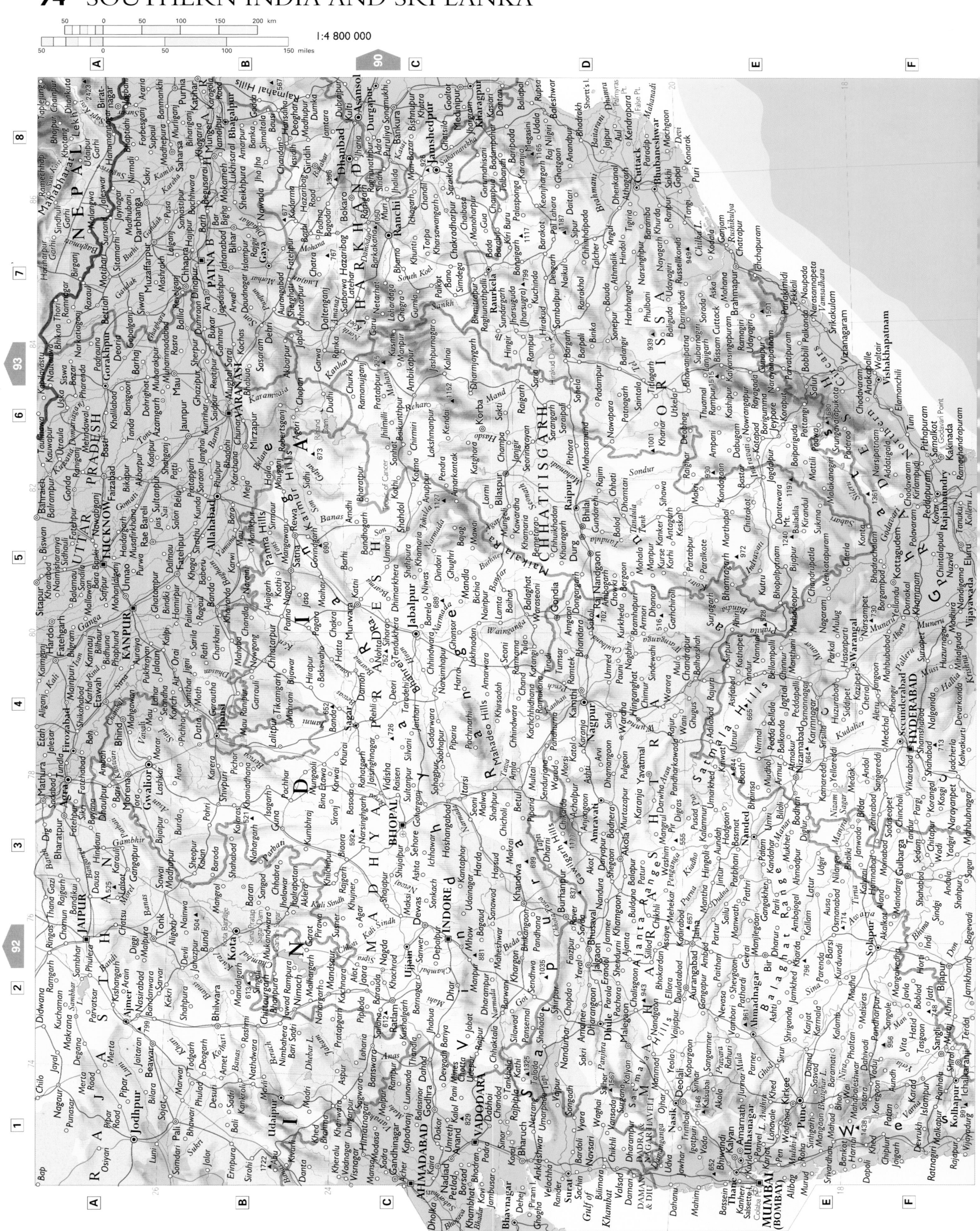

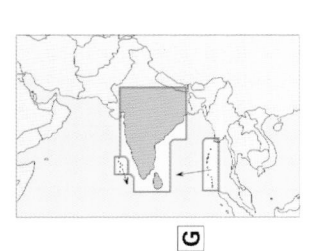

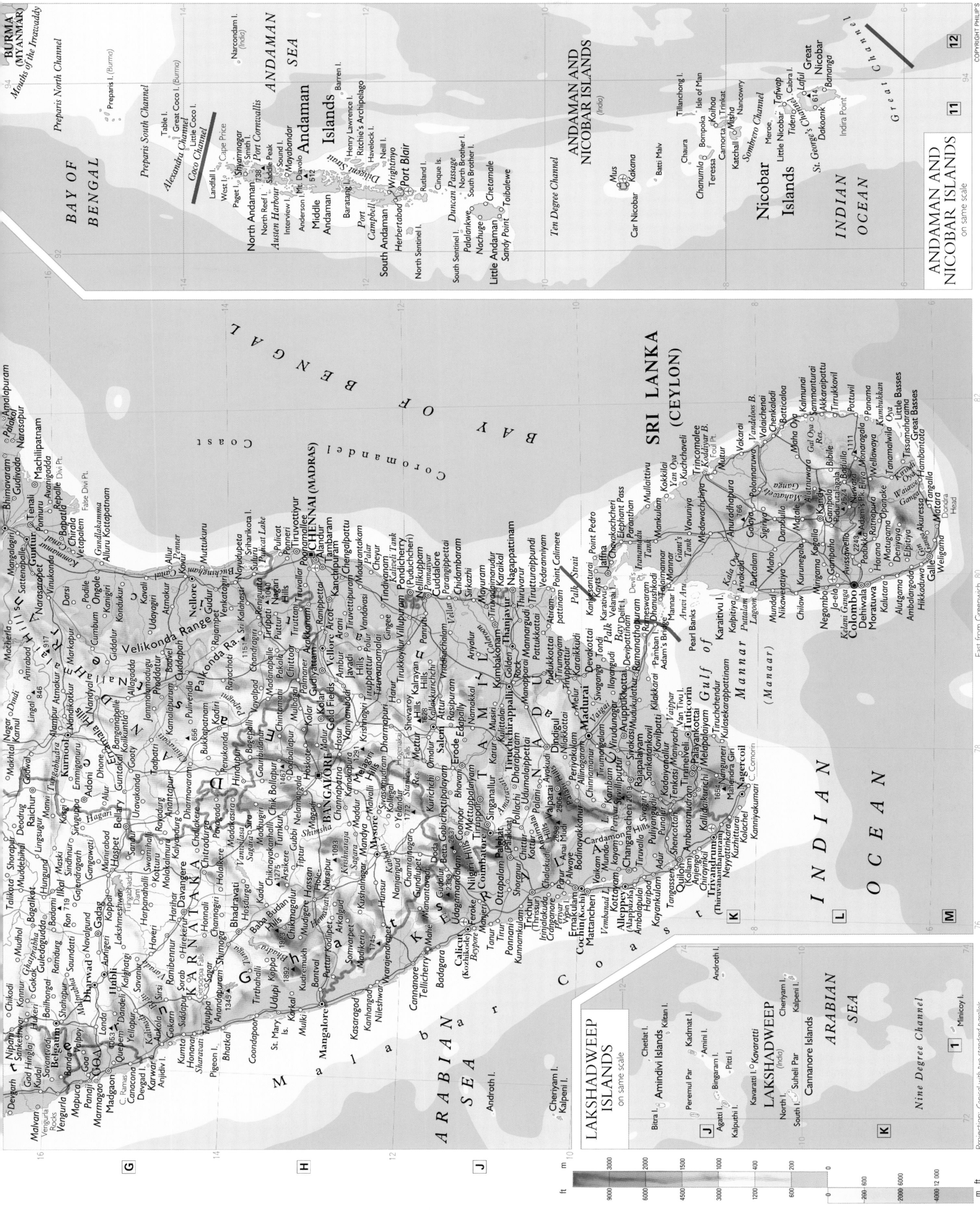

BAY OF BENGAL
ARABIAN SEA
INDIAN OCEAN
SRI LANKA (CEYLON)
ANDAMAN AND NICOBAR ISLANDS
on same scale
LAKSHADWEEP ISLANDS
on same scale
ANDAMAN SEA
BURMA (MYANMAR)
Andaman Islands
Nicobar Islands
Ten Degree Channel
Nine Degree Channel
Coromandel Coast
Malabar Coast
Gulf of Mannar
Palk Strait
CHENNAI (MADRAS)
BANGALORE
Colombo
Port Blair
KARNATAKA
East from Greenwich
Projection: Conical with two standard parallels
COPYRIGHT PHILIP'S

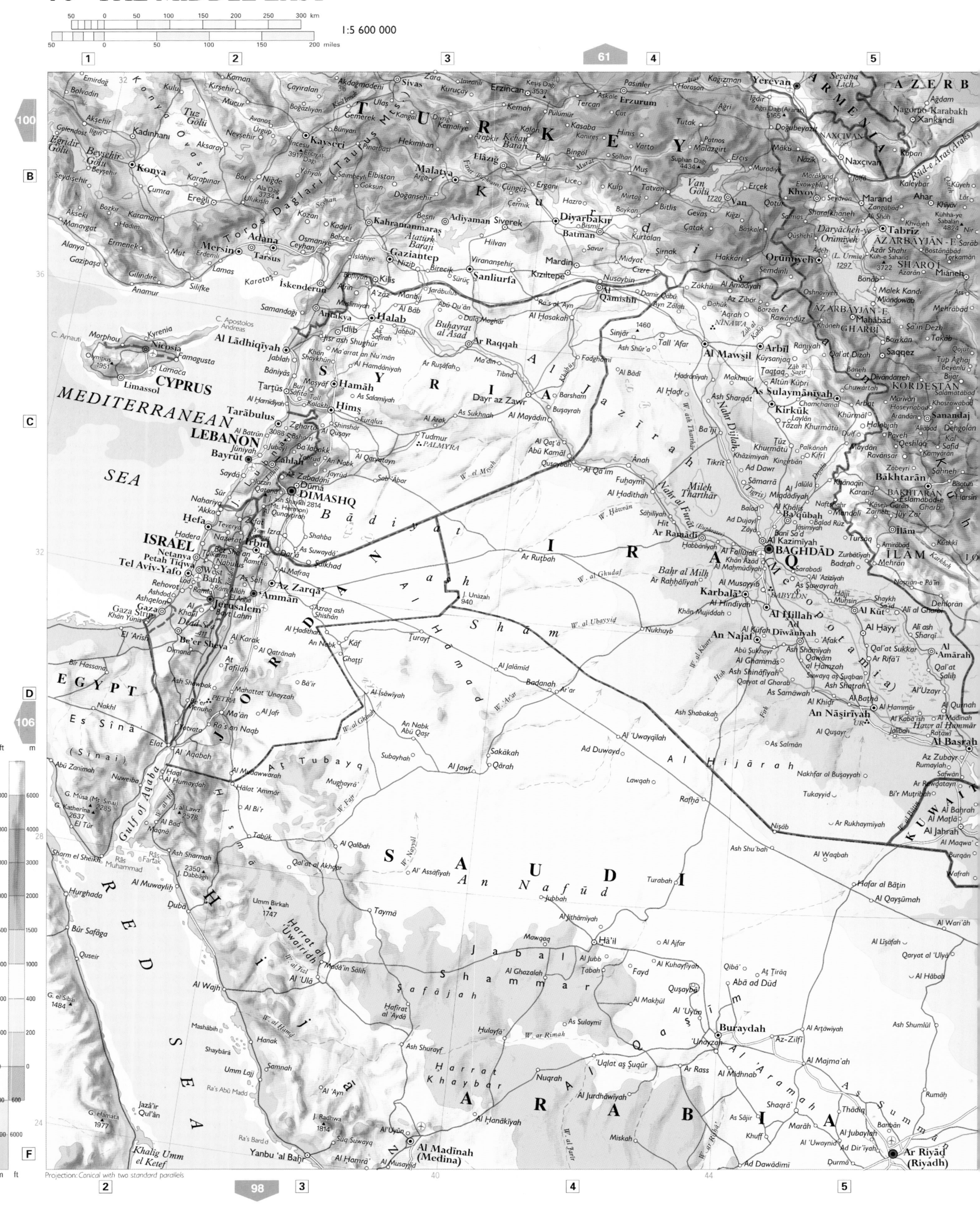

1:5 600 000

Projection: Conical with two standard parallels

6
7
8
9
10
B
C
D
E
F
91
99
TURKMENISTAN
Kara Kum
Kopet Dagh
CASPIAN SEA
Bakı
Türkmenbashi
Cheleken Yarymadasy
Ostrov Ogurchinskiy
Nebitdag
Gazanjyk
Gyzylarbat
Ashgabat
Mary
Bayramaly
Yoloten
Tejen
Dushak
Serakhs
Chärjew
Amudarya
Gyzyletrek
Ardabīl
Rasht
Gīlān
Zanjān
Qazvin
Tehrān
Karaj
Tajrish
Rey
Damāvand
Reshteh-ye Kūhhā-ye Alborz
Māzandarān
Sārī
Bābol
Āmol
Qā'emshahr
Gorgān
Gonbad-e Kāvūs
Bojnūrd
Shirvān
Qūchān
Mashhad
Kūh-e Bīnālūd
Neyshābūr
Sabzevār
Semnān
Dāmghān
Shāhrūd
Qom
Daryācheh-ye Namak
Dasht-e Kavīr
Kāshān
Arāk
Hamadān
Malāyer
Borūjerd
Khorramābād
Khorāsān
Kāshmar
Torbat-e Heydarīyeh
Torbat-e Jām
Tabas
Ferdows
Gonābād
Qāyen
Bīrjand
Afghanistan
Herāt
Farāh
Safīd Kūh
Daryācheh-ye Namakzar
Dasht-e Lūt
Eşfahān
Najafābād
Shahr-e Kord
Yazd
Ardakān
Nā'īn
Zāgros
Kūhhā-ye Zāgros
Dezfūl
Ahvāz
Khūzestān
Masjed Soleymān
Ābādān
Khorramshahr
Bandar-e Ma'shur
Shatt al Arab
Al Kuwayt
Būbiyān
Kermān
Rafsanjān
Sīrjān
Bam
Shīrāz
Fārs
Persepolis
Jahrom
Būshehr
Sīstān
Zābol
Zāhedān
Dasht-e Mārgow
Nīmrūz
Gowd-e Zirreh
Pakistan
Hāmūn-i Mashkel
Sīstān va Balūchestān
Īrānshahr
Bandar-e Abbas
Hormozgān
Qeshm
Str. of Hormuz
Kūhhā-ye Bashākerd
Makrān
Chāh Bahār
Jāsk
The Gulf
Gulf of Oman
Ras Masandam (Oman)
Ra's al Khaymah
Ash Shāriqah (Sharjah)
Dubayy (Dubai)
Abū Zāby (Abu Dhabi)
Al Fujayrah
Al 'Ayn
Al Ḩajar Al Gharbī
Oman
United Arab Emirates
Qatar
Ad Dawḩah
Bahrain
Al Manāmah
Ad Dammām
Al Hufūf
Al Jubayl
Ra's al Mish'āb
Al Jāfūrah
Tropic of Cancer
East from Greenwich
COPYRIGHT PHILIP'S

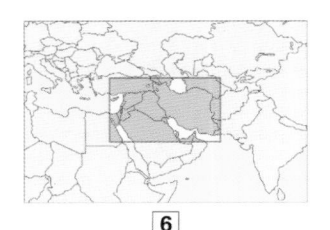

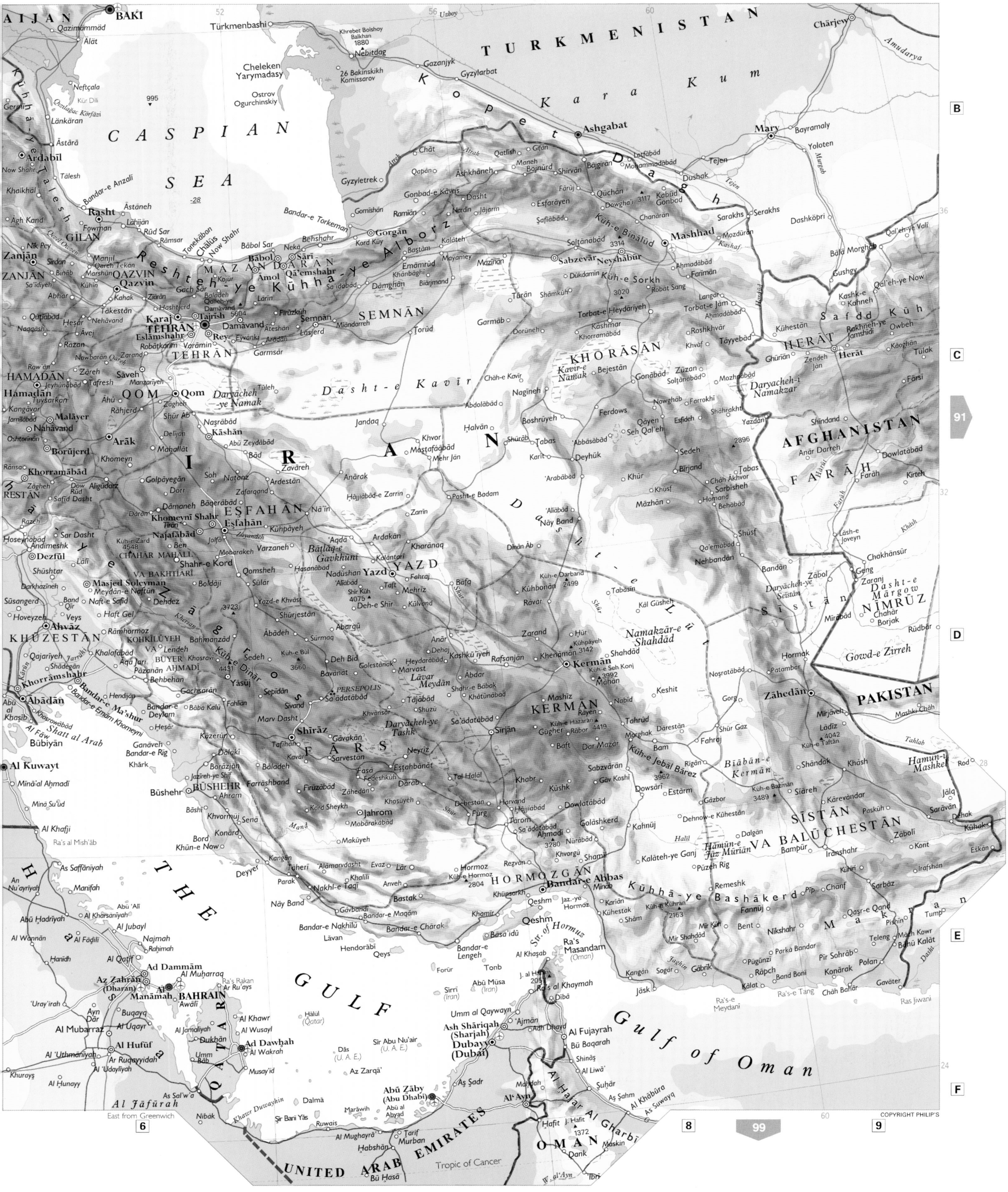

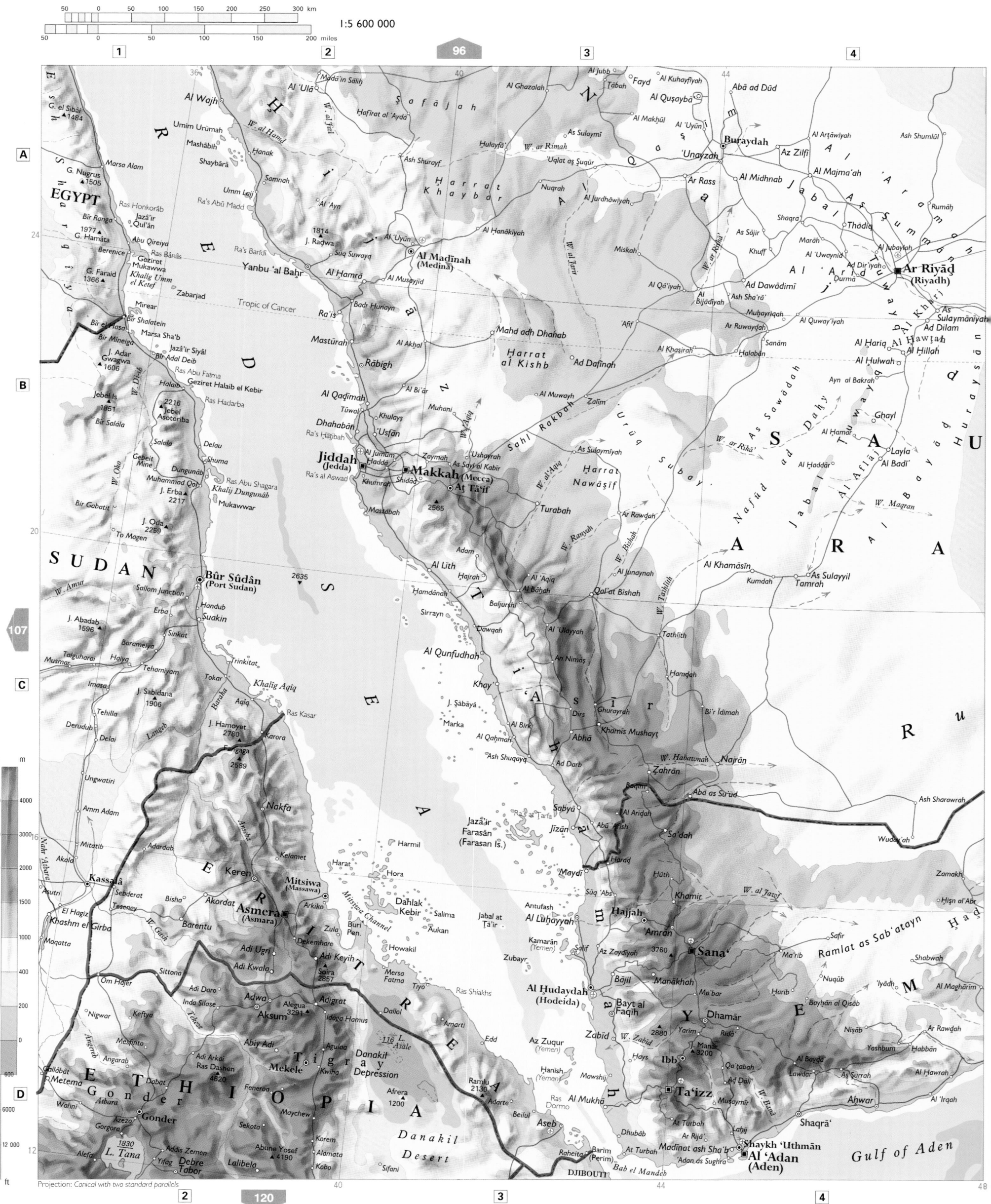

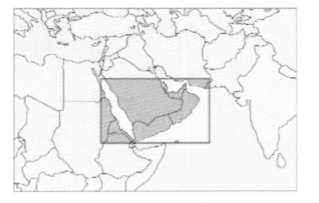

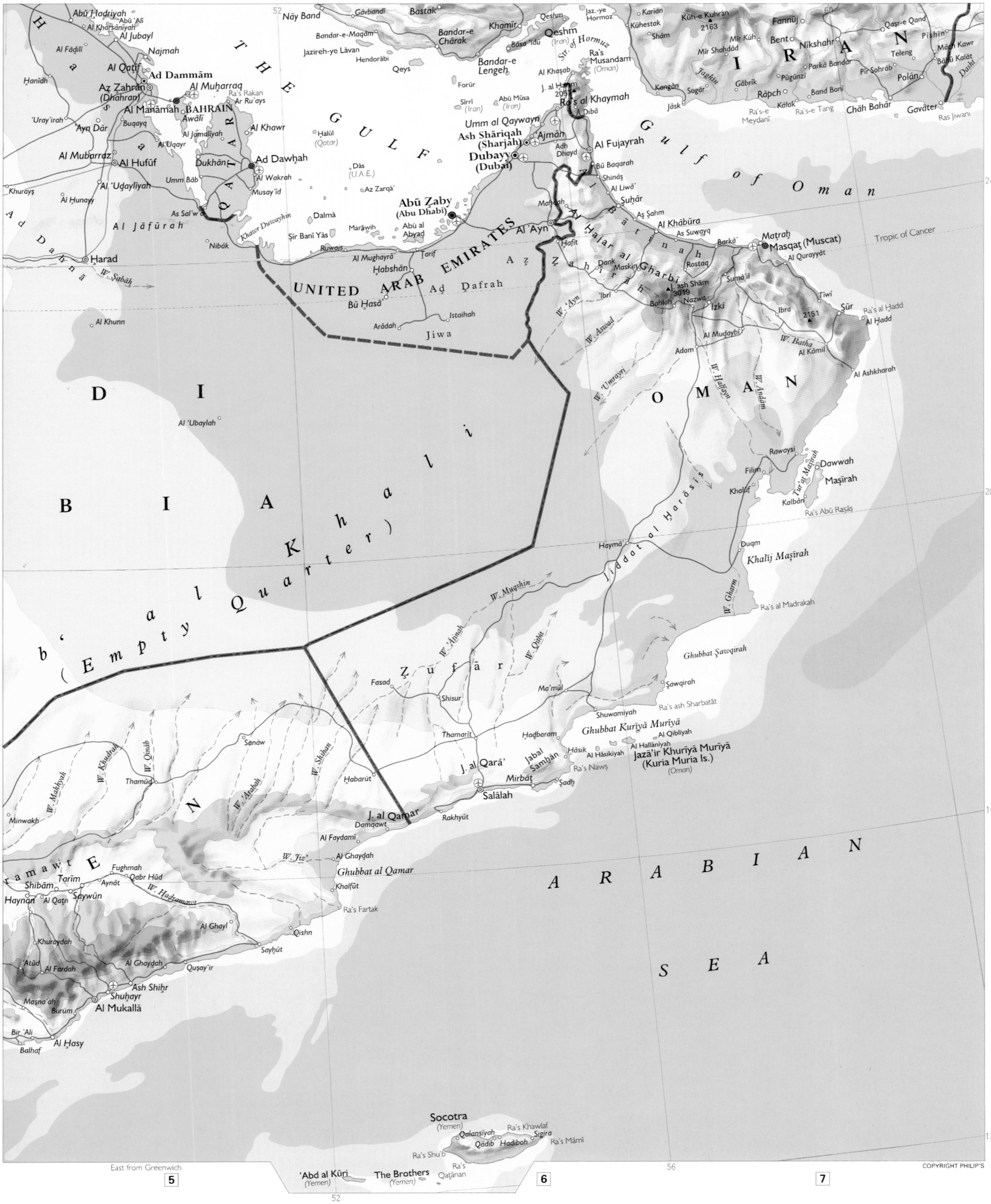

97

5 6 7 8

IRAN

THE GULF

Nāy Band
Gāvbandi
Bastak
Khamir
Jaz-ye Hormoz
Qeshm
Kariān
Kūh-e Kuhrān 2163
Fannūj
Qaṣr-e Qand
Pishīn

Abū Ḥadrīyah
Abū 'Alī
Al Kharsānīyah
Al Jubayl
Najmah
Bandar-e Maqām
Jazireh-ye Lāvan
Bandar-e Chārak
Bāsa 'Idū
Qeshm (Iran)
Str. of Hormuz
Kūhestak
Shām
Mīr Kūh
Mīr Shāhdād
Bent
Nīkshahr
Teleng
Māch Kawr
Bāhū Kalāt
Dahtī

Al Fāḍilī
Ḥanīḍh
Al Qaṭīf
Az Zahrān (Dhahran)
Ad Dammām
Al Muḥarraq
Ra's Rakan
Ar Ru'ays
Hendorābi
Qeys
Ra's Musandam (Oman)
J. al Ḥarīm 2051
Ra's al Khaymah
Jūghīn
Sogar
Jāsk
Gābrīk
Rāpch
Parkā Bandar
Band Boni
Pīr Sohrāb
Polān
Qaṣr-e Qand

'Uray'irah
'Ayn Dār
Al Manāmah
BAHRAIN
Awālī
Buqayq
Forūr
Sīrrī (Iran)
Al Khaṣab
Dibā
Ra's-e Meydani
Ra's-e Tang
Chāh Bahār
Gavāter
Ras Jīwani

Al Mubarraz
Al Hufūf
Umm al Qaywayn
Ash Shāriqah (Sharjah)
Ajmān
Adh Dhayd
Al Fujayrah
Bū Baqarah

Khurays
Al Ḥunayy
'Al 'Uqayr
'Al 'Udaylīyah
Umm Bāb
Das (U.A.E.)
Az Zarqā'
Dubayy (Dubai)
Shinās
Ṣuḥār
As Suwayq

QATAR
Dukhān
Ad Dawḥah
Al Wakrah
Musay'īd
Dalmā
Marāwih
Abū al Abyaḍ
Abū Zaby (Abu Dhabi)
Maḥḍah
Al Liwā'
Aṣ Ṣaḥm
Al Khābūra
Barkā
Matraḥ
Maskat (Muscat)

Ad Dahnā
Al Jāfūrah
As Sal'wa'
Khawr Duwayhin
Nībāk
Şīr Banī Yās
Ruwais
Tarīf
Al 'Ayn
Ḥafīt
Dank
Maskin
Rostaq
Ash Shām 3019
Bahlah
Nazwa
Izki
Sumā'il
Al Quṣayt
Tropic of Cancer

Ḥarad
W. Şabāh
UNITED ARAB EMIRATES
Ad Dafrah
Al Mughayra
Ḥabshān
Bū Ḥaṣā
Arādah
Istaiḥah
Jiwa
W. 'Ayn
'Ibrī
Adam
Al Muḍaybī
Ibra 2151
Tiwī
Şūr
Ra's al Ḥadd
Al Ḥadd

Al Khunn
Al 'Ubaylah
Al Ashkharah

D I B I A

' R b ' a l K h a l i

(E m p t y   Q u a r t e r)

Rawaysī
Filim
Furīq Maṣīrah
Dawwah
Maṣīrah
Khalūf
Kalbān
Ra's Abū Raşāş

W. Muqshin
Haymā
Duqm
Khalīj Maşīrah
Ra's al Madrakah

Fasad
Shisur
Zufār
W. 'Ainah
W. Qitbit
Ma'mūl
Sawqirah
Ghubbat Şawqirah
Ra's ash Sharbatāt

Şanāw
W. Khuḍrah
W. Qinūb
Thamūd
W. Arabah
W. Shiḥan
Thamarīt
Ḥaḍbaram
Ghubbat Kurīyā Murīyā
Shuwamiyah
Ra's ash Sharbatāt

Minwakh
W. Makhyūb
J. al Qarā
Jabal Samḥān
Hāsik
Al Ḥāsikīyah
Al Hallānīyah
Al Qibliyah
Jazā'ir Khurīyā Murīyā (Kuria Muria Is.) (Oman)

Mirbāt
Şadḥ
Ra's Nawş

YEMEN
Ḥabarūt
J. al Qamar
Damqawt
Salālah
Rakhyūt

Al Faydāmī
Fughmah
Qabr Hūd
Al Ghaydah
W. Jiz'
Ghubbat al Qamar
Khalfūt

ramawt
E
Tarīm
Aynāt
W. Ḥaḍramaut
Saywūn
Shibām
Haynān
Al Qaṭn
Al Ghayl
Qishn
Sayḥūt
Ra's Fartak

Khuraydah
'Atūd
Al Fardah
Al Ghaydah
Quşay'ir

A R A B I A N   S E A

Maşna'ah
Burūm
Ash Shiḥr
Shuhayr
Al Mukallā
Bir 'Ali
Balḥaf
Al Ḥasy

Socotra (Yemen)
Qalansīyah
Qādib
Hadīboh
Ra's Khawlaf
Sīgira
Ra's Māmī
Ra's Shu'b
'Abd al Kūri (Yemen)
The Brothers (Yemen)
Ra's Qaţānan

Gulf of Oman

A
B
C
D

24
20
16
12

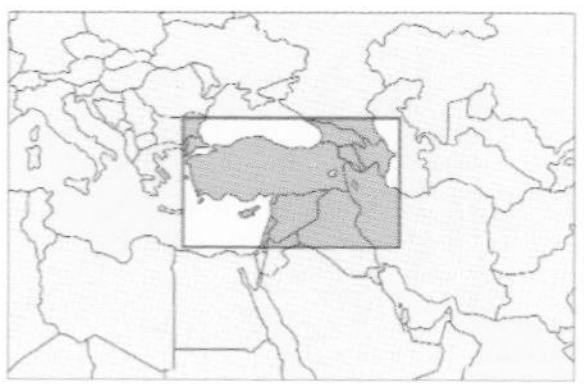

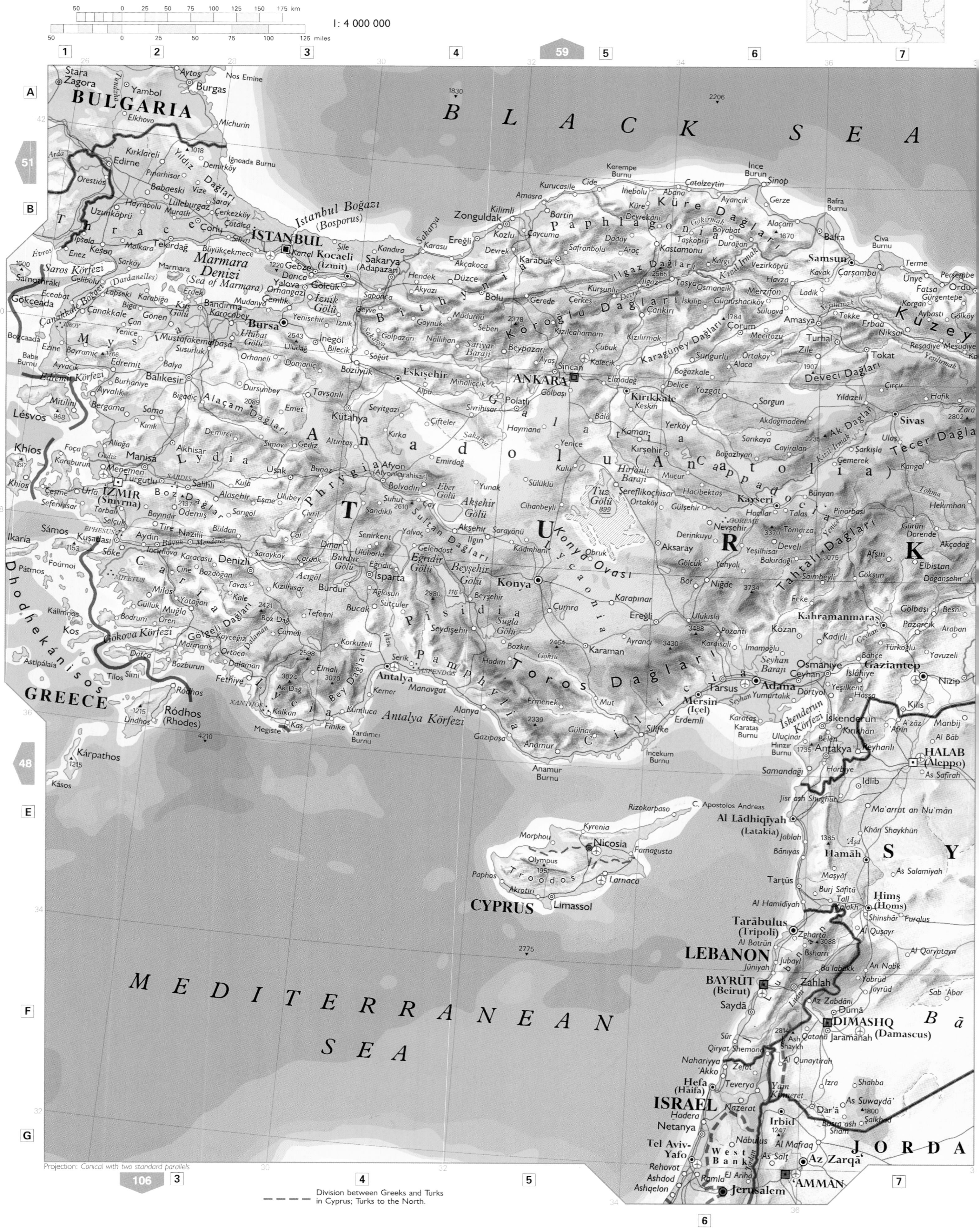

1: 4 000 000

50 25 0 25 50 75 100 125 150 175 km
50 0 25 50 75 100 125 miles

BULGARIA

B L A C K   S E A

Stara Zagora
Yambol
Aytos
Burgas
Nos Emine
Michurin

Kırklareli
Elkhovo
Edirne
Demirköy
İğneada Burnu
Pınarhisar
Babaeski
Vize
Saray
Çerkezköy
Lüleburgaz
Uzunköprü
Muratlı
Çorlu
Keşan
İpsala
Malkara
Tekirdağ
Büyükçekmece
İSTANBUL
Şile
Kocaeli (İzmit)
Kartal
Gebze
Darıca
Yalova
Gölcük
İznik
İznik Gölü

Marmara Denizi (Sea of Marmara)

Kerempe Burnu
Cide
İnebolu
Çatalzeytin
İnce Burun
Sinop
Amasra
Bartın
Küre
Ayancık
Gerze
Zonguldak
Kilimli
Karabük
Safranbolu
Kastamonu
Bafra Burnu
Alaçam
Samsun
Çarşamba
Ünye
Fatsa
Ordu

Küre Dağları
Paphlagonia
Ilgaz Dağları
Köroğlu Dağları

Bolu
Gerede
Çerkeş
Ilgaz
Tosya
Osmancık
Merzifon
Amasya
Tokat
Turhal
Zile

ANKARA
Kırıkkale
Yozgat
Sorgun
Sivas
Yıldızeli

A n a d o l u   (A n a t o l i a)

Cappadocia
Kayseri
Nevşehir
Aksaray
Niğde

T U Z   G Ö L Ü
Konya Ovası
KONYA

Lydia
İZMİR (Smyrna)
Manisa
Turgutlu
Salihli
Aydın
Denizli
Muğla

Caria
Phrygia
Pisidia
Pamphylia
Lycia

Antalya
Antalya Körfezi
Alanya
Anamur

Toros Dağları
Cilicia
Adana
Tarsus
Mersin (İçel)
İskenderun
İskenderun Körfezi
Antakya
Gaziantep
Kilis

HALAB (Aleppo)

LésVOS
Khíos
Dhodhekánisos
GREECE
Ródhos (Rhodes)
Kárpathos
Kásos

M E D I T E R R A N E A N   S E A

CYPRUS
Nicosia
Kyrenia
Morphou
Famagusta
Larnaca
Limassol
Paphos
Akrotiri
Olympus 1951
Troodos

S Y
Al Lādhiqīyah (Latakia)
Jablah
Bāniyās
Hamāh
Ḥimṣ (Homs)
Tartūs
Tarābulus (Tripoli)

LEBANON
BAYRŪT (Beirut)
Saydā

DIMASHQ (Damascus)

ISRAEL
Hefa (Haifa)
Nazeret
Tel Aviv-Yafo
Jerusalem
Netanya

JORDA
AMMÁN
Az Zarqā
Irbid

Projection: Conical with two standard parallels

Division between Greeks and Turks in Cyprus; Turks to the North.

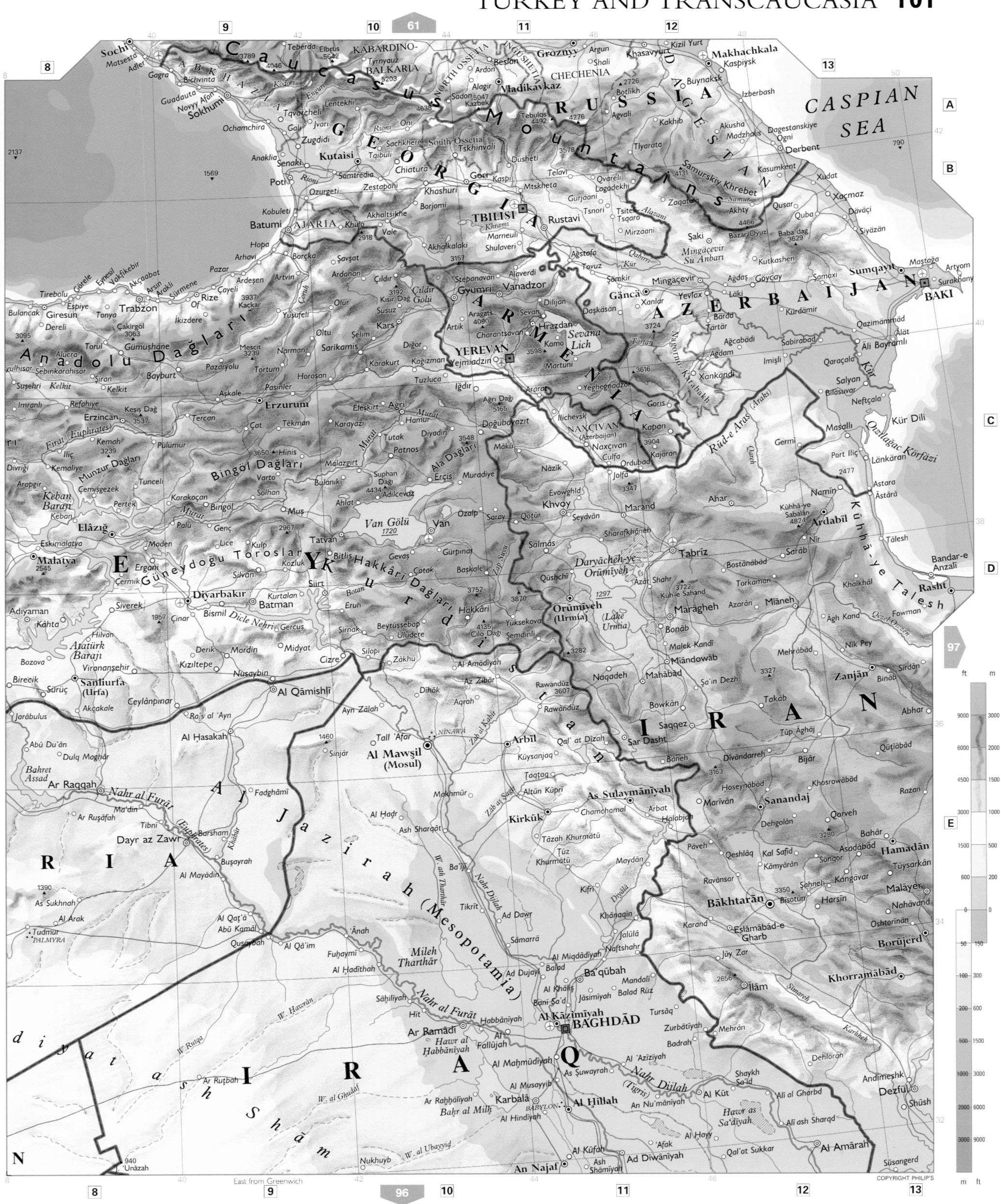

1:12 000 000

100 0 100 200 300 400 500 600 km
100 0 100 200 300 400 miles

Projection : Sanson-Flamsteed's Sinusoidal

East from Greenwich

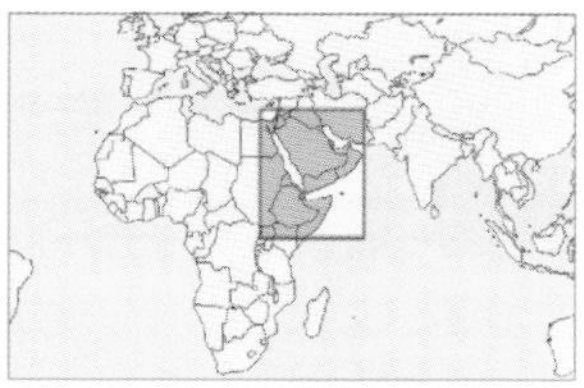

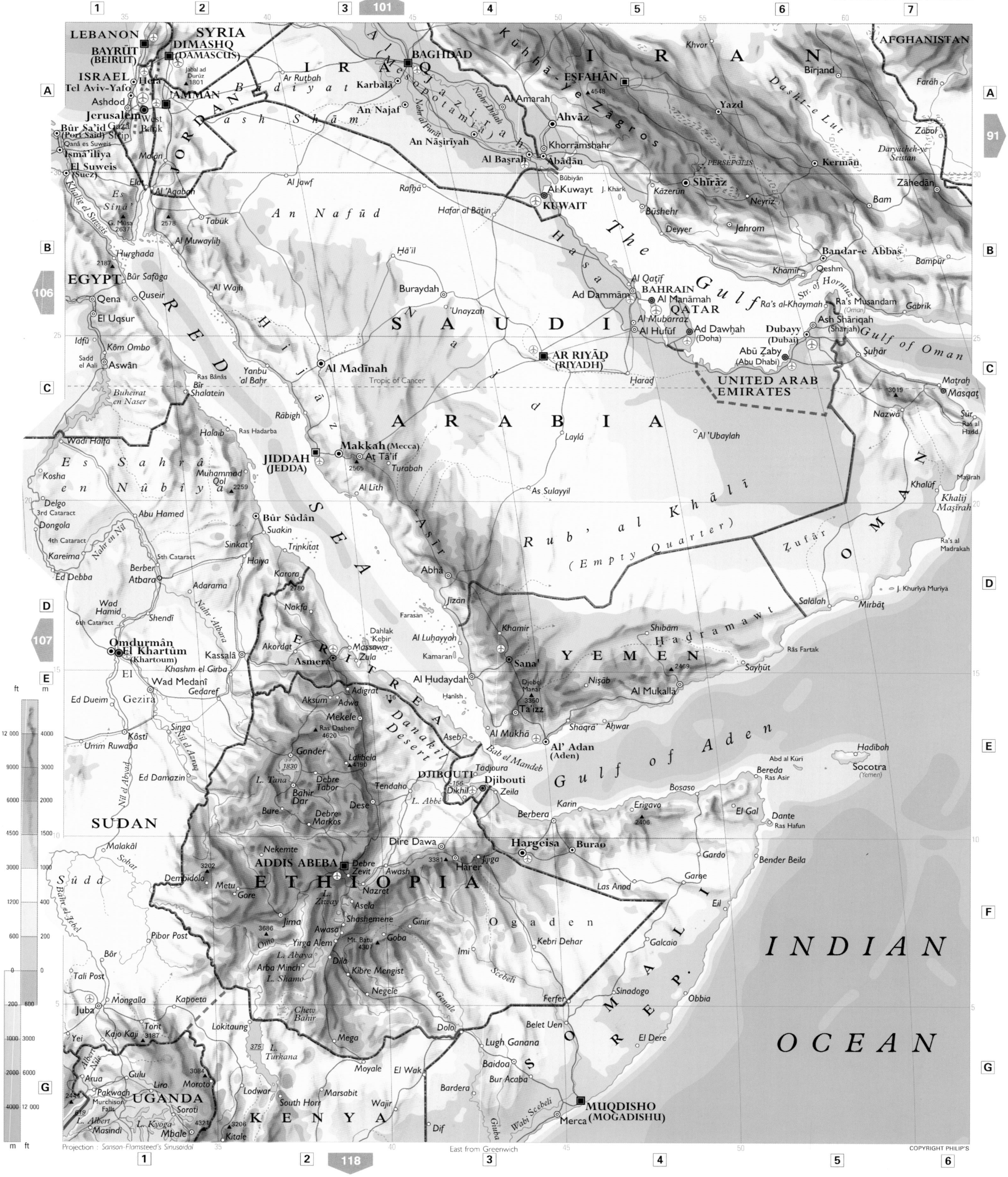

COPYRIGHT PHILIP'S

LEBANON
BAYRŪT (BEIRUT)
SYRIA
DIMASHQ (DAMASCUS)
ISRAEL
Tel Aviv-Yafo
Ashdod
Jerusalem
West Bank
Bûr Sa'îd (Port Said)
Gaza
Qanâ es Suweis
Ismâ'îliya
El Suweis (Suez)
AMMĀN
JORDAN
Haifa
Jabal ad Durūz 1801
Ar Rutbah
Karbalā'
BAGHDĀD
An Najaf
Al Amārah
An Nāşirīyah
Al Başrah
Ābādān
Khorrämshahr
Ahvāz
IRAQ
IRAN
AFGHANISTAN
Khvor
Birjand
Farāh
Yazd
ĘSFAHĀN 4548
Zābol
Daryācheh-ye Seistan
Kermān
Bam
Zāhedān
Ra's Budiyat ash Shām
An Nafūd
Al Jawf
Hafar al Bāṭin
Rafḩā
Al Kuwayt
KUWAIT
J. Khārk
Būbiyān
Bûshehr
Deyyer
Kāzerūn
Shīrāz
Neyriz
Jahrom
PERSEPOLIS
Khamir
Qeshm
Bandar-e Abbas
Bampūr
Gābrik
Ra's al-Khaymah
Ash Shāriqah (Sharjah)
Ra's Musandam (Oman)
Str. of Hormuz
Gulf of Oman
Ma'ān
Elat
Al 'Aqabah
Es Sīnâ'
G. Mûsa 2637
2578
Tabūk
Al Muwaylih
Hā'il
Buraydah
'Unayzah
Ad Dammām
Al Qaṭīf
Al Manāmah
BAHRAIN
QATAR
Al Mubarraz
Al Hufūf
Ad Dawḩah (Doha)
Dubayy (Dubai)
Abū Ƶaby (Abu Dhabi)
Şuḩār
Maṭraḩ
Masqaţ
Şūr
Ra's al Hadd
Hurghada
Bûr Safâga
EGYPT
Qena
Quseir
El Uqsur
Idfû
Kôm Ombo
Aswân
Sadd el Aali
2187
Al Wajh
Yanbu 'al Baḩr
Ras Bānās
Bīr Shalatein
Rābigh
Al Madīnah
AR RIYĀḐ (RIYADH)
SAUDI ARABIA
Tropic of Cancer
Laylá
Al 'Ubaylah
UNITED ARAB EMIRATES
Nazwá
3019
Khalīj Maşīrah
Maşīrah
OMAN
Ra's al Madrakah
Buḩeirat en Naser
Wadi Halfa
Halaib
Ras Hadarba
JIDDAH (JEDDA)
Muhammad Qol 2259
MAKKAH (Mecca)
Aṭ Ṭā'if 2565
Turabah
As Sulayyil
Rub' al Khālī (Empty Quarter)
Ẕufār
Salālah
Mirbāṭ
J. Khurīyā Murīyā
Ra's Fartak
RED SEA
Es Sahrâ en Nûbiya
Kosha
Delgo
3rd Cataract
Dongola
4th Cataract
Kareima
5th Cataract
Ed Debba
Berber
Atbara
Abu Hamed
Bûr Sûdân
Suakin
Sinkat
Trinkitat
Haiya
Karora 2780
Nakfa
Adarama
Al Līth
Abhā
Jīzān
Farasan
Khamir
Shibām
Hadramawt
Al 'Ubaylah
Wad Hamid
6th Cataract
Shendî
Omdurmân
El Khartûm (Khartoum)
Kassalâ
Khashm el Girba
Akordat
Asmera
ERITREA
Massawa
Zula
Dahlak Kebir
Al Luḩayyah
Kamaran
Al Hudaydah
SANA'
Djebel Manar 3350
YEMEN
2469
Nişāb
Al Mukallā
Sayḩūt
Rās Fartak
Hadiboh
Socotra (Yemen)
SUDAN
El Obeid
Wad Medanî
Gedaref
Adigrat
Aksum
Adwa
Mekele
116
Hanīsh
Ta'izz
Al Mukhā
Shaqrā
Ahwar
Al' Adan (Aden)
Bab el Mandeb
Gulf of Aden
Abd al Kūri
Bereda
Ras Asir
Ed Dueim
Umm Ruwaba
Singa
Kôstî
Gezira
Lalibela 4190
Ras Dashen 4620
Gonder
1830
Debre Tabor
Danakil Desert
Aseb
Zula
DJIBOUTI
Tadjoura
Djibouti
Zeila
Berbera
Karin
Bosaso
Erigavo 2406
El Gal
Dante
Ras Hafun
Bahir Dar
L. Tana
Bure
Debre Markos
Dese
Tendaho
L. Abbé
Dikhil 156
INDIAN OCEAN
Ed Damazin
Malakâl
Sobat
L. Shamo
Nekemte
3202
Dembidolo
ADDIS ABEBA
Debre Zeyit
Awash
3381
Harer
Jijiga
Dire Dawa
HARGEISA
Burao
Gardo
Bender Beila
Eil
ETHIOPIA
Metu
Gore
Nazret
Asela
Gardo
Garge
Las Anod
Sûdd
Bahr el Jebel
Jima 3686
Awasa
Shashemene
Ginir
Kebri Dehar
Ogaden
Galcaio
Sinadogo
Obbia
Bôr
Pibor Post
Omo
L. Abaya
Yirga Alem
Dila
Mt. Batu 4307
Goba
Imi
Scebeli
Ferfer
Tali Post
Kibre Mengist
Negele
Genale
Juba
Mongalla
Kapoeta
Chew Bahir
Mega
Dolo
Lugh Ganana
Belet Uen
El Dere
SOMALI REPUBLIC
Yei
Kajo Kaji 3187
Lokitaung
375
L. Turkana
Moyale
El Wak
Bardera
Bur Acaba
Baidoa
MUQDISHO (MOGADISHU)
Merca
Arua
Gulu
3084
Lira
Morota
Lodwar
South Hort
Marsabit
Wajir
Dif
Wabi Scebeli
UGANDA
Pakwach
L. Albert
Murchison Falls
Masindi
L. Kyoga
4321
3206
Soroti
Mbale
Kitale
KENYA

ft / m elevation scale:
12 000 / 4000
9000 / 3000
6000 / 2000
4500 / 1500
3000 / 1000
1200 / 400
600 / 200
0 / 0
200 / 600
1000 / 3000
2000 / 6000
4000 / 12000
m ft

1:2 000 000

10 0 10 20 30 40 50 60 70 80 90 100 km
10 0 10 20 30 40 50 60 miles

1 2 3 4 5 6

MEDITERRANEAN SEA

CYPRUS

Paphos
Episkopi
Limassol
Akrotiri
Episkopi Bay
C. Gata

LEBANON

Al Ḥamīdīyah
Al Mīnā
Tarābulus (Tripoli)
ASH SHAMĀL
Zgharta
Qurnat as Sawdā ▲3088
Bsharri
Al Batrūn
Qartaba
Jubayl
Ibrāhīm
Jūniya
Bikfayyā
2628 ▲ J. Sannīn
BAYRŪT (Beirut)
Ash Shuwayfāt
'Alayh
Ad Dāmūr
JABAL LUBNĀN
1942 ▲ J. al Bārūk
Saydā (Sidon)
Jazzīn
An Nabaṭīyah at Taḥta
AL JANŪB
Sūr (Tyre)
Qiryat Shemona
Nahariyya
Me'ona
'Akko (Acre)
Mifraz Hefa
Qiryat Yam
HAZAFON
Karmi'el
Teverya
Yam Kinneret 210
Hefa (Haifa)
Qiryat Ata
Dāliyat el Karmel
HA KARMEL
TEL MEGIDDO
Nazerat (Nazareth)
Afula
Umm el Faḥm
CAESAREA
Hadera
Pardes
Ḥanna-Karkur
Ṭulkarm
Netanya
HAMERKAZ
SHŌMRŌN
Herzliyya
Kefar Sava
Nābulus
Benē Beraq
Petah Tiqwa
Tel Aviv-Yafo
Ramat Gan
Bat Yam
Rishon le Ziyyon
Yavne
Lod
Ramla
Rehovot
West Bank
SHILO
Ram Allāh
Ashdod
Qiryat Mal'akhi
Bet Shemesh
Jerusalem (Yerushalayim) (Al Quds)
Ashqelon
Qiryat Gat
Bayt Laḥm (Bethlehem)
Gaza
N. Shiqma
N. Besor
ESHKOL
Sederot
Gaza Strip
Khān Yūnis
Rafah
El Daheir
Be'er Sheva (Beersheba)
Bor Mashash
Dimona
Arad
Sedom
HADAROM

ISRAEL

Al Khalīl (Hebron)
Aẓ Ẓāhirīyah
HAR YEHUDA
MIDBAR YEHUDA

SYRIA

Ḥimṣ (Homs)
Tall Kalakh
Shinshār
Furqlus
Halbā
Al Qusayr
HIMŞ
Al Ḥirmil
Al Qaryatayn
2464 ▲
Al Burayj
Bi'r Ghadīr
An Nabk
AL BIQĀ
Ba'labakk
2616 ▲
Al Labwah
Yabrūd
Sirghayā
Khān Abū Shāmat
Zaḥlah
Dumayr
Az Zabadānī
DIMASHQ
Ad Dāmūr
2814 ▲ (Mt Hermon)
Dārayyā
Dūmā
DIMASHQ (Damascus)
Marj 'Uyūn
Al Kiswah
Al Khiyām
Qaṭanā
Al Ḥājānah
Mas'ada
Golan Heights
Al Qunayṭirah
As Sanamayn
Burāq
W. aṣ Ṣafā
Ar Rafīd
DAR'Ā
Izra
Shahbā
AS SUWAYDĀ
1800 ▲
As Suwaydā
JABAL AD DURUZ
Zefat
Shaykh Miskīn
Saḥam al Jawlān
Malaḥ
Ṣālah
Kimmul
Dar'ā
Yarmūk
IRBID
Busrā ash Shām
Salkhad
Tayiba
Bet She'an
Ar Ramthā
Jenin
AJLŪN
J. Umm ad Daraj
Umm al Qiṭṭayn
Tūbās
SAMARIA
Ajlūn
Jarash
Al Mafraq
W. al Far'ah
1247 ▲
JARASH
AL MAFRAQ
Nā'ūr
Karama
N. az Zarqā
AL BALQĀ
As Salt
Wādī as Sīr
AMMĀN
Azraq ash Shīshān
AMM
AZ ZARQĀ
El Arīḥā (Jericho)
Ma'dāba
Dead Sea -411
MA'DĀBA
At Tunayb
'AMMĀN
Ḥuydān
Dhībān
Al Hadithah
W. al Mawjib
W. al Ghadaf

JORDAN

Al Karak
AL KARAK
1305 ▲
Al Mazar
W. al Ḥasa
W. al Mabhaj
At Ṭafīlah
AT TAFĪLAH
Nijil
1072 ▲
J. ash Shawmari
Mahaṭṭat 'Unayzah
Rujm Ṭabal al Jamāl
173 ▲
PETRA
Wādī Mūsā
Ma'ān
173 ▲
Qa'el Jafr
MA'ĀN
Al Jafr
Bā'ir
W. Bā'ir

EGYPT

Bûr Sa'îd (Port Said)
Bûr Fu'ad
Râs Burûn
Khalig el Tîna
Sabkhet el Bardawîl
Bîr el 'Abd
Qanal es Suweis (Suez Canal)
Râmâni
Bîr Qaṭia
Bîr el Duweidar
El Qantara
Bîr el Jafir
Wâḥid
Bîr Madkûr
Bîr Kaseiba
Bîr Lahfân
Bîr el Garârât
SHAMÂL SÎNÎ
W. el 'Arîsh
El 'Arîsh
Ismâ'ilîya
Talâta
ISMÂ'ILÎYA
Khamsa
El Buheirat el Murrat el Kubra (Great Bitter L.)
Bîr el Mālḥi
892 ▲
Bîr Ḥasana
Muweilih
El Quṣeima
G.Yi 'Allaq 1094 ▲
Mizpe Ramon
Qezi'ot
Birein
Sedé Boqér
Hanegev
12 ▲
Bîr Beiḍa
Bîr Gebeil Hisn
W. el Brûk
El 'Agrûd
N. Paran
N. Ḥiyyon
Mamarr Mitla
W. el Kid
El Suweis (Suez)
Bûr Taufîq
Adabiya
Uyûn Mûsa
Nakhl
W. el 'Aqaba
EGYPT
ES SÎNÂ' (Sinai)
Ain Sudr
W. Ruaq
W. Maḥash
W. Giráfi
El Kuntilla
Yotvata
AL 'AQABAH
Ra's an Naqb
948 ▲ G. el Kabrit
Bîr Abu Muḥammad
'En Yvrona
Bîr al Butayyiḥât
Bîr al Qattar
Mahaṭṭat ash Shidīyah
Gineifa
Gebel el Tîh
El Thamad
1435 ▲
Ghubbet el Bûs
Ras Maṭarma
G. el Kabrit
El Wabeira
1592 ▲
1754 ▲
WADI RUM
Baṭn al Ghûl
Râs Sudr
JANÛB SÎNÎ
Elat
Rum
Al 'Aqabah
W. Abu Ga'da
Bîr el Biarât
Bîr Ṭaba
1272 ▲ EL SUWEIS
W. Abu el Gân
Bî'r Wuseit
1165 ▲
Bǐr Ḥeisi
Gulf of Aqaba
W. an Nirḍb
Ḥaql
Al Mudawwarah

SAUDI ARABIA

At Ṭubayq
AŢ ŢUBAYQ

Projection: Polyconic
East from Greenwich
COPYRIGHT PHILIP'S

ft m
9000 3000
6000 2000
4500 1500
3000 1000
1200 400
600 200
0 0
200 600
2000 6000
m ft

- - - 1974 Cease Fire Lines   ▭ National Parks

1:33 600 000

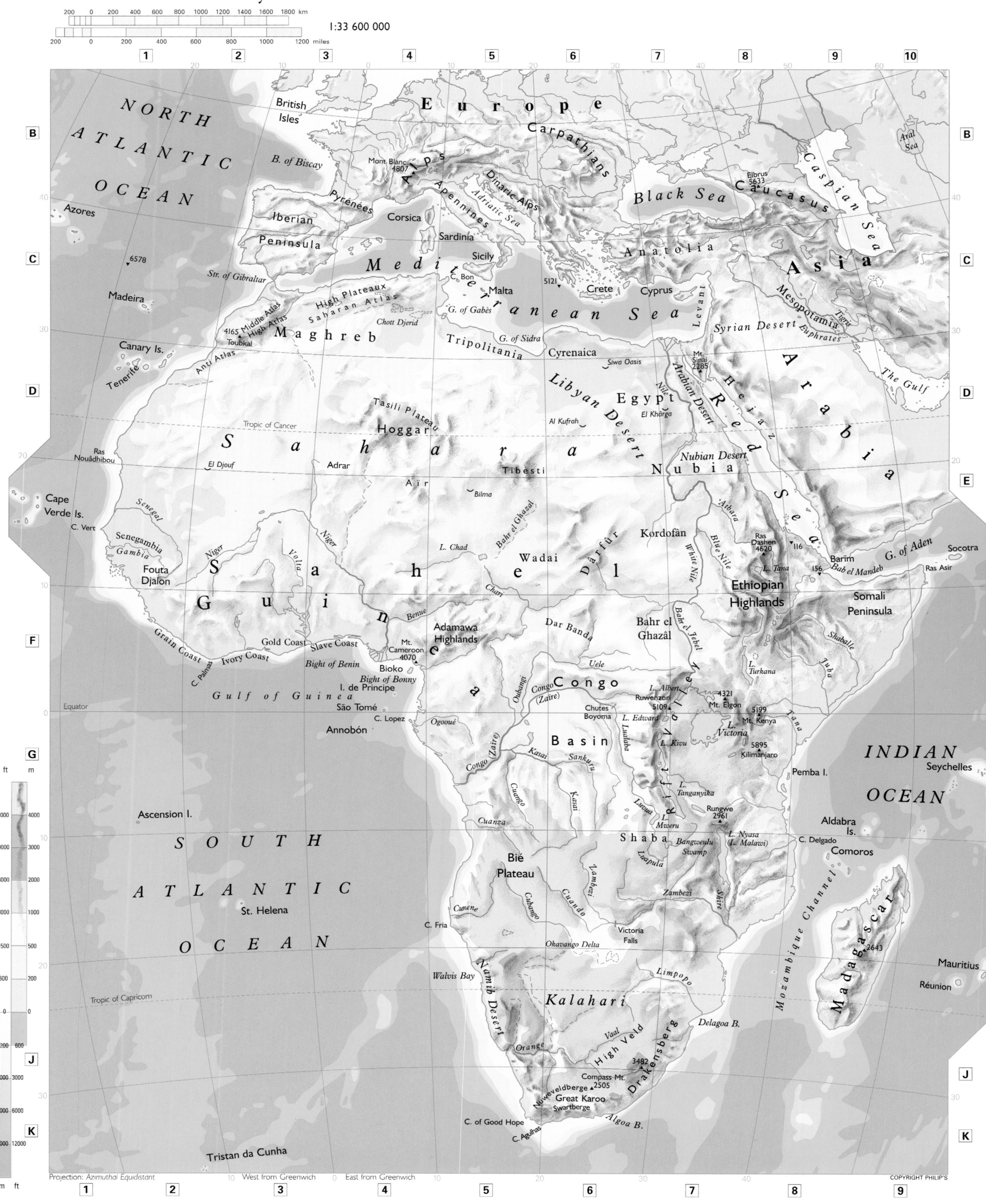

Projection: *Azimuthal Equidistant*

West from Greenwich   East from Greenwich

COPYRIGHT PHILIP'S

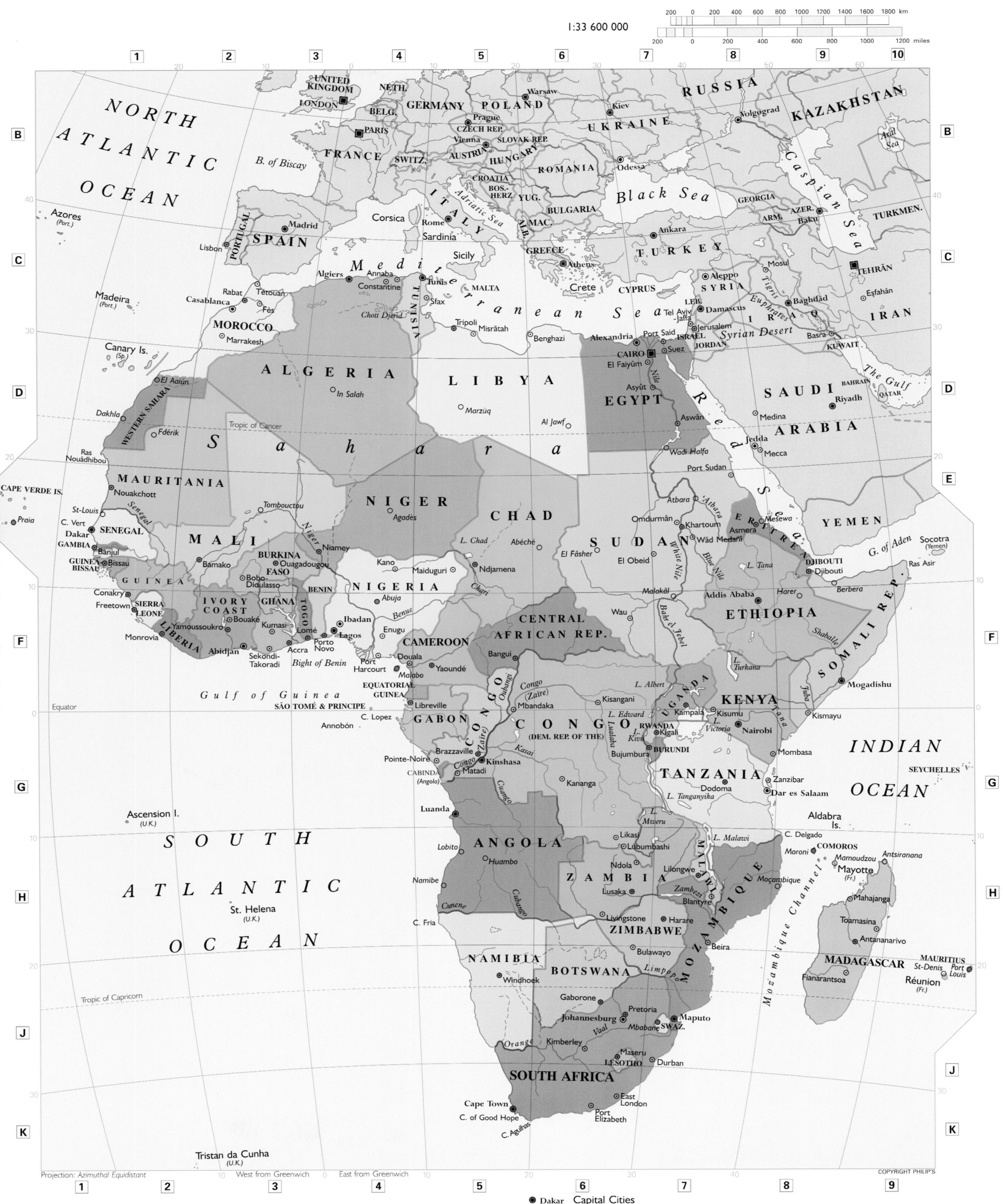

1:33 600 000

200 0 200 400 600 800 1000 1200 1400 1600 1800 km

200 0 200 400 600 800 1000 1200 miles

North Atlantic Ocean

RUSSIA
KAZAKHSTAN

UNITED KINGDOM
LONDON
NETH.
BELG.
Warsaw
GERMANY
POLAND
PRAGUE
Prague
Kiev
Volgograd
UKRAINE
Aral Sea

B. of Biscay
FRANCE
PARIS
CZECH REP.
Vienna
SWITZ.
AUSTRIA
SLOVAK REP.
HUNGARY
ROMANIA
Odessa
GEORGIA
Caspian Sea

CROATIA
BOS.-HERZ.
YUG.
BULGARIA
Black Sea
ARM.
AZER.
Baku
TURKMEN.

ITALY
Corsica
Rome
Sardinia
ALB.
MAC.
GREECE
Athens
ANKARA
Ankara
TURKEY
Mosul
Esfahan
TEHRAN

Madrid
PORTUGAL
SPAIN
Lisbon
Sicily
MALTA
Crete
CYPRUS
SYRIA
Aleppo
Baghdad
IRAN

Azores
(Port.)

Madeira
(Port.)
Algiers
Annaba
Constantine
TUNISIA
Tunis
Sfax
Mediterranean Sea
Tripoli
Misrātah
Benghazi
Alexandria
Port Said
Tel Aviv-Jaffa
ISRAEL
Jerusalem
JORDAN
Damascus
LEB.
Syrian Desert
Basra
KUWAIT
The Gulf

Rabat
Tétouan
Casablanca
Fès
MOROCCO
Marrakesh
CAIRO
El Faiyûm
Suez
SAUDI
Medina
BAHRAIN
Riyadh
QATAR

Canary Is.
(Sp.)
El Aaiún
WESTERN SAHARA
Tropic of Cancer
Fdérik
ALGERIA
In Salah
LIBYA
Marzūq
Al Jawf
EGYPT
Asyût
Aswân
Wadi Halfa
ARABIA
Jedda
Mecca

Dakhla
Ras Nouâdhibou
Sahara
Port Sudan

CAPE VERDE IS.
St-Louis
Nouakchott
MAURITANIA
Tombouctou
NIGER
Agadès
CHAD
Abéché
L. Chad
Ndjamena
SUDAN
Omdurmân
Khartoum
Atbara
Wâd Medani
ERITREA
Mesewa
Asmera
YEMEN
G. of Aden
Socotra
(Yemen)

Praia
C. Vert
Dakar
SENEGAL
GAMBIA
Banjul
Senegal
Bamako
MALI
Niamey
BURKINA FASO
Ouagadougou
Kano
NIGERIA
Maiduguri
Chari
El Fâsher
El Obeid
White Nile
Blue Nile
L. Tana
DJIBOUTI
Djibouti
Ras Asir
Berbera

GUINEA-BISSAU
Bissau
GUINEA
Conakry
Freetown
SIERRA LEONE
Bobo-Dioulasso
BENIN
Abuja
Ibadan
Enugu
CENTRAL AFRICAN REP.
Wau
Malakâl
Addis Ababa
Harer
ETHIOPIA
Shabelle
SOMALI REP.

IVORY COAST
Yamoussoukro
Bouaké
Kumasi
GHANA
TOGO
Lomé
Lagos
CAMEROON
Bangui
Bahr el Yebel

Monrovia
LIBERIA
Abidjan
Sekondi-Takoradi
Accra
Porto Novo
Bight of Benin
Port Harcourt
Douala
Yaoundé
Ubangui
L. Turkana
Mogadishu

Gulf of Guinea
EQUATORIAL GUINEA
Malabo
SÃO TOMÉ & PRINCIPE
Libreville
CONGO
Congo (Zaïre)
Mbandaka
Kisangani
L. Albert
UGANDA
Kampala
KENYA
Kisumu
Nairobi
Kismayu

Equator
GABON
C. Lopez
Annobón
CONGO (DEM. REP. OF THE)
Kasai
RWANDA
Kigali
L. Edward
L. Kivu
BURUNDI
Bujumbura
L. Victoria
Mombasa

Brazzaville
Pointe-Noire
CABINDA (Angola)
Kinshasa
Matadi
Congo
Kananga
TANZANIA
Zanzibar
Dodoma
Dar es Salaam
SEYCHELLES

Luanda
Lobito
ANGOLA
Huambo
Likasi
Lubumbashi
Ndola
ZAMBIA
L. Mweru
L. Tanganyika
L. Malawi
MALAWI
Lilongwe
C. Delgado
Moçambique
COMOROS
Moroni
Mamoudzou
Mayotte (Fr.)
Antsiranana

Indian Ocean

Ascension I.
(U.K.)
Namibe
C. Fria
Cunene
Cubango
Lusaka
Zambezi
Blantyre
MOZAMBIQUE
Mahajanga

South Atlantic Ocean

St. Helena
(U.K.)
Livingstone
Harare
Beira
ZIMBABWE
Bulawayo
Limpopo
MADAGASCAR
Antananarivo
MAURITIUS
St-Denis
Port Louis
Réunion (Fr.)

NAMIBIA
Windhoek
BOTSWANA
Gaborone
Johannesburg
Pretoria
Maputo
Fianarantsoa

Tropic of Capricorn
Vaal
Mbabane
SWAZ.
Kimberley
Maseru
LESOTHO
Durban

SOUTH AFRICA
Orange
Cape Town
C. of Good Hope
C. Agulhas
East London
Port Elizabeth

Tristan da Cunha
(U.K.)

Projection: Azimuthal Equidistant
West from Greenwich
East from Greenwich
COPYRIGHT PHILIP'S

● Dakar Capital Cities

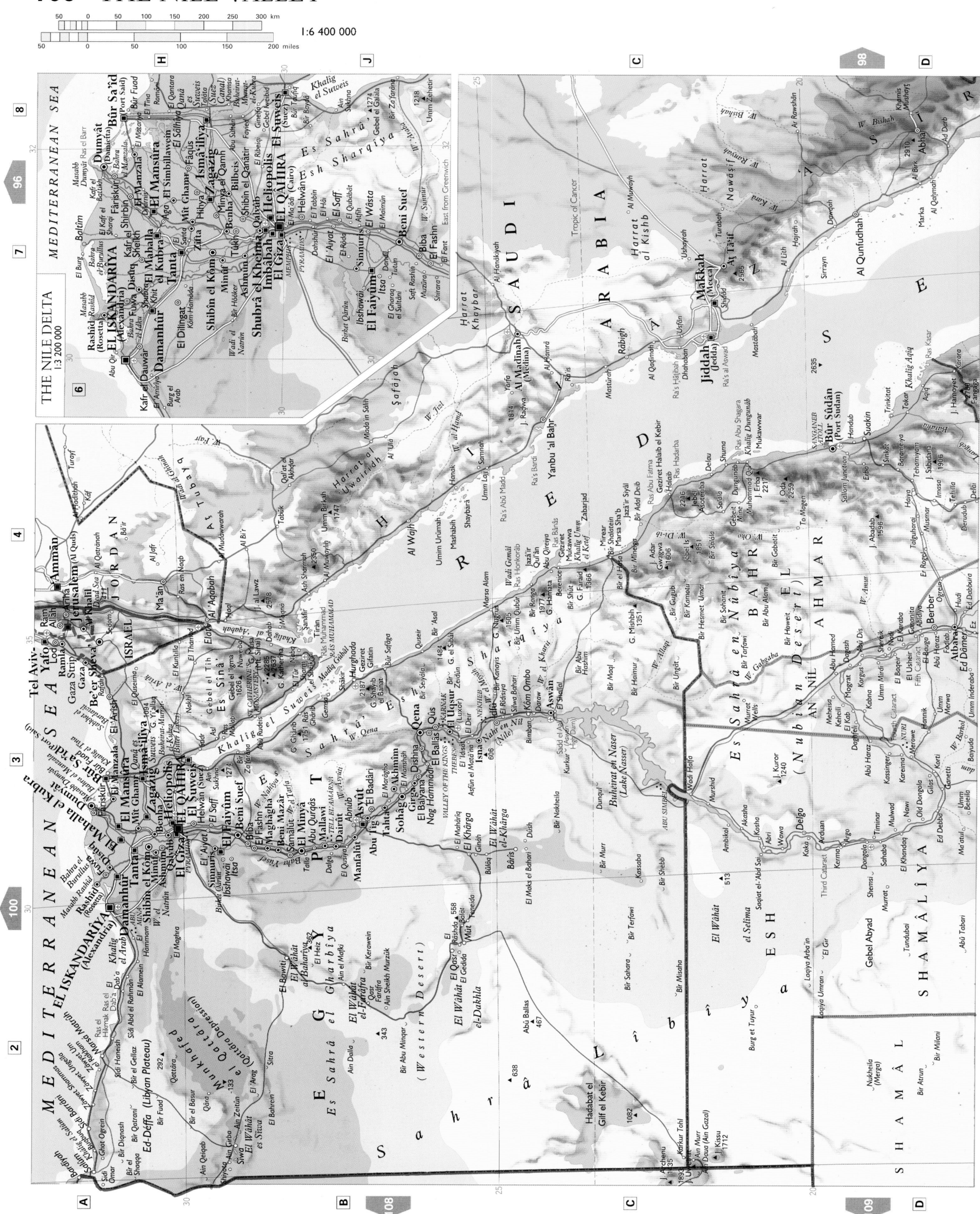

50 0 50 100 150 200 250 300 km

1:6 400 000

50 0 50 100 150 200 miles

THE NILE DELTA
1:3 200 000

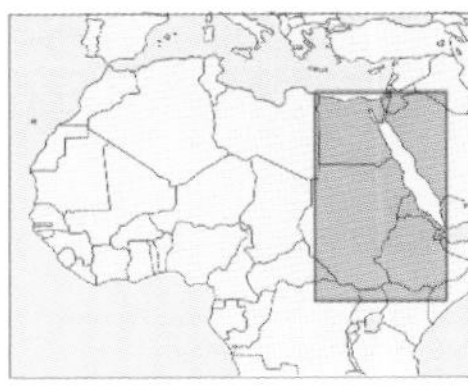

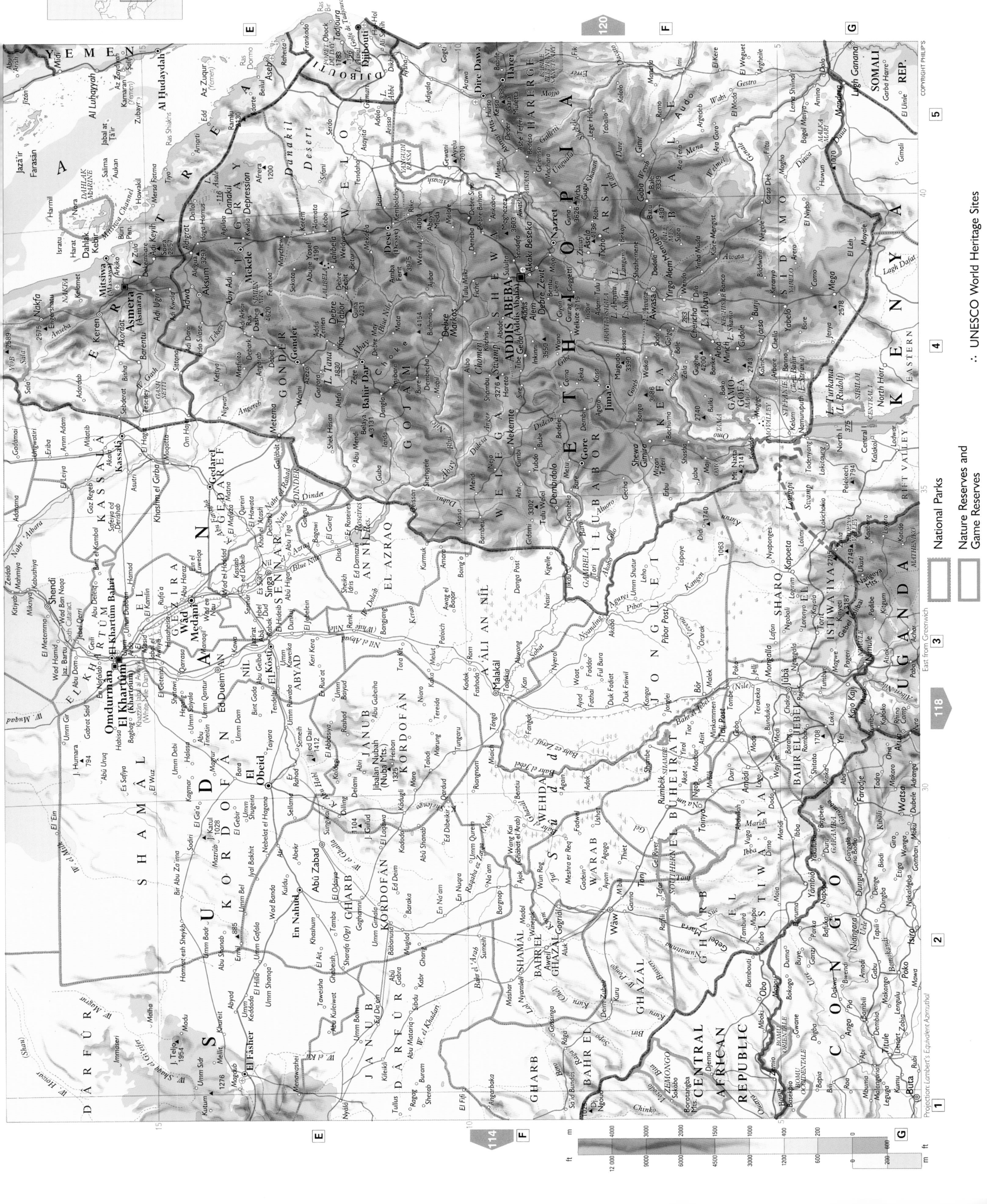

National Parks
Nature Reserves and Game Reserves
UNESCO World Heritage Sites
SUDAN
ETHIOPIA
ERITREA
YEMEN
DJIBOUTI
SOMALI REP.
KENYA
UGANDA
CONGO
CENTRAL AFRICAN REPUBLIC
El Khartûm (Khartoum)
Omdurmân
ADDIS ABEBA
Asmera (Asmara)
Djibouti
Juba
L. Tana
L. Turkana (L. Rudolf)
Projection: Lambert's Equivalent Azimuthal
COPYRIGHT PHILIP'S
East from Greenwich

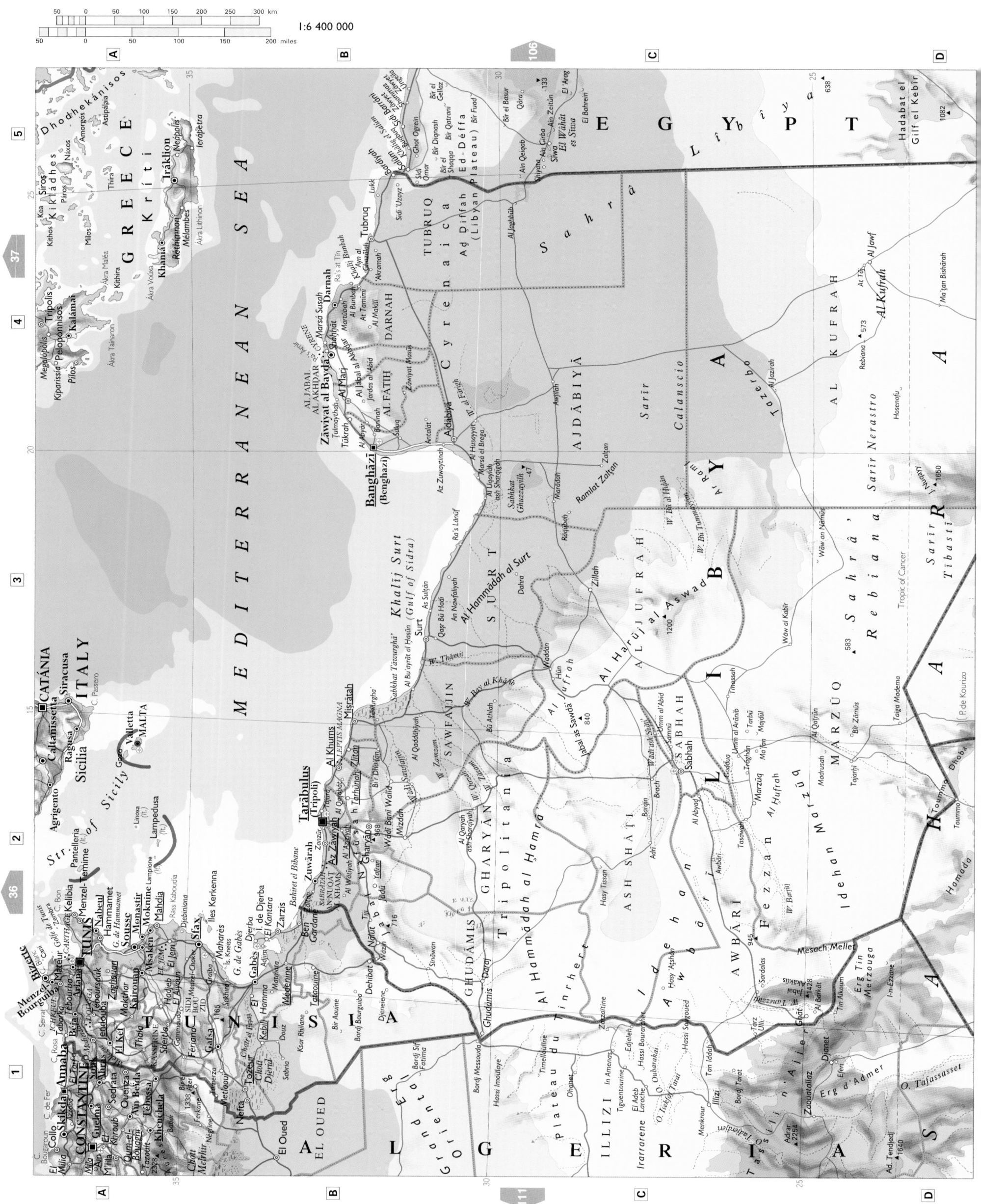

1:6 400 000

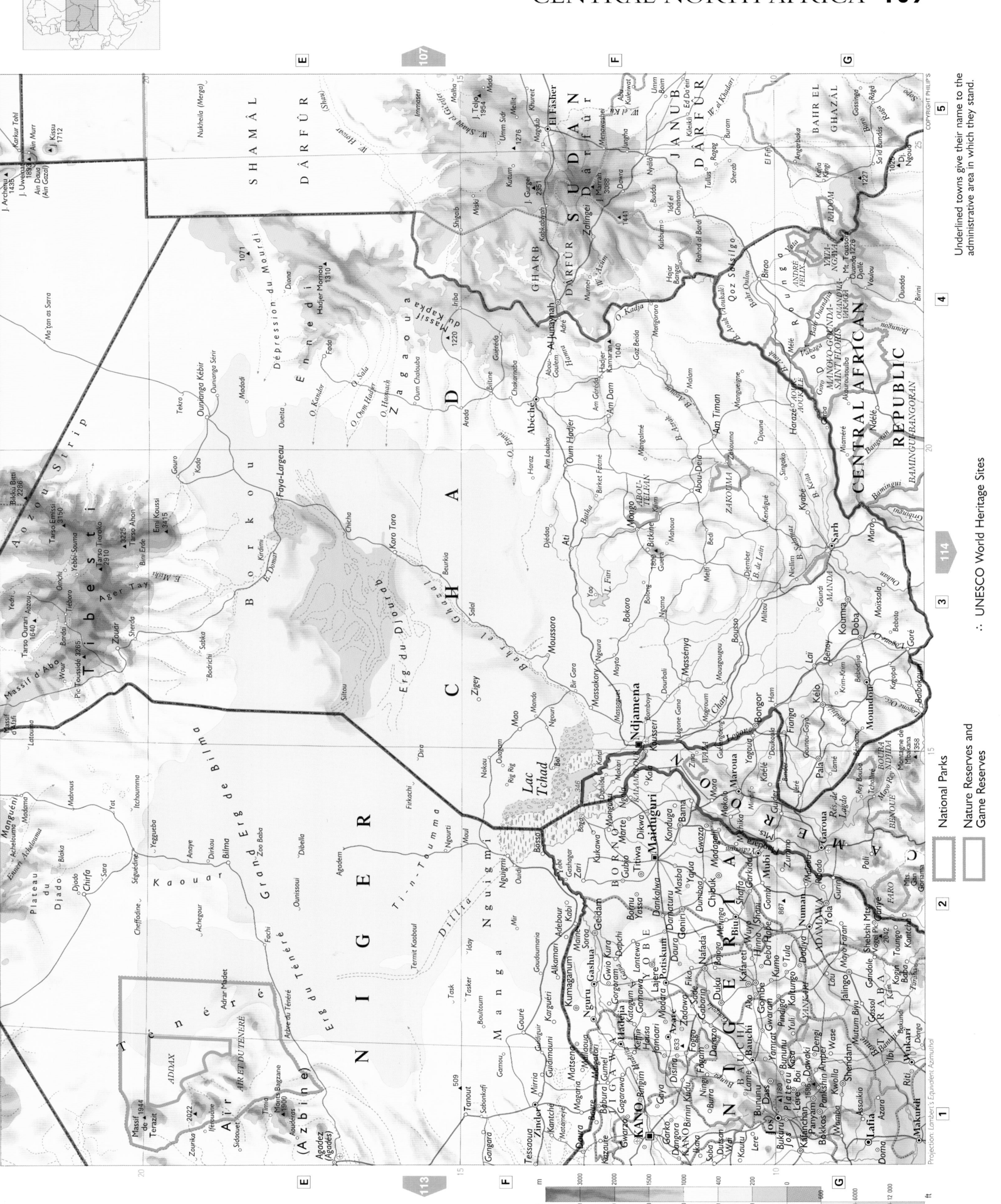

Projection: Lambert's Equivalent Azimuthal

COPYRIGHT PHILIP'S

Underlined towns give their name to the
administrative area in which they stand.

∴ UNESCO World Heritage Sites

National Parks

Nature Reserves and
Game Reserves

SUDAN

GHARB DÂRFÛR

JANUB DÂRFÛR

BAHR EL GHAZAL

CENTRAL AFRICAN REPUBLIC

C H A D

N I G E R

N I G E R I A

C A M E R O O N

Lac Tchad

T i b e s t i

Aozou Strip

A ï r

(Azbine)

Ténéré

B o r k o u

E n n e d i

D Â R F Û R

SHAMÂL DÂRFÛR

Ndjamena

Maiduguri

KANO

El Fasher

Abéché

Agadez (Agadès)

Zinder

Garoua

Faya-Largeau

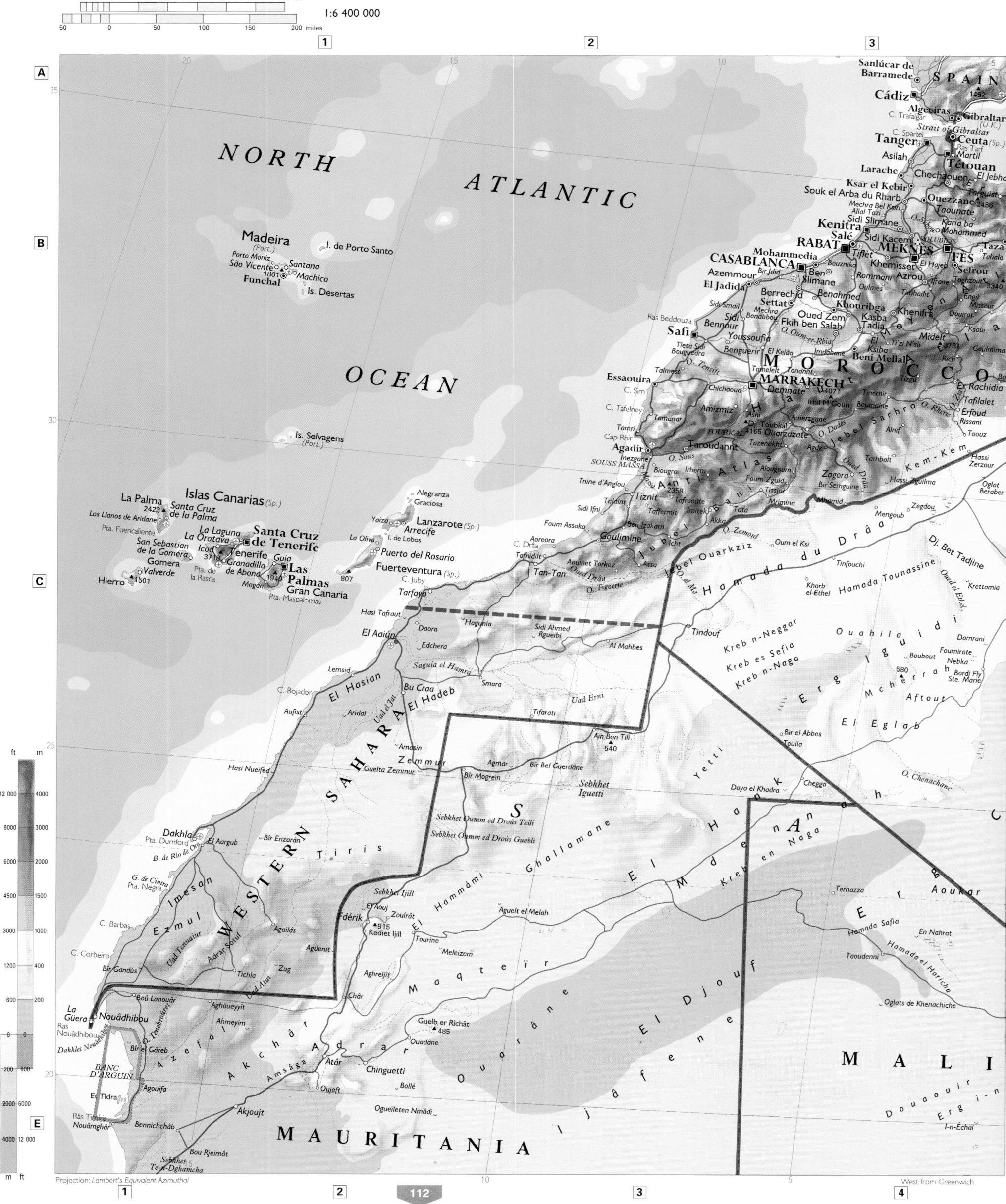

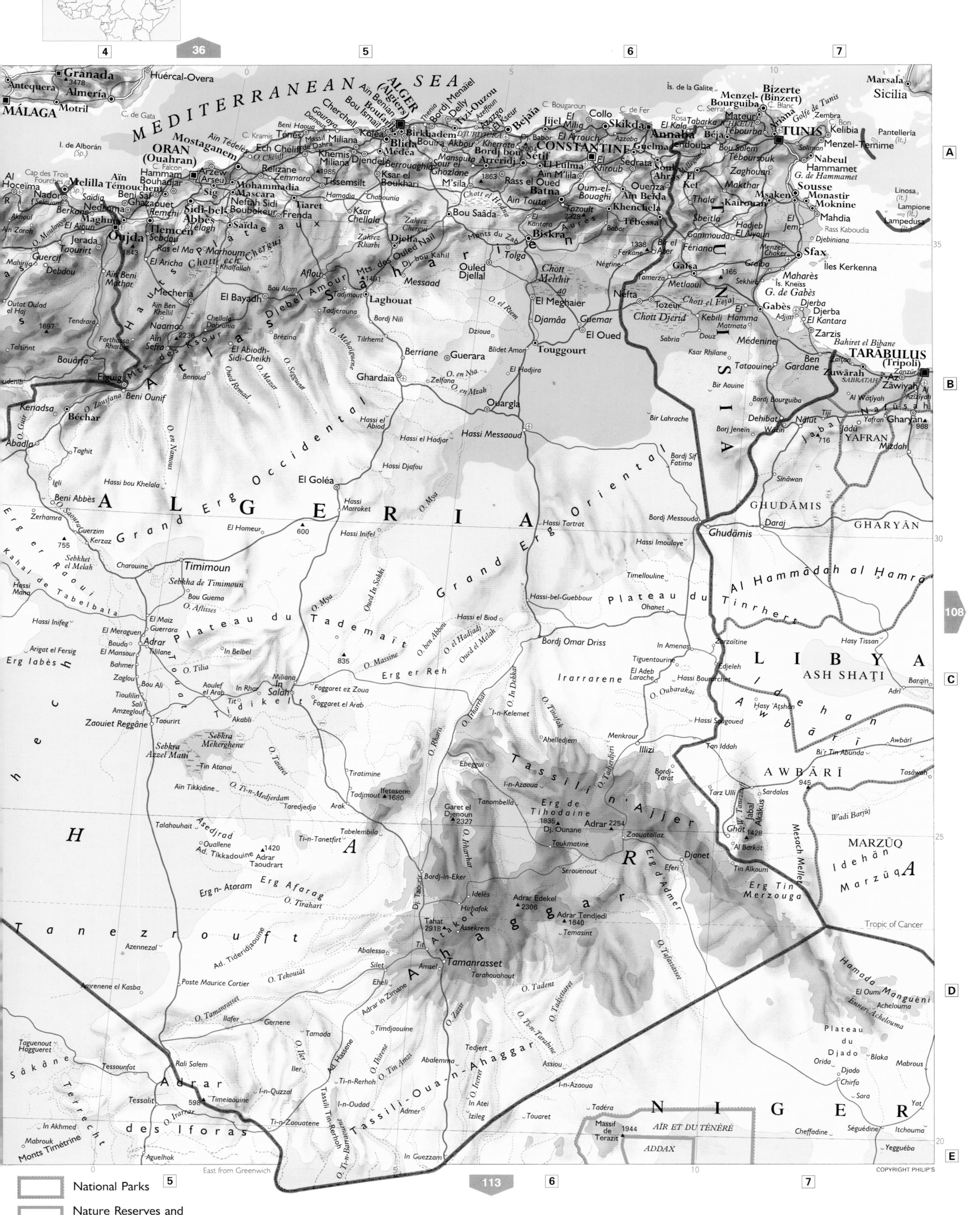

MEDITERRANEAN SEA

MÁLAGA Motril

Granada 3478
Antequera Almería Huércal-Overa

Marsala
Sicilia

Î. de la Galite
Bizerte (Binzert)
Menzel-Bourguiba
Mateur Ariana
Tabarka Béja **TUNIS**
Golfe de Tunis
Zembra
Kelibia
Pantelleria (It.)
Menzel-Temime

C. de Gata
I. de Alborán (Sp.)
ORAN (Ouahran)
C. Falcon
Arzew Arzeu

ALGER (Algiers)
Aïn Benian
Bou Boufarik
 Bordj Menaiel
Delly
Tizi-Ouzou
Azeffoun
C. Bougaroun
Collo
Skikda
Azzaba
C. de Fer
Annaba
Guelma

Constantine
Sétif
El Eulma
El Kroub
Souk Ahras

A

Al Hoceima Cap des Trois Fourches
Melilla (Sp.)
Nador
Saïdia
Aïn Témouchent
Beni Saf
Ghazaouet
Remchi
Tlemcen
Maghnia
Oujda
1843

Mohammadia
Mascara
Neftah Sidi
Sig
Tiaret
Frenda
Hamadia
Saïda
Chabounia
Bou Saâda

Batna
Aïn Touta
Oum-el-Bouaghi
Aïn Beïda
Khenchela
Tébessa

Sfax
Îles Kerkenna

35

Guercif Debdou
Taourirt
Jerada
El Aïoun
Aïn Zorah
El Aricha
Marhoum
Djelfa
Ouled Naïl
Biskra
Tolga

Gafsa
Metlaoui
Maharès
Î. Kneiss
G. de Gabès
Djerba

El Bayadh
Aflou
Laghouat
El Meghaier
El Oued
Nefta
Tozeur
Chott Djerid
Kebili Hamma
Gabès

Naama
Aïn Sefra
2236
Brézina
Messaad
Chott Melrhir
El Oued
Sabria
Douz
Médenine
Zarzis

Béchar
Beni Ounif
Figuig
Taghit
Ghardaïa
Touggourt
El Hadjira
Bir Rhilane
Ben Gardane

B

Abadla
Hassi el Abiod
Ouargla
Bir Lahrache
Zuwārah
Az Zāwiyah

TARABULUS (Tripoli)

Hassi Messaoud

A L G E R I A

Béni Abbès
El Goléa
Hassi Marroket
GHUDĀMIS
Ghudāmis
GHARYĀN

30

Timimoun
Sebkha de Timimoun
600
Hassi Inifel
Hassi Tartrat
Bordj Messouda

Al Hammādah al Hamrā

Plateau du Tinrhert

108

Adrar
In Salah
Bordj Omar Driss
In Amenas
L I B Y A
ASH SHAŢI
C

Erg er Reh
Irrararene

AWBĀRĪ
MARZŪQ
Idehān
Marzūq

Illizi

Tassili-n-'Ajjer

Ghat
1428

25

H O G G A R

Bordj-in-Eker
Idelès
Ad. Tikkadouine
Adrar
Taoudrart
Djanet
Tin Alkoum

Tamanrasset
Tahat 2918
Assekrem

Tropic of Cancer

Hamada
Manguéni
D

Adrar des Iforas
Tessalit

A H A G G A R

Plateau du Djado

N I G E R

Massif de Terazit 1944
AÏR ET DU TÉNÉRÉ
ADDAX

E

East from Greenwich
113
COPYRIGHT PHILIP'S

National Parks

Nature Reserves and Game Reserves

⬦ UNESCO World Heritage Sites

1:6 400 000

ATLANTIC OCEAN

GULF

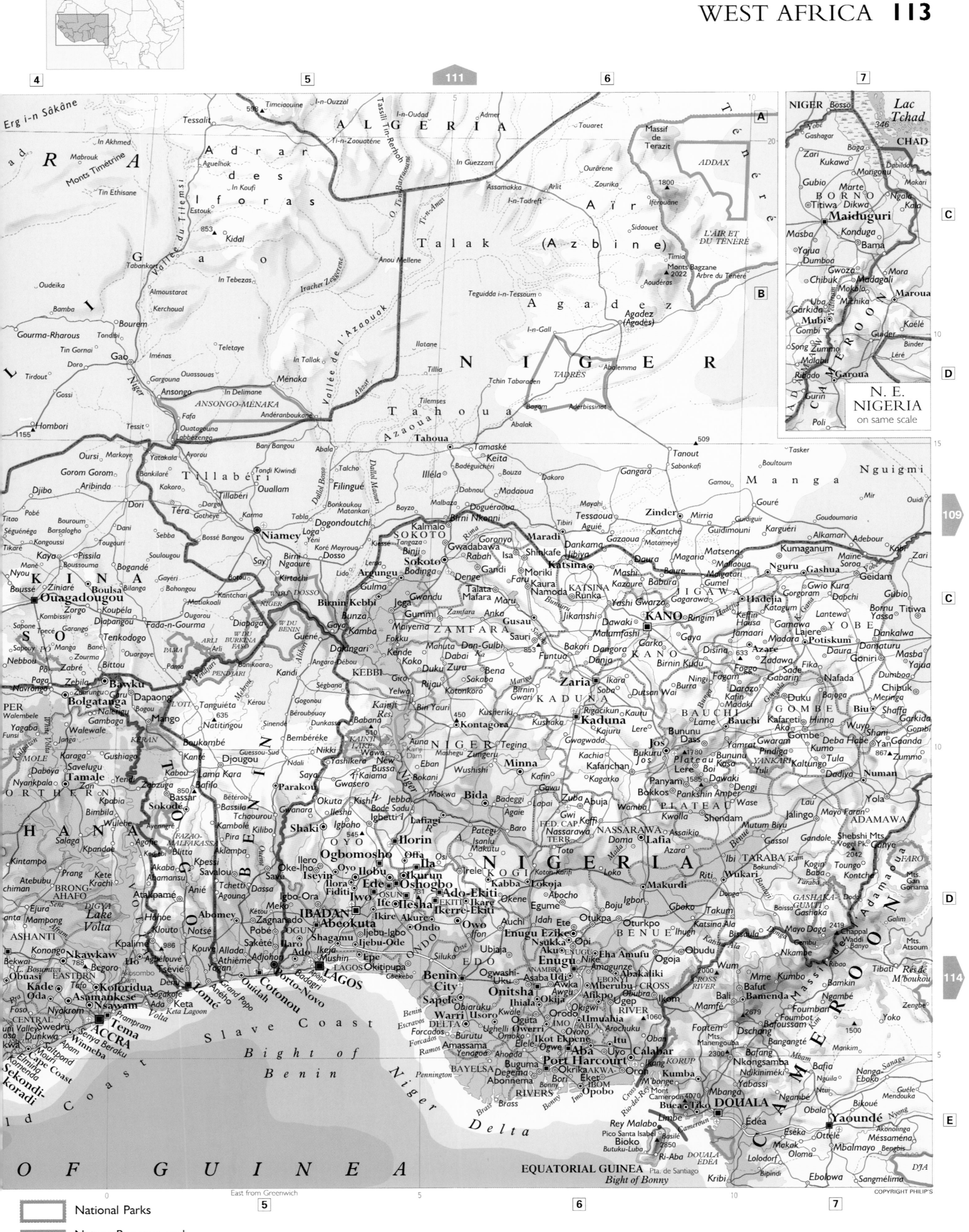

National Parks

Nature Reserves and
Game Reserves

∴ UNESCO World Heritage Sites

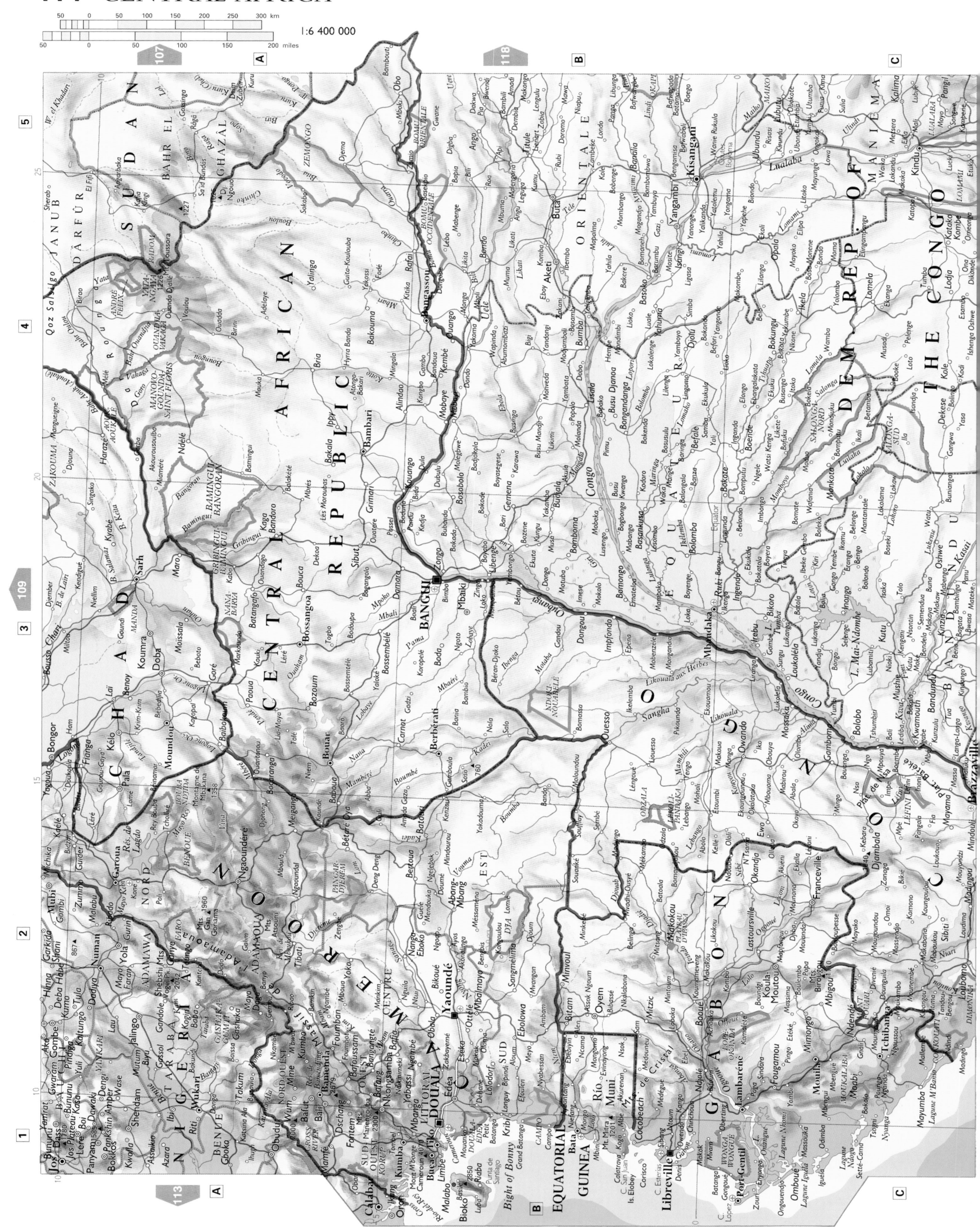

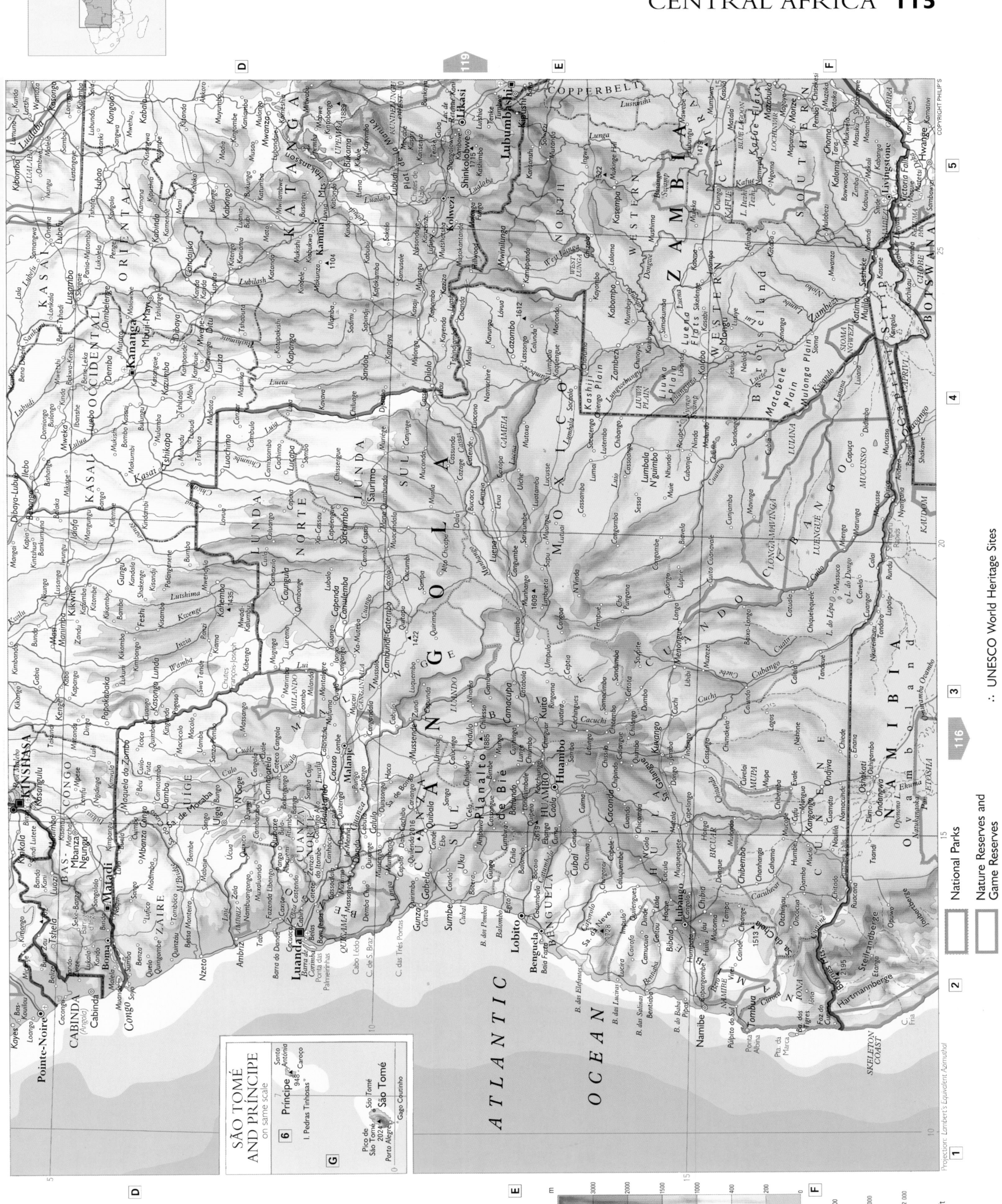

119

116

CENTRAL AFRICA

ATLANTIC OCEAN

COPPERBELT

ZAMBIA

KATANGA

KASAI ORIENTAL

KASAI OCCIDENTAL

CONGO

ZAIRE

BAS-CONGO

CABINDA (Angola)

Kinshasa

Malanji

Luanda

Benguela

Lobito

Lubango

Namibe

ANGOLA

NAMIBIA

BOTSWANA

Lubumbashi

Likasi

Kananga

Mbanza Ngungu

Boma

Matadi

Pointe-Noire

LUNDA NORTE

LUNDA SUL

MOXICO

CUANDO CUBANGO

CUNENE

HUÍLA

HUAMBO

BIÉ

MALANJE

UÍGE

ZAIRE

CUANZA NORTE

CUANZA SUL

BENGUELA

NAMIBE

Planalto de Bié

Caprivi Strip

Barotseland

Okavango

Zambezi

SÃO TOMÉ AND PRÍNCIPE
on same scale

Príncipe
Santo Antonio
I. Pedras Tinhosas
São Tomé
Pico de São Tomé 2024
Porto Alegre
Gago Coutinho

National Parks

Nature Reserves and
Game Reserves

∴ UNESCO World Heritage Sites

Projection: Lambert's Equivalent Azimuthal

m
3000
2000
1500
1000
400
200
0

ft
9000
6000
4500
3000
1200
600
0

ft
200-600
600
6000
4000 12 000

m
200 600
6000

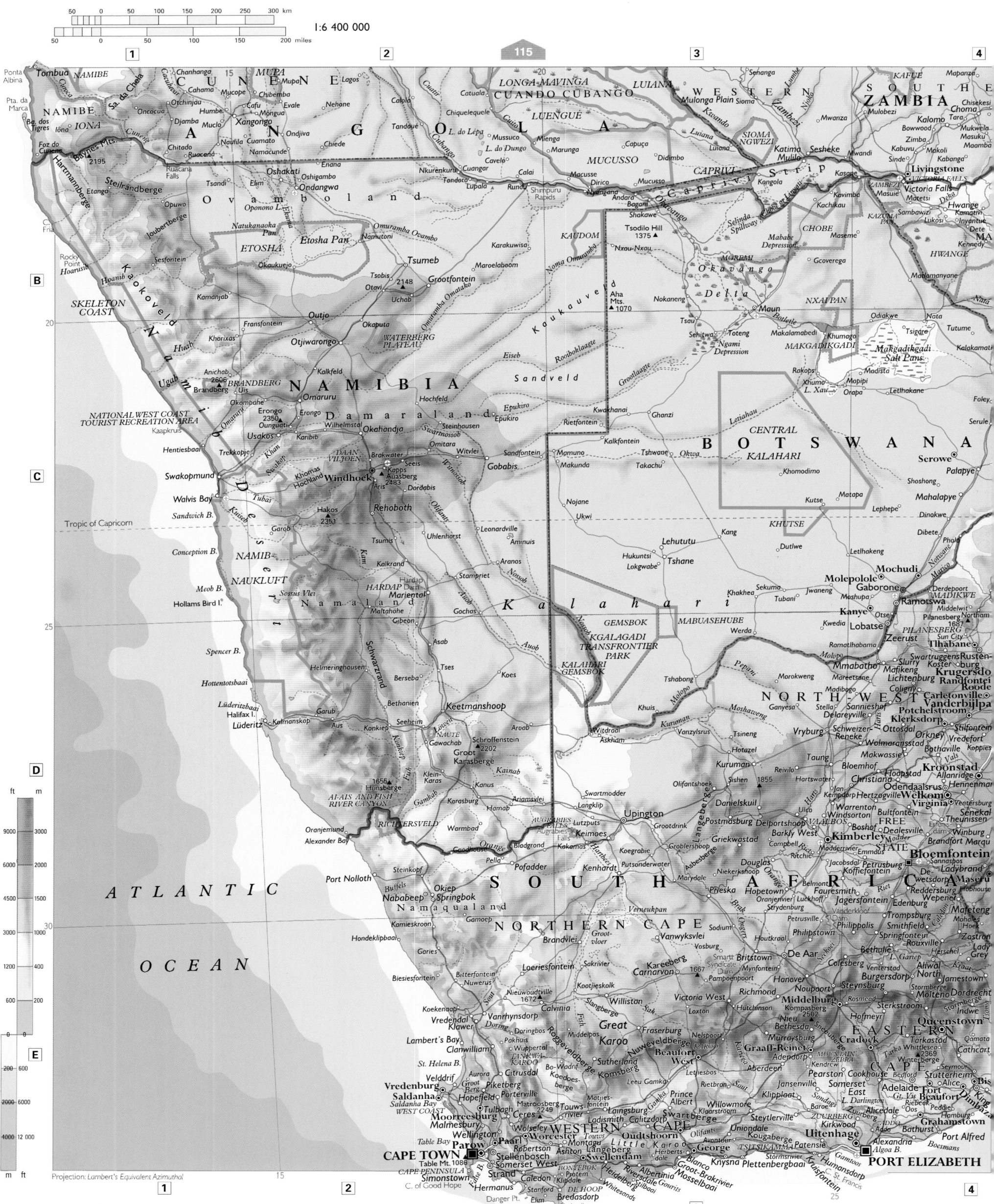

National Parks

Nature Reserves and Game Reserves

△ UNESCO World Heritage Sites

MADAGASCAR

on same scale

COPYRIGHT PHILIP'S

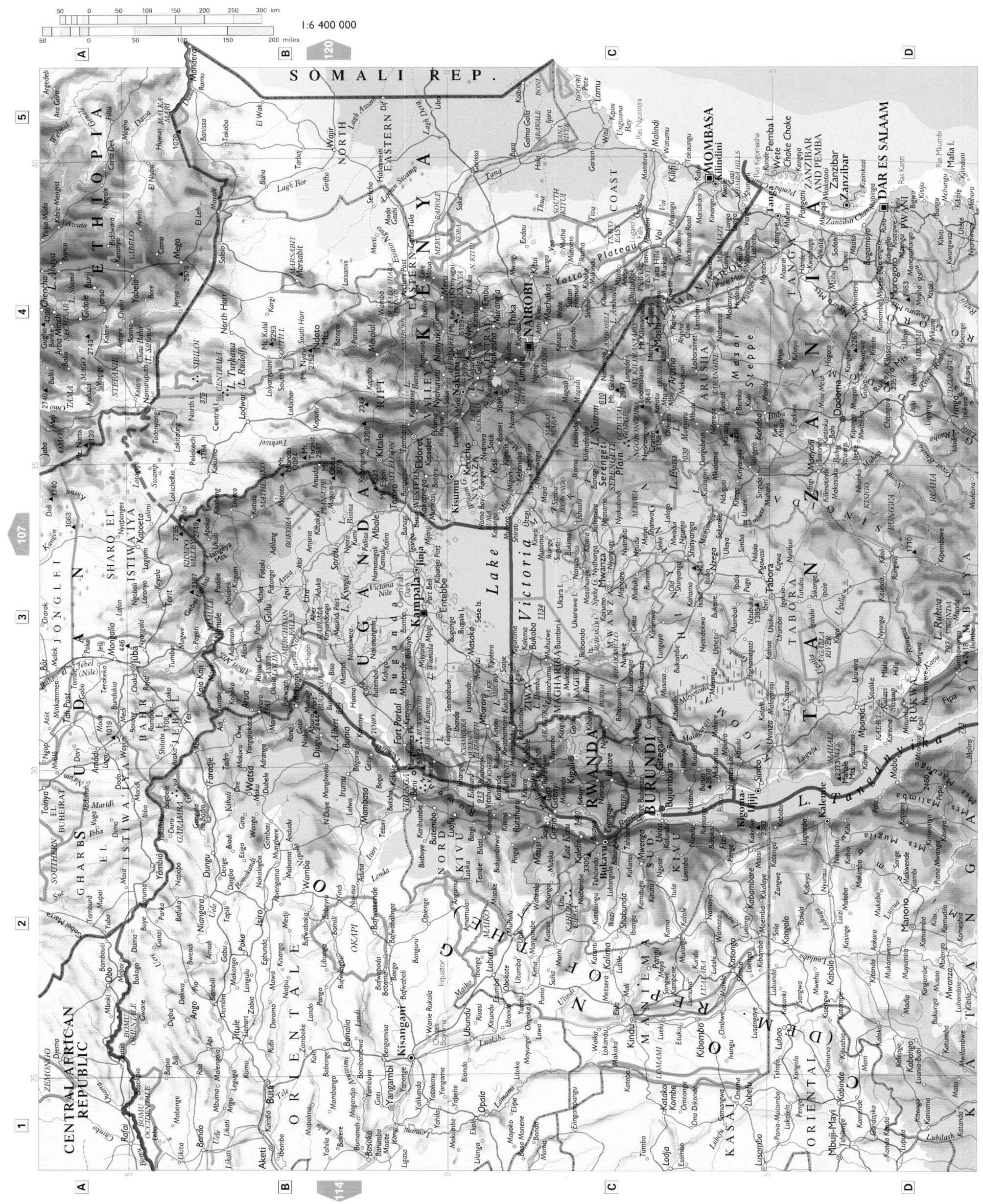

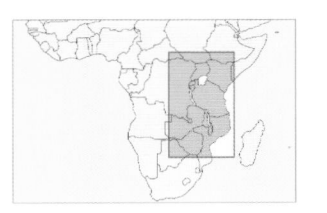

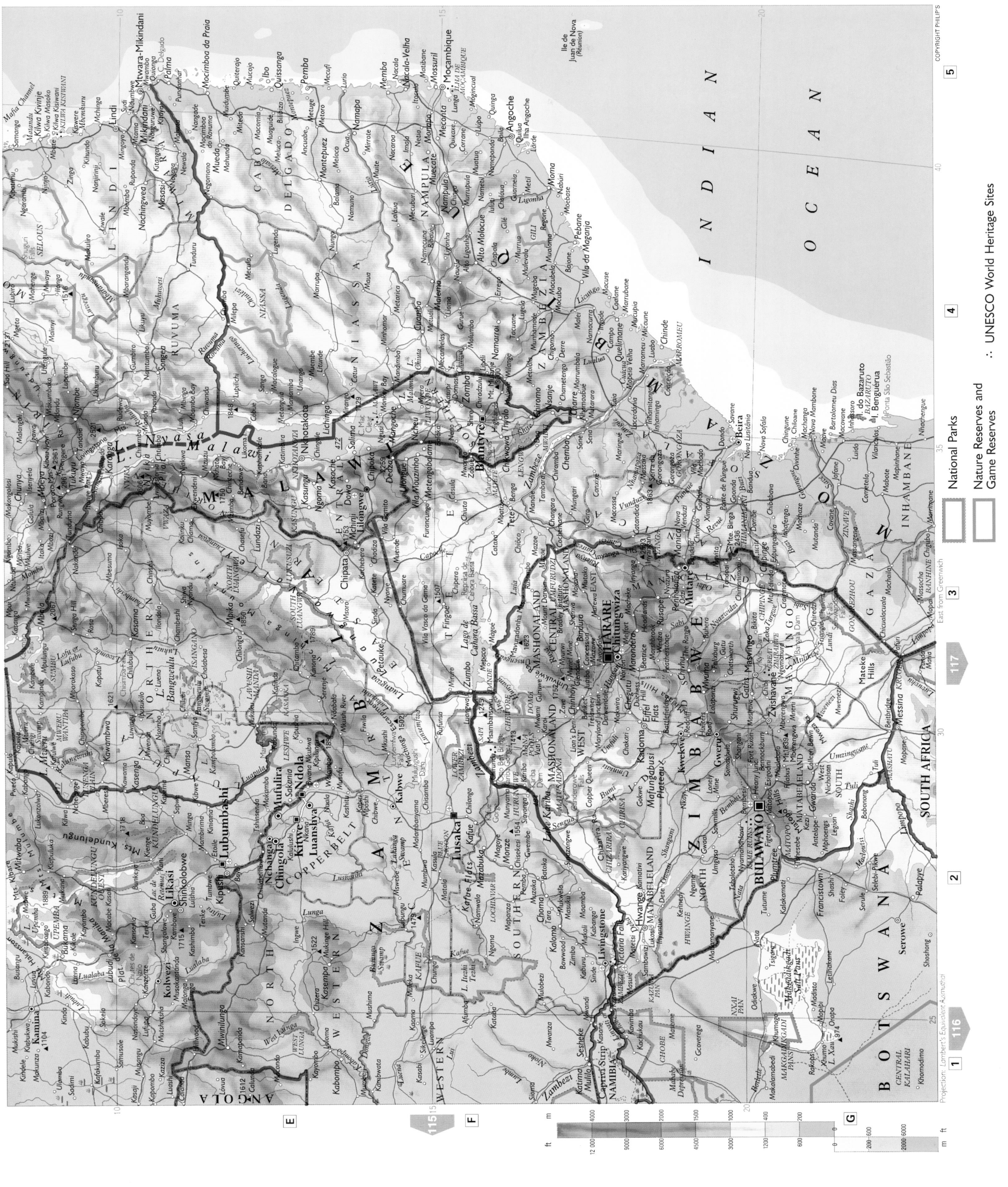
INDIAN OCEAN
MOZAMBIQUE
ZAMBIA
ZIMBABWE
MALAWI
BOTSWANA
SOUTH AFRICA
NAMIBIA
ANGOLA
L. Nyasa / L. Malawi
Lusaka
Harare
Lilongwe
Blantyre
Bulawayo
Beira
Mutare
Ndola
Kitwe
Lubumbashi
Likasi
Kolwezi
Livingstone
Victoria Falls
Lake Kariba
Lago de Cahora Bassa
Zambezi
Quelimane
Nampula
Moçambique
Pemba
Mtwara-Mikindani
Lindi
Tete
Chipata
Kasama
Mansa
Kabwe
Gweru
Masvingo
Francistown
Serowe
Makgadikgadi Salt Pans
Kamina
National Parks
Nature Reserves and Game Reserves
UNESCO World Heritage Sites
Projection: Lambert's Equivalent Azimuthal
COPYRIGHT PHILIP'S
East from Greenwich

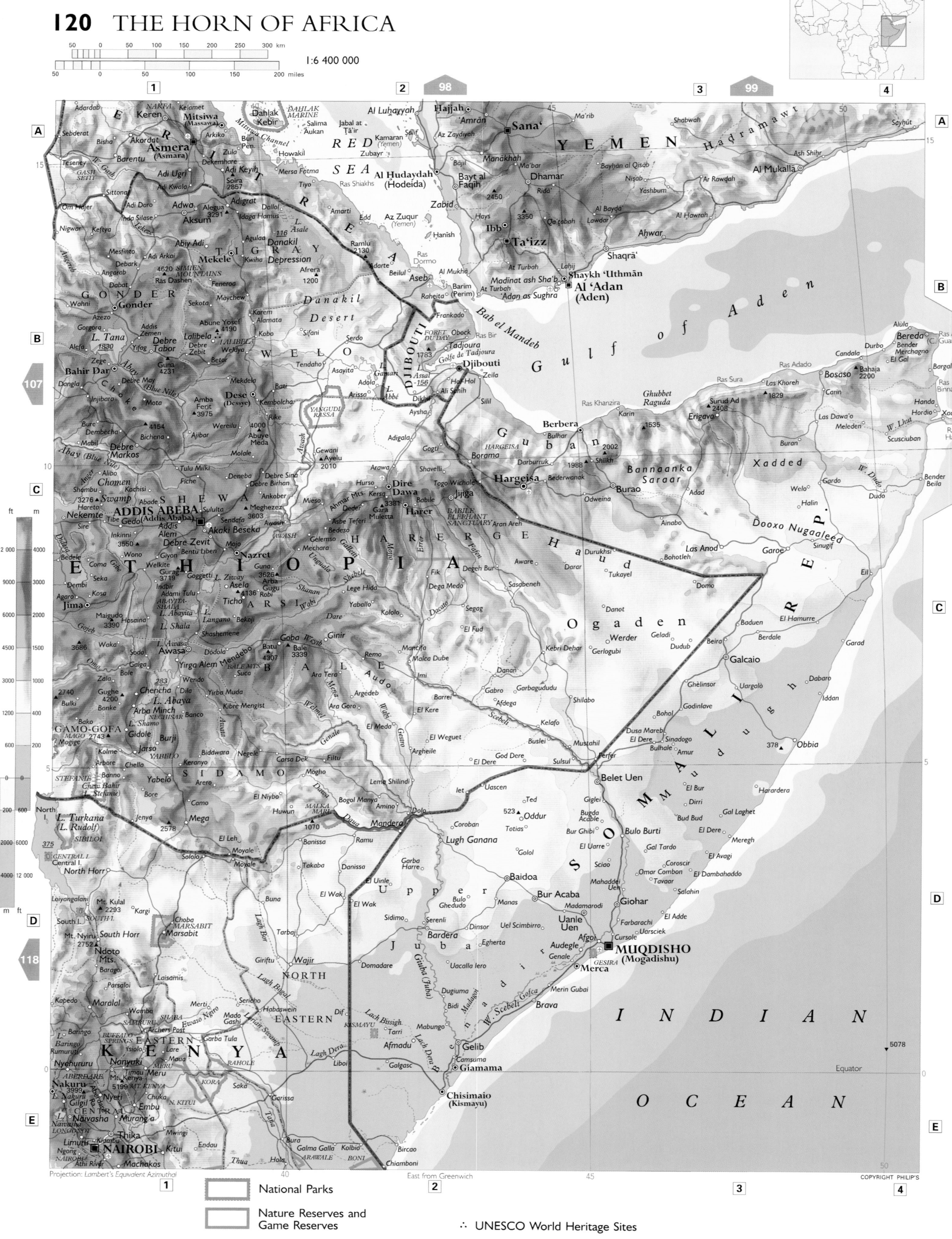

1:6 400 000

National Parks

Nature Reserves and Game Reserves

⋄ UNESCO World Heritage Sites

Projection: Lambert's Equivalent Azimuthal

East from Greenwich

COPYRIGHT PHILIP'S

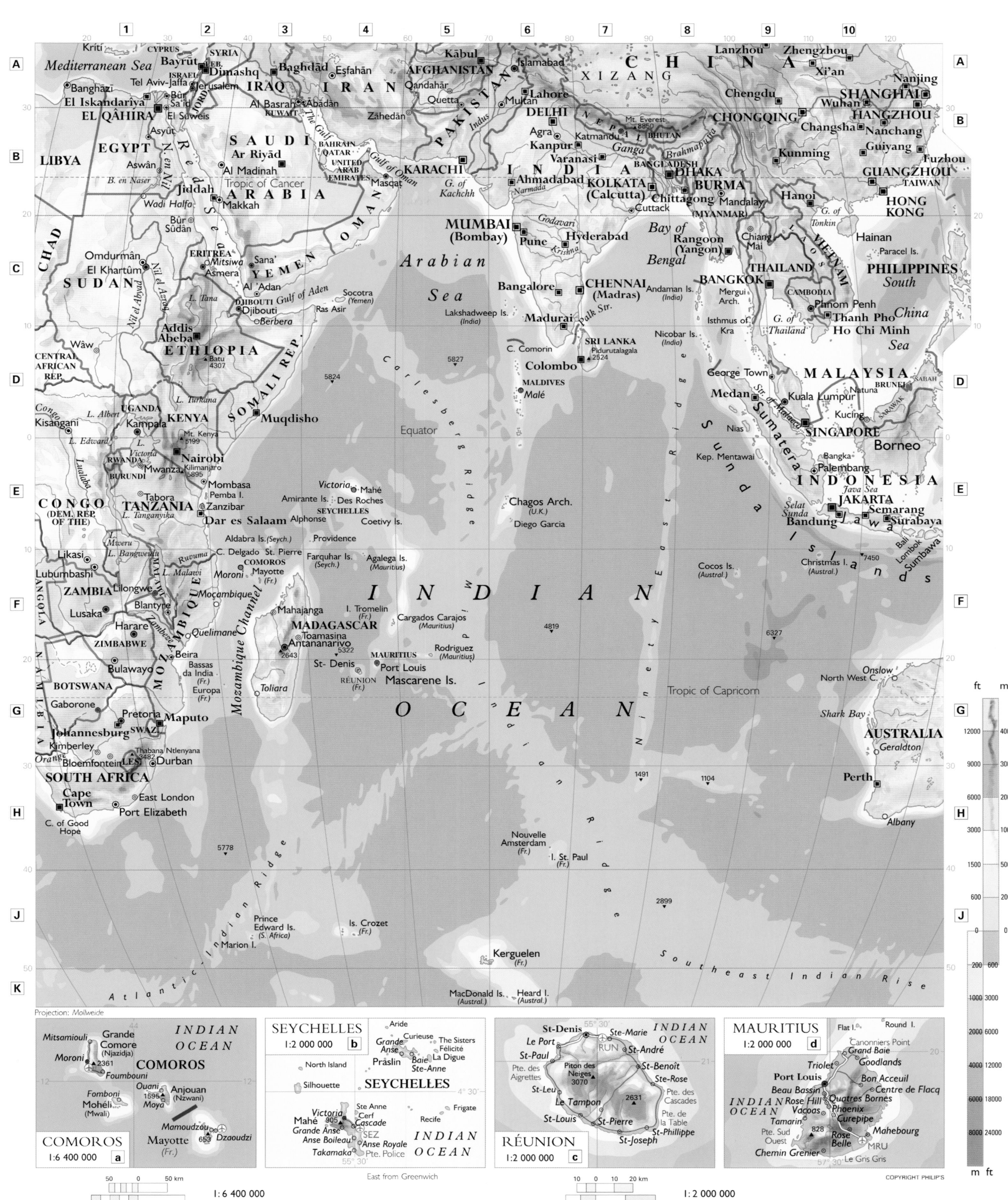

1 **2** **3** **4** **5** **6** **7** **8** **9** **10**

A

Mediterranean Sea   Kríti   CYPRUS   SYRIA   Kābul   Islamabad   C H I N A   Lanzhou   Zhengzhou
Banghāzī   Bayrūt LEB.   Dimashq   Baghdād   Eşfahān   AFGHANISTAN   X I Z A N G   Chengdu   Xi'an   Nanjing
Tel Aviv-Jaffa   ISRAEL   JORDAN   IRAQ   I R A N   Qandahār   Quetta   Mt. Everest   CHONGQING   SHANGHAI   Wuhan   HANGZHOU

B

El Iskandarīya   Jerusalem   Būr Sa'īd   Al Başrah   Ābadān   PAKISTAN   Lahore   8850   Chengdu   Changsha   Nanchang
EL QÂHIRA   El Suweis   KUWAIT   Zāhedān   Multan   DELHI   Katmandu   NEPAL   BHUTAN   Kunming   Guiyang
LIBYA   EGYPT   SAUDI   Ar Riyād   BAHRAIN   United   Zāhedān   Agra   Kanpur   Ganga   BANGLADESH   DHAKA   GUANGZHOU   Fuzhou
Aswân   ARABIA   QATAR   ARAB   Masqat   Indus   Varanasi   Brahmaputra   BURMA   Hanoi   TAIWAN
B. en Naser   Al Madinah   EMIRATES   G. of   KARACHI   I N D I A   KOLKATA   (Calcutta)   Mandalay   HONG

C

Tropic of Cancer   Jiddah   Makkah   Kachchh   Ahmadabad   Narmada   Chittagong   (MYANMAR)   KONG
Wadi Halfa   OMAN   Cuttack   Rangoon   Chiang   G. of
Bûr   Sana'   Godavari   MUMBAI   (Yangon)   Mai   Tonkin
Omdurmân   Sûdân   YEMEN   Masqat   (Bombay)   Pune   Hyderabad   Bay of   LAOS   Hainan
El Khartûm   ERITREA   Mitsiwa   Al 'Adan   Socotra   Arabian   Krishna   Bengal   Paracel Is.
CHAD   SUDAN   Āsmera   Gulf of Aden   (Yemen)   Bangalore   CHENNAI   Andaman Is.   Mergui   THAILAND   PHILIPPINES
WÂw   DJIBOUTI   Djibouti   Ras Asir   S e a   (Madras)   (India)   Arch.   BANGKOK   South

D

CENTRAL   Addis   Berbera   Lakshadweep Is.   Madurai   Isthmus of   Phnom Penh   China
AFRICAN   Abeba   Batu   (India)   Dalk Str.   Kra   CAMBODIA   Thanh Pho
REP.   ETHIOPIA   4307   5827   Pidurutalagala   SRI LANKA   Nicobar Is.   G. of   Ho Chi Minh
Kisangani   L. Turkana   5824   Colombo   2524   (India)   Thailand   Sea
Congo   L. Albert   UGANDA   Carlsberg   MALDIVES   George Town   MALAYSIA   SABAH
L. Edward   Kampala   KENYA   SOMALI REP.   Muqdisho   Ridge   Malé   Medan   Kuala Lumpur   BRUNEI
RWANDA   Victoria   Mt. Kenya   Equator   Nias   Kucing   SARAWAK

E

Mwanza   5199   Victoria   Mahé   Chagos Arch.   Str. of Malacca   SINGAPORE   Borneo
Kilimanjaro   Amirante Is.   Des Roches   (U.K.)   Sumatera   Bangka
BURUNDI   5895   Nairobi   SEYCHELLES   Diego Garcia   Kep. Mentawai   Palembang
Mombasa   Alphonse   Coetivy Is.   INDONESIA   Java Sea
C O N G O   Pemba I.   Selat   JAKARTA   Semarang
(DEM. REP.   Tabora   Zanzibar   Aldabra Is.(Seych.)   St. Pierre   Sunda   Bandung   Surabaya
OF THE)   TANZANIA   Dar es Salaam   Providence   J   a   v   a   Bali
Likasi   L. Tanganyika   C. Delgado   COMOROS   Farquhar Is.   Agalega Is.   Cocos Is.   Lombok
L. Mweru   Ruvuma   Moroni   Mayotte   (Seych.)   (Mauritius)   (Austral.)   Christmas I.   Sumbawa

F

Lubumbashi   L. Bangweulu   (Fr.)   I N D I A N   7450   (Austral.)
ZAMBIA   Lilongwe   Mahajanga   I. Tromelin   Cargados Carajos   4819   6327
Lusaka   Blantyre   MALAWI   (Fr.)   (Mauritius)
ANGOLA   MADAGASCAR   Toamasina   Rodriguez

G

Harare   MOZAMBIQUE   Mocambique   Antananarivo   MAURITIUS   (Mauritius)   Onslow
ZIMBABWE   Quelimane   2643   5322   St-Denis   Port Louis   Tropic of Capricorn   North West C.
Bulawayo   Beira   Mozambique Channel   Mascarene Is.   RÉUNION   Shark Bay
BOTSWANA   Bassas   Toliara   (Fr.)   I N D I A N
Gaborone   da India   Europa   O C E A N
Pretoria   Maputo   (Fr.)   (Fr.)

H

Johannesburg   SWAZ.   AUSTRALIA
Kimberley   Orange   Thabana Ntlenyana   Geraldton
Bloemfontein LES.   3482   Durban   1491   1104   Perth
SOUTH AFRICA   East London   Nouvelle   Albany
Cape   Port Elizabeth   5778   Amsterdam   I. St. Paul
Town   C. of Good   (Fr.)   (Fr.)
Hope

J

Prince   Is. Crozet   2899
Edward Is.   (Fr.)
(S. Africa)
Marion I.

K

Atlantic Indian Ridge   Kerguelen   Southeast Indian Rise
(Fr.)
MacDonald Is.   Heard I.
(Austral.)   (Austral.)

Projection: Moilweide   East from Greenwich   COPYRIGHT PHILIP'S

ft   m

12000   4000
9000   3000
6000   2000
3000   1000
1500   500
600   200
0   0
200   600
1000   3000
2000   6000
4000   12000
6000   18000
8000   24000
m   ft

INDIAN   OCEAN
Mitsamiouli   Grande   44
Comore
Moroni   (Njazidja)
COMOROS
Foumbouni
Fomboni   Ouani   1595   Anjouan
Mohéli   Moya   (Nzwani)
(Mwali)   Mamoudzou
Mayotte   Dzaoudzi
(Fr.)   653

COMOROS   1:6 400 000   **a**

SEYCHELLES   Aride
1:2 000 000   **b**   Curieuse
Grande   The Sisters
Félicité
North Island   Praslin   Baie   La Digue
Ste-Anne
Silhouette   Frigate
Recife
Victoria   905   Ste Anne
Mahé   Cerf
Grande Anse   Cascade
Anse Boileau   SEZ
Takamaka   Anse Royale
Pte. Police
55° 30'   INDIAN
OCEAN

St-Denis   55° 30'   Ste-Marie   INDIAN
Le Port   RUN   St-André   OCEAN
St-Paul   Piton des   St-Benoît
Pte. des   Neiges   Ste-Rose   21
Aigrettes   3070   Pte. des
St-Leu   2631   Cascades
Le Tampon   Pte. de
St-Louis   la Table
St-Pierre   St-Phillippe
St-Joseph

RÉUNION   1:2 000 000   **c**

MAURITIUS   Flat I.   Round I.
1:2 000 000   **d**
Cannoniers Point
Grand Baie
Triolet   Goodlands
Port Louis   Bon Acceuil
Beau Bassin   Centre de Flacq
INDIAN   Rose Hill
OCEAN   Vacoas   Phoenix
Tamarin   Curepipe
Pte. Sud   828   Mahebourg
Ouest   Rose
Chemin Grenier   Belle   MRU
57° 30'   Le Gris Gris

---

50   0   50 km
1: 6 400 000
50   0   50 miles

10   0   10   20 km
1: 2 000 000
10   0   10   20 miles

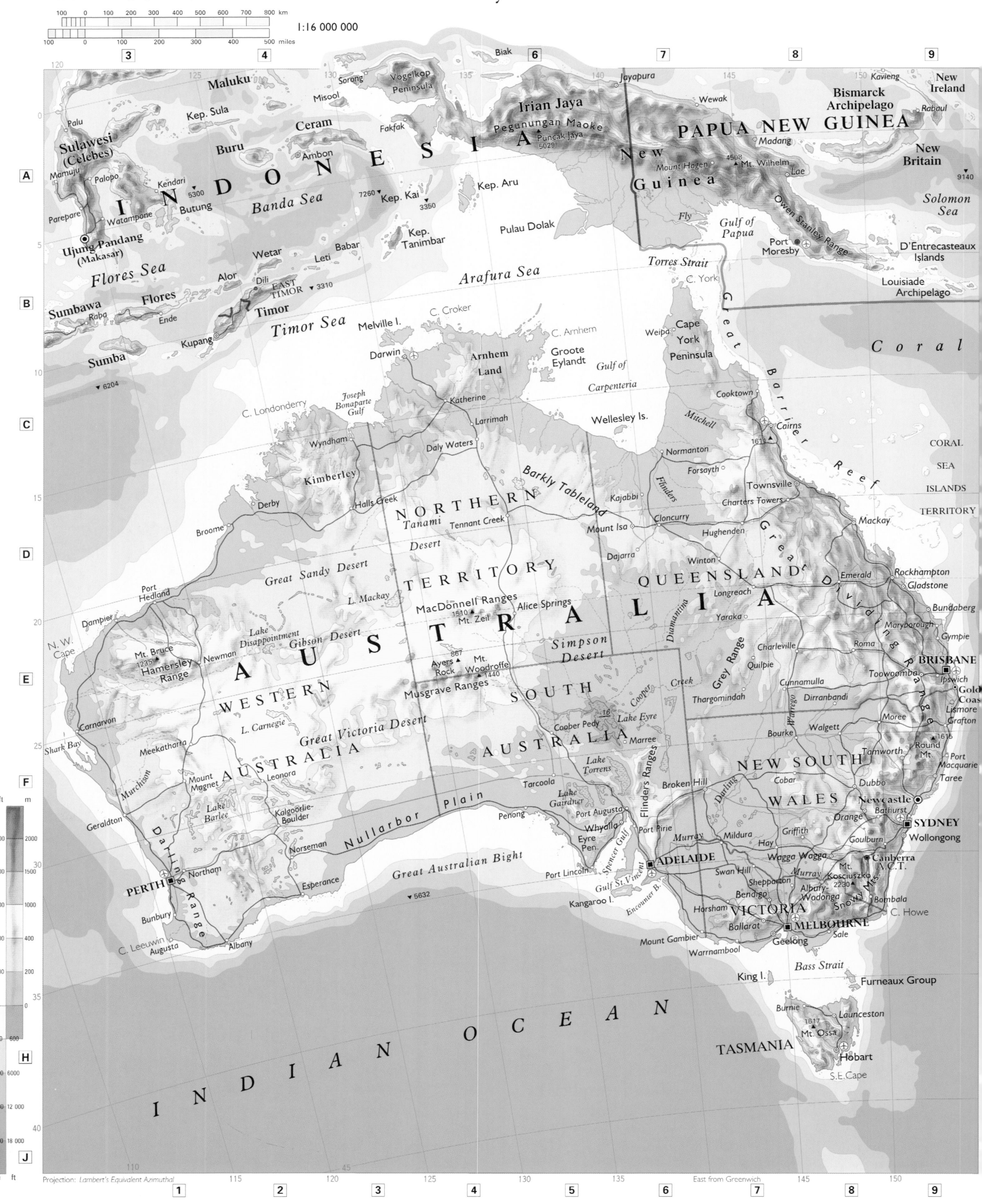

1:16 000 000

Projection: Lambert's Equivalent Azimuthal

East from Greenwich

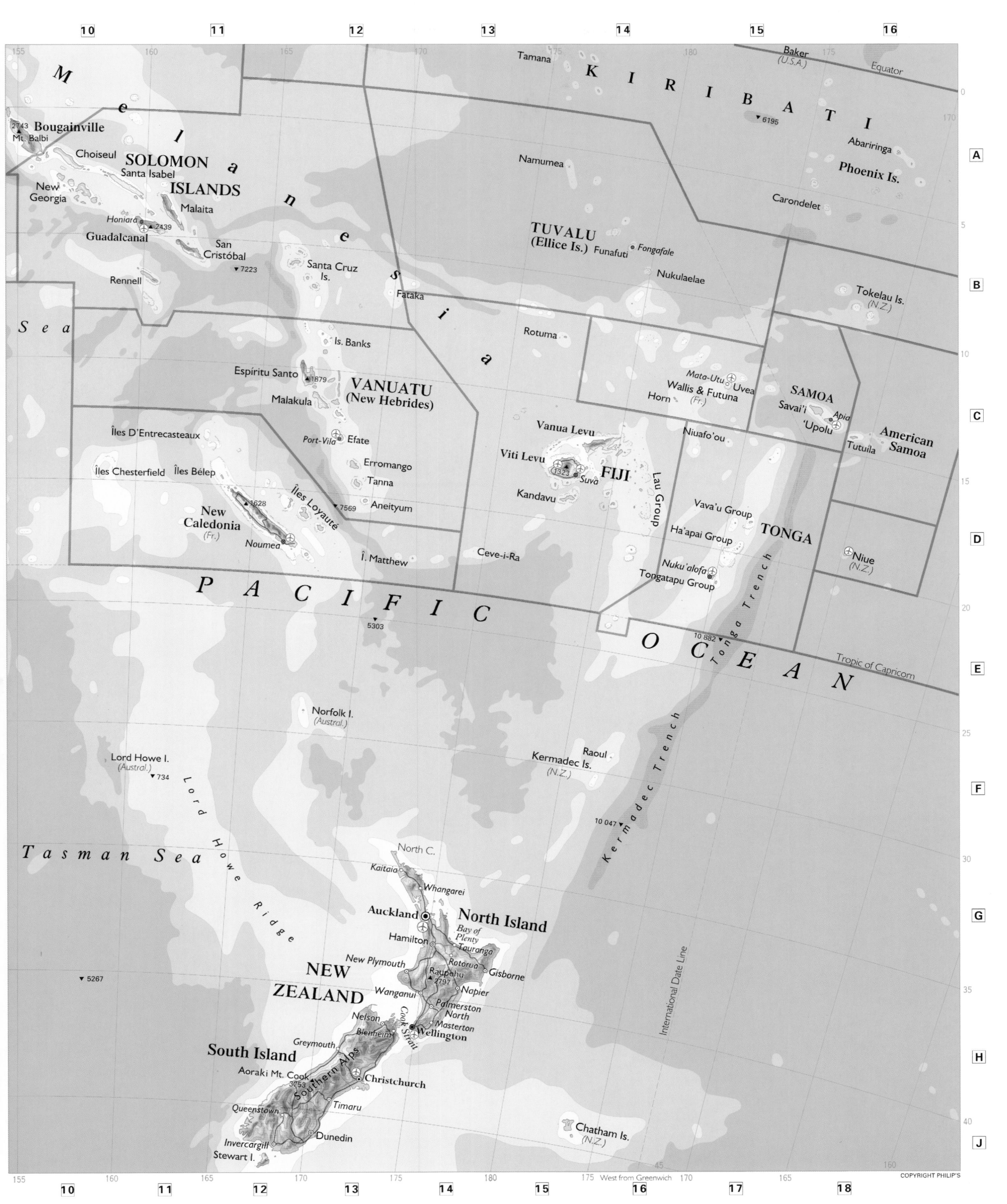

Baker
(U.S.A.)
Equator

M e l a n e s i a

K I R I B A T I

Tamana

▼6195

Abariringa

Phoenix Is.

2743 Bougainville
▲ Mt. Balbi

Choiseul

SOLOMON
Santa Isabel

New
Georgia

ISLANDS

Malaita

Honiara ⊕ ▲2439

Guadalcanal

San
Cristóbal

Namumea

Carondelet

Rennell

▼7223

Santa Cruz
Is.

TUVALU
(Ellice Is.) Funafuti ⊙ Fongafale

Nukulaelae

Tokelau Is.
(N.Z.)

S e a

Fataka

Rotuma

M e l a n e s i a

Is. Banks

Espíritu Santo ⊕ ▲1879

VANUATU
(New Hebrides)

Malakula

Mata-Utu ⊕ Uvea
Wallis & Futuna
Horn   (Fr.)

SAMOA
Savai'i

Apia
'Upolu ⊕

American
Samoa

Tutuila

Îles D'Entrecasteaux

Port-Vila ⊕ Efate

Erromango

Tanna

Vanua Levu

Viti Levu
▲1323 FIJI

Niuafo'ou

Îles Chesterfield Îles Bélep

Îles Loyauté

New
Caledonia
(Fr.)

▲1628

Noumea ⊕

Î. Matthew

▼7569

Aneityum

Suva

Kandavu

Ceve-i-Ra

Lau Group

Vava'u Group

Ha'apai Group

TONGA

Niue
(N.Z.)

P A C I F I C

▼5303

Nuku'alofa ⊕
Tongatapu Group

10 882 ▼

T o n g a   T r e n c h

O C E A N

Tropic of Capricorn

Norfolk I.
(Austral.)

Lord Howe I.
(Austral.)
▼734

Raoul

Kermadec Is.
(N.Z.)

K e r m a d e c   T r e n c h

10 047 ▼

T a s m a n   S e a

L o r d   H o w e   R i d g e

North C.

Kaitaia

Whangarei

Auckland ⊙

North Island

▼5267

Hamilton

Bay of
Plenty
Tauranga

NEW

New Plymouth

Rotorua

Gisborne

ZEALAND

Wanganui

Raupahu
▲2797

Napier

Palmerston
North

Masterton

Nelson

Cook
Strait

Wellington ⊙

South Island

Blenheim

Greymouth

Aoraki Mt. Cook
▲3753

Christchurch

Southern Alps

Queenstown

Timaru

International Date Line

Chatham Is.
(N.Z.)

Invercargill
Stewart I.

Dunedin

West from Greenwich

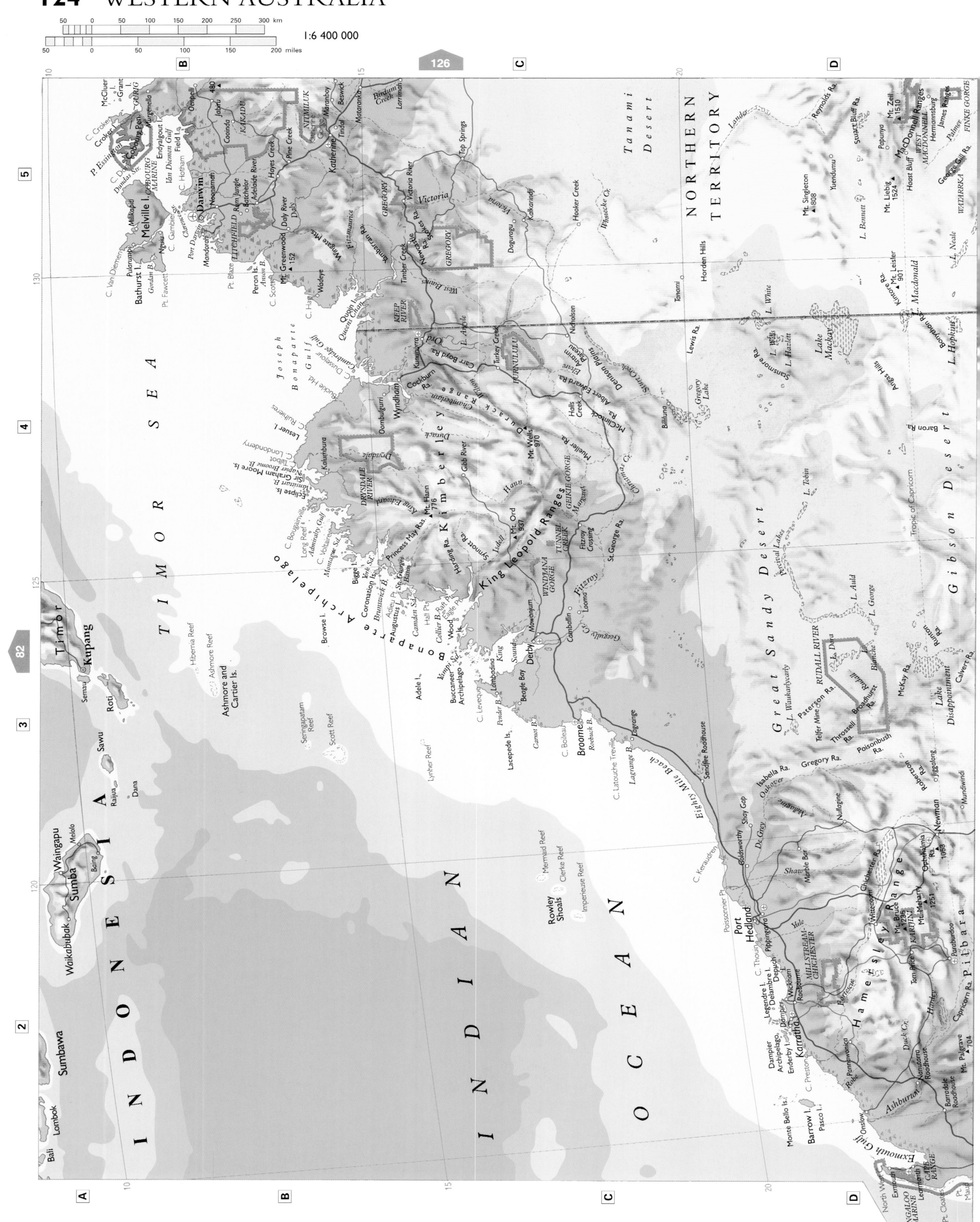

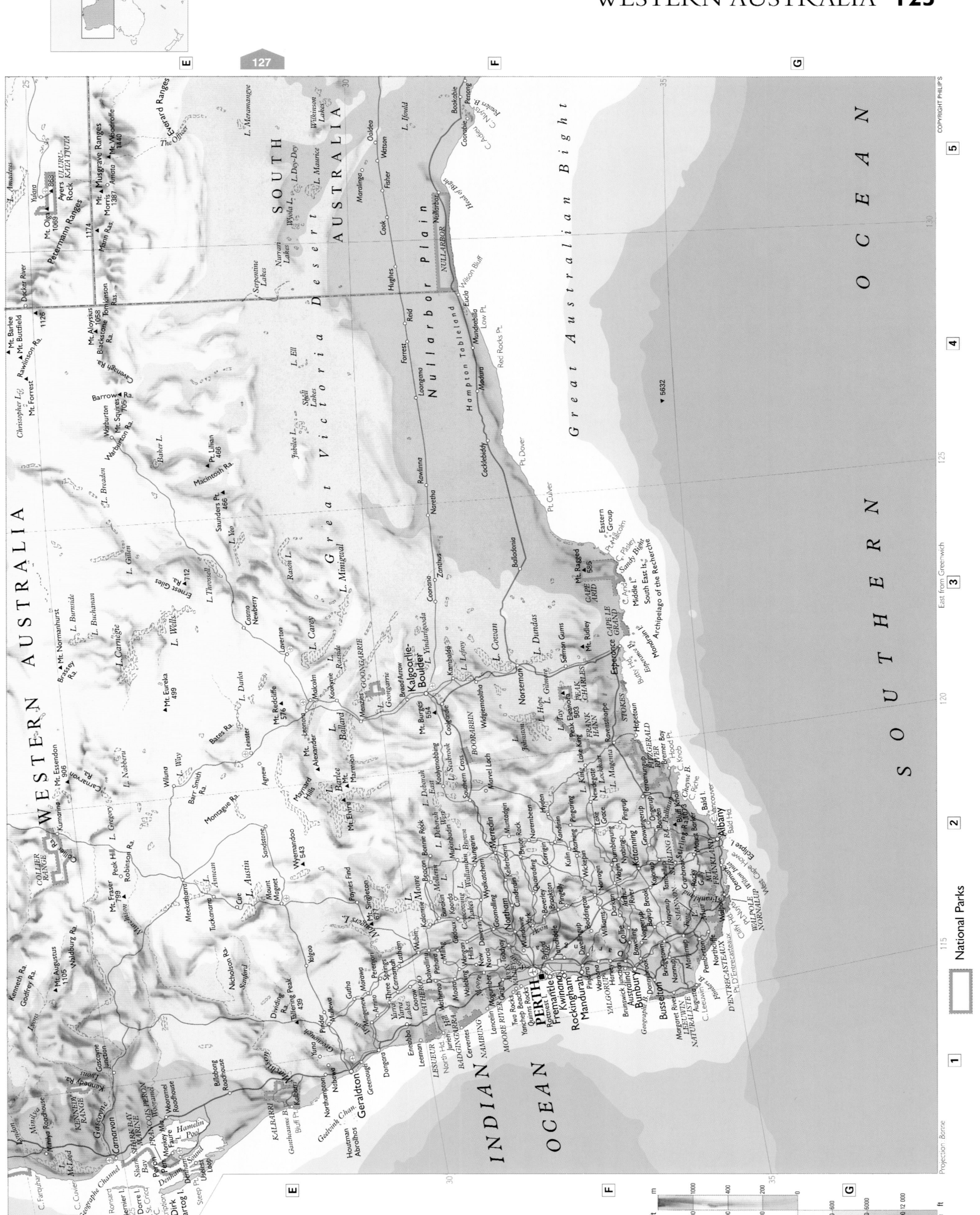

National Parks

E 5

F 5

G 5

E 4

F 4

G 4

3

2

1

WESTERN AUSTRALIA

SOUTH AUSTRALIA

Great Victoria Desert

Nullarbor Plain

NULLARBOR

Hampton Tableland

Great Australian Bight

SOUTHERN OCEAN

INDIAN OCEAN

OCEAN

PERTH

Fremantle

Rockingham

Mandurah

Bunbury

Busselton

Geraldton

Carnarvon

Albany

Kalgoorlie-Boulder

Esperance

Norseman

Kambalda

Coolgardie

Menzies

Leonora

Laverton

Wiluna

Meekatharra

Mount Magnet

Ayers Rock

Uluru-Kata Tjuta

Mt. Olga 1069

Petermann Ranges

Mt. Woodroffe 1440

Amata

Morris 1387

The Officer

Everard Ranges

Mann Ra.

Mt. Augustus 1105

Mt. Bruce

Projection: Bonne

COPYRIGHT PHILIP'S

East from Greenwich

ft 3000 1200 600 0 200-600 2000/6000 4000/12 000 m
m 1000 400 200 0 200-600 2000 1 000 ft

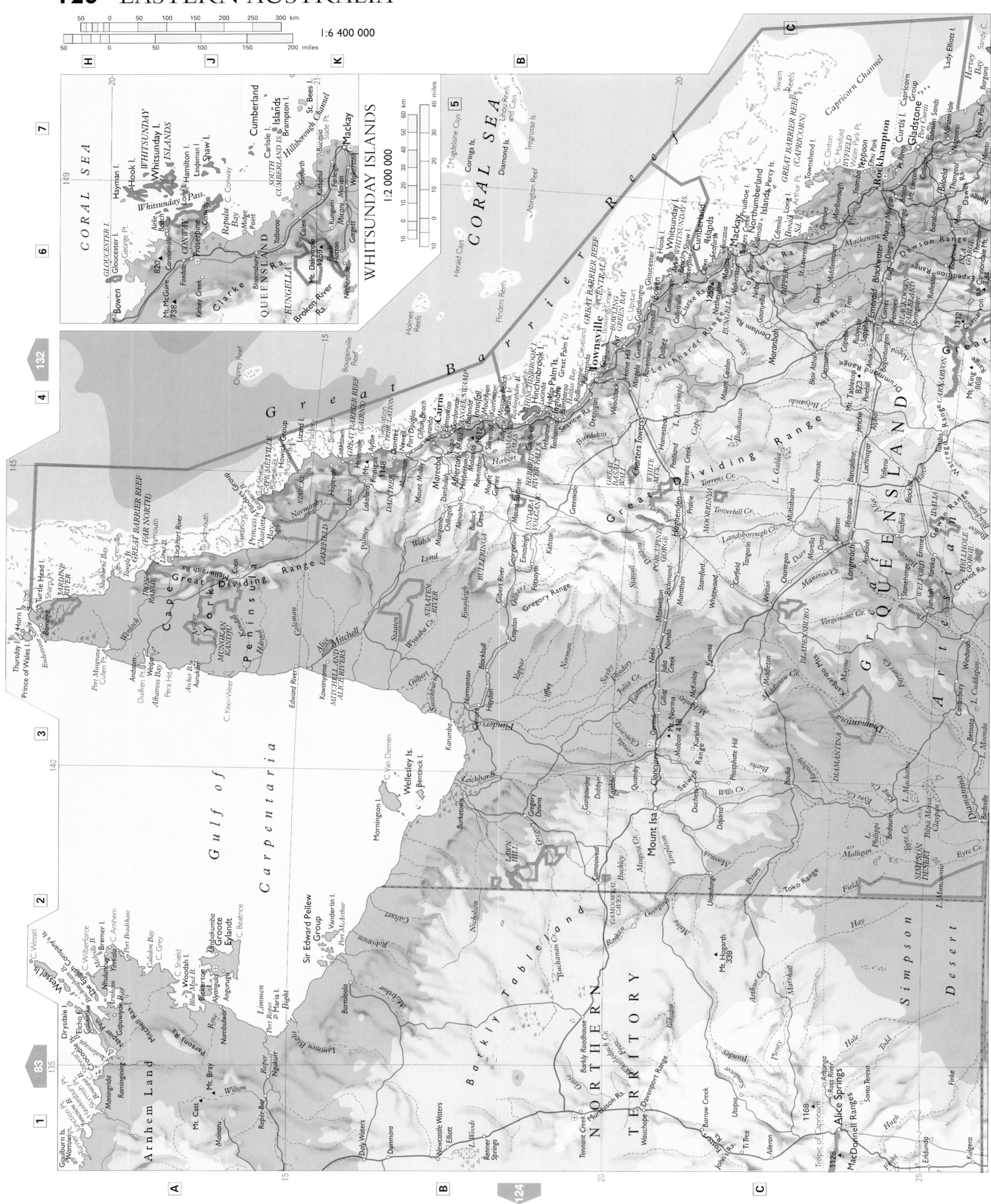

1:6 400 000

50 0 50 100 150 200 250 300 km
50 0 50 100 150 200 miles

WHITSUNDAY ISLANDS

1:2 000 000

10 0 10 20 30 40 50 60 km
10 0 10 20 30 40 miles

CORAL SEA

QUEENSLAND

NORTHERN TERRITORY

Gulf of Carpentaria

Arnhem Land

Barkly Tableland

Simpson Desert

Great Dividing Range

Cape York Peninsula

Great Barrier Reef

Townsville

Cairns

Mackay

Rockhampton

Gladstone

Mount Isa

Cloncurry

Alice Springs

Tropic of Capricorn

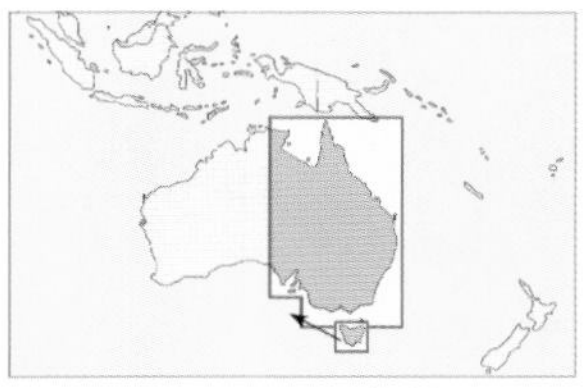

COPYRIGHT PHILIP'S

TASMAN SEA

SOUTH AUSTRALIA

NEW SOUTH WALES

QUEENSLAND

(AUSTRALIAN CAPITAL TERRITORY)

BRISBANE
Gold Coast
Tweed Heads
Newcastle
SYDNEY
Gosford
Wollongong
CANBERRA
MELBOURNE
ADELAIDE

Darling Range
Great Dividing Range
Grey Range
Barrier Range
Flinders Ranges
Gammon Ranges
Blue Mts.
Snowy Mts.
Mt. Kosciuszko 2230

LAKE EYRE
Lake Eyre
Lake Eyre South
Lake Torrens
Lake Gairdner
Lake Frome
Lake Blanche
Lake Callabonna
Lake Gregory

Bundaberg
Maryborough
Hervey Bay
Gympie
Caloundra
Caboolture
Ipswich
Toowoomba
Warwick
Grafton
Coffs Harbour
Port Macquarie
Taree
Tamworth
Armidale
Dubbo
Orange
Bathurst
Parkes
Forbes
Goulburn
Wagga Wagga
Albury
Wodonga
Shepparton
Bendigo
Ballarat
Geelong
Warrnambool
Mount Gambier
Horsham
Mildura
Broken Hill
Bourke
Cobar
Port Augusta
Port Pirie
Whyalla
Port Lincoln
Eyre Peninsula
Yorke Peninsula
Kangaroo I.

Spencer Gulf
Gulf St. Vincent

Darling River
Murray River
Murrumbidgee R.
Cooper Cr.

King Island
Flinders Island
Furneaux Group
Cape Barren I.
Deal I.
Hogan Group
Kent Group
Wilsons Promontory

Bass Strait

National Parks

East from Greenwich

on same scale

TASMANIA

Launceston
Devonport
Burnie
Hobart
Bass Strait
King Island
Flinders Island
Furneaux Group
Cape Barren I.

Projection Bonne

20 0 20 40 60 80 100 120 140 160 km
1:3 200 000
20 0 20 40 60 80 100 miles

2 **3** **4** 127 **5**

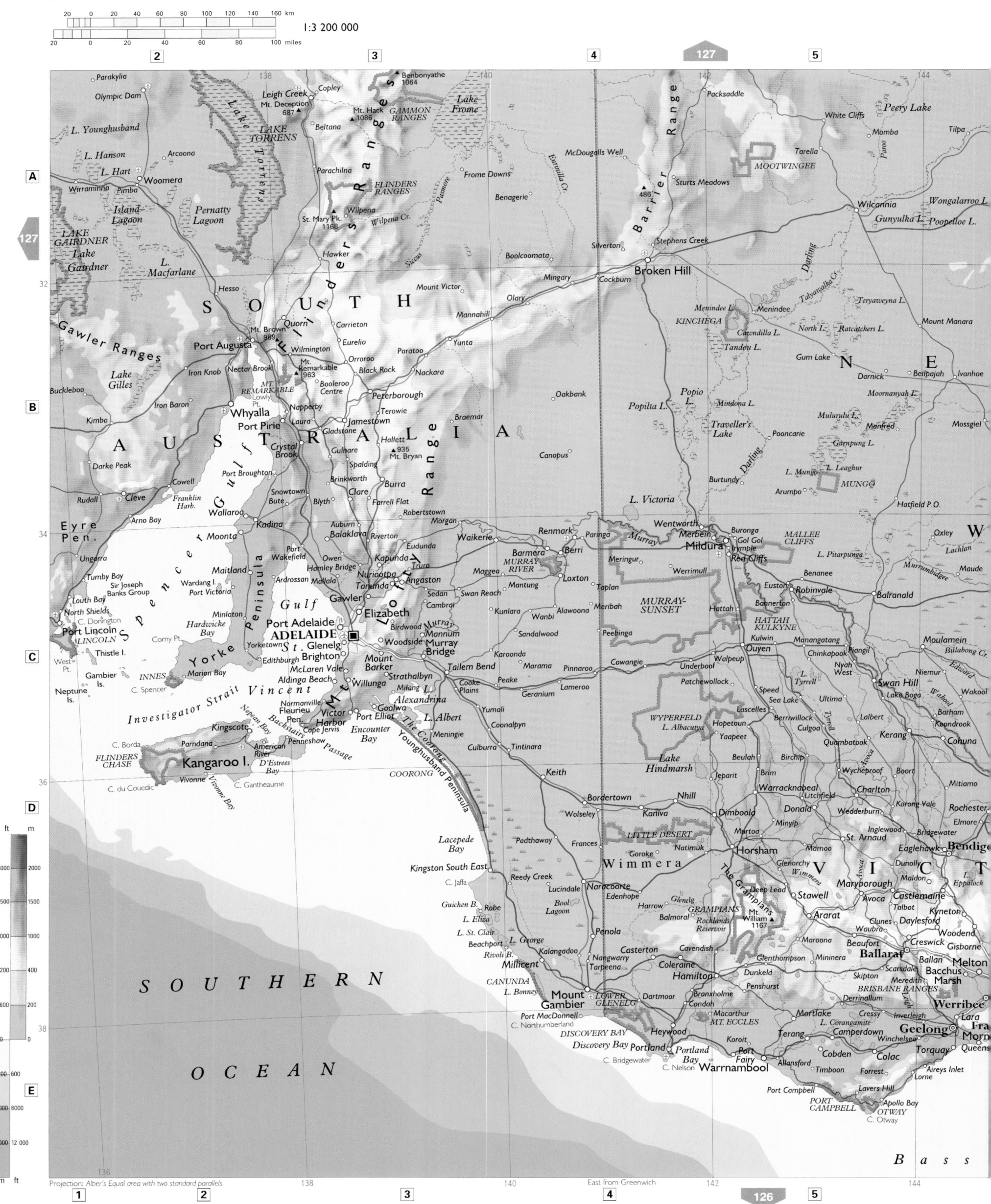

A 127

ft m
6000 2000
4500 1500
3000 1000
1200 400
600 200
0 0
200 600
2000 6000
4000 12 000
m ft

Projection: Alber's Equal area with two standard parallels

1 **2** **3** 140 East from Greenwich **4** 142 **5** 144

126

Parakylia
Olympic Dam
Leigh Creek
Mt. Deception 687
Copley
Benbonyathe 1064
Packsaddle
White Cliffs
Peery Lake
L. Younghusband
Beltana
Mt. Hack 1086
GAMMON RANGES
Lake Frome
MOOTWINGEE
Momba
Tilpa
L. Hanson
Arcoona
Parachilna
McDougalls Well
Tarella
L. Hart
FLINDERS RANGES
Eurilla Cr.
Sturts Meadows
Wilcannia
Wirraminna
Woomera
Pimba
Wilpena
Frome Downs
486
Wongalarroo L.
Island Lagoon
Pernatty Lagoon
St. Mary Pk. 1168
Wilpena Cr.
Benagerie
Barrier Range
Poopelloe L.
LAKE GAIRDNER
Lake Gairdner
Hesso
Hawker
Sicus
Boolcoomata
Silverton
Stephens Creek
Gunyulka L.
L. Macfarlane
Mount Victor
Broken Hill
SOUTH
Quorn
Carrieton
Mannahill
Cockburn
Menindee L.
Menindee
Teryaweyna L.
Gawler Ranges
Mt. Brown 989
Wilmington
Eurelia
Olary
North L.
Ratcatchers L.
Mount Manara
Port Augusta
Orroroo
Paratoo
Yunta
KINCHEGA
Cawndilla L.
Tandou L.
Gum Lake
Iron Knob
Nectar Brook
Mt. Remarkable 963
Black Rock
Nackara
Oakbank
Popilta L.
Darnick
Beilpajah
Ivanhoe
Lake Gilles
Booleroo Centre
Peterborough
Canopus
Popio L.
Mindona L.
Mulurulu L.
Moornanyah L.
Mossgiel
Buckleboo
MT REMARKABLE Lowly Pt.
Napperby
Terowie
Braemar
Traveller's Lake
Manfred
Whyalla
Laura
Jamestown
Pooncarie
Garnpung L.
Kimba
Port Pirie
Gladstone
Hallett 935 Mt. Bryan
Burtundy
L. Mungo
L. Leaghur
MUNGO
Darke Peak
AUSTRALIA
Crystal Brook
Gulnare
Spalding
Arumpo
Hatfield P.O.
Iron Baron
Port Broughton
Brinkworth
Clare
Burra
L. Victoria
Cowell
Snowtown
Robertstown
Wentworth
Buronga
MALLEE CLIFFS
Oxley
Rudall
Cleve
Franklin Harb.
Bute
Blyth
Farrell Flat
Morgan
Renmark
Paringa
Murray
Merbein
Gol Gol
W
Arno Bay
Kadina
Auburn
Balaklava
Riverton
Waikerie
Barmera
Berri
Meringur
Mildura
Red Cliffs
L. Pitarpunga
Eyre Pen.
Moonta
Owen
Eudunda
Kapunda
MURRAY RIVER
Loxton
Taplan
Werrimull
Benanee
Murrumbidgee
Maude
Ungarra
Wardang I.
Port Wakefield
Hamley Bridge
Truro
Maggea
Swan Reach
Kunlara
Wanbi
MURRAY-SUNSET
Euston
Robinvale
Balranald
Tumby Bay
Sir Joseph Banks Group
Maitland
Mallala
Nuriootpa
Tanunda
Angaston
Sedan
Cambrai
Meribah
Hattah
Lachlan
Louth Bay
Minlaton
Ardrossan
Port Victoria
Gawler
Birdwood
Murray
Alawoona
Sandalwood
HATTAH KULKYNE
Kulwin
Manangatang
Moulamein
North Shields
Gulf
Elizabeth
Woodside
Murray Bridge
Karoonda
Cowangie
Underbool
Ouyen
Chinkapook
Piangil
Billabong Cr.
Port Lincoln
LINCOLN
Hardwicke Bay
Port Adelaide
ADELAIDE
St. Glenelg
Brighton
Tailem Bend
Marama
Peake
Pinnaroo
Walpeup
Speed
Nyah West
Niemir
Edward
West Pt.
Corny Pt.
Edithburgh
Mount Barker
Strathalbyn
Cooke Plains
Geranium
Lameroo
Patchewollock
Sea Lake
L. Tyrrell
Ultima
Swan Hill
Lake Boga
Wakool
Gambier Is.
INNES
Marion Bay
Aldinga Beach
McLaren Vale
Willunga
Milang
L. Alexandrina
Yumali
Coonalpyn
WYPERFELD
Lascelles
Berriwillock
Lalbert
Kerang
Cohuna
Neptune Is.
C. Spencer
Yorke
Victor Harbor
Port Elliot
Goolwa
L. Albert
Meningie
Tintinara
L. Albacutya
Hopetoun
Yaapeet
Beulah
Birchip
Quambatook
Koondrook
Normanville
Fleurieu Pen.
Cape Jervis
Encounter Bay
The Coorong
Culburra
Lake Hindmarsh
Jeparit
Brim
Warracknabeal
Wycheproof
Boort
Mitiamo
Kingscote
Backstairs
Penneshaw
Passage
Younghusband Peninsula
Keith
Bordertown
Nhill
Dimboola
Donald
Wedderburn
Korong Vale
Charlton
Rochester
Elmore
C. Borda
Parndana
American River
D'Estrees Bay
COORONG
Wolseley
Kaniva
Minyip
St. Arnaud
Inglewood
Bridgewater
Kangaroo I.
FLINDERS CHASE
C. du Couedic
Vivonne Bay
Lacepede Bay
Padthaway
Frances
LITTLE DESERT
Goroke
Natimuk
Horsham
Marnoo
Maryborough
Dunolly
Maldon
Bendigo
Eaglehawk
C. Gantheaume
Kingston South East
C. Jaffa
Reedy Creek
Lucindale
Naracoorte
Edenhope
Harrow
Balmoral
WIMMERA
Wimmera
Glenorchy
Deep Lead
Stawell
Avoca
Castlemaine
Kyneton
VICT
Guichen B.
Robe
L. Eliza
Bool Lagoon
GRAMPIANS
Rochlands Reservoir
William 1167
Ararat
Clunes
Waubra
Daylesford
Woodend
L. Eppalock
L. St. Clair
Beachport
Penola
Maroona
Beaufort
Creswick
Gisborne
Rivoli B.
Kalangadoo
Casterton
Cavendish
Glenthompson
Mininera
Ballarat
Ballan
Bacchus Marsh
Melton
Millicent
Nangwarry
Tarpeena
Coleraine
Hamilton
Dunkeld
Skipton
Meredith
Derrinallum
Werribee
CANUNDA
L. Bonney
Mount Gambier
LOWER GLENELG
Dartmoor
Branxholme
Condah
Macarthur
MT. ECCLES
Mortlake
L. Corangamite
Camperdown
Cressy
Inverleigh
Geelong
Lara
Fra
Morn
Port MacDonnell
C. Northumberland
DISCOVERY BAY
Heywood
Terang
Koroit
Cobden
Colac
Winchelsea
Torquay
Queens
Discovery Bay
Portland
Portland Bay
C. Bridgewater
C. Nelson
Port Fairy
Warrnambool
Koroit
Port Campbell
Allansford
Timboon
Forrest
Aireys Inlet
Lorne
PORT CAMPBELL
Lavers Hill
Apollo Bay
OTWAY
C. Otway

SOUTHERN OCEAN

B a s s

National Parks

10 0 20 40 60 80 100 120 140 km
10 0 20 40 60 80 100 miles

1:2 800 000

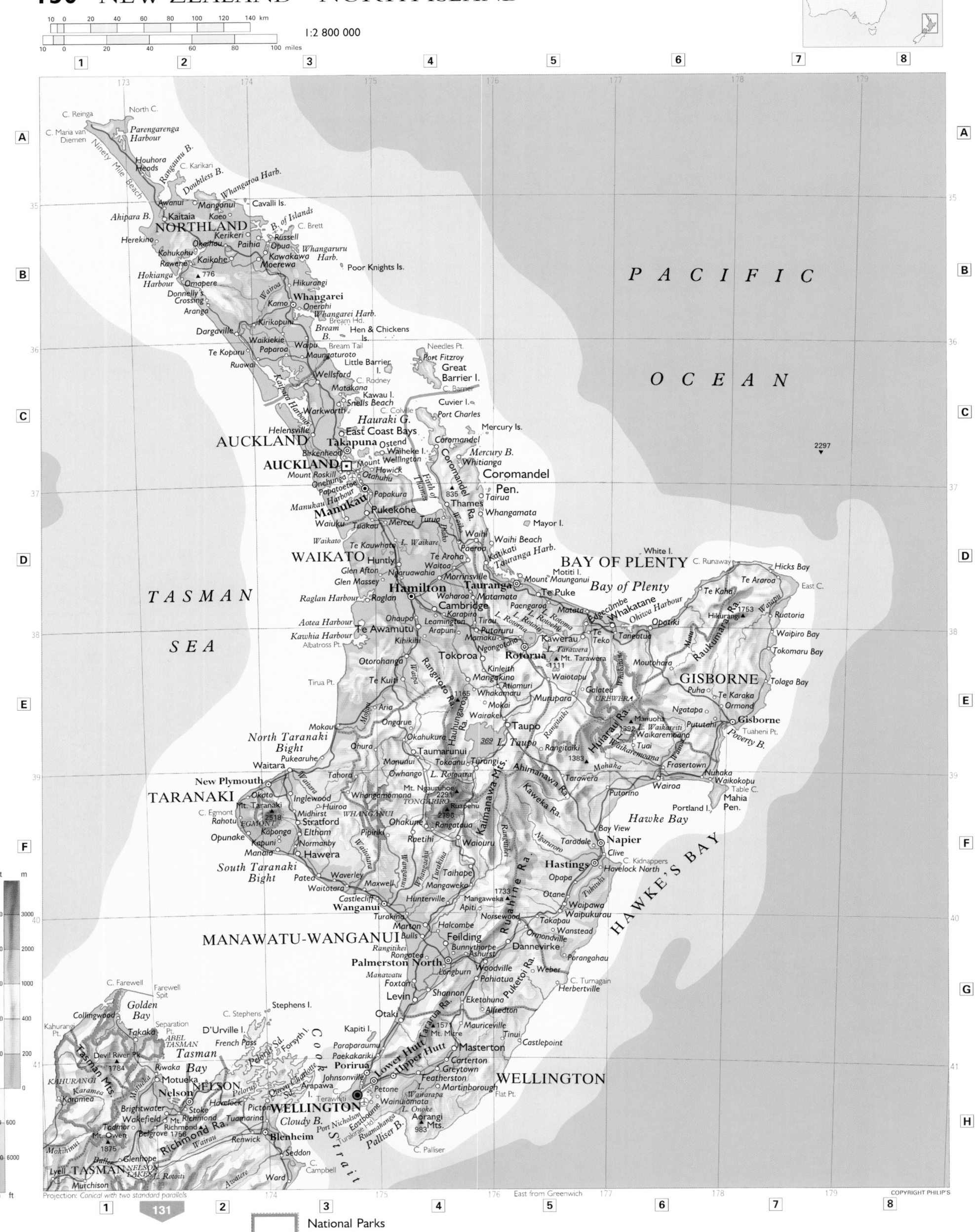

National Parks

COPYRIGHT PHILIP'S

1:2 800 000

10 0 20 40 60 80 100 120 140 km
10 0 20 40 60 80 100 miles

130

Grid columns: 1 2 3 4 5 6 7 8 9
Grid rows: A B C D E F G H

167 168 169 170 171 172 173 174

TASMAN SEA

C. Farewell
Farewell Spit
Golden Bay
Collingwood
Takaka
Kahurangi Pt.
Separation Pt.
C. Stephens
Stephens I.
D'Urville I.
French Pass
Forsyth I.
Jackson
Pelorus Sd.
Queen Charlotte Sd.
Arapawa I.
Tasman Bay
ABEL TASMAN
Riwaka
Motueka
NELSON
Nelson
Moutere
KAHURANGI
Tasman Mts.
1784
Karamea
Karamea
Brightwater
Wakefield
Stoke
Havelock
Picton
Cloudy B.
Tuamarina
Blenheim
Karamea Bight
Waimarie
Seddonville
Granity
Waimangaroa
Millerton
Westport
C. Foulwind
Mokihinui
Matiri Ra.
Mt. Owen 1875
Glenhope
Tadmor
Belgrove
Mt. Richmond 1756
Richmond
Richmond Ra.
Renwick
Wairau
MARLBOROUGH
Seddon
C. Campbell
Ward
Wharanui
Lyell
Buller
Inangahua
Murchison
Gowan
Rotoroa
L. Rotoroa
TASMAN
Mt. Travers 2337
NELSON LAKES
St. Arnaud
St. Arnaud Ra.
L. Rotoiti
Molesworth
Awatere
Clarence
Inland Kaikoura Ra.
Tapuaenuku 2885
Seaward Kaikoura Ra.
Manakau 2610
Kaikoura
PAPAROA
Paparoa Ra.
Reefton
Ikamatua
Mt. Franklyn 2359
Spenser Mts.
Grey
Blackball
Runanga
Greymouth
Taramakau
Brunner
Mt. Ajax 1832
Hanmer Springs
Lewis Pass
Kaikoura Pen.
Hokitika
Kumara
Jacksons
Otira
Otira Gorge
Mt. Crossley 1972
ARTHUR'S PASS
Arthur's Pass 926
L. Kaniere
Ross
L. Sumner
Culverden
Waiau
Hurunui
Parnassus
Domett
Scargill
WESTLAND BIGHT
Wanganui
Abut Hd.
Whataroa
Harihari
Mt. Murchison 2400
Whitcombe Pass
Mt. Arrowsmith 2795
Lake Coleridge
L. Coleridge
Springfield
Sheffield
Waikari
Waipara
Amberley
Ashley
L. Sefton
Oxford
Rangiora
Kaiapoi
Belfast
Riccarton
New Brighton
CHRISTCHURCH
Sumner
Lyttelton
Banks Pen.
Little River 919
Akaroa
Akaroa Harbour
Pegasus Bay
Okarito
L. Mapourika
Whataroa
Gillespies Pt.
WESTLAND
Bruce B.
Titiira Hd.
Mt. Tasman 3497
Aoraki Mount Cook 3753
Mount Cook
Mt. Taylor 2330
Mount Somers
Rakaia
Methven
Darfield
Whitecliffs
Highbank
Rolleston
Hornby
Leeston
Lincoln
Southbridge
L. Ellesmere
Jackson
Jackson Hd. B.
Okuru
Haast
Haast
Glenmary 2609
Mt. Sefton
L. Tekapo
Lake Tekapo
Two Thumbs Ra.
South Branch
Rangitata
Geraldine
Hinds
Ashburton
Tinwald
CANTERBURY PLAINS
Canterbury Bight
Cascade Pt.
SOUTHERN ALPS
Ben Ohau Ra.
Barrier Ra.
L. Pukaki
Mackenzie Plains
Fairlie
Winchester
Temuka
Pleasant Point
Timaru
Awarua Pt.
Awarua B.
MOUNT ASPIRING
Mt. Aspiring 3030
Young Ra.
Hunter
L. Ohau
Lake Pukaki
Ohau
Waitaki Plains 1863
Benmore Pk.
Kirkliston Ra.
The Hunters Hills
Hunter
St. Andrews
Studholme
Waimate
Yates Pt.
Milford Sd.
Mt. Tutoko 2097
Olivine Ra.
Humboldt Mts.
Mt. Earnslaw 2819
Richardson Mts.
Harris Mts.
Pisa Ra.
Wanaka
L. Wanaka
Hawea
Hawea Flat
L. Hawea
Dunstan Mts.
Hawkdun Ra.
St. Bathan's 2087
Mt. St. Bathan's
Hakataramea
Kurow
Duntroon
Waihao
Morven
Glenavy
Tokarahi
Maheno
Waihao Downs
Ngapara Downs
Mitre Peak 1692
Milford Sd.
Sutherland Falls
Franklin Mts.
Glenorchy
Arrowtown
Queenstown
Stuart Mts.
Bligh Sound
George Sound
Caswell Sound
Charles Sound
Thompson Sd.
Secretary I.
Doubtful Sd.
Dagg Sd.
Livingstone Mts.
L. Te Anau
Te Anau
Eyre Mts.
Garvie Mts.
The Remarkables
2342
Double Cone 2324
L. Wakatipu
Kingston
Cromwell
Clyde
Alexandra
Rough Ridge
Naseby
Ranfurly
Windsor
Pukeuri
Oamaru
Maheno
OTAGO
Hyde
Dunback
Hampden
Palmerston
Shag Pt.
Waikouaiti
Waikouaiti Downs
Breaksea Sd.
Resolution I.
Dusky Sd.
FIORDLAND
Murchison Mts.
Mt. Lyall 1905
Kepler Mts.
L. Manapouri
Manapouri
Hunter Mts.
Mossburn
Lumsden
Waikaia
Monowai
L. Monowai
Birchwood
Dipton
Ohai
Nightcaps
Roxburgh
Middlemarch
Sutton
Miller's Flat
Beaumont
Warrington
Port Chalmers
Otago Harbour
Mosgiel
DUNEDIN
Allanton
St. Clair
Otago Pen.
C. Saunders
Providence
Chalky Inlet
Preservation Inlet
Puysegur Pt.
Caroline Pk. 1722
L. Hauroko
Tuatapere
Orawia
Otautau
Winton
Gore
Mataura
Hedgehope
Edendale
Wyndham
Waipahi
Clinton
Balclutha
Stirling
Kaitangata
Owaka
Nugget Pt.
Milton
Waihola
L. Waihola
SOUTHLAND
Clifden
Cameron Mts.
Kaherekoau Mts.
Waiau
Waimea Plain
Waikaka
Kelso
Tapanui
Lawrence
Clutha
Mataura
Riversdale
Waikaia
Long Pt.
Chaslands Mistake
Solander I.
Te Waewae B.
Pahia Pt.
Riverton
Wallacetown
Glenham
Makarewa
Thornbury
South Invercargill
Invercargill
Fortrose
Tokanui
Toetoes
Waipapa Pt.
Bluff
Bluff Harbour
Foveaux Str.
Mt. Anglem 980
Codfish I.
Ruapuke I.
Mason B.
Halfmoon Bay
Paterson Inlet
Doughboy B.
Southwest C.
Port Pegasus
Stewart I.

PACIFIC OCEAN

Projection: Conical with two standard parallels

East from Greenwich

COPYRIGHT PHILIP'S

National Parks

Elevation scale (ft / m):
9000 / 3000
6000 / 2000
3000 / 1000
1200 / 400
600 / 200
0 / 0
200 / 600
2000 / 6000
4000 / 12 000

50   0   50   100   150   200 km
1:5 200 000
50   0   50   100   150 miles

COPYRIGHT PHILIP'S

A   B   C   D   E   F   G

NORTH SOLOMONS

P A C I F I C   O C E A N

Lyra Reef
Nuguria Is.
Sable I.
Kilinailau Is.
C. L'Averdy
Tinputz
Buka I.
Hutjena
Mt. Bibi
2715
Torokina
Sohano
Kunua
Kieta
Arawa
Panguna
Buin
Boku
Matupena Pt.
Toki
Mt. Takuan
2251
Shortland I.
Treasury Is.
(Solomon Is.)

Bougainville I.

S o l o m o n   I s l a n d s

Bougainville Trench   9140

NORTH MATTHIAS GROUP
Mussau I.
Tabalo
Eloaua I.
Emirau I.

NEW HANOVER
Tingwon Group

St. Matthias Group

N E W   I R E L A N D

Lyra Reef
Green Is.
C. Harpan
Lemankoa

Tanga Is.
Boang I.
Malendok I.
Feni Is.
Ambitle I.
Babase I.
Tatau I.
Simberi I.
Tabar
Tabar Is.
Lihir Group
Lihir I.
Namatanai
Konos
Schleinitz 1481
Lakuramau
Kavieng
North C.
Tench I.

Lihir
Hans Meyer Ra.
Verron Ra.
Lambom
C. St. George
St. George's Channel

B i s m a r c k   A r c h i p e l a g o

Ysabel Channel

B i s m a r c k   S e a

N E W   B R I T A I N
Watom I.
Rabaul
Kokopo
Keravat
Gazelle Peninsula
Mt. Snewit 2438
Ulamona
Lolobau I.
Talasea
Kimbe Bay
Kimbe
Hoskins
Ewasse
Willaumez Pen.
2027
Whiteman Ra.
Nukuhu
Kandrian
Gasmata
C. Anukur
C. Kabungu

Whirlwind Reef
Witu Is.
Garove I.
Unea I.
Ottilien Reef
Waku
Sag Sog
Arawe Is.
Aumo I.
C. Gloucester
Gloucester

W E S T   N E W   B R I T A I N

W E S T   S O L O M O N   S e a

8320

B i s m a r c k   S e a

Admiralty Islands
Hermit Is.
Ninigo Group
Aua I.
Wyvulu I.
Kaniet
Sori
Lorengau
Momote
Manus I.
Rambutyo I.
Tong I.
Baluan I.
Los Negros I.
South West Pt.

M A N U S

Circular Reef
Sherburne Reef

Tolokiwa I.
Sakar I.
Umboi I.
Long I.
Siassi Is.
Tami Is.
Crown I.
Saidor
Finschhafen
C. Cretin
Vitiaz Strait
Dampier Strait
Wasu

M A D A N G
C. Girgir
Wotam
Bogia
Manam I.
Karkar I.
Bagabag I.
Matuka I.
Madang
Bibi
Amimon
Adelbert Range
Finisterre Ra.
Dumpu
Amanberg
Ajome

N E W   G U I N E A
W E S T   S E P I K
Wutung
Vanimo
Pagei
Aitape
Sissano
Torricelli Mts.
Lumi
Nuku
Amanab
Green River
West Ra.
Mt. Capella 3993
Mt. Aiyang 3505
Victor Emanuel Ra.
Telefomin
Oksapmin
Mt. Ayamaru
Tabubil

E A S T   S E P I K
Wewak
Vokeo I.
Muschu I.
Kairiru I.
Walis I.
Tarawai I.
Dagua
Maprik
Dreikikir
Boikin
Bainyik
Ambunti
Pagwi
Angoram
Chambri
April
Yuat
Keram
Ramu
Sepik
Karawari

E N G A
Wabag
Wapenamanda
Laiagam
Porgera
Lake Kopiago

W E S T E R N   H I G H L A N D S
Mount Hagen
Baiyer River
Banz
Minj
Mt. Giluwe 4368
Tambul
Kagua

S O U T H E R N   H I G H L A N D S
Mendi
Nipa
Koroba
Tari
Kutubu
L. Kutubu
Mt. Bosavi 2507
Muller
Lake Murray

C H I M B U
Kerowagi
Kundiawa
Kagawa
Mt. Wilhelm 4508
Crater Mt. 3647
4359
Gumine
3231

E A S T E R N   H I G H L A N D S
Goroka
Mt. Michael
Henganofi
Kainantu
Okapa
Obura

P A P U A   N E W   G U I N E A

M O R O B E
Saruwaged Ra.
Kabwum
Mt. Bangeta 4121
Erap
Lae
Markham
Nadzab
Bulolo
Wau
Menyamya
Kaindi
Aseki
Mumeng
Wasu
Huon Peninsula
Huon Gulf
Salamaua
Lasanga I.

B o w u t u   M t s.

N O R T H E R N
Mt. Albert Edward 3989
Mt. Victoria 4035
Popondetta
Buna
Gona
Afore
Sibium
Kokoda
Mt. Suckling 3676
Sariri
Dyke Ackland Bay
Tufi
C. Nelson

G U L F
Kerema
Ihu
Baimuru
Kikori
Kukipi
Iokea
Malalaua

W E S T E R N
Daru
Balimo
Morehead
Lake Murray
Bensbach
Fly
Strickland
Aramia
Bamu
Turama
Kiunga
Tabubil
Wasua
Aworro
Wando
Emeti
Nomad

G u l f   o f   P a p u a

D e c e p t i o n   B a y

Blackwood Bay

Bristow I.
Parama I.
Kiwai I.
Daru
Bobo
Wabuda I.
Purutu I.
Umuda I.

C E N T R A L
Port Moresby
Owen Stanley Range
Mt. Scratchley
Kwikila
Hula
Hood Pt.
Kalo
Kapa Kapa
Abau
Domara
Mullins Harbour

T o r r e s   S t r a i t

INDONESIA

AUSTRALIA
Cape York Peninsula
Saibai I.
Boigu I.
(Australia)
Badu I.
Moa I.
Wednesday I.
Thursday I.
Horn I.
Prince of Wales I.
Turtle Head I.
C. York
Sharp Pt.
Endeavour Strait
Shelburne Bay
Temple Bay
C. Grenville
Wenlock
Cullen Pt.

Great Barrier Reef

C o r a l   S e a

Louisiade Archipelago
Pocklington Reef
Rossel I.
Tagula
Tagula I.
Sudest I.
Misima I.
Bwagaoia
The Calvados Chain
Tawa Tawa Mai Reef
Deboyne Is.
Conflict Group
Egum Atoll
Woodlark I.
Guasopa
Marshall Bennett Is.
Madau I.
Kulumadau
Kiriwina I.
Kaileuna I.
Losuia
Vakuta I.
Ktava I.
Trobriand Islands
Lusancay Is. and Reefs
Kitava I.

D'Entrecasteaux Islands
Goodenough
Bolubolu
Fergusson I.
Sanaroa I.
Normanby I.
Nuakata I.
Basilaki I.
Dumoulin Is.
East C.
Samarai
Ahioma
Alotau
Suau
Mt. Singapore 2883

M I L N E   B A Y

Ward Hunt Strait
C. Ward Hunt

Projection: Lambert Conformal Conic
East from Greenwich

-- -- Tracks

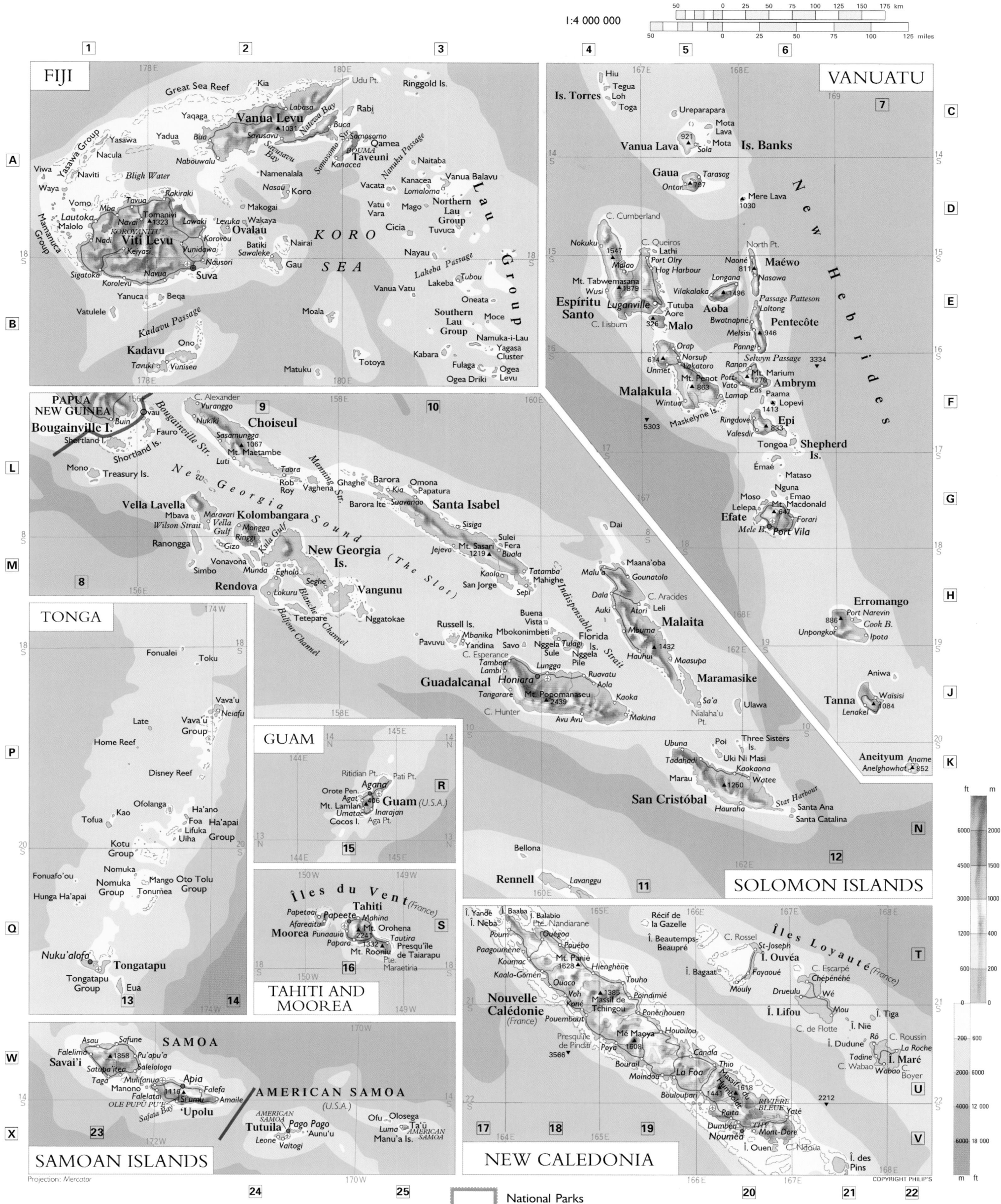

1:4 000 000

50   0   25   50   75 100 125 150 175 km
50   0   25   75   100   125 miles

FIJI

Great Sea Reef   Kia   Udu Pt.   Ringgold Is.
Yaqaga   Labasa   Rabi
Vanua Levu   1031▲   Buca   Samosomo
Savusavu   Samosomo Str.   Qamea
Yadua   Bua   BOUMA   Taveuni
Nabouwalu   Kanacea   Naitaba
Namenalala   Nasau   Koro   Vacata   Vanua Balavu
Makogai   Wakaya   Kanacea   Lomaloma
Levuka   Nairai   Cicia   Northern Lau Group
Ovalau   Batiki   Sawaleke   Tuvuca
Viti Levu   Nausori   Gau   Nayau
Suva   Lakeba Passage   Tubou
Lakeba
Vanua Vatu   Oneata
Moala   Moce
Southern Lau Group   Namuka-i-Lau   Yagasa Cluster
Kadavu   Ono   Kabara   Fulaga
Tavuki   Vunisea   Totoya   Ogea Levu   Ogea Driki
Matuku

KORO SEA

Lau Group

VANUATU

Hiu   167 E   168 E   169
Is. Torres   Tegua   Loh   Toga   Ureparapara   7
Mota Lava   Mota
Vanua Lava   921   Sola   Is. Banks
Gaua   Tarasag   Mere Lava   1030
Ontar   797
C. Cumberland
Nokuku   1547   C. Queiros   Lathi   North Pt.   Naoné   811   Maéwo
Malao   Port Olry   Longana   Nasawa
Mt. Tabwemasana   Hog Harbour   Vilakalaka   1496   Passage Patteson
1879   Wusi   Tutuba   Aoba   Loltong
Espíritu Santo   Luganville   Aore   Bwatnapné   Melsisi   946   Pentecôte
C. Lisburn   326   Malo   Panngi
Orap   Norsup   Selwyn Passage   3334
674   Unmet   Lakatoro   Ranon   Mt. Marium   1278
Malakula   Vato   Ambrym
863   Lamap   Eas   Paama
Wintua   Lopevi   1413
Maskelyne Is.   Ringdove   Epi   833
5303   Valesdir
Tongoa   Shepherd Is.
Émaé   Mataso
Moso   Nguna
Efate   Lelepa   Emao   Mt. Macdonald   647
Mele B.   Port Vila   Forari

New Hebrides

PAPUA NEW GUINEA   C. Alexander   9   10
Buin   Ovau   Vuranggo   Nukiki   158 E   160 E
Bougainville I.   Fauro   Choiseul
Shortland I.   Sasamungga   1067
Mono   Shortland Is.   Mt. Maetambe
Treasury Is.   Luti   Taora
New Georgia Sound   Rob   Vaghena Str.   Ghaghe   Barora   Kia   Omona   Papatura
Vella Lavella   Roy   Barora Ite   Suavanao
Mbava   Maravari   Kolombangara   Santa Isabel
Vella Gulf   Mongga   Ringgi   Sisiga
Ranongga   Vonavona   Kula Gulf   Jejevo   Sulei   Fera
Gizo   Munda   New Georgia Is.   Mt. Sasari   Buala
Simbo   Egholo   Kaolo   1219   Tatamba   Mahighe
Rendova   Lokuru   Seghe   Vangunu   San Jorge   Sepi
Tetepare   Ngatokae   Dai
Blanche Channel   Russell Is.   Buena Vista   Maana'oba   Gounatolo
Balfour Channel   Mbanika   Mbokonimbeti   Malu'u   Dala   C. Aracides
Pavuvu   Yandina   Savo   Nggela Sule   Auki   Atori   Leli
Florida   Nggela Pile   Malaita   Mbuma   1432
C. Esperance   Tambea   Tulagi   Ruavatu   Hauhui   Maasupa
Guadalcanal   Lambi   Lungga   Aola   Maramasike
Honiara   Tangarare   Mt. Popomanaseu   Kaoka   Sa'a   Ulawa
2439   Makina   Nialaha'u Pt.
C. Hunter   Avu Avu

Indispensable Strait

The Slot

TONGA   174 W
Fonualei   Toku
Vava'u   Neiafu   Vava'u Group
Late   Home Reef
Disney Reef
Tofua   Ofolanga   Ha'ano
Kao   Foa   Lifuka   Ha'apai Group
Kotu Group   Uiha
Nomuka   Ha'apai
Fonuafo'ou   Nomuka Group   Mango   Oto Tolu Group
Hunga Ha'apai   Tonumea
Nuku'alofa   Tongatapu
Tongatapu Group   Eua
13   14

GUAM   14 N   145 E
Ritidian Pt.   Pati Pt.
Orote Pen.   Agana
Agat   406   Guam (U.S.A.)
Mt. Lamlan   Inarajan   R
Umatac   Cocos I.   Aga Pt.
13 N   144 E   145 E   13 N
15

TAHITI AND MOOREA   150 W   149 W
Îles du Vent (France)
Papetoai   Papeete   Tahiti
Afareaitu   Mahina
Moorea   Punaauia   Mt. Orohena   S
Papara   2241   Tautira
1332   Presqu'île de Taiarapu
Mt. Rooniu   Pte.
Maraetiria   Pte.
16

Ubuna   Poi   Three Sisters Is.
Tadahadi   Uki Ni Masi   Aniwa   Waisisi
Marau   Kaokaona   Tanna   1084
1250   Watee   Lenakel
San Cristóbal   Haurahu   Star Harbour   Santa Ana   Santa Catalina
Aneityum   Aname   12
Anelghowhat   852   N
Bellona   SOLOMON ISLANDS
Rennell   160 E   Lavanggu   11
162 E

Erromango
886   Port Narevin   Cook B.
Unpongkor   Ipota

SAMOA
Asau   Safune
Falelima   1858   Pu'apu'a
Savai'i   Satupa'itea   Salelologa
Taga   Mulifanua   Apia   Falefa
Manono   1116   Siumu   Amaile
Falelatai   'Upolu
OLE PUPU PU'E   AMERICAN SAMOA (U.S.A.)
Safata Bay
AMERICAN SAMOA   Ofu   Olosega
Tutuila   Pago Pago   Ta'ü
Leone   'Aunu'u   Luma   Manu'a Is.
Vaitogi   AMERICAN SAMOA
23

SAMOAN ISLANDS

Projection: Mercator

NEW CALEDONIA   165 E   166 E   167 E   168 E
Î. Yandé   Î. Baaba   Balabio   Récif de la Gazelle
Î. Neba   Poum   Pte. Nandiarane
Paagoumène   Ouégoa   Î. Beautemps-Beaupré
Koumac   Pouébo   C. Rossel   Î. Ouvéa
Kaala-Gómen   Mt. Panié   Hienghène   St-Joseph   Fayaoué   Mouly
Ouaco   1628   Touho   Î. Bagaat   Drueulu
Voh   Koné   Poindimié   Wé   Î. Lifou
Nouvelle Calédonie (France)   1385   Ponérihouen   C. Escarpé   Chépénéhé
Massif de Tchingou   Houailou   C. de Flotte   Î. Nié
Pouembout   Mé Maoya   Î. Tiga
Presqu'île de Pindaï   1608   Canala   Rô   Î. Dudune
Poya   C. Roussin
3566   Bourail   Thio   Tadine   La Roche
Moindou   Massif Humboldt   1618   C. Wabao   Î. Maré
La Foa   1618   RIVIÈRE BLEUE   2212   C. Boyer
Boulouparis   1441   Yaté   U
Dumbéa   THY   Mont-Dore
Nouméa   Païta   V
Î. Ouen   C. Ndoua   Î. des Pins

COPYRIGHT PHILIP'S

National Parks

ft   m
6000   2000
4500   1500
3000   1000
1200   400
600   200
0   0
200   600
2000   6000
4000   12 000
6000   18 000
m   ft

RUSSIA

KAZAKHSTAN
MONGOLIA
CHINA
Bering Sea
Sea of Okhotsk
Sea of Japan
JAPAN
NORTH KOREA
SOUTH KOREA
TOKYO
Yellow Sea
East China Sea
TAIWAN
PHILIPPINES
South China Sea
INDONESIA
MALAYSIA
BORNEO
PAPUA NEW GUINEA
NORTHERN MARIANAS (U.S.A.)
GUAM (U.S.A.)
FEDERATED STATES OF MICRONESIA
MARSHALL IS.
PALAU
NAURU
SOLOMON IS.
TUVALU
VANUATU
FIJI
SAMOA
TONGA
NEW CALEDONIA
AUSTRALIA
NEW ZEALAND
Coral Sea
Tasman Sea
INDIAN OCEAN
PACIFIC

MOSKVA, Yekaterinburg, Tomsk, Novosibirsk, Irkutsk, Chita, Astana (Aqmola), Semey, Ulaanbaatar, Khabarovsk, Blagoveshchensk, Harbin, Changchun, SHENYANG, Vladivostok, Sapporo, Hakodate, Okhotsk, Petropavlovsk-Kamchatskiy, Poluostrov Kamchatka, Komandorskiye Ostrova (Russia)

BEIJING, TIANJIN, Taiyuan, Dalian, SOUL, Nagoya, Kyōto, Osaka, Yokohama, Sendai, Lanzhou, Xi'an, Nanjing, CHONGQING, Wuhan, SHANGHAI, HANGZHOU, Changsha, Kunming, Fuzhou, Taipei, GUANGZHOU, HONG KONG, Macau, Hanoi, Hainan

DELHI, Kanpur, KOLKATA (Calcutta), DHAKA, BURMA, Mandalay, Rangoon, BANGKOK, THAILAND, CAMBODIA, Phnom Penh, VIETNAM, Thanh Pho Ho Chi Minh, MANILA, Luzon, Mindoro, Samar, Palawan, Mindanao, SINGAPORE, JAKARTA, Surabaya, Palembang, Ujung Pandang

Midway Is. (U.S.A.), Lisianski I. (U.S.A.), Wake I. (U.S.A.), Saipan, Yap, Koror, Truk, Pohnpei, Palikir, Tarawa, Gilbert Is., Butaritari, Banaba, Howland I. (U.S.A.), Baker I. (U.S.A.), Phoenix Is., Enderbury, Abariringa

PORT MORESBY, New Guinea, New Britain, New Ireland, Bougainville, Rabaul, Lae, Honiara, Guadalcanal, Santa Cruz Is., Espiritu Santo, Port Vila, Nouméa, Suva, Nuku'alofa, Fongafale, Apia, Tokelau Is. (N.Z.)

Darwin, Cairns, Townsville, Rockhampton, Brisbane, Alice Springs, Mount Isa, L. Eyre, Perth, Geraldton, Albany, Adelaide, Melbourne, Sydney, Canberra, Mt Kosciuszko 2237, Hobart, Tasmania, Auckland, Wellington, Christchurch, Dunedin, Invercargill, Aoraki Mt Cook 3753

Bay of Bengal, Andaman Sea, Java Sea, Flores Sea, Banda Sea, Arafura Sea, Gulf of Carpentaria, Great Australian Bight, Celebes Sea, Sulu Sea, Timor, EAST TIMOR

Mariana Trench 11,022, Japan Trench 10,554, Kuril Trench 10,542, Tonga Trench 10,822, Kermadec Trench 10,047, Mindanao Trench 10,497

Projection: Mollweide's Homolographic East from Greenwich

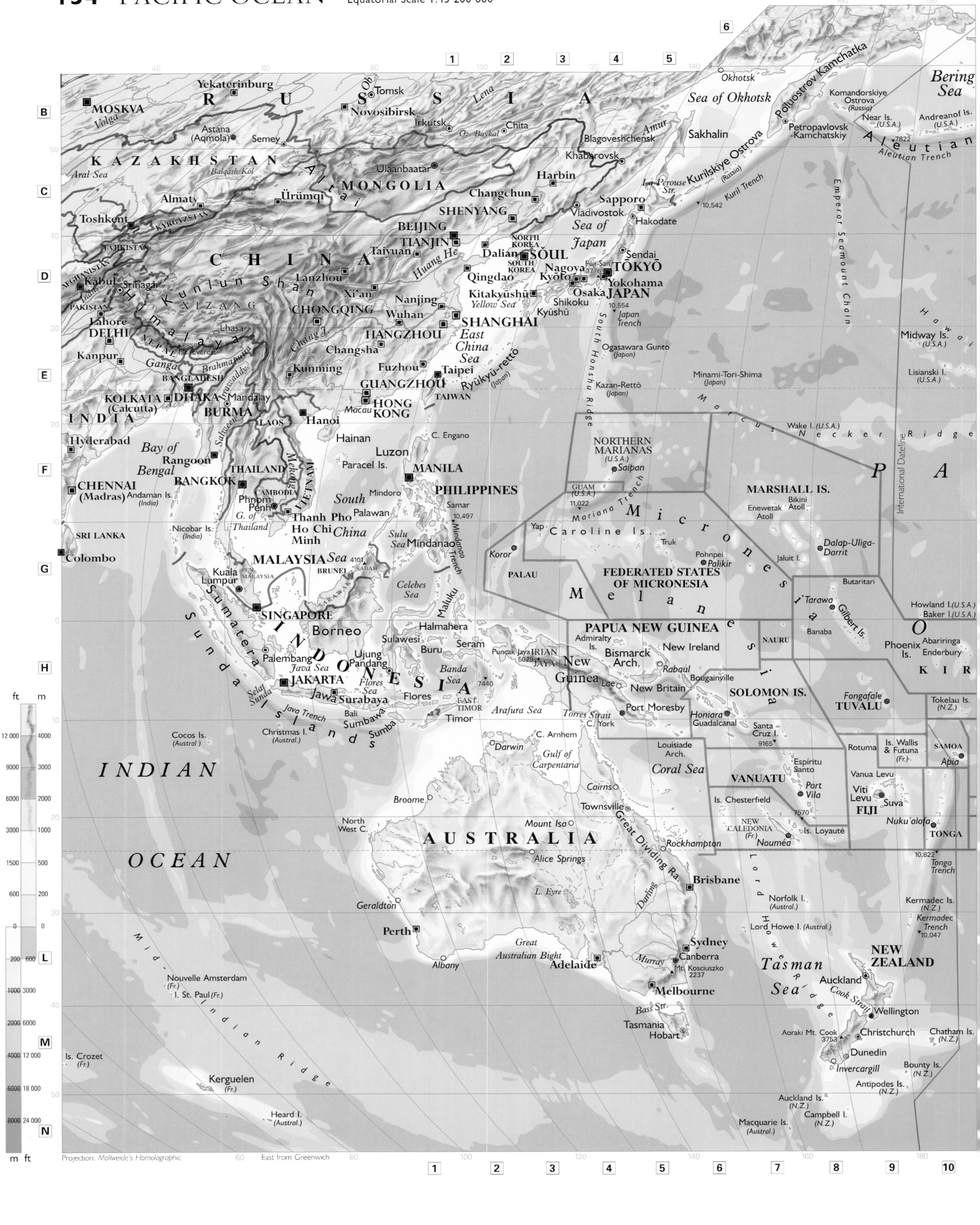

Arctic Circle

ALASKA
(U.S.A.)
Anchorage
5959
Juneau

Bristol Bay
Gulf of Alaska
Is. (U.S.A.)
Prince of Wales I.
(U.S.A.) Prince Rupert
Queen Charlotte Is.
(Canada)

C A N A D A

Edmonton
L. Winnipeg
Newfoundland

Calgary
Winnipeg
Regina

Vancouver
Vancouver I.
Victoria
Seattle
Portland
Boise

L. Superior
Québec
St. John's

N O R T H

St. Lawrence
Montréal
Ottawa
Minneapolis
Toronto
L. Huron
L. Michigan
Detroit
L. Ontario
Buffalo
Boston

Salt Lake
City
Denver
CHICAGO
Pittsburgh
L. Erie
Cincinnati
NEW YORK CITY
PHILADELPHIA
Baltimore
Washington D.C.

A T L A N T I C

C. Mendocino
Sacramento
SAN FRANCISCO
4418
Snake
Colorado

UNITED STATES
Kansas City
St. Louis
Oklahoma City
Memphis
Atlanta
C. Hatteras

Bermuda
(U.K.)

O C E A N

LOS ANGELES
San Diego
Phoenix
Dallas
Houston
San Antonio
New
Orleans
Jacksonville

Guadalupe
(Mex.)
Ciudad
Juárez
Baja California
Golfo de California
Monterrey
Gulf of Mexico
Miami
Florida Str.
BAHAMAS

Sargasso Sea

Tropic of Cancer

6741

C. San Lucas

M E X I C O

La Habana
CUBA

West Indies

Honolulu
Oahu
4205
HAWAIIAN IS.
(U.S.A.)
Hawaii

Is. Revilla Gigedo
(Mex.)
Guadalajara
5610
MEXICO
Puebla
Mérida
7680
HAITI
Kingston
9200
DOMINICAN REP.
PUERTO
RICO
(U.S.A.)
Leeward
Is.

Johnston I.
(U.S.A.)

C I F I C

Acapulco
BELIZE
Canal de Yucatán
JAMAICA

Caribbean Sea
BARBADOS
Windward Is.

North West Christmas I. Ridge

Palmyra Is.
(U.S.A.)
Teraina
Tabuaeran
Kiritimati

I. Clipperton
(Fr.)
GUATEMALA
Guatemala
San Salvador
EL SALVADOR
HONDURAS
NICARAGUA
Managua
San José
COSTA RICA
Colón Panama
PANAMA
Barranquilla
San
Maracaíbo
Caracas
Orinoco
VENEZUELA

O C E A N

Jarvis I.
(U.S.A.)

I. del Coco
(Costa Rica)
Medellín
I. de Malpelo
(Colombia)
Bogotá
Cali
COLOMBIA

K I R I B A T I
Line Is.

Malden I.
Starbuck I.

Equator

Galápagos
(Ecuador)
Quito
ECUADOR

Amazonas

Tongareva

Pukapuka
Manihiki

Vostok I.
Caroline I.
(Millennium I.)
Flint I.

Is. Marquises

Guayaquil
C. Paliñas
Iquitos

BRAZIL

AMER.
SAMOA
(U.S.A.)
Suwarrow Is.

Is. de la
Société
Papeete Tahiti

Is. Tuamotu

Trujillo
6369
PERU

East Pacific Ridge

Niue
(N.Z.)
Cook Is.
(N.Z.)
Rarotonga

Austral / Seamount Chain

FRENCH POLYNESIA

Mururoa
Is. Tubuai
Rapa

Tuamotu Ridge

LIMA
Cuzco
L. Titicaca
Arequipa
Nevada Ancohuma
6550
6866
Peru-
Arica
Iquique
Chile
La Paz
BOLIVIA

Tropic of Capricorn

Ducie I.
Pitcairn I.
(U.K.)

Sala-y-Gómez
(Chile)
I. de Pascua
(Chile)

San Felix
(Chile)
San Ambrosio
(Chile)

8050
Trench
Antofagasta

San Miguel
de Tucumán

PARAGUAY
Asunción

URUGUAY

Arch. de
Juan Fernández
(Chile)
Valparaíso
Aconcagua
6962
Córdoba
Rosario
Porto
Alegre

SANTIAGO
Concepción
BUENOS
AIRES
Montevideo
Río de la Plata

Chile Rise

ARGENTINA

S O U T H

Patagonia

A T L A N T I C

Pacific-Antarctic Ridge

6212
O C E A N

Punta Arenas
Est. de Magallanes
Tierra del Fuego
Falkland Is.
(U.K.)
South Georgia
(U.K.)

C. de Hornos

100 0   200   400   600   800   1000   1200   1400 km
100 0   200   400   600   800   1000 miles

1:28 000 000

Projection: Bonne

West from Greenwich

COPYRIGHT PHILIP'S

Asia

ARCTIC OCEAN

Greenland

Iceland

Petermann's Peak 2940

Mt. Forel 3360

Denmark Strait

Bering Strait

St. Lawrence I.

C. Dezhneva

Bering Sea

Nunivak I.

Barrow Pt.

Beaufort Sea

C. Prince of Wales

Brooks Ra.

Alaska

Yukon

Mt. McKinley

Alaska Range

Alaska Peninsula

Kodiak I.

Gulf of Alaska

Mt. S. Elias 5489

Mt. Logan 5950

Arctic Circle

Mackenzie Mts.

Liard

Mackenzie

Back

Dubawnt

Porcupine

C. Bathurst

Banks I.

M'Clure Strait

Melville I.

Viscount Melville Sd.

Prince of Wales

Gulf of Boothia

Boothia Pen.

Victoria I.

Melville Pen.

Foxe Basin

Foxe Channel

Southampton I.

Parry Is.

Sverdrup Is.

Axel Heiberg I.

Queen Elizabeth Is.

Bathurst

Devon I.

Ellesmere I.

Kane Basin

Nares Str.

Lancaster Sd.

Somerset I.

Bylot I.

Baffin Bay

Baffin Island

Disko I.

Davis Strait

Cape Farewell

Cumberland Sd.

Frobisher B.

C. Chidley

Hudson Strait

Wolstenholme

Ungava Peninsula

Belcher Is.

C. Henrietta Maria

James Bay

Eastmain

Labrador Sea

Coast of Labrador

Hamilton Inlet

Str. of Belle Isle

Newfoundland

C. Race

Great Bear L.

Great Slave L.

Athabasca

Reindeer L.

Churchill

Nelson

L. Winnipeg

Saskatchewan

Peace

Athabasca

Fraser

Skeena

Stikine

Queen Charlotte Islands

Alexander Archipelago

Mt. Waddington 3994

Queen Charlotte Str.

Vancouver I.

Juan de Fuca Str.

C. Flattery

Mt. Rainier 4392

Columbia

Coast Ranges

Cascade Range

Mt. Shasta 4317

C. Blanco

C. Mendocino

Sacramento

Sierra Nevada

San Joaquin

Mt. Whitney 4418

Death Valley 86

Great Basin

Great Salt Lake

Wasatch Ra.

Snake

Selkirk Mts.

Mt. Robson 3954

Rocky Mountains

Mt. Elbert 4399

Blanca Peak 4378

Colorado Plateau

Grand Canyon

Colorado

Gila

Missouri

Platte

Arkansas

Red

Missouri

Mississippi

Great Plains

Great Lakes

L. Superior

L. Michigan

L. Huron

L. Erie

L. Ontario

Niagara Falls

Laurentian Plateau

Hudson

Ohio

Ozark Plateau

Cumberland Plateau

Tennessee

Allegheny Mts.

Blue Ridge Mts.

Appalachian Mts.

Mt. Washington 1917

Long I.

C. Cod

Nantucket I.

C. Sable

Nova Scotia

Cape Breton

Sable I.

B. of Fundy

Pt. Edward

Gulf of St. Lawrence

St. Lawrence

C. Charles

Chesapeake B.

C. Hatteras

Bermuda

NORTH ATLANTIC OCEAN

Sargasso Sea

Bahamas

Florida

Florida Strait

C. San Lucas

Gulf of California

Lower California

Guadalupe

PACIFIC OCEAN

Clarion Fracture Zone

Tropic of Cancer

Revilla Gigedo Is.

C. Corrientes

Western Sierra Madre

Eastern Sierra Madre

Mexican Plateau

Santiago

Balsas

Rio Grande

Mississippi River Delta

Gulf of Mexico

Gulf of Campeche

Yucatán

Yucatán Peninsula

Yucatán Channel

Popocatepetl 5452

Pico de Orizaba 5610

Isthmus of Tehuantepec

G. de Tehuantepec

Guatemala Trench

Central America

Cuba

Greater Antilles

Jamaica

Cayman Trough

Yucatán Basin

G. of Honduras

C. Gracias a Dios

Coco

G. of Panamá

G. of Darién

Hispaniola 9200

Puerto Rico

Antilles

Caribbean Sea

Colombian Basin

Sierra Nevada de Santa Marta 5800

Cord. de Mérida

G. de Venezuela

Maracaibo

Magdalena

Andes

ft   m

9000 3000
6000 2000
3000 1000
1500   500
600   200
200   0
0
200   600
1000 3000
2000 6000
4000 12000
6000 18000
8000 24000

m   ft

1:28 000 000

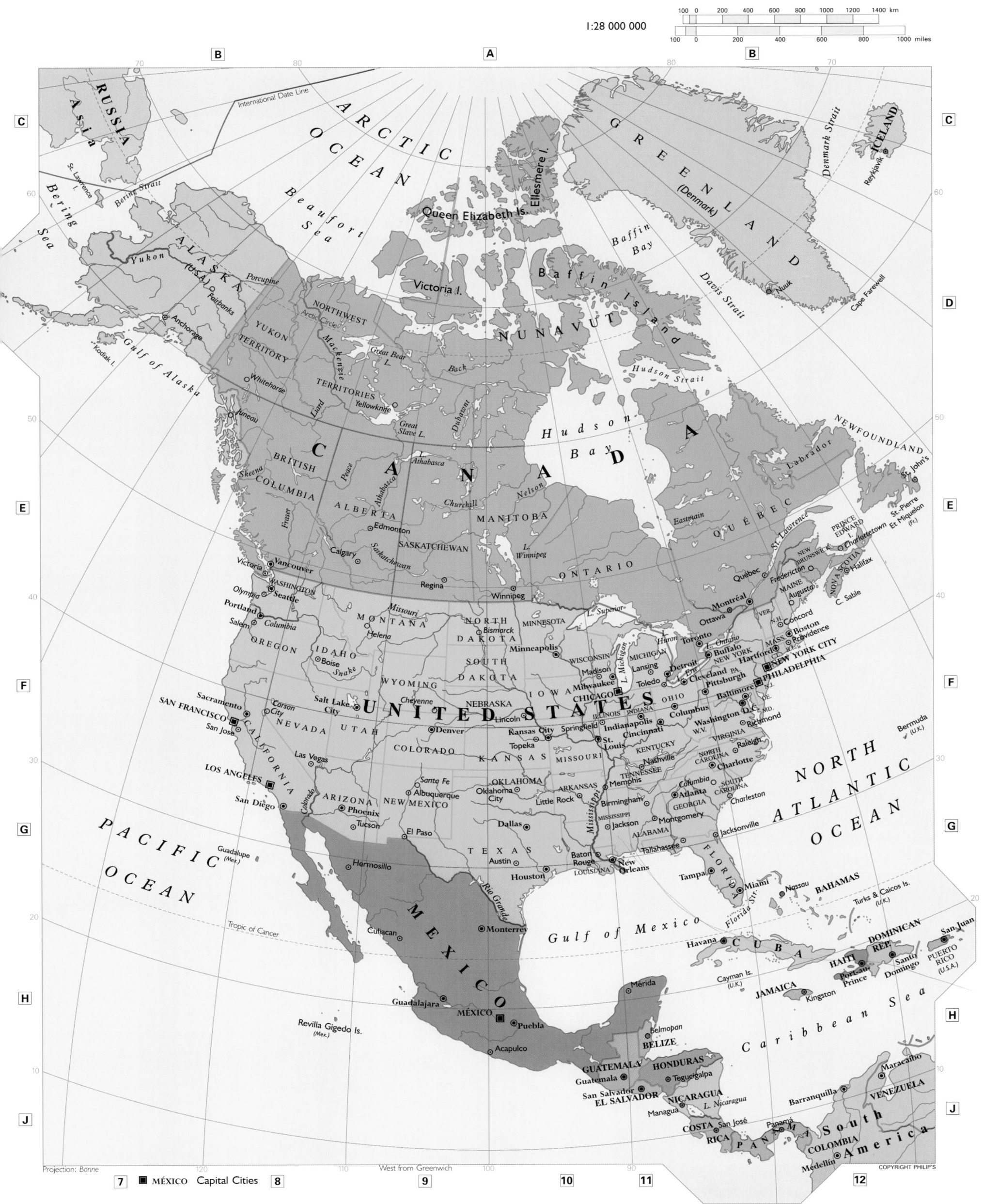

■ MÉXICO Capital Cities

1:12 000 000

Projection : Bonne

ALASKA
1:24 000 000

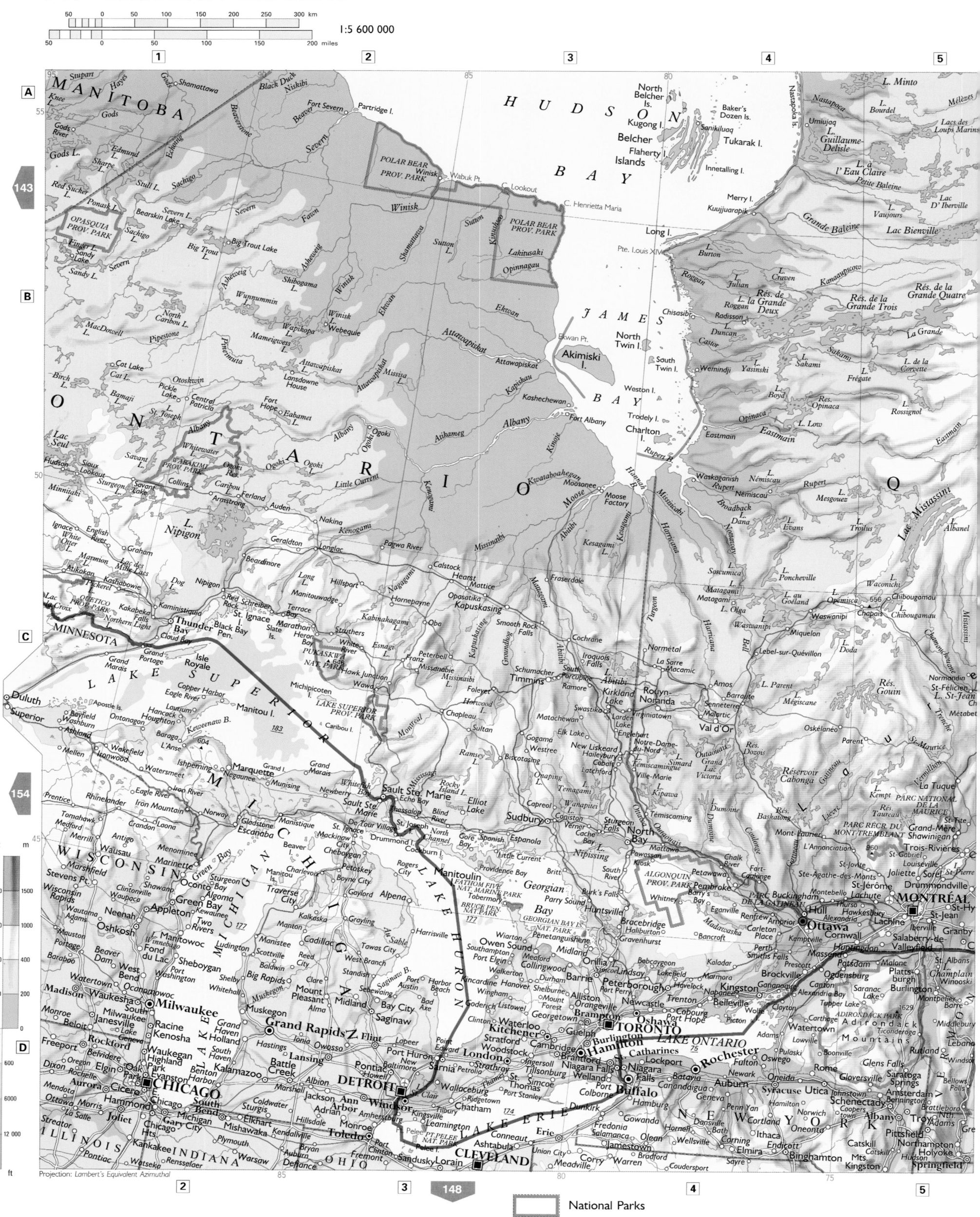

1:5 600 000

National Parks

Projection: Lambert's Equivalent Azimuthal

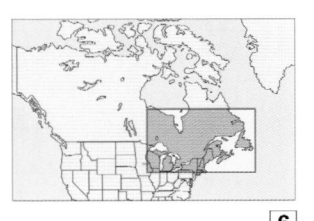

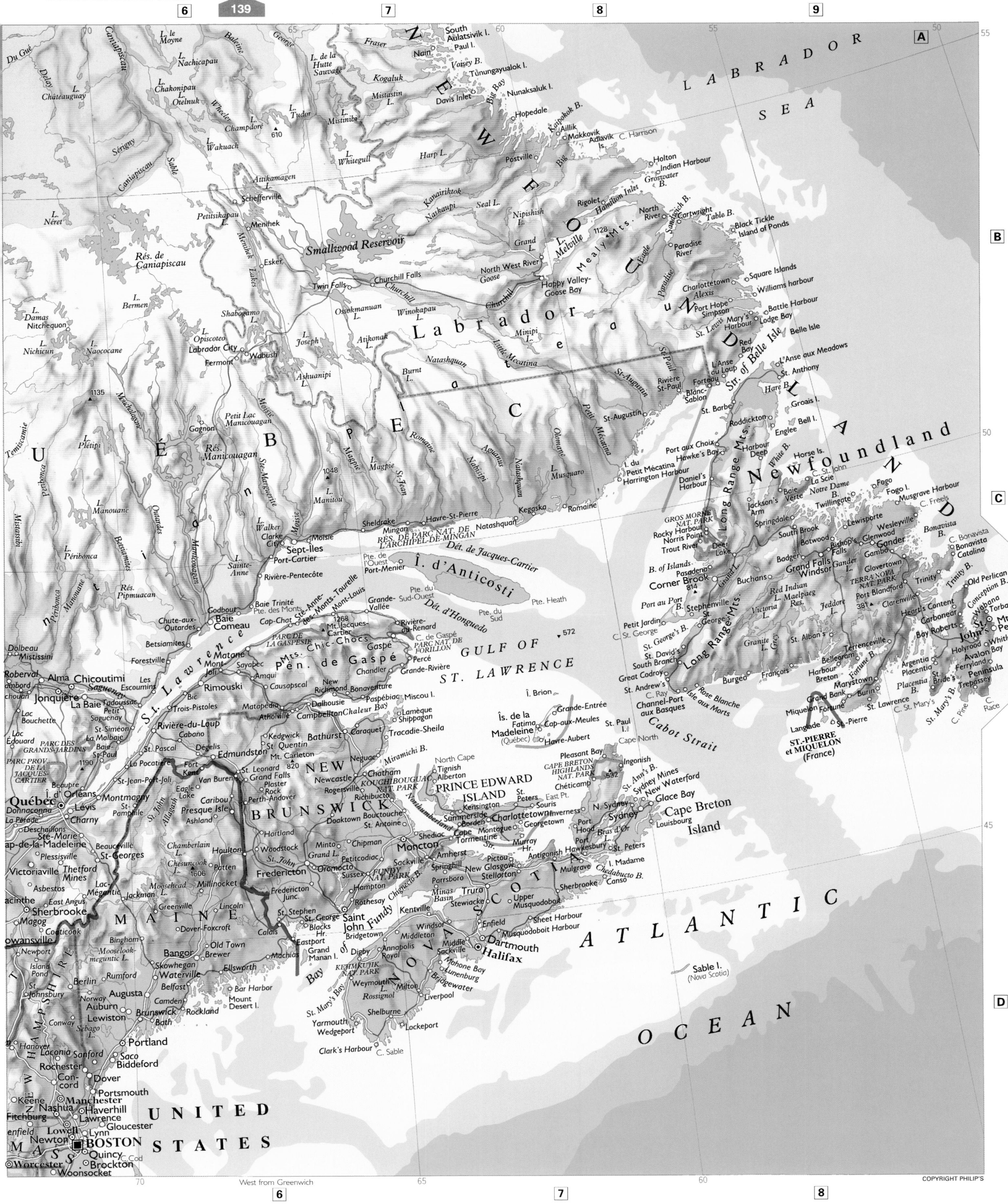
6
139
7
8
9
A
B
C
D
LABRADOR SEA
NEWFOUNDLAND
Labrador
QUÉBEC
GULF OF ST. LAWRENCE
ATLANTIC OCEAN
UNITED STATES
NEW BRUNSWICK
NOVA SCOTIA
PRINCE EDWARD ISLAND
MAINE
Newfoundland
Cape Breton Island
Î. d'Anticosti
Smallwood Reservoir
Rés. de Caniapiscau
Rés. Manicouagan
Pén. de Gaspé
Mts. Chic-Chocs
Mealy Mts.
Long Range Mts.
Cabot Strait
Str. of Belle Isle
Bay of Fundy
St. Lawrence
Schefferville
Labrador City
Wabush
Fermont
Churchill Falls
Happy Valley-Goose Bay
North West River
Nain
Hopedale
Makkovik
Postville
Cartwright
Sept-Îles
Port-Cartier
Baie Comeau
Havre-St-Pierre
Natashquan
Blanc-Sablon
St. Anthony
L'Anse aux Meadows
Corner Brook
Deer Lake
Stephenville
Grand Falls Windsor
Gander
Botwood
Lewisporte
Clarenville
Carbonear
St. John's
Mt. Pearl
Channel-Port aux Basques
Marystown
Burin
ST.-PIERRE et MIQUELON (France)
Miquelon
St.-Pierre
Îs. de la Madeleine (Québec)
Gaspé
Percé
Matane
Rimouski
Rivière-du-Loup
Chicoutimi
Jonquière
La Baie
Alma
Roberval
Québec
Lévis
Charny
Montmagny
Thetford Mines
Victoriaville
Sherbrooke
Magog
Campbellton
Bathurst
Edmundston
Chatham
Newcastle
Moncton
Fredericton
Saint John
St. Stephen
Charlottetown
Summerside
Souris
Sydney
Glace Bay
Louisbourg
Truro
Amherst
New Glasgow
Antigonish
Kentville
Windsor
Dartmouth
Halifax
Lunenburg
Bridgewater
Liverpool
Yarmouth
Digby
Sable I. (Nova Scotia)
Bangor
Augusta
Waterville
Portland
Lewiston
Auburn
Concord
Manchester
Nashua
Portsmouth
Dover
Lowell
Lawrence
Haverhill
Lynn
Gloucester
BOSTON
Quincy
Brockton
Worcester
Woonsocket
Fitchburg
Keene
C. Cod
Presque Isle
Houlton
Caribou
Calais
Eastport
Mt. Katahdin 1606
West from Greenwich
70
65
60
55
50
45

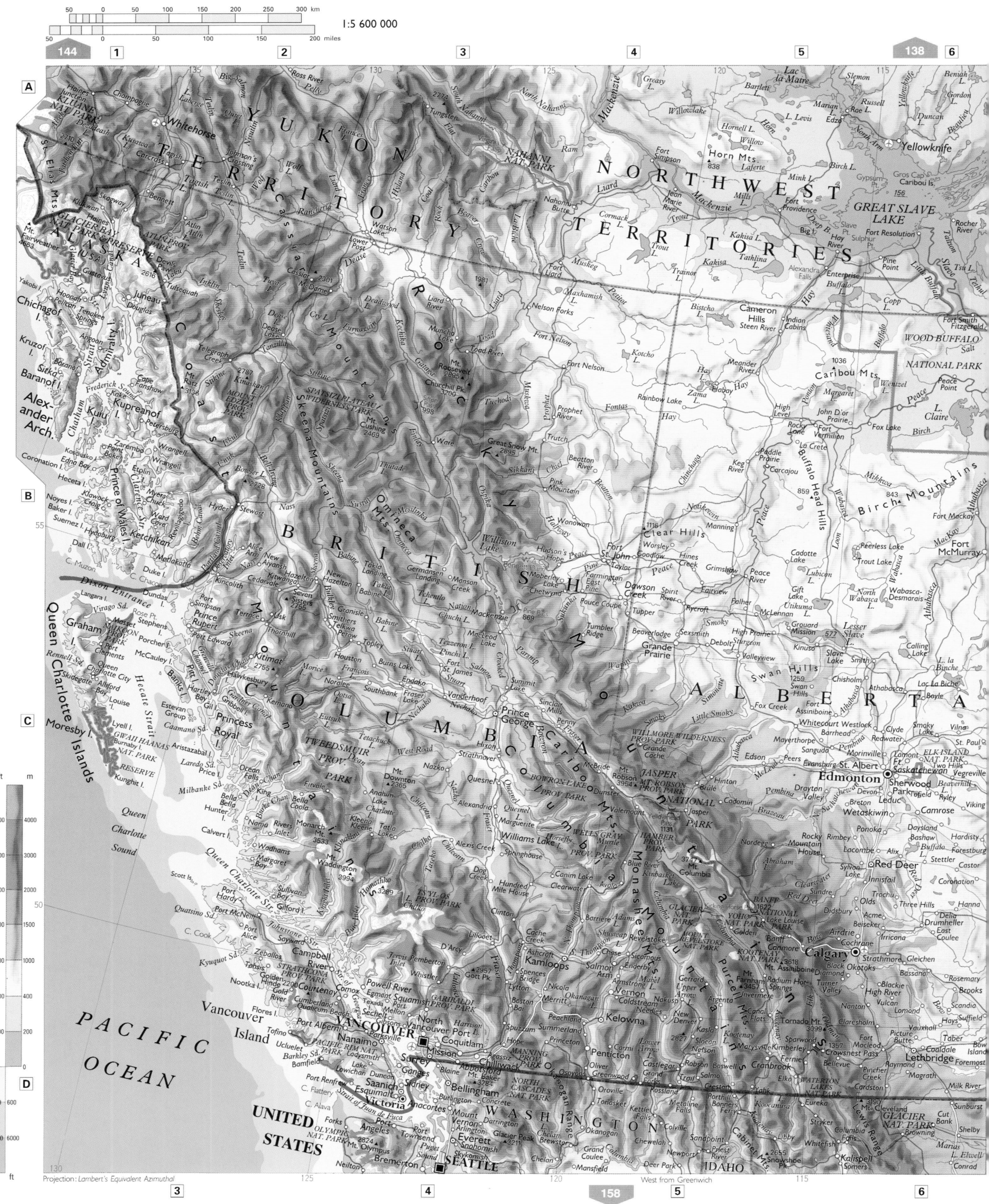

1:5 600 000

Projection: Lambert's Equivalent Azimuthal

West from Greenwich

HUDSON

BAY

NUNAVUT

SASKATCHEWAN

MANITOBA

ONTARIO

MONTANA

NORTH DAKOTA

MINNESOTA

National Parks

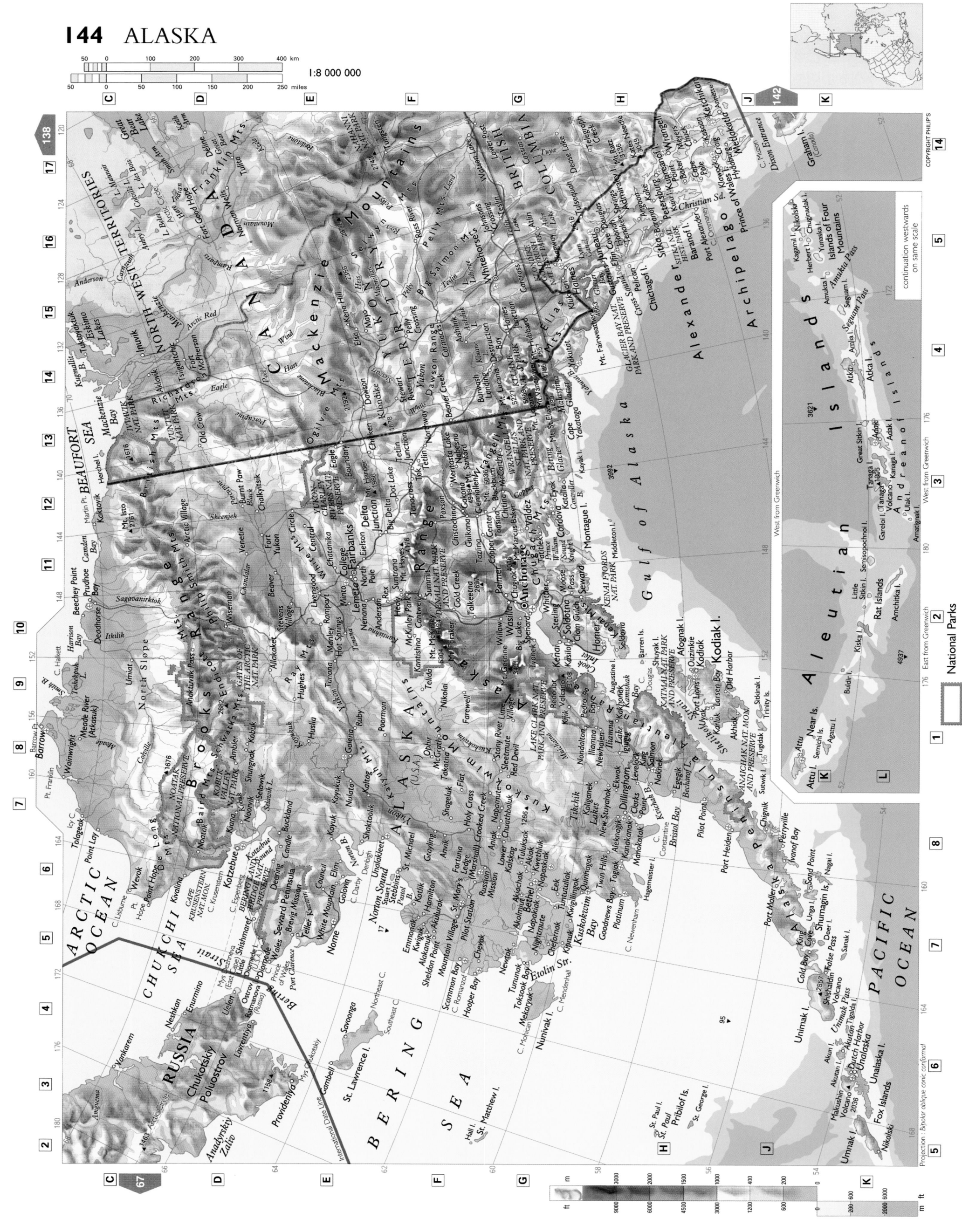

1:8 000 000

National Parks

continuation westwards
on same scale

COPYRIGHT PHILIP'S

Projection: Bipolar oblique conic conformal

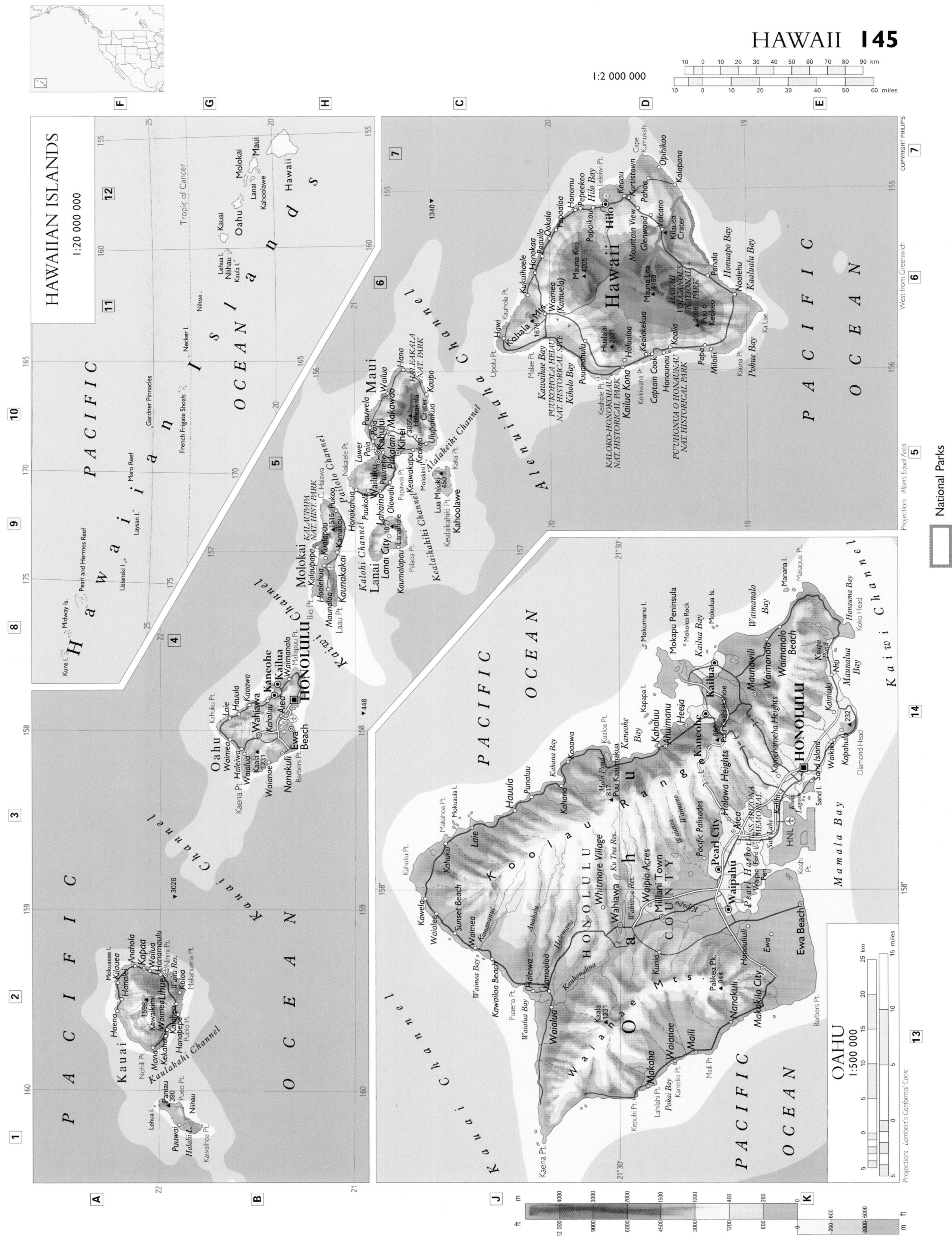

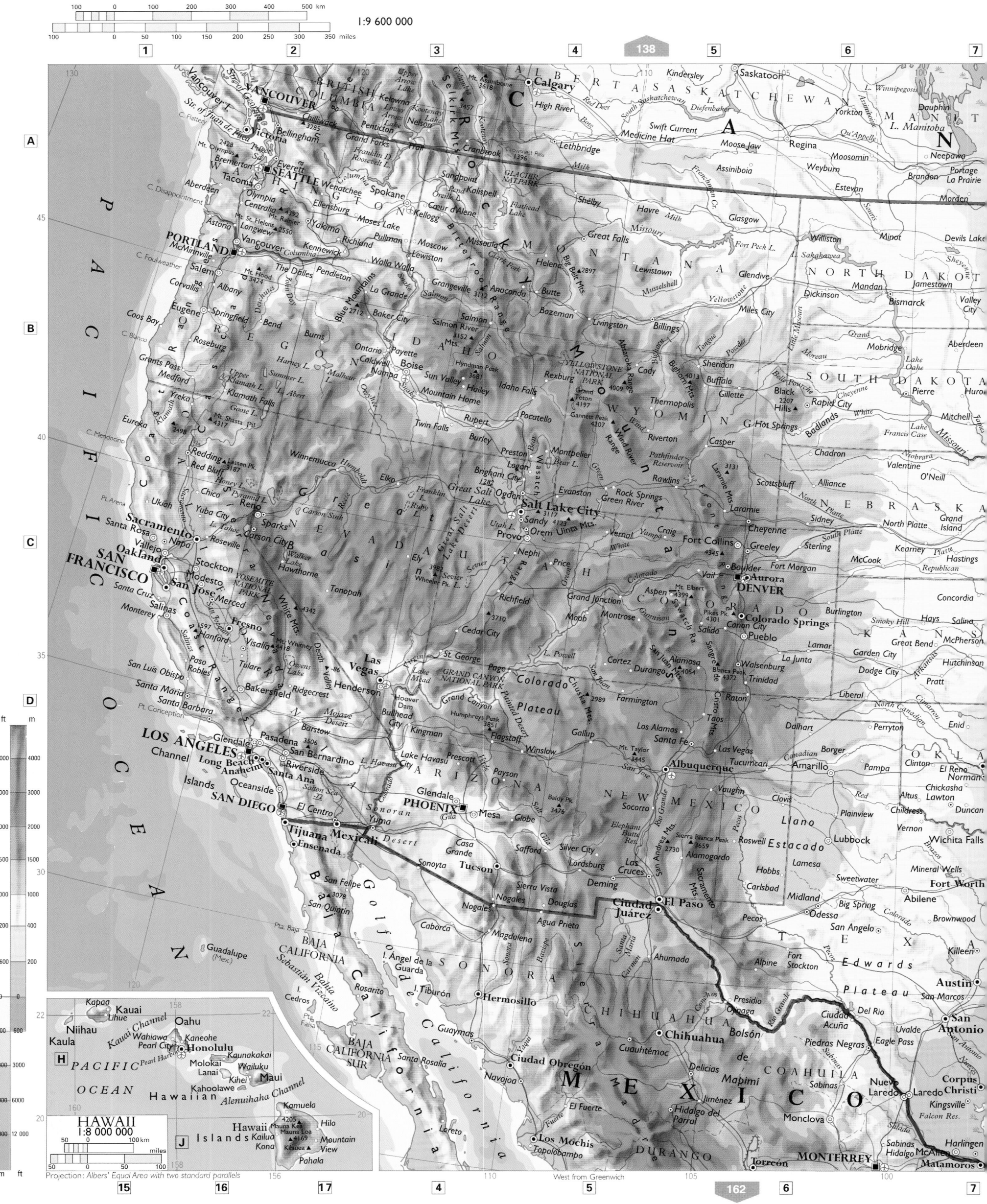

8
9
10
11
12
139
13
A
B
C
D
E
F
163
164
CANADA
Lake Winnipeg
Winnipeg
Lake of the Woods
Lake Nipigon
Thunder Bay
Lake Superior
Sault Ste. Marie
Lake Michigan
Lake Huron
Georgian Bay
Lake Ontario
Lake Erie
Moosonee
Chibougamau
Québec
MONTREAL
Ottawa
TORONTO
Hamilton
London
Kitchener
DETROIT
Windsor
CLEVELAND
Buffalo
Rochester
Syracuse
Albany
BOSTON
Providence
Hartford
NEW YORK
PHILADELPHIA
BALTIMORE
WASHINGTON D.C.
PITTSBURGH
Columbus
Cincinnati
Indianapolis
CHICAGO
Milwaukee
Minneapolis
St. Paul
Duluth
Des Moines
Omaha
Kansas City
ST. LOUIS
Louisville
Nashville
Memphis
Little Rock
Tulsa
Oklahoma City
Wichita
DALLAS
Arlington
HOUSTON
Galveston
New Orleans
Baton Rouge
Jackson
Birmingham
ATLANTA
Charlotte
Raleigh
Norfolk
Virginia Beach
Richmond
Charleston
Savannah
Jacksonville
Orlando
TAMPA
St. Petersburg
West Palm Beach
Fort Lauderdale
MIAMI
Key West
Florida Keys
Straits of Florida
BAHAMAS
Nassau
Andros I.
Grand Bahama I.
Great Abaco I.
Eleuthera I.
Cat I.
Long I.
MINNESOTA
WISCONSIN
IOWA
ILLINOIS
INDIANA
OHIO
MICHIGAN
PENNSYLVANIA
NEW YORK
VERMONT
NEW HAMPSHIRE
MAINE
NEW BRUNSWICK
New England
WEST VIRGINIA
KENTUCKY
TENNESSEE
MISSOURI
ARKANSAS
MISSISSIPPI
ALABAMA
GEORGIA
NORTH CAROLINA
SOUTH CAROLINA
LOUISIANA
FLORIDA
Midwest
Ozark Plateau
Appalachian Mts.
Cumberland Plateau
Allegheny Mts.
Mississippi River Delta
GULF OF MEXICO
ATLANTIC OCEAN
Chesapeake Bay
Delaware B.
Albemarle Sd.
Pamlico Sd.
C. Hatteras
C. Canaveral
C. Sable
Florida Bay
Apalachee B.
Brownsville
Rio Grande

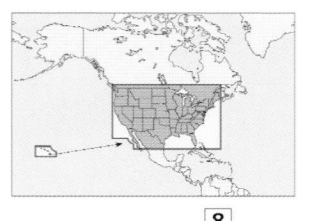

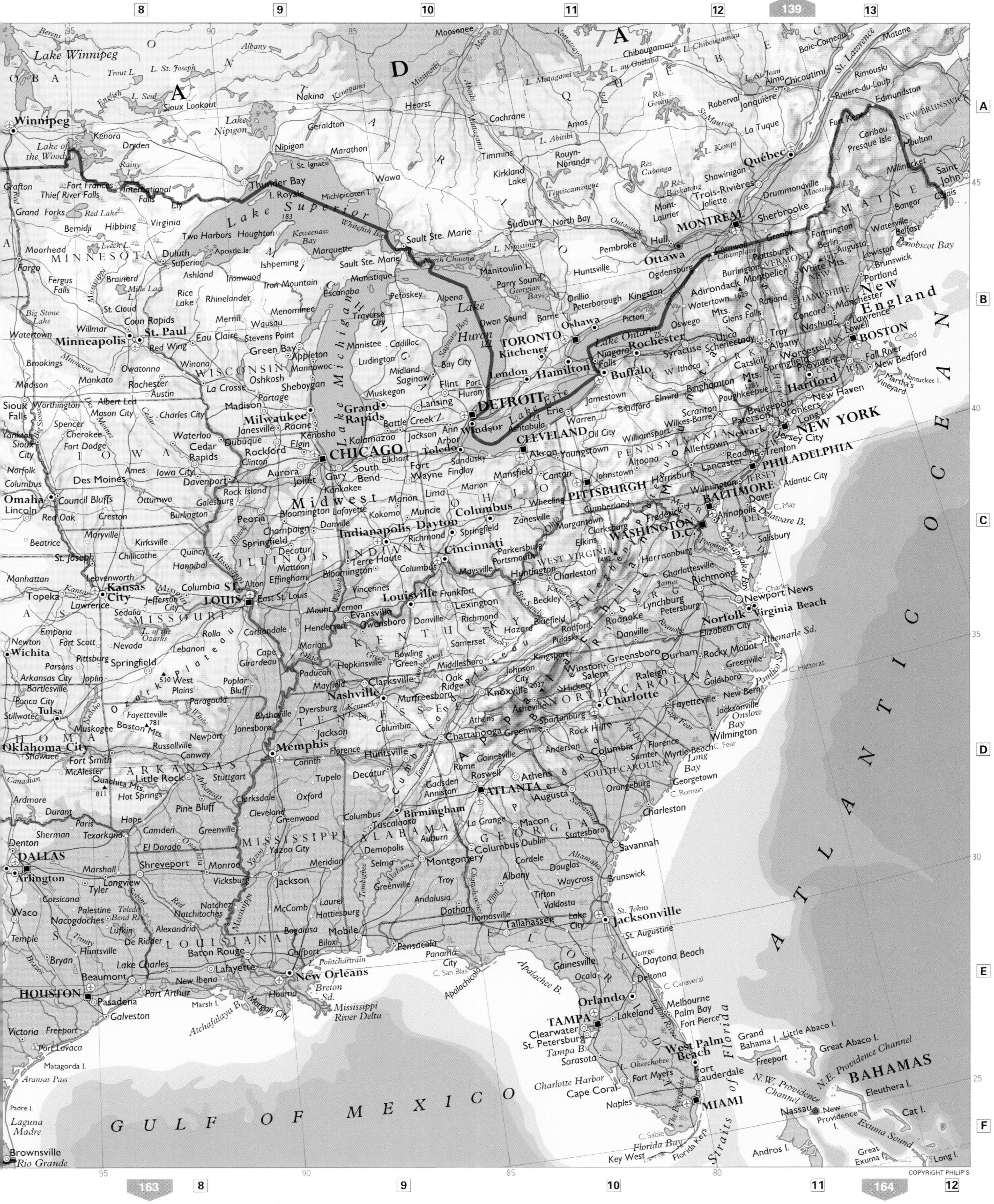

1:4 800 000

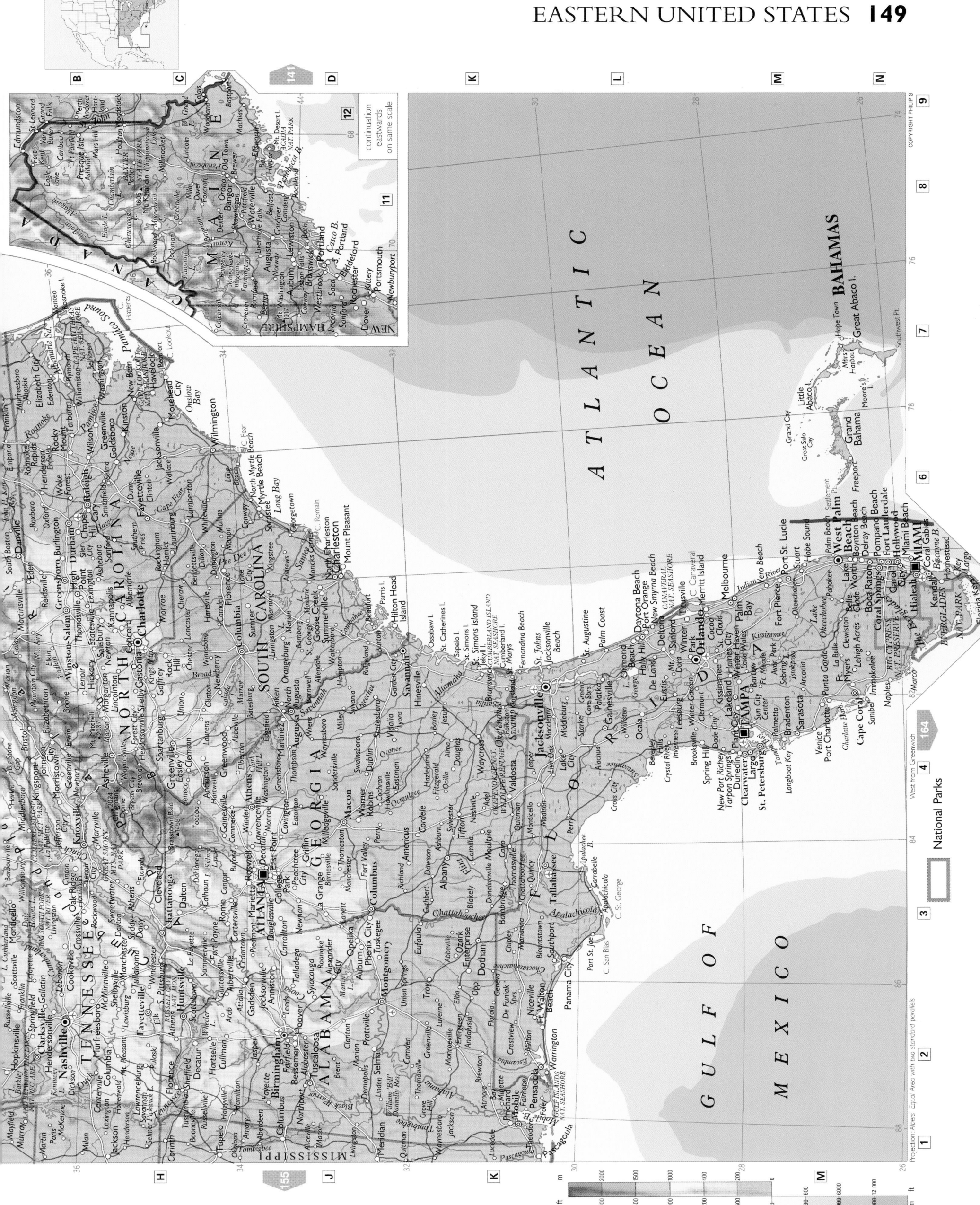

ATLANTIC OCEAN

GULF OF MEXICO

BAHAMAS

National Parks

Projection: Albers' Equal Area with two standard parallels

continuation eastwards on same scale

West from Greenwich

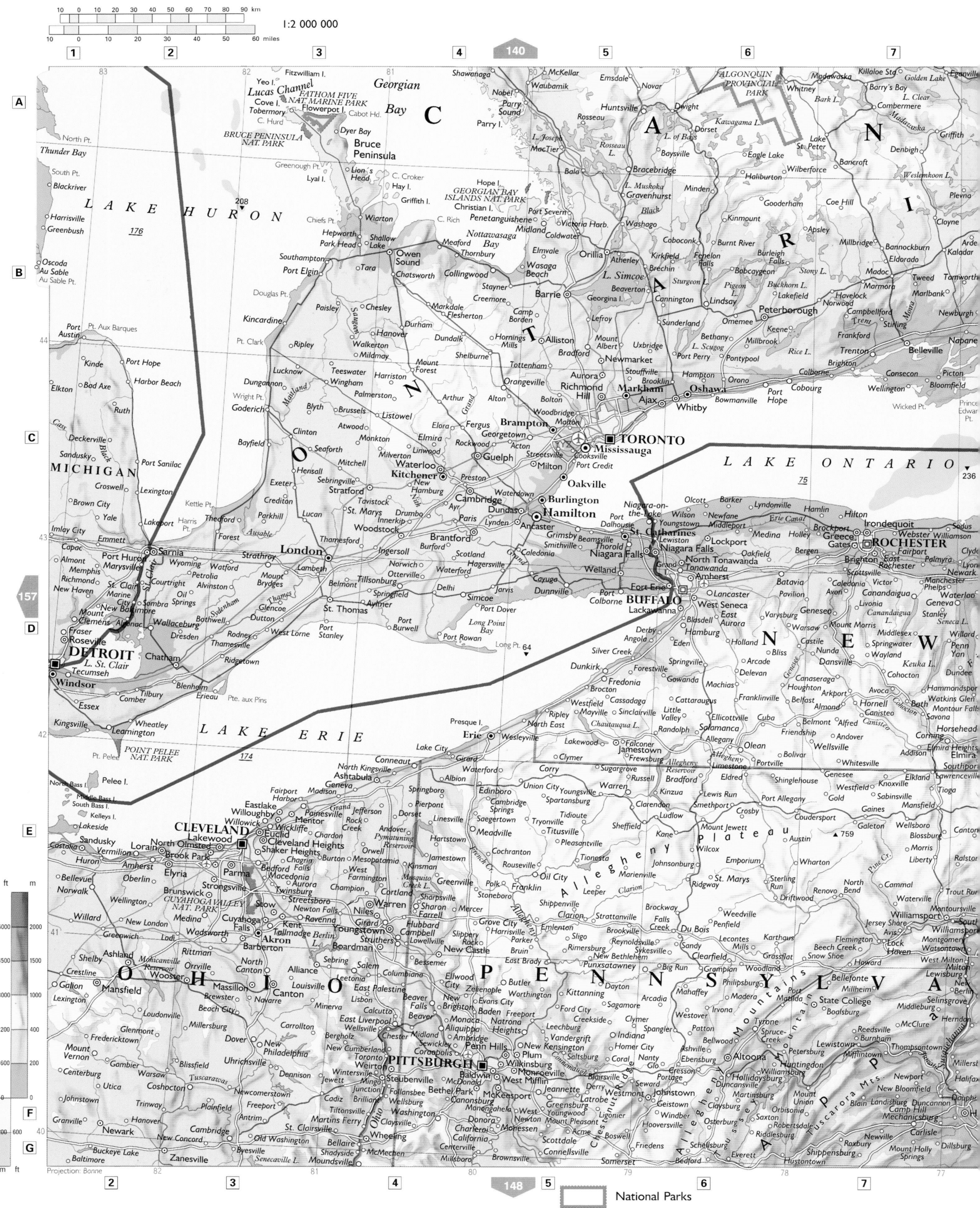

1:2 000 000

National Parks

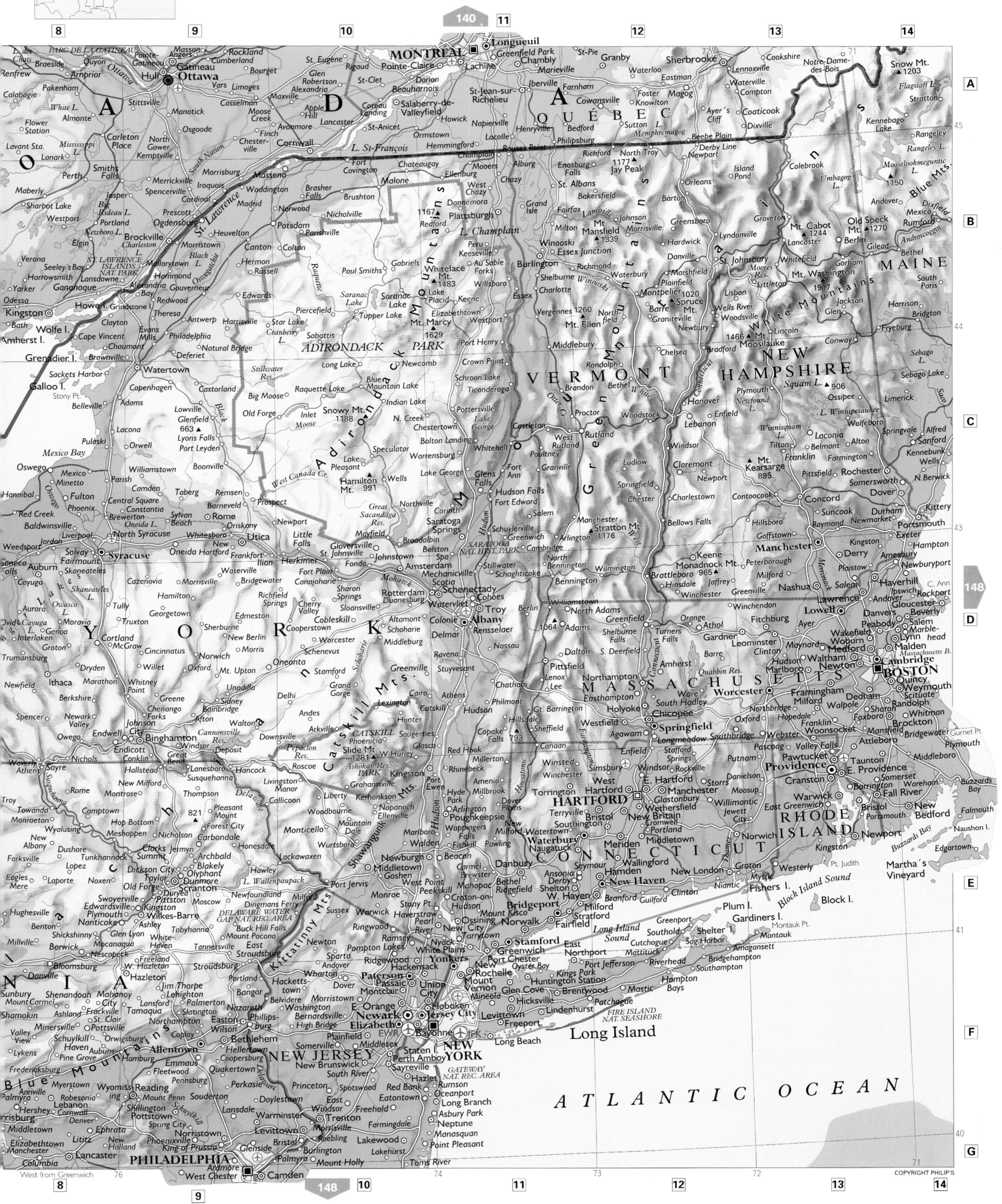

1:2 000 000

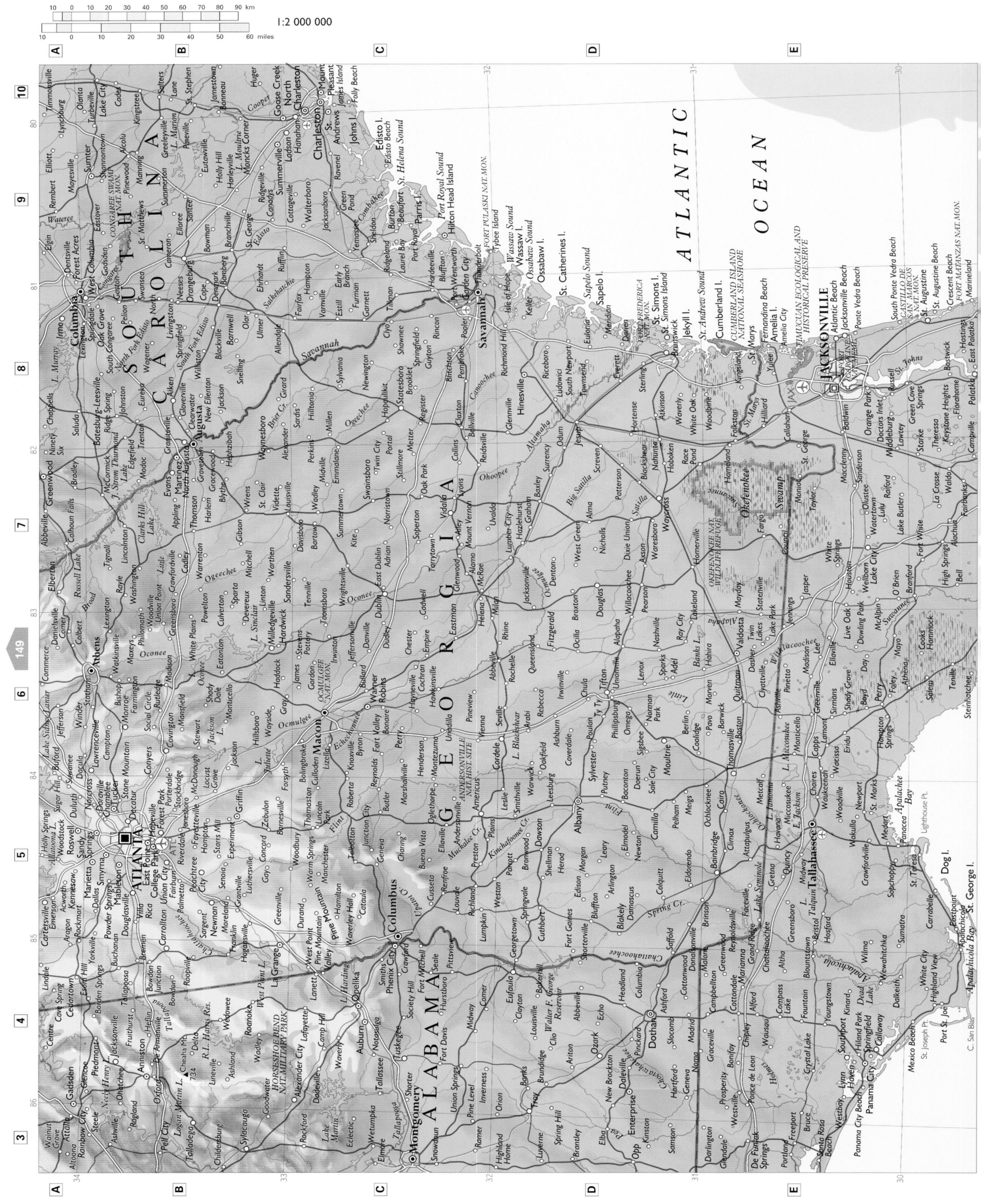

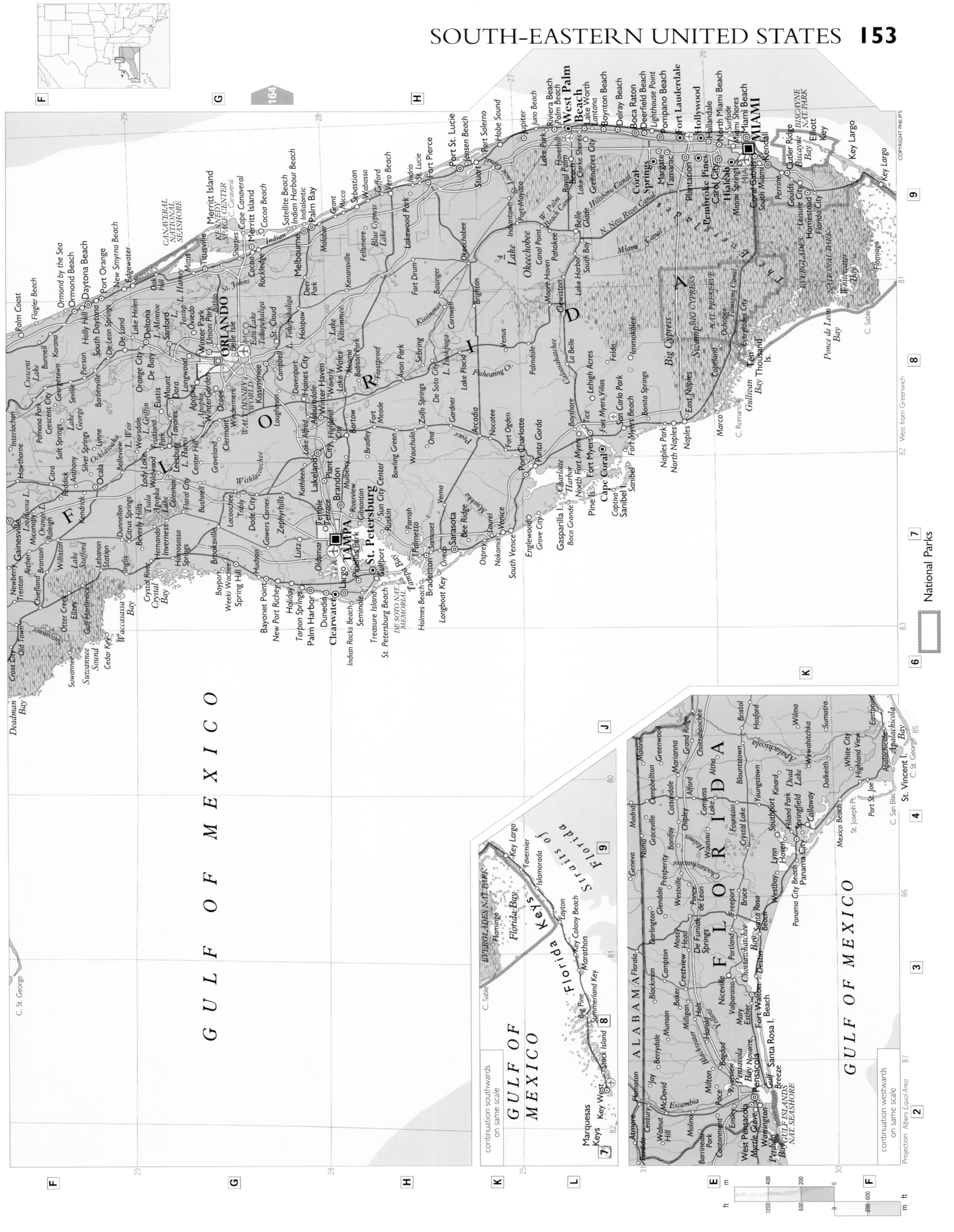

1:4 800 000

States and major geographic labels shown on the map:

CANADA

LAKE SUPERIOR

WISCONSIN
MICHIGAN
MINNESOTA
NORTH DAKOTA
SOUTH DAKOTA
NEBRASKA
IOWA
ILLINOIS
MISSOURI
KANSAS
WYOMING
COLORADO

Thunder Bay, Duluth, Superior, Minneapolis, St Paul, Milwaukee, Chicago, St Louis, Des Moines, Sioux City, Sioux Falls, Omaha, Lincoln, Kansas City, Topeka, Denver, Colorado Springs, Pueblo, Bismarck, Fargo, Rapid City, Grand Island, Madison, Green Bay, Rochester

Mississippi, Missouri, Red, James, Platte, North Platte, South Platte, Niobrara

BADLANDS NAT. PARK, THEODORE ROOSEVELT NAT. MEM. PARK, BLACK HILLS, SAND HILLS, ISLE ROYALE NAT. PARK, VOYAGEURS PARK, APOSTLE ISLANDS NAT. LAKESHORE

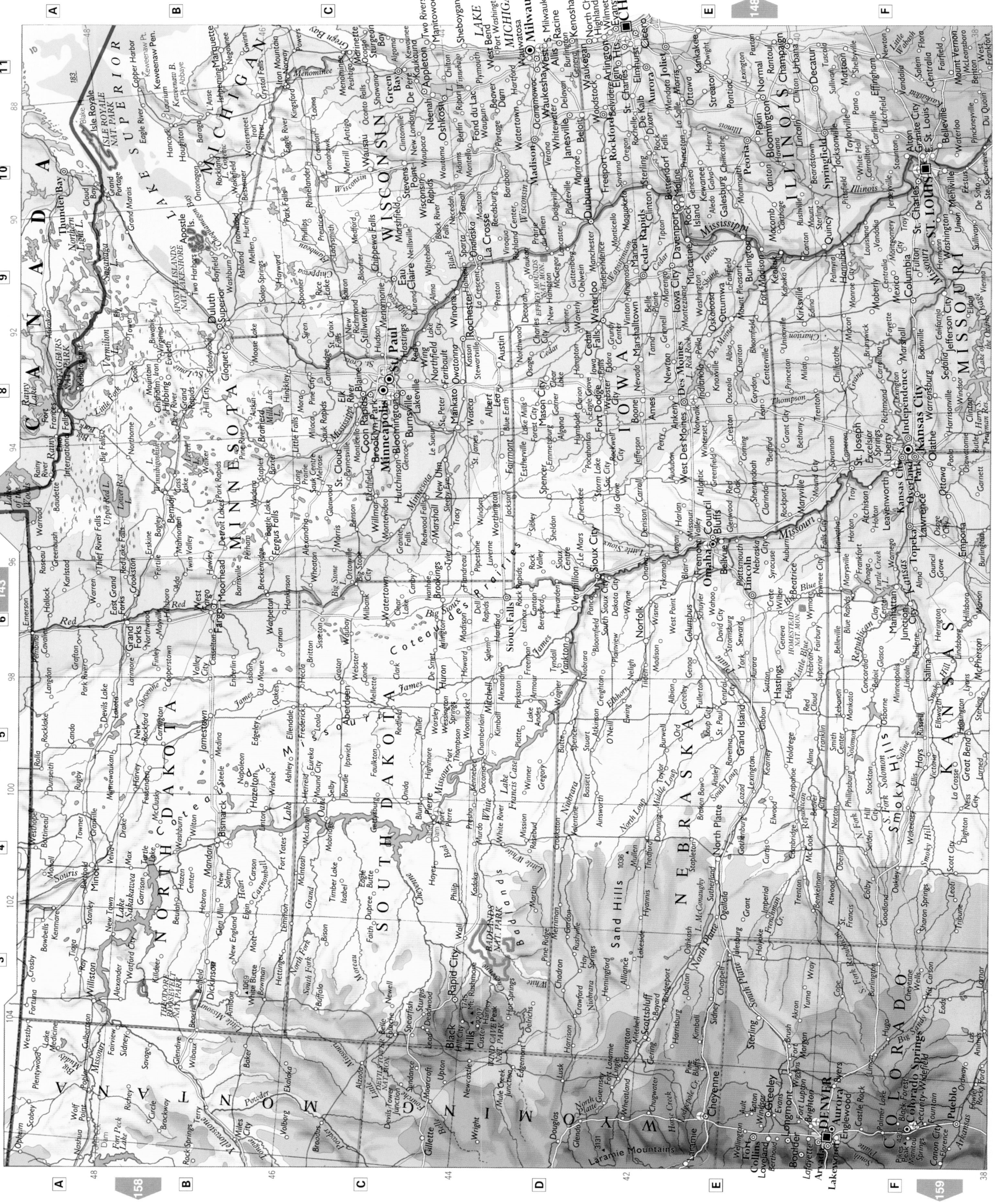

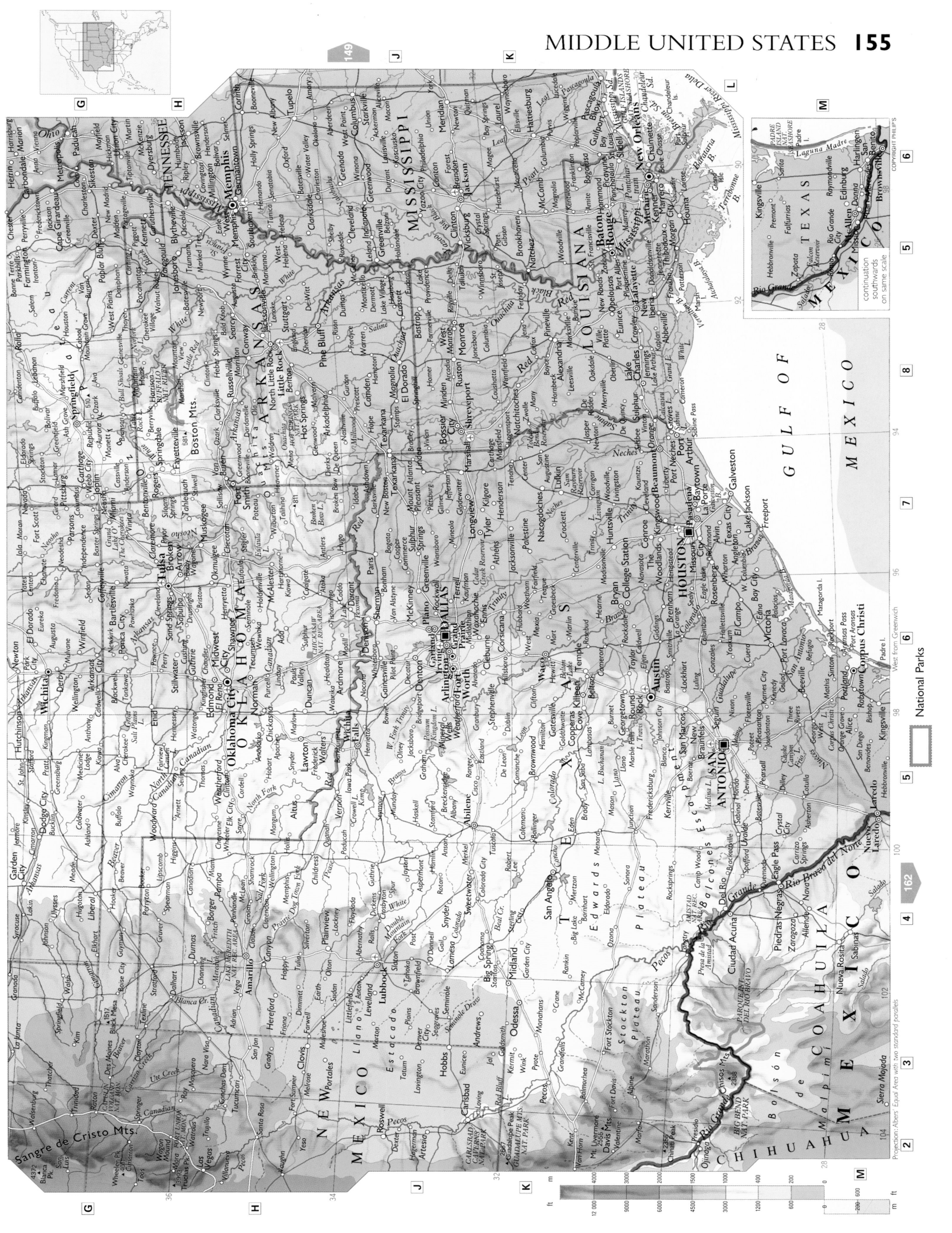

National Parks

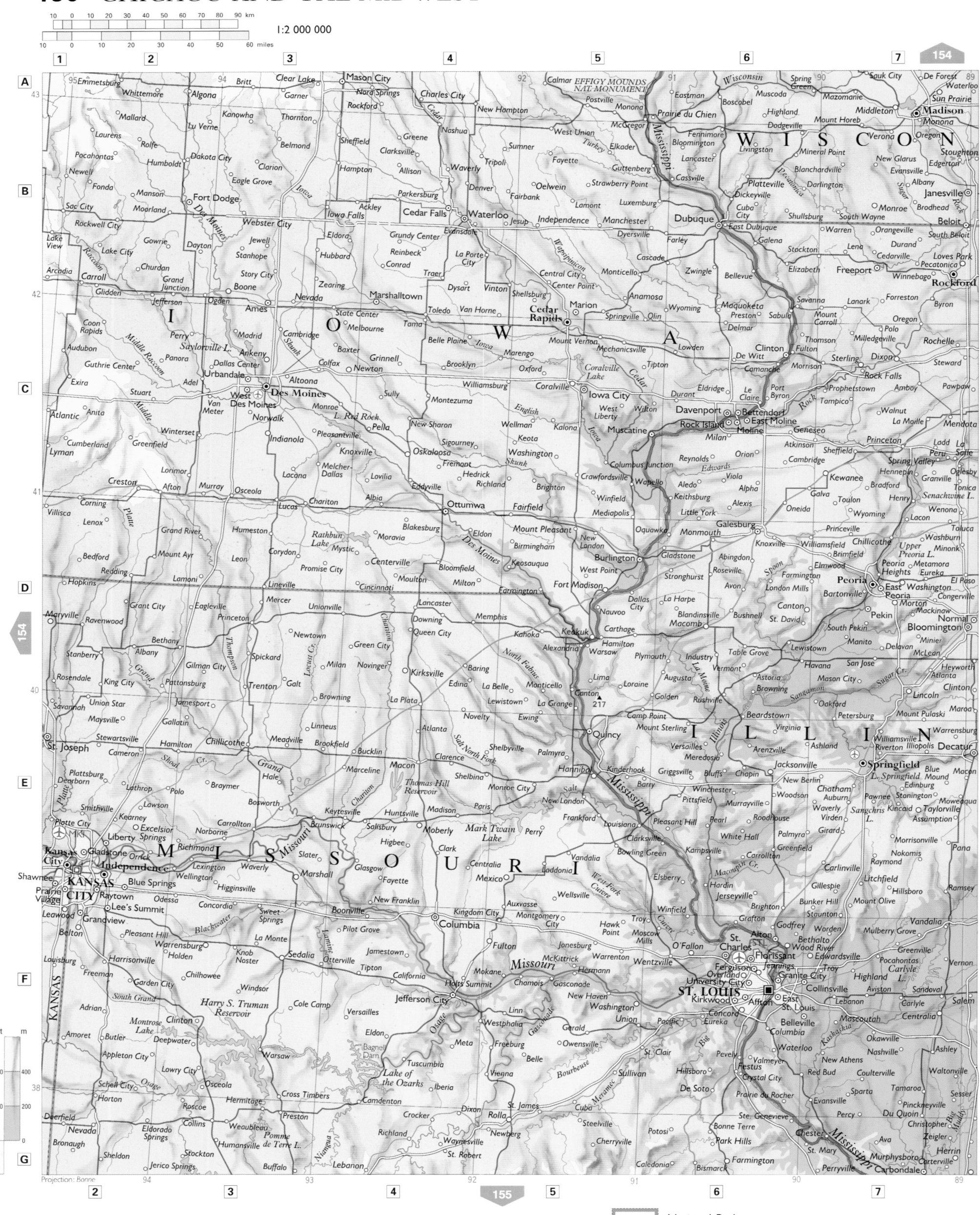

National Parks

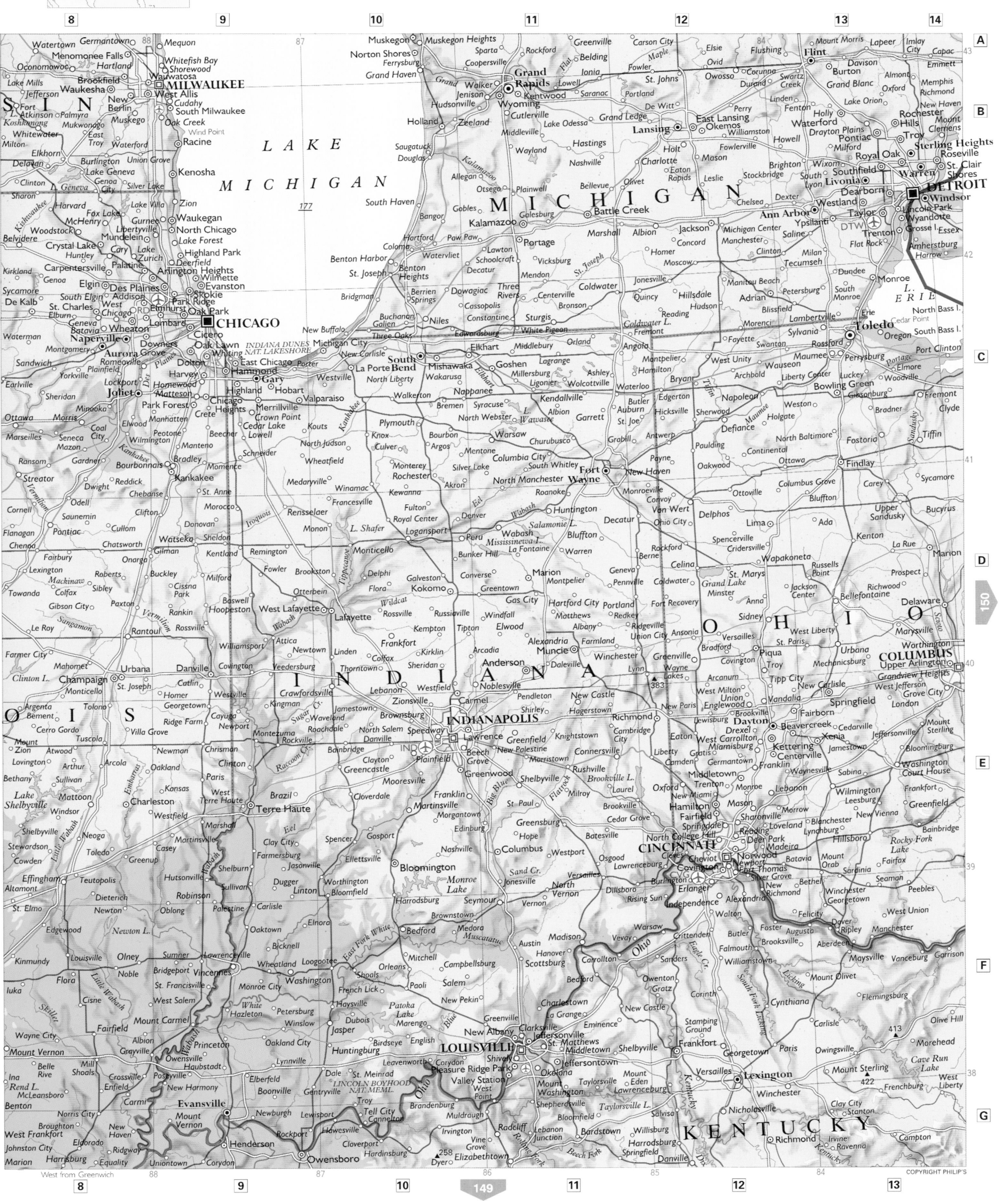

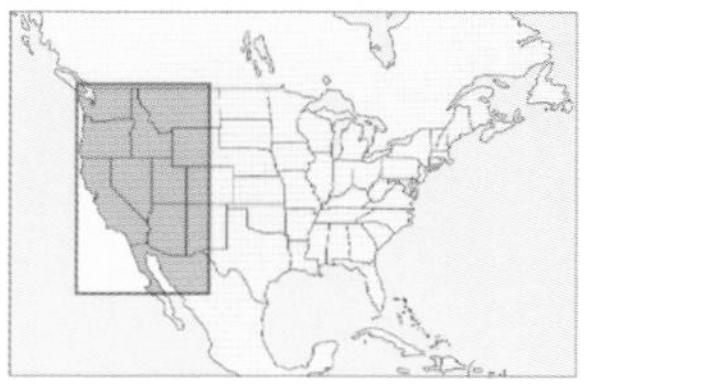

1:4 800 000

50 0 50 100 150 200 km
50 0 50 100 150 miles

154

142

Major states / regions: SASKATCHEWAN · ALBERTA · BRITISH COLUMBIA · MONTANA · WYOMING · IDAHO · WASHINGTON · OREGON · NEVADA · UTAH

Selected places: VANCOUVER · Seattle · PORTLAND · Salt Lake City · Sacramento · Spokane · Helena · Great Falls · Billings · Casper · Boise · Reno · Carson City

Physical features: Rocky Mountains · Bighorn Mountains · Medicine Bow Mts. · Wind River Range · Absaroka Range · Bitterroot Range · Cascade Range · Sierra Nevada · Coast Ranges · Columbia Plateau · Great Salt Lake · Great Salt Lake Desert · Snake River · Columbia River · Missouri River · Strait of Juan de Fuca · Puget Sound · Olympic Mts.

Grid references: A B C D E F · 1 2 3 4 5 6 7 8 9 10

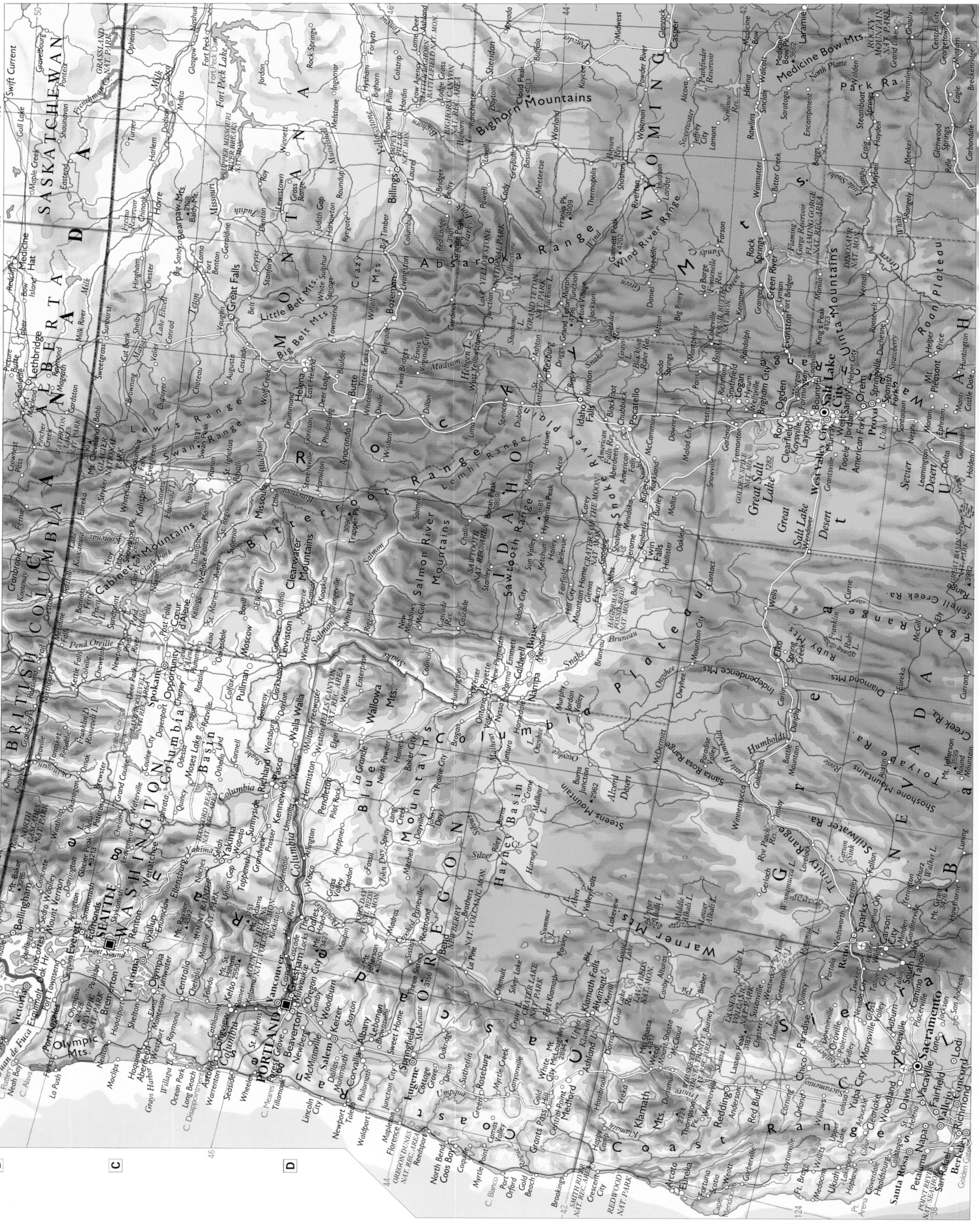

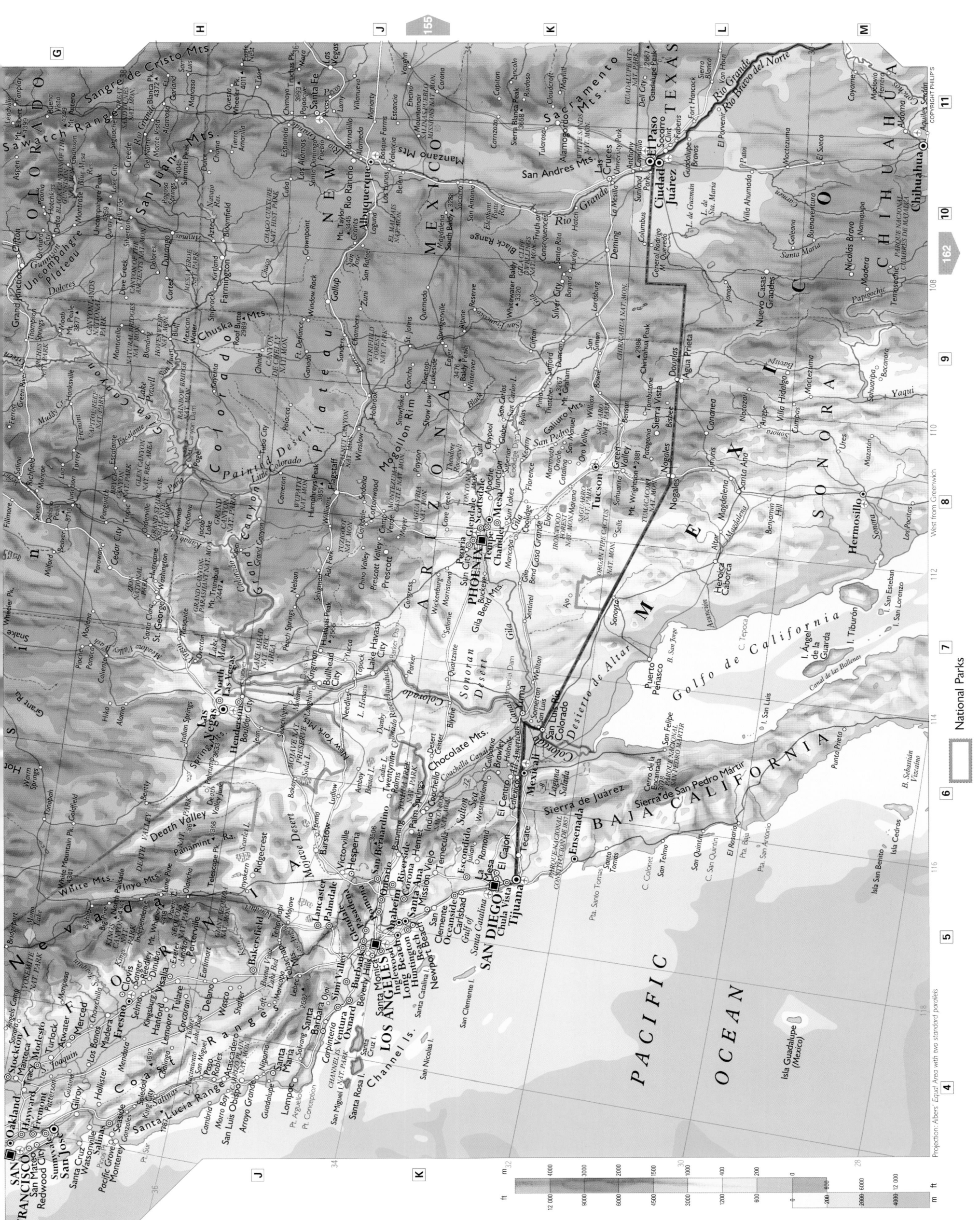

National Parks

Projection: Albers' Equal Area with two standard parallels

10 0 10 20 30 40 50 60 70 80 90 km

10 0 10 20 30 40 50 60 miles

1:2 000 000

159

WESTERN WASHINGTON REGION on same scale

BRITISH COLUMBIA

Vancouver Island

Strait of Georgia

Strait of Juan de Fuca

PACIFIC RIM NATIONAL PARK

PACIFIC OCEAN

OLYMPIC Mountains NATIONAL PARK

WASHINGTON

MT RAINIER NAT PARK

MT ST. HELENS NATIONAL VOLCANIC MONUMENT

OREGON

PORTLAND

SEATTLE
Bellevue
Tacoma
Lakewood
Olympia

VANCOUVER

Victoria

Everett

White Mts.

Inyo Mts.

Pahute Mesa

DEATH VALLEY

Pana

Sierra Nevada

YOSEMITE NATIONAL PARK

KINGS CANYON NATIONAL PARK

SEQUOIA NATIONAL PARK

Reno
Sparks

Lake Tahoe

Carson City

Sacramento Valley

SACRAMENTO

Stockton
Modesto

Merced

Fresno
Clovis

Visalia

San Joaquin Valley

San Francisco

Oakland

San Jose

Santa Cruz

Monterey

Santa Lucia Range

Diablo Range

Santa Rosa

Napa

50   0   50   100   150   200   250   300 km

1:6 400 000

50   0   50   100   150   200 miles

159   155

Projection: Bi-polar oblique Conical Orthomorphic

West from Greenwich

National Parks

State names in Central Mexico

1 DISTRITO FEDERAL
2 AGUASCALIENTES
3 GUANAJUATO
4 HIDALGO
5 MÉXICO
6 MORELOS
7 QUERÉTARO
8 TLAXCALA

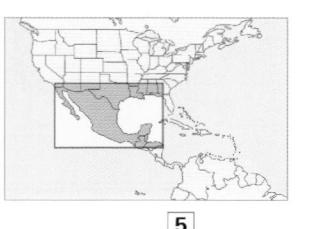

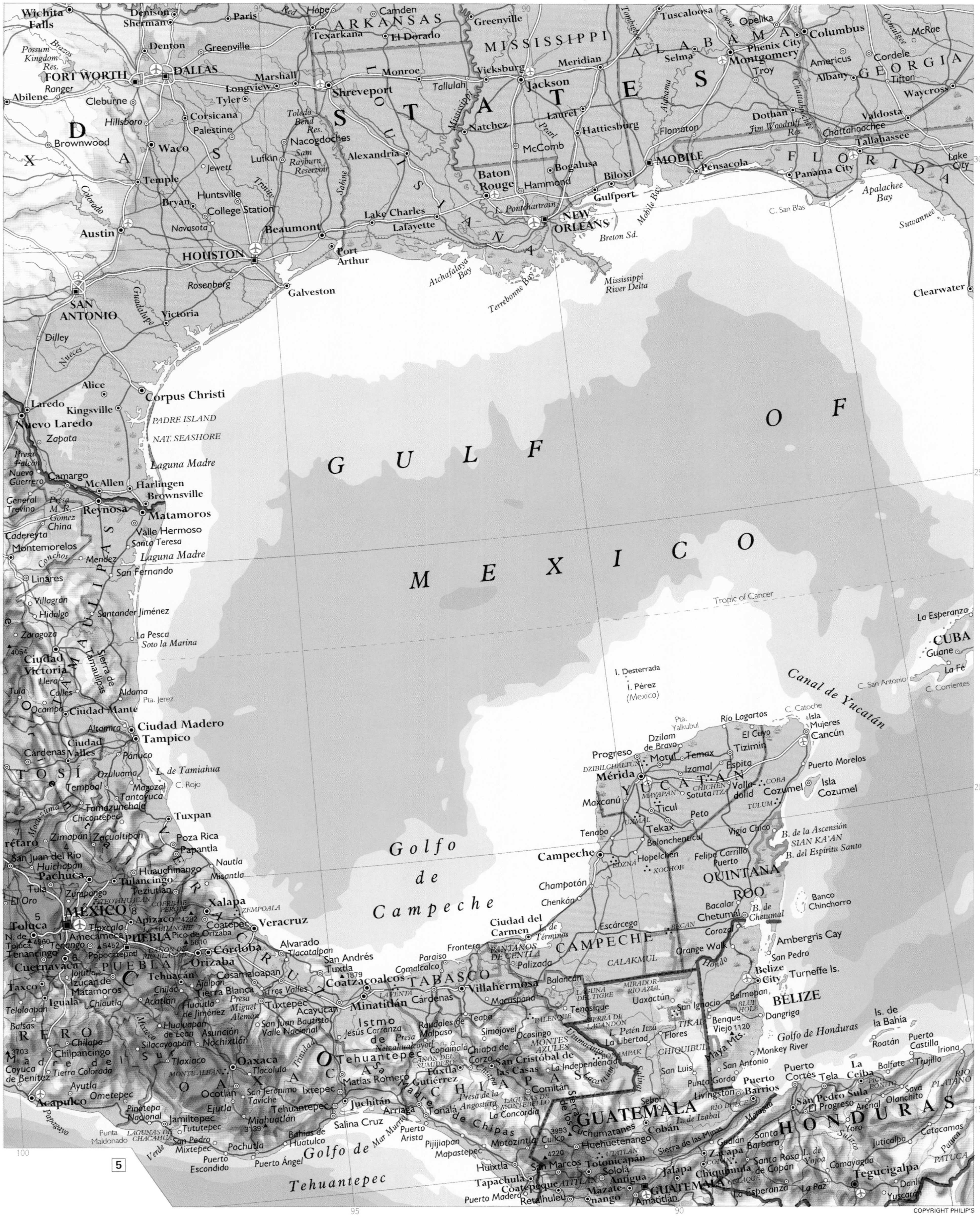

PUERTO RICO 1:2 400 000 [d]

ATLANTIC OCEAN

PUERTO RICO (U.S.A.)

Pta. Agujereada
Isabela
Aguadilla
Arecibo
Barceloneta
Vega Baja
Manati
SAN JUAN
Rio Grande
Bayamón
Carolina
Caguas
Fajardo
Pta. Culebra
Dewey
Mayagüez
San Sebastián
Adjuntas
Utuado
Cordillera Central
Cerro 1338 de Punta
Cayey
Humacoa
Naguabo
Vieques
Esperanza
San German
Yauco
Urayon Mts.
Coamo
Yabucoa
Pta. Aguila
Guanica
Ponce
Guayama
I. Caja de Muertos

VIRGIN ISLANDS 1:1 600 000 [e]

Rufling Pt.
The Settlement
Anegada
East Pt.
Virgin Islands (U.K.)
Jost Van Dyke I.
Great Camanoe
Hans Lollik I.
Guana I.
Virgin Gorda
Virgin Is. (U.S.A.)
Tortola
Beef I.
Spanish Town
Road Town
Peter I.
Charlotte Amalie
Cruz Bay
St. John I.
St. Thomas I.
VIRGIN IS.

ST. LUCIA 1:800 000 [f]

Cap Point
Pte. Hardy
Esperance Bay
Gros Islet
Castries
Marquis
Babonneau
L'Anse la Raye
Dennery
Canaries
Millet
Soufrière
Mt. Gimie 950
Trou Gras Pt.
Soufrière Bay
Petit Piton 750
Micoud
Gros Piton Pt.
Gros Piton 796
Vierge Pt.
Choiseul
Laborie
Vieux Fort
ST. LUCIA
C. Moule à Chique

BARBADOS 1:800 000 [g]

Crabhill
North Point
Spring Hall
Fustic
Boscobelle
Portland
245 Bellepaine
Speightstown
BARBADOS
Westmoreland
Bathsheba
Hillcrest
Holetown
Alleynes Bay
Mt. Hillaby 340
Martin's Bay
Jackson
Bridgefield
Mossiah
Black Rock
Ellerton
Edey
Six Cross Roads
Bridgetown
Ivy
The Crane
Carlisle Bay
Oistins
St. Martins
Worthing
Chancery Lane
Oistins Bay
South Point
BGI

AMAS

ATLANTIC OCEAN

Arthur's Town
The Bight
Cat I.
San Salvador I.
Conception I.
Rum Cay
Long I.
Tropic of Cancer
Sandy Cay
Clarence Town
Samana Cay
Cay Verde
Crooked I.
Plana Cays
Albert Town
Snug Corner
Mayaguana I.
Cay Santa Domingo
Acklins I.
Mira por vos Cay
Hogsty Reef
Little Inagua I.
Turks & Caicos (U.K.)
Caicos Is.
Cockburn Town
Banes
Lake Rose
Turks Is.
Antilla
INAGUA
Great Inagua I.
Mayari
Moa
Matthew Town
Baracoa
Maisi
Pta. de Maisi
Guantanamo
GUANTANAMO BAY (U.S.A.)
Paso de los Vientos

Î. de la Tortue
Monte Cristi
LA ISABELA
Santiago de los Cabelleros
Milwaukee Deep 9200
Puerto Rico Trench
Cap-Haïtien
Puerto Plata
La Vega
Nagua
Samana
Jean Rabel
Fort Liberté
Gonaïves
Coro
Central
Sánchez
Sabana de la Mar
St-Marc
Hinche
Pico Duarte 3175
LOS
C. Engaño
Jérémie
Î. de la Gonâve
San Pedro
Hato Mayor
Bayamón
SAN JUAN
Carolina
St. Thomas
Anegada
Virgin Is.
Sombrero (U.K.)
Navassa I. (U.S.A.)
PORT-AU-PRINCE
San Juan
La Romana
Arecibo
Road Town
Anguilla (U.K.)
Dame Marie
Massif de la Hotte
HAITI
DOMINICAN REP
Azua
de Macorís
Higüey
Aguadilla
Fajardo
Charlotte Amalie
St.-Martin (Fr.)
Les Cayes
Aquin
Goâve
Jacmel
2280
SIERRA DE BAHORUCO
Barahona
Bani
San Cristóbal
SANTO DOMINGO
Mayagüez
Ponce
Caguas
Guayama
Virgin Is. (U.S.A.)
St.-Barthélemy (Fr.)
Pointe-à-Gravois
Î. à Vache
L. Enriquillo
PUERTO RICO (U.S.A.)
Christiansted
Saba (Neth.)
Barbuda
Pedernales
Isla Mona (U.S.A.)
Frederiksted
St. Croix (U.S.A.)
St. Eustatius (Neth.)
ST. KITTS & NEVIS
ANTIGUA & BARBUDA
Hispaniola
I. Beata
C. Beata
Basseterre
St. John's
Antigua
Nevis
Redonda
Montserrat (U.K.)

Antilles
Leeward Islands
Ste.-Rose
Moule
La Désirade
GUADELOUPE (Fr.) 1467
Pointe-à-Pitre
Marie-Galante (Fr.)
Basse-Terre
I. des Saintes (Fr.)
Grand-Bourg
Portsmouth
Dominica Passage
Roseau 1447
DOMINICA
MORNE TROIS PITONS
I. de Aves (Venezuela)
Martinique Passage
Mt. Pelée 1397
Ste.-Marie
Fort-de-France
Le François
Rivière-Pilote
MARTINIQUE (Fr.)
St. Lucia Channel
Castries
ST. LUCIA
Soufrière

BEAN SEA (CARIBBEAN SEA)

Lesser Antilles
St. Vincent Passage
Soufrière 1234
St. Vincent
Speightstown
Kingstown
Bridgetown
BARBADOS
Hillsborough
ST. VINCENT & THE GRENADINES
Grenadines
St. George's
GRENADA

Lesser Antilles

Oranjestad
Aruba (Neth.)
Curaçao
Bonaire
Pta. Gallinas
MACUIRA
C. San Román
Pen. de Paraguaná
NETH. ANTILLES
ARC. LOS ROQUES
I. Blanquilla (Ven.)
Tobago
Willemstad
Is. Las Aves (Ven.)
I. Orchila (Ven.)
Is. Los Hermanos (Ven.)
Scarborough
COLOMBIA
Pen. de la Guajira
Punto Fijo
Is. Los Roques (Ven.)
I. Los Testigos (Ven.)
Galera Point
Port of Spain
SANTA MARTA
Ríohacha
Uribia
Golfo de Venezuela
Punta Cardón
MÉDANOS DE CORO
Puerto Cumarebo
NUEVA ESPARTA
I. de Margarita
La Asunción
Pen. de Paria
Trinidad
BARRAN-QUILLA
TAYRONA
GUAJIRA
San Rafael
Coro
La Vela de Coro
Porlamar
Carúpano
Río Claro
Baranoa
Soledad
Ciénaga
ISLA DE SALAMANCA
Sierra Nevada de Santa Marta 5800
FALCÓN
Tucacas
HENRI PITTIER
Maiquetía
La Guaira
Maracay
CARACAS
VARGAS
I. La Tortuga (Ven.)
Cumaná
LAGUNA DE LA RESTINGA
Arima
TRINIDAD & TOBAGO
Sabanalarga
Fundación
Calamar
Santa Rita
Mene de Mauroa
Baragua
CORO
San Felipe
CARABOBO
Los Teques
MIRANDA
Río Chico
Puerto La Cruz
Güira
San Fernando
MAGDALENA
Plato
Zambrano
MARACAIBO
La Concepción
Cabimas
LARA
Carora
ARAGUY
Valencia
Villa de Cura
San Juan de los Morros
Altagracia de Orituco
Barcelona
Caripito
Caicara
NA
Corozal
Sincé-lejo
Magangué
El Banco
Ciudad Ojeda
Lago de Maracaibo
Mene Grande
TRUJILLO
COJEDES
Calabozo
Valle de la Pascua
Anaco
Maturín
SUCRE
MONAGAS
DELTA
Tucupita
Sahagún
ZULIA
SIERRA DE PERIJÁ
Machiques
CIÉNAGAS DEL CATATUMBO
Betijoque
Valera
El Guache
El Sombrero
Aragua de Barcelona
Cantaura
El Tigre
ANZOÁTEGUI
AMACURO
San Marcos
Planeta Rica
BOLÍVAR
El Banco
CÉSAR
Agustín Codazzi
San Carlos del Zulia
Trujillo
PORTUGUESA
Guanare
El Baúl
GUÁRICO
Ciudad Guayana
Los Barrancos
Libano
Ayapel
Simití
NORTE DE SANTANDER
Ocaña
MÉRIDA
Barinas
San Fernando de Apure
El Sombrero
Santa María de Ipire
Pariaguán
El Tigre
Sierra Imataca
Doba
Caucasia
Cúcuta
TÁCHIRA
Mérida
San Carlos del Bolivia
BARINAS
Achaguas
Cantaura
Ciudad Bolívar
El Pao
Upata
Caicara
Embalse de Guri
El Callao
Tumeremo
Guasipati

VENEZUELA

West from Greenwich
COPYRIGHT PHILIP'S

Please refer to page 169 for inset map of Trinidad and Tobago.

National Parks

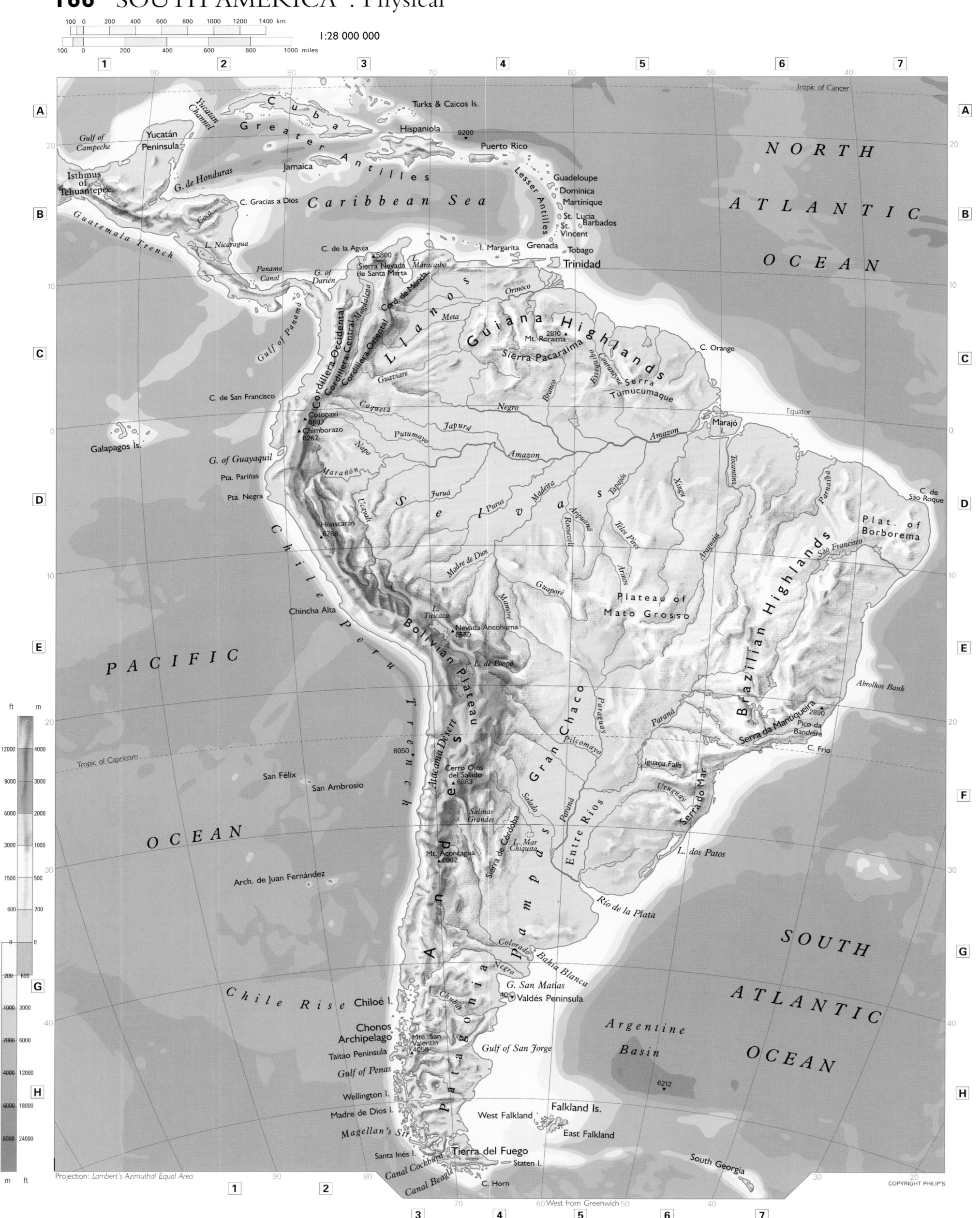

1:28 000 000

100 0 200 400 600 800 1000 1200 1400 km
100 200 400 600 800 1000 miles

Projection: Lambert's Azimuthal Equal Area

COPYRIGHT PHILIP'S

1:28 000 000

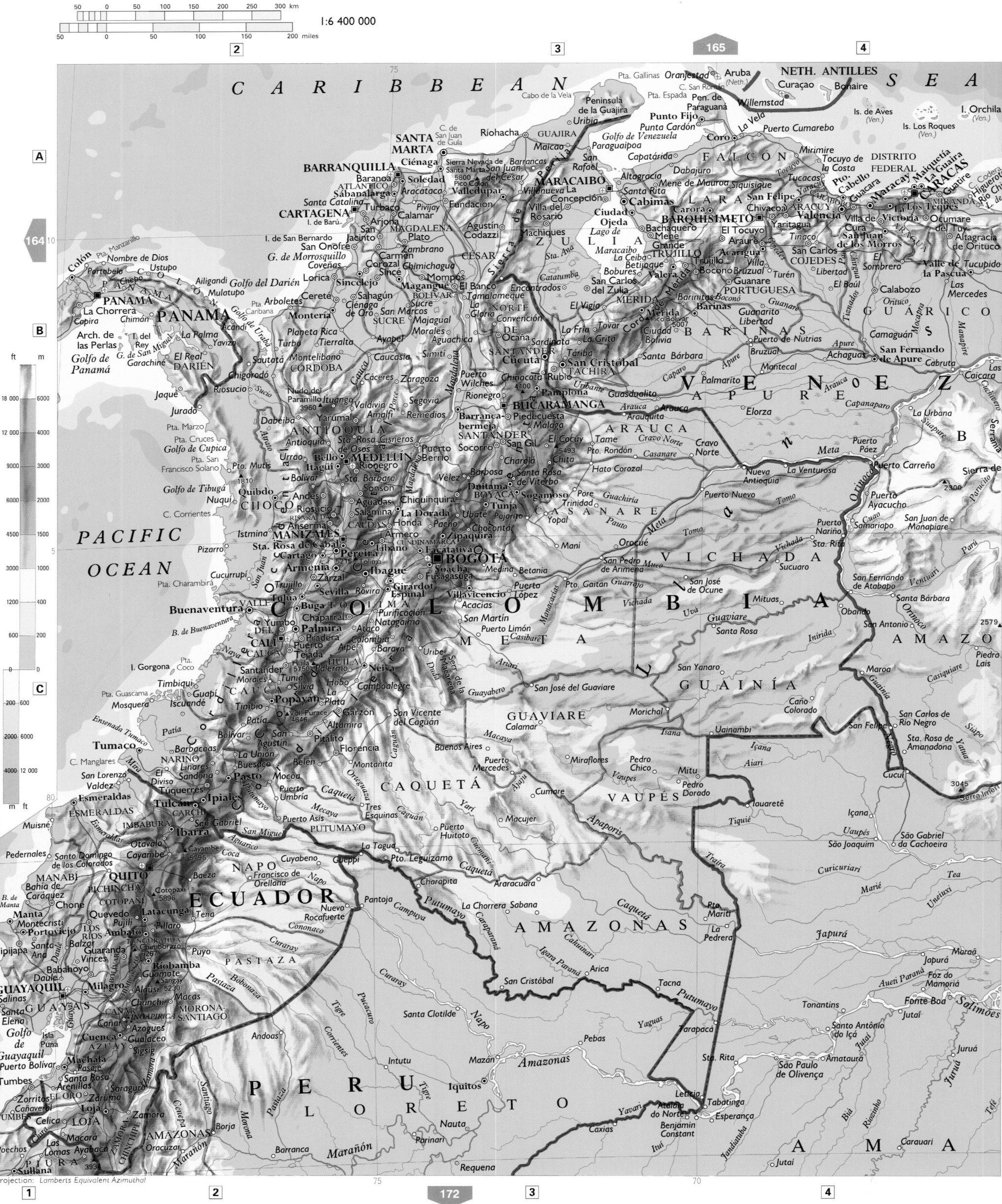

1:6 400 000

Projection: Lamberts Equivalent Azimuthal

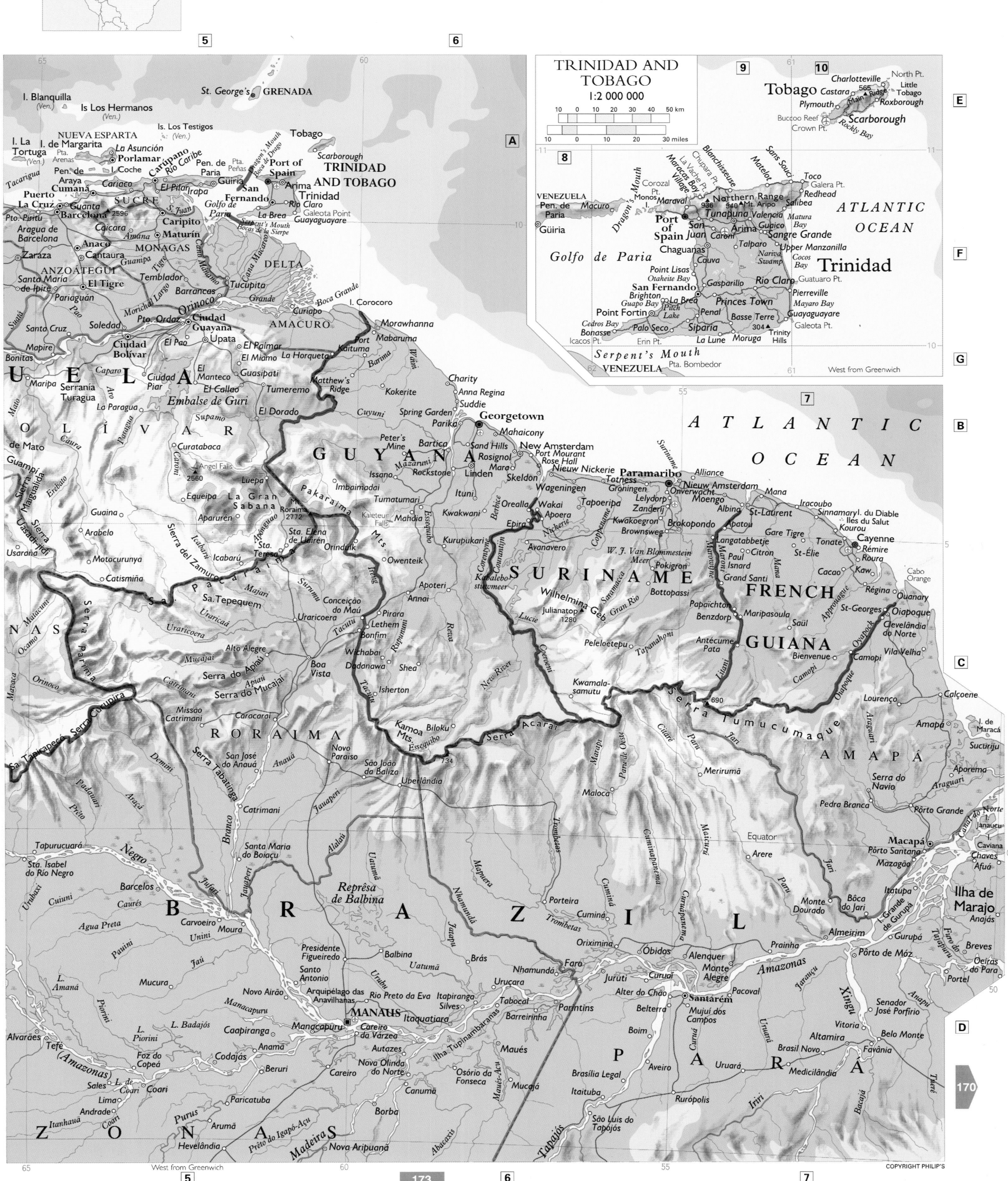

1:6 400 000

ATLANTIC OCEAN

ATLANTIC OCEAN
BAHIA
MINAS GERAIS
GOIÁS
SÃO PAULO
PARANÁ
ESPÍRITO SANTO
RIO DE JANEIRO
DISTRITO FEDERAL
BRASÍLIA
BELO HORIZONTE
SALVADOR (Bahia)
SÃO PAULO
RIO DE JANEIRO
CURITIBA
GOIÂNIA
CAMPINAS
SANTOS
NITERÓI
Tropic of Capricorn
West from Greenwich
Projection: Lambert's Equivalent Azimuthal
COPYRIGHT PHILIP'S
175

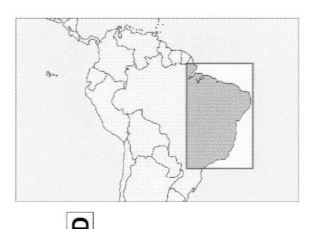

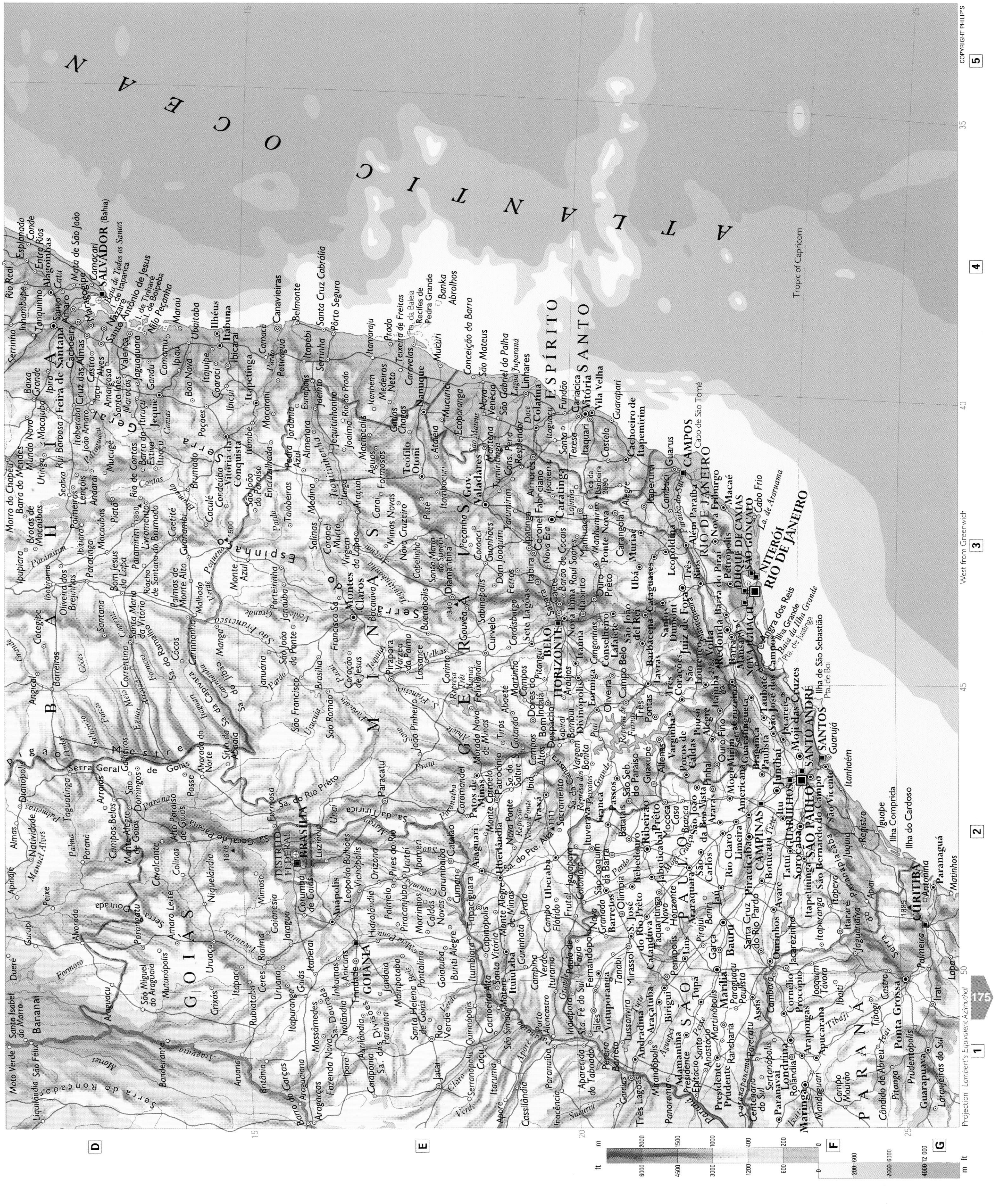

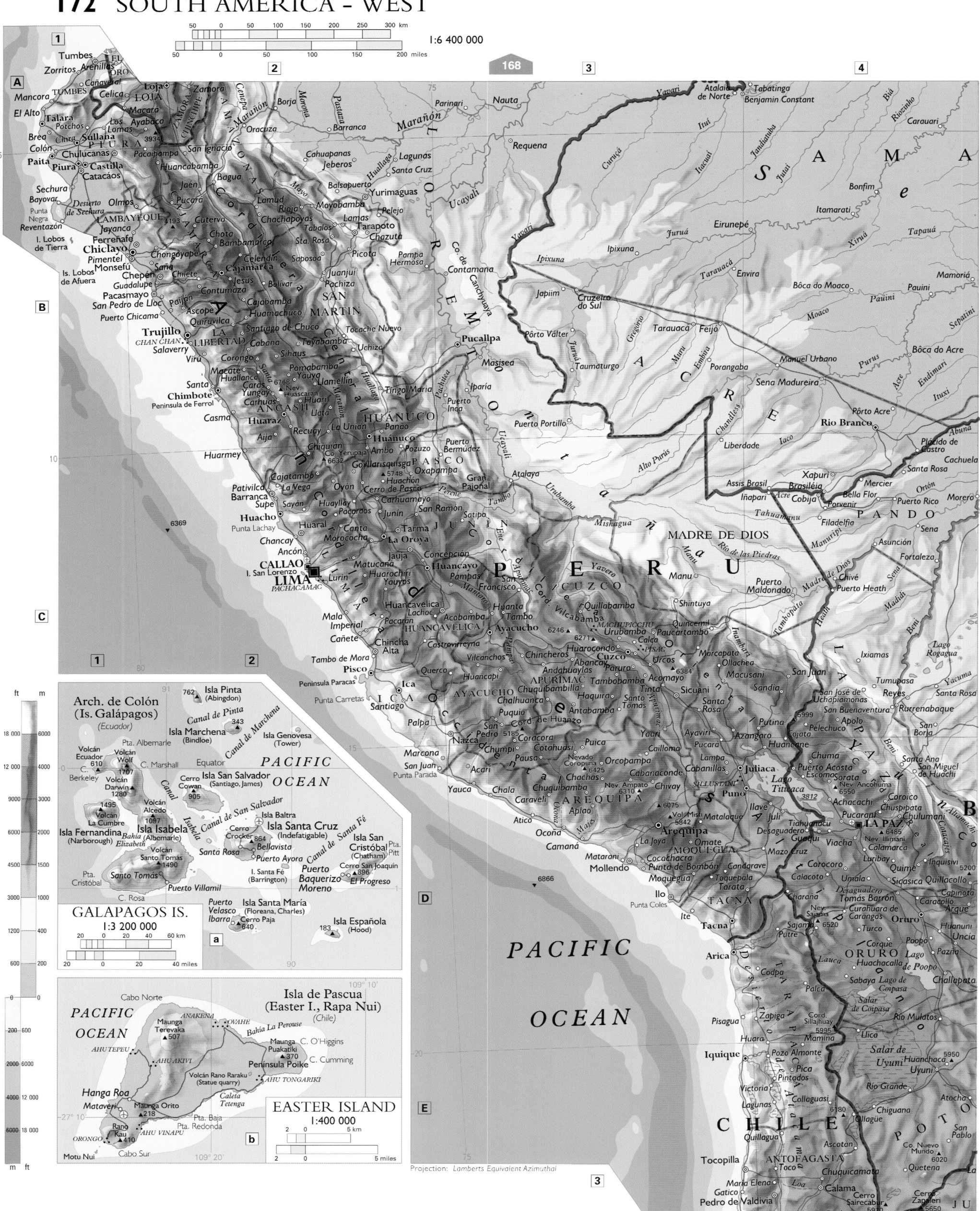

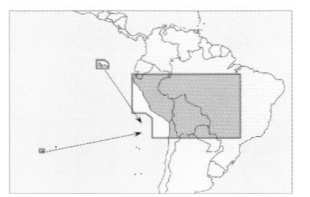

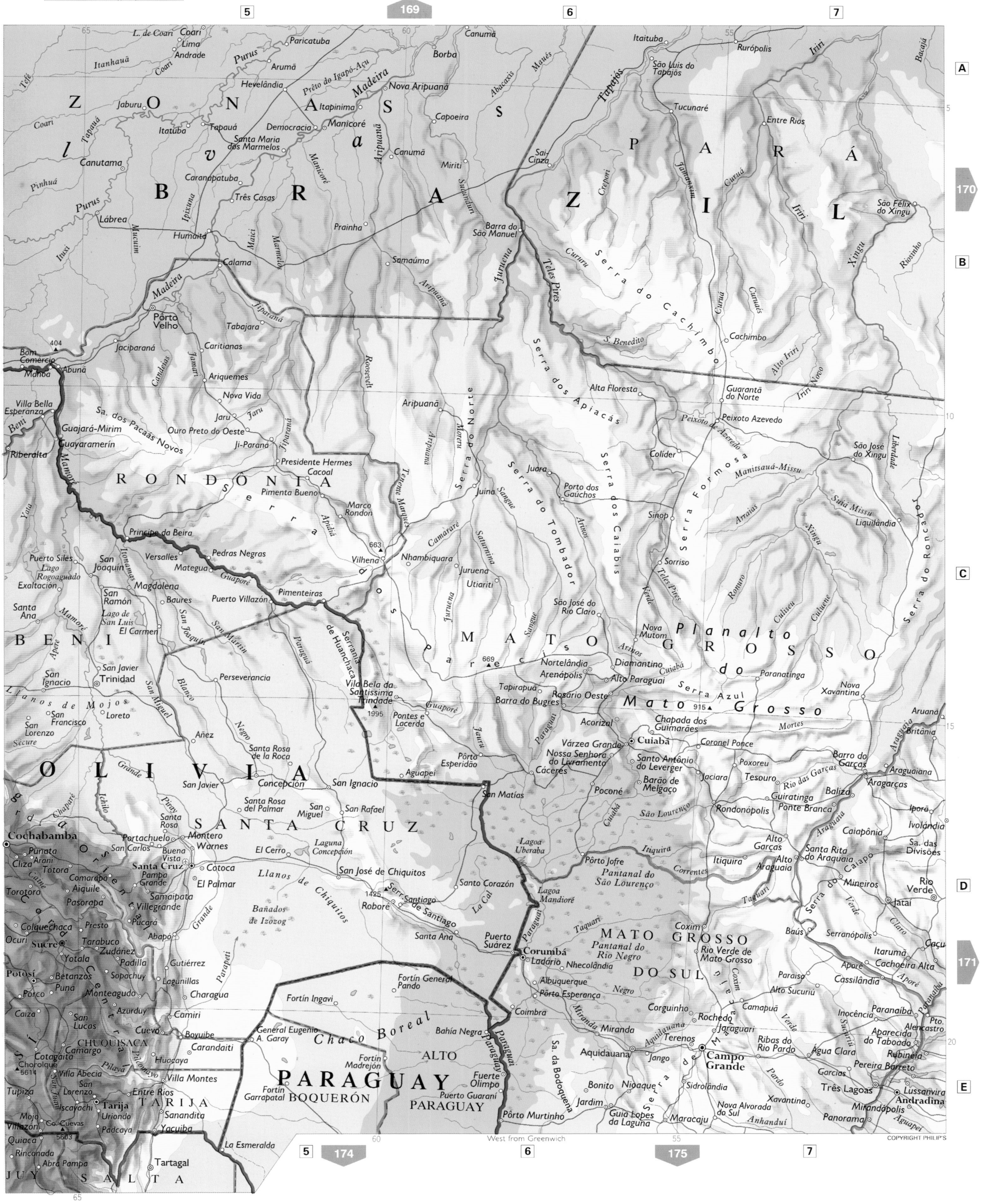

169
170
171
174
175
A
B
C
D
E
5
6
7
L. de Coari
Coari
Lima
Andrade
Paricatuba
Canumã
Borba
Itaituba
Rurópolis
Iriri
Bacajá
Tefé
Itanhauã
Coari
Purus
Arumã
Prêto do Igapó-Açu
Madeira
Nova Aripuanã
Maués
Abacaxis
Tapajós
São Luís do Tapajós
Hevelândia
Jaburu
Itapinima
Manicoré
Capoeira
Tucunaré
Entre Rios
Tapauá
Itatuba
Democracia
Santa Maria dos Marmelos
Canumã
Aripuanã
Canutama
Caranapatuba
Três Casas
Miriti
Sai-Cinza
Crepori
Jamanxim
Curuá
Pinhuã
Purus
Lábrea
Humaitá
Ipixuna
Maici
Marmelos
Manicoré
Prainha
Sucunduri
Barra do São Manuel
São Félix do Xingu
Xingu
Riozinho
Iriri
Mucuim
Ituxi
Calama
Samaúma
Juruena
Teles Pires
Cururu
Serra do Cachimbo
Curuá
Curuaés
Madeira
Pôrto Velho
Tabajara
Jiparaná
Aripuanã
S. Benedito
Cachimbo
404
Bom Comércio
Manoa
Abunã
Jaciparaná
Caritianas
Jamari
Candeias
Ariquemes
Roosevelt
Serra dos Apiacás
Alto Iriri
Iriri Novo
Alta Floresta
Guarantã do Norte
Villa Bella
Esperanza
Beni
Riberalta
Nova Vida
Jaru
Sa. dos Pacaás Novos
Guajará-Mirim
Guayaramerín
Ouro Preto do Oeste
Ji-Paraná
Aripuanã
Moreru
Serra do Norte
Peixoto de Azevedo
Peixoto Azevedo
Colíder
São José do Xingu
Liberdade
Mamoré
Presidente Hermes
Cacoal
Pimenta Bueno
Juara
Porto dos Gaúchos
Serra dos Caiabis
Serra do Tombador
Serra Formosa
Manitsauá-Missu
RONDÔNIA
Tenente Marques
Juína
Sangue
Arinos
Sinop
Suiá Missu
Liquilândia
Yata
Marco Rondon
Apidiá
Serra dos Parecis
Camararé
Saturnina
Arraias
Xingu
Príncipe da Beira
663
Vilhena
Nhambiquara
Juruena
Utiariti
Sorriso
Serra do Roncador
Puerto Siles
Lago Rogoaguado
Exaltación
San Joaquín
Itonamas
Versalles
Pedras Negras
Mategua
Guaporé
Magdalena
Teles Pires
Verde
Ronuro
Culuene
Culiseu
Santa Ana
San Ramón
Baures
Puerto Villazón
Pimenteiras
Lago de San Luis
El Carmen
Mamoré
São José do Rio Claro
Juruena
Sangue
Nova Mutum
Planalto do Mato Grosso
BENI
Apere
San Joaquín
San Martín
Paraguá
Serranía de Huanchaca
669
MATO GROSSO
Arinos
Diamantino
San Javier
Trinidad
San Ignacio
Perseverancia
Blanco
San Miguel
Nortelândia
Arenápolis
Alto Paraguai
Cuiabá
Paranatinga
Serra Azul
Nova Xavantina
Llanos de Mojos
San Francisco
Loreto
San Lorenzo
Sécure
Vila Bela da Santíssima Trindade
1995
Guaporé
Pontes e Lacerda
Tapirapuã
Barra do Bugres
Rosário Oeste
915
Mato Grosso
Aruanã
Chapada dos Guimarães
Mortes
Britânia
Araguaia
Negro
Añez
Santa Rosa de la Roca
Jauru
Paraguai
Acorizal
Cuiabá
Várzea Grande
Nossa Senhora do Livramento
Coronel Ponce
Santo Antônio do Leverger
Pôrto Esperidião
Cáceres
Poxoreu
Barro do Garças
Araguaiana
BOLIVIA
Grande
San Javier
Concepción
San Ignacio
Aguapeí
San Matías
Barão de Melgaço
Poconé
Jaciara
Tesouro
Rio das Garças
Aragarças
Santa Rosa del Palmar
San Miguel
San Rafael
Guiratinga
Baliza
Iporá
Ichilo
Piray
Santa Rosa
SANTA CRUZ
Cuiabá
São Lourenço
Rondonópolis
Ponte Branca
Ivolândia
Cochabamba
Portachuelo
Montero
Warnes
Laguna Concepción
Lagoa Uberaba
Alto Garças
Caiapônia
Punata
Arani
Cliza
Totora
San Carlos
Buena Vista
El Cerro
Itiquira
Alto Araguaia
Santa Rita do Araguaia
Sa. das Divisões
Santa Cruz
Cotoca
Pampa Grande
Comarapa
Aiquile
Tarata
El Palmar
Llanos de Chiquitos
San José de Chiquitos
Santo Corazón
Pôrto Jofre
Pantanal do São Lourenço
Correntes
Serra do Caiapó
Mineiros
Rio Verde
Pasorapa
Samaipata
Villegrande
1425
Serr. Santiago
Roboré
Lagoa Mandioré
Taquari
Jataí
Colquechaca
Presto
Pucará
Bañados de Izozog
Serra de Santiago
La Cal
Coxim
Baús
Serranópolis
Ocurí
Sucre
Tarabuco
Zudáñez
Abapó
Grande
Santa Ana
Puerto Suárez
Corumbá
Pantanal do Rio Negro
MATO GROSSO DO SUL
Rio Verde de Mato Grosso
Itarumã
Caçu
Yotala
Padilla
Gutiérrez
Parapetí
Ladário
Nhecolândia
Aporé
Cachoeira Alta
Potosí
Betanzos
Sopachuy
Lagunillas
Fortín General Pando
Albuquerque
Pôrto Esperança
Negro
Paraíso
Cassilândia
Porco
Puna
Monteagudo
Charagua
Fortín Ingavi
Alto Sucuriú
Azurduy
Camiri
Coimbra
Corguinho
Camapuã
Paranaíba
Inocência
Pto. Alencastro
Caiza
San Lucas
Cuevo
Boyuibe
General Eugenio A. Garay
Chaco Boreal
Bahía Negra
Miranda
Rochedo
Jaraguari
Aparecida do Taboado
CHUQUISACA
Camargo
Carandaiti
Terenos
Ribas do Rio Pardo
Cotagaita
Huacaya
Fortín Madrejón
ALTO PARAGUAY
Aquidauana
Jango
Campo Grande
Água Clara
Rubinéia
Chorolque
5614
Villa Abecia
Pilaya
Villa Montes
PARAGUAY
Fuerte Olimpo
Sa. da Bodoquena
Pardo
Garcias
Pereira Barreto
Tupiza
San Lorenzo
Entre Ríos
TARIJA
Fortín Garrapatal
BOQUERÓN
Puerto Guaraní
Bonito
Nioaque
Sidrolândia
Três Lagoas
Lussanvira
Andradina
Iscayachi
Tarija
Uriondo
Sanandita
Jardim
Serra de Maracaju
Nova Alvorada do Sul
Xavantina
Mirandópolis
Mojo
Villazón
Cuevas
Padcaya
Yacuiba
Pôrto Murtinho
Guia Lopes da Laguna
Maracaju
Anhanduí
Panorama
Aguapeí
Quiaca
5603
Rinconada
Abra Pampa
La Esmeralda
Tartagal
JUJUY
SALTA
65
60
55
West from Greenwich
COPYRIGHT PHILIP'S

1:6 400 000

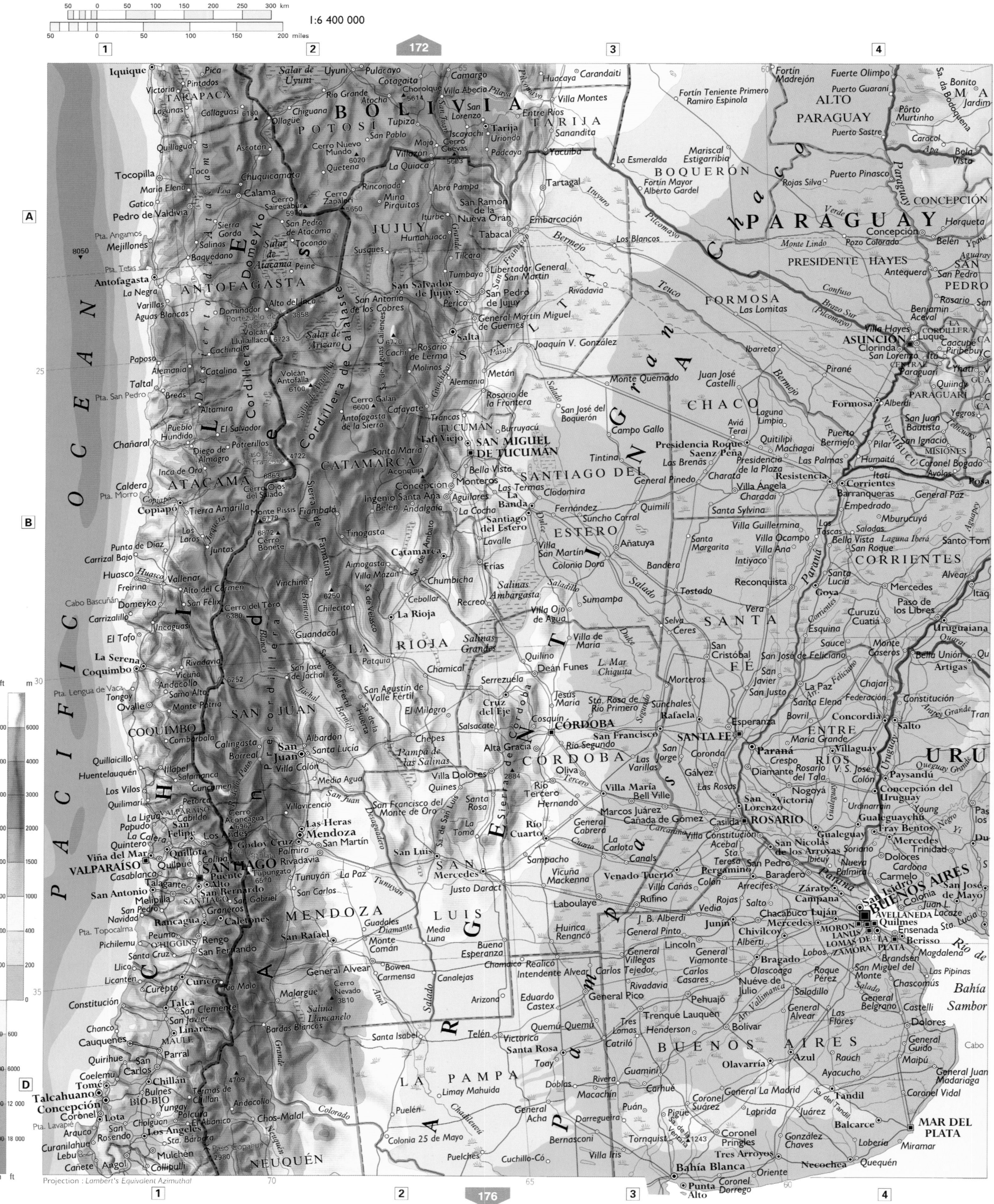

Projection : Lambert's Equivalent Azimuthal

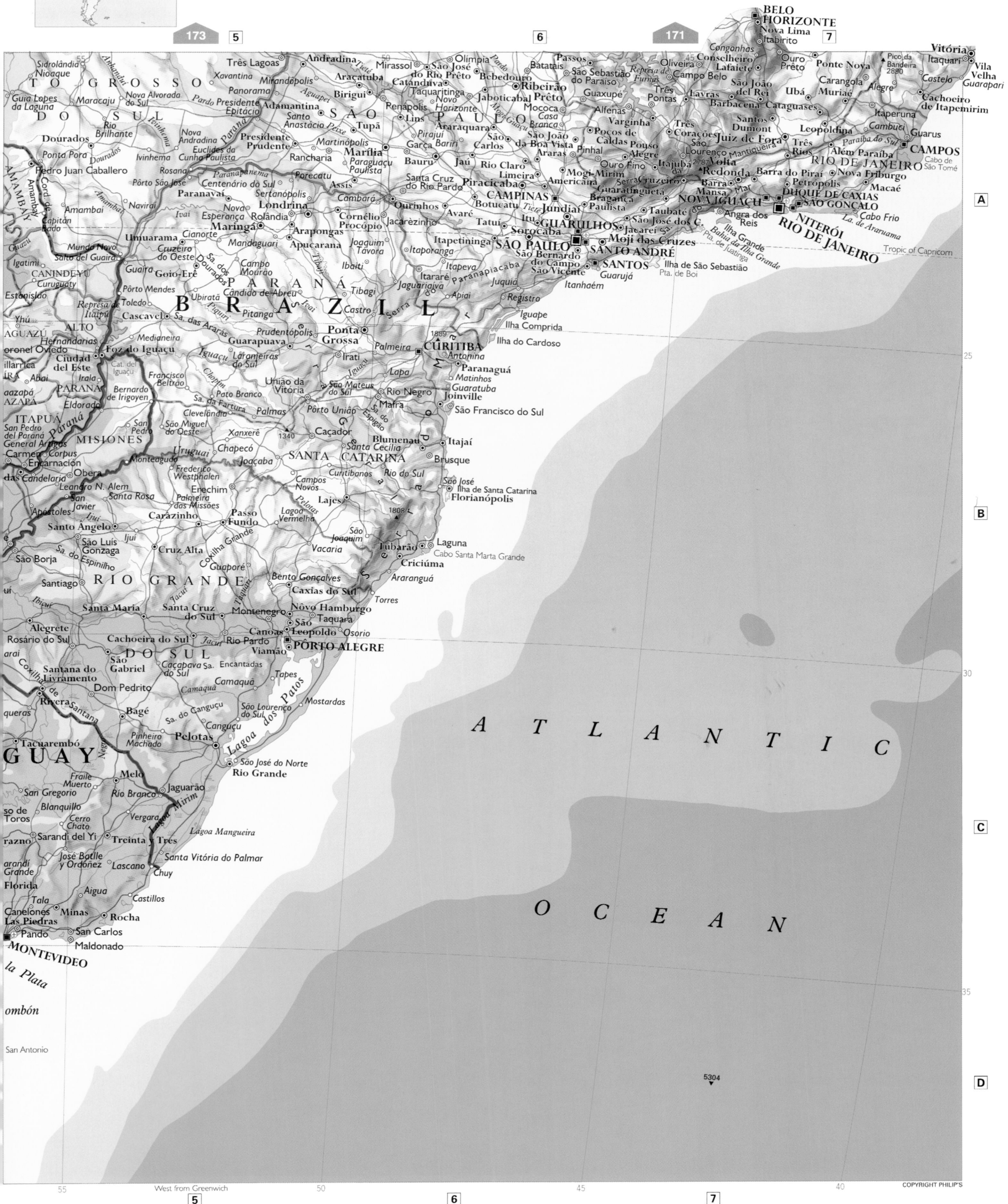

BELO HORIZONTE
Nova Lima
Itabirito
Vitória
Itaquari
Vila Velha
Guarapari

Sidrolândia
Nioaque
Três Lagoas
Andradina
Mirassol
Olímpia
São José do Rio Prêto
Passos
Batatais
São Sebastião do Paraíso
Oliveira
Conselheiro Lafaiete
Congonhas
Ouro Prêto
Ponte Nova
Carangola
Cachoeiro de Itapemirim

Guia Lopes da Laguna
Maracaju
Xavantina
Mirandópolis
Aracatuba
Catanduva
Bebedouro
Ribeirão Prêto
Mococa
Guaxupé
Campo Belo
São João del Rei
Ubá
Muriaé

TO GROSSO
Nova Alvorada do Sul
Presidente Epitácio
Adamantina
Panorama
Penápolis
SÃO
Novo Horizonte
Casa Branca
Alfenas
Varginha
Três Corações
Barbacena
Cataguases
Itaperuna
Cambuí
Guarus

DO SUL
Rio Brilhante
Santo Anastácio
Tupã
Lins
Araraquara
São João da Boa Vista
Poços de Caldas
Pouso Alegre
São Lourenço
Leopoldina
CAMPOS

Dourados
Nova Andradina
Euclides da Cunha Paulista
PAULO
Bauru
Jau
Rio Claro
Americana
Ouro Fino
Itajubá
Volta Redonda
Além Paraíba

Ponta Pora
Dourados
Presidente Prudente
Marília
Bariri
São Carlos
Piracicaba
Mogi-Mirim
Serra
Barra
Barra do Piraí
Nova Friburgo
Macaé

Pedro Juan Caballero
Ivinhema
Rancharia
Paraguaçu Paulista
Garça
CAMPINAS
Jundiaí
Bragança
NOVA IGUAÇU
DUQUE DE CAXIAS
Petrópolis

AMAMBAY
Rosana
Paranapanema
Assis
Cambará
Ourinhos
Botucatu
Paulista
São José dos C.
RIO DE JANEIRO
Cabo Frio

Amambaí
Capitán Bado
Naviraí
Centenário do Sul
Sertanópolis
Avaré
Tatuí
ITU
GUARULHOS
Angra dos Reis
NITERÓI
La. de Araruama

Mundo Novo
Salto del Guairá
PARANÁ
Londrina
Jacarèzinho
Itapetininga
SÃO PAULO
SÃO PAULO
Moji das Cruzes
Ilha Grande
RIO DE JANEIRO

CANINDEYU
Guaíra
Goio-Erê
Maringá
Arapongas
Apucarana
Joaquim Távora
Itararé
São Bernardo do Campo
SANTO ANDRÉ
Ilha da Ilha Grande
Bahía de Ilha Grande

Curuguaty
Umuarama
Cruzeiro do Oeste
Campo Mourão
Mandaguari
Ibaiti
Itaporanga
Apiaí
São Vicente
SANTOS
Guarujá
Pta. de Boi

Estanislao
Cianorte
Cândido de Abreu
Itapeva
Itanhaém
Tropic of Capricorn

ALTO AGUAZÚ
Pôrto Mendes
Toledo
Ubiratã
Pitanga
Jaguariaíva
Paranapiacaba
Juquiá
Registro

Yhú
Represa de Itaipú
Cascavel
Sa. das Araras
Prudentópolis
Ponta Grossa
Palmeira
Iguape
Ilha Comprida

coronel Oviedo
Medianeira
Guarapuava
Irati
CURITIBA
Ilha do Cardoso

villarrica
Ciudad del Este
Foz do Iguaçú
Cat. del Iguaçú
Iguaçu
Laranjeiras do Sul
Lapa
Antonina
Paranaguá

IRA
Irala
Francisco Beltrão
Chopim
Pato Branco
União da Vitória
Matinhos
Guaratuba

aazapá
Abaí
PARANÁ
Bernardo de Irigoyen
Sa. da Fartura
Palmas
São Mateus do Sul
Joinville

AZAPÁ
Eldorado
Cleveland
Xanxerê
Pôrto União
Mafra
São Francisco do Sul

ITAPUA
San Pedro del Parana
General Artigas
San Miguel do Oeste
1340
Caçador
Blumenau
Itajaí

San Pedro del Parana
MISIONES
São Miguel do Oeste
Chapecó
Santa Cecília
Brusque

Carmen
Corpus
Frederico Westphalen
Joaçaba
SANTA CATARINA
São José de Santa Catarina

Encarnación
Obera
Palmeira das Missões
Campos Novos
Rio do Sul
Ilha de Santa Catarina

das Candelaria
Leandro N. Alem
Erechim
Curitibanos
Florianópolis

Apóstoles
San Javier
Santa Rosa
Lajes

Santo Angelo
Ijuí
Carazinho
1808
São Joaquim

São Luis Gonzaga
Cruz Alta
Passo Fundo
Vacaria
Laguna

São Borja
Sa. do Espinilho
Guaporé
Tubarão
Cabo Santa Marta Grande

Santiago
RIO GRANDE
Bento Gonçalves
Criciúma
Ararangúa

Santa Maria
Santa Cruz do Sul
Caxias do Sul
Torres

Alegrete
Montenegro
Nôvo Hamburgo
Taquara

Rosário do Sul
Cachoeira do Sul
Canoas
São Leopoldo
Osorio

Santana do Livramento
São Gabriel
DO SUL
Rio Pardo
Viamão
PÔRTO ALEGRE

Rivera
Dom Pedrito
Caçapava Sa.
Encantadas
Tapes

Bagé
Camaquã
Tapes

Pinheiro Machado
Camaquã
Mostardas

Tacuarembó
Pelotas
Lagoa dos Patos
São Lourenço do Sul

Melo
Jaguarão
São José do Norte
Rio Grande

San Gregorio
Blanquillo
Rio Branco
Vergara

Cerro Chato
Sarandí del Yi
Treinta y Tres
Lagoa Mangueira

José Batlle y Ordóñez
Lascano
Santa Vitória do Palmar
Chuy

Florida
Aigua
Castillos

Tala
Minas
Rocha
Canelones
Las Piedras
San Carlos

MONTEVIDEO
Pando
Maldonado

la Plata
ombón

San Antonio

BRAZIL
PARANÁ
SÃO PAULO
RIO GRANDE DO SUL

ATLANTIC
OCEAN

5304

55 West from Greenwich 50 45 40

25
30
35

A
B
C
D

COPYRIGHT PHILIP'S

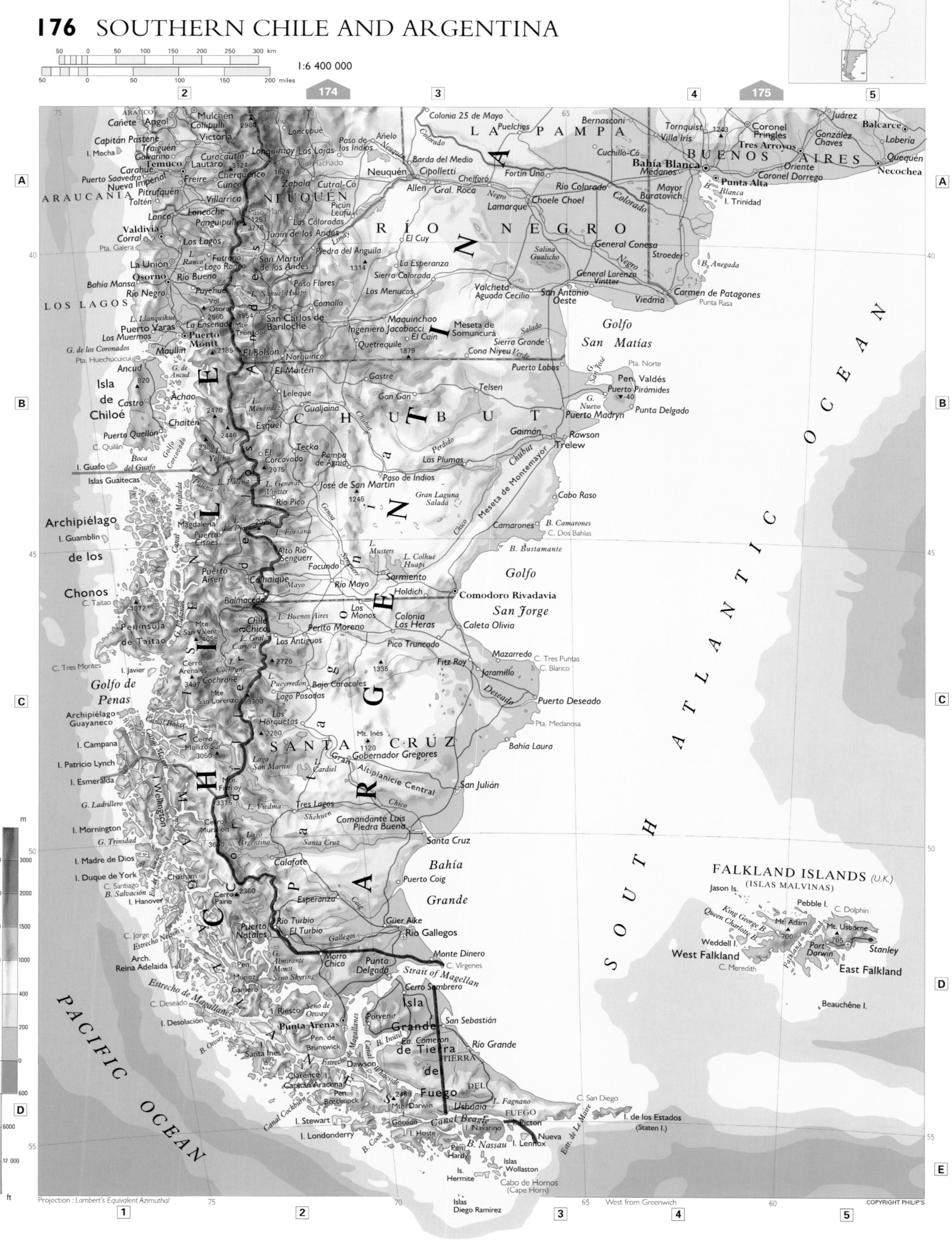

1:6 400 000

50   0   50 100 150 200 250 300 km
50   0   50   100   150   200 miles

ARAUCO
Cañete Angol
Capitán Pastene
Galvarino
Carahue Temuco
Puerto Saavedra
Nueva Imperial Pitrufquén
Toltén

Mulchén
Collipulli
Victoria 2986
Loncopué
Las Lajas
Traiguén
Curacautín Lautaro
Lonquimay Las Lajas
Freire Cherquenco
Cunco
Villarrica
Loncoche Panguipulli
Lanco

Colonia 25 de Mayo
Puelches
Bernasconi
Tornquist 1243
Villa Iris
Coronel
Juárez
Balcarce
González
Chaves
Loberia

LA PAMPA
Paso de los Indios
Añelo
Neuquén
Barda del Medio
Cipolletti
Chelforó
Fortín Uno
Medanos
Bahía Blanca
Coronel
Pringles
Tres Arroyos
BUENOS AIRES
Necochea
Quequén

NEUQUEN
Picún Leufú
Zapala
Cutral-Có
Allen Gral. Roca
Negro
Río Colorado
Choele Choel
Lamarque
Colorado
General Conesa
Stroeder
Carmen de Patagones
Punta Alta
B. Blanca
I. Trinidad
Mayor Buratovich
Coronel Dorrego
Oriente

Valdivia
Corral
Los Lagos
Junín de los Andes
San Martín de los Andes
Las Coloradas
El Cuy
La Esperanza
RÍO NEGRO
Viedma
Punta Rasa

La Unión
Osorno
Río Bueno
Futrono Lago Ranco
Piedra del Anguila
Sierra Colorada
Valcheta
Aguada Cecilio
San Antonio
Oeste
Golfo
San Matías
Pta. Norte

LOS LAGOS
Bahía Mansa
Río Negro
Puyehue
Vol.
Osorno 3954
Comallo
Maquinchao
Meseta de
Somuncurá
Sierra Grande
Cona Niyeu
Puerto Lobos
Pen. Valdés
Puerto Pirámides
Punta Delgado

G. de los Coronados
Los Muermos
Puerto Varas
Maullín
Mte.
Tronador 3554
San Carlos de
Bariloche
Ingeniero Jacobacci
El Caín
Gastre
Telsen
Gaimán
Puerto Madryn

Ancud
Isla
de
Chiloé
Castro
Achao
Chaitén
El Bolsón
El Maitén
Norquinco
Gualjaina
Gan Gan
Rawson
Trelew

CHUBUT
Esquel
Tecka
Perdido
Pampa
de Agnia
Las Plumas
Chubut

El
Corcovado 2075
José de San Martín
Paso de Indios
Camarones
B. Camarones
C. Dos Bahías

Archipiélago
de los
Chonos
Puerto
Cisnes
Río Pico
Gran Laguna
Salada
Chico
Cabo Raso
B. Bustamante

Puerto
Aisen
Coyhaique
Balmaceda
Alto Río
Senguerr
Facundo
Sarmiento
Holdich
Comodoro Rivadavia

Peninsula
de Taitao
Chile
Chico
Los Monos
Colonia
Las Heras
San Jorge
Caleta Olivia

Perito Moreno
Los Antiguos
Pico Truncado
Mazarredo
C. Tres Puntas
C. Blanco

Cochrane
Lago Posadas
Bajo Caracoles
Fitz Roy
Jaramillo
Deseado
Puerto Deseado
Pta. Medanosa

SANTA CRUZ
Las
Hórquetas
Mt. Inés
Gobernador Gregores
Bahía Laura

Gran
Altiplanicie Central
San Julián

Tres Lagos
Comandante Luis
Piedra Buena
Chico
Santa Cruz

Calafate
Puerto Coig
Bahía
Grande

Esperanza
Río Turbio
El Turbio
Puerto
Natales
Güer Aike
Río Gallegos

Monte Dinero
C. Vírgenes
Punta
Delgada
Strait of Magellan

Punta Arenas
Porvenir
Cerro Sombrero
San Sebastián
Isla
Grande
de Tierra
del
Fuego
Río Grande

Ushuaia
Canal Beagle
C. San Diego
I. de los Estados
(Staten I.)

PACIFIC OCEAN

SOUTH ATLANTIC OCEAN

FALKLAND ISLANDS (U.K.)
(ISLAS MALVINAS)
Jason Is.
Pebble I.
C. Dolphin
King George B.
Mt. Adam
Queen Charlotte B.
Weddell I.
Mt. Usborne 705
West Falkland
Port Darwin
Stanley
C. Meredith
East Falkland
Beauchêne I.

Cabo de Hornos
(Cape Horn)
Islas
Diego Ramírez

INDEX TO WORLD MAPS

How to use the index

The index contains the names of all the principal places and features shown on the World Maps. Each name is followed by an additional entry in italics giving the country or region within which it is located. The alphabetical order of names composed of two or more words is governed primarily by the first word and then by the second. This is an example of the rule:

Mīr Kūh, *Iran* .... **97 E8** 26 22N 58 55 E
Mīr Shahdād, *Iran* .... **97 E8** 26 15N 58 29 E
Mira, *Italy* .... **45 C9** 45 26N 12 8 E
Mira por vos Cay, *Bahamas* .. **165 B5** 22 9N 74 30W
Miraj, *India* .... **94 F2** 16 50N 74 45 E

Physical features composed of a proper name (Erie) and a description (Lake) are positioned alphabetically by the proper name. The description is positioned after the proper name and is usually abbreviated:

Erie, L., *N. Amer.* **150 D4** 42 15N 81 0W

Where a description forms part of a settlement or administrative name however, it is always written in full and put in its true alphabetic position:

Mount Olive, *U.S.A.* **156 E7** 39 4N 89 44W

Names beginning with M' and Mc are indexed as if they were spelled Mac. Names beginning St. are alphabetised under Saint, but Sankt, Sint, Sant', Santa and San are all spelt in full and are alphabetised accordingly. If the same place name occurs two or more times in the index and all are in the same country, each is followed by the name of the administrative subdivision in which it is located.

The number in bold type which follows each name in the index refers to the number of the map page where that feature or place will be found. This is usually the largest scale at which the place or feature appears.

The letter and figure which are in bold type immediately after the page number give the grid square on the map page, within which the feature is situated. The letter represents the latitude and the figure the longitude. A lower case letter immediately after the page number refers to an inset map on that page.

In some cases the feature itself may fall within the specified square, while the name is outside. This is usually the case only with features which are larger than a grid square.

The geographical co-ordinates which follow the letter-figure references give the latitude and longitude of each place. The first co-ordinate indicates latitude – the distance north of the Equator. The second co-ordinate indicates longitude – the distance east or west of the Greenwich Meridian. Both latitude and longitude are measured in degrees and minutes (there are 60 minutes in a degree).

The latitude is followed by N(orth) or S(outh) and the longitude by E(ast) or W(est).

Rivers are indexed to their mouths or confluences, and carry the symbol → after their names. The following symbols are also used in the index: ■ country, ▨ overseas territory or dependency, □ first order administrative area, △ national park, ⌓ other park (provincial park, nature reserve or game reserve), ✈ (LHR) principal airport (and location identifier).

How to pronounce place names

English-speaking people usually have no difficulty in reading and pronouncing correctly English place names. However, foreign place name pronunciations may present many problems. Such problems can be minimised by following some simple rules. However, these rules cannot be applied to all situations, and there will be many exceptions.

1. In general, stress each syllable equally, unless your experience suggests otherwise.
2. Pronounce the letter 'a' as a broad 'a' as in 'arm'.
3. Pronounce the letter 'e' as a short 'e' as in 'elm'.
4. Pronounce the letter 'i' as a cross between a short 'i' and long 'e', as the two 'i's in 'California'.
5. Pronounce the letter 'o' as an intermediate 'o' as in 'soft'.
6. Pronounce the letter 'u' as an intermediate 'u' as in 'sure'.
7. Pronounce consonants hard, except in the Romance-language areas where 'g's are likely to be pronounced softly like 'j' in 'jam'; 'j' itself may be pronounced as 'y'; and 'x's may be pronounced as 'h'.
8. For names in mainland China, pronounce 'q' like the 'ch' in 'chin', 'x' like the 'sh' in 'she', 'zh' like the 'j' in 'jam', and 'z' as if it were spelled 'dz'. In general pronounce 'a' as in 'father', 'e' as in 'but', 'i' as in 'keep', 'o' as in 'or', and 'u' as in 'rule'.

Moreover, English has no diacritical marks (accent and pronunciation signs), although some languages do. The following is a brief and general guide to the pronunciation of those most frequently used in the principal Western European languages.

		Pronunciation as in
French	é	day and shows that the e is to be pronounced; e.g. Orléans.
	è	mare
	î	used over any vowel and does not affect pronunciation; shows contraction of the name, usually omission of 's' following a vowel.
	ç	's' before 'a', 'o' and 'u'.
	ë, ï, ü	over 'e', 'i' and 'u' when they are used with another vowel and shows that each is to be pronounced.
German	ä	fate
	ö	fur
	ü	no English equivalent; like French 'tu'
Italian	à, é	over vowels and indicates stress.
Portuguese	ã, õ	vowels pronounced nasally.
	ç	boss
	á	shows stress
	ô	shows that a vowel has an 'i' or 'u' sound combined with it.
Spanish	ñ	canyon
	ü	pronounced as w and separately from adjoining vowels.
	á	usually indicates that this is a stressed vowel.

Abbreviations

A.C.T. – Australian Capital Territory
A.R. – Autonomous Region
Afghan. – Afghanistan
Afr. – Africa
Ala. – Alabama
Alta. – Alberta
Amer. – America(n)
Arch. – Archipelago
Ariz. – Arizona
Ark. – Arkansas
Atl. Oc. – Atlantic Ocean
B. – Baie, Bahía, Bay, Bucht, Bugt
B.C. – British Columbia
Bangla. – Bangladesh
Barr. – Barrage
Bos.-H. – Bosnia-Herzegovina
C. – Cabo, Cap, Cape, Coast
C.A.R. – Central African Republic
C. Prov. – Cape Province
Calif. – California
Cat. – Catarata
Cent. – Central
Chan. – Channel
Colo. – Colorado
Conn. – Connecticut
Cord. – Cordillera
Cr. – Creek
Czech. – Czech Republic
D.C. – District of Columbia
Del. – Delaware
Dem. – Democratic
Dep. – Dependency
Des. – Desert
Dét. – Détroit
Dist. – District
Dj. – Djebel
Domin. – Dominica
Dom. Rep. – Dominican Republic
E. – East
E. Salv. – El Salvador
Eq. Guin. – Equatorial Guinea
Est. – Estrecho
Falk. Is. – Falkland Is.
Fd. – Fjord
Fla. – Florida
Fr. – French
G. – Golfe, Golfo, Gulf, Guba, Gebel
Ga. – Georgia
Gt. – Great, Greater
Guinea-Biss. – Guinea-Bissau
H.K. – Hong Kong
H.P. – Himachal Pradesh
Hants. – Hampshire
Harb. – Harbor, Harbour
Hd. – Head
Hts. – Heights
I.(s). – Île, Ilha, Insel, Isla, Island, Isle
Ill. – Illinois
Ind. – Indiana
Ind. Oc. – Indian Ocean
Ivory C. – Ivory Coast
J. – Jabal, Jebel
Jaz. – Jazīrah
Junc. – Junction
K. – Kap, Kapp
Kans. – Kansas
Kep. – Kepulauan
Ky. – Kentucky
L. – Lac, Lacul, Lago, Lagoa, Lake, Limni, Loch, Lough
La. – Louisiana
Ld. – Land
Liech. – Liechtenstein
Lux. – Luxembourg
Mad. P. – Madhya Pradesh
Madag. – Madagascar
Man. – Manitoba
Mass. – Massachusetts
Md. – Maryland
Me. – Maine
Medit. S. – Mediterranean Sea
Mich. – Michigan
Minn. – Minnesota
Miss. – Mississippi
Mo. – Missouri
Mont. – Montana
Mozam. – Mozambique
Mt.(s) – Mont, Montaña, Mountain
Mte. – Monte
Mti. – Monti
N. – Nord, Norte, North, Northern, Nouveau
N.B. – New Brunswick
N.C. – North Carolina
N. Cal. – New Caledonia
N. Dak. – North Dakota
N.H. – New Hampshire
N.I. – North Island
N.J. – New Jersey
N. Mex. – New Mexico
N.S. – Nova Scotia
N.S.W. – New South Wales
N.W.T. – North West Territory
N.Y. – New York
N.Z. – New Zealand
Nac. – Nacional
Nat. – National
Nebr. – Nebraska
Neths. – Netherlands
Nev. – Nevada
Nfld. – Newfoundland
Nic. – Nicaragua
O. – Oued, Ouadi
Occ. – Occidentale
Okla. – Oklahoma
Ont. – Ontario
Or. – Orientale
Oreg. – Oregon
Os. – Ostrov
Oz. – Ozero
P. – Pass, Passo, Pasul, Pulau
P.E.I. – Prince Edward Island
Pa. – Pennsylvania
Pac. Oc. – Pacific Ocean
Papua N.G. – Papua New Guinea
Pass. – Passage
Peg. – Pegunungan
Pen. – Peninsula, Péninsule
Phil. – Philippines
Pk. – Peak
Plat. – Plateau
Prov. – Province, Provincial
Pt. – Point
Pta. – Ponta, Punta
Pte. – Pointe
Qué. – Québec
Queens. – Queensland
R. – Rio, River
R.I. – Rhode Island
Ra. – Range
Raj. – Rajasthan
Recr. – Recreational, Récréatif
Reg. – Region
Rep. – Republic
Res. – Reserve, Reservoir
Rhld-Pfz. – Rheinland-Pfalz
S. – South, Southern, Sur
Si. Arabia – Saudi Arabia
S.C. – South Carolina
S. Dak. – South Dakota
S.I. – South Island
S. Leone – Sierra Leone
Sa. – Serra, Sierra
Sask. – Saskatchewan
Scot. – Scotland
Sd. – Sound
Sev. – Severnaya
Sib. – Siberia
Sprs. – Springs
St. – Saint
Sta. – Santa
Ste. – Sainte
Sto. – Santo
Str. – Strait, Stretto
Switz. – Switzerland
Tas. – Tasmania
Tenn. – Tennessee
Terr. – Territory, Territoire
Tex. – Texas
Tg. – Tanjung
Trin. & Tob. – Trinidad & Tobago
U.A.E. – United Arab Emirates
U.K. – United Kingdom
U.S.A. – United States of America
Ut. P. – Uttar Pradesh
Va. – Virginia
Vdkhr. – Vodokhranilishche
Vdskh. – Vodoskhovyshche
Vf. – Vírful
Vic. – Victoria
Vol. – Volcano
Vt. – Vermont
W. – Wadi, West
W. Va. – West Virginia
Wall. & F. Is. – Wallis and Futuna Is.
Wash. – Washington
Wis. – Wisconsin
Wlkp. – Wielkopolski
Wyo. – Wyoming
Yorks. – Yorkshire
Yug. – Yugoslavia

A

A 'Âli an Nîl □, *Sudan* **107 F3** 9 30N 33 0 E
A Baña, *Spain* **42 C2** 42 58N 8 46W
A Cañiza, *Spain* **42 C2** 42 13N 8 16W
A Coruña, *Spain* **42 B2** 43 20N 8 25W
A Estrada, *Spain* **42 C2** 42 43N 8 27W
A Fonsagrada, *Spain* **42 B3** 43 8N 7 4W
A Guarda, *Spain* **42 D2** 41 56N 8 52W
A Gudiña, *Spain* **42 C3** 42 4N 7 8W
A Rúa, *Spain* **42 C3** 42 24N 7 6W
Aachen, *Germany* **30 E2** 50 45N 6 6 E
Aadorf, *Switz.* **33 B7** 47 30N 8 55 E
Aalborg = Ålborg, *Denmark* **17 G3** 57 2N 9 54 E
Aalen, *Germany* **31 G6** 48 51N 10 6 E
Aalst, *Belgium* **24 D4** 50 56N 4 2 E
Aalten, *Neths.* **24 C6** 51 56N 6 35 E
Aalter, *Belgium* **24 C3** 51 5N 3 28 E
Äänekoski, *Finland* **15 E21** 62 36N 25 44 E
Aarau, *Switz.* **32 B6** 47 23N 8 4 E
Aarberg, *Switz.* **32 B4** 47 2N 7 16 E
Aarburg, *Switz.* **32 B5** 47 19N 7 54 E
Aare →, *Switz.* **32 A6** 47 33N 8 14 E
Aargau □, *Switz.* **32 B6** 47 26N 8 10 E
Aarhus = Århus, *Denmark* **17 H4** 56 8N 10 11 E
Aarlen = Arlon, *Belgium* **24 E5** 49 42N 5 49 E
Aarschot, *Belgium* **24 D4** 50 59N 4 49 E
Aarwangen, *Switz.* **32 B5** 47 15N 7 46 E
Aasiaat, *Greenland* **10 D5** 68 43N 52 56W
Ab-i-Istada, *Afghan.* **91 B2** 32 29N 67 55 E
Ab-i-Panja = Pyandzh →, *Asia* **65 E4** 37 6N 68 20 E
Aba, *China* **76 A3** 32 59N 101 42 E
Aba, *Dem. Rep. of the Congo* **118 B3** 3 58N 30 17 E
Aba, *Nigeria* **113 D6** 5 10N 7 19 E
Âbâ, Jazîrat, *Sudan* **107 E3** 13 30N 32 31 E
Abacaxis →, *Brazil* **169 D6** 3 54 S 58 47W
Abadab, J., *Sudan* **106 D4** 18 54N 35 56 E
Ābādān, *Iran* **97 D6** 30 22N 48 20 E
Abade, *Ethiopia* **107 F4** 9 22N 38 3 E
Ābādeh, *Iran* **97 D7** 31 8N 52 40 E
Abadin, *Spain* **42 B3** 43 21N 7 29W
Abadla, *Algeria* **111 B4** 31 2N 2 45W
Abaeté, *Brazil* **171 E2** 19 9 S 45 27W
Abaeté →, *Brazil* **171 E2** 18 2 S 45 12W
Abaetetuba, *Brazil* **170 B2** 1 40 S 48 50W
Abagnar Qi, *China* **74 C9** 43 52N 116 2 E
Abah, Tanjung, *Indonesia* **79 K18** 8 46 S 115 38 E
Abai, *Paraguay* **175 B4** 25 58 S 55 54W
Abak, *Nigeria* **113 E6** 4 58N 7 50 E
Abakaliki, *Nigeria* **113 D6** 6 22N 8 2 E
Abakan, *Russia* **67 D10** 53 40N 91 10 E
Abala, *Congo* **114 C3** 1 17 S 15 35 E
Abala, *Niger* **113 C5** 14 56N 3 22 E
Abalak, *Niger* **113 B6** 15 22N 6 21 E
Abalemma, *Algeria* **111 D6** 20 51N 5 59 E
Abalemma, *Niger* **113 B6** 16 12N 7 50 E
Abalessa, *Algeria* **111 D5** 22 58N 4 47 E
Abana, *Turkey* **100 B6** 41 59N 34 1 E
Abancay, *Peru* **172 C3** 13 35 S 72 55W
Abanga →, *Gabon* **114 C2** 0 29N 10 30 E
Abano Terme, *Italy* **45 C8** 45 22N 11 46 E
Abapó, *Bolivia* **173 D5** 18 48 S 63 25W
Abarán, *Spain* **41 G3** 38 12N 1 23W
Abariringa, *Kiribati* **134 H10** 2 50 S 171 40W
Abarqū, *Iran* **97 D7** 31 10N 53 20 E
Abashiri, *Japan* **70 B12** 44 0N 144 15 E
Abashiri-Wan, *Japan* **70 C12** 44 0N 144 30 E
Abau, *Papua N. G.* **132 F5** 10 11 S 148 46 E
Abaújszántó, *Hungary* **52 B6** 48 16N 21 12 E
Abava →, *Latvia* **54 A8** 57 6N 21 54 E
Ābay = Nîl el Azraq →, *Sudan* **107 D3** 15 38N 32 31 E
Abay, *Kazakhstan* **66 E8** 49 38N 72 53 E
Abaya, L., *Ethiopia* **107 F4** 6 30N 37 50 E
Abaya-Shala Lakes Nat. Park △, *Ethiopia* **107 F4** 7 40N 38 37 E
Abaza, *Russia* **66 D9** 52 39N 90 6 E
Abba, *C.A.R.* **114 A3** 5 20N 15 11 E
Abbadia di Fiastra, Riserva Statale ⌂, *Italy* **45 E10** 43 12N 13 24 E
Abbadia San Salvatore, *Italy* **45 F8** 42 53N 11 41 E
'Abbāsābād, *Iran* **97 C8** 33 34N 58 23 E
Abbay = Nîl el Azraq →, *Sudan* **107 D3** 15 38N 32 31 E
Abbaye, Pt., *U.S.A.* **148 B1** 46 58N 88 8W
Abbé, L., *Ethiopia* **107 E5** 11 8N 41 47 E
Abbeville, *France* **27 B8** 50 6N 1 49 E
Abbeville, *Ala., U.S.A.* **152 D4** 31 34N 85 15W
Abbeville, *Ga., U.S.A.* **152 D6** 31 59N 83 18W
Abbeville, *La., U.S.A.* **155 L8** 29 58N 92 8W
Abbeville, *S.C., U.S.A.* **152 A7** 34 11N 82 23W
Abbiategrasso, *Italy* **44 C5** 45 24N 8 54 E
Abbot Ice Shelf, *Antarctica* **7 D16** 73 0 S 92 0W
Abbottabad, *Pakistan* **92 B5** 34 10N 73 15 E
Abbou, O. ben →, *Algeria* **111 C5** 28 32N 5 14 E
Abd al Kūrī, *Yemen* **99 D6** 12 5N 52 20 E
Ābdar, *Iran* **97 D7** 30 16N 55 19 E
'Abdolābād, *Iran* **97 C8** 34 12N 56 30 E
Abdulino, *Russia* **64 E4** 53 42N 53 40 E
Abdulpur, *Bangla.* **90 C2** 24 15N 88 59 E
Abéché, *Chad* **109 F4** 13 50N 20 35 E
Abejar, *Spain* **40 D2** 41 48N 2 47W
Abekr, *Sudan* **107 E2** 12 45N 28 50 E
Abel Tasman Nat. Park △, *N.Z.* **131 A8** 40 59 S 173 3 E
Abemarre, *Indonesia* **83 C6** 7 1 S 140 9 E
Abengourou, *Ivory C.* **112 D4** 6 42N 3 27W
Abenójar, *Spain* **43 G6** 38 53N 4 21W
Åbenrå, *Denmark* **17 J3** 55 3N 9 25 E
Abensberg, *Germany* **31 G7** 48 48N 11 51 E
Abeokuta, *Nigeria* **113 D5** 7 3N 3 19 E
Aber, *Uganda* **118 B3** 2 12N 32 25 E
Aberaeron, *U.K.* **21 E3** 52 15N 4 15W
Aberayron = Aberaeron, *U.K.* **21 E3** 52 15N 4 15W
Aberchirder, *U.K.* **22 D6** 57 34N 2 37W
Abercorn = Mbala, *Zambia* **119 D3** 8 46 S 31 24 E
Abercorn, *Australia* **127 D5** 25 12 S 151 5 E
Aberdare, *U.K.* **21 F4** 51 43N 3 27W
Aberdare Nat. Park △, *Kenya* **118 C4** 0 22 S 36 44 E
Aberdare Ra., *Kenya* **118 C4** 0 15 S 36 50 E
Aberdeen, *Australia* **129 B9** 32 9 S 150 56 E
Aberdeen, *Canada* **143 C7** 52 20N 106 8W
Aberdeen, *China* **69 G11** 22 15N 114 9 E
Aberdeen, *S. Africa* **116 E3** 32 28 S 24 2 E
Aberdeen, *U.K.* **22 D6** 57 9N 2 5W
Aberdeen, *Ala., U.S.A.* **149 J1** 33 49N 88 33W
Aberdeen, *Idaho, U.S.A.* **158 E7** 42 57N 112 50W
Aberdeen, *Md., U.S.A.* **148 F7** 39 31N 76 10W
Aberdeen, *Ohio, U.S.A.* **157 F13** 38 39N 83 46W
Aberdeen, *S. Dak., U.S.A.* **154 C5** 45 28N 98 29W
Aberdeen, *Wash., U.S.A.* **160 D3** 46 59N 123 50W
Aberdeen, City of □, *U.K.* **22 D6** 57 10N 2 10W
Aberdeenshire □, *U.K.* **22 D6** 57 17N 2 36W
Aberdovey = Aberdyfi, *U.K.* **21 E3** 52 33N 4 3W
Aberdyfi, *U.K.* **21 E3** 52 33N 4 3W
Aberfeldy, *U.K.* **22 E5** 56 37N 3 51W
Aberfoyle, *U.K.* **22 E4** 56 11N 4 23W
Abergavenny, *U.K.* **21 F4** 51 49N 3 1W
Abergele, *U.K.* **20 D4** 53 17N 3 35W
Abernathy, *U.S.A.* **155 J4** 33 50N 101 51W
Abert, L., *U.S.A.* **158 E3** 42 38N 120 14W
Aberystwyth, *U.K.* **21 E3** 52 25N 4 5W
Abhā, *Si. Arabia* **98 C3** 18 0N 42 34 E
Abhar, *Iran* **97 B6** 36 9N 49 13 E
Abhayapuri, *India* **90 B3** 26 24N 90 38 E
Abia □, *Nigeria* **113 D6** 5 30N 7 35 E
Abide, *Turkey* **49 C11** 38 55N 29 20 E
Abidiya, *Sudan* **106 D3** 18 18N 34 3 E
Abidjan, *Ivory C.* **112 D4** 5 26N 3 58W
Abilene, *Kans., U.S.A.* **154 F6** 38 55N 97 13W
Abilene, *Tex., U.S.A.* **155 J5** 32 28N 99 43W
Abingdon, *U.K.* **21 F6** 51 40N 1 17W
Abingdon, *Ill., U.S.A.* **156 D6** 40 48N 90 24W
Abingdon, *Va., U.S.A.* **149 G5** 36 43N 81 59W
Abingdon, I. = Pinta, I., *Ecuador* **172 a** 0 35N 90 44W
Abington Reef, *Australia* **126 B4** 18 0 S 149 35 E
Abitau →, *Canada* **143 B7** 59 53N 109 3W
Abitibi →, *Canada* **140 B3** 51 3N 80 55W
Abitibi, L., *Canada* **140 C4** 48 40N 79 40W
Abiy Adi, *Ethiopia* **107 E4** 13 39N 39 3 E
Abkhaz Republic = Abkhazia □, *Georgia* **61 J5** 43 12N 41 5 E
Abkhazia □, *Georgia* **61 J5** 43 12N 41 5 E
Abminga, *Australia* **127 D1** 26 8 S 134 51 E
Abnûb, *Egypt* **106 B3** 27 18N 31 4 E
Åbo = Turku, *Finland* **15 F20** 60 30N 22 19 E
Abo, Massif d', *Chad* **109 D3** 21 41N 16 8 E
Abocho, *Nigeria* **113 D6** 7 35N 6 56 E
Abohar, *India* **92 D6** 30 10N 74 10 E
Aboisso, *Ivory C.* **112 D4** 5 30N 3 5W
Abolo, *Congo* **114 B2** 0 8N 14 16 E
Abomey, *Benin* **113 D5** 7 10N 2 5 E
Abong-Mbang, *Cameroon* **114 B2** 4 0N 13 8 E
Abongabong, *Indonesia* **84 B1** 4 15N 96 48 E
Abonnema, *Nigeria* **113 E6** 4 41N 6 49 E
Abony, *Hungary* **52 C5** 47 12N 20 3 E
Abor Hills, *India* **90 A5** 28 25N 94 46 E
Aborlan, *Phil.* **81 G2** 9 26N 118 33 E
Aboso, *Ghana* **112 D4** 5 23N 1 57W
Abou-Deïa, *Chad* **109 F3** 11 20N 19 20 E
Abou-Goulem, *Chad* **109 F4** 13 37N 21 38 E
Abou-Telfan, Réserve de Faune de l' ⌂, *Chad* **109 F3** 12 2N 18 58 E
Aboyne, *U.K.* **22 D6** 57 4N 2 47W
Abra □, *Phil.* **80 C3** 17 35N 120 45 E
Abra de Ilog, *Phil.* **80 E3** 13 27N 120 44 E
Abra Pampa, *Argentina* **174 A2** 22 43 S 65 42W
Abraham L., *Canada* **142 C5** 52 15N 116 35W
Abrantes, *Portugal* **43 F2** 39 24N 8 7W
Abreojos, Pta., *Mexico* **162 B2** 26 50N 113 40W
Abri, *Esh Shamâliya, Sudan* **106 C3** 20 50N 30 27 E
Abri, *Janub Kordofân, Sudan* **107 E3** 11 40N 30 21 E
Abrolhos, Banka, *Brazil* **171 E4** 18 0 S 38 0W
Abrud, *Romania* **52 D8** 46 19N 23 5 E
Abruzzo □, *Italy* **45 F10** 42 15N 14 0 E
Absaroka Range, *U.S.A.* **158 D9** 44 45N 109 50W
Abtenau, *Austria* **34 D6** 47 33N 13 21 E
Abu, *India* **92 G5** 24 41N 72 50 E
Abū al Abyaḍ, *U.A.E.* **97 E7** 24 11N 53 50 E
Abū al Khaṣīb, *Iraq* **97 D6** 30 25N 48 0 E
Abū 'Alī, *Si. Arabia* **97 E6** 27 20N 49 27 E
Abū 'Alī →, *Lebanon* **103 A4** 34 25N 35 50 E
Abū 'Arīsh, *Si. Arabia* **98 C3** 16 53N 42 48 E
Abu Ballas, *Egypt* **106 C2** 24 26N 27 36 E
Abu Deleiq, *Sudan* **107 D3** 15 57N 33 48 E
Abu Dhabi = Abū Ẓāby, *U.A.E.* **97 E7** 24 28N 54 22 E
Abu Dis, *Sudan* **106 D3** 19 12N 33 38 E
Abu Dom, *Sudan* **107 D3** 16 18N 32 25 E
Abū Du'ān, *Syria* **101 D8** 36 25N 38 15 E
Abu el Gairi, W. →, *Egypt* **103 F2** 29 35N 33 30 E
Abu Fatma, Ras, *Sudan* **106 C4** 22 25N 36 25 E
Abu Gabra, *Sudan* **107 E2** 11 2N 26 50 E
Abu Ga'da, W. →, *Egypt* **103 F1** 29 15N 32 53 E
Abu Gelba, *Sudan* **107 E3** 13 11N 31 52 E
Abu Gubeiha, *Sudan* **107 E3** 11 30N 31 15 E
Abu Habl, Khawr →, *Sudan* **107 E3** 12 37N 31 0 E
Abū Ḥadrīyah, *Si. Arabia* **97 E6** 27 20N 48 58 E
Abu Hamed, *Sudan* **106 D3** 19 32N 33 13 E
Abu Haraz, *An Nîl el Azraq, Sudan* **106 D3** 18 1N 33 58 E
Abu Haraz, *El Gezira, Sudan* **107 E3** 14 35N 33 30 E
Abu Haraz, *Esh Shamâliya, Sudan* **106 D3** 19 8N 32 18 E
Abu Higar, *Sudan* **107 E3** 12 50N 33 59 E
Abū Kamāl, *Syria* **101 E9** 34 30N 41 0 E
Abu Kuleiwat, *Sudan* **107 E2** 12 20N 26 0 E
Abū Madd, Ra's, *Si. Arabia* **96 E3** 24 50N 37 7 E
Abu Matariq, *Sudan* **107 E2** 10 59N 26 9 E
Abu Mendi, *Ethiopia* **107 E4** 11 48N 35 42 E
Abū Mūsā, *U.A.E.* **97 E7** 25 52N 55 3 E
Abū Qaşr, *Si. Arabia* **96 D3** 30 21N 38 34 E
Abu Qir, *Egypt* **106 H7** 31 18N 30 0 E
Abu Qireiya, *Egypt* **106 C4** 24 5N 35 28 E
Abu Qurqâs, *Egypt* **106 B3** 28 1N 30 44 E
Abū Raṣāṣ, Ra's, *Oman* **99 B7** 20 10N 58 38 E
Abu Shagara, Ras, *Sudan* **106 C4** 21 4N 37 19 E
Abu Shanab, *Sudan* **107 E2** 13 58N 27 49 E
Abu Simbel, *Egypt* **106 C3** 22 18N 31 40 E
Abū Şukhayr, *Iraq* **101 G11** 31 54N 44 30 E
Abu Sultân, *Egypt* **106 H8** 30 24N 32 21 E
Abu Tabari, *Sudan* **106 D2** 17 32N 28 32 E
Abu Tig, *Egypt* **106 B3** 27 4N 31 15 E
Abu Tiga, *Sudan* **107 E3** 12 47N 34 12 E
Abu Tineitin, *Sudan* **107 E3** 14 24N 31 1 E
Abu Uruq, *Sudan* **106 D3** 15 52N 30 25 E
Abu Zabad, *Sudan* **107 E2** 12 25N 29 10 E
Abū Ẓāby, *U.A.E.* **97 E7** 24 28N 54 22 E
Abū Zeydābād, *Iran* **97 C6** 33 54N 51 45 E
Abufari, *Brazil* **173 B5** 5 25 S 62 59W
Abuja, *Nigeria* **113 D6** 9 5N 7 32 E
Abukuma-Gawa →, *Japan* **70 E10** 38 6N 140 52 E
Abukuma-Sammyaku, *Japan* **70 F10** 37 30N 140 45 E
Abulug, *Phil.* **80 B3** 18 27N 121 27 E
Abumombazi, *Dem. Rep. of the Congo* **114 B4** 3 42N 22 10 E
Abunã, *Brazil* **173 B4** 9 40 S 65 20W
Abunã →, *Brazil* **173 B4** 9 41 S 65 20W
Abune Yosef, *Ethiopia* **107 E4** 12 5N 39 12 E
Aburatsu, *Japan* **72 F3** 31 34N 131 24 E
Aburo, *Dem. Rep. of the Congo* **118 B3** 2 4N 30 53 E
Abut Hd., *N.Z.* **131 D5** 43 7 S 170 15 E
Abuye Meda, *Ethiopia* **107 E4** 10 30N 39 49 E
Abuyog, *Phil.* **81 F5** 10 45N 125 0 E
Abwong, *Sudan* **107 F3** 9 2N 32 14 E
Åby, *Sweden* **17 F10** 58 40N 16 10 E
Aby, Lagune, *Ivory C.* **112 D4** 5 15N 3 14W
Abyad, *Sudan* **107 E2** 13 47N 26 24 E
Åbybro, *Denmark* **17 G3** 57 10N 9 44 E
Acacías, *Colombia* **168 C3** 3 59N 73 46W
Acadia Nat. Park △, *U.S.A.* **149 C11** 44 20N 68 13W
Acajutla, *El Salv.* **164 D2** 13 36N 89 50W
Açailândia, *Brazil* **170 C2** 5 0 S 47 30W
Acámbaro, *Mexico* **162 D4** 20 0N 100 40W
Acanthus, *Greece* **50 F7** 40 27N 23 47 E
Acaponeta, *Mexico* **162 C3** 22 30N 105 20W
Acapulco, *Mexico* **163 D5** 16 51N 99 56W
Acará, *Brazil* **170 B2** 1 57 S 48 11W
Acarai, Serra, *Brazil* **169 C6** 1 50N 57 50W
Acaraú, *Brazil* **170 B3** 2 53 S 40 7W
Acari, *Brazil* **170 C4** 6 31 S 36 38W
Acarí, *Peru* **172 D3** 15 25 S 74 36W
Acarigua, *Venezuela* **168 B4** 9 33N 69 12W
Acatlán, *Mexico* **163 D5** 18 10N 98 3W
Acayucan, *Mexico* **163 D6** 17 59N 94 58W
Accéglio, *Italy* **44 D4** 44 28N 7 0 E
Accomac, *U.S.A.* **148 G8** 37 43N 75 40W
Accous, *France* **28 E3** 43 0N 0 36W
Accra, *Ghana* **113 D4** 5 35N 0 6W
Accrington, *U.K.* **20 D5** 53 45N 2 22W
Acebal, *Argentina* **174 C3** 33 20 S 60 50W
Aceh □, *Indonesia* **84 B1** 4 15N 97 30 E
Acerra, *Italy* **47 B7** 40 57N 14 22 E
Aceuchal, *Spain* **43 G4** 38 39N 6 30W
Achacachi, *Bolivia* **172 D4** 16 3 S 68 43W
Achaguas, *Venezuela* **168 B4** 7 46N 68 14W
Achalpur, *India* **94 D3** 21 22N 77 32 E
Achao, *Chile* **176 B2** 42 28 S 73 30W
Achegour, *Niger* **109 E2** 19 10N 11 54 E
Achelouma, *Niger* **109 D2** 22 12N 12 50 E
Achelouma, E. →, *Niger* **109 D2** 21 55N 13 35 E
Acheng, *China* **75 B14** 45 30N 126 58 E
Achenkirch, *Austria* **34 D4** 47 32N 11 45 E
Achensee, *Austria* **34 D4** 47 26N 11 45 E
Acher, *India* **92 H5** 23 10N 72 32 E
Achern, *Germany* **31 G4** 48 37N 8 4 E
Acheron →, *N.Z.* **131 C8** 42 16 S 173 4 E
Achill Hd., *Ireland* **23 C1** 53 58N 10 15W
Achill I., *Ireland* **23 C1** 53 58N 10 1W
Achim, *Germany* **30 B5** 53 1N 9 3 E
Achinsk, *Russia* **67 D10** 56 20N 90 20 E
Achisay = Ashchysay, *Kazakhstan* **65 B4** 43 35N 68 53 E
Achit, *Russia* **64 C6** 56 48N 57 54 E
Achouka, *Gabon* **114 C2** 0 52 S 9 45 E
Acıgöl, *Turkey* **49 D11** 37 50N 29 50 E
Acıpayam, *Turkey* **49 D11** 37 26N 29 22 E
Acireale, *Italy* **47 E8** 37 37N 15 10 E
Ackerman, *U.S.A.* **155 J10** 33 19N 89 11W
Ackley, *U.S.A.* **156 B3** 42 33N 93 3W
Acklins I., *Bahamas* **165 B5** 22 30N 74 0W
Acme, *Canada* **142 C6** 51 33N 113 30W
Acme, *U.S.A.* **150 F5** 40 8N 79 26W
Acobamba, *Peru* **172 C3** 12 52 S 74 35W
Acomayo, *Peru* **172 C3** 13 55 S 71 38W
Aconcagua, Cerro, *Argentina* **174 C2** 32 39 S 70 0W
Aconquija, Mt., *Argentina* **174 B2** 27 0 S 66 0W
Acopiara, *Brazil* **170 C4** 6 6 S 39 27W
Açores, Is. dos, *Atl. Oc.* **9 D1** 38 0N 27 0W
Acorizal, *Brazil* **173 D6** 15 12 S 56 22W
Acornhoek, *S. Africa* **117 C5** 24 37 S 31 2 E
Acquapendente, *Italy* **45 F8** 42 44N 11 52 E
Acquasanta Terme, *Italy* **45 F10** 42 46N 13 24 E
Acquasparta, *Italy* **45 F9** 42 41N 12 33 E
Acquaviva delle Fonti, *Italy* **47 B9** 40 54N 16 50 E
Ácqui Terme, *Italy* **44 D5** 44 41N 8 28 E
Acraman, L., *Australia* **127 E2** 32 2 S 135 23 E
Acre = 'Akko, *Israel* **103 C4** 32 55N 35 4 E
Acre □, *Brazil* **172 B3** 9 1 S 71 0W
Acre →, *Brazil* **172 B4** 8 45 S 67 22W
Acri, *Italy* **47 C9** 39 29N 16 23 E
Acs, *Hungary* **52 C3** 47 42N 18 2 E
Actaeon Mt., *St. Helena* **9 h** 15 58 S 5 42W
Actium, *Greece* **39 B2** 38 57N 20 45 E
Acton, *Canada* **150 C4** 43 38N 80 3W
Açu, *Brazil* **170 C4** 5 34 S 36 54W
Acuña, *Mexico* **162 B4** 29 18N 100 55W
Acworth, *U.S.A.* **152 A5** 34 4N 84 41W
Ad Dafinah, *Si. Arabia* **98 B3** 23 18N 41 58 E
Ad Dafrah, *U.A.E.* **99 B6** 23 30N 54 30 E
Ad Dahnā, *Si. Arabia* **99 A5** 24 30N 48 10 E
Ad Ḍāli', *Yemen* **98 D4** 13 42N 44 44 E
Ad Dammām, *Si. Arabia* **97 E6** 26 20N 50 5 E
Ad Dāmūr, *Lebanon* **103 B4** 33 44N 35 27 E
Ad Darb, *Si. Arabia* **98 C3** 16 28N 43 7 E
Ad Dawādimī, *Si. Arabia* **96 E5** 24 35N 44 15 E
Ad Dawḥah, *Qatar* **97 E6** 25 15N 51 35 E
Ad Dawr, *Iraq* **101 E10** 34 27N 43 47 E
Ad Diffah, *Libya* **108 B4** 30 30N 24 30 E
Ad Dilam, *Si. Arabia* **98 B4** 23 55N 47 10 E
Ad Dir'īyah, *Si. Arabia* **96 E5** 24 44N 46 35 E
Ad Dīwānīyah, *Iraq* **101 F11** 32 0N 45 0 E
Ad Dujayl, *Iraq* **101 F11** 33 51N 44 14 E
Ad Duwayd, *Si. Arabia* **96 D4** 30 15N 42 17 E
Ada, *Ghana* **113 D5** 5 44N 0 40 E
Ada, *Serbia, Yug.* **52 E5** 45 49N 20 9 E
Ada, *Minn., U.S.A.* **154 B6** 47 18N 96 31W
Ada, *Ohio, U.S.A.* **157 D13** 40 46N 83 49W
Ada, *Okla., U.S.A.* **155 H6** 34 46N 96 41W
Adabiya, *Egypt* **103 F1** 29 53N 32 28 E
Adad, *Somali Rep.* **120 C3** 9 27N 46 49 E
Adair, C., *Canada* **139 A12** 71 31N 71 24W
Adaja →, *Spain* **42 D6** 41 32N 4 52W
Adak, *U.S.A.* **144 L3** 51 45N 176 45W
Adak I., *U.S.A.* **144 L3** 51 45N 176 45W
Ådalsbruk, *Norway* **18 D8** 60 43N 11 19 E
Adam, *Oman* **99 B7** 22 15N 57 28 E
Adam, Mt., *Falk. Is.* **9 f** 51 34 S 60 4W
Adamantina, *Brazil* **171 F1** 21 42 S 51 4W
Adamaoua, Massif de l', *Cameroon* **113 D7** 7 20N 12 20 E
Adamawa □, *Nigeria* **113 D7** 9 20N 12 30 E
Adamawa Highlands = Adamaoua, Massif de l', *Cameroon* **113 D7** 7 20N 12 20 E
Adamello, Mte., *Italy* **44 B7** 46 9N 10 30 E
Adamello, Parco dell' ⌂, *Italy* **44 B7** 46 4N 10 28 E
Adami Tulu, *Ethiopia* **107 F4** 7 53N 38 41 E
Adaminaby, *Australia* **129 D8** 36 0 S 148 45 E
Adamovka, *Russia* **64 F7** 51 32N 59 56 E
Adams, *Mass., U.S.A.* **151 D11** 42 38N 73 7W
Adams, *N.Y., U.S.A.* **151 C8** 43 49N 76 1W
Adams, *Wis., U.S.A.* **154 D10** 43 57N 89 49W
Adams, Mt., *U.S.A.* **160 D5** 46 12N 121 30W
Adam's Bridge, *Sri Lanka* **95 K4** 9 15N 79 40 E
Adams L., *Canada* **142 C5** 51 10N 119 40W
Adam's Peak, *Sri Lanka* **95 L5** 6 48N 80 30 E
Adamuz, *Spain* **43 G6** 38 2N 4 32W
Adana, *Turkey* **100 D6** 37 0N 35 16 E
Adanero, *Spain* **42 E6** 40 56N 4 36W
Adapazarı = Sakarya, *Turkey* **100 B4** 40 48N 30 25 E
Adar Gwagwa, J., *Sudan* **106 C4** 22 15N 35 20 E
Adarama, *Sudan* **107 D3** 17 10N 34 52 E
Adare, C., *Antarctica* **7 D11** 71 0 S 171 0 E
Adarte, *Eritrea* **107 E5** 13 18N 42 8 E
Adaut, *Indonesia* **83 C4** 8 8 S 131 7 E
Adavale, *Australia* **127 D3** 25 52 S 144 32 E
Adda →, *Italy* **44 C6** 45 8N 9 53 E
Addatigala, *India* **94 F6** 17 31N 82 3 E
Addax, Réserve Naturelle ⌂, *Niger* **109 E1** 19 17N 9 22 E
Addis Ababa = Addis Abeba, *Ethiopia* **107 F4** 9 2N 38 42 E
Addis Abeba, *Ethiopia* **107 F4** 9 2N 38 42 E
Addis Alem, *Ethiopia* **107 F4** 9 0N 38 17 E
Addis Zemen, *Ethiopia* **107 E4** 12 7N 37 47 E
Addison, *Ill., U.S.A.* **157 C8** 41 55N 88 0W
Addison, *N.Y., U.S.A.* **150 D7** 42 1N 77 14W
Addo, *S. Africa* **116 E4** 33 32 S 25 45 E
Addo Elephant Nat. Park △, *S. Africa* **116 E4** 33 30 S 25 50 E
Adebour, *Niger* **113 C7** 13 17N 11 50 E
Ādeh, *Iran* **96 B5** 37 42N 45 11 E
Adel, *Ga., U.S.A.* **152 D6** 31 8N 83 25W
Adel, *Iowa, U.S.A.* **156 C2** 41 37N 94 1W
Adelaide, *Australia* **128 C3** 34 52 S 138 30 E
Adelaide, *Bahamas* **9 b** 25 4N 77 31W
Adelaide, *S. Africa* **116 E4** 32 42 S 26 20 E
Adelaide I., *Antarctica* **7 C17** 67 15 S 68 30W
Adelaide Pen., *Canada* **138 B10** 68 15N 97 30W
Adelaide River, *Australia* **124 B5** 13 15 S 131 7 E
Adelanto, *U.S.A.* **161 L9** 34 35N 117 22W
Adelaye, *C.A.R.* **114 A4** 7 7N 22 49 E
Adelboden, *Switz.* **32 D5** 46 29N 7 33 E
Adele I., *Australia* **124 C3** 15 32 S 123 9 E
Adélie, Terre, *Antarctica* **7 C10** 68 0 S 140 0 E
Adélie Land = Adélie, Terre, *Antarctica* **7 C10** 68 0 S 140 0 E
Adelong, *Australia* **129 C8** 35 16 S 148 4 E
Ademuz, *Spain* **40 E3** 40 5N 1 13W
Aden = Al 'Adan, *Yemen* **98 D4** 12 45N 45 0 E
Aden, G. of, *Asia* **88 D3** 12 30N 47 30 E
Adendorp, *S. Africa* **116 E3** 32 15 S 24 30 E
Aderbissinat, *Niger* **113 B6** 15 34N 7 54 E
Adh Dhayd, *U.A.E.* **97 E7** 25 17N 55 53 E
Adhoi, *India* **92 H4** 23 26N 70 32 E
Adi, *Indonesia* **83 B4** 4 15 S 133 30 E
Adi Arkai, *Ethiopia* **107 E4** 13 35N 37 57 E
Adi Daro, *Ethiopia* **107 E4** 14 20N 38 14 E
Adi Keyih, *Eritrea* **107 E4** 14 51N 39 22 E
Adi Kwala, *Eritrea* **107 E4** 14 38N 38 48 E
Adi Ugri, *Eritrea* **107 E4** 14 58N 38 48 E
Adieu, C., *Australia* **125 F5** 32 0 S 132 10 E
Adieu Pt., *Australia* **124 C3** 15 14 S 124 35 E
Adigala, *Ethiopia* **107 E5** 10 24N 42 15 E
Adige →, *Italy* **45 C9** 45 9N 12 20 E
Adigrat, *Ethiopia* **107 E4** 14 20N 39 26 E
Adıgüzel Barajı, *Turkey* **49 C11** 38 13N 29 14 E
Adilabad, *India* **94 E4** 19 33N 78 20 E
Adilcevaz, *Turkey* **101 C10** 38 47N 42 43 E
Adirondack Mts., *U.S.A.* **151 C10** 44 0N 74 0W
Adirondack Park ⌂, *U.S.A.* **151 C10** 44 0N 74 20W
Adıyaman, *Turkey* **101 D8** 37 45N 38 16 E
Adjim, *Tunisia* **108 B2** 33 47N 10 50 E
Adjohon, *Benin* **113 D5** 6 41N 2 32 E
Adjud, *Romania* **53 D12** 46 7N 27 10 E
Adjumani, *Uganda* **118 B3** 3 20N 31 50 E
Adjuntas, *Puerto Rico* **165 d** 18 10N 66 43W
Adlavik Is., *Canada* **141 B8** 55 0N 58 40W
Adler, *Russia* **61 J4** 43 28N 39 52 E
Adliswil, *Switz.* **33 B7** 47 19N 8 32 E
Admer, *Algeria* **111 D6** 20 21N 5 27 E
Admer, Erg d', *Algeria* **111 D6** 24 0N 9 5 E
Admiralty G., *Australia* **124 B4** 14 20 S 125 55 E
Admiralty I., *U.S.A.* **142 B2** 57 30N 134 30W
Admiralty Is., *Papua N. G.* **132 B4** 2 0 S 147 0 E
Adnan Menderes, Izmir ✕ (ADB), *Turkey* **49 C9** 38 23N 27 6 E
Ado, *Nigeria* **113 D5** 6 36N 2 56 E
Ado-Ekiti, *Nigeria* **113 D6** 7 38N 5 12 E
Adok, *Sudan* **107 F3** 8 10N 30 20 E
Adola, *Ethiopia* **107 E5** 11 14N 41 44 E
Adonara, *Indonesia* **82 C2** 8 15 S 123 5 E
Adoni, *India* **95 G3** 15 33N 77 18 E
Adony, *Hungary* **52 C3** 47 6N 18 52 E
Adour →, *France* **28 E2** 43 32N 1 32W
Adra, *India* **93 H12** 23 30N 86 42 E
Adra, *Spain* **43 J7** 36 43N 3 3W
Adrano, *Italy* **47 E7** 37 40N 14 50 E
Adrar des Iforas, *Algeria* **111 C4** 27 51N 0 11 E
Adrar Madet, *Niger* **109 E2** 18 54N 10 35 E
Adrasman, *Tajikistan* **65 C4** 40 38N 69 58 E
Adré, *Chad* **109 F4** 13 40N 22 20 E
Adrī, *Libya* **108 C2** 27 32N 13 2 E
Ádria, *Italy* **45 C9** 45 3N 12 3 E
Adrian, *Ga., U.S.A.* **152 C7** 32 33N 82 35W
Adrian, *Mich., U.S.A.* **157 C12** 41 54N 84 2W
Adrian, *Mo., U.S.A.* **156 F2** 38 24N 94 21W
Adrian, *Tex., U.S.A.* **155 H3** 35 16N 102 40W
Adrianople = Edirne, *Turkey* **51 E10** 41 40N 26 34 E
Adriatic Sea, *Medit. S.* **12 G9** 43 0N 16 0 E
Adua, *Indonesia* **83 B3** 1 45 S 129 50 E
Adula-Gruppe, *Switz.* **33 D8** 46 30N 9 3 E
Adung Long, *Burma* **90 A6** 28 7N 97 42 E
Adur, *India* **95 K3** 9 8N 76 40 E
Adwa, *Ethiopia* **107 E4** 14 15N 38 52 E
Adygea □, *Russia* **61 H5** 45 0N 40 0 E
Adzhar Republic = Ajaria □, *Georgia* **61 K6** 41 30N 42 0 E
Adzopé, *Ivory C.* **112 D4** 6 7N 3 49W
Ægean Sea, *Medit. S.* **49 C7** 38 30N 25 0 E
Aerhtai Shan, *Mongolia* **68 B4** 46 40N 92 45 E
Ærø, *Denmark* **17 K4** 54 52N 10 25 E
Ærøskøbing, *Denmark* **17 K4** 54 53N 10 24 E
Aesch, *Switz.* **32 B5** 47 28N 7 36 E
Aëtós, *Greece* **48 D3** 37 15N 21 50 E
Afafi, Massif d', *Niger* **109 D3** 22 11N 15 10 E
'Afak, *Iraq* **101 F11** 32 4N 45 15 E
Afándou, *Greece* **38 E12** 36 18N 28 12 E
Afarag, Erg, *Algeria* **111 D5** 23 50N 2 47 E
Afareaitu, *Tahiti* **133 S16** 17 33 S 149 47W
Åfarnes, *Norway* **18 B4** 62 40N 7 32 E
Afdega, *Ethiopia* **120 C2** 6 4N 43 30 E
Affoltern, *Switz.* **33 B6** 47 17N 8 27 E
Affreville = Khemis Miliana, *Algeria* **111 A5** 36 11N 2 14 E
Affton, *U.S.A.* **156 F6** 38 33N 90 20W
Afghanistan ■, *Asia* **91 B2** 33 0N 65 0 E
Afgoi, *Somali Rep.* **120 D2** 2 7N 44 59 E
'Afif, *Si. Arabia* **98 B3** 23 53N 42 56 E
Afikpo, *Nigeria* **113 D6** 5 53N 7 54 E
Aflisses, O. →, *Algeria* **111 C5** 28 40N 0 50 E
Aflou, *Algeria* **111 B5** 34 7N 2 3 E
Afmadu, *Somali Rep.* **120 D2** 0 31N 42 4 E
Afogados da Ingàzeira, *Brazil* **170 C4** 7 45 S 37 39W
Afognak I., *U.S.A.* **144 G9** 58 15N 152 30W
Afore, *Papua N. G.* **132 E5** 9 8 S 148 23 E
Afragóla, *Italy* **47 B7** 40 55N 14 18 E
Afram →, *Ghana* **113 D4** 7 0N 0 52W
Afrera, *Ethiopia* **107 E5** 13 16N 41 5 E
Africa **104 E6** 10 0N 20 0 E
'Afrīn, *Syria* **100 D7** 36 32N 36 50 E
Afşin, *Turkey* **100 C7** 38 14N 36 55 E
Afton, *Iowa, U.S.A.* **156 C2** 41 2N 94 12W
Afton, *N.Y., U.S.A.* **151 D9** 42 14N 75 32W
Afton, *Wyo., U.S.A.* **158 E8** 42 44N 110 56W
Aftout, *Algeria* **110 C4** 26 50N 3 45W
Afuá, *Brazil* **169 D7** 0 15 S 50 20W
'Afula, *Israel* **103 C4** 32 37N 35 17 E
Afumba, *Zambia* **119 E2** 15 38 S 24 56 E
Afyon, *Turkey* **49 C12** 38 45N 30 33 E
Afyon □, *Turkey* **49 C12** 38 25N 30 30 E
Afyonkarahisar = Afyon, *Turkey* **49 C12** 38 45N 30 33 E
Aga, *Egypt* **106 H7** 30 55N 31 10 E
Aga Pt., *Guam* **133 R15** 13 15N 144 43 E
Agadem, *Niger* **109 E2** 16 50N 13 11 E
Agadès = Agadez, *Niger* **113 B6** 16 58N 7 59 E
Agadez, *Niger* **113 B6** 16 58N 7 59 E
Agadir, *Morocco* **110 B3** 30 28N 9 55W
Agaete, *Canary Is.* **9 e1** 28 6N 15 43W
Agaie, *Nigeria* **113 D6** 9 1N 6 18 E
Agaïlás, *Mauritania* **110 D2** 22 37N 14 22W
Again, *Sudan* **107 F2** 8 28N 29 55 E
Agalás, *Greece* **39 D2** 37 43N 20 47 E
Agalega Is., *Mauritius* **121 F4** 11 0 S 57 0 E
Agana, *Guam* **133 R15** 13 28N 144 45 E
Ağapınar, *Turkey* **49 B12** 39 48N 30 47 E
Agar, *India* **92 H7** 23 40N 76 2 E
Agar →, *India* **94 D6** 21 0N 82 57 E
Agaro, *Ethiopia* **107 F4** 7 50N 36 38 E
Agartala, *India* **90 D3** 23 50N 91 23 E
Agăş, *Romania* **53 D11** 46 28N 26 15 E
Agassiz, *Canada* **142 D4** 49 14N 121 46W
Agat, *Guam* **133 R15** 13 25N 144 40 E
Agats, *Indonesia* **83 C5** 5 33 S 138 0 E
Agatti I., *India* **95 J1** 10 50N 72 12 E
Agattu I., *U.S.A.* **144 K4** 52 25N 173 35 E
Agawam, *U.S.A.* **151 D12** 42 5N 72 37W
Agbélouvé, *Togo* **113 D5** 6 35N 1 14 E
Agboville, *Ivory C.* **112 D4** 5 55N 4 15W
Ağcabädi, *Azerbaijan* **61 K8** 40 5N 47 27 E
Ağdam, *Azerbaijan* **61 L8** 40 0N 46 58 E
Ağdaş, *Azerbaijan* **61 K8** 40 44N 47 22 E
Agde, *France* **28 E7** 43 19N 3 28 E

Agde, C. d', *France* . . . . **28 E7** 43 16N 3 28 E
Agdz, *Morocco* **110 B3** 30 47N 6 30W
Agdzhabedi = Ağcabädi, *Azerbaijan* **61 K8** 40 5N 47 27 E
Agen, *France* . . . . **28 D4** 44 12N 0 38 E
Ageo, *Japan* . . . . **73 B11** 35 58N 139 36 E
Ager Tay, *Chad* . . . . **109 E3** 20 0N 17 41 E
Agerbæk, *Denmark* . . . . **17 J2** 55 36N 8 48 E
Agersø, *Denmark* . . . . **17 J5** 55 13N 11 12 E
Ageyevo, *Russia* . . . . **58 E9** 54 10N 36 27 E
Aggteleki Nemzeti Park △, *Hungary* **52 B5** 48 27N 20 36 E
Āgh Kand, *Iran* . . . . **97 B6** 37 15N 48 4 E
Aghireşu, *Romania* . . . . **53 D8** 46 53N 23 15 E
Aghoueyyît, *Mauritania* **110 D1** 21 10N 15 6W
Aghreïjît, *Mauritania* **110 D2** 21 58N 12 11W
Aginskoye, *Russia* . . . . **67 D12** 51 6N 114 32 E
Ağlasun, *Turkey* . . . . **49 D12** 37 39N 30 31 E
Agly →, *France* . . . . **28 F7** 42 46N 3 3 E
Agmar, *Mauritania* **110 C2** 25 18N 10 50W
Agnew, *Australia* . . . . **125 E3** 28 1 S 120 31 E
Agnibilékrou, *Ivory C.* **112 D4** 7 10N 3 11W
Agnita, *Romania* . . . . **53 E9** 45 59N 24 40 E
Agno →, *Switz.* . . . . **33 E7** 45 59N 8 53 E
Agnone, *Italy* . . . . **45 G11** 41 48N 14 22 E
Ago, *Japan* . . . . **73 C8** 34 20N 136 51 E
Agofie, *Ghana* . . . . **113 D5** 8 27N 0 15 E
Agogna →, *Italy* . . . . **42 C5** 45 4N 8 54 E
Agogo, *Sudan* . . . . **107 F2** 7 50N 28 45 E
Agön, *Sweden* . . . . **16 C11** 61 34N 17 23 E
Agon Coutainville, *France* **26 C5** 49 2N 1 34W
Agoo, *Phil.* . . . . **80 C3** 16 20N 120 22 E
Agordo, *Italy* . . . . **45 B9** 46 18N 12 2 E
Agori, *India* . . . . **93 G10** 24 33N 82 57 E
Agouna, *Benin* . . . . **113 D5** 7 39N 1 47 E
Agout →, *France* . . . . **28 E5** 43 47N 1 41 E
Agra, *India* . . . . **92 F7** 27 17N 77 58 E
Agrakhanskiuy Poluostrov, *Russia* . **61 J8** 43 42N 47 36 E
Agram = Zagreb, *Croatia* . . . . **45 C12** 45 50N 15 58 E
Agramunt, *Spain* . . . . **40 D6** 41 48N 1 6 E
Agreda, *Spain* **40 D3** 41 51N 1 55W
Agri, *Turkey* . . . . **101 C10** 39 44N 43 3 E
Agri →, *Italy* . . . . **47 B9** 40 13N 16 44 E
Ağri Daği, *Turkey* . . . . **101 C11** 39 50N 44 15 E
Ağri Karakose = Ağri, *Turkey* . . **101 C10** 39 44N 43 3 E
Agriá, *Greece* . . . . **48 B5** 39 20N 23 1 E
Agrigento, *Italy* . . . . **46 E6** 37 19N 13 34 E
Agrínion, *Greece* . . . . **48 C3** 38 37N 21 27 E
Agrópoli, *Italy* . . . . **47 B7** 40 21N 14 59 E
Ağstafa, *Azerbaijan* . . . . **61 K7** 41 7N 45 27 E
Água Branca, *Brazil* . . . . **170 C3** 5 0 S 42 40W
Agua Caliente, *Baja Calif., Mexico* . **161 N10** 32 29N 116 59W
Agua Caliente, *Sinaloa, Mexico* . . **162 B3** 26 30N 108 20W
Agua Caliente Springs, *U.S.A.* . . **161 N10** 32 56N 116 19W
Água Clara, *Brazil* . . . . **173 E7** 20 25 S 52 45W
Agua Fria Nat. Monument △, *U.S.A.* **159 J8** 34 14N 112 0W
Agua Hechicero, *Mexico* **161 N10** 32 26N 116 14W
Agua Preta →, *Brazil* . . . . **169 D5** 1 4 S 63 48W
Agua Prieta, *Mexico* **162 A3** 31 20N 109 32W
Aguachica, *Colombia* **168 B3** 8 19N 73 38W
Aguada Cecilio, *Argentina* . . . . **176 B3** 40 51 S 65 51W
Aguadas, *Colombia* **168 B2** 5 40N 75 38W
Aguadilla, *Puerto Rico* . . . . **165 d** 18 26N 67 10W
Aguadulce, *Panama* **164 E3** 8 15N 80 20W
Aguanga, *U.S.A.* **161 M10** 33 27N 116 51W
Aguanish, *Canada* **141 B7** 50 14N 62 2W
Aguanus →, *Canada* **141 B7** 50 13N 62 5W
Aguapeí, *Brazil* . . . . **173 D6** 16 12 S 59 43W
Aguapeí →, *Brazil* . . . . **171 F1** 21 0 S 51 0W
Aguapey →, *Argentina* . . . . **174 B4** 29 7 S 56 36W
Aguaray Guazú →, *Paraguay* . . . **174 A4** 24 47 S 57 19W
Aguarico →, *Ecuador* . . . . **168 D2** 0 59 S 75 11W
Aguaro-Guariquito, Parque Nac. △.,
Venezuela **165 E6** 8 30N 66 45W
Aguas →, *Spain* **40 D4** 41 20N 0 30W
Aguas Blancas, *Chile* . . . . **174 A2** 24 15 S 69 55W
Aguas Calientes, Sierra de, *Argentina* **174 B2** 25 26 S 66 40W
Águas Formosas, *Brazil* . . . . **171 E3** 17 5 S 40 57W
Aguascalientes, *Mexico* **162 C4** 21 53N 102 12W
Aguascalientes □, *Mexico* **162 C4** 22 0N 102 20W
Agudo, *Spain* **43 G6** 38 59N 4 52W
Águeda, *Portugal* **42 E2** 40 34N 8 27W
Águeda →, *Spain* **42 D4** 41 2N 6 56W
Aguelhok, *Mali* . . . . **113 B5** 19 29N 0 52 E
Aguelt el Melah, *Mauritania* **110 D2** 23 3N 8 28W
Agüenit, *W. Sahara* **110 D2** 22 11N 13 8W
Aguié, *Niger* . . . . **113 C6** 13 31N 7 46 E
Aguila, Punta, *Puerto Rico* . . . . **165 d** 17 57N 67 13W
Aguilafuente, *Spain* **42 D6** 41 13N 4 7W
Aguilar, *Spain* **43 H6** 37 31N 4 40W
Aguilar de Campoo, *Spain* **42 C6** 42 47N 4 15W
Aguilares, *Argentina* . . . . **174 B2** 27 26 S 65 35W
Aguilas, *Spain* **41 H3** 37 23N 1 35W
Agüimes, *Canary Is.* **9 e1** 27 58N 15 27W
Aguja, C. de la, *Colombia* **168 A3** 11 18N 74 12W
Agujereada, Pta., *Puerto Rico* . . **165 d** 18 30N 67 8W
Agulaa, *Ethiopia* . . . . **107 E4** 13 40N 39 40 E
Agulhas, C., *S. Africa* . . . . **116 E3** 34 52 S 20 0 E
Agulo, *Canary Is.* **9 e1** 28 11N 17 12W
Agung, Gunung, *Indonesia* . . . . **85 D5** 8 20 S 115 28 E
Agur, *Uganda* . . . . **118 B3** 2 28N 32 55 E
Agusan →, *Phil.* . . . . **81 G5** 9 0N 125 30 E
Agusan del Norte □, *Phil.* . . . . **81 G5** 9 20N 125 10 E
Agusan del Sur □, *Phil.* . . . . **81 G5** 8 30N 125 30 E
Agustín Codazzi, *Colombia* **168 A3** 10 2N 73 14W
Agutaya I., *Phil.* . . . . **81 F3** 11 9N 120 58 E
Agvali, *Russia* . . . . **51 E13** 41 8N 89 51 E
Agvali, *Russia* . . . . **61 J8** 42 36N 46 8 E
Aha Mts., *Botswana* . . . . **116 B3** 19 45 S 21 0 E
Ahaggar, *Algeria* . . . . **111 D6** 23 0N 6 30 E
Ahamansu, *Ghana* . . . . **113 D5** 7 38N 0 35 E
Ahar, *Iran* . . . . **101 C12** 38 35N 47 0 E
Ahat, *Turkey* . . . . **49 C11** 38 39N 29 47 E
Ahaura →, *N.Z.* . . . . **131 C6** 42 21 S 171 34 E
Ahaus, *Germany* . . . . **30 C2** 52 4N 7 0 E
Åheim, *Norway* . . . . **18 B2** 62 2N 5 13 E
Ahelledjem, *Algeria* . . . . **111 C6** 26 37N 6 58 E
Ahioma, *Papua N. G.* . . . . **132 F6** 10 20 S 150 33 E
Ahipara B., *N.Z.* . . . . **130 B2** 35 5 S 173 5 E
Ahir Daği, *Turkey* . . . . **49 C12** 38 45N 30 10 E
Ahiri, *India* . . . . **94 E5** 19 30N 80 0 E
Ahlat, *Turkey* . . . . **101 C10** 38 45N 42 29 E
Ahlen, *Germany* . . . . **30 D3** 51 45N 7 53 E
Ahmad Wal, *Pakistan* . . . . **92 E1** 29 18N 65 58 E
Ahmadabad, *India* . . . . **92 H5** 23 0N 72 40 E
Ahmadābād, *Khorāsān, Iran* . . . . **97 C9** 35 3N 60 50 E
Ahmadābād, *Khorāsān, Iran* . . . . **97 C8** 35 49N 59 42 E
Ahmadī, *Iran* . . . . **97 E8** 27 56N 56 42 E
Ahmadnagar, *India* . . . . **94 E2** 19 7N 74 46 E
Ahmadpur, *India* . . . . **94 E3** 18 40N 76 57 E
Ahmadpur, *Pakistan* . . . . **92 E4** 29 12N 71 10 E
Ahmadpur Lamma, *Pakistan* . . . . **92 E4** 28 19N 70 3 E
Ahmar, *Ethiopia* . . . . **107 F5** 9 20N 41 15 E
Ahmedabad = Ahmadabad, *India* . **92 H5** 23 0N 72 40 E
Ahmednagar = Ahmadnagar, *India* **94 E2** 19 7N 74 46 E
Ahmetbey, *Turkey* . . . . **51 E11** 41 26N 27 34 E
Ahmetler, *Turkey* . . . . **49 C11** 38 28N 29 5 E
Ahmetli, *Turkey* . . . . **49 C9** 38 32N 27 57 E
Ahmeyim, *Mauritania* **110 D2** 20 5N 14 25W
Ahoada, *Nigeria* . . . . **113 D6** 5 8N 6 36 E
Ahome, *Mexico* **162 B3** 25 55N 109 11W
Ahon, Tarso, *Chad* . . . . **109 D3** 20 23N 18 18 E
Ahoskie, *U.S.A.* **149 G7** 36 17N 76 59W
Ahr →, *Germany* . . . . **30 E3** 50 32N 7 16 E
Ahram, *Iran* . . . . **97 D6** 28 52N 51 16 E

Ahrax Pt., *Malta* . . . . **38 F7** 36 0N 14 22 E
Ahrensbök, *Germany* . . . . **30 A6** 54 2N 10 33 E
Ahrensburg, *Germany* . . . . **30 B6** 53 40N 10 13 E
Āhū, *Iran* . . . . **97 C6** 34 33N 50 2 E
Ahu Akivi, *Chile* . . . . **172 b** 27 7 S 109 22W
Ahu Tepeu, *Chile* . . . . **172 b** 27 6 S 109 25W
Ahu Tongariki, *Chile* . . . . **172 b** 27 7 S 109 17W
Ahu Vinapu, *Chile* . . . . **172 b** 27 10 S 109 25W
Ahuachapán, *El Salv.* **164 D2** 13 54N 89 52W
Ahun, *France* . . . . **27 F9** 46 4N 2 5 E
Ahuriri →, *N.Z.* . . . . **131 E5** 44 31 S 170 12 E
Ahvāz, *Iran* . . . . **97 D6** 31 20N 48 40 E
Ahvenanmaa = Åland, *Finland* . . **15 F19** 60 15N 20 0 E
Ahwar, *Yemen* . . . . **98 D4** 13 30N 46 40 E
Ahzar →, *Mali* . . . . **113 B5** 15 30N 3 20 E
Ai →, *India* . . . . **90 B3** 26 26N 90 44 E
Ai-Ais, *Namibia* . . . . **116 D2** 27 54 S 17 59 E
Ai-Ais and Fish River Canyon Nat.
Park △, *Namibia* . . . . **116 C2** 24 45 S 17 15 E
Aiari →, *Brazil* **168 C4** 1 22N 68 36W
Aichach, *Germany* . . . . **31 G7** 48 27N 11 8 E
Aichi □, *Japan* . . . . **73 C9** 35 0N 137 15 E
Aiduna, *Indonesia* . . . . **83 B4** 4 0 S 134 6 E
Aiduna, *Indonesia* . . . . **83 B5** 4 27 S 135 15 E
Aiea, *U.S.A.* **145 K14** 21 23N 157 56W
Aigle, *Switz.* . . . . **32 D3** 46 18N 6 58 E
Aignay-le-Duc, *France* . . . . **27 E11** 47 40N 4 43 E
Aigoual, Mt., *France* . . . . **28 D7** 44 8N 3 35 E
Aigre, *France* . . . . **28 C4** 45 54N 0 1 E
Aigrettes, Pte. des, *Réunion* . . . **121 c** 21 3 S 55 13 E
Aigua, *Uruguay* . . . . **175 C5** 34 13 S 54 46W
Aigueperse, *France* . . . . **27 F10** 46 3N 3 13 E
Aigues →, *France* . . . . **29 D8** 44 7N 4 43 E
Aigues-Mortes, *France* . . . . **29 E8** 43 35N 4 12 E
Aigues-Mortes, G. d', *France* . . . **29 E8** 43 31N 4 3 E
Aigües Tortes i Lago San Mauricio,
Parque Nac. de △, *Spain* **40 C4** 42 38N 0 31W
Aiguilles, *France* . . . . **29 D10** 44 47N 6 51 E
Aiguillon, *France* . . . . **28 D4** 44 18N 0 21 E
Aigurande, *France* . . . . **27 F8** 46 27N 1 49 E
Aihui, *China* . . . . **69 A7** 50 10N 127 30 E
Aija, *Peru* . . . . **172 B2** 9 50 S 77 45W
Aikawa, *Japan* . . . . **70 E9** 38 2N 138 15 E
Aiken, *U.S.A.* **152 B8** 33 34N 81 43W
Ailao Shan, *China* . . . . **76 F3** 24 0N 101 20 E
Aileron, *Australia* . . . . **126 C1** 22 39 S 133 20 E
Ailey, *U.S.A.* **152 C7** 32 11N 82 34W
Ailigandi, *Panama* **168 B2** 9 14N 78 1W
Aillant-sur-Tholon, *France* . . . . . . **27 E10** 47 52N 3 20 E
Aillik, *Canada* **141 A8** 55 11N 59 18W
Ailsa Craig, *U.K.* **22 F3** 55 15N 5 6W
Ailuluai, *Papua N. G.* . . . . **132 E6** 9 38 S 150 35 E
Aim, *Russia* . . . . **67 D14** 59 0N 133 55 E
Aimere, *Indonesia* . . . . **79 F6** 8 45 S 121 3 E
Aimogasta, *Argentina* . . . . **174 B2** 28 33 S 66 50W
Aimorés, *Brazil* . . . . **171 E3** 19 30 S 41 4W
Ain □, *France* . . . . **27 F12** 46 5N 5 20 E
Ain →, *France* . . . . **29 C9** 45 45N 5 11 E
Aïn Beïda, *Algeria* . . . . **111 A6** 35 50N 7 29 E
Aïn Ben Khellil, *Algeria* **111 B4** 33 15N 0 49W
Aïn Ben Tili, *Mauritania* **110 C3** 25 59N 9 27W
Aïn Beni Mathar, *Morocco* **111 B4** 34 1N 2 0W
Aïn Benian, *Algeria* . . . . **111 A5** 36 48N 2 55 E
Aïn Dalla, *Egypt* . . . . **106 B2** 27 20N 27 23 E
Aïn el Mafki, *Egypt* . . . . **106 B2** 27 30N 28 15 E
Aïn Girba, *Egypt* . . . . **106 B2** 29 20N 25 14 E
Aïn M'lila, *Algeria* . . . . **111 A6** 36 2N 6 35 E
Aïn Mokra = Berrahal, *Algeria* . . **111 A6** 36 54N 7 33 E
Aïn Murr, *Sudan* . . . . **106 C2** 21 50N 25 9 E
Aïn Qeiqab, *Egypt* . . . . **106 B1** 29 42N 24 55 E
Aïn Salah = In Salah, *Algeria* . . **111 C5** 27 10N 2 32 E
Aïn Sefra, *Algeria* **111 B4** 32 47N 0 37W
Aïn Sheikh Murzūk, *Egypt* . . . . . . **106 B2** 26 47N 27 45 E
Aïn Sudr, *Egypt* . . . . **103 F2** 29 50N 33 6 E
Aïn Sukhna, *Egypt* . . . . **106 J8** 29 32N 32 20 E
Aïn Tédelès, *Algeria* . . . . **111 A5** 36 0N 0 21 E
Aïn Témouchent, *Algeria* **111 A4** 35 16N 1 8W
Aïn Tikkidine, *Algeria* . . . . **111 C5** 25 33N 1 24 E
Aïn Touta, *Algeria* . . . . **111 A6** 35 26N 5 54 E
Aïn Zeitûn, *Egypt* . . . . **106 B2** 29 10N 25 48 E
Aïn Zorah, *Morocco* **111 B4** 34 37N 3 32W
Ainabo, *Somali Rep.* . . . . **120 C3** 9 0N 46 25 E
Ainaži, *Latvia* . . . . **15 H21** 57 50N 24 24 E
Aínos Óros, *Greece* . . . . **39 C2** 38 9N 20 48 E
Ainsworth, *U.S.A.* **154 D5** 42 33N 99 52W
Aioi, *Japan* . . . . **72 C6** 34 48N 134 28 E
Aiome, *Papua N. G.* . . . . **132 C3** 5 8 S 144 44 E
Aipe, *Colombia* **168 C2** 3 13N 75 15W
Aiquile, *Bolivia* . . . . **173 D4** 18 10 S 65 10W
Air, *Niger* . . . . **113 B6** 18 30N 8 0 E
Aïr et du Ténéré, Réserve Naturelle
de L', *Niger* . . . . **109 E1** 18 12N 9 56 E
Air Force I., *Canada* **139 B12** 67 58N 74 5W
Air Hitam, *Malaysia* . . . . **87 M4** 1 55N 103 11 E
Aira, *Japan* . . . . **72 F2** 31 43N 130 43 E
Airaines, *France* . . . . **27 C8** 49 58N 1 55 E
Airão, *Brazil* . . . . **169 D5** 1 56 S 61 22W
Airdrie, *Canada* **142 C6** 51 18N 114 2W
Airdrie, *U.K.* **22 F5** 55 52N 3 57W
Aire →, *France* . . . . **27 C11** 49 18N 4 49 E
Aire →, *U.K.* **20 D7** 53 43N 0 55W
Aire, I. de l', *Spain* . . . . **38 B5** 39 48N 4 16 E
Aire-sur-la-Lys, *France* . . . . **27 B9** 50 37N 2 22 E
Aire-sur-l'Adour, *France* **28 E3** 43 42N 0 15W
Aireys Inlet, *Australia* . . . . **128 E6** 38 29 S 144 5 E
Airlie Beach, *Australia* . . . . **126 J6** 20 16 S 148 43 E
Airmadidi, *Indonesia* . . . . **82 A3** 1 25N 125 0 E
Airolo, *Switz.* . . . . **33 C7** 46 32N 8 37 E
Airvault, *France* . . . . **26 F6** 46 50N 0 8 E
Aisch →, *Germany* . . . . **31 F6** 49 49N 10 58 E
Aisen □, *Chile* . . . . **176 C2** 46 30 S 73 0W
Aisne □, *France* . . . . **27 C10** 49 42N 3 52 E
Aisne →, *France* . . . . **27 C9** 49 26N 2 50 E
Ait, *India* . . . . **93 G8** 25 54N 79 14 E
Aitana, Sierra de, *Spain* **41 G4** 38 35N 0 24W
Aitape, *Papua N. G.* . . . . **132 B2** 3 11 S 142 22 E
Aitkin, *U.S.A.* **154 B8** 46 32N 93 42W
Aitolía Kai Akarnanía □, *Greece* . **48 C3** 38 45N 21 18 E
Aitolikón, *Greece* . . . . **48 C3** 38 26N 21 21 E
Aiuaba, *Brazil* . . . . **170 C3** 6 38 S 40 7W
Aiud, *Romania* . . . . **53 D8** 46 19N 23 44 E
Aix-en-Provence, *France* . . . . **29 E9** 43 32N 5 27 E
Aix-la-Chapelle = Aachen, *Germany* **30 E2** 50 45N 6 6 E
Aix-les-Bains, *France* . . . . **29 C9** 45 41N 5 53 E
Aixe-sur-Vienne, *France* . . . . **28 C5** 45 47N 1 9 E
Aiyang, Mt., *Papua N. G.* . . . . . . **132 C1** 5 10 S 141 20 E
Aíyina, *Greece* . . . . **48 D5** 37 45N 23 26 E
Aíyínion, *Greece* . . . . **50 F6** 40 28N 22 28 E
Aíyion, *Greece* . . . . **48 C4** 38 15N 22 5 E
Aizawl, *India* . . . . **90 D4** 23 40N 92 44 E
Aizenay, *France* **26 F5** 46 44N 1 38W
Aizkraukle, *Latvia* . . . . **15 H21** 56 36N 25 11 E
Aizpute, *Latvia* . . . . **15 H19** 56 43N 21 40 E
Aizuwakamatsu, *Japan* . . . . **70 F9** 37 30N 139 56 E
Ajaccio, *France* . . . . **29 G12** 41 55N 8 40 E
Ajaccio, G. d', *France* . . . . **29 G12** 41 52N 8 40 E
Ajai Game Reserve △, *Uganda* . . **118 B3** 2 52N 31 25 E
Ajaigarh, *India* . . . . **93 G9** 24 52N 80 16 E
Ajalpan, *Mexico* . . . . **163 D5** 18 22N 97 15 E
Ajanta Ra., *India* . . . . **94 D2** 20 30N 75 48 E
Ajari Rep. = Ajaria □, *Georgia* . . **61 K6** 41 30N 42 0 E

Ajaria □, *Georgia* . . . . **61 K6** 41 30N 42 0 E
Ajax, *Canada* **150 C5** 43 50N 79 1W
Ajax, Mt., *N.Z.* . . . . **131 C7** 42 35 S 172 1 E
Ajdábiyá, *Libya* . . . . **108 B4** 30 54N 20 4 E
Ajdovščina, *Slovenia* . . . . **45 C10** 45 54N 13 54 E
Ajibar, *Ethiopia* . . . . **107 E4** 10 35N 38 36 E
Ajka, *Hungary* . . . . **52 C2** 47 4N 17 31 E
'Ajlūn, *Jordan* . . . . **103 C4** 32 18N 35 47 E
'Ajlūn □, *Jordan* . . . . **103 C4** 32 18N 35 47 E
'Ajmān, *U.A.E.* . . . . **97 E7** 25 25N 55 30 E
Ajmer, *India* . . . . **92 F6** 26 28N 74 37 E
Ajnala, *India* . . . . **92 D6** 31 50N 74 48 E
Ajo, *U.S.A.* **159 K7** 32 22N 112 52W
Ajo, C. de, *Spain* **42 B7** 43 31N 3 35W
Ajoie, *Switz.* . . . . **32 B4** 47 22N 7 0 E
Ajok, *Sudan* . . . . **107 F2** 9 15N 28 28 E
Ajuda, Pta. da, *Azores* **9 d3** 37 52N 25 19W
Ajuy, *Phil.* . . . . **81 F4** 11 10N 123 1 E
Ak Dağ, *Turkey* . . . . **49 E11** 36 30N 29 32 E
Ak Dağları, *Muğla, Turkey* . . . . . . **49 E11** 36 30N 29 30 E
Ak Dağları, *Sivas, Turkey* . . . . . . **100 C7** 39 30N 36 0 E
Ak-Mtuz, *Kyrgyzstan* . . . . **65 C8** 41 45N 76 10 E
Ak-Tüz, *Kyrgyzstan* . . . . **65 B8** 42 54N 76 7 E
Akaba, *Togo* . . . . **113 D5** 8 10N 1 2 E
Akabira, *Japan* . . . . **70 C11** 43 33N 142 5 E
Akabli, *Algeria* . . . . **111 C5** 26 49N 1 31 E
Akagera, Parc Nat. d' △, *Rwanda* . **118 C3** 1 31 S 30 33 E
Akaishi-Dake, *Japan* . . . . **73 B10** 35 27N 138 9 E
Akaishi-Sammyaku, *Japan* . . . . . . **73 B10** 35 25N 138 10 E
Akaki Beseka, *Ethiopia* . . . . **107 F4** 8 55N 38 45 E
Akākūs, Jabal, *Libya* . . . . **111 C7** 25 0N 10 30 E
Akala, *Sudan* . . . . **107 D4** 15 39N 36 13 E
Akalkot, *India* . . . . **94 F3** 17 32N 76 13 E
Akamas, *Cyprus* . . . . **39 E8** 35 3N 32 18 E
Akanthou, *Cyprus* . . . . **39 E9** 35 22N 33 45 E
Akarca, *Turkey* . . . . **49 C11** 38 35N 29 35 E
Akaroa, *N.Z.* . . . . **131 D7** 43 49 S 172 59 E
Akaroa Harbour, *N.Z.* . . . . **131 D7** 43 50 S 172 55 E
Akasha, *Sudan* . . . . **106 C3** 21 10N 30 32 E
Akashi, *Japan* . . . . **72 C6** 34 45N 134 58 E
Akbarpur, Bihar, *India* . . . . **93 G10** 24 39N 83 58 E
Akbarpur, Ut. P., *India* . . . . **93 F10** 26 25N 82 32 E
Akbou, *Algeria* . . . . **111 A5** 36 31N 4 31 E
Akçaabat, *Turkey* . . . . **101 B8** 41 1N 39 34 E
Akçadağ, *Turkey* . . . . **100 C7** 38 27N 37 43 E
Akçakale, *Turkey* . . . . **101 D8** 36 41N 38 56 E
Akçakoca, *Turkey* . . . . **100 B4** 41 5N 31 5 E
Akçaova, *Turkey* . . . . **51 E13** 41 3N 29 57 E
Akçay, *Turkey* . . . . **49 E11** 36 36N 29 45 E
Akçay →, *Turkey* . . . . **49 D10** 37 30N 28 55 E
Akchâr, *Mauritania* **110 D2** 20 20N 14 28W
Akdağ, *Turkey* . . . . **49 C10** 38 33N 26 30 E
Akdağmadeni, *Turkey* . . . . **100 C6** 39 39N 35 53 E
Akechi, *Japan* . . . . **73 B9** 35 18N 137 23 E
Akelamo, *Indonesia* . . . . **83 C7** 1 35N 129 40 E
Akernes, *Norway* . . . . **18 F4** 58 45N 7 30 E
Åkers styckebruk, *Sweden* . . . . . . **16 E11** 59 15N 17 5 E
Åkersberga, *Sweden* . . . . **16 E12** 59 29N 18 18 E
Åkershus □, *Norway* . . . . **18 D8** 60 0N 11 10 E
Akeru →, *India* . . . . **94 F5** 17 25N 80 5 E
Aketi, Dem. Rep. of the Congo . . . **114 B4** 2 38N 23 47 E
Akhaïa □, *Greece* . . . . **48 C3** 38 5N 21 45 E
Akhalkalaki, *Georgia* . . . . **61 K6** 41 27N 43 25 E
Akhaltsikhe, *Georgia* . . . . **61 K6** 41 40N 43 0 E
Akharnaí, *Greece* . . . . **48 C5** 38 5N 23 44 E
Akhelóös →, *Greece* . . . . **48 C3** 38 19N 21 7 E
Akhendriá, *Greece* . . . . **49 G7** 34 59N 25 3 E
Akhiok, *U.S.A.* **144 H9** 56 57N 154 10W
Akhisar, *Turkey* . . . . **49 C9** 38 56N 27 48 E
Akhladhókambos, *Greece* . . . . . . **48 D4** 37 31N 22 35 E
Akhmim, *Egypt* . . . . **106 B3** 26 31N 31 47 E
Akhtopol, *Bulgaria* . . . . **51 D11** 42 6N 27 56 E
Akhtuba →, *Russia* . . . . **61 G8** 47 41N 46 55 E
Akhtubinsk, *Russia* . . . . **61 F8** 48 13N 46 7 E
Akhty, *Russia* . . . . **61 K8** 41 30N 47 45 E
Akhtyrka = Okhtyrka, *Ukraine* . . **59 G8** 50 25N 35 0 E
Aki, *Japan* . . . . **72 D5** 33 30N 134 0 E
Aki-Nada, *Japan* . . . . **72 C4** 34 5N 132 40 E
Akiachak, *U.S.A.* **144 F7** 60 55N 161 26W
Akiak, *U.S.A.* **144 F7** 60 55N 161 13W
Akiéni, *Gabon* . . . . **114 C2** 1 1 S 13 53 E
Akimiski I., *Canada* **140 B3** 52 50N 81 30W
Akimovka, *Ukraine* . . . . **59 J8** 46 44N 35 0 E
Åkirkeby, *Denmark* . . . . **17 J8** 55 4N 14 55 E
Akita, *Japan* . . . . **70 E10** 39 45N 140 7 E
Akita □, *Japan* . . . . **70 E10** 39 40N 140 30 E
Akjoujt, *Mauritania* **112 B2** 19 45N 14 15W
Akka, *Morocco* **112 H4** 21 5N 4 11W
Akka, *Morocco* **110 C3** 29 22N 8 9W
Akkaraipattu, Sri Lanka . . . . **95 L5** 7 13N 81 51 E
Akkaya Tepesi, *Turkey* . . . . **49 D11** 37 31N 30 18 E
Akkeshi, *Japan* . . . . **70 C12** 43 2N 144 51 E
'Akko, *Israel* . . . . **103 C4** 32 55N 35 4 E
Akkol = Aqköl, *Kazakhstan* . . . . . . **65 A7** 45 0N 75 39 E
Akkol = Aqköl, *Kazakhstan* . . . . . . **65 B8** 43 36N 70 45 E
Akköy, *Turkey* . . . . **49 D9** 37 29N 27 15 E
Aklampa, *Benin* . . . . **113 D5** 8 15N 2 10 E
Aklan □, *Phil.* . . . . **81 F4** 11 50N 122 30 E
Aklavik, *Canada* **138 B6** 68 12N 135 0W
Aklera, *India* . . . . **92 G7** 24 26N 76 32 E
Akmené, *Lithuania* . . . . **54 B8** 56 15N 22 37 E
Akmenrags, *Latvia* . . . . **54 B8** 56 50N 21 4 E
Akmeqit, *China* . . . . **64 F5** 37 5N 76 55 E
Akmolinsk = Astana, *Kazakhstan* . **66 D8** 51 10N 71 30 E
Akmonte = Almonte, *Spain* **43 H4** 37 13N 6 38W
Aknoul, *Morocco* **111 B4** 34 40N 3 55W
Akō, *Japan* . . . . **72 C6** 34 45N 134 24 E
Ako, *Nigeria* . . . . **113 C7** 10 19N 10 48 E
Akôbô, *Sudan* . . . . **107 F3** 7 47N 33 1 E
Akobo →, *Ethiopia* . . . . **107 F3** 7 48N 33 3 E
Akola, *Maharashtra, India* . . . . . . **94 D3** 30 42N 77 2 E
Akola, *Maharashtra, India* . . . . . . **94 E2** 19 32N 74 3 E
Akolmiut, *U.S.A.* **144 F7** 60 55N 162 20W
Akonolinga, *Cameroon* . . . . **113 E7** 3 50N 12 18 E
Akor, *Mali* **112 C3** 14 59N 6 48W
Akordat, *Eritrea* . . . . **107 D4** 15 30N 37 40 E
Akosombo Dam, *Ghana* . . . . **113 D5** 6 20N 0 5 E
Akot, *India* . . . . **94 D3** 21 10N 77 10 E
Akot, *Sudan* . . . . **107 F3** 6 31N 30 9 E
Akoupé, *Ivory C.* **112 D4** 6 23N 3 54W
Akourousoulba, *C.A.R.* . . . . **114 A4** 8 58N 20 46 E
Akpatok I., *Canada* **139 B13** 60 25N 68 8W
Åkrahamn, *Norway* . . . . **18 E2** 59 15N 5 10 E
'Akramah, *Libya* . . . . **108 B4** 32 2N 21 31 E
Akreijit, *Mauritania* **112 B3** 18 19N 11 9W
Akrítas Venétiko, Ákra, *Greece* . . **48 E3** 36 43N 21 54 E
Akron, *Colo., U.S.A.* **154 E3** 40 10N 103 13W
Akron, *Ohio, U.S.A.* **150 E3** 41 5N 81 31W
Akrotiri, *Cyprus* . . . . **39 E8** 34 36N 32 57 E
Akrotíri, Ákra, *Greece* . . . . **51 F9** 40 26N 25 27 E
Akrotiri Bay, *Cyprus* . . . . **39 F9** 34 35N 33 10 E
Aksai Chin, *China* . . . . **93 B8** 35 15N 79 55 E
Aksaray, *Turkey* . . . . **100 C6** 38 25N 34 2 E
Akşehir, *Turkey* . . . . **100 C4** 38 18N 31 30 E
Akşehir Gölü, *Turkey* . . . . **100 C4** 38 30N 31 25 E
Akstafa = Ağstafa, *Azerbaijan* . . **61 K7** 41 7N 45 27 E
Aksu, *China* . . . . **68 B3** 41 5N 80 10 E
Aksu →, *Turkey* . . . . **100 D4** 36 52N 30 57 E
Aksum, *Ethiopia* . . . . **107 E4** 14 5N 38 40 E

Aktash, *Russia* . . . . **60 C11** 55 2N 52 3 E
Aktöbe, *Uzbekistan* . . . . **65 D2** 39 55N 65 55 E
Aktasty, *Kazakhstan* . . . . **64 F8** 50 42N 61 42 E
Aktion, *Greece* . . . . **39 B2** 38 57N 20 46 E
Akto, *China* . . . . **65 D7** 39 5N 75 56 E
Aktogay, *Kazakhstan* . . . . **66 E8** 46 57N 79 40 E
Aktsyabrski, *Belarus* . . . . **59 B8** 52 38N 28 53 E
Aktyubinsk = Aqtöbe, *Kazakhstan* . **57 D10** 50 17N 57 10 E
Aktyuz = Ak-Tüz, *Kyrgyzstan* . . . **65 B8** 42 54N 76 7 E
Aku, *Nigeria* . . . . **113 D6** 6 40N 7 18 E
Akula, Dem. Rep. of the Congo . . . **114 B4** 2 22N 20 12 E
Akulurak, *U.S.A.* **144 E6** 63 33N 164 33W
Akun I., *U.S.A.* **144 J6** 54 11N 165 32W
Akune, *Japan* . . . . **72 E2** 32 1N 130 12 E
Akure, *Nigeria* . . . . **113 D6** 7 15N 5 5 E
Akurenan, Eq. Guin. . . . . **114 B2** 1 2N 10 40 E
Akuressa, Sri Lanka . . . . **95 L5** 6 5N 80 29 E
Akureyri, Iceland **11 B8** 65 40N 18 6W
Akuseki-Shima, *Japan* . . . . **71 K4** 29 27N 129 37 E
Akutan, *U.S.A.* **144 J6** 54 8N 165 46W
Akutan I., *U.S.A.* **144 J6** 54 7N 165 55W
Akwa-Ibom □, *Nigeria* . . . . **113 E6** 4 30N 7 9 E
Akyab = Sittwe, *Burma* . . . . **90 E4** 20 18N 92 45 E
Akyazı, *Turkey* . . . . **100 B4** 40 40N 30 38 E
Ål, *Norway* . . . . **18 D5** 60 38N 8 33 E
Al Abyad, *Libya* . . . . **108 C2** 26 49N 14 1 E
Al Abyār, *Libya* . . . . **108 B4** 32 9N 20 29 E
Al 'Adan, *Yemen* . . . . **98 D4** 12 45N 45 0 E
Al Aḥsā = Hasa □, *Si. Arabia* . . . **97 E6** 25 50N 49 0 E
Al Ajfar, *Si. Arabia* . . . . **96 E4** 27 26N 43 0 E
Al Amādīyah, *Iraq* . . . . **101 D10** 37 5N 43 30 E
Al 'Amārah, *Iraq* . . . . **101 G12** 31 55N 47 15 E
Al 'Aqabah, *Jordan* . . . . **103 F4** 29 31N 35 0 E
Al 'Aqabah □, *Jordan* . . . . **103 F4** 29 30N 35 0 E
Al 'Aqīq, Si. Arabia . . . . **98 B3** 20 9N 41 25 E
Al Arak, *Syria* . . . . **101 E8** 34 38N 38 35 E
Al 'Aramah, *Si. Arabia* . . . . **96 E5** 25 30N 46 0 E
Al 'Arīḍah, *Si. Arabia* . . . . **96 E5** 17 35N 43 25 E
Al 'Arṭāwiyah, *Si. Arabia* . . . . **96 E5** 26 31N 45 20 E
Al Ashkhara, *Oman* . . . . **99 B7** 21 50N 59 30 E
Al 'Asimah □ = 'Ammān □, *Jordan* **103 D5** 31 40N 36 30 E
Al 'Assāfiyah, *Si. Arabia* . . . . **96 D3** 28 17N 38 59 E
Al 'Ayn, *Si. Arabia* . . . . **96 E3** 25 4N 38 6 E
Al 'Ayn, *U.A.E.* . . . . **97 E7** 24 15N 55 45 E
Al 'Azīzīyah, *Iraq* . . . . **101 F11** 32 54N 45 4 E
Al 'Azīzīyah, *Libya* . . . . **108 B2** 32 30N 13 1 E
Al Bāb, *Syria* . . . . **100 D7** 36 23N 37 29 E
Al Bad', *Si. Arabia* . . . . **96 D2** 28 28N 35 1 E
Al Bādī, *Iraq* . . . . **96 C4** 35 56N 41 32 E
Al Bāhah, *Si. Arabia* . . . . **98 B4** 22 0N 46 35 E
Al Baḥrah, *Kuwait* . . . . **96 D5** 29 40N 47 52 E
Al Baḥral Mayyit = Dead Sea, *Asia* **103 D4** 31 30N 35 30 E
Al Balqā' □, *Jordan* . . . . **103 C4** 32 5N 35 45 E
Al Barkāt, *Libya* . . . . **108 C2** 24 56N 10 14 E
Al Bārūk, J., *Lebanon* . . . . **103 B4** 33 39N 35 40 E
Al Başrah, *Iraq* . . . . **97 D5** 30 30N 47 50 E
Al Baţḥā, *Iraq* . . . . **96 D5** 31 6N 45 53 E
Al Bāținah, *Oman* . . . . **99 A7** 24 10N 56 50 E
Al Batrūn, *Lebanon* . . . . **103 A4** 34 15N 35 40 E
Al Bayḍā, *Si. Arabia* . . . . **98 B4** 22 10N 47 0 E
Al Bayḍā, *Libya* . . . . **108 B4** 32 50N 21 44 E
Al Bayḍā', *Yemen* . . . . **98 D4** 14 5N 45 42 E
Al Bi'ār, *Si. Arabia* . . . . **98 B2** 22 39N 39 40 E
Al Biqā, *Lebanon* . . . . **103 A5** 34 10N 36 10 E
Al Bi'r, *Si. Arabia* . . . . **96 D3** 28 51N 36 16 E
Al Birk, *Si. Arabia* . . . . **98 C3** 18 13N 41 33 E
Al Bu'ayrāt al Ḥasūn, *Libya* . . . . . . **108 B3** 31 24N 15 44 E
Al Bunbah, *Libya* . . . . **108 B4** 32 24N 23 8 E
Al Burayj, *Syria* . . . . **103 A5** 34 15N 36 46 E
Al Fadlī, *Si. Arabia* . . . . **97 E6** 26 58N 49 10 E
Al Fallūjah, *Iraq* . . . . **101 F10** 33 20N 43 55 E
Al Fāṭil □, *Libya* . . . . **108 B2** 31 0N 21 0 E
Al Fāw, *Iraq* . . . . **97 D6** 30 0N 48 30 E
Al Faydamī, *Yemen* . . . . **99 C6** 16 25N 52 26 E
Al Fujayrah, *U.A.E.* . . . . **97 E8** 25 7N 56 18 E
Al Ghadaf, W. →, *Jordan* . . . . **103 D5** 31 26N 36 43 E
Al Ghammās, *Iraq* . . . . **96 D5** 31 45N 44 37 E
Al Gharīb, *Libya* . . . . **108 B4** 32 35N 21 11 E
Al Ghaydah, *Yemen* . . . . **99 C6** 16 13N 52 11 E
Al Ghazālah, *Si. Arabia* . . . . **99 D5** 15 30N 50 54 E
Al Ghayl, *Yemen* . . . . **99 D5** 15 30N 50 54 E
Al Ghazālah, *Si. Arabia* . . . . **96 E4** 26 48N 41 19 E
Al Ḥadd, *Oman* . . . . **99 B7** 22 35N 59 48 E
Al Ḥadīthah, *Iraq* . . . . **101 E10** 34 0N 41 13 E
Al Ḥadīthah, *Si. Arabia* . . . . **103 D6** 31 28N 37 8 E
Al Ḥadr, *Iraq* . . . . **101 E10** 35 35N 42 44 E
Al Ḥāmad, *Si. Arabia* . . . . **96 D3** 31 30N 39 30 E
Al Ḥamar, *Si. Arabia* . . . . **98 B4** 22 26N 46 12 E
Al Ḥamdānīyah, *Syria* . . . . **96 C3** 35 25N 36 50 E
Al Ḥamīdīyah, *Syria* . . . . **103 A4** 34 42N 35 57 E
Al Ḥammār, *Iraq* . . . . **96 D5** 30 57N 46 51 E
Al Ḥanākīyah, *Si. Arabia* . . . . **96 E4** 24 51N 40 31 E
Al Ḥarīq, *Si. Arabia* . . . . **98 B4** 23 29N 46 27 E
Al Ḥarīr, W. →, *Syria* . . . . **103 C4** 32 44N 35 59 E
Al Ḥarūj al Aswad, *Libya* . . . . **108 C3** 27 0N 17 10 E
Al Ḥasā, W. →, *Jordan* . . . . **103 D4** 31 4N 35 29 E
Al Ḥasakah, *Syria* . . . . **101 D9** 36 35N 40 45 E
Al Ḥayy, *Iraq* . . . . **96 C5** 32 5N 46 5 E
Al Ḥaydān, W. →, *Jordan* . . . . . . **103 D4** 31 29N 35 58 E
Al Ḥayy, *Iraq* . . . . **101 F12** 32 5N 46 5 E
Al Ḥijarah, Asia . . . . **96 D4** 30 0N 44 0 E
Al Ḥillah, *Iraq* . . . . **101 F11** 32 30N 44 25 E
Al Ḥindīyah, *Iraq* . . . . **101 F11** 32 30N 44 10 E
Al Hirmil, *Lebanon* . . . . **103 A5** 34 26N 36 24 E
Al Hoceïma, *Morocco* **110 A4** 35 8N 3 58W
Al Ḥudaydah, *Yemen* . . . . **98 D3** 14 50N 43 0 E
Al Ḥufrah, *Libya* . . . . **108 C3** 25 30N 14 0 E
Al Ḥufūf, *Si. Arabia* . . . . **97 E6** 25 25N 49 45 E
Al Ḥulwah, *Si. Arabia* . . . . **98 B4** 23 24N 46 48 E
Al Ḥunayy, *Si. Arabia* . . . . **97 E6** 25 58N 48 45 E
Al Ḥuṣayn, *Libya* . . . . **108 B4** 30 24N 20 37 E
Al 'Irqah, *Yemen* . . . . **99 E4** 13 39N 47 8 E
Al Isāwīyah, *Si. Arabia* . . . . **96 D3** 30 43N 37 59 E
Al Ittihad = Madīnat ash Sha'b,
Yemen . . . . **98 D4** 12 50N 45 0 E
Al Jabal al Akhdar □, *Libya* . . . . . . **108 B4** 32 30N 21 30 E
Al Jafr, *Jordan* . . . . **103 E5** 30 18N 36 14 E
Al Jāfūrah, *Si. Arabia* . . . . **97 E7** 25 0N 50 15 E
Al Jaghbūb, *Libya* . . . . **108 C4** 29 42N 24 38 E
Al Jahrah, *Kuwait* . . . . **96 D5** 29 25N 47 40 E
Al Jalāmīd, *Si. Arabia* . . . . **96 D3** 31 20N 39 45 E
Al Jamalīyah, *Qatar* . . . . **97 E6** 25 37N 51 5 E
Al Janūb □, *Lebanon* . . . . **103 B4** 33 20N 35 20 E
Al Jawf, *Libya* . . . . **108 D4** 24 10N 23 24 E
Al Jazirah, *Iraq* . . . . **101 E10** 33 30N 44 0 E
Al Jithāmīyah, *Si. Arabia* . . . . **96 E4** 27 41N 41 43 E
Al Jubayl, *Si. Arabia* . . . . **97 E6** 27 0N 49 50 E
Al Jubaylah, *Si. Arabia* . . . . **96 E5** 24 55N 46 25 E
Al Jubb, *Si. Arabia* . . . . **96 E4** 27 11N 42 17 E

Al Jufrah, Libya ... 108 C3 29 10N 16 0 E
Al Jufrah □, Libya ... 108 C3 27 30N 17 30 E
Al Junaynah, Sudan ... 109 F4 13 27N 22 45 E
Al Jumūm, Si. Arabia ... 98 B2 21 37N 39 42 E
Al Kabā'ish, Iraq ... 96 D5 30 58N 47 0 E
Al Kāmil, Oman ... 99 B7 22 13N 59 12 E
Al Karak, Jordan ... 103 D4 31 11N 35 42 E
Al Karak □, Jordan ... 103 E5 31 0N 36 0 E
Al Kāẓimīyah, Iraq ... 101 F11 33 22N 44 18 E
Al Khābūra, Oman ... 97 F8 23 57N 57 5 E
Al Khafjī, Si. Arabia ... 97 E6 28 24N 48 29 E
Al Khalīl, West Bank ... 103 D4 31 32N 35 6 E
Al Khālis, Iraq ... 101 F11 33 49N 44 32 E
Al Khamāsīn, Si. Arabia ... 98 B4 20 29N 44 46 E
Al Kharj, Si. Arabia ... 98 B4 24 0N 47 0 E
Al Kharsānīyah, Si. Arabia ... 97 E6 27 13N 49 18 E
Al Khaṣab, Oman ... 97 E8 26 14N 56 15 E
Al Khāṣirah, Si. Arabia ... 98 B3 23 30N 43 47 E
Al Khawr, Qatar ... 97 E6 25 41N 51 30 E
Al Khiḍr, Iraq ... 96 D5 31 12N 45 33 E
Al Khiyām, Lebanon ... 103 B4 33 20N 35 36 E
Al Khums, Libya ... 108 B2 32 40N 14 17 E
Al Khums □, Libya ... 108 B2 31 20N 14 10 E
Al Kiswah, Syria ... 103 B5 33 23N 36 14 E
Al Kūfah, Iraq ... 101 F11 32 2N 44 24 E
Al Kufrah, Libya ... 108 D4 24 17N 23 15 E
Al Kuhayfīyah, Si. Arabia ... 96 E4 27 12N 43 3 E
Al Kūt, Iraq ... 101 F11 32 30N 46 0 E
Al Kuwayt, Kuwait ... 96 D5 29 30N 48 0 E
Al Labwah, Lebanon ... 103 A5 34 11N 36 20 E
Al Lādhiqīyah, Syria ... 100 C3 35 30N 35 45 E
Al Līth, Si. Arabia ... 98 B3 20 9N 40 15 E
Al Liwā', Oman ... 97 E8 24 31N 56 36 E
Al Luḥayyah, Yemen ... 98 D3 15 45N 42 40 E
Al Madīnah, Iraq ... 96 D5 30 57N 47 16 E
Al Madīnah, Si. Arabia ... 96 E3 24 35N 39 52 E
Al Mafraq, Jordan ... 103 C5 32 17N 36 14 E
Al Mafraq □, Jordan ... 103 C5 32 17N 36 15 E
Al Maghārīm, Yemen ... 98 D4 15 1N 47 49 E
Al Mahbes, W. Sahara ... 110 C3 27 10N 9 50W
Al Maḥmūdīyah, Iraq ... 101 F11 33 3N 44 21 E
Al Majma'ah, Si. Arabia ... 96 E5 25 57N 45 22 E
Al Makhrūq, W. →, Jordan ... 103 D6 31 28N 37 0 E
Al Makhūl, Si. Arabia ... 96 E4 26 37N 42 39 E
Al Makīlī, Libya ... 108 B4 32 10N 22 17 E
Al Manāmah, Bahrain ... 97 E6 26 10N 50 30 E
Al Maqwa', Kuwait ... 96 D5 29 10N 47 59 E
Al Marj, Libya ... 108 B4 32 25N 20 30 E
Al Maṭlā, Kuwait ... 96 D5 29 24N 47 40 E
Al Mawjib, W. →, Jordan ... 103 D4 31 28N 35 36 E
Al Mawṣil, Iraq ... 101 D10 36 15N 43 5 E
Al Mayādin, Syria ... 101 E9 35 1N 40 27 E
Al Mazār, Jordan ... 103 D4 31 4N 35 41 E
Al Midhnab, Si. Arabia ... 96 E5 25 50N 44 18 E
Al Minā', Lebanon ... 103 A4 34 24N 35 49 E
Al Miqdādīyah, Iraq ... 101 E11 34 0N 45 0 E
Al Mubarraz, Si. Arabia ... 97 E6 25 30N 49 40 E
Al Mudawwarah, Jordan ... 103 F5 29 19N 36 0 E
Al Mughayrā', U.A.E. ... 97 E7 24 5N 53 32 E
Al Muḥarraq, Bahrain ... 97 E6 26 15N 50 40 E
Al Mukallā, Yemen ... 99 D5 14 33N 49 2 E
Al Mukhā, Yemen ... 98 D3 13 18N 43 15 E
Al Musayyid, Si. Arabia ... 96 E3 24 5N 39 5 E
Al Musayyib, Iraq ... 101 F11 32 49N 44 20 E
Al Muwayh, Si. Arabia ... 106 C5 22 41N 41 37 E
Al Muwayliḥ, Si. Arabia ... 96 E2 27 40N 35 30 E
Al Owuho = Otukpa, Nigeria ... 113 D6 7 9N 7 41 E
Al Qaḍḍāḥīyah, Libya ... 108 B3 31 15N 15 9 E
Al Qaḍīmah, Si. Arabia ... 98 B2 22 20N 39 13 E
Al Qaḥmah, Si. Arabia ... 98 C3 18 0N 41 41 E
Al Qā'im, Iraq ... 101 E9 34 21N 41 7 E
Al Qalībah, Si. Arabia ... 96 D3 28 24N 37 42 E
Al Qāmishlī, Syria ... 101 D9 37 2N 41 14 E
Al Qaryah ash Sharqīyah, Libya ... 108 B2 30 28N 13 40 E
Al Qaryatayn, Syria ... 103 A6 34 12N 37 13 E
Al Qaṣabāt, Libya ... 108 B2 32 39N 14 1 E
Al Qaṣīm, Si. Arabia ... 96 E4 26 0N 43 0 E
Al Qaṭ'ā, Syria ... 101 E9 34 40N 40 48 E
Al Qaṭīf, Si. Arabia ... 97 E6 26 35N 50 0 E
Al Qaṭn, Yemen ... 99 D5 15 51N 48 26 E
Al Qaṭrānah, Jordan ... 103 D5 31 12N 36 6 E
Al Qaṭrūn, Libya ... 108 D3 24 56N 15 3 E
Al Qayṣūmah, Si. Arabia ... 96 D5 28 20N 46 7 E
Al Qiblīyah, Oman ... 99 C7 17 30N 56 20 E
Al Quds = Jerusalem, Israel ... 103 D4 31 47N 35 10 E
Al Qunayṭirah, Syria ... 103 C4 32 55N 35 45 E
Al Qunfudhah, Si. Arabia ... 98 C3 19 3N 41 4 E
Al Qurḥ, Yemen ... 99 C5 16 44N 51 29 E
Al Qurnah, Iraq ... 96 D5 31 1N 47 25 E
Al Quṣayr, Iraq ... 96 D5 30 39N 45 50 E
Al Quṣayr, Syria ... 103 A5 34 31N 36 34 E
Al Quṭayfah, Syria ... 103 B5 33 44N 36 36 E
Al Quwayʿīyah, Si. Arabia ... 98 A4 24 3N 45 15 E
Al 'Ubaylah, Si. Arabia ... 99 B5 21 59N 50 57 E
Al 'Udayliyah, Si. Arabia ... 97 E6 25 8N 49 18 E
Al 'Ulā, Si. Arabia ... 96 E3 26 35N 38 0 E
Al 'Ulayyah, Si. Arabia ... 98 C3 19 39N 41 54 E
Al Uqaylah ash Sharqīgah, Libya ... 108 B3 30 12N 19 10 E
Al 'Uqayr, Si. Arabia ... 97 E6 25 40N 50 15 E
Al 'Uwaynid, Si. Arabia ... 96 E5 24 50N 46 0 E
Al 'Uwayqīlah, Si. Arabia ... 96 D4 30 30N 42 10 E
Al 'Uyūn, Ḥijāz, Si. Arabia ... 96 E3 24 33N 39 35 E
Al 'Uyūn, Najd, Si. Arabia ... 96 E4 26 30N 43 50 E
Al 'Uzayr, Iraq ... 96 D5 31 35N 47 25 E
Al Wajh, Si. Arabia ... 96 E3 26 10N 36 30 E
Al Wakrah, Qatar ... 97 E6 25 10N 51 40 E
Al Waqbah, Si. Arabia ... 96 D5 28 48N 45 33 E
Al Wari'āh, Si. Arabia ... 96 E5 27 51N 47 25 E
Al Wāṭiyah, Libya ... 108 B2 32 28N 11 57 E
Ala, Italy ... 44 C8 45 45N 11 0 E
Ala-Buka, Kyrgyzstan ... 65 C5 41 23N 71 30 E
Ala Dağ, Turkey ... 96 B2 37 44N 35 9 E
Ala Dağları, Turkey ... 101 C10 39 15N 43 33 E
Ala Tau Shankou = Dzungarian
 Gates, Asia ... 68 B3 45 0N 82 0 E
Alabama □, U.S.A. ... 149 J2 33 0N 87 0W
Alabama →, U.S.A. ... 149 K2 31 8N 87 57W
Alabaster, U.S.A. ... 149 J2 33 15N 86 49W
Alabat I., Phil. ... 80 D4 14 7N 122 3 E
Alabel, Phil. ... 81 H5 6 4N 125 16 E
Alabule →, Papua N. G. ... 132 E4 8 31 S 146 56 E
Alaca, Turkey ... 100 B6 40 10N 34 51 E
Alacaatlı, Turkey ... 89 B10 39 15N 28 3 E
Alaçam, Turkey ... 100 B6 41 36N 35 36 E
Alaçam Dağları, Turkey ... 49 B10 39 18N 28 49 E
Alaçatı, Turkey ... 49 C8 38 15N 26 22 E
Alachua, U.S.A. ... 152 F7 29 47N 82 30W
Alaejos, Spain ... 42 D5 41 18N 5 13W
Alaérma, Greece ... 38 E11 36 9N 27 57 E
Alagir, Russia ... 61 J7 43 1N 44 14 E
Alagna Valsésia, Italy ... 44 C4 45 51N 7 56 E
Alagoa Grande, Brazil ... 170 C4 7 3 S 35 35W
Alagoas □, Brazil ... 170 D4 9 0 S 36 0W
Alagoinhas, Brazil ... 171 D4 12 7 S 38 20W
Alagón, Spain ... 40 D3 41 46N 1 12W
Alagón →, Spain ... 42 F4 39 44N 6 53W
Alagyoz = Aragats, Armenia ... 61 K7 40 30N 44 15 E
Alai Range, Asia ... 65 D5 39 45N 72 0 E
Alaior, Spain ... 38 B5 39 57N 4 8 E
Alajero, Canary Is. ... 9 e1 28 3N 17 13W
Alajuela, Costa Rica ... 164 D3 10 2N 84 8W
Alakamisy, Madag. ... 117 C8 21 19 S 47 14 E
Alakanuk, U.S.A. ... 144 E6 62 41N 164 37W

Alaknanda →, India ... 93 D8 30 8N 78 36 E
Alakurtti, Russia ... 56 A5 67 0N 30 30 E
Alalakeiki Channel, U.S.A. ... 145 C5 20 30N 156 30W
Alalapura, Suriname ... 169 C6 2 29N 56 25W
Alalaú →, Brazil ... 169 D5 0 30 S 61 9W
Alamarvdasht, Iran ... 97 E7 27 37N 52 59 E
Alamata, Ethiopia ... 107 E4 12 25N 39 33 E
Alameda, Calif., U.S.A. ... 160 H4 37 46N 122 15W
Alameda, N. Mex., U.S.A. ... 159 J10 35 11N 106 37W
Alaminos, Phil. ... 80 C2 16 10N 119 59 E
Alamo, Ga., U.S.A. ... 152 C7 32 9N 82 47W
Alamo, Nev., U.S.A. ... 161 J11 37 22N 115 10W
Alamo Crossing, U.S.A. ... 161 L13 34 16N 113 33W
Alamogordo, U.S.A. ... 159 K11 32 54N 105 57W
Alamos, Mexico ... 162 B3 27 0N 109 0W
Alamosa, U.S.A. ... 159 H11 37 28N 105 52W
Alampur, India ... 95 G4 15 55N 78 6 E
Åland, Finland ... 15 F19 60 15N 20 0 E
Alandi, India ... 94 F3 17 36N 76 35 E
Alandroal, Portugal ... 43 G3 38 41N 7 24W
Ålands hav, Sweden ... 15 F18 60 0N 19 30 E
Alandur, India ... 95 H5 13 0N 80 15 E
Alange, Presa de, Spain ... 43 G4 38 45N 6 18W
Alania = North Ossetia □, Russia ... 61 J7 43 30N 44 30 E
Alanís, Spain ... 43 G5 38 3N 5 43W
Alanya, Turkey ... 100 D5 36 38N 32 0 E
Alaotra, Farihin', Madag. ... 117 B8 17 30 S 48 30 E
Alapaha, U.S.A. ... 152 D6 31 23N 83 13W
Alapayevsk, Russia ... 64 C8 57 52N 61 42 E
Alappuzha = Alleppey, India ... 95 K3 9 30N 76 28 E
Alar del Rey, Spain ... 42 C6 42 38N 4 20W
Alaraz, Spain ... 42 E5 40 45N 5 17W
Alarcón, Embalse de, Spain ... 40 F2 39 36N 2 10W
Alarobia-Vohiposa, Madag. ... 117 C8 20 59 S 47 9 E
Alaşehir, Turkey ... 49 C10 38 23N 28 30 E
Alaska □, U.S.A. ... 144 E9 64 0N 154 0W
Alaska, G. of, Pac. Oc. ... 144 G11 58 0N 145 0W
Alaska Peninsula, U.S.A. ... 144 J8 56 0N 159 0W
Alaska Range, U.S.A. ... 144 F10 62 50N 151 0W
Alássio, Italy ... 44 E5 44 0N 8 10 E
Ālāt, Azerbaijan ... 61 L9 39 58N 49 25 E
Alat, Uzbekistan ... 65 D1 39 24N 63 47 E
Alatri, Italy ... 45 G10 41 43N 13 21 E
Alatyr, Russia ... 60 C8 54 55N 46 35 E
Alatyr →, Russia ... 60 C8 54 52N 46 36 E
Alausi, Ecuador ... 168 D2 2 0 S 78 50W
Alava □, Spain ... 40 C2 42 48N 2 28W
Alava, C., U.S.A. ... 158 B1 48 10N 124 44W
Alaverdi, Armenia ... 61 K7 41 15N 44 37 E
Alavus, Finland ... 15 E20 62 35N 23 36 E
Alawoona, Australia ... 128 C4 34 45 S 140 30 E
'Alayh, Lebanon ... 103 B4 33 46N 35 33 E
Alaykuu = Kögart, Kyrgyzstan ... 65 C7 40 15N 74 25 E
Alazani →, Azerbaijan ... 61 K8 41 5N 46 40 E
Alba, Italy ... 44 D5 44 42N 8 2 E
Alba □, Romania ... 53 D8 46 10N 23 30 E
Alba Adriática, Italy ... 45 F10 42 50N 13 56 E
Alba de Tormes, Spain ... 42 E5 40 50N 5 30W
Alba-Iulia, Romania ... 53 D8 46 8N 23 39 E
Albac, Romania ... 52 D7 46 28N 22 58 E
Albacete, Spain ... 41 F3 39 0N 1 50W
Albacete □, Spain ... 41 G3 38 50N 2 0W
Albacutya, L., Australia ... 128 C4 35 45 S 141 58 E
Ålbæk, Denmark ... 17 G4 57 36N 10 25 E
Ålbæk Bugt, Denmark ... 17 G4 57 35N 10 40 E
Albaida, Spain ... 41 G4 38 51N 0 31W
Albalate de las Nogueras, Spain ... 40 E2 40 22N 2 18W
Albalate del Arzobispo, Spain ... 40 D4 41 6N 0 31W
Alban, France ... 28 E6 43 53N 2 28 E
Albanel, L., Canada ... 140 B5 50 55N 73 12W
Albania ■, Europe ... 50 E4 41 0N 20 0 E
Albano Laziale, Italy ... 45 G9 41 44N 12 39 E
Albany, Australia ... 125 G2 35 1 S 117 58 E
Albany, Ga., U.S.A. ... 152 D5 31 35N 84 10W
Albany, Ind., U.S.A. ... 157 D11 40 18N 85 14W
Albany, Mo., U.S.A. ... 156 D2 40 15N 94 20W
Albany, N.Y., U.S.A. ... 151 D11 42 39N 73 45W
Albany, Oreg., U.S.A. ... 158 D2 44 38N 123 6W
Albany, Tex., U.S.A. ... 155 J5 32 44N 99 18W
Albany, Wis., U.S.A. ... 156 B7 42 43N 89 26W
Albany →, Canada ... 140 B3 52 17N 81 31W
Albardón, Argentina ... 174 C2 31 20 S 68 30W
Albarracín, Spain ... 40 E3 40 25N 1 26W
Albarracín, Sierra de, Spain ... 40 E3 40 30N 1 30W
Albatera, Spain ... 41 G4 38 11N 0 52W
Albatross B., Australia ... 126 A3 12 45 S 141 30 E
Albatross Pt., N.Z. ... 130 E3 38 7 S 174 44 E
Albay □, Phil. ... 80 E4 13 13N 123 33 E
Albegna →, Italy ... 45 F8 42 30N 11 11 E
Albemarle, U.S.A. ... 149 H5 35 21N 80 11W
Albemarle, I. = Isabela, I., Ecuador ... 172 a 0 30 S 91 4W
Albemarle, Pta., Ecuador ... 172 a 0 11N 91 21W
Albemarle Sd., U.S.A. ... 149 H7 36 5N 76 0W
Albenga, Italy ... 44 D5 44 3N 8 13 E
Alberche →, Spain ... 42 F6 39 58N 4 46W
Alberdi, Paraguay ... 174 B4 26 14 S 58 20W
Alberes, Mts., France ... 28 F6 42 28N 2 56 E
Ålberga, Sweden ... 17 F10 58 44N 16 35 E
Albersdorf, Germany ... 30 A5 54 8N 9 17 E
Albert, France ... 27 C9 50 0N 2 38 E
Albert, L., Africa ... 118 B3 1 30N 31 0 E
Albert, L., Australia ... 128 C3 35 30 S 139 10 E
Albert Edward, Mt., Papua N. G. ... 132 E4 8 20 S 147 24 E
Albert Edward Ra., Australia ... 124 C4 18 17 S 127 57 E
Albert Lea, U.S.A. ... 154 D8 43 39N 93 22W
Albert Nile →, Uganda ... 118 B3 3 36N 32 2 E
Albert Town, Bahamas ... 165 B5 22 37N 74 33W
Alberta □, Canada ... 142 C6 54 40N 115 0W
Alberti, Argentina ... 174 D3 35 1 S 60 16W
Albertinia, S. Africa ... 116 E3 34 11 S 21 34 E
Albertirsa, Hungary ... 57 C11 47 14N 19 37 E
Alberton, Canada ... 141 C7 46 50N 64 0W
Albertville = Kalemie, Dem. Rep. of
 the Congo ... 118 D2 5 55 S 29 9 E
Albertville, France ... 29 C10 45 40N 6 22 E
Albertville, U.S.A. ... 149 H2 34 16N 86 13W
Albi, France ... 28 E6 43 56N 2 9 E
Albia, U.S.A. ... 156 C4 41 2N 92 48W
Albina, Suriname ... 169 B7 5 37N 54 15W
Albina, Ponta, Angola ... 116 B1 15 52 S 11 44 E
Albino, Italy ... 44 C6 45 46N 9 47 E
Albion, Ill., U.S.A. ... 157 F8 38 23N 88 4W
Albion, Ind., U.S.A. ... 157 C11 41 24N 85 25W
Albion, Mich., U.S.A. ... 157 B12 42 15N 84 45W
Albion, Nebr., U.S.A. ... 154 E6 41 42N 98 0W
Albion, Pa., U.S.A. ... 150 E4 41 53N 80 22W
Albocácer, Spain ... 40 E5 40 21N 0 1 E
Albolote, Spain ... 43 H7 37 14N 3 39W
Alborán, Medit. S. ... 43 K7 35 57N 3 0W
Ålborg, Denmark ... 17 G3 57 2N 9 54 E
Ålborg Bugt, Denmark ... 17 H4 56 50N 10 35 E
Alborz, Reshteh-ye Kūhhā-ye, Iran ... 97 C7 36 0N 52 0 E
Albosaggia, Italy ... 33 D9 46 8N 9 51 E
Albox, Spain ... 41 H2 37 23N 2 8W
Albuera, Phil. ... 81 F5 10 55N 124 42 E
Albufeira, Portugal ... 43 H2 37 5N 8 15W
Albula →, Switz. ... 33 C8 46 38N 9 28 E
Albuñol, Spain ... 43 J7 36 48N 3 11W
Albuquerque, Brazil ... 173 D6 19 23 S 79 23W
Albuquerque, U.S.A. ... 159 J10 35 5N 106 39W
Albuquerque, Cayos de, Caribbean ... 164 D3 12 10N 81 50W
Alburg, U.S.A. ... 151 B11 44 59N 73 18W
Alburno, Mte., Italy ... 47 B8 40 33N 15 17 E

Alburquerque, Spain ... 43 F4 39 15N 6 59W
Albury = Albury-Wodonga,
 Australia ... 129 D7 36 3 S 146 56 E
Albury-Wodonga, Australia ... 129 D7 36 3 S 146 56 E
Alcácer do Sal, Portugal ... 43 G2 38 22N 8 33W
Alcáçovas, Portugal ... 43 G2 38 23N 8 9W
Alcalá, Phil. ... 80 C3 17 54N 121 39 E
Alcalá de Chivert, Spain ... 40 E5 40 19N 0 13 E
Alcalá de Guadaira, Spain ... 43 H5 37 20N 5 50W
Alcalá de Henares, Spain ... 42 E7 40 28N 3 22W
Alcalá de los Gazules, Spain ... 43 J5 36 29N 5 43W
Alcalá del Júcar, Spain ... 41 F3 39 12N 1 26W
Alcalá del Río, Spain ... 43 H5 37 31N 5 59W
Alcalá del Valle, Spain ... 43 J5 36 54N 5 10W
Alcalá la Real, Spain ... 43 H7 37 27N 3 57W
Álcamo, Italy ... 46 E5 37 59N 12 55 E
Alcanadre, Spain ... 40 C2 42 24N 2 7W
Alcanadre →, Spain ... 40 D4 41 43N 0 12W
Alcanar, Spain ... 40 E5 40 33N 0 28 E
Alcanede, Portugal ... 43 F2 39 25N 8 49W
Alcanena, Portugal ... 43 F2 39 27N 8 40W
Alcañices, Spain ... 42 D4 41 41N 6 21W
Alcañiz, Spain ... 40 D4 41 2N 0 8W
Alcântara, Brazil ... 170 B3 2 20 S 44 30W
Alcántara, Spain ... 42 F4 39 41N 6 57W
Alcántara, Embalse de, Spain ... 42 F4 39 44N 6 50W
Alcantarilla, Spain ... 41 H3 37 59N 1 12W
Alcaracejos, Spain ... 43 G6 38 24N 4 58W
Alcaraz, Spain ... 41 G2 38 40N 2 29W
Alcaraz, Sierra de, Spain ... 41 G2 38 40N 2 20W
Alcaudete, Spain ... 43 H6 37 35N 4 5W
Alcázar de San Juan, Spain ... 43 F7 39 24N 3 12W
Alcázarquivir = Ksar el Kebir,
 Morocco ... 110 B3 35 0N 6 0W
Alcedo, Volcán, Ecuador ... 172 a 0 24 S 91 6W
Alchevsk, Ukraine ... 59 H10 48 30N 38 45 E
Alcira = Alzira, Spain ... 41 F4 39 9N 0 30W
Alcoa, U.S.A. ... 153 H8 35 47N 83 59W
Alcobaça, Portugal ... 43 F2 39 32N 8 58W
Alcobendas, Spain ... 42 E7 40 32N 3 38W
Alcolea del Pinar, Spain ... 40 D2 41 2N 2 28W
Alcoma, U.S.A. ... 153 H8 27 54N 81 29W
Alcora, Spain ... 40 E4 40 5N 0 14W
Alcorcón, Spain ... 42 E7 40 20N 3 51W
Alcorisa, Spain ... 43 H3 37 25N 7 28W
Alcoutim, Portugal ... 43 H3 37 25N 7 28W
Alcova, U.S.A. ... 158 E10 42 34N 106 43W
Alcoy, Spain ... 41 G4 38 43N 0 30W
Alcúdia, Spain ... 40 A4 41 45N 0 22W
Alcúdia, B. d', Spain ... 38 B4 39 47N 3 15 E
Alcudia, Sierra de la, Spain ... 43 G6 38 34N 4 30W
Aldabra Is., Seychelles ... 121 E3 9 22 S 46 28 E
Aldama, Mexico ... 163 C5 23 0N 98 4W
Aldan, Russia ... 67 D13 58 40N 125 30 E
Aldan →, Russia ... 67 C13 63 28N 129 35 E
Aldea, Pta. de la, Canary Is. ... 9 e1 28 0N 15 50W
Aldeburgh, U.K. ... 21 E9 52 10N 1 37 E
Alden, Norway ... 18 C1 61 19N 4 45 E
Alder Pk., U.S.A. ... 160 K5 35 53N 121 22W
Alderney, U.K. ... 21 H5 49 42N 2 11W
Aldershot, U.K. ... 21 F7 51 15N 0 44W
Aldinga Beach, Australia ... 128 C3 35 17 S 138 27 E
Åled, Sweden ... 17 H6 56 44N 12 57 E
Aledo, U.S.A. ... 156 C6 41 12N 90 45W
Alefa, Ethiopia ... 107 E4 11 55N 36 55 E
Aleg, Mauritania ... 112 B2 17 3N 13 55W
Alegranza, Canary Is. ... 110 C2 29 23N 13 32W
Alegranza, I., Canary Is. ... 9 e2 29 23N 13 32W
Alegre, Brazil ... 171 F3 20 50 S 41 30W
Alegrete, Brazil ... 175 B4 29 40 S 55 30W
Aleisk, Russia ... 66 D9 52 40N 83 0 E
Aleknagik, U.S.A. ... 144 G8 59 17N 158 36W
Aleksandriya = Oleksandriya,
 Kirovohrad, Ukraine ... 59 H7 48 42N 33 3 E
Aleksandriya = Oleksandriya, Rivne,
 Ukraine ... 59 G4 50 37N 26 19 E
Aleksandriyskaya, Russia ... 61 J8 43 58N 47 14 E
Aleksandrov, Russia ... 58 D10 56 23N 38 44 E
Aleksandrov Gay, Russia ... 60 E9 50 9N 48 34 E
Aleksandrovac, Serbia, Yug. ... 50 C5 43 28N 21 3 E
Aleksandrovac, Serbia, Yug. ... 50 B5 44 28N 21 13 E
Aleksandrovka = Oleksandrivka,
 Ukraine ... 59 H7 48 55N 32 20 E
Aleksandrovo, Bulgaria ... 51 C8 43 14N 24 51 E
Aleksandrovsk = Belogorsk, Russia ... 67 D13 51 0N 128 20 E
Aleksandrovsk, Russia ... 64 B6 59 9N 57 33 E
Aleksandrovsk-Sakhalinskiy, Russia ... 67 D15 50 50N 142 20 E
Aleksandrów Kujawski, Poland ... 55 F5 52 53N 18 43 E
Aleksandrów Łódzki, Poland ... 55 G6 51 49N 19 17 E
Alekseyevka, Samara, Russia ... 60 D10 52 35N 51 17 E
Alekseyevka, Voronezh, Russia ... 59 G10 50 43N 38 40 E
Aleksin, Russia ... 58 E9 54 31N 37 9 E
Aleksinac, Serbia, Yug. ... 50 C6 43 31N 21 42 E
Além Paraíba, Brazil ... 171 F3 21 52 S 42 41W
Alemania, Argentina ... 174 B2 25 40 S 65 30W
Alemania, Chile ... 174 B2 25 10 S 69 55W
Alen, Eq. Guin. ... 114 B2 1 58N 11 19 E
Alençon, France ... 26 D7 48 27N 0 4 E
Alenuihaha Channel, U.S.A. ... 145 C6 20 30N 156 0W
Alépé, Ivory C. ... 112 D4 5 30N 3 40W
Aleppo = Ḩalab, Syria ... 100 D7 36 10N 37 15 E
Aléria, France ... 29 F13 42 5N 9 26 E
Aleru, India ... 94 F4 17 39N 79 3 E
Alès, France ... 29 D8 44 9N 4 5 E
Aleşd, Romania ... 52 C7 47 3N 22 22 E
Alessándria, Italy ... 44 D5 44 54N 8 37 E
Ålestrup, Denmark ... 17 H3 56 42N 9 29 E
Ålesund, Norway ... 18 B3 62 28N 6 12 E
Alet-les-Bains, France ... 28 F6 42 59N 2 14 E
Aleutian Is., Pac. Oc. ... 138 C2 52 0N 175 0W
Aleutian Range, U.S.A. ... 144 G9 60 0N 154 0W
Aleutian Trench, Pac. Oc. ... 138 C10 48 0N 180 0 E
Alexander, Ga., U.S.A. ... 152 B8 33 1N 81 53W
Alexander, N. Dak., U.S.A. ... 154 B3 47 51N 103 39W
Alexander, C., Solomon Is. ... 133 L9 6 34 S 156 32 E
Alexander, Mt., Australia ... 125 E3 28 58 S 120 16 E
Alexander Arch., U.S.A. ... 144 J14 56 0N 136 0W
Alexander Bay, S. Africa ... 116 D2 28 40 S 16 30 E
Alexander City, U.S.A. ... 152 C4 32 56N 85 58W
Alexander I., Antarctica ... 7 C17 69 0 S 70 0W
Alexandra, Australia ... 126 D6 37 8 S 145 40 E
Alexandra, N.Z. ... 131 F4 45 14 S 169 25 E
Alexandra Channel, Burma ... 95 G11 14 7N 93 13 E
Alexandra Falls, Canada ... 142 A5 60 29N 116 18W
Alexandretta = İskenderun, Turkey ... 100 D7 36 32N 36 10 E
Alexandria = El Iskandarîya, Egypt ... 106 H7 31 13N 29 58 E
Alexandria, B.C., Canada ... 142 C4 52 35N 122 27W
Alexandria, Ont., Canada ... 140 C5 45 19N 74 38W
Alexandria, Romania ... 53 G10 43 57N 25 24 E
Alexandria, S. Africa ... 116 E4 33 38 S 26 28 E
Alexandria, U.K. ... 22 C7 55 59N 4 35W
Alexandria, Ind., U.S.A. ... 157 D11 40 16N 85 41W
Alexandria, Ky., U.S.A. ... 156 F3 38 58N 84 23W
Alexandria, La., U.S.A. ... 155 K8 31 18N 92 27W
Alexandria, Minn., U.S.A. ... 154 C7 45 53N 95 22W
Alexandria, Mo., U.S.A. ... 156 D5 40 27N 91 28W
Alexandria, S. Dak., U.S.A. ... 154 D6 43 39N 97 47W
Alexandria, Va., U.S.A. ... 148 F7 38 48N 77 3W
Alexandria Bay, U.S.A. ... 151 B9 44 20N 75 55W
Alexandrina, L., Australia ... 128 C3 35 25 S 139 10 E
Alexandroúpolis, Greece ... 51 F9 40 50N 25 54 E
Alexis →, Canada ... 141 B8 52 33N 56 8W

Alexis Creek, Canada ... 142 C4 52 10N 123 20W
Alfabia, Spain ... 38 B3 39 44N 2 44 E
Alfambra, Spain ... 40 E3 40 33N 1 5W
Alfândega da Fé, Portugal ... 42 D4 41 20N 6 59W
Alfaro, Spain ... 40 C3 42 10N 1 50W
Alfatar, Bulgaria ... 51 C11 43 59N 27 13 E
Alfaz del Pi, Spain ... 41 G4 38 35N 0 5W
Alfeld, Germany ... 30 D5 51 59N 9 50 E
Alfenas, Brazil ... 175 A6 21 20 S 46 10W
Alfiós →, Greece ... 48 D3 37 40N 21 33 E
Alföld, Hungary ... 52 D5 47 0N 20 30 E
Alfonsine, Italy ... 45 D9 44 30N 12 3 E
Alfonso XIII = Quezon, Phil. ... 81 G1 9 15N 117 59 E
Alford, Aberds., U.K. ... 22 D6 57 14N 2 41W
Alford, Lincs., U.K. ... 20 D8 53 15N 0 10 E
Alford, U.S.A. ... 152 E4 30 42N 85 24W
Ålfotbreen, Norway ... 18 C2 61 45N 5 39 E
Ålfoten, Norway ... 18 C2 61 51N 5 41 E
Alfred, Maine, U.S.A. ... 151 C14 43 29N 70 43W
Alfred, N.Y., U.S.A. ... 150 D7 42 16N 77 48W
Alfreton, U.K. ... 20 D6 53 6N 1 24W
Alfta, Sweden ... 16 C10 61 21N 16 4 E
Alga, Kazakhstan ... 57 E10 49 53N 57 20 E
Algaida, Spain ... 38 B3 39 33N 2 53 E
Algar, Spain ... 43 J5 36 40N 5 39W
Ålgård, Norway ... 18 F2 58 46N 5 53 E
Algarinejo, Spain ... 43 H6 37 19N 4 9W
Algarve, Portugal ... 43 J2 36 58N 8 20W
Algeciras, Spain ... 43 J5 36 9N 5 28W
Algemesí, Spain ... 41 F4 39 11N 0 27W
Alger, Algeria ... 111 A5 36 42N 3 8 E
Algeria ■, Africa ... 111 C5 28 30N 2 0 E
Alghero, Italy ... 46 B1 40 33N 8 19 E
Ålghult, Sweden ... 17 G9 57 0N 15 35 E
Algiers = Alger, Algeria ... 111 A5 36 42N 3 8 E
Algiers ✈ (ALG), Algeria ... 41 J8 36 39N 3 13 E
Algoa B., S. Africa ... 116 E4 33 50 S 25 45 E
Algodonales, Spain ... 43 J5 36 54N 5 24W
Algodor →, Spain ... 42 F7 39 55N 3 53W
Algoma, U.S.A. ... 148 C2 44 36N 87 26W
Algona, U.S.A. ... 156 A2 43 4N 94 14W
Algonac, U.S.A. ... 150 D2 42 37N 82 32W
Algonquin Prov. Park □, Canada ... 140 C4 45 50N 78 30W
Alhama de Almería, Spain ... 43 J8 36 57N 2 34W
Alhama de Aragón, Spain ... 40 D3 41 18N 1 54W
Alhama de Granada, Spain ... 43 H7 37 0N 3 59W
Alhama de Murcia, Spain ... 41 H3 37 51N 1 25W
Alhambra, U.S.A. ... 161 L8 34 8N 118 6W
Alhaurín el Grande, Spain ... 43 J6 36 39N 4 41W
Alhucemas = Al Hoceïma, Morocco ... 110 A4 35 8N 3 58W
'Alī al Gharbī, Iraq ... 101 F12 32 30N 46 45 E
'Alī ash Sharqī, Iraq ... 101 F12 32 7N 46 44 E
Ali Bayramlı, Azerbaijan ... 61 L9 39 59N 48 52 E
'Alī Khēl, Afghan. ... 91 B3 33 57N 69 43 E
Ali Sāḩih, Djibouti ... 107 E5 11 10N 42 44 E
Ali Shāh, Iran ... 96 B5 38 9N 45 50 E
'Ālia, Italy ... 46 E6 37 47N 13 43 E
Ālīābād, Khorāsān, Iran ... 97 B8 32 30N 57 30 E
Ālīābād, Kordestān, Iran ... 96 C5 35 4N 46 58 E
Ālīābād, Yazd, Iran ... 97 D7 31 41N 53 49 E
Aliaga, Spain ... 40 E4 40 40N 0 42W
Aliağa, Turkey ... 49 C8 38 47N 26 59 E
Aliákmon →, Greece ... 50 F6 40 30N 22 36 E
Alibag, India ... 94 E1 18 38N 72 56 E
Alibo, Ethiopia ... 107 F4 9 52N 37 5 E
Alibori →, Benin ... 113 C5 11 56N 3 17 E
Alibunar, Serbia, Yug. ... 52 E5 45 5N 20 57 E
Alicante, Spain ... 41 G4 38 23N 0 30W
Alicante □, Spain ... 41 G4 38 30N 0 37W
Alicante ✈ (ALC), Spain ... 41 G4 38 14N 0 36W
Alice, S. Africa ... 116 E4 32 48 S 26 55 E
Alice, U.S.A. ... 155 M5 27 45N 98 5W
Alice →, Queens., Australia ... 126 C3 24 2 S 144 50 E
Alice →, Queens., Australia ... 126 B3 15 35 S 142 20 E
Alice →, Papua N. G. ... 132 D1 6 10 S 143 15 E
Alice, Punta, Italy ... 47 C10 39 24N 17 9 E
Alice Arm, Canada ... 142 B3 55 29N 129 31W
Alice Springs, Australia ... 126 C1 23 40 S 133 50 E
Alicedale, S. Africa ... 116 E4 33 15 S 26 4 E
Aliceville, U.S.A. ... 149 J1 33 8N 88 9W
Alichur, Tajikistan ... 65 F8 37 45N 73 33 E
Alicia, Bohol, Phil. ... 81 G5 9 54N 124 26 E
Alicia, Isabela, Phil. ... 80 C3 16 46N 121 42 E
Alicudi, Italy ... 47 D7 38 33N 14 20 E
Aliganj, India ... 93 F8 27 30N 79 10 E
Aligarh, Raj., India ... 92 G7 25 55N 76 15 E
Aligarh, Ut. P., India ... 92 F8 27 55N 78 10 E
Aligūdarz, Iran ... 97 C6 33 25N 49 45 E
Alijó, Portugal ... 42 D3 41 16N 7 27W
Alikanás, Greece ... 39 D2 37 51N 20 47 E
Alima →, Congo ... 114 C3 1 35 S 16 37 E
Alimniá, Greece ... 88 E11 36 16N 27 43 E
Alimodian, Phil. ... 81 F4 10 49N 122 26 E
Alindao, C.A.R. ... 114 A4 5 2N 21 13 E
Alingsås, Sweden ... 17 G6 57 56N 12 31 E
Alipur, Pakistan ... 92 E4 29 25N 70 55 E
Alipur Duar, India ... 90 B2 26 30N 89 35 E
Aliquippa, U.S.A. ... 150 F4 40 37N 80 15W
Alishan, Taiwan ... 77 F13 23 31N 120 48 E
Aliste →, Spain ... 42 D5 41 34N 5 58W
Alitus = Alytus, Lithuania ... 15 J21 54 24N 24 3 E
Alivérion, Greece ... 48 C6 38 24N 24 2 E
Aliwal North, S. Africa ... 116 E4 30 45 S 26 45 E
Alix, Canada ... 142 C6 52 24N 113 11W
Aljezur, Portugal ... 43 H2 37 18N 8 49W
Aljustrel, Portugal ... 43 H2 37 55N 8 10W
Alkmaar, Neths. ... 24 B4 52 37N 4 45 E
All American Canal, U.S.A. ... 159 K6 32 45N 115 15W
Allacapan, Phil. ... 80 B3 18 15N 121 35 E
Allada, Benin ... 113 D5 6 41N 2 9 E
Allagadda, India ... 95 G4 15 8N 78 30 E
Allagash →, U.S.A. ... 149 B11 47 5N 69 3W
Allah Dad, Pakistan ... 92 G2 25 38N 67 34 E
Allahabad, India ... 93 G9 25 25N 81 58 E
Allakaket, U.S.A. ... 144 C9 66 34N 152 39W
Allal Tazi, Morocco ... 110 B3 34 30N 6 20W
Allan, Canada ... 143 C7 51 53N 106 4W
Allanche, France ... 28 C6 45 14N 2 57 E
Allanmyo, Burma ... 90 F5 19 30N 95 17 E
Allanridge, S. Africa ... 116 D4 27 45 S 26 40 E
Allansford, Australia ... 128 E5 38 26 S 142 39 E
Allanton, N.Z. ... 131 F5 45 55 S 170 15 E
Allaqi, Wadi →, Egypt ... 106 C3 22 7N 32 47 E
Allariz, Spain ... 42 C3 42 11N 7 50W
Allassac, France ... 28 C5 45 15N 1 29 E
Allatoona L., U.S.A. ... 152 A5 34 10N 84 44W
Ålleberg, Sweden ... 17 F7 58 10N 13 36 E
Allegan, U.S.A. ... 157 B11 42 32N 85 51W
Allegany, U.S.A. ... 150 D6 42 6N 78 30W
Allegheny →, U.S.A. ... 150 F4 40 27N 80 1W
Allegheny Mts., U.S.A. ... 148 G6 38 15N 80 10W
Allegheny Reservoir, U.S.A. ... 150 E6 41 50N 79 0W
Allègre, France ... 28 C7 45 12N 3 41 E
Allègre, Pte., Guadeloupe ... 164 b 16 22N 61 46W
Allen, Argentina ... 176 A3 38 58 S 67 50W
Allen, Phil. ... 80 E5 12 30N 124 17 E
Allen, Bog of, Ireland ... 23 C5 53 15N 7 0W
Allen, L., Ireland ... 23 B3 54 8N 8 4W
Allendale, U.S.A. ... 152 B8 33 1N 81 18W
Allende, Mexico ... 162 B4 28 20N 100 50W
Allensbach, Germany ... 33 A8 47 43N 9 4 E
Allenstein = Olsztyn, Poland ... 54 E7 53 48N 20 29 E

Allentown, U.S.A. 151 F9   40 37N 75 29W
Allentsteig, Austria .... 34 C8   48 41N 15 20 E
Alleppey, India .... 95 K3   9 30N 76 28 E
Allepuz, Spain 40 E4   40 29N 0 44W
Aller →, Germany .... 30 C5   52 56N 9 12 E
Alleynes B., Barbados .... 165 g   13 13N 59 39W
Alliance, Suriname 169 B7   5 50N 54 50W
Alliance, Nebr., U.S.A. 154 D3   42 6N 102 52W
Alliance, Ohio, U.S.A. 150 F3   40 55N 81 6W
Allier □, France .... 27 F10   46 25N 2 40 E
Allier →, France .... 27 F10   46 57N 3 4 E
Alliford Bay, Canada 142 C2   53 12N 131 58W
Alligator Pond, Jamaica .... 164 a   17 52N 77 34W
Allinagaram, India .... 95 J3   10 2N 77 30 E
Allinge, Denmark .... 17 J8   55 17N 14 50 E
Allison, U.S.A. 156 B4   42 45N 92 48W
Alliston, Canada 140 D4   44 9N 79 52W
Alloa, U.K. 22 E5   56 7N 3 47W
Allones, France .... 26 D8   48 20N 1 40 E
Allora, Australia .... 127 D5   28 2S 152 0 E
Allos, France .... 29 D10   44 15N 6 38 E
Alluitsup Paa, Greenland 10 E6   60 30N 45 35W
Allur, India .... 95 G5   14 40N 80 4 E
Alluru Kottapatnam, India ..... 95 G5   15 24N 80 7 E
Alma, Canada 141 C5   48 35N 71 40W
Alma, Ga., U.S.A. 152 D7   31 33N 82 28W
Alma, Kans., U.S.A. 154 F6   39 1N 96 17W
Alma, Mich., U.S.A. 154 D3   43 23N 84 39W
Alma, Nebr., U.S.A. 154 E5   40 6N 99 22W
Alma Ata = Almaty, Kazakhstan . 65 B8   43 15N 76 57 E
Almacelles, Spain .... 40 D5   41 43N 0 27 E
Almada, Portugal 43 G1   38 40N 9 9W
Almaden, Australia .... 126 B3   17 22 S 144 40 E
Almadén, Spain 43 G6   38 49N 4 52W
Almalyk = Olmaliq, Uzbekistan . 65 C4   40 50N 69 35 E
Almanor, L., U.S.A. 158 F3   40 14N 121 9W
Almansa, Spain 41 G3   38 51N 1 5W
Almanza, Spain 42 C5   42 39N 5 3W
Almanzor, Pico, Spain 42 E5   40 15N 5 18W
Almanzora →, Spain 41 H3   37 14N 1 46W
Almas, Brazil .... 171 D2   11 33 S 47 9W
Almaş, Munţii, Romania .... 52 F7   44 49N 22 12 E
Almassora, Spain 40 F4   39 57N 0 3W
Almaty, Kazakhstan .... 65 B8   43 15N 76 57 E
Almazán, Spain 40 D2   41 30N 2 30W
Almeirim, Brazil .... 169 D7   1 30 S 52 34W
Almeirim, Portugal 43 F2   39 12N 8 37W
Almelo, Neths. .... 24 B6   52 22N 6 42 E
Almenar de Soria, Spain 40 D2   41 43N 2 12W
Almenara, Brazil .... 171 E3   16 11 S 40 42W
Almenara, Spain 40 F4   39 46N 0 14W
Almenara, Sierra de la, Spain .. 41 H3   37 34N 1 32W
Almendra, Embalse de, Spain ... 42 D4   41 10N 6 5W
Almendralejo, Spain 43 G4   38 41N 6 26W
Almere-Stad, Neths. .... 24 B5   52 20N 5 15 E
Almería, Spain 41 J8   36 52N 2 27W
Almería □, Spain 41 H2   37 20N 2 20W
Almería, G. de, Spain 41 J2   36 41N 2 28W
Almetyevsk, Russia .... 60 C11   54 53N 52 20 E
Älmhult, Sweden .... 17 H8   56 33N 14 8 E
Almirante, Panama 164 E3   9 10N 82 30W
Almirante Montt, G., Chile ..... 176 D2   51 52 S 72 50W
Almiropótamos, Greece .... 48 C6   38 16N 24 11 E
Almirós, Greece .... 48 B4   39 11N 22 45 E
Almiroú, Kólpos, Greece .... 49 E5   35 23N 24 20 E
Almodôvar, Portugal 43 H2   37 31N 8 2W
Almodóvar del Campo, Spain 43 G6   38 43N 4 10W
Almodóvar del Río, Spain 43 H5   37 48N 5 1W
Almond, U.S.A. 150 D7   42 19N 77 44W
Almont, U.S.A. 150 D1   42 55N 83 3W
Almonte, Canada 151 A8   45 14N 76 12W
Almonte →, Spain 43 H4   39 13N 6 38W
Almora, India .... 93 E8   29 38N 79 40 E
Almoradí, Spain 41 G4   38 7N 0 46W
Almorox, Spain 42 E6   40 14N 4 24W
Almoustarat, Mali .... 113 B5   17 35N 0 8 E
Almsta, Sweden .... 17 F12   59 58N 18 50 E
Almudévar, Spain 40 C4   42 3N 0 35W
Almuñécar, Spain 43 J7   36 43N 3 41W
Almunge, Sweden .... 16 E12   59 53N 18 3 E
Almuradiel, Spain 43 G7   38 32N 3 28W
Alness, U.K. 22 D4   57 41N 4 16W
Alnif, Morocco 110 B3   31 10N 5 8W
Alnmouth, U.K. 20 B6   55 24N 1 37W
Alnwick, U.K. 20 B6   55 24N 1 42W
Aloi, Uganda .... 118 B3   2 16N 33 10 E
Alon, Burma .... 90 D5   22 12N 95 5 E
Along, India .... 90 A5   28 20N 94 46 E
Alónnisos-Northern Sporades △,
   Greece .... 48 B6   39 15N 24 5 E
Alor, Indonesia .... 82 C2   8 15 S 124 30 E
Alor Setar, Malaysia .... 87 J3   6 7N 100 22 E
Alora, Spain 43 J6   36 49N 4 46W
Alosno, Spain 43 H3   37 33N 7 7W
Alost = Aalst, Belgium .... 24 D4   50 56N 4 2 E
Alot, India .... 92 H6   23 56N 75 40 E
Alotau, Papua N. G. .... 132 F6   10 16 S 150 30 E
Alougoum, Morocco 110 B3   30 17N 6 56W
Aloum, Cameroon .... 114 B2   2 16N 10 34 E
Aloysius, Mt., Australia .... 125 E4   26 0 S 128 38 E
Alpaugh, U.S.A. 160 K7   35 53N 119 29W
Alpe Apuane, Parco □, Italy .... 44 D7   44 14N 10 15 E
Alpedrinha, Portugal 42 E3   40 6N 7 27W
Alpena, U.S.A. 148 C4   45 4N 83 27W
Alpercatas →, Brazil .... 170 C3   6 2 S 44 19W
Alpes-de-Haute-Provence □, France 29 D10   44 8N 6 10 E
Alpes-Maritimes □, France ..... 29 E11   43 55N 7 10 E
Alpha, Australia .... 126 C4   23 39 S 146 37 E
Alpha, U.S.A. 156 C6   41 12N 90 23W
Alphen aan den Rijn, Neths. .... 24 B4   52 7N 4 40 E
Alphonse, Seychelles .... 121 E4   7 0 S 52 45 E
Alpiarça, Portugal 43 F2   39 15N 8 35W
Alpine, Ariz., U.S.A. 159 K9   33 51N 109 9W
Alpine, Calif., U.S.A. 161 N10   32 50N 116 46W
Alpine, Tex., U.S.A. 155 K3   30 22N 103 40W
Alpine Nat. Park △, Australia .. 129 D7   37 15 S 146 45 E
Alpnach Dorf, Switz. .... 33 C6   46 57N 8 17 E
Alps, Europe .... 36 E5   46 30N 9 30 E
Alpu, Turkey .... 100 C4   39 36N 30 58 E
Alqueta, Barragem do, Portugal . 43 G3   38 20N 7 25W
Alrø, Denmark .... 17 J4   55 52N 10 5 E
Als, Denmark .... 17 K3   54 59N 9 55 E
Alsace, France .... 27 D14   48 15N 7 25 E
Alsask, Canada 143 C7   51 21N 109 59W
Alsasua, Spain 40 C2   42 54N 2 10W
Alsek →, U.S.A. 132 B1   59 10N 138 12W
Alsfeld, Germany .... 30 E5   50 44N 9 16 E
Alsten, Norway .... 14 D15   65 58N 12 40 E
Alstermo, Sweden .... 17 H9   56 56N 15 38 E
Alston, U.K. 20 C5   54 49N 2 25W
Alta, Norway .... 14 B20   69 57N 23 10 E
Alta, Sierra, Spain 40 E3   40 31N 1 30W
Alta Floresta, Brazil .... 173 B6   9 57 S 55 58W
Alta Gracia, Argentina .... 174 C3   31 40 S 64 30W
Alta Sierra, U.S.A. 161 K8   35 42N 118 33W
Altaelva →, Norway .... 14 B20   69 54N 23 17 E
Altafjorden, Norway .... 14 A20   70 5N 23 5 E
Altagracia, Venezuela 168 A3   10 45N 71 30W
Altagracia de Orituco, Venezuela 168 B4   9 52N 66 23W
Altai = Aerhtai Shan, Mongolia .. 68 B4   46 40N 92 45 E
Altamachi →, Bolivia .... 172 D4   16 8 S 66 50W
Altamaha →, U.S.A. 152 D8   31 20N 81 20W
Altamira, Brazil .... 169 D7   3 12 S 52 10W
Altamira, Chile .... 174 B2   25 47 S 69 51W

Altamira, Colombia 168 C2   2 3N 75 47W
Altamira, Mexico 163 C5   22 24N 97 55W
Altamira, Cuevas de, Spain 42 B6   43 20N 4 5W
Altamont, Ill., U.S.A. 157 E8   39 4N 88 45W
Altamont, N.Y., U.S.A. 151 D10   42 43N 74 3W
Altamura, Italy .... 47 B9   40 49N 16 33 E
Altanbulag, Mongolia .... 68 A5   50 16N 106 30 E
Altar, Mexico 162 A2   30 40N 111 50W
Altar, Desierto de, Mexico 162 B2   30 10N 112 0W
Altata, Mexico 162 C3   24 30N 108 0W
Altavas, Phil. .... 81 F4   11 32N 122 29 E
Altavista, U.S.A. 148 G6   37 6N 79 17W
Altay, China .... 68 B3   47 48N 88 10 E
Altay, China .... 33 C7   46 52N 8 36 E
Alte Mellum, Germany .... 30 B4   53 43N 8 10 E
Altea, Spain 41 G4   38 38N 0 2W
Altenberg, Germany .... 30 E9   50 45N 13 45 E
Altenbruch, Germany .... 30 B4   53 49N 8 46 E
Altenburg, Germany .... 30 E8   50 59N 12 25 E
Altenkirchen,
   Mecklenburg-Vorpommern,
   Germany .... 30 A9   54 38N 13 22 E
Altenkirchen, Rhld-Pfz., Germany . 30 E3   50 41N 7 39 E
Altenmarkt, Austria .... 34 D7   47 43N 14 39 E
Alter do Chão, Brazil .... 169 D6   2 31 S 54 57W
Alter do Chão, Portugal 43 F3   39 12N 7 40W
Altha, U.S.A. 152 K4   30 34N 85 8W
Altınoluk, Turkey .... 49 B8   39 34N 26 45 E
Altınova, Turkey .... 49 B8   39 12N 26 47 E
Altıntaş, Turkey .... 49 B12   39 4N 30 7 E
Altınyaka, Turkey .... 49 E12   36 33N 30 20 E
Altınyayla, Turkey .... 49 D11   37 0N 29 33 E
Altiplano, Bolivia .... 172 D4   17 0 S 68 0W
Altkirch, France .... 27 E14   47 37N 7 15 E
Altmark, Germany .... 30 C7   52 45N 11 30 E
Altmühl →, Germany .... 31 G7   48 54N 11 52 E
Altmühltal, Naturpark △, Germany 31 G7   48 55N 11 15 E
Altmunster, Austria .... 34 D6   47 54N 13 45 E
Alto Adige = Trentino-Alto
   Adige □, Italy .... 45 B8   46 30N 11 20 E
Alto Alegre, Brazil 169 C5   2 50N 61 20W
Alto Araguaia, Brazil .... 173 D7   17 15 S 53 20W
Alto Chicapa, Angola .... 115 E3   10 52 S 19 17 E
Alto Cuchumatanes =
   Cuchumatanes, Sierra de los,
   Guatemala 164 C1   15 35N 91 25W
Alto Cuito = Tempué, Angola ... 115 E3   13 27 S 18 49 E
Alto del Carmen, Chile .... 174 B1   28 46 S 70 30W
Alto del Inca, Chile .... 174 A2   24 10 S 68 10W
Alto Garças, Brazil .... 173 D7   16 56 S 53 30W
Alto Garda Bresciano, Parco □, Italy 44 C7   45 42N 10 38 E
Alto Iriri →, Brazil .... 173 B7   8 50 S 53 25W
Alto Ligonha, Mozam. .... 119 F4   15 30 S 38 11 E
Alto Molocue, Mozam. .... 119 F4   15 50 S 37 35 E
Alto Paraguai, Brazil .... 173 C6   14 30 S 56 31W
Alto Paraguay □, Paraguay ..... 174 A4   21 0 S 58 30W
Alto Paraiso de Goiás, Brazil ... 171 D2   14 7 S 47 31W
Alto Paraná □, Paraguay .... 175 B5   25 30 S 54 50W
Alto Parnaíba, Brazil .... 170 C2   9 6 S 45 57W
Alto Purús →, Peru .... 172 B3   9 12 S 70 38W
Alto Río Senguerr, Argentina ... 176 C2   45 2 S 70 50W
Alto Santo, Brazil .... 170 C4   5 31 S 38 15W
Alto Sucuriú, Brazil .... 173 D7   19 19 S 52 47W
Alto Turi, Brazil .... 170 B2   2 54 S 45 38W
Alton, Canada 150 C4   43 54N 80 5W
Alton, U.K. 21 F7   51 9N 0 59W
Alton, Ill., U.S.A. 156 F6   38 53N 90 11W
Alton, N.H., U.S.A. 151 C13   43 27N 71 13W
Altona, Canada 143 D9   49 6N 97 33W
Altoona, Ala., U.S.A. 152 A3   34 2N 86 20W
Altoona, Iowa, U.S.A. 156 C3   41 39N 93 28W
Altoona, Pa., U.S.A. 150 F6   40 31N 78 24W
Altos, Brazil .... 170 C3   5 3 S 42 28W
Altötting, Germany .... 31 G8   48 12N 12 39 E
Altstätten, Switz. .... 33 B9   47 22N 9 33 E
Altún Küprī, Iraq .... 101 E11   35 45N 44 9 E
Altun Shan, China .... 68 C3   38 30N 88 0 E
Alturas, U.S.A. 158 F3   41 29N 120 32W
Altus, U.S.A. 155 H5   34 38N 99 20W
Alubijid, Phil. .... 81 G5   8 35N 124 29 E
Alucra, Turkey .... 107 F2   51 9N 30 12 E
Aluk, Sudan .... 107 F2   8 25N 27 30 E
Alūksne, Latvia .... 15 H22   57 24N 27 3 E
Alùla, Somali Rep. .... 120 B4   11 50N 50 45 E
Alunda, Sweden .... 16 D12   60 4N 18 5 E
Alunite, U.S.A. 161 K12   35 59N 114 55W
Aluoro →, Ethiopia .... 107 F3   8 26N 33 24 E
Alupka, Ukraine .... 59 K8   44 23N 34 2 E
Alur, India .... 95 G3   15 24N 77 15 E
Alur Gajah, Malaysia .... 84 B2   2 23N 102 13 E
Alushta, Ukraine .... 59 K8   44 40N 34 25 E
Alusi, Indonesia .... 83 C4   7 35 S 131 40 E
Alustante, Spain 40 E3   40 36N 1 40W
Alutgama, Sri Lanka .... 95 L4   6 26N 79 59 E
Alutnuwara, Sri Lanka .... 95 L5   7 19N 80 59 E
Alva, U.S.A. 155 G5   36 48N 98 40W
Alvaiázere, Portugal 42 F2   39 49N 8 23W
Älvängen, Sweden .... 17 G6   57 58N 12 8 E
Alvão, Parque Natural □, Portugal 42 D3   41 22N 7 48W
Alvarado, Mexico 163 D5   18 40N 95 50W
Alvarado, U.S.A. 155 J6   32 24N 97 13W
Alvarães, Brazil .... 169 D5   3 12 S 64 50W
Alvaro Obregón, Presa, Mexico .. 162 B3   27 55N 109 52W
Alvdal, Norway .... 18 B7   62 6N 10 37 E
Älvdalen, Sweden .... 16 C8   61 13N 14 4 E
Alvear, Argentina .... 174 B4   29 5 S 56 30W
Alverca, Portugal 43 G1   38 56N 9 1W
Alvesta, Sweden .... 17 H8   56 54N 14 35 E
Alvik, Norway .... 18 D3   60 26N 6 26 E
Alvin, U.S.A. 155 L7   29 26N 95 15W
Alvinston, Canada 150 D3   42 49N 81 52W
Alvito, Portugal 43 G3   38 15N 7 58W
Älvkarleby, Sweden .... 16 D11   60 34N 17 26 E
Alvorada, Brazil .... 171 D2   12 28 S 49 6W
Alvord Desert, U.S.A. 158 E4   42 30N 118 25W
Älvros, Sweden .... 16 B8   62 3N 14 38 E
Älvsbyn, Sweden .... 14 D19   65 40N 21 0 E
Alwar, India .... 92 F7   27 38N 76 34 E
Alwaye, India .... 95 J3   10 8N 76 24 E
Alxa Zuoqi, China .... 74 E3   38 50N 105 40 E
Alyangula, Australia .... 126 A2   13 55 S 136 30 E
Alyata = Älät, Azerbaijan ..... 61 L9   39 58N 49 25 E
Alyth, U.K. 22 E5   56 38N 3 13W
Alytus, Lithuania .... 15 J21   54 24N 24 3 E
Alzada, U.S.A. 154 C2   45 2N 104 25W
Alzey, Germany .... 31 F4   49 45N 8 7 E
Alzira, Spain 41 F4   39 9N 0 30W
Am Dam, Chad .... 109 F4   12 40N 20 35 E
Am Géréda, Chad .... 109 F4   12 53N 21 14 E
Am Loubia, Chad .... 109 F4   13 39N 20 8 E
Am Timan, Chad .... 109 F4   11 0N 20 10 E
Amada Gaza, C.A.R. .... 114 B3   4 46N 15 9 E
Amadeus, L., Australia .... 125 D5   24 54 S 131 0 E
Amadi, Dem. Rep. of the Congo . 118 B2   3 40N 26 40 E
Amâdi, Sudan .... 107 F3   5 29N 30 25 E
Amadjuak L., Canada 139 B12   65 0N 71 8W
Amadora, Portugal 43 G1   38 45N 9 13W
Amagansett, U.S.A. 151 F12   40 59N 72 9W
Amager, Denmark .... 17 J6   55 37N 12 35 E
Amagi, Japan .... 72 D2   33 25N 130 39 E
Amagunze, Nigeria .... 113 D6   6 20N 7 40 E
Amahai, Indonesia .... 83 C3   3 20 S 128 55 E

Amaile, Samoa .... 133 W24   13 59 S 171 22W
Amaimon, Papua N. G. .... 132 C3   5 12 S 145 30 E
Amakusa-Nada, Japan .... 72 E2   32 35N 130 5 E
Amakusa-Shotō, Japan .... 72 E2   32 15N 130 10 E
Åmål, Sweden .... 16 E6   59 3N 12 42 E
Amalapuram, India .... 95 F5   16 35N 81 55 E
Amalfi, Colombia 168 B2   6 55N 75 4W
Amalfi, Italy .... 47 B7   40 38N 14 36 E
Amaliás, Greece .... 48 D3   37 47N 21 22 E
Amalner, India .... 94 D2   21 5N 75 5 E
Amamapare, Indonesia .... 83 B5   4 53 S 136 38 E
Amambaí, Brazil .... 175 A4   23 5 S 55 13W
Amambaí →, Brazil .... 175 A5   23 22 S 53 56W
Amambay □, Paraguay .... 175 A4   23 0 S 56 0W
Amambay, Cordillera de, S. Amer. 175 A4   23 0 S 55 45W
Amami-Guntō, Japan .... 71 L4   27 16N 129 21 E
Amami-Ō-Shima, Japan .... 71 L4   28 0N 129 0 E
Aman, Pulau, Malaysia .... 87 c   5 16N 100 24 E
Amana →, Venezuela 169 B5   9 45N 62 39W
Amaná, L., Brazil .... 169 D5   2 35 S 64 40W
Amanab, Papua N. G. .... 132 B1   3 40 S 141 14 E
Amanat →, India .... 93 G11   24 7N 84 4 E
Amanda Park, U.S.A. 160 C3   47 28N 123 55W
Amangeldy, Kazakhstan .... 66 D7   50 10N 65 10 E
Amantea, Italy .... 47 C9   39 8N 16 4 E
Amapá, Brazil 169 C7   2 5N 50 50W
Amapá □, Brazil 169 C7   1 40N 52 0W
Amapari, Brazil 169 C7   0 37N 51 39W
Amara, Sudan .... 107 E3   10 25N 34 10 E
Amarante, Brazil .... 170 C3   6 14 S 42 50W
Amarante, Portugal 42 D2   41 16N 8 5W
Amarante do Maranhão, Brazil .. 170 C2   5 36 S 46 45W
Amaranth, Canada 143 C9   50 36N 98 43W
Amarapura, Burma .... 90 E6   21 54N 96 3 E
Amaravati →, India .... 95 J4   10 N 78 15 E
Amareleja, Portugal 43 G3   38 12N 7 13W
Amargosa, Brazil .... 171 D4   13 2 S 39 36W
Amargosa →, U.S.A. 161 J10   36 14N 116 51W
Amargosa Range, U.S.A. 161 J10   36 20N 116 45W
Amári, Greece .... 39 E5   35 13N 24 40 E
Amarillo, U.S.A. 155 H4   35 13N 101 50W
Amarkantak, India .... 93 H9   22 40N 81 45 E
Amârna, Tell el', Sudan .... 106 B3   27 38N 30 52 E
Amarnath, India .... 94 E1   19 12N 73 22 E
Amaro, Mte., Italy .... 45 F11   42 5N 14 5 E
Amaro Leite, Brazil .... 171 D2   13 58 S 49 9W
Amarpur, Bihar, India .... 93 G12   25 5N 87 0 E
Amarpur, Tripura, India .... 90 D3   23 31N 91 39 E
Amarti, Eritrea .... 107 E5   14 17N 41 6 E
Amarwara, India .... 93 H8   22 18N 79 10 E
Amasin, W. Sahara 110 C2   25 45N 13 20W
Amasra, Turkey .... 100 B5   41 45N 32 23 E
Amassama, Nigeria .... 113 D6   5 1N 6 2 E
Amasya, Turkey .... 100 B6   40 40N 35 50 E
Amasya □, Turkey .... 57 F6   40 40N 35 50 E
Amata, Australia .... 125 E5   26 9 S 131 9 E
Amataurá, Brazil .... 168 D4   3 29 S 68 6W
Amatignak I., U.S.A. 144 L3   51 16N 179 6W
Amatikulu, S. Africa .... 117 D5   29 3 S 31 33 E
Amatitlán, Guatemala 164 D1   14 29N 90 38W
Amatrice, Italy .... 45 F10   42 38N 13 17 E
Amau, Papua N. G. .... 132 C7   10 2 S 148 34 E
Amay, Belgium .... 24 D5   50 33N 5 19 E
Amazon = Amazonas →, S. Amer. 169 D7   0 5 S 50 0W
Amazonas □, Brazil .... 173 B5   5 0 S 65 0W
Amazonas □, Peru .... 172 B2   5 0 S 78 0W
Amazonas □, Venezuela 168 C4   3 30N 66 0W
Amazonas →, S. Amer. .... 169 D7   0 5 S 50 0W
Amba Ferit, Ethiopia .... 107 E4   10 55N 38 50 E
Ambad, India .... 94 E2   19 38N 75 50 E
Ambagarh Chowki, India ...... 94 D5   20 47N 80 43 E
Ambah, India .... 92 F8   26 43N 78 13 E
Ambahakily, Madag. .... 117 C7   21 36 S 43 41 E
Ambahita, Madag. .... 117 C8   24 1 S 46 16 E
Ambajogal, India .... 94 E3   18 44N 76 23 E
Ambala, India .... 92 D7   30 23N 76 56 E
Ambalangoda, Sri Lanka .... 95 L5   6 15N 80 5 E
Ambalapulai, India .... 95 K3   9 25N 76 25 E
Ambalavao, Madag. .... 117 C8   21 50 S 46 56 E
Ambam, Cameroon .... 114 B2   2 20N 11 15 E
Ambanja, Madag. .... 117 A8   13 40 S 48 27 E
Ambararata, Madag. .... 117 B8   15 3 S 48 33 E
Ambarchik, Russia .... 67 C17   69 40N 162 20 E
Ambarijeby, Madag. .... 117 A8   14 56 S 47 41 E
Ambaro, Helodranon', Madag. .. 117 A8   13 23 S 48 38 E
Ambasamudram, India .... 95 K3   8 43N 77 25 E
Ambato, Ecuador .... 168 D2   1 5 S 78 42W
Ambato, Madag. .... 117 A8   13 24 S 48 29 E
Ambato, Sierra de, Argentina .. 174 B2   28 25 S 66 10W
Ambato Boeny, Madag. .... 117 B8   16 28 S 46 43 E
Ambatofinandrahana, Madag. .. 117 C8   20 33 S 46 48 E
Ambatolampy, Madag. .... 117 B8   19 20 S 47 35 E
Ambatomainty, Madag. .... 117 B8   17 41 S 45 40 E
Ambatomanoina, Madag. ...... 117 B8   18 18 S 47 37 E
Ambatondrazaka, Madag. ...... 117 B8   17 55 S 48 28 E
Ambatosoratra, Madag. .... 117 B8   17 37 S 48 31 E
Ambelau, Indonesia .... 82 B3   3 51 S 127 12 E
Ambelón, Greece .... 48 B4   39 45N 22 22 E
Ambenja, Madag. .... 117 B8   15 17 S 46 58 E
Amberg, Germany .... 31 F7   49 26N 11 52 E
Ambergris Cay, Belize 163 D7   18 0N 88 0W
Ambérieu-en-Bugey, France .... 29 C9   45 57N 5 20 E
Amberley, N.Z. .... 131 D7   43 9 S 172 44 E
Ambert, France .... 28 C7   45 33N 3 44 E
Ambidédi, Mali 112 C2   14 35N 11 47W
Ambikapur, India .... 93 H10   23 15N 83 15 E
Ambikol, Sudan .... 106 C3   21 20N 30 50 E
Ambilobé, Madag. .... 117 A8   13 10 S 49 3 E
Ambinanindrano, Madag. ...... 117 C8   20 5 S 48 23 E
Ambinanitelo, Madag. .... 117 B8   15 21 S 49 35 E
Ambinda, Madag. .... 117 B8   16 25 S 45 52 E
Ambitle I., Papua N. G. .... 132 C7   4 5 S 153 37 E
Amble, U.K. 20 B6   55 20N 1 36W
Ambler, U.S.A. 144 C8   67 5N 157 52W
Ambleside, U.K. 20 C5   54 26N 2 58W
Ambo, Peru .... 172 C2   10 5 S 76 10W
Amboahangy, Madag. .... 117 C8   24 15 S 46 22 E
Ambodifototra, Madag. .... 117 B8   16 59 S 49 52 E
Ambodilazana, Madag. .... 117 B8   18 6 S 49 10 E
Ambodiriana, Madag. .... 117 B8   17 55 S 49 18 E
Ambohidratrimo, Madag. ...... 117 B8   18 50 S 47 26 E
Ambohidray, Madag. .... 117 B8   18 36 S 48 18 E
Ambohimahamasina, Madag. ... 117 C8   21 56 S 47 11 E
Ambohimahasoa, Madag. ...... 117 C8   21 7 S 47 13 E
Ambohimanga, Madag. .... 117 C8   20 52 S 47 36 E
Ambohimitombo, Madag. ...... 117 C8   20 43 S 47 26 E
Ambohitra, Madag. .... 117 A8   12 30 S 49 10 E
Amboise, France .... 26 E8   47 24N 1 2 E
Amboiva, Angola .... 115 E2   11 33 S 14 43 E
Ambon, Indonesia .... 83 B3   3 43 S 128 12 E
Ambondro, Madag. .... 117 D8   25 13 S 45 44 E
Amboseli, L., Kenya .... 118 C4   2 40 S 37 10 E
Amboseli Nat. Park △, Kenya .. 118 C4   2 37 S 37 13 E
Ambositra, Madag. .... 117 C8   20 31 S 47 25 E
Ambovombe, Madag. .... 117 D8   25 11 S 46 5 E
Amboy, Calif., U.S.A. 161 L11   34 33N 115 45W
Amboy, Ill., U.S.A. 156 C7   41 44N 89 20W
Ambridge, U.S.A. 150 F4   40 36N 80 14W
Ambriz, Angola .... 115 D2   7 56 S 10 27 E
Ambriz, Reserva □, Angola ..... 115 D2   7 50 S 13 08 E
Ambrolauri, Georgia .... 61 J6   42 33N 43 09 E
Ambrym, Vanuatu .... 133 K6   16 15 S 168 10 E
Ambunti, Papua N. G. .... 132 C2   4 13 S 142 52 E
Ambur, India .... 95 H4   12 48N 78 43 E

Amchitka I., U.S.A. .... 144 L2   51 32N 179 0 E
Amderma, Russia .... 66 C7   69 45N 61 30 E
Amdhi, India .... 93 H9   23 51N 81 27 E
Ameca, Mexico 162 C4   20 30N 104 0W
Ameca →, Mexico 162 C3   20 40N 105 15W
Amecameca, Mexico 163 D5   19 7N 98 46W
Ameland, Neths. .... 24 A5   53 27N 5 45 E
Amélia, Italy .... 45 F9   42 33N 12 25 E
Amelia City, U.S.A. 152 E8   30 35N 81 28W
Amelia I., U.S.A. 152 E8   30 40N 81 25W
Amendolara, Italy .... 47 C9   39 57N 16 35 E
Amenia, U.S.A. 151 E11   41 51N 73 33W
American Falls, U.S.A. 158 E7   42 47N 112 51W
American Falls Reservoir, U.S.A. 158 E7   42 47N 112 52W
American Fork, U.S.A. 158 F8   40 23N 111 48W
American Highland, Antarctica .. 7 D6   73 0 S 75 0 E
American River, Australia ...... 128 C2   35 47 S 137 51 E
American Samoa □, Pac. Oc. ... 133 X24   14 20 S 170 40W
American Samoa, Nat. Park of △,
   Amer. Samoa .... 133 X24   14 15 S 170 28W
Americana, Brazil .... 175 A6   22 45 S 47 20W
Americus, U.S.A. 152 C5   32 4N 84 14W
Amerigo Vespucci, Florence ✈
   (FLR), Italy .... 44 E8   43 49N 11 13 E
Amersfoort, Neths. .... 24 B5   52 9N 5 23 E
Amersfoort, S. Africa .... 117 D4   26 59 S 29 53 E
Amery Ice Shelf, Antarctica .... 7 C6   69 30 S 72 0 E
Amersgane, Morocco 110 B3   31 1N 7 14W
Ames, U.S.A. 42 C2   42 54N 8 38W
Ames, U.S.A. 156 C3   42 2N 93 37W
Amesbury, U.S.A. 151 D14   42 51N 70 56W
Amet, India .... 92 G5   25 18N 73 56 E
Amfíklia, Greece .... 48 C4   38 38N 22 35 E
Amfilokhía, Greece .... 48 C3   38 52N 21 9 E
Amfípolis, Greece .... 50 F7   40 48N 23 52 E
Ámfissa, Greece .... 48 C4   38 32N 22 22 E
Amga, Russia .... 67 C14   60 50N 132 0 E
Amga →, Russia .... 67 C14   62 38N 134 32 E
Amgaon, India .... 94 D5   21 22N 80 22 E
Amgu, Russia .... 67 E14   45 45N 137 15 E
Amgun →, Russia .... 67 D14   52 56N 139 38 E
Amherst, Canada 141 C7   45 48N 64 8W
Amherst, Mass., U.S.A. 151 D12   42 23N 72 31W
Amherst, N.Y., U.S.A. 150 D6   42 59N 78 48W
Amherst, Ohio, U.S.A. 150 E2   41 24N 82 14W
Amherst I., Canada 151 B8   44 8N 76 43W
Amherstburg, Canada 140 D3   42 6N 83 6W
Amiata, Mte., Italy .... 45 F8   42 53N 11 37 E
Amidon, U.S.A. 154 B3   46 29N 103 19W
Amiens, France .... 27 C9   49 54N 2 16 E
Amili, India .... 90 A5   28 25N 95 52 E
Amindaion, Greece .... 50 F5   40 42N 21 42 E
Amindivi Is., India .... 95 J1   11 23N 72 23 E
Amingaon, India .... 90 B3   26 11N 91 40 E
Amini I., India .... 95 J1   11 6N 72 45 E
Aminne, Sweden .... 17 G7   57 7N 14 0 E
Amino, Ethiopia .... 107 G5   4 25N 41 52 E
Aminuis, Namibia .... 116 C2   23 43 S 19 21 E
Åmir, Ra's, Libya .... 108 B4   32 57N 21 43 E
Amīrābād, Iran .... 121 E4   6 0 S 53 0 E
Amirante Is., Seychelles ...... 121 E4   6 0 S 53 0 E
Amisk L., Canada 143 C8   54 35N 102 15W
Amisk Prov. Park □, Canada ... 143 B9   56 43N 98 0W
Amistad, Presa de la, Mexico ... 162 B4   29 24N 101 0W
Amistad Nat. Recr. Area □, U.S.A. 155 L4   29 32N 101 12W
Amite, U.S.A. 155 K9   30 44N 90 30W
Amizmiz, Morocco 110 B3   31 12N 8 15W
Amla, India .... 92 J8   21 56N 78 7 E
Amlapura = Karangasem, Indonesia 79 J18   8 27 S 115 37 E
Åmli, Norway .... 18 F5   58 45N 8 32 E
Amlia I., U.S.A. 144 K4   52 4N 173 30W
Amlwch, U.K. 20 D3   53 24N 4 20W
Amm Adam, Sudan .... 107 D4   16 20N 36 1 E
'Ammān, Jordan .... 103 D4   31 57N 35 52 E
'Ammān □, Jordan .... 103 D5   31 40N 36 30 E
'Ammān ✈ (AMM), Jordan .... 103 D5   31 45N 36 2 E
Ammanford, U.K. 21 F4   51 48N 3 59W
Ammassalik = Tasiilaq, Greenland 10 D7   65 40N 37 20W
Ammerän →, Sweden .... 16 A10   63 9N 16 13 E
Ammersee, Germany .... 31 G7   48 0N 11 7 E
Ammochostos = Famagusta, Cyprus 39 E9   35 8N 33 55 E
Ammon, U.S.A. 158 E8   43 28N 111 58W
Amnat Charoen, Thailand ...... 86 E5   15 51N 104 38 E
Amnura, Bangla. .... 93 G13   24 37N 88 25 E
Amo Jiang →, China .... 76 F3   23 0N 101 50 E
Āmol, Iran .... 97 B7   36 23N 52 20 E
Amoret, U.S.A. 156 F2   38 15N 94 35W
Amorgós, Greece .... 49 E7   36 50N 25 57 E
Amory, U.S.A. 149 J1   33 59N 88 29W
Amos, Canada 140 C4   48 35N 78 5W
Åmot, Buskerud, Norway ...... 18 E6   59 57N 9 54 E
Åmot, Oppland, Norway .... 18 E5   59 10N 10 2 E
Åmot, Telemark, Norway ...... 18 E5   59 34N 8 0 E
Åmotfors, Sweden .... 16 E6   59 47N 12 22 E
Åmotsdal, Norway .... 18 E5   59 37N 8 26 E
Amour, Djebel, Algeria .... 111 B5   33 42N 1 37 E
Amoy = Xiamen, China .... 77 E12   24 25N 118 4 E
Ampanavoana, Madag. .... 117 B9   15 41 S 50 22 E
Ampang, Malaysia .... 87 L3   3 8N 101 45 E
Ampangalana, Lakandranon',
   Madag. .... 117 C8   22 48 S 47 50 E
Ampani, India .... 94 E6   19 35N 82 38 E
Ampanihy, Madag. .... 117 C7   24 40 S 44 45 E
Amparafaravola, Madag. .... 117 B8   17 35 S 48 13 E
Amparihy, Madag. .... 117 C8   20 31 S 48 0 E
Amparo, India .... 91 H9   24 0N 92 45 E
Ampasinambo, Madag. .... 117 C8   20 31 S 48 0 E
Ampasindava, Helodranon', Madag. 117 A8   13 40 S 48 15 E
Ampasindava, Saikanosy, Madag. 117 A8   13 42 S 47 55 E
Ampato, Nevado, Peru .... 172 D3   15 40 S 71 56W
Ampenan, Indonesia .... 85 D3   8 34 S 116 4 E
Amper, Nigeria .... 113 D6   9 25N 9 40 E
Amper →, Germany .... 31 G7   48 29N 11 55 E
Ampezzo, Italy .... 45 B9   46 25N 12 48 E
Amphoe Kathu, Thailand ...... 87 a   7 55N 98 21 E
Amphoe Thalang, Thailand .... 87 a   8 1N 98 20 E
Ampitsikinana, Réunion .... 123 b   12 57 S 49 49 E
Ampombiantambo, Madag. ..... 117 A8   12 42 S 48 57 E
Amposta, Spain .... 40 E5   40 43N 0 34 E
Ampotaka, Madag. .... 117 D7   25 3 S 44 41 E
Ampoza, Madag. .... 117 C7   22 20 S 44 44 E
Amqui, Canada 141 C6   48 28N 67 27W
'Amrābād, India .... 95 F4   16 23N 78 50 E
'Amrān, Yemen .... 98 D3   15 41N 43 55 E
Amraoti = Amravati, India ..... 94 D4   20 55N 77 45 E
Amravati, India .... 94 D4   20 55N 77 45 E
Amreli, India .... 92 J4   21 35N 71 17 E
Amrenene el Kasba, Algeria .... 111 D5   22 10N 0 30 E
Amritsar, India .... 92 G4   31 35N 74 57 E
Amroha, India .... 93 E8   28 53N 78 30 E
Amrum, Germany .... 30 A4   54 38N 8 21 E
Amsâga, Mauritania 110 D2   20 7N 14 10W
Amsel, Algeria .... 111 D6   22 47N 5 29 E
Amsterdam, Neths. .... 24 B4   52 23N 4 54 E
Amsterdam, U.S.A. 151 D10   42 56N 74 11W
Amsterdam, I. = Nouvelle-
   Amsterdam, I., Ind. Oc. ...... 121 H6   38 30 S 77 30 E
Amstetten, Austria .... 34 C7   48 7N 14 51 E
Amudarya →, Turkmenistan .... 65 E2   37 53N 65 15 E
Amudarya →, Uzbekistan ...... 66 E6   43 58N 59 34 E
Amukta Pass, U.S.A. 144 L5   52 0N 171 16W
Amulung, Phil. .... 80 C3   17 50N 121 43 E
Amundsen Gulf, Canada 138 A7   71 0N 124 0W

Amundsen Sea, *Antarctica* .... 7 D15 72 0 S 115 0W
Amungen, *Sweden* .... 16 C9 61 10N 15 40 E
Amuntai, *Indonesia* .... 85 C5 2 28 S 115 25 E
Amur, *Somali Rep.* .... 120 C3 3 5N 41 45 E
Amur →, *Russia* .... 67 D15 52 56N 141 10 E
Amur, W. →, *Sudan* .... 106 D3 18 56N 33 34 E
Amurang, *Indonesia* .... 82 A2 1 5N 124 40 E
Amurrio, *Spain* 40 B1 43 3N 3 0W
Amursk, *Russia* .... 67 D14 50 14N 136 54 E
Amusco, *Spain* 42 C6 42 10N 4 28W
Amvrakikós Kólpos, *Greece* .... 48 C2 39 0N 20 55 E
Amvrosiyivka, *Ukraine* .... 59 J10 47 43N 38 30 E
Amyderya = Amudarya →, *Uzbekistan* .... 66 E6 43 58N 59 34 E
Amzeglouf, *Algeria* .... 111 C5 26 50N 0 1 E
An, *Burma* .... 90 F5 19 48N 94 0 E
An Bien, *Vietnam* .... 87 H5 9 45N 105 0 E
An Hoa, *Vietnam* .... 86 E7 15 40N 108 5 E
An Nabatiyah at Tahta, *Lebanon* .... 103 B4 33 23N 35 27 E
An Nabk, *Si. Arabia* .... 96 D3 31 20N 37 20 E
An Nabk, *Syria* .... 103 A5 34 2N 36 44 E
An Nafūd, *Si. Arabia* .... 96 D4 28 15N 41 0 E
An Najaf, *Iraq* .... 101 G11 32 3N 44 15 E
An Nāşiriyah, *Iraq* .... 96 D5 31 0N 46 15 E
An Nawfaliyah, *Libya* .... 108 B3 30 54N 17 58 E
An Nîl □, *Sudan* .... 106 D3 19 30N 33 0 E
An Nîl el Abyad □, *Sudan* .... 107 E3 14 0N 32 15 E
An Nîl el Azraq □, *Sudan* .... 107 E3 11 30N 34 30 E
An Nimāş, *Si. Arabia* .... 98 D3 19 7N 42 8 E
An Nu'ayrīyah, *Si. Arabia* .... 97 E6 27 30N 48 30 E
An Nu'mānīyah, *Iraq* .... 101 F11 32 32N 45 25 E
An Nuwayb'i, W. →, *Si. Arabia* .... 103 F3 29 18N 34 57 E
An Thoi, Dao, *Vietnam* .... 87 H4 9 58N 104 0 E
An Uaimh, *Ireland* 23 C5 53 39N 6 41W
Āna-Sira, *Norway* .... 18 F3 58 17N 6 25 E
Anabanua, *Indonesia* .... 82 B2 3 57 S 120 4 E
Anabar →, *Russia* .... 67 B12 73 8N 113 36 E
'Anabtā, *West Bank* .... 103 C4 32 19N 35 7 E
Anaco, *Venezuela* 169 B5 9 27N 64 28W
Anaconda, *U.S.A.* 158 C7 46 8N 112 57W
Anacortes, *U.S.A.* 160 B4 48 30N 122 37W
Anacuao, Mt., *Phil.* .... 80 C3 16 16N 121 53 E
Anadarko, *U.S.A.* 155 H5 35 4N 98 15W
Anadia, *Brazil* .... 170 C4 9 42 S 36 18W
Anadia, *Portugal* 42 E2 40 26N 8 27W
Anadolu, *Turkey* .... 100 C5 39 0N 30 0 E
Anadyr, *Russia* .... 67 C18 64 35N 177 20 E
Anadyr →, *Russia* .... 67 C18 64 55N 176 5 E
Anadyrskiy Zaliv, *Russia* .... 67 C19 64 0N 180 0 E
Anáfi, *Greece* .... 49 E7 36 22N 25 48 E
Anafónitria, *Greece* .... 39 D2 37 51N 20 39 E
Anafópoulo, *Greece* .... 49 E7 36 17N 25 50 E
Anaga, Pta. de, *Canary Is.* 9 e1 28 34N 16 9W
Anagni, *Italy* .... 45 G10 41 44N 13 9 E
'Ānah, *Iraq* .... 101 E10 34 25N 42 0 E
Anahulu □, *U.S.A.* 145 J13 21 37N 158 6W
Anaheim, *U.S.A.* 161 M9 33 50N 117 55W
Anahim Lake, *Canada* 142 C3 52 28N 125 18W
Anahola, *U.S.A.* 145 A2 22 9N 159 19W
Anáhuac, *Mexico* 162 B4 27 14N 100 9W
Anai Mudi, *India* .... 95 J3 10 12N 77 4 E
Anaichak Nat. Monument and Preserve △, *U.S.A.* 144 H8 56 40N 157 50W
Anaimalai Hills, *India* .... 95 J3 10 20N 76 40 E
Anajás, *Brazil* .... 170 B2 0 59 S 49 57W
Anajatuba, *Brazil* .... 170 B3 3 16 S 44 37W
Anakapalle, *India* .... 94 F6 17 42N 83 6 E
Anakena, *Chile* .... 172 b 27 5 S 109 20W
Anakie, *Australia* .... 126 C4 23 32 S 147 45 E
Anaklia, *Georgia* .... 61 J5 42 22N 41 35 E
Anaktuvuk Pass, *U.S.A.* 144 B10 68 8N 151 45W
Analalava, *Madag.* .... 117 A8 14 35 S 48 0 E
Analavoka, *Madag.* .... 117 C8 22 23 S 46 30 E
Análipsis, *Greece* .... 38 B9 39 36N 19 55 E
Anamã, *Brazil* .... 169 D5 3 35 S 61 22W
Anambar →, *Pakistan* .... 92 D3 30 15N 68 50 E
Anambas, Kepulauan, *Indonesia* .... 84 B3 3 20N 106 30 E
Anambas Is. = Anambas, Kepulauan, *Indonesia* .... 84 B3 3 20N 106 30 E
Anambra □, *Nigeria* .... 113 D6 6 20N 7 0 E
Aname, *Vanuatu* .... 133 K7 20 8 S 169 47 E
Anamosa, *U.S.A.* 156 B5 42 7N 91 17W
Anamur, *Turkey* .... 100 D5 36 8N 32 58 E
Anamur Burnu, *Turkey* .... 100 D5 36 2N 32 47 E
Anan, *Japan* .... 72 D6 33 54N 134 40 E
Anand, *India* .... 92 H5 22 32N 72 59 E
Anandapuram, *India* .... 95 G2 14 5N 75 12 E
Anandpur, *India* .... 94 D8 21 16N 86 13 E
Anánes, *Greece* .... 48 E6 36 33N 24 9 E
Anantapur, *India* .... 95 G3 14 39N 77 42 E
Anantnag, *India* .... 93 C6 33 45N 75 10 E
Ananyevo, *Kyrgyzstan* .... 65 B8 42 45N 77 40 E
Anapa, *Russia* .... 59 K4 44 55N 37 25 E
Anápodhárs →, *Greece* .... 49 F7 34 59N 25 20 E
Anápolis, *Brazil* .... 171 E2 16 15 S 48 50W
Anapu →, *Brazil* .... 169 D7 1 53 S 50 53W
Anār, *Iran* .... 97 D7 30 55N 55 13 E
Anār Darreh, *Afghan.* .... 91 B1 32 46N 61 39 E
Anārak, *Iran* .... 97 C7 33 25N 53 40 E
Anarisfjällen, *Sweden* .... 16 A7 63 6N 13 10 E
Anas →, *India* .... 92 H5 23 26N 74 0 E
Anatolia = Anadolu, *Turkey* .... 100 C5 39 0N 30 0 E
Anatsogno, *Madag.* .... 117 C7 23 33 S 43 46 E
Añatuya, *Argentina* .... 174 B3 28 20 S 62 50W
Anauá →, *Brazil* 169 C5 0 58N 61 21W
Anaunethad L., *Canada* 143 A8 60 55N 104 25W
Anavilhanas, Arquipélago das, *Brazil* 169 D5 2 42 S 60 45W
Anaye, *Niger* .... 109 E2 19 15N 12 50 E
Anbyŏn, *N. Korea* .... 75 E14 39 1N 127 35 E
Ancares, Reserva Nac. de □, *Spain* 42 C4 42 50N 6 40W
Ancares, Sierra de, *Spain* 42 C4 42 51N 6 52W
Ancash □, *Peru* .... 172 B2 9 30 S 77 45W
Ancaster, *Canada* 150 C5 43 13N 79 59W
Ancenis, *France* 26 E5 47 21N 1 10W
Ancho, Canal, *Chile* .... 176 D2 50 0 S 74 50W
Anchor Bay, *U.S.A.* 160 G3 38 48N 123 34W
Anchorage, *U.S.A.* 144 F10 61 13N 149 54W
Anci, *China* .... 74 E9 39 20N 116 40 E
Ancohuma, Nevada, *Bolivia* .... 172 D4 16 0 S 68 50W
Ancón, *Peru* .... 172 C2 11 50 S 77 10W
Ancona, *Italy* .... 45 E10 43 38N 13 30 E
Ancud, *Chile* .... 176 B2 42 0 S 73 50W
Ancud, G. de, *Chile* .... 176 B2 42 0 S 73 0W
Ancy-le-Franc, *France* .... 27 E11 47 46N 4 10 E
Anda, *China* .... 69 B7 46 24N 125 19 E
Anda, *Phil.* .... 80 C2 16 17N 119 57 E
Andacollo, *Argentina* .... 174 D1 37 10 S 70 42W
Andacollo, *Chile* .... 174 C1 30 14 S 71 6W
Andahuaylas, *Peru* .... 172 C3 13 40 S 73 25W
Andaingo, *Madag.* .... 117 B8 18 12 S 48 17 E
Andalgalá, *Argentina* .... 174 B2 27 40 S 66 30W
Ándalsnes, *Norway* .... 18 B4 62 35N 7 43 E
Andalucía □, *Spain* 43 H6 37 35N 5 0W
Andalusia = Andalucía □, *Spain* 43 H6 37 35N 5 0W
Andalusia, *U.S.A.* 149 K2 31 18N 86 29W
Andaman & Nicobar Is. □, *India* .... 95 K11 10 0N 93 0 E
Andaman Is., *Ind. Oc.* .... 95 H11 12 30N 92 45 E
Andaman Sea, *Ind. Oc.* .... 78 B1 13 0N 96 0 E
Andamooka Opal Fields, *Australia* .... 127 E2 30 27 S 137 9 E
Andapa, *Madag.* .... 117 A8 14 39 S 49 39 E
Andara, *Namibia* .... 116 B3 18 2 S 21 9 E
Andaraí, *Brazil* .... 171 D3 12 48 S 41 20W

Andeer, *Switz.* .... 33 C8 46 36N 9 26 E
Andelfingen, *Switz.* .... 33 A7 47 36N 8 41 E
Andelot-Blancheville, *France* .... 27 D12 48 15N 5 18 E
Andenes, *Norway* .... 14 B17 69 19N 16 18 E
Andenne, *Belgium* .... 24 D5 50 28N 5 5 E
Andéranboukane, *Mali* .... 113 B5 15 26N 3 2 E
Andermatt, *Switz.* .... 33 C7 46 38N 8 35 E
Andernach, *Germany* .... 30 E3 50 26N 7 24 E
Andernos-les-Bains, *France* 28 D2 44 44N 1 6W
Anderslöv, *Sweden* .... 17 J7 55 26N 13 19 E
Anderson, *Alaska, U.S.A.* 144 D10 64 25N 149 15W
Anderson, *Calif., U.S.A.* 158 F2 40 27N 122 18W
Anderson, *Ind., U.S.A.* 157 D11 40 10N 85 41W
Anderson, *Mo., U.S.A.* 155 G7 36 39N 94 27W
Anderson, *S.C., U.S.A.* 149 H4 34 31N 82 39W
Anderson →, *Canada* 138 B7 69 42N 129 0W
Anderson I., *India* .... 95 H11 12 46N 92 43 E
Andersonville, *U.S.A.* 152 C5 32 12N 84 9W
Andersonville Nat. Historic Site △, *U.S.A.* 152 C5 32 12N 84 8W
Anderstorp, *Sweden* .... 17 G7 57 19N 13 9 E
Andes, *Colombia* 168 B2 5 39N 75 54W
Andes, *U.S.A.* 151 D10 42 12N 74 47W
Andes, Cord. de los, *S. Amer.* .... 172 C3 20 0 S 68 0W
Andfjorden, *Norway* .... 14 B17 69 10N 16 20 E
Andhra, L., *India* .... 94 E1 18 54N 73 32 E
Andhra Pradesh □, *India* .... 95 F4 18 0N 79 0 E
Andijon, *Uzbekistan* .... 65 C6 41 10N 72 15 E
Andikíthira, *Greece* .... 48 F5 35 52N 23 15 E
Andilamena, *Madag.* .... 117 B8 17 1 S 48 35 E
Andîmeshk, *Iran* .... 97 C6 32 27N 48 21 E
Andímilos, *Greece* .... 48 E6 36 47N 24 12 E
Andíparos, *Greece* .... 49 D7 37 0N 25 3 E
Andípaxoi, *Greece* .... 48 B2 39 9N 20 13 E
Andípsara, *Greece* .... 49 C7 38 30N 25 29 E
Andírrion, *Greece* .... 48 C3 38 20N 21 46 E
Andizhan = Andijon, *Uzbekistan* .... 65 C6 41 10N 72 15 E
Andkhvoy, *Afghan.* .... 66 E2 36 52N 65 8 E
Andoain, *Spain* 40 B2 43 13N 2 1W
Andoany, *Madag.* .... 117 A8 13 25 S 48 16 E
Andoas, *Peru* .... 168 D2 2 55 S 76 25W
Andohahela, Réserve Naturelle Intégrale d' △, *Madag.* .... 117 C8 24 4 S 46 44 E
Andol, *India* .... 94 F4 17 51N 78 4 E
Andola, *India* .... 94 F3 16 57N 76 50 E
Andong, *S. Korea* .... 75 F15 36 40N 128 43 E
Andongwei, *China* .... 75 G10 35 6N 119 20 E
Andoom, *Australia* .... 126 A3 12 25 S 141 53 E
Andorra ■, *Europe* 40 E4 40 5N 0 28W
Andorra ■, *Europe* .... 28 F5 42 30N 1 30 E
Andorra La Vella, *Andorra* .... 28 F5 42 31N 1 32 E
Andover, *U.K.* 21 F6 51 12N 1 29W
Andover, *Maine, U.S.A.* 151 B14 44 38N 70 45W
Andover, *Mass., U.S.A.* 151 D13 42 40N 71 8W
Andover, *N.J., U.S.A.* 151 F10 40 59N 74 45W
Andover, *N.Y., U.S.A.* 150 D7 42 10N 77 48W
Andover, *Ohio, U.S.A.* 150 E4 41 36N 80 34W
Andøya, *Norway* .... 14 B16 69 10N 15 50 E
Andrade, *Brazil* .... 169 D5 4 40 S 63 45W
Andradina, *Brazil* .... 171 F1 20 54 S 51 23W
Andraharý, Mt., *Madag.* .... 117 A8 13 37 S 49 17 E
Andramasina, *Madag.* .... 117 B8 19 11 S 47 35 E
Andranopasy, *Madag.* .... 117 C7 21 17 S 43 44 E
Andranovory, *Madag.* .... 117 C7 23 8 S 44 10 E
Andratx, *Spain* .... 38 B9 39 39N 2 25 E
André Félix, Parc Nat. d' △, *C.A.R.* .... 114 A4 9 29N 23 8 E
Andreanof Is., *U.S.A.* 144 L1 51 30N 176 0W
Andreapol, *Russia* .... 58 D7 56 40N 32 17 E
Andrée Land, *Greenland* 10 C8 73 40N 26 0W
Andrews, *S.C., U.S.A.* 149 J6 33 27N 79 34W
Andrews, *Tex., U.S.A.* 155 J3 32 19N 102 33W
Andreyevka, *Russia* .... 60 D10 52 19N 51 55 E
Ándria, *Italy* .... 47 A9 41 13N 16 17 E
Andriamena, *Madag.* .... 117 B8 17 26 S 47 30 E
Andriandampy, *Madag.* .... 117 C8 22 45 S 45 41 E
Andriba, *Madag.* .... 117 B8 17 30 S 46 58 E
Andrijevica, *Montenegro, Yug.* .... 50 D3 42 45N 19 48 E
Andringitra, Réserve Naturelle Intégrale d' △, *Madag.* .... 117 C8 22 13 S 46 5 E
Andritsaina, *Greece* .... 48 D3 37 29N 21 52 E
Androka, *Madag.* .... 117 C7 24 58 S 44 2 E
Andropov = Rybinsk, *Russia* .... 58 C10 58 5N 38 50 E
Andros, *Greece* .... 48 D6 37 50N 24 57 E
Andros I., *Bahamas* 164 B4 24 30N 78 0W
Andros Town, *Bahamas* 164 B4 24 43N 77 47W
Androscoggin →, *U.S.A.* 151 C14 43 58N 70 0W
Androth I., *India* .... 95 J1 10 50N 73 41 E
Andrychów, *Poland* .... 55 J6 49 51N 19 18 E
Andselv, *Norway* .... 14 B18 69 4N 18 34 E
Andújar, *Spain* 43 G6 38 3N 4 5W
Andulo, *Angola* .... 115 E3 11 25 S 16 45 E
Âneby, *Norway* .... 18 D7 60 5N 10 51 E
Aneby, *Sweden* .... 17 G8 57 48N 14 49 E
Anegada, B., *Argentina* .... 176 B4 40 20 S 62 20W
Anegada I., *Br. Virgin Is.* .... 165 e 18 45N 64 20W
Anegada Passage, *W. Indies* 165 C7 18 15N 63 45W
Aneho, *Togo* .... 113 D5 6 12N 1 34 E
Aneityum, *Vanuatu* .... 133 K7 20 12 S 169 45 E
Anelghowhat, *Vanuatu* .... 133 K7 20 19 S 169 43 E
Añelo, *Argentina* .... 176 A3 38 20 S 68 45W
Anenni-Noi, *Moldova* .... 53 D14 46 53N 29 15 E
Aneto, Pico de, *Spain* .... 40 C5 42 37N 0 40 E
Añez, *Bolivia* .... 173 D5 15 40 S 63 10W
Anfu, *China* .... 77 D10 27 21N 114 40 E
Ang Kong Marine Nat. Park △, *Thailand* .... 87 H2 9 40N 99 43 E
Ang Mo Kio, *Singapore* .... 87 d 1 23N 103 50 E
Ang Thong, *Thailand* .... 86 E3 14 35N 100 31 E
Ang Thong, Ko, *Thailand* .... 87 b 9 37N 99 41 E
Agadanan, *Phil.* .... 80 C3 16 45N 121 45 E
Angamos, Punta, *Chile* .... 174 A1 23 1 S 70 32W
Angara →, *Russia* .... 67 D10 58 5N 94 20 E
Angara-Débou, *Benin* .... 113 C5 11 19N 3 3 E
Angarab, *Ethiopia* .... 107 E4 13 11N 37 7 E
Angarbaka, *Sudan* .... 107 F1 9 44N 24 44 E
Angarsk, *Russia* .... 67 D11 52 30N 104 0 E
Angas Hills, *Australia* .... 124 D4 23 0 S 127 50 E
Angaston, *Australia* .... 128 C3 34 30 S 139 8 E
Angat, *Phil.* .... 80 D3 14 56N 121 2 E
Ånge, *Sweden* .... 16 B9 62 31N 15 35 E
Ángel, Salto = Angel Falls, *Venezuela* 169 B5 5 57N 62 30W
Ángel de la Guarda, I., *Mexico* 162 B2 29 30N 113 30W
Angel Falls, *Venezuela* 169 B5 5 57N 62 30W
Ángeles, *Phil.* .... 80 D3 15 9N 120 33 E
Ängelholm, *Sweden* .... 17 H6 56 15N 12 58 E
Angels Camp, *U.S.A.* 160 G6 38 4N 120 32W
Ängelsberg, *Sweden* .... 16 E10 59 58N 16 0 E
Anger →, *Ethiopia* .... 107 F4 9 37N 36 6 E
Angereb →, *Ethiopia* .... 107 E4 13 45N 36 40 E
Ångermanälven →, *Sweden* .... 16 B11 62 40N 18 0 E
Ångermanland, *Sweden* .... 14 E18 63 36N 17 45 E
Angermünde, *Germany* .... 30 B9 53 1N 14 0 E
Angers, *Canada* 151 A9 45 31N 75 29W
Angers, *France* 26 E6 47 30N 0 35W
Angerville, *France* .... 25 D9 48 19N 2 0 E
Ängesån →, *Sweden* .... 14 C20 66 16N 22 47 E
Angical, *Brazil* .... 171 D3 12 0 S 44 42W
Angikuni L., *Canada* 143 A9 62 0N 100 0W
Anglem, Mt., *N.Z.* .... 131 G2 46 45 S 167 53 E
Anglès, *Spain* .... 40 D7 41 57N 2 38 E
Anglesey, Isle of □, *U.K.* 20 D3 53 16N 4 18W
Anglet, *France* 28 E2 43 29N 1 31W

Angleton, *U.S.A.* 155 L7 29 10N 95 26W
Anglin →, *France* .... 28 B4 46 42N 0 52 E
Anglisidhes, *Cyprus* .... 39 F9 34 51N 33 27 E
Anglure, *France* .... 27 D10 48 35N 3 50 E
Angmagssalik = Tasiilaq, *Greenland* 10 D7 65 40N 37 20W
Ango, *Dem. Rep. of the Congo* .... 118 B2 4 10N 26 5 E
Angoche, *Mozam.* .... 119 F4 16 8 S 39 55 E
Angoche, I., *Mozam.* .... 119 F4 16 20 S 39 50 E
Angol, *Chile* .... 174 D1 37 56 S 72 45W
Angola, *Ind., U.S.A.* 157 C12 41 38N 85 0W
Angola, *N.Y., U.S.A.* 150 D5 42 38N 79 2W
Angola ■, *Africa* .... 115 E3 12 0 S 18 0 E
Angoon, *U.S.A.* 144 H14 57 30N 134 35W
Angora = Ankara, *Turkey* .... 100 C5 39 57N 32 54 E
Angoram, *Papua N. G.* .... 132 C3 4 4 S 144 4 E
Angoulême, *France* .... 28 C4 45 39N 0 10 E
Angoumois, *France* .... 28 C4 45 50N 0 25 E
Angra do Heroísmo, *Azores* 9 d1 38 39N 27 13W
Angra dos Reis, *Brazil* .... 175 A7 23 0 S 44 10W
Angren, *Uzbekistan* .... 65 C5 41 1N 70 12 E
Angtassom, *Cambodia* .... 87 G5 11 1N 104 41 E
Angu, *Dem. Rep. of the Congo* .... 118 B1 3 23N 24 30 E
Anguang, *China* .... 75 B12 45 15N 123 45 E
Anguilla ☑, *W. Indies* 165 C7 18 14N 63 5W
Anguo, *China* .... 74 E8 38 28N 115 15 E
Angurugu, *Australia* .... 126 A2 14 0 S 136 25 E
Angus □, *U.K.* 22 E6 56 46N 2 56W
Angwa →, *Zimbabwe* .... 117 F2 16 0 S 30 23 E
Anhandui →, *Brazil* .... 175 A5 21 46 S 52 9W
Anholt, *Denmark* .... 17 H5 56 42N 11 33 E
Anhua, *China* .... 77 C8 28 23N 111 12 E
Anhui □, *China* .... 77 B11 32 0N 117 0 E
Anhwei = Anhui □, *China* .... 77 B11 32 0N 117 0 E
Aniak, *U.S.A.* 144 F8 61 35N 159 32W
Anichab, *Namibia* .... 116 C1 21 0 S 14 46 E
Anicuns, *Brazil* .... 171 E1 16 28 S 49 58W
Ánidhros, *Greece* .... 49 E7 36 38N 25 43 E
Anié, *Togo* .... 113 D5 7 42N 1 8 E
Anil, *Brazil* .... 170 B3 2 32 S 44 14W
Animas →, *U.S.A.* 159 H9 36 43N 108 13W
Anina, *Romania* .... 52 E6 45 6N 21 51 E
Anini-y, *Phil.* .... 81 F3 10 25N 121 55 E
Aninoasa, *Romania* .... 53 F9 44 47N 24 10 E
Anita, *U.S.A.* 156 C2 41 27N 94 46W
Anivorano, *Madag.* .... 117 B8 18 44 S 48 58 E
Aniwa, *Vanuatu* .... 133 17 19 17 S 169 35 E
Anjalankoski, *Finland* .... 15 F22 60 45N 26 51 E
Anjangaon, *India* .... 94 D3 21 10N 77 20 E
Anjar, *India* .... 92 H4 23 6N 70 10 E
Anjengo, *India* .... 95 K3 8 40N 76 46 E
Anji, *China* .... 77 B12 30 46N 119 40 E
Anjidiv I., *India* .... 95 G2 14 40N 74 10 E
Anjō, *Japan* .... 73 C9 34 57N 137 5 E
Anjou, *France* 26 E6 47 20N 0 15W
Anjouan, *Comoros Is.* .... 121 a 12 15 S 44 20 E
Anjozorobe, *Madag.* .... 117 B8 18 22 S 47 52 E
Anju, *N. Korea* .... 75 E13 39 36N 125 40 E
Anka, *Nigeria* .... 113 C6 12 13 S 5 58 E
Ankaboa, Tanjona, *Madag.* .... 117 C7 21 58 S 43 20 E
Ankang, *China* .... 74 H5 32 40N 109 1 E
Ankara, *Turkey* .... 100 C5 39 57N 32 54 E
Ankarafantsika, Réserve Naturelle Intégrale d' △, *Madag.* .... 117 B8 16 8 S 47 5 E
Ankaramena, *Madag.* .... 117 C8 21 57 S 46 39 E
Ankarsrum, *Sweden* .... 17 G10 57 41N 16 20 E
Ankasakasa, *Madag.* .... 117 B7 16 21 S 44 52 E
Ankavandra, *Madag.* .... 117 B8 18 46 S 45 18 E
Ankazoabo, *Madag.* .... 117 C7 22 18 S 44 31 E
Ankazobe, *Madag.* .... 117 B8 18 20 S 47 10 E
Ankeny, *U.S.A.* 156 E2 41 44N 93 36W
Ankilimalinika, *Madag.* .... 117 C7 22 58 S 43 45 E
Ankilizato, *Madag.* .... 117 C8 20 25 S 45 1 E
Ankisabe, *Madag.* .... 117 B8 19 17 S 46 29 E
Anklam, *Germany* .... 30 B9 53 51N 13 41 E
Ankleshwar, *India* .... 94 D1 21 38N 73 3 E
Ankober, *Ethiopia* .... 107 F4 9 35N 39 40 E
Ankola, *India* .... 95 G2 14 40N 74 18 E
Ankoro, *Dem. Rep. of the Congo* .... 118 D2 6 45 S 26 55 E
Ankororoka, *Madag.* .... 117 D8 25 30 S 45 11 E
Anlong, *China* .... 76 E5 25 2N 105 27 E
Anlu, *China* .... 77 B9 31 15N 113 45 E
Anmyŏn-do, *S. Korea* .... 75 F14 36 25N 126 25 E
Änn, *Sweden* .... 16 A6 63 16N 12 34 E
Ann, C., *U.S.A.* 151 D14 42 38N 70 35W
Ann Arbor, *U.S.A.* 152 D4 42 17N 83 45W
Anna, *Russia* .... 60 E5 51 28N 40 23 E
Anna, *Ill., U.S.A.* 155 G10 37 28N 89 15W
Anna, *Ohio, U.S.A.* 157 D12 40 24N 84 11W
Anna Regina, *Guyana* 169 B6 7 10N 58 30W
Annaba, *Algeria* .... 111 A6 36 50N 7 46 E
Annaberg-Buchholz, *Germany* .... 30 E9 50 34N 13 0 E
Annai, *Guyana* 169 C6 3 57N 59 8W
Annaka, *Japan* .... 73 A10 36 19N 138 54 E
Annalee →, *Ireland* 23 B4 54 2N 7 24W
Annam, *Vietnam* .... 86 E7 16 0N 108 0 E
Annamitique, Chaîne, *Asia* .... 86 E7 17 0N 106 0 E
Annan, *U.K.* 22 G5 54 59N 3 16W
Annan →, *U.K.* 22 G5 54 58N 3 16W
Annapolis, *U.S.A.* 148 F7 38 59N 76 30W
Annapolis Royal, *Canada* 141 D6 44 44N 65 32W
Annapurna, *Nepal* .... 93 E10 28 34N 83 50 E
Annean, L., *Australia* .... 125 E2 26 54 S 118 14 E
Anneberg, *Sweden* .... 17 G8 57 44N 14 49 E
Annecy, *France* .... 29 C10 45 55N 6 8 E
Annecy, Lac d', *France* .... 27 F13 45 52N 6 10 E
Annemasse, *France* .... 29 C10 46 12N 6 16 E
Annette I., *U.S.A.* 142 C2 55 3N 131 28W
Anning, *China* .... 76 E4 24 55N 102 26 E
Anniston, *U.S.A.* 152 B4 33 39N 85 50W
Annobón, *Atl. Oc.* .... 105 G4 1 25 S 5 36 E
Annonay, *France* .... 29 C8 45 15N 4 40 E
Annot, *France* .... 29 E10 43 58N 6 38 E
Annotto Bay, *Jamaica* .... 164 a 18 17N 76 45W
Ánnsjön, *Sweden* .... 16 A6 63 19N 12 34 E
Annville, *U.S.A.* 151 F8 40 20N 76 31W
Annweiler, *Germany* .... 31 F3 49 12N 7 58 E
Áno Arkhánai, *Greece* .... 49 F7 35 16N 25 11 E
Áno Porróia, *Greece* .... 50 E7 41 17N 23 2 E
Áno Síros, *Greece* .... 48 D6 37 29N 24 56 E
Áno Viánnos, *Greece* .... 39 E6 35 2N 25 21 E
Anorotsangana, *Madag.* .... 117 A8 13 56 S 47 55 E
Anosibe, *Madag.* .... 117 B8 19 26 S 48 13 E
Anou Mellene, *Mali* .... 113 B5 17 25N 0 35 E
Anoumaba, *Ivory C.* 112 D4 6 23N 4 38W
Anoyí, *Greece* .... 38 C2 38 25N 20 41 E
Anóyia, *Greece* .... 39 E5 35 16N 24 52 E
Anping, *Hebei, China* .... 74 E8 38 15N 115 30 E
Anping, *Liaoning, China* .... 75 D12 41 5N 123 30 E
Anpu Gang, *China* .... 76 G7 21 25N 109 56 E
Anqing, *China* .... 77 B11 30 30N 117 3 E
Anqiu, *China* .... 75 F10 36 25N 119 10 E
Anren, *China* .... 77 D9 26 43N 113 18 E
Ansager, *Denmark* .... 17 J2 55 43N 8 45 E
Ansai, *China* .... 74 F5 36 50N 109 20 E
Ansbach, *Germany* .... 31 F6 49 28N 10 34 E
Anse Boileau, *Seychelles* .... 121 b 4 43 S 55 29 E
Anse Royale, *Seychelles* .... 121 b 4 44 S 55 31 E
Anseba →, *Eritrea* .... 107 D4 16 0N 38 30 E
Anserma, *Colombia* 168 B2 5 13N 75 48W

Ansfelden, *Austria* .... 34 C7 48 12N 14 17 E
Anshan, *China* .... 75 D12 41 5N 122 58 E
Anshun, *China* .... 76 D5 26 18N 105 57 E
Ansião, *Portugal* 42 F2 39 56N 8 27W
Ansley, *U.S.A.* 154 E5 41 18N 99 23W
Ansó, *Spain* 40 C4 42 51N 0 48W
Ansoain, *Spain* 40 C4 42 50N 1 38W
Anson, *U.S.A.* 155 J5 32 45N 99 54W
Anson B., *Australia* .... 124 B5 13 20 S 130 6 E
Ansongo, *Mali* .... 113 B5 15 25N 0 35 E
Ansongo-Ménaka, Réserve d' △, *Mali* .... 113 B5 15 3N 1 37 E
Ansonia, *Conn., U.S.A.* 151 E11 41 21N 73 5W
Ansonia, *Ohio, U.S.A.* 157 D12 40 13N 84 38W
Anstruther, *U.K.* 22 E6 56 14N 2 41W
Asudu, *Indonesia* .... 83 B5 2 11 S 139 22 E
Ansus, *Indonesia* .... 83 B5 1 44 S 135 48 E
Antabamba, *Peru* .... 172 C3 14 40 S 73 0W
Antagarh, *India* .... 94 D5 20 6N 81 9 E
Antakya, *Turkey* .... 100 D7 36 14N 36 10 E
Antalaha, *Madag.* .... 117 A9 14 57 S 50 20 E
Antalât, *Libya* .... 108 B4 31 8N 20 42 E
Antalya, *Turkey* .... 100 D4 36 52N 30 45 E
Antalya □, *Turkey* .... 49 E12 36 30N 30 0 E
Antalya Körfezi, *Turkey* .... 100 D4 36 15N 31 30 E
Antambohobe, *Madag.* .... 117 C8 22 20 S 46 47 E
Antanambao-Manampotsy, *Madag.* .... 117 B8 19 29 S 48 34 E
Antanambe, *Madag.* .... 117 B8 16 26 S 49 52 E
Antananarivo, *Madag.* .... 117 B8 18 55 S 47 31 E
Antananarivo □, *Madag.* .... 117 B8 19 0 S 47 0 E
Antanifotsy, *Madag.* .... 117 B8 19 39 S 47 19 E
Antanimbaribe, *Madag.* .... 117 C7 21 30 S 44 48 E
Antanimora, *Madag.* .... 117 C8 24 49 S 45 40 E
Antarctic Pen., *Antarctica* .... 7 C18 67 0 S 60 0W
Antarctica .... 7 E3 90 0 S 0 0W
Antécume Pata, *Fr. Guiana* 169 C7 3 17N 54 4W
Antelope, *Zimbabwe* .... 119 G2 21 2 S 28 31 E
Antenor Navarro, *Brazil* .... 170 C4 6 44 S 38 27W
Antequera, *Paraguay* .... 174 A4 24 8 S 57 7W
Antequera, *Spain* 43 H6 37 5N 4 33W
Antero, Mt., *U.S.A.* 159 G10 38 41N 106 15W
Antevamena, *Madag.* .... 117 C7 21 2 S 44 8 E
Anthemoús, *Greece* .... 50 F7 40 31N 23 15 E
Anthony, *Fla., U.S.A.* 153 F7 29 18N 82 7W
Anthony, *Kans., U.S.A.* 155 G5 37 9N 98 2W
Anthony, *N. Mex., U.S.A.* 159 K10 32 0N 106 36W
Anti Atlas, *Morocco* 110 C3 30 0N 8 30W
Anti-Lebanon = Ash Sharqi, Al Jabal, *Lebanon* .... 103 B5 33 40N 36 10 E
Antibes, *France* .... 29 E11 43 34N 7 6 E
Antibes, C. d', *France* .... 29 E11 43 31N 7 7 E
Anticosti, Î. d', *Canada* 141 C7 49 30N 63 0W
Antifer, C. d', *France* .... 26 C7 49 41N 0 10 E
Antigo, *U.S.A.* 154 C10 45 9N 89 9W
Antigonish, *Canada* 141 C7 45 38N 61 58W
Antigua, *Canary Is.* 9 e2 28 24N 14 1W
Antigua, *Guatemala* 164 D1 14 34N 90 41W
Antigua, *W. Indies* 165 C7 17 0N 61 50W
Antigua & Barbuda ■, *W. Indies* 165 C7 17 20N 61 48W
Antilla, *Cuba* 164 B4 20 40N 75 50W
Antilles = West Indies, *Cent. Amer.* 165 D7 15 0N 65 0W
Antioch = Antakya, *Turkey* .... 100 D7 36 14N 36 10 E
Antioch, *U.S.A.* 160 G5 38 1N 121 48W
Antioche, Pertuis d', *France* 28 B2 46 1 20W
Antioquia, *Colombia* 168 B2 6 40N 75 55W
Antioquia □, *Colombia* 168 B2 7 0N 75 0W
Antipodes Is., *Pac. Oc.* .... 134 M9 49 45 S 178 40 E
Antipolo, *Phil.* .... 80 D3 14 35N 121 10 E
Antique □, *Phil.* .... 81 F4 11 10N 122 5 E
Antlers, *U.S.A.* 155 H7 34 14N 95 37W
Antoetra, *Madag.* .... 117 C8 20 46 S 47 20 E
Antofagasta, *Chile* .... 174 A1 23 50 S 70 30W
Antofagasta □, *Chile* .... 174 A2 24 0 S 69 0W
Antofagasta de la Sierra, *Argentina* .... 174 B2 26 5 S 67 20W
Antofalla, *Argentina* .... 174 B2 25 30 S 68 5W
Antofalla, Salar de, *Argentina* .... 174 B2 25 40 S 67 45W
Anton, *U.S.A.* 155 J3 33 49N 102 10W
Antongila, Helodrano, *Madag.* .... 117 B8 15 30 S 49 50 E
Antonibé, *Madag.* .... 117 A8 14 55 S 47 20 E
Antonina, *Brazil* .... 175 B6 25 26 S 48 42W
António Enes = Angoche, *Mozam.* .... 119 F4 16 8 S 39 55 E
Antrain, *France* 26 D5 48 28N 1 30W
Antrim, *U.K.* 23 B5 54 43N 6 14W
Antrim, *U.S.A.* 150 F3 40 7N 81 21W
Antrim □, *U.K.* 23 B5 54 56N 6 25W
Antrim, Mts. of, *U.K.* 23 A5 55 3N 6 14W
Antrim Plateau, *Australia* .... 124 C4 18 8 S 128 20 E
Antrodoco, *Italy* .... 45 F10 42 25N 13 5 E
Antropovo, *Russia* .... 60 A6 58 24N 43 6 E
Antsakabary, *Madag.* .... 117 B8 15 3 S 48 56 E
Antsalova, *Madag.* .... 117 B7 18 40 S 44 37 E
Antsenavolo, *Madag.* .... 117 C8 21 24 S 48 3 E
Antsiafabositra, *Madag.* .... 117 B8 17 18 S 46 57 E
Antsirabe, *Antananarivo, Madag.* .... 117 B8 19 55 S 47 2 E
Antsirabe, *Antsiranana, Madag.* .... 117 A8 14 0 S 49 59 E
Antsirabe, *Mahajanga, Madag.* .... 117 B8 15 57 S 48 58 E
Antsiranana, *Madag.* .... 117 A8 12 25 S 49 20 E
Antsiranana □, *Madag.* .... 117 A8 12 16 S 49 17 E
Antsohihy, *Madag.* .... 117 A8 14 50 S 47 59 E
Antsohimbondrona Seranana, *Madag.* .... 117 A8 13 7 S 48 48 E
Antu, *China* .... 75 C15 42 30N 128 20 E
Antufash, *Yemen* .... 98 D3 15 42 S 42 25 E
Antwerp = Antwerpen, *Belgium* .... 24 C4 51 13N 4 25 E
Antwerp, *N.Y., U.S.A.* 151 B9 44 12N 75 37W
Antwerp, *Ohio, U.S.A.* 157 C12 41 11N 84 45W
Antwerpen, *Belgium* .... 24 C4 51 13N 4 40 E
Antwerpen □, *Belgium* .... 24 C4 51 15N 4 40 E
Anukur, C., *Papua N. G.* .... 132 D5 6 18N 147 57 E
Anupgarh, *India* .... 92 E5 29 10N 73 10 E
Anuppur, *India* .... 93 H9 23 6N 81 41 E
Anuradhapura, *Sri Lanka* .... 95 K5 8 22N 80 28 E
Anveh, *Iran* .... 97 E7 27 23N 54 11 E
Anvers = Antwerpen, *Belgium* .... 24 C4 51 13N 4 25 E
Anvers I., *Antarctica* .... 7 C17 64 30 S 63 40W
Anvik, *U.S.A.* 144 F7 62 39N 160 13W
Anwen, *China* .... 77 C13 29 4N 120 26 E
Anxi, *Fujian, China* .... 77 E12 25 2N 118 12 E
Anxi, *Gansu, China* .... 68 B4 40 30N 95 43 E
Anxian, *China* .... 76 B5 31 40N 104 25 E
Anxious B., *Australia* .... 127 E1 33 24 S 134 45 E
Anyama, *Ivory C.* 112 D4 5 30N 4 3W
Anyang, *China* .... 74 F8 36 5N 114 21 E
Anyer, *Indonesia* .... 84 D3 6 4 S 105 53 E
Anyer-Kidul, *Indonesia* .... 79 G11 6 4 S 105 53 E
Anyi, *Jiangxi, China* .... 77 C10 28 49N 115 25 E
Anyi, *Shanxi, China* .... 74 G6 35 2N 111 2 E
Anyuan, *China* .... 77 E10 25 9N 115 21 E
Anyue, *China* .... 76 B5 30 9N 105 50 E
Anza, *U.S.A.* 161 M10 33 35N 116 39W
Anze, *China* .... 74 F7 36 10N 112 12 E
Anzhero-Sudzhensk, *Russia* .... 66 D9 56 10N 86 0 E
Ánzio, *Italy* .... 46 A5 41 27N 12 37 E
Anzoátegui □, *Venezuela* 169 B5 9 0N 64 30W
Ao Makham, *Thailand* .... 87 a 7 50N 98 24 E
Ao Phangnga Nat. Park △, *Thailand* .... 87 a 8 15N 98 30 E
Aoba, *Vanuatu* .... 133 E5 15 25 S 167 50 E
Aoga-Shima, *Japan* .... 73 E11 32 28N 139 46 E
Aoiz, *Spain* 40 C3 42 46N 1 22W
Aola, *Solomon Is.* .... 133 M11 9 31 S 160 27 E
Aomen = Macau, *China* .... 69 G10 22 12N 113 33 E
Aomori, *Japan* .... 70 D10 40 45N 140 45 E

Aomori □, *Japan* . . . . **70 D10** 40 45N 140 40 E
Aonla, *India* . . . . **93 E8** 28 16N 79 11 E
Aono-Yama, *Japan* . . . . **72 C3** 34 28N 131 48 E
Aoraki Mount Cook, *N.Z.* . . . **131 D5** 43 36 S 170 9 E
Aorangi Mts., *N.Z.* . . . . **130 H4** 41 28 S 175 22 E
Aore, *Vanuatu* . . . . **133 E5** 15 35 S 167 10 E
Aoreora, *Morocco* **110 C2** 28 51N 10 53W
Aosta, *Italy* . . . . **44 C4** 45 45N 7 20 E
Aotea Harbour, *N.Z.* . . . . **130 D3** 38 0 S 174 50 E
Aoudéras, *Niger* . . . . **113 B6** 17 45N 8 20 E
Aouinet Torkoz, *Morocco* . . . **110 C3** 28 31N 9 46W
Aouk, Bahr ➤, *Africa* . . . . . . **109 G3** 8 51N 18 53 E
Aouk-Aoukalé, Réserve de Faune de
l' ⌂, *C.A.R.* . . . . **114 A4** 9 52N 21 25 E
Aoukar, *Mali* **110 D4** 23 50N 2 45W
Aoukâr, *Mauritania* **112 B3** 17 40N 10 0W
Aoulef el Arab, *Algeria* . . . . **111 C5** 26 55N 1 2 E
Aozou, *Chad* . . . . **109 D3** 21 45N 17 28 E
Aozou Strip, *Chad* . . . . **109 D3** 20 0N 17 15 E
Apa ➤, *S. Amer.* . . . . **174 A4** 22 6 S 58 2W
Apache, *U.S.A.* **155 H5** 34 54N 98 22W
Apache Junction, *U.S.A.* **159 K8** 33 25N 111 33W
Apalachee B., *U.S.A.* **152 E5** 30 0N 84 0W
Apalachicola, *U.S.A.* **152 F5** 29 43N 84 59W
Apalachicola ➤, *U.S.A.* **152 F5** 29 43N 84 58W
Apalachicola B., *U.S.A.* **152 F3** 29 40N 85 0W
Apam, *Ghana* **113 D4** 5 19N 0 42W
Apapa, *Nigeria* . . . . **113 D5** 6 25N 3 25 E
Apaporis ➤, *Colombia* . . . . . **168 D4** 1 23 S 69 25W
Aparecida do Taboado, *Brazil* . **171 F1** 20 5 S 51 0W
Aparri, *Phil.* . . . . **80 B3** 18 22N 121 38 E
Aparurén, *Venezuela* **169 B5** 5 6N 62 8W
Apateu, *Romania* . . . . **52 D6** 46 36N 21 47 E
Apatin, *Serbia, Yug.* . . . . **52 E4** 45 40N 19 0 E
Apatity, *Russia* . . . . **56 A5** 67 34N 33 22 E
Apatou, *Fr. Guiana* **169 B7** 5 9N 54 20W
Apatzingán, *Mexico* **162 D4** 19 0N 102 20W
Apauwar, *Indonesia* . . . . **83 B5** 1 39 S 138 11 E
Apayao □, *Phil.* . . . . **80 B3** 18 10N 121 10 E
Apeldoorn, *Neths.* . . . . **24 B5** 52 13N 5 57 E
Apen, *Germany* . . . . **30 B3** 53 13N 7 48 E
Apennines = Appennini, *Italy* . **44 E7** 44 0N 10 0 E
Apenrade = Aabenrå, *Denmark* . **17 J3** 55 3N 9 25 E
Apere ➤, *Bolivia* . . . . **173 C4** 13 44 S 65 18W
Aphrodisias, *Turkey* . . . . **49 D10** 37 42N 28 46 E
Apiacás, Serra dos, *Brazil* . . . **173 B6** 9 50 S 57 0W
Apiaí, *Brazil* . . . . **171 F2** 24 31 S 48 50W
Apiaú ➤, *Brazil* **169 C5** 2 30N 61 12W
Apiaú, Serra do, *Brazil* **169 C5** 2 30N 61 0W
Apidiá ➤, *Brazil* . . . . **173 C5** 11 8 S 61 11W
Apies ➤, *S. Africa* . . . . **117 D4** 25 15 S 28 8 E
Apinajé, *Brazil* . . . . **171 D2** 11 31 S 48 18W
Apiti, *N.Z.* . . . . **130 F4** 39 58 S 175 54 E
Apizaco, *Mexico* **163 D5** 19 26N 98 9W
Aplao, *Peru* . . . . **172 D3** 16 0 S 72 40W
Apo, Mt., *Phil.* . . . . **81 H5** 6 53N 125 14 E
Apo East Pass, *Phil.* . . . . **80 E3** 12 40N 120 40 E
Apo Reef Marine Park ⌂, *Phil.* . **80 E3** 12 50N 120 50 E
Apo West Pass, *Phil.* . . . . . . **80 E3** 12 31N 120 22 E
Apodi, *Brazil* . . . . **170 C4** 5 39 S 37 48W
Apoera, *Suriname* **169 B6** 5 12N 57 10W
Apolakkiá, *Greece* . . . . **38 E11** 36 5N 27 48 E
Apolakkiá, Órmos, *Greece* . . . **38 E11** 36 5N 27 47 E
Apolda, *Germany* . . . . **30 D7** 51 2N 11 32 E
Apollo Bay, *Australia* . . . . . . **128 E5** 38 45 S 143 40 E
Apollonia = Marsá Susah, *Libya* . **108 B4** 32 52N 21 59 E
Apollonia, *Greece* . . . . **48 E6** 36 58N 24 43 E
Apolo, *Bolivia* . . . . **172 C4** 14 30 S 68 30W
Apónguao ➤, *Venezuela* **169 C5** 4 48N 61 36W
Apopka, *U.S.A.* **153 G8** 28 40N 81 31W
Apopka L., *U.S.A.* **153 G8** 28 38N 81 38W
Aporé ➤, *Brazil* . . . . **173 D7** 18 58 S 52 1W
Aporé ➤, *Brazil* . . . . **171 E1** 19 27 S 50 57W
Aporema, *Brazil* **170 A1** 1 14N 50 49W
Apostle Is., *U.S.A.* **154 B9** 47 0N 90 40W
Apostle Islands Nat. Lakeshore,
U.S.A. **154 B9** 46 57N 90 53W
Apóstoles, *Argentina* . . . . . . **175 B4** 28 0 S 56 0W
Apostolos Andreas, C., *Cyprus* . **39 E10** 35 42N 34 35 E
Apostolovo, *Ukraine* . . . . **59 J7** 47 39N 33 39 E
Apoteri, *Guyana* **169 C6** 4 2N 58 32W
Appalachian Mts., *U.S.A.* . . . **148 G6** 38 0N 80 0W
Äppelbo, *Sweden* . . . . **16 D8** 60 29N 14 1 E
Appennini, *Italy* . . . . **44 E7** 44 0N 10 0 E
Appennino Ligure, *Italy* . . . . **44 D6** 44 30N 9 0 E
Appenzell, *Switz.* . . . . **33 B8** 47 20N 9 25 E
Appenzell-Ausser Rhoden □, *Switz.* . **33 B8** 47 23N 9 23 E
Appenzell-Inner Rhoden □, *Switz.* . **33 B8** 47 20N 9 25 E
Appiano, *Italy* . . . . **45 B8** 46 28N 11 15 E
Apple Hill, *Canada* **151 A10** 45 13N 74 46W
Apple Valley, *U.S.A.* **161 L9** 34 32N 117 14W
Appleby-in-Westmorland, *U.K.* . **20 C5** 54 35N 2 29W
Appledore, *U.K.* **21 F3** 51 3N 4 13W
Apples, *Switz.* . . . . **32 C2** 46 33N 6 26 E
Appleton, *U.S.A.* **148 C1** 44 16N 88 25W
Appleton City, *U.S.A.* **156 F2** 38 11N 94 2W
Appling, *U.S.A.* **152 B7** 33 33N 82 19W
Approuague ➤, *Fr. Guiana* . . **169 C7** 4 20N 52 0W
Aprica, *Italy* . . . . **33 D10** 46 9N 10 6 E
Apricena, *Italy* . . . . **45 G12** 41 47N 15 27 E
April ➤, *Papua N. G.* . . . . . . **132 C2** 4 18 S 142 26 E
Aprília, *Italy* . . . . **46 A5** 41 36N 12 39 E
Apsheronsk, *Russia* . . . . **61 H4** 44 28N 39 42 E
Apsley, *Canada* **150 B6** 44 45N 78 6W
Apt, *France* . . . . **29 E9** 43 53N 5 24 E
Apuane, Alpi, *Italy* . . . . **44 D7** 44 7N 10 14 E
Apuaú, *Brazil* . . . . **169 D5** 2 25 S 60 53W
Apucarana, *Brazil* . . . . **175 A5** 23 55 S 51 33W
Apulia = Púglia □, *Italy* . . . . **47 A9** 41 15N 16 15 E
Apurauan, *Brazil* . . . . **81 G2** 9 35N 118 20 E
Apure □, *Venezuela* **168 B4** 7 10N 68 50W
Apure ➤, *Venezuela* **168 B4** 7 37N 66 25W
Apurímac □, *Peru* . . . . **172 C3** 14 0 S 73 0W
Apurímac ➤, *Peru* . . . . **172 C3** 12 17 S 73 56W
Apuseni, Munţii, *Romania* . . . **52 D7** 46 30N 22 45 E
Āqā Jarī, *Iran* . . . . **97 D6** 30 42N 49 50 E
Aqaba = Al 'Aqabah, *Jordan* . **103 F4** 29 31N 35 0 E
Aqaba, G. of, *Red Sea* . . . . . . **96 D2** 28 15N 33 20 E
'Aqabah, Khalīj al = Aqaba, G. of,
Red Sea . . . . **96 D2** 28 15N 33 20 E
Aqbaqay, *Kazakhstan* . . . . . . **65 A6** 45 0N 72 47 E
Āqcheh, *Afghan.* . . . . **91 A2** 37 0N 66 5 E
Āqcheh, *Afghan.* . . . . **65 E3** 36 56N 66 11 E
'Aqdā, *Iran* . . . . **97 C7** 32 26N 53 37 E
Aqïq, *Sudan* . . . . **106 D4** 18 14N 38 12 E
Aqïq, Khalïg, *Sudan* . . . . **106 D4** 18 0N 38 10 E
'Aqïq, W. al ➤, *Si. Arabia* . . . **98 B3** 20 16N 41 40 E
Aqköl, *Kazakhstan* . . . . **65 A7** 45 0N 75 45 E
Aqköl, *Kazakhstan* . . . . **65 A7** 46 0N 70 45 E
Aqmola = Astana, *Kazakhstan* . **66 D8** 51 10N 71 30 E
Aqqum, *Kazakhstan* . . . . **65 B6** 44 55N 69 18 E
'Aqrah, *Iraq* . . . . **101 D10** 36 46N 43 45 E
Aqsū, *Kazakhstan* . . . . **65 B8** 43 59N 74 14 E
Aqsū, *Kazakhstan* . . . . **65 B4** 42 25N 69 50 E
Aqsūgek, *Kazakhstan* . . . . . . **65 A7** 44 37N 74 30 E
Aqsūmbe, *Kazakhstan* . . . . . . **65 A3** 44 26N 67 33 E
Aqtaū, *Kazakhstan* . . . . **66 E6** 43 55N 51 10 E
Aqtöbe, *Kazakhstan* . . . . **57 D10** 50 17N 57 10 E
Aquidauana, *Brazil* . . . . **173 E6** 20 30 S 55 50W
Aquidauana ➤, *Brazil* . . . . . **173 D6** 19 44 S 56 50W
Aquiles Serdán, *Mexico* **162 B3** 28 37N 105 54W
Aquin, *Haiti* **165 C5** 18 16N 73 24W
Aquitain, Bassin, *France* **25 D3** 44 0N 0 30W

Aquitaine □, *France* **28 D3** 44 25N 0 30W
Aqviligjuaq = Pelly Bay, *Canada* . **139 B11** 68 38N 89 50W
Aqyrtöbe, *Kazakhstan* . . . . . . **65 B6** 42 59N 72 7 E
Aqzhar, *Kazakhstan* . . . . **65 B8** 43 8N 71 37 E
Ar Rachidiya = Er Rachidia,
Morocco **110 B4** 31 58N 4 20W
Ar Rafid, *Syria* . . . . **103 C4** 32 57N 35 52 E
Ar Raḩḩālīyah, *Iraq* . . . . **101 C4** 32 44N 43 23 E
Ar Ramādī, *Iraq* . . . . **101 F10** 33 25N 43 20 E
Ar Raml, *Libya* . . . . **108 C3** 26 45N 19 40 E
Ar Ramthā, *Jordan* . . . . **103 C5** 32 34N 36 0 E
Ar Raqqah, *Syria* . . . . **101 E8** 35 59N 39 8 E
Ar Rass, *Si. Arabia* . . . . **96 E4** 25 50N 43 40 E
Ar Rawḑah, *Si. Arabia* . . . . . **98 B3** 21 16N 42 50 E
Ar Rawḑah, *Yemen* . . . . **90 D4** 14 28N 47 17 E
Ar Rawshān, *Si. Arabia* . . . . . **106 C5** 20 2N 42 36 E
Ar Rifā'ī, *Iraq* . . . . **96 D5** 31 50N 46 10 E
Ar Rijā', *Yemen* . . . . **98 D4** 13 1N 44 35 E
Ar Riyāḑ, *Si. Arabia* . . . . **96 E5** 24 41N 46 42 E
Ar Ru'ays, *Qatar* . . . . **97 E6** 26 8N 51 12 E
Ar Rukhaymīyah, *Iraq* . . . . . **96 D5** 29 22N 45 38 E
Ar Ruşāfah, *Syria* . . . . **101 E8** 35 45N 38 49 E
Ar Ruţbah, *Iraq* . . . . **101 F9** 33 0N 40 15 E
Ar Ruwaydah, *Si. Arabia* . . . . **98 B4** 23 40N 44 40 E
Ara, *India* . . . . **93 G11** 25 35N 84 32 E
Ara Goro, *Ethiopia* . . . . **107 F5** 5 48N 41 18 E
Ara Tera, *Ethiopia* . . . . **107 F5** 6 38N 40 57 E
'Arab, *Iran* **149 H2** 34 19N 86 30W
'Arab, Bahr el ➤, *Sudan* . . . . **107 F2** 9 0N 29 30 E
Arab, Khalīg el, *Egypt* . . . . . **106 A2** 30 55N 29 0 E
Arab, Shatt al ➤, *Asia* . . . . . **97 D6** 30 0N 48 31 E
'Araba, W. ➤, *Egypt* . . . . **106 J8** 28 19N 33 31 E
'Arabābād, *Iran* . . . . **97 C8** 33 2N 57 41 E
'Arabah, W. ➤, *Yemen* . . . . . **99 C5** 18 5N 51 26 E
Araban, *Turkey* . . . . **100 D7** 37 28N 37 44 E
Arabatskaya Strelka, *Ukraine* . **59 K8** 45 40N 35 0 E
Arabba, *Italy* . . . . **45 B8** 46 30N 11 52 E
Arabelo, *Venezuela* **169 C5** 4 55N 64 13W
Arabi, *U.S.A.* **152 D6** 31 50N 83 44W
Arabia, *Asia* . . . . **62 G8** 25 0N 45 0 E
Arabian Desert = Es Sahrâ' Esh
Sharqîya, *Egypt* . . . . **106 B3** 27 30N 32 30 E
Arabian Gulf = Gulf, The, *Asia* . **97 E6** 27 0N 50 0 E
Arabian Sea, *Ind. Oc.* . . . . . . **88 D5** 16 0N 65 0 E
Araç, *Turkey* . . . . **100 B5** 41 15N 33 21 E
Aracaju, *Brazil* . . . . **170 D4** 10 55 S 37 4W
Aracataca, *Colombia* **168 A3** 10 38N 74 9W
Aracati, *Brazil* . . . . **170 B4** 4 30 S 37 44W
Araçatuba, *Brazil* . . . . **175 A5** 21 10 S 50 30W
Araceli, *Phil.* . . . . **81 F2** 10 33N 119 59 E
Aracena, *Spain* **43 H4** 37 53N 6 38W
Aracena, Sierra de, *Spain* . . . **43 H4** 37 50N 6 50W
Aracides, C., *Solomon Is.* . . . **133 M11** 8 21 S 161 0 E
Aračinovo, *Macedonia* . . . . . **50 D5** 42 1N 21 34 E
Araçuaí, *Brazil* . . . . **171 E3** 16 52 S 42 4W
Araçuaí ➤, *Brazil* . . . . **171 E3** 16 46 S 42 2W
'Arad, *Israel* . . . . **103 D4** 31 15N 35 12 E
Arad, *Romania* . . . . **50 D6** 46 10N 21 20 E
Arad □, *Romania* . . . . **52 D6** 46 20N 22 0 E
Arada, *Chad* . . . . **109 F4** 15 0N 20 20 E
Arādān, *Iran* . . . . **97 C7** 35 21N 52 30 E
Aradhippou, *Cyprus* . . . . **39 E9** 34 57N 33 36 E
Arafura Sea, *E. Indies* . . . . . . **83 C5** 9 0 S 135 0 E
Aragarças, *Brazil* . . . . **173 D7** 15 55 S 52 15W
Aragats, *Armenia* . . . . **61 K7** 40 30N 44 15 E
Aragón □, *Spain* **40 D4** 41 25N 0 40W
Aragón ➤, *Spain* **40 C3** 42 13N 1 44W
Aragona, *Italy* . . . . **46 E6** 37 24N 13 27 E
Aragua □, *Venezuela* **168 B4** 10 0N 67 10W
Aragua de Barcelona, *Venezuela* . **169 B5** 9 28N 64 49W
Araguacema, *Brazil* . . . . **171 D2** 8 50 S 49 20W
Araguaçu, *Brazil* . . . . **171 D2** 12 49 S 49 51W
Araguaia ➤, *Brazil* . . . . **170 C2** 5 21 S 48 41W
Araguaiana, *Brazil* . . . . **173 D7** 15 43 S 51 51W
Araguaína, *Brazil* . . . . **170 C2** 7 12 S 48 12W
Araguari, *Brazil* . . . . **171 E2** 18 38 S 48 11W
Araguari ➤, *Brazil* **169 C8** 1 15N 49 55W
Araguatins, *Brazil* . . . . **170 C2** 5 38 S 48 7W
Arain, *India* . . . . **92 F6** 26 27N 75 2 E
Araioses, *Brazil* . . . . **170 B3** 2 53 S 41 55W
Arak, *Algeria* . . . . **111 C5** 25 20N 3 45 E
Arāk, *Iran* . . . . **97 C6** 34 0N 49 40 E
Araka, *Sudan* . . . . **107 G3** 4 20N 30 23 E
Arakan □, *Burma* . . . . **90 F5** 19 0N 94 15 E
Arakan Yoma, *Burma* . . . . . . **90 F5** 20 0N 94 40 E
Arákhova, *Greece* . . . . **48 C4** 38 28N 22 35 E
Arakkonam, *India* . . . . **95 H4** 13 7N 79 43 E
Araklı, *Turkey* . . . . **101 B8** 41 6N 40 2 E
Araks = Aras, Rūd-e ➤, *Asia* . **61 K9** 40 5N 48 29 E
Aral, *Kazakhstan* . . . . **66 E7** 46 41N 61 45 E
Aral Sea, *Asia* . . . . **66 E7** 44 30N 60 0 E
Aral Tengizi = Aral Sea, *Asia* . **66 E7** 44 30N 60 0 E
Aralsk = Aral, *Kazakhstan* . . . **66 E7** 46 41N 61 45 E
Aralskoye More = Aral Sea, *Asia* . **66 E7** 44 30N 60 0 E
Aralsor, Ozero, *Kazakhstan* . . **61 F9** 49 5N 48 42 E
Aramac, *Australia* . . . . **126 C4** 22 58 S 145 14 E
Aramia ➤, *Papua N. G.* . . . . . **132 D2** 7 55 S 143 22 E
Aran ➤, *India* . . . . **94 E4** 19 55N 78 12 E
Aran Arch, *Ethiopia* . . . . **107 F5** 8 43N 43 54 E
Aran Is., *Ireland* **23 A3** 55 0N 8 30W
Aran I., *Ireland* **23 A3** 55 0N 8 30W
Aranda de Duero, *Spain* **42 D7** 41 39N 3 42W
Arandān, *Iran* . . . . **98 A5** 35 23N 46 55 E
Arandelovac, *Serbia, Yug.* . . . **50 B4** 44 18N 20 34 E
Aranga, *N.Z.* . . . . **130 B2** 35 44 S 173 40 E
Arani, *Bolivia* . . . . **173 D4** 17 34 S 65 46W
Arani, *India* . . . . **95 H4** 12 43N 79 19 E
Aranjuez, *Spain* **42 F7** 40 1N 3 40W
Aranos, *Namibia* . . . . **116 C2** 24 9 S 19 7 E
Aransas Pass, *U.S.A.* **155 M6** 27 55N 97 9W
Aranyaprathet, *Thailand* . . . . **86 F4** 13 41N 102 30 E
Arao, *Japan* . . . . **72 E2** 32 59N 130 25 E
Araouane, *Mali* **112 B4** 18 55N 3 30W
Arapahoe, *U.S.A.* **154 E5** 40 18N 99 54W
Arapari, *Brazil* . . . . **170 C2** 5 34 S 49 15W
Arapawa I., *N.Z.* . . . . **131 B9** 41 11 S 174 17 E
Arapey Grande ➤, *Uruguay* . **174 C4** 30 55 S 57 49W
Arapgir, *Turkey* . . . . **101 C8** 39 5N 38 30 E
Arapiraca, *Brazil* . . . . **170 C4** 9 45 S 36 39W
Arapongas, *Brazil* . . . . **175 A5** 23 29 S 51 28W
Arapuni, *N.Z.* . . . . **130 E4** 38 4 S 175 39 E
Ar'ar, *Si. Arabia* . . . . **96 D4** 30 59N 41 2 E
Araracuara, *Colombia* . . . . . . **168 D3** 0 24 S 72 17W
Araranguá, *Brazil* . . . . **175 B6** 29 0 S 49 30W
Araraquara, *Brazil* . . . . **171 F2** 21 50 S 48 0W
Araras, *Brazil* . . . . **171 F2** 22 22 S 47 23W
Araras, Serra das, *Brazil* . . . . **175 C4** 25 0 S 53 10W
Ararat, *Armenia* . . . . **101 C11** 39 48N 44 50 E
Ararat, *Australia* . . . . **128 D5** 37 16 S 143 0 E
Ararat, Mt. = Ağrı Dağı, *Turkey* . **101 C11** 39 50N 44 15 E
Arari, *Brazil* . . . . **170 B3** 3 28 S 44 47W
Araria, *India* . . . . **93 F12** 26 9N 87 33 E
Araripe, Chapada do, *Brazil* . . **170 C3** 7 20 S 40 0W
Araripina, *Brazil* . . . . **170 C3** 7 33 S 40 34W
Araruama, L. de, *Brazil* . . . . . **171 F3** 22 53 S 42 12W
Araruna, *Brazil* . . . . **170 C4** 6 52 S 35 44W
Aras, Rūd-e ➤, *Asia* . . . . **61 K9** 40 5N 48 29 E
Aratãne, *Mauritania* **112 B3** 18 24N 8 32W
Araticu, *Brazil* . . . . **170 B1** 2 10 S 50 10W
Arauca, *Colombia* **168 B3** 7 0N 70 40W
Arauca □, *Colombia* **168 B3** 6 40N 71 0W
Arauca ➤, *Venezuela* **168 B4** 7 24N 66 35W
Arauco, *Chile* . . . . **174 D1** 37 16 S 73 25W

Araújos, *Brazil* . . . . **171 E2** 19 56 S 45 14W
Arauquita, *Colombia* **168 B3** 7 2N 71 25W
Araure, *Venezuela* **168 B4** 9 34N 69 13W
Arawa, *Ethiopia* . . . . **107 F5** 9 57N 41 58 E
Arawale Nat. Reserve ⌂, *Kenya* . **118 C5** 1 24 S 40 9 E
Arawata ➤, *N.Z.* . . . . **131 E3** 44 0 S 168 40 E
Arawe Is., *Papua N. G.* . . . . . **132 D5** 6 6 S 149 0 E
Araxá, *Brazil* . . . . **171 E2** 19 35 S 46 55W
Araya, Pen. de, *Venezuela* . . . **169 A5** 10 40N 64 0W
Arba Gugu, *Ethiopia* . . . . **80 D3** 15 10N 120 46 E
Arba Minch, *Ethiopia* . . . . . . **107 F5** 8 40N 40 15 E
Arbat, *Iraq* . . . . **107 F4** 6 0N 37 30 E
Árbatax, *Italy* . . . . **101 E11** 35 25N 45 35 E
Arbedo, *Switz.* . . . . **46 C2** 39 56N 9 42 E
Arbi, *Ethiopia* . . . . **33 D8** 46 12N 9 3 E
Arbīl, *Iraq* . . . . **107 F4** 9 4N 35 7 E
Arboga, *Sweden* . . . . **101 D11** 36 15N 44 5 E
Arbois, *France* . . . . **16 E9** 59 24N 15 52 E
Arboletes, *Colombia* . . . . **27 F12** 46 55N 5 46 E
Arbon, *Switz.* **168 B2** 8 51N 76 26W
Arbore, *Ethiopia* . . . . **33 A8** 47 31N 9 26 E
Arboréa, *Italy* . . . . **107 F4** 5 3N 36 50 E
Arborfield, *Canada* . . . . **46 C1** 39 46N 8 35 E
Arborg, *Canada* **143 C8** 53 6N 103 39W
Arbroath, *U.K.* **143 C9** 50 54N 97 13W
Arbuckle, *U.S.A.* **22 E6** 56 34N 2 35W
Arbus, *Italy* **160 F4** 39 1N 122 3W
Arc ➤, *France* . . . . **46 C1** 39 30N 8 33 E
Arc-et-Senans, *France* . . . . . . **29 C10** 45 34N 6 12 E
Arc-lès-Gray, *France* . . . . **27 E12** 47 28N 5 34 E
Arcachon, *France* **28 D2** 44 40N 1 10W
Arcachon, Bassin d', *France* . . **28 D2** 44 42N 1 10W
Arcade, Calif., *U.S.A.* **161 L8** 34 2N 118 15W
Arcade, N.Y., *U.S.A.* **150 D6** 42 32N 78 25W
Arcadia, Fla., *U.S.A.* **153 H8** 27 13N 81 52W
Arcadia, Ind., *U.S.A.* **157 D10** 40 11N 86 1W
Arcadia, Iowa, *U.S.A.* **156 B1** 42 5N 95 3W
Arcadia, La., *U.S.A.* **155 J8** 32 33N 92 55W
Arcadia, Pa., *U.S.A.* **150 F6** 40 47N 78 51W
Arcanum, *U.S.A.* **157 E12** 39 59N 84 33W
Arcata, *U.S.A.* **158 F1** 40 52N 124 5W
Arcévia, *Italy* . . . . **45 E9** 43 30N 12 56 E
Archangel = Arkhangelsk, *Russia* . **56 B7** 64 38N 40 36 E
Archar, *Bulgaria* . . . . **50 C7** 43 50N 22 54 E
Archbald, *U.S.A.* **151 E9** 41 30N 75 32W
Archbold, *U.S.A.* **157 C12** 41 31N 84 18W
Archena, *Spain* **41 G3** 38 9N 1 16W
Archenu, J., *Chad* . . . . **109 D4** 22 15N 24 45 E
Archer ➤, *Australia* . . . . **126 A3** 13 28 S 141 41 E
Archer B., *Australia* . . . . **126 A3** 13 20 S 141 30 E
Archer Bend National Park =
Mungkan Kandju Nat. Park △,
Australia . . . . **126 A3** 13 35 S 142 52 E
Archers Post, *Kenya* . . . . **118 B4** 0 35N 37 35 E
Arches Nat. Park △, *U.S.A.* . . **159 G9** 38 45N 109 25W
Archidona, *Spain* **43 H6** 37 6N 4 22W
Archipel-de-Mingan, Réserve de
Parc Nat. de l' △, *Canada* . . **141 B7** 50 13N 63 10W
Archipiélago Chinijo, Parque Nac.
de ○, *Canary Is.* **9 e2** 29 20N 13 30W
Archipiélago Los Roques, Parque
Nac. ○, *Venezuela* **165 D6** 11 50N 66 44W
Arci, Mte., *Italy* . . . . **46 C1** 39 47N 8 45 E
Arcidosso, *Italy* . . . . **45 F8** 42 52N 11 33 E
Arcila = Asilah, *Morocco* **110 A3** 35 29N 6 0W
Arcipelago de la Maddalena, Parco
Nazionale dell' △, *Italy* . . . **46 A2** 41 14N 9 24 E
Arcipelago Toscano, Parco
Nazionale △, *Italy* . . . . **44 F7** 42 45N 10 15 E
Arcis-sur-Aube, *France* . . . . . **27 D11** 48 32N 4 10 E
Arckaringa Cr. ➤, *Australia* . . **127 D2** 28 10 S 135 22 E
Arco, *Italy* . . . . **44 C7** 45 55N 10 54 E
Arco, *U.S.A.* **158 E7** 43 38N 113 18W
Arcola, *U.S.A.* **157 E8** 39 41N 88 19W
Arcoona, *Australia* . . . . **128 A2** 31 2 S 137 1 E
Arcos = Arcos de Jalón, *Spain* . **40 D2** 41 12N 2 16W
Arcos de Jalón, *Spain* **40 D2** 41 12N 2 16W
Arcos de la Frontera, *Spain* . . **43 J5** 36 45N 5 49W
Arcos de Valdevez, *Portugal* . . **42 D2** 41 55N 8 22W
Arcot, *India* . . . . **95 H4** 12 53N 79 20 E
Arcoverde, *Brazil* . . . . **170 C4** 8 25 S 37 4W
Arcozelo, *Portugal* **42 E3** 40 32N 7 47W
Arctic Bay, *Canada* **139 A11** 73 1N 85 7W
Arctic Ocean, *Arctic* **6 B18** 78 0N 160 0W
Arctic Red River = Tsiigehtchic,
Canada **138 B6** 67 15N 134 0W
Arctic Village, *U.S.A.* **144 B11** 68 8N 145 32W
Arda ➤, *Bulgaria* . . . . **49 H11** 41 40N 26 30 E
Arda ➤, *Italy* . . . . **44 C7** 45 2N 10 2 E
Ardabīl, *Iran* . . . . **96 B5** 38 15N 48 18 E
Ardahan, *Turkey* . . . . **101 B10** 41 7N 42 41 E
Ardakān = Sepīdān, *Iran* . . . . **97 D7** 30 20N 52 5 E
Ardakān, *Iran* . . . . **97 C7** 32 19N 53 59 E
Ardala, *Sweden* . . . . **17 F7** 58 22N 13 19 E
Ardales, *Spain* **43 J6** 36 53N 4 51W
Årdalstangen, *Norway* . . . . . . **18 C4** 61 14N 7 43 E
Ardèche □, *France* . . . . **29 D8** 44 42N 4 16 E
Ardèche ➤, *France* . . . . **29 D8** 44 16N 4 39 E
Ardee, *Ireland* **23 C5** 53 52N 6 33W
Arden, *Canada* **150 B8** 44 43N 76 56W
Arden, *Denmark* . . . . **17 H3** 56 46N 9 52 E
Arden, Calif., *U.S.A.* **160 G5** 38 36N 121 33W
Arden, Nev., *U.S.A.* **161 J11** 36 1N 115 14W
Ardenne, *Belgium* . . . . **24 E5** 49 50N 5 5 E
Ardennes = Ardenne, *Belgium* . **24 E5** 49 50N 5 5 E
Ardennes □, *France* . . . . **27 C11** 49 35N 4 40 E
Ardentes, *France* . . . . **27 F8** 46 45N 1 50 E
Arderin, *Ireland* **23 C4** 53 2N 7 39W
Ardeşen, *Turkey* . . . . **101 B9** 41 12N 41 2 E
Ardestān, *Iran* . . . . **97 C7** 33 20N 52 25 E
Ardez, *Switz.* . . . . **33 C10** 46 47N 10 12 E
Árdhas ➤, *Greece* . . . . **51 E10** 41 40N 26 30 E
Ardhéa, *Greece* . . . . **48 D4** 40 58N 22 3 E
Ardila ➤, *Portugal* **43 G3** 38 12N 7 28W
Ardino, *Bulgaria* . . . . **51 F10** 41 34N 25 9 E
Ardivachar Pt., *U.K.* **22 D1** 57 23N 7 26W
Ardlethan, *Australia* . . . . **129 C7** 34 22 S 146 53 E
Ardmore, Okla., *U.S.A.* **155 H6** 34 10N 97 8W
Ardmore, Pa., *U.S.A.* **151 G9** 39 58N 75 18W
Ardnamurchan, Pt. of, *U.K.* . . **22 E2** 56 43N 6 14W
Ardnave Pt., *U.K.* **22 F2** 55 53N 6 20W
Ardon, *Russia* . . . . **61 J7** 43 10N 44 18 E
Ardore, *Italy* . . . . **47 D9** 38 11N 16 10 E
Ardrossan, *Australia* . . . . **128 E2** 34 26 S 137 53 E
Ardrossan, *U.K.* **22 F4** 55 39N 4 49W
Ards Pen., *U.K.* **23 B6** 54 33N 5 34W
Arduan, *Sudan* . . . . **106 D3** 19 54N 30 20 E
Ardud, *Romania* . . . . **52 C7** 47 37N 22 52 E
Åre, *Sweden* . . . . **16 E6** 63 22N 13 15 E
Arecibo, *Puerto Rico* . . . . **165 d** 18 29N 66 43W
Areia Branca, *Brazil* . . . . **170 B4** 5 0 S 37 0W
Arena, Pt., *U.S.A.* **160 G3** 38 57N 123 44W
Arenal, *Honduras* **164 C2** 15 21N 86 50W
Arenales, Cerro, *Chile* . . . . . **176 C2** 47 5 S 73 40W
Arenápolis, *Brazil* . . . . **173 C6** 14 30 S 56 50W
Arenas = Las Arenas, *Spain* . . **42 B6** 43 17N 4 50W
Arenas, Pta., *Venezuela* **169 A5** 10 20N 62 0W
Arenas de San Pedro, *Spain* . . **42 E5** 40 12N 5 5 E
Arendal, *Norway* . . . . **18 E5** 58 28N 8 46 E
Arendsee, *Germany* . . . . **30 C7** 52 52N 11 27 E
Arenillas, *Ecuador* . . . . **168 D1** 3 33 S 80 8W

Arenys de Mar, *Spain* . . . . . . **40 D7** 41 35N 2 33 E
Arenzano, *Italy* . . . . **44 D5** 44 24N 8 41 E
Arenzville, *U.S.A.* **156 E6** 39 53N 90 22W
Areópolis, *Greece* . . . . **48 E4** 36 40N 22 22 E
Arequipa, *Peru* . . . . **172 D3** 16 20 S 71 30W
Arequipa □, *Peru* . . . . **172 D3** 16 0 S 72 50W
Arere, *Brazil* . . . . **169 D7** 0 16 S 53 52W
Arero, *Ethiopia* . . . . **107 G4** 4 41N 38 50 E
Arès, *France* **28 D2** 44 47N 1 8W
Arévalo, *Spain* **42 D6** 41 3N 4 43W
Arezzo, *Italy* . . . . **45 E8** 43 25N 11 53 E
Arga ➤, *Turkey* . . . . **96 B3** 38 21N 37 59 E
Arga ➤, *Spain* **40 C3** 42 18N 1 47W
Argalastí, *Greece* . . . . **48 B5** 39 13N 23 13 E
Argamakmur, *Indonesia* . . . . . **84 C2** 3 35 S 102 0 E
Argamasilla de Alba, *Spain* . . **43 F7** 39 8N 3 5W
Argamasilla de Calatrava, *Spain* . **43 G6** 38 44N 4 4W
Arganda, *Spain* **42 E7** 40 19N 3 26W
Arganil, *Portugal* **42 E2** 40 13N 8 3W
Argao, *Phil.* . . . . **81 G4** 9 52N 123 36 E
Argásion, *Greece* . . . . **39 D2** 37 45N 20 56 E
Argayash, *Russia* . . . . **64 D8** 55 29N 60 52 E
Argedeb, *Ethiopia* . . . . **107 F5** 6 11N 41 13 E
Argelès-Gazost, *France* **28 E3** 43 0N 0 6W
Argelès-sur-Mer, *France* . . . . **28 F7** 42 34N 3 1 E
Argens ➤, *France* . . . . **29 E10** 43 24N 6 44 E
Argent-sur-Sauldre, *France* . . **27 E9** 47 33N 2 25 E
Argenta, *Canada* **142 C5** 50 11N 116 56W
Argenta, *Italy* . . . . **45 D8** 44 37N 11 50 E
Argenta, U.S.A. **157 E8** 39 59N 88 49W
Argentan, *France* **26 D6** 48 45N 0 1W
Argentário, Mte., *Italy* . . . . . . **45 F8** 42 24N 11 9 E
Argentat, *France* . . . . **28 C5** 45 6N 1 56 E
Argentera, *Italy* . . . . **44 D4** 44 12N 7 5 E
Argenteuil, *France* . . . . **27 D9** 48 57N 2 14 E
Argentia, *Canada* **141 C9** 47 18N 53 58W
Argentiera, C. dell', *Italy* . . . **46 B1** 40 44N 8 8 E
Argentière, Aiguilles d', *Switz.* . **32 E4** 45 58N 7 2 E
Argentina ■, *S. Amer.* . . . . . . **174 C2** 35 0 S 66 0W
Argentino, L., *Argentina* . . . . **176 D2** 50 10 S 73 0W
Argenton-Château, *France* . . . **26 F6** 46 59N 0 27W
Argenton-sur-Creuse, *France* . **27 F8** 46 36N 1 30 E
Argeş □, *Romania* . . . . **53 F9** 45 0N 24 45 E
Argeş ➤, *Romania* . . . . **53 F11** 44 5N 26 38 E
Arghandab ➤, *Afghan.* . . . . . **91 C2** 31 30N 64 15 E
Argheile, *Ethiopia* . . . . **107 F5** 5 19N 42 4 E
Argo, *Sudan* . . . . **106 D3** 19 28N 30 30 E
Argolikós Kólpos, *Greece* . . . . **48 D4** 37 20N 22 52 E
Argolís □, *Greece* . . . . **48 D4** 37 38N 22 50 E
Argonne, *France* . . . . **27 C12** 49 10N 5 0 E
Árgos, *Greece* . . . . **48 D4** 37 40N 22 43 E
Argos, *U.S.A.* **157 C10** 41 14N 86 15W
Árgos Orestikón, *Greece* . . . . **50 F5** 40 27N 21 18 E
Argostólion, *Greece* . . . . **39 C2** 38 11N 20 29 E
Argostólion, Kólpos, *Greece* . . **39 C1** 38 10N 20 27 E
Arguedas, *Spain* **40 C3** 42 11N 1 36W
Arguello, Pt., *U.S.A.* **161 L6** 34 35N 120 39W
Argun, *Russia* . . . . **61 J7** 43 18N 45 52 E
Argun ➤, *Russia* . . . . **67 D13** 53 20N 121 28 E
Argungu, *Nigeria* . . . . **113 C5** 12 40N 4 31 E
Arguni, T., *Indonesia* . . . . **83 B4** 3 6 S 133 42 E
Argus Pk., *U.S.A.* **161 K9** 35 52N 117 26W
Argyle, L., *Australia* . . . . **124 C4** 16 20 S 128 40 E
Argyll & Bute □, *U.K.* **22 E3** 56 13N 5 28W
Argyll Forest Park ○, *U.K.* . . **22 E4** 56 6N 5 0W
Arhavi, *Turkey* . . . . **101 B9** 41 21N 41 18 E
Århus, *Denmark* . . . . **17 H4** 56 8N 10 11 E
Århus Amtskommune □, *Denmark* . **17 H4** 56 15N 10 15 E
Aria, *N.Z.* . . . . **130 E4** 38 33 S 175 0 E
Ariadnoye, *Russia* . . . . **70 B7** 45 8N 134 25 E
Ariamsvlei, *Namibia* . . . . **116 D2** 28 9 S 19 51 E
Ariana, *Tunisia* . . . . **108 A2** 36 52N 10 12 E
Ariano Irpino, *Italy* . . . . **47 A8** 41 9N 15 5 E
Ariari ➤, *Colombia* **168 C3** 2 35N 72 47W
Aribinda, *Burkina Faso* **113 C4** 14 17N 0 52W
Arica, *Chile* . . . . **172 D3** 18 32 S 70 20W
Arica, *Colombia* . . . . **168 D3** 2 0 S 71 50W
Arico, *Canary Is.* **9 e1** 28 9N 16 31W
Arid, C., *Australia* . . . . **125 F3** 34 1 S 123 10 E
Arida, *Japan* . . . . **73 C7** 34 5N 135 8 E
Aridal, W. Sahara* **110 C2** 25 59N 13 54W
Aride, *Seychelles* . . . . **121 b** 4 13 S 55 40 E
Ariège □, *France* . . . . **28 F5** 42 56N 1 30 E
Ariège ➤, *France* . . . . **28 E5** 43 30N 1 25 E
Arieş ➤, *Romania* . . . . **53 D8** 46 24N 23 20 E
Arigat el Fersig, *Algeria* **111 C4** 27 35N 2 7W
Arîhã, *Israel* . . . . **106 A4** 31 51N 35 27 E
Arilje, *Serbia, Yug.* . . . . **50 C4** 43 44N 20 7 E
Arília, Ákra, *Greece* . . . . **38 B9** 39 43N 19 39 E
Arima, Trin. & Tob. **169 F9** 10 38N 61 17W
Arinagay, *Phil.* . . . . **80 C3** 16 26N 120 21 E
Arinos ➤, *Brazil* . . . . **173 C6** 10 25 S 58 20W
Ario de Rosales, *Mexico* **162 D4** 19 12N 102 0W
Ariogala, *Lithuania* . . . . **54 C10** 55 16N 23 28 E
Aripo, Mt., Trin. & Tob. **169 F9** 10 45N 61 15W
Aripuanã, *Brazil* . . . . **173 B5** 9 25 S 60 30W
Aripuanã ➤, *Brazil* . . . . **173 B5** 5 7 S 60 25W
Ariquemes, *Brazil* . . . . **173 B5** 9 55 S 63 6W
Arisaig, *U.K.* **22 E3** 56 55N 5 51W
Arîsh, W. el ➤, *Egypt* . . . . . . **106 A3** 31 9N 33 49 E
Arissa, *Ethiopia* . . . . **107 E5** 11 10N 41 35 E
Aristazabal I., *Canada* **142 C3** 52 40N 129 10W
Arita, *Japan* . . . . **72 D1** 33 11N 129 54 E
Aritao, *Phil.* . . . . **80 C3** 16 18N 121 2 E
Ariton, *U.S.A.* **152 D4** 31 36N 85 43W
Arivonimamo, *Madag.* . . . . . . **117 B8** 19 1 S 47 11 E
Ariyalur, *India* . . . . **95 J4** 11 8N 79 8 E
Ariza, *Spain* **40 D2** 41 19N 2 3W
Arizaro, Salar de, *Argentina* . . **174 A2** 24 40 S 67 50W
Arizona, *Argentina* . . . . **174 D2** 35 45 S 65 25W
Arizona □, *U.S.A.* **159 J8** 34 0N 112 0W
Arizpe, *Mexico* **162 A2** 30 20N 110 11W
Årjäng, *Sweden* . . . . **16 E6** 59 24N 12 8 E
Arjeplog, *Sweden* . . . . **14 D18** 66 3N 18 2 E
Arjona, *Colombia* **168 A2** 10 14N 75 22W
Arjona, *Spain* **43 H6** 37 56N 4 4W
Arjuna, *Indonesia* . . . . **85 D4** 7 49 S 112 34 E
Arka, *Russia* . . . . **67 C15** 60 15N 142 0 E
Arkadak, *Russia* . . . . **60 E6** 51 58N 43 30 E
Arkadelphia, *U.S.A.* **155 H8** 34 7N 93 4W
Arkadhía □, *Greece* . . . . **48 D4** 37 30N 22 20 E
Arkaig, L., *U.K.* **22 E3** 56 59N 5 10W
Arkalgud, *India* . . . . **95 H3** 12 46N 76 6 E
Arkalyk = Arqalyk, *Kazakhstan* . **66 D7** 50 13N 66 50 E
Arkansas □, *U.S.A.* **155 H8** 35 0N 92 30W
Arkansas ➤, *U.S.A.* **155 J9** 33 47N 91 4W
Arkansas City, *U.S.A.* **155 G6** 37 4N 97 2W
Arkaroola, *Australia* . . . . **127 E2** 30 20 S 139 22 E
Árkathos ➤, *Greece* . . . . **48 B3** 39 20N 21 4 E
Arkhángelos, Préveza, *Greece* . **39 A2** 39 6N 20 42 E
Arkhángelos, Ródhos, *Greece* . **38 E12** 36 13N 28 7 E
Arkhangelsk, *Russia* . . . . **56 B7** 64 38N 40 36 E
Arkhangelskoye, *Russia* . . . . . **60 E5** 51 32N 40 30 E
Arki, *India* . . . . **92 D7** 31 9N 76 58 E
Arkiko, *Eritrea* . . . . **107 D4** 15 33N 39 30 E
Arklow, *Ireland* **23 D5** 52 48N 6 10W
Árkoi, *Greece* . . . . **49 D9** 37 22N 26 45 E
Arkona, Kap, *Germany* . . . . . . **30 A9** 54 41N 13 26 E
Arkösund, *Sweden* . . . . **17 F10** 58 29N 16 56 E
Arkport, *U.S.A.* **150 D7** 42 24N 77 42W
Arkticheskiy, Mys, *Russia* . . . **67 A10** 81 10N 95 0 E
Arkul, *Russia* . . . . **60 B10** 57 17N 50 3 E

Arkville, U.S.A. ... 151 D10 42 9N 74 37W
Árla, Sweden ... 16 E10 59 17N 16 40 E
Arlanda, Stockholm ✕ (ARN), Sweden ... 16 E11 59 41N 17 56 E
Arlanza →, Spain ... 42 C6 42 6N 4 9W
Arlanzón →, Spain ... 42 C6 42 3N 4 17W
Arlbergpass, Austria ... 34 D3 47 9N 10 12 E
Arles, France ... 29 E8 43 41N 4 40 E
Arlesheim, Switz. ... 32 B5 47 30N 7 37 E
Arli, Burkina Faso ... 113 C5 11 35N 1 28 E
Arli, Parc Nat. de l' △, Burkina Faso ... 113 C5 11 35N 1 28 E
Arlington, S. Africa ... 117 D4 28 1 S 27 53 E
Arlington, Ga., U.S.A. ... 153 D5 31 26N 84 44W
Arlington, N.Y., U.S.A. ... 151 E11 41 42N 73 54W
Arlington, Oreg., U.S.A. ... 158 D3 45 43N 120 12W
Arlington, S. Dak., U.S.A. ... 154 C6 44 22N 97 8W
Arlington, Tex., U.S.A. ... 155 J6 32 44N 97 7W
Arlington, Va., U.S.A. ... 148 F7 38 53N 77 7W
Arlington, Vt., U.S.A. ... 151 C11 43 5N 73 9W
Arlington, Wash., U.S.A. ... 160 B4 48 12N 122 8W
Arlington Heights, U.S.A. ... 157 B9 42 5N 87 59W
Arlon, Belgium ... 24 E5 49 42N 5 49 E
Arltunga, Australia ... 126 C1 23 26 S 134 41 E
Armagh, U.K. ... 23 B5 54 21N 6 39W
Armagh □, U.K. ... 23 B5 54 18N 6 37W
Armagnac, France ... 28 E4 43 50N 0 10 E
Armançon →, France ... 27 E10 47 59N 3 30 E
Armando Bermudez, Parque Nac. △, Dom. Rep. ... 165 C5 19 3N 71 0W
Armatree, Australia ... 129 A8 31 26 S 148 28 E
Armavir, Russia ... 61 H5 45 2N 41 7 E
Armenia, Colombia ... 168 C2 4 35N 75 45W
Armenia ■, Asia ... 61 K7 40 20N 45 0 E
Armeniş, Romania ... 52 F7 45 13N 22 17 E
Armenistís, Ákra, Greece ... 38 E11 36 8N 27 42 E
Armentières, France ... 27 B9 50 40N 2 50 E
Armero, Colombia ... 168 C3 4 58N 74 54W
Armidale, Australia ... 129 A9 30 30 S 151 40 E
Armilla, Spain ... 43 H7 37 9N 3 37W
Armori, India ... 94 D4 20 28N 79 59 E
Armorique, Parc Naturel Régional d' →, France ... 26 D3 48 22N 3 50W
Armour, U.S.A. ... 154 D5 43 19N 98 21W
Armstrong, B.C., Canada ... 142 C5 50 25N 119 10W
Armstrong, Ont., Canada ... 140 B2 50 18N 89 4W
Armur, India ... 94 E4 18 48N 78 16 E
Armutlu, Bursa, Turkey ... 51 F12 40 31N 28 50 E
Armutlu, İzmir, Turkey ... 49 C9 38 24N 27 34 E
Arnaía, Greece ... 50 F7 40 30N 23 38 E
Arnarfjörður, Iceland ... 11 B3 65 48N 23 40W
Arnaud →, Canada ... 139 B12 60 0N 70 0W
Arnauti, C., Cyprus ... 39 E8 35 6N 32 17 E
Arnay-le-Duc, France ... 27 E11 47 10N 4 27 E
Arnedillo, Spain ... 40 C2 42 13N 2 14W
Arnedo, Spain ... 40 C2 42 12N 2 5W
Árnes, Iceland ... 11 A5 66 1N 21 31W
Árnes, Norway ... 18 D8 60 7N 11 28 E
Árnessýsla □, Iceland ... 11 C6 64 15N 20 30W
Arnett, U.S.A. ... 155 G5 36 8N 99 46W
Arnhem, Neths. ... 24 C5 51 58N 5 55 E
Arnhem, C., Australia ... 126 A2 12 20 S 137 30 E
Arnhem, B., Australia ... 126 A2 12 20 S 136 10 E
Arnhem Land, Australia ... 126 A1 13 10 S 134 30 E
Arnissa, Greece ... 50 F5 40 47N 21 49 E
Arno →, Italy ... 44 E7 43 41N 10 17 E
Arno Bay, Australia ... 128 B2 33 54 S 136 34 E
Arnold, U.K. ... 20 D6 53 1N 1 7W
Arnold, U.S.A. ... 160 G6 38 15N 120 20W
Arnoldstein, Austria ... 34 E6 46 33N 13 43 E
Arnon →, France ... 27 E9 47 13N 2 1 E
Arnot, Canada ... 143 B9 55 56N 96 41W
Arnøy, Norway ... 14 A19 70 9N 20 40 E
Arnprior, Canada ... 140 C4 45 26N 76 21W
Arnsberg, Germany ... 30 D4 51 24N 8 5 E
Arnsberger Wald, Naturpark △, Germany ... 30 D4 51 25N 8 20 E
Arnstadt, Germany ... 30 E6 50 50N 10 56 E
Aro →, Venezuela ... 169 B5 8 1N 64 11W
Aroab, Namibia ... 116 D2 26 41 S 19 39 E
Aroánia Óri, Greece ... 48 D4 37 56N 22 12 E
Aroche, Spain ... 43 H4 37 56N 6 57W
Aroeiras, Brazil ... 170 C4 7 31 S 35 41W
Arolla, Switz. ... 32 D4 46 2N 7 29 E
Arolsen, Germany ... 30 D5 51 23N 9 2 E
Aron, India ... 92 G6 25 57N 77 56 E
Aron →, France ... 27 F10 46 50N 3 10 E
Arona, Canary Is. ... 9 e1 28 6N 16 40W
Arona, Italy ... 44 C5 45 46N 8 34 E
Aroroy, Phil. ... 80 E4 12 31N 123 24 E
Arosa, Switz. ... 33 C9 46 47N 9 41 E
Arosa, Ría de, Spain ... 42 C2 42 28N 8 57W
Arøysund, Norway ... 18 E7 59 10N 10 27 E
Arpajon, France ... 27 D9 48 36N 2 15 E
Arpajon-sur-Cère, France ... 28 D6 44 53N 2 28 E
Arpaşu de Jos, Romania ... 53 E9 45 47N 24 37 E
Arqalyk, Kazakhstan ... 66 D7 50 13N 66 50 E
Arque, Bolivia ... 172 D4 17 8 S 66 3W
Arrah = Ara, India ... 93 G11 25 35N 84 32 E
Arrah, Ivory C. ... 112 D4 6 40N 3 58W
Arraias, Brazil ... 171 D2 12 56 S 46 57W
Arraias →, Mato Grosso, Brazil ... 173 C7 11 10 S 53 59W
Arraias →, Pará, Brazil ... 170 C2 7 30 S 49 20W
Arraiolos, Portugal ... 43 G3 38 44N 7 59W
Arran, U.K. ... 22 F3 55 34N 5 12W
Arras, France ... 27 B9 50 17N 2 46 E
Arrats →, France ... 28 D4 44 6N 0 52 E
Arreau, France ... 28 F4 42 54N 0 22 E
Arrecife, Canary Is. ... 9 e2 28 57N 13 37W
Arrecifes, Argentina ... 174 C3 34 6 S 60 9W
Arrée, Mts. d', France ... 26 D3 48 26N 3 55W
Arresø, Denmark ... 17 J6 55 58N 12 6 E
Arriaga, Chiapas, Mexico ... 163 D6 16 15N 93 52W
Arriaga, San Luis Potosí, Mexico ... 162 C4 21 55N 101 23W
Arribes del Duero, Espacio Natural de →, Spain ... 42 D4 41 11N 6 39W
Arrilalah, Australia ... 126 C3 23 43 S 143 54 E
Arrino, Australia ... 125 E2 29 30 S 115 40 E
Arriondas, Spain ... 42 B5 43 23N 5 11W
Arrojado →, Brazil ... 171 D3 13 24 S 44 20W
Arromanches-les-Bains, France ... 26 C6 49 20N 0 38W
Arronches, Portugal ... 43 F3 39 8N 7 16W
Arros →, France ... 28 E3 43 40N 0 2W
Arrow, L., Ireland ... 23 B3 54 3N 8 19W
Arrowhead, L., U.S.A. ... 161 L9 34 16N 117 10W
Arrowsmith, Mt., N.Z. ... 131 D5 43 20 S 170 57 E
Arrowtown, N.Z. ... 131 E3 44 57 S 168 50 E
Arroyo de la Luz, Spain ... 43 F4 39 30N 6 38W
Arroyo Grande, U.S.A. ... 161 K6 35 7N 120 35W
Års, Denmark ... 17 H3 56 48N 9 30 E
Ars, Iran ... 96 B5 37 9N 47 46 E
Ars-sur-Moselle, France ... 27 C13 49 5N 6 4 E
Arsenault L., Canada ... 143 B7 55 6N 108 32W
Arsenev, Russia ... 70 B6 44 10N 133 15 E
Arsi □, Ethiopia ... 107 F4 7 45N 39 0 E
Arsiero, Italy ... 45 C8 45 48N 11 21 E
Arsikere, India ... 95 H3 13 15N 76 15 E
Arsin, Turkey ... 101 B8 41 3N 39 55 E
Arsk, Russia ... 60 B9 56 10N 49 50 E
Arskógssandur, Iceland ... 11 B8 65 56N 18 27W
Ársunda, Sweden ... 16 D10 60 31N 16 45 E
Árta, Greece ... 48 B3 39 8N 21 2 E
Artá, Spain ... 38 B4 39 41N 3 21 E

Árta □, Greece ... 48 B3 39 15N 21 5 E
Arteaga, Mexico ... 162 D4 18 50N 102 20W
Arteche, Phil. ... 80 E5 12 17N 125 22 E
Arteijo = Arteixo, Spain ... 42 B2 43 19N 8 29W
Arteixo, Spain ... 42 B2 43 19N 8 29W
Artem = Artyom, Azerbaijan ... 61 K10 40 28N 50 20 E
Artem, Russia ... 70 C6 43 22N 132 13 E
Artemovsk, Russia ... 67 D10 54 45N 93 35 E
Artemovsk, Ukraine ... 59 H9 48 35N 38 0 E
Artemovskiy, Rostov, Russia ... 61 G5 47 45N 40 16 E
Artemovskiy, Yekaterinburg, Russia ... 64 C8 57 21N 61 54 E
Artenay, France ... 27 D8 48 5N 1 50 E
Artern, Germany ... 30 D7 51 22N 11 18 E
Artesa de Segre, Spain ... 40 D6 41 54N 1 3 E
Artesia = Mosomane, Botswana ... 116 C4 24 2 S 26 19 E
Artesia, U.S.A. ... 155 J2 32 51N 104 24W
Arth, Switz. ... 33 B7 47 4N 8 31 E
Arthington, Liberia ... 112 D2 6 35N 10 45W
Arthur, Canada ... 150 C4 43 50N 80 32W
Arthur, U.S.A. ... 157 E8 39 43N 88 28W
Arthur →, Australia ... 127 D3 41 2 S 144 40 E
Arthur Cr. →, Australia ... 126 C2 22 30 S 136 25 E
Arthur Pt., Australia ... 126 C5 22 7 S 150 3 E
Arthur River, Australia ... 125 F2 33 20 S 117 2 E
Arthur's Pass, N.Z. ... 131 C6 42 54 S 171 35 E
Arthur's Pass Nat. Park △, N.Z. ... 131 C6 42 53 S 171 42 E
Arthur's Town, Bahamas ... 165 B4 24 38N 75 42W
Artigas, Uruguay ... 174 C4 30 20 S 56 30W
Artik, Armenia ... 61 K6 40 38N 43 58 E
Artillery L., Canada ... 143 A7 63 9N 107 52W
Artois, France ... 27 B9 50 20N 2 30 E
Artotína, Greece ... 48 C4 38 42N 22 2 E
Artrutx, C. de, Spain ... 38 B4 39 55N 3 49 E
Artsyz, Ukraine ... 59 J5 46 4N 29 26 E
Artux, China ... 65 D8 39 40N 76 10 E
Artvin, Turkey ... 101 B9 41 14N 41 44 E
Artyom, Azerbaijan ... 61 K10 40 28N 50 20 E
Aru, Kepulauan, Indonesia ... 83 C4 6 0 S 134 30 E
Aru Is. = Aru, Kepulauan, Indonesia ... 83 C4 6 0 S 134 30 E
Arua, Uganda ... 118 B3 3 1N 30 58 E
Aruanã, Brazil ... 171 D1 14 54 S 51 10W
Aruba ☑, W. Indies ... 166 D6 12 30N 70 0W
Arudy, France ... 28 E3 43 7N 0 28W
Arumã, Brazil ... 169 D5 4 44 S 62 8W
Arumpo, Australia ... 128 B5 33 48 S 142 55 E
Arun →, Nepal ... 93 F12 26 55N 87 10 E
Arun →, U.K. ... 21 G7 50 49N 0 33W
Arunachal Pradesh □, India ... 90 A5 28 0N 95 0 E
Aruppukkottai, India ... 95 K4 9 31N 78 8 E
Aruri, Selat, Indonesia ... 83 B5 0 50 S 135 15 E
Arusha, Tanzania ... 118 C4 3 20 S 36 40 E
Arusha □, Tanzania ... 118 C4 4 0 S 36 30 E
Arusha Chini, Tanzania ... 118 C4 3 32 S 37 20 E
Arusha Nat. Park △, Tanzania ... 118 C4 3 16 S 36 47 E
Arut →, Indonesia ... 85 C4 2 42 S 111 34 E
Aruvi →, Sri Lanka ... 95 K4 8 48N 79 53 E
Aruwimi →, Dem. Rep. of the Congo ... 118 B1 1 13N 23 36 E
Arvada, Colo., U.S.A. ... 154 F2 39 48N 105 5W
Arvada, Wyo., U.S.A. ... 158 D10 44 39N 106 8W
Arvakalu, Sri Lanka ... 95 K4 8 20N 79 58 E
Arve →, France ... 27 F13 46 11N 6 8 E
Arvi, Greece ... 39 F6 34 59N 25 28 E
Arvi, India ... 94 D4 20 59N 78 16 E
Arviat, Canada ... 143 A10 61 6N 93 59W
Arvidsjaur, Sweden ... 14 D18 65 35N 19 10 E
Arvika, Sweden ... 16 E6 59 40N 12 36 E
Arvin, U.S.A. ... 161 K8 35 12N 118 50W
Arwal, India ... 93 G11 25 15N 84 41 E
Arxan, China ... 69 B6 47 11N 119 57 E
Åryd, Sweden ... 17 H8 56 49N 14 59 E
Aryirádhes, Greece ... 38 C9 39 27N 19 58 E
Aryiroúpolis, Greece ... 39 E5 35 17N 24 20 E
Arys, Kazakhstan ... 65 B4 42 26N 68 48 E
Arys →, Kazakhstan ... 65 B4 42 45N 68 15 E
Arzachena, Italy ... 46 A2 41 5N 9 23 E
Arzamas, Russia ... 60 C6 55 27N 43 55 E
Arzew, Algeria ... 111 A4 35 50N 0 23W
Arzgir, Russia ... 61 H7 45 18N 44 23 E
Arzignano, Italy ... 45 C8 45 31N 11 20 E
Arzúa, Spain ... 42 C2 42 56N 8 9W
Aš, Czech Rep. ... 30 E7 50 13N 12 12 E
Ås, Norway ... 18 E7 59 40N 10 48 E
Ås, Sweden ... 16 A8 63 15N 14 34 E
As Pontes de García Rodríguez, Spain ... 42 B3 43 27N 7 50W
Aş Şafā, Syria ... 103 B6 33 10N 37 0 E
Aş Şaffānīyah, Si. Arabia ... 97 E6 27 55N 48 50 E
Aş Şafīrah, Syria ... 100 D7 36 5N 37 12 E
Aş Şāhm, Oman ... 97 E8 24 10N 56 53 E
Aş Sājir, Si. Arabia ... 96 E5 25 11N 44 36 E
Aş Salamīyah, Syria ... 100 E7 35 1N 37 2 E
Aş Salmān, Iraq ... 96 D5 30 30N 44 32 E
Aş Salt, Jordan ... 103 C4 32 2N 35 43 E
Aş Sal'w'a, Qatar ... 97 E6 24 23N 50 50 E
Aş Samāwah, Iraq ... 96 D5 31 15N 45 15 E
Aş Sanamayn, Syria ... 103 B5 33 3N 36 10 E
Aş Sawādah, Si. Arabia ... 98 B4 22 24N 44 28 E
Aş Sayl al Kabīr, Si. Arabia ... 98 B3 21 38N 40 25 E
Aş Sohar = Şuḥār, Oman ... 97 E8 24 20N 56 40 E
Aş Sukhnah, Syria ... 100 E8 34 52N 38 52 E
Aş Sulaymānīyah, Iraq ... 101 E11 35 35N 45 29 E
Aş Sulaymānīyah, Si. Arabia ... 98 A4 24 9N 47 18 E
Aş Sulaymī, Si. Arabia ... 96 E4 26 17N 41 21 E
Aş Sulayyil, Si. Arabia ... 98 B4 20 27N 45 34 E
Aş Sultān, Libya ... 108 B3 31 4N 17 8 E
Aş Summān, Si. Arabia ... 96 E5 25 0N 47 0 E
Aş Şurrah, Yemen ... 98 D4 13 57N 46 14 E
Aş Suwaydā', Syria ... 103 C5 32 40N 36 30 E
Aş Suwaydā' □, Syria ... 103 C5 32 45N 36 45 E
Aş Suwayq, Oman ... 97 F8 23 51N 57 26 E
Aş Şuwayrah, Iraq ... 101 F11 32 55N 45 0 E
Asa, Kazakhstan ... 65 B5 43 2N 71 10 E
Åsa, Sweden ... 17 G6 57 21N 12 8 E
Asab, Namibia ... 116 D2 25 30 S 18 0 E
Asaba, Nigeria ... 116 D3 6 12N 6 38 E
Asad, Buḥayrat al, Syria ... 101 D8 36 0N 38 15 E
Asadābād, Iran ... 101 E13 34 47N 48 7 E
Asafo, Ghana ... 112 D4 6 20N 2 40W
Asahi, Japan ... 73 B12 35 43N 140 39 E
Asahi-Gawa →, Japan ... 72 C5 34 36N 133 58 E
Asahigawa, Japan ... 70 C11 43 46N 142 22 E
Asaka, Uzbekistan ... 65 C6 40 38N 72 15 E
Asale, L., Ethiopia ... 107 E5 14 0N 40 20 E
Asama-Yama, Japan ... 73 A10 36 24N 138 31 E
Asamankese, Ghana ... 113 D4 5 50N 0 40W
Āsān →, India ... 92 D8 30 23N 77 24 E
Asansol, India ... 93 H12 23 40N 87 1 E
Åsarna, Sweden ... 16 B8 62 39N 14 22 E
Asau, Samoa ... 133 W23 13 27 S 172 33W
Asayita, Ethiopia ... 107 E5 11 35N 41 23 E
Asbe Teferi, Ethiopia ... 107 F5 9 4N 40 49 E
Asbesberg, S. Africa ... 116 D3 29 0 S 23 0 E
Asbest, Russia ... 64 C8 57 0N 61 30 E
Asbestos, Canada ... 141 C5 45 47N 71 58W
Asbury Park, U.S.A. ... 151 F10 40 13N 74 1W
Ascea, Italy ... 47 B8 40 8N 15 1 E
Ascensión, Mexico ... 162 A3 31 6N 107 59W
Ascensión, B. de la, Mexico ... 163 D7 19 50N 87 20W
Ascension I., Atl. Oc. ... 9 g 7 57 S 14 23W
Aschach an der Donau, Austria ... 34 C7 48 22N 14 2 E
Aschaffenburg, Germany ... 31 F5 49 58N 9 6 E
Aschendorf, Germany ... 30 B3 53 3N 7 19 E
Aschersleben, Germany ... 30 D7 51 45N 11 29 E
Asciano, Italy ... 45 E8 43 14N 11 33 E

Áscoli Piceno, Italy ... 45 F10 42 51N 13 34 E
Áscoli Satriano, Italy ... 47 A8 41 11N 15 32 E
Ascona, Switz. ... 33 D7 46 9N 8 46 E
Ascope, Peru ... 172 B2 7 46 S 79 8W
Ascotán, Chile ... 174 A2 21 45 S 68 17W
Ascuncion, Phil. ... 81 H5 7 35N 125 45 E
Aseb, Eritrea ... 107 E5 13 0N 42 40 E
Āseda, Sweden ... 17 G9 57 10N 15 20 E
Asedjrad, Algeria ... 111 D5 24 51N 1 29 E
Aseki, Papua N. G. ... 132 D4 7 21 S 146 12 E
Asela, Ethiopia ... 107 F4 8 0N 39 0 E
Åsen, Sweden ... 16 C7 61 17N 13 50 E
Asenovgrad, Bulgaria ... 51 D8 42 1N 24 51 E
Aserradero, Mexico ... 162 C3 23 40N 105 43W
Asfeld, France ... 27 C11 49 27N 4 5 E
Asfūn el Matā'na, Egypt ... 106 B3 25 26N 32 30 E
Åsgårdstrand, Norway ... 18 E7 59 22N 10 27 E
Asgata, Cyprus ... 39 E12 34 46N 33 15 E
Ash Fork, U.S.A. ... 159 J7 35 13N 112 29W
Ash Grove, U.S.A. ... 155 G8 37 19N 93 35W
Ash Shabakah, Iraq ... 96 D4 30 49N 43 39 E
Ash Shamāl □, Lebanon ... 103 A5 34 25N 36 0 E
Ash Shāmīyah, Iraq ... 101 G11 31 55N 44 35 E
Ash Sha'rā', Si. Arabia ... 98 A4 24 16N 44 11 E
Ash Shāriqah, U.A.E. ... 97 E7 25 23N 55 26 E
Ash Sharmah, Si. Arabia ... 96 D2 28 1N 35 16 E
Ash Sharqāt, Iraq ... 101 E10 35 27N 43 16 E
Ash Sharqi, Al Jabal, Lebanon ... 103 B5 33 40N 36 10 E
Ash Shāṭi', Libya ... 108 C2 27 30N 12 30 E
Ash Shāṭi □, Libya ... 108 C2 27 30N 13 37 E
Ash Shaṭrah, Iraq ... 96 D5 31 30N 46 10 E
Ash Shawbak, Jordan ... 96 D2 30 32N 35 34 E
Ash Shawmari, J., Jordan ... 103 E5 30 35N 36 35 E
Ash Shiḥr, Yemen ... 99 D5 14 45N 49 36 E
Ash Shināfīyah, Iraq ... 96 D5 31 35N 44 39 E
Ash Shu'bah, Si. Arabia ... 96 D5 28 54N 44 44 E
Ash Shumlūl, Si. Arabia ... 96 E5 26 31N 47 20 E
Ash Shuqayq, Si. Arabia ... 98 C3 17 44N 42 1 E
Ash Shūr'a, Iraq ... 96 C4 35 58N 43 13 E
Ash Shurayf, Si. Arabia ... 96 E3 25 43N 39 14 E
Ash Shuwayfāt, Lebanon ... 103 B4 33 45N 35 30 E
Asha, Russia ... 64 D6 55 0N 57 16 E
Ashanti □, Ghana ... 113 D4 7 30N 1 30W
Ashau, Vietnam ... 86 D6 16 6N 107 22 E
Ashbourne, U.K. ... 20 D6 53 2N 1 43W
Ashburn, U.S.A. ... 152 D6 31 43N 83 39W
Ashburton, N.Z. ... 131 D6 43 53 S 171 48 E
Ashburton →, Australia ... 124 D1 21 40 S 114 56 E
Ashburton, North Branch →, N.Z. ... 131 D6 43 54 S 171 44 E
Ashburton, South Branch →, N.Z. ... 131 D6 43 54 S 171 44 E
Ashchysay, Kazakhstan ... 65 A3 43 35N 68 53 E
Ashcroft, Canada ... 142 C4 50 40N 121 20W
Ashdod, Israel ... 103 D3 31 49N 34 35 E
Ashdown, U.S.A. ... 155 J7 33 40N 94 8W
Asheboro, U.S.A. ... 149 H6 35 43N 79 49W
Åsheim, Norway ... 18 C8 61 42N 11 11 E
Ashern, Canada ... 143 C9 51 11N 98 21W
Asherton, U.S.A. ... 155 L5 28 27N 99 46W
Asheville, U.S.A. ... 149 H4 35 36N 82 33W
Ashewat, Pakistan ... 92 D3 31 22N 68 32 E
Ashewieg →, Canada ... 140 B2 54 17N 87 12W
Ashford, Australia ... 127 D5 29 15 S 151 3 E
Ashford, U.K. ... 21 F8 51 8N 0 53 E
Ashford, U.S.A. ... 152 D4 31 11N 85 14W
Ashgabat, Turkmenistan ... 66 F6 38 0N 57 50 E
Ashibetsu, Japan ... 70 C11 43 31N 142 11 E
Ashikaga, Japan ... 73 A11 36 28N 139 29 E
Ashington, U.K. ... 20 B6 55 11N 1 33W
Ashio, Japan ... 73 A11 36 38N 139 27 E
Ashizuri-Uwakai Nat. Park △, Japan ... 72 E5 32 44N 132 32 E
Ashizuri-Zaki, Japan ... 72 E5 32 44N 133 0 E
Ashkarkot, Afghan. ... 92 C2 33 3N 67 58 E
Ashkhabad = Ashgabat, Turkmenistan ... 66 F6 38 0N 57 50 E
Ắshkhāneh, Iran ... 97 B8 37 26N 56 55 E
Ashland, Ala., U.S.A. ... 152 E3 33 16N 85 50W
Ashland, Ill., U.S.A. ... 156 E7 39 53N 90 1W
Ashland, Kans., U.S.A. ... 155 G5 37 11N 99 46W
Ashland, Ky., U.S.A. ... 148 F4 38 28N 82 38W
Ashland, Mont., U.S.A. ... 158 D10 45 36N 106 16W
Ashland, Ohio, U.S.A. ... 150 F2 40 52N 82 19W
Ashland, Oreg., U.S.A. ... 158 E2 42 12N 122 43W
Ashland, Pa., U.S.A. ... 151 F8 40 45N 76 22W
Ashland, Va., U.S.A. ... 148 G7 37 46N 77 29W
Ashland, Wis., U.S.A. ... 154 B9 46 35N 90 53W
Ashley, Ill., U.S.A. ... 156 F7 38 20N 89 11W
Ashley, Ind., U.S.A. ... 157 C11 41 32N 85 4W
Ashley, N. Dak., U.S.A. ... 154 B5 46 2N 99 22W
Ashley, Pa., U.S.A. ... 151 E9 41 12N 75 55W
Ashley →, N.Z. ... 131 D7 43 17 S 172 44 E
Ashmore and Cartier Is., Australia ... 124 B3 12 14 S 123 5 E
Ashmore Reef, Australia ... 124 B3 12 14 S 123 5 E
Ashmûn, Egypt ... 106 H7 30 18N 30 55 E
Ashmyany, Belarus ... 15 J21 54 26N 25 52 E
Ashokan Reservoir, U.S.A. ... 151 E10 41 56N 74 13W
Ashqelon, Israel ... 103 D3 31 42N 34 35 E
Ashta, India ... 92 H7 23 1N 76 43 E
Ashtabula, U.S.A. ... 150 E4 41 52N 80 47W
Ashti, Maharashtra, India ... 94 D4 21 12N 78 11 E
Ashti, Maharashtra, India ... 94 E2 18 50N 75 15 E
Ashton, S. Africa ... 116 E3 33 50 S 20 5 E
Ashton, U.S.A. ... 158 D8 44 4N 111 27W
Ashuanipi, L., Canada ... 141 B6 52 45N 66 15W
Ashurst, N.Z. ... 130 G4 40 16 S 175 45 E
Ashville, Ala., U.S.A. ... 152 B3 33 50N 86 15W
Ashville, Fla., U.S.A. ... 152 E6 30 37N 83 39W
Ashville, Pa., U.S.A. ... 152 F6 40 34N 78 33W
'Āşī →, Asia ... 100 D6 36 3N 35 59 E
Asia ... 62 E11 45 0N 75 0 E
Asia, Kepulauan, Indonesia ... 83 A4 1 0N 131 13 E
Āsiā Bak, Iran ... 97 C6 35 19N 50 30 E
Asiago, Italy ... 45 C8 45 52N 11 30 E
Asidonhoppo, Suriname ... 169 C6 3 50N 55 30W
Asifabad, India ... 94 E4 19 20N 79 24 E
Asike, Indonesia ... 83 C6 6 39 S 140 24 E
Asilah, Morocco ... 110 A3 35 29N 6 0W
Asinara, Italy ... 46 A1 41 4N 8 16 E
Asinara, G. dell', Italy ... 46 A1 41 0N 8 30 E
Asino, Russia ... 66 D9 57 0N 86 0 E
Asipovichy, Belarus ... 58 F5 53 19N 28 33 E
'Asīr □, Si. Arabia ... 98 C3 18 40N 42 30 E
Asir, Ras, Somali Rep. ... 120 B4 11 55N 51 10 E
Aska, India ... 94 E7 19 2N 84 42 E
Aşkale, Turkey ... 101 C9 39 55N 40 41 E
Askersund, Sweden ... 17 E8 58 53N 14 55 E
Askham, S. Africa ... 116 D3 26 59 S 20 47 E
Askim, Norway ... 18 E7 59 35N 11 10 E
Askja, Iceland ... 11 B10 65 3N 16 48W
Askøy, Norway ... 18 C2 60 29N 5 10 E
Askvoll, Norway ... 18 B1 61 21N 5 4 E
Asl, Egypt ... 106 B3 29 25N 32 53 E
Aslan Burnu, Turkey ... 49 C8 38 44N 26 45 E
Aslanapa, Turkey ... 49 B11 39 13N 29 40 E
Āsmār, Afghan. ... 91 B3 35 10N 71 27 E
Asmera = Asmara, Eritrea ... 107 D4 15 19N 38 55 E
Asmera, Eritrea ... 107 D4 15 19N 38 55 E
Åsnen, Sweden ... 17 H8 56 37N 14 45 E
Asni, Morocco ... 110 B3 31 17N 7 58W
Aso, Japan ... 72 E3 32 55N 131 5 E
Aso Kuju Nat. Park △, Japan ... 72 E3 32 53N 131 6 E
Aso-Zan, Japan ... 72 E3 32 53N 131 6 E
Asola, Italy ... 44 C7 45 13N 10 24 E

Asosa, Ethiopia ... 107 E3 10 3N 34 32 E
Asoteriba, Jebel, Sudan ... 106 C4 21 51N 36 30 E
Aspatria, U.K. ... 20 C4 54 47N 3 19W
Aspe, Spain ... 41 G4 38 20N 0 40W
Aspen, U.S.A. ... 159 G10 39 11N 106 49W
Aspendos, Turkey ... 100 D4 36 54N 31 7 E
Aspermont, U.S.A. ... 155 J4 33 8N 100 14W
Aspet, France ... 28 E4 43 1N 0 48 E
Aspiring, Mt., N.Z. ... 131 E3 44 23 S 168 46 E
Aspres-sur-Buëch, France ... 29 D9 44 32N 5 44 E
Aspromonte, Italy ... 47 D9 38 10N 15 8 E
Aspromonte, Parco Nazionale dell' △, Italy ... 47 D8 38 9N 15 58 E
Aspur, India ... 92 H6 23 58N 73 57 E
Asquith, Canada ... 143 C7 52 8N 107 13W
Assa, Morocco ... 110 C3 28 35N 9 6W
Assab = Aseb, Eritrea ... 107 E5 13 0N 42 40 E
Assâba, Massif de l', Mauritania ... 112 B2 16 10N 11 45W
Assagny, Parc Nat. d' △, Ivory C. ... 112 D4 5 10N 4 48W
Assaikio, Nigeria ... 113 D6 8 34N 8 55 E
Assal, L., Djibouti ... 107 E5 11 40N 42 26 E
Assam □, India ... 90 B4 26 0N 93 0 E
Assamakka, Niger ... 113 B6 19 21N 5 38 E
Assateague Island Nat. Seashore △, U.S.A. ... 148 F8 38 15N 75 10W
Assaye, India ... 94 D2 20 15N 75 34 E
Asse, Belgium ... 24 D4 50 24N 4 10 E
Assekrem, Algeria ... 111 D6 23 16N 5 49 E
Assémini, Italy ... 46 C1 39 17N 9 0 E
Assen, Neths. ... 24 A6 53 0N 6 35 E
Assens, Denmark ... 17 J3 55 16N 9 55 E
Assini, Ivory C. ... 112 D4 5 9N 3 17W
Assiniboia, Canada ... 143 D7 49 40N 105 59W
Assiniboine →, Canada ... 143 D9 49 53N 97 8 E
Assiniboine, Mt., Canada ... 142 C5 50 52N 115 39W
Assiou, Algeria ... 111 D6 21 57N 7 36 E
Assis, Brazil ... 175 A5 22 40 S 50 20W
Assis Brasil, Brazil ... 172 C4 10 55 S 69 32W
Assisi, Italy ... 45 E9 43 4N 12 37 E
Åsskard, Norway ... 18 A5 63 1N 8 30 E
Assok Ngoum, Gabon ... 114 B2 1 45N 11 39 E
Ássos, Greece ... 39 C2 38 22N 20 33 E
Assumption, U.S.A. ... 156 E7 39 31N 89 3W
Assynt, L., U.K. ... 22 C3 58 10N 5 3W
Astaffort, France ... 28 D4 44 4N 0 40 E
Astakidha, Greece ... 49 F8 35 53N 26 50 E
Astakós, Greece ... 39 B3 38 32N 21 5 E
Astana, Kazakhstan ... 66 D8 51 10N 71 30 E
Åstäneh, Iran ... 97 B6 37 17N 49 59 E
Astara, Azerbaijan ... 97 B6 38 30N 48 50 E
Åstârā, Iran ... 101 C13 38 30N 48 52 E
Asterousia, Greece ... 39 F6 34 59N 25 3 E
Asti, Italy ... 44 D5 44 54N 8 12 E
Astipálaia, Greece ... 49 E8 36 32N 26 22 E
Astola I., Pakistan ... 91 D1 25 7N 63 51 E
Astorga, Phil. ... 81 H5 6 54N 125 27 E
Astorga, Spain ... 42 C4 42 29N 6 8W
Astoria, Ill., U.S.A. ... 156 D6 40 14N 90 21W
Astoria, Oreg., U.S.A. ... 160 D3 46 11N 123 50W
Åstorp, Sweden ... 17 H6 56 6N 12 57 E
Astrakhan, Russia ... 61 G8 46 25N 48 5 E
Astudillo, Spain ... 42 C6 42 12N 4 22W
Asturias □, Spain ... 42 B5 43 15N 6 0W
Asturias ✕ (OVD), Spain ... 42 B4 43 33N 6 3W
Asunción, Bolivia ... 172 C1 11 46 S 67 50W
Asunción, Paraguay ... 174 B4 25 10 S 57 30W
Asunción Nochixtlán, Mexico ... 163 D5 17 28N 97 14W
Åsunden, Sweden ... 17 F9 58 0N 15 51 E
Asutri, Sudan ... 107 D4 15 25N 35 45 E
Aswa →, Uganda ... 118 B3 3 43N 31 55 E
Aswa-Lolim Game Reserve △, Uganda ... 118 B3 2 43N 31 35 E
Aswad, Ra's al, Si. Arabia ... 98 B2 21 20N 39 0 E
Aswān, Egypt ... 106 C3 24 4N 32 57 E
Aswân High Dam = Sadd el Aali, Egypt ... 106 C3 23 54N 32 54 E
Asyût, Egypt ... 106 B3 27 11N 31 4 E
Asyûtî, Wadi →, Egypt ... 106 B3 27 11N 31 16 E
Aszód, Hungary ... 52 C4 47 39N 19 28 E
At-Bashy, Kyrgyzstan ... 65 C7 41 10N 75 48 E
At-Bashy Kyrka Tooloru, Kyrgyzstan ... 65 C7 40 50N 75 30 E
At Ṭafīlah, Jordan ... 103 E4 30 45N 35 30 E
At Ṭafīlah □, Jordan ... 103 E4 30 45N 35 30 E
At Ṭā'if, Si. Arabia ... 98 B3 21 5N 40 27 E
At Tāj, Libya ... 108 D4 24 17N 23 18 E
At Tamīmī, Libya ... 108 B4 32 20N 23 4 E
At Ṭirāq, Si. Arabia ... 96 E5 27 19N 44 33 E
At Tubayq, Si. Arabia ... 96 D3 29 30N 37 0 E
At Turbah, Yemen ... 98 D4 13 14N 44 52 E
Atabey, Turkey ... 49 D12 37 57N 30 39 E
Atacama □, Chile ... 174 B2 27 30 S 70 0W
Atacama, Desierto de, Chile ... 174 A2 24 0 S 69 20W
Atacama, Salar de, Chile ... 174 A2 23 30 S 68 20W
Ataco, Colombia ... 168 C2 3 35N 75 23W
Atakor, Algeria ... 111 D6 23 27N 5 31 E
Atakpamé, Togo ... 113 D5 7 31N 1 13 E
Atalaia do Norte, Brazil ... 168 D3 4 20 S 70 12W
Atalándi, Greece ... 48 C4 38 39N 22 58 E
Atalaya, Peru ... 172 C3 10 45 S 73 50W
Atalaya de Femes, Canary Is. ... 9 e2 28 56N 13 47W
Ataléia, Brazil ... 171 E3 18 3 S 41 6W
Atambua, Indonesia ... 82 C2 9 7 S 124 54 E
Atami, Japan ... 73 B11 35 5N 139 4 E
Atankawng, Burma ... 92 C2 9 15N 124 1 E
Atâr, Mauritania ... 110 D2 20 30N 13 5W
Ataram, Erg n-, Algeria ... 111 D5 23 57N 2 0 E
Atarfe, Spain ... 43 H7 37 13N 3 40W
Atari, Pakistan ... 92 D6 30 56N 74 2 E
Atascadero, U.S.A. ... 161 K6 35 29N 120 40W
Atasu, Kazakhstan ... 66 E8 48 30N 71 0 E
Atatürk, Istanbul ✕ (IST), Turkey ... 51 F12 40 59N 28 49 E
Atatürk Baraji, Turkey ... 101 D8 37 28N 38 30 E
Atauro, E. Timor ... 82 C3 8 10 S 125 30 E
'Atbara, Sudan ... 106 D3 17 42N 33 59 E
'Atbara, Nahr →, Sudan ... 106 D3 17 40N 33 56 E
Atbasar, Kazakhstan ... 66 D7 51 48N 68 20 E
Atbashi = At-Bashy, Kyrgyzstan ... 65 C7 41 10N 75 48 E
Atça, Turkey ... 49 D10 37 53N 28 13 E
Atchafalaya B., U.S.A. ... 155 L9 29 25N 91 25W
Atchison, U.S.A. ... 154 F7 39 34N 95 7W
Atebubu, Ghana ... 113 D4 7 47N 1 0W
Ateca, Spain ... 40 D3 41 20N 1 49W
Aterno →, Italy ... 45 F10 42 11N 13 51 E
Ateshān, Iran ... 97 C7 35 35N 52 37 E
Atesine, Alpi, Italy ... 45 B8 46 55N 11 30 E
Atessa, Italy ... 45 F11 42 4N 14 27 E
Atfih, Egypt ... 106 J7 29 25N 31 15 E
Ath, Belgium ... 24 D3 50 38N 3 47 E
Athabasca, Canada ... 142 C6 54 45N 113 20W
Athabasca →, Canada ... 143 B6 58 40N 110 50W
Athabasca, L., Canada ... 143 B7 59 15N 109 15W
Athabasca Sand Dunes Prov. Park △, Canada ... 143 B7 59 4N 108 43W
Athagarh, India ... 94 D7 20 30N 85 37 E
Athboy, Ireland ... 23 C5 53 37N 6 56W
Athenry, Ireland ... 23 C3 53 18N 8 44W
Athens = Athínai, Greece ... 48 D5 37 58N 23 46 E
Athens, Ala., U.S.A. ... 149 H2 34 48N 86 58W
Athens, Ga., U.S.A. ... 152 B6 33 57N 83 23W

Athens, N.Y., U.S.A. ... 151 D11 42 16N 73 49W
Athens, Ohio, U.S.A. ... 148 F4 39 20N 82 6W
Athens, Pa., U.S.A. ... 151 E8 41 57N 76 31W
Athens, Tenn., U.S.A. ... 149 H3 35 27N 84 36W
Athens, Tex., U.S.A. ... 155 J7 32 12N 95 51W
Athens International ✈ (ATH),
  Greece ... 48 D5 37 52N 23 45 E
Athéras, Greece ... 39 C1 38 19N 20 25 E
Atherley, Canada ... 150 B5 44 37N 79 20W
Atherton, Australia ... 126 B4 17 17 S 145 30 E
Athiéme, Benin ... 113 D5 6 37N 1 40 E
Athienou, Cyprus ... 39 E9 35 3N 33 32 E
Athínai, Greece ... 48 D5 37 58N 23 46 E
Athlone, Ireland ... 23 C4 53 25N 7 56W
Athmallik, India ... 94 D7 20 43N 84 32 E
Athna, Cyprus ... 39 E9 35 3N 33 47 E
Athni, India ... 94 F2 16 44N 75 6 E
Athol, N.Z. ... 131 F3 45 30 S 168 35 E
Athol, U.S.A. ... 151 D12 42 36N 72 14W
Athol Is., Bahamas ... 9 b 25 5N 77 16W
Atholl, Forest of, U.K. ... 22 E5 56 51N 3 50W
Atholl, Kap, Greenland ... 10 B4 76 25N 69 30W
Atholville, Canada ... 141 C6 47 59N 66 43W
Áthos, Greece ... 51 F8 40 9N 24 22 E
Athy, Ireland ... 23 C5 53 0N 7 0W
Ati, Chad ... 109 F3 13 13N 18 20 E
Ati, Sudan ... 107 E2 13 5N 29 2 E
Atiak, Uganda ... 118 B3 3 12N 32 2 E
Atiamuri, N.Z. ... 130 E5 38 24 S 176 5 E
Atico, Peru ... 172 D3 16 14 S 73 40W
Atienza, Spain ... 40 D2 41 12N 2 52W
Atiñ, Sudan ... 107 F3 6 10N 30 35 E
Atik L., Canada ... 143 B9 55 15N 96 0W
Atikaki Prov. Wilderness Park △,
  Canada ... 143 C9 51 30N 95 31W
Atikameg ➤, Canada ... 140 B3 52 30N 82 46W
Atikokan, Canada ... 140 C1 48 45N 91 37W
Atikonak L., Canada ... 141 B7 52 40N 64 32W
Atimonan, Phil. ... 80 D3 14 0N 121 55 E
'Atinah, W., Oman ... 99 C6 18 23N 53 28 E
Atirampattinam, India ... 95 J4 10 28N 79 20 E
Atitlán, Parque Nac. △, Cent. Amer. ... 163 E6 14 38N 91 10W
Atka, Russia ... 67 C16 60 50N 151 48 E
Atka, U.S.A. ... 144 K4 52 12N 174 12W
Atka I., U.S.A. ... 144 K4 52 7N 174 30W
Atkarsk, Russia ... 60 E7 51 55N 45 2 E
Atkasuk = Meade River, U.S.A. ... 144 A8 70 28N 157 24W
Atkinson, Ga., U.S.A. ... 152 D8 31 13N 81 47W
Atkinson, Ill., U.S.A. ... 156 C6 41 25N 90 1W
Atkinson, Nebr., U.S.A. ... 154 D5 42 32N 98 59W
Atlanta, Ga., U.S.A. ... 152 B5 33 45N 84 23W
Atlanta, Ill., U.S.A. ... 156 D7 40 16N 89 14W
Atlanta, Mo., U.S.A. ... 156 E4 39 54N 92 29W
Atlanta, Tex., U.S.A. ... 155 J7 33 7N 94 10W
Atlanta Hartsfield International ✈
  (ATL), U.S.A. ... 152 B5 33 38N 84 26W
Atlantic, U.S.A. ... 156 C2 41 24N 95 1W
Atlantic Beach, U.S.A. ... 152 E8 30 20N 81 24W
Atlantic City, U.S.A. ... 148 F8 39 21N 74 27W
Atlantic-Indian Ridge, Atl. Oc. ... 8 M11 53 0 S 5 0W
Atlantic Ocean ... 8 E8 0 0N 20 0W
Atlántico □, Colombia ... 168 A4 10 45N 75 0W
Atlas Mts. = Haut Atlas, Morocco ... 110 B4 32 30N 5 0W
Atlin, Canada ... 142 B2 59 31N 133 41W
Atlin, L., Canada ... 142 B2 59 26N 133 45W
Atlin Prov. Park △, Canada ... 142 B2 59 10N 134 30W
Atløyna, Norway ... 18 C1 61 21N 4 58 E
Atmakur, Andhra Pradesh, India ... 94 E4 18 45N 78 39 E
Atmakur, Andhra Pradesh, India ... 95 G4 14 37N 79 40 E
Atmakur, Andhra Pradesh, India ... 95 G4 15 53N 78 35 E
Atmore, U.S.A. ... 149 K2 31 2N 87 29W
Atna, Norway ... 18 C7 61 44N 10 49 E
Atna ➤, Norway ... 18 C7 61 44N 10 49 E
Atō, Japan ... 72 C3 34 25N 131 40 E
Atocha, Bolivia ... 172 E4 20 56 S 66 14W
Atok, Phil. ... 80 C3 16 35N 120 41 E
Atoka, U.S.A. ... 155 H6 34 23N 96 8W
Átokos Nisís, Greece ... 39 C2 38 26N 20 49 E
Atolia, U.S.A. ... 161 K9 35 19N 117 37W
Atong-Bakari, C.A.R. ... 114 A4 5 49N 21 35 E
Atori, Solomon Is. ... 133 M11 8 42 S 160 59 E
Atrå, Norway ... 18 E5 59 59N 8 45 E
Atrai ➤, Bangla. ... 90 C2 24 7N 89 22 E
Atrak = Atrek ➤, Turkmenistan ... 97 B8 37 35N 53 58 E
Åtran, Sweden ... 17 G6 57 7N 12 57 E
Åtran ➤, Sweden ... 17 H6 56 53N 12 30 E
Atrato ➤, Colombia ... 168 B2 8 17N 76 58W
Atrauli, India ... 92 E8 28 2N 78 20 E
Atrek ➤, Turkmenistan ... 97 B8 37 35N 53 58 E
Atri, Italy ... 45 F10 42 35N 13 58 E
Atsiki, Greece ... 49 B7 39 56N 25 13 E
Atsoum, Mts., Cameroon ... 113 D7 6 41N 12 57 E
Atsugi, Japan ... 73 B11 35 25N 139 21 E
Atsumi, Japan ... 73 C9 34 35N 137 1 E
Atsumi-Wan, Japan ... 73 C9 34 44N 137 13 E
Atsuta, Japan ... 70 C10 43 24N 141 26 E
Atsy, Indonesia ... 83 C5 5 48 S 138 20 E
Attalla, U.S.A. ... 152 A3 34 1N 86 6W
Attapu, Laos ... 86 E6 14 48N 106 50 E
Attapulgus, U.S.A. ... 152 E5 30 45N 84 29W
Attáviros, Greece ... 38 E11 36 12N 27 50 E
Attawapiskat, Canada ... 140 B3 52 56N 82 24W
Attawapiskat ➤, Canada ... 140 B3 52 57N 82 18W
Attawapiskat L., Canada ... 140 B2 52 18N 87 54W
Attersee, Austria ... 34 D6 47 55N 13 32 E
Attica, Ind., U.S.A. ... 157 D9 40 18N 87 15W
Attica, Ohio, U.S.A. ... 150 E2 41 4N 82 53W
Attichy, France ... 27 C10 49 25N 3 3 E
Attigny, France ... 27 C11 49 28N 4 35 E
Attikí □, Greece ... 48 D5 37 10N 23 40 E
Attikamagen L., Canada ... 141 B6 55 0N 66 30W
Attikí □, Greece ... 48 D5 37 10N 23 40 E
Attleboro, U.S.A. ... 151 E13 41 57N 71 17W
Attock, Pakistan ... 92 C5 33 52N 72 20 E
Attopeu = Attapu, Laos ... 86 E6 14 48N 106 50 E
Attu, U.S.A. ... 144 K1 52 56N 173 15 E
Attu I., U.S.A. ... 144 K1 52 55N 172 55 E
Attunga, Australia ... 129 A9 30 55 S 150 50 E
Attur, India ... 95 J4 11 35N 78 30 E
'Atūd, Yemen ... 99 D5 14 53N 48 10 E
Atuel ➤, Argentina ... 174 D2 36 17 S 66 50W
Åtvidaberg, Sweden ... 17 F10 58 12N 16 0 E
Atwater, U.S.A. ... 160 H6 37 21N 120 37W
Atwood, Canada ... 150 C3 43 40N 81 1W
Atwood, Ill., U.S.A. ... 157 E8 39 48N 88 28W
Atwood, Kans., U.S.A. ... 154 F4 39 48N 101 3W
Atyraū, Kazakhstan ... 53 F9 47 5N 52 0 E
Au, Austria ... 34 E3 47 19N 9 59 E
Au Sable ➤, U.S.A. ... 150 B1 44 25N 83 20W
Au Sable ➤, U.S.A. ... 148 C4 44 25N 83 20W
Au Sable Forks, U.S.A. ... 151 B11 44 27N 73 41W
Au Sable Pt., U.S.A. ... 150 B1 44 20N 83 20W
Aubagne, France ... 29 E9 43 17N 5 37 E
Aubarca, C. d', Spain ... 38 C1 39 4N 1 22 E
Aube □, France ... 27 D11 48 15N 4 10 E
Aube ➤, France ... 27 D10 48 34N 3 43 E
Aubenas, France ... 29 D8 44 37N 4 24 E
Aubenton, France ... 27 C11 49 50N 4 12 E
Auberry, U.S.A. ... 160 H7 37 7N 119 29W
Aubigny-sur-Nère, France ... 27 E9 47 30N 2 24 E
Aubin, France ... 28 D6 44 33N 2 15 E
Aubrac, Mts. d', France ... 28 D7 44 40N 3 2 E
Auburn, Australia ... 128 C3 34 1 S 138 42 E
Auburn, Ala., U.S.A. ... 152 C4 32 36N 85 29W

Auburn, Calif., U.S.A. ... 160 G5 38 54N 121 4W
Auburn, Ill., U.S.A. ... 156 E7 39 36N 89 45W
Auburn, Ind., U.S.A. ... 157 C11 41 22N 85 4W
Auburn, Maine, U.S.A. ... 149 C10 44 6N 70 14W
Auburn, N.Y., U.S.A. ... 151 D8 42 56N 76 34W
Auburn, Nebr., U.S.A. ... 154 E7 40 23N 95 51W
Auburn, Wash., U.S.A. ... 160 C4 47 18N 122 14W
Auburn Ra., Australia ... 127 D5 25 15 S 150 30 E
Auburndale, U.S.A. ... 153 G8 28 4N 81 48W
Aubusson, France ... 28 C6 45 57N 2 11 E
Auce, Latvia ... 54 B9 56 28N 22 53 E
Auch, France ... 28 E4 43 39N 0 36 E
Auchi, Nigeria ... 113 D6 7 6N 6 13 E
Auchterarder, U.K. ... 22 E5 56 18N 3 41W
Auchtermuchty, U.K. ... 22 E5 56 18N 3 13W
Auckland, N.Z. ... 130 C3 36 52 S 174 46 E
Auckland □, N.Z. ... 130 E6 36 50 S 175 0 E
Auckland Is., Pac. Oc. ... 124 N8 50 40 S 166 5 E
Aude □, France ... 28 E6 43 8N 2 28 E
Aude ➤, France ... 28 E7 43 13N 3 14 E
Audegle, Somali Rep. ... 120 D2 1 59N 44 50 E
Auden, Canada ... 140 B2 50 14N 87 53W
Auderville, France ... 26 C5 49 43N 1 57W
Audierne, France ... 26 D2 48 1N 4 34W
Audincourt, France ... 27 E13 47 30N 6 50 E
Audo, Ethiopia ... 107 F5 6 20N 41 50 E
Audubon, U.S.A. ... 156 C2 41 43N 94 56W
Auerbach, Germany ... 30 E8 50 35N 12 41 E
Auerbach, Germany ... 30 E8 50 30N 12 24 E
Aueti Paraná ➤, Brazil ... 168 D4 1 51 S 65 37W
Aufist, W. Sahara ... 110 C2 25 44N 14 39W
Augathella, Australia ... 127 D4 25 48 S 146 35 E
Aughnacloy, U.K. ... 23 B5 54 25N 6 59W
Augrabies Falls, S. Africa ... 116 D3 28 35 S 20 20 E
Augrabies Falls Nat. Park △,
  S. Africa ... 116 D3 28 40 S 20 22 E
Augsburg, Germany ... 31 G6 48 25N 10 52 E
Augsburg-Westliche Wälder,
  Naturpark △, Germany ... 31 G6 48 22N 10 40 E
Augusta, Australia ... 125 F2 34 19 S 115 9 E
Augusta, Italy ... 47 E8 37 13N 15 13 E
Augusta, Ark., U.S.A. ... 155 H9 35 17N 91 22W
Augusta, Ga., U.S.A. ... 152 B8 33 28N 81 58W
Augusta, Ill., U.S.A. ... 156 D6 40 14N 90 57W
Augusta, Kans., U.S.A. ... 155 G6 37 41N 96 59W
Augusta, Ky., U.S.A. ... 157 F12 38 47N 84 0W
Augusta, Maine, U.S.A. ... 139 D13 44 19N 69 47W
Augusta, Mont., U.S.A. ... 158 C7 47 30N 112 24W
Augustenborg, Denmark ... 17 K3 54 57N 9 53 E
Augustine I., U.S.A. ... 144 G9 59 22N 153 26W
Augusto Cardosa = Metangula,
  Mozam. ... 119 E3 12 40 S 34 50 E
Augustów, Poland ... 54 E9 53 51N 23 0 E
Augustus, Mt., Australia ... 125 D2 24 20 S 116 50 E
Augustus I., Australia ... 124 C3 15 20 S 124 30 E
Aukan, Eritrea ... 107 D5 15 29N 40 50 E
Auki, Solomon Is. ... 133 M11 8 45 S 160 42 E
Aukra, Norway ... 18 B3 62 47N 6 55 E
Aukrug, Naturpark △, Germany ... 30 A5 54 5N 9 45 E
Aukum, U.S.A. ... 160 G6 38 34N 120 43W
Aul, India ... 94 D8 20 41N 86 39 E
Auld, L., Australia ... 124 D3 22 25 S 123 50 E
Aulla, Italy ... 44 D6 44 12N 9 58 E
Aulnay, France ... 28 B3 46 2N 0 22W
Aulne ➤, France ... 26 D2 48 17N 4 16W
Aulnoye-Aymeries, France ... 27 B10 50 12N 3 50 E
Ault, France ... 26 B8 50 8N 1 26 E
Ault, U.S.A. ... 154 E2 40 35N 104 44W
Aulus-les-Bains, France ... 28 F5 42 49N 1 19 E
'Aunu'u, Amer. Samoa ... 133 X24 14 20 S 170 31W
Auponhia, Indonesia ... 82 B3 1 58 S 125 27 E
Aups, France ... 29 E10 43 37N 6 15 E
Aur, Pulau, Malaysia ... 87 L5 2 35N 104 10 E
Aura, Burma ... 90 B6 26 59N 97 57 E
Auraiya, India ... 93 F8 26 28N 79 33 E
Aurangabad, Bihar, India ... 93 G11 24 45N 84 18 E
Aurangabad, Maharashtra, India ... 94 E2 19 50N 75 23 E
Auray, France ... 26 E4 47 40N 2 59W
Aurdal, Norway ... 18 D6 60 55N 9 26 E
Aure, Norway ... 18 A5 63 16N 8 33 E
Aurès, Algeria ... 111 A6 35 8N 6 30 E
Aurich, Germany ... 30 B3 53 28N 7 28 E
Aurilândia, Brazil ... 171 E1 16 44 S 50 28W
Aurillac, France ... 28 D6 44 55N 2 26 E
Aurlandsfjorden, Norway ... 18 C4 61 3N 7 1 E
Aurlandsvangen, Norway ... 18 D4 60 55N 7 12 E
Auronzo di Cadore, Italy ... 45 B9 46 33N 12 26 E
Aurora = Maéwo, Vanuatu ... 133 E6 15 10 S 168 10 E
Aurora, Canada ... 150 C5 44 0N 79 28W
Aurora = San Francisco, Phil. ... 80 E4 13 21N 122 31 E
Aurora, Isabela, Phil. ... 80 C3 16 59N 121 38 E
Aurora, Zamboanga del S., Phil. ... 81 H4 7 57 S 123 36 E
Aurora, S. Africa ... 116 E2 32 40 S 18 29 E
Aurora, Colo., U.S.A. ... 154 F2 39 44N 104 52W
Aurora, Ill., U.S.A. ... 157 C8 41 45N 88 19W
Aurora, Mo., U.S.A. ... 155 G8 36 58N 93 43W
Aurora, N.Y., U.S.A. ... 151 D8 42 45N 76 42W
Aurora, Nebr., U.S.A. ... 154 E6 40 52N 98 0W
Aurora, Ohio, U.S.A. ... 150 E3 41 21N 81 20W
Aurora Memorial Nat. Park △, Phil. ... 80 D3 15 30N 121 30 E
Aurora Memorial Nat. Park △, Phil. ... 80 D3 15 40N 121 20 E
Aursmoen, Norway ... 18 E8 59 55N 11 26 E
Aursunden, Norway ... 18 B8 62 40N 11 40 E
Aurukun, Australia ... 126 A3 13 20 S 141 45 E
Aus, Namibia ... 116 D2 26 35 S 16 12 E
Ausa, India ... 94 E3 18 15N 76 30 E
Ausable ➤, Canada ... 150 C3 43 19N 81 46W
Auschwitz = Oświęcim, Poland ... 55 H6 50 2N 19 11 E
Aust-Agder □, Norway ... 18 F4 58 45N 8 0 E
Austad, Norway ... 18 F4 58 58N 7 37 E
Austen Harbour, India ... 95 H11 12 55N 92 45 E
Austerlitz = Slavkov u Brna,
  Czech Rep. ... 35 B9 49 10N 16 52 E
Austevoll, Norway ... 18 F2 60 5N 5 13 E
Austin, Ind., U.S.A. ... 157 F11 38 45N 85 49W
Austin, Minn., U.S.A. ... 154 D8 43 40N 92 58W
Austin, Nev., U.S.A. ... 158 G5 39 30N 117 4W
Austin, Pa., U.S.A. ... 150 E6 41 38N 78 6W
Austin, Tex., U.S.A. ... 155 K6 30 17N 97 45W
Austin, L., Australia ... 125 E2 27 40 S 118 0 E
Austin I., Canada ... 143 A10 61 10N 94 0W
Austins, Norway ... 18 D9 60 6N 12 21 E
Austnes, Norway ... 18 B3 62 38N 6 16 E
Austra, Norway ... 14 D14 65 8N 11 55 E
Austral Is. = Tubuai Is., Pac. Oc. ... 135 K13 25 0 S 150 0W
Austral Seamount Chain, Pac. Oc. ... 135 K13 24 0 S 150 0W
Australia ■, Oceania ... 122 E5 23 0 S 135 0 E
Australian Capital Territory □,
  Australia ... 129 C8 35 30 S 149 0 E
Australind, Australia ... 125 F2 33 17 S 115 42 E
Austria ■, Europe ... 34 E7 47 0N 14 0 E
Austvågøy, Norway ... 14 B16 68 20N 14 40 E
Autazes, Brazil ... 169 D6 3 35 S 59 8W

Auterive, France ... 28 E5 43 21N 1 29 E
Authie ➤, France ... 27 B8 50 22N 1 38 E
Authon-du-Perche, France ... 26 D7 48 12N 0 54 E
Autlán, Mexico ... 162 D4 19 40N 104 30W
Autun, France ... 27 F11 46 58N 4 17 E
Auvergne, France ... 28 C7 45 20N 3 15 E
Auvergne, Mts. d', France ... 28 C6 45 20N 2 55 E
Auvézère ➤, France ... 28 C4 45 12N 0 50 E
Auxerre, France ... 27 E10 47 48N 3 32 E
Auxi-le-Château, France ... 27 B9 50 15N 2 8 E
Auxonne, France ... 27 E12 47 10N 5 20 E
Auxvasse, France ... 156 E5 39 1N 91 54W
Auzances, France ... 27 F9 46 2N 2 30 E
Ava, Ill., U.S.A. ... 156 G7 37 53N 89 30W
Ava, Mo., U.S.A. ... 155 G8 36 57N 92 40W
Avaldsnes, Norway ... 18 E2 59 21N 5 20 E
Avallon, France ... 27 E10 47 30N 3 53 E
Avalon, U.S.A. ... 161 M8 33 21N 118 20W
Avalon Pen., Canada ... 141 C9 47 30N 53 20W
Avanavero, Suriname ... 169 C6 4 51N 57 22W
Avanigadda, India ... 95 G5 16 0N 80 56 E
Avannaarsua □, Greenland ... 10 B5 80 0N 55 0W
Avanos, Turkey ... 96 B2 38 43N 34 51 E
Avaré, Brazil ... 175 A6 23 4 S 48 58W
Ávas, Greece ... 51 F9 40 57N 25 56 E
Avawatz Mts., U.S.A. ... 161 K10 35 40N 116 30W
Avdan Daği, Turkey ... 51 F13 40 23N 29 46 E
Avdira, Greece ... 169 D6 3 10 S 5 5W
Aveiro, Brazil ... 42 E2 40 37N 8 38W
Aveiro, Portugal ... 42 E2 40 37N 8 38W
Aveiro □, Portugal ... 42 E2 40 40N 8 35W
Avej, Iran ... 97 C6 35 40N 49 15 E
Avellaneda, Argentina ... 174 C4 34 50 S 58 10W
Avellino, Italy ... 47 B7 40 54N 14 47 E
Avenal, U.S.A. ... 160 K6 36 0N 120 8W
Avenches, Switz. ... 32 C4 46 53N 7 2 E
Averøya, Norway ... 18 A4 63 0N 7 35 E
Aversa, Italy ... 47 B7 40 58N 14 12 E
Avery, U.S.A. ... 158 C6 47 15N 115 49W
Aves, Is. las, Venezuela ... 165 D6 12 0N 67 30W
Avesnes-sur-Helpe, France ... 27 B10 50 8N 3 57 E
Avesnois, Parc Naturel Régional de
  l' △, France ... 27 B10 50 10N 3 45 E
Avesta, Sweden ... 16 D10 60 9N 16 10 E
Aveyron □, France ... 28 D6 44 22N 2 45 E
Aveyron ➤, France ... 28 D5 44 5N 1 16 E
Avezzano, Italy ... 45 F10 42 2N 13 25 E
Avgó, Greece ... 38 E7 35 33N 25 37 E
Aviá Terai, Argentina ... 174 B3 26 45 S 60 50W
Aviano, Italy ... 45 B9 46 4N 12 36 E
Aviemore, U.K. ... 22 D5 57 12N 3 50W
Aviemore, L., N.Z. ... 131 E5 44 37 S 170 18 E
Avigliana, Italy ... 44 C4 45 5N 7 23 E
Avigliano, Italy ... 47 B8 40 44N 15 43 E
Avignon, France ... 29 E8 43 57N 4 50 E
Avila, Spain ... 42 E6 40 39N 4 43W
Ávila □, Spain ... 42 E6 40 30N 5 0W
Ávila, Sierra de, Spain ... 42 E5 40 40N 5 0W
Avila Beach, U.S.A. ... 161 K6 35 11N 120 44W
Avilés, Spain ... 42 B5 43 35N 5 57W
Avintes, Portugal ... 42 D2 41 7N 8 33W
Avionárion, Greece ... 48 C6 38 31N 24 8 E
Avis, Portugal ... 43 F3 39 4N 7 53W
Avis, U.S.A. ... 150 E7 41 11N 77 19W
Avísio ➤, Italy ... 44 B8 46 7N 11 5 E
Avissawella, Sri Lanka ... 95 L5 6 56N 80 11 E
Aviston, U.S.A. ... 156 F7 38 36N 89 36W
Aviz = Avis, Portugal ... 43 F3 39 4N 7 53W
Avize, France ... 27 D11 48 59N 4 1 E
Avlum, Denmark ... 17 H2 56 16N 8 47 E
Avoca, Australia ... 128 D5 37 5 S 143 26 E
Avoca, U.S.A. ... 150 D7 42 25N 77 25W
Avoca ➤, Australia ... 128 C5 35 40 S 143 43 E
Avoca ➤, Ireland ... 23 D5 52 48N 6 10W
Avola, Canada ... 142 C5 51 45N 119 19W
Avola, Italy ... 47 E8 36 56N 15 7 E
Avon, Ill., U.S.A. ... 156 D6 40 40N 90 26W
Avon, N.Y., U.S.A. ... 150 D7 42 55N 77 45W
Avon ➤, Australia ... 125 F2 31 40 S 116 7 E
Avon ➤, Bristol, U.K. ... 21 F5 51 29N 2 41W
Avon ➤, Dorset, U.K. ... 21 G6 50 44N 1 46W
Avon ➤, Warks., U.K. ... 21 E6 52 0N 2 8W
Avon Park, U.S.A. ... 153 H8 27 36N 81 31W
Avondale, Zimbabwe ... 119 F3 17 43 S 30 58 E
Avonlea, Canada ... 143 D8 50 0N 105 0W
Avonmore, Canada ... 151 A10 45 10N 74 58W
Avonmouth, U.K. ... 21 F5 51 30N 2 42W
Avramov, Bulgaria ... 51 D10 42 45N 26 38 E
Avranches, France ... 26 D5 48 40N 1 20W
Avre ➤, France ... 26 D8 48 47N 1 22 E
Avrig, Romania ... 53 E9 45 43N 24 21 E
Avrillé, France ... 26 E6 47 30N 0 35W
Avtovac, Bos.-H. ... 50 C2 43 9N 18 35 E
Avu Avu, Solomon Is. ... 133 M11 9 50 S 160 22 E
Awag el Baqar, Sudan ... 107 E3 10 10N 33 10 E
A'waj ➤, Syria ... 103 B5 33 23N 36 20 E
Awaji, Japan ... 73 C7 34 32N 135 1 E
Awaji-Shima, Japan ... 72 C6 34 30N 134 50 E
'Awālī, Bahrain ... 97 E6 26 0N 50 30 E
Awantipur, India ... 93 C6 33 55N 75 3 E
Awanui, N.Z. ... 130 B2 35 4 S 173 17 E
Awarja ➤, India ... 94 F3 17 5N 76 15 E
Awarua B., N.Z. ... 131 E3 44 28 S 168 1 E
Awarua Pt., N.Z. ... 131 E3 44 15 S 168 5 E
Awasa, Ethiopia ... 107 F4 7 2N 38 28 E
Awasa, L., Ethiopia ... 107 F4 7 0N 38 30 E
Awash, Ethiopia ... 107 F5 9 1N 40 10 E
Awash ➤, Ethiopia ... 107 E5 11 45N 41 5 E
Awash Nat. Park and Reserve △,
  Ethiopia ... 107 F5 9 8N 40 0 E
Awaso, Ghana ... 112 D4 6 15N 2 22W
Awatere ➤, N.Z. ... 131 B9 41 37 S 174 10 E
Awbārī, Libya ... 108 C2 26 46N 12 57 E
Awbārī □, Libya ... 108 C2 26 35N 12 46 E
Awbārī, Idehan, Libya ... 108 C2 27 10N 11 30 E
Awe, L., U.K. ... 22 E3 56 17N 5 16W
Aweil, Sudan ... 107 F2 8 42N 27 20 E
Awgu, Nigeria ... 113 D6 6 4N 7 24 E
Awjilah, Libya ... 108 C4 29 8N 21 7 E
Awka, Nigeria ... 113 D6 6 12N 7 5 E
Aworro, Papua N. G. ... 132 D2 7 43 S 143 11 E
Ax-les-Thermes, France ... 28 F5 42 44N 1 50 E
Axat, France ... 28 F6 42 48N 2 13 E
Axe ➤, U.K. ... 21 F5 50 42N 3 4W
Axel Heiberg I., Canada ... 6 B3 80 0N 90 0W
Axim, Ghana ... 112 E4 4 51N 2 15W
Axinim, Brazil ... 169 D6 4 2 S 59 22W
Axintele, Romania ... 53 F11 44 37N 26 47 E
Axioma, Brazil ... 173 B5 6 45 S 64 31W
Axiós ➤, Greece ... 50 F6 40 57N 22 35 E
Axminster, U.K. ... 21 G4 50 46N 3 0W
Axson, U.S.A. ... 152 D7 31 17N 82 44W
Axvall, Sweden ... 17 F7 58 23N 13 34 E
Ay, France ... 27 C11 49 3N 4 1 E
Ay ➤, Russia ... 64 C6 56 8N 57 40 E
Ayabaca, Peru ... 172 A2 4 40 S 79 53W
Ayabe, Japan ... 73 B7 35 20N 135 20 E
Ayacucho, Argentina ... 174 D4 37 5 S 58 20W
Ayacucho, Peru ... 172 C3 13 0 S 74 0W
Ayaguz, Kazakhstan ... 65 C2 41 12N 65 12 E
Ayakkuduk, Uzbekistan ... 65 C2 41 12N 65 12 E
Ayakudi, India ... 95 J3 10 28N 77 56 E
Ayala, Phil. ... 81 H3 6 57N 121 57 E

Ayamé, Ivory C. ... 112 D4 5 35N 3 9W
Ayamonte, Spain ... 43 H3 37 12N 7 24W
Ayan, Russia ... 67 D14 56 30N 138 16 E
Ayancık, Turkey ... 100 B6 41 57N 34 35 E
Ayapel, Colombia ... 168 B2 8 19N 75 9W
Ayas, Turkey ... 100 B5 40 2N 32 21 E
Ayaviri, Peru ... 172 C3 14 50 S 70 35W
Aybak, Afghan. ... 91 A3 36 15N 68 5 E
Aybastı, Turkey ... 100 B7 40 41N 37 12 E
Aydarkul Ozero, Uzbekistan ... 65 C3 40 50N 67 10 E
Aydın, Turkey ... 47 D9 37 51N 27 51 E
Aydın □, Turkey ... 49 D9 37 50N 28 0 E
Aydın Dağları, Turkey ... 49 D10 37 50N 28 30 E
Aydıncık, Turkey ... 100 D5 36 15N 33 50 E
Aydrlinskiy, Russia ... 64 E7 52 3N 59 50 E
Ayelu, Ethiopia ... 107 E5 10 5N 40 42 E
Ayenngré, Togo ... 113 D5 8 40N 1 1 E
Ayer Hitam, Malaysia ... 87 c 5 24N 100 16 E
Ayerbe, Spain ... 40 C4 42 17N 0 41W
Ayer's Cliff, Canada ... 151 A12 45 10N 72 3W
Ayers Rock, Australia ... 125 E5 25 23 S 131 5 E
Ayiá, Greece ... 48 B4 39 43N 22 45 E
Ayia Aikateríni, Ákra, Greece ... 38 B9 39 50N 19 50 E
Ayia Dhéka, Greece ... 39 E5 35 3N 24 58 E
Ayia Gálini, Greece ... 39 E5 35 6N 24 41 E
Ayia Marína, Kásos, Greece ... 49 F8 35 2N 26 56 E
Ayia Marína, Léros, Greece ... 49 D8 37 11N 26 48 E
Ayia Napa, Cyprus ... 39 F10 34 59N 34 0 E
Ayia Paraskeví, Greece ... 49 B8 39 14N 26 21 E
Ayia Phyla, Cyprus ... 39 F9 34 43N 33 1 E
Ayía Rouméli, Greece ... 39 E4 35 14N 23 58 E
Ayía Varvára, Greece ... 39 E6 35 8N 25 1 E
Ayiássos, Greece ... 49 B8 39 5N 26 23 E
Áyioi Theódhoroi, Greece ... 48 D5 37 55N 23 9 E
Áyion Óros □, Greece ... 51 F8 40 25N 24 6 E
Áyios Amvrósios, Cyprus ... 39 E5 35 20N 33 35 E
Áyios Andréas, Greece ... 48 D4 37 21N 22 45 E
Áyios Evstrátios, Greece ... 49 B6 39 24N 24 58 E
Áyios Ioánnis, Ákra, Greece ... 39 E6 35 20N 25 40 E
Áyios Isídhoros, Greece ... 38 E11 36 9N 27 51 E
Áyios Kírikos, Greece ... 49 D8 37 34N 26 17 E
Áyios Léon, Greece ... 39 D2 37 47N 20 43 E
Áyios Matthaíos, Greece ... 38 C9 39 30N 19 47 E
Áyios Mírono, Greece ... 39 E6 35 15N 25 1 E
Áyios Nikólaos,
  Aitolía kai Akarnanía, Greece ... 39 B2 38 52N 20 48 E
Áyios Nikólaos, Kríti, Greece ... 39 E6 35 11N 25 41 E
Áyios Nikólaos, Levkás, Greece ... 39 B2 38 36N 20 34 E
Áyios Pétros, Greece ... 39 B2 38 40N 20 36 E
Áyios Seryios, Cyprus ... 39 E9 35 12N 33 53 E
Áyios Theodhoros, Cyprus ... 39 E10 35 22N 34 1 E
Áyios Thomás, Greece ... 39 B2 38 58N 20 47 E
Áyios Yeóryios, Greece ... 48 D5 37 28N 23 57 E
Aykathonísi, Greece ... 49 D8 37 28N 27 0 E
Aykino, Russia ... 56 B8 62 15N 49 56 E
Aykırıkçi, Turkey ... 49 B12 39 30N 30 0 E
Aylesbury, U.K. ... 21 F7 51 49N 0 49W
Aylmer, Canada ... 150 D4 42 46N 80 59W
Aylmer, L., Canada ... 138 B8 64 0N 110 8W
'Ayn, Wādī al, Oman ... 97 F7 22 15N 55 28 E
'Ayn al Ghazālah, Libya ... 108 B4 32 10N 23 20 E
Ayn Dār, Si. Arabia ... 97 E7 25 55N 49 10 E
Ayn Zālah, Iraq ... 101 D10 36 45N 42 35 E
Ayna, Spain ... 41 G2 38 34N 2 3W
Aynabulaq, Kazakhstan ... 65 A8 44 36N 77 56 E
Aynāt, Yemen ... 99 C5 16 4N 49 9 E
Ayni, Tajikistan ... 99 D5 39 23N 68 32 E
Ayod, Sudan ... 107 F3 8 N 31 26 E
Ayolas, Paraguay ... 174 B4 27 10 S 56 59W
Ayom, Sudan ... 107 F2 7 49N 28 23 E
Ayon, Ostrov, Russia ... 67 C17 69 50N 169 0 E
Ayora, Spain ... 41 F3 39 3N 1 3W
Ayorou, Niger ... 113 C5 14 53N 1 1 E
Ayos, Cameroon ... 113 B2 3 53N 12 31 E
'Ayoûn el 'Atroûs, Mauritania ... 110 D3 16 38N 9 37W
Ayr, Australia ... 126 B4 19 35 S 147 25 E
Ayr, Canada ... 150 C4 43 17N 80 27W
Ayr, U.K. ... 22 F4 55 28N 4 38W
Ayr ➤, U.K. ... 22 F4 55 28N 4 38W
Ayrancı, Turkey ... 100 D5 37 21N 33 41 E
Ayrancılar, Turkey ... 49 C9 38 15N 27 18 E
Ayre, Pt. of, U.K. ... 20 C1 54 25N 4 21W
Aysha, Ethiopia ... 107 E5 10 50N 42 23 E
Ayton, Australia ... 126 B4 15 56 S 145 22 E
Aytos, Bulgaria ... 51 D11 42 42N 27 16 E
Ayu, Kepulauan, Indonesia ... 83 A4 0 35N 131 5 E
Ayutla, Guatemala ... 164 D1 14 40N 92 10W
Ayutla, Mexico ... 163 D5 16 58N 99 17W
Ayvacık, Turkey ... 100 C2 39 36N 26 24 E
Ayvalık, Turkey ... 49 B8 39 20N 26 46 E
Az Zabadānī, Syria ... 103 B5 33 43N 36 5 E
Az Zāhirīyah, West Bank ... 103 D3 31 25N 34 58 E
Az Zahrān, Si. Arabia ... 97 E6 26 10N 50 7 E
Az Zarqā, Jordan ... 103 C5 32 5N 36 4 E
Az Zarqā, U.A.E. ... 97 E7 24 53N 53 4 E
Az Zarqā □, Jordan ... 103 C5 32 5N 36 4 E
Az Zāwiyah, Libya ... 108 B2 32 52N 12 56 E
Az Zaydīyah, Yemen ... 98 D3 15 20N 43 1 E
Az Zibār, Iraq ... 101 D11 36 52N 44 4 E
Az Zuqur, Yemen ... 98 D3 14 0N 42 45 E
Az Zubayr, Iraq ... 101 D6 30 26N 47 40 E
Az Zuwaytīnah, Libya ... 108 B4 30 58N 20 7 E
Azad Kashmir □, Pakistan ... 93 C5 33 50N 73 50 E
Azambuja, Portugal ... 43 F2 39 4N 8 51W
Azamgarh, India ... 93 F10 26 5N 83 13 E
Azángaro, Peru ... 172 C3 14 55 S 70 13W
Azaoua, Niger ... 113 B5 15 50N 4 0 E
Azaouad, Mali ... 112 B4 19 0N 3 0W
Azaouak, Vallée de l', Mali ... 113 B5 15 50N 3 20 E
Āzār Shahr, Iran ... 101 D11 37 45N 45 59 E
Azara, Nigeria ... 113 D6 8 22N 9 12 E
Azarán, Iran ... 101 D12 37 25N 47 16 E
Azärbayjan = Azerbaijan ■, Asia ... 61 K9 40 20N 48 0 E
Āzarbāyjān-e Gharbī □, Iran ... 96 B5 37 0N 44 30 E
Āzarbāyjān-e Sharqī □, Iran ... 96 B5 37 20N 47 0 E
Azare, Nigeria ... 113 C7 11 55N 10 10 E
Azay-le-Rideau, France ... 26 E7 47 16N 0 30 E
'A'zāz, Syria ... 100 D7 36 36N 37 4 E
Azbine = Aïr, Niger ... 113 B6 18 30N 8 0 E
Azeffal, Mauritania ... 110 D2 21 0N 14 45W
Azefoun, Algeria ... 111 A5 36 51N 4 26 E
Azemmour, Morocco ... 110 B3 33 20N 9 20W
Azennezal, Algeria ... 111 D5 22 58N 0 43 E
Azerbaijan ■, Asia ... 61 K9 40 20N 48 0 E
Azerbaijan = Azerbaijan ■, Asia ... 61 K9 40 20N 48 0 E
Azezo, Ethiopia ... 107 E4 12 28N 37 15 E
Azimganj, India ... 93 G13 24 14N 88 16 E
Aznalcóllar, Spain ... 43 H4 37 32N 6 17W
Azogues, Ecuador ... 172 B3 2 35 S 78 0W
Azores = Açores, Is. dos, Atl. Oc. ... 9 D1 38 0N 27 0W
Azoum ➤, Chad ... 109 F4 10 53N 20 15 E
Azov, Russia ... 61 G4 47 3N 39 25 E
Azov, Sea of, Europe ... 59 J9 46 0N 36 30 E
Azovskoye More = Azov, Sea of,
  Europe ... 59 J9 46 0N 36 30 E
Azpeitia, Spain ... 40 B2 43 12N 2 19W
Azrak, B. ➤, Chad ... 109 F4 10 52N 20 35 E
Azraq ash Shīshān, Jordan ... 103 D5 31 50N 36 49 E
Azrou, Morocco ... 110 B3 33 28N 5 19W

Aztec, *U.S.A.* **159 H10** 36 49N 107 59W
Azúa de Compostela, *Dom. Rep.* **165 C5** 18 25N 70 44W
Azuaga, *Spain* **43 G5** 38 16N 5 39W
Azuara, *Spain* **40 D4** 41 15N 0 53W
Azuay □, *Ecuador* **168 D2** 2 55 S 79 0W
Azuer →, *Spain* **43 F7** 39 8N 3 36W
Azuero, Pen. de, *Panama* **164 E3** 7 30N 80 30W
Azuga, *Romania* **53 E10** 45 27N 25 33 E
Azul, *Argentina* **174 D4** 36 42 S 59 43W
Azul, Lagoa, *Azores* **9 d3** 37 52N 25 47W
Azul, Serra, *Brazil* **173 C7** 14 50 S 54 50W
Azurduy, *Bolivia* **173 D5** 19 59 S 64 29W
Azusa, *U.S.A.* **161 L9** 34 8N 117 52W
Azzaba, *Algeria* **111 A6** 36 48N 7 6 E
Azzano Décimo, *Italy* **45 C9** 45 52N 12 56 E
Azzel Mati, Sebkra, *Algeria* **111 C5** 26 10N 0 43 E

B

Ba Be Nat. Park △, *Vietnam* **86 A5** 22 25N 105 37 E
Ba Don, *Vietnam* **86 D6** 17 45N 106 26 E
Ba Dong, *Vietnam* **87 H6** 9 40N 106 33 E
Ba Ngoi = Cam Lam, *Vietnam* **87 G7** 11 54N 109 10 E
Ba Tri, *Vietnam* **87 G6** 10 2N 106 36 E
Ba Vi Nat. Park △, *Vietnam* **86 B5** 21 1N 105 22 E
Ba Xian = Bazhou, *China* **74 E9** 39 8N 116 22 E
Baa, *Indonesia* **82 D2** 10 50 S 123 0 E
Baaba, Î., *N. Cal.* **133 T18** 20 3 S 163 59 E
Baamonde, *Spain* **42 B3** 43 7N 7 44W
Baao, *Phil.* **80 E4** 13 27N 123 22 E
Baar, *Switz.* **33 B7** 47 12N 8 32 E
Baardeere = Bardera, *Somali Rep.* **120 D2** 2 20N 42 27 E
Baarle-Nassau, *Belgium* **24 C4** 51 27N 4 56 E
Bab el Mandeb, *Red Sea* **98 D3** 12 35N 43 25 E
Baba, *Bulgaria* **50 D7** 42 44N 23 59 E
Baba, B. do, *Angola* **115 E2** 14 50 S 12 14 E
Bābā, Koh-i-, *Afghan.* **91 B2** 34 30N 67 0 E
Baba Budan Hills, *India* **95 H2** 13 30N 75 44 E
Baba Burnu, *Turkey* **49 B8** 39 29N 26 2 E
Baba dag, *Azerbaijan* **61 K9** 41 0N 48 19 E
Bābā Kalū, *Iran* **97 D6** 30 7N 50 49 E
Babaçulândia, *Brazil* **170 C2** 7 13 S 47 46W
Babadag, *Romania* **53 F13** 44 53N 28 44 E
Babadağ, *Turkey* **49 D10** 37 49N 28 52 E
Babadayhan, *Turkmenistan* **66 F7** 37 42N 60 23 E
Babaeski, *Turkey* **51 E11** 41 26N 27 6 E
Babahoyo, *Ecuador* **168 D2** 1 40 S 79 30W
Babai = Sarju →, *India* **93 F9** 27 21N 81 23 E
Babak, *Phil.* **81 H5** 7 8N 125 41 E
Babana, *Nigeria* **113 C5** 10 31N 3 46 E
Babanusa, *Sudan* **107 E2** 11 20N 27 48 E
Babar, *Algeria* **111 A6** 35 10N 7 6 E
Babar, *Indonesia* **83 C3** 8 0 S 129 30 E
Babar, *Pakistan* **92 D3** 31 7N 69 32 E
Babar, Kepulauan, *Indonesia* **83 C4** 8 0 S 131 30 E
Babarkach, *Pakistan* **92 E3** 29 45N 68 0 E
Babase I., *Papua N. G.* **132 B7** 4 0 S 153 42 E
Babayevo, *Russia* **58 C8** 59 24N 35 55 E
Babb, *U.S.A.* **158 B7** 48 51N 113 27W
Babenhausen, *Germany* **31 F4** 49 57N 8 57 E
Băbeni, *Romania* **53 F9** 44 59N 24 11 E
Baberu, *India* **93 G9** 25 33N 80 43 E
Babi Besar, Pulau, *Malaysia* **87 L4** 2 25N 103 59 E
Babia Gora, *Europe* **55 J6** 49 38N 19 38 E
Babian Jiang →, *China* **76 F3** 22 55N 101 47 E
Babile, *Ethiopia* **107 F5** 9 16N 42 11 E
Babile Elephant Sanctuary ⌓, *Ethiopia* **120 C2** 8 45N 42 20 E
Babimost, *Poland* **55 F2** 52 10N 15 49 E
Babinda, *Australia* **126 B4** 17 20 S 145 56 E
Babine, *Canada* **142 B3** 55 22N 126 37W
Babine →, *Canada* **142 B3** 55 45N 127 44W
Babine L., *Canada* **142 C3** 54 48N 126 0W
Babiogórski Park Narodowy △, *Poland* **55 J6** 49 38N 19 39 E
Babo, *Indonesia* **83 B4** 2 30 S 133 30 E
Babócsa, *Hungary* **52 D2** 46 2N 17 21 E
Bābol, *Iran* **97 B7** 36 40N 52 50 E
Bābol Sar, *Iran* **97 B7** 36 45N 52 45 E
Babor, Dj., *Algeria* **111 A6** 36 31N 5 25 E
Baborów, *Poland* **55 H5** 50 7N 18 1 E
Baboua, *C.A.R.* **114 A2** 5 49N 14 58 E
Babruysk, *Belarus* **59 F5** 53 10N 29 15 E
Babson Park, *U.S.A.* **153 H8** 27 49N 81 32W
Babuhri, *India* **92 F3** 26 49N 69 43 E
Babuna, *Macedonia* **50 E5** 41 30N 21 40 E
Babura, *Nigeria* **113 C6** 12 51N 8 59 E
Babusar Pass, *Pakistan* **93 B5** 35 12N 73 59 E
Babušnica, *Serbia, Yug.* **50 C6** 43 7N 22 27 E
Babuyan, *Phil.* **81 F2** 10 0N 118 54 E
Babuyan Chan., *Phil.* **80 B3** 18 40N 121 30 E
Babuyan I., *Phil.* **80 B3** 19 32N 121 57 E
Babuyan Is., *Phil.* **80 B3** 19 10N 121 40 E
Babylon, *Iraq* **101 F11** 32 34N 44 22 E
Bač, *Serbia, Yug.* **52 E4** 45 29N 19 17 E
Bâc →, *Moldova* **53 D14** 46 55N 29 26 E
Bac Can, *Vietnam* **76 F5** 22 8N 105 49 E
Bac Giang, *Vietnam* **76 G6** 21 16N 106 11 E
Bac Lieu, *Vietnam* **87 H5** 9 17N 105 43 E
Bac Ninh, *Vietnam* **76 G6** 21 13N 106 4 E
Bac Phan, *Vietnam* **86 B5** 22 0N 105 0 E
Bac Quang, *Vietnam* **76 F5** 22 30N 104 48 E
Bacabal, *Brazil* **170 B3** 4 15 S 44 45W
Bacacay, *Phil.* **80 E4** 13 18N 123 47 E
Bacajá →, *Brazil* **169 D7** 3 25 S 51 50W
Bacalar, *Mexico* **163 D7** 18 50N 87 27W
Bacan, *Indonesia* **82 B3** 0 50 S 127 30 E
Bacan, Kepulauan, *Indonesia* **82 B3** 0 35 S 127 30 E
Bacarra, *Phil.* **80 B3** 18 15N 120 37 E
Bacău, *Romania* **53 D11** 46 35N 26 55 E
Bacău □, *Romania* **53 D11** 46 30N 26 45 E
Baccarat, *France* **27 D13** 48 28N 6 42 E
Bacchus Marsh, *Australia* **128 D6** 37 43 S 144 27 E
Bacerac, *Mexico* **162 A3** 30 18N 108 50W
Băceşti, *Romania* **53 D12** 46 50N 27 11 E
Bach, *Austria* **33 B10** 47 16N 10 25 E
Bach Long Vi, Dao, *Vietnam* **86 B6** 20 10N 107 40 E
Bach Ma Nat. Park △, *Vietnam* **86 D6** 16 11N 107 49 E
Bachaquero, *Venezuela* **168 B3** 9 56N 71 8W
Bacharach, *Germany* **31 E3** 50 3N 7 44 E
Bachelina, *Russia* **66 D7** 57 45N 67 20 E
Bachhwara, *India* **93 G11** 25 35N 85 54 E
Bachuma, *Ethiopia* **107 F4** 6 48N 35 53 E
Bačina, *Serbia, Yug.* **50 C5** 43 42N 21 23 E
Back →, *Canada* **138 B9** 65 10N 104 0W
Bačka Palanka, *Serbia, Yug.* **52 E4** 45 17N 19 27 E
Bačka Topola, *Serbia, Yug.* **52 E4** 45 49N 19 39 E
Bäckebo, *Sweden* **17 H10** 56 53N 16 4 E
Bäckefors, *Sweden* **17 F6** 58 48N 12 9 E
Bäckhammar, *Sweden* **16 E8** 59 10N 14 11 E
Bački Petrovac, *Serbia, Yug.* **52 E4** 45 29N 19 32 E
Backnang, *Germany* **31 G5** 48 56N 9 26 E
Backstairs Passage, *Australia* **128 C3** 35 40 S 138 5 E
Baco, Mt., *Phil.* **80 E3** 12 49N 121 10 E
Bacolod, *Phil.* **81 F4** 10 40N 122 57 E
Bacon, *Phil.* **80 E5** 13 3N 124 3 E
Baconton, *U.S.A.* **152 D5** 31 23N 84 10W
Bacoor, *Phil.* **80 D3** 14 28N 120 56 E
Bacqueville-en-Caux, *France* **26 C8** 49 47N 1 0 E
Bács-Kiskun □, *Hungary* **52 D4** 46 43N 19 30 E
Bácsalmás, *Hungary* **52 D4** 46 8N 19 17 E
Bacuag = Placer, *Phil.* **81 G5** 9 36N 125 38 E
Bacuk, *Malaysia* **87 J4** 6 4N 102 25 E
Bād, *Iran* **97 C7** 33 41N 52 1 E
Bad →, *U.S.A.* **154 C4** 44 21N 100 22W
Bad Aussee, *Austria* **34 D6** 47 43N 13 45 E
Bad Axe, *U.S.A.* **150 C2** 43 48N 83 0W
Bad Bergzabern, *Germany* **31 F3** 49 6N 7 59 E
Bad Berleburg, *Germany* **30 D4** 51 2N 8 26 E
Bad Bevensen, *Germany* **30 B6** 53 5N 10 35 E
Bad Bramstedt, *Germany* **30 B5** 53 55N 9 53 E
Bad Brückenau, *Germany* **31 E5** 50 18N 9 47 E
Bad Doberan, *Germany* **30 A7** 54 6N 11 53 E
Bad Driburg, *Germany* **30 D5** 51 43N 9 1 E
Bad Ems, *Germany* **31 E3** 50 20N 7 43 E
Bad Frankenhausen, *Germany* **30 D7** 51 21N 11 5 E
Bad Freienwalde, *Germany* **30 C10** 52 46N 14 1 E
Bad Goisern, *Austria* **34 D6** 47 38N 13 38 E
Bad Harzburg, *Germany* **30 D6** 51 52N 10 34 E
Bad Hersfeld, *Germany* **30 E5** 50 52N 9 42 E
Bad Hofgastein, *Austria* **34 D6** 47 17N 13 6 E
Bad Homburg, *Germany* **31 E4** 50 13N 8 38 E
Bad Honnef, *Germany* **30 E3** 50 38N 7 13 E
Bad Iburg, *Germany* **30 C4** 52 10N 8 3 E
Bad Ischl, *Austria* **34 D6** 47 44N 13 38 E
Bad Kissingen, *Germany* **31 E6** 50 11N 10 4 E
Bad Königshofen, *Germany* **31 E6** 50 17N 10 28 E
Bad Kreuznach, *Germany* **31 F3** 49 50N 7 51 E
Bad Krozingen, *Germany* **31 H3** 47 54N 7 42 E
Bad Laasphe, *Germany* **30 E4** 50 56N 8 25 E
Bad Lands, *U.S.A.* **154 D3** 43 40N 102 10W
Bad Langensalza, *Germany* **30 D6** 51 5N 10 38 E
Bad Lauterberg, *Germany* **30 D6** 51 38N 10 28 E
Bad Leonfelden, *Austria* **34 C7** 48 31N 14 18 E
Bad Liebenwerda, *Germany* **30 D9** 51 31N 13 24 E
Bad Mergentheim, *Germany* **31 F5** 49 28N 9 42 E
Bad Münstereifel, *Germany* **30 E2** 50 33N 6 46 E
Bad Nauheim, *Germany* **31 E4** 50 21N 8 43 E
Bad Neuenahr-Ahrweiler, *Germany* **30 E3** 50 32N 7 5 E
Bad Neustadt, *Germany* **31 E6** 50 18N 10 13 E
Bad Oeynhausen, *Germany* **30 C4** 52 12N 8 46 E
Bad Oldesloe, *Germany* **30 B6** 53 48N 10 22 E
Bad Orb, *Germany* **31 E5** 50 12N 9 22 E
Bad Pyrmont, *Germany* **30 D5** 51 59N 9 16 E
Bad Ragaz, *Switz.* **33 C9** 47 0N 9 30 E
Bad Reichenhall, *Germany* **31 H8** 47 43N 12 54 E
Bad Säckingen, *Germany* **31 H3** 47 33N 7 56 E
Bad Salzuflen, *Germany* **30 C4** 52 5N 8 45 E
Bad Salzungen, *Germany* **30 E6** 50 48N 10 14 E
Bad Schwartau, *Germany* **30 B6** 53 55N 10 41 E
Bad Segeberg, *Germany* **30 B6** 53 56N 10 17 E
Bad St. Leonhard, *Austria* **34 E7** 46 58N 14 47 E
Bad Tölz, *Germany* **31 H7** 47 45N 11 34 E
Bad Urach, *Germany* **31 G5** 48 29N 9 23 E
Bad Vöslau, *Austria* **35 D9** 47 58N 16 12 E
Bad Waldsee, *Germany* **31 H5** 47 55N 9 45 E
Bad Wildungen, *Germany* **30 D5** 51 6N 9 7 E
Bad Wimpfen, *Germany* **31 F5** 49 13N 9 11 E
Bad Windsheim, *Germany* **31 F6** 49 36N 10 25 E
Bad Zwischenahn, *Germany* **30 B4** 53 12N 8 1 E
Bada Barabil, *India* **93 H11** 22 7N 85 24 E
Badagara, *India* **95 J2** 11 35N 75 40 E
Badagri, *Nigeria* **113 D5** 6 25N 2 55 E
Badajós, L., *Brazil* **169 D5** 3 15 S 62 50W
Badajoz, *Spain* **43 G4** 38 50N 6 59W
Badajoz □, *Spain* **43 G4** 38 40N 6 30W
Badakhshān □, *Afghan.* **65 E5** 36 30N 71 0 E
Badalona, *Spain* **40 D7** 41 26N 2 15 E
Badalzai, *Afghan.* **92 E1** 29 50N 65 35 E
Badami, *India* **95 G2** 15 55N 75 41 E
Badampahar, *India* **94 C8** 22 10N 86 10 E
Badanah, *Si. Arabia* **96 D4** 30 58N 41 30 E
Badarinath, *India* **93 D8** 30 45N 79 30 E
Badarpur, *India* **90 C4** 24 54N 92 36 E
Badas, Kepulauan, *Indonesia* **84 B3** 0 45N 107 5 E
Baddo →, *Pakistan* **91 D2** 28 0N 64 20 E
Bade, *Indonesia* **83 C5** 7 10 S 139 35 E
Badeggi, *Nigeria* **113 D6** 9 1N 6 8 E
Badéguichéri, *Niger* **113 C6** 14 30N 5 22 E
Baden, *Austria* **35 C9** 48 1N 16 13 E
Baden, *Switz.* **33 B6** 47 28N 8 18 E
Baden, *U.S.A.* **150 F4** 40 38N 80 14W
Baden-Baden, *Germany* **31 G4** 48 44N 8 13 E
Baden-Württemberg □, *Germany* **31 G4** 48 20N 8 40 E
Badgastein, *Austria* **34 D6** 47 7N 13 9 E
Badger, *Canada* **141 C8** 49 0N 56 4W
Badger, *U.S.A.* **160 J7** 36 38N 119 1W
Bādghīs □, *Afghan.* **91 B1** 35 0N 63 0 E
Badgingarra Nat. Park △, *Australia* **125 F2** 30 23 S 115 22 E
Badgom, *India* **93 B6** 34 1N 74 45 E
Badia Polésine, *Italy* **45 C8** 45 5N 11 29 E
Badian, *Phil.* **81 G4** 9 55N 123 24 E
Badiar, Parc Nat. du △, *Guinea* **112 C2** 13 37N 13 11W
Badin, *Pakistan* **91 D3** 24 38N 68 54 E
Badinka, Réserve du ⌓, *Mali* **112 C3** 13 31N 9 28W
Badjokola, *Dem. Rep. of the Congo* **114 B4** 3 54N 20 17 E
Badlands Nat. Park △, *U.S.A.* **154 D3** 43 38N 102 56W
Badnera, *India* **94 D3** 20 48N 77 44 E
Badoc, *Phil.* **80 C3** 17 56N 120 28 E
Badogo, *Mali* **112 C3** 11 2N 8 13W
Badoumbé, *Mali* **112 C2** 13 42N 10 15W
Badr Ḥunayn, *Si. Arabia* **98 B2** 23 44N 38 46 E
Badrah, *Iraq* **101 F11** 33 6N 45 58 E
Badrinath, *India* **93 D8** 30 44N 79 29 E
Badu I., *Papua N. G.* **132 F2** 10 5 S 142 10 E
Baduen, *Somali Rep.* **120 C3** 7 15N 47 40 E
Badulla, *Sri Lanka* **95 L5** 7 1N 81 7 E
Badung, Selat, *Indonesia* **79 K18** 8 40 S 115 22 E
Badupi, *Burma* **90 E4** 21 36N 93 27 E
Badvel, *India* **95 G4** 14 45N 79 3 E
Baena, *Spain* **43 H6** 37 37N 4 20W
Baerami, *Australia* **129 B9** 32 27 S 150 27 E
Baetov, *Kyrgyzstan* **65 C7** 41 13N 74 54 E
Baeza, *Ecuador* **168 D2** 0 25 S 77 53W
Baeza, *Spain* **43 H7** 37 57N 3 25W
Bafang, *Cameroon* **113 D7** 5 9N 10 11 E
Bafatá, *Guinea-Biss.* **112 C2** 12 8N 14 40W
Baffin B., *Canada* **139 A13** 72 0N 64 0W
Baffin I., *Canada* **139 B12** 68 0N 75 0W
Bafia, *Cameroon* **113 E7** 4 40N 11 10 E
Bafilo, *Togo* **113 D5** 9 22N 1 22 E
Bafing →, *Mali* **112 C2** 13 49N 10 50W
Bafing, Parc Nat. du △, *Mali* **112 C2** 12 38N 10 28W
Bafliyūn, *Syria* **96 B3** 36 37N 36 59 E
Bafoulabé, *Mali* **112 C2** 13 50N 10 55W
Bafoussam, *Cameroon* **113 D7** 5 28N 10 25 E
Bāfq, *Iran* **97 D7** 31 40N 55 25 E
Bafra, *Turkey* **100 B6** 41 34N 35 54 E
Bafra Burnu, *Turkey* **100 B7** 41 45N 36 2 E
Bāft, *Iran* **97 D8** 29 15N 56 38 E
Bafut, *Cameroon* **113 D7** 6 6N 10 2 E
Bafwasende, *Dem. Rep. of the Congo* **118 B2** 1 3N 27 5 E
Bagaat, Î., *N. Cal.* **133 K4** 20 40 S 166 15 E
Bagabag, *Phil.* **80 C3** 16 30N 121 15 E
Bagabag I., *Papua N. G.* **132 C4** 4 48 S 146 14 E
Bagac, *Phil.* **80 D3** 14 36N 120 23 E
Bagac Bay, *Phil.* **80 D3** 14 36N 120 20 E
Bagalkot, *India* **95 F2** 16 10N 75 40 E
Bagam, *Niger* **113 B6** 15 43N 6 35 E
Bagamanoc, *Phil.* **80 E5** 13 57N 124 17 E
Bagamoyo, *Tanzania* **118 D4** 6 28 S 38 55 E
Bagan Datoh, *Malaysia* **87 L3** 3 59N 100 47 E
Bagan Serai, *Malaysia* **87 K3** 5 1N 100 32 E
Baganga, *Phil.* **81 H6** 7 34N 126 33 E
Bagani, *Namibia* **116 B3** 18 7 S 21 41 E
Bagansiapiapi, *Indonesia* **84 B2** 2 12N 100 50 E
Bagasra, *India* **92 J4** 21 30N 71 0 E
Bagata, *Dem. Rep. of the Congo* **114 C3** 3 44 S 17 57 E
Bagaud, *India* **92 H6** 22 19N 75 53 E
Bagawi, *Sudan* **107 E3** 12 20N 34 18 E
Bagbag, *Sudan* **107 D3** 15 23N 31 30 E
Bagdad, *Calif., U.S.A.* **161 L11** 34 35N 115 53W
Bagdad, *Fla., U.S.A.* **153 E2** 30 36N 87 2W
Bagdarin, *Russia* **67 D12** 54 26N 113 36 E
Bagé, *Brazil* **175 C5** 31 20 S 54 15W
Bagenalstown = Muine Bheag, *Ireland* **23 D5** 52 42N 6 58W
Bagepalli, *India* **95 H3** 13 47N 77 47 E
Bagevadi, *India* **94 F2** 16 35N 75 58 E
Baggao, *Phil.* **80 C3** 17 56N 121 46 E
Baggs, *U.S.A.* **158 F10** 41 2N 107 39W
Bagh, *Pakistan* **93 C5** 33 59N 73 45 E
Baghain →, *India* **93 G9** 25 32N 81 1 E
Baghdād, *Iraq* **101 F11** 33 20N 44 30 E
Bagherhat, *Bangla.* **90 D2** 22 40N 89 47 E
Bagheria, *Italy* **46 D6** 38 5N 13 30 E
Baghlān, *Afghan.* **91 A3** 32 12N 68 46 E
Baghlān □, *Afghan.* **91 B3** 36 0N 68 30 E
Bagley, *U.S.A.* **154 B7** 47 32N 95 24W
Bagn, *Norway* **18 D6** 60 49N 9 34 E
Bagnara Cálabra, *Italy* **47 D8** 38 17N 15 48 E
Bagnasco, *Italy* **44 D5** 44 18N 8 2 E
Bagnell Dam, *U.S.A.* **156 F4** 38 14N 92 36W
Bagnères-de-Bigorre, *France* **28 E4** 43 5N 0 9 E
Bagnères-de-Luchon, *France* **28 F4** 42 47N 0 38 E
Bagni di Lucca, *Italy* **44 D7** 44 1N 10 35 E
Bagno di Romagna, *Italy* **45 E8** 43 50N 11 57 E
Bagnoles-de-l'Orne, *France* **26 D6** 48 32N 0 25W
Bagnols-sur-Cèze, *France* **29 D8** 44 10N 4 36 E
Bagnorégio, *Italy* **45 F9** 42 37N 12 5 E
Bago = Pegu, *Burma* **90 G6** 17 20N 96 29 E
Bago, *Phil.* **81 F4** 10 32N 122 50 E
Bagodar, *India* **93 G11** 24 5N 85 52 E
Bagrationovsk, *Russia* **15 J19** 54 23N 20 39 E
Bagrdan, *Serbia, Yug.* **50 B5** 44 5N 21 11 E
Bagua, *Peru* **172 B2** 5 35 S 78 22W
Baguio, *Phil.* **80 C3** 16 26N 120 34 E
Bağyurdu, *Turkey* **49 C9** 38 25N 27 41 E
Bagzane, Monts, *Niger* **113 B6** 17 43N 8 45 E
Bah, *India* **93 F8** 26 53N 78 36 E
Bahabón de Esgueva, *Spain* **42 D7** 41 52N 3 43W
Bahadurabad Ghat, *Bangla.* **90 C2** 25 11N 89 44 E
Bahadurganj, *India* **93 F12** 26 16N 87 49 E
Bahadurgarh, *India* **92 E7** 28 40N 76 57 E
Bahama, Canal Viejo de, *W. Indies* **164 B4** 22 10N 77 30W
Bahamas ■, *N. Amer.* **165 B5** 24 0N 75 0W
Bahār, *Iran* **101 E13** 34 54N 48 26 E
Bahārak, *Afghan.* **65 E5** 37 0N 70 53 E
Baharampur, *India* **93 G13** 24 2N 88 27 E
Baharîya, El Wâhât al, *Egypt* **106 B2** 28 0N 28 50 E
Baharu Pandan = Pandan, *Malaysia* **87 d** 1 32N 103 46 E
Bahawalnagar, *Pakistan* **91 C4** 30 0N 73 15 E
Bahawalpur, *Pakistan* **91 C3** 29 24N 71 40 E
Bahçe, *Turkey* **100 D7** 37 13N 36 34 E
Bahçecik, *Turkey* **51 F13** 40 41N 29 44 E
Baheli, *Phil.* **81 F2** 10 0N 118 47 E
Baheri, *India* **93 E8** 28 45N 79 34 E
Bahgul →, *India* **93 F8** 27 45N 79 36 E
Bahi, *Tanzania* **118 D4** 5 58 S 35 21 E
Bahi Swamp, *Tanzania* **118 D4** 6 10 S 35 0 E
Bahía = Salvador, *Brazil* **171 D4** 13 0 S 38 30W
Bahía □, *Brazil* **171 D3** 12 0 S 42 0W
Bahía, Is. de la, *Honduras* **164 C2** 16 45N 86 15W
Bahía Blanca, *Argentina* **174 D3** 38 35 S 62 13W
Bahía de Caráquez, *Ecuador* **168 D1** 0 40 S 80 27W
Bahía Honda, *Cuba* **164 B3** 22 54N 83 10W
Bahía Laura, *Argentina* **176 C3** 48 10 S 66 30W
Bahía Mansa, *Chile* **176 B2** 40 33 S 73 46W
Bahía Negra, *Paraguay* **173 E6** 20 5 S 58 5W
Bahir Dar, *Ethiopia* **107 E4** 11 37N 37 10 E
Bahlah, *Oman* **99 B7** 22 58N 57 18 E
Bahmanzād, *Iran* **97 D6** 31 15N 51 47 E
Bahmer, *Algeria* **111 C4** 27 32N 0 10W
Bahr el Ahmar □, *Sudan* **106 D4** 20 0N 35 0 E
Bahr el Ghazâl □, *Sudan* **107 F2** 7 0N 28 0 E
Bahr el Jabal □, *Sudan* **107 G3** 4 0N 31 0 E
Bahraich, *India* **93 F9** 27 38N 81 37 E
Bahrain ■, *Asia* **97 E6** 26 0N 50 35 E
Bahror, *India* **92 F7** 27 51N 76 20 E
Bāhū Kalāt, *Iran* **97 E9** 25 43N 61 25 E
Bai, *Mali* **112 C4** 13 35N 3 28W
Bai Bung, Mui = Ca Mau, Mui, *Vietnam* **87 H5** 8 38N 104 44 E
Bai Duc, *Vietnam* **86 C5** 18 3N 105 49 E
Bai Thuong, *Vietnam* **86 C5** 19 54N 105 23 E
Baia de Aramă, *Romania* **52 E7** 45 0N 22 50 E
Baía dos Tigres, *Angola* **115 F2** 16 40 S 11 47 E
Baia Farta, *Angola* **115 E2** 12 40 S 13 11 E
Baia Mare, *Romania* **53 C8** 47 40N 23 35 E
Baia-Sprie, *Romania* **53 C8** 47 41N 23 43 E
Baião, *Brazil* **170 B2** 2 40 S 49 40W
Baïbokoum, *Chad* **109 G3** 7 46N 15 43 E
Baicheng, *China* **75 B12** 45 38N 122 42 E
Băicoi, *Romania* **53 E10** 45 3N 25 52 E
Baidoa, *Somali Rep.* **120 D2** 3 8N 43 30 E
Baie Comeau, *Canada* **141 C6** 49 12N 68 10W
Baie-St-Paul, *Canada* **141 C5** 47 28N 70 32W
Baie Ste-Anne, *Seychelles* **121 b** 4 18 S 55 45 E
Baie Trinité, *Canada* **141 C6** 49 25N 67 20W
Baie Verte, *Canada* **141 C8** 49 55N 56 12W
Baignes-Ste-Radegonde, *France* **28 C3** 45 23N 0 25W
Baigneux-les-Juifs, *France* **27 E11** 47 31N 4 39 E
Baihar, *India* **93 H9** 22 6N 80 33 E
Baihe, *China* **74 H6** 32 50N 110 5 E
Ba'ījī, *Iraq* **101 E10** 35 0N 43 30 E
Baijnath, *India* **93 E8** 29 55N 79 37 E
Baikal, L. = Baykal, Oz., *Russia* **67 D11** 53 0N 108 0 E
Baikunthpur, *India* **93 H10** 23 15N 82 33 E
Bailadila, Mt., *India* **94 E5** 18 43N 81 15 E
Baile Atha Cliath = Dublin, *Ireland* **23 C5** 53 21N 6 15W
Băile Govora, *Romania* **53 E9** 45 5N 24 11 E
Băile Herculane, *Romania* **52 F7** 44 53N 22 26 E
Băile Olăneşti, *Romania* **53 E9** 45 12N 24 14 E
Băile Tuşnad, *Romania* **53 D10** 46 9N 25 51 E
Bailén, *Spain* **43 G7** 38 8N 3 48W
Băileşti, *Romania* **53 F8** 44 1N 23 20 E
Bailhongal, *India* **95 G2** 15 55N 74 53 E
Bailique, Ilha, *Brazil* **170 A2** 1 2N 49 58W
Bailugh, *Afghan.* **91 B2** 32 40N 66 47 E
Bailundo, *Angola* **115 E3** 12 10 S 15 50 E
Baima, *China* **76 A3** 33 0N 100 26 E
Baimuru, *Papua N. G.* **132 D3** 7 35 S 144 51 E
Bain-de-Bretagne, *France* **26 E5** 47 50N 1 40W
Bainbridge, *Ga., U.S.A.* **152 E5** 30 55N 84 35W
Bainbridge, *Ind., U.S.A.* **157 E10** 39 46N 86 49W
Bainbridge, *N.Y., U.S.A.* **151 D9** 42 18N 75 29W
Bainbridge, *Ohio, U.S.A.* **157 E13** 39 14N 83 16W
Baing, *Indonesia* **82 D2** 10 14 S 120 34 E
Bainiu, *China* **74 H7** 32 50N 112 15 E
Bainyik, *Papua N. G.* **132 B2** 3 40 S 143 4 E
Baiona, *Spain* **42 C2** 42 6N 8 52W
Bā'ir, *Jordan* **103 E5** 30 45N 36 55 E
Baird Mts., *U.S.A.* **144 C8** 67 0N 160 0W
Bairin Youqi, *China* **75 C10** 43 30N 118 35 E
Bairin Zuoqi, *China* **75 C10** 43 58N 119 15 E
Bairnsdale, *Australia* **129 D7** 37 48 S 147 36 E
Bais, *Phil.* **81 G4** 9 35N 123 7 E
Baisha, *China* **74 G7** 34 20N 112 32 E
Baissa, *Nigeria* **113 D7** 7 14N 10 38 E
Baitadi, *Nepal* **93 E9** 29 35N 80 25 E
Baitarani →, *India* **94 D8** 20 45N 86 48 E
Baixa Grande, *Brazil* **171 D3** 11 57 S 40 11W
Baixa Limia-Sierra do Xurés, Parque Natural de ⌓, *Spain* **42 D2** 41 59N 8 2W
Baixo-Longa, *Angola* **115 F3** 15 41 S 18 45 E
Baiyer River, *Papua N. G.* **132 C3** 5 32 S 144 9 E
Baiyin, *China* **74 F3** 36 45N 104 14 E
Baiyü, *China* **76 B2** 31 16N 98 50 E
Baiyu Shan, *China* **74 F4** 37 15N 107 30 E
Baiyuda, *Sudan* **106 D3** 17 35N 32 7 E
Baj Baj, *India* **93 H13** 22 30N 88 5 E
Baja, *Hungary* **52 D3** 46 12N 18 59 E
Baja, Pta., *Chile* **172 b** 27 10 S 109 22W
Baja, Pta., *Mexico* **162 B1** 29 50N 116 0W
Baja California, *Mexico* **162 A1** 31 10N 115 12W
Baja California □, *Mexico* **162 B2** 30 0N 115 0W
Baja California Sur □, *Mexico* **162 B2** 25 50N 111 50W
Bajag, *India* **93 H9** 22 40N 81 21 E
Bajamar, *Canary Is.* **9 e1** 28 33N 16 20W
Bajana, *India* **92 H4** 23 7N 71 49 E
Bajatrejo, *Indonesia* **79 J17** 8 29 S 114 19 E
Bajawa, *Indonesia* **82 C2** 8 47 S 120 59 E
Bajera, *Indonesia* **79 J18** 8 31 S 115 2 E
Bājgīrān, *Iran* **97 B8** 37 36N 58 24 E
Bājil, *Yemen* **98 D3** 15 4N 43 17 E
Bajimba, Mt., *Australia* **127 D5** 29 17 S 152 6 E
Bajina Bašta, *Serbia, Yug.* **50 C3** 43 58N 19 35 E
Bajmok, *Serbia, Yug.* **52 E4** 45 57N 19 24 E
Bajo Caracoles, *Argentina* **176 C2** 47 27 S 70 56W
Bajo Nuevo, *Caribbean* **164 C4** 15 40N 78 50W
Bajoga, *Nigeria* **113 C7** 10 57N 11 20 E
Bajool, *Australia* **126 C5** 23 40 S 150 35 E
Bak, *Hungary* **52 D1** 46 43N 16 51 E
Bakal, *Russia* **64 D7** 54 56N 58 48 E
Bakala, *C.A.R.* **114 A4** 6 15N 20 20 E
Bakanas = Baqanas, *Kazakhstan* **65 A8** 44 50N 76 15 E
Bakar, *Croatia* **45 C11** 45 18N 14 32 E
Bakel, *Senegal* **112 C2** 14 56N 12 20W
Baker, *Calif., U.S.A.* **161 K10** 35 16N 116 4W
Baker, *Fla., U.S.A.* **153 E3** 30 48N 86 41W
Baker, *Mont., U.S.A.* **154 B2** 46 22N 104 17W
Baker, Canal, *Chile* **176 C2** 47 45 S 74 45W
Baker, L., *Canada* **138 B10** 64 0N 96 0W
Baker, Mt., *U.S.A.* **158 B3** 48 50N 121 49W
Baker City, *U.S.A.* **158 D5** 44 47N 117 50W
Baker I., *Pac. Oc.* **134 G10** 0 10N 176 35W
Baker I., *U.S.A.* **142 B2** 55 20N 133 40W
Baker L., *Australia* **125 E4** 26 54 S 126 5 E
Baker Lake, *Canada* **138 B10** 64 20N 96 3W
Bakere, *Dem. Rep. of the Congo* **114 B4** 1 36N 23 50 E
Bakerhill, *U.S.A.* **152 D4** 31 47N 85 18W
Bakers Creek, *Australia* **126 C4** 21 13 S 149 7 E
Baker's Dozen Is., *Canada* **140 A4** 56 45N 78 45W
Bakersfield, *Calif., U.S.A.* **161 K8** 35 23N 119 1W
Bakersfield, *Vt., U.S.A.* **151 B12** 44 45N 72 48W
Bakhchysaray, *Ukraine* **59 K7** 44 40N 33 45 E
Bakhmach, *Ukraine* **59 G7** 51 10N 32 45 E
Bakhmut = Artemovsk, *Ukraine* **59 H9** 48 35N 38 0 E
Bakht, *Uzbekistan* **65 C4** 40 43N 68 42 E
Bākhtarān, *Iran* **101 E12** 34 23N 47 0 E
Bākhtarān □, *Iran* **96 C5** 34 0N 46 30 E
Bakı, *Azerbaijan* **61 K9** 40 29N 49 56 E
Bakır →, *Turkey* **49 C9** 38 55N 27 0 E
Bakırdaği, *Turkey* **100 C6** 38 13N 35 46 E
Bakkafjörður, *Iceland* **11 A12** 66 2N 14 48W
Bakkaflói, *Iceland* **11 A12** 66 10N 14 45W
Baklan, *Turkey* **49 C11** 38 0N 29 36 E
Bako, *Ethiopia* **107 F4** 5 51N 36 23 E
Bako, *Ivory C.* **112 D3** 9 8N 7 40W
Bakony, *Hungary* **52 C2** 47 10N 17 30 E
Bakony Forest = Bakony, *Hungary* **52 C2** 47 10N 17 30 E
Bakori, *Nigeria* **113 C6** 11 34N 7 25 E
Bakouma, *C.A.R.* **114 A4** 5 40N 22 56 E
Bakpakty = Baqbaqty, *Kazakhstan* **65 A8** 44 35N 76 40 E
Baksan, *Russia* **61 J6** 43 42N 43 32 E
Bakswaho, *India* **93 G8** 24 15N 79 18 E
Baku = Bakı, *Azerbaijan* **61 K9** 40 29N 49 56 E
Bakundi, *Nigeria* **113 D7** 8 2N 10 45 E
Bakutis Coast, *Antarctica* **7 D15** 74 0 S 120 0W
Bakwa-Kenge, *Dem. Rep. of the Congo* **115 C4** 4 51 S 22 4 E
Bakwanga = Mbuji-Mayi, *Dem. Rep. of the Congo* **118 D1** 6 9 S 23 40 E
Baky = Bakı, *Azerbaijan* **61 K9** 40 29N 49 56 E
Bala, *Canada* **150 A5** 45 1N 79 37W
Bala, *Senegal* **112 C2** 14 1N 13 8W
Bâlâ, *Turkey* **100 C5** 39 32N 33 6 E
Bala, *U.K.* **20 E4** 52 54N 3 36W
Bala, L., *U.K.* **20 E4** 52 53N 3 37W
Bālā Morghāb, *Afghan.* **91 B1** 35 35N 63 20 E
Balabac, *Phil.* **81 H1** 7 59N 117 4 E
Balabac I., *Phil.* **81 G1** 8 0N 117 0 E
Balabac Str., *E. Indies* **78 C5** 7 53N 117 5 E
Balabagh, *Afghan.* **92 B4** 34 25N 70 12 E
Ba'labakk, *Lebanon* **103 B5** 34 0N 36 10 E
Balabalangan, Kepulauan, *Indonesia* **85 C5** 2 20 S 117 30 E
Balabio, Î., *N. Cal.* **133 T18** 20 7 S 164 11 E
Bălăciţa, *Romania* **53 F8** 44 23N 23 8 E
Balad, *Iraq* **101 F11** 34 1N 44 9 E
Balad Rūz, *Iraq* **101 F11** 33 42N 45 5 E
Bālādeh, *Fārs, Iran* **97 D6** 29 17N 51 56 E
Bālādeh, *Māzandaran, Iran* **97 B6** 36 12N 51 48 E
Balaghat, *India* **94 D5** 21 49N 80 12 E
Balaghat Ra., *India* **94 E3** 18 50N 76 30 E
Balaguer, *Spain* **40 D5** 41 50N 0 50 E
Balaka, *Dem. Rep. of the Congo* **115 C3** 4 52 S 19 57 E
Balakété, *C.A.R.* **114 A3** 6 56N 19 54 E
Balakhna, *Russia* **60 B6** 56 25N 43 32 E
Balaklava, *Australia* **128 C3** 34 7 S 138 22 E
Balaklava, *Ukraine* **59 K7** 44 30N 33 30 E
Balakliya, *Ukraine* **59 H9** 49 28N 36 55 E
Balakovo, *Russia* **60 D8** 52 4N 47 55 E
Balamau, *India* **93 F9** 27 10N 80 21 E
Balamban, *Phil.* **81 F4** 10 30N 123 43 E
Balambangan, *Malaysia* **85 A5** 7 17N 116 55 E
Bălan, *Romania* **53 D10** 46 39N 25 49 E
Balancán, *Mexico* **163 D6** 17 48N 91 32W
Balanga, *Phil.* **80 D3** 14 41N 120 32 E
Balangala, *Dem. Rep. of the Congo* **114 B3** 0 30N 19 56 E
Balangiga, *Phil.* **81 F5** 11 7N 125 23 E
Balangir, *India* **94 D6** 20 43N 83 35 E
Balaoan, *Phil.* **80 C3** 16 49N 120 24 E
Balapur, *India* **94 D3** 20 40N 76 45 E
Balashov, *Russia* **60 E6** 51 30N 43 10 E
Balasinor, *India* **92 H5** 22 57N 73 23 E
Balasore = Baleshwar, *India* **94 D8** 21 35N 87 3 E
Balassagyarmat, *Hungary* **52 B4** 48 4N 19 15 E
Balât, *Egypt* **106 B2** 25 36N 29 19 E
Balaton, *Hungary* **52 D2** 46 50N 17 40 E
Balaton-Felvidéki Nemzeti Park △, *Hungary* **52 D2** 46 52N 17 30 E
Balatonboglár, *Hungary* **52 D2** 46 46N 17 40 E
Balatonfüred, *Hungary* **52 D2** 46 58N 17 54 E
Balatonszentgyörgy, *Hungary* **52 D2** 46 41N 17 19 E
Balayan, *Phil.* **80 E3** 13 57N 120 44 E
Balazote, *Spain* **41 G2** 38 54N 2 9W
Balbalan, *Phil.* **80 C3** 17 27N 121 12 E
Balbi, Mt., *Papua N. G.* **132 C8** 5 55 S 154 58 E
Balbieriškis, *Lithuania* **54 D10** 54 32N 23 53 E
Balbigny, *France* **29 C8** 45 49N 4 11 E
Balbina, *Brazil* **169 D6** 1 58 S 59 29W
Balbina, Reprêsa de, *Brazil* **169 D6** 2 0 S 59 30W

Balboa, *Panama* **164 E4** 8 57N 79 34W
Balbriggan, *Ireland* **23 C5** 53 37N 6 11W
Balcarce, *Argentina* **174 D4** 38 0 S 58 10W
Balcarres, *Canada* **143 C8** 50 50N 103 35W
Bălceşti, *Romania* **53 F8** 44 37N 23 57 E
Balchik, *Bulgaria* **51 C12** 43 28N 28 11 E
Balclutha, *N.Z.* **131 G4** 46 15 S 169 45 E
Balcones Escarpment, *U.S.A.* **155 L5** 29 30N 99 15W
Balçova, *Turkey* **49 C9** 38 22N 27 4 E
Bald Hd., *Australia* **125 G2** 35 6 S 118 1 E
Bald I., *Australia* **125 F2** 34 57 S 118 27 E
Bald Knob, *U.S.A.* **155 H9** 35 19N 91 34W
Baldock L., *Canada* **143 B9** 56 33N 97 57W
Baldwin, *Fla., U.S.A.* **152 E8** 30 18N 81 59W
Baldwin, *Mich., U.S.A.* **148 D3** 43 54N 85 51W
Baldwin, *Pa., U.S.A.* **150 F5** 40 23N 79 59W
Baldwinsville, *U.S.A.* **151 C8** 43 10N 76 20W
Baldy Mt., *U.S.A.* **158 B9** 48 9N 109 39W
Baldy Peak, *U.S.A.* **159 K9** 33 54N 109 34W
Bale, *Croatia* **45 C10** 45 4N 13 46 E
Bale, *Ethiopia* **107 F5** 6 57N 40 8 E
Bale □, *Ethiopia* **107 F5** 6 20N 41 30 E
Bale Mountains Nat. Park △, *Ethiopia* **107 F4** 6 59N 39 52 E
Baleares, Is., *Spain* **38 B4** 39 30N 3 0 E
Balearic Is. = Baleares, Is., *Spain* **38 B4** 39 30N 3 0 E
Balease, *Indonesia* **82 B2** 2 24 S 120 33 E
Baleia, Pta. da, *Brazil* **171 E4** 17 40 S 39 7W
Baleine = Whale →, *Canada* **141 A6** 58 15N 67 40W
Băleni, *Romania* **53 E12** 45 48N 27 51 E
Baler, *Phil.* **80 D3** 15 46N 121 34 E
Baler Bay, *Phil.* **80 D3** 15 50N 121 35 E
Balerna, *Switz.* **33 E8** 45 52N 9 0 E
Baleshare, *U.K.* **22 D1** 57 31N 7 22W
Baleshwar, *India* **94 D8** 21 35N 87 3 E
Balestrand, *Norway* **18 C3** 61 11N 6 31 E
Balezino, *Russia* **60 B11** 58 2N 53 6 E
Balfate, *Honduras* **164 C2** 15 48N 86 25W
Balfour Channel, *Solomon Is.* **133 M9** 8 43 S 157 27 E
Balharshah, *India* **94 E4** 19 50N 79 23 E
Bali, *Cameroon* **113 D7** 5 54N 10 0 E
Bali, *Dem. Rep. of the Congo* **114 C3** 2 50 S 16 12 E
Balí, *Greece* **39 E5** 35 25N 24 47 E
Bali, *India* **92 G5** 25 11N 73 17 E
Bali, *Indonesia* **79 J17** 8 20 S 115 0 E
Bali □, *Indonesia* **85 D4** 8 20 S 115 0 E
Bali, Selat, *Indonesia* **85 D4** 8 18 S 114 25 E
Bali Sea, *Indonesia* **85 D5** 8 0 S 115 0 E
Balia, *S. Leone* **112 D2** 9 22N 11 1W
Baliapal, *India* **93 J12** 21 40N 87 17 E
Balicuatro Is., *Phil.* **80 E5** 12 39N 124 24 E
Baliem →, *Indonesia* **83 C5** 5 44 S 138 8 E
Baligród, *Poland* **55 J9** 49 20N 22 17 E
Baliguda, *India* **94 D6** 20 12N 83 55 E
Balik Pulau, *Malaysia* **87 c** 5 21N 100 14 E
Balikeşir, *Turkey* **49 B9** 39 39N 27 53 E
Balikeşir □, *Turkey* **49 B9** 39 45N 28 0 E
Balıklıçeşme, *Turkey* **51 F11** 40 18N 27 5 E
Balikpapan, *Indonesia* **85 C5** 1 10 S 116 55 E
Balimbing, *Phil.* **81 J2** 5 5N 119 58 E
Balimo, *Papua N. G.* **132 E2** 8 6 S 142 57 E
Baling, *Malaysia* **87 K3** 5 41N 100 55 E
Balingasag, *Phil.* **81 G5** 8 45N 124 47 E
Balingen, *Germany* **31 G4** 48 16N 8 51 E
Balinţ, *Romania* **52 E6** 45 48N 21 54 E
Balintang Channel, *Phil.* **80 B3** 19 49N 121 40 E
Balintang I., *Phil.* **80 B4** 19 58N 122 9 E
Baliza, *Brazil* **173 D7** 16 0 S 52 20W
Baljurshī, *Si. Arabia* **98 C3** 19 51N 41 33 E
Balkan Mts. = Stara Planina, *Bulgaria* **50 C7** 43 15N 23 0 E
Balkh, *Afghan.* **65 E3** 36 44N 66 47 E
Balkh □, *Afghan.* **65 E3** 36 50N 67 0 E
Balkhash = Balqash, *Kazakhstan* **66 E8** 46 50N 74 50 E
Balkhash, Ozero = Balqash Köl, *Kazakhstan* **66 E8** 46 0N 74 50 E
Balkonda, *India* **94 E4** 18 52N 78 21 E
Ballachulish, *U.K.* **22 E3** 56 41N 5 8W
Balladonia, *Australia* **125 F3** 32 27 S 123 51 E
Ballaghaderreen, *Ireland* **23 C3** 53 55N 8 34W
Ballan, *Australia* **128 D6** 37 35 S 144 13 E
Ballarat, *Australia* **128 D5** 37 33 S 143 50 E
Ballard, L., *Australia* **125 E3** 29 20 S 120 40 E
Ballater, *U.K.* **22 D5** 57 3N 3 3W
Ballé, *Mali* **112 B3** 15 18N 8 33W
Ballena Gris, Parque Natural de la = Ojo de Liebre, Parque Natural ⌓, *Mexico* **162 B2** 27 50N 114 0W
Ballenas, Canal de, *Mexico* **162 B2** 29 10N 113 45W
Balleny Is., *Antarctica* **7 C11** 66 30 S 163 0 E
Balleroy, *France* **26 C6** 49 11N 0 50W
Ballerup, *Denmark* **17 J6** 55 44N 12 21 E
Ballı, *Turkey* **51 F11** 40 50N 27 3 E
Ballia, *India* **93 G11** 25 46N 84 12 E
Ballina, *Australia* **127 D5** 28 50 S 153 31 E
Ballina, *Ireland* **23 B2** 54 7N 9 9W
Ballinasloe, *Ireland* **23 C3** 53 20N 8 13W
Ballinger, *U.S.A.* **155 K5** 31 45N 99 57W
Ballinrobe, *Ireland* **23 C2** 53 38N 9 13W
Ballinskelligs B., *Ireland* **23 E1** 51 48N 10 13W
Ballon, *France* **26 D7** 48 10N 0 14 E
Ballons des Vosges, Parc Naturel Régional des ⌓, *France* **27 E14** 48 0N 7 0 E
Ballsh, *Albania* **50 F3** 40 36N 19 44 E
Ballston Spa, *U.S.A.* **151 D11** 43 0N 73 51W
Ballybunion, *Ireland* **23 D2** 52 31N 9 40W
Ballycastle, *U.K.* **23 A5** 55 12N 6 15W
Ballyclare, *U.K.* **23 B5** 54 46N 6 0W
Ballyhaunis, *Ireland* **23 C3** 53 46N 8 46W
Ballymena, *U.K.* **23 B5** 54 52N 6 17W
Ballymoney, *U.K.* **23 A5** 55 5N 6 31W
Ballymote, *Ireland* **23 B3** 54 5N 8 31W
Ballynahinch, *U.K.* **23 B6** 54 24N 5 54W
Ballyquintin Pt., *U.K.* **23 B6** 54 20N 5 30W
Ballyshannon, *Ireland* **23 B3** 54 30N 8 11W
Balmaceda, *Chile* **176 C2** 46 0 S 71 50W
Balmaseda, *Spain* **40 B1** 43 11N 3 12W
Balmazújváros, *Hungary* **52 C6** 47 37N 21 21 E
Balmertown, *Canada* **143 C10** 51 4N 93 41W
Balmhorn, *Switz.* **32 D5** 46 26N 7 42 E
Balmoral, *Australia* **128 D4** 37 15 S 141 48 E
Balmorhea, *U.S.A.* **155 K3** 30 59N 103 45W
Balochistan = Baluchistan □, *Pakistan* **91 D2** 27 30N 65 0 E
Balod, *India* **94 D5** 20 44N 81 13 E
Balombo, *Angola* **115 E2** 12 21 S 14 46 E
Balombo →, *Angola* **115 E2** 11 57 S 13 46 E
Balonne →, *Australia* **127 D4** 28 47 S 147 56 E
Balotra, *India* **92 G5** 25 50N 72 14 E
Balpyq Bī, *Kazakhstan* **65 A9** 44 52N 78 12 E
Balqash, *Kazakhstan* **66 E8** 46 50N 74 50 E
Balqash Köl, *Kazakhstan* **66 E8** 46 0N 74 50 E
Balrampur, *India* **93 F10** 27 30N 82 20 E
Balranald, *Australia* **128 C5** 34 38 S 143 33 E
Balş, *Romania* **53 F9** 44 22N 24 5 E
Balsapuerto, *Peru* **172 B2** 5 48 S 76 33W
Balsas, *Mexico* **163 D5** 18 0N 99 40W
Balsas →, *Maranhão, Brazil* **170 C3** 7 15 S 44 35W
Balsas →, *Tocantins, Brazil* **170 C2** 9 58 S 47 52W
Balsas →, *Mexico* **162 D4** 17 55N 102 10W
Bålsta, *Sweden* **16 E11** 59 35N 17 30 E
Balsthal, *Switz.* **32 B5** 47 19N 7 41 E
Balston Spa, *U.S.A.* **151 D11** 43 0N 73 52W
Balta, *Romania* **52 F7** 44 54N 22 38 E
Balta, *Ukraine* **59 J5** 48 2N 29 45 E
Baltanás, *Spain* **42 D6** 41 56N 4 15W
Bălţi, *Moldova* **53 C12** 47 48N 27 58 E
Baltic Sea, *Europe* **15 H18** 57 0N 19 0 E
Baltîm, *Egypt* **106 H7** 31 35N 31 10 E
Baltimore, *Ireland* **23 E2** 51 29N 9 22W
Baltimore, *Md., U.S.A.* **148 F7** 39 17N 76 37W
Baltimore, *Ohio, U.S.A.* **150 G2** 39 51N 82 36W
Baltit, *Pakistan* **93 A6** 36 15N 74 40 E
Baltiysk, *Russia* **15 J18** 54 41N 19 58 E
Baltra, I., *Ecuador* **172 a** 0 26 S 90 16W
Baltrum, *Germany* **30 B3** 53 43N 7 24 E
Baluan I., *Papua N. G.* **132 B4** 2 33 S 147 17 E
Baluchistan □, *Pakistan* **91 D2** 27 30N 65 0 E
Balud, *Phil.* **80 E4** 12 2N 123 12 E
Balurghat, *India* **90 C2** 25 15N 88 44 E
Balvi, *Latvia* **15 H22** 57 8N 27 15 E
Balya, *Turkey* **49 B9** 39 44N 27 35 E
Balykchy, *Kyrgyzstan* **65 B8** 42 26N 76 12 E
Balzar, *Ecuador* **168 D2** 2 2 S 79 54W
Bam, *Iran* **97 D8** 29 7N 58 14 E
Bama, *China* **76 E6** 24 8N 107 12 E
Bama, *Nigeria* **113 C7** 11 33N 13 41 E
Bamaga, *Australia* **126 A3** 10 50 S 142 25 E
Bamaji L., *Canada* **140 B1** 51 9N 91 25W
Bamako, *Mali* **112 C3** 12 34N 7 55W
Bamba, *Dem. Rep. of the Congo* **115 D3** 5 45 S 18 23 E
Bamba, *Mali* **113 B4** 17 5N 1 24W
Bambamarca, *Peru* **172 B2** 6 36 S 78 32W
Bambang, *Phil.* **80 C3** 16 23N 121 6 E
Bambannan I., *Phil.* **81 J3** 5 37N 120 17 E
Bambara Maoundé, *Mali* **112 B4** 13 26N 4 3W
Bambari, *C.A.R.* **114 A4** 5 40N 20 35 E
Bambaroo, *Australia* **126 B4** 18 50 S 146 10 E
Bambaya, *Guinea* **112 D2** 10 55N 13 38W
Bamberg, *Germany* **31 F6** 49 54N 10 54 E
Bamberg, *U.S.A.* **152 B8** 33 18N 81 2W
Bambesi, *Ethiopia* **107 F3** 9 45N 34 40 E
Bambey, *Senegal* **112 C1** 14 42N 16 28W
Bambili, *Dem. Rep. of the Congo* **118 B2** 3 40N 26 0 E
Bambinga, *Dem. Rep. of the Congo* **114 C3** 3 43 S 18 53 E
Bambio, *C.A.R.* **114 B3** 3 55N 16 57 E
Bamboi, *Ghana* **112 D4** 8 13N 2 1W
Bambouti, *C.A.R.* **114 A5** 5 24N 27 12 E
Bambuí, *Brazil* **171 F2** 20 1 S 45 58W
Bamburgh, *U.K.* **20 B6** 55 37N 1 43W
Bamenda, *Cameroon* **113 D7** 5 57N 10 11 E
Bamfield, *Canada* **142 D3** 48 45N 125 10W
Bāmīān □, *Afghan.* **91 B2** 35 0N 67 0 E
Bamiancheng, *China* **75 C13** 43 15N 124 2 E
Bamingui, *C.A.R.* **114 A4** 7 34N 20 11 E
Bamingui →, *C.A.R.* **114 A3** 8 33N 19 5 E
Bamingui-Bangoran, Parc Nat. du △, *C.A.R.* **114 A3** 8 30N 19 46 E
Bamkin, *Cameroon* **113 D7** 6 3N 11 27 E
Bampan, *Phil.* **80 D3** 15 40N 120 20 E
Bampūr, *Iran* **97 E9** 27 15N 60 21 E
Bamu →, *Papua N. G.* **132 E2** 8 1 S 143 33 E
Ban, *Burkina Faso* **112 C4** 14 5N 2 27W
Ban Ao Tu Khun, *Thailand* **87 a** 8 9N 98 20 E
Ban Ban, *Laos* **86 C4** 19 31N 103 30 E
Ban Bang Hin, *Thailand* **87 H2** 9 32N 98 35 E
Ban Bang Khu, *Thailand* **87 a** 7 57N 98 23 E
Ban Bang Rong, *Thailand* **87 a** 8 3N 98 25 E
Ban Bo Phut, *Thailand* **87 b** 9 33N 100 2 E
Ban Chaweng, *Thailand* **87 b** 9 32N 100 3 E
Ban Chiang Klang, *Thailand* **86 C3** 19 25N 100 55 E
Ban Chik, *Laos* **86 D4** 17 15N 102 22 E
Ban Choho, *Thailand* **86 E4** 15 2N 102 9 E
Ban Dan Lan Hoi, *Thailand* **86 D2** 17 0N 99 35 E
Ban Don = Surat Thani, *Thailand* **87 H2** 9 6N 99 20 E
Ban Don, *Vietnam* **86 F6** 12 53N 107 48 E
Ban Don, Ao →, *Thailand* **87 H2** 9 20N 99 25 E
Ban Dong, *Thailand* **86 C3** 19 30N 100 59 E
Ban Hong, *Thailand* **86 C2** 18 18N 98 50 E
Ban Hua Thanon, *Thailand* **87 b** 9 26N 100 1 E
Ban Kaeng, *Thailand* **86 D3** 17 29N 100 7 E
Ban Kantang, *Thailand* **87 J2** 7 25N 99 31 E
Ban Karon, *Thailand* **87 a** 7 51N 98 18 E
Ban Kata, *Thailand* **87 a** 7 50N 98 18 E
Ban Keun, *Laos* **86 C4** 18 22N 102 35 E
Ban Khai, *Thailand* **86 F3** 12 46N 101 18 E
Ban Kheun, *Laos* **86 B3** 20 13N 101 7 E
Ban Khlong Khian, *Thailand* **87 a** 8 10N 98 26 E
Ban Khlong Kua, *Thailand* **87 J3** 6 57N 100 8 E
Ban Khuan, *Thailand* **87 a** 8 20N 98 25 E
Ban Khuan Mao, *Thailand* **87 J2** 7 50N 99 37 E
Ban Ko Yai Chim, *Thailand* **87 G2** 11 17N 99 26 E
Ban Kok, *Thailand* **86 D4** 16 40N 103 40 E
Ban Laem, *Thailand* **86 F2** 13 13N 99 59 E
Ban Lamai, *Thailand* **87 b** 9 28N 100 3 E
Ban Lao Ngam, *Laos* **86 E6** 15 28N 106 10 E
Ban Le Kathe, *Thailand* **86 E2** 15 49N 98 53 E
Ban Lo Po Noi, *Thailand* **87 a** 8 1N 98 34 E
Ban Mae Chedi, *Thailand* **86 C2** 19 11N 99 31 E
Ban Mae Laeng, *Thailand* **86 B2** 20 1N 99 17 E
Ban Mae Nam, *Thailand* **87 b** 9 34N 100 0 E
Ban Mae Sariang, *Thailand* **86 C1** 18 10N 97 56 E
Ban Mê Thuôt = Buon Ma Thuot, *Vietnam* **86 F7** 12 40N 108 3 E
Ban Mi, *Thailand* **86 E3** 15 3N 100 32 E
Ban Muong Mo, *Laos* **86 C4** 19 4N 103 58 E
Ban Na Bo, *Thailand* **87 b** 9 19N 99 41 E
Ban Na Mo, *Laos* **86 D5** 17 7N 105 40 E
Ban Na San, *Thailand* **87 H2** 8 53N 99 52 E
Ban Na Tong, *Laos* **86 B3** 20 56N 101 47 E
Ban Nam Bac, *Laos* **86 B4** 20 38N 102 20 E
Ban Nam Ma, *Laos* **86 A3** 22 2N 101 37 E
Ban Ngang, *Laos* **86 E6** 15 59N 106 11 E
Ban Nong Bok, *Laos* **86 D5** 17 5N 104 48 E
Ban Nong Boua, *Laos* **86 E6** 15 40N 106 33 E
Ban Nong Pling, *Thailand* **86 E3** 15 40N 100 10 E
Ban Pak Chan, *Thailand* **87 G2** 10 32N 98 51 E
Ban Patong, *Thailand* **87 a** 7 54N 98 18 E
Ban Phai, *Thailand* **86 D4** 16 4N 102 44 E
Ban Phak Chit, *Thailand* **87 a** 8 0N 98 24 E
Ban Pong, *Thailand* **86 F2** 13 50N 99 55 E
Ban Rawai, *Thailand* **87 a** 7 47N 98 20 E
Ban Ron Phibun, *Thailand* **87 H2** 8 9N 99 51 E
Ban Sakhu, *Thailand* **87 a** 8 4N 98 18 E
Ban Sanam Chai, *Thailand* **87 J3** 7 33N 100 25 E
Ban Sangkha, *Thailand* **86 E4** 14 37N 103 52 E
Ban Tak, *Thailand* **86 D2** 17 2N 99 4 E
Ban Tako, *Thailand* **86 E4** 14 5N 102 40 E
Ban Tha Dua, *Thailand* **86 D2** 17 59N 98 39 E
Ban Tha Li, *Thailand* **86 D3** 17 37N 101 25 E
Ban Tha Nun, *Thailand* **87 a** 8 12N 98 18 E
Ban Tha Rua, *Thailand* **87 a** 7 59N 98 22 E
Ban Tha Yu, *Thailand* **87 a** 8 17N 98 22 E
Ban Thahine, *Laos* **86 E5** 14 12N 105 33 E
Ban Thong Krut, *Thailand* **87 b** 9 25N 99 57 E
Ban Xien Kok, *Laos* **86 B3** 20 54N 100 39 E
Ban Yen Nhan, *Vietnam* **86 B6** 20 57N 106 2 E
Banā, W. →, *Yemen* **98 D4** 13 3N 45 24 E
Banaba, *Kiribati* **134 H8** 0 45 S 169 50 E
Banalia, *Dem. Rep. of the Congo* **118 B2** 1 32N 25 5 E
Banam, *Cambodia* **87 G5** 11 20N 105 17 E
Banamba, *Mali* **112 C3** 13 29N 7 22W
Banana Is., *S. Leone* **112 D2** 8 7N 13 15W
Bananal, I. do, *Brazil* **171 D1** 11 30 S 50 30W
Bananga, *India* **95 L11** 6 57N 93 54 E
Banaras = Varanasi, *India* **93 G10** 25 22N 83 0 E
Banas →, *Gujarat, India* **92 H4** 23 45N 71 25 E
Banas →, *Mad. P., India* **93 G9** 24 15N 81 30 E
Bânâs, Ras, *Egypt* **106 C4** 23 57N 35 59 E
Banaue, *Phil.* **80 C3** 16 55N 121 4 E
Banaz, *Turkey* **49 C11** 38 46N 29 46 E
Banaz →, *Turkey* **49 C11** 38 12N 29 14 E
Banbridge, *U.K.* **23 B5** 54 22N 6 16W
Banbury, *U.K.* **21 E6** 52 4N 1 20W
Banc d'Arguin, Parc Nat. du △, *Mauritania* **110 D1** 20 10N 16 20W
Banchory, *U.K.* **22 D6** 57 3N 2 29W
Banco, *Ethiopia* **107 F4** 6 12N 38 13 E
Bancroft = Chililabombwe, *Zambia* **119 E2** 12 18 S 27 43 E
Bancroft, *Canada* **140 C4** 45 3N 77 51W
Band, *Romania* **53 D9** 46 30N 24 25 E
Band Bonī, *Iran* **97 E8** 25 30N 59 33 E
Band-e Torkestan, *Afghan.* **91 B2** 35 30N 64 0 E
Band Qīr, *Iran* **97 D6** 31 39N 48 53 E
Banda, *Cameroon* **114 B2** 3 58N 14 32 E
Banda, *Mad. P., India* **93 G8** 24 3N 78 57 E
Banda, *Maharashtra, India* **95 G1** 15 49N 73 52 E
Banda, *Ut. P., India* **93 G9** 25 30N 80 26 E
Banda, Kepulauan, *Indonesia* **83 B3** 4 37 S 129 50 E
Banda Aceh, *Indonesia* **84 A1** 5 35N 95 20 E
Banda Banda, Mt., *Australia* **129 A10** 31 10 S 152 28 E
Banda Elat, *Indonesia* **83 C4** 5 40 S 133 5 E
Banda Is. = Banda, Kepulauan, *Indonesia* **83 B3** 4 37 S 129 50 E
Banda Kani, *Dem. Rep. of the Congo* **115 C2** 4 48 S 13 52 E
Banda Sea, *Indonesia* **82 C3** 6 0 S 130 0 E
Bandai-San, *Japan* **70 F10** 37 36N 140 4 E
Bandak, *Norway* **18 E5** 59 23N 8 29 E
Bandama →, *Ivory C.* **112 D3** 6 32N 4 30W
Bandama Blanc →, *Ivory C.* **112 D3** 6 55N 5 30W
Bandama Rouge →, *Ivory C.* **112 D4** 6 55N 5 30W
Bandān, *Iran* **97 D9** 31 23N 60 44 E
Bandanaira, *Indonesia* **83 B3** 4 32 S 129 54 E
Bandanwara, *India* **92 F6** 26 9N 74 38 E
Bandar = Machilipatnam, *India* **95 F5** 16 12N 81 8 E
Bandār-e Abbās, *Iran* **97 E8** 27 15N 56 15 E
Bandar-e Anzalī, *Iran* **97 B6** 37 30N 49 30 E
Bandar-e Bushehr = Būshehr, *Iran* **97 D6** 28 55N 50 55 E
Bandar-e Chārak, *Iran* **97 E7** 26 45N 54 20 E
Bandar-e Deylam, *Iran* **97 D6** 30 5N 50 10 E
Bandar-e Khomeynı, *Iran* **97 D6** 30 30N 49 5 E
Bandar-e Lengeh, *Iran* **97 E7** 26 35N 54 58 E
Bandar-e Maqām, *Iran* **97 E7** 26 56N 53 29 E
Bandar-e Ma'shur, *Iran* **97 D6** 30 35N 49 10 E
Bandar-e Rīg, *Iran* **97 D6** 29 29N 50 38 E
Bandar-e Torkeman, *Iran* **97 B7** 37 0N 54 10 E
Bandar Maharani = Muar, *Malaysia* **87 L4** 2 3N 102 34 E
Bandar Penggaram = Batu Pahat, *Malaysia* **87 M4** 1 50N 102 56 E
Bandar Seri Begawan, *Brunei* **85 B4** 4 52N 115 0 E
Bandar Sri Aman, *Malaysia* **85 B4** 1 15N 111 32 E
Bandawe, *Malawi* **119 E3** 11 58 S 34 5 E
Bande, *Spain* **42 C3** 42 3N 7 58W
Bandeira, Pico da, *Brazil* **171 F3** 20 26 S 41 47W
Bandeirante, *Brazil* **171 D1** 13 41 S 50 48W
Bandera, *Argentina* **174 B3** 28 55 S 62 20W
Banderas, B. de, *Mexico* **162 C3** 20 40N 105 30W
Bandhogarh, *India* **93 H9** 23 40N 81 2 E
Bandi →, *India* **92 F6** 26 12N 75 47 E
Bandia →, *India* **94 E5** 19 2N 80 28 E
Bandiagara, *Mali* **112 C4** 14 12N 3 29W
Bandikui, *India* **92 F7** 27 3N 76 34 E
Bandırma, *Turkey* **51 F11** 40 20N 28 0 E
Bandol, *France* **29 E9** 43 8N 5 46 E
Bandon, *Ireland* **23 E3** 51 44N 8 44W
Bandon →, *Ireland* **23 E3** 51 43N 8 37W
Bandoua, *C.A.R.* **114 B4** 4 39N 21 42 E
Bandula, *Mozam.* **119 F3** 19 0 S 33 7 E
Bandundu, *Dem. Rep. of the Congo* **114 C3** 3 15 S 17 22 E
Bandundu □, *Dem. Rep. of the Congo* **114 C3** 3 30 S 17 30 E
Bandung, *Indonesia* **85 D3** 6 54 S 107 36 E
Bané, *Burkina Faso* **113 C4** 11 42N 0 15W
Băneasa, *Romania* **53 E12** 45 56N 27 55 E
Bāneh, *Iran* **101 E11** 35 59N 45 53 E
Bañeres, *Spain* **41 G4** 38 44N 0 38W
Banes, *Cuba* **165 B4** 21 0N 75 42W
Banff, *Canada* **142 C5** 51 10N 115 34W
Banff, *U.K.* **22 D6** 57 40N 2 33W
Banff Nat. Park △, *Canada* **142 C5** 51 30N 116 15W
Banfora, *Burkina Faso* **112 C4** 10 40N 4 40W
Bang Fai →, *Laos* **86 D5** 16 57N 104 45 E
Bang Hieng →, *Laos* **86 D5** 16 10N 105 10 E
Bang Krathum, *Thailand* **86 D3** 16 34N 100 18 E
Bang Lamung, *Thailand* **86 F3** 13 3N 100 56 E
Bang Mun Nak, *Thailand* **86 D3** 16 2N 100 23 E
Bang Pa In, *Thailand* **86 E3** 14 14N 100 35 E
Bang Rakam, *Thailand* **86 D3** 16 45N 100 7 E
Bang Saphan, *Thailand* **87 G2** 11 14N 99 28 E
Bang Thao, *Thailand* **87 a** 7 59N 98 18 E
Banga, *Angola* **115 D3** 8 43 S 15 13 E
Banga, *Dem. Rep. of the Congo* **115 D4** 5 25 S 20 28 E
Banga, *Aklan, Phil.* **81 F4** 11 38N 122 20 E
Banga, *S. Cotabato, Phil.* **81 H5** 6 21N 124 47 E
Bangaduni I., *India* **90 E2** 21 34N 88 52 E
Bangala Dam, *Zimbabwe* **119 G3** 21 7 S 31 25 E
Bangalore, *India* **95 H3** 12 59N 77 40 E
Banganapalle, *India* **95 G4** 15 19N 78 14 E
Banganga →, *India* **92 F6** 27 6N 77 25 E
Bangangté, *Cameroon* **113 D7** 5 8N 10 32 E
Bangaon, *India* **93 H13** 23 0N 88 47 E
Bangar, *Phil.* **80 C3** 16 54N 120 25 E
Bangassou, *C.A.R.* **114 B4** 4 55N 23 7 E
Bangeta, Mt., *Papua N. G.* **132 D4** 6 21 S 147 3 E
Banggai, *Indonesia* **82 B2** 1 34 S 123 30 E
Banggai, Kepulauan, *Indonesia* **82 B2** 1 40 S 123 30 E
Banggai Arch. = Banggai, Kepulauan, *Indonesia* **82 B2** 1 40 S 123 30 E
Banggi, *Malaysia* **85 A5** 7 17N 117 12 E
Banghāzī, *Libya* **108 B4** 32 11N 20 3 E
Banghāzī □, *Libya* **108 B4** 32 7N 20 4 E
Bangil, *Indonesia* **85 D4** 7 36 S 112 50 E
Bangjang, *Sudan* **107 E3** 11 23N 32 41 E
Bangka, *Sulawesi, Indonesia* **82 A3** 1 50N 125 5 E
Bangka, *Sumatera, Indonesia* **84 C3** 2 0 S 105 50 E
Bangka, Selat, *Indonesia* **84 C3** 2 30 S 105 30 E
Bangkalan, *Indonesia* **85 D4** 7 2 S 112 46 E
Bangkinang, *Indonesia* **84 B2** 0 18N 101 5 E
Bangko, *Indonesia* **84 C2** 2 5 S 102 9 E
Bangkok, *Thailand* **86 F3** 13 45N 100 35 E
Bangladesh ■, *Asia* **90 C3** 24 0N 90 0 E
Bangli, *Indonesia* **79 J18** 8 27 S 115 21 E
Bangolo, *Ivory C.* **112 D3** 7 1N 7 29W
Bangong Co, *India* **93 B8** 35 50N 79 20 E
Bangor, *Down, U.K.* **23 B6** 54 40N 5 40W
Bangor, *Gwynedd, U.K.* **20 D3** 53 14N 4 8W
Bangor, *Maine, U.S.A.* **139 D13** 44 48N 68 46W
Bangor, *Mich., U.S.A.* **157 B10** 42 18N 86 7W
Bangor, *Pa., U.S.A.* **151 F9** 40 52N 75 13W
Bangoran →, *C.A.R.* **114 A3** 8 42N 19 6 E
Bangu, *Dem. Rep. of the Congo* **114 C3** 0 3 S 19 12 E
Bangued, *Phil.* **80 C3** 17 40N 120 37 E
Bangui, *C.A.R.* **114 B3** 4 23N 18 35 E
Bangui, *Phil.* **80 B3** 18 32N 120 46 E
Banguru, *Dem. Rep. of the Congo* **118 B2** 0 30N 27 10 E
Bangweulu, L., *Zambia* **119 E3** 11 0 S 30 0 E
Bangweulu Swamp, *Zambia* **119 E3** 11 20 S 30 15 E
Banhine, Parque Nac. de △, *Mozam.* **117 C5** 22 49 S 32 55 E
Bani, *Dom. Rep.* **165 C5** 18 16N 70 22W
Bani, *Phil.* **80 C2** 16 11N 119 52 E
Bani →, *Mali* **112 C4** 14 30N 4 12W
Bani, Jebel, *Morocco* **110 C3** 29 16N 8 0W
Bani Bangou, *Niger* **113 B5** 15 3N 2 42 E
Banī Sa'd, *Iraq* **101 F11** 33 34N 44 32 E
Bania, *C.A.R.* **114 B3** 4 1N 16 7 E
Bania, *Ivory C.* **112 D4** 9 4N 3 6W
Baniara, *Papua N. G.* **132 E5** 9 44 S 149 54 E
Banihal Pass, *India* **93 C6** 33 30N 75 12 E
Banikoara, *Benin* **113 C5** 11 18N 2 26 E
Banīnah, *Libya* **108 B4** 32 0N 20 12 E
Bāniyās, *Syria* **100 E6** 35 10N 36 0 E
Banja Luka, *Bos.-H.* **52 F2** 44 49N 17 11 E
Banjar, *India* **92 D7** 31 38N 77 21 E
Banjar, *Indonesia* **85 D3** 7 24 S 108 30 E
Banjar →, *India* **93 H9** 22 36N 80 22 E
Banjarmasin, *Indonesia* **85 C4** 3 20 S 114 35 E
Banjarnegara, *Indonesia* **85 D3** 7 24 S 109 42 E
Banjul, *Gambia* **112 C1** 13 28N 16 40W
Banka, *India* **93 G12** 24 53N 86 55 E
Bankas, *Mali* **112 C4** 14 4N 3 31W
Bankeryd, *Sweden* **17 G8** 57 53N 14 6 E
Banket, *Zimbabwe* **119 F3** 17 27 S 30 19 E
Bankilaré, *Niger* **113 C5** 14 35N 0 44 E
Bankot, *India* **94 F1** 17 58N 73 2 E
Banks, *U.S.A.* **152 D4** 31 49N 85 51W
Banks I. = Moa, I., *Papua N. G.* **132 F2** 10 10 S 142 15 E
Banks I., *B.C., Canada* **142 C3** 53 20N 130 0W
Banks I., *N.W.T., Canada* **138 A7** 73 15N 121 30W
Banks Is., *Vanuatu* **133 C5** 13 50 S 167 30 E
Banks L., *U.S.A.* **152 D6** 31 2N 83 6W
Banks Pen., *N.Z.* **131 D8** 43 45 S 173 15 E
Banks Str., *Australia* **127 D4** 40 40 S 148 10 E
Bankumuna, *Dem. Rep. of the Congo* **115 C3** 4 28 S 19 57 E
Bankura, *India* **93 H12** 23 11N 87 18 E
Bankya, *Bulgaria* **50 D7** 42 43N 23 8 E
Banmankhi, *India* **93 G12** 25 53N 87 11 E
Banmauk, *Burma* **90 C5** 24 24N 95 51 E
Bann →, *Arm., U.K.* **23 B5** 54 30N 6 31W
Bann →, *L'derry., U.K.* **23 A5** 55 8N 6 41W
Bannaanka Saraar, *Somali Rep.* **120 C3** 9 25N 46 17 E
Bannalec, *France* **26 E3** 47 57N 3 42W
Bannang Sata, *Thailand* **87 J3** 6 16N 101 16 E
Bannerton, *Australia* **128 C5** 34 42 S 142 47 E
Banning, *U.S.A.* **161 M10** 33 56N 116 53W
Banningville = Bandundu, *Dem. Rep. of the Congo* **114 C3** 3 15 S 17 22 E
Banno, *Ethiopia* **107 G4** 4 51N 37 24 E
Bannockburn, *Canada* **150 B7** 44 39N 77 33W
Bannockburn, *U.K.* **22 E5** 56 5N 3 55W
Bannockburn, *Zimbabwe* **119 G2** 20 17 S 29 48 E
Bannu, *Pakistan* **91 B3** 33 0N 70 18 E
Bano, *India* **93 H11** 22 40N 84 55 E
Bañolas = Banyoles, *Spain* **40 C7** 42 16N 2 44 E
Banon, *France* **29 D9** 44 2N 5 38 E
Baños de la Encina, *Spain* **43 G7** 38 10N 3 46W
Baños de Molgas, *Spain* **42 C3** 42 15N 7 40W
Bánovce nad Bebravou, *Slovak Rep.* **35 C11** 48 44N 18 16 E
Banovići, *Bos.-H.* **52 F3** 44 25N 18 32 E
Bansalan, *Phil.* **81 H5** 6 55N 125 13 E
Bansgaon, *India* **93 F10** 26 33N 83 21 E
Banská Bystrica, *Slovak Rep.* **35 C12** 48 46N 19 14 E
Banská Štiavnica, *Slovak Rep.* **35 C11** 48 25N 18 55 E
Bansko, *Bulgaria* **50 E7** 41 52N 23 28 E
Banskobystrický □, *Slovak Rep.* **35 C12** 48 20N 19 0 E
Banswara, *India* **92 H6** 23 32N 74 24 E
Bantaeng, *Indonesia* **82 C1** 5 32 S 119 56 E
Bantaji, *Nigeria* **113 D7** 8 6N 10 5 E
Bantayan, *Phil.* **81 F4** 11 10N 123 43 E
Bantayan I., *Phil.* **81 F4** 11 13N 123 44 E
Banten, *Indonesia* **84 D3** 6 5 S 106 8 E
Banton I., *Phil.* **80 E4** 12 56N 122 4 E
Bantry, *Ireland* **23 E2** 51 41N 9 27W
Bantry B., *Ireland* **23 E2** 51 37N 9 44W
Bantul, *Indonesia* **85 D4** 7 55 S 110 19 E
Bantva, *India* **92 J4** 21 29N 70 12 E
Bantval, *India* **95 H2** 12 55N 75 0 E
Banya, *Bulgaria* **51 D8** 42 33N 24 50 E
Banyak, Kepulauan, *Indonesia* **84 B1** 2 10N 97 10 E
Banyalbufar, *Spain* **38 B3** 39 42N 2 31 E
Banyo, *Cameroon* **113 D7** 6 52N 11 45 E
Banyoles, *Spain* **40 C7** 42 16N 2 44 E
Banyuls-sur-Mer, *France* **28 F7** 42 28N 3 8 E
Banyumas, *Indonesia* **85 D3** 7 32 S 109 18 E
Banyuwangi, *Indonesia* **85 D4** 8 13 S 114 21 E
Banz, *Papua N. G.* **132 C3** 5 47 S 144 37 E
Banza, *Dem. Rep. of the Congo* **114 B4** 0 28N 20 10 E
Banzare Coast, *Antarctica* **7 C9** 68 0 S 125 0 E
Bao Ha, *Vietnam* **76 F5** 22 11N 104 21 E
Bao Lac, *Vietnam* **86 A5** 22 57N 105 40 E
Bao Loc, *Vietnam* **87 G6** 11 32N 107 48 E
Bao'an = Shenzhen, *China* **69 F10** 22 32N 114 5 E
Baocheng, *China* **74 H4** 33 12N 106 56 E
Baode, *China* **74 E6** 39 1N 111 5 E
Baodi, *China* **75 E9** 39 38N 117 20 E
Baoding, *China* **74 E8** 38 50N 115 28 E
Baoji, *China* **74 G4** 34 20N 107 5 E
Baojing, *China* **76 C7** 28 45N 109 41 E
Baokang, *China* **77 B8** 31 54N 111 12 E
Baoro, *C.A.R.* **114 A3** 5 40N 15 58 E
Baoruco, Sierra de △, *Dom. Rep.* **165 C5** 18 10N 71 25W
Baoshan, *Shanghai, China* **77 B13** 31 27N 121 26 E
Baoshan, *Yunnan, China* **76 E2** 25 10N 99 5 E
Baotou, *China* **74 D6** 40 32N 110 2 E
Baoxing, *China* **76 B4** 30 24N 102 50 E
Baoying, *China* **75 H10** 33 17N 119 20 E
Bap, *India* **92 F5** 27 23N 72 18 E
Bapatla, *India* **95 G5** 15 55N 80 30 E
Bapaume, *France* **27 B9** 50 7N 2 50 E
Baqanas, *Kazakhstan* **65 A8** 44 50N 76 15 E
Baqbaqty, *Kazakhstan* **65 A8** 44 35N 76 40 E
Bāqerābād, *Iran* **97 C6** 33 2N 51 58 E
Ba'qūbah, *Iraq* **101 F11** 33 45N 44 50 E
Baquedano, *Chile* **174 A2** 23 20 S 69 52W
Bar, *Montenegro, Yug.* **50 D3** 42 8N 19 6 E
Bar, *Ukraine* **59 H4** 49 4N 27 40 E
Bar Bigha, *India* **93 G11** 25 21N 85 47 E
Bar Harbor, *U.S.A.* **149 C11** 44 23N 68 13W
Bar-le-Duc, *France* **27 D12** 48 47N 5 10 E
Bar-sur-Aube, *France* **27 D11** 48 14N 4 40 E
Bar-sur-Seine, *France* **27 D11** 48 7N 4 20 E
Bara, *India* **93 G9** 25 16N 81 43 E
Bara, *Indonesia* **82 B3** 3 8 S 126 11 E
Bâra, *Romania* **53 C12** 47 2N 27 3 E
Bara Banki, *India* **93 F9** 26 55N 81 12 E
Barabai, *Indonesia* **85 C5** 2 32 S 115 34 E
Baraboo, *U.S.A.* **154 D10** 43 28N 89 45W
Baracoa, *Cuba* **165 B5** 20 20N 74 30W
Baradā →, *Syria* **103 B5** 33 33N 36 34 E
Baradero, *Argentina* **174 C4** 33 52 S 59 29W
Baradine, *Australia* **129 A8** 30 56 S 149 4 E
Baraga, *U.S.A.* **154 B10** 46 47N 88 30W
Bărăganul, *Romania* **53 F12** 44 49N 27 31 E
Barah →, *India* **92 F6** 27 42N 77 5 E
Barahona, *Dom. Rep.* **165 C5** 18 13N 71 7W
Barahona, *Spain* **40 D2** 41 17N 2 39W
Barail Range, *India* **90 C4** 25 15N 93 20 E
Barajas, Madrid ✕ (MAD), *Spain* **42 E7** 40 26N 3 34W
Barak →, *India* **90 C4** 24 52N 92 30 E
Baraka, *Sudan* **107 E2** 10 59N 27 59 E
Baraka →, *Sudan* **106 D4** 18 13N 37 35 E
Barakaldo, *Spain* **40 B2** 43 18N 2 59W
Barakar →, *India* **93 G12** 24 7N 86 14 E
Barakot, *India* **93 J11** 21 33N 84 59 E
Barakpur, *India* **93 H13** 22 44N 88 30 E
Baralaba, *Australia* **126 C4** 24 13 S 149 50 E
Baralla, *Spain* **42 C3** 42 53N 7 15W

Baralzon L., *Canada* 143 B9   60 0N 98 3W
Baram →, *Malaysia* .... 85 B4   4 35N 113 58 E
Baramati, *India* .... 94 E2   18 11N 74 33 E
Baramba, *India* .... 94 D7   20 25N 85 23 E
Barameiya, *Sudan* .... 106 D4   18 32N 36 38 E
Baramula, *India* .... 93 B6   34 15N 74 20 E
Baran, *India* .... 92 G7   25 9N 76 40 E
Baran →, *Pakistan* .... 92 G3   25 13N 68 17 E
Barañain, *Spain* 40 C3   42 48N 1 40W
Baranavichy, *Belarus* .... 59 F4   53 10N 26 0 E
Barani, *Burkina Faso* 112 C4   13 9N 3 51W
Baranoa, *Colombia* 168 A3   10 48N 74 55W
Baranof, *U.S.A.* 142 B2   57 5N 134 50W
Baranof I., *U.S.A.* 144 H14   57 0N 135 0W
Baranów Sandomierski, *Poland* ... 55 H8   50 29N 21 30 E
Baranya □, *Hungary* .... 52 E3   46 0N 18 15 E
Barão de Cocais, *Brazil* .... 171 E3   19 55 S 43 28W
Barão de Grajaú, *Brazil* .... 170 C3   6 45 S 43 1W
Barão de Melgaço, *Mato Grosso,*
   Brazil .... 173 D6   16 14 S 55 52W
Barão de Melgaço, *Rondônia, Brazil* 173 C5   11 50 S 60 45W
Baraolt, *Romania* .... 53 D10   46 5N 25 34 E
Barapasi, *Indonesia* .... 83 B5   2 15 S 137 5 E
Barapina = Panguna, *Papua N. G.* 132 D8   6 21 S 155 25 E
Baras, *Phil.* .... 80 E5   13 40N 124 22 E
Barasat, *India* .... 93 H13   22 46N 88 31 E
Barat Daya, Kepulauan, *Indonesia* 82 C3   7 30 S 128 0 E
Baratang I., *India* .... 95 H11   12 13N 92 45 E
Barataria B., *U.S.A.* 155 L10   29 20N 89 55W
Barauda, *India* .... 92 H6   23 33N 75 15 E
Baraut, *India* .... 92 E7   29 13N 77 7 E
Baraya, *Colombia* 168 C2   3 10N 75 4W
Barbacan = Roxas, *Phil.* .... 81 F2   10 20N 119 21 E
Barbacena, *Brazil* .... 171 F3   21 15 S 43 56W
Barbacoas, *Colombia* 168 C2   1 45N 78 0W
Barbados ■, *W. Indies* .... 165 g   13 10N 59 30W
Barbalha, *Brazil* .... 170 C4   7 19 S 39 17W
Barban, *Croatia* .... 45 C11   45 5N 14 2 E
Barbària, C. de, *Spain* .... 38 D1   38 39N 1 24 E
Barbaros, *Turkey* .... 51 F11   40 54N 27 27 E
Barbas, C., *W. Sahara* 110 D1   22 20N 16 42W
Barbastro, *Spain* .... 40 C5   42 2N 0 5 E
Barbate = Barbate de Franco, *Spain* 43 J5   36 13N 5 56W
Barbate de Franco, *Spain* 43 J5   36 13N 5 56W
Barbaza, *Phil.* .... 81 F4   11 12N 122 2 E
Barberino di Mugello, *Italy* ... 45 E8   44 0N 11 15 E
Barbers Pt., *U.S.A.* 145 K13   21 18N 158 7W
Barberton, *S. Africa* .... 117 D5   25 42 S 31 2 E
Barberton, *U.S.A.* 150 E3   41 0N 81 39W
Barberville, *U.S.A.* 153 F8   29 11N 81 26W
Barbezieux-St-Hilaire, *France* ... 28 C3   45 28N 0 9W
Barbonneau, *St. Lucia* .... 165 f   13 59N 60 58W
Barbosa, *Colombia* 168 B3   5 57N 73 37W
Barbourville, *U.S.A.* 149 G4   36 52N 83 53W
Barbuda, *W. Indies* 165 C7   17 30N 61 40W
Bârca, *Romania* .... 53 G8   43 59N 23 36 E
Barcaldine, *Australia* .... 126 C4   23 43 S 145 6 E
Barcarena, *Brazil* .... 170 B2   1 30 S 48 40W
Barcarrota, *Spain* 43 G4   38 31N 6 51W
Barce = Al Marj, *Libya* .... 108 B4   32 25N 20 30 E
Barcellona Pozzo di Gotto, *Italy* 47 D8   38 9N 15 13 E
Barcelona, *Spain* .... 40 D7   41 21N 2 10 E
Barcelona, *Venezuela* 169 A5   10 10N 64 40W
Barcelona □, *Spain* .... 40 D7   41 30N 2 0 E
Barcelona ✈ (BCN), *Spain* ... 40 D7   41 18N 2 5 E
Barceloneta, *Puerto Rico* .... 165 d   18 27N 66 32W
Barcelonnette, *France* .... 29 D10   44 23N 6 40 E
Barcelos, *Brazil* .... 169 D5   1 0 S 63 0W
Barcin, *Poland* .... 55 F4   52 52N 17 55 E
Barclayville, *Liberia* 112 E3   4 48N 8 2W
Barcoo →, *Australia* .... 126 D3   25 30 S 142 50 E
Barcs, *Hungary* .... 52 E2   45 58N 17 28 E
Barczewo, *Poland* .... 54 E7   53 50N 20 42 E
Bärdä, *Azerbaijan* .... 61 K8   40 25N 47 10 E
Barda del Medio, *Argentina* ... 176 A3   38 45 S 68 11W
Bardaï, *Chad* .... 109 D3   21 25N 17 0 E
Bardas Blancas, *Argentina* ... 174 D2   35 49 S 69 45W
Bardawîl, Sabkhet el, *Egypt* ... 103 D2   31 10N 33 15 E
Barddhaman, *India* .... 93 H12   23 14N 87 39 E
Bardera, *Somali Rep.* .... 120 D2   2 20N 42 27 E
Barð, *Iceland* 11 A7   66 3N 19 8W
Bárðarbunga, *Iceland* 11 C9   64 38N 17 32W
Barðastrandarsýsla □, *Iceland* ... 11 B3   65 40N 23 0W
Bardi, *Italy* .... 44 D6   44 38N 9 44 E
Bardiyah, *Libya* .... 108 B5   31 45N 25 5 E
Bardoli, *India* .... 94 D1   21 12N 73 5 E
Bardolino, *Italy* .... 44 C7   45 33N 10 43 E
Bardonecchia, *Italy* .... 44 C5   45 5N 6 42 E
Bardsey I., *U.K.* 20 E3   52 45N 4 47W
Bardstown, *U.S.A.* 157 G11   37 49N 85 28W
Bareilly, *India* .... 93 E8   28 22N 79 27 E
Bareli, *India* .... 93 H9   23 6N 80 3 E
Barellan, *Australia* .... 129 C7   34 16 S 146 24 E
Barentin, *France* .... 26 C7   49 33N 0 58 E
Barenton, *France* 26 D6   48 38N 0 50W
Barents Sea, *Arctic* .... 6 B9   73 0N 39 0 E
Barentu, *Eritrea* .... 107 D4   15 2N 37 35 E
Barfleur, *France* 26 C5   49 40N 1 17W
Barfleur, Pte. de, *France* 26 C5   49 42N 1 16W
Barga, *Italy* .... 44 D7   44 4N 10 29 E
Bargal, *Somali Rep.* .... 120 B4   11 25N 51 0 E
Bargara, *Australia* .... 126 C5   24 50 S 152 25 E
Bargarh, *India* .... 94 D6   21 20N 83 37 E
Bargas, *Spain* 42 F6   39 56N 4 3W
Bârgăului Bistriţa, *Romania* ... 53 C9   47 13N 24 46 E
Barge, *Italy* .... 44 D4   44 43N 7 20 E
Bargnop, *Sudan* .... 107 F2   9 32N 28 25 E
Bargo, *Australia* .... 129 C9   34 18 S 150 35 E
Bargteheide, *Germany* .... 30 B6   53 44N 10 14 E
Barguzin, *Russia* .... 67 D11   53 37N 109 37 E
Barh, *India* .... 93 G11   25 29N 85 46 E
Barhaj, *India* .... 93 F10   26 18N 83 44 E
Barham, *Australia* .... 128 C6   35 36 S 144 8 E
Barharwa, *India* .... 93 G12   24 52N 87 47 E
Barhi, *India* .... 93 G11   24 15N 85 25 E
Bari, *Dem. Rep. of the Congo* ... 114 B3   3 20N 13 20 E
Bari, *India* .... 92 F7   26 39N 77 39 E
Bari, *Italy* .... 47 A9   41 8N 16 51 E
Bari Doab, *Pakistan* .... 92 D5   30 20N 73 0 E
Bari Sadri, *India* .... 92 G6   24 28N 74 30 E
Bari Sardo, *Italy* .... 46 C2   39 50N 9 38 E
Barīdī, Ra's, *Si. Arabia* .... 96 E3   24 17N 37 31 E
Barīm, *Yemen* .... 98 D3   12 39N 43 25 E
Barima →, *Guyana* 169 B5   8 33N 60 25W
Barinas, *Venezuela* 168 B3   8 36N 70 15W
Barinas □, *Venezuela* 168 B4   8 10N 69 50W
Baring, *U.S.A.* 156 D4   40 15N 92 12W
Baring, C., *Canada* 138 B8   70 0N 117 30W
Baringa, *Dem. Rep. of the Congo* 114 B4   0 45N 20 52 E
Baringo, L., *Kenya* .... 118 B4   0 47N 36 16 E
Barinitas, *Venezuela* 168 B3   8 45N 70 25W
Baripada, *India* .... 94 D8   21 57N 86 45 E
Bariri, *Brazil* .... 171 F2   22 4 S 48 44W
Bârîs, *Egypt* .... 106 C3   24 42N 30 31 E
Barisal, *Bangla.* .... 93 H17   22 45N 90 20 E
Barisal □, *Bangla.* .... 90 D3   22 45N 90 20 E
Barisan, Bukit, *Indonesia* .... 78 E2   3 30 S 102 15 E
Barito →, *Indonesia* .... 85 C4   4 0 S 114 50 E
Barjac, *France* .... 29 D8   44 20N 4 22 E
Barjols, *France* .... 29 E10   43 34N 6 2 E
Barjūj, Wadi →, *Libya* .... 108 C2   25 26N 12 12 E
Bark L., *Canada* 150 A7   45 27N 77 51W
Barka = Baraka →, *Sudan* ... 106 D4   18 13N 37 35 E

Barkakana, *India* .... 93 H11   23 37N 85 29 E
Barkald, *Norway* .... 18 C7   61 59N 10 53 E
Barkam, *China* .... 76 B4   31 51N 102 28 E
Barker, *U.S.A.* 150 C6   43 20N 78 33W
Barkley, L., *U.S.A.* 149 G2   37 1N 88 14W
Barkley Sound, *Canada* 142 D3   48 50N 125 10W
Barkly East, *S. Africa* .... 116 E4   30 58 S 27 33 E
Barkly Roadhouse, *Australia* ... 126 B2   19 52 S 135 50 E
Barkly Tableland, *Australia* ... 126 B2   17 50 S 136 40 E
Barkly West, *S. Africa* .... 116 D3   28 5 S 24 31 E
Barkol, Wadi →, *Sudan* .... 106 D3   17 40N 32 0 E
Barkol Kazak Zizhixian, *China* ... 68 B4   43 37N 93 2 E
Barla Dağı, *Turkey* .... 49 C12   38 5N 30 40 E
Bârlad, *Romania* .... 53 D12   46 15N 27 38 E
Bârlad →, *Romania* .... 53 E12   45 38N 27 32 E
Barlee, L., *Australia* .... 125 E2   29 15 S 119 30 E
Barlee, Mt., *Australia* .... 125 D4   24 38 S 128 13 E
Barletta, *Italy* .... 47 A9   41 19N 16 17 E
Barlinek, *Poland* .... 55 F2   53 0N 15 1 E
Barlovento, *Canary Is.* 9 e1   28 48N 17 48W
Barlovento, *C. Verde Is.* .... 9 j   17 0N 25 0W
Barlow L., *Canada* 143 A8   62 0N 103 0W
Barmedman, *Australia* .... 129 C7   34 9 S 147 21 E
Barmer, *India* .... 92 G4   25 45N 71 20 E
Barmera, *Australia* .... 128 C4   34 15 S 140 28 E
Barmouth, *U.K.* 20 E3   52 44N 4 4W
Barmstedt, *Germany* .... 30 B5   53 47N 9 46 E
Barn, The, *St. Helena* .... 9 h   15 55 S 5 40W
Barna →, *India* .... 93 G10   25 21N 83 3 E
Barnagar, *India* .... 92 H6   23 7N 75 19 E
Barnala, *India* .... 92 D6   30 23N 75 33 E
Barnard →, *Australia* .... 129 A9   31 34 S 151 25 E
Barnard Castle, *U.K.* 20 C6   54 33N 1 55W
Barnato, *Australia* .... 129 A6   31 38 S 145 0 E
Barnaul, *Russia* .... 66 D9   53 20N 83 40 E
Barnes, *Australia* .... 128 C6   36 2 S 144 49 E
Barnesville, *U.S.A.* 152 B5   33 3N 84 9W
Barnet □, *U.K.* 21 F7   51 38N 0 9W
Barneveld, *Neths.* .... 24 B5   52 7N 5 36 E
Barneveld, *U.S.A.* 151 C9   43 16N 75 14W
Barneville-Cartevert, *France* ... 26 C5   49 23N 1 46W
Barnhart, *U.S.A.* 155 K4   31 8N 101 10W
Barnsley, *U.K.* 20 D6   53 34N 1 27W
Barnstaple, *U.K.* 21 F3   51 5N 4 4W
Barnstaple Bay = Bideford Bay, *U.K.* 21 F3   51 5N 4 20W
Barnsville, *U.S.A.* 154 B6   46 43N 96 28W
Barnwell, *U.S.A.* 153 E5   33 15N 81 23W
Baro, *Nigeria* .... 113 D6   8 35N 6 18 E
Baro →, *Ethiopia* .... 107 F3   8 26N 33 13 E
Barobo, *Phil.* .... 81 G6   8 33N 126 7 E
Baroda = Vadodara, *India* .... 94 H5   22 20N 73 10 E
Baroda, *India* .... 92 G7   25 29N 76 35 E
Baroe, *S. Africa* .... 116 E3   33 13 S 24 33 E
Baron Ra., *Australia* .... 124 D4   23 30 S 127 45 E
Barong, *China* .... 76 B2   31 3N 99 0 E
Barora, *Solomon Is.* .... 133 L10   7 30 S 158 20 E
Barora Ite, *Solomon Is.* .... 133 L10   7 36 S 158 24 E
Barotseland, *Zambia* .... 115 F4   15 0 S 24 0 E
Barouéli, *Mali* 112 C3   13 4N 6 50W
Barpali, *India* .... 94 D6   21 11N 83 35 E
Barpathar, *India* .... 90 B4   26 17N 93 53 E
Barpeta, *India* .... 90 B3   26 20N 91 10 E
Barqin, *Libya* .... 108 C2   27 33N 13 34 E
Barques, Pt. Aux, *U.S.A.* 152 B4   44 4N 82 58W
Barquísimeto, *Venezuela* 168 A4   10 4N 69 19W
Barr, Ras el, *Egypt* .... 106 H7   31 32N 31 50 E
Barr Smith Range, *Australia* ... 125 E3   27 4 S 120 20 E
Barra, *Brazil* .... 170 D3   11 5 S 43 10W
Barra, *U.K.* 22 E1   57 0N 7 29W
Barra, Sd. of, *U.K.* 22 D1   57 4N 7 25W
Barra da Estiva, *Brazil* .... 171 D3   13 38 S 41 19W
Barra de Navidad, *Mexico* ... 162 D4   19 12N 104 41W
Barra do Bugres, *Brazil* .... 173 C6   15 0 S 57 11W
Barra do Corda, *Brazil* .... 170 C2   5 30 S 45 10W
Barra do Dande, *Angola* .... 115 D2   8 28 S 13 22 E
Barra do Mendes, *Brazil* .... 171 D3   11 43 S 42 4W
Barra do Piraí, *Brazil* .... 171 F3   22 30 S 43 50W
Barra Falsa, Pta. da, *Mozam.* ... 117 C6   22 58 S 35 37 E
Barra Hd., *U.K.* 22 E1   56 47N 7 40W
Barra Mansa, *Brazil* .... 171 F3   22 35 S 44 12W
Barraba, *Australia* .... 129 A9   30 21 S 150 35 E
Barracão do Barreto, *Brazil* ... 173 B6   8 48 S 58 24W
Barrackpur = Barakpur, *India* ... 93 H13   22 44N 88 30 E
Barradale Roadhouse, *Australia* ... 124 D1   22 42 S 114 58 E
Barrafranca, *Italy* .... 47 E7   37 22N 14 12 E
Barraigh = Barra, *U.K.* 22 E1   57 0N 7 29W
Barranca, Lima, *Peru* .... 172 C2   10 45 S 77 50W
Barranca, Loreto, *Peru* .... 168 D2   4 50 S 76 50W
Barranca del Cobre, Parque
   Natural →, *Mexico* 162 B3   27 18N 107 40W
Barrancabermeja, *Colombia* ... 168 B3   7 0N 73 50W
Barrancas, *Colombia* 168 A3   10 57N 72 50W
Barrancas, *Venezuela* 169 B5   8 55N 62 5W
Barrancos, *Portugal* 43 G4   38 10N 6 58W
Barranqueras, *Argentina* .... 174 B4   27 30 S 59 0W
Barranquilla, *Colombia* 168 A3   11 0N 74 50W
Barras, *Brazil* .... 170 B3   4 15 S 42 18W
Barras, *Colombia* .... 168 D3   1 45 S 73 13W
Barraute, *Canada* 140 C4   48 26N 77 38W
Barre, Mass., *U.S.A.* 151 D12   42 25N 72 6W
Barre, Vt., *U.S.A.* 151 B12   44 12N 72 30W
Barreal, *Argentina* .... 174 C2   31 33 S 69 28W
Barrei, *Ethiopia* .... 120 C2   6 10N 42 49 E
Barreiras, *Brazil* .... 171 D3   12 8 S 45 0W
Barreirinha, *Brazil* .... 169 D6   2 47 S 57 3W
Barreirinhas, *Brazil* .... 170 B3   2 30 S 42 50W
Barreiro, *Portugal* 43 G1   38 40N 9 6W
Barreiros, *Brazil* .... 170 C4   8 49 S 35 12W
Barrême, *France* .... 29 E10   43 57N 6 23 E
Barren, Nosy, *Madag.* .... 117 B7   18 25 S 43 40 E
Barren I., *India* .... 95 H11   12 16N 93 51 E
Barren Is., *U.S.A.* 144 G9   58 55N 152 15W
Barretos, *Brazil* .... 171 F2   20 30 S 48 35W
Barrhead, *Canada* 142 C6   54 10N 114 24W
Barrie, *Canada* 140 D4   44 24N 79 40W
Barrier, C., *N.Z.* .... 130 C4   36 25 S 175 32 E
Barrier Ra., *Australia* .... 128 A4   31 0 S 141 30 E
Barrier Ra., *Otago, N.Z.* .... 131 E4   44 35 S 169 32 E
Barrier Ra., *W. Coast, N.Z.* .... 131 E3   44 30 S 168 30 E
Barrière, *Canada* 142 C4   51 12N 120 7W
Barrineau Park, *U.S.A.* 153 E2   30 42N 87 26W
Barrington, *U.S.A.* 151 E13   41 44N 71 18W
Barrington, L. = Santa Fé, I., *Ecuador* 172 a
Barrington L., *Canada* 143 B8   56 55N 100 15W
Barrington Tops, *Australia* ... 129 B9   32 6 S 151 28 E
Barrington Tops Nat. Park △,
   Australia .... 129 B9   32 4 S 151 25 E
Barringun, *Australia* .... 127 D4   29 1 S 145 41 E
Barro do Garças, *Brazil* .... 173 D7   15 54 S 52 16W
Barron, *U.S.A.* 154 C9   45 24N 91 51W
Barrow, *U.S.A.* 144 A8   71 18N 156 47W
Barrow →, *Ireland* 23 D5   52 25N 6 58W
Barrow Creek, *Australia* .... 126 C1   21 30 S 133 55 E
Barrow I., *Australia* .... 124 D2   20 45 S 115 20 E
Barrow-in-Furness, *U.K.* 20 C4   54 7N 3 14W
Barrow Pt., *Australia* .... 126 A3   14 20 S 144 40 E
Barrow Ra., *Australia* 144 A8   71 10N 156 20W
Barrow Str., *Canada* 4 B3   74 20N 95 0W
Barry, *U.K.* 21 F4   51 24N 3 16W
Barry, *U.S.A.* 156 E5   39 42N 91 2W
Barry's Bay, *Canada* 140 C4   45 29N 77 41W

Barsalogho, *Burkina Faso* 113 C4   13 25N 1 3W
Barsat, *Pakistan* .... 93 A5   36 10N 72 45 E
Barsham, *Syria* .... 101 E9   35 21N 40 33 E
Barsi, *India* .... 94 E2   18 10N 75 50 E
Barsinghausen, *Germany* .... 30 C5   52 18N 9 28 E
Barskoon, *Kyrgyzstan* .... 65 B8   42 10N 77 37 E
Barth, *Germany* .... 30 A8   54 22N 12 42 E
Barthélemy, Col, *Vietnam* .... 86 C5   19 26N 104 6 E
Bartica, *Guyana* 169 B6   6 25N 58 40W
Bartin, *Turkey* .... 100 B5   41 38N 32 21 E
Bartlesville, *U.S.A.* 155 G7   36 45N 95 59W
Bartlett, *U.S.A.* 160 J8   36 29N 118 2W
Bartlett, L., *Canada* 142 A5   63 5N 118 20W
Bartolomeu Dias, *Mozam.* .... 119 G4   21 10 S 35 8 E
Barton, *Phil.* .... 81 F2   10 24N 119 8 E
Barton, *U.S.A.* 151 B12   44 45N 72 11W
Barton upon Humber, *U.K.* 20 D7   53 41N 0 25W
Bartonville, *U.S.A.* 156 D7   40 39N 89 39W
Bartoszyce, *Poland* .... 54 D7   54 15N 20 55 E
Bartow, Fla., *U.S.A.* 153 H8   27 54N 81 50W
Bartow, Ga., *U.S.A.* 152 C7   32 53N 82 29W
Barú, I. de, *Colombia* 168 A2   10 15N 75 35W
Barú, Volcan, *Panama* 164 E3   8 55N 82 35W
Barumba, *Dem. Rep. of the Congo* 118 B1   1 3N 23 37 E
Barumbu, *Dem. Rep. of the Congo* 114 B4   1 14N 23 31 E
Baruth, *Germany* .... 30 C9   52 4N 13 30 E
Baruunsuu, *Mongolia* .... 74 C3   43 43N 105 35 E
Barvinkove, *Ukraine* .... 59 H9   48 57N 37 0 E
Barwani, *India* .... 92 H6   22 2N 74 57 E
Barwice, *Poland* .... 54 E3   53 44N 16 21 E
Barwick, *U.S.A.* 152 E6   30 54N 83 44W
Barycz →, *Poland* .... 55 G3   51 42N 16 15 E
Barysaw, *Belarus* .... 58 E5   54 17N 28 28 E
Barysh, *Russia* .... 60 D8   53 39N 47 8 E
Barzān, *Iraq* .... 96 B5   36 55N 44 3 E
Bârzava, *Romania* .... 52 D6   46 7N 21 59 E
Bas-Congo □, *Dem. Rep. of*
   the Congo .... 115 D2   5 0 S 15 0 E
Bas-Kouilou, *Congo* .... 115 C2   4 28 S 11 42 E
Bas-Rhin □, *France* .... 27 D14   48 40N 7 30 E
Bašaid, *Serbia, Yug.* .... 52 E5   45 38N 20 25 E
Bāsa'idū, *Iran* .... 97 E7   26 35N 55 20 E
Basal, *Pakistan* .... 92 C5   33 33N 72 13 E
Basankusa, *Dem. Rep. of the Congo* 114 B3   1 5N 19 50 E
Basarabeasca, *Moldova* .... 53 D13   46 21N 28 58 E
Basarabi, *Romania* .... 53 F13   44 10N 28 26 E
Basarabia = Bessarabiya, *Moldova* 59 J5   47 0N 28 10 E
Basauri, *Spain* 40 B2   43 13N 2 53W
Basawa, *Afghan.* .... 91 B3   34 15N 70 50 E
Basco, *Phil.* .... 80 A3   20 27N 121 58 E
Basekpio, *Dem. Rep. of the Congo* 114 B4   4 43N 24 36 E
Basel, *Switz.* .... 32 A5   47 35N 7 35 E
Basel, Euroairport ✈ (BSL), *Europe* 27 E14   47 36N 7 31 E
Basel-Landschaft □, *Switz.* ... 32 B5   47 26N 7 45 E
Basel-Stadt □, *Switz.* .... 32 A5   47 35N 7 35 E
Basento →, *Italy* .... 47 B9   40 20N 16 49 E
Basey, *Phil.* .... 81 F5   11 17N 125 4 E
Bashäkerd, Kühhä-ye, *Iran* ... 97 E8   26 42N 58 35 E
Bashaw, *Canada* 142 C6   52 35N 112 58W
Bāshī, *Iran* .... 97 D6   28 41N 51 4 E
Bashkir Republic =
   Bashkortostan □, *Russia* ... 64 E6   54 0N 57 0 E
Bashkortostan □, *Russia* .... 64 E6   54 0N 57 0 E
Basibasy, *Madag.* .... 117 C7   22 10 S 43 40 E
Basilan I., *Phil.* .... 81 H4   6 33N 122 4 E
Basilan □, *Phil.* .... 81 H4   6 35N 122 0 E
Basilan Str., *Phil.* .... 81 H4   6 50N 122 0 E
Basildon, *U.K.* .... 21 F8   51 34N 0 28 E
Basile, Eq. Guin. .... 113 E6   3 42N 8 48 E
Basilicata □, *Italy* .... 47 B9   40 30N 16 30 E
Basim = Washim, *India* .... 94 D3   20 3N 77 0 E
Basin, *U.S.A.* 158 D9   44 23N 108 2W
Basinger, *U.S.A.* 153 H8   27 23N 81 2W
Basingstoke, *U.K.* 21 F6   51 15N 1 5W
Basirhat, *Bangla.* .... 90 D2   22 40N 88 54 E
Baška, *Croatia* .... 45 D11   44 58N 14 45 E
Başkale, *Turkey* .... 101 C10   38 2N 43 59 E
Baskatong, Rés., *Canada* 140 C4   46 46N 75 50W
Basle = Basel, *Switz.* .... 32 A5   47 35N 7 35 E
Başmakçı, *Turkey* .... 49 D12   37 54N 30 1 E
Basmat, *India* .... 94 E3   19 15N 77 12 E
Basoda, *India* .... 92 H7   23 52N 77 54 E
Basodino, *Switz.* .... 33 D6   46 25N 8 28 E
Basoko, *Dem. Rep. of the Congo* 118 B1   1 16N 23 40 E
Basongo, *Dem. Rep. of the Congo* 115 C4   4 15 S 20 20 E
Basque, Pays, *France* 28 E2   43 15N 1 20W
Basque Provinces = País Vasco □,
   Spain 40 C2   42 50N 2 45W
Basra = Al Başrah, *Iraq* .... 96 D5   30 30N 47 50 E
Bass Str., *Australia* .... 127 C4   39 15 S 146 30 E
Bassano, *Canada* 142 C6   50 48N 112 20W
Bassano del Grappa, *Italy* ... 45 C8   45 46N 11 44 E
Bassar, *Togo* .... 113 D5   9 19N 0 57 E
Bassas da India, *Ind. Oc.* .... 121 G2   22 0 S 39 0 E
Basse-Normandie □, *France* ... 26 D6   48 45N 0 30W
Basse-Pointe, *Martinique* .... 164 c   14 52N 61 8W
Basse Santa-Su, *Gambia* 112 C2   13 13N 14 15W
Basse-Terre, *Guadeloupe* .... 164 b   16 0N 61 44W
Basse Terre, Trin. & Tob. 169 F10   10 7N 61 19W
Bassecourt, *Switz.* .... 32 B4   47 20N 7 15 E
Bassein, Burma .... 90 G5   16 45N 94 30 E
Bassein, India .... 94 E1   19 26N 72 48 E
Basses, Pte. des, *Guadeloupe* ... 164 b   15 52N 61 17W
Basses-Alpes = Alpes-de-Haute-
   Provence □, *France* .... 29 D10   44 8N 6 10 E
Basseterre, *St. Kitts & Nevis* ... 165 C7   17 17N 62 43W
Bassett, *U.S.A.* 154 D5   42 35N 99 32W
Bassi, *India* .... 92 D7   30 44N 76 21 E
Bassigny, *France* .... 27 E12   48 0N 5 30 E
Bassikounou, *Mauritania* 112 B3   15 55N 6 1W
Bassila, *Benin* .... 113 D5   9 1N 1 46 E
Bassum, *Germany* .... 30 C4   52 50N 8 40 E
Båstad, *Sweden* .... 17 H6   56 25N 12 51 E
Bastak, *Iran* .... 97 E7   27 15N 54 25 E
Baştām, *Iran* .... 97 B7   36 29N 55 4 E
Bastar, *India* .... 94 E5   19 15N 81 40 E
Bastelica, *France* .... 29 F13   42 1N 9 3 E
Basti, *India* .... 93 F10   26 52N 82 55 E
Bastia, *France* .... 29 F13   42 40N 9 30 E
Bastogne, *Belgium* .... 24 D5   50 1N 5 43 E
Bastrop, La., *U.S.A.* 155 J9   32 47N 91 55W
Bastrop, Tex., *U.S.A.* 155 K6   30 7N 97 19W
Basud, *Phil.* .... 80 D4   14 4N 122 58 E
Basutoland = Lesotho ■, *Africa* 117 D4   29 40 S 28 0 E
Bat Yam, *Israel* .... 103 C3   32 2N 34 44 E
Bata, *Eq. Guin.* .... 114 B1   1 57N 9 50 E
Bata, *Romania* .... 52 D7   46 1N 22 4 E
Bataan □, *Phil.* .... 80 D3   14 40N 120 25 E
Bataan Nat. Park △, *Phil.* .... 80 D3   14 45N 120 27 E
Batabanó, Cuba 164 B3   22 40N 82 20W
Batabanó, G. de, *Cuba* 164 B3   22 30N 82 30W
Batac, Phil. .... 80 B3   18 3N 120 34 E
Batagai, Russia .... 67 C14   67 38N 134 38 E
Batajnica, Serbia, Yug. .... 50 B4   44 54N 20 17 E
Batak, Bulgaria .... 51 E8   41 57N 24 12 E
Batala, India .... 92 D6   31 48N 75 12 E
Batalha, Portugal 42 F2   39 40N 8 50W
Batam, Indonesia .... 84 B2   1 5N 104 3 E
Batama, Dem. Rep. of the Congo ... 118 B2   0 58N 26 33 E
Batamay, Russia .... 67 C13   63 30N 129 15 E
Batan I., Albay, Phil. .... 80 E4   13 15N 124 0 E

Batan I., Batanes, Phil. .... 80 A3   20 26N 121 58 E
Batanes □, Phil. .... 80 A3   20 40N 121 55 E
Batanes Is., Phil. .... 80 A3   20 30N 122 0 E
Batang, China .... 76 B2   30 1N 99 0 E
Batang, Indonesia .... 85 D3   6 55 S 109 45 E
Batanga, Gabon .... 114 C1   0 21 S 9 18 E
Batangafo, C.A.R. .... 114 A3   7 25N 18 20 E
Batangas, Phil. .... 80 E3   13 35N 121 10 E
Batangas □, Phil. .... 80 E3   13 40N 121 10 E
Batanghari →, Indonesia .... 84 C2   1 36 S 103 37 E
Batanta, Indonesia .... 83 B5   0 55 S 130 40 E
Bataraza, Phil. .... 81 G1   8 40N 117 37 E
Batas I., Phil. .... 81 F2   11 0N 119 36 E
Batatais, Brazil .... 175 A6   20 54 S 47 37W
Batavia = Jakarta, Indonesia .... 84 D3   6 9 S 106 49 E
Batavia, Ill., U.S.A. 157 C8   41 51N 88 19W
Batavia, N.Y., U.S.A. 150 D6   43 0N 78 11W
Batavia, Ohio, U.S.A. 157 E12   39 5N 84 11W
Bataysk, Russia .... 59 J10   47 3N 39 45 E
Batbakara = Amangeldy,
   Kazakhstan .... 66 D7   50 10N 65 10 E
Batchelor, Australia .... 124 B5   13 4 S 131 1 E
Batdambang, Cambodia .... 86 F4   13 7N 103 12 E
Batéké, Plateau, Congo .... 114 C3   3 30 S 15 45 E
Batemans B., Australia .... 129 C9   35 40 S 150 12 E
Batemans Bay, Australia .... 129 C9   35 44 S 150 11 E
Bates Ra., Australia .... 125 E3   27 27 S 121 5 E
Batesburg-Leesville, U.S.A. 152 B8   33 54N 81 33W
Batesville, Ark., U.S.A. 155 H9   35 46N 91 39W
Batesville, Ind., U.S.A. 157 E11   39 18N 85 13W
Batesville, Miss., U.S.A. 155 H10   34 19N 89 57W
Batesville, Tex., U.S.A. 155 L5   28 58N 99 37W
Bath, Canada 151 B8   44 11N 76 47W
Bath, U.K. 21 F5   51 23N 2 22W
Bath, Maine, U.S.A. 149 D11   43 55N 69 49W
Bath, N.Y., U.S.A. 150 D7   42 20N 77 19W
Bath, S.C., U.S.A. 152 B8   33 31N 81 51W
Bath & North East Somerset □, U.K. 21 F5   51 21N 2 27W
Batha →, Chad .... 109 F3   12 47N 17 34 E
Batheay, Cambodia .... 87 G5   11 59N 104 57 E
Bathgate, U.K. 22 F5   55 54N 3 39W
Bathurst = Banjul, Gambia 112 C1   13 28N 16 40W
Bathurst, Australia .... 129 B8   33 25 S 149 31 E
Bathurst, Canada 141 C6   47 37N 65 43W
Bathurst, S. Africa .... 116 E4   33 30 S 26 50 E
Bathurst, C., Canada 138 A7   70 34N 128 0W
Bathurst B., Australia .... 126 A3   14 16 S 144 25 E
Bathurst Harb., Australia .... 127 D4   43 15 S 146 10 E
Bathurst I., Australia .... 124 B5   11 30 S 130 10 E
Bathurst I., Canada 6 B2   76 0N 100 30W
Bathurst Inlet, Canada 138 B9   66 50N 108 1W
Bati, Ethiopia .... 107 E5   11 10N 40 0 E
Batie, Burkina Faso .... 112 D4   9 53 S 2 53W
Batiki, Fiji .... 133 A2   17 48 S 179 10 E
Batlow, Australia .... 129 C8   35 31 S 148 9 E
Batman, Turkey .... 101 D9   37 55N 41 5 E
Baţn al Ghūl, Jordan .... 103 F4   29 36N 35 56 E
Batna, Algeria .... 111 A6   35 34N 6 15 E
Batnfjordsøra, Norway .... 18 B4   62 53N 7 42 E
Bato, Catanduanes, Phil. .... 81 E5   13 36N 124 18 E
Bato, Leyte, Phil. .... 81 F5   10 6N 124 48 E
Bato Bato, Phil. .... 81 J2   5 6N 119 49 E
Batoala, Gabon .... 114 B2   0 48N 13 27 E
Batobato = San Isidro, Phil. .... 81 H6   6 50N 126 5 E
Batočina, Serbia, Yug. .... 50 B5   44 7N 21 5 E
Batoka, Zambia .... 119 F2   16 45 S 27 15 E
Baton Rouge, U.S.A. 155 K9   30 27N 91 11W
Batong, Ko, Thailand .... 87 J2   6 32N 99 12 E
Bátonyterenye, Hungary .... 52 C4   47 59N 19 50 E
Batopilas, Mexico 162 B3   27 0N 107 45W
Batouri, Cameroon .... 114 B2   4 30N 14 25 E
Båtsfjord, Norway .... 14 A23   70 38N 29 39 E
Battambang = Batdambang,
   Cambodia .... 86 F4   13 7N 103 12 E
Batti Malv, India .... 95 K11   8 50N 92 51 E
Batticaloa, Sri Lanka .... 95 L5   7 43N 81 45 E
Battipáglia, Italy .... 47 B7   40 37N 14 58 E
Battle, U.K. .... 21 G8   50 55N 0 30 E
Battle →, Canada 143 C7   52 43N 108 15W
Battle Creek, U.S.A. 157 B11   42 19N 85 11W
Battle Ground, U.S.A. 160 E4   45 47N 122 32W
Battle Harbour, Canada 141 B8   52 16N 55 35W
Battle Lake, U.S.A. 154 B7   46 17N 95 43W
Battle Mountain, U.S.A. 158 F5   40 38N 116 56W
Battlefields, Zimbabwe .... 119 F2   18 37 S 29 47 E
Battleford, Canada 143 C7   52 45N 108 15W
Battonya, Hungary .... 52 D6   46 16N 21 3 E
Batu, Ethiopia .... 107 F4   6 55N 39 45 E
Batu, Bukit, Malaysia .... 85 B4   2 16N 113 43 E
Batu, Kepulauan, Indonesia .... 84 C1   0 30 S 98 25 E
Batu Bora, Bukit, Malaysia .... 85 B4   2 43N 114 43 E
Batu Caves, Malaysia .... 87 L3   3 15N 101 40 E
Batu Ferringhi, Malaysia .... 87 c   5 28N 100 15 E
Batu Gajah, Malaysia .... 87 K3   4 28N 101 3 E
Batu Is. = Batu, Kepulauan,
   Indonesia .... 84 C1   0 30 S 98 25 E
Batu Pahat, Malaysia .... 87 M4   1 50N 102 56 E
Batu Puteh, Gunong, Malaysia ... 84 B2   4 15N 101 30 E
Batuata, Indonesia .... 82 C2   6 12 S 122 42 E
Batugondang, Tanjung, Indonesia ... 79 J17   8 32 S 115 34 E
Batui, Indonesia .... 82 B2   1 17 S 122 33 E
Batukau, Gunung, Indonesia ... 79 J18   8 20 S 115 5 E
Batulaki, Phil. .... 81 J5   5 34N 125 19 E
Batumi, Georgia .... 61 K5   41 39N 41 44 E
Batur, Indonesia .... 79 J18   8 15 S 115 20 E
Batur, Gunung, Indonesia .... 79 J18   8 14 S 115 22 E
Baturaja, Indonesia .... 84 C2   4 11 S 104 15 E
Baturité, Brazil .... 170 B4   4 28 S 38 45W
Baturiti, Indonesia .... 79 J18   8 15 S 115 11 E
Batusangkar, Indonesia .... 84 C2   0 27 S 100 35 E
Bau, Malaysia .... 85 B4   1 25N 110 9 E
Bauang, Phil. .... 80 C3   16 31N 120 20 E
Bauban, Phil. .... 82 C2   5 25 S 122 38 E
Baucau, E. Timor .... 82 C3   8 27 S 126 27 E
Bauchi, Nigeria .... 113 C6   10 22N 9 48 E
Bauchi □, Nigeria .... 113 C7   10 30N 10 0 E
Baud, France 26 E3   47 52N 3 1W
Bauda, India .... 94 D7   20 50N 84 25 E
Baudette, U.S.A. 154 A7   48 43N 94 36W
Bauen, Switz. .... 33 C7   46 56N 8 35 E
Bauhinia, Australia .... 127 E1   32 44 S 134 4 E
Bauhinia, Australia .... 126 C4   24 35 S 149 18 E
Baukau = Baucau, E. Timor ... 82 C3   8 27 S 126 27 E
Bauko, Phil. .... 80 C3   17 0N 120 52 E
Baulal →, Bangla. .... 90 C3   24 22N 91 1 E
Bauld, C., Canada 139 C14   51 38N 55 26W
Bauma, Switz. .... 33 B7   47 23N 8 53 E
Baume-les-Dames, France ... 27 E13   47 22N 6 22 E
Baunatal, Germany .... 30 D5   51 14N 9 24 E
Baunei, Italy .... 46 B2   40 2N 9 40 E
Baure, Nigeria .... 113 C6   12 52N 8 50 E
Baures, Bolivia .... 173 C5   13 35 S 63 30W
Bauru, Brazil .... 175 A6   22 10 S 49 0W
Baús, Brazil .... 173 D7   18 22 S 52 47W
Bausi, India .... 93 G12   24 48N 87 1 E
Bauska, Latvia .... 15 H21   56 24N 24 15 E
Bautino, Kazakhstan .... 61 H10   44 35N 50 14 E
Bautzen, Germany .... 31 D10   51 10N 14 26 E
Bauya, S. Leone 112 D2   7 30N 12 38W
Bāūyrzhan Momyshuly, Kazakhstan 68 B5   42 36N 70 47 E
Bavănăt, Iran .... 97 D7   30 28N 53 27 E
Bavanište, Serbia, Yug. .... 52 F5   44 49N 20 55 E
Bavaria = Bayern □, Germany ... 31 G7   48 50N 12 0 E
Båven, Sweden .... 16 E10   59 0N 16 56 E

Bavispe →, Mexico 162 B3 29 30N 109 11W
Baw Baw Nat. Park △, Australia ... 129 D7 37 50 S 146 17 E
Bawdwin, Burma .... 90 D6 23 5N 97 20 E
Bawe, Indonesia .... 83 B4 2 59 S 134 43 E
Bawean, Indonesia .... 85 D4 5 46 S 112 35 E
Bawku, Ghana 113 C4 11 3N 0 19W
Bawlake, Burma .... 90 F6 19 11N 97 21 E
Bawolung, China .... 76 C3 28 50N 101 16 E
Baxley, U.S.A. 152 D7 31 47N 82 21W
Baxoi, China .... 76 B1 30 1N 96 50 E
Baxter, Iowa, U.S.A. 156 C3 41 49N 93 9W
Baxter, Minn., U.S.A. 154 B7 46 21N 94 17W
Baxter Springs, U.S.A. 155 G7 37 2N 94 44W
Baxter State Park △, U.S.A. 149 B11 46 5N 68 57W
Bay, L. de, Phil. .... 80 D3 14 20N 121 11 E
Bay al Khā'ib, Wādi →, Libya .... 108 B3 30 55N 15 29 E
Bay City, Mich., U.S.A. 148 D4 43 36N 83 54W
Bay City, Tex., U.S.A. 155 L7 28 59N 95 58W
Bay Minette, U.S.A. 149 K2 30 53N 87 46W
Bay of Plenty □, N.Z. .... 130 D5 38 0 S 177 0 E
Bay Roberts, Canada 141 C9 47 36N 53 16W
Bay St. Louis, U.S.A. 155 K10 30 19N 89 20W
Bay Springs, U.S.A. 155 K10 31 59N 89 17W
Bay View, N.Z. .... 130 F5 39 25 S 176 50 E
Baya, Dem. Rep. of the Congo .... 119 E2 11 53 S 27 25 E
Bayambang, Phil. .... 80 D3 15 49N 120 27 E
Bayamo, Cuba 164 B4 20 20N 76 40W
Bayamón, Puerto Rico .... 165 d 18 24N 66 10W
Bayan Har Shan, China .... 68 C4 34 0N 98 0 E
Bayan Hot = Alxa Zuoqi, China .... 74 E3 38 50N 105 40 E
Bayan Lepas, Malaysia .... 87 c 5 17N 100 16 E
Bayan Obo, China .... 74 D5 41 52N 109 59 E
Bayan-Ovoo = Erdenetsogt, Mongolia .... 74 C4 42 55N 106 5 E
Bayana, India .... 92 F7 26 55N 77 18 E
Bayanaūyl, Kazakhstan .... 66 D8 50 45N 75 45 E
Bayandalay, Mongolia .... 74 C2 43 30N 103 29 E
Bayanhongor, Mongolia .... 68 B5 46 8N 102 43 E
Bayard, N. Mex., U.S.A. 159 K9 32 46N 108 8W
Bayard, Nebr., U.S.A. 154 E3 41 45N 103 20W
Bayawan, Phil. .... 81 G4 9 46N 122 45 E
Baybay, Phil. .... 81 F5 10 40N 124 55 E
Bayburt, Turkey .... 101 B9 40 15N 40 20 E
Baydhabo = Baidoa, Somali Rep. .... 120 D2 3 8N 43 30 E
Bayelsa □, Nigeria .... 113 E6 4 30N 6 0 E
Bayerische Alpen, Germany .... 31 H7 47 35N 11 30 E
Bayerische Rhön, Naturpark △, Germany .... 31 E6 50 15N 10 5 E
Bayerischer Spessart, Naturpark △, Germany .... 31 F6 49 58N 10 15 E
Bayerischer Wald, Germany .... 31 G8 48 56N 12 50 E
Bayern □, Germany .... 31 G7 48 50N 12 0 E
Bayeux, France 26 C6 49 17N 0 42W
Bayfield, Canada 150 C3 43 34N 81 42W
Bayfield, U.S.A. 154 B9 46 49N 90 49W
Bāygequm, Kazakhstan .... 65 A3 44 19N 66 27 E
Bayḩān al Qiṣāb, Yemen .... 98 D4 15 48N 45 44 E
Bayındır, Turkey .... 49 C9 38 13N 27 39 E
Baykal, Oz., Russia .... 67 D11 53 0N 108 0 E
Baykan, Turkey .... 96 B4 38 7N 41 44 E
Baykonur = Bayqongyr, Kazakhstan .... 66 E7 47 48N 65 50 E
Baykurt, China .... 65 D7 39 56N 75 33 E
Baymak, Russia .... 64 E7 52 36N 58 19 E
Baymurat, Uzbekistan .... 65 C3 41 46N 58 29 E
Baynes Mts., Namibia .... 116 B1 17 15 S 13 0 E
Bayombong, Phil. .... 80 C3 16 30N 121 10 E
Bayon, France .... 27 D13 48 30N 6 20 E
Bayona = Baiona, Spain 42 C2 42 6N 8 52W
Bayonet Point, U.S.A. 153 G7 28 20N 82 42W
Bayonne, France 28 E2 43 30N 1 28W
Bayonne, U.S.A. 151 F10 40 40N 74 7W
Bayovar, Peru .... 172 B1 5 50 S 81 0W
Bayport, U.S.A. 153 G7 28 32N 82 39W
Bayqongyr, Kazakhstan .... 66 E7 47 48N 65 50 E
Bayram-Ali = Bayramaly, Turkmenistan .... 66 F7 37 37N 62 10 E
Bayramaly, Turkmenistan .... 66 F7 37 37N 62 10 E
Bayramiç, Turkey .... 49 B8 39 48N 26 36 E
Bayreuth, Germany .... 31 F7 49 56N 11 35 E
Bayrischzell, Germany .... 31 H8 47 41N 12 0 E
Bayrūt, Lebanon .... 103 B4 33 53N 35 31 E
Bays, L. of, Canada 150 A5 45 15N 79 4W
Bayshore, U.S.A. 153 J8 26 43N 81 50W
Baysun, Uzbekistan .... 65 D3 38 12N 67 12 E
Baysville, Canada 150 A5 45 9N 79 7W
Bayt al Faqīh, Yemen .... 98 D3 14 31N 43 19 E
Bayt Laḥm, West Bank .... 103 D4 31 43N 35 12 E
Baytown, U.S.A. 155 L7 29 43N 94 59W
Bayugan, Phil. .... 81 G5 8 43N 125 42 E
Bayyrruom, Kazakhstan .... 65 B4 42 7N 68 3 E
Bayzhansay, Kazakhstan .... 65 B4 43 14N 69 54 E
Bayzo, Niger .... 113 C5 13 52N 4 35 E
Baza, Spain 43 H8 37 30N 2 47W
Bazar Dyuzi, Russia .... 61 K8 41 12N 47 50 E
Bazar-Korgon, Kyrgyzstan .... 65 C6 41 0N 72 43 E
Bazardüzü = Bazar Dyuzi, Russia .... 61 K8 41 12N 47 50 E
Bazaruk Karabulak, Russia .... 60 D8 52 20N 46 29 E
Bazarnyy Syzgan, Russia .... 60 D8 53 45N 46 40 E
Bazaruto, I. do, Mozam. .... 117 C6 21 40 S 35 28 E
Bazaruto, Parque Nac. de △, Mozam. .... 117 C6 21 42 S 35 26 E
Bazas, France 28 D3 44 27N 0 13W
Bazhong, China .... 76 B6 31 52N 106 46 E
Bazhou, China .... 74 E9 39 8N 116 22 E
Bazmān, Kūh-e, Iran .... 97 D9 28 4N 60 1 E
Beach, U.S.A. 154 B3 46 58N 104 0W
Beach City, U.S.A. 150 F3 40 39N 81 35W
Beachport, Australia .... 128 D4 37 29 S 140 0 E
Beachy Hd., U.K. .... 21 G8 50 44N 0 15 E
Beacon, Australia .... 125 F2 30 26 S 117 52 E
Beacon, U.S.A. 151 E11 41 30N 73 58W
Beaconsfield, Australia .... 127 D4 41 11 S 146 48 E
Beagle, Canal, S. Amer. .... 176 E3 55 0 S 68 30W
Beagle Bay, Australia .... 124 C3 16 58 S 122 40 E
Bealanana, Madag. .... 117 A8 14 33 S 48 44 E
Beals Cr. →, U.S.A. 155 J4 32 10N 100 51W
Beamsville, Canada 150 C5 43 12N 79 28W
Bear →, Calif., U.S.A. 160 G5 38 56N 121 36W
Bear →, Utah, U.S.A. 146 B4 41 30N 112 8W
Béar, C., France .... 28 F7 42 31N 3 8 E
Bear I., Ireland 23 E2 51 38N 9 50W
Bear L., Canada 143 B9 55 8N 96 0W
Bear L., U.S.A. 158 F8 41 59N 111 21W
Beardmore, Canada 140 C2 49 36N 87 57W
Beardmore Glacier, Antarctica .... 7 E11 84 30 S 170 0 E
Beardstown, U.S.A. 156 E6 40 1N 90 26W
Bearma →, India .... 93 G8 24 20N 79 51 E
Béarn, France 28 E3 43 20N 0 30W
Bearpaw Mts., U.S.A. 158 B9 48 12N 109 30W
Bearskin Lake, Canada 140 B1 53 58N 91 2W
Beas →, India .... 92 D6 31 10N 74 59 E
Beas de Segura, Spain 43 G8 38 15N 2 53W
Beasain, Spain 40 B2 43 3N 2 11W
Beata, C., Dom. Rep. 165 C5 17 40N 71 30W
Beata, I., Dom. Rep. 165 C5 17 34N 71 31W
Beatrice, U.S.A. 154 E6 40 16N 96 45W
Beatrice, Zimbabwe .... 119 F3 18 15 S 30 55 E
Beatrice, C., Australia .... 126 A2 14 20 S 136 55 E
Beatton →, Canada 142 B4 56 15N 120 45W
Beatton River, Canada 142 B4 57 26N 121 20W
Beatty, U.S.A. 160 J10 36 54N 116 46W
Beau Bassin, Mauritius .... 121 d 20 13 S 57 27 E
Beaucaire, France .... 29 E8 43 48N 4 39 E
Beauce, Plaine de la, France .... 27 D8 48 10N 1 45 E

Beauceville, Canada 141 C5 46 13N 70 46W
Beauchêne, I., Falk. Is. .... 9 f 52 55 S 59 15W
Beaudesert, Australia .... 127 D5 27 59 S 153 0 E
Beaufort, Australia .... 128 D5 37 25 S 143 25 E
Beaufort, France .... 29 C10 45 44N 6 34 E
Beaufort, Malaysia .... 85 A5 5 30N 115 40 E
Beaufort, N.C., U.S.A. 149 H7 34 43N 76 40W
Beaufort, S.C., U.S.A. 152 C9 32 26N 80 40W
Beaufort Sea, Arctic 6 B1 72 0N 140 0W
Beaufort West, S. Africa .... 116 E3 32 18 S 22 36 E
Beaugency, France .... 27 E8 47 47N 1 38 E
Beauharnois, Canada 151 A11 45 20N 73 52W
Beaujeu, France .... 27 F11 46 10N 4 35 E
Beaujolais, France .... 27 F11 46 0N 4 22 E
Beaulieu →, Canada 142 A6 62 3N 113 11W
Beaulieu-sur-Dordogne, France .... 28 D5 44 58N 1 50 E
Beaulieu-sur-Mer, France .... 29 E11 43 42N 7 20 E
Beauly, U.K. 22 D4 57 30N 4 28W
Beauly →, U.K. 22 D4 57 29N 4 27W
Beaumaris, U.K. 20 D3 53 16N 4 6W
Beaumont, Belgium .... 25 D4 50 15N 4 14 E
Beaumont, France .... 28 D4 44 45N 0 46 E
Beaumont, N.Z. .... 131 F4 45 50 S 169 33 E
Beaumont, U.S.A. 155 K7 30 5N 94 6W
Beaumont-de-Lomagne, France .... 28 E5 43 53N 1 0 E
Beaumont-le-Roger, France .... 26 C7 49 4N 0 47 E
Beaumont-sur-Sarthe, France .... 26 D7 48 13N 0 8 E
Beaune, France .... 27 E11 47 2N 4 50 E
Beaune-la-Rolande, France .... 27 D9 48 4N 2 25 E
Beaupré, Canada 141 C5 47 3N 70 54W
Beaupréau, France 26 E6 47 12N 1 0W
Beauraing, Belgium .... 25 D4 50 7N 4 57 E
Beaurepaire, France .... 29 C9 45 22N 5 1 E
Beauséjour, Canada 143 C9 50 5N 96 35W
Beautemps-Beaupré, Î., N. Cal. .... 133 K4 20 24 S 166 9 E
Beauvais, France .... 27 C9 49 25N 2 8 E
Beauval, Canada 143 B7 55 9N 107 37W
Beauvoir-sur-Mer, France 26 F4 46 55N 2 2W
Beauvoir-sur-Niort, France 28 B3 46 12N 0 30W
Beaver, Alaska, U.S.A. 144 C11 66 22N 147 24W
Beaver, Okla., U.S.A. 155 G4 36 49N 100 31W
Beaver, Pa., U.S.A. 150 F4 40 42N 80 19W
Beaver, Utah, U.S.A. 159 G7 38 17N 112 38W
Beaver →, B.C., Canada 142 B4 59 52N 124 20W
Beaver →, Ont., Canada 140 A2 55 55N 87 48W
Beaver →, Sask., Canada 143 B7 55 26N 107 45W
Beaver City, U.S.A. 155 G5 36 35N 99 30W
Beaver City, U.S.A. 154 E5 40 8N 99 50W
Beaver Creek, Canada 138 B5 63 0N 141 0W
Beaver Dam, U.S.A. 154 D10 43 28N 88 50W
Beaver Falls, U.S.A. 150 F4 40 46N 80 20W
Beaver Hill L., Canada 143 C10 54 5N 94 50W
Beaver I., U.S.A. 148 C3 45 40N 85 33W
Beavercreek, U.S.A. 157 E12 39 43N 84 11W
Beaverhill L., Canada 142 C6 53 27N 112 32W
Beaverlodge, Canada 142 B5 55 11N 119 29W
Beaverstone →, Canada 140 B2 54 59N 89 25W
Beaverton, Canada 150 B5 44 26N 79 9W
Beaverton, U.S.A. 160 E4 45 29N 122 48W
Beawar, India .... 92 F6 26 3N 74 18 E
Bebedouro, Brazil .... 175 A6 21 0 S 48 25W
Bebera, Tanjung, Indonesia .... 79 K18 8 44 S 115 51 E
Beboa, Madag. .... 117 B7 17 22 S 44 33 E
Bebora, Chad .... 109 G3 8 16N 16 56 E
Bebra, Germany .... 30 E5 50 58N 9 48 E
Becan, Mexico 163 D7 18 31N 89 28W
Beccles, U.K. .... 21 E9 52 27N 1 35 E
Bečej, Serbia, Yug. .... 52 E5 45 36N 20 3 E
Beceni, Romania .... 53 E11 45 23N 26 48 E
Becerreá, Spain 42 C3 42 51N 7 10W
Béchar, Algeria 111 B4 31 38N 2 18W
Becharof L., U.S.A. 144 H8 57 56N 156 23W
Bechuanaland = Botswana ■, Africa .... 116 C3 22 0 S 24 0 E
Bechyně, Czech Rep. .... 32 B7 49 17N 14 29 E
Beckley, U.S.A. 148 G5 37 47N 81 11W
Beckum, Germany .... 30 D4 51 45N 8 2 E
Beclean, Romania .... 53 C9 47 11N 24 11 E
Bečov nad Teplou, Czech Rep. .... 32 A5 50 5N 12 49 E
Bécva →, Czech Rep. .... 35 B10 49 31N 17 20 E
Bédar, Spain 41 H3 37 11N 1 59W
Bédarieux, France .... 28 E7 43 37N 3 10 E
Beddouza, Ras, Morocco 110 B3 32 33N 9 9W
Bedeau = Ras el Ma, Algeria 111 B4 34 26N 0 50W
Bedele, Ethiopia .... 107 F4 8 31N 36 23 E
Bederkesa, Germany .... 30 B4 53 37N 8 50 E
Bederwanak, Somali Rep. .... 120 C2 9 34N 44 23 E
Bedeso, Ethiopia .... 107 F5 9 58N 40 52 E
Bedford, Canada 151 A12 45 7N 72 59W
Bedford, S. Africa .... 116 E4 32 40 S 26 10 E
Bedford, U.K. 21 E7 52 8N 0 28W
Bedford, Ind., U.S.A. 157 F10 38 52N 86 29W
Bedford, Iowa, U.S.A. 156 D2 40 40N 94 44W
Bedford, Ky., U.S.A. 157 F11 38 36N 85 19W
Bedford, Ohio, U.S.A. 150 E3 41 23N 81 32W
Bedford, Pa., U.S.A. 150 F6 40 1N 78 30W
Bedford, Va., U.S.A. 148 G6 37 20N 79 31W
Bedford, C., Australia .... 126 B4 15 14 S 145 21 E
Bedfordshire □, U.K. 21 E7 52 4N 0 28W
Bedi, Chad .... 109 F3 11 6N 18 33 E
Będków, Poland .... 55 G6 51 36N 19 44 E
Bednja →, Croatia .... 45 B13 46 20N 16 52 E
Bednodemyanovsk, Russia .... 60 D6 53 55N 43 15 E
Bedok, Singapore .... 87 d 1 19N 103 56 E
Bedónia, Italy .... 46 D7 44 30N 9 38 E
Bedourie, Australia .... 126 C2 24 30 S 139 30 E
Bedretto, Switz. .... 33 C7 46 31N 8 31 E
Bedti →, India .... 95 G2 14 50N 74 44 E
Bedum, Neths. .... 24 A6 53 18N 6 36 E
Będzin, Poland .... 55 H6 50 19N 19 7 E
Bee Ridge, U.S.A. 153 H7 27 11N 82 29W
Beebe Plain, Canada 151 A12 45 1N 72 9W
Beech Creek, U.S.A. 150 E7 41 5N 77 36W
Beech Fork →, U.S.A. 157 G11 37 46N 85 41W
Beech Grove, U.S.A. 157 E10 39 44N 86 3W
Beecher, U.S.A. 157 E9 41 21N 87 38W
Beechey Point, U.S.A. 144 A10 70 29N 149 9W
Beechworth, Australia .... 129 D7 36 22 S 146 43 E
Beef I., Br. Virgin Is. .... 165 e 18 26N 64 30W
Beelitz, Germany .... 30 C8 52 14N 12 58 E
Beenleigh, Australia .... 127 D5 27 43 S 153 10 E
Be'er Menuḥa, Israel .... 96 D2 30 19N 35 8 E
Be'er Sheva, Israel .... 103 D3 31 15N 34 48 E
Beersheba = Be'er Sheva, Israel .... 103 D3 31 15N 34 48 E
Beeskow, Germany .... 30 C10 52 10N 14 15 E
Beestekraal, S. Africa .... 117 D4 25 23 S 27 38 E
Beeston, U.K. 20 E6 52 56N 1 14W
Beetzendorf, Germany .... 30 C7 52 42N 11 6 E
Beeville, U.S.A. 155 L6 28 24N 97 45W
Befale, Dem. Rep. of the Congo .... 114 B4 0 25N 20 45 E
Befandriana, Mahajanga, Madag. .... 117 B8 15 16 S 48 32 E
Befandriana, Toliara, Madag. .... 117 C7 21 55 S 44 0 E
Befori, Dem. Rep. of the Congo .... 114 B4 0 8N 22 22 E
Befotaka, Antsiranana, Madag. .... 117 A8 13 15 S 48 16 E
Befotaka, Fianarantsoa, Madag. .... 117 C8 23 49 S 47 0 E
Bega, Australia .... 129 D8 36 41 S 149 51 E
Bega, Canalul, Romania .... 52 E5 45 37N 20 46 E
Bégard, France 26 D3 48 38N 3 18W
Beğendik, Turkey .... 51 F10 40 55N 26 34 E
Begna →, Norway .... 8 D14 60 41N 9 46 E
Begoro, Ghana 113 D4 6 23N 0 23W
Begusarai, India .... 93 G12 25 24N 86 9 E
Behābād, Iran .... 97 C8 32 24N 59 47 E
Behala, India .... 93 H13 22 30N 88 20 E

Behara, Madag. .... 117 C8 24 55 S 46 20 E
Behbehān, Iran .... 97 D6 30 30N 50 15 E
Behm Canal, U.S.A. 142 B2 55 10N 131 0W
Behshahr, Iran .... 97 B7 36 45N 53 35 E
Bei Jiang →, China .... 77 F9 23 2N 112 58 E
Bei'an, China .... 69 B7 48 10N 126 20 E
Beibei, China .... 76 C6 29 47N 106 22 E
Beichuan, China .... 76 B5 31 55N 104 39 E
Beihai, China .... 76 G7 21 28N 109 6 E
Beijing, China .... 74 E9 39 55N 116 20 E
Beijing □, China .... 74 E9 39 55N 116 20 E
Beilen, Neths. .... 24 B6 52 52N 6 27 E
Beiliu, China .... 77 F8 22 41N 110 21 E
Beilngries, Germany .... 31 F7 49 2N 11 28 E
Beilpajah, Australia .... 128 B5 32 54 S 143 52 E
Béinamar, Chad .... 109 G3 8 40N 15 23 E
Beinn na Faoghla = Benbecula, U.K. 22 D1 57 26N 7 21W
Beipan Jiang →, China .... 76 E5 25 52N 106 12 E
Beipiao, China .... 75 D11 41 52N 120 32 E
Beira, Mozam. .... 119 F3 19 50 S 34 52 E
Beira, Somali Rep. .... 120 C3 6 57N 47 19 E
Beirut = Bayrūt, Lebanon .... 103 B4 33 53N 35 31 E
Beiseker, Canada 142 C6 51 23N 113 32W
Beitaolaizhao, China .... 75 B13 44 58N 125 58 E
Beitbridge, Zimbabwe .... 119 G3 22 12 S 30 0 E
Beiuş, Romania .... 52 D7 46 40N 22 21 E
Beizhen = Binzhou, China .... 75 D7 37 20N 118 2 E
Beizhen, China .... 75 D11 41 38N 121 54 E
Beizhengzhen, China .... 75 B12 44 31N 123 30 E
Beja, Portugal 43 G3 38 2N 7 53W
Béja, Tunisia .... 108 A1 36 43N 9 12 E
Beja □, Portugal 43 H3 37 55N 7 55W
Bejaïa, Algeria .... 111 A6 36 42N 5 2 E
Béjar, Spain 42 E5 40 23N 5 46W
Bejestān, Iran .... 97 C8 34 30N 58 5 E
Bekaa Valley = Al Biqā, Lebanon .... 103 A5 34 10N 36 10 E
Bekabad, Uzbekistan .... 65 C4 40 13N 69 14 E
Bekasi, Indonesia .... 84 D3 6 14 S 106 59 E
Bekçiler, Turkey .... 49 E11 36 54N 29 26 E
Békés, Hungary .... 52 D6 46 47N 21 9 E
Békés □, Hungary .... 52 D6 46 45N 21 5 E
Békéscsaba, Hungary .... 52 D6 46 40N 21 5 E
Bekily, Madag. .... 117 C8 24 13 S 45 19 E
Bekisopa, Madag. .... 117 C8 21 40 S 45 54 E
Bekitro, Madag. .... 117 C8 24 33 S 45 18 E
Bekodoka, Madag. .... 117 B8 16 58 S 45 7 E
Bekoji, Ethiopia .... 107 F4 7 40N 39 17 E
Bekok, Malaysia .... 87 L4 2 20N 103 7 E
Bekopaka, Madag. .... 117 B7 19 9 S 44 48 E
Bekuli, Indonesia .... 79 J17 8 22 S 114 13 E
Bekwai, Ghana 113 D4 6 30N 1 34W
Bela, India .... 93 G10 25 50N 82 0 E
Bela, Pakistan .... 91 D2 26 12N 66 20 E
Bela Crkva, Serbia, Yug. .... 52 F6 44 55N 21 27 E
Bela Palanka, Serbia, Yug. .... 50 C6 43 13N 22 17 E
Bela Vista, Brazil .... 174 A4 22 12 S 56 20W
Bela Vista, Mozam. .... 117 D5 26 10 S 32 44 E
Bélâbre, France .... 28 B5 46 34N 1 8 E
Belaga, Malaysia .... 85 B4 2 42N 113 47 E
Belalcázar, Spain 43 G5 38 35N 5 10W
Belan →, India .... 93 G9 24 2N 81 45 E
Belang, Indonesia .... 83 C3 0 57N 124 47 E
Belarus ■, Europe .... 58 F4 53 30N 27 0 E
Belas, Angola .... 115 D2 8 55 S 13 9 E
Belau = Palau ■, Pac. Oc. .... 62 J17 7 30N 134 30 E
Belavenona, Madag. .... 117 C8 24 50 S 47 4 E
Belawan, Indonesia .... 84 B1 3 33N 98 32 E
Belaya →, Russia .... 64 D6 54 40N 56 0 E
Belaya Glina, Russia .... 61 G5 46 5N 40 48 E
Belaya Kalitva, Russia .... 61 F5 48 13N 40 50 E
Belaya Kholunitsa, Russia .... 64 B3 58 51N 50 53 E
Belaya Tserkov = Bila Tserkva, Ukraine .... 59 H6 49 45N 30 10 E
Belayan →, Indonesia .... 85 C5 0 14 S 116 36 E
Belcești, Romania .... 53 C12 47 19N 27 7 E
Belchatów, Poland .... 55 G6 51 21N 19 22 E
Belcher Is., Canada 140 A3 56 15N 78 45W
Belchite, Spain 40 D4 41 18N 0 43W
Belden, U.S.A. 160 E5 40 2N 121 17W
Belding, U.S.A. 157 A11 43 6N 85 14W
Belebey, Russia .... 64 D5 54 7N 54 7 E
Beled Weyne = Belet Uen, Somali Rep. .... 120 D3 4 30N 45 5 E
Belém, Brazil .... 170 B2 1 20 S 48 30W
Belém de São Francisco, Brazil .... 170 C4 8 46 S 38 58W
Belén, Argentina .... 174 B2 27 40 S 67 5W
Belén, Colombia .... 174 C2 1 26 S 75 56W
Belén, Paraguay .... 174 A4 23 30 S 57 6W
Belen, U.S.A. 159 J10 34 40N 106 46W
Belene, Bulgaria .... 51 C9 43 39N 25 10 E
Beleni, Turkey .... 100 D7 36 31N 36 10 E
Beles, Is., N. Cal. .... 123 D11 19 45 S 163 40 E
Bélesta, France .... 28 F5 42 55N 1 56 E
Belet Uen, Somali Rep. .... 120 D3 4 30N 45 5 E
Belev, Russia .... 58 F9 53 50N 36 5 E
Belevi, Turkey .... 49 C9 38 0N 27 28 E
Belfair, U.S.A. 160 C4 47 27N 122 50W
Belfast, N.Z. .... 131 D7 43 27 S 172 39 E
Belfast, S. Africa .... 117 D5 25 42 S 30 2 E
Belfast, U.K. 23 B6 54 37N 5 56W
Belfast, Maine, U.S.A. 149 C11 44 26N 69 1W
Belfast, N.Y., U.S.A. 150 D6 42 21N 78 7W
Belfast L., U.K. 23 B6 54 40N 5 50W
Belfield, U.S.A. 154 B3 46 53N 103 12W
Belfort, France .... 27 E13 47 38N 6 50 E
Belfort, Territoire de □, France .... 27 E13 47 40N 6 55 E
Belfry, U.S.A. 158 D9 45 9N 109 1W
Belgaum, India .... 95 G2 15 55N 74 35 E
Belgioioso, Italy .... 44 C6 45 10N 9 19 E
Belgium ■, Europe .... 25 D4 50 30N 5 0 E
Belgodère, France .... 29 F13 42 35N 9 1 E
Belgorod, Russia .... 59 G9 50 35N 36 35 E
Belgorod-Dnestrovskiy = Bilhorod-Dnistrovskyy, Ukraine .... 59 J6 46 11N 30 23 E
Belgrade = Beograd, Serbia, Yug. .... 50 B4 44 50N 20 37 E
Belgrade, U.S.A. 158 D8 45 47N 111 11W
Belgrade × (BEG), Yugoslavia .... 50 C4 43 49N 20 17 E
Belgrove, N.Z. .... 131 B7 41 27 S 172 59 E
Belhaven, U.S.A. 149 H7 35 33N 76 37W
Beli Drim →, Europe .... 50 C5 42 6N 20 25 E
Beli Manastir, Croatia .... 52 E3 45 45N 18 36 E
Beli Timok →, Serbia, Yug. .... 50 C6 43 53N 22 14 E
Bélice →, Italy .... 48 F5 37 35N 12 55 E
Belimbing, Indonesia .... 79 J18 8 24 S 115 2 E
Belinga, Gabon .... 114 B2 1 10N 13 2 E
Belinskiy, Russia .... 60 D6 53 0N 43 25 E
Belinyu, Indonesia .... 84 C3 1 35 S 105 50 E
Beliton Is. = Belitung, Indonesia .... 85 C3 10 S 107 50 E
Belitung, Indonesia .... 85 C3 3 10 S 107 50 E
Beliu, Romania .... 52 D6 46 30N 22 0 E
Belize ■, Cent. Amer. 163 D7 17 0N 88 30W
Belize City, Belize 163 D7 17 25N 88 0W
Beljakovci, Macedonia .... 50 D5 42 6N 21 59 E
Beljanica, Serbia, Yug. .... 50 B6 44 8N 21 43 E
Belkovskiy, Ostrov, Russia .... 67 B14 75 32N 135 44 E
Bell →, Canada 140 C4 49 48N 77 38W
Bell I., Canada 141 B8 50 46N 55 35W

Bell-Irving →, Canada 142 B3 56 12N 129 5W
Bell Peninsula, Canada 139 B11 63 50N 82 0W
Bell Ville, Argentina .... 174 C3 32 40 S 62 40W
Bella, Italy .... 47 B8 40 45N 15 32 E
Bella Bella, Canada 142 C3 52 10N 128 10W
Bella Coola, Canada 142 C3 52 25N 126 40W
Bella Flor, Bolivia .... 172 C4 11 9 S 67 49W
Bella Unión, Uruguay .... 174 C4 30 15 S 57 40W
Bella Vista, Corrientes, Argentina .... 174 B4 28 33 S 59 0W
Bella Vista, Tucuman, Argentina .... 174 B2 27 10 S 65 25W
Bellac, France .... 28 B5 46 7N 1 3 E
Bellágio, Italy .... 44 C6 45 59N 9 15 E
Bellaire, U.S.A. 150 F4 40 1N 80 45W
Bellarion, India .... 95 G3 15 10N 76 56 E
Bellary, India .... 95 G3 15 10N 76 56 E
Bellata, Australia .... 127 D4 29 53 S 149 46 E
Bellavista, Ecuador .... 172 a 0 41 S 90 18W
Belle, U.S.A. 156 F5 38 17N 91 43W
Belle-Chasse, U.S.A. 155 L10 29 51N 89 59W
Belle Fourche, U.S.A. 154 C3 44 40N 103 51W
Belle Fourche →, U.S.A. 154 C3 44 26N 102 18W
Belle Glade, U.S.A. 153 J9 26 41N 80 40W
Belle-Île, France 26 E3 47 20N 3 10W
Belle Isle, Canada 141 B8 51 57N 55 25W
Belle Isle, U.S.A. 153 G8 28 27N 81 21W
Belle Isle, Str. of, Canada 141 B8 51 30N 56 30W
Belle Plaine, U.S.A. 156 C4 41 54N 92 17W
Belle Rive, U.S.A. 158 B4 38 14N 88 45W
Belle Yella, Liberia 112 D3 7 24N 10 0W
Belledonne, France .... 29 C10 45 20N 6 10 E
Bellefontaine, U.S.A. 157 D13 40 22N 83 46W
Bellefonte, U.S.A. 150 F7 40 55N 77 47W
Bellegarde, France .... 27 E9 47 59N 2 26 E
Bellegarde-en-Marche, France .... 28 C6 45 59N 2 18 E
Bellegarde-sur-Valserine, France .... 27 F12 46 4N 5 50 E
Bellême, France .... 26 D7 48 22N 0 34 E
Belleoram, Canada 141 C8 47 31N 55 25W
Belleplaine, Barbados .... 165 g 13 15N 59 34W
Belleville, Canada 140 D4 44 10N 77 23W
Belleville, France .... 27 F11 46 7N 4 45 E
Belleville, Ill., U.S.A. 156 F7 38 31N 89 59W
Belleville, Kans., U.S.A. 154 F6 39 50N 97 38W
Belleville-sur-Vie, France 26 F5 46 46N 1 25W
Bellevue, Canada 142 D6 49 35N 114 22W
Bellevue, Idaho, U.S.A. 158 E6 43 28N 114 16W
Bellevue, Iowa, U.S.A. 156 B6 42 16N 90 26W
Bellevue, Mich., U.S.A. 157 B11 42 27N 85 1W
Bellevue, Nebr., U.S.A. 154 E7 41 8N 95 53W
Bellevue, Ohio, U.S.A. 150 E2 41 17N 82 51W
Bellevue, Wash., U.S.A. 160 C4 47 37N 122 12W
Belley, France .... 29 C9 45 46N 5 41 E
Bellin = Kangirsuk, Canada 139 B13 60 0N 70 0W
Bellinge, Denmark .... 17 J4 55 20N 10 16 E
Bellingen, Australia .... 129 A10 30 25 S 152 50 E
Bellingham, U.S.A. 160 B4 48 46N 122 29W
Bellinzona, Switz. .... 33 D8 46 11N 9 1 E
Bello, Colombia 174 B2 6 20N 75 33W
Bellows Falls, U.S.A. .... 133 C10 11 17 S 159 47 E
Bellows Falls, U.S.A. 151 C12 43 8N 72 27W
Bellpat, Pakistan .... 92 E3 29 0N 68 5 E
Bellpuig d'Urgell, Spain .... 40 D6 41 37N 1 1 E
Belluno, Italy .... 45 B9 46 9N 12 13 E
Bellville, U.S.A. 152 C8 32 9N 81 59W
Bellwood, U.S.A. 150 F6 40 36N 78 20W
Bélmez, Spain 43 G5 38 17N 5 17W
Belmond, U.S.A. 156 B3 42 51N 93 37W
Belmont, Australia .... 129 B9 33 4 S 151 42 E
Belmont, Canada 150 D3 42 53N 81 5W
Belmont, S. Africa .... 116 D3 29 28 S 24 22 E
Belmont, U.S.A. 150 D6 42 14N 78 2W
Belmonte, Brazil .... 171 E4 16 0 S 39 0W
Belmonte, Portugal 42 E3 40 21N 7 20W
Belmonte, Spain 41 F2 39 34N 2 43W
Belmopan, Belize 163 D7 17 18N 88 30W
Belmullet, Ireland 23 B2 54 14N 9 58W
Belo, Dem. Rep. of the Congo .... 114 C4 0 32 S 23 13 E
Belo Horizonte, Brazil .... 171 E3 19 55 S 43 56W
Belo Jardim, Brazil .... 170 C4 8 20 S 36 26W
Belo Monte, Brazil .... 169 D7 3 5 S 51 46W
Belo-sur-Mer, Madag. .... 117 C7 20 42 S 44 0 E
Belo-Tsiribihina, Madag. .... 117 B7 19 40 S 44 30 E
Belogorsk = Bilohirsk, Ukraine .... 59 K8 45 3N 34 35 E
Belogorsk, Russia .... 67 D13 51 0N 128 20 E
Belogradets, Bulgaria .... 51 C11 43 22N 27 18 E
Beloha, Madag. .... 117 D8 25 10 S 45 3 E
Beloit, Kans., U.S.A. 154 F5 39 28N 98 6W
Beloit, Wis., U.S.A. 156 B7 42 31N 89 2W
Belokorovichi, Ukraine .... 59 G5 51 7N 28 2 E
Belomorsk, Russia .... 56 B5 64 35N 34 54 E
Belondo, Dem. Rep. of the Congo .... 114 C3 1 59 S 19 31 E
Belonge, Dem. Rep. of the Congo .... 114 C3 2 7 S 19 33 E
Belonia, India .... 90 D3 23 15N 91 30 E
Belopolye = Bilopillya, Ukraine .... 59 G8 51 14N 34 20 E
Belorechensk, Russia .... 61 H4 44 46N 39 52 E
Beloretsk, Russia .... 64 D7 53 58N 58 24 E
Belorussia = Belarus ■, Europe .... 58 F4 53 30N 27 0 E
Beloslav, Bulgaria .... 51 C11 43 11N 27 42 E
Belovo, Bulgaria .... 50 D8 42 13N 24 1 E
Belovo, Russia .... 66 D9 54 30N 86 0 E
Belovodsk, Ukraine .... 59 H10 49 13N 39 35 E
Beloyarskiy, Russia .... 58 B9 60 10N 37 35 E
Beloye, Ozero, Russia .... 56 A6 60 36N 38 0 E
Beloye More, Russia .... 58 A6 66 30N 38 0 E
Belozem, Bulgaria .... 51 D9 42 12N 25 2 E
Belozersk, Russia .... 58 B9 60 1N 37 45 E
Belp, Switz. .... 32 C5 46 53N 7 30 E
Belpasso, Italy .... 47 E7 37 35N 14 58 E
Belpre, U.S.A. 148 F5 39 17N 81 34W
Belrain, India .... 93 E9 28 23N 80 55 E
Belt, U.S.A. 158 C8 47 23N 110 55W
Beltana, Australia .... 128 A3 30 48 S 138 25 E
Belterra, Brazil .... 169 D7 2 45 S 55 0W
Beltinci, Slovenia .... 45 B13 46 37N 16 20 E
Belton, Mo., U.S.A. 156 F2 38 49N 94 32W
Belton, Tex., U.S.A. 155 K6 31 3N 97 28W
Belton L., U.S.A. 155 K6 31 8N 97 32W
Beltsy = Bălți, Moldova .... 53 C12 47 48N 27 58 E
Belturbet, Ireland 23 B4 54 6N 7 26W
Belukha, Russia .... 66 E9 49 50N 86 50 E
Beluran, Malaysia .... 78 C5 5 48N 117 35 E
Beluŝić, Serbia, Yug. .... 50 C5 43 50N 21 10 E
Belvedere Maríttimo, Italy .... 47 C8 39 37N 15 52 E
Belvès, France .... 28 D5 44 46N 1 0 E
Belvidere, Ill., U.S.A. 154 D10 42 15N 88 50W
Belvidere, N.J., U.S.A. 151 F9 40 50N 75 5W
Belvis de la Jara, Spain 42 F6 39 45N 4 57W
Belyando →, Australia .... 126 C4 21 38 S 146 50 E
Belyy, Russia .... 58 E7 55 49N 33 3 E
Belyy, Ostrov, Russia .... 66 B8 73 30N 71 0 E
Belyy Yar, Russia .... 66 D9 58 26N 84 39 E
Belyye Vody = Aqsū, Kazakhstan .... 65 B4 42 55N 69 50 E
Bełżec, Poland .... 55 H10 50 23N 23 26 E
Belzig, Germany .... 30 C8 52 8N 12 36 E
Belzoni, U.S.A. 155 J9 33 11N 90 29W
Bełżyce, Poland .... 55 G8 51 11N 22 17 E
Bemaraha, Lembalemban' i, Madag. .... 117 B7 18 40 S 44 45 E
Bemarivo, Madag. .... 117 C7 21 45 S 44 45 E
Bemarivo →, Antsiranana, Madag. .... 117 A9 14 9 S 50 9 E
Bemarivo →, Mahajanga, Madag. .... 117 B8 15 27 S 47 40 E

Bemavo, *Madag.* **117 C8** 21 33 S 45 25 E
Bembe, *Angola* **115 D2** 7 3 S 14 25 E
Bembéréke, *Benin* **113 C5** 10 11N 2 43 E
Bembesi, *Zimbabwe* **119 G2** 20 0 S 28 58 E
Bembesi →, *Zimbabwe* **119 F2** 18 57 S 27 47 E
Bembézar →, *Spain* **43 H5** 37 45N 5 13W
Bembibre, *Spain* **42 C4** 42 37N 6 25W
Bemboka Nat. Park △, *Australia* **129 D8** 36 35 S 149 41 E
Bement, *U.S.A.* **157 E8** 39 55N 88 34W
Bemetara, *India* **93 J9** 21 42N 81 32 E
Bemidji, *U.S.A.* **154 B7** 47 28N 94 53W
Bemolanga, *Madag.* **117 B8** 17 44 S 45 6 E
Ben, *Iran* **97 C6** 32 32N 50 45 E
Ben Boyd Nat. Park △, *Australia* **129 D8** 37 0 S 149 55 E
Ben Cruachan, *U.K.* **22 E3** 56 26N 5 8W
Ben Dearg, *U.K.* **22 D4** 57 47N 4 56W
Ben En Nat. Park △, *Vietnam* **86 C5** 19 37N 105 30 E
Ben Gardane, *Tunisia* **108 B2** 33 11N 11 11 E
Ben Hope, *U.K.* **22 C4** 58 25N 4 36W
Ben Lawers, *U.K.* **22 E4** 56 32N 4 14W
Ben Lomond, *N.S.W., Australia* **127 E5** 30 1 S 151 43 E
Ben Lomond, *Tas., Australia* **127 D4** 41 38 S 147 42 E
Ben Lomond, *U.K.* **22 E4** 56 11N 4 38W
Ben Lomond Nat. Park △, *Australia* **127 D4** 41 33 S 147 39 E
Ben Luc, *Vietnam* **87 G6** 10 39N 106 29 E
Ben Macdhui, *U.K.* **22 D5** 57 4N 3 40W
Ben Mhor, *U.K.* **22 D1** 57 15N 7 18W
Ben More, *Arg. & Bute, U.K.* **22 E2** 56 26N 6 1W
Ben More, *Stirl., U.K.* **22 E4** 56 23N 4 32W
Ben More Assynt, *U.K.* **22 C4** 58 8N 4 52W
Ben Nevis, *U.K.* **22 E3** 56 48N 5 1W
Ben Ohau Ra., *N.Z.* **131 E5** 44 1 S 170 4 E
Ben Quang, *Vietnam* **86 D6** 17 3N 106 55 E
Ben Slimane, *Morocco* **110 B3** 33 38N 7 7W
Ben Vorlich, *U.K.* **22 E4** 56 21N 4 14W
Ben Wyvis, *U.K.* **22 D4** 57 40N 4 35W
Bena, *Nigeria* **113 C6** 11 20N 5 50 E
Bena-Dibele, *Dem. Rep. of the Congo* **115 C4** 4 4 S 22 50 E
Bena-Leka, *Dem. Rep. of the Congo* **115 D4** 5 8 S 22 10 E
Bena-Tshadi, *Dem. Rep. of the Congo* **115 C4** 4 40 S 22 49 E
Benadir, *Somali Rep.* **120 D2** 1 30N 44 30 E
Benagerie, *Australia* **128 A4** 31 25 S 140 22 E
Benahmed, *Morocco* **110 B3** 33 4N 7 9W
Benalla, *Australia* **129 D7** 36 30 S 146 0 E
Benalmádena, *Spain* **43 J6** 36 36N 4 34W
Benambra, Mt., *Australia* **129 D7** 36 31 S 147 34 E
Benanee, *Australia* **128 C5** 34 31 S 142 52 E
Benares = Varanasi, *India* **93 G10** 25 22N 83 0 E
Bénat, C., *France* **29 E10** 43 5N 6 22 E
Benavente, *Portugal* **43 G2** 38 59N 8 49W
Benavente, *Spain* **42 C5** 42 2N 5 43W
Benavides, *U.S.A.* **155 M5** 27 36N 98 25W
Benavides de Órbigo, *Spain* **42 C5** 42 30N 5 54W
Benbecula, *U.K.* **22 D1** 57 26N 7 21W
Benbonyathe, *Australia* **128 A3** 30 25 S 139 11 E
Bend, *U.S.A.* **158 D3** 44 4N 121 19W
Bendela, *Dem. Rep. of the Congo* **114 C3** 3 18 S 17 36 E
Bendemeer, *Australia* **129 A9** 30 53 S 151 8 E
Bender Beila, *Somali Rep.* **120 C4** 9 30N 50 48 E
Bender Merchagno, *Somali Rep.* **120 B4** 11 41N 50 34 E
Bendery = Tighina, *Moldova* **53 D14** 46 50N 29 30 E
Bendigo, *Australia* **128 D6** 36 40 S 144 15 E
Bendorf, *Germany* **30 E3** 50 25N 7 35 E
Benē Beraq, *Israel* **103 C3** 32 6N 34 51 E
Beneditinos, *Brazil* **170 C3** 5 27 S 42 22W
Benedito Leite, *Brazil* **170 C3** 7 13 S 44 34W
Bénéna, *Mali* **112 C4** 13 9N 4 17W
Benenitra, *Madag.* **117 C8** 23 27 S 45 5 E
Benešov, *Czech Rep.* **34 B7** 49 46N 14 41 E
Benevento, *Italy* **47 A7** 41 8N 14 45 E
Benfeld, *France* **27 D14** 48 22N 7 34 E
Benga, *Mozam.* **119 F3** 16 11 S 33 40 E
Bengal, Bay of, *Ind. Oc.* **89 D7** 15 0N 90 0 E
Bengbis, *Cameroon* **113 E7** 3 27N 12 36 E
Bengbu, *China* **75 H9** 32 58N 117 20 E
Benghazi = Banghāzī, *Libya* **108 B4** 32 11N 20 3 E
Benghisa Point, *Malta* **38 F8** 35 49N 14 33 E
Bengkalis, *Indonesia* **84 B2** 1 30N 102 10 E
Bengkulu, *Indonesia* **84 C2** 3 50 S 102 12 E
Bengkulu □, *Indonesia* **84 C2** 3 48 S 102 16 E
Bengo, *Dem. Rep. of the Congo* **114 C3** 2 11 S 19 5 E
Bengo □, *Angola* **115 D2** 9 0 S 13 10 E
Bengough, *Canada* **143 D7** 49 25N 105 10W
Bengtsfors, *Sweden* **16 E6** 59 2N 12 14 E
Benguela, *Angola* **115 E2** 12 37 S 13 25 E
Benguela □, *Angola* **115 E2** 13 0 S 13 30 E
Benguerir, *Morocco* **110 B3** 32 16N 7 56W
Benguérua, I., *Mozam.* **117 C6** 21 58 S 35 28 E
Benguet □, *Phil.* **80 C3** 16 30N 120 40 E
Benha, *Egypt* **106 H7** 30 26N 31 8 E
Benham Seamount, *Pac. Oc.* **80 D5** 15 40N 124 30 E
Beni, *Dem. Rep. of the Congo* **118 B2** 0 30N 29 27 E
Beni □, *Bolivia* **173 C4** 14 0 S 65 0W
Beni →, *Bolivia* **173 C4** 10 23 S 65 24W
Beni Abbès, *Algeria* **111 B4** 30 5N 2 5W
Beni Haoua, *Algeria* **111 A5** 36 30N 1 30 E
Beni Mazâr, *Egypt* **106 B3** 28 32N 30 44 E
Beni Mellal, *Morocco* **110 B3** 32 21N 6 21W
Beni Ounif, *Algeria* **111 B4** 32 0N 1 10W
Beni Saf, *Algeria* **111 A4** 35 17N 1 15W
Beni Suef, *Egypt* **106 J7** 29 5N 31 6 E
Beniah L., *Canada* **142 A6** 63 23N 112 17W
Benicarló, *Spain* **40 E5** 40 23N 0 23 E
Benicássim, *Spain* **40 E5** 40 3N 0 4 E
Benicia, *U.S.A.* **160 G4** 38 3N 122 9W
Benidorm, *Spain* **41 G4** 38 33N 0 9W
Benin ■, *Africa* **113 D5** 10 0N 2 0 E
Benin →, *Nigeria* **113 D6** 5 45N 5 4 E
Benin, Bight of, *W. Afr.* **113 E5** 5 0N 3 0 E
Benin City, *Nigeria* **113 D6** 6 20N 5 31 E
Benisa, *Spain* **41 G5** 38 43N 0 3 E
Benitses, *Greece* **38 B9** 39 32N 19 55 E
Benjamin Aceval, *Paraguay* **174 A4** 24 58 S 57 34W
Benjamin Constant, *Brazil* **168 D3** 4 40 S 70 15W
Benjamin Hill, *Mexico* **162 A2** 30 10N 111 10W
Benkelman, *U.S.A.* **154 E4** 40 3N 101 32W
Benkovac, *Croatia* **45 D12** 44 2N 15 37 E
Benmore Pk., *N.Z.* **131 E5** 44 25 S 170 8 E
Bennett, *Canada* **142 B2** 59 56N 134 53W
Bennett, L., *Australia* **124 D5** 22 50 S 131 2 E
Bennetta, Ostrov, *Russia* **67 B15** 76 21N 148 56 E
Bennettsville, *U.S.A.* **149 H6** 34 37N 79 41W
Bennichchâb, *Mauritania* **112 B1** 19 32N 15 12W
Bennington, *N.H., U.S.A.* **151 D11** 43 0N 71 55W
Bennington, *Vt., U.S.A.* **151 D11** 42 53N 73 12W
Beno, *Dem. Rep. of the Congo* **114 C3** 3 41 S 17 49 E
Bénodet, *France* **26 E2** 47 53N 4 7W
Benoni, *S. Africa* **117 D4** 26 11 S 28 18 E
Benoud, *Algeria* **111 B5** 32 20N 0 16 E
Bénoué, Parc Nat. de la △, *Cameroon* **114 A2** 8 30N 13 55 E
Benoy, *Chad* **109 G3** 8 59N 16 19 E
Benque Viejo, *Belize* **163 D7** 17 5N 89 8W
Bensheim, *Germany* **31 F4** 49 40N 8 38 E
Benson, *Ariz., U.S.A.* **159 L8** 31 58N 110 18W
Benson, *Minn., U.S.A.* **154 C7** 45 19N 95 36W
Bent, *Iran* **97 E8** 26 20N 59 31 E
Benteng, *Indonesia* **82 C2** 6 10 S 120 30 E
Bentiaba, *Angola* **115 E2** 14 15 S 12 21 E
Bentinck I., *Australia* **126 B2** 17 3 S 139 35 E
Bentiu, *Sudan* **107 F2** 9 10N 29 55 E
Bento Gonçalves, *Brazil* **175 B5** 29 10 S 51 31W
Benton, *Ark., U.S.A.* **155 H8** 34 34N 92 35W
Benton, *Calif., U.S.A.* **160 H8** 37 48N 118 32W
Benton, *Ill., U.S.A.* **156 G8** 38 0N 88 55W
Benton, *Pa., U.S.A.* **151 E8** 41 12N 76 23W
Benton Harbor, *U.S.A.* **157 B10** 42 6N 86 27W
Benton Heights, *U.S.A.* **157 B10** 42 7N 86 24W
Bentong, *Malaysia* **87 L3** 3 31N 101 55 E
Bentonville, *U.S.A.* **155 G7** 36 22N 94 13W
Bentu Liben, *Ethiopia* **107 F4** 8 32N 38 21 E
Benue □, *Nigeria* **113 D6** 7 20N 8 45 E
Benue →, *Nigeria* **113 D6** 7 48N 6 46 E
Benxi, *China* **75 D12** 41 20N 123 48 E
Benza, *Dem. Rep. of the Congo* **115 D2** 4 49 S 13 17 E
Benzdorp, *Suriname* **169 C7** 3 44N 54 5W
Beo, *Indonesia* **82 A3** 4 25N 126 50 E
Beograd, *Serbia, Yug.* **50 B4** 44 50N 20 37 E
Beoumi, *Ivory C.* **112 D3** 7 45N 5 23W
Bepan Jiang →, *China* **76 E6** 24 55N 106 5 E
Beppu, *Japan* **72 D3** 33 15N 131 30 E
Beppu-Wan, *Japan* **72 D3** 33 18N 131 34 E
Beqa, *Fiji* **133 B2** 18 23 S 178 8 E
Beqaa Valley = Al Biqā, *Lebanon* **103 A5** 34 10N 36 10 E
Ber Mota, *India* **92 H3** 23 27N 68 34 E
Bera, *Bangla.* **90 C2** 24 5N 89 37 E
Berach →, *India* **92 G6** 25 15N 75 2 E
Beraketa, *Madag.* **117 C7** 23 7 S 44 25 E
Béran-Djoko, *Congo* **114 B3** 3 15N 17 0 E
Berane, *Montenegro, Yug.* **50 D3** 42 51N 19 52 E
Berat, *Albania* **50 F3** 40 43N 19 59 E
Berau →, *Indonesia* **85 B5** 2 10N 117 42 E
Berau, Teluk, *Indonesia* **83 B4** 2 30 S 132 30 E
Beravina, *Madag.* **117 B8** 18 10 S 45 14 E
Berber, *Sudan* **106 D3** 18 0N 34 0 E
Berbera, *Somali Rep.* **120 B3** 10 30N 45 2 E
Berbérati, *C.A.R.* **114 B3** 4 15N 15 40 E
Berbice →, *Guyana* **169 B6** 6 20N 57 32W
Berceto, *Italy* **44 D6** 44 31N 9 51 E
Berchidda, *Italy* **46 B2** 40 47N 9 10 E
Berchtesgaden, *Germany* **31 H8** 47 38N 13 0 E
Berchtesgaden, Nationalpark △, *Germany* **31 H8** 47 34N 12 55 E
Berck, *France* **27 B8** 50 25N 1 36 E
Berdale, *Somali Rep.* **120 C3** 7 4N 47 51 E
Berdichev = Berdychiv, *Ukraine* **59 H5** 49 57N 28 30 E
Berdsk, *Russia* **66 D9** 54 47N 83 2 E
Berdyansk, *Ukraine* **59 J9** 46 45N 36 50 E
Berdyaush, *Russia* **64 D7** 55 9N 59 9 E
Berdychiv, *Ukraine* **59 H5** 49 57N 28 30 E
Berea, *U.S.A.* **148 G3** 37 34N 84 17W
Berebere, *Indonesia* **82 A3** 2 25N 128 45 E
Bereda, *Somali Rep.* **120 B4** 11 45N 51 0 E
Berehove, *Ukraine* **59 H2** 48 15N 22 35 E
Bereina, *Papua N. G.* **132 E4** 8 39 S 146 30 E
Berekum, *Ghana* **112 D4** 7 29N 2 34W
Berenice, *Egypt* **106 C4** 24 2N 35 25 E
Berens →, *Canada* **143 C9** 52 25N 97 2W
Berens I., *Canada* **143 C9** 52 18N 97 18W
Berens River, *Canada* **143 C9** 52 25N 97 0W
Beresford, *U.S.A.* **154 D6** 43 5N 96 47W
Berestechko, *Ukraine* **59 G3** 50 22N 25 5 E
Bereşti, *Romania* **53 D12** 46 6N 27 50 E
Beretău →, *Romania* **52 C6** 47 10N 21 50 E
Berettyó →, *Hungary* **52 D6** 46 59N 21 7 E
Berettyóújfalu, *Hungary* **52 C6** 47 13N 21 33 E
Berevo, *Mahajanga, Madag.* **117 B7** 17 14 S 44 17 E
Berevo, *Toliara, Madag.* **117 B7** 19 44 S 44 58 E
Bereza = Byaroza, *Belarus* **59 F3** 52 31N 24 51 E
Berezhany, *Ukraine* **59 H3** 49 26N 24 58 E
Berezina = Byarezina →, *Belarus* **59 F6** 52 33N 30 14 E
Berezivka, *Ukraine* **59 J6** 47 14N 30 55 E
Berezna, *Ukraine* **59 G6** 51 35N 31 46 E
Berezniki, *Russia* **56 B7** 62 51N 42 40 E
Berezniki, *Russia* **64 B6** 59 24N 56 46 E
Berezovo, *Russia* **66 C7** 64 0N 65 0 E
Berga, *Spain* **40 C6** 42 6N 1 48 E
Berga, *Sweden* **17 G10** 57 14N 16 3 E
Bergama, *Turkey* **49 B9** 39 8N 27 11 E
Bergamo, *Italy* **44 C6** 45 41N 9 43 E
Bergaon, *India* **94 D5** 20 41N 80 27 E
Bergara, *Spain* **40 B2** 43 9N 2 28W
Bergby, *Sweden* **16 D11** 60 57N 17 2 E
Bergedorf, *Germany* **30 B6** 53 28N 10 6 E
Bergeforsen, *Sweden* **16 B11** 62 32N 17 23 E
Bergen, *Mecklenburg-Vorpommern, Germany* **30 A9** 54 25N 13 25 E
Bergen, *Niedersachsen, Germany* **30 C5** 52 49N 9 57 E
Bergen, *Neths.* **24 B4** 52 40N 4 43 E
Bergen, *Norway* **18 D2** 60 20N 5 20 E
Bergen, *U.S.A.* **150 C7** 43 5N 77 57W
Bergen ✕ (BGO), *Norway* **18 D2** 60 17N 5 19 E
Bergen op Zoom, *Neths.* **24 C4** 51 28N 4 18 E
Bergerac, *France* **28 D4** 44 51N 0 30 E
Bergheim, *Germany* **30 E2** 50 57N 6 38 E
Bergholz, *U.S.A.* **150 F4** 40 31N 80 53W
Bergisch Gladbach, *Germany* **24 D7** 50 59N 7 8 E
Bergisches Land, Naturpark ⌓, *Germany* **30 E3** 51 0N 7 30 E
Bergkamen, *Germany* **30 D3** 51 37N 7 38 E
Bergkvara, *Sweden* **17 H10** 56 23N 16 5 E
Bergshamra, *Sweden* **16 E12** 59 38N 18 37 E
Bergsjö, *Sweden* **16 C11** 61 59N 17 3 E
Bergstrasse-Odenwald, Naturpark ⌓, *Germany* **31 F1** 49 45N 5 55 E
Bergues, *France* **27 B9** 50 58N 2 24 E
Bergviken, *Sweden* **16 C10** 61 15N 16 40 E
Bergville, *S. Africa* **117 D4** 28 52 S 29 18 E
Berhala, Selat, *Indonesia* **84 C2** 1 0 S 104 15 E
Berhampore = Baharampur, *India* **93 G13** 24 2N 88 27 E
Berhampur = Brahmapur, *India* **94 E7** 19 15N 84 54 E
Berheci →, *Romania* **53 E12** 45 58N 27 28 E
Bering Glacier, *U.S.A.* **144 F12** 60 20N 143 30W
Bering Land Bridge Nat. Preserve ⌓, *U.S.A.* **144 C6** 66 20N 165 0W
Bering Sea, *Pac. Oc.* **138 C1** 58 0N 171 0 E
Bering Strait, *Pac. Oc.* **144 D5** 65 30N 169 0W
Beringen, *Switz.* **33 A7** 47 38N 8 34 E
Beringovskiy, *Russia* **67 C18** 63 3N 179 19 E
Berisso, *Argentina* **174 C4** 34 56 S 57 50W
Berja, *Spain* **43 J8** 36 50N 2 56W
Berkåk, *Norway* **18 B6** 62 50N 10 0 E
Berkane, *Morocco* **111 B4** 34 52N 2 20W
Berkeley, *U.S.A.* **160 H4** 37 52N 122 16W
Berkeley, C., *Ecuador* **172 a** 0 1N 91 35W
Berkner I., *Antarctica* **7 D18** 79 30 S 50 0W
Berkovitsa, *Bulgaria* **50 C7** 43 16N 23 8 E
Berkshire, *U.S.A.* **151 D8** 42 19N 76 11W
Berkshire Downs, *U.K.* **21 F6** 51 33N 1 29W
Berlanga, *Spain* **43 G5** 38 17N 5 50W
Berlenga, I., *Portugal* **43 F1** 39 25N 9 30W
Berlin, *Germany* **30 C9** 52 30N 13 25 E
Berlin, *Ga., U.S.A.* **152 D6** 31 4N 83 37W
Berlin, *Md., U.S.A.* **148 F8** 38 20N 75 13W
Berlin, *N.H., U.S.A.* **151 B13** 44 28N 71 11W
Berlin, *N.Y., U.S.A.* **151 D11** 42 42N 73 23W
Berlin, *Wis., U.S.A.* **148 D1** 43 58N 88 57W
Berlin □, *Germany* **30 C9** 52 30N 13 20 E
Berlin L., *U.S.A.* **150 E4** 41 3N 81 0W
Berlin Tegel ✕ (TXL), *Germany* **30 C9** 52 35N 13 14 E
Bermagui, *Australia* **129 D9** 36 25 S 150 4 E
Bermeja, Sierra, *Spain* **43 J5** 36 30N 5 11W
Bermejo →, *Formosa, Argentina* **174 B4** 26 51 S 58 23W
Bermejo →, *San Juan, Argentina* **174 C2** 32 30 S 67 30W
Bermen, L., *Canada* **141 B6** 53 35N 68 55W
Bermeo, *Spain* **40 B2** 43 25N 2 47W
Bermillo de Sayago, *Spain* **42 D4** 41 22N 6 8W
Bermuda ☒, *Atl. Oc.* **9 a** 32 45N 65 0W
Bermuda International ✕ (BDA), *Bermuda* **9 a** 32 22N 64 41W
Bern, *Switz.* **32 C4** 46 57N 7 28 E
Bern □, *Switz.* **32 C5** 46 45N 7 40 E
Bernalda, *Italy* **47 B9** 40 24N 16 41 E
Bernalillo, *U.S.A.* **159 J10** 35 18N 106 33W
Bernam →, *Malaysia* **84 B2** 3 45N 101 5 E
Bernardo de Irigoyen, *Argentina* **175 B5** 26 15 S 53 40W
Bernardo O'Higgins □, *Chile* **174 C1** 34 15 S 70 45W
Bernardsville, *U.S.A.* **151 F10** 40 43N 74 34W
Bernasconi, *Argentina* **174 D3** 37 55 S 63 44W
Bernau, *Bayern, Germany* **31 H8** 47 47N 12 22 E
Bernau, *Brandenburg, Germany* **30 C9** 52 40N 13 35 E
Bernay, *France* **26 C7** 49 5N 0 35 E
Bernburg, *Germany* **30 D7** 51 47N 11 44 E
Berndorf, *Austria* **34 D9** 47 59N 16 1 E
Berne = Bern, *Switz.* **32 C4** 46 57N 7 28 E
Berne = Bern □, *Switz.* **32 C5** 46 45N 7 40 E
Berne, *U.S.A.* **157 D12** 40 39N 84 57W
Berner Alpen, *Switz.* **32 D5** 46 27N 7 35 E
Berneray, *U.K.* **22 D1** 57 43N 7 11W
Bernese Oberland = Oberland, *Switz.* **32 C5** 46 35N 7 38 E
Bernier I., *Australia* **125 D1** 24 50 S 113 12 E
Bernina, Passo del, *Switz.* **33 D10** 46 25N 10 2 E
Bernina, Piz, *Switz.* **33 D9** 46 20N 9 54 E
Bernkastel-Kues, *Germany* **31 F3** 49 55N 7 3 E
Bero →, *Angola* **115 F2** 15 10 S 12 9 E
Beroroha, *Madag.* **117 C8** 21 40 S 45 10 E
Béroubouay, *Benin* **113 C5** 10 34N 2 46 E
Beroun, *Czech Rep.* **34 B7** 49 57N 14 5 E
Berounka →, *Czech Rep.* **34 B7** 50 0N 14 22 E
Berovo, *Macedonia* **50 E6** 41 38N 22 51 E
Berrahal, *Algeria* **111 A6** 36 54N 7 33 E
Berre, Étang de, *France* **29 E9** 43 27N 5 5 E
Berre-l'Étang, *France* **29 E9** 43 27N 5 10 E
Berrechid, *Morocco* **110 B3** 33 18N 7 36W
Berri, *Australia* **128 C4** 34 14 S 140 35 E
Berriane, *Algeria* **111 B5** 32 50N 3 46 E
Berridale, *Australia* **129 D8** 36 22 S 148 48 E
Berrien Springs, *U.S.A.* **157 C10** 41 57N 86 20W
Berrigan, *Australia* **129 C6** 35 38 S 145 49 E
Berriwillock, *Australia* **128 C5** 35 36 S 142 59 E
Berrouaghia, *Algeria* **111 A5** 36 10N 2 53 E
Berry, *Australia* **129 C9** 34 46 S 150 43 E
Berry, *France* **27 F8** 46 50N 2 0 E
Berry Is., *Bahamas* **164 A4** 25 40N 77 50W
Berrydale, *U.S.A.* **153 E2** 30 53N 87 3W
Berryessa L., *U.S.A.* **160 G4** 38 31N 122 6W
Berryville, *U.S.A.* **155 G8** 36 22N 93 34W
Berseba, *Namibia* **116 D2** 26 0 S 17 46 E
Bersenbrück, *Germany* **30 C3** 52 34N 7 56 E
Bershad, *Ukraine* **59 H5** 48 22N 29 31 E
Berthold, *U.S.A.* **154 A4** 48 19N 101 44W
Berthoud, *U.S.A.* **154 E2** 40 19N 105 5W
Bertincourt, *France* **27 B9** 50 5N 2 58 E
Bertolínia, *Brazil* **170 C3** 7 38 S 43 57W
Bertoua, *Cameroon* **114 B2** 4 30N 13 45 E
Bertraghboy B., *Ireland* **23 C2** 53 22N 9 54W
Berufjörður, *Iceland* **11 C12** 64 48N 14 29W
Berunes, *Iceland* **11 C12** 64 42N 14 16W
Beruri, *Brazil* **169 D5** 3 54 S 61 22W
Berwick, *U.S.A.* **151 E8** 41 3N 76 14W
Berwick-upon-Tweed, *U.K.* **20 B6** 55 46N 2 0W
Berwyn Mts., *U.K.* **20 E4** 52 54N 3 26W
Berysiav, *Ukraine* **59 J7** 46 50N 33 30 E
Berzasca, *Romania* **52 F6** 44 39N 21 58 E
Berzence, *Hungary* **52 D2** 46 12N 17 11 E
Besal, *Pakistan* **93 B5** 35 4N 73 56 E
Besalampy, *Madag.* **117 B7** 16 43 S 44 29 E
Besançon, *France* **27 E13** 47 15N 6 2 E
Besar, *Indonesia* **85 C5** 2 40 S 116 0 E
Besar, Gunong, *Malaysia* **84 A2** 5 10N 101 18 E
Besharyk, *Uzbekistan* **65 C5** 40 26N 70 36 E
Beshenkovichi, *Belarus* **58 E5** 55 2N 29 29 E
Beshkent, *Uzbekistan* **65 D2** 38 49N 65 39 E
Beška, *Serbia, Yug.* **52 E5** 45 8N 20 6 E
Beslan, *Russia* **61 J7** 43 15N 44 28 E
Besna Kobila, *Serbia, Yug.* **50 D6** 42 31N 22 10 E
Besnard L., *Canada* **143 B7** 55 25N 106 0W
Besni, *Turkey* **100 D7** 37 41N 37 52 E
Besor, N. →, *Egypt* **103 D3** 31 28N 34 22 E
Bessa Monteiro, *Angola* **115 D2** 7 7 S 13 44 E
Bessarabiya, *Moldova* **59 J5** 47 0N 28 10 E
Bessarabka = Basarabeasca, *Moldova* **53 D13** 46 21N 28 58 E
Bessèges, *France* **29 D8** 44 18N 4 8 E
Bessemer, *Ala., U.S.A.* **149 J2** 33 24N 86 58W
Bessemer, *Mich., U.S.A.* **156 B6** 46 29N 90 3W
Bessemer, *Pa., U.S.A.* **150 F4** 40 59N 80 30W
Bessin, *France* **26 C6** 49 18N 1 0W
Bessines-sur-Gartempe, *France* **28 B5** 46 6N 1 22 E
Beswick, *Australia* **124 B5** 14 34 S 132 53 E
Bet She'an, *Israel* **103 C4** 32 30N 35 30 E
Bet Shemesh, *Israel* **103 D4** 31 44N 35 0 E
Bet Tadjine, Djebel, *Algeria* **110 C4** 29 0N 3 30W
Betafo, *Madag.* **117 B8** 19 50 S 46 51 E
Betamba, *Dem. Rep. of the Congo* **114 C4** 2 17 S 21 24 E
Betancuria, *Canary Is.* **9 e2** 28 25N 14 3W
Betancuria, Mt., *Canary Is.* **9 e2** 28 25N 14 6W
Betania, *Colombia* **168 C3** 4 22N 72 54W
Betanzos, *Bolivia* **173 D4** 19 34 S 65 27W
Betanzos, *Spain* **42 B2** 43 15N 8 12W
Bétaré Oya, *Cameroon* **114 A2** 5 40N 14 5 E
Betatao, *Madag.* **117 B8** 18 11 S 47 52 E
Bétera, *Spain* **41 F4** 39 35N 0 28W
Bétérou, *Benin* **113 D5** 9 12N 2 16 E
Bethal, *S. Africa* **117 D4** 26 27 S 29 28 E
Bethalto, *U.S.A.* **156 F6** 38 55N 90 2W
Bethanien, *Namibia* **116 D2** 26 31 S 17 8 E
Bethany, *Canada* **150 B6** 44 11N 78 34W
Bethany, *Ill., U.S.A.* **157 E8** 39 39N 88 45W
Bethany, *Mo., U.S.A.* **154 E7** 40 16N 94 2W
Bethel, *Alaska, U.S.A.* **144 F7** 60 48N 161 45W
Bethel, *Conn., U.S.A.* **151 E11** 41 22N 73 25W
Bethel, *Maine, U.S.A.* **151 B14** 44 25N 70 47W
Bethel, *Ohio, U.S.A.* **157 F12** 38 58N 84 5W
Bethel, *Vt., U.S.A.* **151 C12** 43 50N 72 38W
Bethel Park, *U.S.A.* **150 F4** 40 20N 80 1W
Béthenville, *France* **27 C11** 49 18N 4 23 E
Bethlehem = Bayt Lahm, *West Bank* **103 D4** 31 43N 35 12 E
Bethlehem, *S. Africa* **117 D4** 28 14 S 28 18 E
Bethlehem, *U.S.A.* **151 F9** 40 37N 75 23W
Bethulie, *S. Africa* **116 E4** 30 30 S 25 59 E
Béthune, *France* **27 B9** 50 30N 2 38 E
Béthune →, *France* **26 C8** 49 53N 1 4 E
Bethungra, *Australia* **129 C7** 34 45 S 147 51 E
Betijoque, *Venezuela* **168 B3** 9 23N 70 44W
Betioky, *Madag.* **117 C7** 23 48 S 44 20 E
Betong, *Thailand* **87 K3** 5 45N 101 5 E
Betoota, *Australia* **126 D3** 25 45 S 140 42 E
Betor, *Ethiopia* **107 E4** 11 37N 39 2 E
Bétou, *Congo* **114 B3** 3 2N 18 32 E
Betroka, *Madag.* **117 C8** 23 16 S 46 0 E
Betsiamites, *Canada* **141 C6** 48 56N 68 40W
Betsiamites →, *Canada* **141 C6** 48 56N 68 38W
Betsiboka →, *Madag.* **117 B8** 16 3 S 46 36 E
Bettendorf, *U.S.A.* **156 C6** 41 32N 90 30W
Bettiah, *India* **93 F11** 26 48N 84 33 E
Bettna, *Sweden* **17 F10** 58 55N 16 38 E
Bèttola, *Italy* **44 D6** 44 47N 9 36 E
Betul, *India* **94 D3** 21 58N 77 59 E
Betung, *Malaysia* **85 B4** 1 24N 111 31 E
Betws-y-Coed, *U.K.* **20 D4** 53 5N 3 48W
Betxi, *Spain* **40 F4** 39 56N 0 12W
Betzdorf, *Germany* **30 E3** 50 46N 7 52 E
Béu, *Angola* **115 D3** 6 15 S 15 32 E
Beuil, *France* **29 D10** 44 6N 6 59 E
Beulah, *Australia* **128 C5** 35 58 S 142 29 E
Beulah, *Mich., U.S.A.* **148 C2** 44 38N 86 6W
Beulah, *N. Dak., U.S.A.* **154 B4** 47 16N 101 47W
Beurkia, *Chad* **109 E3** 15 20N 17 56 E
Beuvron →, *France* **26 E8** 47 29N 1 15 E
Beveren, *Belgium* **24 C4** 51 12N 4 16 E
Beverley, *Australia* **125 F2** 32 9 S 116 56 E
Beverley, *U.K.* **20 D7** 53 51N 0 26W
Beverley Hills, *U.S.A.* **153 G7** 28 56N 82 28W
Beverly, *U.S.A.* **151 D14** 42 33N 70 53W
Beverly Hills, *U.S.A.* **161 L8** 34 4N 118 25W
Beverungen, *Germany* **30 D5** 51 39N 9 22 E
Bevoalavo, *Madag.* **117 D7** 25 13 S 45 26 E
Bewani, *Papua N. G.* **83 B6** 3 2 S 141 10 E
Bewas →, *India* **93 H8** 23 59N 79 21 E
Bex, *Switz.* **32 D4** 46 15N 7 1 E
Bexhill, *U.K.* **21 G8** 50 51N 0 29 E
Bey Dağları, *Turkey* **49 E12** 36 38N 30 29 E
Beyānlū, *Iran* **96 C5** 36 0N 47 51 E
Beyazköy, *Turkey* **51 E11** 41 21N 27 42 E
Beyçayırı, *Turkey* **51 F10** 40 15N 26 55 E
Beydağ, *Turkey* **49 C10** 38 5N 28 13 E
Beyeğaç, *Turkey* **49 D10** 37 14N 28 53 E
Beyin, *Ghana* **112 D4** 5 1N 2 41W
Beykoz, *Turkey* **51 E13** 41 8N 29 7 E
Beyla, *Guinea* **112 D3** 8 30N 8 38W
Beynat, *France* **28 C5** 45 8N 1 44 E
Beyneu, *Kazakhstan* **57 E10** 45 18N 55 9 E
Beyoba, *Turkey* **49 C9** 38 48N 27 47 E
Beyoğlu, *Turkey* **51 E12** 41 2N 29 0 E
Beypazarı, *Turkey* **100 B4** 40 10N 31 56 E
Beypore →, *India* **95 J2** 11 10N 75 47 E
Beyşehir, *Turkey* **100 D4** 37 41N 31 43 E
Beyşehir Gölü, *Turkey* **100 D4** 37 41N 31 33 E
Beytüşşebap, *Turkey* **101 D10** 37 35N 43 10 E
Bezau, *Austria* **33 B9** 47 23N 9 54 E
Bezdan, *Serbia, Yug.* **52 E3** 45 50N 18 57 E
Bezhetsk, *Russia* **58 D9** 57 47N 36 39 E
Béziers, *France* **28 E7** 43 20N 3 12 E
Bezwada = Vijayawada, *India* **94 F5** 16 31N 80 39 E
Bhabua, *India* **93 G10** 25 3N 83 37 E
Bhadar →, *Gujarat, India* **92 H5** 22 17N 72 20 E
Bhadar →, *Gujarat, India* **92 J3** 21 27N 69 47 E
Bhadarwah, *India* **93 C6** 32 58N 75 46 E
Bhadgaon = Bhaktapur, *Nepal* **93 F11** 27 38N 85 24 E
Bhadohi, *India* **93 G10** 25 25N 82 34 E
Bhadra, *India* **92 E6** 29 8N 75 14 E
Bhadra →, *India* **95 H2** 14 0N 75 20 E
Bhadrachalam, *India* **94 F5** 17 40N 80 53 E
Bhadrakh, *India* **94 D8** 21 10N 86 30 E
Bhadran, *India* **92 H5** 22 19N 72 6 E
Bhadravati, *India* **95 H2** 13 49N 75 40 E
Bhag, *Pakistan* **92 E2** 29 2N 67 49 E
Bhagalpur, *India* **93 G12** 25 10N 87 0 E
Bhagirathi →, *Uttaranchal, India* **93 D8** 30 8N 78 35 E
Bhagirathi →, *W. Bengal, India* **93 H13** 23 25N 88 23 E
Bhainsa, *India* **94 E3** 19 10N 77 58 E
Bhairab →, *Bangla.* **90 D2** 22 51N 89 34 E
Bhairab Bazar, *Bangla.* **90 C3** 24 4N 90 58 E
Bhakkar, *Pakistan* **91 C3** 31 40N 71 5 E
Bhakra Dam, *India* **92 D7** 31 30N 76 45 E
Bhaktapur, *Nepal* **93 F11** 27 38N 85 24 E
Bhalki, *India* **94 E3** 18 2N 77 13 E
Bhamo, *Burma* **90 C6** 24 15N 97 15 E
Bhamragarh, *India* **94 E5** 19 30N 80 40 E
Bhandara, *India* **94 D4** 21 5N 79 42 E
Bhanpura, *India* **92 G6** 24 31N 75 44 E
Bhanrer Ra., *India* **93 H8** 23 40N 79 45 E
Bhaptiahi, *India* **93 F12** 26 19N 86 44 E
Bharat = India ■, *Asia* **89 C6** 20 0N 78 0 E
Bharatpur, *Chhattisgarh, India* **93 H9** 23 44N 81 46 E
Bharatpur, *Raj., India* **92 F7** 27 15N 77 30 E
Bharno, *India* **93 H11** 23 14N 84 53 E
Bharuch, *India* **94 D1** 21 47N 73 0 E
Bhatghar L., *India* **94 E1** 18 10N 73 48 E
Bhatiapara Ghat, *Bangla.* **90 D2** 23 13N 89 42 E
Bhatinda, *India* **92 D6** 30 15N 74 57 E
Bhatkal, *India* **95 H2** 13 58N 74 35 E
Bhatpara, *India* **93 H13** 22 50N 88 25 E
Bhattu, *India* **92 E6** 29 36N 75 19 E
Bhaun, *Pakistan* **92 C5** 32 55N 72 40 E
Bhaunagar = Bhavnagar, *India* **94 D1** 21 45N 72 10 E
Bhavani, *India* **95 J3** 11 27N 77 43 E
Bhavnagar, *India* **94 D1** 21 45N 72 10 E
Bhawanipatna, *India* **94 E5** 19 55N 80 10 E
Bhawari, *India* **92 G5** 25 42N 73 4 E
Bhayavadar, *India* **92 J4** 21 51N 70 15 E
Bhera, *Pakistan* **92 C5** 32 29N 72 57 E
Bhikangaon, *India* **92 J6** 21 52N 75 57 E
Bhilai, *India* **94 D5** 21 13N 81 26 E
Bhilsa = Vidisha, *India* **92 H7** 23 28N 77 53 E
Bhilwara, *India* **92 G6** 25 25N 74 38 E
Bhima →, *India* **94 F3** 16 25N 77 17 E
Bhimavaram, *India* **95 F5** 16 30N 81 30 E
Bhimbar, *Pakistan* **93 C6** 32 59N 74 3 E
Bhind, *India* **93 F8** 26 30N 78 46 E
Bhinga, *India* **93 F9** 27 43N 81 56 E
Bhinmal, *India* **92 G5** 25 0N 72 15 E
Bhiwandi, *India* **94 E1** 19 20N 73 0 E
Bhiwani, *India* **92 E7** 28 50N 76 9 E
Bhogava →, *India* **92 H5** 22 26N 72 20 E
Bhokardan, *India* **94 D2** 20 16N 75 46 E
Bhola, *Bangla.* **90 D3** 22 45N 90 35 E
Bholari, *Pakistan* **92 G3** 25 19N 68 13 E
Bhongir, *India* **94 F4** 17 30N 78 56 E
Bhopal, *India* **92 H7** 23 20N 77 30 E
Bhopalpatnam, *India* **94 E5** 18 52N 80 23 E
Bhor, *India* **94 E1** 18 12N 73 53 E
Bhubaneshwar, *India* **94 D7** 20 15N 85 50 E
Bhuj, *India* **92 H3** 23 15N 69 49 E
Bhusaval, *India* **94 D2** 21 3N 75 46 E
Bhutan ■, *Asia* **90 B3** 27 25N 90 30 E
Biá →, *Brazil* **168 D4** 3 28 S 67 23W
Biafra, B. of = Bonny, Bight of, *Africa* **113 E6** 3 30N 9 20 E
Biak, *Indonesia* **83 B5** 1 10 S 136 6 E
Biała, *Poland* **55 H4** 50 24N 17 40 E
Biała →, *Poland* **55 H7** 50 3N 20 55 E
Biała Piska, *Poland* **54 E9** 53 37N 22 5 E
Biała Podlaska, *Poland* **55 F10** 52 4N 23 6 E
Biała Rawska, *Poland* **55 G7** 51 48N 20 29 E
Białobrzegi, *Poland* **55 G7** 51 39N 20 57 E
Białogard, *Poland* **54 D2** 54 2N 15 58 E
Białowieski Park Narodowy △, *Poland* **55 F10** 52 43N 23 50 E
Białowieża, *Poland* **55 F10** 52 41N 23 49 E
Biały Bór, *Poland* **54 E3** 53 53N 16 51 E
Białystok, *Poland* **55 E10** 53 10N 23 10 E
Bian →, *Indonesia* **83 C5** 8 6 S 139 58 E
Biancavilla, *Italy* **47 E7** 37 38N 14 52 E
Bianco, *Italy* **47 D9** 38 5N 16 9 E
Biankouma, *Ivory C.* **112 D3** 7 50N 7 40W
Biaora, *India* **92 H7** 23 56N 76 56 E
Bīārjmand, *Iran* **97 B7** 36 6N 55 53 E
Biaro, *Indonesia* **82 A3** 2 5N 125 26 E
Biarritz, *France* **28 E2** 43 29N 1 33W
Bias, *Indonesia* **79 J18** 8 24 S 115 36 E
Biasca, *Switz.* **33 D7** 46 22N 8 58 E

Biavela, Angola ... 115 E3 14 43 S 19 47 E
Biba, Egypt ... 106 J7 28 55N 31 0 E
Bibai, Japan ... 70 C10 43 19N 141 52 E
Bibala, Angola ... 115 E2 14 44 S 13 24 E
Bibane, Bahiret el, Tunisia ... 108 B2 33 16N 11 13 E
Bibassé, Gabon ... 114 B2 1 27N 11 37 E
Bibbiena, Italy ... 45 E8 43 42N 11 49 E
Bibby I., Canada ... 143 A10 61 55N 93 0W
Bibel ➤, Spain ... 42 C3 42 24N 7 13W
Biberach, Germany ... 31 G5 48 5N 9 47 E
Biberist, Switz. ... 32 B5 47 11N 7 34 E
Bibi, Papua N. G. ... 132 C4 5 30 S 146 2 E
Bibiani, Ghana ... 112 D4 6 30N 2 8W
Bibile, Sri Lanka ... 95 L5 7 10N 81 25 E
Bibungwa, Dem. Rep. of the Congo ... 118 C2 2 40 S 28 15 E
Bic, Canada ... 141 C6 48 20N 68 41W
Bicaj, Albania ... 50 E4 41 58N 20 25 E
Bicaz, Romania ... 53 D11 46 53N 26 5 E
Bicazu Ardelean, Romania ... 53 D10 46 51N 25 56 E
Biccari, Italy ... 47 A8 41 23N 15 12 E
Bicester, U.K. ... 21 F6 51 54N 1 9W
Bichena, Ethiopia ... 107 E4 10 28N 38 10 E
Bicheno, Australia ... 127 D4 41 52 S 148 18 E
Bichia, India ... 93 H9 22 27N 80 42 E
Bichvinta, Georgia ... 61 J5 43 9N 40 21 E
Bickerton I., Australia ... 126 A2 13 45 S 136 10 E
Bicknell, U.S.A. ... 157 F9 38 47N 87 19W
Bicske, Hungary ... 52 C3 47 29N 18 38 E
Bicuar, Parque Nac. do △, Angola ... 115 F2 15 14 S 14 45 E
Bida, Dem. Rep. of the Congo ... 114 B3 4 55N 19 56 E
Bida, Nigeria ... 113 D6 9 3N 5 58 E
Bidar, India ... 94 F3 17 55N 77 35 E
Biddeford, U.S.A. ... 149 D10 43 30N 70 28W
Biddwara, Ethiopia ... 107 F4 5 11N 38 34 E
Bideford, U.K. ... 21 F3 51 1N 4 13W
Bideford Bay, U.K. ... 21 F3 51 5N 4 20W
Bidhuna, India ... 93 F8 26 49N 79 31 E
Bidon 5 = Poste Maurice Cortier, Algeria ... 111 D5 22 14N 1 2 E
Bidor, Malaysia ... 87 K3 4 6N 101 15 E
Bidzar, Cameroon ... 114 A2 9 54N 14 7 E
Bie, Sweden ... 16 E10 59 5N 16 12 E
Bié □, Angola ... 115 E3 12 30 S 17 0 E
Bié, Planalto de, Angola ... 115 E3 12 0 S 16 0 E
Bieber, U.S.A. ... 158 F3 41 7N 121 8W
Biebrza ➤, Poland ... 55 E9 53 13N 22 25 E
Biebrzański Park Narodowy △, Poland ... 54 E9 53 36N 22 45 E
Biecz, Poland ... 55 J8 49 44N 21 15 E
Biel, Switz. ... 32 B4 47 8N 7 14 E
Bielawa, Poland ... 55 H3 50 43N 16 37 E
Bielefeld, Germany ... 30 C4 52 1N 8 33 E
Bielersee, Switz. ... 32 B4 47 6N 7 5 E
Biella, Italy ... 44 C5 45 34N 8 3 E
Bielsk Podlaski, Poland ... 55 F10 52 47N 23 12 E
Bielsko-Biała, Poland ... 55 J6 49 50N 19 2 E
Bien Hoa, Vietnam ... 87 G6 10 57N 106 49 E
Bienne = Biel, Switz. ... 32 B4 47 8N 7 14 E
Bienno, Italy ... 33 E10 45 56N 10 18 E
Bienvenida, Spain ... 43 G4 38 18N 6 12W
Bienvenue, Fr. Guiana ... 169 C7 3 5N 52 30W
Bienville, L., Canada ... 140 A5 55 5N 72 40W
Bière, Switz. ... 32 C2 46 33N 6 20 E
Bierné, France ... 26 E6 47 48N 0 33W
Bierun, Poland ... 55 H6 50 6N 19 6 E
Bieruców, Poland ... 55 G4 51 7N 17 32 E
Biescas, Spain ... 40 C4 42 37N 0 20W
Biese ➤, Germany ... 30 C7 52 53N 11 46 E
Biescisfontein, S. Africa ... 116 E2 30 57 S 17 58 E
Bieszczadzki Park Narodowy △, Poland ... 55 J9 49 35 N 22 43 E
Bietigheim-Bissingen, Germany ... 31 G5 48 58N 9 8 E
Bieżuń, Poland ... 55 F6 52 58N 19 55 E
Biferno ➤, Italy ... 45 G12 41 59N 15 2 E
Bifoum, Gabon ... 114 C2 0 20 S 10 23 E
Big ➤, Canada ... 141 B8 54 50N 58 55W
Big ➤, U.S.A. ... 156 F6 38 28N 90 37W
Big B., Canada ... 143 A7 55 43N 60 35W
Big Bear City, U.S.A. ... 161 L10 34 16N 116 51W
Big Bear Lake, U.S.A. ... 161 L10 34 15N 116 56W
Big Belt Mts., U.S.A. ... 158 C8 46 30N 111 25W
Big Bend, Swaziland ... 117 D5 26 50 S 31 58 E
Big Bend Nat. Park △, U.S.A. ... 155 L3 29 20N 103 5W
Big Black ➤, U.S.A. ... 155 K9 32 3N 91 4W
Big Blue ➤, Ind., U.S.A. ... 157 E11 39 12N 85 56W
Big Blue ➤, Kans., U.S.A. ... 154 F6 39 35N 96 34W
Big Creek, U.S.A. ... 160 H7 37 11N 119 14W
Big Cypress Nat. Preserve △, U.S.A. ... 153 J8 26 0N 81 10W
Big Cypress Swamp, U.S.A. ... 153 J8 26 15N 81 30W
Big Delta, U.S.A. ... 144 D11 64 10N 145 51W
Big Falls, U.S.A. ... 154 A8 48 12N 93 48W
Big Fork ➤, U.S.A. ... 154 A8 48 31N 93 43W
Big Horn Mts. = Bighorn Mts., U.S.A. ... 158 D10 44 30N 107 30W
Big I., Canada ... 142 A5 51 7N 116 45W
Big Lake, Alaska, U.S.A. ... 144 F10 61 20N 150 20W
Big Lake, Tex., U.S.A. ... 155 K4 31 12N 101 28W
Big Moose, U.S.A. ... 151 C10 43 49N 74 58W
Big Muddy ➤, U.S.A. ... 156 G8 38 0N 89 0W
Big Muddy Cr. ➤, U.S.A. ... 154 A2 48 8N 104 36W
Big Pine, Calif., U.S.A. ... 160 H8 37 10N 118 17W
Big Pine, Fla., U.S.A. ... 153 L8 24 40N 81 21W
Big Piney, U.S.A. ... 158 E8 42 32N 110 7W
Big Rapids, U.S.A. ... 148 D3 43 42N 85 29W
Big Rideau L., Canada ... 151 B8 44 40N 76 15W
Big River, Canada ... 143 C7 53 50N 107 0W
Big Run, U.S.A. ... 150 F6 40 57N 78 55W
Big Sable Pt., U.S.A. ... 148 C2 44 3N 86 1W
Big Salmon ➤, Canada ... 142 A2 61 52N 134 55W
Big Sand L., Canada ... 143 B9 57 45N 99 45W
Big Sandy, U.S.A. ... 158 B8 48 11N 110 7W
Big Sandy ➤, U.S.A. ... 148 F4 38 25N 82 36W
Big Sandy Cr. ➤, U.S.A. ... 154 F3 38 7N 102 29W
Big Satilla ➤, U.S.A. ... 152 D7 31 27N 82 3W
Big Sioux ➤, U.S.A. ... 154 D6 42 29N 96 27W
Big South Fork Nat. River and Recr. Area △, U.S.A. ... 149 G3 36 27N 84 47W
Big Spring, U.S.A. ... 155 J4 32 15N 101 28W
Big Stone City, U.S.A. ... 154 C6 45 18N 96 28W
Big Stone Gap, U.S.A. ... 149 G4 36 52N 82 47W
Big Stone L., U.S.A. ... 154 C6 45 30N 96 35W
Big Sur, U.S.A. ... 160 J5 36 15N 121 48W
Big Timber, U.S.A. ... 158 D9 45 50N 109 57W
Big Trout L., Canada ... 140 B2 53 40N 90 0W
Big Trout Lake, Canada ... 140 B2 53 45N 90 0W
Biğa, Turkey ... 51 F11 40 13N 27 14 E
Biga ➤, Turkey ... 51 F11 40 20N 27 14 E
Bigadiç, Turkey ... 49 B10 39 22N 28 7 E
Biganos, France ... 28 D3 44 39N 0 59W
Biggar, Canada ... 143 C7 52 4N 108 0W
Biggar, U.K. ... 23 F5 55 38N 3 32W
Bigge I., Australia ... 124 B4 14 35 S 125 10 E
Biggenden, Australia ... 127 D5 25 31 S 152 4 E
Biggleswade, U.K. ... 21 E7 52 5N 0 14W
Biggs, U.S.A. ... 160 F5 39 25N 121 43W
Bighorn, U.S.A. ... 158 C10 46 10N 107 28W
Bighorn ➤, U.S.A. ... 158 C10 46 10N 107 28W
Bighorn Canyon Nat. Recr. Area △, U.S.A. ... 158 D9 45 10N 108 0W
Bighorn L., U.S.A. ... 158 D9 44 55N 108 15W
Bighorn Mts., U.S.A. ... 158 D10 44 30N 107 30W
Bigi, Dem. Rep. of the Congo ... 114 B4 3 2N 22 25 E
Bignasco, Switz. ... 33 D7 46 21N 8 37 E
Bignona, Senegal ... 112 C1 12 52N 16 14W

Bigorre, France ... 28 E4 43 10N 0 5 E
Bigstone L., Canada ... 143 C9 53 42N 95 44W
Biguglia, Étang de, France ... 29 F13 42 36N 9 29 E
Bigwa, Tanzania ... 118 D4 7 10 S 39 10 E
Bihać, Bos.-H. ... 45 D12 44 49N 15 57 E
Bihar, India ... 93 G11 25 5N 85 40 E
Bihar □, India ... 93 G12 25 0N 86 0 E
Biharamulo, Tanzania ... 118 C3 2 25 S 31 25 E
Biharamulo Game Reserve △, Tanzania ... 118 C3 2 24 S 31 26 E
Bihariganj, India ... 93 G12 25 44N 86 59 E
Biharkeresztes, Hungary ... 52 C6 47 8N 21 44 E
Bihor □, Romania ... 52 D7 47 0N 22 10 E
Bihor, Munții, Romania ... 52 D7 46 29N 22 47 E
Bijagós, Arquipélago dos, Guinea-Biss. ... 112 C1 11 15N 16 10W
Bijaipur, India ... 92 F7 26 2N 77 20 E
Bijapur, Chhattisgarh, India ... 94 E5 18 50N 80 50 E
Bijapur, Karnataka, India ... 94 F2 16 50N 75 55 E
Bijār, Iran ... 101 E12 35 52N 47 35 E
Bijawar, India ... 93 G8 24 38N 79 30 E
Bijeljina, Bos.-H. ... 52 F4 44 46N 19 14 E
Bijelo Polje, Montenegro, Yug. ... 50 C3 43 1N 19 45 E
Bijie, China ... 76 D5 27 20N 105 16 E
Bijnor, India ... 92 E8 29 27N 78 11 E
Bikaner, India ... 92 E5 28 2N 73 18 E
Bikapur, India ... 93 F10 26 30N 82 7 E
Bikeqi, China ... 74 D6 40 43N 111 20 E
Bikfayyā, Lebanon ... 103 B4 33 55N 35 41 E
Bikié, Congo ... 114 C2 3 7 S 13 52 E
Bikin, Russia ... 67 E14 46 50N 134 20 E
Bikin ➤, Russia ... 70 A7 46 51N 134 2 E
Bikini Atoll, Marshall Is. ... 134 F8 12 0N 167 30 E
Bikita, Zimbabwe ... 117 C5 20 6 S 31 41 E
Bikkū Bīttī, Libya ... 109 D3 22 0N 19 12 E
Bikoro, Dem. Rep. of the Congo ... 114 C3 0 48 S 18 15 E
Bikoué, Cameroon ... 113 E7 3 55N 11 50 E
Bíla Tserkva, Ukraine ... 59 H6 49 45N 30 10 E
Bilanga, Burkina Faso ... 113 C4 12 40N 0 1W
Bilara, India ... 92 F5 26 14N 73 53 E
Bilasipara, India ... 90 B3 26 13N 90 14 E
Bilaspur, Chhattisgarh, India ... 93 H10 22 2N 82 15 E
Bilaspur, Punjab, India ... 92 D7 31 19N 76 50 E
Biläsuvar, Azerbaijan ... 101 C13 39 27N 48 32 E
Bilauk Taungdan, Thailand ... 86 F2 13 0N 99 0 E
Bilbao, Spain ... 40 B2 43 16N 2 56W
Bilbeis, Egypt ... 106 H7 30 25N 31 34 E
Bilbo = Bilbao, Spain ... 40 B2 43 16N 2 56W
Bilbor, Romania ... 53 C10 47 6N 25 30 E
Bilçireşti, Romania ... 53 F10 44 44N 25 48 E
Bildudalur, Iceland ... 11 B3 65 41N 23 36W
Bílé Karpaty, Europe ... 55 B11 49 5N 18 0 E
Bileća, Bos.-H. ... 50 D2 42 53N 18 27 E
Bilecik, Turkey ... 100 B4 40 5N 30 5 E
Bilgoraj, Poland ... 55 H9 50 33N 22 42 E
Bilgram, India ... 93 F9 27 11N 80 2 E
Bilhaur, India ... 93 F9 26 13N 80 5 E
Bilhorod-Dnistrovskyy, Ukraine ... 59 J6 46 11N 30 23 E
Bili ➤, Dem. Rep. of the Congo ... 114 B4 4 9N 22 29 E
Bilibino, Russia ... 67 C17 68 3N 166 20 E
Bilibiza, Mozam. ... 119 E5 12 30 S 40 20 E
Bilíköl, Kazakhstan ... 65 B5 43 5N 70 45 E
Bilimora, India ... 94 D1 20 45N 72 57 E
Bilin, Burma ... 90 G6 17 14N 97 15 E
Biliran □, Phil. ... 81 F5 11 35N 124 28 E
Bilisht, Albania ... 50 F5 40 37N 21 2 E
Bilibalong Roadhouse, Australia ... 125 E2 27 25 S 115 49 E
Billabong Cr. ➤, Australia ... 128 C6 35 5 S 144 2 E
Billdal, Sweden ... 17 G5 57 35N 11 57 E
Billiluna, Australia ... 124 C4 19 37 S 127 41 E
Billings, U.S.A. ... 158 D9 45 47N 108 30W
Billiton Is. = Belitung, Indonesia ... 85 C3 3 10 S 107 50 E
Billsta, Sweden ... 16 A12 63 20N 18 28 E
Billund, Denmark ... 17 J3 55 44N 9 6 E
Bilma, Niger ... 109 E2 18 50N 13 30 E
Bilo Gora, Croatia ... 52 E2 45 53N 17 15 E
Biloela, Australia ... 126 C5 24 24 S 150 31 E
Bilohirsk, Ukraine ... 59 K8 45 1N 34 35 E
Biloku, Guyana ... 169 C6 1 50N 58 25W
Bíloli, India ... 94 E3 18 46N 77 44 E
Bilopillya, Ukraine ... 59 G8 51 11N 34 20 E
Biloxi, U.S.A. ... 155 K10 30 24N 88 53W
Bilpa Morea Claypan, Australia ... 126 D3 25 0 S 140 0 E
Biltine, Chad ... 109 F4 14 40N 20 50 E
Bilugyun, Burma ... 90 G6 16 24N 97 32 E
Bilyarsk, Russia ... 60 C10 54 58N 50 22 E
Bima, Indonesia ... 85 D5 8 25 S 118 49 E
Bimban, Egypt ... 106 C3 24 24N 32 54 E
Bimbe, Angola ... 115 E3 11 50 S 15 50 E
Bimberi Pk., Australia ... 129 C8 35 44 S 148 51 E
Bimbila, Ghana ... 113 D5 8 54N 0 5 E
Bimbo, C.A.R. ... 114 B3 4 15N 18 33 E
Bimini Is., Bahamas ... 164 A4 25 42N 79 25W
Bin Xian, Heilongjiang, China ... 75 B14 45 42N 127 32 E
Bin Xian, Shaanxi, China ... 74 G5 35 2N 108 4 E
Bin Yauri, Nigeria ... 113 C5 10 46N 4 45 E
Bina-Etawah, India ... 92 G8 24 13N 78 14 E
Bināb, Iran ... 97 B6 36 35N 48 41 E
Binaiya, Indonesia ... 83 B3 3 11 S 129 26 E
Binalbagan, Phil. ... 81 F4 10 12N 122 50 E
Binalong, Australia ... 129 C8 34 40 S 148 39 E
Binālūd, Kūh-e, Iran ... 97 B8 36 30N 58 30 E
Binatang = Bintangor, Malaysia ... 85 B4 2 10N 111 40 E
Binche, Belgium ... 24 D4 50 26N 4 10 E
Binchuan, China ... 76 E3 25 42N 100 38 E
Binda, Dem. Rep. of the Congo ... 115 D2 5 52 S 13 14 E
Binder, Chad ... 113 D7 9 56N 14 27 E
Bindki, India ... 93 F9 26 2N 80 36 E
Bindloe, I. = Marchena, I., Ecuador ... 172 a 0 19N 90 29W
Bindoy, Phil. ... 81 G4 9 48N 123 5 E
Bindslev, Denmark ... 17 G4 57 33N 10 11 E
Bindura, Zimbabwe ... 119 F3 17 18 S 31 18 E
Binefar, Spain ... 40 D5 41 51N 0 18 E
Bingara, Australia ... 127 D5 29 52 S 150 36 E
Bingaram I., India ... 95 J11 10 56N 72 17 E
Bingen, Germany ... 31 F3 49 57N 7 53 E
Bingerville, Ivory C. ... 112 D4 5 18N 3 49W
Bingham, U.S.A. ... 149 C11 45 3N 69 53W
Binghamton, U.S.A. ... 151 D9 42 6N 75 55W
Bingo-Ochiai, Japan ... 72 C4 34 59N 133 8 E
Bingöl, Turkey ... 101 C9 38 53N 40 29 E
Bingöl Dağları, Turkey ... 101 C9 39 16N 41 9 E
Bingsjö, Sweden ... 16 C9 61 1N 15 39 E
Binh Dinh = An Nhon, Vietnam ... 86 F7 13 55N 109 7 E
Binh Khe, Vietnam ... 86 F7 13 57N 108 51 E
Binh Son, Vietnam ... 86 E7 15 20N 108 40 E
Binhai, China ... 75 G10 34 2N 119 49 E
Bini Erde, Chad ... 109 D3 16 7N 23 8 E
Binissalem, Spain ... 48 B9 39 41 N 2 50 E
Binic, France ... 26 D4 48 36N 2 49W
Binisatua, Spain ... 38 B5 39 50N 4 11 E
Binjai, Indonesia ... 84 B1 3 20N 98 30 E
Binji, Nigeria ... 113 C5 13 0N 4 55 E
Binka, India ... 94 D6 21 2N 83 48 E
Binnaway, Australia ... 129 A8 31 28 S 149 24 E
Binningen, Switz. ... 32 A5 47 32N 7 34 E
Binongko, Indonesia ... 82 C2 5 57 S 124 2 E
Binscarth, Canada ... 143 C8 50 37N 101 17W
Bint Goda, Sudan ... 107 E3 13 0N 31 33 E
Bintan, Indonesia ... 84 B2 1 0N 104 0 E
Bintangor, Malaysia ... 85 B4 2 10N 111 40 E
Bintuni, Indonesia ... 83 B4 7 S 133 32 E
Bintuni, Teluk, Indonesia ... 83 B4 2 0 S 133 32 E

Binyang, China ... 76 F7 23 12N 108 47 E
Binz, Germany ... 30 A9 54 24N 13 35 E
Binza, Dem. Rep. of the Congo ... 115 C3 4 21 S 15 14 E
Binzert = Bizerte, Tunisia ... 108 A1 37 15N 9 50 E
Binzhou, China ... 75 F10 37 20N 118 2 E
Bío Bío □, Chile ... 174 D1 37 35 S 72 0W
Biograd na Moru, Croatia ... 45 E12 43 56N 15 29 E
Biogradska Gora Nac. Park △, Yugoslavia ... 50 D3 42 55N 19 40 E
Bioko, Eq. Guin. ... 113 E6 3 30N 8 40 E
Biokovo, Croatia ... 45 E14 43 23N 17 0 E
Biougra, Morocco ... 110 B3 30 15N 9 14W
Bipindi, Cameroon ... 113 E7 3 6N 10 30 E
Bir, India ... 94 E2 19 4N 75 46 E
Bir, Ras, Djibouti ... 107 E5 12 0N 43 20 E
Bîr Abu Hashim, Egypt ... 106 C3 23 42N 34 6 E
Bîr Abu Minqar, Egypt ... 106 B2 26 33N 27 33 E
Bîr Abu Muḩammad, Egypt ... 103 F3 29 44N 34 14 E
Bi'r ad Dabbāghāt, Jordan ... 103 E4 30 26N 35 32 E
Bîr Adal Deib, Sudan ... 106 C4 22 35N 36 10 E
Bi'r al Butayyihāt, Jordan ... 103 F4 29 47N 35 20 E
Bi'r al Mārī, Jordan ... 103 E4 30 4N 35 33 E
Bi'r al Qaṭṭār, Jordan ... 103 F4 29 47N 35 32 E
Bir 'Ali, Yemen ... 99 D5 14 1N 48 20 E
Bîr Aouine, Tunisia ... 108 B1 32 25N 9 18 E
Bîr 'Asal, Egypt ... 106 B3 25 55N 34 20 E
Bîr Atrun, Sudan ... 106 D2 18 15N 26 40 E
Bir Beïda, Egypt ... 103 E3 30 25N 34 29 E
Bîr Bel Guerdâne, Mauritania ... 110 C2 25 24N 10 31W
Bîr Beiḩa, Egypt ... 103 E3 30 20N 33 43 E
Bîr Dhu'fân, Libya ... 108 B2 31 59N 14 32 E
Bîr Diqnash, Egypt ... 106 A2 31 3N 25 23 E
Bir el 'Abd, Egypt ... 103 D2 31 2N 33 0 E
Bir el Ater, Algeria ... 111 B6 34 46N 8 3 E
Bîr el Basur, Egypt ... 106 B2 29 51N 26 43 E
Bîr el Biarât, Egypt ... 103 F3 29 30N 34 43 E
Bîr el Duweidar, Egypt ... 103 E1 30 56N 32 32 E
Bîr el Garârât, Egypt ... 103 D2 31 3N 33 34 E
Bîr el Gâreb, Mauritania ... 110 D1 20 33N 16 12W
Bîr el Gellaz, Egypt ... 106 A2 30 50N 26 40 E
Bîr el Heisi, Egypt ... 103 F3 29 22N 34 36 E
Bîr el Jafir, Egypt ... 103 E1 30 50N 32 41 E
Bîr el Mâlḩi, Egypt ... 103 E2 30 38N 33 19 E
Bîr el Shaqqa, Egypt ... 106 A2 30 54N 25 1 E
Bîr el Thamâda, Egypt ... 103 E2 30 12N 33 27 E
Bîr Enzarân, W. Sahara ... 110 D2 23 53N 14 32W
Bîr Fuad, Egypt ... 106 A2 30 35N 26 28 E
Bîr Gandûs, W. Sahara ... 110 D1 21 36N 16 30W
Bîr Gara, Chad ... 109 F3 13 11N 15 58 E
Bîr Gebeil Ḩisn, Egypt ... 103 E2 30 2N 33 18 E
Bîr Haimur, Egypt ... 106 C3 22 45N 33 40 E
Bîr Ḩasana, Egypt ... 103 E2 30 29N 33 46 E
Bîr Hōōker, Egypt ... 106 H7 30 22N 30 21 E
Bi'r Idimah, Si. Arabia ... 98 C4 18 31N 44 12 E
Bîr Jdid, Morocco ... 110 B3 33 26N 8 0W
Bîr Kanayis, Egypt ... 106 C3 24 59N 33 15 E
Bîr Kaseiba, Egypt ... 103 E2 31 0N 33 17 E
Bîr Kerawein, Egypt ... 106 B2 27 10N 28 25 E
Bîr Lahfân, Egypt ... 103 E2 31 0N 33 51 E
Bir Lahrache, Algeria ... 111 B6 32 1N 8 12 E
Bîr Madkûr, Egypt ... 103 E1 30 44N 32 33 E
Bîr Maql, Egypt ... 106 C3 23 7N 33 40 E
Bîr Mîneiga, Sudan ... 106 C4 22 47N 35 12 E
Bîr Misaha, Egypt ... 106 C2 22 12N 27 59 E
Bîr Mogrein, Mauritania ... 110 C2 25 10N 11 25W
Bîr Murr, Egypt ... 106 C3 23 28N 30 10 E
Bi'r Muṭribah, Kuwait ... 96 D5 29 54N 47 17 E
Bîr Nakheila, Egypt ... 106 C3 24 1N 30 50 E
Bîr Qaṭia, Egypt ... 103 E1 30 58N 32 45 E
Bîr Qatrani, Egypt ... 106 A2 30 55N 26 10 E
Bîr Ranga, Egypt ... 106 C4 24 25N 35 15 E
Bîr Sahara, Egypt ... 106 C2 22 54N 28 40 E
Bîr Seiyâla, Egypt ... 106 B3 26 10N 33 50 E
Bîr Semguine, Morocco ... 110 B3 30 1N 5 39W
Bîr Shalatein, Egypt ... 106 C4 23 5N 35 25 E
Bîr Shebb, Egypt ... 106 C2 22 25N 29 40 E
Bîr Shût, Egypt ... 106 C4 23 50N 35 15 E
Bîr Terfawi, Egypt ... 106 C2 22 57N 28 55 E
Bi'r Tin Abunda, Libya ... 111 C7 26 28N 12 27 E
Bîr Umm Qubûr, Egypt ... 106 C3 24 35N 34 2 E
Bîr Za'farâna, Egypt ... 106 B3 29 10N 32 40 E
Bîr Zâmûs, Libya ... 108 D3 24 16N 15 6 E
Bîr Zeidûn, Egypt ... 106 B3 25 45N 33 40 E
Bira, Indonesia ... 83 B4 2 3 S 132 2 E
Biramféro, Guinea ... 112 C3 11 40N 9 10W
Birao, C.A.R. ... 114 A4 10 20N 22 47 E
Biratnagar, Nepal ... 93 F12 26 27N 87 17 E
Birawa, Dem. Rep. of the Congo ... 118 C2 2 20 S 28 48 E
Birch ➤, Canada ... 142 B6 58 28N 112 17W
Birch Hills, Canada ... 143 C7 52 59N 105 25W
Birch I., Canada ... 143 C9 52 26N 99 54W
Birch L., N.W.T., Canada ... 142 A5 62 4N 116 33W
Birch L., Ont., Canada ... 140 B1 51 23N 92 18W
Birch Mts., Canada ... 142 B6 57 30N 113 10W
Birch River, Canada ... 143 C8 52 24N 101 6W
Birchip, Australia ... 128 C5 35 56 S 142 55 E
Birchis, Romania ... 52 E7 45 58N 22 9 E
Birchwood, N.Z. ... 131 F2 45 57 S 167 53 E
Bird, Canada ... 143 B10 56 30N 94 13W
Bird I. = Las Aves, Is., W. Indies ... 165 C7 15 45N 63 55W
Birdseye, U.S.A. ... 157 F10 38 19N 86 42W
Birdsville, Australia ... 126 D2 25 51 S 139 20 E
Birdum Cr. ➤, Australia ... 124 C5 15 14 S 133 0 E
Birdwood, Australia ... 128 C3 34 51 S 138 58 E
Birecik, Turkey ... 101 D8 37 2N 38 0 E
Birein, Israel ... 103 E3 30 50N 34 28 E
Bireuen, Indonesia ... 84 A1 5 14N 96 39 E
Birgu = Vittoriosa, Malta ... 38 F8 35 54N 14 31 E
Biri ➤, Sudan ... 107 F3 6 N 28 51 E
Birifo, Gambia ... 112 C2 13 30N 14 0W
Birigui, Brazil ... 175 A5 21 18 S 50 16W
Birini, C.A.R. ... 114 A4 7 51N 22 24 E
Birjand, Iran ... 97 C8 32 53N 59 13 E
Birkeland, Norway ... 12 E4 58 20N 7 12 E
Birkenfeld, Germany ... 31 F3 49 38N 7 9 E
Birkenhead, N.Z. ... 130 C3 36 49 S 174 46 E
Birkenhead, U.K. ... 20 D4 53 23N 3 2W
Birkerød, Denmark ... 17 J6 55 50N 12 25 E
Birket Fatmé, Chad ... 109 F3 11 N 7 E
Birket Qârûn, Egypt ... 106 J7 29 30N 30 40 E
Birkfeld, Austria ... 34 D8 47 21N 15 45 E
Birkhadem, Algeria ... 111 A5 36 43N 3 3 E
Birkirkara, Malta ... 38 F7 35 54N 14 28 E
Bîrlad = Bârlad, Romania ... 53 D12 46 15N 27 38 E
Birlik, Kazakhstan ... 65 B6 43 40N 73 49 E
Birlik, Kazakhstan ... 66 E8 44 5N 74 31 E
Birmingham, U.K. ... 21 E6 52 29N 1 52W
Birmingham, Ala., U.S.A. ... 149 J2 33 31N 86 48W
Birmingham, Iowa, U.S.A. ... 156 D5 40 53N 91 57W
Birmingham International ✈ (BHX), U.K. ... 21 E6 52 26N 1 48W
Birmitrapur, India ... 94 C7 22 24N 84 46 E
Birni Ngaouré, Niger ... 113 C5 13 5N 2 52 E
Birni Nkonni, Niger ... 113 C6 13 55N 5 15 E
Birnin Gwari, Nigeria ... 113 C6 11 0N 6 45 E
Birnin Kebbi, Nigeria ... 113 C5 12 32N 4 12 E
Birnin Kudu, Nigeria ... 113 C6 11 30N 9 29 E
Birobidzhan, Russia ... 67 E14 48 50N 132 50 E
Birougou, Mts., Gabon ... 114 C2 1 5 S 12 13 E
Birr, Ireland ... 23 C4 53 6N 7 54W
Birrie ➤, Australia ... 127 D4 29 43 S 146 37 E

Birs ➤, Switz. ... 32 B5 47 24N 7 32 E
Birsilpur, India ... 92 E5 28 11N 72 15 E
Birsk, Russia ... 64 D5 55 25N 55 30 E
Biřštonas, Lithuania ... 54 D11 54 37N 24 2 E
Birtle, Canada ... 143 C8 50 30N 101 5W
Biryuchiy, Ukraine ... 59 J8 46 10N 35 0 E
Biržai, Lithuania ... 15 H21 56 11N 24 45 E
Birzebbuga, Malta ... 38 F8 35 50N 14 32 E
Bisa, Indonesia ... 82 B3 1 15 S 127 28 E
Bisáccia, Italy ... 47 A8 41 1N 15 22 E
Bisacquino, Italy ... 46 E6 37 42N 13 15 E
Bisai, Japan ... 73 B8 35 16N 136 44 E
Bisalpur, India ... 93 E8 28 14N 79 48 E
Bisbee, U.S.A. ... 159 L9 31 27N 109 55W
Biscarrosse, France ... 28 D2 44 22N 1 20W
Biscarrosse et de Parentis, Étang de, France ... 28 D2 44 21N 1 10W
Biscay, B. of, Atl. Oc. ... 8 B11 45 0N 2 0W
Biscayne B., U.S.A. ... 153 K9 25 40N 80 12W
Biscayne Nat. Park △, U.S.A. ... 153 K9 25 25N 80 12W
Biscéglie, Italy ... 47 A9 41 14N 16 31 E
Bischheim, France ... 27 D14 48 37N 7 46 E
Bischofshofen, Austria ... 34 D6 47 26N 13 14 E
Bischofswerda, Germany ... 30 D10 51 7N 14 10 E
Bischofszell, Switz. ... 33 B8 47 29N 9 15 E
Bischwiller, France ... 27 D14 48 46N 7 50 E
Biscoe Is., Antarctica ... 7 C17 66 0 S 67 0W
Biscoitos, Azores ... 9 d1 38 47N 27 15W
Biscotasing, Canada ... 140 C3 47 18N 82 9W
Biševo, Croatia ... 45 F13 42 57N 16 3 E
Bisha, Eritrea ... 107 D4 15 30N 37 31 E
Bishah, W. ➤, Si. Arabia ... 98 B3 21 24N 43 26 E
Bishan, China ... 76 C6 29 33N 106 12 E
Bishanga, Dem. Rep. of the Congo ... 115 C4 4 31 S 21 2 E
Bishkek, Kyrgyzstan ... 65 B7 42 54N 74 46 E
Bishnath, India ... 90 B4 26 40N 93 10 E
Bishnupur, India ... 93 H12 23 8N 87 20 E
Bisho, S. Africa ... 117 E4 32 50 S 27 23 E
Bishop, Calif., U.S.A. ... 160 H8 37 22N 118 24W
Bishop, Ga., U.S.A. ... 152 B6 33 49N 83 6W
Bishop, Tex., U.S.A. ... 155 M6 27 35N 97 48W
Bishop Auckland, U.K. ... 20 C6 54 39N 1 40W
Bishop's Falls, Canada ... 141 C8 49 2N 55 30W
Bishop's Stortford, U.K. ... 21 F8 51 52N 0 10 E
Bisignano, Italy ... 47 C9 39 31N 16 17 E
Bisina, L., Uganda ... 118 B3 1 38N 33 56 E
Biskra, Algeria ... 111 B6 34 50N 5 44 E
Biskra, Malta ... 38 F7 35 58N 14 21 E
Biskupiec, Poland ... 54 E7 53 53N 20 58 E
Bismarck, Mo., U.S.A. ... 156 G6 37 46N 90 38W
Bismarck, N. Dak., U.S.A. ... 154 B4 46 48N 100 47W
Bismarck Arch., Papua N. G. ... 132 B5 2 30 S 150 0 E
Bismarck Ra., Papua N. G. ... 132 C3 5 35 S 145 0 E
Bismarck Sea, Papua N. G. ... 132 C4 4 10 S 146 50 E
Bismark, Germany ... 30 C7 52 40N 11 33 E
Bismil, Turkey ... 101 D9 37 51N 40 40 E
Bismo, Norway ... 18 C5 61 54N 8 15 E
Bison, U.S.A. ... 154 C3 45 31N 102 28W
Bisotūn, Iran ... 101 E12 34 23N 47 26 E
Bispgården, Sweden ... 16 A10 63 2N 16 40 E
Bissagos = Bijagós, Arquipélago dos, Guinea-Biss. ... 112 C1 11 15N 16 10W
Bissam Cuttack, India ... 94 E6 19 31N 83 31 E
Bissau, Guinea-Biss. ... 112 C1 11 45N 15 45W
Bissaula, Nigeria ... 113 D7 7 0N 10 2 E
Bissikrima, Guinea ... 112 C2 10 50N 10 58 E
Bissorã, Guinea-Biss. ... 112 C1 12 5N 15 35W
Bistcho L., Canada ... 142 B5 59 45N 118 50W
Bistreţ, Romania ... 53 G8 43 54N 23 23 E
Bistrica = Ilirska-Bistrica, Slovenia ... 45 C11 45 34N 14 14 E
Bistrita, Romania ... 53 C9 47 9N 24 35 E
Bistrița ➤, Romania ... 53 D11 46 30N 26 57 E
Bistrița Năsăud □, Romania ... 53 C9 47 15N 24 30 E
Bistriței, Munții, Romania ... 53 C10 47 15N 25 40 E
Biswan, India ... 93 F9 27 29N 81 2 E
Bisztynek, Poland ... 54 D7 54 8N 20 53 E
Bita ➤, C.A.R. ... 114 A4 6 26N 24 43 E
Bitam, Gabon ... 114 B2 2 5N 11 25 E
Bitburg, Germany ... 31 F2 49 58N 6 31 E
Bitche, France ... 27 C14 49 2N 7 25 E
Bithynia, Turkey ... 153 G8 33 6N 82 18 E
Bitkine, Chad ... 109 F3 11 59N 18 13 E
Bitlis, Turkey ... 101 C10 38 20N 42 3 E
Bitola, Macedonia ... 50 E5 41 1N 21 20 E
Bitolj = Bitola, Macedonia ... 50 E5 41 1N 21 20 E
Bitonto, Italy ... 47 A9 41 6N 16 41 E
Bitra I., India ... 95 J1 11 33N 72 17 E
Bitter Creek, U.S.A. ... 158 F9 41 33N 108 33W
Bitter L. = Buheirat-Murrat-el-Kubra, Egypt ... 106 H8 30 18N 32 26 E
Bitterfeld, Germany ... 30 D8 51 37N 12 20 E
Bitterfontein, S. Africa ... 116 E2 31 1 S 18 32 E
Bitterroot ➤, U.S.A. ... 158 C6 46 52N 114 7W
Bitterroot Range, U.S.A. ... 158 D6 46 0N 114 20W
Bitterwater, U.S.A. ... 160 J6 36 23N 121 0W
Bitti, Italy ... 46 B2 40 29N 9 23 E
Bittou, Burkina Faso ... 113 C4 11 17N 0 18W
Bitung, Indonesia ... 83 A3 1 27N 125 11 E
Biu, Nigeria ... 113 C7 10 40N 12 3 E
Bivolari, Romania ... 53 C12 47 31N 27 27 E
Bivolu, Vf., Romania ... 53 C10 47 16N 25 58 E
Biwa-Ko, Japan ... 73 B8 35 15N 136 10 E
Biwabik, U.S.A. ... 154 B8 47 32N 92 21W
Bixad, Romania ... 53 C8 47 56N 23 28 E
Bixby, U.S.A. ... 155 H7 35 57N 95 53W
Biyang, China ... 74 H7 32 38N 113 21 E
Biysk, Russia ... 66 D9 52 40N 85 0 E
Bizana, S. Africa ... 117 E4 30 50 S 29 52 E
Bizen, Japan ... 72 C6 34 43N 134 8 E
Bjargtangar, Iceland ... 11 B2 65 30N 24 30W
Bjärnum, Sweden ... 17 H7 56 17N 13 43 E
Bjåen, Norway ... 12 E4 59 37N 7 26 E
Bjargtangar, Iceland ... 11 B2 65 30N 24 30W
Bjärka-Säby, Sweden ... 16 A12 63 12N 18 29 E
Bjärnum, Sweden ... 17 H7 56 17N 13 43 E
Bjästa, Sweden ... 16 A12 63 12N 18 29 E
Bjelasica, Montenegro, Yug. ... 50 C3 42 50N 19 40 E
Bjelašnica, Bos.-H. ... 52 G3 43 43N 18 13 E
Bjelland, Norway ... 18 F4 58 23N 7 32 E
Bjelovar, Croatia ... 45 C13 45 56N 16 49 E
Bjerringbro, Denmark ... 17 H3 56 23N 9 39 E
Bjervamoen, Norway ... 18 D5 59 53N 9 38 E
Bjøberg, Norway ... 18 D5 60 56N 8 13 E
Bjørbo, Sweden ... 18 D6 60 27N 14 44 E
Bjørkelangen, Norway ... 18 E8 59 53N 11 34 E
Bjørklinge, Sweden ... 18 D11 60 2N 17 43 E
Bjørklinge, Sweden ... 18 D11 60 2N 17 43 E
Bjørna, Norway ... 18 D2 60 7N 5 8 E
Bjørneborg = Pori, Finland ... 15 F19 61 29N 21 48 E
Bjørneborg, Sweden ... 18 E6 59 14N 14 16 E
Bjørnerøya, Arctic ... 4 B8 74 30N 19 0 E
Bjørnøya, Arctic ... 4 B8 74 30N 19 0 E
Bjursås, Sweden ... 16 D9 60 44N 15 23 E
Bjuv, Sweden ... 17 H6 56 5N 12 55 E
Bla, Mali ... 112 C3 12 56N 5 47W
Blace, Serbia, Yug. ... 50 C6 43 18N 21 17 E
Blachownia, Poland ... 55 H5 50 49N 18 56 E
Black = Da ➤, Vietnam ... 76 G5 21 15N 105 20 E
Black ➤, Canada ... 150 B5 44 42N 79 19W
Black ➤, Alaska, U.S.A. ... 144 C11 66 44N 142 44W
Black ➤, Ariz., U.S.A. ... 159 K8 33 44N 110 13W
Black ➤, Ark., U.S.A. ... 155 H9 35 38N 91 20W
Black ➤, Mich., U.S.A. ... 150 D2 42 59N 82 27W
Black ➤, N.Y., U.S.A. ... 151 C8 43 59N 76 4W

Black ➤, *Wis., U.S.A.* **154 D9** 43 57N 91 22W
Black Bay Pen., *Canada* **140 C2** 48 38N 88 21W
Black Birch L., *Canada* **143 B7** 56 53N 107 45W
Black Canyon of the Gunnison Nat.
  Monument △, *U.S.A.* **159 G10** 38 40N 107 35W
Black Diamond, *Canada* **142 C6** 50 45N 114 14W
Black Duck ➤, *Canada* **140 A2** 56 51N 89 2W
Black Forest = Schwarzwald,
  Germany .... **31 G4** 48 30N 8 20 E
Black Forest, *U.S.A.* **154 F2** 39 0N 104 43W
Black Hd., *Ireland* **23 C2** 53 9N 9 16W
Black Hills, *U.S.A.* **154 D3** 44 0N 103 45W
Black I., *Canada* **143 C9** 51 12N 96 30W
Black L., *Canada* **143 B7** 59 12N 105 15W
Black L., *Mich., U.S.A.* **148 C3** 45 28N 84 16W
Black L., *N.Y., U.S.A.* **151 B9** 44 31N 75 36W
Black Lake, *Canada* **143 B7** 59 11N 105 20W
Black Mesa, *U.S.A.* **155 G3** 36 58N 102 58W
Black Mountain, *Australia* .... **129 A9** 30 18 S 151 39 E
Black Mt. = Mynydd Du, *U.K.* **21 F4** 51 52N 3 50W
Black Mts., *U.K.* **21 F4** 51 55N 3 7W
Black Range, *U.S.A.* **159 K10** 33 15N 107 50W
Black River, *Jamaica* .... **164 a** 18 0N 77 50W
Black River Falls, *U.S.A.* **154 C9** 44 18N 90 51W
Black Rock, *Australia* .... **128 B3** 32 50 S 138 44 E
Black Rock, *Barbados* .... **165 g** 13 7N 59 37W
Black Sea, *Eurasia* .... **57 F6** 43 30N 35 0 E
Black Tickle, *Canada* **141 B8** 53 28N 55 45W
Black Volta ➤, *Africa* **112 D4** 8 41N 1 33W
Black Warrior ➤, *U.S.A.* **149 J2** 32 32N 87 51W
Blackall, *Australia* .... **126 C4** 24 25 S 145 45 E
Blackball, *N.Z.* .... **131 C6** 42 22 S 171 26 E
Blackbull, *Australia* .... **126 B3** 17 55 S 141 45 E
Blackburn, *U.K.* **20 D5** 53 45N 2 29W
Blackburn, Mt., *U.S.A.* **144 F12** 61 44N 143 26W
Blackburn with Darwen □, *U.K.* **20 D5** 53 45N 2 29W
Blackdown Tableland Nat. Park △,
  Australia .... **126 C4** 23 52 S 149 8 E
Blackfoot, *U.S.A.* **158 E7** 43 11N 112 21W
Blackfoot ➤, *U.S.A.* **158 C7** 46 52N 113 53W
Blackfoot River Reservoir, *U.S.A.* **158 E8** 43 0N 111 43W
Blackman, *U.S.A.* **153 E3** 30 56N 86 38W
Blackpool, *U.K.* **20 D4** 53 49N 3 3W
Blackpool □, *U.K.* **20 D4** 53 49N 3 3W
Blackriver, *U.S.A.* **150 B1** 44 46N 83 17W
Blacks Harbour, *Canada* **141 C6** 45 3N 66 49W
Blacksburg, *U.S.A.* **148 G5** 37 14N 80 25W
Blackshear, *U.S.A.* **152 D7** 31 18N 82 14W
Blackshear, L., *U.S.A.* **152 D6** 31 51N 83 56W
Blacksod B., *Ireland* **23 B1** 54 6N 10 0W
Blackstone, *U.S.A.* **148 G7** 37 4N 78 0W
Blackstone Ra., *Australia* .... **125 E4** 26 0 S 128 30 E
Blackville, *U.S.A.* **152 E5** 33 22N 81 16W
Blackwater, *Australia* .... **126 C4** 23 35 S 148 53 E
Blackwater ➤, *Cork, Ireland* **19 E2** 52 5N 9 3W
Blackwater ➤, *Meath, Ireland* **23 C4** 53 39N 6 41W
Blackwater ➤, *Waterford, Ireland* **23 D4** 52 4N 7 52W
Blackwater ➤, *U.K.* **23 B5** 54 31N 6 35W
Blackwater ➤, *Fla., U.S.A.* **153 E2** 30 36N 87 2W
Blackwater ➤, *Mo., U.S.A.* **156 F4** 38 59N 92 59W
Blackwell, *U.S.A.* **155 G6** 36 48N 97 17W
Blackwells Corner, *U.S.A.* **161 K7** 35 37N 119 47W
Blackwood, C., *Papua N.G.* .... **132 D3** 7 49 S 144 31 E
Bladensburg Nat. Park △, *Australia* .... **126 C3** 22 30 S 142 59 E
Blaenau Ffestiniog, *U.K.* **20 E4** 53 0N 3 56W
Blaenau Gwent □, *U.K.* **21 F4** 51 48N 3 12W
Bláfell, *Iceland* **11 C7** 64 30N 19 51W
Bláfjall, *Iceland* **11 B10** 65 26N 16 50W
Blagaj, *Bos.-H.* .... **50 C1** 43 16N 17 55 E
Blagnac, *France* .... **28 E5** 43 37N 1 23 E
Blagnac, Toulouse ✈ (TLS), *France* .... **28 E5** 43 37N 1 22 E
Blagodarnoye = Blagodarnyy, *Russia* .... **61 H6** 45 7N 43 37 E
Blagodarnyy, *Russia* .... **61 H6** 45 7N 43 37 E
Blagoevgrad, *Bulgaria* .... **50 D7** 42 2N 23 5 E
Blagoveshchenka, *Kazakhstan* .... **65 B7** 43 18N 74 12 E
Blagoveshchensk, *Amur, Russia* .... **67 D13** 50 20N 127 30 E
Blagoveshchensk, *Bashkortostan,*
  Russia .... **64 D5** 55 1N 55 59 E
Blahkiuh, *Indonesia* .... **79 J18** 8 31 S 115 12 E
Blain, *France* **26 E5** 47 29N 1 45W
Blain, *U.S.A.* **150 F7** 40 20N 77 31W
Blaine, *Minn., U.S.A.* **154 C8** 45 10N 93 13W
Blaine, *Wash., U.S.A.* **160 B4** 48 59N 122 45W
Blaine Lake, *Canada* **143 C7** 52 51N 106 52W
Blair, *U.S.A.* **154 E6** 41 33N 96 8W
Blair Athol, *Australia* .... **126 C4** 22 42 S 147 31 E
Blair Atholl, *U.K.* **22 E5** 56 46N 3 50W
Blairgowrie, *U.K.* **22 E5** 56 35N 3 21W
Blairsden, *U.S.A.* **160 F6** 39 47N 120 37W
Blairsville, *U.S.A.* **150 F5** 40 26N 79 16W
Blaj, *Romania* .... **53 D8** 46 10N 23 57 E
Blaka, *Niger* .... **109 D2** 21 21N 12 47 E
Blakang Mati, Pulau, *Singapore* .... **87 d** 1 15N 103 50 E
Blake Pt., *U.S.A.* **154 A10** 48 11N 88 25W
Blakely, *Ga., U.S.A.* **152 D5** 31 23N 84 56W
Blakely, *Pa., U.S.A.* **151 E9** 41 28N 75 37W
Blakesburg, *U.S.A.* **156 D4** 40 58N 92 38W
Blakstad, *Norway* .... **18 E5** 58 30N 8 39 E
Blámont, *France* .... **27 D13** 48 35N 6 50 E
Blanc, C., *Spain* .... **38 B3** 39 21N 2 51 E
Blanc, C., *Tunisia* .... **108 A1** 37 15N 9 56 E
Blanc, Mont, *Alps* .... **29 C10** 45 48N 6 50 E
Blanc-Sablon, *Canada* **141 B8** 51 24N 57 12W
Blanca, B., *Argentina* .... **176 A4** 39 10 S 61 30W
Blanca Peak, *U.S.A.* **159 H11** 37 35N 105 29W
Blanchardville, *U.S.A.* **156 B7** 42 49N 89 52W
Blanche, C., *Australia* .... **127 E1** 33 1 S 134 9 E
Blanche, L., *S. Austral., Australia* .... **127 D2** 29 15 S 139 40 E
Blanche, L., *W. Austral., Australia* .... **124 D3** 22 25 S 123 17 E
Blanche Channel, *Solomon Is.* .... **133 M9** 8 30 S 157 30 E
Blanchester, *U.S.A.* **157 E13** 39 17N 83 59W
Blanchisseuse, *Trin. & Tob.* **165 F9** 10 48N 61 18W
Blanco, *S. Africa* .... **116 E3** 33 55 S 22 23 E
Blanco, *U.S.A.* **155 K5** 30 6N 98 25W
Blanco ➤, *Argentina* .... **174 C2** 30 20 S 68 42W
Blanco ➤, *Bolivia* .... **173 C5** 12 30 S 64 18W
Blanco, C., *Costa Rica* **164 E2** 9 34N 85 8W
Blanco, C., *U.S.A.* **158 E1** 42 51N 124 34W
Blanda ➤, *Iceland* **11 B6** 65 37N 20 9W
Blandford Forum, *U.K.* **21 G5** 50 51N 2 9W
Blanding, *U.S.A.* **159 H9** 37 37N 109 29W
Blandinsville, *U.S.A.* **156 D6** 40 33N 90 52W
Blanes, *Spain* .... **40 D7** 41 40N 2 48 E
Blangy-sur-Bresle, *France* .... **27 C8** 49 55N 1 37 E
Blanice ➤, *Czech Rep.* .... **34 B7** 49 10N 14 5 E
Blankaholm, *Sweden* .... **17 G10** 57 36N 16 31 E
Blankenberge, *Belgium* .... **24 C3** 51 20N 3 9 E
Blankenburg, *Germany* .... **30 D6** 51 47N 10 57 E
Blanquefort, *France* **28 D3** 44 55N 0 38W
Blanquilla, I., *Venezuela* **169 A5** 11 51N 64 37W
Blanquillo, *Uruguay* .... **175 C4** 32 53 S 55 37W
Blansko, *Czech Rep.* .... **35 B9** 49 22N 16 40 E
Blantyre, *Malawi* .... **119 F4** 15 45 S 35 0 E
Blarney, *Ireland* **23 E3** 51 56N 8 33W
Blasdell, *U.S.A.* **150 D6** 42 48N 78 50W
Blåsjø, *Norway* .... **18 E3** 59 20N 6 50 E
Blaszki, *Poland* .... **55 G5** 51 38N 18 30 E
Blatná, *Czech Rep.* .... **34 B6** 49 25N 13 52 E
Blato, *Croatia* .... **45 F13** 42 56N 16 48 E
Blatten, *Switz.* .... **32 D5** 46 20N 7 50 E
Blaubeuren, *Germany* .... **31 G5** 48 24N 9 46 E
Blaustein, *Germany* .... **31 G5** 48 25N 9 53 E
Blåvands Huk, *Denmark* .... **17 J2** 55 33N 8 4 E
Blaydon, *U.K.* **20 C6** 54 58N 1 42W

Blaye, *France* **28 C3** 45 8N 0 40W
Blaye-les-Mines, *France* .... **28 D6** 44 1N 2 8 E
Blayney, *Australia* .... **129 B8** 33 32 S 149 14 E
Blaze, Pt., *Australia* .... **124 B5** 12 56 S 130 11 E
Blazowa, *Poland* .... **55 J9** 49 53N 22 7 E
Bleckede, *Germany* .... **30 B6** 53 17N 10 43 E
Bled, *Slovenia* .... **45 B11** 46 27N 14 7 E
Bléfjell, *Norway* .... **18 E6** 59 48N 9 10 E
Blejeşti, *Romania* .... **53 F10** 44 19N 25 27 E
Blekinge, *Sweden* .... **15 H16** 56 25N 15 20 E
Blekinge län □, *Sweden* .... **17 H9** 56 20N 15 20 E
Blenheim, *Canada* **150 D3** 42 20N 82 0W
Blenheim, *N.Z.* .... **131 B8** 41 38 S 173 57 E
Bléone ➤, *France* .... **29 D10** 44 5N 6 0 E
Blérancourt, *France* .... **27 C10** 49 31N 3 9 E
Bletchley, *U.K.* **21 F7** 51 59N 0 44W
Blida, *Algeria* .... **111 A5** 36 30N 2 49 E
Blidet Amor, *Algeria* .... **111 B6** 32 59N 5 58 E
Blido, *Sweden* .... **16 E12** 59 37N 18 53 E
Blidsberg, *Sweden* .... **17 G7** 57 56N 13 30 E
Blieskastel, *Germany* .... **31 F3** 49 14N 7 12 E
Bligh Sound, *N.Z.* .... **131 E2** 44 47 S 167 32 E
Bligh Water, *Fiji* .... **133 A2** 17 0 S 178 0 E
Blind River, *Canada* **140 C3** 46 10N 82 58W
Blinisht, *Albania* .... **50 E3** 41 52N 19 59 E
Blinnenhorn, *Switz.* .... **33 D6** 46 26N 8 19 E
Bliss, *Idaho, U.S.A.* **158 E6** 42 56N 114 57W
Bliss, *N.Y., U.S.A.* **150 D6** 42 34N 78 15W
Blissfield, *Mich., U.S.A.* **157 C13** 41 50N 83 52W
Blissfield, *Ohio, U.S.A.* **150 F3** 40 24N 81 58W
Blitar, *Indonesia* .... **85 D4** 8 5 S 112 11 E
Blitchton, *U.S.A.* **152 C8** 32 12N 81 26W
Blitta, *Togo* .... **113 D5** 8 23N 1 6 E
Block I., *U.S.A.* **151 E13** 41 11N 71 35W
Block Island Sd., *U.S.A.* **151 E13** 41 15N 71 40W
Bloemfontein, *S. Africa* .... **116 D4** 29 6 S 26 7 E
Bloemhof, *S. Africa* .... **116 D4** 27 38 S 25 32 E
Blois, *France* .... **26 E8** 47 35N 1 20 E
Blomskog, *Sweden* .... **16 E6** 59 16N 12 2 E
Blomstermåla, *Sweden* .... **17 H10** 56 59N 16 21 E
Blomvåg, *Norway* .... **18 D1** 60 32N 4 50 E
Blonay, *Switz.* .... **32 D3** 46 28N 6 54 E
Blönduós, *Iceland* **11 B6** 65 40N 20 12W
Blongas, *Indonesia* .... **79 K19** 8 53 S 116 2 E
Błonie, *Poland* .... **55 F7** 52 12N 20 37 E
Bloodvein ➤, *Canada* **143 C9** 51 47N 96 43W
Bloody Foreland, *Ireland* **23 A3** 55 10N 8 17W
Bloomer, *U.S.A.* **154 C9** 45 6N 91 29W
Bloomfield, *Canada* **150 C7** 43 59N 77 14W
Bloomfield, *Australia* .... **126 B4** 15 56 S 145 22 E
Bloomfield, *Ind., U.S.A.* **156 D4** 40 45N 92 25W
Bloomfield, *Ky., U.S.A.* **157 G11** 37 55N 85 19W
Bloomfield, *N. Mex., U.S.A.* **159 H10** 36 43N 107 59W
Bloomfield, *Nebr., U.S.A.* **154 D6** 42 36N 97 39W
Bloomingburg, *U.S.A.* **157 E13** 39 36N 83 24W
Bloomington, *Ill., U.S.A.* **156 D8** 40 28N 89 0W
Bloomington, *Ind., U.S.A.* **157 E10** 39 10N 86 32W
Bloomington, *Minn., U.S.A.* **154 C8** 44 50N 93 17W
Bloomington, *Wis., U.S.A.* **156 B6** 42 53N 90 55W
Bloomsburg, *U.S.A.* **151 F8** 41 0N 76 27W
Bloomsbury, *Australia* .... **126 J6** 20 48 S 148 38 E
Blora, *Indonesia* .... **85 D4** 6 57 S 111 25 E
Blossburg, *U.S.A.* **150 E7** 41 41N 77 4W
Blosseville Kyst, *Greenland* **10 D8** 68 50N 26 30W
Blotzheim, *France* .... **32 A4** 47 36N 7 29 E
Blouberg, *S. Africa* .... **117 C4** 23 8 S 28 59 E
Blountstown, *U.S.A.* **152 E4** 30 27N 85 3W
Bludenz, *Austria* .... **34 D2** 47 10N 9 50 E
Blue ➤, *U.S.A.* **157 F10** 38 11N 86 19W
Blue Cypress L., *U.S.A.* **153 H9** 27 44N 80 45W
Blue Earth, *U.S.A.* **154 D8** 43 38N 94 6W
Blue Hole Nat. Park △, *Belize* **164 C2** 17 24N 88 30W
Blue Lagoon Nat. Park △, *Zambia* .... **119 F2** 15 28 S 27 26 E
Blue Mesa Reservoir, *U.S.A.* **159 G10** 38 28N 107 20W
Blue Mound, *U.S.A.* **156 E7** 39 42N 89 7W
Blue Mountain Lake, *U.S.A.* **151 C10** 43 52N 74 30W
Blue Mountain Pk., *Jamaica* .... **164 a** 18 3N 76 36W
Blue Mountains, The, *Jamaica* .... **164 a** 18 3N 76 36W
Blue Mts., *Australia* .... **129 B9** 33 40 S 150 15 E
Blue Mts., *Maine, U.S.A.* **151 B14** 44 50N 70 35W
Blue Mts., *Oreg., U.S.A.* **158 D4** 45 15N 119 0W
Blue Mts., *Pa., U.S.A.* **151 F8** 40 30N 76 30W
Blue Mts. Nat. Park △, *Australia* .... **129 C9** 34 2 S 150 15 E
Blue Mud B., *Australia* .... **126 A2** 13 33 S 136 0 E
Blue Nile = Nîl el Azraq ➤, *Sudan* .... **107 D3** 15 38N 32 31 E
Blue Rapids, *U.S.A.* **154 F6** 39 41N 96 39W
Blue Ridge Mts., *U.S.A.* **149 G5** 36 30N 80 15W
Blue River, *Canada* **142 C5** 52 6N 119 18W
Blue Springs, *U.S.A.* **156 E2** 39 1N 94 17W
Bluefield, *U.S.A.* **148 G5** 37 15N 81 17W
Bluefields, *Nic.* **164 D3** 12 20N 83 50W
Bluff, *Australia* .... **126 C4** 23 35 S 149 4 E
Bluff, *N.Z.* .... **131 G3** 46 37 S 168 20 E
Bluff, *U.S.A.* **159 H9** 37 17N 109 33W
Bluff Harbour, *N.Z.* .... **131 G3** 46 36 S 168 21 E
Bluff Knoll, *Australia* .... **125 F2** 34 24 S 118 15 E
Bluff Pt., *Australia* .... **125 E1** 27 50 S 114 5 E
Bluffs, *U.S.A.* **156 E6** 39 45N 90 32W
Bluffton, *Ga., U.S.A.* **152 D5** 31 31N 84 52W
Bluffton, *Ind., U.S.A.* **157 D11** 40 44N 85 11W
Bluffton, *Ohio, U.S.A.* **157 D13** 40 54N 83 54W
Bluffton, *S.C., U.S.A.* **152 C9** 32 14N 80 52W
Blumenau, *Brazil* .... **175 B6** 27 0 S 49 0W
Blümisalphorn, *Switz.* .... **32 D5** 46 28N 7 47 E
Blunt, *U.S.A.* **154 C5** 44 31N 99 59W
Bly, *U.S.A.* **158 E3** 42 24N 121 3W
Blyde River Canyon Nature
  Reserve ≈, *S. Africa* .... **117 C5** 24 37 S 31 2 E
Blyth, *Australia* .... **128 B3** 33 49 S 138 28 E
Blyth, *Canada* **150 C3** 43 44N 81 26W
Blyth, *U.K.* **20 B6** 55 8N 1 31W
Blythe, *Calif., U.S.A.* **161 M12** 33 37N 114 36W
Blythe, *Ga., U.S.A.* **152 B7** 33 17N 82 12W
Blytheville, *U.S.A.* **155 H10** 35 56N 89 55W
Bø, *Norway* .... **18 E6** 59 25N 9 3 E
Bo, *S. Leone* **112 D2** 7 55N 11 50W
Bo Duc, *Vietnam* .... **87 G6** 11 58N 106 50 E
Bo Hai, *China* .... **75 E10** 39 0N 119 0 E
Bō-no-Misaki, *Japan* .... **72 F2** 31 15N 130 13 E
Bo Xian = Bozhou, *China* .... **74 H8** 33 55N 115 41 E
Boa Esperança, *Brazil* **169 C5** 3 21N 61 23W
Boa Esperança, Reprêsa, *Brazil* .... **170 C3** 6 50 S 43 50W
Boa Nova, *Brazil* .... **171 D3** 14 22 S 40 10W
Boa Viagem, *Brazil* .... **170 C4** 5 7 S 39 44W
Boa Vista, *Brazil* **169 C5** 2 48N 60 30W
Boa Vista, *C. Verde Is.* .... **9 j** 16 0N 22 49W
Boac, *Phil.* .... **80 E3** 13 27N 121 50 E
Boaco, *Nic.* **164 D2** 12 29N 85 35W
Bo'ai, *China* .... **74 G7** 35 10N 113 3 E
Boal, *Spain* **42 B4** 43 25N 6 49W
Boali, *C.A.R.* .... **114 B3** 4 48N 18 7 E
Boalsburg, *U.S.A.* **150 F7** 40 46N 77 47W
Boane, *Mozam.* .... **117 D5** 26 6 S 32 19 E
Boang I., *Papua N.G.* .... **132 B7** 3 23 S 153 18 E
Boano, *Indonesia* .... **83 D7** 3 0 S 127 56 E
Boardman, *U.S.A.* **150 E4** 41 2N 80 40W
Boath, *India* .... **94 E4** 19 20N 78 20 E
Bobadah, *Australia* .... **129 B7** 32 19 S 146 41 E
Bobai, *China* .... **76 F7** 22 17N 109 59 E
Bobbili, *India* .... **94 C6** 18 35N 83 30 E
Bóbbio, *Italy* .... **44 D6** 44 46N 9 23 E
Bobcaygeon, *Canada* **140 D4** 44 33N 78 33W

Boblad, *India* .... **94 F2** 17 13N 75 26 E
Böblingen, *Germany* .... **31 G5** 48 40N 9 1 E
Bobo-Dioulasso, *Burkina Faso* **112 C4** 11 8N 4 13W
Bobolice, *Poland* .... **54 E3** 53 58N 16 37 E
Bobon, *Phil.* .... **80 E5** 12 32N 124 34 E
Bobonaro, E. *Timor* .... **82 C3** 9 2 S 125 22 E
Bobonaza ➤, *Ecuador* .... **168 D2** 2 36 S 76 38W
Boboshevo, *Bulgaria* .... **50 D7** 42 9N 23 0 E
Bobov Dol, *Bulgaria* .... **50 D6** 42 20N 23 0 E
Bóbr ➤, *Poland* .... **55 F2** 52 4N 15 4 E
Bobraomby, Tanjon' i, *Madag.* .... **117 A8** 12 40 S 49 10 E
Bobrinets, *Ukraine* .... **59 H7** 48 4N 32 5 E
Bobrov, *Russia* .... **60 E5** 51 5N 40 2 E
Bobrovitsa, *Ukraine* .... **59 G6** 50 45N 31 23 E
Bobruysk = Babruysk, *Belarus* .... **59 F5** 53 10N 29 15 E
Boca de Drago, *Venezuela* **169 F9** 11 0N 61 50W
Bôca do Acre, *Brazil* .... **172 B4** 8 50 S 67 27W
Bôca do Jari, *Brazil* .... **169 D7** 1 7 S 51 58W
Bôca do Moaco, *Brazil* .... **172 B4** 7 41 S 68 17W
Boca Grande, *U.S.A.* **153 J7** 26 45N 82 16W
Boca Grande, *Venezuela* **169 B5** 8 40N 60 40W
Boca Raton, *U.S.A.* **153 J9** 26 21N 80 5W
Bocanda, *Ivory C.* **112 D4** 7 0N 4 31W
Bocaranga, *C.A.R.* .... **114 A3** 7 0N 15 35 E
Bocas del Toro, *Panama* **164 E3** 9 15N 82 20W
Boceguillas, *Spain* **42 D7** 41 20N 3 39W
Bochaldino = Belogorsk, *Russia* .... **67 D13** 51 0N 128 20 E
Bochnia, *Poland* .... **55 J7** 49 58N 20 27 E
Bocholt, *Germany* .... **30 D2** 51 50N 6 36 E
Bochum, *Germany* .... **30 D3** 51 28N 7 13 E
Bockenem, *Germany* .... **30 C6** 52 1N 10 8 E
Bočki, *Poland* .... **55 F10** 52 39N 23 3 E
Bocognano, *France* .... **29 F13** 42 5N 9 4 E
Bocoio, *Angola* .... **115 E2** 12 28 S 14 0 E
Boconó, *Venezuela* **168 B3** 9 15N 70 16W
Boconó ➤, *Venezuela* **168 B4** 8 43N 69 34W
Bocoyna, *Mexico* **162 B3** 27 52N 107 35W
Bocşa, *Romania* .... **52 E6** 45 21N 21 47 E
Boda, *C.A.R.* .... **114 B3** 4 19N 17 26 E
Boda, *Dalarnas, Sweden* .... **16 C9** 61 1N 15 13 E
Böda, *Kalmar, Sweden* .... **17 G11** 57 15N 17 3 E
Boda, *Västernorrland, Sweden* .... **16 B10** 62 52N 16 39 E
Bodafors, *Sweden* .... **17 G8** 57 48N 14 23 E
Bodaybo, *Russia* .... **67 D12** 57 50N 114 0 E
Boddam, *U.K.* **22 B7** 59 56N 1 17W
Boddington, *Australia* .... **125 F2** 32 50 S 116 30 E
Bodega Bay, *U.S.A.* **160 G3** 38 20N 123 3W
Boden, *Sweden* .... **8 B19** 65 50N 21 42 E
Bodensee, *Europe* .... **33 A8** 47 35N 9 25 E
Bodenteich, *Germany* .... **30 C6** 52 50N 10 42 E
Bodhan, *India* .... **94 E3** 18 40N 77 44 E
Bodinayakkanur, *India* .... **95 J3** 10 2N 77 10 E
Bodinga, *Nigeria* .... **113 C6** 12 58N 5 10 E
Bodio, *Switz.* .... **33 D7** 46 23N 8 55 E
Bodmin, *U.K.* **21 G3** 50 28N 4 43W
Bodmin Moor, *U.K.* **21 G3** 50 33N 4 36W
Bodø, *Norway* .... **14 C16** 67 17N 14 24 E
Bodoquena, Serra da, *Brazil* .... **173 E6** 21 0 S 56 50W
Bodoupa, *C.A.R.* .... **114 A3** 5 43N 17 36 E
Bodrichi, *Chad* .... **109 E3** 19 11N 15 54 E
Bodrog ➤, *Hungary* .... **52 B6** 48 11N 21 22 E
Bodrum, *Turkey* .... **49 D9** 37 3N 27 30 E
Boduna, *Dem. Rep. of the Congo* .... **114 A3** 5 5N 19 44 E
Bódva ➤, *Hungary* .... **52 B5** 48 19N 20 45 E
Boembé, *Congo* .... **114 C2** 2 54 S 15 9 E
Boën, *France* .... **29 C8** 45 44N 4 1 E
Boende, *Dem. Rep. of the Congo* .... **114 C4** 0 24 S 21 13 E
Boerne, *U.S.A.* **155 L5** 29 47N 98 44W
Boesmans ➤, *S. Africa* .... **116 E4** 33 42 S 26 39 E
Boffa, *Guinea* **112 C2** 10 16N 14 3W
Bofuku, *Dem. Rep. of the Congo* .... **114 C4** 0 57N 20 58 E
Bogale, *Burma* .... **90 G5** 16 17N 95 24 E
Bogalusa, *U.S.A.* **155 K10** 30 47N 89 52W
Bogan ➤, *Australia* .... **129 A7** 30 20 S 146 55 E
Bogan Gate, *Australia* .... **129 B7** 33 7 S 147 49 E
Bogandé, *Burkina Faso* **113 C4** 13 2N 0 8W
Bogangolo, *C.A.R.* .... **114 A3** 5 34N 18 15 E
Bogantungan, *Australia* .... **126 C4** 23 41 S 147 17 E
Bogata, *U.S.A.* **155 J7** 33 28N 95 13W
Bogatić, *Serbia, Yug.* .... **50 B3** 44 51N 19 30 E
Boğazkale, *Turkey* .... **100 D6** 40 2N 34 37 E
Boğazlıyan, *Turkey* .... **100 C6** 39 11N 35 14 E
Bogbonga, *Dem. Rep. of the Congo* .... **114 B3** 1 36N 19 24 E
Bogdanovich, *Russia* .... **64 C9** 56 47N 62 1 E
Bogen, *Sweden* .... **16 D6** 60 4N 12 33 E
Bogense, *Denmark* .... **17 J4** 55 34N 10 5 E
Bogetići, *Montenegro, Yug.* .... **50 D2** 42 41N 18 58 E
Boggabilla, *Australia* .... **127 D5** 28 36 S 150 24 E
Boggabri, *Australia* .... **129 A9** 30 45 S 150 5 E
Boggeragh Mts., *Ireland* **23 D3** 52 2N 8 55W
Bogia, *Papua N.G.* .... **132 C3** 4 9 S 145 0 E
Boglan = Solhan, *Turkey* .... **101 C9** 38 57N 41 3 E
Bognor Regis, *U.K.* **21 G7** 50 47N 0 40W
Bogo, *Phil.* .... **81 F4** 11 3N 124 0 E
Bogodukhov = Bohodukhiv, *Ukraine* .... **59 G8** 50 9N 35 33 E
Bogol Manya, *Ethiopia* .... **107 G5** 4 34N 41 29 E
Bogong, Mt., *Australia* .... **129 D4** 36 47 S 147 17 E
Bogor, *Indonesia* .... **84 D3** 6 36 S 106 48 E
Bogoroditsk, *Russia* .... **58 F10** 53 47N 38 8 E
Bogorodsk, *Russia* .... **60 B6** 56 4N 43 30 E
Bogoso, *Ghana* **112 D4** 5 38N 2 3W
Bogotá, *Colombia* **168 C3** 4 34N 74 0W
Bogotol, *Russia* .... **66 D9** 56 15N 89 50 E
Bogou, *Togo* .... **113 C5** 10 40N 0 12 E
Bogra, *Bangla.* .... **90 C2** 24 51N 89 22 E
Boguchany, *Russia* .... **67 D10** 58 40N 97 30 E
Boguchar, *Russia* .... **59 G6** 49 55N 40 32 E
Bogué, *Mauritania* **111 B2** 16 45N 14 10W
Boguslav, *Ukraine* .... **59 H6** 49 47N 30 56 E
Boguszów-Gorce, *Poland* .... **55 H3** 50 45N 16 12 E
Bohain-en-Vermandois, *France* .... **27 C10** 49 59N 3 28 E
Bohemian Forest = Böhmerwald,
  Germany .... **31 F9** 49 8N 13 14 E
Bohena Cr. ➤, *Australia* .... **129 A8** 30 17 S 149 42 E
Bohinjska Bistrica, *Slovenia* .... **45 B11** 46 17N 14 1 E
Böhmerwald, *Germany* .... **31 F9** 49 8N 13 14 E
Bohmte, *Germany* .... **30 C4** 52 22N 8 19 E
Bohodukhiv, *Ukraine* .... **59 G8** 50 9N 35 33 E
Bohol □, *Phil.* .... **81 G5** 9 50N 124 10 E
Bohol Sea, *Phil.* .... **81 G5** 9 0N 124 0 E
Bohol Str., *Phil.* .... **81 G4** 9 45N 123 40 E
Bohongou, *Burkina Faso* .... **113 C5** 11 30N 0 40 E
Böhönye, *Hungary* .... **52 D2** 46 25N 17 28 E
Bohotleh, *Somali Rep.* .... **120 C3** 8 20N 46 25 E
Bohuslän, *Sweden* .... **17 F5** 58 25N 11 40 E
Boi, *Nigeria* .... **113 D6** 9 35N 9 27 E
Boi, Pta. de, *Brazil* .... **175 A6** 23 55 S 45 15W
Boiaçu, *Brazil* .... **169 D5** 0 27 S 61 46W
Boigu I., *Australia* .... **132 E2** 9 15 S 142 14 E
Boileau, C., *Australia* .... **124 C3** 17 40 S 122 7 E
Boim, *Brazil* .... **169 D6** 2 49 S 55 10W
Boing'o, *Sudan* .... **107 F3** 9 58N 33 44 E
Boipariguda, *India* .... **94 E6** 18 46N 82 26 E
Boipeba, I. de, *Brazil* .... **171 D4** 13 39 S 38 55W
Boiro, *Spain* **42 C2** 42 39N 8 54W
Bois ➤, *Brazil* .... **171 E1** 15 30 S 48 40W
Boise, *U.S.A.* **158 E5** 43 37N 116 13W
Boise City, *U.S.A.* **155 G3** 36 44N 102 31W
Boissevain, *Canada* **143 D8** 49 15N 100 5W
Bôite ➤, *Italy* .... **45 B9** 46 5N 12 5 E

Boitzenburg, *Germany* .... **30 B9** 53 16N 13 35 E
Boizenburg, *Germany* .... **30 B6** 53 23N 10 43 E
Bojador, C., *W. Sahara* **110 C2** 26 0N 14 30W
Bojana ➤, *Albania* .... **50 E3** 41 52N 19 22 E
Bojano, *Italy* .... **47 A7** 41 29N 14 29 E
Bojanowo, *Poland* .... **55 G3** 51 43N 16 42 E
Bøjden, *Denmark* .... **17 J4** 55 6N 10 7 E
Bojnūrd, *Iran* .... **97 B8** 37 30N 57 20 E
Bojonegoro, *Indonesia* .... **85 D4** 7 11 S 111 54 E
Boju, *Nigeria* .... **113 D6** 7 22N 7 55 E
Boka, *Serbia, Yug.* .... **52 E5** 45 22N 20 52 E
Boka Kotorska, *Montenegro, Yug.* .... **50 D2** 42 23N 18 32 E
Bokada, *Dem. Rep. of the Congo* .... **114 B3** 4 8N 19 23 E
Bokala, *Dem. Rep. of the Congo* .... **114 C3** 3 8 S 17 4 E
Bokani, *Nigeria* .... **113 D6** 9 28N 5 10 E
Bokaro, *India* .... **93 H11** 23 46N 85 55 E
Bokatola, *Dem. Rep. of the Congo* .... **114 C3** 0 38 S 18 46 E
Boké, *Guinea* **112 C2** 10 56N 14 17W
Bokela, *Dem. Rep. of the Congo* .... **114 C4** 1 10 S 21 59 E
Bokenda, *Dem. Rep. of the Congo* .... **114 C4** 0 19 S 22 46 E
Bokhara ➤, *Australia* .... **127 D4** 29 55 S 146 42 E
Bokkos, *Nigeria* .... **113 D6** 9 17N 9 1 E
Boknafjorden, *Norway* .... **18 E2** 59 14N 5 40 E
Bokode, *Dem. Rep. of the Congo* .... **114 B3** 3 55N 19 30 E
Bokolo, *Gabon* .... **114 C2** 2 40 S 10 10 E
Bökönbaev, *Kyrgyzstan* .... **65 B8** 42 10N 76 55 E
Bokondo, *Dem. Rep. of the Congo* .... **114 B4** 0 15N 22 32 E
Bokora Game Reserve △, *Uganda* .... **118 B3** 2 12N 31 32 E
Bokoro, *Chad* .... **109 F3** 12 25N 17 14 E
Bokota, *Dem. Rep. of the Congo* .... **114 C4** 0 56 S 22 24 E
Bokote, *Dem. Rep. of the Congo* .... **114 C4** 0 12 S 21 8 E
Bokpyin, *Burma* .... **87 G2** 11 18N 98 42 E
Boksitogorsk, *Russia* .... **58 C7** 59 22N 33 50 E
Bokungu, *Dem. Rep. of the Congo* .... **114 C4** 0 35 S 22 50 E
Bol, *Chad* .... **109 F2** 13 30N 14 40 E
Bol, *Croatia* .... **45 E13** 43 18N 16 38 E
Bolama, *Guinea-Biss.* **112 C1** 11 30N 15 30W
Bolan ➤, *Pakistan* .... **92 E2** 28 38N 67 42 E
Bolan Pass, *Pakistan* .... **91 C2** 29 50N 67 20 E
Bolaños ➤, *Mexico* **162 C4** 21 14N 104 8W
Bolaños de Calatrava, *Spain* **43 G7** 38 54N 3 40W
Bolayir, *Turkey* .... **51 F10** 40 31N 26 45 E
Bolbec, *France* .... **26 C7** 49 30N 0 30 E
Boldāji, *Iran* .... **97 D6** 31 56N 51 3 E
Boldeşti-Scăeni, *Romania* .... **53 E11** 45 3N 26 2 E
Bole, *China* .... **68 B3** 45 11N 81 37 E
Bole, *Ethiopia* .... **107 F4** 6 36N 37 20 E
Bole, *Ghana* **112 D4** 9 2N 2 23W
Bolekhiv, *Ukraine* .... **59 H2** 49 0N 23 57 E
Boleko, *Dem. Rep. of the Congo* .... **114 C3** 1 35 S 19 50 E
Bolesławiec, *Poland* .... **55 G2** 51 17N 15 37 E
Bolgatanga, *Ghana* **113 C4** 10 44N 0 53W
Bolgrad = Bolhrad, *Ukraine* .... **59 K5** 45 40N 28 32 E
Bolhrad, *Ukraine* .... **59 K5** 45 40N 28 32 E
Bolia, *Dem. Rep. of the Congo* .... **114 C3** 1 36 S 18 22 E
Boliden, *Sweden* .... **8 D19** 64 49N 20 24 E
Bolinao, *Phil.* .... **80 C2** 16 23N 119 54 E
Bolinao, C., *Phil.* .... **80 C2** 16 23N 119 55 E
Bolingbroke, *U.S.A.* **152 C6** 32 57N 83 48W
Bolingo, *Dem. Rep. of the Congo* .... **114 C4** 3 31 S 21 43 E
Bolintin-Vale, *Romania* .... **53 F10** 44 27N 25 46 E
Bolívar, *Argentina* .... **174 D3** 36 15 S 60 53W
Bolívar, *Antioquia, Colombia* **168 B2** 5 50N 76 1W
Bolívar, *Cauca, Colombia* **168 C2** 2 0N 77 0W
Bolívar, *Peru* .... **172 B2** 7 8 S 77 43W
Bolívar, *Mo., U.S.A.* **155 G8** 37 37N 93 25W
Bolívar, *N.Y., U.S.A.* **150 D6** 42 4N 78 10W
Bolívar, *Tenn., U.S.A.* **155 H10** 35 12N 89 0W
Bolívar □, *Colombia* **168 B3** 9 0N 74 40W
Bolívar □, *Ecuador* .... **168 D2** 1 15 S 79 5W
Bolívar □, *Venezuela* **169 B5** 6 20N 63 30W
Bolivia ■, *S. Amer.* .... **173 D5** 17 6 S 64 0W
Bolivian Plateau = Altiplano, *Bolivia* .... **172 D5** 17 0 S 68 0W
Boljevac, *Serbia, Yug.* .... **50 C5** 43 51N 21 58 E
Bolkhov, *Russia* .... **58 F9** 53 25N 36 0 E
Bolków, *Poland* .... **55 H3** 50 55N 16 6 E
Bollé, *Mauritania* **110 D2** 20 8N 11 40W
Bollebygd, *Sweden* .... **17 G6** 57 40N 12 35 E
Bollène, *France* .... **29 D8** 44 18N 4 45 E
Bollnäs, *Sweden* .... **16 C10** 61 21N 16 24 E
Bollon, *Australia* .... **127 D4** 28 2 S 147 29 E
Bollstabruk, *Sweden* .... **16 B11** 62 59N 17 40 E
Bolmen, *Sweden* .... **17 H7** 56 55N 13 40 E
Bolobo, *Dem. Rep. of the Congo* .... **114 C3** 2 6 S 16 20 E
Bologna, *Italy* .... **45 D8** 44 29N 11 20 E
Bologna ✈ (BLQ), *Italy* .... **45 D8** 44 44N 11 16 E
Bologoye, *Russia* .... **58 D8** 57 55N 34 5 E
Bolomba, *Dem. Rep. of the Congo* .... **114 B3** 0 35N 19 0 E
Bolombo ➤, *Dem. Rep. of*
  the Congo .... **114 B4** 1 32N 21 14 E
Bolonchenticul, *Mexico* **163 D7** 20 0N 89 49W
Bolondo, *Dem. Rep. of the Congo* .... **114 C3** 2 12 S 18 42 E
Bolong, *Chad* .... **109 F3** 13 1N 17 45 E
Bolong, *Phil.* .... **81 H4** 7 6N 122 14 E
Bolongongo, *Angola* .... **115 D3** 8 28 S 15 16 E
Bolótana, *Italy* .... **46 B1** 40 20N 8 52 E
Bolotovskoye, *Russia* .... **64 A9** 58 35N 62 28 E
Boloven, Cao Nguyen, *Laos* .... **86 E6** 15 10N 106 30 E
Bolpur, *India* .... **93 H12** 23 40N 87 45 E
Bolsena, *Italy* .... **45 F8** 42 39N 11 59 E
Bolsena, L. di, *Italy* .... **45 F8** 42 36N 11 56 E
Bolshaya Chernigovka, *Russia* .... **60 D10** 52 6N 50 52 E
Bolshaya Glushitsa, *Russia* .... **60 D10** 52 28N 50 30 E
Bolshaya Khobda ➤, *Kazakhstan* .... **64 F5** 50 56N 54 34 E
Bolshaya Martynovka, *Russia* .... **61 G5** 47 19N 41 37 E
Bolshaya Vradiyevka, *Ukraine* .... **59 J6** 47 50N 30 40 E
Bolshevik, Ostrov, *Russia* .... **67 B11** 78 30N 102 0 E
Bolshoy Anyuy ➤, *Russia* .... **67 C17** 68 30N 160 49 E
Bolshoy Begichev, Ostrov, *Russia* .... **67 B12** 74 20N 112 30 E
Bolshoy Kavkas = Caucasus
  Mountains, *Eurasia* .... **61 J7** 42 50N 44 0 E
Bolshoy Lyakhovskiy, Ostrov, *Russia* .... **67 B15** 73 35N 142 0 E
Bolshoy Tokmak = Tokmak, *Ukraine* .... **59 J8** 47 16N 35 42 E
Bolshoy Tyuters, Ostrov, *Russia* .... **15 G22** 59 51N 27 13 E
Bólstaðarhlíð, *Iceland* **11 B7** 65 31N 19 49W
Bolsward, *Neths.* .... **24 A5** 53 3N 5 32 E
Bolt Head, *U.K.* **21 G4** 50 12N 3 48W
Boltaña, *Spain* .... **40 C5** 42 28N 0 4 E
Boltigen, *Switz.* .... **32 C4** 46 38N 7 24 E
Bolton, *Canada* **150 C5** 43 54N 79 45W
Bolton, *U.K.* **20 D5** 53 35N 2 26W
Bolton Landing, *U.S.A.* **151 C11** 43 32N 73 35W
Bolu, *Turkey* .... **100 B4** 40 45N 31 35 E
Bolubolu, *Papua N.G.* .... **132 E6** 9 21 S 150 20 E
Bolungavík, *Iceland* **11 A3** 66 9N 23 15W
Boluo, *China* .... **77 F10** 23 3N 114 21 E
Bolvadin, *Turkey* .... **100 C4** 38 45N 31 4 E
Bolzano, *Italy* .... **45 B8** 46 31N 11 22 E
Bom Comércio, *Brazil* .... **173 B4** 9 45 S 65 15W
Bom Conselho, *Brazil* .... **170 C4** 9 10 S 36 41W
Bom Despacho, *Brazil* .... **171 E2** 19 43 S 45 15W
Bom Jesus, *Angola* .... **115 D2** 9 11 S 13 34 E
Bom Jesus, *Brazil* .... **170 C3** 9 4 S 44 22W
Bom Jesus da Gurguéia, Serra, *Brazil* .... **170 C3** 9 0 S 43 0W
Bom Jesus da Lapa, *Brazil* .... **171 D3** 13 15 S 43 25W
Boma, *Dem. Rep. of the Congo* .... **115 D2** 5 50 S 13 4 E
Bomaderry, *Australia* .... **129 C9** 34 52 S 150 37 E
Bomandjokou, *Congo* .... **114 B2** 0 34N 14 23 E
Bomaneh, *Dem. Rep. of the Congo* .... **114 B3** 1 18N 23 47 E
Bomassa, *Congo* .... **114 B3** 2 12N 16 12 E
Bomate, *Dem. Rep. of the Congo* .... **114 C3** 1 24N 23 15 E
Bombala, *Australia* .... **129 D8** 36 56 S 149 15 E
Bombarral, *Portugal* **43 F1** 39 15N 9 9W

Bombay = Mumbai, *India* .... **94 E1** 18 55N 72 50 E
Bombedor, Pta., *Venezuela* **169 G9** 9 53N 61 37W
Bomberai, Semenanjung, *Indonesia* **83 B4** 3 0 S 133 0 E
Bombo Kasani, *Dem. Rep. of*
the Congo .... **115 D4** 5 51 S 21 54 E
Bomboma, *Dem. Rep. of the Congo* **114 B3** 2 25N 18 55 E
Bombombwa, *Dem. Rep. of*
the Congo .... **118 B2** 1 40N 25 40 E
Bomdila, *India* .... **90 B4** 27 18N 92 22 E
Bomdo, *India* .... **90 A5** 28 44N 94 54 E
Bomi Hills, *Liberia* **112 D2** 7 1N 10 38W
Bomili, *Dem. Rep. of the Congo* **118 B2** 1 45N 27 5 E
Bømlo, *Norway* .... **18 E2** 59 37N 5 13 E
Bomokandi →, *Dem. Rep. of*
the Congo .... **118 B2** 3 39N 26 8 E
Bomongo, *Dem. Rep. of the Congo* **114 B3** 1 27N 18 21 E
Bompoka, *India* .... **95 K11** 8 15N 93 13 E
Bomputu, *Dem. Rep. of the Congo* **114 C4** 0 23 S 20 6 E
Bomu →, *C.A.R.* .... **114 B4** 4 40N 22 30 E
Bomu Occidentale, Réserve de
Faune de la △, *Dem. Rep. of*
the Congo .... **114 B4** 4 48N 24 17 E
Bomu Orientale, Réserve de Faune
de la △, *Dem. Rep. of the Congo* **114 B2** 5 0N 25 50 E
Bon, C., *Tunisia* .... **108 A2** 37 1N 11 2 E
Bon Acceuil, *Mauritius* .... **121 d** 20 10 S 57 39 E
Bon Sar Pa, *Vietnam* .... **86 F6** 12 24N 107 35 E
Bonâb, *Iran* .... **101 D12** 37 20N 46 4 E
Bonaduz, *Switz.* .... **33 C8** 46 49N 9 25 E
Bonagarh, *India* .... **93 J11** 21 50N 84 57 E
Bonaire, Neth. Ant. **165 D6** 12 10N 68 15W
Bonaire, *U.S.A.* **152 C6** 32 33N 83 36W
Bonampak, *Mexico* **163 D6** 16 44N 91 5W
Bonang, *Australia* .... **129 D8** 37 11 S 148 41 E
Bonanza, *Nic.* **164 D3** 13 54N 84 35W
Bonaparte Arch., *Australia* .... **124 B3** 14 0 S 124 30 E
Boñar, *Spain* **42 C5** 42 52N 5 19W
Bonar Bridge, *U.K.* **22 D4** 57 54N 4 20W
Bonasse, *Trin. & Tob.* **169 F9** 10 5N 61 54W
Bonaventure, *Canada* **141 C6** 48 5N 65 32W
Bonavista, *Canada* **141 C9** 48 40N 53 5W
Bonavista, C., *Canada* **141 C9** 48 42N 53 5W
Bonavista B., *Canada* **141 C9** 48 45N 53 25W
Bondeno, *Italy* .... **45 D8** 44 53N 11 25 E
Bondo, *Équateur, Dem. Rep. of*
the Congo .... **114 C4** 1 22 S 23 54 E
Bondo, *Orientale, Dem. Rep. of*
the Congo .... **118 B1** 3 55N 23 53 E
Bondoukou, *Ivory C.* **112 D4** 8 2N 2 47W
Bondowoso, *Indonesia* .... **85 D4** 7 55 S 113 49 E
Bône = Annaba, *Algeria* .... **111 A6** 36 50N 7 46 E
Bone, Teluk, *Indonesia* .... **82 B2** 4 10 S 120 50 E
Bonefish Pond, *Bahamas* .... **9 b** 25 59N 77 23W
Bonerate, *Indonesia* .... **82 C2** 7 25 S 121 5 E
Bonerate, Kepulauan, *Indonesia* **82 C2** 6 30 S 121 10 E
Bo'ness, *U.K.* **22 E5** 56 1N 3 37W
Bonete, Cerro, *Argentina* .... **174 B2** 27 55 S 68 40W
Bonfim, *Brazil* **169 C6** 3 33N 59 25W
Bong Son = Hoai Nhon, *Vietnam* **86 E7** 14 28N 109 1 E
Bonga, *Ethiopia* .... **107 F4** 7 15N 36 14 E
Bongabon, *Phil.* .... **80 D3** 15 38N 121 8 E
Bongabong, *Phil.* .... **80 E3** 12 45N 121 29 E
Bongaigaon, *India* .... **90 B3** 26 28N 90 34 E
Bongandanga, *Dem. Rep. of*
the Congo .... **114 B4** 1 24N 21 3 E
Bongao, *Phil.* .... **81 J2** 5 2N 119 46 E
Bongka, *Indonesia* .... **82 B2** 0 58 S 121 27 E
Bongo, *Dem. Rep. of the Congo* **114 C3** 1 47 S 17 41 E
Bongo, Sa. de, *Angola* .... **115 E3** 10 3 S 15 5 E
Bongor, *Chad* .... **109 F3** 10 35N 15 20 E
Bongouanou, *Ivory C.* **112 D4** 6 42N 4 15W
Bonham, *U.S.A.* **155 J6** 33 35N 96 11W
Boni, *Mali* **112 B4** 15 3N 2 10W
Boni Nat. Reserve △, *Kenya* .... **118 C5** 1 35 S 41 18 E
Bonifacio, *France* .... **29 G13** 41 24N 9 10 E
Bonifacio, Bouches de, *Medit. S.* **46 A2** 41 12N 9 15 E
Bonifay, *U.S.A.* **152 K4** 30 47N 85 41W
Bonin Is. = Ogasawara Gunto,
Pac. Oc. .... **62 G18** 27 0N 142 0 E
Bonita Springs, *U.S.A.* **153 M8** 26 21N 81 47W
Bonito, *Brazil* .... **173** 21 8 S 56 28W
Bonke, *Ethiopia* .... **107 F4** 6 5N 37 16 E
Bonkoukou, *Niger* .... **113 C5** 14 0N 3 15 E
Bonn, *Germany* .... **30 E3** 50 46N 7 6 E
Bonnat, *France* .... **27 F8** 46 20N 1 54 E
Bonne Terre, *U.S.A.* **155 G9** 37 55N 90 33W
Bonneau, *U.S.A.* **152 B10** 33 16N 79 58W
Bonners Ferry, *U.S.A.* **158 B5** 48 42N 116 19W
Bonnétable, *France* .... **26 D7** 48 11N 0 25 E
Bonneval, *Eure-et-Loir, France* **26 D8** 48 11N 1 24 E
Bonneval, *Savoie, France* .... **29 C11** 45 22N 7 3 E
Bonneville, *France* .... **27 F13** 46 4N 6 24 E
Bonney, L., *Australia* .... **128 D4** 37 50 S 140 20 E
Bonnie Doon, *Australia* .... **129 D6** 37 2 S 145 53 E
Bonnie Rock, *Australia* .... **125 F2** 30 29 S 118 22 E
Bonny, *Nigeria* .... **113 E6** 4 25N 7 13 E
Bonny →, *Nigeria* .... **113 E6** 4 20N 7 10 E
Bonny, Bight of, *Africa* .... **113 E6** 3 30N 9 20 E
Bonny Hills, *Australia* .... **129 A10** 31 36 S 152 51 E
Bonny-sur-Loire, *France* .... **27 E9** 47 33N 2 50 E
Bonnyrigg, *U.K.* **22 F5** 55 53N 3 6W
Bonnyville, *Canada* **143 C6** 54 20N 110 45W
Bono, *Italy* .... **46 B2** 40 25N 9 2 E
Bonoi, *Indonesia* .... **83 B5** 1 45 S 137 41 E
Bonorva, *Italy* .... **46 B1** 40 25N 8 46 E
Bonsall, *U.S.A.* **161 M9** 33 16N 117 14W
Bontang, *Indonesia* .... **85 B5** 0 10N 117 30 E
Bontebok Nat. Park △, *S. Africa* **116 E3** 34 5 S 20 28 E
Bonthe, *S. Leone* **112 D2** 7 30N 12 33W
Bontoc, *Phil.* .... **80 C3** 17 7N 120 58 E
Bontosunggu, *Indonesia* .... **82 C1** 5 41 S 119 42 E
Bonyeri, *Ghana* **112 D4** 5 1N 2 46W
Bonyhád, *Hungary* .... **52 D3** 46 18N 18 32 E
Bonython Ra., *Australia* .... **124 D4** 23 40 S 128 45 E
Boo, Kepulauan, *Indonesia* .... **83 B3** 1 12 S 129 24 E
Bookabie, *Australia* .... **125 F5** 31 50 S 132 41 E
Booke, *Dem. Rep. of the Congo* **114 C4** 2 34 S 22 3 E
Booker, *U.S.A.* **155 G4** 36 27N 100 32W
Bool Lagoon, *Australia* .... **128 D4** 37 7 S 140 40 E
Boola, *Guinea* .... **112 D3** 8 22N 8 41 E
Boolaboolka L., *Australia* .... **127 E3** 32 38 S 143 10 E
Boolcoomata, *Australia* .... **128 A4** 31 57 S 140 33 E
Booleroo Centre, *Australia* .... **128 B3** 32 53 S 138 21 E
Booligal, *Australia* .... **129 B6** 33 58 S 144 53 E
Boon, *U.S.A.* .... **127 D5** 27 58 S 152 41 E
Boone, *Iowa, U.S.A.* **156 B3** 42 4N 93 53W
Boone, *N.C., U.S.A.* **153 G5** 36 13N 81 41W
Booneville, *Ark., U.S.A.* **155 H8** 35 8N 93 55W
Booneville, *Miss., U.S.A.* **149 H1** 34 39N 88 34W
Boonville, *Calif., U.S.A.* **160 F3** 39 1N 123 22W
Boonville, *Ind., U.S.A.* **157 F9** 38 3N 87 16W
Boonville, *Mo., U.S.A.* **156 F4** 38 58N 92 44W
Boonville, *U.S.A.* **151 C9** 43 29N 75 20W
Boorabbin Nat. Park △, *Australia* **125 F4** 31 30 S 129 57 E
Boorindal, *Australia* .... **127 E4** 30 22 S 146 11 E
Boorowa, *Australia* .... **129 C8** 34 28 S 148 44 E
Boort, *Australia* .... **128 D5** 36 7 S 143 46 E
Boosaaso = Bosaso, *Somali Rep.* **120 B3** 11 12N 49 18 E
Boothia, Gulf of, *Canada* **139 A11** 71 0N 90 0W
Boothia Pen., *Canada* **138 A10** 71 0N 94 0W
Bootle, *U.K.* **20 D4** 53 28N 3 1W
Booué, *Gabon* .... **114 C2** 0 5 S 11 55 E
Bopako, *Dem. Rep. of the Congo* **114 B4** 1 53N 21 13 E

Boppard, *Germany* .... **31 E3** 50 13N 7 35 E
Boquerón □, *Paraguay* .... **173 E5** 23 0 S 60 0W
Boquete, *Panama* **164 E3** 8 46N 82 27W
Boquilla, Presa de la, *Mexico* **162 B3** 27 40N 105 30W
Boquillas del Carmen, *Mexico* **162 B4** 29 17N 102 53W
Bor, *Czech Rep.* .... **34 B5** 49 41N 12 45 E
Bor, *Russia* .... **56 C7** 56 28N 43 59 E
Bor, *Serbia, Yug.* .... **50 B6** 44 5N 22 7 E
Bôr, *Sudan* .... **107 F3** 6 10N 31 40 E
Bor, *Sweden* .... **17 G8** 57 9N 14 10 E
Bor, *Turkey* .... **100 D6** 37 54N 34 32 E
Bor Döbö, *Kyrgyzstan* .... **65 D6** 39 31N 73 16 E
Bor Mashash, *Israel* .... **108 D3** 31 7N 34 50 E
Borah Peak, *U.S.A.* **158 D7** 44 8N 113 47W
Boralday, *Kazakhstan* .... **65 B8** 43 20N 76 51 E
Borama, *Somali Rep.* .... **120 C2** 9 55N 43 7 E
Borang, *Sudan* .... **107 G3** 4 50N 30 59 E
Borangapara, *India* .... **90 C3** 25 14N 90 14 E
Borås, *Sweden* .... **17 G6** 57 43N 12 56 E
Borāzjān, *Iran* .... **97 D6** 29 22N 51 10 E
Borba, *Brazil* .... **169 D6** 4 12 S 59 34W
Borba, *Portugal* **43 G3** 38 50N 7 26W
Borbon, *Phil.* .... **81 F5** 10 50N 124 2 E
Borborema, Planalto da, *Brazil* **170 C4** 7 0 S 37 0W
Borcea, *Romania* .... **53 F12** 44 20N 27 45 E
Borçka, *Turkey* .... **101 B9** 41 25N 41 41 E
Bord Khûn-e Now, *Iran* .... **97 D6** 28 3N 51 28 E
Borda, C., *Australia* .... **128 C2** 35 45 S 136 34 E
Bordeaux, *France* **28 D3** 44 50N 0 36W
Bordeaux ✈ (BOD), *France* .... **125 F2** 34 3 S 118 12 E
Borden, *Australia* .... **141 C7** 34 5N 118 12 E
Borden I., *Canada* **6 B2** 78 30N 111 30W
Borden Pen., *Canada* **139 A11** 73 0N 83 0W
Borden Springs, *U.S.A.* **152 B4** 33 56N 85 28W
Border Ranges Nat. Park △,
Australia .... **127 A5** 28 24 S 152 56 E
Borders = Scottish Borders □, *U.K.* **22 F6** 55 35N 2 50W
Bordertown, *Australia* .... **128 D4** 36 19 S 140 45 E
Borðeyri, *Iceland* **11 B5** 65 12N 21 6W
Bordighera, *Italy* .... **44 E4** 43 46N 7 39 E
Bordj bou Arreridj, *Algeria* .... **111 A5** 36 4N 4 45 E
Bordj Bourguiba, *Tunisia* .... **108 B2** 32 12N 10 2 E
Bordj Fly Ste. Marie, *Algeria* **110 C4** 27 19N 2 32W
Bordj-in-Eker, *Algeria* .... **111 D6** 24 9N 5 3 E
Bordj Menaïel, *Algeria* .... **111 A5** 36 46N 3 43 E
Bordj Messouda, *Algeria* .... **111 B7** 30 12N 9 25 E
Bordj Nili, *Algeria* .... **111 B5** 33 28N 3 2 E
Bordj Omar Driss, *Algeria* .... **111 C6** 28 10N 6 40 E
Bordj Sif Fatima, *Algeria* .... **111 B6** 31 6N 8 41 E
Bordj Tarat, *Algeria* .... **111 C6** 25 55N 9 3 E
Borduttighat, *India* .... **90 B4** 26 57N 93 58 E
Bore, *Ethiopia* .... **107 G4** 4 39N 37 39 E
Borehamwood, *U.K.* **21 F7** 51 40N 0 15W
Borek Wielkopolski, *Poland* .... **55 G4** 51 54N 17 11 E
Borensberg, *Sweden* .... **17 F9** 58 34N 15 17 E
Borgå = Porvoo, *Finland* .... **15 F21** 60 24N 25 40 E
Borgampad, *India* .... **94 F5** 17 39N 80 52 E
Borgarfjarðarsýsla □, *Iceland* **11 C5** 64 30N 21 30W
Borgarfjörður, *Borgarfjarðarsýsla,
Iceland* **11 C4** 64 30N 22 0W
Borgarfjörður, *Norður-Múlasýsla,
Iceland* **14 D7** 65 31N 13 49W
Borgarnes, *Iceland* **11 C5** 64 32N 21 55W
Børgefjellet, *Norway* .... **14 D15** 65 20N 13 45 E
Borger, *Neths.* .... **24 B6** 52 54N 6 44 E
Borger, *U.S.A.* **155 H4** 35 39N 101 24W
Borgholm, *Sweden* .... **17 H10** 56 52N 16 39 E
Borgia, *Italy* .... **47 D9** 38 49N 16 30 E
Borgo San Dalmazzo, *Italy* .... **44 D4** 44 20N 7 30 E
Borgo San Lorenzo, *Italy* .... **45 E8** 43 57N 11 23 E
Borgo Val di Taro, *Italy* .... **44 D6** 44 29N 9 46 E
Borgo Valsugana, *Italy* .... **45 B8** 46 3N 11 27 E
Borgomanero, *Italy* .... **44 C5** 45 42N 8 28 E
Borgorose, *Italy* .... **45 F10** 42 11N 13 13 E
Borgosésia, *Italy* .... **44 C5** 45 43N 8 16 E
Borgund, *Norway* .... **18 C4** 61 3N 7 48 E
Borhoyn Tal, *Mongolia* .... **74 C6** 43 50N 111 58 E
Bori, *Nigeria* .... **113 E6** 4 42N 7 21 E
Borigumma, *India* .... **94 E6** 19 3N 82 33 E
Borikhane, *Laos* .... **86 C4** 18 33N 103 43 E
Borisoglebsk, *Russia* .... **60 E6** 51 27N 42 5 E
Borisov = Barysaw, *Belarus* .... **58 E5** 54 17N 28 28 E
Borisovka, *Russia* .... **59 G9** 50 36N 36 1 E
Borja, *Peru* .... **168 D2** 4 27 S 77 40W
Borja, *Spain* **40 D3** 41 48N 1 34W
Borjas Blancas = Les Borges
Blanques, *Spain* .... **40 D5** 41 31N 0 52 E
Borjomi, *Georgia* .... **61 K6** 41 48N 43 28 E
Børkop, *Denmark* .... **17 J3** 55 39N 9 39 E
Borkou, *Chad* .... **109 E3** 18 15N 18 50 E
Borkum, *Germany* .... **30 B2** 53 34N 6 40 E
Borlänge, *Sweden* .... **16 D9** 60 29N 15 26 E
Borley, C., *Antarctica* .... **7 C5** 66 15 S 52 30 E
Borlu, *Turkey* .... **49 C10** 38 44N 28 27 E
Bormida →, *Italy* .... **44 D5** 44 23N 8 13 E
Bórmio, *Italy* .... **44 B7** 46 28N 10 22 E
Borna, *Germany* .... **30 D8** 51 7N 12 29 E
Borne Sulinowo, *Poland* .... **54 E3** 53 32N 16 36 E
Borneo, E. Indies .... **85 B4** 1 0N 115 0 E
Bornholm, *Denmark* .... **17 J8** 55 10N 15 0 E
Bornholms Amtskommune □,
Denmark .... **17 J8** 55 5N 15 0 E
Bornholmsgattet, *Europe* .... **17 J8** 55 15N 14 20 E
Borno □, *Nigeria* .... **33 E10** 45 56N 10 12 E
Borno □, *Nigeria* .... **113 C7** 11 30N 13 0 E
Bornos, *Spain* **43 J5** 36 48N 5 42W
Bornova, *Turkey* .... **49 C9** 38 27N 27 14 E
Bornu Yassa, *Nigeria* .... **113 C7** 12 14N 12 25 E
Boro →, *Sudan* .... **107 F2** 8 52N 26 11 E
Borobudur, *Indonesia* .... **85 D4** 7 36 S 110 13 E
Borodino, *Russia* .... **58 E8** 55 31N 35 40 E
Borogontsy, *Russia* .... **67 C14** 62 42N 131 8 E
Boromo, *Burkina Faso* **112 C4** 11 45N 2 58W
Boron, *U.S.A.* **161 L9** 35 0N 117 39W
Boronga Is., *Burma* .... **90 F4** 19 58N 93 6 E
Borongan, *Phil.* .... **81 F5** 11 37N 125 26 E
Borotangba Mts., *C.A.R.* .... **107 F2** 6 30N 25 0 E
Borotou, *Ivory C.* **112 D3** 8 46N 7 30W
Borovan, *Bulgaria* .... **50 C7** 43 27N 23 45 E
Borovichi, *Russia* .... **58 C7** 58 25N 33 55 E
Borovsk, *Bereznik, Russia* .... **64 B6** 59 43N 56 40 E
Borovsk, *Moskva, Russia* .... **58 E9** 55 12N 36 24 E
Borrby, *Sweden* .... **17 J8** 55 27N 14 10 E
Borrego Springs, *U.S.A.* **161 M10** 33 15N 116 23W
Borriol, *Spain* **40 E4** 40 4N 0 4W
Borroloola, *Australia* .... **126 B2** 16 4 S 136 17 E
Borşa, *Cluj, Romania* .... **53 D8** 46 56N 23 40 E
Borşa, *Maramureş, Romania* **53 C9** 47 41N 24 50 E
Borsad, *India* .... **92 H5** 22 25N 72 54 E
Borsec, *Romania* .... **53 D10** 46 57N 25 34 E
Borsod-Abaúj-Zemplén □, *Hungary* **54 C5** 48 20N 21 0 E
Bort-les-Orgues, *France* .... **28 C6** 45 24N 2 29 E
Bort, *U.K.* **21 E3** 52 29N 4 2W
Börtnan, *Sweden* .... **16 B7** 62 45N 13 50 E
Börüjerd, *Iran* .... **97 C6** 33 55N 48 50 E
Boryslav, *Ukraine* .... **59 H2** 49 18N 23 28 E
Boryspil, *Ukraine* .... **59 F6** 50 21N 30 59 E
Borzhomi = Borjomi, *Georgia* **61 K6** 41 48N 43 28 E
Borzna, *Ukraine* .... **59 F7** 51 18N 32 26 E
Borzya, *Russia* .... **67 D12** 50 24N 116 31 E
Bosa, *Italy* .... **46 B1** 40 18N 8 30 E
Bosa Monene, *Dem. Rep. of*
the Congo .... **114 C4** 1 16 S 23 40 E

Bosaga, *Turkmenistan* .... **65 E2** 37 33N 65 41 E
Bosambi, *Dem. Rep. of the Congo* **114 B4** 2 24N 22 39 E
Bosanska Dubica, *Bos.-H.* .... **45 C13** 45 10N 16 50 E
Bosanska Gradiška, *Bos.-H.* **52 E2** 45 10N 17 15 E
Bosanska Kostajnica, *Bos.-H.* **45 C13** 45 11N 16 33 E
Bosanska Krupa, *Bos.-H.* .... **45 D13** 44 53N 16 10 E
Bosanski Brod, *Bos.-H.* .... **52 E2** 45 10N 18 0 E
Bosanski Novi, *Bos.-H.* .... **45 C13** 45 2N 16 22 E
Bosanski Petrovac, *Bos.-H.* **45 D13** 44 35N 16 21 E
Bosanski Šamac, *Bos.-H.* .... **52 E3** 45 3N 18 29 E
Bosansko Grahovo, *Bos.-H.* **45 D13** 44 12N 16 26 E
Bosaso, *Somali Rep.* .... **120 B3** 11 12N 49 18 E
Bosavi, Mt., *Papua N. G.* .... **124 A4** 6 30 S 142 49 E
Boscastle, *U.K.* **21 G3** 50 41N 4 42W
Boscobel, *U.S.A.* **156 A6** 43 8N 90 42W
Boscobelle, *Barbados* .... **165 g** 13 16N 59 34W
Bose, *China* .... **76 F6** 23 53N 106 35 E
Boseki, *Dem. Rep. of the Congo* **114 C3** 2 34 S 19 38 E
Boshan, *China* .... **75 F9** 36 28N 117 49 E
Boshof, S. Africa .... **116 D4** 28 31 S 25 13 E
Boshrūyeh, *Iran* .... **97 C8** 33 50N 57 30 E
Bosilegrad, *Serbia, Yug.* .... **50 D6** 42 30N 22 27 E
Boskovice, *Czech Rep.* .... **35 B9** 49 29N 16 40 E
Bosna →, *Bos.-H.* .... **52 E3** 45 4N 18 29 E
Bosna i Hercegovina = Bosnia-
Herzegovina ■, *Europe* .... **52 G2** 44 0N 18 0 E
Bosnia-Herzegovina ■, *Europe* **52 G2** 44 0N 18 0 E
Bosnik, *Indonesia* .... **83 B5** 1 5 S 136 10 E
Bōsō-Hantō, *Japan* .... **73 B12** 35 20N 140 20 E
Bosobolo, *Dem. Rep. of the Congo* **114 B3** 4 15N 19 50 E
Bosque Farms, *U.S.A.* **159 J10** 34 53N 106 40W
Bossangoa, *C.A.R.* .... **114 A3** 6 35N 17 30 E
Bossé Bangou, *Niger* .... **113 C5** 13 20N 1 18 E
Bossembélé, *C.A.R.* .... **114 A3** 5 25N 17 40 E
Bossentélé, *C.A.R.* .... **114 A3** 5 41N 16 38 E
Bossier City, *U.S.A.* **155 J8** 32 31N 93 44W
Bosso, *Niger* .... **113 C7** 13 43N 13 19 E
Bosso, Dallol →, *Niger* .... **113 C5** 12 25N 2 50 E
Bostan, *Pakistan* .... **92 D2** 30 26N 67 2 E
Bosten Hu, *China* .... **68 B3** 41 55N 87 40 E
Boston, *U.K.* **20 E7** 52 59N 0 2W
Boston, *Ga., U.S.A.* **152 E6** 30 47N 83 47W
Boston, *Mass., U.S.A.* **151 D13** 42 22N 71 4W
Boston Bar, *Canada* **142 D4** 49 52N 121 30W
Boston Mts., *U.S.A.* **155 H8** 35 42N 93 15W
Bostwick, *U.S.A.* **152 F8** 29 46N 81 38W
Bosut →, *Croatia* .... **52 E3** 45 20N 18 45 E
Boswell, *Canada* **142 D5** 49 28N 116 45W
Boswell, *Ind., U.S.A.* **157 D9** 40 31N 87 23W
Boswell, *Pa., U.S.A.* **150 F5** 40 10N 79 2W
Bosworth, *U.S.A.* **156 E3** 39 28N 93 20W
Botad, *India* .... **92 H4** 22 15N 71 40 E
Botan →, *Turkey* .... **101 D10** 37 57N 42 1 E
Botene, *Laos* .... **86 D3** 17 35N 101 12 E
Botera, *Angola* .... **115 E2** 11 37 S 14 16 E
Botev, *Bulgaria* .... **50 D8** 42 44N 24 55 E
Botevgrad, *Bulgaria* .... **50 D7** 42 55N 23 47 E
Bothaville, S. Africa .... **116 D4** 27 23 S 26 34 E
Bothnia, G. of, *Europe* .... **14 E19** 63 0N 20 15 E
Bothwell, *Australia* .... **127 D4** 42 20 S 147 1 E
Bothwell, *Canada* **150 D3** 42 38N 81 52W
Boticas, *Portugal* **42 D3** 41 41N 7 40W
Botletle →, *Botswana* .... **116 C3** 20 10 S 23 15 E
Botlikh, *Russia* .... **61 J8** 42 39N 46 11 E
Botna →, *Moldova* .... **53 D14** 46 45N 29 34 E
Botola, *Dem. Rep. of the Congo* **114 C3** 1 17 S 18 13 E
Botolan, *Phil.* .... **80 D3** 15 17N 120 1 E
Botoroaga, *Romania* .... **53 F10** 44 8N 25 32 E
Botoşani, *Romania* .... **53 C11** 47 42N 26 41 E
Botoşani □, *Romania* .... **53 C11** 47 50N 26 50 E
Botou, *Burkina Faso* .... **113 C5** 12 40N 2 3 E
Botricello, *Italy* .... **47 D9** 38 56N 16 51 E
Botro, *Ivory C.* **112 D3** 7 51N 5 19W
Botswana ■, *Africa* .... **116 C3** 22 0 S 24 0 E
Bottineau, *U.S.A.* **154 A4** 48 50N 100 27W
Bottnaryd, *Sweden* .... **17 G7** 57 47N 13 50 E
Bottopassi, *Suriname* **169 C6** 4 14N 55 27W
Bottrop, *Germany* .... **24 C6** 51 31N 6 58 E
Botucatu, *Brazil* .... **175 A6** 22 55 S 48 30W
Botwood, *Canada* **141 C8** 49 6N 55 23W
Bou Alam, *Algeria* **111 C4** 27 11N 0 4W
Bou Ali, *Algeria* **111 C4** 27 11N 0 4W
Bou Guema, *Algeria* .... **111 C5** 28 49N 0 19 E
Bou Ismaïl, *Algeria* .... **111 A5** 36 38N 2 42 E
Bou Izakarn, *Morocco* **110 C3** 29 12N 9 46W
Boû Lanouâr, *Mauritania* **110 D1** 21 12N 16 34W
Bou Rjeïmât, *Mauritania* **112 B1** 19 4N 15 3W
Bou Saâda, *Algeria* .... **111 A5** 35 11N 4 9 E
Bou Salem, *Tunisia* .... **108 A1** 36 45N 9 2 E
Bouaflé, *Ivory C.* **112 D3** 7 1N 5 47W
Bouaké, *Ivory C.* **112 D3** 7 40N 5 2W
Bouanga, *Congo* .... **114 C2** 2 7 S 16 8 E
Bouar, *C.A.R.* .... **114 A3** 6 0N 15 40 E
Bouârfa, *Morocco* .... **111 B4** 32 32N 1 58 E
Bouba Ndjida, Parc Nat. de △,
Cameroon .... **114 A2** 8 50N 14 45 E
Boubout, *Algeria* **110 C4** 27 26N 4 30W
Bouca, *C.A.R.* .... **114 A3** 6 45N 18 25 E
Boucaut B., *Australia* .... **126 A1** 12 0 S 134 25 E
Bouches-du-Rhône □, *France* **29 E9** 43 37N 5 2 E
Boucle de Baoulé, Parc Nat. de la △,
Mali **112 C3** 13 53N 9 0W
Boucles de la Seine Normande, Parc
Naturel Régional de △, *France* **26 C7** 49 32N 0 35 E
Bouctouche, *Canada* **141 C7** 46 30N 64 45W
Bouda, *Algeria* **111 C4** 27 50N 0 27W
Boudenib, *Morocco* **110 B4** 31 59N 3 31W
Boudry, *Switz.* .... **32 C3** 46 57N 6 50 E
Boufarik, *Algeria* .... **111 A5** 36 34N 2 58 E
Bougainville, C., *Australia* **124 B4** 13 57 S 126 4 E
Bougainville I., *Papua N. G.* **133 L8** 6 0 S 155 0 E
Bougainville Reef, *Australia* **126 B4** 15 30 S 147 5 E
Bougainville Str., *Solomon Is.* **133 L9** 6 40 S 156 10 E
Bougaroun, C., *Algeria* .... **111 A6** 37 6N 6 30 E
Bougie = Bejaïa, *Algeria* .... **111 A6** 36 42N 5 2 E
Bougouni, *Mali* **112 C3** 11 30N 7 20W
Bouillon, *Belgium* .... **24 E5** 49 44N 5 3 E
Bouïra, *Algeria* .... **111 A5** 36 20N 3 59 E
Boukombé, *Benin* **113 C5** 11 3N 8 21W
Boulal, *Mali* **112 B3** 15 8N 8 21W
Boulazac, *France* .... **28 C4** 45 10N 0 47 E
Boulder, *Colo., U.S.A.* **154 E2** 40 1N 105 17W
Boulder, *Mont., U.S.A.* **158 C7** 46 14N 112 7W
Boulder City, *U.S.A.* **161 K12** 35 59N 114 50W
Boulder Creek, *U.S.A.* **160 H4** 37 7N 122 7W
Boulder Dam = Hoover Dam, *U.S.A.* **161 K12** 36 1N 114 44W
Boulemane, *Gabon* .... **114 C2** 1 26 S 12 0 E
Bouli, *Mauritania* **112 B2** 15 17N 12 18W
Boulia, *Australia* .... **126 C2** 22 52 S 139 51 E
Bouligny, *France* .... **27 C12** 49 17N 5 45 E
Boulogne →, *France* **26 E5** 47 12N 1 47W
Boulogne-sur-Gesse, *France* **29 E4** 43 18N 0 38 E
Boulogne-sur-Mer, *France* .... **27 B8** 50 42N 1 36 E
Bouloire, *France* .... **26 E7** 47 59N 0 33 E
Boulou →, *C.A.R.* .... **114 A4** 6 45N 24 16 E
Boulouli, *Mali* **112 B3** 15 30N 9 25W
Bouloupari, *N. Cal.* .... **133 U20** 21 52 S 166 4 E
Bouloupesse, *Congo* .... **114 C2** 1 58 S 12 40 E

Boulsa, *Burkina Faso* **113 C4** 12 39N 0 34W
Boultoum, *Niger* .... **113 C7** 14 45N 10 25 E
Bouma Nat. Heritage Park △, *Fiji* **133 A2** 16 50 S 179 52 E
Boumalne, *Morocco* **110 B3** 31 25N 6 0W
Boumba →, *Cameroon* .... **114 B2** 2 2N 15 12 E
Boumbé II →, *C.A.R.* .... **114 B3** 4 4N 15 23 E
Boûmdeïd, *Mauritania* **112 B2** 17 25N 9 50W
Boun Neua, *Laos* .... **86 B3** 21 38N 101 54 E
Boun Tai, *Laos* .... **86 B3** 21 23N 101 58 E
Bouna, *Ivory C.* **112 D4** 9 10N 3 0W
Boundary, *U.S.A.* **144 D12** 64 4N 141 6W
Boundary Peak, *U.S.A.* **160 H8** 37 51N 118 21W
Boundji, *Gabon* .... **114 C2** 1 0N 11 51 E
Boundiali, *Ivory C.* **112 D3** 9 30N 6 20W
Boungou →, *C.A.R.* .... **114 A4** 8 21 S 28 5 E
Bountiful, *U.S.A.* **158 F8** 40 53N 111 53W
Bounty Is., *Pac. Oc.* .... **134 M9** 48 0 S 178 30 E
Boura, *Mali* **112 C4** 12 25N 4 33W
Bourail, N. Cal. .... **133 U19** 21 34 S 165 30 E
Bourbeuse →, *U.S.A.* **156 F6** 38 24N 90 53W
Bourbon, *U.S.A.* **157 C10** 41 18N 86 7W
Bourbon-Lancy, *France* .... **27 F10** 46 37N 3 45 E
Bourbon-l'Archambault, *France* **27 F10** 46 36N 3 4 E
Bourbonnais, *France* .... **27 F10** 46 28N 3 0 E
Bourbonne-les-Bains, *France* **27 E12** 47 54N 5 45 E
Bourbourg, *France* .... **27 B9** 50 56N 2 12 E
Bourdel L., *Canada* **140 A5** 56 43N 74 10W
Bourem, *Mali* **113 B4** 17 0N 0 24W
Bourg, *France* **28 C3** 45 3N 0 34W
Bourg-Argental, *France* .... **29 C8** 45 18N 4 32 E
Bourg-de-Péage, *France* .... **29 C9** 45 2N 5 3 E
Bourg-en-Bresse, *France* .... **27 F12** 46 13N 5 12 E
Bourg-Lastic, *France* .... **28 C6** 45 39N 2 35 E
Bourg-Madame, *France* .... **28 F5** 42 26N 1 55 E
Bourg-St-Andéol, *France* .... **29 D8** 44 23N 4 39 E
Bourg-St-Maurice, *France* .... **29 C10** 45 35N 6 46 E
Bourg-St. Pierre, *Switz.* .... **32 E4** 45 57N 7 12 E
Bourganeuf, *France* .... **28 C5** 45 57N 1 45 E
Bourges, *France* .... **27 E9** 47 9N 2 25 E
Bourget, *Canada* **151 A9** 45 26N 75 9W
Bourget, Lac du, *France* .... **29 C9** 45 44N 5 52 E
Bourgneuf, B. de, *France* **26 E4** 47 3N 2 10W
Bourgneuf-en-Retz, *France* **26 E5** 47 2N 1 58W
Bourgogne, *France* .... **27 F11** 47 0N 4 50 E
Bourgoin-Jallieu, *France* .... **29 C9** 45 36N 5 17 E
Bourgueil, *France* .... **26 E7** 47 17N 0 10 E
Bourke, *Australia* .... **127 E4** 30 8 S 145 55 E
Bourne, *U.K.* **20 E7** 52 47N 0 22W
Bournemouth, *U.K.* **21 G6** 50 43N 1 52W
Bournemouth □, *U.K.* **21 G6** 50 43N 1 52W
Bouroum, *Burkina Faso* **113 C4** 13 37N 0 39W
Bouse, *U.S.A.* **161 M13** 33 56N 114 0W
Boussac, *France* .... **27 F9** 46 22N 2 13 E
Boussé, *Burkina Faso* .... **113 C4** 12 39N 1 53 E
Bousso, *Chad* .... **109 F13** 10 34N 16 52 E
Boussouma, *Burkina Faso* **113 C4** 12 52N 1 13W
Boutilimit, *Mauritania* **112 B2** 17 45N 14 40W
Boutonne →, *France* **28 C3** 45 54N 0 46W
Bouvet I. = Bouvetøya, *Antarctica* **8 M12** 54 26 S 3 24 E
Bouvignes, *Antarctica* .... **8 M12** 54 26 S 3 24 E
Bouxwiller, *France* .... **27 D14** 48 49N 7 27 E
Bouza, *Niger* .... **113 C6** 14 29N 6 2 E
Bouznika, *Morocco* **110 B3** 33 46N 7 6W
Bouzonville, *France* .... **27 C13** 49 17N 6 32 E
Bovalino Marina, *Italy* .... **47 D9** 38 10N 16 10 E
Bovec, *Slovenia* .... **45 B10** 46 20N 13 33 E
Boven Kapuas, Pegunungan,
Malaysia .... **85 B4** 1 25N 113 15 E
Bøverdal, *Norway* .... **18 C5** 61 44N 8 20 E
Bøverfjorden, *Norway* .... **18 A5** 63 1N 8 32 E
Bovill, *U.S.A.* **158 C5** 46 51N 116 24W
Bovino, *Italy* .... **47 A8** 41 15N 15 20 E
Bovril, *Argentina* .... **174 C4** 31 21 S 59 26W
Bow →, *Canada* **142 C6** 49 57N 111 41W
Bow Island, *Canada* **142 D6** 49 50N 111 23W
Bowbells, *U.S.A.* **154 A3** 48 48N 102 15W
Bowdle, *U.S.A.* **154 C5** 45 27N 99 39W
Bowdon, *U.S.A.* **152 B4** 33 32N 85 15W
Bowdon Junction, *U.S.A.* **152 B4** 33 40N 85 10W
Bowelling, *Australia* .... **125 F2** 33 25 S 116 30 E
Bowen, *Argentina* .... **174 D2** 35 0 S 67 31W
Bowen, *Australia* .... **126 J6** 20 0 S 148 16 E
Bowen, Mts., *Australia* .... **129 D7** 37 0 S 147 50 E
Bowie, *Ariz., U.S.A.* **159 K9** 32 19N 109 29W
Bowie, *Tex., U.S.A.* **155 J6** 33 34N 97 51W
Bowkān, *Iran* .... **101 D12** 36 31N 46 12 E
Bowland, Forest of, *U.K.* **20 D5** 54 0N 2 30W
Bowling Green, *Fla., U.S.A.* **153 M5** 27 38N 81 50W
Bowling Green, *Ky., U.S.A.* **148 G2** 36 59N 86 27W
Bowling Green, *Mo., U.S.A.* **156 E5** 39 21N 91 12W
Bowling Green, *Ohio, U.S.A.* **157 C13** 41 23N 83 39W
Bowling Green, C., *Australia* **126 B4** 19 19 S 147 25 E
Bowling Green Bay Nat. Park △,
Australia .... **126 B4** 19 26 S 146 57 E
Bowman, *N. Dak., U.S.A.* **154 B3** 46 11N 103 24W
Bowman, S. C., *U.S.A.* **152 B9** 33 21N 80 41W
Bowman I., *Antarctica* .... **7 C8** 65 0 S 104 0 E
Bowmanville, *Canada* **150 C6** 43 55N 78 41W
Bowmore, *U.K.* **22 F2** 55 45N 6 17W
Bowral, *Australia* .... **129 C9** 34 26 S 150 27 E
Bowraville, *Australia* .... **129 E5** 30 37 S 152 52 E
Bowron →, *Canada* **142 C4** 54 3N 121 50W
Bowron Lake Prov. Park △, *Canada* **142 B3** 53 10N 121 5W
Bowsman, *Canada* **143 C8** 52 14N 101 12W
Bowutu Mts., *Papua N. G.* **132 D4** 7 45 S 147 10 E
Bowwood, *Zambia* .... **119 F12** 17 5 S 26 20 E
Box Cr. →, *Australia* .... **127 E3** 34 10 S 143 50 E
Boxholm, *Sweden* .... **17 F9** 58 12N 15 3 E
Boxmeer, *Neths.* .... **24 C5** 51 38N 5 56 E
Boxtel, *Neths.* .... **24 C5** 51 36N 5 20 E
Boyabat, *Turkey* .... **100 B6** 41 28N 34 47 E
Boyaca □, *Colombia* **168 B3** 5 30N 73 20W
Boyalıca, *Turkey* .... **51 F13** 40 29N 29 33 E
Boyang, *China* .... **77 C11** 29 0N 116 38 E
Boyasanga, *Dem. Rep. of the Congo* **155 K8** 31 23N 92 40W
Boyce, *U.S.A.* **152 E6** 30 11N 83 37W
Boyd, *U.S.A.* **154 C5** 45 27N 99 39W
Boyd L., *Canada* **140 B4** 52 46N 76 42W
Boyenge, *Dem. Rep. of the Congo* **114 C3** 0 33 S 21 2 E
Boyer, C., N. Cal. .... **133 U22** 21 37 S 168 6 E
Boyle, *Canada* **142 C6** 54 35N 112 49W
Boyle, *Ireland* **23 C3** 53 59N 8 18W
Boyne →, *Ireland* **23 C5** 53 43N 6 15W
Boyne City, *U.S.A.* **148 C3** 45 13N 85 1W
Boyni Qara, *Afghan.* .... **91 A2** 36 20N 67 0 E
Boynitsa, *Bulgaria* .... **50 C6** 43 58N 22 32 E
Boynton Beach, *U.S.A.* **153 J9** 26 32N 80 4W
Boyolali, *Indonesia* .... **85 D4** 7 32 S 110 35 E
Boyoma, Chutes, *Dem. Rep. of*
the Congo .... **118 B2** 0 35N 25 23 E
Boysen Reservoir, *U.S.A.* **158 E9** 43 25N 108 11W
Boyup Brook, *Australia* .... **125 F2** 33 50 S 116 23 E
Boz Burun, *Turkey* .... **51 F12** 40 32N 28 46 E
Boz Dağ, *Turkey* .... **49 D11** 37 18N 29 11 E
Boz Dağları, *Turkey* .... **49 C10** 38 20N 28 0 E
Bozan, *Turkey* .... **51 E13** 39 37N 29 7 E
Bozburun, *Turkey* .... **49 E11** 36 49N 28 8 E
Bozcaada, *Turkey* .... **100 C2** 39 49N 26 3 E
Bozdoğan, *Turkey* .... **49 D10** 37 40N 28 17 E

Boze, *Papua N. G.* .... **132 E2**   9 3 S 143 3 E
Bozeman, *U.S.A.* **158 D8** 45 41N 111 2W
Bozen = Bolzano, *Italy* ..... **45 B8** 46 31N 11 22 E
Bozene, *Dem. Rep. of the Congo* **114 B3** 2 56N 19 12 E
Bozhou, *China* .... **74 H8** 33 55N 115 41 E
Bozkır, *Turkey* .... **100 D5** 37 11N 32 14 E
Bozkir, *Turkey* .... **49 D11** 37 50N 29 37 E
Bozkurt, *Turkey* .... **28 D6** 44 28N   2 43 E
Bozoum, *C.A.R.* .... **114 A3** 6 25N 16 35 E
Bozova, *Antalya, Turkey* .... **49 D12** 37 13N 30 18 E
Bozova, *Sanlıurfa, Turkey* .. **101 D8** 37 21N 38 32 E
Bozoviçi, *Romania* .... **52 F7** 44 56N 22 2 E
Bozüyük, *Turkey* .... **49 B12** 39 54N 30 3 E
Bozyazı, *Turkey* .... **44 D4** 44 42N   7 51 E
Bra, *Italy* .... **17 G9** 57 4N 15 3 E
Braås, *Sweden* .... **24 D4** 50 46N   4 30 E
Brabant □, *Belgium* **143 B8** 55 58N 103 43W
Brabant L., *Canada* .... **17 H4** 56 9N 10 7 E
Brabrand, *Denmark* .... **45 E13** 43 20N 16 40 E
Brač, *Croatia* **22 D2** 57 20N   6 30W
Bracadale, L., *U.K.* .... **45 F9** 42 6N 12 10 E
Bracciano, *Italy* .... **45 F9** 42 7N 12 14 E
Bracciano, L. di, *Italy* **140 C4** 45 2N 79 19W
Bracebridge, *Canada* .... **108 C2** 27 31N 14 20 E
Brach, *Libya* .... **26 E8** 47 30N   1 30 E
Bracieux, *France* .... **16 B9** 62 45N 15 26 E
Bräcke, *Sweden* **155 L4** 29 19N 100 25W
Brackettville, *U.S.A.* ...... **45 E13** 43 24N 16 40 E
Brački Kanal, *Croatia* **21 F7** 51 25N   0 43W
Bracknell, *U.K.* **21 F7** 51 25N   0 44W
Bracknell Forest □, *U.K.* ... **52 F7** 46 10N 22 50 E
Brad, *Romania* **153 H7** 27 30N 82 34W
Brádano →, *Italy* .... **47 B9** 40 23N 16 51 E
Bradenton, *U.S.A.* **150 B5** 44 7N 79 34W
Bradford, *Canada* **20 D6** 53 47N   1 45W
Bradford, *U.K.* **156 C7** 41 11N 89 39W
Bradford, *Ill., U.S.A.* **157 D12** 40 8N 84 27W
Bradford, *Ohio, U.S.A.* **150 E6** 41 58N 78 38W
Bradford, *Pa., U.S.A.* **151 C12** 43 59N 72 9W
Bradford, *Vt., U.S.A.* **155 J8** 33 6N 93 39W
Bradley, *Ark., U.S.A.* **160 K6** 35 52N 120 48W
Bradley, *Calif., U.S.A.* **153 H8** 27 48N 81 59W
Bradley, *Fla., U.S.A.* **157 C9** 41 9N 87 52W
Bradley, *Ill., U.S.A.* ...... **119 E3** 17 7 S 31 25 E
Bradley Institute, *Zimbabwe* **157 C13** 41 20N 83 36W
Brádner, *Italy* **155 K5** 31 9N 99 20W
Brady, *U.S.A.* .... **17 J3** 55 58N   9 37 E
Brædstrup, *Denmark* .... **128 B3** 33 12 S 139 35 E
Braemar, *Australia* **151 A8** 45 28N 76 24W
Braeside, *Canada* **42 D2** 41 35N   8 25W
Braga, *Portugal* **42 D2** 41 30N   8 30W
Braga □, *Portugal* .... **53 G10** 43 46N 25 31 E
Bragadiru, *Romania* .... **174 D3** 35 2 S 60 27W
Bragado, *Argentina* .... **170 B2** 1 0 S 47 2W
Bragança, *Brazil* **42 D4** 41 48N   6 50W
Bragança, *Portugal* **42 D4** 41 50N   6 45W
Bragança □, *Portugal* .... **175 A6** 22 55 S 46 32W
Bragança Paulista, *Brazil* .. **14 D21** 64 40N 24 28 E
Brahestad = Raahe, *Finland* . **90 B6** 27 25N 96 22 E
Brahmakund, *India* .... **90 D3** 23 58N 91 15 E
Brahmanbaria, *Bangla.* ...... **90 M8** 24 2N 88 46 E
Brahmani →, *India* .... **94 E7** 19 15N 84 54 E
Brahmapur, *India* .... **68 D3** 23 40N 90 35 E
Brahmaputra →, *Asia* **20 E3** 52 47N   4 46W
Braich-y-pwll, *U.K.* .... **129 C8** 35 27 S 149 49 E
Braidwood, *Australia* .... **53 E12** 45 19N 27 59 E
Brăila, *Romania* .... **53 E12** 45 5N 27 30 E
Brăila □, *Romania* **154 B7** 46 22N 94 12W
Brainerd, *U.S.A.* .... **21 F8** 51 53N   0 34 E
Braintree, *U.K.* **151 D14** 42 13N 71 0W
Braintree, *U.S.A.* .... **116 D3** 29 35 S 22 55 E
Brak →, *S. Africa* .... **30 B4** 53 20N   8 28 E
Brake, *Germany* .... **30 D5** 51 42N   9 11 E
Brakel, *Germany* .... **17 H9** 56 14N 15 6 E
Bräkne-Hoby, *Sweden* .... **116 C2** 22 28 S 17 3 E
Brakwater, *Namibia* .... **17 F6** 58 34N 12 21 E
Brålanda, *Sweden* .... **31 E6** 50 6N 10 40 E
Bramberg, *Germany* .... **17 J3** 55 31N   9 28 E
Bramdrupdam, *Denmark* .... **94 D4** 20 36N 79 52 E
Bramhapuri, *India* .... **17 J2** 55 28N   8 42 E
Bramming, *Denmark* .... **16 B11** 62 14N 17 40 E
Brämön, *Sweden* **140 D4** 43 45N 79 45W
Brampton, *Canada* **20 C5** 54 57N   2 44W
Brampton, *U.K.* .... **30 C3** 52 24N   7 59 E
Bramsche, *Germany* .... **126 J7** 20 50 S 149 17 E
Bramton I., *Australia* **152 B9** 31 35N 80 49W
Branchville, *U.S.A.* .... **169 D5** 1 20 S 61 50W
Branco →, *Brazil* .... **170 C5** 7 9 S 34 47W
Branco, C., *Brazil* .... **116 B2** 21 10 S 14 33 E
Brandberg, *Namibia* ....

Brandberg Nature Reserve △,
Namibia .... **116 C1** 21 10 S 14 30 E
Brandbu, *Norway* .... **18 D7** 60 26N 10 28 E
Brande, *Denmark* .... **17 J3** 55 57N   9 8 E
Brandenburg = Neubrandenburg,
Germany .... **30 B9** 53 33N 13 15 E
Brandenburg, *Germany* .... **30 C8** 52 25N 12 33 E
Brandenburg □, *Germany* **157 G10** 38 0N 86 10W
Brandfort, *S. Africa* .... **30 C9** 52 50N 12 33 E
Brando, *France* .... **116 D4** 28 40 S 26 30 E
Brandon, *Canada* .... **29 F13** 42 47N   9 27 E
Brandon, *Fla., U.S.A.* **143 D9** 49 50N 99 57W
Brandon, *Vt., U.S.A.* **153 H7** 27 56N 82 17W
Brandon B., *Ireland* **151 C11** 43 48N 73 4W
Brandon Mt., *Ireland* **23 D1** 52 17N 10 8W
Brandsen, *Argentina* **23 D1** 52 15N 10 15W
Brandvlei, *S. Africa* .... **174 D4** 35 10 S 58 15W
Brandýs nad Labem, *Czech Rep.* **116 E3** 30 25 S 20 30 E
Brăneşti, *Romania* .... **34 A7** 50 10N 14 40 E
Branford, *Conn., U.S.A.* .... **53 F11** 44 20N 26 20 E
Branford, *Fla., U.S.A.* **151 E12** 41 17N 72 49W
Braniewo, *Poland* **152 F7** 29 58N 82 56W
Bransfield Str., *Antarctica* **54 D6** 54 25N 19 50 E
Brańsk, *Poland* .... **7 C18** 63 0 S 59 0W
Branson, *U.S.A.* .... **55 F9** 52 45N 22 50 E
Brantford, *Canada* **155 G8** 36 39N 93 13W
Brantley, *U.S.A.* **140 D3** 43 10N 80 15W
Brantôme, *France* **152 D3** 31 35N 86 16W
Branxholme, *Australia* ...... **28 C4** 45 22N   0 39 E
Branxton, *Australia* .... **128 D4** 37 52 S 141 49 E
Branzi, *Italy* .... **129 B9** 32 38 S 151 21 E
Brás, *Brazil* .... **45 B8** 46 1N   9 46 E
Bras d'Or L., *Canada* .... **169 D6** 2 5 S 58 10W
Brasher Falls, *U.S.A.* **141 C7** 45 50N 60 50W
Brasil, Planalto, *Brazil* ... **151 B10** 44 49N 74 47W
Brasil Novo, *Brazil* .... **166 E6** 10 0 S 46 30W
Brasiléia, *Brazil* .... **169 D7** 3 19 S 52 38W
Brasília, *Brazil* .... **172 C4** 11 0 S 68 45W
Brasília, *Distrito Federal, Brazil* **171 E2** 15 47 S 47 55W
Brasília, *Minas Gerais, Brazil* **171 E3** 16 23 S 44 26W
Brasília Legal, *Brazil* ..... **169 D6** 3 49 S 55 36W
Braskereidfoss, *Norway* ..... **18 D8** 60 44N 11 46 E
Braslaw, *Belarus* .... **15 J22** 55 38N 27 0 E
Braslovče, *Slovenia* .... **45 B12** 46 21N 15 3 E
Braşov, *Romania* .... **53 E10** 45 38N 25 35 E
Braşov □, *Romania* .... **53 E10** 45 45N 25 15 E
Brass, *Nigeria* .... **113 E6** 4 35N   6 14 E
Brass →, *Nigeria* .... **113 E6** 4 15N   6 13 E
Brassac-les-Mines, *France* .. **28 C7** 45 24N   3 20 E
Brassaht, *Belgium* .... **24 C4** 51 19N   4 27 E
Brassey, *Banjaran, Malaysia* **85 B5** 5 0N 117 15 E
Brassey Ra., *Australia* ..... **125 E3** 25 8 S 122 15 E
Brasstown Bald, *U.S.A.* **149 H4** 34 53N 83 49W
Brastad, *Sweden* .... **17 F5** 58 23N 11 30 E

Brastavăţu, *Romania* .... **53 G9** 43 55N 24 24 E
Bratan = Morozov, *Bulgaria* . **51 D9** 42 30N 25 10 E
Brateş, *Romania* .... **53 E11** 45 50N 26 4 E
Bratislava, *Slovak Rep.* .... **35 C10** 48 10N 17 7 E
Bratislava M.R. Stefanik ✈ (BTS),
Slovak Rep. .... **35 C10** 48 11N 17 9 E
Bratislavský □, *Slovak Rep.* **35 C10** 48 15N 17 20 E
Bratsigovo, *Bulgaria* .... **51 D8** 42 1N 24 22 E
Bratsk, *Russia* .... **67 D11** 56 10N 101 30 E
Brattleboro, *U.S.A.* **151 D12** 42 51N 72 34W
Brattvåg, *Norway* .... **18 B3** 62 37N   6 25 E
Bratunac, *Bos.-H.* .... **52 F4** 44 13N 19 21 E
Braunau, *Austria* .... **34 C6** 48 15N 13 3 E
Braunsberg = Braniewo, *Poland* **54 D6** 54 25N 19 50 E
Braunschweig, *Germany* ...... **30 C6** 52 15N 10 31 E
Braunton, *U.K.* **21 F3** 51 7N   4 10W
Brava, C. *Verde Is.* .... **9 j** 15 0N 24 40W
Brava, *Somali Rep.* .... **120 D2** 1 20N 44 8 E
Bravicea, *Moldova* .... **53 C13** 47 22N   9 35 E
Bråviken, *Sweden* .... **17 F10** 58 38N 16 32 E
Bravo del Norte, Rio = Grande,
Rio →, *U.S.A.* **155 N6** 25 58N 97 9W
Brawley, *U.S.A.* **161 N11** 32 59N 115 31W
Bray, *Ireland* **23 C5** 53 13N   6 7W
Bray, *Mt., Australia* .... **126 A1** 14 0 S 134 30 E
Bray, Pays de, *France* ...... **25 B4** 49 46N   1 26 E
Bray-sur-Seine, *France* ..... **27 D10** 48 25N   3 14 E
Braymer, *U.S.A.* **156 E3** 39 35N 93 48W
Brazeau →, *Canada* **142 C5** 52 55N 115 14W
Brazil, *U.S.A.* **157 E9** 39 32N 87 8W
Brazil ■, *S. Amer.* .... **167 E5** 12 0 S 50 0W
Brazilian Highlands = Brasil,
Planalto, *Brazil* .... **166 E6** 18 0 S 46 30W
Brazo Sur →, *S. Amer.* ...... **174 B4** 25 21 S 57 42W
Brazos →, *U.S.A.* **155 L7** 28 53N 95 23W
Brazzaville, *Congo* .... **115 C3** 4 9 S 15 12 E
Brčko, *Bos.-H.* .... **52 F3** 44 54N 18 46 E
Brda →, *Poland* .... **55 E5** 53 8N 18 8 E
Brdy, *Czech Rep.* .... **34 B6** 49 43N 13 55 E
Brea, *Peru* .... **172 A1** 4 40 S 81 7W
Breaden, L., *Australia* ..... **125 E4** 25 51 S 125 28 E
Breaksea Sd., *N.Z.* .... **131 F1** 45 35 S 166 35 E
Bream B., *N.Z.* .... **130 B3** 35 56 S 174 28 E
Bream Head, *N.Z.* .... **130 B3** 35 51 S 174 36 E
Bream Tail, *N.Z.* .... **130 C3** 36 3 S 174 36 E
Breas, *Chile* .... **174 B1** 25 29 S 70 24W
Breaza, *Romania* .... **53 E10** 45 11N 25 40 E
Brebes, *Indonesia* .... **85 D3** 6 52 S 109 3 E
Brechin, *Canada* **150 B5** 44 32N 79 10W
Brechin, *U.K.* **22 E6** 56 44N   2 39W
Brecht, *Belgium* .... **24 C4** 51 21N   4 38 E
Breckenridge, *Colo., U.S.A.* **158 G10** 39 29N 106 3W
Breckenridge, *Minn., U.S.A.* **154 B6** 46 16N 96 35W
Breckenridge, *Tex., U.S.A.* . **155 J5** 32 45N 98 54W
Breckland, *U.K.* .... **21 E8** 52 30N   0 40 E
Brecknock, Pen., *Chile* ..... **176 D2** 54 35 S 71 30W
Břeclav, *Czech Rep.* .... **35 C9** 48 46N 16 53 E
Brecon, *U.K.* **21 F4** 51 57N   3 23W
Brecon Beacons, *U.K.* **21 F4** 51 53N   3 26W
Brecon Beacons Nat. Park △, *U.K.* **21 F4** 51 50N   3 30W
Breda, *Neths.* .... **24 C4** 51 35N   4 45 E
Bredardyd, *Australia* .... **17 G7** 57 10N 13 45 E
Bredasdorp, *S. Africa* ...... **116 E3** 34 33 S 20 2 E
Bredbo, *Australia* .... **129 C8** 35 58 S 149 10 E
Bredebro, *Denmark* .... **17 J2** 55 4N   8 50 E
Bredstedt, *Germany* .... **30 A4** 54 37N   8 58 E
Bredy, *Russia* .... **64 E8** 52 26N 60 21 E
Bree, *Belgium* .... **24 C5** 51 8N   5 35 E
Bregalnica →, *Macedonia* .... **50 E6** 41 43N 22 9 E
Bregenz, *Austria* .... **34 D2** 47 30N   9 45 E
Bregenzer Wald, *Austria* .... **33 B9** 47 20N 10 0 E
Bregovo, *Bulgaria* .... **50 B6** 44 9N 22 39 E
Bréhal, *France* **26 D5** 48 53N   1 30W
Bréhat, Î. de, *France* **26 D4** 48 51N   3 0W
Breiðafjörður, *Iceland* **11 B3** 65 15N 23 15W
Breiðdalsvik, *Iceland* **11 C13** 64 44N 14 0W
Breil-sur-Roya, *France* ..... **29 E11** 43 56N   7 31 E
Brein, *Norway* .... **18 C3** 61 44N   6 25 E
Breisach, *Germany* .... **31 G3** 48 1N   7 36 E
Brejinho de Nazaré, *Brazil* . **170 D2** 11 1 S 48 34W
Brejo, *Brazil* .... **170 B3** 3 41 S 42 47W
Brekke, *Norway* .... **18 C2** 61 1N   5 26 E
Brekken, *Norway* .... **18 B8** 62 40N 11 51 E
Brekkestø, *Norway* .... **18 F5** 58 11N   8 42 E
Bremanger, *Norway* .... **18 C1** 61 51N   4 58 E
Bremangerlandet, *Norway* .... **18 C1** 61 51N   5 0 E
Bremen, *Germany* .... **30 B4** 53 4N   8 47 E
Bremen, *Ga., U.S.A.* **152 B4** 33 43N 85 9W
Bremen, *Ind., U.S.A.* **157 C10** 41 27N 86 9W
Bremen □, *Germany* .... **30 B4** 53 4N   8 50 E
Bremer Bay, *Australia* ...... **125 F2** 34 21 S 119 20 E
Bremer I., *Australia* .... **126 A2** 12 5 S 136 45 E
Bremerhaven, *Germany* .... **30 B4** 53 33N   8 36 E
Bremerton, *U.S.A.* **160 C4** 47 34N 122 38W
Bremervörde, *Germany* .... **30 B5** 53 29N   9 8 E
Bremgarten, *Switz.* .... **33 B6** 47 22N   8 20 E
Bremnes, *Norway* .... **18 E2** 59 47N   5 8 E
Bremsnes, *Norway* .... **18 A4** 63 6N   7 40 E
Brenes, *Spain* **43 H5** 37 32N   5 54W
Brenham, *U.S.A.* **155 K6** 30 10N 96 24W
Brenne, *France* .... **28 B5** 46 44N   1 14 E
Brenne, Parc Naturel Régional de △,
France .... **28 B5** 46 40N   1 15 E
Brennerpass, *Austria* .... **34 D4** 47 21N 11 30 E
Brennhaug, *Norway* .... **18 C6** 61 54N   9 21 E
Breno, *Italy* .... **44 C7** 45 57N 10 18 E
Brent, *U.S.A.* **149 J2** 32 56N 87 10W
Brenta →, *Italy* .... **45 C9** 45 11N 12 18 E
Brentwood, *U.K.* .... **21 F8** 51 37N   0 19 E
Brentwood, *Calif., U.S.A.* .. **160 H5** 37 56N 121 42W
Brentwood, *N.Y., U.S.A.* **151 F11** 40 47N 73 15W
Bréscia, *Italy* .... **44 C7** 45 33N 10 15 E
Breskens, *Neths.* .... **24 C3** 51 23N   3 33 E
Breslau = Wrocław, *Poland* .. **55 G4** 51 5N 17 5 E
Bresle →, *France* .... **26 B8** 50 4N   1 22 E
Bressanone, *Italy* .... **45 B8** 46 43N 11 39 E
Bressay, *U.K.* **22 A7** 60 9N   1 6W
Bresse, *France* .... **27 F12** 46 50N   5 10 E
Bressuire, *France* **26 F6** 46 51N   0 30W
Brest, *Belarus* .... **59 F2** 52 10N 23 40 E
Brest, *France* **26 D2** 48 24N   4 31W
Brest-Litovsk = Brest, *Belarus* **59 F2** 52 10N 23 40 E
Bretagne, *France* **26 D3** 48 10N   3 0W
Bretanha, Pta. da, *Azores* .. **9 d3** 37 54N 25 47W
Bretçu, *Romania* .... **53 D11** 46 7N 26 18 E
Bretenoux, *France* .... **28 D5** 44 54N   1 51 E
Breteuil, *Eure, France* ..... **26 D7** 48 50N   0 57 E
Breteuil, *Oise, France* ..... **25 C9** 49 38N   2 18 E
Breton, *Canada* **142 C6** 53 7N 114 28W
Breton, Pertuis, *France* **28 B2** 46 17N   1 25W
Breton Sd., *U.S.A.* **155 L10** 29 35N 89 15W
Brett, C., *N.Z.* .... **130 B5** 35 10 S 174 20 E
Bretten, *Germany* .... **31 F4** 49 2N   8 42 E
Breuil-Cervínia, *Italy* ..... **44 C4** 45 56N   7 38 E
Brevard, *U.S.A.* **149 H4** 35 14N 82 44W
Breves, *Brazil* .... **170 B1** 1 40 S 50 29W
Brevig Mission, *U.S.A.* **144 D6** 65 20N 166 29W
Brevik, *Norway* .... **18 E6** 59 4N   9 42 E
Brewarrina, *Australia* ...... **127 E4** 30 0 S 146 51 E
Brewer, *U.S.A.* **149 C11** 44 48N 68 46W
Brewer, Mt., *U.S.A.* **160 J8** 36 44N 118 28W
Brewerville, *Liberia* **112 D2** 6 24N 10 47W
Brewster, *N.Y., U.S.A.* **151 E11** 41 23N 73 37W
Brewster, *Ohio, U.S.A.* **150 F3** 40 43N 81 36W

Brewster, *Wash., U.S.A.* **158 B4** 48 6N 119 47W
Brewster, Kap = Kangikajik,
Greenland **10 C8** 70 7N 22 0W
Brewton, *U.S.A.* **149 K2** 31 7N 87 4W
Breyten, *S. Africa* .... **117 D5** 26 16 S 30 0 E
Breza, *Bos.-H.* .... **52 F3** 44 1N 18 16 E
Brezhnev = Naberezhnyye Chelny,
Russia .... **60 C11** 55 42N 52 19 E
Brežice, *Slovenia* .... **45 C12** 45 54N 15 35 E
Brézina, *Algeria* .... **111 B5** 33 4N   1 14 E
Březnice, *Czech Rep.* .... **34 B6** 49 32N 13 57 E
Breznik, *Bulgaria* .... **50 D6** 42 44N 22 55 E
Brezno, *Slovak Rep.* .... **35 C12** 48 50N 19 40 E
Brezoi, *Romania* .... **53 E9** 45 21N 24 15 E
Brezovica, *Kosovo, Yug.* .... **50 D5** 42 15N 21 3 E
Brezovo, *Bulgaria* .... **51 D9** 42 21N 25 5 E
Bria, *C.A.R.* .... **114 A4** 6 30N 21 58 E
Briançon, *France* .... **29 D10** 44 54N   6 39 E
Briare, *France* .... **27 E9** 47 38N   2 45 E
Briático, *Italy* .... **47 D9** 38 43N 16 2 E
Bribie I., *Australia* .... **127 D5** 27 0 S 153 10 E
Briceni, *Moldova* .... **53 B12** 48 27N 27 6 E
Bricquebec, *France* **26 C5** 49 28N   1 38W
Bridgefield, *Barbados* ...... **165 g** 13 9 S 59 36W
Bridgehampton, *U.S.A.* **151 F12** 40 56N 72 19W
Bridgend, *U.K.* **21 F4** 51 30N   3 4W
Bridgend □, *U.K.* **21 F4** 51 36N   3 36W
Bridgeport, *Calif., U.S.A.* . **160 G7** 38 15N 119 14W
Bridgeport, *Conn., U.S.A.* .. **151 E11** 41 11N 73 12W
Bridgeport, *Nebr., U.S.A.* .. **154 E3** 41 40N 103 6W
Bridgeport, *Tex., U.S.A.* ... **155 J6** 33 13N 97 45W
Bridger, *U.S.A.* **158 D9** 45 18N 108 55W
Bridgeton, *U.S.A.* **148 F8** 39 26N 75 14W
Bridgetown, *Australia* ...... **125 F2** 33 58 S 116 7 E
Bridgetown, *Barbados* .... **165 g** 13 5N 59 30W
Bridgewater, *Australia* ..... **128 D5** 36 36 S 143 59 E
Bridgewater, *Canada* **141 D6** 44 55N 64 31W
Bridgewater, *Mass., U.S.A.* . **151 E14** 41 59N 70 58W
Bridgewater, *N.Y., U.S.A.* .. **151 D9** 42 53N 75 15W
Bridgewater, C., *Australia* . **128 E4** 38 23 S 141 23 E
Bridgewater-Gagebrook, *Australia* **157 C10** 41 57N 86 33W
Bridgman, *U.S.A.* **21 E5** 52 5N   2 25W
Bridgnorth, *U.K.* **151 B14** 44 37N 70 42W
Bridgton, *U.S.A.* **21 F5** 51 8N   2 59W
Bridgwater, *U.K.* **21 F5** 51 15N   3 15W
Bridgwater B., *U.K.* **20 C7** 54 5N   0 12W
Bridlington, *U.K.* **20 C7** 54 6N   0 5W
Bridlington B., *U.K.* .... **127 D4** 40 59 S 147 23 E
Bridport, *Australia* **21 G4** 50 44N   2 45W
Bridport, *U.K.* **26 D2** 48 6N   4 0W
Briec, *France* .... **27 D11** 48 24N   4 30 E
Brienne-le-Château, *France* .. **27 E10** 47 59N   3 38 E
Brienon-sur-Armançon, *France* **32 C6** 46 46N   8 2 E
Brienz, *Switz.* .... **32 C6** 46 48N   8 2 E
Brienzer Rothorn, *Switz.* ... **32 C6** 46 49N   8 4 E
Brienzersee, *Switz.* **152 C8** 32 44N 81 26W
Brier Cr. →, *U.S.A.* ....

Brière, Parc Naturel Régional de △,
France **26 E4** 47 22N   2 13W
Brig, *Switz.* .... **32 D5** 46 18N   7 59 E
Brigg, *U.K.* **20 D7** 53 34N   0 28W
Brigham City, *U.S.A.* **158 F7** 41 31N 112 1W
Bright, *Australia* .... **129 D7** 36 42 S 146 56 E
Brighton, *Australia* .... **128 C3** 35 5 S 138 30 E
Brighton, *Canada* **150 B7** 44 2N 77 44W
Brighton, *Trin. & Tob.* **169 F9** 10 13N 61 39W
Brighton, *U.K.* **21 G7** 50 49N   0 7W
Brighton, *Colo., U.S.A.* **154 F2** 39 59N 104 49W
Brighton, *Fla., U.S.A.* **153 H8** 27 14N 81 6W
Brighton, *Ill., U.S.A.* **156 E6** 39 20N 90 8W
Brighton, *Iowa, U.S.A.* **156 C5** 41 10N 91 49W
Brighton, *Mich., U.S.A.* **157 B13** 42 32N 83 47W
Brignogan-Plage, *France* **26 D2** 48 40N   4 20W
Brignoles, *France* .... **29 E10** 43 25N   6 5 E
Brihuega, *Spain* **40 E2** 40 45N   2 52W
Brikama, *Gambia* **112 C1** 13 15N 16 45W
Brilliant, *U.S.A.* **150 F4** 40 15N 80 39W
Brilon, *Germany* .... **30 D4** 51 23N   8 32 E
Brim, *Australia* .... **128 D5** 36 3 S 142 27 E
Brimfield, *U.S.A.* **156 D7** 40 50N 89 53W
Brindisi, *Italy* .... **47 B10** 40 39N 17 55 E
Brinje, *Croatia* .... **45 D12** 44 59N 15 9 E
Brinkley, *U.S.A.* **155 H9** 34 53N 91 12W
Brinkworth, *Australia* ...... **128 B3** 33 42 S 138 26 E
Brinnon, *U.S.A.* **160 C4** 47 41N 122 54W
Brion, I., *Canada* **141 C7** 47 46N 61 26W
Brionski, *Croatia* .... **45 D10** 44 55N 13 45 E
Brioude, *France* .... **28 C7** 45 18N   3 24 E
Briouze, *France* **26 D6** 48 42N   0 23W
Brisbane, *Australia* .... **127 D5** 27 25 S 153 2 E
Brisbane →, *Australia* ...... **127 D5** 27 24 S 153 9 E
Brisbane Ranges Nat. Park △,
Australia .... **128 D6** 37 47 S 144 16 E
Brisighella, *Italy* .... **45 D8** 44 13N 11 46 E
Brissago, *Switz.* .... **33 D7** 46 7N   8 42 E
Bristol, *U.K.* **21 F5** 51 26N   2 35W
Bristol, *Conn., U.S.A.* **151 E12** 41 40N 72 57W
Bristol, *Fla., U.S.A.* **152 E5** 30 26N 84 59W
Bristol, *Pa., U.S.A.* **151 F10** 40 6N 74 51W
Bristol, *R.I., U.S.A.* **151 E13** 41 40N 71 16W
Bristol, *Tenn., U.S.A.* **149 G4** 36 36N 82 11W
Bristol, City of □, *U.K.* ... **21 F5** 51 27N   2 36W
Bristol B., *U.S.A.* **144 H8** 58 0N 160 0W
Bristol Channel, *U.K.* **21 F3** 51 18N   4 30W
Bristol I., *Antarctica* ..... **7 B1** 58 45 S 28 0W
Bristol L., *U.S.A.* **159 J5** 34 23N 116 50W
Bristow, *U.S.A.* **155 H6** 35 50N 96 23W
Bristow I., *Papua N. G.* .... **132 E2** 9 8 S 143 14 E
Britain = Great Britain, *Europe* **12 E5** 54 0N   2 15W
Britânia, *Brazil* .... **173 D7** 15 15 S 51 9W
British Central Africa = Malawi ■,
Africa .... **119 E3** 11 55 S 34 0 E
British Columbia □, *Canada* . **142 C3** 55 0N 125 15W
British Guiana = Guyana ■, *S. Amer.* **169 B6** 5 0N 59 0W
British Honduras = Belize ■,
Cent. Amer. **163 D7** 17 0N 88 30W
British Indian Ocean Terr. = Chagos
Arch., *Ind. Oc.* .... **121 E6** 6 0 S 72 0 E
British Isles, *Europe* **19 D5** 54 0N   4 0W
British Virgin Is. ☑, *W. Indies* **165 e** 18 30N 64 30W
Brits, *S. Africa* .... **117 D4** 25 37 S 27 48 E
Britstown, *S. Africa* .... **116 E3** 30 37 S 23 30 E
Britt, *Canada* **140 C3** 45 46N 80 34W
Britt, *U.S.A.* **156 A3** 43 6N 93 48W
Brittany = Bretagne, *France* **26 D3** 48 10N   3 0W
Britton, *U.S.A.* **154 C6** 45 48N 97 45W
Brive-la-Gaillarde, *France* . **28 C5** 45 10N   1 32 E
Briviesca, *Spain* **42 C7** 42 32N   3 19W
Brixen = Bressanone, *Italy* . **45 B8** 46 43N 11 39 E
Brixham, *U.K.* **21 G4** 50 23N   3 31W
Brlik = Birlik, *Kazakhstan* . **65 A6** 44 5N 73 31 E
Brlik = Birlik, *Kazakhstan* . **65 A6** 44 5N 73 31 E
Brnaze, *Croatia* .... **45 E13** 43 37N 16 40 E
Brno, *Czech Rep.* .... **35 B9** 49 10N 16 35 E
Broach = Bharuch, *India* .... **94 D1** 21 47N 73 0 E
Broad →, *Ga., U.S.A.* **152 B7** 33 59N 82 39W

Broad →, *S.C., U.S.A.* **149 J5** 34 1N 81 4W
Broad Arrow, *Australia* ..... **125 F3** 30 23 S 121 15 E
Broad B., *U.K.* **22 C2** 58 14N   6 18W
Broad Haven, *Ireland* **23 B2** 54 20N   9 55W
Broad Law, *U.K.* **22 F5** 55 30N   3 21W
Broad Sd., *Australia* .... **126 C4** 22 0 S 149 45 E
Broadalbin, *U.S.A.* **151 C10** 43 4N 74 12W
Broadback →, *Canada* **140 B4** 51 21N 78 52W
Broadford, *Australia* .... **129 D6** 37 14 S 145 4 E
Broadhurst Ra., *Australia* .. **124 D3** 22 30 S 122 30 E
Broads, The, *U.K.* .... **20 E9** 52 45N   1 30 E
Broads Nat. Park △, *U.K.* ... **21 E9** 52 45N   1 30 E
Broadus, *U.S.A.* **154 C2** 45 27N 105 25W
Broager, *Denmark* .... **17 K3** 54 53N   9 40 E
Broby, *Sweden* .... **17 H8** 56 15N 14 4 E
Broc, *Switz.* .... **32 C4** 46 37N   7 6 E
Brocēni, *Latvia* .... **54 B9** 56 42N 22 57 E
Brochet, *Canada* **143 B8** 57 53N 101 40W
Brochet, L., *Canada* **143 B8** 58 36N 101 35W
Brocken, *Germany* .... **30 D6** 51 47N 10 37 E
Brocklehurst, *Australia* .... **129 B8** 32 9 S 148 38 E
Brockport, *U.S.A.* **150 C7** 43 13N 77 56W
Brockton, *U.S.A.* **151 D13** 42 5N 71 1W
Brockville, *Canada* **140 D4** 44 35N 75 41W
Brockway, *Mont., U.S.A.* **154 B2** 47 18N 105 45W
Brockway, *Pa., U.S.A.* **150 E6** 41 15N 78 47W
Brocton, *U.S.A.* **150 D5** 42 23N 79 26W
Brod, *Macedonia* .... **50 E5** 41 32N 21 7 E
Brodarevo, *Serbia, Yug.* .... **50 C3** 43 14N 19 44 E
Brodeur Pen., *Canada* **139 A11** 72 30N 88 10W
Brodhead, *U.S.A.* **156 B7** 42 37N 89 22W
Brodhead, Mt., *U.S.A.* **150 F7** 41 39N 77 47W
Brodick, *U.K.* **22 F3** 55 35N   5 9W
Brodnica, *Poland* .... **55 E6** 53 15N 19 25 E
Brody, *Ukraine* .... **59 G3** 50 5N 25 10 E
Brogan, *U.S.A.* **158 D5** 44 15N 117 31W
Broglie, *France* .... **26 C7** 49 2N   0 30 E
Brok, *Poland* .... **55 F8** 52 43N 21 52 E
Broken Arrow, *U.S.A.* **155 G7** 36 3N 95 48W
Broken Bow, *Nebr., U.S.A.* .. **154 E5** 41 24N 99 38W
Broken Bow, *Okla., U.S.A.* .. **155 H7** 34 2N 94 44W
Broken Bow Lake, *U.S.A.* **155 H7** 34 9N 94 40W
Broken Hill = Kabwe, *Zambia* **119 E2** 14 30 S 28 29 E
Broken Hill, *Australia* ..... **128 A4** 31 58 S 141 29 E
Broken River Ra., *Australia* **126 C4** 21 0 S 148 22 E
Brokind, *Sweden* .... **17 F9** 58 13 S 142 6 E
Brokopondo, *Suriname* **169 B7** 5 3N 54 59W
Bromley □, *U.K.* .... **21 F8** 51 24N   0 2 E
Bromo, *Indonesia* .... **79 G15** 7 55 S 112 55 E
Bromölla, *Sweden* .... **17 H8** 56 5N 14 28 E
Bromsgrove, *U.K.* **21 E5** 52 21N   2 2W
Bronaugh, *U.S.A.* **156 G2** 37 41N 94 28W
Brønderslev, *Denmark* .... **17 G3** 57 16N   9 57 E
Brong-Ahafo □, *Ghana* **112 D4** 7 50N   2 0W
Broni, *Italy* .... **44 C6** 45 4N   9 16 E
Bronkhorstspruit, *S. Africa* **117 D4** 25 46 S 28 45 E
Brønnøysund, *Norway* .... **14 D15** 65 28N 12 14 E
Bronson, *Fla., U.S.A.* **153 F7** 29 27N 82 39W
Bronson, *Mich., U.S.A.* **157 C11** 41 52N 85 12W
Bronte, *Italy* .... **47 E7** 37 47N 14 50 E
Bronte, *U.S.A.* **155 K4** 31 50N 84 22W
Brook Park, *U.S.A.* **150 E3** 51 30N 84 22W
Brooke's Point, *Phil.* ...... **81 G1** 8 47N 117 50 E
Brookfield, *Mo., U.S.A.* **156 E3** 39 47N 93 4W
Brookfield, *Wis., U.S.A.* ... **157 A8** 43 4N 88 9W
Brookhaven, *U.S.A.* **155 K9** 31 35N 90 26W
Brookings, *Oreg., U.S.A.* ... **158 E1** 42 3N 124 17W
Brookings, *S. Dak., U.S.A.* . **154 C6** 44 19N 96 48W
Brooklet, *U.S.A.* **152 C8** 32 23N 81 40W
Brooklin, *Canada* **150 C6** 43 55N 78 55W
Brooklyn, *U.S.A.* **156 C4** 41 44N 92 27W
Brooklyn Park, *U.S.A.* **154 C8** 45 6N 93 23W
Brooks, *Canada* **142 C6** 50 35N 111 55W
Brooks Range, *U.S.A.* **144 C10** 68 0N 152 0W
Brookston, *U.S.A.* **157 D10** 40 36N 86 52W
Brooksville, *Fla., U.S.A.* .. **157 G5** 28 33 S 149 10 E
Brooksville, *Ky., U.S.A.* ... **157 F12** 38 41N 84 4W
Brookville, *Ind., U.S.A.* ... **125 E2** 32 22 S 117 0 E
Brookville, *Ind., U.S.A.* ... **157 E12** 39 25N 85 1W
Brookville, *Ohio, U.S.A.* ... **157 E12** 39 50N 84 27W
Brookville, *Pa., U.S.A.* **150 E5** 41 10N 79 5W
Brookville L., *U.S.A.* **157 E11** 39 28N 85 0W
Broom, L., *U.K.* **22 D3** 57 55N   5 15W
Broome, *Australia* .... **124 C3** 18 0 S 122 15 E
Broons, *France* **26 D4** 48 20N   2 16W
Brora, *U.K.* **22 C5** 58 0N   3 52W
Brora →, *U.K.* **22 C5** 58 0N   3 51W
Brørup, *Denmark* .... **17 J2** 55 29N   9 1 E
Brösarp, *Sweden* .... **17 J8** 55 43N 14 6 E
Brosna →, *Ireland* **23 C4** 53 14N   7 58W
Broşteni, Mehedinţi, *Romania* **52 F7** 44 45N 22 59 E
Broşteni, Suceava, *Romania* . **53 C10** 47 14N 25 43 E
Brostrud, *Norway* .... **18 D5** 60 18N   8 34 E
Brotas de Macaúbas, *Brazil* . **171 D3** 12 0 S 42 38W
Brothers, *U.S.A.* **158 E3** 43 49N 120 36W
Brøttum, *Norway* .... **18 C7** 61 1N 10 34 E
Brou, *France* .... **26 D8** 48 13N   1 11 E
Brouage, *France* **28 C2** 45 52N   1 4W
Brough, *U.K.* **20 C5** 54 32N   2 18W
Brough Hd., *U.K.* **22 B5** 59 8N   3 20W
Broughton, *U.S.A.* **157 G8** 37 56N 88 27W
Broughton Island = Qikiqtarjuaq,
Canada **139 B13** 67 33N 63 0W
Broumov, *Czech Rep.* .... **35 A9** 50 35N 16 20 E
Brovary, *Ukraine* .... **59 G6** 50 34N 30 48 E
Brovst, *Denmark* .... **17 G3** 57 6N   9 31 E
Brown, L., *Australia* .... **125 F2** 31 5 S 118 15 E
Brown, Mt., *Australia* ...... **128 B3** 32 0 S 138 0 E
Brown, Pt., *Australia* ...... **127 E1** 32 32 S 133 50 E
Brown City, *U.S.A.* **150 C2** 43 13N 82 59W
Brown Willy, *U.K.* **21 G3** 50 35N   4 37W
Brownfield, *U.S.A.* **155 J3** 33 11N 102 17W
Browning, *Ill., U.S.A.* **156 D6** 40 8N 90 22W
Browning, *Mo., U.S.A.* **156 D3** 40 3N 93 12W
Browning, *Mont., U.S.A.* **158 B7** 48 34N 113 1W
Brownsburg, *U.S.A.* **157 E10** 39 51N 86 24W
Brownstown, *U.S.A.* **157 F10** 38 53N 86 3W
Brownsville, *Oreg., U.S.A.* . **158 D2** 44 24N 122 59W
Brownsville, *Pa., U.S.A.* ... **150 F5** 40 1N 79 53W
Brownsville, *Tenn., U.S.A.* . **155 H10** 35 36N 89 16W
Brownsville, *Tex., U.S.A.* .. **155 N6** 25 54N 97 30W
Brownsweg, *Suriname* **169 B6** 5 5N 55 15W
Brownville, *U.S.A.* **151 C9** 44 0N 75 59W
Brownwood, *U.S.A.* **155 K5** 31 43N 98 59W
Broxton, *U.S.A.* **155 K5** 31 43N 98 59W
Broye →, *Switz.* **152 D7** 31 38N 82 53W
Bru, *Norway* .... **32 C3** 46 52N   6 58 E
Bruay-la-Buissière, *France* . **27 B9** 50 29N   2 33 E
Bruce, Mt., *Australia* **152 E4** 30 28N 85 58W
Bruce, Mt., *Australia* ...... **124 D2** 22 37 S 118 8 E
Bruce, Mt., *N.Z.* .... **131 D4** 43 35 S 169 42 E
Bruce Peninsula Nat. Park △,
Canada **140 C3** 45 14N 81 36W
Bruce Rock, *Australia* ...... **125 F2** 31 52 S 118 8 E
Bruche →, *France* .... **27 D14** 48 34N   7 43 E
Bruchsal, *Germany* .... **31 F4** 49 7N   8 35 E
Bruck an der Leitha, *Austria* **35 C9** 48 1N 16 47 E
Bruck an der Mur, *Austria* .. **34 D8** 47 24N 15 16 E
Brue →, *U.K.* **21 F5** 51 13N   2 59W
Bruflat, *Norway* .... **18 D6** 60 53N   9 37 E
Bruges = Brugge, *Belgium* ... **24 C3** 51 13N   3 13 E

Brugg, *Switz.* . . . . **32 B6**   47 29N   8 11 E
Brugge, *Belgium* . . . . **24 C3**   51 13N   3 13 E
Bruin, *U.S.A.* **150 E5**   41 3N   79 43W
Bruini, *India* . . . . **90 A6**   29 10N   96 11 E
Brûlé, *Canada* **142 C5**   53 15N 117 58W
Brûlon, *France* **26 E6**   47 58N   0 15W
Brumado, *Brazil* . . . . **171 D3**   14 14 S   41 40W
Brumado ➤, *Brazil* . . . . **171 D3**   14 13 S   41 40W
Brumath, *France* . . . . **27 D14**   48 43N   7 40 E
Brumunddal, *Norway* . . . . . **18 D7**   60 53N   10 56 E
Brundidge, *U.S.A.* **152 D4**   31 43N   85 49W
Bruneau, *U.S.A.* **158 E6**   42 53N 115 48W
Bruneau ➤, *U.S.A.* **158 E6**   42 56N 115 57W
Bruneck = Brunico, *Italy* . . **45 B8**   46 48N   11 56 E
Brunei = Bandar Seri Begawan,
  Brunei . . . . **85 B4**   4 52N 115   0 E
Brunei ■, *Asia* . . . . **85 B4**   4 50N 115   0 E
Brunflo, *Sweden* . . . . **16 A8**   63 5N   14 50 E
Brunico, *Italy* . . . . **45 B8**   46 48N   11 56 E
Brünigpass, *Switz.* . . . . **32 C6**   46 46N   8 8 E
Brünn = Brno, *Czech Rep.* . **35 B9**   49 10N   16 35 E
Brunna, *Sweden* . . . . **16 E11**   59 52N   17 25 E
Brunnen, *Switz.* . . . . **33 C7**   46 59N   8 37 E
Brunner, L., *N.Z.* . . . . **131 C6**   42 37 S 171 27 E
Brunnhöll, *Iceland* **11 C11**   64 17N   15 26W
Brunsbüttel, *Germany* . . . . **30 B5**   53 53N   9 6 E
Brunssum, *Neths.* . . . . **24 D5**   50 57N   5 59 E
Brunswick = Braunschweig,
  Germany . . . . **30 C6**   52 15N   10 31 E
Brunswick, *Ga., U.S.A.* . . . **152 D8**   31 10N   81 30W
Brunswick, *Maine, U.S.A.* . **149 D11** 43 55N   69 58W
Brunswick, *Md., U.S.A.* . . . **148 F7**   39 19N   77 38W
Brunswick, *Mo., U.S.A.* . . . **156 F8**   39 26N   93 8W
Brunswick, *Ohio, U.S.A.* . . **150 E3**   41 14N   81 51W
Brunswick, Pen. de, *Chile* . **176 D2**   53 30 S   71 30W
Brunswick B., *Australia* . . . **124 C3**   15 15 S 124 50 E
Brunswick Junction, *Australia* **125 F2**   33 15 S 115 50 E
Bruntál, *Czech Rep.* . . . . . . **35 B10**   49 59N   17 27 E
Bruny I., *Australia* . . . . **127 D4**   43 20 S 147 15 E
Brus Laguna, *Honduras* . . . **164 C3**   15 47N   84 35W
Brusa = Bursa, *Turkey* . . . . **51 F13**   40 15N   29 5 E
Brusartsi, *Bulgaria* . . . . **50 C7**   43 40N   23 5 E
Brush, *U.S.A.* **154 E3**   40 15N 103 37W
Brushton, *U.S.A.* **151 B10**   44 50N   74 31W
Brusio, *Switz.* . . . . **33 D10**   46 14N   10 8 E
Brusque, *Brazil* . . . . **175 B6**   27 5 S   49 0W
Brussel, *Belgium* . . . . **24 D4**   50 51N   4 21 E
Brussels = Brussel, *Belgium* **24 D4**   50 51N   4 21 E
Brussels, *Canada* **150 C3**   43 44N   81 15W
Brussels Nat. ✈ (BRU), *Belize* **24 D5**   50 54N   5 41 E
Brusy, *Poland* . . . . **54 E4**   53 53N   17 43 E
Bruthen, *Australia* . . . . **129 D7**   37 42 S 147 50 E
Bruvoll, *Norway* . . . . **18 D8**   60 27N   11 29 E
Bruxelles = Brussel, *Belgium* **24 D4**   50 51N   4 21 E
Bruyères, *France* . . . . **27 D13**   48 10N   6 40 E
Bruz, *France* **26 D5**   48 1N   1 46W
Brwinów, *Poland* . . . . **55 F7**   52 9N   20 40 E
Bryagovo, *Bulgaria* . . . . **51 E9**   41 58N   25 8 E
Bryan, *Ohio, U.S.A.* **157 C12** 41 28N   84 33W
Bryan, *Tex., U.S.A.* **155 K6**   30 40N   96 22W
Bryan, Mt., *Australia* . . . . . **128 B3**   33 30 S 139   0 E
Bryanka, *Ukraine* . . . . **59 H10**   48 32N   38 45 E
Bryansk, *Bryansk, Russia* . . **59 F8**   53 13N   34 25 E
Bryansk, *Dagestan, Russia* . **61 H8**   44 20N   47 10 E
Bryanskoye = Bryansk, *Russia* **61 H8**   44 20N   47 10 E
Bryce Canyon Nat. Park △, *U.S.A.* **159 H7**   37 30N 112 10W
Bryne, *Norway* . . . . **18 F2**   58 44N   5 38 E
Bryson City, *U.S.A.* **149 H4**   35 26N   83 27W
Bryukhovetskaya, *Russia* . . **59 K10**   45 48N   39 0 E
Brza Palanka, *Serbia, Yug.* . **50 B6**   44 28N   22 27 E
Brzeg, *Poland* . . . . **55 H4**   50 52N   17 30 E
Brzeg Dolny, *Poland* . . . . . . **55 G3**   51 16N   16 41 E
Brześć Kujawski, *Poland* . . . **55 F5**   52 36N   18 55 E
Brzesko, *Poland* . . . . **55 J7**   49 59N   20 34 E
Brzeziny, *Poland* . . . . **55 G6**   51 49N   19 42 E
Brzozów, *Poland* . . . . **55 J9**   49 41N   22 3 E
Bsharri, *Lebanon* . . . . **103 A5**   34 15N   36 0 E
Bū al Ḥidān, W. ➤, *Libya* . **108 C3**   27 25N   19 22 E
Bū Athlah, *Libya* . . . . **108 B3**   30 9N   15 39 E
Bū Baqarah, *U.A.E.* . . . . . . **97 E8**   25 35N   56 25 E
Bū Craa, *W. Sahara* **110 C2**   26 45N   12 50W
Bū Ḥasā, *U.A.E.* . . . . **97 F7**   23 30N   53 20 E
Bū Tummayim, W. ➤, *Libya* **108 C3**   26 56N   19 13 E
Bua, *Fiji* . . . . **133 A2**   16 48 S 178 37 E
Bua, *Sweden* . . . . **17 G6**   57 14N   12 7 E
Bua Yai, *Thailand* . . . . **86 E4**   15 33N 102 26 E
Buad I., *Phil.* . . . . **81 F5**   11 54N 125 2 E
Buala, *Solomon Is.* . . . . **133 M10**   8 10 S 159 35 E
Buapinang, *Indonesia* . . . . . **82 B2**   4 40 S 121 30 E
Buba, *Guinea-Biss.* **112 C2**   11 40N   14 59W
Bubanda, *Dem. Rep. of the Congo* **114 B3**   4 14N   19 38 E
Bubanza, *Burundi* . . . . **118 C2**   3 6 S   29 23 E
Bubaque, *Guinea-Biss.* **112 C1**   11 16N   15 51W
Bube, *Ethiopia* . . . . **107 F4**   8 46N   35 48 E
Būbiyān, *Kuwait* . . . . **97 D6**   29 45N   48 15 E
Bucak, *Fiji* . . . . **133 A2**   16 38 S 179 52 E
Buca, *Turkey* . . . . **49 C9**   38 22N   27 11 E
Bucaco, *Angola* . . . . **115 E4**   11 26 S   20 10 E
Bucak, *Turkey* . . . . **49 D12**   37 28N   30 36 E
Bucaramanga, *Colombia* . . . **168 B3**   7 0N   73 0W
Bucas Grande I., *Phil.* . . . . . **81 G5**   9 40N 125 57 E
Bucasia, *Australia* . . . . **126 K7**   21 2 S 149 10 E
Bucay, *Phil.* . . . . **80 C3**   17 32N 120 43 E
Buccaneer Arch., *Australia* . **124 C3**   16 7 S 123 20 E
Buccino, *Italy* . . . . **47 B8**   40 38N   15 22 E
Buccoo Reef, *Trin. & Tob.* . **169 E10**   11 10N   60 51W
Bucecea, *Romania* . . . . **53 C11**   47 47N   26 28 E
Bucegi, Parcul Nat. △, *Romania* **53 E10**   45 25N   25 25 E
Bucey-lès-Gy, *France* . . . . . **32 B1**   47 25N   5 51 E
Buchach, *Ukraine* . . . . **59 H3**   49 5N   25 25 E
Buchan, *Australia* . . . . **129 D8**   37 30 S 148 12 E
Buchan, *U.K.* **22 D6**   57 32N   2 21W
Buchan Ness, *U.K.* **22 D7**   57 29N   1 46W
Buchanan, *Canada* **143 C8**   51 40N 102 45W
Buchanan, *Liberia* **112 D2**   5 57N   10 2W
Buchanan, *Ga., U.S.A.* **152 B4**   33 48N   85 11W
Buchanan, *Mich., U.S.A.* . . **157 C10**   41 50N   86 22W
Buchanan, L., *Queens., Australia* **126 C4**   21 35 S 145 52 E
Buchanan, L., *W. Austral., Australia* **125 E3**   25 33 S 123 2 E
Buchanan, L., *U.S.A.* **155 K5**   30 45N   98 25W
Buchanan Cr. ➤, *Australia* . **126 B2**   19 13 S 136 33 E
Buchans, *Canada* **141 C8**   48 50N   56 52W
Bucharest = Bucureşti, *Romania* **53 F11**   44 27N   26 10 E
Bucharest Otopeni ✈ (OTP),
  Romania . . . . **51 B10**   44 30N   26 11 E
Buchen, *Germany* . . . . **31 F5**   49 32N   9 20 E
Buchholz, *Germany* . . . . **30 B5**   53 19N   9 52 E
Buchloe, *Germany* . . . . **31 G6**   48 1N   10 44 E
Buchon, Pt., *U.S.A.* **160 K6**   35 15N 120 54W
Buchs, *Aargau, Switz.* . . . . . **32 B6**   47 23N   8 4 E
Buchs, *St. Galen, Switz.* . . . **33 C8**   47 10N   9 28 E
Buciumi, *Romania* . . . . **52 C8**   47 3N   23 5 E
Buck Hill Falls, *U.S.A.* **151 E9**   41 11N   75 16W
Buckeburg, *Germany* . . . . . **30 C5**   52 16N   9 3 E
Buckeye, *U.S.A.* **159 K7**   33 22N 112 35W
Buckeye Lake, *U.S.A.* **150 G2**   39 55N   82 29W
Buckfastleigh, *U.K.* **21 G4**   50 28N   3 48W
Buckhannon, *U.S.A.* **148 F5**   39 0N   80 8W
Buckhaven, *U.K.* **22 E5**   56 11N   3 3W
Buckhorn L., *Canada* **150 B6**   44 29N   78 23W
Buckie, *U.K.* **22 D6**   57 41N   2 58W
Buckingham, *Canada* **140 C4**   45 37N   75 24W
Buckingham, *U.K.* **21 F7**   51 59N   0 57W
Buckingham B., *Australia* . . **126 A2**   12 10 S 135 40 E
Buckingham Canal, *India* . . **95 H5**   14 0N   80 5 E

Buckinghamshire □, *U.K.* . . **21 F7**   51 53N   0 55W
Buckland, *U.S.A.* **144 D7**   65 59N 161 8W
Buckle Hd., *Australia* . . . . . **124 B4**   14 26 S 127 52 E
Buckleboo, *Australia* . . . . . . **128 B2**   32 54 S 136 12 E
Buckley, *U.K.* **20 D4**   53 10N   3 5W
Buckley, *U.S.A.* **157 D8**   40 36N   88 2W
Buckley ➤, *Australia* . . . . . **126 C2**   20 10 S 138 49 E
Bucklin, *Kans., U.S.A.* **155 G5**   37 33N   99 38W
Bucklin, *Mo., U.S.A.* **156 E4**   39 47N   92 53W
Bucks L., *U.S.A.* **160 F5**   39 54N 121 12W
Buco Zau, *Angola* . . . . **115 C2**   4 46 S   12 33 E
Bucquoy, *France* . . . . **27 B9**   50 9N   2 43 E
Bucureşti, *Romania* . . . . **53 F11**   44 27N   26 10 E
Bucyrus, *U.S.A.* **157 D14**   40 48N   82 59W
Bud, *Norway* . . . . **18 B3**   62 55N   6 55 E
Budacu, Vf., *Romania* . . . . . **53 C10**   47 7N   25 41 E
Budalin, *Burma* . . . . **90 D5**   22 20N   95 10 E
Budaörs, *Hungary* . . . . **52 C3**   47 27N   18 58 E
Budapest, *Hungary* . . . . **52 C4**   47 29N   19 5 E
Budapest □, *Hungary* . . . . . **52 C4**   47 29N   19 5 E
Budapest ✈ (BUD), *Hungary* **52 C4**   47 25N   19 12 E
Budaun, *India* . . . . **93 E8**   28 5N   79 10 E
Budawang Nat. Park △, *Australia* **129 C9**   35 10 S 150 12 E
Budd Coast, *Antarctica* . . . . **7 C8**   68 0 S 112   0 E
Budderoo Nat. Park △, *Australia* **129 C9**   35 40 S 150 41 E
Buddusò, *Italy* . . . . **46 B2**   40 35N   9 15 E
Bude, *U.K.* **21 G3**   50 49N   4 34W
Budennovsk, *Russia* . . . . . . **61 H7**   44 50N   44 10 E
Budeşti, *Romania* . . . . **53 F11**   44 13N   26 30 E
Budge Budge = Baj Baj, *India* **93 H13**   22 30N   88 5 E
Budgewoi, *Australia* . . . . . . **129 B9**   33 13 S 151 34 E
Búðardalur, *Iceland* **11 B5**   65 7N   21 46W
Búðir, *Iceland* **11 C12**   64 56N   14 8W
Budia, *Spain* **42 E2**   40 38N   2 46W
Büdingen, *Germany* . . . . . . **31 E5**   50 16N   9 7 E
Budjala, *Dem. Rep. of the Congo* **114 B3**   2 50N   19 40 E
Budoni, *Italy* . . . . **46 B2**   40 40N   9 45 E
Búðrio, *Italy* . . . . **45 D8**   44 32N   11 32 E
Budva, *Montenegro, Yug.* . . **50 D2**   42 17N   18 50 E
Budweis = České Budějovice,
  Czech Rep. . . . . **34 C7**   48 55N   14 25 E
Budzyń, *Poland* . . . . **55 F3**   52 54N   16 59 E
Bue, *Norway* . . . . **18 F2**   58 40N   5 58 E
Buea, *Cameroon* . . . . **113 E6**   4 10N   9 9 E
Buela, *Angola* . . . . **115 D2**   5 54 S   14 40 E
Buellton, *U.S.A.* **161 L6**   34 37N 120 12W
Buena Esperanza, *Argentina* **174 C2**   34 45 S   65 15W
Buena Park, *U.S.A.* **161 M9**   33 52N 117 59W
Buena Vista, *Bolivia* . . . . . . **171 D5**   17 27 S   63 40W
Buena Vista, *Solomon Is.* . . **133 M11**   8 52 S 160 3 E
Buena Vista, *Colo., U.S.A.* . **159 G10**   38 51N 106 8W
Buena Vista, *Ga., U.S.A.* . . **152 C5**   32 19N   84 31W
Buena Vista, *Va., U.S.A.* . . **148 G6**   37 44N   79 21W
Buena Vista Lake Bed, *U.S.A.* **161 K7**   35 12N 119 18W
Buenaventura, *Colombia* . . . **168 C2**   3 53N   77 4W
Buenaventura, *Mexico* **162 B3**   29 50N 107 30W
Buenaventura, B. de, *Colombia* **168 C2**   3 48N   77 17W
Buendía, Embalse de, *Spain* . **40 E2**   40 25N   2 43W
Buenópolis, *Brazil* . . . . **171 E3**   17 54 S   44 11W
Buenos Aires, *Argentina* . . . **174 C4**   34 30 S   58 20W
Buenos Aires, *Colombia* . . . **168 C3**   1 36N   73 18W
Buenos Aires, *Costa Rica* . . **164 E3**   9 10N   83 20W
Buenos Aires □, *Argentina* . **174 D4**   36 30 S   60 0W
Buenos Aires, L., *Chile* . . . . **176 C2**   46 35 S   72 30W
Buesaco, *Colombia* **168 C2**   1 23N   77 9W
Buet, Mont, *France* . . . . **32 D3**   46 2N   6 52 E
Buffalo, *Mo., U.S.A.* **155 G8**   37 39N   93 6W
Buffalo, *N.Y., U.S.A.* **150 D6**   42 53N   78 53W
Buffalo, *Okla., U.S.A.* **155 G5**   36 50N   99 38W
Buffalo, *S. Dak., U.S.A.* . . . **154 C3**   45 35N 103 33W
Buffalo, *Wyo., U.S.A.* **158 D10**   44 21N 106 42W
Buffalo ➤, *Canada* **142 A5**   60 5N 115 5W
Buffalo ➤, *S. Africa* . . . . . . **117 D5**   28 43 S   30 37 E
Buffalo Head Hills, *Canada* . **142 B5**   57 25 S 115 55W
Buffalo L., *Alta., Canada* . . **142 C6**   52 27N 112 54W
Buffalo L., *N.W.T., Canada* . **142 A5**   60 12N 115 25W
Buffalo Narrows, *Canada* . . **143 B7**   55 51N 108 29W
Buffalo Nat. River △, *U.S.A.* **155 G8**   36 14N   92 36W
Buffalo Springs Nat. Reserve ○,
  Kenya . . . . **118 B4**   0 32N   37 35 E
Buffels ➤, *S. Africa* . . . . . . **116 D2**   29 36 S   17 3 E
Buford, *U.S.A.* **149 H4**   34 10N   84 0W
Bug = Buh ➤, *Ukraine* . . . . **59 J6**   46 59N   31 58 E
Bug ➤, *Poland* . . . . **55 F8**   52 31N   21 5 E
Buga, *Colombia* **168 C2**   4 0N   76 15W
Bugala I., *Uganda* . . . . **118 C3**   0 40 S   32 20 E
Buganda, *Uganda* . . . . **118 C3**   0 0   31 30 E
Buganga, *Uganda* . . . . **118 C3**   0 3 S   32 0 E
Bugasong, *Phil.* . . . . **81 F4**   11 3N 122   4 E
Bugeat, *France* . . . . **28 C5**   45 36N   1 55 E
Bugel, Tanjung, *Indonesia* . . **85 D4**   6 26 S 111   3 E
Buggingen, *Germany* . . . . . . **32 A5**   47 51N   7 38 E
Bugibba, *Malta* . . . . **38 F7**   35 57N   14 25 E
Bugojno, *Bos.-H.* . . . . **52 F2**   44 2N   17 25 E
Bugsuk, *Phil.* . . . . **78 C5**   8 15N 117 15 E
Bugsuk I., *Phil.* . . . . **81 G1**   8 12N 117 18 E
Buguey, *Phil.* . . . . **80 B3**   18 17N 121 50 E
Buguias, *Phil.* . . . . **80 C3**   16 43N 120 50 E
Bugulma, *Russia* . . . . **64 D4**   54 33N   52 48 E
Buguma, *Nigeria* . . . . **113 E6**   4 42N   6 55 E
Bugun Shara, *Mongolia* . . . **68 B5**   49 0N 104   0 E
Bugungu Game Reserve ○, *Uganda* **118 B3**   2 17N   31 50 E
Buguruslan, *Russia* . . . . **64 E4**   53 39N   52 26 E
Buh ➤, *Ukraine* . . . . **59 J6**   46 59N   31 58 E
Buharkent, *Turkey* . . . . **47 D10**   37 58N   28 44 E
Buheirat-Murrat-el-Kubra, *Egypt* **106 H8**   30 18N   32 26 E
Buhera, *Zimbabwe* . . . . **117 B5**   19 18 S   31 29 E
Bühl, *Germany* . . . . **31 G4**   48 40N   8 8 E
Buhl, *U.S.A.* **158 E6**   42 36N 114 46W
Buhuşi, *Romania* . . . . **53 D11**   46 41N   26 45 E
Bui Nat. Park △, *Ghana* . . . **21 E4**   52 9N   3 25W
Builth Wells, *U.K.* **21 E4**   52 9N   3 25W
Buin, *Papua N. G.* . . . . **133 L8**   6 48 S 155 42 E
Buinsk, *Russia* . . . . **33 C10**   46 51N   10 7 E
Buíque, *Brazil* . . . . **170 C4**   8 37 S   37 9W
Buir Nur, *Mongolia* . . . . . . **69 B6**   47 50N 117 42 E
Buis-les-Baronnies, *France* . **29 D9**   44 17N   5 16 E
Buitrago = Buitrago del Lozoya,
  Spain **42 E7**   40 58N   3 38W
Buitrago del Lozoya, *Spain* . **42 E7**   40 58N   3 38W
Bujalance, *Spain* **43 H6**   37 54N   4 23W
Bujanovac, *Serbia, Yug.* . . . **50 D5**   42 28N   21 44 E
Bujaraloz, *Spain* **40 D4**   41 29N   0 10W
Buje, *Croatia* . . . . **45 C10**   45 24N   13 39 E
Buji, *China* . . . . **69 F11**   22 37N 114 5 E
Bujumbura, *Burundi* . . . . . . **118 C2**   3 16 S   29 18 E
Bük, *Hungary* . . . . **52 C1**   47 22N   16 45 E
Buk, *Poland* . . . . **55 F3**   52 21N   16 30 E
Buka I., *Papua N. G.* . . . . . **132 C8**   5 10 S 154 35 E
Bukachacha, *Russia* . . . . . . **67 D12**   52 55N 116 50 E
Bukama, *Dem. Rep. of the Congo* **119 D2**   9 10 S   25 50 E
Bukavu, *Dem. Rep. of the Congo* **118 C2**   2 20 S   28 52 E
Bukene, *Tanzania* . . . . **118 C3**   4 15 S   32 48 E
Bukhara = Bukhoro, *Uzbekistan* **65 D2**   39 48N   64 25 E
Bukhoro, *Uzbekistan* . . . . . . **65 D2**   39 48N   64 25 E
Bukidnon □, *Phil.* . . . . **81 H5**   8 0N 125   0 E
Bukima, *Tanzania* . . . . **118 C3**   1 50 S   33 25 E
Bukit Badung, *Indonesia* . . . **79 K18**   8 49 S 115 10 E
Bukit Kerajaan, *Malaysia* . . **87 c**   5 25N 100 15 E
Bukit Mertajam, *Malaysia* . . **87 c**   5 22N 100 28 E

Bukit Ni, *Malaysia* . . . . **87 d**   1 22N 104 12 E
Bukit Panjang, *Singapore* . . **87 d**   1 23N 103 46 E
Bukit Tengah, *Malaysia* . . . **87 c**   5 22N 100 25 E
Bukittinggi, *Indonesia* . . . . . **84 C2**   0 20 S 100 20 E
Bukkapatnam, *India* . . . . . . **95 G3**   14 14N   77 46 E
Bukoba, *Tanzania* . . . . **118 C3**   1 20 S   31 49 E
Bukrane, *Indonesia* . . . . **83 C4**   7 43 S 131   9 E
Bukum, Pulau, *Singapore* . . **87 d**   1 14N 103 46 E
Bukuru, *Nigeria* . . . . **113 D6**   9 42N   8 48 E
Bukuya, *Uganda* . . . . **118 B3**   0 40N   31 52 E
Būl, Kuh-e, *Iran* . . . . **97 D7**   30 48N   52 45 E
Bula, *Guinea-Biss.* **112 C1**   12 7N   15 43W
Bula, *Indonesia* . . . . **83 B4**   3 6 S 130 30 E
Bula, *Phil.* . . . . **80 E4**   13 28N 123 16 E
Bula-Atumba, *Angola* . . . . . **115 D2**   8 41 S   14 52 E
Bulacan □, *Phil.* . . . . **80 D3**   15 0N 121   5 E
Bûlach, *Switz.* . . . . **33 A7**   47 31N   8 32 E
Bulahdelah, *Australia* . . . . . **129 B10**   32 23 S 152 13 E
Bulalacao, *Phil.* . . . . **80 E3**   12 31N 121 26 E
Bulan, *Phil.* . . . . **80 E4**   12 40N 123 52 E
Bulanash, *Russia* . . . . **64 C9**   57 16N   62 0 E
Bulancak, *Turkey* . . . . **101 B8**   40 56N   38 14 E
Bûland, *Iceland* **11 D8**   63 46N   18 30W
Bulandshahr, *India* . . . . **92 E7**   28 28N   77 51 E
Bulank, *Turkey* . . . . **101 C10**   39 4N   42 14 E
Bulanovo, *Russia* . . . . **64 E5**   52 27N   55 10 E
Bûlâq, *Egypt* . . . . **106 B3**   25 10N   30 38 E
Bulawayo, *Zimbabwe* . . . . . **119 G2**   20 7 S   28 32 E
Buldan, *Turkey* . . . . **49 C10**   38 2N   28 50 E
Buldana, *India* . . . . **94 D3**   20 30N   76 18 E
Buldir I., *U.S.A.* . . . . **144 K1**   52 21N 175 56 E
Buldon, *Phil.* . . . . **81 H5**   7 33N 124 25 E
Bulgar, *Russia* . . . . **60 C9**   54 57N   49 4 E
Bulgaria ■, *Europe* . . . . **51 D9**   42 35N   25 30 E
Bulgheria, Monte, *Italy* . . . . **47 B8**   40 4N   15 26 E
Bulgurca, *Turkey* . . . . **49 C9**   38 9N   27 9 E
Bulhale, *Somali Rep.* . . . . . . **120 C3**   5 20N   46 29 E
Bulhar, *Somali Rep.* . . . . . . **120 B2**   10 25N   44 30 E
Buli, *Indonesia* . . . . **82 A3**   0 53N 128 18 E
Buli, Teluk, *Indonesia* . . . . . **82 A3**   0 48N 128 25 E
Buliluyan, C., *Phil.* . . . . **81 G1**   8 20N 117 15 E
Bulim, *Singapore* . . . . **87 d**   1 22N 103 43 E
Bulki, *Ethiopia* . . . . **107 F4**   6 11N   36 31 E
Bulkley ➤, *Canada* **142 B3**   55 15N 127 40W
Bull Shoals L., *U.S.A.* **155 G8**   36 22N   92 35W
Bullaque ➤, *Spain* **43 G6**   38 59N   4 17W
Bullard, *U.S.A.* **152 C6**   32 38N   83 30W
Bullas, *Spain* **41 G3**   38 2N   1 40W
Bulle, *Switz.* . . . . **32 C4**   46 37N   7 3 E
Buller ➤, *N.Z.* . . . . **131 B6**   41 44 S 171 36 E
Buller, Mt., *Australia* . . . . . **129 D7**   37 10 S 146 28 E
Buller Gorge, *N.Z.* . . . . **131 B7**   41 40 S 172 10 E
Bulleringa Nat. Park △, *Australia* **126 B3**   17 3 S 143 56 E
Bullhead City, *U.S.A.* **161 K12**   35 8N 114 32W
Bulli, *Australia* . . . . **129 C9**   34 15 S 150 57 E
Bullock Creek, *Australia* . . . **126 B3**   17 43 S 144 31 E
Bulloo ➤, *Australia* . . . . **127 D3**   28 43 S 142 30 E
Bulloo L., *Australia* . . . . **127 D3**   28 43 S 142 25 E
Bulls, *N.Z.* . . . . **130 G4**   40 10 S 175 24 E
Bully-les-Mines, *France* . . . . **27 B9**   50 27N   2 44 E
Bulnes, *Chile* . . . . **174 D1**   36 42 S   72 19W
Bulo Burti, *Somali Rep.* . . . **120 D3**   3 50N   45 33 E
Bulo Ghedudo, *Somali Rep.* . **120 D3**   4 0 S   42 42 E
Bulolo, *Papua N. G.* . . . . . . **132 D4**   7 10 S 146 40 E
Bulong, *Dem. Rep. of the Congo* **115 C4**   4 45 S   21 50 E
Bulqizë, *Albania* . . . . **50 E4**   41 30N   20 21 E
Bulsar = Valsad, *India* . . . . **94 D1**   20 40N   72 58 E
Bultfontein, *S. Africa* . . . . . **116 D4**   28 18 S   26 10 E
Buluan, *Phil.* . . . . **81 H5**   6 44N 124 49 E
Buluan, L., *Phil.* . . . . **81 H5**   6 40N 124 49 E
Bulukumba, *Indonesia* . . . . . **82 C2**   5 33 S 120 11 E
Bulun, *Russia* . . . . **67 B13**   70 37N 127 30 E
Bulungkol, *China* . . . . **67 D7**   38 36N   74 58 E
Bulungu, *Dem. Rep. of the Congo* **115 D4**   4 54 S   21 54 E
Bulungur, *Uzbekistan* . . . . . **65 D3**   39 46N   67 16 E
Bulusan, *Phil.* . . . . **80 E5**   12 45N 124   8 E
Bulusan Vol., *Phil.* . . . . **80 E5**   12 46N 124   6 E
Bumba, Bandundu, *Dem. Rep. of
  the Congo* . . . . **115 D3**   6 58 S   19 19 E
Bumba, *Équateur, Dem. Rep. of
  the Congo* . . . . **114 B4**   2 13N   22 30 E
Bumbeşti-Jiu, *Romania* . . . . **53 E8**   45 10N   23 24 E
Bumbiri I., *Tanzania* . . . . . . **118 C3**   1 40 S   31 55 E
Bumbuna, *S. Leone* **112 D2**   9 2N   11 49W
Bumhkang, *Burma* . . . . **90 B6**   26 51N   97 40 E
Bumhpa Bum, *Burma* . . . . . **90 B6**   26 51N   97 14 E
Bumi ➤, *Zimbabwe* . . . . . . **119 F2**   17 0 S   28 20 E
Bumtang ➤, *Bhutan* . . . . . . **90 B3**   26 56N   90 53 E
Buna, *Dem. Rep. of the Congo* **114 C3**   3 14 S   18 59 E
Buna, *Kenya* . . . . **118 B4**   2 58N   39 30 E
Buna, *Papua N. G.* . . . . **132 E5**   8 42 S 148 27 E
Bunama, *Papua N. G.* . . . . . **132 F6**   10 5 S 151   9 E
Bunawan, *Phil.* . . . . **81 G5**   8 12N 125 57 E
Bunazi, *Tanzania* . . . . **118 C3**   1 3 S   31 23 E
Bunbah, Khalīj, *Libya* . . . . . **108 B4**   32 20N   23 15 E
Bunbury, *Australia* . . . . **125 F2**   33 20 S 115 35 E
Bunclody, *Ireland* **23 D5**   52 39N   6 40W
Buncrana, *Ireland* **23 A4**   55 8N   7 27W
Bunda, *Dem. Rep. of the Congo* **115 C3**   5 58 S   14 29 E
Bundaberg, *Australia* . . . . . **127 F5**   24 54 S 152 22 E
Bundanoon, *Australia* . . . . . **129 C9**   34 40 S 150 16 E
Bünde, *Germany* . . . . **30 C4**   52 11N   8 35 E
Bundey ➤, *Australia* . . . . . . **126 C2**   21 46 S 135 37 E
Bundi, *India* . . . . **92 G6**   25 30N   75 35 E
Bundjalung Nat. Park △, *Australia* **127 A5**   29 16 S 153 21 E
Bundoran, *Ireland* **23 B3**   54 28N   8 16W
Bundukia, *Sudan* . . . . **107 F3**   5 14N   30 55 E
Bundure, *Australia* . . . . **129 C7**   35 10 S 146   1 E
Bung Kan, *Thailand* . . . . . . **86 C4**   18 23N 103 37 E
Bunga ➤, *Nigeria* . . . . **113 C6**   11 23N   9 55 E
Bungay, *U.K.* . . . . **21 E9**   52 27N   1 28 E
Bungendore, *Australia* . . . . **129 C8**   35 14 S 149 30 E
Bungil Cr. ➤, *Australia* . . . . **127 D5**   27 5 S 149 5 E
Bungo, *Angola* . . . . **115 D3**   7 25 S   15 33 E
Bungo, Gunong, *Malaysia* . . **85 B4**   1 16N 110   9 E
Bungo-Suidō, *Japan* . . . . . . **72 E4**   33 0N 132 15 E
Bungoma, *Kenya* . . . . **118 B3**   0 34N   34 34 E
Bungotakada, *Japan* . . . . . . **72 D3**   33 35N 131 25 E
Bungu, *Tanzania* . . . . **118 D4**   7 35 S   39 0 E
Bunia, *Dem. Rep. of the Congo* **118 B3**   1 35N   30 20 E
Bunianga, *Dem. Rep. of the Congo* **114 C4**   3 28 S   20 11 E
Bunji, *Pakistan* . . . . **93 B6**   35 45N   74 40 E
Bunker Hill, *Ill., U.S.A.* **156 F7**   39 3N   89 57W
Bunker Hill, *Ind., U.S.A.* . . **157 D10**   40 40N   86 6W
Bunkie, *U.S.A.* **155 K8**   30 57N   92 11W
Bunnell, *U.S.A.* **153 L5**   29 28N   81 16W
Bunnythorpe, *N.Z.* . . . . **130 G4**   40 16 S 175 39 E
Buñol, *Spain* **41 F4**   39 25N   0 47W
Bunsuru, *Nigeria* . . . . **113 C5**   13 1N   5 30 E
Bunta, *Indonesia* . . . . **82 B2**   0 48 S 121 10 E
Buntok, *Indonesia* . . . . **85 C4**   1 40 S 114 58 E
Bununu Dass, *Nigeria* . . . . . **113 C6**   10 5N   9 31 E
Bununu Kasa, *Nigeria* . . . . . **113 D6**   9 51N   9 32 E
Bunya Mts. Nat. Park △, *Australia* **127 A5**   26 51 S 151 34 E
Bünyan, *Turkey* . . . . **100 C6**   38 51N   35 50 E
Bunyu, *Indonesia* . . . . **85 B5**   3 35N 117 50 E
Bunza, *Nigeria* . . . . **113 C5**   12 8N   4 0 E
Buol, *Indonesia* . . . . **82 A2**   1 15N 121 32 E
Buon Brieng, *Vietnam* . . . . . **86 F7**   13 9N 108 12 E
Buon Ma Thuot, *Vietnam* . . **86 F7**   12 40N 108 3 E
Buong Long, *Cambodia* . . . . **86 F6**   13 44N 106 59 E

Buorkhaya, Mys, *Russia* . . . **67 B14**   71 50N 132 40 E
Buqayq, *Si. Arabia* . . . . **97 E6**   26 0N   49 45 E
Buqbuq, *Egypt* . . . . **106 A2**   31 29N   25 29 E
Bur Acaba, *Somali Rep.* . . . **120 D2**   3 12N   44 20 E
Bûr Fuad, *Egypt* . . . . **106 H8**   31 15N   32 20 E
Bur Ghibi, *Somali Rep.* . . . . **120 D3**   3 56N   45 7 E
Bûr Safâga, *Egypt* . . . . **96 E2**   26 43N   33 57 E
Bûr Sa'îd, *Egypt* . . . . **106 H8**   31 16N   32 18 E
Bûr Sûdân, *Sudan* . . . . **106 D4**   19 32N   37 9 E
Bûr Taufîq, *Egypt* . . . . **106 J8**   29 54N   32 32 E
Bura, *Kenya* . . . . **118 C4**   1 4 S   39 58 E
Burakin, *Australia* . . . . **125 F2**   30 31 S 117 10 E
Buram, *Sudan* . . . . **107 E2**   10 51N   25 5 E
Buran, *Somali Rep.* . . . . **120 B3**   10 14N   48 44 E
Burao, *Somali Rep.* . . . . **120 C3**   9 32N   45 32 E
Burāq, *Syria* . . . . **103 B5**   33 11N   36 29 E
Burauen, *Phil.* . . . . **81 F5**   10 58N 124 53 E
Buraydah, *Si. Arabia* . . . . . . **96 E4**   26 20N   43 59 E
Burbank, *U.S.A.* **161 L8**   34 11N 118 19W
Burcher, *Australia* . . . . **129 B7**   33 30 S 147 16 E
Burda, *India* . . . . **92 G6**   25 50N   77 35 E
Burdekin ➤, *Australia* . . . . . **126 B4**   19 38 S 147 25 E
Burdeos Bay, *Phil.* . . . . **80 D4**   14 44N 122 6 E
Burdur, *Turkey* . . . . **49 D12**   37 45N   30 17 E
Burdur □, *Turkey* . . . . **49 D12**   37 45N   30 0 E
Burdur ➤, *Turkey* . . . . **49 D12**   37 44N   30 10 E
Burdur Gölü, *Turkey* . . . . . . **49 D12**   37 45N   30 10 E
Burdwan = Barddhaman, *India* **93 H12**   23 14N   87 39 E
Bure, *Gojam, Ethiopia* . . . . . **107 E4**   10 40N   37 4 E
Bure, *Ilubabor, Ethiopia* . . . **107 F4**   8 19N   35 8 E
Bure ➤, *U.K.* . . . . **20 E9**   52 38N   1 43 E
Büren, *Germany* . . . . **30 D4**   51 33N   8 35 E
Bureya ➤, *Russia* . . . . **67 D7**   49 27N 129 30 E
Burford, *Canada* **150 C4**   43 7N   80 27W
Burg, *Germany* . . . . **30 C7**   52 16N   11 51 E
Burg auf Fehmarn, *Germany* **30 A7**   54 28N   11 9 E
Burg el Arab, *Egypt* . . . . . . **106 H6**   30 54N   29 32 E
Burg et Tuyur, *Sudan* . . . . . **106 C2**   20 55N   27 56 E
Burg Stargard, *Germany* . . . **30 B9**   53 29N   13 18 E
Burgas, *Bulgaria* . . . . **51 D11**   42 33N   27 29 E
Burgas □, *Bulgaria* . . . . **51 D10**   42 30N   26 50 E
Burgaski Zaliv, *Bulgaria* . . . **51 D11**   42 30N   27 39 E
Burgdorf, *Germany* . . . . **30 C6**   52 27N   10 1 E
Burgdorf, *Switz.* . . . . **32 B5**   47 3N   7 37 E
Burgenland □, *Austria* . . . . . **35 D9**   47 20N   16 20 E
Burgeo, *Canada* **141 C8**   47 37N   57 38W
Burgersdorp, *S. Africa* . . . . **116 E4**   31 0 S   26 20 E
Burges, Mt., *Australia* . . . . . **125 F3**   30 50 S 121 5 E
Burghausen, *Germany* . . . . . **31 G8**   48 9N   12 49 E
Burghead, *U.K.* **22 D5**   57 43N   3 30W
Búrgio, *Italy* . . . . **48 E6**   37 36N   13 17 E
Bürglen, *Switz.* . . . . **33 C7**   46 53N   8 40 E
Burglengenfeld, *Germany* . . **31 F8**   49 12N   12 2 E
Burgohondo, *Spain* **42 E6**   40 26N   4 47W
Burgos, *Ilocos N., Phil.* . . . . **80 B3**   18 31N 120 39 E
Burgos, *Pangasinan, Phil.* . . **80 C2**   16 4N 119 52 E
Burgos, *Spain* **42 C7**   42 21N   3 41W
Burgos □, *Spain* **42 C7**   42 21N   3 42W
Burgstädt, *Germany* . . . . . . **30 E8**   50 54N   12 49 E
Burgsvik, *Sweden* . . . . **17 G12**   57 3N   18 19 E
Burguillos del Cerro, *Spain* . **43 G4**   38 23N   6 35W
Burgundy = Bourgogne, *France* **27 F11**   47 0N   4 50 E
Burhaniye, *Turkey* . . . . **49 B8**   39 30N   26 58 E
Burhanpur, *India* . . . . **94 D3**   21 18N   76 14 E
Burhi Gandak ➤, *India* . . . . **93 G12**   25 20N   86 37 E
Burhner ➤, *India* . . . . **93 H9**   22 43N   80 31 E
Buri Pen., *Eritrea* . . . . **107 D4**   15 25N   39 55 E
Burias I., *Phil.* . . . . **80 E4**   12 55N 123 5 E
Burias Pass, *Phil.* . . . . **80 E4**   13 0N 123 15 E
Burica, Pta., *Costa Rica* **164 E3**   8 3N   82 51W
Burien, *U.S.A.* **160 C4**   47 28N 122 21W
Burigi, L., *Tanzania* . . . . . . **118 C3**   2 2 S   31 22 E
Burigi Game Reserve △, *Tanzania* **118 C3**   2 20 S   31 6 E
Burin, *Canada* **141 C8**   47 1N   55 14W
Buriram, *Thailand* . . . . **86 E4**   15 0N 103   0 E
Buriti Alegre, *Brazil* . . . . . . **171 E2**   18 9 S   49 3W
Buriti Bravo, *Brazil* . . . . **170 C3**   5 50 S   43 50W
Buriti dos Lopes, *Brazil* . . . . **170 B3**   3 10 S   41 52W
Burj Sāfitā, *Syria* . . . . **100 F7**   34 49N   36 0 E
Burji, *Ethiopia* . . . . **39 F7**   43 17N   12 8 E
Burkburnett, *U.S.A.* **155 H5**   34 6N   98 34W
Burke ➤, *Australia* . . . . **126 C2**   23 12 S 139 33 E
Burke Chan., *Canada* **142 C3**   52 10N 127 30W
Burketown, *Australia* . . . . . **126 B2**   17 45 S 139 33 E
Burkina Faso ■, *Africa* **112 C4**   12 0N   1 0W
Burlada, *Spain* **40 C3**   42 49N   1 36W
Burleigh Falls, *Canada* **150 B6**   44 33N   78 12W
Burley, *U.S.A.* **158 E7**   42 32N 113 48W
Burli, *Kazakhstan* . . . . **64 F4**   51 25N   52 40 E
Burlingame, *U.S.A.* **160 H4**   37 35N 122 21W
Burlington, *Canada* **140 D4**   43 18N   79 45W
Burlington, *Colo., U.S.A.* . . **154 F3**   39 18N 102 16W
Burlington, *Iowa, U.S.A.* . . . **156 E9**   40 49N   91 14W
Burlington, *Kans., U.S.A.* . . **154 F7**   38 12N   95 45W
Burlington, *N.C., U.S.A.* . . . **149 G6**   36 6N   79 26W
Burlington, *N.J., U.S.A.* **151 F10**   40 4N   74 51W
Burlington, *Vt., U.S.A.* **151 B11**   44 29N   73 12W
Burlington, *Wash., U.S.A.* . . **160 B4**   48 28N 122 19W
Burlington, *Wis., U.S.A.* . . . **157 B8**   42 41N   88 17W
Burlyu-Tyube, *Kazakhstan* . . **66 E8**   46 30N   79 10 E
Burma ■, *Asia* . . . . **90 E6**   21 0N   96 30 E
Burnaby I., *Canada* **142 C2**   52 25N 131 19W
Burnet, *U.S.A.* **155 K5**   30 45N   98 14W
Burney, *U.S.A.* **158 F3**   40 53N 121 40W
Burnham, *U.S.A.* **150 F7**   40 38N   77 34W
Burnham-on-Sea, *U.K.* **21 F5**   51 14N   3 0W
Burnie, *Australia* . . . . **127 D4**   41 4 S 145 56 E
Burnley, *U.K.* **20 D5**   53 47N   2 14W
Burns, *U.S.A.* **158 E4**   43 35N 119 3W
Burns Lake, *Canada* **142 C3**   54 20N 125 45W
Burnside ➤, *Canada* **138 B9**   66 51N 108 4W
Burnside, L., *Australia* . . . . . **125 E3**   25 22 S 123 0 E
Burnsville, *U.S.A.* **154 C8**   44 47N   93 17W
Burnt L., *Canada* **141 B7**   53 35N   64 4W
Burnt Paw, *U.S.A.* **144 C12**   66 54N 143 44W
Burnt River, *Canada* **150 B6**   44 41N   78 42W
Burntwood ➤, *Canada* **143 B9**   56 8N   96 34W
Burntwood L., *Canada* **143 B8**   55 22N 100 26W
Buronga, *Australia* . . . . **128 C5**   34 8 S 142 20 E
Burqān, *Kuwait* . . . . **96 D5**   29 0N   47 57 E
Burqin, *China* . . . . **68 B3**   47 43N   87 0 E
Burra, *Australia* . . . . **128 B3**   33 40 S 138 55 E
Burra, *Nigeria* . . . . **113 C6**   11 0N   8 56 E
Burragorang, L., *Australia* . . **129 B9**   33 52 S 150 37 E
Burray, *U.K.* **22 C6**   58 51N   2 54W
Burrel, *Albania* . . . . **50 E4**   41 36N   20 1 E
Burren Junction, *Australia* . . **129 A8**   30 7 S 148 59 E
Burren Nat. Park △, *Ireland* **23 C3**   53 1N   9 8 58W
Burrendong, L., *Australia* . . **129 B8**   32 45 S 149 10 E
Burriana, *Spain* **40 F4**   39 50N   0 4W
Burrinjuck Res., *Australia* . . **129 C8**   35 0 S 148 36 E
Burro, Serranías del, *Mexico* **162 B4**   29 0N 102 0W
Burrow Pine Mountain Nat. Park △,
  Australia . . . . **129 D7**   36 6 S 147 45 E
Burrum Coast Nat. Park △, *Australia* **127 A5**   25 13 S 152 36 E
Burruyacú, *Argentina* . . . . . **174 B3**   26 30 S   64 40W
Burry Port, *U.K.* **21 F3**   51 41N   4 15W
Bursa, *Turkey* . . . . **51 F13**   40 15N   29 5 E
Burseryd, *Sweden* . . . . **17 G7**   57 12N   13 17 E
Burstall, *Canada* **143 C7**   50 39N 109 54W
Burton, *Mich., U.S.A.* **157 B13**   43 0N   83 40W
Burton, *Ohio, U.S.A.* **150 E3**   41 28N   81 8W

Burton, S.C., U.S.A. 149 J5   32 25N   80 45W
Burton, L., Canada 140 B4   54 45N   78 20W
Burton upon Trent, U.K. 20 E6   52 48N   1 38W
Burtundy, Australia .... 128 B5   33 45 S 142 15 E
Buru, Indonesia .... 82 B3   3 30 S 126 30 E
Buruanga, Phil. .... 81 F3   11 51N 121 53 E
Burūm, Yemen .... 99 D5   14 22N   48 59 E
Burūn, Rās, Egypt .... 103 D2   31 14N   33 7 E
Burunday = Boralday, Kazakhstan 65 B8   43 20N   76 51 E
Bururi, Burundi .... 118 C2   3 15 S   30 0 E
Burundi ■, Africa .... 118 C3   3 15 S   30 0 E
Bururi, Burundi .... 118 C2   3 57 S   29 37 E
Burutu, Nigeria .... 113 D6   5 20N   5 29 E
Burwell, U.S.A. 154 E5   41 47N   99 8W
Burwick, U.K. 22 C5   58 45N   2 58W
Bury, U.K. 20 D5   53 35N   2 17W
Bury St. Edmunds, U.K. .... 21 E8   52 15N   0 43 E
Buryatia □, Russia .... 67 D11   53 0N 110 0 E
Büryltbayat, Kazakhstan .... 65 A7   45 5N   74 1 E
Buryn, Ukraine .... 59 G7   51 13N   33 50 E
Burzenin, Poland .... 55 G5   51 28N   18 47 E
Busa, Mt., Phil. .... 81 H5   6 8N 124 39 E
Busalla, Italy .... 44 D5   44 34N   8 57 E
Busan = Pusan, S. Korea .... 75 G15   35 5N 129 0 E
Busanga, Dem. Rep. of the Congo 114 C4   0 53 S   22 7 E
Busango Swamp, Zambia .... 119 E2   14 15 S   25 45 E
Buşayrah, Syria .... 101 E9   35 9N   40 26 E
Busca, Italy .... 44 D4   44 31N   7 29 E
Bushat, Albania .... 50 E3   41 58N   19 34 E
Büshehr, Iran .... 97 D6   28 55N   50 55 E
Büshehr □, Iran .... 97 D6   28 20N   51 45 E
Bushell, Canada 143 B7   59 31N 108 45W
Bushenyi, Uganda .... 118 C3   0 35 S   30 10 E
Bushimaie →, Dem. Rep. of the Congo 115 D4   6 2 S   23 45 E
Bushire = Büshehr, Iran .... 97 D6   28 55N   50 55 E
Bushnell, Fla., U.S.A. 153 G7   28 40N   82 7W
Bushnell, Ill., U.S.A. 156 D6   40 33N   90 31W
Busie, Ghana 112 C4   10 29N   2 22W
Businga, Dem. Rep. of the Congo 114 B4   3 16N   20 59 E
Busko-Zdrój, Poland .... 55 H7   50 28N   20 42 E
Buskul, Kazakhstan .... 64 E8   53 45N   61 12 E
Buslei, Ethiopia .... 120 C2   5 28N   44 25 E
Busovača, Bos.-H. .... 52 F2   44 6N   17 53 E
Buşra ash Shām, Syria .... 103 C5   32 30N   36 25 E
Busselton, Australia .... 125 F2   33 42 S 115 15 E
Busseri →, Sudan .... 107 F2   7 41N   28 3 E
Busseto, Italy .... 44 D7   44 59N   10 2 E
Bussière-Badil, France .... 28 C4   45 39N   0 36 E
Bussigny, Switz. .... 32 C3   46 33N   6 33 E
Bussolengo, Italy .... 44 C7   45 28N   10 51 E
Bussum, Neths. .... 25 B5   52 16N   5 10 E
Bustamante, B., Argentina ...... 176 C3   45 5 S   66 18W
Buşteni, Romania .... 53 E10   45 24N   25 32 E
Busto, C., Spain 42 B4   43 34N   6 28W
Busto Arsízio, Italy .... 44 C5   45 37N   8 51 E
Busu Djanoa, Dem. Rep. of the Congo 114 B4   1 43N   21 23 E
Busu Kwanga, Dem. Rep. of the Congo 114 B4   1 48N   20 21 E
Busu Mandji, Dem. Rep. of the Congo 114 B4   2 52N   21 14 E
Busuanga, Phil. .... 80 E2   12 14N 119 52 E
Busuanga I., Phil. .... 80 E2   12 10N 120 0 E
Büsum, Germany .... 30 A4   54 7N   8 51 E
Busungbiu, Indonesia .... 79 J17   8 16 S 114 58 E
Buta, Dem. Rep. of the Congo ... 118 B1   2 50N   24 53 E
Butare, Rwanda .... 118 C2   2 31 S   29 52 E
Butaritari, Kiribati .... 134 G9   3 30N 174 0 E
Bute, Australia .... 128 B3   33 51 S 138 2 E
Bute, U.K. 22 F3   53 48N   5 2W
Bute Inlet, Canada 142 C4   50 40N 124 53W
Butemba, Uganda .... 118 B3   1 9N   31 37 E
Butembo, Dem. Rep. of the Congo 118 B2   0 9N   29 18 E
Buteni, Romania .... 52 D7   46 19N   22 7 E
Butera, Italy .... 47 E7   37 11N   14 11 E
Butha Qi, China .... 69 B7   48 0N 122 32 E
Buthidaung, Burma .... 90 E4   20 52N   92 32 E
Butiaba, Uganda .... 118 B3   1 50N   31 20 E
Butler, Ga., U.S.A. 152 C5   32 33N   84 14W
Butler, Ind., U.S.A. 157 C12   41 26N   84 52W
Butler, Ky., U.S.A. 157 F12   38 47N   84 22W
Butler, Mo., U.S.A. 156 F2   38 16N   94 20W
Butler, Pa., U.S.A. 150 F5   40 52N   79 54W
Buton, Indonesia .... 82 C2   5 0 S 122 45 E
Butrintit, L. e, Albania .... 38 B10   39 43N   20 5 E
Bütschwil, Switz. .... 33 B8   47 23N   9 5 E
Butte, Mont., U.S.A. 158 C7   46 0N 112 32W
Butte, Nebr., U.S.A. 154 D5   42 58N   98 51W
Butte Creek →, U.S.A. 160 F5   39 12N 121 56W
Butterworth = Gcuwa, S. Africa 117 E4   32 20 S   28 11 E
Butterworth, Malaysia .... 87 c   5 24N 100 23 E
Buttevant, Ireland 23 D3   52 14N   8 40W
Buttfield, Mt., Australia .... 125 D4   24 45 S 128 9 E
Button B., Canada 143 B10   58 45N   94 23W
Buttonwillow, U.S.A. 161 K7   35 24N 119 28W
Butty Hd., Australia .... 125 F3   33 54 S 121 39 E
Butuan, Phil. .... 81 G5   8 57N 125 33 E
Butuku-Luba, Eq. Guin. .... 113 E6   3 29N   8 33 E
Butung = Buton, Indonesia ...... 82 C2   5 0 S 122 45 E
Buturlinovka, Russia .... 60 E5   50 50N   40 35 E
Butzbach, Germany .... 31 E4   50 25N   8 40 E
Bützow, Germany .... 30 B7   53 50N   11 58 E
Buulobarde = Bulo Burti, Somali Rep. 120 D3   3 50N   45 33 E
Buur Hakaba = Bur Acaba, Somali Rep. 120 D2   3 12N   44 20 E
Buvik, Norway .... 18 A7   63 18N   10 11 E
Buxa Duar, India .... 93 F13   27 45N   89 35 E
Buxar, India .... 93 G10   25 34N   83 58 E
Buxtehude, Germany .... 30 B5   53 28N   9 39 E
Buxton, Guyana 169 B6   6 48N   58 2W
Buxton, U.K. 20 D6   53 16N   1 54W
Buxy, France .... 27 F11   46 44N   4 40 E
Buy, Russia .... 60 A5   58 28N   41 28 E
Buynaksk, Russia .... 61 J8   42 48N   47 7 E
Buyo, Ivory C. 112 D3   6 21N   7 5W
Buyo, L. de, Ivory C. 112 D3   6 16N   7 10W
Büyük Menderes →, Turkey ...... 49 D9   37 28N   27 11 E
Büyükçekmece, Turkey .... 51 E12   41 2N   28 35 E
Büyükkarıştıran, Turkey .... 51 E11   41 18N   27 33 E
Büyükkemikli Burnu, Turkey ... 51 F10   40 18N   26 14 E
Büyükorhan, Turkey .... 49 B10   39 46N   28 56 E
Büyükyoncalı, Turkey .... 51 E11   41 20N   27 55 E
Buzançais, France .... 26 F8   46 54N   1 25 E
Buzău, Romania .... 53 E11   45 10N   26 50 E
Buzău □, Romania .... 53 E11   45 20N   26 30 E
Buzău →, Romania .... 53 E12   45 26N   27 44 E
Buzău, Pasul, Romania .... 53 E11   45 35N   26 12 E
Buzen, Japan .... 72 D3   33 35N 131 5 E
Buzet, Croatia .... 45 C10   45 24N   13 58 E
Buzi →, Mozam. .... 119 F3   19 50 S   34 43 E
Buziaş, Romania .... 52 E6   45 38N   21 36 E
Buzuluk, Russia .... 64 E4   52 48N   52 12 E
Buzuluk →, Russia .... 60 E6   50 15N   42 7 E
Buzzards B., U.S.A. 151 E14   41 45N   70 37W
Buzzards Bay, U.S.A. 151 E14   41 44N   70 37W
Bwagaoia, Papua N. G. .... 132 F7   10 40 S 152 52 E
Bwana Mkubwe, Dem. Rep. of the Congo 119 E2   13 8 S   28 38 E
Bwasa, Dem. Rep. of the Congo 114 C3   3 55 S   18 24 E
Bwatnapné, Vanuatu .... 133 E6   15 41 S 168 9 E

Bwindi Impenetrable Forest Nat.
Park △, Uganda .... 118 C2   1 2 S   29 42 E
Byala, Ruse, Bulgaria .... 51 C9   43 28N   25 44 E
Byala, Varna, Bulgaria .... 51 D11   42 53N   27 55 E
Byala Slatina, Bulgaria .... 50 C7   43 26N   23 58 E
Byarezina →, Belarus .... 59 F6   52 33N   30 14 E
Byaroza, Belarus .... 59 F3   52 31N   24 51 E
Bychawa, Poland .... 55 G9   51 1N   22 36 E
Byczyna, Poland .... 55 G5   51 7N   18 12 E
Bydgoszcz, Poland .... 55 E5   53 10N   18 0 E
Byelarus = Belarus ■, Europe ... 58 F4   53 30N   27 0 E
Byelorussia = Belarus ■, Europe 58 F4   53 30N   27 0 E
Byers, U.S.A. 154 F2   39 43N 104 14W
Byesville, U.S.A. 150 G3   39 58N   81 32W
Byfield Nat. Park △, Australia 126 C5   22 52 S 150 45 E
Byford, Australia .... 125 F2   32 15 S 116 0 E
Bygdin, Norway .... 18 C5   61 21N   8 32 E
Bygland, Norway .... 18 F4   58 50N   7 48 E
Byglandsfjorden, Norway .... 18 F4   58 44N   7 50 E
Bygstad, Norway .... 18 C2   61 23N   5 40 E
Bykhaw, Belarus .... 58 F6   53 31N   30 14 E
Bykhov = Bykhaw, Belarus ...... 58 F6   53 31N   30 14 E
Bykle, Norway .... 18 E4   59 20N   7 22 E
Bykovo, Russia .... 60 F7   49 50N   45 25 E
Bylas, U.S.A. 159 K8   33 8N 110 7W
Bylot, Canada 143 B10   58 25N   94 8W
Bylot I., Canada 139 A12   73 13N   78 34W
Byrock, Australia .... 129 A7   30 40 S 146 27 E
Byron, Ga., U.S.A. 152 C6   32 39N   83 46W
Byron, Ill., U.S.A. 156 B7   42 8N   89 15W
Byron, C., Australia .... 127 D5   28 43 S 153 38 E
Byron Bay, Australia .... 127 D5   28 43 S 153 37 E
Byrranga, Gory, Russia .... 67 B11   75 0N 100 0 E
Byrranga Mts. = Byrranga, Gory, Russia 67 B11   75 0N 100 0 E
Byrum, Denmark .... 17 G5   57 16N   11 0 E
Byske, Sweden .... 14 D19   64 57N   21 11 E
Byske älv →, Sweden .... 14 D19   64 57N   21 13 E
Bystrovka = Kemin, Kyrgyzstan 65 B7   42 47N   75 42 E
Bystrzyca →, Dolnośląskie, Poland 55 G3   51 12N   16 55 E
Bystrzyca →, Lubelskie, Poland 55 G9   51 21N   22 46 E
Bystrzyca Kłodzka, Poland ...... 55 H3   50 19N   16 39 E
Bytča, Slovak Rep. .... 35 B11   49 13N   18 34 E
Bytom, Poland .... 55 H5   50 25N   18 54 E
Bytom Odrzański, Poland ...... 55 G2   51 44N   15 48 E
Bytów, Poland .... 54 D4   54 10N   17 30 E
Byumba, Rwanda .... 118 C3   1 35 S   30 4 E
Bzenec, Czech Rep. .... 35 C10   48 58N   17 18 E
Bzura →, Poland .... 55 F7   52 25N   20 15 E

C

Ca →, Vietnam .... 86 C5   18 45N 105 45 E
Ca Mau, Vietnam .... 87 H5   9 7N 105 8 E
Ca Mau, Mui, Vietnam .... 87 H5   8 38N 104 44 E
Ca Na, Vietnam .... 87 G7   11 20N 108 54 E
Caacupé, Paraguay .... 174 B4   25 23 S   57 5W
Caála, Angola .... 115 E3   12 46 S   15 10 E
Caamaño Sd., Canada 142 C3   52 55N 129 25W
Caapiranga, Brazil .... 169 D5   3 18 S   61 13W
Caazapá, Paraguay .... 174 B4   26 8 S   56 19W
Caazapá □, Paraguay .... 175 B4   26 10 S   56 0W
Cabadbaran, Phil. .... 81 G5   9 10N 125 38 E
Cabagan, Phil. .... 80 C3   17 26N 121 46 E
Cabalian = San Juan, Phil. ...... 81 F5   10 16N 125 10 E
Caballeria, C. de, Spain .... 38 A5   40 5N   4 5 E
Cabana, Peru .... 172 B2   8 25 S   78 5W
Cabana, Spain 42 B2   43 13N   8 54W
Cabanaconde, Peru .... 172 D3   15 38 S   71 58W
Cabañaquinta, Spain 42 B5   43 10N   5 38W
Cabanatuan, Phil. .... 80 D3   15 30N 120 58 E
Cabañeros, Parque Natural de △, Spain 43 F6   39 18N   4 35W
Cabanes, Spain .... 40 E5   40 9N   0 2 E
Cabangan, Phil. .... 80 D3   15 10N 120 3 E
Cabanillas, Peru .... 172 D3   15 5 S   70 28W
Cabano, Canada 141 C6   47 40N   68 56W
Cabar, Croatia .... 45 C11   45 36N   14 39 E
Cabarroguis, Phil. .... 80 C3   16 50N 121 30 E
Cabarruyan I., Phil. .... 80 C2   16 18N 119 52 E
Cabazon, U.S.A. 161 M10   33 55N 116 47W
Cabedelo, Brazil .... 170 C5   7 0 S   34 50W
Cabeza del Buey, Spain 43 G5   38 44N   5 13W
Cabezón de la Sal, Spain 42 B6   43 18N   4 14W
Cabildo, Chile .... 174 C1   32 30 S   71 5W
Cabimas, Venezuela 168 A3   10 23N   71 25W
Cabinda, Angola .... 115 D2   5 33 S   12 11 E
Cabinda □, Angola .... 115 D2   5 0 S   12 30 E
Cabinet Mts., U.S.A. 158 C6   48 0N 115 30W
Cabiri, Angola .... 115 D2   8 52 S   13 39 E
Cable Beach, Bahamas .... 9 b   25 4N   77 24W
Cabo Blanco, Argentina .... 176 C3   47 15 S   65 47W
Cabo de Gata-Níjar, Parque Natural de △, Spain 41 J2   36 51N   2 6W
Cabo Frio, Brazil .... 171 F3   22 51 S   42 3W
Cabo Pantoja, Peru .... 168 D2   1 0 S   75 10W
Cabo Raso, Argentina .... 176 B3   44 20 S   65 10W
Cabonga, Réservoir, Canada ... 140 C4   47 20N   76 40W
Cabool, U.S.A. 155 G8   37 7N   92 6W
Caboolture, Australia .... 127 D5   27 5 S 152 58 E
Cabora Bassa Dam = Cahora Bassa, Reprêsa de, Mozam. 119 F3   15 20 S   32 50 E
Caborca, Mexico 162 A2   30 40N 112 10W
Cabot, Mt., U.S.A. 151 B13   44 30N   71 25W
Cabot Hd., Canada 150 A3   45 14N   81 17W
Cabot Str., Canada 141 C8   47 15N   59 40W
Cabra, Spain 43 H6   37 30N   4 28W
Cabra del Santo Cristo, Spain ... 43 H17   37 42N   3 16W
Cabra I., India .... 95 L11   7 18N   93 50 E
Cábras, Italy .... 46 C1   39 56N   8 32 E
Cabrera, Spain .... 38 B3   39 8N   2 57 E
Cabrera, Parque Nac. de △, Spain 41 F7   39 13N   2 53 E
Cabrera, Sierra, Spain 42 C4   42 12N   6 40W
Cabri, Canada 143 C7   50 35N 108 25W
Cabriel →, Spain 43 F3   39 14N   1 3W
Cabruta, Venezuela 168 B4   7 50N   66 10W
Cabucgayan, Phil. .... 81 F5   11 29N 124 34 E
Cabugao, Phil. .... 80 C3   17 48N 120 27 E
Cabulauan Is., Phil. .... 81 F3   11 25N 120 0 E
Cabulo, Angola .... 115 E3   10 18 S   16 22 E
Caburan = Jose Abad Santos, Phil. 81 J5   5 55N 125 39 E
Cabuta, Angola .... 115 D2   9 48 S   14 58 E
Cabuyaro, Colombia 168 C3   4 18N   72 49W
Cacabelos, Spain 42 C4   42 36N   6 44W
Caçador, Brazil .... 175 B5   26 47 S   51 0W
Čačak, Serbia, Yug. .... 50 C4   43 54N   20 20 E
Cacao, Fr. Guiana 169 C7   4 33N   52 26W
Caçapava do Sul, Brazil .... 175 C5   30 30 S   53 30W
Cáccamo, Italy .... 46 E6   37 56N   13 40 E
Cacém, Portugal 43 G1   38 46N   9 18W
Cáceres, Brazil .... 173 D6   16 5 S   57 40W
Cáceres, Colombia 168 B2   7 35N   75 20W
Cáceres, Spain 43 F4   39 26N   6 23W
Cáceres □, Spain 42 F5   39 45N   6 0W
Cache Cr. →, U.S.A. 160 G5   38 42N 121 42W
Cache Creek, Canada 142 C4   50 48N 121 19W
Cacheu, Guinea-Biss. 112 C1   12 14N   16 8W
Cachi, Argentina .... 174 B2   25 5 S   66 10W

Cachimbo, Brazil .... 173 B7   8 57 S   54 54W
Cachimbo, Serra do, Brazil ...... 173 B6   9 30 S   55 30W
Cachimo, Angola .... 115 D4   8 21 S   21 24 E
Cachinal de la Sierra, Chile ...... 174 A2   24 58 S   69 32W
Cachingues, Angola .... 115 E3   13 5 S   16 43 E
Cachoeira, Brazil .... 171 D4   12 30 S   39 0W
Cachoeira Alta, Brazil .... 171 E1   18 48 S   50 58W
Cachoeira do Sul, Brazil .... 175 C5   30 3 S   52 53W
Cachoeiro de Itapemirim, Brazil 171 F3   20 51 S   41 7W
Cachopo, Portugal 43 H3   37 20N   7 49W
Cachuela Esperanza, Bolivia ... 173 C4   10 32 S   65 38W
Cacine, Guinea-Biss. 112 C1   11 18N   14 57W
Cacoal, Brazil .... 173 C5   11 30 S   61 25W
Cacólo, Angola .... 115 E3   10 9 S   19 21 E
Caconda, Angola .... 115 E3   13 48 S   15 8 E
Cacongo, Angola .... 115 D2   5 11 S   12 5 E
Caçu, Brazil .... 171 E1   18 37 S   51 4W
Cacuaco, Angola .... 115 D2   8 47 S   13 21 E
Cacuchi →, Angola .... 115 E3   14 26 S   16 46 E
Cacula, Angola .... 115 E2   14 29 S   14 10 E
Caculé, Brazil .... 171 D3   14 30 S   42 13W
Caculuvar →, Angola .... 115 F2   16 47 S   14 56 E
Cacuso, Angola .... 115 D3   9 25 S   15 45 E
Čadca, Slovak Rep. .... 35 B11   49 26N   18 45 E
Caddo, U.S.A. 155 H6   34 7N   96 16W
Cadenazzo, Switz. .... 33 D7   46 9N   8 57 E
Cader Idris, U.K. 21 E4   52 42N   3 53W
Cadereyta, Mexico 162 B5   25 36N 100 0W
Cades, U.S.A. 152 B10   33 47N   79 47W
Cadí, Sierra del, Spain .... 40 C6   42 17N   1 42 E
Cadi-Moixeró, Parque Natural de △, Spain 40 C3   42 17N   1 44W
Cadibarrawirracanna, L., Australia 127 D2   28 52 S 135 27 E
Cadillac, France 28 D3   44 38N   0 20W
Cadillac, U.S.A. 148 C3   44 15N   85 24W
Cádiz, Phil. .... 81 F4   10 57N 123 15 E
Cádiz, Spain 43 J4   36 30N   6 20W
Cadiz, Calif., U.S.A. 161 L11   34 30N 115 28W
Cadiz, Ohio, U.S.A. 150 F4   40 22N   81 0W
Cádiz □, Spain 43 J5   36 36N   5 45W
Cádiz, G. de, Spain 43 J3   36 40N   7 0W
Cadiz L., U.S.A. 159 J6   34 18N 115 24W
Cadney Park, Australia .... 127 D1   27 55 S 134 3 E
Cadomin, Canada 142 C5   53 2N 117 20W
Cadotte Lake, Canada 142 B5   56 26N 116 23W
Cadours, France .... 28 E5   43 44N   1 2 E
Cadoux, Australia .... 125 F2   30 46 S 117 7 E
Cadwell, U.S.A. 152 C6   32 16N   83 2W
Caen, France 26 C6   49 10N   0 22W
Caernarfon, U.K. 20 D3   53 8N   4 16W
Caernarfon B., U.K. 20 D3   53 4N   4 40W
Caernarvon = Caernarfon, U.K. ... 20 D3   53 8N   4 16W
Caerphilly, U.K. 21 F4   51 35N   3 13W
Caerphilly □, U.K. 21 F4   51 37N   3 12W
Caesarea, Israel .... 103 C3   32 30N   34 53 E
Caeté, Brazil .... 171 E3   19 55 S   43 40W
Caetité, Brazil .... 171 D3   13 50 S   42 32W
Cafayate, Argentina .... 174 B2   26 2 S   66 0W
Cafu, Angola .... 116 B2   16 30 S   15 8 E
Cagayan □, Phil. .... 80 B3   18 25N 121 42 E
Cagayan de Oro, Phil. .... 81 G5   8 30N 124 40 E
Cagayan Is., Phil. .... 81 G3   9 40N 121 16 E
Cagayan Sulu I., Phil. .... 81 H2   7 1N 118 30 E
Cagli, Italy .... 45 E9   43 33N   12 39 E
Cágliari, Italy .... 46 C2   39 13N   9 7 E
Cágliari, G. di, Italy .... 46 C2   39 8N   9 11 E
Cagnano Varano, Italy .... 45 G12   41 49N   15 47 E
Cagnes-sur-Mer, France .... 29 E11   43 40N   7 9 E
Caguán →, Colombia .... 168 D3   0 8 S   74 18W
Caguas, Puerto Rico .... 165 d   18 14N   66 2W
Caha Mts., Ireland 23 E2   51 45N   9 40W
Cahama, Angola .... 116 B1   16 17 S   14 19 E
Caher, Ireland 23 D4   52 22N   7 56W
Caherciveen, Ireland 23 E1   51 56N   10 14W
Cahora Bassa, L. de, Mozam. ... 119 F3   15 35 S   32 0 E
Cahora Bassa, Reprêsa de, Mozam. 119 F3   15 20 S   32 50 E
Cahore Pt., Ireland 23 D5   52 33N   6 12W
Cahors, France .... 28 D5   44 27N   1 27 E
Cahuapanas, Peru .... 172 B2   5 15 S   77 0W
Cahuinari →, Colombia .... 168 D3   1 21 S   70 44W
Cahul, Moldova .... 53 E13   45 50N   28 15 E
Caì Bau, Dao, Vietnam .... 76 G6   21 10N 107 27 E
Cai Nuoc, Vietnam .... 87 H5   8 56N 105 1 E
Caia, Mozam. .... 119 F4   17 51 S   35 24 E
Caiabis, Serra dos, Brazil ...... 173 C6   11 30 S   56 30W
Caianda, Angola .... 119 E1   11 2 S   23 31 E
Caiapó, Serra do, Brazil .... 173 D7   17 0 S   52 0W
Caiapônia, Brazil .... 171 D7   16 57 S   51 49W
Caibarién, Cuba 164 B4   22 30N   79 30W
Caibiran, Phil. .... 81 F5   11 34N 124 35 E
Caicara = Alvarães, Brazil ...... 169 D5   3 12 S   64 54W
Caicara, Bolívar, Venezuela 168 B4   7 38N   66 10W
Caicara, Monagas, Venezuela ... 169 B5   9 52N   63 38W
Caicó, Brazil .... 170 C4   6 20 S   37 0W
Caicos Is., Turks & Caicos 165 B5   21 40N   71 40W
Caicos Passage, W. Indies 165 B5   22 45N   72 45W
Caidian, China .... 77 B10   30 35N 114 2 E
Cailloma, Peru .... 172 D3   15 12 S   71 45W
Cǎinari, Moldova .... 53 D14   46 41N   29 3 E
Cainde, Angola .... 115 F2   15 59 S   13 24 E
Caine →, Bolivia .... 174 D4   18 23 S   65 21W
Cairn Gorm, U.K. 23 D5   57 7N   3 39W
Cairn Toul, U.K. 22 D5   57 3N   3 42W
Cairngorm Mts., U.K. 23 D5   54 59N   5 1W
Cairnryan, U.K. 22 C4   54 59N   5 1W
Cairns, Australia .... 126 B4   16 57 S 145 45 E
Cairns L., Canada 143 C10   51 42N   94 30W
Cairo = El Qâhira, Egypt ...... 106 H7   30 1N   31 14 E
Cairo, Ga., U.S.A. 152 K3   30 52N   84 13W
Cairo, Ill., U.S.A. 155 G10   37 0N   89 11W
Cairo, N.Y., U.S.A. 151 D11   42 18N   74 0W
Cairo Montenotte, Italy .... 44 D5   44 23N   8 16 E
Cairofa, Angola .... 115 E2   14 3 S   12 54 E
Caithness, U.K. 22 C5   58 25N   3 35W
Caithness, Ord of, U.K. 22 C5   58 8N   3 36W
Caitou, Angola .... 115 F3   14 30 S   17 8 E
Caiundo, Angola .... 115 F3   15 50 S   17 28 E
Caiza, Bolivia .... 174 A3   20 2 S   65 40W
Caja de Muertos, I., Puerto Rico 165 d   17 54N   66 32W
Cajabamba, Peru .... 172 B2   7 38 S   78 4W
Cajamarca, Peru .... 172 B2   6 15 S   78 50W
Cajamarca □, Peru .... 172 B2   7 5 S   78 28W
Cajapió, Brazil .... 170 B3   2 58 S   44 48W
Cajàzeiras, Brazil .... 170 C4   6 52 S   38 30W
Čajetina, Serbia, Yug. .... 50 C3   43 47N   19 42 E
Cajidiocan, Phil. .... 80 E4   12 34N 122 41 E
Cajnice, Bos.-H. .... 52 C4   43 34N   19 5 E
Çakırgol, Turkey .... 49 E12   36 53N   30 33 E
Çakırlar, Turkey .... 49 C11   38 4N   29 23 E
Čakovec, Croatia .... 45 B13   46 23N   16 26 E
Çal, Turkey .... 49 C11   38 9N   29 25 E
Cala, Spain 43 H4   37 59N   6 21W
Cala →, Spain 43 H4   37 38N   6 5W
Cala Cadolar, Punta de = Rotja, Pta., Spain 38 D2   38 38N   1 35 E
Cala d'Or, Spain .... 38 B5   39 23N   3 14 E
Cala en Porter, Spain .... 38 B5   39 52N   4 8 E
Cala Figuera, C. de, Spain ...... 38 B4   39 27N   2 31 E
Cala Forcat, Spain .... 38 B4   40 0N   3 47 E
Cala Major, Spain .... 38 B3   39 33N   2 37 E

Cala Mezquida = Sa Mesquida, Spain 38 B5   39 55N   4 16 E
Cala Millor, Spain .... 38 B4   39 35N   3 22 E
Cala Ratjada, Spain .... 38 B4   39 43N   3 27 E
Cala Santa Galdana, Spain ...... 38 B4   39 56N   3 58 E
Calabanga, Phil. .... 80 E4   13 42N 123 17 E
Calabar, Nigeria .... 113 E6   4 57N   8 20 E
Calabogie, Canada 151 A8   45 18N   76 43W
Calabozo, Venezuela 168 B4   9 0N   67 28W
Calábria □, Italy .... 47 C9   39 0N   16 30 E
Calábria, Parco Nazionale della △, Italy 47 C9   39 6N   16 35 E
Calaburras, Pta. de, Spain 43 J6   36 30N   4 38W
Calaceite, Spain .... 40 D5   41 1N   0 11 E
Calacoto, Bolivia .... 172 D4   17 16 S   68 38W
Calacuccia, France .... 29 F13   42 21N   9 1 E
Calafat, Romania .... 52 G7   43 58N   22 59 E
Calafate, Argentina .... 176 D2   50 19 S   72 15W
Calafell, Spain .... 40 D6   41 11N   1 34 E
Calagua Is., Phil. .... 80 D4   14 30N 122 55 E
Calahorra, Spain 40 C3   42 18N   1 59W
Calai, Angola .... 115 F3   17 47 S   19 41 E
Calais, France .... 27 B8   50 57N   1 56 E
Calais, U.S.A. 149 C12   45 11N   67 17W
Calakmul, Reserva de La Biósfera △, Mexico 163 D7   18 14N   89 48W
Calalaste, Cord. de, Argentina ... 174 B2   25 0 S   67 0W
Calama, Brazil .... 173 B5   8 0 S   62 50W
Calama, Chile .... 174 A2   22 30 S   68 55W
Calamar, Bolívar, Colombia ...... 168 A3   10 15 S   74 55W
Calamar, Vaupés, Colombia 168 C3   1 58N   72 32W
Calamarca, Bolivia .... 172 D4   16 55 S   68 9W
Calamba, Cavite, Phil. .... 80 D3   14 13N 121 10 E
Calamba, Mis. Occ., Phil. ...... 81 G4   8 35N 123 39 E
Calamian Group, Phil. .... 81 F2   11 50N 119 55 E
Calamocha, Spain 40 E3   40 50N   1 17W
Calamonte, Spain 43 G4   38 53N   6 23W
Cǎlan, Romania .... 52 E7   45 44N   22 59 E
Calañas, Spain 43 H4   37 40N   6 53W
Calanda, Spain 40 E4   40 56N   0 15W
Calandagan I., Phil. .... 81 F3   10 39N 120 15 E
Calandula, Angola .... 115 D3   9 3 S   15 57 E
Calang, Indonesia .... 84 B1   4 37N   95 37 E
Calangiánus, Italy .... 46 B2   40 56N   9 11 E
Calanscio, Sarīr, Libya .... 108 C4   27 30N   22 30 E
Calapan, Phil. .... 80 E3   13 25N 121 7 E
Calarasi, Moldova .... 53 C13   47 16N   28 19 E
Cǎlǎraşi, Romania .... 53 F11   44 12N   27 20 E
Cǎlǎraşi □, Romania .... 53 F12   44 10N   27 0 E
Calasparra, Spain 41 G3   38 14N   1 41W
Calatafimi, Italy .... 46 E5   37 55N   12 52 E
Calatagan, Phil. .... 80 E3   13 50N 120 38 E
Calatayud, Spain 40 D3   41 20N   1 40W
Cǎlǎţele, Romania .... 52 D8   46 46N   23 1 E
Calato = Kálathos, Greece ...... 38 E12   36 9N   28 8 E
Calatrava, Eq. Guin. .... 114 B1   1 6N   9 25 E
Calauag, Phil. .... 80 E4   13 55N 122 15 E
Calavá, C., Italy .... 47 D7   38 11N   14 55 E
Calavite, C., Phil. .... 80 E3   13 26N 120 20 E
Calavite Pass, Phil. .... 80 E3   13 20N 120 10 E
Calayan, Phil. .... 80 B3   19 16N 121 28 E
Calayan I., Phil. .... 80 B3   19 20N 121 30 E
Ca lbayog, Phil. .... 80 E5   12 4N 124 38 E
Calbiga, Phil. .... 81 F5   11 38N 125 0 E
Calca, Peru .... 172 C3   13 22 S   72 0W
Calcasieu L., U.S.A. 155 L8   29 55N   93 18W
Calcutta = Kolkata, India ...... 93 H13   22 36N   88 24 E
Calcutta, U.S.A. 150 F4   40 40N   80 34W
Caldaro, Italy .... 45 B8   46 25N   11 14 E
Caldas □, Colombia 168 B2   5 15N   75 30W
Caldas da Rainha, Portugal 43 F1   39 24N   9 4W
Caldas de Reis, Spain 42 C2   42 36N   8 39W
Caldas Novas, Brazil .... 171 E2   17 45 S   48 38W
Calder →, U.K. 20 D6   53 44N   1 22W
Caldera, Chile .... 174 B1   27 5 S   70 55W
Caldera de Taburiente, Parque Nac. de △, Canary Is. 9 e1   28 43N   17 52W
Caldwell, Idaho, U.S.A. 158 E5   43 40N 116 41W
Caldwell, Kans., U.S.A. 155 G6   37 2N   97 37W
Caldwell, Tex., U.S.A. 155 K6   30 32N   96 42W
Caledon, S. Africa .... 116 E2   34 14 S   19 26 E
Caledon →, S. Africa .... 116 E4   30 31 S   26 5 E
Caledon B., Australia .... 126 A2   12 45 S 137 0 E
Caledonia, Canada 150 C5   43 7N   79 58W
Caledonia, Minn., U.S.A. 156 D9   37 45N   90 46W
Caledonia, N.Y., U.S.A. 150 D7   42 58N   77 51W
Calella, Spain .... 40 D7   41 37N   2 40 E
Calemba, Angola .... 116 B2   16 0 S   15 44 E
Calen, Australia .... 126 J6   20 56 S 148 48 E
Calenzana, France .... 29 F12   42 31N   8 51 E
Caleta Olivia, Argentina ...... 176 C3   46 25 S   67 25W
Caletones, Chile .... 174 C1   34 6 S   70 27W
Calexico, U.S.A. 161 N11   32 40N 115 30W
Calf of Man, U.K. 20 C3   54 3N   4 48W
Calgary, Canada 142 C6   51 0N 114 10W
Calheta, Azores 9 d1   38 36N   28 1W
Calheta, Madeira .... 9 c   32 44N   17 11W
Calheta de Nesquim, Azores ... 9 d1   38 24N   28 5W
Calhoun, U.S.A. 149 H3   34 30N   84 57W
Calhoun Falls, U.S.A. 152 A7   34 6N   82 36W
Cali, Colombia 168 C2   3 25N   76 35W
Calicut, India .... 95 J2   11 15N   75 43 E
Caliente, U.S.A. 159 H6   37 37N 114 31W
California, Mo., U.S.A. 156 F8   38 38N   92 34W
California, Pa., U.S.A. 150 F5   40 4N   79 54W
California □, U.S.A. 160 H7   37 30N 119 30W
California, Baja, Mexico 162 A1   32 10N 115 12W
California, Baja, T.N. = Baja California □, Mexico 162 B2   30 0N 115 0W
California, Baja, T.S. = Baja California Sur □, Mexico ... 162 B2   25 50N 111 50W
California, G. de, Mexico 162 B2   27 0N 111 0W
California City, U.S.A. 161 K9   35 10N 117 55W
California Hot Springs, U.S.A. ... 161 K8   35 51N 118 41W
Cǎlimǎneşti, Romania .... 53 E9   45 14N   24 20 E
Cǎlimani, Munţii, Romania ...... 53 C10   47 12N   25 0 E
Calingasta, Argentina .... 174 C2   31 15 S   69 30W
Calinog, Phil. .... 81 F4   11 7N 122 32 E
Calintaan, Phil. .... 80 E3   12 35N 120 57 E
Calipatria, U.S.A. 161 M11   33 8N 115 31W
Calistoga, U.S.A. 160 G4   38 35N 122 35W
Calitri, Italy .... 47 B8   40 54N   15 26 E
Calitzdorp, S. Africa .... 116 E3   33 33 S   21 42 E
Callabonna, L., Australia ...... 127 D3   29 40 S 140 5 E
Callac, France 26 D3   48 25N   3 27W
Callahan, U.S.A. 152 E8   30 34N   81 50W
Callan, Ireland 23 D4   52 32N   7 24W
Callander, U.K. 22 E4   56 15N   4 13W
Callao, Peru .... 172 C2   12 0 S   77 0W
Callaway, U.S.A. 152 E4   30 8N   85 36W
Calles, Mexico 163 C5   23 2N   98 42W
Callicoon, U.S.A. 151 E9   41 46N   75 3W
Calling Lake, Canada 142 B6   55 15N 113 12W
Calliope, Australia .... 126 C5   24 0 S 151 16 E
Callosa de Ensarriá, Spain 41 G4   38 40N   0 8W
Callosa de Segura, Spain 41 G4   38 7N   0 53W
Calmar, U.S.A. 156 A5   43 11N   91 52W
Calne, U.K. 21 F6   51 26N   2 0W
Calola, Angola .... 116 B2   16 25 S   17 48 E
Calolbon = San Andres, Phil. ... 80 E5   13 36N 124 6 E
Calonge, Spain .... 40 D8   41 52N   3 10 E
Caloocan, Phil. .... 80 D3   14 39N 120 58 E
Caloosahatchee →, U.S.A. 153 J7   26 31N   82 1W
Calore →, Italy .... 47 A7   41 11N   14 28 E
Caloundra, Australia .... 127 D5   26 45 S 153 10 E

Calpe, *Spain* .... **41 G5** 38 39N 0 3 E
Calpella, *U.S.A.* **160 F3** 39 14N 123 12W
Calpine, *U.S.A.* **160 F6** 39 40N 120 27W
Calstock, *Canada* **140 C3** 49 47N 84 9W
Caltabellotta, *Italy* .... **46 E6** 37 34N 13 13 E
Caltagirone, *Italy* .... **47 E7** 37 14N 14 31 E
Caltanissetta, *Italy* .... **47 E7** 37 29N 14 4 E
Caltılıbük, *Turkey* .... **51 G12** 39 57N 28 36 E
Caluango, *Angola* .... **115 D3** 8 20 S 19 39 E
Calubian, *Phil.* .... **81 F5** 11 27N 124 26 E
Calucinga, *Angola* .... **115 E3** 11 18 S 16 12 E
Caluire-et-Cuire, *France* .. **27 G11** 45 48N 4 52 E
Calulo, *Angola* .... **115 E2** 10 1 S 14 56 E
Calunda, *Angola* .... **115 E4** 12 7 S 23 36 E
Caluquembe, *Angola* ...... **115 E2** 13 47 S 14 44 E
Caluso, *Italy* .... **44 C4** 45 18N 7 53 E
Caluya I., *Phil.* .... **81 F3** 11 55N 121 34 E
Calvados □, *France* **26 C6** 49 5N 0 15W
Calvert →, *Australia* ...... **126 B2** 16 17 S 137 44 E
Calvert I., *Canada* **142 C3** 51 30N 128 0W
Calvert Ra., *Australia* ..... **124 D3** 24 0 S 122 30 E
Calvi, *France* .... **29 F12** 42 34N 8 45 E
Calviá, *Spain* .... **38 B3** 39 34N 2 31 E
Calvillo, *Mexico* **162 C4** 21 51N 102 43W
Calvinia, *S. Africa* .... **116 E2** 31 28 S 19 45 E
Calvo = Calvo, Mte., *Italy* . **45 G12** 41 44N 15 46 E
Calvo, Mte., *Italy* .... **45 G12** 41 44N 15 46 E
Calwa, *U.S.A.* **160 J7** 36 42N 119 46W
Calzada Almuradiel = Almuradiel,
 Spain **43 G7** 38 32N 3 28W
Calzada de Calatrava, *Spain* **43 G7** 38 42N 3 46W
Cam →, *U.K.* .... **21 E8** 52 21N 0 16 E
Cam Lam, *Vietnam* .... **87 G7** 11 54N 109 10 E
Cam Pha, *Vietnam* .... **76 G6** 21 7N 107 18 E
Cam Ranh, *Vietnam* ...... **87 G7** 11 54N 109 12 E
Cam Xuyen, *Vietnam* ..... **86 C6** 18 15N 106 0 E
Camabatela, *Angola* ...... **115 D3** 8 20 S 15 26 E
Camacã, *Brazil* .... **171 E4** 15 24 S 39 30W
Camaçari, *Brazil* .... **171 E4** 12 41 S 38 18W
Camacha, *Madeira* .... **9 c** 32 41N 16 49W
Camacho, *Mexico* **162 C4** 24 25N 102 18W
Camacupa, *Angola* .... **115 E3** 11 58 S 17 22 E
Camaguán, *Venezuela* **168 B4** 8 6N 67 36W
Camagüey, *Cuba* **164 B4** 21 20N 78 0W
Camaiore, *Italy* .... **44 E7** 43 56N 10 18 E
Camamu, *Brazil* .... **171 D4** 13 57 S 39 7W
Camaná, *Peru* .... **172 D3** 16 30 S 72 50W
Camanche, *U.S.A.* **156 C6** 41 47N 90 15W
Camanche Reservoir, *U.S.A.* **160 G6** 38 14N 121 1W
Camapuã, *Brazil* .... **173 D7** 19 30 S 54 9W
Camaquã, *Brazil* .... **175 C5** 30 51 S 51 49W
Camaquã →, *Brazil* .... **175 C5** 31 17 S 51 47W
Câmara de Lobos, *Madeira* . **9 c** 32 39N 16 59W
Camararé →, *Brazil* .... **173 C6** 12 15 S 58 55W
Camarat, C., *France* .... **29 E10** 43 12N 6 41 E
Camarès, *France* .... **28 E6** 43 49N 2 53 E
Camaret-sur-Mer, *France* .. **26 D2** 48 16N 4 37W
Camargo, *Bolivia* .... **173 E4** 20 38 S 65 15W
Camargo, *Mexico* **163 B5** 26 19N 98 50W
Camargue, *France* .... **29 E8** 43 34N 4 34 E
Camargue, Parc Naturel Régional
 de →, *France* .... **29 E8** 43 30N 4 40 E
Camarillo, *U.S.A.* **161 L7** 34 13N 119 2W
Camariñas, *Spain* **42 B1** 43 8N 9 12W
Camarines Norte □, *Phil.* .. **80 D4** 14 10N 122 45 E
Camarines Sur □, *Phil.* .... **80 E4** 13 40N 123 20 E
Camarón, C., *Honduras* **164 C2** 16 0N 85 5W
Camarones, *Argentina* ..... **176 B3** 44 50 S 65 40W
Camarones, B., *Argentina* .. **176 B3** 44 45 S 65 35W
Camas, *Spain* **43 H4** 37 24N 6 2W
Camas, *U.S.A.* **160 E4** 45 35N 122 24W
Camas Valley, *U.S.A.* **160 E2** 43 2N 123 40W
Camatambo, *Angola* ...... **115 D3** 6 31 S 15 21 E
Camaxilo, *Angola* .... **115 D3** 8 21 S 18 56 E
Camba Cassai, *Angola* ..... **115 D3** 9 47 S 19 9 E
Cambará, *Brazil* .... **173 E4** 23 2 S 50 5W
Cambay = Khambhat, *India* . **92 H5** 22 23N 72 33 E
Cambay, G. of = Khambhat, G. of,
 India .... **89 C6** 20 45N 72 30 E
Cambil, *Spain* **43 H7** 37 40N 3 33W
Cambo, *Angola* .... **115 D3** 10 55 S 20 6 E
Cambo-les-Bains, *France* ... **28 E2** 43 22N 1 23W
Cambodia ■, *Asia* .... **86 F5** 12 15N 105 0 E
Camborne, *U.K.* **23 G2** 50 12N 5 19W
Cambrai, *Australia* .... **128 C3** 34 40 S 139 16 E
Cambrai, *France* .... **27 B10** 50 11N 3 14 E
Cambre, *Spain* **42 B2** 43 17N 8 20W
Cambria, *U.S.A.* **160 K5** 35 34N 121 5W
Cambrian Mts., *U.K.* **21 E4** 52 3N 3 57W
Cambridge, *Canada* **140 D3** 43 23N 80 15W
Cambridge, *Jamaica* .... **164 a** 18 18N 77 54W
Cambridge, *N.Z.* .... **130 D4** 37 54 S 175 29 E
Cambridge, *U.K.* .... **21 E8** 52 12N 0 8 E
Cambridge, *Ill., U.S.A.* **156 C6** 41 18N 90 12W
Cambridge, *Iowa, U.S.A.* .. **156 C3** 41 54N 93 32W
Cambridge, *Mass., U.S.A.* .. **151 D13** 42 22N 71 6W
Cambridge, *Minn., U.S.A.* .. **154 C8** 45 34N 93 13W
Cambridge, *N.Y., U.S.A.* ... **151 C11** 43 2N 73 22W
Cambridge, *Nebr., U.S.A.* .. **154 E4** 40 17N 100 10W
Cambridge, *Ohio, U.S.A.* .. **150 F3** 40 2N 81 35W
Cambridge Bay = Ikaluktutiak,
 Canada **138 B9** 69 10N 105 0W
Cambridge City, *U.S.A.* **157 E11** 39 49N 85 10W
Cambridge G., *Australia* ... **124 B4** 14 55 S 128 15 E
Cambridge Springs, *U.S.A.* . **150 E4** 41 48N 80 4W
Cambridgeshire □, *U.K.* ... **21 E7** 52 25N 0 7W
Cambrils, *Spain* .... **40 D6** 41 8N 1 3 E
Cambuci, *Brazil* .... **171 F3** 21 35 S 41 55W
Cambulo, *Angola* .... **115 D4** 7 49 S 21 15 E
Cambundi-Catembo, *Angola* **115 E3** 10 10 S 17 35 E
Camden, *Australia* .... **129 C9** 34 1 S 150 43 E
Camden, *Ala., U.S.A.* **149 K2** 31 59N 87 17W
Camden, *Ark., U.S.A.* **155 J8** 33 35N 92 50W
Camden, *Maine, U.S.A.* **149 C11** 44 13N 69 4W
Camden, *N.J., U.S.A.* **151 G9** 39 56N 75 7W
Camden, *N.Y., U.S.A.* **151 C9** 43 20N 75 45W
Camden, *Ohio, U.S.A.* **157 E12** 39 38N 84 39W
Camden, *S.C., U.S.A.* **149 H5** 34 16N 80 36W
Camden Bay, *U.S.A.* **144 A11** 70 10N 145 15W
Camden Sd., *Australia* .... **124 C3** 15 27 S 124 25 E
Camdenton, *U.S.A.* **155 F8** 38 1N 92 45W
Cameia, Parque Nac. da △, *Angola* **115 E4** 12 5 S 21 40 E
Camelford, *U.K.* **21 G3** 50 37N 4 42W
Çameli, *Turkey* .... **49 D11** 37 3N 29 24 E
Camenca, *Moldova* .... **53 B13** 48 3N 28 42 E
Camerino, *Italy* .... **45 E10** 43 8N 13 4 E
Cameron, *Ariz., U.S.A.* **159 J8** 35 53N 111 25W
Cameron, *La., U.S.A.* **155 L8** 29 48N 93 20W
Cameron, *Mo., U.S.A.* **156 E2** 39 44N 94 14W
Cameron, *S.C., U.S.A.* **152 B9** 33 34N 80 43W
Cameron, *Tex., U.S.A.* **155 K6** 30 51N 96 59W
Cameron Highlands, *Malaysia* **87 K3** 4 27N 101 22 E
Cameron Hills, *Canada* **142 M5** 59 48N 118 0W
Cameron Mts., *N.Z.* ...... **131 G1** 46 1 S 167 0 E
Cameroon ■, *Africa* ...... **114 A2** 6 0N 12 30 E
Camerota, *Italy* .... **47 B8** 40 2N 15 22 E
Cameroun →, *Cameroon* ... **113 E6** 4 0N 9 35 E
Cameroun, Mt., *Cameroon* . **113 E6** 4 13N 9 10 E
Cametá, *Brazil* .... **170 B2** 2 12 S 49 30W
Çamiçi Gölü, *Turkey* ...... **49 D9** 37 29N 27 28 E
Camiguin □, *Phil.* .... **81 G5** 9 11N 124 42 E
Camiguin I., *Phil.* .... **80 B3** 18 56N 121 55 E

Camiling, *Phil.* .... **80 D3** 15 42N 120 24 E
Camilla, *U.S.A.* **152 D5** 31 14N 84 12W
Caminha, *Portugal* **42 D2** 41 50N 8 50W
Camino, *U.S.A.* **160 G6** 38 44N 120 41W
Camira Creek, *Australia* ... **127 D5** 29 15 S 152 58 E
Camiranga, *Brazil* .... **170 B2** 1 48 S 46 17W
Camiri, *Bolivia* .... **173 E5** 20 3 S 63 31W
Camissombo, *Angola* ...... **115 D4** 8 7 S 20 38 E
Cammal, *U.S.A.* **150 E7** 41 24N 77 28W
Camocim, *Brazil* .... **170 B3** 2 55 S 40 50W
Camooweal, *Australia* ..... **126 B2** 19 56 S 138 7 E
Camooweal Caves Nat. Park △,
 Australia .... **126 C2** 20 1 S 138 11 E
Camopi, *Fr. Guiana* **169 C7** 3 12N 52 17W
Camopi →, *Fr. Guiana* **169 C7** 3 10N 52 20W
Camorta, *India* .... **95 K11** 8 8N 93 30 E
Camotes Is., *Phil.* .... **81 F5** 10 40N 124 24 E
Camotes Sea, *Phil.* .... **81 F5** 10 30N 124 15 E
Camp Borden, *Canada* **150 B5** 44 18N 79 56W
Camp Hill, *Ala., U.S.A.* ... **152 C4** 32 48N 85 39W
Camp Hill, *Pa., U.S.A.* **150 F8** 40 14N 76 55W
Camp Nelson, *U.S.A.* **161 J8** 36 8N 118 39W
Camp Pendleton, *U.S.A.* .. **161 M9** 33 16N 117 23W
Camp Point, *U.S.A.* **156 D5** 40 3N 91 4W
Camp Verde, *U.S.A.* **159 J8** 34 34N 111 51W
Camp Wood, *U.S.A.* **155 L5** 29 40N 100 1W
Campagna, *Italy* .... **47 B8** 40 40N 15 6 E
Campana, *Argentina* ...... **174 C4** 34 10 S 58 55W
Campana, I., *Chile* .... **176 C1** 48 20 S 75 20W
Campanário, *Madeira* ..... **9 c** 32 39N 17 2W
Campanario, *Spain* **43 G5** 38 52N 5 36W
Campánia □, *Italy* .... **47 B7** 41 0N 14 30 E
Campbell, *S. Africa* .... **116 D3** 28 48 S 23 44 E
Campbell, *Calif., U.S.A.* ... **160 H5** 37 17N 121 57W
Campbell, *Fla., U.S.A.* **153 G8** 28 16N 81 27W
Campbell, *Ohio, U.S.A.* ... **150 E4** 41 5N 80 37W
Campbell, C., *N.Z.* .... **131 B9** 41 47 S 174 18 E
Campbell I., *Pac. Oc.* ..... **134 N8** 52 30 S 169 0 E
Campbell L., *Canada* **143 A7** 63 14N 106 55W
Campbell River, *Canada* ... **142 C3** 50 5N 125 20W
Campbell Town, *Australia* . **127 D4** 41 52 S 147 30 E
Campbellford, *Canada* **150 B7** 44 18N 77 48W
Campbellpur, *Pakistan* .... **92 C5** 33 46N 72 26 E
Campbellsburg, *U.S.A.* **157 F10** 38 39N 86 16W
Campbellsville, *U.S.A.* **148 G3** 37 21N 85 20W
Campbellton, *Canada* **141 C6** 47 57N 66 43W
Campbellton, *U.S.A.* **152 E4** 30 57N 85 24W
Campbelltown, *Australia* .. **129 C9** 34 4 S 150 49 E
Campbeltown, *U.K.* **22 F3** 55 26N 5 36W
Campeche, *Mexico* **163 D6** 19 50N 90 32W
Campeche □, *Mexico* **163 D6** 19 50N 90 32W
Campeche, Golfo de, *Mexico* **163 D6** 19 30N 93 0W
Campello, *Spain* **41 G4** 38 26N 0 24W
Campeonia, *Romania* ...... **52 D8** 46 22N 23 3 E
Camperdown, *Australia* ... **128 E5** 38 14 S 143 9 E
Camperville, *Canada* **143 C8** 51 59N 100 9W
Campi Salentina, *Italy* .... **47 B11** 40 24N 18 1 E
Câmpia Turzii, *Romania* ... **53 D8** 46 34N 23 53 E
Campidano, *Italy* .... **46 C1** 39 30N 8 47 E
Campíglia Maríttima, *Italy* . **44 E7** 43 4N 10 37 E
Campillo de Altobuey, *Spain* **41 F3** 39 36N 1 49W
Campillos, *Spain* **43 H6** 37 4N 4 51W
Câmpina, *Romania* .... **53 E10** 45 10N 25 45 E
Campina Grande, *Brazil* ... **170 C4** 7 20 S 35 47W
Campina Verde, *Brazil* .... **171 E2** 19 31 S 49 28W
Campinas, *Brazil* .... **175 A6** 22 50 S 47 0W
Campli, *Italy* .... **45 F10** 42 43N 13 41 E
Campo = Ntem →, *Cameroon* **114 B2** 2 21N 9 49 E
Campo, *Cameroon* .... **114 B1** 2 22N 9 50 E
Campo, *Spain* .... **40 C5** 42 25N 0 24 E
Campo, Réserve de →, *Cameroon* **114 B2** 2 23N 10 5 E
Campo Belo, *Brazil* .... **171 F2** 20 52 S 45 16W
Campo de Criptana, *Spain* . **43 F7** 39 24N 3 7W
Campo de Diauarum, *Brazil* **173 C7** 11 12 S 53 14W
Campo de Gibraltar, *Spain* . **43 J5** 36 15N 5 25W
Campo Flórido, *Brazil* ..... **171 E2** 19 46 S 48 35W
Campo Formoso, *Brazil* .... **170 D3** 10 30 S 40 20W
Campo Grande, *Brazil* ..... **173 E7** 20 25 S 54 40W
Campo Maior, *Brazil* ...... **170 B3** 4 50 S 42 12W
Campo Maior, *Portugal* **43 F3** 39 2N 7 7W
Campo Mourão, *Brazil* .... **175 A5** 24 3 S 52 22W
Campo Tencia, *Switz.* ..... **33 D7** 46 26N 8 43 E
Campo Túres, *Italy* .... **45 B8** 46 53N 11 55 E
Campoalegre, *Colombia* ... **168 C2** 2 41N 75 20W
Campobasso, *Italy* .... **47 A7** 41 34N 14 39 E
Campobello di Licata, *Italy* . **46 E6** 37 15N 13 55 E
Campobello di Mazara, *Italy* **46 E5** 37 38N 12 45 E
Campofelice di Roccella, *Italy* **46 E6** 37 59N 13 53 E
Campomarino, *Italy* .... **45 G12** 41 57N 15 2 E
Camporeale, *Italy* .... **46 E6** 37 54N 13 6 E
Camporrobles, *Spain* **40 F3** 39 39N 1 24W
Campos, *Brazil* .... **171 F3** 21 50 S 41 20W
Campos Altos, *Brazil* ...... **171 E2** 19 47 S 46 10W
Campos Belos, *Brazil* ...... **171 D2** 13 10 S 47 3W
Campos del Port, *Spain* ... **38 B4** 39 26N 3 1 E
Campos Novos, *Brazil* ..... **175 B5** 27 21 S 51 50W
Campos Sales, *Brazil* ...... **170 C3** 7 4 S 40 23W
Camprodón, *Spain* .... **40 C7** 42 19N 2 23 E
Campton, *Fla., U.S.A.* **153 E3** 30 53N 86 31W
Campton, *Ga., U.S.A.* **152 B6** 33 52N 83 43W
Camptonville, *U.S.A.* **157 G13** 37 44N 83 33W
Camptown, *U.S.A.* **160 F5** 39 27N 121 3W
Câmpulung, *Argeș, Romania* **151 E8** 41 44N 76 14W
Câmpulung, *Suceava, Romania* **53 C10** 45 17N 25 3 E
Câmpuri, *Romania* .... **53 D11** 46 0N 26 56 E
Campuya →, *Peru* .... **168 D3** 1 40 S 73 30W
Campville, *U.S.A.* **152 F7** 29 40N 82 7W
Camrose, *Canada* **142 C6** 53 0N 112 50W
Camsell Portage, *Canada* .. **143 B7** 59 37N 109 15W
Camucuio, *Angola* .... **115 E2** 14 7 S 13 15 E
Çamyuva, *Turkey* .... **49 E12** 36 30N 30 30 E
Çan, *Turkey* .... **51 F11** 40 2N 27 3 E
Can Clavo, *Spain* .... **38 D1** 38 57N 1 27 E
Can Creu, *Spain* .... **38 D1** 38 58N 1 28 E
Can Gio, *Vietnam* .... **87 G6** 10 25N 106 58 E
Can Tho, *Vietnam* .... **87 G5** 10 2N 105 46 E
Canaan, *U.S.A.* **151 D11** 42 2N 73 20W
Canacona, *India* .... **95 G2** 15 1N 74 4 E
Canada ■, *N. Amer.* **138 C10** 60 0N 100 0W
Cañada de Gómez, *Argentina* **174 C3** 32 40 S 61 30W
Canadian, *U.S.A.* **155 H4** 35 55N 100 23W
Canadian →, *U.S.A.* **155 H7** 35 28N 95 3W
Canadys, *U.S.A.* **152 B9** 33 0N 80 37W
Canajoharie, *U.S.A.* **151 D10** 42 54N 74 35W
Canakkale, *Turkey* .... **51 F10** 40 8N 26 24 E
Çanakkale □, *Turkey* ..... **51 F10** 40 10N 26 25 E
Çanakkale Boğazı, *Turkey* . **51 F10** 40 17N 26 32 E
Canal Flats, *Canada* **142 C5** 50 10N 115 48W
Canal Point, *U.S.A.* **153 J9** 26 52N 80 38W
Canala, *N. Cal.* .... **133 U19** 21 32 S 165 57 E
Canalejas, *Argentina* ...... **174 D2** 35 15 S 66 34W
Canals, *Argentina* .... **174 C3** 33 35 S 62 53W
Canals, *Spain* **41 G4** 38 58N 0 35W
Canandaigua, *U.S.A.* **150 D7** 42 54N 77 17W
Canandaigua L., *U.S.A.* ... **150 D7** 42 47N 77 19W
Cananea, *Mexico* **162 A2** 31 0N 110 20W
Canapiscau →, *Canada* **141 A6** 56 40N 69 30W
Canapiscau, Rés. de, *Canada* **141 B6** 54 10N 69 55W
Cañar, *Ecuador* .... **168 D2** 2 33 S 78 56W
Cañar □, *Ecuador* .... **168 D2** 2 40 S 79 0W
Canarias, Is., *Atl. Oc.* **9 e1** 28 30N 16 0W
Canaries, *St. Lucia* .... **165 f** 13 55N 61 4W
Canarreos, Arch. de los, *Cuba* **164 B3** 21 35N 81 40W
Canary Is. = Canarias, Is., *Atl. Oc.* **9 e1** 28 30N 16 0W

Canaseraga, *U.S.A.* **150 D7** 42 27N 77 45W
Canastra, Serra da, *Brazil* . **171 F2** 20 0 S 46 20W
Canatlán, *Mexico* **162 C4** 24 31N 104 47W
Cañaveral, *Peru* .... **168 D1** 3 56 S 80 39W
Cañaveral, C., *U.S.A.* **153 G9** 28 27N 80 32W
Canaveral Nat. Seashore △, *U.S.A.* **153 G9** 28 28N 80 34W
Cañaveruelas, *Spain* **40 E2** 40 24N 2 38W
Canaveiras, *Brazil* .... **171 E4** 15 39 S 39 0W
Canbelego, *Australia* ...... **129 A7** 31 32 S 146 18 E
Canberra, *Australia* .... **129 C8** 35 15 S 149 8 E
Canby, *Calif., U.S.A.* **158 F3** 41 27N 120 52W
Canby, *Minn., U.S.A.* **154 C6** 44 43N 96 16W
Canby, *Oreg., U.S.A.* **160 E4** 45 16N 122 42W
Cancale, *France* **26 D5** 48 40N 1 50W
Canche →, *France* .... **27 B8** 50 30N 1 40 E
Canchyuaya, Cordillera de, *Peru* **172 B3** 7 30 S 74 0W
Cancún, *Mexico* **163 C7** 21 8N 86 44W
Candala, *Somali Rep.* ..... **120 B3** 11 30N 49 58 E
Candanchu, *Spain* **40 C4** 42 47N 0 32W
Candarave, *Peru* .... **172 D3** 17 15 S 70 13W
Çandarlı, *Turkey* .... **49 C8** 38 56N 26 56 E
Çandarlı Körfezi, *Turkey* .. **49 C8** 38 52N 26 55 E
Candas, *Spain* **42 B5** 43 35N 5 45W
Candé, *France* **26 E5** 47 34N 1 2W
Candeias →, *Brazil* .... **173 B5** 8 39 S 63 31W
Candela, *Italy* .... **47 A8** 41 8N 15 31 E
Candelaria, *Argentina* ..... **175 B4** 27 29 S 55 44W
Candelaria, *Canary Is.* **9 e1** 28 22N 16 22W
Candelaria, *Phil.* .... **80 E3** 13 56N 121 25 E
Candelario, Parque Natural de △,
 Spain **42 E5** 40 20N 5 46W
Candeleda, *Spain* **42 E5** 40 10N 5 14W
Candelo, *Australia* .... **129 D8** 36 47 S 149 43 E
Candi Dasa, *Indonesia* .... **79 J18** 8 30 S 115 34 E
Candia = Iráklion, *Greece* . **49 E6** 35 20N 25 12 E
Candia, Sea of = Crete, Sea of,
 Greece .... **49 E7** 36 0N 25 0 E
Cândido de Abreu, *Brazil* . **171 F1** 24 35 S 51 20W
Cândido Mendes, *Brazil* .. **170 B2** 1 27 S 45 43W
Candle, *U.S.A.* **144 D7** 65 55N 161 56W
Candle L., *Canada* **143 C7** 53 50N 105 18W
Candlemas I., *Antarctica* .. **7 B1** 57 3 S 26 40W
Cando, *U.S.A.* **154 A5** 48 32N 99 12W
Candon, *Phil.* .... **80 C3** 17 12N 120 27 E
Canea = Khaniá, *Greece* ... **49 E5** 35 30N 24 4 E
Canela, *Brazil* .... **170 D2** 10 15 S 48 25W
Canelli, *Italy* .... **44 D5** 44 43N 8 17 E
Canelones, *Uruguay* ...... **175 C4** 34 32 S 56 17W
Canet-Plage, *France* ...... **28 F7** 42 41N 3 2 E
Cañete, *Chile* .... **174 D1** 37 50 S 73 30W
Cañete, *Peru* .... **172 C2** 13 8 S 76 30W
Cañete, *Spain* **40 E3** 40 3N 1 54W
Cañete de las Torres, *Spain* **43 H6** 37 53N 4 19W
Cangamba, *Angola* .... **115 E3** 13 40 S 19 54 E
Cangandala, *Angola* .... **115 D3** 9 45 S 16 33 E
Cangandala, Parque Nac. da △,
 Angola .... **115 D3** 9 53 S 16 42 E
Cangas, *Spain* **42 C2** 42 16N 8 47W
Cangas de Narcea, *Spain* .. **42 B4** 43 10N 6 32W
Cangas de Onís, *Spain* **42 B5** 43 21N 5 8W
Cangnan, *China* .... **77 D13** 27 30N 120 23 E
Cangoa, *Angola* .... **115 E3** 13 8 S 18 30 E
Cangola, *Angola* .... **115 D3** 7 58 S 15 53 E
Cangolo, *Angola* .... **115 E3** 15 0 S 13 52 E
Cangombe, *Angola* .... **115 E3** 14 24 S 19 59 E
Cangonga, *Angola* .... **115 D3** 9 24 S 17 30 E
Canguaretama, *Brazil* ..... **170 C4** 6 20 S 35 5W
Canguçu, *Brazil* .... **175 C5** 31 22 S 52 40W
Canguçu, Serra do, *Brazil* . **175 C5** 31 20 S 52 40W
Cangumbe, *Angola* .... **115 E3** 11 58 S 19 12 E
Cangwu, *China* .... **77 F8** 23 25N 111 17 E
Cangxi, *China* .... **76 B5** 31 47N 105 59 E
Cangyuan, *China* .... **74 D4** 23 12N 99 14 E
Cangzhou, *China* .... **74 E9** 38 19N 116 52 E
Canhoca, *Angola* .... **115 D2** 9 15 S 14 41 E
Cani, I., *Tunisia* .... **108 A2** 36 21N 10 5 E
Caniapiscau →, *Canada* ... **141 A6** 56 40N 69 30W
Caniapiscau, Rés. de, *Canada* **141 B6** 54 10N 69 55W
Canicatti, *Italy* .... **46 E6** 37 21N 13 51 E
Canicattini Bagni, *Italy* ... **47 E8** 37 2N 15 4 E
Canigao Channel, *Phil.* .... **81 F5** 10 15N 124 42 E
Caniles, *Spain* **43 H8** 37 26N 2 43W
Canim Lake, *Canada* **142 C4** 51 47N 120 54W
Canindé, *Brazil* .... **170 B4** 4 35 S 39 19W
Canindé →, *Brazil* .... **170 C3** 6 15 S 42 52W
Canindeyú □, *Paraguay* ... **175 A4** 24 10 S 55 0W
Canino, *Italy* .... **45 F8** 42 28N 11 45 E
Canisteo, *U.S.A.* **150 D7** 42 16N 77 36W
Canisteo →, *U.S.A.* **150 D7** 42 7N 77 8W
Cañitas, *Mexico* **162 C4** 23 36N 102 43W
Cañizal, *Spain* **42 D5** 41 12N 5 22W
Canjáyar, *Spain* **43 H8** 37 1N 2 44W
Canjinge, *Angola* .... **115 E4** 10 12 S 21 17 E
Çankırı, *Turkey* .... **100 B5** 40 40N 33 37 E
Cankuzo, *Burundi* .... **118 C3** 3 10 S 30 31 E
Canlaon, *Phil.* .... **81 F4** 10 22N 123 12 E
Canlaon Volcano, *Phil.* .... **81 F4** 10 25N 123 8 E
Canmore, *Canada* **142 C5** 51 7N 115 18W
Cann River, *Australia* ..... **129 D8** 37 35 S 149 7 E
Canna, *U.K.* **22 D2** 57 3N 6 33W
Cannanore, *India* .... **95 J3** 11 53N 75 27 E
Cannanore Is., *India* ...... **95 J1** 10 30N 72 30 E
Cannelton, *U.S.A.* **157 G10** 37 55N 86 45W
Cannes, *France* .... **29 E11** 43 32N 7 1 E
Canning Town = Port Canning, *India* **93 H13** 22 23N 88 40 E
Cannington, *Canada* **150 B5** 44 20N 79 2W
Cannóbio, *Italy* .... **44 B5** 46 4N 8 42 E
Cannock, *U.K.* **21 E5** 52 41N 2 1W
Cannon Ball →, *U.S.A.* ... **154 B4** 46 20N 100 38W
Cannondale Mt., *Australia* . **126 D4** 25 13 S 148 57 E
Cannonsville Reservoir, *U.S.A.* **151 D9** 42 4N 75 22W
Cannonvale, *Australia* .... **126 J6** 20 17 S 148 43 E
Caño Colorado, *Colombia* . **168 C4** 2 18N 68 22W
Canoas, *Brazil* .... **175 B5** 29 56 S 51 11W
Canoe L., *Canada* **143 B7** 55 10N 108 15W
Canon City, *U.S.A.* **154 F2** 38 27N 105 14W
Cañón de Río Blanco, Parque
 Nac. △, *Mexico* **163 D5** 18 43N 97 15W
Cañón del Río Lobos, Parque
 Natural de △, *Spain* **42 D7** 41 46N 3 28W
Cañón del Sumidero, Parque Nac. △,
 Mexico **163 D5** 17 32N 96 24W
Canonniers Pt., *Mauritius* . **121 d** 20 2 S 57 32 E
Canoochee →, *U.S.A.* **152 D8** 31 59N 81 19W
Canopus, *Australia* .... **128 B4** 33 29 S 140 42 E
Canora, *Canada* **143 C8** 51 40N 102 30W
Canosa di Púglia, *Italy* .... **47 A9** 41 13N 16 4 E
Canowindra, *Australia* .... **129 B8** 33 35 S 148 38 E
Canso, *Canada* **141 C7** 45 20N 61 0W
Canta, *Peru* .... **172 C2** 11 29 S 76 37W
Cantabria □, *Spain* **42 B7** 43 10N 4 0W
Cantabrian Mts. = Cantábrica,
 Cordillera, *Spain* **42 C5** 43 0N 5 10W
Cantábrica, Cordillera, *Spain* **42 C5** 43 0N 5 10W
Cantal □, *France* .... **28 C6** 45 5N 2 45 E
Cantal, Plomb du, *France* .. **28 C6** 45 3N 2 45 E
Cantanhede, *Portugal* **42 E2** 40 20N 8 36W
Cantaura, *Venezuela* **169 B5** 9 19N 64 21W
Cantavieja, *Spain* **40 E4** 40 31N 0 25W
Čantavir, *Serbia, Yug.* .... **52 E4** 45 55N 19 46 E
Cantemir, *Moldova* .... **53 D13** 46 17N 28 14 E
Canterbury, *Australia* ..... **126 D3** 25 23 S 141 53 E
Canterbury, *U.K.* .... **21 F9** 51 16N 1 6 E

Canterbury □, *N.Z.* .... **131 D6** 43 45 S 171 19 E
Canterbury Bight, *N.Z.* .... **131 E6** 44 16 S 171 55 E
Canterbury Plains, *N.Z.* ... **131 D6** 43 55 S 171 22 E
Cantil, *U.S.A.* **161 K9** 35 18N 117 58W
Cantilan, *Phil.* .... **81 G5** 9 20N 125 58 E
Cantillana, *Spain* **43 H5** 37 36N 5 49W
Canto do Buriti, *Brazil* .... **170 C3** 8 7 S 42 58W
Canton = Guangzhou, *China* **77 F9** 23 5N 113 10 E
Canton, *Ga., U.S.A.* **149 H3** 34 14N 84 29W
Canton, *Ill., U.S.A.* **156 D6** 40 33N 90 2W
Canton, *Miss., U.S.A.* **155 J9** 32 37N 90 2W
Canton, *Mo., U.S.A.* **156 D5** 40 8N 91 32W
Canton, *N.Y., U.S.A.* **151 B9** 44 36N 75 10W
Canton, *Ohio, U.S.A.* **150 F3** 40 48N 81 23W
Canton, *Pa., U.S.A.* **150 E8** 41 39N 76 51W
Canton, *S. Dak., U.S.A.* ... **154 D6** 43 18N 96 35W
Canton L., *U.S.A.* **155 G5** 36 6N 98 35W
Cantonment, *U.S.A.* **153 E2** 30 37N 87 20W
Cantù, *Italy* .... **44 C6** 45 44N 9 8 E
Cantwell, *U.S.A.* **144 E10** 63 24N 148 57W
Canudos, *Brazil* .... **173 B6** 7 13 S 58 5W
Canudos, *Brazil* .... **170 D6** 4 2 S 59 4W
Canumã, *Amazonas, Brazil* **173 B5** 6 8 S 60 10W
Canumã, *Amazonas, Brazil* **173 D6** 3 55 S 59 10W
Canumã →, *Brazil* .... **173 A4** 6 5 S 59 40W
Canunda Nat. Park △, *Australia* **128 C4** 37 42 S 140 16 E
Canutama, *Brazil* .... **173 B5** 6 30 S 64 20W
Canutillo, *U.S.A.* **159 L10** 31 55N 106 36W
Canvey, *U.K.* .... **21 F8** 51 31N 0 37 E
Canyon, *U.S.A.* **155 H4** 34 59N 101 55W
Canyon De Chelly Nat.
 Monument △, *U.S.A.* **159 H9** 36 10N 109 20W
Canyon of the Ancients Nat.
 Monument △, *U.S.A.* **159 H9** 37 30N 108 50W
Canyonlands Nat. Park △, *U.S.A.* **159 G9** 38 15N 110 0W
Canyonville, *U.S.A.* **158 E2** 42 56N 123 17W
Canzar, *Angola* .... **115 D4** 7 35 S 21 34 E
Cao Bang, *Vietnam* .... **76 A6** 22 40N 106 15 E
Cao He →, *China* .... **75 D13** 40 10N 124 32 E
Cao Lanh, *Vietnam* .... **87 G5** 10 27N 105 38 E
Cao Xian, *China* .... **74 G8** 34 50N 115 35 E
Caombo, *Angola* .... **115 D3** 8 42 S 16 33 E
Cáorle, *Italy* .... **45 C9** 45 36N 12 53 E
Cap-aux-Meules, *Canada* .. **141 C7** 47 23N 61 52W
Cap-Chat, *Canada* **141 C6** 49 6N 66 40W
Cap-de-la-Madeleine, *Canada* **140 C5** 46 22N 72 31W
Cap-Haïtien, *Haiti* **165 C5** 19 40N 72 20W
Cap I., *Phil.* .... **81 J3** 5 57N 120 6 E
Cap Pt., *St. Lucia* .... **165 f** 14 7N 60 57W
Capac, *U.S.A.* **150 C2** 43 1N 82 56W
Cápaccio, *Italy* .... **47 B8** 40 25N 15 5 E
Capaci, *Italy* .... **46 D6** 38 10N 13 14 E
Capanaparo →, *Venezuela* . **168 B4** 7 1N 67 7W
Capanema, *Brazil* .... **170 B2** 1 12 S 47 11W
Capão Bonito, *Brazil* ..... **175 A6** 24 3 S 48 58W
Caparo →, *Barinas, Venezuela* **168 B3** 7 48 S 70 23W
Caparo →, *Bolívar, Venezuela* **169 B5** 7 30N 64 0W
Capatárida, *Venezuela* **168 A3** 11 11N 70 37W
Capayas, *Phil.* .... **81 F2** 10 28N 119 39 E
Capbreton, *France* **28 E2** 43 39N 1 26W
Capdenac, *France* .... **28 D6** 44 34N 2 5 E
Capdepera, *Spain* .... **38 B4** 39 42N 3 26 E
Cape →, *Australia* .... **126 C4** 20 59 S 146 51 E
Cape Arid Nat. Park △, *Australia* **125 F3** 33 54 S 122 26 E
Cape Barren I., *Australia* .. **127 D4** 40 25 S 148 15 E
Cape Breton Highlands Nat.
 Park △, *Canada* **141 C7** 46 50N 60 40W
Cape Breton I., *Canada* ... **141 C7** 46 0N 60 30W
Cape Canaveral, *U.S.A.* ... **153 G9** 28 24N 80 36W
Cape Charles, *U.S.A.* **148 G8** 37 16N 76 1W
Cape Coast, *Ghana* **113 D4** 5 5N 1 15W
Cape Cod Nat. Seashore △, *U.S.A.* **148 E10** 41 56N 70 6W
Cape Coral, *U.S.A.* **153 J8** 26 33N 81 57W
Cape Dorset, *Canada* **139 B12** 64 14N 76 32W
Cape Fear →, *U.S.A.* **149 H6** 33 53N 78 1W
Cape Girardeau, *U.S.A.* ... **155 G10** 37 19N 89 32W
Cape Hatteras Nat. Seashore △,
 U.S.A. **149 H8** 35 30N 75 28W
Cape Jervis, *Australia* ..... **128 C3** 35 40 S 138 5 E
Cape Krusenstern Nat.
 Monument △, *U.S.A.* **144 C7** 67 30N 163 30W
Cape Lee Nat. Park △, *Australia* **125 F3** 33 54 S 122 26 E
Cape Lisburne = Wevok, *U.S.A.* **144 B6** 68 53N 166 13W
Cape Lookout Nat. Seashore △,
 U.S.A. **149 H7** 33 45N 76 25W
Cape May, *U.S.A.* **148 F8** 38 56N 74 56W
Cape May Point, *U.S.A.* .. **148 F8** 38 56N 74 58W
Cape Melville Nat. Park △, *Australia* **126 A3** 14 26 S 144 28 E
Cape Mount Park △, *Liberia* **112 D2** 6 44N 11 24W
Cape Peninsula Nat. Park △,
 S. Africa .... **116 E2** 34 20 S 18 28 E
Cape Pole, *U.S.A.* **144 J14** 55 58N 133 48W
Cape Range Nat. Park △, *Australia* **124 D1** 22 3 S 111 0 E
Cape Tormentine, *Canada* . **141 C7** 46 8N 63 47W
Cape Town, *S. Africa* ..... **116 E2** 33 55 S 18 22 E
Cape Tribulation Nat. Park △,
 Australia .... **126 B4** 16 5 S 145 25 E
Cape Verde ■, *Atl. Oc.* ... **9 j** 16 0N 24 0W
Cape Vincent, *U.S.A.* **151 B8** 44 8N 76 20W
Cape Yakataga, *U.S.A.* **144 F12** 60 4N 142 26W
Cape York Peninsula, *Australia* **126 A3** 12 0 S 142 30 E
Capela, *Brazil* .... **170 D4** 10 30 S 37 0W
Capela de Campo, *Brazil* .. **170 B3** 4 40 S 41 55W
Capelas, *Azores* **9 d3** 37 50N 25 41W
Capele, *Angola* .... **115 E2** 13 39 S 14 53 E
Capelinha, *Brazil* .... **171 E3** 17 42 S 42 31W
Capelinhos, Pta. dos, *Azores* **9 d1** 38 36N 28 50W
Capella, *Australia* .... **126 C4** 23 2 S 148 1 E
Capella, Mt., *Papua N. G.* . **132 C** 5 4 S 141 8 E
Capelongo, *Angola* .... **115 E3** 14 54 S 15 8 E
Capenda Camulemba, *Angola* **115 D3** 9 24 S 18 27 E
Capernaum = Kefar Nahum, *Israel* **108 F6** 32 54N 35 34 E
Capertree, *Australia* ...... **129 B8** 33 6 S 149 58 E
Capestang, *France* .... **28 E7** 43 20N 3 2 E
Capesterre, *Guadeloupe* ... **164 b** 15 53N 61 14W
Capesterre-Belle-Eau, *Guadeloupe* **164 b** 16 4N 61 36W
Capim, *Brazil* .... **170 B2** 1 40 S 47 47W
Capim →, *Brazil* .... **170 B2** 1 40 S 47 47W
Capinópolis, *Brazil* .... **171 E2** 18 41 S 49 35W
Capinota, *Bolivia* .... **172 D4** 17 43 S 66 14W
Capira, *Panama* **168 B2** 8 45N 79 53W
Capistrello, *Italy* .... **45 G10** 41 57N 13 23 E
Capitan, *U.S.A.* **159 K11** 33 35N 105 35W
Capitán Aracena, I., *Chile* . **176 J2** 54 10 S 71 20W
Capitán Bermúdez, *Chile* .. **176 A2** 33 53 S 71 1W
Capitol Reef Nat. Park △, *U.S.A.* **159 G8** 38 15N 111 10W
Capitola, *U.S.A.* **160 J5** 36 59N 121 57W
Capivara, Serra da, *Brazil* . **171 D3** 3 3 S 42 20W
Capivari →, *Brazil* .... **81 F4** 11 35N 122 30 E
Capizzi, *Italy* .... **47 E7** 37 51N 14 26 E
Capoche →, *Mozam.* ...... **119 F3** 15 35 S 33 0 E
Capodichino, Naples ✈ (NAP), *Italy* **47 B7** 40 53N 14 16 E
Capoeira, *Angola* .... **115 E2** 13 9 S 14 7 E
Capolo, *Angola* .... **115 E2** 10 20 S 14 7 E
Caporetto = Kobarid, *Slovenia* **45 B10** 46 15N 13 30 E
Caporolo →, *Angola* ...... **115 E2** 12 56 S 12 58 E
Capoterra, *Italy* .... **46 C1** 39 11N 8 58 E
Cappadocia, *Turkey* ...... **100 C6** 39 0N 35 0 E
Capps, *U.S.A.* **152 E6** 30 24N 83 54W
Capraia, *Italy* .... **44 E6** 43 2N 9 50 E
Caprara, Pta., *Italy* .... **46 A1** 41 7N 8 19 E

Caprarola, Italy	45 F9	42 19N 12 14 E
Capreol, Canada	140 C3	46 43N 80 56W
Caprera, Italy	46 A2	41 12N 9 28 E
Capri, Italy	47 B7	40 33N 14 14 E
Capricorn Group, Australia	124 C5	23 30 S 151 55 E
Capricorn Ra., Australia	124 D2	23 20 S 116 50 E
Caprino Veronese, Italy	44 C7	45 36N 10 47 E
Caprivi Game Park △, Namibia	116 B3	17 55 S 22 37 E
Caprivi Strip, Namibia	116 B3	18 0 S 23 0 E
Caps et Marais d'Opale, Parc Naturel		
Régional des △, France	27 B9	50 40N 2 0 E
Captain Cook, U.S.A.	145 D6	19 30N 155 55W
Captain's Flat, Australia	129 C8	35 35 S 149 27 E
Captieux, France	28 D3	44 18N 0 16W
Captiva, U.S.A.	153 J7	26 31N 82 11W
Capuça, Angola	115 F4	17 22 S 21 18 E
Capul I., Phil.	80 E5	12 26N 124 10 E
Capulin Volcano Nat. Monument △,		
U.S.A.	155 G3	36 47N 103 58W
Capunda, Angola	115 E3	10 41 S 17 23 E
Caquetá □, Colombia	168 C3	1 0N 74 0W
Caquetá →, Colombia	168 D4	1 15 S 69 15W
Car Nicobar, India	95 K11	9 10N 92 47 E
Carabao I., Phil.	80 E3	12 4N 121 56 E
Carabobo □, Venezuela	168 A4	10 10N 68 5W
Caracal, Romania	53 F9	44 8N 24 22 E
Caracaraí, Brazil	169 C5	1 50N 61 8W
Caracas, Venezuela	168 A5	10 30N 66 55W
Caracol, Mato Grosso do Sul, Brazil	174 A4	22 18 S 57 1W
Caracol, Piauí, Brazil	170 C3	9 15 S 43 22W
Caracollo, Bolivia	172 D4	17 39 S 67 10W
Caraga, Phil.	81 H6	7 20N 126 34 E
Caragabal, Australia	129 B7	33 49 S 147 45 E
Carággio, Italy	44 D4	44 25N 7 26 E
Carahue, Chile	176 A2	38 43 S 73 12W
Caraí, Brazil	171 E3	17 12 S 41 42W
Carajás, Brazil	170 C1	6 0 S 51 30W
Carajás, Serra dos, Brazil	170 C1	6 0 S 51 30W
Caramoan, Phil.	80 E4	13 46N 123 52 E
Caramoran, Phil.	80 D5	14 0N 124 8 E
Caranapatuba, Brazil	173 B5	6 38 S 62 34W
Carandaiti, Bolivia	173 E5	20 45 S 63 4W
Carangola, Brazil	171 F3	20 44 S 42 5W
Caransebeş, Romania	52 E7	45 28N 22 18 E
Carantec, France	26 D3	48 40N 3 55W
Caraparaná →, Colombia	168 D3	1 45 S 73 13W
Caraquet, Canada	141 C6	47 48N 64 57W
Caras, Peru	172 B2	9 3 S 77 47W
Caraş Severin □, Romania	52 E7	45 10N 22 10 E
Caraşova, Romania	52 E6	45 11N 21 51 E
Caratasca, L., Honduras	164 C3	15 20N 83 40W
Caratinga, Brazil	171 E3	19 50 S 42 10W
Caraúbas, Brazil	168 D4	4 52 S 66 54W
Caraúbas, Brazil	170 C4	5 43 S 37 33W
Caravaca = Caravaca de la Cruz,		
Spain	41 G3	38 8N 1 52W
Caravaca de la Cruz, Spain	41 G3	38 8N 1 52W
Caravággio, Italy	44 C6	45 30N 9 38 E
Caravela, Guinea-Biss.	112 C1	11 30N 16 30W
Caravelas, Brazil	171 E4	17 45 S 39 15W
Caraveli, Peru	172 D3	15 45 S 73 25W
Caravelle, Presqu'île de la,		
Martinique	164 c	14 46N 60 48W
Caràzinho, Brazil	175 B5	28 16 S 52 46W
Carballino = O Carballiño, Spain	42 C2	42 26N 8 5W
Carballo, Spain	42 B2	43 13N 8 41W
Carberry, Canada	143 D9	49 50N 99 25W
Carbó, Mexico	162 B2	29 42N 110 58W
Carbonara, C., Italy	46 C2	39 6N 9 31 E
Carbondale, Colo., U.S.A.	158 G10	39 24N 107 13W
Carbondale, Ill., U.S.A.	155 G10	37 44N 89 13W
Carbondale, Pa., U.S.A.	151 E9	41 35N 75 30W
Carbonear, Canada	141 C9	47 42N 53 13W
Carboneras, Spain	41 J3	36 59N 1 53W
Carboneras de Guadazaón, Spain	40 F3	39 54N 1 50W
Carbónia, Italy	46 C1	39 10N 8 30 E
Carcabuey, Spain	43 H6	37 27N 4 17W
Carcagente = Carcaixent, Spain	41 F4	39 8N 0 28W
Carcaixent, Spain	41 F4	39 8N 0 28W
Carcajou, Canada	142 B5	57 47N 117 6W
Carcar, Phil.	81 F4	10 6N 123 38 E
Carcarana →, Argentina	174 C3	32 27 S 60 48W
Carcasse, C., Haiti	165 C5	18 30N 74 28W
Carcassonne, France	29 E6	43 13N 2 20 E
Carchi □, Ecuador	168 C2	0 45N 78 0W
Carcoar, Australia	129 B8	33 36 S 149 8 E
Carcross, Canada	142 A2	60 13N 134 45W
Çardak, Çanakkale, Turkey	51 F10	40 2N 26 43 E
Çardak, Denizli, Turkey	49 D11	37 49N 29 39 E
Cardamon Hills, India	95 K3	9 30N 77 15 E
Cardeña, Spain	43 G6	38 16N 4 20W
Cárdenas, Cuba	164 B3	23 0N 81 30W
Cárdenas, San Luis Potosí, Mexico	163 C5	22 0N 99 41W
Cárdenas, Tabasco, Mexico	163 D6	17 59N 93 21W
Cardenete, Spain	40 F3	39 46N 1 41W
Cardiel, L., Argentina	176 C2	48 55 S 71 10W
Cardiff, U.K.	21 F4	51 29N 3 10W
Cardiff, U.K.	21 F4	51 31N 3 12W
Cardiff-by-the-Sea, U.S.A.	161 M9	33 1N 117 17W
Cardigan, U.K.	21 E3	52 5N 4 40W
Cardigan B., U.K.	21 E3	52 30N 4 30W
Cardinal, Canada	151 B9	44 47N 75 23W
Cardón, Punta, Venezuela	168 A3	11 37N 70 14W
Cardona, Spain	40 D6	41 56N 1 40 E
Cardona, Uruguay	174 C4	33 53 S 57 18W
Cardoner →, Spain	40 D6	41 41N 1 51 E
Cardoso, Ilha do, Brazil	175 B5	25 8 S 47 58W
Cardston, Canada	142 D6	49 15N 113 20W
Cardwell, Australia	126 B4	18 14 S 146 2 E
Careen L., Canada	143 B7	57 0N 108 11W
Carei, Romania	52 C7	47 40N 22 29 E
Careiro, Brazil	169 D6	3 12 S 59 45W
Careme = Ciremay, Indonesia	85 D3	6 55 S 108 27 E
Carentan, France	26 C5	49 19N 1 15W
Carey, Idaho, U.S.A.	158 E7	43 19N 113 57W
Carey, Ohio, U.S.A.	157 D13	40 57N 83 23W
Carey, L., Australia	125 E3	29 0 S 122 15 E
Carey L., Canada	143 A8	62 12N 102 55W
Careysburg, Liberia	112 D2	6 34N 10 30W
Cargados Garajos, Ind. Oc.	121 F4	17 0 S 59 0 E
Cargèse, France	29 F12	42 7N 8 35 E
Carhaix-Plouguer, France	26 D3	48 18N 3 36W
Carhuamayo, Peru	172 C2	10 51 S 76 4W
Carhuas, Peru	172 B2	9 15 S 77 39W
Carhué, Argentina	174 D3	37 10 S 62 50W
Caria, Turkey	49 D10	37 20N 28 10 E
Cariacica, Brazil	171 F3	20 16 S 40 25W
Cariaco, Venezuela	169 A5	10 29N 63 33W
Cariango, Angola	115 E3	10 37 S 15 20 E
Cariati, Italy	47 C9	39 30N 16 57 E
Caribbean Sea, W. Indies	165 D5	15 0N 75 0W
Cariboo Mts., Canada	142 C4	53 0N 121 0W
Caribou, U.S.A.	149 B12	46 52N 68 1W
Caribou →, Man., Canada	143 B10	59 20N 94 44W
Caribou →, N.W.T., Canada	142 A3	61 27N 125 45W
Caribou L., Canada	140 C2	47 22N 85 49W
Caribou Is., Canada	142 A6	61 55N 113 15W
Caribou L., Man., Canada	143 B9	59 21N 96 10W
Caribou L., Ont., Canada	140 B2	50 25N 89 5W
Caribou Mts., Canada	142 B5	59 12N 115 40W
Caribou River Park Reserve △,		
Canada	143 B9	59 35N 96 35W
Caribrod = Dimitrovgrad,		
Serbia, Yug.	50 C6	43 2N 22 48 E
Carichic, Mexico	162 B3	27 56N 107 3W
Carigara, Phil.	81 F5	11 18N 124 41 E
Carignan, France	27 C12	49 38N 5 10 E
Carignano, Italy	44 D4	44 55N 7 40 E
Carillo, Mexico	162 B4	26 50N 103 55W
Carin, Somali Rep.	120 B3	10 59N 49 13 E
Carinda, Australia	129 A7	30 28 S 147 41 E
Cariñena, Spain	40 D3	41 20N 1 13W
Carinhanha, Brazil	171 D3	14 15 S 44 46W
Carinhanha →, Brazil	171 D3	14 20 S 43 47W
Carini, Italy	46 D6	38 8N 13 11 E
Cariño, Spain	42 B3	43 45N 7 52W
Carínola, Italy	46 A6	41 11N 13 58 E
Carinthia = Kärnten □, Austria	34 E6	46 52N 13 30 E
Caripito, Venezuela	169 A5	10 8N 63 6W
Cariré, Brazil	170 B3	3 57 S 40 27W
Caritianas, Brazil	173 B5	9 20 S 63 6W
Carles, Phil.	81 F4	11 34N 123 8 E
Carlsberg Ridge, Ind. Oc.	121 D5	1 0N 66 0 E
Carlet, Spain	41 F4	39 14N 0 31W
Carleton, Mt., Canada	141 C6	47 23N 66 53W
Carleton Place, Canada	140 C4	45 8N 76 9W
Carletonville, S. Africa	116 D4	26 23 S 27 22 E
Cârlibaba, Romania	53 C10	47 35N 25 8 E
Carlin, U.S.A.	158 F5	40 43N 116 7W
Carlingford L., U.K.	23 B5	54 3N 6 9W
Carlinville, U.S.A.	156 E7	39 17N 89 53W
Carlisle, U.K.	20 C5	54 54N 2 56W
Carlisle, Ind., U.S.A.	157 F9	38 58N 87 24W
Carlisle, Ky., U.S.A.	157 F12	38 19N 84 1W
Carlisle, Pa., U.S.A.	150 F7	40 12N 77 12W
Carlisle B., Barbados	165 g	13 5N 59 37W
Carlisle I., Australia	126 J7	20 49 S 149 18 E
Carlit, Pic, France	28 F5	42 35N 1 55 E
Carloforte, Italy	46 C1	39 8N 8 18 E
Carlos Casares, Argentina	174 D3	35 32 S 61 20W
Carlos Chagas, Brazil	171 E3	17 43 S 40 45W
Carlos Tejedor, Argentina	174 D3	35 25 S 62 25W
Carlow, Ireland	23 D5	52 50N 6 56W
Carlow □, Ireland	23 D5	52 43N 6 50W
Carlsbad = Karlovy Vary, Czech Rep.	34 A5	50 13N 12 51 E
Carlsbad, Calif., U.S.A.	161 M9	33 10N 117 21W
Carlsbad, N. Mex., U.S.A.	155 J2	32 25N 104 14W
Carlsbad Caverns Nat. Park △,		
U.S.A.	155 J2	32 10N 104 35W
Carluke, Canada	143 D8	49 40N 102 20W
Carlyle, U.S.A.	156 F7	38 37N 89 22W
Carlyle L., U.S.A.	156 F7	38 37N 89 21 E
Carmacks, Canada	138 B6	62 5N 136 16W
Carmagnola, Italy	44 D4	44 51N 7 43 E
Carman, Canada	143 D9	49 30N 98 0W
Carmarthen, U.K.	21 F3	51 52N 4 19W
Carmarthen B., U.K.	21 F3	51 40N 4 30W
Carmarthenshire □, U.K.	21 F3	51 55N 4 13W
Carmaux, France	28 D6	44 3N 2 10 E
Carmel, Ind., U.S.A.	157 E10	39 59N 86 8W
Carmel, N.Y., U.S.A.	151 E11	41 26N 73 41W
Carmel-by-the-Sea, U.S.A.	160 J5	36 33N 121 55W
Carmel Valley, U.S.A.	160 J5	36 29N 121 43W
Carmelo, Uruguay	174 C4	34 0 S 58 20W
Carmen, Bolivia	172 C4	11 40 S 67 51W
Carmen, Colombia	168 B2	9 43N 75 8W
Carmen, Paraguay	175 B4	27 13 S 56 12W
Carmen, Bohol, Phil.	81 G5	9 50N 124 12 E
Carmen, Cebu, Phil.	81 F5	10 35N 124 1 E
Carmen, Cotabato, Phil.	81 H5	7 13N 124 45 E
Carmen, Venezuela	168 C4	1 16N 66 52W
Carmen →, Mexico	162 A3	30 42N 106 29W
Carmen, I., Mexico	162 B2	26 0N 111 20W
Carmen de Patagones, Argentina	176 B4	40 50 S 63 0W
Cármenes, Spain	42 C5	42 58N 5 34W
Carmensa, Argentina	174 D2	35 15 S 67 40W
Carmi, Canada	142 D5	49 36N 119 8W
Carmi, U.S.A.	157 F8	38 5N 88 10W
Carmichael, U.S.A.	160 G5	38 38N 121 19W
Carmichael Village, Bahamas	9 b	25 0N 77 26W
Carmila, Australia	126 C4	21 55 S 149 24 E
Carmona, Costa Rica	164 E2	10 0N 85 15W
Carmona, Spain	43 H5	37 28N 5 42W
Carn Ban, U.K.	22 D4	57 7N 4 15W
Carn Eige, U.K.	22 D3	57 17N 5 8W
Carnac, France	25 C2	47 35N 3 6W
Carnamah, Australia	125 E2	29 41 S 115 53 E
Carnarvon, Australia	125 D1	24 51 S 113 42 E
Carnarvon, S. Africa	116 E3	30 56 S 22 8 E
Carnarvon Nat. Park △, Australia	126 C4	24 54 S 148 2 E
Carnarvon Ra., Queens., Australia	126 D4	25 15 S 148 30 E
Carnarvon Ra., W. Austral., Australia	125 E3	25 20 S 120 45 E
Carnatic, India	95 K3	9 40N 77 50 E
Carnation, U.S.A.	160 C5	47 39N 121 55W
Carndonagh, Ireland	23 A4	55 16N 7 15W
Carnduff, Canada	143 D8	49 10N 101 50W
Carnegie, U.S.A.	150 F4	40 24N 80 5W
Carnegie, L., Australia	125 E3	26 5 S 122 30 E
Carnic Alps = Karnische Alpen,		
Europe	34 E6	46 36N 13 0 E
Carniche Alpi = Karnische Alpen,		
Europe	34 E6	46 36N 13 0 E
Carnot, C.A.R.	114 B3	4 59N 15 56 E
Carnot, C., Australia	127 E2	34 57 S 135 38 E
Carnot B., Australia	124 C3	17 20 S 122 15 E
Carnoustie, U.K.	22 E6	56 30N 2 42W
Caro, U.S.A.	148 D4	43 29N 83 24W
Caroço, São Tomé & Principe	115 G6	1 32N 7 27 E
Carol City, U.S.A.	153 K9	25 56N 80 16W
Carolina, Brazil	170 C2	7 10 S 47 30W
Carolina, Puerto Rico	165 d	18 23 S 65 58W
Carolina, S. Africa	117 D5	26 5 S 30 6 E
Caroline I., Kiribati	135 H12	9 58 S 150 13W
Caroline Is., Micronesia	62 J17	8 0N 150 0 E
Caroline, Pk., N.Z.	131 F2	45 57 S 167 15 E
Carondelet, Kiribati	123 B16	5 33 S 173 50 E
Caroni, Trin. & Tob.	169 F9	10 34N 61 23W
Caroni →, Venezuela	169 B5	8 21N 62 43W
Caronie = Nébrodi, Monti, Italy	47 E7	37 54N 14 35 E
Caroona, Australia	129 A9	31 24 S 150 26 E
Carora, Venezuela	168 A3	10 11N 70 5W
Carpathians, Europe	37 D11	49 30N 21 0 E
Carpații Meridionali, Romania	53 E9	45 30N 25 0 E
Carpentaria, G. of, Australia	126 A2	14 0 S 139 0 E
Carpentersville, U.S.A.	157 B8	42 6N 88 17W
Carpentras, France	29 D9	44 3N 5 2 E
Carpi, Italy	44 D7	44 47N 10 53 E
Carpina, Brazil	170 C4	7 51 S 35 15W
Cărpineni, Moldova	53 D13	46 46N 28 22 E
Carpinteria, U.S.A.	161 L7	34 24N 119 31W
Carpio, Spain	42 D5	41 13N 5 7W
Carr Boyd Ra., Australia	124 C4	16 15 S 128 35 E
Carrabelle, U.S.A.	153 F5	29 51N 84 40W
Carral, Spain	42 B2	43 14N 8 21W
Carrangan, Phil.	80 D3	15 58N 121 4 E
Carranza, Presa V., Mexico	162 B4	27 20N 100 50W
Carrara, Italy	44 D7	44 5N 10 6 E
Carrascosa del Campo, Spain	40 E2	40 2N 2 45W
Carrauntoohill, Ireland	23 D2	52 0N 9 45W
Carretas, Punta, Peru	172 C2	14 12 S 76 17W
Carrick-on-Shannon, Ireland	23 C3	53 57N 8 5W
Carrick-on-Suir, Ireland	23 D4	52 21N 7 24W
Carrickfergus, U.K.	23 B6	54 43N 5 49W
Carrickmacross, Ireland	23 C5	53 59N 6 43W
Carrieton, Australia	128 B3	32 25 S 138 31 E
Carrington, U.S.A.	154 B5	47 27N 99 8W
Carrión →, Spain	42 D6	41 53N 4 32W
Carrión de los Condes, Spain	42 C6	42 20N 4 37W
Carrizal Bajo, Chile	174 B1	28 5 S 71 20W
Carrizalillo, Chile	174 B1	29 5 S 71 30W
Carrizo Cr. →, U.S.A.	155 H3	36 55N 103 55W
Carrizo Plain Nat. Monument △,		
U.S.A.	160 K7	35 12N 119 48W
Carrizo Springs, U.S.A.	155 L5	28 31N 99 52W
Carrizozo, U.S.A.	159 K11	33 38N 105 53W
Carroll, U.S.A.	156 D7	42 4N 94 52W
Carrollton, Ga., U.S.A.	152 B4	33 35N 85 5W
Carrollton, Ill., U.S.A.	156 F6	39 18N 90 24W
Carrollton, Ky., U.S.A.	157 F11	38 41N 85 11W
Carrollton, Mo., U.S.A.	156 E3	39 22N 93 30W
Carrollton, Ohio, U.S.A.	150 F3	40 34N 81 5W
Carron →, U.K.	22 A7	57 53N 4 22W
Carron, L., U.K.	22 D3	57 22N 5 35W
Carrot →, Canada	143 C8	53 50N 101 17W
Carrot River, Canada	143 C8	53 17N 103 35W
Carrouges, France	26 D6	48 34N 0 10W
Carrù, Italy	44 D4	44 29N 7 52 E
Carruthers, Canada	143 C7	52 52N 109 16W
Carsa Dek, Ethiopia	107 F4	5 13N 39 50 E
Çarşamba, Turkey	100 B7	41 11N 36 44 E
Cársoli, Italy	45 F10	42 6N 13 5 E
Carson, Calif., U.S.A.	161 M8	33 48N 118 17W
Carson, N. Dak., U.S.A.	154 B4	46 25N 101 34W
Carson →, U.S.A.	160 F8	39 45N 118 40W
Carson City, Mich., U.S.A.	9 A12	43 11N 84 51W
Carson City, Nev., U.S.A.	160 F7	39 10N 119 46W
Carson Sink, U.S.A.	160 G4	39 50N 118 25W
Cartagena, Colombia	168 A2	10 25N 75 33W
Cartagena, Spain	41 H4	37 38N 0 59W
Cartago, Colombia	168 C2	4 45N 75 55W
Cartago, Costa Rica	164 E3	9 50N 83 55W
Cártama, Spain	43 J6	36 43N 4 39W
Cartaxo, Portugal	43 F2	39 10N 8 47W
Cartaya, Spain	43 H3	37 16N 7 9W
Cartersville, U.S.A.	152 A5	34 10N 84 48W
Carterton, N.Z.	130 H4	41 2 S 175 31 E
Carterville, U.S.A.	156 G7	37 46N 89 5W
Carthage, Tunisia	95 A7	36 50N 10 21 E
Carthage, Ill., U.S.A.	156 D5	40 25N 91 8W
Carthage, Mo., U.S.A.	156 G7	37 11N 94 19W
Carthage, N.Y., U.S.A.	148 D8	43 59N 75 37W
Carthage, Tex., U.S.A.	155 J7	32 9N 94 20W
Cartier I., Australia	124 B3	12 31 S 123 29 E
Cartwright, Canada	141 B8	53 41N 56 58W
Caruaru, Brazil	170 C4	8 15 S 35 55W
Carúpano, Venezuela	169 A5	10 39N 63 15W
Caruray, Phil.	81 F2	10 20N 119 0 E
Carutapera, Brazil	170 B2	1 13 S 46 1W
Caruthersville, U.S.A.	155 G10	36 11N 89 39W
Carvalho, Brazil	169 D7	2 16 S 51 29W
Carvin, France	27 B9	50 30N 2 57 E
Carvoeiro, Brazil	169 D5	1 30 S 61 59W
Carvoeiro, C., Portugal	43 F1	39 21N 9 24W
Cary, Ill., U.S.A.	157 B8	42 13N 88 14W
Cary, N.C., U.S.A.	149 H6	35 47N 78 46W
Casa, Pas de la = Envalira, Port d',		
Europe	40 C6	42 33N 1 43 E
Casa Branca, Brazil	171 F2	21 46 S 47 4W
Casa Branca, Portugal	43 G2	38 29N 8 12W
Casa Grande, U.S.A.	159 K8	32 53N 111 45W
Casablanca, Chile	174 C1	33 20 S 71 25W
Casablanca, Morocco	110 B3	33 36N 7 36W
Casacalenda, Italy	45 G11	41 44N 14 51 E
Casalbordino, Italy	45 F11	42 9N 14 35 E
Casale Monferrato, Italy	44 C5	45 8N 8 27 E
Casalmaggiore, Italy	44 D7	44 59N 10 26 E
Casalpusterlengo, Italy	44 C6	45 11N 9 39 E
Casamance →, Senegal	112 C1	12 33N 16 46W
Casanare □, Colombia	168 B3	5 30N 72 0W
Casanare →, Colombia	168 B4	6 2N 69 51W
Casarano, Italy	47 B11	40 0N 18 10 E
Casares, Spain	43 J5	36 27N 5 16W
Casas Ibáñez, Spain	41 F3	39 17N 1 30W
Casasimarro, Spain	41 F2	39 22N 2 3W
Casatejada, Spain	42 F5	39 54N 5 40W
Casavieja, Spain	42 E6	40 17N 4 46W
Cascada de Basaseachic, Parque		
Nac. △, Mexico	162 B3	28 9N 108 15W
Cascade, Seychelles	121 b	4 39 S 55 29 E
Cascade, Idaho, U.S.A.	158 D5	44 31N 116 2W
Cascade, Iowa, U.S.A.	156 D9	42 18N 91 0W
Cascade, Mont., U.S.A.	158 C8	47 16N 111 42W
Cascade Locks, U.S.A.	160 E5	45 40N 121 54W
Cascade Pt., N.Z.	131 E3	44 1 S 168 20 E
Cascade Ra., U.S.A.	160 D5	47 0N 121 30W
Cascade Reservoir, U.S.A.	158 D5	44 32N 116 3W
Cascades, Pte. des, Réunion	121 c	21 9 S 55 51 E
Cascais, Portugal	43 G1	38 41N 9 25W
Cascavel, Ceará, Brazil	170 B4	4 7 S 38 14W
Cascavel, Paraná, Brazil	175 A5	24 57 S 53 28W
Cáscina, Italy	44 E7	43 41N 10 33 E
Casco B., U.S.A.	149 D10	43 45N 70 0W
Caselle Torinese, Italy	44 C4	45 10N 7 39 E
Caserta, Italy	47 A7	41 4N 14 20 E
Casey, U.S.A.	157 E9	39 18N 87 59W
Caseyr, Raas = Asir, Ras,		
Somali Rep.	120 B4	11 55N 51 10 E
Cashel, Ireland	23 D4	52 30N 7 53W
Casibare →, Colombia	168 C3	3 48N 72 18W
Casiguran, Phil.	80 C3	16 22N 122 7 E
Casiguran Sound, Phil.	80 C3	16 6N 121 58 E
Casilda, Argentina	174 C3	33 5 S 61 10W
Casimcea, Romania	53 F13	44 45N 28 23 E
Casino, Australia	129 D5	28 52 S 153 3 E
Casiquiare →, Venezuela	168 C4	2 1N 67 7W
Casitas, Peru	172 A1	3 54 S 80 39W
Casma, Peru	172 B2	9 30 S 78 20W
Casmalia, U.S.A.	161 L6	34 50N 120 32W
Cásola Valsénio, Italy	45 D8	44 12N 11 40 E
Cásoli, Italy	45 F11	42 7N 14 18 E
Caspe, Spain	40 D4	41 14N 0 1W
Casper, U.S.A.	158 E10	42 51N 106 19W
Caspian Depression, Eurasia	61 G9	47 0N 48 0 E
Caspian Sea, Eurasia	61 G9	43 0N 50 0 E
Cass Lake, U.S.A.	154 B7	47 23N 94 37W
Cassà de la Selva, Spain	40 D7	41 53N 2 52 E
Cassadaga, U.S.A.	150 D5	42 20N 79 19W
Cassai →, Angola	115 E4	10 33 S 21 59 E
Cassano allo Iónio, Italy	47 C9	39 47N 16 20 E
Casse, Grande, France	29 C10	45 24N 6 40 E
Cassel, France	27 B9	50 48N 2 30 E
Casselman, Canada	151 A9	45 19N 75 5W
Casselton, U.S.A.	154 B6	46 54N 97 13W
Cassiar, Canada	138 B3	59 16N 129 40W
Cassiar Mts., Canada	142 B2	59 30N 130 30W
Cassilândia, Brazil	173 D7	19 9 S 51 45W
Cassinga, Angola	115 F3	15 5 S 16 4 E
Cássino, Italy	46 A6	41 30N 13 49 E
Cassis, France	29 E9	43 14N 5 32 E
Cassoalala, Angola	115 E4	9 30 S 14 2 E
Cassongue, Angola	115 E4	13 42 S 20 56 E
Cassopolis, U.S.A.	157 C10	41 55N 86 1W
Cassundi, Angola	115 E4	10 57 S 21 5 E
Cassville, Mo., U.S.A.	155 G8	36 41N 93 52W
Cassville, Wis., U.S.A.	156 B6	42 43N 90 59W
Castagneto Carducci, Italy	44 E7	43 9N 10 36 E
Castaic, U.S.A.	161 L8	34 30N 118 38W
Castalia, U.S.A.	150 E2	41 24N 82 49W
Castanhal, Brazil	169 E10	1 18 S 47 55W
Castara, Trin. & Tob.	169 D10	11 17N 60 42W
Castasegna, Switz.	33 D9	46 20N 9 31 E
Castéggio, Italy	44 C6	45 0N 9 7 E
Castejón de Monegros, Spain	40 D4	41 37N 0 15W
Castèl di Sangro, Italy	45 G11	41 47N 14 6 E
Castèl San Giovanni, Italy	44 C6	45 4N 9 26 E
Castèl San Pietro Terme, Italy	45 D8	44 24N 11 35 E
Castelbuono, Italy	47 E7	37 56N 14 5 E
Castelfidardo, Italy	45 E10	43 28N 13 33 E
Castelfiorentino, Italy	44 E7	43 36N 10 58 E
Castelfranco Emília, Italy	44 D8	44 37N 11 3 E
Castelfranco Véneto, Italy	45 C8	45 40N 11 55 E
Casteljaloux, France	28 D4	44 19N 0 6 E
Castellabate, Italy	47 B7	40 17N 14 57 E
Castellammare, G. di, Italy	46 D5	38 8N 12 54 E
Castellammare del Golfo, Italy	46 D5	38 1N 12 53 E
Castellammare di Stábia, Italy	47 B7	40 42N 14 29 E
Castellamonte, Italy	44 C4	45 23N 7 42 E
Castellane, France	29 E10	43 50N 6 31 E
Castellaneta, Italy	47 B9	40 38N 16 56 E
Castelli, Argentina	174 D4	36 7 S 57 47W
Castelló de la Plana, Spain	40 F4	39 58N 0 3W
Castellón de la Plana □, Spain	40 E4	40 15N 0 5W
Castellote, Spain	40 E4	40 48N 0 15W
Castelmáuro, Italy	45 G11	41 50N 14 43 E
Castelnau-de-Médoc, France	28 C3	45 2N 0 48W
Castelnau-Magnoac, France	28 E4	43 17N 0 31 E
Castelnaudary, France	28 E5	43 20N 1 58 E
Castelnovo ne' Monti, Italy	44 D7	44 26N 10 24 E
Castelnuovo di Val di Cécina, Italy	44 E7	43 12N 10 59 E
Castelo, Brazil	171 F3	20 33 S 41 14W
Castelo, Pta. do, Azores	9 d4	36 56N 25 1W
Castelo Branco, Azores	9 d1	38 31N 28 44W
Castelo Branco, Portugal	42 F3	39 50N 7 31W
Castelo Branco □, Portugal	42 F3	39 52N 7 45W
Castelo de Paiva, Portugal	42 D2	41 2N 8 16W
Castelo de Vide, Portugal	42 F3	39 25N 7 27W
Castelo do Piauí, Brazil	170 C3	5 20 S 41 33W
Castelsardo, Italy	46 B1	40 55N 8 43 E
Castelsarrasin, France	28 D5	44 2N 1 7 E
Casteltérmini, Italy	46 E6	37 32N 13 39 E
Castelvetrano, Italy	46 E5	37 41N 12 47 E
Castendo, Angola	115 D2	8 39 S 14 10 E
Casterton, Australia	128 D4	37 30 S 141 30 E
Castets, France	28 E2	43 52N 1 6W
Castiglion Fiorentino, Italy	45 E8	43 20N 11 55 E
Castiglione del Lago, Italy	45 E9	43 7N 12 3 E
Castiglione della Pescáia, Italy	44 F7	42 46N 10 53 E
Castiglione delle Stiviere, Italy	44 C7	45 23N 10 29 E
Castilblanco, Spain	43 F5	39 17N 5 5W
Castile, U.S.A.	150 D6	42 38N 78 3W
Castilla, Peru	172 B1	5 12 S 80 38W
Castilla, Playa de, Spain	43 J4	37 0N 6 33W
Castilla-La Mancha □, Spain	12 H5	39 30N 3 30W
Castilla y León □, Spain	42 D6	42 0N 5 0W
Castillo de Locubín, Spain	43 H7	37 35N 3 56W
Castillo de San Marcos Nat.		
Monument △, U.S.A.	152 F8	29 54N 81 19W
Castillon-en-Couserans, France	28 F5	42 56N 1 1 E
Castillonès, France	28 D4	44 39N 0 37 E
Castillos, Uruguay	175 C5	34 12 S 53 52W
Castle Dale, U.S.A.	158 G8	39 13N 111 1W
Castle Douglas, U.K.	22 G5	54 56N 3 56W
Castle Harbour, Bermuda	9 a	32 21N 64 40W
Castle Rock, Colo., U.S.A.	154 F2	39 22N 104 51W
Castle Rock, Wash., U.S.A.	160 D4	46 17N 122 54W
Castle Rock Pt., St. Helena	9 h	16 1 S 5 45W
Castlebar, Ireland	23 C2	53 52N 9 18W
Castlebay, U.K.	22 E1	56 57N 7 31W
Castleblaney, Ireland	23 B5	54 7N 6 44W
Castlecliff, N.Z.	130 H3	39 57 S 174 59 E
Castlederg, U.K.	23 B4	54 42N 7 35W
Castleford, U.K.	20 D6	53 43N 1 21W
Castlegar, Canada	142 D5	49 20N 117 40W
Castlemaine, Australia	129 D6	37 2 S 144 12 E
Castlepoint, N.Z.	130 G5	40 54 S 176 15 E
Castlepollard, Ireland	23 C4	53 41N 7 19W
Castlerea, Ireland	23 C3	53 46N 8 29W
Castlereagh →, Australia	129 A7	30 12 S 147 32 E
Castlereagh B., Australia	126 A2	12 10 S 135 10 E
Castleton, U.S.A.	151 C11	43 37N 73 11W
Castletown, U.K.	20 C3	54 5N 4 38W
Castletown Bearhaven, Ireland	23 E2	51 39N 9 55W
Castor, Canada	142 C6	52 15N 111 50W
Castor →, Canada	140 B4	53 24N 78 58W
Castorland, U.S.A.	151 C9	43 53N 75 31W
Castres, France	28 E6	43 37N 2 13 E
Castricum, Neths.	24 B4	52 33N 4 40 E
Castries, St. Lucia	165 f	14 2N 60 58W
Castril, Spain	43 H8	37 48N 2 46W
Castro, Brazil	175 A6	24 45 S 50 0W
Castro, Chile	176 B2	42 30 S 73 50W
Castro Alves, Brazil	171 D4	12 46 S 39 33W
Castro del Río, Spain	43 H6	37 41N 4 29W
Castro-Urdiales, Spain	42 B7	43 23N 3 11W
Castro Verde, Portugal	43 H2	37 41N 8 4W
Castrojeriz, Spain	42 C6	42 17N 4 9W
Castropol, Spain	42 B3	43 32N 7 0W
Castroreale, Italy	47 D8	38 6N 15 12 E
Castrovillari, Italy	47 C9	39 49N 16 12 E
Castroville, U.S.A.	160 J5	36 46N 121 45W
Castrovirreyna, Peru	172 C2	13 20 S 75 18W
Castuera, Spain	43 G5	38 43N 5 37W
Caswell Sound, N.Z.	131 E2	44 59 S 167 8 E
Çat, Turkey	101 C9	39 40N 41 3 E
Cat Ba, Dao, Vietnam	86 B6	20 50N 107 0 E
Cat Ba Nat. Park △, Vietnam	86 B6	20 47N 107 3 E
Cat I., Bahamas	165 B4	24 30N 75 30W
Cat L., Canada	140 B1	51 40N 91 50W
Cat Lake, Canada	140 B1	51 40N 91 50W
Cat Tien Nat. Park △, Vietnam	87 G6	11 25N 107 17 E
Čata, Slovak Rep.	35 D11	47 58N 18 38 E
Catabola, Angola	115 E3	12 9 S 17 16 E
Catacamas, Honduras	164 D2	14 54N 85 56W
Catacáos, Peru	172 B1	5 20 S 80 45W
Cataguases, Brazil	171 F3	21 23 S 42 39W
Catagupan, Phil.	81 G1	8 1N 116 58 E
Cataingan, Phil.	80 E4	12 0N 124 0 E
Catak, Turkey	101 C10	38 1N 43 8 E
Catalão, Brazil	171 E2	18 10 S 47 57W
Çatalca, Turkey	51 E12	41 8N 28 27 E
Catalina, Chile	174 B2	25 13 S 69 43W
Catalina, U.S.A.	159 K8	32 30N 110 50W
Catalonia = Cataluña □, Spain	40 D6	41 40N 1 15 E
Cataluña □, Spain	40 D6	41 40N 1 15 E
Catalzeytin, Turkey	100 B6	41 58N 34 12 E
Catamarca, Argentina	174 B2	28 30 S 65 50W
Catamarca □, Argentina	174 B2	27 0 S 65 50W
Catanauan, Phil.	80 E4	13 36N 122 16 E
Catanduanes □, Phil.	80 E5	13 50N 124 20 E
Catanduva, Brazil	175 A6	21 5 S 48 58W
Catánia, Italy	47 E8	37 30N 15 6 E
Catánia, G. di, Italy	47 E8	37 24N 15 9 E
Catanzaro, Italy	47 D9	38 54N 16 35 E
Cataratas del Iguazú = Iguazú, Cat.		
del, Argentina		
Catarman, Camiguin, Phil.	81 G5	9 8N 124 40 E
Catarman, N. Samar, Phil.	80 E5	12 28N 124 35 E
Catatumbo →, Venezuela	168 B3	9 21N 71 45W

Catatumbo-Bari, Parque Nac. △,
  Colombia 165 E5   9 3N 73 12W
Cataula, U.S.A. 152 C5   32 39N 84 52W
Catbalogan, Phil. .... 81 F5   11 46N 124 53 E
Cateco Cangola, Angola .... 115 D3   8 28 S 15 51 E
Cateel, Phil. .... 81 H6   7 47N 126 24 E
Cateel Bay, Phil. .... 81 H6   7 54N 126 25 E
Catembe, Mozam. .... 117 D5   26 0 S 32 33 E
Catende, Angola .... 115 E4   11 14 S 21 30 E
Catende, Brazil .... 170 C4   8 40 S 35 43W
Caterham, U.K. 21 F7   51 15N 0 4W
Catete, Angola .... 115 D2   9 6 S 13 43 E
Cathcart, Australia .... 129 D8   36 52 S 149 24 E
Cathcart, S. Africa .... 116 E4   32 18 S 27 10 E
Cathlamet, U.S.A. 160 D3   46 12N 123 23W
Catio, Guinea-Biss. 112 C1   11 17N 15 15W
Catismiña, Venezuela 169 C5   4 5N 63 40W
Catita, Brazil .... 170 C3   9 31 S 43 1W
Catlettsburg, U.S.A. 148 F4   38 25N 82 36W
Catlin, U.S.A. 157 D9   40 4N 87 42W
Çatma Dağı, Turkey .... 49 C11   38 25N 29 50 E
Catmon, Phil. .... 81 F5   10 43N 124 1 E
Catoche, C., Mexico 163 C7   21 40N 87 8W
Catolé do Rocha, Brazil .... 170 C4   6 21 S 37 45W
Catota, Angola .... 115 E3   13 57 S 17 30 E
Cátria, Mte., Italy .... 45 E9   43 28N 12 42 E
Catriló, Argentina .... 174 D3   36 26 S 63 24W
Catrimani, Brazil 169 C5   0 27N 61 41W
Catrimani →, Brazil 169 C5   0 28N 61 44W
Catskill, U.S.A. 151 D11 42 14N 73 52W
Catskill Mts., U.S.A. 151 D10 42 10N 74 25W
Catskill Park △, U.S.A. ... 151 D10 42 7N 74 39W
Catt, Mt., Australia .... 126 A1   13 49 S 134 23 E
Cattaraugus, U.S.A. 150 D6   42 22N 78 52W
Cattaro = Kotor, Montenegro, Yug. .. 50 D2   42 25N 18 47 E
Catterick, U.K. 20 C6   54 23N 1 37W
Cáttólica, Italy .... 45 E9   43 58N 12 44 E
Cáttólica Eraclea, Italy ... 46 E6   37 26N 13 24 E
Catu, Brazil .... 171 D4   12 21 S 38 23W
Catuala, Angola .... 116 B2   16 25 S 19 2 E
Catuane, Mozam. .... 117 D5   26 48 S 32 18 E
Catubig, Phil. .... 80 E5   12 24N 125 3 E
Catumbela, Angola .... 115 E2   12 25 S 13 34 E
Catumbela →, Angola ..... 115 E2   12 29 S 13 28 E
Catur, Mozam. .... 119 E4   13 45 S 35 30 E
Catwick Is., Vietnam ...... 87 G7   10 0N 109 0 E
Cauayan, Isabela, Phil. .... 80 C3   16 56N 121 46 E
Cauayan, Neg. Occ., Phil. .. 81 G5   10 58N 122 37 E
Cauca □, Colombia 168 C2   2 30N 76 50W
Cauca →, Colombia 168 B3   8 54N 74 28W
Caucaia, Brazil .... 170 B4   3 40 S 38 35W
Caucasia, Colombia 168 B2   8 0N 75 12W
Caucasus Mountains, Eurasia .. 61 J7   42 50N 44 0 E
Caudete, Spain 41 G3   38 42N 1 2W
Caudry, France .... 27 B10   50 7N 3 22 E
Caulnes, France 26 D4   48 18N 2 10W
Caulónia, Italy .... 47 D9   38 23N 16 24 E
Caungula, Angola .... 115 D3   8 26 S 18 38 E
Cauquenes, Chile .... 174 D1   36 0 S 72 22W
Caura →, Venezuela 169 B5   7 38N 64 53W
Caurés →, Brazil .... 169 D5   1 21 S 62 20W
Cauresi →, Mozam. .... 119 F3   17 8 S 33 0 E
Căuşani, Moldova .... 53 D14   46 38N 29 25 E
Causapscal, Canada 141 C6   48 19N 67 12W
Caussade, France .... 26 D5   44 10N 1 33 E
Causse-Méjean, France .... 28 D7   44 18N 3 42 E
Causses du Quercy, Parc Naturel
  Régional des △, France . 28 D5   44 35N 1 35 E
Cauterets, France 28 F3   42 52N 0 8W
Caux, Pays de, France ..... 26 C7   49 38N 0 35 E
Cava de' Tirreni, Italy .... 47 B7   40 42N 14 42 E
Cávado →, Portugal 42 D2   41 32N 8 48W
Cavagrande del Cassibile, Riserva
  Naturale △, Italy ...... 47 F8   36 58N 15 6 E
Cavaillon, France .... 29 E9   43 50N 5 2 E
Cavalaire-sur-Mer, France . 29 E10   43 10N 6 33 E
Cavalcante, Brazil .... 171 D2   13 48 S 47 30W
Cavalese, Italy .... 45 B8   46 17N 11 27 E
Cavalier, U.S.A. 154 A6   48 48N 97 37W
Cavalla = Cavally →, Africa . 112 E3   4 22N 7 32W
Cavalli Is., N.Z. .... 130 B2   35 0 S 173 58 E
Cavallo, I. de, France ..... 29 G13   41 22N 9 16 E
Cavally →, Africa 112 E3   4 22N 7 32W
Cavan, Ireland 23 B4   54 0N 7 22W
Cavan □, Ireland 23 C4   54 1N 7 16W
Cavárzere, Italy .... 45 C9   45 8N 12 5 E
Çavdarhisar, Turkey ...... 49 B11   39 12N 29 37 E
Çavdır, Turkey .... 49 D11   37 10N 29 42 E
Cave Creek, U.S.A. 159 K7   33 50N 111 57W
Cave Run L., U.S.A. 157 F13   38 5N 83 56W
Cave Spring, U.S.A. 152 A4   34 6N 85 20W
Cavenagh Ra., Australia ... 125 E4   26 12 S 127 55 E
Cavendish, Australia ...... 128 D5   37 31 S 142 2 E
Caviana, I., Brazil 169 C7   0 10N 50 10W
Cavite, Phil. .... 80 D3   14 29N 120 55 E
Cavite □, Phil. .... 80 D3   14 15N 120 50 E
Cavnic, Romania .... 53 C8   47 40N 23 52 E
Cavour, Italy .... 44 D4   44 47N 7 22 E
Cavtat, Croatia .... 50 D2   42 35N 18 13 E
Cawayan, Phil. .... 81 F4   11 56N 123 46 E
Cawndilla L., Australia ... 128 B5   32 30 S 142 15 E
Cawnpore = Kanpur, India . 93 F9   26 28N 80 20 E
Caxias, Brazil .... 170 B3   4 55 S 43 20W
Caxias do Sul, Brazil ..... 175 B5   29 10 S 51 10W
Caxito, Angola .... 115 D2   8 30 S 13 30 E
Caxopa, Angola .... 115 E4   11 52 S 20 52 E
Çay, Turkey .... 100 C4   38 35N 31 1 E
Cay Pt., Bahamas .... 9 b   25 59N 77 25W
Cay Sal Bank, Bahamas ... 164 B4   23 45N 80 0W
Cayambe, Napo, Ecuador ... 168 C2   0 2N 77 59W
Cayambe, Quito, Ecuador .. 100 B5   0 3N 78 8W
Çaycuma, Turkey .... 100 B5   41 25N 32 4 E
Çayeli, Turkey .... 101 B9   41 5N 40 45 E
Cayenne, Fr. Guiana 169 B7   5 5N 52 18W
Cayenne □, Fr. Guiana 169 B7   5 5N 52 18W
Cayey, Puerto Rico .... 165 d   18 7N 66 10W
Caygören Baraji, Turkey ... 49 B10   39 15N 28 12 E
Cayiralan, Turkey .... 100 C6   39 17N 35 38 E
Caylus, France .... 28 D5   44 15N 1 47 E
Cayman Brac, Cayman Is. .. 164 C4   19 43N 79 49W
Cayman Is. ☑, W. Indies .. 164 C3   19 40N 80 30W
Cayo Romano, Cuba 164 B4   22 0N 78 0W
Cayres, France .... 28 D7   44 55N 3 48 E
Cayuga, Canada 150 D5   42 59N 79 50W
Cayuga, Ind., U.S.A. 157 E9   39 57N 87 28W
Cayuga, N.Y., U.S.A. 151 D8   42 54N 76 44W
Cayuga L., U.S.A. 151 D8   42 41N 76 41W
Cazage, Angola .... 115 E4   11 2 S 20 45 E
Cazalla de la Sierra, Spain . 43 H5   37 56N 5 43W
Căzăneşti, Romania .... 53 F12   44 36N 27 3 E
Cazaubon, France 28 E3   43 56N 0 3W
Cazaux et de Sanguinet, Étang de,
  France 28 D2   44 29N 1 10W
Cazenovia, U.S.A. 151 D9   42 56N 75 51W
Cazères, France .... 28 E5   43 13N 1 5 E
Cazin, Bos.-H. .... 45 D12   44 57N 15 57 E
Čazma, Croatia .... 45 C13   45 45N 16 39 E
Cazombo, Angola .... 115 E4   11 54 S 22 56 E
Cazorla, Spain 43 H7   37 55N 3 2W
Cazorla, Sierra de, Spain .. 43 G8   38 5N 2 55W
Cea →, Spain 42 C5   42 0N 5 36W
Ceamurlia de Jos, Romania . 53 F14   44 43N 28 47 E
Ceanannus Mor, Ireland ... 23 C5   53 44N 6 53W
Ceará = Fortaleza, Brazil .. 170 B4   3 45 S 38 35W

Ceará □, Brazil .... 170 C4   5 0 S 40 0W
Ceará Mirim, Brazil .... 170 C4   5 38 S 35 25W
Cearu, L., Romania .... 53 F8   44 58N 23 11 E
Cebaco, I. de, Panama 164 E3   7 33N 81 9W
Cebollar, Argentina ...... 174 B2   29 10 S 66 35W
Cebollera, Sierra de, Spain . 40 D2   42 0N 2 30W
Cebreros, Spain 42 E6   40 27N 4 28W
Cebu, Phil. .... 81 F4   10 18N 123 54 E
Cebu □, Phil. .... 81 F4   10 20N 123 40 E
Čečava, Bos.-H. .... 52 F2   44 42N 17 44 E
Ceccano, Italy .... 46 A6   41 34N 13 20 E
Cece, Hungary .... 52 D3   46 46N 18 39 E
Cechi, Ivory C. 112 D4   6 15N 4 25W
Cecil Plains, Australia .... 127 D5   27 30 S 151 11 E
Cécina, Italy .... 44 E7   43 18N 10 33 E
Cécina →, Italy .... 44 E7   43 18N 10 29 E
Ceclavín, Spain 42 F4   39 50N 6 45W
Cedar →, U.S.A. 156 C5   41 17N 91 21W
Cedar City, U.S.A. 159 H7   37 41N 113 4W
Cedar Creek Reservoir, U.S.A. .. 155 J6   32 11N 96 4W
Cedar Falls, Iowa, U.S.A. .. 156 B4   42 32N 92 27W
Cedar Falls, Wash., U.S.A. . 160 C5   47 25N 121 45W
Cedar Grove, U.S.A. 157 E12   39 22N 84 56W
Cedar Key, U.S.A. 153 F6   29 8N 83 2W
Cedar L., Canada 143 C9   53 10N 100 0W
Cedar Point, U.S.A. 157 C13   41 44N 83 21W
Cedar Rapids, U.S.A. 156 C5   41 59N 91 40W
Cedartown, U.S.A. 152 A4   34 1N 85 15W
Cedarvale, Canada 142 B3   55 1N 128 22W
Cedarville, S. Africa ...... 117 E4   30 23 S 29 3 E
Cedarville, Ill., U.S.A. 156 B7   42 23N 89 38W
Cedarville, Ohio, U.S.A. ... 157 E13   39 44N 83 49W
Cedeira, Spain 42 B2   43 39N 8 2W
Cedral, Mexico 162 C4   23 50N 100 42W
Cedrino →, Italy .... 46 B2   40 11N 9 41 E
Cedro, Brazil .... 170 C4   6 34 S 39 3W
Cedros, Azores 9 d1   38 38N 28 42W
Cedros, I. de, Mexico 162 B1   28 10N 115 20W
Cedros B., Trin. & Tob. ... 169 F9   10 16N 61 54W
Ceduna, Australia .... 127 E1   32 7 S 133 46 E
Cedynia, Poland .... 55 F1   52 53N 14 12 E
Cée, Spain 42 C1   42 57N 9 10W
Ceel Dheere = El Dere, Somali Rep. .. 120 C3   5 22N 46 11 E
Ceerigaabo = Erigavo, Somali Rep. . 120 B3   10 35N 47 20 E
Cefalù, Italy .... 47 D7   38 2N 14 1 E
Cega →, Spain 42 D6   41 33N 4 46W
Cegléd, Hungary .... 52 C4   47 11N 19 47 E
Céglie Messápico, Italy .... 47 B10   40 39N 17 31 E
Cehegín, Spain 41 G3   38 6N 1 48W
Cheng, China .... 76 E5   24 58N 105 48 E
Cehu-Silvaniei, Romania .. 53 C8   47 24N 23 9 E
Ceica, Romania .... 52 D7   46 53N 22 10 E
Ceira →, Portugal 42 E2   40 13N 8 16W
Cekik, Indonesia .... 79 J17   8 12 S 114 27 E
Cela, Angola .... 115 E3   11 25 S 15 7 E
Čelákovice, Czech Rep. ... 34 A7   50 10N 14 46 E
Celano, Italy .... 45 F10   42 5N 13 33 E
Celanova, Spain 42 C3   42 9N 7 58W
Celaque, Parque Nac. △, Honduras .. 164 D2   14 30N 88 43W
Celaya, Mexico 162 C4   20 31N 100 37W
Celebes = Sulawesi □, Indonesia .. 83 B2   2 0 S 120 0 E
Celebes Sea, Indonesia .... 83 A2   3 0N 123 0 E
Celendín, Peru .... 172 B2   6 52 S 78 10W
Čelić, Bos.-H. .... 52 F3   44 43N 18 49 E
Celica, Ecuador .... 168 D2   4 7 S 79 59W
Celina, U.S.A. 157 D12   40 33N 84 35W
Celinac, Bos.-H. .... 52 F2   44 44N 17 22 E
Celje, Slovenia .... 45 B12   46 16N 15 18 E
Celldömölk, Hungary ..... 52 C2   47 16N 17 10 E
Celle, Germany .... 30 C6   52 37N 10 4 E
Celorico da Beira, Portugal . 42 E3   40 38N 7 24W
Celtic Sea, Atl. Oc. 8 A11   50 9N 9 34W
Çeltikçi, Turkey .... 49 D12   37 32N 30 29 E
Çemişgezek, Turkey ...... 101 C8   39 3N 38 56 E
Cenderwasih, Teluk, Indonesia . 79 E10   3 0 S 135 20 E
Cenepa →, Peru .... 168 D2   4 40 S 78 10W
Cengong, China .... 76 D7   27 13N 108 44 E
Ceno →, Italy .... 44 D7   44 43N 10 5 E
Centallo, Italy .... 44 D4   44 30N 7 35 E
Centelles, Spain .... 40 D7   41 50N 2 14 E
Centenário do Sul, Brazil .. 171 F1   22 48 S 51 36W
Center, N. Dak., U.S.A. ... 154 B4   47 7N 101 18W
Center, Tex., U.S.A. 155 K7   31 48N 94 11W
Center Hill, U.S.A. 153 G7   28 38N 82 3W
Center Point, U.S.A. 156 B5   42 12N 91 46W
Centerburg, U.S.A. 150 F2   40 18N 82 42W
Centerville, Calif., U.S.A. .. 160 J7   36 44N 119 30W
Centerville, Iowa, U.S.A. .. 156 D4   40 44N 92 52W
Centerville, Mich., U.S.A. . 157 C11   41 55N 85 32W
Centerville, Ohio, U.S.A. .. 157 E12   39 38N 84 9W
Centerville, Pa., U.S.A. ... 150 F5   40 3N 79 59W
Centerville, Tenn., U.S.A. . 149 H2   35 47N 87 28W
Centerville, Tex., U.S.A. ... 155 K7   31 16N 95 59W
Cento, Italy .... 45 D8   44 43N 11 17 E
Central □, Ghana 113 D4   5 30N 1 0W
Central □, Kenya .... 118 C4   0 30 S 37 30 E
Central □, Malawi .... 119 E3   13 30 S 33 30 E
Central □, Papua N. G. ... 132 F5   10 0 S 148 0 E
Central □, U.S.A. 144 D11   65 35N 144 48W
Central, Cordillera, Bolivia . 173 D5   18 30 S 64 55W
Central, Cordillera, Colombia . 168 C2   5 0N 75 0W
Central, Cordillera, Costa Rica . 164 D3   10 10N 84 5W
Central, Cordillera, Dom. Rep. .. 165 C5   19 15N 71 0W
Central, Cordillera, Peru .. 172 B2   7 0 S 77 30W
Central, Cordillera, Phil. .. 80 C3   17 20N 120 57 E
Central, Cordillera, Puerto Rico . 165 d   18 8N 66 35W
Central African Rep. ■, Africa . 114 A4   7 0N 20 0 E
Central America, America .. 136 H11   12 0N 85 0W
Central Butte, Canada 143 C7   50 48N 106 31W
Central City, Colo., U.S.A. . 158 G11   39 48N 105 31W
Central City, Iowa, U.S.A. . 156 B5   42 12N 91 32W
Central City, Ky., U.S.A. .. 148 G2   37 18N 87 7W
Central City, Nebr., U.S.A. . 154 E6   41 7N 98 0W
Central I., Kenya .... 118 B4   3 30N 36 0 E
Central Island Nat. Park △, Kenya . 118 B4   2 33N 36 1 E
Central Kalahari Game Reserve △,
  Botswana .... 116 C3   22 35 S 23 58 E
Central Makran Range, Pakistan . 91 D2   26 30N 64 15 E
Central Patricia, Canada .. 140 B1   51 30N 90 9W
Central Point, U.S.A. 158 E2   42 23N 122 55W
Central Ra., Papua N. G. .. 132 C2   5 0 S 143 0 E
Central Russian Uplands, Europe . 12 E13   54 0N 36 0 E
Central Siberian Plateau, Russia . 62 C14   65 0N 105 0 E
Central Square, U.S.A. 151 C8   43 17N 76 9W
Centralia, Ill., U.S.A. 156 F7   38 32N 89 8W
Centralia, Mo., U.S.A. 156 F4   39 13N 92 8W
Centralia, Wash., U.S.A. .. 160 D4   46 43N 122 58W
Centre, U.S.A. 152 A4   34 9N 85 41W
Centre □, France .... 25 F8   47 55N 1 0 E
Centre de Flacq, Mauritius . 121 d   20 12 S 57 43 E
Century, U.S.A. 153 E22   30 58N 87 16W
Cenxi, China .... 77 F8   22 30N 110 57 E
Čeotina →, Bos.-H. ...... 50 C2   43 36N 18 50 E
Cephalonia = Kefallinía, Greece . 52 E3   38 15N 20 30 E
Cepin, Croatia .... 52 E3   45 32N 18 34 E
Ceprano, Italy .... 46 A6   41 33N 13 31 E
Ceptia, Angola .... 115 E3   12 56 S 17 35 E
Ceptura, Romania .... 53 E11   45 1N 26 21 E
Cepu, Indonesia .... 85 D4   7 9 S 111 35 E
Ceram = Seram, Indonesia . 83 B3   3 10 S 129 0 E
Ceram Sea = Seram Sea, Indonesia . 82 B3   2 30 S 128 30 E
Cerbère, France .... 28 F7   42 26N 3 10 E

Cerbicales, Is., France .... 29 G13   41 33N 9 22 E
Cercal, Portugal 43 H2   37 48N 8 40W
Cerdaña, Spain .... 40 C6   42 22N 1 35 E
Cère →, France .... 28 D5   44 55N 1 49 E
Cerea, Italy .... 45 C8   45 12N 11 13 E
Ceredigion □, U.K. 21 E3   52 16N 4 15W
Ceres, Argentina .... 174 B3   29 55 S 61 55W
Ceres, Brazil .... 171 E2   15 17 S 49 35W
Ceres, S. Africa .... 116 E2   33 21 S 19 18 E
Ceres, U.S.A. 160 H6   37 35N 120 57W
Céret, France .... 28 F6   42 30N 2 42 E
Cereté, Colombia 168 B2   8 53N 75 48W
Cerf, Seychelles .... 121 b   4 38 S 55 40 E
Cergy, France .... 27 C9   49 2N 2 4 E
Cerignola, Italy .... 49 A8   41 17N 15 53 E
Cerigo = Kíthira, Greece ... 48 E5   36 8N 23 0 E
Cérilly, France .... 27 F9   46 37N 2 50 E
Cerisiers, France .... 27 D10   48 8N 3 30 E
Cerizay, France 26 F6   46 50N 0 40W
Çerkeş, Turkey .... 100 B5   40 49N 32 52 E
Çerkezköy, Turkey .... 51 E12   41 17N 28 0 E
Cerknica, Slovenia .... 45 C11   45 48N 14 21 E
Cerkovica, Bulgaria ...... 51 C8   43 41N 24 50 E
Cermerno, Serbia, Yug. ... 50 C4   43 35N 20 25 E
Çermik, Turkey .... 101 C8   38 8N 39 26 E
Cerna, Romania .... 53 E13   45 4N 28 17 E
Cerna →, Romania .... 53 F8   44 38N 23 58 E
Cernavodă, Romania ..... 53 F13   44 22N 28 3 E
Cernay, France .... 27 E14   47 44N 7 10 E
Cernik, Croatia .... 52 E2   45 17N 17 22 E
Cerralvo, I., Mexico 162 C3   24 20N 109 45W
Cerritos, Mexico 162 C4   22 27N 100 20W
Cerro Chato, Uruguay .... 175 C4   33 6 S 55 8W
Cerro El Copey, Parque Nac. △,
  Venezuela 165 D7   11 0N 63 52W
Cerro Gordo, U.S.A. 157 E8   39 53N 88 44W
Cerro Hoya, Parque Nac. △, Panama . 164 E3   7 17N 80 45W
Cerro Saoche, Parque Nac. △,
  Venezuela 165 D6   10 8N 69 38W
Cerro Sombrero, Chile .... 176 D3   52 45 S 69 15W
Certaldo, Italy .... 44 E8   43 33N 11 2 E
Cervantes, Phil. .... 80 C3   17 0N 120 44 E
Cervantes, Australia ..... 125 F2   30 31 S 115 3 E
Cervaro →, Italy .... 47 A8   41 30N 15 52 E
Cervati, Monte, Italy ..... 47 B8   40 17N 15 29 E
Cervera, Spain .... 40 D6   41 40N 1 16 E
Cervera de Pisuerga, Spain . 42 C6   42 51N 4 30W
Cervera del Río Alhama, Spain . 40 C3   42 2N 1 58W
Cervéteri, Italy .... 45 F9   42 0N 12 6 E
Cérvia, Italy .... 45 D9   44 15N 12 22 E
Cervignano del Friuli, Italy . 45 C10   45 49N 13 20 E
Cervione, France .... 29 F13   42 20N 9 29 E
Cervinara, Italy .... 47 A7   41 1N 14 37 E
Cervo, Spain 42 B3   43 40N 7 24W
César □, Colombia 168 B3   9 0N 73 30W
Cesaro, Italy .... 47 E7   37 50N 14 38 E
Cesena, Italy .... 45 D9   44 9N 12 15 E
Cesenático, Italy .... 45 D9   44 12N 12 24 E
Cēsis, Latvia .... 15 H21   57 18N 25 15 E
Česká Lípa, Czech Rep. ... 34 A7   50 45N 14 30 E
České Budějovice, Czech Rep. . 35 B9   49 54N 16 27 E
České Velenice, Czech Rep. . 34 C7   48 45N 14 57 E
Českomoravská Vrchovina,
  Czech Rep. .... 34 B8   49 30N 15 40 E
Český Brod, Czech Rep. ... 34 A7   50 4N 14 52 E
Český Krumlov, Czech Rep. . 34 C7   48 43N 14 21 E
Český Těšín, Czech Rep. ... 35 B11   49 45N 18 39 E
Çeşme, Turkey .... 49 C8   38 20N 26 23 E
Cessnock, Australia ...... 129 B9   32 50 S 151 21 E
Cesson-Sévigné, France ... 26 D5   48 7N 1 36W
Cestas, France 28 D3   44 44N 0 41W
Cestos →, Liberia 112 D3   5 40N 9 10W
Cestos Sehnkwehn Nat. Park △,
  Liberia 112 D3   5 40N 9 10W
Cetate, Romania .... 52 F8   44 7N 23 2 E
Cetin Grad, Croatia ...... 45 C12   45 9N 15 45 E
Cetina →, Croatia .... 45 E13   43 26N 16 42 E
Cetinje, Montenegro, Yug. . 50 D2   42 23N 18 59 E
Cetraro, Italy .... 47 C8   39 31N 15 55 E
Ceuta, N. Afr. 110 A3   35 52N 5 18W
Ceva, Italy .... 44 D5   44 23N 8 2 E
Ceve-i-Ra, Fiji .... 123 E13   21 46 S 174 31 E
Cévennes, France .... 28 D7   44 10N 3 50 E
Cévennes, Parc Nat. des △, France . 28 D7   44 15N 3 40 E
Cevio, Switz. .... 33 D7   46 19N 8 36 E
Ceyhan, Turkey .... 100 D6   37 4N 35 47 E
Ceyhan →, Turkey ...... 100 D6   36 38N 35 40 E
Ceylânpınar, Turkey ..... 101 D9   36 50N 40 2 E
Ceylon = Sri Lanka ■, Asia . 95 L5   7 30N 80 50 E
Cha-am, Thailand .... 86 F2   12 48N 99 58 E
Cha Pa, Vietnam .... 86 A4   22 20N 103 47 E
Chá Pungana, Angola .... 115 E3   13 44 S 18 39 E
Chabanais, France .... 28 C4   45 52N 0 48 E
Chabeuil, France .... 29 D9   44 54N 5 3 E
Chablais, France .... 27 F13   46 20N 6 36 E
Chablis, France .... 27 E10   47 47N 3 48 E
Chabounia, Algeria ...... 111 A5   35 30N 2 38 E
Chacabuco, Argentina .... 174 C3   34 40 S 60 27W
Chachapoyas, Peru ...... 172 B2   6 15 S 77 50W
Chachasp, Peru .... 172 D3   15 30 S 72 15W
Chachoengsao, Thailand .. 86 F3   13 42N 101 5 E
Chachro, Pakistan .... 92 G4   25 5N 70 15 E
Chaco □, Argentina ...... 174 B3   26 30 S 61 0W
Chaco □, U.S.A. 159 H9   36 46N 108 39W
Chaco Culture Nat. Historical
  Park △, U.S.A. 159 H10   36 3N 107 58W
Chacon, C., U.S.A. 142 C2   54 42N 132 0W
Chad ■, Africa .... 109 F3   15 0N 17 15 E
Chad, L. = Tchad, L., Chad . 109 F2   13 30N 14 30 E
Chadan, Russia .... 67 D10   51 17N 91 35 E
Chadileuvú →, Argentina . 174 D2   37 46 S 66 0W
Chadiza, Zambia .... 119 E3   14 45 S 32 27 E
Chadron, U.S.A. 154 D3   42 50N 103 0W
Chadyr-Lunga = Ciadâr-Lunga,
  Moldova .... 53 D13   46 3N 28 51 E
Chae Hom, Thailand ..... 86 C2   18 43N 99 35 E
Chae Son Nat. Park △, Thailand . 86 C2   18 42N 99 20 E
Chaek, Kyrgyzstan ...... 65 C7   41 55N 74 30 E
Chaem →, Thailand ..... 86 C2   18 11N 98 38 E
Chaeryŏng, N. Korea .... 75 E13   38 24N 125 36 E
Chagai Hills = Chāh Gay Hills,
  Afghan. .... 91 C1   29 30N 64 0 E
Chagda, Russia .... 67 D14   58 45N 130 38 E
Chaghcharān, Afghan. ... 91 B2   34 31N 65 15 E
Chagny, France .... 27 F11   46 57N 4 45 E
Chagoda, Russia .... 58 C8   59 10N 35 15 E
Chagos Arch., Ind. Oc. ... 121 E6   6 0 S 72 0 E
Chagres, Parque Nac. △, Panama . 164 E4   9 29N 79 30W
Chagrin Falls, U.S.A. 150 E3   41 26N 81 24W
Chaguanas, Trin. & Tob. .. 169 F9   10 30N 61 30W
Chāh Akhvor, Iran ...... 97 C8   32 41N 59 40 E
Chāh Bahar, Iran .... 97 E9   25 20N 60 40 E
Chāh-e Āb, Afghan. ..... 65 E4   37 23N 69 48 E
Chāh-e Kavīr, Iran ...... 97 C8   34 29N 56 52 E
Chāhār Borjak, Afghan. .. 91 C1   30 17N 62 3 E
Chāhār Mahāll va Bakhtīarī □, Iran . 97 C6   32 0N 49 0 E
Chahtung, Burma .... 90 B7   26 41N 98 10 E

Chai Wan, China .... 69 G11   22 16N 114 14 E
Chaillé-les-Marais, France . 28 B2   46 25N 1 2W
Chainat, Thailand .... 86 E3   15 11N 100 8 E
Chaires, U.S.A. 152 E5   30 26N 84 7W
Chaitén, Chile .... 176 B2   42 55 S 72 43W
Chaiya, Thailand .... 87 H2   9 23N 99 14 E
Chaiyaphum, Thailand ... 86 E4   15 48N 102 2 E
Chaj Doab, Pakistan ..... 92 C5   32 15N 73 0 E
Chajari, Argentina ...... 174 C4   30 42 S 58 0W
Chak Amru, Pakistan .... 92 C6   32 22N 75 11 E
Chaka, Sudan .... 107 G3   4 49N 31 14 E
Chakar →, Pakistan ..... 92 E3   29 29N 68 2 E
Chakari, Zimbabwe ...... 117 B4   18 5 S 29 51 E
Chakaria, Bangla. .... 90 E4   21 45N 92 5 E
Chakarnaba, Chad .... 109 F4   14 13N 20 51 E
Chake Chake, Tanzania ... 118 D4   5 15 S 39 45 E
Chakhānsūr, Afghan. ..... 91 C1   31 10N 62 0 E
Chakonipau, L., Canada .. 141 A6   56 18N 68 30W
Chakradharpur, India .... 93 H11   22 45N 85 40 E
Chakrata, India .... 92 D7   30 42N 77 51 E
Chakwadam, Burma ..... 90 B7   27 29N 98 31 E
Chakwal, Pakistan ...... 91 B4   32 56N 72 53 E
Chala, Peru .... 172 D3   15 48 S 74 20W
Chalais, France .... 28 C4   45 16N 0 3 E
Chalakudi, India .... 95 J3   10 18N 76 20 E
Chalchihuites, Mexico 162 C4   23 29N 103 53W
Chalcis = Khalkís, Greece . 48 C5   38 27N 23 42 E
Châlette-sur-Loing, France . 27 D9   48 1N 2 44 E
Chaleur B., Canada 141 C6   47 55N 65 30W
Chalfant, U.S.A. 160 H8   37 32N 118 21W
Chalhuanca, Peru .... 172 C3   14 15 S 73 15W
Chalindrey, France ...... 27 E12   47 43N 5 26 E
Chaling, China .... 77 D9   26 58N 113 30 E
Chalisgaon, India .... 94 D2   20 30N 75 10 E
Chalk River, Canada 140 C4   46 1N 77 27W
Chalkar = Shalkar, Kazakhstan . 64 F3   50 40N 51 52 E
Chalkar, Ozero = Shalkar, Ozero,
  Kazakhstan .... 64 F3   50 35N 51 47 E
Chalky Inlet, N.Z. ...... 131 G1   46 3 S 166 31 E
Chalkyitsik, U.S.A. 144 C12   66 39N 143 43W
Challakere, India .... 95 G3   14 19N 76 39 E
Challans, France 26 F5   46 50N 1 52W
Challapata, Bolivia ...... 173 G5   18 53 S 66 50W
Challis, U.S.A. 158 D6   44 30N 114 14W
Chalmette, U.S.A. 155 L10   29 56N 89 58W
Chalon-sur-Saône, France . 27 F11   46 48N 4 50 E
Chalonnes-sur-Loire, France . 26 E6   47 20N 0 45W
Châlons-en-Champagne, France . 27 D11   48 58N 4 20 E
Chālus, France .... 28 C4   45 39N 0 58 E
Chālūs, Iran .... 97 B6   36 38N 51 26 E
Cham, Germany .... 31 F8   49 13N 12 39 E
Cham, Switz. .... 33 B6   47 11N 8 28 E
Cham, Cu Lao, Vietnam .. 86 E7   15 57N 108 30 E
Chama, U.S.A. 159 H10   36 54N 106 35W
Chamah, Gunong, Malaysia . 84 A2   5 13N 101 35 E
Chamaicó, Argentina .... 174 D3   35 3 S 64 58W
Chaman, Pakistan .... 91 C2   30 58N 66 25 E
Chamba, India .... 92 C7   32 35N 76 10 E
Chamba, Tanzania ...... 119 E4   11 37 S 37 0 E
Chambal →, India ...... 93 F8   26 29N 79 15 E
Chamberlain, U.S.A. 154 D5   43 49N 99 20W
Chamberlain →, Australia . 124 C4   15 30 S 127 54 E
Chamberlain L., U.S.A. .. 149 B11   46 14N 69 19W
Chambers, U.S.A. 159 J9   35 11N 109 26W
Chambersburg, U.S.A. ... 148 F7   39 56N 77 40W
Chambéry, France ...... 29 C9   45 34N 5 55 E
Chamblee, U.S.A. 152 B5   33 53N 84 18W
Chambly, Canada 151 A11   45 27N 73 17W
Chambord, Canada 141 C5   48 25N 72 6W
Chambouline, France .... 28 C5   45 26N 1 42 E
Chambri L., Papua N. G. . 132 C2   4 15 S 143 10 E
Chamchamal, Iraq ...... 101 C11   35 32N 44 50 E
Chamela, Mexico 162 D3   19 32N 105 5W
Chamical, Argentina .... 174 C2   30 22 S 66 27W
Chamkar Luong, Cambodia . 87 G4   11 0N 103 45 E
Chamois, U.S.A. 156 F8   38 41N 91 46W
Chamoli, India .... 93 D8   30 24N 79 21 E
Chamonix-Mont Blanc, France . 29 C10   45 55N 6 51 E
Chamoson, Switz. ...... 32 D4   46 12N 7 13 E
Chamouchouane →, Canada . 140 C5   48 37N 72 20W
Champa, India .... 93 H10   22 2N 82 43 E
Champagne, Canada 142 A1   60 49N 136 30W
Champagne, France ..... 27 D11   48 40N 4 20 E
Champagnole, France .... 27 F12   46 45N 5 55 E
Champaign, U.S.A. 157 E9   40 7N 88 15W
Champassak, Laos ...... 86 E5   14 53N 105 52 E
Champaubert, France .... 27 D10   48 50N 3 45 E
Champawat, India ...... 93 E9   29 20N 80 6 E
Champdeniers-St-Denis, France . 28 B3   46 29N 0 25W
Champdoré, L., Canada .. 141 A6   55 55N 65 49W
Champeix, France ...... 28 C7   45 37N 3 8 E
Champéry, Switz. ...... 32 D3   46 11N 6 52 E
Champion, U.S.A. 150 E4   41 19N 80 51W
Champlain, U.S.A. 151 B11   44 59N 73 27W
Champlain, L., U.S.A. .. 151 B11   44 40N 73 20W
Champlitte, France ..... 27 E12   47 37N 5 31 E
Champotón, Mexico 163 D6   19 20N 90 50W
Champua, India .... 93 H11   22 5N 85 40 E
Chamrajnagar, India .... 95 J3   11 52N 76 52 E
Chamusca, Portugal 43 F2   39 21N 8 29W
Chan Chan, Peru .... 172 B2   8 7 S 79 0W
Chana, Thailand .... 87 J3   6 55N 100 44 E
Chañaral, Chile .... 174 B1   26 23 S 70 40W
Chanārān, Iran .... 97 B8   36 39N 59 6 E
Chanasma, India .... 92 H5   23 44N 72 5 E
Chancay, Peru .... 172 C2   11 32 S 77 2W
Chancery Lane, Barbados . 165 g   13 3N 59 30W
Chanco, Chile .... 174 D1   35 44 S 72 32W
Chancy, Switz. .... 32 D1   46 8N 5 58 E
Chand, India .... 93 J8   21 57N 79 7 E
Chandalar, U.S.A. 144 C11   67 30N 148 29W
Chandan, India .... 93 G12   24 38N 86 40 E
Chandan Chauki, India .. 93 E9   28 33N 80 47 E
Chandannagar, India ... 93 H13   22 52N 88 24 E
Chandausi, India ...... 93 E8   28 27N 78 49 E
Chandeleur Is., U.S.A. .. 155 L10   29 55N 88 57W
Chandeleur Sd., U.S.A. . 155 L10   29 55N 89 0W
Chandigarh, India ..... 92 D7   30 43N 76 47 E
Chandil, India .... 93 H12   22 58N 86 3 E
Chandler, Australia .... 127 D1   27 0 S 133 19 E
Chandler, Canada 141 C7   48 18N 64 46W
Chandler, Ariz., U.S.A. . 159 K8   33 18N 111 50W
Chandler, Okla., U.S.A. . 155 H6   35 42N 96 53W
Chandless →, Brazil ... 172 B4   9 53 S 69 31W
Chandod, India .... 92 J5   21 59N 73 28 E
Chandpur, Bangla. ..... 90 D3   23 8N 90 45 E
Chandragiri, India ..... 95 H4   13 35N 79 19 E
Chandrapur, India ..... 94 E3   19 57N 79 25 E
Chandrupatla, India .... 94 E5   18 33N 80 24 E
Chānf, Iran .... 97 E9   26 38N 60 29 E
Chang, Pakistan .... 92 F3   26 59N 68 30 E
Chang, Ko, Thailand ... 87 G4   12 0N 102 23 E
Ch'ang Chiang = Chang Jiang →,
  China .... 77 B13   31 48N 121 10 E
Chang Jiang →, China .. 77 B13   31 48N 121 10 E
Changan = Xi'an, China . 93 C7   34 15N 109 0 E
Changan, China .... 69 F10   23 18N 113 48 E
Changanacheri, India ... 95 K3   9 25N 76 31 E
Changane →, Mozam. .. 117 C5   24 30 S 33 30 E
Changbai, China ...... 75 D15   41 25N 128 5 E
Changbai Shan, China .. 75 C15   42 20N 129 0 E
Changchiak'ou = Zhangjiakou,
  China .... 74 D8   40 48N 114 55 E

Ch'angchou = Changzhou, China .. 77 B12 31 47N 119 58 E
Changchun, China .... 75 C13 43 57N 125 17 E
Changchunling, China .... 75 B13 45 18N 125 27 E
Changde, China .... 77 C8 29 4N 111 35 E
Changdo-ri, N. Korea .... 75 E14 38 30N 127 40 E
Changfeng, China .... 77 A11 32 28N 117 10 E
Changhai = Shanghai, China .. 77 B13 31 15N 121 26 E
Changhua, China .... 77 B12 30 12N 119 12 E
Changhua, Taiwan .... 77 E13 24 2N 120 30 E
Changhŭng, S. Korea .... 75 G14 34 41N 126 52 E
Changhŭngni, N. Korea ...... 75 D15 40 24N 128 19 E
Changi, Malaysia .... 84 B2 1 23N 103 59 E
Changi, Singapore .... 87 d 1 23N 103 59 E
Changi, Singapore ✈ (SIN), Singapore . 87 M4 1 23N 103 59 E
Changjiang, China .... 86 C7 19 20N 108 55 E
Changjiang Shuiku, China .... 69 G10 22 29N 113 27 E
Changjin, N. Korea .... 75 D14 40 23N 127 15 E
Changjin-chŏsuji, N. Korea ... 75 D14 40 30N 127 15 E
Changle, China .... 77 E12 25 59N 119 27 E
Changli, China .... 75 E10 39 40N 119 13 E
Changling, China .... 75 B12 44 20N 123 58 E
Changlun, Malaysia .... 87 J3 6 25N 100 26 E
Changning, Hunan, China .... 77 D9 26 28N 112 22 E
Changning, Sichuan, China ... 76 C5 28 40N 104 56 E
Changning, Yunnan, China ... 76 E2 24 45N 99 30 E
Changping, China .... 74 D9 40 14N 116 12 E
Changsha, China .... 77 C9 28 12N 113 0 E
Changshan, China .... 77 C12 28 55N 118 27 E
Changshu, China .... 77 B13 31 38N 120 43 E
Changshun, China .... 76 D6 26 3N 106 25 E
Changtai, China .... 77 E11 24 35N 117 42 E
Changting, China .... 77 E11 25 50N 116 22 E
Changwu, China .... 74 G4 35 10N 107 45 E
Changxing, China .... 77 B12 31 0N 119 55 E
Changyang, China .... 77 B8 30 30N 111 10 E
Changyi, China .... 75 F10 36 40N 119 30 E
Changyŏn, N. Korea .... 75 E13 38 15N 125 6 E
Changyuan, China .... 74 G8 35 15N 114 42 E
Changzhi, China .... 74 F7 36 10N 113 6 E
Changzhou, China .... 77 B12 31 47N 119 58 E
Chanhanga, Angola .... 116 B1 16 0 S 14 8 E
Chania = Khaniá, Greece ..... 39 E5 35 30N 24 4 E
Chanlar = Xanlar, Azerbaijan 61 K8 40 37N 46 12 E
Channagiri, India .... 95 G2 14 2N 75 56 E
Channapatna, India .... 95 H3 12 40N 77 15 E
Channel Is., U.K. 21 H5 49 19N 2 24W
Channel Is., U.S.A. 161 M7 33 40N 119 15W
Channel Islands Nat. Park △, U.S.A. 161 L7 34 0N 119 24W
Channel-Port aux Basques, Canada 141 C8 47 30N 59 9W
Channel Tunnel, Europe ...... 21 F9 51 0N 1 30 E
Channing, U.S.A. 155 H3 35 41N 102 20W
Chantada, Spain 42 C3 42 36N 7 46W
Chanthaburi, Thailand .... 86 F4 12 38N 102 12 E
Chantilly, France .... 27 C9 49 12N 2 29 E
Chantonnay, France 26 F5 46 40N 1 3W
Chantrey Inlet, Canada 138 B10 67 48N 96 20W
Chanumla, India .... 95 K11 8 19N 93 5 E
Chanute, U.S.A. 155 G7 37 41N 95 27W
Chanza →, Spain 43 H3 37 32N 7 30W
Chao Hu, China .... 77 B11 31 30N 117 30 E
Chao Phraya →, Thailand .... 86 F3 13 32N 100 36 E
Chao Phraya Lowlands, Thailand 86 E3 15 30N 100 0 E
Chaocheng, China .... 74 F8 36 4N 115 37 E
Chaohu, China .... 77 B11 31 38N 117 50 E
Chaoyang, Guangdong, China 77 F11 23 17N 116 30 E
Chaoyang, Liaoning, China ... 75 D11 41 35N 120 22 E
Chaozhou, China .... 77 F11 23 42N 116 32 E
Chapada dos Guimarães, Brazil 173 D6 15 26 S 55 45W
Chapais, Canada 140 C5 49 47N 74 51W
Chapala, Mozam. .... 119 F4 15 50 S 37 35 E
Chapala, L. de, Mexico 162 C4 20 10N 103 20W
Chaparé →, Bolivia .... 173 D5 15 58 S 64 42W
Chaparmukh, India .... 90 B4 26 12N 92 31 E
Chaparral, Colombia 168 C2 3 43N 75 28W
Chapayev, Kazakhstan .... 60 E10 50 25N 51 10 E
Chapayevsk, Russia .... 60 D9 53 0N 49 40 E
Chapecó, Brazil .... 175 B5 27 14 S 52 41W
Chapel Hill, U.S.A. 149 H6 35 55N 79 4W
Chapetsk →, Russia .... 64 B3 58 36N 50 4 E
Chapin, U.S.A. 156 E6 39 46N 90 24W
Chapleau, Canada 140 C3 47 50N 83 24W
Chaplin, Canada 143 C7 50 28N 106 40W
Chaplin L., Canada 143 C7 50 22N 106 36W
Chaplino, Ukraine .... 59 H9 48 8N 36 15 E
Chaplygin, Russia .... 58 F11 53 15N 40 0 E
Chappell, U.S.A. 154 E3 41 6N 102 28W
Chappells, U.S.A. 152 A8 34 11N 81 52W
Chapra = Chhapra, India ..... 93 G11 25 48N 84 44 E
Châr, Mauritania 110 D2 21 32N 12 45W
Chara, Russia .... 67 D12 56 54N 118 20 E
Charadai, Argentina .... 174 B4 27 35 S 59 55W
Charagua, Bolivia .... 173 D5 19 45 S 63 10W
Charalá, Colombia 168 B3 6 17N 73 10W
Charambirá, Punta, Colombia 168 C2 4 16N 77 32W
Charaña, Bolivia .... 172 D4 17 30 S 69 25W
Charantsavan, Armenia ...... 61 K7 40 35N 44 41 E
Charanwala, India .... 92 F5 27 51N 72 10 E
Charapita, Colombia .... 168 D3 0 37 S 74 21W
Charata, Argentina .... 174 B3 27 13 S 61 14W
Charcas, Mexico 162 C4 23 10N 101 20W
Chard, U.K. 21 G5 50 52N 2 58W
Chardon, U.S.A. 150 E3 41 35N 81 12W
Charduar, India .... 90 B4 26 51N 92 46 E
Chardzhou = Chärjew, Turkmenistan 65 D1 39 6N 63 34 E
Charente □, France .... 28 C4 45 50N 0 16 E
Charente →, France 28 C3 45 57N 1 5W
Charente-Maritime □, France 28 C3 45 45N 0 45W
Charenton-du-Cher, France ... 27 F9 46 44N 2 39 E
Chari →, Chad .... 109 F2 12 58N 14 31 E
Chārīkār, Afghan. .... 91 B3 35 0N 69 10 E
Charing, U.S.A. 152 C5 32 28N 84 22W
Chariton, U.S.A. 156 C3 41 1N 93 19W
Chariton →, U.S.A. 156 E4 39 19N 92 58W
Charity, Guyana 169 B6 7 24N 58 36W
Chärjew, Turkmenistan ...... 65 D1 39 6N 63 34 E
Charkhari, India .... 93 G8 25 24N 79 45 E
Charkhi Dadri, India .... 92 E7 28 37N 76 17 E
Charleroi, Belgium .... 24 D4 50 24N 4 27 E
Charleroi, U.S.A. 150 F5 40 9N 79 57W
Charles, C., U.S.A. 148 G8 37 7N 75 58W
Charles, I. = Santa María, I., Ecuador 172 a 1 17 S 90 26W
Charles City, U.S.A. 156 A4 43 4N 92 41W
Charles de Gaulle, Paris ✈ (CDG), France 27 D9 48 59N 2 32 E
Charles L., Canada 143 B6 59 50N 110 33W
Charles Sound, N.Z. .... 131 F2 45 2 S 167 4 E
Charles Town, U.S.A. 148 F7 39 17N 77 52W
Charleston, Ill., U.S.A. 157 E8 39 30N 88 10W
Charleston, Miss., U.S.A. 155 H9 34 1N 90 4W
Charleston, Mo., U.S.A. 155 G10 36 55N 89 21W
Charleston, S.C., U.S.A. 152 C10 32 46N 79 56W
Charleston, W. Va., U.S.A. ... 148 F5 38 21N 81 38W
Charleston L., Canada 151 B9 44 32N 76 0W
Charleston Peak, U.S.A. 161 J11 36 16N 115 42W
Charlestown, Ireland 23 C3 53 58N 8 48W
Charlestown, S. Africa .... 117 D4 27 26 S 29 53 E
Charlestown, Ind., U.S.A. 157 F11 38 27N 85 40W
Charlestown, N.H., U.S.A. 151 C12 43 14N 72 25W
Charlestown of Aberlour, U.K. 22 D5 57 28N 3 14W
Charleville = Rath Luirc, Ireland 23 D3 52 21N 8 40W
Charleville, Australia .... 127 D4 26 24 S 146 15 E
Charleville-Mézières, France . 27 C11 49 44N 4 40 E
Charlevoix, U.S.A. 148 C3 45 19N 85 16W

Charlieu, France .... 27 F11 46 10N 4 10 E
Charlotte, Mich., U.S.A. 157 B12 42 34N 84 50W
Charlotte, N.C., U.S.A. 149 H5 35 13N 80 51W
Charlotte, Vt., U.S.A. 151 B11 44 19N 73 14W
Charlotte Amalie, U.S. Virgin Is. 165 e 18 21N 64 56W
Charlotte Harbor, U.S.A. 153 J7 26 50N 82 10W
Charlotte L., Canada 142 C3 52 12N 125 19W
Charlottenberg, Sweden ..... 16 E6 59 54N 12 17 E
Charlottesville, U.S.A. 148 F6 38 2N 78 30W
Charlottetown, Nfld., Canada 141 B8 52 46N 56 7W
Charlottetown, P.E.I., Canada 141 C7 46 14N 63 8W
Charlotteville, Trin. & Tob. ... 169 E10 11 20N 60 33W
Charlton, Australia .... 128 D5 36 16 S 143 24 E
Charlton, U.S.A. 154 E8 40 59N 93 20W
Charlton I., Canada 140 B4 52 0N 79 20W
Charmes, France .... 27 D13 48 22N 6 17 E
Charmey, Switz. .... 32 C4 46 37N 7 0 E
Charny, Canada 141 C5 46 43N 71 15W
Charolles, France .... 27 F11 46 27N 4 16 E
Chârost, France .... 27 F9 47 0N 2 7 E
Charouine, Algeria 111 C4 29 0N 0 15W
Charre, Mozam. .... 119 F4 17 13 S 35 10 E
Charroux, France .... 28 B4 46 9N 0 25 E
Charsadda, Pakistan .... 92 B4 34 7N 71 45 E
Charshanga, Turkmenistan .. 65 E3 37 30N 66 1 E
Charters Towers, Australia .. 126 C4 20 5 S 146 13 E
Chartres, France .... 26 D8 48 29N 1 30 E
Chartreuse, Parc Naturel Régional de □, France 29 C9 45 22N 5 42 E
Charvakskoye Vdkhr., Uzbekistan 65 C5 41 35N 70 0 E
Chascomús, Argentina ...... 174 D4 35 30 S 58 0W
Chascfu, Zambia .... 119 E3 11 55 S 33 8 E
Chashma Barrage, Pakistan .. 91 B3 32 27N 71 20 E
Chaslands Mistake, N.Z. ..... 131 G4 46 38 S 169 22 E
Chasseneuil-sur-Bonnieure, France . 28 C4 45 52N 0 29 E
Chasseron, Switz. .... 32 C3 46 52N 6 32 E
Chāt, Iran .... 97 B7 37 59N 55 16 E
Chatal Balkan = Udvoy Balkan, Bulgaria 51 D10 42 50N 26 50 E
Chatanika, U.S.A. 144 D11 65 7N 147 28W
Château-Arnoux, France ..... 29 D10 44 6N 6 0 E
Château-Chinon, France ..... 27 E10 47 4N 3 56 E
Château d'Oex, Switz. .... 32 D4 46 28N 7 8 E
Château-d'Olonne, France ... 28 B2 46 30N 1 44W
Château-du-Loir, France ..... 26 E7 47 40N 0 25 E
Château-Gontier, France 26 E6 47 50N 0 48W
Château-la-Vallière, France .. 26 E7 47 30N 0 20 E
Château-Landon, France ..... 27 D9 48 8N 2 40 E
Château-Renault, France ..... 26 E7 47 36N 0 56 E
Château-Salins, France ...... 27 D13 48 50N 6 30 E
Château-Thierry, France ..... 27 C10 49 3N 3 20 E
Châteaubourg, France 26 D5 48 7N 1 25W
Châteaubriant, France 26 E5 47 43N 1 23W
Châteaudun, France .... 26 D8 48 3N 1 20 E
Chateaugay, U.S.A. 151 B10 44 56N 74 5W
Châteaugiron, France 26 D5 48 3N 1 30W
Châteauguay, L., Canada 141 A5 56 26N 70 3W
Châteaulin, France 26 D2 48 11N 4 8W
Châteaumeillant, France ..... 27 F9 46 35N 2 12 E
Châteauneuf-sur-Charente, France . 28 C3 45 36N 0 3W
Châteauneuf-sur-Cher, France . 27 F9 46 52N 2 18 E
Châteauneuf-sur-Loire, France . 27 E9 47 52N 2 13 E
Châteaurenard, Bouches-du-Rhône, France 29 E8 43 53N 4 51 E
Châteaurenard, Loiret, France . 27 E9 47 56N 2 55 E
Châteauroux, France .... 27 F8 46 50N 1 40 E
Châteaux, Pte. des, Guadeloupe 164 b 16 15N 61 10W
Châtel-St-Denis, Switz. ...... 32 C3 46 32N 6 54 E
Châtelaillon-Plage, France ... 28 B2 46 5N 1 5W
Châtelguyon, France .... 28 C7 45 55N 3 4 E
Châtellerault, France .... 26 F7 46 50N 0 30 E
Châtelus-Malvaleix, France .. 27 F9 46 18N 2 1 E
Chatham = Miramichi, Canada 141 C6 47 2N 65 28W
Chatham, Canada 140 D3 42 24N 82 11W
Chatham, U.K. .... 21 F8 51 22N 0 32 E
Chatham, Ill., U.S.A. 156 E7 39 40N 89 42W
Chatham, N.Y., U.S.A. 151 D11 42 21N 73 36W
Chatham, I. = San Cristóbal, I., Ecuador 172 a 0 50 S 89 26W
Chatham I., Chile .... 176 D2 50 40 S 74 25W
Chatham Is., Pac. Oc. .... 134 M10 44 0 S 176 40W
Chatham-Kent = Chatham, Canada 140 D3 42 24N 82 11W
Châtillon, Italy .... 44 C4 45 45N 7 37 E
Châtillon-Coligny, France .... 27 E9 47 50N 2 51 E
Châtillon-en-Diois, France ... 29 D9 44 41N 5 29 E
Châtillon-sur-Indre, France .. 26 F8 46 59N 1 10 E
Châtillon-sur-Loire, France ... 27 E9 47 35N 2 44 E
Châtillon-sur-Seine, France .. 27 E11 47 50N 4 33 E
Chatkal →, Uzbekistan ...... 65 C5 41 30N 70 1 E
Chatkal Kyrka Tooloru, Kyrgyzstan 65 C5 41 30N 70 45 E
Chatmohar, Bangla. .... 93 G13 24 15N 89 15 E
Chatra, India .... 93 G11 24 12N 84 56 E
Chatrapur, India .... 94 E7 19 22N 85 2 E
Chats, L. des, Canada 151 A8 45 30N 76 20W
Chatsu, India .... 92 F6 26 36N 75 57 E
Chatsworth, Canada 150 B4 44 27N 80 54W
Chatsworth, U.S.A. 157 D8 40 45N 88 18W
Chatsworth, Zimbabwe ...... 119 F3 19 38 S 31 13 E
Chatta-Hantō, Japan .... 73 C8 34 45N 136 55 E
Chattahoochee, U.S.A. 152 E5 30 42N 84 51W
Chattahoochee →, U.S.A. ... 152 E5 30 54N 84 57W
Chattanooga, U.S.A. 149 H3 35 3N 85 19W
Chatteris, U.K. .... 21 E8 52 28N 0 2 E
Chaturat, Thailand .... 86 E3 15 40N 101 51 E
Chatyr-Köl, Kyrgyzstan ...... 65 C7 40 40N 75 18 E
Chatyr-Tash, Kyrgyzstan .... 65 C8 40 55N 76 25 E
Chau Doc, Vietnam .... 87 G5 10 42N 105 7 E
Chaudes-Aigues, France ..... 28 D7 44 51N 3 1 E
Chauffailles, France .... 27 F11 46 13N 4 20 E
Chauk, Burma .... 90 E5 20 53N 94 49 E
Chaukan Pass, Burma .... 90 B6 27 8N 97 10 E
Chaumont, France .... 27 D12 48 7N 5 8 E
Chaumont-en-Vexin, France . 27 C8 49 16N 1 53 E
Chaumont-sur-Loire, France . 26 E8 47 29N 1 11 E
Chaunay, France .... 28 B4 46 13N 0 9 E
Chauny, France .... 27 C10 49 37N 3 12 E
Chaura, India .... 95 K11 8 27N 93 2 E
Chausey, Îs., France 26 D5 48 52N 1 49W
Chaussin, France .... 27 F12 46 59N 5 22 E
Chautauqua L., U.S.A. 150 D5 42 10N 79 24W
Chauvay, Kyrgyzstan .... 65 C6 40 8N 72 8 E
Chauvigny, France .... 26 F7 46 34N 0 39 E
Chauvin, Canada 143 C6 52 45N 110 10W
Chavakachcheri, Sri Lanka .. 95 K5 9 39N 80 9 E
Chavanges, France .... 27 D11 48 30N 4 35 E
Chavantina, Brazil .... 173 C7 14 40 S 52 21W
Chaves, Brazil .... 170 B2 0 15 S 49 55W
Chaves, Portugal 42 D3 41 45N 7 32W
Chavuma, Zambia .... 115 E4 13 4 S 22 40 E
Chawang, Thailand .... 87 H2 8 25N 99 30 E
Chayan = Shayan, Kazakhstan 65 A4 43 5N 69 22 E
Chaykovskiy, Russia .... 64 C5 56 47N 54 9 E
Chazelles-sur-Lyon, France .. 29 C8 45 39N 4 22 E
Chazuta, Peru .... 172 B2 6 30 S 76 0W
Chazy, U.S.A. 151 B11 44 53N 73 26W
Cheaha Mt., U.S.A. 152 B4 33 29N 85 49W
Cheb, Czech Rep. .... 34 A5 50 9N 12 28 E
Chebanse, U.S.A. 157 D9 41 0N 87 54W
Cheboksarskoye Vdkhr., Russia . 60 B8 56 13N 46 58 E
Cheboksary, Russia .... 60 B8 56 8N 47 12 E

Cheboygan, U.S.A. 148 C3 45 39N 84 29W
Chebsara, Russia .... 58 C10 59 10N 38 59 E
Chech, Erg, Africa 110 D4 25 0N 2 15W
Chechaouen, Morocco 110 A3 35 9N 5 15W
Chechen, Ostrov, Russia .... 61 H8 43 59N 47 40 E
Chechenia □, Russia .... 61 J7 43 30N 45 29 E
Checheno-Ingush Republic = Chechenia □, Russia 61 J7 43 30N 45 29 E
Chechnya = Chechenia □, Russia 61 J7 43 30N 45 29 E
Chech'ŏn, S. Korea .... 75 F15 37 8N 128 12 E
Chęciny, Poland .... 55 H7 50 46N 20 28 E
Checotah, U.S.A. 155 H7 35 28N 95 31W
Chedabucto B., Canada 141 C7 45 25N 61 8W
Cheduba I., Burma .... 90 F4 18 45N 93 40 E
Cheepie, Australia .... 127 D4 26 33 S 145 1 E
Chef-Boutonne, France 28 B3 46 7N 0 4W
Cheffadine, Niger .... 109 D2 19 57N 12 11 E
Chefornak, U.S.A. 144 F6 60 13N 164 12W
Chegdomyn, Russia .... 67 D14 51 7N 133 1 E
Chegga, Mauritania 110 C3 25 27N 5 40W
Chegutu, Zimbabwe .... 119 F3 18 10 S 30 14 E
Chehalis, U.S.A. 160 D4 46 40N 122 58W
Chehalis →, U.S.A. 160 D3 46 57N 123 50W
Cheile Nerei-Beusnita, Parcul Nat. △, Romania 52 F6 44 56N 21 52 E
Cheiron, Mt., France .... 29 E10 43 49N 6 58 E
Cheju, S. Korea .... 75 H14 33 29N 126 34 E
Cheju do, S. Korea .... 75 H14 33 29N 126 34 E
Chekalin, Russia .... 58 E9 54 10N 36 10 E
Chekiang = Zhejiang □, China 77 C13 29 0N 120 0 E
Chekla = Kuru, Bahr el →, Sudan 114 B1 8 10N 26 50 E
Chela, Sa. da, Angola .... 116 B1 16 20 S 13 20 E
Chelan, U.S.A. 158 C4 47 51N 120 1W
Chelan, L., U.S.A. 158 B3 48 11N 120 30W
Chelek, Uzbekistan .... 65 D3 39 55N 66 51 E
Cheleken, Turkmenistan ..... 57 G9 39 34N 53 16 E
Cheleken Yarymadasy, Turkmenistan 97 B7 39 30N 53 15 E
Chelforó, Argentina .... 176 A3 39 0 S 66 33W
Chelkar = Shalqar, Kazakhstan 66 E6 47 48N 59 39 E
Chelkar Tengiz, Solonchak, Kazakhstan 66 E7 48 5N 63 7 E
Chella, Ethiopia .... 107 F4 5 0N 37 26 E
Chellala Dahrania, Algeria ... 111 B5 33 2N 0 1 E
Chelles, France .... 27 D9 48 52N 2 33 E
Chełm, Poland .... 55 G10 51 8N 23 30 E
Chełmno, Poland .... 55 B5 53 20N 18 30 E
Chelmsford, U.K. .... 21 F8 51 44N 0 29 E
Chełmza, Poland .... 55 B5 53 10N 18 39 E
Chelsea, Australia .... 129 E6 38 5 S 145 8 E
Chelsea, Mich., U.S.A. 157 B12 42 19N 84 1W
Chelsea, Vt., U.S.A. 151 C12 43 59N 72 27W
Cheltenham, U.K. 21 F5 51 54N 2 4W
Chelva, Spain 40 F4 39 45N 1 0W
Chelyabinsk, Russia .... 64 D8 55 10N 61 24 E
Chelyuskin, C., Russia ...... 68 B11 77 30N 103 0 E
Chemainus, Canada 160 B3 48 55N 123 42W
Chembar = Belinskiy, Russia 60 D6 53 0N 43 25 E
Chemillé, France 26 E6 47 14N 0 45W
Chemin Grenier, Mauritius .. 121 d 20 29 S 57 28 E
Chemnitz, Germany .... 30 E8 50 51N 12 54 E
Chemulpo = Inch'ŏn, S. Korea 75 F14 37 27N 126 40 E
Chemult, U.S.A. 158 E3 43 14N 121 47W
Chen, Gora, Russia .... 67 C15 65 16N 141 50 E
Chenab →, Pakistan .... 91 C3 30 23N 71 2 E
Chenachane →, Algeria 110 C4 25 20N 3 20W
Chenango Forks, U.S.A. 151 D9 42 15N 75 51W
Chencha, Ethiopia .... 107 F4 6 15N 37 32 E
Chenchiang = Zhenjiang, China 77 A12 32 11N 119 26 E
Cheney, U.S.A. 158 C5 47 30N 117 35W
Cheng Xian, China .... 76 H4 12 42N 79 58 E
Chengalpattu, India .... 95 H4 12 42N 79 58 E
Chengbu, China .... 77 D8 26 18N 110 16 E
Chengcheng, China .... 77 D8 26 18N 110 16 E
Chengchou = Zhengzhou, China 74 G7 34 45N 113 34 E
Chengdong Hu, China ...... 77 A11 32 15N 116 20 E
Chengde, China .... 76 B5 30 38N 104 2 E
Chengdu, China .... 90 A6 28 47N 96 16 E
Chenggong, China .... 76 E4 24 52N 102 56 E
Chenggu, China .... 74 H4 33 10N 107 21 E
Chenghai, China .... 77 F11 23 29N 116 42 E
Chengjiang, China .... 76 E4 24 39N 103 0 E
Chengkou, China .... 76 B7 31 54N 108 31 E
Ch'engmai, China .... 86 C7 19 50N 109 58 E
Chengwu, China .... 74 G8 34 58N 115 50 E
Chengxi Hu, China .... 77 A11 32 15N 116 10 E
Chengyang, China .... 75 F11 36 18N 120 21 E
Chenjiagang, China .... 75 G10 34 23N 119 47 E
Chenkán, Mexico 163 D6 19 8N 90 58W
Chennai, India .... 95 H5 13 8N 80 19 E
Chenôve, France .... 27 E12 47 16N 5 1 E
Chenxi, China .... 77 C8 28 2N 110 12 E
Chenzhou, China .... 77 E9 25 47N 113 1 E
Cheo Reo, Vietnam .... 86 F7 13 25N 108 28 E
Cheom Ksan, Cambodia ..... 86 E5 14 13N 104 56 E
Chepelare, Bulgaria .... 51 E8 41 44N 24 40 E
Chepén, Peru .... 172 B2 7 15 S 79 23W
Chépénéhé, Vanuatu .... 133 K5 20 47 S 167 9 E
Chepes, Argentina .... 174 C2 31 20 S 66 35W
Chepo, Panama 164 E4 9 10N 79 6W
Chepstow, U.K. 21 F5 51 38N 2 41W
Cheptsa = Chapetsk →, Russia 64 B3 58 36N 50 4 E
Chequamegon B., U.S.A. 154 B9 46 40N 90 30W
Cher □, France .... 27 E9 47 10N 2 30 E
Cher →, France .... 26 E7 47 21N 0 29 E
Chéradi, Italy .... 47 B10 40 27N 17 10 E
Cherán, India .... 28 B4 25 45N 90 44 E
Cherasco, Italy .... 44 D4 44 39N 7 51 E
Cheraw, U.S.A. 149 H6 34 42N 79 53W
Cherbourg, France 26 C5 49 39N 1 40W
Cherchell, Algeria .... 111 A5 36 35N 2 12 E
Cherdakly, Russia .... 60 C9 54 25N 48 50 E
Cherdyn, Russia .... 64 A6 60 24N 56 29 E
Cheremkhovo, Russia .... 67 D11 53 8N 103 1 E
Cherepanovo, Russia .... 66 D9 54 15N 83 30 E
Cherepovets, Russia .... 58 C9 59 5N 37 55 E
Chergui, Chott ech, Algeria .. 111 B5 34 21N 0 25 E
Chergui, Zahrez, Algeria .... 111 B5 35 11N 3 31 E
Cherial, India .... 94 F4 17 55N 78 59 E
Cheribon = Cirebon, Indonesia 85 D3 6 45 S 108 32 E
Cherikov = Cherykaw, Belarus 59 F7 53 32N 31 20 E
Cheriyam I., India .... 95 J1 10 9N 73 40 E
Cherkasy, Ukraine .... 59 H7 49 27N 32 4 E
Cherkessk, Russia .... 61 H6 44 15N 42 5 E
Cherla, India .... 94 E5 18 5N 80 49 E
Cherlak, Russia .... 66 D8 54 15N 74 24 E
Chermoz, Russia .... 64 B6 58 46N 56 10 E
Chernak = Shornak, Kazakhstan 67 B9 70 30N 89 10 E
Chernaya Kholunitsa, Russia 64 B3 58 57N 51 34 E
Cherni, Bulgaria .... 50 D7 42 35N 23 18 E
Chernigov = Chernihiv, Ukraine 59 G6 51 28N 31 20 E
Chernihiv, Ukraine .... 59 G6 51 28N 31 20 E
Chernivtsi, Ukraine .... 59 G6 51 20N 30 15 E
Chernobyl = Chornobyl, Ukraine 59 G6 51 20N 30 15 E
Chernomorskoye = Chornomorske, Ukraine 59 K7 45 31N 32 40 E
Chernovtsy = Chernivtsi, Ukraine 59 H3 48 15N 25 52 E
Chernushka, Russia .... 64 C6 56 29N 56 3 E

Chernyakhovsk, Russia ..... 15 J19 54 36N 21 48 E
Chernyanka, Russia .... 59 G9 50 56N 37 49 E
Chernysheyskiy, Russia ..... 67 C12 63 0N 112 30 E
Chernyy Otrog, Russia ...... 64 F6 51 53N 56 0 E
Chernyye Zemli, Russia ..... 61 H8 46 10N 46 0 E
Cherokee, Iowa, U.S.A. 154 D7 42 45N 95 33W
Cherokee, Okla., U.S.A. 155 G5 36 45N 98 21W
Cherokee Village, U.S.A. 155 G9 36 17N 91 30W
Cherokees, Grand Lake O' The, U.S.A. 155 G7 36 28N 95 2W
Cherquenco, Chile .... 176 A2 38 35 S 72 0W
Cherrapunji, India .... 90 C3 25 17N 91 47 E
Cherry Valley, Calif., U.S.A. . 163 M10 33 59N 116 57W
Cherry Valley, N.Y., U.S.A. .. 151 D10 42 48N 74 45W
Cherryville, U.S.A. 156 G5 37 51N 91 16W
Cherskiy, Russia .... 67 C17 68 45N 161 18 E
Cherskogo Khrebet, Russia .. 67 C15 65 0N 143 0 E
Chertkovo, Russia .... 59 H11 49 25N 40 19 E
Cherven, Belarus .... 58 F5 53 45N 28 28 E
Cherven-Bryag, Bulgaria .... 51 C8 43 17N 24 7 E
Chervonohrad, Ukraine ..... 59 G3 50 25N 24 10 E
Cherwell →, U.K. 21 F6 51 44N 1 14W
Cherykaw, Belarus .... 58 F6 53 32N 31 20 E
Chesapeake, U.S.A. 148 G7 36 50N 76 17W
Chesapeake B., U.S.A. 148 G7 38 0N 76 10W
Cheshire □, U.K. 20 D5 53 14N 2 30W
Cheshskaya Guba, Russia ... 56 A8 67 20N 47 0 E
Cheshunt, U.K. 21 F7 51 43N 0 1W
Chesil Beach, U.K. 21 G5 50 37N 2 33W
Chesley, Canada 150 B3 44 17N 81 5W
Cheste, Spain 41 F4 39 30N 0 41W
Chester, U.K. 20 D5 53 12N 2 53W
Chester, Calif., U.S.A. 158 F3 40 19N 121 14W
Chester, Ga., U.S.A. 152 C6 32 24N 83 9W
Chester, Ill., U.S.A. 155 G10 37 55N 89 49W
Chester, Mont., U.S.A. 158 B8 48 31N 110 58W
Chester, Pa., U.S.A. 148 F8 39 51N 75 22W
Chester, S.C., U.S.A. 149 H5 34 43N 81 12W
Chester, Vt., U.S.A. 151 C12 43 16N 72 36W
Chester, W. Va., U.S.A. 150 F4 40 37N 80 34W
Chester-le-Street, U.K. 20 C6 54 51N 1 34W
Chesterfield, U.K. 20 D6 53 15N 1 25W
Chesterfield, Is., N. Cal. .... 134 J7 19 52 S 158 15 E
Chesterfield Inlet = Igluligaarjuk, Canada 139 B10 63 21N 90 42W
Chesterfield Inlet, Canada .. 138 B10 63 30N 90 45W
Chesterfield Ra., Australia .. 127 D4 25 30 S 147 27 E
Chesterton Range Nat. Park △, Australia 127 A4 26 16 S 147 22 E
Chestertown, U.S.A. 151 C11 43 73 48W
Chesterville, Canada 151 A9 45 6N 75 14W
Chestnut Ridge, U.S.A. 150 F5 40 20N 79 10W
Chesuncook L., U.S.A. 149 C11 46 0N 69 21W
Chetamale, India .... 95 J11 10 43N 92 33 E
Chéticamp, Canada 141 C7 46 37N 60 59W
Chetlat I., India .... 95 J1 11 42N 72 42 E
Chetrosu, Moldova .... 53 B12 48 5N 27 54 E
Chetumal, Mexico 163 D7 18 30N 88 20W
Chetumal, B. de, Mexico 163 D7 18 40N 88 10W
Chetwynd, Canada 142 B4 55 45N 121 36W
Chevak, U.S.A. 144 F6 61 32N 165 35W
Chevanceaux, France 28 C3 45 18N 0 25W
Cheviot, The, U.K. 20 B5 55 29N 2 9W
Cheviot Hills, U.K. 20 B5 55 20N 2 30W
Cheviot Ra., Australia ...... 126 D3 25 20 S 143 45 E
Chew Bahir, Ethiopia .... 107 G4 4 40N 36 50 E
Chewelah, U.S.A. 158 B5 48 17N 117 43W
Chewore Safari Area △, Zimbabwe 119 F2 16 0 S 29 52 E
Cheyenne, Okla., U.S.A. 155 H5 35 37N 99 40W
Cheyenne, Wyo., U.S.A. 154 C4 41 8N 104 49W
Cheyenne →, U.S.A. 154 C4 44 41N 101 18W
Cheyenne Wells, U.S.A. 154 F3 38 49N 102 21W
Cheyne B., Australia .... 125 F2 34 35 S 118 50 E
Cheyur, India .... 95 H5 12 21N 80 0 E
Chhabra, India .... 92 G7 24 40N 76 54 E
Chhaktala, India .... 92 H6 22 6N 74 11 E
Chhapra, India .... 93 G11 25 48N 84 44 E
Chhata, India .... 92 F7 27 42N 77 30 E
Chhatak, Bangla. .... 90 C3 25 5N 91 37 E
Chhatarpur, Jharkhand, India 93 G11 24 23N 84 11 E
Chhatarpur, Mad. P., India . 93 G8 24 55N 79 35 E
Chhati, India .... 90 D3 20 47N 81 40 E
Chhattisgarh □, India ...... 93 J10 22 0N 82 0 E
Chhaygaon, India .... 90 B3 26 3N 91 24 E
Chhep, Cambodia .... 86 F5 13 45N 105 24 E
Chhindwara, Mad. P., India 93 H8 22 3N 79 29 E
Chhindwara, Mad. P., India 93 H8 22 2N 78 59 E
Chhinhdipada, India .... 94 D7 21 6N 84 52 E
Chhlong, Cambodia .... 87 F5 12 15N 105 58 E
Chhota Tawa →, India ...... 92 H7 22 14N 76 36 E
Chhoti Kali Sindh →, India . 92 G6 24 2N 75 31 E
Chhuikhadan, India .... 93 J9 21 32N 80 59 E
Chhuk, Cambodia .... 87 G5 10 46N 104 28 E
Chi →, Thailand .... 86 E5 15 11N 104 43 E
Chiai, Taiwan .... 77 F13 23 29N 120 25 E
Chiali, Taiwan .... 77 F13 23 10N 120 11 E
Chiamussu = Jiamusi, China 69 B8 46 40N 130 26 E
Chianciano Terme, Italy .... 45 E8 43 3N 11 49 E
Chiang Dao, Thailand ...... 86 C2 19 22N 98 58 E
Chiang Kham, Thailand ..... 76 G3 19 32N 100 18 E
Chiang Khan, Thailand ..... 86 D3 17 52N 101 36 E
Chiang Khong, Thailand .... 76 G3 20 17N 100 24 E
Chiang Mai, Thailand ...... 86 C2 18 47N 98 59 E
Chiang Rai, Thailand .... 76 H2 19 52N 99 50 E
Chiang Saen, Thailand ..... 76 G3 20 16N 100 5 E
Chiange, Angola .... 115 F2 15 35 S 13 40 E
Chiapa →, Mexico 163 D6 16 42N 93 0W
Chiapa de Corzo, Mexico ... 163 D6 16 42N 93 0W
Chiapas □, Mexico 163 D6 17 0N 92 45W
Chiaramonte Gulfi, Italy .... 49 E7 37 3N 14 42 E
Chiaravalle, Italy .... 45 E10 43 36N 13 19 E
Chiaravalle Centrale, Italy .. 47 D9 38 41N 16 25 E
Chiari, Italy .... 44 C6 45 32N 9 56 E
Chiasso, Switz. .... 33 E8 45 50N 9 2 E
Chiatura, Georgia .... 61 J6 42 15N 43 17 E
Chiautla, Mexico 163 D5 18 18N 98 34W
Chiávari, Italy .... 44 D6 44 19N 9 19 E
Chiavenna, Italy .... 44 B6 46 19N 9 24 E
Chiba, Japan .... 73 B12 35 30N 140 7 E
Chiba □, Japan .... 73 B12 35 30N 140 20 E
Chibabava, Mozam. .... 117 C5 20 17 S 33 35 E
Chibemba, Cunene, Angola 115 F2 15 48 S 14 8 E
Chibemba, Huíla, Angola ... 116 B2 16 20 S 15 20 E
Chibia, Zimbabwe .... 115 F2 15 10 S 13 42 E
Chibougamau, Canada 140 C5 49 56N 74 24W
Chibougamau, L., Canada ... 140 C5 49 50N 74 20W
Chibuk, Nigeria .... 113 C7 10 52N 12 50 E
Chibuto, Mozam. .... 117 C5 24 40 S 33 33 E
Chic-Chocs, Mts., Canada ... 141 C6 48 55N 66 0W
Chicacole = Srikakulam, India 94 E6 18 14N 83 58 E
Chicago, U.S.A. 157 C9 41 52N 87 38W
Chicago Heights, U.S.A. 157 C9 41 30N 87 38W
Chicago O'Hare International ✈ (ORD), U.S.A. 157 C9 41 59N 87 54W
Chicapa →, Dem. Rep. of the Congo 115 D4 10 25 S 20 48 E
Chicha, Chad .... 109 E3 16 57N 18 34 E
Chichagof I., U.S.A. 144 H14 57 30N 135 30W
Chichaoua, Morocco 110 B3 31 32N 8 44W
Chichén-Itzá, Mexico 163 C7 20 40N 88 36W
Chichén-Itzá, Ruinas, Mexico 163 C7 20 40N 88 36W
Chicheng, China .... 74 D8 40 55N 115 55 E

Chichester, U.K. 21 G7 50 50N 0 47W
Chichester Ra., Australia ...... 124 D2 22 12 S 119 15 E
Chichibu, Japan .... 73 A11 35 59N 139 10 E
Chichibu-Tama Nat. Park △, Japan 73 B10 35 52N 138 42 E
Ch'ich'ihaerh = Qiqihar, China .. 67 E13 47 26N 124 0 E
Chicholi, India .... 92 H8 22 1N 77 40 E
Chickasaw Nat. Recr. Area △, U.S.A. 155 H6 34 26N 97 0W
Chickasha, U.S.A. 155 H6 35 3N 97 58W
Chicken, U.S.A. 144 D12 64 5N 141 56W
Chiclana de la Frontera, Spain .. 43 J4 36 26N 6 9W
Chiclayo, Peru .... 172 B2 6 42 S 79 50W
Chico, U.S.A. 160 F5 39 44N 121 50W
Chico →, Chubut, Argentina ..... 176 B3 44 0 S 67 0W
Chico →, Santa Cruz, Argentina . 176 C3 50 0 S 68 30W
Chicomba, Angola .... 115 E2 14 10 S 14 52 E
Chicomo, Mozam. .... 117 C5 24 31 S 34 6 E
Chicomostoc, Mexico 162 C4 22 28N 102 49W
Chicontepec, Mexico 163 C5 20 58N 98 10W
Chicopee, U.S.A. 151 D12 42 9N 72 37W
Chicoutimi, Canada 141 C5 48 28N 71 5W
Chicualacuala, Mozam. .... 117 C5 22 6 S 31 42 E
Chicuma, Angola .... 115 E2 13 26 S 14 50 E
Chidambaram, India .... 95 J4 11 20N 79 45 E
Chidenguele, Mozam. .... 117 C5 24 55 S 34 11 E
Chidley, C., Canada 139 B13 60 23N 64 26W
Chiducuane, Mozam. .... 117 C5 24 35 S 34 25 E
Chiede, Angola .... 116 B2 17 15 S 16 22 E
Chiefland, U.S.A. 153 F7 29 29N 82 52W
Chiefs Pt., Canada 150 B3 44 41N 81 18W
Chiem Hoa, Vietnam .... 86 A5 22 12N 105 17 E
Chiemsee, Germany .... 31 H8 47 53N 12 28 E
Chiengi, Zambia .... 119 D2 8 45 S 29 10 E
Chiengmai = Chiang Mai, Thailand 86 C2 18 47N 98 59 E
Chiengo, Angola .... 115 E4 13 20 S 21 55 E
Chienti →, Italy .... 45 E10 43 18N 13 45 E
Chieri, Italy .... 44 C4 45 1N 7 49 E
Chiers →, France .... 27 C11 49 39N 4 59 E
Chiesa in Valmalenco, Italy .... 44 B6 46 16N 9 51 E
Chiese →, Italy .... 44 C7 45 8N 10 25 E
Chieti, Italy .... 45 F11 42 21N 14 10 E
Chifeng, China .... 75 C10 42 18N 118 58 E
Chigasaki, Japan .... 73 B11 35 19N 139 24 E
Chigirin, Ukraine .... 59 H7 49 4N 32 38 E
Chignecto B., Canada 141 C7 45 30N 64 40W
Chignik, U.S.A. 144 H8 56 18N 158 24W
Chigorodó, Colombia 168 B2 7 41N 76 42W
Chiguana, Bolivia .... 174 A2 21 0 S 67 58W
Chigwell, U.K. .... 21 F8 51 37N 0 5 E
Chiha-ri, N. Korea .... 75 E14 38 40N 126 30 E
Chihli, G. of = Bo Hai, China .. 75 E10 39 0N 119 0 E
Chihuahua, Mexico 162 B3 28 40N 106 3W
Chihuahua □, Mexico 162 B3 28 40N 106 3W
Chiili = Shīeli, Kazakhstan .... 65 A3 44 20N 66 15 E
Chik Bollapur, India .... 95 H3 13 25N 77 45 E
Chikalda, India .... 94 D3 21 24N 77 19 E
Chikhli, Ahmadabad, India ...... 94 D1 20 45N 73 4 E
Chikhli, Maharashtra, India .... 94 D3 20 20N 76 18 E
Chikmagalur, India .... 95 H2 13 15N 75 45 E
Chiknayakanhalli, India .... 95 H3 13 26N 76 37 E
Chikodi, India .... 95 F2 16 26N 74 38 E
Chikugo, Japan .... 72 D2 33 14N 130 28 E
Chikuma-Gawa →, Japan .... 73 A10 36 59N 138 35 E
Chikushino, Japan .... 72 D2 33 30N 130 30 E
Chikwawa, Malawi .... 119 F3 16 2 S 34 50 E
Chila, Angola .... 115 E2 12 3 S 14 22 E
Chilac, Mexico 163 D5 18 20N 97 24W
Chilam Chavki, Pakistan .... 93 B6 35 5N 75 5 E
Chilanga, Zambia .... 119 F2 15 33 S 28 16 E
Chilapa, Mexico 163 D5 17 40N 99 11W
Chilas, Pakistan .... 93 B6 35 5N 74 5 E
Chilaw, Sri Lanka .... 95 L4 7 30N 79 50 E
Chilcotin →, Canada 142 C4 51 44N 122 23W
Childers, Australia .... 127 D5 25 15 S 152 17 E
Childers, U.S.A. 152 B3 31 5N 91 21W
Childress, U.S.A. 155 H4 34 25N 100 13W
Chile ■, S. Amer. .... 174 C1 35 0 S 72 0W
Chile Chico, Chile .... 176 C2 46 33 S 71 44W
Chile Rise, Pac. Oc. .... 135 L18 38 0 S 92 0W
Chilecito, Argentina .... 174 B2 29 10 S 67 30W
Chilessa, Angola .... 115 E3 11 35 S 16 34 E
Chilete, Peru .... 172 B2 7 10 S 78 50W
Chilhowee, U.S.A. 156 F3 38 36N 93 51W
Chilia, Brațul →, Romania ...... 53 E14 45 14N 29 42 E
Chilik = Shelek, Kazakhstan .... 65 B9 43 33N 78 17 E
Chililabombwe, Zambia .... 119 E2 12 18 S 27 43 E
Chilin = Jilin, China .... 75 C14 43 44N 126 30 E
Chilka L., India .... 94 E7 19 40N 85 25 E
Chilko →, Canada 142 C4 52 0N 123 40W
Chilko L., Canada 142 C4 51 20N 124 10W
Chillagoe, Australia .... 126 B3 17 7 S 144 33 E
Chillán, Chile .... 174 D1 36 40 S 72 10W
Chillicothe, Ill., U.S.A. 156 D7 40 55N 89 29W
Chillicothe, Mo., U.S.A. 156 E3 39 48N 93 33W
Chillicothe, Ohio, U.S.A. 148 F4 39 20N 82 59W
Chilliwack, Canada 142 D4 49 10N 121 54W
Chilo, India .... 92 E3 27 25N 73 32 E
Chiloane, I., Mozam. .... 117 C5 20 40 S 34 55 E
Chiloé, I. de, Chile .... 176 B2 42 30 S 73 50W
Chilonda, Angola .... 115 E3 11 19 S 16 12 E
Chilongo, Angola .... 115 E3 13 55 S 16 35 E
Chilpancingo, Mexico 163 D5 17 30N 99 30W
Chiltern, Australia .... 129 D7 36 10 S 146 36 E
Chiltern Hills, U.K. 21 F7 51 40N 0 53W
Chilton, U.S.A. 148 C1 44 2N 88 10W
Chiluage, Angola .... 115 D4 9 30 S 21 50 E
Chilubi, Zambia .... 119 E2 11 5 S 29 58 E
Chilubula, Zambia .... 119 E3 10 14 S 30 51 E
Chilumba, Malawi .... 119 E3 10 28 S 34 12 E
Chilung, Taiwan .... 77 E13 25 3N 121 45 E
Chilwa, L., Malawi .... 119 F4 15 15 S 35 40 E
Chimakela, Angola .... 115 E3 15 24 S 16 58 E
Chimakudi, India .... 90 C4 25 47N 93 48 E
Chimaltitán, Mexico 162 C4 21 46N 103 50W
Chimán, Panama 164 E4 8 45N 78 40W
Chimanimani, Zimbabwe .... 117 B5 19 48 S 32 52 E
Chimanimani Nat. Park △,
   Zimbabwe .... 119 F3 19 48 S 33 0 E
Chimay, Belgium .... 24 D4 50 3N 4 20 E
Chimayo, U.S.A. 159 H11 36 0N 105 56W
Chimbay, Uzbekistan .... 66 E6 42 57N 59 47 E
Chimborazo, Ecuador .... 168 D2 1 29 S 78 55W
Chimborazo □, Ecuador .... 168 D2 1 0 S 78 40W
Chimbote, Peru .... 172 B2 9 0 S 78 35W
Chimbu □, Papua N. G. .... 132 D3 6 15 S 144 50 E
Chimichagua, Colombia 168 B3 9 15N 73 49W
Chimion, Uzbekistan .... 65 C5 40 15N 71 32 E
Chimkent = Shymkent, Kazakhstan 65 B8 42 18N 69 36 E
Chimoio, Mozam. .... 119 F3 19 4 S 33 30 E
Chimpembe, Zambia .... 119 E2 9 31 S 29 33 E
Chimur, India .... 94 D4 20 30N 79 23 E
Chin □, Burma .... 90 D4 22 0N 93 0 E
Chin Hills, Burma .... 90 D4 22 30N 93 30 E
Chin Ling Shan = Qinling Shandi,
   China .... 74 H5 33 50N 108 10 E
China, Mexico 163 B5 25 40N 99 20W
China ■, Asia .... 69 C6 30 0N 110 0 E
China Lake, U.S.A. 161 K9 35 44N 117 37W
Chinacota, Colombia 168 B3 7 37N 72 36W
Chinan = Jinan, China .... 74 F9 36 38N 117 1 E
Chinandega, Nic. 164 D2 12 35N 87 12W
Chinati Peak, U.S.A. 155 L2 29 57N 104 29W
Chinaz, Uzbekistan .... 65 C4 40 56N 68 46 E
Chincha Alta, Peru .... 172 C2 13 25 S 76 7W
Chinchaga →, Canada 142 B5 58 53N 118 20W

Chincheros, Peru .... 172 C3 13 30 S 73 44W
Chinchilla, Australia .... 127 D5 26 45 S 150 38 E
Chinchilla de Monte Aragón, Spain 41 G3 38 53N 1 40W
Chincholi, India .... 94 E3 17 28N 77 26 E
Chinchorro, Banco, Mexico 163 D7 18 35N 87 20W
Chinchou = Jinzhou, China ...... 75 D11 41 5N 121 3 E
Chinchoua, Gabon .... 114 B1 0 1N 9 48 E
Chincoteague, U.S.A. 148 G8 37 56N 75 23W
Chindo, S. Korea .... 75 G14 34 28N 126 15 E
Chinde, Mozam. .... 119 F4 18 35 S 36 30 E
Chindwin →, Burma .... 90 E5 21 26N 95 15 E
Chineni, India .... 93 C6 33 2N 75 15 E
Chinga, Mozam. .... 119 F4 15 13 S 38 35 E
Chingirlau, Kazakhstan .... 64 F5 51 7N 54 7 E
Chingola, Zambia .... 119 E2 12 31 S 27 53 E
Chingole, Malawi .... 119 E3 13 4 S 34 17 E
Chingoroi, Angola .... 115 E2 13 31 S 14 21 E
Ch'ingtao = Qingdao, China ..... 75 F11 36 5N 120 20 E
Chinguar, Angola .... 115 E3 12 25 S 16 45 E
Chinguetti, Mauritania 110 D2 20 25N 12 24W
Chingune, Mozam. .... 117 C5 20 33 S 34 58 E
Chinhae, S. Korea .... 75 G15 35 9N 128 47 E
Chinhanguanine, Mozam. .... 117 D5 25 21 S 32 30 E
Chinhoyi, Zimbabwe .... 119 F3 17 20 S 30 8 E
Chini, India .... 92 D8 31 32N 78 15 E
Chiniot, Pakistan .... 91 C4 31 45N 73 0 E
Chínipas, Mexico 162 B3 27 22N 108 32W
Chinji, Pakistan .... 92 C5 32 42N 72 22 E
Chinju, S. Korea .... 75 G15 35 12N 128 2 E
Chinkai, Afghan. .... 91 C2 31 57N 67 26 E
Chinkapook, Australia .... 128 C5 35 11 S 142 57 E
Chinko →, C.A.R. .... 114 B4 4 50N 23 53 E
Chinle, U.S.A. 159 H9 36 9N 109 33W
Chinmen, Taiwan .... 77 E13 24 26N 118 19 E
Chinmen Tao, Taiwan .... 77 E12 24 27N 118 23 E
Chinnamanur, India .... 95 K3 9 50N 77 24 E
Chinnampo = Namp'o, N. Korea ... 75 E13 38 52N 125 10 E
Chinnur, India .... 94 E4 18 57N 79 49 E
Chino, Japan .... 73 B10 35 59N 138 9 E
Chino, U.S.A. 161 L9 34 1N 117 41W
Chino Valley, U.S.A. 159 J7 34 45N 112 27W
Chinon, France .... 26 E7 47 10N 0 15 E
Chinook, U.S.A. 158 B9 48 35N 109 14W
Chinoya, Zambia .... 115 E4 13 55 S 23 16 E
Chinsali, Zambia .... 119 E3 10 30 S 32 2 E
Chintalapudi, India .... 94 F5 17 4N 80 59 E
Chióggia, Italy .... 45 C9 45 13N 12 17 E
Chíos = Khíos, Greece .... 49 C8 38 27N 26 9 E
Chipata, Zambia .... 119 E3 13 38 S 32 28 E
Chiperceni, Moldova .... 53 C13 47 31N 28 50 E
Chipindo, Angola .... 115 E3 13 49 S 15 48 E
Chipinge, Zimbabwe .... 119 G3 20 13 S 32 28 E
Chipinge Safari Area △, Zimbabwe 119 G3 20 14 S 33 0 E
Chipiona, Spain 43 J4 36 44N 6 26W
Chipley, U.S.A. 152 E4 30 47N 85 32W
Chiplun, India .... 94 F1 17 31N 73 34 E
Chipman, Canada 141 C6 46 6N 65 53W
Chipoka, Malawi .... 119 E3 13 57 S 34 28 E
Chippenham, U.K. 21 F5 51 27N 2 6W
Chippewa →, U.S.A. 154 C8 44 25N 92 5W
Chippewa Falls, U.S.A. 154 C9 44 56N 91 24W
Chipping Norton, U.K. 21 F6 51 56N 1 32W
Chiprovtsi, Bulgaria .... 50 C6 43 24N 22 52 E
Chiputneticook Lakes, U.S.A. ... 149 C11 45 35N 67 35W
Chiquelquele, Angola .... 115 F3 16 44 S 19 5 E
Chiquián, Peru .... 172 C2 10 10 S 77 0W
Chiquibul Nat. Park △, Belize .. 164 C2 16 49N 88 52W
Chiquimula, Guatemala 164 D2 14 51N 89 37W
Chiquinquira, Colombia 168 B3 5 37N 73 50W
Chiquitos, Llanos de, Bolivia .. 173 D5 18 0 S 61 30W
Chir →, Russia .... 61 F6 48 30N 43 0 E
Chira →, Peru .... 168 D1 4 54 S 81 8W
Chirala, India .... 95 G5 15 50N 80 26 E
Chiramba, Mozam. .... 119 F3 16 55 S 34 39 E
Chirawa, India .... 92 E6 28 14N 75 42 E
Chirayinkil, India .... 95 K3 8 41N 76 49 E
Chirchiq, Uzbekistan .... 65 C4 41 29N 69 35 E
Chiredzi, Zimbabwe .... 117 C5 21 0 S 31 38 E
Chirfa, Niger .... 109 D2 20 55N 12 22 E
Chirgua →, Venezuela 168 B4 8 54N 67 58W
Chiricahua Nat. Monument △,
   U.S.A. 159 K9 32 0N 109 20W
Chiricahua Peak, U.S.A. 159 L9 31 51N 109 18W
Chiriquí, G. de, Panama 164 E3 8 0N 82 10W
Chiriquí, L. de, Panama 164 E3 9 10N 82 0W
Chirisa Safari Area △, Zimbabwe 119 F2 17 53 S 28 15 E
Chirivira Falls, Zimbabwe ...... 119 G3 21 10 S 32 12 E
Chirnogi, Romania .... 53 F11 44 7N 26 32 E
Chirripó Grande, Cerro, Costa Rica 164 E3 9 29N 83 29W
Chirundu, Zimbabwe .... 117 B4 16 3 S 28 50 E
Chisamba, Zambia .... 119 E2 14 55 S 28 20 E
Chisasibi, Canada 140 B4 53 50N 79 0W
Ch'ishan, Taiwan .... 77 F13 22 44N 120 31 E
Chishmy, Russia .... 64 D5 54 35N 55 23 E
Chisholm, Canada 142 C6 54 55N 114 10W
Chisholm, U.S.A. 154 B8 47 29N 92 53W
Chishtian Mandi, Pakistan ...... 92 E5 29 50N 72 55 E
Chishui, China .... 76 C5 28 30N 105 42 E
Chishui He →, China .... 76 C5 28 49N 105 50 E
Chisimaio, Somali Rep. .... 120 E2 0 22 S 42 32 E
Chisimba Falls, Zambia .... 119 E3 10 12 S 30 56 E
Chișinău, Moldova .... 53 C13 47 2N 28 50 E
Chișinău-Criş, Romania .... 52 D6 46 32N 21 37 E
Chisone →, Italy .... 44 D4 44 49N 7 25 E
Chisos Mts., U.S.A. 155 L3 29 5N 103 15W
Chissengue, Angola .... 115 D4 9 13 S 20 34 E
Chissibuca, Mozam. .... 117 C5 22 48 S 35 18 E
Chistochina, U.S.A. 144 E11 62 34N 144 40W
Chistopol, Russia .... 60 C10 55 25N 50 38 E
Chita, Colombia 168 B3 6 11N 72 28W
Chita, Russia .... 67 D12 52 0N 113 35 E
Chitado, Angola .... 115 F2 17 10 S 14 8 E
Chitanda →, Angola .... 115 F3 16 1 S 15 12 E
Chitapur, India .... 94 F3 17 10N 77 5 E
Chitembo, Angola .... 115 E3 13 30 S 16 50 E
Chitina, U.S.A. 144 F11 61 31N 144 26W
Chitipa, Malawi .... 119 D3 9 41 S 33 19 E
Chitose, Japan .... 70 C10 42 49N 141 39 E
Chitradurga, India .... 95 G3 14 14N 76 24 E
Chitrakoot, India .... 94 E5 19 10N 81 40 E
Chitral, Pakistan .... 91 B3 35 50N 71 56 E
Chitravati →, India .... 95 G4 14 45N 78 15 E
Chitré, Panama 164 E3 7 59N 80 27W
Chittagong, Bangla. .... 90 D3 22 19N 91 48 E
Chittagong □, Bangla. .... 90 C3 24 5N 91 0 E
Chittaurgarh, India .... 92 G6 24 52N 74 38 E
Chittoor, India .... 95 H4 13 15N 79 5 E
Chittur, India .... 95 J3 10 40N 76 45 E
Chitungwiza, Zimbabwe .... 119 F3 18 0 S 31 6 E
Chiumbe →, Dem. Rep. of
   the Congo .... 115 D4 6 59 S 21 12 E
Chiumbo, Angola .... 115 E3 12 29 S 16 8 E
Chiume, Angola .... 115 F4 15 3 S 21 14 E
Chiuro, Italy .... 33 D9 46 10N 9 59 E
Chiusi, Italy .... 45 E8 43 1N 11 57 E
Chiva, Spain 41 F4 39 27N 0 41W
Chivacoa, Venezuela 168 A4 10 10N 68 54W
Chivay, Peru .... 172 D3 15 43 S 71 43W
Chivé, Bolivia .... 172 C4 12 23 S 68 35W
Chivhu, Zimbabwe .... 119 F3 19 2 S 30 52 E

Chivilcoy, Argentina .... 174 C4 34 55 S 60 0W
Chiwanda, Tanzania .... 119 E3 11 23 S 34 55 E
Chixi, China .... 77 G9 22 0N 112 58 E
Chizarira, Zimbabwe .... 119 F2 17 36 S 27 45 E
Chizarira Nat. Park △, Zimbabwe 119 F2 17 44 S 27 52 E
Chizela, Zambia .... 115 E4 13 8 S 25 0 E
Chizera, Zambia .... 119 E2 13 10 S 25 0 E
Chizu, Japan .... 72 B6 35 16N 134 14 E
Chkalov = Orenburg, Russia ..... 64 F5 51 45N 55 6 E
Chkolovsk, Russia .... 60 B6 56 50N 43 10 E
Chloride, U.S.A. 161 K12 35 25N 114 12W
Chlumec nad Cidlinou, Czech Rep. 34 A8 50 9N 15 29 E
Chmielnik, Poland .... 55 H7 50 37N 20 43 E
Cho Bo, Vietnam .... 76 G5 20 46N 105 10 E
Cho Phuoc Hai, Vietnam .... 87 G6 10 26N 107 18 E
Choa Chu Kang, Singapore .... 87 d 1 22N 103 41 E
Choba, Kenya .... 118 B4 2 30N 38 5 E
Chobe Nat. Park △, Botswana .... 116 B4 18 37 S 24 23 E
Choch'iwŏn, S. Korea .... 75 F14 36 37N 127 18 E
Chochiwŏn, S. Korea .... 75 F14 36 37N 127 18 E
Chociwel, Poland .... 54 E2 53 29N 15 21 E
Chocó □, Colombia 168 B2 6 0N 77 0W
Chocolate Mts., U.S.A. 161 M11 33 15N 115 15W
Choconta, Colombia 168 B3 5 9N 73 41W
Choctawhatchee →, U.S.A. 152 E3 30 25N 86 8W
Choctawhatchee B., U.S.A. 153 E3 30 20N 86 20W
Chodavaram, Andhra Pradesh, India 94 F6 17 50N 82 57 E
Chodavaram, Andhra Pradesh, India 94 F6 17 27N 81 46 E
Chodecz, Poland .... 55 F6 52 24N 19 2 E
Chodov, Czech Rep. .... 34 A5 50 15N 12 45 E
Chodziez, Poland .... 55 F3 52 58N 16 58 E
Choele Choel, Argentina .... 176 A3 39 11 S 65 40W
Chōfu, Japan .... 73 B11 35 39N 139 33 E
Choisul, St. Lucia .... 165 f 13 47N 61 3W
Choiseul, Solomon Is. .... 133 L9 7 0 S 156 40 E
Choix, Mexico 162 B3 26 40N 108 23W
Chojna, Poland .... 55 F1 52 58N 14 25 E
Chojnice, Poland .... 54 E4 53 42N 17 32 E
Chojnów, Poland .... 55 G2 51 18N 15 58 E
Chok-Tal, Kyrgyzstan .... 65 B8 42 35N 76 45 E
Chōkai-San, Japan .... 70 E10 39 6N 140 3 E
Choke, Ethiopia .... 107 E4 11 18N 37 15 E
Choke Canyon L., U.S.A. 155 L5 28 30N 98 20W
Chokurdakh, Russia .... 67 B15 70 38N 147 55 E
Cholame, U.S.A. 160 K6 35 44N 120 18W
Cholet, France 26 E6 47 4N 0 52W
Cholguan, Chile .... 174 D1 37 10 S 72 3W
Cholpon-Ata, Kyrgyzstan .... 65 B8 42 40N 77 6 E
Choluteca, Honduras 164 D2 13 20N 87 14W
Choluteca →, Honduras 164 D2 13 0N 87 20W
Chom Bung, Thailand .... 86 F2 13 37N 99 36 E
Chom Thong, Thailand .... 86 C2 18 25N 98 41 E
Choma, Zambia .... 119 F2 16 48 S 26 59 E
Chomen Swamp, Ethiopia .... 107 F4 9 20N 37 10 E
Chomun, India .... 92 F6 27 15N 75 40 E
Chomutov, Czech Rep. .... 34 A6 50 28N 13 23 E
Chon Buri, Thailand .... 86 F3 13 21N 101 1 E
Chon Thanh, Vietnam .... 87 G6 11 24N 106 36 E
Ch'onan, S. Korea .... 75 F14 36 48N 127 9 E
Chone, Ecuador .... 168 D2 0 40 S 80 0W
Chong Kai, Cambodia .... 86 F4 13 57N 103 35 E
Chong Mek, Thailand .... 86 E5 15 10N 105 27 E
Chong Phangan, Thailand .... 87 b 9 39N 100 0 E
Chong Samui, Thailand .... 87 b 9 21N 99 50 E
Chongde, China .... 77 B13 30 32N 120 26 E
Chŏngdo, S. Korea .... 75 G15 35 38N 128 42 E
Chŏngha, S. Korea .... 75 F15 36 12N 129 21 E
Ch'ŏngjin, N. Korea .... 75 D15 41 47N 129 50 E
Chŏngju, N. Korea .... 75 E13 39 40N 125 5 E
Chŏngju, S. Korea .... 75 F14 36 39N 127 27 E
Chongli, China .... 76 B4 28 41N 106 36 E
Chongming, China .... 77 B13 31 40N 121 30 E
Chongming Dao, China .... 77 B13 31 40N 121 30 E
Chongoyape, Peru .... 172 B2 6 35 S 79 25W
Chongqing, Chongqing, China .... 76 C6 29 35N 106 25 E
Chongqing, Sichuan, China ...... 76 B4 30 38N 108 5 E
Chongqing Shi □, China .... 76 C6 30 0N 108 0 E
Chongren, China .... 77 D11 27 46N 116 3 E
Chŏngup, S. Korea .... 75 G14 35 35N 126 50 E
Chongyi, China .... 77 E10 25 45N 114 29 E
Chongzuo, China .... 76 F6 22 23N 107 20 E
Chŏnju, S. Korea .... 75 G14 35 50N 127 4 E
Chonos, Arch. de los, Chile .... 176 C2 45 0 S 75 0W
Chop, Ukraine .... 59 H2 48 26N 22 12 E
Chopda, India .... 94 D2 21 20N 75 15 E
Chopim →, Brazil .... 175 B5 25 35 S 53 5W
Chor, Pakistan .... 92 G3 25 31N 69 46 E
Chorbat La, India .... 93 B7 34 42N 76 37 E
Chorley, U.K. 20 D5 53 39N 2 38W
Chornobyl, Ukraine .... 59 G6 51 20N 30 15 E
Chornomorske, Ukraine .... 59 K7 45 31N 32 46 E
Choroque, Cerro, Bolivia .... 174 A2 20 59 S 66 5W
Choroszcz, Poland .... 55 E9 53 10N 22 59 E
Chorregon, Australia .... 126 C3 22 40 S 143 32 E
Chortkiv, Ukraine .... 59 H3 49 2N 25 46 E
Ch'ŏrwon, S. Korea .... 75 E14 38 15N 127 10 E
Chorzele, Poland .... 55 E7 53 15N 20 55 E
Chorzów, Poland .... 55 H5 50 18N 18 57 E
Chos-Malal, Argentina .... 174 D1 37 20 S 70 15W
Ch'osan, N. Korea .... 75 D13 40 50N 125 47 E
Chōshi, Japan .... 73 B12 35 45N 140 51 E
Choszczno, Poland .... 55 E2 53 7N 15 25 E
Chota, Peru .... 172 B2 6 33 S 78 39W
Choteau, U.S.A. 158 C7 47 49N 112 11W
Chotěboř, Czech Rep. .... 34 B8 49 43N 15 40 E
Chotila, India .... 92 H4 22 23N 71 15 E
Chotta Udepur, India .... 92 H6 22 19N 74 1 E
Chowchilla, U.S.A. 160 H6 37 7N 120 16W
Choybalsan, Mongolia .... 69 B6 48 4N 114 30 E
Chrisman, U.S.A. 157 E9 39 48N 87 41W
Christchurch, N.Z. .... 131 D7 43 33 S 172 47 E
Christchurch, U.K. 21 G6 50 44N 1 47W
Christian I., Canada 150 B4 44 50N 80 12W
Christian Sd., U.S.A. 144 J14 55 56N 134 40W
Christiana, S. Africa .... 124 D4 27 52 S 25 8 E
Christiansfeld, Denmark .... 17 J3 55 21N 9 29 E
Christianshåb = Qasigiannguit,
   Greenland 10 D5 68 50N 51 18W
Christiansted, U.S. Virgin Is. . 165 C7 17 45N 64 42W
Christie B., Canada 143 A6 62 32N 111 10W
Christina →, Canada 143 B6 56 40N 111 3W
Christmas Cr. →, Australia ..... 124 C4 18 29 S 125 23 E
Christmas I. = Kiritimati, Kiribati 135 G12 1 58N 157 27W
Christmas I., Ind. Oc. .... 121 F9 10 30 S 105 40 E
Christopher, U.S.A. 157 F9 37 59N 89 3W
Christopher L., Australia ...... 125 D4 24 49 S 127 42 E
Christyakovo = Thorez, Ukraine . 59 H10 48 4N 38 34 E
Chrudim, Czech Rep. .... 34 B8 49 58N 15 43 E
Chrzanów, Poland .... 55 H6 50 10N 19 21 E
Chtimba, Malawi .... 119 E3 10 35 S 34 13 E
Chu = Shū, Kazakhstan .... 65 B6 43 36N 73 42 E
Chu →, Vietnam .... 86 C5 19 53N 105 45 E
Chu Lai, Vietnam .... 86 E7 15 28N 108 45 E
Chuadanga, Bangla. .... 90 D2 23 38N 88 51 E
Chuak, Ko, Thailand .... 87 b 9 28N 99 41 E
Ch'uanchou = Quanzhou, China ... 77 E12 24 55N 118 34 E
Chuankou, China .... 74 G6 34 20N 110 59 E
Chuanthaburi, India .... 87 F8 61 40N 159 15 E
Chubbuck, U.S.A. 158 E7 42 55N 112 28W
Chubu □, Japan .... 73 A9 36 45N 137 30 E
Chubu-Sangaku Nat. Park △, Japan 73 A9 36 30N 137 40 E
Chubut □, Argentina .... 176 B3 43 30 S 69 0W

Chubut →, Argentina .... 176 B3 43 20 S 65 5W
Chuchi L., Canada 142 B4 55 12N 124 30W
Chudovo, India .... 92 H4 22 29N 71 41 E
Chudovo, Russia .... 58 C6 59 10N 31 41 E
Chugach Mts., U.S.A. 144 F11 60 45N 147 0W
Chugiak, U.S.A. 144 F10 61 24N 149 29W
Chuginadak I., U.S.A. 144 K5 52 50N 169 45W
Chūgoku □, Japan .... 72 C5 35 0N 133 0 E
Chūgoku-Sanchi, Japan .... 72 C5 35 0N 133 0 E
Chuguyev = Chuhuyiv, Ukraine ... 59 H9 49 55N 36 45 E
Chugwater, U.S.A. 154 E2 41 46N 104 50W
Chuhuyiv, Ukraine .... 59 H9 49 55N 36 45 E
Chukchi Sea, Russia .... 67 C19 68 0N 175 0 E
Chukotskoye Nagorye, Russia .... 67 C18 68 0N 175 0 E
Chula, U.S.A. 152 D6 31 33N 83 32W
Chula Vista, U.S.A. 161 N9 32 39N 117 5W
Chulakkurgan = Sholaqqorghan,
   Kazakhstan .... 65 A3 43 46N 69 9 E
Chulband →, India .... 94 D4 20 40N 79 54 E
Chulucanas, Peru .... 172 B1 5 8 S 80 10W
Chulumani, Bolivia .... 172 D4 16 24 S 67 31W
Chulym →, Russia .... 66 D9 57 43N 83 51 E
Chum Phae, Thailand .... 86 D4 16 40N 102 6 E
Chum Saeng, Thailand .... 86 E3 15 55N 100 15 E
Chuma, Bolivia .... 172 D4 15 24 S 68 56W
Chumar, India .... 93 C8 32 40N 78 35 E
Chumbicha, Argentina .... 174 B2 29 0 S 66 10W
Chumerna, Bulgaria .... 51 D9 42 45N 25 55 E
Chumikan, Russia .... 67 D14 54 40N 135 10 E
Chumphon, Thailand .... 87 G2 10 35N 99 14 E
Chumpi, Peru .... 172 D3 15 1 S 73 46W
Chumuare, Mozam. .... 119 E3 14 31 S 31 50 E
Chumunjin, S. Korea .... 75 F15 37 55N 128 54 E
Chuna →, Russia .... 67 D10 57 47N 94 37 E
Chun'an, China .... 77 C12 29 35N 119 3 E
Ch'unch'ŏn, S. Korea .... 75 F14 37 58N 127 44 E
Chunchura, India .... 93 H13 22 53N 88 27 E
Chunga, Zambia .... 119 F2 15 0 S 26 2 E
Chunggang-ŭp, N. Korea .... 75 D14 41 48N 126 48 E
Chunghwa, N. Korea .... 75 E13 38 52N 125 47 E
Ch'ungju, S. Korea .... 75 F14 36 58N 127 58 E
Chungking = Chongqing, China ... 76 C6 29 35N 106 25 E
Chungli, Taiwan .... 77 E13 24 57N 121 6 E
Ch'ungmu, S. Korea .... 75 G15 34 50N 128 20 E
Chungt'iaoshan = Zhongtiao Shan,
   China .... 74 G6 35 0N 111 10 E
Chungyang Shanmo, Taiwan .... 77 F13 23 10N 121 0 E
Chunian, Pakistan .... 90 D5 30 57N 74 0 E
Chunya, Tanzania .... 119 D3 8 30 S 33 27 E
Chunyang, China .... 75 C15 43 38N 129 23 E
Chupara Pt., Trin. & Tob. 169 D9 10 49N 61 22W
Chuquibamba, Peru .... 172 D3 15 47 S 72 44W
Chuquibambilla, Peru .... 172 C3 14 7 S 72 41W
Chuquicamata, Chile .... 174 A2 22 15 S 69 0W
Chuquisaca □, Bolivia .... 173 E5 20 30 S 63 30W
Chur, Switz. .... 33 C9 46 52N 9 32 E
Churachandpur, India .... 90 C4 24 20N 93 40 E
Church Stretton, U.K. 21 E5 52 32N 2 48W
Churchill, Australia .... 129 E7 38 19 S 146 25 E
Churchill, Canada 143 B10 58 47N 94 11W
Churchill →, Man., Canada 143 B10 58 47N 94 12W
Churchill →, Nfld., Canada 141 B7 53 19N 60 10W
Churchill, C., Canada 143 B10 58 46N 93 12W
Churchill Falls, Canada 141 B7 53 36N 64 19W
Churchill L., Canada 143 B7 55 55N 108 20W
Churchill Pk., Canada 142 B3 58 10N 125 10W
Churdan, U.S.A. 156 E2 42 9N 94 29W
Churfisten, Switz. .... 33 B8 47 8N 9 17 E
Churki, India .... 93 H10 23 50N 83 12 E
Churu, India .... 92 E6 28 20N 74 50 E
Churubusco, U.S.A. 157 C11 41 14N 85 19W
Churún Merú = Angel Falls,
   Venezuela 169 B5 5 57N 62 30W
Churwalden, Switz. .... 33 C9 46 47N 9 33 E
Chushal, India .... 93 C8 33 40N 78 40 E
Chuska Mts., U.S.A. 159 H9 36 15N 108 50W
Chusovaya →, Russia .... 64 B6 58 12N 56 50 E
Chusovoy, Russia .... 64 B6 58 22N 57 50 E
Chuspipata, Bolivia .... 172 D4 16 18 S 67 48W
Chust, Uzbekistan .... 65 C5 41 0N 71 13 E
Chute-aux-Outardes, Canada 141 C6 49 7N 68 24W
Chuuronjang, N. Korea .... 75 D15 41 35N 129 40 E
Chuvash Republic = Chuvashia □,
   Russia .... 60 C8 55 30N 47 0 E
Chuvashia □, Russia .... 60 C8 55 30N 47 0 E
Chuwārtah, Iraq .... 96 C5 35 43N 45 34 E
Chuxiong, China .... 76 E3 25 2N 101 28 E
Chüy = Shū →, Kazakhstan .... 65 A3 45 0N 67 44 E
Chüy □, Kyrgyzstan .... 65 A8 42 55N 75 15 E
Chuy, Uruguay .... 175 C5 33 41 S 53 27W
Chuzenji-Ko, Japan .... 73 A11 36 44N 139 27 E
Ci Xian, China .... 74 F8 36 20N 114 25 E
Ciacova, Romania .... 52 E6 45 35N 21 10 E
Ciadâr-Lunga, Moldova .... 53 D13 46 3N 28 51 E
Ciamis, Indonesia .... 85 D3 7 20 S 108 21 E
Cianjur, Indonesia .... 84 D3 6 49 S 107 8 E
Cianorte, Brazil .... 175 A5 23 37 S 52 37W
Cibola, U.S.A. 161 M12 33 17N 114 42W
Cicero, U.S.A. 157 C9 41 50N 87 45W
Cícero Dantas, Brazil .... 171 F11 10 36 S 38 23W
Cicia, Fiji .... 133 A3 17 45 S 179 18W
Cidacos →, Spain 40 C3 42 21N 1 38W
Cide, Turkey .... 100 B5 41 53N 33 1 E
Ciénagas del Cataumbo, Parque
   Nac. △, Venezuela 165 E5 9 25N 71 54W
Ciechanów, Poland .... 55 F7 52 52N 20 38 E
Ciechanowiec, Poland .... 55 F9 52 40N 22 31 E
Ciechocinek, Poland .... 55 F5 52 53N 18 45 E
Ciego de Avila, Cuba 166 B4 21 50N 78 50W
Ciénaga, Colombia 168 A3 11 1N 74 15W
Ciénaga de Oro, Colombia 168 B2 8 53N 75 37W
Cienfuegos, Cuba 164 B3 22 10N 80 30W
Cierp, France .... 28 F4 42 55N 0 40 E
Cíes, Is., Spain 42 C2 42 12N 8 55W
Cieszanów, Poland .... 55 H10 50 14N 23 8 E
Cieszyn, Poland .... 55 J5 49 45N 18 35 E
Cieza, Spain 41 G3 38 17N 1 23W
Çifteler, Turkey .... 100 C4 39 22N 31 2 E
Cifuentes, Spain 40 E2 40 47N 2 37W
Çihanbeyli, Turkey .... 100 C5 38 40N 32 55 E
Cihuatlán, Mexico 162 D4 19 14N 104 35W
Cijara, Embalse de, Spain 43 F6 39 18N 4 52W
Cijara, Parque Natural de △, Spain 43 F6 39 18N 4 52W
Cijulang, Indonesia .... 79 G13 7 42 S 108 27 E
Cilacap, Indonesia .... 85 D3 7 43 S 109 0 E
Çıldır, Turkey .... 101 B10 41 7N 43 8 E
Çıldır Gölü, Turkey .... 101 B10 41 5N 43 15 E
Cilento e Vallo di Diano, Parco
   Nazionale del △, Italy ...... 47 B8 40 15N 15 20 E
Cili, China .... 77 C8 29 30N 111 8 E
Cilibia, Romania .... 53 E12 45 4N 27 4 E
Cilicia, Turkey .... 100 D5 36 30N 34 0 E
Cill Chainnigh = Kilkenny, Ireland 23 D4 52 39N 7 15W
Cilo Dağı, Turkey .... 101 D10 37 28N 43 55 E
Cima, U.S.A. 161 K11 35 14N 115 30W
Cimarron, Kans., U.S.A. 155 G4 37 48N 100 21W
Cimarron, N. Mex., U.S.A. 155 G2 36 31N 104 55W
Cimarron →, U.S.A. 155 G6 36 10N 96 17W
Cimișlia, Moldova .... 53 D13 46 34N 28 44 E
Cimone, Mte., Italy .... 44 D7 44 12N 10 42 E
Cimpu, Indonesia .... 82 B2 3 25 S 120 22 E
Çınar, Turkey .... 101 D9 37 46N 40 19 E

Çınarcık, Turkey 51 F13 40 38N 29 5 E
Cinca →, Spain 40 D5 41 26N 0 21 E
Cincar, Bos.-H. 52 G2 43 55N 17 5 E
Cincinnati, Iowa, U.S.A. 156 D4 40 38N 92 56W
Cincinnati, Ohio, U.S.A. 157 E12 39 6N 84 31W
Cincinnati-Northern Kentucky
  International ✈ (CVG), U.S.A. 157 E12 39 3N 84 40W
Cincinnatus, U.S.A. 151 D9 42 33N 75 54W
Çine, Turkey 49 D10 37 37N 28 2 E
Ciney, Belgium 24 D5 50 18N 5 5 E
Cíngoli, Italy 45 E10 43 23N 13 10 E
Cinigiano, Italy 45 F8 42 53N 11 24 E
Cinque I., India 95 J11 11 16N 92 42 E
Cinto, Mte., France 29 F12 42 24N 8 54 E
Cintra, G. de, W. Sahara 110 D1 23 0N 16 15W
Cintruénigo, Spain 40 C3 42 5N 1 49W
Ciocile, Romania 53 F12 44 45N 27 14 E
Ciolănești din Deal, Romania 53 F10 44 19N 25 5 E
Ciorani, Romania 53 F11 44 45N 26 25 E
Ciovo, Croatia 45 E13 43 30N 16 17 E
Cipó, Brazil 170 D4 11 6 S 38 31W
Cipolletti, Argentina 176 A3 38 56 S 67 59W
Circeo, Mte., Italy 46 A6 41 14N 13 3 E
Çırçır, Turkey 100 C7 36 5N 36 47 E
Circle, Alaska, U.S.A. 144 D11 65 50N 144 4W
Circle, Mont., U.S.A. 154 B2 47 25N 105 35W
Circleville, U.S.A. 148 F4 39 36N 82 57W
Cicular Reef, Papua N. G. 132 B4 3 25 S 147 47 E
Cirebon, Indonesia 85 D3 6 45 S 108 32 E
Ciremay, Indonesia 85 D3 6 55 S 108 27 E
Cirencester, U.K. 21 F6 51 43N 1 57W
Cireșu, Romania 52 F7 44 47N 22 31 E
Cirey-sur-Vezouze, France 27 D13 48 35N 6 57 E
Ciriè, Italy 44 C4 45 14N 7 36 E
Cirium, Cyprus 39 F8 34 40N 32 53 E
Cirò, Italy 47 C10 39 23N 17 4 E
Cirò Marina, Italy 47 C10 39 22N 17 8 E
Ciron →, France 28 D3 44 36N 0 18W
Cisco, U.S.A. 155 J5 32 23N 98 59W
Cislău, Romania 53 E11 45 14N 26 20 E
Cisna, Poland 55 J9 49 12N 22 20 E
Cisnădie, Romania 53 E9 45 42N 24 9 E
Cisne, Romania 157 F8 38 31N 88 26W
Cisneros, Colombia 168 B2 6 33N 75 4W
Cissna Park, U.S.A. 157 D9 40 34N 87 54W
Cisterna di Latina, Italy 46 A5 41 35N 12 49 E
Cisternino, Italy 47 B10 40 44N 17 25 E
Cistierna, Spain 42 C5 42 48N 5 7W
Citaré →, Brazil 169 C7 1 11N 54 41W
Citeli-Ckaro = Tsiteli-Tsqaro,
  Georgia 61 K8 41 33N 46 0 E
Citlaltépetl = Orizaba, Pico de,
  Mexico 163 D5 19 0N 97 20W
Citra, U.S.A. 153 F7 29 25N 82 7W
Citron, Fr. Guiana 169 C7 4 44N 53 57W
Citrus Heights, U.S.A. 160 G5 38 42N 121 17W
Citrus Springs, U.S.A. 153 F7 29 0N 82 27W
Citrusdal, S. Africa 116 E2 32 35 S 19 0 E
Città della Pieve, Italy 45 F9 42 57N 12 1 E
Città di Castello, Italy 45 E9 43 27N 12 14 E
Città Sant' Angelo, Italy 45 F11 42 32N 14 5 E
Cittadella, Italy 45 C8 45 39N 11 47 E
Cittaducale, Italy 45 F9 42 23N 12 57 E
Cittanova, Italy 47 D9 38 21N 16 5 E
Ciuc, Munții, Romania 53 D11 46 25N 26 5 E
Ciucaș, Vf., Romania 53 E10 45 31N 25 56 E
Ciucea, Romania 52 D7 46 57N 22 49 E
Ciuciulea, Moldova 53 C12 47 40N 27 29 E
Ciuciuleni, Moldova 53 C13 47 2N 28 25 E
Ciudad Altamirano, Mexico 162 D4 18 20N 100 40W
Ciudad Bolívar, Venezuela 169 B5 8 5N 63 36W
Ciudad Camargo, Mexico 162 B3 27 41N 105 10W
Ciudad de Valles, Mexico 163 C5 22 0N 99 0W
Ciudad del Carmen, Mexico 163 D6 18 38N 91 50W
Ciudad del Este, Paraguay 175 B5 25 30 S 54 50W
Ciudad Delicias = Delicias, Mexico 162 B3 28 10N 105 30W
Ciudad Guayana, Venezuela 169 B5 8 0N 62 30W
Ciudad Guerrero, Mexico 162 B3 28 33N 107 28W
Ciudad Guzmán, Mexico 162 D4 19 40N 103 30W
Ciudad Juárez, Mexico 162 A3 31 40N 106 28W
Ciudad Madero, Mexico 163 C5 22 19N 97 50W
Ciudad Mante, Mexico 163 C5 22 50N 99 0W
Ciudad Obregón, Mexico 162 B3 27 28N 109 59W
Ciudad Ojeda, Venezuela 168 A3 10 12N 71 19W
Ciudad Piar, Venezuela 169 B5 7 27N 63 19W
Ciudad Real, Spain 43 G7 38 59N 3 55W
Ciudad Real □, Spain 43 G7 38 50N 4 0W
Ciudad Rodrigo, Spain 42 E4 40 35N 6 32W
Ciudad Trujillo = Santo Domingo,
  Dom. Rep. 165 C6 18 30N 69 59W
Ciudad Victoria, Mexico 163 C5 23 41N 99 9W
Ciudadela, Spain 38 B4 40 0N 3 50 E
Ciulnița, Romania 53 F12 44 26N 27 22 E
Ciumeghiu, Romania 52 D6 46 44N 21 35 E
Ciuperceni, Romania 52 F8 44 54N 23 4 E
Civa Burnu, Turkey 100 B7 41 21N 36 38 E
Cividale del Friuli, Italy 45 B10 46 6N 13 25 E
Civita Castellana, Italy 45 F9 42 18N 12 24 E
Civitanova Marche, Italy 45 E10 43 18N 13 44 E
Civitavécchia, Italy 45 F8 42 6N 11 48 E
Civray, France 28 B4 46 10N 0 17 E
Çivril, Turkey 49 C12 38 20N 29 43 E
Cixerri →, Italy 46 C1 39 17N 8 59 E
Cixi, China 77 B13 30 17N 121 9 E
Cizre, Turkey 101 D10 37 19N 42 10 E
Cizur Mayor, Spain 40 C3 42 47N 1 41W
Clackmannanshire □, U.K. 22 E5 56 10N 3 43W
Clacton-on-Sea, U.K. 21 F9 51 47N 1 11 E
Clain →, France 26 F7 46 47N 0 33 E
Claire, L., Canada 142 B6 58 35N 112 5W
Clairton, U.S.A. 150 F5 40 18N 79 53W
Clairvaux-les-Lacs, France 27 F12 46 35N 5 45 E
Claise →, France 28 B5 46 56N 0 42 E
Clallam Bay, U.S.A. 160 B2 48 15N 124 16W
Clam Gulch, U.S.A. 144 F10 60 15N 151 23W
Clamecy, France 27 E10 47 28N 3 30 E
Clanton, U.S.A. 149 J2 32 51N 86 38W
Clanwilliam, S. Africa 116 E2 32 11 S 18 52 E
Clara, Ireland 23 C4 53 21N 7 37W
Claraville, U.S.A. 161 K8 35 24N 118 20W
Clare, Australia 128 B3 33 50 S 138 37 E
Clare, U.S.A. 148 D3 43 49N 84 46W
Clare □, Ireland 23 D3 52 45N 9 0W
Clare →, Ireland 23 C2 53 20N 9 2W
Clare I., Ireland 23 C1 53 49N 10 0W
Claremont, Calif., U.S.A. 161 L9 34 6N 117 43W
Claremont, N.H., U.S.A. 151 C12 43 23N 72 20W
Claremont Pt., Australia 126 A3 14 1 S 143 41 E
Claremore, U.S.A. 155 G7 36 19N 95 36W
Claremorris, Ireland 23 C3 53 45N 9 0W
Clarence →, Australia 127 D5 29 25 S 153 22 E
Clarence →, N.Z. 131 K4 42 10 S 173 56 E
Clarence, I., Chile 178 G2 54 0 S 72 0W
Clarence, Port, U.S.A. 144 D6 65 15N 166 40W
Clarence I., Antarctica 5 C18 61 10 S 54 0W
Clarence Str., Australia 124 B5 12 0 S 131 0 E
Clarence Town, Bahamas 165 B5 23 6N 74 59W
Clarendon, U.S.A. 150 E5 41 47N 79 6W
Clarendon, Tex., U.S.A. 155 H4 34 56N 100 53W
Clarenville, Canada 141 C9 48 10N 54 1W
Claresholm, Canada 142 D6 50 0N 113 33W
Clarie Coast, Antarctica 7 C9 68 0 S 135 0 E

Clarinda, U.S.A. 154 E7 40 44N 95 2W
Clarion, Iowa, U.S.A. 156 B3 42 44N 93 44W
Clarion, Pa., U.S.A. 150 E5 41 13N 79 23W
Clarion →, U.S.A. 150 E5 41 7N 79 41W
Clark, Mo., U.S.A. 156 E4 39 17N 92 21W
Clark, S. Dak., U.S.A. 154 C6 44 53N 97 44W
Clark Fork, U.S.A. 158 B5 48 9N 116 11W
Clark Fork →, U.S.A. 158 B5 48 9N 116 15W
Clarkdale, U.S.A. 159 J7 34 46N 112 3W
Clarke City, Canada 141 B6 50 12N 66 38W
Clarke I., Australia 127 D4 40 32 S 148 10 E
Clarke Ra., Australia 126 J6 20 40 S 148 30 E
Clark's Fork →, U.S.A. 158 D9 45 39N 108 43W
Clark's Harbour, Canada 141 D6 43 25N 65 38W
Clarks Hill L., U.S.A. 152 B7 33 40N 82 12W
Clarks Point, U.S.A. 144 G8 58 51N 158 33W
Clarks Summit, U.S.A. 151 E9 41 30N 75 42W
Clarksburg, U.S.A. 148 F5 39 17N 80 30W
Clarksdale, U.S.A. 155 H9 34 12N 90 35W
Clarksville, Ark., U.S.A. 155 H8 35 28N 93 28W
Clarksville, Ind., U.S.A. 157 F11 38 17N 85 45W
Clarksville, Iowa, U.S.A. 156 B4 42 47N 92 40W
Clarksville, Tenn., U.S.A. 149 G2 36 32N 87 21W
Clarksville, Tex., U.S.A. 155 J7 33 37N 95 3W
Claro →, Brazil 171 E1 19 8 S 50 40W
Claskanie, U.S.A. 160 D3 46 6N 123 12W
Claude, U.S.A. 155 H4 35 7N 101 22W
Claveria, Cagayan, Phil. 80 B3 18 37N 121 4 E
Claveria, Masbate, Phil. 80 E4 12 54N 123 15 E
Claveria, Mis. Or., Phil. 81 G5 8 38N 124 55 E
Clavering Ø, Greenland 10 C8 74 15N 21 0W
Claxton, U.S.A. 152 C8 32 10N 81 55W
Clay, U.S.A. 160 G5 38 17N 121 10W
Clay Center, U.S.A. 154 F6 39 23N 97 8W
Clay City, Ind., U.S.A. 157 E9 39 17N 87 7W
Clay City, Ky., U.S.A. 157 G13 37 52N 83 55W
Claypool, U.S.A. 159 K8 33 25N 110 51W
Claysburg, U.S.A. 150 F6 40 17N 78 27W
Claysville, U.S.A. 150 F4 40 7N 80 25W
Clayton, Ala., U.S.A. 152 D4 31 53N 85 27W
Clayton, Ind., U.S.A. 157 E10 39 41N 86 31W
Clayton, N. Mex., U.S.A. 155 G3 36 27N 103 11W
Clayton, N.Y., U.S.A. 151 B8 44 14N 76 5W
Clear, C., Ireland 23 E2 51 25N 9 32W
Clear, L., Canada 150 A7 45 26N 77 12W
Clear Hills, Canada 142 B5 56 40N 119 30W
Clear I., Ireland 23 E2 51 26N 9 30W
Clear L., U.S.A. 160 F4 39 2N 122 47W
Clear Lake, Iowa, U.S.A. 156 A3 43 8N 93 23W
Clear Lake, S. Dak., U.S.A. 154 C6 44 45N 96 41W
Clear Lake Reservoir, U.S.A. 158 F3 41 56N 121 5W
Clearfield, Pa., U.S.A. 150 E6 41 2N 78 27W
Clearfield, Utah, U.S.A. 158 F8 41 7N 112 2W
Clearlake, U.S.A. 158 G2 38 57N 122 38W
Clearlake Highlands, U.S.A. 160 G4 38 57N 122 38W
Clearwater, Canada 142 C4 51 38N 120 2W
Clearwater, U.S.A. 153 H17 27 58N 82 48W
Clearwater →, Alta., Canada 142 C6 52 22N 114 57W
Clearwater →, Alta., Canada 143 B6 56 44N 111 23W
Clearwater L., Canada 143 C8 53 9N 120 21W
Clearwater Mts., U.S.A. 158 C6 46 5N 115 20W
Clearwater Prov. Park △, Canada 143 C8 54 0N 101 0W
Clearwater River Prov. Park △,
  Canada 143 B7 56 55N 109 10W
Cleburne, U.S.A. 155 J6 32 21N 97 23W
Clee Hills, U.K. 21 E5 52 26N 2 35W
Cleethorpes, U.K. 20 D7 53 33N 0 3W
Cleeve Cloud, U.K. 21 F6 51 56N 2 0W
Clelles, France 29 D9 44 50N 5 38 E
Clemson, U.S.A. 149 H4 34 41N 82 50W
Cleopatra Needle, Phil. 81 F2 10 7N 118 58 E
Clerke Reef, Australia 124 C2 17 22 S 119 20 E
Clermont, Australia 126 C4 22 49 S 147 39 E
Clermont, France 27 C9 49 23N 2 24 E
Clermont, U.S.A. 153 G8 28 33N 81 46W
Clermont-en-Argonne, France 27 C12 49 5N 5 4 E
Clermont-Ferrand, France 28 C7 45 46N 3 4 E
Clermont-l'Hérault, France 28 E7 43 38N 3 26 E
Clerval, France 27 E13 47 25N 6 30 E
Clervaux, Lux. 24 D6 50 4N 6 2 E
Cles, Italy 44 B8 46 21N 11 2 E
Cleve, Australia 128 B2 33 43 S 136 30 E
Clevedon, U.K. 21 F5 51 26N 2 52W
Cleveland, Miss., U.S.A. 155 J9 33 45N 90 43W
Cleveland, Ohio, U.S.A. 150 E3 41 30N 81 42W
Cleveland, Okla., U.S.A. 155 G6 36 19N 96 28W
Cleveland, Tenn., U.S.A. 149 H3 35 10N 84 53W
Cleveland, Tex., U.S.A. 155 K7 30 21N 95 5W
Cleveland, C., Australia 126 B4 19 11 S 147 1 E
Cleveland, Mt., U.S.A. 158 B7 48 56N 113 51W
Cleveland Heights, U.S.A. 150 E3 41 30N 81 34W
Clevelândia, Brazil 175 B5 26 24 S 52 23W
Clevelândia do Norte, Brazil 169 C7 3 49N 51 52W
Cleves, U.S.A. 157 E12 39 10N 84 45W
Clew B., Ireland 23 C2 53 50N 9 49W
Clewiston, U.S.A. 153 J9 26 45N 80 56W
Clifden, Ireland 23 C1 53 29N 10 1W
Clifden, N.Z. 131 G2 46 1 S 167 42 E
Cliffdell, U.S.A. 160 D5 46 56N 121 5W
Cliffy Hd., Australia 125 G2 35 1 S 116 29 E
Clifton, Australia 127 D5 27 59 S 151 53 E
Clifton, Ariz., U.S.A. 159 K9 33 3N 109 18W
Clifton, Colo., U.S.A. 159 G9 39 7N 108 25W
Clifton, Ill., U.S.A. 157 D9 40 56N 87 56W
Clifton, Tex., U.S.A. 155 K6 31 47N 97 35W
Clifton Beach, Australia 126 B4 16 46 S 145 39 E
Clifton Pt., Bahamas 9 b 25 1N 77 34W
Climax, Canada 143 D7 49 10N 108 20W
Climax, U.S.A. 152 E5 30 53N 84 26W
Clinch →, U.S.A. 149 H3 35 53N 84 29W
Clingmans Dome, U.S.A. 149 H4 35 34N 83 30W
Clint, U.S.A. 159 L10 31 35N 106 14W
Clinton, B.C., Canada 142 C4 51 6N 121 35W
Clinton, Ont., Canada 140 D3 43 37N 81 32W
Clinton, N.Z. 131 G4 46 12 S 169 23 E
Clinton, Ark., U.S.A. 155 H8 35 36N 92 28W
Clinton, Conn., U.S.A. 151 E12 41 17N 72 32W
Clinton, Ill., U.S.A. 156 E9 40 9N 88 57W
Clinton, Ind., U.S.A. 157 E9 39 40N 87 24W
Clinton, Iowa, U.S.A. 156 C6 41 51N 90 12W
Clinton, Mass., U.S.A. 151 D13 42 25N 71 41W
Clinton, Mich., U.S.A. 157 B13 42 4N 83 58W
Clinton, Miss., U.S.A. 155 J9 32 20N 90 20W
Clinton, Mo., U.S.A. 156 F8 38 22N 93 46W
Clinton, N.C., U.S.A. 149 H6 35 0N 78 22W
Clinton, Okla., U.S.A. 155 H5 35 31N 98 58W
Clinton, S.C., U.S.A. 149 H5 34 29N 81 53W
Clinton, Tenn., U.S.A. 149 G3 36 6N 84 8W
Clinton, Wash., U.S.A. 160 C4 47 59N 122 21W
Clinton, Wis., U.S.A. 157 B8 42 34N 88 52W
Clinton, C., Australia 126 C5 22 30 S 150 45 E
Clinton Colden L., Canada 138 B9 63 58N 107 27W
Clinton, U.S.A. 157 D8 40 15N 88 45W
Clintonville, U.S.A. 154 C10 44 37N 88 46W
Clio, U.S.A. 152 D4 31 43N 85 37W
Clipperton, I., Pac. Oc. 135 F17 10 18N 109 13W
Clisham, U.K. 22 D2 57 57N 6 49W
Clisson, France 26 E5 47 5N 1 16W
Clitheroe, U.K. 20 D5 53 53N 2 22W
Clive, N.Z. 130 F5 39 36 S 176 58 E
Cliza, Bolivia 173 D4 17 36 S 65 56W
Clo-oose, Canada 160 B2 48 39N 124 49W

Cloates, Pt., Australia 124 D1 22 43 S 113 40 E
Clocolan, S. Africa 117 D4 28 55 S 27 34 E
Clodomira, Argentina 174 B3 27 35 S 64 14W
Clogher Hd., Ireland 23 C5 53 48N 6 14W
Clonakilty, Ireland 23 E3 51 37N 8 53W
Clonakilty B., Ireland 23 E3 51 35N 8 51W
Cloncurry, Australia 126 C3 20 40 S 140 28 E
Cloncurry →, Australia 126 B3 18 37 S 140 40 E
Clondalkin, Ireland 23 C5 53 19N 6 25W
Clones, Ireland 23 B4 54 11N 7 15W
Clonmel, Ireland 23 D4 52 21N 7 42W
Cloppenburg, Germany 30 C4 52 51N 8 1 E
Cloquet, U.S.A. 154 B8 46 43N 92 28W
Clorinda, Argentina 174 B4 25 16 S 57 45W
Cloud Bay, Canada 140 C2 48 5N 89 26W
Cloud Peak, U.S.A. 158 D10 44 23N 107 11W
Cloudcroft, U.S.A. 159 K11 32 58N 105 45W
Cloudy B., N.Z. 131 B9 41 25 S 174 10 E
Cloverdale, Calif., U.S.A. 160 G4 38 48N 123 1W
Cloverdale, Ind., U.S.A. 157 E10 39 31N 86 48W
Cloverport, U.S.A. 157 G10 37 50N 86 38W
Clovis, Calif., U.S.A. 160 J7 36 49N 119 42W
Clovis, N. Mex., U.S.A. 155 H3 34 24N 103 12W
Cloyes-sur-le-Loir, France 26 E8 48 0N 1 14 E
Cloyne, Canada 150 B7 44 49N 77 11W
Club Terrace, Australia 129 D8 37 35 S 148 58 E
Cluj □, Romania 53 D8 46 45N 23 30 E
Cluj-Napoca, Romania 53 D8 46 47N 23 38 E
Clunes, Australia 128 D5 37 20 S 143 45 E
Cluny, France 27 F11 46 26N 4 38 E
Cluses, France 27 F13 46 5N 6 35 E
Clusone, Italy 44 C6 45 53N 9 57 E
Clutha →, N.Z. 131 G4 46 20 S 169 49 E
Clwyd □, U.K. 20 D4 53 19N 3 31W
Clwyd →, U.K. 20 D4 53 19N 3 30W
Clyattville, U.S.A. 153 F6 30 42N 83 19W
Clyde, Canada 142 C6 54 9N 113 39W
Clyde, N.Z. 131 F4 45 12 S 169 20 E
Clyde, N.Y., U.S.A. 150 C8 43 5N 76 52W
Clyde, Ohio, U.S.A. 157 C14 41 18N 82 59W
Clyde →, U.K. 22 F4 55 55N 4 30W
Clyde, Firth of, U.K. 22 F3 55 22N 5 1W
Clyde Muirshiel Forest Park △, U.K. 22 F4 55 50N 4 23W
Clyde River, Canada 139 A13 70 30N 68 30W
Clydebank, U.K. 22 F4 55 54N 4 23W
Clyderdale, U.S.A. 150 D5 41 19N 79 37W
Clymer, Pa., U.S.A. 150 D5 40 40N 79 1W
Clyo, U.S.A. 152 C8 32 29N 81 16W
Ćmielów, Poland 55 H8 50 53N 21 31 E
Côa →, Portugal 42 D3 41 5N 7 6W
Coachella, U.S.A. 161 M10 33 41N 116 10W
Coachella Canal, U.S.A. 161 N12 32 43N 114 57W
Coahoma, U.S.A. 155 J4 32 18N 101 18W
Coahuayana →, Mexico 162 D4 18 41N 103 45W
Coahuila □, Mexico 162 B4 27 0N 103 0W
Coal →, Canada 142 B3 59 39N 126 57W
Coal City, U.S.A. 157 C8 41 17N 88 17W
Coal I., N.Z. 131 G1 46 8 S 166 40 E
Coalane, Mozam. 119 F4 17 48 S 37 2 E
Coalcomán, Mexico 162 D4 18 40N 103 10W
Coaldale, Canada 142 D6 49 45N 112 35W
Coalgate, U.S.A. 155 H6 34 32N 96 13W
Coalinga, U.S.A. 160 J6 36 9N 120 21W
Coalisland, U.K. 23 B5 54 33N 6 42W
Coalville, U.K. 20 E6 52 44N 1 23W
Coalville, U.S.A. 158 F8 40 55N 111 24W
Coamo, Puerto Rico 165 d 18 5N 66 22W
Coaraci, Brazil 171 D4 14 38 S 39 32W
Coari, Brazil 169 D5 4 8 S 63 7W
Coari →, Brazil 169 D5 4 30 S 63 33W
Coari, L. de, Brazil 169 D5 4 5 S 63 0W
Coast □, Kenya 118 C4 2 40 S 39 45 E
Coast Mts., Canada 142 C3 55 0N 129 20W
Coast Ranges, U.S.A. 160 G4 39 0N 123 0W
Coatbridge, U.K. 22 F4 55 52N 4 6W
Coatepec, Mexico 163 D5 19 27N 96 58W
Coatepeque, Guatemala 164 D1 14 46N 91 55W
Coatesville, U.S.A. 148 F8 39 59N 75 50W
Coaticook, Canada 141 C5 45 10N 71 46W
Coats I., Canada 139 B11 62 30N 83 0W
Coats Land, Antarctica 7 D1 77 0 S 25 0W
Coatzacoalcos, Mexico 163 D6 18 7N 94 25W
Coba, Mexico 163 C7 20 31N 87 39W
Cobadin, Romania 53 F13 44 5N 28 13 E
Cobalt, Canada 140 C4 47 25N 79 42W
Cobán, Guatemala 164 C1 15 30N 90 21W
Çobanlar, Turkey 49 C12 38 41N 30 47 E
Cobar, Australia 129 A6 31 27 S 145 48 E
Cobargo, Australia 129 D8 36 20 S 149 55 E
Cobbannah, Australia 129 D7 37 37 S 147 13 E
Cobberas, Mt., Australia 129 D8 36 53 S 148 12 E
Cobden, Canada 128 E5 38 20N 143 3 E
Cóbh, Ireland 23 E3 51 51N 8 17W
Cobija, Bolivia 172 C4 11 0 S 68 50W
Cobleskill, U.S.A. 151 D10 42 41N 74 29W
Coboconk, Canada 150 B6 44 39N 78 48W
Cobourg, Canada 140 D4 43 58N 78 10W
Cobourg Marine Park ≏, Australia 124 B5 11 26 S 131 58 E
Cobourg Pen., Australia 124 B5 11 20 S 132 15 E
Cobram, Australia 129 C6 35 54 S 145 40 E
Cóbué, Mozam. 119 E3 12 0 S 34 58 E
Coburg, Germany 31 E6 50 15N 10 58 E
Coca, Spain 42 D6 41 13N 4 32W
Coca →, Ecuador 168 D2 0 29 S 76 58W
Cocachacra, Peru 172 D3 17 5 S 71 45W
Cocal, Brazil 170 B3 3 35 S 41 34W
Cochabamba = Kakinada, India 94 F6 16 57N 82 11 E
Cocentaina, Spain 41 G4 38 45N 0 27W
Cochabamba, Bolivia 173 D4 17 26 S 66 10W
Coche, I., Venezuela 169 A5 10 47N 63 56W
Cochem, Germany 31 E3 50 9N 7 9 E
Cochemane, Mozam. 119 F3 17 0 S 32 54 E
Cochin, India 95 K3 9 58N 76 20 E
Cochin China = Nam-Phan, Vietnam 87 G6 10 30N 106 0 E
Cochran, U.S.A. 152 D4 32 23N 83 21W
Cochrane, Alta., Canada 142 C6 51 11N 114 30W
Cochrane, Ont., Canada 140 C3 49 0N 81 0W
Cochrane, Chile 176 C2 47 15 S 72 0W
Cochrane →, Canada 143 B8 59 0N 103 40W
Cochrane, L., Chile 176 C2 47 10 S 72 0W
Cochranton, U.S.A. 150 E4 41 31N 80 3W
Cockburn, Australia 128 B4 32 5 S 141 0 E
Cockburn, Canal, Chile 178 G2 54 30 S 72 0W
Cockburn I., Canada 140 C3 45 55N 83 22W
Cockburn Ra., Australia 124 C4 15 46 S 128 0 E
Cockermouth, U.K. 20 C4 54 40N 3 22W
Cocklebiddy, Australia 125 F4 32 0 S 126 3 E
Cockpit Country, The, Jamaica 164 a 18 15N 77 45W
Côco →, Brazil 170 C2 9 27 S 50 2W
Coco →, Cent. Amer. 164 D3 15 0N 83 8W
Coco, I. del, Pac. Oc. 135 G19 5 25N 87 55W
Coco Channel, Asia 95 H11 14 N 93 10 E
Cocoa, U.S.A. 153 G9 28 21N 80 44W
Cocoa Beach, U.S.A. 153 G9 28 19N 80 37W
Cocobeach, Gabon 114 B1 0 59N 9 34 E
Cocoparra Nat. Park ≏, Australia 129 C4 34 5 S 146 12 E
Cocora, Romania 53 F12 44 45N 27 3 E
Côcos, Brazil 171 D3 14 10 S 44 15W
Côcos, Brazil 171 D3 12 46 S 44 48W
Cocos, B. de, Trin. & Tob. 169 D10 10 25N 61 2W
Cocos I., Guam 121 F8 12 10 S 96 55 E
Cocos Is., Ind. Oc. 121 F8 12 10 S 96 55 E
Cod, C., U.S.A. 148 D10 42 5N 70 10W
Codajás, Brazil 169 D5 3 55 S 62 0W

Codera, C., Venezuela 168 A4 10 35N 66 4W
Codfish I., N.Z. 131 G2 46 47 S 167 38 E
Codigoro, Italy 45 D9 44 49N 12 8 E
Codlea, Romania 53 E10 45 42N 25 27 E
Codó, Brazil 170 B3 4 30 S 43 55W
Codogno, Italy 44 C6 45 9N 9 42 E
Codpa, Chile 172 D4 18 50 S 69 44W
Codróipo, Italy 45 C10 45 58N 13 0 E
Codru, Munții, Romania 52 D7 46 30N 22 15 E
Cody, U.S.A. 158 D9 44 32N 109 3W
Coe Hill, Canada 150 B7 44 52N 77 50W
Coelemu, Chile 176 D1 36 30 S 72 48W
Coelho Neto, Brazil 170 B3 4 15 S 43 2W
Coen, Australia 126 A3 13 52 S 143 12 E
Coeroeni →, Suriname 169 C6 3 21N 57 31W
Coesfeld, Germany 30 D3 51 56N 7 10 E
Coëtivy Is., Seychelles 121 E4 7 8 S 56 16 E
Coeur d'Alene, U.S.A. 158 C5 47 45N 116 51W
Coeur d'Alene L., U.S.A. 158 C5 47 32N 116 48W
Coevorden, Neths. 24 B6 52 40N 6 44 E
Cofete, Canary Is. 9 e2 28 6N 14 23W
Coffeyville, U.S.A. 155 G7 37 2N 95 37W
Coffin B., Australia 127 E2 34 38 S 135 28 E
Coffin Bay, Australia 127 E2 34 37 S 135 29 E
Coffin Bay Nat. Park △, Australia 127 E2 34 34 S 135 19 E
Coffin Bay Peninsula, Australia 127 E2 34 32 S 135 15 E
Coffs Harbour, Australia 129 A10 30 16 S 153 5 E
Cofre de Perote, Parque Nac. △,
  Mexico 163 D5 19 29N 97 8W
Cofrentes, Spain 41 F3 39 13N 1 5W
Cogalnic →, Moldova 53 E14 45 49N 29 40 E
Cogealac, Romania 53 F13 44 36N 28 36 E
Coghinas →, Italy 46 B1 40 55N 8 48 E
Coghinas, L. del, Italy 46 B2 40 46N 9 3 E
Cognac, France 28 C3 45 41N 0 20W
Cogne, Italy 44 C4 45 37N 7 21 E
Cogolludo, France 29 E10 43 15N 6 32 E
Cogolludo, Spain 40 E1 40 59N 3 10W
Cohocton, U.S.A. 150 D7 42 30N 77 30W
Cohocton →, U.S.A. 150 D7 42 9N 77 6W
Cohoes, U.S.A. 151 D11 42 46N 73 42W
Cohuna, Australia 128 C6 35 45 S 144 15 E
Coiba, I., Panama 164 E3 7 30N 81 40W
Coig →, Argentina 176 D3 51 0 S 69 10W
Coigeach, Rubha, U.K. 22 C3 58 6N 5 26W
Coihaique, Chile 176 C2 45 30 S 71 45W
Coimbatore, India 95 J3 11 2N 76 59 E
Coimbra, Brazil 173 D6 19 55 S 57 48W
Coimbra, Portugal 42 E2 40 15N 8 27W
Coimbra □, Portugal 42 E2 40 12N 8 25W
Coín, Spain 43 J6 36 40N 4 48W
Coipasa, L. de, Bolivia 172 D4 19 12 S 68 7W
Coipasa, Salar de, Bolivia 172 D4 19 26 S 68 9W
Cojata, Peru 172 D4 15 2 S 69 25W
Cojedes □, Venezuela 168 B4 9 20N 68 20W
Cojedes →, Venezuela 168 B4 8 34N 68 5W
Cojimies, Ecuador 168 C1 0 20N 80 0W
Cojocna, Romania 53 D8 46 45N 23 50 E
Cojutepequé, El Salv. 164 D2 13 41N 88 54W
Çoka, Serbia, Yug. 52 E5 45 57N 20 12 E
Cokeville, U.S.A. 158 E8 42 5N 110 57W
Colaba Pt., India 94 E1 18 54N 72 53 E
Colac, Australia 128 E5 38 21 S 143 35 E
Colachel = Kolachel, India 95 K3 8 10N 77 15 E
Colatina, Brazil 171 E3 19 32 S 40 37W
Colbeck, C., Antarctica 7 D13 77 6 S 157 48W
Colbert, U.S.A. 152 A6 34 3N 83 13W
Colborne, Canada 150 C7 44 0N 77 53W
Colby, U.S.A. 154 F4 39 24N 101 3W
Colchester, U.K. 21 F8 51 54N 0 55 E
Cold Bay, U.S.A. 144 J7 55 12N 162 42W
Cold L., Canada 143 C7 54 33N 110 5W
Coldstream, Canada 142 C5 50 13N 119 11W
Coldstream, U.K. 22 F6 55 39N 2 15W
Coldwater, Canada 150 B5 44 42N 79 40W
Coldwater, Kans., U.S.A. 155 G5 37 16N 99 20W
Coldwater, Mich., U.S.A. 157 C11 41 57N 85 0W
Coldwater, Ohio, U.S.A. 157 D12 40 29N 84 38W
Coldwater, L., U.S.A. 157 C12 41 48N 84 39W
Cole Camp, U.S.A. 156 F3 38 28N 93 12W
Coleambally, Australia 129 C6 34 49 S 145 52 E
Colebrook, U.S.A. 151 B13 44 54N 71 30W
Coleman, Fla., U.S.A. 153 G7 28 48N 82 4W
Coleman, Tex., U.S.A. 155 K5 31 50N 99 26W
Coleman →, Australia 126 B3 15 6 S 141 38 E
Colenso, S. Africa 117 D4 28 44 S 29 50 E
Coleraine, Australia 128 D4 37 36 S 141 40 E
Coleraine, U.K. 23 A5 55 8N 6 41W
Coleridge, L., N.Z. 131 D6 43 17 S 171 30 E
Coleroon →, India 95 J4 11 25N 79 50 E
Colesberg, S. Africa 116 E4 30 45 S 25 5 E
Coleville, U.S.A. 160 G7 38 34N 119 30W
Colfax, Calif., U.S.A. 160 F6 39 6N 120 57W
Colfax, Ill., U.S.A. 157 D8 40 34N 88 37W
Colfax, Ind., U.S.A. 157 D10 40 12N 86 40W
Colfax, Iowa, U.S.A. 156 C3 41 41N 93 14W
Colfax, La., U.S.A. 155 K8 31 31N 92 42W
Colfax, Wash., U.S.A. 158 C5 46 53N 117 22W
Colhué Huapi, L., Argentina 176 C3 45 30 S 69 0W
Colibași, Moldova 53 E13 45 43N 28 41 E
Colibași, Romania 53 F9 44 56N 24 54 E
Cólico, Italy 44 B6 46 8N 9 22 E
Colíder, Brazil 173 C6 10 45 S 55 25W
Coligny, France 27 F12 46 23N 5 21 E
Coligny, S. Africa 117 D4 26 17 S 26 15 E
Colima, Mexico 162 D4 19 10N 103 40W
Colima □, Mexico 162 D4 19 10N 103 40W
Colima, Nevado de, Mexico 162 D4 19 35N 103 45W
Colina, Chile 174 C1 33 13 S 70 45W
Colina do Norte, Guinea-Biss. 112 C2 12 28N 15 0W
Colinas, Goiás, Brazil 171 D2 14 15 S 48 2W
Colinas, Maranhão, Brazil 170 C3 6 0 S 44 10W
Colindres, Spain 42 B7 43 24N 3 27W
Coll, U.K. 22 E2 56 39N 6 34W
Collaguasi, Chile 174 A2 21 5 S 68 45W
Collarada, Peña, Spain 40 C4 42 43N 0 29W
Collarenebri, Australia 127 D4 29 33 S 148 34 E
Colle di Val d'Elsa, Italy 44 E8 43 25N 11 7 E
Colléchio, Italy 44 D7 44 45N 10 13 E
Colleen Bawn, Zimbabwe 119 G2 21 0 S 29 12 E
College, U.S.A. 144 D11 64 52N 147 49W
College Park, U.S.A. 152 B3 33 40N 84 27W
College Station, U.S.A. 155 K6 30 37N 96 21W
Collesalvetti, Italy 44 E7 43 34N 10 27 E
Colli Euganei, Parco Regionale
  dei ≏, Italy 45 C8 45 18N 11 43 E
Collie, N.S.W., Australia 129 A8 31 41 S 148 18 E
Collie, W. Austral., Australia 125 F2 33 22 S 116 8 E
Collier B., Australia 124 C3 16 10 S 124 15 E
Collier Ra., Australia 125 D2 24 39 S 119 7 E
Collier Range Nat. Park △, Australia 125 D2 24 39 S 119 7 E
Collina, Passo di, Italy 44 D7 44 2N 10 56 E
Collingwood, Canada 140 D3 44 29N 80 13W
Collingwood, N.Z. 131 A7 40 41 S 172 42 E
Collins, Canada 140 B2 50 17N 89 27W
Collins, Mo., U.S.A. 152 C2 32 11N 82 7W
Collins, Mo., U.S.A. 156 G3 37 54N 93 37W
Collinsville, Australia 126 C4 20 30 S 147 56 E
Collinsville, U.S.A. 156 F7 38 40N 89 59W
Collipulli, Chile 174 D1 37 55 S 72 30W
Collo, Algeria 111 A6 36 58N 6 37 E
Collooney, Ireland 23 B3 54 11N 8 29W
Colmar, France 27 D14 48 5N 7 20 E
Colmars, France 29 D10 44 11N 6 39 E

Colmenar, Spain 43 J6 36 54N 4 20W
Colmenar de Oreja, Spain 42 E7 40 6N 3 25W
Colmenar Viejo, Spain 42 E7 40 39N 3 47W
Colo ◂, Australia ...... 129 B9 33 25 S 150 52 E
Cologne = Köln, Germany ...... 30 E2 50 56N 6 57 E
Colom, I. d'en, Spain ...... 38 B5 39 58N 4 16 E
Coloma, Calif., U.S.A. 160 G6 38 48N 120 53W
Coloma, Mich., U.S.A. 157 B10 42 11N 86 19W
Colomb-Béchar = Béchar, Algeria .. 111 B4 31 38N 2 18W
Colombey-les-Belles, France ...... 27 D12 48 32N 5 54 E
Colombey-les-Deux-Églises, France . 27 D11 48 13N 4 50 E
Colômbia, Brazil ...... 171 F2 20 10 S 48 40W
Colombia ■, S. Amer. 168 C3 3 45N 73 0W
Colombian Basin, S. Amer. 136 H12 14 0N 76 0W
Colombier, Switz. ...... 32 C3 46 58N 6 53 E
Colombo, Sri Lanka ...... 95 L4 6 56N 79 58 E
Colomiers, France ...... 28 E5 43 36N 1 21 E
Colón, Buenos Aires, Argentina .. 174 C3 33 53 S 61 7W
Colón, Entre Ríos, Argentina .. 174 C4 32 12 S 58 10W
Colón, Cuba 164 B3 22 42N 80 54W
Colón, Panama 164 E4 9 20N 79 54W
Colón, Peru ...... 172 A1 5 0 S 81 0W
Colón, Arch. de, Ecuador ...... 172 a 0 0 91 0W
Colonia 25 de Mayo, Argentina .. 176 A3 37 45 S 67 41W
Colònia de Sant Jordi, Spain ...... 38 B3 39 19N 2 59 E
Colonia del Sacramento, Uruguay .. 174 C4 34 25 S 57 50W
Colonia Dora, Argentina ...... 174 B3 28 34 S 62 59W
Colonia Las Heras, Argentina .. 176 C3 46 33 S 68 57W
Colonial Beach, U.S.A. 148 F7 38 15N 76 58W
Colonie, U.S.A. 151 D11 42 43N 73 50W
Colonna, C., Italy ...... 47 C10 39 2N 17 12 E
Colonsay, Canada 143 C7 51 59N 105 52W
Colonsay, U.K. 22 E2 56 5N 6 12W
Colorado ▢, U.S.A. 159 G10 39 30N 105 30W
Colorado ◂, Argentina ...... 176 A4 39 50 S 62 8W
Colorado ◂, N. Amer. 159 L6 31 45N 114 40W
Colorado ◂, U.S.A. 155 L7 28 36N 95 59W
Colorado City, U.S.A. 155 J4 32 24N 100 52W
Colorado Plateau, U.S.A. 159 H8 37 0N 111 0W
Colorado River Aqueduct, U.S.A. . 161 L12 34 17N 114 10W
Colorado Springs, U.S.A. 154 F2 38 50N 104 49W
Colorno, Italy ...... 44 D7 44 56N 10 23 E
Colotlán, Mexico 162 C4 22 6N 103 16W
Colquechaca, Bolivia ...... 173 D4 18 40 S 66 1W
Colquitt, U.S.A. 152 D5 31 10N 84 44W
Colstrip, U.S.A. 158 D10 45 53N 106 38W
Colton, U.S.A. 151 B10 44 33N 74 56W
Columbia, Ala., U.S.A. 152 D4 31 18N 85 7W
Columbia, Ill., U.S.A. 156 F6 38 27N 90 12W
Columbia, Ky., U.S.A. 148 G3 37 6N 85 18W
Columbia, La., U.S.A. 155 J8 32 6N 92 5W
Columbia, Miss., U.S.A. 155 K10 31 15N 89 50W
Columbia, Mo., U.S.A. 156 F4 38 57N 92 20W
Columbia, Pa., U.S.A. 151 F8 40 2N 76 30W
Columbia, S.C., U.S.A. 152 A8 34 0N 81 2W
Columbia, Tenn., U.S.A. 149 H2 35 37N 87 2W
Columbia ◂, N. Amer. 6 A4 83 0N 70 0W
Columbia, C., Canada 6 A4 83 0N 70 0W
Columbia, District of □, U.S.A. .. 148 F7 38 55N 77 0W
Columbia, Mt., Canada 142 C5 52 8N 117 20W
Columbia Basin, U.S.A. 158 C4 46 45N 119 5W
Columbia City, U.S.A. 157 C11 41 10N 85 29W
Columbia Falls, U.S.A. 158 B6 48 23N 114 11W
Columbia Mts., Canada 142 C5 52 0N 119 0W
Columbia Plateau, U.S.A. 158 D5 44 0N 117 30W
Columbiana, U.S.A. 150 F4 40 53N 80 42W
Columbretes, Is., Spain ...... 40 F5 39 50N 0 50 E
Columbus, Ga., U.S.A. 152 C5 32 28N 84 59W
Columbus, Ind., U.S.A. 157 E11 39 13N 85 55W
Columbus, Kans., U.S.A. 155 G7 37 10N 94 50W
Columbus, Miss., U.S.A. 149 J1 33 30N 88 25W
Columbus, Mont., U.S.A. 158 D9 45 38N 109 15W
Columbus, N. Mex., U.S.A. 159 L10 31 50N 107 38W
Columbus, Nebr., U.S.A. 154 E6 41 26N 97 22W
Columbus, Ohio, U.S.A. 157 E13 39 58N 83 0W
Columbus, Tex., U.S.A. 155 L6 29 42N 96 33W
Columbus Grove, U.S.A. 157 D12 40 55N 84 4W
Columbus Junction, U.S.A. 156 C5 41 17N 91 22W
Colunga, Spain 42 B5 43 29N 5 16W
Colusa, U.S.A. 160 F4 39 13N 122 1W
Colville, U.S.A. 158 B5 48 33N 117 54W
Colville ◂, U.S.A. 144 A10 70 25N 150 30W
Colville, C., N.Z. ...... 130 C4 36 29 S 175 21 E
Colwood, Canada 160 B3 48 26N 123 29W
Colwyn Bay, U.K. 20 D4 53 18N 3 44W
Coma, Ethiopia ...... 107 F4 8 29N 36 53 E
Comácchio, Italy ...... 45 D9 44 42N 12 11 E
Comalcalco, Mexico 163 D6 18 16N 93 13W
Comallo, Argentina ...... 176 B2 41 0 S 70 5W
Comana, Romania ...... 53 F11 44 10N 26 10 E
Comanche, U.S.A. 155 K5 31 54N 98 36W
Comandante Luis Piedrabuena,
  Argentina ...... 176 C3 49 59 S 68 54W
Comăneşti, Romania ...... 53 D11 46 25N 26 26 E
Comarapa, Bolivia ...... 173 D5 17 54 S 64 29W
Comarnic, Romania ...... 53 E10 45 15N 25 38 E
Comayagua, Honduras 164 D2 14 25N 87 37W
Combahee ◂, U.S.A. 149 J5 32 30N 80 31W
Combara, Australia ...... 129 A8 31 10 S 148 22 E
Combarbalá, Chile ...... 174 C1 31 11 S 71 2W
Combe Martin, U.K. 21 F3 51 12N 4 3W
Combeaufontaine, France ...... 27 E12 47 38N 5 54 E
Comber, Canada 150 D2 42 14N 82 33W
Comber, U.K. 23 B6 54 33N 5 45W
Combermere, Canada 150 A7 45 22N 77 37W
Combermere Bay, Burma ...... 90 F4 19 37N 93 34 E
Comblain-au-Pont, Belgium ...... 24 D5 50 29N 5 35 E
Combourg, France 26 D5 48 25N 1 46W
Comboyne, Australia ...... 129 A10 31 34 S 152 27 E
Combrailles, France ...... 27 F9 46 8N 2 8 E
Combronde, France ...... 28 C7 45 58N 3 5 E
Comer, Ala., U.S.A. 152 C4 32 2N 85 23W
Comer, Ga., U.S.A. 152 A6 34 4N 83 8W
Comeragh Mts., Ireland 23 D4 52 18N 7 34W
Comet, Australia ...... 126 C4 23 36 S 148 38 E
Comilla, Bangla. ...... 90 D3 23 28N 91 10 E
Comino, Malta ...... 38 E7 36 1N 14 20 E
Cómino, C., Italy ...... 46 B2 40 32N 9 49 E
Cómiso, Italy ...... 47 F7 36 56N 14 36 E
Comitán, Mexico 163 D6 16 18N 92 9W
Commentry, France ...... 27 F9 46 20N 2 46 E
Commerce, Ga., U.S.A. 149 H4 34 12N 83 28W
Commerce, Tex., U.S.A. 155 J7 33 15N 95 54W
Commercy, France ...... 27 D12 48 43N 5 34 E
Commissioner's Pt., Bermuda ...... 9 a 32 19N 64 49W
Committee B., Canada 139 B11 68 30N 86 30W
Commonwealth B., Antarctica .... 7 C10 67 0 S 144 0 E
Commoron Cr. ◂, Australia ...... 127 D5 28 22 S 150 8 E
Communism Pk. = Kommunizma,
  Pik, Tajikistan ...... 65 D6 39 0N 72 2 E
Como, Italy ...... 44 C6 45 47N 9 5 E
Como, Lago di, Italy ...... 44 B6 46 0N 9 11 E
Comodoro Rivadavia, Argentina .. 176 C3 45 50 S 67 40W
Comoé, Parc Nat. de la △, Ivory C. .. 110 D4 9 0N 3 35W
Comorâste, Romania ...... 52 E6 45 10N 21 35 E
Comorin, C., India ...... 95 K3 8 3N 77 40 E
Comoro Is. = Comoros ■, Ind. Oc. . 121 a 12 10 S 44 15 E
Comoros ■, Ind. Oc. ...... 121 a 12 10 S 44 15 E
Comox, Canada 142 D4 49 42N 124 55W
Compass Lake, U.S.A. 152 K4 30 36N 85 24W
Compiègne, France ...... 27 C9 49 24N 2 50 E
Comporta, Portugal 43 G2 38 22N 8 46W
Compostela, Mexico 162 C4 21 15N 104 53W
Compostela, Phil. ...... 81 H6 7 40N 126 2 E

Comprida, I., Brazil ...... 175 A6 24 50 S 47 42W
Compton, Canada 151 A13 45 14N 71 49W
Compton, U.S.A. 161 M8 33 54N 118 13W
Comrat, Moldova ...... 53 D13 46 18N 28 40 E
Con Cuong, Vietnam ...... 86 C5 19 2N 104 54 E
Con Dao Nat. Park △, Vietnam .. 87 H6 8 42N 106 35 E
Con Son, Vietnam ...... 87 H6 8 41N 106 37 E
Cona Niyeu, Argentina ...... 176 B3 41 58 S 67 0W
Conakry, Guinea 112 D2 9 29N 13 49W
Conara, Australia ...... 127 D4 41 50 S 147 26 E
Conargo, Australia ...... 129 C6 35 16 S 145 10 E
Concarneau, France 26 E3 47 52N 3 56W
Conceição, Brazil ...... 170 C4 7 33 S 38 31W
Conceição, Mozam. ...... 119 F4 18 47 S 36 7 E
Conceição da Barra, Brazil ...... 171 E4 18 35 S 39 45W
Conceição do Araguaia, Brazil .... 170 C2 8 0 S 49 2W
Conceição do Canindé, Brazil .... 170 C3 7 54 S 41 34W
Conceição do Maú, Brazil 169 C6 3 35N 59 53W
Concepción, Argentina ...... 173 D5 16 15 S 62 8W
Concepción, Bolivia ...... 173 D5 16 15 S 62 8W
Concepción, Chile ...... 176 D1 36 50 S 73 0W
Concepción, Mexico 163 D6 18 15N 90 5W
Concepción, Paraguay ...... 174 A4 23 22 S 57 26W
Concepción, Peru ...... 172 C2 11 54 S 75 19W
Concepción □, Chile ...... 176 D1 37 0 S 72 30W
Concepción ◂, Mexico 162 A2 30 32N 113 2W
Concepción, Est. de, Chile ...... 176 D2 50 30 S 74 55W
Concepción, L., Bolivia ...... 173 D5 17 20 S 61 20W
Concepción, Punta, Mexico 162 B2 26 55N 111 59W
Concepción del Oro, Mexico 162 C4 24 40N 101 30W
Concepción del Uruguay, Argentina 174 C4 32 35 S 58 20W
Conception, Pt., U.S.A. 161 L6 34 27N 120 28W
Conception B., Canada 141 C9 47 45N 53 0W
Conception B., Namibia ...... 116 C1 23 55 S 14 22 E
Conception I., Bahamas 165 B4 23 52N 75 9W
Concession, Zimbabwe ...... 119 F3 17 27 S 30 56 E
Conchas Dam, U.S.A. 155 H2 35 22N 104 11W
Concho, U.S.A. 159 J9 34 28N 109 36W
Concho ◂, U.S.A. 155 K5 31 34N 99 43W
Conchos ◂, Chihuahua, Mexico .. 162 B4 29 32N 105 0W
Conchos ◂, Tamaulipas, Mexico .. 163 B5 25 9N 98 35W
Concise, Switz. ...... 32 C3 46 51N 6 43 E
Concord, Calif., U.S.A. 160 H4 37 59N 122 2W
Concord, Ga., U.S.A. 152 B5 33 5N 84 27W
Concord, Mich., U.S.A. 157 B12 42 11N 84 38W
Concord, Mo., U.S.A. 156 F6 38 32N 90 23W
Concord, N.C., U.S.A. 149 H5 35 25N 80 35W
Concord, N.H., U.S.A. 151 C13 43 12N 71 32W
Concordia, Argentina ...... 174 C4 31 20 S 58 2W
Concórdia, Brazil ...... 168 D4 4 36 S 66 36W
Concordia, Mexico 162 C3 23 18N 106 2W
Concordia, Kans., U.S.A. 154 F6 39 34N 97 40W
Concordia, Mo., U.S.A. 156 F8 38 59N 93 34W
Concrete, U.S.A. 158 B3 48 32N 121 45W
Cunda, Angola ...... 116 E2 11 9 S 14 20 E
Condah, Australia ...... 128 D4 37 57 S 141 44 E
Condamine, Australia ...... 127 D5 26 56 S 150 9 E
Condat, France ...... 28 C6 45 21N 2 46 E
Condé, Angola ...... 115 E2 10 50 S 14 37 E
Conde, Brazil ...... 171 D4 11 49 S 37 37W
Condé-sur-Noireau, France 26 D6 48 51N 0 33W
Condeúba, Brazil ...... 171 D3 14 52 S 42 0W
Condobolin, Australia ...... 129 B7 33 4 S 147 6 E
Condom, France ...... 28 E4 43 57N 0 22 E
Condon, U.S.A. 158 D3 45 14N 120 11W
Conegliano, Italy ...... 45 C9 45 53N 12 18 E
Conejera, I. = Conills, I. des, Spain . 38 B3 39 11N 2 58 E
Conejos, Mexico 162 B4 26 14N 103 53W
Conero, Parco del △, Italy ...... 45 E10 43 32N 13 35 E
Conflict Group, Papua N. G. ...... 132 F6 10 47 S 151 45 E
Confolens, France ...... 28 B4 46 2N 0 40 E
Confuso ◂, Paraguay ...... 174 B4 25 9 S 57 34W
Congaree ◂, U.S.A. 152 B9 33 44N 80 38W
Congaree Swamp Nat. Monument △,
  U.S.A. 152 B9 33 47N 80 47W
Congaz, Moldova ...... 53 D13 46 7N 28 36 E
Congerville, U.S.A. 156 D7 40 38N 89 11W
Conghua, China ...... 77 F9 23 36N 113 51 E
Congjiang, China ...... 76 E7 25 43N 108 52 E
Congleton, U.K. 20 D5 53 10N 2 13W
Congo, Brazil ...... 170 C4 7 48 S 36 40W
Congo (Kinshasa) = Congo, Dem.
  Rep. of the ■, Africa ...... 115 C4 3 0 S 23 0 E
Congo ■, Africa ...... 114 C3 1 0 S 16 0 E
Congo ◂, Africa ...... 115 D2 6 4 S 12 24 E
Congo, Dem. Rep. of the ■, Africa . 115 C4 3 0 S 23 0 E
Congo Basin, Africa ...... 104 G6 0 10 S 24 30 E
Congonhas, Brazil ...... 171 F3 20 30 S 43 52W
Congress, U.S.A. 159 J7 34 9N 112 51W
Conil = Conil de la Frontera, Spain . 43 J4 36 17N 6 10W
Conil de la Frontera, Spain 43 J4 36 17N 6 10W
Conills, I. des, Spain ...... 38 B3 39 11N 2 58 E
Coniston, Canada 140 C3 46 29N 80 51W
Conjeeveram = Kanchipuram, India 95 H4 12 52N 79 45 E
Conklin, Canada 143 B6 55 38N 111 5W
Conklin, U.S.A. 151 D9 42 2N 75 49W
Conkouati, Réserve de Faune de △,
  Congo ...... 114 C2 3 50 S 11 28 E
Conlea, Australia ...... 129 B6 30 7 S 144 35 E
Conn, L., Ireland 23 B2 54 3N 9 15W
Connacht □, Ireland 23 C2 53 43N 9 12W
Conneaut, U.S.A. 150 E4 41 57N 80 34W
Connecticut □, U.S.A. 151 E12 41 30N 72 45W
Connecticut ◂, U.S.A. 151 E12 41 16N 72 20W
Connell, U.S.A. 158 C4 46 40N 118 52W
Connellsville, U.S.A. 150 F5 40 1N 79 35W
Connemara, Ireland 23 C2 53 29N 9 45W
Connemara Nat. Park △, Ireland .. 23 C2 53 32N 9 52W
Connemaugh ◂, U.S.A. 150 F5 40 28N 79 19W
Conner, Phil. ...... 80 C3 17 48N 121 19 E
Connerré, France ...... 26 D7 48 3N 0 30 E
Connersville, U.S.A. 157 E11 39 39N 85 8W
Connors Ra., Australia ...... 126 C4 21 40 S 149 10 E
Conoble, Australia ...... 129 B6 32 55 S 144 33 E
Cononaco ◂, Ecuador ...... 168 D2 1 32 S 75 35W
Conques, France ...... 28 D6 44 36N 2 23 E
Conquest, Canada 143 C7 51 32N 107 14W
Conrad, Iowa, U.S.A. 156 D8 42 14N 92 52W
Conrad, Mont., U.S.A. 158 B8 48 10N 111 57W
Conran, C., Australia ...... 129 D8 37 49 S 148 44 E
Conroe, U.S.A. 155 K7 30 19N 95 27W
Consecon, Canada 150 C7 44 0N 77 31W
Conselheiro Lafaiete, Brazil ...... 171 F3 20 40 S 43 48W
Conselheiro Pena, Brazil ...... 171 E3 19 10 S 41 30W
Conselve, Italy ...... 45 C8 45 14N 11 52 E
Consett, U.K. 20 C6 54 51N 1 50W
Consort, Canada 143 C6 52 1N 110 46W
Constance = Konstanz, Germany .. 31 H5 47 40N 9 10 E
Constance, L. = Bodensee, Europe .. 33 A8 47 35N 9 25 E
Constanţa, Romania ...... 53 F13 44 14N 28 38 E
Constanţa □, Romania ...... 53 F13 44 15N 28 15 E
Constantia, U.S.A. 151 C8 43 15N 76 1W
Constantina, Spain 43 H5 37 51N 5 40W
Constantine, Algeria ...... 111 A6 36 25N 6 42 E
Constantine, U.S.A. 157 C11 41 50N 85 40W
Constitución, Chile 144 G8 58 24N 158 54W
Constitución, Uruguay ...... 174 C4 31 0 S 57 50W
Constitucion de 1857, Parque Nac. △,
  Mexico 162 A1 32 4N 115 55W
Consuegra, Spain 43 F7 39 28N 3 36W

Consul, Canada 143 D7 49 20N 109 30W
Contact, U.S.A. 158 F6 41 46N 114 45W
Contai, India ...... 93 J12 21 54N 87 46 E
Contamana, Peru ...... 172 B3 7 19 S 74 55W
Contarina, Italy ...... 45 C9 45 1N 12 13 E
Contas ◂, Brazil ...... 171 D4 14 17 S 39 1W
Contes, France ...... 29 E11 43 49N 7 19 E
Conthey, Switz. ...... 32 D4 46 14N 7 18 E
Continental, U.S.A. 157 C12 41 6N 84 16W
Contoocook, U.S.A. 151 C13 43 13N 71 45W
Contra Costa, Mozam. ...... 117 D5 25 9 S 33 30 E
Contres, France ...... 26 E8 47 24N 1 26 E
Contrexéville, France ...... 27 D12 48 10N 5 53 E
Controller B., U.S.A. 144 F11 60 7N 144 15W
Contumazá, Peru ...... 172 B2 7 23 S 78 57W
Contwoyto L., Canada 138 B8 65 42N 110 50W
Convención, Colombia 168 B3 8 28N 73 21W
Conversano, Italy ...... 47 B10 40 58N 17 7 E
Converse, U.S.A. 157 D11 40 35N 85 52W
Convoy, U.S.A. 157 D12 40 55N 84 43W
Conway = Conwy, U.K. 20 D4 53 17N 3 50W
Conway = Conwy ◂, U.K. 20 D4 53 17N 3 50W
Conway, Australia ...... 126 J6 20 24 S 148 46 E
Conway, Ark., U.S.A. 155 H8 35 5N 92 26W
Conway, N.H., U.S.A. 151 C13 43 59N 71 7W
Conway, S.C., U.S.A. 149 J6 33 51N 79 3W
Conway, C., Australia ...... 126 J6 20 34 S 148 46 E
Conway, L., Australia ...... 127 D2 28 17 S 135 35 E
Conwy, U.K. 20 D4 53 17N 3 50W
Conwy □, U.K. 20 D4 53 10N 3 44W
Conwy ◂, U.K. 20 D4 53 17N 3 50W
Conyers, U.S.A. 152 B5 33 40N 84 1W
Coober Pedy, Australia ...... 127 D1 29 1 S 134 43 E
Cooch Behar = Koch Bihar, India . 90 B2 26 22N 89 29 E
Cooinda, Australia ...... 124 B5 13 15 S 130 5 E
Cook, Australia ...... 125 F5 30 37 S 130 25 E
Cook, U.S.A. 154 B8 47 49N 92 39W
Cook, B., Chile ...... 176 E2 55 10 S 70 0W
Cook, C., Canada 142 C3 50 8N 127 55W
Cook, Mt. = Aoraki Mount Cook,
  N.Z. ...... 131 D5 43 36 S 170 9 E
Cook B., Vanuatu ...... 133 H7 18 46 S 169 15 E
Cook Inlet, U.S.A. 144 G10 60 0N 152 0W
Cook Is., Pac. Oc. ...... 135 J12 17 0 S 160 0W
Cook Strait, N.Z. ...... 130 H3 41 15 S 174 29 E
Cooke Plains, Australia ...... 128 C3 35 23 S 139 34 E
Cookeville, U.S.A. 149 G3 36 10N 85 30W
Cookhouse, S. Africa ...... 116 E4 32 44 S 25 47 E
Cooks Hammock, U.S.A. 152 F6 29 56N 83 17W
Cookshire, Canada 151 A13 45 25N 71 38W
Cookstown, U.K. 23 B5 54 39N 6 45W
Cooksville, Canada 150 C5 43 36N 79 35W
Cooktown, Australia ...... 126 B4 15 30 S 145 16 E
Coolabah, Australia ...... 129 A7 31 1 S 146 43 E
Cooladdi, Australia ...... 127 D4 26 37 S 145 23 E
Coolah, Australia ...... 129 A8 31 48 S 149 41 E
Coolamon, Australia ...... 129 C7 34 46 S 147 8 E
Coolgardie, Australia ...... 125 F3 30 55 S 121 8 E
Coolidge, Ariz., U.S.A. 159 K8 32 59N 111 31W
Coolidge, Ga., U.S.A. 152 D6 31 1N 83 52W
Coolidge Dam, U.S.A. 159 K8 33 0N 110 20W
Cooloola Nat. Park △, Australia .. 127 D5 26 3 S 153 2 E
Cooma, Australia ...... 129 D8 36 12 S 149 8 E
Coon Rapids, Iowa, U.S.A. 156 C2 41 53N 94 41W
Coon Rapids, Minn., U.S.A. 154 C8 45 9N 93 19W
Coonabarabran, Australia ...... 129 A8 31 14 S 149 18 E
Coonalpyn, Australia ...... 128 C3 35 43 S 139 52 E
Coonamble, Australia ...... 129 A8 30 56 S 148 27 E
Coonana, Australia ...... 125 F3 31 0 S 123 0 E
Coondapoor, India ...... 95 H2 13 42N 74 40 E
Coonimie, L., Australia ...... 127 D2 26 4 S 139 59 E
Coonoor, India ...... 95 J3 11 21N 76 45 E
Cooper ◂, Australia ...... 125 J7 33 23N 95 42 E
Cooper Cr. ◂, Australia ...... 128 D2 28 29 S 137 46 E
Cooperstown, N. Dak., U.S.A. 154 B5 47 27N 98 8W
Cooperstown, N.Y., U.S.A. 151 D10 42 42N 74 56W
Coopersville, U.S.A. 157 A11 43 4N 85 57W
Coopracambra Nat. Park △,
  Australia ...... 129 D8 37 20 S 149 20 E
Coorabie, Australia ...... 125 F5 31 54 S 132 18 E
Coorong, The, Australia ...... 128 C3 35 50 S 139 20 E
Coorong Nat. Park △, Australia .. 125 E2 29 53 S 116 2 E
Cooroy, Australia ...... 127 D5 26 22 S 152 54 E
Coos Bay, U.S.A. 158 E1 43 22N 124 13W
Coosa ◂, U.S.A. 149 J2 32 30N 86 16W
Cootamundra, Australia ...... 129 C8 34 36 S 148 1 E
Cootehill, Ireland 23 B4 54 4N 7 5W
Copahue Paso, Argentina ...... 174 D1 37 49 S 71 8W
Copake Falls, U.S.A. 151 D11 42 7N 73 31W
Copán, Honduras 164 D2 14 50N 89 9W
Copatana, Brazil ...... 168 D4 2 48 S 67 4W
Cope, Colo., U.S.A. 154 F3 39 40N 102 51W
Cope, S.C., U.S.A. 152 B8 33 23N 81 0W
Cope, C., Spain 41 H3 37 26N 1 28W
Copeland, U.S.A. 153 K8 25 57N 81 22W
Copenhagen = København, Denmark 17 J6 55 41N 12 34 E
Copenhagen, U.S.A. 151 C9 43 54N 75 41W
Copenhagen ✈ (CPH), Denmark .. 17 J6 55 37N 12 39 E
Cupertino, Italy ...... 47 B11 40 16N 18 3 E
Copiapó, Chile ...... 174 B1 27 30 S 70 20W
Copiapó ◂, Chile ...... 174 B1 27 19 S 70 56W
Coplay, U.S.A. 151 F9 40 44N 75 29W
Copley, Australia ...... 128 A3 30 36 S 138 26 E
Copp L., Canada 142 A6 60 14N 114 40W
Copparo, Italy ...... 45 D8 44 54N 11 49 E
Coppename ◂, Suriname 169 B6 5 48N 55 55W
Copper ◂, U.S.A. 144 F11 60 18N 145 3W
Copper Center, U.S.A. 144 F11 61 58N 145 18W
Copper Harbor, U.S.A. 148 B2 47 28N 87 53W
Copper Queen, Zimbabwe ...... 119 F2 17 29 S 29 18 E
Copperas Cove, U.S.A. 155 K6 31 8N 97 54W
Copperbelt □, Zambia ...... 119 E2 13 15 S 27 30 E
Coppermine = Kugluktuk, Canada . 138 B8 67 50N 115 5W
Coppermine ◂, Canada 138 B8 67 49N 116 4W
Copperopolis, U.S.A. 160 H6 37 58N 120 38W
Coppet, Switz. ...... 32 D2 46 19N 6 12 E
Copsa Mică, Romania ...... 53 D9 46 7N 24 15 E
Coquet ◂, U.K. 20 B6 55 20N 1 32W
Coquilhatville = Mbandaka,
  Dem. Rep. of the Congo ...... 114 B3 0 1N 18 18 E
Coquille, U.S.A. 158 E1 43 11N 124 11W
Coquimbo, Chile ...... 174 B1 30 0 S 71 20W
Coquimbo □, Chile ...... 174 C1 31 0 S 71 0W
Corabia, Romania ...... 53 G9 43 48N 24 30 E
Coração de Jesus, Brazil ...... 171 E3 16 43 S 44 22W
Coracora, Peru ...... 172 D3 15 5 S 73 45W
Coraki, Australia ...... 127 D5 28 59 S 153 17 E
Coral, U.S.A. 150 F5 40 29N 79 10W
Coral Bay, Phil. ...... 81 G1 8 25N 117 20 E
Coral Gables, U.S.A. 153 K9 25 45N 80 16W
Coral Harbour = Salliq, Canada .. 139 B11 64 8N 83 10W
Coral Heights, Bahamas ...... 9 b 25 1N 77 27W
Coral Hts., Bahamas ...... 9 b 25 1N 77 33W
Coral Sea, Pac. Oc. ...... 130 C4 15 0 S 150 0 E
Coral Springs, U.S.A. 153 J9 26 16N 80 13W
Coralville, U.S.A. 156 C5 41 40N 91 34W
Coralville L., U.S.A. 156 C5 41 50N 91 40W
Corangamite, L., Australia ...... 128 E5 38 5 S 143 30 E
Corantijn ◂, Suriname 169 B6 5 50N 57 8W

Coraopolis, U.S.A. 150 F4 40 31N 80 10W
Corato, Italy ...... 47 A9 41 9N 16 25 E
Corbeil-Essonnes, France ...... 27 D9 48 36N 2 26 E
Corbeiro, C., W. Sahara 110 D1 21 50N 17 0W
Corbie, France ...... 27 C9 49 54N 2 30 E
Corbières, France ...... 28 F6 42 55N 2 35 E
Corbigny, France ...... 27 E10 47 16N 3 40 E
Corbin, U.S.A. 148 G3 36 57N 84 6W
Corbones ◂, Spain 43 H5 37 36N 5 39W
Corby, Romania ...... 53 F13 44 25N 28 39 E
Corby, U.K. 21 E7 52 30N 0 41W
Corcaigh = Cork, Ireland 23 E3 51 54N 8 29W
Corcoran, U.S.A. 160 J7 36 6N 119 33W
Corcovado, Parque Nac. △,
  Costa Rica 164 E3 8 33N 83 35W
Cordele, U.S.A. 152 D6 31 58N 83 47W
Cordell, U.S.A. 155 H5 35 17N 98 59W
Cordenòns, Italy ...... 45 C9 45 59N 12 42 E
Cordes, France ...... 28 D5 44 5N 1 57 E
Cordisburgo, Brazil ...... 171 E3 19 7 S 44 21W
Córdoba, Mexico 163 D5 18 53N 96 56W
Córdoba, Argentina 174 C3 31 20N 64 10W
Córdoba, Spain 43 H6 37 50N 4 50W
Córdoba □, Argentina ...... 174 C3 31 22 S 64 15W
Córdoba □, Colombia 168 B2 8 20N 75 40W
Córdoba □, Spain 43 G6 38 5N 5 0W
Córdoba, Sierra de, Argentina .... 174 C3 31 10 S 64 25W
Cordon, Phil. ...... 80 C3 16 42N 121 32 E
Cordova, U.S.A. 144 F11 60 33N 145 45W
Corella, Spain 40 C3 42 7N 1 53W
Corella ◂, Australia ...... 126 B3 19 34 S 140 47 E
Coremas, Brazil ...... 170 C4 7 1 S 37 58W
Corentyne ◂, Guyana 169 B6 5 50N 57 8W
Corfield, Australia ...... 126 C3 21 40 S 143 21 E
Corfu = Kérkira, Greece ...... 38 B9 39 38N 19 50 E
Corfu ✈ (CFU), Greece ...... 48 B1 39 35N 19 54 E
Corgo = O Corgo, Spain 42 C3 42 56N 7 25W
Corguinho, Brazil ...... 173 D7 19 53 S 54 52W
Cori, Italy ...... 46 A5 41 39N 12 55 E
Coria, Spain 42 F4 39 58N 6 33W
Coria del Río, Spain 43 H4 37 16N 6 3W
Corigliano Cálabro, Italy ...... 47 C9 39 36N 16 31 E
Coringa, Barra de, Angola ...... 115 D2 8 52 S 13 9 E
Coringa Is., Australia ...... 126 B4 16 58 S 149 58 E
Corinth = Kórinthos, Greece ...... 48 D4 37 56N 22 55 E
Corinth, Ky., U.S.A. 157 F12 38 30N 84 34W
Corinth, Miss., U.S.A. 149 H1 34 56N 88 31W
Corinth, N.Y., U.S.A. 151 C11 43 15N 73 49W
Corinth, G. of = Korinthiakós
  Kólpos, Greece ...... 48 C4 38 16N 22 30 E
Corinth Canal, Greece ...... 48 D4 37 58N 23 0 E
Corinto, Brazil ...... 171 E3 18 20 S 44 30W
Corinto, Nic. 164 D2 12 30N 87 10W
Corisco, Eq. Guin. ...... 114 B1 0 55N 9 18 E
Cork, Ireland 23 E3 51 54N 8 29W
Cork □, Ireland 23 E3 51 57N 8 40W
Cork Harbour, Ireland 23 E3 51 47N 8 16W
Corlay, France 26 D3 48 20N 3 5W
Corleone, Italy ...... 46 E6 37 49N 13 18 E
Corleto Perticara, Italy ...... 47 B9 40 23N 16 2 E
Çorlu, Turkey ...... 51 E11 41 11N 27 42 E
Cormack L., Canada 142 A4 60 56N 121 37W
Cormòns, Italy ...... 45 C10 45 58N 13 28 E
Cormorant, Canada 143 C8 54 14N 100 35W
Cormorant L., Canada 143 C8 54 15N 100 50W
Corn Is. = Maíz, Is. del, Nic. 164 D3 12 15N 83 4W
Cornalvo, Parque Natural de △,
  Spain 43 F4 39 1N 6 13W
Cornélio Procópio, Brazil ...... 175 A5 23 7 S 50 40W
Cornell, U.S.A. 157 D10 41 0N 88 44W
Corner Brook, Canada 141 C8 48 57N 57 58W
Corner Inlet, Australia ...... 129 E7 38 45 S 146 20 E
Corneşti, Moldova ...... 53 C13 47 21N 28 1 E
Cornigliio, Italy ...... 44 D7 44 29N 10 5 E
Corning, Ark., U.S.A. 155 G9 36 25N 90 35W
Corning, Calif., U.S.A. 158 G2 39 56N 122 11W
Corning, Iowa, U.S.A. 156 D2 40 59N 94 44W
Corning, N.Y., U.S.A. 150 D7 42 9N 77 3W
Corno Grande, Italy ...... 45 F10 42 28N 13 34 E
Cornwall, Canada 140 C5 45 2N 74 44W
Cornwall, U.S.A. 151 F8 40 17N 76 25W
Cornwall □, U.K. 21 G3 50 26N 4 40W
Cornwell, U.S.A. 153 H8 27 15N 81 6W
Corny Pt., Australia ...... 128 C2 34 55 S 137 0 E
Coro, Venezuela 168 A4 11 25N 69 41W
Coroaci, Brazil ...... 171 E3 18 35 S 42 17W
Coroatá, Brazil ...... 170 B3 4 8 S 44 0W
Coroban, Somali Rep. ...... 106 D2 8 58N 42 44 E
Corocoro, Bolivia ...... 172 D4 17 15 S 68 28W
Coroco I., Venezuela 169 B5 8 30N 60 10W
Coroico, Bolivia ...... 172 D4 16 0 S 67 50W
Coromandel, Brazil ...... 171 E2 18 28 S 47 13W
Coromandel, N.Z. ...... 130 C4 36 45 S 175 31 E
Coromandel Coast, India ...... 95 H5 12 30N 81 0 E
Coromandel Pen., N.Z. ...... 130 C4 37 0 S 175 40 E
Coromandel Ra., N.Z. ...... 130 C4 37 0 S 175 40 E
Coron, Phil. ...... 80 E12 12N 120 12 E
Coron Bay, Phil. ...... 81 F3 11 55N 120 2 E
Coron I., Phil. ...... 81 F3 11 55N 120 14 E
Corona, Calif., U.S.A. 161 M9 33 53N 117 34W
Corona, N. Mex., U.S.A. 159 J11 34 15N 105 36W
Coronach, Canada 143 D7 49 7N 105 31W
Coronado, U.S.A. 161 N9 32 41N 117 11W
Coronado, B. de, Costa Rica 164 E3 9 0N 83 40W
Coronados, G. de los, Chile ...... 176 B2 41 40 S 74 0W
Coronados, Is. los, U.S.A. 161 N9 32 25N 117 15W
Coronation, Canada 142 C6 52 5N 111 27W
Coronation Gulf, Canada 138 B8 68 25N 110 0W
Coronation I., Antarctica ...... 7 C18 60 45 S 46 0W
Coronation Is., Australia ...... 124 B3 14 57 S 124 55 E
Coronda, Argentina ...... 174 C3 31 58 S 60 56W
Coronel, Chile ...... 174 D1 37 0 S 73 10W
Coronel Bogado, Paraguay ...... 174 B4 27 11 S 56 18W
Coronel Dorrego, Argentina ...... 174 D3 38 40 S 61 10W
Coronel Fabriciano, Brazil ...... 171 E3 19 31 S 42 38W
Coronel Murta, Brazil ...... 171 E3 16 37 S 42 11W
Coronel Oviedo, Paraguay ...... 174 B4 25 24 S 56 30W
Coronel Ponce, Brazil ...... 173 D7 15 46 S 54 58W
Coronel Pringles, Argentina ...... 174 D3 38 0 S 61 30W
Coronel Suárez, Argentina ...... 174 D3 37 30 S 61 52W
Coronel Vidal, Argentina ...... 174 D4 37 28 S 57 45W
Corongo, Peru ...... 172 B2 8 30 S 77 53W
Coropuna, Nevado, Peru ...... 172 D3 15 30 S 72 41W
Çorovodë, Albania ...... 50 F4 40 31N 20 14 E
Corowa, Australia ...... 129 C7 35 58 S 146 21 E
Corozal, Belize 163 D7 18 23N 88 23W
Corozal, Colombia 168 B2 9 19N 75 18W
Corozal Pt., Trin. & Tob. 169 F9 10 44N 61 40W
Corps, France ...... 29 D9 44 50N 5 56 E
Corpus, Argentina ...... 175 B4 27 10 S 55 30W
Corpus Christi, U.S.A. 155 M6 27 47N 97 24W
Corpus Christi, L., U.S.A. 155 L6 28 2N 97 52W
Corque, Bolivia ...... 172 D4 18 20 S 67 41W
Corral, Chile ...... 176 A2 39 52 S 73 26W
Corral de Almaguer, Spain 42 F7 39 45N 3 10W
Corralejo, Canary Is. 9 e2 28 43N 13 53W
Corrandibby Ra., Australia ...... 125 E1 24 45 S 114 20 E
Correntes, C. das, Mozam. ...... 117 C6 24 6 S 35 34 E
Corrente, Brazil ...... 170 D2 10 27 S 45 10W
Corrente ◂, Brazil ...... 171 D3 13 8 S 43 28W
Corrientes, Brazil ...... 171 D4 17 38 S 55 8W
Corrientes □, Brazil ...... 174 B4 27 30 S 58 45W

Correntina, Brazil .... 171 D3 13 20 S 44 39W
Corrèze □, France .... 28 C5 45 20N 1 45 E
Corrèze →, France .... 28 C5 45 10N 1 28 E
Corrib, L., Ireland 23 C2 53 27N 9 16W
Corridónia, Italy .... 45 E10 43 15N 13 30 E
Corrientes, Argentina ...... 174 B4 27 30 S 58 45W
Corrientes □, Argentina .... 174 B4 28 0 S 57 0W
Corrientes →, Argentina .... 174 C4 30 42 S 59 38W
Corrientes →, Peru .... 168 D3 3 43 S 74 35W
Corrientes, C., Colombia 168 B2 5 30N 77 34W
Corrientes, C., Cuba 164 B3 21 43N 84 30W
Corrientes, C., Mexico 162 C3 20 25N 105 42W
Corrigan, U.S.A. 155 K7 31 0N 94 52W
Corrigin, Australia .... 125 F2 32 20 S 117 53 E
Corry, U.S.A. 150 E5 41 55N 79 39W
Corryong, Australia .... 129 F7 36 12 S 147 53 E
Corse, France .... 29 G13 42 0N 9 0 E
Corse, C., France .... 29 E13 43 1N 9 25 E
Corse, Parc Naturel Régional de △,
  France .... 29 F13 42 14N 9 10 E
Corse-du-Sud □, France .... 29 G13 41 45N 9 0 E
Corsica = Corse, France .... 29 G13 42 0N 9 0 E
Corsicana, U.S.A. 155 J6 32 6N 96 28W
Corte, France .... 29 F13 42 19N 9 11 E
Corte Pinto, Portugal 43 H3 37 42N 7 29W
Cortegana, Spain 43 H4 37 52N 6 49W
Cortes, Phil. .... 81 G6 9 17N 126 11 E
Cortez, U.S.A. 159 H9 37 21N 108 35W
Cortina d'Ampezzo, Italy .... 45 B9 46 32N 12 8 E
Cortland, N.Y., U.S.A. 151 D8 42 36N 76 11W
Cortland, Ohio, U.S.A. 150 E4 41 20N 80 44W
Cortona, Italy .... 45 E8 43 16N 11 59 E
Corubal →, Guinea-Biss. 112 C2 11 57N 15 5W
Coruche, Portugal 43 G2 38 57N 8 30W
Çoruh →, Turkey .... 61 K5 41 38N 41 38 E
Çorum, Turkey .... 100 B6 40 30N 34 57 E
Corumbá, Brazil .... 173 D6 19 0 S 57 30W
Corumbá →, Brazil .... 171 E2 18 19 S 48 55W
Corumbá de Goiás, Brazil .... 171 E2 16 0 S 48 50W
Corumbaíba, Brazil .... 171 E2 18 9 S 48 34W
Çoruñna = A Coruña, Spain .. 42 B2 43 20N 8 25W
Corunna, U.S.A. 157 B12 42 59N 84 7W
Corvallis, U.S.A. 158 D2 44 34N 123 16W
Corvette, L. de la, Canada .. 140 B5 53 25N 74 3W
Corvo, Azores 9 d2 39 42N 31 6W
Corydon, Ind., U.S.A. 157 F10 38 13N 86 7W
Corydon, Iowa, U.S.A. 156 D3 40 46N 93 19W
Corydon, Ky., U.S.A. 157 G9 37 44N 87 42W
Cosalá, Mexico 162 C3 24 28N 106 40W
Cosamaloapan, Mexico 163 D5 18 23N 95 50W
Cosenza, Italy .... 47 C9 39 18N 16 15 E
Coşereni, Romania .... 53 F11 44 38N 26 35 E
Coshocton, U.S.A. 150 F3 40 16N 81 51W
Cosmo Newberry, Australia .. 125 E3 28 0 S 122 54 E
Cosne-Cours-sur-Loire, France .. 27 E9 47 24N 2 54 E
Coso Junction, U.S.A. 161 J9 36 3N 117 57W
Coso Pk., U.S.A. 161 J9 36 13N 117 44W
Cospeito, Spain 42 B3 43 12N 7 34W
Cosquín, Argentina .... 174 C3 31 15 S 64 30W
Cossato, Italy .... 44 C5 45 34N 8 10 E
Cossé-le-Vivien, France 26 E6 47 57N 0 54W
Cosson →, France .... 26 E8 47 30N 1 15 E
Costa Blanca, Spain 41 G4 38 25N 0 10W
Costa Brava, Spain .... 40 D8 41 30N 3 0 E
Costa del Sol, Spain 43 J6 36 30N 4 30W
Costa Dorada, Spain ...... 40 D6 41 12N 1 15 E
Costa Mesa, U.S.A. 161 M9 33 38N 117 55W
Costa Rica ■, Cent. Amer. .. 164 E3 10 0N 84 0W
Costa Smeralda, Italy ...... 46 A2 41 5N 9 35 E
Costermansville = Bukavu,
  Dem. Rep. of the Congo .. 118 C2 2 20 S 28 52 E
Costeşti, Romania .... 53 F9 44 40N 24 53 E
Costigliole d'Asti, Italy .... 44 D5 44 47N 8 11 E
Cosumnes →, U.S.A. 160 G5 38 16N 121 26W
Coswig, Sachsen, Germany .. 30 D9 51 7N 13 34 E
Coswig, Sachsen-Anhalt, Germany .. 30 D8 51 53N 12 27 E
Cotabato, Phil. .... 81 H5 7 14N 124 15 E
Cotabato □, Phil. .... 81 H5 7 0N 124 0 E
Cotacajes →, Bolivia ...... 172 D4 16 0 S 67 1W
Cotagaita, Bolivia .... 174 A2 20 45 S 65 40W
Cotahuasi, Peru .... 172 D3 15 12 S 72 50W
Côte-d'Ivoire, France ...... 29 E11 43 25N 7 10 E
Côte-d'Ivoire = Ivory Coast ■,
  Africa 112 D4 7 30N 5 0W
Côte-d'Or □, France .... 27 E11 47 10N 4 50 E
Côte-d'Or □, France .... 27 E11 47 30N 4 50 E
Coteau des Prairies, U.S.A. .. 154 C6 45 20N 97 50W
Coteau du Missouri, U.S.A. .. 154 B4 47 0N 100 0W
Coteau Landing, Canada 151 A10 45 15N 74 13W
Cotentin, France 26 C5 49 15N 1 30W
Côtes-d'Armor □, France 26 D4 48 25N 2 40W
Côtes de Meuse, France .... 27 C12 49 15N 5 22 E
Côtes-du-Nord = Côtes-d'Armor □,
  France 26 D4 48 25N 2 40W
Cotiella, Spain .... 40 C5 42 31N 0 19 E
Cotillo, Canary Is. 9 e2 28 41N 14 1W
Cotiujeni, Moldova .... 53 C13 47 51N 28 33 E
Cotoca, Bolivia .... 173 D5 17 49 S 63 3W
Cotonou, Benin .... 113 D5 6 20N 2 25 E
Cotopaxi, Ecuador .... 168 D2 0 40 S 78 30W
Cotopaxi □, Ecuador ...... 168 D2 0 5 S 78 55W
Cotronei, Italy .... 47 C9 39 9N 16 47 E
Cotswold Hills, U.K. 21 F5 51 42N 2 10W
Cottage Grove, U.S.A. 158 E2 43 48N 123 3W
Cottageville, U.S.A. 152 C9 32 56N 80 29W
Cottbus, Germany .... 30 D10 51 45N 14 20 E
Cottondale, U.S.A. 152 K4 30 48N 85 23W
Cottonwood, Ala., U.S.A. 152 D4 31 3N 85 18W
Cottonwood, Ariz., U.S.A. .. 159 J7 34 45N 112 1W
Cotulla, U.S.A. 155 L5 28 26N 99 14W
Coubre, Pte. de la, France .. 28 C2 45 42N 1 15W
Couches, France .... 27 F11 46 53N 4 30 E
Couço, Portugal 43 G2 38 59N 8 17W
Coudersport, U.S.A. 150 E6 41 46N 78 1W
Couedic, C. du, Australia .... 129 D2 36 5 S 136 40 E
Couëron, France 26 E5 47 13N 1 44W
Couesnon →, France 26 D5 48 38N 1 32W
Couhé, France .... 28 B4 46 17N 0 11 E
Coulanges-sur-Yonne, France .. 27 E10 47 31N 3 33 E
Coulee City, U.S.A. 158 C4 47 37N 119 17W
Coulman I., Antarctica .... 7 D11 73 35 S 170 0 E
Coulommiers, France ...... 27 D10 48 50N 3 3 E
Coulon →, France .... 29 E9 43 51N 5 E
Coulonge →, Canada 140 C4 45 52N 76 46W
Coulonges-sur-l'Autize, France .. 28 B3 46 29N 0 36W
Coulounieix-Chamiers, France .. 28 C4 45 11N 0 42 E
Coulterville, Calif., U.S.A. .. 160 H6 37 43N 120 12W
Coulterville, Ill., U.S.A. 156 F7 38 11N 89 36W
Council, Alaska, U.S.A. 144 B7 64 53N 163 41W
Council, Idaho, U.S.A. 158 D5 44 44N 116 26W
Council Bluffs, U.S.A. 156 E7 41 16N 95 52W
Council Grove, U.S.A. 154 F6 38 40N 96 29W
Coupeville, U.S.A. 160 B4 48 13N 122 41W
Courantyne →, S. Amer. 169 B6 5 55N 57 5W
Courcelles, Belgium ...... 24 D4 50 28N 4 22 E
Courçon, France 28 B3 46 15N 0 50W
Courmayeur, Italy .... 44 C3 45 47N 6 58 E
Couronne, C., France ...... 29 E9 43 19N 5 3 E
Cours-la-Ville, France ...... 27 F11 46 7N 4 19 E
Coursan, France .... 28 E7 43 14N 3 4 E
Courseulles-sur-Mer, France .. 26 C6 49 20N 0 29W

Courtenay, Canada 142 D4 49 45N 125 0W
Courtenay, France .... 27 D10 48 2N 3 3 E
Courtland, U.S.A. 160 G5 38 20N 121 34W
Courtrai = Kortrijk, Belgium .. 24 D3 50 50N 3 17 E
Courtright, Canada 150 D2 42 49N 82 28W
Coushatta, U.S.A. 155 J8 32 1N 93 21W
Coutances, France 26 C5 49 3N 1 28W
Coutras, France 28 C3 45 3N 0 8W
Coutts Crossing, Australia .. 127 D5 29 49 S 152 55 E
Couva, Trin. & Tob. 169 F9 10 24N 61 30W
Couvet, Switz. .... 32 C3 46 57N 6 38 E
Couvin, Belgium .... 24 D4 50 3N 4 29 E
Covarrubias, Spain 42 C7 42 4N 3 31W
Cove I., Canada 150 A3 45 17N 81 44W
Coveñas, Colombia 168 B2 9 24N 75 44W
Coventry, U.K. 21 E6 52 25N 1 28W
Coverdale, U.S.A. 152 D6 31 38N 83 58W
Covilhã, Portugal 42 E3 40 17N 7 31W
Covington, Ga., U.S.A. .... 152 B6 28 40 S 49 23W
Covington, Ind., U.S.A. 157 D9 40 9N 87 24W
Covington, Ky., U.S.A. 157 F12 39 5N 84 31W
Covington, Ohio, U.S.A. 157 E12 40 7N 84 21W
Covington, Okla., U.S.A. 155 G6 36 18N 97 35W
Covington, Tenn., U.S.A. 155 H10 35 34N 89 39W
Covington, Va., U.S.A. 148 G5 37 47N 79 59W
Cowal, L., Australia ...... 129 B7 33 40 S 147 25 E
Cowan, Cerro, Ecuador .... 172 a 0 12 S 90 48W
Cowan, L., Australia ...... 125 F3 31 45 S 121 45 E
Cowan L., Canada 143 C7 54 0N 107 15W
Cowangie, Australia ...... 128 C4 35 12 S 141 26 E
Cowansville, Canada 140 C5 45 14N 72 46W
Coward Springs, Australia .. 127 D2 29 24 S 136 49 E
Cowcowing Lakes, Australia .. 125 F2 30 55 S 117 20 E
Cowden, U.S.A. 157 E8 39 15N 88 52W
Cowdenbeath, U.K. 22 E5 56 7N 3 21W
Cowell, Australia .... 128 B2 33 39 S 136 56 E
Cowes, Australia .... 129 E6 38 28 S 145 14 E
Cowes, U.K. 21 G6 50 45N 1 18W
Cowichan L., Canada 160 B2 48 53N 124 17W
Cowlitz →, U.S.A. 160 D4 46 6N 122 55W
Cowra, Australia .... 129 B8 33 49 S 148 42 E
Cox, Spain 41 G4 38 8N 0 53W
Coxilha Grande, Brazil .... 175 B5 28 18 S 51 30W
Coxim, Brazil .... 173 D7 18 30 S 54 55W
Coxim →, Brazil .... 173 D7 18 34 S 54 46W
Cox's Bazar, Bangla. ...... 90 E3 21 26N 91 59 E
Coyote Wells, U.S.A. 161 N11 32 44N 115 58W
Coyuca de Benítez, Mexico .. 163 D4 17 1N 100 8W
Coyuca de Catalan, Mexico .. 163 D4 18 18N 100 41W
Cozad, U.S.A. 154 E5 40 52N 99 59W
Cozes, France 28 C3 45 34N 0 49W
Cozumel, Mexico 163 C7 20 31N 86 55W
Cozumel, Isla, Mexico 163 C7 20 30N 86 40W
Crabhill, Barbados .... 165 g 13 19N 59 38W
Cracow = Kraków, Poland .. 55 H16 50 4N 19 57 E
Cracow, Australia .... 127 D5 25 17 S 150 17 E
Cradle Mt.-Lake St. Clair Nat.
  Park △, Australia ...... 127 D4 41 49 S 147 56 E
Cradock, Australia .... 127 E2 32 6 S 138 31 E
Cradock, S. Africa .... 124 E4 32 8 S 25 36 E
Craig, Alaska, U.S.A. 144 J14 55 29N 133 9W
Craig, Colo., U.S.A. 158 F10 40 31N 107 33W
Craigavon, U.K. 23 B5 54 27N 6 23W
Craigieburn, Australia .... 129 D6 37 36 S 144 56 E
Craigmore, Zimbabwe ...... 119 G3 20 28 S 32 50 E
Craik, Canada 143 C7 51 3N 105 49W
Crailsheim, Germany ...... 31 F6 49 8N 10 5 E
Craiova, Romania .... 53 F8 44 21N 23 48 E
Cramsie, Australia .... 126 C3 23 20 S 144 15 E
Cranberry L., U.S.A. 151 B10 44 11N 74 50W
Cranberry Portage, Canada .. 143 C8 54 35N 101 23W
Cranbrook, Australia ...... 125 F2 34 18 S 117 33 E
Cranbrook, Canada 142 D5 49 30N 115 46W
Crandon, U.S.A. 154 C10 45 34N 88 54W
Crane, Oreg., U.S.A. 158 E4 43 25N 118 35W
Crane, Tex., U.S.A. 155 K3 31 24N 102 21W
Cranganore, India .... 95 J3 10 13N 76 13 E
Cranston, U.S.A. 151 E13 41 47N 71 26W
Craon, France 26 E6 47 50N 0 58W
Craonne, France .... 27 C10 49 27N 3 46 E
Craponne-sur-Arzon, France .. 27 C8 45 19N 3 51 E
Crasna, Romania .... 53 D12 46 32N 27 51 E
Crasna →, Romania ...... 52 C7 47 44N 22 35 E
Crasnei, Munţii, Romania .. 53 C8 47 0N 23 20 E
Crater L., U.S.A. 158 E2 42 56N 122 6W
Crater Lake Nat. Park △, U.S.A. .. 158 E2 42 55N 122 10W
Crater Mt., Papua N. G. .... 132 D3 6 37 S 145 7 E
Crater Pt., Papua N. G. .... 132 C7 5 25 S 152 9 E
Craters of the Moon Nat. Park △,
  U.S.A. 158 E7 43 25N 113 30W
Crateús, Brazil .... 170 C3 5 10 S 40 39W
Crati →, Italy .... 47 C9 39 43N 16 31 E
Crato, Brazil .... 170 C4 7 10 S 39 25W
Crato, Portugal 43 F3 39 16N 7 39W
Craven, L., Canada 140 B4 54 20N 76 56W
Cravo Norte, Colombia 168 B3 6 18N 70 12W
Cravo Norte →, Colombia .. 168 B3 6 18N 70 12W
Crawford, Ala., U.S.A. 152 C4 32 27N 85 11W
Crawford, Nebr., U.S.A. 154 D3 42 41N 103 25W
Crawfordsville, Ind., U.S.A. .. 157 D10 40 2N 86 54W
Crawfordville, Iowa, U.S.A. .. 156 C4 41 12N 91 32W
Crawfordville, Fla., U.S.A. .. 152 E5 30 11N 84 23W
Crawfordville, Ga., U.S.A. .. 152 C5 33 33N 82 54W
Crawley, U.K. 21 F7 51 7N 0 11W
Crazy Mts., U.S.A. 158 C8 46 12N 110 20W
Crean L., Canada 143 C7 54 5N 106 9W
Crécy-en-Ponthieu, France .. 27 B8 50 15N 1 53 E
Crediton, Canada 150 C3 43 17N 81 33W
Crediton, U.K. 21 G4 50 47N 3 40W
Cree →, Canada 143 B7 58 57N 105 47W
Cree →, U.K. 22 G4 54 55N 4 25W
Cree L., Canada 143 B7 57 30N 106 30W
Creede, U.S.A. 159 H10 37 51N 106 56W
Creekside, U.S.A. 150 F5 40 40N 79 11W
Creel, Mexico 162 B3 27 45N 107 38W
Creemore, Canada 150 B4 44 19N 80 6W
Creighton, Canada 143 C8 54 45N 101 54W
Creighton, U.S.A. 154 D6 42 28N 97 54W
Creil, France .... 27 C9 49 15N 2 29 E
Crema, Italy .... 44 C7 45 22N 9 41 E
Cremona, Italy .... 44 C7 45 7N 10 2 E
Crepaja, Serbia, Yug. ...... 52 E5 45 1N 20 38 E
Crepori →, Brazil .... 173 B6 5 42 S 57 8W
Crépy, France .... 27 C10 49 35N 3 32 E
Crépy-en-Valois, France .... 27 C9 49 14N 2 54 E
Cres, Croatia .... 45 D11 44 58N 14 25 E
Crescent Beach, U.S.A. 152 F8 29 46N 81 15W
Crescent City, Calif., U.S.A. .. 158 F1 41 45N 124 12W
Crescent City, Fla., U.S.A. .. 153 F8 29 26N 81 31W
Crescent Hd., Australia .... 129 A10 31 11 S 152 59 E
Crescent L., U.S.A. 153 F8 29 28N 81 35W
Crescentino, Italy .... 44 C5 45 11N 8 6 E
Crespo, Argentina .... 174 C3 32 2 S 60 19W
Cresson, U.S.A. 150 F6 40 28N 78 36W
Cressy, Australia .... 128 E5 38 2 S 143 40 E
Crest, France .... 29 D9 44 44N 5 2 E
Cresta, Mt., Phil. .... 80 C4 17 1N 122 6 E
Crestline, Calif., U.S.A. 161 L9 34 14N 117 18W
Crestline, Ohio, U.S.A. 150 F2 40 47N 82 44W
Creston, Canada 142 D5 49 10N 116 31W
Creston, Calif., U.S.A. 160 K6 35 32N 120 33W
Creston, Iowa, U.S.A. 156 C2 41 4N 94 22W

Crestview, Calif., U.S.A. 160 H8 37 46N 118 58W
Crestview, Fla., U.S.A. 153 K3 30 46N 86 34W
Creswick, Australia ...... 128 D5 37 25 S 143 58 E
Crêt de la Neige, France .... 27 F12 46 16N 5 58 E
Crete = Kríti, Greece ...... 39 E6 35 15N 25 0 E
Crete, Ill., U.S.A. 157 C9 41 27N 87 38W
Crete, Nebr., U.S.A. 154 E6 40 38N 96 58W
Crete, Sea of, Greece ...... 49 E7 36 0N 25 0 E
Créteil, France .... 27 D9 48 47N 2 28 E
Cretin, C., Papua N. G. .... 132 D4 6 40 S 147 53 E
Creus, C. de, Spain ...... 40 C8 42 20N 3 19 E
Creuse □, France .... 27 F9 46 10N 2 0 E
Creuse →, France .... 28 B4 47 0N 0 34 E
Creutzwald, France ...... 27 C13 49 21N 6 42 E
Creuzburg, Germany ...... 30 D6 51 3N 10 14 E
Crèvecœur-le-Grand, France .. 27 C9 49 37N 2 5 E
Crevillente, Spain 41 G4 38 12N 0 48W
Crewe, U.K. 20 D5 53 6N 2 26W
Crewkerne, U.K. 21 G5 50 53N 2 48W
Crianlarich, U.K. 22 E4 56 24N 4 37W
Criciúma, Brazil .... 175 B6 28 40 S 49 23W
Cricova, Moldova .... 53 C13 47 8N 28 52 E
Cridersville, U.S.A. 157 D12 40 39N 84 9W
Crieff, U.K. 22 E5 56 22N 3 50W
Crikvenica, Croatia ...... 45 C11 45 11N 14 40 E
Crimea □, Ukraine .... 59 K8 45 30N 33 10 E
Crimean Pen. = Krymskyy Pivostriv,
  Ukraine .... 59 K8 45 0N 34 0 E
Crimmitschau, Germany .... 30 E8 50 48N 12 24 E
Cristal, Mts. de, Gabon .... 114 B2 30 0N 10 30 E
Cristalândia, Brazil ...... 170 D2 10 36 S 49 11W
Cristino Castro, Brazil .... 170 C3 8 49 S 44 13W
Cristóbal, Pta., Ecuador .... 172 a 0 54 S 91 31W
Cristuru Secuiesc, Romania .. 53 D10 46 17N 25 2 E
Crişul Alb →, Romania .... 52 D6 46 42N 21 17 E
Crişul Negru →, Romania .. 52 D6 46 42N 21 16 E
Crişul Repede →, Romania .. 52 D6 46 55N 20 59 E
Crittenden, U.S.A. 157 F12 38 47N 84 36W
Crivitz, Germany .... 30 B7 53 34N 11 39 E
Crixás, Brazil .... 171 D1 14 27 S 49 10 E
Crna →, Macedonia ...... 50 E5 41 33N 21 59 E
Crna Gora = Montenegro □,
  Yugoslavia .... 50 D3 42 40N 19 20 E
Crna Gora, Macedonia .... 50 D5 42 10N 21 30 E
Crna Reka = Crna →, Macedonia .. 50 E5 41 33N 21 59 E
Crna Trava, Serbia, Yug. .... 50 C6 42 49N 22 19 E
Crni Drim →, Macedonia .. 50 E4 41 17N 20 40 E
Crni Timok →, Serbia, Yug. .. 50 C6 43 53N 22 15 E
Crnoljeva Planina, Kosovo, Yug. .. 50 D5 42 20N 21 0 E
Črnomelj, Slovenia ...... 45 C12 45 33N 15 10 E
Croagh Patrick, Ireland 23 C2 53 46N 9 40W
Croajingolong Nat. Park △, Australia .. 129 F8 37 45 S 149 26 E
Croatia ■, Europe ...... 45 C13 45 20N 16 0 E
Crocker, Canada 156 G4 37 57N 92 16W
Crocker, Banjaran, Malaysia .. 85 A5 5 40N 116 30 E
Crocker, Cerro, Ecuador .... 172 a 0 36 S 90 21W
Crockett, U.S.A. 155 K7 31 19N 95 27W
Crocodile = Krokodil →, Mozam. .. 117 D5 25 14 S 32 18 E
Crocodile Is., Australia .... 126 A1 11 43 S 134 58 E
Crocq, France .... 28 C6 45 52N 2 21 E
Crodo, Italy .... 44 B5 46 13N 8 19 E
Crohy Hd., Ireland 23 B3 54 55N 8 26W
Croisette, C., France ...... 29 E9 43 14N 5 22 E
Croisic, Pte. du, France 26 E4 47 19N 2 31W
Croix, L. La, Canada 140 C1 48 20N 92 15W
Croker, C., Australia ...... 124 B5 10 58 S 132 35 E
Croker, C., Canada 150 B4 44 58N 80 59W
Croker I., Australia ...... 124 B5 11 12 S 132 32 E
Cromarty, U.K. 22 D4 57 40N 4 2W
Cromer, U.K. .... 20 E9 52 56N 1 17 E
Cromwell, N.Z. .... 131 F4 45 3 S 169 14 E
Cromwell, U.S.A. 151 E12 41 36N 72 39W
Cronat, France .... 27 F10 46 43N 3 40 E
Crook, U.K. 20 C6 54 43N 1 45W
Crooked →, Canada 142 C4 54 50N 122 54W
Crooked →, U.S.A. 158 D3 44 32N 121 16W
Crooked Creek, U.S.A. 144 F8 61 52N 158 7W
Crooked I., Bahamas 165 B5 22 50N 74 10W
Crooked Island Passage, Bahamas .. 165 B5 22 55N 74 35W
Crookston, Minn., U.S.A. .. 154 B6 47 47N 96 37W
Crookston, Nebr., U.S.A. .. 154 D4 42 56N 100 45W
Crookwell, Australia ...... 129 E8 34 28 S 149 24 E
Cropane-Micone, Riserva Statale △,
  Italy .... 47 D9 38 31N 16 18 E
Crosby, N. Dak., U.S.A. 154 A3 48 55N 103 18W
Crosby, Pa., U.S.A. 150 E6 41 45N 78 23W
Crosbyton, U.S.A. 155 J4 33 40N 101 14W
Crosía, Italy .... 47 C9 39 35N 16 45 E
Cross →, Nigeria .... 113 E6 4 42N 8 21 E
Cross City, U.S.A. 153 F6 29 38N 83 7W
Cross Fell, U.K. 20 C5 54 43N 2 28W
Cross L., Canada 143 C9 54 45N 97 30W
Cross Lake, Canada 143 C9 54 37N 97 47W
Cross River □, Nigeria .... 113 D6 6 0N 8 0 E
Cross River Nat. Park △, Nigeria .. 113 D6 5 50N 9 50 E
Cross Sound, U.S.A. 144 H14 58 0N 135 0W
Cross Timbers, U.S.A. 156 F3 38 1N 93 14W
Crossett, U.S.A. 155 J9 33 8N 91 58W
Crosshaven, Ireland 23 E3 51 47N 8 17W
Crossley, Mt., N.Z. ...... 131 C7 42 50 S 172 5 E
Crossville, Ill., U.S.A. 157 F8 38 10N 88 4W
Crossville, Tenn., U.S.A. .. 149 G3 35 57N 85 2W
Croswell, U.S.A. 150 C2 43 16N 82 37W
Croton-on-Hudson, U.S.A. .. 151 E11 41 12N 73 55W
Crotone, Italy .... 47 C10 39 5N 17 8 E
Crow →, Canada 142 B4 59 41N 124 20W
Crow Agency, U.S.A. 158 D10 45 36N 107 28W
Crow Hd., Ireland 23 E1 51 35N 10 9W
Crowdy Bay Nat. Park △, Australia .. 129 A10 31 45 S 152 45 E
Crowell, U.S.A. 155 J5 33 59N 99 43W
Crowl Cr. →, Australia .... 129 B6 32 0 S 145 30 E
Crowley, U.S.A. 155 K8 30 13N 92 22W
Crowley, L., U.S.A. 160 H8 37 35N 118 42W
Crown I., Papua N. G. .... 132 C4 5 7 S 145 8 E
Crown Point, Ind., U.S.A. .. 157 C9 41 25N 87 22W
Crown Point, N.Y., U.S.A. .. 151 C11 43 57N 73 26W
Crown Pt., Trin. & Tob. 169 E10 11 18N 60 51W
Crownpoint, U.S.A. 159 J9 35 41N 108 9W
Crows Landing, U.S.A. 160 H5 37 23N 121 6W
Crows Nest, Australia .... 127 D5 27 16 S 152 4 E
Crowsnest Pass, Canada .. 142 D6 49 40N 114 40W
Croydon, Australia ...... 126 B3 18 13 S 142 14 E
Croydon □, U.K. 21 F7 51 22N 0 5W
Crozet, Is., Ind. Oc. ...... 121 J4 46 27 S 52 0 E
Crozon, France 26 D2 48 15N 4 30W
Cruces, Punta, Colombia .. 168 B2 6 39N 77 32W
Cruz, C., Cuba 164 C4 19 50N 77 50W
Cruz Alta, Brazil .... 175 B5 28 45 S 53 40W
Cruz Bay, U.S. Virgin Is. .. 165 e 18 20N 64 48W
Cruz das Almas, Brazil .... 171 D4 12 0 S 39 6W
Cruz de Incio, Spain 42 C3 42 34N 7 21W
Cruz del Eje, Argentina .... 174 C3 30 45 S 64 50W
Cruzeiro, Brazil .... 171 F2 22 33 S 45 0W
Cruzeiro do Oeste, Brazil .. 173 A5 23 46 S 53 4W
Cruzeiro do Sul, Brazil .... 172 B3 7 35 S 72 35W
Cry L., Canada 142 B3 58 45N 129 0W
Crystal B., U.S.A. 153 G7 28 50N 82 45W
Crystal Bay, U.S.A. 160 F7 39 15N 120 0W
Crystal Brook, Australia .. 128 B3 33 21 S 138 12 E
Crystal City, Mo., U.S.A. .. 156 F6 38 13N 90 23W
Crystal City, Tex., U.S.A. .. 155 L5 28 41N 99 50W

Crystal Falls, U.S.A. 148 B1 46 5N 88 20W
Crystal Lake, Fla., U.S.A. .. 152 E4 30 26N 85 42W
Crystal Lake, Ill., U.S.A. .. 157 B8 42 14N 88 19W
Crystal River, U.S.A. 153 G7 28 54N 82 35W
Crystal Springs, U.S.A. 155 K9 31 59N 90 21W
Csenger, Hungary .... 52 C7 47 50N 22 42 E
Csongrád, Hungary ...... 52 D5 46 43N 20 12 E
Csongrád □, Hungary .... 52 D5 46 32N 20 15 E
Csorna, Hungary .... 52 C2 47 38N 17 18 E
Csurgo, Hungary .... 52 D2 46 16N 17 9 E
Cu Lao Hon, Vietnam ...... 87 G7 10 54N 108 18 E
Cua Rao, Vietnam .... 86 C5 19 16N 104 27 E
Cuácua →, Mozam. ...... 119 F4 17 54 S 37 0 E
Cuále, Angola .... 115 D3 8 22 S 16 10 E
Cuale →, Angola .... 115 D3 8 29 S 15 1 E
Cuamato, Angola .... 116 B2 17 2 S 15 7 E
Cuamba, Mozam. .... 119 E4 14 45 S 36 22 E
Cuando, Angola .... 115 E3 14 34 S 19 1 E
Cuando →, Angola ...... 115 F4 17 30 S 23 15 E
Cuando Cubango □, Angola .. 116 B3 16 25 S 20 0 E
Cuangar, Angola .... 116 B2 17 36 S 18 39 E
Cuango = Kwango →, Dem. Rep. of
  the Congo .... 114 C3 3 14 S 17 22 E
Cuango, Lunda Norte, Angola .. 115 D3 9 8 S 18 3 E
Cuango, Mexico, Angola .. 115 E3 6 20 S 16 42 E
Cuango, Uíge, Angola .... 115 D3 6 15 S 16 42 E
Cuanza →, Angola ...... 115 D2 9 21 S 13 9 E
Cuanza Norte □, Angola .. 115 D2 8 50 S 14 30 E
Cuanza Sul □, Angola .... 115 E2 10 50 S 14 50 E
Cuao →, Venezuela 168 C4 4 55N 67 40W
Cuarto →, Argentina ...... 174 C3 33 25 S 63 2W
Cuatir →, Angola .... 115 F3 17 1 S 18 56 E
Cuatrociénegas, Mexico .. 162 B4 26 59N 102 5W
Cuauhtémoc, Mexico 162 B3 28 25N 106 52W
Cuba, Portugal 43 G3 38 10N 7 54W
Cuba, N.J., U.S.A. 156 F8 38 4N 91 24W
Cuba, N. Mex., U.S.A. 159 J10 36 1N 107 4W
Cuba, N.Y., U.S.A. 150 D6 42 13N 78 17W
Cuba ■, W. Indies 164 B4 22 0N 79 0W
Cuba City, U.S.A. 156 B6 42 36N 90 26W
Cubal, Angola .... 115 E2 12 26 S 14 3 E
Cubal →, Angola .... 115 E2 12 13 S 13 39 E
Cubango →, Africa ...... 116 B3 18 50 S 22 25 E
Cubanja, Angola .... 115 E4 14 49 S 21 20 E
Cubia, Angola .... 115 F4 15 53 S 22 13 E
Çubuk, Turkey .... 100 B5 40 14N 33 3 E
Cuc Phuong Nat. Park △, Vietnam .. 86 B5 20 17N 105 38 E
Cuchi, Angola .... 115 E3 14 37 S 16 58 E
Cuchi →, Angola .... 115 F3 15 13 S 17 20 E
Cuchillo-Có, Argentina .... 176 A4 38 20 S 64 37W
Cuchivero →, Venezuela .. 168 B4 5 40N 66 10W
Cuchumatanes, Sierra de los,
  Guatemala 164 C1 15 35N 91 25W
Cuckfield, U.K. 21 F7 51 1N 0 8W
Cucui, Brazil 168 C4 1 12N 66 50W
Cucumbi, Angola .... 115 E3 10 17 S 19 1 E
Cucurpe, Mexico 162 A2 30 20N 110 43W
Cucurrupí, Colombia 168 C2 4 23N 76 56W
Cúcuta, Colombia 168 B3 7 54N 72 31W
Cudahy, U.S.A. 157 B9 42 58N 87 52W
Cudalbi, Romania .... 53 E12 45 46N 27 41 E
Cuddalore, India .... 95 J4 11 46N 79 45 E
Cuddapah, India .... 95 G4 14 30N 78 47 E
Cuddapan, L., Australia .. 126 D3 25 45 S 141 26 E
Cudgewa, Australia ...... 129 D7 36 10 S 147 42 E
Cudillero, Spain 42 B4 43 33N 6 9W
Cue, Australia .... 125 E2 27 25 S 117 54 E
Cuebe →, Angola .... 115 F3 15 46 S 17 32 E
Cuéllar, Spain 42 D6 41 23N 4 21W
Cuemba, Angola .... 115 E3 11 50 S 17 42 E
Cuenca, Ecuador .... 168 D2 2 50 S 79 9W
Cuenca, Spain 40 E2 40 5N 2 10W
Cuenca □, Spain 40 F3 40 0N 2 0W
Cuenca, Serranía de, Spain .. 40 F3 39 55N 1 50W
Cuenca Alta del Manzanares, Parque
  Regional de △, Spain .. 42 E7 40 40N 3 55W
Cuerdo del Pozo, Embalse de la,
  Spain 40 D2 41 51N 2 44W
Cuernavaca, Mexico 163 D5 18 55N 99 15W
Cuero, U.S.A. 155 L6 29 6N 97 17W
Cuers, France .... 29 E10 43 14N 6 5 E
Cueva de la Quebrado del Toro,
  Parque Nac. △, Venezuela .. 165 D6 10 46N 69 3W
Cuevas, Cerro, Bolivia .... 173 E4 22 0 S 65 12W
Cuevas del Almanzora, Spain .. 41 H3 37 18N 1 58W
Cuevo, Bolivia .... 173 E5 20 15 S 63 30W
Cugir, Romania .... 53 E8 45 48N 23 25 E
Cugnaux, France .... 28 E5 43 32N 1 20 E
Cuhai-Bakony →, Hungary .. 52 C2 47 35N 17 54 E
Cuiabá, Brazil .... 173 D6 15 30 S 56 0W
Cuiabá →, Brazil .... 173 D6 17 5 S 56 36W
Cuihangcun, China ...... 69 G10 22 29N 113 32 E
Cuijk, Neths. .... 24 C5 51 44N 5 50 E
Cuilco, Guatemala 164 C1 15 24N 91 58W
Cuillin Hills, U.K. 22 D2 57 13N 6 15W
Cuillin Sd., U.K. 22 D2 57 4N 6 20W
Cuilo = Kwilu →, Dem. Rep. of
  the Congo .... 115 C3 3 22 S 17 22 E
Cuilo, Angola .... 115 D3 8 12 S 19 28 E
Cuilo-Futa, Angola ...... 115 D3 6 23 S 18 55 E
Cuíma, Angola .... 115 E3 13 25 S 15 45 E
Cuiseaux, France .... 27 F12 46 30N 5 22 E
Cuité, Brazil .... 170 C4 6 29 S 36 9W
Cuito →, Angola .... 116 B3 18 1 S 20 48 E
Cuito Cuanavale, Angola .. 115 F3 15 10 S 19 10 E
Cuitzeo, L. de, Mexico 162 D4 19 55N 101 5W
Cuiuni →, Brazil .... 169 D5 0 45 S 63 7W
Cuivre →, U.S.A. 156 F6 39 8N 90 44W
Cuivre, West Fork →, U.S.A. .. 156 E6 39 2N 90 58W
Cujmir, Romania .... 52 F7 44 13N 22 57 E
Cukai, Malaysia .... 87 K4 4 13N 103 25 E
Culasi, Phil. .... 81 F4 11 26N 122 3 E
Culbertson, U.S.A. 154 A2 48 9N 104 31W
Culburra, N.S.W., Australia .. 129 C9 34 56 S 150 46 E
Culburra, S. Austral., Australia .. 129 C3 35 41 S 147 3 E
Culcairn, Australia ...... 129 C8 35 41 S 147 3 E
Culebra, Isla de, Puerto Rico .. 165 d 18 19N 65 18W
Culebra, Sierra de la, Spain .. 42 D4 41 55N 6 20W
Culfa, Azerbaijan .... 101 C11 38 57N 45 38 E
Culgoa →, Australia ...... 128 C5 34 44 S 143 6 E
Culgoa, Australia .... 127 D4 29 56 S 146 20 E
Culgoa Flood Plain Nat. Park △,
  Australia .... 127 A4 28 58 S 147 5 E
Culiacán, Mexico 162 C3 24 50N 107 23W
Culiacán →, Mexico 162 C3 24 30N 107 42W
Culik, Indonesia .... 79 J18 8 21 S 115 37 E
Culion, Phil. .... 81 F3 11 54N 119 58 E
Culion I., Phil. .... 81 F2 11 50N 120 0 E
Culiseu →, Brazil .... 173 C7 12 14 S 53 17W
Cúllar, Spain 43 H8 37 35N 2 34W
Cullarin Ra., Australia .... 129 C8 34 30 S 149 30 E
Cullen, U.K. 22 D6 57 42N 2 49W
Cullen Bullen, Australia .. 129 C9 33 18 S 150 2 E
Cullen Pt., Australia ...... 126 A3 11 57 S 141 54 E
Cullera, Spain 41 F4 39 9N 0 17W
Cullman, U.S.A. 149 H2 34 11N 86 51W
Culloden, U.S.A. 152 C5 32 52N 84 6W
Cullom, U.S.A. 157 D8 40 53N 88 16W
Cullompton, U.K. 21 G4 50 51N 3 24W
Culo →, Angola .... 115 D3 6 13 S 15 34 E
Culoz, France .... 29 C9 45 47N 5 46 E
Culpeper, U.S.A. 148 F7 38 30N 78 0W
Culuene →, Brazil .... 173 C7 12 56 S 52 51W

Culver, *U.S.A.* **157 C10** 41 13N 86 25W
Culver, Pt., *Australia* .... **125 F3** 32 54 S 124 43 E
Culverden, *N.Z.* .... **131 C7** 42 47 S 172 49 E
Culverton, *U.S.A.* **152 B7** 33 19N 82 54W
Cuma, *Angola* .... **115 E3** 12 52 S 15 5 E
Cumaná, *Venezuela* **169 A5** 10 30N 64 5W
Cumaovası, *Turkey* .... **49 C9** 38 15N 27 9 E
Cumare, *Colombia* .... **168 C3** -0'49N 72 32W
Cumari, *Brazil* .... **171 E2** 18 16 S 48 11W
Cumberland, *B.C., Canada* ... **142 D4** 49 40N 125 0W
Cumberland, *Ont., Canada* ... **151 A9** 45 29N 75 24W
Cumberland, *Iowa, U.S.A.* ... **156 C2** 41 16N 94 52W
Cumberland, *Md., U.S.A.* **148 F6** 39 39N 78 46W
Cumberland →, *U.S.A.* **149 G2** 36 15N 87 0W
Cumberland, C., *Vanuatu* .... **133 D4** 14 39 S 166 37 E
Cumberland, L., *U.S.A.* **149 G3** 36 57N 84 55W
Cumberland Gap Nat. Historic
  Park △, *U.S.A.* **149 G4** 36 36N 83 40W
Cumberland I., *U.S.A.* **152 E8** 30 50N 81 25W
Cumberland Is., *Australia* .... **126 J7** 20 35 S 149 10 E
Cumberland Island Nat. Seashore △,
  U.S.A. **152 E8** 30 12N 81 24W
Cumberland L., *Canada* **143 C8** 54 3N 102 18W
Cumberland Pen., *Canada* **139 B13** 67 0N 64 0W
Cumberland Plateau, *U.S.A.* . **149 H3** 36 0N 85 0W
Cumberland Sd., *Canada* **139 B13** 65 30N 66 0W
Cumbernauld, *U.K.* **22 F5** 55 57N 3 58W
Cumbira, *Angola* .... **115 E3** 12 11 S 15 8 E
Cumborah, *Australia* .... **127 D4** 29 40 S 147 45 E
Cumbres de Majalca, Parque Nac. △,
  Mexico **162 B3** 28 52N 106 24W
Cumbres de Monterrey, Parque
  Nac. △, *Mexico* **162 B4** 25 40N 100 35W
Cumbres Mayores, *Spain* **43 G4** 38 4N 6 39W
Cumbria □, *U.K.* **20 C5** 54 42N 2 52W
Cumbrian Mts., *U.K.* **20 C5** 54 30N 3 0W
Cumbum, *India* .... **95 G4** 15 40N 79 10 E
Cuminá, *Brazil* .... **169 D6** 1 57 S 56 2W
Cuminá, *Brazil* .... **169 D6** 1 30 S 56 0W
Cuminapanema →, *Brazil* ..... **170 D7** 1 9 S 54 54W
Cumming, C., *Chile* .... **172 b** 27 6 S 109 14W
Cummings Mt., *U.S.A.* **161 K8** 35 2N 118 34W
Cummins, *Australia* .... **127 E2** 34 16 S 135 43 E
Cumnock, *Australia* .... **129 B8** 32 59 S 148 46 E
Cumnock, *U.K.* **22 F4** 55 28N 4 17W
Cumpas, *Mexico* **162 B3** 30 0N 109 48W
Cumplida, Pta., *Canary Is.* .. **9 e1** 28 50N 17 48W
Çumra, *Turkey* .... **100 D5** 37 34N 32 45 E
Cuncumén, *Chile* .... **172 C1** 31 53 S 70 38W
Cunderdin, *Australia* .... **125 F2** 31 37 S 117 12 E
Cundinamarca □, *Colombia* ... **168 C3** 5 0N 74 0W
Cunene □, *Angola* .... **115 F3** 16 30 S 15 0 E
Cunene →, *Angola* .... **116 B1** 17 20 S 11 50 E
Cúneo, *Italy* .... **44 D4** 44 23N 7 32 E
Çüngüş, *Turkey* .... **96 B3** 38 13N 39 17 E
Cunhinga, *Angola* .... **115 E3** 12 11 S 16 47 E
Cunillera, I. = Sa Conillera, *Spain* ... **38 D1** 38 59N 1 13 E
Cunjamba, *Angola* .... **115 F4** 15 27 S 20 10 E
Cunlhat, *France* .... **28 C7** 45 38N 3 32 E
Cunnamulla, *Australia* .... **127 D4** 28 2 S 145 38 E
Cunningham, *Bahamas* .... **9 b** 25 5N 77 26W
Cuorgnè, *Italy* .... **44 C4** 45 23N 7 39 E
Cupar, *Canada* **143 C8** 50 57N 104 10W
Cupar, *U.K.* **22 E5** 56 19N 3 1W
Cupcini, *Moldova* .... **53 B12** 48 6N 27 23 E
Cupica, G. de, *Colombia* **168 B2** 6 25N 77 30W
Ćuprija, *Serbia, Yug.* .... **50 C5** 43 57N 21 26 E
Curaçá, *Brazil* .... **170 C4** 8 59 S 39 54W
Curaçao, *Neth. Ant.* **165 D6** 12 10N 69 0W
Curacautín, *Chile* .... **176 A2** 38 26 S 71 53W
Curahuara de Carangas, *Bolivia* **172 D4** 17 52 S 68 26W
Curanilahue, *Chile* .... **174 D1** 37 29 S 73 28W
Curaray →, *Peru* .... **168 D3** 2 20 S 74 5W
Curatabaca, *Venezuela* **169 B5** 6 19N 62 51W
Cure →, *France* .... **27 E10** 47 40N 3 41 E
Curepipe, *Mauritius* .... **121 d** 20 19 S 57 31 E
Curepto, *Chile* .... **174 D1** 35 8 S 72 1W
Curiapo, *Venezuela* **169 B5** 8 33N 61 5W
Curicó, *Chile* .... **174 C1** 34 55 S 71 20W
Curicuriari →, *Brazil* .... **168 D4** 0 10 S 66 50W
Curieuse, *Seychelles* .... **121 b** 4 15 S 55 44 E
Curimatá, *Brazil* .... **170 D3** 10 3 S 44 17W
Curinga, *Italy* .... **47 D9** 38 49N 16 19 E
Curiplaya, *Colombia* **168 C3** 0 16N 74 52W
Curitiba, *Brazil* .... **175 B6** 25 20 S 49 10W
Curitibanos, *Brazil* .... **175 B5** 27 18 S 50 36W
Curlewis, *Australia* .... **129 A9** 31 7 S 150 16 E
Curoca →, *Angola* .... **115 F2** 15 43 S 11 55 E
Currabubula, *Australia* ...... **129 A9** 31 16 S 150 44 E
Currais Novos, *Brazil* .... **170 C4** 6 13 S 36 30W
Curral Velho, *C. Verde Is.* ... **9 j** 16 8N 22 48W
Curralinho, *Brazil* .... **170 B2** 1 45 S 49 46W
Currant, *U.S.A.* **158 G6** 38 51N 115 32W
Curraweena, *Australia* .... **129 A6** 30 47 S 145 54 E
Currawinya Nat. Park △, *Australia* **127 D3** 28 55 S 144 27 E
Current →, *U.S.A.* **155 G9** 36 15N 90 55W
Currie, *Australia* .... **127 C3** 39 56 S 143 53 E
Currie, *U.S.A.* **158 F6** 40 16N 114 45W
Cursole, *Somali Rep.* .... **120 D3** 2 14N 45 25 E
Curtea de Argeş, *Romania* .... **53 E9** 45 12N 24 42 E
Curtici, *Romania* .... **52 D6** 46 21N 21 18 E
Curtis, *U.S.A.* **154 E4** 40 38N 100 31W
Curtis Group, *Australia* ...... **127 C4** 39 30 S 146 37 E
Curtis I., *Australia* .... **126 C5** 23 35 S 151 10 E
Curuá →, *Pará, Brazil* .... **169 D7** 2 24 S 54 5W
Curuá →, *Pará, Brazil* .... **173 B7** 5 23 S 54 22W
Curuá, I., *Brazil* **170 A1** 0 48N 50 10W
Curuaés →, *Brazil* .... **173 B7** 7 10 S 54 45W
Curuaí, *Brazil* .... **169 D6** 2 15 S 55 29W
Curuápanema →, *Brazil* ...... **169 D6** 2 25 S 55 2W
Curuçá, *Brazil* .... **170 B2** 0 43 S 47 50W
Curuçá →, *Brazil* .... **172 B3** 4 27 S 71 23W
Curuguaty, *Paraguay* .... **175 A4** 24 31 S 55 42W
Çürük, *Indonesia* .... **84 C2** 4 26 S 102 13 E
Curupira, Serra, *S. Amer.* **169 C5** 1 25N 64 30W
Cururu →, *Brazil* .... **173 B6** 7 12 S 58 3W
Cururupu, *Brazil* .... **170 B3** 1 50 S 44 50W
Curuzú Cuatiá, *Argentina* .... **174 B4** 29 50 S 58 5W
Curvelo, *Brazil* .... **171 E3** 18 45 S 44 27W
Cushing, *U.S.A.* **155 H6** 35 59N 96 46W
Cushing, Mt., *Canada* **142 B3** 57 35N 126 57W
Cusihuiriáchic, *Mexico* **162 B3** 28 10N 106 50W
Cusna, Mte., *Italy* .... **44 D7** 44 17N 10 23 E
Cussabat = Al Qaşabāt, *Libya* . **108 B2** 32 39N 14 1 E
Cusset, *France* .... **27 F10** 46 8N 3 28 E
Cusseta, *U.S.A.* **152 C5** 32 18N 84 47W
Cusso, Sa. do, *Angola* .... **115 D2** 6 50 S 16 5 E
Custer, *U.S.A.* **154 D3** 43 46N 103 36W
Cut Bank, *U.S.A.* **158 B7** 48 38N 112 20W
Cutchogue, *U.S.A.* **151 E12** 41 1N 72 30W
Cuervo, *Peru* .... **172 B2** 6 25 S 78 55W
Cuthbert, *U.S.A.* **152 D5** 31 46N 84 48W
Cutler, *U.S.A.* **160 J7** 36 31N 119 17W
Cutler Ridge, *U.S.A.* **153 K9** 25 35N 80 20W
Cutlerville, *U.S.A.* **157 B11** 42 50N 85 40W
Cutral-Có, *Argentina* .... **176 A3** 38 36 S 69 15W
Cutro, *Italy* .... **47 C9** 39 2N 16 59 E
Cuttaburra →, *Australia* ..... **127 D3** 29 43 S 144 22 E
Cuttack, *India* .... **94 D7** 20 25N 85 57 E
Cuva →, *Angola* .... **115 E2** 11 52 S 14 52 E
Cuvier, C., *Australia* .... **125 D1** 24 20 S 113 40 E
Cuvier I., *N.Z.* .... **130 C4** 36 27 S 175 50 E
Cuxhaven, *Germany* .... **30 B4** 53 51N 8 41 E

Cuyabeno, *Ecuador* .... **168 D2** 0 16 S 75 53W
Cuyahoga Falls, *U.S.A.* **150 E3** 41 8N 81 29W
Cuyahoga Valley Nat. Park △,
  U.S.A. **150 E3** 41 15N 81 33W
Cuyapo, *Phil.* .... **80 D3** 15 46N 120 40 E
Cuyo, *Phil.* .... **81 F3** 10 50N 121 5 E
Cuyo East Pass, *Phil.* .... **81 F3** 10 48N 121 28 E
Cuyo I., *Phil.* .... **81 F3** 10 51N 121 2 E
Cuyo Islands, *Phil.* .... **81 F3** 11 4N 120 57 E
Cuyo West Pass, *Phil.* .... **81 F3** 11 0N 120 30 E
Cuyuni →, *Guyana* **169 B6** 6 23N 58 41W
Cuzco, *Bolivia* .... **172 E4** 20 0 S 66 50W
Cuzco, *Peru* .... **172 C3** 13 32 S 72 0W
Cuzco □, *Peru* .... **172 C3** 13 31 S 71 59W
Cvrsnica, *Bos.-H.* .... **42 G2** 43 36N 17 35 E
Cwmbran, *U.K.* **21 F4** 51 39N 3 2W
Cyangugu, *Rwanda* .... **118 C2** 2 29 S 28 54 E
Cybinka, *Poland* .... **55 F1** 52 12N 14 46 E
Cyclades = Kikládhes, *Greece* . **48 E6** 37 0N 24 30 E
Cygnet, *Australia* .... **127 D4** 43 8 S 147 1 E
Cynthiana, *U.S.A.* **157 F12** 38 23N 84 18W
Cypress Hills, *Canada* **143 D7** 49 40N 109 30W
Cypress Hills Prov. Park ⌂, *Canada* **143 D7** 49 40N 109 30W
Cyprus ■, *Asia* .... **39 F9** 35 0N 33 0 E
Cyrenaica, *Libya* .... **108 B4** 27 0N 23 0 E
Cyrene = Shaḥḥāt, *Libya* ..... **108 B4** 32 48N 21 54 E
Cyrene, *Libya* .... **108 B4** 32 48N 21 54 E
Czaplinek, *Poland* .... **54 E3** 53 34N 16 14 E
Czar, *Canada* **143 C6** 52 27N 110 50W
Czarna →, *Łódzkie, Poland* .. **55 G6** 51 18N 19 55 E
Czarna →, *Świętokrzyskie, Poland* **55 H8** 50 28N 21 11 E
Czarna Białostocka, *Poland* .. **55 E10** 53 18N 23 17 E
Czarna Woda, *Poland* .... **54 E5** 53 51N 18 6 E
Czarne, *Poland* .... **54 E3** 53 42N 16 58 E
Czarnków, *Poland* .... **55 F3** 52 55N 16 38 E
Czech Rep. ■, *Europe* .... **34 B8** 50 0N 15 0 E
Czechowice-Dziedzice, *Poland* **55 J5** 49 54N 18 59 E
Czempiń, *Poland* .... **55 F3** 52 9N 16 43 E
Czeremcha, *Poland* .... **55 F10** 52 31N 23 21 E
Czerniejewo, *Poland* .... **55 F4** 52 26N 17 30 E
Czernowitz = Chernivtsi, *Ukraine* **59 H3** 48 15N 25 52 E
Czersk, *Poland* .... **54 E4** 53 46N 17 58 E
Czerwień, *Poland* .... **55 F2** 52 1N 15 23 E
Czerwionka-Leszczyny, *Poland* . **55 H5** 50 7N 18 37 E
Częstochowa, *Poland* .... **55 H6** 50 49N 19 7 E
Człopa, *Poland* .... **54 E3** 53 6N 16 6 E
Człuchów, *Poland* .... **54 E4** 53 41N 17 22 E
Czyżew-Osada, *Poland* .... **55 F9** 52 48N 22 19 E

D

Da →, *Vietnam* .... **76 G5** 21 15N 105 20 E
Da Hinggan Ling, *China* ...... **69 B7** 48 0N 121 0 E
Da Lat, *Vietnam* .... **87 G7** 11 56N 108 25 E
Da Nang, *Vietnam* .... **86 D7** 16 4N 108 13 E
Da Qaidam, *China* .... **68 C4** 37 50N 95 15 E
Da Yunhe →, *China* .... **75 G11** 34 25N 120 5 E
Da'an, *China* .... **75 B13** 45 30N 124 7 E
Daan Viljoen Game Park △,
  Namibia .... **116 C2** 22 2 S 16 45 E
Daanbantayan, *Phil.* .... **81 F5** 11 17N 124 2 E
Dab'a, Ras el, *Egypt* .... **106 H6** 31 3N 28 31 E
Daba Shan, *China* .... **74 B7** 32 0N 109 0 E
Dabai, *Nigeria* .... **113 C6** 11 25N 5 15 E
Dabajuro, *Venezuela* **168 A3** 11 2N 70 40W
Dabakala, *Ivory C.* **112 D4** 8 15N 4 20W
Dabaro, *Somali Rep.* .... **120 C3** 6 21N 48 43 E
Dabas, *Hungary* .... **52 C4** 47 11N 19 19 E
Dabat, *Ethiopia* .... **107 E4** 12 58N 37 41 E
Dabbagh, Jabal, *Si. Arabia* ... **96 E2** 27 52N 35 45 E
Dabeiba, *Colombia* **168 B2** 7 1N 76 16W
Dabhoi, *India* .... **92 H5** 22 10N 73 20 E
Dąbie, *Poland* .... **55 F5** 52 5N 18 50 E
Dabie Shan, *China* .... **77 B10** 31 20N 115 20 E
Dabilda, *Cameroon* .... **113 C7** 12 45N 14 35 E
Dabilda, Cent. Amer. .... **109 F2** 12 14N 14 34 E
Dabnou, *Niger* .... **113 C6** 14 10N 5 22 E
Dabo = Pasirkuning, *Indonesia* **84 C2** 0 30 S 104 33 E
Dabola, *Guinea* **112 C2** 10 50N 11 5W
Dabou, *Ivory C.* **112 D4** 5 20N 4 23W
Daboya, *Ghana* **113 D4** 9 30N 1 20W
Dąbrowa Białostocka, *Poland* . **54 E10** 53 40N 23 21 E
Dąbrowa Górnicza, *Poland* ... **55 H6** 50 15N 19 10 E
Dąbrowa Tarnowska, *Poland* .. **55 H7** 50 10N 20 59 E
Dabu, *China* .... **77 E11** 24 22N 116 41 E
Dabugam, *India* .... **94 E6** 19 27N 82 26 E
Dabung, *Malaysia* .... **87 K4** 5 23N 102 1 E
Dabus →, *Ethiopia* .... **107 E4** 10 48N 35 10 E
Dacato →, *Ethiopia* .... **107 F5** 7 25N 42 40 E
Dacca = Dhaka, *Bangla.* ..... **90 D3** 23 43N 90 26 E
Dacca = Dhaka □, *Bangla.* ... **90 C3** 24 25N 90 25 E
Dachau, *Germany* .... **31 G7** 48 15N 11 26 E
Dachstein, Hoher, *Austria* .... **34 D6** 47 28N 13 35 E
Dačice, *Czech Rep.* .... **33 F8** 49 5N 15 26 E
Dacula, *U.S.A.* **152 B6** 33 59N 83 54W
Dadanawa, *Guyana* **169 C6** 2 50N 59 30W
Daday, *Turkey* .... **100 B5** 41 28N 33 27 E
Dade City, *U.S.A.* **153 G7** 28 22N 82 11W
Dadès, Oued →, *Morocco* **110 B3** 30 58N 6 44W
Dadeville, *U.S.A.* **152 C4** 32 50N 85 46W
Dadhar, *Pakistan* .... **92 E2** 29 28N 67 39 E
Dadiya, *Nigeria* .... **113 D7** 9 35N 11 24 E
Dadra = Achalpur, *India* ...... **94 D3** 21 22N 77 32 E
Dadra & Nagar Haveli □, *India* **91 D1** 20 5N 73 0 E
Dadri = Charkhi Dadri, *India* . **92 E7** 28 37N 76 17 E
Dadu, *Pakistan* .... **91 D2** 26 45N 67 45 E
Dadu He →, *China* .... **76 C4** 29 31N 103 46 E
Daet, *Phil.* .... **80 D4** 14 2N 122 55 E
Dafang, *China* .... **76 D5** 27 9N 105 39 E
Dağ, *Turkey* .... **49 D12** 37 12N 30 31 E
Dagali, *Norway* .... **18 D5** 60 25N 8 28 E
Dagana, *Senegal* **112 B1** 16 30N 15 35W
Dagash, *Sudan* .... **106 D3** 19 19N 33 25 E
Dagestan □, *Russia* .... **61 J8** 42 30N 47 0 E
Dagestanskiye Ogni, *Russia* ... **61 J9** 42 6N 48 12 E
Dagg Sd., *N.Z.* .... **131 F1** 45 23 S 166 45 E
Daggett, *U.S.A.* **161 L10** 34 52N 116 52W
Daghestan Republic = Dagestan □,
  Russia .... **106 D3** 42 30N 47 0 E
Daghfeli, *Sudan* .... **106 D3** 19 18N 32 40 E
Dağlıq Qarabağ = Nagorno-
  Karabakh □, *Azerbaijan* ..... **101 C12** 39 55N 46 45 E
Dagmersellen, *Switz.* .... **32 B5** 47 13N 7 59 E
Dagö = Hiiumaa, *Estonia* ..... **15 G20** 58 50N 22 45 E
Dagua, Papua N. G. .... **132 B2** 3 27 S 143 20 E
Daguan, *China* .... **76 D4** 27 43N 103 56 E
Dagupan, *Phil.* .... **80 D3** 16 3N 120 20 E
Daguragu, *Australia* .... **124 C5** 17 33 S 130 30 E
Dahab, *Egypt* .... **106 J8** 28 30N 34 31 E
Dahanu, *India* .... **94 E1** 19 58N 72 44 E
Dahivadi, *India* .... **94 F2** 17 45N 74 33 E
Dahlak Kebir, *Eritrea* .... **107 D5** 15 50N 40 10 E
Dahlak Marine Nat. Park △, *Eritrea* **107 D5** 15 40N 40 10 E
Dahlenburg, *Germany* .... **30 B6** 53 11N 10 44 E
Dahlonega, *U.S.A.* **149 H4** 34 32N 83 59W
Dahme, *Germany* .... **30 D9** 51 52N 13 25 E
Dahod, *India* .... **92 H6** 22 50N 74 15 E
Dahomey = Benin ■, *Africa* △ **113 D5** 10 0N 2 0 E
Dahong Shan, *China* .... **77 B9** 31 25N 113 0 E

Dahra, *Libya* .... **108 C3** 29 30N 17 50 E
Dahra, *Senegal* **112 B1** 15 22N 15 30W
Dahra, Massif de, *Algeria* .... **111 A5** 36 7N 1 21 E
Dahshûr, *Egypt* .... **106 J7** 29 45N 31 14 E
Dahūk, *Iraq* .... **101 D10** 36 50N 43 1 E
Daby, Nafūd ad, *Si. Arabia* ... **98 B4** 22 0N 45 25 E
Dai, *Solomon Is.* .... **133 L11** 7 54 S 160 40 E
Dai Hao, *Vietnam* .... **86 C6** 18 1N 106 25 E
Dai Shan, *China* .... **77 B14** 30 25N 122 10 E
Dai Xian, *China* .... **74 E7** 39 4N 112 58 E
Daicheng, *China* .... **74 E9** 38 42N 116 38 E
Daigo, *Japan* .... **73 A12** 36 46N 140 21 E
Daik-u, *Burma* .... **90 G6** 17 47N 96 40 E
Daimanji-San, *Japan* .... **72 A5** 36 14N 133 20 E
Daimiel, *Spain* **43 F7** 39 5N 3 35W
Daingean, *Ireland* **23 C4** 53 18N 7 17W
Dainkog, *China* .... **76 A1** 32 30N 97 58 E
Daintree, *Australia* .... **126 B4** 16 20 S 145 20 E
Daintree Nat. Park △, *Australia* **126 B4** 16 8 S 145 2 E
Daiō-Misaki, *Japan* .... **73 C8** 34 15N 136 45 E
Dair, J. ed, *Sudan* .... **107 E3** 12 27N 30 42 E
Dairût, *Egypt* .... **106 B3** 27 34N 30 43 E
Daisen-Oki Nat. Park △, *Japan* **72 B5** 35 23N 133 34 E
Daisetsu-Zan, *Japan* .... **70 C11** 43 30N 142 57 E
Daitari, *India* .... **94 D7** 21 10N 85 46 E
Daito, *Japan* .... **72 B4** 35 19N 132 58 E
Dajarra, *Australia* .... **126 C2** 21 42 S 139 30 E
Dajin Chuan →, *China* ...... **76 B3** 31 16N 101 59 E
Dak Dam, *Cambodia* .... **86 F6** 12 20N 107 21 E
Dak Nhe, *Vietnam* .... **86 E6** 15 28N 107 48 E
Dak Pek, *Vietnam* .... **86 E6** 15 4N 107 44 E
Dak Song, *Vietnam* .... **87 F6** 12 19N 107 35 E
Dak Sui, *Vietnam* .... **86 E6** 14 55N 107 43 E
Dakar, *Senegal* **112 C1** 14 34N 17 29W
Dakhin, *Bangla.* .... **90 D3** 22 30N 90 45 E
Dakhla, *W. Sahara* **110 D1** 23 50N 15 53W
Dakhla, El Wâhât el-, *Egypt* .. **106 B2** 25 30N 28 50 E
Dakingari, *Nigeria* .... **113 C5** 11 37N 4 1 E
Dakoank, *India* .... **95 L11** 7 2N 93 43 E
Dakor, *India* .... **92 H5** 22 45N 73 11 E
Dakoro, *Niger* .... **113 C6** 14 31N 6 46 E
Dakota City, *Iowa, U.S.A.* **156 B2** 42 43N 94 12W
Dakota City, *Nebr., U.S.A.* ... **154 D6** 42 25N 96 25W
Đakovica, *Kosovo, Yug.* ...... **50 D4** 42 22N 20 26 E
Đakovo, *Croatia* .... **52 E3** 45 19N 18 24 E
Dala, Lunda Sul, *Angola* ...... **115 E4** 11 3 S 20 17 E
Dala, Uíge, *Angola* .... **115 D3** 8 5 S 15 49 E
Dala, *Solomon Is.* .... **133 M11** 8 30 S 160 41 E
Dala-Cachibo, *Angola* .... **115 E2** 10 30 S 14 41 E
Dalaas, *Austria* .... **33 B10** 47 7N 10 0 E
Dalaba, *Guinea* **112 C2** 10 47N 12 12W
Dalachi, *China* .... **74 F3** 36 48N 105 0 E
Dalaguete, *Phil.* .... **81 G4** 9 46 S 123 30 E
Dalai Nur, *China* .... **74 C9** 43 20N 116 45 E
Dālakī, *Iran* .... **97 D6** 29 26N 51 17 E
Dalaman, *Turkey* .... **49 E10** 36 48N 28 47 E
Dalaman →, *Turkey* .... **49 E10** 36 41N 28 43 E
Dalandzadgad, *Mongolia* ..... **74 C3** 43 27N 104 30 E
Dalanganem Is., *Phil.* .... **81 F3** 10 40N 120 17 E
Dalap-Uliga-Darrit, *Marshall Is.* **134 G9** 7 7N 171 24 E
Dalarna, *Sweden* .... **16 D8** 61 0N 14 0 E
Dalarnas län □, *Sweden* ...... **16 C8** 61 0N 14 15 E
Dalasýsla □, *Iceland* .... **11 B4** 65 15 S 22 0W
Dalat, *Malaysia* .... **85 B4** 2 44N 111 56 E
Đălbandīn, *Pakistan* .... **91 C2** 29 0N 64 23 E
Dalbeattie, *U.K.* **22 G5** 54 56N 3 50W
Dalbeg, *Australia* .... **126 C4** 20 16 S 147 18 E
Dalbosjön, *Sweden* .... **17 F6** 58 40N 12 45 E
Dalby, *Australia* .... **127 D5** 27 10 S 151 17 E
Dalby, *Sweden* .... **17 J7** 55 40N 13 22 E
Dalby Söderskog Nationalpark △,
  Sweden .... **17 J7** 55 41N 13 21 E
Dale, *Norway* .... **18 C2** 61 22N 5 23 E
Dale, *U.S.A.* **157 F10** 38 10N 86 59W
Dale City, *U.S.A.* **148 F7** 38 38N 77 18W
Dale Hollow L., *U.S.A.* **149 G3** 36 32N 85 27W
Dalen, *Norway* .... **18 E4** 59 26N 8 0 E
Dalet, *Burma* .... **90 E4** 21 36N 93 51 E
Daletme, *Burma* .... **90 E4** 21 36N 92 46 E
Daleville, Ala., *U.S.A.* **152 D4** 31 19N 85 43W
Daleville, Ind., *U.S.A.* **157 D11** 40 7N 85 33W
Dalga, *Egypt* .... **106 B3** 27 39N 30 41 E
Dalgān, *Iran* .... **97 E8** 27 31N 59 19 E
Dalhart, *U.S.A.* **155 G3** 36 4N 102 31W
Dalhousie, *Canada* **141 C6** 48 5N 66 26W
Dalhousie, *India* .... **92 C6** 32 38N 75 58 E
Dali, Shaanxi, *China* .... **74 G5** 34 48N 109 58 E
Dali, Yunnan, *China* .... **76 E3** 25 40N 100 10 E
Dalian, *China* .... **75 E11** 38 50N 121 40 E
Daliang Shan, *China* .... **76 D4** 28 0N 102 45 E
Daling He →, *China* .... **75 D11** 40 55N 121 40 E
Dāliyat el Karmel, *Israel* ..... **103 C4** 32 43N 35 2 E
Dalj, *Croatia* .... **52 E3** 45 29N 18 59 E
Dalkeith, *U.K.* **22 F5** 55 54N 3 4W
Dallas, Ga., *U.S.A.* **152 B5** 33 55N 84 51W
Dallas, Oreg., *U.S.A.* **158 D2** 44 55N 123 19W
Dallas, Tex., *U.S.A.* **155 J6** 32 47N 96 49W
Dallas Center, *U.S.A.* **156 C2** 41 41N 93 58W
Dallas City, *U.S.A.* **156 D5** 40 38N 91 10W
Dalli, *Ethiopia* .... **107 E5** 14 14N 40 17 E
Dalmã, U.A.E. .... **97 E7** 24 30N 52 20 E
Dalmacija, *Croatia* .... **45 E13** 43 20N 17 0 E
Dalmas, L., *Canada* **45 E13** 43 20N 71 50W
Dalmatovo, *Russia* .... **64 C9** 56 16N 62 56 E
Dalmau, *India* .... **93 F9** 26 4N 81 2 E
Dalmellington, *U.K.* **22 F4** 55 19N 4 23W
Dalmeny, *Australia* .... **129 D9** 36 10 S 150 8 E
Dalnegorsk, *Russia* .... **67 E14** 44 32N 135 33 E
Dalnerechensk, *Russia* .... **67 E14** 45 50N 133 40 E
Daloa, *Ivory C.* **112 D3** 7 0N 6 30W
Dalou Shan, *China* .... **76 C6** 28 15N 107 0 E
Dalry, *U.K.* **22 F4** 55 42N 4 43W
Dalrymple, L., *Australia* ...... **126 C4** 20 40 S 147 0 E
Dalrymple, Mt., *Australia* .... **126 K6** 21 1 S 148 39 E
Dalsland, *Sweden* .... **17 F6** 58 50N 12 15 E
Dalsmynni, *Iceland* **11 C5** 64 48N 21 29W
Daltenganj, *India* .... **93 H11** 24 0N 84 4 E
Dalton, Ga., *U.S.A.* **149 H3** 34 46N 84 58W
Dalton, Mass., *U.S.A.* **151 D11** 42 28N 73 11W
Dalton, Nebr., *U.S.A.* **154 E3** 41 25N 102 58W
Dalton, Kap, *Greenland* **10 D8** 69 25N 24 3W
Dalton-in-Furness, *U.K.* **20 C4** 54 10N 3 11W
Dalupiri I., Cagayan, *Phil.* .... **80 B3** 19 5N 121 12 E
Dalupiri I., N. Samar, *Phil.* ... **81 E6** 12 25N 124 16 E
Dalvík, *Iceland* **11 B8** 65 58N 18 32W
Dalwallinu, *Australia* .... **125 F2** 30 17 S 116 40 E
Daly →, *Australia* .... **124 B5** 13 35 S 130 19 E
Daly City, *U.S.A.* **160 H4** 37 42N 122 28W
Daly L., *Canada* **143 B7** 56 32N 105 39W
Daly River, *Australia* .... **124 B5** 13 46 S 130 42 E
Daly Waters, *Australia* .... **126 B1** 16 15 S 133 24 E
Dalyan, *Turkey* .... **49 E10** 36 50N 28 38 E

Dāmaneh, *Iran* .... **97 C6** 33 1N 50 29 E
Damanganga →, *India* .... **94 D1** 20 25N 72 56 E
Damanhûr, *Egypt* .... **106 H7** 31 0N 30 30 E
Damant L., *Canada* **143 A7** 61 45N 105 5W
Damanzhuang, *China* .... **74 E9** 38 5N 116 35 E
Damar, *Indonesia* .... **82 C3** 7 7 S 128 40 E
Damara, *C.A.R.* .... **114 B3** 4 58N 18 42 E
Damaraland, *Namibia* .... **116 C2** 20 0 S 15 0 E
Damascus = Dimashq, *Syria* ... **103 B5** 33 30N 36 18 E
Damascus, *U.S.A.* **152 D5** 31 18N 84 43W
Damaturu, *Nigeria* .... **113 C7** 11 45N 11 55 E
Damāvand, *Iran* .... **97 C7** 35 47N 52 0 E
Damāvand, Qolleh-ye, *Iran* ... **97 C7** 35 56N 52 10 E
Damba, *Angola* .... **115 D3** 6 44 S 15 20 E
Dâmbovicioara, *Romania* ..... **53 E10** 45 0N 25 30 E
Dâmbovița □, *Romania* ...... **53 F11** 44 12N 26 26 E
Dâmbovița →, *Romania* ...... **53 F10** 44 28N 26 26 E
Dambulla, *Sri Lanka* .... **95 L5** 7 51N 80 39 E
Dame Marie, *Haiti* **165 C5** 18 36N 74 26W
Damergou, *Niger* .... **113 C6** 14 15N 9 0 E
Dāmghān, *Iran* .... **97 B7** 36 10N 54 17 E
Dămienesti, *Romania* .... **53 D11** 46 44N 26 59 E
Damietta = Dumyât, *Egypt* ... **106 H7** 31 24N 31 48 E
Daming, *China* .... **74 F8** 36 15N 115 6 E
Damīr Qābū, *Syria* .... **96 B4** 36 58N 41 51 E
Dammai I., *Phil.* .... **81 J3** 5 47N 120 25 E
Dammam = Ad Dammām, *Si. Arabia* **97 E6** 26 20N 50 5 E
Dammarie-les-Lys, *France* .... **27 D9** 48 31N 2 39 E
Dammartin-en-Goële, *France* . **27 C9** 49 3N 2 41 E
Dammastock, *Switz.* .... **33 C6** 46 38N 8 24 E
Damme, *Germany* .... **30 C4** 52 32N 8 11 E
Damoh, *India* .... **93 H12** 23 17N 87 35 E
Damodar →, *India* .... **93 H8** 23 50N 79 28 E
Damous, *Algeria* .... **111 A5** 36 31N 1 42 E
Dampier, *Australia* .... **124 D2** 20 41 S 116 42 E
Dampier, Selat, *Indonesia* .... **83 B4** 0 40 S 131 0 E
Dampier Arch., *Australia* ..... **124 D2** 20 38 S 116 32 E
Dampier Str., *Papua N. G.* ... **132 C5** 5 50 S 148 0 E
Dampier-sur-Salon, *France* ... **32 A1** 47 33 S 5 41 E
Damqawt, *Yemen* .... **99 C6** 16 34N 52 50 E
Damrani, *Algeria* **110 C4** 27 5N 2 56W
Damrei, Chuor Phnum, *Cambodia* **87 G4** 11 30N 103 0 E
Damroh, *India* .... **90 A5** 28 26N 95 14 E
Damūls, *Austria* .... **33 B9** 47 17N 9 53 E
Damvillers, *France* .... **27 C12** 49 20N 5 21 E
Dan-Gulbi, *Nigeria* .... **113 C6** 11 40N 6 15 E
Dan Xian, *China* .... **86 C7** 19 31N 109 33 E
Dana, *Indonesia* .... **82 D2** 11 0 S 122 52 E
Dana, L., *Canada* **140 B4** 50 53N 77 20W
Dana, Mt., *U.S.A.* **160 H7** 37 54N 119 12W
Danakil Desert, *Ethiopia* ..... **107 E5** 12 45N 41 0 E
Danané, *Ivory C.* **112 D3** 7 16N 8 9W
Danao, *Phil.* .... **81 F5** 10 31N 124 1 E
Danau Poso, *Indonesia* .... **79 E6** 1 52 S 120 35 E
Danba, *China* .... **76 B3** 30 54N 101 48 E
Danbury, *U.S.A.* **151 E11** 41 24N 73 28W
Danby L., *U.S.A.* **159 J6** 34 13N 115 5W
Dand, *Afghan.* .... **91 C2** 32 38N 65 32 E
Dande →, *Angola* .... **115 D2** 6 15 S 15 34 E
Dande Safari Area △, *Zimbabwe* **119 F3** 15 56 S 30 16 E
Dandeldhura, *Nepal* .... **93 E9** 29 20N 80 35 E
Dandeli, *India* .... **95 G2** 15 5N 74 30 E
Dandenong, *Australia* .... **129 E6** 38 0 S 145 15 E
Dandil, *Egypt* .... **106 J7** 29 10N 31 2 E
Dandong, *China* .... **75 D13** 40 10N 124 20 E
Danfeng, *China* .... **74 H6** 33 45N 110 25 E
Dangan Liedao, *China* .... **77 F10** 22 0N 114 0 E
Dangara, *Tajikistan* .... **65 D4** 38 6N 69 22 E
Dange, *Angola* .... **115 D3** 7 56 S 15 3 E
Dangé-St-Romain, *France* ..... **28 B4** 46 56N 0 36 E
Dăngeni, *Romania* .... **53 C11** 47 51N 26 58 E
Danger Is. = Pukapuka, *Cook Is.* **135 J11** 10 53 S 165 49W
Danger Pt., *S. Africa* .... **116 E2** 34 40 S 19 17 E
Danginpuri, *Indonesia* .... **79 K18** 8 40 S 115 13 E
Dangla, *Ethiopia* .... **107 E4** 11 18N 36 56 E
Dangora, *Nigeria* .... **113 C6** 11 30N 8 7 E
Dangouadougou, *Burkina Faso* . **112 D4** 10 9N 4 56W
Dangrek, Phnom, *Thailand* .... **86 E5** 14 15N 105 0 E
Dangriga, *Belize* **163 D7** 17 0N 88 13W
Dangshan, *China* .... **74 G9** 34 27N 116 22 E
Dangtu, *China* .... **77 B12** 31 32N 118 25 E
Dangyang, *China* .... **77 B8** 30 52N 111 44 E
Dani, *Burkina Faso* **113 C4** 13 43N 0 10W
Daniel, *U.S.A.* **158 E8** 42 52N 110 4W
Daniel's Harbour, *Canada* **141 B8** 50 13N 57 35W
Danielskuil, *S. Africa* .... **116 D3** 28 11 S 23 33 E
Danielson, *U.S.A.* **151 E13** 41 48N 71 53W
Danielsville, *U.S.A.* **152 A6** 34 8N 83 13W
Danilov, *Russia* .... **58 C11** 58 16N 40 13 E
Danilovgrad, Montenegro, *Yug.* **60 E7** 50 25N 44 12 E
Danilovka, *Russia* .... **74 F6** 36 28N 110 45 E
Danja, *Nigeria* .... **113 C6** 11 21N 7 30 E
Danje-la-Menha, *Angola* ..... **115 D2** 9 32 S 14 39 E
Danjiangkou, *China* .... **77 A8** 32 31N 111 30 E
Danjiangkou Shuiku, *China* ... **77 A8** 32 37N 111 30 E
Dank, *Oman* .... **97 F8** 23 33N 56 16 E
Dankalwa, *Nigeria* .... **113 C7** 12 12N 12 12 E
Dankama, *Nigeria* .... **113 C6** 13 20N 7 44 E
Dankov, *Russia* .... **58 F10** 53 20N 39 15 E
Danleng, *China* .... **76 B4** 30 1N 103 31 E
Danlí, *Honduras* **164 D2** 14 4N 86 35W
Danmark Fjord, *Greenland* **10 A8** 81 30N 22 0W
Danmarkshavn, *Greenland* **10 B9** 76 45N 18 50W
Dannemora, *U.S.A.* **151 B11** 44 43N 73 44W
Dannenberg, *Germany* .... **30 B7** 53 6N 11 5 E
Dannevirke, *N.Z.* .... **130 G5** 40 12 S 176 8 E
Dannhauser, *S. Africa* .... **117 D5** 28 0 S 30 3 E
Danot, *Ethiopia* .... **120 C3** 7 33N 45 17 E
Dansville, *U.S.A.* **150 D7** 42 34N 77 42W
Danta, *India* .... **92 G5** 24 11N 72 46 E
Dantan, *India* .... **93 J12** 21 57N 87 20 E
Dantewara, *India* .... **94 E5** 18 54N 81 21 E
Danube = Dunărea →, *Europe* . **53 E14** 45 20N 29 40 E
Danubyu, *Burma* .... **90 G5** 17 15N 95 35 E
Danvers, *U.S.A.* **151 D14** 42 34N 70 56W
Danville, Ga., *U.S.A.* **152 C6** 32 36N 83 15W
Danville, Ill., *U.S.A.* **157 D10** 40 8N 87 37W
Danville, Ind., *U.S.A.* **156 E9** 39 46N 86 32W
Danville, Ky., *U.S.A.* **157 G12** 37 39N 84 46W
Danville, Va., *U.S.A.* **149 G6** 36 36N 79 23W
Danville, Vt., *U.S.A.* **151 B12** 44 25N 72 9W
Danyang, *China* .... **77 B12** 32 0N 119 31 E
Danzig = Gdańsk, *Poland* ..... **54 D5** 54 22N 18 40 E
Dao, *Phil.* .... **81 F3** 10 30N 121 57 E
Dao = Tobias Fornier, *Phil.* ... **81 F4** 11 24N 122 1 E
Dao, *Portugal* **42 E2** 40 20N 8 11W
Dao Xian, *China* .... **77 E8** 25 36N 111 31 E
Daocheng, *China* .... **76 C3** 29 3N 100 10 E
Daora, W. Sahara .... **110 C2** 7 5 S 128 40 E
Daoud = Aïn Beïda, *Algeria* .. **111 A6** 35 50N 7 29 E
Daoukro, *Ivory C.* **112 D4** 7 0N 3 58W
Dapa, *Phil.* .... **81 G6** 9 46N 126 3 E
Dapaong, *Togo* .... **113 C5** 10 55N 0 16 E
Dapchi, *Nigeria* .... **113 C7** 12 30N 11 31 E
Dapiak, Mt., *Phil.* .... **81 G4** 8 15N 123 28 E
Dapitan, *Phil.* .... **81 G4** 8 39N 123 25 E
Dapoli, *India* .... **94 F1** 17 40N 73 9 E
Daqing Shan, *China* .... **74 D6** 40 40N 111 0 E
Daqu Shan, *China* .... **77 B14** 30 25N 122 20 E
Dar Banda, *Africa* .... **104 F6** 8 0N 23 0 E
Dar el Beida = Casablanca, *Morocco* **110 B3** 33 36N 7 36W

Dar es Salaam, Tanzania ... 118 D4 6 50 S 39 12 E
Dar Mazār, Iran ... 97 D8 29 14N 57 20 E
Dar Rounga, C.A.R. ... 114 A4 0 45N 22 20 E
Dar'ā, Syria ... 103 C5 32 36N 36 7 E
Dar'ā □, Syria ... 103 C5 32 55N 36 10 E
Dārāb, Iran ... 97 D7 28 50N 54 30 E
Daraban, Pakistan ... 92 D4 31 44N 70 20 E
Darabani, Romania ... 53 B11 48 10N 26 39 E
Darai Hills, Papua N. G. ... 132 D2 7 8 S 143 33 E
Daraina, Madag. ... 117 A8 13 12 S 49 40 E
Daraj, Libya ... 108 B2 30 10N 10 28 E
Daram, Phil. ... 81 F5 11 38N 124 48 E
Dārān, Iran ... 97 C6 32 59N 50 24 E
Daraut Kurgan = Daroot-Korgan,
  Kyrgyzstan ... 65 D6 39 33N 72 11 E
Daravica, Kosovo, Yug. ... 50 A4 42 32N 20 8 E
Daraw, Egypt ... 106 C3 24 22N 32 51 E
Dārayyā, Syria ... 103 B5 33 28N 36 15 E
Darazo, Nigeria ... 113 C7 11 1N 10 24 E
Darband, Pakistan ... 92 B5 34 20N 72 50 E
Darband, Kūh-e, Iran ... 97 D8 31 34N 57 8 E
Darbhanga, India ... 93 F11 26 15N 85 55 E
Darburruk, Somali Rep. ... 120 C2 9 44N 44 31 E
Darby, C., U.S.A. ... 144 D7 64 19N 162 47W
D'Arcy, Canada ... 142 C4 50 27N 122 35W
Darda, Croatia ... 52 E3 45 40N 18 41 E
Dardanelle, Ark., U.S.A. ... 155 H8 35 13N 93 9W
Dardanelle, Calif., U.S.A. ... 160 G7 38 20N 119 50W
Dardanelles = Çanakkale Boğazı,
  Turkey ... 51 F10 40 17N 26 32 E
Dare ↠, Ethiopia ... 107 F5 7 20N 42 11 E
Darende, Turkey ... 100 C7 38 31N 37 30 E
Dārestān, Iran ... 97 D8 29 9N 58 42 E
Darfield, N.Z. ... 131 D7 43 29 S 172 7 E
Darfo, Italy ... 44 C7 45 53N 10 11 E
Dārfūr, Sudan ... 104 E6 13 40N 24 0 E
Dargai, Pakistan ... 92 B4 34 25N 71 55 E
Dargan Ata, Turkmenistan ... 66 E7 40 29N 62 10 E
Dargaville, N.Z. ... 130 B2 35 57 S 173 52 E
Dargol, Niger ... 113 C5 13 54N 1 22 E
Darhan, Mongolia ... 68 B5 49 37N 106 21 E
Darhan Muminggan Lianheqi, China 74 D6 41 40N 110 28 E
Dari, Sudan ... 107 F3 5 48N 30 26 E
Darıca, Turkey ... 100 B3 40 45N 29 23 E
Darien, U.S.A. ... 152 D8 31 23N 81 26W
Darién, G. del, Colombia ... 168 B2 9 0N 77 0W
Darién, Parque Nac. △, Panama ... 164 E4 7 36N 77 57W
Dariganga = Ovoot, Mongolia ... 74 B7 45 21N 113 45 E
Daringbad, India ... 64 E10 19 54N 84 8 E
Darinskoye, Kazakhstan ... 50 E14 51 20N 51 44 E
Darjeeling = Darjiling, India ... 90 B2 27 3N 88 18 E
Darjiling, India ... 90 B2 27 3N 88 18 E
Darkan, Australia ... 125 F2 33 20 S 116 43 E
Darke Peak, Australia ... 128 B2 33 27 S 136 12 E
Darkhana, Pakistan ... 92 D5 30 39N 72 11 E
Darkhazīneh, Iran ... 97 D6 31 54N 48 39 E
Darkot Pass, Pakistan ... 65 E6 36 45N 73 26 E
Darling ↠, Australia ... 128 C4 34 4 S 141 54 E
Darling Downs, Australia ... 127 D5 27 30 S 150 30 E
Darling Ra., Australia ... 125 F2 32 30 S 116 0 E
Darlington, U.K. ... 20 C6 54 32N 1 33W
Darlington, Fla., U.S.A. ... 152 E3 30 57N 86 3W
Darlington, S.C., U.S.A. ... 149 H6 34 18N 79 52W
Darlington, Wis., U.S.A. ... 156 B6 42 41N 90 7W
Darlington □, U.K. ... 20 C6 54 32N 1 33W
Darlington, S. Africa ... 116 E4 33 10 S 25 9 E
Darlington Point, Australia ... 129 C7 34 37 S 146 1 E
Darlot, L., Australia ... 125 E3 27 48 S 121 35 E
Darłowo, Poland ... 54 D3 54 25N 16 25 E
Dărmăneşti, Bacău, Romania ... 53 D11 46 21N 26 33 E
Dărmăneşti, Suceava, Romania ... 53 C11 47 44N 26 9 E
Darmstadt, Germany ... 31 F4 49 51N 8 39 E
Darnah, Libya ... 108 B4 32 45N 22 45 E
Darnah □, Libya ... 108 B4 31 0N 23 40 E
Darnall, S. Africa ... 117 D5 29 23 S 31 18 E
Darney, France ... 27 D13 48 5N 6 2 E
Darnick, Australia ... 128 B5 32 48 S 143 38 E
Darnley, Antarctica ... 7 C6 68 0 S 69 0 E
Darnley B., Canada ... 138 B7 69 30N 123 30W
Daroca, Spain ... 40 D3 41 9N 1 25W
Daroot-Korgan, Kyrgyzstan ... 65 D6 39 33N 72 11 E
Darou-Mousti, Senegal ... 112 B1 15 3N 16 3W
Darr ↠, Australia ... 126 C3 23 39 S 143 50 E
Darra Pezu, Pakistan ... 92 C4 32 19N 70 44 E
Darran Mts., N.Z. ... 131 E1 44 37 S 167 59 E
Darrequeira, Argentina ... 174 D3 37 42 S 63 10W
Darrington, U.S.A. ... 158 B3 48 15N 121 36W
Darsana, Bangla. ... 90 D2 23 35N 88 48 E
Darsi, India ... 95 G4 15 46N 79 44 E
Darsser Ort, Germany ... 30 A8 54 28N 12 32 E
Dart ↠, U.K. ... 21 G4 50 24N 3 39W
Dart, C., Antarctica ... 7 D14 73 6 S 126 20W
Dartford, U.K. ... 21 F8 51 26N 0 13 E
Dartmoor, Australia ... 128 D4 37 56 S 141 19 E
Dartmoor, U.K. ... 21 G4 50 38N 3 57W
Dartmoor Nat. Park △, U.K. ... 21 G4 50 37N 3 59W
Dartmouth, Canada ... 141 D7 44 40N 63 30W
Dartmouth, U.K. ... 21 G4 50 21N 3 36W
Dartmouth, L., Australia ... 129 D7 26 4 S 145 18 E
Dartmouth Res, Australia ... 127 D4 26 4 S 145 18 E
Dartuch = Artrutx, C. de, Spain ... 38 B4 39 55N 3 49 E
Daru, Papua N. G. ... 132 E2 9 3 S 143 13 E
Daruba, Indonesia ... 82 A3 2 5N 128 14 E
Daruvar, Croatia ... 52 E2 45 35N 17 14 E
Darvaza, Turkmenistan ... 66 E6 40 11N 58 24 E
Darvel, Teluk = Lahad Datu, Teluk,
  Malaysia ... 85 B5 4 50N 118 20 E
Darwen, U.K. ... 20 D5 53 42N 2 29W
Darwendale, Zimbabwe ... 117 B5 17 41 S 30 33 E
Darwha, India ... 94 D3 20 15N 77 45 E
Darwin, Australia ... 124 B5 12 25 S 130 51 E
Darwin, U.S.A. ... 161 J9 36 15N 117 35W
Darwin, Mt., Chile ... 176 D3 54 47 S 69 55W
Darwin, Volcán, Ecuador ... 172 a 0 10 S 91 18W
Darya Khan, Pakistan ... 92 D4 31 48N 71 6 E
Daryapur, India ... 94 D3 20 57N 77 17 E
Daryoi Amu = Amudarya ↠,
  Uzbekistan ... 66 E6 43 58N 59 34 E
Dās, U.A.E. ... 97 E7 25 20N 53 30 E
Dashen, Ras, Ethiopia ... 107 E4 13 8N 38 26 E
Dasher, U.S.A. ... 152 E6 30 45N 83 13W
Dashetai, China ... 74 D5 41 0N 109 5 E
Dashhowuz, Turkmenistan ... 66 E6 41 49N 59 58 E
Dashkesan = Daşkäsän, Azerbaijan ... 61 K7 40 25N 46 0 E
Dashköpri, Turkmenistan ... 97 B9 36 16N 62 8 E
Dasht, Iran ... 97 B8 37 17N 56 7 E
Dasht ↠, Pakistan ... 91 D1 25 10N 61 40 E
Dasht-i-Tahlab, Pakistan ... 91 C1 28 40N 62 2 E
Daska, Pakistan ... 92 C6 32 20N 74 20 E
Daşkäsän, Azerbaijan ... 61 K7 40 25N 46 0 E
Dasmariñas, Phil. ... 80 D3 14 20N 120 56 E
Dassa, Benin ... 113 D5 7 46N 2 14 E
Dasuya, India ... 92 D6 31 49N 75 38 E
Datça, Turkey ... 49 E9 36 46N 27 40 E
Datia, India ... 93 G8 25 39N 78 27 E
Datian, China ... 77 E11 25 40N 117 50 E
Datong, Anhui, China ... 77 B11 30 48N 117 44 E
Datong, Shanxi, China ... 74 D7 40 6N 113 18 E
Dattakhel, Pakistan ... 92 C3 32 54N 69 46 E
Dattapur = Dhamangaon, India ... 94 D4 20 48N 78 9 E
Datteln, Germany ... 30 D3 51 39N 7 21 E
Datu, Tanjung, Indonesia ... 85 B3 2 5N 109 39 E
Datu Piang, Phil. ... 81 H5 7 2N 124 30 E

Datuk, Tanjong = Datu, Tanjung,
  Indonesia ... 85 B3 2 5N 109 39 E
Daua = Dawa ↠, Africa ... 107 G5 4 11N 42 6 E
Daud Khel, Pakistan ... 92 C4 32 53N 71 34 E
Daudnagar, India ... 93 G11 25 2N 84 24 E
Daugava ↠, Latvia ... 15 H21 57 4N 24 3 E
Daugavpils, Latvia ... 15 J22 55 53N 26 32 E
Daulatabad, India ... 94 E2 19 57N 75 15 E
Daule, Ecuador ... 168 D2 1 56 S 79 56W
Daule ↠, Ecuador ... 168 D2 2 10 S 79 52W
Daulpur, India ... 92 F7 26 45N 77 59 E
Daun, Germany ... 31 E2 50 11N 6 49 E
Daund, India ... 94 E2 18 26N 74 40 E
Dauphin, Canada ... 143 C8 51 9N 100 5W
Dauphin, U.S.A. ... 150 F8 40 22N 76 56W
Dauphin L., Canada ... 143 C9 51 20N 99 45W
Dauphiné, France ... 29 C9 45 15N 5 25 E
Daura, Borno, Nigeria ... 113 C7 11 31N 11 24 E
Daura, Katsina, Nigeria ... 113 C6 13 2N 8 21 E
Dausa, India ... 92 F7 26 52N 76 20 E
Dāvāçi, Azerbaijan ... 61 K9 41 15N 48 57 E
Davangere, India ... 95 G2 14 25N 75 55 E
Davao, Phil. ... 81 H5 7 0N 125 40 E
Davao □, Phil. ... 81 H5 7 0N 125 40 E
Davao del Sur □, Phil. ... 81 H5 6 30N 125 40 E
Davao G., Phil. ... 81 H5 6 30N 125 48 E
Davao Oriental □, Phil. ... 81 H6 7 10N 126 30 E
Dāvar Panāh, Iran ... 97 E9 27 25N 62 15 E
Davenport, Calif., U.S.A. ... 160 H4 37 1N 122 12W
Davenport, Fla., U.S.A. ... 153 G8 28 10N 81 36W
Davenport, Iowa, U.S.A. ... 156 C6 41 32N 90 35W
Davenport, Wash., U.S.A. ... 158 C4 47 39N 118 9W
Davenport Ra., Australia ... 126 C1 20 28 S 134 0 E
Daventry, U.K. ... 21 E6 52 16N 1 10W
David, Panama ... 164 E3 8 30N 82 30W
David City, U.S.A. ... 154 E6 41 15N 97 8W
David Gorodok = Davyd Haradok,
  Belarus ... 59 F4 52 4N 27 8 E
Davidson, Canada ... 143 C7 51 16N 105 59W
Davis, U.S.A. ... 160 G5 38 33N 121 44W
Davis Dam, U.S.A. ... 161 K12 35 11N 114 34W
Davis Inlet, Canada ... 141 A7 55 50N 60 59W
Davis Mts., U.S.A. ... 155 K2 30 50N 103 55W
Davis Sea, Antarctica ... 7 C7 66 0 S 92 0 E
Davis Str., N. Amer. ... 139 B14 65 0N 58 0W
Davisboro, U.S.A. ... 152 C7 32 59N 82 36W
Davison, U.S.A. ... 157 A13 43 2N 83 31W
Davlekanovo, Russia ... 64 D5 54 13N 55 3 E
Davo ↠, Ivory C. ... 112 D3 5 0N 6 10W
Davos, Switz. ... 33 C9 46 48N 9 49 E
Davutlar, Turkey ... 49 D9 37 43N 27 17 E
Davy L., Canada ... 143 B7 58 53N 108 18W
Davyd Haradok, Belarus ... 59 F4 52 4N 27 8 E
Dawa ↠, Africa ... 107 G5 4 11N 42 6 E
Dawaki, Bauchi, Nigeria ... 113 D6 9 25N 9 33 E
Dawaki, Kano, Nigeria ... 113 C6 12 5N 8 23 E
Dawei = Tavoy, Burma ... 86 E2 14 2N 98 12 E
Dawes Ra., Australia ... 126 C5 24 40 S 150 40 E
Dawlish, U.K. ... 21 G4 50 35N 3 28W
Dawna Ra., Burma ... 86 D2 16 30N 98 30 E
Dawnyein, Burma ... 86 G5 15 54N 95 36 E
Dawqah, Si. Arabia ... 98 C3 19 36N 40 54 E
Dawros Hd., Ireland ... 23 B3 54 50N 8 33W
Dawson, Canada ... 138 B6 64 10N 139 30W
Dawson, U.S.A. ... 152 D5 31 46N 84 27W
Dawson, I., Chile ... 176 D2 53 50 S 70 50W
Dawson B., Canada ... 143 C8 52 53N 100 49W
Dawson Creek, Canada ... 142 B4 55 45N 120 15W
Dawson Inlet, Canada ... 143 A10 61 50N 93 25W
Dawson Ra., Australia ... 126 C4 24 30 S 149 48 E
Dawu, Hubei, China ... 77 B9 31 34N 114 7 E
Dawu, Sichuan, China ... 76 B3 30 55N 101 10 E
Dawwah, Oman ... 99 B7 20 33N 58 48 E
Dawwara, Ras id-, Malta ... 38 F7 35 52N 14 21 E
Dax, France ... 28 E2 43 44N 1 3W
Daxian, China ... 76 B6 31 15N 107 23 E
Daxin, China ... 76 F6 22 50N 107 11 E
Daxindian, China ... 75 F11 37 30N 120 50 E
Daxinggou, China ... 75 C15 43 25N 129 40 E
Daxue Shan, Sichuan, China ... 76 B3 30 30N 101 30 E
Daxue Shan, Yunnan, China ... 76 F2 23 42N 99 48 E
Day, U.S.A. ... 152 E6 30 12N 83 17W
Daya el Khadra, Mauritania ... 110 C3 25 14N 6 2W
Dayao, China ... 76 E3 25 43N 101 20 E
Daye, China ... 77 B10 30 6N 114 58 E
Dayet en Naharat, Mali ... 112 B4 17 39N 3 10W
Dayi, China ... 76 B4 30 41N 103 29 E
Daylesford, Australia ... 128 D6 37 21 S 144 9 E
Dayong, China ... 77 C8 29 11N 110 30 E
Dayr az Zawr, Syria ... 101 E9 35 20N 40 5 E
Daysland, Canada ... 142 C6 52 50N 112 20W
Dayton, Iowa, U.S.A. ... 156 B2 42 14N 94 6W
Dayton, Ky., U.S.A. ... 157 E12 39 47N 84 28W
Dayton, Nev., U.S.A. ... 160 F7 39 14N 119 36W
Dayton, Ohio, U.S.A. ... 148 F3 39 45N 84 12W
Dayton, Pa., U.S.A. ... 150 F5 40 53N 79 15W
Dayton, Tenn., U.S.A. ... 149 H3 35 30N 85 1W
Dayton, Wash., U.S.A. ... 158 C5 46 19N 117 59W
Dayton, Wyo., U.S.A. ... 158 D10 44 53N 107 16W
Daytona Beach, U.S.A. ... 153 F8 29 13N 81 1W
Dayu, China ... 77 E10 25 24N 114 22 E
Dayville, U.S.A. ... 158 D4 44 28N 119 32W
Dazhu, China ... 76 B6 30 41N 107 15 E
Dazu, China ... 76 C5 29 40N 105 42 E
De Aar, S. Africa ... 116 E3 30 39 S 24 0 E
De Armanville, U.S.A. ... 152 B4 33 38N 85 45W
De Bary, U.S.A. ... 153 G8 28 54N 81 18W
De Biesbosch, Nat. Park △, Neths. ... 24 C4 51 45N 4 48 E
De Forest, U.S.A. ... 156 A7 43 15N 89 20W
De Funiak Springs, U.S.A. ... 152 K3 30 43N 86 7W
De Grey ↠, Australia ... 124 D2 20 12 S 119 13 E
De Haan, Belgium ... 24 C3 51 16N 3 2 E
De Hoge Veluwe, Nat. Park △,
  Neths. ... 24 B5 52 5N 5 46 E
De Hoop Nature Reserve ⌂,
  S. Africa ... 116 E3 34 30 S 20 28 E
De Jongs, Tg., Indonesia ... 83 C5 6 55 S 138 30 E
De Kalb, U.S.A. ... 154 E10 41 56N 88 46W
De Kennemerduinen, Nat. Park △,
  Neths. ... 24 B4 52 27N 4 33 E
De Land, U.S.A. ... 153 F8 29 2N 81 18W
De Leon, U.S.A. ... 155 J5 32 7N 98 32W
De Leon Springs, U.S.A. ... 153 F8 29 7N 81 21W
De Long Mts., U.S.A. ... 144 B7 68 30N 163 0W
De Panne, Belgium ... 24 C2 51 6N 2 34 E
De Pere, U.S.A. ... 148 C1 44 27N 88 4W
De Queen, U.S.A. ... 155 H7 34 2N 94 21W
De Quincy, U.S.A. ... 155 K8 30 27N 93 26W
De Ridder, U.S.A. ... 155 K8 30 51N 93 17W
De Smet, U.S.A. ... 154 C6 44 23N 97 33W
De Soto, U.S.A. ... 156 F6 38 8N 90 34W
De Soto City, U.S.A. ... 153 H8 27 27N 81 24W
De Tour Village, U.S.A. ... 148 C4 46 0N 83 56W
De Witt, Ark., U.S.A. ... 155 H9 34 18N 91 20W
De Witt, Iowa, U.S.A. ... 156 C6 41 49N 90 33W
De Witt, Mich., U.S.A. ... 157 B12 42 51N 84 34W
Dead Sea, Asia ... 103 D4 31 30N 35 30 E
Deadman B., U.S.A. ... 153 F6 29 30N 83 30W
Deadwood, U.S.A. ... 154 C3 44 23N 103 44W
Deadwood L., Canada ... 142 B3 59 10N 128 30W

Deal, U.K. ... 21 F9 51 13N 1 25 E
Deal I., Australia ... 127 C4 39 30 S 147 20 E
Dealesville, S. Africa ... 116 D4 28 41 S 25 44 E
De'an, China ... 77 C10 29 21N 115 46 E
Dean ↠, Canada ... 142 C3 52 49N 126 58W
Dean, Forest of, U.K. ... 21 F5 51 45N 2 33W
Dean Chan., Canada ... 142 C3 52 30N 127 15W
Deán Funes, Argentina ... 174 C3 30 20 S 64 20W
Dearborn, Mich., U.S.A. ... 157 B13 42 19N 83 11W
Dearborn, Mo., U.S.A. ... 156 E2 39 32N 94 46W
Dease ↠, Canada ... 142 B3 59 56N 128 32W
Dease L., Canada ... 142 B2 58 40N 130 5W
Dease Lake, Canada ... 142 B2 58 25N 130 6W
Death Valley, U.S.A. ... 161 J10 36 15N 116 50W
Death Valley Junction, U.S.A. ... 161 J10 36 20N 116 25W
Death Valley Nat. Park △, U.S.A. ... 161 J10 36 45N 117 15W
Deauville, France ... 26 C7 49 23N 0 2 E
Deba, Spain ... 40 B2 43 18N 2 21W
Deba Habe, Nigeria ... 113 C7 10 14N 11 20 E
Debak, Malaysia ... 85 B4 1 34N 111 25 E
Debaltsevo, Ukraine ... 59 H10 48 22N 38 26 E
Debao, China ... 76 F6 23 21N 106 46 E
Debar, Macedonia ... 50 A4 41 31N 20 30 E
Debark, Ethiopia ... 107 E4 13 1N 37 48 E
Debden, Canada ... 143 C7 53 30N 106 50W
Dębica, Poland ... 55 H8 50 2N 21 25 E
Dęblin, Poland ... 55 G8 51 34N 21 50 E
Debno, Poland ... 55 F1 52 44N 14 41 E
Dēbo, L., Mali ... 112 B4 15 14N 4 15W
Deboit, Canada ... 142 B5 55 12N 118 1W
Deborah East, L., Australia ... 125 F2 30 45 S 119 0 E
Deborah West, L., Australia ... 125 F2 30 45 S 118 50 E
Deboyne Is., Papua N. G. ... 132 F7 10 43 S 152 22 E
Debre Birhan, Ethiopia ... 107 F4 9 41N 39 31 E
Debre Markos, Ethiopia ... 107 E4 10 20N 37 40 E
Debre May, Ethiopia ... 107 E4 11 20N 37 25 E
Debre Sina, Ethiopia ... 107 F4 9 51N 39 50 E
Debre Tabor, Ethiopia ... 107 E4 11 50N 38 26 E
Debre Zebit, Ethiopia ... 107 E4 11 48N 38 30 E
Debrecen, Hungary ... 52 C6 47 33N 21 42 E
Debrzno, Poland ... 54 E4 53 33N 17 14 E
Dečani, Kosovo, Yug. ... 50 D4 42 30N 20 18 E
Decatur, Ala., U.S.A. ... 149 H2 34 36N 86 59W
Decatur, Ga., U.S.A. ... 152 D5 33 47N 84 18W
Decatur, Ill., U.S.A. ... 156 E8 39 51N 88 57W
Decatur, Ind., U.S.A. ... 157 D12 40 50N 84 56W
Decatur, Mich., U.S.A. ... 157 B11 42 7N 85 58W
Decatur, Tex., U.S.A. ... 155 J6 33 14N 97 35W
Decazeville, France ... 28 D6 44 34N 2 15 E
Deccan, India ... 94 F4 18 0N 79 0 E
Deception, Mt., Australia ... 128 A3 30 42 S 138 16 E
Deception, Papua N. G. ... 132 D3 7 45 S 144 40 E
Deception Bay, Australia ... 127 D5 27 10 S 153 5 E
Deception I., Canada ... 143 B8 56 33N 104 13W
Dechang, China ... 76 D4 27 25N 102 11 E
Dechhu, India ... 92 F5 26 46N 72 20 E
Děčín, Czech Rep. ... 34 A7 50 47N 14 12 E
Decize, France ... 27 F10 46 50N 3 28 E
Deckerville, U.S.A. ... 150 C2 43 32N 82 44W
Decollatura, Italy ... 47 C9 39 2N 16 21 E
Decorah, U.S.A. ... 154 D9 43 18N 91 48W
Deda, Romania ... 53 D9 46 56N 24 50 E
Dedaye, Burma ... 90 G5 16 24N 95 53 E
Dedéagach = Alexandroúpolis,
  Greece ... 51 F9 40 50N 25 54 E
Deder, Ethiopia ... 107 F5 9 19N 41 27 E
Dedham, U.S.A. ... 151 D13 42 15N 71 10W
Dédougou, Burkina Faso ... 112 C4 12 30N 3 25W
Dedovichi, Russia ... 58 D5 57 32N 29 56 E
Dedza, Malawi ... 119 E3 14 20 S 34 20 E
Dee ↠, Aberds., U.K. ... 19 D9 57 9N 2 5W
Dee ↠, Dumf. & Gall., U.K. ... 22 G4 54 51N 4 3W
Dee ↠, Wales, U.K. ... 20 D4 53 22N 3 17W
Deep B. = Chilumba, Malawi ... 119 E3 10 28 S 34 12 E
Deep Bay = Shenzhen Wan, China ... 69 G10 22 27N 113 55 E
Deep Lead, Australia ... 128 D5 37 0 S 142 43 E
Deepwater, Australia ... 127 D5 29 25 S 151 51 E
Deer ↠, Canada ... 143 B10 58 23N 94 13W
Deer I., U.S.A. ... 144 J7 54 55N 162 18W
Deer Lake, Nfld., Canada ... 141 C8 49 11N 57 27W
Deer Lake, Ont., Canada ... 143 C10 52 36N 94 20W
Deer Lodge, U.S.A. ... 158 C7 46 24N 112 44W
Deer Park, Fla., U.S.A. ... 153 G9 28 6N 80 54W
Deer Park, Ohio, U.S.A. ... 157 E12 39 13N 84 23W
Deer Park, Wash., U.S.A. ... 158 C5 47 57N 117 28W
Deer River, U.S.A. ... 154 B8 47 20N 93 48W
Deeragun, Australia ... 126 B4 19 16 S 146 33 E
Deerdeport, S. Africa ... 116 C4 24 37 S 26 27 E
Deerfield, Ill., U.S.A. ... 157 B9 42 10N 87 51W
Deerfield, Mo., U.S.A. ... 156 G2 37 50N 94 30W
Deerfield Beach, U.S.A. ... 153 J9 26 19N 80 6W
Deering, U.S.A. ... 144 C7 66 4N 162 42W
Deferiet, U.S.A. ... 151 B9 44 2N 75 41W
Defiance, U.S.A. ... 157 C11 41 17N 84 22W
Degana, India ... 92 F6 26 50N 74 20 E
Degebe ↠, Portugal ... 43 G3 38 13N 7 29W
Degeberga, Sweden ... 17 J8 55 51N 14 5 E
Degeh Bur, Ethiopia ... 120 C2 8 11N 43 31 E
Dégelis, Canada ... 141 C6 47 30N 68 35W
Degema, Nigeria ... 113 E6 4 50N 6 48 E
Degerfors, Sweden ... 16 E8 59 15N 14 27 E
Degerhamn, Sweden ... 17 H10 56 20N 16 24 E
Degersheim, Switz. ... 33 B8 47 23N 9 12 E
Deggendorf, Germany ... 31 G8 48 50N 12 57 E
Degh ↠, Pakistan ... 92 D5 31 3N 73 21 E
Deh Bīd, Iran ... 97 D7 30 39N 53 11 E
Deh-e Shīr, Iran ... 97 D7 31 29N 53 45 E
Deh Nugaled = Nugaaleed, Dooxo,
  Somali Rep. ... 120 C3 8 35N 48 35 E
Dehaj, Iran ... 97 D7 30 42N 54 53 E
Dehak, Iran ... 91 D7 31 43N 60 47 E
Déhane, Cameroon ... 114 B2 3 30N 10 5 E
Dehdez, Iran ... 97 D6 31 43N 50 17 E
Dehej, India ... 92 J5 21 44N 72 40 E
Dehestān, Iran ... 97 D7 28 30N 55 35 E
Dehglān, Iran ... 101 E12 35 17N 47 25 E
Dehibat, Tunisia ... 108 B2 32 0N 10 47 E
Dehiwala, Sri Lanka ... 95 L4 6 50N 79 51 E
Dehlorān, Iran ... 101 F12 32 41N 47 16 E
Dehnow-e Kūheştān, Iran ... 97 E9 27 58N 58 32 E
Dehra Dun, India ... 92 D8 30 20N 78 4 E
Dehri, India ... 93 G11 24 50N 84 15 E
Dehua, China ... 77 E12 25 23N 118 14 E
Dehui, China ... 75 B13 44 30N 125 40 E
Deim Zubeir, Sudan ... 107 F2 7 49N 26 16 E
Deinze, Belgium ... 24 D3 50 59N 3 32 E
Dej, Romania ... 53 C8 47 10N 23 52 E
Deje, Sweden ... 16 E7 59 35N 13 28 E
Dejiang, China ... 76 C7 28 18N 108 7 E
Deka ↠, Zimbabwe ... 116 B4 18 4 S 26 42 E
Dekemhare, Eritrea ... 107 D4 15 6N 39 0 E
Dekese, Dem. Rep. of the Congo ... 112 E4 3 24 S 21 24 E
Dekoa, C.A.R. ... 114 A3 6 19N 19 4 E
Dekkanabad, Uzbekistan ... 65 D3 38 21N 66 30 E
Del Carmen, Phil. ... 81 G6 9 50N 126 0 E
Del Mar, U.S.A. ... 161 N9 32 58N 117 16W

Del Norte, U.S.A. ... 159 H10 37 41N 106 21W
Del Rio, U.S.A. ... 155 L4 29 22N 100 54W
Delai, Sudan ... 106 D4 17 21N 36 6 E
Delambre I., Australia ... 124 D2 20 26 S 117 5 E
Delami, Sudan ... 107 E3 11 38N 30 23 E
Delano, U.S.A. ... 161 K7 35 46N 119 15W
Delano Peak, U.S.A. ... 159 G7 38 22N 112 22W
Delārām, Afghan. ... 91 B1 32 9N 63 25 E
Delareyville, S. Africa ... 116 D4 26 41 S 25 26 E
Delaronde L., Canada ... 143 C7 54 3N 107 3W
Delavan, Ill., U.S.A. ... 156 D7 40 22N 89 33W
Delavan, Wis., U.S.A. ... 154 D10 42 38N 88 39W
Delaware, U.S.A. ... 148 E4 40 18N 83 4W
Delaware □, U.S.A. ... 148 F8 39 0N 75 20W
Delaware ↠, U.S.A. ... 151 G9 39 15N 75 20W
Delaware B., U.S.A. ... 148 F9 39 0N 75 10W
Delaware Water Gap Nat. Recr.
  Area ⌂, U.S.A. ... 151 E10 41 10N 74 55W
Delay ↠, Canada ... 141 A5 56 56N 71 28W
Delbrück, Germany ... 30 D4 51 46N 8 34 E
Delčevo, Macedonia ... 50 E6 41 58N 22 46 E
Delebio, Italy ... 33 D8 46 8N 9 27 E
Delegate, Australia ... 129 D8 37 4 S 148 56 E
Delémont, Switz. ... 32 B4 47 22N 7 20 E
Delevan, U.S.A. ... 150 D6 42 29N 78 29W
Delft, Neths. ... 24 B4 52 1N 4 22 E
Delft I., Sri Lanka ... 95 K4 9 30N 79 40 E
Delfzijl, Neths. ... 24 A6 53 20N 6 55 E
Delgada, Punta, Chile ... 176 G3 52 28 S 69 32W
Delgado, C., Mozam. ... 119 E5 10 45 S 40 40 E
Delgerhet, Mongolia ... 74 B6 45 50N 110 30 E
Delgo, Sudan ... 106 C3 20 6N 30 40 E
Delhi, Canada ... 150 D4 42 51N 80 30W
Delhi, India ... 92 E7 28 38N 77 17 E
Delhi, La., U.S.A. ... 155 J9 32 28N 91 30W
Delhi, N.Y., U.S.A. ... 151 D10 42 17N 74 55W
Deli Jovan, Serbia, Yug. ... 50 B6 43 13N 22 9 E
Delia, Canada ... 142 C6 51 38N 112 23W
Delice, Turkey ... 100 C6 39 54N 34 2 E
Delicias, Mexico ... 162 B3 28 10N 105 30W
Delījān, Iran ... 97 C6 33 59N 50 40 E
Delimara Point, Malta ... 38 F8 35 49N 14 34 E
Déline, Canada ... 138 B7 65 10N 123 30W
Delisle, Canada ... 143 C7 51 55N 107 8W
Delitzsch, Germany ... 30 D8 51 31N 12 20 E
Dell City, U.S.A. ... 159 L11 31 56N 105 12W
Dell Rapids, U.S.A. ... 154 D6 43 50N 96 43W
Delle, France ... 27 E14 47 30N 7 2 E
Dellys, Algeria ... 111 A5 36 57N 3 57 E
Delmar, Iowa, U.S.A. ... 156 C6 42 0N 90 37W
Delmar, N.Y., U.S.A. ... 151 D11 42 37N 73 47W
Delmenhorst, Germany ... 30 B4 53 3N 8 37 E
Delmiro Gouveia, Brazil ... 170 C4 9 24 S 38 6W
Delnice, Croatia ... 45 C11 45 23N 14 50 E
Delonga, Ostrova, Russia ... 67 B15 76 40N 149 20 E
Deloraine, Australia ... 127 D4 41 30 S 146 40 E
Deloraine, Canada ... 143 D8 49 15N 100 29W
Delphi, Greece ... 48 C4 38 28N 22 30 E
Delphi, U.S.A. ... 157 D10 40 36N 86 41W
Delphos, U.S.A. ... 157 D12 40 51N 84 21W
Delportshoop, S. Africa ... 116 D3 28 22 S 24 20 E
Delray Beach, U.S.A. ... 153 J9 26 28N 80 4W
Delsbo, Sweden ... 16 C10 61 48N 16 32 E
Delta, Ala., U.S.A. ... 152 B4 33 25N 85 42W
Delta, Colo., U.S.A. ... 159 G9 38 44N 108 4W
Delta, Utah, U.S.A. ... 158 G7 39 21N 112 35W
Delta □, Nigeria ... 113 D6 5 30N 6 0 E
Delta Amacuro □, Venezuela ... 169 B5 8 30N 61 30W
Delta del Ebro, Parque Natural
  de △, Spain ... 40 E5 40 43N 0 43 E
Delta del Po, Parco del △, Italy ... 45 D9 44 50N 12 15 E
Delta del Saloum, Parc Nat. du △,
  Senegal ... 112 C1 13 42N 16 43W
Delta Dunării Rezervatie ⌂,
  Romania ... 53 E14 45 15N 29 25 E
Delta Junction, U.S.A. ... 144 D11 64 2N 145 44W
Deltona, U.S.A. ... 153 G8 28 54N 81 16W
Delungra, Australia ... 127 D5 29 39 S 150 51 E
Delvada, India ... 92 J4 20 46N 71 2 E
Delvinákion, Greece ... 48 B2 39 57N 20 32 E
Delvinë, Albania ... 50 G4 39 59N 20 6 E
Demagiri, India ... 90 D4 23 5N 92 28 E
Demak, Indonesia ... 85 G14 6 53 S 110 38 E
Demanda, Sierra de la, Spain ... 40 C2 42 15N 3 0W
Demavend = Damāvand, Iran ... 97 C7 35 47N 52 0 E
Demba, Dem. Rep. of the Congo ... 115 D4 5 28 S 22 15 E
Demba Chio, Angola ... 115 D2 9 43 S 13 41 E
Dembecha, Ethiopia ... 107 E4 10 32N 37 30 E
Dembi, Ethiopia ... 107 F4 8 5N 36 25 E
Dembidolo, Ethiopia ... 107 F3 8 34N 34 50 E
Demchok, India ... 93 C8 32 42N 79 29 E
Demer ↠, Belgium ... 24 D5 50 57N 4 42 E
Demerdzhi, Greece ... 49 D9 38 23N 23 1 E
Demetrias, Greece ... 48 B4 39 22N 22 58 E
Demidov, Russia ... 58 E6 55 16N 31 30 E
Deming, N. Mex., U.S.A. ... 159 K10 32 16N 107 46W
Deming, Wash., U.S.A. ... 160 B4 48 50N 122 13W
Demini ↠, Brazil ... 169 D5 0 46 S 62 56W
Demirci, Turkey ... 49 B10 39 2N 28 38 E
Demirköprü Baraji, Turkey ... 49 C10 38 42N 28 25 E
Demirköy, Turkey ... 51 E11 41 49N 27 45 E
Demmin, Germany ... 30 B9 53 54N 13 2 E
Demnate, Morocco ... 110 B3 31 44N 6 59W
Democracia, Brazil ... 173 B5 5 48 S 61 26W
Demonte, Italy ... 44 D4 44 19N 7 17 E
Demopolis, U.S.A. ... 149 J2 32 31N 87 50W
Dempo, Indonesia ... 84 C2 4 2 S 103 15 E
Demta, Indonesia ... 83 B6 2 20 S 140 8 E
Demyansk, Russia ... 58 D7 57 40N 32 27 E
Den Burg, Neths. ... 24 A4 53 3N 4 47 E
Den Chai, Thailand ... 86 D3 17 59N 100 4 E
Den Haag = 's-Gravenhage, Neths. ... 24 B4 52 7N 4 17 E
Den Helder, Neths. ... 24 B4 52 57N 4 45 E
Den Oever, Neths. ... 24 B5 52 56N 5 2 E
Denain, France ... 27 B10 50 20N 3 22 E
Denair, U.S.A. ... 160 H6 37 32N 120 48W
Denali Nat. Park and Preserve △,
  U.S.A. ... 144 E10 63 30N 152 0W
Denau, Uzbekistan ... 65 - 38 16N 67 54 E
Denbigh, Canada ... 150 A7 45 8N 77 15W
Denbigh, U.K. ... 20 D4 53 12N 3 25W
Denbigh □, U.K. ... 144 D7 64 23N 161 32W
Denbighshire □, U.K. ... 20 D4 53 8N 3 22W
Dendang, Indonesia ... 85 C3 3 7 S 107 56 E
Dendê = Ndindi, Gabon ... 114 C2 3 46 S 11 9 E
Dendermonde, Belgium ... 24 C4 51 2N 4 5 E
Deneba, Ethiopia ... 107 F4 9 47N 39 10 E
Denezhkin Kamen, Gora, Russia ... 64 B7 60 25N 59 32 E
Deng Deng, Cameroon ... 114 A2 5 12N 13 31 E
Dengchuan, China ... 76 E3 25 59N 100 3 E
Denge, Nigeria ... 113 C6 12 52N 12 2 E
Dengfeng, China ... 74 G7 34 25N 113 2 E
Dengi, Nigeria ... 113 D6 9 25N 9 55 E
Dengkou, China ... 74 D4 40 18N 106 55 E
Denham, Australia ... 125 E1 25 56 S 113 31 E
Denham, Mt., Jamaica ... 164 a 18 13N 77 32W
Denham ↠, Australia ... 126 C4 21 55 S 147 46 E
Denham Ra., Australia ... 126 C4 21 55 S 147 46 E
Denham Sd., Australia ... 125 E1 25 45 S 113 15 E
Denholm, Canada ... 143 C7 52 39N 108 1W
Denia, Spain ... 41 G5 38 49N 0 8 E
Denial B., Australia ... 127 E1 32 14 S 133 32 E
Deniliquin, Australia ... 129 C6 35 30 S 144 58 E
Denis, Gabon ... 114 B1 0 19N 9 22 E

Denison, Iowa, U.S.A. **154 E7** 42 1N 95 21W
Denison, Tex., U.S.A. **155 J6** 33 45N 96 33W
Denison Plains, Australia ...... **124 C4** 18 35 S 128 0 E
Deniyaya, Sri Lanka .... **95 L5** 6 21N 80 33 E
Denizli, Turkey .... **49 D11** 37 42N 29 2 E
Denizli □, Turkey .... **49 D11** 37 45N 29 5 E
Denman, Australia .... **129 B9** 32 24 S 150 42 E
Denman Glacier, Antarctica ... **7 C7** 66 45 S 99 25 E
Denmark, Australia .... **125 F2** 34 59 S 117 25 E
Denmark, U.S.A. **152 B8** 33 19N 81 9W
Denmark ■, Europe .... **17 J3** 55 45N 10 0 E
Denmark Str., Atl. Oc. **10 D8** 66 0N 30 0W
Dennery, St. Lucia .... **161 f** 13 55N 60 54W
Dennison, U.S.A. **160 F3** 40 24N 81 19W
Denny, U.K. **22 E5** 56 1N 3 55W
Denpasar, Indonesia .... **79 K18** 8 39 S 115 13 E
Denpasar ✈ (DPS), Indonesia .. **79 K18** 8 44 S 115 10 E
Denton, Ga., U.S.A. **152 D7** 31 44N 82 42W
Denton, Mont., U.S.A. **158 C9** 47 19N 109 57W
Denton, Tex., U.S.A. **155 J6** 33 13N 97 8W
D'Entrecasteaux, Pt., Australia . **125 F2** 34 50 S 115 57 E
D'Entrecasteaux Is., Papua N. G. **132 E6** 9 0 S 151 0 E
D'Entrecasteaux Nat. Park △,
　Australia .... **125 F2** 34 20 S 115 33 E
Dents du Midi, Switz. .... **32 D3** 46 10N 6 56 E
Dentsville, U.S.A. **152 A9** 34 4N 80 58W
Denu, Ghana .... **113 D5** 6 4N 1 8 E
Denver, Colo., U.S.A. **154 F2** 39 44N 104 59W
Denver, Ind., U.S.A. **157 D10** 40 52N 86 5W
Denver, Iowa, U.S.A. **156 B4** 42 40N 92 20W
Denver, Pa., U.S.A. **151 F8** 40 14N 76 8W
Denver City, U.S.A. **155 J3** 32 58N 102 50W
Deoband, India .... **92 E7** 29 42N 77 43 E
Deobhog, India .... **94 E6** 19 53N 82 44 E
Deodrug, India .... **95 F3** 16 26N 76 55 E
Deogarh, Orissa, India .... **94 D7** 21 32N 84 45 E
Deogarh, Raj., India .... **92 G5** 25 32N 73 54 E
Deoghar, India .... **93 G12** 24 30N 86 42 E
Deolali, India .... **94 E1** 19 58N 73 50 E
Deoli = Devli, India .... **92 G6** 25 50N 75 20 E
Déols, France .... **27 F8** 46 50N 1 43 E
Deora, India .... **92 F4** 26 22N 70 55 E
Deoria, India .... **93 H8** 23 24N 79 1 E
Deoria, India .... **93 F10** 26 31N 83 48 E
Deosai Mts., Pakistan .... **93 B6** 35 40N 75 0 E
Deosri, India .... **90 B3** 26 46N 90 29 E
Depalpur, India .... **92 H6** 22 51N 75 33 E
Deping, China .... **75 F9** 37 25N 116 58 E
Deposit, U.S.A. **151 D9** 42 4N 75 25W
Depuch I., Australia .... **124 D2** 20 37 S 117 44 E
Deputatskiy, Russia .... **67 C14** 69 18N 139 54 E
Dêqên, China .... **76 C2** 28 34N 98 51 E
Deqing, China .... **77 F8** 23 8N 111 42 E
Dera Ghazi Khan, Pakistan ... **91 C3** 30 5N 70 43 E
Dera Ismail Khan, Pakistan ... **91 C3** 31 50N 70 50 E
Derabugti, Pakistan .... **92 E3** 29 2N 69 9 E
Derawar Fort, Pakistan .... **92 E4** 28 46N 71 20 E
Derbent, Russia .... **61 J9** 42 5N 48 15 E
Derbent, Turkey .... **49 C10** 38 11N 28 33 E
Derbent, Uzbekistan .... **65 D3** 38 13N 67 1 E
Derby, Australia .... **124 C3** 17 18 S 123 38 E
Derby, U.K. **20 E6** 52 56N 1 28W
Derby, Conn., U.S.A. **151 E11** 41 19N 73 5W
Derby, Kans., U.S.A. **155 G6** 37 33N 97 16W
Derby, N.Y., U.S.A. **150 D6** 42 41N 78 58W
Derby City □, U.K. **20 E6** 52 56N 1 28W
Derby Line, U.S.A. **151 B12** 45 0N 72 6W
Derbyshire □, U.K. **20 D6** 53 11N 1 38W
Đerdap, Nac. Park △, Yugoslavia **50 B6** 44 40N 22 23 E
Derdepoort, S. Africa .... **116 C4** 24 38 S 26 24 E
Derecske, Hungary .... **52 C6** 47 20N 21 33 E
Dereköy, Turkey .... **51 E11** 41 55N 27 21 E
Dereli, Turkey .... **101 B8** 40 44N 38 26 E
Derg →, U.K. **23 B4** 54 44N 7 26W
Derg, L., Ireland **23 D3** 53 0N 8 20W
Dergachi = Derhaci, Ukraine .. **59 G9** 50 9N 36 11 E
Derhaci, Ukraine .... **59 G9** 50 9N 36 11 E
Derik, Turkey .... **101 D9** 37 21N 40 18 E
Derinkuyu, Turkey .... **100 C6** 38 22N 34 45 E
Dermantsi, Bulgaria .... **51 C8** 43 8N 24 17 E
Dermott, U.S.A. **155 J9** 33 32N 91 26W
Dêrong, China .... **76 C2** 28 44N 99 9 E
Derrinallum, Australia .... **128 D5** 37 57 S 143 15 E
Derry = Londonderry, U.K. ... **23 B4** 55 0N 7 20W
Derry = Londonderry □, U.K. . **23 B4** 55 0N 7 20W
Derry, N.H., U.S.A. **151 D13** 42 53N 71 19W
Derry, Pa., U.S.A. **150 F5** 40 20N 79 18W
Derryveagh Mts., Ireland **23 B3** 54 56N 8 11W
Derudub, Sudan .... **106 D4** 17 31N 36 7 E
Derval, France **26 E5** 47 40N 1 41W
Derveni, Greece .... **48 C4** 38 8N 22 25 E
Derventa, Bos.-H. .... **52 F2** 44 59N 17 55 E
Derwent →, Cumb., U.K. **20 C4** 54 39N 3 33W
Derwent →, Derby, U.K. **20 E6** 52 57N 1 28W
Derwent →, N. Yorks., U.K. ... **20 D7** 53 45N 0 58W
Derwent Water, U.K. **20 C4** 54 35N 3 9W
Des Moines, Iowa, U.S.A. **156 C3** 41 35N 93 37W
Des Moines, N. Mex., U.S.A. .. **155 G3** 36 46N 103 50W
Des Moines →, U.S.A. **156 D5** 40 23N 91 25W
Des Plaines, U.S.A. **157 B9** 42 3N 87 54W
Des Plaines →, U.S.A. **157 C8** 41 23N 88 15W
Desa, Romania .... **52 G8** 43 52N 23 2 E
Desaguadero, Peru .... **172 D4** 16 34 S 69 3W
Desaguadero →, Argentina ... **174 C2** 34 30 S 66 46W
Desaguadero →, Bolivia ...... **172 D4** 16 35 S 69 5W
Desar, Malaysia .... **87 d** 1 31N 104 17 E
Descanso, Pta., Mexico **161 N9** 32 21N 117 3W
Descartes, France .... **26 B4** 46 59N 0 42 E
Deschaillons, Canada **141 C5** 46 32N 72 7W
Deschambault L., Canada **143 C8** 54 50N 103 30W
Deschutes →, U.S.A. **158 D3** 45 38N 120 55W
Dese, Ethiopia .... **107 E4** 11 5N 39 40 E
Deseado, C., Chile .... **176 D2** 52 45 S 74 42W
Desenzano del Garda, Italy ... **44 C7** 45 28N 10 32 E
Desert Center, U.S.A. **161 M11** 33 43N 115 24W
Desert Hot Springs, U.S.A. ... **161 M10** 33 58N 116 30W
Desertas, Ilhas, Madeira **110 B1** 32 30N 16 40W
Deset, Norway .... **18 C8** 61 20N 11 26 E
Deshnok, India .... **92 F5** 27 48N 73 21 E
Desierto Central de Baja California,
　Parque Natural del △, Mexico **161 N10** 28 42N 114 43W
Desna →, Ukraine .... **59 G6** 50 33N 30 32 E
Desnăţui →, Romania .... **53 G8** 43 53N 23 55 E
Desolación, I., Chile .... **176 D2** 53 0 S 74 0W
Despeñaperros, Parque Natural
　de △, Spain **43 G7** 38 23N 3 32W
Despeñaperros, Paso, Spain ... **43 G7** 38 24N 3 30W
Despotovac, Serbia, Yug. ..... **50 B5** 44 6N 21 30 E
Dessau, Germany .... **30 D7** 51 51N 12 14 E
Dessye = Dese, Ethiopia ...... **107 E4** 11 5N 39 40 E
Destin, U.S.A. **153 E3** 30 24N 86 30W
D'Estrees B., Australia .... **128 C2** 35 55 S 137 45 E
Desuri, India .... **92 G5** 25 18N 73 35 E
Desvres, France .... **27 B8** 50 40N 1 48 E
Det Udom, Thailand .... **86 E5** 14 54N 105 5 E
Deta, Romania .... **52 E6** 45 24N 21 13 E
Dete, Zimbabwe .... **116 B4** 18 38 S 26 50 E
Đetinja →, Serbia, Yug. .... **50 C4** 43 51N 20 2 E
Detmold, Germany .... **30 D4** 51 56N 8 52 E
Detour, Pt., U.S.A. **156 C2** 45 40N 86 40W
Detroit, U.S.A. **150 D1** 42 20N 83 3W
Detroit Lakes, U.S.A. **154 B7** 46 49N 95 51W
Detroit Wayne County ✈ (DTW),
　U.S.A. **157 B13** 42 13N 83 21W

Dettifoss, Iceland **11 B10** 65 48N 16 24W
Detva, Slovak Rep. .... **35 C12** 48 34N 19 25 E
Deurne, Neths. .... **24 C5** 51 27N 5 49 E
Deutsch Krone = Wałcz, Poland ... **55 E3** 53 17N 16 27 E
Deutsch-Luxemburgischer
　Naturpark △, Germany ..... **31 F2** 49 58N 6 12 E
Deutsche Bucht, Germany ..... **30 A4** 54 15N 8 0 E
Deutschlandsberg, Austria .... **34 E8** 46 49N 15 14 E
Deux-Sèvres □, France **26 F6** 46 35N 0 20W
Deva, Romania .... **52 E7** 45 53N 22 55 E
Deva Nat. Park △, Australia .. **129 C8** 35 55 S 149 48 E
Devakottai, India .... **95 K4** 9 55N 78 45 E
Devaprayag, India .... **93 D8** 30 13N 78 35 E
Devarkonda, India .... **94 F4** 16 42N 78 56 E
Dévaványa, Hungary .... **52 C5** 47 2N 20 59 E
Deveci Dağları, Turkey .... **100 B7** 40 6N 36 15 E
Devecikonağı, Turkey .... **51 G12** 39 55N 28 34 E
Develi, Turkey .... **100 C6** 38 23N 35 29 E
Deventer, Neths. .... **24 B6** 52 15N 6 10 E
Devereux, U.S.A. **152 B6** 33 13N 83 5W
Deveron →, U.K. **22 D6** 57 41N 2 32W
Devesel, Romania .... **52 F7** 44 28N 22 41 E
Devgad I., India .... **95 G2** 14 48N 74 5 E
Devgadh Bariya, India .... **92 H5** 22 40N 73 55 E
Devgarh, India .... **95 F1** 16 23N 73 23 E
Devi →, India .... **94 E8** 19 59N 86 24 E
Devikot, India .... **92 F4** 26 42N 71 12 E
Devil River Pk., N.Z. .... **131 A7** 40 56 S 172 37 E
Devils Den, U.S.A. **160 K7** 35 46N 119 58W
Devils Island, I. = Diable, Île du,
　Fr. Guiana **169 B7** 5 16N 52 34W
Devils Lake, U.S.A. **154 A5** 48 7N 98 52W
Devils Paw, Canada **142 B2** 58 47N 134 0W
Devils Postpile Nat. Monument △,
　U.S.A. **160 H7** 37 37N 119 5W
Devil's Pt., Sri Lanka .... **95 K5** 9 26N 80 6 E
Devils Tower Junction, U.S.A. . **154 C2** 44 31N 104 57W
Devils Tower Nat. Monument,
　U.S.A. **154 C2** 44 35N 104 43W
Devin, Bulgaria .... **51 E8** 41 44N 24 24 E
Devine, U.S.A. **155 L5** 29 8N 98 54W
Devipattinam, India .... **95 K4** 9 29N 78 54 E
Devizes, U.K. **21 F6** 51 22N 1 58W
Devli, India .... **92 G6** 25 50N 75 20 E
Devnya, Bulgaria .... **51 C11** 43 13N 27 33 E
Devoll →, Albania .... **50 F4** 40 57N 20 15 E
Devon, Canada **142 C6** 53 24N 113 44W
Devon □, U.K. **21 G4** 50 50N 3 40W
Devon I., Canada **6 B3** 75 10N 85 0W
Devonport, Australia .... **127 D4** 41 10 S 146 22 E
Devrek, Turkey .... **100 B4** 41 13N 31 57 E
Devrekâni, Turkey .... **100 B5** 41 36N 33 50 E
Devrez →, Turkey .... **100 B6** 41 6N 34 25 E
Devrukh, India .... **94 F1** 17 3N 73 37 E
Dewas, India .... **92 H7** 22 59N 76 3 E
Dewetsdorp, S. Africa .... **116 D4** 29 33 S 26 39 E
Dewey, Puerto Rico .... **165 d** 18 18N 65 18W
Dexing, China .... **77 C11** 28 46N 117 30 E
Dexter, Maine, U.S.A. **149 C11** 45 1N 69 18W
Dexter, Mich., U.S.A. **157 B13** 42 20N 83 53W
Dexter, Mo., U.S.A. **155 G10** 36 48N 89 57W
Dexter, N. Mex., U.S.A. **155 J2** 33 12N 104 22W
Dey-Dey, L., Australia .... **125 E5** 29 12 S 131 4 E
Deyang, China .... **76 B5** 31 3N 104 27 E
Deyhūk, Iran .... **97 C8** 33 15N 57 30 E
Deyyer, Iran .... **97 E6** 27 55N 51 55 E
Dezadeash L., Canada **142 A1** 60 28N 136 58W
Dezfūl, Iran .... **97 C6** 32 20N 48 30 E
Dezhneva, Mys, Russia **67 C19** 66 5N 169 40W
Dezhou, China .... **74 F9** 37 26N 116 18 E
Dhadhar →, India .... **93 G11** 24 56N 85 24 E
Dháfni, Kríti, Greece .... **39 E6** 35 13N 25 3 E
Dháfni, Pelopónnisos, Greece .. **48 D3** 37 48N 22 1 E
Dhafnoúdhi, Ákra, Greece .... **39 C2** 38 28N 20 32 E
Dhahaban, Si. Arabia .... **98 B2** 21 58N 39 3 E
Dhahiriya = Aẓ Ẓāhirīyah,
　West Bank .... **103 D3** 31 25N 34 58 E
Dhahran = Aẓ Ẓahrān, Si. Arabia **97 E6** 26 10N 50 7 E
Dhak, Pakistan .... **92 C5** 32 25N 72 33 E
Dhaka, Bangla. .... **90 D3** 23 43N 90 26 E
Dhaka □, Bangla. .... **90 C3** 24 25N 90 25 E
Dhali, Cyprus .... **39 E9** 35 1N 33 25 E
Dhamangaon, India .... **94 D4** 20 48N 78 9 E
Dhamār, Yemen .... **98 D4** 14 30N 44 20 E
Dhamási, Greece .... **48 B4** 39 43N 22 11 E
Dhampur, India .... **93 E8** 29 19N 78 33 E
Dhamra →, India .... **94 D8** 20 47N 86 58 E
Dhamtari, India .... **94 D3** 20 42N 81 35 E
Dhanbad, India .... **93 H12** 23 50N 86 30 E
Dhankuta, Nepal .... **93 F12** 26 55N 87 40 E
Dhanora, India .... **94 D5** 20 20N 80 22 E
Dhanushkodi, India .... **95 K4** 9 11N 79 24 E
Dhar, India .... **92 H6** 22 35N 75 26 E
Dharampur, Gujarat, India ... **94 D1** 20 32N 73 17 E
Dharampur, Mad. P., India ... **92 H6** 22 13N 75 18 E
Dharamsala = Dharmsala, India **92 C7** 32 16N 76 23 E
Dharangaon, India .... **94 D2** 21 1N 75 16 E
Dharapuram, India .... **95 J3** 10 45N 77 34 E
Dhariwal, India .... **92 D6** 31 57N 75 19 E
Dharla →, Bangla. .... **93 G13** 25 46N 89 42 E
Dharmapuri, India .... **95 H4** 12 10N 78 10 E
Dharmavaram, India .... **95 G3** 14 29N 77 44 E
Dharmjaygarh, India .... **93 H10** 22 28N 83 13 E
Dharmsala, India .... **92 C7** 32 16N 76 23 E
Dharni, India .... **92 J7** 21 33N 76 53 E
Dharug Nat. Park △, Australia . **129 B9** 33 20 S 151 2 E
Dharur, India .... **94 E3** 18 50N 76 13 E
Dharwad, India .... **95 G2** 15 30N 75 4 E
Dhasan →, India .... **93 G8** 25 48N 79 24 E
Dhaulagiri, Nepal .... **93 E10** 28 39N 83 28 E
Dhebar, L., India .... **92 G6** 24 10N 74 0 E
Dheftera, Cyprus .... **39 E9** 35 5N 33 16 E
Dhenkanal, India .... **94 D7** 20 45N 85 35 E
Dhenoúsa, Greece .... **49 D7** 37 8N 25 48 E
Dherinia, Cyprus .... **39 E9** 35 3N 33 57 E
Dheskáti, Greece .... **50 G5** 39 55N 21 49 E
Dhespotikó, Greece .... **48 E6** 36 57N 24 58 E
Dhestina, Greece .... **48 C4** 38 25N 22 31 E
Dhiarrizos →, Cyprus .... **39 F8** 34 41N 32 34 E
Dhíavlos Zakínthou, Greece ... **39 D7** 37 50N 21 0 E
Dhíbān, Jordan .... **103 D4** 31 30N 35 46 E
Dhidhimótikhon, Greece ..... **51 E10** 41 22N 26 29 E
Dhíkti Óros, Greece .... **39 E6** 35 8N 25 30 E
Dhilianáta, Greece .... **39 C2** 38 13N 20 31 E
Dhílos, Greece .... **49 D7** 37 23N 25 15 E
Dhilwan, India .... **92 D6** 31 31N 75 21 E
Dhimarkhera, India .... **93 H9** 23 28N 80 22 E
Dhímitsána, Greece .... **48 D3** 37 36N 22 3 E
Dhírfis Óros, Greece .... **48 C5** 38 40N 23 54 E
Dhodhekánisos □, Greece .... **49 E8** 36 35N 27 0 E
Dhodhekánisos □, Greece .... **49 E8** 36 35N 27 0 E
Dhokós, Greece .... **48 D5** 37 20N 23 20 E
Dholiana, Greece .... **48 B2** 39 54N 20 32 E
Dholka, India .... **92 H5** 22 44N 72 29 E
Dhomokós, Greece .... **48 B4** 39 10N 22 18 E
Dhoraji, India .... **92 J4** 21 45N 70 37 E
Dhoxáton, Greece .... **51 E8** 41 9N 24 16 E
Dragonísti, Greece .... **48 D5** 37 27N 23 29 E
Dhrástis, Ákra, Greece .... **38 B9** 39 48N 19 40 E
Dhrakáta, Greece .... **39 C2** 38 16N 20 35 E
Dhrangadhra, India .... **92 H4** 22 59N 71 31 E
Dhrápanon, Ákra, Greece .... **39 E5** 35 28N 24 14 E

Dhriopís, Greece .... **48 D6** 37 25N 24 26 E
Dhrol, India .... **92 H4** 22 33N 70 25 E
Dhubāb, Yemen .... **98 D3** 12 56N 43 25 E
Dhuburi, India .... **90 B2** 26 2N 89 59 E
Dhule, India .... **94 D2** 20 58N 74 50 E
Dhupdhara, India .... **90 B3** 26 10N 91 3 E
Dhuusa Marreeb = Dusa Mareb,
　Somali Rep. .... **120 C3** 5 30N 46 15 E
Di-ib, W. →, Sudan .... **106 C4** 22 38N 36 6 E
Di Linh, Vietnam .... **87 G7** 11 35N 108 4 E
Di Linh, Cao Nguyen, Vietnam **87 G7** 11 30N 108 0 E
Día, Greece .... **39 E6** 35 28N 25 14 E
Diabakania, Guinea **112 C2** 10 38N 10 58W
Diable, Île du, Fr. Guiana **169 B7** 5 16N 52 34W
Diablo, Mt., U.S.A. **160 H5** 37 53N 121 56W
Diablo Range, U.S.A. **160 J5** 37 20N 121 25W
Diafarabé, Mali **112 C4** 14 9N 4 57W
Diala, Mali **112 C3** 14 10N 9 58W
Dialakoro, Mali **112 C3** 12 18N 7 54W
Dialakoto, Senegal **112 C2** 13 21N 13 19W
Diallassagou, Mali **112 C4** 13 47N 3 41W
Diamante, Argentina .... **174 C3** 32 5 S 60 40W
Diamante →, Argentina ...... **174 C2** 34 30 S 66 46W
Diamantina, Brazil .... **171 E3** 18 17 S 43 40W
Diamantina →, Australia ..... **127 D2** 26 45 S 139 10 E
Diamantina Nat. Park △, Australia **126 C3** 23 33 S 141 23 E
Diamantino, Brazil .... **173 C6** 14 30 S 56 30W
Diamond Bar, U.S.A. **161 L9** 34 1N 117 48W
Diamond Harbour, India ..... **93 H13** 22 11N 88 14 E
Diamond Head, U.S.A. **152 K14** 21 16N 157 49W
Diamond Is., Australia .... **126 B5** 17 25 S 151 5 E
Diamond Mts., U.S.A. **158 G6** 39 50N 115 30W
Diamond Springs, U.S.A. **160 G6** 38 42N 120 49W
Dian Chi, China .... **76 E4** 24 50N 102 43 E
Dianalund, Denmark .... **17 J5** 55 32N 11 30 E
Dianbai, China .... **77 G8** 21 33N 111 0 E
Diancheng, China .... **77 G8** 21 30N 111 4 E
Dianjiang, China .... **76 B6** 30 24N 107 20 E
Diano Marina, Italy .... **44 E5** 43 54N 8 5 E
Dianópolis, Brazil .... **171 D2** 11 38 S 46 50W
Dianra, Ivory C. **112 D3** 8 45N 6 14W
Diapaga, Burkina Faso .... **113 C5** 12 5N 1 46 E
Diapangou, Burkina Faso ..... **113 C5** 12 5N 0 10 E
Diariguila, Guinea **112 C2** 10 35N 10 2W
Diavolo, Mt., India .... **95 H11** 12 40N 92 56 E
Dībā, Oman .... **97 E8** 25 45N 56 16 E
Dibaba, India .... **92 E8** 28 13N 78 15 E
Dibaya, Dem. Rep. of the Congo **115 D4** 6 30 S 22 57 E
Dibaya-Lubue, Dem. Rep. of
　the Congo .... **115 C3** 4 12 S 19 54 E
Dibbeen Nat. Park △, Jordan . **103 C4** 32 20N 35 45 E
Dibella, Niger .... **109 E2** 17 32N 13 6 E
Dibete, Botswana .... **116 C4** 23 45 S 26 32 E
Dibrugarh, India .... **90 B5** 27 29N 94 55 E
Dickens, U.S.A. **155 J4** 33 37N 100 50W
Dickeyville, U.S.A. **156 B6** 42 38N 90 36W
Dickinson, U.S.A. **154 B3** 46 53N 102 47W
Dick's Pt., Bahamas .... **9 b** 25 4N 77 18W
Dickson = Dikson, Russia .... **66 B9** 73 40N 80 5 E
Dickson, U.S.A. **149 G2** 36 5N 87 23W
Dickson City, U.S.A. **151 E9** 41 29N 75 40W
Dicle Nehri →, Turkey .... **100 B9** 37 44N 41 10 E
Dicomano, Italy .... **45 E8** 43 53N 11 31 E
Didcot, U.K. **21 F6** 51 36N 1 14W
Didesa, W. →, Ethiopia .... **107 F4** 10 2N 35 32 E
Didiéni, Mali **112 C3** 13 53N 8 6W
Didimbo, Angola .... **115 F4** 17 30 S 21 45 E
Didsbury, Canada **142 C6** 51 35N 114 10W
Didwana, India .... **92 F6** 27 23N 74 36 E
Die, France .... **29 D9** 44 47N 5 22 E
Diébougou, Burkina Faso **112 C4** 11 0N 3 15W
Diecke, Guinea **112 D3** 7 2N 8 30W
Diefenbaker, L., Canada **143 C7** 51 0N 106 55W
Diego de Almagro, Chile ..... **174 B1** 26 22 S 70 3W
Diego Ramírez, Islas, Chile ... **176 E3** 56 30 S 68 44W
Diekirch, Lux. .... **24 E6** 49 52N 6 10 E
Diéma, Mali **112 C3** 14 32N 9 12W
Diembéring, Senegal **112 C1** 12 29N 16 47W
Diemelsee, Naturpark △, Germany **30 D4** 51 20N 8 40 E
Dien Ban, Vietnam .... **86 E7** 15 53N 108 16 E
Dien Bien, Vietnam .... **76 G4** 21 20N 103 0 E
Dien Khanh, Vietnam .... **87 F7** 12 15N 109 6 E
Diepholz, Germany .... **30 C4** 52 37N 8 22 E
Diepoldsau, Switz. .... **33 B9** 47 23N 9 40 E
Dieppe, France .... **26 C8** 49 54N 1 4 E
Dierks, U.S.A. **155 H8** 34 7N 94 1W
Diessenhofen, Switz. .... **33 A7** 47 42N 8 46 E
Diest, Belgium .... **24 D5** 50 58N 5 4 E
Dieterich, U.S.A. **157 E8** 39 4N 88 23W
Dietikon, Switz. .... **33 B6** 47 24N 8 24 E
Dieulefit, France .... **29 D9** 44 32N 5 4 E
Dieulouard, France .... **27 D13** 48 49N 6 5 E
Dif, Somali Rep. .... **120 D2** 0 59N 40 58 E
Differdange, Lux. .... **24 E5** 49 31N 5 54 E
Diffun, Phil. .... **80 C3** 16 36N 121 33 E
Dig, India .... **92 F7** 27 28N 77 20 E
Digba, Dem. Rep. of the Congo **118 B2** 4 25N 25 48 E
Digboi, India .... **90 B5** 27 29N 95 38 E
Digby, Canada **141 D6** 44 38N 65 50W
Diggi, India .... **92 F6** 26 22N 75 26 E
Dighinala, Bangla. .... **90 D4** 23 15N 92 5 E
Dighton, U.S.A. **154 F4** 38 29N 100 28W
Digne-les-Bains, France ...... **29 D10** 44 5N 6 12 E
Digoin, France .... **27 F11** 46 29N 4 1 E
Digor, Turkey .... **101 B10** 40 22N 43 25 E
Digos, Phil. .... **81 H5** 6 45N 125 20 E
Digranes, Iceland **11 A12** 66 4N 14 44W
Digras, India .... **94 D3** 20 6N 77 45 E
Digul →, Indonesia .... **83 C5** 7 7 S 138 42 E
Dihang = Brahmaputra →, Asia **68 D3** 23 40N 90 35 E
Dijlah, Nahr →, Asia .... **96 D5** 31 0N 47 25 E
Dijon, France .... **27 E12** 47 20N 5 3 E
Dikhil, Djibouti .... **107 E5** 11 8N 42 20 E
Dikili, Turkey .... **49 B8** 39 4N 26 53 E
Dikirnis, Egypt .... **106 H7** 31 6N 31 35 E
Dikkil = Dikhil, Djibouti ..... **107 E5** 11 8N 42 20 E
Dikodougou, Ivory C. **112 D3** 9 6N 5 27W
Diksmuide, Belgium .... **24 C2** 51 2N 2 52 E
Dikson, Russia .... **66 B9** 73 40N 80 5 E
Dikwa, Nigeria .... **113 C7** 12 4N 13 30 E
Dila, Ethiopia .... **107 F4** 6 21N 38 22 E
Dilasag, Phil. .... **80 C4** 16 25N 122 11 E
Dili, E. Timor .... **82 C3** 8 39 S 125 34 E
Diligent Strait, India .... **95 H11** 12 11N 92 57 E
Dilijan, Armenia .... **61 K7** 40 46N 44 57 E
Dilizhan = Dilijan, Armenia .. **61 K7** 40 46N 44 57 E
Dilj, Croatia .... **52 E3** 45 29N 18 1 E
Dillenburg, Germany .... **30 C4** 50 44N 8 17 E
Dilley, U.S.A. **155 L5** 28 40N 99 10W
Dillia →, Niger .... **109 E2** 14 9N 18 24 E
Dilling, Sudan .... **107 E2** 12 3N 29 35 E
Dillingen, Bayern, Germany .. **31 G6** 48 34N 10 29 E
Dillingen, Saarland, Germany . **31 F2** 49 22N 6 43 E
Dillingham, U.S.A. **144 G8** 59 3N 158 28W
Dillon, Canada **143 B7** 55 56N 108 35W
Dillon, Mont., U.S.A. **158 D7** 45 13N 112 38W

Dillon, S.C., U.S.A. **149 H6** 34 25N 79 22W
Dillon →, Canada **143 B7** 55 56N 108 56W
Dillsboro, U.S.A. **157 E11** 39 1N 85 4W
Dillsburg, U.S.A. **150 F7** 40 7N 77 2W
Dilly, Mali **112 C3** 15 1N 7 40W
Dilolo, Dem. Rep. of the Congo **115 E4** 10 28 S 22 18 E
Dimas, Mexico **162 C3** 23 43N 106 47W
Dimapur, India .... **90 C4** 25 54N 93 45 E
Dimashq, Syria .... **103 B5** 33 30N 36 18 E
Dimashq □, Syria .... **103 B5** 33 30N 36 30 E
Dimbaza, S. Africa .... **117 E4** 32 50 S 27 14 E
Dimbelenge, Dem. Rep. of the Congo **115 D4** 5 33 S 23 7 E
Dimbokro, Ivory C. **112 D4** 6 45N 4 46W
Dimboola, Australia .... **128 D5** 36 28 S 142 7 E
Dimbovița = Dâmbovița →,
　Romania .... **53 F11** 44 12N 26 26 E
Dimbulah, Australia .... **126 B4** 17 8 S 145 4 E
Dimitrovgrad, Bulgaria ...... **51 D9** 42 5N 25 35 E
Dimitrovgrad, Russia .... **60 C9** 54 14N 49 39 E
Dimitrovgrad, Serbia, Yug. ... **50 C6** 43 2N 22 48 E
Dimitrovo = Pernik, Bulgaria . **50 D7** 42 35N 23 2 E
Dimmitt, U.S.A. **155 H3** 34 33N 102 19W
Dimo, Sudan .... **107 F2** 5 19N 29 10 E
Dimona, Israel .... **103 D4** 31 2N 35 1 E
Dimonika, Réserve de la Biosphere
　de △, Congo .... **114 C2** 4 13 S 12 21 E
Dimovo, Bulgaria .... **50 C6** 43 43N 22 50 E
Dinagat, Phil. .... **81 F5** 10 10N 125 40 E
Dinaig, Phil. .... **81 H5** 7 11N 124 10 E
Dinajpur, Bangla. .... **90 C2** 25 33N 88 43 E
Dinalupihan, Phil. .... **80 D3** 14 52N 120 28 E
Dinan, France **26 D4** 48 28N 2 2W
Dīnān Āb, Iran .... **97 C8** 32 4N 56 49 E
Dinant, Belgium .... **24 D4** 50 16N 4 55 E
Dinapur, India .... **93 G11** 25 38N 85 5 E
Dinar, Turkey .... **49 C12** 38 5N 30 10 E
Dīnār, Kūh-e, Iran .... **97 D6** 30 42N 51 46 E
Dinara Planina, Croatia ..... **45 D13** 44 0N 16 30 E
Dinard, France **26 D4** 48 38N 2 6W
Dinaric Alps = Dinara Planina,
　Croatia .... **45 D13** 44 0N 16 30 E
Dinas, Phil. .... **81 H4** 7 38N 123 20 E
Dindanko, Mali **112 C3** 14 8N 9 9W
Dinde, Angola .... **115 E2** 14 17 S 13 42 E
Dinder, Nahr ed →, Sudan ... **107 E3** 14 6N 33 40 E
Dindi →, India .... **94 F4** 16 24N 80 5 E
Dindigul, India .... **95 J4** 10 25N 78 0 E
Dindori, India .... **93 H9** 22 57N 81 5 E
Ding Xian = Dingzhou, China **74 E8** 38 30N 114 59 E
Dinga, Dem. Rep. of the Congo **115 D3** 5 17 S 16 42 E
Dinga, Pakistan .... **92 G2** 25 26N 67 10 E
Dingalan, Phil. .... **80 D3** 15 18N 121 25 E
Dingalan Bay, Phil. .... **80 D3** 15 18N 121 25 E
Dingbian, China .... **74 F4** 37 35N 107 32 E
Dingelstädt, Germany .... **30 D6** 51 18N 10 19 E
Dingle, Ireland **23 D1** 52 9N 10 17W
Dingle, Sweden .... **17 F5** 58 32N 11 35 E
Dingle B., Ireland **23 D1** 52 3N 10 20W
Dingli, Malta .... **38 F7** 35 52N 14 23 E
Dingmans Ferry, U.S.A. **151 E10** 41 13N 74 55W
Dingnan, China .... **77 E10** 24 45N 115 0 E
Dingo, Australia .... **126 C4** 23 38 S 149 19 E
Dingolfing, Germany .... **31 G7** 48 38N 12 30 E
Dingras, Phil. .... **80 B3** 18 6N 120 42 E
Dingtao, China .... **74 G8** 35 5N 115 35 E
Dinguira, Mali **112 C2** 14 11N 11 16W
Dinguiraye, Guinea **112 C2** 11 18N 10 49W
Dingwall, U.K. **22 D4** 57 36N 4 26W
Dingxi, China .... **74 G3** 35 30N 104 33 E
Dingxiang, China .... **74 E7** 38 30N 112 58 E
Dingzhou, China .... **74 E8** 38 30N 114 59 E
Dinh, Mui, Vietnam .... **87 G7** 11 22N 109 1 E
Dinh Lap, Vietnam .... **76 G6** 21 33N 107 6 E
Dinhata, India .... **90 B2** 26 8N 89 27 E
Dinira, Parque Nac. △, Venezuela **165 E5** 9 57N 70 6W
Dinokwe, Botswana .... **116 C4** 23 29 S 26 37 E
Dinorwic, Canada **143 D10** 49 41N 92 30W
Dinosaur Nat. Monument △, U.S.A. **158 F9** 40 30N 108 45W
Dinosaur Prov. Park △, Canada **142 C6** 50 47N 111 30W
Dinsor, Somali Rep. .... **120 D2** 2 24N 42 59 E
Dinuba, U.S.A. **160 J7** 36 32N 119 23W
Diö, Sweden .... **17 H8** 56 37N 14 15 E
Dioïla, Mali **112 C3** 12 23N 6 50W
Dioka, Mali **112 C2** 14 57N 10 4W
Diomede, U.S.A. **144 D5** 65 47N 169 0W
Diona, Chad .... **109 E4** 17 51N 22 36 E
Diongoï, Mali **112 C3** 14 38N 8 34W
Diósgyör, Hungary .... **52 B5** 48 7N 20 43 E
Diosig, Romania .... **52 C7** 47 18N 22 2 E
Diouani, Mali **112 C4** 14 19N 2 44W
Dioudiou, Senegal .... **112 C1** 16 12N 14 8 E
Dioura, Mali **112 C3** 14 5N 5 16W
Diourbel, Senegal **112 C1** 14 39N 16 12W
Dipacundo, Phil. .... **80 D3** 15 51N 121 32 E
Dipalpur, Pakistan .... **92 D5** 30 40N 73 39 E
Diplo, Pakistan .... **81 G4** 8 36 S 120 29 E
Dipolog, Phil. .... **81 G4** 8 36N 123 20 E
Dipperu Nat. Park △, Australia **126 C4** 21 56 S 148 42 E
Dipton, N.Z. .... **131 F3** 45 54 S 168 22 E
Dir, Pakistan .... **91 B3** 35 8N 71 59 E
Diré, Mali **112 B4** 16 20N 3 25W
Dire Dawa, Ethiopia .... **107 F5** 9 35N 41 45 E
Diriamba, Nic. **164 D2** 11 51N 86 19W
Dirico, Angola .... **115 F4** 17 50 S 20 42 E
Dirk Hartog I., Australia .... **125 E1** 25 50 S 113 5 E
Dirkou, Niger .... **109 E2** 19 1N 12 53 E
Dirranbandi, Australia ...... **127 D4** 28 33 S 148 17 E
Dirs, Si. Arabia .... **98 C3** 13 22N 43 22 E
Disa, India .... **92 G4** 24 18N 72 10 E
Disa, Sudan .... **107 E3** 12 5N 34 15 E
Disappointment, C., U.S.A. ... **158 C2** 46 18N 124 5W
Disappointment, L., Australia . **124 D3** 23 20 S 122 40 E
Disaster B., Australia .... **129 D8** 37 15 S 149 58 E
Discovery B., Australia ...... **128 D4** 38 10 S 140 40 E
Discovery B., China .... **69 G11** 22 18N 114 1 E
Discovery Bay Nat. Park △, Australia **128 D4** 39 S 141 16 E
Disentis Muster, Switz. ...... **33 C7** 46 42N 8 50 E
Dishna, Egypt .... **106 B3** 26 9N 32 32 E
Disina, Nigeria .... **113 C6** 11 35N 9 50 E
Disko = Qeqertarsuaq, Greenland **10 D5** 69 45N 53 30W
Disko Bugt, Greenland **10 D5** 69 10N 52 0W
Disna = Dzisna →, Belarus ... **58 E5** 55 34N 28 12 E
Disney Reef, Tonga .... **133 P13** 19 17 S 174 7W
Dispur, India .... **90 B3** 26 3N 91 52 E
Diss, U.K. .... **21 E9** 52 23N 1 7 E
Disteghil Sar, Pakistan ...... **93 A6** 36 20N 75 12 E
Distrito Federal □, Brazil .... **171 E2** 15 45 S 47 45W
Distrito Federal □, Mexico ... **163 D5** 19 15N 99 10W
Distrito Federal □, Venezuela . **164 A5** 10 30N 66 55W
Disūq, Egypt .... **106 H7** 31 8N 30 35 E
Diu, India .... **92 J4** 20 45N 70 58 E
Diuata Mts., Phil. .... **81 G5** 9 0N 125 30 E
Diuata Pt., Phil. .... **101 E12** 8 55N 125 47 E
Dīvāndarreh, Iran .... **114 C2** 2 43 S 12 1 E
Divernié □ .... **114 C2** 2 43 S 12 1 E
Dives →, France **26 C6** 49 18N 0 7W
Dives-sur-Mer, France **26 C6** 49 18N 0 8W
Divi Pt., India .... **95 G5** 15 59N 81 2 E
Divichi = Dāvāçi, Azerbaijan .. **61 K9** 41 15N 48 57 E
Divinópolis, Brazil .... **171 F3** 20 10 S 44 54W

Divisões, Serra dos, *Brazil* .... **171 E1** 17 0 S 51 0W
Divjake, *Albania* .... **50 F3** 41 0N 19 32 E
Divnoye, *Russia* .... **61 H6** 45 55N 43 21 E
Divo, *Ivory C.* **112 D3** 5 48N 5 15W
Diviği, *Turkey* .... **101 C8** 39 22N 38 7 E
Diwāl Kol, *Afghan.* .... **91 B2** 34 23N 67 52 E
Dix →, *U.S.A.* **157 G12** 37 49N 84 43W
Dixie Mt., *U.S.A.* **160 F6** 39 55N 120 16W
Dixie Union, *U.S.A.* **152 D7** 31 20N 82 28W
Dixon, *Calif., U.S.A.* **160 G5** 38 27N 121 49W
Dixon, *Ill., U.S.A.* **156 C7** 41 50N 89 29W
Dixon, *Mo., U.S.A.* **156 G4** 37 59N 92 6W
Dixon Entrance, *U.S.A.* **138 C6** 54 30N 132 0W
Dixville, *Canada* **151 A13** 45 4N 71 46W
Diyadin, *Turkey* .... **101 C10** 39 33N 43 40 E
Diyālā □, *Iraq* .... **101 F11** 33 14N 44 31 E
Diyarbakir, *Turkey* .... **101 D9** 37 55N 40 18 E
Diyodar, *India* .... **92 G4** 24 8N 71 50 E
Dja, Réserve du ⌂, *Cameroon* .. **114 B2** 3 10N 12 58 E
Djadié →, *Gabon* .... **114 B2** 0 46N 12 58 E
Djado, *Niger* .... **109 D2** 21 4N 12 14 E
Djado, Plateau du, *Niger* ...... **109 D2** 21 29N 12 21 E
Djakarta = Jakarta, *Indonesia* .. **84 D3** 6 9 S 106 49 E
Djamâa, *Algeria* .... **111 B6** 33 32N 5 59 E
Djamba, *Angola* .... **116 B1** 16 45 S 13 58 E
Djambala, *Congo* .... **114 C2** 2 32 S 14 30 E
Djanet, *Algeria* .... **111 D6** 24 35N 9 32 E
Djaul I., *Papua N. G.* .... **132 B6** 2 58 S 150 57 E
Djawa = Jawa, *Indonesia* ...... **85 D4** 7 0 S 110 0 E
Djebiniana, *Tunisia* .... **108 A2** 35 1N 11 0 E
Djédaa, *Chad* .... **109 F3** 13 31N 18 34 E
Djelfa, *Algeria* .... **111 B5** 34 40N 3 15 E
Djema, *C.A.R.* .... **118 A2** 6 3N 25 15 E
Djember, *Chad* .... **109 F2** 10 25N 17 50 E
Djembo, *Dem. Rep. of the Congo* **115 D4** 9 54 S 22 18 E
Djendel, *Algeria* .... **111 A5** 36 15N 2 25 E
Djeneïene, *Tunisia* .... **108 B2** 31 45N 10 9 E
Djenné, *Mali* **112 C4** 14 0N 4 30W
Djenoun, Garet el, *Algeria* ..... **111 C6** 25 4N 5 31 E
Djerba, *Tunisia* .... **108 B2** 33 52N 10 51 E
Djerba, I. de, *Tunisia* .... **108 B2** 33 50N 10 48 E
Djéréme →, *Cameroon* .... **114 A2** 5 20N 13 24 E
Djerid, Chott, *Tunisia* .... **108 B1** 33 42N 8 30 E
Djiba, *Gabon* .... **114 C2** 1 20 S 13 9 E
Djibo, *Burkina Faso* **113 C4** 14 9N 1 35W
Djibouti, *Djibouti* .... **107 E5** 11 30N 43 5 E
Djibouti ■, *Africa* .... **107 E5** 12 0N 43 0 E
Djolu, *Dem. Rep. of the Congo* . **114 B2** 0 35N 22 5 E
Djouab →, *Gabon* .... **114 B2** 1 13N 13 12 E
Djougou, *Benin* .... **113 D5** 9 40N 1 45 E
Djoum, *Cameroon* .... **114 B2** 2 41N 12 35 E
Djourna, *Chad* .... **109 F4** 10 27N 20 4 E
Djourab, Erg du, *Chad* .... **109 E3** 16 40N 18 50 E
Djugu, *Dem. Rep. of the Congo* **118 B3** 1 55N 30 35 E
Djúpávík, *Iceland* **11 B5** 65 57N 21 34W
Djúpivogur, *Iceland* **11 C12** 64 39N 14 17W
Djupvasshytta, *Norway* .... **18 B4** 62 2N 7 16 E
Djurås, *Sweden* .... **18 D9** 60 36N 15 8 E
Djurdjura, Parc Nat. du ⌂, *Algeria* **111 A5** 35 20N 4 15 E
Djurö Nationalpark ⌂, *Sweden* . **17 F7** 58 52N 13 28 E
Djursland, *Denmark* .... **17 H4** 56 27N 10 45 E
Dmitriya Lapteva, Proliv, *Russia* . **67 B15** 73 0N 140 0 E
Dmitriyev Lgovskiy, *Russia* .... **59 F8** 52 10N 35 0 E
Dmitrov, *Russia* .... **58 D9** 56 25N 37 32 E
Dmitrovsk-Orlovskiy, *Russia* ... **59 F8** 52 29N 35 10 E
Dnepr = Dnipro →, *Ukraine* ... **59 J7** 46 30N 32 18 E
Dneprodzerzhinsk =
Dniprodzerzhynsk, *Ukraine* .... **59 H8** 48 32N 34 37 E
Dneprodzerzhinskoye Vdkhr. =
Dniprodzerzhynske Vdskh.,
Ukraine .... **59 H8** 48 49N 34 8 E
Dnepropetrovsk = Dnipropetrovsk,
Ukraine .... **59 H8** 48 30N 35 0 E
Dneprorudnoye = Dniprorudne,
Ukraine .... **59 J8** 47 21N 34 58 E
Dnestr = Dnister →, *Europe* ... **59 J6** 46 18N 30 17 E
Dnestrovski = Belgorod, *Russia* . **59 G9** 50 35N 36 35 E
Dnieper = Dnipro →, *Ukraine* . **59 J7** 46 30N 32 18 E
Dniester = Dnister →, *Europe* .. **59 J6** 46 18N 30 17 E
Dnipro →, *Ukraine* .... **59 J7** 46 30N 32 18 E
Dniprodzerzhynsk, *Ukraine* .... **59 H8** 48 32N 34 37 E
Dniprodzerzhynske Vdskh., *Ukraine* **59 H8** 48 49N 34 8 E
Dnipropetrovsk, *Ukraine* ...... **59 H8** 48 30N 35 0 E
Dniprorudne, *Ukraine* .... **59 J8** 47 21N 34 58 E
Dnister →, *Europe* .... **59 J6** 46 18N 30 17 E
Dnistrovskyy Lyman, *Ukraine* .. **59 J6** 46 15N 30 17 E
Dno, *Russia* .... **58 D5** 57 50N 29 58 E
Dnyapro = Dnipro →, *Ukraine* . **59 J7** 46 30N 32 18 E
Doabi, *Afghan.* .... **91 A3** 36 1N 69 32 E
Doaktown, *Canada* **141 C6** 46 33N 66 8W
Doan Hung, *Vietnam* .... **76 G5** 21 30N 105 10 E
Doany, *Madag.* .... **117 A8** 14 21 S 49 30 E
Doba, *Chad* .... **109 G3** 8 40N 16 50 E
Dobandi, *Pakistan* .... **92 D2** 31 13N 66 50 E
Dobbiaco, *Italy* .... **45 B9** 46 44N 12 14 E
Dobbyn, *Australia* .... **126 B3** 19 44 S 140 2 E
Dobczyce, *Poland* .... **55 J7** 49 52N 20 5 E
Dobele, *Latvia* .... **15 H20** 56 37N 23 16 E
Dobele □, *Latvia* .... **54 B10** 56 35N 23 5 E
Döbeln, *Germany* .... **30 D9** 51 6N 13 7 E
Doberai, Jazirah, *Indonesia* .... **83 B4** 1 25 S 133 0 E
Dobiegniew, *Poland* .... **55 F2** 52 59N 15 45 E
Doblas, *Argentina* .... **174 D3** 37 5 S 64 0W
Dobo, *Dem. Rep. of the Congo* . **114 B4** 2 20N 22 11 E
Dobo, *Indonesia* .... **83 C4** 5 45 S 134 15 E
Doboj, *Bos.-H.* .... **52 F3** 44 46N 18 4 E
Dobra, *Wielkopolskie, Poland* .. **55 G5** 51 55N 18 37 E
Dobra, Zachodnio-Pomorskie,
Poland .... **54 E2** 53 34N 15 20 E
Dobra, Dîmboviţa, *Romania* ... **53 F10** 44 52N 25 40 E
Dobra, Hunedoara, *Romania* ... **52 E7** 45 54N 22 36 E
Dobre Miasto, *Poland* .... **54 E7** 53 58N 20 26 E
Dobreşti, *Romania* .... **52 D7** 46 51N 22 18 E
Dobrich, *Bulgaria* .... **51 C11** 43 37N 27 49 E
Dobrinishta, *Bulgaria* .... **50 E7** 41 49N 23 34 E
Dobříš, *Czech Rep.* .... **34 B7** 49 46N 14 10 E
Dobrodzień, *Poland* .... **55 H5** 50 45N 18 25 E
Dobropole, *Ukraine* .... **59 H9** 48 25N 37 2 E
Dobruja, *Europe* .... **53 F13** 44 30N 28 15 E
Dobrush, *Belarus* .... **59 F6** 52 25N 31 22 E
Dobrzany, *Poland* .... **54 E2** 53 22N 15 25 E
Dobrzyń nad Wisłą, *Poland* .... **55 F6** 52 39N 19 22 E
Doc, Mui, *Vietnam* .... **86 D6** 17 58N 106 30 E
Doc Can L., *Phil.* .... **81 J2** 5 55N 119 56 E
Doce →, *Brazil* .... **171 E4** 19 37 S 39 49W
Docker River, *Australia* .... **127 D4** 24 52 S 129 5 E
Dockta, *Sweden* .... **16 A12** 63 3N 18 34 E
Doctor Arroyo, *Mexico* **162 C4** 23 40N 100 11W
Doctors Inlet, *U.S.A.* **152 E8** 30 6N 81 47W
Doda, *India* .... **93 C6** 33 10N 75 34 E
Doda, L., *Canada* **140 C4** 49 25N 75 13W
Doda Betta, *India* .... **95 J3** 11 24N 76 44 E
Dodaga, *Indonesia* .... **83 A3** 1 9N 128 11 E
Dodballapur, *India* .... **95 H3** 13 18N 77 32 E
Dodecanese = Dhodhekánisos,
Greece .... **49 E8** 36 35N 27 0 E
Dodge City, *U.S.A.* **155 G5** 37 45N 100 1W
Dodge L., *Canada* **143 B7** 59 50N 105 36W
Dodgeville, *U.S.A.* **156 B6** 42 58N 90 8W
Dodjı, *Cameroon* .... **113 D7** 7 30N 12 3 E
Dodo, *Sudan* .... **107 F2** 5 10N 29 57 E
Dodola, *Ethiopia* .... **107 F4** 6 59N 39 11 E

Dodoma, *Tanzania* .... **118 D4** 6 8 S 35 45 E
Dodoma □, *Tanzania* .... **118 D4** 6 0 S 36 0 E
Dodona, *Greece* .... **48 B2** 39 40N 20 46 E
Dodori Nat. Reserve ⌂, *Kenya* . **118 C5** 1 55 S 41 7 E
Dodsland, *Canada* **143 C7** 51 50N 108 45W
Dodson, *U.S.A.* **158 B9** 48 24N 108 15W
Dodurga, *Turkey* .... **49 B11** 39 49N 29 57 E
Doerun, *U.S.A.* **152 D6** 31 19N 83 55W
Doesburg, *Neths.* .... **24 B6** 52 1N 6 9 E
Doetinchem, *Neths.* .... **24 C6** 51 59N 6 18 E
Dog Creek, *Canada* **142 C4** 51 35N 122 14W
Dog I., *U.S.A.* **152 F5** 29 48N 84 36W
Dog L., *Man., Canada* **143 C9** 51 2N 98 31W
Dog L., *Ont., Canada* **140 C2** 48 48N 89 30W
Doğanşehir, *Turkey* .... **100 C7** 38 5N 37 53 E
Dogliani, *Italy* .... **44 D4** 44 32N 7 56 E
Dôgo, *Japan* .... **72 A5** 36 15N 133 16 E
Dôgo-San, *Japan* .... **72 B5** 35 2N 133 13 E
Dogondoutchi, *Niger* .... **113 C5** 13 38N 4 2 E
Dogran, *Pakistan* .... **92 D5** 31 48N 73 35 E
Doğubayazıt, *Turkey* .... **101 C11** 39 31N 44 5 E
Doguéraoua, *Niger* .... **113 C6** 14 0N 5 31 E
Dogura, *Papua N. G.* .... **132 F6** 10 6 S 150 5 E
Doha = Ad Dawḥah, *Qatar* .... **97 E6** 25 15N 51 35 E
Dohazari, *Bangla.* .... **90 D4** 22 10N 92 5 E
Dohinog = Manukan, *Phil.* .... **81 G4** 8 32N 123 12 E
Dohrighat, *India* .... **93 F10** 26 16N 83 31 E
Dohrn Banke, *Greenland* **10 D8** 65 55N 25 50W
Doi, *Indonesia* .... **82 A3** 2 14N 127 49 E
Doi Inthanon Nat. Park △, *Thailand* **86 C2** 18 33N 98 34 E
Doi Khuntan Nat. Park △, *Thailand* **86 C2** 18 33N 99 14 E
Doi Luang, *Thailand* .... **86 C3** 18 30N 101 0 E
Doi Luang Nat. Park △, *Thailand* **86 C2** 19 22N 99 35 E
Doi Saket, *Thailand* .... **86 C2** 18 52N 99 9 E
Doi Suthep Nat. Park △, *Thailand* **86 C2** 18 49N 98 53 E
Dois Irmãos, Sa., *Brazil* .... **170 C3** 9 0 S 42 30W
Dojransko Jezero, *Macedonia* .. **50 E6** 41 13N 22 44 E
Dokka, *Norway* .... **18 D7** 60 49N 10 7 E
Dokka →, *Norway* .... **18 D7** 60 49N 10 7 E
Dokkum, *Neths.* .... **24 A5** 53 20N 5 59 E
Dokri, *Pakistan* .... **92 F3** 27 25N 68 7 E
Dokuchayevsk, *Ukraine* .... **59 J9** 47 44N 37 40 E
Dol-de-Bretagne, *France* **26 D5** 48 34N 1 47W
Dolac, Kosovo, *Yug.* .... **50 D4** 42 36N 20 36 E
Dolak, Pulau, *Indonesia* ...... **83 C5** 8 0 S 138 30 E
Dolbeau, *Canada* **141 C5** 48 53N 72 18W
Dole, *France* .... **27 E12** 47 7N 5 31 E
Doleib, Wadi →, *Sudan* ...... **107 E3** 12 10N 33 15 E
Dolenji Logatec, *Slovenia* ..... **45 C11** 45 56N 14 15 E
Dolgellau, *U.K.* **20 E4** 52 45N 3 53W
Dolgelley = Dolgellau, *U.K.* ... **20 E4** 52 45N 3 53W
Dolhasca, *Romania* .... **53 C11** 47 26N 26 36 E
Dolianova, *Italy* .... **46 C2** 39 22N 9 10 E
Dolinskaya = Dolynska, *Ukraine* **59 H7** 48 6N 32 46 E
Dolj □, *Romania* .... **53 F8** 44 10N 23 30 E
Dollard, *Neths.* .... **24 A7** 53 20N 7 10 E
Dolna Banya, *Bulgaria* .... **50 D7** 42 18N 23 44 E
Dolni Chiflik, *Bulgaria* .... **51 D12** 42 59N 27 43 E
Dolni Dŭbnik, *Bulgaria* .... **51 C8** 43 24N 24 26 E
Dolnoślaskie □, *Poland* .... **55 G3** 51 10N 16 30 E
Dolný Kubín, *Slovak Rep.* ..... **35 B12** 49 12N 19 18 E
Dolo, *Ethiopia* .... **107 G5** 4 11N 42 3 E
Dolo, *Italy* .... **45 C9** 45 25N 12 5 E
Dolomites = Dolomiti, *Italy* ... **45 B8** 46 23N 11 51 E
Dolomiti, *Italy* .... **45 B8** 46 23N 11 51 E
Dolomiti Bellunesi, Parco
Nazionale △, *Italy* .... **45 B9** 46 10N 12 5 E
Dolomiti d'Ampezzo, Parco Naturale
Regionale delle ⌂, *Italy* ...... **45 B9** 46 37N 12 10 E
Dolomiti di Sesto, Parco Naturale ⌂,
Italy .... **45 B9** 46 36N 12 19 E
Dolores, *Argentina* .... **174 D4** 36 20 S 57 40W
Dolores, *Phil.* .... **80 E5** 12 2N 125 29 E
Dolores, *Uruguay* .... **174 C4** 33 34 S 58 15W
Dolores, *U.S.A.* **159 H9** 37 28N 108 30W
Dolores →, *U.S.A.* **159 G9** 38 49N 109 17W
Dolphin, C., *Falk. Is.* .... **9 f** 51 10 S 59 0W
Dolphin and Union Str., *Canada* **138 B8** 69 5N 114 45W
Dolsk, *Poland* .... **55 G4** 51 59N 17 3 E
Dolton, *U.S.A.* **157 C9** 41 38N 87 36W
Dolungmukh, *India* .... **90 B5** 27 30N 94 18 E
Dolynska, *Ukraine* .... **59 H7** 48 6N 32 46 E
Dolzhanskaya, *Russia* .... **59 J9** 46 37N 37 48 E
Dom, *Switz.* .... **32 D5** 46 6N 7 50 E
Dom Joaquim, *Brazil* .... **171 E3** 18 57 S 43 16W
Dom Pedrito, *Brazil* .... **175 C5** 31 0 S 54 40W
Dom Pedro, *Brazil* .... **170 B3** 4 59 S 44 27W
Doma, *Nigeria* .... **113 D6** 8 25N 8 18 E
Doma Safari Area ⌂, *Zimbabwe* **119 F3** 16 28 S 30 12 E
Domaniç, *Turkey* .... **49 B11** 39 48N 29 36 E
Domar, E. →, *Chad* .... **109 E3** 18 11N 18 4 E
Domariaganj →, *India* .... **93 F10** 26 17N 83 44 E
Domasi, *Malawi* .... **119 F4** 15 15 S 35 22 E
Domat Ems, *Switz.* .... **33 C8** 46 50N 9 27 E
Domažlice, *Czech Rep.* .... **34 B5** 49 28N 12 58 E
Dombarovskiy, *Russia* .... **64 F7** 50 46N 59 32 E
Dombås, *Norway* .... **18 B6** 62 4N 9 8 E
Dombasle-sur-Meurthe, *France* . **27 D13** 48 38N 6 21 E
Dombes, *France* .... **29 C9** 45 58N 5 0 E
Dombóvár, *Hungary* .... **52 D3** 46 21N 18 9 E
Dombrád, *Hungary* .... **52 B6** 48 13N 21 54 E
Dome Fuji, *Antarctica* .... **7 D5** 77 20 S 39 45 E
Domel I. = Letsôk-aw Kyun, *Burma* **87 G2** 11 30N 98 25 E
Domérat, *France* .... **27 F9** 46 21N 2 32 E
Domett, *N.Z.* .... **131 C8** 42 53 S 173 12 E
Domfront, *France* **26 D6** 48 37N 0 40W
Dominador, *Chile* .... **174 A2** 24 21 S 69 20W
Dominica ■, *W. Indies* **165 C7** 15 20N 61 20W
Dominica Passage, *W. Indies* .. **165 C7** 15 10N 61 20W
Dominican Rep. ■, *W. Indies* .. **165 C5** 19 0N 70 30W
Domiongo, *Dem. Rep. of the Congo* **115 C4** 4 37 S 21 15 E
Dömitz, *Germany* .... **30 B7** 53 8N 11 15 E
Domme, *France* .... **28 D5** 44 48N 1 12 E
Domneşti, *Romania* .... **53 E9** 45 12N 24 50 E
Domo, *Ethiopia* .... **120 C3** 7 50N 47 10 E
Domodóssola, *Italy* .... **44 B5** 46 7N 8 17 E
Domogled-Valea Cernei, Parcul
Nat. △, *Romania* .... **52 F7** 44 52N 22 27 E
Dompaire, *France* .... **27 D13** 48 14N 6 14 E
Dompierre-sur-Besbre, *France* . **27 F10** 46 31N 3 41 E
Dompim, *Ghana* **112 D4** 5 10N 2 5W
Dompu, *Indonesia* .... **85 D5** 8 32 S 118 28 E
Domrémy-la-Pucelle, *France* ... **27 D12** 48 26N 5 40 E
Domville, Mt., *Australia* ...... **127 D5** 28 1 S 151 15 E
Domvraína, *Greece* .... **48 C4** 38 15N 22 59 E
Domžale, *Slovenia* .... **45 B11** 46 9N 14 35 E
Don →, *India* .... **95 G3** 16 20N 76 15 E
Don →, *Russia* .... **59 J10** 47 4N 39 18 E
Don →, *Aberds., U.K.* **22 D6** 57 11N 2 5W
Don →, *S. Yorks., U.K.* **20 D7** 53 41N 0 52W
Don, C., *Australia* .... **124 B5** 11 18 S 131 46 E
Don Benito, *Spain* **43 G5** 38 53N 5 51W
Don Figueiro Mts., *Jamaica* .... **164 a** 17 25 S 77 5W
Doña Mencía, *Spain* **43 H6** 37 33N 4 21W
Donaghadee, *U.K.* **23 B6** 54 39N 5 33W
Donald, *Australia* .... **128 D5** 36 23 S 143 0 E
Donaldsonville, *U.S.A.* **155 K9** 30 6N 90 59W
Donalsonville, *U.S.A.* **152 D5** 31 3N 84 53W
Doñana, Parque Nac. de △, *Spain* **43 J4** 36 59N 6 23W

Donau = Dunărea →, *Europe* . **53 E14** 45 20N 29 40 E
Donau →, *Austria* .... **24 D3** 48 10N 17 0 E
Donau Auen, Nationalpark △,
Austria .... **35 C9** 48 8N 16 44 E
Donaueschingen, *Germany* .... **31 H4** 47 56N 8 32 E
Donauwörth, *Germany* .... **31 G6** 48 43N 10 47 E
Doncaster, *U.K.* **20 D6** 53 32N 1 6W
Dondo, *Angola* .... **115 D2** 9 45 S 14 25 E
Dondo, *Dem. Rep. of the Congo* **114 B4** 4 11N 21 39 E
Dondo, *Mozam.* .... **119 F3** 19 33 S 34 46 E
Dondo, Teluk, *Indonesia* ...... **82 A2** 0 50N 120 30 E
Dondra Head, *Sri Lanka* ...... **95 M5** 5 55N 80 40 E
Donduşeni, *Moldova* .... **53 B12** 48 14N 27 36 E
Donegal, *Ireland* **23 B3** 54 39N 8 5W
Donegal □, *Ireland* **23 B4** 54 53N 8 0W
Donegal B., *Ireland* **23 B3** 54 31N 8 49W
Donets →, *Russia* .... **61 G5** 47 33N 40 55 E
Donetsk, *Ukraine* .... **59 J9** 48 0N 37 45 E
Dong Ba Thin, *Vietnam* .... **87 F7** 12 8N 109 13 E
Dong Dang, *Vietnam* .... **76 G6** 21 54N 106 42 E
Dong Giam, *Vietnam* .... **86 C5** 19 25N 105 31 E
Dong Ha, *Vietnam* .... **86 D6** 16 55N 107 8 E
Dong Hene, *Laos* .... **86 D5** 16 40N 105 18 E
Dong Hoi, *Vietnam* .... **86 D6** 17 29N 106 36 E
Dong Jiang →, *China* .... **77 F10** 23 6N 114 0 E
Dong Khe, *Vietnam* .... **86 A6** 22 26N 106 27 E
Dong Ujimqin Qi, *China* ...... **74 B9** 45 32N 116 55 E
Dong Van, *Vietnam* .... **86 A5** 23 16N 105 22 E
Dong Xoai, *Vietnam* .... **87 G6** 11 32N 106 55 E
Donga, *Nigeria* .... **113 D7** 7 45N 10 2 E
Donga →, *Nigeria* .... **113 D7** 8 20N 9 58 E
Dong'an, *China* .... **77 D8** 26 23N 111 12 E
Dongara, *Australia* .... **125 E1** 29 14 S 114 57 E
Dongargarh, *India* .... **94 D5** 21 10N 80 40 E
Dongbei, *China* .... **75 D13** 45 0N 125 0 E
Dongchuan, *China* .... **76 D4** 26 8N 103 1 E
Dongfang, *China* .... **86 C7** 18 50N 108 33 E
Dongfeng, *China* .... **75 C13** 42 40N 125 34 E
Donggala, *Indonesia* .... **82 B1** 0 30 S 119 40 E
Donggan, *China* .... **76 F5** 23 22N 105 9 E
Dongguan, *China* .... **77 F9** 22 58N 113 44 E
Dongguang, *China* .... **77 F9** 37 50N 116 30 E
Donghai Dao, *China* .... **77 G11** 20 45N 110 48 E
Dongjingcheng, *China* .... **75 B15** 44 5N 129 10 E
Dongkou, *China* .... **77 D8** 27 6N 110 35 E
Dongliu, *China* .... **77 B11** 30 13N 116 55 E
Dongmen, *China* .... **76 F6** 22 20N 107 48 E
Dongning, *China* .... **75 B16** 44 2N 131 5 E
Dongnyi, *China* .... **76 C3** 28 3N 100 15 E
Dongo, *Angola* .... **115 E3** 14 36 S 15 48 E
Dongo, *Dem. Rep. of the Congo* **114 B4** 4 35N 23 13 E
Dongola, *Sudan* .... **106 D3** 19 9N 30 22 E
Dongou, *Congo* .... **114 B3** 2 0N 18 5 E
Dongping, *China* .... **77 G9** 35 55N 116 20 E
Dongshan Dao, *China* .... **77 G11** 20 45N 116 43 E
Dongsheng, *China* .... **74 E6** 39 50N 110 0 E
Dongtai, *China* .... **75 H11** 32 51N 120 21 E
Dongting Hu, *China* .... **77 C9** 29 18N 112 45 E
Dongtou, *China* .... **77 D13** 27 51N 121 10 E
Dongwe →, *Zambia* .... **115 E4** 13 59 S 23 53 E
Dongxiang, *China* .... **77 C11** 28 11N 116 34 E
Dongxing, *China* .... **76 G7** 21 34N 108 0 E
Dongyang, *China* .... **77 C13** 29 13N 120 15 E
Dongzhi, *China* .... **77 B11** 30 9N 117 0 E
Donington, C., *Australia* ...... **125 E2** 34 45 S 136 0 E
Doniphan, *U.S.A.* **155 G9** 36 37N 90 50W
Donja Stubica, *Croatia* .... **45 C12** 45 59N 15 59 E
Donji Dušnik, *Serbia, Yug.* .... **50 C6** 43 12N 22 5 E
Donji Miholjac, *Croatia* .... **52 E3** 45 45N 18 10 E
Donji Milanovac, *Serbia, Yug.* .. **50 B6** 44 28N 22 6 E
Donji Vakuf, *Bos.-H.* .... **52 F2** 44 8N 17 24 E
Dønna, *Norway* .... **14 C15** 66 6N 12 30 E
Donna, *U.S.A.* **155 M5** 26 9N 98 4W
Donnaconna, *Canada* **141 C5** 46 41N 71 41W
Donnelly's Crossing, *N.Z.* ..... **130 B2** 35 42 S 173 38 E
Donnybrook, *Australia* .... **125 F2** 33 34 S 115 48 E
Donnybrook, *S. Africa* .... **117 D4** 29 59 S 29 48 E
Donora, *U.S.A.* **150 F5** 40 11N 79 52W
Donostia = Donostia-San Sebastián,
Spain **40 B3** 43 17N 1 58W
Donostia-San Sebastián, *Spain* . **40 B3** 43 17N 1 58W
Donovan, *U.S.A.* **157 D9** 40 53N 87 37W
Donque, *Angola* .... **115 F2** 15 28 S 14 6 E
Donskoy, *Russia* .... **58 F10** 53 55N 38 15 E
Donsol, *Phil.* .... **80 E4** 12 54N 123 36 E
Donzère, *France* .... **29 D8** 44 28N 4 43 E
Donzère-Mondragon, Barrage de,
France .... **27 E10** 47 20N 3 6 E
Donzy, *France* **20 E6** 51 30N 0 58W
Dookie, *Australia* .... **129 D6** 36 20 S 145 41 E
Doon →, *U.K.* **22 F4** 55 27N 4 39W
Doonerak, Mt., *U.S.A.* **136 B5** 67 55N 150 20W
Doorn, *Neths.* .... **24 B5** 52 2N 5 20 E
Dora, L., *Australia* .... **124 D3** 22 0 S 123 0 E
Dora Báltea →, *Italy* .... **44 C5** 45 11N 8 3 E
Dora Ripária →, *Italy* .... **44 C4** 45 5N 7 44 E
Doran L., *Canada* **143 A7** 61 13N 108 6W
Doraville, *U.S.A.* **152 B5** 33 54N 84 17W
Dorchester, *U.K.* **21 G5** 50 42N 2 27W
Dorchester, C., *Canada* **139 B12** 65 27N 77 27W
Dordabis, *Namibia* .... **116 C2** 22 52 S 17 38 E
Dordogne □, *France* .... **28 C4** 45 5N 0 40 E
Dordogne →, *France* **28 C3** 45 2N 0 36W
Dordrecht, *Neths.* .... **24 C4** 51 48N 4 39 E
Dordrecht, *S. Africa* .... **116 E4** 31 20 S 27 3 E
Dore →, *France* .... **29 C7** 45 50N 3 35 E
Dore, Mts., *France* .... **29 C6** 45 32N 2 50 E
Doré L., *Canada* **143 C7** 54 46N 107 17W
Doré Lake, *Canada* **143 C7** 54 38N 107 36W
Dores do Indaiá, *Brazil* .... **171 E2** 19 27 S 45 36W
Dorfen, *Germany* .... **31 G8** 48 15N 12 8 E
Dorgali, *Italy* .... **46 B2** 40 17N 9 35 E
Dori, *Burkina Faso* **113 C4** 14 3N 0 2W
Doring →, *S. Africa* .... **116 E2** 31 54 S 18 39 E
Doringbos, *S. Africa* .... **116 E2** 31 59 S 19 16 E
Dorion, *Canada* **151 A10** 45 23N 74 3W
Dormaa-Ahenkro, *Ghana* **112 D4** 7 15N 2 52W
Dormans, *France* .... **27 C10** 49 4N 3 38 E
Dormo, Ras, *Eritrea* .... **107 E5** 13 14N 42 35 E
Dornbirn, *Austria* .... **34 D2** 47 25N 9 45 E
Dornes, *France* .... **27 F10** 46 48N 3 18 E
Dorneşti, *Romania* .... **53 C11** 47 52N 26 1 E
Dornie, *U.K.* **22 D3** 57 17N 5 31W
Dornoch, *U.K.* **22 D4** 57 53N 4 2W
Dornoch Firth, *U.K.* **22 D4** 57 51N 4 4W
Dornogovi □, *Mongolia* ...... **74 C6** 44 0N 110 0 E
Doro, *Mali* **113 B4** 16 9N 0 51W
Dorog, *Hungary* .... **52 C3** 47 42N 18 45 E
Dorogobuzh, *Russia* .... **58 E8** 54 50N 33 18 E
Dorohoi, *Romania* .... **53 C11** 47 56N 26 30 E
Döröö Nuur, *Mongolia* ...... **74 B4** 48 0N 93 0 E
Dorpat = Tartu, *Estonia* ..... **15 G22** 58 20N 26 44 E
Dorre I., *Australia* .... **125 E1** 25 13 S 113 12 E
Dorrian, *U.S.A.* .... **97 C6** 33 17N 53 38 E
Dorrigo, *Australia* .... **129 E5** 30 20 S 152 44 E
Dorrigo Nat. Park △, *Australia* . **129 A10** 30 22 S 152 47 E
Dorris, *U.S.A.* **158 F3** 41 58N 121 55W
Dorset □, *U.K.* **21 G5** 50 45N 2 26W
Dorset, *Canada* **150 A6** 45 14N 78 54W
Dorset, *U.S.A.* **150 E4** 41 40N 80 40W

Dorset □, *U.K.* **21 G5** 50 45N 2 26W
Dorsten, *Germany* .... **30 D2** 51 40N 6 58 E
Dortmund, *Germany* .... **30 D3** 51 30N 7 28 E
Dortmund-Ems-Kanal →, *Germany* **30 D3** 51 50N 7 26 E
Dörtyol, *Turkey* .... **100 D7** 36 50N 36 13 E
Dorum, *Germany* .... **30 B4** 53 41N 8 34 E
Doruma, *Dem. Rep. of the Congo* **118 B2** 4 42N 27 33 E
Dorūneh, *Iran* .... **97 C8** 35 10N 57 18 E
Dos Bahías, C., *Argentina* .... **176 B3** 44 58 S 65 32W
Dos Hermanas, *Spain* **43 H5** 37 16N 5 55W
Dos Palos, *U.S.A.* **160 J6** 36 59N 120 37W
Döşemealtı, *Turkey* .... **49 D12** 37 4N 30 36 E
Dosso, *Niger* .... **113 C5** 13 0N 3 13 E
Dosso, Réserve Partielle de ⌂, *Niger* **113 C5** 12 36N 2 36 E
Dostuk, *Kyrgyzstan* .... **65 C6** 40 30N 75 0 E
Dot Lake, *U.S.A.* **144 E11** 63 40N 144 4W
Dotnuva, *Lithuania* **152 D4** 31 33N 85 24W
Döttingen, *Switz.* .... **32 A6** 47 34N 8 15 E
Doty, *U.S.A.* **160 D3** 46 38N 123 17W
Douai, *France* .... **27 B10** 50 21N 3 4 E
Douako, *Guinea* **112 D2** 9 45N 10 8W
Douala, *Cameroon* .... **113 E6** 4 0N 9 45 E
Douala-Édéa, Réserve de ⌂,
Cameroon .... **114 B1** 3 20N 9 41 E
Douaouirt, *Mali* **110 D4** 20 45N 3 0W
Douarnenez, *France* **26 D2** 48 6N 4 21W
Doubabougou, *Mali* **112 C3** 14 13N 7 59W
Double Cone, *N.Z.* .... **131 D5** 25 56 S 153 11 E
Double Island Pt., *Australia* ... **127 D5** 25 56 S 153 11 E
Double Mountain Fork →, *U.S.A.* **155 J4** 33 16N 100 0W
Doubrava →, *Czech Rep.* ..... **34 A8** 50 2N 15 20 E
Doubs □, *France* .... **27 E13** 47 10N 6 20 E
Doubs →, *France* .... **27 F12** 46 53N 5 1 E
Doubtful Sd., *N.Z.* .... **131 F1** 45 20 S 166 49 E
Doubtless B., *N.Z.* .... **130 A2** 34 55 S 173 26 E
Doudeville, *France* .... **26 C7** 49 43N 0 47 E
Doué-la-Fontaine, *France* **26 E6** 47 11N 0 16W
Douentza, *Mali* **112 C4** 14 58N 2 48W
Douentza, Réserve de ⌂, *Mali* . **112 B4** 15 40N 2 25W
Dougga, *Tunisia* .... **108 A1** 36 30N 8 55 E
Doughboy B., *N.Z.* .... **131 H2** 47 2 S 167 40 E
Douglas, *S. Africa* .... **116 D3** 29 4 S 23 46 E
Douglas, *U.K.* **20 C3** 54 10N 4 28W
Douglas, *Alaska, U.S.A.* **144 G14** 58 17N 134 24W
Douglas, *Ariz., U.S.A.* **159 L9** 31 21N 109 33W
Douglas, *Ga., U.S.A.* **152 D7** 31 31N 82 51W
Douglas, *Mich., U.S.A.* **157 B10** 42 39N 86 14W
Douglas, *Wyo., U.S.A.* **154 D2** 42 45N 105 24W
Douglas Apsley Nat. Park △,
Australia .... **127 D4** 41 45 S 148 11 E
Douglas C., *Canada* **144 G9** 58 51N 153 15W
Douglas Chan., *Canada* **142 C3** 53 40N 129 20W
Douglas Pt., *Canada* **150 B3** 44 19N 81 37W
Douglasville, *U.S.A.* **152 B5** 33 45N 84 45W
Douirat, *Morocco* **110 B4** 33 2N 4 11W
Doukáton, Ákra, *Greece* ...... **39 B2** 38 34N 20 33 E
Doukoula, *Cameroon* .... **114 A2** 10 10N 15 0 E
Doukoula, *Cent. Amer.* ...... **109 F2** 10 10N 15 0 E
Doulevant-le-Château, *France* . **27 D11** 48 23N 4 55 E
Doullens, *France* .... **27 B9** 50 10N 2 20 E
Doumé, *Cameroon* .... **114 B2** 4 15 S 13 25 E
Doumen, *China* .... **77 F9** 22 10N 113 18 E
Douna, *Mali* **112 C3** 13 13N 6 0W
Dounguia, *Congo* .... **114 C2** 2 53 S 11 58 E
Dourada, Serra, *Brazil* .... **171 D2** 13 10 S 48 45W
Dourados, *Brazil* .... **175 A5** 22 9 S 54 50W
Dourados →, *Brazil* .... **175 A5** 21 58 S 54 18W
Dourados, Serra dos, *Brazil* ... **175 A5** 23 30 S 53 30W
Dourbali, *Chad* .... **109 F3** 11 49N 15 52 E
Dourdan, *France* .... **27 D9** 48 30N 2 1 E
Douro →, *Europe* **42 D2** 41 8N 8 40W
Douvaine, *France* .... **27 F13** 46 19N 6 16 E
Douvres-la-Délivrande, *France* . **26 C6** 49 17N 0 23W
Douz, *Tunisia* .... **108 B1** 33 25N 9 0 E
Douze →, *France* **28 E3** 43 54N 0 30W
Dove →, *U.K.* **20 E6** 52 51N 1 36W
Dove Creek, *U.S.A.* **159 H9** 37 46N 108 54W
Dover, *Australia* .... **127 D4** 43 18 S 147 2 E
Dover, *U.K.* .... **21 F9** 51 7N 1 19 E
Dover, *Del., U.S.A.* **148 F8** 39 10N 75 32W
Dover, *N.H., U.S.A.* **151 C14** 43 12N 70 56W
Dover, *N.J., U.S.A.* **151 F10** 40 53N 74 34W
Dover, *Ohio, U.S.A.* **150 F3** 40 32N 81 29W
Dover, Pt., *Australia* .... **125 F4** 32 32 S 125 32 E
Dover, Str. of, *Europe* .... **21 G9** 51 0N 1 30 E
Dover-Foxcroft, *U.S.A.* **149 C11** 45 11N 69 13W
Dover Plains, *U.S.A.* **151 E11** 41 43N 73 35W
Dovey = Dyfi →, *U.K.* **21 E3** 52 32N 4 3W
Dovre, *Norway* .... **18 C6** 61 58N 9 18 E
Dovrefjell, *Norway* .... **18 B6** 62 15N 9 33 E
Dovrefjell Nasjonalpark △, *Norway* **19 B6** 62 15N 9 33 E
Dowa, *Malawi* .... **119 E3** 13 38N 33 58 E
Dowagiac, *U.S.A.* **157 C10** 41 59N 86 6W
Dowerin, *Australia* .... **125 F2** 31 12 S 117 2 E
Dowgha'i, *Iran* .... **97 B8** 36 54N 58 32 E
Dowlat Yār, *Afghan.* .... **91 B2** 34 30N 65 45 E
Dowlatābād, Farāh, *Afghan.* .. **91 B2** 32 47N 62 40 E
Dowlatābād, Fāryāb, *Afghan.* . **65 E2** 36 26N 64 55 E
Dowlatābād, *Iran* .... **97 D8** 28 20N 56 40 E
Dowling Park, *U.S.A.* **152 E6** 30 15N 83 15W
Dothan, *U.S.A.* **23 B5** 54 23N 6 2W
Downers Grove, *U.S.A.* **157 C8** 41 48N 88 1W
Downey, *Calif., U.S.A.* **161 M8** 33 56N 118 7W
Downey, *Idaho, U.S.A.* **158 E7** 42 26N 112 7W
Downham Market, *U.K.* ...... **21 E8** 52 37N 0 23 E
Downieville, *U.S.A.* **160 F6** 39 34N 120 50W
Downpatrick, *U.K.* **23 B6** 54 20N 5 43W
Downpatrick Hd., *Ireland* **23 B2** 54 20N 9 21W
Downsville, *U.S.A.* **151 D10** 42 5N 75 0W
Downton, Mt., *Canada* **142 C4** 52 42N 124 52W
Dowsārī, *Iran* .... **97 D8** 28 25N 57 59 E
Dowshī, *Afghan.* .... **91 B3** 35 35N 68 43 E
Doyle, *U.S.A.* **160 E6** 40 2N 120 6W
Doylestown, *U.S.A.* **151 F9** 40 21N 75 10W
Dōzen, *Japan* .... **72 A5** 36 5N 133 5 E
Dozois, Rés., *Canada* **140 C4** 47 30N 77 5W
Dra Khel, *Pakistan* .... **92 F2** 27 58N 66 45 E
Drâa, C., *Morocco* **110 C2** 28 47N 11 0W
Drâa, Hamada du, *Algeria* **110 C3** 28 30N 6 30W
Drâa, Oued →, *Morocco* **110 C2** 28 40N 11 10W
Drac →, *France* .... **29 C9** 45 13N 5 41 E
Dračevo, *Macedonia* .... **50 E5** 41 56N 21 31 E
Drachten, *Neths.* .... **24 A6** 53 7N 6 5 E
Drăgăneşti, *Moldova* .... **53 C13** 47 3N 28 51 E
Drăgăneşti-Olt, *Romania* ..... **53 F9** 44 9N 24 32 E
Drăgăneşti-Vlaşca, *Romania* .. **53 F9** 44 5N 25 33 E
Drăgaš, Kosovo, *Yug.* .... **50 D4** 42 5N 20 41 E
Drăgăşani, *Romania* .... **53 F9** 44 39N 24 17 E
Dragichyn, *Belarus* .... **59 F3** 52 15N 25 8 E
Dragocvet, Serbia, *Yug.* ...... **50 B5** 43 58N 21 16 E
Dragon's Mouth = Boca de Drago,
Venezuela **169 F9** 11 0N 61 50W
Dragovishtitsa, *Bulgaria* ...... **50 D6** 42 22N 22 39 E
Draguignan, *France* .... **29 E10** 43 32N 6 27 E
Drain, *U.S.A.* **158 E2** 43 40N 123 19W
Drake, *U.S.A.* **154 B4** 47 55N 100 23W
Drake Passage, *S. Ocean* ..... **7 B17** 58 0 S 68 0W
Drakensberg, *S. Africa* .... **117 D4** 31 0 S 28 0 E
Dráma, *Greece* .... **51 E8** 41 9N 24 10 E
Dráma □, *Greece* .... **51 E8** 41 20N 24 0 E

Drammen, Norway 18 E7 59 42N 10 12 E
Drangajökull, Iceland 11 A4 66 9N 22 15W
Drangedal, Norway 18 E6 59 6N 9 3 E
Drangsnes, Iceland 11 B5 65 41N 21 27W
Dranov, Ostrov, Romania 53 F14 44 55N 29 30 E
Dras, India 93 B6 34 25N 75 48 E
Drau = Drava →, Croatia 52 E3 45 33N 18 55 E
Drava →, Croatia 52 E3 45 33N 18 55 E
Dravograd, Slovenia 45 B12 46 36N 15 5 E
Drawa →, Poland 55 F2 52 52N 15 59 E
Drawieński Park Narodowy △, Poland 55 E2 53 6N 15 58 E
Drawno, Poland 55 E2 53 13N 15 46 E
Drawsko Pomorskie, Poland 54 E2 53 35N 15 50 E
Drayton Plains, U.S.A. 157 B13 42 42N 83 23W
Drayton Valley, Canada 142 C6 53 12N 114 58W
Dreieich, Germany 31 E4 50 1N 8 41 E
Dreikikir, Papua N. G. 132 B2 3 35 S 142 46 E
Dren, Kosovo, Yug. 50 C4 43 8N 20 46 E
Drenthe □, Neths. 24 B6 52 52N 6 40 E
Drepanum, C., Cyprus 39 F8 34 54N 32 19 E
Dresden, Canada 150 D2 42 35N 82 11W
Dresden, Germany 30 D9 51 3N 13 44 E
Dreux, France 26 D8 48 44N 1 23 E
Drevsjø, Norway 18 C9 61 53N 12 1 E
Drexel, U.S.A. 157 E12 39 45N 84 18W
Drezdenko, Poland 55 F2 52 50N 15 49 E
Driffield, U.K. 20 C7 54 0N 0 26W
Driftwood, U.S.A. 150 E6 41 20N 78 8W
Driggs, U.S.A. 158 E8 43 44N 111 6W
Drin →, Albania 50 B3 42 1N 19 38 E
Drin i Zi →, Albania 50 E4 41 37N 20 28 E
Drina →, Bos.-H. 50 B3 44 53N 19 21 E
Drincea →, Romania 52 F7 44 20N 22 55 E
Drinjača →, Bos.-H. 52 F4 44 15N 19 8 E
Drissa = Vyerkhnyadzvinsk, Belarus 58 E4 55 45N 27 58 E
Driva →, Norway 18 B6 62 41N 9 32 E
Drivstua, Norway 18 B6 62 26N 9 47 E
Drniš, Croatia 45 E13 43 51N 16 10 E
Drøbak, Norway 18 E7 59 39N 10 39 E
Drobeta-Turnu Severin, Romania 52 F7 44 39N 22 41 E
Drobin, Poland 55 F6 52 42N 19 58 E
Drochia, Moldova 53 B12 48 2N 27 48 E
Drogheda, Ireland 23 C5 53 43N 6 22W
Drogichin = Dragichyn, Belarus 59 F3 52 15N 25 8 E
Drogobych = Drohobych, Ukraine 59 H2 49 20N 23 30 E
Drohiczyn, Poland 55 F9 52 24N 22 39 E
Drohobych, Ukraine 59 H2 49 20N 23 30 E
Droichead Atha = Drogheda, Ireland 23 C5 53 43N 6 22W
Droichead Nua, Ireland 23 C5 53 11N 6 48W
Droitwich, U.K. 21 E5 52 16N 2 8W
Drôme □, France 29 D9 44 38N 5 15 E
Drôme →, France 29 D8 44 46N 4 46 E
Dromedary, C., Australia 129 D9 36 17 S 150 10 E
Drömling, Naturpark △, Germany 30 C7 52 29N 11 5 E
Dromore, U.K. 23 B4 54 31N 7 28W
Dromore West, Ireland 23 B3 54 15N 8 52W
Dronero, Italy 44 D4 44 28N 7 22 E
Dronfield, U.K. 20 D6 53 19N 1 27W
Dronne →, France 28 C3 45 2N 0 9W
Dronning Ingrid Land, Greenland 10 D5 66 25N 52 5W
Dronning Maud Land, Antarctica 7 D3 72 30 S 12 0 E
Dronninglund, Denmark 17 G4 57 10N 10 19 E
Dronten, Neths. 24 B5 52 32N 5 43 E
Dropt →, France 28 D3 44 35N 0 6W
Drosendorf, Austria 34 C8 48 52N 15 37 E
Drosh, Pakistan 91 B3 35 33N 71 48 E
Droué, France 26 D8 48 3N 1 6 E
Drouin, Australia 129 E6 38 10 S 145 53 E
Drueulu, N. Cal. 133 K5 20 56 S 167 5 E
Drumbo, Canada 150 D3 43 16N 80 35W
Drumheller, Canada 142 C6 51 25N 112 40W
Drummond, U.S.A. 158 C7 46 40N 113 9W
Drummond I., U.S.A. 148 C4 46 1N 83 39W
Drummond Pt., Australia 127 E2 34 9 S 135 16 E
Drummond Ra., Australia 126 C4 23 45 S 147 10 E
Drummondville, Canada 140 C5 45 55N 72 25W
Drumright, U.S.A. 155 H6 35 59N 96 36W
Druskininkai, Lithuania 15 J20 54 3N 23 58 E
Drut →, Belarus 59 F6 53 3N 30 5 E
Druya, Belarus 58 E4 55 45N 27 28 E
Družba, Bulgaria 51 C12 43 15N 28 1 E
Druzhina, Russia 67 C15 68 14N 145 18 E
Drvar, Bos.-H. 45 D13 44 21N 16 23 E
Drvenik, Croatia 45 E13 43 27N 16 3 E
Drwęca →, Poland 55 E5 53 0N 18 42 E
Dry Harbour Mts., Jamaica 164 a 18 19N 77 24W
Dry Tortugas, U.S.A. 164 B3 24 38N 82 55W
Dryanovo, Bulgaria 51 D9 42 59N 25 28 E
Dryden, Canada 143 D10 49 47N 92 50W
Dryden, U.S.A. 151 D8 42 30N 76 18W
Drygalski I., Antarctica 7 C7 66 0 S 92 0 E
Drysdale →, Australia 124 B4 13 59 S 126 51 E
Drysdale I., Australia 126 A2 11 41 S 136 0 E
Drysdale River Nat. Park △, Australia 124 B4 14 56 S 127 2 E
Drzewica, Poland 55 G7 51 27N 20 29 E
Drzewiczka →, Poland 55 G7 51 36N 20 36 E
Dschang, Cameroon 113 D7 5 32N 10 3 E
Du Bois, U.S.A. 150 E6 41 8N 78 46W
Du Gué →, Canada 140 A5 57 21N 70 45W
Du He, China 77 A8 32 48N 110 40 E
Du Quoin, U.S.A. 156 G7 38 1N 89 14W
Du'an, China 76 F7 23 59N 108 3 E
Duanesburg, U.S.A. 151 D10 42 45N 74 11W
Duaringa, Australia 126 C4 23 42 S 149 42 E
Duarte, Pico, Dom. Rep. 165 D5 19 2N 70 59W
Dubā, Si. Arabia 96 E2 27 10N 35 40 E
Dubai = Dubayy, U.A.E. 97 E7 25 18N 55 20 E
Dubăsari, Moldova 53 C14 47 15N 29 10 E
Dubăsari Vdkhr., Moldova 53 C13 47 30N 29 0 E
Dubawnt →, Canada 143 A8 64 33N 100 6W
Dubawnt, L., Canada 143 A8 63 4N 101 42W
Dubayy, U.A.E. 97 E7 25 18N 55 20 E
Dubbo, Australia 129 B8 32 11 S 148 35 E
Dubele, Dem. Rep. of the Congo 118 B2 2 56N 29 35 E
Dübendorf, Switz. 33 B7 47 24N 8 37 E
Dubica, Croatia 45 C13 45 11N 16 48 E
Dublin, Ireland 23 C5 53 21N 6 15W
Dublin, Ga., U.S.A. 152 C7 32 32N 82 54W
Dublin, Tex., U.S.A. 155 J5 32 5N 98 21W
Dublin □, Ireland 23 C5 53 24N 6 20W
Dublin ✈ (DUB), Ireland 23 C5 53 26N 6 15W
Dubna, Russia 58 D9 56 44N 37 10 E
Dubnica nad Váhom, Slovak Rep. 35 C11 48 58N 18 11 E
Dubno, Ukraine 59 G3 50 25N 25 45 E
Dubois, Idaho, U.S.A. 158 D7 44 10N 112 14W
Dubois, Ind., U.S.A. 157 F10 38 27N 86 48W
Dubossary = Dubăsari, Moldova 53 C14 47 15N 29 10 E
Dubossary Vdkhr. = Dubăsari Vdkhr., Moldova 53 C13 47 30N 29 0 E
Dubovka, Russia 61 F7 49 5N 44 50 E
Dubovskoye, Russia 61 G6 47 28N 42 46 E
Dubrajpur, India 93 H12 23 48N 87 25 E
Dubréka, Guinea 112 D2 9 46N 13 31W
Dubrovitsa = Dubrovytsya, Ukraine 59 G4 51 31N 26 35 E
Dubrovnik, Croatia 45 D7 42 39N 18 6 E
Dubrovytsya, Ukraine 59 G4 51 31N 26 35 E
Dubulu, Dem. Rep. of the Congo 114 B4 4 18N 20 16 E
Dubuque, U.S.A. 156 B6 42 30N 90 41W
Dubysa →, Lithuania 54 C10 55 5N 23 26 E
Duchang, China 77 C11 29 18N 116 12 E
Duchesne, U.S.A. 158 F8 40 10N 110 24W
Duchess, Australia 126 C2 21 20 S 139 50 E

Ducie I., Pac. Oc. 135 K15 24 40 S 124 48W
Duck →, U.S.A. 149 G2 36 2N 87 52W
Duck Cr. →, Australia 124 D2 22 37 S 116 53 E
Duck Lake, Canada 143 C7 52 50N 106 16W
Duck Mountain Prov. Park △, Canada 143 C8 51 45N 101 0W
Duckwall, Mt., U.S.A. 160 H6 37 58N 120 7W
Duda →, Colombia 168 C3 2 34N 74 3W
Duderstadt, Germany 30 D6 51 31N 10 15 E
Dudhnai, India 90 C3 25 59N 90 47 E
Dudinka, Russia 67 C9 69 30N 86 13 E
Dudley, U.K. 21 E5 52 31N 2 5W
Dudna →, India 94 E3 19 17N 76 54 E
Dudo, Somali Rep. 120 C4 9 20N 50 12 E
Dudub, Ethiopia 120 C3 6 55N 46 43 E
Dudune, Î., N. Cal. 133 U21 21 21 S 167 46 E
Dudwa, India 93 E9 28 30N 80 41 E
Duékoué, Ivory C. 112 D3 6 40N 7 15W
Duenas, Phil. 81 F4 11 4N 122 37 E
Dueñas, Spain 42 D6 41 52N 4 33W
Dueré, Brazil 171 D2 11 20 S 49 17W
Duero = Douro →, Europe 42 D2 41 8N 8 40W
Dufftown, U.K. 22 D5 57 27N 3 8W
Dufourspitz, Switz. 32 E5 45 56N 7 52 E
Dugger, U.S.A. 157 F9 39 4N 87 18W
Dugi Otok, Croatia 45 D11 44 0N 15 3 E
Dugiuma, Somali Rep. 120 D2 1 15N 42 34 E
Dugo Selo, Croatia 45 C13 45 51N 16 18 E
Duifken Pt., Australia 126 A3 12 33 S 141 38 E
Duisburg, Germany 30 D2 51 26N 6 45 E
Duitama, Colombia 168 B3 5 50N 73 2W
Duiwelskloof, S. Africa 117 C5 23 42 S 30 10 E
Dujiangyan, China 76 B4 31 2N 103 38 E
Duk Fadiat, Sudan 107 F3 7 45N 31 25 E
Duk Faiwil, Sudan 107 F3 7 30N 31 29 E
Dukat, Albania 50 F3 40 16N 19 32 E
Dükdamīn, Iran 97 C8 35 59N 57 43 E
Dukelský Průsmyk, Slovak Rep. 35 B14 49 25N 21 42 E
Dukhān, Qatar 97 E6 25 25N 50 50 E
Dukhovshchina, Russia 58 E7 55 15N 32 27 E
Duki, Pakistan 91 C3 30 14N 68 25 E
Dukla, Poland 55 J8 49 30N 21 35 E
Duku, Bauchi, Nigeria 113 C7 10 43N 10 43 E
Duku, Sokoto, Nigeria 113 C5 11 11N 4 55 E
Dula, Dem. Rep. of the Congo 118 B4 4 40N 20 21 E
Dulag, Phil. 81 F5 10 57N 125 2 E
Dulce, U.S.A. 159 H10 36 56N 107 0W
Dulce →, Argentina 174 C3 30 32 S 62 33W
Dulce, G., Costa Rica 164 E3 8 40N 83 20W
Dulf, Iraq 96 C5 35 7N 45 51 E
Dülgopol, Bulgaria 51 C11 43 3N 27 22 E
Dulit, Banjaran, Malaysia 78 D4 3 15N 114 30 E
Duliu, China 74 E9 39 2N 116 55 E
Dullabchara, India 90 C4 24 30N 92 26 E
Dullewala, Pakistan 90 D4 31 50N 71 25 E
Dullstroom, S. Africa 117 D5 25 27 S 30 7 E
Dülmen, Germany 30 D3 51 49N 7 17 E
Dulovo, Bulgaria 51 C11 43 48N 27 9 E
Dulqelet, Norway 60 D4 60 34N 12 19 E
Dulq Maghār, Syria 101 D8 36 22N 38 39 E
Duluth, Ga., U.S.A. 152 A5 34 0N 84 9W
Duluth, Minn., U.S.A. 156 B8 46 47N 92 6W
Dum Dum, India 93 H13 22 39N 88 33 E
Dum Duma, India 90 B5 27 40N 95 40 E
Dūmā, Syria 103 B5 33 34N 36 24 E
Dumaguete, Phil. 81 G4 9 17N 123 15 E
Dumai, Indonesia 84 B2 1 35N 101 28 E
Dumaran = Araceli, Phil. 81 F2 10 33N 119 59 E
Dumaran, Phil. 81 F2 10 33N 119 51 E
Dumaran I., Phil. 81 F2 10 33N 119 51 E
Dumarao, Phil. 81 F4 11 16N 122 41 E
Dumas, Ark., U.S.A. 155 J9 33 53N 91 29W
Dumas, Tex., U.S.A. 155 H4 35 52N 101 58W
Dumayr, Syria 103 B5 33 39N 36 42 E
Dumbarton, U.K. 22 F4 55 57N 4 33W
Dumbéa, N. Cal. 133 V20 22 10 S 166 27 E
Dumbier, Slovak Rep. 35 C12 48 56N 19 38 E
Dumbleyung, Australia 125 F2 33 17 S 117 42 E
Dumbo, Angola 115 E3 14 6 S 17 24 E
Dumboa, Nigeria 113 C7 11 15N 12 55 E
Dumbrăveni, Romania 53 D9 46 14N 24 34 E
Dumfries, U.K. 22 F5 55 4N 3 37W
Dumfries & Galloway □, U.K. 22 F5 55 9N 3 58W
Dumingag, Phil. 81 G4 8 20N 123 20 E
Dumitreşti, Romania 53 E11 45 33N 26 55 E
Dumka, India 93 G12 24 12N 87 15 E
Dumlupınar, Turkey 49 C12 38 53N 30 0 E
Dümmer, Germany 30 C4 52 31N 8 21 E
Dümmer, Naturpark △, Germany 30 C4 52 31N 8 21 E
Dumoine →, Canada 140 C4 46 13N 77 51W
Dumoine, L., Canada 140 C4 46 55N 77 55W
Dumoulin Is., Papua N. G. 132 F6 10 54 S 150 46 E
Dumpu, Papua N. G. 132 C3 5 53 S 145 44 E
Dumraon, India 93 G11 25 33N 84 8 E
Dumyât, Egypt 106 H7 31 24N 31 48 E
Dumyât, Masabb, Egypt 106 H7 31 28N 31 51 E
Dún Dealgan = Dundalk, Ireland 23 B5 54 1N 6 24W
Dún Laoghaire, Ireland 23 C5 53 17N 6 8W
Dun-le-Palestel, France 27 F8 46 18N 1 39 E
Dun-sur-Auron, France 27 F9 46 53N 2 33 E
Dun-sur-Meuse, France 27 C12 49 23N 5 11 E
Duna = Dunărea →, Europe 53 E14 45 20N 29 40 E
Duna →, Hungary 52 E3 45 51N 18 48 E
Duna-Drava Nemzeti Park △, Hungary 52 D3 46 15N 18 50 E
Duna-völgyi-főcsatorna, Hungary 52 D4 46 40N 19 14 E
Dunaföldvár, Hungary 52 D3 46 50N 18 57 E
Dunagiri, India 93 D8 30 31N 79 52 E
Dunaj = Dunărea →, Europe 53 E14 45 20N 29 40 E
Dunaj →, Poland 55 H7 50 15N 20 44 E
Dunajec →, Poland 55 H7 50 15N 20 44 E
Dunajská Streda, Slovak Rep. 35 C10 48 0N 17 37 E
Dunakeszi, Hungary 52 C4 47 37N 19 8 E
Dunapatáj, Hungary 52 D4 46 39N 19 4 E
Dunărea →, Europe 53 E14 45 20N 29 40 E
Dunaszekcső, Hungary 52 D3 46 6N 18 45 E
Dunaújváros, Hungary 52 D3 46 58N 18 57 E
Dunav = Dunărea →, Europe 53 E14 45 20N 29 40 E
Dunavăţu de Jos, Romania 53 F14 44 59N 29 13 E
Dunavtsi, Bulgaria 50 C7 43 57N 22 53 E
Dunay, Russia 70 C6 42 52N 132 22 E
Dunback, N.Z. 131 F5 45 23 S 170 36 E
Dunbar, U.K. 22 E6 56 0N 2 31W
Dunblane, U.K. 22 E5 56 11N 3 58W
Duncan, Canada 142 D4 48 45N 123 40W
Duncan, Ariz., U.S.A. 159 K9 32 43N 109 6W
Duncan, Okla., U.S.A. 155 H6 34 30N 97 57W
Duncan, L., Canada 140 B4 53 29N 77 58W
Duncan L., Canada 142 A6 62 51N 113 58W
Duncan Passage, India 95 J11 11 0N 92 0 E
Duncan Town, Bahamas 164 B4 22 15N 75 45W
Duncannon, U.S.A. 150 F7 40 23N 77 2W
Duncansby Head, U.K. 23 C5 58 38N 3 1W
Duncansville, U.S.A. 150 F6 40 25N 78 26W
Dundaga, Latvia 54 A9 57 30N 22 20 E
Dundalk, Canada 150 B4 44 10N 80 24W
Dundalk, Ireland 23 B5 54 1N 6 24W
Dundalk, U.S.A. 148 F7 39 16N 76 32W
Dundalk Bay, Ireland 23 C5 53 55N 6 15W

Dundas = Uummannaq, Greenland 10 B4 77 0N 69 0W
Dundas, Canada 150 C5 43 17N 79 59W
Dundas, L., Australia 125 F3 32 35 S 121 50 E
Dundas I., Canada 142 C2 54 30N 130 50W
Dundas Str., Australia 124 B5 11 15 S 131 35 E
Dundee, S. Africa 117 D5 28 11 S 30 15 E
Dundee, U.K. 22 E6 56 28N 2 59W
Dundee, Mich., U.S.A. 157 C13 41 57N 83 40W
Dundee, N.Y., U.S.A. 150 D8 42 32N 76 59W
Dundee City □, U.K. 22 E6 56 30N 2 58W
Dundgovĭ □, Mongolia 74 B4 45 10N 106 0 E
Dundrum, U.K. 23 B6 54 16N 5 52W
Dundrum B., U.K. 23 B6 54 13N 5 47W
Dunedin, N.Z. 131 F5 45 50 S 170 33 E
Dunedin, U.S.A. 153 G7 28 1N 82 47W
Dunedoo, Australia 129 A8 32 0 S 149 25 E
Dunfermline, U.K. 22 E5 56 5N 3 27W
Dungannon, Canada 150 D3 43 51N 81 36W
Dungannon, U.K. 23 B5 54 31N 6 46W
Dungarpur, India 92 H5 23 52N 73 45 E
Dungarvan, Ireland 23 D4 52 5N 7 37W
Dungarvan Harbour, Ireland 23 D4 52 4N 7 35W
Dungeness, U.K. 21 G8 50 54N 0 59 E
Dungo, L. do, Angola 116 B2 17 15 S 19 0 E
Dungog, Australia 129 B9 32 22 S 151 46 E
Dungu, Dem. Rep. of the Congo 118 B2 3 40N 28 32 E
Dungun, Malaysia 87 K4 4 45N 103 25 E
Dungunâb, Sudan 106 C4 21 10N 37 9 E
Dungunâb, Khalîg, Sudan 106 C4 21 5N 37 12 E
Dunhua, China 68 B4 40 8N 94 36 E
Dunk I., Australia 126 B4 17 59 S 146 29 E
Dunkassa, Benin 113 C5 10 21N 3 10 E
Dunkeld, Queens., Australia 127 E4 33 25 S 149 29 E
Dunkeld, Vic., Australia 128 D5 37 40 S 142 22 E
Dunkeld, U.K. 22 E5 56 34N 3 35W
Dunkerque, France 27 A9 51 2N 2 20 E
Dunkery Beacon, U.K. 21 F4 51 9N 3 36W
Dunkirk = Dunkerque, France 27 A9 51 2N 2 20 E
Dunkirk, U.S.A. 150 D5 42 29N 79 20W
Dunkuj, Sudan 107 E3 12 50N 32 49 E
Dunkwa, Central, Ghana 112 D4 6 0N 1 47W
Dunkwa, Central, Ghana 113 D4 5 30N 1 0W
Dúnleary = Dún Laoghaire, Ireland 23 C5 53 17N 6 8W
Dunleer, Ireland 23 C5 53 50N 6 24W
Dunmanus B., Ireland 23 E2 51 31N 9 50W
Dunmanway, Ireland 23 E2 51 43N 9 6W
Dunmara, Australia 126 B1 16 42 S 133 25 E
Dunmore, U.S.A. 151 E9 41 25N 75 38W
Dunmore Hd., Ireland 23 D1 52 10N 10 35W
Dunmore Town, Bahamas 164 A4 25 30N 76 39W
Dunn, U.S.A. 149 H6 35 19N 78 37W
Dunnellon, U.S.A. 153 F7 29 3N 82 28W
Dunnet Hd., U.K. 22 C5 58 40N 3 21W
Dunning, U.S.A. 154 E4 41 50N 100 6W
Dunnville, Canada 150 D5 42 54N 79 36W
Dunolly, Australia 128 D5 36 51 S 143 44 E
Dunoon, U.K. 22 F4 55 57N 4 56W
Dunphy, U.S.A. 158 F5 40 42N 116 31W
Dunqul, Egypt 106 C3 23 26N 31 37 E
Duns, U.K. 22 F6 55 47N 2 20W
Dunseith, U.S.A. 154 A4 48 50N 100 3W
Dunsmuir, U.S.A. 158 F2 41 13N 122 16W
Dunstable, U.K. 21 F7 51 53N 0 32W
Dunstan Mts., N.Z. 131 E4 44 53 S 169 35 E
Dunster, Canada 142 C5 53 8N 119 50W
Duntroon, N.Z. 131 E5 44 51 S 170 40 E
Dunvegan, U.K. 22 D2 57 27N 6 35W
Dunvegan L., Canada 143 A7 60 8N 107 10W
Duolun, China 74 C9 42 12N 116 28 E
Duong Dong, Vietnam 87 G4 10 13N 103 58 E
Dupax, Phil. 80 C3 16 17N 121 5 E
Dupree, U.S.A. 154 C4 45 4N 101 35W
Dupuyer, U.S.A. 158 B7 48 13N 112 30W
Duqm, Oman 99 C7 19 39N 57 42 E
Duque de Caxias, Brazil 171 F2 22 45 S 43 19W
Duque de York, I., Chile 176 D1 50 37 S 75 25W
Durack →, Australia 124 C4 15 33 S 127 52 E
Durack Ra., Australia 124 C4 16 50 S 127 40 E
Durağan, Turkey 100 B6 41 25N 35 3 E
Durak, Turkey 49 B10 39 42N 28 17 E
Durakovac, Kosovo, Yug. 50 D4 42 43N 20 29 E
Durance →, France 29 E8 43 55N 4 45 E
Durand, Ga., U.S.A. 152 C5 32 54N 84 51W
Durand, Ill., U.S.A. 156 B7 42 26N 89 20W
Durand, Mich., U.S.A. 157 B13 42 55N 83 59W
Durand, Wis., U.S.A. 154 C9 44 38N 91 58W
Durango, Mexico 162 C4 24 3N 104 39W
Durango, U.S.A. 159 H10 37 16N 107 53W
Durango □, Mexico 162 C4 25 0N 105 0W
Durankulak, Bulgaria 51 C12 43 41N 28 32 E
Durant, Iowa, U.S.A. 156 E9 41 36N 90 54W
Durant, Miss., U.S.A. 155 J10 33 4N 89 51W
Durant, Okla., U.S.A. 155 J6 33 59N 96 25W
Duratón →, Spain 42 D6 41 37N 4 7W
Durazno, Uruguay 174 C4 33 25 S 56 31W
Durazzo = Durrës, Albania 50 E3 41 19N 19 28 E
Durban, France 28 F6 42 59N 2 49 E
Durban, S. Africa 117 D5 29 49 S 31 1 E
Durbo, Somali Rep. 120 B4 11 37N 50 20 E
Durbuy, Belgium 24 D5 50 21N 5 28 E
Dúrcal, Spain 43 J7 36 59N 3 34W
Düren, Germany 30 E2 50 48N 6 29 E
Durg, India 94 D5 21 15N 81 22 E
Durgapur, India 93 H12 23 30N 87 20 E
Durham, Canada 140 D3 44 10N 80 49W
Durham, U.K. 20 C6 54 47N 1 34W
Durham, Calif., U.S.A. 160 F5 39 39N 121 48W
Durham, N.C., U.S.A. 149 H6 35 59N 78 54W
Durham, N.H., U.S.A. 151 C14 43 8N 70 56W
Durham □, U.K. 20 C6 54 42N 1 45W
Durlești, Moldova 53 C13 47 1N 28 46 E
Durmā, Si. Arabia 96 E5 24 37N 46 8 E
Durmitor, Montenegro, Yug. 50 C3 43 10N 19 0 E
Durmitor Nac. Park △, Yugoslavia 50 C3 43 15N 19 5 E
Durness, U.K. 22 C4 58 34N 4 45W
Durnford, Pta., W. Sahara 110 D1 23 37N 16 0W
Durrës, Albania 50 E3 41 19N 19 28 E
Durrow, Ireland 23 D4 52 51N 7 24W
Dursey I., Ireland 23 E1 51 36N 10 12W
Dursley, U.K. 21 F5 51 40N 2 21W
Dursunbey, Turkey 49 B9 39 35N 28 37 E
Durtal, France 26 E6 47 40N 0 18W
Duru, Dem. Rep. of the Congo 118 B2 4 14N 28 50 E
Duru Gölü, Turkey 51 E12 41 20N 28 35 E
Durusu, Turkey 51 E12 41 17N 28 41 E
Durūz, Jabal ad, Jordan 103 C5 32 35N 36 40 E
D'Urville, Tanjung, Indonesia 83 B5 1 28 S 137 54 E
D'Urville I., N.Z. 131 E3 40 50 S 173 55 E
Dusa Mareb, Somali Rep. 120 C3 5 30N 46 15 E
Dūsh, Egypt 106 C3 24 35N 30 41 E
Dushak, Turkmenistan 66 F7 37 13N 60 1 E
Dushan, China 76 E6 25 48N 107 30 E
Dushanbe, Tajikistan 66 F7 38 33N 68 48 E
Dusheti, Georgia 61 J7 42 10N 44 42 E
Dushore, U.S.A. 151 E8 41 31N 76 24W
Dusky Sd., N.Z. 131 F1 45 47 S 166 30 E
Dussejour, C., Australia 124 B4 14 45 S 128 13 E
Düsseldorf, Germany 30 D2 51 14N 6 47 E
Düsseldorf Rhein-Ruhr ✈ (DUS), Germany 30 D2 51 17N 6 46 E
Dusti, Tajikistan 65 E4 37 20N 68 40 E

Dustlik, Uzbekistan 65 C4 40 31N 68 2 E
Duszniki-Zdrój, Poland 55 H3 50 24N 16 24 E
Dutch Guiana = Suriname ■, S. Amer. 169 C6 4 0N 56 0W
Dutch Harbor, U.S.A. 144 K6 53 53N 166 32W
Dutlwe, Botswana 116 C3 23 58 S 23 46 E
Dutsan Wai, Nigeria 113 C6 10 50N 8 10 E
Dutton, Canada 150 D3 42 39N 81 30W
Dutton →, Australia 126 C3 20 44 S 143 10 E
Duved, Sweden 16 A6 63 24N 12 55 E
Düvertepe, Turkey 49 B10 39 14N 28 27 E
Duwayhin, Khawr, U.A.E. 97 E6 24 20N 51 25 E
Duyun, China 76 D6 26 18N 107 10 E
Düzağaç, Turkey 49 C12 38 48N 30 10 E
Düzce, Turkey 100 B4 40 50N 31 10 E
Duzdab = Zāhedān, Iran 97 D9 29 30N 60 50 E
Dve Mogili, Bulgaria 51 C9 43 35N 25 55 E
Dvina, Severnaya →, Russia 56 B7 64 32N 40 30 E
Dvinsk = Daugavpils, Latvia 15 J22 55 53N 26 32 E
Dvinskaya Guba, Russia 56 B6 65 0N 39 0 E
Dvor, Croatia 45 C13 45 4N 16 22 E
Dvůr Králové nad Labem, Czech Rep. 34 A8 50 27N 15 50 E
Dwarka, India 92 H3 22 18N 69 8 E
Dwellingup, Australia 125 F2 32 43 S 116 4 E
Dwight, Canada 150 A5 45 20N 79 1W
Dwight, U.S.A. 157 C8 41 5N 88 26W
Dyatkovo, Russia 58 F8 53 40N 34 27 E
Dyatlovo = Dzyatlava, Belarus 58 F3 53 28N 25 28 E
Dyce, U.K. 22 D6 57 13N 2 12W
Dyer, U.S.A. 157 G10 37 24N 86 13W
Dyer, C., Canada 139 B13 66 40N 61 0W
Dyer Bay, Canada 150 A3 45 10N 81 20W
Dyer Plateau, Antarctica 7 D17 70 45 S 65 30W
Dyersburg, U.S.A. 155 G10 36 3N 89 23W
Dyersville, U.S.A. 156 B5 42 29N 91 8W
Dyfi →, U.K. 21 E3 52 32N 4 3W
Dyje →, Czech Rep. 35 C9 48 37N 16 56 E
Dyke Ackland B., Papua N. G. 132 E5 9 0 S 148 45 E
Dymer, Ukraine 59 G6 50 47N 30 18 E
Dynów, Poland 55 J9 49 50N 22 11 E
Dyranut, Norway 18 D4 60 22N 7 31 E
Dyrhólaey, Iceland 11 D7 63 24N 19 8W
Dyrnes, Norway 18 A4 63 25N 7 52 E
Dysart, Australia 126 B4 22 10 S 148 23 E
Dysart, U.S.A. 156 D5 42 10N 92 18W
Dyurtyuli, Russia 60 D10 55 18N 54 40 E
Dyushambe = Dushanbe, Tajikistan 65 D4 38 33N 68 48 E
Dzamin Üüd = Borhoyn Tal, Mongolia 74 C6 43 50N 111 58 E
Dzaoudzi, Mayotte 121 a 12 47 S 45 16 E
Dzaudzhikau = Vladikavkaz, Russia 61 J7 43 0N 44 35 E
Dzerzhinsk, Russia 56 B6 56 14N 43 30 E
Dzhalal-Abad = Jalal-Abad, Kyrgyzstan 65 C6 40 56N 73 0 E
Dzhalinda, Russia 67 D13 53 26N 124 0 E
Dzhambeyty, Kazakhstan 64 F4 50 16N 52 35 E
Dzhambul = Taraz, Kazakhstan 65 B5 42 54N 71 22 E
Dzhankoy, Ukraine 59 K8 45 40N 34 20 E
Dzhanybek, Kazakhstan 60 F8 49 25N 46 50 E
Dzhargalantu = Hovd, Mongolia 68 B4 48 2N 91 37 E
Dzharkurgan = Jarqŭrghon, Uzbekistan 65 E3 37 31N 67 25 E
Dzharylhach, Ostriv, Ukraine 59 J7 46 2N 32 55 E
Dzhezkazgan = Zhezqazghan, Kazakhstan 66 E7 47 44N 67 40 E
Dzhibkhalantu = Ulyasutay, Mongolia 68 B4 47 56N 97 28 E
Dzhirgatal, Tajikistan 65 D5 39 13N 71 12 E
Dzhizak = Jizzakh, Uzbekistan 65 C3 40 6N 67 50 E
Dzhugdzur, Khrebet, Russia 67 D14 57 30N 138 0 E
Dzhuma, Uzbekistan 65 D3 39 42N 66 40 E
Dzhungarskiye Vorota = Dzungarian Gates, Asia 68 B3 45 0N 82 0 E
Dzhvari = Jvari, Georgia 61 J6 42 42N 42 4 E
Działdowo, Poland 55 E7 53 15N 20 15 E
Działoszyce, Poland 55 H7 50 22N 20 20 E
Dzibilchaltún, Mexico 163 C7 21 5N 89 36W
Dzibilchaltun, Yucatán, Mexico 163 C7 21 5N 89 36W
Dzierzgoń, Poland 54 E6 53 58N 19 20 E
Dzierżoniów, Poland 55 H3 50 45N 16 39 E
Dzilam de Bravo, Mexico 163 C7 21 24N 88 53W
Dzioua, Algeria 111 B6 33 14N 5 14 E
Dzisna, Belarus 58 E5 55 34N 28 12 E
Dzisna →, Belarus 58 E5 55 34N 28 12 E
Dziwnów, Poland 54 D1 54 2N 14 45 E
Dzungaria = Junggar Pendi, China 68 B3 44 30N 86 0 E
Dzungarian Gates, Asia 68 B3 45 0N 82 0 E
Dzuumod, Mongolia 68 B5 47 45N 106 58 E
Dzyarzhynsk, Belarus 58 F4 53 40N 27 1 E
Dzyatlava, Belarus 58 F3 53 28N 25 28 E

E

Eabamet L., Canada 140 B2 51 30N 87 46W
Eads, U.S.A. 154 F3 38 29N 102 47W
Eagar, U.S.A. 159 J9 34 6N 109 17W
Eagle, Alaska, U.S.A. 144 D12 64 47N 141 12W
Eagle, Colo., U.S.A. 158 G10 39 39N 106 50W
Eagle →, Canada 141 B8 53 36N 57 26W
Eagle Butte, U.S.A. 154 C4 45 0N 101 10W
Eagle Grove, U.S.A. 156 B3 42 40N 93 54W
Eagle L., Canada 143 D10 49 42N 93 13W
Eagle L., Calif., U.S.A. 158 F3 40 39N 120 45W
Eagle L., Maine, U.S.A. 149 B11 46 20N 69 22W
Eagle Lake, Canada 150 A6 45 8N 78 29W
Eagle Lake, Maine, U.S.A. 149 B11 47 3N 68 36W
Eagle Lake, Tex., U.S.A. 155 L6 29 35N 96 20W
Eagle Mountain, U.S.A. 161 M11 33 49N 115 27W
Eagle Nest, U.S.A. 159 H11 36 33N 105 16W
Eagle Pass, U.S.A. 155 L4 28 43N 100 30W
Eagle Pk., U.S.A. 160 G7 38 10N 119 25W
Eagle Pt., Australia 124 C3 16 11 S 124 23 E
Eagle River, Mich., U.S.A. 148 B1 47 24N 88 18W
Eagle River, Wis., U.S.A. 154 C10 45 55N 89 15W
Eaglehawk, N.S.W., Australia 127 E3 36 44 S 144 15 E
Eaglehawk, Vic., Australia 128 D5 36 44 S 144 15 E
Eagles Mere, U.S.A. 151 E8 41 25N 76 33W
Eagleville, U.S.A. 156 D3 40 28N 93 59W
Ealing □, U.K. 21 F7 51 31N 0 20W
Ear Falls, Canada 143 C10 50 38N 93 13W
Earle, U.S.A. 155 H9 35 16N 90 28W
Earlimart, U.S.A. 161 K7 35 53N 119 16W
Earlville, U.S.A. 157 C8 41 35N 88 55W
Early Branch, U.S.A. 152 C9 32 45N 80 55W
Earn →, U.K. 22 E5 56 23N 3 19W
Earn, L., U.K. 22 E4 56 23N 4 13W
Earnslaw, Mt., N.Z. 131 E2 44 32 S 168 27 E
Earth, U.S.A. 155 H3 34 14N 102 24W
Eas, Vanuatu 133 C5 20 36 S 168 15 E
Easley, U.S.A. 149 H4 34 50N 82 36W
East Anglia, U.K. 20 E9 52 30N 1 0 E
East Angus, Canada 141 C5 45 30N 71 40W
East Ayrshire □, U.K. 22 F4 55 26N 4 11W
East Beskids = Vychodné Beskydy, Europe 35 B15 49 20N 22 0 E
East Brady, U.S.A. 150 F5 40 59N 79 36W

East C., N.Z. ...... 130 D7 37 42 S 178 35 E
East C., Papua N. G. ...... 132 F6 10 13 S 150 53 E
East Chicago, U.S.A. 157 C9 41 38N 87 27W
East China Sea, Asia ...... 69 D7 30 0N 126 0 E
East Coast Bays, N.Z. ...... 130 C3 36 46 S 174 46 E
East Coulee, Canada 142 C6 51 23N 112 27W
East Dereham, U.K. ...... 21 E8 52 41N 0 57 E
East Dublin, U.S.A. 152 C7 32 32N 82 52W
East Dubuque, U.S.A. 156 B6 42 30N 90 39W
East Dunbartonshire □, U.K. 22 F4 55 57N 4 13W
East End Pt., Bahamas ...... 9 b 25 3N 77 16W
East Falkland, Falk. Is. ...... 9 f 51 30 S 58 30W
East Grand Forks, U.S.A. 154 B6 47 56N 97 1W
East Greenwich, U.S.A. 151 E13 41 40N 71 27W
East Grinstead, U.K. ...... 21 F8 51 7N 0 0 E
East Hartford, U.S.A. 151 E12 41 46N 72 39W
East Helena, U.S.A. 158 C8 46 35N 111 56W
East Indies, Asia ...... 62 K15 0 0 120 0 E
East Kilbride, U.K. 22 F4 55 47N 4 11W
East Lamma Channel, China ...... 69 G11 22 14N 114 9 E
East Lansing, U.S.A. 157 B12 42 44N 84 29W
East Liverpool, U.S.A. 150 F4 40 37N 80 35W
East London, S. Africa ...... 117 E4 33 0 S 27 55 E
East Lothian □, U.K. 22 F6 55 58N 2 44W
East Main = Eastmain, Canada 140 B4 52 10N 78 30W
East Moline, U.S.A. 156 C6 41 32N 90 26W
East Naples, U.S.A. 153 J8 26 8N 81 46W
East New Britain □, Papua N. G. ...... 132 D7 6 30 S 152 30 E
East Northport, U.S.A. 151 F11 40 53N 73 20W
East Orange, U.S.A. 151 F10 40 46N 74 13W
East Pacific Ridge, Pac. Oc. ...... 135 J17 15 0 S 110 0W
East Pakistan = Bangladesh ■, Asia ...... 90 C3 24 0N 90 0 E
East Palatka, U.S.A. 152 F8 29 39N 81 36W
East Palestine, U.S.A. 150 F4 40 50N 80 33W
East Peoria, U.S.A. 156 D7 40 40N 89 34W
East Pine, Canada 142 B4 55 48N 120 12W
East Point, U.S.A. 152 B5 33 41N 84 27W
East Providence, U.S.A. 151 E13 41 49N 71 23W
East Pt., Br. Virgin Is. ...... 165 e 18 40N 64 18W
East Pt., Canada 141 C7 46 27N 61 58W
East Renfrewshire □, U.K. 22 F4 55 46N 4 21W
East Retford = Retford, U.K. 20 D7 53 19N 0 56W
East Riding of Yorkshire □, U.K. 20 D7 53 55N 0 30W
East Rochester, U.S.A. 150 C7 43 7N 77 29W
East St. Louis, U.S.A. 156 F6 38 37N 90 9W
East Schelde = Oosterschelde →, Neths. ...... 24 C4 51 33N 4 0 E
East Sea = Japan, Sea of, Asia ...... 70 E7 40 0N 135 0 E
East Sepik □, Papua N. G. ...... 132 C2 4 0 S 143 45 E
East Siberian Sea, Russia ...... 67 B17 73 0N 160 0 E
East Stroudsburg, U.S.A. 151 E9 41 1N 75 11W
East Sussex □, U.K. ...... 21 G8 50 56N 0 19 E
East Tawas, U.S.A. 148 C4 44 17N 83 29W
East Timor ■, Asia ...... 82 C3 8 50 S 126 0 E
East Tohopekaliga, Lake, U.S.A. 153 G8 28 18N 81 9W
East Toorale, Australia ...... 127 E4 30 27 S 145 28 E
East Troy, U.S.A. 157 B8 42 47N 88 24W
East Walker →, U.S.A. 160 G7 38 52N 119 10W
East Windsor, U.S.A. 151 F10 40 17N 74 34W
Eastbourne, N.Z. ...... 130 H3 41 19 S 174 55 E
Eastbourne, U.K. ...... 21 G8 50 46N 0 18 E
Eastend, Canada 143 D7 49 32N 108 50W
Easter I. = Pascua, I. de, Chile ...... 172 b 27 7 S 109 23W
Eastern □, Ghana 113 D4 6 30N 0 30W
Eastern □, Kenya ...... 118 C4 0 0 38 30 E
Eastern Cape □, S. Africa ...... 116 E4 32 0 S 26 0 E
Eastern Cr. →, Australia ...... 126 C3 20 40 S 141 35 E
Eastern Ghats, India ...... 95 H4 14 0N 78 50 E
Eastern Group = Lau Group, Fiji ...... 133 A3 17 0 S 178 30W
Eastern Group, Australia ...... 125 F3 33 30 S 124 30 E
Eastern Highlands □, Papua N. G. ...... 132 D3 6 30 S 145 35 E
Eastern Province □, S. Leone 112 D2 8 15N 11 0W
Eastern Samar □, Phil. ...... 81 F5 11 40N 125 40 E
Eastern Transvaal = Mpumalanga □, S. Africa ...... 117 B5 26 0 S 30 0 E
Easterville, Canada 143 C9 53 8N 99 49W
Easthampton, U.S.A. 151 D12 42 16N 72 40W
Eastlake, U.S.A. 150 E3 41 40N 81 26W
Eastland, U.S.A. 155 J5 32 24N 98 49W
Eastleigh, U.K. 21 G6 50 58N 1 21W
Eastmain, U.S.A. 140 B4 52 10N 78 30W
Eastmain →, Canada 140 B4 52 27N 78 26W
Eastman, Canada 151 A12 45 18N 72 19W
Eastman, Ga., U.S.A. 152 C6 32 12N 83 11W
Eastman, Wis., U.S.A. 156 A5 43 10N 91 1W
Easton, Md., U.S.A. 148 F7 38 47N 76 5W
Easton, Pa., U.S.A. 151 F9 40 41N 75 13W
Easton, Wash., U.S.A. 160 C5 47 14N 121 11W
Eastover, U.S.A. 152 B9 33 52N 80 41W
Eastpoint, U.S.A. 152 F5 29 44N 84 53W
Eastpointe, U.S.A. 150 D2 42 27N 82 56W
Eastport, U.S.A. 149 C12 44 56N 67 0W
Eastsound, U.S.A. 160 B4 48 42N 122 55W
Eaton, Colo., U.S.A. 154 E2 40 32N 104 42W
Eaton, Ohio, U.S.A. 157 E12 39 45N 84 38W
Eaton Rapids, U.S.A. 157 B12 42 31N 84 39W
Eatonia, Canada 143 C7 51 13N 109 25W
Eatonton, U.S.A. 152 B6 33 20N 83 23W
Eatontown, U.S.A. 151 F10 40 19N 74 4W
Eatonville, U.S.A. 160 D4 46 52N 122 16W
Eau Claire, Fr. Guiana 169 C7 3 30N 53 40W
Eau Claire, U.S.A. 154 C9 44 49N 91 30W
Eau Claire, L. à l', Canada 140 A5 56 10N 74 25W
Eauze, France ...... 28 E4 43 53N 0 7 E
Eban, Nigeria ...... 113 D5 9 40N 4 42 E
Ebanga, Angola ...... 115 E2 12 45 S 14 45 E
Ebangalakata, Dem. Rep. of the Congo ...... 114 C4 0 29 S 21 29 E
Ebbegebirge, Naturpark ○, Germany ...... 30 D3 51 10N 7 55 E
Ebbw Vale, U.K. 21 F4 51 46N 3 12W
Ebebiyín, Eq. Guin. ...... 114 B2 2 9N 11 20 E
Ebeggui, Algeria ...... 111 C6 26 2N 6 0 E
Ebel, Gabon ...... 114 B2 0 7N 11 5 E
Ebeltoft, Denmark ...... 17 H4 56 12N 10 41 E
Ebeltoft Vig, Denmark ...... 17 H4 56 10N 10 35 E
Ebensburg, U.S.A. 150 F6 40 29N 78 44W
Ebensee, Austria ...... 34 D6 47 48N 13 46 E
Eber Gölü, Turkey ...... 100 C4 38 38N 31 11 E
Eberbach, Germany ...... 31 F4 49 28N 8 59 E
Eberswalde-Finow, Germany ...... 30 C9 52 50N 13 49 E
Ebetsu, Japan ...... 70 C10 43 7N 141 34 E
Ebey's Landing Nat. Historical Reserve ○, U.S.A. 160 B4 48 13N 122 41W
Ebian, China ...... 76 C4 29 11N 103 13 E
Ebikon, Switz. ...... 33 B6 47 5N 8 21 E
Ebingen, Germany ...... 31 G5 48 13N 9 1 E
Ebino, Japan ...... 72 E2 32 2N 130 48 E
Ebnat-Kappel, Switz. ...... 33 B8 47 16N 9 7 E
Ebo, Angola ...... 115 E2 11 40 S 14 40 E
Ebola →, Dem. Rep. of the Congo ...... 114 B4 3 20N 20 57 E
Éboli, Italy ...... 47 B8 40 39N 15 2 E
Ebolowa, Cameroon ...... 113 E7 2 55N 11 10 E
Ebonyi □, Nigeria ...... 113 D6 6 20N 8 0 E
Eboy, Dem. Rep. of the Congo ...... 114 B4 2 50N 23 11 E
Ebrach, Germany ...... 31 F6 49 51N 10 29 E
Ébrié, Lagune, Ivory C. 112 D4 5 12N 4 26W
Ebro →, Spain ...... 40 E5 40 43N 0 54 E
Ebro, Embalse del, Spain 42 C7 43 0N 3 58W
Ebstorf, Germany ...... 30 B6 53 2N 10 24 E
Eccabat, Turkey ...... 51 F10 40 11N 26 21 E
Ech Chéliff, Algeria ...... 111 A5 36 10N 1 20 E
Echallens, Switz. ...... 32 C3 46 38N 6 38 E
Echechonnee →, U.S.A. 152 C6 32 39N 83 36W
Echigo-Sammyaku, Japan ...... 71 F9 36 50N 139 50 E

Échirolles, France ...... 29 C9 45 8N 5 44 E
Echizen-Misaki, Japan ...... 73 B7 35 59N 135 57 E
Echmiadzin = Yejmiadzin, Armenia ...... 61 K7 40 12N 44 19 E
Echo, U.S.A. 152 D4 31 29N 85 28W
Echo Bay, N.W.T., Canada 138 B8 66 5N 117 55W
Echo Bay, Ont., Canada 140 C3 46 29N 84 4W
Echoing →, Canada 140 B1 55 51N 92 5W
Echterdingen, Stuttgart × (STR), Germany ...... 31 G5 48 42N 9 11 E
Echternach, Lux. ...... 24 E6 49 49N 6 25 E
Echuca, Australia ...... 129 D6 36 10 S 144 45 E
Ecija, Spain 43 H5 37 30N 5 10W
Eckental, Germany ...... 31 F7 49 35N 11 12 E
Eckernförde, Germany ...... 30 A5 54 28N 9 50 E
Eclectic, U.S.A. 152 C3 32 38N 86 2W
Eclipse I., Australia ...... 125 G2 35 5 S 117 58 E
Eclipse Is., Australia ...... 124 B4 13 54 S 126 19 E
Eclipse Sd., Canada 139 A11 72 38N 79 0W
Éccommoy, France ...... 26 E7 47 50N 0 17 E
Economy = Ambridge, U.S.A. 150 F4 40 36N 80 14W
Ecoporanga, Brazil ...... 171 E3 18 23 S 40 50W
Écouché, France 26 D6 48 42N 0 10W
Ecrins, Parc Nat. des △, France ...... 29 D10 44 54N 6 18 E
Ecuador ■, S. Amer. ...... 168 D2 2 0 S 78 0W
Ecuador, Volcán, Ecuador ...... 172 a 1 1 S 91 32W
Écueillé, France ...... 26 E8 47 5N 1 21 E
Ed, Sweden ...... 17 F5 58 55N 11 55 E
Ed Dabbura, Sudan ...... 106 D3 17 40N 34 15 E
Ed Da'ein, Sudan ...... 107 E2 11 26N 26 9 E
Ed Dâmer, Sudan ...... 106 D3 17 27N 34 0 E
Ed Debba, Sudan ...... 106 D3 18 0N 30 51 E
Ed-Déffa, Egypt ...... 106 A2 30 40N 26 30 E
Ed Deim, Sudan ...... 107 E2 10 10N 28 20 E
Ed Dueim, Sudan ...... 107 E3 14 0N 32 10 E
Edam, Canada 143 C7 53 11N 108 46W
Edam, Neths. ...... 24 B5 52 31N 5 3 E
Edane, Sweden ...... 16 E6 59 38N 12 49 E
Edapally, India ...... 95 J4 11 19N 78 3 E
Eday, U.K. 22 B6 59 11N 2 47W
Edchera, W. Sahara 110 C2 27 2N 13 4W
Edd, Eritrea ...... 107 E5 14 0N 41 38 E
Eddrachillis B., U.K. 22 C3 58 17N 5 14W
Eddystone, U.K. 21 G3 50 11N 4 16W
Eddystone Pt., Australia ...... 127 D4 40 59 S 148 20 E
Eddyville, U.S.A. 156 C4 41 9N 92 38W
Ede, Neths. ...... 24 B5 52 4N 5 40 E
Ede, Nigeria ...... 113 D5 7 45N 4 29 E
Édéa, Cameroon ...... 113 E7 3 51N 10 9 E
Edebäck, Sweden ...... 16 D7 60 4N 13 32 E
Edehon L., Canada 143 A9 60 25N 97 15W
Edekel, Adrar, Algeria ...... 111 D6 23 56N 6 47 E
Edelény, Hungary ...... 52 B5 48 18N 20 44 E
Eden, Australia ...... 129 D8 37 3 S 149 55 E
Eden, N.C., U.S.A. 149 G6 36 29N 79 53W
Eden, N.Y., U.S.A. 150 D6 42 39N 78 55W
Eden, Tex., U.S.A. 155 K5 31 13N 99 51W
Eden →, U.K. 20 C4 54 57N 3 1W
Edenburg, S. Africa ...... 116 D4 29 43 S 25 58 E
Edendale, N.Z. ...... 131 G3 46 19 S 168 48 E
Edendale, S. Africa ...... 117 D5 29 39 S 30 18 E
Edenderry, Ireland 23 C4 53 21N 7 4W
Edenhope, Australia ...... 128 D4 37 4 S 141 19 E
Edenton, U.S.A. 149 G7 36 4N 76 39W
Edenville, S. Africa ...... 117 D4 27 37 S 27 34 E
Eder →, Germany ...... 30 D5 51 12N 9 28 E
Eder-Stausee, Germany ...... 30 D4 51 10N 8 57 E
Edewecht, Germany ...... 30 B3 53 8N 7 58 E
Edgar, U.S.A. 154 E6 40 22N 97 58W
Edgartown, U.S.A. 151 E14 41 23N 70 31W
Edge Hill, U.K. 21 E6 52 8N 1 26W
Edgecumbe, N.Z. ...... 130 E5 37 59 S 176 47 E
Edgefield, U.S.A. 152 B8 33 47N 81 56W
Edgeley, U.S.A. 154 B5 46 22N 98 43W
Edgemont, U.S.A. 154 D3 43 18N 103 50W
Edgeøya, Svalbard ...... 6 B9 77 45N 22 30 E
Edgerton, Ohio, U.S.A. 157 C12 41 27N 84 45W
Edgerton, Wis., U.S.A. 156 B7 42 50N 89 4W
Edgewater, U.S.A. 153 G9 28 59N 80 54W
Edgewood, U.S.A. 157 F10 38 55N 84 40W
Édhessa, Greece ...... 50 F6 40 48N 22 5 E
Edievale, N.Z. ...... 131 G4 45 49 S 169 22 E
Edina, Liberia 112 D2 6 0N 10 10W
Edina, U.S.A. 156 D4 40 10N 92 11W
Edinboro, U.S.A. 150 E4 41 52N 80 8W
Edinburg, Ill., U.S.A. 156 D7 39 39N 89 23W
Edinburg, Ind., U.S.A. 157 E11 39 21N 85 58W
Edinburg, Tex., U.S.A. 155 M5 26 18N 98 10W
Edinburgh, U.K. 22 F5 55 57N 3 13W
Edinburgh × (EDI), U.K. 22 F5 55 54N 3 22W
Edinburgh, City of □, U.K. 22 F5 55 57N 3 17W
Edineţ, Moldova ...... 53 B12 48 9N 27 18 E
Edirne, Turkey ...... 51 E10 41 40N 26 34 E
Edirne □, Turkey ...... 51 E10 41 12N 26 30 E
Edison, Ga., U.S.A. 152 D5 31 34N 84 44W
Edison, Wash., U.S.A. 160 B4 48 33N 122 27W
Edisto →, U.S.A. 152 C9 32 29N 80 21W
Edisto Beach, U.S.A. 152 C9 32 29N 80 20W
Edisto I., U.S.A. 152 C9 32 34N 80 17W
Edithburgh, Australia ...... 128 C2 35 5 S 137 43 E
Edjeleh, Algeria ...... 111 C6 28 38N 9 50 E
Edmeston, U.S.A. 151 D9 42 42N 75 15W
Edmond, U.S.A. 155 H6 35 39N 97 29W
Edmonds, U.S.A. 160 C4 47 49N 122 23W
Edmonton, Australia ...... 126 B4 17 2 S 145 46 E
Edmonton, Canada 142 C6 53 30N 113 30W
Edmund L., Canada 140 B1 54 45N 93 17W
Edmundston, Canada 141 C6 47 23N 68 20W
Edna, U.S.A. 155 L6 28 59N 96 39W
Edo □, Nigeria ...... 113 D6 6 30N 6 0 E
Edolo, Italy ...... 44 B7 46 10N 10 21 E
Edøy, Norway ...... 18 A5 63 18N 8 10 E
Edremit, Turkey ...... 49 B9 39 34N 27 0 E
Edremit Körfezi, Turkey ...... 49 B8 39 30N 26 45 E
Edsbro, Sweden ...... 16 E12 59 54N 18 29 E
Edsbyn, Sweden ...... 16 C9 61 23N 15 49 E
Edson, Canada 142 C5 53 35N 116 28W
Eduardo Castex, Argentina ...... 174 D3 35 50 S 64 18W
Edward →, Australia ...... 128 C5 35 5 S 143 30 E
Edward, L., Africa ...... 118 C1 0 25 S 29 40 E
Edward River, Australia ...... 126 A3 14 59 S 141 26 E
Edward VII Land, Antarctica ...... 7 E13 80 0 S 150 0W
Edwards, Calif., U.S.A. 161 L9 34 55N 117 51W
Edwards, N.Y., U.S.A. 151 B9 44 20N 75 15W
Edwards →, U.S.A. 156 C6 41 9N 90 59W
Edwards Air Force Base, U.S.A. 161 L9 34 50N 117 40W
Edwards Plateau, U.S.A. 155 K4 30 45N 101 20W
Edwardsburg, U.S.A. 157 C10 41 48N 86 6W
Edwardsville, Ill., U.S.A. 156 F7 38 49N 89 58W
Edwardsville, Pa., U.S.A. 151 E9 41 15N 75 56W
Edxná, Mexico 163 D7 19 35N 90 14W
Edzo, Canada 142 A5 62 49N 116 4W
Eek, U.S.A. 144 F7 60 14N 162 1W
Eeklo, Belgium ...... 24 C3 51 11N 3 33 E
Eel →, Ind., U.S.A. 157 E10 39 7N 86 57W
Eel →, Ind., U.S.A. 157 D10 40 45N 86 22W
Efate, Vanuatu ...... 133 G6 17 40 S 168 25 E
Efate, I., Vanuatu ...... 133 G6 17 40 S 168 25 E
Eferding, Austria ...... 34 C7 48 18N 14 1 E
Eferi, Algeria ...... 111 D6 24 30N 9 28 E
Effigy Mounds Nat. Monument ○, U.S.A. 156 A5 43 5N 91 11W
Effingham, U.S.A. 157 F8 39 7N 88 33W
Effretikon, Switz. ...... 33 B7 47 25N 8 42 E
Eforie, Romania ...... 53 F13 44 1N 28 37 E

Efoulen, Cameroon ...... 114 B2 2 46N 10 43 E
Efteløt, Norway ...... 18 E6 59 33N 9 49 E
Ega →, Spain 40 C3 42 19N 1 55W
Égadi, Ísole, Italy ...... 46 E5 37 55N 12 16 E
Egan Range, U.S.A. 158 G6 39 35N 114 55W
Eganville, Canada 140 C4 45 32N 77 5W
Egedesminde = Aasiaat, Greenland 10 D5 68 43N 52 56W
Egegik, U.S.A. 144 G8 58 13N 157 22W
Eger = Cheb, Czech Rep. ...... 34 A5 50 9N 12 28 E
Eger, Hungary ...... 52 C5 47 53N 20 27 E
Eger →, Hungary ...... 52 C5 47 38N 20 50 E
Egersund, Norway ...... 18 F3 58 26N 6 1 E
Egg, Switz. ...... 33 B9 47 20N 9 54 E
Egg, Switz. ...... 33 B7 47 18N 8 41 E
Egg I., St. Helena ...... 9 h 15 58 S 5 47W
Egg L., Canada 143 B7 55 5N 105 30W
Eggedal, Norway ...... 18 D6 60 1N 9 21 E
Eggegebirge Südlicher Teutoburger Wald, Naturpark ○, Germany ...... 30 D4 51 40N 8 59 E
Eggenburg, Austria ...... 34 C8 48 38N 15 50 E
Eggenfelden, Germany ...... 31 G8 48 23N 12 46 E
Eggiwil, Switz. ...... 32 C5 46 52N 7 47 E
Egherta, Somali Rep. ...... 120 D2 2 4N 43 11 E
Éghezée, Belgium ...... 24 D4 50 35N 4 55 E
Egholo, Solomon Is. ...... 133 M9 8 25 S 157 25 E
Egilsstaðir, Iceland 11 B12 65 16N 14 25W
Égina, Greece ...... 115 E2 12 4 S 13 58 E
Égletons, France ...... 28 C6 45 24N 2 3 E
Eglisau, Switz. ...... 33 A7 47 35N 8 31 E
Egmont, Canada 142 D4 49 45N 123 56W
Egmont, C., N.Z. ...... 130 F2 39 16 S 173 45 E
Egmont, Mt. = Taranaki, Mt., N.Z. ...... 130 F3 39 17 S 174 5 E
Egmont Nat. Park △, N.Z. ...... 130 F3 39 17 S 174 4 E
Egra, India ...... 93 J12 21 54N 87 32 E
Eğridir, Turkey ...... 100 D4 37 52N 30 51 E
Eğridir Gölü, Turkey ...... 100 D4 37 53N 30 50 E
Egtved, Denmark ...... 17 J3 55 38N 9 18 E
Éguas →, Brazil ...... 171 D3 12 26 S 44 14W
Egume, Nigeria ...... 113 D6 7 30N 7 14 E
Egvekinot, Russia 67 C19 66 19N 179 50W
Egyek, Hungary ...... 52 C5 47 39N 20 52 E
Egypt ■, Africa ...... 106 B3 28 0N 31 0 E
Eha Amufu, Nigeria ...... 113 D6 6 30N 7 46 E
Eheli, Algeria ...... 111 D5 22 26N 4 40 E
Ehime □, Japan ...... 73 H6 33 30N 132 40 E
Ehingen, Germany ...... 31 G5 48 16N 9 43 E
Ehrenberg, U.S.A. 161 M12 33 36N 114 31W
Ehrhardt, U.S.A. 152 B8 33 6N 81 1W
Ehrwald, Austria ...... 34 D3 47 24N 10 56 E
Eibar, Spain 40 B2 43 11N 2 28W
Eichstätt, Germany ...... 31 G7 48 54N 11 11 E
Eide, Hordaland, Norway ...... 18 B2 60 31N 6 44 E
Eide, Møre og Romsdal, Norway ...... 18 B4 62 55N 7 27 E
Eider →, Germany ...... 30 A4 54 19N 8 57 E
Eidsbugarden, Norway ...... 18 D4 61 23N 8 16 E
Eidsbygda, Norway ...... 18 B4 62 36N 7 30 E
Eidsdal, Norway ...... 18 B4 62 16N 7 10 E
Eidsvåg, Norway ...... 18 B5 62 46N 8 2 E
Eidsvold, Australia ...... 127 D5 25 25 S 151 12 E
Eidsvoll, Norway ...... 18 D6 60 19N 11 14 E
Eielson, U.S.A. 144 D11 64 40N 147 4W
Eifel, Germany ...... 30 D5 50 15N 6 50 E
Eiffel Flats, Zimbabwe ...... 119 F3 18 20 S 30 0 E
Eiger, Switz. ...... 32 C6 46 34N 8 1 E
Eigg, U.K. 22 E2 56 54N 6 10W
Eighty Mile Beach, Australia ...... 124 C3 19 30 S 120 40 E
Eikefjord, Norway ...... 18 C2 61 35N 5 27 E
Eikelandsosen, Norway ...... 18 F2 60 15N 5 4 E
Eiken, Norway ...... 18 F4 58 29N 7 14 E
Eikeren, Norway ...... 18 E6 59 38N 9 58 E
Eikesdal, Norway ...... 18 B5 62 28N 8 12 E
Eil, Somali Rep. ...... 120 F4 8 0N 49 50 E
Eil, L., U.K. 22 E3 56 51N 5 16W
Eildon, Australia ...... 129 D6 37 14 S 145 55 E
Eildon, L., Australia ...... 129 D7 37 10 S 146 0 E
Eilenburg, Germany ...... 30 D8 51 27N 12 36 E
Ein el Luweiqa, Sudan ...... 107 E3 14 5N 33 50 E
Eina, Norway ...... 18 D7 60 38N 10 35 E
Einasleigh, Australia ...... 126 B3 18 32 S 144 5 E
Einasleigh →, Australia ...... 126 B3 17 30 S 142 17 E
Einbeck, Germany ...... 30 D5 51 49N 9 53 E
Eindhoven, Neths. ...... 24 C5 51 26N 5 28 E
Einsiedeln, Switz. ...... 33 B7 47 7N 8 46 E
Eire ■, Europe 23 C4 53 0N 7 52W
Eiríksjökull, Iceland 11 C6 64 46N 20 24W
Eiríksstaðir, Iceland 11 B11 65 7N 15 25W
Eirunepé, Brazil ...... 172 B4 6 35 S 69 53W
Eiseb →, Namibia ...... 116 C2 20 33 S 20 59 E
Eisenach, Germany ...... 30 D6 50 58N 10 19 E
Eisenberg, Germany ...... 30 E7 50 58N 11 54 E
Eisenerz, Austria ...... 34 D7 47 32N 14 54 E
Eisenhüttenstadt, Germany ...... 30 C10 52 9N 14 38 E
Eisenkappel, Austria ...... 34 E7 46 29N 14 36 E
Eisenstadt, Austria ...... 35 D9 47 51N 16 31 E
Eisfeld, Germany ...... 31 E6 50 25N 10 54 E
Eisleben, Germany ...... 30 D7 51 32N 11 32 E
Eislingen, Germany ...... 31 G5 48 41N 9 42 E
Eivindvik, Norway ...... 18 D2 60 59N 5 12 E
Eivissa, Spain ...... 38 D1 38 54N 1 26 E
Eixe, Serra do, Spain 42 C4 42 16N 6 54W
Ejea de los Caballeros, Spain 40 C3 42 7N 1 9W
Ejeda, Madag. ...... 117 C7 24 20 S 44 31 E
Ejura, Ghana 113 D4 7 23N 1 15W
Ejutla, Mexico 163 D5 16 34N 96 44W
Ekalaka, U.S.A. 154 C2 45 53N 104 33W
Ekalla, Gabon ...... 114 C2 1 27 S 14 0 E
Ekanga, Dem. Rep. of the Congo ...... 114 C4 2 23 S 23 14 E
Ekenässjön, Sweden ...... 17 G8 57 28N 15 1 E
Ekerö, Sweden ...... 16 E11 59 16N 17 45 E
Eket, Nigeria ...... 113 E6 4 38N 7 56 E
Eketahuna, N.Z. ...... 130 G4 40 38 S 175 43 E
Ekhinádhes Nísoi, Greece ...... 39 C3 38 17N 21 2 E
Ekhínos, Greece ...... 51 E9 41 16N 25 1 E
Ekibastuz, Kazakhstan ...... 68 D8 51 50N 75 10 E
Ekiti □, Nigeria ...... 113 D6 7 55 S 5 20 E
Ekoli, Dem. Rep. of the Congo ...... 118 C1 0 25 S 29 40 E
Ekoln, Sweden ...... 16 E11 59 45N 17 37 E
Ekouamou, Congo ...... 114 B3 0 8N 16 31 E
Ekoungoungou, Congo ...... 114 C3 1 10 S 15 52 E
Ekshärad, Sweden ...... 16 D7 60 10N 13 26 E
Eksjö, Sweden ...... 17 G8 57 40N 14 58 E
Ekukola, Dem. Rep. of the Congo ...... 114 C3 0 31 S 18 56 E
Ekuku, Dem. Rep. of the Congo ...... 114 C4 0 41 S 24 22 E
Ekukula, Dem. Rep. of the Congo ...... 114 B4 0 25 S 21 30 E
Ekuma →, Namibia ...... 116 B2 18 40 S 16 2 E
Ekuta, Dem. Rep. of the Congo ...... 114 B3 0 18 S 20 49 E
Ekwan →, Canada 140 B3 53 16N 82 7W
Ekwan Pt., Canada 140 B3 53 16N 82 7W
Ekwok, U.S.A. 144 G8 59 22N 157 30W
El Aaiún, W. Sahara 110 C2 27 9N 13 12W
El Aargub, Mauritania 110 D1 20 25N 15 20W
El Abanico, Chile ...... 174 D1 37 20 S 71 31W
El Abbasiya, Sudan ...... 107 E3 13 7N 29 43 E
El Abiodh-Sidi-Cheikh, Algeria ...... 111 B5 32 53N 0 31 E
El Adde, Somali Rep. ...... 120 D3 3 50N 42 5 E
El 'Agrûd, Egypt ...... 103 E3 30 14N 34 24 E
El Aïoun, Morocco 111 B4 34 33N 2 30W
El Ait, Sudan ...... 107 E2 12 22N 27 27 E
El 'Aiyat, Egypt ...... 106 J7 29 36N 31 15 E
El 'Alamein, Egypt ...... 106 A2 30 48N 28 58 E
El Alto, Peru ...... 172 A1 4 15 S 81 14W

El Aouj, Mauritania 110 D2 22 53N 12 49W
El 'Aqaba, W. →, Egypt ...... 103 E2 30 7N 33 54 E
El 'Arag, Egypt ...... 106 B2 28 40N 26 20 E
El Arahal, Algeria 43 H5 37 15N 5 33W
El Aricha, Algeria 111 B4 34 13N 1 10W
El Arīḥā, West Bank ...... 103 D4 31 52N 35 27 E
El 'Arîsh, Egypt ...... 103 D2 31 8N 33 50 E
El 'Arîsh, W. →, Egypt ...... 103 D2 31 8N 33 47 E
El Arrouch, Algeria ...... 111 A6 36 10N 1 20 E
El Asnam = Ech Chéliff, Algeria ...... 111 A5 36 10N 1 20 E
El Astillero, Spain 42 B7 43 24N 3 49W
El Badâri, Egypt ...... 106 B3 27 4N 31 25 E
El Bahrein, Egypt ...... 106 B2 28 30N 26 25 E
El Ballâs, Egypt ...... 106 B3 26 2N 32 43 E
El Balyana, Egypt ...... 106 B3 26 10N 32 3 E
El Banco, Colombia 168 B3 9 0N 73 58W
El Baqeir, Sudan ...... 106 D3 18 40N 33 40 E
El Barco de Ávila, Spain 42 E5 40 21N 5 31W
El Barco de Valdeorras = O Barco, Spain 42 C4 42 23N 6 58W
El Bauga, Sudan ...... 106 D3 18 18N 33 52 E
El Baúl, Venezuela 168 B4 8 57N 68 17W
El Bawiti, Egypt ...... 106 B2 28 25N 28 45 E
El Bayadh, Algeria ...... 111 B5 33 40N 1 1 E
El Bierzo, Spain 42 C4 42 45N 6 30W
El Bluff, Nic. 164 D3 11 59N 83 40W
El Bolsón, Argentina ...... 176 B2 41 55 S 71 30W
El Bonillo, Spain 41 G2 38 57N 2 35W
El Brûk, W. →, Egypt ...... 103 E2 30 15N 33 50 E
El Buheirat □, Sudan ...... 107 F3 7 0N 30 0 E
El Bur, Somali Rep. ...... 120 D3 4 40N 46 37 E
El Burgo de Osma, Spain 40 D1 41 35N 3 4W
El Caín, Argentina ...... 176 B3 41 38 S 68 19W
El Cajon, U.S.A. 161 N10 32 48N 116 58W
El Callao, Venezuela 169 B5 7 18N 61 50W
El Campo, U.S.A. 155 L6 29 12N 96 16W
El Carmen, Bolivia ...... 173 C5 13 40 S 63 55W
El Centro, U.S.A. 161 N11 32 48N 115 34W
El Cerro, Bolivia ...... 173 D5 17 30 S 61 40W
El Cerro de Andévalo, Spain 43 H4 37 45N 6 57W
El Cocuy, Colombia 168 B3 6 25N 72 27W
El Compadre, Mexico 161 N10 32 20N 116 14W
El Corcovado, Argentina ...... 176 B2 43 25 S 71 35W
El Coronil, Spain 43 H5 37 5N 5 38W
El Cuy, Argentina ...... 176 B3 39 55 S 68 25W
El Cuyo, Mexico 163 C7 21 30N 87 40W
El Dab'a, Egypt ...... 106 H6 31 0N 28 27 E
El Daheir, Egypt ...... 103 D3 31 13N 34 10 E
El Dambadelio, Somali Rep. ...... 120 D3 3 17N 46 40 E
El Dátil, Mexico 162 B2 30 7N 112 15W
El Deir, Egypt ...... 106 B3 25 25N 32 20 E
El Dere, Somali Rep. ...... 120 C2 5 6N 43 5 E
El Dere, Somali Rep. ...... 120 D3 3 50N 47 8 E
El Dere, Somali Rep. ...... 120 C3 5 22N 46 11 E
El Descanso, Mexico 161 N10 32 12N 116 58W
El Desemboque, Mexico 162 A2 30 30N 112 57W
El Dilingat, Egypt ...... 106 H7 30 50N 30 31 E
El Diviso, Colombia 168 C2 1 22N 78 14W
El Djouf, Mauritania 104 D3 20 0N 9 0W
El Dorado, Ark., U.S.A. 155 J8 33 12N 92 40W
El Dorado, Kans., U.S.A. 155 G6 37 49N 96 52W
El Dorado, Venezuela 169 B5 6 55N 61 37W
El Eglab, Algeria 110 C4 26 20N 4 30W
El 'Ein, Sudan ...... 107 E2 16 35N 29 22 E
El Ejido, Spain 43 J8 36 47N 2 49W
El Escorial, Spain 42 E6 40 35N 4 7W
El Espinar, Spain 42 D6 41 43N 4 15W
El Eulma, Algeria ...... 111 A6 36 9N 5 42 E
El Faiyûm, Egypt ...... 106 J7 29 19N 30 50 E
El Fâsher, Sudan ...... 107 E2 13 33N 25 26 E
El Fashn, Egypt ...... 106 J7 28 50N 30 54 E
El Ferrol = Ferrol, Spain 42 B2 43 29N 8 15W
El Fifi, Sudan ...... 107 E2 10 4N 25 0 E
El Fud, Ethiopia ...... 120 C2 7 15N 42 52 E
El Fuerte, Mexico 162 B3 26 30N 108 40W
El Ga'a, Sudan ...... 107 E2 14 16N 29 59 E
El Gal, Somali Rep. ...... 120 D4 11 15N 49 58 E
El Garef, Sudan ...... 107 E3 14 19 E
El Geneina = Al Junaynah, Sudan ...... 109 F4 13 27N 22 45 E
El Geteina, Sudan ...... 107 E3 14 50N 32 27 E
El Gezira □, Sudan ...... 106 D2 15 0N 33 0 E
El Gîr, Sudan ...... 106 D3 19 50N 28 18 E
El Gîza, Egypt ...... 106 J7 30 0N 31 10 E
El Gogorron, Parque Nac. △, Mexico 162 C4 21 50N 100 50W
El Goléa, Algeria ...... 111 B5 30 30N 2 50 E
El Grau, Spain 41 G4 39 0N 0 7W
El Guácharo, Parque Nac. △, Venezuela 165 D7 10 8N 63 21W
El Guache, Parque Nac. △, Venezuela 165 E6 9 45N 69 30W
El Hadeb, W. Sahara 110 C2 25 51N 13 0W
El Hadjira, Algeria ...... 111 B6 32 36N 5 30 E
El Hagiz, Sudan ...... 107 D4 15 15N 35 50 E
El Hâi, Egypt ...... 106 B3 29 39N 31 18 E
El Hajeb, Morocco 110 B3 33 43N 5 13W
El Hamma, Tunisia ...... 108 B1 33 54N 9 48 E
El Hammam, Egypt ...... 106 A2 30 52N 29 25 E
El Hammâmi, Mauritania 110 D2 23 3N 11 30W
El Hamurre, Somali Rep. ...... 120 C3 7 13N 48 54 E
El Hank, Mauritania 110 D3 24 30N 7 0W
El Hasian, W. Sahara 110 C2 26 20N 14 0W
El Hawata, Sudan ...... 107 E3 13 25N 34 42 E
El Heiz, Egypt ...... 106 B2 27 50N 28 40 E
El Hideib, Sudan ...... 107 E3 13 0N 32 50 E
El Hilla, Sudan ...... 107 E2 13 24N 27 2 E
El Hôçeima, Morocco ...... 111 C5 29 43N 1 45 E
El 'Idisat, Egypt ...... 106 B3 25 30N 32 35 E
El Iskandarîya, Egypt ...... 106 H7 31 13N 29 58 E
El Jadida, Morocco 110 B3 33 11N 8 17W
El Jardal, Honduras 164 D2 14 54N 88 50W
El Jebelein, Sudan ...... 107 E3 12 40N 32 55 E
El Jem, Tunisia ...... 108 A2 35 18N 10 42 E
El Kab, Sudan ...... 106 D3 19 27N 32 46 E
El Kabrît, G., Egypt ...... 103 F2 29 42N 33 16 E
El Kafr el Sharqi, Egypt ...... 106 H7 31 16N 31 10 E
El Kala, Algeria ...... 111 A6 36 50N 8 30 E
El Kamlin, Sudan ...... 107 D3 15 3N 33 11 E
El Kantara, Algeria ...... 111 B6 35 14N 5 45 E
El Kantara, Tunisia ...... 108 B2 33 45N 10 58 E
El Kef, Tunisia ...... 108 A1 36 12N 8 47 E
El Kelâa, Morocco 110 B3 32 4N 7 27W
El Kere, Ethiopia ...... 107 F5 5 50N 42 5 E
El Khandaq, Sudan ...... 106 D3 18 30N 30 33 E
El Khârga, Egypt ...... 106 B3 25 30N 30 33 E
El Khartûm, Sudan ...... 107 D3 15 31N 32 35 E
El Khartûm □, Sudan ...... 107 D3 16 0N 33 0 E
El Khartûm Bahrî, Sudan ...... 107 D3 15 40N 32 31 E
El Khroub, Algeria ...... 111 A6 36 10N 6 55 E
El Ksabi, Algeria 110 B3 32 20N 4 29W
El Ksiba, Morocco 110 B3 32 45N 6 1W
El Kuntilla, Egypt ...... 103 E3 30 1N 34 45 E
El Laqâwa, Sudan ...... 107 E2 11 25N 29 1 E
El Leh, Ethiopia ...... 107 G4 3 46N 39 13 E
El Maestrazgo, Spain 40 E4 40 30N 0 25W
El Mafâza, Sudan ...... 107 E3 13 38N 34 30 E
El Maghra, Egypt ...... 106 A2 30 15N 28 55 E
El Mahalla el Kubra, Egypt ...... 106 H7 31 0N 31 0 E
El Mahârîq, Egypt ...... 106 B3 25 35N 30 35 E
El Maïmûn, Egypt ...... 106 J7 29 14N 31 12 E

El Maitén, Argentina ... 176 B2 42 3 S 71 10W
El Maiz, Algeria ... 111 C4 28 19N 0 9W
El Maks el Bahari, Egypt ... 106 C3 24 30N 30 40 E
El Malpais Nat. Monument △, U.S.A. ... 159 J10 34 53N 108 0W
El Manshâh, Egypt ... 106 B3 26 26N 31 50 E
El Mansour, Algeria ... 111 C4 27 47N 0 14W
El Mansûra, Egypt ... 106 H7 31 0N 31 19 E
El Manteco, Venezuela ... 169 B5 7 38N 62 45W
El Manzala, Egypt ... 106 H7 31 10N 31 50 E
El Marâgha, Egypt ... 106 B3 26 35N 31 10 E
El Masid, Sudan ... 107 D3 15 15N 33 0 E
El Masnou, Spain ... 40 D7 41 28N 2 20 E
El Matariya, Egypt ... 106 H8 31 15N 32 0 E
El Meda, Ethiopia ... 107 F5 5 39N 41 47 E
El Medano, Canary Is. ... 9 e1 28 3N 16 32W
El Meghaier, Algeria ... 111 B6 33 55N 5 58 E
El Meraguen, Algeria ... 111 C4 28 0N 0 7W
El Metemma, Sudan ... 107 D3 16 50N 33 10 E
El Miamo, Venezuela ... 169 B5 7 39N 61 46W
El Milagro, Argentina ... 174 C2 30 59 S 65 59W
El Milia, Algeria ... 111 A6 36 51N 6 13 E
El Minyâ, Egypt ... 106 B3 28 7N 30 33 E
El Monte, U.S.A. ... 161 L8 34 4N 118 1W
El Montseny, Spain ... 40 D7 41 55N 2 25 E
El Mreyye, Mauritania ... 112 B3 18 0N 6 0W
El Nido, Phil. ... 81 F2 11 10N 119 25 E
El Niybo, Ethiopia ... 107 G4 4 40N 39 55 E
El Obeid, Sudan ... 107 E3 13 8N 30 10 E
El Odaiya, Sudan ... 107 E2 12 8N 28 12 E
El Oro, Mexico ... 163 D4 19 48N 100 8W
El Oro □, Ecuador ... 168 D2 3 30 S 79 50W
El Oued, Algeria ... 111 B6 33 20N 6 58 E
El Oumi, Niger ... 111 D7 20 11N 0 15 E
El Palmar, Bolivia ... 173 D5 17 50 S 63 9W
El Palmar, Venezuela ... 169 B5 7 58N 61 53W
El Palmito, Presa, Mexico ... 162 B3 25 40N 105 30W
El Paso, Ill., U.S.A. ... 156 D7 40 44N 89 1W
El Paso, Tex., U.S.A. ... 159 L10 31 45N 106 29W
El Paso Robles, U.S.A. ... 160 K6 35 38N 120 41W
El Pedernoso, Spain ... 41 F2 39 29N 2 45W
El Pedroso, Spain ... 43 H5 37 51N 5 45W
El Pilar, Venezuela ... 169 A5 10 32N 63 9W
El Pinacate y Gran Desierto de Altar = Gran Desierto del Pinacate, Parque Natural △, Mexico ... 162 A2 31 51N 113 32W
El Pobo de Dueñas, Spain ... 40 E3 40 46N 1 39W
El Portal, U.S.A. ... 160 H7 37 41N 119 47W
El Porvenir, Mexico ... 162 A3 31 15N 105 51W
El Prat de Llobregat, Spain ... 40 D7 41 18N 2 3 E
El Progreso, Ecuador ... 172 a 0 54 S 89 33W
El Progreso, Honduras ... 164 C2 15 26N 87 51W
El Pueblito, Mexico ... 162 B3 29 3N 105 4W
El Pueblo, Canary Is. ... 9 e1 28 36N 17 47W
El Puente del Arzobispo, Spain ... 42 F5 39 48N 5 10W
El Puerto de Santa María, Spain ... 43 J4 36 36N 6 13W
El Qâhira, Egypt ... 106 H7 30 1N 31 14 E
El Qantara, Egypt ... 103 E1 30 51N 32 20 E
El Qaşr, Egypt ... 106 B2 25 44N 28 42 E
El Qubâbât, Egypt ... 106 J7 29 28N 31 16 E
El Quseima, Egypt ... 106 B3 30 40N 34 15 E
El Quşîya, Egypt ... 106 B3 27 29N 30 44 E
El Râshda, Egypt ... 106 B2 25 36N 28 57 E
El Reno, U.S.A. ... 155 H6 35 32N 97 57W
El Ridisiya, Egypt ... 106 C3 24 56N 32 51 E
El Rio, U.S.A. ... 161 L7 34 14N 119 10W
El Ronquillo, Spain ... 43 H4 37 44N 6 10W
El Roque, Pta., Canary Is. ... 9 e1 28 10N 15 25W
El Rosarito, Mexico ... 162 B2 28 38N 114 4W
El Rubio, Spain ... 43 H5 37 22N 5 0W
El Saff, Egypt ... 106 J7 29 34N 31 16 E
El Saheira, W. →, Egypt ... 103 E2 30 5N 33 25 E
El Salto, Mexico ... 162 C3 23 47N 105 22W
El Salvador ■, Cent. Amer. ... 164 D2 13 50N 89 0W
El Sauce, Nic. ... 164 D2 13 0N 86 40W
El Saucejo, Spain ... 43 H5 37 4N 5 6W
El Shallal, Egypt ... 106 C3 24 0N 32 53 E
El Simbillawein, Egypt ... 106 H7 30 48N 31 13 E
El Sombrero, Venezuela ... 168 B4 9 23N 67 3W
El Sueco, Mexico ... 162 B3 29 54N 106 24W
El Suweis, Egypt ... 106 J8 29 58N 32 31 E
El Tabbin, Egypt ... 106 J7 29 47N 31 16 E
El Tamarâni, W. →, Egypt ... 103 E3 30 7N 34 43 E
El Thamad, Egypt ... 103 F3 29 40N 34 28 E
El Tigre, Venezuela ... 169 B5 8 44N 64 15W
El Tîh, Gebal, Egypt ... 103 F2 29 40N 33 50 E
El Tina, Egypt ... 106 H8 31 3N 32 22 E
El Tîna, Khalîg, Egypt ... 103 D1 31 10N 32 40 E
El Tocuyo, Venezuela ... 168 B4 9 47N 69 48W
El Tofo, Chile ... 174 B1 29 22 S 71 18W
El Tránsito, Chile ... 174 B1 28 52 S 70 17W
El Tûr, Egypt ... 96 D2 28 14N 33 36 E
El Turbio, Argentina ... 176 D2 51 45 S 72 5W
El Uinle, Somali Rep. ... 75 G3 3 4N 41 42 E
El Uqsur, Egypt ... 106 B3 25 41N 32 38 E
El Valle, Parque Natural de △, Spain ... 41 H3 37 56N 1 6W
El Venado, Mexico ... 162 C4 22 56N 101 10W
El Vendrell, Spain ... 40 D6 41 10N 1 30 E
El Vergel, Mexico ... 162 B3 26 28N 106 22W
El Vigía, Venezuela ... 168 B3 8 38N 71 39W
El Viso del Alcor, Spain ... 43 H5 37 23N 5 43W
El Wabeira, Egypt ... 103 F2 29 34N 33 6 E
El Wak, Kenya ... 118 B5 2 49N 40 56 E
El Wak, Somali Rep. ... 120 D2 2 44N 41 1 E
El Waqf, Egypt ... 106 B3 25 45N 32 15 E
El Weguet, Ethiopia ... 107 F5 5 28N 42 17 E
El Wuz, Sudan ... 107 D3 15 5N 30 7 E
Elafónisos, Greece ... 48 E4 36 29N 22 56 E
Elamanchili, India ... 94 F6 17 33N 82 50 E
Élancourt, France ... 27 D8 48 47N 1 58 E
Elands, Australia ... 129 A10 31 37 S 152 20 E
Elassa, Greece ... 49 F8 35 18N 26 21 E
Elassón, Greece ... 48 B4 39 53N 22 12 E
Elat, Israel ... 103 F3 29 30N 34 56 E
Eláthia, Greece ... 48 C4 38 37N 22 46 E
Eláti Óros, Greece ... 39 B2 38 43N 21 41 E
Elâzğ, Turkey ... 101 C8 38 37N 39 14 E
Elba, Italy ... 44 F7 42 46N 10 17 E
Elba, U.S.A. ... 152 D3 31 25N 86 4W
Elbasan, Albania ... 50 E4 41 9N 20 9 E
Elbe, U.S.A. ... 160 D4 46 45N 122 10W
Elbe →, Europe ... 30 B4 53 50N 9 0 E
Elbe-Seitenkanal, Germany ... 30 C6 52 45N 10 32 E
Elberfeld, U.S.A. ... 157 F9 38 10N 87 27W
Elbert, Mt., U.S.A. ... 159 G10 39 7N 106 27W
Elberton, U.S.A. ... 152 A7 34 7N 82 52W
Elbeuf, France ... 26 C8 49 17N 1 2 E
Elbidtan, Turkey ... 100 C7 38 13N 37 12 E
Elbing = Elbląg, Poland ... 54 D6 54 10N 19 25 E
Elbistan, Turkey ... 100 C7 38 13N 37 15 E
Elbląg, Poland ... 54 D6 54 10N 19 25 E
Elbow, Canada ... 143 C7 51 7N 106 35W
Elbow, Pta., W. Sahara ... 110 D1 21 15N 17 35W
Elbrus, Asia ... 61 J6 43 21N 42 30 E
Elbufer-Drawehn, Naturpark △, Germany ... 30 B6 53 8N 10 58 E
Elburn, U.S.A. ... 157 C8 41 54N 88 28W
Elburz Mts. = Alborz, Reshteh-ye Kūhhā-ye, Iran ... 97 C7 36 0N 52 0 E
Elche, Spain ... 41 G4 38 15N 0 42W
Elche de la Sierra, Spain ... 41 G2 38 27N 2 3W
Elcho I., Australia ... 126 A2 11 55 S 135 45 E
Elda, Spain ... 41 G4 38 29N 0 47W

Elde →, Germany ... 30 B7 53 7N 11 15 E
Eldon, Iowa, U.S.A. ... 156 D4 40 55N 92 13W
Eldon, Mo., U.S.A. ... 156 F4 38 21N 92 35W
Eldon, Wash., U.S.A. ... 160 C3 47 33N 123 3W
Eldora, U.S.A. ... 156 B3 42 22N 93 5W
Eldorado, Argentina ... 175 B5 26 28 S 54 43W
Eldorado, Canada ... 150 B7 44 35N 77 31W
Eldorado, Mexico ... 162 C3 24 20N 107 22W
Eldorado, Ill., U.S.A. ... 157 G8 37 49N 88 26W
Eldorado, Tex., U.S.A. ... 155 K4 30 52N 100 36W
Eldorado Springs, U.S.A. ... 155 G8 37 52N 94 1W
Eldorendo, U.S.A. ... 152 D5 31 3N 84 39W
Eldoret, Kenya ... 118 B4 0 30N 35 17 E
Eldred, U.S.A. ... 156 C6 41 58N 78 23W
Eldridge, U.S.A. ... 156 B5 41 39N 90 35W
Elea, C., Cyprus ... 39 E10 35 19N 34 4 E
Eleanora, Pk., Australia ... 125 F3 32 57 S 121 9 E
Elefantes →, Africa ... 117 C5 24 10 S 32 40 E
Elefantes, B. das, Angola ... 115 E2 13 13 S 12 44 E
Elefantes, G., Chile ... 176 C2 46 28 S 73 49W
Elefantes do Maputo, Reserva de △, Mozam. ... 117 D5 26 23 S 32 48 E
Elektrogorsk, Russia ... 58 E10 55 56N 38 50 E
Elektrostal, Russia ... 58 E10 55 41N 38 32 E
Elele, Nigeria ... 113 D6 5 5N 6 50 E
Elena, Bulgaria ... 51 D9 42 55N 25 53 E
Elephant Butte Reservoir, U.S.A. ... 159 K10 33 9N 107 11W
Elephant I., Antarctica ... 7 C18 61 0 S 55 0W
Elephant Pass, Sri Lanka ... 95 K5 9 35N 80 25 E
Elesbão Veloso, Brazil ... 170 C3 6 13 S 42 8W
Eleshnitsa, Bulgaria ... 50 E7 41 52N 23 36 E
Eleşkirt, Turkey ... 101 C10 39 50N 42 50 E
Eleuthera, Bahamas ... 164 B4 25 0N 76 20W
Elevsís, Greece ... 48 C5 38 4N 23 26 E
Elevtheroúpolis, Greece ... 51 F8 40 52N 24 20 E
Elfin Cove, U.S.A. ... 144 G13 58 12N 136 22W
Elfros, Canada ... 143 C7 51 12N 104 0W
Elgå, Norway ... 18 B8 62 10N 11 56 E
Elgepiggen, Norway ... 18 B8 62 10N 11 21 E
Elgg, Switz. ... 33 B7 47 29N 8 52 E
Elgin, Canada ... 151 B8 44 36N 76 13W
Elgin, U.K. ... 22 D5 57 39N 3 19W
Elgin, Ill., U.S.A. ... 157 B8 42 2N 88 17W
Elgin, N. Dak., U.S.A. ... 154 B4 46 24N 101 51W
Elgin, Oreg., U.S.A. ... 160 D5 45 34N 117 55W
Elgin, S.C., U.S.A. ... 152 A9 34 10N 80 48W
Elgin, Tex., U.S.A. ... 155 K6 30 21N 97 22W
Elgoibar, Spain ... 40 B2 43 13N 2 24W
Elgon, Mt., U.S.A. ... 118 B3 1 10N 34 30 E
Eliase, Indonesia ... 83 C4 8 21 S 130 48 E
Elikón, Greece ... 48 C4 38 18N 22 45 E
Elim, Namibia ... 116 B2 17 48 S 15 31 E
Elim, S. Africa ... 116 E2 34 35 S 19 45 E
Elim, U.S.A. ... 144 D7 64 37N 162 15W
Elin Pelin, Bulgaria ... 50 D7 42 40N 23 36 E
Elingampangu, Dem. Rep. of the Congo ... 114 C4 2 0 S 24 4 E
Elipa, Dem. Rep. of the Congo ... 114 C4 1 3 S 24 20 E
Eliseu Martins, Brazil ... 170 C3 8 13 S 43 42W
Elista, Russia ... 61 G7 46 16N 44 14 E
Eliza, L., Australia ... 128 D3 37 15 S 139 50 E
Elizabeth, Australia ... 128 C3 34 42 S 138 41 E
Elizabeth, Ill., U.S.A. ... 156 B6 42 19N 90 13W
Elizabeth, N.J., U.S.A. ... 151 F10 40 40N 74 13W
Elizabeth, B., Ecuador ... 172 a 0 36 S 91 12W
Elizabeth City, U.S.A. ... 149 G7 36 18N 76 14W
Elizabethton, U.S.A. ... 149 G4 36 21N 82 13W
Elizabethtown, Ky., U.S.A. ... 157 G11 37 42N 85 52W
Elizabethtown, N.Y., U.S.A. ... 151 B11 44 13N 73 36W
Elizabethtown, Pa., U.S.A. ... 151 F8 40 9N 76 36W
Elizabethville = Lubumbashi, Dem. Rep. of the Congo ... 119 E2 11 40 S 27 28 E
Elizondo, Spain ... 40 B3 43 12N 1 30W
Elk, Poland ... 54 E9 53 50N 22 21 E
Elk →, Canada ... 142 C5 49 11N 115 14W
Elk →, Poland ... 54 E9 53 41N 22 28 E
Elk →, U.S.A. ... 149 H2 34 46N 87 16W
Elk City, U.S.A. ... 155 H5 35 25N 99 25W
Elk Creek, U.S.A. ... 160 F4 39 36N 122 32W
Elk Grove, U.S.A. ... 160 G5 38 25N 121 22W
Elk Island Nat. Park △, Canada ... 142 C6 53 35N 112 59W
Elk Lake, Canada ... 148 A3 47 40N 80 25W
Elk Point, Canada ... 143 C6 53 54N 110 55W
Elk River, Idaho, U.S.A. ... 160 C5 46 47N 116 11W
Elk River, Minn., U.S.A. ... 154 C8 45 18N 93 35W
Elkader, U.S.A. ... 156 B5 42 51N 91 24W
Elkedra →, Australia ... 126 C2 21 8 S 136 22 E
Elkhart, Ind., U.S.A. ... 157 C11 41 41N 85 58W
Elkhart, Kans., U.S.A. ... 155 G4 37 0N 101 54W
Elkhart →, U.S.A. ... 157 F11 38 22N 85 11W
Elkhorn, Canada ... 143 D8 49 59N 101 14W
Elkhorn, U.S.A. ... 157 B8 42 40N 88 33W
Elkhorn →, U.S.A. ... 154 E6 41 8N 96 19W
Elkhovo, Bulgaria ... 51 D10 42 10N 26 35 E
Elkin, U.S.A. ... 149 G5 36 15N 80 51W
Elkins, U.S.A. ... 148 F6 38 55N 79 51W
Elkland, U.S.A. ... 150 E7 41 59N 77 19W
Elko, Canada ... 142 D5 49 20N 115 10W
Elko, U.S.A. ... 158 F6 40 50N 115 46W
Elkton, U.S.A. ... 150 C1 43 49N 83 11W
Ell, L., Australia ... 125 E4 29 13 S 127 46 E
Ellaville, Fla., U.S.A. ... 152 E6 30 23N 83 10W
Ellaville, Ga., U.S.A. ... 152 E3 32 14N 84 19W
Ellef Ringnes I., Canada ... 6 B2 78 30N 102 2W
Ellen, Mt., U.S.A. ... 151 B12 44 9N 72 56W
Ellenburg, U.S.A. ... 151 B11 44 54N 73 48W
Ellendale, U.S.A. ... 154 B5 46 0N 98 32W
Ellensburg, U.S.A. ... 158 C3 46 59N 120 34W
Ellenville, U.S.A. ... 151 E10 41 43N 74 24W
Ellerton, Barbados ... 165 g 13 7N 59 33W
Ellery, Mt., Australia ... 129 D8 37 28 S 148 47 E
Ellesmere, N.Z. ... 131 H7 43 47 S 172 28 E
Ellesmere I., Canada ... 6 B4 79 30N 80 0W
Ellesmere Port, U.K. ... 20 D5 53 17N 2 54W
Ellettsville, U.S.A. ... 157 E10 39 14N 86 38W
Ellice Is. = Tuvalu ■, Pac. Oc. ... 134 H9 8 0 S 178 0 E
Ellicottville, U.S.A. ... 150 D6 42 17N 78 40W
Ellinikón, Athens ✈ (ATH), Greece ... 48 D5 37 52N 23 45 E
Elliot, Australia ... 126 B1 17 33 S 133 32 E
Elliot, S. Africa ... 117 E4 31 22 S 27 48 E
Elliot Lake, Canada ... 140 C3 46 25N 82 35W
Elliotdale = Xhora, S. Africa ... 117 E4 31 55 S 28 38 E
Elliott, Australia ... 152 A9 34 6N 80 10W
Elliott Key, U.S.A. ... 155 K9 25 27N 80 12W
Ellis, U.S.A. ... 154 F5 38 56N 99 34W
Elliston, Australia ... 127 E1 33 39 S 134 53 E
Ellisville, U.S.A. ... 155 K10 31 36N 89 12W
Ellon, U.K. ... 22 D6 57 22N 2 4W
Ellora, India ... 94 D2 20 1N 75 10 E
Ellore = Eluru, India ... 94 F5 16 48N 81 8 E
Elloree, U.S.A. ... 152 B9 33 30N 80 34W
Ellsworth, Kans., U.S.A. ... 154 F5 38 44N 98 14W
Ellsworth, Maine, U.S.A. ... 149 C11 44 33N 68 25W
Ellsworth Land, Antarctica ... 7 D16 76 0 S 89 0W
Ellsworth Mts., Antarctica ... 7 D16 78 30 S 85 0W
Ellwangen, Germany ... 31 G6 48 57N 10 8 E
Ellwood City, U.S.A. ... 150 F4 40 52N 80 17W
Ellzey, U.S.A. ... 153 F7 29 19N 82 48W
Elm, Switz. ... 33 C8 46 54N 9 10 E
Elm-Lappwald, Naturpark △, Germany ... 30 C6 52 15N 10 50 E
Elma, Canada ... 143 D9 49 52N 95 55W
Elma, U.S.A. ... 160 C2 47 0N 123 25W
Elmadağ, Turkey ... 100 C5 39 55N 33 14 E
Elmalı, Turkey ... 49 E11 36 44N 29 56 E

Elmhurst, U.S.A. ... 157 C9 41 53N 87 56W
Elmina, Ghana ... 113 D4 5 5N 1 21W
Elmira, Canada ... 150 C4 43 36N 80 33W
Elmira, U.S.A. ... 150 D8 42 6N 76 48W
Elmira Heights, U.S.A. ... 150 D8 42 8N 76 50W
Elmodel, U.S.A. ... 152 D5 31 21N 84 29W
Elmore, Australia ... 128 D6 36 30 S 144 37 E
Elmore, Ala., U.S.A. ... 152 C3 32 32N 86 19W
Elmore, Calif., U.S.A. ... 161 M11 33 7N 115 49W
Elmore, Minn., U.S.A. ... 157 C13 41 29N 83 18W
Elmshorn, Germany ... 30 B5 53 43N 9 40 E
Elmvale, Canada ... 150 B5 44 35N 79 52W
Elmwood, U.S.A. ... 156 D7 40 47N 89 58W
Elne, France ... 28 F6 42 36N 2 58 E
Elnesvågen, Norway ... 18 B4 62 52N 7 10 E
Elnora, U.S.A. ... 157 F9 38 53N 87 5W
Eloaua I., Papua N. G. ... 132 A5 1 38 S 149 40 E
Elobey, Is., Eq. Guin. ... 114 B1 1 1N 9 29 E
Elongo, Dem. Rep. of the Congo ... 114 C4 0 19 S 21 39 E
Elora, Canada ... 150 C4 43 41N 80 26W
Elorza, Venezuela ... 168 B4 7 3N 69 31W
Elos, Greece ... 48 E4 36 46N 22 43 E
Eloúnda, Greece ... 39 E6 35 16N 25 43 E
Eloy, U.S.A. ... 159 K8 32 45N 111 33W
Éloyes, France ... 27 D13 48 6N 6 36 E
Elrose, Canada ... 143 C7 51 12N 108 0W
Elsberry, U.S.A. ... 156 E6 39 10N 90 47W
Elsdorf, Germany ... 30 E2 50 55N 6 34 E
Elsie, Mich., U.S.A. ... 157 A12 43 5N 84 23W
Elsie, Oreg., U.S.A. ... 160 E3 45 52N 123 36W
Elsinore = Helsingør, Denmark ... 17 H6 56 2N 12 35 E
Elster →, Germany ... 30 D7 51 25N 11 57 E
Elsterwerda, Germany ... 30 D9 51 27N 13 31 E
Eltham, N.Z. ... 130 F3 39 26 S 174 19 E
Elton, Russia ... 61 F8 49 5N 46 52 E
Elton, Ozero, Russia ... 61 F8 49 5N 46 42 E
Eltville, Germany ... 31 E4 50 2N 8 7 E
Eluru, India ... 94 F5 16 48N 81 8 E
Elvas, Portugal ... 43 G3 38 50N 7 10W
Elven, France ... 26 E4 47 44N 2 36W
Elverum, Norway ... 18 D8 60 53N 11 34 E
Elvire →, Australia ... 124 C4 17 51 S 128 11 E
Elvire, Mt., Australia ... 125 E2 29 22 S 119 36 E
Elvo →, Italy ... 44 C5 45 23N 8 21 E
Elwell, L., U.S.A. ... 158 B8 48 22N 111 17W
Elwood, Ill., U.S.A. ... 157 C8 41 24N 88 7W
Elwood, Ind., U.S.A. ... 157 D11 40 17N 85 50W
Elwood, Nebr., U.S.A. ... 154 E5 40 36N 99 52W
Elx = Elche, Spain ... 41 G4 38 15N 0 42W
Ely, U.K. ... 21 E8 52 24N 0 16 E
Ely, Minn., U.S.A. ... 154 B9 47 55N 91 51W
Ely, Nev., U.S.A. ... 158 G6 39 15N 114 54W
Elyria, U.S.A. ... 150 E2 41 22N 82 7W
Elyrus, Greece ... 48 F5 35 15N 23 45 E
Elz →, Germany ... 31 G3 48 18N 7 44 E
Emådalen, Sweden ... 16 C8 61 20N 14 44 E
Émaé, Vanuatu ... 133 C6 17 4 S 168 24 E
Emāmrūd, Iran ... 97 B7 36 30N 55 0 E
Emån →, Sweden ... 17 G10 57 8N 16 30 E
Emao, Vanuatu ... 133 C6 17 29 S 168 30 E
Emateloa, Dem. Rep. of the Congo ... 114 B3 1 16N 18 42 E
Emba, Kazakhstan ... 66 E6 48 50N 58 8 E
Emba →, Kazakhstan ... 65 B7 46 55N 53 28 E
Embarcación, Argentina ... 174 A3 23 10 S 64 0W
Embarras Portage, Canada ... 143 B6 58 27N 111 28W
Embetsu, Japan ... 70 B10 44 44N 141 47 E
Embi = Emba, Kazakhstan ... 66 E6 48 50N 58 8 E
Embi = Emba →, Kazakhstan ... 57 E9 46 55N 53 28 E
Embira →, Brazil ... 172 B3 7 19 S 70 15W
Embóna, Greece ... 38 E11 36 13N 27 51 E
Embrach, Switz. ... 33 B7 47 30N 8 36 E
Embrun, France ... 29 D10 44 34N 6 30 E
Embu, Kenya ... 118 C4 0 32 S 37 38 E
Emden, Germany ... 30 B3 53 21N 7 12 E
Emecik, Turkey ... 49 E9 36 46N 27 49 E
Emerald, Queens., Australia ... 126 C4 23 32 S 148 10 E
Emerald, Vic., Australia ... 129 G18 37 56 S 145 29 E
Emerson, Canada ... 143 D9 49 0N 97 10W
Emerson, U.S.A. ... 152 A5 34 8N 84 45W
Emet, Turkey ... 49 B11 39 20N 29 15 E
Emeti, Papua N. G. ... 132 D2 7 53 S 143 15 E
Emi Koussi, Chad ... 109 E3 19 45N 18 55 E
Emília-Romagna □, Italy ... 44 D8 44 45N 11 0 E
Emilius, Mte., Italy ... 44 C4 45 45N 7 20 E
Eminabad, Pakistan ... 92 C6 32 2N 74 8 E
Emine, Nos, Bulgaria ... 51 D11 42 40N 27 56 E
Eminence, U.S.A. ... 157 F11 38 22N 85 11W
Emirau I., Papua N. G. ... 132 A6 1 40 S 150 0 E
Emirdağ, Turkey ... 100 C4 39 2N 31 8 E
Emissi, Tarso, Chad ... 109 D3 21 27N 18 36 E
Emlenton, U.S.A. ... 150 E5 41 11N 79 43W
Emlichheim, Germany ... 30 C2 52 37N 6 51 E
Emmaboda, Sweden ... 17 H9 56 37N 15 32 E
Emmalane, U.S.A. ... 152 C7 32 46N 82 0W
Emmaus, S. Africa ... 116 D4 29 2 S 25 15 E
Emmaus, U.S.A. ... 151 F9 40 32N 75 30W
Emme →, Switz. ... 32 B5 47 14N 7 32 E
Emmeloord, Neths. ... 24 B5 52 44N 5 46 E
Emmen, Neths. ... 24 B6 52 48N 6 57 E
Emmen, Switz. ... 31 H4 47 5N 8 18 E
Emmenbrücke, Switz. ... 33 B6 47 4N 8 16 E
Emmendingen, Germany ... 31 G3 48 6N 7 51 E
Emmental, Switz. ... 32 C4 46 55N 7 40 E
Emmerich, Germany ... 30 D2 51 50N 6 14 E
Emmet, Australia ... 126 C3 24 45 S 144 30 E
Emmetsburg, U.S.A. ... 156 A2 43 7N 94 41W
Emmett, Idaho, U.S.A. ... 158 E5 43 52N 116 30W
Emmett, Mich., U.S.A. ... 150 D2 42 59N 82 46W
Emmiganuru, India ... 95 E3 15 43N 77 28 E
Emmonak, U.S.A. ... 144 E6 62 46N 164 30W
Emo, Canada ... 143 D10 48 38N 93 50W
Emöd, Hungary ... 52 C5 47 57N 20 47 E
Emona, Bulgaria ... 51 D11 42 43N 27 53 E
Empalme, Mexico ... 162 B2 28 1N 110 49W
Empangeni, S. Africa ... 117 D5 28 50 S 31 52 E
Empedrado, Argentina ... 174 B4 28 0 S 58 46W
Emperor Seamount Chain, Pac. Oc. ... 136 C9 40 0N 170 0 E
Empoli, Italy ... 44 E7 43 43N 10 57 E
Emporia, Kans., U.S.A. ... 154 F6 38 25N 96 11W
Emporia, Va., U.S.A. ... 149 G7 36 42N 77 32W
Emporium, U.S.A. ... 150 E6 41 31N 78 14W
Empress, Canada ... 143 C7 50 57N 110 0W
Empty Quarter = Rub' al Khālī, Si. Arabia ... 99 C5 19 0N 48 0 E
Ems →, Germany ... 30 B3 53 20N 7 12 E
Emsdale, Canada ... 150 A5 45 32N 79 19W
Emsdetten, Germany ... 30 C3 52 10N 7 32 E
Emu, China ... 75 C15 43 40N 128 6 E
Emu Park, Australia ... 126 C5 23 13 S 150 50 E
'En 'Avrona, Israel ... 103 F4 29 43N 35 0 E
En Nahrat, Mali ... 107 E2 22 55N 3 36W
En Nahud, Sudan ... 107 E2 12 45N 28 25 E
En Nofalab, Sudan ... 107 D3 15 52N 32 32 E
Ena, Japan ... 73 B9 35 25N 137 25 E
Ena-San, Japan ... 73 B9 35 26N 137 36 E
Enambú, Colombia ... 168 C3 1 1N 70 17W
Enana, Namibia ... 116 B2 17 30 S 16 23 E
Enånger, Sweden ... 16 C11 61 30N 17 9 E
Enard B., U.K. ... 22 C3 58 5N 5 20W
Enare = Inarijärvi, Finland ... 14 B22 69 0N 28 0 E
Enarotali, Indonesia ... 83 B5 3 55 S 136 21 E

Enbekshi, Kazakhstan ... 65 C4 41 22N 68 3 E
Encampment, U.S.A. ... 158 F10 41 12N 106 47W
Encantadas, Serra, Brazil ... 175 C5 30 40 S 53 0W
Encarnación, Paraguay ... 175 B4 27 15 S 55 50W
Encarnación de Diaz, Mexico ... 162 C4 21 30N 102 13W
Enchi, Ghana ... 112 D4 5 53N 2 48W
Encinitas, U.S.A. ... 161 M9 33 3N 117 17W
Encino, U.S.A. ... 159 J11 34 39N 105 28W
Encontrados, Venezuela ... 168 B3 9 3N 72 14W
Encounter B., Australia ... 128 C3 35 45 S 138 45 E
Encruzilhada, Brazil ... 171 E3 15 31 S 40 54W
Encs, Hungary ... 52 B6 48 20N 21 8 E
Endako, Canada ... 142 C3 54 6N 125 2W
Endau →, Malaysia ... 85 B4 2 30N 103 30 E
Endeavour Str., Australia ... 126 A3 10 45 S 142 0 E
Endelave, Denmark ... 17 J4 55 46N 10 18 E
Enden, Norway ... 18 C7 61 47N 10 15 E
Enderbury I., Kiribati ... 134 H10 3 8 S 171 5W
Enderby, Canada ... 142 C5 50 35N 119 10W
Enderby I., Australia ... 124 D2 20 35 S 116 30 E
Enderby Land, Antarctica ... 7 C5 66 0 S 53 0 E
Enderlin, U.S.A. ... 154 B6 46 38N 97 36W
Endicott, U.S.A. ... 151 D8 42 6N 76 4W
Endicott Mts., U.S.A. ... 144 C10 68 0N 152 0W
Endimari →, Brazil ... 172 B4 8 46 S 66 7W
Endwell, U.S.A. ... 151 D8 42 6N 76 1W
Endyalgout I., Australia ... 124 B5 11 40 S 132 35 E
Ene →, Peru ... 172 C3 11 10 S 74 18W
Eneabba, Australia ... 125 E2 29 49 S 115 16 E
Energetichéskiy, Kazakhstan ... 64 F7 51 45N 58 45 E
Energetik, Russia ... 65 B8 42 35N 77 1 E
Enewetak Atoll, Marshall Is. ... 134 F8 11 30N 162 15 E
Enez, Turkey ... 51 F10 40 45N 26 5 E
Enfer, Pte. d', Martinique ... 164 c 14 22N 60 54W
Enfida, Tunisia ... 111 A7 36 22N 10 25 E
Enfield, Canada ... 141 D7 44 56N 63 32W
Enfield, Conn., U.S.A. ... 151 E12 41 58N 72 36W
Enfield, Ill., U.S.A. ... 157 F8 38 6N 88 20W
Enfield, N.H., U.S.A. ... 151 C12 43 39N 72 9W
Enga □, Papua N. G. ... 132 C2 5 30 S 143 30 E
Engadin, Switz. ... 31 J6 46 45N 10 10 E
Engan, Norway ... 18 A5 63 8N 8 31 E
Engaño, C., Dom. Rep. ... 165 C6 18 30N 68 20W
Engaño, C., Phil. ... 80 B4 18 35N 122 23 E
Engaru, Japan ... 70 B11 44 3N 143 31 E
Engcobo, S. Africa ... 117 E4 31 37 S 28 0 E
Engelberg, Switz. ... 33 C6 46 48N 8 25 E
Engels, Russia ... 61 D8 51 28N 46 6 E
Engemann L., Canada ... 143 B7 58 0N 106 55W
Engerdal, Norway ... 18 C8 61 45N 11 58 E
Engershatu, Eritrea ... 107 D4 16 7N 38 34 E
Enggano, Indonesia ... 84 D2 5 20 S 102 40 E
Engil, Morocco ... 110 B4 33 12N 4 32W
Engineer Group, Papua N. G. ... 132 F6 10 35 S 151 10 E
Engkilili, Malaysia ... 85 B4 1 3N 111 42 E
England, U.S.A. ... 155 H9 34 33N 91 58W
England □, U.K. ... 21 E5 52 0N 2 0W
Englee, Canada ... 141 B8 50 45N 56 5W
Englehart, Canada ... 140 C4 47 49N 79 52W
Englewood, Colo., U.S.A. ... 154 F2 39 39N 104 59W
Englewood, Fla., U.S.A. ... 153 J7 26 58N 82 21W
Englewood, Ohio, U.S.A. ... 157 E12 39 53N 84 18W
English, U.S.A. ... 157 F10 38 20N 86 28W
English →, U.S.A. ... 143 C10 50 35N 93 30W
English ~, U.S.A. ... 156 C5 41 29N 91 32W
English B., Ascension I. ... 9 g 7 54 S 14 23W
English Bazar = Ingraj Bazar, India ... 93 G13 24 58N 88 10 E
English Channel, Europe ... 21 G6 50 0N 2 0W
English River, Canada ... 140 C1 49 14N 91 0W
Engures ezers, Latvia ... 54 A10 57 16N 23 6 E
Enguri →, Georgia ... 61 J5 42 27N 41 38 E
Enid, U.S.A. ... 155 G6 36 24N 97 53W
Enipévs →, Greece ... 48 B4 39 22N 22 17 E
Enkhuizen, Neths. ... 24 B5 52 42N 5 17 E
Enköping, Sweden ... 16 E11 59 37N 17 4 E
Enle, China ... 76 F3 24 0N 101 9 E
Enna, Italy ... 47 E7 37 34N 14 16 E
Ennadai, Canada ... 143 A8 61 8N 100 53W
Ennadai L., Canada ... 143 A8 61 0N 101 0W
Enné →, Chad ... 109 F4 12 44N 18 45 E
Ennedi, Chad ... 109 E4 17 15N 22 0 E
Enneri Achelouma →, Niger ... 111 D7 21 55N 13 35 E
Enngonia, Australia ... 127 D4 29 21 S 145 50 E
Ennigerloh, Germany ... 30 D4 51 50N 8 2 E
Ennis, Ireland ... 23 D3 52 51N 8 59W
Ennis, Mont., U.S.A. ... 158 D8 45 21N 111 44W
Ennis, Tex., U.S.A. ... 155 J6 32 20N 96 38W
Enniscorthy, Ireland ... 23 D5 52 30N 6 34W
Enniskillen, U.K. ... 23 B4 54 21N 7 39W
Ennistimon, Ireland ... 23 D2 52 57N 9 17W
Enns, Austria ... 34 C7 48 12N 14 28 E
Enns →, Austria ... 34 C7 48 14N 14 32 E
Enontekiö, Finland ... 14 B20 68 23N 23 37 E
Enping, China ... 77 F9 22 16N 112 21 E
Enrekang, Indonesia ... 82 B1 3 34 S 119 47 E
Enrile, Phil. ... 80 C3 17 34N 121 48 E
Enriquillo, L., Dom. Rep. ... 165 C5 18 20N 72 5W
Enschede, Neths. ... 24 B6 52 13N 6 53 E
Ensenada, Argentina ... 174 C4 34 55 S 57 55W
Ensenada, Mexico ... 162 A1 31 50N 116 50W
Ensenada de los Muertos, Mexico ... 162 C2 23 59N 109 50W
Enshi, China ... 76 B7 30 18N 109 29 E
Enshū-Nada, Japan ... 73 C9 34 27N 137 38 E
Ensiola, Pta. de n', Spain ... 38 B3 39 7N 2 55 E
Ensisheim, France ... 27 E14 47 52N 7 20 E
Ensley, U.S.A. ... 153 E2 30 32N 87 16W
Entebbe, Uganda ... 118 B3 0 4N 32 28 E
Enterprise, Canada ... 142 A5 60 47N 115 45W
Enterprise, Ala., U.S.A. ... 152 D4 31 19N 85 51W
Enterprise, Oreg., U.S.A. ... 158 D5 45 25N 117 17W
Entlebuch, Switz. ... 32 C6 46 59N 8 4 E
Entorno de Doñana, Parque Natural de △, Spain ... 43 J4 37 0N 6 26W
Entraygues-sur-Truyère, France ... 28 D6 44 38N 2 35 E
Entre Ríos, Bolivia ... 174 A3 21 30 S 64 25W
Entre Rios, Bahia, Brazil ... 171 D4 11 56 S 38 5W
Entre Ríos, Pará, Brazil ... 173 B7 5 24 S 54 21W
Entre Ríos □, Argentina ... 174 C4 30 30 S 58 30W
Entrepeñas, Embalse de, Spain ... 40 E2 40 34N 2 42W
Entroncamento, Portugal ... 43 F2 39 28N 8 28W
Enugu, Nigeria ... 113 D6 6 30N 7 30 E
Enugu □, Nigeria ... 113 D6 6 30N 7 45 E
Enugu Ezike, Nigeria ... 113 D6 7 0N 7 29 E
Enumclaw, U.S.A. ... 160 C5 47 12N 121 59W
Envalira, Port d', Europe ... 40 C6 42 33N 1 43 E
Envermeu, France ... 26 C8 49 53N 1 15 E
Envigado, Colombia ... 168 B2 6 10N 75 35W
Enviken, Sweden ... 16 D9 60 49N 15 46 E
Envira, Brazil ... 172 B3 7 18 S 70 13W
Enying, Hungary ... 42 D3 46 54N 18 15 E
Enyonga, Gabon ... 114 C1 0 59 S 9 22 E
Enza →, Italy ... 44 D7 44 54N 10 31 E
Enzan, Japan ... 73 B10 35 42N 138 44 E
Éolie, Is., Italy ... 47 D7 38 30N 14 57 E
Epalinges, Switz. ... 32 C3 46 33N 6 40 E
Epanomí, Greece ... 40 F6 40 25N 22 59 E
Epe, Neths. ... 24 B5 52 21N 5 59 E
Epe, Nigeria ... 113 D5 6 36N 3 59 E
Épernay, France ... 27 C10 49 3N 3 56 E
Épernon, France ... 27 D8 48 35N 1 40 E
Ephesus, Turkey ... 49 D9 37 55N 27 22 E
Ephraim, U.S.A. ... 158 G8 39 22N 111 35W
Ephrata, Pa., U.S.A. ... 151 F8 40 11N 76 11W

Ephrata, *Wash., U.S.A.* **158 C4** 47 19N 119 33W
Epi, *Vanuatu* .... **133 F6** 16 43 S 168 15 E
Epidaurus Limera, *Greece* ...... **48 E5** 36 46N 23 0 E
Épila, *Spain* **40 D3** 41 36N 1 17W
Épinac, *France* .... **27 F11** 46 59N 4 31 E
Épinal, *France* .... **27 D13** 48 10N 6 27 E
Epira, *Guyana* .... **169 B6** 5 N 57 20W
Episkopí, *Cyprus* .... **39 F8** 34 40N 32 54 E
Episkopí, *Greece* .... **39 E5** 35 20N 24 20 E
Episkopi Bay, *Cyprus* .... **39 F8** 34 35N 32 50 E
Epitálion, *Greece* .... **48 D3** 37 37N 21 30 E
Eppalock, L., *Australia* .... **128 D6** 36 52 S 144 34 E
Eppan = Appiano, *Italy* .... **48 B8** 46 28N 11 15 E
Eppingen, *Germany* .... **31 F4** 49 8N 8 53 E
Epsom, *U.K.* **21 F7** 51 19N 0 16W
Epukiro, *Namibia* .... **116 C2** 21 40 S 19 9 E
Equality, *U.S.A.* **157 G8** 37 44N 88 20W
Équateur □, *Dem. Rep. of the Congo* **114 B4** 2 0N 21 0 E
Equatorial Guinea ■, *Africa* ... **114 B1** 2 0N 8 0 E
Equeipa, *Venezuela* **169 B5** 5 22N 62 43W
Er Hai, *China* .... **76 E3** 25 48N 100 11 E
Er Rachidia, *Morocco* **110 B4** 31 58N 4 20W
Er Rahad, *Sudan* .... **107 E3** 12 45N 30 32 E
Er Rif, *Morocco* **111 A4** 35 1N 4 1W
Er Rogel, *Sudan* .... **106 D4** 18 10N 35 25 E
Er Roseires, *Sudan* .... **107 E3** 11 55N 34 30 E
Er Rua'at, *Sudan* .... **107 E3** 12 21N 32 17 E
Eracléa, *Italy* .... **45 C9** 45 35N 12 40 E
Eran, *Phil.* .... **81 G1** 9 4N 117 42 E
Erandol, *India* .... **94 D2** 20 56N 75 20 E
Eranga, *Dem. Rep. of the Congo* **114 C3** 1 52 S 18 56 E
Erap, *Papua N. G.* .... **132 D4** 6 37 S 146 51 E
Erave, *Papua N. G.* .... **132 D2** 6 39 S 144 0 E
Erave →, *Papua N. G.* .... **132 D3** 6 54 S 144 47 E
Erāwadī Myit = Irrawaddy →,
Burma .... **90 G5** 15 50N 95 6 E
Erāwadī Myitwanya = Irrawaddy,
Mouths of the, *Burma* .... **90 H5** 15 30N 95 0 E
Erba, *Italy* .... **44 C6** 45 48N 9 15 E
Erba, *Sudan* .... **106 D4** 19 5N 36 51 E
Erba, J., *Sudan* .... **106 C4** 20 48N 36 47 E
Erbaa, *Turkey* .... **100 B7** 40 42N 36 36 E
Erbeskopf, *Germany* .... **31 F3** 49 44N 7 2 E
Erbil = Arbīl, *Iraq* .... **101 D11** 36 15N 44 5 E
Erbu, *Ethiopia* .... **107 E3** 6 44N 34 53 E
Ercan, Nicosia ✕ (ECN), *Cyprus* **39 E9** 35 10N 33 30 E
Erçek, *Turkey* .... **96 B4** 38 39N 43 36 E
Erçiş, *Turkey* .... **101 C10** 39 2N 43 21 E
Erciyaş Dağı, *Turkey* .... **57 G6** 38 30N 35 30 E
Érd, *Hungary* .... **52 C3** 47 22N 18 56 E
Erdao Jiang →, *China* .... **75 C14** 43 0N 127 0 E
Erdek, *Turkey* .... **51 F11** 40 23N 27 47 E
Erdemli, *Turkey* .... **100 D6** 36 36N 34 19 E
Erdene = Ulaan-Uul, *Mongolia* ... **74 B6** 44 13N 111 10 E
Erdenet, *Mongolia* .... **68 B5** 49 2N 104 5 E
Erdenetsogt, *Mongolia* .... **74 C4** 42 55N 106 5 E
Erding, *Germany* .... **31 G7** 48 18N 11 54 E
Erdre →, *France* **26 E5** 47 13N 1 32W
Erebato →, *Venezuela* **169 B5** 5 54N 64 16W
Erebus, Mt., *Antarctica* .... **7 D11** 77 35 S 167 0 E
Erechim, *Brazil* .... **175 B5** 27 35 S 52 15W
Ereğli, *Konya, Turkey* .... **100 D6** 37 31N 34 4 E
Ereğli, *Zonguldak, Turkey* .... **100 B4** 41 15N 31 24 E
Erei, Monti, *Italy* .... **47 E7** 37 20N 14 20 E
Erenhot, *China* .... **74 C7** 43 48N 112 2 E
Erenköy = Kokkina, *Cyprus* .... **39 E8** 35 11N 32 36 E
Eresma →, *Spain* **42 D6** 41 26N 4 45W
Eressós, *Greece* .... **49 B7** 39 11N 25 57 E
Erfenisdam, *S. Africa* .... **116 D4** 28 30 S 26 50 E
Erfjord, *Norway* .... **18 E3** 59 20N 6 14 E
Erfoud, *Morocco* **110 B4** 31 30N 4 15W
Erfstadt, *Germany* .... **30 E2** 50 50N 6 50 E
Erft →, *Germany* .... **30 D2** 51 11N 6 44 E
Erfurt, *Germany* .... **30 E7** 50 58N 11 2 E
Ergani, *Turkey* .... **101 C8** 38 17N 39 49 E
Ergel, *Mongolia* .... **74 C5** 43 8N 109 5 E
Ergene →, *Turkey* .... **51 E10** 41 1N 26 22 E
Ergeni Vozvyshennost, *Russia* ... **61 G7** 47 0N 44 0 E
Érgli, *Latvia* .... **15 H21** 56 54N 25 38 E
Erhlin, *Taiwan* .... **77 F13** 23 54N 120 22 E
Eria →, *Spain* **42 C5** 42 3N 5 44W
Eriba, *Sudan* .... **107 D4** 16 40N 36 10 E
Eriboll, L., *U.K.* **22 C4** 58 30N 4 42W
Érice, *Italy* .... **46 D5** 38 2N 12 35 E
Eridu, *Iraq* **152 E6** 30 18N 83 45W
Erie, *Mich., U.S.A.* **157 C13** 41 47N 83 31W
Erie, *Pa., U.S.A.* **150 D4** 42 8N 80 5W
Erie, L., *N. Amer.* **150 D4** 42 15N 81 0W
Erie Canal, *U.S.A.* **150 C7** 43 5N 78 43W
Erieau, *Canada* **150 D3** 42 16N 81 57W
Erigavo, *Somali Rep.* .... **120 B3** 10 35N 47 20 E
Erikoúsa, *Greece* .... **38 B9** 39 53N 19 34 E
Eriksdale, *Canada* **143 C9** 50 52N 98 7W
Erímanthos, *Greece* .... **48 D3** 37 57N 21 50 E
Erimo-misaki, *Japan* .... **70 D11** 41 50N 143 15 E
Erin Pt., *Trin. & Tob.* **169 F9** 10 13N 61 40W
Erinpura, *India* .... **92 G5** 25 9N 73 3 E
Eriskay, *U.K.* **22 D1** 57 4N 7 18W
Eriswil, *Switz.* .... **32 B5** 47 5N 7 46 E
Erithraí, *Greece* .... **48 C5** 38 13N 23 20 E
Eritrea ■, *Africa* .... **107 E4** 14 0N 38 30 E
Erjas →, *Portugal* **42 F3** 39 40N 7 1W
Erkech-Tam, *Kyrgyzstan* .... **65 D6** 39 41N 73 55 E
Erkelenz, *Germany* .... **30 D2** 51 4N 6 19 E
Erkner, *Germany* .... **30 C9** 52 25N 13 44 E
Erlangen, *Germany* .... **31 F6** 49 36N 11 0 E
Erlanger, *U.S.A.* **157 E12** 39 1N 84 36W
Erldunda, *Australia* .... **126 D1** 25 14 S 133 12 E
Ermelo, *Neths.* .... **24 B5** 52 18N 5 35 E
Ermelo, *S. Africa* .... **117 D4** 26 31 S 29 59 E
Ermenek, *Turkey* .... **100 D5** 36 38N 33 0 E
Ermil, *Sudan* .... **107 E2** 13 35N 27 40 E
Ermióni, *Greece* .... **48 D5** 37 23N 23 15 E
Ermones, *Greece* .... **38 B9** 39 37N 19 46 E
Ermoúpolis = Síros, *Greece* ... **48 D6** 37 28N 24 57 E
Erne →, *Ireland* **23 B3** 54 30N 8 16W
Erne, Lower L., *U.K.* **23 B4** 54 28N 7 47W
Erne, Upper L., *U.K.* **23 B4** 54 14N 7 32W
Ernée, *France* **26 D6** 48 18N 0 56W
Ernest Giles Ra., *Australia* ... **125 E3** 27 0 S 123 45 E
Ernstberg, *Germany* .... **31 E2** 50 13N 6 47 E
Erode, *India* .... **95 J3** 11 24N 77 45 E
Eromanga, *Australia* .... **127 D3** 26 40 S 143 11 E
Erongo, *Namibia* .... **116 C2** 21 39 S 15 58 E
Erquy, *France* **26 D4** 48 38N 2 29W
Err, Piz d', *Switz.* .... **33 C9** 46 34N 9 43 E
Erramala Hills, *India* .... **95 G4** 15 30N 78 15 E
Errer →, *Ethiopia* .... **107 F5** 7 32N 42 35 E
Errigal, *Ireland* **23 A3** 55 2N 8 6W
Errinundra Nat. Park △, *Australia* **129 D8** 37 20 S 148 47 E
Erris Hd., *Ireland* **23 B1** 54 19N 10 0W
Erromango, *Vanuatu* .... **133 H7** 18 45 S 169 5 E
Ersekë, *Albania* .... **50 F4** 40 22N 20 40 E
Erskine, *U.S.A.* **154 B7** 47 40N 96 0W
Erstein, *France* .... **27 D14** 48 25N 7 38 E
Ertfeld, *Switz.* .... **33 C7** 46 50N 8 38 E
Erthólmene, *Denmark* .... **17 J9** 55 19N 15 11 E
Ertil, *Russia* .... **60 C5** 51 55N 40 50 E
Ertis = Irtysh →, *Russia* .... **66 C7** 61 4N 68 52 E
Ertvågøy, *Norway* .... **18 A3** 63 0N 12 0 E
Eruh, *Turkey* .... **101 D10** 37 46N 42 13 E
Eruwa, *Nigeria* .... **113 D5** 7 33N 3 26 E
Ervy-le-Châtel, *France* .... **27 D10** 48 2N 3 55 E

Erwin, *U.S.A.* **149 G4** 36 9N 82 25W
Eryuan, *China* .... **76 D2** 26 7N 99 57 E
Erzgebirge, *Germany* .... **30 E8** 50 27N 12 55 E
Erzin, *Russia* .... **67 D10** 50 15N 95 10 E
Erzincan, *Turkey* .... **101 C8** 39 46N 39 30 E
Erzurum, *Turkey* .... **101 C9** 39 57N 41 15 E
Es Caló, *Spain* .... **38 D2** 38 40N 1 30 E
Es Canar, *Spain* .... **38 C2** 39 2N 1 36 E
Es Mercadal, *Spain* .... **38 B5** 39 59N 4 5 E
Es Migjorn Gran, *Spain* .... **38 B5** 39 57N 4 3 E
Es Safiya, *Sudan* .... **107 D3** 15 31N 30 7 E
Es Sahrā' Esh sharqīya, *Egypt* ... **106 B3** 27 30N 32 30 E
Es Sînâ', *Egypt* .... **103 F3** 29 0N 34 0 E
Es Sûkî, *Sudan* .... **107 E3** 13 20N 33 58 E
Es Vedrà, *Spain* .... **38 D1** 38 52N 1 12 E
Esa'ala, *Papua N. G.* .... **132 E6** 9 45 S 150 49 E
Esambo, *Dem. Rep. of the Congo* **118 C1** 3 48 S 23 30 E
Esan-Misaki, *Japan* .... **70 D10** 41 40N 141 10 E
Esashi, *Hokkaidō, Japan* ..... **70 B11** 44 56N 142 35 E
Esashi, *Hokkaidō, Japan* ..... **70 D10** 41 52N 140 7 E
Esbjerg, *Denmark* .... **17 J2** 55 29N 8 29 E
Escada, *Brazil* .... **170 C4** 8 22 S 35 8W
Escalante, *U.S.A.* **159 H8** 37 47N 111 36W
Escalante →, *U.S.A.* **159 H8** 37 24N 110 57W
Escalante, *Phil.* .... **81 F4** 10 50N 123 33 E
Escalón, *Mexico* **162 B4** 26 46N 104 20W
Escambia →, *U.S.A.* **152 K2** 30 32N 87 11W
Escanaba, *U.S.A.* **148 C2** 45 45N 87 4W
Escarpada Pt., *Phil.* .... **80 B4** 18 31N 122 3 E
Escarpé, C., *Vanuatu* .... **133 K5** 20 41 S 167 13 E
Esch-sur-Alzette, *Lux.* .... **24 E6** 49 32N 6 0 E
Eschede, *Germany* .... **30 C6** 52 44N 10 14 E
Escholzmatt, *Switz.* .... **32 C5** 46 55N 7 56 E
Eschwege, *Germany* .... **30 D6** 51 11N 10 2 E
Eschweiler, *Germany* .... **30 E2** 50 49N 6 15 E
Escoma, *Bolivia* .... **172 D4** 15 40 S 69 8W
Escondido, *U.S.A.* **161 M9** 33 7N 117 5W
Escravos →, *Nigeria* .... **113 D6** 5 35N 5 10 E
Escuinapa, *Mexico* **162 C3** 22 50N 105 50W
Escuintla, *Guatemala* **164 D1** 14 20N 90 48W
Ésero →, *Cameroon* .... **113 E7** 3 41N 10 44 E
Eşen →, *Turkey* .... **49 E11** 36 27N 29 16 E
Esenguly, *Turkmenistan* .... **66 F6** 37 37N 53 59 E
Esens, *Germany* .... **30 B3** 53 38N 7 36 E
Esenyurt, *Turkey* .... **51 E12** 41 3N 28 48 E
Esera →, *Spain* .... **40 C5** 42 6N 0 15 E
Eşfahān, *Iran* .... **97 C6** 32 39N 51 43 E
Eşfahān □, *Iran* .... **97 C6** 32 50N 51 50 E
Esfarāyen, *Iran* .... **97 B8** 37 4N 57 30 E
Esfideh, *Iran* .... **97 C8** 33 39N 59 46 E
Esgueva →, *Spain* **42 D6** 41 40N 4 43W
Esh Sham = Dimashq, *Syria* ... **103 B5** 33 30N 36 18 E
Esh Shamālīya □, *Sudan* ..... **106 D2** 19 0N 29 0 E
Esha Ness, *U.K.* **22 A7** 60 29N 1 38W
Eshan, *China* .... **76 E4** 24 11N 102 24 E
Esher, *U.K.* **21 F7** 51 21N 0 20W
Eshkāshem = Ishkashim, *Tajikistan* **65 E5** 36 44N 71 37 E
Eshkol Nat. Park △, *Israel* ... **103 D3** 31 20N 34 30 E
Eshowe, *S. Africa* .... **117 D5** 28 50 S 31 30 E
Esiama, *Ghana* **112 E4** 4 56N 2 25W
Esigodini, *Zimbabwe* .... **117 C4** 20 18 S 28 56 E
Esik, *Kazakhstan* .... **65 B8** 43 21N 77 27 E
Esil = Ishim →, *Russia* .... **66 D8** 57 45N 71 10 E
Esino →, *Italy* .... **45 E10** 43 39N 13 22 E
Esira, *Madag.* .... **117 C8** 24 20 S 46 42 E
Esk →, *Cumb., U.K.* **22 G5** 54 58N 3 2W
Esk →, *N. Yorks., U.K.* **20 C7** 54 30N 0 37W
Eskān, *Iran* .... **91 D1** 26 48N 63 9 E
Esker, *Canada* **141 B6** 53 53N 66 25W
Eski-Nookat, *Kyrgyzstan* ..... **65 C6** 40 16N 72 36 E
Eskifjörður, *Iceland* **11 B13** 65 3N 13 55W
Eskilsäter, *Sweden* .... **17 F7** 58 57N 13 10 E
Eskilstuna, *Sweden* .... **16 E10** 59 22N 16 32 E
Eskimo Pt. = Arviat, *Canada* ... **138 B10** 61 10N 94 15W
Eskişehir, *Turkey* .... **49 B12** 39 50N 30 30 E
Eskişehir □, *Turkey* .... **49 B12** 39 40N 31 0 E
Esla →, *Spain* **42 D4** 41 29N 6 3W
Eslāmābād-e Gharb, *Iran* ..... **101 E12** 34 10N 46 30 E
Eslāmshahr, *Iran* .... **97 C6** 35 40N 51 10 E
Eslöv, *Sweden* .... **17 J7** 55 50N 13 20 E
Eşme, *Turkey* .... **49 C10** 38 23N 28 58 E
Esmeralda, I., *Chile* .... **176 C1** 48 55 S 75 25W
Esmeraldas, *Ecuador* **168 C2** 1 0N 79 40W
Esmeraldas □, *Ecuador* **168 C2** 0 40N 79 30W
Esmeraldas →, *Ecuador* **168 C2** 0 58N 79 38W
Esnagi L., *Canada* **140 C3** 48 36N 84 33W
Esom Hill, *U.S.A.* **152 B3** 33 57N 85 23W
Espa, *Norway* .... **18 D8** 60 34N 11 16 E
Espada, Pta., *Colombia* **168 A3** 12 5N 71 7W
Espalion, *France* .... **28 D6** 44 32N 2 47 E
Espanola, *Canada* **140 C3** 46 15N 81 46W
Espanola, *U.S.A.* **159 H10** 35 59N 106 5W
Española, I., *Ecuador* .... **172 a** 1 23 S 89 39W
Esparreguera, *Spain* .... **40 D6** 41 33N 1 52 E
Esparta, *Costa Rica* **164 E3** 9 59N 84 40W
Espeland, *Norway* .... **18 D2** 60 23N 5 28 E
Espelkamp, *Germany* .... **30 C4** 52 24N 8 36 E
Espenberg, C., *U.S.A.* **144 C7** 66 33N 163 36W
Esperança, *Amazonas, Brazil* ... **168 D4** 4 24 S 69 52W
Esperança, *Paraíba, Brazil* ... **170 C4** 7 1 S 35 51W
Esperance, *Australia* .... **125 F3** 33 45 S 121 55 E
Esperance →, *Solomon Is.* ..... **133 M10** 9 15 S 159 43 E
Esperance B., *Australia* .... **125 F3** 33 48 S 121 55 E
Esperance B., *St. Lucia* .... **165 f** 14 4N 60 55W
Esperantinópolis, *Brazil* ..... **170 B3** 4 53 S 44 53W
Esperanza, *Santa Cruz, Argentina* **176 D2** 51 1 S 70 49W
Esperanza, *Santa Fe, Argentina* **174 C3** 31 29 S 61 3W
Esperanza, *Agusan del S., Phil.* **81 G5** 8 43N 125 36 E
Esperanza, *Masbate, Phil.* ..... **81 F5** 11 45N 124 3 E
Esperanza, *Puerto Rico* .... **165 d** 18 6N 65 28W
Espéraza, *France* .... **29 F6** 42 56N 2 14 E
Espevær, *Norway* .... **18 E2** 59 35N 5 7 E
Espichel, C., *Portugal* **43 G1** 38 22N 9 16W
Espiel, *Spain* **43 G5** 38 11N 5 1W
Espigão, Serra do, *Brazil* ..... **175 B5** 26 35 S 50 30W
Espinal, *Colombia* **168 C3** 4 9N 74 53W
Espinar, *Peru* .... **172 C3** 14 51 S 71 24W
Espinazo, Sierra del = Espinhaço,
Serra do, *Brazil* .... **171 E3** 17 30 S 43 30W
Espinhaço, Serra do, *Brazil* ... **171 E3** 17 30 S 43 30W
Espinho, *Portugal* **42 D2** 41 1N 8 38W
Espinilho, Serra do, *Brazil* ... **175 B5** 28 30 S 55 0W
Espinosa de los Monteros, *Spain* **42 B7** 43 5N 3 34W
Espírito Santo □, *Brazil* ..... **171 F3** 20 0 S 40 45W
Espírito Santo, *Vanuatu* ..... **133 E4** 15 15 S 166 50 E
Espíritu Santo, B. del, *Mexico* ... **163 D7** 19 15N 87 0W
Espíritu Santo, I., *Mexico* **162 C2** 24 30N 110 23W
Espita, *Mexico* **163 C7** 21 1N 88 19W
Espiye, *Turkey* .... **101 B8** 40 56N 38 43 E
Esplanada, *Brazil* .... **171 D4** 11 47 S 37 57W
Espluga de Francolí, *Spain* ... **40 D6** 41 24N 1 7 E
Espoo, *Finland* .... **15 F21** 60 12N 24 40 E
Esprels, *France* .... **32 A2** 47 32N 6 22 E
Espuña, Sierra, *Spain* **41 H3** 37 51N 1 35W
Espungabera, *Mozam.* .... **117 C5** 20 29 S 32 45 E
Esquel, *Argentina* .... **176 B2** 42 55 S 71 20W
Esquimalt, *Canada* **142 D4** 48 26N 123 25W
Esquina, *Argentina* .... **174 C4** 30 0 S 59 30W
Essandsjøen, *Norway* .... **18 A8** 63 0N 12 0 E
Essaouira, *Morocco* **110 B3** 31 32N 9 42W
Essebie, *Dem. Rep. of the Congo* **118 B3** 2 58N 30 40 E
Essen, *Belgium* .... **24 C4** 51 28N 4 28 E

Essen, *Germany* .... **30 D3** 51 28N 7 2 E
Essendon, Mt., *Australia* ..... **125 E3** 25 0 S 120 29 E
Essequibo →, *Guyana* **169 B6** 6 50N 58 30W
Essex, *Canada* **150 D2** 42 10N 82 49W
Essex, *Calif., U.S.A.* **161 L11** 34 44N 115 15W
Essex, *N.Y., U.S.A.* **151 B11** 44 19N 73 21W
Essex □, *U.K.* .... **21 F8** 51 54N 0 27 E
Essex Junction, *U.S.A.* **151 B11** 44 29N 73 7W
Esslingen, *Germany* .... **31 G5** 48 44N 9 18 E
Essonne □, *France* .... **27 D9** 48 30N 2 20 E
Estaca de Bares, C. de, *Spain* ... **42 A3** 43 46N 7 42W
Estadilla, *Spain* .... **40 C5** 42 4N 0 16 E
Estados, I. de Los, *Argentina* ... **176 D4** 54 40 S 64 30W
Estagel, *France* .... **28 F6** 42 47N 2 40 E
Eşţahbānāt, *Iran* .... **97 D7** 29 8N 54 4 E
Estância, *Brazil* .... **170 D4** 11 16 S 37 26W
Estancia, *U.S.A.* **159 J10** 34 46N 106 4W
Estancia Cameron, *Chile* ..... **176 D3** 53 38 S 69 39W
Estārm, *Iran* .... **97 D8** 28 21N 58 21 E
Estarreja, *Portugal* **42 E2** 40 45N 8 35W
Estats, Pic d', *Spain* .... **40 C6** 42 40N 1 24 E
Estavayer-le-Lac, *Switz.* ..... **32 C3** 46 51N 6 51 E
Estcourt, *S. Africa* .... **117 D4** 29 0 S 29 53 E
Este, *Italy* .... **45 C8** 45 14N 11 39 E
Este, Parque Nac. del △, *Dom. Rep.* **165 C6** 18 14N 68 42W
Estelí, *Nic.* **164 D2** 13 9N 86 22W
Estella, *Spain* **40 C2** 42 40N 2 2W
Estellencs, *Spain* .... **38 B3** 39 39N 2 29 E
Estena →, *Spain* **43 F6** 39 23N 4 44W
Estepa, *Spain* **43 H6** 37 17N 4 52W
Estepona, *Spain* **43 J5** 36 24N 5 7W
Esterhazy, *Canada* **143 C8** 50 37N 102 5W
Esterías, C., *Gabon* .... **114 B1** 0 40N 9 20 E
Esternay, *France* .... **27 D10** 48 44N 3 33 E
Esterri d'Aneu, *Spain* .... **40 C6** 42 38N 1 5 E
Estevan, *Canada* **143 D8** 49 10N 102 59W
Estevan Group, *Canada* **142 C3** 53 3N 129 38W
Estherville, *U.S.A.* **154 D7** 43 24N 94 50W
Estill, *U.S.A.* **152 C8** 32 45N 81 15W
Estissac, *France* .... **27 D10** 48 16N 3 48 E
Eston, *Canada* **143 C7** 51 8N 108 40W
Estonia ■, *Europe* .... **15 G21** 58 30N 25 30 E
Estoril, *Portugal* **43 G1** 38 42N 9 23W
Estouk, *Mali* .... **113 B5** 18 14N 1 2 E
Estrada, Serra da, *Portugal* ... **42 E3** 40 10N 7 45W
Estrela, *Spain* **43 G7** 38 25N 3 35W
Estremoz, *Portugal* **43 G3** 38 51N 7 39W
Estrondo, Serra do, *Brazil* ... **170 C2** 7 20 S 48 0W
Esztergom, *Hungary* .... **52 C3** 47 47N 18 44 E
Et Tîdra, *Mauritania* **112 B1** 19 45N 16 20W
Etah, *India* .... **93 F8** 27 35N 78 40 E
Étain, *France* .... **27 C12** 49 13N 5 38 E
Étampes, *France* .... **27 D9** 48 26N 2 10 E
Etanga, *Namibia* .... **116 B1** 17 55 S 13 0 E
Étaples, *France* .... **27 B8** 50 30N 1 39 E
Etawah, *India* .... **93 F8** 26 48N 79 6 E
Etawney L., *Canada* **143 B9** 57 50N 96 50W
Ete, *Nigeria* .... **113 D6** 7 2N 7 28 E
Étel, *France* **26 E3** 47 39N 3 12W
Etelhem, *Sweden* .... **17 H13** 57 26N 18 29 E
Ethel, *U.S.A.* **160 D4** 46 32N 122 46W
Ethel, Oued el →, *Algeria* **110 C4** 28 31N 3 37W
Ethelbert, *Canada* **143 C8** 51 32N 100 25W
Ethiopia ■, *Africa* .... **102 F3** 8 0N 40 0 E
Ethiopian Highlands, *Ethiopia* ... **62 J7** 10 0N 37 0 E
Etili, *Turkey* .... **51 G10** 39 59N 26 54 E
Etive, L., *U.K.* **23 E3** 56 29N 5 10W
Etna, *Italy* .... **47 E7** 37 50N 14 55 E
Etna, *Norway* .... **18 E2** 60 49N 10 7 E
Etne, *Norway* .... **18 E2** 59 40N 5 58 E
Etoile, *Dem. Rep. of the Congo* ... **119 E2** 11 33 S 27 30 E
Etolin I., *U.S.A.* **144 F6** 56 6N 132 21W
Etosha Nat. Park △, *Namibia* ... **116 B2** 19 0 S 16 0 E
Etosha Pan, *Namibia* .... **116 B2** 18 40 S 16 30 E
Etoumbi, *Congo* .... **114 C2** 0 1 S 14 57 E
Etowah, *U.S.A.* **149 H3** 35 20N 84 32W
Étréchy, *France* .... **27 D9** 48 30N 2 12 E
Étrépagny, *France* .... **27 C8** 49 18N 1 36 E
Étretat, *France* .... **26 C7** 49 42N 0 12 E
Étropole, *Bulgaria* .... **51 D8** 42 50N 24 0 E
Ettelbruck, *Lux.* .... **24 E6** 49 51N 6 5 E
Ettlingen, *Germany* .... **31 G4** 48 58N 8 25 E
Ettrick Water →, *U.K.* **22 F6** 55 31N 2 55W
Etuku, *Dem. Rep. of the Congo* ... **118 C2** 3 42 S 25 45 E
Etulia, *Moldova* .... **53 E13** 45 32N 28 27 E
Etzatlán, *Mexico* **162 C4** 20 48N 104 5W
Etzná, *Mexico* **163 D6** 19 35N 90 15W
Etzná-Tixmucuy = Edzná, *Mexico* **163 D6** 19 35N 90 15W
Eu, *France* .... **26 B8** 50 3N 1 26 E
Eua, *Tonga* .... **123 Q13** 21 22 S 174 45 E
Eubenangee Swamp Nat. Park △,
Australia .... **126 B4** 16 25 S 146 1 E
Euboea = Évvoia, *Greece* ..... **48 C6** 38 30N 24 0 E
Eucha, *U.S.A.* **155 G7** 36 27N 94 49W
Euchareena, *Australia* .... **129 B8** 32 57 S 149 6 E
Eucla, *Australia* .... **125 F4** 31 41 S 128 52 E
Euclid, *U.S.A.* **150 E3** 41 34N 81 32W
Euclides da Cunha, *Brazil* ..... **170 D4** 10 31 S 39 1W
Eucumbene, L., *Australia* ..... **129 D8** 36 2 S 148 40 E
Eudora, *U.S.A.* **155 J9** 33 7N 91 16W
Eudunda, *Australia* .... **128 C3** 34 12 S 139 7 E
Eufaula, *Ala., U.S.A.* **152 D3** 31 54N 85 9W
Eufaula, *Okla., U.S.A.* **155 H7** 35 17N 95 35W
Eufaula L., *U.S.A.* **155 H7** 35 18N 95 21W
Eugene, *U.S.A.* **158 E2** 44 5N 123 4W
Eugowra, *Australia* .... **129 B8** 33 22 S 148 24 E
Eulo, *Australia* .... **129 D4** 28 10 S 145 3 E
Eulonia, *U.S.A.* **153 D8** 31 32N 81 26W
Eumungerie, *Australia* .... **129 A8** 31 56 S 148 36 E
Eungella Nat. Park △, *Australia* **126 C4** 20 57 S 148 40 E
Eunice, La., *U.S.A.* **155 K8** 30 30N 92 25W
Eunice, N. Mex., U.S.A.* **155 J3** 32 26N 103 10W
Eupen, *Belgium* .... **24 D6** 50 37N 6 3 E
Euphrates = Furāt, Nahr al →, *Asia* **96 D5** 31 0N 47 25 E
Eure □, *France* .... **26 C8** 49 6N 1 0 E
Eure →, *France* .... **26 C8** 49 18N 1 12 E
Eure-et-Loir □, *France* .... **26 D8** 48 22N 1 30 E
Eureka, *Canada* **6 B3** 80 0N 85 56W
Eureka, *Calif., U.S.A.* **158 F1** 40 47N 124 9W
Eureka, *Ill., U.S.A.* **156 D7** 40 43N 89 16W
Eureka, *Kans., U.S.A.* **155 G6** 37 49N 96 17W
Eureka, *Mo., U.S.A.* **156 F6** 38 30N 90 38W
Eureka, *Mont., U.S.A.* **158 B6** 48 53N 115 3W
Eureka, *Nev., U.S.A.* **158 G5** 39 31N 115 58W
Eureka, *S.C., U.S.A.* **152 B8** 33 42N 81 46W
Eureka, S. Dak., U.S.A.* **154 C5** 45 46N 99 38W
Eureka, Mt., *Australia* .... **125 E3** 26 35 S 121 35 E
Eurelia, *Australia* .... **128 B3** 32 33 S 138 35 E
Euroa, *Australia* .... **129 D6** 36 44 S 145 35 E
Europa, Île, *Ind. Oc.* .... **121 G2** 22 20 S 40 22 E
Europa, Picos de, *Spain* **42 B6** 43 10N 4 49W
Europa, Pta. de, *Gib.* **43 J5** 36 3N 5 21W
Europe .... **24 C4** 51 57N 4 10 E
Europoort, *Neths.* .... **24 C4** 51 57N 4 10 E
Euskirchen, *Germany* .... **30 E2** 50 38N 6 48 E
Eustis, *U.S.A.* **153 G8** 28 51N 81 41W
Euston, *Australia* .... **128 C4** 34 30 S 142 46 E
Eutaw, *U.S.A.* **152 E2** 32 50N 87 53W
Eutawville, *U.S.A.* **152 B9** 33 24N 80 21W
Eutin, *Germany* .... **30 A6** 54 7N 10 37 E
Eutsuk L., *Canada* **142 C3** 53 20N 126 45W
Eva, *Brazil* .... **169 D6** 3 9 S 59 6W
Evale, *Angola* .... **116 B2** 16 33 S 15 44 E
Evangelist *Norway* .... **18 D3** 60 39N 6 7 E
Evans, *U.S.A.* **154 E2** 40 23N 104 41W
Evans, L., *Canada* **140 B4** 50 50N 77 0W

Evans City, *U.S.A.* **150 F4** 40 46N 80 4W
Evans Head, *Australia* .... **127 D5** 29 7 S 153 27 E
Evans Mills, *U.S.A.* **151 B9** 44 6N 75 48W
Evansburg, *Canada* **142 C5** 53 36N 114 59W
Evansdale, *U.S.A.* **156 B4** 42 30N 92 17W
Evanston, *Ill., U.S.A.* **157 B9** 42 3N 87 41W
Evanston, *Wyo., U.S.A.* **158 F8** 41 16N 110 58W
Evansville, *Ind., U.S.A.* **157 G9** 37 58N 87 35W
Evansville, *Wis., U.S.A.* **156 B7** 42 47N 89 18W
Évaux-les-Bains, *France* .... **29 B6** 46 12N 2 29 E
Evaz, *Iran* .... **97 E7** 27 46N 53 59 E
Eveleen, *Afyon, Turkey* .... **49 C11** 38 4N 29 54 E
Eveleer, *Çanakkale, Turkey* ... **49 B8** 39 47N 26 44 E
Eveleth, *U.S.A.* **154 B8** 47 28N 92 32W
Evensk, *Russia* .... **67 C16** 62 12N 159 30 E
Evenstad, *Norway* .... **18 C8** 61 25N 11 7 E
Everard, L., *Australia* .... **127 E1** 31 30 S 135 0 E
Everard Ranges, *Australia* ... **125 E5** 27 5 S 132 28 E
Everest, Mt., *Nepal* .... **93 E12** 28 5N 86 58 E
Everett, *Ga., U.S.A.* **152 D8** 31 24N 81 38W
Everett, *Pa., U.S.A.* **150 F6** 40 1N 78 23W
Everett, *Wash., U.S.A.* **160 C4** 47 59N 122 12W
Everglades, The, *U.S.A.* **153 K9** 25 50N 81 0W
Everglades City, *U.S.A.* **153 K8** 25 52N 81 23W
Everglades Nat. Park △, *U.S.A.* **149 K2** 25 30N 80 57W
Evergreen, *Ala., U.S.A.* **152 K2** 31 26N 86 57W
Evergreen, *Mont., U.S.A.* **158 B6** 48 9N 114 13W
Everöd, *Sweden* .... **17 J8** 55 53N 14 5 E
Everton, *Australia* .... **129 D7** 36 25 S 146 33 E
Evertsberg, *Sweden* .... **16 C7** 61 8N 13 58 E
Evesham, *U.K.* **21 E6** 52 6N 1 56W
Evfimía, Ayía, *Greece* .... **39 C2** 38 18N 20 36 E
Évian-les-Bains, *France* ..... **27 F13** 46 24N 6 35 E
Evinayong, *Eq. Guin.* .... **114 B2** 1 26N 10 35 E
Évinos →, *Greece* .... **48 C3** 38 27N 21 40 E
Évisa, *France* .... **29 F12** 42 15N 8 48 E
Evolène, *Switz.* .... **32 D4** 46 7N 7 30 E
Évora, *Portugal* **43 G3** 38 33N 7 57W
Évora □, *Portugal* **43 G3** 38 33N 7 50W
Evowghlī, *Iran* .... **101 C11** 38 43N 45 13 E
Evreux, *France* .... **26 C8** 49 3N 1 8 E
Evritanía □, *Greece* .... **48 B3** 39 5N 21 30 E
Évron, *France* **26 D6** 48 10N 0 24W
Évros □, *Greece* .... **51 E10** 41 10N 26 0 E
Évros →, *Greece* .... **100 B2** 41 40N 26 34 E
Évrótas →, *Greece* .... **48 E4** 36 50N 22 40 E
Évry, *France* .... **27 D9** 48 38N 2 27 E
Évvoia, *Greece* .... **48 C6** 38 40N 23 40 E
Évvoia □, *Greece* .... **48 C5** 38 40N 23 40 E
Evxinoúpolis, *Greece* .... **48 B4** 39 12N 22 42 E
Ewa, *U.S.A.* **145 K13** 21 20N 158 1W
Ewa Beach, *U.S.A.* **145 K13** 21 19N 158 1W
Ewasse, *Papua N. G.* .... **132 C6** 5 19 S 151 1 E
Ewe, L., *U.K.* **22 D3** 57 49N 5 38W
Ewing, Mo., U.S.A.* **156 E5** 40 6N 91 43W
Ewing, Nebr., U.S.A.* **154 D5** 42 16N 98 21W
Ewo, *Congo* .... **114 C2** 0 48 S 14 45 E
Exaltación, *Bolivia* .... **172 C4** 13 10 S 65 20W
Excelsior Springs, *U.S.A.* **156 E2** 39 20N 94 13W
Excideuil, *France* .... **28 C5** 45 20N 1 4 E
Exe →, *U.K.* **21 G4** 50 41N 3 29W
Exeter, *Canada* **150 C3** 43 21N 81 29W
Exeter, *U.K.* **21 G4** 50 43N 3 31W
Exeter, *Calif., U.S.A.* **160 J7** 36 18N 119 9W
Exeter, *N.H., U.S.A.* **151 D14** 42 59N 70 57W
Exira, *U.S.A.* **156 C2** 41 35N 94 52W
Exmoor, *U.K.* **21 F4** 51 12N 3 45W
Exmoor Nat. Park △, *U.K.* **21 F4** 51 8N 3 42W
Exmouth, *Australia* .... **124 D1** 21 54 S 114 10 E
Exmouth, *U.K.* **21 G4** 50 37N 3 25W
Exmouth G., *Australia* .... **124 D1** 22 15 S 114 15 E
Expedition Nat. Park △, *Australia* **127 A4** 25 41 S 149 7 E
Expedition Ra., *Australia* ... **126 C4** 24 30 S 149 12 E
Experiment, *U.S.A.* **152 B8** 33 17N 84 17W
Extremadura □, *Spain* **43 F4** 39 30N 6 5W
Exuma Sound, *Bahamas* **164 B4** 24 30N 76 20W
Eyak, *U.S.A.* **144 F11** 60 32N 145 36W
Eyasi, L., *Tanzania* .... **118 C3** 3 30 S 35 0 E
Eydehamn, *Norway* .... **18 F5** 58 30N 8 53 E
Eye Pen., *U.K.* **22 C2** 58 13N 6 10W
Eyemouth, *U.K.* **22 E6** 55 52N 2 5W
Eygurande, *France* .... **27 G9** 45 40N 2 26 E
Eyjafjallajökull, *Iceland* **11 D7** 63 38N 19 36W
Eyjafjarðarsýsla □, *Iceland* ... **11 B6** 65 30N 18 30W
Eyjafjörður, *Iceland* **11 A6** 66 15N 18 30W
Eymet, *France* .... **28 D4** 44 40N 0 25 E
Eymoutiers, *France* .... **28 C5** 45 40N 1 45 E
Eynesil, *Turkey* .... **101 B8** 41 4N 39 8 E
Eyrarbakki, *Iceland* **11 D3** 63 52N 21 9W
Eyre (North), L., *Australia* ... **127 D2** 28 30 S 137 20 E
Eyre (South), L., *Australia* ... **127 D2** 29 18 S 137 25 E
Eyre, L., *Australia* .... **122 F6** 29 30 S 137 26 E
Eyre Mts., N.Z.* .... **131 F3** 45 25 S 168 25 E
Eyre Pen., *Australia* .... **127 E2** 33 30 S 136 17 E
Eysturoy, *Færoe Is.* **14 E9** 62 13N 6 54W
Eyvānkī, *Iran* .... **97 C6** 35 24N 51 56 E
Ez Zeidab, *Sudan* .... **106 D3** 17 25N 33 55 E
Ezcaray, *Spain* **40 C1** 42 19N 3 0W
Ežerėlis, *Lithuania* .... **54 D10** 54 53N 23 37 E
Ezhou, *China* .... **77 B10** 30 23N 114 50 E
Ezine, *Turkey* .... **49 B8** 39 48N 26 20 E
Ezmul, *Mauritania* **110 D1** 22 15N 16 30W
Ezouza →, *Cyprus* .... **39 F8** 34 44N 32 27 E

F

F.Y.R.O.M. = Macedonia ■, *Europe* **50 E5** 41 53N 21 40 E
Fabala, *Guinea* **112 D3** 9 44N 9 5W
Fabens, *U.S.A.* **159 L10** 31 30N 106 10W
Fåberg, *Norway* .... **18 C7** 61 10N 10 25 E
Fabero, *Spain* **42 C4** 42 46N 6 31W
Fåborg, *Denmark* .... **17 J4** 55 6N 10 15 E
Fabriano, *Italy* .... **45 E9** 43 20N 12 54 E
Fabrichnyy, *Kazakhstan* .... **65 B8** 43 9N 76 24 E
Făcăeni, *Romania* .... **53 F12** 44 32N 27 53 E
Facatativá, *Colombia* **168 C3** 4 49N 74 22W
Faceville, *U.S.A.* **152 E5** 30 45N 84 38W
Fachi, *Niger* .... **109 E7** 18 6N 11 34 E
Facundo, *Argentina* .... **176 C3** 45 18 S 69 58W
Fada, *Chad* .... **109 E4** 17 13N 21 34 E
Fada-n-Gourma, *Burkina Faso* ... **113 C5** 12 10N 0 30 E
Fadd, *Hungary* .... **52 D3** 46 28N 18 49 E
Faddeyevskiy, Ostrov, *Russia* ... **67 B15** 76 0N 144 0 E
Faddor, *Sudan* .... **107 F3** 8 7N 32 17 E
Fadghāmī, *Syria* .... **101 E9** 35 53N 40 52 E
Fadlab, *Sudan* .... **106 D3** 17 42N 34 2 E
Faenza, *Italy* .... **45 D8** 44 17N 11 53 E
Færingehavn = Kangerluarsoruseq,
Greenland **10 E5** 63 45N 51 27W
Færoe Is. = Føroyar, *Atl. Oc.* ... **14 F9** 62 0N 7 0W
Fafa, *Mali* .... **113 B5** 15 22N 0 48 E
Fafe, *Portugal* **42 D2** 41 27N 8 11W
Fagam, *Nigeria* .... **113 C7** 11 1N 10 1 E
Făgăras, *Romania* .... **53 E9** 45 48N 24 58 E
Fagaras, Munții, *Romania* ..... **53 E9** 45 40N 24 40 E
Fågelmara, *Sweden* .... **17 H9** 56 16N 15 58 E
Fagerheim, *Norway* .... **18 D4** 60 26N 7 46 E
Fagerhult, *Sweden* .... **17 G9** 57 8N 15 40 E

Name	Ref	Lat	Long
Fagernes, *Norway*	18 D6	60 59N	9 14 E
Fagersta, *Sweden*	16 D9	60 1N	15 46 E
Făget, *Romania*	52 E7	45 52N	22 10 E
Făget, Munţii, *Romania*	53 C8	47 40N	23 10 E
Fagnano, L., *Argentina*	176 D3	54 30 S	68 0W
Fagnières, *France*	27 D11	48 58N	4 20 E
Faguibine, L., *Mali*	112 B4	16 45N	4 0W
Fahlīān, *Iran*	97 D6	30 11N	51 28 E
Fahraj, *Kermān, Iran*	97 D8	29 0N	59 0 E
Fahraj, *Yazd, Iran*	97 D7	31 46N	54 36 E
Fai Tsi Long Archipelago, *Vietnam*	76 G6	21 0N	107 30 E
Faial, *Azores*	9 d1	38 34N	28 42W
Faial, *Madeira*	9 c	32 47N	16 53W
Faial, Canal do, *Azores*	9 d1	38 33N	28 35W
Faido, *Switz.*	33 D7	46 29N	8 48 E
Fair Haven, *U.S.A.*	148 D9	43 36N	73 16W
Fair Hd., *U.K.*	23 A5	55 14N	6 9W
Fair Isle, *U.K.*	19 B6	59 30N	1 40W
Fair Oaks, *U.S.A.*	160 G5	38 39N	121 16W
Fairbank, *U.S.A.*	156 B4	42 38N	92 3W
Fairbanks, *Alaska, U.S.A.*	144 D11	64 51N	147 43W
Fairbanks, *Fla., U.S.A.*	152 F7	29 44N	82 16W
Fairborn, *U.S.A.*	157 E12	39 49N	84 2W
Fairburn, *U.S.A.*	152 B5	33 34N	84 35W
Fairbury, *Ill., U.S.A.*	157 D8	40 45N	88 31W
Fairbury, *Nebr., U.S.A.*	154 E6	40 8N	97 11W
Fairfax, *Ohio, U.S.A.*	157 E13	39 5N	83 37W
Fairfax, *S.C., U.S.A.*	152 C8	32 59N	81 15W
Fairfax, *Vt., U.S.A.*	151 B11	44 40N	73 1W
Fairfield, *Australia*	129 B9	33 53 S	150 57 E
Fairfield, *Ala., U.S.A.*	149 J2	33 29N	86 55W
Fairfield, *Calif., U.S.A.*	160 G4	38 15N	122 3W
Fairfield, *Conn., U.S.A.*	151 E11	41 9N	73 16W
Fairfield, *Idaho, U.S.A.*	158 E6	43 21N	114 44W
Fairfield, *Ill., U.S.A.*	157 F8	38 23N	88 22W
Fairfield, *Iowa, U.S.A.*	156 D5	40 56N	91 57W
Fairfield, *Ohio, U.S.A.*	157 E12	39 21N	84 34W
Fairfield, *Tex., U.S.A.*	155 K7	31 44N	96 10W
Fairford, *Canada*	143 C9	51 37N	98 38W
Fairhope, *U.S.A.*	149 K2	30 31N	87 54W
Fairlie, *N.Z.*	131 E5	44 5 S	170 49 E
Fairmead, *U.S.A.*	160 H6	37 5N	120 10W
Fairmont, *Minn., U.S.A.*	154 D7	43 39N	94 28W
Fairmont, *W. Va., U.S.A.*	148 F5	39 29N	80 9W
Fairmount, *Calif., U.S.A.*	161 L8	34 45N	118 26W
Fairmount, *N.Y., U.S.A.*	151 C8	43 5N	76 12W
Fairplay, *U.S.A.*	159 G11	39 15N	106 2W
Fairport, *U.S.A.*	150 C7	43 6N	77 27W
Fairport Harbor, *U.S.A.*	150 E3	41 45N	81 17W
Fairview, *Canada*	142 B5	56 5N	118 25W
Fairview, *Mont., U.S.A.*	154 B2	47 51N	104 3W
Fairview, *Okla., U.S.A.*	155 G5	36 16N	98 29W
Fairweather, Mt., *U.S.A.*	142 B1	58 55N	137 32W
Faisalabad, *Pakistan*	91 C4	31 30N	73 5 E
Faith, *U.S.A.*	154 C3	45 2N	102 2W
Faizabad, *India*	93 F10	26 45N	82 10 E
Faizpur, *India*	94 D2	21 14N	75 49 E
Fajã Grande, *Azores*	9 d	39 27N	31 16W
Fajardo, *Puerto Rico*	165 d	18 20N	65 39W
Fajr, W. →, *Si. Arabia*	96 D3	29 10N	38 10 E
Fakenham, *U.K.*	20 E8	52 51N	0 51 E
Fåker, *Sweden*	16 A8	63 0N	14 34 E
Fakfak, *Indonesia*	83 B4	2 55 S	132 18 E
Fakfak, Peg., *Indonesia*	83 B4	2 50 S	132 0 E
Fakiya, *Bulgaria*	51 D11	42 10N	27 6 E
Fakobli, *Ivory C.*	112 D3	7 23N	7 23W
Fakse, *Denmark*	17 J6	55 15N	12 8 E
Fakse Bugt, *Denmark*	17 J6	55 11N	12 15 E
Fakse Ladeplads, *Denmark*	17 J6	55 11N	12 9 E
Faku, *China*	75 C12	42 32N	123 21 E
Falaba, *S. Leone*	112 D2	9 54N	11 22W
Falaise, *France*	26 D6	48 54N	0 12W
Falaise, Mui, *Vietnam*	86 C5	19 6N	105 45 E
Falakrón Óros, *Greece*	50 E7	41 15N	23 58 E
Falam, *Burma*	90 D4	23 0N	93 45 E
Falces, *Spain*	40 C3	42 24N	1 48W
Fălciu, *Romania*	53 D13	46 17N	28 7 E
Falcó, C. des, *Spain*	38 B1	38 50N	1 23 E
Falcón □, *Venezuela*	168 A4	11 0N	69 50W
Falcon, C., *Algeria*	111 A4	35 50N	0 50W
Falcón, Presa, *Mexico*	163 B5	26 35N	99 10W
Falcon Lake, *Canada*	143 D9	49 42N	95 15W
Falcon Reservoir, *U.S.A.*	155 M5	26 34N	99 10W
Falconara Maríttima, *Italy*	45 E10	43 37N	13 24 E
Falcone, C. del, *Italy*	46 B1	40 58N	8 12 E
Falconer, *U.S.A.*	150 D5	42 7N	79 13W
Faléa, *Mali*	112 C2	12 16N	11 17W
Falefa, *Samoa*	133 W24	13 54 S	171 31W
Falelatai, *Samoa*	133 W24	13 55 S	171 59W
Falelima, *Samoa*	133 W23	13 32 S	172 41W
Falémé →, *Senegal*	112 C2	14 46N	12 14W
Falenki, *Russia*	64 B3	58 22N	51 35 E
Falerum, *Sweden*	17 F10	58 8N	16 13 E
Faleshty = Fălești, *Moldova*	53 C12	47 32N	27 44 E
Fălești, *Moldova*	53 C12	47 32N	27 44 E
Falfurrias, *U.S.A.*	155 M5	27 14N	98 9W
Falher, *Canada*	142 B5	55 44N	117 15W
Falirakí, *Greece*	38 E12	36 22N	28 12 E
Falkenberg, *Germany*	30 D9	51 35N	13 14 E
Falkenberg, *Sweden*	17 H6	56 54N	12 30 E
Falkensee, *Germany*	30 C9	52 34N	13 4 E
Falkirk, *U.K.*	22 F5	56 0N	3 47W
Falkirk □, *U.K.*	22 F5	56 0N	3 49W
Falkland, *U.K.*	22 E5	56 16N	3 12W
Falkland, East, I., *Falk. Is.*	176 D5	51 40 S	58 30W
Falkland, West, I., *Falk. Is.*	176 D4	51 40 S	60 0W
Falkland Is. □, *Atl. Oc.*	9f	51 30 S	59 0W
Falkland Sd., *Falk. Is.*	9f	52 0 S	60 0W
Falkonéra, *Greece*	48 E5	36 50N	23 52 E
Falköping, *Sweden*	17 F7	58 12N	13 33 E
Fall River, *U.S.A.*	151 E13	41 43N	71 10W
Fällanden, *Switz.*	33 B7	47 22N	8 38 E
Fallbrook, *U.S.A.*	161 M9	33 23N	117 14W
Fallon, *U.S.A.*	158 G4	39 28N	118 47W
Falls City, *U.S.A.*	154 E7	40 3N	95 36W
Falls Creek, *U.S.A.*	150 E6	41 9N	78 48W
Falmouth, *Jamaica*	164 a	18 30N	77 40W
Falmouth, *U.K.*	21 G2	50 9N	5 5W
Falmouth, *Ky., U.S.A.*	157 F12	38 41N	84 20W
Falmouth, *Mass., U.S.A.*	151 E14	41 33N	70 37W
Falsa, Pta., *Mexico*	162 B1	27 51N	115 3W
False B., *S. Africa*	116 E2	34 15 S	18 40 E
False Divi Pt., *India*	95 G5	15 43N	80 50 E
False Pass, *U.S.A.*	144 J7	54 51N	163 25W
False Pt., *India*	93 J8	20 18N	86 48 E
Falso, C., *Honduras*	164 C3	15 12N	83 21W
Falster, *Denmark*	17 K5	54 45N	11 55 E
Falsterbo, *Sweden*	15 J15	55 23N	12 50 E
Fălticeni, *Romania*	53 C11	47 21N	26 20 E
Falun, *Sweden*	16 D9	60 37N	15 37 E
Famagusta, *Cyprus*	39 E9	35 8N	33 55 E
Famagusta Bay, *Cyprus*	39 E10	35 15N	34 0 E
Famatina, Sierra de, *Argentina*	174 B2	27 30 S	68 0W
Family L., *Canada*	143 C9	51 54N	95 27W
Famoso, *U.S.A.*	161 K7	35 37N	119 12W
Fan Xian, *China*	74 G8	35 55N	115 38 E
Fana, *Mali*	112 C3	13 0N	6 56W
Fanad Hd., *Ireland*	23 A4	55 17N	7 38W
Fanahammaren, *Norway*	16 E10	60 16N	5 20 E
Fanárion, *Greece*	48 B3	39 24N	21 47 E
Fandriana, *Madag.*	117 C8	20 14 S	47 21 E
Fânes-Sénnes e Braies, Parco Naturale △, *Italy*	45 B9	46 38N	12 4 E
Fang, *Thailand*	76 H2	19 55N	99 13 E
Fang Xian, *China*	77 A8	32 3N	110 40 E
Fangaga, *Sudan*	106 D4	17 40N	37 50 E
Fangaga, *Sudan*	107 F3	9 4N	30 53 E
Fangchang, *China*	77 B12	31 5N	118 4 E
Fangcheng, *China*	74 H7	33 18N	112 59 E
Fangchenggang, *China*	76 G7	21 42N	108 21 E
Fangliao, *Taiwan*	77 F13	22 22N	120 38 E
Fangshan, *China*	74 E6	38 3N	111 25 E
Fangzi, *China*	75 F10	36 33N	119 10 E
Fani i Madh →, *Albania*	50 E4	41 56N	20 16 E
Fanjakana, *Madag.*	117 C8	21 10 S	46 53 E
Fanjiatun, *China*	75 C13	43 40N	125 15 E
Fanling, *China*	69 F11	22 30N	114 8 E
Fannich, L., *U.K.*	22 D4	57 38N	4 59W
Fannrem, *Norway*	18 A6	63 16N	9 50 E
Fannūj, *Iran*	97 E8	26 35N	59 38 E
Fanø, *Denmark*	17 J2	55 25N	8 25 E
Fano, *Italy*	45 E10	43 50N	13 1 E
Fanshi, *China*	74 E7	39 12N	113 20 E
Fao = Al Fāw, *Iraq*	97 D6	30 0N	48 30 E
Faqirwali, *Pakistan*	92 E5	29 27N	73 0 E
Fâqûs, *Egypt*	106 H7	30 44N	31 47 E
Far East, *Asia*	62 E16	40 0N	130 0 E
Fara in Sabina, *Italy*	45 F9	42 12N	12 43 E
Faradje, *Dem. Rep. of the Congo*	118 B2	3 50N	29 45 E
Farafangana, *Madag.*	117 C8	22 49 S	47 50 E
Farāfra, El Wâhât el-, *Egypt*	106 B2	27 15N	28 20 E
Farāh, *Afghan.*	91 B1	32 20N	62 7 E
Farāh □, *Afghan.*	91 B1	32 25N	62 10 E
Farāh →, *Afghan.*	88 B5	31 27N	61 28 E
Farahalana, *Madag.*	117 A9	14 26 S	50 10 E
Faraid, Gebel, *Egypt*	106 C4	23 33N	35 19 E
Farako, *Ivory C.*	112 D4	10 45N	6 50W
Faramana, *Burkina Faso*	112 C4	11 56N	4 45W
Faranah, *Guinea*	112 C2	10 3N	10 45W
Farap, *Turkmenistan*	65 D1	39 9N	63 36 E
Farasān, Jazā'ir, *Si. Arabia*	98 C3	16 45N	41 55 E
Farasan Is. = Farasān, Jazā'ir, *Si. Arabia*	98 C3	16 45N	41 55 E
Faratsiho, *Madag.*	117 B8	19 24 S	46 57 E
Farborachi, *Somali Rep.*	120 D3	3 20N	45 30 E
Fardes →, *Spain*	43 H7	37 35N	3 0W
Fareham, *U.K.*	21 G6	50 51N	1 11W
Farewell, *U.S.A.*	144 E9	62 31N	153 54W
Farewell, C., *N.Z.*	131 A7	40 29 S	172 43 E
Farewell C. = Nunap Isua, *Greenland*	10 F6	59 48N	43 55W
Farewell Spit, *N.Z.*	131 A8	40 35 S	173 0 E
Färgelanda, *Sweden*	17 F5	58 34N	12 0 E
Farghona, *Uzbekistan*	65 C5	40 23N	71 19 E
Farghonskaya Dolina, *Uzbekistan*	65 C5	40 50N	71 30 E
Fargo, *Ga., U.S.A.*	152 F7	30 41N	82 34W
Fargo, *N. Dak., U.S.A.*	154 B6	46 53N	96 48W
Fār'iah, W. al →, *West Bank*	103 C4	32 12N	35 27 E
Faribault, *U.S.A.*	154 C8	44 18N	93 16W
Faridabad, *India*	92 D6	28 26N	77 19 E
Faridkot, *India*	92 D6	30 44N	74 45 E
Faridpur, *Bangla.*	90 D2	23 15N	89 55 E
Faridpur, *India*	93 E8	28 13N	79 33 E
Farīgh, W. al →, *Libya*	108 B3	30 20N	20 44 E
Fārila, *Sweden*	16 C9	61 48N	15 50 E
Farim, *Guinea-Biss.*	112 C1	12 27N	15 9W
Farīmān, *Iran*	97 C8	35 40N	59 49 E
Farina, *Australia*	127 E2	30 3 S	138 15 E
Farinha →, *Brazil*	170 C2	6 51 S	47 30W
Fariones, Pta., *Canary Is.*	9 e2	29 13N	13 28W
Fâriskûr, *Egypt*	106 H7	31 20N	31 43 E
Färjestaden, *Sweden*	17 H10	56 39N	16 27 E
Farkadhón, *Greece*	48 B4	39 36N	22 4 E
Farkhor = Parkhar, *Tajikistan*	65 E4	37 30N	69 34 E
Farleigh, *Australia*	126 K7	21 4 S	149 8 E
Farley, *U.S.A.*	156 B6	42 27N	91 0W
Farmakonisi, *Greece*	49 D9	37 17N	27 5 E
Farmer City, *U.S.A.*	157 D8	40 15N	88 39W
Farmersburg, *U.S.A.*	157 E9	39 15N	87 23W
Farmerville, *U.S.A.*	155 J8	32 47N	92 24W
Farmingdale, *U.S.A.*	151 F10	40 12N	74 10W
Farmington, *Canada*	142 B4	55 54N	120 30W
Farmington, *Calif., U.S.A.*	160 H6	37 55N	120 59W
Farmington, *Ga., U.S.A.*	152 B6	33 47N	83 26W
Farmington, *Ill., U.S.A.*	156 D7	40 42N	90 0W
Farmington, *Iowa, U.S.A.*	156 D5	40 38N	91 44W
Farmington, *Maine, U.S.A.*	149 C10	44 40N	70 9W
Farmington, *Mo., U.S.A.*	155 G9	37 47N	90 25W
Farmington, *N.H., U.S.A.*	151 C13	43 24N	71 4W
Farmington, *N. Mex., U.S.A.*	159 H9	36 44N	108 12W
Farmington, *Utah, U.S.A.*	158 F8	41 0N	111 12W
Farmington →, *U.S.A.*	151 E12	41 51N	72 38W
Farmland, *U.S.A.*	157 D11	40 15N	85 5W
Farmville, *U.S.A.*	148 G6	37 18N	78 24W
Färnäs, *Sweden*	16 D8	61 0N	14 39 E
Farne Is., *U.K.*	20 B6	55 38N	1 37W
Färnebofjärden Nationalpark △, *Sweden*	16 D10	60 10N	16 48 E
Farnham, *Canada*	151 A12	45 17N	72 59W
Farnham, Mt., *Canada*	142 C5	50 29N	116 30W
Faro, *Brazil*	169 D6	2 10 S	56 39W
Faro, *Canada*	138 B6	62 11N	133 22W
Faro, *Portugal*	43 H3	37 2N	7 55W
Fårö, *Sweden*	15 H18	57 55N	19 5 E
Faro □, *Cameroon*	113 D7	8 0N	12 30 E
Faro □, *Portugal*	43 H2	37 12N	8 10W
Faro ✈ (FAO), *Portugal*	43 H3	37 2N	7 57W
Faro, Réserve de △, *Cameroon*	114 A2	8 15N	12 37 E
Fårösund, *Sweden*	17 G13	57 52N	19 2 E
Farquhar, C., *Australia*	125 D1	23 50 S	113 36 E
Farquhar Is., *Seychelles*	126 D3	25 35 S	140 43 E
Farrars Cr. →, *Australia*	126 D3	25 35 S	140 43 E
Farrāshband, *Iran*	97 D7	28 57N	52 5 E
Farrell, *U.S.A.*	150 E4	41 13N	80 30W
Farrell Flat, *Australia*	128 B3	33 48 S	138 48 E
Farrokhī, *Iran*	97 C8	33 50N	59 31 E
Farruch, C. = Ferrutx, C., *Spain*	38 B4	39 47N	3 21 E
Fārs □, *Iran*	97 D7	29 30N	55 0 E
Fársala, *Greece*	48 B4	39 17N	22 23 E
Fārsī, *Afghan.*	91 B1	33 47N	63 15 E
Farsø, *Denmark*	17 H3	56 46N	9 19 E
Farson, *U.S.A.*	158 E9	42 6N	109 27W
Farsund, *Norway*	18 F5	58 5N	6 55 E
Fartak, Rās, *Si. Arabia*	96 D2	28 5N	34 34 E
Fartak, Ra's, *Yemen*	99 D6	15 38N	52 15 E
Fărțănești, *Romania*	53 E12	45 49N	27 59 E
Fartura, Serra da, *Brazil*	175 B5	26 21 S	52 52W
Faru, *Nigeria*	113 C6	12 48N	6 12 E
Fārūj, *Iran*	97 B8	37 14N	58 14 E
Farum, *Denmark*	17 H3	55 49N	9 31 E
Farvel, Kap = Nunap Isua, *Greenland*	10 F6	59 48N	43 55W
Farwell, *U.S.A.*	155 H3	34 23N	103 2W
Fāryāb □, *Afghan.*	65 E2	36 0N	65 0 E
Fasā, *Iran*	97 D7	29 0N	53 39 E
Fasano, *Italy*	47 B10	40 50N	17 22 E
Fashoda, *Sudan*	107 F3	9 50N	32 2 E
Fassa, *Mali*	112 C3	13 26N	8 15 E
Fastiv, *Ukraine*	59 G5	50 7N	29 57 E
Fastnet Rock, *Ireland*	23 E2	51 22N	9 37W
Fastov = Fastiv, *Ukraine*	59 G5	50 7N	29 57 E
Fatagar, Tanjung, *Indonesia*	83 B4	2 46 S	131 57 E
Fataka, *Solomon Is.*	123 C12	11 55 S	170 12 E
Fatehabad, *Haryana, India*	92 E6	29 31N	75 27 E
Fatehabad, *Ut. P., India*	93 F8	27 25N	79 35 E
Fatehgarh, *India*	93 F8	27 25N	79 35 E
Fatehpur, *Bihar, India*	93 G11	24 38N	85 14 E
Fatehpur, *Raj., India*	93 F6	28 0N	74 40 E
Fatehpur, *Raj., India*	93 G9	25 56N	81 13 E
Fatehpur, *Ut. P., India*	93 F9	27 10N	81 13 E
Fatehpur Sikri, *India*	92 F6	27 6N	77 40 E
Fatesh, *Russia*	59 F8	52 8N	35 57 E
Fathai, *Sudan*	107 F3	8 5N	31 48 E
Fathom Five Nat. Marine Park △, *Canada*	140 C3	45 17N	81 40W
Fatick, *Senegal*	112 C1	14 19N	16 27W
Fatima, *Canada*	141 C7	47 24N	61 53W
Fátima, *Portugal*	43 F2	39 37N	8 39W
Fatoya, *Guinea*	112 C3	11 37N	9 10W
Fatsa, *Turkey*	100 B7	41 2N	37 31 E
Faucille, Col de la, *France*	27 F13	46 22N	6 2 E
Faulkton, *U.S.A.*	154 C5	45 2N	99 8W
Faulquemont, *France*	27 C13	49 3N	6 36 E
Faure I., *Australia*	125 E1	25 52 S	113 50 E
Fǎurei, *Romania*	53 E12	45 6N	27 19 E
Fauresmith, *S. Africa*	116 D4	29 44 S	25 17 E
Fauro, *Solomon Is.*	133 L9	6 55 S	156 7 E
Fauske, *Norway*	14 C16	67 17N	15 25 E
Fåvang, *Norway*	18 C7	61 27N	10 11 E
Favara, *Italy*	46 E6	37 19N	13 39 E
Faváritx, C. de, *Spain*	38 B5	40 0N	4 15 E
Faverges, *France*	29 C10	45 45N	6 17 E
Favignana, *Italy*	46 E5	37 56N	12 20 E
Favignana, I., *Italy*	46 E5	37 56N	12 19 E
Fawcett, Pt., *Australia*	124 B5	11 46 S	130 2 E
Fawn →, *Canada*	140 A2	55 20N	87 35W
Fawnskin, *U.S.A.*	161 L10	34 16N	116 56W
Faxaflói, *Iceland*	11 C3	64 29N	23 0W
Faxälven →, *Sweden*	16 A10	63 13N	17 13 E
Faya-Largeau, *Chad*	109 E3	17 58N	19 6 E
Fayaoué, *Vanuatu*	133 K4	20 38 S	166 33 E
Fayd, *Si. Arabia*	96 E4	27 1N	42 52 E
Fayence, *France*	29 E10	43 38N	6 42 E
Fayette, *Ala., U.S.A.*	149 J2	33 41N	87 50W
Fayette, *Iowa, U.S.A.*	156 B5	42 51N	91 48W
Fayette, *Mo., U.S.A.*	156 F4	39 9N	92 41W
Fayette, *Ohio, U.S.A.*	157 C12	41 40N	84 20W
Fayetteville, *Ark., U.S.A.*	155 G7	36 4N	94 10W
Fayetteville, *Ga., U.S.A.*	152 B5	33 27N	84 27W
Fayetteville, *N.C., U.S.A.*	149 H6	35 3N	78 53W
Fayetteville, *Tenn., U.S.A.*	149 H2	35 9N	86 34W
Fayied, *Egypt*	106 H8	30 18N	32 16 E
Fayón, *Spain*	40 D5	41 15N	0 20 E
Fazao-Malfakassa, Parc Nat. de △, *Togo*	113 D5	8 45N	0 50 E
Fazenda Libongo, *Angola*	115 D2	8 24 S	13 24 E
Fazenda Nova, *Brazil*	171 E1	16 11 S	50 48W
Fazilka, *India*	92 D6	30 27N	74 2 E
Fazilpur, *Pakistan*	92 E4	29 18N	70 29 E
Fdérik, *Mauritania*	110 D2	22 40N	12 45W
Feale →, *Ireland*	23 D2	52 27N	9 37W
Fear, C., *U.S.A.*	149 J7	33 50N	77 58W
Feather →, *U.S.A.*	158 G3	38 47N	121 36W
Feather Falls, *U.S.A.*	160 F5	39 36N	121 16W
Featherston, *N.Z.*	130 H4	41 6 S	175 20 E
Featherstone, *Zimbabwe*	119 F3	18 42 S	30 55 E
Fécamp, *France*	26 C7	49 45N	0 22 E
Feda, *Norway*	18 F3	58 17N	6 50 E
Fedala = Mohammedia, *Morocco*	110 B3	33 44N	7 21W
Federación, *Argentina*	174 C4	31 0 S	57 55W
Federal Capital Terr. □, *Nigeria*	113 D6	9 0N	7 10 E
Federal Way, *U.S.A.*	160 C4	47 18N	122 19W
Fedeshküh, *Iran*	97 D7	28 49N	53 50 E
Fedje, *Norway*	18 E1	60 47N	4 43 E
Fehérgyarmat, *Hungary*	52 C7	47 58N	22 30 E
Fehmarn, *Germany*	30 A7	54 27N	11 7 E
Fehmarn Bælt, *Europe*	17 K5	54 35N	11 20 E
Fehmarn Belt = Fehmarn Bælt, *Europe*	17 K5	54 35N	11 20 E
Fei Xian, *China*	75 G9	35 18N	117 59 E
Feijó, *Brazil*	172 B3	8 9 S	70 21W
Feilding, *N.Z.*	130 G4	40 13 S	175 35 E
Feira de Santana, *Brazil*	171 D4	12 15 S	38 57W
Feiring, *Norway*	18 D6	60 30N	11 10 E
Feixi, *China*	77 B11	31 43N	117 59 E
Feixiang, *China*	74 F8	36 30N	114 45 E
Feke, *Turkey*	100 D6	37 48N	35 56 E
Fekete →, *Hungary*	52 E3	45 47N	18 15 E
Felanitx, *Spain*	38 B4	39 28N	3 9 E
Felda →, *U.S.A.*	153 J8	26 34N	81 26W
Feldbach, *Austria*	34 E8	46 57N	15 52 E
Feldberg, *Baden-W., Germany*	31 H3	47 52N	8 0 E
Feldberg, *Mecklenburg-Vorpommern, Germany*	30 B9	53 20N	13 25 E
Feldkirch, *Austria*	34 E7	47 15N	9 37 E
Feldkirchen, *Austria*	34 E7	46 44N	14 6 E
Felicité, *Seychelles*	121 h	4 19 S	55 52 E
Felicity, *U.S.A.*	157 F12	38 51N	84 6W
Felipe Carrillo Puerto, *Mexico*	163 D7	19 38N	88 3W
Felixburg, *Zimbabwe*	117 B5	19 29 S	30 51 E
Felixlândia, *Brazil*	171 E3	18 47 S	44 55W
Felixstowe, *U.K.*	21 F9	51 58N	1 23 E
Felletin, *France*	28 C6	45 53N	2 11 E
Fellingsbro, *Sweden*	16 E9	59 26N	15 37 E
Fellsmere, *U.S.A.*	153 H9	27 46N	80 36W
Felton, *U.S.A.*	160 H4	37 3N	122 4W
Feltre, *Italy*	45 B8	46 1N	11 54 E
Femer Bælt = Fehmarn Bælt, *Europe*	17 K5	54 35N	11 20 E
Femø, *Denmark*	17 K5	54 58N	11 35 E
Femunden, *Norway*	18 B8	62 10N	11 53 E
Femundsmarka Nasjonalpark △, *Norway*	18 B9	62 18N	12 6 E
Fen He →, *China*	74 G6	35 36N	110 42 E
Fene, *Spain*	42 B2	43 27N	8 9W
Fenelon Falls, *Canada*	150 B6	44 32N	78 45W
Fener Burnu, *Turkey*	49 E9	36 58N	27 18 E
Feneroa, *Ethiopia*	107 E4	13 5N	39 3 E
Feng Xian, *Jiangsu, China*	74 G9	34 43N	116 35 E
Feng Xian, *Shaanxi, China*	74 H4	33 54N	106 40 E
Fengári, *Greece*	51 F9	40 25N	25 42 E
Fengcheng, *Jiangxi, China*	77 C10	28 12N	115 48 E
Fengcheng, *Liaoning, China*	75 D13	40 28N	124 5 E
Fengfeng, *China*	74 F8	36 28N	114 8 E
Fenggang, *China*	76 D7	27 57N	107 42 E
Fenghua, *China*	77 C13	29 40N	121 25 E
Fenghuang, *China*	77 C7	27 57N	109 29 E
Fengkai, *China*	77 F8	23 24N	111 30 E
Fengkang, *Taiwan*	77 F13	22 12N	120 42 E
Fengle, *China*	77 B9	31 29N	112 29 E
Fengning, *Taiwan*	77 F13	23 45N	121 26 E
Fengqing, *China*	74 D9	41 10N	116 33 E
Fengning, *China*	74 D9	41 10N	116 33 E
Fengqing, *China*	76 E2	24 38N	99 55 E
Fengqiu, *China*	74 G8	35 2N	114 25 E
Fengrun, *China*	75 E10	39 48N	118 8 E
Fengshan, *Guangxi Zhuangzu, China*	76 E6	24 31N	107 3 E
Fengshan, *Guangxi Zhuangzu, China*	76 E6	24 31N	107 3 E
Fengshan, *Taiwan*	77 F13	22 38N	120 21 E
Fengshun, *China*	77 F11	23 46N	116 10 E
Fengtai, *Anhui, China*	77 A11	32 50N	116 18 E
Fengtai, *Beijing, China*	74 E9	39 50N	116 18 E
Fengxian, *China*	74 G4	34 29N	107 25 E
Fengxiang, *China*	74 G4	34 29N	107 25 E
Fengyang, *China*	75 H9	32 51N	117 29 E
Fengyi, *China*	76 E3	25 55N	100 35 E
Fengyüan, *Taiwan*	74 D7	40 25N	113 2 E
Feni Is., *Papua N. G.*	132 C7	4 0 S	153 40 E
Fennimore, *U.S.A.*	156 B6	42 59N	90 39W
Fenny, *Bangla.*	90 D3	22 55N	91 32 E
Feno, C. de, *France*	29 G12	41 58N	8 33 E
Fenoarivo, *Fianarantsoa, Madag.*	117 C8	21 43 S	46 24 E
Fenoarivo, *Fianarantsoa, Madag.*	117 C8	20 52 S	46 53 E
Fenoarivo Afovoany, *Madag.*	117 B8	18 26 S	46 34 E
Fenoarivo Atsinanana, *Madag.*	117 B8	17 22 S	49 25 E
Fens, The, *U.K.*	20 E7	52 38N	0 2W
Fensmark, *Denmark*	17 J5	55 17N	11 48 E
Fenton, *U.S.A.*	157 B13	42 48N	83 42W
Fenxi, *China*	74 F6	36 40N	111 31 E
Fenyang, *China*	74 F6	37 18N	111 48 E
Fenyang, *China*	77 D10	27 45N	114 47 E
Feodosiya, *Ukraine*	59 K8	45 2N	35 16 E
Fer, C. de, *Algeria*	111 A6	37 3N	7 10 E
Fera, *Solomon Is.*	133 M10	8 6 S	159 37 E
Ferdows, *Iran*	97 C8	33 58N	58 2 E
Fère-Champenoise, *France*	27 D10	48 45N	3 59 E
Fère-en-Tardenois, *France*	27 C10	49 10N	3 30 E
Ferentino, *Italy*	45 G10	41 42N	13 15 E
Ferfer, *Somali Rep.*	120 C3	5 4N	45 9 E
Fergana = Farghona, *Uzbekistan*	65 C5	40 23N	71 19 E
Fergana Range, *Asia*	65 C6	41 0N	73 50 E
Ferganskaya Dolina = Farghonskaya Dolina, *Uzbekistan*	65 C5	40 50N	71 30 E
Fergus, *Canada*	150 C4	43 43N	80 24W
Fergus Falls, *U.S.A.*	154 B6	46 17N	96 4W
Fergusson I., *Papua N. G.*	132 E6	9 30 S	150 45 E
Fériana, *Tunisia*	108 B1	34 59N	8 33 E
Feričanci, *Croatia*	52 E2	45 32N	18 0 E
Ferihegy, Budapest ✈ (BUD), *Hungary*	52 C4	47 25N	19 12 E
Ferkane, *Algeria*	111 B6	34 37N	7 26 E
Ferkéssédougou, *Ivory C.*	112 D3	9 35N	5 6W
Ferlach, *Austria*	34 E7	46 32N	14 18 E
Ferland, *Canada*	140 B2	50 19N	88 27W
Ferlo, Vallée du, *Senegal*	112 B2	15 15N	14 15W
Ferlo-Nord, Réserve de Faune du △, *Senegal*	112 B2	15 43N	14 0W
Ferlo-Sud, Réserve de Faune du △, *Senegal*	112 B2	15 43N	14 0W
Fermanagh □, *U.K.*	23 B4	54 21N	7 40W
Fermo, *Italy*	45 E10	43 9N	13 43 E
Fermont, *Canada*	141 B6	52 47N	67 5W
Fermoselle, *Spain*	42 D4	41 19N	6 27W
Fermoy, *Ireland*	23 D3	52 9N	8 16W
Fernán Núñez, *Spain*	43 H6	37 40N	4 44W
Fernández, *Argentina*	174 B3	27 55 S	63 50W
Fernandina I., *Ecuador*	172 a	0 25 S	91 30W
Fernandina Beach, *U.S.A.*	152 E8	30 40N	81 27W
Fernando de Noronha, *Brazil*	170 B5	4 0 S	33 10W
Fernando Póo = Bioko, *Eq. Guin.*	113 E6	3 30N	8 40 E
Fernandópolis, *Brazil*	171 F1	20 16 S	50 14W
Ferndale, *U.S.A.*	160 B4	48 51N	122 36W
Fernie, *Canada*	142 D5	49 30N	115 5W
Fernlees, *Australia*	126 C4	23 51 S	148 7 E
Fernley, *U.S.A.*	158 G4	39 36N	119 15W
Feroke, *India*	95 J2	11 9N	75 46 E
Ferozepore = Firozpur, *India*	92 D6	30 55N	74 40 E
Férrai, *Greece*	51 F10	40 53N	26 10 E
Ferrandina, *Italy*	47 B9	40 29N	16 27 E
Ferrara, *Italy*	45 D8	44 50N	11 35 E
Ferrato, C., *Italy*	46 C2	39 18N	9 38 E
Ferreira do Alentejo, *Portugal*	43 G2	38 4N	8 6W
Ferreñafe, *Peru*	172 E2	6 42 S	79 50W
Ferret, C., *France*	28 D2	44 38N	1 15W
Ferrette, *France*	27 E14	47 30N	7 20 E
Ferriday, *U.S.A.*	155 K9	31 38N	91 33W
Ferriere, *Italy*	44 D6	44 40N	9 30 E
Ferrières, *France*	27 D9	48 5N	2 48 E
Ferro, Capo, *Italy*	46 A2	41 9N	9 31 E
Ferrol, *Spain*	42 B2	43 29N	8 15W
Ferrol, Pen. de, *Peru*	172 E2	9 10 S	78 35W
Ferron, *U.S.A.*	159 G8	39 5N	111 8W
Ferros, *Brazil*	171 E3	19 14 S	43 2W
Ferrutx, C., *Spain*	38 B4	39 47N	3 21 E
Ferryland, *Canada*	141 C9	47 2N	52 53W
Ferrysburg, *U.S.A.*	157 A10	43 5N	86 13W
Fertile, *U.S.A.*	154 B6	47 32N	96 17W
Fertőszentmiklós, *Hungary*	52 C1	47 35N	16 53 E
Fertöszentmiklós, *Hungary*	52 C1	47 35N	16 53 E
Fertőd Nemzeti Park △, *Hungary*	52 C1	47 25N	16 50 E
Fès, *Morocco*	110 B4	34 0N	5 0W
Feshi, *Dem. Rep. of the Congo*	115 D3	6 8 S	18 10 E
Fessenden, *U.S.A.*	154 B5	47 39N	99 38W
Festøy, *Norway*	18 B3	62 22N	6 19 E
Festus, *U.S.A.*	156 F6	38 13N	90 24W
Fetai Bowé, *Senegal*	112 C2	14 56N	13 58W
Fetești, *Romania*	53 F12	44 22N	27 51 E
Fethiye, *Turkey*	49 E11	36 36N	29 6 E
Fethiye Körfezi, *Turkey*	49 E10	36 40N	28 50 E
Fetlar, *U.K.*	22 A8	60 36N	0 52W
Fetsund, *Norway*	18 E8	59 56N	11 10 E
Feuchten, *Austria*	33 B10	47 3N	10 44 E
Feuerthalen, *Switz.*	33 A7	47 37N	8 38 E
Feuilles →, *Canada*	139 C12	58 47N	70 4W
Feurs, *France*	29 C8	45 45N	4 13 E
Fevik, *Norway*	18 F5	58 22N	8 39 E
Feyzābād, *Badakhshān, Afghan.*	65 E5	37 7N	70 33 E
Feyzābād, *Fāryāb, Afghan.*	91 A2	36 17N	64 52 E
Fez = Fès, *Morocco*	110 B4	34 0N	5 0W
Fezzan, *Libya*	108 C2	27 0N	13 0 E
Fia, *Congo*	114 C2	3 25 S	14 49 E
Fiambalá, *Argentina*	174 B2	27 45 S	67 37W
Fianarantsoa, *Madag.*	117 C8	21 26 S	47 5 E
Fianarantsoa □, *Madag.*	117 B8	19 30 S	47 0 E
Fianga, *Cameroon*	109 G3	9 55N	15 9 E
Fiche, *Ethiopia*	107 F4	9 50N	38 46 E
Fichtelgebirge, *Germany*	31 E7	50 2N	11 55 E
Fichtelgebirge, Naturpark △, *Germany*	31 E8	50 8N	12 0 E
Ficksburg, *S. Africa*	117 D4	28 51 S	27 53 E
Fidenza, *Italy*	44 D7	44 52N	10 3 E
Fiditi, *Nigeria*	113 D5	7 45N	3 53 E
Fidjeland, *Norway*	18 F3	58 57N	6 56 E
Field →, *Australia*	126 C2	23 48 S	138 0 E
Field I., *Australia*	124 B5	12 5 S	132 23 E
Fieni, *Romania*	53 E10	45 8N	25 25 E
Fier, *Albania*	50 F4	40 43N	19 33 E
Fierzë, *Albania*	50 D4	42 15N	20 1 E
Fiesch, *Switz.*	32 D6	46 25N	8 8 E
Fife □, *U.K.*	22 E5	56 16N	3 1W
Fife Forest Park △, *U.K.*	22 E5	56 16N	3 15W
Fife Ness, *U.K.*	22 E6	56 17N	2 35W
Fifth Cataract, *Sudan*	106 D3	18 22N	33 50 E
Figari, *France*	29 G13	41 29N	9 7 E
Figeac, *France*	28 D6	44 37N	2 2 E
Figeholm, *Sweden*	17 G10	57 22N	16 33 E
Figline Valdarno, *Italy*	45 E8	43 37N	11 28 E
Figtree, *Zimbabwe*	119 G2	20 22 S	28 20 E
Figueira Castelo Rodrigo, *Portugal*	42 E4	40 57N	6 58W
Figueira da Foz, *Portugal*	42 E2	40 7N	8 54W
Figueira dos Vinhos, *Portugal*	42 F2	39 55N	8 16W
Figueres, *Spain*	40 C7	42 18N	2 58 E
Figuig, *Morocco*	111 B4	32 5N	1 11W
Fihaonana, *Madag.*	117 B8	18 36 S	47 12 E
Fiherenana, *Madag.*	117 C8	18 29 S	48 24 E
Fiherenana →, *Madag.*	117 C7	23 19 S	43 37 E
Fiji ■, *Pac. Oc.*	133 A2	17 20 S	179 0 E
Fik, *Ethiopia*	107 F5	8 10N	42 19 E
Fika, *Nigeria*	113 C8	11 15N	11 13 E
Filabres, Sierra de los, *Spain*	43 H8	37 13N	2 20W
Filabusi, *Zimbabwe*	117 C4	20 34 S	29 20 E

Filadelfia, *Bolivia* .... 172 C4 11 20 S 68 46W
Filadélfia, *Brazil* .... 170 C2 7 21 S 47 30W
Filadélfia, *Italy* .... 47 D9 38 47N 16 17 E
Fil'akovo, *Slovak Rep.* .... 35 C12 48 17N 19 50 E
Filey, *U.K.* 20 C7 54 12N 0 18W
Filey B., *U.K.* 20 C7 54 12N 0 15W
Filfla, *Malta* .... 38 F7 35 47N 14 24 E
Filiaşi, *Romania* .... 53 F8 44 32N 23 31 E
Filiátes, *Greece* .... 38 B10 39 38N 20 16 E
Filiatrá, *Greece* .... 48 D3 37 9N 21 35 E
Filicudi, *Italy* .... 47 D7 38 35N 14 33 E
Filim, *Oman* .... 99 B7 20 37N 58 12 E
Filingué, *Niger* .... 113 C5 14 21N 3 22 E
Filioúri →, *Greece* .... 51 E9 41 15N 25 40 E
Filipstad, *Sweden* .... 16 E8 59 43N 14 9 E
Filisur, *Switz.* .... 33 C9 46 41N 9 40 E
Fillefjell, *Norway* .... 18 C5 61 8N 8 10 E
Fillmore, *Calif., U.S.A.* 161 L8 34 24N 118 55W
Fillmore, *Utah, U.S.A.* 159 G7 38 58N 112 20W
Filótion, *Greece* .... 49 D7 37 3N 25 30 E
Filottrano, *Italy* .... 45 E10 43 26N 13 21 E
Filtu, *Ethiopia* .... 107 F5 5 8N 40 35 E
Fimi →, *Dem. Rep. of the Congo* 114 C3 1 1S 16 58 E
Fina, Réserve de ◯, *Mali* 112 C3 13 15N 8 46W
Finale Emilia, *Italy* .... 44 D8 44 50N 11 18 E
Finale Ligure, *Italy* .... 44 D5 44 10N 8 20 E
Fiñana, *Spain* 43 H8 37 10N 2 50W
Finch, *Canada* 151 A9 45 11N 75 7W
Finch Hatton, *Australia* .... 126 K6 20 25 S 148 39 E
Findhorn →, *U.K.* 22 D5 57 38N 3 38W
Findlay, *U.S.A.* 157 C13 41 2N 83 39W
Finger L., *Canada* 140 B1 53 33N 93 30W
Finger Lakes, *U.S.A.* 151 D8 42 40N 76 30W
Fíngoè, *Mozam.* .... 119 E3 15 5 S 31 50 E
Finike, *Turkey* .... 49 E12 36 21N 30 10 E
Finike Körfezi, *Turkey* .... 49 E12 36 17N 30 16 E
Finiq, *Albania* .... 50 G4 39 54N 20 3 E
Finistère □, *France* 26 D3 48 20N 4 0W
Finisterre = Fisterra, *Spain* 42 C1 42 54N 9 16W
Finisterre, C. = Fisterra, C., *Spain* 42 C1 42 50N 9 19W
Finisterre Ra., *Papua N. G.* .... 132 D4 6 0 S 146 30 E
Finke, *Australia* .... 126 D1 25 34 S 134 35 E
Finke Gorge Nat. Park △, *Australia* .... 124 D5 24 8 S 132 49 E
Finland ■, *Europe* .... 14 E22 63 0N 27 0 E
Finland, G. of, *Europe* .... 15 G21 60 0N 26 0 E
Finlay →, *Canada* 142 B3 57 0N 125 10W
Finley, *Australia* .... 129 C6 35 38 S 145 35 E
Finley, *U.S.A.* 154 B6 47 31N 97 50W
Finn →, *Ireland* 23 B4 54 51N 7 28W
Finnerödja, *Sweden* .... 17 F8 58 57N 14 24 E
Finnigan, Mt., *Australia* .... 126 B4 15 49 S 145 17 E
Finniss, C., *Australia* .... 127 E1 33 8 S 134 51 E
Finnmark, *Norway* .... 14 B20 69 37N 23 57 E
Finnsnes, *Norway* .... 14 B18 69 14N 18 0 E
Finschhafen, *Papua N. G.* .... 132 D4 6 33 S 147 50 E
Finse, *Norway* .... 18 D4 60 36N 7 30 E
Finspång, *Sweden* .... 17 F9 58 43N 15 47 E
Finsteraarhorn, *Switz.* .... 32 C6 46 31N 8 10 E
Finsterwalde, *Germany* .... 30 D9 51 37N 13 42 E
Fiora →, *Italy* .... 45 F8 42 20N 11 34 E
Fiordland Nat. Park △, *N.Z.* .... 131 F2 45 46 S 167 0 E
Fiorenzuola d'Arda, *Italy* .... 44 D6 44 56N 9 55 E
Fíq, *Syria* .... 103 C4 32 46N 35 41 E
Firat = Furãt, Nahr al →, *Asia* .... 96 D5 31 0N 47 25 E
Fire Island Nat. Seashore ◯, *U.S.A.* 151 F11 40 38N 73 8W
Firebag →, *Canada* 143 B6 57 45N 111 21W
Firebaugh, *U.S.A.* 160 J6 36 52N 120 27W
Firedrake L., *Canada* 143 A8 61 25N 104 30W
Firenze, *Italy* .... 45 E8 43 46N 11 15 E
Firenzuola, *Italy* .... 45 D8 44 7N 11 23 E
Firk →, *Iraq* .... 96 D5 30 59N 44 34 E
Firkachi, *Niger* .... 109 E2 15 40N 14 20 E
Firmi, *France* .... 28 D6 44 23N 2 19 E
Firminy, *France* .... 29 C8 45 23N 4 18 E
Firozabad, *India* .... 93 F8 27 10N 78 25 E
Firozpur, *India* .... 92 D6 30 55N 74 40 E
Firozpur-Jhirka, *India* .... 92 F7 27 48N 76 57 E
Fīrūzābād, *Iran* .... 97 D7 28 52N 52 35 E
Fīrūzkūh, *Iran* .... 97 C7 35 50N 52 50 E
Firvale, *Canada* 142 C3 52 27N 126 13W
Fish →, *Namibia* .... 116 D2 28 7 S 17 10 E
Fish →, *S. Africa* .... 116 E3 31 30 S 20 16 E
Fish River Canyon, *Namibia* .... 116 D2 27 40 S 17 35 E
Fisheating Cr. →, *U.S.A.* 153 J8 26 57N 81 7W
Fisher, *Australia* .... 125 F5 30 30 S 131 0 E
Fisher B., *Canada* 143 C9 51 35N 97 13W
Fishers I., *U.S.A.* 151 E13 41 15N 72 0W
Fishguard, *U.K.* 21 E3 52 0N 4 58W
Fishing L., *Canada* 143 C9 52 10N 95 24W
Fishkill, *U.S.A.* 151 E11 41 32N 73 53W
Fiskárdho, *Greece* .... 39 C2 38 28N 20 35 E
Fiskenesset = Qeqertarsuatsiaat, *Greenland* 10 E5 63 5N 50 45W
Fismes, *France* .... 27 C10 49 20N 3 40 E
Fisterra, *Spain* 42 C1 42 54N 9 16W
Fisterra, C., *Spain* 42 C1 42 50N 9 19W
Fitchburg, *U.S.A.* 151 D13 42 35N 71 48W
Fitjar, *Iceland* 11 C5 64 26N 21 18W
Fitjar, *Norway* .... 18 E2 59 55N 5 17 E
Fitri, L., *Chad* .... 109 F3 12 50N 17 28 E
Fitz Roy, *Argentina* .... 176 C3 47 0 S 67 0W
Fitzgerald, *Canada* 142 B6 59 51N 111 36W
Fitzgerald, *U.S.A.* 152 D6 31 43N 83 15W
Fitzgerald River Nat. Park △, *Australia* .... 125 F3 33 53 S 120 3 E
Fitzmaurice →, *Australia* .... 124 B5 14 45 S 130 5 E
Fitzroy →, *Queens., Australia* .... 126 C5 23 32 S 150 52 E
Fitzroy →, *W. Austral., Australia* .... 124 C3 17 31 S 123 35 E
Fitzroy Crossing, *Australia* .... 124 C4 18 9 S 125 38 E
Fitzwilliam I., *Canada* 150 A3 45 30N 81 45W
Fiuggi, *Italy* .... 45 G10 41 48N 13 13 E
Fiume = Rijeka, *Croatia* .... 45 C11 45 20N 14 21 E
Fiumicino, Rome ✈ (FCO), *Italy* .... 45 G9 41 48N 12 15 E
Five Points, *U.S.A.* 160 J6 36 26N 120 6W
Fivizzano, *Italy* .... 44 D7 44 14N 10 8 E
Fizi, *Dem. Rep. of the Congo* .... 118 C2 4 17 S 28 55 E
Fjæra, *Norway* .... 18 E3 59 52N 6 22 E
Fjærland, *Norway* .... 18 C3 61 24N 6 43 E
Fjällbacka, *Sweden* .... 17 F5 58 36N 11 17 E
Fjärdhundra, *Sweden* .... 16 E10 59 47N 16 56 E
Fjellerup, *Denmark* .... 16 H4 56 29N 10 34 E
Fjerritslev, *Denmark* .... 17 G3 57 5N 9 15 E
Fjugesta, *Sweden* .... 16 E8 59 11N 14 52 E
Fkih ben Salah, *Morocco* 110 B3 32 32N 6 45W
Flå, *Norway* .... 18 D6 60 25N 9 28 E
Flagler Beach, *U.S.A.* 153 F8 29 29N 81 8W
Flagstaff, *U.S.A.* 159 J8 35 12N 111 39W
Flagstaff B., *St. Helena* .... 9 h 15 54 S 5 41W
Flagstaff L., *U.S.A.* 149 C10 45 12N 70 18W
Flaherty I., *Canada* 140 A4 56 15N 79 15W
Flåm, *Norway* .... 18 D4 60 50N 7 7 E
Flamatt, *Switz.* .... 32 C4 46 53N 7 19 E
Flambeau →, *U.S.A.* 154 C9 45 18N 91 14W
Flamborough Hd., *U.K.* 20 C7 54 7N 0 7W
Flamengos, *Azores* 9 d1 38 33N 28 39W
Fláming, *Germany* .... 30 C8 52 0N 13 0 E
Flaming Gorge Nat. Recr. Area ◯, *U.S.A.* 158 F9 41 10N 109 25W
Flaming Gorge Reservoir, *U.S.A.* 158 F9 41 10N 109 25W
Flamingo, *U.S.A.* 153 K9 25 8N 80 57W
Flamingo, Teluk, *Indonesia* .... 83 C5 5 30 S 138 0 E
Flanagan, *U.S.A.* 157 D8 40 53N 88 52W
Flanders = Flandre, *Europe* .... 27 B9 50 50N 2 30 E
Flandre, *Europe* .... 27 B9 50 50N 2 30 E

Flandre Occidentale = West-Vlaanderen □, *Belgium* .... 24 D2 51 0N 3 0 E
Flandre Orientale = Oost-Vlaanderen □, *Belgium* .... 24 C3 51 5N 3 50 E
Flandreau, *U.S.A.* 154 C6 44 3N 96 36W
Flanigan, *U.S.A.* 160 E7 40 10N 119 53W
Flannan Is., *U.K.* 22 C1 58 9N 7 52W
Flåsjön, *Sweden* .... 14 D16 64 5N 15 40 E
Flat →, *Canada* 144 E8 62 28N 158 1W
Flat →, *Canada* 142 A3 61 33N 125 18W
Flat →, *U.S.A.* 157 B11 42 56N 85 20W
Flat I., *Mauritius* .... 121 d 19 53 S 57 35 E
Flat Pt., *N.Z.* .... 130 H4 41 14 S 175 57 E
Flat Rock, *U.S.A.* 157 B13 42 6N 83 17W
Flateby, *Norway* .... 18 E8 59 50N 11 10 E
Flateyri, *Iceland* 11 A3 66 3N 23 31W
Flathead L., *U.S.A.* 158 C7 47 51N 114 8W
Flatrock →, *U.S.A.* 157 F10 39 12N 85 56W
Flattery, C., *Australia* .... 126 A4 14 58 S 145 21 E
Flattery, C., *U.S.A.* 160 B2 48 23N 124 29W
Flatts Village, *Bermuda* .... 9 a 32 18N 64 43W
Flatwoods, *U.S.A.* 148 F4 38 31N 82 43W
Flawil, *Switz.* .... 33 B8 47 26N 9 11 E
Flecha Pt., *Phil.* .... 81 H4 7 22N 123 24 E
Flechas Pt., *Phil.* .... 81 F2 10 22N 119 34 E
Fleetwood, *U.K.* 20 D4 53 55N 3 1W
Fleetwood, *U.S.A.* 151 F9 40 27N 75 49W
Flekke, *Norway* .... 18 C2 61 19N 5 20 E
Flekkefjord, *Norway* .... 18 F3 58 18N 6 39 E
Flemingsburg, *U.S.A.* 157 F13 38 25N 83 45W
Flemington, *U.S.A.* 150 E7 41 7N 77 28W
Flemish Cap, *Atl. Oc.* 8 B7 47 0N 45 0W
Flen, *Sweden* .... 16 E10 59 4N 16 35 E
Flensburg, *Germany* .... 30 A5 54 47N 9 27 E
Flers, *France* 26 D6 48 47N 0 33W
Flesberg, *Norway* .... 18 E6 59 51N 9 27 E
Flesherton, *Canada* 150 B4 44 16N 80 33W
Flesko, Tanjung, *Indonesia* .... 82 A2 0 29N 124 30 E
Fleurance, *France* .... 28 E4 43 52N 0 40 E
Fleurier, *Switz.* .... 32 C3 46 54N 6 35 E
Fleurieu Pen., *Australia* .... 128 C3 35 40 S 138 5 E
Flevoland □, *Neths.* .... 24 B5 52 30N 5 30 E
Flims, *Switz.* .... 33 C8 46 50N 9 17 E
Flin Flon, *Canada* 143 C8 54 46N 101 53W
Flinders →, *Australia* .... 126 B3 17 36 S 140 36 E
Flinders B., *Australia* .... 125 F2 34 19 S 115 19 E
Flinders Chase Nat. Park △, *Australia* .... 128 C2 35 50 S 136 42 E
Flinders Group, *Australia* .... 126 A3 14 11 S 144 15 E
Flinders I., *S. Austral., Australia* .... 127 E1 33 44 S 134 41 E
Flinders I., *Tas., Australia* .... 127 D4 40 0 S 148 0 E
Flinders Ranges, *Australia* .... 128 B2 31 30 S 138 30 E
Flinders Ranges Nat. Park △, *Australia* .... 128 A3 31 30 S 138 40 E
Flinders Reefs, *Australia* .... 126 B4 17 37 S 148 31 E
Flint, *U.K.* 20 D4 53 15N 3 8W
Flint, *U.S.A.* 157 A13 43 1N 83 41W
Flint →, *U.S.A.* 152 F5 30 57N 84 34W
Flint I., *Kiribati* .... 135 J12 11 26 S 151 48W
Flintshire □, *U.K.* 20 D4 53 17N 3 17W
Flirsch, *Austria* .... 33 B10 47 9N 10 24 E
Flisa, *Norway* .... 18 D9 60 37N 12 0 E
Flisa →, *Norway* .... 18 D9 60 37N 12 0 E
Fliseryd, *Sweden* .... 17 G10 57 6N 16 15 E
Flix, *Spain* .... 40 D5 41 14N 0 32 E
Flixecourt, *France* .... 27 B9 50 1N 2 5 E
Floby, *Sweden* .... 17 F7 58 8N 13 20 E
Floda, *Sweden* .... 17 G6 57 49N 12 22 E
Flodden, *U.K.* 20 B5 55 37N 2 8W
Flogny-la-Chapelle, *France* .... 27 E10 47 57N 3 57 E
Floodwood, *U.S.A.* 154 B8 46 55N 92 55W
Flora, *Phil.* .... 80 B3 18 14N 121 5 E
Flora, *Ill., U.S.A.* 156 F8 38 40N 88 29W
Flora, *Ind., U.S.A.* 157 D10 40 33N 86 31W
Florac, *France* .... 28 D7 44 20N 3 37 E
Florahome, *U.S.A.* 152 F8 29 44N 81 54W
Floral City, *U.S.A.* 153 C7 28 45N 82 17W
Florala, *U.S.A.* 149 K2 31 0N 86 20W
Florânia, *Brazil* .... 170 C4 6 8 S 36 49W
Floreana, I. = Santa María, I., *Ecuador* .... 172 a 1 20 S 90 25W
Florence = Firenze, *Italy* .... 45 E8 43 46N 11 15 E
Florence, *Ala., U.S.A.* 149 H2 34 48N 87 41W
Florence, *Ariz., U.S.A.* 159 K8 33 2N 111 23W
Florence, *Colo., U.S.A.* 154 F2 38 23N 105 8W
Florence, *Oreg., U.S.A.* 158 E1 43 58N 124 7W
Florence, *S.C., U.S.A.* 149 H6 34 12N 79 46W
Florence, L., *Australia* .... 127 D2 28 53 S 138 9 E
Florence Amerigo Vespucci ✈ (FLR), *Italy* .... 44 E8 43 49N 11 13 E
Florence Bay = Chitmba, *Malawi* 119 E3 10 35 S 34 13 E
Florence Pisa ✈ (PSA), *Italy* .... 44 E7 43 40N 10 22 E
Florencia, *Colombia* 168 C2 1 36N 75 36W
Florennes, *Belgium* .... 24 D4 50 15N 4 35 E
Florensac, *France* .... 28 E7 43 23N 3 28 E
Florenville, *Belgium* .... 24 E5 49 40N 5 19 E
Flores, *Azores* 9 d2 39 26N 31 13W
Flores, *Brazil* .... 170 C4 7 51 S 37 59W
Flores, *Guatemala* 164 C2 16 59N 89 50W
Flores, *Indonesia* .... 83 F2 8 35 S 121 0 E
Flores I., *Canada* 142 D3 49 20N 126 10W
Flores Sea, *Indonesia* 83 L8 24 40N 81 0W
Floresta, *Brazil* .... 170 C4 8 40 S 37 26W
Floreşti, *Moldova* .... 53 C13 47 53N 28 17 E
Floresville, *U.S.A.* 155 L5 29 8N 98 10W
Floriano, *Brazil* .... 170 C3 6 50 S 43 0W
Florianópolis, *Brazil* .... 175 B6 27 30 S 48 30W
Florida, *Cuba* 164 B4 21 32N 78 14W
Florida, *Uruguay* .... 175 C4 34 7 S 56 10W
Florida □, *U.S.A.* 149 L5 28 0N 82 0W
Florida, Straits of, *U.S.A.* 164 B4 25 0N 80 0W
Florida B., *U.S.A.* 164 B3 25 0N 80 45W
Florida City, *U.S.A.* 153 K9 25 27N 80 29W
Florida Is., *Solomon Is.* .... 133 M11 9 55 S 160 15 E
Florida Keys, *U.S.A.* 153 L8 24 40N 81 0W
Floridablanca, *Phil.* .... 80 D3 14 59N 120 31 E
Flóridia, *Italy* .... 47 E8 37 5N 15 9 E
Flórina, *Greece* .... 50 F5 40 48N 21 26 E
Flórina □, *Greece* .... 50 F5 40 45N 21 20 E
Florissant, *U.S.A.* 156 F6 38 48N 90 20W
Florø, *Norway* .... 18 C2 61 35N 5 1 E
Flotte, C. de, N. Cal. .... 133 U21 21 10 S 167 25 E
Flower Station, *Canada* 151 A8 45 10N 76 41W
Flowerpot I., *Canada* 150 A3 45 18N 81 38W
Floydada, *U.S.A.* 155 J4 33 59N 101 20W
Fludir, *Iceland* 11 C6 64 7N 20 6W
Flüelapass, *Switz.* .... 33 C9 46 46N 9 56 E
Flugumyri, *Iceland* 11 B7 65 34N 19 19W
Fluk, *Indonesia* .... 82 B3 1 42 S 127 44 E
Flúmen →, *Spain* 40 D4 41 43N 0 9W
Flumendosa →, *Italy* .... 46 C2 39 26N 9 37 E
Fluminimaggiore, *Italy* .... 46 C1 39 26N 8 30 E
Flushing = Vlissingen, *Neths.* .... 24 C3 51 26N 3 34 E
Flushing, *U.S.A.* 157 A13 43 4N 83 51W
Fluvià →, *Spain* .... 40 C8 42 12N 3 7 E
Fly →, *Papua N. G.* .... 83 C6 8 25 S 143 0 E
Flying Fish, C., *Antarctica* .... 7 D15 72 6 S 102 29W
Foam Lake, *Canada* 143 C8 51 40N 103 32W
Foça, *Turkey* .... 49 C8 38 39N 26 46 E
Fochabers, *U.K.* 22 D5 57 37N 3 6W
Focşani, *Romania* .... 53 E12 45 41N 27 15 E
Fodé, *C.A.R.* .... 114 A4 5 29N 23 18 E

Fodécontéa, *Guinea* 112 C2 10 50N 14 22W
Fogang, *China* .... 79 F9 23 52N 113 30 E
Foggaret el Arab, *Algeria* .... 111 C5 27 13N 2 49 E
Foggaret ez Zoua, *Algeria* .... 111 C5 27 20N 2 53 E
Fóggia, *Italy* .... 47 A8 41 27N 15 34 E
Foggo, *Nigeria* .... 113 C6 11 21N 9 57 E
Foglia →, *Italy* .... 45 E9 43 55N 12 54 E
Fogo, *Canada* 141 C9 49 43N 54 17W
Fogo, C. Verde Is. .... 9 j 15 5N 24 20W
Fogo I., *Canada* 141 C9 49 40N 54 5W
Fohnsdorf, *Austria* .... 34 D7 47 12N 14 40 E
Föhr, *Germany* .... 30 A4 54 43N 8 30 E
Foia, *Portugal* 43 H2 37 19N 8 37W
Foix, *France* .... 28 E5 42 58N 1 38 E
Fojnica, Bos.-H. .... 42 G2 43 59N 17 51 E
Fokís □, *Greece* .... 48 C4 38 30N 22 15 E
Fokku, *Nigeria* .... 113 C5 11 36N 4 32 E
Fokstua, *Norway* .... 18 B6 62 7N 9 17 E
Folda, Nord-Trøndelag, *Norway* .... 14 D14 64 32N 10 30 E
Folda, Nordland, *Norway* .... 14 C16 67 38N 14 50 E
Földeák, *Hungary* .... 52 D5 46 19N 20 30 E
Folégandros, *Greece* .... 48 E6 36 40N 24 55 E
Foley, *Botswana* .... 116 C4 21 34 S 27 21 E
Foley, *Ala., U.S.A.* 149 K2 30 24N 87 41W
Foley, *Fla., U.S.A.* 152 E3 30 4N 83 32W
Foleyet, *Canada* 140 C3 48 15N 82 25W
Folgefonni, *Norway* .... 18 D3 60 3N 6 23 E
Foligno, *Italy* .... 45 F9 42 57N 12 42 E
Folkestad, *Norway* .... 18 B3 62 7N 6 1 E
Folkestone, *U.K.* .... 21 F9 51 5N 1 12 E
Folkston, *U.S.A.* 152 E7 30 50N 82 0W
Folla →, *Norway* .... 18 B7 62 7N 10 37 E
Follansbee, *U.S.A.* 150 F4 40 19N 80 35W
Folldal, *Norway* .... 18 B7 62 8N 10 0 E
Follebu, *Norway* .... 18 C7 61 13N 10 16 E
Follónica, *Italy* .... 44 F7 42 55N 10 45 E
Follónica, G. di, *Italy* .... 44 F7 42 50N 10 43 E
Folsom L., *U.S.A.* 160 G5 38 42N 121 9W
Folteşti, *Romania* .... 53 E13 45 45N 28 5 E
Fomboni, *Comoros Is.* .... 121 a 12 18 S 43 46 E
Fomm er-Rîh Bay, *Malta* .... 38 F7 35 54N 14 20 E
Fond-du-Lac, *Canada* 143 B7 59 19N 107 12W
Fond-du-Lac →, *Canada* 143 B8 59 17N 106 0W
Fond du Lac, *U.S.A.* 156 D10 43 47N 88 27W
Fonda, *Iowa, U.S.A.* 156 B2 42 35N 94 51W
Fonda, *N.Y., U.S.A.* 151 D10 42 57N 74 22W
Fondi, *Italy* .... 46 A6 41 21N 13 25 E
Fonfría, *Spain* 42 D4 41 37N 6 9W
Fongafale, *Tuvalu* .... 134 H9 8 31 S 179 13 E
Fongen, *Norway* .... 18 B8 63 11N 11 38 E
Fonni, *Italy* .... 46 B2 40 7N 9 15 E
Fonsagrada = A Fonsagrada, *Spain* 42 B3 43 8N 7 4W
Fonseca, G. de, Cent. Amer. 164 D2 13 10N 87 40W
Font-Romeu, *France* .... 28 F5 42 31N 2 3 E
Fontaine-Française, *France* .... 27 E12 47 32N 5 21 E
Fontainebleau, *France* .... 27 D9 48 24N 2 40 E
Fontana, *U.S.A.* 161 L9 34 6N 117 26W
Fontana, L., *Argentina* .... 176 B2 44 55 S 71 30W
Fontas →, *Canada* 142 B4 58 14N 121 48W
Fonte Boa, *Brazil* .... 168 D4 2 33 S 66 0W
Fontem, *Cameroon* .... 113 D6 5 32N 9 52 E
Fontenay-le-Comte, *France* 28 B3 46 28N 0 48W
Fontenelle Reservoir, *U.S.A.* 158 E8 42 1N 110 3W
Fontur, *Iceland* 14 C6 66 23N 14 32W
Fonuafo'ou, *Tonga* .... 133 Q13 20 19 S 175 25W
Fonualei, *Tonga* .... 133 P13 18 1 S 174 19W
Fonyód, *Hungary* .... 52 D2 46 44N 17 33 E
Foochow = Fuzhou, *China* .... 77 D12 26 5N 119 16 E
Foping, *China* .... 74 H5 33 41N 108 0 E
Fora →, *Norway* .... 18 B7 62 57N 10 40 E
Foraker, Mt., *U.S.A.* 144 E10 62 58N 151 24W
Forari, *Vanuatu* .... 133 G6 17 40 S 168 31 E
Forbach, *France* .... 27 C13 49 10N 6 52 E
Forbes, *Australia* .... 129 B8 33 22 S 148 5 E
Forbesganj, *India* .... 93 F12 26 17N 87 18 E
Forcados, *Nigeria* .... 113 D6 5 26N 5 26 E
Forcados →, *Nigeria* .... 113 D6 5 25N 5 19 E
Forcalquier, *France* .... 29 E9 43 58N 5 47 E
Forchheim, *Germany* .... 31 F7 49 43N 11 2 E
Forclaz, Col de la, *Switz.* .... 32 D4 46 3N 7 2 E
Ford City, *Calif., U.S.A.* 161 K7 35 9N 119 27W
Ford City, *Pa., U.S.A.* 150 F5 40 46N 79 32W
Ford I., *U.S.A.* 145 K14 21 22N 157 58W
Fordate, *Indonesia* .... 83 C4 7 0 S 131 58 E
Førde, Hordaland, *Norway* .... 18 E2 59 36N 5 27 E
Førde, Sogn og Fjordane, *Norway* .... 18 C2 61 27N 5 53 E
Førdefjorden, *Norway* .... 18 C2 61 30N 5 18 E
Førdesfjord, *Norway* .... 18 E2 59 25N 5 20 E
Ford's Bridge, *Australia* .... 129 A4 29 41 S 145 29 E
Fordyce, *U.S.A.* 155 J8 33 49N 92 25W
Forécariah, *Guinea* 112 D2 9 28N 13 10W
Forel, Mt., *Greenland* 10 D7 66 52N 36 55W
Foremost, *Canada* 142 D6 49 26N 111 34W
Forest, *Canada* 150 C3 43 6N 82 0W
Forest, *U.S.A.* 155 J10 32 22N 89 29W
Forest Acres, *U.S.A.* 152 A9 34 1N 80 58W
Forest City, *Iowa, U.S.A.* 156 B3 43 16N 93 39W
Forest City, *N.C., U.S.A.* 149 H5 35 20N 81 52W
Forest City, *Pa., U.S.A.* 151 E9 41 39N 75 28W
Forest Grove, *U.S.A.* 160 E3 45 31N 123 7W
Forest Park, *U.S.A.* 152 B5 33 37N 84 22W
Forestburg, *Canada* 142 C6 52 35N 112 1W
Foreste Casentinesi-Monte Falterona-Campigna, Parco Nazionale delle △, *Italy* .... 45 E8 43 50N 11 48 E
Foresthill, *U.S.A.* 160 F6 39 1N 120 49W
Forestier Pen., *Australia* .... 127 D4 43 0 S 148 0 E
Forestville, *Canada* 141 C6 48 48N 69 2W
Forestville, *Calif., U.S.A.* 160 G4 38 28N 122 54W
Forestville, *N.Y., U.S.A.* 150 D5 42 28N 79 10W
Forêt d'Orient, Parc Naturel Régional de la △, *France* .... 27 D11 48 16N 4 25 E
Forêt du Day, Parc Nat. du △, *Djibouti* .... 111 E4 11 56N 42 40 E
Forez, Mts. du, *France* .... 28 C7 45 40N 3 50 E
Forfar, *U.K.* 22 E6 56 39N 2 53W
Forggensee, *Germany* .... 33 A11 47 35N 10 44 E
Forillon, Parc Nat. du △, *Canada* 141 C7 48 46N 64 12W
Forks, *U.S.A.* 160 C2 47 57N 124 23W
Forksville, *U.S.A.* 151 E8 41 29N 76 35W
Forlì, *Italy* .... 45 D9 44 13N 12 3 E
Forman, *U.S.A.* 154 B6 46 7N 97 38W
Formazza, *Italy* .... 44 B6 46 23N 8 26 E
Formby Pt., *U.K.* 20 D4 53 33N 3 6W
Formentera, *Spain* .... 39 B1 38 43N 1 27 E
Formentor, C. de, *Spain* .... 38 B4 39 58N 3 13 E
Former Yugoslav Republic of Macedonia = Macedonia ■, *Europe* .... 50 E5 41 53N 21 40 E
Fórmia, *Italy* .... 46 A6 41 15N 13 37 E
Formiga, *Brazil* .... 171 F2 20 27 S 45 25W
Formígine, *Italy* .... 44 D7 44 37N 10 51 E
Formosa = Taiwan ■, *Asia* .... 77 F13 23 30N 121 0 E
Formosa, *Argentina* .... 174 B4 26 15 S 58 10W
Formosa, *Brazil* .... 171 E2 15 32 S 47 20W
Formosa □, *Argentina* .... 174 B4 25 0 S 60 0W
Formosa, Serra, *Brazil* .... 169 F8 12 0 S 55 0W
Formosa B. = Ungwana B., *Kenya* .... 118 C5 2 40 S 40 20 E
Formosa Strait = Taiwan Strait, *Asia* .... 77 E12 24 40N 120 0 E
Formoso →, *Brazil* .... 171 D2 10 34 S 49 50W
Fornells, *Spain* .... 38 A5 40 3N 4 7 E
Fornos de Algodres, *Portugal* 42 E3 40 38N 7 32W
Fornovo di Taro, *Italy* .... 44 D7 44 42N 10 6 E

Føroyar, Atl. Oc. 14 F9 62 0N 7 0W
Forres, *U.K.* 22 D5 57 37N 3 37W
Forrest, Vic., Australia .... 128 E5 38 33 S 143 47 E
Forrest, W. Austral., Australia .... 125 F4 30 51 S 128 6 E
Forrest, Mt., *Australia* .... 125 D4 24 48 S 127 45 E
Forrest City, *U.S.A.* 155 H9 35 1N 90 47W
Forreston, *U.S.A.* 156 B7 42 8N 89 35W
Fors, *Sweden* .... 16 D10 60 14N 16 21 E
Forsand, *Norway* .... 18 B3 58 54N 6 5 E
Forsayth, *Australia* .... 126 B3 18 33 S 143 34 E
Forshaga, *Sweden* .... 16 E7 59 33N 13 29 E
Förslöv, *Sweden* .... 17 H6 56 21N 12 48 E
Forsmo, *Sweden* .... 16 A11 63 16N 17 54 E
Forssa, *Finland* .... 15 F20 60 49N 23 38 E
Forst, *Germany* .... 30 D10 51 45N 14 37 E
Forster, *Australia* .... 129 B10 32 12 S 152 31 E
Forsvik, *Sweden* .... 17 F8 58 35N 14 26 E
Forsyth, Ga., U.S.A. 152 B6 33 2N 83 56W
Forsyth, Mont., U.S.A. 158 C10 46 16N 106 41W
Forsyth I., *N.Z.* .... 131 A9 40 58 S 174 5 E
Fort Abbas, *Pakistan* .... 92 E5 29 12N 72 52 E
Fort Albany, *Canada* 140 B3 52 15N 81 35W
Fort Ann, *U.S.A.* 151 C11 43 25N 73 30W
Fort Assiniboine, *Canada* 142 C5 54 20N 114 45W
Fort Atkinson, *U.S.A.* 157 B8 42 56N 88 50W
Fort Augustus, *U.K.* 22 D4 57 9N 4 42W
Fort Beaufort, S. Africa .... 116 E4 32 46 S 26 40 E
Fort Benton, *U.S.A.* 158 C8 47 49N 110 40W
Fort Bragg, *U.S.A.* 158 G2 39 26N 123 48W
Fort Bridger, *U.S.A.* 158 F8 41 19N 110 23W
Fort Caroline Nat. Memorial ◯, *U.S.A.* 152 E8 30 23N 81 30W
Fort Chipewyan, *Canada* 143 B6 58 42N 111 8W
Fort Clatsop Nat. Memorial ◯, *U.S.A.* 160 D3 46 8N 123 53W
Fort Collins, *U.S.A.* 154 E2 40 35N 105 5W
Fort-Coulonge, *Canada* 140 C4 45 50N 76 45W
Fort Covington, *U.S.A.* 151 B10 44 59N 74 29W
Fort Davis, Ala., U.S.A. 152 J3 32 15N 85 43W
Fort Davis, Tex., U.S.A. 155 K3 30 35N 103 54W
Fort-de-France, *Martinique* .... 166 c 14 36N 61 2W
Fort de Polignac = Illizi, Algeria 111 C6 26 31N 8 32 E
Fort Defiance, *U.S.A.* 159 J9 35 45N 109 5W
Fort Dodge, *U.S.A.* 156 B2 42 30N 94 11W
Fort Drum, *U.S.A.* 153 H9 27 32N 80 48W
Fort Edward, *U.S.A.* 151 C11 43 16N 73 35W
Fort Erie, *Canada* 150 D6 42 54N 78 56W
Fort Fairfield, *U.S.A.* 149 B12 46 46N 67 50W
Fort Flatters = Bordj Omar Driss, Algeria .... 111 C6 28 10N 6 40 E
Fort Frances, *Canada* 143 D10 48 36N 93 24W
Fort Frederica Nat. Monument ◯, *U.S.A.* 152 D8 31 13N 81 23W
Fort Gaines, *U.S.A.* 152 D4 31 36N 85 3W
Fort Garland, *U.S.A.* 159 H11 37 26N 105 26W
Fort George = Chisasibi, *Canada* 140 B4 53 50N 79 0W
Fort Good-Hope, *Canada* 138 B7 66 14N 128 40W
Fort Hancock, *U.S.A.* 159 L11 31 18N 105 51W
Fort Hertz = Putao, *Burma* .... 90 B6 27 28N 97 30 E
Fort Hill = Chitipa, *Malawi* .... 119 D3 9 41 S 33 19 E
Fort Hope, *Canada* 140 B2 51 30N 88 0W
Fort Irwin, *U.S.A.* 161 K10 35 16N 116 34W
Fort Kent, *U.S.A.* 149 B11 47 15N 68 36W
Fort Klamath, *U.S.A.* 158 E3 42 42N 122 0W
Fort Laramie, *U.S.A.* 154 D2 42 13N 104 31W
Fort Lauderdale, *U.S.A.* 153 J9 26 7N 80 8W
Fort Liard, *Canada* 142 A4 60 14N 123 30W
Fort Liberté, *Haiti* 165 C5 19 42N 71 51W
Fort Lupton, *U.S.A.* 154 E2 40 5N 104 49W
Fort Mackay, *Canada* 142 B6 57 12N 111 41W
Fort Macleod, *Canada* 142 D6 49 45N 113 30W
Fort McMurray, *Canada* 142 B6 56 44N 111 7W
Fort McPherson, *Canada* 138 B6 67 30N 134 55W
Fort Madison, *U.S.A.* 156 E9 40 38N 91 27W
Fort Manning = Mchinji, *Malawi* .... 119 E3 13 47 S 32 58 E
Fort Matanzas Nat. Monument ◯, *U.S.A.* 152 F8 29 43N 81 14W
Fort Meade, *U.S.A.* 153 H8 27 45N 81 48W
Fort Mitchell, *U.S.A.* 152 C4 32 20N 85 1W
Fort Morgan, *U.S.A.* 154 E3 40 15N 103 48W
Fort Myers, *U.S.A.* 153 J8 26 39N 81 52W
Fort Myers Beach, *U.S.A.* 153 J8 26 33N 81 52W
Fort Myers Villas, *U.S.A.* 153 J8 26 33N 81 52W
Fort Nelson, *Canada* 142 B4 58 50N 122 44W
Fort Nelson →, *Canada* 142 B4 59 32N 124 0W
Fort Norman = Tulita, *Canada* 138 B7 64 57N 125 30W
Fort Ogden, *U.S.A.* 153 H8 27 5N 81 57W
Fort Payne, *U.S.A.* 149 H3 34 26N 85 43W
Fort Peck, *U.S.A.* 158 B10 48 1N 106 27W
Fort Peck Dam, *U.S.A.* 158 C10 48 0N 106 26W
Fort Peck L., *U.S.A.* 158 C10 48 0N 106 26W
Fort Pierce, *U.S.A.* 153 H9 27 27N 80 20W
Fort Pierre, *U.S.A.* 154 C4 44 21N 100 22W
Fort Pierre Bordes = Ti-n-Zaouatene, Algeria .... 111 E5 19 55N 2 55 E
Fort Plain, *U.S.A.* 151 D10 42 56N 74 37W
Fort Portal, *Uganda* .... 118 B3 0 40N 30 20 E
Fort Providence, *Canada* 142 A5 61 3N 117 40W
Fort Pulaski Nat. Monument ◯, *U.S.A.* 152 C9 32 2N 80 56W
Fort Qu'Appelle, *Canada* 143 C8 50 45N 103 50W
Fort Recovery, *U.S.A.* 157 D12 40 25N 84 47W
Fort Resolution, *Canada* 142 A6 61 10N 113 40W
Fort Rixon, *Zimbabwe* .... 119 G2 20 2 S 29 17 E
Fort Ross, *U.S.A.* 160 G3 38 32N 123 13W
Fort Rupert = Waskaganish, *Canada* 140 B4 51 30N 78 40W
Fort St. James, *Canada* 142 C4 54 30N 124 10W
Fort St. John, *Canada* 142 B4 56 15N 120 50W
Fort Saskatchewan, *Canada* 142 C6 53 40N 113 15W
Fort Scott, *U.S.A.* 155 G7 37 50N 94 42W
Fort Severn, *Canada* 140 A2 56 0N 87 40W
Fort Shevchenko, *Kazakhstan* .... 61 H10 44 35N 50 23 E
Fort Simpson, *Canada* 142 A4 61 45N 121 15W
Fort Smith, *Canada* 142 B6 60 0N 111 51W
Fort Smith, *U.S.A.* 155 H7 35 23N 94 25W
Fort Stockton, *U.S.A.* 155 K3 30 53N 102 53W
Fort Sumner, *U.S.A.* 155 H2 34 28N 104 15W
Fort Thomas, *U.S.A.* 157 E12 39 5N 84 27W
Fort Thompson, *U.S.A.* 154 C5 44 3N 99 26W
Fort Union Nat. Monument ◯, *U.S.A.* 155 H2 35 54N 105 1W
Fort Valley, *U.S.A.* 152 C6 32 33N 83 53W
Fort Vermilion, *Canada* 142 B5 58 24N 116 0W
Fort Walton Beach, *U.S.A.* 153 E3 30 25N 86 36W
Fort Wayne, *U.S.A.* 157 C11 41 4N 85 9W
Fort White, *U.S.A.* 152 F7 29 55N 82 43W
Fort William, *U.K.* 22 E3 56 49N 5 7W
Fort Worth, *U.S.A.* 155 J6 32 45N 97 18W
Fort Yates, *U.S.A.* 154 B4 46 5N 100 38W
Fort Yukon, *U.S.A.* 144 C11 66 34N 145 16W
Fortaleza, *Bolivia* .... 172 C4 12 6 S 66 49W
Fortaleza, *Brazil* .... 170 B4 3 45 S 38 35W
Forteau, *Canada* 141 B8 51 28N 56 58W
Fortescue →, *Australia* .... 124 D2 21 0 S 116 4 E
Forth →, *U.K.* 22 E5 56 9N 3 50W
Forth, Firth of, *U.K.* 22 E6 56 5N 2 55W
Forthassa Rharbia, *Algeria* 111 B4 32 52N 1 18W
Fortín Garrapatal, *Paraguay* .... 173 E2 20 57 S 61 50W
Fortín General Pando, *Paraguay* .... 173 D6 19 45 S 59 47W
Fortín Ingavi, *Paraguay* .... 173 D6 19 45 S 60 7W
Fortín Madrejón, *Paraguay* .... 173 D6 20 10 S 59 54W
Fortín Uno, *Argentina* .... 176 A3 38 50 S 65 18W
Fortore →, *Italy* .... 45 G12 41 55N 15 17 E
Fortrose, *N.Z.* .... 131 G3 46 38 S 168 45 E

Fortrose, *U.K.* **22 D4** 57 35N 4 9W
Fortuna, *Spain* **41 G3** 38 11N 1 7W
Fortuna, *Calif., U.S.A.* **158 F1** 40 36N 124 9W
Fortuna, *N. Dak., U.S.A.* **154 A3** 48 55N 103 47W
Fortuna Ledge, *U.S.A.* **144 F7** 61 53N 162 5W
Fortune, *Canada* **141 C8** 47 4N 55 50W
Fortune B., *Canada* **141 C8** 47 30N 55 22W
Forūr, *Iran* .... **97 E7** 26 17N 54 32 E
Fos-sur-Mer, *France* .... **29 E8** 43 26N 4 56 E
Foshan, *China* .... **77 F9** 23 4N 113 5 E
Fosna, *Norway* .... **14 E14** 63 50N 10 20 E
Fosnavåg, *Norway* .... **18 B2** 62 22N 5 38 E
Foso, *Ghana* **113 D4** 5 43N 1 15W
Fossano, *Italy* .... **44 D4** 44 33N 7 43 E
Foss, *Iceland* **11 D9** 63 51N 17 52W
Fossil, *U.S.A.* **158 D3** 45 0N 120 9W
Fossil Butte Nat. Mon. ◻, *U.S.A.* .. **158 F8** 41 50N 110 27W
Fossombrone, *Italy* .... **45 E9** 43 41N 12 48 E
Fossvellir, *Iceland* **11 B12** 65 27N 14 37W
Foster, *Australia* .... **129 E7** 38 40 S 146 15 E
Foster, *Canada* **151 A12** 45 17N 72 30W
Foster, *U.S.A.* **157 F12** 38 48N 84 13W
Foster ➤, *Canada* **143 B7** 55 47N 105 49W
Fosters Ra., *Australia* .... **126 C1** 21 35 S 133 48 E
Fostoria, *U.S.A.* **157 C13** 41 10N 83 25W
Fotadrevo, *Madag.* .... **117 C8** 24 3 S 45 1 E
Fouesnant, *France* **26 E2** 47 53N 4 1W
Fougamou, *Gabon* .... **114 C2** 1 16 S 10 30 E
Fougères, *France* **26 D5** 48 21N 1 14W
Foul Pt., *Sri Lanka* .... **95 K5** 8 35N 81 18 E
Foula, *U.K.* **22 A6** 60 10N 2 5W
Foulalaba, *Mali* **112 C3** 10 40N 7 20W
Foulness I., *U.K.* .... **21 F8** 51 36N 0 55 E
Foulpointe, *Madag.* .... **117 B8** 17 41 S 49 31 E
Foulweather, C., *U.S.A.* **146 B2** 44 50N 124 5W
Foulwind, C., *N.Z.* .... **131 B6** 41 45 S 171 28 E
Foum Assaka, *Morocco* **110 C2** 29 8N 10 24W
Foum Zguid, *Morocco* **110 B3** 30 2N 6 59W
Foumban, *Cameroon* .... **113 D7** 5 45N 10 50 E
Foumbot, *Cameroon* .... **113 D7** 5 31N 10 28 E
Foumbouni, *Comoros Is.* .... **121 a** 11 52 S 43 32 E
Foumirate, *Algeria* **110 C4** 27 30N 3 12W
Foundiougne, *Senegal* **112 C1** 14 5N 16 32W
Fountain, *Colo., U.S.A.* **154 F2** 38 41N 104 42W
Fountain, *Fla., U.S.A.* **152 K4** 30 29N 85 25W
Fountain Springs, *U.S.A.* **161 K8** 35 54N 118 51W
Four Mountains, Is. of, *U.S.A.* .. **144 K5** 53 0N 170 0W
Fourchambault, *France* .... **27 E10** 47 2N 3 3 E
Fouriesburg, *S. Africa* .... **116 D4** 28 38 S 28 14 E
Fourmies, *France* .... **27 B11** 50 1N 4 2 E
Fournás, *Greece* .... **48 B3** 39 3N 21 52 E
Foúrnoi, *Greece* .... **49 D8** 37 36N 26 32 E
Fours, *France* .... **27 F10** 46 50N 3 42 E
Fourth Cataract, *Sudan* .... **106 D3** 18 47N 32 3 E
Fouta Djalon, *Guinea* **112 C2** 11 20N 12 10W
Foux, Cap-à-, *Haiti* **165 C5** 19 43N 73 27W
Foveaux Str., *N.Z.* .... **131 G3** 46 42 S 168 10 E
Fowey, *U.K.* **21 G3** 50 20N 4 39W
Fowler, *Calif., U.S.A.* **160 J7** 36 38N 119 41W
Fowler, *Colo., U.S.A.* **154 F3** 38 8N 104 2W
Fowler, *Ind., U.S.A.* **157 D9** 40 37N 87 19W
Fowler, *Mich., U.S.A.* **157 B12** 43 0N 84 45W
Fowlers B., *Australia* .... **125 F5** 31 59 S 132 34 E
Fowlerville, *U.S.A.* **157 B12** 42 40N 84 4W
Fowman, *Iran* .... **97 B6** 37 13N 49 19 E
Fox ➤, *Canada* **143 B10** 56 3N 93 18W
Fox Creek, *Canada* **142 C5** 54 24N 116 48W
Fox Is., *U.S.A.* **144 K6** 53 0N 168 0W
Fox Lake, *Canada* **142 B6** 58 28N 114 31W
Fox Lake, *U.S.A.* **157 B8** 42 24N 88 11W
Fox Valley, *Canada* **143 C7** 50 30N 109 25W
Foxboro, *U.S.A.* **151 D13** 42 4N 71 16W
Foxdale, *Australia* .... **126 J6** 20 22 S 148 35 E
Foxe Basin, *Canada* **139 B12** 66 0N 77 0W
Foxe Chan., *Canada* **139 B11** 65 0N 80 0W
Foxe Pen., *Canada* **139 B12** 65 0N 76 0W
Foxton, *N.Z.* .... **130 G4** 40 29 S 175 18 E
Foyle, Lough, *U.K.* **23 A4** 55 7N 7 4W
Foynes, *Ireland* **23 D2** 52 37N 9 7W
Foz, *Spain* **42 B3** 43 33N 7 20W
Foz do Copeá, *Brazil* .... **169 D5** 3 52 S 63 19W
Foz do Cunene, *Angola* .... **116 B1** 17 15 S 11 48 E
Foz do Gregório, *Brazil* .... **172 B3** 6 47 S 70 44W
Foz do Iguaçu, *Brazil* .... **175 B5** 25 30 S 54 30W
Foz do Mamoriá, *Brazil* .... **168 D4** 2 27 S 66 32W
Foz do Riosinho, *Brazil* .... **172 B3** 7 11 S 71 50W
Frackville, *U.S.A.* **151 F8** 40 47N 76 14W
Fraga, *Spain* .... **40 D5** 41 32N 0 21 E
Fraile Muerto, *Uruguay* .... **175 C5** 32 31 S 54 32W
Framingham, *U.S.A.* **151 D13** 42 17N 71 25W
Framnes, *Iceland* **11 A6** 66 1N 20 26W
Frampol, *Poland* .... **55 H9** 50 41N 22 40 E
Franca, *Brazil* .... **171 F2** 20 33 S 47 30W
Francavilla al Mare, *Italy* ...... **45 F11** 42 25N 14 17 E
Francavilla Fontana, *Italy* ...... **47 B10** 40 32N 17 35 E
France ■, *Europe* .... **25 C5** 47 0N 3 0 E
Frances, *Australia* .... **128 D4** 36 41 S 140 55 E
Frances ➤, *Canada* **142 A3** 60 16N 129 10W
Frances L., *Canada* **142 A3** 61 23N 129 30W
Francesville, *U.S.A.* **157 D10** 40 59N 86 53W
Franceville, *Gabon* .... **114 C2** 1 40 S 13 32 E
Franche-Comté, *France* .... **27 F12** 46 50N 5 55 E
Franches Montagnes, *Switz.* .... **32 B4** 47 10N 7 0 E
Francis Case, L., *U.S.A.* **154 D5** 43 4N 98 34W
Francisco Beltrão, *Brazil* .... **175 B5** 26 5 S 53 4W
Francisco de Orellana, *Ecuador* .. **168 D2** 0 28 S 76 58W
Francisco I. Madero, Coahuila,
  Mexico **162 B4** 25 48N 103 18W
Francisco I. Madero, Durango,
  Mexico **162 C4** 24 32N 104 22W
Francisco Sá, *Brazil* .... **171 E3** 16 28 S 43 30W
Francistown, *Botswana* .... **117 C4** 21 7 S 27 33 E
Francofonte, *Italy* .... **47 E7** 37 14N 14 53 E
François, *Canada* **141 C8** 47 35N 56 45W
François-Joseph, Chutes, *Dem. Rep.
  of the Congo* .... **115 D3** 7 37 S 17 17 E
François L., *Canada* **142 C3** 54 0N 125 30W
François Peron Nat. Park △,
  Australia .... **125 E1** 25 42 S 113 33 E
Franeker, *Neths.* .... **24 A5** 53 12N 5 33 E
Frank Hann Nat. Park △, *Australia* .. **125 F3** 32 52 S 120 19 E
Frankado, *Djibouti* .... **107 E5** 12 30N 43 12 E
Frankenberg, *Germany* .... **30 D4** 51 3N 8 48 E
Frankenhöhe, Naturpark ◻,
  Germany .... **31 F6** 49 20N 10 25 E
Frankenwald, *Germany* .... **31 E7** 50 20N 11 30 E
Frankenwald, Naturpark ◻,
  Germany .... **31 E7** 50 15N 11 30 E
Frankford, *Canada* **150 B7** 44 12N 77 36W
Frankford, *U.S.A.* **156 E5** 39 29N 91 19W
Frankfort, *S. Africa* .... **117 D4** 27 17 S 28 30 E
Frankfort, *Ind., U.S.A.* **157 D10** 40 17N 86 31W
Frankfort, *Kans., U.S.A.* **154 F6** 39 42N 96 25W
Frankfort, *Ky., U.S.A.* **157 F12** 38 12N 84 52W
Frankfort, *N.Y., U.S.A.* **151 C9** 43 2N 75 4W
Frankfort, *Ohio, U.S.A.* **157 E13** 39 24N 83 11W
Frankfurt, Brandenburg, *Germany* .. **30 C10** 52 20N 14 32 E
Frankfurt, Hessen, *Germany* .... **31 E4** 50 7N 8 41 E
Frankfurt International ✈ (FRA),
  Germany .... **31 E4** 50 1N 8 34 E
Fränkische Alb, *Germany* .... **31 F7** 49 10N 11 23 E
Fränkische Rezat ➤, *Germany* .. **31 F7** 49 11N 11 1 E
Fränkische Saale ➤, *Germany* .. **31 E5** 50 3N 9 42 E

Fränkische Schweiz, *Germany* ... **31 F7** 49 50N 11 16 E
Fränkische Schweiz-Veldensteiner
  Forst, Naturpark ◻, *Germany* .. **31 F7** 49 45N 11 22 E
Frankland ➤, *Australia* .... **125 G2** 35 0 S 116 48 E
Franklin, *Ga., U.S.A.* **152 B4** 33 17N 85 6W
Franklin, *Ind., U.S.A.* **157 E10** 39 29N 86 3W
Franklin, *Ky., U.S.A.* **149 G2** 36 43N 86 35W
Franklin, *La., U.S.A.* **155 L9** 29 48N 91 30W
Franklin, *Mass., U.S.A.* **151 D13** 42 5N 71 24W
Franklin, *N.H., U.S.A.* **151 C13** 43 27N 71 39W
Franklin, *Nebr., U.S.A.* **154 E5** 40 6N 98 57W
Franklin, *Ohio, U.S.A.* **157 E12** 39 34N 84 18W
Franklin, *Pa., U.S.A.* **150 E5** 41 24N 79 50W
Franklin, *Va., U.S.A.* **149 G7** 36 41N 76 56W
Franklin, *W. Va., U.S.A.* **148 F6** 38 39N 79 20W
Franklin, Pt., *U.S.A.* **144 A8** 70 55N 158 48W
Franklin B., *Canada* **138 B7** 69 45N 126 0W
Franklin D. Roosevelt L., *U.S.A.* .. **158 B4** 48 18N 118 9W
Franklin-Gordon Wild Rivers Nat.
  Park △, *Australia* .... **127 D4** 42 19 S 145 51 E
Franklin Harb., *Australia* .... **128 B2** 33 43 S 136 55 E
Franklin I., *Antarctica* .... **7 D11** 76 10 S 168 30 E
Franklin L., *U.S.A.* **158 F6** 40 25N 115 22W
Franklin Mts., *Canada* **138 A10** 72 0N 96 0W
Franklin Mts., *N.Z.* .... **131 E2** 44 55 S 167 45 E
Franklin Str., *Canada* **138 A10** 72 0N 96 0W
Franklinton, *U.S.A.* **155 K9** 30 51N 90 9W
Franklinville, *U.S.A.* **150 D6** 42 20N 78 27W
Franklyn Mt., *N.Z.* .... **131 C7** 42 4 S 172 42 E
Franks Pk., *U.S.A.* **158 E9** 43 58N 109 18W
Frankston, *Australia* .... **129 E6** 38 8 S 145 8 E
Frånö, *Sweden* .... **16 B11** 62 55N 17 56 E
Fransfontein, *Namibia* .... **116 C2** 20 12 S 15 1 E
Fränsta, *Sweden* .... **16 B10** 62 30N 16 11 E
Frantsa Iosifa, Zemlya, *Russia* .. **66 A6** 82 0N 55 0 E
Franz, *Canada* **140 C3** 48 25N 84 30W
Franz Josef Land = Frantsa Iosifa,
  Zemlya, *Russia* .... **66 A6** 82 0N 55 0 E
Franz Josef Strauss, Munich ✈
  (MUC), *Germany* .... **31 G7** 48 20N 11 50 E
Franzburg, *Germany* .... **30 A8** 54 11N 12 51 E
Frascati, *Italy* .... **45 G9** 41 48N 12 41 E
Fraser, *U.S.A.* **150 D2** 42 32N 82 57W
Fraser ➤, *B.C., Canada* **142 D4** 49 7N 123 11W
Fraser ➤, *Nfld., Canada* **141 A7** 56 39N 62 10W
Fraser, Mt., *Australia* .... **125 E2** 25 35 S 118 20 E
Fraser I., *Australia* .... **127 D5** 25 15 S 153 10 E
Fraser Lake, *Canada* **142 C4** 54 0N 124 50W
Fraser Nat. Park △, *Australia* ... **129 D6** 37 9 S 145 51 E
Fraserburg, *S. Africa* .... **116 E3** 31 55 S 21 30 E
Fraserburg Road = Leeu Gamka,
  S. Africa .... **116 E3** 32 47 S 21 59 E
Fraserburgh, *U.K.* **22 D6** 57 42N 2 1W
Fraserdale, *Canada* **140 C3** 49 55N 81 37W
Frasertown, *N.Z.* .... **130 E6** 38 58 S 177 28 E
Frashër, *Albania* .... **50 F4** 40 23N 20 30 E
Frasne, *France* .... **27 F13** 46 50N 6 10 E
Frătești, *Romania* .... **53 G10** 43 58N 25 58 E
Frauenfeld, *Switz.* .... **33 A7** 47 34N 8 54 E
Fray Bentos, *Uruguay* .... **174 C4** 33 10 S 58 15W
Frechilla, *Spain* **42 C6** 42 8N 4 50W
Fredericia, *Denmark* .... **17 J3** 55 34N 9 45 E
Frederick, *Md., U.S.A.* **148 F7** 39 25N 77 25W
Frederick, *Okla., U.S.A.* **155 H5** 34 23N 99 1W
Frederick, *S. Dak., U.S.A.* **154 C5** 45 50N 98 31W
Frederick E. Hyde Fjord, *Greenland* .. **10 A8** 83 25N 29 0W
Fredericksburg, *Pa., U.S.A.* **151 F8** 40 27N 76 26W
Fredericksburg, *Tex., U.S.A.* **155 K5** 30 16N 98 52W
Fredericksburg, *Va., U.S.A.* **148 F7** 38 18N 77 28W
Fredericktown, *Mo., U.S.A.* **155 G9** 37 34N 90 18W
Fredericktown, *Ohio, U.S.A.* **150 F2** 40 29N 82 33W
Frederico I. Madero, Presa, *Mexico* .. **162 B3** 28 7N 105 40W
Frederico Westphalen, *Brazil* ... **175 B5** 27 22 S 53 24W
Fredericton, *Canada* **141 C6** 45 57N 66 40W
Fredericton Junction, *Canada* ... **141 C6** 45 41N 66 40W
Frederiksborg Amtskommune ◻,
  Denmark .... **17 J6** 55 50N 12 10 E
Frederikshåb = Paamiut, *Greenland* .. **10 E6** 62 0N 49 43W
Frederikshald = Halden, *Norway* .. **18 E9** 59 9N 11 23 E
Frederikshavn, *Denmark* .... **17 G4** 57 28N 10 31 E
Frederikssund, *Denmark* .... **17 J6** 55 50N 12 3 E
Frederiksted, *U.S. Virgin Is.* **165 C7** 17 43N 64 53W
Frederiksværk, *Denmark* .... **17 J6** 55 58N 12 4 E
Fredonia, *Ariz., U.S.A.* **159 H7** 36 57N 112 32W
Fredonia, *Kans., U.S.A.* **155 G7** 37 32N 95 49W
Fredonia, *N.Y., U.S.A.* **150 D5** 42 26N 79 20W
Fredriksberg, *Sweden* .... **16 D8** 60 8N 14 23 E
Fredrikstad, *Norway* .... **18 E7** 59 13N 10 57 E
Free State ◻, *S. Africa* .... **116 D4** 28 30 S 27 0 E
Freeburg, *U.S.A.* **156 F8** 38 19N 91 56W
Freehold, *U.S.A.* **151 F10** 40 16N 74 17W
Freel Peak, *U.S.A.* **160 G7** 38 52N 119 54W
Freeland, *U.S.A.* **151 E9** 41 1N 75 54W
Freels, C., *Canada* **141 C9** 49 15N 53 30W
Freeman, *Calif., U.S.A.* **161 K9** 35 35N 117 53W
Freeman, *Mo., U.S.A.* **156 F7** 38 37N 94 30W
Freeman, *S. Dak., U.S.A.* **154 D6** 43 21N 97 26W
Freeport, *Bahamas* **164 A4** 26 30N 78 47W
Freeport, *Fla., U.S.A.* **152 E3** 30 30N 86 8W
Freeport, *Ill., U.S.A.* **156 B7** 42 23N 89 38W
Freeport, *N.Y., U.S.A.* **151 F11** 40 39N 73 35W
Freeport, *Ohio, U.S.A.* **150 F3** 40 12N 81 15W
Freeport, *Pa., U.S.A.* **150 F5** 40 41N 79 41W
Freeport, *Tex., U.S.A.* **155 L7** 28 57N 95 21W
Freetown, *S. Leone* **112 D2** 8 30N 13 17W
Frégate, L., *Canada* **140 B5** 53 15N 74 45W
Fregenal de la Sierra, *Spain* **43 G4** 38 10N 6 39W
Fregene, *Italy* .... **45 G9** 41 51N 12 12 E
Fréhel, C., *France* **26 D4** 48 40N 2 20W
Freiberg, *Germany* .... **30 E9** 50 55N 13 20 E
Freibourg = Fribourg, *Switz.* .... **32 C4** 46 49N 7 9 E
Freiburg, Baden-W., *Germany* ... **31 H3** 47 59N 7 51 E
Freiburg, Niedersachsen, *Germany* .. **30 B5** 53 49N 9 16 E
Freiburger Alpen, *Switz.* .... **32 C4** 46 37N 7 10 E
Freilassing, *Germany* .... **31 H8** 47 50N 12 58 E
Freire, *Chile* .... **176 A2** 38 54 S 72 38W
Freirina, *Chile* .... **174 B1** 28 30 S 71 10W
Freising, *Germany* .... **31 G7** 48 24N 11 45 E
Freistadt, *Austria* .... **34 C7** 48 30N 14 30 E
Freital, *Germany* .... **30 D9** 51 1N 13 39 E
Fréjus, *France* .... **29 E10** 43 25N 6 44 E
Fremantle, *Australia* .... **125 F2** 32 7 S 115 47 E
Fremont, *Calif., U.S.A.* **160 H4** 37 32N 121 57W
Fremont, *Ind., U.S.A.* **157 C12** 41 44N 84 56W
Fremont, *Iowa, U.S.A.* **156 C4** 41 13N 92 26W
Fremont, *Mich., U.S.A.* **148 D3** 43 28N 85 57W
Fremont, *Nebr., U.S.A.* **154 E6** 41 26N 96 30W
Fremont, *Ohio, U.S.A.* **157 C13** 41 21N 83 7W
Fremont ➤, *U.S.A.* **159 G8** 38 24N 110 42W
Fremont Camp, *U.S.A.* **160 H5** 37 53N 121 16W
French Creek ➤, *U.S.A.* **150 E5** 41 24N 79 50W
French Frigate Shoals, *U.S.A.* ... **145 G10** 23 45N 166 10W
French Guiana ☑, *S. Amer.* **169 C7** 4 0N 53 0W
French Lick, *U.S.A.* **157 F10** 38 33N 86 37W
French Pass, *N.Z.* .... **131 A8** 40 55 S 173 55 E
French Polynesia ☑, *Pac. Oc.* ... **135 K13** 20 0 S 145 0W
French Territory of the Afars and
  Issas = Djibouti ■, *Africa* ..... **107 E5** 12 0N 43 0 E
Frenchman Cr. ➤, *N. Amer.* **158 B10** 48 31N 107 10W
Frenchman Cr. ➤, *U.S.A.* **154 E4** 40 14N 100 50W
Frenda, *Algeria* .... **111 A5** 35 2N 1 1 E
Frenstát pod Radhoštěm, *Czech Rep.* .. **35 B11** 49 35N 18 13 E

Fresco, *Ivory C.* **112 D3** 5 3N 5 31W
Fresco ➤, *Brazil* .... **173 B7** 7 15 S 51 30W
Freshfield, C., *Antarctica* .... **7 C10** 68 25 S 151 10 E
Fresnay-sur-Sarthe, *France* ..... **26 D7** 48 17N 0 1 E
Fresnillo, *Mexico* **162 C4** 23 10N 103 0W
Fresno, *U.S.A.* **160 J7** 36 44N 119 47W
Fresno Alhandiga, *Spain* **42 E5** 40 42N 5 37W
Fresno Reservoir, *U.S.A.* **158 B9** 48 36N 109 57W
Fresvik, *Norway* .... **18 C3** 61 4N 6 55 E
Freudenstadt, *Germany* .... **31 G4** 48 27N 8 24 E
Frévent, *France* .... **27 B9** 50 15N 2 17 E
Frew ➤, *Australia* .... **126 C2** 20 0 S 135 38 E
Frewsburg, *U.S.A.* **150 D5** 42 3N 79 10W
Freycinet Nat. Park △, *Australia* .. **127 D4** 42 11 S 148 19 E
Freycinet Pen., *Australia* .... **127 D4** 42 10 S 148 25 E
Freyming-Merlebach, *France* .... **27 C13** 49 8N 6 48 E
Freyung, *Germany* .... **31 G9** 48 48N 13 31 E
Fria, *Guinea* **112 C2** 10 27N 13 38W
Fria, C., *Namibia* .... **116 B1** 18 0 S 12 0 E
Frías, *Argentina* .... **174 B2** 28 40 S 65 5W
Fribourg, *Switz.* .... **32 C4** 46 49N 7 9 E
Fribourg ◻, *Switz.* .... **32 C4** 46 40N 7 0 E
Frick, *Switz.* .... **32 A6** 47 31N 8 1 E
Fridafors, *Sweden* .... **17 H8** 56 25N 14 39 E
Friday Harbor, *U.S.A.* **160 B3** 48 32N 123 1W
Friedberg, Bayern, *Germany* .... **31 G6** 48 21N 10 59 E
Friedberg, Hessen, *Germany* .... **31 E4** 50 19N 8 45 E
Friedens, *U.S.A.* **150 F6** 40 3N 78 59W
Friedland, *Germany* .... **30 B9** 53 40N 13 33 E
Friedrichshafen, *Germany* ...... **31 H5** 47 39N 9 30 E
Friedrichskoog, *Germany* .... **30 A4** 54 1N 8 53 E
Friedrichstadt, *Germany* .... **30 A5** 54 23N 9 6 E
Friendly Is. = Tonga ■, *Pac. Oc.* .. **133 P13** 19 50 S 174 30W
Friendship, *U.S.A.* **150 D6** 42 12N 78 8W
Friesack, *Germany* .... **34 E7** 46 57N 14 24 E
Friesack, *Germany* .... **30 C8** 52 44N 12 34 E
Friesland ◻, *Neths.* .... **24 A5** 53 5N 5 50 E
Friesoythe, *Germany* .... **30 B3** 53 1N 7 51 E
Frigate, *Seychelles* .... **121 b** 4 35 S 55 56 E
Friggesund, *Sweden* .... **16 B10** 61 54N 16 33 E
Frillesås, *Sweden* .... **17 G6** 57 20N 12 12 E
Frinnaryd, *Sweden* .... **17 G8** 57 55N 14 59 E
Frio ➤, *U.S.A.* **155 L5** 28 26N 98 11W
Frio, C., *Brazil* .... **166 F6** 22 50 S 41 50W
Friol, *Spain* **42 B3** 43 2N 7 47W
Friona, *U.S.A.* **155 H3** 34 38N 102 43W
Fristad, *Sweden* .... **17 G6** 57 50N 13 0 E
Fritch, *U.S.A.* **155 H4** 35 38N 101 36W
Fritsla, *Sweden* .... **17 G6** 57 33N 12 47 E
Fritzlar, *Germany* .... **30 D5** 51 7N 9 16 E
Friuli-Venézia Giulia ◻, *Italy* ... **45 B9** 46 0N 13 0 E
Frobisher B., *Canada* **139 B13** 62 30N 66 0W
Frobisher Bay = Iqaluit, *Canada* .. **139 B13** 63 44N 68 31W
Frobisher L., *Canada* **143 B7** 56 20N 108 15W
Frohavet, *Norway* .... **14 E13** 64 0N 9 30 E
Frohnleiten, *Austria* .... **34 D8** 47 16N 15 19 E
Frolovo, *Russia* .... **60 F6** 49 45N 43 40 E
Frombork, *Poland* .... **54 D6** 54 21N 19 41 E
Frome, *U.K.* **21 F5** 51 14N 2 19W
Frome ➤, *U.K.* **21 G5** 50 41N 2 6W
Frome, L., *Australia* .... **128 A3** 30 45 S 139 45 E
Frome Downs, *Australia* .... **128 A3** 31 13 S 139 45 E
Frómista, *Spain* **42 C6** 42 16N 4 25W
Front Range, *U.S.A.* **146 C5** 40 25N 105 45W
Front Royal, *U.S.A.* **148 F6** 38 55N 78 12W
Fronteira, *Portugal* **43 F3** 39 3N 7 39W
Fronteiras, *Brazil* .... **170 C3** 7 5 S 40 37W
Frontera, *Canary Is.* **e1** 27 47N 17 59W
Frontera, *Mexico* **163 D6** 18 30N 92 40W
Fronteras, *Mexico* **162 A3** 30 56N 109 31W
Frontignan, *France* .... **28 E7** 43 27N 3 45 E
Frosinone, *Italy* .... **46 A6** 41 38N 13 19 E
Frostburg, *U.S.A.* **148 F6** 39 39N 78 56W
Frostisen, *Norway* .... **14 B17** 68 14N 17 10 E
Frostproof, *U.S.A.* **153 H8** 27 45N 81 32W
Frouard, *France* .... **27 D13** 48 47N 6 8 E
Frövi, *Sweden* .... **16 E9** 59 28N 15 24 E
Frøya, *Norway* .... **14 E13** 63 43N 8 40 E
Fruithurst, *U.S.A.* **152 B4** 33 44N 85 26W
Fruitland Park, *U.S.A.* **153 G8** 28 51N 81 54W
Frumoasa, *Romania* .... **53 D10** 46 28N 25 48 E
Frunze = Bishkek, *Kyrgyzstan* ... **65 B7** 42 54N 74 46 E
Frunze, *Kyrgyzstan* .... **65 C5** 40 7N 71 44 E
Fruška Gora, Serbia, Yug. .... **52 E4** 45 7N 19 30 E
Fruška Gora Nac. Park △,
  Yugoslavia .... **50 A3** 45 8N 19 40 E
Frutal, *Brazil* .... **171 F2** 20 0 S 49 0W
Frutigen, *Switz.* .... **32 C5** 46 35N 7 38 E
Frýdek-Místek, *Czech Rep.* ..... **35 B11** 49 40N 18 20 E
Frýdlant, *Czech Rep.* .... **34 A8** 50 56N 15 9 E
Fryeburg, *U.S.A.* **151 B14** 44 1N 70 59W
Fryvaldov = Jeseník, *Czech Rep.* .. **35 A10** 50 14N 17 8 E
Fthiótis ◻, *Greece* .... **48 C4** 38 50N 22 25 E
Fu Jiang ➤, *China* .... **76 C6** 30 0N 106 16 E
Fu Xian = Wafangdian, *China* ... **75 E11** 39 38N 121 58 E
Fu Xian, *China* .... **74 G5** 36 0N 109 20 E
Fu'an, *China* .... **77 D12** 27 11N 119 36 E
Fubian, *China* .... **76 B4** 31 17N 102 22 E
Fucécchio, *Italy* .... **44 E7** 43 44N 10 48 E
Fucheng, *China* .... **74 F9** 37 50N 116 10 E
Fuchou = Fuzhou, *China* .... **77 D12** 26 5N 119 16 E
Fuchū, *Hiroshima, Japan* .... **72 G5** 34 34N 133 14 E
Fuchū, *Tōkyō, Japan* .... **73 B11** 35 40N 139 29 E
Fuchuan, *China* .... **77 E8** 24 50N 111 5 E
Fuchun Jiang ➤, *China* .... **77 B13** 30 5N 120 5 E
Fúcino, Piana del, *Italy* .... **45 F10** 42 1N 13 31 E
Fuding, *China* .... **77 D13** 27 20N 120 12 E
Fuencaliente, *Canary Is.* **9 e1** 28 28N 17 50W
Fuencaliente, *Spain* **43 G6** 38 25N 4 18W
Fuencaliente, Pta., *Canary Is.* ... **9 e1** 28 27N 17 51W
Fuengirola, *Spain* **43 J6** 36 32N 4 41W
Fuenlabrada, *Spain* **42 E7** 40 17N 3 48W
Fuensalida, *Spain* **42 E6** 40 3N 4 12W
Fuente-Álamo, *Spain* **41 G3** 38 44N 1 24W
Fuente-Álamo de Murcia, *Spain* .. **41 H3** 37 42N 1 6W
Fuente de Cantos, *Spain* **43 G4** 38 15N 6 18W
Fuente del Maestre, *Spain* **43 G4** 38 15N 6 18W
Fuente el Fresno, *Spain* **43 F7** 39 14N 3 46W
Fuente Obejuna, *Spain* **43 G5** 38 15N 5 25W
Fuente Palmera, *Spain* **43 H5** 37 42N 5 6W
Fuentes de Andalucía, *Spain* **43 H5** 37 28N 5 20W
Fuentes de Ebro, *Spain* **40 D4** 41 31N 0 38W
Fuentes de León, *Spain* **43 G4** 38 5N 6 32W
Fuentes de Oñoro, *Spain* **42 E4** 40 33N 6 52W
Fuentesaúco, *Spain* **42 D5** 41 15N 5 30W
Fuerte ➤, *Mexico* **162 B3** 25 50N 109 25W
Fuerte Olimpo, *Paraguay* .... **174 A4** 21 0 S 57 51W
Fuerteventura, *Canary Is.* **9 e2** 28 30N 14 0W
Fuerteventura ✈ (FUE), *Canary Is.* .. **9 e2** 28 24N 13 52W
Fufeng, *China* .... **74 G5** 34 22N 108 0 E
Fuga I., *Phil.* .... **80 B3** 18 52N 121 20 E
Fughmah, *Yemen* .... **99 C5** 16 9N 49 26 E
Fugong, *China* .... **76 D2** 27 5N 98 47 E
Fugou, *China* .... **74 G8** 34 3N 114 25 E
Fugu, *China* .... **74 E6** 39 2N 111 3 E
Fuhai, *China* .... **68 B3** 47 2N 87 25 E
Fuhaymī, *Iraq* .... **101 E10** 34 16N 42 10 E
Fuhlbüttel, Hamburg ✈ (HAM),
  Germany .... **30 B5** 53 35N 9 59 E
Fuji, *Japan* .... **73 B10** 35 9N 138 39 E
Fuji-Hakone-Izu Nat. Park △, *Japan* .. **73 B10** 35 15N 138 45 E
Fuji-San, *Japan* .... **73 B10** 35 22N 138 44 E
Fuji-Yoshida, *Japan* .... **73 B10** 35 30N 138 46 E
Fujian ◻, *China* .... **77 E12** 26 0N 118 0 E

Fujieda, *Japan* .... **73 C10** 34 52N 138 16 E
Fujinomiya, *Japan* .... **73 B10** 35 10N 138 40 E
Fujioka, *Japan* .... **73 A11** 36 15N 139 5 E
Fujisawa, *Japan* .... **73 B11** 35 22N 139 29 E
Fujiyama, Mt. = Fuji-San, *Japan* .. **73 B10** 35 22N 138 44 E
Fukaya, *Japan* .... **73 A11** 36 12N 139 12 E
Fukien = Fujian ◻, *China* .... **77 E12** 26 0N 118 0 E
Fukue, *Japan* .... **73 B7** 35 19N 135 9 E
Fukue-Shima, *Japan* .... **71 H4** 32 40N 128 45 E
Fukui, *Japan* .... **73 A8** 36 5N 136 10 E
Fukui ◻, *Japan* .... **73 B8** 36 0N 136 12 E
Fukuma, *Japan* .... **72 D2** 33 46N 130 28 E
Fukuoka, *Japan* .... **72 D2** 33 39N 130 21 E
Fukuoka ◻, *Japan* .... **72 D2** 33 30N 131 0 E
Fukuoka International ✈ (FUK),
  Japan .... **72 D2** 33 36N 130 27 E
Fukuroi, *Japan* .... **73 C9** 34 45N 137 55 E
Fukushima, *Japan* .... **70 F10** 37 44N 140 28 E
Fukushima ◻, *Japan* .... **70 F10** 37 30N 140 15 E
Fukuyama, *Japan* .... **72 C5** 34 35N 133 20 E
Fulacunda, *Guinea-Biss.* **112 C1** 11 44N 15 3W
Fulaga, *Fiji* .... **133 B3** 19 8 S 178 33W
Fulda, *Germany* .... **30 E5** 50 32N 9 40 E
Fulda ➤, *Germany* .... **30 D5** 51 25N 9 39 E
Fulford Harbour, *Canada* **160 B3** 48 47N 123 27W
Fuliang, *China* .... **77 C11** 29 23N 117 14 E
Fullerton, *Calif., U.S.A.* **161 M9** 33 53N 117 56W
Fullerton, *Nebr., U.S.A.* **154 E6** 41 22N 97 58W
Fulongquan, *China* .... **75 B13** 44 20N 124 42 E
Fülöpszállás, *Hungary* .... **52 D4** 46 49N 19 15 E
Fulton, *Ill., U.S.A.* **156 C6** 41 52N 90 11W
Fulton, *Ind., U.S.A.* **157 D10** 40 57N 86 16W
Fulton, *Mo., U.S.A.* **156 F5** 38 52N 91 57W
Fulton, *N.Y., U.S.A.* **151 C8** 43 19N 76 25W
Fulufjället, *Sweden* .... **16 C6** 61 32N 12 41 E
Fumay, *France* .... **27 C11** 49 58N 4 40 E
Fumel, *France* .... **28 D4** 44 30N 0 58 E
Fumin, *China* .... **76 E4** 25 10N 102 20 E
Funabashi, *Japan* .... **73 B12** 35 45N 140 0 E
Funafuti = Fongafale, *Tuvalu* ... **134 H9** 8 31 S 179 13 E
Funäsdalen, *Sweden* .... **16 B6** 62 32N 12 58 E
Funchal, *Madeira* .... **9 c** 32 38N 16 54W
Funchal ✈ (FNC), *Madeira* ..... **9 c** 32 42N 16 45W
Fundación, *Colombia* **168 A3** 10 31N 74 11W
Fundão, *Brazil* .... **171 E3** 19 55 S 40 24W
Fundão, *Portugal* **42 E3** 40 8N 7 30W
Fundu Moldovei, *Romania* ..... **53 C10** 47 32N 25 24 E
Fundulea, *Romania* .... **53 F11** 44 28N 26 31 E
Fundy, B. of, *Canada* **141 D6** 45 0N 66 0W
Fundy Nat. Park △, *Canada* **141 C6** 45 35N 65 10W
Fünfkirchen = Pécs, *Hungary* ... **52 D3** 46 5N 18 15 E
Funhalouro, *Mozam.* .... **117 C5** 23 3 S 34 25 E
Funing, Hebei, China .... **75 E10** 39 53N 119 12 E
Funing, Jiangsu, China .... **75 H10** 33 45N 119 50 E
Funing, Yunnan, China .... **76 F5** 23 35N 105 45 E
Funiu Shan, *China* .... **74 H7** 33 30N 112 20 E
Funsi, *Ghana* **112 C4** 10 21N 1 54W
Funtua, *Nigeria* .... **113 C6** 11 30N 7 18 E
Fuping, Hebei, China .... **74 E8** 38 48N 114 12 E
Fuping, Shaanxi, China .... **74 G5** 34 42N 109 10 E
Fuqing, *China* .... **77 E12** 25 41N 119 21 E
Fuquan, *China* .... **76 D6** 26 40N 107 50 E
Furano, *Japan* .... **70 C11** 43 21N 142 23 E
Furāt, Nahr al ➤, *Asia* .... **96 D5** 31 0N 47 25 E
Fürg, *Iran* .... **97 D7** 28 18N 55 13 E
Furkapass, *Switz.* .... **33 C7** 46 34N 8 35 E
Furkating, *India* .... **90 B4** 26 28N 93 59 E
Furman, *U.S.A.* **152 C8** 32 41N 81 11W
Furmanov, *Russia* .... **60 B5** 57 10N 41 9 E
Furmanovo, *Kazakhstan* .... **60 F9** 49 42N 49 25 E
Furnas, *Azores* **9 d3** 37 46N 25 19W
Furnás, *Spain* .... **38 C2** 39 1N 1 32 E
Furnas, Reprêsa de, *Brazil* ..... **171 E2** 20 50 S 45 30W
Furneaux Group, *Australia* ..... **127 D4** 40 10 S 147 50 E
Furqlus, *Syria* .... **103 A6** 34 36N 37 8 E
Fürstenau, *Germany* .... **30 C3** 52 31N 7 40 E
Fürstenberg =
  Eisenhüttenstadt, *Germany* .... **30 C10** 52 9N 14 38 E
Fürstenberg, *Germany* .... **30 B9** 53 10N 13 8 E
Fürstenfeld, *Austria* .... **34 D9** 47 3N 16 3 E
Fürstenfeldbruck, *Germany* ..... **31 G7** 48 11N 11 15 E
Fürstenwalde, *Germany* .... **30 C10** 52 22N 14 3 E
Fürth, *Germany* .... **31 F6** 49 28N 10 59 E
Furth im Wald, *Germany* .... **31 F8** 49 18N 12 50 E
Furtwangen, *Germany* .... **31 G4** 48 2N 8 12 E
Furudal, *Sweden* .... **16 C9** 61 10N 15 11 E
Furukawa, Gifu, Japan .... **73 A9** 36 14N 137 11 E
Furukawa, Miyagi, Japan .... **70 E10** 38 34N 140 58 E
Furulund, *Sweden* .... **17 J7** 55 46N 13 6 E
Fury and Hecla Str., *Canada* **139 B11** 69 56N 84 0W
Fusagasuga, *Colombia* **168 C3** 4 21N 74 22W
Fuscaldo, *Italy* .... **47 C9** 39 25N 16 2 E
Fushan, Shandong, China .... **75 F11** 37 30N 121 15 E
Fushan, Shanxi, China .... **74 G6** 35 58N 111 51 E
Fushë Arrëz, *Albania* .... **50 D4** 42 4N 20 2 E
Fushë Krujë, *Albania* .... **50 E3** 41 29N 19 43 E
Fushun, Liaoning, China .... **75 D12** 41 50N 123 56 E
Fushun, Sichuan, China .... **76 C5** 29 13N 104 52 E
Fusio, *Switz.* .... **33 D7** 46 27N 8 40 E
Fusong, *China* .... **75 C14** 42 20N 127 15 E
Füssen, *Germany* .... **31 H6** 47 34N 10 42 E
Fustic, *Barbados* .... **165 g** 13 16N 59 38W
Fusui, *China* .... **76 F6** 22 40N 107 56 E
Futago-Yama, *Japan* .... **72 D3** 33 31N 131 36 E
Futian, *China* .... **69 F11** 22 32N 114 4 E
Futog, Yugoslavia .... **52 E4** 45 15N 19 42 E
Futrono, *Chile* .... **176 B2** 40 8 S 72 24W
Futtsu, *Japan* .... **73 B10** 35 18N 139 49 E
Futuna, Wall. & F. Is. .... **134 J9** 14 25 S 178 20W
Fuwa, *Egypt* .... **106 H7** 31 12N 30 33 E
Fuxian Hu, *China* .... **76 E4** 24 30N 102 53 E
Fuxin, *China* .... **75 C11** 42 5N 121 48 E
Fuyang, Anhui, China .... **74 H8** 33 0N 115 48 E
Fuyang, Zhejiang, China .... **77 B12** 30 5N 119 57 E
Fuyang ➤, *China* .... **74 E9** 38 12N 117 0 E
Fuyang Dao, *China* .... **77 D13** 26 34N 120 9 E
Fuyong, *China* .... **69 F10** 22 41N 113 48 E
Fuyu, *China* .... **75 B13** 45 12N 124 43 E
Fuyuan, *China* .... **76 E5** 25 40N 104 16 E
Füzesgyarmat, *Hungary* .... **77 D12** 26 5N 119 16 E
Fuzhou, *China* .... **77 D12** 26 5N 119 16 E
Fylde, *U.K.* **20 D5** 53 50N 2 58W
Fyn, *Denmark* .... **17 J4** 55 20N 10 30 E
Fyne, L., *U.K.* **22 F3** 55 59N 5 23W
Fyns Amtskommune ◻, *Denmark* .. **17 J4** 55 15N 10 30 E
Fynshav, *Denmark* .... **17 K3** 54 59N 9 59 E
Fyresdal, *Norway* .... **18 E5** 59 11N 8 5 E
Fyresvatn, *Norway* .... **18 E5** 59 6N 8 10 E
Fyzabad = Faizabad, *India* ...... **93 F10** 26 45N 82 10 E

G

Ga, *Ghana* **112 D4** 9 47N 2 30W
Gaanda, *Nigeria* .... **113 C7** 10 10N 12 27 E
Gabarin, *Nigeria* .... **113 C7** 11 8N 10 27 E
Gabas ➤, *France* **28 E3** 43 46N 0 42W
Gabela, *Angola* .... **115 E2** 11 0 S 14 24 E
Gabès, *Tunisia* .... **108 B2** 33 53N 10 2 E

Gabès, G. de, Tunisia ... 108 B2 34 0N 10 30 E
Gabgaba, W. →, Egypt ... 106 C3 22 10N 33 5 E
Gabia, Dem. Rep. of the Congo 115 C3 4 37 S 17 14 E
Gąbin, Poland ... 55 F6 52 23N 19 41 E
Gabon ■, Africa ... 114 C2 0 10 S 10 0 E
Gabon →, Gabon ... 114 B1 0 25N 9 20 E
Gaborone, Botswana ... 116 C4 24 45 S 25 57 E
Gabriels, U.S.A. ... 151 B10 44 26N 74 12W
Gäbrīk, Iran ... 97 E8 25 44N 58 28 E
Gabro, Ethiopia ... 120 C2 6 18N 43 16 E
Gabrovo, Bulgaria ... 51 D9 42 52N 25 19 E
Gacé, France ... 26 D7 48 49N 0 20 E
Gāch Sār, Iran ... 97 B6 36 7N 51 19 E
Gachsārān, Iran ... 97 D6 30 15N 50 45 E
Gacko, Bos.-H. ... 50 C2 43 10N 18 33 E
Gad Hinglaj, India ... 95 F2 16 14N 74 21 E
Gadag, India ... 95 G2 15 30N 75 45 E
Gadaisu, Papua N. G. ... 132 F5 10 22 S 149 46 E
Gadamai, Sudan ... 107 D4 17 11N 36 10 E
Gadap, Pakistan ... 92 G2 25 5N 67 28 E
Gadarwara, India ... 93 H8 22 50N 78 50 E
Gadebusch, Germany ... 30 B7 53 42N 11 7 E
Gadein, Sudan ... 107 F2 8 10N 28 45 E
Gadhada, India ... 92 J4 22 0N 71 35 E
Gadmen, Switz. ... 33 C6 46 45N 8 16 E
Gádor, Sierra de, Spain ... 43 J8 36 57N 2 45W
Gadra, Pakistan ... 92 G4 25 40N 70 38 E
Gadsden, Ala., U.S.A. ... 152 A3 34 1N 86 1W
Gadsden, S.C., U.S.A. ... 152 B9 33 51N 80 46W
Gadwal, India ... 95 F3 16 10N 77 50 E
Gadyach = Hadyach, Ukraine 59 G8 50 21N 34 0 E
Gadzi, C.A.R. ... 114 B3 4 47N 16 42 E
Găeşti, Romania ... 53 F10 44 48N 25 19 E
Gaeta, Italy ... 46 A6 41 12N 13 35 E
Gaeta, G. di, Italy ... 46 A6 41 6N 13 30 E
Gaffney, U.S.A. ... 149 H5 35 5N 81 39W
Gafsa, Tunisia ... 108 B1 34 24N 8 43 E
Gag, Indonesia ... 83 B3 0 27 S 129 52 E
Gagarawa, Nigeria ... 113 C6 12 25N 9 32 E
Gagaria, India ... 92 G4 25 43N 70 46 E
Gagarin, Russia ... 58 E8 55 38N 35 0 E
Gagarin, Uzbekistan ... 65 C4 40 39N 68 10 E
Găgăuzia □, Moldova ... 53 D13 46 10N 28 40 E
Gaggenau, Germany ... 31 G4 48 48N 8 18 E
Gaghamni, Sudan ... 107 E2 11 41N 28 19 E
Gagino, Russia ... 60 C7 55 15N 45 1 E
Gagliano del Capo, Italy ... 47 C11 39 50N 18 22 E
Gagnef, Sweden ... 16 D9 60 36N 15 5 E
Gagnoa, Ivory C. ... 112 D3 6 56N 5 16W
Gagnon, Canada ... 141 B6 51 50N 68 5W
Gagnon, L., Canada ... 143 A6 62 3N 110 27W
Gago Coutinho,
São Tomé & Principe ... 115 G6 0 1 S 6 32 E
Gagra, Georgia ... 61 J5 43 20N 40 10 E
Gahini, Rwanda ... 118 C3 1 50 S 30 30 E
Gahmar, India ... 93 G10 25 27N 83 49 E
Gai Xian = Gaizhou, China ... 75 D12 40 22N 122 20 E
Gaibanda, Bangla. ... 90 C2 25 20N 89 36 E
Gaïdhouronísi, Greece ... 39 F6 34 53N 25 41 E
Gail, U.S.A. ... 155 J4 32 46N 101 27W
Gail →, Austria ... 34 E6 46 36N 13 53 E
Gaillac, France ... 28 E5 43 54N 1 54 E
Gaillimh = Galway, Ireland ... 23 C2 53 17N 9 3W
Gaillon, France ... 26 C8 49 10N 1 20 E
Gaimán, Argentina ... 176 B3 43 10 S 65 25W
Gaines, U.S.A. ... 150 E7 41 46N 77 35W
Gainesville, Fla., U.S.A. ... 153 F7 29 40N 82 20W
Gainesville, Ga., U.S.A. ... 149 H4 34 18N 83 50W
Gainesville, Mo., U.S.A. ... 155 G8 36 36N 92 26W
Gainesville, Tex., U.S.A. ... 155 J6 33 38N 97 8W
Gainsborough, U.K. ... 20 D7 53 24N 0 46W
Gairdner, L., Australia ... 128 A2 31 30 S 136 0 E
Gairloch, U.K. ... 22 D3 57 43N 5 41W
Gairloch, L., U.K. ... 22 D3 57 43N 5 45W
Gais, Switz. ... 33 B8 47 22N 9 27 E
Gaizhou, China ... 75 D12 40 22N 122 20 E
Gaj, Croatia ... 52 E2 45 28N 17 3 E
Gaj →, Pakistan ... 92 F2 26 26N 67 21 E
Gajendragarh, India ... 95 G2 15 45N 75 59 E
Gakona, U.S.A. ... 144 E11 62 18N 145 18W
Gakuch, Pakistan ... 93 A5 36 7N 73 45 E
Gal Laghet, Somali Rep. ... 120 D3 4 9N 47 10 E
Gal Oya Res., Sri Lanka ... 95 L5 7 5N 81 30 E
Gal Tardo, Somali Rep. ... 120 D3 3 34N 45 58 E
Galaasiya, Uzbekistan ... 65 D2 39 51N 64 26 E
Galachipa, Bangla. ... 90 D3 22 8N 90 26 E
Galala, Gebel el, Egypt ... 106 J8 29 21N 32 22 E
Galán, Cerro, Argentina ... 174 B2 25 55 S 66 52W
Galana →, Kenya ... 118 C5 3 9 S 40 8 E
Galangue, Angola ... 115 E3 13 42 S 16 9 E
Galangue, Serra, Angola ... 115 E3 14 18 S 15 52 E
Galanta, Slovak Rep. ... 35 C10 48 11N 17 45 E
Galápagar, Spain ... 42 E7 40 36N 3 58W
Galápagos = Colón, Arch. de,
Ecuador ... 172 a 0 0 91 0W
Galashiels, U.K. ... 22 F6 55 37N 2 49W
Galatás, Greece ... 48 D5 37 30N 23 26 E
Galatea, N.Z. ... 130 E5 38 24 S 176 45 E
Galați, Romania ... 53 E13 45 27N 28 2 E
Galați □, Romania ... 53 E12 45 45N 27 30 E
Galatia, Turkey ... 100 C5 39 30N 33 0 E
Galatina, Italy ... 47 B11 40 10N 18 10 E
Galátone, Italy ... 47 B11 40 9N 18 4 E
Galax, U.S.A. ... 149 G5 36 40N 80 56W
Galaxídhion, Greece ... 48 C4 38 22N 22 23 E
Galcaio, Somali Rep. ... 120 C3 6 30N 47 30 E
Galdhøpiggen, Norway ... 18 C5 61 38N 8 18 E
Galeana, Chihuahua, Mexico ... 162 A3 30 7N 107 38W
Galeana, Nuevo León, Mexico ... 162 A3 24 50N 100 4W
Galegu, Sudan ... 107 E4 12 36N 35 2 E
Galela, Indonesia ... 82 A3 1 50N 127 49 E
Galena, Alaska, U.S.A. ... 144 D8 64 44N 156 56W
Galena, Ill., U.S.A. ... 156 B6 42 25N 90 26W
Galeota Pt., Trin. & Tob. ... 169 F10 10 8N 60 59W
Galera, Spain ... 41 H2 37 45N 2 33W
Galera, Pta. de, Chile ... 176 A2 39 59 S 73 43W
Galera, Pta. da, Azores ... 9 d3 37 42N 25 36W
Galera Pt., Trin. & Tob. ... 169 F10 10 49N 60 54W
Galesburg, Ill., U.S.A. ... 156 D6 40 57N 90 22W
Galesburg, Mich., U.S.A. ... 157 B11 42 17N 85 26W
Galeton, U.S.A. ... 150 E7 41 44N 77 39W
Galga, Ethiopia ... 107 F4 6 39N 37 47 E
Galgasc, Somali Rep. ... 120 D2 0 11N 41 38 E
Galheirão →, Brazil ... 171 D2 12 23 S 45 5W
Galheiros, Brazil ... 171 D2 13 18 S 46 25W
Gali, Georgia ... 61 J5 42 37N 41 46 E
Galicea Mare, Romania ... 53 F8 44 4N 23 19 E
Galich, Russia ... 60 A6 58 22N 42 24 E
Galiche, Bulgaria ... 50 C7 43 34N 23 53 E
Galicia □, Spain ... 42 C3 42 43N 7 45W
Galičica, Nac. Park △, Macedonia 50 E4 41 2N 20 55 E
Galien, U.S.A. ... 157 C1 41 48N 86 30W
Galilee = Hagalil, Israel ... 103 C4 32 53N 35 18 E
Galilee, L., Australia ... 126 C4 22 20 S 145 50 E
Galilee, Sea of = Yam Kinneret,
Israel ... 103 C4 32 45N 35 35 E
Galim, Cameroon ... 113 D7 7 6N 12 25 E
Galina Pt., Jamaica ... 164 a 18 24N 76 58W
Galinoporni, Cyprus ... 39 E10 35 31N 34 18 E
Galion, U.S.A. ... 150 F2 40 44N 82 47W
Galite, Îs. de la, Tunisia ... 111 A6 37 30N 8 59 E
Galiuro Mts., U.S.A. ... 159 K8 32 30N 110 20W
Galiwinku, Australia ... 126 A2 12 5 S 135 34 E
Gallabat, Sudan ... 107 E4 12 58N 36 11 E

Gallan Hd., U.K. ... 22 C1 58 15N 7 2W
Gallarate, Italy ... 44 C5 45 40N 8 48 E
Gallatin, Mo., U.S.A. ... 156 E3 39 55N 93 58W
Gallatin, Tenn., U.S.A. ... 149 G2 36 24N 86 27W
Galle, Sri Lanka ... 95 L5 6 5N 80 10 E
Gállego →, Spain ... 40 D4 41 39N 0 51W
Gallegos →, Argentina ... 176 D3 51 35 S 69 0W
Galletti →, Ethiopia ... 107 F5 8 46N 41 10 E
Galley Hd., Ireland ... 23 E3 51 32N 8 55W
Galliate, Italy ... 44 C5 45 29N 8 42 E
Gallinas, Pta., Colombia ... 168 A3 12 28N 71 40W
Gallipoli = Gelibolu, Turkey ... 51 F10 40 28N 26 43 E
Gallípoli, Italy ... 47 B10 40 3N 17 58 E
Gallipolis, U.S.A. ... 148 F4 38 49N 82 12W
Gällivare, Sweden ... 14 C19 67 9N 20 40 E
Gallneukirchen, Austria ... 34 C7 48 21N 14 25 E
Gällö, Sweden ... 16 B9 62 55N 15 13 E
Gallo, C., Italy ... 46 D6 38 13N 13 19 E
Gallocanta, L. de, Spain ... 40 E3 40 58N 1 30W
Galloo I., U.S.A. ... 151 C8 43 55N 76 25W
Galloway, U.K. ... 22 F4 55 1N 4 29W
Galloway, Mull of, U.K. ... 22 G4 54 39N 4 52W
Galloway Forest Park △, U.K. ... 22 F4 55 3N 4 20W
Gallup, U.S.A. ... 159 J9 35 32N 108 45W
Gallur, Spain ... 40 D3 41 52N 1 19W
Gallyaaral, Uzbekistan ... 65 C3 40 2N 67 35 E
Galong, Australia ... 129 C8 34 37 S 148 34 E
Galoya, Sri Lanka ... 95 K5 8 10N 80 55 E
Galt, Calif., U.S.A. ... 160 G5 38 15N 121 18W
Galt, Mo., U.S.A. ... 156 D3 40 8N 93 23W
Galten, Denmark ... 17 H3 56 9N 9 54 E
Galtür, Austria ... 34 E3 46 58N 10 11 E
Galty Mts., Ireland ... 23 D3 52 22N 8 10W
Galtymore, Ireland ... 23 D3 52 21N 8 11W
Galva, U.S.A. ... 156 C6 41 10N 90 3W
Galvarino, Chile ... 176 A2 38 24 S 72 47W
Galve de Sorbe, Spain ... 40 D1 41 13N 3 10W
Galveston, U.S.A. ... 157 D10 40 35N 86 11W
Galveston, Tex., U.S.A. ... 155 L7 29 18N 94 48W
Galveston B., U.S.A. ... 155 L7 29 36N 94 50W
Gálvez, Argentina ... 174 C3 32 0 S 61 14W
Galway, Ireland ... 23 C2 53 17N 9 3W
Galway □, Ireland ... 23 C2 53 22N 9 1W
Galway B., Ireland ... 23 C2 53 13N 9 10W
Gam, Indonesia ... 83 B4 0 27 S 130 36 E
Gam →, Vietnam ... 86 B5 21 55N 105 12 E
Gamagōri, Japan ... 73 C9 34 50N 137 14 E
Gamari, L., Ethiopia ... 107 E5 11 32N 41 40 E
Gamawa, Nigeria ... 113 C7 12 10N 10 31 E
Gamay, Phil. ... 80 E5 12 23N 125 18 E
Gamay Bay, Phil. ... 80 E5 12 21N 125 21 E
Gamba, Angola ... 115 B3 11 42 S 17 14 E
Gambaga, Ghana ... 113 C4 10 30N 0 28W
Gambat, Pakistan ... 92 F3 27 17N 68 26 E
Gambela, Ethiopia ... 107 F3 8 14N 34 38 E
Gambela Nat. Park △, Ethiopia ... 107 F3 8 0N 34 0 E
Gambell, U.S.A. ... 144 E5 63 47N 171 45W
Gambhir →, India ... 92 F6 26 58N 77 27 E
Gambia ■, W. Afr. ... 112 C1 13 25N 16 0W
Gambia →, W. Afr. ... 112 C1 13 28N 16 34W
Gambier, U.S.A. ... 150 F2 40 22N 82 23W
Gambier, C., Australia ... 124 B5 11 56 S 130 57 E
Gambier Is., Australia ... 128 C2 35 3 S 136 30 E
Gambier Village, Bahamas ... 9 b 25 4N 77 30W
Gambo, C.A.R. ... 114 B4 4 39N 22 16 E
Gambo, Canada ... 141 C9 48 47N 54 13W
Gamboli, Pakistan ... 92 E3 29 53N 68 24 E
Gamboma, Congo ... 114 C3 1 55 S 15 52 E
Gamboula, C.A.R. ... 114 B3 4 8N 15 9 E
Gambuta, Indonesia ... 82 A2 0 30N 123 20 E
Gamka →, S. Africa ... 116 E3 33 18 S 21 39 E
Gamkab →, Namibia ... 116 D2 28 4 S 17 54 E
Gamla Uppsala, Sweden ... 16 E11 59 54N 17 40 E
Gamlakarleby = Kokkola, Finland 14 E20 63 50N 23 8 E
Gamleby, Sweden ... 17 G10 57 54N 16 20 E
Gammon →, Canada ... 143 C9 51 24N 95 44W
Gammouda, Tunisia ... 108 A1 35 3N 9 39 E
Gamo-Gofa □, Ethiopia ... 107 F4 5 40N 36 40 E
Gamoda-Saki, Japan ... 72 D6 33 50N 134 45 E
Gamou, Niger ... 113 C6 14 20N 9 55 E
Gampaha, Sri Lanka ... 95 L4 7 5N 79 59 E
Gampel, Switz. ... 32 D5 46 19N 7 44 E
Gampola, Sri Lanka ... 95 L5 7 10N 80 34 E
Gams, Switz. ... 33 B8 47 12N 9 26 E
Gamtoos →, S. Africa ... 116 E4 33 58 S 25 1 E
Gan, France ... 28 E3 43 12N 0 27W
Gan Goriama, Mts., Cameroon ... 113 D7 7 44N 12 45 E
Gan Jiang →, China ... 77 C11 29 15N 116 0 E
Ganado, U.S.A. ... 159 J9 35 43N 109 33W
Gananita, Sudan ... 106 D3 18 22N 33 50 E
Gananoque, Canada ... 140 D4 44 20N 76 10W
Ganassi, Phil. ... 81 H5 7 49N 124 6 E
Gäncä, Azerbaijan ... 61 K8 40 45N 46 20 E
Gancheng, China ... 86 C7 18 51N 108 37 E
Gand = Gent, Belgium ... 24 C3 51 2N 3 42 E
Ganda, Angola ... 115 E2 13 3 S 14 35 E
Gandajika, Dem. Rep. of the Congo 115 D4 6 46 S 23 58 E
Gandak →, India ... 93 G11 25 39N 85 13 E
Gandava, Pakistan ... 92 C2 28 32N 67 32 E
Gander, Canada ... 141 C9 48 58N 54 35W
Gander L., Canada ... 141 C9 48 58N 54 35W
Ganderkesee, Germany ... 30 B4 53 2N 8 32 E
Ganderowe Falls, Zimbabwe ... 119 F2 17 20 S 29 10 E
Gandesa, Spain ... 40 D5 41 3N 0 26 E
Gandhi Sagar, India ... 92 G6 24 40N 75 40 E
Gandhinagar, India ... 92 H5 23 15N 72 45 E
Gandi, Nigeria ... 113 C6 12 55N 5 49 E
Gandía, Spain ... 41 G4 38 58N 0 9W
Gandino, Italy ... 44 C6 45 49N 9 54 E
Gando, Pta., Canary Is. ... 9 e1 27 55N 15 22W
Gandole, Nigeria ... 113 D7 8 28N 11 35 E
Gandou, Congo ... 114 B3 2 25N 17 25 E
Gandrí, Brazil ... 171 D4 13 45 S 39 30W
Găneb, Mauritania ... 112 B2 18 29N 10 8W
Ganedidalem = Gani, Indonesia ... 82 B3 0 48 S 128 14 E
Ganetti, Sudan ... 106 D3 18 0N 31 10 E
Ganga →, India ... 93 H14 23 20N 90 30 E
Ganga Sagar, India ... 93 J13 21 38N 88 5 E
Gangafani, Mali ... 112 C4 14 20N 2 20W
Gangakher, India ... 94 E3 18 57N 76 45 E
Ganganagar, India ... 92 E5 29 56N 73 56 E
Gangapur, Maharashtra, India ... 94 E2 19 41N 75 1 E
Gangapur, Raj., India ... 92 F7 26 32N 76 49 E
Gangara, Niger ... 113 C6 14 35N 8 29 E
Gangaw, Burma ... 90 D5 22 5N 94 5 E
Gangaw Taungdan, Burma ... 90 C6 24 55N 96 35 E
Gangawati, India ... 95 G3 15 30N 76 36 E
Ganges = Ganga →, India ... 93 H14 23 20N 90 30 E
Ganges, Canada ... 142 D4 48 51N 123 31W
Ganges, France ... 28 E7 43 56N 3 42 E
Ganges, Mouths of the, India ... 93 J14 21 30N 90 0 E
Gânghester, Sweden ... 17 G7 57 42N 13 1 E
Gângiova, Romania ... 53 G8 43 54N 23 50 E
Gangoh, India ... 92 E7 29 46N 77 18 E
Gangtok, India ... 90 B2 27 20N 88 37 E
Gangu, China ... 74 G3 34 40N 105 15 E
Gangwa, Dem. Rep. of the Congo 114 C4 3 30 S 20 54 E
Gangyao, China ... 75 B14 44 12N 126 37 E

Gani, Indonesia ... 82 B3 0 48 S 128 14 E
Ganj, India ... 93 F8 27 45N 78 57 E
Ganjam, India ... 94 E7 19 23N 85 4 E
Ganluc, China ... 76 C4 28 58N 102 59 E
Ganmain, Australia ... 129 C7 34 47 S 147 1 E
Gannat, France ... 27 F10 46 7N 3 11 E
Gannett Peak, U.S.A. ... 158 E9 43 11N 109 39W
Ganquan, China ... 74 F5 36 20N 109 20 E
Gänserdorf, Austria ... 35 C9 48 20N 16 43 E
Gansu □, China ... 74 G3 36 0N 104 0 E
Ganta, Liberia ... 112 D3 7 15N 8 59W
Gantheaume, C., Australia ... 128 C2 36 4 S 137 32 E
Gantheaume B., Australia ... 125 E1 27 40 S 114 10 E
Gantsevichi = Hantsavichy, Belarus 59 F4 52 49N 26 30 E
Ganye, Nigeria ... 113 D7 8 25N 12 4 E
Ganyem = Genyem, Indonesia ... 83 B6 2 46 S 140 12 E
Ganyu, China ... 75 G10 34 50N 119 8 E
Ganyushkino, Kazakhstan ... 61 G9 46 35N 49 20 E
Ganzhou, China ... 77 E10 25 51N 114 56 E
Gao, Mali ... 113 B4 16 15N 0 5W
Gao Xian, China ... 76 C5 28 21N 104 32 E
Gao'an, China ... 77 C10 28 26N 115 17 E
Gaochun, China ... 77 B12 31 20N 118 49 E
Gaohe, China ... 77 F9 22 46N 112 57 E
Gaohebu, China ... 77 B11 30 43N 116 49 E
Gaokeng, China ... 77 D9 27 40N 113 58 E
Gaolan Dao, China ... 77 G10 21 55N 113 10 E
Gaoligong Shan, China ... 76 E2 24 45N 98 45 E
Gaomi, China ... 75 F10 36 20N 119 42 E
Gaoming, China ... 77 F9 36 N 113 1 E
Gaoping, China ... 74 G7 35 45N 112 55 E
Gaotang, China ... 74 F9 36 50N 116 15 E
Gaoua, Burkina Faso ... 112 C4 10 20N 3 8W
Gaoual, Guinea ... 112 C2 11 45N 13 25W
Gaoxiong = Kaohsiung, Taiwan ... 77 F13 22 35N 120 16 E
Gaoyang, China ... 74 E8 38 40N 115 45 E
Gaoyou, China ... 77 F9 23 3N 113 15 E
Gaoyou Hu, China ... 75 H10 32 45N 119 20 E
Gaozhou, China ... 77 G8 21 58N 110 50 E
Gap, France ... 29 D10 44 33N 6 5 E
Gapan, Phil. ... 80 D3 15 19N 120 57 E
Gapat →, India ... 93 G10 24 30N 82 28 E
Gapuwiyak, Australia ... 126 A2 12 25 S 135 43 E
Gar, China ... 78 C2 32 10N 79 58 E
Garabekewül, Turkmenistan ... 65 D2 38 30N 64 8 E
Garabogazköl Aylagy, Turkmenistan 57 F9 41 0N 53 30 E
Garachico, Canary Is. ... 9 e1 28 22N 16 48W
Garachiné, Panama ... 164 E4 8 0N 78 12W
Garad, Somali Rep. ... 120 C3 6 57N 49 24 E
Garafia, Canary Is. ... 9 e1 28 48N 17 57W
Garah, Australia ... 127 D4 29 5 S 149 38 E
Garaina, Papua N. G. ... 132 D4 7 53 S 147 8 E
Garajonay, Canary Is. ... 9 e1 28 7N 17 14W
Garamba, Parc Nat. de la △,
Dem. Rep. of the Congo ... 118 B2 4 10N 29 40 E
Garango, Burkina Faso ... 113 C4 11 48N 0 34W
Garanhuns, Brazil ... 170 C4 8 50 S 36 30W
Garautha, India ... 93 G8 25 34N 79 18 E
Garavuti, Tajikistan ... 65 E4 37 34N 68 26 E
Garawe, Liberia ... 112 E3 4 35N 8 0W
Garba Harre, Somali Rep. ... 120 D2 3 19N 42 13 E
Garba Tula, Kenya ... 118 B4 0 30N 38 32 E
Garbagudullu, Ethiopia ... 120 C2 6 12N 43 50 E
Garbaharreey = Garba Harre,
Somali Rep. ... 120 D2 3 19N 42 13 E
Garberville, U.S.A. ... 158 F2 40 6N 123 48W
Garbiyang, India ... 93 D9 30 8N 80 54 E
Garbsen, Germany ... 30 C5 52 26N 9 31 E
Garça, Brazil ... 171 F2 22 14 S 49 37W
Garças →, Mato Grosso, Brazil ... 173 D7 15 54 S 52 16W
Garças →, Pernambuco, Brazil ... 170 C4 8 43 S 39 41W
Garchitorena, Phil. ... 80 E4 13 52N 123 40 E
Garcia Hernandez, Phil. ... 81 G5 9 37N 124 18 E
Garcias, Brazil ... 173 E7 20 34 S 52 13W
Gard □, France ... 29 D8 44 2N 4 10 E
Gard →, France ... 29 E8 43 51N 4 37 E
Garda, L. di, Italy ... 44 C7 45 40N 10 41 E
Gardanne, France ... 29 E9 43 27N 5 27 E
Gårdby, Sweden ... 17 H10 56 36N 16 38 E
Garde L., Canada ... 143 A7 62 50N 106 13W
Gardelegen, Germany ... 30 C7 52 32N 11 24 E
Garden City, Ga., U.S.A. ... 153 C8 32 6N 81 9W
Garden City, Kans., U.S.A. ... 155 G4 37 58N 100 53W
Garden City, Mo., U.S.A. ... 156 F2 38 34N 94 12W
Garden City, Tex., U.S.A. ... 155 K4 31 52N 101 29W
Garden Grove, U.S.A. ... 161 M9 33 47N 117 55W
Garderen, Neths. ... 24 D7 52 7N 5 40 E
Gardez, Afghan. ... 91 B3 33 37N 69 9 E
Gardhíki, Greece ... 48 C3 38 50N 21 55 E
Gardiner, Maine, U.S.A. ... 149 C11 44 14N 69 47W
Gardiner, Mont., U.S.A. ... 158 D8 45 2N 110 22W
Gardiners I., U.S.A. ... 151 E12 41 6N 72 6W
Gardner, Fla., U.S.A. ... 153 H8 27 21N 81 48W
Gardner, Mass., U.S.A. ... 151 D13 42 34N 71 59W
Gardner Canal, Canada ... 142 C3 53 27N 128 8W
Gardner Pinnacles, U.S.A. ... 123 E11 25 0N 167 55W
Gardnerville, U.S.A. ... 160 G7 38 56N 119 45W
Gardo, Somali Rep. ... 120 C3 9 30N 49 6 E
Gardone Val Trómpia, Italy ... 44 C7 45 41N 10 11 E
Gárdony, Hungary ... 52 C3 47 12N 18 39 E
Gare Tigre, Fr. Guiana ... 169 C7 4 58N 53 9W
Garelol I., U.S.A. ... 144 L3 51 48N 178 48W
Garešnica, Croatia ... 45 C13 45 36N 16 56 E
Garéssio, Italy ... 44 D5 44 12N 8 2 E
Garey, U.S.A. ... 161 L6 34 53N 120 19W
Garfield, U.S.A. ... 158 C5 47 1N 117 9W
Gargaliánoi, Greece ... 48 D3 37 4N 21 38 E
Gargan, Mt., France ... 28 C5 45 37N 1 39 E
Gargano, Parco Nazionale del △,
Italy ... 45 G12 41 43N 15 52 E
Gargett, Australia ... 126 K6 21 9 S 148 46 E
Gargouna, Mali ... 113 B5 15 56N 0 13 E
Gargždai, Lithuania ... 9 J19 55 43N 21 24 E
Garhchiroli, India ... 94 D5 20 10N 80 0 E
Gari, Russia ... 84 B9 59 26N 62 21 E
Garibaldi Prov. Park △, Canada ... 142 D4 49 50N 122 40W
Gariep, L., S. Africa ... 116 E4 30 40 S 25 40 E
Garies, S. Africa ... 116 E2 30 32 S 17 59 E
Garigliano →, Italy ... 46 A6 41 13N 13 45 E
Garissa, Kenya ... 118 C4 0 25 S 39 40 E
Garkida, Nigeria ... 113 C6 10 27N 12 36 E
Garko, Nigeria ... 113 C6 11 45N 8 35 E
Garland, Tex., U.S.A. ... 155 J6 32 55N 96 38W
Garland, Utah, U.S.A. ... 158 F7 41 47N 112 10W
Garlasco, Italy ... 44 C5 45 11N 8 55 E
Garliava, Lithuania ... 9 J20 54 49N 23 52 E
Garm, Tajikistan ... 65 D5 39 0N 70 20 E
Garmāb, Iran ... 97 C8 35 25N 56 45 E
Garmisch-Partenkirchen, Germany 31 H7 47 30N 11 6 E
Garmo, Qullai = Kommunizma, Pik,
Tajikistan ... 65 D6 39 0N 72 2 E
Garmsār, Iran ... 97 C7 35 20N 52 25 E
Garner, U.S.A. ... 156 D8 43 6N 93 36W
Garnett, U.S.A. ... 154 F7 38 17N 95 14W
Garnpung L., Australia ... 128 B5 33 25 S 143 10 E
Garo Hills, India ... 90 C3 25 30N 90 30 E

Garoe, Somali Rep. ... 120 C3 8 25N 48 33 E
Garonne →, France ... 28 C3 45 2N 0 36W
Garonne, Canal Latéral à la, France 28 D4 44 45N 0 18 E
Garot, India ... 92 G6 24 19N 75 41 E
Garoua, Cameroon ... 113 D7 9 19N 13 21 E
Garove I., Papua N. G. ... 132 C5 4 42 S 149 30 E
Garpenberg, Sweden ... 16 D10 60 19N 16 12 E
Garphyttan, Sweden ... 16 E8 59 18N 14 56 E
Garrauli, India ... 93 G8 25 5N 79 22 E
Garrel, Germany ... 30 C4 52 57N 8 0 E
Garrett, U.S.A. ... 157 C11 41 21N 85 8W
Garrigue = Garrigues, France ... 28 E7 43 40N 3 55 E
Garrigues, France ... 28 E7 43 40N 3 55 E
Garrison, Ky., U.S.A. ... 157 F13 38 36N 83 10W
Garrison, Mont., U.S.A. ... 158 C7 46 31N 112 49W
Garrison, N. Dak., U.S.A. ... 154 B4 47 40N 101 25W
Garrison Res. = Sakakawea, L.,
U.S.A. ... 154 B4 47 30N 101 25W
Garrovillas, Spain ... 43 F4 39 40N 6 33W
Garrucha, Spain ... 41 H3 37 11N 1 49W
Garry →, U.K. ... 22 E5 56 44N 3 47W
Garry, L., Canada ... 138 B9 65 58N 100 18W
Garsen, Kenya ... 118 C5 2 20 S 40 5 E
Gärsnäs, Sweden ... 17 J8 55 32N 14 10 E
Garson L., Canada ... 143 B6 56 19N 110 2W
Garstang, U.K. ... 20 D5 53 55N 2 46W
Gartempe →, France ... 28 B4 46 47N 0 49 E
Gartz, Germany ... 30 B10 53 13N 14 22 E
Garu, Ghana ... 113 C4 10 55N 0 11W
Garu, India ... 93 H11 23 40N 84 14 E
Garub, Namibia ... 116 D2 26 37 S 16 0 E
Garut, Indonesia ... 85 D3 7 14 S 107 53 E
Garvão, Portugal ... 43 H2 37 42N 8 21W
Garvie Mts., N.Z. ... 131 F3 45 30 S 168 50 E
Garwa = Garoua, Cameroon ... 113 D7 9 19N 13 21 E
Garwa, India ... 93 G10 24 11N 83 47 E
Garwolin, Poland ... 55 G8 51 55N 21 38 E
Gary, U.S.A. ... 157 C9 41 36N 87 20W
Garz, Germany ... 30 A9 54 19N 13 20 E
Garzê, China ... 76 B3 31 38N 100 1 E
Garzón, Colombia ... 168 C2 2 10N 75 40W
Gas City, U.S.A. ... 157 D11 40 29N 85 37W
Gas-San, Japan ... 70 E10 38 32N 140 1 E
Gasan, Phil. ... 80 E3 13 19N 121 51 E
Gasan Kuli = Esenguly,
Turkmenistan ... 66 F6 37 37N 53 59 E
Gaschurn, Austria ... 33 C10 46 59N 10 2 E
Gascogne, France ... 28 E4 43 45N 0 20 E
Gascogne, G. de, Europe ... 28 E2 44 0N 2 0W
Gasconade →, U.S.A. ... 156 F5 38 40N 91 34W
Gascony = Gascogne, France ... 28 E4 43 45N 0 20 E
Gascoyne →, Australia ... 125 D1 24 52 S 113 37 E
Gascoyne Junction, Australia ... 125 E2 25 2 S 115 17 E
Gascueña, Spain ... 40 E2 40 18N 2 31W
Gash, Wadi →, Ethiopia ... 107 D4 16 48N 35 51 E
Gash-Setit Wildlife Reserve △,
Eritrea ... 107 D4 15 12N 36 58 E
Gashagar, Nigeria ... 113 C7 13 22N 12 47 E
Gashaka, Nigeria ... 113 D7 7 20N 11 29 E
Gashaka-Gumti Nat. Park △, Nigeria 113 D7 7 23N 11 34 E
Gasherbrum, Pakistan ... 93 B7 35 40N 76 40 E
Gashua, Nigeria ... 113 C7 12 54N 11 0 E
Gasmata, Papua N. G. ... 132 D6 6 17 S 150 20 E
Gasparilla I., U.S.A. ... 153 J7 26 46N 82 16W
Gasparillo, Trin. & Tob. ... 169 F9 10 18N 61 26W
Gaspé, Canada ... 141 C7 48 52N 64 30W
Gaspé, C. de, Canada ... 141 C7 48 48N 64 7W
Gaspé, Pén. de, Canada ... 141 C6 48 45N 65 40W
Gaspésie, Parc de Conservation de
la △, Canada ... 141 C6 48 55N 65 50W
Gassan, Burkina Faso ... 112 C4 12 49N 3 12W
Gassol, Nigeria ... 113 D7 8 34N 10 25 E
Gasteiz = Vitoria-Gasteiz, Spain ... 40 C2 42 50N 2 41W
Gaston, U.S.A. ... 152 B8 33 49N 81 5W
Gastonia, U.S.A. ... 149 H5 35 16N 81 11W
Gastoúni, Greece ... 48 D3 37 51N 21 15 E
Gastoúri, Greece ... 38 B9 39 34N 19 54 E
Gastre, Argentina ... 176 B3 42 20 S 69 15W
Gästrikland, Sweden ... 16 D10 60 45N 16 40 E
Gata, C., Cyprus ... 39 F9 34 34N 33 2 E
Gata, C. de, Spain ... 41 J2 36 41N 2 13W
Gata, Sierra de, Spain ... 42 E4 40 20N 6 45W
Gataga →, Canada ... 142 B3 58 35N 126 59W
Gatchina, Russia ... 58 B6 59 35N 30 9 E
Gatehouse of Fleet, U.K. ... 22 G4 54 53N 4 12W
Gates, U.S.A. ... 150 C7 43 9N 77 42W
Gates of the Arctic Nat. Park and
Preserve △, U.S.A. ... 144 C10 67 20N 152 0W
Gateshead, U.K. ... 20 C6 54 57N 1 35W
Gatesville, U.S.A. ... 155 K6 31 26N 97 45W
Gateway Nat. Recr. Area △, U.S.A. 151 F11 40 26N 73 59W
Gaths, Zimbabwe ... 119 G3 20 2 S 30 32 E
Gatico, Chile ... 174 A1 22 29 S 70 20W
Gâtinais, France ... 27 D9 48 5N 2 46 E
Gâtine, Hauteurs de, France ... 28 B3 46 35N 0 45W
Gatineau, Canada ... 151 A9 45 29N 75 38W
Gatineau →, Canada ... 140 C4 45 40N 75 42W
Gattaran, Phil. ... 80 B3 18 4N 121 38 E
Gattinara, Italy ... 44 C5 45 37N 8 22 E
Gatton, Australia ... 127 D5 27 32 S 152 17 E
Gatun, L., Panama ... 164 E4 9 7N 79 56W
Gatwick, London × (LGW), U.K. ... 21 F7 51 10N 0 11W
Gatyana, S. Africa ... 117 E4 32 16 S 28 31 E
Gau, Fiji ... 133 B2 18 2 S 179 18 E
Gaucín, Spain ... 43 J5 36 31N 5 19W
Gauer L., Canada ... 143 B9 57 0N 97 50W
Gauhati = Guwahati, India ... 90 B3 26 10N 91 45 E
Gauja →, Latvia ... 15 H21 57 10N 24 16 E
Gaula →, Norway ... 18 A7 63 21N 10 14 E
Gaupne, Norway ... 18 C4 61 31N 7 17 E
Gausdak = Gowārdak, Turkmenistan 65 E3 37 50N 66 4 E
Gauri Phanta, India ... 93 E10 28 41N 80 36 E
Gauribidanur, India ... 95 H3 13 37N 77 32 E
Gausta, Norway ... 18 E5 59 48N 8 40 E
Gauteng □, S. Africa ... 117 D4 26 0 S 28 0 E
Gāv Koshī, Iran ... 97 D8 28 38N 57 12 E
Gāvakān, Iran ... 97 D7 29 37N 53 10 E
Gavarnie, France ... 28 F3 42 44N 0 1W
Gavāter, Iran ... 97 E9 25 10N 61 31 E
Gāvbandī, Iran ... 97 E7 27 12N 53 4 E
Gavdhopoúla, Greece ... 39 F5 34 56N 24 0 E
Gávdhos, Greece ... 39 F5 34 50N 24 5 E
Gavi, Italy ... 44 D5 44 41N 8 49 E
Gavião, Portugal ... 43 F3 39 28N 7 56W
Gaviota, U.S.A. ... 161 L6 34 29 S 120 13W
Gāvkhūnī, Bāţlāq-e, Iran ... 97 C7 32 6N 52 52 E
Gävle, Sweden ... 16 D11 60 40N 17 9 E
Gävleborgs län □, Sweden ... 16 D11 61 30N 16 15 E
Gavorrano, Italy ... 44 F8 42 55N 10 54 E
Gavray, France ... 26 D5 48 55N 1 20W
Gavrilov Yam, Russia ... 58 D10 57 18N 39 49 E
Gávrion, Greece ... 48 D6 37 54N 24 44 E
Gawachab, Namibia ... 116 D2 27 4 S 17 55 E
Gawai, Burma ... 90 B6 27 56N 97 30 E
Gawilgarh Hills, India ... 94 D3 21 15N 76 45 E
Gawler, Australia ... 128 C3 34 30 S 138 42 E

Gawler Ranges, Australia ... 128 B2 32 20 S 136 0 E
Gawu, Nigeria ... 113 D6 9 14N 6 52 E
Gaxun Nur, China ... 68 B5 42 22N 100 30 E
Gay, Russia ... 64 F7 51 27N 58 27 E
Gay, U.S.A. ... 152 B5 33 6N 84 35W
Gaya, India ... 93 G11 24 47N 85 4 E
Gaya, Niger ... 113 C5 11 52N 3 28 E
Gaya, Nigeria ... 113 C6 11 57N 9 0 E
Gayéri, Burkina Faso ... 113 C5 12 39N 0 29 E
Gaylord, U.S.A. ... 148 C3 45 2N 84 41W
Gayndah, Australia ... 127 D5 25 35 S 151 32 E
Gayny, Russia ... 64 A5 60 18N 54 19 E
Gaysin = Haysyn, Ukraine ... 59 H5 48 57N 29 25 E
Gayvoron = Hayvoron, Ukraine ... 59 H5 48 22N 29 52 E
Gaza, Gaza Strip ... 103 D3 31 30N 34 28 E
Gaza □, Mozam. ... 117 C5 23 10 S 32 45 E
Gaza Strip □, Asia ... 103 D3 31 29N 34 25 E
Gazalkent, Uzbekistan ... 65 C4 41 33N 69 46 E
Gazanjyk, Turkmenistan ... 97 B7 39 16N 55 32 E
Gazaoua, Niger ... 113 C6 13 32N 7 55 E
Gázbor, Iran ... 97 D8 28 5N 58 51 E
Gazelle, Récif de la, N. Cal. ... 133 T19 20 10 S 165 30 E
Gazelle Pen., Papua N. G. ... 132 C6 4 40 S 152 0 E
Gazi, Dem. Rep. of the Congo ... 118 B1 1 3N 24 30 E
Gaziantep, Turkey ... 100 D7 37 6N 37 23 E
Gazimağosa = Famagusta, Cyprus ... 39 E9 35 8N 33 55 E
Gazipaşa, Turkey ... 100 D5 36 16N 32 18 E
Gbarnga, Liberia ... 112 D3 7 19N 9 13W
Gbekebo, Nigeria ... 113 D5 6 20N 4 56 E
Gboko, Nigeria ... 113 D6 7 17N 9 4 E
Gbongan, Nigeria ... 113 D5 7 28N 4 20 E
Gcoverega, Botswana ... 116 B3 19 8 S 24 18 E
Gcuwa, S. Africa ... 117 E4 32 20 S 28 11 E
Gdańsk, Poland ... 54 D5 54 22N 18 40 E
Gdańsk ✈ (GDN), Poland ... 54 D5 54 22N 18 30 E
Gdańska, Zatoka, Poland ... 54 D6 54 30N 19 20 E
Gdov, Russia ... 15 G22 58 48N 27 55 E
Gdynia, Poland ... 54 D5 54 35N 18 33 E
Geba →, Guinea-Biss. ... 112 C1 11 46N 15 36W
Gebe, Indonesia ... 83 A3 0 5N 129 25 E
Gebeciler, Turkey ... 49 C12 38 46N 30 46 E
Gebeit Mine, Sudan ... 106 C4 21 3N 36 29 E
Gebel Abyad, Sudan ... 106 D2 19 0N 26 0 E
Gebel Iweibid, Egypt ... 106 H8 30 8N 32 13 E
Gebze, Turkey ... 51 F13 40 47N 29 25 E
Gecha, Ethiopia ... 107 F4 7 30N 35 18 E
Gedaref, Sudan ... 107 E4 14 2N 35 28 E
Gedaref □, Sudan ... 107 E4 14 0N 35 0 E
Gede, Tanjung, Indonesia ... 84 D3 6 46 S 105 12 E
Gediz, Turkey ... 49 B11 39 1N 29 24 E
Gediz →, Turkey ... 49 C8 38 35N 26 48 E
Gedo, Ethiopia ... 107 F4 9 2N 37 25 E
Gèdre, France ... 28 F4 42 47N 0 2 E
Gedser, Denmark ... 17 K5 54 35N 11 55 E
Gedung, Pulau, Malaysia ... 87 c 5 17N 100 23 E
Geegully Cr. →, Australia ... 124 C3 18 32 S 123 41 E
Geel, Belgium ... 24 C4 51 10N 4 59 E
Geelong, Australia ... 128 E6 38 10 S 144 22 E
Geelvink B. = Cenderawasih, Teluk, Indonesia ... 79 E9 3 0 S 135 20 E
Geelvink Chan., Australia ... 125 E1 28 30 S 114 0 E
Geesthacht, Germany ... 30 B6 53 26N 10 22 E
Geidam, Nigeria ... 113 C7 12 57N 11 57 E
Geikie →, Canada ... 143 B8 57 45N 103 52W
Geikie Gorge Nat. Park △, Australia ... 124 C4 18 3 S 125 41 E
Geilenkirchen, Germany ... 30 E2 50 57N 6 8 E
Geili, Sudan ... 107 D3 16 1N 32 37 E
Geilo, Norway ... 18 D5 60 32N 8 14 E
Geisingen, Germany ... 31 H4 47 54N 8 38 E
Geislingen, Germany ... 31 G5 48 37N 9 50 E
Geistown, U.S.A. ... 150 F6 40 18N 78 52W
Geita, Tanzania ... 118 C3 2 48 S 32 12 E
Geitastrand, Norway ... 18 A6 63 22N 9 56 E
Geithus, Norway ... 18 E6 59 57N 9 59 E
Gejiu, China ... 76 F4 23 20N 103 10 E
Gel →, Sudan ... 107 F2 7 5N 29 10 E
Gel, Meydān-e, Iran ... 97 D7 29 4N 54 50 E
Gel River, Sudan ... 107 F2 7 5N 29 10 E
Gela, Italy ... 47 F7 37 4N 14 15 E
Gela, G. di, Italy ... 47 F7 37 0N 14 20 E
Geladi, Ethiopia ... 120 C3 6 59N 46 30 E
Gelahun, Liberia ... 112 D2 7 55N 10 28W
Gelang Patah, Malaysia ... 87 d 1 27N 103 35 E
Gelderland □, Neths. ... 24 B6 52 5N 6 10 E
Geldern, Germany ... 30 D2 51 31N 6 20 E
Geldrop, Neths. ... 24 C5 51 25N 5 32 E
Geleen, Neths. ... 24 D5 50 57N 5 49 E
Gelehun, S. Leone ... 112 D2 8 20N 11 40W
Gelembe, Turkey ... 49 B9 39 10N 27 51 E
Gelemso, Ethiopia ... 107 F5 8 49N 40 31 E
Gelendost, Turkey ... 100 C4 38 7N 31 1 E
Gelendzhik, Russia ... 59 K10 44 33N 38 10 E
Gelib, Somali Rep. ... 120 D2 0 29N 42 46 E
Gelibolu, Turkey ... 51 F10 40 28N 26 43 E
Gelibolu Yarımadası, Turkey ... 51 F10 40 20N 26 30 E
Gelidonya Burnu, Turkey ... 100 D4 36 12N 30 24 E
Gelnhausen, Germany ... 31 E5 50 11N 9 11 E
Gelnica, Slovak Rep. ... 35 C13 48 51N 20 55 E
Gelsenkirchen, Germany ... 30 D3 51 32N 7 6 E
Gelterkinden, Switz. ... 32 B5 47 28N 7 51 E
Gelting, Germany ... 30 A5 54 45N 9 53 E
Gelugur, Malaysia ... 87 c 5 22N 100 18 E
Gemas, Malaysia ... 87 L4 2 37N 102 36 E
Gembloux, Belgium ... 24 D4 50 34N 4 43 E
Gembu, Nigeria ... 113 D7 6 42N 11 10 E
Gemena, Dem. Rep. of the Congo ... 114 B3 3 13N 19 48 E
Gemerek, Turkey ... 100 C7 39 15N 36 10 E
Gemla, Sweden ... 17 H8 56 52N 14 39 E
Gemlik, Turkey ... 51 F13 40 26N 29 9 E
Gemlik Körfezi, Turkey ... 51 F12 40 25N 28 55 E
Gemona del Friuli, Italy ... 45 B10 46 16N 13 9 E
Gemsa, Egypt ... 106 B3 27 39N 33 35 E
Gemsbok Nat. Park △, Botswana ... 116 D3 25 5 S 21 1 E
Gemünden, Germany ... 31 E5 50 3N 9 42 E
Genale, Somali Rep. ... 120 D2 1 48N 44 42 E
Genale →, Ethiopia ... 107 F4 6 2N 39 1 E
Genç, Turkey ... 101 C9 38 44N 40 34 E
Gençay, France ... 28 B4 46 23N 0 23 E
Geneina, Gebel, Egypt ... 106 B3 29 2N 33 56 E
General Acha, Argentina ... 174 D3 37 20 S 64 38W
General Alvear, Buenos Aires, Argentina ... 174 D4 36 0 S 60 0W
General Alvear, Mendoza, Argentina ... 174 D2 35 0 S 67 40W
General Artigas, Paraguay ... 174 B4 26 52 S 56 16W
General Belgrano, Argentina ... 174 D4 36 35 S 58 47W
General Cabrera, Argentina ... 174 C3 32 53 S 63 52W
General Carrera, L., Chile ... 176 C2 46 35 S 72 0W
General Cepeda, Mexico ... 162 B4 25 23N 101 27W
General Conesa, Argentina ... 176 B4 40 6 S 64 25W
General Eugenio A. Garay, Paraguay ... 173 E5 20 31 S 62 8W
General Guido, Argentina ... 174 D4 36 40 S 57 50W
General Juan Madariaga, Argentina ... 174 D4 37 0 S 57 0W
General La Madrid, Argentina ... 174 D3 37 17 S 61 20W
General Lorenzo Vintter, Argentina ... 176 B4 40 45 S 64 26W
General Luna, Phil. ... 80 E4 13 15N 122 35 E
General MacArthur, Phil. ... 81 F5 11 18N 125 28 E
General Martin Miguel de Güemes, Argentina ... 174 A3 24 50 S 65 0W
General Paz, Argentina ... 174 B4 27 45 S 57 36W
General Pico, Argentina ... 174 D3 35 45 S 63 50W
General Pinedo, Argentina ... 174 B3 27 15 S 61 20W
General Pinto, Argentina ... 174 C3 34 45 S 61 50W
General Sampaio, Brazil ... 170 B4 4 2 S 39 29W

General Santos, Phil. ... 81 H5 6 5N 125 14 E
General Tinio, Phil. ... 80 D3 15 39N 121 10 E
General Toshevo, Bulgaria ... 51 C12 43 42N 28 6 E
General Trevino, Mexico ... 163 B5 26 14N 99 29W
General Trías, Mexico ... 162 B3 28 21N 106 22W
General Viamonte, Argentina ... 174 D3 35 1 S 61 3W
General Villegas, Argentina ... 174 D3 35 5 S 63 0W
General Vintter, L., Argentina ... 176 B2 43 55 S 71 40W
Generoso, Mte., Switz. ... 33 E8 45 56N 9 2 E
Genesee, Idaho, U.S.A. ... 158 C5 46 33N 116 56W
Genesee, Pa., U.S.A. ... 150 E7 41 59N 77 54W
Genesee →, U.S.A. ... 150 C7 43 16N 77 36W
Geneseo, Ill., U.S.A. ... 156 C6 41 27N 90 9W
Geneseo, N.Y., U.S.A. ... 150 D7 42 48N 77 49W
Geneva = Genève, Switz. ... 32 D2 46 12N 6 9 E
Geneva, Ala., U.S.A. ... 152 D4 31 2N 85 52W
Geneva, Ga., U.S.A. ... 152 C5 32 35N 84 33W
Geneva, Ill., U.S.A. ... 157 C8 41 53N 88 18W
Geneva, Ind., U.S.A. ... 157 D12 40 36N 84 58W
Geneva, N.Y., U.S.A. ... 150 D8 42 52N 76 59W
Geneva, Nebr., U.S.A. ... 156 E6 40 32N 97 36W
Geneva, Ohio, U.S.A. ... 150 E4 41 48N 80 57W
Geneva (GVA), Switz. ... 32 D2 46 14N 6 11 E
Geneva, L. = Léman, L., Europe ... 27 F13 46 26N 6 30 E
Geneva, L., U.S.A. ... 154 D10 42 38N 88 30W
Genève, Switz. ... 32 D2 46 12N 6 9 E
Genève □, Switz. ... 32 D2 46 10N 6 10 E
Geng, Afghan. ... 91 C1 31 22N 61 28 E
Gengenbach, Germany ... 31 G4 48 24N 8 1 E
Gengma, China ... 76 F2 23 32N 99 20 E
Genichesk = Henichesk, Ukraine ... 59 J8 46 12N 34 50 E
Genil →, Spain ... 41 H5 37 42N 5 19W
Genk, Belgium ... 24 D5 50 58N 5 32 E
Genkai-Nada, Japan ... 72 D2 34 0N 130 0 E
Genlis, France ... 27 E12 47 11N 5 12 E
Gennargentu, Mti. del, Italy ... 46 B2 40 1N 9 19 E
Gennes, France ... 26 E6 47 20N 0 17W
Genoa = Génova, Italy ... 44 D5 44 25N 8 57 E
Genoa, Australia ... 129 D8 37 29 S 149 35 E
Genoa, Ill., U.S.A. ... 157 B8 42 6N 88 42W
Genoa, N.Y., U.S.A. ... 151 D8 42 40N 76 32W
Genoa, Nebr., U.S.A. ... 154 E6 41 27N 97 44W
Genoa, Nev., U.S.A. ... 160 F7 39 2N 119 50W
Genoa →, Argentina ... 176 B2 44 55 S 70 5W
Genoa ✈ (GOA), Italy ... 44 D5 44 25N 8 56 E
Genoa City, U.S.A. ... 157 B8 42 30N 88 20W
Génova, Italy ... 44 D5 44 25N 8 57 E
Génova, G. di, Italy ... 44 E6 44 0N 9 0 E
Genovesa, I., Ecuador ... 172 a 0 20N 89 58W
Genriyetty, Ostrov, Russia ... 67 B16 77 6N 156 30 E
Gent, Belgium ... 24 C3 51 2N 3 42 E
Genteng, Bali, Indonesia ... 79 J17 8 22 S 114 9 E
Genteng, Jawa, Indonesia ... 79 G12 7 22 S 106 24 E
Genthin, Germany ... 30 C8 52 25N 12 9 E
Gentio do Ouro, Brazil ... 170 D3 11 25 S 42 30W
Gentryville, U.S.A. ... 157 F9 38 6N 87 2W
Genyem, Indonesia ... 83 B6 2 46 S 140 12 E
Genzano di Lucánia, Italy ... 47 B9 40 51N 16 2 E
Genzano di Roma, Italy ... 45 G9 41 42N 12 41 E
Geoagiu, Romania ... 53 A5 55N 23 12 E
Geographe B., Australia ... 125 F2 33 30 S 115 15 E
Geographe Chan., Australia ... 125 D1 24 30 S 113 0 E
Geokchay = Göyçay, Azerbaijan ... 61 K8 40 42N 47 43 E
Georga, Zemlya, Russia ... 66 A5 80 30N 49 0 E
George, S. Africa ... 116 E3 33 58 S 22 29 E
George →, Canada ... 141 A6 58 49N 66 10W
George, L., N.S.W., Australia ... 129 C8 35 10 S 149 25 E
George, L., S. Austral., Australia ... 128 D4 37 25 S 140 0 E
George, L., W. Austral., Australia ... 124 D3 22 45 S 123 40 E
George, L., Uganda ... 118 B3 0 5N 30 10 E
George, L., Fla., U.S.A. ... 153 F8 29 17N 81 36W
George, L., N.Y., U.S.A. ... 151 C11 43 37N 73 33W
George, L., S. Austral., Australia ... 124 D5 24 22 S 131 45 E
George L, St. Helena ... 9 h 15 58 S 5 38W
George Pt., Australia ... 126 J6 20 6 S 148 36 E
George River = Kangiqsualujjuaq, Canada ... 139 C13 58 30N 65 59W
George Sound, N.Z. ... 131 E2 44 52 S 167 25 E
George Town, Australia ... 127 D4 41 6 S 146 49 E
George Town, Bahamas ... 164 B4 23 33N 75 47W
George Town, Cayman Is. ... 164 C3 19 20N 81 24W
George Town, Malaysia ... 87 c 5 25N 100 20 E
George V Land, Antarctica ... 7 C10 69 0 S 148 0 E
George VI Sound, Antarctica ... 7 D17 71 0 S 68 0W
George West, U.S.A. ... 155 L5 28 20N 98 7W
Georgetown, Ascension I. ... 9 g 7 56 S 14 25W
Georgetown, Australia ... 126 B3 18 17 S 143 33 E
Georgetown, Ont., Canada ... 140 D4 43 40N 79 56W
Georgetown, P.E.I., Canada ... 141 C7 46 13N 62 24W
Georgetown, Gambia ... 112 C2 13 30N 14 47W
Georgetown, Guyana ... 169 B6 6 50N 58 12W
Georgetown, Calif., U.S.A. ... 160 G6 38 54N 120 50W
Georgetown, Colo., U.S.A. ... 158 G11 39 42N 105 42W
Georgetown, Fla., U.S.A. ... 153 F8 29 23N 81 38W
Georgetown, Ga., U.S.A. ... 152 C3 31 53N 85 6W
Georgetown, Ill., U.S.A. ... 157 E9 39 59N 87 38W
Georgetown, Ky., U.S.A. ... 157 F12 38 13N 84 33W
Georgetown, N.Y., U.S.A. ... 151 D9 42 46N 75 44W
Georgetown, Ohio, U.S.A. ... 157 F13 38 52N 83 54W
Georgetown, S.C., U.S.A. ... 153 J6 33 23N 79 17W
Georgetown, Tex., U.S.A. ... 155 K6 30 38N 97 41W
Georgia □, U.S.A. ... 152 C6 32 50N 83 15W
Georgia ■, Asia ... 61 J6 42 0N 43 0 E
Georgia, Str. of, Canada ... 142 D4 49 25N 124 0W
Georgian B., Canada ... 140 C3 45 15N 81 0W
Georgian Bay Islands Nat. Park △, Canada ... 140 D4 44 53N 79 52W
Georgina →, Australia ... 126 C2 23 30 S 139 47 E
Georgina I., Canada ... 150 B5 44 22N 79 17W
Georgiu-Dezh = Liski, Russia ... 59 G10 51 3N 39 30 E
Georgiyevsk, Russia ... 61 H6 44 12N 43 28 E
Georgsmarienhütte, Germany ... 30 C4 52 13N 8 3 E
Gera, Germany ... 30 E8 50 53N 12 4 E
Geraardsbergen, Belgium ... 24 D3 50 45N 3 53 E
Geral, Serra, Bahia, Brazil ... 171 D3 14 0 S 41 0W
Geral, Serra, Goiás, Brazil ... 170 D2 11 15 S 46 30W
Geral, Serra, Sta. Catarina, Brazil ... 175 B6 26 25 S 50 0W
Geral de Goiás, Serra, Brazil ... 171 D2 12 0 S 46 0W
Geral do Paraná, Serra, Brazil ... 171 E2 15 0 S 47 30W
Gerald, U.S.A. ... 156 F5 38 24N 91 20W
Geraldine, N.Z. ... 131 E6 44 5 S 171 15 E
Geraldine, U.S.A. ... 158 C8 47 36N 110 16W
Geraldton, Australia ... 125 E1 28 48 S 114 32 E
Geraldton, Canada ... 140 C2 49 44N 86 59W
Geranium, Australia ... 128 C4 35 23 S 140 11 E
Gérardmer, France ... 27 D13 48 3N 6 50 E
Gerçüş, Turkey ... 101 D9 37 34N 41 23 E
Gerdine, Mt., U.S.A. ... 148 F9 61 35N 152 27W
Gerede, Turkey ... 100 B5 40 45N 32 10 E
Gerês, Sierra do, Portugal ... 40 D3 41 48N 8 0W
Gereshk, Afghan. ... 91 C2 31 47N 64 35 E
Geretsried, Germany ... 31 H7 47 51N 11 28 E
Gérgal, Spain ... 41 H2 37 7N 2 31W
Gerik, Malaysia ... 87 K3 5 50N 101 15 E
Gering, U.S.A. ... 154 E3 41 50N 103 40W
Gerlach, U.S.A. ... 158 F4 40 39N 119 21W
Gerlachovský štít, Slovak Rep. ... 35 B13 49 11N 20 7 E
Gerlogubi, Ethiopia ... 120 C3 6 53N 45 3 E
German East Africa = Tanzania ■, Africa ... 118 D3 6 0 S 34 0 E
German Planina, Macedonia ... 50 D6 42 20N 22 0 E
Germania Land, Greenland ... 10 B9 77 5N 19 30W
Germansen Landing, Canada ... 142 B4 55 43N 124 40W
Germantown, Ohio, U.S.A. ... 157 E12 39 38N 84 22W

Germantown, Tenn., U.S.A. ... 155 M10 35 5N 89 49W
Germantown, Wis., U.S.A. ... 157 A8 43 14N 88 6W
Germany ■, Europe ... 30 E6 51 0N 10 0 E
Germencik, Turkey ... 49 D9 37 52N 27 37 E
Germering, Germany ... 31 G7 48 8N 11 22 E
Germershelm, Germany ... 31 F4 49 12N 8 22 E
Germí, Iran ... 97 B6 39 1N 48 3 E
Germiston, S. Africa ... 117 D4 26 15 S 28 10 E
Gernene, Algeria ... 111 D5 21 40N 2 24 E
Gernsheim, Germany ... 31 F4 49 45N 8 30 E
Gero, Japan ... 73 B9 35 48N 137 14 E
Gerogery, Australia ... 129 C7 35 50 S 147 1 E
Gerokgak, Indonesia ... 79 J17 8 11 S 114 27 E
Gerolzhofen, Germany ... 31 F6 49 54N 10 21 E
Gerona = Girona, Spain ... 40 D7 41 58N 2 46 E
Gerrard, Canada ... 142 C5 50 30N 117 17W
Gerringong, Australia ... 129 C9 34 46 S 150 47 E
Gers □, France ... 28 E4 43 35N 0 30 E
Gers →, France ... 28 D4 44 9N 0 39 E
Gersoppa Falls, India ... 95 G2 14 12N 74 46 E
Gerstofen, Germany ... 31 G6 48 25N 10 53 E
Gertak Sanggul, Malaysia ... 87 c 5 17N 100 12 E
Gertak Sanggul, Tanjung, Malaysia ... 87 c 5 16N 100 11 E
Gerung, Indonesia ... 79 K19 8 43 S 116 7 E
Géryville = El Bayadh, Algeria ... 111 B5 33 40N 1 1 E
Gerzat, France ... 28 C7 45 48N 3 8 E
Gerze, Turkey ... 100 B6 41 48N 35 12 E
Geseke, Germany ... 30 D4 51 38N 8 31 E
Geser, Indonesia ... 83 B4 3 50 S 130 54 E
Gesira Nat. Park △, Somali Rep. ... 120 D2 1 58N 44 59 E
Gesso →, Italy ... 44 D4 44 24N 7 33 E
Gestro, Wabi →, Ethiopia ... 107 G5 4 12N 42 2 E
Getafe, Spain ... 42 E7 40 18N 3 44W
Getinge, Sweden ... 17 H6 56 49N 12 44 E
Gettysburg, Pa., U.S.A. ... 148 F7 39 50N 77 14W
Gettysburg, S. Dak., U.S.A. ... 154 C5 45 1N 99 57W
Getxo, Spain ... 40 B2 43 21N 2 59W
Getz Ice Shelf, Antarctica ... 7 D14 75 0 S 130 0W
Geureudong, Gunong, Indonesia ... 84 B1 4 13N 96 42 E
Geurie, Australia ... 129 B8 32 22 S 148 50 E
Gevaş, Turkey ... 101 C10 38 15N 43 6 E
Gévaudan, France ... 28 D7 44 40N 3 40 E
Gevgelija, Macedonia ... 50 E6 41 9N 22 30 E
Gévora →, Spain ... 43 G4 38 53N 6 57W
Gevrai, India ... 94 E2 19 16N 75 45 E
Gewani, Ethiopia ... 107 E5 10 12N 40 40 E
Gex, France ... 27 F13 46 21N 6 3 E
Geyikli, Turkey ... 49 B8 39 48N 26 12 E
Geyser, U.S.A. ... 158 C8 47 16N 110 30W
Geyserville, U.S.A. ... 160 G4 38 42N 122 54W
Geysir, Iceland ... 11 C6 64 19N 20 18W
Geyve, Turkey ... 100 B4 40 30N 30 18 E
Ghàbat el Arab = Wang Kai, Sudan ... 107 F2 9 3N 29 23 E
Ghabeish, Sudan ... 107 E2 12 22N 27 21 E
Ghafurov, Tajikistan ... 65 C4 40 13N 69 43 E
Ghaggar →, India ... 92 E6 29 30N 74 53 E
Ghaghara →, India ... 93 G11 25 45N 84 40 E
Ghaghat →, Bangla. ... 90 C2 25 19N 89 38 E
Ghaghe, Solomon Is. ... 133 L10 7 24 S 158 15 E
Ghagra, India ... 93 H11 23 17N 84 33 E
Ghagra →, India ... 93 F9 27 29N 81 9 E
Ghajn Tuffieha Bay, Malta ... 38 E7 35 56N 14 21 E
Ghajnsielem, Malta ... 38 E7 36 2N 14 17 E
Ghalla, Wadi el →, Sudan ... 107 E2 10 25N 27 32 E
Ghana ■, W. Afr. ... 113 D4 8 0N 1 0W
Ghansor, India ... 93 H9 22 39N 80 1 E
Ghanzi, Botswana ... 116 C3 21 50 S 21 34 E
Gharb, Malta ... 38 E6 36 4N 14 13 E
Gharb el Istiwa'iya □, Sudan ... 107 G3 5 0N 30 0 E
Gharb Kordofân, Sudan ... 107 E2 12 0N 28 0 E
Gharbîya, Es Sahrâ el, Egypt ... 106 B2 27 40N 26 30 E
Ghardaïa, Algeria ... 111 B5 32 20N 3 37 E
Ghârib, G., Egypt ... 106 B3 28 6N 33 3 E
Gharig, Sudan ... 107 E2 10 47N 27 33 E
Gharm, W. →, Oman ... 99 C7 19 57N 57 38 E
Gharyān, Libya ... 108 B2 32 10N 13 0 E
Gharyān □, Libya ... 108 B2 30 35N 12 0 E
Ghat, Libya ... 108 D2 24 59N 10 11 E
Ghatal, India ... 93 H12 22 40N 87 46 E
Ghatampur, India ... 93 F9 26 8N 80 13 E
Ghatgaon, India ... 95 J14 21 24N 85 53 E
Ghatsila, India ... 93 H12 22 36N 86 31 E
Ghaṭṭī, Si. Arabia ... 94 E3 31 16N 37 31 E
Ghawdex = Gozo, Malta ... 38 E7 36 3N 14 15 E
Ghayl, Si. Arabia ... 98 B4 21 40N 46 20 E
Ghazal, Bahr el →, Chad ... 109 F3 13 0N 15 47 E
Ghazâl, Bahr el →, Sudan ... 107 F3 9 31N 30 25 E
Ghazaouet, Algeria ... 111 A4 35 8N 1 50W
Ghaziabad, India ... 92 E7 28 42N 77 26 E
Ghazipur, India ... 93 G10 25 38N 83 35 E
Ghaznī, Afghan. ... 91 B3 33 30N 68 28 E
Ghaznī □, Afghan. ... 91 B3 32 10N 68 20 E
Ghedi, Italy ... 44 C7 45 24N 10 16 E
Ghelari, Romania ... 52 E7 45 38N 22 45 E
Ghèlinsor, Somali Rep. ... 120 C3 6 28N 46 39 E
Ghent = Gent, Belgium ... 24 C3 51 2N 3 42 E
Gheorghe Gheorghiu-Dej = Oneşti, Romania ... 53 D11 46 17N 26 47 E
Gheorgheni, Romania ... 53 D10 46 43N 25 41 E
Gherla, Romania ... 53 C8 47 2N 23 57 E
Ghidigeni, Romania ... 53 D12 46 3N 27 30 E
Ghiffa, Italy ... 44 C6 45 58N 8 37 E
Ghilarza, Italy ... 46 B1 40 7N 8 50 E
Ghîmeş-Făget, Romania ... 53 D11 46 35N 26 2 E
Ghînah, Wādī →, Si. Arabia ... 96 D3 30 27N 38 14 E
Ghisonaccia, France ... 29 F13 42 1N 9 26 E
Ghisoni, France ... 29 F13 42 7N 9 12 E
Ghizao, Afghan. ... 91 B3 33 20N 65 44 E
Ghizar →, Pakistan ... 93 A5 36 15N 73 43 E
Ghod →, India ... 94 E2 18 32N 74 33 E
Ghogha, India ... 94 D1 21 40N 72 20 E
Ghot Ogrein, Egypt ... 106 A2 31 10N 25 20 E
Ghotaru, India ... 92 F4 27 20N 70 1 E
Ghotki, Pakistan ... 92 E3 28 5N 69 21 E
Ghowr □, Afghan. ... 91 B2 34 0N 64 20 E
Ghudaf, W. al →, Iraq ... 101 F10 32 56N 43 30 E
Ghudāmis, Libya ... 108 B2 30 11N 9 29 E
Ghudāmis □, Libya ... 108 B2 30 10N 10 25 E
Ghughri, India ... 93 H9 22 39N 80 41 E
Ghugus, India ... 94 E4 19 58N 79 12 E
Ghulam Mohammad Barrage, Pakistan ... 92 G3 25 30N 68 20 E
Ghurayrah, Si. Arabia ... 98 C3 18 37N 42 41 E
Ghūrīān, Afghan. ... 91 B1 34 17N 61 25 E
Ghuzzayil, Sabkhat, Libya ... 108 C3 29 30N 19 30 E
Gia Dinh, Vietnam ... 87 G6 10 49N 106 42 E
Gia Lai = Plei Ku, Vietnam ... 86 F7 13 57N 108 0 E
Gia Nghia, Vietnam ... 86 F7 11 58N 107 42 E
Gia Ngoc, Vietnam ... 86 E7 14 50N 108 58 E
Gia Vuc, Vietnam ... 86 E7 14 42N 108 34 E
Giamama, Somali Rep. ... 120 D2 0 4N 42 44 E
Giannutri, Italy ... 44 F8 42 15N 11 6 E
Giant Forest, U.S.A. ... 160 J8 36 36N 118 43W
Giant Mts. = Krkonoše, Czech Rep. ... 34 A8 50 50N 15 35 E
Giant Sequoia National Monument △, U.S.A. ... 160 K8 36 0N 118 32W
Giants Causeway, U.K. ... 23 A5 55 16N 6 29W
Giant's Tank, Sri Lanka ... 95 K5 8 51N 80 2 E
Gianyar, Indonesia ... 79 K18 8 32 S 115 20 E
Giarabub = Al Jaghbūb, Libya ... 108 C4 29 42N 24 38 E
Giarre, Italy ... 47 E8 37 43N 15 11 E

Giaveno, Italy ... 44 C4 45 2N 7 21 E
Gibara, Cuba ... 164 B4 21 9N 76 11W
Gibb River, Australia ... 124 C4 16 26 S 126 26 E
Gibbon, U.S.A. ... 154 E5 40 45N 98 51W
Gibe →, Ethiopia ... 107 F4 7 20N 37 36 E
Gibellina Nuova, Italy ... 46 E5 37 48N 12 52 E
Gibeon, Namibia ... 116 D2 25 9 S 17 43 E
Gibraléon, Spain ... 43 H4 37 23N 6 58W
Gibraltar ☑, Europe ... 43 J5 36 7N 5 22W
Gibraltar, Str. of, Medit. S. ... 43 K5 35 55N 5 40W
Gibraltar Range Nat. Park △, Australia ... 127 A5 29 31 S 152 19 E
Gibson, U.S.A. ... 152 B7 33 14N 82 36W
Gibson City, U.S.A. ... 157 D8 40 28N 88 22W
Gibson Desert, Australia ... 124 D4 24 0 S 126 0 E
Gibsonburg, U.S.A. ... 157 C13 41 23N 83 19W
Gibsons, U.S.A. ... 142 D4 49 24N 123 32W
Gibsonville, U.S.A. ... 160 F6 39 46N 120 54W
Giddalur, India ... 95 G4 15 20N 78 57 E
Giddings, U.S.A. ... 155 K6 30 11N 96 56W
Gidole, Ethiopia ... 107 F4 5 40N 37 25 E
Giebnegáisi = Kebnekaise, Sweden ... 14 C18 67 53N 18 33 E
Gien, France ... 27 E9 47 40N 2 36 E
Giengen, Germany ... 31 G6 48 37N 10 14 E
Giessen, Germany ... 30 E4 50 34N 8 41 E
Gifān, Iran ... 97 B8 37 54N 57 28 E
Gifatin, Geziret, Egypt ... 106 B3 27 10N 33 50 E
Gifford, U.S.A. ... 153 H9 27 40N 80 25W
Gifhorn, Germany ... 30 C6 52 30N 10 33 E
Gift Lake, Canada ... 142 B5 55 53N 115 49W
Gifu, Japan ... 73 B8 35 30N 136 45 E
Gifu □, Japan ... 73 B9 35 40N 137 0 E
Gigant, Russia ... 61 G5 46 28N 41 0 E
Giganta, Sa. de la, Mexico ... 162 B2 25 30N 111 30W
Gigen, Bulgaria ... 51 C8 43 40N 24 28 E
Gigha, U.K. ... 22 F3 55 42N 5 44W
Giglei, Somali Rep. ... 120 C3 5 23N 46 20 E
Giglio, Italy ... 44 F7 42 20N 10 52 E
Gignac, France ... 28 E7 43 39N 3 32 E
Gignod, Italy ... 32 E4 45 47N 7 17 E
Gigüela →, Spain ... 43 F7 39 8N 3 44W
Gijón, Spain ... 42 B5 43 32N 5 42W
Gila →, U.S.A. ... 159 K6 32 43N 114 33W
Gila Bend, U.S.A. ... 159 K7 32 57N 112 43W
Gila Bend Mts., U.S.A. ... 159 K7 33 10N 113 0W
Gila Cliff Dwellings Nat. Monument △, U.S.A. ... 159 K9 33 2N 108 16W
Gīlān □, Iran ... 97 B6 37 0N 50 0 E
Gilău, Romania ... 53 D8 46 45N 23 23 E
Gilbert →, Australia ... 126 B3 16 35 S 141 15 E
Gilbert Is., Kiribati ... 134 G9 1 0N 172 0 E
Gilbert River, Australia ... 126 B3 18 9 S 142 52 E
Gilbert Plains, Canada ... 143 C8 51 9N 100 28W
Gilead, U.S.A. ... 151 B14 44 24N 70 59W
Gilford I., Canada ... 142 C3 50 40N 126 30W
Gilgandra, Australia ... 129 A8 31 43 S 148 39 E
Gilgil, Kenya ... 118 C4 0 30 S 36 20 E
Gilgit, India ... 93 B6 35 50N 74 15 E
Gilgit →, Pakistan ... 93 B6 35 44N 74 37 E
Gilgunnia, Australia ... 129 B7 32 26 S 146 2 E
Gili, Reserva do →, Mozam. ... 119 F4 16 39 S 39 45 E
Gilimanuk, Indonesia ... 79 J17 8 10 S 114 26 E
Giljeva Planina, Serbia, Yug. ... 50 C3 43 9N 20 0 E
Gili Pt., St. Helena ... 9 h 15 58 S 5 38W
Gillam, Canada ... 143 B10 56 20N 94 40W
Gilleleje, Denmark ... 17 H6 56 8N 12 19 E
Gillen, L., Australia ... 125 E3 26 11 S 124 38 E
Gilles, L., Australia ... 128 B2 32 50 S 136 45 E
Gillespie, U.S.A. ... 156 F7 39 8N 89 49W
Gillespies Pt., N.Z. ... 131 D4 43 24 S 169 49 E
Gillette, U.S.A. ... 154 C2 44 18N 105 30W
Gilliat, Australia ... 126 C3 20 40 S 141 28 E
Gillingham, U.K. ... 21 F8 51 23N 0 33 E
Gilman, U.S.A. ... 157 D9 40 46N 88 0W
Gilman City, U.S.A. ... 156 D3 40 8N 93 53W
Gilmer, U.S.A. ... 155 J7 32 44N 94 57W
Gilmore, L., Australia ... 125 F3 32 29 S 121 37 E
Gilo →, Ethiopia ... 107 F3 8 10N 33 15 E
Gilort →, Romania ... 53 F8 44 38N 23 32 E
Gilroy, U.S.A. ... 160 H5 37 1N 121 34W
Giluwe, Mt., Papua N. G. ... 132 D2 6 8 S 143 52 E
Gimbi, Ethiopia ... 107 F4 9 3N 35 42 E
Gimie, Mt, St. Lucia ... 165 f 13 54N 61 0W
Gimli, Canada ... 143 C9 50 40N 97 0W
Gimo, Sweden ... 16 D12 60 11N 18 12 E
Gimone →, France ... 28 E5 44 0N 1 6 E
Gimont, France ... 28 E4 43 38N 0 52 E
Gimpu, Indonesia ... 82 B2 1 36 S 120 2 E
Gin →, Sri Lanka ... 95 L5 6 5N 80 7 E
Gin Gin, Australia ... 127 D5 25 0 S 151 58 E
Ginâh, Egypt ... 106 B3 25 21N 30 30 E
Ginatilan, Phil. ... 81 G4 9 34N 123 19 E
Gineifa, Egypt ... 106 H8 30 12N 32 25 E
Gingee, India ... 95 H4 12 15N 79 25 E
Gingin, Australia ... 125 F2 31 22 S 115 54 E
Gingindlovu, S. Africa ... 117 D5 29 2 S 31 30 E
Gingoog, Phil. ... 81 G5 8 50N 125 7 E
Ginir, Ethiopia ... 107 F5 7 6N 40 40 E
Gino, Pizzo di, Italy ... 44 D6 46 9N 9 10 E
Ginosa, Italy ... 47 B9 40 35N 16 45 E
Ginzo de Limia = Xinzo de Limia, Spain ... 42 C3 42 3N 7 47W
Gioia, Golfo di, Italy ... 47 D8 38 30N 15 45 E
Gioia del Colle, Italy ... 47 B9 40 48N 16 55 E
Gioia Táuro, Italy ... 47 D8 38 26N 15 54 E
Gioiosa Iónica, Italy ... 47 D9 38 20N 16 18 E
Gioiosa Marea, Italy ... 47 D7 38 10N 14 54 E
Gióna, Óros, Greece ... 48 C4 38 38N 22 14 E
Giovi, Passo dei, Italy ... 44 D5 44 33N 8 57 E
Giovinazzo, Italy ... 47 A9 41 11N 16 40 E
Gippsland, Australia ... 129 D7 37 52 S 147 0 E
Gir Hills, India ... 92 J4 21 0N 71 0 E
Girab, India ... 92 F3 26 2N 70 38 E
Girâfi, W. →, Egypt ... 103 F3 29 58N 34 39 E
Giraltovce, Slovak Rep. ... 35 B14 49 7N 21 32 E
Girard, Ill., U.S.A. ... 156 E7 39 27N 89 47W
Girard, Kans., U.S.A. ... 155 G7 37 31N 94 51W
Girard, Ohio, U.S.A. ... 150 E4 41 9N 80 42W
Girard, Pa., U.S.A. ... 150 E4 42 0N 80 19W
Girardot, Colombia ... 168 C3 4 18N 74 48W
Girdle Ness, U.K. ... 22 D6 57 9N 2 3W
Giresun, Turkey ... 101 B8 40 55N 38 30 E
Girga, Egypt ... 106 B3 26 17N 31 55 E
Girgenti = Agrigento, Italy ... 46 E6 37 19N 13 34 E
Girgir, C., Papua N. G. ... 132 B3 3 50 S 144 35 E
Giri →, Dem. Rep. of the Congo ... 114 B3 0 30N 17 59 E
Giri, India ... 92 D7 30 28N 77 41 E
Giridih, India ... 93 G12 24 10N 86 21 E
Girifalco, Italy ... 47 D9 38 49N 16 26 E
Girilambone, Australia ... 129 A7 31 16 S 146 57 E
Giro, Nigeria ... 113 C5 11 7N 4 42 E
Giron = Kyrenia, Cyprus ... 113 C5 35 20N 33 19 E
Giromagny, France ... 27 E13 47 45N 6 50 E
Girona, Spain ... 40 D7 41 58N 2 46 E
Girona □, Spain ... 40 C7 42 11N 2 30 E
Gironde □, France ... 28 C3 44 45N 0 30W
Gironde →, France ... 28 C2 45 32N 1 7W
Gironella, Spain ... 40 C6 42 2N 1 53 E
Girraween Nat. Park △, Australia ... 127 A5 28 46 S 151 54 E

Giru, *Australia* . . . . 126 B4   19 30 S 147 5 E
Girvan, *U.K.* 22 F4   55 14N 4 51W
Gisborne, *Australia* . . . . 128 D6   37 29 S 144 36 E
Gisborne, *N.Z.* . . . . 130 E7   38 39 S 178 5 E
Gisborne □, *N.Z.* . . . . 130 E6   38 30 S 178 0 E
Gisenyi, *Rwanda* . . . . 118 C2   1 41 S 29 15 E
Gislaved, *Sweden* . . . . 17 G7   57 19N 13 32 E
Gisors, *France* . . . . 27 C8   49 15N 1 47 E
Gissarskiy Khrebet, *Tajikistan* . 65 D4   39 0N 69 0 E
Giswil, *Switz.* . . . . 32 C6   46 50N 8 11 E
Gitega, *Burundi* . . . . 118 C2   3 26 S 29 56 E
Giuba →, *Somali Rep.* . . . . . . 120 D2   1 30N 42 35 E
Giubiasco, *Switz.* . . . . 33 D8   46 11N 9 1 E
Giugliano in Campania, *Italy* . . 47 B7   40 56N 14 12 E
Giulianova, *Italy* . . . . 45 F10   42 45N 13 57 E
Giurgeni, *Romania* . . . . 53 F12   44 45N 27 48 E
Giurgiu, *Romania* . . . . 53 G10   43 52N 25 57 E
Giurgiu □, *Romania* . . . . 53 F10   44 20N 26 0 E
Giurgiuleşti, *Moldova* . . . . . . 53 E13   45 29N 28 12 E
Give, *Denmark* . . . . 17 J3   55 51N 9 13 E
Givet, *France* . . . . 27 B11   50 8N 4 49 E
Givors, *France* . . . . 29 C8   45 35N 4 45 E
Givry, *France* . . . . 27 F11   46 41N 4 46 E
Giyon, *Ethiopia* . . . . 107 F4   8 33N 38 1 E
Giza = El Gîza, *Egypt* . . . . . . 106 J7   30 0N 31 10 E
Gizhduvan, *Uzbekistan* . . . . . 65 C2   40 6N 64 41 E
Gizhiga, *Russia* . . . . 67 C17   62 3N 160 30 E
Gizhiginskaya Guba, *Russia* . . 67 C16   61 0N 158 0 E
Gizo, *Solomon Is.* . . . . 133 M9   8 5 S 156 50 E
Giżycko, *Poland* . . . . 54 D8   54 2N 21 48 E
Gizzeria, *Italy* . . . . 47 D9   38 59N 16 12 E
Gjalicë e Lumës, Mal., *Albania* . 50 D4   42 2N 20 25 E
Gjegjan, *Albania* . . . . 50 E4   41 58N 20 3 E
Gjendesheim, *Norway* . . . . . . 18 C5   61 30N 8 48 E
Gjerstad, *Norway* . . . . 18 F6   58 54N 9 1 E
Gjevilvatnet, *Norway* . . . . 18 B6   62 43N 9 23 E
Gjirokastër, *Albania* . . . . 50 F4   40 7N 20 10 E
Gjoa Haven, *Canada* 138 B10   68 20N 96 8W
Gjøra, *Norway* . . . . 18 B6   62 33N 9 4 E
Gjøvik, *Norway* . . . . 18 D7   60 47N 10 43 E
Gjuhës, Kepi i, *Albania* . . . . . 50 F3   40 28N 19 15 E
Glace Bay, *Canada* 141 C8   46 11N 59 58W
Glacier Bay, *U.S.A.* 144 G14   58 40N 136 0W
Glacier Bay Nat. Park and
  Preserve △, *U.S.A.* 142 B1   58 45N 136 30W
Glacier Nat. Park △, *Canada* . 142 C5   51 15N 117 30W
Glacier Nat. Park △, *U.S.A.* . . 158 B7   48 30N 113 18W
Glacier Peak, *U.S.A.* 158 B3   48 7N 121 7W
Gladewater, *U.S.A.* 155 J7   32 33N 94 56W
Gladstone, *Queens., Australia* . 126 C5   23 52 S 151 16 E
Gladstone, *S. Austral., Australia* . 128 B3   33 15 S 138 22 E
Gladstone, *Canada* 143 C9   50 13N 98 57W
Gladstone, *Ill., U.S.A.* 156 D6   40 52N 90 57W
Gladstone, *Mich., U.S.A.* 148 C2   45 51N 87 1W
Gladstone, *Mo., U.S.A.* 156 E2   39 14N 94 35W
Gladwin, *U.S.A.* 148 D13   43 59N 84 29W
Glafsfjorden, *Sweden* . . . . . . 16 E6   59 30N 12 37 E
Glagah, *Indonesia* . . . . 79 J17   8 13 S 114 18 E
Głagów Małopolski, *Poland* . . 55 H8   50 10N 21 56 E
Glâma = Glomma →, *Norway* . 18 E7   59 12N 10 57 E
Glåma, *Iceland* 11 B4   65 48N 23 0W
Glamis, *U.S.A.* 161 N11   32 55N 115 5W
Glamoč, *Bos.-H.* . . . . 45 D13   44 3N 16 51 E
Glamorgan, Vale of □, *U.K.* . . 21 F4   51 28N 3 25W
Glåmos, *Norway* . . . . 18 B8   62 41N 11 25 E
Glamsbjerg, *Denmark* . . . . . . 17 J4   55 17N 10 6 E
Gland, *Switz.* . . . . 32 D2   46 26N 6 16 E
Glarner Alpen, *Switz.* . . . . . . 33 C8   46 50N 9 0 E
Glärnisch, *Switz.* . . . . 33 C8   47 0N 9 0 E
Glarus, *Switz.* . . . . 33 B8   47 3N 9 4 E
Glarus □, *Switz.* . . . . 33 C8   47 0N 9 5 E
Glasco, *Kans., U.S.A.* 154 E6   39 22N 97 50W
Glasco, *N.Y., U.S.A.* 151 D11   42 3N 73 57W
Glasgow, *U.K.* 22 F4   55 51N 4 15W
Glasgow, *Ky., U.S.A.* 148 G3   37 0N 85 55W
Glasgow, *Mo., U.S.A.* 156 E4   39 14N 92 51W
Glasgow, *Mont., U.S.A.* 158 B10   48 12N 106 38W
Glasgow, City of □, *U.K.* 22 F4   55 51N 4 12W
Glasgow International ✈ (GLA),
  U.K. 22 F4   55 51N 4 21W
Glaslyn, *Canada* 143 C7   53 22N 108 21W
Glastonbury, *U.K.* 21 F5   51 9N 2 43W
Glastonbury, *U.S.A.* 151 E12   41 43N 72 37W
Glatt →, *Switz.* . . . . 33 B7   47 28N 8 32 E
Glattfelden, *Switz.* . . . . 33 A7   47 33N 8 32 E
Glauchau, *Germany* . . . . 30 E8   50 49N 12 33 E
Glava, *Sweden* . . . . 16 E6   59 33N 12 35 E
Glavice, *Croatia* . . . . 45 E13   43 43N 16 41 E
Glazov, *Russia* . . . . 60 A11   58 9N 52 40 E
Gleichen, *Canada* 142 C6   50 52N 113 3W
Gleisdorf, *Austria* . . . . 34 D8   47 6N 15 44 E
Gleiwitz = Gliwice, *Poland* . . 55 H5   50 22N 18 41 E
Glen, *U.S.A.* 151 B13   44 7N 71 11W
Glen Affric, *U.K.* 22 D3   57 17N 5 1W
Glen Afton, *N.Z.* . . . . 130 D4   37 37 S 175 4 E
Glen Canyon, *U.S.A.* 159 H8   37 30N 110 40W
Glen Canyon Dam, *U.S.A.* . . . 159 H8   36 57N 111 29W
Glen Canyon Nat. Recr. Area △,
  U.S.A. 159 H8   37 15N 111 0W
Glen Coe, *U.K.* 22 E3   56 40N 5 0W
Glen Cove, *U.S.A.* 151 F11   40 52N 73 38W
Glen Garry, *U.K.* 22 D3   57 3N 5 7W
Glen Innes, *Australia* . . . . 127 D5   29 44 S 151 44 E
Glen Lyon, *U.S.A.* 151 E8   41 10N 76 5W
Glen Massey, *N.Z.* . . . . 130 D4   37 38 S 175 2 E
Glen Mor, *U.K.* 22 D4   57 9N 4 37W
Glen More Forest Park △, *U.K.* . 22 D5   57 8N 3 40W
Glen Moriston, *U.K.* 22 D4   57 11N 4 52W
Glen Robertson, *Canada* 151 A10   45 22N 74 30W
Glen Spean, *U.K.* 22 E4   56 53N 4 40W
Glen Ullin, *U.S.A.* 154 B4   46 49N 101 50W
Glénan, Îs. de, *France* 26 E3   47 42N 4 0W
Glenariff Nat. Park △, *Ireland* . 23 A5   55 2N 6 10W
Glenavy, *N.Z.* . . . . 131 K6   44 54 S 171 7 E
Glenburn, *Australia* . . . . 129 D6   37 27 S 145 26 E
Glencoe, *Canada* 150 D3   42 45N 81 43W
Glencoe, *S. Africa* . . . . 117 D5   28 11 S 30 11 E
Glencoe, *Ala., U.S.A.* 153 J2   33 57N 85 56W
Glencoe, *Minn., U.S.A.* 154 C7   44 46N 94 9W
Glendale, *Ariz., U.S.A.* 159 K7   33 32N 112 11W
Glendale, *Calif., U.S.A.* 161 L8   34 9N 118 15W
Glendale, *Fla., U.S.A.* 152 E3   30 52N 86 7W
Glendale, *Zimbabwe* . . . . 119 F3   17 22 S 31 5 E
Glendive, *U.S.A.* 154 B2   47 7N 104 43W
Glendo, *U.S.A.* 154 D2   42 30N 105 2W
Glenelg, *Australia* . . . . 128 C3   34 58 S 138 31 E
Glenelg →, *Australia* . . . . 128 E4   38 4 S 140 59 E
Glenfield, *U.S.A.* 151 C9   43 43N 75 24W
Glengarriff, *Ireland* 23 E2   51 45N 9 34W
Glenham, *N.Z.* . . . . 131 G3   46 26 S 168 52 E
Glenhope, *N.Z.* . . . . 131 B7   41 40 S 172 34 E
Glenmary, Mt., *N.Z.* . . . . 131 D4   43 58 S 169 55 E
Glenmont, *U.S.A.* 150 F2   40 31N 82 6W
Glenmorgan, *Australia* . . . . . . 127 D4   27 14 S 149 42 E
Glenn, *U.S.A.* 160 F4   39 31N 122 1W
Glennallen, *U.S.A.* 144 E11   62 7N 145 33W
Glennamaddy, *Ireland* 23 C3   53 37N 8 33W
Glenns Ferry, *U.S.A.* 158 E6   42 57N 115 18W
Glennville, *U.S.A.* 152 D8   31 56N 81 56W
Glenorchy, *Australia* . . . . 128 D5   36 55 S 142 41 E
Glenorchy, *N.Z.* . . . . 131 E3   44 51 S 168 24 E
Glenore, *Australia* . . . . 126 B3   17 50 S 141 12 E
Glenreagh, *Australia* . . . . 127 E5   30 2 S 153 1 E

Glenrock, *U.S.A.* 158 E11   42 52N 105 52W
Glenrothes, *U.K.* 22 E5   56 12N 3 10W
Glenrowan, *Australia* . . . . 129 D7   36 29 S 146 13 E
Glens Falls, *U.S.A.* 151 C11   43 19N 73 39W
Glenside, *U.S.A.* 151 F9   40 6N 75 9W
Glenthompson, *Australia* . . . . 128 D5   37 38 S 142 38 E
Glenties, *Ireland* 23 B3   54 49N 8 16W
Glenveagh Nat. Park △, *Ireland* . 23 A3   55 3N 8 1W
Glenville, *U.S.A.* 148 F5   38 56N 80 50W
Glenwood, *Canada* 141 C9   49 0N 54 58W
Glenwood, *Ark., U.S.A.* 155 H8   34 20N 93 33W
Glenwood, *Ga., U.S.A.* 152 C7   32 11N 82 40W
Glenwood, *Hawaii, U.S.A.* . . . 145 D6   19 29N 155 9W
Glenwood, *Iowa, U.S.A.* 154 E7   41 3N 95 45W
Glenwood, *Minn., U.S.A.* 154 C7   45 39N 95 23W
Glenwood, *Wash., U.S.A.* . . . 160 D5   46 1N 121 17W
Glenwood Springs, *U.S.A.* . . . 158 G10   39 33N 107 19W
Gletsch, *Switz.* . . . . 33 C6   46 34N 8 22 E
Glettinganes, *Iceland* 11 B13   65 30N 13 37W
Glidden, *U.S.A.* 156 B2   42 4N 94 44W
Glifádha, *Greece* . . . . 48 D5   37 52N 23 45 E
Glimåkra, *Sweden* . . . . 17 H8   56 19N 14 7 E
Glina, *Croatia* . . . . 45 C13   45 20N 16 6 E
Glinojeck, *Poland* . . . . 55 F7   52 49N 20 21 E
Glittertind, *Norway* . . . . 18 C5   61 40N 8 32 E
Gliwice, *Poland* . . . . 55 H5   50 22N 18 41 E
Globe, *U.S.A.* 159 K8   33 24N 110 47W
Glodeanu Siliştea, *Romania* . . 53 F11   44 50N 26 48 E
Glodeni, *Moldova* . . . . 53 C12   47 45N 27 31 E
Glödnitz, *Austria* . . . . 34 E7   46 53N 14 7 E
Gloggnitz, *Austria* . . . . 34 D8   47 41N 15 56 E
Głogów, *Poland* . . . . 55 G3   51 37N 16 5 E
Głogówek, *Poland* . . . . 55 H4   50 21N 17 53 E
Glomma →, *Norway* . . . . 18 E7   59 12N 10 57 E
Gloria, *Phil.* . . . . 80 E3   12 59N 121 30 E
Glorieuses, Is., *Ind. Oc.* . . . . . 117 A8   11 30 S 47 20 E
Glóssa, *Greece* . . . . 48 B5   39 10N 23 45 E
Glossop, *U.K.* 20 D6   53 27N 1 56W
Gloucester, *Australia* . . . . 129 B9   32 15 S 151 59 E
Gloucester, *Papua N. G.* . . . . 132 C5   5 31 S 148 31 E
Gloucester, *U.K.* 21 F5   51 53N 2 15W
Gloucester, *U.S.A.* 151 D14   42 37N 70 40W
Gloucester, C., *Papua N. G.* . . 132 C5   5 26 S 148 21 E
Gloucester I., *Australia* . . . . . 126 J6   20 0 S 148 30 E
Gloucester Island Nat. Park △,
  Australia . . . . 126 J6   20 2 S 148 30 E
Gloucester Point, *U.S.A.* 148 G7   37 15N 76 29W
Gloucestershire □, *U.K.* 21 F5   51 46N 2 15W
Gloversville, *U.S.A.* 151 C10   43 3N 74 21W
Glovertown, *Canada* 141 C9   48 40N 54 3W
Gloverville, *U.S.A.* 152 B8   33 32N 81 48W
Głowno, *Poland* . . . . 55 G6   51 59N 19 42 E
Głubczyce, *Poland* . . . . 55 H4   50 13N 17 52 E
Glubokiy, *Russia* . . . . 61 F5   48 35N 40 25 E
Glubokoye = Hlybokaye, *Belarus* . 58 E4   55 10N 27 45 E
Głuchołazy, *Poland* . . . . 55 H4   50 19N 17 24 E
Glücksburg, *Germany* . . . . . . 30 A5   54 50N 9 33 E
Glückstadt, *Germany* . . . . . . 30 B5   53 45N 9 25 E
Glukhov = Hlukhiv, *Ukraine* . . 59 G7   51 40N 33 58 E
Glusk, *Belarus* . . . . 59 F5   52 53N 28 41 E
Głuszyca, *Poland* . . . . 55 H3   50 41N 16 23 E
Glyngøre, *Denmark* . . . . 17 H2   56 46N 8 52 E
Gmünd, *Kärnten, Austria* . . . . 34 E6   46 54N 13 31 E
Gmünd, *Niederösterreich, Austria* . 34 C8   48 45N 15 0 E
Gmunden, *Austria* . . . . 34 D6   47 55N 13 48 E
Gnali, *Gabon* . . . . 114 C2   2 34 S 11 18 E
Gnarp, *Sweden* . . . . 16 B11   62 3N 17 16 E
Gnesta, *Sweden* . . . . 16 E11   59 3N 17 17 E
Gniew, *Poland* . . . . 54 E5   53 50N 18 50 E
Gniewkowo, *Poland* . . . . 55 F5   52 54N 18 25 E
Gniezno, *Poland* . . . . 55 F4   52 30N 17 35 E
Gnjilane, *Kosovo, Yug.* . . . . . 50 D5   42 28N 21 29 E
Gnoien, *Germany* . . . . 30 B8   53 58N 12 41 E
Gnosjö, *Sweden* . . . . 17 G7   57 22N 13 43 E
Gnowangerup, *Australia* . . . . 125 F2   33 58 S 117 59 E
Go Cong, *Vietnam* . . . . 87 G6   10 22N 106 40 E
Gō-Gawa →, *Japan* . . . . 72 B4   35 2N 132 13 E
Gō-no-ura, *Japan* . . . . 72 D1   33 44N 129 40 E
Goa, *India* . . . . 95 G1   15 33N 73 59 E
Goa □, *India* . . . . 95 G1   15 33N 73 59 E
Goalen Hd., *Australia* . . . . . . 129 D9   36 33 S 150 4 E
Goalpara, *India* . . . . 90 B3   26 10N 90 40 E
Goaltor, *India* . . . . 93 H12   22 43N 87 10 E
Goalundo Ghat, *Bangla.* . . . . . 93 H13   23 50N 89 47 E
Goaso, *Ghana* 112 D4   6 48N 2 30W
Goat Fell, *U.K.* 22 F3   55 38N 5 11W
Goba, *Ethiopia* . . . . 107 F4   7 1N 39 59 E
Goba, *Mozam.* . . . . 117 D5   26 15 S 32 13 E
Gobabis, *Namibia* . . . . 116 C2   22 30 S 19 0 E
Gobe, *Papua N. G.* . . . . 132 E5   9 4 S 149 0 E
Göbel, *Turkey* . . . . 51 F12   40 0N 28 9 E
Gobernador Gregores, *Argentina* . 175 F2   48 46 S 70 15W
Gobi, *Asia* . . . . 74 C6   44 0N 110 0 E
Gobichettipalayam, *India* . . . . 95 J3   11 31N 77 21 E
Gobles, *U.S.A.* 157 B11   42 22N 85 53W
Gobō, *Japan* . . . . 73 D7   33 53N 135 10 E
Gobo, *Sudan* . . . . 111 F2   5 40N 31 10 E
Göçbeyli, *Turkey* . . . . 49 B9   39 13N 27 25 E
Goch, *Germany* . . . . 30 D2   51 41N 6 9 E
Gochas, *Namibia* . . . . 116 C2   24 59 S 18 55 E
Godalming, *U.K.* 21 F7   51 11N 0 36W
Godavari →, *India* . . . . 94 F6   16 25N 82 18 E
Godavari Pt., *India* . . . . 94 F6   17 0N 82 20 E
Godbout, *Canada* 141 C6   49 20N 67 38W
Godda, *India* . . . . 93 G12   24 50N 87 13 E
Goddua, *Libya* . . . . 108 C2   26 26N 14 19 E
Godech, *Bulgaria* . . . . 50 C7   43 1N 23 4 E
Goderich, *Canada* 150 D3   43 45N 81 41W
Goderville, *France* . . . . 26 C7   49 38N 0 22 E
Godfrey, *U.S.A.* 156 F6   38 58N 90 11W
Godfrey Ra., *Australia* . . . . . . 125 D2   24 0 S 117 0 E
Godhavn = Qeqertarsuaq, *Greenland* . 10 D5   69 15N 53 38W
Godöğalir, *Iceland* 11 B7   65 20N 19 6W
Godhra, *India* . . . . 92 H5   22 49N 73 40 E
Godinlave, *Somali Rep.* . . . . . 120 C3   5 54N 46 38 E
Gödöllő, *Hungary* . . . . 52 C4   47 38N 19 25 E
Godoy Cruz, *Argentina* . . . . . 174 C2   32 56 S 68 52W
Gods →, *Canada* . . . . 140 A1   56 22N 92 51 E
Gods L., *Canada* 140 B1   54 40N 94 15W
Gods River, *Canada* 143 C10   54 50N 94 5W
Godthåb = Nuuk, *Greenland* . . 10 E5   64 10N 51 35W
Godwin Austen = K2, *Pakistan* . 93 B7   35 58N 76 32 E
Goeie Hoop, Kaap die = Good
  Hope, C. of, *S. Africa* . . . . . 116 E2   34 24 S 18 30 E
Goéland, L. au, *Canada* 140 C4   49 50N 76 48W
Goeree, *Neths.* . . . . 24 C3   51 50N 4 0 E
Goes, *Neths.* . . . . 24 C3   51 30N 3 55 E
Goffstown, *U.S.A.* 151 C13   43 1N 71 36W
Gogama, *Canada* 140 C3   47 35N 81 43W
Gogebic, L., *U.S.A.* 154 B10   46 30N 89 35W
Goggetti, *Ethiopia* . . . . 107 F4   8 11N 38 35 E
Gogolin, *Poland* . . . . 55 H5   50 30N 18 0 E
Gogonou, *Benin* . . . . 113 C5   10 50N 2 50 E
Gogra = Ghaghara →, *India* . . 93 G11   25 45N 84 40 E
Gogrial, *Sudan* . . . . 107 F2   8 30N 28 8 E
Gogti, *Ethiopia* . . . . 107 E5   10 7N 42 51 E
Gohana, *India* . . . . 92 E7   29 8N 76 42 E
Goharganj, *India* . . . . 92 H7   23 1N 77 41 E
Goi →, *India* . . . . 92 H6   22 4N 74 46 E
Goiana, *Brazil* . . . . 170 C5   7 33 S 34 59W
Goianésia, *Brazil* . . . . 171 E2   15 18 S 49 7W
Goiânia, *Brazil* . . . . 171 E2   16 43 S 49 20W

Goiás, *Brazil* . . . . 171 E1   15 55 S 50 10W
Goiás □, *Brazil* . . . . 170 D2   12 10 S 48 0W
Goiatuba, *Brazil* . . . . 171 E2   18 1 S 49 23W
Goio-Erê, *Brazil* . . . . 175 A5   24 12 S 53 1W
Góis, *Portugal* 40 E2   40 10N 8 6W
Gojeb →, *Ethiopia* . . . . 107 F4   10 55N 36 30 E
Gojeb, Wabi →, *Ethiopia* . . . . 107 F4   7 12N 36 40 E
Gojō, *Japan* . . . . 73 C7   34 21N 135 42 E
Gojra, *Pakistan* . . . . 92 D5   31 10N 72 40 E
Gokak, *India* . . . . 95 F2   16 11N 74 52 E
Gokarn, *India* . . . . 95 G2   14 33N 74 17 E
Gökçeada, *Turkey* . . . . 51 F9   40 10N 25 50 E
Gökçedağ, *Turkey* . . . . 49 B10   39 33N 28 8 E
Gökçen, *Turkey* . . . . 49 C9   38 7N 27 53 E
Gökçeören, *Turkey* . . . . 49 C10   38 37N 28 35 E
Gökçeyaz, *Turkey* . . . . 49 B9   39 40N 27 40 E
Gökırmak →, *Turkey* . . . . 100 B6   41 25N 35 8 E
Goksan, *Turkey* . . . . 49 D10   37 1N 28 17 E
Gökova, *Turkey* . . . . 49 D9   37 4N 28 3 E
Gökova Körfezi, *Turkey* . . . . . 49 D9   36 55N 27 50 E
Göksu →, *Turkey* . . . . 100 D6   36 19N 34 5 E
Göksun, *Turkey* . . . . 100 D7   38 2N 36 30 E
Göktepe, *Turkey* . . . . 90 D6   22 26N 97 0 E
Gokteik, *Burma* . . . . 49 D10   37 25N 28 34 E
Gökurt, *Pakistan* . . . . 92 E2   29 40N 67 26 E
Gokwe, *Zimbabwe* . . . . 117 B4   18 7 S 28 58 E
Gol, *Norway* . . . . 18 D5   60 42N 8 55 E
Gol Gol, *Australia* . . . . 128 C5   34 12 S 142 14 E
Gola, *India* . . . . 93 E9   28 3N 80 32 E
Golaghat, *India* . . . . 90 B5   26 30N 94 0 E
Golakganj, *India* . . . . 93 F13   26 8N 89 52 E
Golan Heights = Hagolan, *Syria* . 103 C4   33 0N 35 45 E
Gołańcz, *Poland* . . . . 55 F4   52 57N 17 18 E
Goläshkerd, *Iran* . . . . 97 E8   27 59N 57 16 E
Golaya Pristen = Hola Pristan,
  Ukraine . . . . 59 J7   46 29N 32 32 E
Gölbaşı, *Adıyaman, Turkey* . . 100 D7   37 43N 37 25 E
Gölbaşı, *Ankara, Turkey* . . . . 100 C5   39 47N 32 49 E
Golchikha, *Russia* . . . . 6 B12   71 45N 83 30 E
Golconda, *U.S.A.* 160 F5   40 58N 117 30W
Gölcük, *Kocaeli, Turkey* . . . . . 51 F13   40 42N 29 48 E
Gölcük, *Niğde, Turkey* . . . . . . 100 C6   38 14N 34 47 E
Gold, *U.S.A.* 150 E7   41 52N 77 50W
Gold Beach, *U.S.A.* 158 E1   42 25N 124 25W
Gold Coast, *Australia* . . . . . . 122 F9   28 0 S 153 25 E
Gold Coast, *W. Afr.* 113 E4   4 0N 1 40W
Gold Creek, *U.S.A.* 144 E10   62 46N 149 41W
Gold Hill, *U.S.A.* 158 E2   42 26N 123 3W
Gold River, *Canada* 142 D3   49 46N 126 3W
Goldach, *Switz.* . . . . 33 B8   47 28N 9 28 E
Gołdap, *Poland* . . . . 54 D9   54 19N 22 18 E
Goldau, *Switz.* . . . . 33 B7   47 3N 8 33 E
Goldberg, *Germany* . . . . 30 B8   53 35N 12 4 E
Golden, *Canada* 142 C5   51 20N 116 59W
Golden, *U.S.A.* 156 D5   40 7N 91 1W
Golden B., *N.Z.* . . . . 131 A7   40 40 S 172 50 E
Golden Gate, *U.S.A.* 158 H2   37 54N 122 30W
Golden Gate Highlands Nat. Park △,
  S. Africa . . . . 117 D4   28 40 S 28 40 E
Golden Hinde, *Canada* 142 D3   49 40N 125 44W
Golden Lake, *Canada* 150 A7   45 34N 77 21W
Golden Rock, *India* . . . . 95 J4   10 45N 78 48 E
Golden Spike Nat. Historic Site △,
  U.S.A. 158 F7   41 37N 112 33W
Golden Vale, *Ireland* 23 D3   52 33N 8 17W
Goldendale, *U.S.A.* 158 D3   45 49N 120 50W
Goldfield, *U.S.A.* 159 H5   37 42N 117 14W
Goldsand L., *Canada* 143 B8   57 2N 101 8W
Goldsboro, *U.S.A.* 149 H7   35 23N 77 59W
Goldsmith, *U.S.A.* 155 K3   31 59N 102 37W
Goldsworthy, *Australia* . . . . . 124 D2   20 21 S 119 30 E
Goldthwaite, *U.S.A.* 155 K5   31 27N 98 34W
Golegã, *Portugal* 40 F2   39 24N 8 29W
Goleniów, *Poland* . . . . 54 E1   53 35N 14 50 E
Golestānak, *Iran* . . . . 97 D7   30 36N 54 14 E
Goleta, *U.S.A.* 161 L7   34 27N 119 50W
Golfito, *Costa Rica* 164 E3   8 41N 83 5W
Golfo Aranci, *Italy* . . . . 46 B2   40 59N 9 38 E
Golfo di Orosei e del Gennargentu,
  Parco Nazionale del △, *Italy* . 46 B2   40 5N 9 15 E
Gölgeli Dağları, *Turkey* . . . . . 49 D10   37 10N 28 55 E
Gölhisar, *Turkey* . . . . 49 D11   37 8N 29 32 E
Goliad, *U.S.A.* 155 L6   28 40N 97 23W
Golija, *Montenegro, Yug.* . . . . 50 C4   43 5N 18 45 E
Golija, *Serbia, Yug.* . . . . 50 C4   43 22N 20 15 E
Golina, *Poland* . . . . 55 F5   52 15N 18 4 E
Gölköy, *Turkey* . . . . 100 B7   40 41N 37 37 E
Göllersdorf, *Austria* . . . . 34 C9   48 29N 16 7 E
Gollnow = Goleniów, *Poland* . . 54 E1   53 35N 14 50 E
Gölmarmara, *Turkey* . . . . 49 C9   38 43N 27 55 E
Golo →, *France* . . . . 29 F13   42 31N 9 32 E
Gololcha →, *Somali Rep.* . . . 120 D2   3 38N 43 49 E
Golova, *Turkey* . . . . 49 D11   36 37N 29 38 E
Golovin, *U.S.A.* 144 D7   64 33N 163 2W
Golpäyegän, *Iran* . . . . 97 C6   33 27N 50 18 E
Gölpazarı, *Turkey* . . . . 100 B4   40 16N 30 18 E
Golra, *Pakistan* . . . . 92 C5   33 37N 72 56 E
Golspie, *U.K.* 22 D5   57 58N 3 59W
Golub-Dobrzyń, *Poland* . . . . . 55 E6   53 7N 19 2 E
Golubac, *Serbia, Yug.* . . . . . . 50 B5   44 38N 21 38 E
Golungo Alto, *Angola* . . . . . . 115 D2   9 8 S 14 43 E
Golyam Perelik, *Bulgaria* . . . . 51 E8   41 36N 24 33 E
Golyama Kamchiya →, *Bulgaria* . 51 C11   43 10N 27 30 E
Goma, *Dem. Rep. of the Congo* . 118 C2   1 37 S 29 10 E
Gomal Pass, *Pakistan* . . . . . . 92 D3   31 56N 69 20 E
Gomati →, *India* . . . . 93 G10   25 32N 83 11 E
Gombari, *Dem. Rep. of the Congo* . 118 B2   2 45N 29 3 E
Gombe, *Dem. Rep. of the Congo* . 114 C3   4 38 S 17 36 E
Gombe, *Nigeria* . . . . 113 C7   10 19N 11 2 E
Gombe, *Tanzania* . . . . 118 C3   4 38 S 31 40 E
Gombe □, *Nigeria* . . . . 113 C7   10 0N 11 10 E
Gombe →, *Tanzania* . . . . 118 C3   4 38 S 31 40 E
Gombi, *Nigeria* . . . . 113 C7   10 12N 12 30 E
Gomel = Homyel, *Belarus* . . . 59 F6   52 28N 31 0 E
Gomera, *Canary Is.* 9 e1   28 7N 17 14W
Gómez Palacio, *Mexico* 162 B4   25 40N 104 0W
Gomīshān, *Iran* . . . . 97 B7   37 4N 54 6 E
Gommern, *Germany* . . . . 30 C7   52 4N 11 50 E
Gomogomo, *Indonesia* . . . . . 83 C4   6 39 S 134 43 E
Gomotartsi, *Bulgaria* . . . . 50 B6   44 5N 22 57 E
Gompa = Ganta, *Liberia* 112 D3   7 15N 8 59W
Gomphi, *Greece* . . . . 48 B3   39 26N 21 36 E
Goms, *Switz.* . . . . 32 D6   46 27N 8 15 E
Gonābād, *Iran* . . . . 97 C8   34 15N 58 45 E
Gonaïves, *Haiti* 165 C5   19 20N 72 42W
Gonarezhou Nat. Park △, *Zimbabwe* . 119 G3   21 32 S 31 55 E
Gonâve, G. de la, *Haiti* 165 C5   19 29N 72 42W
Gonâve, I. de la, *Haiti* 165 C5   18 45N 73 0W
Gonbad-e Kāvūs, *Iran* . . . . . . 97 B7   37 20N 55 25 E
Gönc, *Hungary* . . . . 52 B6   48 28N 21 14 E
Gonda, *India* . . . . 93 F9   27 9N 81 58 E
Gondal, *India* . . . . 92 J4   21 58N 70 52 E
Gonder, *Ethiopia* . . . . 107 E4   12 39N 37 30 E
Gonder □, *Ethiopia* . . . . 107 E4   12 55N 37 30 E
Gondia, *India* . . . . 94 D5   21 23N 80 10 E
Gondola, *Mozam.* . . . . 119 F3   19 10 S 33 37 E
Gondomar, *Portugal* 40 D2   41 10N 8 35W
Gondrecourt-le-Château, *France* . 27 D12   48 31N 5 30 E
Gönen, *Balıkesir, Turkey* . . . . 51 F11   40 6N 27 39 E
Gönen, *Isparta, Turkey* . . . . . 49 D12   37 57N 30 31 E
Gönen →, *Turkey* . . . . 51 F11   40 6N 27 39 E
Gong Xian, *China* . . . . 78 C5   28 23N 104 47 E
Gong'an, *China* . . . . 77 B9   30 7N 112 12 E
Gongbei, *China* . . . . 69 G10   22 12N 113 32 E
Gongcheng, *China* . . . . 77 E8   24 50N 110 49 E

Gongga Shan, *China* . . . . 76 C3   29 40N 101 55 E
Gongguan, *China* . . . . 76 G7   21 48N 109 36 E
Gonghe, *China* . . . . 68 C5   36 18N 100 32 E
Gongming, *China* . . . . 69 F10   22 47N 113 53 E
Gongo Yembe, *Dem. Rep. of
  the Congo* . . . . 114 C3   1 58 S 18 40 E
Gongola □, *Nigeria* . . . . 113 D7   9 30N 12 4 E
Gongolgon, *Australia* . . . . . . 127 E4   30 21 S 146 54 E
Gongoué, *Gabon* . . . . 114 C1   0 35 S 9 13 E
Gongshan, *China* . . . . 76 D2   27 43N 98 29 E
Gongtan, *China* . . . . 76 C7   28 56N 108 20 E
Gongzhuling, *China* . . . . 75 C13   43 30N 124 40 E
Goniadz, *Poland* . . . . 54 E9   53 30N 22 44 E
Goniri, *Nigeria* . . . . 113 C7   11 30N 12 15 E
Gonjo, *China* . . . . 76 B2   30 52N 98 17 E
Gonnesa, *Italy* . . . . 46 C1   39 16N 8 28 E
Gónnos, *Greece* . . . . 48 B4   39 52N 22 29 E
Gonnosfanádiga, *Italy* . . . . . . 46 C1   39 29N 8 39 E
Gonzaga, *Phil.* . . . . 80 B4   18 16N 122 0 E
Gonzales, *Calif., U.S.A.* 160 J5   36 30N 121 26W
Gonzales, *Tex., U.S.A.* 155 L6   29 30N 97 27W
González Chaves, *Argentina* . . 174 D3   38 2 S 60 5W
Goobang Nat. Park △, *Australia* . 116 E2   32 34 S 148 30 E
Good Hope, C. of, *S. Africa* . . 116 E2   34 24 S 18 30 E
Goodenough I., *Papua N. G.* . . 132 E6   9 20 S 150 15 E
Gooderham, *Canada* 150 B6   44 54N 78 21W
Goodhouse, *S. Africa* . . . . . . 116 D2   28 57 S 18 13 E
Gooding, *U.S.A.* 158 E6   42 56N 114 43W
Goodland, *U.S.A.* 154 F4   39 21N 101 43W
Goodlands, *Mauritius* . . . . . . 121 d   20 2 S 57 39 E
Goodlow, *Canada* 142 B4   56 20N 120 8W
Goodnews Bay, *U.S.A.* 144 G7   59 7N 161 35W
Goodooga, *Australia* . . . . 127 D4   29 3 S 147 28 E
Goodsprings, *U.S.A.* 161 K11   35 49N 115 27W
Goodwater, *U.S.A.* 152 B3   33 4N 86 3W
Goole, *U.K.* 20 D7   53 42N 0 53W
Goolgowi, *Australia* . . . . 129 B6   33 58 S 145 41 E
Goolwa, *Australia* . . . . 128 C3   35 30 S 138 47 E
Goomalling, *Australia* . . . . . . 125 F2   31 15 S 116 49 E
Goombalie, *Australia* . . . . 127 D5   26 12 S 152 6 E
Goonda, *Mozam.* . . . . 119 F3   19 48 S 33 57 E
Goondiwindi, *Australia* . . . . . 127 D5   28 30 S 150 21 E
Goongarrie, L., *Australia* . . . . 125 E3   30 3 S 121 9 E
Goongarrie Nat. Park △, *Australia* . 125 F3   30 5 S 121 30 E
Goonyella, *Australia* . . . . 126 C4   21 47 S 147 58 E
Goose →, *Canada* 141 B7   53 20N 60 35W
Goose Creek, *U.S.A.* 152 C9   32 59N 80 2W
Goose L., *U.S.A.* 158 F3   41 56N 120 26W
Gooty, *India* . . . . 95 G3   15 7N 77 41 E
Gopalganj, *Bangla.* . . . . 90 D2   26 5N 84 30 E
Gopalganj, *India* . . . . 93 F11   26 28N 84 30 E
Goppenstein, *Switz.* . . . . 32 D5   46 23N 7 46 E
Göppingen, *Germany* . . . . . . 31 G5   48 42N 9 39 E
Gor, *Spain* 43 H8   37 23N 2 58W
Góra, *Dolnośląskie, Poland* . . 55 G3   51 40N 16 31 E
Góra, *Mazowieckie, Poland* . . 55 F7   52 39N 20 6 E
Góra Kalwaria, *Poland* . . . . . . 55 G8   51 59N 21 14 E
Gorakhpur, *India* . . . . 93 F10   26 47N 83 23 E
Goražde, *Bos.-H.* . . . . 52 G3   43 38N 18 58 E
Gorbatov, *Russia* . . . . 60 B6   56 12N 43 2 E
Gorbea, Peña, *Spain* 40 B2   43 1N 2 50W
Gorczański Park Narodowy △,
  Poland . . . . 55 J7   49 30N 20 10 E
Gorda, *U.S.A.* 160 K5   35 53N 121 26W
Gorda, Pta., *Canary Is.* 9 e1   28 45N 18 0W
Gorda, Pta., *Nic.* 164 D3   14 20N 83 10W
Gordan B., *Australia* . . . . 124 B5   11 35 S 130 10 E
Gördes, *Turkey* . . . . 49 C10   38 54N 28 17 E
Gordon, *Ga., U.S.A.* 152 C5   32 54N 83 20W
Gordon, *Nebr., U.S.A.* 154 D3   42 48N 102 12W
Gordon →, *Australia* . . . . 127 D4   42 27 S 145 30 E
Gordon L., *Alta., Canada* . . . . 176 G3   54 5 S 69 35W
Gordon L., *N.W.T., Canada* . . 142 A6   56 30N 110 25W
Gordonvale, *Australia* . . . . . . 126 B4   17 5 S 145 50 E
Goré, *Chad* . . . . 109 G3   7 59N 16 31 E
Gore, *Ethiopia* . . . . 107 F4   8 12N 35 32 E
Gore, *N.Z.* . . . . 131 G3   46 5 S 168 58 E
Gore Bay, *Canada* 140 C3   45 57N 82 28W
Görele, *Turkey* . . . . 101 B8   41 2N 39 0 E
Goreme, *Turkey* . . . . 100 C6   38 35N 34 52 E
Gorey, *Ireland* 23 D5   52 41N 6 18W
Gorg, *Iran* . . . . 97 D8   29 29N 59 43 E
Gorgān, *Iran* . . . . 88 B4   36 55N 54 30 E
Gorgān →, *Iran* . . . . 97 B7   36 50N 54 29 E
Gorgona, *Italy* . . . . 44 E6   43 26N 9 54 E
Gorgora, *Ethiopia* . . . . 107 E4   12 15N 37 17 E
Gorgoram, *Nigeria* . . . . 113 C7   12 40N 10 45 E
Gori, *Georgia* . . . . 101 B13   44 23N 71 10 E
Gori, *Georgia* . . . . 101 B13   42 0N 44 7 E
Goribidnur = Gauribidanur, *India* . 95 H3   13 37N 77 32 E
Goriganga →, *India* . . . . 93 E9   29 45N 80 23 E
Gorinchem, *Neths.* . . . . 24 C4   51 50N 4 59 E
Gorinhatã, *Brazil* . . . . 171 E2   19 15 S 49 46W
Goris, *Armenia* . . . . 101 C12   39 31N 46 22 E
Goritsy, *Russia* . . . . 58 D9   57 4N 36 43 E
Gorízia, *Italy* . . . . 45 C10   45 56N 13 37 E
Gorj □, *Romania* . . . . 53 E8   45 5N 23 25 E
Gorki = Horki, *Belarus* . . . . . . 58 E6   54 17N 30 59 E
Gorki = Nizhniy Novgorod, *Russia* . 60 B7   21 48N 109 36 E
Gorkiy = Nizhniy Novgorod, *Russia* . 60 B7   56 20N 44 0 E
Gorkovskoye Vdkhr., *Russia* . . 60 B7   57 2N 43 4 E
Gorleston, *U.K.* . . . . 21 E9   52 35N 1 44 E
Gorlice, *Poland* . . . . 55 J8   49 35N 21 11 E
Görlitz, *Germany* . . . . 30 D10   51 9N 14 58 E
Gorlovka = Horlivka, *Ukraine* . 59 H10   48 19N 38 5 E
Gorman, *U.S.A.* 161 L8   34 47N 118 51W
Gorna Dzhumayo = Blagoevgrad,
  Bulgaria . . . . 50 D7   42 2N 23 5 E
Gorna Oryakhovitsa, *Bulgaria* . 51 C9   43 7N 25 40 E
Gornja Radgona, *Slovenia* . . . 45 B13   46 40N 16 2 E
Gornja Tuzla, *Bos.-H.* . . . . 52 F3   44 35N 18 46 E
Gornji Grad, *Slovenia* . . . . . . 45 B11   46 20N 14 52 E
Gornji Milanovac, *Serbia, Yug.* . 50 B4   44 3N 20 29 E
Gornji Vakuf, *Bos.-H.* . . . . 52 G2   43 57N 17 34 E
Gorno Ablanovo, *Bulgaria* . . . 51 C9   43 37N 25 43 E
Gorno-Altaysk, *Russia* . . . . . . 66 D9   51 50N 86 5 E
Gorno-Badakhshan □, *Tajikistan* . 65 F8   38 30N 73 0 E
Gornyatski, *Russia* . . . . 6 B9   67 32N 64 3 E
Gornyatskiy, *Russia* . . . . 61 F6   48 48N 40 56 E
Gornyy, *Saratov, Russia* . . . . . 61 D8   51 50N 48 30 E
Gornyy, *Sib., Russia* . . . . 70 B6   44 57N 133 59 E
Goro, *C.A.R.* . . . . 109 H4   9 41N 21 16 E
Gorodenka = Horodenka, *Ukraine* . 59 H3   48 41N 25 29 E
Gorodets, *Russia* . . . . 60 B6   56 38N 43 28 E
Gorodishche = Horodyshche,
  Ukraine . . . . 59 H6   49 17N 31 27 E
Gorodishche, *Russia* . . . . 60 D7   53 13N 45 40 E
Gorodnya = Horodnya, *Ukraine* . 59 G6   51 55N 31 33 E
Gorodok = Haradok, *Belarus* . 58 E6   55 30N 30 3 E
Gorodok = Horodok, *Ukraine* . 59 H3   49 46N 23 32 E
Gorodok = Zakamensk, *Russia* . 67 D11   50 23N 103 17 E
Gorodovikovsk, *Russia* . . . . . 61 G5   46 5N 41 56 E
Goroka, *Papua N. G.* . . . . 132 D3   6 7 S 145 25 E
Goroke, *Australia* . . . . 128 D4   36 43 S 141 29 E
Gorokhov = Horokhiv, *Ukraine* . 59 G3   50 30N 24 45 E
Gorokhovets, *Russia* . . . . 60 B6   56 13N 42 42 E
Gorom Gorom, *Burkina Faso* . 113 C4   14 26N 0 14W
Goromonzi, *Zimbabwe* . . . . . 119 F3   17 52 S 31 22 E
Gorong, Kepulauan, *Indonesia* . 83 B4   3 59 S 131 25 E
Gorongosa, Parque Nac. de △,
  Mozam. . . . . 117 B5   18 50 S 34 29 E
Gorongose →, *Mozam.* . . . . . 117 C5   20 30 S 34 40 E

Gorongoza, *Mozam.* .... 119 F3   18 44 S   34 2 E
Gorongoza, Sa. da, *Mozam.* ... 119 F3   18 27 S   34 2 E
Gorontalo, *Indonesia* .... 82 A2   0 35N 123 5 E
Goronyo, *Nigeria* .... 113 C6   13 29N   5 39 E
Górowo Iławeckie, *Poland* ..... 54 D7   54 17N 20 30 E
Gorron, *France* 26 D6   48 25N   0 50W
Gorshechnoye, *Russia* .... 59 G10 51 31N 38 2 E
Gort, *Ireland* 23 C3   53 3N   8 49W
Gortis, *Greece* .... 39 E5   35 4N 24 58 E
Gorumahisani, *India* .... 94 C8   22 20N 86 24 E
Góry Bystrzyckie, *Poland* ..... 55 H3   50 16N 16 33 E
Goryachiy Klyuch, *Russia* ..... 61 H4   44 38N 39 8 E
Gorzkowice, *Poland* .... 55 G6   51 13N 19 36 E
Górzno, *Poland* .... 55 E6   53 12N 19 38 E
Gorzów Śląski, *Poland* .... 55 G5   51 3N 18 22 E
Gorzów Wielkopolski, *Poland* .. 55 F2   52 43N 15 15 E
Göschenen, *Switz.* .... 33 C7   46 40N   8 36 E
Gose, *Japan* .... 73 C7   34 27N 135 44 E
Gosford, *Australia* .... 129 B9   33 23 S 151 18 E
Goshen, *Calif., U.S.A.* 160 J7   36 21N 119 25W
Goshen, *Ind., U.S.A.* 157 C11 41 35N 85 50W
Goshen, *N.Y., U.S.A.* 151 E10 41 24N 74 20W
Goshogawara, *Japan* .... 70 D10 40 48N 140 27 E
Gosier, *Guadeloupe* .... 164 b   16 12N 61 30W
Goslar, *Germany* .... 30 D6   51 54N 10 25 E
Gospić, *Croatia* .... 45 D12 44 35N 15 23 E
Gosport, *U.K.* 21 G6   50 48N   1 9W
Gosport, *U.S.A.* 157 E10 39 21N 86 40W
Gossa, *Norway* .... 18 B3   62 52N   6 50 E
Gossas, *Senegal* 112 C1   14 28N 16 0W
Gossau, *Switz.* .... 33 B8   47 25N   9 15 E
Gosse →, *Australia* .... 126 B1   19 32 S 134 37 E
Gossi, *Mali* 113 B4   15 48N   1 20W
Gossinga, *Sudan* .... 107 F2   8 36N 25 59 E
Gostivar, *Macedonia* .... 50 E4   41 48N 20 57 E
Gostyń, *Poland* .... 55 G4   51 50N 17 3 E
Gostynin, *Poland* .... 55 F6   52 26N 19 29 E
Göta älv →, *Sweden* .... 17 G5   57 42N 11 54 E
Göta kanal, *Sweden* .... 17 F9   58 30N 15 58 E
Götaland, *Sweden* .... 17 G8   57 30N 14 30 E
Göteborg, *Sweden* .... 17 G5   57 43N 11 59 E
Götene, *Sweden* .... 73 B10 35 18N 138 56 E
Götene, *Sweden* .... 17 F7   58 32N 13 30 E
Goteşti, *Moldova* .... 53 D13 46 9N 28 10 E
Gotha, *Germany* .... 30 E6   50 56N 10 42 E
Gothenburg = Göteborg, *Sweden* . 17 G5   57 43N 11 59 E
Gothenburg, *U.S.A.* 154 E4   40 56N 100 10W
Gotland, *Sweden* .... 17 G12 57 30N 18 33 E
Gotlands län □, *Sweden* .... 17 G12 57 15N 18 30 E
Gotō-Rettō, *Japan* .... 71 H4   32 55N 129 5 E
Gotse Delchev, *Bulgaria* ...... 50 E7   41 36N 23 46 E
Gotska Sandön, *Sweden* .... 15 G18 58 24N 19 15 E
Gōtsu, *Japan* .... 72 C4   35 0N 132 14 E
Gott Pk., *Canada* 142 C4   50 18N 122 16W
Göttero, Monte, *Italy* .... 44 D6   44 22N   9 42 E
Göttingen, *Germany* .... 30 D5   51 31N   9 55 E
Gottwald = Zmiyiv, *Ukraine* ... 59 H9   49 39N 36 27 E
Gotvaldov = Zlín, *Czech Rep.* . 35 B10 49 14N 17 40 E
Götzis, *Austria* .... 33 B9   47 20N   9 38 E
Goubangzi, *China* .... 75 D11 41 20N 121 52 E
Gouda, *Neths.* .... 24 B4   52 1N   4 42 E
Goúdhoura, Ákra, *Greece* ...... 39 F7   34 59N 26 6 E
Goudiry, *Senegal* 112 C2   14 15N 12 45W
Goudoumaria, *Niger* .... 113 C7   13 40N 11 10 E
Gouéké, *Guinea* 112 D3   8 2N   8 43W
Gough I., *Atl. Oc.* .... 8 L11   40 10 S 9 45W
Gouin, Rés., *Canada* 140 C5   48 35N 74 40W
Gouitafla, *Ivory C.* 112 D3   7 30N   5 53W
Goulburn, *Australia* .... 129 C8   34 44 S 149 44 E
Goulburn Is., *Australia* ...... 126 A1   11 40 S 133 20 E
Goulburn River Nat. Park △,
   Australia .... 129 B9   32 19 S 150 10 E
Goulds, *U.S.A.* 153 K9   25 33N 80 23W
Goulia, *Ivory C.* 112 C3   10 1N   7 11W
Goulimine, *Morocco* 110 C3   28 56N 10 0W
Goulmima, *Morocco* 110 B4   31 41N   4 57W
Goumbou, *Mali* 112 B3   15 2N   7 25W
Gouménissa, *Greece* .... 50 F6   40 56N 22 37 E
Gounatolo, *Solomon Is.* .... 133 M11 8 25 S 160 52 E
Goundam, *Mali* 112 B4   16 27N   3 40W
Goundi, *Chad* .... 109 G3   9 22N 17 21 E
Gounou-Gaya, *Chad* .... 109 G3   9 38N 15 31 E
Goúra, *Greece* .... 48 D4   37 56N 22 20 E
Gouraya, *Algeria* .... 111 A5   36 31N   1 56 E
Gourbassi, *Mali* 112 C2   13 24N 11 38W
Gourdon, *France* .... 28 D5   44 44N   1 23 E
Gouré, *Niger* .... 113 C7   14 0N 10 10 E
Gouri, *Chad* .... 109 E3   18 50N 16 49 E
Gourin, *France* 26 D3   48 8N   3 37W
Gouris →, *S. Africa* .... 116 E3   34 21 S 21 52 E
Gourma-Rharous, *Mali* 113 B4   16 55N   1 50W
Gournais, *Greece* .... 39 E6   35 19N 25 16 E
Gournay-en-Bray, *France* ...... 27 C8   49 29N   1 44 E
Gouro, *Chad* .... 109 E3   19 36N 19 36 E
Gourock, *U.K.* 22 F4   55 57N   4 49W
Gourock Ra., *Australia* .... 129 D8   36 0 S 149 25 E
Goursi, *Burkina Faso* 112 C4   12 42N   2 37W
Gouvêa, *Brazil* .... 171 E3   18 27 S 43 44W
Gouverneur, *U.S.A.* 151 B9   44 20N 75 28W
Gouviá, *Greece* .... 38 B9   39 39N 19 50 E
Gouzon, *France* .... 27 F9   46 12N   2 14 E
Governador Valadares, *Brazil* . 171 E3   18 15 S 41 57W
Governor Generoso, *Phil.* ..... 81 H6   6 39N 126 5 E
Governor's Harbour, *Bahamas* .. 164 A4   25 10N 76 14W
Govindgarh, *India* .... 93 G9   24 23N 81 18 E
Gowan Ra., *Australia* .... 126 D4   25 0 S 145 0 E
Gowanda, *U.S.A.* 150 D6   42 28N 78 56W
Gower, *U.K.* 21 F3   51 35N   4 10W
Gowers Corner, *U.S.A.* 153 G7   28 20N 82 30W
Gowna, L., *Ireland* 23 C4   53 51N   7 34W
Gowrie, *U.S.A.* 156 B2   42 17N 94 17W
Gowurdak, *Turkmenistan* .... 65 E3   37 50N 66 4 E
Goya, *Argentina* .... 174 B4   29 10 S 59 10W
Göyçay, *Azerbaijan* .... 61 K8   40 42N 47 43 E
Goyder Lagoon, *Australia* ..... 127 D2   27 3 S 138 58 E
Goyllarisquizga, *Peru* .... 172 C2   10 31 S 76 24W
Göynük, *Antalya, Turkey* ...... 49 E12 36 41N 30 33 E
Göynük, *Bolu, Turkey* .... 100 B4   40 24N 30 48 E
Goz Beïda, *Chad* .... 109 F4   12 10N 21 20 E
Goz Regeb, *Sudan* .... 107 D4   16 3N 35 33 E
Gozdnica, *Poland* .... 55 G2   51 28N 15 4 E
Gozo, *Malta* .... 38 F2   36 3N 14 15 E
Graaff-Reinet, *S. Africa* ..... 116 E3   32 13 S 24 32 E
Grabill, *U.S.A.* 157 C12 41 13N 84 57W
Grabo, *Ivory C.* 112 D3   4 57N   7 30W
Grabow, *Germany* .... 30 B7   53 17N 11 34 E
Grabów nad Prosną, *Poland* .... 55 G5   51 31N 18 7 E
Grabs, *Switz.* .... 33 B8   47 11N   9 27 E
Gračac, *Croatia* .... 45 D12 44 18N 15 57 E
Gračanica, *Bos.-H.* .... 52 F3   44 43N 18 18 E
Graçay, *France* .... 27 E8   47 10N   1 50 E
Graceville, *U.S.A.* 152 E4   30 58N 85 31W
Gracewood, *U.S.A.* 152 B7   33 22N 82 2W
Gracias a Dios, C., *Honduras* . 164 D3   15 0N 83 10W
Graciosa, *Azores* 9 d1   39 4N 28 0W
Graciosa, I., *Canary Is.* 9 e2   29 15N 13 32W
Grad Sofiya □, *Bulgaria* ...... 50 D7   42 35N 23 20 E
Gradac, *Montenegro, Yug.* ..... 52 C3   43 23N 19 9 E
Gradačac, *Bos.-H.* .... 52 F3   44 52N 18 26 E
Gradaús, *Brazil* .... 170 C1   7 43 S 51 11W
Gradaús, Serra dos, *Brazil* ... 170 C1   8 0 S 50 45W
Gradeška Planina, *Macedonia* .. 50 E6   41 30N 22 15 E

Gradets, *Bulgaria* .... 51 D10 42 46N 26 30 E
Gradiške, *Slovenia* .... 45 B12 46 37N 15 52 E
Grădiştea de Munte, *Romania* .. 53 E8   45 37N 23 13 E
Grado, *Italy* .... 45 C10 45 40N 13 23 E
Grado, *Spain* 42 B4   43 23N   6 4W
Grady, *U.S.A.* 155 H3   34 49N 103 19W
Graeca, Lacul, *Romania* .... 53 F11 44 5N 26 10 E
Grafarnes, *Iceland* 11 C3   64 55N 23 16W
Grafenau, *Germany* .... 31 G9   48 51N 13 22 E
Gräfenberg, *Germany* .... 31 F7   49 39N 11 14 E
Grafham Water, *U.K.* 21 E7   52 19N   0 18W
Grafton, *Australia* .... 127 D5   29 38 S 152 58 E
Grafton, *Ill., U.S.A.* 156 F6   38 58N 90 26W
Grafton, *N. Dak., U.S.A.* 154 A6   48 25N 97 25W
Grafton, *W. Va., U.S.A.* 148 F5   39 21N 80 2W
Graham, *Canada* 140 C1   49 20N 90 30W
Graham, *Ga., U.S.A.* 152 D7   31 50N 82 30W
Graham, *Tex., U.S.A.* 155 J5   33 6N 98 35W
Graham, Mt., *U.S.A.* 159 K9   32 42N 109 52W
Graham Bell, Ostrov = Greem-Bell,
   Ostrov, *Russia* .... 66 A7   81 0N 62 0 E
Graham I., *Canada* 142 C2   53 40N 132 30W
Graham Land, *Antarctica* ...... 7 C17   65 0 S 64 0W
Grahamstown, *S. Africa* .... 116 E4   33 19 S 26 31 E
Grahamsville, *U.S.A.* 151 E10 41 51N 74 33W
Grahovo, *Montenegro, Yug.* .... 52 D2   42 40N 18 40 E
Graiba, *Tunisia* .... 108 B2   34 30N 10 13 E
Graie, Alpi, *Europe* .... 29 C11 45 30N   7 10 E
Grain Coast, *W. Afr.* 112 E3   4 20N 10 0W
Grajagan, *Indonesia* .... 79 K17   8 35 S 114 13 E
Grajagan, Teluk, *Indonesia* ... 79 K17   8 40 S 114 18 E
Grajaú, *Brazil* .... 170 C2   5 50 S 46 4W
Grajaú →, *Brazil* .... 170 B3   3 41 S 44 48W
Grajewo, *Poland* .... 54 E9   53 39N 22 30 E
Gramada, *Bulgaria* .... 50 C6   43 49N 22 39 E
Gramat, *France* .... 28 D5   44 48N   1 43 E
Grammichele, *Italy* .... 47 E7   37 13N 14 38 E
Grámmos, Óros, *Greece* .... 50 F4   40 18N 20 47 E
Grampian, *U.S.A.* 150 F6   40 58N 78 37W
Grampian Highlands = Grampian
   Mts., *U.K.* 22 E5   56 50N   4 0W
Grampian Mts., *U.K.* 22 E5   56 50N   4 0W
Grampians, The, *Australia* .... 128 D5   37 0 S 142 20 E
Grampians Nat. Park △, *Australia* . 128 D5   37 15 S 142 28 E
Gramsh, *Albania* .... 50 F4   40 52N 20 12 E
Gran, *Norway* .... 18 D7   60 23N 10 31 E
Gran →, *Suriname* 169 C6   4 1N 55 30W
Gran Altiplanicie Central, *Argentina* . 176 C3   49 0 S 69 30W
Gran Canaria, *Canary Is.* 9 e1   27 55N 15 35W
Gran Chaco, *S. Amer.* .... 174 B3   25 0 S 61 0W
Gran Desierto del Pinacate, Parque
   Natural △, *Mexico* 162 A2   31 51N 113 32W
Gran Laguna Salada, *Argentina* . 176 B3   44 24 S 67 23W
Gran Pajonal, *Peru* .... 172 C3   10 45 S 74 30W
Gran Paradiso, *Italy* .... 44 C4   45 33N   7 17 E
Gran Sasso d'Itália, *Italy* ... 45 F10 42 27N 13 42 E
Gran Sasso e Monti Della Laga,
   Parco Nazionale del △, *Italy* . 45 F10 42 32N 13 22 E
Granada, *Nic.* 164 D2   11 58N 86 0W
Granada, *Spain* 43 H7   37 10N   3 35W
Granada, *U.S.A.* 155 F3   38 4N 102 19W
Granada □, *Spain* 43 H7   37 18N   3 0W
Granadilla de Abona, *Canary Is.* . 9 e1   28 7N 16 33W
Granard, *Ireland* 23 C4   53 47N   7 30W
Granbury, *U.S.A.* 155 J6   32 27N 97 47W
Granby, *Canada* 140 C5   45 25N 72 45W
Granby, *U.S.A.* 158 F11 40 5N 105 56W
Grand →, *Canada* 150 D5   42 51N 79 34W
Grand →, *Mich., U.S.A.* 157 A10 43 4N 86 15W
Grand →, *Mo., U.S.A.* 156 F3   39 23N 93 7W
Grand →, *S. Dak., U.S.A.* 154 C4   45 40N 100 45W
Grand Anse, *Seychelles* .... 121 b   4 18 S 55 45 E
Grand Bahama, *Bahamas* 164 A4   26 40N 78 30W
Grand Baie, *Mauritius* .... 121 d   20 0 S 57 35 E
Grand Bank, *Canada* 141 C8   47 6N 55 48W
Grand Banks, *Atl. Oc.* 8 B6   45 0N 52 0W
Grand Bassam, *Ivory C.* 112 D4   5 10N   3 49W
Grand Batanga, *Cameroon* ...... 114 B1   2 50N   9 55 E
Grand Béréby, *Ivory C.* 112 E3   4 38N   6 55W
Grand Blanc, *U.S.A.* 157 B13 42 56N 83 38W
Grand-Bourg, *Guadeloupe* ...... 164 b   15 53N 61 19W
Grand Canal = Yun Ho →, *China* . 75 E9   39 10N 117 10 E
Grand Canyon, *U.S.A.* 159 H7   36 3N 112 9W
Grand Canyon Nat. Park △, *U.S.A.* . 159 H7   36 15N 112 30W
Grand Canyon-Parashant Nat.
   Monument △, *U.S.A.* 159 H7   36 30N 113 20W
Grand Cayman, *Cayman Is.* 164 C3   19 20N 81 20W
Grand Centre, *Canada* 143 C6   54 25N 110 13W
Grand Cess, *Liberia* 112 E3   4 40N   8 12W
Grand Coulee, *U.S.A.* 158 C4   47 57N 119 0W
Grand Coulee Dam, *U.S.A.* 158 C4   47 57N 118 59W
Grand Erg de Bilma, *Niger* .... 109 E2   18 30N 14 0 E
Grand Falls, *Canada* 141 C6   47 3N 67 44W
Grand Falls-Windsor, *Canada* .. 141 C8   48 56N 55 40W
Grand Forks, *Canada* 142 D5   49 0N 118 30W
Grand Forks, *U.S.A.* 154 B6   47 55N 97 3W
Grand Gorge, *U.S.A.* 151 D10 42 21N 74 29W
Grand Haven, *U.S.A.* 157 A10 43 4N 86 13W
Grand I., *Mich., U.S.A.* 148 B2   46 31N 86 40W
Grand I., *N.Y., U.S.A.* 150 D6   43 0N 78 58W
Grand Island, *U.S.A.* 154 E5   40 55N 98 21W
Grand Isle, *La., U.S.A.* 155 L9   29 14N 90 0W
Grand Isle, *Vt., U.S.A.* 151 B11 44 43N 73 18W
Grand Junction, *Colo., U.S.A.* . 159 G9   39 4N 108 33W
Grand Junction, *Iowa, U.S.A.* . 156 D2   42 2N 94 14W
Grand L., *N.B., Canada* 141 C6   45 57N 66 7W
Grand L., *Nfld., Canada* 141 C8   49 0N 57 30W
Grand L., *Nfld., Canada* 141 B7   53 40N 60 30W
Grand L., *Ohio, U.S.A.* 157 D12 40 32N 84 25W
Grand Lahou, *Ivory C.* 112 D3   5 10N   5 5W
Grand Lake, *U.S.A.* 158 F11 40 15N 105 49W
Grand Ledge, *U.S.A.* 157 B10 42 45N 84 45W
Grand-Lieu, L. de, *France* 26 E5   47 6N   1 40W
Grand Manan I., *Canada* 141 D6   44 45N 66 52W
Grand Marais, *Canada* 154 B9   47 45N 90 25W
Grand Marais, *U.S.A.* 148 B3   46 40N 85 59W
Grand-Mère, *Canada* 140 C5   46 36N 72 40W
Grand Popo, *Benin* .... 113 D5   6 15N   1 57 E
Grand Portage, *U.S.A.* 154 B10 47 58N 89 41W
Grand Prairie, *U.S.A.* 155 J6   32 47N 97 0W
Grand Rapids, *Canada* 143 C9   53 12N 99 19W
Grand Rapids, *Mich., U.S.A.* .. 157 B10 42 58N 85 40W
Grand Rapids, *Minn., U.S.A.* .. 154 B8   47 14N 93 31W
Grand Ridge, *U.S.A.* 152 K4   30 43N 85 1W
Grand River, *U.S.A.* 156 D3   40 49N 93 58W
Grand St-Bernard, Col du, *Europe* . 32 E4   45 50N   7 10 E
Grand Santi, *Fr. Guiana* 169 C7   4 20N 54 24W
Grand Staircase-Escalante Nat.
   Monument △, *U.S.A.* 159 H8   37 5N 112 0W
Grand Teton, *U.S.A.* 158 E8   43 54N 111 50W
Grand Teton Nat. Park △, *U.S.A.* . 158 D8   43 50N 110 50W
Grand Union Canal, *U.K.* 21 E7   52 7N   0 53W
Grand View, *Canada* 143 C8   51 10N 100 42W
Grand-Vigie, Pte. de la, *Guadeloupe* . 164 b   16 32N 61 27W
Grandas de Salime, *Spain* 42 B4   43 13N   6 53W
Grande →, *Jujuy, Argentina* ... 174 A2   24 20 S 65 2W
Grande →, *Mendoza, Argentina* . 174 D2   36 52 S 69 45W
Grande →, *Bolivia* .... 173 D5   15 51 S 64 39W
Grande →, *Bahia, Brazil* ...... 170 D3   11 30 S 44 30W
Grande →, *Minas Gerais, Brazil* . 171 F1   20 6 S 51 4W
Grande →, *Venezuela* 169 B5   8 36N 61 39W
Grande, B., *Argentina* .... 176 D3   50 30 S 68 20W
Grande, I., *Brazil* .... 171 F3   23 9 S 44 14W

Grande, Rio →, *U.S.A.* 155 N6   25 58N 97 9W
Grande, Serra, *Piauí, Brazil* . 170 C2   8 0 S 45 10W
Grande, Serra, *Tocantins, Brazil* . 170 D2   11 15 S 46 30W
Grande Anse, *Seychelles* ...... 121 b   4 40 S 55 26 E
Grande Baleine, R. de la →, *Canada* . 140 A4   55 16N 77 47W
Grande Cache, *Canada* 142 C5   53 53N 119 8W
Grande Comore, *Comoros Is.* ... 121 a   11 35 S 43 20 E
Grande-Entrée, *Canada* 141 C7   47 30N 61 40W
Grande Prairie, *Canada* 142 B5   55 10N 118 50W
Grande-Rivière, *Canada* 141 C7   48 26N 64 30W
Grande-Terre, I., *Guadeloupe* . 164 b   16 20N 61 25W
Grande-Vallée, *Canada* 141 C6   49 14N 65 8W
Grandfalls, *U.S.A.* 155 K3   31 20N 102 51W
Grândola, *Portugal* 43 G2   38 12N   8 35W
Grandpré, *France* .... 27 C11 49 20N   4 50 E
Grands Causses, Parc Naturel
   Régional des △, *France* .. 28 D6   44 5N   2 58 E
Grands-Jardins, Parc des △, *Canada* . 141 C5   47 41N 70 51W
Grandson, *Switz.* .... 32 C3   46 49N   6 39 E
Grandview, *Mo., U.S.A.* 156 F2   38 53N 94 32W
Grandview, *Wash., U.S.A.* 158 C4   46 15N 119 54W
Grandview Heights, *U.S.A.* 157 E13 39 58N 83 2W
Grandvilliers, *France* .... 27 C8   49 40N   1 57 E
Graneros, *Chile* .... 174 C1   34 5 S 70 45W
Grangemouth, *U.K.* 22 E5   56 1N   3 42W
Granger, *U.S.A.* 158 F9   41 35N 109 58W
Grängesberg, *Sweden* .... 16 D9   60 6N 15 1 E
Grangeville, *U.S.A.* 158 D5   45 56N 116 7W
Gransle, *Canada* 142 C3   54 53N 126 13W
Granite City, *U.S.A.* 156 F6   38 42N 90 9W
Granite Falls, *U.S.A.* 154 C7   44 49N 95 33W
Granite L., *Canada* 141 C8   48 8N 57 5W
Granite Mt., *U.S.A.* 161 M10 33 5N 116 28W
Granite Pk., *U.S.A.* 158 D9   45 10N 109 48W
Graniteville, *S.C., U.S.A.* ... 152 B8   33 34N 81 49W
Graniteville, *Vt., U.S.A.* 151 B12 44 8N 72 29W
Granitogorsk, *Kazakhstan* ..... 65 B6   42 44N 73 28 E
Granitola, C., *Italy* .... 46 E5   37 34N 12 39 E
Granity, *N.Z.* .... 131 B6   41 39 S 171 51 E
Granja, *Brazil* .... 170 B3   3 7 S 40 50W
Granja de Moreruela, *Spain* ... 42 D5   41 48N   5 44W
Granja de Torrehermosa, *Spain* . 43 G5   38 19N   5 35W
Gränna, *Sweden* .... 17 F8   58 1N 14 28 E
Granollers, *Spain* .... 40 D7   41 39N   2 18 E
Gransee, *Germany* .... 30 B9   53 1N 13 8 E
Grant, *Fla., U.S.A.* 153 H9   27 56N 80 32W
Grant, *Nebr., U.S.A.* 154 E4   40 53N 101 42W
Grant, Mt., *U.S.A.* 158 G4   38 34N 118 48W
Grant City, *U.S.A.* 156 D2   40 29N 94 25W
Grant I., *Australia* .... 124 B5   11 10 S 132 52 E
Grant Range, *U.S.A.* 159 G6   38 30N 115 25W
Grantham, *U.K.* 20 E7   52 55N   0 38W
Grantown-on-Spey, *U.K.* 22 D5   57 20N   3 36W
Grants, *U.S.A.* 159 J10 35 9N 107 52W
Grants Pass, *U.S.A.* 158 E2   42 26N 123 19W
Grantsville, *U.S.A.* 158 F7   40 36N 112 28W
Granville, *France* 26 D5   48 50N   1 35W
Granville, *Ill., U.S.A.* 156 C7   41 16N 89 14W
Granville, *N. Dak., U.S.A.* ... 154 A4   48 16N 100 47W
Granville, *N.Y., U.S.A.* 151 C11 43 24N 73 16W
Granville, *Ohio, U.S.A.* 150 F2   40 4N 82 31W
Granville L., *Canada* 143 B8   56 18N 100 30W
Granvin, *Norway* .... 18 D3   60 33N   6 45 E
Graskop, *S. Africa* .... 117 C5   24 56 S 30 49 E
Gräsö, *Sweden* .... 16 D12 60 28N 18 35 E
Grass →, *Canada* 143 B9   56 3N 96 33W
Grass Range, *U.S.A.* 158 C9   47 0N 109 0W
Grass River Prov. Park △, *Canada* . 143 C8   54 40N 100 50W
Grass Valley, *Calif., U.S.A.* . 160 F6   39 13N 121 4W
Grass Valley, *Oreg., U.S.A.* .. 158 D3   45 22N 120 47W
Grassano, *Italy* .... 47 B9   40 38N 16 17 E
Grasse, *France* .... 29 E10 43 38N   6 56 E
Grassflat, *U.S.A.* 150 F6   41 0N 78 6W
Grasslands Nat. Park △, *Canada* . 143 D7   49 11N 107 38W
Grassy, *Australia* .... 127 D3   40 3 S 144 5 E
Gråsten, *Denmark* .... 17 K3   54 55N   9 35 E
Grästorp, *Sweden* .... 17 F6   58 20N 12 40 E
Gratia, *U.S.A.* 157 E12 39 38N 84 32W
Gratkorn, *Austria* .... 34 D8   47 8N 15 21 E
Gratz, *U.S.A.* 157 F12 38 28N 84 57W
Graubünden □, *Switz.* .... 33 C9   46 45N   9 30 E
Graulhet, *France* .... 28 E5   43 45N   1 59 E
Graus, *Spain* .... 40 C5   42 11N   0 20 E
Gravatá, *Brazil* .... 170 C4   8 10 S 35 29W
Gravberget, *Norway* .... 18 D9   60 53N 12 14 E
Grave, Pte. de, *France* 28 C2   45 34N   1 4W
Gravelbourg, *Canada* 143 D7   49 50N 106 35W
Gravelines, *France* .... 27 A9   51 1N   2 10 E
's-Gravenhage, *Neths.* .... 24 B4   52 7N   4 17 E
Gravenhurst, *Canada* 140 D4   44 52N 79 20W
Gravesend, *Australia* .... 127 D5   29 35 S 150 20 E
Gravesend, *U.K.* .... 21 F8   51 26N   0 22 E
Gravina in Púglia, *Italy* ..... 47 B9   40 49N 16 25 E
Gravois, Pointe-à-, *Haiti* 165 C5   18 15N 73 56W
Gravone →, *France* .... 29 G12 41 58N   8 45 E
Gray, *France* .... 27 E12 47 27N   5 35 E
Gray, *U.S.A.* 152 B6   33 1N 83 32W
Grayling, *Alaska, U.S.A.* 144 E7   62 57N 160 3W
Grayling, *Mich., U.S.A.* 148 C3   44 40N 84 43W
Grays, *U.K.* .... 21 F8   51 28N   0 21 E
Grays Harbor, *U.S.A.* 158 C1   46 59N 124 1W
Grays L., *U.S.A.* 158 E8   43 4N 111 26W
Grays River, *U.S.A.* 160 D3   46 21N 123 37W
Grayson, *U.S.A.* 157 F9   38 16N 88 0W
Grayville, *U.S.A.* 156 F8   38 16N 88 0W
Grayvoron, *Russia* .... 59 G8   50 29N 35 41 E
Graz, *Austria* .... 34 D8   47 4N 15 27 E
Grdelica, *Serbia, Yug.* .... 50 D6   42 55N 22 3 E
Greåker, *Norway* .... 18 E8   59 16N 11 12 E
Greasy L., *Canada* 142 A4   62 55N 122 12W
Great Abaco I., *Bahamas* 164 A4   26 25N 77 10W
Great Artesian Basin, *Australia* . 126 C3   23 0 S 144 0 E
Great Australian Bight, *Australia* . 125 F5   33 30 S 130 0 E
Great Bahama Bank, *Bahamas* ... 164 B4   23 15N 78 0W
Great Barrier I., *N.Z.* .... 130 C4   36 11 S 175 25 E
Great Barrier Reef, *Australia* . 126 B4   18 0 S 146 50 E
Great Barrier Reef Commonwealth
   Marine △, *Australia* ..... 126 B4   20 0 S 150 0 E
Great Barrington, *U.S.A.* 151 D11 42 12N 73 22W
Great Basalt Wall Nat. Park △,
   Australia .... 126 B4   19 52 S 145 43 E
Great Basin, *U.S.A.* 158 G5   40 0N 117 0W
Great Basin Nat. Park △, *U.S.A.* . 158 G6   38 55N 114 14W
Great Basses, *Sri Lanka* ...... 95 L5   6 11N 81 29 E
Great Bear →, *Canada* 138 B7   65 0N 124 0W
Great Bear L., *Canada* 138 B7   65 30N 120 0W
Great Belt = Store Bælt, *Denmark* . 17 J4   55 20N 11 0 E
Great Bend, *Kans., U.S.A.* 154 F5   38 22N 98 46W
Great Bend, *Pa., U.S.A.* 151 E9   41 58N 75 45W
Great Blasket I., *Ireland* 23 D1   52 6N 10 32W
Great Britain, *Europe* 12 E5   54 0N   2 15W
Great Camanoe, *Br. Virgin Is.* . 165 e   18 30N 64 35W
Great Channel, *Asia* .... 95 L11 6 0N 94 0 E
Great Coco I., *Burma* .... 95 G11 14 7N 93 22 E
Great Codroy, *Canada* 141 C8   47 51N 59 16W
Great Dividing Ra., *Australia* . 126 C4   23 0 S 146 0 E
Great Driffield = Driffield, *U.K.* . 20 C7   54 0N   0 26W
Great Exuma I., *Bahamas* 164 B4   23 30N 75 50W
Great Falls, *U.S.A.* 158 C8   47 30N 111 17W
Great Fish = Groot Vis →, *S. Africa* . 116 E4   33 28 S 27 5 E
Great Guana Cay, *Bahamas* 164 B4   24 0N 76 20W
Great Inagua I., *Bahamas* 165 B5   21 0N 73 20W

Great Indian Desert = Thar Desert,
   India .... 92 F5   28 0N 72 0 E
Great Karoo, *S. Africa* .... 116 E3   31 55 S 21 0 E
Great Lake, *Canada* .... 127 D4   41 50 S 146 40 E
Great Lakes, *N. Amer.* 136 E11 46 0N 84 0W
Great Malvern, *U.K.* 21 E5   52 7N   2 18W
Great Miami →, *U.S.A.* 148 F3   39 20N 84 40W
Great Nicobar, *India* .... 95 L11 7 0N 93 50 E
Great Ormes Head, *U.K.* 20 D4   53 20N   3 52W
Great Ouse →, *U.K.* .... 20 E8   52 48N   0 21 E
Great Palm I., *Australia* ..... 126 B4   18 45 S 146 40 E
Great Pedro Bluff, *Jamaica* ... 164 a   17 51N 77 44W
Great Plains, *N. Amer.* 136 E9   47 0N 105 0W
Great Ruaha →, *Tanzania* ...... 118 D4   7 56 S 37 52 E
Great Sacandaga Res., *U.S.A.* . 151 C10 43 6N 74 16W
Great Saint Bernard Pass = Grand
   St-Bernard, Col du, *Europe* . 32 E4   45 50N   7 10 E
Great Salt L., *U.S.A.* 158 F7   41 15N 112 40W
Great Salt Lake Desert, *U.S.A.* . 158 F7   40 50N 113 30W
Great Salt Plains L., *U.S.A.* . 155 G5   36 45N 98 8W
Great Sand Dunes Nat.
   Monument △, *U.S.A.* 159 H11 37 48N 105 45W
Great Sandy Desert, *Australia* . 124 D3   21 0 S 124 0 E
Great Sandy Nat. Park △, *Australia* . 127 A5   26 13 S 153 2 E
Great Sangi = Sangihe, Pulau,
   Indonesia .... 82 A3   3 35N 125 30 E
Great Scarcies →, *S. Leone* ... 112 D2   9 0N 13 0W
Great Sd., *Bermuda* .... 9 a   32 17N 64 51W
Great Sea Reef, *Fiji* .... 133 A2   16 15 S 179 0 E
Great Sitkin I., *U.S.A.* 144 K3   52 3N 176 6W
Great Skellig, *Ireland* 23 E1   51 47N 10 33W
Great Slave L., *Canada* 142 A5   61 23N 115 38W
Great Smoky Mts. Nat. Park △,
   U.S.A. 149 H4   35 40N 83 40W
Great Snow Mt., *Canada* 142 B4   57 26N 124 0W
Great Stour = Stour →, *U.K.* .. 21 F9   51 18N   1 22 E
Great Victoria Desert, *Australia* . 125 E4   29 30 S 126 30 E
Great Wall, *China* .... 74 E5   38 30N 109 30 E
Great Whale River = Kuujjuarapik,
   Canada 140 A4   55 20N 77 35W
Great Whernside, *U.K.* 20 C6   54 10N   1 58W
Great Yarmouth, *U.K.* .... 21 E9   52 37N   1 44 E
Great Zimbabwe, *Zimbabwe* ..... 119 G3   20 16 S 30 54 E
Greater Antilles, *W. Indies* .. 165 C5   17 40N 74 0W
Greater London □, *U.K.* 21 F7   51 31N   0 6W
Greater Manchester □, *U.K.* ... 20 D5   53 30N   2 15W
Greater St Lucia Wetlands Park △,
   S. Africa .... 117 D5   28 6 S 32 27 E
Greater Sunda Is., *Indonesia* . 78 F4   7 0 S 112 0 E
Grebbestad, *Sweden* .... 17 F5   58 42N 11 15 E
Grebenka = Hrebenka, *Ukraine* . 59 G7   50 9N 32 22 E
Greco, C., *Cyprus* .... 39 F10 34 57N 34 5 E
Greco, Mte., *Italy* .... 45 G10 41 48N 13 58 E
Gredos, Sierra de, *Spain* 42 E6   40 20N   5 0W
Greece, *U.S.A.* 150 C7   43 13N 77 41W
Greece ■, *Europe* .... 48 B3   40 0N 23 0 E
Greeley, *Colo., U.S.A.* 154 E2   40 25N 104 42W
Greeley, *Nebr., U.S.A.* 154 E5   41 33N 98 32W
Greeleyville, *U.S.A.* 152 B10 33 40N 79 59W
Greem-Bell, Ostrov, *Russia* ... 66 A7   81 0N 62 0 E
Green →, *Ky., U.S.A.* 148 G2   37 54N 87 30W
Green →, *Utah, U.S.A.* 159 G9   38 11N 109 53W
Green B., *U.S.A.* 148 C2   45 0N 87 30W
Green Bay, *U.S.A.* 148 C2   44 31N 88 0W
Green C., *Australia* .... 129 D9   37 13 S 150 1 E
Green City, *U.S.A.* 156 D4   40 16N 92 57W
Green Cove Springs, *U.S.A.* ... 152 F8   29 59N 81 40W
Green Is., *Papua N. G.* .... 132 C8   4 35 S 154 10 E
Green Island Bay, *Phil.* ...... 81 F2   10 13N 119 16 E
Green Lake, *Canada* 143 C7   54 17N 107 47W
Green Mts., *U.S.A.* 151 C12 43 45N 72 45W
Green Pond, *U.S.A.* 152 C9   32 44N 80 37W
Green River, *Papua N. G.* ..... 132 B1   3 54 S 141 11 E
Green River, *Utah, U.S.A.* 159 G8   38 59N 110 10W
Green River, *Wyo., U.S.A.* 158 F9   41 32N 109 28W
Green Valley, *U.S.A.* 159 L8   31 52N 110 56W
Greenacres City, *U.S.A.* 153 J9   26 38N 80 7W
Greenbank, *U.S.A.* 160 B4   48 6N 122 34W
Greenbush, *Mich., U.S.A.* 150 B1   44 35N 83 19W
Greenbush, *Minn., U.S.A.* 154 A6   48 42N 96 11W
Greencastle, *U.S.A.* 157 E10 39 38N 86 52W
Greene, *Iowa, U.S.A.* 156 B4   42 54N 92 48W
Greene, *N.Y., U.S.A.* 151 D9   42 20N 75 46W
Greenfield, *Calif., U.S.A.* ... 160 J5   36 19N 121 15W
Greenfield, *Calif., U.S.A.* ... 161 K8   35 15N 119 0W
Greenfield, *Ill., U.S.A.* 156 F6   39 21N 90 12W
Greenfield, *Ind., U.S.A.* 157 E11 39 47N 85 46W
Greenfield, *Iowa, U.S.A.* 156 C2   41 18N 94 28W
Greenfield, *Mass., U.S.A.* 151 D12 42 35N 72 36W
Greenfield, *Mo., U.S.A.* 155 G8   37 25N 93 51W
Greenfield, *Ohio, U.S.A.* 157 E13 39 21N 83 23W
Greenfield Park, *Canada* 151 A11 45 29N 73 29W
Greenland ☑, *N. Amer.* 10 D6   66 0N 45 0W
Greenland Sea, *Arctic* 10 B10 73 0N 10 0W
Greenock, *U.K.* 22 F4   55 57N   4 46W
Greenore, *Ireland* 23 B5   54 2N   6 8W
Greenore Pt., *Ireland* 23 D5   52 14N   6 19W
Greenough, *Australia* .... 125 E1   28 58 S 114 43 E
Greenough →, *Australia* .... 125 E1   28 51 S 114 38 E
Greenough Pt., *Canada* 150 B3   44 58N 81 26W
Greenport, *U.S.A.* 151 E12 41 6N 72 22W
Greensboro, *Fla., U.S.A.* 152 K3   30 34N 84 45W
Greensboro, *Ga., U.S.A.* 152 B6   33 35N 83 11W
Greensboro, *N.C., U.S.A.* 149 G6   36 4N 79 48W
Greensboro, *Vt., U.S.A.* 151 B12 44 36N 72 18W
Greensburg, *Ind., U.S.A.* 157 E11 39 20N 85 29W
Greensburg, *Kans., U.S.A.* 155 G5   37 36N 99 18W
Greensburg, *Pa., U.S.A.* 150 F5   40 18N 79 33W
Greenstone Pt., *U.K.* 22 D3   57 55N   5 37W
Greentown, *U.S.A.* 157 D11 40 29N 85 58W
Greenup, *U.S.A.* 157 E8   39 15N 88 10W
Greenvale, *Australia* .... 126 B4   18 59 S 145 7 E
Greenville, *Liberia* 112 D3   5 1N   9 6W
Greenville, *Ala., U.S.A.* 149 K2   31 50N 86 38W
Greenville, *Calif., U.S.A.* ... 160 E6   40 8N 120 57W
Greenville, *Fla., U.S.A.* 152 F6   30 28N 83 38W
Greenville, *Ga., U.S.A.* 152 B5   33 2N 84 43W
Greenville, *Ill., U.S.A.* 156 F7   38 53N 89 25W
Greenville, *Ind., U.S.A.* 157 F11 38 22N 85 59W
Greenville, *Maine, U.S.A.* 149 C11 45 28N 69 35W
Greenville, *Mich., U.S.A.* 148 D3   43 11N 85 15W
Greenville, *Miss., U.S.A.* 155 J9   33 24N 91 4W
Greenville, *Mo., U.S.A.* 155 G9   37 8N 90 27W
Greenville, *N.C., U.S.A.* 149 H7   35 37N 77 23W
Greenville, *N.H., U.S.A.* 151 D13 42 46N 71 49W
Greenville, *N.Y., U.S.A.* 151 D10 42 25N 74 1W
Greenville, *Ohio, U.S.A.* 157 D12 40 6N 84 38W
Greenville, *Pa., U.S.A.* 150 E4   41 24N 80 23W
Greenville, *S.C., U.S.A.* 149 H4   34 51N 82 24W
Greenville, *Tenn., U.S.A.* 149 G4   36 13N 82 51W
Greenville, *Tex., U.S.A.* 155 J6   33 8N 96 7W
Greenwater Lake Prov. Park △,
   Canada 143 C8   52 32N 103 30W
Greenwich, *Conn., U.S.A.* 151 E11 41 2N 73 38W
Greenwich, *N.Y., U.S.A.* 151 C11 43 5N 73 30W
Greenwich, *Ohio, U.S.A.* 150 E2   41 2N 82 31W
Greenwood, *Canada* 142 D5   49 10N 118 40W
Greenwood, *Ark., U.S.A.* 155 H7   35 13N 94 16W
Greenwood, *Ind., U.S.A.* 157 E10 39 37N 86 7W
Greenwood, *Miss., U.S.A.* 155 J9   33 31N 90 11W
Greenwood, *S.C., U.S.A.* 149 H4   34 12N 82 10W

Greenwood, Mt., *Australia* **124 B5** 13 48 S 130 4 E
Gregbe, *Ivory C.* **112 D3** 6 48N 6 43W
Gregório →, *Brazil* **172 B3** 6 50 S 70 46W
Gregory, *U.S.A.* **154 D5** 43 14N 99 20W
Gregory →, *Australia* **126 B2** 17 53 S 139 17 E
Gregory, L., *S. Austral., Australia* **127 D2** 28 55 S 139 0 E
Gregory, L., *W. Austral., Australia* **125 E2** 25 38 S 119 58 E
Gregory Downs, *Australia* **126 B2** 18 35 S 138 45 E
Gregory L., *Australia* **124 D4** 20 0 S 127 40 E
Gregory Nat. Park △, *Australia* **124 C5** 15 38 S 131 15 E
Gregory Ra., *Queens., Australia* **126 B3** 19 30 S 143 40 E
Gregory Ra., *W. Austral., Australia* **124 D3** 21 20 S 121 12 E
Greiffenberg, *Germany* **30 B9** 53 5N 13 57 E
Greifswald, *Germany* **30 A9** 54 5N 13 23 E
Greifswalder Bodden, *Germany* **30 A9** 54 12N 13 35 E
Grein, *Austria* **34 C7** 48 14N 14 51 E
Greiz, *Germany* **30 E8** 50 39N 12 10 E
Gremikha, *Russia* **56 A6** 67 59N 39 47 E
Gremyachinsk, *Russia* **64 B6** 58 34N 57 51 E
Grenå, *Denmark* **17 H4** 56 25N 10 53 E
Grenada, *U.S.A.* **155 J10** 33 47N 89 49W
Grenada ■, *W. Indies* **165 D7** 12 10N 61 40W
Grenade, *France* **28 E5** 43 47N 1 17 E
Grenadier I., *U.S.A.* **151 B8** 44 3N 76 22W
Grenadines, *St. Vincent* **165 D7** 12 40N 61 20W
Grenchen, *Switz.* **32 B4** 47 12N 7 24 E
Grenen, *Denmark* **17 G4** 57 44N 10 40 E
Grenfell, *Australia* **129 B8** 33 52 S 148 8 E
Grenfell, *Canada* **143 C8** 50 30N 102 56W
Grenivík, *Iceland* **11 B8** 65 57N 18 11W
Grenjaðarstaður, *Iceland* **11 B9** 65 49N 17 21W
Grenoble, *France* **29 C9** 45 12N 5 42 E
Grenville, C., *Australia* **126 A3** 12 0 S 143 13 E
Grenville Chan., *Canada* **142 C3** 53 40N 129 46W
Gréoux-les-Bains, *France* **29 E9** 43 45N 5 52 E
Gresham, *U.S.A.* **160 E4** 45 30N 122 26W
Gresik, *Indonesia* **85 D4** 7 13 S 112 38 E
Gressan, *Italy* **32 E4** 45 43N 7 17 E
Gretna, *U.K.* **22 F5** 55 0N 3 3W
Gretna, *U.S.A.* **152 E5** 30 37N 84 40W
Greven, *Germany* **30 C3** 52 6N 7 37 E
Grevená, *Greece* **50 F5** 40 4N 21 25 E
Grevená □, *Greece* **50 F5** 40 2N 21 25 E
Grevenbroich, *Germany* **30 D2** 51 5N 6 35 E
Grevenmacher, *Lux.* **24 E6** 49 41N 6 26 E
Grevesmühlen, *Germany* **30 B7** 53 52N 11 12 E
Grevestrand, *Denmark* **17 J6** 55 36N 12 19 E
Grey →, *Canada* **141 C8** 47 34N 57 6W
Grey →, *N.Z.* **131 C6** 42 27 S 171 12 E
Grey, C., *Australia* **126 A2** 13 0 S 136 35 E
Grey Ra., *Australia* **127 D3** 27 0 S 143 30 E
Greybull, *U.S.A.* **158 D9** 44 30N 108 3W
Greymouth, *N.Z.* **131 C6** 42 29 S 171 13 E
Greystones, *Ireland* **23 C5** 53 9N 6 5W
Greytown, *N.Z.* **130 H4** 41 5 S 175 29 E
Greytown, *S. Africa* **117 D5** 29 1 S 30 36 E
Gribanovskiy, *Russia* **60 E5** 51 28N 41 50 E
Gribbell I., *Canada* **142 C3** 53 23N 129 0W
Gribës, Mal i, *Albania* **50 F3** 40 17N 19 45 E
Gribingui →, *C.A.R.* **114 A3** 8 33N 19 5 E
Gribingui-Bamingui, Réserve de Faune du ⌂, *C.A.R.* **114 A3** 7 45N 19 17 E
Gridley, *U.S.A.* **160 F5** 39 22N 121 42W
Griebeg, Ras il-, *Malta* **38 F7** 35 58N 14 23 E
Griekwastad, *S. Africa* **116 D3** 28 49 S 23 15 E
Griesheim, *Germany* **31 F4** 49 51N 8 33 E
Grieskirchen, *Austria* **34 C6** 48 16N 13 48 E
Griffin, *U.S.A.* **152 B5** 33 15N 84 16W
Griffin, L., *U.S.A.* **153 G8** 28 52N 81 51W
Griffith, *Australia* **129 C7** 34 18 S 146 2 E
Griffith, *Canada* **150 A7** 45 15N 77 10W
Griffith I., *Canada* **150 B4** 44 50N 80 55W
Griggsville, *U.S.A.* **156 E6** 39 43N 90 43W
Grignols, *France* **28 D3** 44 23N 0 2W
Grigoriopol, *Moldova* **53 C14** 47 9N 29 18 E
Grimari, *C.A.R.* **114 A4** 5 43N 20 6 E
Grimaylov = Hrymayliv, *Ukraine* **59 H4** 49 20N 26 5 E
Grimes, *U.S.A.* **160 F5** 39 4N 121 54W
Grimma, *Germany* **30 D8** 51 14N 12 43 E
Grimmen, *Germany* **30 A9** 54 7N 13 3 E
Grimsay, *U.K.* **22 D1** 57 29N 7 14W
Grimsby, *Canada* **150 C5** 43 12N 79 34W
Grimsby, *U.K.* **20 D7** 53 34N 0 5W
Grimselpass, *Switz.* **33 C6** 46 34N 8 23 E
Grímsey, *Iceland* **11 A9** 66 33N 17 58W
Grimshaw, *Canada* **142 B5** 56 10N 117 40W
Grimslöv, *Sweden* **17 H8** 56 44N 14 34 E
Grímsstaðir, *Iceland* **11 B10** 65 39N 16 7W
Grimstad, *Norway* **18 F5** 58 20N 8 35 E
Grímsvötn, *Iceland* **11 C9** 64 26N 17 22W
Grindavík, *Iceland* **11 D4** 63 50N 22 26W
Grindelwald, *Switz.* **32 C6** 46 38N 8 2 E
Grindsted, *Denmark* **17 J2** 55 46N 8 55 E
Grindstone I., *Canada* **151 B8** 44 43N 76 14W
Grindu, *Romania* **53 F11** 44 44N 26 50 E
Grinnell, *U.S.A.* **156 C4** 41 45N 92 43W
Grintavec, *Slovenia* **45 B11** 46 22N 14 32 E
Gris-Nez, C., *France* **27 B8** 50 52N 1 35 E
Grisolles, *France* **28 E5** 43 49N 1 19 E
Grisons = Graubünden □, *Switz.* **33 C9** 46 45N 9 30 E
Grisslehamn, *Sweden* **16 D12** 60 5N 18 49 E
Grmeč Planina, *Bos.-H.* **45 D13** 44 43N 16 16 E
Groais I., *Canada* **141 B8** 50 55N 55 35W
Grobiņa, *Latvia* **54 B8** 56 33N 21 10 E
Groblersdal, *S. Africa* **117 D4** 25 15 S 29 25 E
Grobming, *Austria* **34 D6** 47 27N 13 54 E
Grocka, *Serbia, Yug.* **50 B4** 44 40N 20 42 E
Gródek, *Poland* **55 E10** 53 6N 23 40 E
Grodków, *Poland* **55 H4** 50 43N 17 21 E
Grodno = Hrodna, *Belarus* **58 F2** 53 42N 23 52 E
Grodzisk Mazowiecki, *Poland* **55 F7** 52 7N 20 37 E
Grodzisk Wielkopolski, *Poland* **55 F3** 52 15N 16 22 E
Grodzyanka = Hrodzyanka, *Belarus* **58 F5** 53 31N 28 42 E
Groesbeck, *U.S.A.* **155 K6** 31 31N 96 31W
Groix, *France* **26 E3** 47 38N 3 29W
Groix, Î. de, *France* **26 E3** 47 38N 3 28W
Grójec, *Poland* **55 G7** 51 50N 20 58 E
Gronau, *Niedersachsen, Germany* **30 C5** 52 5N 9 47 E
Gronau, *Nordrhein-Westfalen, Germany* **30 C3** 52 12N 7 2 E
Grong, *Norway* **14 D15** 64 25N 12 8 E
Grönhögen, *Sweden* **17 H10** 56 16N 16 24 E
Groningen, *Neths.* **24 A6** 53 15N 6 35 E
Groningen, *Suriname* **169 B6** 5 48N 55 28W
Groningen □, *Neths.* **24 A6** 53 16N 6 40 E
Grønnedal = Kangilinnguit, *Greenland* **10 E6** 61 20N 47 57W
Groom, *U.S.A.* **155 H4** 35 12N 101 6W
Groot →, *S. Africa* **116 E3** 33 45 S 24 36 E
Groot Berg →, *S. Africa* **116 E2** 32 47 S 18 8 E
Groot-Brakrivier, *S. Africa* **116 E3** 34 2 S 22 18 E
Groot Karasberge, *Namibia* **116 D2** 27 20 S 18 40 E
Groot-Kei →, *S. Africa* **117 E4** 32 41 S 28 22 E
Groot Vis →, *S. Africa* **116 E4** 33 28 S 27 5 E
Grootdrink, *S. Africa* **116 D3** 28 33 S 21 42 E
Groote Eylandt, *Australia* **126 A2** 14 0 S 136 40 E
Grootfontein, *Namibia* **116 B2** 19 31 S 18 6 E
Grootlaagte →, *Africa* **116 C3** 20 55 S 21 27 E
Grootvloer →, *S. Africa* **116 E3** 30 0 S 20 40 E
Gros C., *Canada* **142 A6** 61 59N 113 32W
Gros Islet, *St. Lucia* **165 f** 14 5N 60 58W
Gros Morne Nat. Park △, *Canada* **141 C8** 49 40N 57 50W
Gros Piton, *St. Lucia* **165 f** 13 49N 61 5W
Gros Piton Pt., *St. Lucia* **165 f** 13 49N 61 5W
Grósio, *Italy* **44 B7** 46 18N 10 16 E
Grosne →, *France* **27 F11** 46 42N 4 56 E
Grosotto, *Italy* **33 D10** 46 17N 10 15 E
Grossa, Pta., *Spain* **38 C2** 39 6N 1 36 E
Grosse I., *U.S.A.* **157 B13** 42 8N 83 9W
Grossenbrode, *Germany* **30 A7** 54 21N 11 4 E
Grossenhain, *Germany* **30 D9** 51 17N 13 32 E
Grosser Arber, *Germany* **31 F9** 49 6N 13 8 E
Grosser Plöner See, *Germany* **30 A6** 54 10N 10 22 E
Grosseto, *Italy* **45 F8** 42 46N 11 8 E
Grossgerungs, *Austria* **34 C7** 48 34N 14 57 E
Grossglockner, *Austria* **34 D5** 47 5N 12 40 E
Grosswardein = Oradea, *Romania* **52 C6** 47 2N 21 58 E
Groswater B., *Canada* **141 B8** 54 20N 57 40W
Grotli, *Norway* **18 B4** 62 2N 7 42 E
Groton, *Conn., U.S.A.* **151 E12** 41 21N 72 5W
Groton, *N.Y., U.S.A.* **151 D8** 42 36N 76 22W
Groton, *S. Dak., U.S.A.* **154 C5** 45 27N 98 6W
Grottáglie, *Italy* **47 B10** 40 32N 17 26 E
Grottaminarda, *Italy* **47 A8** 41 4N 15 2 E
Grottammare, *Italy* **45 F10** 42 59N 13 52 E
Grouard Mission, *Canada* **142 B5** 55 33N 116 9W
Grouin, Pte. du, *France* **26 D5** 48 43N 1 51W
Groundhog →, *Canada* **140 C3** 48 45N 82 58W
Grouw, *Neths.* **24 A5** 53 5N 5 51 E
Grove City, *Fla., U.S.A.* **153 J7** 26 56N 82 19W
Grove City, *Ohio, U.S.A.* **157 E13** 39 53N 83 6W
Grove City, *Pa., U.S.A.* **150 E4** 41 10N 80 5W
Grove Hill, *U.S.A.* **149 K2** 31 42N 87 47W
Groveland, *Calif., U.S.A.* **160 H6** 37 50N 120 14W
Groveland, *Fla., U.S.A.* **153 G8** 28 34N 81 51W
Grover City, *U.S.A.* **161 K6** 35 7N 120 37W
Groves, *U.S.A.* **155 L8** 29 57N 93 54W
Groveton, *U.S.A.* **151 B13** 44 36N 71 31W
Grovetown, *U.S.A.* **152 B7** 33 27N 82 12W
Grožnjan, *Croatia* **45 C10** 45 22N 13 43 E
Groznyy, *Russia* **61 J7** 43 20N 45 45 E
Grua, *Norway* **18 D7** 60 16N 10 40 E
Grubišno Polje, *Croatia* **52 E2** 45 44N 17 12 E
Grudovo, *Bulgaria* **51 D11** 42 21N 27 10 E
Grudusk, *Poland* **55 E7** 53 3N 20 38 E
Grudziądz, *Poland* **54 E5** 53 30N 18 47 E
Gruinard B., *U.K.* **22 D3** 57 56N 5 35W
Gruissan, *France* **28 E7** 43 8N 3 7 E
Grumo Áppula, *Italy* **47 A9** 41 1N 16 42 E
Grums, *Sweden* **16 E7** 59 22N 13 5 E
Grünberg, *Germany* **30 E4** 50 35N 8 58 E
Grund, *Iceland* **11 B8** 65 31N 18 9W
Gründau, *Germany* **31 E5** 50 10N 9 9 E
Grundy Center, *U.S.A.* **156 B4** 42 22N 92 47W
Grungedal, *Norway* **18 E4** 59 44N 7 43 E
Grünstadt, *Germany* **31 F4** 49 34N 8 9 E
Gruppo di Tessa, Parco Naturale ⌂, *Italy* **44 B8** 46 47N 11 0 E
Gruvberget, *Sweden* **16 C10** 61 6N 16 10 E
Gruver, *U.S.A.* **155 G4** 36 16N 101 24W
Gruyères, *Switz.* **32 C4** 46 35N 7 4 E
Gruža, *Serbia, Yug.* **50 C4** 43 54N 20 46 E
Gryazi, *Russia* **59 F10** 52 30N 39 58 E
Gryazovets, *Russia* **58 C11** 58 50N 40 10 E
Grybów, *Poland* **55 J7** 49 36N 20 55 E
Grycksbo, *Sweden* **16 D9** 60 40N 15 29 E
Gryfice, *Poland* **54 E2** 53 55N 15 13 E
Gryfino, *Poland* **55 E1** 53 16N 14 29 E
Gryfów Śląski, *Poland* **55 G2** 51 2N 15 24 E
Grythyttan, *Sweden* **16 E8** 59 41N 14 32 E
Gstaad, *Switz.* **32 D4** 46 28N 7 18 E
Gua Musang, *Malaysia* **87 K3** 4 53N 101 58 E
Guacanayabo, G. de, *Cuba* **164 B4** 20 40N 77 20W
Guacara, *Venezuela* **168 A4** 10 14N 67 53W
Guachípas →, *Argentina* **174 B2** 25 40 S 65 30W
Guachiría →, *Colombia* **168 B3** 5 27N 70 36W
Guadajoz →, *Spain* **43 H6** 37 50N 4 51W
Guadalajara, *Mexico* **162 C4** 20 40N 103 20W
Guadalajara, *Spain* **40 E1** 40 37N 3 12W
Guadalajara □, *Spain* **40 E2** 40 47N 2 30W
Guadalcanal, *Solomon Is.* **133 M11** 9 32 S 160 12 E
Guadalcanal, *Spain* **43 G5** 38 5N 5 52W
Guadalén →, *Spain* **43 G7** 38 5N 3 32W
Guadales, *Argentina* **174 C2** 34 30 S 67 55W
Guadalete →, *Spain* **43 J4** 36 35N 6 13W
Guadalimar →, *Spain* **43 G7** 38 5N 3 28W
Guadalmena →, *Spain* **43 G8** 38 19N 2 56W
Guadalmez →, *Spain* **43 G5** 38 46N 5 4W
Guadalope →, *Spain* **40 D4** 41 15N 0 3W
Guadalquivir →, *Spain* **43 J4** 36 47N 6 22W
Guadalupe = Guadeloupe ⊠, *W. Indies* **164 b** 16 20N 61 40W
Guadalupe, *Brazil* **170 C3** 6 44 S 43 47W
Guadalupe, *Mexico* **161 N10** 32 4N 116 32W
Guadalupe, *Spain* **43 F5** 39 27N 5 17W
Guadalupe, *U.S.A.* **161 L6** 34 59N 120 33W
Guadalupe →, *Mexico* **161 N10** 32 6N 116 51W
Guadalupe →, *U.S.A.* **155 L6** 28 27N 96 47W
Guadalupe, Sierra de, *Spain* **43 F5** 39 28N 5 30W
Guadalupe Bravos, *Mexico* **162 A3** 31 20N 106 10W
Guadalupe I., *Pac. Oc.* **136 G8** 29 0N 118 50W
Guadalupe Mts. Nat. Park △, *U.S.A.* **155 K2** 32 0N 104 30W
Guadalupe Peak, *U.S.A.* **155 K2** 31 50N 104 52W
Guadalupe y Calvo, *Mexico* **162 B3** 26 6N 106 58W
Guadarrama, Sierra de, *Spain* **42 E7** 41 0N 4 0W
Guadauta, *Georgia* **61 J5** 43 7N 40 32 E
Guadeloupe ⊠, *W. Indies* **164 b** 16 20N 61 40W
Guadeloupe, Parque Nat. de la △, *Guadeloupe* **164 b** 16 10N 61 40W
Guadeloupe Mts. Nat. Park △, *U.S.A.* **155 K2** 31 40N 104 20W
Guadeloupe Passage, *W. Indies* **165 C7** 16 50N 62 15W
Guadelupe, *Peru* **172 B2** 7 15 S 79 29W
Guadiamar →, *Spain* **43 J4** 36 55N 6 24W
Guadiana →, *Portugal* **43 H3** 37 14N 7 22W
Guadiana Menor →, *Spain* **43 H7** 37 56N 3 15W
Guadiaro →, *Spain* **43 J5** 36 17N 5 17W
Guadiato →, *Spain* **43 H5** 37 48N 5 5W
Guadiela →, *Spain* **40 E2** 40 22N 2 49W
Guadix, *Spain* **43 H7** 37 18N 3 11W
Guafo, Boca del, *Chile* **176 B2** 43 35 S 74 0W
Guafo, I., *Chile* **176 B2** 43 35 S 74 50W
Guaico, *Trin. & Tob.* **169 F9** 10 35N 61 9W
Guainía □, *Colombia* **168 C4** 2 30N 69 0W
Guainía →, *Colombia* **168 C4** 2 1N 67 7W
Guaíra, *Brazil* **175 A5** 24 5 S 54 10W
Guaíra □, *Paraguay* **174 B4** 25 45 S 56 30W
Guaitecas, Is., *Chile* **176 B2** 44 0 S 74 30W
Guajará-Mirim, *Brazil* **173 C4** 10 50 S 65 20W
Guajira □, *Colombia* **168 A3** 11 30N 72 30W
Guajira, Pen. de la, *Colombia* **168 A3** 12 0N 72 0W
Gualaceo, *Ecuador* **168 D2** 2 54 S 78 47W
Gualán, *Guatemala* **164 C2** 15 8N 89 22W
Gualdo Tadino, *Italy* **45 E9** 43 14N 12 47 E
Gualeguay, *Argentina* **174 C4** 33 10 S 59 14W
Gualeguaychú, *Argentina* **174 C4** 33 3 S 59 31W
Gualequay →, *Argentina* **174 C4** 33 19 S 59 39W
Gualicho, Salina, *Argentina* **176 B3** 40 25 S 65 20W
Gualjaina, *Argentina* **176 B2** 42 45 S 70 30W
Guam ⊠, *Pac. Oc.* **133 R15** 13 27N 144 45 E
Guamá, *Brazil* **170 B2** 1 37 S 47 29W
Guamá →, *Brazil* **170 B2** 1 29 S 48 30W
Guamblin, I., *Chile* **176 B1** 44 50 S 75 0W
Guaminí, *Argentina* **174 D3** 37 1 S 62 28W
Guamote, *Ecuador* **168 D2** 1 56 S 78 43W
Guampí, Sierra de, *Venezuela* **169 B4** 6 0N 65 35W
Guamúchil, *Mexico* **162 B3** 25 25N 108 3W
Guana I., *Br. Virgin Is.* **165 e** 18 30N 64 30W
Guanabacoa, *Cuba* **164 B3** 23 8N 82 18W
Guanacaste , Parque Nac. △, *Costa Rica* **164 D2** 10 57N 85 30W
Guanacaste, Cordillera del, *Costa Rica* **164 D2** 10 40N 85 4W
Guanacevi, *Mexico* **162 B3** 25 40N 106 0W
Guanahani = San Salvador I., *Bahamas* **165 B5** 24 0N 74 40W
Guanajay, *Cuba* **164 B3** 22 56N 82 42W
Guanajuato, *Mexico* **162 C4** 21 0N 101 20W
Guanajuato □, *Mexico* **162 C4** 20 40N 101 20W
Guanambi, *Brazil* **171 D3** 14 13 S 42 47W
Guanare, *Venezuela* **168 B4** 8 42N 69 12W
Guanare →, *Venezuela* **168 B4** 8 13N 67 46W
Guandacol, *Argentina* **174 B2** 29 30 S 68 40W
Guane, *Cuba* **164 B3** 22 10N 84 7W
Guang'an, *China* **76 B6** 30 28N 106 35 E
Guangchang, *China* **77 D11** 26 50N 116 21 E
Guangde, *China* **77 B12** 30 54N 119 25 E
Guangdong □, *China* **77 F9** 23 0N 113 0 E
Guangfeng, *China* **77 C12** 28 20N 118 15 E
Guanghan, *China* **76 B5** 30 58N 104 17 E
Guangling, *China* **74 E8** 39 47N 114 22 E
Guangnan, *China* **76 E5** 24 5N 105 4 E
Guangning, *China* **77 F9** 23 40N 112 22 E
Guangrao, *China* **75 F10** 37 5N 118 25 E
Guangshui, *China* **77 B9** 31 37N 114 0 E
Guangshun, *China* **76 D6** 26 8N 106 21 E
Guangwu, *China* **74 F3** 37 48N 105 57 E
Guangxi Zhuangzu Zizhiqu □, *China* **76 F7** 24 0N 109 0 E
Guangyuan, *China* **76 A5** 32 26N 105 51 E
Guangze, *China* **77 D11** 27 30N 117 12 E
Guangzhou, *China* **77 F9** 23 5N 113 10 E
Guanhães, *Brazil* **171 E3** 18 47 S 42 57W
Guanica, *Puerto Rico* **165 d** 17 59N 66 55W
Guanipa →, *Venezuela* **169 B5** 9 56N 62 26W
Guanling, *China* **76 E5** 25 56N 105 35 E
Guannan, *China* **75 G10** 34 8N 119 21 E
Guanta, *Venezuela* **169 A5** 10 14N 64 36W
Guantánamo, *Cuba* **165 B4** 20 10N 75 14W
Guantánamo B., *Cuba* **165 C4** 19 59N 75 10W
Guantao, *China* **74 F8** 36 42N 115 25 E
Guanyang, *China* **77 E8** 25 30N 111 8 E
Guanyun, *China* **75 G10** 34 20N 119 18 E
Guapí, *Colombia* **168 C2** 2 36N 77 54W
Guápiles, *Costa Rica* **164 D3** 10 10N 83 46W
Guapo B., *Trin. & Tob.* **169 F9** 10 12N 61 41W
Guaporé, *Brazil* **175 B5** 28 51 S 51 54W
Guaporé →, *Brazil* **173 C4** 11 55 S 65 4W
Guaqui, *Bolivia* **172 D4** 16 41 S 68 54W
Guara, Sierra de, *Spain* **40 C4** 42 19N 0 15W
Guarabira, *Brazil* **170 C4** 6 51 S 35 29W
Guaramacal, Parque Nac. △, *Venezuela* **165 E5** 9 10N 70 10W
Guaranda, *Ecuador* **168 D2** 1 36 S 79 0W
Guarapari, *Brazil* **171 F3** 20 40 S 40 30W
Guarapuava, *Brazil* **171 G1** 25 20 S 51 30W
Guaratinguetá, *Brazil* **175 A6** 22 49 S 45 9W
Guaratuba, *Brazil* **175 B6** 25 53 S 48 38W
Guarda, *Portugal* **42 E3** 40 32N 7 20W
Guarda □, *Portugal* **42 E3** 40 40N 7 20W
Guardafui, C. = Asir, Ras, *Somali Rep.* **120 B4** 11 55N 51 10 E
Guardamar del Segura, *Spain* **41 G4** 38 5N 0 39W
Guardavalle, *Italy* **47 D9** 38 30N 16 30 E
Guárdia Sanframondi, *Italy* **47 A7** 41 15N 14 36 E
Guardiagrele, *Italy* **45 F11** 42 11N 14 13 E
Guardo, *Spain* **42 C6** 42 47N 4 50W
Guareña, *Spain* **43 G4** 38 51N 6 6W
Guareña →, *Spain* **42 D5** 41 29N 5 23W
Guari, *Papua N. G.* **132 E4** 8 3 S 146 52 E
Guárico □, *Venezuela* **168 B4** 8 40N 66 35W
Guarrojo →, *Colombia* **168 C3** 4 6N 70 42W
Guarujá, *Brazil* **175 A6** 24 2 S 46 25W
Guarulhos, *Brazil* **175 A6** 23 29 S 46 33W
Guarus, *Brazil* **171 F3** 21 44 S 41 20W
Guasave, *Mexico* **162 B3** 25 34N 108 27W
Guascama, Pta., *Colombia* **168 C2** 2 32N 78 24W
Guasdualito, *Venezuela* **168 B3** 7 15N 70 44W
Guasipati, *Venezuela* **169 B5** 7 28N 61 54W
Guasopa, *Papua N. G.* **132 E7** 9 12 S 152 56 E
Guastalla, *Italy* **44 D7** 44 55N 10 39 E
Guatemala, *Guatemala* **164 D1** 14 40N 90 22W
Guatemala ■, *Cent. Amer.* **164 C1** 15 40N 90 30W
Guatire, *Venezuela* **168 A4** 10 28N 66 32W
Guatopo, Parque Nac. △, *Venezuela* **165 D6** 10 5N 66 30W
Guatuaro Pt., *Trin. & Tob.* **169 F10** 10 19N 60 59W
Guavi →, *Papua N. G.* **132 D2** 7 48 S 143 16 E
Guaviare □, *Colombia* **168 C3** 2 0N 72 30W
Guaviare →, *Colombia* **168 C4** 4 3N 67 44W
Guaxupé, *Brazil* **175 A6** 21 10 S 47 5W
Guayabero →, *Colombia* **168 C3** 2 36N 72 47W
Guayaguayare, *Trin. & Tob.* **169 F9** 10 12N 61 3W
Guayama, *Puerto Rico* **165 d** 17 59N 66 7W
Guayaneco, Arch., *Chile* **176 C1** 47 45 S 75 10W
Guayaquil, *Ecuador* **168 D2** 2 15 S 79 52W
Guayaquil, G. de, *Ecuador* **168 D1** 3 10 S 81 0W
Guayaramerín, *Bolivia* **173 C4** 10 48 S 65 23W
Guayas →, *Ecuador* **168 D2** 2 36 S 79 52W
Guaymas, *Mexico* **162 B2** 27 59N 110 54W
Guba, *Dem. Rep. of the Congo* **119 E2** 10 38 S 26 27 E
Guba, *Ethiopia* **107 E4** 11 17N 35 20 E
Gubakha, *Russia* **64 B6** 58 52N 57 36 E
Gûbâl, Madîq, *Egypt* **106 B3** 27 30N 34 0 E
Gubam, *Papua N. G.* **132 E1** 8 39 S 141 53 E
Guban, *Somali Rep.* **120 B1** 10 30N 44 0 E
Gubat, *Phil.* **80 E5** 12 55N 124 7 E
Gubbi, *India* **95 H3** 13 19N 76 56 E
Gúbbio, *Italy* **45 E9** 43 21N 12 35 E
Guben, *Germany* **30 D10** 51 57N 14 42 E
Gubin, *Poland* **55 G1** 51 57N 14 43 E
Gubio, *Nigeria* **113 C7** 12 30N 12 42 E
Gubkin, *Russia* **59 G9** 51 17N 37 32 E
Guča, *Serbia, Yug.* **50 C4** 43 46N 20 15 E
Gucheng, *China* **77 A8** 32 20N 111 30 E
Gudå, *Norway* **18 A8** 63 27N 11 36 E
Gudalur, *India* **95 J3** 11 30N 76 29 E
Gudata = Guadauta, *Georgia* **61 J5** 43 7N 40 32 E
Gudbrandsdalen, *Norway* **15 F14** 61 33N 10 10 E
Gudenå →, *Denmark* **17 H4** 56 29N 10 13 E
Gudermes, *Russia* **61 J8** 43 24N 46 5 E
Gudhjem, *Denmark* **17 J8** 55 12N 14 58 E
Gudivada, *India* **95 F5** 16 30N 81 3 E
Gudiyattam, *India* **95 H4** 12 57N 78 55 E
Gudur, *India* **95 G4** 14 12N 79 55 E
Gudvangen, *Norway* **18 D3** 60 52N 6 49 E
Guebwiller, *France* **27 E14** 47 55N 7 12 E
Guecho = Getxo, *Spain* **40 B2** 43 21N 2 59W
Guékédou, *Guinea* **112 D2** 8 40N 10 5W
Guelb er Rîchât, *Mauritania* **110 D2** 21 7N 11 24W
Guéle Mendouka, *Cameroon* **113 E7** 4 23N 12 55 E
Guélengdeng, *Chad* **109 F3** 10 55N 15 31 E
Guelma, *Algeria* **111 A6** 36 25N 7 29 E
Guelmine = Goulimine, *Morocco* **110 C3** 28 56N 10 0W
Guelph, *Canada* **140 D3** 43 35N 80 20W
Guelta Zemmur, *W. Sahara* **110 C2** 25 8N 12 22W
Guemar, *Algeria* **111 B6** 33 30N 6 49 E
Guéméné-Penfao, *France* **26 E5** 47 38N 1 50W
Guéméné-sur-Scorff, *France* **26 D3** 48 4N 3 13W
Guéné, *Benin* **113 C5** 11 44N 3 16 E
Güeppí, *Peru* **168 D2** 0 7 S 75 15W
Guer, *France* **26 E4** 47 54N 2 8W
Güer Aike, *Argentina* **176 D3** 51 39 S 69 35W
Guera, *Chad* **109 F3** 11 55N 18 12 E
Guérande, *France* **26 E4** 47 20N 2 26W
Guerara, *Algeria* **111 B5** 32 51N 4 22 E
Guercif, *Morocco* **111 B4** 34 14N 3 21W
Guéréda, *Chad* **109 F4** 14 31N 22 5 E
Guéret, *France* **27 F8** 46 11N 1 51 E
Guérigny, *France* **27 E10** 47 6N 3 10 E
Guerneville, *U.S.A.* **160 G4** 38 30N 123 0W
Guernica = Gernika-Lumo, *Spain* **40 B2** 43 19N 2 40W
Guernsey, *U.K.* **21 H5** 49 26N 2 35W
Guernsey, *U.S.A.* **154 D2** 42 19N 104 45W
Guerrara, *Algeria* **111 C4** 28 5N 0 8W
Guerrero □, *Mexico* **163 D5** 17 30N 100 0W
Guerzim, *Algeria* **111 C4** 29 39N 1 40W
Guessou-Sud, *Benin* **113 C5** 10 3N 2 38 E
Gueugnon, *France* **27 F11** 46 36N 4 4 E
Guéyo, *Ivory C.* **112 D3** 5 25N 6 5W
Gufuðalur, *Iceland* **11 B4** 65 34N 22 25W
Gughe, *Ethiopia* **107 F4** 6 12N 37 30 E
Gügher, *Iran* **99 D8** 29 28N 56 27 E
Guglionesi, *Italy* **45 G11** 41 55N 14 55 E
Guhakolak, Tanjung, *Indonesia* **79 G11** 6 50 S 105 14 E
Gui Jiang →, *China* **77 F8** 23 30N 111 15 E
Guia, *Canary Is.* **9 e1** 28 8N 15 38W
Guia de Isora, *Canary Is.* **9 e1** 28 12N 16 46W
Guia Lopes da Laguna, *Brazil* **175 A4** 21 26 S 56 7W
Guiana, *Venezuela* **169 B5** 5 9N 63 36W
Guiana Highlands, *S. Amer.* **166 C4** 5 10N 60 40W
Guibéroua, *Ivory C.* **112 D3** 6 14N 6 10W
Guichen B., *Australia* **128 D3** 37 10 S 139 45 E
Guichi, *China* **77 B11** 30 39N 117 27 E
Guider, *Cameroon* **113 D7** 9 56N 13 57 E
Guidiguir, *Niger* **113 C6** 13 40N 9 50 E
Guidimouni, *Niger* **113 C6** 13 42N 9 31 E
Guiding, *China* **76 D6** 26 34N 107 11 E
Guidong, *China* **77 D9** 26 7N 113 57 E
Guidónia-Montecélio, *Italy* **45 F9** 42 1N 12 45 E
Guiers, L. de, *Senegal* **112 B1** 16 10N 15 50W
Guigang, *China* **76 F7** 23 8N 109 35 E
Guiglo, *Ivory C.* **112 D3** 6 45N 7 30W
Guihulñgan, *Phil.* **81 F5** 10 7N 123 16 E
Guijá, *Mozam.* **117 C5** 24 27 S 33 0 E
Guijuelo, *Spain* **42 E5** 40 33N 5 40W
Guildford, *U.K.* **21 F7** 51 14N 0 34W
Guilford, *U.S.A.* **151 E12** 41 17N 72 41W
Guilin, *China* **77 E8** 25 18N 110 15 E
Guillaume-Delisle L., *Canada* **140 A4** 56 15N 76 17W
Guillaumes, *France* **29 D10** 44 5N 6 52 E
Guillestre, *France* **29 D10** 44 39N 6 40 E
Guilvinec, *France* **26 E2** 47 48N 4 17W
Güimar, *Canary Is.* **9 e1** 28 18N 16 24W
Guimarães, *Brazil* **170 B3** 2 9 S 44 42W
Guimarães, *Portugal* **42 D2** 41 28N 8 24W
Guimaras □, *Phil.* **81 F4** 10 35N 122 37 E
Guimba, *Phil.* **80 D3** 15 40N 120 46 E
Guinayangan, *Phil.* **80 E4** 13 54N 122 27 E
Guinda, *U.S.A.* **160 G4** 38 50N 122 12W
Guindulman, *Phil.* **81 G5** 9 46N 124 29 E
Guinea, *Africa* **104 F4** 8 0N 8 0 E
Guinea ■, *W. Afr.* **112 C2** 10 20N 11 30W
Guinea, Gulf of, *Atl. Oc.* **112 C2** 3 0N 2 30 E
Guinea-Bissau ■, *Africa* **112 C2** 12 0N 15 0W
Güines, *Cuba* **164 B3** 22 50N 82 0W
Guingamp, *France* **26 D3** 48 34N 3 10W
Guinguinéo, *Senegal* **112 C1** 14 20N 15 57W
Guinobatan, *Phil.* **80 E4** 13 11N 123 36 E
Guipavas, *France* **26 D2** 48 26N 4 29W
Guiping, *China* **77 F8** 23 21N 110 2 E
Guipúzcoa □, *Spain* **40 B2** 43 12N 2 15W
Guir, *Mali* **112 B4** 18 52N 2 52W
Guir, O. →, *Algeria* **111 B4** 31 29N 2 17W
Guiratinga, *Brazil* **173 D7** 16 21 S 53 45W
Guirel, *Mauritania* **112 B3** 15 30N 7 3W
Güiria, *Venezuela* **169 F8** 10 32N 62 18W
Guiscard, *France* **27 C10** 49 40N 3 1 E
Guise, *France* **27 C10** 49 52N 3 35 E
Guita-Koulouba, *C.A.R.* **114 A4** 5 58N 23 21 E
Guitiriz, *Spain* **42 B3** 43 11N 7 50W
Guitri, *Ivory C.* **112 D3** 5 30N 5 14W
Guiuan, *Phil.* **81 F5** 11 5N 125 55 E
Guixi, *China* **77 C11** 28 16N 117 15 E
Guiyang, *Guizhou, China* **76 D6** 26 32N 106 40 E
Guiyang, *Hunan, China* **77 E9** 25 46N 112 42 E
Guizhou □, *China* **76 D6** 27 0N 107 0 E
Gujan-Mestras, *France* **28 D2** 44 38N 1 4W
Gujar Khan, *Pakistan* **92 C5** 33 16N 73 19 E
Gujarat □, *India* **92 H4** 23 20N 71 0 E
Gujiang, *China* **77 D10** 27 11N 114 47 E
Gujranwala, *Pakistan* **91 B4** 32 10N 74 12 E
Gujrat, *Pakistan* **91 B4** 32 40N 74 2 E
Gukovo, *Russia* **61 F5** 48 1N 39 58 E
Gulargambone, *Australia* **129 A8** 31 20 S 148 30 E
Gulbarga, *India* **94 F3** 17 20N 76 50 E
Gulbene, *Latvia* **15 H22** 57 8N 26 52 E
Gulcha, *Kyrgyzstan* **65 C6** 40 19N 73 26 E
Guledagudda, *India* **95 F2** 16 3N 75 48 E
Gulf □, *Papua N. G.* **132 D3** 8 0 S 145 0 E
Gulf, The, *Asia* **97 E6** 27 0N 50 0 E
Gulf Breeze, *U.S.A.* **153 E2** 30 21N 87 9W
Gulf Hammock, *U.S.A.* **153 F7** 29 15N 82 43W
Gulf Islands Nat. Seashore ⌂, *U.S.A.* **153 K2** 30 10N 87 10W
Gulfport, *Fla., U.S.A.* **153 H7** 27 44N 82 43W
Gulfport, *Miss., U.S.A.* **155 K10** 30 22N 89 6W
Gulgong, *Australia* **129 B8** 32 20 S 149 49 E
Gulin, *China* **76 C5** 28 1N 105 50 E
Gulistan, *Pakistan* **92 D2** 30 30N 66 35 E
Guliston, *Uzbekistan* **65 C4** 40 29N 68 46 E
Gulkana, *U.S.A.* **144 E11** 62 16N 145 23W
Gull Lake, *Canada* **143 C7** 50 10N 108 29W
Gullbrå, *Norway* **18 D3** 60 50N 6 17 E
Gullbrandstorp, *Sweden* **17 H6** 56 42N 12 43 E
Gullbringusýsla □, *Iceland* **11 D4** 64 0N 22 0W
Gullfoss, *Iceland* **11 C6** 64 20N 20 8W
Gullhaug, *Norway* **18 E7** 59 30N 10 15 E
Gullivan B., *U.S.A.* **153 K8** 25 45N 81 40W
Gullspång, *Sweden* **17 F8** 58 59N 14 6 E
Gullstein, *Norway* **18 A5** 63 13N 8 9 E
Güllük, *Turkey* **49 D9** 37 14N 27 35 E
Gulluk Daği Milli Parki △, *Turkey* **49 E12** 37 0N 30 30 E
Güllük Korfezi, *Turkey* **49 D9** 37 12N 27 30 E
Gulma, *Nigeria* **113 C5** 12 40N 4 23 E
Gulmarg, *India* **93 B6** 34 3N 74 25 E
Gülnar, *Turkey* **100 D5** 36 19N 33 24 E
Gulnare, *Australia* **128 B3** 33 27 S 138 27 E
Gülpınar, *Turkey* **49 B8** 39 32N 26 7 E
Gülşehir, *Turkey* **100 C6** 38 44N 34 37 E
Gulshad, *Kazakhstan* **66 E8** 46 45N 74 25 E
Gulsvik, *Norway* **18 D6** 60 24N 9 38 E
Gulu, *Uganda* **118 B3** 2 48N 32 17 E
Gŭlŭbovo, *Bulgaria* **51 D9** 42 8N 25 55 E
Gulud, J., *Sudan* **107 E2** 11 31N 29 31 E
Gulwe, *Tanzania* **118 D4** 6 30 S 36 25 E
Gulyaypole = Hulyaypole, *Ukraine* **59 J9** 47 45N 36 21 E
Gum Lake, *Australia* **128 B5** 32 42 S 143 9 E
Gumaca, *Phil.* **80 E4** 13 55N 122 6 E
Gumal →, *Pakistan* **92 D4** 31 40N 71 50 E
Gumbaz, *Pakistan* **92 D3** 30 2N 69 0 E
Gumel, *Nigeria* **113 C6** 12 39N 9 22 E
Gumiel de Hizán, *Spain* **42 D7** 41 46N 3 41W
Gumla, *India* **93 H11** 23 3N 84 33 E
Gumlu, *Australia* **126 B4** 19 53 S 147 41 E
Gumma □, *Japan* **73 A10** 36 30N 138 20 E
Gummersbach, *Germany* **30 D3** 51 2N 7 34 E
Gummi, *Nigeria* **113 C6** 12 4N 5 9 E
Gümüldür, *Turkey* **49 C9** 38 6N 27 0 E

INDEX TO WORLD MAPS Hampshire Downs 221

Gümüşçay, *Turkey* **51 F11** 40 16N 27 17 E
Gümüşhaciköy, *Turkey* **100 B6** 40 50N 35 18 E
Gümüşhane, *Turkey* **101 B8** 40 30N 39 30 E
Gümüşsu, *Turkey* **49 C11** 38 14N 29 1 E
Gumzai, *Indonesia* **83 C4** 5 28 S 134 42 E
Guna, *Ethiopia* **107 F4** 8 18N 39 52 E
Guna, *India* **92 G7** 24 40N 77 19 E
Gundagai, *Australia* **129 C8** 35 3 S 148 6 E
Gundarehi, *India* **94 D5** 20 57N 81 17 E
Gundelfingen, *Germany* **31 G6** 48 34N 10 22 E
Gundih, *Indonesia* **85 D4** 7 10 S 110 56 E
Gundlakamma →, *India* **95 G5** 15 30N 80 15 E
Gundlupet, *India* **95 J3** 11 48N 76 41 E
Gunebang, *Australia* **129 B7** 33 1 S 146 38 E
Güney, *Burdur, Turkey* **49 D11** 37 29N 29 34 E
Güney, *Denizli, Turkey* **49 C11** 38 10N 29 4 E
Güneydoğu Toroslar, *Turkey* **101 C9** 38 20N 40 30 E
Gungal, *Australia* **129 B9** 32 17 S 150 32 E
Gungo, *Angola* **115 E2** 10 58 S 15 30 E
Gungu, *Dem. Rep. of the Congo* **115 D3** 5 43 S 19 20 E
Gunisao →, *Canada* **143 C9** 53 56N 97 53W
Gunisao L., *Canada* **143 C9** 53 33N 96 15W
Gunjyal, *Pakistan* **92 C4** 32 20N 71 55 E
Günlüce, *Turkey* **49 E10** 36 50N 28 20 E
Gunnarskog, *Sweden* **16 E6** 59 49N 12 34 E
Gunnbjørn Fjeld, *Greenland* **10 D8** 68 55N 29 47W
Gunnebo, *Sweden* **17 G10** 57 44N 16 32 E
Gunnedah, *Australia* **129 A9** 30 59 S 150 15 E
Gunnewin, *Australia* **127 D4** 25 59 S 148 33 E
Gunningbar Cr. →, *Australia* **129 A7** 31 14 S 147 6 E
Gunnison, *Colo., U.S.A.* **159 G10** 38 33N 106 56W
Gunnison, *Utah, U.S.A.* **158 G8** 39 9N 111 49W
Gunnison →, *U.S.A.* **159 G9** 39 4N 108 35W
Gunpowder, *Australia* **126 B2** 19 42 S 139 22 E
Guntakal, *India* **95 G3** 15 11N 77 27 E
Guntersville, *U.S.A.* **149 H2** 34 21N 86 18W
Guntong, *Malaysia* **87 K3** 4 36N 101 3 E
Guntur, *India* **95 F5** 16 23N 80 30 E
Gunungapi, *Indonesia* **82 C3** 6 45 S 126 30 E
Gunungsitoli, *Indonesia* **84 B1** 1 15N 97 30 E
Gunupur, *India* **94 E6** 19 5N 83 50 E
Günz →, *Germany* **31 G6** 48 27N 10 16 E
Gunza, *Angola* **115 E2** 10 50 S 13 50 E
Günzburg, *Germany* **31 G6** 48 26N 10 17 E
Gunzenhausen, *Germany* **31 F6** 49 7N 10 44 E
Guo He →, *China* **75 H9** 32 59N 117 10 E
Guoyang, *China* **74 H9** 33 32N 116 12 E
Gupis, *Pakistan* **93 A5** 36 15N 73 20 E
Gura Humorului, *Romania* **53 C10** 47 35N 25 53 E
Gura-Teghii, *Romania* **53 E11** 45 30N 26 25 E
Gurag, *Ethiopia* **107 F4** 8 20N 38 20 E
Gurahonţ, *Romania* **52 D7** 46 16N 22 21 E
Gurdaspur, *India* **92 C6** 32 5N 75 31 E
Gurdon, *U.S.A.* **155 J8** 33 55N 93 9W
Güre, *Balıkesir, Turkey* **49 B8** 39 36N 26 54 E
Güre, *Uşak, Turkey* **49 C11** 38 39N 29 10 E
Gurgaon, *India* **92 E7** 28 27N 77 1 E
Gürgentepe, *Turkey* **100 B7** 40 51N 37 50 E
Gurghiu, Munţii, *Romania* **53 D10** 46 41N 25 15 E
Gurgueia →, *Brazil* **170 C3** 6 50 S 43 24W
Gurha, *India* **92 G4** 25 12N 71 39 E
Guri, Embalse de, *Venezuela* **169 B5** 7 50N 62 52W
Gurig Nat. Park △, *Australia* **124 B5** 11 36 S 132 7 E
Gurimatu, *Papua N. G.* **132 D3** 6 45 S 144 45 E
Gurin, *Nigeria* **113 D7** 9 5N 12 54 E
Gurinhatã, *Brazil* **171 E2** 19 14 S 49 48W
Gurjaani, *Georgia* **61 K7** 41 43N 45 52 E
Gurk →, *Austria* **34 E7** 46 35N 14 31 E
Gurkha, *Nepal* **93 E11** 28 5N 84 40 E
Gurley, *Australia* **127 D4** 29 45 S 149 48 E
Gurnee, *U.S.A.* **157 B9** 42 22N 87 55W
Gurnet Point, *U.S.A.* **151 D14** 42 1N 70 34W
Guro, *Mozam.* **119 F3** 17 26 S 32 30 E
Gürpınar, *İst., Turkey* **51 F12** 40 59N 28 37 E
Gürpınar, *Van, Turkey* **101 C10** 38 18N 43 25 E
Gürsu, *Turkey* **51 F13** 40 13N 29 11 E
Gurué, *Mozam.* **119 F4** 15 25 S 36 58 E
Gurun, *Malaysia* **87 K3** 5 49N 100 27 E
Gürün, *Turkey* **100 C7** 38 43N 37 15 E
Gurupá, *Brazil* **169 D7** 1 25 S 51 35W
Gurupá, I. Grande de, *Brazil* **169 D7** 1 25 S 51 45W
Gurupi, *Brazil* **171 D2** 11 43 S 49 4W
Gurupi →, *Brazil* **170 B2** 1 13 S 46 6W
Gurupi, Serra do, *Brazil* **170 C2** 5 0 S 47 50W
Guruwe, *Zimbabwe* **117 B5** 16 40 S 30 42 E
Guryev = Atyraū, *Kazakhstan* **57 E9** 47 5N 52 0 E
Gus-Khrustalnyy, *Russia* **60 C5** 55 42N 40 44 E
Gusau, *Nigeria* **113 C6** 12 12N 6 40 E
Gusev, *Russia* **15 J20** 54 35N 22 10 E
Gushan, *China* **75 E12** 39 50N 123 35 E
Gushgy, *Turkmenistan* **66 F7** 35 20N 62 18 E
Gushi, *China* **77 A10** 32 11N 115 41 E
Gushiago, *Ghana* **113 D4** 9 55N 0 15W
Gusinje, *Montenegro, Yug.* **50 D3** 42 35N 19 50 E
Gusinoozersk, *Russia* **67 D11** 51 16N 106 27 E
Gúspini, *Italy* **46 C1** 39 32N 8 37 E
Güssing, *Austria* **35 D9** 47 3N 16 20 E
Gustav Holm, Kap, *Greenland* **10 D7** 66 36N 34 15W
Gustavsberg, *Sweden* **16 E12** 59 19N 18 23 E
Gustavus, *U.S.A.* **142 B1** 58 25N 135 44W
Gustine, *U.S.A.* **160 H6** 37 16N 121 0W
Güstrow, *Germany* **30 B8** 53 47N 12 10 E
Gusum, *Sweden* **17 F10** 58 16N 16 30 E
Guta = Kolárovo, *Slovak Rep.* **35 D10** 47 54N 18 0 E
Gütersloh, *Germany* **30 D4** 51 54N 8 24 E
Gutha, *Australia* **125 E2** 28 58 S 115 55 E
Guthalungra, *Australia* **126 B4** 19 52 S 147 50 E
Guthrie, *Okla., U.S.A.* **155 H6** 35 53N 97 25W
Guthrie, *Tex., U.S.A.* **155 J4** 33 37N 100 19W
Guthrie Center, *U.S.A.* **156 C2** 41 41N 94 30W
Gutian, *China* **77 D12** 26 32N 118 43 E
Gutiérrez, *Bolivia* **173 D5** 19 25 S 63 34W
Guttannen, *Switz.* **33 C6** 46 38N 8 18 E
Guttenberg, *U.S.A.* **156 B5** 42 47N 91 6W
Gutu, *Zimbabwe* **117 B5** 19 41 S 31 9 E
Gutulia Nasjonalpark △, *Norway* **18 B9** 62 2N 12 11 E
Guwahati, *India* **90 B3** 26 10N 91 45 E
Guy Fawkes River Nat. Park △, *Australia* **127 B5** 30 0 S 152 20 E
Guyana ■, *S. Amer.* **169 B6** 5 0N 59 0W
Guyane française = French Guiana ⊠, *S. Amer.* **169 C7** 4 0N 53 0W
Guyang, *China* **74 D6** 41 0N 110 5 E
Guyenne, *France* **28 D4** 44 30N 0 40 E
Guymon, *U.S.A.* **155 G4** 36 41N 101 29W
Guyotville = Aïn Benian, *Algeria* **111 A5** 36 48N 2 55 E
Guyra, *Australia* **127 E5** 30 15 S 151 40 E
Guyton, *U.S.A.* **152 C8** 32 20N 81 24W
Guyuan, *Hebei, China* **74 D8** 41 37N 115 40 E
Guyuan, *Ningxia Huizu, China* **74 G4** 36 0N 106 20 E
Guzar, *Uzbekistan* **65 D3** 38 36N 66 15 E
Güzelbahçe, *Turkey* **49 C8** 38 21N 26 54 E
Güzelyurt = Morphou, *Cyprus* **39 E8** 35 12N 32 59 E
Guzhang, *China* **76 C7** 28 42N 109 58 E
Guzhen, *China* **75 H9** 33 22N 117 18 E
Guzmán, L. de, *Mexico* **162 A3** 31 25N 107 25W
Gvardeysk, *Russia* **15 J19** 54 39N 21 5 E
Gvardeyskoye, *Ukraine* **59 K8** 45 7N 34 1 E
Gvarv, *Norway* **18 E6** 59 23N 9 9 E
Gwa, *Burma* **90 G5** 17 36N 94 34 E
Gwaai, *Zimbabwe* **119 F2** 19 15 S 27 45 E
Gwaai →, *Zimbabwe* **119 F2** 17 59 S 26 52 E
Gwabegar, *Australia* **129 A8** 30 31 S 149 0 E
Gwadabawa, *Nigeria* **113 C6** 13 28N 5 15 E
Gwādar, *Pakistan* **91 D1** 25 10N 62 18 E
Gwagwada, *Nigeria* **113 C6** 10 15N 7 15 E
Gwaii Haanas Nat. Park Reserve △, *Canada* **142 C2** 52 21N 131 26W
Gwalior, *India* **92 F8** 26 12N 78 10 E
Gwanara, *Nigeria* **113 D5** 8 55N 3 9 E
Gwanda, *Zimbabwe* **119 G2** 20 55 S 29 0 E
Gwandu, *Nigeria* **113 C5** 12 30N 4 41 E
Gwane, *Dem. Rep. of the Congo* **118 B2** 4 45N 25 48 E
Gwaram, *Nigeria* **113 C7** 10 15N 10 25 E
Gwarzo, *Nigeria* **113 C6** 12 20N 8 55 E
Gwasero, *Nigeria* **113 D5** 9 29N 3 30 E
Gwda →, *Poland* **55 E3** 53 3N 16 44 E
Gweebarra B., *Ireland* **23 B3** 54 51N 8 23W
Gweedore, *Ireland* **23 A3** 55 3N 8 13W
Gweru, *Zimbabwe* **119 F2** 19 28 S 29 45 E
Gwi, *Nigeria* **113 D6** 9 0N 7 10 E
Gwinn, *U.S.A.* **148 B2** 46 19N 87 27W
Gwio Kura, *Nigeria* **113 C7** 12 40N 11 2 E
Gwoza, *Nigeria* **113 C7** 11 5N 13 40 E
Gwydir →, *Australia* **127 D4** 29 27 S 149 48 E
Gwynedd □, *U.K.* **20 E3** 52 52N 4 10W
Gyandzha = Gäncä, *Azerbaijan* **61 K8** 40 45N 46 20 E
Gyaring Hu, *China* **68 C4** 34 50N 97 40 E
Gydanskiy Poluostrov, *Russia* **66 C8** 70 0N 78 0 E
Gyl, *Norway* **18 B5** 62 57N 8 7 E
Gyldenløve Fjord, *Greenland* **10 E6** 64 15N 40 30W
Gympie, *Australia* **127 D5** 26 11 S 152 38 E
Gyobingauk, *Burma* **90 F5** 18 13N 95 39 E
Gyōda, *Japan* **73 A11** 36 10N 139 30 E
Gyomaendrőd, *Hungary* **52 D5** 46 56N 20 50 E
Gyöngyös, *Hungary* **52 C4** 47 48N 19 56 E
Győr, *Hungary* **52 C2** 47 41N 17 40 E
Győr-Moson-Sopron □, *Hungary* **52 C2** 47 40N 17 20 E
Gypsum Pt., *Canada* **142 A6** 61 53N 114 35W
Gypsumville, *Canada* **143 C9** 51 45N 98 40W
Gyueshevo, *Bulgaria* **50 D6** 42 14N 22 28 E
Gyula, *Hungary* **52 D6** 46 38N 21 17 E
Gyumri, *Armenia* **61 K6** 40 47N 43 50 E
Gyzylarbat, *Turkmenistan* **66 F6** 39 4N 56 23 E
Gyzyletrek, *Turkmenistan* **97 B7** 37 36N 54 46 E
Gzhatsk = Gagarin, *Russia* **58 E8** 55 38N 35 0 E
Gzira, *Malta* **38 F7** 35 54N 14 29 E

H

Ha 'Arava →, *Israel* **103 E4** 30 50N 35 20 E
Ha Coi, *Vietnam* **76 G6** 21 26N 107 46 E
Ha Dong, *Vietnam* **76 G5** 20 58N 105 46 E
Ha Giang, *Vietnam* **76 F5** 22 50N 104 59 E
Ha Karmel Nat. Park △, *Israel* **103 C4** 32 45N 35 5 E
Ha Tien, *Vietnam* **87 G5** 10 23N 104 29 E
Ha Tinh, *Vietnam* **86 C5** 18 20N 105 54 E
Ha Trung, *Vietnam* **86 C5** 19 58N 105 50 E
Ha Yaek Chalong, *Thailand* **87 a** 7 50N 98 22 E
Haaksbergen, *Neths.* **24 B6** 52 9N 6 45 E
Ha'ano, *Tonga* **133 P13** 19 41 S 174 18W
Ha'apai Group, *Tonga* **133 P13** 19 47 S 174 27W
Haapsalu, *Estonia* **15 G20** 58 56N 23 30 E
Haarlem, *Neths.* **24 B4** 52 23N 4 39 E
Haast, *N.Z.* **131 D4** 43 51 S 169 1 E
Haast →, *N.Z.* **131 D4** 43 50 S 169 2 E
Haast Bluff, *Australia* **124 D5** 23 22 S 132 0 E
Haast Pass, *N.Z.* **131 E4** 44 6 S 169 21 E
Hab →, *Pakistan* **92 G3** 24 53N 66 41 E
Hab Nadi Chauki, *Pakistan* **92 G2** 25 0N 66 50 E
Ḩabarūt, *Yemen* **99 C6** 17 18N 52 44 E
Habaswein, *Kenya* **118 B4** 1 2N 39 30 E
Ḩabawnah, W. →, *Si. Arabia* **98 C4** 17 57N 44 58 E
Habay, *Canada* **142 B5** 58 50N 118 44W
Ḩabbān, *Yemen* **98 D4** 14 21N 47 5 E
Ḩabbānīyah, *Iraq* **101 F10** 33 17N 43 29 E
Ḩabbānīyah, Hawr al, *Iraq* **101 F10** 33 17N 43 29 E
Habichtswald, Naturpark ⌂, *Germany* **30 D5** 51 15N 9 15 E
Habiganj, *Bangla.* **90 C3** 24 24N 91 30 E
Habo, *Sweden* **17 G8** 57 55N 14 6 E
Haboro, *Japan* **70 B10** 44 22N 141 42 E
Ḩabshān, *U.A.E.* **97 F7** 23 50N 53 37 E
Hachenburg, *Germany* **30 E3** 50 40N 7 49 E
Hachi, *India* **90 B5** 27 48N 94 2 E
Hachijō-Jima, *Japan* **73 D11** 33 5N 139 45 E
Hachiman, *Japan* **73 B8** 35 45N 136 57 E
Hachinohe, *Japan* **70 D10** 40 30N 141 29 E
Hachiōji, *Japan* **73 B11** 35 40N 139 20 E
Hachŏn, *N. Korea* **75 D15** 41 29N 129 2 E
Hacıbektaş, *Turkey* **100 C6** 38 56N 34 33 E
Hacılar, *Turkey* **100 C6** 38 38N 35 26 E
Hack, Mt., *Australia* **128 A3** 30 45 S 138 55 E
Hackås, *Sweden* **16 B8** 62 56N 14 30 E
Hackensack, *U.S.A.* **151 F10** 40 53N 74 3W
Hackettstown, *U.S.A.* **151 F10** 40 51N 74 50W
Haco, *Angola* **115 E3** 10 15 S 15 44 E
Hadali, *Pakistan* **92 C5** 32 16N 72 11 E
Hadano, *Japan* **73 B11** 35 22N 139 14 E
Hadarba, Ras, *Sudan* **106 C4** 22 4N 36 51 E
Hadarom □, *Israel* **103 E4** 31 0N 35 0 E
Ḩadbaram, *Oman* **99 C6** 17 27N 55 15 E
Ḩadd, Ra's al, *Oman* **99 B7** 22 35N 59 50 E
Ḩaddā, *Si. Arabia* **98 B2** 21 27N 39 34 E
Haddington, *U.K.* **22 F6** 55 57N 2 47W
Haddock, *U.S.A.* **152 B6** 33 2N 83 26W
Haded Plain = Xadded, *Somali Rep.* **120 C3** 9 46N 48 2 E
Hadejia, *Nigeria* **113 C7** 12 30N 10 5 E
Hadejia →, *Nigeria* **113 C7** 12 50N 10 51 E
Ḩadera, *Israel* **103 C3** 32 27N 34 55 E
Ḩadera, N. →, *Israel* **103 C3** 32 28N 34 52 E
Haderslev, *Denmark* **17 J3** 55 15N 9 30 E
Hadgaon, *India* **94 E3** 19 30N 77 40 E
Hadhramaut = Ḩaḑramawt, *Yemen* **99 D5** 15 30N 49 30 E
Hadiboh, *Yemen* **99 D6** 12 39N 54 2 E
Hadım, *Turkey* **100 D5** 36 58N 32 26 E
Hadjadj, O. el →, *Algeria* **111 C6** 28 18N 5 20 E
Hadjeb El Aïoun, *Tunisia* **108 A1** 35 21N 9 32 E
Hadjer Kamaran, *Chad* **109 F4** 12 41N 21 46 E
Hadjer Mornou, *Chad* **109 E4** 17 12N 23 8 E
Hadong, *S. Korea* **75 G14** 35 5N 127 44 E
Ḩaḑramawt, *Yemen* **99 D5** 15 30N 49 30 E
Ḩaḑramawt, W. →, *Yemen* **99 D5** 15 10N 51 8 E
Ḩadrānīyah, *Iraq* **96 C4** 35 38N 43 14 E
Hadrian's Wall, *U.K.* **20 B5** 55 0N 2 30W
Hadsten, *Denmark* **17 H4** 56 19N 10 3 E
Hadsund, *Denmark* **17 H4** 56 44N 10 8 E
Hadyach, *Ukraine* **59 G8** 50 21N 34 0 E
Hægeland, *Norway* **18 F4** 58 22N 7 45 E
Haeju, *N. Korea* **75 E13** 38 3N 125 45 E
Haena, *U.S.A.* **145 A2** 22 14N 159 34W
Haenam, *S. Korea* **75 G14** 34 34N 126 35 E
Haenertsburg, *S. Africa* **117 C4** 24 0 S 29 50 E
Haerhpin = Harbin, *China* **75 B14** 45 48N 126 40 E
Hafar al Bāţin, *Si. Arabia* **96 D5** 28 32N 45 52 E
Hafik, *Turkey* **100 C7** 39 51N 37 23 E
Ḩafīrat al 'Aydā, *Si. Arabia* **96 E3** 26 26N 39 12 E
Ḩafit, *Oman* **97 F7** 23 59N 55 49 E
Hafizabad, *Pakistan* **92 C5** 32 5N 73 40 E
Haflong, *India* **90 C4** 25 10N 93 5 E
Hafnarfjörður, *Iceland* **11 C5** 64 4N 21 57W
Hafnir, *Iceland* **11 D4** 63 56N 22 41W
Hafslo, *Norway* **18 C4** 61 19N 7 10 E
Haft Gel, *Iran* **97 D6** 31 30N 49 32 E
Hafun, Ras, *Somali Rep.* **102 E5** 10 29N 51 30 E
Hagalil, *Israel* **103 C4** 32 53N 35 18 E
Hagari →, *India* **95 G3** 15 40N 77 0 E
Hagby, *Sweden* **17 H10** 56 34N 16 11 E
Hagemeister I., *U.S.A.* **144 G7** 58 39N 160 54W
Hagen, *Germany* **30 D3** 51 21N 7 27 E
Hagenow, *Germany* **30 B7** 53 26N 11 12 E
Hagerman, *U.S.A.* **155 J2** 33 7N 104 20W
Hagerman Fossil Beds Nat. Monument ⌂, *U.S.A.* **158 E6** 42 48N 114 57W
Hagerstown, *Ind., U.S.A.* **157 E11** 39 55N 85 10W
Hagerstown, *Md., U.S.A.* **148 F7** 39 39N 77 43W
Hagersville, *Canada* **150 D4** 42 58N 80 3W
Hagetmau, *France* **28 E3** 43 39N 0 37W
Hagfors, *Sweden* **16 D7** 60 3N 13 45 E
Hagi, *Iceland* **11 B3** 65 28N 23 25W
Hagi, *Japan* **72 C3** 34 30N 131 22 E
Hagolan, *Syria* **103 C4** 33 0N 35 45 E
Hagondange, *France* **27 C13** 49 16N 6 11 E
Hagonoy, *Phil.* **80 D3** 14 50N 120 44 E
Hags Hd., *Ireland* **23 D2** 52 57N 9 28W
Hague, C. de la, *France* **26 C5** 49 44N 1 56W
Hague, The = 's-Gravenhage, *Neths.* **24 B4** 52 7N 4 17 E
Haguenau, *France* **27 D14** 48 49N 7 47 E
Hagunía, *W. Sahara* **110 C2** 27 26N 12 24W
Hahira, *U.S.A.* **152 E6** 30 59N 83 22W
Hai Duong, *Vietnam* **76 G6** 20 56N 106 19 E
Hai'an, *Guangdong, China* **76 G8** 20 18N 110 11 E
Hai'an, *Jiangsu, China* **77 A13** 32 37N 120 27 E
Haicheng, *Fujian, China* **77 E11** 24 23N 117 48 E
Haicheng, *Liaoning, China* **75 D12** 40 50N 122 45 E
Haidar Khel, *Afghan.* **92 C3** 33 58N 68 38 E
Haidargarh, *India* **93 F9** 26 37N 81 22 E
Haifa = Ḩefa, *Israel* **103 C4** 32 46N 35 0 E
Haifeng, *China* **77 F10** 22 58N 115 10 E
Haiger, *Germany* **30 E4** 50 43N 8 12 E
Haikou, *China* **69 D6** 20 1N 110 16 E
Ḩā'il, *Si. Arabia* **96 E4** 27 28N 41 45 E
Hailakandi, *India* **90 C4** 24 42N 92 34 E
Hailar, *China* **69 B6** 49 10N 119 38 E
Hailey, *U.S.A.* **158 E6** 43 31N 114 19W
Haileybury, *Canada* **140 C4** 47 30N 79 38W
Hailin, *China* **75 B15** 44 37N 129 30 E
Hailing Dao, *China* **77 G8** 21 35N 111 47 E
Hailong, *China* **75 C13** 42 32N 125 40 E
Hailuoto, *Finland* **14 D21** 65 3N 24 45 E
Haimen, *Guangdong, China* **77 F11** 23 15N 116 38 E
Haimen, *Jiangsu, China* **77 B13** 31 52N 121 10 E
Hainan □, *China* **86 C7** 19 0N 109 30 E
Hainaut □, *Belgium* **24 D4** 50 30N 4 0 E
Hainburg, *Austria* **35 C9** 48 9N 16 56 E
Haines, *Alaska, U.S.A.* **142 B1** 59 14N 135 26W
Haines, *Oreg., U.S.A.* **158 D5** 44 55N 117 56W
Haines City, *U.S.A.* **153 G8** 28 7N 81 38W
Haines Junction, *Canada* **142 A1** 60 45N 137 30W
Hainfeld, *Austria* **34 C8** 48 3N 15 48 E
Haining, *China* **77 B13** 30 28N 120 40 E
Haiphong, *Vietnam* **76 G6** 20 47N 106 41 E
Haitan Dao, *China* **77 E12** 25 30N 119 45 E
Haiti ■, *W. Indies* **165 C5** 19 0N 72 30W
Haiya, *Sudan* **106 D4** 18 20N 36 21 E
Haiyan, *China* **77 B13** 30 28N 120 58 E
Haiyang, *China* **75 F11** 36 47N 121 9 E
Haiyuan, *Guangxi Zhuangzu, China* **76 F6** 22 8N 107 35 E
Haiyuan, *Ningxia Huizu, China* **74 F3** 36 35N 105 52 E
Haizhou, *China* **75 G10** 34 37N 119 7 E
Haizhou Wan, *China* **75 G10** 34 50N 119 20 E
Hajar Bangar, *Sudan* **109 F4** 10 40N 22 45 E
Hajdú-Bihar □, *Hungary* **52 C6** 47 30N 21 30 E
Hajdúböszörmény, *Hungary* **52 C6** 47 40N 21 30 E
Hajdúdorog, *Hungary* **52 C6** 47 48N 21 30 E
Hajdúhadház, *Hungary* **52 C6** 47 40N 21 40 E
Hajdúnánás, *Hungary* **52 C6** 47 50N 21 26 E
Hajdúsámson, *Hungary* **52 C6** 47 37N 21 42 E
Hajdúszoboszló, *Hungary* **52 C6** 47 27N 21 22 E
Hajiganj, *Bangla.* **90 D3** 23 15N 90 50 E
Hajipur, *India* **93 G11** 25 45N 85 13 E
Ḩajjah, *Yemen* **98 D3** 15 42N 43 36 E
Ḩājjī Muḩsin, *Iraq* **96 C5** 32 35N 45 29 E
Ḩājjīābād, *Iran* **97 D7** 28 19N 55 55 E
Ḩājjīābād-e Zarrīn, *Iran* **97 C7** 33 9N 54 51 E
Hajnówka, *Poland* **55 F10** 52 47N 23 35 E
Ḩajrah, *Si. Arabia* **98 B3** 20 14N 41 3 E
Haka, *Burma* **90 D4** 22 39N 93 37 E
Hakansson, Mts., *Dem. Rep. of the Congo* **119 D2** 8 40 S 25 45 E
Hakataramea, *N.Z.* **131 E5** 44 43 S 170 30 E
Hakkâri, *Turkey* **101 D10** 37 34N 43 44 E
Hakkâri Dağları, *Turkey* **101 C10** 38 2N 42 58 E
Hakken-Zan, *Japan* **73 C7** 34 10N 135 54 E
Hakodate, *Japan* **70 D10** 41 45N 140 44 E
Hakos, *Namibia* **116 C2** 23 13 S 16 21 E
Hakota, *Japan* **73 A12** 36 5N 140 30 E
Håksberg, *Sweden* **16 D9** 60 11N 15 12 E
Haku-San, *Japan* **73 A8** 36 9N 136 46 E
Haku-San Nat. Park △, *Japan* **73 A8** 36 15N 136 45 E
Hakuba, *Japan* **73 A9** 36 42N 137 51 E
Hakui, *Japan* **71 F8** 36 53N 136 47 E
Hakun, *Burma* **90 B5** 26 46N 95 42 E
Hala, *Pakistan* **91 D3** 25 43N 68 20 E
Ḩalab, *Syria* **100 D7** 36 10N 37 15 E
Ḩalaban, *Si. Arabia* **98 B4** 23 29N 44 23 E
Ḩalabjah, *Iraq* **101 E11** 35 10N 45 58 E
Halach, *Turkmenistan* **65 D2** 38 4N 64 52 E
Halaib, *Sudan* **106 C4** 22 12N 36 30 E
Halalii L., *U.S.A.* **145 B1** 21 52N 160 11W
Halasa, *Sudan* **107 E3** 14 26N 30 39 E
Hālat 'Ammār, *Si. Arabia* **96 D3** 29 10N 36 4 E
Halawa, C., *U.S.A.* **145 B5** 21 10N 156 43W
Halawa Heights, *U.S.A.* **145 K14** 21 23N 157 55W
Halbā, *Lebanon* **103 A5** 34 34N 36 6 E
Halberstadt, *Germany* **30 D7** 51 54N 11 3 E
Halcombe, *N.Z.* **130 G4** 40 8 S 175 30 E
Halcon, *Phil.* **79 B6** 13 0N 121 30 E
Halcon, Mt., *Phil.* **80 E3** 13 16N 121 0 E
Halden, *Norway* **18 E8** 59 9N 11 23 E
Haldensleben, *Germany* **30 C7** 52 17N 11 24 E
Haldwani, *India* **93 E8** 29 31N 79 30 E
Hale, *U.S.A.* **156 E3** 39 36N 93 20W
Hale →, *Australia* **126 C2** 24 56 S 135 53 E
Haleakala Crater, *U.S.A.* **145 C5** 20 43N 156 16W
Haleakala Nat. Park △, *U.S.A.* **145 C5** 20 40N 156 15W
Haleiwa, *U.S.A.* **145 J13** 21 36N 158 6W
Halesowen, *U.K.* **21 E5** 52 27N 2 3W
Halesworth, *U.K.* **21 E9** 52 20N 1 31 E
Haleyville, *U.S.A.* **152 B3** 34 14N 87 37W
Half Assini, *Ghana* **112 D4** 5 1N 2 50W
Halfmoon Bay, *N.Z.* **131 G3** 46 50 S 168 5 E
Halfway →, *Canada* **142 B4** 56 12N 121 32W
Halia, *India* **93 G10** 24 50N 82 19 E
Haliburton, *Canada* **140 C4** 45 3N 78 30W
Halifax, *Australia* **126 B4** 18 32 S 146 22 E
Halifax, *Canada* **141 D7** 44 38N 63 35W
Halifax, *U.K.* **20 D6** 53 43N 1 52W
Halifax, *U.S.A.* **150 F8** 40 25N 76 55W
Halifax B., *Australia* **126 B4** 18 50 S 147 0 E
Halifax I., *Namibia* **116 D2** 26 38 S 15 4 E
Halīl →, *Iran* **97 E8** 27 40N 58 30 E
Halin, *Somali Rep.* **120 C3** 9 6N 48 37 E
Halkett, C., *U.S.A.* **144 A9** 70 48N 152 11W
Halkirk, *U.K.* **22 C5** 58 30N 3 29W
Hall Beach = Sanirajak, *Canada* **139 B11** 68 46N 81 12W
Hall I., *U.S.A.* **144 F4** 60 40N 173 6W
Hall in Tirol, *Austria* **34 D4** 47 17N 11 30 E
Hall Pen., *Canada* **139 B13** 63 30N 66 0W
Hall Pt., *Australia* **124 C3** 15 40 S 124 23 E
Hallabro, *Sweden* **17 H9** 56 22N 15 5 E
Halland, *Sweden* **15 H15** 57 8N 12 47 E
Hallandale, *U.S.A.* **153 K9** 25 59N 80 8W
Hallands län □, *Sweden* **17 H6** 57 0N 12 40 E
Hallands Väderö, *Sweden* **17 H6** 56 27N 12 34 E
Hallandsås, *Sweden* **17 H7** 56 22N 13 0 E
Hallaskar, *Norway* **18 D4** 60 15N 7 9 E
Hällbybrunn, *Sweden* **16 E10** 59 24N 16 25 E
Halle, *Belgium* **24 D4** 50 44N 4 13 E
Halle, *Nordrhein-Westfalen, Germany* **30 C4** 52 3N 8 22 E
Halle, *Sachsen-Anhalt, Germany* **30 D7** 51 30N 11 56 E
Hällefors, *Sweden* **16 E8** 59 47N 14 31 E
Hälleforsnäs, *Sweden* **16 E10** 59 10N 16 30 E
Hallein, *Austria* **34 D6** 47 40N 13 5 E
Hällekis, *Sweden* **17 F7** 58 38N 13 27 E
Hallen, *Sweden* **16 A8** 63 11N 14 4 E
Hallett, *Australia* **128 B3** 33 25 S 138 55 E
Hallettsville, *U.S.A.* **155 L6** 29 27N 96 57W
Hallia →, *India* **94 F4** 16 55N 79 20 E
Hallim, *S. Korea* **75 H14** 33 24N 126 15 E
Hallingby, *Norway* **18 D7** 60 7N 10 10 E
Hallingdal, *Norway* **18 D6** 60 40N 9 8 E
Hallingdalselvi →, *Norway* **18 D6** 60 23N 9 35 E
Hallingskarvet, *Norway* **18 D4** 60 36N 7 47 E
Hallingskeid, *Norway* **18 D4** 60 40N 7 17 E
Hallock, *U.S.A.* **154 A6** 48 47N 96 57W
Hallormsstaður, *Iceland* **11 B12** 65 6N 14 45W
Halls Creek, *Australia* **124 C4** 18 16 S 127 38 E
Hallsberg, *Sweden* **16 E9** 59 5N 15 7 E
Hallstahammar, *Sweden* **16 E10** 59 38N 16 15 E
Hallstatt, *Austria* **34 D6** 47 33N 13 38 E
Hallstavik, *Sweden* **16 D12** 60 5N 18 37 E
Hallstead, *U.S.A.* **151 E9** 41 58N 75 45W
Halmahera, *Indonesia* **82 A3** 0 40N 128 0 E
Halmahera Sea, *Indonesia* **83 B3** 0 0 129 0 E
Halmeu, *Romania* **52 C8** 47 57N 23 2 E
Halmstad, *Sweden* **17 H6** 56 41N 12 52 E
Halq el Oued, *Tunisia* **108 A2** 36 53N 10 18 E
Hals, *Denmark* **17 H4** 57 0N 10 18 E
Halsa, *Norway* **18 A5** 63 3N 8 14 E
Halsafjorden, *Norway* **18 A5** 63 5N 8 10 E
Hälsingborg = Helsingborg, *Sweden* **17 H6** 56 3N 12 42 E
Hälsingland, *Sweden* **16 C10** 61 40N 16 5 E
Halstead, *U.K.* **21 F8** 51 57N 0 40 E
Haltdalen, *Norway* **18 B8** 62 56N 11 8 E
Haltern, *Germany* **30 D3** 51 44N 7 11 E
Halti, *Finland* **14 B19** 69 17N 21 18 E
Halton □, *U.K.* **20 D5** 53 22N 2 45W
Haltwhistle, *U.K.* **20 C5** 54 58N 2 26W
Ḩālūl, *Qatar* **97 E7** 25 40N 52 40 E
Halvad, *India* **92 H4** 23 1N 71 11 E
Ḩalvān, *Iran* **97 C8** 33 57N 56 15 E
Ham, *Chad* **109 F3** 10 1N 15 35 E
Ham, *France* **27 C10** 49 45N 3 4 E
Ham Tan, *Vietnam* **87 G6** 10 40N 107 45 E
Ham Yen, *Vietnam* **86 A5** 22 4N 105 3 E
Hamab, *Namibia* **116 D2** 28 7 S 19 16 E
Hamad, *Sudan* **107 D3** 15 20N 33 32 E
Hamada, *Japan* **72 C4** 34 56N 132 4 E
Hamadān, *Iran* **97 C6** 34 52N 48 32 E
Hamadān □, *Iran* **97 C6** 35 0N 49 0 E
Hamadia, *Algeria* **111 A5** 35 28N 1 57 E
Hamāh, *Syria* **100 E7** 35 5N 36 40 E
Hamakita, *Japan* **73 C9** 34 45N 137 47 E
Hamamatsu, *Japan* **73 C9** 34 45N 137 45 E
Hamar, *Norway* **18 D8** 60 48N 11 7 E
Hamâta, Gebel, *Egypt* **96 E2** 24 17N 35 0 E
Hambantota, *Sri Lanka* **95 L5** 6 10N 81 10 E
Hamber Prov. Park ⌂, *Canada* **142 C5** 52 20N 118 0W
Hamburg, *Germany* **30 B5** 53 33N 9 59 E
Hamburg, *Ark., U.S.A.* **155 J9** 33 14N 91 48W
Hamburg, *N.Y., U.S.A.* **150 D6** 42 43N 78 50W
Hamburg, *Pa., U.S.A.* **151 F9** 40 33N 75 59W
Hamburg □, *Germany* **30 B5** 53 30N 10 0 E
Hamburg Fuhlsbüttel ✈ (HAM), *Germany* **30 B5** 53 35N 9 59 E
Ḩamḑ, W. al →, *Si. Arabia* **96 E3** 24 55N 36 20 E
Ḩamḑah, *Si. Arabia* **98 C3** 19 2N 43 36 E
Ḩamdānah, *Si. Arabia* **98 C3** 19 59N 40 34 E
Hamden, *U.S.A.* **151 E12** 41 23N 72 54W
Hamdibey, *Turkey* **49 B9** 39 50N 27 15 E
Häme, *Finland* **15 F20** 61 38N 25 10 E
Hämeenlinna, *Finland* **15 F21** 61 0N 24 28 E
Hamélé, *Ghana* **112 C4** 10 56N 2 45W
Hamelin Pool, *Australia* **125 E1** 26 22 S 114 20 E
Hameln, *Germany* **30 C5** 52 6N 9 21 E
Hamerkaz □, *Israel* **103 C3** 32 15N 34 55 E
Hamersley Ra., *Australia* **124 D2** 22 0 S 117 45 E
Hamhung, *N. Korea* **75 E14** 39 54N 127 30 E
Hami, *China* **68 B4** 42 55N 93 25 E
Hamilton = Churchill →, *Canada* **141 B7** 53 19N 60 10W
Hamilton, *Australia* **128 D5** 37 45 S 142 2 E
Hamilton, *Bermuda* **9 a** 32 17N 64 47W
Hamilton, *Canada* **140 D4** 43 15N 79 50W
Hamilton, *N.Z.* **130 D4** 37 47 S 175 19 E
Hamilton, *U.K.* **22 F4** 55 46N 4 2W
Hamilton, *Ala., U.S.A.* **149 H1** 34 9N 87 59W
Hamilton, *Alaska, U.S.A.* **144 E7** 62 54N 163 53W
Hamilton, *Ga., U.S.A.* **152 C5** 32 45N 84 53W
Hamilton, *Ill., U.S.A.* **156 D5** 40 24N 91 21W
Hamilton, *Ind., U.S.A.* **157 C12** 41 33N 84 56W
Hamilton, *Mo., U.S.A.* **156 E2** 39 45N 94 0W
Hamilton, *Mont., U.S.A.* **158 C6** 46 15N 114 10W
Hamilton, *N.Y., U.S.A.* **151 D9** 42 50N 75 33W
Hamilton, *Ohio, U.S.A.* **157 E12** 39 24N 84 34W
Hamilton, *Tex., U.S.A.* **155 K5** 31 42N 98 7W
Hamilton →, *Australia* **126 C2** 23 30 S 139 47 E
Hamilton City, *U.S.A.* **160 F4** 39 45N 122 1W
Hamilton I., *Australia* **126 J6** 20 21 S 148 56 E
Hamilton Inlet, *Canada* **141 B8** 54 0N 57 30W
Hamilton Mt., *U.S.A.* **151 C10** 43 25N 74 22W
Hamina, *Finland* **15 F22** 60 34N 27 12 E
Hamirpur, *H.P., India* **92 D7** 31 41N 76 31 E
Hamirpur, *Ut. P., India* **93 G9** 25 57N 80 9 E
Hamitabat, *Turkey* **51 E11** 41 30N 27 17 E
Hamlet, *U.S.A.* **149 H6** 34 53N 79 42W
Hamley Bridge, *Australia* **128 C3** 34 17 S 138 35 E
Hamlin = Hameln, *Germany* **30 C5** 52 6N 9 21 E
Hamlin, *N.Y., U.S.A.* **150 C7** 43 17N 77 55W
Hamlin, *Tex., U.S.A.* **155 J4** 32 53N 100 8W
Hamm, *Germany* **30 D3** 51 40N 7 50 E
Hammam Bouhadjar, *Algeria* **111 A4** 35 23N 0 58W
Hammamet, *Tunisia* **108 A2** 36 24N 10 38 E
Hammamet, G. de, *Tunisia* **108 A2** 36 10N 10 48 E
Ḩammār, Hawr al, *Iraq* **96 D5** 30 50N 47 10 E
Hammarstrand, *Sweden* **16 A10** 63 7N 16 20 E
Hammelburg, *Germany* **31 E5** 50 6N 9 53 E
Hammeren, *Denmark* **17 J8** 55 18N 14 47 E
Hammerfest, *Norway* **14 A20** 70 39N 23 41 E
Hammerum, *Denmark* **17 H3** 56 8N 9 3 E
Hamminkeln, *Germany* **30 D2** 51 43N 6 35 E
Hammond, *Ind., U.S.A.* **157 C9** 41 38N 87 30W
Hammond, *La., U.S.A.* **155 K9** 30 30N 90 28W
Hammond, *N.Y., U.S.A.* **151 B9** 44 27N 75 42W
Hammondsport, *U.S.A.* **150 D7** 42 25N 77 13W
Hammonton, *U.S.A.* **148 F8** 39 39N 74 48W
Hamneda, *Sweden* **17 H7** 56 41N 13 51 E
Hamoyet, Jebel, *Sudan* **106 D4** 17 33N 38 2 E
Hampden, *N.Z.* **131 F5** 45 18 S 170 50 E
Hampshire □, *U.K.* **21 F6** 51 7N 1 23W
Hampshire Downs, *U.K.* **21 F6** 51 15N 1 10W

Hampton, *N.B., Canada* 141 C6   45 32N   65 51W
Hampton, *Ont., Canada* 150 C6   43 58N   78 45W
Hampton, *Ark., U.S.A.* 155 J8   33 32N   92 28W
Hampton, *Ga., U.S.A.* 152 B5   33 23N   84 17W
Hampton, *Iowa, U.S.A.* 156 B3   42 45N   93 13W
Hampton, *N.H., U.S.A.* 151 D14   42 57N   70 50W
Hampton, *S.C., U.S.A.* 152 C8   32 52N   81 7W
Hampton, *Va., U.S.A.* 148 G7   37 2N   76 21W
Hampton Bays, *U.S.A.* 151 F12   40 53N   72 30W
Hampton Springs, *U.S.A.* 152 E6   30 5N   83 40W
Hampton Tableland, *Australia* .... 125 F4   32 0S 127 0 E
Hamra, *Sweden* .... 16 C8   61 39N   14 59 E
Hamra ~, *Chad* .... 109 E4   12 52N   21 15 E
Hamrat esh Sheykh, *Sudan* .... 107 E2   14 38N   27 55 E
Hamrun, *Malta* .... 38 F8   35 53N   14 29 E
Hamtik, *Phil.* .... 81 F3   10 42N 121 59 E
Hamur, *Turkey* .... 101 C10   39 37N   43 3 E
Hamyang, *S. Korea* .... 75 G14   35 32N 127 42 E
Han Jiang ~, *China* .... 77 F11   23 25N 116 40 E
Han Shui ~, *China* .... 76 A7   30 34N 114 17 E
Han Shui ~, *China* .... 77 B10   30 35N 114 18 E
Hana, *U.S.A.* 145 C6   20 45N 155 59W
Hanahan, *U.S.A.* 152 C10   32 55N   80 0W
Hanak, *Si. Arabia* .... 96 E3   25 32N   37 0 E
Hanalei, *U.S.A.* 145 A2   22 12N 159 30W
Hanamaki, *Japan* .... 70 E10   39 23N 141 7 E
Hanamaulu, *U.S.A.* 145 B2   21 59N 159 22W
Hanang, *Tanzania* .... 118 C4   4 30 S   35 25 E
Hanapepe, *U.S.A.* 145 B2   21 55N 159 35W
Hanau, *Germany* .... 31 E4   50 7N   8 56 E
Hanauma B., *U.S.A.* 145 K14   21 15N 157 40W
Hanbogd = Ihbulag, *Mongolia* .... 74 C4   43 11N 107 10 E
Hançalar, *Turkey* .... 49 C11   38 8N   29 24 E
Hânceşti, *Moldova* .... 53 D13   46 50N   28 36 E
Hancheng, *China* .... 74 G6   35 31N 110 25 E
Hanchuan, *China* .... 77 B9   30 40N 113 50 E
Hancock, *Mich., U.S.A.* 154 B10   47 8N   88 35W
Hancock, *N.Y., U.S.A.* 151 E9   41 57N   75 17W
Handa, *Japan* .... 73 C8   34 53N 136 55 E
Handa, *Somali Rep.* .... 120 B4   10 37N   51 2 E
Handan, *China* .... 74 F8   36 35N 114 28 E
Handeni, *Tanzania* .... 118 D4   5 25 S   38 2 E
Handlová, *Slovak Rep.* .... 35 C11   48 45N   18 35 E
Handub, *Sudan* .... 106 D4   19 15N   37 16 E
Handwara, *India* .... 93 B6   34 21N   74 20 E
Haneda, Tokyo ✈ (HND), *Japan* .... 73 B11   35 33N 139 46 E
Hanegev, *Israel* .... 103 E4   30 50N   35 0 E
Hanford, *U.S.A.* 160 J7   36 20N 119 39W
Hanford Reach Nat. Recr. Area △,
   U.S.A. 158 C4   46 40N 119 28W
Hang Chat, *Thailand* .... 86 C2   18 20N   99 21 E
Hang Dong, *Thailand* .... 86 C2   18 41N   98 55 E
Hanga Roa, *Chile* .... 172 b   27 8 S 109 26W
Hangang ~, *S. Korea* .... 75 F14   37 50N 126 30 E
Hangayn Nuruu, *Mongolia* .... 68 B4   47 30N   99 0 E
Hangchou = Hangzhou, *China* .... 77 B13   30 18N 120 11 E
Hanggin Houqi, *China* .... 74 D4   40 58N 107 4 E
Hanggin Qi, *China* .... 74 E5   39 52N 108 50 E
Hangu, *China* .... 75 E9   39 18N 117 53 E
Hangzhou, *China* .... 77 B13   30 18N 120 11 E
Hangzhou Wan, *China* .... 77 B13   30 15N 120 45 E
Hanhongor, *Mongolia* .... 74 C3   43 55N 104 28 E
Hanīdh, *Si. Arabia* .... 97 E6   26 35N   48 38 E
Hanish, *Yemen* .... 98 D3   13 45N   42 46 E
Haniska, *Slovak Rep.* .... 35 C14   48 37N   21 15 E
Hanjiang, *China* .... 77 E12   25 26N 119 6 E
Hankinson, *U.S.A.* 154 B6   46 4N   96 54W
Hanko, *Finland* .... 15 G20   59 50N   22 57 E
Hankou, *China* .... 77 B10   30 35N 114 30 E
Hanksville, *U.S.A.* 159 G8   38 22N 110 43W
Hanle, *India* .... 93 C8   32 42N   79 4 E
Hanmer Springs, *N.Z.* .... 131 C7   42 32 S 172 50 E
Hann ~, *Australia* .... 124 C4   17 26 S 126 17 E
Hann, Mt., *Australia* .... 124 C4   15 45 S 126 0 E
Hanna, *Canada* 142 C6   51 40N 111 54W
Hanna, *U.S.A.* 158 F10   41 52N 106 34W
Hannah B., *Canada* 140 B4   51 40N   80 0W
Hannibal, *Mo., U.S.A.* 156 F8   39 42N   91 22W
Hannibal, *N.Y., U.S.A.* 151 C8   43 19N   76 35W
Hannik, *Sudan* .... 106 D3   18 12N   32 20 E
Hannover, *Germany* .... 30 C5   52 22N   9 46 E
Hanö, *Sweden* .... 17 H8   56 1N   14 50 E
Hanöbukten, *Sweden* .... 17 J8   55 35N   14 30 E
Hanoi, *Vietnam* .... 76 G5   21 5N 105 55 E
Hanover = Hannover, *Germany* .... 30 C5   52 22N   9 46 E
Hanover, *Canada* 140 D3   44 9N   81 2W
Hanover, *S. Africa* .... 116 E3   31 4 S   24 29 E
Hanover, *Ind., U.S.A.* 157 F11   38 43N   85 28W
Hanover, *N.H., U.S.A.* 151 C12   43 42N   72 17W
Hanover, *Ohio, U.S.A.* 150 F2   40 4N   82 16W
Hanover, *Pa., U.S.A.* 148 F7   39 48N   76 59W
Hanover, I., *Chile* .... 176 G2   51 0 S   74 50W
Hans Lollik I., *U.S. Virgin Is.* .... 165 e   18 24N   64 53W
Hans Meyer Ra., *Papua N. G.* .... 132 C7   4 20 S 152 55 E
Hansdiha, *India* .... 93 G12   24 36N   87 5 E
Hanshou, *China* .... 77 C8   28 56N 111 50 E
Hansi, *India* .... 92 E6   29 10N   75 57 E
Hanson, L., *Australia* .... 128 A2   31 0 S 136 15 E
Hanstholm, *Denmark* .... 17 G2   57 7N   8 36 E
Hantsavichy, *Belarus* .... 59 F4   52 49N   26 30 E
Hanumangarh, *India* .... 92 E6   29 35N   74 19 E
Hanyin, *China* .... 76 A7   32 54N 108 28 E
Hanyū, *Japan* .... 73 A11   36 10N 139 32 E
Hanyuan, *China* .... 76 C4   29 21N 102 40 E
Hanzhong, *China* .... 74 H4   33 10N 107 1 E
Hanzhuang, *China* .... 75 G9   34 33N 117 23 E
Haora, *India* .... 93 H13   22 37N   88 20 E
Haouach, O. ~, *Chad* .... 109 E4   16 45N   19 35 E
Haoxue, *China* .... 77 B9   30 3N 112 27 E
Haparanda, *Sweden* .... 14 D21   65 52N   24 8 E
Hapeville, *U.S.A.* 152 B5   33 40N   84 25W
Happy, *U.S.A.* 155 H4   34 45N 101 52W
Happy Camp, *U.S.A.* 158 F2   41 48N 123 23W
Happy Valley-Goose Bay, *Canada* 141 B7   53 15N   60 20W
Hapsu, *N. Korea* .... 75 D15   41 13N 128 51 E
Hapur, *India* .... 92 E7   28 45N   77 45 E
Haql, *Si. Arabia* .... 103 F3   29 10N   34 58 E
Haquira, *Peru* .... 172 C3   14 14 S   72 12W
Har, *Indonesia* .... 83 C4   5 16 S 133 14 E
Har-Ayrag, *Mongolia* .... 74 B5   45 47N 109 16 E
Har Hu, *China* .... 68 C4   38 20N   97 38 E
Har Us Nuur, *Mongolia* .... 68 B4   48 0N   92 0 E
Har Yehuda, *Israel* .... 103 D3   31 35N   34 57 E
Harad, *Si. Arabia* .... 99 A5   24 22N   49 0 E
Harad, *Yemen* .... 98 C3   16 26N   43 5 E
Haradok, *Belarus* .... 58 E6   55 30N   30 3 E
Härädsbäck, *Sweden* .... 17 H8   56 32N   14 26 E
Haranomachi, *Japan* .... 70 F10   37 38N 140 58 E
Harardera, *Somali Rep.* .... 120 D3   4 33N   47 38 E
Harare, *Zimbabwe* .... 119 F3   17 43 S   31 2 E
Harāsīs, Jiddat al, *Oman* .... 99 C7   19 30N   56 0 E
Harat, *Eritrea* .... 107 D4   16 5N   39 26 E
Haraz, *Chad* .... 109 F3   14 20N   19 12 E
Harazé, *Chad* .... 109 G4   9 57N   20 48 E
Harbhanga, *India* .... 94 D7   20 38N   84 36 E
Harbin, *China* .... 75 B14   45 48N 126 40 E
Harbiye, *Turkey* .... 100 D7   36 10N   36 8 E
Harbo, *Sweden* .... 16 D11   60 7N   17 12 E
Harboør, *Denmark* .... 17 H2   56 38N   8 10 E
Harbor Beach, *U.S.A.* 150 C2   43 51N   82 39W
Harbour Breton, *Canada* 141 C8   47 29N   55 50W
Harbour Deep, *Canada* 141 B8   50 25N   56 32W
Harburg, *Germany* .... 30 B5   53 27N   9 58 E

Harburger Berge, Naturpark △,
   Germany .... 30 B5   53 26N   9 51 E
Hårby, *Denmark* .... 17 J4   55 13N   10 7 E
Harda, *India* .... 92 H7   22 27N   77 5 E
Hardangerfjorden, *Norway* .... 18 D3   60 5N   6 0 E
Hardangerjøkulen, *Norway* .... 18 D4   60 30N   7 27 E
Hardangervidda, *Norway* .... 18 D4   60 7N   7 20 E
Hardangervidda Nasjonalpark △,
   Norway .... 18 D4   60 10N   7 25 E
Hardap Dam, *Namibia* .... 116 C2   24 32 S   17 50 E
Hardap Recr. Resort △, *Namibia* .... 116 C2   24 29 S   17 45 E
Hardeeville, *U.S.A.* 152 C8   32 17N   81 5W
Harden, *Australia* .... 129 C8   34 32 S 148 24 E
Hardenberg, *Neths.* .... 24 B6   52 34N   6 37 E
Harderwijk, *Neths.* .... 24 B5   52 21N   5 38 E
Hardey ~, *Australia* .... 124 D2   22 45 S 116 8 E
Hardin, *Ill., U.S.A.* 156 F6   39 10N   90 37W
Hardin, *Mont., U.S.A.* 158 D10   45 44N 107 37W
Harding, *S. Africa* .... 117 E4   30 35 S   29 55 E
Harding, L., *U.S.A.* 152 C4   32 40N   85 5W
Harding Ra., *Australia* .... 124 C3   16 17 S 124 55 E
Hardinsburg, *U.S.A.* 157 G10   37 47N   86 28W
Hardisty, *Canada* 142 C6   52 40N 111 18W
Hardoi, *India* .... 93 F9   27 26N   80 6 E
Hardwar = Haridwar, *India* .... 92 E8   29 58N   78 9 E
Hardwick, *Ga., U.S.A.* 152 B6   33 4N   83 14W
Hardwick, *Vt., U.S.A.* 151 B12   44 30N   72 22W
Hardwicke B., *Australia* .... 128 C2   34 55 S 137 20 E
Hardy, *Pen., Chile* .... 176 E3   55 30 S   68 20W
Hardy, Pte., *St. Lucia* .... 165 f   14 6N   60 56W
Hare B., *Canada* 141 B8   51 15N   55 45W
Hareid, *Norway* .... 18 B3   62 22N   6 1 E
Haren, *Germany* .... 30 C3   52 47N   7 13 E
Harer, *Ethiopia* .... 107 F5   9 20N   42 8 E
Harerge □, *Ethiopia* .... 107 F5   7 12N   42 0 E
Harestua, *Norway* .... 18 D7   60 11N   10 44 E
Hareto, *Ethiopia* .... 107 F4   9 23N   37 6 E
Harfleur, *France* .... 26 C7   49 30N   0 10 E
Hargeisa, *Somali Rep.* .... 120 C2   9 30N   44 2 E
Hargeisa Game Park △, *Somali Rep.* .... 120 B2   10 2N   44 2 E
Harghita □, *Romania* .... 53 D10   46 30N   25 30 E
Harghita, Munţii, *Romania* .... 53 D10   46 25N   25 35 E
Hargshamn, *Sweden* .... 16 D12   60 12N   18 30 E
Hari ~, *Indonesia* .... 84 C2   1 16 S 104 5 E
Haria, *Canary Is.* 9 e2   29 8N   13 32W
Harib, *Yemen* .... 98 D4   14 56N   45 30 E
Haricha, Hamada el, *Mali* 110 D4   22 40N   3 15W
Haridwar, *India* .... 92 E8   29 58N   78 9 E
Harihari, *India* .... 95 G2   14 32N   75 44 E
Harihari, *N.Z.* .... 131 D5   43 9 S 170 33 E
Harim, Jabal al, *Oman* .... 97 E8   25 58N   56 14 E
Harima-Nada, *Japan* .... 72 C6   34 30N 134 35 E
Haringhata ~, *Bangla.* .... 90 E2   22 0N   89 58 E
Haripad, *India* .... 95 K3   9 14N   76 28 E
Harīrūd ~, *Asia* .... 91 A1   37 24N   60 38 E
Harlan, *Iowa, U.S.A.* 154 E7   41 39N   95 19W
Harlan, *Ky., U.S.A.* 149 G4   36 51N   83 19W
Hârlău, *Romania* .... 53 C11   47 23N   26 55 E
Harlech, *U.K.* 21 E3   52 52N   4 6W
Harlem, *Ga., U.S.A.* 152 B7   33 25N   82 19W
Harlem, *Mont., U.S.A.* 158 B9   48 32N 108 47W
Hårlev, *Denmark* .... 17 J6   55 21N   12 14 E
Harleyville, *U.S.A.* 152 B9   33 13N   80 27W
Harlingen, *Neths.* .... 24 A5   53 11N   5 25 E
Harlingen, *U.S.A.* 155 M6   26 12N   97 42W
Harlow, *U.K.* .... 21 F8   51 46N   0 8 E
Harlowton, *U.S.A.* 158 C9   46 26N 109 50W
Harmancık, *Turkey* .... 49 B11   39 41N   29 9 E
Harmånger, *Sweden* .... 16 C11   61 55N   17 20 E
Harmil, *Eritrea* .... 107 D5   16 30N   40 10 E
Harnai, *India* .... 94 F1   17 48N   73 6 E
Harnai, *Pakistan* .... 92 D2   30 6N   67 56 E
Harney, *U.S.A.* 153 G8   28 45N   81 3W
Harney Basin, *U.S.A.* 158 E4   43 30N 119 0W
Harney L., *U.S.A.* 158 E4   43 14N 119 8W
Harney Peak, *U.S.A.* 154 D3   43 52N 103 32W
Härnön, *Sweden* .... 16 B12   62 36N   18 0 E
Härnösand, *Sweden* .... 16 B11   62 38N   17 55 E
Haro, *Spain* 40 C2   42 35N   2 55W
Harold, *U.S.A.* 153 E3   30 40N   86 53W
Harold Pond, *Bahamas* .... 9 b   25 2N   77 22W
Haroldswick, *U.K.* 22 A8   60 48N   0 50W
Harp L., *Canada* 141 A7   55 5N   61 50W
Harpanahalli, *India* .... 95 G3   14 47N   76 2 E
Harper, *Liberia* 112 E3   4 25N   7 43W
Harper, Mt., *U.S.A.* 144 D12   64 14N 143 51W
Harplinge, *Sweden* .... 17 H6   56 45N   12 45 E
Harr, *Mauritania* 112 B2   15 20N   12 28W
Harrai, *India* .... 93 H8   22 37N   79 13 E
Harrand, *Pakistan* .... 92 E4   29 28N   70 3 E
Harrat Khaybar, *Si. Arabia* .... 106 B5   25 30N   39 45 E
Harrat Nawāsif, *Si. Arabia* .... 106 C5   21 0N   42 0 E
Harricana ~, *Canada* 140 B4   50 56N   79 32W
Harriman, *U.S.A.* 149 H3   35 56N   84 33W
Harrington, *Australia* .... 129 A10   31 52 S 152 42 E
Harrington Harbour, *Canada* 141 B8   50 31N   59 30W
Harrington Sd., *Bermuda* .... 9 a   32 20N   64 44W
Harris, *U.K.* 22 D2   57 50N   6 55W
Harris, L., *U.S.A.* 153 G8   28 47N   81 49W
Harris, Sd. of, *U.K.* 22 D1   57 44N   7 6W
Harris L., *Australia* .... 127 E2   31 10 S 135 10 E
Harris Mts., *N.Z.* .... 131 E3   44 49 S 168 49 E
Harris Pt., *Canada* 150 C2   43 6N   82 9W
Harrisburg, *Ill., U.S.A.* 155 G10   37 44N   88 32W
Harrisburg, *Nebr., U.S.A.* 154 E3   41 33N 103 44W
Harrisburg, *Pa., U.S.A.* 150 F8   40 16N   76 53W
Harrismith, *S. Africa* .... 117 D4   28 15 S   29 8 E
Harrison, *Ark., U.S.A.* 155 G8   36 14N   93 7W
Harrison, *Maine, U.S.A.* 151 B14   44 7N   70 39W
Harrison, *Nebr., U.S.A.* 154 D3   42 41N 103 53W
Harrison, C., *Canada* 141 B8   54 55N   57 55W
Harrison Bay, *U.S.A.* 144 A10   70 40N 151 0W
Harrison L., *Canada* 142 D4   49 33N 121 50W
Harrisonburg, *U.S.A.* 148 F6   38 27N   78 52W
Harrisonville, *U.S.A.* 156 F6   38 39N   94 21W
Harriston, *Canada* 150 C4   43 57N   80 53W
Harrisville, *Mich., U.S.A.* 150 B1   44 39N   83 17W
Harrisville, *N.Y., U.S.A.* 151 B9   44 9N   75 19W
Harrisville, *Pa., U.S.A.* 150 E5   41 8N   80 0W
Harrodsburg, *Ind., U.S.A.* 157 E10   39 1N   86 33W
Harrodsburg, *Ky., U.S.A.* 157 G12   37 46N   84 51W
Harrogate, *U.K.* 20 C6   54 0N   1 33W
Harrow, *Australia* .... 128 D4   37 9 S 141 35 E
Harrow, *Canada* 157 B14   42 2N   82 55W
Harrow □, *U.K.* 21 F7   51 35N   0 21W
Harrowsmith, *Canada* 151 B8   44 24N   76 40W
Harry S. Truman Reservoir, *U.S.A.* 156 F3   38 16N   93 24W
Harsefeld, *Germany* .... 30 B5   53 27N   9 30 E
Harsewinkel, *Germany* .... 30 D4   51 56N   8 14 E
Harsin, *Iran* .... 101 E12   34 18N   47 33 E
Hârşova, *Romania* .... 53 F12   44 40N   27 59 E
Harstad, *Norway* .... 14 B17   68 48N   16 30 E
Harsud, *India* .... 92 H7   22 6N   76 44 E
Hart, *India* 148 D2   43 42N   86 22W
Hart, L., *Australia* .... 128 A2   31 10 S 136 25 E
Hartbees ~, *S. Africa* .... 116 D3   28 45 S   20 32 E
Hartberg, *Austria* .... 34 D8   47 17N   15 58 E
Hårteigen, *Norway* .... 18 D4   60 11N   7 3 E
Hartford, *Ala., U.S.A.* 152 D4   31 6N   85 42W
Hartford, *Conn., U.S.A.* 151 E12   41 46N   72 41W
Hartford, *Ky., U.S.A.* 148 G2   37 27N   86 55W
Hartford, *Mich., U.S.A.* 157 B10   42 13N   86 10W
Hartford, *S. Dak., U.S.A.* 154 D6   43 38N   96 57W

Hartford, *Wis., U.S.A.* 154 D10   43 19N   88 22W
Hartford City, *U.S.A.* 157 D11   40 27N   85 22W
Hartland, *Canada* 141 C6   46 20N   67 32W
Hartland, *U.S.A.* 157 A8   45 6N   88 21W
Hartland Pt., *U.K.* 21 F3   51 1N   4 32W
Hartlepool, *U.K.* 20 C6   54 42N   1 13W
Hartlepool □, *U.K.* 20 C6   54 42N   1 17W
Hartley Bay, *Canada* 142 C3   53 25N 129 15W
Hartmannberge, *Namibia* .... 116 B1   17 0 S   13 0 E
Hartney, *Canada* 143 D8   49 30N 100 35W
Hârtop, *Moldova* .... 53 D13   46 39N   28 40 E
Harts ~, *S. Africa* .... 116 D3   28 24 S   24 17 E
Hartselle, *U.S.A.* 149 H2   34 27N   86 56W
Hartshorne, *U.S.A.* 155 H7   34 51N   95 34W
Hartstown, *U.S.A.* 150 E4   41 33N   80 23W
Hartsville, *U.S.A.* 149 H5   34 23N   80 4W
Hartswater, *S. Africa* .... 116 D3   27 34 S   24 43 E
Hartwell, *U.S.A.* 149 H4   34 21N   82 56W
Haruku, *Indonesia* .... 83 B3   3 34 S 128 29 E
Harunabad, *Pakistan* .... 92 E5   29 35N   73 8 E
Harur, *India* .... 95 H4   12 3N   78 29 E
Hārūt ~, *Afghan.* .... 91 C1   31 29N   61 24 E
Harvand, *Iran* .... 97 D7   28 25N   55 43 E
Harvard, *U.S.A.* 157 B8   42 25N   88 37W
Harvey, *Australia* .... 125 F2   33 5 S 115 54 E
Harvey, *U.S.A.* 157 C9   41 36N   87 50W
Harvey, *N. Dak., U.S.A.* 154 B5   47 47N   99 56W
Harwich, *U.K.* .... 21 F9   51 56N   1 17 E
Haryana □, *India* .... 92 E7   29 0N   76 10 E
Haryn ~, *Belarus* .... 59 F4   52 7N   27 17 E
Harz, *Germany* .... 30 D6   51 38N   10 44 E
Harz Nationalpark △, *Germany* .... 30 D6   51 40N   10 18 E
Harzgerode, *Germany* .... 30 D7   51 38N   11 8 E
Hasa □, *Si. Arabia* .... 97 E6   25 50N   49 0 E
Hasaheisa, *Sudan* .... 107 E3   14 44N   33 20 E
Hasalbag, *China* .... 65 E8   37 52N   76 42 E
Hasanābād, *Iran* .... 97 C7   32 8N   52 44 E
Hasanparti, *India* .... 94 B4   18 4N   79 32 E
Hasdo ~, *India* .... 93 J10   21 44N   82 44 E
Häselgehr, *Austria* .... 33 B10   47 19N   10 30 E
Haselünne, *Germany* .... 30 C3   52 40N   7 29 E
Hashima, *Japan* .... 73 B8   35 20N 136 40 E
Hashimoto, *Japan* .... 73 C7   34 19N 135 37 E
Hashtjerd, *Iran* .... 97 C6   35 52N   50 40 E
Hasi Nueifed, *W. Sahara* 110 D2   24 54N   14 49W
Hasik, *Oman* .... 99 C6   17 22N   55 17 E
Haskell, *U.S.A.* 155 J5   33 10N   99 44W
Hasköy, *Turkey* .... 51 E10   41 38N   26 52 E
Haslach, *Germany* .... 31 G4   48 16N   8 1 E
Hasle, *Denmark* .... 17 J8   55 11N   14 44 E
Haslemere, *U.K.* 21 F7   51 5N   0 43W
Haslev, *Denmark* .... 17 J6   55 18N   11 57 E
Hasparren, *France* 28 E2   43 24N   1 18W
Hassa, *Turkey* .... 100 D7   36 48N   36 29 E
Hassan, *India* .... 95 H3   13 0N   76 5 E
Hassberge, Naturpark △, *Germany* .... 31 E6   50 8N   10 45 E
Hassela, *Sweden* .... 16 B10   62 7N   16 42 E
Hasselt, *Belgium* .... 24 D5   50 56N   5 21 E
Hassen, Adrar, *Algeria* .... 111 D5   21 0N   4 0 E
Hassfurt, *Germany* .... 31 E6   50 2N   10 30 E
Hassi bou Khelala, *Algeria* 111 B4   30 17N   0 18W
Hassi Bourachet, *Algeria* .... 111 C6   27 26N   9 19 E
Hassi Djafou, *Algeria* .... 111 B5   30 5 S   3 35 E
Hassi el Abiod, *Algeria* .... 111 C6   31 47N   3 37 E
Hassi el Biod, *Algeria* .... 111 C6   28 30N   6 0 E
Hassi el Hadjar, *Algeria* .... 111 B5   31 28N   4 45 E
Hassi Imoulaye, *Algeria* .... 111 C6   29 54N   9 10 E
Hassi Inifeg, *Algeria* 111 C4   28 15N   1 30W
Hassi Inifel, *Algeria* .... 111 C5   29 50N   3 41 E
Hassi Mana, *Algeria* 111 C4   28 48N   2 24W
Hassi Messaoud, *Algeria* .... 111 B6   31 51N   6 1 E
Hassi Sougoued, *Algeria* .... 111 C6   26 50N   9 28 E
Hassi Zguilma, *Algeria* 111 B4   30 2N   2 19W
Hässleholm, *Sweden* .... 17 H7   56 10N   13 46 E
Hassloch, *Germany* .... 31 F4   49 22N   8 16 E
Hästholmen, *Sweden* .... 17 F8   58 17N   14 38 E
Hastings, *Australia* .... 129 E6   38 18 S 145 12 E
Hastings, *N.Z.* .... 130 F5   39 39 S 176 52 E
Hastings, *U.K.* .... 21 G8   50 51N   0 35 E
Hastings, *Fla., U.S.A.* 153 F8   29 43N   81 31W
Hastings, *Mich., U.S.A.* 157 B11   42 39N   85 17W
Hastings, *Minn., U.S.A.* 154 C8   44 44N   92 51W
Hastings, *Nebr., U.S.A.* 154 E5   40 35N   98 23W
Hastings Ra., *Australia* .... 129 A10   31 15 S 152 14 E
Hästveda, *Sweden* .... 17 H7   56 17N   13 55 E
Hasy 'Aṭshān, *Libya* .... 108 C2   27 20N   10 25 E
Hasy Tissan, *Libya* .... 111 C7   28 14N   12 26 E
Hat Yai, *Thailand* .... 85 J3   7 1N 100 27 E
Hatanbulag = Ergel, *Mongolia* .... 74 C5   43 8N 109 5 E
Hatay = Antalya, *Turkey* .... 100 D4   36 52N   30 45 E
Hatch, *U.S.A.* 159 K10   32 40N 107 9W
Hatchet L., *Canada* 143 B8   58 36N 103 40W
Hateg, *Romania* .... 52 E7   45 36N   22 55 E
Hateruma-Shima, *Japan* .... 71 M1   24 3N 123 47 E
Hatfield P.O., *Australia* .... 128 B5   33 54 S 143 49 E
Hatgal, *Mongolia* .... 68 A5   50 26N 100 9 E
Hathras, *India* .... 92 F7   27 36N   78 6 E
Hatia, *Bangla.* .... 90 D3   22 30N   91 5 E
Hatia Is., *Bangla.* .... 90 D3   22 30N   91 0 E
Ḥāṭibah, Ra's, *Si. Arabia* .... 106 C4   21 55N   38 57 E
Hatid, *India* .... 94 F2   17 17N   75 3 E
Hato Corozal, *Colombia* 168 B3   6 11N   71 45W
Hato Mayor, *Dom. Rep.* 165 C6   18 46N   69 15W
Hatsukaichi, *Japan* .... 72 C4   34 22N 132 22 E
Hatta, *India* .... 93 G8   24 7N   79 36 E
Hattah, *Australia* .... 128 C5   34 48 S 142 17 E
Hattah Kulkyne Nat. Park △,
   Australia .... 128 C5   35 40 S 142 22 E
Hatteras, C., *U.S.A.* 149 H8   35 14N   75 32W
Hattiesburg, *U.S.A.* 155 K10   31 20N   89 17W
Hatvan, *Hungary* .... 52 C4   47 40N   19 45 E
Hau Bon = Cheo Reo, *Vietnam* .... 78 B3   13 25N 108 28 E
Hau Duc, *Vietnam* .... 86 E7   15 20N 108 13 E
Haubstadt, *U.S.A.* 157 F9   38 12N   87 34W
Haud, *Ethiopia* .... 120 C2   8 10N   45 0 E
Hauganes, *Iceland* 11 B8   65 55N   18 18W
Haugastøl, *Norway* .... 18 D4   60 30N   7 50 E
Hauge, *Norway* .... 18 E2   58 23N   6 15 E
Haugesund, *Norway* .... 18 E2   59 23N   5 13 E
Hauhui, *Solomon Is.* .... 133 M11   9 10 S 160 59 E
Hauhungaroa Ra., *N.Z.* .... 130 E4   38 42 S 175 40 E
Haukeligrend, *Norway* .... 18 E3   59 45N   7 25 E
Haukipudas, *Finland* .... 14 D21   65 12N   25 20 E
Haultain ~, *Canada* 143 B7   55 51N 106 46W
Haungpa, *Burma* .... 90 C6   25 29N   96 7 E
Hauraha, *Solomon Is.* .... 133 N11   10 46 S 161 59 E
Hauraki G., *N.Z.* .... 130 C4   36 35 S 175 5 E
Hauroko L., *N.Z.* .... 131 F2   45 59 S 167 21 E
Hausruck, *Austria* .... 34 C6   48 6N   13 30 E
Hausstock, *Switz.* .... 33 C8   46 53N   9 3 E
Haut Atlas, *Morocco* 110 B4   32 30N   5 0W
Haut-Jura, Parc Naturel Régional
   du ~, *France* .... 27 F9   46 23N   2 23 E
Haut-Languedoc, Parc Naturel
   Régional des ~, *France* .... 28 E6   43 30N   2 43 E
Haut Niger, Parc Nat. du △, *Guinea* 112 C2   10 20N   10 20W
Haut-Rhin □, *France* .... 27 E14   48 0N   7 15 E
Haut-Zaïre = Orientale □,
   Dem. Rep. of the Congo .... 118 B2   2 20N   26 0 E
Haute-Corse □, *France* .... 29 F13   42 30N   9 30 E
Haute-Garonne □, *France* .... 28 E5   43 30N   1 30 E

Haute-Loire □, *France* .... 28 C7   45 5N   3 50 E
Haute-Marne □, *France* .... 27 D12   48 10N   5 20 E
Haute-Normandie □, *France* .... 26 C7   49 20N   1 0 E
Haute-Saône □, *France* .... 27 E13   47 45N   6 10 E
Haute-Savoie □, *France* .... 29 C10   46 0N   6 20 E
Haute-Vienne □, *France* .... 28 C5   45 50N   1 10 E
Hautes-Alpes □, *France* .... 29 D10   44 42N   6 20 E
Hautes Fagnes = Hohe Venn,
   Belgium .... 24 D6   50 30N   6 5 E
Hautes Fagnes, Parc Nat. des =
   Hohes Venn-Eifel, Naturpark △,
   Europe .... 30 E2   50 30N   6 10 E
Hautes-Pyrénées □, *France* .... 28 F4   43 0N   0 10 E
Hauteville-Lompnès, *France* .... 29 C9   45 58N   5 36 E
Hautmont, *France* .... 27 B10   50 15N   3 55 E
Hauts-de-Seine □, *France* .... 27 D9   48 52N   2 15 E
Hauts Plateaux, *Algeria* .... 111 B5   35 0N   1 0 E
Hauula, *U.S.A.* 145 J14   21 37N 157 55W
Hauzenberg, *Germany* .... 31 G9   48 40N   13 37 E
Havana = La Habana, *Cuba* 164 B3   23 8N   82 22W
Havana, *Fla., U.S.A.* 152 E5   30 37N   84 25W
Havana, *Ill., U.S.A.* 156 D6   40 18N   90 4W
Havant, *U.K.* 21 G7   50 51N   0 58W
Havârna, *Romania* .... 53 B11   48 4N   26 43 E
Havasor = Kıʒıl, *Turkey* .... 96 B4   38 18N   43 25 E
Havasu, L., *U.S.A.* 161 L12   34 18N 114 28W
Havdhem, *Sweden* .... 17 G12   57 10N   18 20 E
Havel ~, *Germany* .... 30 C8   52 50N   12 3 E
Havelian, *Pakistan* .... 92 B5   34 2N   73 10 E
Havelock, *Canada* 140 D4   44 26N   77 53W
Havelock, *N.Z.* .... 131 B8   41 17 S 173 48 E
Havelock, *U.S.A.* 149 H7   34 53N   76 54W
Havelock I., *India* .... 95 J11   11 58N   93 0 E
Havelock North, *N.Z.* .... 130 F5   39 40 S 176 53 E
Haverfordwest, *U.K.* 21 F3   51 48N   4 58W
Haverhill, *U.K.* .... 21 E8   52 5N   0 28 E
Haverhill, *Fla., U.S.A.* 153 J9   26 42N   80 7W
Haverhill, *Mass., U.S.A.* 151 D13   42 47N   71 5W
Haveri, *India* .... 95 G2   14 53N   75 24 E
Haverstraw, *U.S.A.* 151 E11   41 12N   73 58W
Håverud, *Sweden* .... 17 F6   58 50N   12 28 E
Havirga, *Mongolia* .... 74 B7   45 41N 113 5 E
Havlíčkův Brod, *Czech Rep.* .... 34 B8   49 36N   15 33 E
Havnby, *Denmark* .... 17 J2   55 5N   8 34 E
Havran, *Turkey* .... 49 B9   39 33N   27 6 E
Havre, *U.S.A.* 158 B9   48 33N 109 41W
Havre-Aubert, *Canada* 141 C7   47 12N   61 56W
Havre-St.-Pierre, *Canada* 141 B7   50 18N   63 33W
Havsa, *Turkey* .... 51 E10   41 31N   26 48 E
Havza, *Turkey* .... 100 B6   41 0N   35 35 E
Haw ~, *U.S.A.* 149 H6   35 36N   79 3W
Hawaii, *U.S.A.* 145 M8   19 30N 155 30W
Hawaii □, *U.S.A.* 145 D5   19 30N 156 30W
Hawaii I., *Pac. Oc.* 146 J17   20 55N   155 0W
Hawaii Volcanoes Nat. Park △,
   U.S.A. 145 D6   19 23N 155 17W
Hawaiian Is., *Pac. Oc.* 135 D10   20 30N 156 0W
Hawaiian Ridge, *Pac. Oc.* 135 E11   24 0N 165 0W
Hawarden, *Canada* 143 C7   51 25N 106 36W
Hawarden, *U.S.A.* 154 D6   43 0N   96 29W
Hawea, L., *N.Z.* .... 131 E4   44 28 S 169 19 E
Hawea Flat, *N.Z.* .... 131 E4   44 40 S 169 19 E
Hawera, *N.Z.* .... 130 F3   39 35 S 174 19 E
Hawesville, *U.S.A.* 157 G10   37 54N   86 45W
Hawi, *U.S.A.* 145 C6   20 14N 155 50W
Hawick, *U.K.* 22 F6   55 26N   2 47W
Hawk Junction, *Canada* 140 C3   48 5N   84 38W
Hawk Point, *U.S.A.* 156 F5   38 58N   91 8W
Hawkdun Ra., *N.Z.* .... 131 E3   44 53 S 170 5 E
Hawke B., *N.Z.* .... 130 F6   39 25 S 177 20 E
Hawker, *Australia* .... 128 A3   31 59 S 138 22 E
Hawke's Bay, *N.Z.* .... 130 F5   39 45 S 176 35 E
Hawkesbury, *Canada* 140 C5   45 37N   74 37W
Hawkesbury ~, *Australia* 142 C3   53 37N 129 3W
Hawkesbury Pt., *Australia* .... 126 A1   11 55 S 134 5 E
Hawkinsville, *U.S.A.* 152 D6   32 17N   83 28W
Hawks Nest, *Australia* .... 129 E10   32 41 S 152 11 E
Hawley, *Minn., U.S.A.* 154 B6   46 53N   96 19W
Hawley, *Pa., U.S.A.* 151 E9   41 28N   75 11W
Ḥawrān, W. ~, *Iraq* .... 101 F10   33 58N   42 34 E
Hawsh Mūssá, *Lebanon* .... 103 B4   33 45N   35 55 E
Hawthorne, *Fla., U.S.A.* 153 F7   29 36N   82 5W
Hawthorne, *Nev., U.S.A.* 158 G4   38 32N 118 38W
Hay, *Australia* .... 129 C6   34 30 S 144 51 E
Hay ~, *Australia* .... 126 C2   24 50 S 138 0 E
Hay ~, *Canada* 142 A5   60 50N 116 26W
Hay, C., *Australia* .... 124 B4   14 5 S 129 29 E
Hay I., *Canada* 150 B4   44 53N   80 58W
Hay L., *Canada* 142 B5   58 50N 118 50W
Hay-on-Wye, *U.K.* 21 E4   52 5N   3 8W
Hay River, *Canada* 142 A5   60 51N 115 44W
Hay Springs, *U.S.A.* 154 D3   42 41N 102 41W
Haya = Tehoru, *Indonesia* .... 83 B3   3 23 S 129 30 E
Hayachine-San, *Japan* .... 70 E10   39 34N 141 29 E
Hayange, *France* .... 27 C13   49 20N   6 2 E
Hayato, *Japan* .... 72 J5   31 40N 130 43 E
Haydarlı, *Turkey* .... 49 C12   38 16N   30 23 E
Hayden, *U.S.A.* 158 F10   40 30N 107 16W
Haydon, *Australia* .... 126 B3   18 0 S 141 30 E
Hayes, *U.S.A.* 154 C4   44 23N 101 1W
Hayes ~, *Canada* 140 A1   57 3N   92 12W
Hayes, Mt., *U.S.A.* 144 E11   63 37N 146 43W
Hayes Creek, *Australia* .... 124 B5   13 43 S 131 22 E
Hayle, *U.K.* 21 G2   50 11N   5 26W
Haymana, *Turkey* .... 100 C5   39 26N   32 42 E
Haymen I., *Australia* .... 126 J6   20 4 S 148 58 E
Haymen, *Yemen* .... 99 D5   15 50N   48 18 E
Haynesville, *U.S.A.* 155 J8   33 2N   93 8W
Hayrabolu, *Turkey* .... 51 E11   41 12N   27 5 E
Hays, *Canada* 142 C6   50 6N 111 48W
Hays, *U.S.A.* 154 F5   38 53N   99 20W
Hays, *Yemen* .... 98 D3   13 56N   43 29 E
Haysville, *U.S.A.* 157 F10   38 28N   86 55W
Haysyn, *Ukraine* .... 59 H5   48 57N   29 25 E
Hayvoron, *Ukraine* .... 59 H5   48 22N   29 52 E
Hayward, *Calif., U.S.A.* 160 H4   37 40N 122 5W
Hayward, *Wis., U.S.A.* 154 B9   46 1N   91 29W
Haywards Heath, *U.K.* 21 G7   51 0N   0 5W
Ḥazafon □, *Israel* .... 103 C4   32 40N   35 20 E
Hazārān, Kūh-e, *Iran* .... 97 D8   29 35N   57 20 E
Hazard, *U.S.A.* 148 G4   37 15N   83 12W
Hazaribag, *India* .... 93 H11   23 58N   85 26 E
Hazaribag Road, *India* .... 93 G11   24 12N   85 57 E
Hazebrouck, *France* .... 27 B9   50 42N   2 31 E
Hazelton, *Canada* 142 B3   55 20N 127 42W
Hazelton, *U.S.A.* 154 B4   46 29N 100 17W
Hazen, *U.S.A.* 154 B4   47 18N 101 38W
Hazlehurst, *Ga., U.S.A.* 152 D7   31 52N   82 36W
Hazlehurst, *Miss., U.S.A.* 155 K9   31 52N   90 24W
Hazlet, *U.S.A.* 151 F10   40 25N   74 12W
Hazleton, *Pa., U.S.A.* 151 F9   40 57N   75 59W
Hazlett, L., *Australia* .... 124 D4   21 30 S 128 48 E
Hazro, *Turkey* .... 96 B4   38 15N   40 47 E
He Xian, *Anhui, China* .... 77 B12   31 45N 118 30 E
He Xian, *Guangxi Zhuangzu, China* .... 77 E8   24 27N 111 30 E
Head of Bight, *Australia* .... 125 F5   31 30 S 131 25 E
Headland, *U.S.A.* 152 D4   31 21N   85 21W
Headlands, *Zimbabwe* .... 119 F3   18 15 S   32 2 E
Healdsburg, *U.S.A.* 160 G4   38 37N 122 52W
Healdton, *U.S.A.* 155 H6   34 14N   97 29W
Healesville, *Australia* .... 129 D6   37 35 S 145 30 E
Healy, *U.S.A.* 144 E10   63 52N 148 58W

Heany Junction, *Zimbabwe* .... 117 C4 20 6 S 28 54 E
Heard I., *Ind. Oc.* .... 121 K6 53 0 S 74 0 E
Hearne, *Canada* 155 K6 30 53N 96 36W
Hearst, *Canada* 140 C3 49 40N 83 41W
Heart ➤, *U.S.A.* 154 B4 46 46N 100 50W
Heart's Content, *Canada* 141 C9 47 54N 53 27W
Heath ➤, *Bolivia* .... 172 C4 12 31 S 68 38W
Heath Mts., *N.Z.* .... 131 F2 45 39 S 167 9 E
Heath Pt., *Canada* 141 C7 49 8N 61 40W
Heathcote, *Australia* .... 129 D6 36 56 S 144 45 E
Heathrow, London ✈ (LHR), *U.K.* . 21 F7 51 28N 0 27W
Heavener, *U.S.A.* 155 H7 34 53N 94 36W
Hebbronville, *U.S.A.* 155 M5 27 18N 98 41W
Hebei □, *China* .... 74 E9 39 0N 116 0 E
Hebel, *Australia* .... 127 D4 28 58 S 147 47 E
Heber, *U.S.A.* 161 N11 32 44N 115 32W
Heber City, *U.S.A.* 158 F8 40 31N 111 25W
Heber Springs, *U.S.A.* 155 H9 35 30N 92 2W
Hebert, *Canada* 143 C7 50 30N 107 10W
Hebgen L., *U.S.A.* 158 D8 44 52N 111 20W
Hebi, *China* .... 74 G8 35 57N 114 7 E
Hebrides, *U.K.* 12 D4 57 30N 7 0W
Hebrides, Sea of the, *U.K.* 22 D2 57 5N 7 0W
Hebron = Al Khalīl, *West Bank* .... 103 D4 31 32N 35 6 E
Hebron, *Canada* 139 C13 58 5N 62 30W
Hebron, N. Dak., *U.S.A.* 154 B3 46 54N 102 3W
Hebron, Nebr., *U.S.A.* 154 E6 40 10N 97 35W
Heby, *Sweden* .... 16 E10 59 56N 16 53 E
Hecate Str., *Canada* 142 C2 53 10N 130 30W
Heceta I., *U.S.A.* 142 B2 55 46N 133 40W
Hechi, *China* .... 76 E7 24 40N 108 2 E
Hechingen, *Germany* .... 31 G4 48 21N 8 57 E
Hechuan, *China* .... 76 B6 30 2N 106 12 E
Hecla, *U.S.A.* 154 C5 45 53N 98 9W
Hecla I., *Canada* 143 C9 51 10N 96 43W
Hedal, *Norway* .... 18 D6 60 37N 9 41 E
Heddal, *Norway* .... 18 E6 59 36N 9 9 E
Hédé, *France* 26 D5 48 18N 1 49W
Hede, *Sweden* .... 16 B7 62 23N 13 30 E
Hedemora, *Sweden* .... 16 D9 60 18N 15 58 E
Hedensted, *Denmark* .... 17 J3 55 46N 9 42 E
Hedesunda, *Sweden* .... 16 D10 60 23N 17 0 E
Hedgehope, *N.Z.* .... 131 G3 46 12 S 168 34 E
Hedmark □, *Norway* .... 18 C8 61 17N 11 40 E
Hedrick, *U.S.A.* 156 C4 41 11N 92 19W
Heerde, *Neths.* .... 24 B6 52 24N 6 2 E
Heerenveen, *Neths.* .... 24 B5 52 57N 5 55 E
Heerhugowaard, *Neths.* .... 24 B4 52 40N 4 51 E
Heerlen, *Neths.* .... 24 D5 50 55N 5 58 E
Hefa, *Israel* .... 103 C4 32 46N 35 0 E
Hefa □, *Israel* .... 103 C4 32 40N 35 0 E
Hefei, *China* .... 77 B11 31 52N 117 18 E
Hefeng, *China* .... 77 C8 29 55N 109 52 E
Heflin, *U.S.A.* 152 B4 33 39N 85 35W
Hegalig, *Sudan* .... 107 E3 14 36N 31 54 E
Hegang, *China* .... 69 B8 47 20N 130 19 E
Heggenes, *Norway* .... 18 C6 61 9N 9 4 E
Hegra, *Norway* .... 18 A8 63 27N 11 8 E
Hei Ling Chau, *China* .... 69 G11 22 15N 114 2 E
Heiban, *Sudan* .... 107 E3 11 13N 30 31 E
Heichengzhen, *China* .... 74 F4 36 24N 106 3 E
Heidal, *Norway* .... 18 C6 61 45N 9 19 E
Heide, *Germany* .... 30 A5 54 11N 9 6 E
Heidelberg, *Germany* .... 31 F4 49 24N 8 42 E
Heidelberg, S. Africa .... 116 E3 34 6 S 20 59 E
Heidenau, *Germany* .... 30 E9 50 57N 13 52 E
Heidenheim, *Germany* .... 31 G6 48 41N 10 9 E
Heigun-Tō, *Japan* .... 72 D4 33 47N 132 14 E
Heijing, *China* .... 76 E3 25 22N 101 44 E
Heijo = P'yŏngyang, N. Korea ...... 75 E13 39 0N 125 30 E
Heilbad Heiligenstadt, *Germany* .. 30 D6 51 22N 10 8 E
Heilbron, S. Africa .... 117 D4 27 16 S 27 59 E
Heilbronn, *Germany* .... 31 F5 49 9N 9 13 E
Heiligenblut, *Austria* .... 34 D5 47 2N 12 51 E
Heiligenhafen, *Germany* .... 30 A6 54 22N 10 59 E
Heilongjiang □, *China* .... 69 B7 48 0N 126 0 E
Heilprin Land, *Greenland* 10 A7 82 5N 33 0W
Heilunkiang = Heilongjiang □, China 69 B7 48 0N 126 0 E
Heim, *Norway* .... 18 A6 63 26N 9 5 E
Heimaey, *Iceland* 11 D6 63 26N 20 17W
Heimdal, *Norway* .... 18 A7 63 21N 10 22 E
Heinola, *Finland* .... 15 F22 61 13N 26 2 E
Heinsberg, *Germany* .... 30 D2 51 3N 6 5 E
Heinsun, *Burma* .... 90 C5 25 52N 95 35 E
Heinze Kyun, *Burma* .... 86 E1 14 25N 97 45 E
Heirnkut, *Burma* .... 90 C5 25 14N 94 44 E
Heishan, *China* .... 75 D12 41 40N 122 5 E
Heishui, Liaoning, China .... 75 C10 42 8N 119 30 E
Heishui, Sichuan, China .... 76 A4 32 4N 103 2 E
Hejaz = Ḥijāz □, Si. Arabia .... 96 E3 24 0N 40 0 E
Hejian, *China* .... 74 E9 38 25N 116 5 E
Hejiang, *China* .... 76 C5 28 43N 105 46 E
Hejin, *China* .... 74 G6 35 35N 110 42 E
Hekimhan, *Turkey* .... 100 C7 38 50N 37 55 E
Hekinan, *Japan* .... 73 C9 34 52N 137 0 E
Hekla, *Iceland* 11 D7 63 56N 19 35W
Hekou, Guangdong, China .... 77 F9 23 13N 112 45 E
Hekou, Yunnan, China .... 76 F4 22 30N 103 59 E
Hel, *Poland* .... 54 D5 54 4N 18 47 E
Helagsfjället, *Sweden* .... 16 B6 62 54N 12 25 E
Helan Shan, *China* .... 74 E3 38 30N 105 55 E
Helechosa, *Spain* 43 F6 39 22N 4 53W
Helemano ➤, *U.S.A.* 145 J13 21 35N 158 7W
Helen Atoll, *Pac. Oc.* .... 83 A4 2 40N 132 0 E
Helena, Ark., *U.S.A.* 155 H9 34 32N 90 36W
Helena, Ga., *U.S.A.* 152 C7 32 5N 82 55W
Helena, Mont., *U.S.A.* 158 C7 46 36N 112 2W
Helendale, *U.S.A.* 161 L9 34 44N 117 19W
Helensburgh, Australia .... 129 C9 34 11 S 151 1 E
Helensburgh, *U.K.* 22 E4 56 1N 4 43W
Helensville, *N.Z.* .... 130 C3 36 41 S 174 29 E
Helenvale, Australia .... 126 B4 15 43 S 145 14 E
Helgasjön, *Sweden* .... 17 H8 56 55N 14 50 E
Helgeland, *Norway* .... 14 C15 66 7N 13 29 E
Helgeland, *Germany* .... 30 A3 54 10N 7 53 E
Heligoland = Helgoland, Germany . 30 A3 54 10N 7 53 E
Heligoland B. = Deutsche Bucht,
     Germany .... 30 A4 54 15N 8 0 E
Heliopolis, *Egypt* .... 106 H7 30 6N 31 17 E
Hell, *Norway* .... 18 A7 63 26N 10 54 E
Hella, *Iceland* 11 D6 63 50N 20 24W
Helleland, *Norway* .... 18 F3 58 33N 6 7 E
Hellertown, *U.S.A.* 151 F9 40 35N 75 21W
Hellespont = Çanakkale Boğazı,
     Turkey .... 51 F10 40 17N 26 32 E
Hellesylt, *Norway* .... 18 B3 62 6N 6 51 E
Hellevoetsluis, *Neths.* .... 24 C4 51 50N 4 8 E
Hellhole Gorge Nat. Park △,
     Australia .... 126 D3 25 31 S 144 12 E
Hellín, *Spain* 41 G3 38 31N 1 40W
Hellissandur, *Iceland* 11 C3 64 55N 23 54W
Hells Canyon Nat. Recr. Area △,
     U.S.A. 158 D5 45 30N 117 45W
Hell's Gate Nat. Park △, Kenya ... 118 C4 0 54 S 36 27 E
Hellvik, *Norway* .... 18 F2 58 32N 5 52 E
Helmand □, Afghan. .... 91 C2 31 20N 64 0 E
Helmand ➤, Afghan. .... 91 C1 31 12N 61 34 E
Helme ➤, Germany .... 30 D7 51 20N 11 21 E
Helmeringhausen, Namibia .... 116 D2 25 54 S 16 57 E
Helmond, *Neths.* .... 24 C5 51 29N 5 41 E
Helmsdale, *U.K.* 23 C5 58 7N 3 39W
Helmsdale ➤, *U.K.* 23 C5 58 7N 3 40W
Helmstedt, *Germany* .... 30 C7 52 12N 11 0 E
Helong, *China* .... 75 C15 42 40N 129 0 E

Helper, *U.S.A.* 158 G8 39 41N 110 51W
Helsingborg, *Sweden* .... 17 H6 56 3N 12 42 E
Helsinge, *Denmark* .... 17 H6 56 2N 12 12 E
Helsingfors = Helsinki, Finland ..... 15 F21 60 15N 25 3 E
Helsingør, *Denmark* .... 17 H6 56 2N 12 35 E
Helsinki, *Finland* .... 15 F21 60 15N 25 3 E
Helska, Mierzeja, Poland .... 54 D5 54 45N 18 40 E
Helston, *U.K.* 21 G2 50 6N 5 17W
Helvellyn, *U.K.* 20 C4 54 32N 3 1W
Helwân, *Egypt* .... 106 J7 29 50N 31 20 E
Hemel Hempstead, *U.K.* 21 F7 51 44N 0 28W
Hemet, *U.S.A.* 161 M10 33 45N 116 58W
Hemingford, *U.S.A.* 154 D3 42 19N 103 4W
Hemmingford, Canada 151 A11 45 3N 73 35W
Hempstead, *U.S.A.* .... 114 B4 1 54N 22 42 E
Hempstead, *U.S.A.* 155 K6 30 6N 96 5W
Hemse, *Sweden* .... 17 G12 57 15N 18 22 E
Hemsedal, *Norway* .... 18 D5 60 53N 8 30 E
Hemsön, *Sweden* .... 16 B12 62 42N 18 5 E
Hen, *Norway* .... 18 D7 60 13N 10 14 E
Hen and Chickens Is., N.Z. .... 130 B3 35 58 S 174 45 E
Henan, *Sweden* .... 17 F5 58 14N 11 40 E
Henan □, China .... 74 H8 34 0N 114 0 E
Henares ➤, Spain 42 E7 40 24N 3 30W
Henashi-Misaki, Japan .... 70 D9 40 37N 139 51 E
Hendaye, *France* 28 E2 43 23N 1 47W
Hendek, *Turkey* .... 100 B4 40 48N 30 44 E
Henderson, Argentina .... 174 D3 36 18 S 61 43W
Henderson, Ga., *U.S.A.* 152 C6 32 21N 83 47W
Henderson, Ky., *U.S.A.* 157 G9 37 50N 87 35W
Henderson, N.C., *U.S.A.* 149 G6 36 20N 78 25W
Henderson, Nev., *U.S.A.* 161 J12 36 2N 114 59W
Henderson, Tenn., *U.S.A.* 149 H1 35 26N 88 38W
Henderson, Tex., *U.S.A.* 155 J7 32 9N 94 48W
Hendersonville, N.C., *U.S.A.* 149 H4 35 19N 82 28W
Hendersonville, Tenn., *U.S.A.* 149 G2 36 18N 86 37W
Hendijān, Iran .... 97 D6 30 14N 49 43 E
Hendorābī, Iran .... 97 E7 26 40N 53 37 E
Heng Jiang, China .... 76 C5 28 40N 104 25 E
Heng Xian, China .... 76 F7 22 40N 109 17 E
Henganofi, Papua N. G. .... 132 D3 6 15 S 145 38 E
Hengcheng, China .... 74 E4 38 18N 106 28 E
Hengchun, Taiwan .... 77 F13 22 0N 120 44 E
Hengdaohezi, China .... 75 B15 44 52N 129 0 E
Hengelo, *Neths.* .... 24 B6 52 16N 6 48 E
Hengfeng, China .... 77 C10 28 12N 115 48 E
Henggang, China .... 69 F11 22 39N 114 12 E
Hengmen, China .... 69 F10 22 33N 113 35 E
Hengqin Dao, China .... 69 G10 22 7N 113 34 E
Hengshan, Hunan, China .... 77 D9 27 16N 112 45 E
Hengshan, Shaanxi, China .... 74 F5 37 58N 109 5 E
Hengshui, China .... 74 F8 37 41N 115 40 E
Hengyang, China .... 77 D9 26 59N 112 22 E
Henichesk, Ukraine .... 59 J8 46 12N 34 50 E
Henima, India .... 90 C4 25 22N 93 36 E
Hénin-Beaumont, France .... 27 B9 50 25N 2 58 E
Henley-on-Thames, U.K. 21 F7 51 32N 0 54W
Henlopen, C., U.S.A. 148 F8 38 48N 75 6W
Hennan, Sweden .... 16 B9 62 2N 15 54 E
Hennebont, France 26 E3 47 49N 3 19W
Hennenman, S. Africa .... 116 D4 27 59 S 27 1 E
Hennepin, U.S.A. 156 C7 41 15N 89 21W
Hennessey, U.S.A. 155 G6 36 6N 97 54W
Hennigsdorf, Germany .... 30 C9 52 38N 13 12 E
Henri Pittier, Parque Nac. △,
     Venezuela 165 D6 10 27N 67 40W
Henrietta, U.S.A. 155 J5 33 49N 98 12W
Henrietta, Ostrov = Genriyetty,
     Ostrov, Russia .... 67 B16 77 6N 156 30 E
Henrietta Maria, C., Canada 140 A3 55 9N 82 20W
Henry, U.S.A. 156 C7 41 7N 89 22W
Henry Lawrence I., India .... 95 H11 12 9N 93 5 E
Henryetta, U.S.A. 155 H7 35 27N 95 59W
Henryville, Canada 151 A11 45 8N 73 11W
Hensall, Canada 150 C3 43 26N 81 30W
Henstedt-Ulzburg, Germany .... 30 B6 53 47N 10 0 E
Hentiesbaai, Namibia .... 116 C1 22 8 S 14 8 E
Hentiyn Nuruu, Mongolia .... 69 B5 48 30N 108 30 E
Henty, Australia .... 129 C7 35 30 S 147 0 E
Henzada, Burma .... 90 G5 17 38N 95 26 E
Hephaestia, Greece .... 49 B7 39 55N 25 14 E
Hephzibah, U.S.A. 152 B7 33 19N 82 6W
Heping, China .... 77 E10 24 29N 115 0 E
Heppner, U.S.A. 158 D4 45 21N 119 33W
Hepu, China .... 76 G7 21 40N 109 12 E
Hepworth, Canada 150 B3 44 37N 81 9W
Heqing, China .... 76 D3 26 37N 100 11 E
Hequ, China .... 74 E6 39 20N 111 15 E
Héraðsflói, Iceland 11 B12 65 42N 14 12W
Héraðsvötn ➤, Iceland 11 B7 65 45N 19 25W
Heradsbygd, Norway .... 18 D8 60 49N 11 39 E
Heraklion = Iráklion, Greece .... 49 E6 35 20N 25 12 E
Herald Cays, Australia .... 126 B4 16 58 S 149 9 E
Herand, Norway .... 18 D3 60 20N 6 2 E
Herāt, Afghan. .... 91 B1 34 20N 62 7 E
Herāt □, Afghan. .... 91 B1 35 0N 62 0 E
Hérault □, France .... 28 E7 43 34N 3 15 E
Hérault ➤, France .... 28 E7 43 17N 3 26 E
Herbault, France .... 26 E8 47 36N 1 8 E
Herbert ➤, Australia .... 126 B4 18 31 S 146 17 E
Herbert I., U.S.A. 144 K5 52 45N 170 7W
Herbert River Falls Nat. Park △,
     Australia .... 126 B4 18 15 S 145 32 E
Herbertabad, India .... 95 J11 11 43N 92 37 E
Herberton, Australia .... 126 B4 17 20 S 145 25 E
Herbertsdale, S. Africa .... 116 E3 34 1 S 21 46 E
Herbertville, N.Z. .... 130 G5 40 30 S 176 33 E
Herbignac, France 26 E4 47 27N 2 18W
Herborn, Germany .... 30 E4 50 40N 8 19 E
Herby, Poland .... 55 H5 50 45N 18 50 E
Herceg-Novi, Montenegro, Yug. ... 50 D2 42 30N 18 33 E
Herchmer, Canada 143 B10 57 22N 94 10W
Herðubreið, Iceland 11 B10 65 11N 16 21W
Hereford, U.K. 21 E5 52 4N 2 43W
Hereford, U.S.A. 155 H3 34 49N 102 24W
Herefordshire □, U.K. 21 E5 52 8N 2 40W
Herefoss, Norway .... 18 F5 58 32N 8 23 E
Herehogna, Sweden .... 18 C9 61 44N 12 8 E
Hereke, Turkey .... 51 F13 40 47N 29 38 E
Herekino, N.Z. .... 130 B2 35 18 S 173 11 E
Herencia, Spain 43 F7 39 21N 3 22W
Herentals, Belgium .... 24 C4 51 12N 4 51 E
Herford, Germany .... 30 C4 52 7N 8 39 E
Héricourt, France .... 27 E13 47 32N 6 45 E
Herington, U.S.A. 154 F6 38 40N 96 57W
Herisau, Switz. .... 33 B8 47 22N 9 17 E
Hérisson, France .... 27 F9 46 32N 2 42 E
Herlong, U.S.A. 160 F6 40 8N 120 8W
Herm, U.K. 21 H5 49 30N 2 28W
Hermann, U.S.A. 156 F5 38 42N 91 27W
Hermannsburg, Australia .... 124 D5 23 57 S 132 45 E
Hermannsburg, Germany .... 30 C6 52 50N 10 5 E
Hermannstadt = Sibiu, Romania ... 53 E9 45 45N 24 9 E
Hermansverk, Norway .... 18 D3 61 10N 6 58 E
Hermanus, S. Africa .... 116 E2 34 27 S 19 12 E
Herment, France .... 28 C6 45 45N 2 24 E
Hermidale, Australia .... 129 A7 31 30 S 146 42 E
Hermiston, U.S.A. 158 D4 45 51N 119 17W
Hermit Is., Papua N. G. .... 132 A3 1 32 S 145 5 E
Hermitage, U.S.A. 156 G3 36 56N 93 19W
Hermite, I., Chile .... 176 H3 55 50 S 68 0W
Hermon, U.S.A. 151 B9 44 28N 75 14W

Hermon, Mt. = Shaykh, J. ash,
     Lebanon .... 103 B4 33 25N 35 50 E
Hermosillo, Mexico 162 B2 29 10N 111 0W
Hernád ➤, Hungary .... 52 C6 47 56N 21 8 E
Hernandarias, Paraguay .... 175 B5 25 20 S 54 40W
Hernandez, U.S.A. 160 J6 36 24N 120 46W
Hernando, Argentina .... 174 C3 32 28 S 63 40W
Hernando, Fla., U.S.A. 153 G7 28 54N 82 23W
Hernando, Miss., U.S.A. 155 H10 34 50N 90 0W
Hernani, Spain 40 B3 43 16N 1 58W
Herndon, U.S.A. 150 F8 40 43N 76 51W
Herne, Germany .... 24 C7 51 32N 7 14 E
Herne Bay, U.K. .... 21 F9 51 21N 1 8 E
Herning, Denmark .... 17 H2 56 8N 8 58 E
Herod, U.S.A. 152 D5 31 42N 84 26W
Heroica = Caborca, Mexico 162 A2 30 40N 112 10W
Heroica Nogales = Nogales, Mexico 162 A2 31 20N 110 56W
Heron Bay, Canada 140 C2 48 40N 86 25W
Herradura, Pta. de la, Canary Is. .. 48 F5 28 26N 14 8W
Herre, Norway .... 18 E6 59 6N 9 34 E
Herreid, U.S.A. 154 C4 45 50N 100 4W
Herrenberg, Germany .... 31 G4 48 35N 8 52 E
Herrera, Spain 43 H6 37 26N 4 55W
Herrera de Alcántara, Spain 43 F3 39 39N 7 25W
Herrera de Pisuerga, Spain 42 C6 42 35N 4 20W
Herrera del Duque, Spain 43 F5 39 10N 5 3W
Herrestad, Sweden .... 17 F5 58 21N 11 50 E
Herrin, U.S.A. 155 G10 37 48N 89 2W
Herriot, Canada 143 B8 56 22N 101 16W
Herrljunga, Sweden .... 17 F7 58 5N 13 1 E
Hersbruck, Germany .... 31 F7 49 30N 11 26 E
Hershey, U.S.A. 151 F8 40 17N 76 39W
Herstal, Belgium .... 24 D5 50 40N 5 38 E
Hertford, U.K. 21 F7 51 48N 0 4W
Hertfordshire □, U.K. 21 F7 51 51N 0 5W
's-Hertogenbosch, Neths. .... 24 C5 51 42N 5 17 E
Hertzogville, S. Africa .... 116 D4 28 9 S 25 30 E
Hervás, Spain 42 E5 40 16N 5 52W
Hervey B., Australia .... 126 C5 25 0 S 152 52 E
Herzberg, Brandenburg, Germany . 30 D9 51 41N 13 14 E
Herzberg, Niedersachsen, Germany 30 D6 51 38N 10 20 E
Herzliyya, Israel .... 103 C3 32 10N 34 50 E
Herzogenbuchsee, Switz. .... 32 B5 47 11N 7 42 E
Herzogenburg, Austria .... 34 C8 48 17N 15 41 E
Ḩeşār, Fārs, Iran .... 97 D6 29 52N 50 16 E
Ḩeşār, Markazī, Iran .... 97 C6 35 50N 49 12 E
Heshan, China .... 76 F7 23 50N 108 53 E
Heshui, China .... 74 G5 35 48N 108 0 E
Heshun, China .... 74 F7 37 22N 113 32 E
Heskestad, Norway .... 18 F3 58 28N 6 22 E
Hesperia, U.S.A. 161 L9 34 25N 117 18W
Hessdalen, Norway .... 18 B8 62 48N 11 10 E
Hesse = Hessen □, Germany ...... 30 E4 50 30N 9 0 E
Hessen □, Germany .... 30 E4 50 30N 9 0 E
Hessenreuther und Manteler Wald,
     Naturpark △, Germany .... 31 F8 49 45N 12 1 E
Hesso, Australia .... 128 B2 32 8 S 137 27 E
Hesteyri, Iceland 11 A4 66 20N 22 53W
Hestra, Sweden .... 17 G7 57 26N 13 35 E
Hetch Hetchy Aqueduct, U.S.A. ... 160 H5 37 29N 122 19W
Hettinger, U.S.A. 154 C3 46 0N 102 42W
Hettstedt, Germany .... 30 D7 51 39N 11 31 E
Heuvelton, U.S.A. 151 B9 44 37N 75 25W
Hevelândia, Brazil .... 169 E5 5 12 S 61 50W
Heves □, Hungary .... 52 C5 47 50N 20 0 E
Heves, Hungary .... 52 C5 47 36N 20 17 E
Hewitt, U.S.A. 155 K6 31 27N 97 11W
Hexham, U.K. 20 C5 54 58N 2 4W
Hexi, Yunnan, China .... 76 E4 24 9N 102 38 E
Hexi, Zhejiang, China .... 77 D12 27 58N 119 38 E
Hexigten Qi, China .... 75 C9 43 18N 117 30 E
Heydarābād, Iran .... 97 D7 30 33N 55 38 E
Heyfield, Australia .... 129 D7 37 59 S 146 47 E
Heysham, U.K. 20 C5 54 3N 2 53W
Heyuan, China .... 77 F10 23 49N 114 45 E
Heywood, Australia .... 128 E4 38 8 S 141 37 E
Heyworth, U.S.A. 156 D8 40 19N 88 59W
Heze, China .... 74 G8 35 14N 115 20 E
Hezhang, China .... 76 D5 27 8N 104 41 E
Hi, Ko, Thailand .... 87 a 7 44N 98 22 E
Hi-no-Misaki, Japan .... 73 B6 35 26N 132 38 E
Hi Vista, U.S.A. 161 L9 34 45N 117 46W
Hialeah, U.S.A. 153 K9 25 50N 80 17W
Hiawatha, U.S.A. 154 F7 39 51N 95 32W
Hibbing, U.S.A. 154 B8 47 25N 92 56W
Hibbs B., Australia .... 127 D4 42 35 S 145 15 E
Hibernia Reef, Australia .... 124 B3 12 0 S 123 23 E
Hibiki-Nada, Japan .... 72 D2 34 0N 130 0 E
Hickman, U.S.A. 155 G10 36 34N 89 11W
Hickory, U.S.A. 149 H5 35 44N 81 21W
Hicks, Pt., Australia .... 129 D8 37 49 S 149 17 E
Hicks Bay, N.Z. .... 130 D7 37 34 S 178 21 E
Hicks L., Canada 143 A9 61 25N 100 0W
Hicksville, N.Y., U.S.A. 151 F11 40 46N 73 32W
Hicksville, Ohio, U.S.A. 157 C12 41 18N 84 46W
Hida, Romania .... 53 D8 47 10N 23 19 E
Hida-Gawa ➤, Japan .... 73 B9 35 26N 137 3 E
Hida-Sammyaku, Japan .... 73 A9 36 30N 137 40 E
Hida-Sanchi, Japan .... 73 A9 36 10N 137 0 E
Hidaka, Japan .... 72 B6 35 30N 134 44 E
Hidaka-Sammyaku, Japan .... 70 C11 42 35N 142 45 E
Hidalgo, Mexico 163 C5 24 15N 99 26W
Hidalgo □, Mexico 163 C5 20 30N 99 10W
Hidalgo, Presa M., Mexico 162 B3 26 30N 108 35W
Hidalgo del Parral, Mexico 162 B3 26 58N 105 40W
Hiddensee, Germany .... 30 A9 54 32N 13 6 E
Hidrolândia, Brazil .... 171 E2 17 0 S 49 15W
Hieflau, Austria .... 34 D7 47 36N 14 46 E
Hiendelaencina, Spain 40 D2 41 5N 3 0W
Hienghène, N. Cal. .... 133 T18 20 41 S 164 56 E
Hierro, Canary Is. 48 G1 27 44N 18 0W
Higashi-Hiroshima, Japan .... 72 C4 34 25N 132 45 E
Higashi-Matsuyama, Japan .... 73 A11 36 2N 139 25 E
Higashiajima-San, Japan .... 70 F10 37 40N 140 10 E
Higashiōsaka, Japan .... 73 C7 34 40N 135 37 E
Higasi-Suidō, Japan .... 72 D1 34 0N 129 30 E
Higbee, U.S.A. 156 E4 39 19N 92 31W
Higgins, U.S.A. 155 G4 36 7N 100 2W
Higgins Corner, U.S.A. 160 F5 39 2N 121 5W
Higginsville, U.S.A. 156 E3 39 4N 93 43W
High Atlas = Haut Atlas, Morocco . 110 B4 32 30N 5 0W
High Bridge, U.S.A. 151 F10 40 40N 74 54W
High Island Res., China .... 69 G11 22 22N 114 21 E
High Level, Canada 142 B5 58 31N 117 8W
High Peak, Phil. .... 80 D3 15 29N 120 7 E
High Pk., St. Helena .... 9 h 15 58 S 5 44W
High Point, U.S.A. 149 H6 35 57N 80 0W
High Prairie, Canada 142 B5 55 30N 116 30W
High River, Canada 142 C6 50 30N 113 50W
High Springs, U.S.A. 152 F7 29 50N 82 36W
High Tatra = Tatry, Slovak Rep. ... 35 B13 49 20N 20 0 E
High Veld, Africa .... 104 J6 27 0 S 27 0 E
High Wycombe, U.K. 21 F7 51 37N 0 45W
Highbank, N.Z. .... 131 D6 43 37 S 171 45 E
Highland, Ill., U.S.A. 156 F7 38 44N 89 41W
Highland, Ind., U.S.A. 157 C9 41 33N 87 28W
Highland, Wis., U.S.A. 156 A6 43 5N 90 22W
Highland □, U.K. 22 D4 57 17N 4 21W
Highland City, U.S.A. 153 H8 27 58N 81 53W
Highland Home, U.S.A. 152 D3 31 57N 86 19W
Highland Mills = Experiment, U.S.A. 152 B5 33 17N 84 17W
Highland Park, U.S.A. 157 B9 42 11N 87 48W
Highland View, U.S.A. 152 F4 29 50N 85 19W

Highmore, U.S.A. 154 C5 44 31N 99 27W
Highrock L., Man., Canada 143 B8 55 45N 100 30W
Highrock L., Sask., Canada 143 B7 57 5N 105 32W
Higüey, Dom. Rep. 165 C6 18 37N 68 42W
Hihya, Egypt .... 106 H7 30 40N 31 36 E
Hiiumaa, Estonia .... 15 G20 58 50N 22 45 E
Hijar, Spain 40 D4 41 10N 0 27W
Ḥijāz □, Si. Arabia .... 96 E3 24 0N 40 0 E
Hijo = Tagum, Phil. .... 81 H5 7 33N 125 53 E
Hiji, Japan .... 72 D3 33 22N 131 32 E
Hikari, Japan .... 72 D3 33 58N 131 58 E
Hiketa, Japan .... 72 C6 34 13N 134 24 E
Hikkaduwa, Sri Lanka .... 95 L5 6 8N 80 6 E
Hikmak, Ras el, Egypt .... 106 A2 31 15N 27 51 E
Hiko, U.S.A. 160 H11 37 32N 115 14W
Hikone, Japan .... 73 B8 35 15N 136 10 E
Hikurangi, Gisborne, N.Z. .... 130 E5 37 55 S 178 4 E
Hikurangi, Northland, N.Z. .... 130 B3 35 36 S 174 17 E
Hiland Park, U.S.A. 152 F4 30 12N 85 33W
Hilawng, Burma .... 90 E4 21 23N 93 48 E
Hildburghausen, Germany .... 30 E6 50 25N 10 42 E
Hildesheim, Germany .... 30 C5 52 9N 9 56 E
Hilðærendi, Iceland 11 D7 63 44N 19 57W
Hill ➤, Australia .... 125 F2 30 23 S 115 3 E
Hill City, Idaho, U.S.A. 158 E6 43 18N 115 3W
Hill City, Kans., U.S.A. 154 F5 39 22N 99 51W
Hill City, S. Dak., U.S.A. 154 D3 43 56N 103 35W
Hill Island L., Canada 143 A7 60 30N 109 50W
Hillaby, Mt., Barbados .... 165 g 13 12N 59 35W
Hillared, Sweden .... 17 G7 57 37N 13 10 E
Hillcrest, Barbados .... 165 g 13 13N 59 32W
Hillcrest Center, U.S.A. 161 K8 35 23N 118 57W
Hillegom, Neths. .... 24 B4 52 18N 4 35 E
Hillerød, Denmark .... 17 J6 55 56N 12 19 E
Hillerstorp, Sweden .... 17 G7 57 20N 13 52 E
Hilli, Bangla. .... 90 C2 25 17N 89 1 E
Hilliard, U.S.A. 152 E8 30 41N 81 55W
Hillsboro, Ga., U.S.A. 152 B6 33 11N 83 38W
Hillsboro, Kans., U.S.A. 154 F6 38 21N 97 12W
Hillsboro, Mo., U.S.A. 156 F6 38 14N 90 34W
Hillsboro, N. Dak., U.S.A. 154 B6 47 26N 97 3W
Hillsboro, N.H., U.S.A. 151 C13 43 7N 71 54W
Hillsboro, Ohio, U.S.A. 157 E13 39 12N 83 37W
Hillsboro, Oreg., U.S.A. 160 E4 45 31N 122 59W
Hillsboro, Tex., U.S.A. 155 J6 32 1N 97 8W
Hillsboro Canal, U.S.A. 153 J9 26 30N 80 15W
Hillsborough, Grenada 165 D7 12 28N 61 28W
Hillsborough Channel, Australia ... 126 J7 20 56 S 149 15 E
Hillsdale, Mich., U.S.A. 157 C12 41 56N 84 38W
Hillsdale, N.Y., U.S.A. 151 D11 42 11N 73 30W
Hillsport, Canada 140 C2 49 27N 85 34W
Hillston, Australia .... 129 B6 33 30 S 145 31 E
Hilltonia, U.S.A. 152 C8 32 53N 81 40W
Hilo, U.S.A. 145 D6 19 44N 155 5W
Hilo B., U.S.A. 145 D6 19 45N 155 5W
Hilton, U.S.A. 150 C7 43 17N 77 48W
Hilton Head Island, U.S.A. 153 C9 32 13N 80 45W
Hilvan, Turkey .... 101 D8 37 34N 38 58 E
Hilversum, Neths. .... 24 B5 52 14N 5 10 E
Hilzingen, Germany .... 33 A7 47 46N 8 47 E
Himachal Pradesh □, India .... 92 D7 31 30N 77 0 E
Himalaya, Asia .... 93 E11 29 0N 84 0 E
Himamaylan, Phil. .... 81 F4 10 6N 122 52 E
Himarë, Albania .... 50 F3 40 8N 19 43 E
Hime-Jima, Japan .... 72 D3 33 43N 131 40 E
Himeji, Japan .... 72 C6 34 50N 134 40 E
Himi, Japan .... 73 A8 36 50N 136 55 E
Himmerland, Denmark .... 17 H3 56 45N 9 30 E
Ḩimṣ, Syria .... 103 A5 34 40N 36 45 E
Ḩimṣ □, Syria .... 103 A6 34 30N 37 0 E
Hinatuan, Phil. .... 81 G6 8 23N 126 20 E
Hinatuan Passage, Phil. .... 81 G5 9 45N 125 47 E
Hinche, Haiti 165 C5 19 9N 72 1W
Hinchinbrook I., Australia .... 126 B4 18 20 S 146 15 E
Hinchinbrook Island Nat. Park △,
     Australia .... 126 B4 18 14 S 146 6 E
Hinckley, U.K. 21 E6 52 33N 1 22W
Hinckley, U.S.A. 154 B8 46 1N 92 56W
Hindaun, India .... 92 F7 26 44N 77 5 E
Hindmarsh, L., Australia .... 128 D4 36 5 S 141 55 E
Hindoli, India .... 94 D7 20 40N 85 10 E
Hinds, N.Z. .... 131 D6 43 59 S 171 36 E
Hindsholm, Denmark .... 17 J4 55 30N 10 40 E
Hindu Bagh, Pakistan .... 91 C2 30 56N 67 50 E
Hindu Kush, Asia .... 65 E5 36 0N 71 0 E
Hindupur, India .... 94 D3 13 49N 77 32 E
Hines Creek, Canada 142 B5 56 20N 118 40W
Hinesville, U.S.A. 152 D8 31 51N 81 36W
Hinganghat, India .... 94 D4 20 30N 78 52 E
Hingham, U.S.A. 158 B8 48 33N 110 25W
Hingir, India .... 93 J10 21 57N 83 41 E
Hingoli, India .... 94 E3 19 41N 77 15 E
Hinigaran, Phil. .... 81 F4 10 16N 122 50 E
Hinis, Turkey .... 101 C9 39 22N 41 43 E
Hinna = Imi, Ethiopia .... 107 F5 6 28N 42 10 E
Hinna, Norway .... 11 H4 56 55N 14 50 E
Hinnerup, Denmark .... 17 H4 56 16N 10 4 E
Hinnøya, Norway .... 14 B16 68 35N 15 50 E
Hino, Japan .... 73 C8 35 0N 136 15 E
Hinoba-an, Phil. .... 81 G4 9 35N 122 28 E
Hinojosa del Duque, Spain 43 G5 38 30N 5 9W
Hinokage, Japan .... 72 E3 32 39N 131 24 E
Hinsdale, U.S.A. 151 D12 42 47N 72 29W
Hinterrhein ➤, Switz. .... 33 C8 46 40N 9 25 E
Hinton, Canada 142 C5 53 26N 117 34W
Hinton, U.S.A. 148 G5 37 40N 80 54W
Hinuangan, Phil. .... 81 F5 10 25N 125 12 E
Hinzir Burnu, Turkey .... 100 D6 36 19N 35 46 E
Hirado, Japan .... 72 D1 33 22N 129 33 E
Hirado-Shima, Japan .... 72 D1 33 20N 129 30 E
Hirakata, Japan .... 73 C7 34 48N 135 40 E
Hirakud, India .... 94 D6 21 32N 83 51 E
Hirakud Dam, India .... 94 D6 21 32N 83 45 E
Hiran ➤, India .... 93 H8 23 6N 79 21 E
Hirapur, India .... 93 H8 24 22N 79 13 E
Hirata, Japan .... 72 B4 35 24N 132 49 E
Hiratsuka, Japan .... 73 B11 35 19N 139 21 E
Hirekerur, India .... 95 G2 14 28N 75 23 E
Hirfanlı Barajı, Turkey .... 100 C5 39 18N 33 31 E
Hirhafok, Algeria .... 111 D6 23 49N 5 45 E
Hiromi, Japan .... 72 D4 33 13N 132 36 E
Hiroo, Japan .... 70 C11 42 17N 143 19 E
Hirosaki, Japan .... 70 D10 40 34N 140 28 E
Hiroshima, Japan .... 72 C4 34 24N 132 30 E
Hiroshima □, Japan .... 72 C3 34 50N 133 0 E
Hirson, France .... 27 C11 49 55N 4 4 E
Hirschberg = Jelenia Góra, Poland 55 H2 50 50N 15 45 E
Hirson, France .... 27 C11 49 55N 4 4 E
Hirtshals, Denmark .... 17 G3 57 36N 9 57 E
Hisai, Japan .... 73 C8 34 40N 136 28 E
Hisar, India .... 92 E6 29 12N 75 45 E
Hisarcık, Turkey .... 49 B11 39 15N 29 14 E
Hisaria, Bulgaria .... 51 D8 42 30N 24 42 E
Hisb ➤, Iraq .... 96 D5 31 45N 44 17 E
Ḩismá, Si. Arabia .... 96 D3 28 30N 36 0 E
Ḩisn al 'Abr, Yemen .... 98 C4 16 8N 47 14 E
Hişn al 'Abr, Tajikistan .... 66 B1 68 33 E
Hispaniola, W. Indies 165 C5 19 0N 71 0W
Ḩīt, Iraq .... 101 F10 33 38N 42 49 E
Hita, Japan .... 72 D3 33 20N 130 58 E
Hitachi, Japan .... 73 A12 36 36N 140 39 E

Hitachi-Ōta, *Japan* .... **73 A12** 36 30N 140 30 E
Hitchin, *U.K.* **21 F7** 51 58N 0 16W
Hitoyoshi, *Japan* .... **72 E2** 32 13N 130 45 E
Hitra, *Norway* .... **18 A5** 63 30N 8 45 E
Hittisau, *Austria* .... **33 B9** 47 28N 9 58 E
Hitzacker, *Germany* .... **30 B7** 53 9N 11 2 E
Hiu, *Vanuatu* .... **133 C4** 13 10 S 166 35 E
Hiuchi-Nada, *Japan* .... **72 C5** 34 5N 133 20 E
Hixon, *Canada* **142 C4** 53 25N 122 35W
Ḥiyyon, N. →, *Israel* .... **103 E4** 30 25N 35 10 E
Hjalmar L., *Canada* **143 A7** 61 33N 109 25W
Hjälmaren, *Sweden* .... **16 E9** 59 18N 15 40 E
Hjältevad, *Sweden* .... **17 G9** 57 38N 15 20 E
Hjartdal, *Norway* .... **18 E5** 59 37N 8 41 E
Hjelmelandsvågen, *Norway* .... **18 E3** 59 14N 6 10 E
Hjelset, *Norway* .... **18 B4** 62 48N 7 30 E
Hjerkinn, *Norway* .... **18 B6** 62 13N 9 33 E
Hjo, *Sweden* .... **17 F8** 58 22N 14 17 E
Hjørring, *Denmark* .... **17 G3** 57 29N 9 59 E
Hjortkvarn, *Sweden* .... **17 F9** 58 54N 15 26 E
Hjukse, *Norway* .... **18 E6** 59 31N 9 19 E
Hkakabo Razi, *Burma* .... **90 B6** 28 17N 97 46 E
Hko-lam, *Burma* .... **90 E7** 21 7N 98 5 E
Hko-ut, *Burma* .... **90 E7** 20 58N 98 2 E
Hkyenhpa, *Burma* .... **90 B6** 27 43N 97 25 E
Hlaingbwe, *Burma* .... **90 G6** 17 8N 97 50 E
Hlinsko, *Czech Rep.* .... **34 B8** 49 45N 15 54 E
Hlobane, *S. Africa* .... **117 D5** 27 42 S 31 0 E
Hlohovec, *Slovak Rep.* .... **35 C10** 48 26N 17 49 E
Hlučín, *Czech Rep.* .... **35 B11** 49 54N 18 11 E
Hluhluwe, *S. Africa* .... **117 D5** 28 1 S 32 15 E
Hluhluwe Game Reserve △,
  S. Africa .... **117 C5** 22 10 S 32 5 E
Hlukhiv, *Ukraine* .... **59 G7** 51 40N 33 58 E
Hlwaze, *Burma* .... **90 F6** 18 54N 96 37 E
Hlyboka, *Ukraine* .... **59 H3** 48 5N 25 56 E
Hlybokaye, *Belarus* .... **58 E4** 55 10N 27 45 E
Hnappadalssýsla □, *Iceland* **11 C4** 64 50N 22 30W
Hnífsdalur, *Iceland* **11 A3** 66 7N 23 8W
Hnúšt'a, *Slovak Rep.* .... **35 C12** 48 35N 19 58 E
Ho, *Ghana* .... **113 D5** 6 37N 0 27 E
Ho Chi Minh City = Thanh Pho Ho
  Chi Minh, *Vietnam* .... **87 G6** 10 58N 106 40 E
Ho Thuong, *Vietnam* .... **86 C5** 19 32N 105 48 E
Hoa Binh, *Vietnam* .... **76 G5** 20 50N 105 20 E
Hoa Da, *Vietnam* .... **87 G7** 11 16N 108 40 E
Hoa Hiep, *Vietnam* .... **87 G5** 11 34N 105 51 E
Hoai Nhon, *Vietnam* .... **86 E7** 14 28N 109 1 E
Hoang Lien Son, *Vietnam* .... **76 F4** 22 0N 104 0 E
Hoanib →, *Namibia* .... **116 B2** 19 27 S 12 46 E
Hoare B., *Canada* **139 B13** 65 17N 62 30W
Hoarusib →, *Namibia* .... **127 G4** 42 50 S 147 21 E
Hobart, *Australia* .... **127 G4** 42 50 S 147 21 E
Hobart, *Ind., U.S.A.* **157 C9** 41 32N 87 15W
Hobart, *Okla., U.S.A.* **155 H5** 35 1N 99 6W
Hobbs, *U.S.A.* **155 J3** 32 42N 103 8W
Hobbs Coast, *Antarctica* .... **7 D14** 74 50 S 131 0W
Hobe Sound, *U.S.A.* **153 H9** 27 4N 80 8W
Hobo, *Colombia* **168 C2** 2 35N 75 30W
Hoboken, *Ga., U.S.A.* **152 D7** 31 11N 82 8W
Hoboken, *N.J., U.S.A.* **151 F10** 40 45N 74 4W
Hobro, *Denmark* .... **17 H3** 56 39N 9 46 E
Hoburgen, *Sweden* .... **17 H12** 56 55N 18 7 E
Hocalar, *Turkey* .... **49 C11** 38 36N 30 0 E
Hochdorf, *Switz.* .... **33 B6** 47 10N 8 17 E
Hochfeld, *Namibia* .... **116 C2** 21 28 S 17 58 E
Hochharz, Nationalpark △, *Germany* **30 D6** 51 48N 10 38 E
Hochschwab, *Austria* .... **33 D8** 47 35N 15 0 E
Hochstadt, *Germany* .... **31 F6** 49 42N 10 47 E
Hochtaunus, Naturpark △, *Germany* **31 E4** 50 20N 8 30 E
Hockenheim, *Germany* .... **31 F4** 49 19N 8 32 E
Hodaka-Dake, *Japan* .... **73 A9** 36 17N 137 39 E
Hodeida = Al Ḥudaydah, *Yemen* ... **98 D3** 14 50N 43 0 E
Hodgeville, *Canada* **143 C7** 50 7N 106 58W
Hodgson, *Canada* **143 C9** 51 13N 97 36W
Hódmezővásárhely, *Hungary* ...... **52 D5** 46 28N 20 22 E
Hodna, Chott el, *Algeria* .... **111 A6** 35 26N 4 43 E
Hodna, Monts du, *Algeria* .... **111 A5** 35 52N 4 42 E
Hodonín, *Czech Rep.* .... **35 C10** 48 50N 17 10 E
Hodzhambas, *Turkmenistan* .... **65 D2** 38 7N 65 0 E
Hœdic, Î. de, *France* **26 E4** 47 20N 2 52W
Hoek van Holland, *Neths.* .... **24 C4** 52 0N 4 7 E
Hoengsŏng, *S. Korea* .... **75 F14** 37 29N 127 59 E
Hoeryong, *N. Korea* .... **75 C15** 42 30N 129 45 E
Hoeyang, *N. Korea* .... **75 E14** 38 43N 127 36 E
Hof, *Germany* .... **31 E7** 50 19N 11 55 E
Hof, *Norður-Múlasýsla, Iceland* ... **11 B11** 66 53N 15 0W
Hof, *Suður-Múlasýsla, Iceland* **11 C12** 64 33N 14 40W
Hof, *Norway* .... **18 E7** 59 32N 10 5 E
Hoffell, *Iceland* **11 C11** 64 23N 15 20W
Hofgeismar, *Germany* .... **30 D5** 51 29N 9 23 E
Hofheim, *Germany* .... **31 E4** 50 5N 8 27 E
Hofmeyr, *S. Africa* .... **116 E4** 31 39 S 25 50 E
Höfn, *Iceland* **11 C11** 64 15N 15 13W
Hofors, *Sweden* .... **16 D10** 60 31N 16 15 E
Hofsjökull, *Iceland* **11 C8** 64 49N 18 48W
Hofsós, *Iceland* **11 B7** 65 53N 19 26W
Hōfu, *Japan* .... **72 C3** 34 3N 131 34 E
Hog Harbour, *Vanuatu* .... **133 E5** 15 8 S 167 6 E
Hogan Group, *Australia* .... **127 F4** 39 13 S 147 1 E
Höganäs, *Sweden* .... **17 H6** 56 12N 12 33 E
Hogansville, *U.S.A.* **152 B5** 33 10N 84 55W
Hogarth, Mt., *Australia* .... **126 C2** 21 48 S 136 58 E
Hogenakkal Falls, *India* .... **95 H3** 12 6N 77 50 E
Hoggar = Ahaggar, *Algeria* .... **111 D6** 23 0N 6 30 E
Högsäter, *Sweden* .... **17 F6** 58 38N 12 5 E
Högsby, *Sweden* .... **17 G10** 57 10N 16 1 E
Högsjö, *Sweden* .... **16 E9** 59 4N 15 44 E
Hogsty Reef, *Bahamas* **165 B5** 21 41N 73 48W
Hoh →, *U.S.A.* **160 C2** 47 45N 124 29W
Hohe Acht, *Germany* .... **31 E3** 50 22N 7 0 E
Hohe Tauern, *Austria* .... **34 D5** 47 11N 12 40 E
Hohe Tauern, Nationalpark △,
  Austria .... **34 D5** 47 15N 12 20 E
Hohe Venn, *Belgium* .... **24 D6** 50 30N 6 5 E
Hohenau, *Austria* .... **35 C9** 48 36N 16 55 E
Hohenems, *Austria* .... **34 D2** 47 22N 9 42 E
Hohenlohe Ebene, *Germany* ...... **31 F5** 49 8N 9 36 E
Hohenwald, *U.S.A.* **149 H2** 35 33N 87 33W
Hohenwestedt, *Germany* .... **30 A5** 54 5N 9 40 E
Hoher Freschen, *Austria* .... **33 B9** 47 18N 9 46 E
Hoher Rhön = Rhön, *Germany* ..... **30 E5** 50 24N 9 58 E
Hoher Vogelsberg, Naturpark △,
  Germany .... **30 D5** 51 45N 9 35 E
Hohes Venn-Eifel, Naturpark △,
  Europe .... **30 E2** 50 30N 6 10 E
Hohhot, *China* .... **74 D6** 40 52N 111 40 E
Hóhlakas, *Greece* .... **38 F11** 35 57N 27 53 E
Hohoe, *Ghana* .... **113 D5** 7 8N 0 32 E
Hoi An, *Vietnam* .... **86 E7** 15 30N 108 19 E
Hoi Xuan, *Vietnam* .... **76 C5** 20 25N 105 9 E
Hoisington, *U.S.A.* **154 F5** 38 31N 98 47W
Hojai, *India* .... **90 B4** 26 0N 92 54 E
Højer, *Denmark* .... **17 K2** 54 58N 8 42 E
Hōjō, *Japan* .... **72 C6** 33 58N 132 46 E
Hok, *Sweden* .... **17 G8** 57 31N 14 16 E
Hökensås, *Sweden* .... **17 G8** 58 0N 14 5 E
Hökerum, *Sweden* .... **17 G7** 57 51N 13 16 E
Hokianga Harbour, *N.Z.* .... **131 C5** 35 31 S 173 22 E
Hokitika, *N.Z.* .... **131 K3** 42 42 S 171 0 E
Hokkaidō □, *Japan* .... **70 C11** 43 30N 143 0 E
Hokksund, *Norway* .... **18 E6** 59 48N 9 54 E
Hol-Hol, *Djibouti* .... **107 E5** 11 20N 42 50 E

Hola Pristan, *Ukraine* .... **59 J7** 46 29N 32 32 E
Holalkere, *India* .... **95 G3** 14 2N 76 11 E
Hólar, *Iceland* **11 B7** 65 44N 19 8W
Holbæk, *Denmark* .... **17 J5** 55 43N 11 43 E
Holbrook, *Australia* .... **129 C7** 35 42 S 147 18 E
Holbrook, *U.S.A.* **159 J8** 34 54N 110 10W
Holden, *Mo., U.S.A.* **156 F3** 38 43N 94 0W
Holden, *Utah, U.S.A.* **158 G7** 39 6N 112 16W
Holdenville, *U.S.A.* **155 H6** 35 5N 96 24W
Holdich, *Argentina* .... **176 C3** 45 57 S 68 13W
Holdrege, *U.S.A.* **154 E5** 40 26N 99 23W
Hole-Narsipur, *India* .... **95 H3** 12 48N 76 16 E
Holešov, *Czech Rep.* .... **35 B10** 49 20N 17 35 E
Holetown, *Barbados* .... **165 g** 13 11N 59 38W
Holgate, *U.S.A.* **157 C12** 41 15N 84 8W
Holguín, *Cuba* **164 B4** 20 50N 76 20W
Holič, *Slovak Rep.* .... **35 C10** 48 49N 17 10 E
Holice, *Czech Rep.* .... **34 A8** 50 5N 16 0 E
Holiday, *U.S.A.* **153 G7** 28 13N 82 43W
Höljes, *Sweden* .... **16 D6** 60 50N 12 35 E
Hollabrunn, *Austria* .... **34 C9** 48 34N 16 5 E
Hollams Bird I., *Namibia* .... **116 C1** 24 40 S 14 30 E
Holland, *Mich., U.S.A.* **157 B10** 42 47N 86 7W
Holland, *N.Y., U.S.A.* **150 D6** 42 38N 78 32W
Hollandale, *U.S.A.* **155 J9** 33 10N 90 51W
Hollandia = Jayapura, *Indonesia* ... **83 B6** 2 28 S 140 38 E
Holley, *U.S.A.* **150 C6** 43 14N 78 2W
Hollfeld, *Germany* .... **31 F7** 49 56N 11 18 E
Hollidaysburg, *U.S.A.* **150 F6** 40 26N 78 24W
Hollis, *U.S.A.* **155 H5** 34 41N 99 55W
Hollister, *Calif., U.S.A.* **160 J5** 36 51N 121 24W
Hollister, *Idaho, U.S.A.* **158 E6** 42 21N 114 35W
Höllviken = Höllviksnäs, *Sweden* .. **17 J6** 55 26N 12 58 E
Höllviksnäs, *Sweden* .... **17 J6** 55 26N 12 58 E
Holly, *U.S.A.* **157 B13** 42 48N 83 38W
Holly Hill, *Fla., U.S.A.* **153 F8** 29 16N 81 3W
Holly Hill, *S.C., U.S.A.* **152 B9** 33 19N 80 25W
Holly Springs, *Ga., U.S.A.* **152 A5** 34 10N 84 30W
Holly Springs, *Miss., U.S.A.* **155 H10** 34 46N 89 27W
Hollywood, *U.S.A.* **153 J9** 26 1N 80 9W
Holman, *Canada* **138 A8** 70 44N 117 44W
Hólmavík, *Iceland* **11 B5** 65 42N 21 40W
Holmen, *Norway* .... **18 D7** 60 40N 10 22 E
Holmen, *U.S.A.* **154 D9** 43 58N 91 15W
Holmes →, *U.S.A.* **152 E4** 30 30N 85 50W
Holmes Beach, *U.S.A.* **153 H7** 27 31N 82 43W
Holmes Reefs, *Australia* .... **126 B4** 16 27 S 148 0 E
Holmestrand, *Norway* .... **18 E7** 59 31N 10 14 E
Holmsjö, *Sweden* .... **17 H9** 56 25N 15 32 E
Holmsjön, *Västernorrland, Sweden* **16 B10** 62 41N 16 23 E
Holmsjön, *Västernorrland, Sweden* **16 B9** 62 26N 15 20 E
Holmsland Klit, *Denmark* .... **17 J2** 56 0N 8 5 E
Holmsund, *Sweden* .... **14 E19** 63 41N 20 20 E
Holod, *Romania* .... **52 D7** 46 49N 22 8 E
Holopaw, *U.S.A.* **153 G8** 28 8N 81 5W
Holøydal, *Norway* .... **18 B8** 62 12N 11 27 E
Holroyd →, *Australia* .... **126 A3** 14 10 S 141 36 E
Holstebro, *Denmark* .... **17 H2** 56 22N 8 37 E
Holsteinische Schweiz, Naturpark △,
  Germany .... **30 A6** 54 8N 10 30 E
Holsteinsborg = Sisimiut, *Greenland* **10 D5** 66 40N 53 30W
Holsworthy, *U.K.* **21 G3** 50 48N 4 22W
Holt, *Iceland* .... **11 D7** 63 33N 19 48 E
Holt, *Fla., U.S.A.* **153 E3** 30 43N 86 45W
Holt, *Mich., U.S.A.* **157 B12** 42 39N 84 31W
Holton, *Canada* **141 B8** 54 31N 57 12W
Holton, *U.S.A.* **154 F7** 39 28N 95 44W
Holts Summit, *U.S.A.* **156 F4** 38 38N 92 7W
Holtville, *U.S.A.* **161 N11** 32 49N 115 23W
Holualoa, *U.S.A.* **145 D6** 19 37N 155 57W
Holum, *Norway* .... **18 F4** 58 6N 7 32 E
Holwerd, *Neths.* .... **24 A5** 53 22N 5 54 E
Holy Cross, *U.S.A.* **144 E8** 62 12N 159 46W
Holy I., *Angl., U.K.* **20 D3** 53 17N 4 37W
Holy I., *Northumb., U.K.* **20 B6** 55 40N 1 47W
Holyhead, *U.K.* **20 D3** 53 18N 4 38W
Holyoke, *Colo., U.S.A.* **154 E3** 40 35N 102 18W
Holyoke, *Mass., U.S.A.* **151 D12** 42 12N 72 37W
Holyrood, *Canada* **141 C9** 47 27N 53 8W
Holzkirchen, *Germany* .... **31 H7** 47 52N 11 42 E
Holzminden, *Germany* .... **30 D5** 51 50N 9 28 E
Homa Bay, *Kenya* .... **118 C3** 0 36 S 34 30 E
Homalin, *Burma* .... **90 C8** 24 55N 95 0 E
Homand, *Iran* .... **97 C8** 32 28N 59 37 E
Homathko →, *Canada* **142 C4** 51 0N 124 56W
Homberg, *Germany* .... **30 D5** 51 2N 9 25 E
Hombori, *Mali* **113 B4** 15 20N 1 38W
Homburg, *Germany* .... **31 F3** 49 28N 7 18 E
Home B., *Canada* **139 B13** 68 40N 67 10W
Home Hill, *Australia* .... **126 B4** 19 43 S 147 25 E
Home Reef, *Tonga* .... **133 P13** 18 59 S 174 47W
Homedale, *U.S.A.* **158 E5** 43 37N 116 56W
Homeland, *U.S.A.* **152 E7** 30 51N 82 1W
Homer, *Alaska, U.S.A.* **144 G10** 59 39N 151 33W
Homer, *Ill., U.S.A.* **157 D9** 40 4N 87 57W
Homer, *La., U.S.A.* **155 J8** 32 48N 93 4W
Homer, *Mich., U.S.A.* **157 B12** 42 9N 84 49W
Homer City, *U.S.A.* **150 F5** 40 32N 79 10W
Homert, Naturpark △, *Germany* ... **30 D4** 51 15N 8 0 E
Homerville, *U.S.A.* **152 D7** 31 2N 82 45W
Homestead, *Australia* .... **126 C4** 20 20 S 145 40 E
Homestead, *U.S.A.* **153 K9** 25 28N 80 29W
Homestead Nat. Monument of
  America △, *U.S.A.* **154 E6** 40 17N 96 50W
Homewood, *Calif., U.S.A.* **160 F6** 39 4N 120 8W
Homewood, *Ill., U.S.A.* **157 C9** 41 34N 87 40W
Hommelvik, *Norway* .... **18 A7** 63 25N 10 48 E
Hommersåk, *Norway* .... **18 F2** 58 56N 5 50 E
Homnabad, *India* .... **94 F3** 17 45N 77 11 E
Homoine, *Mozam.* .... **117 C6** 23 55 S 35 8 E
Homoljske Planina, *Serbia, Yug.* ... **50 B5** 44 10N 21 45 E
Homonhon I., *Phil.* .... **83 F6** 10 44N 125 43 E
Homorod, *Romania* .... **53 D10** 46 5N 25 15 E
Homosassa Springs, *U.S.A.* **153 G7** 28 48N 82 35W
Homs = Al Khums, *Libya* .... **108 B2** 32 40N 14 17 E
Homs = Ḥimṣ, *Syria* .... **103 A5** 34 40N 36 45 E
Homyel, *Belarus* .... **59 F6** 52 28N 31 0 E
Hon Chong, *Vietnam* .... **87 G5** 10 25N 104 30 E
Hon Me, *Vietnam* .... **86 C5** 19 23N 105 56 E
Honan = Henan □, *China* .... **74 H8** 34 0N 114 0 E
Honaunau, *U.S.A.* **145 D6** 19 26N 155 55W
Honavar, *India* .... **95 G2** 14 17N 74 27 E
Honaz, *Turkey* .... **49 D11** 37 46N 29 18 E
Honbetsu, *Japan* .... **70 C11** 43 7N 143 37 E
Honcut, *U.S.A.* **160 F5** 39 20N 121 32W
Honda, *Colombia* **168 B3** 5 12N 74 45W
Honda Bay, *Phil.* .... **81 G2** 9 53N 118 49 E
Hondarribia, *Spain* **40 B3** 43 22N 1 47W
Hondeklipbaai, *S. Africa* .... **116 E2** 30 19 S 17 17 E
Hondo, *Japan* .... **72 C2** 32 27N 130 12 E
Hondo, *U.S.A.* **155 L5** 29 21N 99 9W
Hondo →, *Belize* **163 D7** 18 25N 88 10W
Honduras ■, *Cent. Amer.* **164 D2** 14 40N 86 30W
Honduras, G. de, *Caribbean* **164 C2** 16 50N 87 0W
Hønefoss, *Norway* .... **18 D7** 60 10N 10 18 E
Honesdale, *U.S.A.* **151 E9** 41 34N 75 16W
Honey L., *U.S.A.* **160 E6** 40 15N 120 19W
Honfleur, *France* .... **26 C7** 49 25N 0 13 E
Høng, *Denmark* .... **17 J5** 55 31N 11 18 E
Hong →, *Vietnam* .... **76 F5** 22 0N 104 0 E
Hong Gai, *Vietnam* .... **76 G6** 20 57N 107 5 E
Hong He →, *China* .... **74 H8** 32 25N 115 35 E
Hong Hu, *China* .... **77 C9** 29 54N 113 0 E
Hong Kong □, *China* .... **69 G11** 22 11N 114 14 E
Hong Kong I., *China* .... **69 G11** 22 16N 114 12 E
Hong Kong International ✈ (HKG),
  China .... **69 G10** 22 19N 113 57 E
Honga, *Angola* .... **115 F3** 15 9 S 15 12 E
Hong'an, *China* .... **77 B10** 31 20N 114 40 E
Hongch'ŏn, *S. Korea* .... **75 F14** 37 44N 127 53 E
Honghai Wan, *China* .... **77 F10** 22 40N 115 0 E
Honghe, *China* .... **76 F4** 23 25N 102 25 E
Honghu, *China* .... **77 C9** 29 50N 113 30 E
Hongjiang, *China* .... **76 D7** 27 7N 109 59 E
Hongliu He →, *China* .... **74 F5** 38 0N 109 50 E
Hongor, *Mongolia* .... **74 B7** 45 45N 112 50 E
Hongsa, *Laos* .... **86 C3** 19 43N 101 20 E
Hongshui He →, *China* .... **76 F7** 23 48N 109 30 E
Hongsŏng, *S. Korea* .... **75 F14** 36 37N 126 38 E
Hongtong, *China* .... **74 F6** 36 16N 111 40 E
Honguedo, Détroit d', *Canada* **141 C7** 49 15N 64 0W
Hongwon, *N. Korea* .... **75 E14** 40 0N 127 56 E
Hongya, *China* .... **76 C4** 29 57N 103 22 E
Hongyuan, *China* .... **76 A4** 32 51N 102 40 E
Hongze Hu, *China* .... **77 H10** 33 15N 118 35 E
Honiara, *Solomon Is.* .... **133 M10** 9 27 S 159 57 E
Honiton, *U.K.* **21 G4** 50 47N 3 11W
Honjō, *Akita, Japan* .... **70 E10** 39 23N 140 3 E
Honjō, *Gumma, Japan* .... **73 A11** 36 14N 139 18 E
Honkawane, *Japan* .... **73 B10** 35 5N 138 5 E
Honkorâb, Ras, *Egypt* .... **106 C4** 24 35N 35 10 E
Honnali, *India* .... **95 G2** 14 15N 75 40 E
Honningsvåg, *Norway* .... **14 A21** 70 59N 25 59 E
Hönö, *Sweden* .... **17 G5** 57 41N 11 39 E
Honoka'a, *U.S.A.* **145 C6** 20 5N 155 28W
Honokahua, *U.S.A.* **145 C5** 21 0N 156 40W
Honolulu, *U.S.A.* **145 C5** 21 19N 157 52W
Honolulu International ✈ (HNL),
  U.S.A. **145 B4** 21 19N 157 55W
Honomu, *U.S.A.* **145 C6** 19 52N 155 7W
Honouliuli, *U.S.A.* **145 K13** 21 22N 158 2W
Honshū, *Japan* .... **72 G8** 36 0N 138 0 E
Hontoria del Pinar, *Spain* **40 D1** 41 50N 3 10W
Honuapo B., *U.S.A.* **145 D6** 19 5N 155 25W
Hood, I. = Española, I., *Ecuador* ... **172 a** 1 23 S 89 39W
Hood, Mt., *U.S.A.* **158 D3** 45 23N 121 42W
Hood, Pt., *Australia* .... **125 F2** 34 23 S 119 34 E
Hood Pt., *Papua N. G.* .... **132 F4** 10 4 S 147 45 E
Hood River, *U.S.A.* **158 D3** 45 43N 121 31W
Hoodsport, *U.S.A.* **160 C4** 47 24N 123 9W
Hooge, *Germany* .... **30 A4** 54 34N 8 33 E
Hoogeveen, *Neths.* .... **24 B6** 52 44N 6 28 E
Hoogezand-Sappemeer, *Neths.* .... **24 A6** 53 9N 6 45 E
Hooghly = Hugli →, *India* .... **93 H13** 21 56N 88 4 E
Hooghly-Chinsura = Chunchura,
  India .... **93 H13** 22 53N 88 27 E
Hook Hd., *Ireland* **23 D5** 52 7N 6 56W
Hook I., *Australia* .... **126 J6** 20 4 S 149 0 E
Hook of Holland = Hoek van
  Holland, *Neths.* .... **24 C4** 52 0N 4 7 E
Hooker, *U.S.A.* **155 G4** 36 52N 101 13W
Hooker Creek, *Australia* .... **124 C5** 18 23 S 130 38 E
Hoolehua, *U.S.A.* **145 C5** 21 10N 157 5W
Hoonah, *U.S.A.* **142 B1** 58 7N 135 27W
Hooper Bay, *U.S.A.* **144 F6** 61 32N 166 6W
Hoopeston, *U.S.A.* **157 D9** 40 28N 87 40W
Hoopstad, *S. Africa* .... **116 D4** 27 50 S 25 55 E
Hoorn, *Neths.* .... **24 B5** 52 38N 5 4 E
Hoover, *U.S.A.* **149 J2** 33 20N 86 11W
Hoover Dam, *U.S.A.* **161 K12** 36 1N 114 44W
Hooversville, *U.S.A.* **150 F6** 40 9N 78 55W
Hop Bottom, *U.S.A.* **151 E9** 41 42N 75 46W
Hopa, *Turkey* .... **101 B9** 41 28N 41 30 E
Hope, *Canada* **142 D4** 49 25N 121 25W
Hope, *Ariz., U.S.A.* **161 M13** 33 43N 113 42W
Hope, *Ark., U.S.A.* **155 J8** 33 40N 93 36W
Hope, *Ind., U.S.A.* **157 E11** 39 18N 85 46W
Hope, L., *S. Austral., Australia* .... **127 D2** 28 24 S 139 18 E
Hope, L., *W. Austral., Australia* .... **125 F3** 32 35 S 120 15 E
Hope, Pt., *U.S.A.* **144 B6** 68 21N 166 47W
Hope I., *Canada* **150 B4** 44 55N 80 11W
Hope Town, *Bahamas* **164 A4** 26 35N 76 57W
Hopedale, *Canada* **141 A7** 55 28N 60 13W
Hopedale, *U.S.A.* **151 D13** 42 8N 71 33W
Hopefield, *S. Africa* .... **116 E2** 33 3 S 18 22 E
Hopei = Hebei □, *China* .... **74 E9** 39 0N 116 0 E
Hopelchén, *Mexico* **163 D7** 19 46N 89 50W
Hopetoun, *Vic., Australia* .... **128 C5** 35 42 S 142 22 E
Hopetoun, *W. Austral., Australia* .. **125 F3** 33 57 S 120 7 E
Hopetown, *S. Africa* .... **116 D3** 29 34 S 24 3 E
Hopevale, *Australia* .... **126 B4** 15 16 S 145 20 E
Hopewell, *U.S.A.* **152 G7** 37 18N 77 17W
Hopfgarten, *Austria* .... **34 D5** 47 27N 12 10 E
Hopkins, *U.S.A.* .... **90 C6** 24 58N 96 30 E
Hopkins, *U.S.A.* **154 F7** 40 33N 94 49W
Hopkins →, *Australia* .... **128 D4** 24 15 S 128 35 E
Hopkinsville, *U.S.A.* **149 G2** 36 52N 87 29W
Hopland, *U.S.A.* **160 G3** 38 58N 123 7W
Hopong, *Burma* .... **90 E6** 20 47N 97 11 E
Hoquiam, *U.S.A.* **160 C3** 46 59N 123 53W
Hōrai, *Japan* .... **73 C9** 34 58N 137 32 E
Horasan, *Turkey* .... **101 B10** 40 3N 42 11 E
Horažd'ovice, *Czech Rep.* .... **34 B6** 49 19N 13 42 E
Horb, *Germany* .... **31 G4** 48 26N 8 47 E
Hörby, *Sweden* .... **17 J7** 55 51N 13 40 E
Horcajo de Santiago, *Spain* **40 F1** 39 50N 3 1W
Hordabø, *Norway* .... **18 D1** 60 42N 4 54 E
Hordaland □, *Norway* .... **18 D3** 60 25N 6 15 E
Horden Hills, *Australia* .... **124 D5** 20 15 S 130 0 E
Hordio, *Somali Rep.* .... **120 B4** 10 33N 51 6 E
Horezu, *Romania* .... **53 E8** 45 6N 24 0 E
Horgen, *Switz.* .... **33 B7** 47 15N 8 35 E
Horgoš, *Serbia, Yug.* .... **52 D4** 46 10N 20 0 E
Horice, *Czech Rep.* .... **34 A8** 50 21N 15 39 E
Horinger, *China* .... **74 D6** 40 28N 111 48 E
Horki, *Belarus* .... **58 E6** 54 17N 30 59 E
Horlick Mts., *Antarctica* .... **7 E15** 84 0 S 102 0W
Horlivka, *Ukraine* .... **59 H10** 48 19N 38 5 E
Hormak, *Iran* .... **97 D9** 29 58N 60 51 E
Hormoz, *Iran* .... **97 E7** 27 35N 55 0 E
Hormoz, Jaz-ye, *Iran* .... **97 E8** 27 8N 56 28 E
Hormozgān □, *Iran* .... **97 E8** 27 30N 56 0 E
Hormuz, Kūh-e, *Iran* .... **97 E7** 27 27N 55 10 E
Hormuz, Str. of, *The Gulf* .... **97 E8** 26 30N 56 30 E
Horn, *Austria* .... **34 C8** 48 39N 15 40 E
Horn, *Iceland* **11 C2** 66 28N 22 28W
Horn, *Sweden* .... **17 G9** 57 54N 15 51 E
Horn →, *Canada* **142 A5** 61 30N 118 1W
Horn, Cape = Hornos, C. de, *Chile* . **176 E3** 55 50 S 67 30W
Horn, Is., *Wall. & F. Is.* .... **123 C15** 14 16 S 178 6W
Horn Head, *Ireland* **23 A3** 55 14N 8 0W
Horn Mts., *Canada* **142 A5** 61 30N 118 1W
Hornachuelos, *Spain* **43 H5** 37 50N 5 14W
Hornavan, *Sweden* .... **14 C17** 66 15N 17 30 E
Hornbeck, *U.S.A.* **155 K8** 31 20N 93 24W
Hornbjarg, *Iceland* **11 A4** 66 28N 22 28W
Hornbrook, *U.S.A.* **158 F2** 41 55N 122 33W
Hornburg, *Germany* .... **30 C6** 52 2N 10 36 E
Horncastle, *U.K.* **20 D7** 53 13N 0 7W
Horndal, *Sweden* .... **16 D10** 60 18N 16 23 E
Hornell, *U.S.A.* **150 D7** 42 20N 77 40W
Hornell L., *Canada* **142 A5** 62 20N 119 25W
Hornepayne, *Canada* **140 C3** 49 14N 84 48W

Horní Planá, *Czech Rep.* .... **34 C7** 48 46N 14 2 E
Hornindal, *Norway* .... **18 C3** 61 58N 6 28 E
Hornings Mills, *Canada* **150 B4** 44 9N 80 12W
Hornitos, *U.S.A.* **160 H6** 37 30N 120 14W
Hornos, C. de, *Chile* .... **176 E3** 55 50 S 67 30W
Hornos Is., *Papua N. G.* .... **132 B4** 2 12 S 147 45 E
Hornoy-le-Bourg, *France* .... **27 C8** 49 50N 1 54 E
Hornsby, *Australia* .... **129 B9** 33 42 S 151 2 E
Hornsea, *U.K.* **20 D7** 53 55N 0 11W
Hornsjø, *Norway* .... **18 C7** 61 19N 10 38 E
Hornslandet, *Sweden* .... **16 C11** 61 35N 17 37 E
Hörnum, *Germany* .... **30 A4** 54 45N 8 18 E
Horobetsu = Noboribetsu, *Japan* .. **70 C10** 42 24N 141 6 E
Horodenka, *Ukraine* .... **59 H3** 48 41N 25 29 E
Horodnya, *Ukraine* .... **59 G6** 51 55N 31 33 E
Horodok, Khmelnytskyy, *Ukraine* .. **59 H4** 49 10N 26 34 E
Horodok, Lviv, *Ukraine* .... **59 H2** 49 46N 23 32 E
Horodyshche, *Ukraine* .... **59 H6** 49 17N 31 27 E
Horokhiv, *Ukraine* .... **59 G3** 50 30N 24 45 E
Horodnoye Youyi Qianqi, *China* ... **75 A12** 46 5N 122 3 E
Horqueta, *Paraguay* .... **174 A4** 23 15 S 56 55W
Horred, *Sweden* .... **17 G6** 57 22N 12 28 E
Horse Creek, *U.S.A.* **154 E3** 41 57N 105 10W
Horse I., *Canada* **143 C9** 53 20N 99 6W
Horse Is., *Canada* **141 B8** 50 15N 55 50W
Horsefly L., *Canada* **142 C4** 52 25N 121 0W
Horseheads, *U.S.A.* **150 D8** 42 10N 76 49W
Horsens, *Denmark* .... **17 J3** 55 52N 9 51 E
Horseshoe Bend Nat. Military
  Park △, *U.S.A.* **152 C4** 32 59N 85 44W
Horsham, *Australia* .... **128 D5** 36 44 S 142 13 E
Horsham, *U.K.* **21 F7** 51 4N 0 20W
Horšovský Týn, *Czech Rep.* .... **34 B5** 49 31N 12 58 E
Horta, *Azores* **9 d1** 38 32N 28 38W
Horten, *Norway* .... **18 E7** 59 25N 10 32 E
Hortense, *U.S.A.* **152 D8** 31 20N 81 57W
Horti, *India* .... **94 F2** 17 7N 75 47 E
Hortobágy →, *Hungary* .... **52 C6** 47 30N 21 6 E
Hortobágyi Nemzeti Park △,
  Hungary .... **52 C6** 47 36N 21 10 E
Horton, *Kans., U.S.A.* **154 F7** 39 40N 95 32W
Horton, *U.S.A.* **156 G2** 37 58N 94 22W
Horton →, *Canada* **138 B7** 69 56N 126 52W
Horw, *Switz.* .... **33 B6** 47 1N 8 19 E
Horwood L., *Canada* **140 C3** 48 5N 82 20W
Hosaina, *Ethiopia* .... **107 F4** 7 30N 37 47 E
Hosdurga, *India* .... **95 H3** 13 49N 76 17 E
Hose, Gunung-Gunung, *Malaysia* .. **108 D4** 2 5N 114 6 E
Hosenofabad, *Khuzestān, Iran* ..... **97 C6** 32 45N 48 20 E
Hoseynābād, *Kordestān, Iran* ...... **101 E12** 35 33N 47 8 E
Hosford, *U.S.A.* **152 E5** 30 24N 84 48W
Hoshangabad, *India* .... **92 H7** 22 45N 77 45 E
Hoshiarpur, *India* .... **92 D6** 31 30N 75 58 E
Hoskins, *Papua N. G.* .... **132 C6** 5 29 S 150 27 E
Hoskote, *India* .... **95 H3** 13 4N 77 48 E
Hospental, *Switz.* .... **33 C7** 46 37N 8 34 E
Hospet, *India* .... **95 G3** 15 15N 76 20 E
Hospitalet de l'Infant = l'Hospitalet de
  l'Infant, *Spain* .... **42 C6** 40 57N 0 58 E
Hosston, *U.S.A.* **155 J8** 32 53N 93 52W
Hoste, I., *Chile* .... **176 E3** 55 0 S 69 0W
Hostens, *France* **28 D3** 44 30N 0 40W
Hosur, *India* .... **95 H3** 12 45N 77 49 E
Hot, *Thailand* .... **86 C2** 18 8N 98 29 E
Hot Creek Range, *U.S.A.* **158 G6** 38 40N 116 20W
Hot Springs = Truth or
  Consequences, *U.S.A.* **159 K10** 33 8N 107 15W
Hot Springs, *Ark., U.S.A.* **155 H8** 34 31N 93 3W
Hot Springs, *S. Dak., U.S.A.* **154 D3** 43 26N 103 29W
Hot Springs Nat. Park △, *U.S.A.* .. **155 H8** 34 32N 93 4W
Hotagen, *Sweden* .... **14 E16** 63 50N 14 30 E
Hotan, *China* .... **68 C2** 37 25N 79 55 E
Hotazel, *S. Africa* .... **116 D3** 27 17 S 22 58 E
Hotchkiss, *U.S.A.* **159 G10** 38 48N 107 43W
Hotham, C., *Australia* .... **124 B5** 12 2 S 131 18 E
Hoti, *Indonesia* .... **83 B4** 3 0 S 130 22 E
Hoting, *Sweden* .... **14 D17** 64 8N 16 15 E
Hotolisht, *Albania* .... **50 A1** 41 10N 20 25 E
Hotte, Massif de la, *Haiti* **165 C5** 18 30N 73 45W
Hottentotsbaai, *Namibia* .... **116 D1** 26 8 S 14 59 E
Hou Hai, *China* .... **69 F10** 22 32N 113 56 E
Houailou, *N. Cal.* .... **133 U19** 21 17 S 165 38 E
Houat, Î. de, *France* **26 E4** 47 24N 2 58W
Houck, *U.S.A.* **158 J9** 35 18N 109 8W
Houei Sai, *Laos* .... **76 G3** 20 18N 100 26 E
Houeillès, *France* .... **28 D4** 44 12N 0 2 E
Houffalize, *Belgium* .... **24 D5** 50 8N 5 48 E
Houghton, *Mich., U.S.A.* **154 B10** 47 7N 88 34W
Houghton, *N.Y., U.S.A.* **150 D6** 42 25N 78 10W
Houghton L., *U.S.A.* **148 C3** 44 21N 84 44W
Houghton-le-Spring, *U.K.* **20 C6** 54 51N 1 28W
Houhora Heads, *N.Z.* .... **130 A2** 34 49 S 173 9 E
Houlton, *U.S.A.* **149 B12** 46 8N 67 51W
Houma, *U.S.A.* **155 L9** 29 36N 90 43W
Houmt Souk = Djerba, *Tunisia* .... **108 B2** 33 52N 10 51 E
Houndé, *Burkina Faso* **112 C4** 11 34N 3 31W
Hourtin, *France* **28 C2** 45 11N 1 4W
Hourtin-Carcans, Étang d', *France* . **28 C2** 45 10N 1 6W
Housatonic →, *U.S.A.* **151 E11** 41 10N 73 7W
Houston, *Canada* **142 C3** 54 25N 126 39W
Houston, *Fla., U.S.A.* **152 B5** 30 15N 82 54W
Houston, *Mo., U.S.A.* **156 G9** 37 22N 91 58W
Houston, *Tex., U.S.A.* **155 L7** 29 46N 95 22W
Hout →, *S. Africa* .... **117 C4** 23 4 S 29 36 E
Houtkraal, *S. Africa* .... **116 E3** 30 23 S 24 5 E
Houtman Abrolhos, *Australia* ..... **125 E1** 28 43 S 113 48 E
Hov, *Norway* .... **18 D7** 60 42N 10 20 E
Hovd, *Mongolia* .... **68 B4** 48 2N 91 37 E
Hovda, *Norway* .... **18 D4** 60 53N 9 11 E
Hovden, *Aust-Agder, Norway* ..... **18 E4** 59 33N 7 22 E
Hovden, *Sogn & Fjordane, Norway* **18 C1** 61 41N 4 52 E
Hove, *U.K.* **21 G7** 50 50N 0 10W
Hovenweep Nat. Monument △,
  U.S.A. **159 H9** 37 20N 109 0W
Hoveyzeh, *Iran* .... **18 D6** 60 38N 8 8 E
Hoveyzeh, *Iran* .... **97 D6** 31 27N 48 4 E
Hovgaard Ø, *Greenland* **10 B9** 79 25N 18 50W
Hovin, *Norway* .... **18 E6** 59 35N 9 9 E
Hovmantorp, *Sweden* .... **17 H9** 56 47N 15 7 E
Hövsgöl, *Mongolia* .... **74 C5** 43 37N 109 39 E
Hövsgöl Nuur, *Mongolia* .... **68 A5** 51 0N 100 30 E
Hovsta, *Sweden* .... **16 E9** 59 22N 15 15 E
Howakil, *Eritrea* .... **107 D5** 15 10N 40 16 E
Howar, Wadi →, *Sudan* .... **105 E11** 17 30N 27 8 E
Howard, *Australia* .... **127 D5** 25 16 S 152 32 E
Howard, *Pa., U.S.A.* **150 F7** 41 1N 77 40W
Howard, *S. Dak., U.S.A.* **154 C6** 44 1N 97 32W
Howe, *U.S.A.* **158 E7** 43 48N 113 0W
Howe, C., *Australia* .... **129 D9** 37 30 S 150 0 E
Howe I., *Canada* **151 B8** 44 16N 76 17W
Howell, *U.S.A.* **157 B13** 42 36N 83 56W
Howick, *N.Z.* .... **130 C3** 36 54 S 174 56 E
Howick, *S. Africa* .... **117 D5** 29 28 S 30 14 E
Howick Group, *Australia* .... **126 A4** 14 20 S 145 30 E
Howitt, L., *Australia* .... **127 D2** 27 40 S 138 40 E
Howland I., *Pac. Oc.* **134 G10** 0 48N 176 38W
Howlong, *Australia* .... **129 C7** 35 59 S 146 38 E
Howrah = Haora, *India* .... **93 H13** 22 37N 88 20 E
Howth Hd., *Ireland* **23 C5** 53 22N 6 4W
Höxter, *Germany* .... **30 D5** 51 46N 9 22 E
Hoy, *U.K.* **22 C5** 58 50N 3 15W
Hoya, *Germany* .... **30 C5** 52 49N 9 8 E
Høyanger, *Norway* .... **18 D3** 61 13N 6 4 E
Hoyerswerda, *Germany* .... **30 D10** 51 26N 14 14 E

Hoylake, *U.K.* **20 D4** 53 24N   3 10W
Hōyo-Kaikyō, *Japan* .... **72 D3** 33 20N 131 58 E
Hoyos, *Spain* **42 E4** 40 9N   6 45W
Hpa-an = Pa-an, *Burma* .... **90 G6** 16 51N 97 40 E
Hpawlum, *Burma* .... **90 B7** 27 12N 98 12 E
Hpettintha, *Burma* .... **90 C5** 24 14N 95 23 E
Hpizow, *Burma* .... **90 B7** 26 57N 98 24 E
Hpunan Pass, *India* .... **90 A6** 28 9N 97 20 E
Hradec Králové, *Czech Rep.* ... **34 A8** 50 15N 15 50 E
Hrádek, *Czech Rep.* .... **35 C9** 48 46N 16 16 E
Hranice, *Czech Rep.* .... **35 B10** 49 34N 17 45 E
Hrazdan, *Armenia* .... **61 K7** 40 30N 44 46 E
Hrebenka, *Ukraine* .... **59 G7** 50 9N 32 22 E
Hrífunes, *Iceland* **11 D8** 63 38N 18 30W
Hrísey, *Iceland* **11 B8** 66 0N 18 23W
Hrodna, *Belarus* .... **58 F2** 53 42N 23 52 E
Hrodzyanka, *Belarus* .... **58 F5** 53 31N 28 42 E
Hron →, *Slovak Rep.* .... **35 D11** 47 49N 18 45 E
Hrubieszów, *Poland* .... **55 H10** 50 49N 23 51 E
Hrubý Jeseník, *Czech Rep.* .... **35 A10** 50 5N 17 10 E
Hrvatska = Croatia ■, *Europe* . **45 C13** 45 20N 16 0 E
Hrymayliv, *Ukraine* .... **59 H4** 49 20N 26 5 E
Hsa-paw, *Burma* .... **90 F6** 19 1N 97 30 E
Hsenwi, *Burma* .... **90 D6** 23 22N 97 55 E
Hsi-hkip, *Burma* .... **90 E6** 20 25N 96 42 E
Hsiamen = Xiamen, *China* ...... **77 E12** 24 25N 118 4 E
Hsian = Xi'an, *China* .... **74 G5** 34 15N 109 0 E
Hsinchu, *Taiwan* .... **77 E13** 24 48N 120 58 E
Hsinhailien = Lianyungang, *China* **75 G10** 34 40N 119 11 E
Hsinying, *Taiwan* .... **77 F13** 23 18N 120 19 E
Hsipaw, *Burma* .... **90 D6** 22 37N 97 18 E
Hsopket, *Burma* .... **76 F2** 23 11N 98 26 E
Hsüchou = Xuzhou, *China* ...... **75 G9** 34 18N 117 10 E
Htawgaw, *Burma* .... **90 C7** 25 57N 98 23 E
Hu Xian, *China* .... **74 G5** 34 8N 108 42 E
Hua Hin, *Thailand* .... **86 F2** 12 34N 99 58 E
Hua Xian, *Henan, China* .... **74 G8** 35 30N 114 30 E
Hua Xian, *Shaanxi, China* ..... **74 G5** 34 30N 109 48 E
Hua'an, *China* .... **77 E11** 25 1N 117 32 E
Huab →, *Namibia* .... **116 B2** 20 52 S 13 25 E
Huacaya, *Bolivia* .... **173 E5** 20 45 S 63 43W
Huachacalla, *Bolivia* .... **172 D4** 18 45 S 68 17W
Huacheng, *China* .... **77 E10** 24 4N 115 37 E
Huachinera, *Mexico* **162 A3** 30 9N 108 55W
Huacho, *Peru* .... **172 C2** 11 10 S 77 35W
Huachón, *Peru* .... **172 C2** 10 35 S 76 0W
Huade, *China* .... **74 D7** 41 55N 113 59 E
Huadian, *China* .... **75 C14** 43 0N 126 40 E
Huadu, *China* .... **77 F9** 23 22N 113 12 E
Huai Had Nat. Park △, *Thailand* **86 D5** 16 52N 104 17 E
Huai He →, *China* .... **77 A12** 33 0N 118 30 E
Huai Nam Dang Nat. Park △, *Thailand* **86 C2** 19 30N 98 30 E
Huai Yot, *Thailand* .... **87 J2** 7 45N 99 37 E
Huai'an, *Hebei, China* .... **74 D8** 40 30N 114 20 E
Huai'an, *Jiangsu, China* ...... **75 H10** 33 30N 119 10 E
Huaibei, *China* .... **74 G9** 34 0N 116 48 E
Huaibin, *China* .... **77 A10** 32 32N 115 20 E
Huaide = Gongzhuling, *China* .. **75 C13** 43 30N 124 40 E
Huaidezhen, *China* .... **75 C13** 43 48N 124 50 E
Huaihua, *China* .... **76 D7** 27 32N 109 57 E
Huaiji, *China* .... **77 F9** 23 55N 112 12 E
Huainan, *China* .... **77 A11** 32 38N 116 58 E
Huaining, *China* .... **77 B11** 30 24N 116 40 E
Huairen, *China* .... **74 E7** 39 48N 113 20 E
Huairou, *China* .... **74 D9** 40 20N 116 35 E
Huaiyang, *China* .... **74 H8** 33 40N 114 52 E
Huaiyin, *China* .... **75 H10** 33 30N 119 2 E
Huaiyuan, *Anhui, China* .... **77 A11** 32 55N 117 10 E
Huaiyuan, *Guangxi Zhuangzu, China* **76 E7** 24 31N 108 22 E
Huajianzi, *China* .... **75 D13** 41 23N 125 20 E
Huajuapan de Leon, *Mexico* **163 D5** 17 50N 97 48W
Hualalai, *U.S.A.* **145 D6** 19 42N 155 52W
Hualapai Peak, *U.S.A.* **159 J7** 35 5N 113 54W
Hualien, *Taiwan* .... **77 E13** 24 0N 121 30 E
Huallaga →, *Peru* .... **172 B2** 5 15 S 75 30W
Huallanca, *Peru* .... **172 B2** 8 50 S 77 56W
Huamachuco, *Peru* .... **172 B2** 7 50 S 78 5W
Huambo, *Angola* .... **115 E3** 12 42 S 15 54 E
Huambo □, *Angola* .... **115 E3** 13 0 S 16 0 E
Huan Jiang →, *China* .... **74 G5** 34 28N 109 0 E
Huan Xian, *China* .... **74 F4** 36 33N 107 7 E
Huancabamba, *Peru* .... **172 B2** 5 10 S 79 15W
Huancane, *Peru* .... **172 D4** 15 10 S 69 44W
Huancapi, *Peru* .... **172 C3** 13 40 S 74 0W
Huancavelica, *Peru* .... **172 C2** 12 50 S 75 0W
Huancavelica □, *Peru* .... **172 C3** 13 0 S 75 0W
Huancayo, *Peru* .... **172 C2** 12 5 S 75 12W
Huanchaca, *Bolivia* .... **172 E4** 20 15 S 66 40W
Huanchaca, Serranía de, *Bolivia* **173 C5** 14 30 S 60 39W
Huang Hai = Yellow Sea, *China* **75 G12** 35 0N 123 0 E
Huang He →, *China* .... **75 F10** 37 55N 118 50 E
Huang Xian, *China* .... **75 F11** 37 38N 120 30 E
Huangchuan, *China* .... **77 A10** 32 15N 115 10 E
Huanggang, *China* .... **77 B10** 30 29N 114 52 E
Huangguoshu, *China* .... **76 E5** 26 0N 105 40 E
Huangling, *China* .... **74 G5** 35 34N 109 15 E
Huanglong, *China* .... **74 G5** 35 30N 109 59 E
Huanglongtan, *China* .... **77 A8** 32 40N 110 33 E
Huangmei, *China* .... **77 B10** 30 5N 115 56 E
Huangpi, *China* .... **77 B10** 30 50N 114 22 E
Huangping, *China* .... **76 D6** 26 52N 107 54 E
Huangshan, *China* .... **77 C12** 29 42N 118 25 E
Huangshi, *China* .... **77 B10** 30 10N 115 3 E
Huangsongdian, *China* .... **75 C14** 43 45N 127 25 E
Huangyan, *China* .... **77 C13** 28 38N 121 19 E
Huangyangsi, *China* .... **76 D8** 26 33N 111 39 E
Huaning, *China* .... **76 E4** 24 17N 102 56 E
Huanjiang, *China* .... **76 E7** 24 50N 108 18 E
Huanta, *Peru* .... **172 C3** 12 55 S 74 20W
Huantai, *China* .... **75 F9** 36 58N 117 56 E
Huánuco, *Peru* .... **172 B2** 9 55 S 76 15W
Huánuco □, *Peru* .... **172 B2** 9 55 S 76 14W
Huanuni, *Bolivia* .... **172 D4** 18 16 S 66 51W
Huanzo, Cordillera de, *Peru* .. **172 C3** 14 35 S 73 20W
Huaping, *China* .... **76 D3** 26 46N 101 25 E
Huara, *Chile* .... **172 C2** 19 59 S 69 47W
Huaral, *Peru* .... **172 C2** 11 32 S 77 11W
Huaraz, *Peru* .... **172 B2** 9 30 S 77 32W
Huari, *Peru* .... **172 B2** 9 55 S 77 14W
Huarmey, *Peru* .... **172 C2** 10 5 S 78 5W
Huarochiri, *Peru* .... **172 C2** 12 9 S 76 15W
Huarocondo, *Peru* .... **172 C3** 13 26 S 72 14W
Huarong, *China* .... **77 C9** 29 29N 112 30 E
Huascarán, *Peru* .... **172 B2** 9 7 S 77 36W
Huascarán, Nevado, *Peru* ...... **172 B2** 9 7 S 77 37W
Huasco, *Chile* .... **174 B1** 28 30 S 71 15W
Huasco →, *Chile* .... **174 B1** 28 27 S 71 13W
Huasna, *U.S.A.* **161 K6** 35 6N 120 24W
Huatabampo, *Mexico* **162 B3** 26 50N 109 50W
Huauchinango, *Mexico* **163 C5** 20 11N 98 3W
Huautla de Jiménez, *Mexico* ... **163 D5** 18 8N 96 51W
Huaxi, *China* .... **76 D6** 26 25N 106 40 E
Huay Namota, *Mexico* **162 C4** 21 56N 104 30W
Huayin, *China* .... **74 G6** 34 35N 110 5 E
Huayllay, *Peru* .... **172 C2** 11 3 S 76 21W
Huayuan, *China* .... **76 C7** 28 37N 109 29 E
Huayun, *China* .... **76 B6** 30 14N 106 40 E
Huazhou, *China* .... **77 G8** 21 33N 110 53 E
Hubbard, *Iowa, U.S.A.* **156 B3** 42 18N 93 18W
Hubbard, *Ohio, U.S.A.* **150 E4** 41 9N 80 34W
Hubbard, *Tex., U.S.A.* **155 K6** 31 51N 96 48W
Hubbart Pt., *Canada* **143 B10** 59 21N 94 41W

Hubei □, *China* .... **77 B9** 31 0N 112 0 E
Hubli, *India* .... **95 G2** 15 22N 75 15 E
Huch'ang, *N. Korea* .... **75 D14** 41 25N 127 2 E
Hucknall, *U.K.* **20 D6** 53 3N   1 13W
Huddersfield, *U.K.* **20 D6** 53 39N   1 47W
Hude, *Germany* .... **30 B4** 53 7N   8 26 E
Hudi, *Sudan* .... **106 D3** 17 43N 34 18 E
Hudiksvall, *Sweden* .... **16 C11** 61 43N 17 10 E
Hudson, *Canada* **140 B1** 50 6N 92 9W
Hudson, *Fla., U.S.A.* **153 G7** 28 22N 82 42W
Hudson, *Mass., U.S.A.* **151 D13** 42 23N 71 34W
Hudson, *Mich., U.S.A.* **157 C12** 41 51N 84 21W
Hudson, *N.Y., U.S.A.* **151 D11** 42 15N 73 46W
Hudson, *Wis., U.S.A.* **154 C8** 44 58N 92 45W
Hudson, *Wyo., U.S.A.* **158 E9** 42 54N 108 35W
Hudson →, *U.S.A.* **151 F10** 40 42N 74 2W
Hudson Bay, *Nunavut, Canada* .. **139 C11** 60 0N 86 0W
Hudson Bay, *Sask., Canada* **143 C8** 52 51N 102 23W
Hudson Falls, *U.S.A.* **151 C11** 43 18N 73 35W
Hudson Mts., *Antarctica* ...... **7 D16** 74 32 S 99 20W
Hudson Str., *Canada* **139 B13** 62 0N 70 0W
Hudson's Hope, *Canada* **142 B4** 56 0N 121 54W
Hudsonville, *U.S.A.* **157 B11** 42 52N 85 52W
Hue, *Vietnam* .... **86 D6** 16 30N 107 35 E
Huebra →, *Spain* **42 D4** 41 2N   6 48W
Huechucuicui, Pta., *Chile* .... **176 B2** 41 48 S 74 2W
Huedin, *Romania* .... **52 D8** 46 52N 23 2 E
Huehuetenango, *Guatemala* **164 C1** 15 20N 91 28W
Huejúcar, *Mexico* **162 C4** 22 21N 103 13W
Huélamo, *Spain* **40 E3** 40 17N   1 48W
Huelgoat, *France* **26 D3** 48 22N   3 46W
Huelma, *Spain* **43 H7** 37 39N   3 28W
Huelva, *Spain* **43 H4** 37 18N   6 57W
Huelva □, *Spain* **43 H4** 37 40N   7 0W
Huelva →, *Spain* **43 H5** 37 27N   6 0W
Huentelauquén, *Chile* .... **174 C1** 31 38 S 71 33W
Huerva-Overa, *Spain* **41 H3** 37 23N   1 57W
Huerta, Sa. de la, *Argentina* . **174 C2** 31 10 S 67 30W
Huertas, C. de las, *Spain* **41 G4** 38 21N   0 24W
Huerva →, *Spain* **40 C4** 41 39N   0 52W
Huesca, *Spain* **40 C4** 42 8N   0 25W
Huesca □, *Spain* .... **40 C4** 42 0N   0 1 E
Huéscar, *Spain* **41 H2** 37 44N   2 35W
Huetamo, *Mexico* **162 D4** 18 36N 100 54W
Huete, *Spain* **40 E2** 40 10N   2 43W
Huger, *U.S.A.* **152 B10** 33 6N 79 48W
Hugh →, *Australia* .... **126 D1** 25 1 S 134 1 E
Hughenden, *Australia* .... **126 C3** 20 52 S 144 10 E
Hughes, *Australia* .... **125 F4** 30 42 S 129 31 E
Hughes, *U.S.A.* **144 C9** 66 3N 154 15W
Hughesville, *U.S.A.* **151 E8** 41 14N 76 44W
Hugli →, *India* .... **93 J13** 21 56N 88 4 E
Hugo, *Colo., U.S.A.* **156 F3** 39 8N 103 28W
Hugo, *Okla., U.S.A.* **155 H7** 34 1N 95 31W
Hugoton, *U.S.A.* **155 G4** 37 11N 101 21W
Hui Xian = Huixian, *China* .... **74 G7** 35 27N 113 12 E
Hui Xian, *China* .... **74 H4** 33 50N 106 4 E
Hui'an, *China* .... **77 E12** 25 1N 118 43 E
Hui'anbu, *China* .... **74 F4** 37 28N 106 38 E
Huiarau Ra., *N.Z.* .... **130 E5** 38 45 S 176 55 E
Huichang, *China* .... **77 E10** 25 32N 115 45 E
Huichapán, *Mexico* **163 C5** 20 24N 99 40W
Huidong, *Guangdong, China* .... **77 F10** 22 58N 114 43 E
Huidong, *Sichuan, China* ...... **76 D4** 26 34N 102 35 E
Huifa →, *China* .... **75 C14** 43 0N 127 50 E
Huíla, *Angola* .... **115 F2** 15 4 S 13 32 E
Huíla □, *Angola* .... **115 E2** 14 0 S 15 0 E
Huila □, *Colombia* **168 C2** 2 30N 75 45W
Huila, Nevado del, *Colombia* .. **168 C2** 3 0N 76 0W
Huilai, *China* .... **77 F11** 23 0N 116 18 E
Huili, *China* .... **76 D4** 26 35N 102 17 E
Huimin, *China* .... **75 F9** 37 27N 117 28 E
Huinan, *China* .... **75 C14** 42 40N 126 2 E
Huinca Renancó, *Argentina* .... **174 C3** 34 51 S 64 22W
Huining, *China* .... **74 G3** 35 38N 105 0 E
Huinong, *China* .... **74 E4** 39 5N 106 35 E
Huiroa, *N.Z.* .... **130 F3** 39 15 S 174 30 E
Huisache, *Mexico* **162 C4** 22 55N 100 25W
Huishui, *China* .... **76 D6** 26 7N 106 38 E
Huisne →, *France* .... **26 E7** 47 59N   0 1 E
Huiting, *China* .... **74 G9** 34 5N 116 5 E
Huitong, *China* .... **76 D7** 26 51N 109 45 E
Huixian, *China* .... **74 G7** 35 27N 113 12 E
Huixtla, *Mexico* **163 D6** 15 9N 92 28W
Huize, *China* .... **76 D4** 26 24N 103 15 E
Huizhou, *China* .... **77 F10** 23 0N 114 23 E
Hukeri, *India* .... **95 F2** 16 14N 74 36 E
Hukou, *China* .... **77 C11** 29 45N 116 21 E
Hŭksan-chedo, *S. Korea* .... **75 G13** 34 40N 125 30 E
Hukuntsi, *Botswana* .... **116 C3** 23 58 S 21 45 E
Hula, *Papua N. G.* .... **132 F4** 10 5 S 147 43 E
Hulayfā', *Si. Arabia* .... **96 E4** 25 58N 40 45 E
Huld = Ulaanjirem, *Mongolia* .. **74 B3** 45 5N 105 30 E
Hulin He →, *China* .... **75 B12** 45 0N 122 10 E
Hull = Kingston upon Hull, *U.K.* **20 D7** 53 45N   0 21W
Hull, *Canada* **140 C4** 45 25N 75 44W
Hull →, *U.K.* **20 D7** 53 44N   0 20W
Hulst, *Neths.* .... **24 C4** 51 17N   4 2 E
Hultsfred, *Sweden* .... **17 G9** 57 30N 15 52 E
Hulun = Hailar, *China* .... **75 B6** 49 10N 119 38 E
Hulun Nur, *China* .... **69 B6** 49 0N 117 30 E
Hulyaypole, *Ukraine* .... **59 J9** 47 45N 36 21 E
Huma, Tanjung, *Malaysia* ...... **87 c** 5 29N 100 16 E
Humacao, *Puerto Rico* .... **165 d** 18 9N 65 50W
Humahuaca, *Argentina* .... **174 A2** 23 10 S 65 25W
Humaitá, *Brazil* .... **173 B5** 7 35 S 63 1W
Humaitá, *Paraguay* .... **174 B4** 27 2 S 58 31W
Humansdorp, *S. Africa* .... **116 E3** 34 2 S 24 46 E
Humansville, *U.S.A.* **156 G3** 37 48N 93 35W
Humara, J., *Sudan* .... **107 D3** 16 16N 30 59 E
Humbe, *Angola* .... **116 B1** 16 40 S 14 55 E
Humber →, *U.K.* **20 D7** 53 42N   0 7W
Humboldt, *Canada* **143 C7** 52 15N 105 9W
Humboldt, *Iowa, U.S.A.* **156 B2** 42 44N 94 13W
Humboldt, *Tenn., U.S.A.* **155 H10** 35 50N 88 55W
Humboldt →, *U.S.A.* **158 F4** 39 59N 118 36W
Humboldt, Massif du, *N. Cal.* . **133 U20** 21 53 S 166 25 E
Humboldt Gletscher = Sermersuaq, *Greenland* **10 B4** 79 30N 62 0W
Humboldt Mts., *N.Z.* .... **131 E3** 44 30 S 168 15 E
Hume, *U.S.A.* **160 J8** 36 48N 118 54W
Hume, L., *Australia* .... **129 D7** 36 0 S 147 5 E
Humen, *China* .... **69 F10** 22 50N 113 40 E
Humenné, *Slovak Rep.* .... **35 C14** 48 55N 21 50 E
Humeston, *U.S.A.* **156 D3** 40 52N 93 30W
Hummelsta, *Sweden* .... **16 E10** 59 34N 16 58 E
Hummelvik, *Norway* .... **18 A5** 63 39N   8 19 E
Humpata, *Angola* .... **115 F2** 15 2 S 13 24 E
Humphreys, Mt., *U.S.A.* **160 H8** 37 17N 118 40W
Humphreys Peak, *U.S.A.* **159 J8** 35 21N 111 41W
Humpolec, *Czech Rep.* .... **34 B8** 49 31N 15 20 E
Humptulips, *U.S.A.* **160 C3** 47 14N 123 57W
Humula, *Australia* .... **129 C7** 35 31 S 147 46 E
Hūn, *Libya* .... **108 C3** 29 2N 16 0 E
Hun Jiang →, *China* .... **75 D13** 40 50N 125 38 E
Húnaflói, *Iceland* **11 B6** 65 50N 20 50W
Hunan □, *China* .... **77 D9** 27 30N 112 0 E
Hunasavadhanahalli □, *Iceland* **11 B6** 65 30N 20 2 E
Hunchun, *China* .... **75 C16** 42 52N 130 28 E
Hundested, *Denmark* .... **17 J5** 55 58N 11 52 E
Hundewali, *Pakistan* .... **92 D5** 31 55N 72 38 E
Hundorp, *Norway* .... **18 D4** 61 33N   9 58 E
Hundred Islands Nat. Park △, *Phil.* **80 C3** 16 10N 120 2 E
Hundred Mile House, *Canada* ... **142 C4** 51 38N 121 18W

Hundvåg, *Norway* .... **18 E2** 59 0N   5 43 E
Hunedoara, *Romania* .... **52 E7** 45 40N 22 50 E
Hunedoara □, *Romania* .... **52 E7** 45 50N 22 54 E
Hünfeld, *Germany* .... **30 E5** 50 39N   9 46 E
Hung Yen, *Vietnam* .... **76 G6** 20 39N 106 4 E
Hunga Ha'apai, *Tonga* .... **133 Q13** 20 41 S 175 7W
Hungary ■, *Europe* .... **35 D12** 47 20N 19 20 E
Hungary, Plain of, *Europe* .... **12 F10** 47 0N 20 0 E
Hŭngnam, *N. Korea* .... **75 E14** 39 49N 127 45 E
Hungt'ou Hsü, *Taiwan* .... **77 G13** 22 0N 121 30 E
Hungund, *India* .... **95 F3** 16 4N 76 3 E
Huni Valley, *Ghana* **112 D4** 5 33N   1 56W
Hunneberg, *Sweden* .... **17 F6** 58 18N 12 30 E
Hunnebostrand, *Sweden* .... **17 F5** 58 27N 11 18 E
Hunsberge, *Namibia* .... **116 D2** 27 45 S 17 12 E
Hunstanton, *U.K.* .... **20 E8** 52 56N   0 29 E
Hunsur, *India* .... **95 H3** 12 16N 76 16 E
Hunter →, *Germany* .... **30 B4** 53 14N   8 28 E
Hunter, *N.Z.* .... **131 A6** 44 36 S 171 2 E
Hunter, *U.S.A.* **151 D10** 42 13N 74 13W
Hunter →, *Australia* .... **129 B9** 32 52 S 151 46 E
Hunter →, *N.Z.* .... **131 E4** 44 21 S 169 27 E
Hunter, C., *Solomon Is.* ...... **133 M10** 9 48 S 159 50 E
Hunter I., *Australia* .... **127 D3** 40 30 S 144 45 E
Hunter I., *Canada* **142 C3** 51 55N 128 0W
Hunter Mts., *N.Z.* .... **131 F2** 45 43 S 167 25 E
Hunter Ra., *Australia* .... **129 B9** 32 45 S 150 15 E
Hunters Road, *Zimbabwe* .... **119 F2** 19 9 S 29 49 E
Hunterville, *N.Z.* .... **130 F4** 39 56 S 175 35 E
Huntingburg, *U.S.A.* **157 F10** 38 18N 86 57W
Huntingdon, *Canada* **140 C5** 45 6N 74 10W
Huntingdon, *U.K.* **21 E7** 52 20N   0 11W
Huntingdon, *U.S.A.* **150 F6** 40 30N 78 1W
Huntington, *Ind., U.S.A.* **157 D11** 40 53N 85 30W
Huntington, *Oreg., U.S.A.* **158 D5** 44 21N 117 16W
Huntington, *Utah, U.S.A.* **158 G8** 39 20N 110 58W
Huntington, *W. Va., U.S.A.* ... **148 F4** 38 25N 82 27W
Huntington Beach, *U.S.A.* **161 M9** 33 40N 118 5W
Huntington Station, *U.S.A.* ... **151 F11** 40 52N 73 26W
Huntley, *U.S.A.* **157 B8** 42 10N 88 26W
Huntly, *N.Z.* .... **130 D4** 37 34 S 175 11 E
Huntly, *U.K.* **22 D6** 57 27N   2 47W
Huntsville, *Canada* **140 C4** 45 20N 79 14W
Huntsville, *Ala., U.S.A.* **149 H2** 34 44N 86 35W
Huntsville, *Mo., U.S.A.* **156 E4** 39 26N 92 33W
Huntsville, *Tex., U.S.A.* **155 K7** 30 43N 95 33W
Hunyani →, *Zimbabwe* .... **119 F3** 15 57 S 30 39 E
Hunyuan, *China* .... **74 E7** 39 42N 113 42 E
Hunza →, *India* .... **93 B6** 35 54N 74 20 E
Huo Xian = Huozhou, *China* .... **74 F6** 36 36N 111 42 E
Huo Pen., *Papua N. G.* .... **132 D4** 7 0 S 147 30 E
Huong Hoa, *Vietnam* .... **86 D6** 16 37N 106 45 E
Huong Khe, *Vietnam* .... **86 C5** 18 13N 105 41 E
Huonville, *Australia* .... **127 D4** 43 0 S 147 5 E
Huoqiu, *China* .... **77 A11** 32 20N 116 12 E
Huoshan, *Anhui, China* .... **77 B11** 32 28N 118 30 E
Huoshan, *Anhui, China* .... **77 B11** 31 25N 116 20 E
Huoshao Dao = Lü-Tao, *Taiwan* . **77 F13** 22 40N 121 30 E
Huozhou, *China* .... **74 F6** 36 36N 111 42 E
Hupeh = Hubei □, *China* .... **77 B9** 31 0N 112 0 E
Ḩūr, *Iran* .... **97 D8** 30 50N 57 7 E
Hurbanovo, *Slovak Rep.* .... **35 D11** 47 51N 18 11 E
Hurd, C., *Canada* **150 A3** 45 13N 81 44W
Hure Qi, *China* .... **75 C11** 42 45N 121 45 E
Hurezani, *Romania* .... **53 F8** 44 49N 23 40 E
Hurghada, *Egypt* .... **106 B3** 27 15N 33 50 E
Hurley, N. Mex., *U.S.A.* **159 K9** 32 42N 108 38W
Hurley, Wis., *U.S.A.* **154 B9** 46 27N 90 11W
Huron, *Calif., U.S.A.* **160 J6** 36 12N 120 6W
Huron, *Ohio, U.S.A.* **150 E2** 41 24N 82 33W
Huron, *S. Dak., U.S.A.* **156 C5** 44 22N 98 13W
Huron, L., *U.S.A.* **150 B2** 44 30N 82 40W
Hurricane, *U.S.A.* **159 H7** 37 11N 113 17W
Hurso, *Ethiopia* .... **107 F5** 9 35N 41 33 E
Hurstboro, *U.S.A.* **149 J3** 32 17N 85 25W
Hurunui →, *N.Z.* .... **131 C8** 42 54 S 173 18 E
Hurup, *Denmark* .... **17 H2** 56 46N   8 25 E
Húsafell, *Iceland* **11 C6** 64 42N 20 58W
Húsavík, *Iceland* **11 A9** 66 3N 17 21W
Ḩuşi, *Romania* .... **53 D13** 46 41N 28 7 E
Huskisson, *Australia* .... **129 C9** 35 2 S 150 41 E
Huskvarna, *Sweden* .... **17 G8** 57 47N 14 15 E
Huslia, *U.S.A.* **144 B8** 65 41N 156 24W
Husnes, *Norway* .... **18 E2** 59 52N   5 45 E
Hustad, *Norway* .... **18 B4** 62 57N   7 0 E
Hustadvika, *Norway* .... **18 A3** 63 0N   7 0 E
Hustontown, *U.S.A.* **150 F6** 40 3N 78 2W
Hustopeče, *Czech Rep.* .... **35 C9** 48 57N 16 43 E
Husum, *Germany* .... **30 A5** 54 28N   9 4 E
Husum, *Sweden* .... **16 A13** 63 21N 19 12 E
Hutchinson, *Minn., U.S.A.* **154 C7** 44 54N 94 22W
Hutchinson, *Kans., U.S.A.* **155 F6** 38 5N 97 56W
Huṯḥ, *Yemen* .... **98 C3** 16 41N 43 58 E
Hutjena, *Papua N. G.* .... **132 C8** 5 23 S 154 42 E
Hutsonville, *U.S.A.* **157 E9** 39 7N 87 40W
Hutte Sauvage, L. de la, *Canada* **141 A7** 56 15N 64 45W
Hüttenberg, *Austria* .... **34 E7** 46 56N 14 33 E
Hüttenberg Berge, Naturpark △, *Germany* **30 A5** 54 24N   9 40 E
Hutton, Mt., *Australia* .... **127 D4** 25 51 S 148 20 E
Huttwil, *Switz.* .... **32 B5** 47 7N   7 50 E
Huwun, *Ethiopia* .... **107 G5** 4 23N 40 6 E
Huy, *Belgium* .... **24 D5** 50 31N   5 15 E
Huzhou, *China* .... **77 B13** 30 51N 120 8 E
Huzurabad, *India* .... **94 E4** 18 12N 79 25 E
Huzurnagar, *India* .... **94 F4** 16 54N 79 53 E
Hvalpsund, *Denmark* .... **17 H3** 56 42N   9 11 E
Hvammsfjörður, *Iceland* **11 B4** 65 4N 22 5W
Hvammstangi, *Iceland* **11 B6** 65 24N 20 57W
Hvammur, Mýrasýsla, *Iceland* .. **11 B7** 64 51N 21 19 E
Hvammur, Skagafjarðarsýsla, *Iceland* **11 B7** 65 33N 19 51W
Hvannadalshnúkur, *Iceland* **11 C6** 64 1N 16 41W
Hvanneyri, *Iceland* **11 C5** 64 34N 21 36W
Hvar, *Croatia* .... **45 E13** 43 11N 16 28 E
Hvarski Kanal, *Croatia* .... **45 E13** 43 15N 16 35 E
Hveragerði, *Iceland* **11 C5** 64 0N 21 12W
Hvítá, *Iceland* **11 C5** 64 37N 19 50W
Hvítárvatn, *Iceland* **11 C7** 64 37N 19 50W
Hvittingfoss, *Norway* .... **18 E7** 59 29N 10 0 E
Hvolsvöllur, *Iceland* **11 D6** 63 45N 20 14W
Hwachŏn-chŏsuji, *S. Korea* .... **75 E14** 38 5N 127 50 E
Hwang Ho = Huang He →, *China* . **75 F10** 37 55N 118 50 E
Hwange, *Zimbabwe* .... **119 F2** 18 18 S 26 30 E
Hwange Nat. Park △, *Zimbabwe* . **116 B4** 19 0 S 26 30 E
Hwekum, *Burma* .... **90 D5** 22 39N 94 44 E
Hyaing, *Burma* .... **90 D5** 22 39N 94 44 E
Hyannis, *Mass., U.S.A.* **148 E10** 41 39N 70 17W
Hyannis, *Nebr., U.S.A.* **154 E4** 42 0N 101 46W
Hyargas Nuur, *Mongolia* .... **66 B4** 49 0N 93 0 E
Hybo, *Sweden* .... **16 C10** 61 49N 16 15 E
Hydaburg, *U.S.A.* **144 C2** 55 15N 132 50W
Hyde, *N.Z.* .... **131 F5** 45 18 S 170 16 E
Hyde Park, *Guyana* **169 B6** 6 30N 58 16W
Hyde Park, *U.S.A.* **151 E11** 41 47N 73 56W
Hyden, *Australia* .... **125 F2** 32 24 S 118 53 E
Hyder, *U.S.A.* **142 B2** 55 55N 130 5W
Hyderabad, *India* .... **94 F4** 17 22N 78 29 E
Hyderabad, *Pakistan* .... **91 D3** 25 23N 68 24 E
Hyen, *Norway* .... **18 C2** 61 44N   5 56 E
Hyères, *France* .... **29 E10** 43 8N   6 9 E

Hyères, Îs. d', *France* .... **29 F10** 43 0N   6 20 E
Hyesan, *N. Korea* .... **75 D15** 41 20N 128 10 E
Hyland →, *Canada* **142 B3** 59 52N 128 12W
Hylestad, *Norway* .... **18 E4** 59 6N   7 29 E
Hyllestad, *Norway* .... **18 C2** 61 10N   5 17 E
Hyltebruk, *Sweden* .... **17 H7** 56 59N 13 15 E
Hymia, *India* .... **93 C8** 33 40N 78 2 E
Hyndman Peak, *U.S.A.* **158 E6** 43 45N 114 8W
Hynnekleiv, *Norway* .... **18 F5** 58 36N   8 25 E
Hyōgo □, *Japan* .... **72 B6** 35 15N 134 50 E
Hyrra Banda, *C.A.R.* .... **114 A4** 5 58N 22 1 E
Hyrum, *U.S.A.* **158 F8** 41 38N 111 51W
Hysham, *U.S.A.* **158 C10** 46 18N 107 14W
Hythe, *U.K.* .... **21 F9** 51 4N   1 5 E
Hyūga, *Japan* .... **72 E3** 32 25N 131 35 E
Hyvinge = Hyvinkää, *Finland* .. **15 F21** 60 38N 24 50 E
Hyvinkää, *Finland* .... **15 F21** 60 38N 24 50 E

I

I-n-Azaoua, *Illizi, Algeria* .. **111 C6** 25 42N   6 54 E
I-n-Azaoua, *Tamanrasset, Algeria* **111 D6** 20 46N   7 32 E
I-n-Échaï, *Mali* **110 D4** 20 10N   2 5W
I-n-Gall, *Niger* .... **113 B6** 16 51N   7 1 E
I-n-Kelemet, *Algeria* .... **111 C6** 26 57N   5 47 E
I-n-Oudad, *Algeria* .... **111 D5** 20 17N   4 38 E
I-n-Ouzzal, *Algeria* .... **113 A5** 20 40N   2 35 E
I-n-Ouzzal, *Algeria* .... **111 D5** 20 41N   2 34 E
I-n-Tadreft, *Niger* .... **113 B6** 19 5N   6 38 E
Iabès, Erg, *Algeria* **111 C4** 27 30N   2 2W
Iablaniţa, *Romania* .... **52 F7** 44 57N 22 19 E
Iaco →, *Brazil* .... **172 B4** 9 3 S 68 34W
Iacobeni, *Romania* .... **53 C10** 47 25N 25 20 E
Iaçu, *Brazil* .... **171 D3** 12 45 S 40 13W
Iakora, *Madag.* .... **117 C8** 23 6 S 46 40 E
Ialibu, *Papua N. G.* .... **132 D2** 6 15 S 143 59 E
Ialomiţa □, *Romania* .... **53 F12** 44 30N 27 30 E
Ialomiţa →, *Romania* .... **53 F12** 44 42N 27 51 E
Ialoveni, *Moldova* .... **53 D13** 46 56N 28 47 E
Ialpug →, *Moldova* .... **53 E15** 45 41N 28 53 E
Iamonia L., *U.S.A.* **152 E5** 30 38N 84 14W
Ianca, *Romania* .... **53 E12** 45 6N 27 29 E
Iara, *Romania* .... **53 D8** 46 31N 23 35 E
Iarda, *Ethiopia* .... **107 E4** 11 9N 35 53 E
Iargara, *Moldova* .... **53 D13** 46 24N 28 23 E
Iaşi, *Romania* .... **53 C12** 47 10N 27 40 E
Iaşi □, *Romania* .... **53 C12** 47 20N 27 0 E
Iasmos, *Greece* .... **51 E9** 41 8N 25 1 E
Iauaretê, *Colombia* **168 C4** 0 36N 69 12W
Ib →, *India* .... **93 J10** 21 34N 83 48 E
Iba, *Phil.* .... **80 D2** 15 22N 120 0 E
Ibadan, *Nigeria* .... **113 C5** 7 22N   3 58 E
Ibagué, *Colombia* **168 C2** 4 20N 75 20W
Ibaití, *Brazil* .... **171 F1** 23 50 S 50 10W
Ibajay, *Phil.* .... **81 F4** 11 49N 122 10 E
Iballë, *Albania* .... **50 D4** 42 12N 20 2 E
Ibăneşti, *Botoşani, Romania* .. **53 B11** 48 4N 26 22 E
Ibăneşti, *Mureş, Romania* ..... **53 D9** 46 45N 24 57 E
Ibanshe, Dem. Rep. of the Congo **115 C4** 4 58 S 21 30 E
Ibar →, *Serbia, Yug.* .... **50 C4** 43 43N 20 45 E
Ibara, *Japan* .... **72 C5** 34 36N 133 28 E
Ibaraki, *Japan* .... **73 C7** 34 49N 135 34 E
Ibaraki □, *Japan* .... **73 A12** 36 10N 140 10 E
Ibarra, *Ecuador* **168 C2** 0 21N 78 7W
Ibb, *Yemen* .... **98 D4** 14 2N 44 10 E
Ibba, *Sudan* .... **107 G2** 4 49N 29 2 E
Ibba, Bahr el →, *Sudan* .... **107 F2** 5 30N 28 55 E
Ibbenbüren, *Germany* .... **30 C3** 52 16N   7 43 E
Ibeke Gembo, Dem. Rep. of the Congo **114 C3** 1 24 S 18 51 E
Ibembo, Dem. Rep. of the Congo . **118 B1** 2 35 S 23 35 E
Ibenga →, *Congo* .... **114 B3** 1 19 S 18 10 E
Ibera, L., *Argentina* .... **174 B4** 28 30 S 57 9W
Iberia, *Peru* **156 F4** 58 5N 92 18W
Iberian Peninsula, *Europe* **12 H5** 40 0N   5 0W
Iberville, *Canada* **140 C5** 45 19N 73 17W
Iberville, Lac d', *Canada* **140 B5** 55 55N 73 15W
Ibi, *Nigeria* .... **113 D6** 8 15N   9 44 E
Ibi, *Spain* **41 G4** 38 38N   0 34W
Ibiá, *Brazil* .... **171 E2** 19 30 S 46 30W
Ibiapaba, Sa. da, *Brazil* ..... **170 B3** 4 0 S 41 30W
Ibicaraí, *Brazil* .... **171 D4** 14 51 S 39 36W
Ibicuí, *Brazil* .... **171 E4** 14 51 S 39 59W
Ibicuy →, *Brazil* .... **171 B4** 29 25 S 56 47W
Ibicuy, *Argentina* .... **174 C4** 33 55 S 59 10W
Ibipetuba, *Brazil* .... **170 D3** 11 0 S 44 32W
Ibitiara, *Brazil* .... **171 D3** 12 39 S 42 13W
Ibiza = Eivissa, *Spain* .... **38 D1** 38 54N   1 26 E
Ibiza ✈ (IBZ), *Spain* .... **41 G6** 38 53N   1 22 E
Iblei, Monti, *Italy* .... **47 E7** 37 15N 14 45 E
Ibo, *Mozam.* .... **119 E5** 12 22 S 40 40 E
Ibonma, *Indonesia* .... **83 B4** 3 29 S 133 31 E
Ibotirama, *Brazil* .... **171 D3** 12 13 S 43 12W
Ibrāhīm →, *Lebanon* .... **103 A4** 34 4N 35 38 E
'Ibrī, *Oman* .... **97 F8** 23 14N 56 30 E
Ibriktepe, *Turkey* .... **51 F10** 41 0N 26 30 E
Ibu, *Indonesia* .... **83 A3** 1 35N 127 33 E
Ibuki-Sanchi, *Japan* .... **73 B8** 35 25N 136 18 E
Ibusuki, *Japan* .... **72 F2** 31 12N 130 40 E
Ica, *Peru* .... **172 C2** 14 0 S 75 48W
Ica □, *Peru* .... **172 C2** 14 30 S 75 30W
Iça →, *Brazil* .... **172 A4** 2 55 S 67 58W
Icabarú, *Venezuela* **169 C5** 4 20N 61 45W
Icabarú →, *Venezuela* **169 C5** 4 45N 62 15W
Icacos Pt., *Trin. & Tob.* **169 F9** 10 3N 61 57W
Içana, *Brazil* **168 C4** 0 21N 67 19W
Içana →, *Brazil* **168 C4** 0 26N 67 19W
Icatu, *Brazil* .... **170 B3** 2 46 S 44 4W
İçel = Mersin, *Turkey* .... **100 D6** 36 51N 34 36 E
Iceland ■, *Europe* **11 C8** 64 45N 19 0W
Ichalkaranji, *India* .... **94 F2** 16 40N 74 33 E
Ich'ang = Yichang, *China* ..... **77 B8** 30 40N 111 20 E
Ichchapuram, *India* .... **94 E7** 19 10N 84 40 E
Ichhawar, *India* .... **92 H7** 23 1N 77 1 E
Ichihara, *Japan* .... **73 B12** 35 28N 140 5 E
Ichikawa, *Japan* .... **73 B11** 35 44N 139 55 E
Ichilo →, *Bolivia* .... **173 D5** 15 57 S 64 50W
Ichinohe, *Japan* .... **70 D10** 40 13N 141 17 E
Ichinomiya, Gifu, *Japan* ...... **73 B8** 35 18N 136 48 E
Ichinomiya, Kumamoto, *Japan* .. **72 E3** 32 55N 131 5 E
Ichinoseki, *Japan* .... **70 E10** 38 55N 141 8 E
Ichkeul Nat. Park △, *Tunisia* . **108 A1** 37 5N   9 37 E
Ichnya, *Ukraine* .... **59 G7** 50 52N 32 24 E
Icht, *Morocco* **110 C3** 29 6N   8 54W
Icó, *Brazil* .... **170 C4** 6 24 S 38 51W
Icod, Canary Is. .... **115 D3** 0 52 S 16 43E
Icod, *Canary Is.* **9 e1** 28 22N 16 43W
Icoraci, *Brazil* .... **170 B2** 1 48 S 48 29W
Icy C., *U.S.A.* **144 A7** 70 20N 161 52W
Ida Grove, *U.S.A.* **154 D7** 42 21N 95 28W
Ida Valley, *Australia* .... **125 E3** 28 42 S 120 29 E
Idabel, *U.S.A.* **155 J7** 33 54N 94 50W
Idah, *Nigeria* .... **113 D6** 7 5N   6 40 E
Idaho □, *U.S.A.* **158 D6** 45 0N 115 0W
Idaho City, *U.S.A.* **158 E6** 43 50N 115 50W
Idaho Falls, *U.S.A.* **158 E7** 43 30N 112 2W
Idalia △, *Australia* .... **126 C3** 24 49 S 144 36 E
Idanha-a-Nova, *Portugal* **42 F3** 39 50N   7 15W
Idar-Oberstein, *Germany* ...... **31 F3** 49 43N   7 16 E

Iday, Niger .... 109 F2 14 54N 11 33 E
'Idd el Ghanam, Sudan .... 109 F4 11 30N 24 19 E
Iddan, Somali Rep. .... 120 C3 6 10N 48 55 E
Idelès, Algeria .... 111 D6 23 50N 5 53 E
Idfû, Egypt .... 106 C3 24 55N 32 49 E
Idhi Oros, Greece .... 39 E5 35 15N 24 45 E
Idhra, Greece .... 48 D5 37 20N 23 28 E
Idi, Indonesia .... 84 A1 5 2N 97 37 E
Idi Amin Dada, L. = Edward, L.,
  Africa .... 118 C2 0 25 S 29 40 E
Idiofa, Dem. Rep. of the Congo . 115 C3 4 55 S 19 42 E
Idkerberget, Sweden .... 16 D9 60 22N 15 15 E
Idku, Bahra el, Egypt .... 106 H7 31 18N 30 18 E
Idlib, Syria .... 100 E7 35 55N 36 36 E
Idre, Sweden .... 16 C6 61 52N 12 42 E
Idria, U.S.A. 160 J6 36 25N 120 41W
Idrija, Slovenia .... 45 C11 46 0N 14 5 E
Idritsa, Russia .... 58 D5 56 17N 28 53 E
Idro, Italy .... 33 E10 45 44N 10 29 E
Idutywa, S. Africa .... 117 E4 32 8 S 28 18 E
Ieper, Belgium .... 24 D2 50 51N 2 53 E
Ierápetra, Greece .... 39 F6 35 1N 25 44 E
Ierissós, Greece .... 50 F7 40 22N 23 52 E
Ierissoú Kólpos, Greece .... 50 F7 40 27N 23 57 E
Iernut, Romania .... 53 D9 46 27N 24 15 E
Ieshima-Shotō, Japan .... 72 C6 34 40N 134 32 E
Iesi, Italy .... 45 E10 43 31N 13 14 E
Iésolo, Italy .... 45 C9 45 32N 12 38 E
Ifach, Peñón de, Spain .... 41 G5 38 38N 0 5 E
'Ifâl, W. al →, Si. Arabia ...... 96 D2 28 7N 35 3 E
Ifanadiana, Madag. .... 117 C8 21 19 S 47 39 E
Ife, Nigeria .... 113 D5 7 30N 4 31 E
Iférouâne, Niger .... 113 B6 19 5N 8 24 E
Ifetesene, Algeria .... 111 C5 26 0N 4 33 E
Iffley, Australia .... 126 B3 18 53 S 141 12 E
Ifon, Nigeria .... 113 D6 6 58N 5 40 E
Iforas, Adrar des, Africa .... 111 D5 19 40N 1 40 E
Ifould, L., Australia .... 125 F5 30 52 S 132 6 E
Ifrane, Morocco 110 B3 33 33N 5 7W
Ifugao □, Phil. .... 80 C3 16 40N 121 10 E
Iga, Japan .... 73 C8 34 45N 136 10 E
Iganga, Uganda .... 118 B3 0 37N 33 28 E
Igara Paraná →, Colombia 168 D3 2 9S 71 47W
Igarapava, Brazil .... 171 F2 20 3 S 47 47W
Igarapé, Brazil 170 B2 1 4S 47 33W
Igarapé-Açu, Brazil 170 B2 1 4S 47 33W
Igarapé-Mirim, Brazil .... 170 B2 1 59 S 48 58W
Igarka, Russia .... 66 C9 67 30N 86 33 E
Igatimi, Paraguay .... 175 A4 24 5 S 55 40W
Igatpuri, India .... 94 E1 19 40N 73 35 E
Igbetti, Nigeria .... 113 D5 8 44N 4 8 E
Igbo-Ora, Nigeria .... 113 D5 7 29N 3 15 E
Igboho, Nigeria .... 113 D5 8 53N 3 50 E
Igbor, Nigeria .... 113 D6 7 27N 8 34 E
Iğdır, Turkey .... 101 C11 39 55N 44 2 E
Igelfors, Sweden .... 17 F9 58 52N 15 41 E
Iggesund, Sweden .... 16 C11 61 39N 17 10 E
Ighil Izane = Relizane, Algeria .. 111 A5 35 44N 0 31 E
Igiugig, U.S.A. 144 G9 59 20N 155 55W
Iglésias, Italy .... 46 C1 39 19N 8 32 E
Igli, Algeria 111 B4 30 25N 2 19W
Igloolik, Canada .... 64 D6 54 50N 56 26 E
Igloolik, Canada 139 B11 69 20N 81 49W
Iglulligaarjuk, Canada 139 B10 63 21N 90 42W
Iglulik = Igloolik, Canada 139 B11 69 20N 81 49W
'Igma, Gebel el, Egypt .... 106 B3 28 55N 34 0 E
Ignace, Canada 140 C1 49 30N 91 40W
Iğneada, Turkey .... 51 E11 41 52N 27 59 E
Iğneada Burnu, Turkey .... 41 E37 41 53N 28 2 E
Igoumenítsa, Greece .... 38 B10 39 32N 20 18 E
Igra, Russia .... 60 B11 57 33N 53 7 E
Iguaçu →, Brazil .... 175 B5 25 36 S 54 36W
Iguaçu, Cat. del, Brazil .... 175 B5 25 41 S 54 26W
Iguaçu Falls = Iguaçu, Cat. del,
  Brazil .... 175 B5 25 41 S 54 26W
Iguala, Mexico 163 D5 18 20N 99 40W
Igualada, Spain .... 40 D6 41 37N 1 37 E
Iguape, Brazil .... 171 F2 24 43 S 47 33W
Iguassu = Iguaçu →, Brazil ..... 175 B5 25 36 S 54 36W
Iguatu, Brazil .... 170 C4 6 20 S 39 18W
Iguéla, Gabon .... 114 C1 2 0 S 9 16 E
Iguéla, Lagune, Gabon .... 114 C2 1 48 S 9 16 E
Iguetti, Sebkhet, Mauritania .... 110 C3 25 N 5 50W
Iguig, Phil. .... 80 C3 17 45N 121 44 E
Iharana, Madag. .... 117 A9 13 25 S 50 0 E
Ihbulag, Mongolia .... 74 C4 43 11N 107 10 E
Iheya-Shima, Japan .... 71 L3 27 4N 127 58 E
Ihiala, Nigeria .... 113 D6 5 51N 6 55 E
Ihirene →, Algeria .... 111 D5 20 28N 4 37 E
Ihosy, Madag. .... 117 C8 22 24 S 46 8 E
Ihotry, Farihy, Madag. .... 117 C7 21 56 S 43 41 E
Ihu, Papua N. G. .... 132 D3 7 55 S 145 24 E
Ihugh, Nigeria .... 113 D6 7 9N 9 0 E
Ii, Finland .... 14 D21 65 19N 25 22 E
Ii-Shima, Japan .... 71 L3 26 43N 127 47 E
Iida, Japan .... 73 B9 35 35N 137 50 E
Iijoki →, Finland .... 14 D21 65 20N 25 20 E
Iisalmi, Finland .... 14 E22 63 32N 27 10 E
Iiyama, Japan .... 71 F9 36 51N 138 22 E
Iizuka, Japan .... 72 D2 33 38N 130 42 E
Ijâfene, Mauritania 110 D3 20 40N 8 0W
Ijebu-Igbo, Nigeria .... 113 D5 6 56N 4 1 E
Ijebu-Ode, Nigeria .... 113 D5 6 47N 3 58 E
Ijill, Sebkhet, Mauritania 110 D2 22 47N 12 53W
IJmuiden, Neths. .... 24 B4 52 28N 4 35 E
IJssel →, Neths. .... 24 B5 52 35N 5 50 E
IJsselmeer, Neths. .... 24 B5 52 45N 5 20 E
Ijuí, Brazil .... 175 B5 28 23 S 53 55W
Ijuí →, Brazil .... 175 B4 27 58 S 55 20W
Ijûin, Japan .... 72 F2 31 37N 130 24 E
Ik →, Russia .... 64 D4 55 41N 53 29 E
Ikalamavony, Madag. .... 117 C8 21 9 S 46 35 E
Ikale, Nigeria .... 113 D6 7 40N 5 37 E
Ikali, Dem. Rep. of the Congo ... 114 C4 2 2S 21 4 E
Ikaluktutiak, Canada 138 B9 69 10N 105 0W
Ikamatua, N.Z. .... 131 C6 42 16 S 171 41 E
Ikang, Nigeria .... 113 E6 4 49N 8 30 E
Ikara, Nigeria .... 113 C6 11 12N 8 15 E
Ikare, Nigeria .... 113 D6 7 32N 5 40 E
Ikaría, Greece .... 49 D8 37 35N 26 10 E
Ikast, Denmark .... 17 H3 56 8N 9 10 E
Ikeda, Japan .... 72 C5 34 1N 133 48 E
Ikeja, Nigeria .... 113 D5 6 36N 3 23 E
Ikela, Dem. Rep. of the Congo ... 114 C4 1 6S 23 6 E
Ikélemba, Congo .... 114 B3 1 12N 16 38 E
Ikélemba →, Dem. Rep. of
  the Congo .... 114 B3 0 7N 18 17 E
Ikengo, Dem. Rep. of the Congo . 114 C3 0 8S 18 8 E
Ikerre-Ekiti, Nigeria .... 113 D6 7 25N 5 19 E
Ikhtiman, Bulgaria .... 50 D7 42 27N 23 48 E
Iki, Japan .... 72 D1 33 45N 129 42 E
Iki-Kaikyō, Japan .... 72 D1 33 40N 129 45 E
Ikimba L., Tanzania .... 118 C3 1 30 S 31 20 E
Ikire, Nigeria .... 113 D5 7 23N 4 15 E
Ikitsuki-Shima, Japan .... 72 D1 33 23N 129 26 E
Ikizdere, Turkey .... 101 B9 40 46N 40 32 E
Iko, Nigeria .... 113 C5 5 16 0 E
Ikom, Nigeria .... 113 D6 6 0N 8 42 E
Ikomu, Dem. Rep. of the Congo . 114 C4 5 14 S 19 40 E
Ikongo, Madag. .... 117 C8 21 52 S 47 27 E
Ikopa →, Madag. .... 117 B8 16 45 S 46 40 E
Ikorongo Game Reserve △,
  Tanzania .... 118 C3 1 50 S 34 53 E
Ikot Ekpene, Nigeria .... 113 D6 5 12N 7 40 E
Ikungu, Tanzania .... 118 C3 1 33 S 33 42 E

Ikuno, Japan .... 72 B6 35 10N 134 48 E
Ikurun, Nigeria .... 113 D5 7 54N 4 40 E
Il-Kullana, Malta .... 38 F7 35 50N 14 24 E
Il-Muxnar, Malta .... 38 F8 35 51N 14 34 E
Ila, Dem. Rep. of the Congo .... 114 C4 2 53 S 21 7 E
Ila, Nigeria .... 113 D5 8 0N 4 39 E
Ilafer, Algeria .... 111 D5 21 40N 1 58 E
Ilagan, Phil. .... 80 C3 17 7N 121 53 E
Ilaka, Madag. .... 117 B8 19 33 S 48 52 E
Ilâm, Iran .... 101 F12 33 36N 46 36 E
Ilam, Nepal .... 93 F12 26 58N 87 58 E
Ilam □, Iran .... 96 C5 33 0N 47 0 E
Ilan, Taiwan .... 77 E13 24 45N 121 44 E
Ilanskiy, Russia .... 67 D10 56 14N 96 3 E
Ilanz, Switz. .... 33 C8 46 46N 9 12 E
Ilaro, Nigeria .... 113 D5 6 53N 3 3 E
Ilatane, Niger .... 113 B5 16 30N 4 45 E
Ilave, Peru 172 D4 16 5 69 40W
Iława, Poland .... 55 B6 53 36N 19 34 E
Ilayangudi, India .... 95 K4 9 34N 78 37 E
Ile →, Kazakhstan .... 66 E8 45 53N 77 10 E
Ile-à-la-Crosse, Canada 143 B7 55 27N 107 53W
Ile-à-la-Crosse, Lac, Canada 143 B7 55 40N 107 45W
Ile-de-France □, France .... 27 D9 49 0N 2 20 E
Ileanda, Romania .... 53 C8 47 20N 23 38 E
Ilebo, Dem. Rep. of the Congo .. 115 C4 4 17 S 20 55 E
Ilek, Russia .... 64 F4 51 32N 53 21 E
Ilek →, Russia .... 64 F4 51 30N 53 22 E
Iler, Algeria .... 111 D5 20 57N 3 21 E
Iler, O. →, Algeria .... 111 D5 20 59N 3 14 E
Ilero, Nigeria .... 113 D5 8 0N 3 20 E
Ilesha, Kwara, Nigeria .... 113 D5 8 57N 3 28 E
Ilesha, Oyo, Nigeria .... 113 D5 7 37N 4 40 E
Ilford, Canada 143 B9 56 4N 95 35W
Ilfracombe, Australia .... 126 C3 23 30 S 144 30 E
Ilfracombe, U.K. 21 F3 51 12N 4 8W
Ilgaz, Turkey .... 100 B5 40 55N 33 37 E
Ilgaz Dağları, Turkey .... 100 B5 41 10N 33 50 E
Ilgın, Turkey .... 100 C4 38 16N 31 55 E
Ilha, Pta. da, Azores 9 d1 38 25N 28 3W
Ilha de Moçambique, Mozam. ... 119 F5 15 4S 40 52 E
Ilha Grande, Brazil .... 169 D4 0 27 S 65 2W
Ilha Grande, B. da, Brazil 171 F3 23 9S 44 30W
Ílhavo, Portugal 42 E2 40 33N 8 43W
Ilhéus, Brazil .... 171 D4 14 49 S 39 2W
Ili = Ile →, Kazakhstan .... 66 E8 45 53N 77 10 E
Ilia, Romania .... 52 E7 45 57N 22 40 E
Ilía □, Greece .... 48 D3 37 45N 21 35 E
Iliamna, U.S.A. 144 G9 59 45N 154 55W
Iliamna L., U.S.A. 144 G9 59 30N 155 0W
Ilian, Mt., Phil. .... 81 F2 10 26N 119 33 E
Iliç, Turkey .... 101 C8 39 27N 38 33 E
Ilıca, Turkey .... 49 B9 39 52N 27 46 E
Ilich, Kazakhstan .... 65 C4 40 50N 68 27 E
Ilichevsk, Azerbaijan .... 101 C11 39 22N 45 5 E
Iligan, Phil. .... 81 G5 8 12N 124 13 E
Iligan Bay, Phil. .... 81 G5 8 25N 124 0 E
Iligan Pt., Phil. .... 80 B4 18 25N 122 25 E
Ilíkí, L., Greece .... 48 C5 38 24N 23 15 E
Ilin I., Phil. .... 80 E3 12 14N 121 5 E
Ilio Pt., U.S.A. 145 B4 21 13N 157 16W
Iliodhrómia, Greece .... 48 B5 39 12N 23 50 E
Ilion, U.S.A. 151 D9 43 1N 75 2W
Ilirska-Bistrica, Slovenia ...... 45 C11 45 34N 14 14 E
Ilkal, India .... 95 G3 15 57N 76 8 E
Ilkeston, U.K. 20 E6 52 58N 1 19W
Ilkley, U.K. 20 D6 53 56N 1 48W
Illampu = Ancohuma, Nevada,
  Bolivia .... 172 D4 16 0 S 68 50W
Illana B., Phil. .... 81 H4 7 35N 123 45 E
Illapel, Chile .... 174 C1 32 0 S 71 10W
Ille-et-Vilaine □, France 26 D5 48 10N 1 30W
Ille-sur-Têt, France .... 28 F6 42 40N 2 38 E
Illéla, Niger .... 113 C6 14 32N 5 20 E
Iller →, Germany .... 31 G5 48 23N 9 58 E
Illertissen, Germany .... 31 G6 48 12N 10 7 E
Illescas, Spain 42 E7 40 8N 3 51W
Illetas, Spain .... 38 B3 39 32N 2 35 E
Illichivsk, Ukraine .... 59 J6 46 20N 30 35 E
Illiers-Combray, France .... 26 D8 48 18N 1 15 E
Illimani, Nevado, Bolivia ...... 172 D4 16 30 S 67 50W
Illinois □, U.S.A. 156 D7 40 15N 89 30W
Illinois →, U.S.A. 156 F6 38 58N 90 28W
Illiopolis, U.S.A. 156 E7 39 51N 89 15W
Illium = Troy, Turkey .... 49 B8 39 57N 26 12 E
Illizi, Algeria .... 111 C6 26 31N 8 32 E
Illkirch-Graffenstaden, France .. 27 D14 48 34N 7 42 E
Íllora, Spain 43 H7 37 17N 3 53W
Illulissat, Greenland 10 D5 69 12N 51 10W
Ilm →, Germany .... 30 D7 51 6N 11 40 E
Ilmajoki, Finland .... 15 E20 62 44N 22 34 E
Ilmen, Ozero, Russia .... 58 C6 58 15N 31 10 E
Ilmenau, Germany .... 30 E6 50 41N 10 54 E
Ilo, Peru .... 172 D3 17 40 S 71 20W
Ilobu, Nigeria .... 113 D5 7 45N 4 25 E
Ilocos Norte □, Phil. .... 80 B3 18 10N 120 45 E
Ilocos Sur □, Phil. .... 80 C3 17 20N 120 35 E
Iloilo, Phil. .... 81 F4 10 45N 122 33 E
Iloilo □, Phil. .... 81 F4 11 0N 122 40 E
Ilora, Nigeria .... 113 D5 7 45N 3 50 E
Ilorin, Nigeria .... 113 D5 8 30N 4 35 E
Ilovatka, Russia .... 60 E7 50 30N 45 50 E
Ilovlya, Russia .... 61 F7 49 15N 44 2 E
Ilovlya →, Russia .... 61 F7 49 14N 44 0 E
Iłowa, Poland .... 55 G2 51 30N 15 10 E
Ilubabor □, Ethiopia .... 107 F4 7 25N 35 0 E
Ilva Mică, Romania .... 53 C9 47 17N 24 40 E
Ilwaco, U.S.A. 160 D2 46 19N 124 3W
Ilwaki, Indonesia .... 82 C3 7 55 S 126 30 E
Ilyichevsk = Illichivsk, Ukraine . 59 J6 46 20N 30 35 E
Iłża, Poland .... 55 G8 51 10N 21 15 E
Ilzanka →, Poland .... 55 G8 51 14N 21 48 E
Imabari, Japan .... 72 C5 34 4N 133 0 E
Imaichi, Japan .... 73 A11 36 43N 139 46 E
Imaloto →, Madag. .... 117 C8 23 27 S 45 13 E
Imamoğlu, Turkey .... 100 D6 37 15N 35 38 E
Imandra, Ozero, Russia .... 56 A5 67 30N 33 0 E
Imanombo, Madag. .... 117 C8 24 26 S 45 49 E
Imari, Japan .... 72 D1 33 15N 129 52 E
Imasa, Sudan .... 106 D4 18 0N 36 12 E
Imathía □, Greece .... 50 F6 40 30N 22 15 E
Imatra, Finland .... 58 B5 61 12N 28 48 E
Imazu, Japan .... 73 B8 35 24N 136 2 E
Imbabura □, Ecuador 168 C2 0 30N 78 45W
Imbaimadai, Guyana 169 B5 5 44N 60 17W
Imbil, Australia .... 127 D5 26 22 S 152 32 E
Imbonga, Dem. Rep. of the Congo 114 C3 0 43 S 19 44 E
Imdahane, Morocco 110 B3 32 8N 7 0W
Iménas, Mali .... 113 B5 16 20N 0 40 E
imeni 26 Bakinskikh Komissarov =
  Neftçala, Azerbaijan .... 97 B6 39 19N 49 12 E
imeni 26 Bakinskikh Komissarov,
  Turkmenistan .... 97 B7 39 22N 54 10 E
Imeri, Serra, Brazil 168 C4 0 50N 65 25W
Imerimandroso, Madag. .... 117 B8 17 26 S 48 35 E
Imesan, Mauritania 110 D1 22 5N 15 30W
Imese, Dem. Rep. of the Congo .. 114 B3 2 6N 18 9 E
Imi, Ethiopia .... 107 F5 6 28N 42 10 E
Imishli = Imişli, Azerbaijan .... 61 L9 39 55N 48 4 E
Imişli, Azerbaijan .... 61 L9 39 55N 48 4 E
Imitek, Morocco 110 C3 29 43N 8 10W
Imlay, U.S.A. 158 F4 40 40N 118 9W
Imlay City, U.S.A. 150 D1 43 2N 83 5W
Immenstadt, Germany .... 31 H6 47 33N 10 13 E
Immingham, U.K. 20 D7 53 37N 0 13W
Immokalee, U.S.A. 153 J8 26 25N 81 25W
Imo □, Nigeria .... 113 E6 5 30N 7 10 E
Imo →, Nigeria .... 113 E6 4 36N 7 35 E
Imola, Italy .... 45 D8 44 20N 11 42 E
Imotski, Croatia .... 45 E14 43 27N 17 12 E
Impé, Congo .... 114 C3 2 45 S 15 16 E
Imperatriz, Amazonas, Brazil ... 172 B4 5 18 S 67 11W
Imperatriz, Maranhão, Brazil ... 170 C2 5 30 S 47 29W
Impéria, Italy .... 44 E5 43 53N 8 3 E
Imperial, Canada 143 C7 51 21N 105 28W
Imperial, Peru 172 C2 13 4S 76 21W
Imperial, Calif., U.S.A. 161 N11 32 51N 115 34W
Imperial, Nebr., U.S.A. 154 E4 40 31N 101 39W
Imperial Beach, U.S.A. 161 N9 32 35N 117 8W
Imperial Dam, U.S.A. 161 N12 32 55N 114 25W
Imperial Reservoir, U.S.A. 161 N12 32 53N 114 28W
Imperial Valley, U.S.A. 161 N11 33 0N 115 30W
Imperieuse Reef, Australia ..... 124 C2 17 36 S 118 50 E
Impfondo, Congo .... 114 B3 1 40N 18 0 E
Imphal, India .... 90 C4 24 48N 93 56 E
Imphy, France .... 27 F10 46 55N 3 16 E
Impulo, Angola .... 115 E2 13 51 S 13 39 E
Imranlı, Turkey .... 101 C8 39 54N 38 7 E
Imroz = Gökçeada, Turkey ..... 51 F9 40 10N 25 50 E
Imroz, Turkey .... 51 F9 40 10N 25 55 E
Imst, Austria .... 34 D3 47 15N 10 44 E
Imuris, Mexico 162 A2 30 47N 110 52W
Imuruan B., Phil. .... 80 E3 10 40N 119 10 E
Imus, Phil. .... 80 D3 14 26N 120 56 E
In Akhmed, Mali 113 B4 19 49N 0 56W
In Alei, Mali 112 B4 17 42N 2 33W
In Amenas, Algeria .... 111 C6 28 5N 9 33 E
In Atei, Algeria .... 111 D6 20 33N 6 4 E
In Belbel, Algeria .... 111 C5 27 55N 1 12 E
In Dekkar, O. →, Algeria ...... 111 C6 27 12N 6 16 E
In Delimane, Mali .... 113 B5 15 52N 1 31 E
In Guezzam, Algeria .... 111 E6 19 37N 5 52 E
In Koufi, Mali .... 113 B5 19 11N 1 25 E
In Rhar, Algeria .... 111 C5 27 10N 1 59 E
In Salah, Algeria .... 111 C5 27 10N 2 32 E
In Tallak, Mali .... 113 B5 16 19N 3 15 E
In Tebezas, Mali .... 113 B5 17 49N 3 15 E
Ina, Japan .... 73 B9 35 50N 137 55 E
Ina, U.S.A. 157 F8 38 9N 88 54W
Ina-Bonchi, Japan .... 73 B9 35 45N 137 58 E
Inabanga, Phil. .... 81 F5 10 2N 124 4 E
Inagauan, Phil. .... 81 G2 9 33N 118 39 E
Inagua Nat. Park △, Bahamas ... 165 B5 21 5N 73 24W
Inajá, Brazil .... 170 C4 8 54 S 37 49W
Inambari →, Peru .... 172 C4 12 41 S 69 44W
Inamgahua, N.Z. .... 131 B6 41 52 S 171 59 E
Inanwatan, Indonesia .... 83 B4 2 8S 132 10 E
Inarajan, Guam .... 133 R15 13 16N 144 45 E
Inari, Finland .... 14 B22 68 54N 27 5 E
Inarijärvi, Finland .... 14 B22 69 0N 28 0 E
Inawashiro-Ko, Japan .... 70 F10 37 29N 140 6 E
Inazawa, Japan .... 73 B8 35 15N 136 47 E
Inbin, Burma .... 90 F5 18 6N 95 16 E
Inca, Spain .... 38 B3 39 43N 2 54 E
Inca de Oro, Chile .... 174 B2 26 45 S 69 54W
Incaguasi, Chile .... 174 B1 29 12 S 71 5W
Ince Burun, Turkey .... 100 A6 42 7N 34 56 E
Incekum Burnu, Turkey .... 100 D5 36 13N 33 57 E
Incesu, Turkey .... 100 C6 38 38N 35 11 E
Inch'ŏn, S. Korea .... 75 F14 37 27N 126 40 E
Incio = Cruz de Incio, Spain 42 C3 42 39N 7 21W
Incirliova, Turkey .... 49 D9 37 50N 27 41 E
Incline Village, U.S.A. 158 G4 39 10N 119 58W
Incomáti →, Mozam. .... 117 D5 25 46 S 32 43 E
Inda Silase, Ethiopia .... 107 E4 14 10N 38 15 E
Indal, Sweden .... 16 B11 62 35N 17 5 E
Indalsälven →, Sweden .... 16 B11 62 36N 17 30 E
Indaw, Burma .... 90 C6 24 15N 96 5 E
Indawgyi In, Burma .... 90 C6 25 8N 96 20 E
Indbir, Ethiopia .... 107 F4 8 7N 37 52 E
Indefatigable, I. = Santa Cruz, I.,
  Ecuador .... 172 a 0 38 S 90 23W
Independence, Calif., U.S.A. ... 160 J8 36 48N 118 12W
Independence, Iowa, U.S.A. 156 B5 42 28N 91 54W
Independence, Kans., U.S.A. ... 155 G7 37 14N 95 42W
Independence, Ky., U.S.A. 157 F12 38 57N 84 33W
Independence, Mo., U.S.A. 156 E2 39 6N 94 25W
Independence Fjord, Greenland . 10 A8 82 10N 29 0W
Independence Mts., U.S.A. 158 F5 41 20N 116 0W
Independência, Brazil .... 170 C3 5 23 S 40 19W
Independenţa, Romania .... 53 E12 45 25N 27 42 E
Index, U.S.A. 160 C5 47 50N 121 33W
Indi, India .... 94 F2 17 10N 75 58 E
India ■, Asia .... 89 C6 20 0N 78 0 E
Indialantic, U.S.A. 153 G9 28 6N 80 34W
Indian →, U.S.A. 153 G9 27 59N 80 34W
Indian Cabins, Canada 142 B5 59 52N 117 40W
Indian Harbour, Canada 141 B8 54 27N 57 13W
Indian Head, Canada 143 C8 50 30N 103 41W
Indian Lake, U.S.A. 151 C10 43 47N 74 16W
Indian Ocean .... 121 E6 5 0 S 75 0 E
Indian Rocks Beach, U.S.A. ... 153 H7 27 53N 82 51W
Indian Springs, U.S.A. 161 J11 36 35N 115 40W
Indiana, U.S.A. 150 F5 40 37N 79 9W
Indiana □, U.S.A. 157 E11 40 0N 86 0W
Indianapolis, U.S.A. 157 E10 39 46N 86 9W
Indianapolis International ✈ (IND),
  U.S.A. 157 E10 39 43N 86 17W
Indianola, Iowa, U.S.A. 156 C3 41 22N 93 34W
Indianola, Miss., U.S.A. 155 J9 33 27N 90 39W
Indiantown, U.S.A. 153 M9 27 1N 80 28W
Indiapora, Brazil .... 171 E1 19 57 S 50 17W
Indiga, Russia .... 56 A8 67 50N 48 50 E
Indigirka →, Russia .... 67 B15 70 48N 148 54 E
Indija, Serbia, Yug. .... 52 E5 45 6N 20 7 E
Indio, U.S.A. 161 M10 33 43N 116 13W
Indira Pt., India .... 95 L11 6 44N 93 49 E
Indispensable Strait, Solomon Is. 133 M11 9 0 S 160 30 E
Indo-China, Asia .... 62 H14 15 0N 102 0 E
Indonesia ■, Asia .... 78 E4 5 0 S 115 0 E
Indore, India .... 92 H6 22 42N 75 53 E
Indramayu, Indonesia .... 85 D3 6 20 S 108 19 E
Indravati →, India .... 93 K12 19 20N 80 20 E
Indre □, France .... 27 F8 46 50N 1 39 E
Indre →, France .... 26 E7 47 16N 0 11 E
Indre Arna, Norway .... 18 D2 60 26N 5 30 E
Indre-et-Loire □, France ...... 26 E7 47 20N 0 40 E
Indrio, U.S.A. 153 H9 27 31N 80 21W
Indulkana, Australia .... 127 D1 26 58 S 133 5 E
Indungo, Angola .... 117 C5 14 48 S 16 17 E
Indus →, Pakistan .... 91 G2 24 20N 67 47 E
Indus, Mouths of the, Pakistan .. 91 H3 24 0N 68 0 E
Industry, U.S.A. 156 D6 40 20N 90 36W
Inebolu, Turkey .... 100 B5 41 55N 33 40 E
Inecik, Turkey .... 51 F11 40 55N 27 14 E
İnegöl, Turkey .... 51 F13 40 5N 29 31 E
Inés, Mt., Argentina .... 176 F3 48 54 S 67 13W
Ineu, Romania .... 52 D6 46 26N 21 51 E
Inezgane, Morocco 110 B4 30 28N 9 29W
Infanta, Phil. .... 80 D3 14 45N 121 39 E
Infantes = Villanueva de los Infantes,
  Spain 43 G7 38 43N 3 1W
Infiernillo, Presa del, Mexico ... 162 D4 18 9N 102 0W

Infiesto, Spain 42 B5 43 21N 5 21W
Inga, Barrage d', Dem. Rep. of
  the Congo .... 115 D2 5 39 S 13 39 E
Ingabu, Burma .... 90 G5 17 37N 95 20 E
Inganda, Dem. Rep. of the Congo 114 C4 0 5S 20 57 E
Ingapirca, Ecuador .... 168 D2 2 38 S 78 56W
Ingelstad, Sweden .... 17 H8 56 45N 14 56 E
Ingende, Dem. Rep. of the Congo 114 C3 0 12 S 18 57 E
Ingeniero Jacobacci, Argentina . 176 B3 41 20 S 69 36W
Ingenio, Canary Is. 9 e1 27 55N 15 26W
Ingenio Santa Ana, Argentina .. 174 B2 27 25 S 65 40W
Ingersoll, Canada 140 D3 43 4N 80 55W
Ingham, Australia .... 126 B4 18 43 S 146 10 E
Ingichka, Uzbekistan .... 65 D2 39 47N 65 58 E
Ingleborough, U.K. 20 C5 54 10N 2 22W
Inglefield Land, Greenland 10 B4 78 30N 70 0W
Inglewood, Queens., Australia .. 127 D5 28 25 S 151 2 E
Inglewood, Vic., Australia ..... 128 D5 36 29 S 143 53 E
Inglewood, N.Z. .... 130 F3 39 9 S 174 14 E
Inglewood, U.S.A. 161 M8 33 58N 118 21W
Inglis, U.S.A. 153 F7 29 2N 82 40W
Ingolf Fjord, Greenland 10 A9 80 35N 17 30W
Ingólfshöfði, Iceland 14 E5 63 48N 16 39W
Ingolstadt, Germany .... 31 G7 48 46N 11 26 E
Ingomar, U.S.A. 158 C10 46 35N 107 23W
Ingonish, Canada 141 C7 46 42N 60 18W
Ingore, Guinea-Biss. 112 C1 12 24N 15 48W
Ingraj Bazar, India .... 93 G13 24 58N 88 10 E
Ingrid Christensen Coast, Antarctica
  .... 7 C6 69 30 S 76 0 E
Ingul = Inhul →, Ukraine ..... 59 J7 46 50N 32 0 E
Ingulec = Inhulec, Ukraine .... 59 J7 47 42N 33 14 E
Inguletz = Inhulets →, Ukraine . 59 J7 46 46N 32 47 E
Inguri = Enguri →, Georgia .... 61 J5 42 27N 41 38 E
Ingushetia □, Russia .... 61 J7 43 20N 44 50 E
Ingwavuma, S. Africa .... 117 D5 27 9 S 31 59 E
Inhaca, Mozam. .... 117 D5 26 1S 32 57 E
Inhafenga, Mozam. .... 117 C5 20 36 S 33 53 E
Inhambane, Mozam. .... 117 C6 23 54 S 35 30 E
Inhambane □, Mozam. .... 117 C5 22 30 S 34 20 E
Inhambupe, Brazil .... 171 D4 11 47 S 38 21W
Inhaminga, Mozam. .... 119 F4 18 26 S 35 0 E
Inharrime, Mozam. .... 117 C6 24 30 S 35 0 E
Inharrime →, Mozam. .... 117 C6 24 30 S 35 0 E
Inhisar, Turkey .... 49 A12 40 3N 30 23 E
Inhul →, Ukraine .... 59 J7 46 50N 32 0 E
Inhulec, Ukraine .... 59 J7 47 42N 33 14 E
Inhulets →, Ukraine .... 59 J7 46 46N 32 47 E
Inhuma, Brazil .... 170 C3 6 40 S 41 42W
Inhumas, Brazil .... 171 E2 16 22 S 49 30W
Iniesta, Spain 41 F3 39 27N 1 45W
Ining = Yining, China .... 66 E9 43 58N 81 10 E
Inini □, Fr. Guiana 169 C7 4 0N 53 0W
Inírida →, Colombia 168 C4 3 55N 67 52W
Inishbofin, Ireland 23 C1 53 37N 10 13W
Inisheer, Ireland 23 C2 53 3N 9 32W
Inishfree B., Ireland 23 A3 55 4N 8 23W
Inishkea North, Ireland 23 B1 54 9N 10 11W
Inishkea South, Ireland 23 B1 54 7N 10 12W
Inishmaan, Ireland 23 C2 53 5N 9 35W
Inishmore, Ireland 23 C2 53 8N 9 45W
Inishowen Pen., Ireland 23 A4 55 14N 7 15W
Inishshark, Ireland 23 C1 53 37N 10 16W
Inishturk, Ireland 23 C1 53 42N 10 7W
Inishvickillane, Ireland 23 D1 52 3N 10 37W
Injibara, Ethiopia .... 107 E4 10 59N 36 55 E
Injune, Australia .... 127 D4 25 53 S 148 32 E
Inklin →, Canada 142 B2 58 50N 133 10W
Inland Kaikoura Ra., N.Z. ..... 131 B8 41 59 S 173 41 E
Inland Sea = Setonaikai, Japan . 72 C5 34 20N 133 30 E
Inle L., Burma .... 90 E6 20 30N 96 58 E
Inlet, U.S.A. 151 C10 43 45N 74 48W
Inn →, Austria .... 34 C6 48 35N 13 28 E
Innamincka, Australia .... 127 D3 27 44 S 140 46 E
Innbygda, Norway .... 18 C9 61 19N 12 17 E
Inner Hebrides, U.K. 22 E2 57 0N 6 30W
Inner Mongolia = Nei Monggol
  Zizhiqu □, China .... 74 D7 42 0N 112 0 E
Inner Sound, U.K. 22 D3 57 30N 5 55W
Innerkip, Canada 150 C4 43 13N 80 42W
Innerkirchen, Switz. .... 32 C6 46 43N 8 14 E
Innes Nat. Park △, Australia ... 128 C2 35 52 S 136 53 E
Innetalling I., Canada 140 A4 56 0N 79 0W
Innisfail, Australia .... 126 B4 17 33 S 146 5 E
Innisfail, Canada 142 C6 52 0N 113 57W
In'noshima, Japan .... 72 C5 34 19N 133 10 E
Innsbruck, Austria .... 34 D4 47 16N 11 23 E
Innviertel, Austria .... 34 C6 48 15N 13 15 E
Innvik, Norway .... 18 C3 61 51N 6 37 E
Inny →, Ireland 23 C4 53 30N 7 50W
Ino, Japan .... 72 D5 33 33N 133 26 E
Inobonto, Indonesia .... 83 A2 0 52N 123 57 E
Inocência, Brazil .... 171 E1 19 55 S 51 48W
Inongo, Dem. Rep. of the Congo 114 C3 1 55 S 18 30 E
Inoni, Congo .... 114 C3 3 4S 15 39 E
İnönü, Turkey .... 49 B12 39 48N 30 9 E
Inoucdjouac = Inukjuak, Canada 139 C12 58 25N 78 15W
Inowrocław, Poland .... 55 F5 52 50N 18 12 E
Inpundong, N. Korea .... 75 D14 41 25N 126 34 E
Inquisivi, Bolivia .... 172 D4 16 50 S 67 10W
Ins, Switz. .... 32 B4 47 1N 7 7 E
Inscription, C., Australia ...... 125 E1 25 29 S 112 59 E
Insein, Burma .... 90 G6 16 50N 96 5 E
Insjön, Sweden .... 16 D9 60 41N 15 2 E
Ińsko, Poland .... 54 E2 53 25N 15 32 E
Insterberg = Chernyakhovsk, Russia 15 J19 54 36N 21 48 E
Insurăţei, Romania .... 53 F12 44 50N 27 40 E
Inta, Russia .... 56 A11 66 5N 60 8 E
Intendente Alvear, Argentina .. 174 D3 35 12 S 63 32W
Intepe, Turkey .... 49 A8 40 1N 26 18 E
Interlachen, U.S.A. 153 F8 29 37N 81 53W
Interlaken, Switz. .... 32 C5 46 41N 7 50 E
Interlaken, U.S.A. 151 D8 42 37N 76 44W
International Falls, U.S.A. 154 A8 48 36N 93 25W
Interview I., India .... 95 H11 12 55N 92 43 E
Intiyaco, Argentina .... 174 B3 28 43 S 60 5W
Intorsura Buzăului, Romania ... 53 E11 45 41N 26 2 E
Intragna, Switz. .... 33 D7 46 11N 8 42 E
Intutu, Peru .... 168 D3 3 32 S 74 48W
Inubō-Zaki, Japan .... 73 B12 35 42N 140 52 E
Inukjuak, Canada 139 C12 58 25N 78 15W
Inútil, B., Chile .... 176 D2 53 30 S 70 15W
Inuvik, Canada 138 B6 68 16N 133 40W
Inuyama, Japan .... 73 B8 35 23N 136 56 E
Inveraray, U.K. 22 E3 56 14N 5 5W
Inverbervie, U.K. 22 E6 56 51N 2 17W
Invercargill, N.Z. .... 131 G3 46 24 S 168 24 E
Inverclyde □, U.K. 22 F4 55 55N 4 49W
Inverell, Australia .... 127 D5 29 45 S 151 8 E
Invergordon, U.K. 22 D4 57 41N 4 10W
Inverleigh, Australia .... 128 E6 38 6S 144 3 E
Inverloch, Australia .... 128 F7 38 38 S 145 45 E
Invermere, Canada 142 C5 50 30N 116 2W
Inverness, Canada 141 C7 46 15N 61 19W
Inverness, U.K. 22 D4 57 29N 4 13W
Inverness, Ala., U.S.A. 153 E11 30 21N 85 17W
Inverness, Fla., U.S.A. 153 G7 28 50N 82 20W
Inverurie, U.K. 22 D6 57 17N 2 23W
Investigator Group, Australia .. 127 E1 34 45 S 134 20 E
Investigator Str., Australia .... 128 C2 35 30 S 137 0 E
Inya, Russia .... 66 D9 50 28N 86 37 E
Inyanga, Zimbabwe .... 119 F3 18 12 S 32 40 E
Inyangani, Zimbabwe .... 119 F3 18 5S 32 50 E
Inyantue, Zimbabwe .... 116 B4 18 33 S 26 39 E

Inyo Mts., *U.S.A.* **160 J9** 36 40N 118 0W
Inyokern, *U.S.A.* **161 K9** 35 39N 117 49W
Inywa, *Burma* **90 D6** 23 56N 96 17 E
Inza, *Russia* **60 D8** 53 55N 46 25 E
Inzer, *Russia* **64 D6** 54 14N 57 34 E
Inzhavino, *Russia* **60 D6** 52 22N 42 30 E
Inzia →, *Dem. Rep. of the Congo* **115 C3** 3 45 S 17 57 E
Iō-Jima, *Japan* **71 J5** 30 48N 130 18 E
Ioánnina, *Greece* **48 B2** 39 42N 20 47 E
Ioánnina □, *Greece* **48 B2** 39 39N 20 57 E
Iokea, *Papua N. G.* **132 E4** 8 25 S 146 16 E
Iola, *U.S.A.* **155 G7** 37 55N 95 24W
Ioma, *Papua N. G.* **132 E4** 8 19 S 147 52 E
Ion Corvin, *Romania* **53 F12** 44 7N 27 50 E
Iôna, *Angola* **115 F2** 16 54 S 12 34 E
Iona, *U.K.* **22 E2** 56 20N 6 25W
Iona, Parque Nac. do △, *Angola* **115 F2** 16 47 S 12 20 E
Ione, *U.S.A.* **160 G6** 38 21N 120 56W
Iongo, *Angola* **115 D3** 9 11 S 17 45 E
Ionia, *U.S.A.* **157 B11** 42 59N 85 4W
Ionian Is. = Iónioi Nísoi, *Greece* **39 B1** 38 40N 20 0 E
Ionian Sea, *Medit. S.* **12 H9** 37 30N 17 30 E
Iónioi Nísoi, *Greece* **39 B1** 38 40N 20 0 E
Iónioi Nísoi □, *Greece* **39 B2** 38 40N 20 0 E
Íos, *Greece* **49 E7** 36 41N 25 20 E
Iowa □, *U.S.A.* **156 C3** 42 18N 93 30W
Iowa →, *U.S.A.* **156 C5** 41 10N 91 1W
Iowa City, *U.S.A.* **156 C5** 41 40N 91 32W
Iowa Falls, *U.S.A.* **156 B3** 42 31N 93 16W
Iowa Park, *U.S.A.* **155 J5** 33 57N 98 40W
Ipala, *Tanzania* **118 C3** 4 30 S 32 52 E
Ipameri, *Brazil* **171 E2** 17 44 S 48 9W
Ipanema, *Brazil* **171 E3** 19 47 S 41 44W
Iparía, *Peru* **172 B3** 9 17 S 74 29W
Ipáti, *Greece* **48 C4** 38 52N 22 14 E
Ipatinga, *Brazil* **171 E3** 19 32 S 42 30W
Ipatovo, *Russia* **61 H6** 45 45N 42 50 E
Ipel' →, *Europe* **35 D11** 47 48N 18 53 E
Ipiales, *Colombia* **168 C2** 0 50N 77 37W
Ipiaú, *Brazil* **171 D4** 14 8 S 39 44W
Ipil, *Phil.* **81 H4** 7 47N 122 35 E
Ipin = Yibin, *China* **76 C5** 28 45N 104 32 E
Ipirá, *Brazil* **171 D4** 12 10 S 39 44W
Ipiranga, *Brazil* **168 D4** 3 13 S 65 57W
Ípiros □, *Greece* **48 B2** 39 30N 20 30 E
Ipixuna, *Brazil* **172 B3** 7 0 S 71 40W
Ipixuna →, *Amazonas, Brazil* **172 B3** 7 11 S 71 51W
Ipixuna →, *Amazonas, Brazil* **173 B5** 5 45 S 63 2W
Ipoh, *Malaysia* **87 K3** 4 35N 101 5 E
Iporá, *Brazil* **173 D7** 16 28 S 51 7W
Ipota, *Vanuatu* **133 H7** 18 52 S 169 20 E
Ippy, *C.A.R.* **114 A4** 6 5N 21 7 E
İpsala, *Turkey* **51 F10** 40 55N 26 23 E
Ipsárion, Óros, *Greece* **51 F8** 40 40N 24 40 E
Ipsos, *Greece* **38 B9** 39 43N 19 48 E
Ipswich, *Australia* **127 D5** 27 35 S 152 40 E
Ipswich, *U.K.* **21 E9** 52 4N 1 10 E
Ipswich, *Mass., U.S.A.* **151 D14** 42 41N 70 50W
Ipswich, *S. Dak., U.S.A.* **154 C5** 45 27N 99 2W
Ipu, *Brazil* **170 B3** 4 23 S 40 44W
Ipueiras, *Brazil* **170 B3** 4 33 S 40 43W
Ipupiara, *Brazil* **171 D3** 11 49 S 42 37W
Iqaluit, *Canada* **139 B13** 63 44N 68 31W
Iquique, *Chile* **172 E3** 20 19 S 70 5W
Iquitos, *Peru* **168 D3** 3 45 S 73 10W
Irabu-Jima, *Japan* **71 M2** 24 50N 125 10 E
Iracoubo, *Fr. Guiana* **169 B7** 5 30N 53 10W
Īrafshān, *Iran* **97 E9** 26 42N 61 56 E
Irahuan, *Phil.* **81 G2** 9 48N 118 41 E
Iráklia, *Kikládhes, Greece* **49 E7** 36 50N 25 28 E
Iráklia, *Sérrai, Greece* **50 E7** 41 10N 23 16 E
Iráklion, *Greece* **39 E6** 35 20N 25 12 E
Iráklion □, *Greece* **39 E6** 35 10N 25 10 E
Iraklion ✈ (HER), *Greece* **39 E6** 35 20N 25 15 E
Irako-Zaki, *Japan* **73 C9** 34 35N 137 1 E
Irala, *Paraguay* **175 B5** 25 55 S 54 35W
Iran ■, *Asia* **97 C7** 33 0N 53 0 E
Iran, Gunung-Gunung, *Malaysia* **85 B4** 2 20N 114 50 E
Iran, Plateau of, *Asia* **62 F9** 32 0N 55 0 E
Iran Ra. = Iran, Gunung-Gunung,
Malaysia **85 B4** 2 20N 114 50 E
Iranamadu Tank, *Sri Lanka* **95 K5** 9 23N 80 29 E
Īrānshahr, *Iran* **97 E9** 27 15N 60 40 E
Irapa, *Venezuela* **169 A5** 10 34N 62 35W
Irapuato, *Mexico* **162 C4** 20 40N 101 30W
Iraq ■, *Asia* **101 F10** 33 0N 44 0 E
Irarrar, O. →, *Mali* **111 E5** 20 0N 1 30 E
Irarrarene, *Algeria* **111 C6** 27 37N 7 30 E
Irati, *Brazil* **175 B5** 25 25 S 50 38W
Irbes saurums, *Latvia* **54 A9** 57 45N 22 5 E
Irbid, *Jordan* **103 C4** 32 35N 35 48 E
Irbid □, *Jordan* **103 C5** 32 15N 36 35 E
Irbit, *Russia* **64 C9** 57 41N 63 3 E
Irebu, *Dem. Rep. of the Congo* **114 C3** 0 40 S 17 46 E
Irecê, *Brazil* **170 D3** 11 18 S 41 52W
Iregua →, *Spain* **40 C7** 42 27N 2 24 E
Ireland ■, *Europe* **23 C4** 53 50N 7 52W
Ireland I., *Bermuda* **9 a** 32 19N 64 50W
Irele, *Nigeria* **113 D6** 7 40N 5 40 E
Iremel, Gora, *Russia* **64 D7** 54 33N 58 50 E
Ireng →, *Brazil* **169 C6** 3 33N 59 51W
Irerrer, O. →, *Algeria* **111 E6** 19 25N 5 47 E
Irgiz, Bolshaya →, *Russia* **60 D9** 52 10N 49 10 E
Irharrhar, O. →, *Algeria* **111 C6** 28 3N 6 15 E
Irherm, *Morocco* **110 B3** 30 7N 8 18W
Irhil M'Goun, *Morocco* **110 B3** 31 30N 6 28W
Irhyangdong, *N. Korea* **75 D15** 41 15N 129 30 E
Iri, *S. Korea* **75 G14** 35 59N 127 0 E
Irian Jaya □, *Indonesia* **83 B5** 4 0 S 137 0 E
Iriba, *Chad* **109 E4** 15 7N 22 15 E
Irié, *Guinea* **112 D3** 8 15N 9 10W
Iriga, *Phil.* **80 E4** 13 25N 123 25 E
Iriklinskiy, *Russia* **64 F7** 51 39N 58 38 E
Iriklinskoye Vdkhr., *Russia* **64 F7** 52 0N 59 0 E
Iringa, *Tanzania* **118 D4** 7 48 S 35 43 E
Iringa □, *Tanzania* **118 D4** 7 48 S 35 43 E
Irinjalakuda, *India* **95 J3** 10 21N 76 14 E
Iriomote-Jima, *Japan* **71 M1** 24 19N 123 48 E
Iriona, *Honduras* **164 C2** 15 57N 85 11W
Iriri →, *Brazil* **169 D7** 3 52 S 52 37W
Iriri Novo →, *Brazil* **173 B7** 8 46 S 53 22W
Irish Republic ■, *Europe* **23 C4** 53 50N 7 52W
Irish Sea, *U.K.* **19 E4** 53 38N 4 48W
Irkeshtam = Erkech-Tam,
Kyrgyzstan **65 D6** 39 41N 73 55 E
Irkutsk, *Russia* **67 D11** 52 18N 104 20 E
Irlığanlı, *Turkey* **49 D11** 37 53N 29 12 E
Irma, *Canada* **143 C6** 52 55N 111 14W
Irō-Zaki, *Japan* **73 C10** 34 36N 138 51 E
Iroise, Mer d', *France* **26 D2** 48 15N 4 45W
Iron Baron, *Australia* **128 B2** 32 58 S 137 11 E
Iron Gate = Portile de Fier, *Europe* **52 F7** 44 44N 22 30 E
Iron Knob, *Australia* **128 B2** 32 46 S 137 8 E
Iron Mountain, *U.S.A.* **148 C1** 45 49N 88 4W
Iron Range Nat. Park △, *Australia* **126 A3** 12 34 S 143 18 E
Iron River, *U.S.A.* **154 B10** 46 6N 88 39W
Irondequoit, *U.S.A.* **150 C7** 43 13N 77 35W
Ironton, *Mo., U.S.A.* **155 G9** 37 36N 90 38W
Ironton, *Ohio, U.S.A.* **148 F4** 38 32N 82 41W
Ironwood, *U.S.A.* **154 B9** 46 27N 90 9W
Ironwood Forest Nat. Monument ⌓,
U.S.A. **159 K8** 32 28N 111 36W
Iroquois, *Canada* **151 B9** 44 51N 75 19W
Iroquois →, *U.S.A.* **157 C9** 41 5N 87 49W
Iroquois Falls, *Canada* **140 C3** 48 46N 80 41W
Irosin, *Phil.* **80 E5** 12 42N 124 2 E
Irpin, *Ukraine* **59 G6** 50 30N 30 15 E
Irqieqa, Ras I-, *Malta* **38 F7** 35 56N 14 29 E
Irrara Cr. →, *Australia* **127 D4** 29 35 S 145 31 E
Irrawaddy □, *Burma* **90 G5** 17 0N 95 0 E
Irrawaddy →, *Burma* **90 G5** 15 50N 95 6 E
Irrawaddy, Mouths of the, *Burma* **90 H5** 15 30N 95 0 E
Irricana, *Canada* **142 C6** 51 19N 113 37W
Irsina, *Italy* **47 B9** 40 45N 16 14 E
Irtysh →, *Russia* **66 C7** 61 4N 68 52 E
Irumu, *Dem. Rep. of the Congo* **118 B2** 1 32N 29 53 E
Irún, *Spain* **40 B3** 43 20N 1 52W
Irunea = Pamplona, *Spain* **40 C3** 42 48N 1 38W
Irurzun, *Spain* **40 C3** 42 55N 1 50W
Irvine, *U.K.* **22 F4** 55 37N 4 41W
Irvine, *Calif., U.S.A.* **161 M9** 33 41N 117 46W
Irvine, *Ky., U.S.A.* **157 G13** 37 42N 83 58W
Irvinestown, *U.K.* **23 B4** 54 28N 7 39W
Irving, *U.S.A.* **155 J6** 32 49N 96 56W
Irvington, *U.S.A.* **157 G10** 37 53N 86 17W
Irvona, *U.S.A.* **150 F6** 40 46N 78 33W
Irwin →, *Australia* **125 E1** 29 15 S 114 54 E
Irwinton, *U.S.A.* **152 C6** 32 49N 83 10W
Irwinville, *U.S.A.* **152 D6** 31 39N 83 23W
Irymple, *Australia* **128 C5** 34 14 S 142 8 E
Is, Jebel, *Sudan* **106 C4** 22 3N 35 28 E
Is-sur-Tille, *France* **27 E12** 47 30N 5 8 E
Isa, *Nigeria* **113 C6** 13 14N 6 24 E
Isa Khel, *Pakistan* **92 C4** 32 41N 71 17 E
Isaac →, *Australia* **126 C4** 22 55 S 149 20 E
Isabel, *U.S.A.* **154 C4** 45 24N 101 26W
Isabela, *Basilan, Phil.* **81 H3** 6 40N 121 59 E
Isabela, *Negros, Phil.* **81 F4** 10 12N 122 59 E
Isabela, *Puerto Rico* **165 d** 18 30N 67 2W
Isabela □, *Phil.* **80 C4** 17 0N 122 0 E
Isabela, Canal, *Ecuador* **172 a** 0 20 S 90 55W
Isabela, I., *Ecuador* **172 a** 0 30 S 91 4W
Isabela, I., *Mexico* **162 C3** 21 51N 105 55W
Isabelia, Cord., *Nic.* **164 D2** 13 30N 85 25W
Isabella Ra., *Australia* **124 D3** 21 0 S 121 4 E
Isaccea, *Romania* **53 E13** 45 16N 28 28 E
Ísafjarðardjúp, *Iceland* **11 A3** 66 10N 23 0W
Ísafjarðarsýsla □, *Iceland* **11 B3** 66 0N 23 0W
Ísafjörður, *Iceland* **11 A3** 66 5N 23 9W
Isagarh, *India* **92 G7** 24 48N 77 51 E
Isahaya, *Japan* **72 E2** 32 52N 130 2 E
Isaka, *Dem. Rep. of the Congo* **114 C3** 2 33 S 18 54 E
Isaka, *Tanzania* **118 C3** 3 56 S 32 59 E
Isakly, *Russia* **60 C10** 54 8N 51 32 E
Işalniţa, *Romania* **53 F8** 44 24N 23 44 E
Isalo, Parc Nat. de l' △, *Madag.* **117 C8** 22 23 S 45 16 E
Isan →, *India* **93 F9** 26 51N 80 7 E
Isana = Içana →, *Brazil* **168 C4** 0 26N 67 19W
Isandja, *Dem. Rep. of the Congo* **114 C4** 2 59 S 21 59 E
Isangano Nat. Park △, *Zambia* **119 E3** 11 8 S 30 35 E
Isangi, *Dem. Rep. of the Congo* **114 B4** 0 52N 24 10 E
Isanlu Makutu, *Nigeria* **113 D6** 8 20N 5 50 E
Isar →, *Germany* **31 G8** 48 48N 12 57 E
Isarco →, *Italy* **45 B8** 46 27N 11 18 E
Ísari, *Greece* **48 D3** 37 22N 22 0 E
Isarog, Mt., *Phil.* **80 E4** 13 39N 123 23 E
Íscar, *Spain* **42 D6** 41 22N 4 32W
Iscayachi, *Bolivia* **173 E4** 21 31 S 65 3W
İscehisar, *Turkey* **49 C12** 38 51N 30 45 E
Ischgl, *Austria* **33 B10** 47 1N 10 17 E
Íschia, *Italy* **46 B6** 40 44N 13 57 E
Iscuandé, *Colombia* **168 C2** 2 28N 77 59W
Isdell →, *Australia* **124 C3** 16 27 S 124 51 E
Ise, *Japan* **73 C8** 34 25N 136 45 E
Ise-Shima Nat. Park △, *Japan* **73 C8** 34 25N 136 48 E
Ise-Wan, *Japan* **73 C8** 34 43N 136 43 E
Isefjord, *Denmark* **17 J5** 55 53N 11 50 E
Isel →, *Austria* **34 E5** 46 50N 12 47 E
Iseltwald, *Switz.* **32 C5** 46 43N 7 58 E
Isenthal, *Switz.* **33 C7** 46 55N 8 34 E
Iseo, *Italy* **44 C7** 45 39N 10 3 E
Iseo, L. d', *Italy* **44 C7** 45 43N 10 4 E
Iseramagazi, *Tanzania* **118 C3** 4 37 S 32 10 E
Isère □, *France* **29 C9** 45 15N 5 40 E
Isère →, *France* **29 D8** 44 59N 4 51 E
Iserlohn, *Germany* **30 D3** 51 22N 7 41 E
Isérnia, *Italy* **47 A7** 41 36N 14 14 E
Isesaki, *Japan* **73 A11** 36 19N 139 12 E
Iseyin, *Nigeria* **113 D5** 8 0N 3 36 E
Isfahan = Eşfahān, *Iran* **97 C6** 32 39N 51 43 E
Isfana, *Kyrgyzstan* **65 D4** 39 50N 69 31 E
Isfara, *Tajikistan* **65 C5** 40 7N 70 38 E
Isfjorden, *Norway* **18 B4** 62 35N 7 49 E
Ishëm, *Albania* **50 E3** 41 33N 19 34 E
Ishenga Oshwe, *Dem. Rep. of*
the Congo **114 C4** 3 57 S 22 33 E
Isherton, *Guyana* **169 C6** 2 20N 59 25W
Ishigaki-Shima, *Japan* **71 M2** 24 20N 124 10 E
Ishikari-Gawa →, *Japan* **70 C10** 43 15N 141 23 E
Ishikari-Sammyaku, *Japan* **70 C11** 43 30N 143 0 E
Ishikari-Wan, *Japan* **70 C10** 43 25N 141 1 E
Ishikawa □, *Japan* **73 A8** 36 30N 136 30 E
Ishim, *Russia* **66 D7** 56 10N 69 30 E
Ishim →, *Russia* **66 D8** 57 45N 71 10 E
Ishimbay, *Russia* **64 E6** 53 28N 56 2 E
Ishinomaki, *Japan* **70 E10** 38 32N 141 20 E
Ishioka, *Japan* **73 A12** 36 11N 140 16 E
Ishizuchi-Yama, *Japan* **72 D5** 33 45N 133 6 E
Ishkashim, *Tajikistan* **65 E5** 36 44N 71 37 E
Ishkuman, *Pakistan* **93 A5** 36 30N 73 50 E
Ishpeming, *U.S.A.* **148 B2** 46 29N 87 40W
Ishtykhan, *Uzbekistan* **65 D3** 39 58N 66 29 E
Ishurdi, *Bangla.* **90 C2** 24 9N 89 3 E
Isigny-sur-Mer, *France* **26 C5** 49 19N 1 6W
Isıklar Dağı, *Turkey* **51 F11** 40 45N 27 15 E
Işıklı, *Turkey* **49 C11** 38 19N 29 51 E
Isil Kul, *Russia* **66 D8** 54 55N 71 16 E
Ísili, *Italy* **46 C2** 39 44N 9 6 E
Isiolo, *Kenya* **118 B4** 0 24N 37 33 E
Isiro, *Dem. Rep. of the Congo* **118 B2** 2 53N 27 40 E
Isisford, *Australia* **126 C3** 24 15 S 144 21 E
Iskandar, *Uzbekistan* **65 C4** 41 36N 69 41 E
İskenderun, *Turkey* **100 D7** 36 32N 36 10 E
İskenderun Körfezi, *Turkey* **100 D6** 36 40N 35 50 E
Iski-Naukat = Eski-Nookat,
Kyrgyzstan **65 C6** 40 16N 72 36 E
İskilip, *Turkey* **100 B6** 40 45N 34 29 E
Iskŭr →, *Bulgaria* **51 C8** 43 45N 24 25 E
Iskŭr, Yazovir, *Bulgaria* **50 D7** 42 23N 23 30 E
Iskut →, *Canada* **142 B2** 56 45N 131 49W
Isla →, *U.K.* **22 E5** 56 32N 3 20W
Isla Coiba, Parque Nac. △, *Panama* **164 E3** 7 33N 81 36W
Isla Cristina, *Spain* **43 H3** 37 13N 7 17W
Isla de Salamanca, Parque Nac. △,
Colombia **165 D5** 10 59N 74 40W
Isla Gorge Nat. Park △, *Australia* **126 D4** 25 10 S 149 57 E
Isla Tiburón y San Estebán, Reserva
Ecológica ⌓, *Mexico* **162 B2** 29 0N 112 27W
Isla Vista, *U.S.A.* **161 L7** 34 25N 119 53W
İslâhiye, *Turkey* **100 D7** 37 0N 36 35 E
Islam Headworks, *Pakistan* **92 E5** 29 49N 72 33 E
Islamabad, *Pakistan* **91 B4** 33 40N 73 10 E
Islamgarh, *Pakistan* **92 F4** 27 51N 70 48 E
Islamkot, *Pakistan* **92 G4** 24 42N 70 13 E
Islamorada, *U.S.A.* **153 L9** 24 56N 80 37W
Islampur, *Bihar, India* **93 G11** 25 9N 85 12 E
Islampur, *Maharashtra, India* **94 F2** 17 2N 74 20 E
Island Bay, *Phil.* **81 G2** 9 6N 118 10 E
Island L., *Canada* **143 C10** 53 47N 94 25W
Island Lagoon, *Australia* **128 A2** 31 30 S 136 40 E
Island Pond, *U.S.A.* **151 B13** 44 49N 71 53W
Islands, B. of, *Canada* **141 C8** 49 11N 58 15W
Islands, B. of, *N.Z.* **130 B3** 35 15 S 174 6 E
Islay, *U.K.* **22 F2** 55 46N 6 10W
Isle →, *France* **28 D3** 44 55N 0 15W
Isle aux Morts, *Canada* **141 C8** 47 35N 59 0W
Isle of Hope, *U.S.A.* **152 D8** 31 58N 81 5W
Isle of Wight □, *U.K.* **21 G6** 50 41N 1 17W
Isle Royale Nat. Park △, *U.S.A.* **148 B1** 48 0N 88 55W
Isleton, *U.S.A.* **160 G5** 38 10N 121 37W
Ismail = Izmayil, *Ukraine* **59 K5** 45 22N 28 46 E
Ismâ'ilîya, *Egypt* **106 H8** 30 37N 32 18 E
Ismaning, *Germany* **31 G7** 48 13N 11 40 E
Isna, *Egypt* **106 B3** 25 17N 32 30 E
Isoanala, *Madag.* **117 C8** 23 50 S 45 44 E
Isogstalo, *India* **93 B8** 34 15N 78 46 E
Ísola del Liri, *Italy* **45 G10** 41 41N 13 34 E
Ísola della Scala, *Italy* **44 C7** 45 16N 11 0 E
Ísola di Capo Rizzuto, *Italy* **47 D10** 38 58N 17 6 E
İsparta, *Turkey* **49 D12** 37 47N 30 30 E
Isperikh, *Bulgaria* **51 C10** 43 43N 26 50 E
Íspica, *Italy* **47 F7** 36 47N 14 55 E
Israel ■, *Asia* **103 D3** 32 0N 34 50 E
Isratu, *Eritrea* **107 D4** 16 20N 39 53 E
Issano, *Guyana* **169 B6** 5 49N 59 26W
Issia, *Ivory C.* **112 D3** 6 33N 6 33W
Issoire, *France* **28 C7** 45 32N 3 15 E
Issoudun, *France* **27 F8** 46 57N 1 59 E
Issyk-Kul = Balykchy, *Kyrgyzstan* **65 B8** 42 26N 76 12 E
Issyk-Kul, Ozero = Ysyk-Köl,
Kyrgyzstan **65 B8** 42 25N 77 15 E
Ist, *Croatia* **45 D11** 44 17N 14 47 E
Istaihah, *U.A.E.* **99 B6** 23 19N 54 4 E
Istállós-kő, *Hungary* **52 B5** 48 4N 20 26 E
İstanbul, *Turkey* **51 E12** 41 0N 29 0 E
İstanbul □, *Turkey* **51 E12** 41 0N 29 0 E
Istanbul ✈ (IST), *Turkey* **51 F12** 40 59N 28 49 E
İstanbul Boğazı, *Turkey* **51 E13** 41 10N 29 10 E
Isteren, *Norway* **18 B8** 61 58N 11 47 E
Istiaía, *Greece* **48 C5** 38 57N 23 9 E
Istmina, *Colombia* **168 B2** 5 10N 76 39W
Isto, Mt., *U.S.A.* **144 B12** 69 12N 143 48W
Istok, *Kosovo, Yug.* **50 D4** 42 45N 20 24 E
Istokpoga, L., *U.S.A.* **153 H8** 27 23N 81 17W
Istra, *Croatia* **45 C10** 45 10N 14 0 E
Istres, *France* **29 E8** 43 31N 4 59 E
Istria = Istra, *Croatia* **45 C10** 45 10N 14 0 E
Isugod, *Phil.* **81 G2** 9 19N 118 5 E
Isulan, *Phil.* **81 H5** 6 30N 124 29 E
Itá, *Paraguay* **174 B4** 25 29 S 57 21W
Itabaiana, *Paraíba, Brazil* **170 C4** 7 18 S 35 19W
Itabaiana, *Sergipe, Brazil* **170 D4** 10 41 S 37 37W
Itabaianinha, *Brazil* **170 D4** 11 16 S 37 47W
Itaberaba, *Brazil* **171 D3** 12 32 S 40 18W
Itaberaí, *Brazil* **171 E2** 16 2 S 49 48W
Itabira, *Brazil* **171 E3** 19 37 S 43 13W
Itabirito, *Brazil* **171 F3** 20 15 S 43 48W
Itaboca, *Brazil* **169 D5** 4 50 S 62 40W
Itabuna, *Brazil* **171 D4** 14 48 S 39 16W
Itacajá, *Brazil* **170 C2** 8 19 S 47 46W
Itacaunas →, *Brazil* **170 C2** 5 21 S 49 8W
Itacuaí →, *Brazil* **172 A3** 4 20 S 70 12W
Itaguaçu, *Brazil* **171 E3** 19 48 S 40 51W
Itaguari →, *Brazil* **171 D3** 14 11 S 44 40W
Itaguatins, *Brazil* **170 C2** 5 47 S 47 29W
Itaim →, *Brazil* **170 C3** 7 2 S 42 2W
Itainópolis, *Brazil* **170 C3** 7 24 S 41 31W
Itaipú, Reprêsa de, *Brazil* **175 B5** 25 30 S 54 30W
Itaituba, *Brazil* **169 D6** 4 10 S 55 50W
Itajaí, *Brazil* **175 B6** 27 50 S 48 39W
Itajubá, *Brazil* **171 F2** 22 24 S 45 30W
Itajuípe, *Brazil* **171 D4** 14 41 S 39 22W
Itaka, *Tanzania* **119 D3** 8 50 S 32 49 E
Itako, *Japan* **73 B12** 35 56N 140 33 E
Itala Nature Reserve ⌓, *S. Africa* **117 D5** 27 30 S 31 7 E
Italy ■, *Europe* **13 G8** 42 0N 13 0 E
Itamaraju, *Brazil* **171 E4** 17 4 S 39 32W
Itamarati, *Brazil* **172 B4** 6 24 S 68 15W
Itamataré, *Brazil* **170 B2** 2 16 S 46 24W
Itambacuri, *Brazil* **171 E3** 18 1 S 41 42W
Itambé, *Brazil* **171 E3** 15 15 S 40 37W
Itami, *Japan* **73 C7** 34 46N 135 25 E
Itampolo, *Madag.* **117 C7** 24 41 S 43 57 E
Itandrano, *Madag.* **117 C8** 21 47 S 45 17 E
Itanhaém, *Brazil* **171 F2** 24 11 S 46 47W
Itanhauã →, *Brazil* **169 D5** 4 45 S 63 48W
Itanhém, *Brazil* **171 E3** 17 9 S 40 20W
Itano, *Japan* **72 C6** 34 7N 134 28 E
Itapaci, *Brazil* **171 D2** 14 57 S 49 34W
Itapagé, *Brazil* **170 B4** 3 41 S 39 34W
Itaparica, I. de, *Brazil* **171 D4** 12 54 S 38 42W
Itapebi, *Brazil* **171 E4** 15 56 S 39 32W
Itapecuru-Mirim, *Brazil* **170 B3** 3 24 S 44 20W
Itaperuna, *Brazil* **171 F3** 21 10 S 41 54W
Itapetinga, *Brazil* **171 E3** 15 15 S 40 15W
Itapetininga, *Brazil* **175 A6** 23 36 S 48 7W
Itapeva, *Brazil* **175 A6** 23 59 S 48 59W
Itapicuru →, *Bahia, Brazil* **170 D4** 11 47 S 37 32W
Itapicuru →, *Maranhão, Brazil* **170 B3** 2 52 S 44 12W
Itapinima, *Brazil* **173 B5** 5 25 S 60 44W
Itapipoca, *Brazil* **170 B4** 3 30 S 39 35W
Itapiranga, *Brazil* **169 D6** 2 45 S 58 1W
Itapiúna, *Brazil* **170 B4** 4 33 S 38 57W
Itaporanga, *Paraíba, Brazil* **170 C4** 7 18 S 38 0W
Itaporanga, *São Paulo, Brazil* **171 F2** 23 42 S 49 29W
Itapuá □, *Paraguay* **175 B4** 26 40 S 55 40W
Itapuranga, *Brazil* **171 E2** 15 40 S 49 59W
Itaquari, *Brazil* **171 F3** 20 20 S 40 25W
Itaquatiara, *Brazil* **169 D6** 2 58 S 58 30W
Itaquí, *Brazil* **174 B4** 29 8 S 56 30W
Itararé, *Brazil* **175 A6** 24 6 S 49 23W
Itarsi, *India* **92 H7** 22 36N 77 51 E
Itarumã, *Brazil* **171 E1** 18 42 S 51 25W
Itatí, *Argentina* **174 B4** 27 16 S 58 15W
Itatira, *Brazil* **170 B4** 4 30 S 39 37W
Itatuba, *Brazil* **173 B5** 5 46 S 63 20W
Itatupa, *Brazil* **169 D7** 0 37 S 51 12W
Itaueira, *Brazil* **170 C3** 7 36 S 43 2W
Itaueira →, *Brazil* **170 C3** 6 41 S 42 55W
Itaúna, *Brazil* **171 F3** 20 4 S 44 34W
Itbayat, *Phil.* **80 A3** 20 47N 121 51 E
Itbayat I., *Phil.* **80 A3** 20 45N 121 50 E
Itchen →, *U.K.* **21 G6** 50 55N 1 22W
Itchouma, *Niger* **111 D7** 20 14N 13 32 E
Itchoumma, *Niger* **109 D2** 20 14N 13 32 E
Ite, *Peru* **172 D3** 17 55 S 70 57W
Itéa, *Greece* **48 C4** 38 25N 22 25 E
Itezhi Tezhi, L., *Zambia* **119 F2** 15 30 S 25 30 E
Ithaca = Itháki, *Greece* **39 C2** 38 25N 20 40 E
Ithaca, *U.S.A.* **151 D8** 42 27N 76 30W
Itháki, *Greece* **39 C2** 38 25N 20 40 E
Íti △, *Greece* **48 C4** 38 50N 22 15 E
Itinga, *Brazil* **171 E3** 16 36 S 41 47W
Itiquira, *Brazil* **173 D7** 17 12 S 54 7W
Itiquira →, *Brazil* **173 D6** 17 18 S 56 44W
Itiruçu, *Brazil* **171 D3** 13 31 S 40 9W
Itiúba, *Brazil* **170 D4** 10 43 S 39 51W
Itkilik →, *U.S.A.* **144 A10** 70 9N 150 56W
Itō, *Japan* **73 C11** 34 58N 139 5 E
Itogon, *Phil.* **80 C3** 16 22N 120 41 E
Itoigawa, *Japan* **71 F8** 37 2N 137 51 E
Itoko, *Dem. Rep. of the Congo* **114 C4** 1 0 S 21 48 E
Iton →, *France* **26 C8** 49 9N 1 12 E
Itonamas →, *Bolivia* **173 C5** 12 28 S 64 24W
Itri, *Italy* **46 A6** 41 17N 13 32 E
Itsa, *Egypt* **106 J7** 29 15N 30 47 E
Itsuki, *Japan* **72 E2** 32 24N 130 50 E
Íttiri, *Italy* **46 B1** 40 36N 8 34 E
Ittoqqortoormiit, *Greenland* **10 C8** 70 20N 23 0W
Itu, *Brazil* **175 A6** 23 17 S 47 15W
Itu, *Nigeria* **113 D6** 5 10N 7 58 E
Itu Aba I., *S. China Sea* **78 B4** 10 23N 114 21 E
Ituaçu, *Brazil* **171 D3** 13 50 S 41 18W
Ituango, *Colombia* **168 B2** 7 4N 75 45W
Ituí →, *Brazil* **168 D3** 4 38 S 70 19W
Ituiutaba, *Brazil* **171 E2** 19 0 S 49 25W
Itumbiara, *Brazil* **171 E2** 18 20 S 49 10W
Ituna, *Canada* **143 C8** 51 10N 103 24W
Itunge Port, *Tanzania* **119 D3** 9 40 S 33 55 E
Ituni, *Guyana* **169 B6** 5 28N 58 15W
Itupiranga, *Brazil* **170 C2** 5 9 S 49 20W
Iturama, *Brazil* **171 E1** 19 44 S 50 11W
Iturbe, *Argentina* **174 A2** 23 0 S 65 25W
Ituri →, *Dem. Rep. of the Congo* **118 B2** 1 40N 27 1 E
Iturup, Ostrov, *Russia* **67 E15** 45 0N 148 0 E
Ituverava, *Brazil* **171 F2** 20 20 S 47 47W
Ituxi →, *Brazil* **173 B5** 7 18 S 64 51W
Ituyuro →, *Argentina* **174 A3** 22 40 S 63 50W
Itzehoe, *Germany* **30 B5** 53 55N 9 31 E
Iuka, *U.S.A.* **157 F8** 38 37N 88 47W
Ivahona, *Madag.* **117 C8** 23 27 S 46 10 E
Ivaí →, *Brazil* **175 A5** 23 18 S 53 42W
Ivalo, *Finland* **14 B22** 68 38N 27 35 E
Ivalojoki →, *Finland* **14 B22** 68 40N 27 40 E
Ivanava, *Belarus* **59 F3** 52 7N 25 29 E
Ivančice, *Czech Rep.* **35 B9** 49 6N 16 23 E
Ivăneşti, *Romania* **53 D12** 46 39N 27 27 E
Ivangorod, *Russia* **58 C5** 59 27N 28 13 E
Ivanhoe, *N.S.W., Australia* **128 B6** 32 56 S 144 20 E
Ivanhoe, *Vic., Australia* **129 D6** 37 46 S 145 2 E
Ivanhoe, *Calif., U.S.A.* **160 J7** 36 23N 119 13W
Ivanhoe, *Minn., U.S.A.* **154 C6** 44 28N 96 15W
Ivanić Grad, *Croatia* **45 C13** 45 41N 16 25 E
Ivanjica, *Serbia, Yug.* **50 C4** 43 35N 20 12 E
Ivanjska, *Bos.-H.* **52 F2** 44 55N 17 4 E
Ivankoyskoye Vdkhr., *Russia* **58 D9** 56 37N 36 32 E
Ivano-Frankivsk, *Ukraine* **59 H3** 48 40N 24 40 E
Ivano-Frankovsk = Ivano-Frankivsk,
Ukraine **59 H3** 48 40N 24 40 E
Ivanof Bay, *U.S.A.* **144 J8** 55 54N 159 29W
Ivanovka, *Kyrgyzstan* **65 B7** 42 53N 75 6 E
Ivanovo = Ivanava, *Belarus* **59 F3** 52 7N 25 29 E
Ivanovo, *Russia* **58 D11** 57 5N 41 0 E
Ivanšćica, *Croatia* **45 B13** 46 12N 16 13 E
Ivato, *Madag.* **117 C8** 20 37 S 47 10 E
Ivatsevichy, *Belarus* **59 F3** 52 43N 25 21 E
Ivaylovgrad, *Bulgaria* **51 E10** 41 32N 26 8 E
Ivdel, *Russia* **56 B11** 60 42N 60 24 E
Ivindo →, *Gabon* **114 C2** 0 9 S 12 9 E
Ivinheima →, *Brazil* **175 A5** 23 14 S 53 42W
Ivinhema, *Brazil* **175 A5** 22 10 S 53 37W
Ivittuut, *Greenland* **10 E6** 61 14N 48 12W
Iviza = Eivissa, *Spain* **38 D1** 38 54N 1 26 E
Ivohibe, *Madag.* **117 C8** 22 31 S 46 57 E
Ivolândia, *Brazil* **171 E1** 16 34 S 50 51W
Ivory Coast, *W. Afr.* **112 E4** 4 20N 5 0W
Ivory Coast ■, *Africa* **112 D4** 7 30N 5 0W
Ivösjön, *Sweden* **17 H8** 56 8N 14 25 E
Ivrea, *Italy* **44 C4** 45 28N 7 52 E
İvrindi, *Turkey* **49 B9** 39 34N 27 30 E
Ivujivik, *Canada* **139 B12** 62 24N 77 55W
Ivvavik Nat. Park △, *Canada* **144 B13** 69 6N 139 30W
Ivybridge, *U.K.* **21 G4** 50 23N 3 56W
Iwai-Jima, *Japan* **72 D3** 33 47N 131 58 E
Iwaizumi, *Japan* **70 E10** 39 50N 141 45 E
Iwaki, *Japan* **71 F10** 37 3N 140 55 E
Iwakuni, *Japan* **72 C4** 34 15N 132 8 E
Iwami, *Japan* **72 B6** 35 32N 134 15 E
Iwamizawa, *Japan* **70 C10** 43 12N 141 46 E
Iwanai, *Japan* **70 C10** 42 58N 140 30 E
Iwase, *Japan* **73 A12** 36 21N 140 6 E
Iwata, *Japan* **73 C9** 34 42N 137 51 E
Iwate □, *Japan* **70 E10** 39 30N 141 30 E
Iwate-San, *Japan* **70 E10** 39 51N 141 0 E
Iwo, *Nigeria* **113 D5** 7 39N 4 9 E
Iwonicz-Zdrój, *Poland* **55 J8** 49 37N 21 47 E
Iwungu, *Dem. Rep. of the Congo* **115 D3** 5 16 S 19 17 E
Ixiamas, *Bolivia* **172 C4** 13 50 S 68 5W
Ixopo, *S. Africa* **117 E5** 30 11 S 30 5 E
Ixtepec, *Mexico* **163 D5** 16 32N 95 10W
Ixtlán del Río, *Mexico* **162 C4** 21 5N 104 21W
'Iyādh, *Yemen* **98 D4** 14 59N 46 51 E
Iyal Bakhit, *Sudan* **107 E2** 13 20N 28 39 E
Iyo, *Japan* **72 D4** 33 45N 132 45 E
Iyo-Mishima, *Japan* **72 D5** 33 58N 133 30 E
Iyo-Nada, *Japan* **72 D4** 33 40N 132 20 E
Izabal, L. de, *Guatemala* **164 C2** 15 30N 89 10W
Izamal, *Mexico* **163 C7** 20 56N 89 1W
Izberbash, *Russia* **61 J8** 42 35N 47 52 E
Izbica, *Poland* **55 H10** 50 53N 23 10 E
Izbica Kujawska, *Poland* **55 F5** 52 25N 18 40 E
Izbiceni, *Romania* **53 G9** 43 45N 24 40 E
Izena-Shima, *Japan* **71 L3** 26 56N 127 56 E
Izgrev, *Bulgaria* **51 C10** 43 36N 26 58 E
Izh →, *Russia* **64 C4** 56 9N 53 0 E
Izhevsk, *Russia* **64 C4** 56 51N 53 14 E
Izhma →, *Russia* **56 A9** 65 19N 52 54 E
Izileg, *Algeria* **111 D6** 20 20N 6 4 E
Izkī, *Oman* **99 B7** 22 56N 57 46 E
Izmayil, *Ukraine* **59 K5** 45 22N 28 46 E
İzmir, *Turkey* **49 C9** 38 25N 27 8 E
İzmir □, *Turkey* **49 C9** 38 15N 27 40 E
İzmir Adnan Menderes ✈ (ADB),
Turkey **49 C9** 38 23N 27 6 E
İzmir Körfezi, *Turkey* **49 C8** 38 30N 26 50 E
İzmit = Kocaeli, *Turkey* **51 F13** 40 45N 29 50 E
Iznájar, *Spain* **43 H6** 37 15N 4 19W
Iznalloz, *Spain* **43 H7** 37 24N 3 30W
İznik, *Turkey* **100 B3** 40 23N 29 46 E
İznik Gölü, *Turkey* **51 F13** 40 27N 29 30 E
Izobil'nyy, *Russia* **61 H5** 45 25N 41 44 E
Izola, *Slovenia* **45 C10** 45 32N 13 39 E
Izozog, Bañados de, *Bolivia* **173 D5** 18 48 S 62 10W
Izra, *Syria* **103 C5** 32 51N 36 15 E
Iztochni Rodopi, *Bulgaria* **51 E9** 41 45N 25 30 E
Izu-Hantō, *Japan* **73 C11** 34 45N 139 0 E
Izu-Shotō, *Japan* **71 G10** 34 30N 140 0 E
Izúcar de Matamoros, *Mexico* **163 D5** 18 36N 98 28W
Izuhara, *Japan* **72 C1** 34 12N 129 17 E
Izumi, *Kagoshima, Japan* **72 E2** 32 5N 130 22 E
Izumi, *Ōsaka, Japan* **73 C7** 34 28N 135 24 E
Izumi-Sano, *Japan* **73 C7** 34 23N 135 18 E
Izumo, *Japan* **72 B4** 35 20N 132 46 E
Izyaslav, *Ukraine* **59 G4** 50 5N 26 50 E
Izyum, *Ukraine* **59 H9** 49 12N 37 19 E

J

J.F. Rodrigues, *Brazil* **170 B1** 2 55 S 50 20W
J.P. Koch Fjord, *Greenland* **10 A6** 82 45N 44 0W
Ja-ela, *Sri Lanka* **95 L4** 7 5N 79 53 E
Jaba, *Ethiopia* **107 F4** 6 20N 35 7 E
Jabal at Tā'ir, *Red Sea* **107 D5** 15 35N 41 52 E
Jabalón →, *Spain* **43 G6** 38 53N 4 5W

Jabalpur, India ... 93 H8 23 9N 79 58 E
Jabbūl, Syria ... 96 B3 36 4N 37 30 E
Jabiru, Australia ... 124 B5 12 40 S 132 53 E
Jablah, Syria ... 100 E6 35 20N 36 0 E
Jablanac, Croatia ... 45 D11 44 42N 14 56 E
Jablanica, Bos.-H. ... 52 G2 43 40N 17 45 E
Jablonec nad Nisou, Czech Rep. ... 34 A8 50 43N 15 10 E
Jablonica, Slovak Rep. ... 35 C10 48 37N 17 26 E
Jabłonowo Pomorskie, Poland ... 54 E6 53 23N 19 10 E
Jablunkov, Czech Rep. ... 35 B11 49 35N 18 46 E
Jaboatão, Brazil ... 170 C4 8 7 S 35 1W
Jabonga, Phil. ... 81 G5 9 20N 125 32 E
Jaboticabal, Brazil ... 175 A6 21 15 S 48 17W
Jabukovac, Serbia, Yug. ... 50 B6 44 22N 22 21 E
Jaburu, Brazil ... 173 B5 5 30 S 64 0W
Jaca, Spain ... 40 C4 42 35N 0 33W
Jacaré →, Brazil ... 170 D3 10 3 S 42 13W
Jacareí, Brazil ... 175 A6 23 20 S 46 0W
Jacarèzinho, Brazil ... 175 A6 23 5 S 49 58W
Jaciara, Brazil ... 173 D7 15 59 S 54 57W
Jacinto, Brazil ... 171 E3 16 10 S 40 17W
Jaciparaná, Brazil ... 173 B5 9 15 S 64 23W
Jackman, U.S.A. ... 149 C10 45 35N 70 17W
Jacksboro, U.S.A. ... 155 J5 33 14N 98 15W
Jackson, Barbados ... 165 g 13 7N 59 36W
Jackson, Ala., U.S.A. ... 149 K2 31 31N 87 53W
Jackson, Calif., U.S.A. ... 160 G6 38 21N 120 46W
Jackson, Ga., U.S.A. ... 152 B6 33 20N 83 57W
Jackson, Ky., U.S.A. ... 148 G4 37 33N 83 23W
Jackson, Mich., U.S.A. ... 157 B12 42 15N 84 24W
Jackson, Minn., U.S.A. ... 154 D7 43 37N 95 1W
Jackson, Miss., U.S.A. ... 155 J9 32 18N 90 12W
Jackson, Mo., U.S.A. ... 155 G10 37 23N 89 40W
Jackson, N.H., U.S.A. ... 151 B13 44 10N 71 11W
Jackson, Ohio, U.S.A. ... 148 F4 39 3N 82 39W
Jackson, S.C., U.S.A. ... 152 B8 33 20N 81 47W
Jackson, Tenn., U.S.A. ... 149 H1 35 37N 88 49W
Jackson, Wyo., U.S.A. ... 158 E8 43 29N 110 46W
Jackson, C., N.Z. ... 131 A9 40 59 S 174 20 E
Jackson B., N.Z. ... 131 D3 43 58 S 168 42 E
Jackson Center, U.S.A. ... 157 D12 40 27N 84 4W
Jackson Hd., N.Z. ... 131 D3 43 58 S 168 37 E
Jackson L., Fla., U.S.A. ... 152 E5 30 30N 84 17W
Jackson L., Ga., U.S.A. ... 152 B6 33 19N 83 50W
Jackson L., Wyo., U.S.A. ... 158 E8 43 52N 110 36W
Jacksons, N.Z. ... 131 C6 42 46 S 171 32 E
Jackson's Arm, Canada ... 141 C8 49 52N 56 47W
Jacksonville, Ala., U.S.A. ... 152 B4 33 49N 85 46W
Jacksonville, Ark., U.S.A. ... 155 H8 34 52N 92 7W
Jacksonville, Calif., U.S.A. ... 160 H6 37 52N 120 24W
Jacksonville, Fla., U.S.A. ... 152 E8 30 20N 81 39W
Jacksonville, Ga., U.S.A. ... 152 D7 31 49N 82 59W
Jacksonville, Ill., U.S.A. ... 156 E6 39 44N 90 14W
Jacksonville, N.C., U.S.A. ... 149 H7 34 45N 77 26W
Jacksonville, Tex., U.S.A. ... 155 K7 31 58N 95 17W
Jacksonville Beach, U.S.A. ... 152 E8 30 17N 81 24W
Jacksonville International ✈ (JAX), U.S.A. ... 152 E8 30 30N 81 41W
Jacmel, Haiti ... 165 C5 18 14N 72 32W
Jacob Lake, U.S.A. ... 159 H7 36 43N 112 13W
Jacobabad, Pakistan ... 91 C3 28 20N 68 29 E
Jacobina, Brazil ... 170 D3 11 11 S 40 30W
Jacques Cartier, Dét. de, Canada ... 141 C7 50 0N 63 30W
Jacques Cartier, Mt., Canada ... 141 C6 48 57N 66 0W
Jacques Cartier, Parc Prov. ⌂, Canada ... 141 C5 47 15N 71 33W
Jacqueville, Ivory C. ... 112 D4 5 12N 4 25W
Jacuí →, Brazil ... 175 C5 30 2 S 51 15W
Jacumba, U.S.A. ... 161 N10 32 37N 116 11W
Jacundá →, Brazil ... 170 B1 1 57 S 50 26W
Jadcherla, India ... 94 F4 16 46N 78 9 E
Jade, Germany ... 30 B4 53 22N 8 14 E
Jadebusen, Germany ... 30 B4 53 29N 8 12 E
Jadotville = Likasi, Dem. Rep. of the Congo ... 119 E2 10 55 S 26 48 E
Jadovnik, Serbia, Yug. ... 50 C3 43 20N 19 45 E
Jadraque, Spain ... 40 E2 40 55N 2 55W
Jādū, Libya ... 108 B2 32 0N 12 0 E
Jaén, Peru ... 172 B2 5 25 S 78 40W
Jaén, Spain ... 43 H7 37 44N 3 43W
Jaén □, Spain ... 43 H7 37 50N 3 30W
Jæren, Norway ... 18 F2 58 42N 5 47 E
Jærens rev, Norway ... 18 F2 58 45N 5 45 E
Jafarabad, India ... 92 J4 20 52N 71 22 E
Jafène, Africa ... 110 D3 20 35N 5 30 E
Jaffa = Tel Aviv-Yafo, Israel ... 103 C3 32 4N 34 48 E
Jaffa, C., Australia ... 128 D3 36 58 S 139 40 E
Jaffna, Sri Lanka ... 95 K5 9 45N 80 2 E
Jaffray, Canada ... 143 D10 49 47N 94 26W
Jaffrey, U.S.A. ... 151 D12 42 49N 72 2W
Jagadhri, India ... 92 D7 30 10N 77 20 E
Jagadishpur, India ... 93 G11 25 30N 84 21 E
Jagdalpur, India ... 94 E6 19 3N 82 0 E
Jagersfontein, S. Africa ... 124 D4 29 44 S 25 27 E
Jaghīn →, Iran ... 97 E8 27 17N 57 13 E
Jagna, Phil. ... 81 G5 9 39N 124 22 E
Jagodina, Serbia, Yug. ... 50 B5 44 5N 21 15 E
Jagst →, Germany ... 31 F5 49 14N 9 10 E
Jagtial, India ... 94 E4 18 50N 79 0 E
Jaguaquara, Brazil ... 171 D4 13 32 S 39 58W
Jaguariaíva, Brazil ... 175 A6 24 10 S 49 50W
Jaguaribe, Brazil ... 170 C4 5 53 S 38 37W
Jaguaribe →, Brazil ... 170 B4 4 25 S 37 45W
Jaguaruana, Brazil ... 170 B4 4 50 S 37 47W
Jagüey Grande, Cuba ... 164 B3 22 35N 81 7W
Jagungal, Mt., Australia ... 129 D8 36 8 S 148 22 E
Jahanabad, India ... 93 G11 25 13N 84 59 E
Jahazpur, India ... 92 G6 25 37N 75 17 E
Jahrom, Iran ... 97 D7 28 30N 53 31 E
Jaicós, Brazil ... 170 C3 7 21 S 41 8W
Jaigarh, India ... 94 F1 17 17N 73 13 E
Jaijon, India ... 92 D7 31 21N 76 9 E
Jailolo, Indonesia ... 82 A3 1 5N 127 30 E
Jailolo, Selat, Indonesia ... 83 A3 0 5N 129 5 E
Jaintiapur, Bangla. ... 90 C4 25 8N 92 24 E
Jaipur, Assam, India ... 90 B5 27 16N 95 24 E
Jaipur, Raj., India ... 92 F6 27 0N 75 50 E
Jais, India ... 93 F9 26 15N 81 32 E
Jaisalmer, India ... 92 F4 26 55N 70 54 E
Jaisinghnagar, India ... 93 H8 23 38N 78 34 E
Jaitaran, India ... 92 F5 26 12N 73 56 E
Jaithari, India ... 93 H8 23 14N 78 37 E
Jājarm, Iran ... 97 B8 36 58N 56 27 E
Jajce, Bos.-H. ... 52 F2 44 19N 17 17 E
Jajpur, India ... 94 D8 20 53N 86 22 E
Jakam →, India ... 92 H6 23 54N 74 13 E
Jakarta, Indonesia ... 84 F3 6 9 S 106 49 E
Jakhal, India ... 92 E6 29 48N 75 50 E
Jakhau, India ... 92 H3 23 13N 68 43 E
Jakobshavn = Illulissat, Greenland ... 10 D5 69 12N 51 10W
Jakobstad = Pietarsaari, Finland ... 14 E20 63 40N 22 43 E
Jakupica, Macedonia ... 50 E5 41 45N 21 22 E
Jal, U.S.A. ... 155 J3 32 7N 103 12W
Jalal-Abad, Kyrgyzstan ... 65 C6 40 56N 73 0 E
Jalālābād, Afghan. ... 91 B3 34 30N 70 29 E
Jalalabad, India ... 93 F8 27 41N 79 42 E
Jalalpur Jattan, Pakistan ... 92 C6 32 38N 74 11 E
Jalama, U.S.A. ... 161 L6 34 29N 120 29W
Jalapa, Guatemala ... 164 D2 14 39N 89 59W
Jalapa Enríquez = Xalapa, Mexico ... 163 D5 19 32N 96 55W
Jalasjärvi, Finland ... 15 E20 62 29N 22 47 E
Jalaun, India ... 93 F8 26 8N 79 25 E
Jalāzīn, Afghan. ... 65 E2 37 2N 64 49 E
Jaldak, Afghan. ... 91 C2 31 58N 66 43 E

Jaldhaka →, Bangla. ... 90 B2 26 16N 89 16 E
Jales, Brazil ... 171 F1 20 10 S 50 33W
Jalesar, India ... 92 F8 27 29N 78 19 E
Jaleswar, Nepal ... 93 F11 26 38N 85 48 E
Jalgaon, India ... 94 D2 21 0N 75 42 E
Jalībah, Iraq ... 96 D5 30 35N 46 32 E
Jalingo, Nigeria ... 113 D7 8 55N 11 25 E
Jalisco □, Mexico ... 162 D4 20 0N 104 0W
Jalkot, Pakistan ... 93 B5 35 14N 73 24 E
Jallas →, Spain ... 42 C1 42 54N 9 8W
Jalna, India ... 94 E2 19 48N 75 38 E
Jalón →, Spain ... 40 D3 41 47N 1 4W
Jalor, India ... 92 G5 25 21N 72 37 E
Jalpa, Mexico ... 162 C4 21 38N 102 58W
Jalpaiguri, India ... 90 B2 26 32N 88 46 E
Jālq, Iran ... 91 D1 27 35N 62 46 E
Jaluit I., Marshall Is. ... 134 G8 6 0N 169 30 E
Jalūlā, Iraq ... 101 E11 34 16N 45 10 E
Jamaame = Giamama, Somali Rep. ... 120 D2 0 4N 42 44 E
Jamaari, Nigeria ... 113 C6 11 44N 9 53 E
Jamaica ■, W. Indies ... 164 a 18 10N 77 30W
Jamalpur, Bangla. ... 90 C2 24 52N 89 56 E
Jamalpur, India ... 93 G12 25 18N 86 28 E
Jamalpurganj, India ... 93 H13 23 2N 87 59 E
Jamanxim →, Brazil ... 173 A6 4 43 S 56 18W
Jamari, Brazil ... 173 B5 8 45 S 63 27W
Jamari →, Brazil ... 173 B5 8 27 S 63 30W
Jamba, Angola ... 118 E3 14 40 S 16 2 E
Jambewangi, Indonesia ... 79 J17 8 17 S 114 7 E
Jambi, Indonesia ... 84 C2 1 38 S 103 30 E
Jambi □, Indonesia ... 84 C2 1 30 S 102 30 E
Jambusar, India ... 92 H5 22 3N 72 51 E
James, U.S.A. ... 132 C5 32 58N 83 29W
James →, S. Dak., U.S.A. ... 154 D6 42 52N 97 18W
James →, Va., U.S.A. ... 148 G7 36 56N 76 27W
James, I. = San Salvador, I., Ecuador ... 172 a 0 16 S 90 42W
James Island, U.S.A. ... 152 C10 32 45N 79 55W
James Ranges, Australia ... 124 D5 24 10 S 132 30 E
James Ross I., Antarctica ... 7 C18 63 58 S 57 50W
Jamesabad, Pakistan ... 92 G3 25 17N 69 15 E
Jameson Land, Greenland ... 10 C8 71 0N 24 30W
Jamesport, U.S.A. ... 156 E3 39 58N 93 48W
Jamestown, S. Africa ... 124 B3 31 6 S 26 45 E
Jamestown, Ind., U.S.A. ... 157 E10 39 56N 86 38W
Jamestown, Mo., U.S.A. ... 156 F4 38 48N 92 30W
Jamestown, N. Dak., U.S.A. ... 154 B5 46 54N 98 42W
Jamestown, N.Y., U.S.A. ... 150 D5 42 6N 79 14W
Jamestown, Ohio, U.S.A. ... 157 E13 39 39N 83 33W
Jamestown, Pa., U.S.A. ... 150 E4 41 29N 80 27W
Jamestown, S.C., U.S.A. ... 152 B10 33 17N 79 42W
Jamīlābād, Iran ... 97 C6 34 24N 48 28 E
Jamiltepec, Mexico ... 163 D5 16 17N 97 49W
Jamira →, India ... 93 J13 21 35N 88 28 E
Jāmjō, Sweden ... 17 H9 56 12N 15 49 E
Jamkhandi, India ... 94 F2 16 30N 75 15 E
Jamkhed, India ... 94 E2 18 43N 75 19 E
Jammalamadugu, India ... 95 G4 14 51N 78 25 E
Jammerbugt, Denmark ... 17 G3 57 15N 9 20 E
Jammu, India ... 92 C6 32 43N 74 54 E
Jammu & Kashmir □, India ... 93 B7 34 25N 77 0 E
Jamnagar, India ... 92 H4 22 30N 70 6 E
Jamner, India ... 94 D2 20 45N 75 52 E
Jamni →, India ... 93 G8 25 13N 78 35 E
Jampur, Pakistan ... 91 C3 29 39N 70 40 E
Jamrud, Pakistan ... 92 C4 33 59N 71 24 E
Jämsä, Finland ... 15 F21 61 53N 25 10 E
Jamshedpur, India ... 93 H12 22 44N 86 12 E
Jamtara, India ... 93 H12 23 59N 86 49 E
Jämtland, Sweden ... 14 E15 63 31N 14 0 E
Jämtlands län □, Sweden ... 16 B7 62 40N 13 50 E
Jamuna →, India ... 90 D2 23 51N 89 45 E
Jamunamukh, India ... 90 B4 26 1N 92 44 E
Jamurki, Bangla. ... 90 C3 24 9N 90 2 E
Jan L., Canada ... 143 C8 54 56N 102 55W
Jan Mayen, Arctic ... 6 B7 71 0N 9 0W
Janakkala, Finland ... 15 F21 60 54N 24 36 E
Janaúba, Brazil ... 171 E3 15 48 S 43 19W
Janaucu, I., Brazil ... 170 A1 0 30N 50 10W
Jand, Pakistan ... 92 C5 33 30N 72 6 E
Jandaia, Brazil ... 171 E1 17 6 S 50 7W
Jandaq, Iran ... 97 C7 34 3N 54 22 E
Jandía, Canary Is. ... 9 e2 28 6N 14 21W
Jandía, Parque Nac. de △, Canary Is. ... 9 e2 28 4N 14 19W
Jandía, Pta. de, Canary Is. ... 9 e2 28 3N 14 31W
Jandiatuba →, Brazil ... 168 D4 3 28 S 68 42W
Jandola, Pakistan ... 92 C4 32 20N 70 9 E
Jandowae, Australia ... 127 D5 26 45 S 151 7 E
Jándula →, Spain ... 43 G6 38 3N 4 6W
Jane Pk., N.Z. ... 131 F3 45 15 S 168 20 E
Janesville, U.S.A. ... 156 B7 42 41N 89 1W
Janga, Ghana ... 117 C6 10 5N 1 0W
Jangamo, Mozam. ... 117 C6 24 6 S 35 21 E
Janghai, India ... 93 G10 25 33N 82 19 E
Jango, Brazil ... 173 E6 20 27 S 55 29W
Jangoon, India ... 94 F4 17 44N 79 5 E
Jangy-Bazar, Kyrgyzstan ... 65 C5 41 40N 70 53 E
Jangy-Jol, Kyrgyzstan ... 65 C6 41 36N 72 9 E
Janhtang Ga, Burma ... 90 B6 26 32N 96 38 E
Jani Khel, Afghan. ... 91 B3 32 46N 68 24 E
Janikowo, Poland ... 55 F5 52 45N 18 7 E
Janin = Ioánnina □, Greece ... 48 B2 39 39N 20 57 E
Janiuay, Phil. ... 81 F4 10 58N 122 30 E
Janja, Bos.-H. ... 52 F4 44 40N 19 14 E
Janjevo, Kosovo, Yug. ... 50 D5 42 35N 21 19 E
Janjgir, India ... 93 J10 22 1N 82 34 E
Janjina, Croatia ... 45 F14 42 58N 17 25 E
Janos, Mexico ... 162 A3 30 45N 108 10W
Jánoshalma, Hungary ... 52 D4 46 18N 19 21 E
Jánosháza, Hungary ... 52 C2 47 8N 17 12 E
Jánossomorja, Hungary ... 52 C2 47 47N 17 11 E
Janów, Poland ... 55 H6 50 44N 19 27 E
Janów Lubelski, Poland ... 55 H9 50 48N 22 23 E
Janów Podlaski, Poland ... 55 F10 52 11N 23 11 E
Janowiec Wielkopolski, Poland ... 55 F4 52 45N 17 30 E
Januária, Brazil ... 171 E3 15 25 S 44 25W
Janub Dārfūr □, Sudan ... 107 E2 11 0N 25 0 E
Janub Kordofān □, Sudan ... 107 E3 12 0N 30 0 E
Janūb Sīnī □, Egypt ... 103 F2 29 30N 33 50 E
Janubio, Canary Is. ... 9 e2 28 56N 13 50W
Janville, France ... 27 D8 48 10N 1 50 E
Janwada, India ... 94 E3 18 0N 77 29 E
Janzé, France ... 26 E5 47 55N 1 28W
Jaora, India ... 92 H6 23 40N 75 10 E
Japan ■, Asia ... 71 G8 36 0N 136 0 E
Japan, Sea of, Asia ... 70 E7 40 0N 135 0 E
Japan Trench, Pac. Oc. ... 62 F18 32 0N 142 0 E
Japen = Yapen, Indonesia ... 83 B5 1 50 S 136 0 E
Japiim, Brazil ... 172 B3 7 2 S 72 54W
Japla, India ... 93 G11 24 33N 84 1 E
Japurá, Brazil ... 168 D4 1 48 S 66 34W
Japurá →, Brazil ... 168 D4 3 8 S 65 46W
Jaquarão, Brazil ... 175 C5 32 34 S 53 23W
Jaqué, Panama ... 164 E4 7 27N 78 8W
Jarābulus, Syria ... 100 B3 36 49N 38 1 E
Jaraguá, Brazil ... 171 E2 15 45 S 49 20W
Jaraguari, Brazil ... 173 E6 20 30 S 54 35W
Jaraicejo, Spain ... 43 F5 39 40N 5 49W
Jaraíz de la Vera, Spain ... 42 E5 40 4N 5 45W
Jarama →, Spain ... 42 E7 40 24N 3 32W
Jaramānah, Syria ... 100 F7 33 29N 36 21 E

Jaramillo, Argentina ... 176 C3 47 10 S 67 7W
Jarandilla, Spain ... 42 E5 40 8N 5 39W
Jaranwala, Pakistan ... 91 C4 31 15N 73 26 E
Jarash, Jordan ... 103 C4 32 17N 35 54 E
Jarash □, Jordan ... 103 C4 32 17N 35 54 E
Jarauçu →, Brazil ... 169 D7 1 48 S 52 22W
Järbo, Sweden ... 16 D10 60 43N 16 36 E
Jardas al 'Abīd, Libya ... 108 B4 32 18N 20 59 E
Jardim, Brazil ... 174 A4 21 28 S 56 2W
Jardín →, Spain ... 41 G2 38 50N 2 10W
Jardine River Nat. Park △, Australia ... 126 A3 11 9 S 142 21 E
Jardines de la Reina, Arch. de los, Cuba ... 164 B4 20 50N 78 50W
Jargalang, China ... 75 C12 43 5N 122 55 E
Jargalant = Hovd, Mongolia ... 68 B4 48 2N 91 37 E
Jari →, Brazil ... 169 D7 1 9 S 51 54W
Jaria Janjail, Bangla. ... 90 C3 25 0N 90 40 E
Jarīr, W. al →, Si. Arabia ... 96 E4 25 38N 42 30 E
Järlåsa, Sweden ... 16 E11 59 53N 17 12 E
Jarmen, Germany ... 30 B9 53 54N 13 20 E
Järna, Dalarna, Sweden ... 16 D8 60 33N 14 26 E
Järna, Stockholm, Sweden ... 16 E11 59 6N 17 34 E
Jarnac, France ... 27 C12 49 5N 5 53 E
Jarny, France ... 27 C12 49 9N 5 53 E
Jaro, Phil. ... 81 F5 11 11N 124 47 E
Jarocin, Poland ... 55 G4 51 59N 17 29 E
Jaroměř, Czech Rep. ... 34 A8 50 22N 15 52 E
Jarosław, Poland ... 55 H9 50 2N 22 42 E
Järpås, Sweden ... 17 F6 58 23N 12 57 E
Järpen, Sweden ... 16 A7 63 21N 13 26 E
Jarqūrghon, Uzbekistan ... 65 E3 37 31N 67 25 E
Jarrahdale, Australia ... 125 F2 32 24 S 116 5 E
Jarrahi →, Iran ... 97 D6 30 49N 48 48 E
Jarres, Plaine des, Laos ... 86 C4 19 27N 103 10 E
Jarso, Ethiopia ... 107 F4 5 15N 37 30 E
Jartai, China ... 74 E3 39 45N 105 48 E
Jaru, Brazil ... 173 C5 10 26 S 62 28W
Jaru →, Brazil ... 173 C5 10 5 S 61 59W
Jarud Qi, China ... 75 B11 44 28N 120 50 E
Järvenpää, Finland ... 15 F21 60 29N 25 5 E
Jarvis, Canada ... 150 D4 42 53N 80 6W
Jarvis I., Pac. Oc. ... 135 H12 0 15 S 160 5W
Jarvornik, Czech Rep. ... 35 A10 50 23N 17 2 E
Järvsö, Sweden ... 16 C10 61 43N 16 10 E
Järwa, India ... 93 F10 27 38N 82 30 E
Jaša Tomić, Serbia, Yug. ... 52 E5 45 26N 20 50 E
Jasaan, Phil. ... 81 G5 8 39N 124 45 E
Jasdan, India ... 92 H4 22 2N 71 12 E
Jashpurnagar, India ... 93 H11 22 54N 84 9 E
Jasidih, India ... 93 G12 24 31N 86 39 E
Jasień, Poland ... 55 G2 51 46N 15 0 E
Jāsimīyah, Iraq ... 101 F11 33 45N 44 41 E
Jasin, Malaysia ... 87 L4 2 20N 102 26 E
Jāsk, Iran ... 97 E8 25 38N 57 45 E
Jasło, Poland ... 55 J8 49 45N 21 30 E
Jasmund, Germany ... 30 A9 54 32N 13 35 E
Jasmund, Nationalpark △, Germany ... 30 A9 54 31N 13 38 E
Jaso, India ... 93 G9 24 30N 80 29 E
Jason Is., Falk. Is. ... 9 f 51 0 S 61 0W
Jasonville, U.S.A. ... 157 E9 39 10N 87 12W
Jasper, Alta., Canada ... 142 C5 52 55N 118 5W
Jasper, Ont., Canada ... 151 B9 44 52N 75 57W
Jasper, Ala., U.S.A. ... 149 J2 33 50N 87 17W
Jasper, Fla., U.S.A. ... 152 E7 30 31N 82 57W
Jasper, Ind., U.S.A. ... 157 F10 38 24N 86 56W
Jasper, Tex., U.S.A. ... 155 K8 30 56N 94 1W
Jasper Nat. Park △, Canada ... 142 C5 52 50N 118 8W
Jasrasar, India ... 92 F5 27 43N 73 49 E
Jassey = Iaşi, Romania ... 53 C12 47 10N 27 40 E
Jastarnia, Poland ... 54 D5 54 42N 18 40 E
Jastrebarsko, Croatia ... 45 C12 45 41N 15 39 E
Jastrowie, Poland ... 54 E3 53 26N 16 49 E
Jastrzębie Zdrój, Poland ... 55 J5 49 57N 18 35 E
Jász-Nagykun-Szolnok □, Hungary ... 52 C5 47 15N 20 30 E
Jászapáti, Hungary ... 52 C5 47 32N 20 10 E
Jászárokszállás, Hungary ... 52 C4 47 39N 19 58 E
Jászberény, Hungary ... 52 C4 47 30N 19 55 E
Jászkisér, Hungary ... 52 C5 47 27N 20 20 E
Jászladány, Hungary ... 52 C5 47 23N 20 18 E
Jataí, Brazil ... 171 E1 17 58 S 51 48W
Jatapu →, Brazil ... 169 D6 2 13 S 58 17W
Jath, India ... 94 F2 17 3N 75 13 E
Jati, Pakistan ... 92 G3 24 20N 68 19 E
Jatibarang, Indonesia ... 85 D3 6 28 S 108 18 E
Jatiluwih, Indonesia ... 79 J18 8 23 S 115 6 E
Jatinegara, Indonesia ... 84 D3 6 13 S 106 52 E
Játiva = Xàtiva, Spain ... 41 G4 38 59N 0 32W
Jättendal, Sweden ... 16 C11 61 58N 17 15 E
Jaú, Angola ... 115 F2 15 12 S 13 31 E
Jaú, Brazil ... 175 A6 22 10 S 48 30W
Jaú →, Brazil ... 169 D5 1 54 S 61 26W
Jauaperí →, Brazil ... 169 D5 1 54 S 61 26W
Jauja, Peru ... 172 C2 11 45 S 75 15W
Jaunpur, India ... 93 G10 25 46N 82 44 E
Jaur →, Brazil ... 173 D6 16 2 S 57 46W
Java = Jawa, Indonesia ... 85 D4 7 0 S 110 0 E
Java Barat □, Indonesia ... 79 G12 7 0 S 107 0 E
Java Sea, Indonesia ... 85 C3 4 35 S 107 15 E
Java Tengah □, Indonesia ... 79 G14 7 0 S 110 0 E
Java Timur □, Indonesia ... 79 G15 8 0 S 113 0 E
Java Trench, Ind. Oc. ... 84 D7 9 0 S 105 0 E
Javadi Hills, India ... 95 H4 12 40N 78 40 E
Javalambre, Sa. de, Spain ... 40 E4 40 6N 1 0W
Jávea, Spain ... 41 G5 38 48N 0 10 E
Javhlant = Ulyasutay, Mongolia ... 68 B4 47 56N 97 28 E
Javier, I., Chile ... 176 C2 47 5 S 74 25W
Javla, India ... 94 F2 17 18N 75 9 E
Jawa, Indonesia ... 85 D4 7 0 S 110 0 E
Jawad, India ... 92 G6 24 36N 74 51 E
Jawar, W. al →, Yemen ... 98 D4 15 50N 45 58 E
Jawhar, India ... 94 E1 19 55N 73 14 E
Jawor, Poland ... 55 G3 51 4N 16 11 E
Jaworzno, Poland ... 55 H6 50 13N 19 11 E
Jaworzyna Śląska, Poland ... 55 H3 50 55N 16 28 E
Jay, U.S.A. ... 153 E20 44 55N 72 30W
Jaya, Puncak, Indonesia ... 83 B5 3 57 S 137 17 E
Jayanca, Peru ... 172 B2 6 20 S 79 55W
Jayanti, India ... 93 26 45N 89 40 E
Jayapura, Indonesia ... 83 B6 2 28 S 140 38 E
Jayawijaya, Pegunungan, Indonesia ... 83 B5 5 0 S 139 0 E
Jayrūd, Syria ... 100 F7 33 49N 36 44 E
Jayton, U.S.A. ... 155 J4 33 15N 100 34W
Jāzireh-ye Shīf, Iran ... 97 E8 27 20N 58 55 E
Jazminal, Mexico ... 162 C4 24 56N 101 25W
Jazzīn, Lebanon ... 103 B4 33 31N 35 14 E
Jean, U.S.A. ... 161 K11 35 47N 115 20W
Jean Marie River, Canada ... 142 A4 61 32N 120 38W
Jean Rabel, Haiti ... 165 C5 19 50N 73 5W
Jeanerette, U.S.A. ... 155 L9 29 55N 91 40W
Jeanette, Ostrov = Zhannetty, Ostrov, Russia ... 67 B16 76 43N 158 0 E
Jeannette, U.S.A. ... 150 F5 40 20N 79 36W
Jebāl Bārez, Kūh-e, Iran ... 97 D8 28 30N 58 20 E
Jebba, Nigeria ... 113 D5 9 9N 4 48 E
Jebel, Bahr el →, Sudan ... 107 F3 9 30N 30 25 E
Jebel Dud, Sudan ... 107 E3 13 20N 33 58 E
Jebel Qerri, Sudan ... 107 D3 16 16N 32 50 E
Jeberos, Peru ... 172 B2 5 20 S 76 20W
Jedburgh, U.K. ... 22 F6 55 29N 2 33W
Jedda = Jiddah, Si. Arabia ... 98 B2 21 29N 39 10 E
Jeddore L., Canada ... 141 C8 48 3N 55 55W
Jedlicze, Poland ... 55 J8 49 43N 21 40 E

Jędrzejów, Poland ... 55 H7 50 35N 20 15 E
Jedwabne, Poland ... 55 E9 53 17N 22 18 E
Jeetzel →, Germany ... 30 B7 53 9N 11 3 E
Jefferson, Iowa, U.S.A. ... 156 B2 42 1N 94 23W
Jefferson, Ohio, U.S.A. ... 150 E4 41 44N 80 46W
Jefferson, Tex., U.S.A. ... 155 J7 32 46N 94 21W
Jefferson, Wis., U.S.A. ... 157 B8 43 0N 88 48W
Jefferson, Mt., Nev., U.S.A. ... 158 G5 38 51N 117 0W
Jefferson, Mt., Oreg., U.S.A. ... 158 D3 44 41N 121 48W
Jefferson City, Mo., U.S.A. ... 156 F5 38 34N 92 10W
Jefferson City, Tenn., U.S.A. ... 149 G4 36 7N 83 30W
Jeffersontown, U.S.A. ... 157 F11 38 12N 85 35W
Jeffersonville, Ga., U.S.A. ... 152 C6 32 41N 83 20W
Jeffersonville, Ind., U.S.A. ... 157 F11 38 17N 85 44W
Jeffersonville, Ohio, U.S.A. ... 157 E13 39 39N 83 34W
Jeffrey City, U.S.A. ... 158 E10 42 30N 107 49W
Jega, Nigeria ... 113 C5 12 15N 4 23 E
Jejevo, Solomon Is. ... 133 M10 8 6 S 159 8 E
Jēkabpils, Latvia ... 15 H21 56 29N 25 57 E
Jekyll I., U.S.A. ... 152 D8 31 4N 81 25W
Jelcz-Laskowice, Poland ... 55 G4 51 2N 17 19 E
Jelenia Góra, Poland ... 55 H2 50 50N 15 45 E
Jelgava, Latvia ... 15 H20 56 41N 23 49 E
Jelgava □, Latvia ... 54 B10 56 35N 23 45 E
Jelica, Serbia, Yug. ... 50 C4 43 50N 20 17 E
Jelli, Sudan ... 107 F3 5 25N 31 45 E
Jelšava, Slovak Rep. ... 35 C13 48 37N 20 15 E
Jemaja, Indonesia ... 87 L5 3 5N 105 45 E
Jemaluang, Malaysia ... 87 L4 2 16N 103 52 E
Jember, Indonesia ... 85 D4 8 11 S 113 41 E
Jembongan, Malaysia ... 78 C5 6 45N 117 20 E
Jena, Germany ... 30 E7 50 54N 11 35 E
Jena, U.S.A. ... 155 K8 31 41N 92 8W
Jenbach, Austria ... 34 D4 47 24N 11 47 E
Jendouba, Tunisia ... 108 A1 36 29N 8 47 E
Jenīn, West Bank ... 103 C4 32 28N 35 18 E
Jenison, U.S.A. ... 157 B11 42 54N 85 47W
Jenkins, U.S.A. ... 148 G4 37 10N 82 38W
Jenner, U.S.A. ... 160 G3 38 27N 123 7W
Jennings, Fla., U.S.A. ... 152 E6 30 36N 83 6W
Jennings, La., U.S.A. ... 155 K8 30 13N 92 40W
Jennings, Mo., U.S.A. ... 156 F6 38 43N 90 16W
Jensen Beach, U.S.A. ... 153 H9 27 15N 80 14W
Jepara, Indonesia ... 85 D3 7 40 S 109 14 E
Jeparit, Australia ... 128 D5 36 8 S 142 1 E
Jequié, Brazil ... 171 D3 13 51 S 40 5W
Jequitaí →, Brazil ... 171 E3 17 4 S 44 50W
Jequitinhonha, Brazil ... 171 E3 16 30 S 41 0W
Jequitinhonha →, Brazil ... 171 E4 15 51 S 38 53W
Jerada, Morocco ... 111 B4 34 17N 2 10W
Jerantut, Malaysia ... 87 L4 3 56N 102 22 E
Jerejak, Pulau, Malaysia ... 87 c 5 19N 100 19 E
Jérémie, Haiti ... 165 C5 18 40N 74 10W
Jeremoabo, Brazil ... 170 D4 10 4 S 38 21W
Jerez, Punta, Mexico ... 163 C5 22 58N 97 40W
Jerez de García Salinas, Mexico ... 162 C4 23 39N 103 0W
Jerez de la Frontera, Spain ... 43 J4 36 41N 6 7W
Jerez de los Caballeros, Spain ... 43 G4 38 20N 6 45W
Jericho = El Arīḩā, West Bank ... 103 D4 31 52N 35 27 E
Jericho, Australia ... 126 C4 23 38N 146 6 E
Jerichow, Germany ... 30 C8 52 30N 12 1 E
Jerico Springs, U.S.A. ... 156 G2 37 37N 94 1W
Jerid, Chott el = Djerid, Chott, Tunisia ... 108 B1 33 42N 8 30 E
Jerilderie, Australia ... 129 C6 35 20 S 145 41 E
Jermyn, U.S.A. ... 151 E9 41 31N 75 31W
Jerome, U.S.A. ... 158 E6 42 44N 114 31W
Jerramungup, Australia ... 125 F2 33 55 S 118 55 E
Jersey, U.K. ... 21 H5 49 11N 2 7W
Jersey City, U.S.A. ... 151 F10 40 44N 74 4W
Jersey Shore, U.S.A. ... 150 E7 41 12N 77 15W
Jerseyville, U.S.A. ... 156 E6 39 7N 90 20W
Jerumenha, Brazil ... 170 C3 7 5 S 43 0W
Jerusalem, Israel ... 103 D4 31 47N 35 10 E
Jervis B., Australia ... 129 C9 35 8 S 150 46 E
Jervis Inlet, Canada ... 142 C4 50 0N 123 57W
Jesenice, Slovenia ... 46 C2 39 47N 13 1 E
Jeseník, Czech Rep. ... 35 A10 50 14N 17 8 E
Jesenké, Slovak Rep. ... 35 C13 48 20N 20 10 E
Jesi = Iesi, Italy ... 45 E10 43 31N 13 14 E
Jesselton = Kota Kinabalu, Malaysia ... 85 A5 6 0N 116 4 E
Jessheim, Norway ... 18 D8 60 9N 11 10 E
Jessnitz, Germany ... 30 D8 51 40N 12 18 E
Jessore, Bangla. ... 90 D2 23 10N 89 10 E
Jessup, L., U.S.A. ... 153 G8 28 43N 81 14W
Jesup, Ga., U.S.A. ... 152 D8 31 36N 81 53W
Jesup, Iowa, U.S.A. ... 156 B4 42 29N 92 4W
Jesús, Peru ... 172 B2 7 15 S 78 25W
Jesús Carranza, Mexico ... 163 D5 17 28N 95 1W
Jesús María, Argentina ... 174 C3 30 59 S 64 5W
Jetmore, U.S.A. ... 155 F5 38 4N 99 54W
Jetpur, India ... 92 J4 21 45N 70 10 E
Jeumont, France ... 27 B11 50 18N 4 6 E
Jevnaker, Norway ... 18 D8 60 15N 10 26 E
Jewell, U.S.A. ... 156 B3 42 20N 93 39W
Jewett, U.S.A. ... 150 F3 40 22N 81 2W
Jewett City, U.S.A. ... 151 E13 41 36N 72 0W
Jeyḩūnābād, Iran ... 97 C6 34 58N 48 59 E
Jeypore, India ... 94 E6 18 50N 82 38 E
Jezioro, Jezioro, Poland ... 54 E6 53 40N 19 35 E
Jeziorany, Poland ... 54 E7 53 58N 20 46 E
Jeziorka →, Poland ... 55 F8 52 8N 21 9 E
Jha Jha, India ... 93 G12 24 46N 86 22 E
Jhaarkand = Jharkhand □, India ... 93 H11 24 0N 85 50 E
Jhabua, India ... 92 H6 22 46N 74 36 E
Jhajjar, India ... 92 E7 28 37N 76 42 E
Jhal, Pakistan ... 91 D2 28 17N 67 27 E
Jhal Jhao, Pakistan ... 91 D2 26 20N 65 35 E
Jhalakati, Bangla. ... 90 D3 22 39N 90 12 E
Jhalawar, India ... 92 G7 24 40N 76 10 E
Jhalida, India ... 93 H11 23 22N 85 58 E
Jhalrapatan, India ... 92 G7 24 33N 76 10 E
Jhang Maghiana, Pakistan ... 91 C4 31 15N 72 22 E
Jhansi, India ... 93 G8 25 30N 78 36 E
Jhargram, India ... 93 H12 22 27N 86 59 E
Jharia, India ... 93 H12 23 45N 86 26 E
Jharkhand □, India ... 93 H11 24 0N 85 50 E
Jharsuguda, India ... 94 D7 21 56N 84 5 E
Jhelum, Pakistan ... 91 B4 33 0N 73 45 E
Jhelum →, Pakistan ... 93 H10 23 24N 82 51 E
Jhilmilli, India ... 93 H10 23 24N 82 51 E
Jhudo, Pakistan ... 92 G3 24 58N 69 18 E
Jhunjhunu, India ... 92 E6 28 10N 75 30 E
Ji-Paraná, Brazil ... 173 C5 10 52 S 62 57W
Ji Xian, Hebei, China ... 74 F8 37 35N 115 30 E
Ji Xian, Henan, China ... 74 G8 35 22N 114 5 E
Ji Xian, Shanxi, China ... 74 F6 36 7N 110 40 E
Jia Xian, Henan, China ... 74 H7 33 59N 113 12 E
Jia Xian, Shaanxi, China ... 74 E6 38 12N 110 28 E
Jiading, China ... 77 B13 31 23N 121 15 E
Jiahe, China ... 77 E9 25 38N 112 19 E
Jialing Jiang →, China ... 76 C6 29 30N 106 20 E
Jiamusi, China ... 69 B8 46 40N 130 26 E
Ji'an, Jiangxi, China ... 77 D10 27 6N 114 59 E
Ji'an, Jilin, China ... 75 D14 41 5N 126 10 E
Jianchang, China ... 75 D11 40 55N 120 35 E
Jianchangying, China ... 75 D10 40 10N 118 50 E
Jianchuan, China ... 76 D2 26 38N 99 55 E
Jiande, China ... 77 C12 29 23N 119 15 E
Jiang'an, China ... 76 C5 28 40N 105 3 E
Jiangbei, China ... 76 C6 29 40N 106 34 E
Jiangcheng, China ... 76 F3 22 36N 101 52 E

Jiangchuan, China . . . . 76 E4 24 8N 102 39 E
Jiangdi, China . . . . 76 D4 26 57N 103 37 E
Jiangdu, China . . . . 77 A12 32 27N 119 36 E
Jiange, China . . . . 76 A5 32 4N 105 32 E
Jianghua, China . . . . 77 E8 25 0N 111 47 E
Jiangjin, China . . . . 76 C6 29 14N 106 14 E
Jiangkou, China . . . . 76 D7 27 40N 108 49 E
Jiangle, China . . . . 77 D11 26 42N 117 23 E
Jiangling, China . . . . 77 B9 30 25N 112 12 E
Jiangmen, China . . . . 77 F9 22 32N 113 0 E
Jiangning, China . . . . 77 B12 31 55N 118 50 E
Jiangshan, China . . . . 77 C12 28 40N 118 37 E
Jiangsu □, China . . . . 75 H11 33 0N 120 0 E
Jiangxi □, China . . . . 77 D11 27 30N 116 0 E
Jiangyan, China . . . . 77 A13 32 30N 120 7 E
Jiangyin, China . . . . 77 B13 31 54N 120 17 E
Jiangyong, China . . . . 77 E8 25 20N 111 22 E
Jiangyou, China . . . . 76 B5 31 44N 104 43 E
Jianhe, China . . . . 76 D7 26 37N 108 31 E
Jianning, China . . . . 77 C9 29 46N 112 56 E
Jian'ou, China . . . . 77 D11 26 50N 116 50 E
Jianshi, China . . . . 77 D12 27 3N 118 17 E
Jianshui, China . . . . 76 B7 30 37N 109 38 E
Jianyang, Fujian, China . . . . 77 D12 27 20N 118 5 E
Jianyang, Sichuan, China . . . . . . 76 B5 30 24N 104 33 E
Jiao Xian = Jiaozhou, China . . . . 75 F11 36 18N 120 1 E
Jiaohe, Hebei, China . . . . 74 E9 38 2N 116 20 E
Jiaohe, Jilin, China . . . . 75 C14 43 40N 127 22 E
Jiaojiang, China . . . . 77 C13 28 40N 121 24 E
Jiaoling, China . . . . 77 E11 24 41N 116 12 E
Jiaozhou, China . . . . 75 F11 36 18N 120 1 E
Jiaozhou Wan, China . . . . 75 F11 36 5N 120 10 E
Jiaozuo, China . . . . 74 G7 35 16N 113 12 E
Jiashan, China . . . . 77 B13 30 55N 120 55 E
Jiashi, China . . . . 65 D8 39 29N 76 39 E
Jiawang, China . . . . 75 G9 34 28N 117 26 E
Jiaxiang, China . . . . 74 G9 35 25N 116 20 E
Jiaxing, China . . . . 77 B13 30 49N 120 45 E
Jiayi = Chiai, Taiwan . . . . 77 F13 23 29N 120 25 E
Jiayu, China . . . . 77 C9 29 55N 113 55 E
Jibão, Serra do, Brazil . . . . 171 D3 14 48 S 45 0W
Jibiya, Nigeria . . . . 113 C6 13 5N 7 12 E
Jibou, Romania . . . . 53 C8 47 15N 23 17 E
Jibuti = Djibouti ■, Africa . . . . . 107 E5 12 0N 43 0 E
Jicarón, I., Panama 164 E3 7 10N 81 50W
Jičín, Czech Rep. . . . . 34 A8 50 25N 15 28 E
Jiddah, Si. Arabia . . . . 98 B2 21 29N 39 10 E
Jido, India . . . . 90 A5 29 2N 94 58 E
Jieshou, China . . . . 74 H8 33 18N 115 22 E
Jiexiu, China . . . . 74 F6 37 2N 111 55 E
Jieyang, China . . . . 77 F11 23 35N 116 21 E
Jigawa □, Nigeria . . . . 113 C6 12 0N 9 45 E
Jiggalong, Australia . . . . 124 D3 23 21 S 120 47 E
Jigni, India . . . . 93 G8 25 45N 79 25 E
Jihlava, Czech Rep. . . . . 34 B8 49 28N 15 35 E
Jihlava ➤, Czech Rep. . . . . 35 C9 48 55N 16 36 E
Jihlavský □, Czech Rep. . . . . . . 34 B8 49 30N 15 30 E
Jihočeský □, Czech Rep. . . . . . . 34 B7 49 0N 14 35 E
Jihomoravský □, Czech Rep. . . . 35 B9 49 5N 16 30 E
Jijel, Algeria . . . . 111 A6 36 52N 5 50 E
Jijiga, Ethiopia . . . . 120 C2 9 20N 42 50 E
Jikamshi, Nigeria . . . . 113 C6 12 12N 7 45 E
Jikau, Sudan . . . . 107 F3 8 28N 33 47 E
Jilib = Gelib, Somali Rep. . . . . . 120 D2 0 29N 42 46 E
Jilin, China . . . . 75 C14 43 44N 126 30 E
Jilin □, China . . . . 75 C14 44 0N 127 0 E
Jiloca ➤, Spain 40 D3 41 21N 1 39W
Jilong = Chilung, Taiwan . . . . . . 77 E13 25 3N 121 45 E
Jim Thorpe, U.S.A. 151 F9 40 52N 75 44W
Jima, Ethiopia . . . . 107 F4 7 40N 36 47 E
Jimbaran, Teluk, Indonesia . . . . 79 K18 8 46 S 115 2 E
Jimbolia, Romania . . . . 52 E5 45 47N 20 43 E
Jimena de la Frontera, Spain . . . 43 J5 36 27N 5 24W
Jiménez, Mexico 162 B4 27 10N 104 54W
Jimenez, Phil. . . . . 81 G4 8 20N 123 50 E
Jimo, China . . . . 75 F11 36 23N 120 30 E
Jin, Kepulauan, Indonesia . . . . . 83 C4 6 50 S 134 40 E
Jin Jiang ➤, China . . . . 77 C10 28 24N 115 48 E
Jin Xian = Jinzhou, China . . . . . 74 E8 38 2N 115 2 E
Jin Xian, China . . . . 75 E11 38 55N 121 42 E
Jinan, China . . . . 74 F9 36 38N 117 1 E
Jincheng, China . . . . 68 C5 35 30N 112 10 E
Jinchuan, China . . . . 74 G7 35 29N 112 50 E
Jind, India . . . . 76 B4 31 30N 102 3 E
Jindabyne, Australia . . . . 92 E7 29 19N 76 22 E
Jinding, China . . . . 129 D8 36 25 S 148 35 E
Jindřichův Hradec, Czech Rep. . . 69 G10 22 22N 113 33 E
Jing He ➤, China . . . . 34 B8 49 10N 15 2 E
Jing Shan, China . . . . 74 G5 34 27N 109 4 E
Jing Xian, China . . . . 77 B8 31 20N 112 50 E
Jingbian, China . . . . 77 B12 30 58N 118 25 E
Jingchuan, China . . . . 77 C10 28 50N 115 17 E
Jingde, China . . . . 74 F5 37 20N 108 30 E
Jingdezhen, China . . . . 76 G4 35 20N 107 20 E
Jingdong, China . . . . 77 B12 30 15N 118 27 E
Jinggangshan, China . . . . 77 C11 29 20N 117 11 E
Jinggu, China . . . . 76 E3 24 23N 100 47 E
Jinghai, China . . . . 77 D10 26 58N 114 15 E
Jinghong, China . . . . 76 F3 23 35N 100 41 E
Jingjiang, China . . . . 74 E9 38 55N 116 55 E
Jingle, China . . . . 77 A13 32 2N 120 16 E
Jingmen, China . . . . 74 E6 38 20N 111 55 E
Jingning, China . . . . 77 B9 31 0N 112 10 E
Jingpo Hu, China . . . . 74 G3 35 30N 105 43 E
Jingshan, China . . . . 75 C15 43 55N 128 55 E
Jingtai, China . . . . 77 B9 31 1N 113 7 E
Jingxi, China . . . . 74 F3 37 10N 104 6 E
Jingxing, China . . . . 76 F6 23 8N 106 27 E
Jingyang, China . . . . 74 E8 38 2N 114 8 E
Jingyu, China . . . . 74 G5 34 30N 108 50 E
Jingyuan, China . . . . 75 C14 42 25N 126 45 E
Jingzhou, China . . . . 74 F3 36 30N 104 40 E
Jinhua, China . . . . 76 D7 26 33N 109 40 E
Jining, Nei Monggol Zizhiqu, China 74 H6 33 15N 111 0 E
Jining, Shandong, China . . . . . . 77 C12 29 18N 119 38 E
Jinja, Uganda . . . . 74 D7 41 5N 113 0 E
Jinjang, Malaysia . . . . 118 B3 0 25N 33 12 E
Jinji, China . . . . 87 L3 3 13N 101 39 E
Jinjiang, Fujian, China . . . . 74 F4 37 58N 106 8 E
Jinjiang, Yunnan, China . . . . 77 E12 24 43N 118 33 E
Jinjini, Ghana . . . . 76 D3 26 14N 100 34 E
Jinju, S. Korea 112 D4 7 26N 2 42W
Jinkouhe, China . . . . 77 B10 30 20N 114 4 E
Jinmen Dao, China . . . . 76 C4 29 18N 103 4 E
Jinning, China . . . . 77 E12 24 25N 118 25 E
Jinotega, Nic. . . . . 76 E4 24 38N 102 38 E
Jinotepe, Nic. 164 D2 13 6N 85 59W
Jinping, Guizhou, China 164 D2 11 50N 86 10W
Jinping, Yunnan, China . . . . 76 D7 26 41N 109 10 E
Jinsha, China . . . . 76 F4 22 45N 103 18 E
Jinsha Jiang ➤, China . . . . 76 D6 27 29N 106 38 E
Jinshan, China . . . . 76 C5 28 50N 104 36 E
Jinshi, China . . . . 77 B13 30 55N 104 49 E
Jintan, China . . . . 77 C8 29 40N 111 50 E
Jintotolo Channel, Phil. . . . . 77 B12 31 42N 119 36 E
Jintur, India . . . . 81 F4 11 48N 123 5 E
Jinxi, Jiangxi, China . . . . 94 E3 19 37N 76 42 E
Jinxi, Liaoning, China . . . . 77 D11 27 56N 116 45 E
Jinxian, China . . . . 75 D11 40 52N 120 50 E
Jinxiang, China . . . . 77 C11 28 26N 116 17 E
Jinyang, China . . . . 74 G9 35 5N 116 22 E

Jinyang, China . . . . 76 D4 27 28N 103 5 E
Jinyun, China . . . . 77 C13 28 35N 120 5 E
Jinzhai, China . . . . 77 B10 31 40N 115 53 E
Jinzhou, Hebei, China . . . . 74 E8 38 2N 115 2 E
Jinzhou, Liaoning, China . . . . . . 75 D11 41 5N 121 3 E
Jiparaná, Brazil . . . . 173 B5 8 3 S 62 52W
Jipijapa, Ecuador . . . . 168 D1 1 0 S 80 40W
Jiquilpan, Mexico 162 D4 19 57N 102 42W
Jishan, China . . . . 74 G6 35 34N 110 58 E
Jishou, China . . . . 76 C7 28 21N 109 43 E
Jishui, China . . . . 77 D10 27 12N 115 8 E
Jisr ash Shughūr, Syria . . . . 100 E7 35 49N 36 18 E
Jitarning, Australia . . . . 125 F2 32 48 S 117 57 E
Jitra, Malaysia . . . . 87 J3 6 16N 100 25 E
Jiu ➤, Romania . . . . 53 G8 43 47N 23 48 E
Jiudengkou, China . . . . 74 E4 39 56N 106 40 E
Jiujiang, Guangdong, China . . . . 77 F9 22 50N 113 0 E
Jiujiang, Jiangxi, China . . . . 77 C10 29 42N 115 58 E
Jiuling Shan, China . . . . 77 C10 28 40N 114 40 E
Jiulong = Kowloon, China . . . . . 69 G11 22 19N 114 11 E
Jiulong, China . . . . 76 C4 28 57N 101 31 E
Jiutai, China . . . . 75 B13 44 10N 125 50 E
Jiuxincheng, China . . . . 74 E8 39 17N 115 59 E
Jiuyuhang, China . . . . 77 B12 30 18N 119 56 E
Jiwa, U.A.E. . . . . 99 B6 23 0N 54 10 E
Jiwani, Ras, Pakistan . . . . 91 D1 25 1N 61 44 E
Jixi, Anhui, China . . . . 77 B12 30 15N 118 34 E
Jixi, Heilongjiang, China . . . . . . 75 B16 45 20N 130 50 E
Jiyang, China . . . . 75 F9 37 0N 117 12 E
Jiyuan, China . . . . 74 G7 35 7N 112 57 E
Jiz', W. ➤, Yemen . . . . 99 C6 16 12N 52 14 E
Jīzān, Si. Arabia . . . . 98 C3 17 0N 42 20 E
Jize, China . . . . 74 F8 36 54N 114 56 E
Jizera ➤, Czech Rep. . . . . 34 A7 50 10N 14 43 E
Jizl, Wādī al ➤, Si. Arabia . . . . . 96 E3 25 39N 38 25 E
Jizō-Zaki, Japan . . . . 72 B5 35 34N 133 20 E
Jizzakh, Uzbekistan . . . . 65 C3 40 6N 67 50 E
Joaçaba, Brazil . . . . 175 B5 27 5 S 51 31W
Joaíma, Brazil . . . . 171 E3 16 39 S 41 2W
Joal Fadiout, Senegal 112 C1 14 9N 16 50W
João Amaro, Brazil . . . . 171 D3 12 46 S 40 22W
João Câmara, Brazil . . . . 170 C4 5 32 S 35 48W
João Pessoa, Brazil . . . . 171 E2 7 10 S 34 52W
João Pinheiro, Brazil . . . . 171 E2 17 45 S 46 10W
Joaquim Távora, Brazil . . . . 171 F2 23 30 S 49 58W
Joaquín V. González, Argentina . 174 B3 25 10 S 64 0W
Jobat, India . . . . 92 H6 22 25N 74 34 E
Jobourg, Nez de, France 26 C5 49 41N 1 57W
Jódar, Spain 43 H7 37 50N 3 21W
Jodhpur, India . . . . 92 F5 26 23N 73 8 E
Jodiya, India . . . . 92 H4 22 42N 70 18 E
Joensuu, Finland . . . . 56 B4 62 37N 29 49 E
Jõetsu, Japan . . . . 71 F9 37 12N 138 10 E
Jœuf, France . . . . 27 C12 49 12N 6 0 E
Jofane, Mozam. . . . . 117 C5 21 15 S 34 18 E
Jogbani, India . . . . 93 F12 26 25N 87 15 E
Jõgeva, Estonia . . . . 15 G22 58 45N 26 24 E
Jogjakarta = Yogyakarta, Indonesia 85 D4 7 49 S 110 22 E
Jõhana, Japan . . . . 73 A8 36 30N 136 57 E
Johannesburg, S. Africa . . . . . . 117 D4 26 10 S 28 2 E
Johannesburg, U.S.A. 161 K9 35 22N 117 38W
Johansfors, Sweden . . . . 17 H9 56 42N 15 32 E
Johilla ➤, India . . . . 93 H9 23 37N 81 14 E
John Crow Mts., Jamaica . . . . . 164 a 18 5N 76 25W
John Day, U.S.A. 158 D4 44 25N 118 57W
John Day ➤, U.S.A. 158 D3 45 44N 120 39W
John Day Fossil Beds Nat. Mon. △,
  U.S.A. 158 D4 44 33N 119 38W
John D'Or Prairie, Canada 142 B5 58 30N 115 8W
John F. Kennedy International, New
  York ✈ (JFK), U.S.A. 151 F11 40 38N 73 47W
John F. Kennedy Space Center =
  Kennedy Space Center, U.S.A. . 153 G9 28 40N 80 42W
John H. Kerr Reservoir, U.S.A. . . 149 G6 36 36N 78 18W
John o' Groats, U.K. 22 C5 58 38N 3 4W
John's Ra., Australia . . . . 126 C1 21 55 S 133 23 E
Johnson, Kans., U.S.A. 155 G4 37 34N 101 45W
Johnson, Vt., U.S.A. 151 B12 44 38N 72 41W
Johnson City, N.Y., U.S.A. 151 D9 42 7N 75 58W
Johnson City, Tenn., U.S.A. 149 G4 36 19N 82 21W
Johnson City, Tex., U.S.A. 155 K5 30 17N 98 25W
Johnsonburg, U.S.A. 150 E6 41 29N 78 41W
Johnsondale, U.S.A. 161 K8 35 58N 118 32W
Johnson's Crossing, Canada . . . 142 A2 60 29N 133 18W
Johnsonville, N.Z. . . . . 130 H3 41 13 S 174 48 E
Johnston, U.S.A. 152 B8 33 50N 81 48W
Johnston, L., Australia . . . . 125 F3 32 25 S 120 30 E
Johnston City, U.S.A. 156 G8 37 49N 88 56W
Johnston Falls = Mambilima Falls,
  Zambia . . . . 119 E2 10 31 S 28 45 E
Johnstone Str., Canada 135 F11 17 10N 169 8W
Johnstown, Ireland 23 C8 52 28N 126 0W
Johnstown, N.Y., U.S.A. 151 C10 43 0N 74 22W
Johnstown, Ohio, U.S.A. 150 F2 40 9N 82 41W
Johnstown, Pa., U.S.A. 150 F6 40 20N 78 55W
Johor □, Malaysia . . . . 84 B2 2 5N 103 20 E
Johor, Selat, Asia . . . . 87 d 1 28N 103 47 E
Johor Baharu, Malaysia . . . . . . 87 d 1 28N 103 46 E
Jõhvi, Estonia . . . . 15 G22 59 22N 27 27 E
Joigny, France . . . . 27 E10 47 58N 3 20 E
Joinville, Brazil . . . . 175 B6 26 15 S 48 55W
Joinville, France . . . . 27 D12 48 27N 5 10 E
Joinville I., Antarctica . . . . 7 C18 65 0 S 55 30W
Jojutla, Mexico 163 D5 18 37N 99 11W
Jokkmokk, Sweden . . . . 8 C18 66 35N 19 50 E
Jökulsá á Bru ➤, Iceland 11 B12 65 40N 14 16W
Jökulsá á Fjöllum ➤, Iceland . . . 11 A10 66 10N 16 30W
Jökulsárlþjúfur △, Iceland 11 B10 65 56N 16 31W
Jolfa, Ázarbājān-e Sharqí, Iran . . 101 C11 38 57N 45 38 E
Jolfa, Eşfahan, Iran . . . . 101 C6 32 58N 51 37 E
Joliet, U.S.A. 157 C8 41 32N 88 5W
Joliette, Canada 140 C5 46 3N 73 24W
Jolo, Phil. . . . . 81 H3 6 0N 121 0 E
Jolo Group, Phil. . . . . 81 J3 6 0N 121 9 E
Jolon, U.S.A. 160 K5 35 58N 121 9W
Jølstravatnet, Norway . . . . 18 C3 61 32N 6 23 E
Jomalig I., Phil. . . . . 80 D4 14 42N 122 22 E
Jombang, Indonesia . . . . 85 D4 7 33 S 112 14 E
Jomda, China . . . . 76 B2 31 28N 98 18 E
Jona, Switz. . . . . 33 B7 47 14N 8 51 E
Jonava, Lithuania . . . . 12 J21 55 8N 24 12 E
Jondal, Norway . . . . 18 D3 60 16N 6 15 E
Jones, Phil. . . . . 80 C3 16 33N 121 42 E
Jones Sound, Canada 6 B3 76 0N 85 0W
Jonesboro, Ark., U.S.A. 155 H9 35 50N 90 42W
Jonesboro, Ga., U.S.A. 152 B5 33 31N 84 22W
Jonesboro, La., U.S.A. 155 J8 32 15N 92 43W
Jonesville, Ind., U.S.A. 157 E11 39 5N 85 54W
Jonesville, Mich., U.S.A. 157 C12 41 59N 84 40W
Jong ➤, S. Leone 112 D2 7 32N 12 23W
Jonglei, Sudan . . . . 107 F3 6 25N 30 50 E
Jonglei □, Sudan . . . . 107 F3 7 30N 32 30 E
Joniškis, Lithuania . . . . 15 H20 56 13N 23 35 E
Jönköping, Sweden . . . . 17 G8 57 45N 14 8 E
Jönköpings län □, Sweden . . . . . 17 G8 57 45N 14 10 E
Jonquière, Canada 141 C5 48 27N 71 14W
Jonsered, Sweden . . . . 17 G6 57 45N 12 10 E
Jonzac, France 28 C3 45 27N 0 28W
Joplin, U.S.A. 155 G7 37 6N 94 31W
Jora, India . . . . 92 F6 26 20N 77 49 E
Jordan, Phil. . . . . 81 F4 10 40N 122 35 E

Jordan, Mont., U.S.A. 158 C10 47 19N 106 55W
Jordan, N.Y., U.S.A. 151 C8 43 4N 76 29W
Jordan ■, Asia . . . . 103 E5 31 0N 36 0 E
Jordan ➤, Asia . . . . 103 D4 31 48N 35 32 E
Jordan Valley, U.S.A. 158 E5 42 59N 117 3W
Jordânia, Brazil . . . . 171 E3 15 55 S 40 11W
Jordanów, Poland . . . . 55 J6 49 41N 19 49 E
Jordet, Norway . . . . 18 C9 61 25N 12 8 E
Jorge, C., Chile . . . . 176 D1 51 40 S 75 35W
Jorgen Brønlund Fjord, Greenland 10 A8 82 30N 29 0W
Jorhat, India . . . . 90 B5 26 45N 94 12 E
Jorm, Afghan. . . . . 65 E5 36 50N 70 52 E
Jörn, Sweden . . . . 14 D19 65 4N 20 1 E
Jorong, Indonesia . . . . 85 C4 3 58 S 114 56 E
Jørpeland, Norway . . . . 18 E3 59 3N 6 1 E
Jorquera ➤, Chile . . . . 174 B2 28 3 S 69 58W
Jos, Nigeria . . . . 113 D6 9 53N 8 51 E
Jos Plateau, Nigeria . . . . 113 D6 9 55N 9 0 E
Jošanička Banja, Serbia, Yug. . . 50 C4 43 24N 20 47 E
José Abad Santos, Phil. . . . . 81 J5 5 55N 125 39 E
José Batlle y Ordóñez, Uruguay . 175 C4 33 20 S 55 10W
José de San Martín, Argentina . . 176 B2 44 4 S 70 26W
Jose Panganiban, Phil. . . . . 80 D4 14 17N 122 41 E
Joseni, Romania . . . . 53 D10 46 42N 25 29 E
Joseph, L., Nfld., Canada 141 B6 52 45N 65 18W
Joseph, L., Ont., Canada 150 A5 45 10N 79 44W
Joseph Bonaparte G., Australia . 124 B4 14 35 S 128 50 E
Joseph Bonaparte G., Australia . 93 D8 30 34N 79 34 E
Joshinetsu-Kōgen Nat. Park △,
  Japan . . . . 73 A10 36 42N 138 32 E
Joshua Tree, U.S.A. 161 L10 34 8N 116 19W
Joshua Tree Nat. Park △, U.S.A. . 161 M10 33 55N 116 0W
Josselin, France 26 E4 47 57N 2 33W
Jost Van Dyke, Br. Virgin Is. . . . 165 e 18 29N 64 47W
Jostedal, Norway . . . . 18 C4 61 35N 7 15 E
Jostedalsbreen, Norway . . . . . . 18 C3 61 40N 6 59 E
Jotunheimen, Norway . . . . 18 C5 61 35N 8 25 E
Jotunheimen Nasjonalpark △,
  Norway . . . . 18 C5 61 32N 8 25 E
Joubertberge, Namibia . . . . 116 B1 18 30 S 14 0 E
Joué-lès-Tours, France . . . . 26 E7 47 21N 0 40 E
Jourdanton, U.S.A. 155 L5 28 55N 98 33W
Joutseno, Finland . . . . 58 B5 61 7N 28 30 E
Joutsijärvi, Finland . . . . 8 C23 66 40N 27 45 E
Jovellanos, Cuba 164 B3 22 40N 81 10W
Jowai, Phil. . . . . 80 E4 13 4N 123 36 E
Jowai, India . . . . 90 C4 25 26N 92 12 E
Jowhar = Giohar, Somali Rep. . . 120 D3 2 48N 45 30 E
Jowzjān □, Afghan. . . . . 65 E3 36 10N 66 0 E
Joyeuse, France . . . . 29 D8 44 29N 4 16 E
Jõyõ, Japan . . . . 73 C7 34 50N 135 47 E
Józefów, Lubelskie, Poland . . . . 55 H10 50 28N 23 2 E
Józefów, Mazowieckie, Poland . . 55 F8 52 10N 21 11 E
Ju Xian, China . . . . 75 F10 35 35N 118 20 E
Juan Aldama, Mexico 162 C4 24 20N 103 23W
Juan Bautista Alberdi, Argentina 174 C3 34 6 S 61 5W
Juan de Fuca Str., Canada 160 B3 48 15N 124 0W
Juan de Nova, Ind. Oc. . . . . 117 B7 17 3 S 43 45 E
Juan Fernández, Arch. de, Pac. Oc. 135 L20 33 50 S 80 0W
Juan José Castelli, Argentina . . . 174 B3 25 7 S 60 57W
Juan L. Lacaze, Uruguay . . . . . . 175 C4 34 26 S 57 25W
Juanjuí, Peru . . . . 172 E2 7 10 S 76 45W
Juankoski, Finland . . . . 14 E23 63 3N 28 19 E
Juara, Brazil . . . . 173 C6 11 20 S 57 25W
Juárez, Argentina . . . . 174 D4 37 40 S 59 43W
Juárez, Mexico 161 N11 32 20N 115 57W
Juárez, Sierra de, Mexico 162 A1 32 0N 116 0W
Juàzeiro, Brazil . . . . 170 C3 9 30 S 40 30W
Juàzeiro do Norte, Brazil . . . . . . 170 C4 7 10 S 39 18W
Juba = Giuba ➤, Somali Rep. . . 120 D2 1 42 S 51 25 E
Juba, Sudan . . . . 107 G3 4 50N 31 35 E
Jubayl, Lebanon . . . . 103 A4 34 5N 35 39 E
Jubbah, Si. Arabia . . . . 96 D4 28 2N 40 56 E
Jubbal, India . . . . 92 D7 31 5N 77 40 E
Jubbulpore = Jabalpur, India . . . 93 H8 23 9N 79 58 E
Jūbek, Germany . . . . 30 A5 54 33N 9 22 E
Jubga, Russia . . . . 61 H4 44 19N 38 48 E
Jubilee L., Australia . . . . 125 E4 29 0 S 126 50 E
Juby, C., Morocco 110 C2 28 0N 12 59W
Júcar = Xúquer ➤, Spain 41 F4 39 5N 0 10W
Júcaro, Cuba 164 B4 21 37N 78 51W
Juchitán, Mexico 163 D5 16 27N 95 5W
Judaberg, Norway . . . . 18 E2 59 10 S 5 51 E
Judaea = Har Yehuda, Israel . . . 103 D3 31 35N 34 57 E
Judenburg, Austria . . . . 34 D7 47 12N 14 38 E
Judith ➤, U.S.A. 158 C9 47 44N 109 39W
Judith, Pt., U.S.A. 151 E13 41 22N 71 29W
Judith Gap, U.S.A. 158 C9 46 41N 109 45W
Juelsminde, Denmark . . . . 17 J4 55 43N 10 1 E
Jufari ➤, Brazil . . . . 169 D5 1 13 S 62 0W
Jugoslavia = Yugoslavia ■, Europe 50 C4 43 20N 20 0 E
Juigalpa, Nic. 164 D2 12 6N 85 26W
Juillac, France . . . . 28 C5 45 20N 1 19 E
Juist, Germany . . . . 30 B2 53 40N 6 59 E
Juiz de Fora, Brazil . . . . 171 F3 21 43 S 43 19W
Jujuy □, Argentina . . . . 174 A2 23 20 S 65 40W
Julesburg, U.S.A. 154 E3 40 59N 102 16W
Juli, Peru . . . . 172 D4 16 10 S 69 25W
Julia Cr. ➤, Australia . . . . 126 C3 20 0 S 141 11 E
Julia Creek, Australia . . . . 126 C3 20 39 S 141 44 E
Juliaca, Peru . . . . 172 D3 15 25 S 70 10W
Julian, U.S.A. 161 M10 33 4N 116 38W
Julian Alps = Julijske Alpe, Slovenia 45 B11 46 15N 14 1 E
Julian L., Canada 140 B4 54 25N 77 57W
Julianatop, Suriname 169 C6 3 40N 56 30W
Julianehåb = Qaqortoq, Greenland 10 E6 60 43N 46 0W
Jülich, Germany . . . . 30 E2 50 55N 6 22 E
Julierpass, Switz. . . . . 33 D9 46 28N 9 32 E
Juliette, L., U.S.A. 152 B6 33 2N 83 50W
Julijske Alpe, Slovenia . . . . 45 B11 46 15N 14 1 E
Julimes, Mexico 162 B3 28 25N 105 27W
Jullundur, India . . . . 92 D6 31 20N 75 40 E
Julu, China . . . . 74 F8 37 15N 115 2 E
Jumbo, Zimbabwe . . . . 119 F3 17 30 S 30 58 E
Jumbo Pk., U.S.A. 161 J12 36 12N 114 11W
Jumentos Cays, Bahamas 164 B4 23 0N 75 40W
Jumilla, Spain 41 G3 38 28N 1 19W
Jumla, Nepal . . . . 93 E10 29 15N 82 13 E
Jumna = Yamuna ➤, India . . . . . 93 G9 25 30N 81 53 E
Junagadh, India . . . . 92 J4 21 30N 70 30 E
Junction, Tex., U.S.A. 155 K5 30 29N 99 46W
Junction, Utah, U.S.A. 159 G7 38 14N 112 13W
Junction B., Australia . . . . 126 A1 11 52 S 133 55 E
Junction City, Kans., U.S.A. 154 F6 39 2N 96 50W
Junction City, Oreg., U.S.A. 158 D2 44 13N 123 12W
Junction Pt., Australia . . . . 126 A1 11 45 S 133 50 E
Jundah, Australia . . . . 126 C3 24 46 S 143 2 E
Jundiaí, Brazil . . . . 175 A6 24 30 S 47 0W
Juneau, U.S.A. 142 B2 58 18N 134 25W
Junee, Australia . . . . 129 C7 34 53 S 147 35 E
Jungfrau, Switz. . . . . 32 C5 46 32N 7 58 E
Junggar Pendi, China . . . . 68 B3 44 30N 86 0 E
Jungshahi, Pakistan . . . . 92 G2 24 52N 67 44 E
Juniata ➤, U.S.A. 150 F7 40 30N 77 40W
Junín, Argentina . . . . 174 C3 34 33 S 60 57W
Junín, Peru . . . . 172 C2 11 10 S 76 0W
Junín □, Peru . . . . 172 C3 11 30 S 75 0W
Junín de los Andes, Argentina . . 176 A2 39 45 S 71 0W
Jūniyah, Lebanon . . . . 103 B4 33 59N 35 38 E
Junlian, China . . . . 76 C5 28 8N 104 29 E
Junnar, India . . . . 94 E1 19 12N 73 58 E
Juno Beach, U.S.A. 153 J9 26 52N 80 3W

Juntas, Chile . . . . 174 B2 28 24 S 69 58W
Juntura, U.S.A. 158 E4 43 45N 118 5W
Juparanã, L., Brazil . . . . 171 E3 19 16 S 40 8W
Jupiter, U.S.A. 153 J9 26 57N 80 6W
Juquiá, Brazil . . . . 171 F2 24 19 S 47 38W
Jur ➤, Sudan . . . . 107 F2 8 45N 29 15 E
Jura = Jura, Mts. du, Europe . . . 27 F13 46 40N 6 5 E
Jura = Schwäbische Alb, Germany 31 G5 48 20N 9 30 E
Jura, U.K. 22 F3 56 0N 5 50W
Jura □, France . . . . 27 F12 46 47N 5 45 E
Jura □, Switz. . . . . 31 H3 47 20N 7 20 E
Jura ➤, France . . . . 27 F13 46 40N 6 5 E
Jura ➤, Lithuania . . . . 54 C9 55 3N 22 9 E
Jura, Mts. du, Europe . . . . 27 F13 46 40N 6 5 E
Jura, Sd. of, U.K. 22 F3 55 57N 5 45W
Jura Suisse, Switz. . . . . 32 B4 47 10N 7 0 E
Jurado, Colombia 168 B2 7 7N 77 46W
Jurbarkas, Lithuania . . . . 15 J20 55 4N 22 46 E
Jurien, Australia . . . . 125 F2 30 18 S 115 2 E
Jurilovca, Romania . . . . 53 F13 44 46N 28 52 E
Jūrmala, Latvia . . . . 15 H20 56 58N 23 34 E
Jurong, China . . . . 77 B12 31 57N 119 9 E
Jurong, Singapore . . . . 87 d 1 19N 103 42 E
Juruá, Brazil . . . . 168 D4 3 25 S 66 2W
Juruá ➤, Brazil . . . . 168 D4 2 37 S 65 44W
Juruena, Brazil . . . . 173 C6 13 0 S 58 10W
Juruena ➤, Brazil . . . . 173 B6 7 20 S 58 3W
Juruti, Brazil . . . . 169 D6 2 9 S 56 4W
Jussey, France . . . . 27 E13 47 50N 5 55 E
Justo Daract, Argentina . . . . . . 174 C2 33 52 S 65 12W
Jutaí, Amazonas, Brazil . . . . 168 D4 2 44 S 66 57W
Jutaí, Amazonas, Brazil . . . . 172 B4 5 11 S 68 54W
Jutaí ➤, Brazil . . . . 168 D4 2 43 S 66 57W
Jüterbog, Germany . . . . 30 D9 51 59N 13 5 E
Juticalpa, Honduras 164 D2 14 40N 86 12W
Jutland = Jylland, Denmark . . . . 17 H3 56 25N 9 30 E
Juventud, I. de la, Cuba 164 B3 21 40N 82 40W
Juvigny-sous-Andaine, France . . 26 D6 48 32N 0 30W
Jüy Zar, Iran . . . . 101 F12 33 50N 46 18 E
Juye, China . . . . 74 G9 35 22N 116 5 E
Juzennecourt, France . . . . 27 D11 48 10N 4 58 E
Jvari, Georgia . . . . 61 J6 42 42N 42 4 E
Jyderup, Denmark . . . . 17 J5 55 40N 11 26 E
Jylland, Denmark . . . . 17 H3 56 25N 9 30 E
Jyväskylä, Finland . . . . 15 E21 62 14N 25 50 E

K

K2, Pakistan . . . . 93 B7 35 58N 76 32 E
Ka ➤, Nigeria . . . . 113 C5 11 40N 4 10 E
Ka Lae, U.S.A. 145 E6 18 55N 155 41W
Kaawawa, U.S.A. 145 J14 21 31N 158 9W
Kaala, U.S.A. 145 J13 21 31N 158 9W
Kaala-Gomén, N. Cal. . . . . 133 T18 20 40 S 164 25 E
Kaap Plateau, S. Africa . . . . 116 D3 28 30 S 24 0 E
Kaapkruis, Namibia . . . . 116 C1 21 55 S 13 57 E
Kaapstad = Cape Town, S. Africa 116 E2 33 55 S 18 22 E
Kaatoan, Mt., Phil. . . . . 81 G5 8 10N 124 52 E
Kaba, Guinea 112 C2 10 9N 11 40W
Kabacan, Phil. . . . . 81 H5 7 8N 124 49 E
Kabaena, Indonesia . . . . 82 C2 5 15 S 122 0 E
Kabala, S. Leone 112 D2 9 38N 11 37W
Kabale, Uganda . . . . 118 C3 1 15 S 30 0 E
Kabalebostuwmeer, Suriname . . 169 C6 4 45N 57 30W
Kabale, Dem. Rep. of the Congo . 118 D2 6 0 S 26 58 E
Kabambare, Dem. Rep. of the Congo 118 C2 4 41 S 27 39 E
Kabango, Dem. Rep. of the Congo 119 D2 8 35 S 28 30 E
Kabanjahe, Indonesia . . . . 84 B1 3 6N 98 30 E
Kabara, Fiji . . . . 133 E3 18 59 S 178 56W
Kabara, Mali 112 B4 16 40N 2 50W
Kabardinka, Russia . . . . 83 B4 0 4 S 130 58 E
Kabardinka, Russia . . . . 59 K10 44 40N 37 57 E
Kabardino-Balkar Republic =
  Kabardino-Balkaria □, Russia . 61 J6 43 30N 43 30 E
Kabardino-Balkaria □, Russia . . 61 J6 43 30N 43 30 E
Kabarega Falls = Murchison Falls,
  Uganda . . . . 118 B3 2 15N 31 30 E
Kabasalan, Phil. . . . . 81 H4 7 47N 122 44 E
Kabat, Indonesia . . . . 79 J17 8 16 S 114 19 E
Kabba, Nigeria . . . . 113 D6 7 50N 6 3 E
Kabbani ➤, India . . . . 95 H3 12 13N 76 54 E
Kabetogama, U.S.A. 154 A8 48 28N 92 59W
Kabi, Niger . . . . 113 C7 13 30N 12 35 E
Kabin Buri, Thailand . . . . 86 F3 13 57N 101 43 E
Kabinakagami L., Canada 140 C3 48 54N 84 25W
Kabinda, Dem. Rep. of the Congo 118 D1 6 19 S 24 20 E
Kablūbīyah, Sudan . . . . 109 H4 13 0N 24 0 E
Kablungu, C., Papua N. G. . . . . . 133 L8 6 19 S 150 1 E
Kabna, Sudan . . . . 106 D3 19 6N 32 40 E
Kabo, C.A.R. . . . . 114 A3 7 35N 18 38 E
Kabompo, Zambia . . . . 119 E1 13 36 S 24 14 E
Kabompo ➤, Zambia . . . . 115 E4 14 11 S 23 11 E
Kabondo, Dem. Rep. of the Congo 119 D2 8 58 S 25 40 E
Kabongo, Dem. Rep. of the Congo 118 D2 7 22 S 25 33 E
Kabot, Guinea 112 C2 10 48N 14 57W
Kabou, Togo . . . . 113 D5 9 55 E
Kaboudia, Rass, Tunisia . . . . . . 108 A2 35 13N 11 10 E
Kabr, Sudan . . . . 107 E2 10 54N 26 50 E
Kabrousse, Senegal 112 C1 12 25N 16 45W
Kabubu, Dem. Rep. of the Congo 115 D4 9 42 S 24 40 E
Kabūd Gonbad, Iran . . . . 97 B8 37 5N 59 45 E
Kabugao, Phil. . . . . 80 B3 18 2N 121 11 E
Kābul, Afghan. . . . . 93 B3 34 28N 69 1 E
Kabul □, Afghan. . . . . 91 B3 34 30N 69 0 E
Kābul ➤, Pakistan . . . . 91 B4 33 55N 72 14 E
Kabuli, Papua N. G. . . . . 132 B4 2 5 S 146 40 E
Kabunga, Dem. Rep. of the Congo 118 C2 1 38 S 28 3 E
Kaburuang, Indonesia . . . . 82 A3 3 50N 126 30 E
Kabushiya, Sudan . . . . 107 D3 16 54N 33 41 E
Kabwanga, Dem. Rep. of the Congo 115 D4 7 2 S 27 26 E
Kabwe, Zambia . . . . 119 E2 14 30 S 28 29 E
Kabwum, Papua N. G. . . . . 132 D4 6 13 S 147 15 E
Kačanik, Kosovo, Yug. . . . . 50 D5 42 13N 21 12 E
Kačerginė, Lithuania . . . . 54 D10 54 56N 23 42 E
Kachchh, Gulf of, India . . . . 92 H3 22 50N 69 15 E
Kachchh, Rann of, India . . . . . . 92 H4 24 0N 70 0 E
Kachchhidhana, India . . . . 93 J8 21 44N 78 46 E
Kachebera, Zambia . . . . 119 E3 13 50 S 32 50 E
Kachia, Nigeria . . . . 113 D6 9 59N 7 55 E
Kachikau, Botswana . . . . 116 B3 18 8 S 24 26 E
Kachin □, Burma . . . . 90 G6 26 0N 97 30 E
Kachira, L., Uganda . . . . 118 C3 0 40 S 31 7 E
Kachiry, Kazakhstan . . . . 66 D8 53 10N 75 50 E
Kachisi, Ethiopia . . . . 107 F4 9 40N 37 50 E
Kachnar, India . . . . 92 H6 23 50N 75 6 E
Kacholi, Cambodia . . . . 87 B3 11 30N 103 3 E
Kachnara, India . . . . 99 E10 30 1N 79 20 E
Kaçkar, Turkey . . . . 101 B9 40 45N 41 10 E
Kada, Chad . . . . 114 B2 14 29N 19 39 E
Kadaingti, Burma . . . . 90 G6 17 37N 97 32 E
Kadaiyanallur, India . . . . 95 K3 9 3N 77 22 E
Kadan, Czech Rep. . . . . 34 A6 50 23N 13 16 E
Kadan Kyun, Burma . . . . 86 F2 12 30N 98 20 E
Kadanai ➤, Afghan. . . . . 92 D1 31 22N 65 45 E
Kadarkút, Hungary . . . . 52 D2 46 13N 17 39 E
Kadavu, Fiji . . . . 133 E2 19 0 S 178 15 E
Kadavu Passage, Fiji . . . . 133 E2 18 45 S 178 0 E
Kade, Ghana 113 D4 6 7N 0 56W
Kadei ➤, C.A.R. . . . . 114 B3 3 31N 16 3 E

Kadi, *India* .... 92 H5   23 18N   72 23 E
Kadina, *Australia* .... 128 B2   33 55 S 137 43 E
Kadınhanı, *Turkey* ...... 100 C5   38 14N   32 13 E
Kadiolo, *Mali* 112 C3   10 35N   7 41W
Kadipur, *India* .... 93 F10   26 10N   82 23 E
Kadirabad, *India* .... 94 E2   19 51N   75 54 E
Kadiri, *India* .... 95 G4   14 12N   78 13 E
Kadirli, *Turkey* .... 100 D7   37 23N   36 5 E
Kadiyevka = Stakhanov, *Ukraine*   59 H10   48 35N   38 40 E
Kadja, O. →, *Chad* ..... 109 F4   12   2N   22 28 E
Kadmat I., *India* .... 95 J1   11 14N   72 47 E
Kadodo, *Sudan* .... 107 E2   11   4N   29 31 E
Kadoka, *U.S.A.* 154 D4   43 50N 101 31W
Kadom, *Russia* .... 60 C6   54 37N   42 30 E
Kadoma, *Zimbabwe* ..... 119 F2   18 20 S   29 52 E
Kâdugli, *Sudan* .... 107 E2   11   0N   29 45 E
Kaduna, *Nigeria* .... 113 C6   10 30N   7 21 E
Kaduna □, *Nigeria* ..... 113 C6   10   0N   7 30 E
Kadur, *India* .... 95 H3   13 34N   76   1 E
Kaduy, *Russia* .... 58 C9   59 12N   37   9 E
Kaédi, *Mauritania* 112 B2   16   9N   13 28W
Kaélé, *Cameroon* .... 113 C7   10   7N   14 27 E
Kaena Pt., *U.S.A.* 145 J13   21 35N 158 17W
Kaeng Khoi, *Thailand* .. 86 E3   14 35N 101   0 E
Kaeng Kra Chan Nat. Park △,
  Thailand .... 86 F2   12 57N   99 23 E
Kaeng Tana Nat. Park △, *Thailand*   86 E5   15 25N 105 32 E
Kaeo, *N.Z.* .... 130 B2   35   6 S 173 49 E
Kaesŏng, *N. Korea* ..... 75 F14   37 58N 126 35 E
Kāf, *Si. Arabia* .... 104 D3   31 25N   37 29 E
Kafakumba, *Dem. Rep. of the Congo*   115 D4   9 38 S   23 46 E
Kafan = Kapan, *Armenia*   101 C12   39 18N   46 27 E
Kafanchan, *Nigeria* .... 113 D6   9 40N   8 20 E
Kafareti, *Nigeria* ..... 113 C7   10 25N   11 12 E
Kaffrine, *Senegal* 112 C1   14   8N   15 36W
Kafia Kingi, *Sudan* .... 114 A4   9 20N   24 25 E
Kafin, *Nigeria* .... 113 D6   9 30N   7   4 E
Kafin Madaki, *Nigeria* . 113 C6   10 41N   9 46 E
Kafinda, *Zambia* .... 119 E3   12 32 S   30 20 E
Kafirévs, Ákra, *Greece* . 48 C6   38   9N   24 38 E
Kafr el Battikh, *Egypt* . 106 H7   31 25N   31 44 E
Kafr el Dauwâr, *Egypt* .. 106 H7   31   8N   30   8 E
Kafr el Sheikh, *Egypt* .. 106 H7   31 15N   30 50 E
Kafue, *Zambia* .... 119 F2   15 46 S   28   9 E
Kafue Flats, *Zambia* .... 119 F2   15 40 S   27 25 E
Kafue Nat. Park △, *Zambia*   119 F2   15 12 S   25 38 E
Kafulwe, *Zambia* .... 119 D2   9   0 S   29   1 E
Kafumba, *Dem. Rep. of the Congo*   115 D3   5 23 S   18 55 E
Kaga, *Afghan.* .... 92 B4   34 14N   70 10 E
Kaga, *Japan* .... 73 A8   36 16N 136 15 E
Kaga Bandoro, *C.A.R.* .. 114 A3   7   0N   19 10 E
Kagamil I., *U.S.A.* 144 K5   53   0N 169 43W
Kagan, *Uzbekistan* ..... 65 D2   39 43N   64 33 E
Kagarko, *Nigeria* ...... 113 D6   9 28N   7 36 E
Kagawa □, *Japan* .... 72 C6   34 15N 134   0 E
Kagera = Ziwa Maghariba □,
  Tanzania .... 118 C3   2   0 S   31 30 E
Kagera →, *Uganda* ...... 118 C3   0 57 S   31 47 E
Kağızman, *Turkey* ...... 101 B10   40   5N   43 10 E
Kagmar, *Sudan* .... 107 E3   14 24N   30 25 E
Kagopal, *Chad* .... 109 G3   8 16N   16 23 E
Kagoshima, *Japan* ...... 72 F2   31 35N 130 33 E
Kagoshima □, *Japan* .... 72 F2   31 30N 130 30 E
Kagoshima-Wan, *Japan* .. 72 F2   31 25N 130 40 E
Kagua, *Papua N. G.* ... 132 D2   6 26 S 143 48 E
Kagul = Cahul, *Moldova*   53 E13   45 50N   28 15 E
Kahak, *Iran* .... 97 B6   36   6N   49 46 E
Kahalu‘u, *U.S.A.* 145 K14   21 28N 157 50W
Kahama, *Tanzania* ...... 118 C3   4   8 S   32 30 E
Kahan, *Pakistan* .... 92 E3   29 18N   68 54 E
Kahana, *U.S.A.* 145 J14   21 34N 157 53W
Kahana B., *U.S.A.* 145 J14   21 35N 157 50W
Kahang, *Malaysia* ...... 87 L4   2 12N 103 32 E
Kahayan →, *Indonesia* .. 85 C4   3 40 S 114   0 E
Kahe, *Tanzania* .... 118 C4   3 30 S   37 25 E
Kahemba, *Dem. Rep. of the Congo*   115 D3   7 18 S   18 55 E
Kaherekoau Mts., *N.Z.* .. 131 F2   45 15 S 167 15 E
Kahil, Djebel bou, *Algeria*   111 B5   34 26N   4   0 E
Kahnūj, *Iran* .... 97 E8   27 55N   57 40 E
Kahoka, *U.S.A.* 156 D5   40 25N   91 44W
Kahoolawe, *U.S.A.* 145 C5   20 33N 156 37W
Kahramanmaraş, *Turkey* . 100 D7   37 37N   36 53 E
Kâhta, *Turkey* .... 101 D8   37 46N   38 36 E
Kahuku, *U.S.A.* 145 J14   21 41N 157 57W
Kahuku Pt., *U.S.A.* 145 J14   21 43N 157 59W
Kahului, *U.S.A.* 145 C5   20 54N 156 28W
Kahurangi Nat. Park △, *N.Z.*   131 B7   41 10 S 172 32 E
Kahurangi Pt., *N.Z.* ... 131 A7   40 50 S 172 10 E
Kahuta, *Pakistan* ...... 92 C5   33 35N   73 24 E
Kahuzi-Biega, Parc Nat. du △,
  Dem. Rep. of the Congo   118 C2   1 50 S   27 55 E
Kai, Kepulauan, *Indonesia*   83 C4   5 55 S 132 45 E
Kai Besar, *Indonesia* .. 83 C4   5 35 S 133   0 E
Kai Is. = Kai, Kepulauan, *Indonesia*   83 C4   5 55 S 132 45 E
Kai Kecil, *Indonesia* .. 83 C4   5 45 S 132 40 E
Kai Xian, *China* .... 76 B7   31 11N 108 21 E
Kaiama, *Nigeria* .... 113 D5   9 36N   4   1 E
Kaiapit, *Papua N. G.* . 132 D4   6 18 S 146 18 E
Kaiapoi, *N.Z.* .... 131 D7   43 24 S 172 40 E
Kaieteur Falls, *Guyana* . 169 B6   5 1N   59 10W
Kaifeng, *China* .... 74 G8   34 48N 114 21 E
Kaihua, *China* .... 77 C12   29 12N 118 20 E
Kaijiang, *China* .... 76 B6   31   7N 107 55 E
Kaikohe, *N.Z.* .... 130 B2   35 25 S 173 49 E
Kaikoura, *N.Z.* .... 131 C8   42 25 S 173 43 E
Kaikoura Pen., *N.Z.* ... 131 C8   42 25 S 173 43 E
Kailahun, *S. Leone* 112 D2   8 18N   10 39W
Kailashahar, *India* .... 90 C4   24 19N   92   0 E
Kaileuna I., *Papua N. G.*   132 E6   8 32 S 150 57 E
Kaili, *China* .... 76 D6   26 33N 107 59 E
Kailu, *China* .... 75 C11   43 38N 121 18 E
Kailua, *U.S.A.* 145 K14   21 24N 157 44W
Kailua B., *U.S.A.* 145 K14   21 24N 157 44W
Kailua Kona, *U.S.A.* ... 145 D6   19 39N 155 59W
Kaim →, *Papua N. G.* .. 132 D1   5 55 S 141 33 E
Kaimana, *Indonesia* .... 83 C5   5 32 S 138 48 E
Kaimana, *Indonesia* .... 83 B4   3 59 S 133 45 E
Kaimanawa Mts., *N.Z.* .. 130 F4   39 15 S 175 56 E
Kaimata, *N.Z.* .... 131 C6   42 34 S 171 28 E
Kaimganj, *India* .... 93 F8   27 33N   79 24 E
Kaimon-Dake, *Japan* .... 72 F2   31 11N 130 32 E
Kaimuki, *U.S.A.* 145 K14   21 17N 157 48W
Kaimur Hills, *India* ... 93 G10   24 30N   82   0 E
Kainab →, *Namibia* ..... 116 D2   28 32 S   19 34 E
Kainan, *Japan* .... 73 C7   34   9N 135 12 E
Kainantu, *Papua N. G.* . 132 D3   6 18 S 145 52 E
Kainji Dam, *Nigeria* ... 113 D5   9 55N   4 35 E
Kainji Lake Nat. Park △, *Nigeria*   113 C5   10   5N   4   6 E
Kainji Res., *Nigeria* .. 113 C5   10 1N   4 40 E
Kainuu, *Finland* .... 14 D23   64 30N   29 7 E
Kaipara Harbour, *N.Z.* . 130 C3   36 25 S 174 14 E
Kaiping, *China* .... 77 F9   22 23N 112 42 E
Kaipokok B., *Canada* ... 141 B8   54 54N   59 47W
Kaira, *India* .... 92 H5   22 45N   72 50 E
Kairana, *India* .... 92 E7   29 24N   77 15 E
Kairiru I., *Papua N. G.*   132 B2   3 21 S 143 34 E
Kairomi, *Indonesia* .... 83 B4   0 47 S 133 40 E
Kairouan, *Tunisia* ..... 108 A2   35 45N   10 5 E
Kairuku, *Papua N. G.* .. 132 E4   8 51 S 146 35 E
Kaiserslautern, *Germany*   31 G3   49 26N   7 45 E
Kaiserstuhl, *Germany* .. 72 C4   34 22N 131   0 E
Kaita, *Japan* .... 72 C4   34 22N 132 34 E
Kaitaia, *N.Z.* .... 130 B2   35   8 S 173 17 E
Kaitangata, *N.Z.* ...... 131 G4   46 17 S 169 51 E

Kaithal, *India* .... 92 E7   29 48N   76 26 E
Kaitu →, *Pakistan* ..... 92 C4   33 10N   70 30 E
Kaiwi Channel, *U.S.A.* . 145 K14   21 15N 157 30W
Kaiyang, *China* .... 76 D6   27   4N 106 59 E
Kaiyuan, *Liaoning, China*   75 C13   42 28N 124   1 E
Kaiyuan, *Yunnan, China* . 76 F4   23 40N 103 12 E
Kaiyuh Mts., *U.S.A.* ... 144 D8   64 30N 158   0W
Kajaani, *Finland* ...... 14 D22   64 17N   27 46 E
Kajabbi, *Australia* .... 126 C3   20   0 S 140   1 E
Kajana = Kajaani, *Finland*   14 D22   64 17N   27 46 E
Kajang, *Malaysia* ...... 87 L3   2 59N 101 48 E
Kajaran, *Armenia* ...... 101 C12   39 10N   46   7 E
Kajiado, *Kenya* .... 118 C4   1 53 S   36 48 E
Kajo Kaji, *Sudan* ...... 107 G3   3 58N   31 40 E
Kajuru, *Nigeria* .... 113 C6   10 15N   7 34 E
Kajy-Say, *Kyrgyzstan* .. 65 B8   42   8N   77 10 E
Kaka, *Sudan* .... 107 E3   10 38N   32 10 E
Kaka Pt., *U.S.A.* 145 C5   20 31N 156 33W
Kakabeka Falls, *Canada* . 140 C2   48 24N   89 37W
Kakamas, *S. Africa* .... 116 D3   28 45 S   20 33 E
Kakamega, *Kenya* .... 118 B3   0 20N   34 46 E
Kakamigahara, *Japan* ... 73 B8   35 28N 136 48 E
Kakana, *India* .... 95 K11   9 7N   92 48 E
Kakanj, *Bos.-H.* .... 52 F3   44   4N   18   4 E
Kakanui Mts., *N.Z.* .... 131 F5   45 10 S 170 30 E
Kakata, *Liberia* 112 D2   6 35N   10 20W
Kakdwip, *India* .... 93 J13   21 53N   88 11 E
Kake, *Japan* .... 72 C4   34 36N 132 19 E
Kake, *U.S.A.* 142 B2   56 59N 133 57W
Kakegawa, *Japan* .... 73 C10   34 45N 138   1 E
Kakeroma-Jima, *Japan* .. 71 K4   28   8N 129 14 E
Kakhib, *Russia* .... 61 J8   42 28N   46 34 E
Kakhonak, *U.S.A.* 144 G9   59 26N 154 51W
Kakhovka, *Ukraine* ..... 59 J7   46 45N   33 30 E
Kakhovske Vdskh., *Ukraine*   59 J7   47   5N   34   0 E
Kakinada, *India* .... 94 F6   16 57N   82 11 E
Kakisa →, *Canada* 142 A5   61   3N 118 10W
Kakisa L., *Canada* 142 A5   60 56N 117 43W
Kakogawa, *Japan* .... 72 C6   34 46N 134 51 E
Kaktovik, *U.S.A.* 144 A12   70   8N 143 38W
Kakuma, *Kenya* .... 118 B3   3 43N   34 52 E
Kakum Nat. Park △, *Ghana*   113 H4   5 24N   1 28W
Kakwa →, *Canada* 142 C5   54 37N 118 28W
Kāl Gūsheh, *Iran* ...... 97 D8   30 59N   58 12 E
Kāl Safīd, *Iran* .... 101 E12   34 52N   47 23 E
Kala, *Nigeria* .... 113 C7   12   2N   14 40 E
Kala Oya →, *Sri Lanka* . 95 K4   8 20N   79 45 E
Kalaa-Kebira, *Tunisia* . 108 A2   35 59N   10 32 E
Kalaallit Nunaat = Greenland ☒,
  N. Amer. 10 D6   66   0N   45   0W
Kalabagh, *Pakistan* .... 92 C4   33   0N   71 28 E
Kalabahi, *Indonesia* ... 82 C2   8 13 S 124 31 E
Kalabáka, *Greece* ...... 48 B3   39 42N   21 39 E
Kalabana, *Mali* 112 C3   14 10N   8 35W
Kalabo, *Zambia* .... 115 E4   14 58 S   22 40 E
Kalach, *Russia* .... 60 E5   50 22N   41   0 E
Kalach na Donu, *Russia* . 61 F6   48 43N   43 32 E
Kaladan →, *Burma* ...... 90 E4   20 20N   93   5 E
Kaladar, *Canada* 140 D4   44 37N   77   5W
Kalahari, *Africa* ...... 116 C3   24   0 S   21 30 E
Kalahari Gemsbok Nat. Park △,
  S. Africa .... 116 D3   25 30 S   20 30 E
Kalaheo, *U.S.A.* 145 B2   21 56N 159 32W
Kalaikhum, *Tajikistan* . 65 D5   38 28N   70 46 E
Kalajoki, *Finland* ..... 14 D20   64 12N   24 10 E
Kālak, *Iran* .... 97 E8   25 29N   59 22 E
Kalakamati, *Botswana* .. 117 C4   20 40 S   27 25 E
Kalakan, *Russia* .... 67 D12   55 15N 116 45 E
K'alak'unlun Shank'ou = Karakoram
  Pass, *Asia* .... 93 B7   35 33N   77 50 E
Kalam, *Pakistan* .... 93 B5   35 34N   72 30 E
Kalama, *Dem. Rep. of the Congo*   118 C2   2 52 S   28 35 E
Kalama, *U.S.A.* 160 E4   46   1N 122 51W
Kálamai, *Greece* .... 48 D4   37   3N   22 10 E
Kalamaloué, Parc Nat. de △,
  Cameroon .... 109 F2   12   9N   14 58 E
Kalamansig, *Phil.* ..... 81 H5   6 33N 124   3 E
Kalamariá, *Greece* ..... 50 F6   40 33N   22 55 E
Kalamata = Kálamai, *Greece*   48 D4   37   3N   22 10 E
Kalamazoo, *U.S.A.* 157 B11   42 17N   85 35W
Kalamazoo →, *U.S.A.* ... 157 B10   42 40N   86 10W
Kalamb, *India* .... 94 E2   18   3N   74 48 E
Kalambo Falls, *Tanzania*   119 D3   8 37 S   31 35 E
Kalamítsi, *Greece* ..... 39 B2   38 45N   20 36 E
Kalamnuri, *India* ...... 94 E3   19 40N   77 20 E
Kálamos, *Attikí, Greece*   48 C5   38 17N   23 52 E
Kálamos, *Levkás, Greece*   39 B2   38 37N   20 55 E
Kálamos Nísís, *Greece* . 39 B2   38 37N   20 55 E
Kalan, *Turkey* .... 96 B3   39 7N   39 32 E
Kalangadoo, *Australia* . 128 D4   37 34 S 140 41 E
Kalankalan, *Guinea* 112 C3   10   7N   8 54W
Kalannie, *Australia* ... 125 F2   30 22 S 117   5 E
Kalāntarī, *Iran* .... 97 C7   32 10N   54   8 E
Kalao, *Indonesia* ...... 82 C2   7 21 S 121   0 E
Kalaotoa, *Indonesia* ... 82 C2   7 20 S 121 50 E
Kalapana, *U.S.A.* 145 D7   19 21N 154 59W
Kälarne, *Sweden* .... 16 B10   62 59N   16   5 E
Kalasin, *Thailand* ..... 86 D4   16 26N 103 30 E
Kalat, *Pakistan* .... 91 C2   29 8N   66 31 E
Kalāteh, *Iran* .... 97 B7   36 33N   55 41 E
Kalāteh-ye Ganj, *Iran* . 97 E8   27 31N   57 55 E
Kálathos, *Greece* ...... 38 E12   36   9N   28   8 E
Kalaupapa, *U.S.A.* ..... 81 H5   7 54N 124 50 E
Kalaupapa Nat. Historical Park △,
  U.S.A. 145 B5   21 12N 156 59W
Kalaus →, *Russia* ...... 61 H7   45 40N   44 7 E
Kalávrita, *Greece* ..... 48 C4   38   3N   22   8 E
Kalaw, *Burma* .... 90 E6   20 38N   96 34 E
Kalbān, *Oman* .... 99 B7   20 58N   58 38 E
Kalbarri, *Australia* ... 125 E1   27 40 S 114 10 E
Kalbarri Nat. Park △, *Australia*   125 E1   27 51 S 114 30 E
Kalce, *Slovenia* .... 36 F8   45 54N   14 13 E
Kaldrananes, *Iceland* .. 11 B5   65 45N   21 25W
Kale, *Antalya, Turkey* . 49 E12   36 14N   30   0 E
Kale, *Denizli, Turkey* . 49 D10   37 27N   28 49 E
Kalecik, *Turkey* .... 100 B5   40 4N   33 26 E
Kalehe, *Dem. Rep. of the Congo*   118 C2   2 6 S   28 50 E
Kalema, *Tanzania* ...... 118 C3   1 12 S   31 55 E
Kalemie, *Dem. Rep. of the Congo*   118 C2   5 55 S   29   9 E
Kalemyo, *Burma* .... 90 D5   23 11N   94 4 E
Kalety, *Poland* .... 55 H5   50 35N   18 52 E
Kalewa, *Burma* .... 90 D5   23 10N   94 15 E
Kaleybar, *Iran* .... 96 B5   38 47N   47   2 E
Kálfafell, *Iceland* 11 D9   63 57N   17 41W
Kalgan = Zhangjiakou, *China*   74 D8   40 48N 114 55 E
Kalghatgi, *India* ...... 95 G2   15 11N   74 58 E
Kalgoorlie-Boulder, *Australia*   125 F3   30 40 S 121 22 E
Kalhovd, *Norway* .... 18 D5   60 4N   8 21 E
Kali →, *India* .... 93 F8   27 6N   79 55 E
Kali Sindh →, *India* ... 92 G6   25 32N   76 17 E
Kaliakra, Nos, *Bulgaria*   51 C12   43 21N   28 30 E
Kalianda, *Indonesia* ... 84 D3   5 50 S 105 45 E
Kalibo, *Phil.* .... 81 F4   11 43N 122 22 E
Kaliganj, *Bangla.* ..... 90 D2   22 45N   89 45 E
Kalihi, *U.S.A.* 145 K14   21 20N 157 53W
Kalima, *Dem. Rep. of the Congo*   118 C2   2 33 S   26 32 E
Kalimantan, *Indonesia* . 85 C4   0   0   114   0 E
Kalimantan Barat □, *Indonesia*   85 C4   0   0 110 30 E
Kalimantan Selatan □, *Indonesia*   85 C5   2 30 S 115 30 E
Kalimantan Tengah □, *Indonesia*   85 C4   2 0 S 113 30 E
Kalimantan Timur □, *Indonesia*   85 B5   1 30N 116 30 E
Kálimnos, *Greece* ...... 49 D8   37 0N   27 0 E

Kalimpong, *India* ...... 90 B2   27   4N   88 35 E
Kalinadi →, *India* ..... 95 G2   14 50N   74 7 E
Kalinga □, *Phil.* ...... 80 C3   17 30N 121 20 E
Kalinin = Tver, *Russia* . 58 C8   56 55N   35 55 E
Kaliningrad, *Russia* ... 15 J19   54 42N   20 32 E
Kaliningrad ✈ (KGD), *Russia*   15 J19   54 45N   20 33 E
Kalininsk, *Russia* ..... 60 E7   51 30N   44 40 E
Kalininskoye =
  Kara-Balta, *Kyrgyzstan*   65 B6   42 50N   73 49 E
Kalinkavichy, *Belarus* . 59 F5   52 12N   29 20 E
Kalinkovichi = Kalinkavichy, *Belarus*   59 F5   52 12N   29 20 E
Kalinovik, *Bos.-H.* .... 50 C2   43 31N   18 25 E
Kalipetrovo, *Bulgaria* . 51 B11   44   5N   27 14 E
Kaliro, *Uganda* .... 118 B3   0 56N   33 30 E
Kalírrákhi, *Greece* .... 51 F8   40 40N   24 35 E
Kalispell, *U.S.A.* 158 B6   48 12N 114 19W
Kalisz, *Poland* .... 55 G5   51 45N   18   8 E
Kalisz Pomorski, *Poland*   55 E2   53 17N   15 55 E
Kaliua, *Tanzania* ...... 118 D3   5   5 S   31 48 E
Kaliveli Tank, *India* .. 95 H4   12   5N   79 50 E
Kalívia Thorikoú, *Greece*   48 D5   37 50N   23 55 E
Kalix, *Sweden* .... 14 D20   65 53N   23 12 E
Kalix →, *Sweden* .... 14 D20   65 50N   23 11 E
Kalka, *India* .... 92 D7   30 46N   76 57 E
Kalkali Ghat, *India* ... 90 C4   24 36N   92 20 E
Kalkan, *Turkey* .... 49 E11   36 15N   29 23 E
Kalkarindji, *Australia*   124 C5   17 30 S 130 47 E
Kalkaska, *U.S.A.* 148 C3   44 44N   85 11W
Kalkfeld, *Namibia* ..... 116 C2   20 57 S   16 14 E
Kalkfontein, *Botswana* . 116 C3   22 4 S   20 57 E
Kalkım, *Turkey* .... 49 B9   39 48N   27 13 E
Kalkrand, *Namibia* ..... 116 C2   24 1 S   17 35 E
Kallakkurichchi, *India*   95 J4   11 44N   79 1 E
Kallam, *India* .... 94 E3   18 36N   76 2 E
Kållandsö, *Sweden* ..... 17 F7   58 40N   13 5 E
Kallavesi, *Finland* .... 14 E22   62 58N   27 30 E
Källby, *Sweden* .... 17 F7   58 30N   13 8 E
Kållered, *Sweden* ...... 17 G6   57 32N   12 4 E
Kallidaikurichi, *India*   95 K3   8 38N   77 31 E
Kallimasiá, *Greece* .... 49 C8   38 18N   26 6 E
Kallinge, *Sweden* ...... 17 H9   56 15N   15 18 E
Kallithéa, *Greece* ..... 48 D5   37 55N   23 41 E
Kallmet, *Albania* ...... 50 E3   41 51N   19 41 E
Kalloní, *Greece* .... 49 B8   39 14N   26 12 E
Kallonís, Kólpos, *Greece*   49 B8   39 10N   26 10 E
Kallsjön, *Sweden* ...... 14 E15   63 38N   13 0 E
Kalmalo, *Nigeria* ...... 113 C6   13 40N   5 20 E
Kalmanstunga, *Iceland* . 11 C6   64 44N   20 48W
Kalmar, *Sweden* .... 17 H10   56 40N   16 20 E
Kalmar län □, *Sweden* .. 17 G10   57 25N   16 0 E
Kalmar sund, *Sweden* ... 17 H10   56 40N   16 25 E
Kalmyk Republic = Kalmykia □,
  Russia .... 61 G8   46   5N   46 1 E
Kalmykia □, *Russia* .... 61 G8   46   5N   46 1 E
Kalmykovo, *Kazakhstan* . 57 E9   49 0N   51 47 E
Kalna, *India* .... 93 H13   23 13N   88 25 E
Kalnai, *India* .... 93 H10   22 46N   83 30 E
Kalni →, *Bangla.* ...... 90 C3   24 21N   91 13 E
Kalo, *Papua N. G.* ..... 132 F4   10 1 S 147 48 E
Kalocsa, *Hungary* ...... 52 D4   46 32N   18 59 E
Kalofer, *Bulgaria* ..... 51 D8   42 37N   24 59 E
Kalohi Channel, *U.S.A.*   145 C5   21 0N 157 0W
Kalokhorio, *Cyprus* .... 39 E12   34 51N   33 2 E
Kaloko, *Dem. Rep. of the Congo*   118 D2   6 47 S   25 48 E
Koloko-Honokohau Nat. Historical
  Park △, *U.S.A.* 145 D5   19 40N 156   1W
Kalol, *Gujarat, India* . 92 H5   22 37N   73 31 E
Kalol, *Gujarat, India* . 92 H5   23 15N   72 33 E
Kalolímnos, *Greece* .... 49 D9   37 4N   27 5 E
Kalomo, *Zambia* .... 119 F2   17 0 S   26 30 E
Kalona, *U.S.A.* 156 C5   41 29N   91 43W
Kalpeni I., *India* ..... 95 J1   10 5N   73 38 E
Kalpi, *India* .... 93 F8   26 8N   79 47 E
Kalpitiya, *Sri Lanka* .. 95 K4   8 14N   79 46 E
Kalpuththi I., *India* .. 95 J1   10 49N   72 10 E
Kalrayan Hills, *India* . 95 J4   11 45N   78 40 E
Kalsubai, *India* .... 94 E1   19 35N   73 45 E
Kaltag, *U.S.A.* 144 D8   64 20N 158 43W
Kaltbrunn, *Switz.* ..... 33 B8   47 13N   9 2 E
Kaltern = Caldaro, *Italy*   45 B8   46 25N   11 14 E
Kaltungo, *Nigeria* ..... 113 D7   9 48N   11 19 E
Kalu, *Pakistan* .... 92 G2   25 5N   67 39 E
Kaluga, *Russia* .... 58 D9   54 35N   36 10 E
Kalulong, Bukit, *Malaysia*   85 B4   3 14N 114 39 E
Kalulushi, *Zambia* ..... 119 E2   12 50 S   28 3 E
Kalundborg, *Denmark* ... 17 J5   55 41N   11 5 E
Kalush, *Ukraine* .... 59 H3   49 3N   24 23 E
Kaluszyn, *Poland* ...... 55 F8   52 13N   21 52 E
Kalutara, *Sri Lanka* ... 95 L5   6 35N   80 0 E
Kalya, *Russia* .... 64 A7   60 15N   59 59 E
Kalyan, *Maharashtra, India*   94 D2   20 30N   74 3 E
Kalyan, *Maharashtra, India*   94 E1   19 15N   73 9 E
Kalyandurg, *India* ..... 95 G3   14 33N   77 6 E
Kalyani, *India* .... 94 F3   17 52N   76 57 E
Kalyansingapuram, *India*   94 E6   19 30N   83 19 E
Kalyazin, *Russia* ...... 58 D9   57 15N   37 55 E
Kam, *Albania* .... 50 C4   42 22N   20 20 E
Kam →, *Nigeria* .... 113 D7   8 15N   10 E
Kama, *Burma* .... 90 F5   19 1N   95 4 E
Kama, *Dem. Rep. of the Congo*   118 C2   3 30 S   27 5 E
Kama →, *Russia* .... 64 C5   55 45N   52 0 E
Kamachumu, *Tanzania* ... 118 C3   1 37 S   31 37 E
Kamae, *Japan* .... 72 E3   32 48N 131 56 E
Kamaing, *Burma* .... 90 E10   39 16N 141 53 E
Kamaishi, *Japan* .... 70 E10   39 16N 141 53 E
Kamakou, *U.S.A.* 145 B5   21 7N 156 52W
Kamakura, *Japan* .... 73 B11   35 19N 139 33 E
Kamalapuram, *India* .... 95 G4   14 35N   78 23 E
Kamalété, *Gabon* .... 114 C2   0 43 S   11 49 E
Kamalia, *Pakistan* ..... 92 D5   30 44N   72 42 E
Kaman, *India* .... 92 F6   27 39N   77 16 E
Kaman, *Turkey* .... 100 C5   39 22N   33 44 E
Kamana, *Dem. Rep. of the Congo*   115 D4   5 59 S   24 58 E
Kamanar →, *U.S.A.* 145 J13   21 38N 158 4W
Kamanjab, *Namibia* ..... 116 B2   19 35 S   14 51 E
Kamapanda, *Zambia* ..... 119 E1   12 5 S   24 0 E
Kamaran, *Yemen* .... 98 D3   15 21N   42 35 E
Kamareddi, *India* ...... 94 E4   18 19N   78 21 E
Kamashi, *Uzbekistan* ... 65 D2   38 51N   65 23 E
Kamativi, *Zimbabwe* .... 116 B4   18 15 S   27 27 E
Kamba, *Dem. Rep. of the Congo*   115 C4   4 0 S   22 1 E
Kamba, *Nigeria* .... 113 C5   11 50N   3 45 E
Kambalda, *Australia* ... 125 F3   31 10 S 121 37 E
Kambam, *India* .... 95 K3   9 45N   77 16 E
Kambar, *Pakistan* ...... 91 C2   27 37N   68 1 E
Kambarka, *Russia* ...... 64 C5   56 15N   54 11 E
Kambia, *S. Leone* 112 D2   9 3N   12 53W
Kambos, *Cyprus* .... 39 E8   35 2N   32 44 E
Kambove, *Dem. Rep. of the Congo*   119 E2   10 51 S   26 33 E
Kamchatka, Poluostrov, *Russia*   67 D16   57 0N 160 0 E
Kamchatka Pen. = Kamchatka,
  Poluostrov, *Russia* ... 67 D16   57 0N 160 0 E
Kamchiya →, *Bulgaria* .. 51 C11   43 4N   27 44 E
Kame Ruins, *Zimbabwe* .. 119 G2   20 7 S   28 25 E
Kamehameha Heights, *U.S.A.*   145 K14   21 21N 157 52W

Kamen, *Russia* .... 66 D9   53 50N   81 30 E
Kamen-Rybolov, *Russia* . 70 B6   44 46N 132 2 E
Kamende, *Dem. Rep. of the Congo*   115 D4   6 26 S   24 35 E
Kamenica, *Serbia, Yug.*   50 C6   43 27N   22 27 E
Kamenica, *Serbia, Yug.*   50 B3   44 25N   19 45 E
Kamenice nad Lipou, *Czech Rep.*   34 B8   49 18N   15 2 E
Kamenjak, Rt, *Croatia* . 45 D10   44 47N   13 55 E
Kamenka, *Russia* .... 59 H7   49 3N   32 6 E
Kamenka, *Kazakhstan* ... 59 H7   49 3N   32 6 E
Kamenka = Kaminka, *Ukraine*   59 H7   49 3N   32 6 E
Kamenka, *Arkhangelsk, Russia*   56 A7   65 58N   44 0 E
Kamenka, *Penza, Russia*   60 D6   53 10N   44 5 E
Kamenka, *Voronezh, Russia*   59 G10   50 47N   39 20 E
Kamenka Bugskaya = Kamyanka-
  Buzka, *Ukraine* .... 59 G3   50 8N   24 16 E
Kamenka Dneprovskaya =
  Kamyanka-Dniprovska, *Ukraine*   59 J8   47 29N   34 28 E
Kamennomostskiy, *Russia*   61 H5   44 10 S   40 13 E
Kameno, *Bulgaria* ...... 51 D11   42 34N   27 18 E
Kamenolomni, *Russia* ... 61 G5   47 40N   40 14 E
Kamensk-Shakhtinskiy, *Russia*   61 F5   48 23N   40 20 E
Kamensk Uralskiy, *Russia*   64 C9   56 25N   62 2 E
Kamenskiy, *Russia* ..... 60 E7   50 48N   45 25 E
Kamenskoye, *Russia* .... 51 C17   62 45N 165 30 E
Kamenyak, *Bulgaria* .... 51 C10   43 24N   26 57 E
Kamenz, *Germany* .... 30 D10   51 15N   14 5 E
Kameoka, *Japan* .... 73 C7   35 0N 135 35 E
Kameyama, *Japan* .... 73 C8   34 51N 136 27 E
Kami-Jima, *Japan* ...... 72 E2   32 27N 130 20 E
Kami-Koshiki-Jima, *Japan*   72 F1   31 50N 129 52 E
Kamiagata, *Japan* ...... 72 C1   34 47N 129 24 E
Kamiah, *U.S.A.* 158 C5   46 14N 116   2W
Kamień Krajeński, *Poland*   54 E4   53 32N   17 32 E
Kamień Pomorski, *Poland*   54 E1   53 57N   14 43 E
Kamienna →, *Poland* .... 55 G8   51 6N   21 47 E
Kamienna Góra, *Poland* . 55 H3   50 47N   16 2 E
Kamieńsk, *Poland* ...... 55 G6   51 12N   19 29 E
Kamieskroon, *S. Africa*   116 E2   30 9 S   17 56 E
Kamilukuak, L., *Canada*   143 A8   62 22N 101 40W
Kamin-Kashyrskyy, *Ukraine*   59 G3   51 39N   24 56 E
Kamina, *Dem. Rep. of the Congo*   119 D2   8 45 S   25 0 E
Kaminak L., *Canada* 143 A10   62 10N   95 0W
Kaministiquia, *Canada* . 140 C1   48 32N   89 35W
Kaminka, *Ukraine* ...... 59 H7   49 3N   32 6 E
Kaminoyama, *Japan* ..... 70 E10   38 9N 140 17 E
Kamioka, *Japan* .... 73 A9   36 25N 137 15 E
Kamiros, *Greece* .... 38 E11   36 20N   27 56 E
Kamishak B., *U.S.A.* ... 144 G9   59 15N 153 45W
Kamitsushima, *Japan* ... 72 C1   34 50N 129 28 E
Kamituga, *Dem. Rep. of the Congo*   118 C2   3 2 S   28 10 E
Kamla →, *India* .... 93 G12   25 35N   86 36 E
Kamloops, *Canada* 142 C4   50 40N 120 20W
Kamnik, *Slovenia* ...... 45 B11   46 14N   14 37 E
Kamo, *Armenia* .... 61 K7   40 21N   45 7 E
Kamo, *Japan* .... 70 F9   37 39N 139 3 E
Kamo, *N.Z.* .... 130 B3   35 42 S 174 11 E
Kamoa Mts., *Guyana* 160 C6   1 30N   59 0W
Kamogawa, *Japan* .... 73 B12   35 5N 140 5 E
Kamojima, *Japan* .... 72 C6   34 4N 134 21 E
Kamoke, *Pakistan* ...... 92 C6   32 4N   74 4 E
Kamooloa, *U.S.A.* 145 J13   21 34N 158 7W
Kamp →, *Austria* .... 34 C8   48 23N   15 42 E
Kampala, *Uganda* .... 118 B3   0 20N   32 30 E
Kampong Chhnang, *Cambodia*   87 F5   12 20N 104 35 E
Kampar, *Malaysia* ...... 87 K3   4 18N 101 9 E
Kampar →, *Indonesia* ... 84 B2   0 30N 103 8 E
Kampen, *Neths.* .... 24 B5   52 33N   5 53 E
Kamphaeng Phet, *Thailand*   86 D2   16 28N   99 30 E
Kampinoski Park Narodowy △,
  Poland .... 55 F7   52 21N   20 40 E
Kampolombo, L., *Zambia*   119 E2   11 37 S   29 42 E
Kampong Pengerang, *Malaysia*   87 d   1 22N 104 7 E
Kampong Punggai, *Malaysia*   87 d   1 27N 104 18 E
Kampong Saom, *Cambodia*   87 G4   10 38N 103 30 E
Kampong Saom, Chaak, *Cambodia*   87 G4   10 50N 103 32 E
Kampong Tanjong Langsat, *Malaysia*   87 d   1 28N 104 1 E
Kampong Telok Ramunia, *Malaysia*   87 d   1 26N 104 15 E
Kampong To, *Thailand* .. 87 c   6 3N 101 13 E
Kampot, *Cambodia* ...... 87 G5   10 36N 104 10 E
Kampsville, *U.S.A.* 156 E6   39 18N   90 37W
Kampti, *Burkina Faso* .. 112 C4   10 7N   3 25W
Kampuchea = Cambodia ■, *Asia*   86 F5   12 15N 105 0 E
Kampung Air Putih, *Malaysia*   87 K4   4 15N 103 10 E
Kampung Jerangau, *Malaysia*   87 K4   4 50N 103 10 E
Kampung Raja, *Malaysia*   87 K4   5 45N 102 35 E
Kampungbaru = Tolitoli, *Indonesia*   83 B4   1 5N 120 50 E
Kamrau, Teluk, *Indonesia*   83 B4   3 30 S 133 36 E
Kamsack, *Canada* 143 C8   51 34N 101 54W
Kamsai, *Guinea* 112 C2   10 40N   14 36W
Kamskoye Ustye, *Russia*   60 C9   55 10N   49 20 E
Kamskoye Vdkhr., *Russia*   64 C6   58 41N   56 7 E
Kamthi, *India* .... 94 D4   21 9N   79 19 E
Kamuchawie L., *Canada* . 143 B8   56 18N 101 59W
Kamuela, *U.S.A.* 145 C6   20 1N 155 41W
Kamui-Misaki, *Japan* ... 70 C10   43 20N 140 21 E
Kamundan →, *Indonesia* . 83 B4   2 17 S 132 39 E
Kamyanets-Podilskyy, *Ukraine*   59 H4   48 45N   26 40 E
Kamyanka-Buzka, *Ukraine*   59 G3   50 8N   24 16 E
Kamyanka-Dniprovska, *Ukraine*   59 J8   47 29N   34 28 E
Kāmyārān, *Iran* .... 101 E12   34 47N   46 56 E
Kamyshin, *Russia* ...... 60 E7   50 10N   45 24 E
Kamyshlov, *Russia* ..... 64 C9   56 50N   62 43 E
Kamyzyak, *Russia* ...... 61 G9   46 4N   48 10 E
Kan, *Burma* .... 90 D5   22 25N   94 5 E
Kan, *Sudan* .... 107 F3   9 7N   31 47 E
Kanaaupscow, *Canada* ... 140 B4   54 2N   76 30W
Kanaaupscow →, *Canada* . 139 C12   53 39N   77 9W
Kanab, *U.S.A.* 159 H7   37 3N 112 32W
Kanab →, *U.S.A.* 159 H7   36 24N 112 38W
Kanacea, Lau Group, *Fiji*   133 A3   17 15 S 179 6W
Kanacea, Taveuni, *Fiji*   133 A2   16 59 S 179 56 E
Kanaga I., *U.S.A.* 144 L3   51 45N 177 22W
Kanagawa □, *Japan* ..... 73 B11   35 20N 139 20 E
Kanagi, *Japan* .... 70 D10   40 54N 140 27 E
Kanairiktok →, *Canada* . 141 A7   55 2N   60 18W
Kanakanak, *U.S.A.* 144 G8   59 0N 158 32W
Kanakapura, *India* ..... 95 H3   12 33N   77 28 E
Kanália, *Greece* .... 48 B4   39 30N   22 53 E
Kananga, *Dem. Rep. of the Congo*   115 D4   5 55 S   22 18 E
Kanangra-Boyd Nat. Park △,
  Australia .... 129 B9   33 57 S 150 15 E
Kanash, *Russia* .... 60 C8   55 30N   47 32 E
Kanastraíon, Ákra = Palioúrion,
  Ákra, *Greece* .... 50 G7   39 57N   23 45 E
Kanawha →, *U.S.A.* 148 F4   38 50N   82 9W
Kanazawa, *Japan* .... 73 A8   36 30N 136 38 E
Kanbalu, *Burma* .... 90 D5   23 12N   95 31 E
Kanchanaburi, *Thailand*   86 E2   14 2N   99 31 E
Kanchenjunga, *Nepal* ... 93 F13   27 50N   88 10 E
Kanchipuram, *India* .... 95 H4   12 52N   79 45 E
Kańczuga, *Poland* ...... 55 J9   49 59N   22 25 E
Kanda Kanda, *Dem. Rep. of
  the Congo* .... 115 D4   6 52 S   23 48 E
Kandaghat, *India* ...... 92 D7   30 59N   77 7 E
Kandahar = Qandahār, *Afghan.*   91 C2   31 32N   65 43 E
Kandalaksha, *Russia* ... 94 E3   18 57N   77 12 E
Kandalakshskiy Zaliv, *Russia*   115 D3   6 20 S   19 40 E
Kandalaksha, *Russia* ... 54 A5   67 9N   32 30 E
Kandalakshskiy Zaliv, *Russia*   54 A6   66 0N   35 0 E
Kandangan, *Indonesia* .. 79 G13   2 51 S 108 6 E
Kandanos, *Greece* ...... 39 E4   35 19N   23 44 E
Kandava, *Latvia* .... 54 A9   57 2N   22 46 E
Kandavu = Kadavu, *Fiji*   133 B2   19 0 S 178 15 E

Kandavu Passage = Kadavu Passage,
  Fiji .... **133 B2** 18 45 S 178 0 E
Kandep, *Papua N. G.* .... **132 C2** 5 54 S 143 32 E
Kander →, *Switz.* .... **32 C5** 46 33N 7 38 E
Kandersteg, *Switz.* .... **32 D5** 46 28N 7 40 E
Kandhíla, *Aitolía kai Akarnanía,*
  Greece .... **39 B2** 38 42N 20 56 E
Kandhíla, *Arkadhía, Greece* ..... **48 D4** 37 46N 22 22 E
Kandhkot, *Pakistan* .... **92 E3** 28 16N 69 8 E
Kandhla, *India* .... **92 E7** 29 18N 77 19 E
Kandi, *Benin* .... **113 C5** 11 7N 2 55 E
Kandi, *India* .... **93 H13** 23 58N 88 5 E
Kandiaro, *Pakistan* .... **92 F3** 27 4N 68 13 E
Kandra, *Turkey* .... **100 B4** 41 4N 30 9 E
Kandla, *India* .... **92 H4** 23 0N 70 10 E
Kandor, O. →, *Chad* .... **109 E4** 17 13N 20 52 E
Kandos, *Australia* .... **129 B8** 32 45 S 149 58 E
Kandreho, *Madag.* .... **117 B8** 17 29 S 46 6 E
Kandrian, *Papua N. G.* .... **132 D5** 6 14 S 149 37 E
Kandy, *Sri Lanka* .... **95 L5** 7 18N 80 43 E
Kane, *U.S.A.* **150 E6** 41 40N 78 49W
Kane Basin, *Greenland* **10 B4** 79 1N 70 0W
Kaneilio Pt., *U.S.A.* **145 K13** 21 27N 158 12W
Kanel, *Senegal* **112 B2** 15 30N 13 18W
Kaneohe, *U.S.A.* **145 K14** 21 25N 157 48W
Kaneohe B., *U.S.A.* **145 K14** 21 30N 157 50W
Kanevskaya, *Russia* .... **61 G4** 46 3N 38 57 E
Kanfanar, *Croatia* .... **45 C10** 45 7N 13 50 E
Kang, *Botswana* .... **116 C3** 23 41 S 22 50 E
Kang Krung Nat. Park △, *Thailand* **87 H2** 9 3N 98 32 E
Kangaamiut, *Greenland* **10 D5** 65 50N 53 20W
Kangaba, *Mali* **112 C3** 11 56N 8 25W
Kangal, *Turkey* .... **100 C7** 39 14N 37 23 E
Kangān, *Fārs, Iran* .... **97 E7** 27 50N 52 3 E
Kangān, *Hormozgān, Iran* .... **97 E8** 25 48N 57 28 E
Kangar, *Malaysia* .... **87 J3** 6 27N 100 12 E
Kangaré, *Mali* **112 C3** 11 36N 8 4W
Kangaroo I., *Australia* .... **128 C2** 35 45 S 137 0 E
Kangaroo Mts., *Australia* .... **126 C3** 23 29 S 141 51 E
Kangasala, *Finland* .... **15 F21** 61 28N 24 4 E
Kangāvar, *Iran* .... **97 C6** 34 40N 48 0 E
Kangding, *China* .... **76 B3** 30 1N 101 57 E
Kangdong, *N. Korea* .... **75 E14** 39 9N 126 5 E
Kangean, Kepulauan, *Indonesia* .. **85 D5** 6 55 S 115 23 E
Kangean Is. = Kangean, Kepulauan,
  Indonesia .... **85 D5** 6 55 S 115 23 E
Kangen →, *Sudan* .... **107 F3** 6 47N 33 9 E
Kangerdlugssuak, *Greenland* **10 D7** 68 10N 32 20W
Kangerluarsoruseq, *Greenland* ... **10 E5** 63 45N 51 27W
Kangerluarsoruset =
  Kangerluarsoruseq, *Greenland* ... **10 E5** 63 45N 51 27W
Kangerlussuaq, *Greenland* **10 D5** 66 59N 50 40W
Kanggye, *N. Korea* .... **75 D14** 41 0N 126 35 E
Kanggyōng, *S. Korea* .... **75 F14** 36 10N 127 0 E
Kanghwa, *S. Korea* .... **75 F14** 37 45N 126 30 E
Kangikajik, *Greenland* **10 C8** 70 7N 22 0W
Kangilinnguit, *Greenland* **10 E6** 61 20N 47 57W
Kangiqsliniq = Rankin Inlet, *Canada* **138 B10** 62 30N 93 0W
Kangiqsualujjuaq, *Canada* **139 C13** 58 30N 65 59W
Kangiqsujuaq, *Canada* **139 B12** 61 30N 72 0W
Kangiqtugaapik = Clyde River,
  Canada **139 A13** 70 30N 68 30W
Kangirsuk, *Canada* **139 B13** 60 0N 70 0W
Kangkar Chemaran, *Malaysia* ..... **87 d** 1 34N 104 12 E
Kangkar Sungai Tiram, *Malaysia* . **87 d** 1 35N 103 55 E
Kangkar Teberau, *Malaysia* ...... **87 d** 1 32N 103 51 E
Kangnūng, *S. Korea* .... **75 F15** 37 45N 128 54 E
Kango, *Gabon* .... **114 B2** 0 11N 10 5 E
Kangoya, *Dem. Rep. of the Congo* **115 D4** 9 53 S 22 48 E
Kangping, *China* .... **75 C12** 42 43N 123 18 E
Kangpokpi, *India* .... **90 C4** 25 8N 93 58 E
Kangra, *India* .... **92 C7** 32 6N 76 16 E
Kangyidaung, *Burma* .... **90 G5** 16 56N 94 54 E
Kanhan →, *India* .... **94 D4** 21 4N 79 34 E
Kanhangad, *India* .... **95 H2** 12 21N 74 58 E
Kanhar →, *India* .... **93 G10** 24 28N 83 8 E
Kanheri, *India* .... **94 E1** 19 13N 72 50 E
Kani, Sagaing, *Burma* .... **90 D5** 23 52N 95 22 E
Kani, Sagaing, *Burma* .... **90 D5** 22 26N 94 51 E
Kani, *Ivory C.* **112 D3** 8 29N 6 36W
Kaniama, *Dem. Rep. of the Congo* **118 D1** 7 30 S 24 12 E
Kaniapiskau = Caniapiscau →,
  Canada **141 A6** 56 40N 69 30W
Kaniapiskau, Res. = Caniapiscau,
  Rés. de, *Canada* **141 B6** 54 10N 69 55W
Kaniere, L., *N.Z.* .... **131 C6** 42 50 S 171 10 E
Kanigiri, *India* .... **95 G4** 15 24N 79 31 E
Kanimekh, *Uzbekistan* .... **65 C2** 40 16N 65 7 E
Kanin, Poluostrov, *Russia* ...... **56 A8** 68 0N 45 0 E
Kanin Nos, Mys, *Russia* .... **56 A7** 68 39N 43 32 E
Kanin Pen. = Kanin, Poluostrov,
  Russia .... **56 A8** 68 0N 45 0 E
Kaninë, *Albania* .... **50 F3** 40 23N 19 30 E
Kaniva, *Australia* .... **128 D4** 36 22 S 141 18 E
Kanjiža, *Serbia, Yug.* .... **52 D5** 46 3N 20 4 E
Kanjut Sar, *Pakistan* .... **93 A6** 36 7N 75 25 E
Kankaanpää, *Finland* .... **15 F20** 61 44N 22 50 E
Kankakee, *U.S.A.* **157 C9** 41 7N 87 52W
Kankakee →, *U.S.A.* **157 C8** 41 23N 88 15W
Kankan, *Guinea* **112 C3** 10 23N 9 15W
Kankendy = Xankändi, *Azerbaijan* **101 C12** 39 52N 46 49 E
Kanker, *India* .... **94 D5** 20 10N 81 40 E
Kankesanturai, *Sri Lanka* .... **95 K5** 9 49N 80 2 E
Kankossa, *Mauritania* **112 B2** 15 54N 11 31W
Kankroli, *India* .... **92 G5** 25 4N 73 53 E
Kanmuri-Yama, *Japan* .... **72 C4** 34 30N 132 4 E
Kannabe, *Japan* .... **72 C4** 34 58N 133 23 E
Kannapolis, *U.S.A.* **149 H5** 35 30N 80 37W
Kannauj, *India* .... **93 F8** 27 3N 79 56 E
Kanniyakumari, *India* .... **95 K3** 8 5N 77 34 E
Kano, *Nigeria* .... **113 C6** 12 2N 8 30 E
Kano □, *Nigeria* .... **113 C6** 11 30N 8 30 E
Kan'onji, *Japan* .... **72 C5** 34 7N 133 39 E
Kanoroba, *Ivory C.* **112 D3** 9 7N 6 18W
Kanowha, *U.S.A.* **156 B3** 42 57N 93 47W
Kanowit, *Malaysia* .... **85 B4** 2 14N 112 20 E
Kanoya, *Japan* .... **72 F2** 31 25N 130 50 E
Kanpetlet, *Burma* .... **90 E4** 21 10N 93 59 E
Kanpur, *India* .... **93 F9** 26 28N 80 20 E
Kansai International ✈ (KIX), *Japan* **73 C7** 34 27N 135 12 E
Kansas □, *U.S.A.* **157 E9** 39 33N 87 56W
Kansas □, *U.S.A.* **156 F2** 38 30N 99 0W
Kansas →, *U.S.A.* **154 F7** 39 7N 94 37W
Kansas City, *Kans., U.S.A.* **156 E2** 39 7N 94 38W
Kansas City, *Mo., U.S.A.* **156 E2** 39 6N 94 35W
Kansas City International ✈ (MCI),
  U.S.A. **156 E2** 39 18N 94 43W
Kansenia, *Dem. Rep. of the Congo* **119 E2** 10 20 S 26 0 E
Kansk, *Russia* .... **67 D10** 56 20N 95 37 E
Kansōng, *S. Korea* .... **75 E15** 38 24N 128 30 E
Kansu = Gansu □, *China* .... **74 G3** 36 0N 104 0 E
Kansu, *China* .... **65 D7** 39 46N 75 2 E
Kant, *Kyrgyzstan* .... **65 B7** 42 53N 74 51 E
Kantaphor, *India* .... **92 H7** 22 35N 76 34 E
Kantchari, *Burkina Faso* .... **113 C5** 12 37N 1 37 E
Kantché, *Niger* .... **113 C6** 13 31N 8 30 E
Kanté, *Togo* .... **113 D5** 9 57N 1 3 E
Kantemirovka, *Russia* .... **59 H10** 49 43N 39 55 E
Kantharalak, *Thailand* .... **88 E5** 14 39N 104 39 E
Kantishna, *U.S.A.* **144 E10** 63 31N 150 57W
Kantishna →, *U.S.A.* **144 D10** 64 45N 149 58W
Kantli →, *India* .... **92 E6** 28 20N 75 30 E
Kantō □, *Japan* .... **73 A11** 36 15N 139 30 E

Kantō-Sanchi, *Japan* .... **73 B10** 35 59N 138 50 E
Kantu-long, *Burma* .... **90 F6** 19 57N 97 36 E
Kanturk, *Ireland* **23 D3** 52 11N 8 54W
Kanuma, *Japan* .... **73 A11** 36 34N 139 42 E
Kanus, *Namibia* .... **116 D2** 27 50 S 18 39 E
Kanye, *Botswana* .... **116 C4** 24 55 S 25 28 E
Kanzenze, *Dem. Rep. of the Congo* **119 E2** 10 30 S 25 12 E
Kanzi, Ras, *Tanzania* .... **118 D4** 7 1 S 39 33 E
Kao, *Tonga* .... **133 P13** 19 40 S 175 1W
Kao Phara, *Thailand* .... **87 a** 8 3N 98 22 E
Kaoe, *Indonesia* .... **82 A3** 1 11N 127 54 E
Kaohsiung, *Taiwan* .... **77 F13** 22 35N 120 16 E
Kaoka, *Solomon Is.* .... **133 M11** 9 42 S 160 43 E
Kaokoana, *Solomon Is.* .... **133 N11** 10 27 S 161 56 E
Kaokoveld, *Namibia* .... **116 B1** 19 15 S 14 30 E
Kaolack, *Senegal* **112 C1** 14 5N 16 8W
Kaolan = Lanzhou, *China* .... **74 F2** 36 1N 103 52 E
Kaolo, *Solomon Is.* .... **133 M10** 8 24 S 159 38 E
Kaoma, *Zambia* .... **115 E4** 14 47 S 24 48 E
Kaouar, *Niger* .... **109 E2** 19 5N 12 52 E
Kapaa, *U.S.A.* **145 A2** 22 5N 159 19W
Kapadvanj, *India* .... **92 H5** 23 5N 73 0 E
Kapagere, *Papua N. G.* .... **132 E4** 9 46 S 147 42 E
Kapahulu, *U.S.A.* **145 K14** 21 16N 157 49W
Kapakli, *Turkey* .... **51 E11** 41 19N 27 59 E
Kapan, *Armenia* .... **101 C12** 39 18N 46 27 E
Kapanga, Bandundu, *Dem. Rep. of
  the Congo* .... **115 D3** 5 4 S 16 58 E
Kapanga, Katanga, *Dem. Rep. of
  the Congo* .... **115 D4** 8 30 S 22 40 E
Kapapa I., *U.S.A.* **145 K14** 21 29N 157 48W
Kapatagan, *Phil.* .... **81 H4** 7 52N 123 44 E
Kapchagai = Qapshaghay,
  Kazakhstan .... **65 B8** 43 51N 77 14 E
Kapchagaiskoye Vdkhr. =
  Qapshaghay Bögeni, *Kazakhstan* .. **65 B8** 43 45N 77 50 E
Kapela = Velika Kapela, *Croatia* **45 C12** 45 10N 15 5 E
Kapéllo, Ákra, *Greece* .... **48 E5** 36 9N 23 2 E
Kapema, *Dem. Rep. of the Congo* . **119 E2** 10 45 S 28 22 E
Kapfenberg, *Austria* .... **34 D8** 47 26N 15 18 E
Kapı Dağı, *Turkey* .... **51 F11** 40 28N 27 50 E
Kapia, *Dem. Rep. of the Congo* .. **115 C3** 4 17 S 19 46 E
Kapiri Mposhi, *Zambia* .... **119 E2** 13 59 S 28 43 E
Kapīsā □, *Afghan.* .... **91 B3** 35 0N 69 20 E
Kapiskau →, *Canada* **140 B3** 52 47N 81 55W
Kapit, *Malaysia* .... **85 B4** 2 0N 112 55 E
Kapiti I., *N.Z.* .... **130 G3** 40 50 S 174 56 E
Kapka, Massif du, *Chad* .... **109 E4** 15 7N 21 45 E
Kaplan, *U.S.A.* **155 K8** 30 0N 92 17W
Kaplice, *Czech Rep.* .... **34 C7** 48 42N 14 30 E
Kapoe, *Thailand* .... **87 H2** 9 34N 98 32 E
Kapoeta, *Sudan* .... **107 G3** 4 50N 33 35 E
Kápolnásnyék, *Hungary* .... **52 C3** 47 16N 18 41 E
Kapombo, *Dem. Rep. of the Congo* **115 E4** 10 40 S 23 30 E
Kaponga, *N.Z.* .... **130 F3** 39 29 S 174 9 E
Kapos →, *Hungary* .... **52 D2** 46 25N 17 47 E
Kaposvár, *Hungary* **52 D2** 46 59N 122 13W
Kapowsin, *U.S.A.* **160 D4** 46 59N 122 13W
Kapp, *Norway* .... **18 D7** 60 43N 10 52 E
Kappeln, *Germany* .... **30 A5** 54 40N 9 55 E
Kappelshamn, *Sweden* .... **17 G12** 57 52N 18 47 E
Kapps, *Namibia* .... **116 C2** 22 32 S 17 18 E
Kaprije, *Croatia* .... **45 E12** 43 42N 15 43 E
Kapsan, *N. Korea* .... **75 D15** 41 4N 128 19 E
Kapsukas = Marijampolė, *Lithuania* **15 J20** 54 33N 23 19 E
Kaptai, *Bangla.* .... **90 D4** 22 21N 92 17 E
Kaptai L., *Bangla.* .... **90 D4** 22 40N 92 20 E
Kapuas →, *Indonesia* .... **85 C4** 3 10 S 114 5 E
Kapuas →, *Indonesia* .... **85 C3** 0 25 S 109 20 E
Kapuas Hulu, Pegunungan, *Malaysia* **85 B4** 1 30N 113 30 E
Kapuas Hulu Ra. = Kapuas Hulu,
  Pegunungan, *Malaysia* .... **85 B4** 1 30N 113 30 E
Kapulo, *Dem. Rep. of the Congo* . **119 D2** 8 18 S 29 15 E
Kapunda, *Australia* .... **128 C3** 34 20 S 138 56 E
Kapuni, *N.Z.* .... **130 F3** 39 29 S 174 8 E
Kapurthala, *India* .... **92 D6** 31 23N 75 25 E
Kapuskasing, *Canada* **140 C3** 49 25N 82 30W
Kapuskasing →, *Canada* **140 C3** 49 49N 82 0W
Kaputar, *Australia* .... **129 E5** 30 15N 150 10 E
Kaputir, *Kenya* .... **118 B4** 2 5N 35 28 E
Kapuvár, *Hungary* .... **52 C2** 47 36N 17 1 E
Kaqung, *China* .... **65 E8** 38 0N 76 50 E
Kara, *Russia* .... **66 C7** 69 10N 65 0 E
Karā, W. →, *Si. Arabia* .... **106 C5** 20 45N 41 42 E
Kara Ada, *Turkey* .... **49 E9** 36 58N 27 28 E
Kara-Balta, *Kyrgyzstan* .... **65 B6** 42 50N 73 49 E
Kara Bogaz Gol, Zaliv =
  Garabogazköl Aylagy,
  Turkmenistan .... **57 F9** 41 0N 53 30 E
Kara Burun, *Turkey* .... **49 E9** 36 32N 27 58 E
Kara Kalpak Republic =
  Qoraqalpoghiston □, *Uzbekistan* . **66 E6** 43 0N 58 0 E
Kara-Köl, *Kyrgyzstan* .... **65 C6** 41 40N 72 43 E
Kara-Kulja, *Kyrgyzstan* .... **65 C6** 40 39N 73 26 E
Kara Kum, *Turkmenistan* .... **66 F6** 39 30N 60 0 E
Kara-Saki, *Japan* .... **72 C1** 34 41N 129 30 E
Kara-Say, *Kyrgyzstan* .... **65 C8** 41 33N 77 54 E
Kara-Suu, *Kyrgyzstan* .... **65 C6** 40 44N 72 53 E
Karaadilli, *Turkey* .... **49 C12** 38 30N 30 37 E
Karabash, *Russia* .... **64 D8** 55 29N 60 14 E
Karabekaul = Garabekewül,
  Turkmenistan .... **65 D2** 38 30N 64 8 E
Karabiğa, *Turkey* .... **51 F11** 40 23N 27 17 E
Karabük, *Turkey* .... **100 B5** 41 12N 32 37 E
Karabulak = Qarabulaq, *Kazakhstan* **65 A9** 44 54N 78 30 E
Karabulak, *China* .... **65 C8** 40 48N 77 32 E
Karaburun, *Albania* .... **50 F3** 40 25N 19 20 E
Karaburun, *Turkey* .... **49 C8** 38 41N 26 28 E
Karabutak = Qarabutaq, *Kazakhstan* **64 G8** 49 59N 60 14 E
Karacabey, *Turkey* .... **51 F12** 40 12N 28 21 E
Karacaköy, *Turkey* .... **51 E11** 41 8N 28 22 E
Karacasu, *Turkey* .... **49 D10** 37 43N 28 35 E
Karachala = Qaraçala, *Azerbaijan* **61 L9** 39 45N 48 53 E
Karachayevsk, *Russia* .... **61 J5** 43 50N 41 55 E
Karachey-Cherkessia □, *Russia* .. **61 J5** 43 40N 41 30 E
Karachi, *Pakistan* .... **92 G2** 24 53N 67 0 E
Karad, *India* .... **94 F2** 17 15N 74 10 E
Karadirek, *Turkey* .... **47 C12** 38 34N 30 11 E
Karaga, *Ghana* **113 D4** 9 58N 0 28W
Karaganda = Qaraghandy,
  Kazakhstan .... **66 E8** 49 50N 73 10 E
Karagayly = Qaraghayly,
  Kazakhstan .... **66 E8** 49 26N 76 0 E
Karaginskiy, Ostrov, *Russia* .... **67 D17** 58 45N 164 0 E
Karagiye, Vpadina, *Kazakhstan* .. **57 F9** 43 27N 51 45 E
Karagiye Depression = Karagiye,
  Vpadina, *Kazakhstan* .... **57 F9** 43 27N 51 45 E
Karagola Road, *India* .... **93 G12** 25 29N 87 23 E
Karagüney Dağları, *Turkey* ...... **100 B6** 40 30N 34 40 E
Karaikal, *India* .... **95 J4** 10 59N 79 50 E
Karaikkudi, *India* .... **95 J4** 10 5N 78 45 E
Karaisali, *Turkey* .... **100 D6** 37 16N 35 2 E
Karaj, *Iran* .... **97 C6** 35 48N 51 0 E
Karak, *Malaysia* .... **87 L4** 3 25N 102 2 E
Karakalpakstan =
  Qoraqalpoghiston □, *Uzbekistan* . **66 E6** 43 0N 58 0 E
Karakelong, *Indonesia* .... **82 A3** 4 35N 126 50 E

Karakitang, *Indonesia* .... **82 A3** 3 14N 125 28 E
Karaklis = Vanadzor, *Armenia* ... **61 K7** 40 48N 44 30 E
Karakoçan, *Turkey* .... **101 C9** 38 57N 40 2 E
Karakol, *Kyrgyzstan* .... **65 B9** 42 30N 78 52 E
Karakoram Pass, *Asia* .... **93 B7** 35 33N 77 50 E
Karakoram Ra., *Pakistan* .... **93 B7** 35 30N 77 0 E
Karakul, *Tajikistan* .... **65 D6** 39 2N 73 33 E
Karakul, *Uzbekistan* .... **65 D1** 39 22N 63 40 E
Karakul, Ozero, *Tajikistan* ..... **65 D6** 39 5N 73 25 E
Karakurt, *Turkey* .... **101 B10** 40 10N 42 37 E
Karalon, *Russia* .... **67 D12** 57 5N 115 50 E
Karaman, *Jordan* .... **103 D4** 31 57N 35 35 E
Karaman, *Balıkesir, Turkey* ..... **49 B9** 39 39N 28 0 E
Karaman, *Konya, Turkey* .... **100 D5** 37 14N 33 13 E
Karamanlı, *Turkey* .... **49 D11** 37 23N 29 47 E
Karamay, *China* .... **68 B3** 45 30N 84 58 E
Karambu, *Indonesia* .... **85 C5** 3 53 S 116 6 E
Karamea, *N.Z.* .... **131 B7** 41 14 S 172 6 E
Karamea →, *N.Z.* .... **131 B7** 41 13 S 172 26 E
Karamea Bight, *N.Z.* .... **131 B6** 41 22 S 171 40 E
Karamet Niyaz = Garamätnyyaz,
  Turkmenistan .... **65 E2** 37 45N 64 34 E
Karamnasa →, *India* .... **93 G10** 25 31N 83 52 E
Karamürsel, *Turkey* .... **51 F13** 40 41N 29 36 E
Karand, *Iran* .... **101 E12** 34 16N 46 15 E
Karangana, *Mali* **112 C3** 12 15N 5 4W
Karanganyar, *Indonesia* .... **85 D3** 7 38 S 109 37 E
Karangasem, *Indonesia* .... **79 J18** 8 27 S 115 37 E
Karanja, Maharashtra, *India* .... **94 D4** 21 11N 78 24 E
Karanja, Maharashtra, *India* .... **94 D3** 20 29N 77 31 E
Karanjia, *India* .... **93 J11** 21 47N 85 58 E
Karankasso, *Burkina Faso* **112 C4** 10 50N 3 53W
Karaova, *Turkey* .... **49 D9** 37 5N 27 40 E
Karapınar, *Turkey* .... **100 D5** 37 41N 33 30 E
Karapiro, *N.Z.* .... **130 D4** 37 53 S 175 32 E
Karas, *Indonesia* .... **83 B4** 3 27 S 132 40 E
Karasburg, *Namibia* .... **116 D2** 28 0 S 18 44 E
Karasino, *Russia* .... **66 C9** 66 50N 86 50 E
Karasjok, *Norway* .... **14 B21** 69 27N 25 30 E
Karasu, *Turkey* .... **100 B4** 41 4N 30 46 E
Karasuk, *Russia* .... **66 D8** 53 44N 78 2 E
Karasuyama, *Japan* .... **73 A12** 36 39N 140 9 E
Karataş, Adana, *Turkey* .... **49 C10** 36 36N 35 21 E
Karataş, Manisa, *Turkey* .... **49 C10** 38 35N 28 16 E
Karataş Burnu, *Turkey* .... **100 D6** 36 31N 35 24 E
Karatau, Khrebet = Qarataū,
  Kazakhstan .... **65 B4** 43 30N 69 30 E
Karateki Shan, *China* .... **65 C8** 40 40N 77 50 E
Karativu, *Sri Lanka* .... **95 K4** 8 22N 79 47 E
Karatobe, *Kazakhstan* .... **64 G4** 49 44N 53 30 E
Karatoprak, *Turkey* .... **49 D9** 37 2N 27 15 E
Karatoya →, *India* .... **90 C2** 24 7N 89 36 E
Karatsu, *Japan* .... **72 D1** 33 26N 129 58 E
Karaturuk = Qaratürүq, *Kazakhstan* **65 B8** 43 35N 77 50 E
Karaul, *Russia* .... **66 B9** 70 6N 82 15 E
Karaulbazar, *Uzbekistan* .... **65 D2** 39 30N 64 48 E
Karauli, *India* .... **92 F7** 26 30N 77 4 E
Karavastasë, L. e, *Albania* ..... **50 F3** 40 55N 19 30 E
Karavostási, *Cyprus* .... **39 E8** 35 8N 32 50 E
Karawa, *Dem. Rep. of the Congo* . **116 E3** 3 18N 20 17 E
Karawang, *Indonesia* .... **85 D3** 6 30 S 107 15 E
Karawanken, *Europe* .... **34 E7** 46 30N 14 40 E
Karayazı, *Turkey* .... **101 C10** 39 41N 42 9 E
Karazhal, *Kazakhstan* .... **66 E8** 48 2N 70 49 E
Karbalā', *Iraq* .... **101 F11** 32 36N 44 3 E
Kårböle, *Sweden* .... **16 C9** 61 59N 15 2 E
Karcag, *Hungary* .... **52 C5** 47 19N 20 57 E
Karcha →, *Pakistan* .... **93 B7** 34 45N 76 10 E
Karchana, *India* .... **93 G9** 25 17N 81 56 E
Karczew, *Poland* .... **55 F8** 52 5N 21 15 E
Kardam, *Bulgaria* .... **51 C12** 43 45N 28 6 E
Kardeljevo = Ploče, *Croatia* .... **45 E14** 43 4N 17 26 E
Kardhakata, *Greece* .... **39 C1** 38 17N 20 28 E
Kardhámila, *Greece* .... **48 C8** 38 35N 26 5 E
Kardhámili, *Greece* .... **48 B3** 36 53N 22 13 E
Kardhítsa, *Greece* .... **48 B3** 39 23N 21 54 E
Kardhítsa □, *Greece* .... **48 B3** 39 15N 21 50 E
Kärdla, *Estonia* .... **15 G20** 58 50N 22 40 E
Kareeberge, S. *Africa* .... **116 E3** 30 59 S 21 50 E
Kareha →, *India* .... **93 G12** 25 44N 86 21 E
Kareima, *Sudan* .... **106 D3** 18 30N 31 49 E
Karelia □, *Russia* .... **56 A5** 65 30N 32 30 E
Karelian Republic = Karelia □,
  Russia .... **56 A5** 65 30N 32 30 E
Karema, *Papua N. G.* .... **132 E4** 9 12 S 147 18 E
Karera, *India* .... **92 G8** 25 32N 78 9 E
Kārevāndar, *Iran* .... **97 E9** 27 53N 60 44 E
Kargasok, *Russia* .... **66 D9** 59 3N 80 53 E
Kargi, *Turkey* .... **100 B6** 41 11N 34 30 E
Kargil, *India* .... **93 B7** 34 32N 76 12 E
Kargopol, *Russia* .... **58 B10** 61 30N 38 58 E
Kargowa, *Poland* .... **55 F2** 52 5N 15 51 E
Karguéri, *Niger* .... **113 C7** 13 27N 10 30 E
Karhal, *India* .... **93 F8** 27 1N 78 57 E
Kariá, *Greece* .... **39 B2** 38 45N 20 39 E
Kariba, Zimbabwe* .... **119 F2** 16 28 S 28 50 E
Kariba, L., *Zimbabwe* .... **119 F2** 16 40 S 28 25 E
Kariba Dam, *Zimbabwe* .... **119 F2** 16 30 S 28 35 E
Kariba Gorge, *Zambia* .... **119 F2** 16 30 S 28 50 E
Karibib, *Namibia* .... **116 C2** 22 0 S 15 56 E
Karijini Nat. Park △, *Australia* **124 D2** 23 8 S 118 15 E
Karikari, C., *N.Z.* .... **130 A2** 34 46 S 173 24 E
Karimata, Kepulauan, *Indonesia* . **85 C3** 1 25 S 109 0 E
Karimata, Selat, *Indonesia* ..... **85 C3** 2 0 S 108 40 E
Karimata Is. = Karimata, Kepulauan,
  Indonesia .... **85 C3** 1 25 S 109 0 E
Karimganj, *India* .... **90 C4** 24 52N 92 20 E
Karimnagar, *India* .... **94 E4** 18 26N 79 10 E
Karimun Kecil, Pulau, *Indonesia* **87 d** 1 8N 103 22 E
Karimunjawa, Kepulauan, *Indonesia* **85 D3** 5 50 S 110 30 E
Karin, *Somali Rep.* .... **120 B3** 10 50N 45 52 E
Káristos, *Greece* .... **49 C7** 38 1N 24 29 E
Karīt, *Iran* .... **97 C8** 33 29N 56 55 E
Kariya, *Japan* .... **73 C9** 34 58N 137 1 E
Kariyangwe, *Zimbabwe* .... **117 B4** 18 5 S 27 38 E
Karjala, *Finland* .... **58 A5** 62 0N 30 25 E
Karjat, Maharashtra, *India* ..... **94 E1** 18 33N 73 5 E
Karjat, Maharashtra, *India* ..... **94 E1** 18 55N 73 20 E
Karkal, *India* .... **95 H2** 13 15N 74 56 E
Karkar, Papua N. G.* .... **132 C4** 4 32 S 145 57 E
Karkar I., *Papua N. G.* .... **132 C4** 4 40 S 146 0 E
Karkaralinsk = Qarqaraly,
  Kazakhstan .... **66 E8** 49 26N 75 30 E
Karkheh →, *Iran* .... **96 D5** 31 2N 47 29 E
Karkinitska Zatoka, *Ukraine* .... **59 K7** 45 56N 33 0 E
Karkinitskiy Zaliv = Karkinitska
  Zatoka, *Ukraine* .... **59 K7** 45 56N 33 0 E
Karkur Tohl, *Egypt* .... **106 C2** 22 5N 25 5 E
Karl Liebknecht, *Russia* .... **59 G9** 51 40N 35 36 E
Karl-Marx-Stadt = Chemnitz,
  Germany .... **30 E8** 50 51N 12 54 E
Karlholmsbruk, *Sweden* .... **16 D11** 60 31N 17 37 E
Karlino, *Poland* .... **54 D2** 54 3N 15 53 E
Karlivka, *Ukraine* .... **59 H8** 49 29N 35 8 E
Karlobag, *Croatia* .... **45 D12** 44 32N 15 5 E

Karlovac, *Croatia* .... **45 C12** 45 31N 15 36 E
Karlovarský □, *Czech Rep.* ...... **34 A5** 50 10N 12 50 E
Karlovka = Karlivka, *Ukraine* ... **59 H8** 49 29N 35 8 E
Karlovo, *Bulgaria* .... **51 D8** 42 38N 24 47 E
Karlovy Vary, *Czech Rep.* .... **34 A5** 50 13N 12 51 E
Karlsbad = Karlovy Vary,
  Czech Rep. .... **34 A5** 50 13N 12 51 E
Karlsborg, *Sweden* .... **17 F8** 58 33N 14 33 E
Karlshamn, *Sweden* .... **17 H8** 56 10N 14 51 E
Karlskoga, *Sweden* .... **16 E8** 59 28N 14 33 E
Karlskrona, *Sweden* .... **17 H8** 56 10N 15 35 E
Karlsruhe, *Germany* .... **31 F4** 49 0N 8 23 E
Karlstad = Karlovac, *Croatia* ... **45 C12** 45 31N 15 36 E
Karlstad, *Sweden* .... **16 E7** 59 23N 13 30 E
Karlstad, *U.S.A.* **154 A6** 48 35N 96 31W
Karlstadt, *Germany* .... **31 F5** 49 57N 9 47 E
Karluk, *U.S.A.* **144 H9** 57 34N 154 28W
Karma, *Niger* .... **113 C5** 13 38N 1 52 E
Karmala, *India* .... **94 E2** 18 25N 75 12 E
Karmana, *Uzbekistan* .... **65 C2** 40 8N 65 21 E
Karmėlava, *Lithuania* .... **54 D11** 54 58N 24 4 E
Karmi'el, *Israel* .... **103 C4** 32 55N 35 18 E
Karmøy, *Norway* .... **18 E2** 59 15N 5 15 E
Karnak, *Egypt* .... **106 B3** 25 43N 32 39 E
Karnal, *India* .... **92 E7** 29 42N 77 2 E
Karnali →, *Nepal* .... **93 E9** 28 45N 81 16 E
Karnaphuli Res. = Kaptai L., *Bangla.* **90 D4** 22 40N 92 20 E
Karnaprayag, *India* .... **93 D8** 30 16N 79 15 E
Karnataka □, *India* .... **95 H3** 13 15N 77 0 E
Karnes City, *U.S.A.* **155 L6** 28 53N 97 54W
Karnische Alpen, *Europe* .... **34 E6** 46 36N 13 0 E
Karnobat, *Bulgaria* .... **51 D10** 42 39N 26 59 E
Kärnten □, *Austria* .... **34 E6** 46 52N 13 30 E
Karoi, *Zimbabwe* .... **119 F2** 16 48 S 29 45 E
Karomatan, *Phil.* .... **81 H4** 7 55N 123 44 E
Karon, Ao, *Thailand* .... **87 a** 7 51N 98 17 E
Karonga, *Malawi* .... **119 D3** 9 57 S 33 55 E
Karoonda, *Australia* .... **128 C3** 35 1 S 139 59 E
Karor, *Pakistan* .... **92 D4** 31 15N 70 59 E
Karora, *Sudan* .... **106 D4** 17 44N 38 15 E
Karosa, *Indonesia* .... **82 B1** 1 48 S 119 22 E
Karounga, *Mali* **112 B3** 15 20N 7 35W
Karousádhes, *Greece* .... **38 B9** 39 47N 19 45 E
Karpacz, *Poland* .... **55 H2** 50 46N 15 46 E
Karpasia, *Cyprus* .... **39 E10** 35 34N 34 15 E
Kárpathos, *Greece* .... **49 F9** 35 37N 27 10 E
Kárpathos, Stenón, *Greece* ...... **49 F9** 36 0N 27 30 E
Karpatsky △, *Ukraine* .... **53 B9** 48 20N 24 35 E
Karpenísion, *Greece* .... **48 C3** 38 55N 21 40 E
Karpinsk, *Russia* .... **64 B8** 59 45N 60 1 E
Karpogory, *Russia* .... **56 B7** 64 0N 44 27 E
Karpuz Burnu = Apostolos Andreas,
  C., *Cyprus* .... **39 E10** 35 42N 34 35 E
Karpuzlu, *Turkey* .... **49 D9** 37 33N 27 51 E
Karratha, *Australia* .... **124 D2** 20 53 S 116 40 E
Karrebæk, *Denmark* .... **66 E7** 41 00N 43 5 E
Karsakpay, *Kazakhstan* .... **66 E7** 47 55N 66 40 E
Karsha, *Kazakhstan* .... **60 F10** 49 45N 51 35 E
Karshi = Qarshi, *Uzbekistan* .... **65 D2** 38 53N 65 48 E
Karsiyang, *India* .... **90 B2** 26 56N 88 18 E
Karsog, *India* .... **92 D7** 31 23N 77 12 E
Karst = Kras, *Croatia* .... **45 C10** 45 35N 14 0 E
Kartal, *Turkey* .... **51 F13** 40 53N 29 11 E
Kartál Óros, *Greece* .... **51 F8** 41 15N 25 13 E
Kartaly, *Russia* .... **64 E8** 53 3N 60 40 E
Kartapur, *India* .... **92 D6** 31 27N 75 32 E
Karthaus, *U.S.A.* **150 E6** 41 8N 78 9W
Kartuzy, *Poland* .... **54 D5** 54 22N 18 10 E
Karuah, *Australia* .... **129 B9** 32 37 S 151 56 E
Karufa, *Indonesia* .... **83 B4** 3 50 S 133 20 E
Karuma Game Reserve △, *Uganda* .. **118 B3** 2 5N 32 15 E
Karumai, *Australia* .... **126 B3** 17 31 S 140 50 E
Karumba, *Australia* .... **126 B3** 17 31 S 140 50 E
Karumo, *Tanzania* .... **118 C3** 2 25 S 32 50 E
Karumwa, *Tanzania* .... **118 C3** 3 12 S 32 38 E
Kārūn →, *Iran* .... **97 D6** 30 26N 48 10 E
Karungu, *Kenya* .... **118 C3** 0 50 S 34 10 E
Karup, *Denmark* .... **17 H3** 56 19N 9 10 E
Karur, *India* .... **95 J4** 10 59N 78 2 E
Karviná, *Czech Rep.* .... **35 B11** 49 53N 18 31 E
Karwan →, *India* .... **92 F8** 27 26N 78 4 E
Karwendel, Alpenpark △, *Austria* **34 D4** 47 25N 11 30 E
Karwi, *India* .... **93 G9** 25 12N 80 57 E
Kaş, *Turkey* .... **49 E11** 36 11N 29 37 E
Kasaan, *U.S.A.* **144 J14** 55 32N 132 24W
Kasaba, *Turkey* .... **49 E11** 36 24N 29 40 E
Kasabi, Zambia* .... **115 E4** 14 52 S 23 45 E
Kasaba, *Malawi* .... **119 E3** 13 25 S 34 20 E
Kasai →, *Dem. Rep. of the Congo* **72 C6** 34 55N 134 52 E
Kasai →, *Dem. Rep. of the Congo* **115 C3** 3 30 S 16 10 E
Kasai-Occidental □, *Dem. Rep. of
  the Congo* .... **115 D4** 6 0 S 22 0 E
Kasai-Oriental □, *Dem. Rep. of
  the Congo* .... **118 D1** 5 0 S 24 30 E
Kasaji, *Dem. Rep. of the Congo* . **119 E1** 10 25 S 23 27 E
Kasama, *Japan* .... **73 A12** 36 23N 140 16 E
Kasama, *Zambia* .... **119 E3** 10 16 S 31 9 E
Kasan, *Uzbekistan* .... **65 D2** 39 0N 65 35 E
Kasan-dong, *N. Korea* .... **75 D14** 41 18N 126 55 E
Kasane, *Namibia* .... **116 B3** 17 34 S 24 50 E
Kasanga, *Tanzania* .... **115 D3** 8 30 S 31 10 E
Kasangulu, *Dem. Rep. of the Congo* **115 D3** 4 33 S 15 15 E
Kasanka Nat. Park △, *Zambia* .... **119 E3** 11 34 S 30 15 E
Kasansay, *Uzbekistan* .... **65 C4** 41 15N 71 31 E
Kasaoka, *Japan* .... **72 C5** 34 30N 133 30 E
Kasar, Ras, *Sudan* .... **106 D4** 18 2N 38 36 E
Kasaragod, *India* .... **95 H2** 12 30N 74 58 E
Kasat, *Burma* .... **90 G7** 15 56N 98 13 E
Kasba, *Bangla.* .... **93 H17** 23 45N 91 2 E
Kasba L., *Canada* **143 A8** 60 20N 102 10W
Kasba Tadla, *Morocco* **110 B3** 32 36N 6 17W
Kaschau = Košice, *Slovak Rep.* .. **55 C14** 48 42N 21 15 E
Kāseh Garān, *Iran* .... **101 F12** 34 5N 46 2 E
Kasempa, *Zambia* .... **119 E2** 13 30 S 25 44 E
Kasenga, *Dem. Rep. of the Congo* **119 E2** 10 20 S 28 45 E
Kasese, *Uganda* .... **118 B3** 0 13N 30 3 E
Kasewa, *Zambia* .... **119 E2** 14 28 S 28 53 E
Kasganj, *India* .... **93 F8** 27 48N 78 42 E
Kashabowie, *Canada* **140 C1** 48 40N 90 26W
Kashaf, *Iran* .... **97 C9** 35 58N 61 7 E
Kāshān, *Iran* .... **97 C6** 34 5N 51 30 E
Kashechewan, *Canada* **140 B3** 52 18N 81 37W
Kashgar = Kashi, *China* .... **65 D8** 39 30N 76 2 E
Kashi, *China* .... **65 D8** 39 30N 76 2 E
Kashihara, *Japan* .... **73 C7** 34 27N 135 46 E
Kashiji Plain, *Zambia* .... **114 E3** 13 12 S 22 20 E
Kashima, Ibaraki, *Japan* .... **73 B12** 35 58N 140 38 E
Kashima-Nada, *Japan* .... **73 B12** 36 0N 140 45 E
Kashin, *Dem. Rep. of the Congo* . **118 D2** ....
Kashin, *Russia* .... **58 D9** 57 20N 37 36 E
Kashipur, Orissa, *India* .... **94 E6** 19 16N 83 3 E
Kashipur, Uttaranchal, *India* ... **93 E8** 29 15N 79 0 E
Kashira, *Japan* .... **58 E10** 54 45N 38 10 E
Kashiwazaki, *Japan* .... **72 F22** 56 26N 95 33 E
Kashiwazaki, *Japan* .... **72 F9** 37 22N 138 33 E
Kashk-e Kohneh, *Afghan.* .... **91 B1** 34 55N 62 30 E
Kashkū'īyeh, *Iran* .... **97 D7** 30 31N 55 40 E

Kāshmar, Iran ... 97 C8 35 16N 58 26 E
Kashmir, Asia ... 93 C7 34 0N 76 0 E
Kashmor, Pakistan ... 91 C3 28 28N 69 32 E
Kashpirovka, Russia ... 60 D9 53 0N 48 30 E
Kashun Noerh = Gaxun Nur, China ... 68 B5 42 22N 100 30 E
Kasiari, India ... 93 H12 22 8N 87 14 E
Kasilof, U.S.A. ... 144 F10 60 23N 151 18W
Kasimov, Russia ... 60 C5 54 55N 41 20 E
Kasinge, Dem. Rep. of the Congo ... 118 D2 6 15 S 26 58 E
Kasiruta, Indonesia ... 82 B3 0 25 S 127 12 E
Kaskaskia →, U.S.A. ... 156 G7 37 58N 89 57W
Kaskattama →, Canada ... 143 B10 57 3N 90 4W
Kaskelen = Qaskeleng, Kazakhstan ... 65 B8 43 20N 76 35 E
Kaskinen, Finland ... 15 E19 62 22N 21 15 E
Kaskö = Kaskinen, Finland ... 15 E19 62 22N 21 15 E
Kasli, Russia ... 64 D8 55 53N 60 46 E
Kaslo, Canada ... 142 D5 49 55N 116 55W
Kasmere L., Canada ... 143 B8 59 34N 101 10W
Kasongan, Indonesia ... 85 C4 2 0 S 113 23 E
Kasongo, Dem. Rep. of the Congo ... 118 C2 4 30 S 26 33 E
Kasongo Lunda, Dem. Rep. of
  the Congo ... 115 D3 6 35 S 16 49 E
Kásos, Greece ... 49 F8 35 20N 26 55 E
Kásos, Stenón, Greece ... 49 F8 35 30N 26 30 E
Kaspi, Georgia ... 61 K7 41 59N 44 26 E
Kaspichan, Bulgaria ... 51 C11 43 18N 27 11 E
Kaspiysk, Russia ... 61 J8 42 52N 47 40 E
Kaspiyskiy, Russia ... 61 H8 45 22N 47 23 E
Kassab ed Doleib, Sudan ... 107 E3 13 30N 33 35 E
Kassaba, Egypt ... 106 C2 22 40N 29 55 E
Kassalâ, Sudan ... 107 D4 15 30N 36 0 E
Kassalâ □, Sudan ... 107 D4 15 20N 36 26 E
Kassándra, Greece ... 50 F7 40 0N 23 30 E
Kassándrinon, Greece ... 50 F7 40 1N 23 27 E
Kassel, Germany ... 30 D5 51 18N 9 26 E
Kassinger, Sudan ... 106 D3 18 46N 31 51 E
Kassiópi, Greece ... 38 B9 39 48N 19 53 E
Kasson, U.S.A. ... 154 C8 44 2N 92 45W
Kastamonu, Turkey ... 100 B5 41 25N 33 43 E
Kastav, Croatia ... 45 C11 45 22N 14 20 E
Kastéli, Greece ... 49 E4 35 29N 23 38 E
Kastéllion, Greece ... 39 E6 35 12N 25 20 E
Kastellórizon = Megíste, Greece ... 49 E11 36 8N 29 34 E
Kástellos, Greece ... 49 E9 36 16N 27 49 E
Kastéllou, Ákra, Greece ... 49 F9 35 30N 27 15 E
Kasterlee, Belgium ... 24 C4 51 15N 4 59 E
Kastlösa, Sweden ... 17 H10 56 26N 16 25 E
Kastóri, Greece ... 48 D4 37 10N 22 17 E
Kastoría, Greece ... 50 F5 40 30N 21 19 E
Kastoría □, Greece ... 50 F5 40 30N 21 15 E
Kastorías, Límni, Greece ... 50 F5 40 30N 21 20 E
Kastornoye, Russia ... 59 G10 51 55N 38 2 E
Kastós, Greece ... 39 B2 38 34N 20 55 E
Kastós Nísis, Greece ... 39 B2 38 35N 20 55 E
Kastrosikiá, Greece ... 39 A2 39 6N 20 38 E
Kastrup, Copenhagen ✈ (CPH),
  Denmark ... 17 J6 55 37N 12 39 E
Kastsyukovichy, Belarus ... 58 F7 53 20N 32 4 E
Kasuga, Japan ... 72 D2 33 32N 130 26 E
Kasugai, Japan ... 73 B8 35 12N 136 59 E
Kasukabe, Japan ... 73 B11 35 58N 139 49 E
Kasulu, Tanzania ... 118 C3 4 37 S 30 5 E
Kasumi, Japan ... 72 B6 35 38N 134 38 E
Kasumiga-Ura, Japan ... 73 B12 36 0N 140 25 E
Kasumkent, Russia ... 61 K9 41 47N 48 15 E
Kasungu, Malawi ... 119 E3 13 0 S 33 29 E
Kasungu Nat. Park △, Malawi ... 119 E3 12 53 S 33 9 E
Kasur, Pakistan ... 91 C4 31 5N 74 25 E
Kataba, Zambia ... 119 F2 16 5 S 25 10 E
Katagum, Nigeria ... 113 C7 12 18N 10 21 E
Katahdin, Mt., U.S.A. ... 149 C11 45 54N 68 56W
Katako Kombe, Dem. Rep. of
  the Congo ... 118 C1 3 25 S 24 20 E
Katákolon, Greece ... 48 D3 37 38N 21 19 E
Katale, Tanzania ... 118 C3 4 52 S 31 7 E
Katalla, U.S.A. ... 144 F11 60 12N 144 31W
Katamatite, Australia ... 129 D6 36 6 S 145 41 E
Katanda, Katanga, Dem. Rep. of
  the Congo ... 118 D1 7 52 S 24 13 E
Katanda, Nord-Kivu, Dem. Rep. of
  the Congo ... 118 C2 0 55 S 29 21 E
Katanga □, Dem. Rep. of the Congo ... 118 D2 8 0 S 25 0 E
Katangi, India ... 94 D4 21 56N 79 50 E
Katanning, Australia ... 125 F2 33 40 S 117 33 E
Katapakishi, Dem. Rep. of the Congo ... 115 D4 8 15 S 22 49 E
Katastári, Greece ... 39 D2 37 50N 20 45 E
Katav Ivanovsk, Russia ... 64 D7 54 45N 58 12 E
Katavi Nat. Park △, Tanzania ... 118 D3 6 51 S 31 3 E
Katavi Swamp, Tanzania ... 118 D3 6 50 S 31 10 E
Kataysk, Russia ... 64 C9 56 20N 62 30 E
Katchall, India ... 95 L11 7 57N 93 22 E
Katchiungo, Angola ... 115 E3 12 35 S 16 13 E
Katerini, Greece ... 50 F6 40 18N 22 37 E
Katghora, India ... 93 H10 22 30N 82 33 E
Katha, Burma ... 90 C6 24 10N 96 30 E
Katherîna, Gebel, Egypt ... 96 D2 28 30N 33 57 E
Katherine, Australia ... 124 B5 14 27 S 132 20 E
Katherine →, Australia ... 122 C5 14 40 S 131 42 E
Katherine Gorge, Australia ... 124 B5 14 18 S 132 28 E
Kathi, India ... 92 J6 21 47N 74 3 E
Kathiawar, India ... 92 H4 22 20N 71 0 E
Kathikas, Cyprus ... 39 E11 34 55N 32 25 E
Kathleen, U.S.A. ... 153 G7 28 7N 82 2W
Kathmandu = Katmandu, Nepal ... 93 F11 27 45N 85 20 E
Kathua, India ... 92 C6 32 23N 75 34 E
Kati, Mali ... 112 C3 12 41N 8 4W
Katihar, India ... 93 G12 25 34N 87 36 E
Katikati, N.Z. ... 130 D4 37 32 S 175 57 E
Katima Mulilo, Zambia ... 116 B3 17 28 S 24 13 E
Katimbira, Malawi ... 119 E3 12 40 S 34 0 E
Katingan = Mendawai →, Indonesia ... 85 C4 3 30 S 113 0 E
Katiola, Ivory C. ... 112 D3 8 10N 5 10W
Katipunan, Phil. ... 81 G4 8 31N 123 17 E
Katla, Iceland ... 11 D7 63 36N 19 7W
Katlanovo, Macedonia ... 50 E5 41 52N 21 40 E
Katmai Nat. Park and Preserve △,
  U.S.A. ... 144 G9 58 20N 155 0W
Katmandu, Nepal ... 93 F11 27 45N 85 20 E
Katni, India ... 93 H9 23 51N 80 24 E
Káto Akhaïa, Greece ... 48 C3 38 8N 21 33 E
Káto Arkhánai, Greece ... 39 E6 35 15N 25 10 E
Káto Khorió, Greece ... 39 E6 35 3N 25 47 E
Káto Pyrgos, Cyprus ... 39 E8 35 11N 32 41 E
Káto Stavros, Greece ... 50 F7 40 39N 23 43 E
Katokhí, Greece ... 48 C3 38 8N 21 7 E
Katol, India ... 94 D4 21 17N 78 38 E
Katompe, Dem. Rep. of the Congo ... 118 D2 6 2 S 26 23 E
Katong, Singapore ... 87 d 1 18N 103 53 E
Katonga →, Uganda ... 118 B3 0 34N 31 50 E
Katoomba, Australia ... 129 B9 33 41 S 150 19 E
Katoúna, Greece ... 48 C3 38 47N 21 7 E
Katowice, Poland ... 55 H6 50 17N 19 5 E
Katranci Daği, Turkey ... 49 D12 37 27N 30 0 E
Katrine, L., U.K. ... 22 E4 56 15N 4 30W
Katrineholm, Sweden ... 17 F10 59 9N 16 12 E
Katsepe, Madag. ... 117 B8 15 45 S 46 15 E
Katsina, Nigeria ... 113 C6 13 0N 7 32 E
Katsina □, Nigeria ... 113 C6 12 30N 7 30 E
Katsina Ala, Nigeria ... 113 D6 7 10N 9 30 E
Katsina Ala →, Nigeria ... 113 D6 7 10N 9 20 E
Katsumoto, Japan ... 72 D1 33 51N 129 42 E
Katsuta, Japan ... 73 A12 36 25N 140 31 E
Katsuura, Japan ... 73 B12 35 10N 140 20 E

Katsuyama, Fukui, Japan ... 73 A8 36 3N 136 30 E
Katsuyama, Okayama, Japan ... 72 B5 35 3N 133 41 E
Kattakúrgan, Uzbekistan ... 65 D3 39 55N 66 15 E
Kattaviá, Greece ... 38 F11 35 57N 27 46 E
Kattegat, Denmark ... 17 H5 56 40N 11 20 E
Katthammarsvik, Sweden ... 17 G12 57 26N 18 51 E
Katul, J., Sudan ... 107 E2 14 12N 29 25 E
Katumba, Dem. Rep. of the Congo ... 118 D2 7 40 S 25 17 E
Katwa, India ... 93 H13 23 30N 88 5 E
Katwijk, Neths. ... 24 B4 52 12N 4 24 E
Kąty Wrocławskie, Poland ... 55 G3 51 2N 16 45 E
Kauai, U.S.A. ... 145 A2 22 3N 159 30W
Kauai Channel, U.S.A. ... 145 B3 21 45N 158 50W
Kaub, Germany ... 31 E3 50 5N 7 46 E
Kaudom Game Reserve ○, Namibia ... 116 B3 18 45 S 20 51 E
Kaufbeuren, Germany ... 31 H6 47 53N 10 37 E
Kaufman, U.S.A. ... 155 J6 32 35N 96 19W
Kauhajoki, Finland ... 15 E20 62 25N 22 10 E
Kauhola Pt., U.S.A. ... 145 C6 20 15N 155 47W
Kaukauna, U.S.A. ... 148 C1 44 17N 88 17W
Kaukonahua →, U.S.A. ... 145 J13 21 35N 158 7W
Kaula I., U.S.A. ... 145 B1 21 40N 160 33W
Kalakahi Channel, U.S.A. ... 145 B2 22 0N 159 55W
Kaumalapau, U.S.A. ... 145 C5 20 47N 156 59W
Kauna Pt., U.S.A. ... 145 D6 19 2N 155 53W
Kaunakakai, U.S.A. ... 145 B4 21 6N 157 1W
Kaunas, Lithuania ... 15 J20 54 54N 23 54 E
Kaunas ✈ (KUN), Lithuania ... 54 D11 54 57N 24 3 E
Kaunghein, Burma ... 90 C5 25 41N 95 26 E
Kaunia, Bangla. ... 90 C2 25 46N 89 26 E
Kaunos, Turkey ... 49 E10 36 49N 28 39 E
Kaupalatmada, Indonesia ... 82 B3 3 30 S 126 10 E
Kaupangur, Iceland ... 11 B8 65 38N 18 2W
Kaura Namoda, Nigeria ... 113 C6 12 37N 6 33 E
Kauru, Nigeria ... 113 C6 10 33N 8 12 E
Kautokeino, Norway ... 14 B20 69 0N 23 4 E
Kauwapur, India ... 93 F10 27 31N 82 18 E
Kavacha, Russia ... 67 C17 60 16N 169 51 E
Kavadarci, Macedonia ... 50 E6 41 26N 22 3 E
Kavajë, Albania ... 50 E3 41 11N 19 33 E
Kavak, Turkey ... 100 B7 41 4N 36 3 E
Kavak Daği, Turkey ... 49 D10 37 10N 28 2 E
Kavaklı, Turkey ... 51 E11 41 39N 27 10 E
Kavaklıdere, Turkey ... 49 D10 37 27N 28 21 E
Kavalerovo, Russia ... 70 B7 44 15N 135 4 E
Kavali, India ... 95 G5 14 55N 80 1 E
Kaválla, Greece ... 51 F8 40 57N 24 28 E
Kaválla □, Greece ... 51 E8 41 5N 24 30 E
Kaválla Kólpos, Greece ... 51 F8 40 50N 24 25 E
Kavár, Iran ... 97 D7 29 11N 52 44 E
Kavaratti, India ... 95 J1 10 34N 72 37 E
Kavaratti I., India ... 95 J1 10 33N 72 38 E
Kavarna, Bulgaria ... 51 C12 43 26N 28 22 E
Kavava, Dem. Rep. of the Congo ... 115 D4 8 52 S 27 19 E
Kavi, India ... 92 H5 22 12N 72 38 E
Kavieng, Papua N. G. ... 132 B6 2 36 S 150 51 E
Kavimba, Botswana ... 116 B3 18 2 S 24 38 E
Kavîr, Dasht-e, Iran ... 97 C7 34 30N 55 0 E
Kavkaz, Russia ... 59 K9 45 20N 36 40 E
Kävlinge, Sweden ... 17 J7 55 47N 13 9 E
Kavos, Greece ... 38 C10 39 23N 20 3 E
Kavoúsi, Greece ... 39 E6 35 7N 25 51 E
Kavungo, Angola ... 115 E4 11 31 S 23 3 E
Kaw, Fr. Guiana ... 169 C7 4 30N 52 15W
Kawa, Sudan ... 107 E3 13 42N 32 34 E
Kawachi-Nagano, Japan ... 73 C7 34 28N 135 31 E
Kawagama L., Canada ... 150 A6 45 18N 78 45W
Kawagoe, Japan ... 73 B11 35 55N 139 29 E
Kawaguchi, Japan ... 73 B11 35 52N 139 45 E
Kawaihae B., U.S.A. ... 145 D6 20 0N 155 50W
Kawaihoa Pt., U.S.A. ... 145 B1 21 47N 160 12W
Kawaikini, U.S.A. ... 145 A2 22 5N 159 29W
Kawaloa Beach, U.S.A. ... 145 J13 21 37N 158 5W
Kawakawa, N.Z. ... 130 B3 35 23 S 174 6 E
Kawambwa, Zambia ... 119 D2 9 48 S 29 3 E
Kawanabe, Japan ... 72 F2 31 23N 130 24 E
Kawanoe, Japan ... 72 C5 34 1N 133 34 E
Kawardha, India ... 93 J9 22 0N 81 17 E
Kawasaki, Japan ... 73 B11 35 31N 139 43 E
Kawasi, Indonesia ... 82 B3 1 38 S 127 28 E
Kawau I., N.Z. ... 130 C3 36 25 S 174 52 E
Kaweka Ra., N.Z. ... 130 F5 39 17 S 176 19 E
Kawela, U.S.A. ... 145 J13 21 42N 158 1W
Kawerau, N.Z. ... 130 E5 38 7 S 176 42 E
Kawhia Harbour, N.Z. ... 130 E3 38 5 S 174 51 E
Kawio, Kepulauan, Indonesia ... 79 D7 4 30N 125 30 E
Kawkareik, Burma ... 90 G7 16 33N 98 14 E
Kawlin, Burma ... 90 D5 23 47N 95 41 E
Kawthaung, Burma ... 87 H2 10 5N 98 36 E
Kawthoolei = Kayin □, Burma ... 90 C5 24 50N 94 58 E
Kawthule = Kayin □, Burma ... 90 C5 24 50N 94 58 E
Kawya, Burma ... 90 C5 24 50N 94 58 E
Kaxholmen, Sweden ... 17 G8 57 51N 14 19 E
Kay, Russia ... 64 B4 59 57N 52 59 E
Kaya, Burkina Faso ... 113 C4 13 4N 1 10W
Kayah □, Burma ... 90 F6 19 15N 97 15 E
Kayak I., U.S.A. ... 144 G11 59 56N 144 23W
Kayalıköy Baraji, Turkey ... 51 E11 41 50N 27 5 E
Kayan, Burma ... 90 G6 16 54N 96 34 E
Kayan →, Indonesia ... 85 B5 2 55N 117 35 E
Kayankulam, India ... 95 K3 9 10N 76 33 E
Kayasa, Indonesia ... 82 A3 0 47N 127 38 E
Kaycee, U.S.A. ... 158 E10 43 43N 106 38W
Kayeli, Indonesia ... 82 B3 3 20 S 127 10 E
Kayenda, Dem. Rep. of Congo ... 115 E4 10 48 S 23 6 E
Kayenta, U.S.A. ... 159 H8 36 44N 110 15W
Kayes, Congo ... 115 C2 4 25 S 11 41 E
Kayes, Mali ... 112 C2 14 25N 11 30W
Kayı, Turkey ... 49 B12 39 12N 30 46 E
Kayima, S. Leone ... 112 D2 8 54N 11 15W
Kayin □, Burma ... 90 G6 18 0N 97 30 E
Kaymakçı, Turkey ... 49 C10 38 10N 28 8 E
Kayoa, Indonesia ... 82 A3 0 1N 127 28 E
Kayomba, Zambia ... 119 E1 13 11 S 24 2 E
Kayombo, Zambia ... 115 E4 13 3 S 23 51 E
Kayrakkumskoye Vdkhr., Tajikistan ... 65 C4 40 20N 70 0 E
Kaysatskoye, Russia ... 60 F8 49 47N 46 49 E
Kayseri, Turkey ... 100 C6 38 45N 35 30 E
Kaysville, U.S.A. ... 158 F8 41 2N 111 56W
Kayts, Sri Lanka ... 95 K4 9 42N 79 51 E
Kayuagung, Indonesia ... 84 C2 3 24 S 104 50 E
Kayyngdy, Kyrgyzstan ... 65 B6 42 49N 73 41 E
Kaz Daği, Turkey ... 49 B8 39 42N 26 50 E
Kazachye, Russia ... 67 B14 70 52N 135 58 E
Kazakhstan ■, Asia ... 66 E7 50 0N 70 0 E
Kazan, Russia ... 60 C9 55 50N 49 10 E
Kazan →, Canada ... 143 A9 64 3N 95 35W
Kazan-Kuygan, Kyrgyzstan ... 65 C7 41 34N 75 42 E
Kazan-Rettô, Pac. Oc. ... 134 E6 25 0N 141 0 E
Kazanlŭk, Bulgaria ... 51 D9 42 38N 25 20 E
Kazanskaya, Russia ... 60 F5 49 50N 41 10 E
Kazarman, Kyrgyzstan ... 65 C6 41 24N 73 59 E
Kazatin = Kozyatyn, Ukraine ... 59 H5 49 45N 28 50 E
Kazaure, Nigeria ... 113 C6 12 42N 8 28 E
Kazbek, Russia ... 61 J7 42 42N 44 30 E
Kâzerûn, Iran ... 97 D6 29 38N 51 40 E
Kazhim, Russia ... 64 B8 60 20N 51 32 E
Kazi Magomed = Qazimämmäd,
  Azerbaijan ... 61 K9 40 3N 49 0 E
Kazimierz Dolny, Poland ... 55 G8 51 19N 21 57 E
Kazimierza Wielka, Poland ... 55 H7 50 15N 20 30 E

Kazincbarcika, Hungary ... 52 B5 48 17N 20 36 E
Kazipet, India ... 94 F4 17 58N 79 30 E
Kaziza, Dem. Rep. of the Congo ... 115 E4 10 42 S 23 52 E
Kazlų Rūda, Lithuania ... 54 D10 54 46N 23 30 E
Kazo, Japan ... 73 A11 36 7N 139 36 E
Kaztalovka, Kazakhstan ... 60 F9 49 47N 48 43 E
Kazu, Burma ... 90 C6 25 27N 97 46 E
Kazuma Pan Nat. Park △, Zimbabwe ... 119 F2 18 20 S 25 48 E
Kazumba, Dem. Rep. of the Congo ... 115 D4 6 25 S 22 5 E
Kazuno, Japan ... 70 D10 40 10N 140 45 E
Kazym →, Russia ... 66 C7 63 54N 65 50 E
Kcynia, Poland ... 55 F4 53 0N 17 30 E
Ke-hsi Mansam, Burma ... 90 E6 21 56N 97 50 E
Ké-Macina, Mali ... 112 C3 13 58N 5 22W
Kéa, Greece ... 48 D6 37 35N 24 22 E
Keaau, U.S.A. ... 145 D6 19 37N 155 2W
Keady, U.K. ... 23 B5 54 15N 6 42W
Keahi Pt., U.S.A. ... 145 K14 21 19N 157 59W
Keahole Pt., U.S.A. ... 145 D5 19 44N 156 3W
Kealaikahiki Channel, U.S.A. ... 145 C5 20 35N 156 50W
Kealaikahiki Pt., U.S.A. ... 145 C5 20 32N 156 42W
Kealakekua, U.S.A. ... 145 D6 19 31N 155 55W
Kealia, U.S.A. ... 145 D6 19 24N 155 53W
Kearney, Mo., U.S.A. ... 156 E22 39 22N 94 22W
Kearney, Nebr., U.S.A. ... 154 E5 40 42N 99 5W
Kearny, U.S.A. ... 159 K8 33 3N 110 55W
Kearsarge, Mt., U.S.A. ... 151 C13 43 22N 71 50W
Keban, Turkey ... 101 C8 38 50N 38 50 E
Keban Baraji, Turkey ... 101 C8 38 41N 38 33 E
Kebara, Congo ... 114 C2 2 27 S 14 25 E
Kebbi, Ivory C. ... 112 D3 9 18N 6 37W
Kebbi, Mayo →, Cameroon ... 114 A2 9 18N 13 5 E
Kebbi □, Nigeria ... 113 C5 11 35N 4 0 E
Kebili, Tunisia ... 108 B1 33 47N 9 0 E
Kebnekaise, Sweden ... 14 C18 67 53N 18 33 E
Kebri Dehar, Ethiopia ... 120 C2 6 45N 44 17 E
Kebumen, Indonesia ... 85 D3 7 42 S 109 40 E
Kecel, Hungary ... 52 D4 46 31N 19 16 E
Kechika →, Canada ... 142 B3 59 41N 127 12 E
Keçiborlu, Turkey ... 49 D12 37 57N 30 18 E
Kecskemét, Hungary ... 52 D4 46 57N 19 42 E
Kedada, Ethiopia ... 107 F4 5 25N 35 58 E
Kedah □, Malaysia ... 84 A2 5 50N 100 40 E
Kėdainiai, Lithuania ... 15 J21 55 15N 24 2 E
Kedarnath, India ... 93 D8 30 44N 79 4 E
Kedgwick, Canada ... 141 C6 47 40N 67 20W
Kédhros Óros, Greece ... 39 E5 35 11N 24 37 E
Kediet Ijill, Mauritania ... 110 D2 22 38N 12 35W
Kediri, Indonesia ... 85 D4 7 51 S 112 1 E
Kedja, Dem. Rep. of the Congo ... 114 B3 4 50N 19 16 E
Kedjebi, Ghana ... 113 D5 8 12N 0 25 E
Kédougou, Senegal ... 112 C2 12 35N 12 10W
Kędzierzyn-Koźle, Poland ... 55 H5 50 20N 18 12 E
Keehi Lagoon, U.S.A. ... 145 K14 21 17N 157 55W
Keeler, U.S.A. ... 161 J8 36 29N 117 52W
Keeley L., Canada ... 143 C7 54 54N 108 8W
Keeling Is. = Cocos Is., Ind. Oc. ... 125 E8 12 10 S 96 55 E
Keelung = Chilung, Taiwan ... 77 E13 25 3N 121 45 E
Keen, Mt., U.K. ... 22 D5 56 58N 2 54W
Keene, Canada ... 150 B6 44 15N 78 10W
Keene, Calif., U.S.A. ... 161 K8 35 13N 118 33W
Keene, N.H., U.S.A. ... 151 D12 42 56N 72 17W
Keene, N.Y., U.S.A. ... 151 B11 44 16N 73 46W
Keep River Nat. Park △, Australia ... 124 C4 15 49 S 129 8 E
Keeper Hill, Ireland ... 23 D3 52 45N 8 16W
Keepit, L., Australia ... 129 A9 30 50 S 150 30 E
Keer-Weer, C., Australia ... 126 A3 14 0 S 141 32 E
Keeseville, U.S.A. ... 151 B11 44 29N 73 30W
Keetmanshoop, Namibia ... 116 D2 26 35 S 18 8 E
Keewatin, Canada ... 143 D10 49 46N 94 34W
Keewatin →, Canada ... 143 B8 56 29N 100 46W
Kefa □, Ethiopia ... 107 F4 6 55N 36 30 E
Kefallinía, Greece ... 39 C2 38 15N 20 30 E
Kefallinía □, Greece ... 39 C2 38 20N 20 30 E
Kefallinía ✈ (EFL), Greece ... 39 C1 38 10N 20 30 E
Kéfalos, Greece ... 49 E8 36 45N 26 59 E
Kefamenanu, Indonesia ... 83 C2 9 28 S 124 29 E
Kefar Sava, Israel ... 103 C3 32 11N 34 54 E
Keffi, Nigeria ... 113 D6 8 55N 7 43 E
Keffin Hausa, Nigeria ... 113 C6 12 13N 9 59 E
Keflavík, Iceland ... 11 C4 64 2N 22 35W
Keflavík ✈ (KEF), Iceland ... 11 C4 64 0N 22 45W
Keftya, Ethiopia ... 107 E4 13 54N 37 7 E
Keg River, Canada ... 142 B5 57 54N 117 55W
Kegalla, Sri Lanka ... 95 L5 7 15N 80 21 E
Kegaska, Canada ... 141 B7 50 9N 61 18W
Keheili, Sudan ... 106 D3 19 25N 32 50 E
Kehl, Germany ... 31 G3 48 34N 7 50 E
Keighley, U.K. ... 20 D6 53 52N 1 54W
Keijo = Sŏul, S. Korea ... 75 F14 37 31N 126 58 E
Keila, Estonia ... 15 G21 59 18N 24 25 E
Keimoes, S. Africa ... 116 D3 28 41 S 20 59 E
Keita, Niger ... 113 C6 14 46N 5 56 E
Keita, B. →, Chad ... 109 G3 9 14N 18 21 E
Keitele, Finland ... 14 E22 63 10N 26 20 E
Keith, Australia ... 128 D4 36 6 S 140 20 E
Keith, U.K. ... 22 D6 57 32N 2 57W
Keithsburg, U.S.A. ... 156 C6 41 6N 90 56W
Keiyasi, Fiji ... 133 A1 17 53 S 177 46 E
Keizer, U.S.A. ... 158 D2 44 57N 123 1W
Kejimkujik Nat. Park △, Canada ... 141 D6 44 25N 65 25W
Kekaha, U.S.A. ... 145 B2 21 58N 159 43W
Kekri, India ... 92 G6 26 0N 75 10 E
Kelam, Ethiopia ... 107 G4 4 48N 35 58 E
Kelamet, Eritrea ... 107 D4 16 0N 38 30 E
Kelan, China ... 74 E6 38 43N 111 31 E
Kelang, Indonesia ... 82 B3 3 12 S 127 6 E
Kelang, Malaysia ... 87 L3 3 2N 101 26 E
Kelani Ganga →, Sri Lanka ... 95 L4 6 58N 79 50 E
Kelantan □, Malaysia ... 84 A2 5 10N 102 0 E
Kelantan →, Malaysia ... 87 J4 6 13N 102 14 E
Kělcyrě, Albania ... 50 F4 40 20N 20 12 E
Kelekçi, Turkey ... 49 D11 37 15N 29 29 E
Keles, Turkey ... 51 G13 39 54N 29 14 E
Keles, Uzbekistan ... 65 C4 41 24N 69 12 E
Keleti-főcsatorna, Hungary ... 52 C5 47 45N 21 20 E
Kelheim, Germany ... 31 G7 48 54N 11 52 E
Kelibia, Tunisia ... 108 A2 36 50N 11 3 E
Kelkit, Turkey ... 101 B8 40 7N 39 16 E
Kelkit →, Turkey ... 100 B7 40 45N 36 32 E
Kellé, Congo ... 114 C2 0 8 S 14 38 E
Keller, U.S.A. ... 152 D8 31 50N 81 15W
Kellerberrin, Australia ... 125 F2 31 36 S 117 38 E
Kellett, C., Canada ... 6 B1 72 0N 126 0W
Kelleys I., U.S.A. ... 150 E2 41 36N 82 42W
Kellogg, U.S.A. ... 158 C5 47 32N 116 7W
Kells = Ceanannus Mor, Ireland ... 23 C5 53 44N 6 53W
Kelmė, Lithuania ... 54 C9 55 38N 22 56 E
Kélo, Chad ... 109 G3 9 10N 15 45 E
Kelokedhara, Cyprus ... 39 F8 34 48N 32 39 E
Kelowna, Canada ... 142 D5 49 50N 119 25W
Kelsey Creek, Australia ... 126 J6 20 26 S 148 31 E
Kelso, N.Z. ... 131 F4 45 54 S 169 15 E
Kelso, U.K. ... 22 F6 55 36N 2 26W
Kelso, U.S.A. ... 160 D4 46 9N 122 54W
Keluang, Malaysia ... 87 L4 2 3N 103 18 E
Kelvington, Canada ... 143 C8 52 10N 103 30W
Kem, Russia ... 56 B5 65 0N 34 38 E
Kem →, Russia ... 56 B5 64 57N 34 41 E
Kem-Kem, Morocco ... 110 B4 30 40N 4 30W

Kema, Indonesia ... 79 D7 1 22N 125 8 E
Kemah, Turkey ... 101 C8 39 32N 39 5 E
Kemaliye, Erzincan, Turkey ... 101 C8 39 16N 38 29 E
Kemaliye, Manisa, Turkey ... 49 C10 38 27N 28 25 E
Kemalpaşa, Turkey ... 49 C9 38 27N 27 27 E
Kemaman, Malaysia ... 78 D2 4 12N 103 18 E
Kemano, Canada ... 142 C3 53 35N 128 0W
Kemapyu, Burma ... 90 F6 18 49N 97 19 E
Kemasik, Malaysia ... 87 K4 4 25N 103 27 E
Kembé, C.A.R. ... 114 B4 4 36N 21 58 E
Kembolcha, Ethiopia ... 107 E4 11 2N 39 42 E
Kemer, Antalya, Turkey ... 49 E12 36 36N 30 34 E
Kemer, Burdur, Turkey ... 49 D12 37 21N 30 4 E
Kemer, Muğla, Turkey ... 49 E11 36 40N 29 22 E
Kemer Baraji, Turkey ... 49 D10 37 30N 28 37 E
Kemerovo, Russia ... 66 D9 55 20N 86 5 E
Kemeru Nac. Parks △, Latvia ... 54 B10 56 58N 23 25 E
Kemi, Finland ... 14 D21 65 44N 24 34 E
Kemi älv = Kemijoki →, Finland ... 14 D21 65 47N 24 32 E
Kemijärvi, Finland ... 14 C22 66 43N 27 22 E
Kemijoki →, Finland ... 14 D21 65 47N 24 32 E
Kemin, Kyrgyzstan ... 65 B7 42 47N 75 42 E
Kemmerer, U.S.A. ... 158 F8 41 48N 110 32W
Kemmuna = Comino, Malta ... 38 E7 36 1N 14 20 E
Kemp, L., U.S.A. ... 155 J5 33 46N 99 9W
Kemp Land, Antarctica ... 7 C5 69 0 S 55 0 E
Kempas, Malaysia ... 87 d 1 33N 103 42 E
Kempsey, Australia ... 129 A10 31 1 S 152 50 E
Kempt, L., Canada ... 140 C5 47 25N 74 22W
Kempten, Germany ... 31 H6 47 45N 10 17 E
Kempton, Australia ... 127 D4 42 31 S 147 12 E
Kempton, U.S.A. ... 157 D10 40 17N 86 14W
Kemptville, Canada ... 140 D4 45 0N 75 38W
Ken →, India ... 93 G9 25 13N 80 27 E
Kenadsa, Algeria ... 111 B4 31 48N 2 26W
Kenai, U.S.A. ... 144 F10 60 33N 151 16W
Kenai Fjords Nat. Park △, U.S.A. ... 144 F10 59 40N 149 50W
Kenai Mts., U.S.A. ... 144 G10 60 0N 150 0W
Kendai, India ... 93 H10 22 45N 82 37 E
Kendal, Indonesia ... 85 D4 6 56 S 110 14 E
Kendal, U.K. ... 20 C5 54 20N 2 44W
Kendall, Australia ... 129 A10 31 35 S 152 44 E
Kendall, U.S.A. ... 153 K9 25 41N 80 19W
Kendall →, Australia ... 126 A3 14 4 S 141 35 E
Kendallville, U.S.A. ... 157 C11 41 27N 85 16W
Kendari, Indonesia ... 82 B2 3 50 S 122 30 E
Kendawangan, Indonesia ... 85 C4 2 32 S 110 17 E
Kende, Nigeria ... 113 C5 11 30N 4 12 E
Kendi, Pulau, Malaysia ... 87 c 5 13N 100 11 E
Kendrapara, India ... 94 D8 20 35N 86 30 E
Kendrew, S. Africa ... 116 E3 32 32 S 24 30 E
Kendrick, U.S.A. ... 158 C5 46 37N 116 39W
Kene Thao, Laos ... 86 D3 17 44N 101 10 E
Kenedy, U.S.A. ... 155 L6 28 49N 97 51W
Kenema, S. Leone ... 112 D2 7 50N 11 14W
Keng Kok, Laos ... 86 D5 16 26N 105 12 E
Keng Tawng, Burma ... 90 E7 20 45N 98 18 E
Keng Tung, Burma ... 76 G2 21 0N 99 30 E
Kengani, Dem. Rep. of the Congo ... 114 C2 2 59 S 17 36 E
Kenge, Dem. Rep. of the Congo ... 115 C3 4 50 S 17 4 E
Kengeja, Tanzania ... 118 D4 5 26 S 39 45 E
Kenhardt, S. Africa ... 116 D3 29 19 S 21 12 E
Kéniéba, Mali ... 112 C2 12 54N 11 17W
Kenitra, Morocco ... 110 B3 34 15N 6 40W
Kenli, China ... 75 F10 37 30N 118 20 E
Kenmare, Ireland ... 23 E2 51 53N 9 36W
Kenmare, U.S.A. ... 154 A3 48 41N 102 5W
Kenmare River, Ireland ... 23 E2 51 48N 9 51W
Kennebago Lake, U.S.A. ... 151 A14 45 4N 70 40W
Kennebec, U.S.A. ... 154 D5 43 54N 99 52W
Kennebec →, U.S.A. ... 149 D11 43 45N 69 46W
Kennebunk, U.S.A. ... 151 C14 43 23N 70 33W
Kennedy, Zimbabwe ... 116 B4 18 52 S 27 10 E
Kennedy Kanal, Arctic ... 10 A4 80 50N 66 0W
Kennedy Ra., Australia ... 125 D2 24 45 S 115 10 E
Kennedy Range Nat. Park △,
  Australia ... 125 D2 24 34 S 115 2 E
Kennedy Space Center, U.S.A. ... 153 G9 28 40N 80 42W
Kenner, U.S.A. ... 155 L9 29 59N 90 15W
Kennesaw, U.S.A. ... 152 A5 34 1N 84 37W
Kennet →, U.K. ... 21 F7 51 27N 0 57W
Kenneth Ra., Australia ... 125 D2 23 50 S 117 8 E
Kennett, U.S.A. ... 155 G9 36 14N 90 3W
Kennewick, U.S.A. ... 158 C4 46 12N 119 7W
Kenogami →, Canada ... 140 B3 51 6N 84 28W
Kenogami L., Canada ... 148 A3 48 9N 80 7W
Kenora, Canada ... 143 D10 49 47N 94 29W
Kenosha, U.S.A. ... 157 D9 42 35N 87 49W
Kensington, Canada ... 141 C7 46 28N 63 34W
Kent, Ohio, U.S.A. ... 150 E3 41 9N 81 22W
Kent, Tex., U.S.A. ... 155 K2 31 4N 104 13W
Kent, Wash., U.S.A. ... 160 C4 47 23N 122 14W
Kent □, U.K. ... 21 F8 51 12N 0 40 E
Kent Group, Australia ... 127 C4 39 30 S 147 20 E
Kent Pen., Canada ... 138 B9 68 30N 107 0W
Kentaū, Kazakhstan ... 65 B4 43 32N 68 36 E
Kentland, U.S.A. ... 157 D9 40 46N 87 27W
Kenton, U.S.A. ... 157 D13 40 39N 83 37W
Kentucky □, U.S.A. ... 148 G3 37 0N 84 0W
Kentucky →, U.S.A. ... 156 F11 38 41N 85 11W
Kentucky L., U.S.A. ... 149 G2 37 1N 88 16W
Kentville, Canada ... 141 C7 45 6N 64 29W
Kentwood, La., U.S.A. ... 155 K9 30 56N 90 31W
Kentwood, Mich., U.S.A. ... 157 H11 42 52N 85 37W
Kenya ■, Africa ... 118 B4 1 0N 38 0 E
Kenya, Mt., Kenya ... 118 C4 0 10 S 37 18 E
Kenzou, Cameroon ... 114 B3 4 10N 15 2 E
Keo Neua, Deo, Vietnam ... 86 C5 18 23N 105 10 E
Keokea, U.S.A. ... 145 C5 20 43N 156 22W
Keokuk, U.S.A. ... 156 D5 40 24N 91 24W
Keonjhargarh, India ... 93 J11 21 28N 85 35 E
Keosauqua, U.S.A. ... 156 D5 40 44N 91 58W
Keota, U.S.A. ... 156 C5 41 22N 91 57W
Kep, Cambodia ... 87 G5 10 29N 104 19 E
Kep, Vietnam ... 86 B6 21 24N 106 16 E
Kepala Batas, Malaysia ... 87 c 5 31N 100 26 E
Kepez, Turkey ... 51 F10 40 5N 26 24 E
Kepi, Indonesia ... 83 C5 6 32 S 139 19 E
Kępice, Poland ... 54 B4 54 16N 16 51 E
Kepler Mts., N.Z. ... 131 F2 45 25 S 167 20 E
Kepno, Poland ... 55 G4 51 18N 17 58 E
Keppel Pt., Papua N. G. ... 132 F4 10 10 S 147 58 E
Kepsut, Turkey ... 49 B10 39 40N 28 9 E
Kepuhi Pt., U.S.A. ... 145 K13 21 29N 158 14W
Kerala □, India ... 95 J3 11 0N 76 15 E
Keram →, Papua N. G. ... 132 C3 4 7 S 144 5 E
Kerama-Rettô, Japan ... 71 L3 26 5N 127 15 E
Keran, Pakistan ... 93 B5 34 35N 73 59 E
Keran, Parc Nat. de la △, Togo ... 113 C5 10 0N 0 41 E
Kerang, Australia ... 128 C5 35 40 S 143 55 E
Keranji, Ethiopia ... 107 F4 9 48N 36 6 E
Kerao →, Sudan ... 107 E3 11 0N 32 41 E
Keratéa, Greece ... 48 D5 37 48N 23 58 E
Keraudren, C., Australia ... 124 C2 19 58 S 119 45 E
Kerava, Finland ... 15 F21 60 25N 25 5 E
Keravat, Papua N. G. ... 132 C7 4 17 S 152 2 E
Kerch, Ukraine ... 65 C5 45 20N 36 20 E
Kerchenskiy Proliv, Black Sea ... 59 K9 45 10N 36 30 E
Kerchoual, Mali ... 113 B5 17 12N 0 20 E
Kerema, Papua N. G. ... 132 D3 7 58 S 145 50 E

Kerempe Burnu, *Turkey* **100 A5** 42 2N 33 20 E
Keren, *Eritrea* **107 D4** 15 45N 38 28 E
Kerewan, *Gambia* **112 C1** 13 29N 16 10W
Kerguelen, *Ind. Oc.* **121 J5** 49 15 S 69 10 E
Keri, *Greece* **39 D2** 37 40N 20 49 E
Keri Kera, *Sudan* **107 E3** 12 21N 32 42 E
Kericho, *Kenya* **118 C4** 0 22 S 35 15 E
Kerikeri, *N.Z.* **130 B2** 35 12 S 173 59 E
Kerinci, *Indonesia* **84 C2** 1 40 S 101 15 E
Kerkenna, Is., *Tunisia* **108 B2** 34 48N 11 11 E
Kerki, *Turkmenistan* **65 E2** 37 50N 65 12 E
Kerkinítis, Límni, *Greece* **50 E7** 41 12N 23 10 E
Kérkira, *Greece* **38 B9** 39 38N 19 50 E
Kérkira □, *Greece* **38 B9** 39 37N 19 50 E
Kérkira ✗ (CFU), *Greece* **48 B1** 39 35N 19 54 E
Kerkouane, *Tunisia* **46 F4** 36 58N 11 2 E
Kerkrade, *Neths.* **24 D6** 50 53N 6 4 E
Kerma, *Sudan* **106 D3** 19 33N 30 32 E
Kermadec Is., *Pac. Oc.* **134 L10** 30 0 S 178 15W
Kermadec Trench, *Pac. Oc.* **134 L10** 30 30 S 176 0W
Kermān, *Iran* **97 D8** 30 15N 57 1 E
Kerman, *U.S.A.* **160 J6** 36 43N 120 4W
Kermān □, *Iran* **97 D8** 30 0N 57 0 E
Kermān, Bīābān-e, *Iran* **97 D8** 28 45N 59 45 E
Kermānshāh = Bākhtarān, *Iran* **101 E12** 34 23N 47 0 E
Kermen, *Bulgaria* **51 D10** 42 30N 26 16 E
Kermit, *U.S.A.* **155 K3** 31 52N 103 6W
Kern →, *U.S.A.* **161 K7** 35 16N 119 18W
Kernhof, *Austria* **34 D8** 47 49N 15 32 E
Kernow = Cornwall □, *U.K.* **21 G3** 50 26N 4 40W
Kerns, *Switz.* **33 C6** 46 54N 8 17 E
Kernville, *U.S.A.* **161 K8** 35 45N 118 26W
Keroh, *Malaysia* **87 K3** 5 43N 101 1 E
Kérou, *Benin* **113 C5** 10 50N 2 5 E
Kérouane, *Guinea* **112 D3** 9 15N 9 0W
Kerowagi, *Papua N. G.* **132 C3** 5 51 S 144 51 E
Kerpen, *Germany* **30 E2** 50 51N 6 41 E
Kerrera, *U.K.* **22 E3** 56 24N 5 33W
Kerrobert, *Canada* **143 C7** 51 56N 109 8W
Kerrville, *U.S.A.* **155 K5** 30 3N 99 8W
Kerry □, *Ireland* **23 D2** 52 7N 9 35W
Kerry Hd., *Ireland* **23 D2** 52 25N 9 56W
Kersa, *Ethiopia* **107 F5** 9 28N 41 48 E
Kertosono, *Indonesia* **85 D4** 7 38 S 112 9 E
Kerulen →, *Asia* **69 B6** 48 48N 117 0 E
Kerzaz, *Algeria* **111 C4** 29 29N 1 37W
Kerzers, *Switz.* **32 C4** 46 59N 7 12 E
Kesagami →, *Canada* **140 B4** 51 40N 79 45W
Kesagami L., *Canada* **140 B3** 50 23N 80 15W
Keşan, *Turkey* **51 F10** 40 49N 26 38 E
Kesch, Piz, *Switz.* **33 C9** 46 38N 9 53 E
Kesennuma, *Japan* **70 E10** 38 54N 141 35 E
Keshit, *Iran* **97 D8** 29 43N 58 17 E
Kesigi = Kosgi, *India* **95 G3** 15 51N 77 16 E
Keşiş Dağ, *Turkey* **101 C8** 39 47N 39 46 E
Keskal, *India* **94 D5** 20 5N 81 35 E
Keskin, *Turkey* **100 C5** 39 40N 33 36 E
Kestell, *S. Africa* **117 D4** 28 17 S 28 42 E
Kestenga, *Russia* **56 A5** 65 50N 31 45 E
Keswick, *U.K.* **20 C4** 54 36N 3 8W
Keszthely, *Hungary* **52 D2** 46 50N 17 15 E
Ket →, *Russia* **66 D9** 58 55N 81 32 E
Keta, *Ghana* **113 D5** 5 49N 1 0 E
Keta Lagoon, *Ghana* **113 D5** 5 55N 1 0 E
Ketapang, *Bali, Indonesia* **79 J17** 8 9 S 114 23 E
Ketapang, *Kalimantan, Indonesia* **85 C4** 1 55 S 110 0 E
Ketchikan, *U.S.A.* **142 B2** 55 21N 131 39W
Ketchum, *U.S.A.* **158 E6** 43 41N 114 22W
Kete Krachi, *Ghana* **113 D4** 7 46N 0 1W
Ketef, Khalîg Umm el, *Egypt* **96 F2** 23 40N 35 35 E
Keti Bandar, *Pakistan* **92 G2** 24 8N 67 27 E
Kétou, *Benin* **113 D5** 7 25N 2 45 E
Ketri, *India* **92 E6** 28 1N 75 50 E
Kętrzyn, *Poland* **54 D8** 54 7N 21 22 E
Kettering, *U.K.* **21 E7** 52 24N 0 43W
Kettering, *U.S.A.* **157 E12** 39 41N 84 10W
Kettle →, *Canada* **143 B11** 56 40N 89 34W
Kettle Falls, *U.S.A.* **158 B4** 48 37N 118 3W
Kettle Pt., *Canada* **150 C2** 43 13N 82 1W
Kettleman City, *U.S.A.* **160 J7** 36 1N 119 58W
Kęty, *Poland* **55 J6** 49 51N 19 16 E
Keuka L., *U.S.A.* **150 D7** 42 30N 77 9W
Keuruu, *Finland* **15 E21** 62 16N 24 41 E
Kevelaer, *Germany* **30 D2** 51 36N 6 15 E
Kewanee, *U.S.A.* **156 C7** 41 14N 89 56W
Kewanna, *U.S.A.* **157 C10** 41 1N 86 25W
Kewaunee, *U.S.A.* **148 C2** 44 27N 87 31W
Keweenaw B., *U.S.A.* **148 B1** 47 0N 88 15W
Keweenaw Pen., *U.S.A.* **148 B2** 47 30N 88 0W
Keweenaw Pt., *U.S.A.* **148 B2** 47 25N 87 43W
Key Colony Beach, *U.S.A.* **153 L9** 24 45N 80 57W
Key Largo, *U.S.A.* **153 K9** 25 5N 80 27W
Key West, *U.S.A.* **153 L8** 24 33N 81 48W
Keyala, *Sudan* **107 G3** 4 27N 32 52 E
Keynsham, *U.K.* **21 F5** 51 24N 2 29W
Keyser, *U.S.A.* **148 F6** 39 26N 78 59W
Keystone Heights, *U.S.A.* **152 F7** 29 47N 82 1W
Keytesville, *U.S.A.* **156 E4** 39 26N 92 56W
Kez, *Russia* **64 C4** 57 55N 53 46 E
Kezhma, *Russia* **67 D11** 58 59N 101 9 E
Kezi, *Zimbabwe* **117 C4** 20 58 S 28 32 E
Kežmarok, *Slovak Rep.* **35 B13** 49 10N 20 28 E
Kgalagadi Transfrontier Park ⌓, *Africa* **116 D3** 25 10 S 21 0 E
Khabarovsk, *Russia* **67 E14** 48 30N 135 5 E
Khabr, *Iran* **97 D8** 28 51N 56 22 E
Khābūr →, *Syria* **101 E9** 35 17N 40 35 E
Khachmas = Xaçmaz, *Azerbaijan* **61 K9** 41 31N 48 42 E
Khachrod, *India* **92 H6** 23 25N 75 20 E
Khadari, W. el →, *Sudan* **107 E2** 10 29N 27 15 E
Khadro, *Pakistan* **92 F3** 26 11N 68 50 E
Khadyzhensk, *Russia* **61 H4** 44 26N 39 32 E
Khadzhilyangar, *China* **93 B8** 35 45N 79 20 E
Khaga, *India* **93 G9** 25 47N 81 7 E
Khagaria, *India* **93 G12** 25 30N 86 32 E
Khaipur, *Pakistan* **92 E5** 29 34N 72 17 E
Khair, *India* **92 F7** 27 57N 77 46 E
Khairabad, *India* **93 F9** 27 33N 80 47 E
Khairagarh, *India* **93 J9** 21 27N 81 2 E
Khairpur, *Pakistan* **91 D3** 27 32N 68 49 E
Khairpur Nathan Shah, *Pakistan* **92 F2** 27 6N 67 44 E
Khairwara, *India* **92 H5** 23 58N 73 38 E
Khaisor →, *Pakistan* **92 D3** 31 17N 68 59 E
Khajuri Kach, *Pakistan* **92 C3** 32 4N 69 51 E
Khāk Dow, *Afghan.* **91 B2** 34 57N 67 16 E
Khakassia □, *Russia* **66 D9** 53 0N 90 0 E
Khakhea, *Botswana* **116 C3** 24 48 S 23 22 E
Khalafābād, *Iran* **97 D6** 30 54N 49 24 E
Khalfallah, *Algeria* **111 B5** 34 20N 0 16 E
Khalfūt, *Yemen* **99 D6** 15 52N 52 10 E
Khalilabad, *India* **93 F10** 26 48N 83 5 E
Khalīlī, *Iran* **97 E7** 27 38N 53 17 E
Khalkhāl, *Iran* **97 B6** 37 37N 48 32 E
Khálki, *Dhodhekánisos, Greece* **49 E9** 36 17N 27 35 E
Khálki, *Thessalía, Greece* **48 B4** 39 36N 22 30 E
Khalkidhikí □, *Greece* **50 F7** 40 25N 23 20 E
Khalkís, *Greece* **48 C5** 38 27N 23 42 E
Khalmer-Sede = Tazovskiy, *Russia* **66 C8** 67 30N 78 44 E
Khalmer Yu, *Russia* **66 C7** 67 58N 65 1 E
Khalturin, *Russia* **64 B2** 58 40N 48 50 E
Khalūf, *Oman* **102 C6** 20 30N 58 13 E
Kham Keut, *Laos* **86 C5** 18 15N 104 43 E
Khamaria, *India* **93 H9** 23 5N 80 48 E
Khambhaliya, *India* **92 H3** 22 14N 69 41 E
Khambhat, *India* **92 H5** 22 23N 72 33 E
Khambhat, G. of, *India* **89 C6** 20 45N 72 30 E
Khamgaon, *India* **94 D3** 20 42N 76 37 E
Khamilonísion, *Greece* **49 F8** 35 50N 26 15 E
Khamīr, *Iran* **97 E7** 26 57N 55 36 E
Khamir, *Yemen* **98 C3** 16 2N 44 0 E
Khamīs Mushayṭ, *Si. Arabia* **98 C3** 18 18N 42 44 E
Khammam, *India* **94 F5** 17 11N 80 6 E
Khamsa, *Egypt* **103 E1** 30 27N 32 23 E
Khamza, *Uzbekistan* **65 C5** 40 25N 71 29 E
Khan →, *Namibia* **116 C2** 22 37 S 14 56 E
Khān Abū Shāmat, *Syria* **103 B5** 33 39N 36 53 E
Khān Azād, *Iraq* **96 C5** 33 7N 44 22 E
Khān Mujiddah, *Iraq* **96 C4** 32 21N 43 48 E
Khān Shaykhūn, *Syria* **100 E7** 35 26N 36 38 E
Khān Yūnis, *Gaza Strip* **103 D3** 31 21N 34 18 E
Khānābād, *Afghan.* **65 E4** 36 45N 69 5 E
Khanabad, *Uzbekistan* **65 C6** 40 47N 73 0 E
Khanai, *Pakistan* **92 D2** 30 30N 67 8 E
Khānaqīn, *Iraq* **101 E11** 34 23N 45 25 E
Khānbāghī, *Iran* **97 B7** 36 10N 55 25 E
Khandrá, *Greece* **49 F8** 35 3N 26 8 E
Khandūd, *Afghan.* **65 E6** 36 57N 72 19 E
Khandwa, *India* **94 D3** 21 49N 76 22 E
Khandyga, *Russia* **67 C14** 62 42N 135 35 E
Khāneh, *Iran* **96 B5** 36 41N 45 8 E
Khanewal, *Pakistan* **91 C3** 30 20N 71 55 E
Khangah Dogran, *Pakistan* **92 D5** 31 50N 73 37 E
Khanh Duong, *Vietnam* **86 F7** 12 44N 1[illegible] 44 E
Khaniá, *Greece* **39 E5** 35 30N 24 4 E
Khaniá □, *Greece* **39 E5** 35 30N 24 0 E
Khanía ✗ (CHQ), *Greece* **39 E5** 35 30N 24 6 E
Khaniadhana, *India* **92 G8** 25 1N 78 8 E
Khaníon, Kólpos, *Greece* **39 E4** 35 33N 23 55 E
Khanka, L., *Asia* **67 E14** 45 0N 132 24 E
Khankendy = Xankändi, *Azerbaijan* **101 C12** 39 52N 46 49 E
Khanna, *India* **92 D7** 30 42N 76 16 E
Khanozai, *Pakistan* **92 D2** 30 37N 67 19 E
Khanpur, *Pakistan* **91 C3** 28 42N 70 35 E
Khantaū, *Kazakhstan* **65 A6** 44 13N 73 48 E
Khanty-Mansiysk, *Russia* **66 C7** 61 0N 69 0 E
Khao Laem Nat. Park △, *Thailand* **86 E2** 14 56N 98 31 E
Khao Luang Nat. Park △, *Thailand* **87 H2** 8 34N 99 42 E
Khao Phlu, *Thailand* **87 b** 9 29N 99 59 E
Khao Pu-Khao Ya Nat. Park △, *Thailand* **87 J2** 7 26N 99 57 E
Khao Sam Roi Yot Nat. Park △, *Thailand* **87 F2** 12 13N 99 57 E
Khao Sok Nat. Park △, *Thailand* **87 H2** 8 55N 98 38 E
Khao Yai Nat. Park △, *Thailand* **86 E3** 14 21N 101 29 E
Khaoen Si Nakarin Nat. Park △, *Thailand* **86 E2** 14 47N 99 0 E
Khapalu, *Pakistan* **93 B7** 35 10N 76 20 E
Khapcheranga, *Russia* **67 E12** 49 42N 112 24 E
Kharabali, *Russia* **61 G8** 47 25N 47 15 E
Kharaghoda, *India* **92 H4** 23 11N 71 46 E
Kharagpur, *India* **93 H12** 22 20N 87 25 E
Khárakas, *Greece* **39 E6** 35 1N 25 7 E
Kharan Kalat, *Pakistan* **91 C2** 28 34N 65 21 E
Kharānaq, *Iran* **97 C7** 32 20N 54 45 E
Kharda, *India* **94 E2** 18 40N 75 34 E
Khardung La, *India* **93 B7** 34 20N 77 43 E
Khârga, El Wâhât-el, *Egypt* **106 B3** 25 10N 30 35 E
Khargon, *India* **94 D2** 21 45N 75 40 E
Khari →, *India* **92 G6** 25 54N 74 31 E
Kharian, *Pakistan* **92 C5** 32 49N 73 52 E
Khariar, *India* **94 D6** 20 17N 82 46 E
Kharit, Wadi el →, *Egypt* **106 C3** 24 26N 33 3 E
Khārk, Jazīreh-ye, *Iran* **97 D6** 29 15N 50 28 E
Kharkiv, *Ukraine* **59 H9** 49 58N 36 20 E
Kharkov = Kharkiv, *Ukraine* **59 H9** 49 58N 36 20 E
Kharmanli, *Bulgaria* **51 E9** 41 55N 25 55 E
Kharovsk, *Russia* **58 C11** 59 56N 40 13 E
Kharsawangarh, *India* **93 H11** 22 48N 85 50 E
Kharta, *Turkey* **100 B3** 40 55N 29 7 E
Khartoum = El Khartûm, *Sudan* **107 D3** 15 31N 32 35 E
Khasan, *Russia* **70 C5** 42 25N 130 40 E
Khasavyurt, *Russia* **61 J8** 43 16N 46 40 E
Khāsh, *Iran* **91 C1** 28 15N 61 15 E
Khāsh, Dasht-e, *Afghan.* **91 C1** 31 50N 62 30 E
Khashm el Girba, *Sudan* **107 E4** 14 59N 35 58 E
Khashum, *Sudan* **107 E2** 12 27N 28 2 E
Khashuri, *Georgia* **61 J6** 42 3N 43 35 E
Khasi Hills, *India* **90 C3** 25 30N 91 30 E
Khaskovo, *Bulgaria* **51 E9** 41 56N 25 30 E
Khaskovo □, *Bulgaria* **51 E9** 42 0N 25 40 E
Khatanga, *Russia* **67 B11** 72 0N 102 20 E
Khatanga →, *Russia* **67 B11** 72 55N 106 0 E
Khatauli, *India* **92 E7** 29 17N 77 43 E
Khatra, *India* **93 H12** 22 59N 86 51 E
Khātūnābād, *Iran* **97 D7** 30 1N 55 25 E
Khatyrka, *Russia* **67 C18** 62 3N 175 15 E
Khavast, *Uzbekistan* **65 C4** 40 10N 68 49 E
Khavda, *India* **92 H3** 23 51N 69 43 E
Khavdháta, *Greece* **39 D1** 38 12N 20 23 E
Khawlaf, Ra's, *Yemen* **99 D6** 12 40N 54 7 E
Khay', *Si. Arabia* **98 C3** 18 45N 41 24 E
Khaybar, Ḥarrat, *Si. Arabia* **96 E4** 25 45N 40 0 E
Khaydarken, *Kyrgyzstan* **65 D5** 39 57N 71 20 E
Khāzimiyah, *Iraq* **96 C4** 34 46N 43 37 E
Khazzān Jabal al Awliyā, *Sudan* **107 D3** 15 24N 32 20 E
Khe Bo, *Vietnam* **86 C5** 19 8N 104 41 E
Khe Long, *Vietnam* **86 B5** 21 29N 104 46 E
Khed, *Maharashtra, India* **94 F1** 17 43N 73 27 E
Khed, *Maharashtra, India* **94 E1** 18 51N 73 56 E
Khekra, *India* **92 E7** 28 52N 77 20 E
Khemarak Phouminville, *Cambodia* **87 G4** 11 37N 102 59 E
Khemis Miliana, *Algeria* **111 A5** 36 11N 2 14 E
Khemisset, *Morocco* **110 B3** 33 50N 6 1W
Khemmarat, *Thailand* **86 D5** 16 10N 105 15 E
Khenāmān, *Iran* **97 D8** 30 27N 56 29 E
Khenchela, *Algeria* **111 A6** 35 28N 7 11 E
Khenifra, *Morocco* **110 B3** 32 58N 5 46W
Kherrata, *Algeria* **111 A6** 36 27N 5 13 E
Khersān →, *Iran* **97 D6** 31 33N 50 22 E
Khérson, *Greece* **50 E6** 41 5N 22 47 E
Kherson, *Ukraine* **59 J7** 46 35N 32 35 E
Khersónisos Akrotíri, *Greece* **39 E5** 35 30N 24 10 E
Kheta →, *Russia* **67 B11** 71 54N 102 6 E
Khewari, *Pakistan* **92 F3** 26 36N 68 52 E
Khilchipur, *India* **92 G7** 24 2N 76 34 E
Khiliomódhion, *Greece* **48 D4** 37 48N 22 51 E
Khilok, *Russia* **67 D12** 51 30N 110 45 E
Khimki, *Russia* **58 E9** 55 50N 37 20 E
Khíos, *Greece* **49 C8** 38 27N 26 9 E
Khíos □, *Greece* **49 C8** 38 27N 26 9 E
Khirsadoh, *India* **93 H8** 22 11N 78 47 E
Khiuma = Hiiumaa, *Estonia* **15 G20** 58 50N 22 45 E
Khiva, *Uzbekistan* **66 E7** 41 30N 60 18 E
Khīyāv, *Iran* **96 B5** 38 30N 47 45 E
Khlebarovo, *Bulgaria* **51 C10** 43 37N 26 15 E
Khlong Khlung, *Thailand* **86 D2** 16 12N 99 43 E
Khmelnik, *Ukraine* **59 H4** 49 33N 27 58 E
Khmelnitskiy = Khmelnytskyy, *Ukraine* **59 H4** 49 23N 27 0 E
Khmelnytskyy, *Ukraine* **59 H4** 49 23N 27 0 E
Khmer Rep. = Cambodia ■, *Asia* **86 F5** 12 15N 105 0 E
Khoai, Hon, *Vietnam* **87 H5** 8 26N 104 50 E
Khodoriv, *Ukraine* **59 H3** 49 24N 24 19 E
Khodzent = Khŭjand, *Tajikistan* **65 C4** 40 17N 69 37 E
Khojak Pass, *Afghan.* **91 C2** 30 51N 66 34 E
Khok Kloi, *Thailand* **87 a** 8 17N 98 19 E
Khok Pho, *Thailand* **87 J3** 6 43N 101 6 E
Khokhropār, *Pakistan* **91 D3** 25 42N 70 12 E
Kholm, *Afghan.* **65 E3** 36 45N 67 40 E
Kholm, *Russia* **58 D6** 57 10N 31 15 E
Kholmsk, *Russia* **67 E15** 47 40N 142 5 E
Khomas Hochland, *Namibia* **116 C2** 22 40 S 16 0 E
Khombole, *Senegal* **112 C1** 14 43N 16 42W
Khomeyn, *Iran* **97 C6** 33 40N 50 7 E
Khomeynī Shahr, *Iran* **97 C6** 32 41N 51 31 E
Khomodino, *Botswana* **116 C3** 22 46 S 23 52 E
Khon Kaen, *Thailand* **86 D4** 16 30N 102 47 E
Khong →, *Cambodia* **86 F5** 13 32N 105 58 E
Khong Sedone, *Laos* **86 E5** 15 34N 105 49 E
Khonuu, *Russia* **67 C15** 66 30N 143 12 E
Khoper →, *Russia* **60 F6** 49 30N 42 20 E
Khor el 'Atash, *Sudan* **107 E3** 13 20N 34 15 E
Khóra, *Greece* **48 D3** 37 3N 21 42 E
Khóra Sfakíon, *Greece* **39 E5** 35 15N 24 9 E
Khorāsān □, *Iran* **97 C8** 34 0N 58 0 E
Khorat = Nakhon Ratchasima, *Thailand* **86 E4** 14 59N 102 12 E
Khorat, Cao Nguyen, *Thailand* **86 E4** 15 30N 102 50 E
Khorb el Ethel, *Algeria* **110 C3** 28 30N 6 17W
Khorixas, *Namibia* **116 C1** 20 16 S 14 59 E
Khorol, *Ukraine* **59 H7** 49 48N 33 15 E
Khorramābād, *Khorāsān, Iran* **97 C8** 35 6N 57 57 E
Khorramābād, *Lorestān, Iran* **97 C6** 33 30N 48 25 E
Khorrāmshahr, *Iran* **97 D6** 30 29N 48 15 E
Khorugh, *Tajikistan* **65 E5** 37 30N 71 36 E
Khosravī, *Iran* **97 D6** 30 48N 51 28 E
Khosrowābād, *Khuzestān, Iran* **97 D6** 30 10N 48 25 E
Khosrowābād, *Kordestān, Iran* **101 E12** 35 31N 47 38 E
Khost, *Pakistan* **92 D2** 30 13N 67 35 E
Khosūyeh, *Iran* **97 D7** 28 32N 54 26 E
Khotan = Hotan, *China* **68 C2** 37 25N 79 55 E
Khotyn, *Ukraine* **59 H4** 48 31N 26 27 E
Khouribga, *Morocco* **110 B3** 32 58N 6 57W
Khowai, *Bangla.* **90 C3** 24 5N 91 40 E
Khowst, *Afghan.* **91 B3** 33 22N 69 58 E
Khoyniki, *Belarus* **59 G5** 51 54N 29 55 E
Khrami →, *Georgia* **61 K7** 41 25N 45 0 E
Khrenovoye, *Russia* **60 E5** 51 4N 40 16 E
Khrisoúpolis, *Greece* **51 F8** 40 58N 24 42 E
Khristianá, *Greece* **49 E7** 36 14N 25 13 E
Khromtau, *Kazakhstan* **64 F7** 50 17N 58 27 E
Khrysokhou B., *Cyprus* **39 E8** 35 6N 32 25 E
Khtapodhiá, *Greece* **49 D7** 37 24N 25 34 E
Khu Khan, *Thailand* **86 E5** 14 42N 104 12 E
Khuan Wa, *Thailand* **87 a** 7 53N 98 17 E
Khudrah, W. →, *Yemen* **99 C5** 18 10N 50 20 E
Khudzhand = Khŭjand, *Tajikistan* **65 C4** 40 17N 69 37 E
Khuff, *Si. Arabia* **96 E5** 24 55N 44 53 E
Khūgīānī, *Afghan.* **91 C2** 31 34N 66 32 E
Khuis, *Botswana* **116 D3** 26 40 S 21 49 E
Khuiyala, *India* **92 F4** 27 9N 70 25 E
Khŭjand, *Tajikistan* **65 C4** 40 17N 69 37 E
Khujner, *India* **92 H7** 23 47N 76 36 E
Khulayş, *Si. Arabia* **98 B2** 22 9N 39 19 E
Khulna, *Bangla.* **90 D2** 22 45N 89 34 E
Khulna □, *Bangla.* **90 D2** 22 25N 89 35 E
Khulo, *Georgia* **61 K6** 41 33N 42 19 E
Khumago, *Botswana* **116 C3** 20 26 S 24 32 E
Khumrah, *Si. Arabia* **98 B2** 21 22N 39 13 E
Khunjerab Pass = Kinjirap Daban, *Asia* **91 A6** 36 40N 75 25W
Khūnsorkh, *Iran* **97 E8** 27 9N 56 7 E
Khunti, *India* **93 H11** 23 5N 85 17 E
Khūr, *Iran* **97 C8** 32 55N 58 18 E
Khurai, *India* **92 G8** 24 3N 78 23 E
Khuraydah, *Yemen* **99 D5** 15 33N 48 18 E
Khurayş, *Si. Arabia* **97 E6** 25 6N 48 2 E
Khurda, *India* **94 D7** 20 11N 85 37 E
Khureit, *Sudan* **107 E2** 13 59N 26 3 E
Khurīyā Murīyā, Ghubbat, *Oman* **99 C6** 17 40N 55 45 E
Khurīyā Murīyā, Jazā'ir, *Oman* **99 C6** 17 30N 55 58 E
Khurja, *India* **92 E7** 28 15N 77 58 E
Khūrmāl, *Iraq* **96 C5** 35 18N 46 2 E
Khurr, Wādī al, *Iraq* **96 C4** 32 3N 43 52 E
Khūsf, *Iran* **97 C8** 32 46N 58 53 E
Khushab, *Pakistan* **91 B4** 32 20N 72 20 E
Khust, *Ukraine* **59 H2** 48 10N 23 18 E
Khutse Game Reserve ⌓, *Botswana* **116 C3** 23 31 S 24 12 E
Khuzdar, *Pakistan* **91 D2** 27 52N 66 30 E
Khūzestān □, *Iran* **97 D6** 31 0N 49 0 E
Khvāf, *Iran* **97 C9** 34 33N 60 8 E
Khvājeh, *Iran* **96 B5** 38 9N 46 35 E
Khvājeh Moḥammad, Kūh-e, *Afghan.* **65 E5** 36 22N 70 17 E
Khvalynsk, *Russia* **60 D9** 52 30N 48 2 E
Khvānsār, *Iran* **97 D7** 29 56N 54 8 E
Khvatovka, *Russia* **60 D8** 52 24N 46 32 E
Khvor, *Iran* **97 C7** 33 45N 55 0 E
Khvorgū, *Iran* **97 E8** 27 34N 56 27 E
Khvormūj, *Iran* **97 D6** 28 40N 51 30 E
Khvoy, *Iran* **101 C11** 38 35N 45 0 E
Khvoynaya, *Russia* **58 C8** 58 58N 34 28 E
Khyber Pass, *Afghan.* **91 B3** 34 10N 71 8 E
Kia, *Fiji* **133 A2** 16 16 S 179 8 E
Kia, *Solomon Is.* **133 L10** 7 32 S 158 26 E
Kiabukwa, *Dem. Rep. of the Congo* **119 D1** 8 40 S 24 48 E
Kiadho →, *India* **94 E3** 19 37N 77 40 E
Kiama, *Australia* **129 C9** 34 40 S 150 50 E
Kiama, *Dem. Rep. of the Congo* **115 D3** 7 19 S 17 49 E
Kiamba, *Phil.* **81 H5** 6 2N 124 46 E
Kiambi, *Dem. Rep. of the Congo* **118 D2** 7 15 S 28 0 E
Kiambu, *Kenya* **118 C4** 1 8 S 36 50 E
Kiana, *U.S.A.* **144 C7** 66 58N 160 26W
Kiang West Nat. Park △, *Gambia* **112 C1** 13 25N 15 50W
Kiangara, *Madag.* **117 B8** 17 58 S 47 2 E
Kiangsi = Jiangxi □, *China* **77 D11** 27 30N 116 0 E
Kiangsu = Jiangsu □, *China* **75 H11** 33 0N 120 0 E
Kiáton, *Greece* **48 C4** 38 1N 22 45 E
Kibæk, *Denmark* **17 H2** 56 2N 8 51 E
Kibale Nat. Park △, *Uganda* **118 B3** 0 16N 30 18 E
Kibanga Port, *Uganda* **118 B3** 0 10N 32 58 E
Kibangou, *Congo* **114 C2** 3 26 S 12 22 E
Kibara, *Tanzania* **118 C3** 2 8 S 33 30 E
Kibare, Mts., *Dem. Rep. of the Congo* **118 D2** 8 25 S 27 10 E
Kibawe, *Phil.* **81 H5** 7 34N 125 0 E
Kibenga, *Dem. Rep. of the Congo* **115 D3** 7 56 S 17 30 E
Kibira, Parc Nat. de △, *Burundi* **118 C3** 3 6 S 30 24 E
Kibombo, *Dem. Rep. of the Congo* **118 C2** 3 57 S 25 53 E
Kibondo, *Tanzania* **118 C3** 3 35 S 30 45 E
Kibray, *Uzbekistan* **65 C4** 41 23N 69 27 E
Kibre Mengist, *Ethiopia* **107 F4** 5 54N 38 59 E
Kibumbu, *Burundi* **118 C2** 3 32 S 29 45 E
Kibungo, *Rwanda* **118 C3** 2 10 S 30 32 E
Kibuye, *Burundi* **118 C2** 3 39 S 29 59 E
Kibuye, *Rwanda* **118 C2** 2 3 S 29 21 E
Kibwesa, *Tanzania* **118 D2** 6 30 S 29 58 E
Kibwezi, *Kenya* **118 C4** 2 27 S 37 57 E
Kicasalih, *Turkey* **51 E10** 41 23N 26 48 E
Kičevo, *Macedonia* **50 E4** 41 34N 20 59 E
Kichha, *India* **93 E8** 28 53N 79 30 E
Kichha →, *India* **93 E8** 28 41N 79 18 E
Kichmengskiy Gorodok, *Russia* **56 B8** 59 59N 45 48 E
Kicking Horse Pass, *Canada* **142 C5** 51 28N 116 16W
Kidal, *Mali* **113 B5** 18 26N 1 22 E
Kidapawan, *Phil.* **81 H5** 7 1N 125 3 E
Kidderminster, *U.K.* **21 E5** 52 24N 2 15W
Kidepo Valley Nat. Park △, *Uganda* **118 B3** 3 52N 33 50 E
Kidete, *Tanzania* **118 D4** 6 25 S 37 17 E
Kidira, *Senegal* **112 C2** 14 28N 12 13W
Kidnappers, C., *N.Z.* **130 F6** 39 38 S 177 5 E
Kidsgrove, *U.K.* **20 D5** 53 5N 2 14W
Kidston, *Australia* **126 B3** 18 52 S 144 8 E
Kidugallo, *Tanzania* **118 D4** 6 49 S 38 15 E
Kidurong, Tanjong, *Malaysia* **85 B4** 3 16N 113 3 E
Kiel, *Germany* **30 A6** 54 19N 10 8 E
Kiel Canal = Nord-Ostsee-Kanal, *Germany* **30 A5** 54 12N 9 32 E
Kielce, *Poland* **55 H7** 50 52N 20 42 E
Kielder Water, *U.K.* **20 B5** 55 11N 2 31W
Kieler Bucht, *Germany* **30 A6** 54 35N 10 25 E
Kiembara, *Burkina Faso* **112 C4** 13 15N 2 44W
Kien Binh, *Vietnam* **87 H5** 9 55N 105 19 E
Kien Tan, *Vietnam* **87 G5** 10 7N 105 17 E
Kienge, *Dem. Rep. of the Congo* **119 E2** 10 30 S 27 30 E
Kiessé, *Niger* **113 C5** 13 29N 4 1 E
Kieta, *Papua N. G.* **132 D8** 6 12 S 155 36 E
Kiev = Kyyiv, *Ukraine* **59 G6** 50 30N 30 28 E
Kifaya, *Guinea* **112 C2** 12 10N 13 4W
Kiffa, *Mauritania* **112 B2** 16 37N 11 24W
Kifisiá, *Greece* **48 C5** 38 4N 23 49 E
Kifissós →, *Greece* **48 C5** 38 35N 23 20 E
Kifrī, *Iraq* **101 E11** 34 45N 45 0 E
Kigali, *Rwanda* **118 C3** 1 59 S 30 4 E
Kigarama, *Tanzania* **118 C3** 1 1 S 31 50 E
Kigelle, *Sudan* **107 F3** 8 40N 34 2 E
Kigezi Game Reserve ⌓, *Uganda* **118 C2** 0 34 S 29 55 E
Kigoma □, *Tanzania* **118 D3** 5 0 S 30 0 E
Kigoma-Ujiji, *Tanzania* **118 C2** 4 55 S 29 36 E
Kigomasha, Ras, *Tanzania* **118 C4** 4 58 S 38 58 E
Kığzı, *Turkey* **96 B4** 38 18N 43 25 E
Kihei, *U.S.A.* **145 C5** 20 47N 156 28W
Kihikihi, *N.Z.* **130 E4** 38 2 S 175 22 E
Kihnu, *Estonia* **15 G21** 58 9N 24 1 E
Kiholo B., *U.S.A.* **145 D6** 19 50N 155 55W
Kii-Hantō, *Japan* **73 D7** 34 0N 135 45 E
Kii-Nagashima, *Japan* **73 C8** 34 12N 136 20 E
Kii-Sanchi, *Japan* **73 C8** 34 20N 136 0 E
Kii-Suidō, *Japan* **72 D6** 33 40N 134 45 E
Kiire, *Japan* **72 F2** 31 22N 130 33 E
Kijik, *U.S.A.* **144 F9** 60 20N 154 20W
Kikaiga-Shima, *Japan* **71 K4** 28 19N 129 59 E
Kikinda, *Serbia, Yug.* **52 E5** 45 50N 20 30 E
Kikládhes, *Greece* **48 E6** 37 0N 24 30 E
Kikládhes □, *Greece* **48 D6** 37 0N 25 0 E
Kikoira, *Australia* **129 B7** 33 39 S 146 40 E
Kikombo, *Bandundu, Dem. Rep. of the Congo* **115 D3** 5 37 S 18 50 E
Kikombo, *Bandundu, Dem. Rep. of the Congo* **115 D3** 5 49 S 17 45 E
Kikongo, *Dem. Rep. of the Congo* **115 C3** 4 16 S 17 17 E
Kikori, *Papua N. G.* **132 D3** 7 25 S 144 15 E
Kikori →, *Papua N. G.* **132 D3** 7 38 S 144 20 E
Kikuchi, *Japan* **72 E2** 32 59N 130 47 E
Kikwit, *Dem. Rep. of the Congo* **115 D3** 5 0 S 18 45 E
Kil, *Sweden* **16 E7** 59 30N 13 20 E
Kilafors, *Sweden* **16 C10** 61 14N 16 36 E
Kilakkarai, *India* **95 K4** 9 12N 78 47 E
Kilar, *India* **92 C7** 33 6N 76 25 E
Kilauea, *U.S.A.* **145 A2** 22 13N 159 25W
Kilauea Crater, *U.S.A.* **145 D6** 19 25N 155 17W
Kilbrannan Sd., *U.K.* **22 F3** 55 37N 5 26W
Kilchberg, *Switz.* **33 B7** 47 18N 8 33 E
Kilchu, *N. Korea* **75 D15** 40 57N 129 25 E
Kilcoy, *Australia* **127 D5** 26 59 S 152 30 E
Kildare, *Ireland* **23 C5** 53 9N 6 55W
Kildare □, *Ireland* **23 C5** 53 10N 6 50W
Kileikli, *Sudan* **107 E2** 11 25N 25 31 E
Kilembe, *Dem. Rep. of the Congo* **115 D3** 5 42 S 19 55 E
Kilen, *Norway* **18 E5** 59 20N 8 49 E
Kilfinnane, *Ireland* **23 D3** 52 21N 8 28W
Kilgore, *U.S.A.* **155 J7** 32 23N 94 53W
Kilibo, *Benin* **113 D5** 8 32N 2 38 E
Kilifi, *Kenya* **118 C4** 3 40 S 39 48 E
Kilimanjaro, *Tanzania* **118 C4** 3 7 S 37 20 E
Kilimanjaro □, *Tanzania* **118 C4** 4 0 S 38 0 E
Kilimli, *Turkey* **100 B4** 41 28N 31 50 E
Kilinailau Is., *Papua N. G.* **132 C8** 4 45 S 155 20 E
Kilindini, *Kenya* **118 C4** 4 4 S 39 40 E
Kilis, *Turkey* **100 D7** 36 42N 37 6 E
Kiliya, *Ukraine* **59 K5** 45 28N 29 16 E
Kilkee, *Ireland* **23 D2** 52 41N 9 39W
Kilkeel, *U.K.* **23 B5** 54 4N 6 0W
Kilkenny, *Ireland* **23 D4** 52 39N 7 15W
Kilkenny □, *Ireland* **23 D4** 52 35N 7 15W
Kilkieran B., *Ireland* **23 C2** 53 20N 9 41W
Kilkís, *Greece* **50 F6** 40 58N 22 57 E
Kilkís □, *Greece* **50 E6** 41 5N 22 50 E
Killala, *Ireland* **23 B2** 54 13N 9 12W
Killala B., *Ireland* **23 B2** 54 16N 9 8W
Killaloe, *Ireland* **23 D3** 52 48N 8 28W
Killaloe Station, *Canada* **150 A7** 45 33N 77 25W
Killarney, *Australia* **127 D5** 28 20 S 152 18 E
Killarney, *Canada* **143 D9** 49 10N 99 40W
Killarney, *Ireland* **23 D2** 52 4N 9 30W
Killarney, L., *Bahamas* **9 b** 25 3N 77 27W
Killarney Nat. Park △, *Ireland* **23 D2** 52 0N 9 33W
Killary Harbour, *Ireland* **23 C2** 53 38N 9 52W
Killdeer, *U.S.A.* **154 B3** 47 26N 102 48W
Killeberg, *Sweden* **17 H8** 56 29N 14 5 E
Killeen, *U.S.A.* **155 K6** 31 7N 97 44W
Killin, *U.K.* **22 E4** 56 28N 4 19W
Killíni, *Ilía, Greece* **39 D3** 37 55N 21 8 E
Killíni, *Korinthía, Greece* **48 D4** 37 54N 22 25 E
Killíni, Ákra, *Greece* **39 D3** 37 57N 21 8 E
Killorglin, *Ireland* **23 D2** 52 6N 9 47W
Killybegs, *Ireland* **23 B3** 54 38N 8 26W
Kilmarnock, *U.K.* **22 F4** 55 37N 4 29W
Kilmez, *Russia* **60 B10** 56 58N 50 55 E
Kilmez →, *Russia* **60 B10** 56 58N 50 28 E
Kilmore, *Australia* **129 D6** 37 25 S 144 53 E
Kilondo, *Tanzania* **119 D3** 9 45 S 34 20 E
Kilosa, *Tanzania* **118 D4** 6 48 S 37 0 E
Kilrush, *Ireland* **23 D2** 52 38N 9 29W
Kiltan I., *India* **95 J1** 11 29N 73 0 E
Kilwa Kisiwani, *Tanzania* **119 D4** 8 58 S 39 32 E
Kilwa Kivinje, *Tanzania* **119 D4** 8 45 S 39 25 E
Kilwa Masoko, *Tanzania* **119 D4** 8 55 S 39 30 E
Kilwinning, *U.K.* **22 F4** 55 39N 4 43W
Kim, *U.S.A.* **155 G3** 37 15N 103 21W
Kim →, *Cameroon* **113 D7** 5 28N 11 7 E
Kimaam, *Indonesia* **83 C5** 7 58 S 138 53 E
Kimamba, *Tanzania* **118 D4** 6 45 S 37 10 E
Kimba, *Australia* **128 B2** 33 8 S 136 23 E
Kimball, *Nebr., U.S.A.* **154 E3** 41 14N 103 40W
Kimball, *S. Dak., U.S.A.* **154 D5** 43 45N 98 57W
Kimbanda, *Dem. Rep. of the Congo* **115 C3** 4 16 S 18 30 E
Kimbe, *Papua N. G.* **132 C6** 5 33 S 150 11 E
Kimbe B., *Papua N. G.* **132 C6** 5 15 S 150 30 E
Kimberley, *Australia* **124 C4** 16 20 S 127 0 E
Kimberley, *Canada* **142 D5** 49 40N 115 59W
Kimberley, *S. Africa* **116 D3** 28 43 S 24 46 E
Kimberly, *U.S.A.* **158 E6** 42 32N 114 22W
Kimbongo, *Dem. Rep. of the Congo* **115 D3** 6 8 S 18 1 E
Kimch'aek, *N. Korea* **75 D15** 40 40N 129 10 E
Kimch'ŏn, *S. Korea* **75 F15** 36 11N 128 4 E
Kími, *Greece* **48 C6** 38 38N 24 6 E
Kimitsu, *Japan* **73 B10** 35 19N 139 54 E
Kimje, *S. Korea* **75 G14** 35 48N 126 45 E
Kimmirut, *Canada* **139 B13** 62 50N 69 50W
Kímolos, *Greece* **48 E6** 36 48N 24 37 E
Kimongo, *Congo* **115 C2** 4 27 S 12 53 E
Kimovsk, *Moskva, Russia* **58 E9** 55 21N 37 28 E
Kimovsk, *Tula, Russia* **58 E10** 54 0N 38 29 E
Kimpangu, *Dem. Rep. of the Congo* **115 D3** 5 52 S 15 3 E
Kimparana, *Mali* **112 C4** 12 48N 5 0W
Kimry, *Russia* **58 D9** 56 55N 37 15 E

Kimstad, Sweden 17 F9 58 35N 15 58 E
Kimvula, Dem. Rep. of the Congo 115 D3 5 44 S 15 58 E
Kin, Burma 90 D5 22 46N 94 42 E
Kin-u, Burma 90 D5 22 46N 95 37 E
Kinabalu, Gunong, Malaysia 85 A5 6 3N 116 14 E
Kinard, U.S.A. 152 E4 30 16N 85 15W
Kínaros, Greece 49 E8 36 59N 26 15 E
Kinaskan L., Canada 142 B2 57 38N 130 8W
Kinbasket L., Canada 142 C5 52 0N 118 10W
Kincaid, U.S.A. 156 E7 39 35N 89 25W
Kincardine, Canada 140 D3 44 10N 81 40W
Kinchafoonee Cr. →, U.S.A. 152 D5 31 38N 84 10W
Kinchega Nat. Park △, Australia 128 B5 32 27 S 142 15 E
Kincolith, Canada 142 B3 55 0N 129 57W
Kinda, Kasai-Or., Dem. Rep. of the Congo 119 D2 9 18 S 25 4 E
Kinda, Katanga, Dem. Rep. of the Congo 115 C4 4 47 S 21 48 E
Kindambi, Dem. Rep. of the Congo 115 D4 5 6 S 18 14 E
Kindberg, Austria 34 D8 47 30N 15 27 E
Kinde, U.S.A. 150 C2 43 56N 83 0W
Kindele, Dem. Rep. of the Congo 115 D4 8 39 S 24 10 E
Kinder Scout, U.K. 20 D6 53 24N 1 52W
Kinderhook, U.S.A. 156 E5 39 42N 91 10W
Kindersley, Canada 143 C7 51 30N 109 10W
Kindia, Guinea 112 D2 10 0N 12 52W
Kindley U.S.A.F. Base, Bermuda 9 a 32 22N 64 42W
Kindongo, Dem. Rep. of the Congo 114 C3 3 58 S 17 30 E
Kindu, Dem. Rep. of the Congo 118 C2 2 55 S 25 50 E
Kinel, Russia 60 D10 53 15N 50 40 E
Kineshma, Russia 60 B6 57 30N 42 5 E
Kinesi, Tanzania 118 C3 1 25 S 33 50 E
King, L., Australia 125 F2 33 10 S 119 35 E
King, Mt., Australia 126 D4 25 10 S 147 30 E
King City, Calif., U.S.A. 160 J5 36 13N 121 8W
King City, Mo., U.S.A. 156 D2 40 3N 94 31W
King Cove, U.S.A. 144 J7 55 3N 162 19W
King Cr. →, Australia 126 C2 24 35 S 139 30 E
King Edward →, Australia 124 B4 14 14 S 126 35 E
King Frederick VI Land = Kong Frederik VI Kyst, Greenland 10 E6 63 0N 43 0W
King George B., Falk. Is. 9 f 51 30 S 60 30W
King George I., Antarctica 7 C18 60 0 S 60 0W
King George Is., Canada 139 C11 57 20N 80 30W
King I. = Kadan Kyun, Burma 86 F2 12 30N 98 20 E
King I., Australia 127 C3 39 50 S 144 0 E
King I., Canada 142 C3 52 10N 127 40W
King Leopold Ranges, Australia 124 C4 17 30 S 125 45 E
King of Prussia, U.S.A. 151 F9 40 5N 75 23W
King Salmon, U.S.A. 144 G8 58 42N 156 40W
King Sd., Australia 124 C3 16 50 S 123 20 E
King William I., Canada 138 B10 69 10N 97 25W
King William's Town, S. Africa 116 E4 32 51 S 27 22 E
Kingaok = Bathurst Inlet, Canada 138 B9 66 50N 108 1W
Kingaroy, Australia 127 D5 26 32 S 151 51 E
Kingdom City, U.S.A. 156 F5 38 56N 91 56W
Kingfisher, U.S.A. 155 H6 35 52N 97 56W
Kingirbān, Iraq 96 C5 34 40N 44 54 E
Kingisepp = Kuressaare, Estonia 15 G20 58 15N 22 30 E
Kingisepp, Russia 58 C5 59 25N 28 40 E
Kingking = Pantukan, Phil. 81 H5 7 9N 125 54 E
Kinglake Nat. Park △, Australia 129 D6 37 30 S 145 22 E
Kingman, Ariz., U.S.A. 161 K12 35 12N 114 4W
Kingman, Ind., U.S.A. 150 E9 39 58N 87 18W
Kingman, Kans., U.S.A. 155 G5 37 39N 98 7W
Kingoonya, Australia 127 E2 30 55 S 135 19 E
Kingri, Pakistan 92 D3 30 27N 69 49 E
Kings →, U.S.A. 160 J7 36 3N 119 50W
Kings Canyon Nat. Park △, U.S.A. 160 J8 36 50N 118 40W
King's Lynn, U.K. 20 E8 52 45N 0 24 E
Kings Mountain, U.S.A. 149 H5 35 15N 81 20W
Kings Park, U.S.A. 151 F11 40 53N 73 16W
King's Peak, U.S.A. 158 F8 40 46N 110 27W
Kingsbridge, U.K. 21 G4 50 17N 3 47W
Kingsburg, U.S.A. 160 J7 36 31N 119 33W
Kingscote, Australia 128 C2 35 40 S 137 38 E
Kingscourt, Ireland 23 C5 53 55N 6 48W
Kingsford, U.S.A. 148 C1 45 48N 88 4W
Kingsland, U.S.A. 152 D5 30 48N 81 41W
Kingsley, U.S.A. 154 D7 42 35N 95 58W
Kingsport, U.S.A. 149 G4 36 33N 82 33W
Kingston, Canada 140 D4 44 14N 76 30W
Kingston, Jamaica 164 a 18 0N 76 50W
Kingston, N.Z. 131 F3 45 20 S 168 43 E
Kingston, N.H., U.S.A. 151 D13 42 56N 71 3W
Kingston, N.Y., U.S.A. 151 E11 41 56N 73 59W
Kingston, Pa., U.S.A. 151 E9 41 56N 75 54W
Kingston, R.I., U.S.A. 151 E13 41 29N 71 30W
Kingston Pk., U.S.A. 161 K11 35 45N 115 54W
Kingston South East, Australia 128 D3 36 51 S 139 55 E
Kingston upon Hull, U.K. 20 D7 53 45N 0 21W
Kingston upon Hull □, U.K. 20 D7 53 45N 0 21W
Kingston-upon-Thames □, U.K. 21 F7 51 24N 0 17W
Kingstown, Australia 129 A9 30 29 S 151 6 E
Kingstown, St. Vincent 165 D7 13 10N 61 10W
Kingstree, U.S.A. 152 B10 33 40N 79 50W
Kingsville, Canada 140 D3 42 2N 82 45W
Kingsville, U.S.A. 155 M6 27 31N 97 52W
Kingunda, Dem. Rep. of the Congo 115 D3 6 36 S 16 58 E
Kingussie, U.K. 22 D4 57 6N 4 2W
Kingwood, U.S.A. 155 K7 29 54N 95 18W
Kınık, Antalya, Turkey 49 E11 36 20N 29 20 E
Kınık, Izmir, Turkey 49 B9 39 6N 27 24 E
Kinistino, Canada 143 C7 52 57N 105 2W
Kinjirap Daban, Asia 91 A6 36 40N 75 25W
Kinkala, Congo 115 C2 4 18 S 14 49 E
Kinki □, Japan 73 D8 33 45N 136 0 E
Kinleith, N.Z. 131 D4 38 20 S 175 56 E
Kinlochleven, U.K. 22 E4 56 43N 5 0W
Kinmount, Canada 150 B6 44 48N 78 45W
Kinmundy, U.S.A. 157 F8 38 46N 88 51W
Kinn, Norway 18 C1 61 34N 4 45 E
Kinna, Sweden 17 G6 57 32N 12 42 E
Kinnairds Hd., U.K. 22 D6 57 43N 2 1W
Kinnared, Sweden 17 G7 57 2N 13 7 E
Kinnarodden, Norway 12 A11 71 8N 27 40 E
Kinnarp, Sweden 17 F7 58 5N 13 32 E
Kinneviken, Sweden 17 F7 58 35N 13 15 E
Kinngait = Cape Dorset, Canada 139 B12 64 14N 76 32W
Kino, Mexico 162 B2 28 45N 111 59W
Kinogitan, Phil. 81 G5 9 0N 124 48 E
Kinoje →, Canada 140 B3 52 8N 81 25W
Kinomoto, Japan 73 B8 35 30N 136 13 E
Kinoni, Uganda 118 C3 0 41 S 30 28 E
Kinoosao, Canada 143 B8 57 5N 102 1W
Kinross, U.K. 22 E5 56 13N 3 25W
Kinsale, Ireland 23 E3 51 42N 8 31W
Kinsale, Old Hd. of, Ireland 23 E3 51 37N 8 33W
Kinsarvik, Norway 18 D3 60 22N 6 43 E
Kinsha = Chang Jiang →, China 77 B13 31 48N 121 10 E
Kinsley, U.S.A. 155 G5 37 55N 99 25W
Kinsman, U.S.A. 150 E4 41 26N 80 35W
Kinston, Ala., U.S.A. 152 D3 31 13N 86 10W
Kinston, N.C., U.S.A. 149 H7 35 16N 77 35W
Kintamani, Indonesia 79 J18 8 14 S 115 19 E
Kintampo, Ghana 113 D4 8 5N 1 41W
Kintap, Indonesia 85 C5 3 51 S 115 13 E
Kintore, U.K. 22 D6 57 14N 2 20W
Kintore Ra., Australia 124 D4 23 15 S 128 47 E
Kintshua, Dem. Rep. of the Congo 115 C3 4 27 S 19 38 E
Kintyre, U.K. 22 F3 55 30N 5 35W
Kintyre, Mull of, U.K. 22 F3 55 17N 5 47W
Kinu-Gawa →, Japan 73 B11 35 36N 139 57 E

Kinushseo →, Canada 140 A3 55 15N 83 45W
Kinuso, Canada 142 B5 55 20N 115 25W
Kinwat, India 94 E4 19 38N 78 12 E
Kinyangiri, Tanzania 118 C3 4 25 S 34 37 E
Kinzia, Dem. Rep. of the Congo 114 C3 3 36 S 18 26 E
Kinzig →, Germany 31 G3 48 36N 7 49 E
Kinzua, U.S.A. 150 E6 41 52N 78 58W
Kinzua Dam, U.S.A. 150 E6 41 53N 79 0W
Kióni, Greece 39 C2 38 27N 20 41 E
Kiosk, Canada 140 C4 46 6N 78 53W
Kiowa, Kans., U.S.A. 155 G5 37 1N 98 29W
Kiowa, Okla., U.S.A. 155 H7 34 43N 95 54W
Kipahigan L., Canada 143 B8 55 20N 101 55W
Kipanga, Tanzania 118 D4 6 15 S 35 20 E
Kipapa →, U.S.A. 145 K13 21 24N 158 1W
Kiparissía, Greece 48 D3 37 15N 21 40 E
Kiparissiakós Kólpos, Greece 48 D3 37 25N 21 25 E
Kipawa, L., Canada 140 C4 46 50N 79 0W
Kipembawe, Tanzania 118 D3 7 38 S 33 27 E
Kipengere Ra., Tanzania 119 D3 9 12 S 34 15 E
Kipili, Tanzania 118 D3 7 28 S 30 32 E
Kipini, Kenya 118 C5 2 30 S 40 32 E
Kipling, Canada 143 C8 50 6N 102 38W
Kipnuk, U.S.A. 144 G6 59 56N 164 3W
Kippure, Ireland 23 C5 53 11N 6 21W
Kipushi, Dem. Rep. of the Congo 119 E2 11 48 S 27 12 E
Kirandul, India 94 E5 18 33N 81 10 E
Kirane, Mali 112 B2 15 20N 10 20W
Kiranomena, Madag. 117 B8 18 17 S 46 2 E
Kiraz, Turkey 49 C10 38 14N 28 13 E
Kirazh, Turkey 51 F10 40 2N 26 41 E
Kirchberg, Bern, Switz. 32 B5 47 5N 7 35 E
Kirchberg, St. Galen, Switz. 33 B8 47 25N 9 2 E
Kirchhain, Germany 30 E4 50 47N 8 56 E
Kirchheim, Germany 31 G5 48 39N 9 27 E
Kirchheimbolanden, Germany 31 F3 49 40N 8 0 E
Kirchschlag, Austria 35 D9 47 30N 16 19 E
Kirdimi, Chad 109 E3 18 11N 18 31 E
Kireç, Turkey 49 B10 39 32N 28 45 E
Kirensk, Russia 67 D11 57 50N 107 55 E
Kirghiz Range, Asia 65 B6 42 40N 73 40 E
Kirghizia = Kyrgyzstan ■, Asia 65 C6 42 0N 75 0 E
Kirghizstan = Kyrgyzstan ■, Asia 65 C6 42 0N 75 0 E
Kirgiziya Steppe, Eurasia 57 E10 50 0N 55 0 E
Kiri, Dem. Rep. of the Congo 114 C3 1 29 S 19 0 E
Kiri Buru, India 94 D7 22 0N 85 0 E
Kiribati ■, Pac. Oc. 134 H10 5 0 S 180 0 E
Kırıkhan, Turkey 100 D7 36 31N 36 21 E
Kırıkkale, Turkey 100 C5 39 51N 33 32 E
Kirikopuni, N.Z. 130 B3 35 50 S 174 1 E
Kirin = Jilin, China 75 C14 43 44N 126 30 E
Kirindi Oya →, Sri Lanka 95 L5 6 15N 81 20 E
Kirinyaga = Kenya, Mt., Kenya 118 C4 0 10 S 37 18 E
Kirishi, Russia 58 C7 59 28N 31 59 E
Kirishima-Yama, Japan 72 J5 31 58N 130 55 E
Kiritimati, Kiribati 135 G12 1 58N 157 27W
Kiriwina I., Papua N. G. 132 E6 8 40 S 151 6 E
Kırka, Turkey 49 B12 39 17N 30 33 E
Kırkağaç, Turkey 49 B9 39 6N 27 40 E
Kirkby, U.K. 20 D5 53 30N 2 54W
Kirkby-in-Ashfield, U.K. 20 D6 53 6N 1 14W
Kirkby Lonsdale, U.K. 20 C5 54 12N 2 36W
Kirkby Stephen, U.K. 20 C5 54 29N 2 21W
Kirkcaldy, U.K. 22 E5 56 7N 3 9W
Kirkcudbright, U.K. 22 G4 54 50N 4 2W
Kirkee, India 94 E1 18 34N 73 56 E
Kirkehamn, Norway 18 F3 58 14N 6 31 E
Kirkenær, Norway 18 D9 60 27N 12 3 E
Kirkenes, Norway 14 B23 69 40N 30 5 E
Kirkfield, Canada 150 B6 44 34N 78 59W
Kirkintilloch, U.K. 22 F4 55 56N 4 8W
Kirkjubæjarklaustur, Iceland 11 D8 63 47N 18 4W
Kirkkonummi, Finland 15 F21 60 8N 24 26 E
Kirkland, U.S.A. 157 B8 42 6N 88 51W
Kirkland Lake, Canada 140 C3 48 9N 80 2W
Kırklareli, Turkey 51 E11 41 44N 27 15 E
Kırklareli □, Turkey 51 E11 41 45N 27 15 E
Kirklin, U.S.A. 157 D10 40 12N 86 22W
Kirkliston Ra., N.Z. 131 E5 44 25 S 170 34 E
Kirksville, U.S.A. 156 D4 40 12N 92 35W
Kirkūk, Iraq 101 E11 35 30N 44 21 E
Kirkwall, U.K. 22 C6 58 59N 2 58W
Kirkwood, S. Africa 116 E4 33 22 S 25 15 E
Kirkwood, U.S.A. 156 F6 38 35N 90 24W
Kirlampudi, India 94 E5 17 12N 82 12 E
Kirn, Germany 31 F3 49 47N 7 26 E
Kirov, Kaluga, Russia 58 E8 54 3N 34 20 E
Kirov, Kirov, Russia 64 B2 58 35N 49 40 E
Kirovabad = Gäncä, Azerbaijan 61 K8 40 45N 46 20 E
Kirovakan = Vanadzor, Armenia 61 K7 40 48N 44 30 E
Kirovo = Kirovohrad, Ukraine 59 H7 48 35N 32 20 E
Kirovo-Chepetsk, Russia 64 B3 58 28N 50 0 E
Kirovograd = Kirovohrad, Ukraine 59 H7 48 35N 32 20 E
Kirovohrad, Ukraine 59 H7 48 35N 32 20 E
Kirovsk = Babadayhan, Turkmenistan 66 F7 37 42N 60 23 E
Kirovsk, Russia 56 A5 67 32N 33 41 E
Kirovskiy = Balpyq Bi, Kazakhstan 65 A9 44 52N 78 12 E
Kirovskiy, Astrakhan, Russia 61 H9 45 51N 48 11 E
Kirovskiy, Kamchatka, Russia 67 D16 54 27N 155 42 E
Kirovskiy, Primorsk, Russia 70 B6 45 7N 133 30 E
Kirriemuir, U.K. 22 E5 56 41N 3 1W
Kirs, Russia 64 B4 59 21N 52 14 E
Kirsanov, Russia 60 D6 52 35N 42 40 E
Kırşehir, Turkey 100 C6 39 14N 34 5 E
Kirtachi, Niger 113 C5 12 52N 2 30 E
Kirteh, Afghan. 93 H1 32 15N 65 0 E
Kirthar Range, Pakistan 91 D2 27 0N 67 0 E
Kirtland, U.S.A. 163 H9 36 44N 108 21W
Kiruna, Sweden 14 C19 67 52N 20 15 E
Kirundu, Dem. Rep. of the Congo 118 C2 0 50 S 25 35 E
Kirya, Russia 60 C8 55 8N 46 55 E
Kiryū, Japan 73 A11 36 24N 139 20 E
Kisa, Sweden 17 G9 58 0N 15 39 E
Kisaga, Tanzania 118 C3 4 30 S 34 23 E
Kisalaya, Nic. 164 D3 14 40N 84 3W
Kisalföld, Hungary 52 C2 47 30N 17 0 E
Kisambo, Dem. Rep. of the Congo 115 D3 6 25 S 18 14 E
Kisámou, Kólpos, Greece 39 E4 35 30N 23 38 E
Kisandji, Dem. Rep. of the Congo 115 D3 6 18 S 19 16 E
Kisanga, Dem. Rep. of the Congo 118 B2 2 30N 26 35 E
Kisangani, Dem. Rep. of the Congo 118 B2 0 35N 25 15 E
Kisantu, Dem. Rep. of the Congo 115 D3 5 7 S 15 5 E
Kisar, Indonesia 83 C3 8 5 S 127 10 E
Kisaran, Indonesia 84 B1 3 0N 99 37 E
Kisarawe, Tanzania 118 D4 6 53 S 39 0 E
Kisarazu, Japan 73 B11 35 23N 139 55 E
Kisber, Hungary 52 C3 47 30N 18 0 E
Kishanganga →, Pakistan 93 B5 34 18N 73 28 E
Kishanganj, India 90 B2 26 3N 88 14 E
Kishangarh, Raj., India 92 F6 26 34N 74 52 E
Kishangarh, Raj., India 92 F4 27 50N 70 30 E
Kishb, Ḥarrat al, Si. Arabia 98 B3 22 30N 40 15 E
Kishi, Nigeria 113 D5 9 1N 3 52 E
Kishinev = Chişinău, Moldova 53 C13 47 2N 28 50 E
Kishiwada, Japan 73 D7 34 28N 135 22 E
Kishorganj, Bangla. 90 C3 24 26N 90 40 E
Kishtwar, India 93 C6 33 20N 75 48 E
Kishwaukee →, U.S.A. 156 B7 42 12N 89 8W
Kisielice, Poland 55 E6 53 36N 19 16 E
Kisigo Game Reserve △, Tanzania 118 D3 6 27 S 34 17 E
Kisii, Kenya 118 C3 0 40 S 34 45 E

Kisiju, Tanzania 118 D4 7 23 S 39 19 E
Kisir, Turkey 101 B10 41 0N 43 5 E
Kisizi, Uganda 118 C2 1 0 S 29 58 E
Kiska I., U.S.A. 144 L2 51 59N 177 30 E
Kiskomárom = Zalakomár, Hungary 52 D2 46 33N 17 10 E
Kiskőrei-víztároló, Hungary 52 C5 47 31N 20 36 E
Kiskőrös, Hungary 52 D4 46 37N 19 20 E
Kiskundorozsma, Hungary 52 D5 46 16N 20 5 E
Kiskunfélegyháza, Hungary 52 D4 46 42N 19 53 E
Kiskunhalas, Hungary 52 D4 46 28N 19 37 E
Kiskunmajsa, Hungary 52 D4 46 30N 19 48 E
Kiskunsági Nemzeti Park △, Hungary 52 D4 46 35N 19 30 E
Kislovodsk, Russia 61 J6 43 50N 42 45 E
Kismayu = Chisimaio, Somali Rep. 120 E2 0 22 S 42 32 E
Kismayu Nat. Park △, Somali Rep. 120 D2 1 25N 41 30 E
Kiso-Gawa →, Japan 73 B8 35 20N 136 45 E
Kiso-Sammyaku, Japan 73 B9 35 45N 137 45 E
Kisofukushima, Japan 73 B9 35 52N 137 43 E
Kisoro, Uganda 118 C2 1 17 S 29 48 E
Kissidougou, Guinea 112 D2 9 5N 10 5W
Kissimmee, U.S.A. 153 G8 28 18N 81 24W
Kissimmee →, U.S.A. 153 H8 27 9N 80 52W
Kissimmee, L., U.S.A. 153 H8 27 55N 81 17W
Kississing L., Canada 143 B8 55 10N 101 20W
Kissónerga, Cyprus 39 E11 34 49N 32 24 E
Kissu, J., Sudan 106 C2 21 37N 25 10 E
Kistanje, Croatia 41 E12 43 58N 15 55 E
Kisújszállás, Hungary 52 C5 47 12N 20 50 E
Kisuki, Japan 72 B4 35 17N 132 54 E
Kisumu, Kenya 118 C3 0 3 S 34 45 E
Kisvárda, Hungary 52 B7 48 14N 22 4 E
Kiswani, Tanzania 118 C4 4 5 S 37 57 E
Kiswere, Tanzania 119 D4 9 27 S 39 30 E
Kit Carson, U.S.A. 154 F3 38 46N 102 48W
Kita, Mali 112 C3 13 5N 9 25W
Kita-Ura, Japan 73 B12 36 0N 140 34 E
Kitaa □, Greenland 10 C6 70 0N 47 0W
Kitab, Uzbekistan 65 D3 39 7N 66 52 E
Kitaibaraki, Japan 71 F10 36 50N 140 45 E
Kitakami, Japan 70 E10 39 20N 141 10 E
Kitakami-Gawa →, Japan 70 E10 38 25N 141 19 E
Kitakami-Sammyaku, Japan 70 E10 39 30N 141 30 E
Kitakata, Japan 70 F9 37 39N 139 52 E
Kitakyūshū, Japan 72 D2 33 50N 130 50 E
Kitale, Kenya 118 B4 1 0N 35 0 E
Kitami, Japan 70 C11 43 48N 143 54 E
Kitami-Sammyaku, Japan 70 B11 44 22N 142 43 E
Kitangiri, L., Tanzania 118 C3 4 5 S 34 20 E
Kitaya, Tanzania 119 E5 10 38 S 40 8 E
Kitchener, Canada 140 D3 43 27N 80 29W
Kitee, Finland 58 A6 62 5N 30 9 E
Kitega = Gitega, Burundi 118 C2 3 26 S 29 56 E
Kitengo, Dem. Rep. of the Congo 118 D1 7 26 S 24 8 E
Kitgum, Uganda 118 B3 3 17N 32 52 E
Kithira, Greece 48 E5 36 8N 23 0 E
Kíthnos, Greece 49 F9 37 26N 24 27 E
Kiti, Cyprus 39 E9 34 50N 33 34 E
Kiti, C., Cyprus 39 E9 34 48N 33 36 E
Kitimat, Canada 142 C3 54 3N 128 38W
Kitinen →, Finland 14 C22 67 14N 27 27 E
Kitiyab, Sudan 107 D13 17 13N 33 35 E
Kitombe, Dem. Rep. of the Congo 115 D3 5 22 S 18 59 E
Kítros, Greece 50 F6 40 22N 22 34 E
Kitsuki, Japan 72 D3 33 25N 131 37 E
Kittakittaooloo, L., Australia 127 D2 28 3 S 138 14 E
Kittanning, U.S.A. 150 F5 40 49N 79 31W
Kittatinny Mts., U.S.A. 151 F10 41 0N 75 0W
Kittery, U.S.A. 149 D10 43 5N 70 45W
Kittilä, Finland 14 C21 67 40N 24 51 E
Kitui, Kenya 118 C4 1 17 S 38 0 E
Kitwanga, Canada 142 B3 55 6N 128 4W
Kitwe, Zambia 119 E2 12 54 S 28 13 E
Kitzbühel, Austria 34 D5 47 27N 12 24 E
Kitzbüheler Alpen, Austria 34 D5 47 20N 12 15 E
Kitzingen, Germany 31 F6 49 44N 10 9 E
Kiunga, Papua N. G. 132 D1 6 7 S 141 18 E
Kivalina, U.S.A. 144 C6 67 44N 164 33W
Kivarli, India 92 F5 24 33N 72 46 E
Kivertsi, Ukraine 59 G3 50 50N 25 28 E
Kividhes, Cyprus 39 E11 34 46N 32 51 E
Kivik, Sweden 17 J8 55 41N 14 13 E
Kivotós, Greece 50 F5 40 13N 21 26 E
Kivu, L., Dem. Rep. of the Congo 118 C2 1 48 S 29 0 E
Kiwai I., Papua N. G. 132 E2 8 35 S 143 30 E
Kiyev = Kyyiv, Ukraine 59 G6 50 30N 30 28 E
Kiyevskoye Vdkhr. = Kyyivske Vdskh., Ukraine 59 G6 51 0N 30 25 E
Kıyıköy, Turkey 51 E12 41 38N 28 5 E
Kizel, Russia 64 B6 59 3N 57 40 E
Kizema, Russia 60 B8 61 9N 44 52 E
Kızıl Adalar, Turkey 51 F13 40 52N 29 5 E
Kızıl Irmak →, Turkey 100 B6 41 44N 35 58 E
Kizil Jilga, China 93 B8 35 26N 78 50 E
Kizil Yurt, Russia 61 J8 43 13N 46 54 E
Kızılcabölük, Turkey 49 D11 37 37N 29 1 E
Kızılcahamam, Turkey 100 B5 40 30N 32 30 E
Kızılhisar, Turkey 100 D3 37 23N 29 17 E
Kızılırmak, Turkey 100 B5 40 20N 33 59 E
Kızılkaya, Turkey 49 D12 37 18N 30 27 E
Kızılören, Turkey 49 D12 38 15N 30 10 E
Kizilskoye, Russia 64 E7 52 44N 58 54 E
Kızıltepe, Turkey 100 D7 37 12N 40 35 E
Kizimkazi, Tanzania 118 D4 6 28 S 39 30 E
Kızlyar, Russia 61 J8 43 51N 46 40 E
Kizyl-Arvat = Gyzylarbat, Turkmenistan 66 F6 39 4N 56 23 E
Kjellerup, Denmark 17 H3 56 17N 9 26 E
Kjellmyra, Norway 18 D9 60 39N 12 1 E
Kjølen, Norway 8 C16 66 0N 14 0 E
Kjölur, Iceland 11 C5 64 50N 19 25W
Kjósarsýsla □, Iceland 11 C5 64 15N 21 30W
Kladanj, Bos.-H. 52 F3 44 14N 18 42 E
Kladnica, Serbia, Yug. 50 D4 43 23N 20 2 E
Kladno, Czech Rep. 34 A7 50 10N 14 7 E
Kladovo, Serbia, Yug. 50 B6 44 36N 22 33 E
Klæbu, Norway 18 A7 63 18N 10 29 E
Klaeng, Thailand 86 F3 12 47N 101 39 E
Klagan, Malaysia 85 A5 5 58N 117 27 E
Klagenfurt, Austria 34 E7 46 38N 14 18 E
Klaipėda, Lithuania 15 J19 55 43N 21 10 E
Klaipėda □, Lithuania 15 J19 55 43N 21 7 E
Klaksvík, Faroe Is. 11 E9 62 14N 6 35W
Klamath →, U.S.A. 158 F1 41 33N 124 5W
Klamath Falls, U.S.A. 158 E3 42 13N 121 46W
Klamath Mts., U.S.A. 158 F2 41 20N 123 0W
Klamono, Indonesia 83 B4 1 8 S 131 30 E
Klang, Malaysia 84 B2 3 2N 101 26 E
Klangklang, Burma 90 D4 22 41N 93 26 E
Klanjec, Croatia 41 B12 46 3N 15 45 E
Klappan →, Canada 142 B3 58 0N 129 43W
Klara →, Sweden 17 G12 59 23N 13 32 E
Klarälven →, Sweden 16 E7 59 23N 13 32 E
Klässbol, Sweden 17 F6 59 19N 12 53 E
Klaten, Indonesia 85 D4 7 43 S 110 36 E
Klatovy, Czech Rep. 34 B6 49 23N 13 18 E
Klausenburg = Cluj-Napoca, Romania 53 D8 46 47N 23 38 E
Klawer, S. Africa 116 E2 31 44 S 18 36 E
Klawock, U.S.A. 144 J14 55 33N 133 6W

Klazienaveen, Neths. 24 B6 52 44N 7 0 E
Klé, Mali 112 C3 12 0N 6 28W
Kłecko, Poland 55 F4 52 38N 17 25 E
Kleczew, Poland 55 F5 52 22N 18 9 E
Kleena Kleene, Canada 142 C4 52 0N 124 59W
Klein-Karas, Namibia 116 D2 27 33 S 18 7 E
Klein-Karas, Macedonia 50 E4 41 32N 20 49 E
Klenoec, Macedonia 50 E4 41 32N 20 49 E
Klenovec, Slovak Rep. 35 C12 48 36N 19 54 E
Klerksdorp, S. Africa 116 D4 26 53 S 26 38 E
Kleszczele, Poland 55 E10 52 35N 23 19 E
Kletnya, Russia 58 E7 53 23N 33 12 E
Kletsk = Klyetsk, Belarus 59 F4 53 5N 26 45 E
Kletskiy, Russia 61 F6 49 16N 43 11 E
Kleve, Germany 30 D2 51 47N 6 11 E
Klickitat, U.S.A. 158 D3 45 49N 121 9W
Klickitat →, U.S.A. 160 E5 45 42N 121 17W
Klidhes, Cyprus 39 E10 35 42N 34 36 E
Klimovichi, Belarus 58 F6 53 36N 32 0 E
Klin, Russia 58 D9 56 20N 36 48 E
Klina, Kosovo, Yug. 50 D4 42 37N 20 35 E
Klinaklini →, Canada 142 C3 51 21N 125 40W
Klintehamn, Sweden 17 G12 57 24N 18 12 E
Klintsy, Russia 59 F7 52 50N 32 10 E
Klip →, S. Africa 117 D4 27 3 S 29 3 E
Klipdale, S. Africa 116 E2 34 19 S 19 57 E
Klippan, Sweden 17 H7 56 8N 13 6 E
Klipplaat, S. Africa 116 E3 33 1 S 24 22 E
Klisura, Bulgaria 51 D8 42 40N 24 28 E
Kljajićevo, Serbia, Yug. 52 E4 45 45N 19 17 E
Ključ, Bos.-H. 45 D13 44 32N 16 48 E
Kłobuck, Poland 55 H5 50 55N 18 55 E
Klockestrand, Sweden 16 B11 62 53N 17 55 E
Kłodawa, Poland 55 F5 52 15N 18 55 E
Kłodzko, Poland 55 H3 50 28N 16 38 E
Kløfta, Norway 18 D6 60 4N 11 9 E
Klondike Goldrush Nat. Historical Park △, U.S.A. 144 E14 59 27N 135 19W
Klong Wang Chao Nat. Park △, Thailand 86 D2 16 20N 99 9 E
Klos, Albania 50 E4 41 28N 20 10 E
Klosterneuburg, Austria 35 C9 48 18N 16 19 E
Klosters, Switz. 33 C9 46 52N 9 52 E
Kloten, Switz. 33 B7 47 27N 8 35 E
Klötze, Germany 30 C7 52 37N 11 10 E
Klouto, Togo 113 D5 6 57N 0 44 E
Kluane L., Canada 138 B6 61 15N 138 40W
Kluane Nat. Park △, Canada 142 A1 60 45N 139 30W
Kluczbork, Poland 55 H5 50 58N 18 12 E
Klukwan, U.S.A. 142 B1 59 24N 135 54W
Klungkung, Indonesia 79 K18 8 32 S 115 24 E
Klyetsk, Belarus 59 F4 53 5N 26 45 E
Klyuchevskaya, Gora, Russia 67 D17 55 50N 160 30 E
Knaben, Norway 18 F4 58 40N 7 4 E
Knappavellir, Iceland 11 D10 63 54N 16 36W
Knared, Sweden 17 H7 56 31N 13 19 E
Knaresborough, U.K. 20 C6 54 1N 1 28W
Knarvik, Norway 18 D2 60 32N 5 19 E
Knee L., Man., Canada 140 A1 55 3N 94 45W
Knee L., Sask., Canada 143 B7 55 51N 107 0W
Kneiss, Is., Tunisia 108 B2 34 22N 10 18 E
Knezha, Bulgaria 51 C8 43 30N 24 5 E
Knić, Serbia, Yug. 50 C4 43 53N 20 42 E
Knight I., U.S.A. 144 F11 60 21N 147 45W
Knight Inlet, Canada 142 C3 50 45N 125 40W
Knighton, U.K. 21 E4 52 21N 3 3W
Knights Ferry, U.S.A. 160 H6 37 50N 120 40W
Knights Landing, U.S.A. 160 G5 38 48N 121 43W
Knightstown, U.S.A. 157 E11 39 48N 85 32W
Knin, Croatia 45 D13 44 2N 16 17 E
Knislinge, Sweden 17 H8 56 12N 14 5 E
Knittelfeld, Austria 34 D7 47 13N 14 51 E
Knivsta, Sweden 16 E11 59 43N 17 48 E
Knjaževac, Serbia, Yug. 50 C6 43 35N 22 18 E
Knob, C., Australia 125 F2 34 32 S 119 16 E
Knob Noster, U.S.A. 156 F3 38 46N 93 33W
Knock, Ireland 23 C3 53 48N 8 55W
Knockmealdown Mts., Ireland 23 D4 52 14N 7 56W
Knokke-Heist, Belgium 24 C3 51 21N 3 17 E
Knossós, Greece 39 E6 35 16N 25 10 E
Knowlton, Canada 151 A12 45 13N 72 31W
Knox, U.S.A. 157 C10 41 18N 86 37W
Knox Coast, Antarctica 7 C8 66 30 S 108 0 E
Knoxville, Ga., U.S.A. 152 C6 32 47N 83 59W
Knoxville, Ill., U.S.A. 156 D6 40 55N 90 17W
Knoxville, Iowa, U.S.A. 156 C4 41 19N 93 6W
Knoxville, Pa., U.S.A. 150 E7 41 57N 77 27W
Knoxville, Tenn., U.S.A. 149 H4 35 58N 83 55W
Knud Rasmussen Land, Greenland 10 B4 79 0N 60 0W
Knysna, S. Africa 116 E3 34 2 S 23 2 E
Knyszyn, Poland 54 E9 53 20N 22 56 E
Ko Kha, Thailand 86 C2 18 11N 99 24 E
Kō-Saki, Japan 72 C1 34 5N 129 13 E
Ko Yao, Thailand 87 J2 6 31N 99 26 E
Ko Tarutao Nat. Park △, Thailand 87 J2 6 31N 99 26 E
Koartac = Quaqtaq, Canada 139 B13 60 55N 69 40W
Koba, Aru, Indonesia 83 C4 6 37 S 134 37 E
Koba, Bangka, Indonesia 84 C3 2 26 S 106 14 E
Kobarid, Slovenia 45 B10 46 15N 13 30 E
Kobayashi, Japan 72 F2 31 56N 130 59 E
Kobdo = Hovd, Mongolia 68 B4 48 2N 91 37 E
Kobe, Indonesia 82 A3 0 20N 127 54 E
Kōbe, Japan 73 C7 34 45N 135 10 E
Kobelyaky, Ukraine 59 H8 49 11N 34 12 E
København, Denmark 17 J6 55 41N 12 34 E
Københavns Amtskommune □, Denmark 17 J6 55 42N 12 21 E
Kobenni, Mauritania 112 B3 15 50N 9 24W
Kōbi-Sho, Japan 71 M1 25 56N 123 41 E
Koblenz, Germany 31 E3 50 21N 7 36 E
Koblenz, Switz. 32 A6 47 37N 8 14 E
Kobo, Dem. Rep. of the Congo 115 C3 4 54 S 17 9 E
Kobo, Ethiopia 107 E4 12 2N 39 56 E
Kobroor, Indonesia 83 C4 6 10 S 134 30 E
Kobryn, Belarus 59 F3 52 15N 24 22 E
Kobuchizawa, Japan 73 B10 35 52N 138 19 E
Kobuk, U.S.A. 144 C8 66 54N 156 53W
Kobuk →, U.S.A. 144 C7 66 54N 160 38W
Kobuk Valley Nat. Park △, U.S.A. 144 C8 67 0N 160 0W
Kobuleti, Georgia 61 K5 41 55N 41 45 E
Kobylin, Poland 55 G4 51 43N 17 12 E
Kobyłka, Poland 55 F8 52 21N 21 10 E
Kobylkino, Russia 60 C6 54 8N 43 12 E
Koca →, Turkey 51 E11 40 8N 27 57 E
Kocabaş, Turkey 49 D11 37 49N 29 20 E
Kocaeli, Turkey 51 F13 40 45N 29 55 E
Kocaeli □, Turkey 51 F13 40 45N 29 50 E
Kočane, Serbia, Yug. 50 C5 43 12N 21 52 E
Kočani, Macedonia 50 E6 41 55N 22 25 E
Koçarlı, Turkey 49 D9 37 45N 27 43 E
Kočevje, Slovenia 45 C11 45 39N 14 50 E
Koch Bihar, India 90 B2 26 22N 89 29 E
Kochang, S. Korea 75 G14 35 41N 127 55 E
Kochas, India 93 G10 25 15N 83 56 E
Kocher →, Germany 31 F5 49 14N 9 12 E
Kochi = Cochin, India 95 K3 9 58N 76 20 E
Kōchi, Japan 72 D5 33 30N 133 35 E
Kōchi □, Japan 72 D5 33 40N 133 30 E
Kochiu = Gejiu, China 76 F4 23 20N 103 10 E
Kochkor, Kyrgyzstan 65 B7 42 13N 75 46 E
Kochkor-Ata, Kyrgyzstan 65 C6 41 1N 72 29 E
Kock, Poland 55 G9 51 38N 22 27 E
Kodaira, Japan 73 B11 35 44N 139 29 E

Kodala, India ... 94 E7 19 38N 84 57 E
Kodarma, India ... 93 G11 24 28N 85 36 E
Koddiyar B., Sri Lanka ... 95 K5 8 33N 81 15 E
Kode, Sweden ... 17 G5 57 57N 11 51 E
Kodi, Dem. Rep. of the Congo ... 114 C4 3 34 S 22 12 E
Kodi, Indonesia ... 82 C1 9 33 S 119 0 E
Kodiak, U.S.A. ... 144 H9 57 47N 152 24W
Kodiak I., U.S.A. ... 144 H9 57 30N 152 45W
Kodinar, India ... 92 J4 20 46N 70 46 E
Kodlipet, India ... 95 H2 12 48N 75 53 E
Kodok, Sudan ... 107 F3 9 53N 32 7 E
Kodori →, Georgia ... 95 J5 42 47N 41 10 E
Kodoro, Dem. Rep. of the Congo ... 114 B4 1 16N 20 6 E
Koedoesberge, S. Africa ... 116 E3 32 40 S 20 11 E
Koes, Namibia ... 116 D2 26 0 S 19 15 E
Kofarnikhon, Tajikistan ... 65 D4 38 34N 69 1 E
Kofçaz, Turkey ... 51 E11 41 58N 27 12 E
Koffiefontein, S. Africa ... 116 D4 29 30 S 25 0 E
Kofiau, Indonesia ... 83 B3 1 11 S 129 50 E
Köflach, Austria ... 34 D8 47 4N 15 4 E
Koforidua, Ghana ... 113 D4 6 3N 0 17W
Kōfu, Japan ... 73 B10 35 40N 138 30 E
Koga, Japan ... 73 A11 36 11N 139 43 E
Kogaluk →, Canada ... 141 A7 56 12N 61 44W
Kögart, Kyrgyzstan ... 65 C7 40 15N 74 25 E
Køge, Denmark ... 17 J6 55 27N 12 11 E
Køge Bugt, Denmark ... 17 J6 55 30N 12 20 E
Kogi □, Nigeria ... 113 D6 7 45N 6 45 E
Kogin Baba, Nigeria ... 113 D7 7 55N 11 35 E
Kogo, Eq. Guin. ... 114 B1 1 5N 9 42 E
Koh-i-Khurd, Afghan. ... 91 B2 33 30N 65 59 E
Koh-i-Maran, Pakistan ... 92 E2 29 18N 66 50 E
Kohala Mts., U.S.A. ... 145 C6 20 5N 155 45W
Kohat, Pakistan ... 91 B3 33 40N 71 29 E
Kohima, India ... 90 C5 25 35N 94 10 E
Kohkīlūyeh va Būyer Aḥmadī □, Iran ... 97 D6 31 30N 50 30 E
Kohler Ra., Antarctica ... 7 D15 77 0 S 110 0W
Kohlu, Pakistan ... 92 E3 29 54N 69 15 E
Kohtla-Järve, Estonia ... 15 G22 59 20N 27 20 E
Kohukohu, N.Z. ... 130 B2 35 22 S 173 38 E
Koihoa, India ... 95 K11 8 12N 93 29 E
Koilkuntla, India ... 95 G4 15 14N 78 19 E
Koillismaa, Finland ... 14 D23 65 44N 28 36 E
Koin-dong, N. Korea ... 75 D14 40 28N 126 18 E
Koinare, Bulgaria ... 51 C8 43 21N 24 8 E
Koindu, S. Leone ... 112 D2 8 26N 10 19W
Kojetín, Czech Rep. ... 35 B10 49 21N 17 20 E
Kojŏ, N. Korea ... 75 E14 38 58N 127 58 E
Kojonup, Australia ... 125 F2 33 48 S 117 10 E
Kojūr, Iran ... 97 B6 36 23N 51 43 E
Kök-Aygyr, Kyrgyzstan ... 65 C7 40 42N 75 32 E
Kök-Janggak, Kyrgyzstan ... 65 C6 41 2N 73 12 E
Koka, Sudan ... 106 C3 20 5N 30 35 E
Kokand = Qŭqon, Uzbekistan ... 65 C5 40 30N 70 57 E
Kokas, Indonesia ... 83 B4 2 42 S 132 26 E
Kokava, Slovak Rep. ... 35 C12 48 35N 19 50 E
Kokcha →, Afghan. ... 91 A3 37 9N 69 24 E
Kokchetav = Kökshetaū, Kazakhstan ... 66 D7 53 20N 69 25 E
Kokemäenjoki →, Finland ... 15 F19 61 32N 21 44 E
Kokra, Guyana ... 169 B6 7 12N 59 35W
Kokhma, Russia ... 60 B5 56 57N 41 8 E
Koki, Senegal ... 112 B1 15 30N 15 59W
Kokkilai, Sri Lanka ... 95 K5 9 0N 80 57 E
Kokkina, Cyprus ... 39 E8 35 11N 32 36 E
Kokkola, Finland ... 14 E20 63 50N 23 8 E
Kokko, Nigeria ... 113 C5 11 28N 4 29 E
Koko Head, U.S.A. ... 145 K14 21 16N 157 43W
Kokoda, Papua N. G. ... 132 E4 8 54 S 147 47 E
Kokolopozo, Ivory C. ... 112 D3 5 8N 6 5W
Kokomo, U.S.A. ... 157 D10 40 29N 86 8W
Kokonau, Indonesia ... 83 B5 4 43 S 136 26 E
Kokopo, Papua N. G. ... 132 C7 4 22 S 152 19 E
Kokoro, Niger ... 113 C5 14 12N 0 55 E
Koksan, N. Korea ... 75 E14 38 46N 126 40 E
Köksaray, Kazakhstan ... 65 B4 42 38N 68 9 E
Kökshetaū, Kazakhstan ... 66 D7 53 20N 69 25 E
Koksoak →, Canada ... 139 C13 58 30N 68 10W
Kokstad, S. Africa ... 117 E4 30 32 S 29 29 E
Köksū, Kazakhstan ... 65 C4 41 28N 68 1 E
Köktal, Kazakhstan ... 65 B5 43 16N 70 18 E
Kokubu, Japan ... 72 F2 31 44N 130 46 E
Kokyar, China ... 65 E8 37 23N 77 10 E
Kola, Indonesia ... 83 C4 5 35 S 134 30 E
Kola, Russia ... 56 A5 68 45N 33 8 E
Kola Pen. = Kolskiy Poluostrov, Russia ... 56 A6 67 30N 38 0 E
Kolachel, India ... 95 K3 8 10N 77 15 E
Kolachi →, Pakistan ... 92 F2 27 8N 67 2 E
Kolahoi, India ... 93 B6 34 12N 75 22 E
Kolahun, Liberia ... 112 D2 8 15N 10 4W
Kolaka, Indonesia ... 82 B2 4 3 S 121 46 E
Kolar, India ... 95 H4 13 12N 78 15 E
Kolar Gold Fields, India ... 95 H4 12 58N 78 16 E
Kolaras, India ... 92 G6 25 14N 77 36 E
Kolari, Finland ... 14 C20 67 20N 23 48 E
Kolarovgrad = Shumen, Bulgaria ... 51 C10 43 18N 26 55 E
Kolárovo, Slovak Rep. ... 35 D10 47 54N 18 0 E
Kolašin, Montenegro, Yug. ... 50 D3 42 50N 19 31 E
Kolbäck, Sweden ... 16 E10 59 34N 16 15 E
Kolbäcksån →, Sweden ... 16 E10 59 36N 16 16 E
Kolbeinsstaðir, Iceland ... 11 C4 64 59N 22 16W
Kolberg = Kołobrzeg, Poland ... 54 D2 54 10N 15 35 E
Kolbermoor, Germany ... 31 H8 47 51N 12 4 E
Kolbu, Norway ... 18 D7 60 39N 10 45 E
Kolbuszowa, Poland ... 55 H8 50 25N 22 5 E
Kolchugino = Leninsk-Kuznetskiy, Russia ... 66 D9 54 44N 86 10 E
Kolchugino, Russia ... 58 D10 56 17N 39 22 E
Kolda, Senegal ... 112 C2 12 55N 14 57W
Koldegi, Sudan ... 107 E3 12 3N 30 16 E
Kolding, Denmark ... 17 J3 55 30N 9 29 E
Kole, Dem. Rep. of the Congo ... 114 C4 3 16 S 22 42 E
Koléa, Algeria ... 111 A5 36 38N 2 46 E
Kolepom = Dolak, Pulau, Indonesia ... 83 C5 8 0 S 138 30 E
Kolguyev, Ostrov, Russia ... 56 A8 69 20N 48 30 E
Kolhapur, India ... 94 F2 16 43N 74 15 E
Kolia, Ivory C. ... 112 D3 9 46N 6 28W
Koliganek, U.S.A. ... 144 G8 59 48N 157 25W
Kolín, Czech Rep. ... 34 A8 50 2N 15 9 E
Kolind, Denmark ... 17 H4 56 21N 10 34 E
Kolkas rags, Latvia ... 15 H20 57 46N 22 37 E
Kolkata, India ... 93 H13 22 36N 88 24 E
Kolkhozobod, Tajikistan ... 65 E4 37 35N 68 40 E
Kollam = Quilon, India ... 95 K3 8 50N 76 38 E
Kölleda, Germany ... 30 D7 51 11N 11 15 E
Kollegal, India ... 95 H3 12 9N 77 9 E
Kolleru L., India ... 94 F5 16 40N 81 10 E
Kollum, Neths. ... 24 A6 53 17N 6 10 E
Kolmanskop, Namibia ... 116 D2 26 45 S 15 14 E
Köln, Germany ... 30 E2 50 56N 6 57 E
Kolno, Poland ... 54 E8 53 25N 21 56 E
Koło, Poland ... 55 F5 52 14N 18 40 E
Koloa, U.S.A. ... 145 B22 51 59N 159 28W
Kołobrzeg, Poland ... 54 D2 54 10N 15 35 E
Kolokani, Mali ... 112 C3 13 35N 7 45W
Koloko, Burkina Faso ... 112 C3 11 5N 5 19W
Kololo, Ethiopia ... 107 F5 7 29N 41 58 E
Kolombangara, Solomon Is. ... 133 M9 8 0 S 157 5 E
Kolomna, Russia ... 58 E10 55 8N 38 45 E
Kolomyya, Ukraine ... 59 H3 48 31N 25 2 E
Kolondiéba, Mali ... 112 C3 11 5N 6 54W
Kolonodale, Indonesia ... 82 B2 2 0 S 121 19 E
Kolonowskie, Poland ... 55 H5 50 53N 18 22 E

Kolosib, India ... 90 C4 24 15N 92 45 E
Kolpashevo, Russia ... 66 D9 58 20N 83 5 E
Kolpino, Russia ... 58 C6 59 44N 30 39 E
Kolpny, Russia ... 59 F9 52 17N 37 1 E
Kolskiy Poluostrov, Russia ... 56 A6 67 30N 38 0 E
Kolskiy Zaliv, Russia ... 56 A5 69 23N 34 0 E
Kolsva, Sweden ... 16 E9 59 36N 15 51 E
Kolubara →, Serbia, Yug. ... 50 B4 44 35N 20 15 E
Koluszki, Poland ... 55 G6 51 45N 19 46 E
Kolwezi, Dem. Rep. of the Congo ... 119 E2 10 40 S 25 25 E
Kolyma →, Russia ... 67 C16 69 30N 161 0 E
Kolymskoye Nagorye, Russia ... 67 C16 63 0N 157 0 E
Kôm Hamâda, Egypt ... 106 H7 30 46N 30 41 E
Kôm Ombo, Egypt ... 106 C3 24 25N 32 52 E
Komadugu Gana →, Nigeria ... 113 C7 13 5N 12 24 E
Komagane, Japan ... 73 B9 35 44N 137 58 E
Komaki, Japan ... 73 B8 35 17N 136 55 E
Komandorskiye Is. = Komandorskiye Ostrova, Russia ... 67 D17 55 0N 167 0 E
Komandorskiye Ostrova, Russia ... 67 D17 55 0N 167 0 E
Kománro, Slovak Rep. ... 35 D11 47 49N 18 5 E
Komárom, Hungary ... 52 C3 47 43N 18 7 E
Komárom-Esztergom □, Hungary ... 52 C3 47 35N 18 20 E
Komatipoort, S. Africa ... 117 D5 25 25 S 31 55 E
Komatou Yialou, Cyprus ... 39 E13 35 25N 34 8 E
Komatsu, Japan ... 73 A8 36 25N 136 30 E
Komatsushima, Japan ... 72 D6 34 0N 134 35 E
Komba, Dem. Rep. of the Congo ... 114 B4 2 52N 24 3 E
Kombissiri, Burkina Faso ... 113 C4 12 4N 1 20W
Kombo, Gabon ... 114 C2 0 20 S 12 22 E
Kombong, India ... 90 A5 28 7N 94 51 E
Kombori, Burkina Faso ... 112 C4 13 26N 3 56W
Kombóti, Greece ... 48 B3 39 6N 21 5 E
Komen, Slovenia ... 45 C10 45 49N 13 45 E
Komenda, Ghana ... 113 D4 5 4N 1 28W
Komi □, Russia ... 56 B10 64 0N 55 0 E
Komiža, Croatia ... 45 E13 43 3N 16 11 E
Komló, Hungary ... 52 D3 46 15N 18 16 E
Kommamur Canal, India ... 95 G5 16 0N 80 25 E
Kommunarsk = Alchevsk, Ukraine ... 59 H10 48 30N 38 45 E
Kommunizma, Pik, Tajikistan ... 65 D6 39 0N 72 2 E
Komodo, Indonesia ... 82 C1 8 37 S 119 20 E
Komoé →, Ivory C. ... 112 D4 5 12N 3 44W
Komono, Congo ... 114 C2 3 10 S 13 20 E
Komoran, Pulau, Indonesia ... 83 C5 8 18 S 138 45 E
Komoro, Japan ... 73 A10 36 19N 138 26 E
Komotini, Greece ... 51 E9 41 9N 25 26 E
Komovi, Montenegro, Yug. ... 50 D3 42 41N 19 39 E
Kompasberg, S. Africa ... 116 E3 31 45 S 24 32 E
Kompong Bang, Cambodia ... 87 F5 12 24N 104 40 E
Kompong Cham, Cambodia ... 87 F5 12 0N 105 30 E
Kompong Chhnang = Kampong Chhnang, Cambodia ... 87 F5 12 20N 104 35 E
Kompong Chikreng, Cambodia ... 86 F5 13 5N 104 18 E
Kompong Kleang, Cambodia ... 86 F5 13 6N 104 8 E
Kompong Luong, Cambodia ... 87 G5 11 49N 104 48 E
Kompong Pranak, Cambodia ... 86 F5 13 35N 104 55 E
Kompong Som = Kampong Saom, Cambodia ... 87 G4 10 38N 103 30 E
Kompong Som, Chhung = Kampong Saom, Chaak, Cambodia ... 87 G4 10 50N 103 32 E
Kompong Speu, Cambodia ... 87 G5 11 26N 104 32 E
Kompong Sralau, Cambodia ... 86 E5 14 5N 105 46 E
Kompong Thom, Cambodia ... 86 F5 12 35N 104 51 E
Kompong Trabeck, Cambodia ... 86 F5 13 6N 105 14 E
Kompong Trabeck, Cambodia ... 87 G5 11 9N 105 28 E
Kompong Trach, Cambodia ... 87 G5 11 25N 105 48 E
Kompong Tralach, Cambodia ... 87 F5 11 54N 104 47 E
Komrat = Comrat, Moldova ... 53 D13 46 18N 28 40 E
Komsberg, S. Africa ... 116 E3 32 40 S 20 45 E
Komsomolabad, Tajikistan ... 65 D4 38 50N 69 55 E
Komsomolets, Kazakhstan ... 64 E9 53 45N 62 2 E
Komsomolets, Ostrov, Russia ... 67 A10 80 30N 95 0 E
Komsomolsk, Amur, Russia ... 67 D14 50 30N 137 0 E
Komsomolsk, Ivanovo, Russia ... 58 D11 57 2N 40 20 E
Komsomolsk, Turkmenistan ... 65 B5 39 2N 63 33 E
Komsomolskiy, Russia ... 60 C7 54 27N 45 33 E
Kômür Burnu, Turkey ... 49 C8 38 39N 26 12 E
Kon Tum, Vietnam ... 86 E7 14 24N 108 0 E
Kon Tum, Plateau du, Vietnam ... 86 E7 14 30N 108 30 E
Kona, Mali ... 112 C4 14 57N 3 53W
Konakovo, Russia ... 58 D9 56 52N 36 51 E
Konarak, India ... 92 K9 19 54N 86 7 E
Konarhā □, Afghan. ... 91 B3 34 30N 71 3 E
Konāri, Iran ... 97 D6 28 13N 51 36 E
Konch, India ... 93 G8 26 0N 79 10 E
Konda →, Indonesia ... 83 B4 1 34 S 131 57 E
Kondagaon, India ... 94 E5 19 35N 81 35 E
Konde, Tanzania ... 118 C3 4 57 S 39 45 E
Kondiá, Greece ... 49 B7 39 49N 25 10 E
Kondinin, Australia ... 125 F2 32 34 S 118 8 E
Kondoa, Tanzania ... 118 C4 4 55 S 35 50 E
Kondókali, Greece ... 38 A9 39 38N 19 51 E
Kondopaga, Russia ... 58 A8 62 12N 34 17 E
Konâratyevo, Russia ... 67 D10 57 22N 98 15 E
Kondrovo, Russia ... 58 E8 54 48N 35 56 E
Konduga, Nigeria ... 113 C7 11 35N 13 26 E
Kondukur, India ... 95 G4 15 12N 79 57 E
Koné, N. Cal. ... 133 U18 21 4 S 164 52 E
Köneürgench, Turkmenistan ... 66 E6 42 19N 59 10 E
Konevo, Russia ... 58 A10 62 8N 39 20 E
Kong = Khong →, Cambodia ... 86 F5 13 32N 105 58 E
Kong, Ivory C. ... 112 D4 8 54N 4 36W
Kong, Koh, Cambodia ... 87 G4 11 20N 103 0 E
Kong Christian IX Land, Greenland ... 10 D7 68 0N 36 0W
Kong Christian X Land, Greenland ... 10 C8 74 0N 29 0W
Kong Frederik IX Land, Greenland ... 10 D5 67 0N 52 0W
Kong Frederik VI Kyst, Greenland ... 10 D5 63 0N 43 0W
Kong Frederik VIII Land, Greenland ... 10 B8 78 30N 26 0W
Kong Oscar Fjord, Greenland ... 10 C8 72 20N 24 0W
Kongbo, C.A.R. ... 114 B4 4 44N 21 23 E
Kongeå →, Denmark ... 17 J2 55 23N 8 39 E
Kongerslev, Denmark ... 17 H4 56 54N 10 6 E
Kongju, S. Korea ... 75 F14 36 30N 127 0 E
Kongkemul, Indonesia ... 85 B4 1 52N 112 11 E
Konglu, Burma ... 90 B6 27 13N 97 57 E
Kongola, Namibia ... 116 B3 17 45 S 23 20 E
Kongolo, Kasai-Or., Dem. Rep. of the Congo ... 118 D1 5 26 S 24 49 E
Kongolo, Katanga, Dem. Rep. of the Congo ... 118 D2 5 22 S 27 0 E
Kongor, Sudan ... 107 F3 7 1N 31 27 E
Kongoulou, Cameroon ... 113 B8 2 59N 11 7 E
Kongoussi, Burkina Faso ... 113 C4 13 19N 1 32W
Kongsberg, Norway ... 18 E6 59 39N 9 39 E
Kongsvinger, Norway ... 18 D9 60 12N 12 2 E
Kongwa, Tanzania ... 118 D4 6 11 S 36 26 E
Koni, Dem. Rep. of the Congo ... 119 E2 10 40 S 27 11 E
Koni, Mts., Dem. Rep. of the Congo ... 119 E2 10 36 S 27 10 E
Koniakari, Mali ... 112 C2 14 35N 10 50W
Koniecpol, Poland ... 55 H6 50 46N 19 40 E
Königs Wusterhausen, Germany ... 30 C9 52 19N 13 38 E
Königsberg = Kaliningrad, Russia ... 15 J19 54 42N 20 32 E
Königsbrunn, Germany ... 31 G6 48 16N 10 54 E
Königslutter, Germany ... 30 C6 52 15N 10 49 E
Konin, Poland ... 55 F5 52 12N 18 15 E
Konispol, Albania ... 38 B10 39 42N 20 10 E
Kónitsa, Greece ... 48 A2 40 5N 20 48 E
Köniz, Switz. ... 32 C4 46 56N 7 25 E
Konjic, Bos.-H. ... 52 G2 43 42N 17 58 E
Konkiep, Namibia ... 116 D2 26 49 S 17 15 E
Konkö, Japan ... 72 C4 34 34N 133 36 E

Konkouré →, Guinea ... 112 D2 9 50N 13 42W
Könnern, Germany ... 30 D7 51 41N 11 47 E
Konnur, India ... 95 F2 16 14N 74 49 E
Kono, S. Leone ... 112 D2 8 30N 11 5W
Konogogo, Papua N. G. ... 132 B7 3 29 S 152 10 E
Konolfingen, Switz. ... 32 C5 46 54N 7 38 E
Konongo, Ghana ... 113 D4 6 40N 1 15W
Konos, Papua N. G. ... 132 B6 3 10 S 151 44 E
Konosha, Russia ... 58 B11 61 0N 40 5 E
Kōnosu, Japan ... 73 A11 36 3N 139 31 E
Konotop, Ukraine ... 59 G7 51 12N 33 7 E
Konsankoro, Guinea ... 112 D3 9 2N 9 0W
Końskie, Poland ... 55 G7 51 15N 20 23 E
Konsmo, Norway ... 18 F4 58 16N 7 23 E
Konstancin-Jeziorna, Poland ... 55 F8 52 5N 21 7 E
Konstantinovka = Kostyantynivka, Ukraine ... 59 H9 48 32N 37 39 E
Konstantinovsk, Russia ... 61 G5 47 33N 41 10 E
Konstantynów Łódźki, Poland ... 55 G6 51 45N 19 20 E
Konstanz, Germany ... 31 H5 47 40N 9 10 E
Kont, Iran ... 97 E9 26 55N 61 50 E
Konta, India ... 94 F5 17 48N 81 23 E
Kontagora, Nigeria ... 113 C6 10 23N 5 27 E
Kontcha, Cameroon ... 113 D7 7 59N 12 15 E
Konya, Turkey ... 100 D5 37 52N 32 35 E
Konya Ovası, Turkey ... 100 D5 38 9N 33 5 E
Konyin, Burma ... 90 D5 22 58N 94 42 E
Konz, Germany ... 31 F2 49 42N 6 34 E
Konza, Kenya ... 118 C4 1 45 S 37 7 E
Konzhakovskiy Kamen, Gora, Russia ... 64 B7 59 38N 59 8 E
Koo-wee-rup, Australia ... 129 E6 38 13 S 145 28 E
Koocanusa, L., Canada ... 158 B6 49 20N 115 15W
Kookynie, Australia ... 125 E3 29 17 S 121 22 E
Koolan Range, U.S.A. ... 145 J14 21 35N 157 50W
Koolyanobbing, Australia ... 125 F2 30 48 S 119 36 E
Koondrook, Australia ... 128 C6 35 33 S 144 8 E
Koonibba, Australia ... 127 E1 31 54 S 133 25 E
Koorawatha, Australia ... 129 C8 34 2 S 148 33 E
Koorda, Australia ... 125 F2 30 48 S 117 35 E
Kooskia, U.S.A. ... 158 C6 46 9N 115 59W
Kootenay →, U.S.A. ... 142 D5 49 19N 117 39W
Kootenay L., Canada ... 142 D5 49 45N 116 50W
Kootenay Nat. Park △, Canada ... 142 C5 51 0N 116 0W
Kootingal, Australia ... 129 A9 31 1 S 151 3 E
Kootjieskolk, S. Africa ... 116 E3 31 15 S 20 21 E
Kopaonik, Yugoslavia ... 50 C4 43 10N 20 50 E
Kopaonik Nac. Park △, Yugoslavia ... 50 C4 43 20N 20 50 E
Kopargaon, India ... 94 E2 19 51N 74 28 E
Kópasker, Iceland ... 11 A6 66 18N 16 27W
Kópavogur, Iceland ... 11 C5 64 6N 21 55W
Koper, Slovenia ... 45 C10 45 31N 13 44 E
Kopervik, Norway ... 18 E2 59 17N 5 17 E
Kopet Dagh, Asia ... 97 B8 38 0N 58 0 E
Kopi, Australia ... 127 E2 33 24 S 135 40 E
Köping, Sweden ... 16 E10 59 31N 16 3 E
Köpingsvik, Sweden ... 17 H10 56 53N 16 43 E
Kopište, Croatia ... 45 F13 42 48N 16 42 E
Koplik, Albania ... 50 D3 42 15N 19 25 E
Köpmanholmen, Sweden ... 16 A12 63 10N 18 35 E
Koppa, India ... 95 H2 13 33N 75 21 E
Koppal, India ... 95 G3 15 23N 76 5 E
Koppang, Norway ... 18 C8 61 34N 11 3 E
Kopparberg, Sweden ... 16 E9 59 52N 15 0 E
Kopperå, Norway ... 16 A6 63 24N 11 50 E
Koppies, S. Africa ... 117 D4 27 20 S 27 30 E
Koppom, Sweden ... 16 E5 59 43N 12 10 E
Koprivlen, Bulgaria ... 50 E7 41 31N 23 53 E
Koprivnica, Croatia ... 45 B13 46 12N 16 45 E
Kopřivnice, Czech Rep. ... 35 B11 49 36N 18 9 E
Koprivshtitsa, Bulgaria ... 51 D8 42 40N 24 19 E
Köprübaşı, Turkey ... 49 C10 38 43N 28 23 E
Kopychyntsi, Ukraine ... 59 H3 49 7N 25 58 E
Kora Nat. Park △, Kenya ... 118 C4 0 14 S 38 44 E
Korab, Macedonia ... 50 E4 41 44N 20 40 E
Korákiana, Greece ... 38 B9 39 42N 19 45 E
Koral, India ... 92 J5 21 50N 73 12 E
Korangal, India ... 94 E3 17 6N 77 38 E
Koraput, India ... 94 E6 18 50N 82 40 E
Korarou, L., Mali ... 112 B4 15 15N 3 15W
Korba, India ... 93 H10 22 20N 82 45 E
Korbach, Germany ... 30 D4 51 16N 8 52 E
Korbu, G., Malaysia ... 87 K3 4 41N 101 18 E
Korçë, Albania ... 50 F4 40 37N 20 50 E
Korčula, Croatia ... 45 F13 42 56N 16 57 E
Korčulanski Kanal, Croatia ... 45 E13 43 3N 16 40 E
Kord Kūy, Iran ... 97 B7 36 48N 54 7 E
Kord Sheykh, Iran ... 97 D7 28 31N 52 53 E
Korday, Kazakhstan ... 65 B7 43 1N 74 43 E
Kordestān □, Iran ... 96 C5 36 0N 47 0 E
Koré Mayroua, Niger ... 113 C5 13 18N 3 55 E
Korea, North ■, Asia ... 75 E14 40 0N 127 0 E
Korea, South ■, Asia ... 75 G15 36 0N 128 0 E
Korea Bay, Korea ... 75 E13 39 0N 124 0 E
Korea Strait, Asia ... 75 H15 34 0N 129 30 E
Koregaon, India ... 94 F2 17 40N 74 10 E
Korem, Ethiopia ... 107 E4 12 30N 39 32 E
Korenevo, Russia ... 59 G8 51 27N 34 55 E
Korenovsk, Russia ... 61 H4 45 30N 39 22 E
Korets, Ukraine ... 59 G4 50 40N 27 5 E
Korfantów, Poland ... 55 H4 50 29N 17 34 E
Korgan, Turkey ... 100 B7 40 44N 37 13 E
Korgus, Sudan ... 106 D3 19 16N 33 29 E
Korhogo, Ivory C. ... 112 D3 9 29N 5 28W
Koribundu, S. Leone ... 112 D2 7 41N 11 46W
Korienzé, Mali ... 112 B4 15 22N 3 50W
Korinós, Greece ... 48 A4 40 31N 22 34 E
Korinthía □, Greece ... 48 C4 38 16N 22 30 E
Korinthiakós Kólpos, Greece ... 48 C4 38 16N 22 30 E
Korinthos, Greece ... 48 D4 37 56N 22 55 E
Korioumé, Mali ... 112 B4 16 35N 3 0W
Kórissa, Límni, Greece ... 38 C9 39 27N 19 53 E
Korithi, Greece ... 39 D2 37 55N 20 42 E
Kōriyama, Japan ... 70 F10 37 24N 140 23 E
Korkino, Russia ... 64 D8 54 54N 61 23 E
Korkuteli, Turkey ... 100 D4 37 45N 30 14 E
Korla, China ... 68 B3 41 45N 86 4 E
Kormakiti, C., Cyprus ... 39 E8 35 23N 32 56 E
Körmend, Hungary ... 52 C1 47 5N 16 35 E
Kornat, Croatia ... 45 E12 43 50N 15 20 E
Kornat, Nac. Park △, Croatia ... 45 E12 43 50N 15 12 E
Kornešty = Corneşti, Moldova ... 53 C13 47 21N 28 1 E
Korneuburg, Austria ... 35 C9 48 20N 16 20 E
Kórnik, Poland ... 55 F3 52 15N 17 6 E
Kornsjø, Norway ... 18 E8 58 57N 11 39 E
Koro, Fiji ... 133 A2 17 19 S 179 23 E
Koro, Ivory C. ... 112 D3 8 32N 7 30W
Koro, Mali ... 112 C4 14 1N 2 58W
Koro Sea, Fiji ... 133 A3 17 30 S 179 45W
Koroba, Papua N. G. ... 132 C2 5 44 S 142 47 E
Koroča, Russia ... 59 G9 50 55N 37 19 E
Köroğlu Dağları, Turkey ... 100 B5 40 38N 33 0 E
Korogwe, Tanzania ... 118 D4 5 5 S 38 25 E
Koroit, Australia ... 128 E5 38 18 S 142 22 E
Korolevu, Fiji ... 133 B1 18 12 S 177 46 E
Korona, U.S.A. ... 153 F8 29 20N 81 30W
Koronadal, Phil. ... 81 H5 6 12N 125 1 E
Korong Vale, Australia ... 128 E3 36 22 S 143 45 E
Koróni, Greece ... 48 E3 36 48N 21 57 E
Korónia, Limni, Greece ... 50 F7 40 47N 23 10 E

Koronís, Greece ... 49 D7 37 12N 25 35 E
Koronowo, Poland ... 55 E4 53 19N 17 55 E
Koropelé, C.A.R. ... 114 B3 4 44N 17 11 E
Koror, Palau ... 134 G5 7 20N 134 28 E
Körös →, Hungary ... 52 D5 46 43N 20 12 E
Körös Maros Nemzeti Park △, Hungary ... 52 C5 47 8N 20 52 E
Köröstarcsa, Hungary ... 52 D6 46 53N 21 3 E
Korosten, Ukraine ... 59 G5 50 54N 28 36 E
Korostyshev, Ukraine ... 59 G5 50 19N 29 4 E
Korotoyak, Russia ... 59 G10 51 1N 39 2 E
Korovou, Fiji ... 133 A2 17 47 S 178 32 E
Koroyanitu Nat. Heritage Park △, Fiji ... 133 A1 17 40 S 177 50 E
Korraraika, Helodrano' i, Madag. ... 117 B7 17 45 S 43 57 E
Korsakov, Russia ... 67 E15 46 36N 142 42 E
Korsberga, Sweden ... 17 G9 57 19N 15 1 E
Korshunovo, Russia ... 67 D12 58 37N 110 10 E
Korsør, Denmark ... 17 J5 55 20N 11 9 E
Korsze, Poland ... 54 D8 54 11N 21 9 E
Korti, Sudan ... 106 D3 18 6N 31 33 E
Kortrijk, Belgium ... 24 D3 50 50N 3 17 E
Korucu, Turkey ... 49 B9 39 28N 27 22 E
Korumburra, Australia ... 129 E6 38 26 S 145 50 E
Korwai, India ... 92 G8 24 7N 78 5 E
Koryakskoye Nagorye, Russia ... 67 C18 61 0N 171 0 E
Koryŏng, S. Korea ... 75 G15 35 44N 128 15 E
Koryukovka, Ukraine ... 59 G6 51 46N 32 16 E
Kos, Greece ... 49 E9 36 50N 27 15 E
Kosa, Ethiopia ... 107 F4 7 50N 36 50 E
Kosa, Russia ... 64 A5 60 11N 55 51 E
Kosa →, Russia ... 64 A5 59 56N 55 0 E
Kosai, Japan ... 73 C9 34 42N 137 32 E
Kosaya Gora, Russia ... 58 E9 54 10N 37 30 E
Koschagyl, Kazakhstan ... 57 E9 46 40N 54 0 E
Kościan, Poland ... 55 F3 52 5N 16 40 E
Kościerzyna, Poland ... 54 D4 54 8N 17 59 E
Kosciusko, U.S.A. ... 155 J10 33 4N 89 35W
Kosciusko Nat. Park △, Australia ... 129 D8 36 30 S 148 20 E
Kosciuszko, Mt., Australia ... 129 D8 36 27 S 148 16 E
Kösély →, Hungary ... 52 C6 47 25N 21 5 E
Kosgi, Andhra Pradesh, India ... 94 F3 16 58N 77 43 E
Kosgi, Andhra Pradesh, India ... 95 G3 15 51N 77 16 E
Kosha, Sudan ... 106 C3 20 50N 30 30 E
Koshava, Bulgaria ... 50 B7 44 4N 23 2 E
Koshigaya, Japan ... 73 B11 35 54N 139 48 E
K'oshih = Kashi, China ... 65 D8 39 30N 76 2 E
Koshiki-Rettō, Japan ... 72 F1 31 45N 129 49 E
Koshkonong L., U.S.A. ... 157 B8 42 52N 88 58W
Kōshoku, Japan ... 73 A10 36 38N 138 6 E
Koshrabad, Uzbekistan ... 65 C4 40 18N 66 32 E
Kosi, India ... 92 F7 27 48N 77 29 E
Kosi →, India ... 93 E8 28 41N 78 57 E
Košice, Slovak Rep. ... 35 C14 48 42N 21 15 E
Kosjerić, Serbia, Yug. ... 50 B3 44 0N 19 55 E
Kŏsk, Turkey ... 49 D10 37 50N 28 3 E
Koskinoú, Greece ... 38 E12 36 23N 28 13 E
Koslan, Russia ... 56 B8 63 34N 49 14 E
Koslin = Koszalin, Poland ... 54 D3 54 11N 16 8 E
Košong, N. Korea ... 75 E15 38 40N 128 22 E
Kosovo □, Yugoslavia ... 50 D5 42 30N 21 0 E
Kosovo Polje, Kosovo, Yug. ... 50 D5 42 40N 21 5 E
Kosovska Kamenica, Kosovo, Yug. ... 50 D5 42 35N 21 35 E
Kosovska Mitrovica, Kosovo, Yug. ... 50 D4 42 54N 20 52 E
Kosrap, China ... 65 E8 38 0N 76 12 E
Kossou, L. de, Ivory C. ... 112 D3 6 59N 5 31W
Kosta, Sweden ... 17 H9 56 51N 15 24 E
Kostajnica, Croatia ... 45 C13 45 17N 16 30 E
Kostanjevica, Slovenia ... 45 C12 45 51N 15 27 E
Kostenets, Bulgaria ... 50 D7 42 15N 23 52 E
Koster, S. Africa ... 116 D4 25 52 S 26 54 E
Kôstî, Sudan ... 107 E3 13 8N 32 43 E
Kostinbrod, Bulgaria ... 50 D7 42 49N 23 13 E
Kostolac, Serbia, Yug. ... 50 B5 44 37N 21 15 E
Kostopil, Ukraine ... 59 G4 50 51N 26 22 E
Kostroma, Russia ... 58 D11 57 50N 40 58 E
Kostromskoye Vdkhr., Russia ... 58 D11 57 52N 40 49 E
Kostrzyn, Lubuskie, Poland ... 55 F1 52 35N 14 39 E
Kostrzyn, Wielkopolskie, Poland ... 55 F4 52 24N 17 14 E
Kostyantynivka, Ukraine ... 59 H9 48 32N 37 39 E
Kostyukovichi = Kastsyukovichy, Belarus ... 58 F7 53 20N 32 4 E
Koszalin, Poland ... 54 D3 54 11N 16 8 E
Kőszeg, Hungary ... 52 C1 47 23N 16 33 E
Kot Addu, Pakistan ... 91 C3 30 30N 71 0 E
Kot Kapura, Pakistan ... 92 D6 30 35N 74 50 E
Kot Moman, Pakistan ... 92 C5 32 13N 73 0 E
Kot Sultan, Pakistan ... 92 D4 30 46N 70 56 E
Kota, India ... 92 G6 25 14N 75 49 E
Kota Baharu, Malaysia ... 87 J4 6 7N 102 14 E
Kota Barrage, India ... 92 G6 25 6N 75 51 E
Kota Belud, Malaysia ... 85 A5 6 21N 116 26 E
Kota Kinabalu, Malaysia ... 85 A5 6 0N 116 4 E
Kota Kubu Baharu, Malaysia ... 87 L3 3 34N 101 39 E
Kota Tinggi, Malaysia ... 87 M4 1 44N 103 53 E
Kotaagung, Indonesia ... 84 D2 5 38 S 104 29 E
Kotabaru, Indonesia ... 85 C5 3 20 S 116 20 E
Kotabumi, Indonesia ... 84 D2 4 49 S 104 54 E
Kotagede, Indonesia ... 83 G14 7 54 S 110 26 E
Kotamobagu, Indonesia ... 82 A2 0 57N 124 31 E
Kotapad, India ... 94 E6 19 9N 82 21 E
Kotawaringin, Indonesia ... 85 C4 2 28 S 111 27 E
Kotcho L., Canada ... 142 B4 59 7N 121 12W
Kotdwara, India ... 93 E8 29 45N 78 32 E
Kotel, Bulgaria ... 51 D10 42 52N 26 26 E
Kotelnich, Russia ... 60 A9 58 22N 48 24 E
Kotelnikovo, Russia ... 61 G6 47 38N 43 8 E
Kotelnyy, Ostrov, Russia ... 67 B14 75 10N 139 0 E
Kothagudam, India ... 94 F5 17 30N 80 40 E
Kothapet, India ... 94 E4 19 21N 79 28 E
Kothari →, India ... 92 G6 25 20N 75 4 E
Köthen, Germany ... 30 D7 51 45N 11 59 E
Kothi, Chhattisgarh, India ... 93 H10 23 21N 82 3 E
Kothi, Mad. P., India ... 93 G9 24 45N 80 40 E
Kotiro, Pakistan ... 92 F2 26 17N 67 13 E
Kotka, Finland ... 15 F22 60 28N 26 58 E
Kotlas, Russia ... 56 B8 61 17N 46 43 E
Kotlenska Planina, Bulgaria ... 51 D10 42 56N 26 30 E
Kotli, Pakistan ... 92 C5 33 30N 73 55 E
Kotlik, U.S.A. ... 144 F7 63 2N 163 33W
Kotma, India ... 93 H9 23 12N 81 58 E
Kotmul, Pakistan ... 93 B6 35 32N 75 10 E
Kotonu, Japan ... 72 C4 34 11N 133 49 E
Koton-Karifi, Nigeria ... 113 D6 9 0N 6 48 E
Kotor, Montenegro, Yug. ... 50 D3 42 25N 18 47 E
Kotor Varoš, Bos.-H. ... 52 F2 44 38N 17 22 E
Kotoriba, Croatia ... 45 B13 46 23N 16 48 E
Kotovo, Russia ... 60 C7 50 22N 44 45 E
Kotovsk, Russia ... 60 D5 52 36N 41 32 E
Kotovsk, Ukraine ... 59 H5 47 45N 29 35 E
Kotputli, India ... 92 F7 27 43N 76 12 E
Kotri, Pakistan ... 91 D3 25 22N 68 22 E
Kotri →, India ... 94 E5 19 15N 80 35 E
Kótronas, Greece ... 48 E4 36 38N 22 29 E
Kötschach-Mauthen, Austria ... 34 E6 46 41N 13 1 E
Kottayam, India ... 95 K3 9 35N 76 33 E
Kotturu, India ... 95 G3 14 45N 76 10 E
Kotto →, C.A.R. ... 114 B4 4 14N 22 2 E
Kotuy →, Russia ... 67 B11 71 54N 102 6 E
Kottur, India ... 95 J3 10 34N 76 56 E

Kotu Group, *Tonga* .... 133 Q14 20 0 S 173 35 E
Kotuy →, *Russia* .... 67 B11 71 54N 102 6 E
Kotzebue, *U.S.A.* 144 C7 66 53N 162 39W
Kotzebue Sound, *U.S.A.* 144 C7 66 20N 163 0W
Kouango, *C.A.R.* .... 114 B4 5 0N 20 10 E
Kouchibouguac Nat. Park △, *Canada* 141 C6 46 50N 65 20W
Koudougou, *Burkina Faso* 112 C4 12 10N 2 20W
Koufonísi, *Greece* .... 39 F7 34 56N 26 8 E
Koufonísia, *Greece* .... 49 E7 36 57N 25 35 E
Kougaberge, *S. Africa* .... 116 E3 33 48 S 23 50 E
Kouibli, *Ivory C.* 112 D3 7 15N 7 14W
Kouilou →, *Congo* .... 115 C2 4 10 S 12 5 E
Koukl = Kulen, *Cambodia* .... 86 F5 13 50N 104 40 E
Koula Moutou, *Gabon* .... 114 C2 1 15 S 12 25 E
Koulen = Kulen, *Cambodia* .... 86 F5 13 50N 104 40 E
Koulikoro, *Mali* 112 C3 12 40N 7 50W
Kouloúra, *Greece* .... 38 B9 39 42N 19 54 E
Koúm-bournoú, Ákra, *Greece* .... 38 E12 36 15N 28 11 E
Koumac, *N. Cal.* .... 133 T18 20 33 S 164 17 E
Koumala, *Australia* .... 126 C4 21 38 S 149 15 E
Koumameveng, *Gabon* .... 114 B2 0 11N 11 51 E
Koumankou, *Mali* 112 C3 11 58N 6 6W
Koumbia, *Burkina Faso* 112 C4 11 10N 3 50W
Koumbia, *Guinea* 112 C2 11 48N 13 29W
Koumboum, *Guinea* 112 C2 10 25N 13 0W
Koumra, *Chad* .... 109 G3 8 50N 17 35 E
Koun-Fao, *Ivory C.* 112 D4 7 30N 3 15W
Koundara, *Guinea* 112 C2 12 29N 13 18W
Koundé, *C.A.R.* .... 114 A2 7 6N 14 38 E
Koundian, *Guinea* 112 C3 13 10N 10 35W
Koungheul, *Senegal* 112 C2 14 0N 14 50W
Koungoulou, *Congo* .... 114 C2 3 31 S 13 20 E
Kounradskiy, *Kazakhstan* .... 66 E8 46 59N 75 0 E
Kountze, *U.S.A.* 155 K7 30 22N 94 19W
Koupéla, *Burkina Faso* 113 C4 12 11N 0 21W
Kourémalé, *Mali* 112 C3 11 59N 8 42W
Kouris →, *Cyprus* .... 39 F8 34 38N 32 54 E
Kourizo, P. de, *Chad* .... 108 D3 22 28N 15 27 E
Kourou, *Fr. Guiana* 169 B7 5 9N 52 39W
Kourouba, *Mali* 112 C3 13 22N 10 57W
Kouroukoto, *Mali* 112 C2 12 35N 10 5W
Kourouma, *Burkina Faso* 112 C4 11 35N 4 50W
Kourouninkoto, *Mali* 112 C3 13 52N 9 53W
Kouroussa, *Guinea* 112 C3 10 45N 9 45W
Koussanar, *Senegal* 112 C2 13 52N 14 5W
Koussané, *Mali* 112 C2 14 53N 11 14W
Koussane, *Senegal* 112 C2 14 10N 12 22W
Kousseri, *Cameroon* .... 109 F2 12 0N 14 55 E
Koutiala, *Mali* 112 C3 12 25N 5 23W
Kouto, *Ivory C.* 112 D3 9 53N 6 25W
Kouts, *U.S.A.* 157 C9 41 19N 87 2W
Kouvé, *Togo* .... 113 D5 6 25N 1 25 E
Kouyi, *Congo* .... 114 C2 2 29 S 12 25 E
Kouyou →, *Congo* .... 114 C3 0 44 S 16 38 E
Kovačica, *Serbia, Yug.* .... 52 E5 45 5N 20 38 E
Kovdor, *Russia* .... 56 A5 67 34N 30 24 E
Kovel, *Ukraine* .... 59 G3 51 11N 24 38 E
Kovilpatti, *India* .... 95 K3 9 10N 77 50 E
Kovin, *Serbia, Yug.* .... 52 F5 44 44N 20 59 E
Kovrov, *Russia* .... 60 B6 56 25N 41 25 E
Kovur, *Andhra Pradesh, India* .... 94 F5 17 3N 81 39 E
Kovur, *Andhra Pradesh, India* .... 95 G5 14 30N 80 1 E
Kowal, *Poland* .... 55 F6 52 32N 19 7 E
Kowalewo Pomorskie, *Poland* .... 55 E5 53 10N 18 52 E
Kowanyama, *Australia* .... 126 B3 15 29 S 141 44 E
Kowlīnī, *Afghan.* .... 65 E2 37 39N 65 58 E
Kowloon, *China* .... 69 G11 22 19N 114 11 E
Kowŏn, *N. Korea* .... 75 E14 39 26N 127 14 E
Kōyama, *Japan* .... 72 F2 31 20N 130 56 E
Köyceğiz, *Turkey* .... 49 E10 36 57N 28 40 E
Köyceğz Gölü, *Turkey* .... 49 E10 36 56N 28 42 E
Koytash, *Uzbekistan* .... 65 C3 40 11N 67 19 E
Koyuk, *U.S.A.* 144 D7 64 56N 161 9W
Koyukuk, *U.S.A.* 144 D8 64 55N 157 32W
Koyukuk →, *U.S.A.* 144 D8 64 55N 157 32W
Koyulhisar, *Turkey* .... 100 B7 40 20N 37 52 E
Koyunyeri, *Turkey* .... 51 F10 40 50N 26 26 E
Koza, *Japan* .... 71 L3 26 19N 127 46 E
Kozak, *Turkey* .... 49 B9 39 15N 27 6 E
Kozan, *Turkey* .... 100 D6 37 26N 35 50 E
Kozáni, *Greece* .... 50 F5 40 19N 21 47 E
Kozáni □, *Greece* .... 50 F5 40 18N 21 45 E
Kozara, *Bos.-H.* .... 45 D14 45 0N 17 0 E
Kozara, Nac. Park △, *Bos.-H.* .... 52 F2 45 0N 17 0 E
Kozarac, *Bos.-H.* .... 45 D13 44 58N 16 48 E
Kozelets, *Ukraine* .... 59 G6 50 55N 31 7 E
Kozelsk, *Russia* .... 58 E8 54 2N 35 48 E
Kozhikode = Calicut, *India* .... 95 J2 11 15N 75 43 E
Kozhva, *Russia* .... 56 A10 65 10N 57 0 E
Koziegłowy, *Poland* .... 55 H6 50 37N 19 8 E
Kozienice, *Poland* .... 55 G8 51 35N 21 34 E
Kozje, *Slovenia* .... 45 B12 46 5N 15 35 E
Kozloduy, *Bulgaria* .... 50 C7 43 45N 23 42 E
Kozlovets, *Bulgaria* .... 51 C9 43 30N 25 20 E
Kozlovka, *Russia* .... 60 C9 55 52N 48 14 E
Kozlu, *Turkey* .... 100 B4 41 26N 31 45 E
Kozluk, *Turkey* .... 101 C9 38 11N 41 31 E
Koźmin, *Poland* .... 55 G4 51 48N 17 27 E
Kozmodemyansk, *Russia* .... 60 B8 56 20N 46 36 E
Kōzu-Shima, *Japan* .... 73 C11 34 13N 139 10 E
Kożuchów, *Poland* .... 55 G2 51 45N 15 31 E
Kozyatyn, *Ukraine* .... 59 H5 49 45N 28 50 E
Kpabia, *Ghana* 113 D4 9 10N 0 20W
Kpalimé, *Togo* .... 113 D5 6 57N 0 44 E
Kpandae, *Ghana* 113 D4 8 30N 0 2W
Kpessi, *Togo* .... 113 D5 8 4N 1 16 E
Kra, Isthmus of = Kra, Kho Khot, *Thailand* .... 87 G2 10 15N 99 30 E
Kra, Kho Khot, *Thailand* .... 87 G2 10 15N 99 30 E
Kra Buri, *Thailand* .... 87 G2 10 22N 98 46 E
Kraai →, *S. Africa* .... 116 E4 30 40 S 26 45 E
Krabi, *Thailand* .... 87 H2 8 4N 98 55 E
Kracheh, *Cambodia* .... 86 F6 12 32N 106 10 E
Kragan, *Indonesia* .... 85 D4 6 43 S 111 38 E
Kragerø, *Norway* .... 18 F6 58 52N 9 25 E
Kragujevac, *Serbia, Yug.* .... 50 B4 44 2N 20 56 E
Krajenka, *Poland* .... 55 E3 53 18N 16 59 E
Krajina, *Bos.-H.* .... 45 D13 44 45N 16 35 E
Krakatau = Rakata, Pulau, *Indonesia* .... 84 D3 6 10 S 105 20 E
Krakatoa = Rakata, Pulau, *Indonesia* .... 84 D3 6 10 S 105 20 E
Krakor, *Cambodia* .... 86 F5 12 32N 104 12 E
Kraków, *Poland* .... 55 H6 50 4N 19 57 E
Kraków ✈ (KRK), *Poland* .... 55 H6 50 5N 19 52 E
Kraksaan, *Indonesia* .... 84 D3 7 43 S 113 23 E
Kralanh, *Cambodia* .... 86 F4 13 35N 103 25 E
Králíky, *Czech Rep.* .... 35 A9 50 6N 16 45 E
Kraljevo, *Serbia, Yug.* .... 50 C4 43 44N 20 41 E
Královéhradecký □, *Czech Rep.* .... 34 A8 50 25N 15 50 E
Královský Chlmec, *Slovak Rep.* .... 35 C14 48 27N 22 0 E
Kralupy nad Vltavou, *Czech Rep.* .... 34 A7 50 13N 14 20 E
Kramatorsk, *Ukraine* .... 59 H9 48 50N 37 30 E
Kramfors, *Sweden* .... 16 B11 62 55N 17 48 E
Kramis, C., *Algeria* .... 111 A5 36 26N 0 45 E
Kraniá, *Greece* .... 50 G5 39 53N 21 18 E
Kranía Elassónas, *Greece* .... 48 B4 39 57N 22 2 E
Kranídhion, *Greece* .... 48 D5 37 20N 23 10 E
Kranj, *Slovenia* .... 45 B11 46 16N 14 22 E
Kranjska Gora, *Slovenia* .... 45 B10 46 29N 13 48 E
Krapina, *Croatia* .... 45 B11 46 10N 15 52 E
Krapina →, *Croatia* .... 45 C12 45 50N 15 50 E
Krapkowice, *Poland* .... 55 H4 50 29N 17 56 E

Kras, *Croatia* .... 45 C10 45 35N 14 0 E
Krasavino, *Russia* .... 56 B8 60 58N 46 29 E
Krashyy Klyuch, *Russia* .... 64 D6 55 23N 56 39 E
Kraskino, *Russia* .... 67 E14 42 44N 130 48 E
Kräslava, *Latvia* .... 58 E4 55 54N 27 10 E
Kraslice, *Czech Rep.* .... 34 A5 50 19N 12 31 E
Krasnaya Gorbatka, *Russia* .... 60 C5 55 52N 41 45 E
Krasnaya Polyana, *Russia* .... 61 J5 43 40N 40 13 E
Kraśnik, *Poland* .... 55 H9 50 55N 22 15 E
Krasnoarmeisk, *Ukraine* .... 59 H9 48 18N 37 11 E
Krasnoarmeysk, *Russia* .... 60 E7 51 0N 45 42 E
Krasnoarmeyskiy, *Russia* .... 61 G6 47 0N 42 12 E
Krasnobrod, *Poland* .... 55 H10 50 33N 23 12 E
Krasnodar, *Russia* .... 61 H4 45 5N 39 0 E
Krasnodon, *Ukraine* .... 59 H10 48 17N 39 44 E
Krasnogorskiy, *Russia* .... 60 B9 56 10N 48 28 E
Krasnograd = Krasnohrad, *Ukraine* .... 59 H8 49 27N 35 27 E
Krasnogvardeysk = Bulungur, *Uzbekistan* .... 65 D3 39 46N 67 16 E
Krasnogvardeyskoye, *Russia* .... 61 H5 45 52N 41 33 E
Krasnogvardyesk, *Ukraine* .... 59 K8 45 32N 34 16 E
Krasnohrad, *Ukraine* .... 59 H8 49 27N 35 27 E
Krasnokamsk, *Russia* .... 64 B5 58 4N 55 48 E
Krasnokutsk, *Ukraine* .... 59 G8 50 10N 34 50 E
Krasnolesnyy, *Russia* .... 59 G10 51 53N 39 35 E
Krasnoperekopsk, *Ukraine* .... 59 J7 46 0N 33 54 E
Krasnorechenskiy, *Russia* .... 70 B7 44 41N 135 14 E
Krasnoselkup, *Russia* .... 66 C9 65 20N 82 10 E
Krasnoslobodsk, *Mordvinia, Russia* .... 60 C6 54 25N 43 45 E
Krasnoslobodsk, *Volgograd, Russia* .... 61 F7 48 42N 44 33 E
Krasnoturinsk, *Russia* .... 64 B8 59 46N 60 12 E
Krasnoufimsk, *Russia* .... 64 C6 56 36N 57 38 E
Krasnouralsk, *Russia* .... 64 B8 58 21N 60 3 E
Krasnousolskiy, *Russia* .... 64 C6 53 54N 56 27 E
Krasnovishersk, *Russia* .... 64 A6 60 23N 57 3 E
Krasnovodsk = Türkmenbashi, *Turkmenistan* .... 57 G9 40 5N 53 5 E
Krasnoyarsk, *Russia* .... 67 D10 56 8N 93 0 E
Krasnoyarskiy, *Russia* .... 64 F7 51 58N 59 55 E
Krasnoye = Krasnyy, *Russia* .... 58 E6 54 25N 31 30 E
Krasnoye, *Russia* .... 64 B1 59 15N 47 40 E
Krasnozavodsk, *Russia* .... 58 D10 56 27N 38 25 E
Krasny Sulin, *Russia* .... 59 J11 47 52N 40 8 E
Krasnystaw, *Poland* .... 55 H10 50 57N 23 5 E
Krasnyy, *Russia* .... 58 E6 54 25N 31 30 E
Krasnyy Kholm, *Orenburg, Russia* .... 64 F5 51 35N 54 9 E
Krasnyy Kholm, *Tver, Russia* .... 58 C9 58 10N 37 10 E
Krasnyy Kut, *Russia* .... 60 E8 50 50N 47 0 E
Krasnyy Liman, *Ukraine* .... 59 H9 48 58N 37 50 E
Krasnyy Luch, *Ukraine* .... 59 H10 48 13N 39 0 E
Krasnyy Profintern, *Russia* .... 58 D11 57 45N 40 27 E
Krasnyy Yar, *Astrakhan, Russia* .... 61 G9 46 43N 48 23 E
Krasnyy Yar, *Samara, Russia* .... 60 D10 53 30N 50 22 E
Krasnyy Yar, *Volgograd, Russia* .... 60 E7 50 42N 44 45 E
Krasnyye Baki, *Russia* .... 60 B7 57 8N 45 10 E
Krasnyyoskolske Vdskh., *Ukraine* .... 59 H9 49 27N 37 40 E
Kraszna →, *Hungary* .... 52 B7 48 4N 22 20 E
Kratie = Kracheh, *Cambodia* .... 86 F6 12 32N 106 10 E
Kratke Ra., *Papua N. G.* .... 132 D3 6 45 S 146 0 E
Kratovo, *Macedonia* .... 50 D6 42 6N 22 10 E
Krau, *Indonesia* .... 79 E10 3 19 S 140 5 E
Kraulshavn = Nuussuaq, *Greenland* 10 C5 74 8N 57 5W
Kravanh, Chuor Phnum, *Cambodia* .... 87 G4 12 0N 103 32 E
Kreb es Sefia, *Algeria* 110 C3 27 12N 7 11W
Kreb n-Naga, *Algeria* 110 C3 27 3N 7 9W
Kreb n-Neggar, *Algeria* 110 C3 27 20N 7 15W
Krefeld, *Germany* .... 30 D2 51 20N 6 33 E
Krémaston, Límni, *Greece* .... 48 C3 38 52N 21 30 E
Kremen, *Croatia* .... 45 D12 44 28N 15 53 E
Kremenchuk, *Ukraine* .... 59 H7 49 5N 33 25 E
Kremenchuksk Vdskh., *Ukraine* .... 59 H7 49 20N 32 30 E
Kremenets, *Ukraine* .... 59 G3 50 8N 25 43 E
Kremennaya, *Ukraine* .... 59 H10 49 1N 38 10 E
Kremges = Svitlovodsk, *Ukraine* .... 59 H7 49 5N 33 24 E
Kremmen, *Germany* .... 30 C9 52 45N 13 1 E
Kremmling, *U.S.A.* 158 F10 40 4N 106 24W
Kremnica, *Slovak Rep.* .... 35 C11 48 45N 18 50 E
Krems, *Austria* .... 34 C8 48 25N 15 36 E
Kremsmünster, *Austria* .... 34 C7 48 3N 14 8 E
Kretinga, *Lithuania* .... 15 J19 55 53N 21 15 E
Krettamia, *Algeria* 110 C4 28 47N 3 27W
Krettsy, *Russia* .... 58 C7 58 15N 32 30 E
Kreuzberg, *Germany* .... 31 E5 50 22N 9 58 E
Kreuzlingen, *Switz.* .... 33 A8 47 38N 9 10 E
Kreuztal, *Germany* .... 30 E4 50 57N 8 0 E
Kría Vrísi, *Greece* .... 50 F6 40 41N 22 18 E
Kribi, *Cameroon* .... 113 E6 2 57N 9 56 E
Krichem, *Bulgaria* .... 51 D8 42 8N 24 28 E
Krichev = Krychaw, *Belarus* .... 58 F6 53 40N 31 41 E
Kriens, *Switz.* .... 33 B6 47 2N 8 17 E
Krim, *Slovenia* .... 45 C11 45 53N 14 30 E
Krim-Krim, *Chad* .... 109 G3 9 0N 15 24 E
Kriós, Ákra, *Greece* .... 39 E4 35 13N 23 34 E
Krishna →, *India* .... 95 G5 15 57N 80 59 E
Krishnagiri, *India* .... 95 H4 12 32N 78 16 E
Krishnanagar, *India* .... 93 H13 23 24N 88 33 E
Krishnaraja Sagara, *India* .... 95 H3 12 20N 76 30 E
Kristdala, *Sweden* .... 17 G10 57 24N 16 13 E
Kristiansand, *Norway* .... 18 F5 58 8N 8 1 E
Kristianstad, *Sweden* .... 17 H8 56 2N 14 9 E
Kristiansund, *Norway* .... 18 A4 63 7N 7 45 E
Kristiinankaupunki, *Finland* .... 15 E19 62 16N 21 21 E
Kristinehamn, *Sweden* .... 16 E8 59 18N 14 7 E
Kristinestad = Kristiinankaupunki, *Finland* .... 15 E19 62 16N 21 21 E
Krithotí, Ákra, *Greece* .... 39 B3 38 30N 21 2 E
Kríti, *Greece* .... 39 E6 35 15N 25 0 E
Kritsá, *Greece* .... 39 E6 35 10N 25 41 E
Kriva →, *Macedonia* .... 50 D5 42 5N 21 47 E
Kriva Palanka, *Macedonia* .... 50 D6 42 11N 22 19 E
Krivaja →, *Bos.-H.* .... 52 F3 44 27N 18 9 E
Krivelj, *Serbia, Yug.* .... 50 B6 44 10N 22 5 E
Křivoklátsko □, *Czech Rep.* .... 34 A6 50 1N 13 51 E
Krivoy Rog = Kryvyy Rih, *Ukraine* .... 59 J7 47 51N 33 20 E
Křiževci, *Croatia* .... 45 B13 46 3N 16 32 E
Krk, *Croatia* .... 45 C11 45 8N 14 40 E
Krka →, *Slovenia* .... 45 C12 45 50N 15 30 E
Krka, Nac. Park △, *Croatia* .... 45 E12 43 53N 15 56 E
Krknoše, *Czech Rep.* .... 34 A8 50 50N 15 35 E
Krkonoše Národní Park △, *Czech Rep.* .... 34 A8 50 43N 15 39 E
Krnov, *Czech Rep.* .... 35 A10 50 5N 17 40 E
Krobia, *Poland* .... 55 G3 51 47N 16 59 E
Krøderen, *Norway* .... 18 D6 60 9N 9 49 E
Krokeaí, *Greece* .... 48 E4 36 53N 22 32 E
Krokek, *Sweden* .... 17 F10 58 40N 16 24 E
Krokodil →, *Mozam.* .... 117 D5 25 14 S 32 18 E
Krokom, *Sweden* .... 16 A8 63 20N 14 30 E
Krokowa, *Poland* .... 54 D5 54 47N 18 9 E
Króksfjarðarnes, *Iceland* 11 B5 65 27N 21 56W
Krokstadelva, *Norway* .... 18 E7 59 56N 10 1 E
Krolevets, *Ukraine* .... 59 G7 51 35N 33 20 E
Kroměříž, *Czech Rep.* .... 35 C9 49 18N 17 21 E
Krompachy, *Slovak Rep.* .... 35 C13 48 54N 20 52 E
Kromy, *Russia* .... 59 F8 52 48N 35 48 E
Kronach, *Germany* .... 31 E7 50 14N 11 19 E
Krong Kaoh Kong, *Cambodia* .... 78 B2 11 35N 103 0 E
Kronobergs län □, *Sweden* .... 17 H8 56 45N 14 30 E
Kronprins Christian Land, *Greenland* 10 A8 80 30N 22 0W
Kronprins Frederik Land, *Greenland* 10 B5 79 0N 55 0W
Kronshtadt, *Russia* .... 58 C5 59 57N 29 51 E
Kronprins Olav Kyst, *Antarctica* .... 7 C5 69 0 S 42 0 E
Kroonstad, *S. Africa* .... 116 D4 27 43 S 27 19 E
Kröpelin, *Germany* .... 30 A7 54 4N 11 47 E

Kropotkin, *Russia* .... 61 H5 45 28N 40 28 E
Kropp, *Germany* .... 30 A5 54 24N 9 31 E
Krosna, *Lithuania* .... 54 D10 54 23N 23 33 E
Krośniewice, *Poland* .... 55 F6 55 5N 19 11 E
Krosno, *Poland* .... 55 J8 49 42N 21 46 E
Krosno Odrzańskie, *Poland* .... 55 F2 52 3N 15 7 E
Krotoszyn, *Poland* .... 55 G4 51 42N 17 23 E
Krotovka, *Russia* .... 60 D10 53 18N 51 10 E
Kroussón, *Greece* .... 39 E5 35 13N 24 59 E
Krrabë, *Albania* .... 50 E3 41 13N 20 0 E
Krško, *Slovenia* .... 45 C12 45 57N 15 30 E
Krstača, *Serbia, Yug.* .... 50 D4 42 57N 20 8 E
Kruger Nat. Park △, *S. Africa* .... 117 C5 24 50 S 31 40 E
Krugersdorp, *S. Africa* .... 117 D4 26 5 S 27 46 E
Kruisfontein, *S. Africa* .... 116 E3 33 59 S 24 43 E
Krujë, *Albania* .... 50 E3 41 32N 19 46 E
Krulevshchina = Krulyewshchyna, *Belarus* .... 58 E4 55 5N 27 45 E
Krulyewshchyna, *Belarus* .... 58 E4 55 5N 27 45 E
Krumbach, *Germany* .... 31 G6 48 13N 10 22 E
Krumë, *Albania* .... 50 D4 42 14N 20 28 E
Krumovgrad, *Bulgaria* .... 51 E9 41 29N 25 38 E
Krung Thep = Bangkok, *Thailand* .... 86 F3 13 45N 100 35 E
Krupanj, *Serbia, Yug.* .... 50 B3 44 25N 19 22 E
Krupina, *Slovak Rep.* .... 35 C12 48 22N 19 5 E
Krupinica →, *Slovak Rep.* .... 35 C11 48 4N 18 55 E
Krupki, *Belarus* .... 58 E5 54 19N 29 8 E
Krusenstern, C., *U.S.A.* 144 C7 67 0N 163 45W
Kruševac, *Serbia, Yug.* .... 50 C5 43 35N 21 28 E
Kruševo, *Macedonia* .... 50 E5 41 23N 21 19 E
Kruszwica, *Poland* .... 55 F5 52 40N 18 20 E
Krychaw, *Belarus* .... 58 F6 53 40N 31 41 E
Krymsk, *Russia* .... 59 K10 44 50N 38 0 E
Krymskiy Poluostrov = Krymskyy Pivostriv, *Ukraine* .... 59 K8 45 0N 34 0 E
Krymskyy Pivostriv, *Ukraine* .... 59 K8 45 0N 34 0 E
Krynica, *Poland* .... 55 J7 49 25N 20 57 E
Krynica Morska, *Poland* .... 54 D6 54 23N 19 25 E
Krynki, *Poland* .... 55 E10 53 17N 23 43 E
Kryvyy Rih, *Ukraine* .... 59 J7 47 51N 33 20 E
Krzepice, *Poland* .... 55 H5 50 58N 18 50 E
Krzeszów, *Poland* .... 55 H10 50 24N 22 21 E
Krzna →, *Poland* .... 55 F10 52 8N 23 32 E
Krzywiń, *Poland* .... 55 G3 51 58N 16 50 E
Krzyż Wielkopolski, *Poland* .... 55 F2 52 52N 16 0 E
Ksabi, *Morocco* 110 B4 32 51N 4 13W
Ksar Chellala, *Algeria* .... 111 A5 35 13N 2 19 E
Ksar el Boukhari, *Algeria* .... 110 B5 35 51N 2 52 E
Ksar el Kebir, *Morocco* 110 B3 35 0N 6 0W
Ksar es Souk = Er Rachidia, *Morocco* 110 B4 31 58N 4 20W
Ksar Rhilane, *Tunisia* .... 108 B1 33 0N 9 39 E
Ksiąz Wielkopolski, *Poland* .... 55 F4 52 4N 17 8 E
Ksour, Mts. des, *Algeria* 111 B4 32 45N 0 30W
Kstovo, *Russia* .... 60 B7 56 12N 44 13 E
Ku, W. el →, *Sudan* .... 107 E2 13 37N 25 15 E
Ku-Ring-Gai Chase Nat. Park △, *Australia* .... 129 B9 33 39 S 151 14 E
Ku Tree Reservoir, *U.S.A.* 145 K14 21 30N 157 59W
Kuah, *Malaysia* .... 87 J2 6 19N 99 51 E
Kuala Belait, *Malaysia* .... 84 B3 4 35N 114 11 E
Kuala Berang, *Malaysia* .... 87 K4 5 5N 103 1 E
Kuala Dungun = Dungun, *Malaysia* .... 87 K4 4 45N 103 25 E
Kuala Kangsar, *Malaysia* .... 87 K3 4 46N 100 56 E
Kuala Kelawang, *Malaysia* .... 87 L4 2 56N 102 5 E
Kuala Kerai, *Malaysia* .... 87 K4 5 30N 102 12 E
Kuala Kerian, *Malaysia* .... 87 c 5 10N 100 25 E
Kuala Lipis, *Malaysia* .... 87 K4 4 10N 102 3 E
Kuala Lumpur, *Malaysia* .... 87 L3 3 9N 101 41 E
Kuala Nerang, *Malaysia* .... 87 J3 6 16N 100 37 E
Kuala Pilah, *Malaysia* .... 87 L4 2 45N 102 15 E
Kuala Rompin, *Malaysia* .... 87 L4 2 49N 103 29 E
Kuala Selangor, *Malaysia* .... 87 L3 3 20N 101 15 E
Kuala Sepetang, *Malaysia* .... 87 K3 4 49N 100 28 E
Kuala Terengganu, *Malaysia* .... 87 K4 5 20N 103 8 E
Kualajelai, *Indonesia* .... 85 C4 2 58 S 110 46 E
Kualakapuas, *Indonesia* .... 85 C4 2 55 S 114 20 E
Kualakurun, *Indonesia* .... 85 C4 1 10 S 113 50 E
Kualapembuang, *Indonesia* .... 85 C4 3 14 S 112 38 E
Kualasimpang, *Indonesia* .... 84 B1 4 17N 98 3 E
Kualoa Pt., *U.S.A.* 145 J14 21 31N 157 50W
Kuamut, *Malaysia* .... 85 A5 5 13N 117 30 E
Kuancheng, *China* .... 75 D10 40 37N 118 30 E
Kuandang, *Indonesia* .... 82 A2 0 56N 123 1 E
Kuandian, *China* .... 75 D13 40 45N 124 45 E
Kuangchou = Guangzhou, *China* .... 77 F9 23 5N 113 10 E
Kuanshan, *Taiwan* .... 77 F13 23 2N 121 3 E
Kuantan, *Malaysia* .... 87 L4 3 49N 103 20 E
Kuapa Pond, *U.S.A.* 145 K14 21 17N 157 43W
Kuba = Quba, *Azerbaijan* .... 61 K9 41 21N 48 32 E
Kuban →, *Russia* .... 59 K9 45 20N 37 30 E
Kuban Lowlands = Prikubanskaya Nizmennost, *Russia* .... 61 H4 45 30N 38 33 E
Kubenskoye, Ozero, *Russia* .... 58 C10 59 40N 39 25 E
Kublis, *Switz.* .... 33 C9 46 54N 9 45 E
Kubokawa, *Japan* .... 72 E3 33 12N 133 8 E
Kubor, Mt., *Papua N. G.* .... 132 D3 6 10 S 144 44 E
Kubrat, *Bulgaria* .... 51 C10 43 49N 26 31 E
Kubu, *Indonesia* .... 79 J18 8 16 S 115 35 E
Kubutambahan, *Indonesia* .... 79 J18 8 5 S 115 10 E
Kucar, Tanjung, *Indonesia* .... 79 K18 8 39 S 114 34 E
Kučevo, *Serbia, Yug.* .... 50 B5 44 30N 21 40 E
Kucha Gompa, *India* .... 93 B7 34 25N 76 56 E
Kuchaman, *India* .... 92 F6 27 13N 74 47 E
Kuchchaveli, *Sri Lanka* .... 95 K5 8 49N 81 6 E
Kuchinda, *India* .... 95 A3 47 7N 10 12 E
Kuchenspitze, *Austria* .... 93 H11 21 44N 84 21 E
Kuchinda, *Malaysia* .... 85 B4 1 33N 110 25 E
Kuchino-eruba-Jima, *Japan* .... 71 J5 30 28N 130 12 E
Kuchino-Shima, *Japan* .... 71 K4 29 57N 129 55 E
Kuchinotsu, *Japan* .... 72 E2 32 36N 130 11 E
Kuchl, *Austria* .... 34 D6 47 37N 13 9 E
Küchnay Darvīshān, *Afghan.* .... 92 D3 30 59N 64 10 E
Kucing = Kuching, *Malaysia* .... 85 B4 1 33N 110 25 E
Kuçovë, *Albania* .... 50 F3 40 47N 19 57 E
Küçükbahçe, *Turkey* .... 49 C8 38 33N 26 24 E
Küçükköy, *Turkey* .... 49 B9 39 16N 26 42 E
Küçükkuyu, *Turkey* .... 49 B8 39 32N 26 36 E
Küçükmenderes →, *Turkey* .... 49 D9 37 57N 27 16 E
Kud →, *Pakistan* .... 92 F2 26 5N 66 20 E
Kudal, *India* .... 95 F1 16 2N 73 41 E
Kudalier →, *India* .... 94 C4 18 35N 79 48 E
Kudamatsu, *Japan* .... 72 D3 34 0N 131 52 E
Kudara, *Tajikistan* .... 65 D6 38 21N 72 37 E
Kudat, *Malaysia* .... 85 A5 6 55N 116 55 E
Kudirkos Naumiestis, *Lithuania* .... 54 D9 54 46N 22 53 E
Kudowa-Zdrój, *Poland* .... 55 H3 50 27N 16 15 E
Kudremukh, *India* .... 95 H2 13 15N 75 20 E
Kudus, *Indonesia* .... 85 D4 6 48 S 110 51 E
Kudymkar, *Russia* .... 56 C3 59 1N 54 39 E
Kueiyang = Guiyang, *China* .... 76 D6 26 32N 106 40 E
Kufra Oasis = Al Kufrah, *Libya* .... 107 D3 24 17N 23 15 E
Kufstein, *Austria* .... 34 D5 47 35N 12 11 E
Kuglugtuk, *Canada* 138 B8 67 50N 115 5W
Kühak, *Iran* .... 91 D1 27 12N 63 10 E
Kuhan, *Pakistan* .... 92 E2 28 19N 67 14 E
Kühbonān, *Iran* .... 91 D8 31 23N 56 19 E
Kūhestak, *Iran* .... 97 E8 26 47N 57 2 E
Kühestān, *Afghan.* .... 91 A9 34 39N 61 12 E
Kuhin, *Iran* .... 97 B6 36 22N 49 40 E
Kūhīrī, *Iran* .... 97 E9 26 55N 61 2 E

Kuhnsdorf, *Austria* .... 34 E7 46 37N 14 38 E
Kūhpāyeh, *Esfahan, Iran* .... 97 C7 32 44N 52 20 E
Kūhpāyeh, *Kermān, Iran* .... 97 D8 30 35N 57 15 E
Kührān, Kūh-e, *Iran* .... 97 E8 26 46N 58 12 E
Kui Buri, *Thailand* .... 87 F2 12 3N 99 52 E
Kuichong, *China* .... 69 F11 22 38N 114 25 E
Kuiseb →, *Namibia* .... 116 B2 22 59 S 14 31 E
Kuito, *Angola* .... 115 G3 12 22 S 16 55 E
Kuiu I., *U.S.A.* .... 75 E14 39 57N 126 1 E
Kujang, *N. Korea* .... 75 E14 39 57N 126 1 E
Kujawsko-Pomorskie □, *Poland* .... 54 E5 53 20N 18 30 E
Kuji, *Japan* .... 70 D10 40 11N 141 46 E
Kujū-San, *Japan* .... 72 D3 33 5N 131 15 E
Kukavica, *Serbia, Yug.* .... 50 D5 42 48N 21 57 E
Kukawa, *Nigeria* .... 113 C7 12 58N 13 27 E
Kukës, *Albania* .... 50 D4 42 5N 20 27 E
Kuki, *Japan* .... 73 A11 36 4N 139 40 E
Kukipi, *Papua N. G.* .... 132 E4 8 10 S 146 6 E
Kukmor, *Russia* .... 60 B10 56 11N 50 54 E
Kukuihaele, *U.S.A.* 145 C6 20 5N 155 35W
Kukup, *Malaysia* .... 87 d 1 20N 103 27 E
Kukup, Pulau, *Malaysia* .... 87 d 1 18N 103 25 E
Kukvidze, *Russia* .... 60 E6 50 40N 43 0 E
Kula, *Bulgaria* .... 50 C6 43 52N 22 36 E
Kula, *Serbia, Yug.* .... 52 E4 45 37N 19 32 E
Kula, *Turkey* .... 49 C10 38 32N 28 40 E
Kula Gulf, *Solomon Is.* .... 133 M9 8 5 S 157 18 E
Kulachi, *Pakistan* .... 92 D4 31 56N 70 27 E
Kulai, *Malaysia* .... 87 M4 1 44N 103 35 E
Kulaly, Ostrov, *Kazakhstan* .... 61 H10 45 0N 50 0 E
Kulanak, *Kyrgyzstan* .... 65 C7 41 22N 75 30 E
Kulasekarappattinam, *India* .... 95 K4 8 20N 78 5 E
Kulassein I., *Phil.* .... 81 H3 6 25N 120 41 E
Kulaura, *Bangla.* .... 90 C4 24 32N 92 3 E
Kulautuva, *Lithuania* .... 54 D10 54 56N 23 36 E
Kuldīga, *Latvia* .... 15 H19 56 58N 21 59 E
Kuldīga □, *Latvia* .... 54 B8 56 55N 22 0 E
Kuldja = Yining, *China* .... 66 E9 43 58N 81 10 E
Kuldu, *Sudan* .... 107 E2 12 50N 28 30 E
Kulebaki, *Russia* .... 60 C6 55 22N 42 3 E
Kulen, *Cambodia* .... 86 F5 13 50N 104 40 E
Kulen Vakuf, *Bos.-H.* .... 45 D13 44 35N 16 2 E
Kulgam, *India* .... 93 C6 33 36N 75 2 E
Kulgera, *Australia* .... 126 D1 25 50 S 133 18 E
Kulim, *Malaysia* .... 87 K3 5 22N 100 34 E
Kulin, *Australia* .... 125 F2 32 40 S 118 2 E
Kulittalai, *India* .... 95 J4 10 55N 78 25 E
Kullen, *Sweden* .... 17 H6 56 18N 12 26 E
Kulmbach, *Germany* .... 31 E7 50 6N 11 26 E
Kŭlob, *Tajikistan* .... 65 E4 37 55N 69 50 E
Kulp, *Turkey* .... 101 C9 38 29N 41 2 E
Kulpawn →, *Ghana* 113 D4 10 20N 1 5W
Kulsary, *Kazakhstan* .... 57 E9 46 59N 54 1 E
Kulti, *India* .... 93 H12 23 43N 86 50 E
Kulu, *India* .... 92 D7 31 58N 77 6 E
Kulu, *Turkey* .... 100 C5 39 5N 33 4 E
Kulumadau, *Papua N. G.* .... 132 E7 9 3 S 152 43 E
Kulunda, *Russia* .... 66 D8 52 35N 78 57 E
Kulungar, *Afghan.* .... 92 C3 34 0N 69 2 E
Kulwin, *Australia* .... 97 D7 31 21N 54 35 E
Kulwin, *Australia* .... 128 C5 35 0 S 142 42 E
Kulyab = Kŭlob, *Tajikistan* .... 65 E4 37 55N 69 50 E
Kuma, *Japan* .... 72 E3 33 39N 132 54 E
Kuma →, *Russia* .... 61 H8 44 55N 47 0 E
Kumafsarı, *Turkey* .... 49 D11 37 19N 29 32 E
Kumagaya, *Japan* .... 73 A11 36 9N 139 22 E
Kumai, *Indonesia* .... 85 C4 2 44 S 111 43 E
Kumak, *Russia* .... 64 F8 51 10N 60 8 E
Kumalar Dağı, *Turkey* .... 49 C12 38 15N 30 20 E
Kumamba, Kepulauan, *Indonesia* .... 83 B5 1 36 S 138 45 E
Kumamoto, *Japan* .... 72 E2 32 45N 130 45 E
Kumamoto □, *Japan* .... 72 E2 32 55N 130 55 E
Kumano, *Japan* .... 73 D8 33 54N 136 5 E
Kumano-Nada, *Japan* .... 73 D8 33 47N 136 20 E
Kumanovo, *Macedonia* .... 50 D5 42 9N 21 42 E
Kumara, *N.Z.* .... 91 B3 34 30N 70 28 E
Kumara, *N.Z.* .... 131 K3 42 37 S 171 12 E
Kumarina, *Australia* .... 125 D2 24 41 S 119 32 E
Kumarkhali, *Bangla.* .... 90 D2 23 51N 89 15 E
Kumasi, *Ghana* 112 D4 6 41N 1 38W
Kumayri = Gyumri, *Armenia* .... 61 K6 40 47N 43 50 E
Kumba, *Cameroon* .... 113 E6 4 36N 9 24 E
Kumbağ, *Turkey* .... 51 F11 40 51N 27 27 E
Kumbakonam, *India* .... 127 D5 27 15 S 150 55 E
Kumbarilla, *Australia* .... 127 D5 27 15 S 150 55 E
Kumbe, *Indonesia* .... 83 C6 8 21 S 140 13 E
Kumbhraj, *India* .... 92 G7 24 22N 77 3 E
Kumbia, *Australia* .... 127 D5 26 41 S 151 39 E
Kumbo, *Cameroon* .... 113 D7 6 15N 10 36 E
Kumbukkan Oya →, *Sri Lanka* .... 95 L5 6 35N 81 40 E
Kümch'ŏn, *N. Korea* .... 75 E14 38 10N 126 29 E
Kumdah, *Si. Arabia* .... 98 B4 20 23N 30 12 E
Kumdok, *India* .... 93 C8 33 32N 78 10 E
Kume-Shima, *Japan* .... 73 B10 26 20N 126 47 E
Kumeny, *Russia* .... 60 A9 58 10N 49 47 E
Kumertau, *Russia* .... 64 E5 52 45N 55 57 E
Kumharsain, *India* .... 92 D7 31 19N 77 27 E
Kŭmhwa, *S. Korea* .... 75 E14 38 17N 127 28 E
Kumi, *Uganda* .... 118 B3 1 30N 33 58 E
Kumkale, *Turkey* .... 51 G10 39 59N 26 11 E
Kumkurgan = Qumqŭrghan, *Uzbekistan* .... 65 E3 37 49N 67 35 E
Kumla, *Sweden* .... 16 E9 59 8N 15 10 E
Kumluca, *Turkey* .... 49 E12 36 22N 30 20 E
Kummerower See, *Germany* .... 30 B8 53 49N 12 51 E
Kumo, *Nigeria* .... 90 B6 26 30N 97 15 E
Kumon Bum, *Burma* .... 73 B10 35 18N 138 57 E
Kumori-Yama, *Japan* .... 95 G2 14 29N 74 32 E
Kumta, *India* .... 132 E5 9 45 S 148 13 E
Kumukahi, C., *U.S.A.* 145 D7 19 31N 154 49W
Kumusi →, *Papua N. G.* .... 132 E5 9 18 S 148 13 E
Kumylzhenskaya, *Russia* .... 60 F6 49 51N 42 38 E
Kunágota, *Hungary* .... 52 D6 46 26N 21 2 E
Kunak, *Malaysia* .... 85 B5 4 41N 118 15 E
Kunashir, Ostrov, *Russia* .... 67 E15 44 0N 146 0 E
Kunda, *Estonia* .... 15 G22 59 30N 26 34 E
Kunda, *India* .... 93 G9 25 43N 81 31 E
Kundelungu, Parc de △, *Dem. Rep. of the Congo* .... 119 E2 10 30 S 27 40 E
Kundelungu Ouest, Parc Nat. de △, *Dem. Rep. of the Congo* .... 119 D2 9 55 S 27 17 E
Kundian, *Pakistan* .... 92 C4 32 27N 71 28 E
Kundiawa, *Papua N. G.* .... 132 D3 6 2 S 145 1 E
Kundla, *India* .... 92 J4 21 21N 71 25 E
Kundur, *Indonesia* .... 84 C3 3 35 S 107 48 E
Kung, Ao, *Thailand* .... 87 a 8 5N 98 24 E
Kunga →, *Bangla.* .... 90 K2 21 46N 89 30 E
Kungälv, *Sweden* .... 17 G5 57 53N 11 59 E
Kunghit I., *Canada* 142 C2 52 6N 131 3W
Kungrad = Qŭnghirot, *Uzbekistan* .... 65 E3 42 44N 59 7 E
Kungsängen, *Sweden* .... 16 E11 59 29N 17 45 E
Kungsbacka, *Sweden* .... 17 H6 57 30N 12 5 E
Kungsgården, *Sweden* .... 16 D10 60 37N 16 35 E
Kungsör, *Sweden* .... 16 E10 59 25N 16 5 E
Kungur, *Dem. Rep. of the Congo* .... 114 B3 2 47N 19 12 E
Kungur, *Russia* .... 64 C6 57 25N 56 57 E
Kungurri, *Australia* .... 126 K6 21 3 S 148 45 E
Kungyangon, *Burma* .... 90 M7 16 27N 96 20 E
Kunhar →, *Pakistan* .... 93 B5 34 20N 73 30 E

Kunhegyes, Hungary 52 C5 47 22N 20 36 E
Kunia, U.S.A. 145 K13 21 28N 158 4W
Kunimi-Dake, Japan 72 E3 32 33N 131 1 E
Kuningan, Indonesia 85 D3 6 59 S 108 29 E
Kunisaki, Japan 72 D3 33 33N 131 45 E
Kunjirap Daban, Pakistan 65 E7 36 52N 75 27 E
Kunlara, Australia 128 C3 34 54 S 139 55 E
Kunlong, Burma 76 F2 23 20N 98 50 E
Kunlun Shan, Asia 68 C3 36 0N 86 30 E
Kunmadaras, Hungary 52 C5 47 28N 20 45 E
Kunming, China 76 E4 25 1N 102 41 E
Kunnamkulam, India 95 J3 10 38N 76 7 E
Kunów, Poland 55 H8 50 57N 21 17 E
Kunsan, S. Korea 75 G14 35 59N 126 45 E
Kunshan, China 77 B13 31 22N 120 58 E
Kunszentmárton, Hungary 52 D5 46 50N 20 20 E
Kunszentmiklós, Hungary 52 C4 47 2N 19 8 E
Kuntaur, Senegal 112 C2 13 40N 14 48W
Kunua, Papua N. G. 132 C8 5 46 S 154 43 E
Kununurra, Australia 124 C4 15 40 S 128 50 E
Kunwari →, India 93 F8 26 26N 79 11 E
Kunya-Urgench = Köneürgench, Turkmenistan 66 E6 42 19N 59 10 E
Künzelsau, Germany 31 F5 49 17N 9 42 E
Kunzulu, Dem. Rep. of the Congo 114 C3 3 28 S 16 12 E
Kuopio, Finland 14 E22 62 53N 27 35 E
Kupa →, Croatia 45 C13 45 28N 16 24 E
Kupang, Indonesia 82 D2 10 19 S 123 39 E
Kupiano, Papua N. G. 132 F5 10 4 S 148 14 E
Kupreanof I., U.S.A. 142 B2 56 50N 133 30W
Kupres, Bos.-H. 52 G2 43 56N 17 15 E
Kupyansk, Ukraine 59 H9 49 52N 37 35 E
Kupyansk-Uzlovoi, Ukraine 59 H9 49 40N 37 43 E
Kuqa, China 68 B3 41 35N 82 30 E
Kur, Indonesia 83 C4 5 20 S 132 0 E
Kür →, Azerbaijan 101 C13 39 29N 49 15 E
Kur →, Bhutan 90 B3 26 50N 91 0 E
Kür Dili, Azerbaijan 97 B6 39 3N 49 13 E
Kura = Kür →, Azerbaijan 101 C13 39 29N 49 15 E
Kurahashi-Jima, Japan 72 C4 34 8N 132 31 E
Kuranda, Australia 126 B4 16 48 S 145 35 E
Kuranga, India 92 H3 22 4N 69 10 E
Kurashiki, Japan 72 C5 34 40N 133 50 E
Kurayoshi, Japan 72 B5 35 26N 133 50 E
Kürdämir, Azerbaijan 61 K9 40 25N 48 3 E
Kurday = Qorday, Kazakhstan 65 B7 43 21N 74 59 E
Kurdistan, Asia 101 D10 37 20N 43 30 E
Kurduvadi, India 94 E2 18 8N 75 29 E
Kŭrdzhali, Bulgaria 51 E9 41 38N 25 21 E
Kure, Japan 72 C4 34 14N 132 32 E
Küre, Turkey 100 B5 41 48N 33 43 E
Küre Dağları, Turkey 100 B6 41 50N 34 10 E
Kure I., U.S.A. 145 F8 28 25N 178 25W
Kuressaare, Estonia 15 G20 58 15N 22 30 E
Kurgan, Russia 66 D7 55 26N 65 18 E
Kurgan-Tyube = Qŭrghonteppa, Tajikistan 65 E4 37 50N 68 47 E
Kurganinsk, Russia 61 H5 44 54N 40 34 E
Kurgannaya = Kurganinsk, Russia 61 H5 44 54N 40 34 E
Kuri, India 92 F4 26 37N 70 43 E
Kuria Maria Is. = Khurīyā Murīyā, Jazā'ir, Oman 99 C6 17 30N 55 58 E
Kurichchi, India 95 J3 11 36N 77 35 E
Kuridala, Australia 126 C3 21 16 S 140 29 E
Kurigram, Bangla. 90 C2 25 49N 89 39 E
Kurik, Indonesia 83 C5 8 9 S 139 59 E
Kurikka, Finland 15 E20 62 36N 22 24 E
Kuril Is. = Kurilskiye Ostrova, Russia 67 E15 45 0N 150 0 E
Kuril Trench, Pac. Oc. 62 E19 44 0N 153 0 E
Kurilsk, Russia 67 E15 45 14N 147 53 E
Kurilskiye Ostrova, Russia 67 E15 45 0N 150 0 E
Kurino, Japan 72 F2 31 57N 130 43 E
Kurinskaya Kosa = Kür Dili, Azerbaijan 97 B6 39 3N 49 13 E
Kurkheda, India 94 D5 20 37N 80 12 E
Kurkur, Egypt 106 C3 23 50N 32 0 E
Kurla, India 94 E1 19 5N 72 52 E
Kurlovskiy, Russia 60 C5 55 25N 40 40 E
Kurmuk, Sudan 107 E3 10 33N 34 21 E
Kurnool, India 95 G4 15 45N 78 0 E
Kuro-Shima, Kagoshima, Japan 71 J4 30 50N 129 57 E
Kuro-Shima, Okinawa, Japan 71 M2 24 14N 124 1 E
Kurobe-Gawe →, Japan 73 A9 36 55N 137 25 E
Kurogi, Japan 72 D2 33 12N 130 40 E
Kuror, J., Sudan 106 C3 20 27N 31 30 E
Kurow, N.Z. 131 E5 44 44 S 170 29 E
Kurów, Poland 55 G9 51 23N 22 12 E
Kurrajong, Australia 129 B9 33 33 S 150 42 E
Kurram →, Pakistan 91 B3 32 36N 71 20 E
Kurri Kurri, Australia 129 B9 32 50 S 151 28 E
Kurrimine, Australia 126 B4 17 47 S 146 6 E
Kursavka, Russia 61 H6 44 29N 42 32 E
Kurse Korhi, India 94 D5 20 14N 80 46 E
Kurshskaya Kosa ⌓, Russia 54 C7 55 7N 20 45 E
Kurshskiy Zaliv, Russia 15 J19 55 9N 21 6 E
Kuršių Nerijos Nac. Parkas △, Lithuania 54 C8 55 30N 21 6 E
Kursk, Russia 59 G9 51 42N 36 11 E
Kuršumlija, Serbia, Yug. 50 C5 43 9N 21 19 E
Kuršumlijska Banja, Serbia, Yug. 50 C5 43 3N 21 11 E
Kurşunlu, Bursa, Turkey 51 F13 40 3N 29 40 E
Kurşunlu, Çankırı, Turkey 100 B5 40 51N 33 15 E
Kurtalan, Turkey 101 D9 37 56N 41 44 E
Kurtbey, Turkey 51 E10 41 9N 26 35 E
Kürti →, Kazakhstan 65 A8 44 16N 76 42 E
Kurtistown, U.S.A. 145 D6 19 36N 155 4W
Kuru, Sudan 107 F2 7 43N 26 31 E
Kuru, Bahr el →, Sudan 107 F2 8 10N 26 50 E
Kurucaşile, Turkey 100 B5 41 49N 32 42 E
Kuruçay, Turkey 96 B3 39 39N 38 29 E
Kuruktag, China 68 B3 41 0N 89 0 E
Kuruman, S. Africa 116 D3 27 28 S 23 28 E
Kuruman →, S. Africa 116 D3 26 56 S 20 39 E
Kurume, Japan 72 D2 33 15N 130 30 E
Kurun →, Sudan 107 F3 5 30N 34 17 E
Kurunegala, Sri Lanka 95 L5 7 30N 80 23 E
Kurupukari, Guyana 169 C6 4 43N 58 37W
Kurya, Russia 56 B10 61 42N 57 9 E
Kus Gölü, Turkey 51 F11 40 10N 27 55 E
Kusa, Russia 64 D7 55 20N 59 29 E
Kuşadası, Turkey 100 D2 37 52N 27 15 E
Kuşadası Körfezı, Turkey 49 D8 37 56N 27 0 E
Kusamba, Indonesia 79 K18 8 34 S 115 27 E
Kusatsu, Gumma, Japan 73 A10 36 37N 138 36 E
Kusatsu, Shiga, Japan 73 C7 34 58N 135 57 E
Kusawa L., Canada 142 A1 60 20N 136 13W
Kusel, Germany 31 F3 49 32N 7 24 E
Kushaka, Nigeria 113 C6 10 32N 6 48 E
Kushalgarh, India 92 H6 23 10N 74 27 E
Kushalnagar, India 95 H2 12 14N 75 57 E
Kushchevskaya, Russia 61 G4 46 33N 39 35 E
Kusheriki, Nigeria 113 C6 10 33N 6 28 E
Kushikino, Japan 72 F2 31 44N 130 16 E
Kushima, Japan 72 F3 31 29N 131 14 E
Kushimoto, Japan 73 D7 33 28N 135 47 E
Kushiro, Japan 70 C12 43 0N 144 25 E
Kushiro-Gawa →, Japan 70 C12 42 59N 144 23 E
Kūshk, Iran 97 D8 28 46N 56 51 E
Kushka = Gushgy, Turkmenistan 66 F7 35 20N 62 18 E
Kūshkī, Iran 96 C5 33 31N 47 13 E
Kushnarenkovo, Russia 64 D5 55 6N 55 22 E
Kushol, India 93 C7 33 40N 76 36 E
Kushrabat = Koshrabad, Uzbekistan 65 C3 40 18N 66 32 E
Kushtia, Bangla. 90 D2 23 55N 89 5 E
Kushum →, Kazakhstan 60 F10 49 20N 50 30 E
Kushva, Russia 64 B7 58 18N 59 45 E
Kuskokwim →, U.S.A. 144 F7 60 5N 162 25W
Kuskokwim B., U.S.A. 144 G7 59 45N 162 25W
Kuskokwim Mts., U.S.A. 144 E9 62 30N 156 0W
Kusmi, India 93 H10 23 17N 83 55 E
Küsnacht, Switz. 33 B7 47 19N 8 35 E
Kussharo-Ko, Japan 70 C12 43 38N 144 21 E
Küssnacht, Switz. 33 B6 47 5N 8 26 E
Kustanay = Qostanay, Kazakhstan 66 D7 53 10N 63 35 E
Küstenje = Constanţa, Romania 53 F13 44 14N 28 38 E
Kusu, Indonesia 82 A3 0 53N 127 43 E
Kusu, Japan 72 D3 33 16N 131 9 E
Kut, Ko, Thailand 87 G4 11 40N 102 35 E
Kuta, Indonesia 79 K18 8 43 S 115 11 E
Kutacane, Indonesia 84 B1 3 50N 97 50 E
Kütahya, Turkey 49 B12 39 30N 30 2 E
Kütahya □, Turkey 49 B11 39 10N 29 30 E
Kutaisi, Georgia 61 J6 42 19N 42 40 E
Kutaraja = Banda Aceh, Indonesia 84 A1 5 35N 95 20 E
Kutch, Gulf of = Kachchh, Gulf of, India 92 H3 22 50N 69 15 E
Kutch, Rann of = Kachchh, Rann of, India 92 H4 24 0N 70 0 E
Kutina, Croatia 45 C13 45 29N 16 48 E
Kutiyana, India 92 J4 21 36N 70 2 E
Kutjevo, Croatia 52 E2 45 23N 17 55 E
Kutkai, Burma 90 D6 23 27N 97 56 E
Kutkashen, Azerbaijan 61 K8 40 58N 47 47 E
Kutná Hora, Czech Rep. 34 B8 49 57N 15 16 E
Kutno, Poland 55 F6 52 15N 19 23 E
Kutru, India 94 E5 19 5N 80 46 E
Kutse, Botswana 116 C3 21 7 S 22 16 E
Kuttabul, Australia 126 K6 21 1 S 148 54 E
Kutu, Dem. Rep. of the Congo 114 C3 2 40 S 18 11 E
Kutu Moke, Dem. Rep. of the Congo 114 C3 3 12 S 17 21 E
Kutum, Sudan 107 E1 14 10N 24 40 E
Kúty, Slovak Rep. 35 C10 48 40N 17 3 E
Kuujjuaq, Canada 139 C13 58 6N 68 15W
Kuujjuarapik, Canada 140 A4 55 20N 77 35W
Kuŭp-tong, N. Korea 75 D14 40 45N 126 1 E
Kuusamo, Finland 14 D23 65 57N 29 8 E
Kuusankoski, Finland 15 F22 60 55N 26 38 E
Kuvandyk, Russia 64 F6 51 28N 57 21 E
Kuvango, Angola 115 E3 14 28 S 16 20 E
Kuvasay, Uzbekistan 65 C5 40 18N 71 59 E
Kuvshinovo, Russia 58 D8 57 2N 34 11 E
Kuwait = Al Kuwayt, Kuwait 96 D5 29 30N 48 0 E
Kuwait ■, Asia 96 D5 29 30N 47 30 E
Kuwana, Japan 73 B8 35 5N 136 43 E
Kuwana →, India 93 F10 26 25N 83 15 E
Kuybyshev = Samara, Russia 60 D10 53 8N 50 6 E
Kuybyshev, Russia 66 D8 55 27N 78 19 E
Kuybyshevka-Vostochnaya = Belogorsk, Russia 67 D13 51 0N 128 20 E
Kuybyshevo, Ukraine 59 J9 47 25N 36 40 E
Kuybyshevskiy, Tajikistan 65 E4 37 52N 68 44 E
Kuybyshevskoye Vdkhr., Russia 60 C9 55 2N 49 30 E
Kuye He →, China 74 E6 38 23N 110 46 E
Kūyeh, Iran 96 B5 38 45N 47 57 E
Kuylyuk, Uzbekistan 65 C4 41 14N 69 17 E
Kūysanjaq, Iraq 101 D11 36 5N 44 38 E
Kuyto, Ozero, Russia 56 B5 65 6N 31 20 E
Kuyucak, Turkey 49 D10 37 55N 28 28 E
Kuyumba, Russia 67 C10 60 58N 96 59 E
Kuzey Anadolu Dağları, Turkey 100 B7 41 30N 35 0 E
Kuzhitturai, India 95 K3 8 18N 77 11 E
Kuzino, Russia 64 C7 57 1N 59 27 E
Kuzitrin →, U.S.A. 144 D6 65 10N 165 25W
Kuzmin, Serbia, Yug. 52 E4 45 2N 19 25 E
Kuznetsk, Russia 60 D8 53 12N 46 40 E
Kuzomen, Russia 56 A6 66 22N 36 50 E
Kvænangen, Norway 14 A19 70 5N 21 15 E
Kværndrup, Denmark 17 J4 55 10N 10 31 E
Kvaløy, Norway 14 B18 69 40N 18 30 E
Kvam, Norway 18 C6 61 40N 9 42 E
Kvänum, Sweden 17 F7 58 18N 13 11 E
Kvareli = Qvareli, Georgia 61 K7 41 57N 45 47 E
Kvarner, Croatia 45 D11 44 50N 14 10 E
Kvarnerič, Croatia 45 D11 44 43N 14 37 E
Kvås, Norway 18 F4 58 16N 7 14 E
Kvernaland, Norway 18 F2 58 47N 5 45 E
Kvichak B., U.S.A. 144 G8 58 48N 157 30W
Kvicksund, Sweden 16 E10 59 27N 16 19 E
Kvikne, Norway 18 B7 62 35N 10 16 E
Kvillsfors, Sweden 17 G9 57 24N 15 29 E
Kvina →, Norway 18 F3 58 19N 6 55 E
Kvinlog, Norway 18 F3 58 31N 6 55 E
Kvismare kanal, Sweden 16 E9 59 11N 15 35 E
Kvissleby, Sweden 16 B11 62 18N 17 22 E
Kviteseid, Norway 18 E5 59 24N 8 29 E
Kwabhaca, S. Africa 117 E4 30 51 S 29 0 E
Kwakhanai, Botswana 116 C3 21 39 S 21 16 E
Kwakoegron, Suriname 169 B6 5 12N 55 25W
Kwale, Kenya 118 C4 4 15 S 39 31 E
Kwale, Nigeria 113 D6 5 46N 6 26 E
Kwamalasamutu, Suriname 169 C6 2 20N 56 47W
KwaMashu, S. Africa 117 D5 29 45 S 30 58 E
Kwamouth, Dem. Rep. of the Congo 114 C3 3 9 S 16 12 E
Kwando →, Africa 116 B3 18 27 S 23 32 E
Kwangchow = Guangzhou, China 77 F9 23 5N 113 10 E
Kwangdaeri, N. Korea 75 D14 40 31N 127 32 E
Kwangju, S. Korea 75 G14 35 9N 126 54 E
Kwango →, Dem. Rep. of the Congo 114 C3 3 14 S 17 22 E
Kwangsi-Chuang = Guangxi Zhuangzu Zizhiqu □, China 76 F7 24 0N 109 0 E
Kwangtung = Guangdong □, China 77 F9 23 0N 113 0 E
Kwara □, Nigeria 113 D6 8 45N 4 30 E
Kwataboahegan →, Canada 140 B3 51 9N 80 50W
Kwatisore, Indonesia 83 B4 3 18 S 134 50 E
KwaZulu Natal □, S. Africa 117 D5 29 0 S 30 0 E
Kweichow = Guizhou □, China 76 D6 27 0N 107 0 E
Kwekwe, Zimbabwe 119 F2 18 58 S 29 48 E
Kwenge →, Dem. Rep. of the Congo 115 C3 4 50 S 18 44 E
Kwethluk, U.S.A. 144 F7 60 49N 161 26W
Kwidzyn, Poland 54 E5 53 44N 18 55 E
Kwigillingok, U.S.A. 144 G7 59 51N 163 8W
Kwiguk, U.S.A. 144 E6 62 46N 164 30W
Kwiha, Ethiopia 107 E4 13 29N 39 32 E
Kwikila, Papua N. G. 132 E4 9 49 S 147 38 E
Kwilu →, Dem. Rep. of the Congo 115 C3 3 22 S 17 22 E
Kwinana New Town, Australia 125 F2 32 15 S 115 47 E
Kwinbet, Burma 90 G5 16 20N 94 14 E
Kwisa →, Poland 55 G2 51 34N 15 24 E
Kwoka, Indonesia 83 B4 0 31 S 132 27 E
Kwolla, Nigeria 113 D6 9 0N 9 15 E
Kwun Tong, China 69 G11 22 19N 114 13 E
Kya-in-Seikkyi, Burma 90 G7 16 2N 98 8 E
Kyabé, Chad 109 G3 9 30N 19 0 E
Kyabra Cr. →, Australia 127 D3 25 36 S 142 55 E
Kyabram, Australia 129 D6 36 19 S 145 4 E
Kyaikkami, Burma 90 G6 16 4N 97 34 E
Kyaiklat, Burma 90 G5 16 25N 95 40 E
Kyaikmaraw, Burma 90 G6 16 23N 97 44 E
Kyaikthin, Burma 90 D5 23 32N 95 40 E
Kyaikto, Burma 86 D1 17 20N 97 3 E
Kyakhta, Russia 67 D11 50 30N 106 25 E
Kyambura Game Reserve ⌓, Uganda 118 C3 0 7 S 30 9 E
Kyancutta, Australia 127 E2 33 8 S 135 33 E
Kyangin, Burma 90 F5 18 20N 95 20 E
Kyaukhnyat, Burma 90 F6 18 15N 97 31 E
Kyaukki, Burma 90 F6 18 27N 96 56 E
Kyaukkyi, Burma 90 F5 18 15N 94 29 E
Kyaukme, Burma 90 D6 22 32N 97 2 E
Kyaukpadaung, Burma 90 E5 20 52N 95 8 E
Kyaukpyu, Burma 90 F4 19 28N 93 30 E
Kyaukse, Burma 90 E6 21 36N 96 10 E
Kyauktaga, Burma 90 F6 18 10N 96 37 E
Kyauktan, Burma 90 G6 16 38N 96 19 E
Kyauktaw, Burma 90 E4 20 51N 92 59 E
Kyaunggon, Burma 90 G5 17 6N 95 11 E
Kyawkku, Burma 90 E6 21 48N 96 56 E
Kybartai, Lithuania 54 D9 54 39N 22 45 E
Kyburz, U.S.A. 160 G6 38 47N 120 18W
Kyeintali, Burma 90 G5 18 0N 94 29 E
Kyelang, India 92 C7 32 35N 77 2 E
Kyenjojo, Uganda 118 B3 0 40N 30 37 E
Kyidaunggan, Burma 90 F6 19 53N 96 12 E
Kyjov, Czech Rep. 35 B10 49 1N 17 7 E
Kyle, Canada 143 C7 50 50N 108 2W
Kyle Dam, Zimbabwe 119 G3 20 15 S 31 0 E
Kyle of Lochalsh, U.K. 22 D3 57 17N 5 44W
Kyll →, Germany 31 F2 49 48N 6 41 E
Kyllburg, Germany 31 E2 50 2N 6 34 E
Kymijoki →, Finland 15 F22 60 30N 26 55 E
Kyneton, Australia 128 D6 37 10 S 144 29 E
Kynuna, Australia 126 C3 21 37 S 141 55 E
Kyō-ga-Saki, Japan 73 B7 35 45N 135 15 E
Kyoga, L., Uganda 118 B3 1 35N 33 0 E
Kyogle, Australia 127 D5 28 40 S 153 0 E
Kyom →, Sudan 107 F2 8 58N 28 13 E
Kyongju, S. Korea 75 G15 35 51N 129 14 E
Kyŏngsŏng, N. Korea 75 D15 41 35N 129 36 E
Kyōto, Japan 73 C7 35 0N 135 45 E
Kyōto □, Japan 73 B7 35 15N 135 45 E
Kyparissovouno, Cyprus 39 E9 35 19N 33 10 E
Kyperounda, Cyprus 39 F8 34 56N 32 58 E
Kyrenia, Cyprus 39 E9 35 20N 33 20 E
Kyrgyzstan ■, Asia 65 C6 42 0N 75 0 E
Kyritz, Germany 30 C8 52 56N 12 24 E
Kyrkhult, Sweden 17 H8 56 22N 14 34 E
Kyrksæterøra, Norway 18 A6 63 18N 9 5 E
Kyrönjoki →, Finland 14 E19 63 14N 21 45 E
Kyshtym, Russia 64 D8 55 42N 60 34 E
Kystatyam, Russia 67 C13 67 20N 123 10 E
Kysucké Nové Mesto, Slovak Rep. 35 B11 49 18N 18 47 E
Kythréa, Cyprus 39 E9 35 15N 33 29 E
Kytlym, Russia 64 B7 59 30N 59 12 E
Kyu-hkok, Burma 90 C7 24 4N 98 4 E
Kyunhla, Burma 90 D5 23 25N 95 15 E
Kyuquot Sound, Canada 142 D3 50 2N 127 22W
Kyurdamir = Kürdämir, Azerbaijan 61 K9 40 25N 48 3 E
Kyūshū, Japan 72 E3 33 0N 131 0 E
Kyūshū □, Japan 72 E3 33 0N 131 0 E
Kyūshū-Sanchi, Japan 72 E3 32 35N 131 17 E
Kyustendil, Bulgaria 50 D6 42 16N 22 41 E
Kyusyur, Russia 67 B13 70 19N 127 30 E
Kywong, Australia 129 C7 34 58 S 146 44 E
Kyyiv, Ukraine 59 G6 50 30N 30 28 E
Kyyivske Vdskh., Ukraine 59 G6 51 0N 30 25 E
Kyzyl, Russia 67 D10 51 50N 94 30 E
Kyzyl-Adyr, Kyrgyzstan 65 B5 42 39N 71 35 E
Kyzyl Kum, Uzbekistan 65 B2 42 30N 65 0 E
Kyzyl-Kyya, Kyrgyzstan 65 C6 40 16N 72 8 E
Kyzyl-Orda = Qyzylorda, Kazakhstan 65 A2 44 48N 65 28 E
Kyzyl-Suu, Kyrgyzstan 65 B9 42 20N 78 0 E
Kyzyl-Suu →, Kyrgyzstan 65 D6 38 50N 70 0 E
Kyzyltepa, Uzbekistan 65 C2 40 1N 64 51 E

L

La Albuera, Spain 43 G4 38 45N 6 49W
La Alcarria, Spain 40 E2 40 31N 2 45W
La Almarcha, Spain 40 F2 39 41N 2 24W
La Almunia de Doña Godina, Spain 40 D3 41 29N 1 23W
La Amistad, Parque Internacional △, America 164 E3 9 28N 83 18W
La Asunción, Venezuela 169 A5 11 2N 63 53W
La Baie, Canada 141 C5 48 19N 70 53W
La Banda, Argentina 174 B3 27 45 S 64 10W
La Bañeza, Spain 42 C5 42 17N 5 54W
La Barca, Mexico 162 C4 20 20N 102 40W
La Barge, U.S.A. 158 E8 42 16N 110 12W
La Bastide-Puylaurent, France 28 D7 44 35N 3 55 E
La Baule-Escoubiac, France 26 E4 47 17N 2 24W
La Belle, Fla., U.S.A. 153 J8 26 46N 81 26W
La Belle, Mo., U.S.A. 156 D5 40 7N 91 55W
La Biche →, Canada 142 B4 59 57N 123 50W
La Biche, L., Canada 142 C6 54 50N 112 5W
La Bisbal d'Empordà, Spain 40 D8 41 58N 3 2 E
La Bomba, Mexico 162 A1 31 53N 115 2W
La Brea, Trin. & Tob. 169 F9 10 15N 61 37W
La Brède, France 28 D3 44 41N 0 32W
La Bresse, France 27 D13 48 2N 6 53 E
La Bureba, Spain 42 C7 42 36N 3 24W
La Cal →, Bolivia 173 D6 17 27 S 58 15W
La Calera, Chile 174 C1 32 50 S 71 10W
La Calle = El Kala, Algeria 111 A6 36 50N 8 30 E
La Campiña, Spain 43 H6 37 45N 4 45W
La Canal = Sa Canal, Spain 38 D1 38 51N 1 23 E
La Cañiza = A Cañiza, Spain 42 C2 42 13N 8 16W
La Canourgue, France 28 D7 44 26N 3 13 E
La Capelle, France 27 C10 49 59N 3 50 E
La Carlota, Argentina 174 C3 33 30 S 63 20W
La Carlota, Phil. 81 F4 10 25N 122 55 E
La Carlota, Spain 43 H6 37 40N 4 56W
La Carolina, Spain 43 G7 38 17N 3 38W
La Castellana, Phil. 81 F4 10 20N 123 3 E
La Cavalerie, France 28 D7 44 1N 3 10 E
La Ceiba, Honduras 164 C2 15 40N 86 50W
La Ceiba, Venezuela 168 C3 9 28N 71 4W
La Chaise-Dieu, France 28 C7 45 18N 3 42 E
La Chapelle d'Angillon, France 27 E9 47 21N 2 25 E
La Chapelle-St-Luc, France 27 D11 48 20N 4 3 E
La Chapelle-sur-Erdre, France 26 E5 47 18N 1 34W
La Charité-sur-Loire, France 27 E10 47 10N 3 1 E
La Chartre-sur-le-Loir, France 26 E7 47 44N 0 34 E
La Châtaigneraie, France 28 B3 46 39N 0 44W
La Châtre, France 27 F9 46 35N 2 0 E
La Chaux-de-Fonds, Switz. 32 B3 47 7N 6 50 E
La Chorrera, Colombia 168 D3 0 44 S 73 1W
La Chorrera, Panama 164 E4 8 53N 79 47W
La Ciotat, France 29 E9 43 10N 5 37 E
La Clayette, France 27 F11 46 17N 4 19 E
La Cocha, Argentina 174 B2 27 50 S 65 40W
La Concepción = Ri-Aba, Eq. Guin. 113 E6 3 28N 8 40 E
La Concepción, Panama 164 E3 8 31N 82 37W
La Concepción, Venezuela 168 A3 10 30N 71 50W
La Concordia, Mexico 163 D6 16 8N 92 38W
La Coruña = A Coruña, Spain 42 B2 43 20N 8 25W
La Coruña □, Spain 42 B2 43 10N 8 30W
La Côte, Switz. 32 D2 46 25N 6 15 E
La Côte-St-André, France 29 C9 45 24N 5 15 E
La Courtine-le-Trucq, France 28 C6 45 41N 2 15 E
La Crau, Bouches-du-Rhône, France 29 E8 43 32N 4 40 E
La Crau, Var, France 29 E10 43 9N 6 4 E
La Crescent, U.S.A. 154 D9 43 50N 91 18W
La Crete, Canada 142 B5 58 11N 116 24W
La Crosse, Fla., U.S.A. 152 F7 29 51N 82 24W
La Crosse, Kans., U.S.A. 154 F5 38 32N 99 18W
La Crosse, Wis., U.S.A. 154 D9 43 48N 91 15W
La Cruz, Costa Rica 164 D2 11 4N 85 39W
La Cruz, Mexico 162 C3 23 55N 106 54W
La Cumbre, Volcán, Ecuador 172 a 0 21 S 91 32W
La Désirade, Guadeloupe 164 b 16 18N 61 3W
La Digue, Seychelles 121 b 4 20 S 55 51 E
La Dorada, Colombia 168 B3 5 30N 74 40W
La Ensenada, Chile 176 B2 41 12 S 72 33W
La Escondida, Mexico 162 C5 24 6N 99 55W
La Esmeralda, Paraguay 174 A3 22 16 S 62 33W
La Esperanza, Argentina 176 B3 40 26 S 68 32W
La Esperanza, Cuba 164 B3 22 46N 83 44W
La Esperanza, Honduras 164 D2 14 15N 88 10W
La Estrada = A Estrada, Spain 42 C2 42 43N 8 27W
La Faouët, France 26 D3 48 2N 3 30W
La Fayette, U.S.A. 149 H3 34 42N 85 17W
La Fé, Cuba 164 B3 22 2N 84 15W
La Fère, France 27 C10 49 39N 3 21 E
La Ferté-Bernard, France 26 D7 48 10N 0 40 E
La Ferté-Gaucher, France 27 D10 48 47N 3 19 E
La Ferté-Macé, France 26 D6 48 35N 0 22W
La Ferté-St-Aubin, France 27 E8 47 42N 1 57 E
La Ferté-sous-Jouarre, France 27 D10 48 56N 3 8 E
La Ferté-Vidame, France 26 D7 48 37N 0 53 E
La Flèche, France 26 E6 47 42N 0 4W
La Foa, N. Cal. 133 U19 21 43 S 165 50 E
La Follette, U.S.A. 149 G3 36 23N 84 7W
La Fontaine, U.S.A. 157 D11 40 40N 85 43W
La Fregeneda, Spain 42 E4 40 58N 6 54W
La Fría, Venezuela 168 B3 8 13N 72 15W
La Fuente de San Esteban, Spain 42 E4 40 49N 6 15W
La Gacilly, France 26 E4 47 45N 2 8W
La Gineta, Spain 41 F2 39 8N 2 1W
La Gloria, Colombia 168 B3 8 37N 73 48W
La Goulette = Halq el Oued, Tunisia 108 A2 36 53N 10 18 E
La Gran Sabana, Venezuela 169 B5 5 30N 61 30W
La Grand-Combe, France 29 D8 44 13N 4 2 E
La Grande, U.S.A. 158 D4 45 20N 118 5W
La Grande →, Canada 140 B5 53 50N 79 0W
La Grande Deux, Rés., Canada 140 B4 53 40N 76 55W
La Grande-Motte, France 29 E8 43 23N 4 5 E
La Grande Quatre, Rés., Canada 140 B5 54 0N 73 15W
La Grande Trois, Rés., Canada 140 B4 53 40N 75 10W
La Grange, Calif., U.S.A. 160 H6 37 42N 120 27W
La Grange, Ga., U.S.A. 152 B4 33 2N 85 2W
La Grange, Ky., U.S.A. 148 F3 38 25N 85 23W
La Grange, Ky., U.S.A. 157 F11 38 24N 85 22W
La Grange, Mo., U.S.A. 156 D5 40 3N 91 35W
La Grange, Tex., U.S.A. 155 L6 29 54N 96 52W
La Grave, France 29 C10 45 3N 6 18 E
La Grita, Venezuela 168 B3 8 8N 71 59W
La Guaira, Venezuela 168 A4 10 36N 66 56W
La Guardia = A Guarda, Spain 42 D2 41 56N 8 52W
La Gudiña = A Gudiña, Spain 42 C3 42 4N 7 8W
La Güera, Mauritania 110 D1 20 51N 17 0W
La Guerche-de-Bretagne, France 26 E5 47 57N 1 16W
La Guerche-sur-l'Aubois, France 27 F9 46 58N 2 56 E
La Habana, Cuba 164 B3 23 8N 82 22W
La Harpe, U.S.A. 156 D6 40 35N 90 58W
La Haute Vallée de Chevreuse, Parc Naturel Régional de ⌓, France 27 D8 48 35N 1 58 E
La Haye-du-Puits, France 26 C5 49 17N 1 33W
La Horqueta, Venezuela 169 B5 7 55N 60 20W
La Horra, Spain 42 D7 41 44N 3 53W
La Independencia, Mexico 163 D6 16 31N 91 47W
La Isabela, Dom. Rep. 165 C5 19 58N 71 2W
La Jonquera, Spain 40 C7 42 25N 2 53 E
La Joya, Peru 172 D3 16 43 S 71 52W
La Junta, U.S.A. 155 F3 37 59N 103 33W
La Laguna, Canary Is. 9 e1 28 28N 16 18W
La Libertad, Guatemala 164 C1 16 47N 90 7W
La Libertad, Mexico 162 B2 29 55N 112 41W
La Libertad □, Peru 172 B2 8 0 S 78 30W
La Ligua, Chile 174 C1 32 30 S 71 16W
La Línea de la Concepción, Spain 43 J5 36 15N 5 23W
La Loche, Canada 143 B7 56 29N 109 26W
La Londe-les-Maures, France 29 E10 43 8N 6 14 E
La Lora, Spain 42 C7 42 45N 4 0W
La Loupe, France 26 D8 48 29N 1 0 E
La Louvière, Belgium 24 D4 50 27N 4 10 E
La Lune, Trin. & Tob. 169 F9 10 3N 61 22W
La Machine, France 27 F10 46 54N 3 27 E
La Maddalena, Italy 46 A2 41 13N 9 24 E
La Malbaie, Canada 141 C5 47 40N 70 10W
La Malinche, Parque Nac. △, Mexico 163 D5 19 15N 98 3W
La Mancha, Spain 41 F2 39 10N 2 54W
La Mariña, Spain 42 B3 43 30N 7 40W
La Martre, L., Canada 142 A5 63 15N 117 55W
La Mesa, U.S.A. 161 N9 32 46N 117 3W
La Misión, Mexico 162 A1 32 5N 116 50W
La Moille, U.S.A. 156 C7 41 32N 89 17W
La Moine →, U.S.A. 156 E6 39 59N 90 31W
La Monte, U.S.A. 156 F3 38 46N 93 26W
La Mothe-Achard, France 26 F5 46 37N 1 40W
La Motte, France 29 D10 44 20N 6 3 E
La Motte-Chalançon, France 29 D9 44 30N 5 21 E
La Motte-Servolex, France 29 C9 45 35N 5 53 E
La Moure, U.S.A. 154 B5 46 21N 98 18W
La Muela, Spain 40 D3 41 36N 1 7W
La Mure, France 29 D9 44 55N 5 48 E
La Negra, Chile 174 A1 23 46 S 70 18W
La Neuveville, Switz. 32 B4 47 4N 7 6 E
La Oliva, Canary Is. 9 e2 28 36N 13 57W
La Oraya, Peru 172 C2 11 32 S 75 54W
La Orotava, Canary Is. 9 e1 28 22N 16 31W
La Oroya, Peru 172 C2 11 32 S 75 54W
La Pacaudière, France 27 F10 46 11N 3 52 E
La Palma, Canary Is. 9 e1 28 40N 17 50W
La Palma, Panama 164 E4 8 15N 78 0W
La Palma del Condado, Spain 43 H4 37 21N 6 38W
La Paloma, Chile 174 C1 30 35 S 71 0W
La Pampa □, Argentina 174 D2 36 50 S 66 0W
La Paragua, Venezuela 169 B5 6 50N 63 20W
La Paz, Entre Ríos, Argentina 174 C4 30 50 S 59 45W
La Paz, San Luis, Argentina 174 C2 33 30 S 67 20W
La Paz, Bolivia 172 D4 16 20 S 68 10W
La Paz, Honduras 164 D2 14 20N 87 47W
La Paz, Mexico 162 C2 24 10N 110 20W
La Paz, Abra, Phil. 80 C3 17 40N 120 41 E
La Paz, Tarlac, Phil. 80 D3 15 26N 120 45 E
La Paz □, Bolivia 172 D4 15 30 S 68 0W
La Paz Centro, Nic. 164 D2 12 20N 86 41W
La Pedrera, Colombia 168 D4 1 18 S 69 43W
La Pérade, Canada 141 C5 46 35N 72 12W
La Perouse, Bahía, Chile 172 b 27 5 S 109 18W
La Perouse Str., Asia 70 B11 45 40N 142 0 E
La Pesca, Mexico 163 C5 23 46N 97 47W
La Piedad, Mexico 162 C4 20 20N 102 1W
La Pine, U.S.A. 158 E3 43 40N 121 30W
La Plata, Argentina 174 D4 35 0 S 57 55W
La Plata, Colombia 168 C2 2 23N 75 53W
La Plata, U.S.A. 156 D4 40 2N 92 29W
La Plata, L., Argentina 176 B2 44 55 S 71 50W
La Pobla de Lillet, Spain 40 C6 42 16N 1 59 E
La Pocatière, Canada 141 C5 47 22N 70 2W
La Pola de Gordón, Spain 42 C5 42 51N 5 41W
La Porta, France 29 F13 42 25N 9 21 E
La Porte, Ind., U.S.A. 157 C10 41 36N 86 43W
La Porte, Tex., U.S.A. 155 L7 29 39N 95 1W
La Porte City, U.S.A. 156 B4 42 19N 92 12W
La Presanella, Italy 44 B7 46 13N 10 40 E
La Puebla = Sa Pobla, Spain 38 B4 39 46N 3 1 E
La Puebla de Cazalla, Spain 43 H5 37 10N 5 20W
La Puebla de los Infantes, Spain 43 H5 37 47N 5 24W
La Puebla de Montalbán, Spain 42 F6 39 52N 4 22W
La Puebla del Río, Spain 43 H4 37 16N 6 3W
La Puerta de Segura, Spain 43 G8 38 22N 2 45W

La Punt, *Switz.* . . . . 33 C9   46 35N   9 56 E
La Purísima, *Mexico* 162 B2   26 10N 112 4W
La Push, *U.S.A.* 160 C2   47 55N 124 38W
La Quiaca, *Argentina* . . . . 174 A2   22 5 S 65 35W
La Réole, *France* 28 D3   44 35N 0 1W
La Restinga, *Canary Is.* 9 e1   27 38N 17 59W
La Rioja, *Argentina* . . . . 174 B2   29 20 S 67 0W
La Rioja □, *Argentina* . . . . 174 B2   29 30 S 67 0W
La Rioja □, *Spain* 40 C2   42 20N 2 20W
La Robla, *Spain* 42 C5   42 50N 5 41W
La Roche, *N. Cal.* . . . . 133 U22   21 26 S 168 2 E
La Roche, *Switz.* . . . . 32 C4   46 57N 7 7 E
La Roche-Bernard, *France* 26 E4   47 31N 2 19W
La Roche-Canillac, *France* . . . . . 28 C5   45 12N 1 57 E
La Roche-en-Ardenne, *Belgium* . . 24 D5   50 11N 5 35 E
La Roche-sur-Foron, *France* . . . 27 F13   46 4N 6 19 E
La Roche-sur-Yon, *France* 26 F5   46 40N 1 25W
La Rochefoucauld, *France* . . . . . 28 C4   45 44N 0 24 E
La Rochelle, *France* 28 B2   46 10N 1 9W
La Roda, *Spain* 41 F2   39 13N 2 15W
La Roda de Andalucía, *Spain* . . 43 H6   37 12N 4 46W
La Romana, *Dom. Rep.* 165 C6   18 27N 68 57W
La Ronge, *Canada* 143 B7   55 5N 105 20W
La Rue, *U.S.A.* 157 D13   40 35N 83 23W
La Rumorosa, *Mexico* 161 N10   32 33N 116 4W
La Sabina = Sa Savina, *Spain* . . 38 D1   38 44N 1 25 E
La Sagra, *Spain* 41 H2   37 57N 2 35W
La Salle, *U.S.A.* 156 C7   41 20N 89 6W
La Sanabria, *Spain* 42 C4   42 0N 6 30W
La Santa, *Canary Is.* 9 e2   29 5N 13 40W
La Sarraz, *Switz.* . . . . 32 C3   46 38N 6 32 E
La Sarre, *Canada* 140 C4   48 45N 79 15W
La Scie, *Canada* 141 C8   49 57N 55 36W
La Selva, *Spain* . . . . 40 C7   42 0N 2 45 E
La Selva Beach, *U.S.A.* 160 J5   36 56N 121 51W
La Selva del Camp, *Spain* . . . . . 40 D6   41 13N 1 8 E
La Serena, *Chile* . . . . 174 B1   29 55 S 71 10W
La Serena, *Spain* 43 G5   38 45N 5 40W
La Seu d'Urgell, *Spain* . . . . 40 C6   42 22N 1 23 E
La Seyne-sur-Mer, *France* . . . . . 29 E9   43 7N 5 52 E
La Sila, *Italy* . . . . 47 C9   39 15N 16 35 E
La Solana, *Spain* 43 G7   38 59N 3 14W
La Souterraine, *France* . . . . 27 F8   46 15N 1 30 E
La Spézia, *Italy* . . . . 44 D6   44 7N 9 50 E
La Suze-sur-Sarthe, *France* . . . . . 26 E7   47 53N 0 2 E
La Tagua, *Colombia* 168 C3   0 3N 74 40W
La Teste, *France* 28 D2   44 37N 1 8W
La Tortuga, *Venezuela* 169 A4   11 0N 65 22W
La Tour de Peilz, *Switz.* . . . . 32 D3   46 27N 6 52 E
La Tour-du-Pin, *France* . . . . 29 C9   45 33N 5 27 E
La Tournette, *France* . . . . 32 E2   45 36N 6 30 E
La Tranche-sur-Mer, *France* 26 F5   46 20N 1 27W
La Tremblade, *France* 28 C2   45 46N 1 8W
La Trinidad, *Phil.* . . . . 80 C3   16 28N 120 35 E
La Trinité, *Martinique* . . . . 164 c   14 43N 60 58W
La Tuque, *Canada* 140 C5   47 30N 72 50W
La Unión, *Chile* . . . . 176 B2   40 10 S 73 0W
La Unión, *Colombia* 168 C2   1 35N 77 5W
La Unión, *El Salv.* 164 D2   13 20N 87 50W
La Unión, *Mexico* 162 D4   17 58N 101 49W
La Unión, *Peru* . . . . 172 D2   9 43 S 76 45W
La Unión, *Spain* 41 H4   37 38N 0 53W
La Unión □, *Phil.* . . . . 80 C3   16 30N 120 25 E
La Urbana, *Venezuela* 168 B4   7 8N 66 56W
La Vache Pt., *Trin. & Tob.* 169 F9   10 47N 61 37W
La Vall d'Uixó, *Spain* 40 F4   39 49N 0 15W
La Vecilla de Curveño, *Spain* . . 42 C5   42 51N 5 27W
La Vega, *Dom. Rep.* 165 C5   19 20N 70 30W
La Vega, *Peru* . . . . 172 C2   10 41 S 77 44W
La Vela de Coro, *Venezuela* . . . 168 A4   11 27N 69 34W
La Veleta, *Spain* 43 H7   37 1N 3 22W
La Venta, *Mexico* 163 D6   18 8N 94 3W
La Ventura, *Mexico* 162 C4   24 38N 100 54W
La Venturosa, *Colombia* 168 B4   6 8N 68 48W
La Victoria, *Venezuela* 168 A4   10 14N 67 20W
La Voulte-sur-Rhône, *France* . . . 29 D8   44 48N 4 46 E
Laa an der Thaya, *Austria* . . . . . 35 C9   48 43N 16 23 E
Laaber, Grosse →, *Germany* . . . 31 G8   48 55N 12 30 E
Laage, *Germany* . . . . 30 B8   53 55N 12 21 E
Laas Caanood = Las Anod,
  Somali Rep. . . . . 120 C3   8 26N 47 19 E
Laatzen, *Germany* . . . . 30 C5   52 19N 9 48 E
Laau Pt., *U.S.A.* 145 B4   21 6N 157 19W
Laba →, *Russia* . . . . 61 H4   45 11N 39 42 E
Laban, *Burma* . . . . 90 C6   25 52N 96 40 E
Labasa, *Fiji* . . . . 133 A2   16 30 S 179 27 E
Labason, *Phil.* . . . . 81 G4   8 4N 122 31 E
Labastide-Murat, *France* . . . . . . 28 D5   44 39N 1 33 E
Labastide-Rouairoux, *France* . . . 28 E6   43 28N 2 39 E
Labbézenga, *Mali* . . . . 113 B5   15 2N 0 48 E
Labdah = Leptis Magna, *Libya* . 108 B2   32 40N 14 12 E
Labe = Elbe →, *Europe* . . . . . . 30 B4   53 50N 9 0 E
Labé, *Guinea* 112 C2   11 24N 12 16W
Laberge, L., *Canada* 142 A1   61 11N 135 12W
Labian, Tanjong, *Malaysia* . . . . . 85 A5   5 9N 119 13 E
Labig Pt. = Iligan Pt., *Phil.* . . . . 80 B4   18 25N 122 15 E
Labin, *Croatia* . . . . 45 C11   45 5N 14 8 E
Labinsk, *Russia* . . . . 61 H5   44 40N 40 48 E
Labis, *Malaysia* . . . . 87 L4   2 22N 103 2 E
Łabiszyn, *Poland* . . . . 55 F4   52 57N 17 54 E
Labo, *Phil.* . . . . 80 D4   14 9N 122 51 E
Laboe, *Germany* . . . . 30 A6   54 24N 10 13 E
Laboka, *Gabon* . . . . 114 B2   0 19N 11 32 E
Labouheyre, *France* 28 D3   44 13N 0 55W
Laboulaye, *Argentina* . . . . 174 C3   34 10 S 63 30W
Labrador, *Canada* 141 B7   53 20N 61 0W
Labrador City, *Canada* 141 B6   52 57N 66 55W
Labrador Sea, *Atl. Oc.* 139 C14   57 0N 54 0W
Lábrea, *Brazil* . . . . 173 B5   7 15 S 64 51W
Labruguière, *France* . . . . 28 E6   43 31N 2 16 E
Labuan, *Malaysia* . . . . 85 A5   5 20N 115 14 E
Labuan, Pulau, *Malaysia* . . . . . . 85 A5   5 21N 115 13 E
Labuha, *Indonesia* . . . . 83 B3   0 30 S 127 30 E
Labuhan, *Indonesia* . . . . 84 D3   6 22 S 105 50 E
Labuhanbajo, *Indonesia* . . . . 82 C2   8 28 S 119 54 E
Labuk, Telok, *Malaysia* . . . . 85 A5   6 10N 117 50 E
Labutta, *Burma* . . . . 90 G5   16 9N 94 46 E
Labyrinth, L., *Australia* . . . . 127 E2   30 40 S 135 11 E
Labytnangi, *Russia* . . . . 66 C7   66 39N 66 21 E
Laç, *Albania* . . . . 50 E3   41 38N 19 43 E
Lac Bouchette, *Canada* 141 C5   48 16N 72 11W
Lac Édouard, *Canada* 140 C5   47 40N 72 16W
Lac La Biche, *Canada* 142 C6   54 45N 111 58W
Lac la Martre = Wha Ti, *Canada* 138 B8   63 8N 117 16W
Lac La Ronge Prov. Park △, *Canada* 143 B7   55 9N 104 41W
Lac-Mégantic, *Canada* 141 C5   45 35N 70 53W
Lac Thien, *Vietnam* . . . . 86 F7   12 25N 108 11 E
Lacanau, *France* 28 D2   44 58N 1 5W
Lacanau, Étang de, *France* 28 D2   44 58N 1 5W
Lacantún →, *Mexico* 163 D6   16 36N 90 40W
Lacara →, *Spain* 42 G4   38 55N 6 25W
Lacaune, *France* . . . . 28 E6   43 43N 2 40 E
Lacaune, Mts. de, *France* . . . . . 28 E6   43 43N 2 43 E
Laccadive Is. = Lakshadweep Is.,
  India . . . . 95 J1   10 0N 72 30 E
Lacepede B., *Australia* . . . . 128 D3   36 40 S 139 40 E
Lacepede Is., *Australia* . . . . 124 C3   16 55 S 122 0 E
Lacerdónia, *Mozam.* . . . . 119 F4   18 3 S 35 35 E
Lacey, *U.S.A.* 160 C4   47 7N 122 49W
Lachay, Pta., *Peru* . . . . 172 C2   11 17 S 77 44W
Lachen, *India* . . . . 90 B2   27 46N 88 36 E

Lachen, *Switz.* . . . . 33 B7   47 12N 8 51 E
Lachhmangarh, *India* . . . . 92 F6   27 50N 75 4 E
Lachi, *Pakistan* . . . . 92 C4   33 25N 71 20 E
Lachine, *Canada* 140 C5   45 30N 73 40W
Lachlan →, *Australia* . . . . 128 C5   34 22 S 143 55 E
Lachoc, *Peru* . . . . 172 C2   12 50 S 75 6W
Lachute, *Canada* 140 C5   45 39N 74 21W
Lackawanna, *U.S.A.* 150 D6   42 50N 78 50W
Lackawaxen, *U.S.A.* 151 E10   41 29N 74 59W
Lacolle, *Canada* 151 A11   45 5N 73 22W
Lacon, *U.S.A.* 156 C7   41 2N 89 24W
Lacona, *Iowa, U.S.A.* 156 C3   41 12N 93 23W
Lacona, *N.Y., U.S.A.* 151 C8   43 39N 76 10W
Láconi, *Italy* . . . . 46 C2   39 54N 9 4 E
Laconia, *U.S.A.* 151 C13   43 32N 71 28W
Lacochee, *U.S.A.* 153 G7   28 28N 82 11W
Lacq, *France* 28 E3   43 25N 0 35W
Ladakh Ra., *India* . . . . 93 C8   34 0N 78 0 E
Ladário, *Brazil* . . . . 173 D6   19 1 S 57 35W
Ladd, *U.S.A.* 156 C7   41 23N 89 13W
Laddonia, *U.S.A.* 156 E5   39 15N 91 39W
Lądek-Zdrój, *Poland* . . . . 55 H3   50 21N 16 53 E
Ládhon →, *Greece* . . . . 48 D3   37 40N 21 50 E
Ladik, *Turkey* . . . . 100 B6   40 57N 35 58 E
Ladismith, *S. Africa* . . . . 116 E3   33 28 S 21 15 E
Ladíspoli, *Italy* . . . . 45 G9   41 56N 12 5 E
Lādīz, *Iran* . . . . 97 D9   28 55N 61 15 E
Ladnun, *India* . . . . 92 F6   27 38N 74 25 E
Ladoga, L. = Ladozhskoye Ozero,
  Russia . . . . 58 B6   61 15N 30 30 E
Ladozhskoye Ozero, *Russia* . . . 58 B6   61 15N 30 30 E
Ladrillero, G., *Chile* . . . . 176 C1   49 20 S 75 35W
Ladson, *U.S.A.* 152 C9   32 59N 80 6W
Lady Elliot I., *Australia* . . . . . 126 C5   24 7 S 152 42 E
Lady Grey, *S. Africa* . . . . 116 E4   30 43 S 27 13 E
Lady Lake, *U.S.A.* 153 G8   28 55N 81 55W
Ladybrand, *S. Africa* . . . . 116 D4   29 9 S 27 29 E
Ladysmith, *Canada* 142 D4   49 0N 123 49W
Ladysmith, *S. Africa* . . . . 117 D4   28 32 S 29 46 E
Ladysmith, *U.S.A.* 154 C9   45 28N 91 12W
Lae, *Papua N. G.* . . . . 132 D4   6 40 S 147 2 E
Laem Hin Khom, *Thailand* . . . . 87 b   9 25N 99 56 E
Laem Khat, *Thailand* . . . . 87 a   8 6N 98 26 E
Laem Nga, *Thailand* . . . . 87 a   7 55N 98 27 E
Laem Ngop, *Thailand* . . . . 87 F4   12 10N 102 26 E
Laem Phan Wa, *Thailand* . . . . . 87 a   7 47N 98 25 E
Laem Pho, *Thailand* . . . . 87 J3   6 55N 101 19 E
Laem Phrom Thep, *Thailand* . . . 87 a   7 45N 98 19 E
Laem Riang, *Thailand* . . . . 87 a   8 7N 98 27 E
Laem Sam Rong, *Thailand* . . . . . 87 b   9 35N 100 4 E
Laem Son, *Thailand* . . . . 87 a   7 59N 98 16 E
Laem Yamu, *Thailand* . . . . 87 a   7 59N 98 26 E
Lærdalsøyri, *Norway* . . . . 18 C4   61 6N 7 28 E
Læsø, *Denmark* . . . . 17 G5   57 15N 11 5 E
Læsø Rende, *Denmark* . . . . 17 G4   57 20N 10 45 E
Lafayette, *Ala., U.S.A.* 153 C4   32 54N 85 24W
Lafayette, *Colo., U.S.A.* 154 F2   39 58N 105 12W
Lafayette, *Ind., U.S.A.* 157 D10   40 25N 86 54W
Lafayette, *La., U.S.A.* 155 K9   30 14N 92 1W
Lafayette, *Tenn., U.S.A.* 149 G2   36 31N 86 2W
Laferte →, *Canada* 142 A5   61 53N 117 44W
Lafia, *Nigeria* . . . . 113 D6   8 30N 8 34 E
Lafiagi, *Nigeria* . . . . 113 D6   8 52N 5 20 E
Laflèche, *Canada* 143 D7   49 45N 106 40W
Lafon, *Sudan* . . . . 107 F3   5 5N 32 29 E
Laful, *India* . . . . 95 L11   7 10N 93 52 E
Lagaip →, *Papua N. G.* . . . . . . 132 C2   5 4 S 142 52 E
Lagan, *Sweden* . . . . 17 H7   56 56N 13 58 E
Lagan →, *Sweden* . . . . 17 H6   56 30N 12 58 E
Lagan →, *U.K.* 23 B6   54 36N 5 55W
Laganás, *Greece* . . . . 49 D2   37 44N 20 53 E
Lagangilang, *Phil.* . . . . 80 C3   17 37N 120 44 E
Lagarfljót →, *Iceland* 11 B12   65 40N 14 18W
Lagarto, *Brazil* . . . . 170 D4   10 54 S 37 41W
Lagawe, *Phil.* . . . . 80 C3   16 49N 121 6 E
Lagdo, Rés. de, *Cameroon* . . . . 114 A2   8 40N 14 0 E
Lage, *Germany* . . . . 30 D4   51 59N 8 48 E
Lagen = Opplandelva →, *Norway* 18 D4   61 8N 10 25 E
Lågen →, *Vestfold, Norway* . . . 18 E7   59 3N 10 3 E
Lägerdorf, *Germany* . . . . 30 B5   53 53N 9 34 E
Laghmān □, *Afghan.* . . . . 91 B3   34 20N 70 0 E
Laghouat, *Algeria* . . . . 111 B5   33 50N 2 59 E
Lagnieu, *France* . . . . 29 C9   45 55N 5 20 E
Lagny-sur-Marne, *France* . . . . . 27 D9   48 52N 2 44 E
Lago, *Italy* . . . . 47 C9   39 10N 16 9 E
Lago de Sanabria y Entorno, Parque
  Natural de ○, *Spain* 42 C4   42 9N 6 45W
Lago Posadas, *Argentina* . . . . . 176 C2   47 30 S 71 40W
Lago Ranco, *Chile* . . . . 176 B2   40 19 S 72 30W
Lagoa, *Azores* 9 d3   37 45N 25 20W
Lagôa, *Portugal* 43 H2   37 8N 8 27W
Lagoa Vermelha, *Brazil* . . . . . . 175 B5   28 13 S 51 32W
Lagoaça, *Portugal* 42 D4   41 11N 6 44W
Lagodekhi, *Georgia* . . . . 61 K8   41 50N 46 22 E
Lagonegro, *Italy* . . . . 47 B8   40 8N 15 45 E
Lagonoy G., *Phil.* . . . . 80 E4   13 35N 123 50 E
Lagos, *Angola* . . . . 115 H4   16 3 S 16 35 E
Lagos, *Nigeria* . . . . 113 D5   6 25N 3 27 E
Lagos, *Portugal* 43 H2   37 5N 8 41W
Lagos □, *Nigeria* . . . . 113 D5   6 28N 3 25 E
Lagos de Moreno, *Mexico* . . . 162 C4   21 21N 101 55W
Lagrange, *U.S.A.* . . . . 124 C3   18 45 S 121 43 E
Lagrange, *U.S.A.* 157 C11   41 39N 85 25W
Lagrange B., *Australia* . . . . . . 124 C3   18 38 S 121 42 E
Laguardia, *Spain* 40 C2   42 33N 2 35W
Laguépie, *France* . . . . 28 D5   44 8N 1 57 E
Laguna, *Brazil* . . . . 175 B6   28 30 S 48 50W
Laguna, *U.S.A.* 159 J10   35 2N 107 25W
Laguna □, *Phil.* . . . . 80 D3   14 10N 121 20 E
Laguna Beach, *U.S.A.* 161 M9   33 33N 117 47W
Laguna de Duera, *Spain* 42 D6   41 35N 4 43W
Laguna de La Restinga, Parque
  Nac. △, *Venezuela* 165 D7   10 58N 64 0W
Laguna del Tigre, Parque Nac. △,
  Guatemala 164 C1   17 32N 90 56W
Laguna Limpia, *Argentina* . . . . 174 B4   26 32 S 59 45W
Lagunas, *Chile* . . . . 174 A2   21 0 S 69 45W
Lagunas, *Peru* . . . . 172 B2   5 10 S 75 35W
Lagunas de Chacahua, Parque
  Nac. △, *Mexico* 163 D5   16 0N 97 43W
Lagunas de Montebello, Parque
  Nac. △, *Mexico* 163 D6   16 6N 91 41W
Lagunas de Ruidera, Parque Natural
  de ○, *Spain* 41 G2   38 57N 2 52W
Lagunillas, *Bolivia* . . . . 173 D5   19 38 S 63 43W
Lahad Datu, *Malaysia* . . . . 85 A5   5 0N 118 20 E
Lahad Datu, Teluk, *Malaysia* . . 85 B5   4 50N 118 20 E
Lahaina, *U.S.A.* 145 C5   20 53N 156 41W
Lahan Sai, *Thailand* . . . . 86 E4   14 25N 102 52 E
Lahanam, *Laos* . . . . 86 D5   16 16N 105 16 E
Lahar, *India* . . . . 93 F8   26 12N 78 57 E
Laharpur, *India* . . . . 93 F9   27 43N 80 56 E
Lahat, *Indonesia* . . . . 84 C2   3 45 S 103 30 E
Lahe, *Burma* . . . . 90 B5   26 20N 95 20 E
Lahewa, *Indonesia* . . . . 84 D1   1 22N 97 12 E
Lahijan, *Iran* . . . . 98 B4   13 4N 44 53 E
Lāhījān, *Iran* . . . . 97 B6   37 10N 50 6 E
Lahilahi Pt., *U.S.A.* 145 K13   21 28N 158 13W
Lahn →, *Germany* . . . . 31 E3   50 19N 7 37 E
Lahnstein, *Germany* . . . . 31 E3   50 19N 7 37 E
Laholm, *Sweden* . . . . 17 H7   56 30N 13 2 E
Laholmsbukten, *Sweden* . . . . . . 17 H6   56 30N 12 45 E
Lahore, *Pakistan* . . . . 91 C4   31 32N 74 22 E

Lahpongsel, *Burma* . . . . 90 B7   27 7N 98 25 E
Lahr, *Germany* . . . . 31 G3   48 20N 7 53 E
Lahri, *Pakistan* . . . . 92 E3   29 11N 68 13 E
Lahti, *Finland* . . . . 15 F21   60 58N 25 40 E
Lahtis = Lahti, *Finland* . . . . . . 15 F21   60 58N 25 40 E
Laï, *Chad* . . . . 109 G3   9 25N 16 18 E
Lai Chau, *Vietnam* . . . . 76 F4   22 5N 103 3 E
Lai-hka, *Burma* . . . . 90 E6   21 16N 97 40 E
Laiagam, *Papua N. G.* . . . . . . 132 C2   5 33 S 143 30 E
Lai`an, *China* . . . . 77 A12   32 28N 118 30 E
Laibach = Ljubljana, *Slovenia* . 45 B11   46 4N 14 33 E
Laibin, *China* . . . . 76 F7   23 42N 109 20 E
Laie, *U.S.A.* 145 J14   21 39N 157 56W
Laifeng, *China* . . . . 76 C7   29 27N 109 20 E
L'Aigle, *France* . . . . 26 D7   48 46N 0 38 E
L'Aiguillon-sur-Mer, *France* . . . 28 B2   46 20N 1 18W
Laila = Layla, *Si. Arabia* . . . . . 98 B4   22 10N 46 40 E
Laingsburg, *S. Africa* . . . . 116 E3   33 9 S 20 52 E
Lainio älv →, *Sweden* . . . . 14 C20   67 35N 22 40 E
Lairg, *U.K.* 22 C4   58 2N 4 24W
Laïri, B. de, *Chad* . . . . 109 F3   12 28N 16 45 E
Lais, *Phil.* . . . . 81 H5   6 20N 125 8 E
Laishui, *China* . . . . 74 E8   39 23N 115 45 E
Laissac, *France* . . . . 28 D6   44 23N 2 50 E
Láives, *Italy* . . . . 45 B8   46 26N 11 20 E
Laiwu, *China* . . . . 75 F9   36 15N 117 40 E
Laixi, *China* . . . . 75 F11   36 50N 120 31 E
Laiyang, *China* . . . . 75 F11   36 59N 120 45 E
Laizhou, *China* . . . . 75 F10   37 8N 119 57 E
Laizhou Wan, *China* . . . . 75 F10   37 30N 119 30 E
Laja →, *Mexico* 162 C4   20 55N 100 46W
Lajedo, *Azores* 9 d1   39 24N 31 15W
Lajere, *Nigeria* . . . . 113 C7   12 10N 11 25 E
Lajes, *Azores* 9 d1   38 46N 27 6W
Lajes, Rio Grande do N., *Brazil* 170 C4   5 41 S 36 14W
Lajes, Sta. Catarina, *Brazil* . . . 175 B5   27 48 S 50 20W
Lajes das Flores, *Azores* 9 d2   39 23N 31 10W
Lajes do Pico, *Azores* 9 d1   38 24N 28 16W
Lajinha, *Brazil* . . . . 171 F3   20 9 S 41 37W
Lajkovac, *Serbia, Yug.* . . . . 50 B4   44 27N 20 14 E
Lajosmizse, *Hungary* . . . . 52 C4   47 3N 19 32 E
Lak Sao, *Laos* . . . . 86 C5   18 11N 104 59 E
Láka, *Greece* . . . . 38 C10   39 17N 20 9 E
Lakamané, *Mali* 112 C3   14 35N 9 44W
Lakatoro, *Vanuatu* . . . . 133 F5   16 6 S 167 25 E
Lake Alfred, *U.S.A.* 153 G8   28 6N 81 44W
Lake Alpine, *U.S.A.* 160 G7   38 29N 120 0W
Lake Andes, *U.S.A.* 154 D5   43 9N 98 32W
Lake Arthur, *U.S.A.* 155 K8   30 5N 92 41W
Lake Bindegolly Nat. Park △,
  Australia . . . . 127 A3   28 0 S 144 12 E
Lake Boga, *Australia* . . . . 128 C5   35 26 S 143 38 E
Lake Butler, *U.S.A.* 152 E7   30 1N 82 21W
Lake Cargelligo, *Australia* . . . 129 B7   33 15 S 146 22 E
Lake Charles, *U.S.A.* 155 K8   30 14N 93 13W
Lake City, *Colo., U.S.A.* 159 G10   38 2N 107 19W
Lake City, *Fla., U.S.A.* 152 E7   30 11N 82 38W
Lake City, *Iowa, U.S.A.* 156 B2   42 16N 94 44W
Lake City, *Mich., U.S.A.* 148 C3   44 20N 85 13W
Lake City, *Minn., U.S.A.* 154 C8   44 27N 92 16W
Lake City, *S.C., U.S.A.* 153 J6   33 52N 79 45W
Lake Clark Nat. Park and
  Preserve △, *U.S.A.* 144 D9   61 0N 154 0W
Lake Clarke Shores, *U.S.A.* . . 153 J9   26 39N 80 5W
Lake Coleridge, *N.Z.* . . . . 131 D6   43 17 S 171 30 E
Lake Cowichan, *Canada* 142 D4   48 49N 124 3W
Lake District Nat. Park △, *U.K.* 20 C4   54 30N 3 21W
Lake Elsinore, *U.S.A.* 161 M9   33 38N 117 20W
Lake Eyre Nat. Park △, *Australia* 127 A2   28 40 S 137 31 E
Lake Forest, *U.S.A.* 157 B9   42 15N 87 50W
Lake Gairdner Nat. Park △,
  Australia . . . . 127 B2   31 41 S 135 51 E
Lake Geneva, *U.S.A.* 157 B8   42 36N 88 26W
Lake George, *U.S.A.* 151 C11   43 26N 73 43W
Lake Grace, *Australia* . . . . . . 125 F2   33 7 S 118 28 E
Lake Harbor, *U.S.A.* 153 J9   26 42N 80 48W
Lake Harbour = Kimmirut, *Canada* 139 B13   62 50N 69 50W
Lake Havasu City, *U.S.A.* . . . 161 L12   34 27N 114 22W
Lake Helen, *U.S.A.* 153 G8   28 59N 81 14W
Lake Hughes, *U.S.A.* 161 L8   34 41N 118 26W
Lake Isabella, *U.S.A.* 161 K8   35 38N 118 28W
Lake Jackson, *U.S.A.* 155 L7   29 3N 95 27W
Lake Junction, *U.S.A.* 158 D8   44 35N 110 28W
Lake King, *Australia* . . . . 125 F2   33 5 S 119 45 E
Lake Kopiago, *Papua N. G.* . . 132 C2   5 23 S 142 31 E
Lake Kutubu, *Papua N. G.* . . . 132 D2   6 20 S 143 18 E
Lake Lenore, *Canada* 143 C8   52 24N 104 59W
Lake Louise, *Canada* 142 C5   51 30N 116 10W
Lake Malawi Nat. Park △, *Malawi* 119 E3   14 2 S 34 53 E
Lake Mburo Nat. Park △, *Uganda* 118 C3   0 33 S 30 56 E
Lake Mead Nat. Recr. Area △,
  U.S.A. 161 K12   36 15N 114 30W
Lake Meredith Nat. Recr. Area ○,
  U.S.A. 155 H4   35 50N 101 50W
Lake Mills, *Iowa, U.S.A.* 154 D8   43 25N 93 32W
Lake Mills, *Wis., U.S.A.* 154 A8   43 5N 88 55W
Lake Murray, *Papua N. G.* . . . 132 D1   6 48 S 141 29 E
Lake Nakuru Nat. Park △, *Kenya* 118 C4   0 21 S 36 8 E
Lake Naujan Nat. Park △, *Phil.* 80 E3   13 9N 121 20 E
Lake Odessa, *U.S.A.* 157 B11   42 47N 85 8W
Lake Orion, *U.S.A.* 157 B13   42 47N 83 14W
Lake Park, *Fla., U.S.A.* 153 J9   26 48N 80 3W
Lake Park, *Ga., U.S.A.* 153 H5   30 41N 83 11W
Lake Placid, *Fla., U.S.A.* 153 H8   27 18N 81 22W
Lake Placid, *N.Y., U.S.A.* . . . 151 B11   44 17N 73 59W
Lake Pleasant, *U.S.A.* 151 C10   43 28N 74 25W
Lake Providence, *U.S.A.* 155 J9   32 48N 91 10W
Lake Pukaki, *N.Z.* . . . . 131 E5   44 11 S 170 8 E
Lake Roosevelt Nat. Recr. Area ○,
  U.S.A. 158 C4   47 57N 118 59W
Lake St. Peter, *Canada* 150 A6   45 18N 78 2W
Lake Superior Prov. Park ○, *Canada* 140 C3   47 45N 84 45W
Lake Tekapo, *N.Z.* . . . . 131 D5   44 0 S 170 30 E
Lake View, *U.S.A.* 156 B1   42 18N 95 3W
Lake Villa, *U.S.A.* 157 B8   42 25N 88 4W
Lake Village, *U.S.A.* 155 J9   33 20N 91 17W
Lake Wales, *U.S.A.* 153 H8   27 54N 81 35W
Lake Worth, *U.S.A.* 153 J9   26 37N 80 3W
Lake Zurich, *U.S.A.* 157 B8   42 12N 88 5W
Lakeba, *Fiji* . . . . 133 B3   18 13 S 178 47W
Lakeba Passage, *Fiji* . . . . 133 B3   18 5 S 178 47W
Lakefield, *Canada* 140 D4   44 25N 78 16W
Lakefield Nat. Park △, *Australia* 126 B3   15 24 S 144 26 E
Lakehurst, *U.S.A.* 151 F10   40 1N 74 19W
Lakeland, *Australia* . . . . 126 B3   15 49 S 144 57 E
Lakeland, *Fla., U.S.A.* 153 G8   28 3N 81 57W
Lakeland, *Ga., U.S.A.* 152 D6   31 2N 83 4W
Lakemba = Lakeba, *Fiji* . . . . . 133 B3   18 13 S 178 47W
Lakeport, *Calif., U.S.A.* 160 F4   39 3N 122 55W
Lakeport, *Mich., U.S.A.* 157 B13   43 7N 82 30W
Lakes Entrance, *Australia* . . . 129 D8   37 50 S 148 0 E
Lakeside, *Ariz., U.S.A.* 159 J9   34 9N 109 58W
Lakeside, *Calif., U.S.A.* 161 N10   32 52N 116 55W
Lakeside, *Nebr., U.S.A.* 154 D3   42 3N 102 26W
Lakeside, *Ohio, U.S.A.* 150 E2   41 32N 82 46W
Lakeview, *U.S.A.* 158 E3   42 11N 120 21W
Lakewood, *Colo., U.S.A.* 154 C2   39 44N 105 5W
Lakewood, *N.J., U.S.A.* 151 F10   40 6N 74 13W
Lakewood, *N.Y., U.S.A.* 150 D5   42 6N 79 19W

Lakewood, *Ohio, U.S.A.* 150 E3   41 29N 81 48W
Lakewood, *Wash., U.S.A.* . . . 160 C4   47 11N 122 32W
Lakewood Park, *U.S.A.* 153 H9   27 30N 80 23W
Lakha, *India* . . . . 92 F4   26 9N 70 54 E
Lakhaniá, *Greece* . . . . 38 F11   35 58N 27 54 E
Lakhimpur, *India* . . . . 93 F9   27 57N 80 46 E
Lakhipur, *Assam, India* . . . . . . 90 C4   24 48N 93 0 E
Lakhipur, *Assam, India* . . . . . . 90 B3   26 2N 90 18 E
Lakhnadon, *India* . . . . 93 H8   22 36N 79 36 E
Lakhonpheng, *Laos* . . . . 86 E5   15 54N 105 34 E
Lakhpat, *India* . . . . 92 H3   23 48N 68 47 E
Läki, *Azerbaijan* . . . . 61 K8   40 34N 47 22 E
Laki, *Iceland* 11 E4   64 4N 18 14W
Lakitusaki →, *Canada* 140 B3   54 21N 82 25W
Lakki, *Pakistan* . . . . 92 C4   32 36N 70 55 E
Lákkoi, *Greece* . . . . 39 E4   35 24N 23 57 E
Lakonía □, *Greece* . . . . 48 E4   36 55N 22 30 E
Lakonikós Kólpos, *Greece* . . . . 48 E4   36 40N 22 40 E
Lakor, *Indonesia* . . . . 83 C3   8 15 S 128 17 E
Lakota, *Ivory C.* 112 D3   5 50N 5 30W
Lakota, *U.S.A.* 154 A5   48 2N 98 21W
Laksar, *India* . . . . 92 E8   29 46N 78 3 E
Laksefjorden, *Norway* . . . . 14 A22   70 45N 26 50 E
Lakselv, *Norway* . . . . 14 A21   70 2N 25 0 E
Laksettipet, *India* . . . . 94 E4   18 52N 79 13 E
Lakshadweep □, *India* . . . . 95 J1   10 0N 72 30 E
Lakshadweep Is., *India* . . . . . . 95 J1   10 0N 72 30 E
Laksham, *Bangla.* . . . . 90 D3   23 14N 91 14 E
Lakshimpur, *Bangla.* . . . . 93 H10   22 58N 83 3 E
Lakshmeshwar, *India* . . . . 95 G2   15 9N 75 28 E
Lakshmikantapur, *India* . . . . . 93 H13   22 5N 88 20 E
Lakuramau, *Papua N. G.* . . . . 132 B2   2 54 S 151 15 E
Lal-lo, *Phil.* . . . . 80 B3   18 12N 121 40 E
Lala, *Dem. Rep. of the Congo* . 115 C4   4 10 S 20 30 E
Lala Musa, *Pakistan* . . . . 81 H4   7 59N 123 46 E
Lalaghat, *India* . . . . 92 C5   32 40N 73 57 E
Lalago, *Tanzania* . . . . 90 C4   24 30N 92 40 E
Lalapanzi, *Zimbabwe* . . . . 118 C3   3 28 S 33 58 E
Lalapaşa, *Turkey* . . . . 119 F3   19 20 S 30 15 E
Lalbenque, *France* . . . . 51 E10   41 49N 26 44 E
Lalibela, *Ethiopia* . . . . 28 D5   44 19N 1 34 E
Lalín, *Spain* . . . . 107 E4   12 33N 39 0 E
Lalín, *China* . . . . 75 B14   45 12N 127 0 E
Lalín He →, *China* 42 C2   42 40N 8 5W
Lalinde, *France* . . . . 75 B13   45 32N 125 40 E
Lalitapur, *Nepal* . . . . 28 D4   44 50N 0 44 E
Lalitpur, *India* . . . . 93 F11   27 40N 85 20 E
Lalkua, *India* . . . . 93 G8   24 42N 78 28 E
Lalm, *Norway* . . . . 93 E8   29 5N 79 31 E
Lalsot, *India* . . . . 18 C6   61 50N 9 17 E
Lam, *Vietnam* . . . . 92 F7   26 34N 76 20 E
Lam Pao Res., *Thailand* . . . . . 86 B6   21 21N 106 31 E
Lama Kara, *Togo* . . . . 86 D4   16 50N 103 15 E
Lamag, *Malaysia* . . . . 113 D5   9 30N 1 15 E
Lamap, *Vanuatu* . . . . 85 A5   5 30N 117 49 E
Lamar, *Colo., U.S.A.* . . . . . . 133 F5   16 26 S 167 43 E
Lamar, *Mo., U.S.A.* 154 F3   38 5N 102 37W
Lamarque, *Argentina* 155 G7   37 30N 94 16W
Lamas, *Peru* . . . . 176 A3   39 24 S 65 40W
Lamastre, *France* . . . . 172 B2   6 28 S 76 31W
Lambach, *Austria* . . . . 29 D8   44 59N 4 35 E
Lamballe, *France* . . . . 34 C6   48 6N 13 51 E
Lambaréné, *Gabon* 26 D4   48 29N 2 31W
Lambasa = Labasa, *Fiji* . . . . . . 114 C2   0 41 S 10 12 E
Lambay I., *Ireland* . . . . 133 A2   16 30 S 179 27 E
Lambayeque □, *Peru* 23 C5   53 29N 6 1W
Lambert, C., *Papua N. G.* . . . 172 B2   6 45 S 80 0W
Lambert Glacier, *Antarctica* . . 132 C6   4 1 S 151 31 E
Lambert-St. Louis International
  (STL), *U.S.A.* 156 F6   38 45N 90 22W
Lambert's Bay, *S. Africa* . . . . 116 E2   32 5 S 18 17 E
Lambertville, *U.S.A.* 157 C13   41 46N 83 35W
Lambesc, *France* . . . . 29 E9   43 39N 5 16 E
Lambeth, *Canada* 150 D3   42 54N 81 18W
Lambi, *Solomon Is.* . . . . 133 M10   9 22 S 159 39 E
Lámbia, *Greece* . . . . 48 D3   37 52N 21 53 E
Lambomakondro, *Madag.* . . . . 117 C7   22 41 S 44 44 E
Lambon, *Papua N. G.* . . . . . . 132 C4   4 45 S 152 48 E
Lambro →, *Italy* . . . . 44 C6   45 8N 9 32 E
Lambu, *Papua N. G.* . . . . 132 B6   3 18 S 151 43 E
Lambunao, *Phil.* . . . . 81 F4   11 3N 122 29 E
Lamé, *Chad* . . . . 109 G2   9 19N 14 32 E
Lame, *Nigeria* . . . . 113 C6   10 30N 9 20 E
Lame Deer, *U.S.A.* 158 D10   45 37N 106 40W
Lamego, *Portugal* 42 D3   41 5N 7 52W
Lamèque, *Canada* 141 C7   47 45N 64 38W
Lameroo, *Australia* . . . . 128 C3   35 19 S 140 33 E
Lamesa, *U.S.A.* 155 J4   32 44N 101 58W
Lamía, *Greece* . . . . 48 C4   38 55N 22 26 E
Lamigan Pt., *Phil.* . . . . 81 H6   6 48N 126 21 E
Lamine →, *U.S.A.* 156 F4   38 59N 92 51W
Lamington Nat. Park △, *Australia* 127 A5   28 13 S 153 12 E
Lamitan, *Phil.* . . . . 81 H4   6 39N 122 8 E
Lamlan, Mt., *Guam* . . . . 133 R15   13 22N 144 41 E
Lamma I., *China* . . . . 69 G11   22 12N 114 8 E
Lammermuir Hills, *U.K.* 22 F6   55 50N 2 40W
Lammhult, *Sweden* . . . . 17 G8   57 10N 14 35 E
Lamoille, *U.S.A.* 151 B11   44 38N 73 13W
Lamon B., *Phil.* . . . . 80 D4   7 7 S 122 25 E
Lamongan, *Indonesia* . . . . 84 D4   7 5N 112 25 E
Lamoni, *U.S.A.* 156 D3   40 37N 93 56W
Lamont, *Canada* 142 C6   53 46N 112 50W
Lamont, *Calif., U.S.A.* 161 K8   35 15N 118 55W
Lamont, *Fla., U.S.A.* 152 E6   30 23N 83 49W
Lamont, *Iowa, U.S.A.* 156 B5   42 35N 91 40W
Lamont, *Wyo., U.S.A.* 158 E10   42 13N 107 29W
Lamotte-Beuvron, *France* . . . . 27 E9   47 36N 2 2 E
Lampa, *Peru* . . . . 172 D3   15 22 S 70 22W
Lampang, *Thailand* . . . . 86 C2   18 16N 99 32 E
Lampasas, *U.S.A.* 155 K5   31 4N 98 11W
Lampazos de Naranjo, *Mexico* . 162 B4   27 2N 100 32W
Lampedusa, *Medit. S.* . . . . . . 111 A7   35 36N 12 40 E
Lampertheim, *Germany* . . . . . 31 F4   49 35N 8 27 E
Lampeter, *U.K.* 21 E3   52 7N 4 4W
Lampione, *Medit. S.* . . . . 108 A2   35 33N 12 20 E
Lampman, *Canada* 143 D8   49 25N 102 50W
Lamprechtshausen, *Austria* . . . 34 D2   48 0N 12 58 E
Lampung □, *Indonesia* . . . . . . 84 D2   5 30 S 104 30 E
Lamta, *India* . . . . 93 H9   22 8N 80 7 E
Lamu, *Burma* . . . . 90 F5   19 14N 94 10 E
Lamu, *Kenya* . . . . 118 C5   2 16 S 40 55 E
Lamud, *Peru* . . . . 172 B2   6 10 S 77 57W
Lamy, *U.S.A.* 159 J11   35 29N 105 53W
Lan Xian, *China* . . . . 74 E6   38 15N 111 35 E
Lan Yu = Hungt'ou Hsü, *Taiwan* 77 G13   22 0N 121 30 E
Lanai, *U.S.A.* 145 C5   20 50N 156 55W
Lanai City, *U.S.A.* 145 C5   20 50N 156 55W
Lanaihale, *U.S.A.* 145 C5   20 49N 156 53W
Lanak La, *India* . . . . 93 B8   34 27N 79 32 E
Lanak'o Shank'ou = Lanak La,
  China . . . . 93 B8   34 27N 79 32 E
Lanao, L., *Phil.* . . . . 81 H5   7 52N 124 15 E
Lanao del Norte □, *Phil.* . . . . 81 H5   8 0N 124 0 E
Lanao del Sur □, *Phil.* . . . . . . 81 H5   7 40N 124 15 E
Lanark, *Canada* 151 A8   45 1N 76 22W

Lanark, *U.K.* **22 F5** 55 40N 3 47W
Lanark, *U.S.A.* **156 B7** 42 6N 89 50W
Lanbi Kyun, *Burma* .... **87 G2** 10 50N 98 20 E
Lancang, *China* .... **76 F2** 22 36N 99 58 E
Lancang Jiang ➤, *China* .. **76 G3** 21 40N 101 10 E
Lancashire □, *U.K.* **20 D5** 53 50N 2 48W
Lancaster, *Canada* **151 A10** 45 10N 74 30W
Lancaster, *U.K.* **20 C5** 54 3N 2 48W
Lancaster, Calif., *U.S.A.* ... **161 L8** 34 42N 118 8W
Lancaster, Ky., *U.S.A.* **148 G3** 37 37N 84 35W
Lancaster, Mo., *U.S.A.* **156 D4** 40 31N 92 32W
Lancaster, N.H., *U.S.A.* **151 B13** 44 29N 71 34W
Lancaster, N.Y., *U.S.A.* **150 D6** 42 54N 78 40W
Lancaster, Ohio, *U.S.A.* ... **148 F4** 39 43N 82 36W
Lancaster, Pa., *U.S.A.* **151 F8** 40 2N 76 19W
Lancaster, S.C., *U.S.A.* **149 H5** 34 43N 80 46W
Lancaster, Wis., *U.S.A.* **156 D9** 42 51N 90 43W
Lancaster Sd., *Canada* **139 A11** 74 13N 84 0W
Lancelin, *Australia* .... **125 F2** 31 0 S 115 18 E
Lanchow = Lanzhou, *China* . **74 F2** 36 1N 103 52 E
Lanciano, *Italy* .... **45 F11** 42 14N 14 23 E
Lanco, *Chile* .... **176 A2** 39 24 S 72 46W
Lancones, *Peru* .... **172 A1** 4 30 S 80 30W
Lancun, *China* .... **75 F11** 36 25N 120 10 E
Łańcut, *Poland* .... **55 H9** 50 10N 22 13 E
Lancy, *Switz.* .... **32 D2** 46 12N 6 8 E
Land Between the Lakes Nat. Recr.
   Area △, *U.S.A.* **149 G1** 36 55N 88 7W
Landau, Bayern, *Germany* ... **31 G8** 48 40N 12 41 E
Landau, Rhld-Pfz., *Germany* . **31 F4** 49 12N 8 6 E
Landay, *Afghan.* .... **91 C1** 30 31N 63 47 E
Landeck, *Austria* .... **34 D3** 47 9N 10 34 E
Lander, *U.S.A.* **158 E9** 42 50N 108 44W
Lander ➤, *Australia* .... **124 D5** 22 0 S 132 0 E
Landerneau, *France* **26 D2** 48 28N 4 17W
Landeryd, *Sweden* .... **17 G7** 57 7N 13 15 E
Landes, *France* **28 D2** 44 0N 1 0W
Landes □, *France* **28 E3** 43 57N 0 48W
Landes de Gascogne, Parc Naturel
   Régional des △, *France* . **28 D3** 44 23N 0 50W
Landete, *Spain* **40 F3** 39 56N 1 25W
Landfall I., *India* .... **95 H11** 13 40N 93 2 E
Landi Kotal, *Pakistan* ...... **92 B4** 34 7N 71 6 E
Landsborg, *U.S.A.* **150 F7** 40 21N 77 19W
Landivisiau, *France* **26 D2** 48 31N 4 6W
Landquart, *Switz.* .... **33 C9** 46 58N 9 32 E
Landquart ➤, *Switz.* .... **33 C9** 46 50N 9 47 E
Landrecies, *France* .... **27 B10** 50 7N 3 40 E
Land's End, *U.K.* **21 G2** 50 4N 5 44W
Landsberg, *Germany* .... **31 G6** 48 2N 10 53 E
Landsborough Cr. ➤, *Australia* **126 C3** 22 28 S 144 35 E
Landsbro, *Sweden* .... **17 G8** 57 24N 14 56 E
Landshut, *Germany* .... **31 G8** 48 34N 12 8 E
Landskrona, *Sweden* .... **17 J6** 55 53N 12 50 E
Landstuhl, *Germany* .... **31 F3** 49 24N 7 33 E
Landvetter, *Sweden* .... **17 G6** 57 41N 12 17 E
Lane, *U.S.A.* **152 B10** 33 32N 79 53W
Lanesboro, *U.S.A.* **151 E9** 41 57N 75 34W
Lanester, *France* **26 E3** 47 46N 3 22W
Lanett, *U.S.A.* **152 C4** 32 52N 85 12W
Lang Qua, *Vietnam* .... **86 A5** 22 16N 104 27 E
Lang Shan, *China* .... **74 D4** 41 0N 106 30 E
Lang Son, *Vietnam* .... **76 G6** 21 52N 106 42 E
Lang Suan, *Thailand* .... **87 H2** 9 57N 99 4 E
Langå, *Denmark* .... **17 H3** 56 23N 9 54 E
Langa-Langa, Dem. Rep. of
   the *Congo* .... **114 C3** 3 50 S 15 59 E
Lángadhás, *Greece* .... **50 F7** 40 46N 23 6 E
Langádhia, *Greece* .... **48 D4** 37 43N 22 1 E
Långan ➤, *Sweden* .... **16 A8** 63 19N 14 44 E
Langanes, *Iceland* **11 A12** 66 20N 14 53W
Langano, L., *Ethiopia* ...... **107 F4** 7 36N 38 43 E
Langar, *Afghan.* .... **65 E6** 37 2N 73 47 E
Langar, *Iran* .... **97 C9** 35 23N 60 25 E
Langara I., *Canada* **142 C2** 54 14N 133 1W
Långås, *Sweden* .... **17 H6** 56 58N 12 26 E
Langatabbetje, *Suriname* ... **169 C7** 4 59N 54 28W
Langdai, *China* .... **76 D5** 26 6N 105 21 E
Langdon, *U.S.A.* **154 A5** 48 45N 98 22W
Länge Jan = Ölands södra udde,
   Sweden .... **17 H10** 56 12N 16 23 E
Langeac, *France* .... **28 C7** 45 7N 3 29 E
Langeais, *France* .... **26 E7** 47 20N 0 24 E
Langeb Baraka ➤, *Sudan* ... **106 D4** 17 28N 36 50 E
Langeberg, S. *Africa* .... **116 E3** 33 55 S 21 0 E
Langeberge, S. *Africa* ...... **116 D3** 28 15 S 22 33 E
Langeland, *Denmark* .... **17 K4** 54 56N 10 48 E
Langelands Bælt, *Denmark* .. **17 K4** 54 50N 10 55 E
Langen, *Austria* .... **33 B10** 47 8N 10 7 E
Langen, Hessen, *Germany* ... **31 F4** 49 59N 8 40 E
Langen, Niedersachsen, *Germany* . **30 B4** 53 36N 8 36 E
Langenargen, *Germany* ...... **33 A9** 47 36N 9 33 E
Langenburg, *Canada* **143 C8** 50 51N 101 43W
Langeneß, *Germany* .... **30 A4** 54 38N 8 36 E
Langenlois, *Austria* .... **34 C8** 48 29N 15 40 E
Langenthal, *Switz.* .... **32 B5** 47 13N 7 47 E
Langeoog, *Germany* .... **30 B3** 53 45N 7 32 E
Langeskov, *Denmark* .... **17 J4** 55 22N 10 35 E
Langesund, *Norway* .... **18 F6** 59 0N 9 45 E
Langevåg, *Norway* .... **18 B3** 62 26N 6 13 E
Länghem, *Sweden* .... **17 G7** 57 36N 13 14 E
Langhirano, *Italy* .... **44 D7** 44 37N 10 16 E
Langholm, *U.K.* **22 F5** 55 9N 3 0W
Langisjór, *Iceland* **11 C6** 64 11N 18 55W
Langjökull, *Iceland* **11 C6** 64 39N 20 12W
Langkawi, Pulau, *Malaysia* .. **87 J2** 6 25N 99 45 E
Langklip, S. *Africa* .... **116 D3** 28 12 S 20 20 E
Langkon, *Malaysia* .... **85 A5** 6 30N 116 40 E
Langlade, St- P. & M. **141 C8** 46 50N 56 20W
Langley, *Canada* **160 A4** 49 7N 122 39W
Langnau, *Switz.* .... **32 C5** 46 56N 7 47 E
Langogne, *France* .... **28 D7** 44 43N 3 50 E
Langon, *France* **28 D3** 44 33N 0 16W
Langøya, *Norway* .... **14 B16** 68 45N 14 50 E
Langres, *France* .... **42 B5** 47 52N 5 20 E
Langres, Plateau de, *France* . **27 E12** 47 45N 5 3 E
Langsa, *Indonesia* .... **84 B1** 4 30N 97 57 E
Långsele, *Sweden* .... **16 A11** 63 12N 17 4 E
Långshyttan, *Sweden* .... **16 D10** 60 27N 16 2 E
Langtao, *Burma* .... **90 B6** 27 15N 97 34 E
Langting, *India* .... **90 C4** 25 31N 93 7 E
Langtry, *U.S.A.* **155 L4** 29 49N 101 34W
Langu, *Thailand* .... **87 J2** 6 53N 99 47 E
Langue de Barbarie, Parc Nat. de
   la △, *Senegal* **112 C1** 14 54N 16 30W
Languedoc, *France* .... **28 E7** 43 58N 3 55 E
Languedoc-Roussillon □, *France* . **28 E6** 43 25N 3 0 E
Langwang, *China* .... **69 F9** 22 38N 113 27 E
Langwies, *Switz.* .... **33 C9** 46 50N 9 44 E
Langxi, *China* .... **77 B12** 31 10N 119 12 E
Langxiangzhen, *China* .... **74 E9** 39 43N 116 8 E
Langzhong, *China* .... **76 B5** 31 38N 105 58 E
Lanigan, *Canada* **143 C7** 51 51N 105 2W
Lanigarh, *India* .... **94 E6** 19 43N 83 23 E
Lanjigarh, *India* .... **94 E6** 19 43N 83 23 E
Lanjian, *China* .... **74 G8** 34 48N 114 50 E
Länkäran, *Azerbaijan* .... **97 B6** 38 48N 48 52 E
Lanmeur, *France* **26 D3** 48 39N 3 43W
Lannemezan, *France* .... **28 E4** 43 8N 0 23 E
Lannilis, *France* **26 D2** 48 35N 4 32W
Lannion, *France* **26 D3** 48 46N 3 29W
L'Annonciation, *Canada* **140 C5** 46 25N 74 55W
Lanouaille, *France* .... **28 C5** 45 24N 1 9 E
Lanping, *China* .... **76 D2** 26 28N 99 12 E

Lansdale, *U.S.A.* **151 F9** 40 14N 75 17W
Lansdowne, *Australia* .... **129 A10** 31 48 S 152 30 E
Lansdowne, *Canada* **151 B8** 44 24N 76 1W
Lansdowne, *India* .... **93 E8** 29 50N 78 41 E
Lansdowne House, *Canada* .. **140 B2** 52 14N 87 53W
L'Anse, *U.S.A.* **148 B1** 46 45N 88 27W
L'Anse au Loup, *Canada* **141 B8** 51 32N 56 50W
L'Anse aux Meadows, *Canada* . **141 B8** 51 36N 55 32W
L'Anse la Raye, St. *Lucia* ... **165 f** 13 55N 61 19W
Lansford, *U.S.A.* **151 F9** 40 50N 75 53W
Lanshan, *China* .... **77 E9** 25 24N 112 10 E
Lansing, *U.S.A.* **157 B12** 42 44N 84 33W
Lanslebourg-Mont-Cenis, *France* . **29 C10** 45 17N 6 52 E
Lanta Yai, Ko, *Thailand* .... **87 J2** 7 35N 99 3 E
Lantana, *U.S.A.* **153 J9** 26 35N 80 3W
Lantau I., *China* .... **69 G10** 22 15N 113 56 E
Lantewa, *Nigeria* .... **113 C7** 12 16N 11 44 E
Lantian, *China* .... **74 G5** 34 11N 109 20 E
Lanus, *Argentina* .... **174 C4** 34 44 S 58 27W
Lanusei, *Italy* .... **46 C2** 39 52N 9 34 E
Lanuza, *Phil.* .... **81 G6** 9 16N 126 4 E
Lanxi, *China* .... **77 C12** 29 13N 119 28 E
Lanzarote, Canary Is. **9 e2** 29 0N 13 40W
Lanzarote ✈ (ACE), Canary Is. . **9 e2** 28 57N 13 40W
Lanzhou, *China* .... **74 F2** 36 1N 103 52 E
Lanzo Torinese, *Italy* .... **44 C4** 45 16N 7 28 E
Lao ➤, *Italy* .... **47 C8** 39 47N 15 48 E
Lao Bao, *Laos* .... **86 D6** 16 35N 106 30 E
Lao Cai, *Vietnam* .... **76 F4** 22 30N 103 57 E
Laoag, *Phil.* .... **80 B3** 18 7N 120 34 E
Laoang, *Phil.* .... **80 E5** 12 32N 125 8 E
Laoha He ➤, *China* .... **75 C11** 43 25N 120 35 E
Laohekou, *China* .... **77 A8** 32 22N 111 38 E
Laois □, *Ireland* **23 D4** 52 57N 7 36W
Laon, *France* .... **27 C10** 49 33N 3 35 E
Laona, *U.S.A.* **148 C1** 45 34N 88 40W
Lapa, *Brazil* .... **175 B6** 25 46 S 49 44W
Lapac I., *Phil.* .... **81 J3** 5 32N 120 47 E
Lapai, *Nigeria* .... **113 D6** 9 5N 6 32 E
Lapalisse, *France* .... **27 F10** 46 15N 3 38 E
Lapara I., *Phil.* .... **81 J2** 5 57N 120 0 E
Lapeer, *U.S.A.* **157 A13** 43 3N 83 19W
Lapeyrade, *France* **28 D3** 44 4N 0 3W
Lapithos, *Cyprus* .... **39 E9** 35 21N 33 11 E
Lapland = Lappland, *Europe* . **14 B21** 68 7N 24 0 E
Laporte, *U.S.A.* **151 E8** 41 25N 76 30W
Lapovo, Serbia, *Yug.* .... **50 B5** 44 10N 21 7 E
Lappeenranta, *Finland* ...... **15 F23** 61 3N 28 12 E
Lappland, *Europe* .... **14 B21** 68 7N 24 0 E
Laprida, *Argentina* .... **174 D3** 37 34 S 60 45W
Lâpseki, *Turkey* .... **51 F10** 40 20N 26 41 E
Laptev Sea, *Russia* .... **67 B13** 76 0N 125 0 E
Lapu-Lapu, *Phil.* .... **81 F4** 10 20N 123 55 E
Lapua, *Finland* .... **14 E20** 62 58N 23 0 E
Lăpuş ➤, *Romania* .... **53 C8** 47 25N 23 40 E
Lăpuş, Munţii, *Romania* .... **53 C8** 47 20N 23 50 E
Lăpuşna, *Moldova* .... **53 D13** 46 53N 28 25 E
Łapy, *Poland* .... **55 F9** 52 59N 22 52 E
Laqiya Arba'in, *Sudan* ...... **106 C2** 20 1N 28 1 E
Laqiya Umran, *Sudan* .... **106 D2** 19 55N 28 18 E
L'Áquila, *Italy* .... **45 F10** 42 22N 13 22 E
Lār, Azarbájan-e Sharqi, *Iran* . **96 B5** 38 30N 47 52 E
Lār, Fárs, *Iran* .... **97 E7** 27 40N 54 14 E
Lara, *Australia* .... **128 E6** 38 2 S 144 26 E
Lara □, *Venezuela* **168 A4** 10 10N 69 50W
Larabanga, *Ghana* **112 D4** 9 16N 1 56W
Larache, *Morocco* **110 A3** 35 10N 6 5W
Laragne-Montéglin, *France* .. **29 D9** 44 18N 5 49 E
Laramie, *U.S.A.* **154 E2** 41 19N 105 35W
Laramie ➤, *U.S.A.* **158 F11** 42 13N 104 33W
Laramie Mts., *U.S.A.* **154 E2** 42 0N 105 30W
Laranjeiras, *Brazil* .... **170 D4** 10 48 S 37 10W
Laranjeiras do Sul, *Brazil* .. **175 B5** 25 23 S 52 23W
Larantuka, *Indonesia* .... **82 C2** 8 21 S 122 55 E
Larat, *Indonesia* .... **83 C4** 7 0 S 132 0 E
L'Arbresle, *France* .... **29 C8** 45 50N 4 36 E
Lärbro, *Sweden* .... **17 G12** 57 47N 18 50 E
Lårdal, *Norway* .... **18 E5** 59 25N 8 10 E
Larde, *Mozam.* .... **119 F4** 16 28 S 39 43 E
Larder Lake, *Canada* **140 C4** 48 5N 79 40W
Lardhos, Ákra = Líndhos, Ákra,
   Greece .... **38 C10** 36 4N 28 10 E
Lárdhos, Órmos, *Greece* .... **38 C10** 36 4N 28 2 E
Laredo, *Spain* **42 B7** 43 26N 3 28W
Laredo, *U.S.A.* **155 M5** 27 30N 99 30W
Laredo Sd., *Canada* **142 C3** 52 30N 128 53W
Larena, *Phil.* .... **81 G4** 9 15N 123 35 E
Largentière, *France* .... **29 D8** 44 34N 4 18 E
L'Argentière-la-Bessée, *France* . **29 D10** 44 47N 6 33 E
Largo, *U.S.A.* **153 H7** 27 55N 82 47W
Largo, Key, *U.S.A.* **153 K9** 25 5N 80 15W
Largs, *U.K.* **22 F4** 55 47N 4 52W
Lari, *Italy* .... **44 E7** 43 34N 10 35 E
Lariang, *Indonesia* .... **82 B1** 1 26 S 119 17 E
Larimore, *U.S.A.* **154 B6** 47 54N 97 38W
Lārīn, *Iran* .... **97 C7** 35 55N 52 19 E
Larino, *Italy* .... **45 G11** 41 48N 14 54 E
Lárisa, *Greece* .... **48 B4** 39 36N 22 27 E
Lárisa □, *Greece* .... **48 B4** 39 39N 22 24 E
Larkana, *Pakistan* .... **91 D3** 27 32N 68 18 E
Larnaca, *Cyprus* .... **39 F9** 34 55N 33 38 E
Larnaca ✈ (LCA), *Cyprus* .... **39 F9** 34 50N 33 34 E
Larnaca Bay, *Cyprus* .... **39 F9** 34 53N 33 45 E
Larne, *U.K.* **23 B6** 54 51N 5 51W
Larned, *U.S.A.* **154 F5** 38 11N 99 6W
Laroquebrou, *France* .... **28 D6** 44 58N 2 12 E
Larose, *U.S.A.* **155 L9** 29 34N 90 23W
Larrimah, *Australia* .... **124 C5** 15 35 S 133 12 E
Larsen Bay, *U.S.A.* **144 H9** 57 32N 153 59W
Larsen Ice Shelf, *Antarctica* . **7 C17** 67 0 S 62 0W
Laruns, *France* **28 F3** 43 0N 0 26W
Larvik, *Norway* .... **18 E7** 59 4N 10 2 E
Larzac, Causse du, *France* ... **28 E7** 43 50N 3 17 E
Las Alpujarras, *Spain* **41 J1** 36 55N 3 20W
Las Animas, *U.S.A.* **154 F3** 38 4N 103 13W
Las Anod, Somali *Rep.* ...... **108 D3** 8 26N 47 19 E
Las Arenas, *Spain* **42 B6** 43 17N 4 50W
Las Aves, Is., W. *Indies* **165 C7** 15 45N 63 55W
Las Batuecas, Reserva Nac. de △,
   Spain **42 E4** 40 32N 6 5W
Las Bonitas, *Venezuela* **168 B4** 7 52N 65 40W
Las Breñas, *Argentina* ...... **174 B3** 27 5 S 61 7W
Las Cabezas de San Juan, *Spain* . **43 J5** 36 57N 5 58W
Las Cañadas del Teide, Parque Nac.
   de △, Canary Is. **9 e1** 28 15N 16 37W
Las Chimeneas, *Mexico* **161 N10** 32 8N 116 5W
Las Coloradas, *Argentina* ... **176 A2** 39 34 S 70 36W
Las Cruces, *U.S.A.* **159 K10** 32 19N 106 47W
Las Flores, *Argentina* .... **174 D4** 36 10 S 59 7W
Las Heras, *Argentina* .... **174 C2** 32 51 S 68 49W
Las Horquetas, *Argentina* ... **176 C2** 48 14 S 71 11W
Las Khoreh, Somali *Rep.* .... **108 C4** 11 10N 48 20 E
Las Lajas, *Argentina* .... **176 A2** 38 30 S 70 25W
Las Lomas, *Peru* .... **172 A1** 4 40 S 80 10W
Las Lomitas, *Argentina* ..... **174 A3** 24 43 S 60 35W
Las Marismas, *Spain* **43 H4** 37 5N 6 20W
Las Mercedes, *Venezuela* **168 B4** 9 39N 66 24W
Las Minas, *Spain* **41 G3** 38 20N 1 41W
Las Navas de la Concepción, *Spain* . **43 H5** 37 56N 5 30W
Las Navas del Marqués, *Spain* . **42 E6** 40 36N 4 20W
Las Nieves, *Phil.* .... **81 G5** 8 46N 125 34 E
Las Palmas, *Argentina* ...... **174 B4** 27 8 S 58 45W
Las Palmas, Canary Is. **9 e1** 28 7N 15 26W

Las Palmas ➤, *Mexico* **161 N10** 32 26N 116 54W
Las Palmas ✈ (LPA), Canary Is. . **9 e1** 27 55N 15 25W
Las Pedroñas, *Spain* **41 F2** 39 26N 2 40W
Las Piedras, *Uruguay* .... **175 C4** 34 44 S 56 14W
Las Pipinas, *Argentina* ..... **174 D4** 35 30 S 57 19W
Las Plumas, *Argentina* ...... **176 B3** 43 40 S 67 15W
Las Rosas, *Argentina* .... **174 C3** 32 30 S 61 35W
Las Rozas, *Spain* **42 E7** 40 29N 3 52W
Las Tablas, *Panama* **164 E3** 7 49N 80 14W
Las Termas, *Argentina* ...... **174 B3** 27 29 S 64 52W
Las Toscas, *Argentina* ...... **174 B4** 28 21 S 59 18W
Las Truchas, *Mexico* **162 D4** 17 57N 102 13W
Las Varillas, *Argentina* ..... **174 C3** 31 50 S 62 50W
Las Vegas, N. *Mex., U.S.A.* .. **159 J11** 35 36N 105 13W
Las Vegas, Nev., *U.S.A.* **161 J11** 36 10N 115 9W
Las Vegas McCarran International ✈
   (LAS), *U.S.A.* **161 J11** 36 5N 115 9W
Lasanga I., Papua N. G. ...... **132 D4** 7 25 S 147 15 E
Lasarte, *Spain* **40 B2** 43 16N 2 1W
Lascano, *Uruguay* .... **175 C5** 33 35 S 54 12W
Lascelles, *Australia* .... **128 C5** 35 34 S 142 34 E
Lash-e Joveyn, *Afghan.* ..... **91 C1** 31 45N 61 30 E
Lashburn, *Canada* **143 C7** 53 10N 109 40W
Lashio, *Burma* .... **90 D6** 22 56N 97 45 E
Lashkar, *India* .... **92 F8** 26 10N 78 10 E
Lashkar Gāh, *Afghan.* .... **91 C2** 31 35N 64 21 E
Łasin, *Poland* .... **54 E6** 53 30N 19 2 E
Lasíthi, *Greece* .... **39 E6** 35 11N 25 31 E
Lasíthi □, *Greece* .... **39 E6** 35 5N 25 50 E
Lāsjerd, *Iran* .... **97 C7** 35 24N 53 4 E
Lask, *Poland* .... **55 G6** 51 34N 19 8 E
Łaskarzew, *Poland* .... **55 G8** 51 48N 21 36 E
Laško, *Slovenia* .... **45 B12** 46 10N 15 16 E
Lassance, *Brazil* .... **171 E3** 17 54 S 44 34W
Lassay-les-Châteaux, *France* . **26 D6** 48 27N 0 30W
Lassen Pk., *U.S.A.* **158 F3** 40 29N 121 31W
Lassen Volcanic Nat. Park △, *U.S.A.* . **158 F3** 40 30N 121 20W
Lassongo, *Angola* .... **115 E4** 12 5 S 22 46 E
Last Mountain L., *Canada* ... **143 C7** 51 5N 105 14W
Lastchance Cr. ➤, *U.S.A.* ... **160 E5** 40 2N 121 15W
Lastoursville, *Gabon* .... **114 C2** 0 55 S 12 38 E
Lastovo, *Croatia* .... **45 F13** 42 46N 16 55 E
Lastovski Kanal, *Croatia* .... **45 F14** 42 50N 17 0 E
Lat Yao, *Thailand* .... **86 E2** 15 45N 99 48 E
Latacunga, *Ecuador* .... **168 D2** 0 50 S 78 35W
Latakia = Al Lādhiqīyah, *Syria* . **100 E6** 35 30N 35 45 E
Latchford, *Canada* **140 C4** 47 20N 79 50W
Late, *Tonga* .... **133 P13** 18 48 S 174 39W
Latehar, *India* .... **93 H11** 23 45N 84 30 E
Laterza, *Italy* .... **47 B9** 40 37N 16 48 E
Latham, *Australia* .... **125 E2** 29 44 S 116 20 E
Lathen, *Germany* .... **30 C3** 52 52N 7 19 E
Lathi, *India* .... **92 F4** 27 43N 71 23 E
Lathrop, *U.S.A.* **156 E2** 39 33N 94 20W
Lathrop Wells, *U.S.A.* **161 J10** 36 39N 116 24W
Latiano, *Italy* .... **47 B10** 40 33N 17 43 E
Latina, *Italy* .... **46 A5** 41 28N 12 52 E
Latisana, *Italy* .... **45 C10** 45 47N 13 0 E
Latium = Lazio □, *Italy* ..... **45 F9** 42 10N 12 30 E
Laton, *U.S.A.* **160 J7** 36 26N 119 41W
Latorytsya ➤, Slovak *Rep.* ... **35 C14** 48 28N 21 50 E
Latouche Treville, C., *Australia* . **124 C3** 18 27 S 121 49 E
Latouma, *Niger* .... **109 D2** 22 10N 14 50 E
Látrar, *Iceland* **11 A3** 66 24N 23 2W
Latrobe, *Australia* .... **127 D4** 41 14 S 146 30 E
Latrobe, *U.S.A.* **150 F5** 40 19N 79 23W
Latrónico, *Italy* .... **47 B9** 40 5N 16 1 E
Latur, *India* .... **94 E3** 18 25N 76 40 E
Latvia ■, *Europe* .... **15 H20** 56 50N 24 0 E
Lau, *Nigeria* .... **113 D7** 9 11N 11 19 E
Lau Fau Shan, *China* .... **69 G10** 22 28N 113 59 E
Lau Group, *Fiji* .... **133 A3** 17 0 S 178 30W
Lauca ➤, *Bolivia* .... **172 D4** 19 9 S 68 10W
Lauchhammer, *Germany* ..... **30 D9** 51 29N 13 47 E
Lauda-Königshofen, *Germany* . **31 F5** 49 33N 9 42 E
Laudal, *Norway* .... **18 F4** 58 15N 7 30 E
Lauenburg, *Germany* .... **30 B6** 53 22N 10 32 E
Lauenburgische Seen, Naturpark △,
   Germany .... **30 B6** 53 38N 10 45 E
Lauf, *Germany* .... **31 F7** 49 30N 11 16 E
Laufás, *Iceland* **11 B8** 65 53N 18 4W
Läufelfingen, *Switz.* .... **32 B5** 47 24N 7 52 E
Laufen, *Switz.* .... **32 B5** 47 25N 7 30 E
Laugar, *Iceland* **11 B5** 65 15N 21 48W
Laugarás, *Iceland* **11 C6** 64 7N 20 30W
Laugarbakki, *Iceland* **11 B6** 65 20N 20 55W
Laugarvatn, *Iceland* **11 C6** 64 13N 20 45W
Laughlin, *U.S.A.* **159 J6** 35 8N 114 35W
Laujar de Andarax, *Spain* ... **41 H2** 37 0N 2 54W
Laukaa, *Finland* .... **15 E21** 62 24N 25 56 E
Launceston, *Australia* ...... **127 D4** 41 24 S 147 8 E
Launceston, *U.K.* **21 G3** 50 38N 4 22W
Laune ➤, *Ireland* **23 D2** 52 7N 9 47W
Launglon Bok, *Burma* .... **86 F1** 13 50N 97 54 E
Laupheim, *Germany* .... **31 G5** 48 14N 9 52 E
Laura, Queens., *Australia* ... **126 B3** 15 32 S 144 32 E
Laura, S. *Austral., Australia* . **128 E2** 33 10 S 138 18 E
Laureana di Borrello, *Italy* .. **47 D9** 38 30N 16 5 E
Laurel, Fla., *U.S.A.* **153 H7** 27 8N 82 27W
Laurel, Ind., *U.S.A.* **157 E11** 39 31N 85 11W
Laurel, Miss., *U.S.A.* **155 K10** 31 41N 89 8W
Laurel, Mont., *U.S.A.* **158 D9** 45 40N 108 46W
Laurel Bay, *U.S.A.* **152 C9** 32 27N 80 47W
Laurencekirk, *U.K.* **22 E6** 56 50N 2 28W
Laurens, Iowa, *U.S.A.* **156 B2** 42 51N 94 52W
Laurens, S.C., *U.S.A.* **149 H4** 34 30N 82 1W
Laurentian Plateau, *Canada* . **141 B6** 52 0N 70 0W
Lauria, *Italy* .... **47 B8** 40 2N 15 50 E
Laurie L., *Canada* **143 B8** 56 35N 101 57W
Laurinburg, *U.S.A.* **149 H6** 34 47N 79 28W
Laurium, *U.S.A.* **148 B1** 47 14N 88 27W
Lausanne, *Switz.* .... **32 C3** 46 32N 6 38 E
Laut, *Indonesia* .... **84 C3** 4 45N 108 0 E
Laut, Pulau, *Indonesia* ...... **85 C5** 3 40 S 116 10 E
Laut Kecil, Kepulauan, *Indonesia* . **85 C5** 4 45 S 115 40 E
Lautaro, *Chile* .... **176 A2** 38 31 S 72 27W
Lautem, E. *Timor* .... **83 C3** 8 22 S 126 54 E
Lauterbach, *Germany* .... **30 E5** 50 37N 9 24 E
Lauterbrunnen, *Switz.* .... **32 C5** 46 36N 7 55 E
Lauterecken, *Germany* ...... **31 F3** 49 38N 7 35 E
Lautoka, *Fiji* .... **133 A1** 17 37 S 177 27 E
Lauzès, *France* .... **28 D5** 44 34N 1 35 E
Lava Beds Nat. Monument △, *U.S.A.* . **158 F3** 41 40N 121 30W
Lavagh More, *Ireland* **23 B3** 54 46N 8 6W
Lavagna, *Italy* .... **44 D6** 44 18N 9 22 E
Laval, *France* **26 D6** 48 4N 0 48W
Lavalle, *Argentina* .... **174 B2** 28 15 S 65 15W
Lavanggu, Solomon Is. .... **133 N11** 11 36 S 160 16 E
Lavant Station, *Canada* **151 A8** 45 3N 76 42W
Lāvar Meydān, *Iran* .... **97 D7** 30 20N 54 30 E
Lavardac, *France* .... **28 D4** 44 12N 0 20 E
Lavaur, *France* .... **28 E5** 43 40N 1 49 E
Lavaux, *Switz.* .... **32 D3** 46 30N 6 45 E
Lavelanet, *France* .... **28 F5** 42 57N 1 51 E
L'Averdy, C., Papua N. G. .... **132 C8** 5 33 S 155 4 E
Lavers Hill, *Australia* .... **128 E5** 38 40 S 143 25 E
Laverton, *Australia* .... **125 E3** 28 44 S 122 29 E
Lavik, *Norway* .... **18 C2** 61 6N 5 25 E
Lavis, *Italy* .... **44 B8** 46 8N 11 7 E
Lávkos, *Greece* .... **48 B5** 39 9N 23 14 E

Lavos, *Portugal* **42 E2** 40 6N 8 49W
Lavradio, *Portugal* **43 G1** 38 40N 9 3W
Lavras, *Brazil* .... **171 F3** 21 20 S 45 0W
Lavre, *Portugal* **43 G2** 38 46N 8 22W
Lávrion, *Greece* .... **48 D6** 37 40N 24 4 E
Lávris, *Greece* .... **39 E5** 35 25N 24 40 E
Lavumisa, *Swaziland* .... **117 D5** 27 20 S 31 55 E
Lavushi Manda Nat. Park △, *Zambia* . **119 E3** 12 46 S 31 10 E
Lawa, *Phil.* .... **81 H5** 6 12N 125 41 E
Lawa-an, *Phil.* .... **81 F5** 11 51N 125 5 E
Lawaki, *Fiji* .... **133 A2** 17 40 S 178 35 E
Lawas, *Malaysia* .... **85 B5** 4 55N 115 25 E
Lawdar, *Yemen* .... **98 D4** 13 53N 45 52 E
Lawele, *Indonesia* .... **82 C2** 5 13 S 122 57 E
Lawksawk, *Burma* .... **90 E6** 21 15N 96 52 E
Lawn Hill Nat. Park △, *Australia* . **126 B2** 18 15 S 138 6 E
Lawowa, *Indonesia* .... **82 B2** 4 26 S 122 56 E
Lawqah, Si. *Arabia* .... **96 D4** 29 49N 42 45 E
Lawra, *Ghana* **112 C4** 10 39N 2 51W
Lawrence, *N.Z.* .... **131 F4** 45 55 S 169 41 E
Lawrence, Ind., *U.S.A.* **157 E10** 39 50N 86 2W
Lawrence, Kans., *U.S.A.* **154 F7** 38 58N 95 14W
Lawrence, Mass., *U.S.A.* **151 D13** 42 43N 71 10W
Lawrenceburg, Ind., *U.S.A.* .. **157 E12** 39 6N 84 52W
Lawrenceburg, Ky., *U.S.A.* ... **157 F12** 38 2N 84 54W
Lawrenceburg, Tenn., *U.S.A.* . **149 H2** 35 14N 87 20W
Lawrenceville, Ga., *U.S.A.* .. **152 B6** 33 57N 83 59W
Lawrenceville, Ill., *U.S.A.* ... **157 F9** 38 44N 87 41W
Lawrenceville, Pa., *U.S.A.* ... **150 E7** 41 59N 77 8W
Laws, *U.S.A.* **160 H8** 37 24N 118 20W
Lawson, *U.S.A.* **156 E2** 39 26N 94 12W
Lawtey, *U.S.A.* **152 E7** 30 3N 82 5W
Lawton, Mich., *U.S.A.* **157 B11** 42 10N 85 50W
Lawton, Okla., *U.S.A.* **155 H5** 34 37N 98 25W
Lawu, *Indonesia* .... **85 G14** 7 40 S 111 13 E
Lawz, J. al, Si. *Arabia* ...... **106 H4** 28 39N 35 18 E
Laxá, *Sweden* .... **17 F8** 58 59N 14 37 E
Laxamýri, *Iceland* **11 B9** 65 58N 17 24W
Laxford, L., *U.K.* **22 C3** 58 24N 5 6W
Laxou, *France* .... **27 D13** 48 41N 6 8 E
Lay ➤, *France* **28 B2** 46 18N 1 17W
Layla, Si. *Arabia* .... **98 B4** 22 10N 46 40 E
Laylān, *Iraq* .... **96 C5** 35 18N 44 31 E
Layon ➤, *France* **26 E6** 47 20N 0 45W
Laysan I., *U.S.A.* **145 F9** 25 50N 171 50W
Layton, Fla., *U.S.A.* **153 L9** 24 50N 80 47W
Layton, Utah, *U.S.A.* **158 F7** 41 4N 111 58W
Laytonville, *U.S.A.* **158 G2** 39 41N 123 29W
Laza, *Burma* .... **90 B6** 26 30N 97 38 E
Lazardia, *Brazil* .... **39 B2** 38 47N 20 40 E
Lazarevac, Serbia, *Yug.* ..... **50 B4** 44 23N 20 17 E
Lazarevskoye, *Russia* .... **61 J4** 43 55N 39 21 E
Lazarivo, *Madag.* .... **117 C8** 23 54 S 44 59 E
Lazdijai, *Lithuania* .... **54 D10** 54 14N 23 31 E
Lazi, *Phil.* .... **81 G4** 9 8N 123 38 E
Lazio □, *Italy* .... **45 F9** 42 10N 12 30 E
Lazo, *Moldova* .... **53 C13** 47 33N 28 2 E
Lazo, *Russia* .... **70 C6** 43 25N 133 55 E
Le Beausset, *France* .... **29 E9** 43 12N 5 48 E
Le Blanc, *France* .... **28 B5** 46 37N 1 3 E
Le Bleymard, *France* .... **28 D7** 44 30N 3 42 E
Le Bourgneuf-la-Forêt, *France* . **26 D6** 48 10N 0 59W
Le Brassus, *Switz.* .... **32 C2** 46 35N 6 13 E
Le Bugue, *France* .... **28 D4** 44 55N 0 56 E
Le Canourgue = La Canourgue,
   France .... **28 D7** 44 26N 3 13 E
Le Cateau Cambrésis, *France* . **27 B10** 50 7N 3 32 E
Le Caylar, *France* .... **28 E7** 43 51N 3 19 E
Le Châble, *Switz.* .... **32 D4** 46 5N 7 12 E
Le Chambon-Feugerolles, *France* . **29 C8** 45 24N 4 19 E
Le Châtelard, *France* .... **32 D3** 46 4N 6 57 E
Le Châtelet, *France* .... **27 F9** 46 38N 2 16 E
Le Chesne, *France* .... **27 C11** 49 30N 4 45 E
Le Cheylard, *France* .... **29 D8** 44 55N 4 25 E
Le Claire, *U.S.A.* **156 C6** 41 36N 90 21W
Le Conquet, *France* **26 D2** 48 21N 4 46W
Le Creusot, *France* .... **27 F11** 46 48N 4 24 E
Le Croisic, *France* **26 E4** 47 18N 2 30W
Le Donjon, *France* .... **27 F10** 46 22N 3 48 E
Le Dorat, *France* .... **28 B5** 46 14N 1 5 E
Le François, *Martinique* .... **164 c** 14 38N 60 57W
Le Grand-Lucé, *France* ..... **26 E7** 47 52N 0 28 E
Le Grand-Pressigny, *France* . **26 F7** 46 55N 0 48 E
Le Grand-Quevilly, *France* .. **26 C8** 49 24N 1 3 E
Le Gris Gris, *Mauritius* ..... **121 d** 20 31 S 57 32 E
Le Havre, *France* .... **26 C7** 49 30N 0 5 E
Le Lamentin, *Martinique* ... **164 c** 14 35N 61 2W
Le Lavandou, *France* .... **29 E10** 43 8N 6 22 E
Le Lion-d'Angers, *France* ... **26 E6** 47 37N 0 43W
Le Locle, *Switz.* .... **32 B3** 47 3N 6 44 E
Le Louroux-Béconnais, *France* . **26 E6** 47 30N 0 55W
Le Luc, *France* .... **29 E10** 43 23N 6 21 E
Le Lude, *France* .... **26 E7** 47 39N 0 9 E
Le Maire, Estr. de, *Argentina* . **176 D4** 54 50 S 65 0W
Le Mans, *France* .... **26 E7** 48 0N 0 10 E
Le Marin, *Martinique* .... **164 c** 14 27N 60 55W
Le Mars, *U.S.A.* **154 D6** 42 47N 96 10W
Le Mayet-de-Montagne, *France* . **27 F10** 46 4N 3 40 E
Le Mêle-sur-Sarthe, *France* . **26 D7** 48 31N 0 22 E
Le Moléson, *Switz.* .... **32 C4** 46 33N 7 1 E
Le Monastier-sur-Gazeille, *France* . **28 D7** 44 57N 3 59 E
Le Monêtier-les-Bains, *France* . **29 D10** 44 58N 6 30 E
Le Mont-Dore, *France* ...... **28 C6** 45 35N 2 49 E
Le Mont-St-Michel, *France* .. **26 D5** 48 40N 1 30W
Le Muy, *France* .... **29 E10** 43 28N 6 34 E
Le Palais, *France* **26 E3** 47 20N 3 9W
Le Perthus, *France* .... **28 F6** 42 30N 2 53 E
Le Pont, *Switz.* .... **32 C2** 46 41N 6 19 E
Le Port, *Réunion* .... **121 c** 20 56 S 55 18 E
Le Prêcheur, *Martinique* .... **164 c** 14 50N 61 12W
Le Puy-en-Velay, *France* ..... **28 C7** 45 3N 3 52 E
Le Robert, *Martinique* ...... **164 c** 14 40N 60 56W
Le Roy, *U.S.A.* **157 D8** 38 5N 88 46W
Le St-Esprit, *Martinique* .... **164 c** 14 34N 60 56W
Le Sentier, *Switz.* .... **32 C2** 46 37N 6 15 E
Le Sueur, *U.S.A.* **154 C8** 44 28N 93 55W
Le Tampon, *Réunion* .... **121 c** 21 16 S 55 32 E
Le Teil, *France* .... **29 D8** 44 33N 4 40 E
Le Teilleul, *France* **26 D6** 48 32N 0 53W
Le Theil, *France* .... **26 D7** 48 16N 0 42 E
Le Thillot, *France* .... **27 E13** 47 53N 6 46 E
Le Thuy, *Vietnam* .... **86 D6** 17 14N 106 49 E
Le Touquet-Paris-Plage, *France* . **27 B8** 50 30N 1 36 E
Le Tréport, *France* .... **26 B8** 50 3N 1 20 E
Le Val-d'Ajol, *France* .... **27 E13** 47 55N 6 30 E
Le Verdon-sur-Mer, *France* .. **28 C2** 45 33N 1 4W
Le Vigan, *France* .... **28 E7** 43 59N 3 36 E
Lea ➤, *U.K.* .... **21 F8** 51 31N 0 1 E
Lea Lea, Papua N. G. .... **132 E4** 9 17 S 146 59 E
Leach, *Cambodia* .... **87 F4** 12 21N 103 46 E
Lead, *U.S.A.* **154 C3** 44 21N 103 46W
Leader, *Canada* **143 C7** 50 50N 109 30W
Leadhills, *U.K.* **22 F5** 55 25N 3 47W
Leadville, *U.S.A.* **159 G10** 39 15N 106 18W
Leaf ➤, *U.S.A.* **155 K10** 30 59N 88 44W
Leaf Rapids, *Canada* **143 B9** 56 30N 99 59W
Leaghur L., *Australia* .... **128 E3** 33 35 S 143 3 E
Lealui, *Zambia* .... **115 F4** 15 10 S 23 2 E
Leamington, *Canada* **140 D3** 42 3N 82 36W
Leamington, *N.Z.* .... **130 H4** 37 55 S 175 30 E
Leamington, *U.S.A.* **158 G7** 39 32N 112 17W
Leamington Spa = Royal
   Leamington Spa, *U.K.* ... **21 E6** 52 18N 1 31W
Le'an, *China* .... **77 D10** 27 22N 115 48 E
Leandro Norte Alem, *Argentina* . **175 B4** 27 34 S 55 15W

Leane, L., Ireland 23 D2 52 2N 9 32W
Learmonth, Australia 124 D1 22 13 S 114 10 E
Leary, U.S.A. 152 D5 31 29N 84 31W
Leask, Canada 143 C7 53 5N 106 45W
Leatherhead, U.K. 21 F7 51 18N 0 20W
Leavenworth, Ind., U.S.A. 157 F10 38 12N 86 21W
Leavenworth, Kans., U.S.A. 154 F7 39 19N 94 55W
Leavenworth, Wash., U.S.A. 158 C3 47 36N 120 40W
Leawood, U.S.A. 156 F2 38 57N 94 37W
Łeba, Poland 54 D4 54 45N 17 32 E
Łeba →, Poland 54 D4 54 46N 17 33 E
Lebach, Germany 31 F2 49 25N 6 54 E
Lebak, Phil. 81 H5 6 32N 124 5 E
Lebam, U.S.A. 160 D3 46 34N 123 33W
Lebane, Serbia, Yug. 50 D5 42 56N 21 44 E
Lebango, Congo 114 B2 0 39N 14 21 E
Lebango →, Congo 114 B2 0 2N 14 52 E
Lebanon, Ill., U.S.A. 156 F7 38 38N 89 49W
Lebanon, Ind., U.S.A. 157 D10 40 3N 86 28W
Lebanon, Kans., U.S.A. 154 F5 39 49N 98 33W
Lebanon, Ky., U.S.A. 148 G3 37 34N 85 15W
Lebanon, Mo., U.S.A. 155 G8 37 41N 92 40W
Lebanon, N.H., U.S.A. 151 C12 43 39N 72 15W
Lebanon, Ohio, U.S.A. 157 E12 39 26N 84 13W
Lebanon, Oreg., U.S.A. 158 D2 44 32N 122 55W
Lebanon, Pa., U.S.A. 151 F8 40 20N 76 26W
Lebanon, Tenn., U.S.A. 149 G2 36 12N 86 18W
Lebanon ■, Asia 103 B5 34 0N 36 0 E
Lebanon Junction, U.S.A. 157 G11 37 50N 85 44W
Lebanon Station, U.S.A. 153 F7 29 10N 82 37W
Lebec, U.S.A. 161 L8 34 50N 118 52W
Lebedyan, Russia 59 F10 53 0N 39 10 E
Lebedyn, Ukraine 59 G8 50 35N 34 30 E
Lebel-sur-Quévillon, Canada 140 C4 49 3N 76 59W
Lebo, Dem. Rep. of the Congo 114 B4 4 30N 23 58 E
Lebomboberge, S. Africa 117 C5 24 30 S 32 0 E
Lębork, Poland 54 D4 54 33N 17 46 E
Lebrija, Spain 43 J4 36 53N 6 5W
Łebsko, Jezioro, Poland 54 D4 54 40N 17 25 E
Lebu, Chile 174 D1 37 40 S 73 47W
Leca da Palmeira, Portugal 42 D2 41 12N 8 42W
Lecce, Italy 47 B11 40 23N 18 11 E
Lecco, Italy 44 C6 45 51N 9 23 E
Lecco, L. di, Italy 44 C6 45 51N 9 19 E
Lécera, Spain 40 D4 41 13N 0 43W
Lech, Austria 34 D3 47 13N 10 9 E
Lech →, Germany 31 G6 48 43N 10 56 E
Lechang, China 77 E9 25 10N 113 20 E
Lechtaler Alpen, Austria 34 D3 47 15N 10 30 E
Léconi, Gabon 114 C2 1 35 S 14 14 E
Léconi →, Gabon 114 C2 1 11 S 13 16 E
Lecontes Mills, U.S.A. 150 E6 41 5N 78 17W
Lectoure, France 28 E4 43 56N 0 38 E
Łęczna, Poland 55 F9 51 18N 22 53 E
Łęczyca, Poland 55 F6 52 5N 19 15 E
Ledang, Gunong, Malaysia 84 B2 2 22N 102 37 E
Ledesma, Spain 42 D5 41 6N 5 59W
Lediba, Dem. Rep. of the Congo 114 C3 3 1 S 16 34 E
Lédo, Cabo, Angola 115 D2 9 43 S 13 12 E
Ledong, China 86 C7 18 41N 109 5 E
Leduc, Canada 142 C6 53 15N 113 30W
Lee, Fla., U.S.A. 152 E6 30 25N 83 18W
Lee, Mass., U.S.A. 151 D11 42 19N 73 15W
Lee →, Ireland 23 E3 51 53N 8 56W
Lee Vining, U.S.A. 160 H7 37 58N 119 7W
Leech L., U.S.A. 154 B7 47 10N 94 24W
Leechburg, U.S.A. 150 F5 40 37N 79 36W
Leeds, U.K. 20 D6 53 48N 1 33W
Leeds, U.S.A. 149 J2 33 33N 86 33W
Leek, Neths. 24 A6 53 10N 6 24 E
Leek, U.K. 20 D5 53 7N 2 1W
Leeman, Australia 125 E1 29 57 S 114 58 E
Leeper, U.S.A. 150 E5 41 22N 79 18W
Leer, Germany 30 B3 53 13N 7 26 E
Lee's Summit, U.S.A. 156 F2 38 55N 94 23W
Leesburg, Fla., U.S.A. 153 G8 28 49N 81 53W
Leesburg, Ga., U.S.A. 152 D5 31 44N 84 10W
Leesburg, Ohio, U.S.A. 157 E13 39 21N 83 33W
Leeston, N.Z. 131 D7 43 45 S 172 19 E
Leesville, U.S.A. 155 K8 31 9N 93 16W
Leeton, Australia 129 C7 34 33 S 146 23 E
Leetonia, U.S.A. 150 F4 40 53N 80 45W
Leeu Gamka, S. Africa 116 E3 32 47 S 21 59 E
Leeuwarden, Neths. 24 A5 53 15N 5 48 E
Leeuwin, C., Australia 125 F2 34 20 S 115 9 E
Leeuwin Naturaliste Nat. Park △,
   Australia 125 F2 34 6 S 115 3 E
Leeward Is., Atl. Oc. 165 C7 16 30N 63 30W
Léfini, Congo 114 C3 2 55 S 15 39 E
Léfini →, Congo 114 C3 2 56 S 16 9 E
Léfini, Réserve de Chasse de la △,
   Congo 114 C3 2 55 S 15 20 E
Lefka, Cyprus 39 E8 35 6N 32 51 E
Lefkoniko, Cyprus 39 E9 35 18N 33 44 E
Lefroy, Canada 150 B5 44 16N 79 34W
Lefroy, L., Australia 125 F3 31 21 S 121 40 E
Łeg →, Poland 55 H8 50 42N 21 50 E
Leganés, Spain 42 E7 40 19N 3 45W
Legazpi, Phil. 80 E4 13 10N 123 45 E
Lège-Cap-Ferret, France 28 D2 44 48N 1 9W
Lege Hida, Ethiopia 107 F5 7 56N 41 4 E
Legendre I., Australia 124 D2 20 22 S 116 55 E
Leghorn = Livorno, Italy 44 E7 43 33N 10 19 E
Legionowo, Poland 55 F7 52 25N 20 50 E
Legnago, Italy 45 C8 45 11N 11 18 E
Legnano, Italy 44 C5 45 36N 8 54 E
Legnica, Poland 55 G3 51 12N 16 10 E
Legrad, Croatia 45 B13 46 17N 16 51 E
Leh, India 93 B7 34 9N 77 35 E
Lehigh Acres, U.S.A. 153 J8 26 36N 81 39W
Lehighton, U.S.A. 151 F9 40 50N 75 43W
Lehliu, Romania 53 F11 44 29N 26 50 E
Lehrte, Germany 30 C5 52 22N 9 58 E
Lehua I., U.S.A. 145 A1 22 1N 160 6W
Lehututu, Botswana 116 C3 23 54 S 21 55 E
Lei Shui →, China 77 D9 26 55N 112 35 E
Leiah, Pakistan 91 D4 30 58N 70 58 E
Leibnitz, Austria 34 E8 46 47N 15 34 E
Leibo, China 76 C4 28 11N 103 34 E
Leicester, U.K. 21 E6 52 38N 1 8W
Leicester City □, U.K. 21 E6 52 38N 1 8W
Leicestershire □, U.K. 21 E6 52 41N 1 17W
Leichhardt →, Australia 126 B2 17 35 S 139 48 E
Leichhardt Ra., Australia 126 C4 20 46 S 147 40 E
Leiden, Neths. 24 B4 52 9N 4 30 E
Leie →, Belgium 24 C3 51 2N 3 45 E
Leifers = Láives, Italy 45 B8 46 26N 11 20 E
Leigh →, Australia 128 E6 38 4 S 144 2 E
Leigh Creek, Australia 128 A3 30 38 S 138 26 E
Leikanger, Sogn og Fjordane,
   Norway 18 B2 62 8N 5 18 E
Leikanger, Sogn og Fjordane,
   Norway 18 C2 61 10N 6 51 E
Leikong, Norway 18 B2 62 15N 5 47 E
Leikthó, Burma 90 F6 19 13N 96 35 E
Leimen, Germany 31 F4 49 21N 8 41 E
Leine →, Germany 30 C5 52 43N 9 36 E
Leinefelde, Germany 30 D6 51 23N 10 19 E
Leinster, Australia 125 E3 27 51 S 120 36 E
Leinster □, Ireland 23 C4 53 3N 7 8W
Leinster, Mt., Ireland 23 D5 52 37N 6 46W
Leipalingis, Lithuania 54 D10 54 5N 23 51 E
Leipzig, Germany 30 D8 51 18N 12 22 E

Leira, Norway 18 D6 60 58N 9 17 E
Leira, Portugal 42 F2 39 46N 8 53W
Leiria □, Portugal 42 F2 39 46N 8 53W
Leirvåssbu, Norway 18 C5 61 33N 8 13 E
Leirvik, Norway 18 E2 59 47N 5 28 E
Leishan, China 76 D7 26 15N 108 20 E
Leisler, Mt., Australia 124 D4 23 23 S 129 20 E
Leisure City, U.S.A. 153 K9 25 31N 80 26W
Leith, U.K. 22 F5 55 59N 3 11W
Leith Hill, U.K. 21 F7 51 11N 0 22W
Leitha →, Europe 35 D10 47 50N 17 15 E
Leitrim, Ireland 23 B3 54 0N 8 5W
Leitrim □, Ireland 23 B4 54 8N 8 0W
Leitza, Spain 40 B3 43 5N 1 55W
Leiyang, China 77 D9 26 27N 112 45 E
Leizhou, China 77 G8 20 52N 110 8 E
Leizhou Bandao, China 76 G7 21 0N 110 0 E
Leizhou Wan, China 77 G8 20 50N 110 20 E
Lek →, Neths. 24 C4 51 54N 4 35 E
Leka, Norway 14 D14 65 5N 11 35 E
Lukáni, Greece 51 E8 41 10N 24 35 E
Lekbibaj, Albania 50 D3 42 17N 19 56 E
Lekeitio, Spain 40 B2 43 20N 2 32W
Lekhainá, Greece 48 D3 37 57N 21 16 E
Lekitobi, Indonesia 83 B2 1 58 S 124 33 E
Lékoli-Pandaka, Réserve de Faune
   de la △, Congo 114 B2 0 41N 14 50 E
Lekoui, Burkina Faso 112 C4 12 37N 3 40W
Leksand, Sweden 16 D9 60 44N 15 1 E
Leksula, Indonesia 82 B3 3 46 S 126 31 E
Lékva Óros, Greece 39 E5 35 18N 24 3 E
Leland, Mich., U.S.A. 148 C3 45 1N 85 45W
Leland, Miss., U.S.A. 155 J9 33 24N 90 54W
Lelång, Sweden 16 E6 59 10N 12 5 E
Leleiwi Pt., U.S.A. 145 D7 19 44N 155 0W
Lelepa, Vanuatu 133 G6 17 35 S 168 11 E
Leleque, Argentina 176 B2 42 28 S 71 0W
Lelewau, Indonesia 82 B2 3 25 S 124 33 E
Leli, Solomon Is. 133 M11 8 42 S 161 4 E
Lelu, Burma 90 F5 19 4N 95 0 E
Lelydorp, Surinam 169 B6 5 42N 55 14W
Lelystad, Neths. 24 B5 52 30N 5 25 E
Lem, Denmark 17 H2 56 1N 8 24 E
Lema, Nigeria 113 C5 12 58N 4 13 E
Lema Shilindi, Ethiopia 107 G5 4 50N 42 6 E
Léman, L., Europe 27 F13 46 26N 6 30 E
Lemankoa, Papua N. G. 132 C8 5 3 S 154 34 E
Lembar, Indonesia 79 K19 8 45 S 116 4 E
Lemberg = Lviv, Ukraine 59 H3 49 50N 24 0 E
Lembuak, Indonesia 79 K19 8 36 S 116 11 E
Lemera, Dem. Rep. of the Congo 118 C2 3 0 S 28 55 E
Lemery, Phil. 80 E3 13 51N 120 56 E
Lemeta, U.S.A. 144 D11 64 52N 147 44W
Lemhi, Dem. Rep. of the Congo 115 D3 5 18 S 15 13 E
Lemhi Ra., U.S.A. 158 D7 44 30N 113 30W
Lemmer, Neths. 24 B5 52 51N 5 43 E
Lemmon, U.S.A. 154 C3 45 57N 102 10W
Lemon Grove, U.S.A. 161 N9 32 45N 117 2W
Lemoore, U.S.A. 160 J7 36 18N 119 46W
Lempdes, France 28 C7 45 22N 3 17 E
Lemsid, W. Sahara 110 C2 26 33N 13 51W
Lemvig, Denmark 17 H2 56 33N 8 20 E
Lemyethna, Burma 90 G5 17 36N 95 9 E
Lena, U.S.A. 156 B7 42 23N 89 49W
Lena →, Russia 67 B13 72 52N 126 40 E
Lenakel, Vanuatu 133 J7 19 38 S 169 16 E
Lenart, Slovenia 45 B12 46 36N 15 48 E
Lenartovce, Slovak Rep. 35 C13 48 18N 20 19 E
Lencloître, France 26 F7 46 50N 0 20 E
Lençóis, Brazil 171 D3 12 35 S 41 24W
Lendas, Greece 39 E5 34 56N 24 56 E
Lendava, Slovenia 45 B13 46 35N 16 25 E
Lendeh, Iran 97 D6 30 58N 50 25 E
Lendinara, Italy 45 C8 45 5N 11 36 E
Lenger, Kazakhstan 65 B4 42 12N 69 54 E
Lengerich, Germany 30 C3 52 11N 7 52 E
Lenggong, Malaysia 87 K3 5 6N 100 58 E
Lenggries, Germany 31 H7 47 41N 11 35 E
Léngoué →, Congo 114 B3 1 15N 15 38 E
Lengshuijiang, China 77 D8 27 40N 111 26 E
Lengshuitan, China 77 D8 26 27N 111 35 E
Lengua de Vaca, Pta., Chile 174 C1 30 14 S 71 38W
Lengwe Nat. Park △, Malawi 119 F3 16 14 S 34 45 E
Lengyeltóti, Hungary 52 D2 46 40N 17 40 E
Lenhovda, Sweden 17 G9 57 0N 15 16 E
Lenina, Kanal →, Russia 61 J7 43 44N 45 17 E
Lenina, Pik, Kyrgyzstan 65 D6 39 20N 72 55 E
Leninabad = Khüjand, Tajikistan 65 C4 40 17N 69 37 E
Leninakan = Gyumri, Armenia 61 K6 40 47N 43 50 E
Leningrad = Sankt-Peterburg, Russia 58 C5 59 55N 30 20 E
Leningradskiy, Tajikistan 65 D5 38 0N 70 1 E
Lenino = Leninsk-Kuznetskiy, Russia 66 D9 54 44N 86 10 E
Lenino, Ukraine 59 K8 45 17N 35 46 E
Leninogorsk, Kazakhstan 66 D9 50 20N 83 30 E
Leninogorsk, Russia 64 D4 54 36N 52 30 E
Leninpol, Kyrgyzstan 65 B5 42 29N 71 55 E
Leninsk = Asaka, Uzbekistan 65 C6 40 38N 72 15 E
Leninsk, Russia 61 F7 48 40N 45 15 E
Leninsk-Kuznetskiy, Russia 66 D9 54 44N 86 10 E
Leninskiy, Tajikistan 65 D4 38 26N 68 46 E
Leninskoye, Kyrgyzstan 65 C6 40 40N 73 9 E
Leninskoye = Qazyghurt,
   Kazakhstan 65 C4 41 45N 69 23 E
Leninskoye, Kazakhstan 64 F6 50 44N 57 53 E
Leninskoye, Russia 60 A8 58 23N 47 3 E
Lenk, Switz. 32 D4 46 27N 7 28 E
Lenkoran = Länkäran, Azerbaijan 97 B6 38 48N 48 52 E
Lenmalu, Indonesia 83 B4 1 45 S 130 15 E
Lenne →, Germany 30 D3 51 25N 7 29 E
Lennestadt, Germany 30 D4 51 8N 8 2 E
Lennox, U.S.A. 154 D6 43 21N 96 53W
Lennox, I., Chile 176 E3 55 18 S 66 50W
Lennoxville, Canada 151 A13 45 22N 71 51W
Leno, Italy 44 C7 45 22N 10 13 E
Lenoir, U.S.A. 149 H5 35 55N 81 32W
Lenoir City, U.S.A. 149 H3 35 48N 84 16W
Lenore L., Canada 143 C8 52 30N 104 59W
Lenox, Ga., U.S.A. 153 D6 31 16N 83 28W
Lenox, Iowa, U.S.A. 156 E7 40 53N 94 34W
Lenox, Mass., U.S.A. 151 D11 42 22N 73 17W
Lens, France 27 B9 50 26N 2 50 E
Lensahn, Germany 30 A6 54 13N 10 53 E
Lensk, Russia 67 C12 60 48N 114 55 E
Lensvik, Norway 18 A6 63 31N 9 48 E
Lentekhi, Georgia 61 J6 42 47N 42 45 E
Lenti, Hungary 52 D1 46 37N 16 33 E
Lentini, Italy 47 E8 37 17N 15 0 E
Lenwood, U.S.A. 161 L9 34 53N 117 7W
Lenya, Burma 78 B1 11 33N 98 57 E
Lenzburg, Switz. 32 B6 47 23N 8 11 E
Lenzen, Germany 30 B7 53 5N 11 27 E
Lenzerheide, Switz. 33 C9 46 44N 9 34 E
Léo, Burkina Faso 112 C4 11 3N 2 2W
Leoben, Austria 34 D8 47 22N 15 5 E
Leobschütz = Głubczyce, Poland 55 H4 50 13N 17 52 E
Leodhas = Lewis, U.K. 22 C2 58 9N 6 40W
Leola, U.S.A. 154 C5 45 43N 98 56W
Leominster, U.K. 21 E5 52 14N 2 43W
Leominster, U.S.A. 151 D13 42 32N 71 46W
León, France 28 E2 43 53N 1 18W
León, Mexico 162 C4 21 7N 101 40W
León, Nic. 164 D2 12 20N 86 51W
León, Spain 42 C5 42 38N 5 34W
León, U.S.A. 156 E8 40 44N 93 45W

León □, Spain 42 C5 42 40N 5 55W
León →, U.S.A. 155 K6 31 14N 97 28W
León, Montes de, Spain 42 C4 42 30N 6 18W
Leonardo da Vinci, Rome ✈ (FCO),
   Italy 45 G9 41 48N 12 15 E
Leonardtown, U.S.A. 148 F7 38 17N 76 38W
Leonardville, Namibia 116 C2 23 29 S 18 49 E
Leonberg, Germany 31 G5 48 48N 9 1 E
Leonding, Austria 34 C7 48 16N 14 15 E
Leone, Amer. Samoa 133 X24 14 23 S 170 48W
Leones, Italy 45 F9 42 34N 12 58 E
Leonforte, Italy 47 E7 37 38N 14 23 E
Leongatha, Australia 129 E6 38 30 S 145 58 E
Leonia, U.S.A. 152 E3 30 55N 86 1W
Leonídhion, Greece 48 D4 37 9N 22 52 E
Leonora, Australia 125 E3 28 49 S 121 19 E
Leopold II, L. = Mai-Ndombe, L.,
   Dem. Rep. of the Congo 114 C3 2 0 S 18 20 E
Leopoldina, Brazil 171 F3 21 28 S 42 40W
Leopoldo Bulhões, Brazil 171 E2 16 37 S 48 46W
Leopoldsburg, Belgium 24 C5 51 7N 5 13 E
Leopoldville = Kinshasa, Dem. Rep.
   of the Congo 115 C3 4 20 S 15 15 E
Leoti, U.S.A. 154 F4 38 29N 101 21W
Leova, Moldova 53 D13 46 28N 28 15 E
Leoville, Canada 143 C7 53 39N 107 33W
Lepe, Spain 43 H3 37 15N 7 12W
Lepel = Lyepyel, Belarus 58 E5 54 50N 28 40 E
Lepenoú, Greece 48 C3 38 42N 21 17 E
Leping, China 77 C11 28 47N 117 7 E
Lépo, L. do, Angola 116 B2 17 0 S 19 0 E
Lepontine, Alpi, Italy 33 D6 46 22N 8 27 E
Leppävirta, Finland 15 E22 62 29N 27 46 E
Lepsény, Hungary 52 D3 47 0N 18 15 E
Leptis Magna, Libya 108 B2 32 40N 14 12 E
Lequeitio = Lekeitio, Spain 40 B2 43 20N 2 32W
Lercara Friddi, Italy 46 E6 37 45N 13 36 E
Lerdo, Mexico 162 B4 25 32N 103 32W
Léré, C.A.R. 114 A3 6 46N 17 25 E
Léré, Chad 113 D7 9 39N 14 13 E
Léré, Mali 112 B4 15 45N 4 55W
Lere, Bauchi, Nigeria 113 D6 9 43N 9 18 E
Lere, Kaduna, Nigeria 113 C6 10 23N 8 35 E
Leribe, Lesotho 117 D4 28 51 S 28 3 E
Lérici, Italy 44 D6 44 4N 9 55 E
Lérida = Lleida, Spain 40 D5 41 37N 0 39 E
Lérins, Îs. de, France 29 E11 43 31N 7 3 E
Lerma, Spain 42 C7 42 0N 3 47W
Léros, Greece 49 D8 37 10N 26 50 E
Lérouville, France 27 D12 48 44N 5 30 E
Lerum, Sweden 17 G6 57 46N 12 16 E
Lerwick, U.K. 22 A7 60 9N 1 9W
Les, Romania 53 D6 46 58N 21 50 E
Les Abrets, France 29 C9 45 32N 5 35 E
Les Andelys, France 26 C8 49 15N 1 25 E
Les Bois, Switz. 32 B3 47 11N 6 50 E
Les Borges Blanques, Spain 40 D5 41 30N 0 52 E
Les Cayes, Haiti 165 C5 18 15N 73 46W
Les Diablerets, Switz. 32 D4 46 23N 7 10 E
Les Essarts, France 26 F5 46 47N 1 12W
Les Herbiers, France 26 F5 46 52N 1 1W
Les Minquiers, Plateau des, Chan. Is. 26 C4 48 58N 2 8W
Les Mouboas, C.A.R. 114 A4 6 11N 20 13 E
Les Pieux, France 26 C5 49 30N 1 48W
Les Ponts-de-Cé, France 26 E6 47 25N 0 30W
Les Riceys, France 27 E11 47 59N 4 22 E
Les Sables-d'Olonne, France 28 B2 46 30N 1 45W
Les Vans, France 29 D8 44 25N 4 2 E
Les Verrières, Switz. 32 C2 46 55N 6 28 E
Lesbos = Lésvos, Greece 49 B8 39 10N 26 20 E
L'Escala, Spain 40 C8 42 7N 3 8 E
Leshan, China 76 C4 29 33N 103 41 E
Leshukonskoye, Russia 56 B8 64 54N 45 46 E
Leshwe, Demaliques de △,
   Dem. Rep. of the Congo 119 E2 12 45 S 29 30 E
Lésina, Italy 45 G12 41 52N 15 21 E
Lésina, L. di, Italy 45 G12 41 53N 15 26 E
Lesjaskog, Norway 18 B5 62 14N 8 22 E
Lesjaverk, Norway 18 B5 62 8N 8 34 E
Lesjöfors, Sweden 16 E8 59 58N 14 11 E
Lesko, Poland 55 J9 49 30N 22 23 E
Leskov I., Antarctica 7 B1 56 0 S 28 0W
Leskovac, Serbia, Yug. 50 D6 43 0N 21 58 E
Leskovik, Albania 50 F4 40 10N 20 34 E
Leslie, Ga., U.S.A. 152 D5 31 57N 84 5W
Leslie, Mich., U.S.A. 157 B12 42 27N 84 26W
Leśna, Poland 55 G2 51 1N 15 15 E
Lesneven, France 26 D2 48 35N 4 20W
Leśnica, Poland 55 H5 50 26N 18 11 E
Leśnica, Serbia, Yug. 50 B4 44 39N 19 20 E
Lesnoy, Russia 64 B4 59 47N 52 9 E
Lesnoye, Russia 58 B9 58 15N 35 18 E
Lesopilnoye, Russia 70 A7 46 44N 134 20 E
Lesotho ■, Africa 117 D4 29 40 S 28 0 E
Lesozavodsk, Russia 67 E14 45 30N 133 29 E
Lesparre-Médoc, France 28 C3 45 18N 0 57W
Lessay, France 26 C5 49 14N 1 30W
Lesse →, Belgium 24 D4 50 15N 4 54 E
Lesse et Lomme, Parc Nat. de △,
   Belize 24 D5 50 8N 5 9 E
Lessebo, Sweden 17 H9 56 45N 15 16 E
Lesser Antilles, W. Indies 165 D7 15 0N 61 0W
Lesser Slave L., Canada 142 B5 55 30N 115 25W
Lesser Sunda Is., Indonesia 82 C1 8 0 S 120 0 E
Lessines, Belgium 24 D3 50 42N 3 50 E
Lester, U.S.A. 160 C5 47 12N 121 29W
Lester B. Pearson International,
   Toronto ✈ (YYZ), Canada 150 C5 43 40N 79 34W
Lestock, Canada 143 C8 51 19N 103 59W
Lesueur I., Australia 124 B4 13 50 S 127 17 E
Lesueur Nat. Park △, Australia 125 F2 30 11 S 115 10 E
Lésvos, Greece 49 B8 39 10N 26 20 E
Leszno, Poland 55 G3 51 50N 16 30 E
Letaba, S. Africa 117 C5 23 59 S 31 50 E
Letälven, Sweden 16 E8 59 5N 14 4 E
Letchworth, U.K. 21 F7 51 59N 0 13W
Letea, Ostrov, Romania 53 E14 45 18N 29 20 E
Lethbridge, Canada 142 D6 49 45N 112 45W
Lethem, Guyana 169 C6 3 20N 59 50W
Leti, Kepulauan, Indonesia 83 C3 8 10 S 128 0 E
Leti Is. = Leti, Kepulauan, Indonesia 82 C3 8 10 S 128 0 E
Letiahau →, Botswana 116 C3 21 16 S 24 0 E
Leticia, Colombia 168 D4 4 9 S 70 0W
Leting, China 75 E10 39 23N 118 55 E
Letjiesbos, S. Africa 116 E3 32 34 S 22 16 E
Letlhakane, Botswana 116 C4 21 27 S 25 30 E
Letlhakeng, Botswana 116 C4 24 0 S 24 59 E
Letong, Indonesia 78 D3 2 58N 105 42 E
Letpadan, Burma 90 G5 17 45N 95 45 E
Letpan, Burma 90 F5 19 28N 94 10 E
Letsôk-aw Kyun, Burma 79 G2 11 37N 98 59 E
Letterkenny, Ireland 23 B4 54 57N 7 45W
Leu, Romania 53 F8 44 10N 24 0 E
Leua, Angola 115 D4 11 34 S 20 32 E
Leucadia, U.S.A. 161 M9 33 4N 117 18W
Leucate, France 28 F7 42 56N 3 3 E
Leucate, Étang de, France 28 F7 42 50N 3 0 E
Leuchars, U.K. 22 E6 56 24N 2 53W
Leuk, Switz. 32 D5 46 19N 7 37 E
Leukerbad, Switz. 32 D5 46 24N 7 37 E
Leuşeni, Moldova 53 D13 46 49N 28 12 E
Leuser, G., Indonesia 84 B1 3 46N 97 12 E

Leutkirch, Germany 31 H6 47 49N 10 1 E
Leuven, Belgium 24 D4 50 52N 4 42 E
Leuze-en-Hainaut, Belgium 24 D3 50 36N 3 37 E
Lev Tolstoy, Russia 58 F10 53 13N 39 29 E
Levádhia, Greece 48 C4 38 27N 22 54 E
Levan, Albania 50 F3 40 40N 19 28 E
Levanger, Norway 14 E14 63 45N 11 19 E
Levant, Î. du, France 29 E10 43 3N 6 28 E
Lévanto, Italy 44 D6 44 10N 9 38 E
Lévanzo, Italy 46 D5 38 0N 12 20 E
Leveld, Norway 18 D5 60 44N 8 33 E
Levelland, U.S.A. 155 J3 33 35N 102 23W
Leven, U.K. 22 E6 56 12N 3 0W
Leven, L., U.K. 22 E5 56 12N 3 22W
Leven, Toraka, Madag. 117 A8 12 30 S 47 45 E
Leveque C., Australia 124 C3 16 20 S 123 0 E
Leverano, Italy 30 D3 50 1N 7 1 E
Leverkusen, Germany 35 C11 48 13N 18 35 E
Levice, Slovak Rep. 45 C8 46 0N 11 18 E
Lévico Terme, Italy 29 G13 41 40N 9 7 E
Levie, France 27 F13 46 58N 6 42 E
Levier, France 130 G4 40 37 S 175 18 E
Levin, N.Z. 141 C5 46 48N 71 9W
Lévis, Canada 142 A5 62 37N 117 58W
Levis, L., Canada 49 D8 37 0N 26 28 E
Levítha, Greece 151 F11 40 44N 73 31W
Levittown, N.Y., U.S.A. 151 F10 40 9N 74 51W
Levittown, Pa., U.S.A. 51 E10 41 52N 26 15 E
Levka, Bulgaria 39 B2 38 40N 20 43 E
Levkás, Greece 38 C10 39 25N 20 3 E
Levkímmi, Greece 39 B2 38 45N 20 40 E
Levkímmi, Ákra, Greece 39 E9 35 18N 33 25 E
Levkôsia = Nicosia, Cyprus 35 H3 49 21N 20 35 E
Levoča, Slovak Rep. 27 F8 46 59N 1 38 E
Levroux, France 51 C11 43 42N 24 38 E
Levski, Bulgaria 51 D8 42 38N 24 47 E
Levskigrad = Karlovo, Bulgaria 133 A2 17 34 S 179 0 E
Levuka, Fiji 90 F6 19 38N 96 7 E
Lewe, Burma 21 G8 50 52N 0 1 E
Lewes, U.K. 148 F8 38 46N 75 9W
Lewes, U.S.A. 55 H4 50 45N 17 37 E
Lewin Brzeski, Poland 22 C2 58 9N 6 40W
Lewis, U.K. 160 E4 45 51N 122 48W
Lewis →, U.S.A. 22 C2 58 31N 6 16W
Lewis, Butt of, U.K. 131 C7 42 11 S 172 11 E
Lewis Pass, N.Z. 124 D4 20 3 S 128 50 E
Lewis Ra., Australia 158 C7 45 8N 113 5W
Lewis Range, U.S.A. 150 E6 41 52N 78 40W
Lewis Run, U.S.A. 157 E12 39 51N 84 40W
Lewisburg, Ohio, U.S.A. 150 F8 40 58N 76 54W
Lewisburg, Pa., U.S.A. 149 H2 35 27N 86 48W
Lewisburg, Tenn., U.S.A. 148 G5 37 48N 80 27W
Lewisburg, W. Va., U.S.A. 157 G10 39 21N 84 25W
Lewisport, Canada 141 C8 49 15N 55 3W
Lewiston, Idaho, U.S.A. 158 C5 46 25N 117 1W
Lewiston, Maine, U.S.A. 149 C11 44 6N 70 13W
Lewiston, N.Y., U.S.A. 150 C5 43 11N 79 3W
Lewistown, Ill., U.S.A. 156 D6 40 24N 90 9W
Lewistown, Mont., U.S.A. 158 C9 47 4N 109 26W
Lewistown, Pa., U.S.A. 150 F7 40 36N 77 34W
Lexington, Ga., U.S.A. 152 B6 33 52N 83 7W
Lexington, Ill., U.S.A. 154 E10 40 39N 88 47W
Lexington, Ky., U.S.A. 157 F12 38 3N 84 30W
Lexington, Mich., U.S.A. 150 C2 43 16N 82 32W
Lexington, Mo., U.S.A. 156 F3 39 11N 93 52W
Lexington, N.C., U.S.A. 149 H5 35 49N 80 15W
Lexington, N.Y., U.S.A. 151 D10 42 15N 74 22W
Lexington, Nebr., U.S.A. 154 E5 40 47N 99 45W
Lexington, Ohio, U.S.A. 150 F2 40 41N 82 35W
Lexington, S.C., U.S.A. 152 B8 33 59N 81 11W
Lexington, Tenn., U.S.A. 149 H1 35 39N 88 24W
Lexington, Va., U.S.A. 148 G6 37 47N 79 27W
Lexington Park, U.S.A. 148 F7 38 16N 76 27W
Leyburn, U.K. 20 C6 54 19N 1 48W
Leye, China 76 E6 24 48N 106 29 E
Leyland, U.K. 20 D5 53 42N 2 43W
Leyre →, France 28 D2 44 39N 1 1W
Leysin, Switz. 32 D4 46 21N 7 1 E
Leyte, Phil. 81 F5 10 30N 125 0 E
Leyte □, Phil. 81 F5 10 50N 125 0 E
Leyte Gulf, Phil. 55 F6 50 16N 22 25 E
Lezajsk, Poland 50 E3 41 47N 19 39 E
Lezhë, Albania 76 B5 30 19N 104 58 E
Lezhi, China 28 E6 43 13N 2 43 E
Lézignan-Corbières, France 59 G8 51 42N 35 16 E
Lezoux, France 68 D3 29 5N 90 58 E
Lgov, Russia 68 D3 29 5N 87 38 E
Lhasa, China 84 B1 4 55N 95 24 E
Lhazê, China 84 A1 5 10N 97 10 E
Lhokkruet, Indonesia 40 D3 42 16N 2 6 E
Lhokseumawe, Indonesia 90 B3 27 39N 91 10 E
L'Hospitalet de Llobregat, Spain 86 D2 17 48N 98 57 E
Lhuntsi Dzong, Bhutan 77 C9 29 24N 112 1 E
Li, Thailand 74 G3 34 0N 113 0 E
Li Shui →, China 74 B8 38 30N 115 35 E
Li Xian, Gansu, China 77 C8 29 36N 111 42 E
Li Xian, Hebei, China 74 D7 40 28N 112 25 E
Li Xian, Hunan, China 75 D9 36 20N 119 37 E
Lia-Moya, C.A.R. 74 H4 33 56N 106 18 E
Liádhoi, Greece 76 C7 29 1N 108 44 E
Lian, Phil. 78 B6 30 38N 107 47 E
Liancheng, China 77 D9 26 5N 107 6 E
Lianga, Phil. 77 C9 28 50N 112 1 E
Lianga Bay, Phil. 77 G8 21 40N 110 20 E

Liangcheng, Nei Monggol Zizhiqu,
   China 74 D7 40 28N 112 25 E
Liangcheng, Shandong, China 75 G10 35 32N 119 37 E
Lianghe, China 76 E2 24 44N 98 19 E
Lianghekou, China 76 C7 29 11N 108 44 E
Liangping, China 76 B6 30 38N 107 47 E
Liangpran, Indonesia 78 D4 1 4N 114 23 E
Lianhua, China 77 D9 27 3N 113 54 E
Lianjiang, Fujian, China 77 D12 26 12N 119 27 E
Lianjiang, Guangdong, China 77 G8 21 40N 110 20 E
Lianping, China 77 E10 24 28N 114 30 E
Lianshan, China 77 E9 24 38N 112 8 E
Lianshanguan, China 75 D12 40 53N 123 43 E
Lianshui, China 75 H10 33 42N 119 20 E
Lianyuan, China 77 D8 27 40N 111 38 E
Lianyungang, China 75 G10 34 40N 119 11 E
Lianzhou, China 77 E9 24 51N 112 2 E
Liao He →, China 75 D11 41 0N 121 50 E
Liaocheng, China 74 F8 36 28N 115 58 E
Liaodong Bandao, China 75 E12 40 0N 122 30 E
Liaodong Wan, China 75 D11 40 20N 121 10 E
Liaoning □, China 75 D12 41 40N 122 30 E
Liaoyang, China 75 D12 41 15N 122 58 E
Liaoyuan, China 75 C13 42 58N 125 2 E
Liaozhong, China 75 D12 41 23N 122 50 E
Liapádes, Greece 38 B9 39 42N 19 40 E
Liard →, Canada 142 A4 61 51N 121 18W
Liard River, Canada 142 B3 59 25N 126 5W
Liari, Pakistan 92 G2 25 37N 66 30 E
Líbano, Colombia 168 C2 5 3N 75 4W
Libau = Liepāja, Latvia 15 H19 56 30N 21 0 E
Libby, U.S.A. 158 B6 48 23N 115 33W
Libenge, Dem. Rep. of the Congo 114 B3 3 40N 18 55 E
Liberal, U.S.A. 155 G4 37 3N 100 55W

Liberdade, Brazil .... 172 C3   10 5 S 70 20W
Liberdade →, Brazil .... 173 B7   9 40 S 52 17W
Liberec, Czech Rep. .... 34 A8   50 47N 15 7 E
Liberecký □, Czech Rep. ...... 34 A8   50 45N 15 0 E
Liberia, Costa Rica 164 D2   10 40N 85 30W
Liberia ■, W. Afr. 112 D3   6 30N   9 30W
Libertad, Phil. .... 81 F3   11 46N 121 55 E
Libertad, Venezuela 168 B4   8 20N 69 37W
Liberty, Ind., U.S.A. 157 E12   39 38N 84 56W
Liberty, Mo., U.S.A. 156 E2   39 15N 94 25W
Liberty, N.Y., U.S.A. 151 E10   41 48N 74 45W
Liberty, Pa., U.S.A. 150 E7   41 34N 77 6W
Liberty, Tex., U.S.A. 155 K7   30 3N 94 48W
Liberty Center, U.S.A. 157 C12   41 27N 84 1W
Libertyville, U.S.A. 157 B9   42 18N 87 57W
Libiąż, Poland .... 55 H6   50 7N 19 21 E
Libibi, Angola .... 115 E3   14 42 S 17 44 E
Lībīya, Sahrā', Africa .... 108 C4   25 0N 25 0 E
Libjo, Phil. .... 81 F5   10 12N 125 32 E
Libmanan, Phil. .... 80 E4   13 42N 123 4 E
Libo, China .... 76 E6   25 22N 107 53 E
Libobo, Tanjung, Indonesia ... 82 B3   0 54 S 128 28 E
Libode, S. Africa .... 117 E4   31 33 S 29 2 E
Libohovë, Albania .... 50 F4   40 3N 20 10 E
Libona, Phil. .... 81 G5   8 20N 124 44 E
Libonda, Zambia .... 115 E4   14 28 S 23 12 E
Libourne, France 28 D3   44 55N   0 14W
Libramont, Belgium .... 24 E5   49 55N   5 23 E
Librazhd, Albania .... 50 E4   41 12N 20 22 E
Libreville, Gabon .... 114 B1   0 25N   9 26 E
Libya ■, N. Afr. .... 108 C3   27 0N 17 0 E
Libyan Desert = Lībīya, Sahrā',
  Africa .... 108 C4   25 0N 25 0 E
Libyan Plateau = Ed-Déffa, Egypt . 106 A2 30 40N 26 30 E
Licantén, Chile .... 174 D1   35 55 S 72 0W
Licata, Italy .... 46 E6   37 6N 13 56 E
Lice, Turkey .... 101 C9   38 27N 40 39 E
Licheng, China .... 74 F7   36 28N 113 20 E
Lichfield, U.K. 21 E6   52 41N   1 49W
Lichinga, Mozam. .... 119 E4   13 13 S 35 11 E
Lichtenburg, S. Africa .... 116 D4   26 8 S 26 8 E
Lichtenfels, Germany .... 31 E7   50 8N 11 4 E
Lichuan, Hubei, China .... 76 B7   30 18N 108 57 E
Lichuan, Jiangxi, China ...... 77 D11   27 18N 116 55 E
Licking →, U.S.A. 157 E12   39 6N 84 30W
Licosa, Punta, Italy .... 47 B7   40 15N 14 54 E
Licungo →, Mozam. .... 119 F4   17 40 S 37 15 E
Lida, Belarus .... 15 K21   53 53N 25 15 E
Liden, Sweden .... 16 B10   62 42N 16 48 E
Lidhoríkion, Greece .... 48 C4   38 32N 22 12 E
Lidhult, Sweden .... 17 H7   56 50N 13 27 E
Lidköping, Sweden .... 17 F7   58 31N 13 7 E
Lido, Italy .... 45 C4   45 25N 12 22 E
Lido, Niger .... 113 C5   12 54N   3 44 E
Lido di Roma = Ostia, Lido di, Italy . 45 G9 41 43N 12 17 E
Lidzbark, Poland .... 55 E6   53 15N 19 49 E
Lidzbark Warmiński, Poland ... 54 D7   54 7N 20 34 E
Liebenwalde, Germany .... 30 C9   52 52N 13 24 E
Lieberose, Germany .... 30 D10   51 59N 14 17 E
Liebig, Mt., Australia .... 124 D5   23 18 S 131 22 E
Liebling, Romania .... 52 E6   45 36N 21 20 E
Liechtenstein ■, Europe ...... 33 B9   47 8N   9 35 E
Liège, Belgium .... 24 D5   50 38N   5 35 E
Liège □, Belgium .... 24 D5   50 32N   5 35 E
Liegnitz = Legnica, Poland ... 55 G3   51 12N 16 10 E
Lienart, Dem. Rep. of the Congo . 118 B2   3 3N 25 31 E
Lienyünchiangshih = Lianyungang,
  China .... 75 G10   34 40N 119 11 E
Lienz, Austria .... 34 E5   46 50N 12 46 E
Liepāja, Latvia .... 15 H19   56 30N 21 0 E
Liepāja □, Latvia .... 54 B8   56 30N 21 30 E
Liepājas ezers, Latvia .... 54 B8   56 27N 21 3 E
Lier, Belgium .... 24 C4   51 7N   4 34 E
Liernais, France .... 27 E11   47 13N   4 16 E
Liestal, Switz. .... 32 B5   47 29N   7 44 E
Liești, Romania .... 53 E12   45 38N 27 34 E
Liévin, France .... 27 B9   50 24N   2 47 E
Lièvre →, Canada 140 C4   45 31N 75 26W
Liezen, Austria .... 34 D7   47 34N 14 15 E
Liffey →, Ireland 23 C5   53 21N   6 13W
Lifford, Ireland 23 B4   54 51N   7 29W
Liffré, France 26 D5   48 12N   1 30W
Lifjell, Norway .... 18 E5   59 27N   8 45 E
Lifou, I., N. Cal. .... 133 K5   20 53 S 167 13 E
Lifudzin, Russia .... 70 B7   44 21N 134 58 E
Lifuka, Tonga .... 133 P13   19 48 S 174 21W
Ligao, Phil. .... 80 E4   13 14N 123 32 E
Ligasa, Dem. Rep. of the Congo . 114 B4   0 44N 23 49 E
Lighthouse Point, U.S.A. 153 J9   26 15N 80 7W
Lighthouse Pt., U.S.A. 152 F5   29 54N 84 21W
Lightning Ridge, Australia ... 127 D4   29 22 S 148 0 E
Lignano Sabbiadoro, Italy .... 45 C10   45 42N 13 9 E
Ligny-en-Barrois, France ..... 27 D12   48 36N   5 20 E
Ligonha →, Mozam. .... 119 F4   16 54 S 39 9 E
Ligonier, Ind., U.S.A. 157 C11   41 28N 85 35W
Ligonier, Pa., U.S.A. 150 F5   40 15N 79 14W
Ligourion, Greece .... 48 D5   37 37N 23 4 E
Ligueil, France .... 26 E7   47 2N   0 49 E
Liguria □, Italy .... 44 D5   44 30N   8 50 E
Ligurian Sea, Medit. S. ...... 12 G7   43 20N   9 0 E
Lihir Group, Papua N. G. ..... 132 B7   3 0 S 152 35 E
Lihir I., Papua N. G. .... 132 B7   3 5 S 152 35 E
Lihou Reefs and Cays, Australia . 126 B5 17 25 S 151 40 E
Lihue, U.S.A. 145 B2   21 59N 159 23W
Lijiang, China .... 76 D3   26 55N 100 20 E
Likasi, Dem. Rep. of the Congo . 119 E2 10 55 S 26 48 E
Likati, Dem. Rep. of the Congo . 114 B4   3 20N 24 0 E
Likati →, Dem. Rep. of the Congo . 114 B4 3 20N 24 0 E
Likenäs, Sweden .... 16 D8   60 37N 13 3 E
Likete, Dem. Rep. of the Congo . 114 C4   0 48 S 23 31 E
Likhoslavl, Russia .... 58 D8   57 12N 35 30 E
Likhovskoy, Russia .... 59 H11   48 10N 40 10 E
Likimi, Dem. Rep. of the Congo . 114 B4   2 44N 20 47 E
Likisia = Liquica, E. Timor .. 82 C3   8 36 S 125 19 E
Likita, Dem. Rep. of the Congo . 114 B4   3 23 S 23 36 E
Liknes, Norway .... 18 F3   58 19N   6 59 E
Likokou, Gabon .... 114 C2   0 12 S 12 48 E
Likoma I., Malawi .... 119 E3   12 3 S 34 45 E
Likouala □, Congo .... 114 C3   0 2N 14 53 E
Likouala aux Herbes →, Congo . 114 C3   0 52 S 17 8 E
Likumburu, Tanzania .... 119 D4   9 43 S 35 8 E
Lilanga, Dem. Rep. of the Congo . 114 C4   0 34 S 23 56 E
L'Île-Bouchard, France .... 26 E7   47 7N   0 26 E
L'Île-Rousse, France .... 29 F12   42 38N   8 57 E
Lilenga, Dem. Rep. of the Congo . 114 B4   1 4N   22 2 E
Liling, China .... 77 D9   27 42N 113 29 E
Lilla Edet, Sweden .... 17 F6   58 8N 12 8 E
Lille, France .... 27 B10   50 38N   3 3 E
Lille Bælt, Denmark .... 17 J3   55 20N   9 45 E
Lillebonne, France .... 26 C7   49 30N   0 32 E
Lillehammer, Norway .... 18 C7   61 8N 10 30 E
Lillesand, Norway .... 18 F5   58 15N   8 23 E
Lillestrøm, Norway .... 18 E8   59 58N 11 5 E
Lillhärdal, Sweden .... 16 C8   61 51N 14 5 E
Lillian Pt., Australia .... 125 E4   27 40 S 126 6 E
Lillo, Spain 42 F7   39 45N   3 20W
Lillooet, Canada 142 C4   50 44N 121 57W
Lillooet →, Canada 142 D4   49 15N 121 57W
Lilongwe, Malawi .... 119 E3   14 0 S 33 48 E
Liloy, Phil. .... 81 G4   8 4N 122 39 E
Lim →, Bos.-H. .... 50 C3   43 45N 19 15 E
Lim Chu Kang, Singapore ...... 87 d   1 26N 103 43 E
Lima, Brazil .... 169 D5   4 36 S 63 40W
Lima, Indonesia .... 82 B3   3 39 S 127 58 E
Lima, Peru .... 172 C2   12 0 S 77 0W
Lima, Ill., U.S.A. 156 D5   40 11N 91 23W
Lima, Mont., U.S.A. 158 D7   44 38N 112 36W
Lima, Ohio, U.S.A. 157 D12   40 44N 84 6W
Lima □, Peru .... 172 C2   12 3 S 77 3W
Lima →, Portugal 42 D2   41 41N   8 50W
Liman, Indonesia .... 79 G14   7 48 S 111 45 E
Liman, Russia .... 61 H8   45 45N 47 12 E
Limanowa, Poland .... 55 J7   49 42N 20 22 E
Limassol, Cyprus .... 39 F9   34 42N 33 1 E
Limavady, U.K. 23 A5   55 3N   6 56W
Limay →, Argentina .... 176 A3   39 0 S 68 0W
Limay Mahuida, Argentina ..... 174 D2   37 10 S 66 45W
Limbang, Brunei .... 85 B5   4 42N 115 6 E
Limbara, Mte., Italy .... 46 B2   40 51N   9 10 E
Limbaži, Latvia .... 15 H21   57 31N 24 42 E
Limbdi, India .... 92 H4   22 34N 71 51 E
Limbe, Cameroon .... 113 E6   4 1N   9 10 E
Limboto, Indonesia .... 82 A2   0 37N 122 57 E
Limbueta, Angola .... 115 E3   12 30 S 18 42 E
Limburg, Germany .... 31 E4   50 22N   8 4 E
Limburg □, Belgium .... 24 C5   51 2N   5 25 E
Limburg □, Neths. .... 24 C5   51 20N   5 55 E
Lime Village, U.S.A. 144 F9   61 21N 155 28W
Limedsforsen, Sweden .... 16 D7   60 52N 13 25 E
Limeira, Brazil .... 175 A6   22 35 S 47 28W
Limenária, Greece .... 51 F8   40 38N 24 32 E
Limerick, Ireland 23 D3   52 40N   8 37W
Limerick, U.S.A. 151 C14   43 41N 70 48W
Limerick □, Ireland 23 D3   52 30N   8 50W
Limestone, U.S.A. 150 D6   42 2N 78 38W
Limestone →, Canada 143 B10   56 31N 94 7W
Limfjorden, Denmark .... 17 H3   56 55N   9 0 E
Limia = Lima →, Portugal 42 D2   41 41N   8 50W
Limín Khersónísou, Greece .... 39 E6   35 18N 25 21 E
Limingen, Norway .... 14 D15   64 48N 13 35 E
Limmared, Sweden .... 17 G7   57 34N 13 20 E
Limmat →, Switz. .... 33 B6   47 26N   8 20 E
Limmen Bight, Australia ...... 126 A2   14 40 S 135 35 E
Limmen Bight →, Australia .... 126 B2   15 7 S 135 44 E
Límni, Greece .... 48 C5   38 43N 23 18 E
Límni Voulkariá, Greece ...... 39 B2   38 52N 20 50 E
Límnos, Greece .... 49 B7   39 50N 25 5 E
Limoeiro, Brazil .... 170 C4   7 52 S 35 27W
Limoeiro do Norte, Brazil .... 170 C4   5 5 S 38 0W
Limoges, Canada 151 A9   45 20N 75 16W
Limoges, France .... 28 C5   45 50N   1 15 E
Limón, Costa Rica 164 E3   10 0N 83 2W
Limon, U.S.A. 154 F3   39 16N 103 41W
Limone Piemonte, Italy .... 44 D4   44 12N   7 34 E
Limousin, France .... 28 C5   45 30N   1 30 E
Limousin, Plateaux du, France . 28 C5   45 45N   1 15 E
Limoux, France .... 28 E6   43 4N   2 12 E
Limpopo = Northern □, S. Africa . 117 C4 24 5 S 29 0 E
Limpopo →, Africa .... 117 D5   25 5 S 33 30 E
Limuru, Kenya .... 118 C4   1 2 S 36 35 E
Lin Xian, China .... 74 F6   37 57N 110 58 E
Lin'an, China .... 77 B12   30 15N 119 42 E
Linao Pt., Phil. .... 81 H4   6 46N 123 58 E
Linapacan I., Phil. .... 81 F2   11 30N 119 52 E
Linapacan Str., Phil. .... 81 F2   11 27N 119 49 E
Linapacan I., Phil. .... 81 F2   11 37N 119 56 E
Linares, Chile .... 174 D1   35 50 S 71 40W
Linares, Colombia 168 C2   1 23N 77 31W
Linares, Mexico 163 C5   24 50N 99 40W
Linares, Spain 43 G7   38 10N   3 40W
Linaro, Capo, Italy .... 45 F8   42 2N 11 50 E
Línas Mte., Italy .... 46 C1   39 25N   8 38 E
Linate, Milan ✈ (LIN), Italy . 44 C6   45 27N   9 16 E
Lincang, China .... 76 F3   23 58N 100 1 E
Lincheng, China .... 74 F8   37 25N 114 30 E
Linchuan, China .... 77 D11   27 57N 116 15 E
Lincoln, Argentina .... 174 C3   34 55 S 61 30W
Lincoln, N.Z. .... 131 D7   43 38 S 172 30 E
Lincoln, U.K. 20 D7   53 14N   0 32W
Lincoln, Calif., U.S.A. 160 G5   38 54N 121 17W
Lincoln, Ill., U.S.A. 156 D7   40 9N 89 22W
Lincoln, Kans., U.S.A. 154 F5   39 3N 98 9W
Lincoln, Maine, U.S.A. 149 C11   45 22N 68 30W
Lincoln, N.H., U.S.A. 151 B13   44 3N 71 40W
Lincoln, N. Mex., U.S.A. 159 K11   33 30N 105 23W
Lincoln, Nebr., U.S.A. 154 E6   40 49N 96 41W
Lincoln Boyhood Nat. Memorial △,
  U.S.A. 157 F10   38 7N 86 58W
Lincoln City, U.S.A. 158 D1   44 57N 124 1W
Lincoln Hav = Lincoln Sea, Arctic . 10 A5 84 0N 55 0W
Lincoln Park, Ga., U.S.A. 152 C5   32 52N 84 20W
Lincoln Park, Mich., U.S.A. .. 157 B13   42 15N 83 11W
Lincoln Sea, Arctic 10 A5   84 0N 55 0W
Lincolnshire □, U.K. 20 D7   53 14N   0 32W
Lincolnshire Wolds, U.K. 20 D7   53 26N   0 13W
Lincolnton, Ga., U.S.A. 153 B7   33 48N 82 29W
Lincolnton, N.C., U.S.A. 149 H5   35 29N 81 16W
L'Incudine, France .... 29 G13   41 50N   9 12 E
Lind, U.S.A. 158 C4   46 58N 118 37W
Linda, U.S.A. 160 F5   39 8N 121 34W
Lindale, U.S.A. 152 A4   34 11N 85 11W
Lindås, Norway .... 18 D2   60 44N   5 9 E
Lindau, Germany .... 31 H5   47 33N   9 41 E
Lindeman I., Australia .... 126 J7   20 27 S 149 3 E
Linden, Guyana 169 B6   6 0N   58 10W
Linden, Ala., U.S.A. 149 J2   32 18N 87 48W
Linden, Calif., U.S.A. 160 G5   38 1N 121 5W
Linden, Ind., U.S.A. 157 D10   40 11N 86 54W
Linden, Mich., U.S.A. 157 B13   42 49N 83 47W
Linden, Tex., U.S.A. 155 J7   33 1N 94 22W
Lindenhurst, U.S.A. 151 F11   40 41N 73 23W
Lindenow Fjord, Greenland 10 E6   60 30N 43 25W
Lindesberg, Sweden .... 16 E9   59 36N 15 15 E
Lindesnes, Norway .... 9 G13   57 58N   7 3 E
Líndhos, Greece .... 38 E12   36 6N 28 4 E
Líndhos, Ákra, Greece .... 38 E12   36 4N 28 10 E
Lindi, Tanzania .... 119 D4   9 58 S 39 38 E
Lindi □, Tanzania .... 119 D4   9 40 S 38 30 E
Lindi →, Dem. Rep. of the Congo . 118 B2 0 33N 25 5 E
Lindö, Sweden .... 17 F10   58 37N 16 15 E
Lindome, Sweden .... 17 G6   57 35N 12 5 E
Lindoso, Portugal 42 D2   41 52N   8 11W
Lindow, Germany .... 30 C8   52 58N 12 59 E
Lindsay, Canada 140 D4   44 22N 78 43W
Lindsay, Calif., U.S.A. 160 J7   36 12N 119 5W
Lindsay, Okla., U.S.A. 155 H6   34 50N 97 38W
Lindsborg, U.S.A. 154 F6   38 35N 97 40W
Lindsdal, Sweden .... 17 H10   56 44N 16 18 E
Linesville, U.S.A. 150 E4   41 39N 80 26W
Lineville, Ala., U.S.A. 152 A3   33 18N 85 45W
Lineville, Iowa, U.S.A. 156 E8   40 35N 93 32W
Linfen, China .... 74 F6   36 3N 111 30 E
Ling Xian, Hunan, China ...... 77 D9   26 29N 113 48 E
Ling Xian, Shandong, China ... 74 F9   37 22N 116 30 E
Lingal, India .... 95 F4   16 17N 78 31 E
Lingao, China .... 86 C7   19 56N 109 42 E
Lingayen, Phil. .... 80 C3   16 10N 120 14 E
Lingayen G., Phil. .... 80 C3   16 10N 120 15 E
Lingbi, China .... 75 H9   33 33N 117 33 E
Lingbo, Sweden .... 16 C10   61 3N 16 41 E
Lingchuan, Guangxi Zhuangzu,
  China .... 77 E8   25 26N 110 21 E
Lingchuan, Shanxi, China ..... 74 G7   35 45N 113 12 E
Lingding Yang, China .... 69 G10   22 25N 113 44 E
Lingen, Germany .... 30 C3   52 31N   7 19 E
Lingga, Indonesia .... 84 C2   0 12 S 104 37 E
Lingga, Kepulauan, Indonesia . 84 C2   0 10 S 104 30 E
Lingga Arch. = Lingga, Kepulauan,
  Indonesia .... 84 C2   0 10 S 104 30 E
Linghem, Sweden .... 17 F9   58 26N 15 47 E
Lingig, Phil. .... 81 G6   8 2N 126 24 E
Lingle, U.S.A. 154 D2   42 8N 104 21W
Lingomo, Dem. Rep. of the Congo . 114 B4 0 38N 22 3 E
Lingshan, China .... 76 F7   22 25N 109 18 E
Lingshi, China .... 74 F6   36 48N 111 48 E
Lingshou, China .... 74 E8   38 20N 114 20 E
Lingshui, China .... 86 C8   18 27N 110 0 E
Lingsugur, India .... 95 F3   16 10N 76 31 E
Lingtai, China .... 74 G4   35 0N 107 40 E
Linguère, Senegal 112 B1   15 25N 15 5W
Lingui, China .... 77 E8   25 12N 110 2 E
Lingunda, Dem. Rep. of the Congo . 114 C3 0 49N 21 8 E
Lingwu, China .... 74 E4   38 6N 106 20 E
Lingyuan, China .... 75 D10   41 10N 119 15 E
Lingyun, China .... 76 E6   25 2N 106 35 E
Linhai, China .... 77 C13   28 50N 121 8 E
Linhares, Brazil .... 171 E3   19 25 S 40 4W
Linhe, China .... 74 D4   40 48N 107 20 E
Linjiang, China .... 75 D14   41 50N 127 0 E
Linköping, Sweden .... 17 F9   58 28N 15 36 E
Linkou, China .... 75 B16   45 15N 130 18 E
Linli, China .... 77 C8   29 27N 111 30 E
Linn, China 156 F5   38 29N 91 51W
Linneus, U.S.A. 156 E3   39 53N 93 11W
Linnhe, L., U.K. 22 E3   56 36N   5 25W
Linosa, Medit. S. .... 108 A2   35 51N 12 50 E
Linqi, China .... 74 G7   35 45N 113 52 E
Linqing, China .... 74 F8   36 50N 115 42 E
Linqu, China .... 75 F10   36 25N 118 30 E
Linru, China .... 74 G7   34 11N 112 52 E
Lins, Brazil .... 175 A6   21 40 S 49 44W
Linshui, China .... 76 B6   30 21N 106 57 E
Linstead, Jamaica .... 164 a   18 8N 77 2W
Linta →, Madag. .... 117 D7   25 2 S 44 5 E
Linth →, Switz. .... 31 H5   47 7N   9 7 E
Linthal, Switz. .... 33 C8   46 54N   9 0 E
Linton, Ind., U.S.A. 157 F9   39 2N 87 10W
Linton, N. Dak., U.S.A. 154 B4   46 16N 100 14W
Lintong, China .... 74 G5   34 20N 109 10 E
Linwood, Canada 150 C4   43 35N 80 43W
Linwu, China .... 77 E9   25 19N 112 31 E
Linxi, China .... 75 C10   43 36N 118 2 E
Linxia, China .... 74 C5   35 36N 103 10 E
Linxiang, China .... 77 C9   29 28N 113 23 E
Linyanti →, Africa .... 116 B4   17 50 S 25 5 E
Linyi, China .... 75 G10   35 5N 118 21 E
Linz, Austria .... 34 C7   48 18N 14 18 E
Linz, Germany .... 30 E3   50 34N   7 17 E
Linzhenzhen, China .... 74 F5   36 30N 109 59 E
Linzi, China .... 75 F10   36 50N 118 20 E
Lioko, Équateur, Dem. Rep. of
  the Congo .... 114 B4   0 2N   22 4 E
Lioko, Orientale, Dem. Rep. of
  the Congo .... 114 B4   1 25N 23 7 E
Liomseter, Norway .... 18 C6   61 15N   9 35 E
Lion, G. du, France .... 28 E7   43 10N   4 0 E
Lionárisso, Cyprus .... 39 E10   35 28N 34 8 E
Lioni, Italy .... 47 B8   40 52N 15 11 E
Lions, G. of = Lion, G. du, France . 28 E7 43 10N   4 0 E
Lion's Den, Zimbabwe .... 119 F3   17 15 S 30 5 E
Lion's Head, Canada 150 B3   44 58N 81 15W
Liouesso, Congo .... 114 B3   1 2N 15 43 E
Liozno = Lyozna, Belarus ..... 58 E6   55 0N 30 50 E
Lipa, Phil. .... 80 E3   13 57N 121 10 E
Lipali, Mozam. .... 119 F4   15 50 S 35 50 E
Lipany, Slovak Rep. .... 35 B13   49 9N 20 58 E
Lípari, Italy .... 47 D7   38 26N 14 58 E
Lípari, I., Italy .... 47 D7   38 29N 14 56 E
Lípari, Is. = Eólie, Ís., Italy . 47 D7 38 30N 14 57 E
Lipcani, Moldova .... 53 B11   48 14N 26 48 E
Lipetsk, Russia .... 59 F10   52 37N 39 35 E
Lipiany, Poland .... 55 E1   53 2N 14 58 E
Liping, China .... 76 D7   26 15N 109 7 E
Lipkany = Lipcani, Moldova ... 53 B11   48 14N 26 48 E
Lipljan, Kosovo, Yug. .... 50 D5   42 31N 21 7 E
Lipník nad Bečvou, Czech Rep. . 55 F6   49 32N 17 36 E
Lipno, Poland .... 55 E6   52 49N 19 15 E
Lipova, Romania .... 52 D6   46 8N 21 42 E
Lipovcy Manzovka, Russia ..... 70 B6   44 12N 131 33 E
Lipovets, Ukraine .... 59 H5   49 12N 29 1 E
Lippe →, Germany .... 30 D2   51 39N   6 38 E
Lippstadt, Germany .... 30 D4   51 41N   8 22 E
Lipscomb, U.S.A. 155 G4   36 14N 100 16W
Lipsk, Poland .... 54 E10   53 44N 23 24 E
Lipsko, Poland .... 55 G8   51 9N   21 40 E
Lipsói, Greece .... 49 D8   37 19N 26 50 E
Liptovský Hrádok, Slovak Rep. . 35 B12   49 2N 19 44 E
Liptovský Mikuláš, Slovak Rep. . 35 B12 49 6N 19 35 E
Liptrap C., Australia .... 129 E6   38 50 S 145 55 E
Lipu, China .... 77 E8   24 30N 110 22 E
Liquica, E. Timor .... 82 C3   8 36 S 125 19 E
Liquillo, Sierra de, Puerto Rico . 165 d 18 20N 65 47W
Lira, Uganda .... 118 B3   2 17N 32 57 E
Liranga, Congo .... 114 C3   0 43 S 17 32 E
Liri →, Italy .... 46 A6   41 25N 13 52 E
Liria = Lliria, Spain 41 F4   39 37N   0 35W
Lisakovsk, Kazakhstan .... 64 E9   52 33N 62 37 E
Lisala, Dem. Rep. of the Congo . 114 B4 2 12N 21 38 E
Lisboa, Portugal 43 G1   38 42N   9 10W
Lisboa □, Portugal 43 F1   39 0N   9 12W
Lisbon = Lisboa, Portugal 43 G1   38 42N   9 10W
Lisbon, N. Dak., U.S.A. 154 B6   46 27N 97 41W
Lisbon, N.H., U.S.A. 151 B13   44 13N 71 55W
Lisbon, Ohio, U.S.A. 150 F4   40 46N 80 46W
Lisbon Falls, U.S.A. 149 D10   44 0N 70 4W
Lisburn, U.K. 23 B5   54 31N   6 3W
Lisburn, C., U.S.A. 144 B3   68 53N 166 13W
Liscannor B., Ireland 23 D2   52 55N   9 24W
Liscia →, Italy .... 46 A2   41 11N   9 9 E
Lishe Jiang →, China .... 76 E3   24 35N 101 35 E
Lishi, China .... 74 F6   37 31N 111 8 E
Lishu, China .... 75 C13   43 20N 124 18 E
Lishui, Jiangsu, China .... 77 B12   31 38N 119 2 E
Lishui, Zhejiang, China ...... 77 C12   28 28N 119 54 E
Lisianski I., Pac. Oc. 145 F9   26 2N 174 0W
Lisichansk = Lysychansk, Ukraine . 59 H10 48 55N 38 30 E
Lisieux, France .... 26 C7   49 10N   0 12 E
Liski, Russia .... 59 G10   51 3N 39 30 E
L'Isle-Jourdain, Gers, France . 28 E5   43 36N   1 5 E
L'Isle-Jourdain, Vienne, France . 28 B4 46 13N   0 31 E
L'Isle-Mont-la-Ville, Switz. . 32 C2   46 37N   6 25 E
L'Isle-sur-la-Sorgue, France . 29 E9   43 54N   5 2 E
Lisle-sur-Tarn, France .... 28 E5   43 52N   1 49 E
Lismore, Australia .... 129 D5   28 44 S 153 21 E
Lismore, Ireland 23 D4   52 8N   7 55W
Lista, Norway .... 18 F3   58 7N   6 39 E
Lister, Mt., Antarctica ...... 7 D11   78 0 S 162 0 E
Liston, Australia .... 127 D5   28 39 S 152 6 E
Listowel, Canada 140 D3   43 44N 80 58W
Listowel, Ireland 23 D2   52 27N   9 29W
Lit, Sweden .... 16 A8   63 19N 14 51 E
Litang, Guangxi Zhuangzu, China . 76 F7 23 12N 109 8 E
Litang, Sichuan, China .... 76 B3   30 1N 100 17 E
Litang, Malaysia .... 85 A5   5 27N 118 31 E
Litang Qu →, China .... 76 C3   28 4N 101 32 E
Litani →, Lebanon .... 103 B4   33 20N 35 15 E
Litchfield, Australia .... 128 D5   36 18 S 142 52 E
Litchfield, Calif., U.S.A. ... 160 E6   40 24N 120 23W
Litchfield, Conn., U.S.A. 151 E11   41 45N 73 11W
Litchfield, Ill., U.S.A. 156 E7   39 11N 89 39W
Litchfield, Minn., U.S.A. 154 C7   45 8N 94 32W
Litchfield Nat. Park △, Australia . 124 B5 13 14 S 131 1 E
Liteni, Romania .... 53 C11   47 32N 26 32 E
Lithakiá, Greece .... 39 D2   37 43N 20 50 E
Lithgow, Australia .... 129 B9   33 25 S 150 8 E
Líthinon, Ákra, Greece .... 39 F5   34 55N 24 44 E
Lithuania ■, Europe .... 15 J20   55 30N 24 0 E
Litija, Slovenia .... 45 B11   46 3N 14 50 E
Lititz, U.S.A. 151 F8   40 9N 76 18W
Litókhoron, Greece .... 50 F6   40 8N 22 34 E
Litoko, Dem. Rep. of the Congo . 114 C4 1 13 S 24 47 E
Litoměřice, Czech Rep. .... 34 A7   50 33N 14 10 E
Litomyšl, Czech Rep. .... 34 B9   49 52N 16 20 E
Litschau, Austria .... 34 C8   48 58N 15 4 E
Little Abaco I., Bahamas 164 A4   26 50N 77 30W
Little Andaman I., India ..... 95 J11   10 45N 92 30 E
Little Barrier I., N.Z. ...... 130 C4   36 12 S 175 8 E
Little Basses, Sri Lanka ..... 95 L5   6 24N 81 43 E
Little Belt Mts., U.S.A. 158 C8   46 40N 110 45W
Little Bighorn Battlefield Nat.
  Monument △, U.S.A. 158 D10   45 34N 107 26W
Little Blue →, U.S.A. 154 F6   39 42N 96 41W
Little Buffalo →, Canada 142 A6   61 0N 113 46W
Little Cayman, Cayman Is. 164 C3   19 41N 80 3W
Little Churchill →, Canada ... 143 B9   57 30N 95 22W
Little Coco I., Burma .... 95 H11   14 0N 93 13 E
Little Colorado →, U.S.A. 159 H8   36 12N 111 48W
Little Current, Canada 140 C3   45 55N 82 0W
Little Current →, Canada 140 B3   50 57N 84 36W
Little Desert Nat. Park △, Australia . 128 D3 36 25 S 141 30 E
Little Diomede I., U.S.A. 144 D5   65 45N 168 56W
Little Falls, Minn., U.S.A. .. 154 C7   45 59N 94 22W
Little Falls, N.Y., U.S.A. ... 151 C10   43 3N 74 51W
Little Fork →, U.S.A. 154 A8   48 31N 93 35W
Little Grand Rapids, Canada .. 143 C9   52 0N 95 29W
Little Humboldt →, U.S.A. 158 F5   41 1N 117 43W
Little Inagua I., Bahamas 165 B5   21 40N 73 50W
Little Karoo, S. Africa ...... 116 E3   33 45 S 21 0 E
Little Lake, U.S.A. 161 K9   35 56N 117 55W
Little Laut Is. = Laut Kecil,
  Kepulauan, Indonesia .... 85 C5   4 45 S 115 40 E
Little Mecatina = Petit-Mécatina →,
  Canada 141 B8   50 40N 59 30W
Little Minch, U.K. 22 D2   57 35N   6 45W
Little Missouri →, U.S.A. 154 B3   47 36N 102 25W
Little Nicobar, India .... 95 L11   7 20N 93 40 E
Little Ouse →, U.K. .... 21 E9   52 22N   1 12 E
Little Rann, India .... 92 H4   23 25N 71 25 E
Little Red →, U.S.A. 155 H9   35 11N 91 27W
Little River, N.Z. .... 131 D7   43 45 S 172 49 E
Little Rock, U.S.A. 155 H8   34 45N 92 17W
Little Ruaha →, Tanzania ..... 118 D4   7 57 S 37 53 E
Little Sable Pt., U.S.A. 148 D2   43 38N 86 33W
Little Scarcies →, S. Leone .. 112 D2   8 50N 13 10W
Little Sioux →, U.S.A. 154 E6   41 48N 96 4W
Little Sitkin I., U.S.A. ..... 144 L2   51 57N 178 31 E
Little Smoky →, Canada 142 C5   54 44N 117 11W
Little Snake →, U.S.A. 158 F9   40 27N 108 26W
Little Sound, Bermuda .... 9 a   32 15N 64 50W
Little Tobago, Trin. & Tob. .. 169 E10   11 18N 60 30W
Little Valley, U.S.A. 150 D6   42 15N 78 48W
Little Wabash →, U.S.A. 157 G8   37 55N 88 5W
Little White →, U.S.A. 154 D4   43 40N 100 40W
Little York, U.S.A. 156 C6   41 10N 90 45W
Littlefield, U.S.A. 155 J3   33 55N 102 20W
Littlehampton, U.K. 21 G7   50 49N   0 32W
Littleton, U.S.A. 151 B13   44 18N 71 46W
Litunga, Angola .... 115 E3   13 19 S 16 48 E
Litvinov, Czech Rep. .... 34 A6   50 36N 13 37 E
Liu He →, China .... 75 D11   40 55N 121 35 E
Liu Jiang →, China .... 76 F7   23 55N 109 30 E
Liuba, China .... 74 H4   33 38N 106 55 E
Liucheng, China .... 76 E7   24 38N 109 14 E
Liugou, China .... 75 D10   40 57N 118 15 E
Liuhe, China .... 75 C13   42 17N 125 43 E
Liuheng Dao, China .... 77 C14   29 40N 122 5 E
Liujiang, China .... 76 E7   24 26N 109 11 E
Liukang Tenggaja = Sabalana,
  Kepulauan, Indonesia .... 82 C1   6 45 S 118 50 E
Liuli, Tanzania .... 119 E3   11 3 S 34 38 E
Liuwa Plain, Zambia .... 115 E4   14 20 S 22 30 E
Liuwa Plain Nat. Park △, Zambia . 115 E4 14 45 S 22 35 E
Liuyang, China .... 77 C9   28 10N 113 37 E
Liuzhou, China .... 76 E7   24 22N 109 22 E
Liuzhuang, China .... 75 H11   33 12N 120 18 E
Livada, Romania .... 53 C8   47 52N 23 5 E
Livadherón, Greece .... 50 F5   40 2N 21 57 E
Livadhia, Cyprus .... 39 F9   34 57N 33 38 E
Livádhion, Greece .... 48 A4   40 8N 22 9 E
Livadhje, Albania .... 38 B10   39 47N 20 7 E
Livarot, France .... 26 D7   48 58N   0 9 E
Live Oak, Calif., U.S.A. 160 F5   39 17N 121 40W
Live Oak, Fla., U.S.A. 153 F6   30 18N 82 59W
Livengood, U.S.A. 144 D10   65 32N 148 33W
Liveras, Cyprus .... 39 E8   35 23N 32 57 E
Livermore, U.S.A. 160 H5   37 41N 121 47W
Livermore, Mt., U.S.A. 155 K2   30 38N 104 11W
Livermore Falls, U.S.A. 149 C11   44 29N 70 9W
Liverpool, Australia .... 129 B9   33 54 S 150 58 E
Liverpool, Canada 141 D7   44 5N 64 41W
Liverpool, U.K. 20 D4   53 25N   3 0W
Liverpool Bay, U.K. 20 D4   53 30N   3 20W
Liverpool Plains, Australia .. 129 A9   31 15 S 150 15 E
Liverpool Ra., Australia ..... 129 A9   31 50 S 150 30 E
Livigno, Italy .... 44 B7   46 35N 10 10 E
Livingston, Guatemala 164 C2   15 50N 88 50W
Livingston, U.K. 22 F5   55 54N   3 30W
Livingston, Ala., U.S.A. 149 J1   32 35N 88 11W
Livingston, Calif., U.S.A. ... 160 H6   37 23N 120 43W
Livingston, Mont., U.S.A. 158 D8   45 40N 110 34W
Livingston, S.C., U.S.A. 149 J5   33 32N 80 53W
Livingston, Tenn., U.S.A. 149 G3   36 23N 85 19W
Livingston, Tex., U.S.A. 155 K7   30 43N 94 56W
Livingston, Wis., U.S.A. 156 F6   42 54N 90 26W
Livingston, L., U.S.A. 155 K7   30 50N 95 10W
Livingston Manor, U.S.A. 151 E10   41 54N 74 50W
Livingstone, Zambia .... 119 F2   17 46 S 25 52 E
Livingstone Mts., N.Z. .... 131 F3   45 15 S 168 9 E
Livingstone Mts., Tanzania ... 119 D3   9 40 S 34 20 E
Livingstonia, Malawi .... 119 E3   10 38 S 34 5 E
Livno, Bos.-H. .... 52 G2   43 50N 17 1 E
Livny, Russia .... 59 F9   52 30N 37 30 E
Livonia, Mich., U.S.A. 157 B13   42 23N 83 23W
Livonia, N.Y., U.S.A. 150 D7   42 49N 77 40W
Livorno, Italy .... 44 E7   43 33N 10 19 E
Livradois-Forez, Parc Naturel
  Régional du, France .... 28 E7   45 0N   3 0 E
Livramento, Brazil .... 175 C4   30 55 S 55 30W
Livramento do Brumado, Brazil . 171 D3 13 39 S 41 50W
Livron-sur-Drôme, France ..... 29 D8   44 46N   4 51 E
Liwale, Tanzania .... 119 D4   9 48 S 37 58 E
Liwiec →, Poland .... 55 F8   52 36N 21 34 E
Liwonde Nat. Park △, Malawi .. 119 E4   14 48 S 35 20 E
Lixi, China .... 76 D3   26 23N 101 59 E
Lixian, China .... 76 B4   31 13N 103 12 E
Lixoúrion, Greece .... 39 C2   38 12N 20 26 E
Liyang, China .... 77 B12   31 26N 119 28 E
Lizard I., Australia .... 126 A4   14 42 S 145 30 E
Lizard Pt., U.K. 21 H2   49 57N   5 13W
Lizarda, Brazil .... 170 C2   9 36 S 46 41W
Lizella, U.S.A. 152 C6   32 48N 83 49W

Lizzano, *Italy* 47 B10 40 23N 17 27 E
Ljig, *Serbia, Yug.* 50 B4 44 13N 20 18 E
Ljøra →, *Norway* 18 C9 61 24N 12 35 E
Ljørdal, *Norway* 18 C9 61 23N 12 41 E
Ljosland, *Norway* 18 F4 58 47N 7 22 E
Ljubija, *Bos.-H.* 45 D13 44 55N 16 35 E
Ljubinje, *Bos.-H.* 50 D2 42 58N 18 5 E
Ljubljana, *Slovenia* 45 B11 46 4N 14 33 E
Ljubljana ✕ (LJU), *Slovenia* 45 B11 46 14N 14 33 E
Ljubno, *Slovenia* 45 B11 46 25N 14 46 E
Ljubovija, *Serbia, Yug.* 50 B3 44 11N 19 22 E
Ljugarn, *Sweden* 17 G12 57 20N 18 43 E
Ljung, *Sweden* 17 G7 57 59N 13 3 E
Ljungan →, *Sweden* 16 B11 62 18N 17 23 E
Ljungaverk, *Sweden* 16 B10 62 30N 16 5 E
Ljungby, *Sweden* 15 H15 56 49N 13 55 E
Ljungbyholm, *Sweden* 17 H10 56 39N 16 5 E
Ljungdalen, *Sweden* 16 B6 62 51N 12 47 E
Ljungsbro, *Sweden* 17 F9 58 31N 15 30 E
Ljungskile, *Sweden* 17 F5 58 14N 11 55 E
Ljusdal, *Sweden* 16 C10 61 46N 16 3 E
Ljusfallshammar, *Sweden* 17 F9 58 48N 15 30 E
Ljusnan →, *Sweden* 16 C11 61 12N 17 8 E
Ljusne, *Sweden* 16 C11 61 13N 17 7 E
Ljutomer, *Slovenia* 45 B13 46 31N 16 11 E
Llagostera, *Spain* 40 D7 41 50N 2 54 E
Llamellín, *Peru* 172 B2 9 0 S 76 54W
Llancanelo, Salina, *Argentina* 174 D2 35 40 S 69 8W
Llandeilo, *U.K.* 21 F4 51 53N 3 59W
Llandovery, *U.K.* 21 F4 51 59N 3 48W
Llandrindod Wells, *U.K.* 21 E4 52 14N 3 22W
Llandudno, *U.K.* 20 D4 53 19N 3 50W
Llanelli, *U.K.* 21 F3 51 41N 4 10W
Llanes, *Spain* 42 B6 43 25N 4 50W
Llangollen, *U.K.* 20 E4 52 58N 3 11W
Llanidloes, *U.K.* 21 E4 52 27N 3 31W
Llano, *U.S.A.* 155 K5 30 45N 98 41W
Llano →, *U.S.A.* 155 K5 30 39N 98 26W
Llano Estacado, *U.S.A.* 155 J3 33 30N 103 0W
Llanos, *S. Amer.* 166 C3 5 0N 71 35W
Llanquihue, L., *Chile* 176 B1 41 10 S 72 50W
Llanwrtyd Wells, *U.K.* 21 E4 52 7N 3 38W
Llata, *Peru* 172 B2 9 25 S 76 47W
Llebeig, C. des, *Spain* 38 B3 39 33N 2 18 E
Lleida, *Spain* 40 D5 41 37N 0 39 E
Lleida □, *Spain* 40 C6 42 6N 1 0 E
Llentrisca, C., *Spain* 38 D1 38 52N 1 15 E
Llera, *Mexico* 163 C5 23 19N 99 1W
Llerena, *Spain* 43 G5 38 17N 6 0W
Lleyn Peninsula, *U.K.* 20 E3 52 51N 4 36W
Llica, *Bolivia* 172 D4 19 52 S 68 16W
Llico, *Chile* 174 C1 34 46 S 72 5W
Lliria, *Spain* 41 F4 39 37N 0 35W
Llobregat →, *Spain* 40 D7 41 19N 2 9 E
Llodio, *Spain* 40 B2 43 9N 2 58W
Llorente, *Phil.* 81 F5 11 25N 125 33 E
Lloret de Mar, *Spain* 40 D7 41 41N 2 53 E
Lloyd B., *Australia* 126 A3 12 45 S 143 27 E
Lloyd L., *Canada* 143 B7 57 22N 108 57W
Lloydminster, *Canada* 143 C7 53 17N 110 0W
Llucena del Cid, *Spain* 40 E4 40 9N 0 17W
Llucmajor, *Spain* 38 B3 39 29N 2 53 E
Llullaillaco, Volcán, *S. Amer.* 174 A2 24 43 S 68 30W
Lo →, *Vietnam* 86 B5 21 18N 105 25 E
Loa, *U.S.A.* 159 G8 38 24N 111 39W
Loa →, *Chile* 174 A1 21 26 S 70 41W
Loaita I., *S. China Sea* 78 B4 10 41N 114 25 E
Loange →, *Dem. Rep. of the Congo* 115 C4 4 17 S 20 2 E
Loango, *Congo* 115 C2 4 38 S 11 50 E
Loano, *Italy* 44 D5 44 8N 8 15 E
Loay, *Phil.* 81 G5 9 36N 124 1 E
Lobatse, *Botswana* 116 D4 25 12 S 25 40 E
Löbau, *Germany* 30 D10 51 5N 14 40 E
Lobaye →, *C.A.R.* 114 B3 3 41N 18 35 E
Lobenstein, *Germany* 30 E7 50 25N 11 39 E
Lobería, *Argentina* 174 D4 38 10 S 58 40W
Löberöd, *Sweden* 17 J7 55 47N 13 31 E
Łobez, *Poland* 54 E2 53 38N 15 39 E
Lobito, *Angola* 115 E2 12 18 S 13 35 E
Lobo, *Indonesia* 83 B4 3 45 S 134 5 E
Lobo, *Phil.* 80 E3 13 39N 121 13 E
Lobo →, *Ivory C.* 112 D3 6 2N 6 45W
Lobos, *Argentina* 174 D4 35 10 S 59 0W
Lobos, I., *Mexico* 162 B2 27 15N 110 30W
Lobos, I. de, *Canary Is.* 9 e2 28 45N 13 50W
Lobos de Afuera, Islas, *Peru* 172 B1 6 57 S 80 42W
Lobos de Tierra, I., *Peru* 172 B1 6 27 S 80 52W
Lobva, *Russia* 64 B8 59 10N 60 30 E
Lobva →, *Russia* 64 B8 59 8N 60 48 E
Łobżenica, *Poland* 55 E4 53 18N 17 15 E
Loc Binh, *Vietnam* 86 B6 21 46N 106 54 E
Loc Ninh, *Vietnam* 87 G6 11 50N 106 34 E
Locarno, *Switz.* 33 D7 46 10N 8 47 E
Loch Baghasdail = Lochboisdale, *U.K.* 22 D1 57 9N 7 20W
Loch Garman = Wexford, *Ireland* 23 D5 52 20N 6 28W
Loch Lomond and the Trossachs Nat. Park △, *U.K.* 22 E4 56 10N 4 40W
Loch Nam Madadh = Lochmaddy, *U.K.* 22 D1 57 36N 7 10W
Lochaber, *U.K.* 22 E3 56 59N 5 1W
Locharbriggs, *U.K.* 22 F5 55 7N 3 35W
Lochboisdale, *U.K.* 22 D1 57 9N 7 20W
Loche, L. La, *Canada* 143 B7 56 30N 109 30W
Lochem, *Neths.* 24 B6 52 9N 6 26 E
Loches, *France* 26 E7 47 7N 1 0 E
Lochgilphead, *U.K.* 22 E3 56 2N 5 26W
Lochinvar Nat. Park △, *Zambia* 119 F2 15 55 S 27 15 E
Lochinver, *U.K.* 22 C3 58 9N 5 14W
Lochloosa L., *U.S.A.* 153 F7 29 30N 82 7W
Lochmaddy, *U.K.* 22 D1 57 36N 7 10W
Lochnagar, *Australia* 126 C4 23 33 S 145 38 E
Lochnagar, *U.K.* 22 E5 56 57N 3 15W
Łochów, *Poland* 55 F8 52 33N 21 42 E
Lochy, L., *U.K.* 22 E4 57 0N 4 53W
Lock, *Australia* 127 E2 33 34 S 135 46 E
Lock Haven, *U.S.A.* 150 E7 41 8N 77 28W
Lockeford, *U.S.A.* 160 G5 38 10N 121 9W
Lockeport, *Canada* 141 D6 43 47N 65 4W
Lockerbie, *U.K.* 22 F5 55 7N 3 21W
Lockhart, *Australia* 129 C7 35 14 S 146 40 E
Lockhart, *U.S.A.* 155 L6 29 53N 97 40W
Lockhart, L., *Australia* 125 F2 33 15 S 119 3 E
Lockhart River, *Australia* 126 A3 12 58 S 143 30 E
Lockney, *U.S.A.* 155 H4 34 7N 101 27W
Lockport, *Ill., U.S.A.* 157 C8 41 35N 88 3W
Lockport, *N.Y., U.S.A.* 150 C6 43 10N 78 42W
Locminé, *France* 26 E4 47 54N 2 51W
Locri, *Italy* 47 D9 38 14N 16 16 E
Locronan, *France* 26 D2 48 7N 4 15W
Locust Cr. →, *U.S.A.* 156 E3 39 40N 93 17W
Locust Grove, *U.S.A.* 152 B5 33 21N 84 7W
Lod, *Israel* 103 D3 31 57N 34 54 E
Lodalskåpa, *Norway* 18 C4 61 47N 7 13 E
Lodeinoye Pole, *Russia* 58 B7 60 44N 33 33 E
Lodève, *France* 28 E7 43 44N 3 19 E
Lodge Bay, *Canada* 141 B8 52 14N 55 51W
Lodge Grass, *U.S.A.* 158 D10 45 19N 107 22W
Lodgepole Cr. →, *U.S.A.* 154 E2 41 20N 104 30W
Lodhran, *Pakistan* 92 E4 29 32N 71 30 E
Lodi, *Italy* 44 C6 45 19N 9 30 E
Lodi, *Calif., U.S.A.* 160 G5 38 8N 121 16W
Lodi, *Ohio, U.S.A.* 150 E3 41 2N 82 0W
Lodja, *Dem. Rep. of the Congo* 118 C1 3 30 S 23 23 E
Lodosa, *Spain* 40 C2 42 25N 2 4W
Lödöse, *Sweden* 17 F6 58 2N 12 9 E
Lodwar, *Kenya* 118 B4 3 10N 35 40 E
Łódź, *Poland* 55 G6 51 45N 19 27 E
Łódzkie □, *Poland* 55 G6 51 30N 19 30 E
Loei, *Thailand* 86 D3 17 29N 101 35 E
Loengo, *Dem. Rep. of the Congo* 118 C2 4 48 S 26 30 E
Loeriesfontein, *S. Africa* 116 E2 31 0 S 19 26 E
Lofa →, *Liberia* 113 D2 6 35N 11 8W
Lofa Mano Nat. Park △, *Liberia* 112 D2 7 55N 10 25W
Lofer, *Austria* 34 D5 47 35N 12 41 E
Lofoten, *Norway* 14 B15 68 30N 14 0 E
Lofsdalen, *Sweden* 16 B7 62 10N 13 20 E
Lofsen →, *Sweden* 16 B7 62 7N 13 57 E
Loftahammar, *Sweden* 17 G10 57 54N 16 41 E
Loga, *Niger* 113 C5 13 40N 3 15 E
Logan, *Iowa, U.S.A.* 154 E7 41 39N 95 47W
Logan, *Ohio, U.S.A.* 148 F4 39 32N 82 25W
Logan, *Utah, U.S.A.* 158 F8 41 44N 111 50W
Logan, *W. Va., U.S.A.* 148 G5 37 51N 81 59W
Logan, Mt., *Canada* 138 B5 60 31N 140 22W
Logan Martin L., *U.S.A.* 152 B3 33 26N 86 20W
Logandale, *U.S.A.* 161 J12 36 36N 114 29W
Logansport, *Ind., U.S.A.* 157 D10 40 45N 86 22W
Logansport, *La., U.S.A.* 155 K8 31 58N 94 0W
Logirim, *Sudan* 107 G3 4 43N 33 14 E
Logo, *Sudan* 107 F3 5 20N 30 18 E
Logone →, *Chad* 109 F3 12 6N 15 2 E
Logone Gana, *Chad* 109 F3 11 36N 15 4 E
Logone Occidental →, *Chad* 109 G3 8 50N 16 0 E
Logone Orientale →, *Chad* 109 G3 9 7N 16 26 E
Logroño, *Spain* 40 C2 42 28N 2 27W
Logrosán, *Spain* 43 F5 39 20N 5 32W
Løgstør, *Denmark* 17 H3 56 58N 9 14 E
Logtak Lake, *India* 90 C4 24 33N 93 50 E
Løgumkloster, *Denmark* 17 J2 55 4N 8 57 E
Loh, *Vanuatu* 133 C4 13 21 S 166 38 E
Lohals, *Denmark* 17 J4 55 8N 10 55 E
Lohardaga, *India* 93 H11 23 27N 84 45 E
Loharia, *India* 92 H6 23 45N 74 14 E
Loharu, *India* 92 E6 28 27N 75 49 E
Lohja, *Finland* 15 F21 60 12N 24 5 E
Löhne, *Germany* 30 C4 52 11N 8 40 E
Lohr, *Germany* 31 F5 49 59N 9 35 E
Lohri Wah →, *Pakistan* 92 F2 27 27N 67 37 E
Loi-kaw, *Burma* 90 F6 19 40N 97 17 E
Loi-lem, *Burma* 90 E6 20 52N 97 28 E
Loimaa, *Finland* 15 F20 60 50N 23 5 E
Loir →, *France* 26 E6 47 33N 0 32W
Loir-et-Cher □, *France* 26 E8 47 40N 1 20 E
Loire □, *France* 29 C8 45 40N 4 5 E
Loire →, *France* 26 E4 47 16N 2 10W
Loire Anjou Touraine, Parc Naturel Régional de ⌂, *France* 26 E6 47 14N 0 5W
Loire-Atlantique □, *France* 26 E5 47 25N 1 40W
Loiret □, *France* 27 E9 47 55N 2 30 E
Loitz, *Germany* 30 B9 53 58N 13 8 E
Loja, *Ecuador* 172 A2 3 59 S 79 16W
Loja, *Spain* 43 H6 37 10N 4 10W
Loja □, *Ecuador* 168 D2 4 0 S 79 13W
Loje →, *Angola* 115 D2 7 49 S 13 6 E
Loji = Kawasi, *Indonesia* 82 B3 1 38 S 127 28 E
Løjt Kirkeby, *Denmark* 17 J3 55 7N 9 26 E
Lojung, *China* 76 E7 24 27N 109 36 E
Loka, *Dem. Rep. of the Congo* 114 B3 0 22N 18 2 E
Loka, *Sudan* 107 G3 4 13N 31 0 E
Lokandu, *Dem. Rep. of the Congo* 118 C2 2 30 S 25 45 E
Lokaw, *Dem. Rep. of the Congo* 114 C4 2 40 S 20 12 E
Løken, *Norway* 18 E8 59 48N 11 29 E
Lokeren, *Belgium* 24 C3 51 6N 3 59 E
Lokgwabe, *Botswana* 116 C3 24 10 S 21 50 E
Lokhvitsa, *Ukraine* 59 G7 50 25N 33 18 E
Lokichokio, *Kenya* 118 B3 4 19N 34 13 E
Lokitaung, *Kenya* 118 B4 4 12N 35 48 E
Lokkan tekojärvi, *Finland* 14 C22 67 55N 27 35 E
Løkken, *Denmark* 17 G3 57 22N 9 41 E
Løkken, *Norway* 18 A6 63 9N 9 41 E
Loknya, *Russia* 58 D6 56 49N 30 4 E
Loko, *C.A.R.* 114 B3 3 38N 18 2 E
Loko, *Nigeria* 113 D6 8 1N 7 53 E
Lokoja, *Nigeria* 113 D6 7 47N 6 45 E
Lokolama, *Dem. Rep. of the Congo* 114 C3 2 35 S 19 50 E
Lokolenge, *Dem. Rep. of the Congo* 114 B4 1 12N 22 38 E
Lokolo →, *Dem. Rep. of the Congo* 114 C3 0 43 S 19 40 E
Lokoro →, *Dem. Rep. of the Congo* 114 C3 1 43 S 18 23 E
Lokot, *Russia* 59 F8 52 34N 34 36 E
Lokuru, *Solomon Is.* 133 M9 8 20 S 157 0 E
Lol →, *Sudan* 107 F2 9 13N 26 30 E
Lola, *Angola* 115 E2 14 19 S 13 37 E
Lola, *Guinea* 112 D3 7 52N 8 29W
Lola, Mt., *U.S.A.* 160 F6 39 26N 120 22W
Lolibai, Gebel, *Sudan* 107 G3 3 50N 33 0 E
Lolimi, *Sudan* 107 G3 4 35N 34 0 E
Loliondo, *Tanzania* 118 C4 2 2 S 35 39 E
Lolland, *Denmark* 17 K5 54 45N 11 30 E
Lollar, *Germany* 30 E4 50 37N 8 43 E
Lolo, *U.S.A.* 158 C6 46 45N 114 5W
Lolo →, *Eq. Guin.* 114 B1 1 36N 9 37 E
Lolo →, *Gabon* 114 C2 0 18 S 12 18 E
Lolobau I., *Papua N. G.* 132 C6 4 55 S 151 10 E
Lolodorf, *Cameroon* 113 E7 3 16N 10 49 E
Loloma, *Zambia* 115 E4 13 24 S 24 21 E
Loltong, *Vanuatu* 133 E6 15 32 S 168 10 E
Lom, *Bulgaria* 50 C7 43 48N 23 12 E
Lom, *Norway* 18 C5 61 50N 8 34 E
Lom →, *Bulgaria* 50 C7 43 45N 23 15 E
Lom →, *Cameroon* 114 A2 5 20N 13 24 E
Lom Kao, *Thailand* 86 D3 16 53N 101 14 E
Lom Sak, *Thailand* 86 D3 16 47N 101 15 E
Loma, *U.S.A.* 158 C8 47 56N 110 30W
Loma Linda, *U.S.A.* 161 L9 34 3N 117 16W
Lomako →, *Dem. Rep. of the Congo* 114 B4 0 50N 20 50 E
Lomaloma, *Fiji* 133 A3 17 17 S 178 59W
Lomami →, *Dem. Rep. of the Congo* 118 B1 0 46N 24 16 E
Lomas de Zamóra, *Argentina* 174 C4 34 45 S 58 25W
Lombadina, *Australia* 124 C3 16 31 S 122 54 E
Lombard, *U.S.A.* 157 C8 41 53N 88 1W
Lombárdia □, *Italy* 44 C6 45 40N 9 30 E
Lombardy = Lombárdia □, *Italy* 44 C6 45 40N 9 30 E
Lombe, *Angola* 115 D3 9 27 S 16 13 E
Lombez, *France* 28 E4 43 29N 0 55 E
Lomblen, *Indonesia* 82 C2 8 30 S 123 32 E
Lombok, *Indonesia* 85 D5 8 45 S 116 30 E
Lombok, Selat, *Indonesia* 79 K18 8 30 S 115 50 E
Lomé, *Togo* 113 D5 6 9N 1 20 E
Lomela, *Dem. Rep. of the Congo* 114 C4 2 19 S 23 15 E
Lomela →, *Dem. Rep. of the Congo* 114 C4 0 15 S 20 40 E
Lomianki, *Poland* 55 F7 52 21N 20 54 E
Lomié, *Cameroon* 114 B2 3 13N 13 38 E
Lomma, *Sweden* 17 J7 55 43N 13 6 E
Lommel, *Belgium* 24 C5 51 14N 5 19 E
Lomond, *Canada* 142 C6 50 24N 112 36W
Lomond, L., *U.K.* 22 E4 56 8N 4 38W
Lomphat, *Cambodia* 86 F6 13 30N 106 59 E
Lompobatang, *Indonesia* 82 C1 5 24 S 119 56 E
Lompoc, *U.S.A.* 161 L6 34 38N 120 28W
Lomsegga, *Norway* 18 C5 61 49N 8 21 E
Łomża, *Poland* 55 E9 53 10N 22 2 E
Lon, Ko, *Thailand* 87 a 7 47N 98 23 E
Lonavale, *India* 94 E1 18 46N 73 29 E
Loncoche, *Chile* 176 A2 39 20 S 72 50W
Loncopuè, *Argentina* 176 A2 38 4 S 70 37W
Londa, *India* 95 G2 15 30N 74 30 E
Londiani, *Kenya* 118 C4 0 10 S 35 33 E
Londinières, *France* 26 C8 49 50N 1 25 E
London, *Canada* 140 D3 42 59N 81 15W
London, *U.K.* 21 F7 51 30N 0 3W
London, *Ky., U.S.A.* 148 G3 37 8N 84 5W
London, *Ohio, U.S.A.* 157 E13 39 53N 83 27W
London, Greater □, *U.K.* 21 F7 51 36N 0 5W
London Gatwick ✕ (LGW), *U.K.* 21 F7 51 10N 0 11W
London Heathrow ✕ (LHR), *U.K.* 21 F7 51 28N 0 27W
London Mills, *U.S.A.* 156 D6 40 43N 90 11W
London Stansted ✕ (STN), *U.K.* 21 F8 51 54N 0 14 E
Londonderry, *U.K.* 23 B4 55 0N 7 20W
Londonderry □, *U.K.* 23 B4 55 0N 7 20W
Londonderry, C., *Australia* 124 B4 13 45 S 126 55 E
Londonderry, I., *Chile* 176 E2 55 0 S 71 0W
Londrina, *Brazil* 175 A5 23 18 S 51 10W
Londuimbale, *Angola* 115 E3 12 15 S 15 19 E
Lone Pine, *U.S.A.* 160 J8 36 36N 118 4W
Lonely Mine, *Zimbabwe* 117 B4 19 30 S 28 49 E
Long Akah, *Malaysia* 85 B4 3 19N 114 47 E
Long B., *U.S.A.* 149 J6 33 35N 78 45W
Long Beach, *Calif., U.S.A.* 161 M8 33 47N 118 11W
Long Beach, *N.Y., U.S.A.* 151 F11 40 35N 73 39W
Long Beach, *Wash., U.S.A.* 160 D2 46 21N 124 3W
Long Branch, *U.S.A.* 151 F11 40 18N 74 0W
Long Cay, *Bahamas* 9 b 25 6N 77 22W
Long Creek, *U.S.A.* 158 D4 44 43N 119 6W
Long Eaton, *U.K.* 20 E6 52 53N 1 15W
Long I., *Australia* 126 J6 20 22 S 148 51 E
Long I., *Bahamas* 165 B4 23 20N 75 10W
Long I., *Canada* 140 B4 54 50N 79 20W
Long I., *Ireland* 23 E2 51 30N 9 34W
Long I., *Papua N. G.* 132 C4 5 20 S 147 5 E
Long I., *U.S.A.* 151 F11 40 45N 73 30W
Long Island Sd., *U.S.A.* 151 E12 41 10N 73 0W
Long L., *Canada* 140 C2 49 30N 86 50W
Long Lake, *U.S.A.* 151 C10 43 58N 74 25W
Long Point B., *Canada* 150 D4 42 40N 80 10W
Long Prairie →, *U.S.A.* 154 C7 46 20N 94 36W
Long Pt., *Bahamas* 9 b 25 1N 77 20W
Long Pt., *Canada* 150 D4 42 35N 80 2W
Long Pt., *N.Z.* 131 G4 46 34 S 169 36 E
Long Range Mts., *Canada* 141 C8 49 30N 57 30W
Long Reef, *Australia* 124 B4 14 1 S 125 48 E
Long Spruce, *Canada* 143 B10 56 24N 94 21W
Long Str. = Longa, Proliv, *Russia* 6 C16 70 0N 175 0 E
Long Thanh, *Vietnam* 87 G6 10 47N 106 57 E
Long Xian, *China* 74 G4 34 55N 106 55 E
Long Xuyen, *Vietnam* 87 G5 10 19N 105 28 E
Longa, *Angola* 115 E3 14 42 S 18 32 E
Longá, *Greece* 48 E3 36 53N 21 55 E
Longa →, *Angola* 115 E2 10 14 S 13 29 E
Longa, Proliv, *Russia* 6 C16 70 0N 175 0 E
Longa Mavinga, Coutada Pública do ⌂, *Angola* 115 F4 16 20 S 20 15 E
Long'an, *China* 76 F6 23 10N 107 40 E
Longana, *Vanuatu* 133 E5 15 18 S 168 0 E
Longarone, *Italy* 45 B9 46 16N 12 18 E
Longbenton, *U.K.* 20 B6 55 1N 1 31W
Longboat Key, *U.S.A.* 153 H7 27 23N 82 39W
Longburn, *N.Z.* 130 G4 40 23 S 175 35 E
Longchang, *China* 76 C5 29 18N 105 15 E
Longchi, *China* 76 C4 29 25N 103 24 E
Longchuan, *Guangdong, China* 77 E10 24 5N 115 17 E
Longchuan, *Yunnan, China* 76 E1 24 23N 97 58 E
Longde, *China* 74 G4 35 30N 106 20 E
Longeau, *France* 27 E12 47 47N 5 20 E
Longford, *Australia* 127 D4 41 32 S 147 3 E
Longford, *Ireland* 23 C4 53 43N 7 49W
Longford □, *Ireland* 23 C4 53 42N 7 45W
Longhai, *China* 77 E11 24 25N 117 46 E
Longhua, *Guangdong, China* 69 F11 22 39N 114 0 E
Longhua, *Hebei, China* 75 D9 41 18N 117 45 E
Longhui, *China* 77 D8 27 7N 111 2 E
Longido, *Tanzania* 118 C4 2 43 S 36 42 E
Longiram, *Indonesia* 85 C5 0 5 S 115 45 E
Longkou, *Jiangxi, China* 77 D10 26 8N 115 10 E
Longkou, *Shandong, China* 75 F11 37 40N 120 18 E
Longlac, *Canada* 140 C2 49 45N 86 25W
Longli, *China* 76 D6 26 25N 106 58 E
Longlin, *China* 76 E5 24 47N 105 20 E
Longling, *China* 76 E2 24 37N 98 39 E
Longmeadow, *U.S.A.* 151 D12 42 3N 72 34W
Longmen, *China* 77 F10 23 40N 114 18 E
Longming, *China* 76 F6 22 59N 107 7 E
Longmont, *U.S.A.* 154 E2 40 10N 105 6W
Longnan, *China* 77 E10 24 55N 114 47 E
Longnawan, *Indonesia* 85 B4 1 51N 114 55 E
Longobucco, *Italy* 47 C9 39 27N 16 37 E
Longonot Nat. Park △, *Kenya* 120 E1 0 55 S 36 28 E
Longos, *Greece* 38 C10 39 16N 20 7 E
Longquan, *China* 77 C12 28 7N 119 10 E
Longreach, *Australia* 126 C3 23 28 S 144 14 E
Longshan, *China* 76 C7 29 29N 109 25 E
Longsheng, *China* 77 E8 25 48N 110 0 E
Longué-Jumelles, *France* 26 E6 47 22N 0 8W
Longueau, *France* 27 C9 49 52N 2 21 E
Longueuil, *Canada* 151 A11 45 32N 73 28W
Longuy, *Cameroon* 114 B1 3 5N 9 58 E
Longuyon, *France* 27 C12 49 27N 5 35 E
Longvic, *France* 27 E12 47 17N 5 4 E
Longview, *Tex., U.S.A.* 155 J7 32 30N 94 44W
Longview, *Wash., U.S.A.* 160 D4 46 8N 122 57W
Longwood, *St. Helena* 9 h 15 57 S 5 41W
Longwood, *U.S.A.* 153 G8 28 42N 81 21W
Longwy, *France* 27 C12 49 30N 5 46 E
Longxi, *China* 74 G3 34 53N 104 40 E
Longxue Dao, *China* 69 F10 22 41N 113 38 E
Longyan, *China* 77 E11 25 10N 117 0 E
Longyou, *China* 77 C12 29 1N 119 8 E
Longzhou, *China* 76 F6 22 22N 106 50 E
Lonigo, *Italy* 45 C8 45 23N 11 23 E
Löningen, *Germany* 30 C3 52 44N 7 46 E
Lonja →, *Croatia* 45 C13 45 22N 16 40 E
Lonkala, *Dem. Rep. of the Congo* 115 C4 4 37 S 23 14 E
Lonkin, *Burma* 90 C6 25 39N 96 22 E
Lonoke, *U.S.A.* 155 H9 34 47N 91 54W
Lonquimay, *Chile* 176 A2 38 26 S 71 14W
Lons-le-Saunier, *France* 27 F12 46 40N 5 31 E
Lönsboda, *Sweden* 17 H8 56 24N 14 20 E
Lønset, *Norway* 18 B4 62 46N 7 24 E
Lonton, *Burma* 90 C6 25 6N 96 17 E
Looe, *U.K.* 21 G3 50 22N 4 28W
Loogootee, *U.S.A.* 157 F10 38 41N 86 55W
Lookout, C., *Canada* 140 A3 55 18N 83 56W
Lookout, C., *U.S.A.* 149 H7 34 35N 76 32W
Loolmalasin, *Tanzania* 118 C4 3 0 S 35 53 E
Loon →, *Alta., Canada* 142 B5 57 8N 115 3W
Loon →, *Man., Canada* 143 B8 55 53N 101 59W
Loon Lake, *Canada* 143 C7 54 2N 109 10W
Loongana, *Australia* 125 F4 30 52 S 127 5 E
Loop Hd., *Ireland* 23 D2 52 34N 9 56W
Lop Buri, *Thailand* 86 E3 14 48N 100 37 E
Lop Nor = Lop Nur, *China* 68 B4 40 20N 90 10 E
Lop Nur, *China* 68 B4 40 20N 90 10 E
Lopare, *Bos.-H.* 52 F3 44 39N 18 46 E
Lopatin, *Russia* 61 J8 43 50N 47 35 E
Lopatina, Gora, *Russia* 67 D15 50 47N 143 10 E
Lopaye, *Sudan* 107 F3 6 37N 33 40 E
Lopé-Okanda, Réserve de ⌂, *Gabon* 114 C2 0 45 S 11 34 E
Lopevi, *Vanuatu* 133 F6 16 30 S 168 21 E
Lopez, *Phil.* 80 E4 13 53N 122 15 E
Lopez, *U.S.A.* 151 E8 41 27N 76 20W
Lopez, C., *Gabon* 114 C1 0 47 S 8 40 E
Lopori →, *Dem. Rep. of the Congo* 114 B3 1 14N 19 49 E
Lopphavet, *Norway* 14 A19 70 27N 21 15 E
Lora, *Norway* 18 B5 62 8N 8 45 E
Lora →, *Afghan.* 91 C2 31 35N 66 32 E
Lora →, *Norway* 18 B5 62 8N 8 42 E
Lora, Hāmūn-i-, *Pakistan* 91 C2 29 38N 64 58 E
Lora Cr. →, *Australia* 127 D2 28 10 S 135 22 E
Lora del Río, *Spain* 43 H5 37 39N 5 33W
Lorain, *U.S.A.* 150 E2 41 28N 82 11W
Loraine, *U.S.A.* 156 D5 40 9N 91 13W
Loralai, *Pakistan* 91 C3 30 20N 68 41 E
Lorca, *Spain* 41 H3 37 41N 1 42W
Lord Howe I., *Pac. Oc.* 134 L7 31 33 S 159 6 E
Lord Howe Ridge, *Pac. Oc.* 134 L8 30 0 S 162 30 E
Lordsburg, *U.S.A.* 159 K9 32 21N 108 43W
Lorengau, *Papua N. G.* 132 B4 2 1 S 147 15 E
Lorestan □, *Iran* 97 C6 33 30N 48 40 E
Loreto, *Bolivia* 173 D5 15 13 S 64 40W
Loreto, *Brazil* 170 C2 7 5 S 45 10W
Loreto, *Italy* 45 E10 43 26N 13 36 E
Loreto, *Mexico* 162 B2 26 1N 111 21W
Loreto, *Phil.* 81 F5 10 21N 125 34 E
Loreto □, *Peru* 168 D3 5 0 S 75 0W
Lorgues, *France* 29 E10 43 28N 6 22 E
Lorhosso, *Burkina Faso* 112 C4 10 17N 3 38W
Lorica, *Colombia* 168 B2 9 14N 75 49W
Lorient, *France* 26 E3 47 45N 3 23W
Lorimor, *U.S.A.* 156 C2 41 8N 94 3W
Lőrinci, *Hungary* 52 C4 47 44N 19 41 E
Lormi, *India* 93 H9 22 17N 81 41 E
Lorn, *U.K.* 22 E3 56 26N 5 10W
Lorn, Firth of, *U.K.* 22 E3 56 20N 5 40W
Lorne, *Australia* 128 E5 38 33 S 143 59 E
Loronyo, *Sudan* 107 G3 4 38N 32 38 E
Lorovouno, *Cyprus* 39 E8 35 8N 32 36 E
Lörrach, *Germany* 31 H3 47 36N 7 40 E
Lorraine □, *France* 27 D13 48 53N 6 0 E
Lorraine, Parc Naturel Régional de ⌂, *France* 27 D12 48 55N 5 50 E
Los, *Sweden* 16 C9 61 45N 15 10 E
Los, Îles de, *Guinea* 112 D2 9 30N 13 50W
Los Alamos, *Calif., U.S.A.* 161 L6 34 44N 120 17W
Los Alamos, *N. Mex., U.S.A.* 159 J10 35 53N 106 19W
Los Alcornocales, Parque Natural de ⌂, *Spain* 43 J5 36 21N 5 32W
Los Altos, *U.S.A.* 160 H4 37 23N 122 7W
Los Andes, *Chile* 174 C1 32 50 S 70 40W
Los Angeles, *Chile* 174 D1 37 28 S 72 23W
Los Angeles, *U.S.A.* 161 L8 34 4N 118 15W
Los Angeles, Bahia de, *Mexico* 162 B2 28 56N 113 34W
Los Angeles Aqueduct, *U.S.A.* 161 K9 35 22N 118 5W
Los Angeles International ✕ (LAX), *U.S.A.* 161 M8 33 57N 118 25W
Los Antiguos, *Argentina* 176 C2 46 35 S 71 40W
Los Banos, *U.S.A.* 160 H6 37 4N 120 51W
Los Barrios, *Spain* 43 J5 36 11N 5 30W
Los Blancos, *Argentina* 174 A3 23 40 S 62 30W
Los Chiles, *Costa Rica* 164 D3 11 2N 84 43W
Los Corrales de Buelna, *Spain* 42 B6 43 16N 4 4W
Los Cristianos, *Canary Is.* 9 e1 28 3N 16 42W
Los Gallardos, *Spain* 41 H3 37 10N 1 57W
Los Gatos, *U.S.A.* 160 H5 37 14N 121 59W
Los Haïtises, Parque Nac. △, *Dom. Rep.* 165 C6 19 4N 69 36W
Los Hermanos Is., *Venezuela* 169 A5 11 45N 64 25W
Los Islotes, *Canary Is.* 9 e2 29 4N 13 44W
Los Lagos, *Chile* 176 A2 39 51 S 72 50W
Los Llanos de Aridane, *Canary Is.* 9 e1 28 38N 17 54W
Los Lomas, *Peru* 172 A1 4 40 S 80 10W
Los Loros, *Chile* 174 B1 27 50 S 70 6W
Los Lunas, *U.S.A.* 159 J10 34 48N 106 44W
Los Menucos, *Argentina* 176 B3 40 50 S 68 10W
Los Mochis, *Mexico* 162 B3 25 45N 108 57W
Los Monegros, *Spain* 40 D4 41 29N 0 13W
Los Monos, *Argentina* 176 C3 46 1 S 69 36W
Los Muermos, *Chile* 176 B2 41 24 S 73 29W
Los Nietos, *Spain* 41 H4 37 39N 0 47W
Los Olivos, *U.S.A.* 161 L6 34 40N 120 7W
Los Palacios, *Cuba* 164 B3 22 35N 83 15W
Los Palacios y Villafranca, *Spain* 43 H5 37 10N 5 55W
Los Reyes, *Mexico* 162 D4 19 34N 102 30W
Los Ríos □, *Ecuador* 168 D2 1 30 S 79 25W
Los Roques Is., *Venezuela* 165 D6 11 50N 66 45W
Los Santos de Maimona, *Spain* 43 G4 38 27N 6 22W
Los Teques, *Venezuela* 168 A4 10 21N 67 2W
Los Testigos, Is., *Venezuela* 169 A5 11 23N 63 6W
Los Vilos, *Chile* 174 C1 32 10 S 71 30W
Los Yébenes, *Spain* 43 F7 39 36N 3 55W
Łosice, *Poland* 55 F9 52 13N 22 43 E
Lošinj, *Croatia* 36 F8 44 30N 14 30 E
Loskop Dam, *S. Africa* 117 D4 25 23 S 29 20 E
Løsning, *Denmark* 17 J3 55 48N 9 42 E
Losombo, *Dem. Rep. of the Congo* 114 B3 1 2N 19 4 E
Losone, *Switz.* 33 D7 46 10N 8 45 E
Lossiemouth, *U.K.* 22 D5 57 42N 3 17W
Lostwithiel, *U.K.* 21 G3 50 24N 4 41W
Losuia, *Papua N. G.* 132 E6 8 30 S 151 4 E
Lot □, *France* 28 D5 44 39N 1 40 E
Lot →, *France* 28 D4 44 18N 0 20 E
Lot-et-Garonne □, *France* 28 D4 44 22N 0 30 E
Lota, *Chile* 174 D1 37 5 S 73 10W
Lotagipi Swamp, *Sudan* 107 G3 4 36N 34 55 E
Løten, *Norway* 18 D8 60 51N 11 21 E
Lotfābād, *Iran* 97 B8 37 32N 59 20 E
Lothair, *S. Africa* 117 D5 26 22 S 30 27 E
Loto, *Dem. Rep. of the Congo* 114 C4 2 48 S 22 3 E
Lotoi →, *Dem. Rep. of the Congo* 114 C3 1 35 S 18 30 E
Lotorp, *Sweden* 17 F9 58 44N 15 50 E
Lötschbergtunnel, *Switz.* 32 D5 46 26N 7 43 E
Löttorp, *Sweden* 17 G11 57 10N 17 0 E
Lotung, *Taiwan* 77 E13 24 41N 121 46 E
Lotzwil, *Switz.* 32 B5 47 12N 7 48 E
Lou I., *Papua N. G.* 132 B4 2 25 S 147 22 E
Loubomo, *Congo* 114 C2 4 9 S 12 47 E
Loudéac, *France* 26 D4 48 11N 2 47W
Loudi, *China* 77 D8 27 42N 111 59 E
Loudima, *Congo* 114 C2 4 6 S 13 5 E
Loudonville, *U.S.A.* 150 F2 40 38N 82 14W
Loudun, *France* 26 E7 47 3N 0 5 E
Loue →, *France* 27 E12 47 1N 5 28 E
Louga, *Senegal* 112 B1 15 45N 16 5W
Loughborough, *U.K.* 20 E6 52 47N 1 11W
Loughman, *U.S.A.* 153 G8 28 14N 81 34W
Loughrea, *Ireland* 23 C3 53 12N 8 33W
Loughros More B., *Ireland* 23 B3 54 48N 8 32W
Louhans, *France* 27 F12 46 38N 5 12 E
Louis Trichardt, *S. Africa* 117 C4 23 1 S 29 43 E
Louis XIV, Pte., *Canada* 140 B4 54 37N 79 45W
Louisa, *U.S.A.* 148 F4 38 7N 82 36W
Louisbourg, *Canada* 141 C8 45 55N 60 0W
Louisburg, *U.S.A.* 156 F2 38 37N 94 41W
Louise I., *Canada* 142 C2 52 55N 131 50W
Louiseville, *Canada* 140 C5 46 20N 72 56W
Louisiade Arch., *Papua N. G.* 132 F7 11 10 S 153 0 E
Louisiana, *U.S.A.* 156 E6 39 27N 91 3W
Louisiana □, *U.S.A.* 155 K9 30 50N 92 0W
Louisville, *Ala., U.S.A.* 152 D4 31 47N 85 33W
Louisville, *Ga., U.S.A.* 152 B7 33 0N 82 25W
Louisville, *Ill., U.S.A.* 157 F8 38 46N 88 30W
Louisville, *Ky., U.S.A.* 157 F11 38 15N 85 46W
Louisville, *Miss., U.S.A.* 155 J10 33 7N 89 3W
Louisville, *Ohio, U.S.A.* 150 F3 40 50N 81 16W
Loukoléla, *Congo* 114 C3 1 4 S 17 10 E
Loukouo, *Congo* 114 C2 3 38 S 14 39 E

Loulay, France 28 B3 46 3N 0 30W
Loulé, Portugal 43 H3 37 9N 8 0W
Louny, Czech Rep. 34 A6 50 20N 13 48 E
Loup City, U.S.A. 154 E5 41 17N 98 58W
Lourdes, France 28 E3 43 6N 0 3W
Lourenço, Brazil 169 C7 2 30N 51 40W
Lourinhã, Portugal 43 F1 39 14N 9 17W
Loúros, Greece 39 A2 39 3N 20 47 E
Lousã, Portugal 42 E2 40 7N 8 14W
Louta, Burkina Faso 112 C4 13 30N 3 10W
Louth, Australia 129 A6 30 30 S 145 8 E
Louth, Ireland 23 C5 53 58N 6 32W
Louth, U.K. 20 D7 53 22N 0 1W
Louth □, Ireland 23 C5 53 56N 6 34W
Louth Bay, Australia 128 C1 34 33 S 135 56 E
Loutrá Aidhipsoú, Greece 48 C5 38 54N 23 2 E
Loutrá Killínis, Greece 39 D3 37 52N 21 7 E
Loutráki, Greece 48 D4 37 58N 22 57 E
Louvain = Leuven, Belgium 24 D4 50 52N 4 42 E
Louvale, U.S.A. 152 C5 32 10N 84 50W
Louviers, France 26 C8 49 12N 1 10 E
Louwsburg, S. Africa 117 D5 27 37 S 31 7 E
Lovat →, Russia 58 C6 58 14N 31 28 E
Lovćen, Montenegro, Yug. 50 D2 42 23N 18 51 E
Lovćen Nac. Park △, Yugoslavia 50 D2 42 20N 18 50 E
Lovech, Bulgaria 51 C8 43 8N 24 42 E
Lovech □, Bulgaria 51 C8 43 15N 24 45 E
Loveland, Colo., U.S.A. 154 E2 40 24N 105 5W
Loveland, Ohio, U.S.A. 157 E12 39 16N 84 16W
Lovell, U.S.A. 158 D9 44 50N 108 24W
Lovelock, U.S.A. 156 F4 40 11N 118 28W
Lóvere, Italy 44 C7 45 49N 10 4 E
Loves Park, U.S.A. 156 B7 42 19N 89 3W
Lövestad, Sweden 17 J7 55 40N 13 54 E
Loviisa, Finland 15 F22 60 28N 26 12 E
Lovilia, U.S.A. 156 C4 41 8N 92 55W
Loving, U.S.A. 155 J2 32 17N 104 6W
Lovington, Ill., U.S.A. 157 E8 39 43N 88 38W
Lovington, N. Mex., U.S.A. 155 J3 32 57N 103 21W
Lovisa = Loviisa, Finland 15 F22 60 28N 26 12 E
Lovosice, Czech Rep. 34 A7 50 30N 14 2 E
Lovran, Croatia 45 C11 45 18N 14 15 E
Lovrin, Romania 52 E5 45 58N 20 48 E
Lövstabruk, Sweden 16 D11 60 25N 17 53 E
Lövstabuken, Sweden 16 D11 60 35N 17 45 E
Lóvua, Lunda Norte, Angola 115 D4 7 19 S 20 12 E
Lóvua, Moxico, Angola 115 E4 11 33 S 23 33 E
Lóvua →, Dem. Rep. of the Congo 115 D4 6 6 S 20 37 E
Low, L., Canada 140 B4 52 29N 76 17W
Low Pt., Australia 125 F4 32 25 S 127 25 E
Low Tatra = Nízké Tatry, Slovak Rep. 35 C12 48 55N 19 30 E
Lowa, Dem. Rep. of the Congo 118 C2 1 25 S 25 47 E
Lowa →, Dem. Rep. of the Congo 118 C2 1 24 S 25 51 E
Lowden, U.S.A. 156 C6 41 52N 90 56W
Lowell, Ind., U.S.A. 157 C9 41 18N 87 25W
Lowell, Mass., U.S.A. 151 D13 42 38N 71 19W
Lowell, Mich., U.S.A. 157 B11 42 56N 85 20W
Lowellville, U.S.A. 150 E4 41 2N 80 32W
Löwen →, Namibia 116 D2 26 51 S 18 17 E
Lower Alkali L., U.S.A. 158 F3 41 16N 120 2W
Lower Arrow L., Canada 142 D5 49 40N 118 5W
Lower Austria = Niederösterreich □, Austria 34 C8 48 25N 15 40 E
Lower California = Baja California, México 162 A1 31 10N 115 12W
Lower Glenelg Nat. Park △, Australia 128 E4 38 4 S 141 41 E
Lower Hutt, N.Z. 130 H3 41 10 S 174 55 E
Lower Kalskag, U.S.A. 144 F7 61 31N 160 22W
Lower Lake, U.S.A. 160 G4 38 55N 122 37W
Lower Manitou L., Canada 143 D10 49 15N 93 0W
Lower Paia, U.S.A. 145 C5 20 55N 156 23W
Lower Post, Canada 142 B3 59 58N 128 30W
Lower Red L., U.S.A. 154 B7 47 58N 95 0W
Lower Saxony = Niedersachsen □, Germany 30 C4 52 50N 9 0 E
Lower Tunguska = Tunguska, Nizhnyaya →, Russia 67 C9 65 48N 88 4 E
Lower Zambezi Nat. Park △, Zambia 119 F2 15 25 S 29 40 E
Lowestoft, U.K. 21 E9 52 29N 1 45 E
Lowgar □, Afghan. 91 B3 34 0N 69 0 E
Łowicz, Poland 55 F6 52 6N 19 55 E
Lowly, Pt., Australia 128 B2 33 0 S 137 46 E
Lowry City, U.S.A. 156 F3 38 8N 93 44W
Lowville, U.S.A. 151 C9 43 47N 75 29W
Loxton, Australia 128 C4 34 28 S 140 31 E
Loxton, S. Africa 116 E3 31 30 S 22 22 E
Loyalton, U.S.A. 160 F6 39 41N 120 14W
Loyalty Is. = Loyauté, Îs., N. Cal. 133 K4 20 50 S 166 30 E
Loyang = Luoyang, China 74 G7 34 40N 112 26 E
Loyauté, Îs., N. Cal. 133 K4 20 50 S 166 30 E
Loyev = Loyew, Belarus 59 G6 51 56N 30 40 E
Loyew, Belarus 59 G6 51 56N 30 46 E
Loyoro, Uganda 118 B3 3 22N 34 14 E
Lož, Slovenia 45 C11 45 43N 14 30 E
Lozère □, France 28 D7 44 35N 3 30 E
Loznica, Serbia, Yug. 50 B3 44 32N 19 12 E
Lozova, Ukraine 59 H9 49 0N 36 20 E
Lozva →, Russia 64 B9 59 36N 62 20 E
Lu, India 90 B5 26 58N 95 14 E
Lü Shan, China 77 C11 29 30N 115 55 E
Lü-Tao, Taiwan 77 F13 22 40N 121 30 E
Lu Verne, U.S.A. 156 B2 42 55N 94 5W
Lu Wo, China 69 F11 22 33N 114 6 E
Lua →, Dem. Rep. of the Congo 114 B3 2 46N 18 26 E
Lua Makiki, U.S.A. 145 C5 20 33N 156 37W
Luachimo, Angola 115 D4 7 23 S 20 48 E
Luacono, Angola 115 E4 11 15 S 21 37 E
Luajan →, India 93 G11 24 44N 85 1 E
Lualaba →, Dem. Rep. of the Congo 118 B2 0 26N 25 20 E
Luale, Dem. Rep. of the Congo 114 B4 1 9N 23 5 E
Luampa, Zambia 119 F1 15 4 S 24 20 E
Lu'an, China 77 B11 31 45N 116 29 E
Luan Chau, Vietnam 76 G4 21 38N 103 24 E
Luan He →, China 75 E10 39 20N 119 5 E
Luan Xian, China 75 E10 39 40N 118 40 E
Luancheng, Guangxi Zhuangzu, China 76 F7 22 48N 108 55 E
Luancheng, Hebei, China 74 F8 37 53N 114 40 E
Luanco, Spain 42 B5 43 37N 5 48W
Luanda, Angola 115 D2 8 50 S 13 15 E
Luando, Reserva Natural Integral do △, Angola 115 E3 11 0 S 17 32 E
Luang, Thale, Thailand 87 J3 7 30N 100 15 E
Luang Prabang, Laos 76 H4 19 52N 102 10 E
Luanginga →, Zambia 115 E4 15 11 S 22 55 E
Luangwa, Zambia 119 F3 15 35 S 30 16 E
Luangwa →, Zambia 119 F3 14 25 S 30 25 E
Luangwa Valley, Zambia 119 E3 13 30 S 31 30 E
Luania-Bubi, Dem. Rep. of the Congo 115 D4 7 28 S 24 49 E
Luanne, China 75 D9 40 55N 117 40 E
Luanping, China 75 D9 40 53N 117 23 E
Luanshya, Zambia 119 E2 13 3 S 28 28 E
Luapula □, Zambia 119 E2 11 0 S 29 0 E
Luapula →, Africa 119 D2 9 26 S 28 33 E
Luarca, Spain 42 B4 43 32N 6 32W
Luashi, Dem. Rep. of the Congo 119 E1 10 50 S 23 36 E
Luatamba, Angola 115 E3 12 52 S 17 14 E
Luatira, Angola 115 E4 10 40 S 22 10 E
Luau, Angola 115 E4 10 40 S 22 10 E
Luba, Phil. 80 C3 17 19N 120 42 E

Lubaczów, Poland 55 H10 50 10N 23 8 E
Lubalo, Angola 115 D3 9 10 S 19 15 E
Lubamiti, Dem. Rep. of the Congo 114 C3 2 28 S 17 47 E
Lubań, Poland 55 G2 51 5N 15 15 E
Lubana, Ozero = Lubānas Ezers, Latvia 15 H22 56 45N 27 0 E
Lubānas Ezers, Latvia 15 H22 56 45N 27 0 E
Lubang, Phil. 80 E3 13 52N 120 7 E
Lubang Is., Phil. 80 E3 13 50N 120 12 E
Lubango, Angola 115 E2 14 55 S 13 30 E
Lubao, Dem. Rep. of the Congo 118 D2 5 17 S 25 42 E
Lubartów, Poland 55 G9 51 28N 22 42 E
Lubawa, Poland 54 E6 53 30N 19 48 E
Lübbecke, Germany 30 C4 52 18N 8 37 E
Lübben, Germany 30 D9 51 56N 13 54 E
Lübbenau, Germany 30 D9 51 52N 13 57 E
Lubbock, U.S.A. 155 J4 33 35N 101 51W
Lübeck, Germany 30 B6 53 52N 10 40 E
Lübecker Bucht, Germany 30 A6 54 5N 10 54 E
Lubefu, Dem. Rep. of the Congo 118 C1 4 47 S 24 27 E
Lubefu →, Dem. Rep. of the Congo 118 C1 4 10 S 23 0 E
Lubelskie □, Poland 55 G9 51 20N 22 50 E
Lubero = Luofu, Dem. Rep. of the Congo 118 C2 0 10 S 29 15 E
Luberon, Parc Naturel Régional du △, France 29 E9 43 52N 5 25 E
Lubersac, France 28 C5 45 26N 1 23 E
Lubicon L., Canada 142 B5 56 23N 115 56W
Lubień Kujawski, Poland 55 F6 52 23N 19 9 E
Lubilash →, Dem. Rep. of the Congo 115 D4 6 2 S 23 45 E
Lubin, Poland 55 G3 51 24N 16 11 E
Lublin, Poland 55 G9 51 12N 22 38 E
Lubliniec, Poland 55 H5 50 43N 18 45 E
Lubnän, Jabal, Lebanon 103 B4 33 45N 35 40 E
Lubniewice, Poland 55 F2 52 31N 15 15 E
Lubny, Ukraine 59 G7 50 3N 32 58 E
Lubomierz, Poland 55 G2 51 1N 15 31 E
Luboń, Poland 55 F3 52 21N 16 51 E
Lubondaie, Dem. Rep. of the Congo 115 D4 8 1 S 26 32 E
Lubongola, Dem. Rep. of the Congo 118 C2 2 35 S 27 50 E
L'ubotín, Slovak Rep. 35 B13 49 17N 20 53 E
Lubraniec, Poland 55 F5 52 33N 18 50 E
Lubsko, Poland 55 G1 51 45N 14 57 E
Lübtheen, Germany 30 B7 53 18N 11 5 E
Lubuagan, Phil. 80 C3 17 21N 121 10 E
Lubudi, Dem. Rep. of the Congo 115 D4 6 51 S 21 18 E
Lubudi →, Kasai-Occ., Dem. Rep. of the Congo 115 C4 4 19 S 20 23 E
Lubudi →, Katanga, Dem. Rep. of the Congo 119 D2 9 0 S 25 35 E
Lubuklinggau, Indonesia 84 C2 3 15 S 102 55 E
Lubuksikaping, Indonesia 84 B2 0 10N 100 15 E
Lubumbashi, Dem. Rep. of the Congo 119 E2 11 40 S 27 28 E
Lubunda, Dem. Rep. of the Congo 118 D2 5 12 S 26 41 E
Lubungu, Zambia 119 E2 14 35 S 26 24 E
Lubuskie □, Poland 55 F2 52 10N 15 20 E
Lubutu, Dem. Rep. of the Congo 118 C2 0 45 S 26 30 E
Luc An Chau, Vietnam 86 A5 22 6N 104 43 E
Luc-en-Diois, France 29 D9 44 36N 5 28 E
Lucala, Angola 115 D3 9 7 S 15 58 E
Lucala →, Angola 115 D2 9 38 S 14 14 E
Lucan, Canada 150 C3 43 11N 81 24W
Lucania, Mt., Canada 138 B5 61 1N 140 29W
Lucapa, Angola 115 D4 8 25 S 20 45 E
Lucas, U.S.A. 156 F5 39 3N 98 32W
Lucas Channel, Canada 150 A3 45 21N 81 45W
Lucban, Phil. 80 D3 14 6N 121 33 E
Lucca, Italy 44 E7 43 50N 10 29 E
Lucé, France 28 D8 48 26N 1 27 E
Luce Bay, U.K. 22 G4 54 45N 4 48W
Lucea, Jamaica 164 a 18 25N 78 10W
Lucedale, U.S.A. 149 K1 30 56N 88 35W
Lucena, Phil. 80 E3 13 56N 121 37 E
Lucena, Spain 43 H6 37 27N 4 31W
Lučenec, Slovak Rep. 35 C12 48 18N 19 42 E
Lucens, Switz. 32 C3 46 43N 6 51 E
Lucera, Italy 47 A8 41 30N 15 20 E
Lucerne = Luzern, Switz. 33 B6 47 3N 8 18 E
Lucerne, U.S.A. 160 F4 39 6N 122 48W
Lucerne Valley, U.S.A. 161 L10 34 27N 116 57W
Lucero, Mexico 162 A3 30 49N 106 30W
Luchena →, Spain 41 H3 37 44N 1 50W
Lucheng, China 74 F7 36 20N 113 11 E
Lucheringo →, Mozam. 119 E4 11 43 S 36 17 E
Lüchow, Germany 30 C7 52 58N 11 8 E
Luchuan, China 77 F8 22 21N 110 12 E
Lucia, U.S.A. 160 J5 36 2N 121 33W
Lucie →, Suriname 169 C6 3 35N 57 38W
Lucinda, Australia 126 B4 18 32 S 146 20 E
Lucindale, Australia 128 D4 36 58 S 140 26 E
Lucira, Angola 115 E2 14 0 S 12 35 E
Luciras, B. das, Angola 115 E2 13 52 S 12 31 E
Luckau, Germany 30 D9 51 50N 13 42 E
Luckenwalde, Germany 30 C9 52 5N 13 10 E
Luckey, U.S.A. 157 C13 41 27N 83 29W
Luckhoff, S. Africa 116 D3 29 44 S 24 43 E
Lucknow, Canada 150 C3 43 57N 81 31W
Lucknow, India 93 F9 26 50N 81 0 E
Luçon, France 28 B2 46 28N 1 10W
Lucusse, Angola 115 E4 12 32 S 20 48 E
Lüda = Dalian, China 75 E11 38 50N 121 40 E
Luda Kamchiya →, Bulgaria 51 C11 43 3N 27 29 E
Ludbreg, Croatia 45 B13 46 15N 16 38 E
Lüdenscheid, Germany 30 D3 51 13N 7 37 E
Lüderitz, Namibia 116 D2 26 41 S 15 8 E
Lüderitzbaai, Namibia 116 D2 26 36 S 15 8 E
Ludhiana, India 92 D6 30 57N 75 56 E
Ludian, China 76 D4 27 10N 103 33 E
Luding Qiao, China 76 C4 29 53N 102 12 E
Lüdinghausen, Germany 30 D3 51 46N 7 27 E
Ludington, U.S.A. 148 D2 43 57N 86 27W
Ludlow, U.K. 21 E5 52 22N 2 42W
Ludlow, Calif., U.S.A. 161 L10 34 43N 116 10W
Ludlow, Pa., U.S.A. 150 E6 41 43N 78 56W
Ludlow, Vt., U.S.A. 151 C12 43 24N 72 42W
Ludowici, U.S.A. 152 D8 31 43N 81 45W
Ludus, Romania 53 D9 46 29N 24 5 E
Ludvika, Sweden 16 D9 60 8N 15 14 E
Ludwigsburg, Germany 31 G5 48 53N 9 11 E
Ludwigsdorf, Germany 30 C9 52 17N 13 17 E
Ludwigshafen, Germany 31 F4 49 29N 8 26 E
Ludwigslust, Germany 30 B7 53 19N 11 30 E
Ludza, Latvia 58 D4 56 32N 27 43 E
Lue, Australia 129 B8 32 38 S 149 50 E
Luebo, Dem. Rep. of the Congo 115 D4 5 21 S 21 23 E
Lueki, Dem. Rep. of the Congo 118 C2 3 20 S 25 48 E
Luena, Angola 115 E3 12 13 S 19 51 E
Luena, Dem. Rep. of the Congo 119 D2 9 28 S 25 43 E
Luena, Zambia 119 E3 10 40 S 30 25 E
Luena →, Zambia 115 E4 12 30 S 22 34 E
Luena →, Zambia 119 E2 14 46 S 23 30 E
Luena Flats, Zambia 115 E4 14 47 S 22 17 E
Luengué, Coutada Pública do △, Angola 115 F3 16 55 S 19 55 E
Luenha = Ruenya →, Africa 119 F3 16 24 S 33 48 E
Luepa, Venezuela 169 B5 5 43N 61 31W
Luete →, Zambia 115 F4 15 46 S 23 10 E
Lüeyang, China 74 H4 33 22N 106 10 E
Lufeng, Guangdong, China 77 F10 22 57N 115 38 E
Lufeng, Yunnan, China 76 E4 25 0N 102 5 E
Lufico, Angola 115 D2 6 24 S 13 2 E
Lufira →, Dem. Rep. of the Congo 119 D2 9 30 S 27 0 E

Lufkin, U.S.A. 155 K7 31 21N 94 44W
Lufupa, Dem. Rep. of the Congo 119 E1 10 37 S 24 56 E
Luga, Russia 58 C5 58 40N 29 55 E
Luga →, Russia 58 C5 59 40N 28 18 E
Lugano, Switz. 33 E7 46 1N 8 57 E
Lugano, L. di, Switz. 33 E8 46 0N 9 0 E
Luganville, Vanuatu 133 E5 15 27 S 167 10 E
Lugard's Falls, Kenya 118 C4 3 6 S 38 41 E
Lugela, Mozam. 119 F4 16 25 S 36 43 E
Lugenda →, Mozam. 119 E4 11 25 S 38 33 E
Lugh Ganana = Luuq, Somali Rep. 120 D2 3 48N 42 34 E
Lugnaquilla, Ireland 23 D5 52 58N 6 28W
Lugo, Italy 45 D8 44 25N 11 54 E
Lugo, Spain 42 B3 43 2N 7 35W
Lugo □, Spain 42 C3 43 0N 7 30W
Lugoj, Romania 52 E6 45 42N 21 57 E
Lugovoy = Qulan, Kazakhstan 65 B6 42 55N 72 43 E
Lugus I., Phil. 81 J3 5 41N 120 50 E
Luhe, China 77 A12 32 19N 118 50 E
Luhe →, Germany 30 B6 53 23N 10 13 E
Luhit →, India 90 B5 27 48N 95 28 E
Luhuo, China 76 B3 31 21N 100 48 E
Lui →, Zambia 115 D3 8 21 S 17 33 E
Lui →, Zambia 115 F3 16 18 S 23 17 E
Luia, Angola 115 D4 8 10 S 21 32 E
Luia →, Angola 115 D4 8 32 S 21 47 E
Luiana, Angola 116 B3 17 25 S 22 59 E
Luiana →, Angola 115 F4 17 24 S 23 3 E
Luiana, Coutada Pública do △, Angola 115 F4 16 55 S 22 20 E
Luilaka →, Dem. Rep. of the Congo 114 C4 0 52 S 20 12 E
Luimneach = Limerick, Ireland 23 D3 52 40N 8 37W
Luing, U.K. 22 E3 56 14N 5 39W
Luino, Italy 44 C5 45 59N 8 44 E
Luio →, Angola 115 E4 13 17 S 21 37 E
Luís Correia, Brazil 170 B3 3 0 S 41 35W
Luís Gonçalves, Brazil 170 C1 5 37 S 50 25W
Luitpold Coast, Antarctica 7 D1 78 30 S 32 0W
Luiza, Dem. Rep. of the Congo 115 D4 7 40 S 22 30 E
Luizi, Dem. Rep. of the Congo 118 D2 6 0 S 27 25 E
Luján, Argentina 174 C4 34 45 S 59 5W
Lujiang, China 77 B11 31 20N 117 15 E
Lukala, Dem. Rep. of the Congo 115 D2 5 31 S 14 32 E
Lukang, Taiwan 77 E13 24 1N 120 22 E
Lukanga, Bandundu, Dem. Rep. of the Congo 114 C3 1 41 S 18 9 E
Lukanga, Équateur, Dem. Rep. of the Congo 114 C3 1 0 S 18 45 E
Lukanga Swamp, Zambia 119 E2 14 30 S 27 40 E
Lukavac, Bos.-H. 52 F3 44 33N 18 32 E
Lukenie →, Dem. Rep. of the Congo 114 C3 3 0 S 18 50 E
Lukhisaral, India 93 G12 25 11N 86 5 E
Lüki, Bulgaria 51 E8 41 50N 24 43 E
Lukk, Libya 108 B4 32 1N 24 46 E
Lukolela, Équateur, Dem. Rep. of the Congo 114 C3 1 10 S 17 12 E
Lukolela, Kasai-Or., Dem. Rep. of the Congo 118 D1 5 23 S 24 32 E
Lukosi, Zimbabwe 119 F2 18 30 S 26 30 E
Lukovë, Albania 50 G3 39 59N 19 54 E
Lukovit, Bulgaria 51 C8 43 13N 24 11 E
Łuków, Poland 55 G9 51 55N 22 23 E
Lukoyanov, Russia 60 C7 55 2N 44 29 E
Luksefjell, Norway 18 E6 59 23N 9 34 E
Lukumi, Dem. Rep. of the Congo 118 C2 1 43 S 24 32 E
Lukusuzi Nat. Park △, Zambia 119 E3 12 43 S 32 36 E
Lula, Dem. Rep. of the Congo 115 D3 5 22 S 16 2 E
Lule älv →, Sweden 14 D10 65 35N 22 10 E
Luleå, Sweden 14 D20 65 35N 22 10 E
Lüleburgaz, Turkey 51 E11 41 23N 27 22 E
Luliang, China 76 E4 25 0N 103 40 E
Luling, U.S.A. 155 L6 29 41N 97 39W
Lulonga →, Dem. Rep. of the Congo 114 B3 1 0N 18 10 E
Lulu, U.S.A. 152 E7 30 7N 82 29W
Lulu →, Dem. Rep. of the Congo 114 B4 1 58N 23 42 E
Lulua →, Dem. Rep. of the Congo 115 C4 4 30 S 20 30 E
Luluaburg = Kananga, Dem. Rep. of the Congo 115 D4 5 55 S 22 18 E
Luma, Amer. Samoa 133 X25 14 15 S 169 33W
Lumai, Angola 115 E4 13 13 S 21 25 E
Lumajang, Indonesia 85 D4 8 8 S 113 13 E
Lumaku, Gunong, Malaysia 85 B5 4 52N 115 38 E
Lumbala, Angola 115 E4 12 39 S 22 35 E
Lumbala Kaquengue, Angola 115 E4 14 18 S 21 18 E
Lumbala N'guimbo, Angola 115 E4 14 18 S 21 18 E
Lumbe →, Zambia 115 F4 16 44 S 23 41 E
Lumber City, U.S.A. 152 D7 31 56N 82 41W
Lumberton, U.S.A. 149 H6 34 37N 79 0W
Lumding, India 90 C4 25 46N 93 10 E
Lumi, Papua N. G. 132 B2 3 30 S 142 2 E
Lumpkin, U.S.A. 152 C5 32 3N 84 48W
Lumsden, Canada 143 C8 50 39N 104 52W
Lumsden, N.Z. 131 G3 45 44 S 168 27 E
Lumut, Malaysia 87 K3 4 13N 100 37 E
Lumut, Tanjung, Indonesia 84 C3 3 50 S 105 58 E
Luna, India 92 H3 23 43N 69 16 E
Luna, Phil. 80 B3 18 18N 121 21 E
Lunan, China 76 E4 24 40N 103 18 E
Lunavada, India 92 H5 23 8N 73 37 E
Lunca, Romania 53 C10 47 22N 25 1 E
Lunca Corbului, Romania 53 F9 44 42N 24 45 E
Lund, Sweden 17 J7 55 44N 13 12 E
Lunda Norte □, Angola 115 D3 8 0 S 20 0 E
Lunda Sul □, Angola 115 D4 10 0 S 20 0 E
Lundamo, Norway 18 A7 63 9N 10 19 E
Lundazi, Zambia 119 E3 12 20 S 33 7 E
Lunderskov, Denmark 17 J3 55 29N 9 19 E
Lundi →, Zimbabwe 119 G3 21 43 S 32 34 E
Lundu, Malaysia 85 B3 1 40N 109 50 E
Lundy, U.K. 21 F3 51 10N 4 41W
Lune →, U.K. 20 C5 54 0N 2 51W
Lüneburg, Germany 30 B6 53 15N 10 24 E
Lüneburg Heath = Lüneburger Heide, Germany 30 B6 53 10N 10 12 E
Lüneburger Heide, Germany 30 B6 53 10N 10 12 E
Lunel, France 29 E8 43 39N 4 9 E
Lünen, Germany 30 D3 51 37N 7 32 E
Lunenburg, Canada 141 D7 44 22N 64 18W
Lunéville, France 27 D13 48 36N 6 30 E
Lunga →, Zambia 119 E2 14 34 S 26 25 E
Lunga →, Zambia 119 E2 13 13 S 16 7 E
Lunge, Angola 115 E3 12 13 S 16 7 E
Lungern, Switz. 32 C6 46 48N 8 10 E
Lungga, Solomon Is. 133 M11 9 25 S 160 3 E
Lungi Airport, S. Leone 112 D2 8 40N 13 17W
Lunglei, India 93 H18 22 55N 92 45 E
Lungngo, Burma 90 E4 21 57N 93 36 E
Lungwebungu →, Zambia 115 E4 14 20 S 23 15 E
Luni, India 92 G5 26 0N 73 6 E
Luni →, India 92 G4 24 41N 71 14 E
Luninets = Luninyets, Belarus 59 F4 52 15N 26 50 E
Luning, U.S.A. 158 G4 38 30N 118 11W
Lunino, Russia 60 F7 53 35N 45 6 E
Luninyets, Belarus 59 F4 52 15N 26 50 E
Lunkaransar, India 92 E5 28 29N 73 44 E
Lunner, Norway 18 D7 60 19N 10 35 E
Lunsemfwa →, Zambia 119 E3 14 54 S 30 12 E
Lunsemfwa Falls, Zambia 119 E2 14 30 S 29 6 E
Luo He →, China 74 G6 34 35N 110 20 E
Luocheng, China 76 E7 24 48N 108 53 E
Luochuan, China 74 G5 35 45N 109 26 E

Luoci, China 76 E4 25 19N 102 18 E
Luodian, China 76 E6 25 24N 106 43 E
Luoding, China 77 F8 22 45N 111 40 E
Luofu, Dem. Rep. of the Congo 118 C2 0 10 S 29 15 E
Luohe, China 74 H8 33 32N 114 2 E
Luojiang, China 76 B5 31 18N 104 33 E
Luonan, China 74 G6 34 5N 110 10 E
Luoning, China 74 G6 34 35N 111 40 E
Luoshan, China 77 A10 32 13N 114 30 E
Luotian, China 77 B10 30 46N 115 22 E
Luoxiao Shan, China 77 D10 26 30N 114 1 E
Luoyang, China 74 G7 34 40N 112 26 E
Luoyuan, China 77 D12 26 28N 119 30 E
Luozi, Dem. Rep. of the Congo 115 C2 4 54 S 14 0 E
Luozigou, China 75 C16 43 42N 130 18 E
Lupanshui, China 76 D5 26 38N 104 48 E
Lupeni, Romania 53 E8 45 21N 23 13 E
Lupilichi, Mozam. 119 E4 11 47 S 35 13 E
Łupire, Angola 115 E4 13 36 S 19 29 E
Łupków, Poland 55 J9 49 15N 22 4 E
Lupoing, China 76 E5 24 53N 104 21 E
Lupon, Phil. 81 H6 6 54N 126 0 E
Luputa, Dem. Rep. of the Congo 115 D4 7 7 S 23 43 E
Luqa, Malta 38 F7 35 52N 14 29 E
Luquan, China 76 E4 25 35N 102 25 E
Luque, Paraguay 174 B4 25 19 S 57 25W
Luquembo, Angola 115 E3 10 44 S 17 43 E
Lúras, Italy 46 B2 40 56N 9 10 E
Luray, U.S.A. 148 F6 38 40N 78 28W
Lure, France 27 E13 47 40N 6 30 E
Luremo, Angola 115 D3 8 30 S 17 50 E
Lurgan, U.K. 23 B5 54 28N 6 19W
Luribay, Bolivia 172 G4 17 6 S 67 39W
Lurín, Peru 172 C2 12 17 S 76 52W
Lusaka, Zambia 119 F2 15 28 S 28 16 E
Lusambo, Dem. Rep. of the Congo 118 C1 4 58 S 23 28 E
Lusancay Is. and Reefs, Papua N. G. 132 E6 8 30 S 150 30 E
Lusangaye, Dem. Rep. of the Congo 118 C2 4 54 S 26 0 E
Luseland, Canada 143 C7 52 5N 109 24W
Lusenga Plain Nat. Park △, Zambia 119 D2 9 22 S 29 14 E
Lusengo, Dem. Rep. of the Congo 114 B3 1 47N 19 31 E
Lushan, Henan, China 74 H7 33 45N 112 55 E
Lushan, Sichuan, China 76 B4 30 12N 102 52 E
Lushi, China 74 G6 34 3N 111 3 E
Lushnjë, Albania 50 F3 40 55N 19 41 E
Lushoto, Tanzania 118 C4 4 47 S 38 20 E
Lushui, China 76 E2 25 58N 98 44 E
Lüshun, China 75 E11 38 45N 121 15 E
Lusignan, France 28 B4 46 26N 0 8 E
Lusigny-sur-Barse, France 27 D11 48 16N 4 15 E
Lusiye, Zambia 119 E4 16 30 S 27 5 E
Lusk, U.S.A. 154 D2 42 46N 104 27W
Lussac-les-Châteaux, France 28 B4 46 24N 0 43 E
Lustenau, Austria 34 D2 47 26N 9 39 E
Lustrafjorden, Norway 18 C4 61 23N 7 25 E
Lüt, Dasht-e, Iran 97 D8 31 30N 58 0 E
Luta = Dalian, China 75 E11 38 50N 121 40 E
Lutembo, Angola 115 E4 13 26 S 21 16 E
Lutherstadt Wittenberg, Germany 30 D8 51 53N 12 39 E
Luthersville, U.S.A. 152 B5 33 13N 84 45W
Luti, Solomon Is. 133 L9 7 14 S 157 0 E
Luton, U.K. 21 F7 51 53N 0 24W
Luton □, U.K. 21 F7 51 53N 0 24W
Lutong, Malaysia 85 B4 4 28N 114 0 E
Lutry, Switz. 32 C3 46 31N 6 42 E
Eutselk'e, Canada 143 A6 62 24N 110 44W
Lutshima →, Dem. Rep. of the Congo 115 D3 5 22 S 18 59 E
Lutsk, Ukraine 59 G3 50 50N 25 15 E
Lutuai, Angola 115 E4 12 41 S 20 7 E
Lutz, U.S.A. 153 G7 28 9N 82 28W
Lützow Holmbukta, Antarctica 7 C4 69 10 S 37 30 E
Lutzputs, S. Africa 116 D3 28 3 S 20 40 E
Luuk, Phil. 81 J3 5 58N 121 18 E
Luuq = Lugh Ganana, Somali Rep. 120 D2 3 48N 42 34 E
Luverne, Ala., U.S.A. 152 D3 31 43N 86 16W
Luverne, Minn., U.S.A. 154 D6 43 39N 96 13W
Luvo, Angola 115 D2 5 51 S 14 5 E
Lúvua, Angola 115 E4 8 49 S 25 19 E
Luvua, Dem. Rep. of the Congo 119 D2 8 48 S 25 17 E
Luvuvhu →, S. Africa 117 C5 22 25 S 31 18 E
Luwegu →, Tanzania 119 D4 8 31 S 37 23 E
Luwuk, Indonesia 83 B2 0 56 S 122 47 E
Luxembourg, Lux. 24 E6 49 37N 6 9 E
Luxembourg □, Belgium 24 E5 49 58N 5 30 E
Luxembourg ■, Europe 25 B7 49 45N 6 10 E
Luxembourg ✈ (LUX), Lux. 24 E6 49 37N 6 10 E
Luxemburg, U.S.A. 156 B5 32 36N 91 5W
Luxi, Hunan, China 77 C8 28 20N 110 7 E
Luxi, Yunnan, China 76 E4 24 40N 103 55 E
Luxi, Yunnan, China 76 E2 24 27N 98 36 E
Luxor = El Uqsur, Egypt 106 B3 25 41N 32 38 E
Luy-de-Béarn →, France 28 E3 43 39N 0 48W
Luy-de-France →, France 28 E3 43 39N 0 48W
Luz, Azores 9 d1 39 1N 28 0W
Luz-St-Sauveur, France 28 F4 42 53N 0 0W
Luza, Russia 56 B8 60 39N 47 10 E
Luzern, Switz. 33 B6 47 3N 8 18 E
Luzern □, Switz. 32 B5 47 2N 7 55 E
Luzhai, China 76 E7 24 29N 109 42 E
Luzhi, China 76 D5 26 21N 105 16 E
Luzhou, China 76 C5 28 52N 105 20 E
Luziânia, Brazil 171 E2 16 20 S 48 0W
Luzilândia, Brazil 170 B3 3 28 S 42 22W
Lužnice →, Czech Rep. 34 B7 49 14N 14 23 E
Luzon, Phil. 80 C3 16 0N 121 0 E
Luzy, France 27 F10 46 47N 3 58 E
Luzzi, Italy 47 C9 39 27N 16 17 E
Lviv, Ukraine 59 H3 49 50N 24 0 E
Lvov = Lviv, Ukraine 59 H3 49 50N 24 0 E
Lwówek, Poland 55 C2 51 7N 15 38 E
Lwówek Śląski, Poland 55 G2 51 7N 15 38 E
Lyakhavichy, Belarus 59 F4 53 2N 26 32 E
Lyakhovskiye, Ostrova, Russia 67 B15 73 40N 141 0 E
Lyaki = Läki, Azerbaijan 61 K8 40 34N 47 22 E
Lyall Mt., N.Z. 131 F2 45 16 S 167 32 E
Lyallpur = Faisalabad, Pakistan 91 C4 31 30N 73 5 E
Lyalya →, Russia 64 B8 59 9N 61 29 E
Lyangar, Tajikistan 65 C6 37 3N 72 40 E
Lyaskovets, Bulgaria 51 C9 43 6N 25 44 E
Lybster, U.K. 23 C5 58 18N 3 15W
Lycaonia, Turkey 100 D5 38 0N 33 0 E
Lychen, Germany 30 B9 53 12N 13 18 E
Lychkova, Russia 58 D7 57 55N 32 24 E
Lycia, Turkey 49 E11 36 30N 29 30 E
Lyckeby, Sweden 17 H9 56 12N 15 39 E
Lycksele, Sweden 14 D18 64 38N 18 40 E
Lycosura, Greece 38 D3 37 24N 22 3 E
Lydda = Lod, Israel 104 C3 31 57N 34 54 E
Lydenburg, S. Africa 117 D5 25 10 S 30 29 E
Lydia, Turkey 49 C10 38 48N 28 19 E
Łydynia →, Poland 55 F7 52 43N 20 42 E
Lyell, N.Z. 131 B7 41 48 S 172 4 E
Lyell I., Canada 142 C2 52 40N 131 35W
Lyepyel, Belarus 58 E5 54 50N 28 40 E
Lyford Cay, Bahamas 9 b 25 2N 77 33W

Lyme B., U.K. 21 G4 50 42N 2 53W
Lyme Regis, U.K. 21 G5 50 43N 2 57W
Lymington, U.K. 21 G6 50 45N 1 32W
Łyna →, Poland 15 J19 54 37N 21 14 E
Lynchburg, Ohio, U.S.A. 157 E13 39 15N 83 48W
Lynchburg, S.C., U.S.A. 152 A9 34 3N 80 4W
Lynchburg, Va., U.S.A. 148 G6 37 25N 79 9W
Lynd →, Australia 126 B3 16 28 S 143 18 E
Lynd Ra., Australia 127 D4 25 30 S 149 20 E
Lynden, Canada 150 C4 43 14N 80 9W
Lynden, U.S.A. 160 B4 48 57N 122 27W
Lyndhurst, Australia 127 E2 30 15 S 138 18 E
Lyndon →, Australia 125 D1 23 29 S 114 6 E
Lyndonville, N.Y., U.S.A. 150 C6 43 20N 78 23W
Lyndonville, Vt., U.S.A. 151 B12 44 31N 72 1W
Lyngdal, Buskerud, Norway 18 E6 59 54N 9 32 E
Lyngdal, Vest-Agder, Norway 18 F4 58 8N 7 7 E
Lyngen, Norway 14 B19 69 45N 20 30 E
Lyngør, Norway 18 F6 58 38N 9 8 E
Lynn, Ind., U.S.A. 157 D12 40 3N 84 56W
Lynn, Mass., U.S.A. 151 D14 42 28N 70 57W
Lynn Canal, U.S.A. 144 G14 58 50N 135 15W
Lynn Haven, U.S.A. 152 E4 30 15N 85 39W
Lynn Lake, Canada 143 B8 56 51N 101 3W
Lynne, U.S.A. 153 F8 29 12N 81 55W
Lynnville, U.S.A. 157 F9 38 12N 87 19W
Lynnwood, U.S.A. 160 C4 47 49N 122 19W
Lynton, U.K. 21 F4 51 13N 3 50W
Lyntupy, Belarus 15 J22 55 4N 26 23 E
Lynx L., Canada 143 A7 62 25N 106 15W
Lyon, France 29 C6 45 46N 4 50 E
Lyon St-Exupéry ✈ (LYS), France 29 C9 45 44N 5 2 E
Lyonnais, France 29 C8 45 45N 4 15 E
Lyonnais = Lyon = France 29 C8 45 46N 4 50 E
Lyons, Ga., U.S.A. 152 C7 32 12N 82 19W
Lyons, Kans., U.S.A. 154 F5 38 21N 98 12W
Lyons, N.Y., U.S.A. 150 C8 43 5N 77 0W
Lyons →, Australia 125 E2 25 2 S 115 9 E
Lyons Falls, U.S.A. 151 C9 43 37N 75 22W
Lyozna, Belarus 58 E6 55 0N 30 50 E
Lyra Reef, Papua N. G. 132 A7 1 50 S 153 35 E
Lys = Leie →, Belgium 24 C3 51 2N 3 45 E
Lysá nad Labem, Czech Rep. 34 A7 50 11N 14 51 E
Lysebotn, Norway 18 E3 59 3N 6 37 E
Lysefjorden, Norway 18 E3 59 0N 6 23 E
Lysekil, Sweden 17 F5 58 17N 11 26 E
Lyskovo, Russia 60 B7 56 0N 45 3 E
Lyss, Switz. 32 B4 47 4N 7 19 E
Lystrup, Denmark 17 H4 56 14N 10 14 E
Lysva, Russia 64 B6 58 7N 57 49 E
Lysvik, Sweden 16 D7 60 1N 13 9 E
Lysychansk, Ukraine 59 H10 48 55N 38 30 E
Lytham St. Anne's, U.K. 20 D4 53 45N 3 0W
Lyttelton, N.Z. 131 D7 43 35 S 172 44 E
Lytton, Canada 142 C4 50 13N 121 31W
Lyuban, Russia 58 C6 59 16N 31 18 E
Lyubcha, Belarus 58 E9 53 39N 37 50 E
Lyubim, Russia 58 C11 58 20N 40 39 E
Lyubimets, Bulgaria 51 E10 41 50N 26 5 E
Lyuboml, Ukraine 59 G3 51 11N 24 4 E
Lyubotyn, Ukraine 59 H8 50 0N 36 0 E
Lyubytino, Russia 58 C7 58 50N 33 16 E
Lyudinovo, Russia 58 F8 53 52N 34 28 E

M

M.R. Gomez, Presa, Mexico 163 B5 26 10N 99 0W
M.R. Stefánik, Bratislava ✈ (BTS), Slovak Rep. 35 C10 48 11N 17 9 E
Ma →, Vietnam 76 H5 19 47N 105 56 E
Ma, O. el →, Algeria 110 C3 27 45N 7 52W
Ma'adaba, Jordan 103 E4 30 43N 35 47 E
Maamba, Zambia 116 B4 17 17 S 26 28 E
Ma'ān, Jordan 103 E5 30 12N 35 44 E
Ma'ān □, Jordan 103 F5 30 0N 36 0 E
Maana'oba, Solomon Is. 133 M11 8 17 S 160 50 E
Maanselkä, Finland 14 C23 63 52N 28 32 E
Ma'anshan, China 77 B12 31 44N 118 29 E
Maarianhamina, Finland 15 F18 60 5N 19 55 E
Maarmorilik, Greenland 10 C5 71 3N 51 0W
Ma'arrat an Nu'mān, Syria 100 E7 35 43N 36 43 E
Maas →, Neths. 24 C4 51 45N 4 32 E
Maaseik, Belgium 24 C5 51 6N 5 45 E
Maasin, Phil. 81 J5 5 52N 125 0 E
Maasin, Phil. 79 B6 10 8N 124 50 E
Maastricht, Neths. 24 D5 50 50N 5 40 E
Maasupa, Solomon Is. 133 M11 9 16 S 161 17 E
Maave, Mozam. 117 C5 21 4 S 34 47 E
Mababe Depression, Botswana 116 B3 18 50 S 24 15 E
Mabaia, Angola 115 D2 7 12 S 14 2 E
Mabalane, Mozam. 117 C5 23 37 S 32 31 E
Mabanga, Dem. Rep. of the Congo 114 B3 1 30N 19 6 E
Ma'bar, Yemen 98 D4 14 48N 44 17 E
Mabaruma, Guyana 169 B6 8 10N 59 50W
Mabein, Burma 90 D6 23 29N 96 37 E
Mabel L., Canada 142 C5 50 35N 118 43W
Mabenge, Dem. Rep. of the Congo 114 C3 3 39 S 18 40 E
Mabenge, Dem. Rep. of the Congo 118 B1 4 15N 24 12 E
Maberly, Canada 151 B8 44 50N 76 32W
Mabian, China 76 C4 28 47N 103 37 E
Mabil, Ethiopia 107 E4 10 26N 36 52 E
Mabinay, Phil. 81 G4 9 48N 122 54 E
Mabirou, Congo 114 C3 1 3 S 15 42 E
Mablethorpe, U.K. 20 D8 53 20N 0 15 E
Mableton, U.S.A. 152 B5 33 49N 84 36W
Mably, France 27 F11 46 5N 4 4 E
Maboma, Dem. Rep. of the Congo 118 B2 2 30N 28 10 E
Mabonto, S. Leone 112 D2 8 33N 11 50W
Maboukou, Congo 114 C2 3 39 S 12 31 E
Mabrouk, Mali 113 B4 19 29N 1 15W
Mabrous, Niger 109 D2 21 14N 13 35 E
Mabuasehube Game Reserve △, Botswana 116 D3 25 5 S 21 10 E
Mabungo, Somali Rep. 120 D2 0 49N 42 35 E
Mac Bac, Vietnam 87 H6 9 46N 106 7 E
Macachín, Argentina 174 D3 37 10 S 63 43W
Macaé, Brazil 171 F3 22 20 S 41 43W
Macael, Spain 41 H2 37 20N 2 18W
Macaíba, Brazil 170 C4 5 51 S 35 21W
Macajuba, Brazil 171 D3 12 9 S 40 22W
McAlester, U.S.A. 155 H7 34 56N 95 46W
McAllen, U.S.A. 155 M5 26 12N 98 14W
McAlpin, U.S.A. 152 F7 30 8N 82 57W
McAlpine L., Canada 138 B9 66 40N 102 50W
Macamic, Canada 140 C4 48 45N 79 0W
Macao = Macau, China 69 G10 22 12N 113 33 E
Macão, Portugal 43 F3 39 35N 7 59W
Macapá, Brazil 169 C7 0 5N 51 4W
Macará, Ecuador 168 D2 4 23 S 79 57W
Macarani, Brazil 171 E3 15 33 S 40 24W
Macarena, Serranía de la, Colombia 168 C3 2 45N 73 55W
Macareo, Caño →, Venezuela 169 B5 9 47N 61 36W
Macarthur, Australia 128 E5 38 5 S 142 0 E
McArthur →, Australia 126 B2 15 54 S 136 40 E
McArthur, Port, Australia 126 B2 16 4 S 136 23 E
Macas, Ecuador 168 D2 2 19 S 78 7W
Macate, Peru 172 B2 8 48 S 78 7W
Macau, Brazil 170 C4 5 15 S 36 40W
Macau, China 69 G10 22 12N 113 33 E

Macaúbas, Brazil 171 D3 13 2 S 42 42W
Macaya →, Colombia 168 C3 0 59N 72 20W
McBride, Canada 142 C4 53 20N 120 19W
McCall, U.S.A. 158 D5 44 55N 116 6W
McCamey, U.S.A. 155 K3 31 8N 102 14W
McCammon, U.S.A. 158 E7 42 39N 112 12W
McCauley I., Canada 142 C2 53 40N 130 15W
McCleary, U.S.A. 160 C3 47 3N 123 16W
Macclenny, U.S.A. 152 F7 30 17N 82 7W
Macclesfield, U.K. 20 D5 53 15N 2 8W
M'Clintock Chan., Canada 138 A9 72 0N 102 0W
McClintock Ra., Australia 124 C4 18 44 S 127 38 E
McCloud, U.S.A. 158 F2 41 15N 122 8W
McCluer I., Australia 124 B5 11 5 S 133 0 E
McClure, U.S.A. 150 F7 40 42N 77 19W
McClure, L., U.S.A. 160 H6 37 35N 120 16W
M'Clure Str., Canada 6 B2 75 0N 119 0W
McClusky, U.S.A. 154 B4 47 29N 100 27W
McComb, U.S.A. 155 K9 31 15N 90 27W
McConaughy, L., U.S.A. 154 E4 41 14N 101 40W
McCook, U.S.A. 154 E4 40 12N 100 38W
McCormick, U.S.A. 152 B7 33 55N 82 17W
McCreary, Canada 143 C9 50 47N 99 29W
McCullough Mt., U.S.A. 161 K11 35 35N 115 13W
McCusker →, Canada 143 B7 55 32N 108 39W
McDame, Canada 142 B3 59 44N 128 59W
McDavid, U.S.A. 153 E2 30 52N 87 19W
McDermitt, U.S.A. 158 F5 41 59N 117 43W
McDonald, U.S.A. 150 F4 40 22N 80 14W
Macdonald, L., Australia 124 D4 23 30 S 129 0 E
Macdonald, Mt., Vanuatu 133 G6 17 36 S 168 23 E
McDonald Is., Ind. Oc. 121 K6 53 0 S 73 0 E
MacDonnell Ranges, Australia 124 D5 23 40 S 133 0 E
McDonough, U.S.A. 152 B5 33 27N 84 9W
McDougalls Well, Australia 128 A4 31 8 S 141 15 E
MacDowell L., Canada 140 B1 52 15N 92 45W
Macduff, U.K. 22 D6 57 40N 2 31W
Maceda, Spain 42 C3 42 16N 7 39W
Macedonia, U.S.A. 150 E3 41 19N 81 31W
Macedonia ■, Europe 50 E5 41 53N 21 40 E
Maceió, Brazil 170 C4 9 40 S 35 41W
Maceira, Portugal 42 F2 39 41N 8 55W
Macenta, Guinea 112 D3 8 35N 9 32W
Macerata, Italy 45 E10 43 18N 13 27 E
McFarland, U.S.A. 161 K7 35 41N 119 14W
McFarlane →, Canada 143 B7 59 12N 107 58W
Macfarlane, L., Australia 128 B2 32 0 S 136 40 E
McGehee, U.S.A. 155 J9 33 38N 91 24W
McGill, U.S.A. 158 G6 39 23N 114 47W
Macgillycuddy's Reeks, Ireland 23 E2 51 58N 9 45W
McGrath, U.S.A. 144 E9 62 58N 155 36W
McGraw, U.S.A. 151 D8 42 36N 76 8W
McGregor, U.S.A. 156 A5 43 1N 91 11W
McGregor →, Canada 127 D3 27 0 S 142 45 E
McGuire, Mt., Australia 126 J6 20 18 S 148 23 E
Mâch Kowr, Iran 97 E9 25 48N 61 28 E
Machacalis, Brazil 171 E3 17 5 S 40 45W
Machado = Jiparaná →, Brazil 173 B5 8 3 S 62 52W
Machagai, Argentina 174 B3 26 56 S 60 2W
Machakos, Kenya 118 C4 1 30 S 37 15 E
Machala, Ecuador 168 D2 3 20 S 79 57W
Machanga, Mozam. 117 C6 20 59 S 35 0 E
Machattie, L., Australia 126 C2 24 50 S 139 48 E
Machault, France 27 C11 49 21N 4 29 E
Machava, Mozam. 117 D5 25 54 S 32 28 E
Machece, Mozam. 119 F4 19 15 S 35 32 E
Machecoul, France 26 F5 47 0N 1 49W
Macheke, Zimbabwe 117 B5 18 5 S 31 51 E
Macheng, China 77 B10 31 12N 115 2 E
McHenry, U.S.A. 157 B8 42 21N 88 16W
Macherla, India 94 F4 16 29N 79 26 E
Machero, Spain 43 F6 39 21N 4 20W
Machgaon, India 94 D8 20 5N 86 17 E
Machhu →, India 92 H4 23 6N 70 46 E
Machias, Maine, U.S.A. 149 C12 44 43N 67 28W
Machias, N.Y., U.S.A. 150 D6 42 25N 78 30W
Machichi →, Canada 143 B10 57 3N 92 6W
Machico, Madeira 9 c 32 43N 16 44W
Machida, Japan 73 B11 35 28N 139 23 E
Machilipatnam, India 95 F5 16 12N 81 8 E
Machiques, Venezuela 168 A3 10 4N 72 34W
Machupicchu, Peru 172 C3 13 8 S 72 30W
Machynlleth, U.K. 21 E4 52 35N 3 50W
Macia, Mozam. 117 D5 25 2 S 33 8 E
Macias Nguema Biyogo = Bioko, Eq. Guin. 113 E6 3 30N 8 40 E
Maciejowice, Poland 55 G8 51 36N 21 26 E
McIlwraith Ra., Australia 126 A3 13 50 S 143 20 E
Măcin, Romania 53 E13 45 16N 28 8 E
Macina, Mali 112 C4 14 50N 5 0W
McInnes L., Canada 143 C10 52 13N 93 45W
McIntosh, U.S.A. 154 C4 45 55N 101 21W
McIntosh L., Canada 143 B8 55 45N 105 0W
Macintosh Ra., Australia 125 E4 27 39 S 125 32 E
Macintyre →, Australia 127 D5 28 37 S 150 47 E
Macizo Galaico, Spain 42 C3 42 30N 7 30W
Mackay, Australia 126 K7 21 8 S 149 11 E
Mackay, U.S.A. 158 E7 43 55N 113 37W
MacKay →, Canada 142 B6 57 10N 111 38W
Mackay, L., Australia 124 D4 22 30 S 129 0 E
McKay Ra., Australia 124 D3 23 0 S 122 30 E
McKeesport, U.S.A. 150 F5 40 21N 79 52W
McKellar, Canada 150 A5 45 30N 79 55W
McKenna, U.S.A. 160 D4 46 56N 122 33W
Mackenzie, Canada 142 B4 55 20N 123 5W
McKenzie, U.S.A. 149 G1 36 8N 88 31W
Mackenzie →, Australia 126 C4 23 38 S 149 46 E
Mackenzie →, Canada 138 B6 69 10N 134 20W
McKenzie →, U.S.A. 158 D2 44 7N 123 6W
Mackenzie Bay, Canada 6 B1 69 0N 137 30W
Mackenzie City = Linden, Guyana 169 B6 6 0N 58 10W
Mackenzie Mts., Canada 138 B6 64 0N 130 0W
Mackenzie Plains, N.Z. 131 E5 44 10 S 170 25 E
Mackinaw →, U.S.A. 156 D7 40 32N 89 21W
Mackinaw →, U.S.A. 156 D7 40 33N 89 44W
Mackinaw City, U.S.A. 148 C3 45 47N 84 44W
Mackinlay, Australia 126 C3 21 16 S 141 18 E
Mackinlay →, Australia 126 C3 20 50 S 141 28 E
McKinley, Mt., U.S.A. 144 E10 63 4N 151 0W
McKinley Park, U.S.A. 144 E10 63 44N 148 55W
McKinley Sea, Arctic 10 A11 82 0N 0 0W
McKinney, U.S.A. 155 J6 33 12N 96 37W
Mackinnon Road, Kenya 118 C4 3 40 S 39 1 E
McKittrick, Calif., U.S.A. 161 K7 35 18N 119 37W
Macklin, Canada 143 C7 52 20N 109 56W
Macksville, Australia 129 A10 30 40 S 152 56 E
McLaren Vale, Australia 128 C3 35 13 S 138 31 E
Maclean, Australia 127 D5 29 26 S 153 16 E
McLean, Ill., U.S.A. 156 D7 40 19N 89 10W
McLean, Tex., U.S.A. 155 H4 35 14N 100 36W
McLeansboro, U.S.A. 154 F10 38 6N 88 32W
Maclear, S. Africa 117 E4 31 2 S 28 23 E
Maclear, C., Malawi 119 E3 13 58 S 34 49 E
McLennan, Canada 142 B5 55 42N 116 50W
Macleod = Lake Mead → ... 129 A10 54 9 S 115 44W
MacLeod, B., Canada 143 A7 62 53N 110 0W
MacLeod, L., Australia 125 D1 24 9 S 113 47 E
MacLeod Lake, Canada 142 C4 54 58N 123 0W
McLoughlin, Mt., U.S.A. 158 E2 42 27N 122 19W

MacMahon = Aïn Touta, Algeria 111 A6 35 26N 5 54 E
McMechen, U.S.A. 150 G4 39 57N 80 44W
McMinnville, Oreg., U.S.A. 158 D2 45 13N 123 12W
McMinnville, Tenn., U.S.A. 149 H3 35 41N 85 46W
McMurdo Sd., Antarctica 7 D11 77 0 S 170 0 E
McMurray = Fort McMurray, Canada 142 B6 56 44N 111 7W
McMurray, U.S.A. 160 B4 48 19N 122 14W
Maco, Phil. 81 H5 7 20N 125 50 E
Macocola, Angola 115 D3 6 47 S 16 8 E
Macocodene, Mozam. 117 C6 23 32 S 35 5 E
Macolo, Angola 115 D3 7 5 S 16 42 E
Macomb, U.S.A. 156 D6 40 27N 90 40W
Macomer, Italy 46 B1 40 16N 8 47 E
Mâcon, France 27 F11 46 19N 4 50 E
Macon, Ga., U.S.A. 152 C6 32 51N 83 38W
Macon, Ill., U.S.A. 156 E8 39 43N 89 0W
Macon, Miss., U.S.A. 149 J1 33 7N 88 34W
Macon, Mo., U.S.A. 156 E4 39 44N 92 28W
Macondo, Angola 115 E4 12 37 S 23 46 E
Macossa, Mozam. 119 F3 17 55 S 33 56 E
Macoun L., Canada 143 B8 56 32N 103 40W
Macoupin Cr. →, U.S.A. 156 E3 39 11N 90 38W
Macovane, Mozam. 117 C6 21 30 S 35 2 E
McPherson, U.S.A. 154 F6 38 22N 97 40W
McPherson Pk., U.S.A. 161 L7 34 53N 119 53W
McPherson Ra., Australia 127 D5 28 15 S 153 15 E
Macquarie →, Australia 129 A7 30 7 S 147 24 E
Macquarie Harbour, Australia 127 D4 42 15 S 145 23 E
Macquarie Is., Pac. Oc. 134 N7 54 36 S 158 55 E
McRae, U.S.A. 152 C7 32 4N 82 54W
MacRobertson Land, Antarctica 7 D6 71 0 S 64 0 E
Macroom, Ireland 23 E3 51 54N 8 57W
MacTier, Canada 150 A5 45 9N 79 46W
Macubela, Mozam. 119 F4 16 53 S 37 49 E
Macugnaga, Italy 44 C4 45 58N 7 58 E
Macuira, Parque Nac. △, Colombia 165 D5 12 9N 71 21W
Macuiza, Mozam. 119 F3 18 7 S 34 29 E
Macujer, Colombia 168 C3 0 24N 73 10W
Macuro, Venezuela 169 F9 10 42N 61 55W
Macusani, Peru 172 C3 14 4 S 70 29W
Macuse, Mozam. 119 F4 17 45 S 37 10 E
Macuspana, Mexico 163 D6 17 46N 92 36W
Macusse, Angola 116 B3 17 48 S 20 23 E
Mada →, Nigeria 113 D6 7 59N 7 55 E
Ma'dabā □, Jordan 103 D4 31 43N 35 47 E
Madadeni, S. Africa 117 D5 27 43 S 30 3 E
Madadi, Chad 109 E4 18 28N 20 45 E
Madagali, Nigeria 113 C7 10 56N 13 33 E
Madagascar ■, Africa 117 C8 20 0 S 47 0 E
Mādā'in Sālih, Si. Arabia 96 E3 26 46N 37 57 E
Madakasira, India 95 H3 13 56N 77 16 E
Madalena, Azores 9 d1 38 32N 28 32W
Madama, Niger 109 D2 22 0N 13 40 E
Madan, Bulgaria 51 E8 41 30N 24 57 E
Madanapalle, India 95 H4 13 33N 78 28 E
Madang, Papua N. G. 132 C3 5 12 S 145 49 E
Madang □, Papua N. G. 132 C3 5 0 S 145 30 E
Madaoua, Niger 113 C6 14 5N 6 27 E
Madaripur, Bangla. 90 C3 23 19N 90 15 E
Madauk, Burma 90 D7 17 56N 96 52 E
Madawaska, Canada 150 A7 45 30N 78 0W
Madawaska →, Canada 150 A7 45 27N 76 21W
Madaya, Burma 90 D6 22 12N 96 10 E
Madbar, Sudan 107 F3 6 17N 30 45 E
Maddalena, Italy 46 A2 41 16N 9 23 E
Maddaloni, Italy 45 A7 41 2N 14 23 E
Maddela, Phil. 80 C3 16 21N 121 41 E
Maddur, India 95 H3 12 36N 77 4 E
Madeira, Atl. Oc. 9 c 32 50N 17 0W
Madeira →, Brazil 169 D6 3 22 S 58 45W
Mädelegabel, Germany 33 B10 47 18N 10 18 E
Madeleine, Îs. de la, Canada 141 C7 47 30N 61 40W
Maden, Turkey 101 C8 38 23N 39 40 E
Madera, Mexico 162 B3 29 12N 108 7W
Madera, Calif., U.S.A. 160 J6 36 57N 120 3W
Madera, Pa., U.S.A. 150 F6 40 49N 78 26W
Madgaon, India 95 G1 15 12N 73 58 E
Madha, India 94 F2 18 0N 75 30 E
Madhavpur, India 92 J3 21 15N 69 58 E
Madhepura, India 93 F12 26 11N 86 23 E
Madhira, India 94 F5 16 55N 80 22 E
Madhubani, India 93 F12 26 21N 86 7 E
Madhugiri, India 95 H3 13 40N 77 12 E
Madhumati →, Bangla. 90 C3 22 33N 89 52 E
Madhupur, India 93 G12 24 16N 86 39 E
Madhya Pradesh □, India 92 J8 22 50N 78 0 E
Madidi →, Bolivia 172 C4 12 32 S 66 52W
Madikeri, India 95 H2 12 30N 75 45 E
Madikwe Game Reserve △, S. Africa 117 D4 24 48 S 26 32 E
Madill, U.S.A. 155 H6 34 6N 96 46W
Madimba, Angola 115 D2 6 36 S 14 23 E
Madīnah, Dem. Rep. of the Congo 115 D3 4 58 S 15 5 E
Ma'din, Syria 101 E8 35 45N 39 36 E
Madina, Mali 112 C3 13 25N 8 30W
Madinani, Ivory C. 112 D3 9 37N 6 57W
Madīnat ash Sha'b, Yemen 98 D4 12 50N 45 0 E
Madingo, Congo 114 C2 4 5 S 11 24 E
Madingou, Congo 114 C2 4 10 S 13 33 E
Madirovalo, Madag. 117 B8 16 26 S 46 32 E
Madison, Calif., U.S.A. 160 G5 38 41N 121 59W
Madison, Fla., U.S.A. 152 F6 30 28N 83 25W
Madison, Ind., U.S.A. 156 F3 38 44N 85 23W
Madison, Nebr., U.S.A. 154 E6 41 50N 97 27W
Madison, Ohio, U.S.A. 150 E3 41 46N 81 3W
Madison, S. Dak., U.S.A. 154 D6 44 0N 97 7W
Madison, Wis., U.S.A. 156 A7 43 4N 89 24W
Madison →, U.S.A. 158 D8 45 56N 111 31W
Madison Heights, U.S.A. 148 G6 37 25N 79 8W
Madisonville, Ky., U.S.A. 148 G2 37 20N 87 30W
Madisonville, Tex., U.S.A. 155 K7 30 57N 95 55W
Madista, Botswana 116 C4 21 15 S 25 6 E
Madiun, Indonesia 85 D4 7 38 S 111 32 E
Madjingo, Gabon 114 C2 1 2 S 13 15 E
Madoc, Canada 150 B7 44 30N 77 28W
Madol, Sudan 107 F2 9 3N 27 45 E
Madon →, France 27 D13 48 36N 6 8 E
Madona, Latvia 15 H22 56 53N 26 5 E
Madonie, Italy 46 E6 37 50N 13 50 E
Madonna di Campiglio, Italy 33 D11 46 14N 10 49 E
Madra Dağı, Turkey 49 B9 39 23N 27 12 E
Madrakah, Ra's al, Oman 99 C7 19 0N 57 50 E
Madras = Chennai, India 95 H5 13 8N 80 19 E
Madras = Tamil Nadu □, India 95 J3 11 0N 77 0 E
Madras, U.S.A. 158 D3 44 38N 121 8W
Madre, Laguna, U.S.A. 155 M6 27 0N 97 30W
Madre, Sierra, Phil. 80 C4 17 0N 122 0 E
Madre de Dios →, Peru 172 C3 12 0 S 70 15W
Madre de Dios □, Bolivia 172 C4 10 59 S 65 49W
Madre de Dios, I., Chile 176 D1 50 20 S 75 10W
Madre del Sur, Sierra, Mexico 162 B3 17 30N 100 0W
Madre Occidental, Sierra, Mexico 162 B3 27 0N 107 0W
Madre Oriental, Sierra, Mexico 162 C5 25 0N 100 0W
Madri, India 92 G5 24 16N 73 32 E
Madrid, Spain 42 E7 40 25N 3 45W
Madrid, Ala., U.S.A. 152 D4 31 2N 85 24W
Madrid, Iowa, U.S.A. 156 C3 41 53N 93 49W

Madrid, N.Y., U.S.A. 151 B9 44 45N 75 8W
Madrid □, Spain 42 E7 40 30N 3 45W
Madrid Barajas ✈ (MAD), Spain 42 E7 40 26N 3 34W
Madridejos, Spain 43 F7 39 28N 3 32W
Madrigal de las Altas Torres, Spain 42 D6 41 5N 5 0W
Madrona, Sierra, Spain 43 G6 38 27N 4 16W
Madroñera, Spain 43 F5 39 26N 5 42W
Madrusah, Libya 108 D2 24 48N 14 32 E
Madu, Sudan 107 E2 14 37N 26 4 E
Maduo, Dem. Rep. of the Congo 114 C4 1 24 S 20 44 E
Madura, Australia 125 F4 31 55 S 127 0 E
Madura, Indonesia 79 G15 7 30 S 114 0 E
Madura, Selat, Indonesia 85 D4 7 30 S 113 20 E
Madurai, India 95 K4 9 55N 78 10 E
Madurantakam, India 95 H4 12 30N 79 50 E
Madzhalis, Russia 61 J8 42 9N 47 47 E
Mae Chan, Thailand 86 B2 20 9N 99 52 E
Mae Hong Son, Thailand 86 C2 19 16N 97 56 E
Mae Khlong →, Thailand 86 F3 13 24N 100 0 E
Mae Phrik, Thailand 86 D2 17 27N 99 7 E
Mae Ping Nat. Park △, Thailand 86 D2 17 37N 98 51 E
Mae Ramat, Thailand 86 D2 16 58N 98 31 E
Mae Rim, Thailand 86 C2 18 54N 98 57 E
Mae Sot, Thailand 86 D2 16 43N 98 34 E
Mae Suai, Thailand 76 H2 19 39N 99 33 E
Mae Tha, Thailand 86 C2 18 28N 99 8 E
Mae Wong Nat. Park △, Thailand 86 E2 15 54N 99 12 E
Mae Yom Nat. Park △, Thailand 86 D2 18 43N 100 15 E
Maebaru, Japan 72 D3 33 33N 130 12 E
Maebashi, Japan 73 A11 36 24N 139 4 E
Maella, Spain 40 D5 41 8N 0 7 E
Maesteg, U.K. 21 F4 51 36N 3 40W
Maestra, Sierra, Cuba 164 B4 20 15N 77 0W
Maestre de Campo I., Phil. 80 E3 12 56N 121 42 E
Maetambe, Mt., Solomon Is. 133 L9 7 3 S 157 1 E
Maevatanana, Madag. 117 B8 16 56 S 46 49 E
Maéwo, Vanuatu 133 E6 15 10 S 168 10 E
Mafa, Indonesia 82 A3 0 3N 127 53 E
Mafeking = Mafikeng, S. Africa 116 D4 25 50 S 25 38 E
Mafeking, Canada 143 C8 52 40N 101 10W
Maféré, Ivory C. 112 D4 5 30N 3 2W
Mafeteng, Lesotho 117 D4 29 51 S 27 15 E
Maffra, Australia 129 D7 37 53 S 146 58 E
Mafia I., Tanzania 118 D4 7 45 S 39 50 E
Mafikeng, S. Africa 116 D4 25 50 S 25 38 E
Mafra, Brazil 175 B6 26 10 S 49 55W
Mafra, Portugal 43 G1 38 55N 9 20W
Mafungabusi Plateau, Zimbabwe 119 F2 18 30 S 29 8 E
Magadan, Russia 67 D16 59 38N 150 50 E
Magadi, India 95 H3 12 58N 77 14 E
Magadi, Kenya 118 C4 1 54 S 36 19 E
Magadi, L., Kenya 118 C4 1 54 S 36 19 E
Magaliesburg, S. Africa 117 D4 26 0 S 27 32 E
Magallanes = Punta Arenas, Chile 176 D2 53 10 S 71 0W
Magallanes □, Chile 176 D2 52 0 S 72 0W
Magallanes, Estrecho de, Chile 176 D2 52 30 S 75 0W
Magaluf, Spain 38 B9 39 29N 2 32 E
Magangué, Colombia 168 B3 9 14N 74 45W
Magarida, Phil. 81 H5 6 51N 124 31 E
Magaria, Niger 113 C6 13 4N 9 5 E
Magarida, Papua N. G. 132 F5 10 18 S 149 20 E
Magburaka, S. Leone 112 D2 8 47N 12 0W
Magdalen Is. = Madeleine, Îs. de la, Canada 141 C7 47 30N 61 40W
Magdalena, Argentina 174 D4 35 5 S 57 30W
Magdalena, Bolivia 173 C5 13 13 S 63 57W
Magdalena, Malaysia 83 B5 4 25N 117 55 E
Magdalena, Mexico 162 A2 30 50N 112 0W
Magdalena, U.S.A. 159 J10 34 7N 107 15W
Magdalena □, Colombia 168 A3 10 0N 74 0W
Magdalena →, Colombia 168 A3 11 6N 74 51W
Magdalena →, Mexico 162 A2 30 40N 112 25W
Magdalena, B., Mexico 162 C2 24 30N 112 10W
Magdalena, I., Mexico 176 B2 44 40 S 73 0W
Magdalena, Llano de la, Mexico 162 C2 25 0N 111 30W
Magdeburg, Germany 30 C7 52 7N 11 38 E
Magdeleine Cays, Australia 126 B5 16 33 S 150 18 E
Magdub, Sudan 107 E2 13 42N 25 5 E
Magee, U.S.A. 155 K10 31 52N 89 44W
Magelang, Indonesia 85 D4 7 29 S 110 13 E
Magellan's Str. = Magallanes, Estrecho de, Chile 176 D2 52 30 S 75 0W
Magenta, Italy 44 C5 45 28N 8 53 E
Magenta, L., Australia 125 F2 33 30 S 119 2 E
Magerøya, Norway 14 A21 71 3N 25 40 E
Maggea, Australia 128 C4 34 28 S 140 2 E
Maggia, Switz. 33 D7 46 15N 8 42 E
Maggia →, Switz. 33 D7 46 18N 8 36 E
Maggiorasca, Mte., Italy 44 D6 44 33 S 9 29 E
Maggiore, Lago, Italy 44 C5 45 57N 8 39 E
Maggotty, Jamaica 164 a 18 9N 77 46W
Maghâgha, Egypt 106 B3 28 38N 30 50 E
Maghama, Mauritania 112 B2 15 32N 12 57W
Magherafelt, U.K. 23 B5 54 45N 6 37W
Maghnia, Algeria 111 B4 34 50N 1 43W
Maghreb, N. Afr. 104 C3 32 0N 5 0W
Magione, Italy 45 E9 43 8N 12 12 E
Magistralnyy, Russia 67 D11 56 16N 107 36 E
Maglaj, Bos.-H. 52 F3 44 33N 18 7 E
Magliano in Toscana, Italy 47 B11 47 0N 18 18 E
Magnac-Laval, France 28 B5 46 13N 1 11 E
Magnetic Pole (North), Canada 6 A2 88 30N 107 0W
Magnetic Pole (South), Antarctica 7 C8 64 8 S 138 8 E
Magnisía □, Greece 48 B5 39 15N 23 0 E
Magnitogorsk, Russia 65 D10 53 27N 59 4 E
Magnolia, Ark., U.S.A. 155 J8 33 16N 93 14W
Magnolia, Miss., U.S.A. 155 K9 31 9N 90 28W
Magnor, Norway 18 E9 59 56N 12 15 E
Magny-en-Vexin, France 27 C8 49 9N 1 47 E
Mago, Fiji 133 A3 17 26 S 179 8W
Mago Nat. Park △, Ethiopia 107 F4 5 40N 36 18 E
Magog, Canada 141 C5 45 18N 72 9W
Magoro, Uganda 118 B3 1 45N 34 12 E
Magosa = Famagusta, Cyprus 49 D12 35 8N 33 55 E
Magouládhes, Greece 38 B9 39 45N 19 42 E
Magoye, Zambia 119 F2 16 1 S 27 30 E
Magozal, Mexico 163 C5 21 34N 97 59W
Magpie, L., Canada 141 B7 51 0N 64 41W
Magrath, Canada 142 D6 49 25N 112 50W
Magre →, Spain 41 F4 39 11N 0 25W
Magrur, Sudan 107 E3 14 1N 30 27 E
Magrur, Wadi →, Sudan 107 D2 16 5N 26 30 E
Magsingal, Phil. 80 C3 17 41N 120 25 E
Maga Lahjar, Mauritania 112 B2 17 18N 14 43W
Maguan, China 76 F5 23 0N 104 21 E
Maguarinho, C., Brazil 170 B2 0 15 S 48 30W
Magude, Mozam. 117 D5 25 2 S 32 40 E
Maguindanao □, Phil. 81 H5 7 5N 124 0 E
Magurski Park Narodowy △, Poland 55 J8 49 35N 21 30 E
Mágusa = Famagusta, Cyprus 39 E9 35 8N 33 55 E
Maguse L., Canada 143 A10 61 40N 95 10W
Maguse Pt., Canada 143 A10 61 20N 93 50W
Magvana, India 92 H3 23 13N 69 22 E
Magwe, Burma 90 E5 20 10N 95 0 E
Magwe, Sudan 107 G3 4 30N 31 17 E
Magwe □, Burma 90 F5 20 0N 95 0 E
Maha Oya, Sri Lanka 95 L5 7 31N 81 10 E
Maha Sarakham, Thailand 86 D4 16 12N 103 16 E
Mahābād, Iran 101 D11 36 50N 45 45 E
Mahabaleshwar, India 94 F1 17 58N 73 43 E
Mahabharat Lekh, Nepal 93 E10 28 30N 82 0 E

Mahabo, *Madag.* . . . . 117 C7 20 23 S 44 40 E
Mahad, *India* . . . . 94 E1 18 6N 73 29 E
Mahaddei Uen, *Somali Rep.* . . . . . 120 D3 2 58N 45 32 E
Mahadeo Hills, *India* . . . . 93 H8 22 20N 78 30 E
Mahadeopur, *India* . . . . 94 E5 18 48N 80 0 E
Mahaffey, *U.S.A.* 150 F6 40 53N 78 44W
Mahagi, *Dem. Rep. of the Congo* . . 118 B3 2 20N 31 0 E
Mahaicony, *Guyana* 169 B6 6 36N 57 48W
Mahajamba →, *Madag.* . . . . 117 B8 15 33 S 47 8 E
Mahajamba, Helodranon' i, *Madag.* 117 B8 15 24 S 47 5 E
Mahajan, *India* . . . . 92 E5 28 48N 73 56 E
Mahajanga, *Madag.* . . . . 117 B8 15 40 S 46 25 E
Mahajanga □, *Madag.* . . . . 117 B8 17 0 S 47 0 E
Mahajilo →, *Madag.* . . . . 117 B8 19 42 S 45 22 E
Mahakam →, *Indonesia* . . . . 85 C5 0 35 S 117 17 E
Mahalapye, *Botswana* . . . . 116 C4 23 1 S 26 51 E
Mahalchhar, *Bangla.* . . . . 90 D4 22 55N 92 2 E
Mahale Mts., *Tanzania* . . . . 118 D3 6 20 S 30 0 E
Mahale Mts. Nat. Park △, *Tanzania* 118 D2 6 10 S 29 50 E
Maḥallāt, *Iran* . . . . 97 C6 33 55N 50 30 E
Māhān, *Iran* . . . . 97 D8 30 5N 57 18 E
Mahan →, *India* . . . . 93 H10 23 30N 82 50 E
Mahanadi →, *India* . . . . 94 D8 20 20N 86 25 E
Mahananda →, *India* . . . . 93 G12 25 12N 87 52 E
Mahanoro, *Madag.* . . . . 117 B8 19 54 S 48 48 E
Mahanoy City, *U.S.A.* 151 F8 40 49N 76 9W
Mahaplag, *Phil.* . . . . 81 F5 10 35N 124 57 E
Maharashtra □, *India* . . . . 94 D2 20 30N 75 30 E
Maharès, *Tunisia* . . . . 108 B2 34 32N 10 29 E
Mahasamund, *India* . . . . 94 D6 21 6N 82 6 E
Mahasham, W. →, *Egypt* . . . . 103 E3 30 15N 34 10 E
Mahasoa, *Madag.* . . . . 117 C8 22 12 S 46 6 E
Mahasolo, *Madag.* . . . . 117 B8 19 7 S 46 22 E
Mahattat ash Shīdīyah, *Jordan* . . . 103 F4 29 55N 35 55 E
Mahattat 'Unayzah, *Jordan* . . . . . . 103 E4 30 30N 35 47 E
Mahavavy →, *Madag.* . . . . 117 B8 15 57 S 45 54 E
Mahaweli Ganga →, *Sri Lanka* . . . 95 K5 8 27N 81 13 E
Mahaxay, *Laos* . . . . 86 D5 17 22N 105 12 E
Mahbubabad, *India* . . . . 94 E5 17 42N 80 2 E
Mahbubnagar, *India* . . . . 94 F3 16 45N 77 59 E
Mahd adh Dhahab, *Si. Arabia* . . . . 98 B3 23 30N 40 52 E
Maḥḍah, *Oman* . . . . 97 E7 24 24N 55 59 E
Mahdia, *Guyana* 169 B6 5 13N 59 8W
Mahdia, *Tunisia* . . . . 108 A2 35 28N 11 0 E
Mahe, *Jammu & Kashmir, India* . . . 93 C8 33 10N 78 32 E
Mahé, *Pondicherry, India* . . . . 95 J2 11 42N 75 34 E
Mahé, *Seychelles* . . . . 121 b 4 40 S 55 30 E
Mahé ✈ (SEZ), *Seychelles* . . . . 121 b 4 40 S 55 31 E
Mahebourg, *Mauritius* . . . . 121 d 20 24 S 57 42 E
Mahendra Giri, *India* . . . . 95 K3 8 20N 77 30 E
Mahendraganj, *India* . . . . 90 C2 25 20N 89 45 E
Mahendragarh, *India* . . . . 92 E7 28 17N 76 14 E
Mahenge, *Tanzania* . . . . 119 D4 8 45 S 36 41 E
Maheno, *N.Z.* . . . . 131 F5 45 10 S 170 50 E
Mahesana, *India* . . . . 92 H5 23 39N 72 26 E
Maheshwar, *India* . . . . 92 H6 22 11N 75 35 E
Mahesana, *India* . . . . 93 F8 26 29N 78 37 E
Mahi →, *India* . . . . 92 H5 22 15N 72 55 E
Mahia Pen., *N.Z.* . . . . 130 F6 39 9 S 177 55 E
Mahighe, *Solomon Is.* . . . . 133 M10 8 30 S 159 58 E
Mahilyow, *Belarus* . . . . 58 F6 53 55N 30 18 E
Mahim, *India* . . . . 94 E1 19 39N 72 44 E
Mahina, *Tahiti* . . . . 133 S16 17 30 S 149 27W
Mahirija, *Morocco* 111 B4 34 0N 3 16W
Mahlaing, *Burma* . . . . 90 E5 21 6N 95 39 E
Mahmiya, *Sudan* . . . . 107 D3 17 12N 33 43 E
Mahmud Kot, *Pakistan* . . . . 92 D4 30 16N 71 0 E
Mahmudia, *Romania* . . . . 53 E14 45 5N 29 5 E
Mahmudiye, *Turkey* . . . . 49 B12 39 48N 30 15 E
Mahmutbey, *Turkey* . . . . 51 E12 41 3N 28 49 E
Mahnomen, *U.S.A.* 154 B7 47 19N 95 58W
Maho, *Sri Lanka* . . . . 95 L5 7 49N 80 16 E
Mahoba, *India* . . . . 93 G8 25 15N 79 55 E
Mahomet, *U.S.A.* 157 D8 40 12N 88 24W
Mahón = Maó, *Spain* . . . . 38 B5 39 53N 4 16 E
Mahón, Menorca ✈ (MAH), *Spain* 40 F9 39 50N 4 16 E
Mahone Bay, *Canada* 141 D7 44 30N 64 20W
Mahopac, *U.S.A.* 151 E11 41 22N 73 45W
Mahoua, *Chad* . . . . 109 F3 11 49N 18 26 E
Mahuta, *Nigeria* . . . . 113 C5 11 32N 4 58 E
Mahuva, *India* . . . . 92 J4 21 5N 71 48 E
Mahya Daği, *Turkey* . . . . 51 E11 41 47N 27 36 E
Mai-Ndombe, L., *Dem. Rep. of the Congo* . . . . 114 C3 2 0 S 18 20 E
Mai-Sai, *Thailand* . . . . 76 C2 20 20N 99 55 E
Mai Thon, Ko, *Thailand* . . . . 87 a 7 40N 98 22 E
Maia, *Azores* 9 d4 36 56N 25 1W
Maia, *Portugal* 42 D2 41 14N 8 37W
Maia, *Spain* 40 B3 43 12N 1 29W
Maials, *Spain* . . . . 40 D5 41 22N 0 30 E
Maihong, *India* . . . . 90 C4 25 18N 93 10 E
Maicao, *Colombia* 168 A3 11 23N 72 13W
Maîche, *France* . . . . 27 E13 47 16N 6 48 E
Maici →, *Brazil* . . . . 173 B5 6 30 S 61 43W
Maicurú →, *Brazil* . . . . 169 D7 2 14 S 54 17W
Máida, *Italy* . . . . 37 D9 38 51N 16 22 E
Maidan Khula, *Afghan.* . . . . 91 B3 33 36N 69 50 E
Maidenhead, *U.K.* 21 F7 51 31N 0 42W
Maidstone, *Canada* 143 C7 53 5N 109 20W
Maidstone, *U.K.* . . . . 21 F8 51 16N 0 32 E
Maiduguri, *Nigeria* . . . . 113 C7 12 0N 13 20 E
Maiella, Parco Nazionale della △, *Italy* . . . . 45 F11 42 5N 14 5 E
Măieruș, *Romania* . . . . 53 E10 45 53N 25 31 E
Maigatari, *Nigeria* . . . . 113 C6 12 46N 9 27 E
Maignelay Montigny, *France* . . . . . 27 C9 49 32N 2 30 E
Maigo, *Phil.* . . . . 81 G4 8 10N 123 50 E
Maigualida, Sierra, *Venezuela* 169 B4 5 30N 65 10W
Maigudo, *Ethiopia* . . . . 107 F4 7 30N 37 8 E
Maihar, *India* . . . . 93 G9 24 16N 80 45 E
Maihara, *Japan* . . . . 73 B8 35 19N 136 17 E
Maijdi, *Bangla.* . . . . 90 D3 22 48N 91 10 E
Maikala Ra., *India* . . . . 94 D5 22 0N 81 0 E
Maiko, Parc Nat. de la △, *Dem. Rep. of the Congo* . . . . 118 C2 0 30 S 27 50 E
Maikoor, *Indonesia* . . . . 83 C4 6 8 S 134 6 E
Mailani, *India* . . . . 93 E9 28 17N 80 21 E
Maili, *U.S.A.* 145 K13 21 25N 158 11W
Maili Pt, *U.S.A.* 145 K13 21 25N 158 11W
Maillezais, *France* 28 B3 46 22N 0 45W
Mailsi, *Pakistan* . . . . 92 E5 29 48N 72 15 E
Maimbung, *Phil.* . . . . 81 J3 5 56N 121 2 E
Main →, *Germany* . . . . 31 F4 50 0N 8 18 E
Main →, *U.K.* 23 B5 54 48N 6 18W
Main Range Nat. Park △, *Australia* 127 A5 28 11 S 152 27 E
Main Ridge, *Trin. & Tob.* 169 L10 11 16N 60 40W
Mainburg, *Germany* . . . . 31 G7 48 38N 11 47 E
Maindargi, *India* . . . . 94 F3 17 28N 76 18 E
Maine, *France* 26 D6 48 20N 0 15W
Maine □, *U.S.A.* 149 C11 45 20N 69 0W
Maine →, *Ireland* 23 D2 52 9N 9 45W
Maine-et-Loire □, *France* 26 E6 47 31N 0 30W
Maïne-Soroa, *Niger* . . . . 113 C7 13 13N 12 2 E
Maingkaing, *Burma* . . . . 90 D4 24 48N 95 16 E
Maingkwan, *Burma* . . . . 90 B6 26 15N 96 37 E
Mainit, *Phil.* . . . . 81 G5 9 32N 125 32 E
Mainit, L., *Phil.* . . . . 81 G5 9 31N 125 30 E
Mainland, *Orkney, U.K.* 22 C5 58 59N 3 8W
Mainland, *Shet., U.K.* 22 A7 60 15N 1 22W
Mainoru, *Australia* . . . . 126 A1 14 0 S 134 6 E
Mainpuri, *India* . . . . 93 F8 27 18N 79 4 E
Maintal, *Germany* . . . . 31 E4 50 7N 8 52 E
Maintenon, *France* . . . . 27 D8 48 35N 1 35 E
Maintirano, *Madag.* . . . . 117 B7 18 3 S 44 1 E

Mainz, *Germany* . . . . 31 E4 50 1N 8 14 E
Maio, C. Verde Is. . . . . 9 j 15 10N 23 10W
Maipú, *Argentina* . . . . 174 D4 36 52 S 57 50W
Maiquetía, *Venezuela* 168 A4 10 36N 66 57W
Máira →, *Italy* . . . . 44 D4 44 49N 7 38 E
Mairabari, *India* . . . . 90 B4 26 30N 92 22 E
Mairipotaba, *Brazil* . . . . 171 E2 17 18 S 49 28W
Maisí, *Cuba* 165 B5 20 17N 74 9W
Maisí, Pta. de, *Cuba* 165 B5 20 10N 74 10W
Maitland, *N.S.W., Australia* . . . . . . 129 B9 32 33 S 151 36 E
Maitland, *S. Austral., Australia* . . . 128 C2 34 23 S 137 40 E
Maitland, *Canada* 150 C3 43 45N 81 43W
Maitland, Banjaran, *Malaysia* . . . . . 85 B5 4 55N 116 37 E
Maitum, *Phil.* . . . . 81 H5 6 2N 124 30 E
Maiyema, *Nigeria* . . . . 113 C5 12 5N 4 25 E
Maiyuan, *China* . . . . 77 E11 25 34N 117 28 E
Maiz, Is. del, *Nic.* 164 D3 12 15N 83 4W
Maizuru, *Japan* . . . . 73 B7 35 25N 135 22 E
Majagual, *Colombia* 168 B3 8 33N 74 38W
Majalengka, *Indonesia* . . . . 85 D3 6 50 S 108 13 E
Majari →, *Brazil* 169 C5 3 29N 60 58W
Majdūl, *Libya* . . . . 108 C3 25 51N 15 7 E
Majene, *Indonesia* . . . . 82 B1 3 38 S 118 57 E
Majes →, *Peru* . . . . 172 D3 16 40 S 72 44W
Majete Game Reserve △, *Malawi* . 119 F3 15 54 S 34 34 E
Majevica, *Bos.-H.* . . . . 52 F3 44 45N 18 50 E
Maji, *Ethiopia* . . . . 107 F4 6 12N 35 30 E
Majiang, *China* . . . . 76 D6 26 28N 107 32 E
Majorca = Mallorca, *Spain* . . . . 38 B4 39 30N 3 0 E
Majors Creek, *Australia* . . . . 129 C8 35 33 S 149 45 E
Majuriã, *Brazil* . . . . 173 B5 7 30 S 64 55W
Maka, *Senegal* 112 C2 13 40N 14 10W
Makaha, *U.S.A.* 145 K13 21 29N 158 13W
Makaha, *Zimbabwe* . . . . 117 B5 17 20 S 32 3 E
Makahoa Pt., *U.S.A.* 145 J14 21 41N 157 56W
Makahuena Pt., *U.S.A.* 145 B2 21 52N 159 27W
Makak, *Cameroon* . . . . 113 E7 3 36N 11 0 E
Makakilo City, *U.S.A.* 145 K13 21 22N 158 5W
Makakou, *Gabon* . . . . 114 C2 0 11 S 12 12 E
Makalamabedi, *Botswana* . . . . 116 C3 20 19 S 23 51 E
Makale, *Indonesia* . . . . 82 B1 3 6 S 119 51 E
Makamba, *Burundi* . . . . 118 C2 4 8 S 29 49 E
Makapuu Pt., *U.S.A.* 145 K14 21 19N 157 39W
Makarewa, *N.Z.* . . . . 131 G3 46 20 S 168 21 E
Makari, *Cameroon* . . . . 113 C7 12 35N 10 27 E
Makari, *Cent. Amer.* . . . . 109 F2 12 35N 10 27 E
Makarikari = Makgadikgadi Salt Pans, *Botswana* . . . . 116 C4 20 40 S 25 45 E
Makarovo, *Russia* . . . . 67 D11 57 40N 107 45 E
Makarska, *Croatia* . . . . 45 E14 43 20N 17 2 E
Makaryev, *Russia* . . . . 60 B6 57 52N 43 50 E
Makasar = Ujung Pandang, *Indonesia* . . . . 82 C1 5 10 S 119 20 E
Makasar, Selat, *Indonesia* . . . . 85 C5 1 0 S 118 20 E
Makasar, Str. of = Makasar, Selat, *Indonesia* . . . . 85 C5 1 0 S 118 20 E
Makat, *Kazakhstan* . . . . 57 E9 47 39N 53 19 E
Makaw, *Dem. Rep. of the Congo* . . 114 C3 3 29 S 18 20 E
Makawao, *U.S.A.* 145 C5 20 52N 156 17W
Makaya, *Dem. Rep. of the Congo* . 114 C3 3 21 S 18 1 E
Makbon, *Indonesia* . . . . 83 B4 0 45 S 131 32 E
Makedonija = Macedonia ■, *Europe* 50 E5 41 53N 21 40 E
Makeni, *S. Leone* 112 D2 8 55N 12 5W
Makeyevka = Makiyivka, *Ukraine* . 59 H9 48 0N 38 0 E
Makgadikgadi Nat. Park △, *Botswana* . . . . 116 C3 20 27 S 24 47 E
Makgadikgadi Salt Pans, *Botswana* . 116 C4 20 40 S 25 45 E
Makhachkala, *Russia* . . . . 61 J8 43 0N 47 30 E
Makhairádhon, *Greece* . . . . 39 D2 37 46N 20 49 E
Makharadze = Ozurgeti, *Georgia* . 61 K5 41 55N 42 2 E
Makhmūr, *Iraq* . . . . 101 E10 35 46N 43 35 E
Makhtal, *India* . . . . 95 E3 16 30N 77 31 E
Makhyah, W. →, *Yemen* . . . . 99 C5 17 40N 49 1 E
Makian, *Indonesia* . . . . 82 A3 0 20N 127 20 E
Makina, *Solomon Is.* . . . . 133 M11 9 50 S 160 50 E
Makindu, *Kenya* . . . . 118 C4 2 18 S 37 49 E
Makinsk, *Kazakhstan* . . . . 68 D8 52 37N 70 26 E
Makiyivka, *Ukraine* . . . . 59 H9 48 0N 38 0 E
Makkah, *Si. Arabia* . . . . 98 B2 21 30N 39 54 E
Makkovik, *Canada* 141 A8 55 10N 59 10W
Makó, *Hungary* . . . . 52 D5 46 14N 20 33 E
Mako, *Senegal* 112 C2 12 50N 12 20W
Makogai, *Fiji* . . . . 133 A2 17 28 S 179 0 E
Makok, *Gabon* . . . . 114 C1 0 1 S 9 35 E
Makokou, *Gabon* . . . . 114 B2 0 40N 12 50 E
Makongo, *Dem. Rep. of the Congo* 118 B2 3 25N 26 17 E
Makoro, *Dem. Rep. of the Congo* . 118 B2 3 10N 29 59 E
Makoua, *Congo* . . . . 114 C3 0 5 S 15 50 E
Maków Mazowiecki, *Poland* . . . . . . 55 F8 52 52N 21 6 E
Maków Podhalański, *Poland* . . . . . . 55 J6 49 43N 19 45 E
Makrá, *Greece* . . . . 49 E7 36 15N 25 54 E
Makran, *Asia* . . . . 91 D1 26 13N 61 30 E
Makran Coast Range, *Pakistan* . . . 91 D2 25 40N 64 0 E
Makrana, *India* . . . . 92 F6 27 2N 74 46 E
Mákri, *Greece* . . . . 51 F9 40 52N 25 40 E
Makri, *India* . . . . 94 E6 19 46N 81 55 E
Makriyialos, *Greece* . . . . 39 E6 35 2N 25 59 E
Maktar, *Tunisia* . . . . 108 A1 35 48N 9 12 E
Mākū, *Iran* . . . . 101 C11 39 15N 44 31 E
Makum, *India* . . . . 90 B5 27 30N 95 23 E
Makumbi, *Dem. Rep. of the Congo* 115 D4 5 50 S 20 43 E
Makunda, *Botswana* . . . . 116 C3 22 30 S 20 7 E
Makung, *Taiwan* . . . . 77 F12 23 34N 119 34 E
Makunza, *Dem. Rep. of the Congo* 115 D4 5 52 S 24 19 E
Makurazaki, *Japan* . . . . 72 F2 31 15N 130 20 E
Makurdi, *Nigeria* . . . . 113 D6 7 43N 8 35 E
Makushin Volcano, *U.S.A.* 144 K6 53 53N 166 55W
Makūyeh, *Iran* . . . . 97 D7 28 7N 53 9 E
Makwassie, S. *Africa* . . . . 116 D4 27 17 S 26 0 E
Makwiro, *Zimbabwe* . . . . 117 B5 17 58 S 30 25 E
Mal, *India* . . . . 90 B2 26 51N 88 45 E
Māl, *Mauritania* 112 B2 16 58N 13 23W
Mal B., *Ireland* 23 D2 52 50N 9 30W
Mala, *Peru* . . . . 172 C2 12 40 S 76 38W
Mala, Pta., *Panama* 164 E3 7 28N 80 2W
Mala Belozërka, *Ukraine* . . . . 59 J8 47 12N 34 56 E
Malá Fatra, Národný Park △, *Slovak Rep.* . . . . 35 B12 49 10N 19 0 E
Mala Kapela, *Croatia* . . . . 45 D12 44 45N 15 30 E
Mała Panew →, *Poland* . . . . 55 H4 50 43N 17 54 E
Mala Vyska, *Ukraine* . . . . 59 H6 48 39N 31 36 E
Malabang, *Phil.* . . . . 81 H5 7 36N 124 3 E
Malabar, *U.S.A.* 153 H9 28 0N 80 34W
Malabar Coast, *India* . . . . 95 J2 11 0N 75 0 E
Malabo = Rey Malabo, *Eq. Guin.* . . 113 E6 3 45N 8 50 E
Malabon, *Phil.* . . . . 80 D3 14 21N 121 0 E
Malabrigo Pt., *Phil.* . . . . 80 E3 13 36N 121 15 E
Malabu, *Nigeria* . . . . 113 D7 9 32N 12 48 E
Malabuñgan, *Phil.* . . . . 81 G1 9 3N 117 38 E
Malacca, Str. of, *Indonesia* . . . . 87 L3 3 0N 101 0 E
Malacky, *Slovak Rep.* . . . . 35 C10 48 27N 17 0 E
Malad City, *U.S.A.* 158 E7 42 12N 112 15W
Maladeta, *Spain* . . . . 40 C5 42 39N 0 39 E
Maladzyechna, *Belarus* . . . . 58 E4 54 20N 26 50 E
Malae Pt., *U.S.A.* 145 C6 20 7N 155 53W
Málaga, *Colombia* 168 B3 6 42N 72 44W
Málaga, *Spain* 43 J6 36 43N 4 23W
Málaga □, *Spain* 43 J6 36 38N 4 58W
Malagarasi, *Tanzania* . . . . 118 D3 5 5 S 30 50 E
Malagarasi →, *Tanzania* . . . . 118 D2 5 12 S 29 47 E
Malagasy Rep. = Madagascar ■, *Africa* . . . . 117 C8 20 0 S 47 0 E
Malagón, *Spain* 43 F7 39 11N 3 52W
Malagón →, *Spain* 43 H3 37 35N 7 29W

Malahide, *Ireland* 23 C5 53 26N 6 9W
Malaimbandy, *Madag.* . . . . 117 C8 20 20 S 45 36 E
Malaita, *Solomon Is.* . . . . 133 M11 9 0 S 161 0 E
Malakâl, *Sudan* . . . . 107 F3 9 33N 31 40 E
Malakanagiri, *India* . . . . 94 E5 18 21N 81 54 E
Malakand, *Pakistan* . . . . 91 B3 34 40N 71 55 E
Malakula, *Vanuatu* . . . . 133 F5 16 15 S 167 30 E
Malakwal, *Pakistan* . . . . 92 C5 32 34N 73 13 E
Malalag, *Phil.* . . . . 81 H5 6 36N 125 24 E
Malalaua, *Papua N. G.* . . . . 132 E4 8 4 S 146 10 E
Malam, *Chad* . . . . 109 F4 11 27N 20 59 E
Malamala, *Indonesia* . . . . 82 B2 3 21 S 120 55 E
Malanda, *Australia* . . . . 126 B4 17 22 S 145 35 E
Malang, *Indonesia* . . . . 85 D4 7 59 S 112 45 E
Malangas, *Phil.* . . . . 81 H4 7 37N 123 1 E
Malange □, *Angola* . . . . 115 D3 9 30 S 16 0 E
Malangen, *Norway* . . . . 14 B18 69 24N 18 37 E
Malanje, *Angola* . . . . 115 D3 9 36 S 16 17 E
Malapatan, *Phil.* . . . . 81 J5 5 59N 125 18 E
Mälaren, *Sweden* . . . . 16 E11 59 30N 17 10 E
Malargüe, *Argentina* . . . . 174 D2 35 32 S 69 30W
Malartic, *Canada* 140 C4 48 9N 78 9W
Malaryta, *Belarus* . . . . 59 G3 51 50N 24 3 E
Malaspina Glacier, *U.S.A.* 144 G12 59 50N 140 30W
Malatya, *Turkey* . . . . 101 C8 38 25N 38 20 E
Malawali, *Malaysia* . . . . 85 A5 7 3N 117 18 E
Malawi ■, *Africa* . . . . 119 E3 11 55 S 34 0 E
Malawi, L. = Nyasa, L., *Africa* . . . . . 119 E3 12 30 S 34 30 E
Malay, *Phil.* . . . . 81 F3 11 54N 121 55 E
Malay Pen., *Asia* . . . . 87 J3 7 25N 100 0 E
Malaya Belozërka = Mala Belozërka, *Ukraine* . . . . 59 J8 47 12N 34 56 E
Malaya Vishera, *Russia* . . . . 58 C7 58 55N 32 25 E
Malaya Viska = Mala Vyska, *Ukraine* 59 H6 48 39N 31 36 E
Malaybalay, *Phil.* . . . . 81 G5 8 5N 125 7 E
Malāyer, *Iran* . . . . 97 C6 34 19N 48 51 E
Malaysia ■, *Asia* . . . . 81 J1 5 0N 110 0 E
Malazgirt, *Turkey* . . . . 101 C10 39 10N 42 33 E
Malbaza, *Niger* . . . . 113 C6 13 59N 5 38 E
Malbon, *Australia* . . . . 126 C3 21 5 S 140 17 E
Malbooma, *Australia* . . . . 127 E1 30 41 S 134 11 E
Malbork, *Poland* . . . . 54 D6 54 3N 19 1 E
Malca Dube, *Ethiopia* . . . . 120 C2 6 47N 42 4 E
Malcésine, *Italy* . . . . 44 C7 45 46N 10 48 E
Malchin, *Germany* . . . . 30 B8 53 44N 12 44 E
Malchow, *Germany* . . . . 30 B8 53 28N 12 25 E
Malcolm, *Australia* . . . . 125 E3 28 51 S 121 25 E
Malcolm, Pt., *Australia* . . . . 125 F3 33 48 S 123 45 E
Malczyce, *Poland* . . . . 55 G3 51 14N 16 29 E
Maldah, *India* . . . . 93 G13 25 2N 88 9 E
Maldegem, *Belgium* . . . . 24 C3 51 14N 3 26 E
Malden, *Mass., U.S.A.* 151 D13 42 26N 71 4W
Malden, *Mo., U.S.A.* 155 G10 36 34N 89 57W
Malden I., *Kiribati* . . . . 135 H12 4 3 S 155 1W
Maldives ■, *Ind. Oc.* . . . . 89 E6 5 0N 73 0 E
Maldon, *Australia* . . . . 128 D6 37 0 S 144 6 E
Maldon, *U.K.* . . . . 21 F8 51 44N 0 42 E
Maldonado, *Uruguay* . . . . 175 C5 34 59 S 55 0W
Maldonado, Punta, *Mexico* 163 D5 16 19N 98 35W
Malè, *Italy* . . . . 44 B7 46 21N 10 55 E
Male, *Maldives* . . . . 89 E6 4 0N 73 28 E
Malé Karpaty, *Slovak Rep.* . . . . 35 C10 48 30N 17 20 E
Maléa, Ákra, *Greece* . . . . 48 E5 36 28N 23 7 E
Malebo, Pool, *Africa* . . . . 115 C3 4 17 S 15 20 E
Malegaon, *India* . . . . 94 D2 20 30N 74 38 E
Malei, *Mozam.* . . . . 119 F4 17 12 S 36 58 E
Malek, *Sudan* . . . . 107 F3 6 4N 31 36 E
Malek Kandī, *Iran* . . . . 101 D12 37 9N 46 6 E
Malela, Bas-Congo, *Dem. Rep. of the Congo* . . . . 115 D2 5 59 S 12 37 E
Malela, Maniema, *Dem. Rep. of the Congo* . . . . 118 C2 4 22 S 26 8 E
Malema, *Mozam.* . . . . 119 E4 14 57 S 37 20 E
Máleme, *Greece* . . . . 39 E4 35 31N 23 49 E
Malendok I., *Papua N. G.* . . . . 132 B7 3 28 S 153 13 E
Maleny, *Australia* . . . . 127 D5 26 45 S 152 52 E
Malerås, *Sweden* . . . . 17 H9 56 54N 15 34 E
Malerkotla, *India* . . . . 92 D6 30 32N 75 58 E
Máles, *Greece* . . . . 39 E6 35 6N 25 35 E
Malesherbes, *France* . . . . 27 D9 48 15N 2 24 E
Maleshevska Planina, *Europe* . . . . . 50 E7 41 38N 23 7 E
Malesína, *Greece* . . . . 48 C5 38 37N 23 14 E
Malestroit, *France* 26 E4 47 49N 2 25W
Malfa, *Italy* . . . . 47 D7 38 35N 14 50 E
Malgobek, *Russia* . . . . 61 J7 43 30N 44 34 E
Malgomaj, *Sweden* . . . . 14 D17 64 40N 16 30 E
Malgrat = Malgrat de Mar, *Spain* . . 40 D7 41 39N 2 46 E
Malgrat de Mar, *Spain* . . . . 40 D7 41 39N 2 46 E
Malha, *Sudan* . . . . 107 D2 15 8N 25 10 E
Malhada, *Brazil* . . . . 171 D3 14 21 S 43 47W
Malhargarh, *India* . . . . 92 G6 24 17N 74 59 E
Malheur →, *U.S.A.* 158 E4 43 20N 116 48W
Malheur L., *U.S.A.* 158 E4 43 20N 118 48W
Mali, *Guinea* 112 C2 12 10N 12 20W
Mali ■, *Africa* 112 B4 17 0N 3 0W
Mali →, *Burma* . . . . 90 C6 25 42N 97 30 E
Mali Kanal, *Serbia, Yug.* . . . . 52 E4 45 36N 19 24 E
Mali Kyun, *Burma* . . . . 86 F2 13 0N 98 20 E
Malibu, *U.S.A.* 161 L8 34 2N 118 41W
Maligaya = Gloria, *Phil.* . . . . 80 E3 12 59N 121 30 E
Maliku, *Indonesia* . . . . 82 B2 0 39 S 123 16 E
Malili, *Indonesia* . . . . 82 B2 2 42 S 121 6 E
Malilla, *Sweden* . . . . 17 G9 57 23N 15 48 E
Malimba, Mts., *Dem. Rep. of the Congo* . . . . 118 D2 7 30 S 29 30 E
Malin Hd., *Ireland* 23 A4 55 23N 7 23W
Malin Pen., *Ireland* 23 A4 55 20N 7 17W
Malindang, Mt., *Phil.* . . . . 81 G4 8 13N 123 38 E
Malindi, *Kenya* . . . . 118 C5 3 12 S 40 5 E
Malines = Mechelen, *Belgium* . . . . 24 C4 51 2N 4 29 E
Malino, *Indonesia* . . . . 82 A2 0 39N 121 0 E
Malinyi, *Tanzania* . . . . 119 D4 8 56 S 36 0 E
Malipo, *China* . . . . 76 F5 23 7N 104 42 E
Maliq, *Albania* . . . . 50 F4 40 45N 20 48 E
Malita, *Phil.* . . . . 81 H5 6 19N 125 39 E
Maliwun, *Burma* . . . . 78 B1 10 17N 98 40 E
Maliya, *India* . . . . 92 H3 23 5N 70 46 E
Maljenik, *Serbia, Yug.* . . . . 50 C5 43 54N 21 43 E
Malka Mari Nat. Park △, *Kenya* . . . 118 B5 4 11N 40 46 E
Malkapur, *India* . . . . 94 D1 20 53N 73 58 E
Malkara, *Turkey* . . . . 51 F10 40 53N 26 53 E
Malkhangiri = Malakanagiri, *India* . 94 E5 18 21N 81 54 E
Malkinia Górna, *Poland* . . . . 55 F9 52 42N 22 5 E
Malko Tŭrnovo, *Bulgaria* . . . . 51 E11 41 59N 27 31 E
Mallacoota, *Australia* . . . . 129 D8 37 34 S 149 40 E
Mallacoota Inlet, *Australia* . . . . 129 D8 37 34 S 149 40 E
Mallaig, *U.K.* 22 D3 57 0N 5 50W
Mallala, *Australia* . . . . 128 C3 34 26 S 138 30 E
Mallaoua, *Niger* . . . . 113 C6 13 16N 8 32 E
Mallard, *U.S.A.* 156 D2 42 56N 94 41W
Mallawan, *India* . . . . 93 F9 27 4N 80 12 E
Mallawi, *Egypt* . . . . 106 B3 27 44N 30 44 E
Mallee Cliffs Nat. Park △, *Australia* 128 C4 34 16 S 142 32 E
Mallemort, *France* . . . . 29 E9 43 43N 5 11 E
Málles Venosta, *Italy* . . . . 44 B7 46 41N 10 32 E
Mállia, *Greece* . . . . 39 E6 35 17N 25 32 E
Mallicolo = Malakula, *Vanuatu* . . . . 133 F5 16 15 S 167 30 E
Mallión, Kólpos, *Greece* . . . . 39 E6 35 19N 25 27 E
Mallorca, *Spain* . . . . 38 B4 39 30N 3 0 E
Mallorytown, *Canada* 151 B9 44 29N 75 53W
Mallow, *Ireland* 23 D3 52 8N 8 39W
Malmbäck, *Sweden* . . . . 17 G8 57 34N 14 28 E
Malmberget, *Sweden* . . . . 14 C19 67 11N 20 40 E

Malmédy, *Belgium* . . . . 24 D6 50 25N 6 2 E
Malmesbury, S. *Africa* . . . . 116 E2 33 28 S 18 41 E
Malmköping, *Sweden* . . . . 16 E10 59 8N 16 44 E
Malmö, *Sweden* . . . . 17 J6 55 36N 12 59 E
Malmslätt, *Sweden* . . . . 17 F9 58 27N 15 33 E
Malmyzh, *Russia* . . . . 60 B10 56 31N 50 41 E
Malnaş, *Romania* . . . . 53 D10 46 2N 25 49 E
Malo, *Vanuatu* . . . . 133 E5 15 40 S 167 11 E
Malo Konare, *Bulgaria* . . . . 51 D8 42 12N 24 24 E
Maloarkhangelsk, *Russia* . . . . 59 F9 52 28N 36 30 E
Maloca, *Brazil* 169 C6 0 43N 55 57W
Maloja, *Switz.* . . . . 33 D9 46 25N 9 55 E
Malojapass, *Switz.* . . . . 33 D9 46 23 S 9 42 E
Malolo, *Fiji* . . . . 133 A1 17 45 S 177 0 E
Malolos, *Phil.* . . . . 80 D3 14 50N 120 49 E
Malolotja Nature Reserve △, *Swaziland* . . . . 117 D5 26 4 S 31 6 E
Malombe L., *Malawi* . . . . 119 E4 14 40 S 35 15 E
Malomice, *Poland* . . . . 55 G2 51 34N 15 29 E
Malomir, *Bulgaria* . . . . 51 D10 42 16N 26 32 E
Malone, *Fla., U.S.A.* 152 K4 30 57N 85 10W
Malone, *N.Y., U.S.A.* 151 B10 44 51N 74 18W
Malong, *China* . . . . 76 E4 25 24N 103 34 E
Malonga, *Dem. Rep. of the Congo* . 115 E4 10 24 S 23 10 E
Malonno, *Italy* . . . . 33 D10 46 7N 10 18 E
Małopolskie □, *Poland* . . . . 55 J7 49 50N 20 20 E
Malorad, *Bulgaria* . . . . 50 C7 43 28N 23 41 E
Måløy, *Norway* . . . . 18 C2 61 57N 5 6 E
Maloyaroslovets, *Russia* . . . . 58 E9 55 2N 36 20 E
Malpartida, *Spain* 43 F4 39 26N 6 30W
Malpaso, *Canary Is.* 9 e1 27 43N 18 3W
Malpelo, I. de, *Colombia* 135 G19 4 3N 81 35W
Malpica de Bergantiños, *Spain* . . . 42 B2 43 19N 8 50W
Malprabha →, *India* . . . . 95 F3 16 20N 76 5 E
Malpur, *India* . . . . 92 H5 23 21N 73 27 E
Malpura, *India* . . . . 92 F6 26 17N 75 23 E
Mals = Málles Venosta, *Italy* . . . . . 44 B7 46 41N 10 32 E
Malsiras, *India* . . . . 94 F2 17 52N 74 55 E
Malta, *Brazil* . . . . 170 C4 6 54 S 37 31W
Malta, *Idaho, U.S.A.* 158 E7 42 18N 113 22W
Malta, *Mont., U.S.A.* 158 B10 48 21N 107 52W
Malta ■, *Europe* . . . . 38 F7 35 55N 14 26 E
Malta ✈ (MLA), *Malta* . . . . 38 F7 35 52N 14 29 E
Maltahöhe, *Namibia* . . . . 116 C2 24 55 S 17 0 E
Maltepe, *Turkey* . . . . 51 F13 40 55N 29 8 E
Malters, *Switz.* . . . . 32 B6 47 3N 8 11 E
Malton, *Canada* 150 C5 43 42N 79 38W
Malton, *U.K.* 20 C7 54 8N 0 49W
Malu'u, *Solomon Is.* . . . . 133 M11 8 20 S 160 38 E
Maluku, *Dem. Rep. of the Congo* . . 114 C3 4 3 S 15 34 E
Maluku, *Indonesia* . . . . 79 E7 1 0 S 127 0 E
Maluku □, *Indonesia* . . . . 82 B3 3 0 S 128 0 E
Maluku Sea = Molucca Sea, *Indonesia* . . . . 82 A3 0 0 125 0 E
Malumfashi, *Nigeria* . . . . 113 C6 11 48N 7 39 E
Malunda, *Indonesia* . . . . 82 B1 3 0 S 118 50 E
Malundo, *Angola* . . . . 115 E4 14 51 S 22 0 E
Malung, *Sweden* . . . . 16 D7 60 42N 13 44 E
Malungon, *Phil.* . . . . 81 H5 6 16N 125 14 E
Malungsfors, *Sweden* . . . . 16 D7 60 44N 13 33 E
Malur, *India* . . . . 95 H3 13 0N 77 55 E
Maluso, *Phil.* . . . . 81 H3 6 33N 121 53 E
Malvan, *Ghana* 112 D4 8 40N 2 1W
Malvaglia, *Switz.* . . . . 33 D7 46 24N 8 59 E
Malvalli, *India* . . . . 95 H3 12 28N 77 8 E
Malvan, *India* . . . . 95 F1 16 2N 73 30 E
Malvern, *U.S.A.* 155 H8 34 22N 92 49W
Malvern Hills, *U.K.* 21 E5 52 0N 2 19W
Malvik, *Norway* . . . . 18 A7 63 25N 10 40 E
Malvinas, Is. = Falkland Is. □, *Atl. Oc.* . . . . 9 f 51 30 S 59 0W
Malý Dunaj →, *Slovak Rep.* . . . . . . 35 D11 47 45N 18 9 E
Malya, *Tanzania* . . . . 118 C3 3 5 S 33 38 E
Malybay, *Kazakhstan* . . . . 65 B9 43 30N 78 25 E
Malyn, *Ukraine* . . . . 59 G5 50 46N 29 3 E
Maly Lyakhovskiy, Ostrov, *Russia* . 67 B15 74 7N 140 36 E
Malyn, *Ukraine* . . . . 67 D12 58 18N 112 54 E
Mamadysh, *Russia* . . . . 60 B9 55 42N 51 10 E
Mamaia, *Romania* . . . . 53 E5 36 5 S 137 50 E
Mamala B., *U.S.A.* 145 K14 21 15N 157 55W
Mamanguape, *Brazil* . . . . 170 C4 6 50 S 35 4W
Mamanuca Group, *Fiji* . . . . 133 A1 17 35 S 177 5 E
Mamarr Mitlā, *Egypt* . . . . 103 E1 30 2N 32 54 E
Mamasa, *Indonesia* . . . . 82 B1 2 55 S 119 20 E
Mambajao, *Phil.* . . . . 81 G5 9 15N 124 43 E
Mambasa, *Dem. Rep. of the Congo* 118 B2 1 22N 29 3 E
Mamberamo →, *Indonesia* . . . . 83 B5 2 0 S 137 50 E
Mambéré →, *C.A.R.* . . . . 114 B3 3 31N 16 3 E
Mambili →, *Congo* . . . . 114 B3 0 16N 16 7 E
Mambilima Falls, *Zambia* . . . . 119 E2 10 31 S 28 45 E
Mambirima, *Dem. Rep. of the Congo* 119 E2 11 25 S 27 33 E
Mambo, *Tanzania* . . . . 118 C4 4 52 S 38 22 E
Mambrui, *Kenya* . . . . 118 C5 3 5 S 40 5 E
Mamburao, *Phil.* . . . . 80 E3 13 13N 120 39 E
Mameigwess L., *Canada* 140 B2 52 35N 87 50W
Mamers, *France* . . . . 26 D7 48 21N 0 22 E
Mamfé, *Cameroon* . . . . 113 D6 5 50N 9 15 E
Mamī, Ra's, *Yemen* . . . . 99 D6 12 32 S 54 13 E
Mamiña, *Chile* . . . . 172 E4 20 5 S 69 14W
Mammoth, *U.S.A.* 159 K8 32 43N 110 39W
Mammoth Cave Nat. Park △, *U.S.A.* 148 G3 37 8N 86 13W
Mamoré →, *Bolivia* . . . . 173 C4 10 23 S 65 53W
Mamou, *Guinea* 112 C2 10 15N 12 0W
Mamoudzou, *Mayotte* . . . . 121 a 12 48 S 45 14 E
Mampatá, *Guinea-Biss.* 112 C2 11 54N 14 53W
Mampikony, *Madag.* . . . . 117 B8 16 6 S 47 38 E
Mampoko, *Dem. Rep. of the Congo* 114 B3 0 51N 18 42 E
Mampong, *Ghana* 113 D4 7 6N 1 26W
Mamry, Jezioro, *Poland* . . . . 54 D8 54 5N 21 50 E
Mamuil Malal, Paso, S. *Amer.* . . . . . 176 A2 39 35 S 71 28W
Mamuju, *Indonesia* . . . . 82 B1 2 41 S 118 50 E
Mamūl, *Oman* . . . . 99 C6 18 58N 55 16 E
Mamuno, *Botswana* . . . . 116 C3 22 16 S 20 1 E
Mamuras, *Albania* . . . . 50 E3 41 34N 19 41 E
Man, *Ivory C.* 112 D3 7 30N 7 40W
Man →, *India* . . . . 94 F2 17 31N 75 32 E
Man, I. of, *India* . . . . 95 K11 8 28N 93 36 E
Man, I. of, *U.K.* 20 C3 54 15N 4 30W
Man-Bazar, *India* . . . . 93 H12 23 4N 86 39 E
Man Na, *Burma* . . . . 90 D7 23 4N 98 1 E
Man Tun, *Burma* . . . . 90 D7 23 52N 98 38 E
Mana, Fr. Guiana 169 B7 5 45N 53 55W
Mana, *U.S.A.* 145 A2 22 2N 159 47W
Mana →, *Guyana* 169 B7 5 45N 53 55W
Mana Pools Nat. Park △, *Zimbabwe* 119 F2 15 56 S 29 25 E
Manaar, G. of = Mannar, G. of, *Asia* 95 K4 8 30N 79 0 E
Manabí □, *Ecuador* . . . . 168 D1 0 40 S 80 5W
Manacacías →, *Colombia* 168 C3 4 23N 72 4W
Manacapuru, *Brazil* . . . . 169 D5 3 16 S 60 37W
Manacor, *Spain* . . . . 38 B4 39 34N 3 13 E
Manadas, *Azores* 9 d1 38 38N 28 6W
Manado, *Indonesia* . . . . 82 A2 1 29N 124 51 E
Managua, *Nic.* 164 D2 12 6N 86 20W
Managua, L. de, *Nic.* 164 D2 12 20N 86 30W
Manaia, *N.Z.* . . . . 130 F3 39 33 S 174 8 E
Manakara, *Madag.* . . . . 117 C8 22 8 S 48 1 E
Manali, *India* . . . . 92 C7 32 16N 77 10 E
Manam I., *Papua N. G.* . . . . 132 C3 4 5 S 145 0 E
Manama = Al Manāmah, *Bahrain* . . 97 E6 26 10N 50 30 E
Manambao →, *Madag.* . . . . 117 B7 17 35 S 44 0 E

Manambato, *Madag.* .... 117 A8   13 43 S   49 7 E
Manambolo ↔, *Madag.* .... 117 B7   19 18 S   44 22 E
Manambolosy, *Madag.* .... 117 B8   16 2 S   49 40 E
Mánamo, Caño ↔, *Venezuela* ... 169 B5   9 55N   62 16W
Manana I., *U.S.A.* 145 K14   21 20N 157 40W
Mananara, *Madag.* .... 117 B8   16 10 S   49 46 E
Mananara ↔, *Madag.* .... 117 C8   23 21 S   47 42 E
Mananara, Réserve Naturelle
  Intégrale de △, *Madag.* ... 117 B8   16 14 S   49 45 E
Manangatang, *Australia* .... 128 C5   35 5 S 142 54 E
Mananjary, *Madag.* .... 117 C8   21 13 S   48 20 E
Manankoro, *Mali* 112 C3   10 28N   7 25W
Manantavadi, *India* .... 95 J3   11 49N   76 1 E
Manantenina, *Madag.* .... 117 C8   24 17 S   47 19 E
Manaos = Manaus, *Brazil* ..... 169 D6   3 0 S   60 0W
Manapala, *Phil.* .... 81 F4   10 58N 123 5 E
Manapire ↔, *Venezuela* 168 B4   7 42N   66 7W
Manapouri, *N.Z.* .... 131 F2   45 34 S 167 39 E
Manapouri, L., *N.Z.* .... 131 F2   45 32 S 167 32 E
Manapparai, *India* .... 95 J4   10 36N   78 25 E
Manaqil, *Sudan* .... 107 E3   14 15N   32 59 E
Manar ↔, *India* .... 94 E3   18 50N   77 20 E
Manār, Jabal, *Yemen* .... 98 D4   14 2N   44 17 E
Manaravolo, *Madag.* .... 117 C8   23 59 S   45 39 E
Manas, *China* .... 68 B3   44 17N   85 56 E
Manas, *Somali Rep.* .... 120 D2   2 57N   43 28 E
Manas ↔, *India* .... 90 B3   26 12N   90 40 E
Manas, Gora, *Kyrgyzstan* ..... 65 B5   42 22N   71 2 E
Manaslu, *Nepal* .... 93 E11   28 33N   84 33 E
Manasquan, *U.S.A.* 151 F10   40 8N   74 3W
Manassa, *U.S.A.* 159 H11   37 11N 105 56W
Manatí, *Puerto Rico* .... 165 d   18 26N   66 29W
Manati B., *St. Helena* .... 9 h   16 0 S   5 46W
Manatuto, *E. Timor* .... 82 C3   8 30 S 126 1 E
Manau, *Papua N. G.* .... 132 E4   8 4 S 148 0 E
Manaung, *Burma* .... 90 F4   18 45N   93 40 E
Manaus, *Brazil* .... 169 D6   3 0 S   60 0W
Manavgat, *Turkey* .... 100 D4   36 47N   31 26 E
Manawan L., *Canada* 143 B8   55 24N 103 14W
Manawatu ↔, *N.Z.* .... 130 G4   40 28 S 175 12 E
Manawatu-Wanganui □, *N.Z.* ... 130 F4   39 50 S 175 30 E
Manay, *Phil.* .... 81 H6   7 17N 126 33 E
Manbij, *Syria* .... 100 D7   36 31N   37 57 E
Mancha Real, *Spain* 43 H7   37 48N   3 39W
Manche □, *France* 26 C5   49 10N   1 20W
Manchegorsk, *Russia* .... 66 C4   67 54N   32 58 E
Manchester, *U.K.* 20 D5   53 29N   2 12W
Manchester, *Calif., U.S.A.* .. 160 G3   38 58N 123 41W
Manchester, *Conn., U.S.A.* ... 151 E12   41 47N   72 31W
Manchester, *Ga., U.S.A.* 152 C5   32 51N   84 37W
Manchester, *Iowa, U.S.A.* 156 B5   42 29N   91 27W
Manchester, *Ky., U.S.A.* 148 G4   37 9N   83 46W
Manchester, *Mich., U.S.A.* ... 157 B12   42 9N   84 2W
Manchester, *N.H., U.S.A.* 151 D13   42 59N   71 28W
Manchester, *N.Y., U.S.A.* 150 D7   42 56N   77 16W
Manchester, *Ohio, U.S.A.* 157 F13   38 41N   83 36W
Manchester, *Pa., U.S.A.* 151 F8   40 4N   76 43W
Manchester, *Tenn., U.S.A.* ... 149 H2   35 29N   86 5W
Manchester, *Vt., U.S.A.* 151 C11   43 10N   73 5W
Manchester International ✈ (MAN),
  U.K. 20 D5   53 21N   2 17W
Manchester L., *Canada* 143 A7   61 28N 107 29W
Manchhar L., *Pakistan* .... 92 F2   26 25N   67 39 E
Manchuria = Dongbei, *China* .. 75 D13   45 0N 125 0 E
Manchurian Plain, *China* ..... 62 E16   47 0N 124 0 E
Manciano, *Italy* .... 45 F8   42 35N   11 31 E
Mancifa, *Ethiopia* .... 107 F5   6 53N   41 50 E
Mancora, *Peru* .... 172 A1   4 9 S   81 1W
Mand ↔, *India* .... 93 J10   21 42N   83 15 E
Mand ↔, *Iran* .... 97 D7   28 20N   52 30 E
Manda, *Ludewe, Tanzania* ..... 119 E3   10 30 S   34 40 E
Manda, *Mbeya, Tanzania* ...... 118 D3   7 58 S   32 29 E
Manda, *Mbeya, Tanzania* ...... 119 D3   8 30 S   32 49 E
Manda, Parc Nat. de △, *Chad* . 109 G3   9 45N   17 52 E
Mandabé, *Madag.* .... 117 C7   21 0 S   44 55 E
Mandaguari, *Brazil* .... 175 A5   23 32 S   51 42W
Mandah = Töhöm, *Mongolia* .... 74 B5   44 27N 108 2 E
Mandal, *Norway* .... 18 F4   58 2N   7 25 E
Mandala, Puncak, *Indonesia* .. 83 B6   4 44 S 140 20 E
Mandalay, *Burma* .... 90 D6   22 0N   96 4 E
Mandalay □, *Burma* .... 90 E5   22 0N   96 5 E
Mandale = Mandalay, *Burma* ... 90 D6   22 0N   96 4 E
Mandalgarh, *India* .... 92 G6   25 12N   75 6 E
Mandalgovi, *Mongolia* .... 74 B4   45 45N 106 10 E
Mandalī, *Iraq* .... 101 F11   33 43N   45 28 E
Mandan, *U.S.A.* 154 B4   46 50N 100 54W
Mandaon, *Phil.* .... 80 E4   12 13N 123 17 E
Mandar, Teluk, *Indonesia* .... 82 B1   3 35 S 119 15 E
Mandara Mts., *Nigeria* .... 109 F2   10 40N   13 40 E
Mándas, *Italy* .... 46 C2   39 40N   9 8 E
Mandasor = Mandsaur, *India* .. 92 G6   24 3N   75 8 E
Mandaue, *Phil.* .... 81 F4   10 20N 123 56 E
Mandelieu-la-Napoule, *France* . 29 E10   43 34N   6 57 E
Mandera, *Kenya* .... 118 B5   3 55N   41 53 E
Mandeville, *Jamaica* .... 164 a   18 2N   77 31W
Mandi, *India* .... 92 D7   31 39N   76 58 E
Mandi Dabwali, *India* .... 92 E6   29 58N   74 42 E
Mandiana, *Guinea* 112 C3   10 37N   8 39W
Mandimba, *Mozam.* .... 119 E4   14 20 S   35 40 E
Mandioli, *Indonesia* .... 83 B3   0 40 S 127 20 E
Mandioré, L., *S. Amer.* ...... 173 D6   18 5 S   57 33W
Mandla, *India* .... 93 H9   22 39N   80 30 E
Mandø, *Denmark* .... 17 J2   55 18N   8 33 E
Mandorah, *Australia* .... 124 B5   12 32 S 130 42 E
Mandoto, *Madag.* .... 117 B8   19 34 S   46 17 E
Mandoúdhion, *Greece* .... 48 C5   38 48N   23 29 E
Mándra, *Greece* .... 48 C5   38 4N   23 30 E
Mandra, *Pakistan* .... 92 C5   33 23N   73 12 E
Mandráki, *Greece* .... 49 E9   36 36N   27 11 E
Mandrare ↔, *Madag.* .... 117 D8   25 10 S   46 30 E
Mandritsara, *Madag.* .... 117 B8   15 50 S   48 49 E
Mandronarivo, *Madag.* .... 117 C8   21 7 S   45 38 E
Mandsaur, *India* .... 92 G6   24 3N   75 8 E
Mandurah, *Australia* .... 125 F2   32 36 S 115 48 E
Mandúria, *Italy* .... 47 B10   40 24N   17 38 E
Mandvi, *India* .... 92 H3   22 51N   69 22 E
Mandya, *India* .... 95 H3   12 30N   77 0 E
Mandzai, *Pakistan* .... 92 D2   30 55N   67 6 E
Mané, *Burkina Faso* 113 C4   12 59N   1 21W
Maneh, *Iran* .... 97 B8   37 39N   57 7 E
Manengouba, Mts., *Cameroon* .. 113 E6   5 0N   9 50 E
Maner ↔, *India* .... 94 E4   18 30N   79 40 E
Manera, *Madag.* .... 117 E7   22 55 S   44 20 E
Manérbio, *Italy* .... 44 C7   45 21N   10 8 E
Maneroo Cr. ↔, *Australia* .... 126 C3   23 21 S 143 53 E
Manfalût, *Egypt* .... 106 B3   27 20N   30 52 E
Manfred, *Australia* .... 128 B5   33 19 S 143 45 E
Manfredónia, *Italy* .... 45 G12   41 38N   15 55 E
Manfredónia, G. di, *Italy* ... 45 G13   41 35N   16 5 E
Manga, *Brazil* .... 171 D3   14 46 S   43 56W
Manga, *Burkina Faso* 113 C4   11 40N   1 4W
Manga, *Congo* .... 114 C3   0 10 S   14 0 E
Manga, *Niger* .... 113 C7   15 0N   14 0 E
Mangabeiras, Chapada das, *Brazil* 170 C2   10 0 S   46 30W
Mangai, *Dem. Rep. of the Congo* 115 C3   4 2 S   19 33 E
Mangakino, *N.Z.* .... 130 E4   38 22 S 175 47 E
Mangal, *Phil.* .... 81 H3   6 25N 121 58 E
Mangalagiri, *India* .... 95 F5   16 26N   80 36 E
Mangaldai, *India* .... 90 B4   26 26N   92 2 E
Mangalia, *Romania* .... 53 G13   43 50N   28 35 E
Mangalmé, *Chad* .... 109 F3   12 0N   18 45 E
Mangalore, *India* .... 95 H2   12 55N   74 47 E
Mangalvedha, *India* .... 94 F2   17 31N   75 28 E

Mangan, *India* .... 90 B2   27 31N   88 32 E
Mangaon, *India* .... 94 E1   18 15N   73 20 E
Mangawan, *India* .... 93 G9   24 41N   81 33 E
Mangaweka, *N.Z.* .... 130 F4   39 48 S 175 47 E
Mangaweka, Mt., *N.Z.* .... 130 F5   39 49 S 176 5 E
Mange, *Dem. Rep. of the Congo* 114 B4   0 54N   20 30 E
Manger, *Norway* .... 18 D2   60 38N   5 3 E
Manggar, *Indonesia* .... 85 C3   2 50 S 108 10 E
Manggawitu, *Indonesia* .... 83 B4   4 8 S 133 32 E
Manggis, *Indonesia* .... 79 J18   8 29 S 115 31 E
Mangin Taungdan, *Burma* ...... 90 C5   24 15N   95 45 E
Mangindrano, *Madag.* .... 117 A8   14 17 S   48 58 E
Mangkalihat, Tanjung, *Indonesia* 85 B5   1 2N 118 59 E
Mangla, *Pakistan* .... 92 C5   33 7N   73 39 E
Mangla Dam, *Pakistan* .... 93 C5   33 9N   73 44 E
Manglares, C., *Colombia* 168 C2   1 36N   79 2W
Manglaur, *India* .... 92 E7   29 44N   77 49 E
Mango, *Togo* .... 113 C5   10 20N   0 30 E
Mango, *Tonga* .... 133 Q14   20 17 S 173 25W
Mangoche, *Malawi* .... 119 E4   14 25 S   35 16 E
Mangoky ↔, *Madag.* .... 117 C7   21 29 S   43 41 E
Mangole, *Indonesia* .... 82 B3   1 50 S 125 55 E
Mangombe, *Dem. Rep. of the Congo* 118 C2   1 20 S   26 48 E
Mangonui, *N.Z.* .... 130 B2   35 1 S 173 32 E
Mangoro ↔, *Madag.* .... 117 B8   20 0 S   48 45 E
Mangrol, *Mad. P., India* ..... 92 J4   21 7N   70 7 E
Mangrol, *Raj., India* .... 92 G6   25 20N   76 31 E
Mangrul Pir, *India* .... 94 D3   20 19N   77 21 E
Mangualde, *Portugal* 42 E3   40 38N   7 48W
Manguchar, *Pakistan* .... 92 E2   28 25N   67 52 E
Manguéigne, *Chad* .... 109 F4   10 30N   21 15 E
Mangueira, L. da, *Brazil* .... 175 C5   33 0 S   52 50W
Manguéni, Hamada, *Niger* ..... 108 D2   22 35N   12 40 E
Mangum, *U.S.A.* 155 H5   34 53N   99 30W
Mangungu, *Dem. Rep. of the Congo* 115 D3   5 16 S   19 36 E
Mangyshlak Poluostrov, *Kazakhstan* 66 E6   44 30N   52 30 E
Manhattan, *U.S.A.* 154 F6   39 11N   96 35W
Manhattan, *U.S.A.* 157 C9   41 26N   87 59W
Manhiça, *Mozam.* .... 117 D5   25 23 S   32 49 E
Manhuaçu, *Brazil* .... 171 F3   20 15 S   42 2W
Manhumirim, *Brazil* .... 171 F3   20 22 S   41 57W
Maní, *Colombia* 168 C3   4 49N   72 17W
Mania ↔, *Madag.* .... 117 B8   19 42 S   45 22 E
Maníago, *Italy* .... 45 B9   46 10N   12 43 E
Manica, *Mozam.* .... 117 B5   18 58 S   32 59 E
Manica □, *Mozam.* .... 117 B5   19 10 S   33 45 E
Manicaland □, *Zimbabwe* ...... 119 F3   19 0 S   32 30 E
Manicoré, *Brazil* .... 173 B5   5 48 S   61 16W
Manicoré ↔, *Brazil* .... 173 B5   5 51 S   61 19W
Manicouagan ↔, *Canada* 141 C6   49 30N   68 30W
Manicouagan, Rés., *Canada* ... 141 B6   51 5N   68 40W
Maniema □, *Dem. Rep. of the Congo* 118 C2   3 0 S   26 0 E
Manīfah, *Si. Arabia* .... 97 E6   27 44N   49 0 E
Manifold, C., *Australia* ..... 126 C5   22 41 S 150 50 E
Maniganggo, *China* .... 76 B2   31 56N   99 10 E
Manigotagan, *Canada* 143 C9   51 6N   96 18W
Manigotagan ↔, *Canada* 143 C9   51 7N   96 20W
Manihari, *India* .... 93 G12   25 21N   87 38 E
Manihiki, *Cook Is.* .... 135 J11   10 24 S 161 1 W
Manitsoq, *Greenland* 10 D5   65 26N   52 55W
Manika, Plateau de la, *Dem. Rep. of*
  the Congo .... 119 E2   10 0 S   25 5 E
Manikchhari, *Bangla.* .... 90 D3   22 51N   91 50 E
Manikganj, *Bangla.* .... 90 D3   23 52N   90 0 E
Manikpur, *India* .... 93 G9   25 4N   81 7 E
Manila, *Phil.* .... 80 D3   14 40N 121 3 E
Manila, *U.S.A.* 158 F9   40 59N 109 43W
Manila B., *Phil.* .... 80 D3   14 40N 120 35 E
Manildra, *Australia* .... 129 B8   33 11 S 148 41 E
Manilla, *Australia* .... 129 A9   30 45 S 150 43 E
Manimpé, *Mali* 112 C3   14 11N   5 28W
Maningrida, *Australia* .... 126 A1   12 3 S 134 13 E
Maninian, *Ivory C.* 112 C3   10 3N   7 52W
Manipa, *Indonesia* .... 82 B3   3 17 S 127 35 E
Manipur □, *India* .... 90 C4   25 0N   94 0 E
Manipur ↔, *Burma* .... 90 D5   23 45N   94 20 E
Manisa, *Turkey* .... 49 C9   38 38N   27 30 E
Manisa □, *Turkey* .... 49 C9   38 40N   28 0 E
Manistee, *U.S.A.* 148 C2   44 15N   86 19W
Manistee ↔, *U.S.A.* 148 C2   44 15N   86 21W
Manistique, *U.S.A.* 148 C2   45 57N   86 15W
Manito, *U.S.A.* 156 D7   40 26N   89 47W
Manito L., *Canada* 143 C7   52 43N 109 43W
Manitoba □, *Canada* 143 B9   55 30N   97 0W
Manitoba, L., *Canada* 143 C9   51 0N   98 45W
Manitoba Beach, *U.S.A.* 157 C12   41 58N   84 19W
Manitou ↔, *Canada* 143 D9   49 15N   98 32W
Manitou, L., *Canada* 141 B6   50 55N   65 17W
Manitou L., *Canada* 143 C7   52 43N 109 43W
Manitou Springs, *U.S.A.* 154 F2   38 52N 104 55W
Manitoulin I., *Canada* 140 C3   45 40N   82 30W
Manitouwadge, *Canada* 140 B2   49 8N   85 48W
Manitowoc, *U.S.A.* 148 C2   44 5N   87 40W
Manitsauá-Missu ↔, *Brazil* .. 173 C7   10 58 S   53 20W
Maniyachi, *India* .... 95 K3   8 51N   77 55 E
Manizales, *Colombia* 168 B2   5 5N   75 32W
Manja, *Madag.* .... 117 C7   21 26 S   44 20 E
Manjacaze, *Mozam.* .... 117 C5   24 45 S   34 0 E
Manjakandriana, *Madag.* ...... 117 B8   18 55 S   47 47 E
Manjeri, *India* .... 95 J3   11 7N   76 11 E
Manjhand, *Pakistan* .... 91 D3   25 50N   68 10 E
Manjil, *Iran* .... 97 B6   36 46N   49 30 E
Manjimup, *Australia* .... 125 F2   34 15 S 116 6 E
Manjlegaon, *India* .... 94 E3   19 9N   76 14 E
Manjra ↔, *India* .... 94 E3   18 49N   77 52 E
Mankato, *Kans., U.S.A.* 154 F5   39 47N   98 13W
Mankato, *Minn., U.S.A.* 154 C8   44 10N   94 0W
Mankayan, *Phil.* .... 80 C3   16 52N 120 47 E
Mankayane, *Swaziland* .... 117 D5   26 40 S   31 4 E
Mankera, *Pakistan* .... 92 D4   31 23N   71 26 E
Mankim, *Cameroon* .... 113 D7   5 6N   12 3 E
Mankono, *Ivory C.* 112 D3   8 1N   6 10W
Mankota, *Canada* 143 D7   49 25N 107 5W
Mankulam, *Sri Lanka* .... 95 K5   9 8N   80 29 E
Manlay = Üydzin, *Mongolia* ... 74 B4   44 9N 107 0 E
Manley Hot Springs, *U.S.A.* .. 144 D10   65 0N 150 38W
Manlleu, *Spain* .... 40 C7   42 2N   2 17 E
Manly, *Australia* .... 129 B9   33 48 S 151 17 E
Manmad, *India* .... 94 D2   20 18N   74 28 E
Mann Ranges, *Australia* ...... 125 E5   26 6 S 130 5 E
Manna, *Indonesia* .... 84 C2   4 25 S 102 55 E
Mannahill, *Australia* .... 128 B4   32 25 S 140 0 E
Mannar, *Sri Lanka* .... 95 K4   9 1N   79 54 E
Mannar, G. of, *Asia* .... 95 K4   8 30N   79 0 E
Mannar I., *Sri Lanka* .... 95 K4   9 5N   79 45 E
Mannargudi, *India* .... 95 J4   10 45N   79 51 E
Männedorf, *Switz.* .... 33 B7   47 15N   8 43 E
Mannheim, *Germany* .... 31 F4   49 29N   8 29 E
Manning, *Canada* 142 B5   56 53N 117 39W
Manning, *Oreg., U.S.A.* ...... 160 E3   45 45 S 123 13W
Manning, *S.C., U.S.A.* 152 B9   33 42N   80 13W
Manning ↔, *Australia* .... 129 A10   31 52 S 152 43 E
Manning Prov. Park □, *Canada* 142 D4   49 5N 120 45W
Manning Str., *Solomon Is.* ... 133 L10   7 30 S 158 0 E
Mannu ↔, *Italy* .... 46 C2   39 16N   9 0 E
Mannu, C., *Italy* .... 46 B1   40 3N   8 21 E
Mannum, *Australia* .... 128 C3   34 50 S 139 20 E
Mano, *S. Leone* .... 112 D2   8 3 S   12 2W
Mano, *Liberia* 112 D2   6 56N   11 30W
Mano River, *Liberia* 112 D2   7 20N   11 6W
Manoa, *Bolivia* .... 173 B4   9 40 S   65 27W
Manoharpur, *India* .... 93 H11   22 23N   85 12 E
Manokotak, *U.S.A.* 144 G8   58 58N 159 3W
Manokwari, *Indonesia* .... 83 B4   0 54 S 134 0 E

Manolás, *Greece* .... 48 C3   38 4N   21 21 E
Manolo Fortich, *Phil.* .... 81 G5   8 28N 124 50 E
Manombo, *Madag.* .... 117 C7   22 57 S   43 28 E
Manono, *Dem. Rep. of the Congo* 118 D2   7 15 S   27 25 E
Manono, *Samoa* .... 133 W23   13 50 S 172 5W
Manoppello, *Italy* .... 45 F11   42 15N   14 3 E
Manosque, *France* .... 29 E9   43 49N   5 47 E
Manotick, *Canada* 151 A9   45 13N   75 41W
Manouane ↔, *Canada* 141 C5   49 30N   71 10W
Manouane, L., *Canada* 141 B5   50 45N   70 45W
Manovo-Gounda Saint Floris, Parc
  Nat. du △, *C.A.R.* ..... 114 A4   9 30N   21 25 E
Manp'o, *N. Korea* .... 75 D14   41 6N 126 24 E
Manpojin = Manp'o, *N. Korea* . 75 D14   41 6N 126 24 E
Manpur, *Chhattisgarh, India* . 90 D3   23 17N   83 35 E
Manpur, *Chhattisgarh, India* . 94 D5   20 22N   80 43 E
Manpur, *Mad. P., India* ...... 92 H6   22 26N   75 37 E
Manresa, *Spain* .... 40 D6   41 48N   1 50 E
Mansa, *Gujarat, India* .... 92 H5   23 27N   72 45 E
Mansa, *Punjab, India* .... 92 E6   30 0N   75 27 E
Mansa, *Zambia* .... 119 E2   11 13 S   28 55 E
Mansalay, *Phil.* .... 80 E3   12 31N 121 26 E
Mánsásen, *Sweden* .... 16 A8   63 5N   14 18 E
Mansehra, *Pakistan* .... 92 B5   34 20N   73 15 E
Mansel I., *Canada* 139 B11   62 0N   80 0W
Mansfield, *Australia* .... 129 D7   37 4 S 146 6 E
Mansfield, *U.K.* 20 D6   53 9N   1 11W
Mansfield, *Ga., U.S.A.* 152 B6   33 31N   83 44W
Mansfield, *La., U.S.A.* 155 J8   32 2N   93 43W
Mansfield, *Mass., U.S.A.* 151 D13   42 2N   71 13W
Mansfield, *Ohio, U.S.A.* 150 F2   40 45N   82 31W
Mansfield, *Pa., U.S.A.* 150 E7   41 48N   77 5W
Mansfield, Mt., *U.S.A.* 151 B12   44 33N   72 49W
Mansi, *Burma* .... 90 C5   24 48N   95 52 E
Mansidão, *Brazil* .... 170 D3   10 43 S   44 2W
Mansilla de las Mulas, *Spain* 42 C5   42 30N   5 25W
Mansle, *France* .... 28 C4   45 52N   0 12 E
Manso ↔, *Brazil* .... 171 D2   13 50 S   47 0W
Mansoa, *Guinea-Biss.* 112 C1   12 0N   15 20W
Manson, *U.S.A.* 156 B2   42 32N   94 32W
Manson Creek, *Canada* 142 B4   55 37N 124 32W
Mansoura, *Algeria* .... 111 A5   36 1N   4 31 E
Manta, *Ecuador* .... 168 D1   1 0 S   80 40W
Manta, B. de, *Ecuador* .... 168 D1   0 54 S   80 44W
Mantalingajan, Mt., *Phil.* ... 81 G1   8 55N 117 45 E
Mantantale, *Dem. Rep. of the Congo* 114 C4   2 10 S   20 11 E
Mantare, *Tanzania* .... 118 C3   2 42 S   33 13 E
Mantaro ↔, *Peru* .... 172 C2   12 16 S   73 57W
Manteca, *U.S.A.* 160 H5   37 48N 121 13W
Mantecal, *Venezuela* 168 B4   7 34N   69 17W
Mantena, *Brazil* .... 171 E3   18 47 S   40 59W
Manteo, *U.S.A.* 149 H8   35 55N   75 40W
Mantes-la-Jolie, *France* ..... 27 D8   48 58N   1 41 E
Mantha, *India* .... 94 E3   19 40N   76 23 E
Manthani, *India* .... 94 E4   18 40N   79 35 E
Manti, *U.S.A.* 158 G8   39 16N 111 38W
Mantiqueira, Serra da, *Brazil* 171 F3   22 0 S   44 0W
Mantorp, *Sweden* .... 17 F9   58 21N   15 20 E
Mántova, *Italy* .... 44 C7   45 9N   10 48 E
Mänttä, *Finland* .... 15 E21   62 0N   24 40 E
Mantua = Mántova, *Italy* ..... 44 C7   45 9N   10 48 E
Mantung, *Australia* .... 128 C4   34 35 S 140 3 E
Manturovo, *Russia* .... 60 A7   58 23N   44 45 E
Manu, *Peru* .... 172 C3   12 10 S   70 51W
Manu ↔, *Peru* .... 172 C3   12 16 S   70 55W
Manu'a Is., *Amer. Samoa* ..... 133 X25   14 13 S 169 35W
Manuel Alves ↔, *Brazil* ..... 171 D2   11 19 S   48 28W
Manuel Alves Grande ↔, *Brazil* 170 C2   7 27 S   47 35W
Manuel Urbano, *Brazil* .... 172 B4   8 53 S   69 18W
Manui, *Indonesia* .... 82 B2   3 35 S 123 5 E
Manukan, *Phil.* .... 81 G4   8 32N 123 12 E
Manukau, *N.Z.* .... 130 D3   37 0 S 174 52 E
Manukau Harbour, *N.Z.* .... 130 D3   37 3 S 174 45 E
Manunui, *N.Z.* .... 130 E4   38 54 S 175 21 E
Manuoha, *N.Z.* .... 130 E6   38 39 S 177 7 E
Manuripi ↔, *Bolivia* .... 172 C4   11 6 S   67 36W
Manus □, *Papua N. G.* .... 132 B4   2 0 S 147 0 E
Manus I., *Papua N. G.* .... 132 B4   2 0 S 147 0 E
Manvi, *India* .... 95 G3   15 57N   76 59 E
Manwath, *India* .... 94 E3   19 19N   76 32 E
Many, *U.S.A.* 155 K8   31 34N   93 29W
Manyara □, *Tanzania* .... 118 C4   3 40 S   35 50 E
Manyas, *Turkey* .... 51 F11   40 2N   27 59 E
Manych ↔, *Russia* .... 61 G5   47 13N   40 40 E
Manych-Gudilo, Ozero, *Russia* 61 G6   46 24N   42 38 E
Manyonga ↔, *Tanzania* .... 118 C3   4 10 S   34 15 E
Manyoni, *Tanzania* .... 118 D3   5 45 S   34 55 E
Manzai, *Pakistan* .... 92 C4   32 12N   70 15 E
Manzala, Bahra el, *Egypt* .... 106 H7   31 10N   31 56 E
Manzanar Nat. Historic Site △,
  U.S.A. 160 J7   36 44N 119 5W
Manzanares, *Spain* 43 F7   39 2N   3 22W
Manzaneda, *Spain* 42 C3   42 12N   7 15W
Manzanillo, *Cuba* 164 B4   20 20N   77 31W
Manzanillo, *Mexico* 162 D4   19 0N 104 20W
Manzanillo, Pta., *Panama* 164 E4   9 30N   79 40W
Manzano Mts., *U.S.A.* 159 J10   34 40N 106 20W
Manzarīyeh, *Iran* .... 97 C6   34 53N   50 50 E
Manzhouli, *China* .... 69 B6   49 35N 117 25 E
Manzini, *Swaziland* .... 117 D5   26 30 S   31 25 E
Mao, *Chad* .... 109 F3   14 4 S   15 19 E
Maó, *Spain* .... 38 B5   39 53N   4 16 E
Maoke, Pegunungan, *Indonesia* 83 B5   3 40 S 137 30 E
Maolin, *China* .... 75 C12   43 58N 123 30 E
Maoming, *China* .... 77 G8   21 50N 110 54 E
Maoxing, *China* .... 77 G13   21 56N 120 43 E
Maoxian, *China* .... 76 B4   31 41N 103 49 E
Maoxing, *China* .... 75 B13   45 28N 124 40 E
Mapalma, *Dem. Rep. of the Congo* 114 B4   2 3N   24 30 E
Mapam Yumco, *China* .... 68 C3   30 45N   81 28 E
Mapastepec, *Mexico* 163 D6   15 26N   92 54W
Mapfongui, *Gabon* .... 114 C2   1 15 S   12 59 E
Maphrao ↔, *Thailand* .... 87 a   7 56N   98 26 E
Mapi ↔, *Indonesia* .... 83 B5   6 55 S 139 14 E
Mapia, Kepulauan, *Indonesia* . 83 A4   0 50N 134 20 E
Mapimí, *Mexico* 162 B4   25 50N 103 50W
Mapimí, Bolsón de, *Mexico* ... 162 B4   27 30N 104 15W
Maping, *China* .... 77 B9   31 34N 113 12 E
Mapinhane, *Mozam.* .... 117 C6   22 20 S   35 0 E
Mapire, *Venezuela* 169 B5   7 45N   64 42W
Mapixari, *Brazil* 157 B12   42 59N   84 57W
Maple Creek, *Canada* 143 D7   49 55N 109 29W
Maple Valley, *U.S.A.* 160 C4   47 25N 122 3W
Mapleton, *U.S.A.* 158 D2   44 2N 123 52W
Mapourika, L., *N.Z.* .... 131 D3   43 16 S 170 12 E
Maprik, *Papua N. G.* .... 132 B2   3 44 S 143 3 E
Mapuca, *India* .... 95 G1   15 36N   73 46 E
Mapuera ↔, *Brazil* .... 169 D6   1 5 S   57 2W
Mapulanguene, *Mozam.* .... 117 C5   24 29 S   32 6 E
Maputo, *Mozam.* .... 117 D5   25 58 S   32 32 E
Maputo □, *Mozam.* .... 117 D5   26 0 S   32 25 E
Maputo, B. de, *Mozam.* .... 117 D5   25 50 S   32 45 E
Maputo Game Reserve = Elefantes
  do Maputo, Reserva de △,
  Mozam. .... 117 D5   26 23 S   32 48 E
Maqiaohe, *China* .... 75 B16   44 40N 130 30 E
Maqnā, *Si. Arabia* .... 96 B2   28 25N   34 50 E
Maqran, W. ↔, *Si. Arabia* ... 98 B4   20 55N   47 12 E
Maqteir, *Mauritania* 110 D2   21 50N   11 40W

Maquan He = Brahmaputra ↔, *Asia* 68 D3   23 40N   90 35 E
Maqueda, *Spain* 42 E6   40 4N   4 22W
Maqueda Channel, *Phil.* ...... 81 E5   13 42N 124 1 E
Maquela do Zombo, *Angola* .... 118 D3   6 0 S   15 15 E
Maquinchao, *Argentina* .... 176 B3   41 15 S   68 50W
Maquoketa, *U.S.A.* 156 B6   42 4N   90 40W
Mar, Serra do, *Brazil* .... 175 B6   25 30 S   49 0W
Mar Chiquita, L., *Argentina* . 174 C3   30 40 S   62 50W
Mar del Plata, *Argentina* .... 174 D4   38 0 S   57 30W
Mar Menor, *Spain* 41 H4   37 40N   0 45W
Mara, *Guyana* 169 B6   6 0N   57 36W
Mara, *India* .... 90 A5   28 11N   94 14 E
Mara, *Tanzania* .... 118 C3   1 30 S   34 32 E
Mara □, *Tanzania* .... 118 C3   1 45 S   34 20 E
Maraã, *Brazil* .... 168 D4   1 52 S   65 25W
Marabá, *Brazil* .... 170 C2   5 20 S   49 5W
Maracá, I. de, *Brazil* 169 C7   2 10N   50 30W
Maracaibo, *Venezuela* 168 A3   10 40N   71 37W
Maracaibo, L. de, *Venezuela* . 168 B3   9 40N   71 30W
Maracaju, *Brazil* .... 175 A4   21 38 S   55 9W
Maracaju, Serra de, *Brazil* .. 173 E6   23 57 S   55 1W
Maracanã, *Brazil* .... 170 B2   0 46 S   47 27W
Maracás, *Brazil* .... 171 D3   13 26 S   40 18W
Maracas Bay Village, *Trin. & Tob.* 169 F9   10 46N   61 28W
Maracay, *Venezuela* 168 A4   10 15N   67 28W
Maracena, *Spain* .... 43 H7   37 12 S   3 38W
Marādah, *Libya* .... 108 C3   29 15N   19 15 E
Maradi, *Niger* .... 113 C6   13 29N   7 20 E
Maraetiria, Pte., *Tahiti* .... 133 S16   17 51 S 149 10W
Marāgheh, *Iran* .... 101 D12   37 30N   46 12 E
Maragogipe, *Brazil* .... 171 D4   12 46 S   38 55W
Marāh, *Si. Arabia* .... 96 E5   25 0N   45 35 E
Marahoue, Parc Nat. de la △,
  Ivory C. 112 D3   8 0N   7 8W
Marais du Cotentin et du Bessin △,
  France 26 C5   49 10N   1 30W
Marais Poitevin, Val de Sèvre et
  Vendée, Parc Naturel Régional
  de △, *France* 28 B3   46 18N   0 35W
Marajó, B. de, *Brazil* .... 170 B2   1 0 S   48 30W
Marajó, I. de, *Brazil* .... 170 B2   1 0 S   49 30W
Marākand, *Iran* .... 96 B5   38 51N   45 16 E
Marakele Nat. Park △, *S. Africa* 117 E4   32 14 S   25 27 E
Maralal, *Kenya* .... 118 B4   1 0N   36 38 E
Maralinga, *Australia* .... 125 F5   30 13 S 131 32 E
Maram, *India* .... 90 A3   25 25N   94 6 E
Marama, *Australia* .... 128 C4   35 10 S 140 10 E
Maramag, *Phil.* .... 81 H5   7 46N 125 0 E
Maramaraereğlisi, *Turkey* .... 51 F11   40 57N   27 57 E
Maramasike, *Solomon Is.* ..... 133 M11   9 30 S 161 25 E
Marampa, *S. Leone* 112 D2   8 45N   12 28W
Maramures □, *Romania* .... 53 C9   47 45N   24 0 E
Maran, *Malaysia* .... 87 L4   3 35N 102 45 E
Marana, *U.S.A.* 159 K8   32 27N 111 13W
Maranboy, *Australia* .... 124 B5   14 40 S 132 39 E
Maranchón, *Spain* 40 D2   41 6N   2 15W
Marand, *Iran* .... 101 C11   38 30N   45 45 E
Marandokhori, *Greece* .... 39 K6   38 38N   20 39 E
Marang, *Malaysia* .... 87 K4   5 12N 103 13 E
Marang, *Malaysia* .... 87 K4   5 12N 103 13 E
Maranhão = São Luís, *Brazil* . 170 B3   2 39 S   44 15W
Maranhão □, *Brazil* .... 170 B2   5 0 S   46 0W
Marano, L. di, *Italy* .... 45 C10   45 44N   13 10 E
Maranoa ↔, *Australia* .... 127 D4   27 50 S 148 37 E
Marañón ↔, *Peru* .... 172 A3   4 30 S   73 35W
Marão, *Brazil* .... 117 C5   24 18 S   34 2 E
Marapi ↔, *Brazil* 169 C6   0 37N   55 58W
Marari, *Brazil* .... 172 B4   5 43 S   67 47W
Maraş = Kahramanmaraş, *Turkey* 100 D7   37 37N   36 53 E
Mărăşești, *Romania* .... 53 E12   45 52N   27 14 E
Maratea, *Italy* .... 47 C8   39 59N   15 43 E
Marateca, *Portugal* 43 G2   38 34N   8 40W
Marathasa, *Cyprus* .... 39 F8   34 59N   32 51 E
Marathás, A'a, *Greece* .... 39 J2   37 39N   20 48 E
Marathókambos, *Greece* .... 49 D8   37 43N   26 42 E
Marathon, *Australia* .... 126 C3   20 51 S 143 32 E
Marathon, *Canada* 140 C2   48 44N   86 23W
Marathón, *Greece* .... 48 C5   38 11N   23 58 E
Marathon, *Fla., U.S.A.* 153 L8   24 43N   81 5W
Marathon, *N.Y., U.S.A.* 151 D8   42 27N   76 2W
Marathon, *Tex., U.S.A.* 155 K3   30 12N 103 15W
Marathóvouno, *Cyprus* .... 39 E9   35 13N   33 37 E
Maratua, *Indonesia* .... 85 B5   2 10N 118 35 E
Maraú, *Brazil* .... 171 D4   14 6 S   39 0W
Marau, *Solomon Is.* .... 133 N11   10 31 S 161 31 E
Maravari, *Solomon Is.* .... 133 L9   7 50 S 156 42 E
Maraval, *Trin. & Tob.* 169 F9   10 43N   61 32W
Maravatío, *Mexico* 162 D4   19 51N 100 25W
Marawi City, *Phil.* .... 81 G5   8 0N 124 21 E
Marāwih, *U.A.E.* .... 97 E7   24 18N   53 18 E
Marbach, *Switz.* .... 32 C5   46 51N   7 53 E
Marbella, *Spain* 43 J6   36 30N   4 57W
Marble Bar, *Australia* .... 124 D2   21 9 S 119 44 E
Marble Falls, *U.S.A.* 155 K5   30 35N   98 16W
Marblehead, *U.S.A.* 151 D14   42 30N   70 51W
Mârburg, *Norway* .... 18 D5   60 11N   8 9 E
Marburg = Maribor, *Slovenia* . 45 B12   46 36N   15 40 E
Marburg, *Germany* .... 30 E4   50 47N   8 46 E
Marcal ↔, *Hungary* .... 52 C2   47 41N   17 40 E
Marcali, *Hungary* .... 52 D2   46 35N   17 25 E
Marcapata, *Peru* .... 172 C3   13 31 S   70 52W
Marcaria, *Italy* .... 44 C7   45 7N   10 32 E
Mărculești, *Moldova* .... 53 B12   48 20N   27 14 E
March, *U.K.* .... 21 E8   52 33N   0 5 E
Marchal, *Dem. Rep. of the Congo* 156 E4   3 49 S   92 57W
Marchand = Rommani, *Morocco* . 110 B3   33 31N   6 40W
Marche, *France* .... 28 B5   46 5N   1 20 E
Marche □, *Italy* .... 45 E10   43 30N   13 15 E
Marche-en-Famenne, *Belgium* .. 24 D5   50 14N   5 19 E
Marchena, *Spain* 43 H5   37 18N   5 23W
Marchena, Canal de, *Ecuador* . 172 a   0 19N   90 12W
Marchena, I., *Ecuador* .... 172 a   0 19N   90 29W
Marches = Marche □, *Italy* ... 45 E10   43 30N   13 15 E
Marchesale, Riserva Statale □, *Italy* 49 B5   38 32N   16 12 E
Marciana Marina, *Italy* ...... 44 F7   42 48N   10 12 E
Marcianise, *Italy* .... 47 A7   41 1N   14 17 E
Marcigny, *France* .... 27 F11   46 17N   4 2 E
Marcillat-en-Combraille, *France* 27 F11   46 10N   2 38 E
Marck, *France* .... 27 B8   50 57N   1 57 E
Marckolsheim, *France* .... 27 D14   48 10N   7 30 E
Marco, *U.S.A.* 153 K8   25 58N   81 44W
Marco Rondon, *Brazil* .... 173 C5   12 6 S   60 56W
Marcona, *Peru* .... 172 C2   15 10 S   75 30W
Marcos Juárez, *Argentina* .... 174 C3   32 42 S   62 5W
Mărculești, *Moldova* .... 53 C13   47 27N   28 15 E
Marcus Baker, Mt., *U.S.A.* ... 144 F11   61 26N 147 45W
Marcus I. = Minami-Tori-Shima,
  Pac. Oc. .... 134 E7   24 20N 153 58 E
Marcus Necker Ridge, *Pac. Oc.* 134 F9   20 0N 175 0 E
Marcy, Mt., *U.S.A.* 151 B11   44 7N   73 56W
Mardan, *Pakistan* .... 91 B4   34 20N   72 0 E
Mardin, *Turkey* .... 101 D9   37 20N   40 43 E
Mårdsjön, *Sweden* .... 16 A9   63 18N   11 30 E
Maré, Î., *N. Cal.* .... 133 U22   21 30 S 168 0 E
Marécchia ↔, *Italy* .... 45 E9   44 4N   12 34 E
Marechal Deodoro, *Brazil* .... 170 C4   9 43 S   35 54W
Maree, L., *U.K.* 22 D3   57 40N   5 26W
Mareeba, *Australia* .... 126 B4   16 59 S 145 28 E
Mareetsane, *S. Africa* .... 116 D4   26 9 S   25 25 E
Marek, *Indonesia* .... 82 B2   4 41 S 120 24 E
Maremma, *Italy* .... 45 F8   42 30N   11 15 E
Maremma, Parco Naturale della △,
  Italy .... 44 F8   42 35N   11 8 E

Maréna, *Kayes, Mali* 112 C2   14 36N   10 45W
Maréna, *Koulikouro, Mali* 112 C3   13 55N   7 20W
Marengo, *Ind., U.S.A.* 157 F10   38 22N   86 21W
Marengo, *Iowa, U.S.A.* 156 C4   41 48N   92   4W
Marennes, *France* 28 C2   45 49N   1   7W
Marerano, *Madag.* .... 117 C7   21 23 S   44 52 E
Marettimo, *Italy* .... 46 E5   37 58N   12   4 E
Mareuil, *France* .... 28 C4   45 26N   0 29 E
Marfa, *U.S.A.* 155 K2   30 19N   104   1W
Marganets = Marhanets, *Ukraine* .. 59 J8   47 40N   34 40 E
Margaret →, *Australia* .... 124 C4   18   9 S 125 41 E
Margaret Bay, *Canada* 142 C3   51 20N 127 35W
Margaret L., *Canada* 142 B5   58 56N 115 25W
Margaret River, *Australia* ...... 125 F2   33 57 S 115   4 E
Margarita, I. de, *Venezuela* 169 A5   11   0N   64   0W
Margarítion, *Greece* .... 48 B2   39 22N   20 26 E
Margaritovo, *Russia* .... 70 C7   43 25N 134 45 E
Margate, *S. Africa* .... 117 E5   30 50 S   30 20 E
Margate, *U.K.* .... 21 F9   51 23N   1 23 E
Margate, *U.S.A.* 153 J9   26 15N   80 12W
Margeride, Mts. de la, *France* ... 28 D7   44 43N   3 38 E
Margherita, *India* .... 90 B5   27 16N   95 40 E
Margherita di Savóia, *Italy* ..... 47 A9   41 22N   16   9 E
Margherita Pk., *Uganda* .... 118 B3   0 22N   29 51 E
Marghilon = Margilan, *Uzbekistan* . 65 C5   40 27N   71 42 E
Marghita, *Romania* .... 52 C7   47 22N   22 22 E
Margilan, *Uzbekistan* .... 65 C5   40 27N   71 42 E
Margonin, *Poland* .... 55 F4   52 58N   17   5 E
Margosatubig, *Phil.* .... 81 H4   7 34N 123 10 E
Mãrgow, Dasht-e, *Afghan.* ...... 91 C1   30 40N   62 30 E
Marguerite, *Canada* 142 C4   52 30N 122 25W
Marhanets, *Ukraine* .... 59 J8   47 40N   34 40 E
Marhoum, *Algeria* 111 B4   34 27N   0 11W
Mari, *Papua N. G.* .... 132 E1   9 11 S 141 42 E
Mari El □, *Russia* .... 60 B8   56 30N   48   0 E
Mari Indus, *Pakistan* .... 92 C4   32 57N   71 34 E
Mari Republic = Mari El □, *Russia* . 60 B8   56 30N   48   0 E
María, Sa. de, *Spain* 41 H2   37 39N   2 14W
Maria Aurora, *Phil.* .... 80 D3   15 48N 121 28 E
María Elena, *Chile* .... 174 A2   22 18 S   69 40W
María Grande, *Argentina* .... 174 C4   31 45 S   59 55W
Maria I., *N. Terr., Australia* .... 126 A2   14 52 S 135 45 E
Maria I., *Tas., Australia* .... 127 D4   42 35 S 148   0 E
Maria Island Nat. Park △, *Australia* . 127 D4   42 38 S 148   5 E
Maria Theresiopel = Subotica,
   Serbia, Yug. .... 52 D4   46   6N   19 39 E
Maria van Diemen, C., *N.Z.* .... 130 A1   34 29 S 172 40 E
Mariager, *Denmark* .... 17 H3   56 40N   9 59 E
Mariager Fjord, *Denmark* .... 17 H4   56 42N   10 19 E
Mariakani, *Kenya* .... 118 C4   3 50 S   39 27 E
Mariala Nat. Park △, *Australia* ... 127 A4   25 57 S 145   2 E
Mariana, *Australia* .... 126 K6   31   9 S 148 57 E
Marian L., *Canada* 142 A5   63   0N 116 15W
Mariana Trench, *Pac. Oc.* ...... 62 H18   13   0N 145   0 E
Marianao, *Cuba* 164 B3   23   8N   82 24W
Mariani, *India* .... 90 B5   26 39N   94 19 E
Marianna, *Ark., U.S.A.* 155 H9   34 46N   90 46W
Marianna, *Fla., U.S.A.* 152 E4   30 46N   85 14W
Mariannelund, *Sweden* .... 17 G9   57 37N   15 35 E
Mariánské Láznĕ, *Czech Rep.* .... 34 B5   49 58N   12 41 E
Marias →, *U.S.A.* 158 C8   47 56N 110 30W
Mariato, Punta, *Panama* 164 E3   7 12N   80 52W
Mariazell, *Austria* .... 34 D8   47 47N   15 19 E
Ma'rib, *Yemen* .... 98 D4   15 25N   45 21 E
Maribo, *Denmark* .... 17 K5   54 48N   11 30 E
Maribor, *Slovenia* .... 45 B12   46 36N   15 40 E
Maricaban I., *Phil.* .... 80 E3   13 39N 120 53 E
Marico →, *Africa* .... 116 C4   23 35 S   26 57 E
Maricopa, *Ariz., U.S.A.* 159 K7   33   4N 112   3W
Maricopa, *Calif., U.S.A.* 161 K7   35   4N 119 24W
Marîdî, *Sudan* .... 107 G2   4 55N   29 25 E
Marîdî, Wadi →, *Sudan* .... 107 F2   6 15N   29 21 E
Marié →, *Brazil* .... 168 D4   0 27 S   66 26W
Marie Byrd Land, *Antarctica* .... 5 D14   79 30 S 125   0W
Marie-Galante, *Guadeloupe* ..... 164 b   15 56N   61 16W
Mariecourt = Kangiqsujuaq, *Canada* . 139 B12   61 10N   72   0W
Mariefred, *Sweden* .... 16 E11   59 15N   17 12 E
Marieholm, *Sweden* .... 17 J7   55 53N   13 10 E
Mariembourg, *Belgium* .... 24 D4   50   6N   4 31 E
Marienbad = Mariánské Láznĕ,
   Czech Rep. .... 34 B5   49 58N   12 41 E
Marienberg, *Germany* .... 30 E9   50 39N   13   9 E
Marienburg = Malbork, *Poland* ... 54 D6   54   3N   19   1 E
Mariental, *Namibia* .... 116 C2   24 36 S   18   0 E
Marienville, *U.S.A.* 150 E5   41 28N   79   8W
Mariestad, *Sweden* .... 17 F7   58 43N   13 50 E
Marietta, *Ga., U.S.A.* 152 B3   33 57N   84 33W
Marietta, *Ohio, U.S.A.* 148 F5   39 25N   81 27W
Marieville, *Canada* 151 A11   45 26N   73 10W
Mariga →, *Nigeria* .... 113 C6   9 40N   5 55 E
Marignane, *France* .... 29 E9   43 25N   5 13 E
Marigny, *France* .... 32 D3   46   6N   6 31 E
Marihatag, *Phil.* .... 81 G6   8 48N 126 18 E
Mariinsk, *Russia* .... 66 D9   56 10N   87 20 E
Mariinskiy Posad, *Russia* .... 60 B8   56 10N   47 45 E
Marijampolé, *Lithuania* .... 15 J20   54 33N   23 19 E
Marijampolés □, *Lithuania* ...... 54 D10   54 34N   23 21 E
Marília, *Brazil* .... 175 A6   22 13 S   50   0W
Marimba, *Angola* .... 115 D3   8 28 S   17   8 E
Marín, *Spain* 42 C2   42 23N   8 42W
Marina, *U.S.A.* 160 J5   36 41N 121 48W
Marinduque, *Phil.* .... 79 B6   13 25N 122   0 E
Marinduque □, *Phil.* .... 80 E4   13 18N 122   0 E
Marine City, *U.S.A.* 150 D2   42 43N   82 30W
Marineland, *U.S.A.* 152 F8   29 40N   81 13W
Marineo, *Italy* .... 46 E6   37 57N   13 25 E
Marinette, *U.S.A.* 148 C2   45   6N   87 38W
Maringá, *Brazil* .... 175 A5   23 26 S   52   2W
Maringa →, *Dem. Rep. of the Congo* . 114 B3   1 14N   19 48 E
Marinha Grande, *Portugal* 42 F2   39 45N   8 56W
Marino, *Italy* .... 45 G9   41 46N   12 39 E
Marion, *Ala., U.S.A.* 149 J2   32 38N   87 19W
Marion, *Ill., U.S.A.* 155 G10   37 44N   88 56W
Marion, *Ind., U.S.A.* 157 D11   40 32N   85 40W
Marion, *Iowa, U.S.A.* 156 B5   42   2N   91 36W
Marion, *Kans., U.S.A.* 154 F6   38 21N   97   1W
Marion, *N.C., U.S.A.* 149 H5   35 41N   82   1W
Marion, *Ohio, U.S.A.* 157 D13   40 35N   83   8W
Marion, *S.C., U.S.A.* 149 H6   34 11N   79 24W
Marion, *Va., U.S.A.* 149 G5   36 50N   81 31W
Marion, *L., U.S.A.* 152 B9   33 28N   80 10W
Marion Bay, *Australia* .... 128 C2   35 12 S 136 59 E
Marion I., *Ind. Oc.* .... 121 J2   47   0 S   38   0 E
Maripa, *Venezuela* .... 169 B4   7 26 S   65   9W
Maripasoula, *Fr. Guiana* 169 C7   3 40N   54   4W
Mariposa, *U.S.A.* 160 H7   37 29N 119 58W
Mariscal Estigarribia, *Paraguay* .. 174 A3   22   3 S   60 40W
Maritime Alps = Maritimes, Alpes,
   Europe .... 29 D11   44 10N   7 10 E
Maritimes, Alpes, *Europe* ...... 29 D11   44 10N   7 10 E
Maritsa = Évros →, *Greece* ..... 100 B2   41 40N   26 34 E
Maritsá, *Greece* .... 49 C10   36 22N   28   8 E
Marium, Mt., *Vanuatu* .... 133 F6   16 15 S 168   7 E
Mariupol, *Ukraine* .... 59 J9   47 5N   37 31 E
Mariusa, Parque Nac. △, *Venezuela* . 165 E7   9 24N   61 27W
Marīvān, *Iran* .... 101 E12   35 30N   46 25 E
Mariveles, *Phil.* .... 80 D3   14 26N 120 29 E
Marj 'Uyūn, *Lebanon* .... 103 B4   33 20N   35 35 E
Marjan = Wazikhwah, *Afghan.* ... 91 B3   32 11N   68 21 E
Mark Twain L., *U.S.A.* 156 F9   39 28N   91 55W
Marka = Merca, *Somali Rep.* .... 120 D2   1 48N   44 50 E
Marka, *Si. Arabia* .... 106 D5   18 14N   41 19 E
Markam, *China* .... 76 C2   29 42N   98 38 E
Markapur, *India* .... 95 G4   15 44N   79 19 E

Markaryd, *Sweden* .... 17 H7   56 28N   13 35 E
Markat, *Albania* .... 38 B10   39 44N   20 12 E
Markdale, *Canada* 150 B4   44 19N   80 39W
Marked Tree, *U.S.A.* 155 H9   35 32N   90 25W
Markelsdorfer Huk, *Germany* .... 30 A7   54 33N   11   4 E
Market Drayton, *U.K.* 20 E5   52 54N   2 29W
Market Harborough, *U.K.* 21 E7   52 29N   0 55W
Market Rasen, *U.K.* 20 D7   53 24N   0 20W
Markham, *Canada* 150 C5   43 52N   79 16W
Markham →, *Papua N. G.* ...... 132 D4   6 41 S 147   2 E
Markham, Mt., *Antarctica* ...... 7 E11   83   0 S 164   0 E
Marki, *Poland* .... 55 F8   52 20N   21   2 E
Märkische Schweiz, Naturpark △,
   Germany .... 30 C10   52 34N   14   2 E
Markit, *China* .... 65 D8   38 53N   77 35 E
Markkleeberg, *Germany* .... 30 D8   51 16N   12 23 E
Markleeville, *U.S.A.* 160 G7   38 42N 119 47W
Markounda, *C.A.R.* .... 114 A3   7 39N   16 55 E
Markoupoulon, *Greece* .... 48 D5   37 53N   23 57 E
Markovac, *Serbia, Yug.* .... 50 B5   44 14N   21   7 E
Markovo, *Russia* .... 67 C17   64 40N 170 24 E
Markoye, *Burkina Faso* .... 113 C5   14 39N   0   2 E
Marks, *Russia* .... 60 E8   51 45N   46 50 E
Marksville, *U.S.A.* 155 K8   31   8N   92   4W
Markt Schwaben, *Germany* ...... 31 G7   48 11N   11 52 E
Marktoberdorf, *Germany* .... 31 H6   47 45N   10 37 E
Marktredwitz, *Germany* .... 31 E8   50   1N   12   5 E
Marl, *Germany* .... 30 D3   51 39N   7   4 E
Marla, *Australia* .... 127 D1   27 19 S 133 33 E
Marlbank, *Canada* 150 B7   44 26N   77   6W
Marlboro, *Mass., U.S.A.* 151 D13   42 19N   71 33W
Marlboro, *N.Y., U.S.A.* 151 E11   41 36N   73 59W
Marlborough, *Australia* .... 126 C4   22 46 S 149 52 E
Marlborough, *U.K.* 21 F6   51 25N   1 43W
Marlborough □, *N.Z.* .... 131 B8   41 40 S 173 50 E
Marlborough Downs, *U.K.* 21 F6   51 27N   1 53W
Marle, *France* .... 27 C10   49 43N   3 47 E
Marlin, *U.S.A.* 155 K6   31 18N   96 54W
Marlow, *Germany* .... 30 A8   54   9N   12 33 E
Marlow, *U.K.* 21 F7   51 34N   0 46W
Marlow, *U.S.A.* 155 H6   34 39N   97 58W
Marly, *Switz.* .... 32 C4   46 47N   7 10 E
Marmagao, *India* .... 95 G1   15 25N   73 56 E
Marmande, *France* .... 28 D4   44 30N   0 10 E
Marmara, *Turkey* .... 51 F11   40 35N   27 34 E
Marmara, Sea of = Marmara Denizi,
   Turkey .... 51 F12   40 45N   28 15 E
Marmara Denizi, *Turkey* .... 51 F12   40 45N   28 15 E
Marmara Gölü, *Turkey* .... 49 C10   38 37N   28   2 E
Marmaris, *Turkey* .... 49 E10   36 50N   28 14 E
Marmaris Limanı, *Turkey* ...... 49 E10   36 50N   28 19 E
Marmelos →, *Brazil* .... 173 B5   6   6 S   61 46W
Marmion, Mt., *Australia* .... 125 E2   29 16 S 119 50 E
Marmion L., *Canada* 140 C1   48 55N   91 20W
Marmolada, Mte., *Italy* .... 45 B8   46 26N   11 51 E
Marmolejo, *Spain* 43 G6   38   3N   4 13W
Marmora, *Canada* 150 B7   44 28N   77 41W
Mármora, La, *Italy* .... 46 C2   39 59N   9 20 E
Marnay, *France* .... 27 E12   47 16N   5 48 E
Marne, *Germany* .... 30 B5   53 56N   9   2 E
Marne □, *France* .... 27 D11   48 50N   4 10 E
Marne →, *France* .... 27 D9   48 48N   2 24 E
Marneuli, *Georgia* .... 61 K7   41 30N   44 48 E
Marnia = Maghnia, *Algeria* 111 B4   34 50N   1 43W
Marnoo, *Australia* .... 128 D5   36 40 S 142 52 E
Maro, *Chad* .... 109 G3   8 30N   19   0 E
Maro Reef, *U.S.A.* 145 F9   25 25N 170 35W
Maroa, *U.S.A.* 156 D8   40   2N   88 57W
Maroa, *Venezuela* 168 C4   2 43N   67 33W
Maroala, *Madag.* .... 117 B8   15 23 S   47 59 E
Maroantsetra, *Madag.* .... 117 B8   15 26 S   49 44 E
Maroelaboom, *Namibia* .... 116 B2   19 15 S   18 53 E
Marofandilia, *Madag.* .... 117 C7   20   7 S   44 34 E
Marojejy, Réserve de △, *Madag.* .. 117 A8   14 26 S   49 21 E
Marolambo, *Madag.* .... 117 C8   20   2 S   48   7 E
Maromandia, *Madag.* .... 117 A8   14 13 S   48   5 E
Maromokotro, *Madag.* .... 117 A8   14   0 S   49   0 E
Marondera, *Zimbabwe* .... 119 F3   18   5 S   31 42 E
Maroni →, *Fr. Guiana* 169 B7   5 30N   54   0W
Marónia, *Greece* .... 51 F9   40 53N   25 30 E
Maronne →, *France* .... 28 C5   45   5N   1 56 E
Maroochydore, *Australia* .... 127 D5   26 29 S 153   5 E
Maroona, *Australia* .... 128 D5   37 27 S 142 54 E
Maros, *Indonesia* .... 82 C1   5   0 S 119 34 E
Maros →, *Hungary* .... 52 D5   46 15N   20 13 E
Marosakoa, *Madag.* .... 117 B8   15 26 S   46 38 E
Maroseranana, *Madag.* .... 117 B8   18 32 S   48 51 E
Maróstica, *Italy* .... 45 C8   45 44N   11 40 E
Marotandrano, *Madag.* .... 117 B8   16 10 S   48 50 E
Marotaolano, *Madag.* .... 117 A8   12 47 S   49 15 E
Maroua, *Cameroon* .... 113 C7   10 40N   14 20 E
Marovato, *Madag.* .... 117 B8   15 48 S   48   5 E
Marovoay, *Madag.* .... 117 B8   16   6 S   46 39 E
Marowijne □, *Suriname* 169 C7   4   0N   55   0W
Marowijne →, *Suriname* 169 B7   5 45N   53 58W
Marquard, *S. Africa* .... 116 D4   28 40 S   27 28 E
Marquesas Is. = Marquises, Is.,
   Pac. Oc. .... 135 H14   9 30 S 140   0W
Marquesas Keys, *U.S.A.* 153 L7   24 35N   82 10W
Marquette, *U.S.A.* 148 B2   46 33N   87 24W
Marquis, *St. Lucia* .... 165 f   14   2N   60 54W
Marquise, *France* .... 27 B8   50 50N   1 40 E
Marquises, Is., *Pac. Oc.* .... 135 H14   9 30 S 140   0W
Marra, Gebel, *Sudan* .... 107 F2   7 20N   27 35 E
Marra Cr. →, *Australia* .... 129 A7   30 5 S 147 5 E
Marra Marra Nat. Park △, *Australia* . 129 B9   33 30 S 151   4 E
Marracuene, *Mozam.* .... 117 D5   25 45 S   32 35 E
Marradi, *Italy* .... 45 D8   44   4N   11 37 E
Marrakech, *Morocco* 110 B3   31   9N   8   0W
Marratxi, *Spain* .... 38 B3   39 39N   2 48 E
Marrawah, *Australia* .... 127 D3   39   5 S 144 42 E
Marrecas, Serra das, *Brazil* ..... 170 C3   9   0 S   41 0W
Marree, *Australia* .... 127 D2   29 39 S 138   1 E
Marrero, *U.S.A.* 155 L9   29 54N   90   6W
Marrimane, *Mozam.* .... 117 C5   22 58 S   33 34 E
Marromeu, *Mozam.* .... 117 B6   18 15 S   36 25 E
Marromeu, Reserva de △, *Mozam.* . 117 B6   19 15 S   36   0 E
Marroquí, Punta, *Spain* 43 K5   36   0N   5 37W
Marrowie Cr. →, *Australia* ..... 129 B6   33 23 S 145 40 E
Marrubane, *Mozam.* .... 119 F4   18   0 S   37   0 E
Marrúbiu, *Italy* .... 46 C1   39 40N   8 35 E
Marrupa, *Mozam.* .... 119 E4   13   8 S   37 30 E
Mars B., *Ascension I.* .... 9 g   7 59 S   14 24W
Mars Hill, *U.S.A.* 149 B12   46 31N   67 52W
Marsá 'Alam, *Egypt* .... 106 C3   25   5N   34 54 E
Marsá el Brega, *Libya* .... 108 B3   30 24N   19 37 E
Marsá Matrûh, *Egypt* .... 106 A2   31 19N   27   9 E
Marsá Sha'b, *Sudan* .... 106 C4   22 52N   35 47 E
Marsá Susah, *Libya* .... 108 A4   32 52N   21 59 E
Marsabit, *Kenya* .... 118 B4   2 18N   38   0 E
Marsabit Nat. Park and Reserve △,
   Kenya .... 118 B4   2 23N   37 56 E
Marsala, *Italy* .... 46 E5   37 48N   12 26 E
Marsalforn, *Malta* .... 38 F1   36   4N   14 16 E
Mârşani, *Romania* .... 53 F9   44   1N   24   1 E
Marsaskala, *Malta* .... 38 F8   35 52N   14 34 E
Marsberg, *Germany* .... 30 D4   51 28N   8 52 E
Marsciano, *Italy* .... 45 F9   42 54N   12 20 E
Marsden, *Australia* .... 128 B10   33 47 S 147 32 E
Marseillan, *France* .... 28 E7   43 23N   3 31 E
Marseille, *France* .... 29 E9   43 18N   5 23 E

Marseille ✈ (MRS), *France* ...... 29 E9   43 26N   5 14 E
Marseilles = Marseille, *France* ... 29 E9   43 18N   5 23 E
Marseilles, *U.S.A.* 157 C8   41 20N   88 43W
Marsh I., *U.S.A.* 155 L9   29 34N   91 53W
Marshall = Fortuna Ledge, *U.S.A.* . 144 F7   61 53N 162   5W
Marshall, *Liberia* 112 D2   6   8N   10 22W
Marshall, *Ark., U.S.A.* 155 H8   35 55N   92 38W
Marshall, *Ill., U.S.A.* 157 E9   39 23N   87 42W
Marshall, *Mich., U.S.A.* 157 B12   42 16N   84 58W
Marshall, *Minn., U.S.A.* 154 C7   44 25N   95 45W
Marshall, *Mo., U.S.A.* 156 F8   39   7N   93 12W
Marshall, *Tex., U.S.A.* 155 J7   32 33N   94 23W
Marshall →, *Australia* .... 126 C2   22 59 S 136 59 E
Marshall, C., *Ecuador* .... 172 a   0   1 S   91 12W
Marshall Bennett Is., *Papua N. G.* . 132 E6   8 50 S 151 55 E
Marshall Is. ■, *Pac. Oc.* .... 134 G9   9 0N 171   0 E
Marshalltown, *U.S.A.* 156 B4   42   3N   92 55W
Marshallville, *U.S.A.* 152 C6   32 27N   83 56W
Marshbrook, *Zimbabwe* .... 117 B5   18 33 S   31   9 E
Marshfield, *Mo., U.S.A.* 155 G8   37 15N   92 54W
Marshfield, *Vt., U.S.A.* 151 B12   44 20N   72 20W
Marshfield, *Wis., U.S.A.* 154 C9   44 40N   90 10W
Marshūn, *Iran* .... 97 B6   36 19N   49 23 E
Mársico Nuovo, *Italy* .... 47 B8   40 25N   15 44 E
Märsta, *Sweden* .... 16 E11   59 37N   17 52 E
Marstal, *Denmark* .... 17 K4   54 51N   10 30 E
Marstrand, *Sweden* .... 17 G5   57 53N   11 35 E
Mart, *U.S.A.* 155 K6   31 33N   96 50W
Marta →, *Italy* .... 45 F8   42 14N   11 42 E
Martaban, *Burma* .... 90 G6   16 30N   97 35 E
Martaban, G. of, *Burma* .... 90 G6   16   5N   96 30 E
Martano, *Italy* .... 47 B11   40 12N   18 18 E
Martapura, *Kalimantan, Indonesia* . 85 C4   3 22 S 114 47 E
Martapura, *Sumatera, Indonesia* .. 84 C2   4 19 S 104 22 E
Marte, *Nigeria* .... 113 C7   12 23N   13 46 E
Martel, *France* .... 28 D5   44 57N   1 37 E
Martelange, *Belgium* .... 24 E5   49 49N   5 43 E
Martés, Sierra, *Spain* 41 F4   39 20N   1   0W
Martfû, *Hungary* .... 52 C5   47   1N   20 17 E
Marthaguy Cr. →, *Australia* .... 129 A7   30 16 S 147 35 E
Marthapal, *India* .... 94 E5   19 20 S   81 37 E
Martha's Vineyard, *U.S.A.* 151 E14   41 25N   70 38W
Martigné-Ferchaud, *France* 26 E5   47 50N   1 20W
Martigny, *Switz.* .... 32 D4   46   6N   7   3 E
Martigues, *France* .... 29 E9   43 24N   5   4 E
Martil, *Morocco* 110 A3   35 36N   5 15W
Martin, *Slovak Rep.* .... 35 B11   49 6N   18 58 E
Martin, *S. Dak., U.S.A.* 154 D4   43 11N 101 44W
Martin, *Tenn., U.S.A.* 155 G10   36 21N   88 51W
Martín →, *Spain* 40 D4   41 18N   0 19W
Martin, *L., U.S.A.* 152 C4   32 41N   85 55W
Martin Pt., *U.S.A.* 144 A12   70   8N 143 16W
Martina Franca, *Italy* .... 47 B10   40 42N   17 20 E
Martinborough, *N.Z.* .... 130 H4   41 14 S 175 29 E
Martinez, *Calif., U.S.A.* 160 G4   38   1N 122   8W
Martinez, *Ga., U.S.A.* 149 J4   33 31N   82   4W
Martinho Campos, *Brazil* ...... 171 E2   19 20 S   45 13W
Martinique ☑, *W. Indies* ...... 165 c   14 40N   61   0W
Martinique Passage, *W. Indies* ... 165 C7   15 15N   61   0W
Martínon, *Greece* .... 48 C5   38 35N   23 12 E
Martinópolis, *Brazil* .... 175 A5   22 11 S   51 12W
Martin's Bay, *Barbados* .... 165 g   13 12N   59 29W
Martins Ferry, *U.S.A.* 150 F4   40   6N   80 44W
Martinsberg, *Austria* .... 34 C8   48 22N   15   9 E
Martinsburg, *Pa., U.S.A.* 150 F6   40 19N   78 20W
Martinsburg, *W. Va., U.S.A.* 148 F7   39 27N   77 58W
Martinsicuro, *Italy* .... 45 F10   42 54N   13 54 E
Martinsville, *Ill., U.S.A.* 157 E9   39 20N   87 53W
Martinsville, *Ind., U.S.A.* 157 E10   39 26N   86 25W
Martinsville, *Va., U.S.A.* 149 G6   36 41N   79 52W
Marton, *N.Z.* .... 130 G4   40   4 S 175 23 E
Martorell, *Spain* .... 40 D6   41 28N   1 56 E
Martos, *Spain* 43 H7   37 44N   3 58W
Martūbah, *Libya* .... 108 B4   32 25N   22 45 E
Martuk, *Kazakhstan* .... 52 E6   50 46N   56 31 E
Marturi, *Armenia* .... 61 K7   40   8N   45 20 E
Maru, *Nigeria* .... 113 C6   12 22N   6 22 E
Marudi, *Malaysia* .... 85 B4   4 11N 114 19 E
Maruf, *Afghan.* .... 91 C2   31 30N   67   6 E
Marugame, *Japan* .... 72 C3   34 15N 133 40 E
Marui = Pagwi, *Papua N. G.* .... 132 C2   4   3 S 143   2 E
Maruim, *Brazil* .... 170 D4   10 45 S   37   5W
Marulan, *Australia* .... 129 C9   34 43 S 150   3 E
Marunga, *Angola* .... 116 B3   17 28 S   20   2 E
Marungu, Mts., *Dem. Rep. of
   the Congo* .... 118 D3   7 30 S   30   0 E
Maruoka, *Japan* .... 73 A8   36   9N 136 16 E
Marv Dasht, *Iran* .... 97 D7   29 50N   52 40 E
Marvast, *Iran* .... 97 D7   30 30N   54 15 E
Marvejols, *France* .... 28 D7   44 33N   3 19 E
Marvel Loch, *Australia* .... 125 F2   31 28 S 119 29 E
Marwar, *India* .... 92 G5   25 43N   73 45 E
Mary, *Turkmenistan* .... 64 F7   37 40N   61 50 E
Mary Esther, *U.S.A.* 153 E3   30 27N   86 38W
Maryborough = Port Laoise, *Ireland* . 23 C4   53   2N   7 18W
Maryborough, *Queens., Australia* . 127 D5   25 31 S 152 37 E
Maryborough, *Vic., Australia* .... 128 D5   37   0 S 143 44 E
Maryfield, *Canada* 143 D8   49 50N 101 35W
Maryland □, *U.S.A.* 148 F7   39   0N   76 30W
Maryland Junction, *Zimbabwe* ... 119 F3   17 45 S   30 31 E
Maryport, *U.K.* 20 C4   54 44N   3 28W
Mary's Harbour, *Canada* 141 B8   52 18N   55 51W
Marystown, *Canada* 141 C8   47 10N   55 10W
Marysvale, *U.S.A.* 159 G7   38 27N 112 14W
Marysville, *Calif., U.S.A.* 160 F5   39   9N 121 35W
Marysville, *Kans., U.S.A.* 154 F6   39 51N   96 39W
Marysville, *Mich., U.S.A.* 150 D2   42 54N   82 29W
Marysville, *Ohio, U.S.A.* 157 D13   40 14N   83 22W
Marysville, *Wash., U.S.A.* 160 B4   48   3N 122 11W
Maryville, *Mo., U.S.A.* 156 E7   40 21N   94 52W
Maryville, *Tenn., U.S.A.* 149 H4   35 46N   83 58W
Marzo, Punta, *Colombia* 168 B2   6 50N   77 42W
Marzuq, *Libya* .... 108 C2   25 53N   13 57 E
Marzuq □, *Libya* .... 108 D3   25   0N   16   0 E
Marzûq, Idehan, *Libya* .... 108 D2   24 50N   13 51 E
Masahunga, *Tanzania* .... 118 C3   2   6 S   33 18 E
Masai, *Malaysia* .... 87 d   1 29N 103 53 E
Masai Mara Nat. Reserve △, *Kenya* . 118 C4   1 25 S   35   5 E
Masai Steppe, *Tanzania* .... 118 C4   4 30 S   36 30 E
Masaka, *Uganda* .... 118 C3   0 21 S   31 45 E
Masalembo, Kepulauan, *Indonesia* . 85 D5   5 35 S 114 30 E
Masalima, Kepulauan, *Indonesia* .. 85 D5   5 4 S 117 5 E
Masallı, *Azerbaijan* .... 101 C13   39   2N   48 40 E
Masamba, *Indonesia* .... 82 B2   2 30 S 120 15 E
Masan, S. Korea .... 75 G15   35 11N 128 32 E
Masandam, Ra's, *Oman* .... 97 E8   26 30N   56 30 E
Masasi, *Tanzania* .... 119 E4   10 45 S   38 52 E
Masaya, *Nic.* 164 D2   12   0N   86   7W
Masba, *Nigeria* .... 113 C7   11 35N   13   1 E
Masbate, *Phil.* .... 80 E4   12 21N 123 36 E
Masbate □, *Phil.* .... 80 E4   12 30N 123 30 E
Masbate Pass, *Phil.* .... 80 E4   12 30N 123 40 E
Mascara, *Algeria* .... 111 A5   35 26N   0 6 E
Mascarene Is., *Ind. Oc.* .... 121 G4   22   0 S   55   0 E
Mascota, *Mexico* 162 C4   20 30N 104 50W
Mascoutah, *U.S.A.* 156 F7   38 29N   89 48W
Masela, *Indonesia* .... 83 C4   8   9 S 129 51 E
Maseru, *Lesotho* .... 116 D4   29 18 S   27 30 E
Masfjorden, *Norway* .... 18 D2   60 48N   5 18 E

Mashaba, *Zimbabwe* .... 119 G3   20   2 S   30 29 E
Mashābih, *Si. Arabia* .... 96 E3   25 35N   36 30 E
Mashan, *China* .... 76 F7   23 40N 108 11 E
Mashar, *Sudan* .... 107 F2   9 16N   26 51 E
Mashatu Game Reserve △, *Botswana* . 117 C4   22   5 S   29   5 E
Mashegu, *Nigeria* .... 113 D6   10   0N   5 35 E
Masherbrum, *Pakistan* .... 93 B7   35 38N   76 18 E
Mashhad, *Iran* .... 97 B8   36 20N   59 35 E
Mashi, *Nigeria* .... 113 C6   13   0N   7 54 E
Mashiki, *Japan* .... 72 E2   32 51N 130 53 E
Mashiz, *Iran* .... 97 D8   29 56N   56 37 E
Mashkal, →, *Pakistan* .... 91 C2   26   2N   65 40 E
Mashkel, Hāmūn-i-, *Pakistan* .... 91 C1   28 20N   62 56 E
Mashki Chāh, *Pakistan* .... 91 C1   29 5N   62 30 E
Mashonaland Central □, *Zimbabwe* . 117 B5   17 30 S   31   0 E
Mashonaland East □, *Zimbabwe* .. 117 B5   18   0 S   32   0 E
Mashonaland West □, *Zimbabwe* .. 117 B4   17 30 S   29 30 E
Mashrakh, *India* .... 93 F11   26   7N   84 48 E
Mashtaga = Maştağa, *Azerbaijan* .. 61 K10   40 35N   49 57 E
Masi Manimba, *Dem. Rep. of
   the Congo* .... 115 C3   4 40 S   17 54 E
Masibi, *Angola* .... 115 E4   11   6 S   22 41 E
Masindi, *Uganda* .... 118 B3   1 40N   31 43 E
Masindi Port, *Uganda* .... 118 B3   1 43N   32   2 E
Masinloc, *Phil.* .... 80 D2   15 32N 119 57 E
Maşīrah, *Oman* .... 99 B7   21   0N   58 50 E
Maşīrah, Khalīj, *Oman* .... 99 B7   20 10N   58 10 E
Maşīrah, Tur'at, *Oman* .... 99 B7   20 30N   58 40 E
Masisea, *Peru* .... 172 B3   8 35 S   74 22W
Masisi, *Dem. Rep. of the Congo* .. 118 C2   1 23 S   28 49 E
Masjed Soleyman, *Iran* .... 97 D6   31 55N   49 18 E
Mask, L., *Ireland* 23 C2   53 36N   9 22W
Maskelyne Is., *Vanuatu* .... 133 F5   16 32 S 167 49 E
Maski, *India* .... 95 G3   15 56N   76 46 E
Maskin, *Oman* .... 97 F8   23 30N   56 50 E
Maslen Nos, *Bulgaria* .... 51 D11   42 18N   27 48 E
Maslinica, *Croatia* .... 45 E13   43 24N   16 13 E
Maşna'ah, *Yemen* .... 99 D5   14 27N   48 17 E
Masnou = El Masnou, *Spain* .... 40 D7   41 28N   2 20 E
Masoala, Parc Nat. de △, *Madag.* . 117 B9   15 30 S   50 12 E
Masoala, Tanjon' i, *Madag.* ..... 117 B9   15 59 S   50 13 E
Masoarivo, *Madag.* .... 117 B7   19   3 S   44 19 E
Masohi = Amahai, *Indonesia* .... 83 C3   3 20 S 128 55 E
Masomeloka, *Madag.* .... 117 C8   20 17 S   48 37 E
Mason, *Mich., U.S.A.* 157 B12   42 35N   84 27W
Mason, *Nev., U.S.A.* 160 G7   38 56N 119   38W
Mason, *Ohio, U.S.A.* 157 E12   39 22N   84 19W
Mason, *Tex., U.S.A.* 155 K5   30 45N   99 14W
Mason B., *N.Z.* .... 131 G2   46 55 S 167 45 E
Mason City, *Ill., U.S.A.* 156 D7   40 12N   89 42W
Mason City, *Iowa, U.S.A.* 156 A3   43   9N   93 12W
Maspalomas, *Canary Is.* 9 e1   27 46N   15 35W
Maspalomas, Pta., *Canary Is.* ... 9 e1   27 43N   15 36W
Masqat, *Oman* .... 99 B7   23 37N   58 36 E
Massa, *Congo* .... 114 C3   3 45 S   15 29 E
Massa, *Italy* .... 44 D7   44   1N   10   9 E
Massa, O. →, *Morocco* 110 B3   30   2N   9 40W
Massa Maríttima, *Italy* .... 44 E7   43   3N   10 52 E
Massachusetts □, *U.S.A.* 151 D13   42 30N   72   0W
Massachusetts B., *U.S.A.* 151 D14   42 20N   70 50W
Massafra, *Italy* .... 47 B10   40 35N   17   7 E
Massaguet, *Chad* .... 109 F3   12 28N   15 26 E
Massakory, *Chad* .... 109 F3   13   0N   15 49 E
Massanella, *Spain* .... 38 B3   39 48N   2 51 E
Massangano, *Angola* .... 115 D3   9 40 S   14 13 E
Massangena, *Mozam.* .... 117 C5   21 34 S   33   0 E
Massango, *Angola* .... 115 D3   8   1 S   16 10 E
Massapê, *Brazil* .... 170 B3   3 31 S   40 19W
Massat, *France* .... 28 F5   42 53N   1 21 E
Massawa = Mitsiwa, *Eritrea* .... 107 D4   15 35N   39 25 E
Massena, *U.S.A.* 151 B10   44 56N   74 54W
Massénya, *Chad* .... 109 F3   11 21N   16   9 E
Masset, *Canada* 142 C2   54   2N 132 10W
Masseube, *France* .... 28 E4   43 25N   0 34 E
Massiac, *France* .... 28 C7   45 15N   3 11 E
Massiah Street, *Barbados* ...... 165 g   13   9N   59 29W
Massif Central, *France* .... 28 D7   44 55N   3   0 E
Massif des Bauges, Parc Naturel
   Régional du △, *France* .... 27 G13   45 40N   6 10 E
Massigui, *Mali* 112 C3   11 48N   6 50W
Massillon, *U.S.A.* 150 F3   40 48N   81 32W
Massima, *Gabon* .... 114 C2   1 27 S   11 33 E
Massine, O. →, *Algeria* .... 111 C5   36 13N   2 12 E
Massinga, *Mozam.* .... 117 C5   23 15 S   35 22 E
Massingir, *Mozam.* .... 117 C5   23 51 S   32 4 E
Mässlingen, *Sweden* .... 16 B6   62 40N   12 50 E
Masson, *Canada* 151 A9   45 32N   75 25W
Masson I., *Antarctica* .... 7 C7   66 10 S   93 20 E
Massoukita, *Gabon* .... 114 C1   1 37 S   9 56 E
Mastábah, *Si. Arabia* .... 61 K10   40 35N   49 57 E
Mastaga, *Azerbaijan* .... 61 K10   40 35N   49 57 E
Mastanli = Momchilgrad, *Bulgaria* . 51 F9   41 33N   25 23 E
Masterton, *N.Z.* .... 130 G4   40 56 S 175 39 E
Mastic, *U.S.A.* 151 F12   40 47N   72 54W
Mástikho, Ákra, *Greece* .... 49 C8   38 10N   26   2 E
Mastuj, *Pakistan* .... 93 A5   36 20N   72 36 E
Mastung, *Pakistan* .... 91 C2   29 50N   66 56 E
Mastūrah, *Si. Arabia* .... 98 B2   23   7N   38 52 E
Masty, *Belarus* .... 58 F3   53 27N   24 38 E
Masuda, *Japan* .... 72 C3   34 40N 131 51 E
Masuika, *Dem. Rep. of the Congo* . 115 D4   7 37 S   22 32 E
Masvingo, *Zimbabwe* .... 119 G3   20   8 S   30 49 E
Masvingo □, *Zimbabwe* .... 119 G3   21   0 S   31 30 E
Maswa Game Reserve △, *Tanzania* . 118 C3   2 58 S   34 19 E
Maşyāf, *Syria* .... 100 E7   35   4N   36 20 E
Maszewo, *Poland* .... 54 E2   53 29N   15   3 E
Mat →, *Albania* .... 38 B4   41 40N   19 35 E
Mata de São João, *Brazil* ...... 171 D4   12 31 S   38 17W
Mata Utu, Wall. & F. Is. .... 123 C15   13 17 S 176   8W
Matabeleland North □, *Zimbabwe* . 119 F2   19   0 S   28   0 E
Matabeleland South □, *Zimbabwe* . 119 G2   21   0 S   29   0 E
Mataboor, *Indonesia* .... 83 B5   1 41 S 138   3 E
Matachel →, *Spain* 43 G4   38 50N   6 17W
Matachewan, *Canada* 140 C3   47 56N   80 39W
Matacuni →, *Venezuela* .... 169 C4   3 27 S   65 49W
Matadi, *Dem. Rep. of the Congo* . 115 C2   5 52 S   13 31 E
Matagalpa, *Nic.* 164 D2   13   0N   85 58W
Matagami, *Canada* 140 C4   49 45N   77 34W
Matagami, L., *Canada* 140 C4   49 50N   77 40W
Matagorda B., *U.S.A.* 155 L6   28 40N   96   0W
Matagorda I., *U.S.A.* 155 L6   28 15N   96 30W
Mataguinao, *Phil.* .... 80 E5   12 5N 124 55 E
Matak, *Indonesia* .... 84 B3   3 18N 106 16 E
Matakana, *Australia* .... 129 B6   32 59 S 145 54 E
Matakana, *N.Z.* .... 130 C5   36 21 S 174 43 E
Matala, *Angola* .... 115 E3   14 46 S   15   4 E
Matala, *Greece* .... 39 F5   34 59N   24 45 E
Matalaque, *Peru* .... 172 D3   16 26 S   70 49W
Matale, *Sri Lanka* .... 95 L5   7 30N   80 37 E
Matam, *Senegal* 112 B2   15 34N   13 17W
Matamata, *N.Z.* .... 130 D4   37 48 S 175 47 E
Matameye, *Niger* .... 113 C6   13 26N   8 28 E
Matamoros, *Campeche, Mexico* .. 161 D6   18 2N 90 50W
Matamoros, *Coahuila, Mexico* ... 162 B4   25 33N 103 15W
Matamoros, *Tamaulipas, Mexico* .. 163 B5   25 50N 97 30W
Ma'tan as Sarra, *Libya* .... 109 D4   21 45N   22 0 E
Matana, Danau, *Indonesia* ..... 82 B2   2 28 S 121 20 E
Matandu →, *Tanzania* .... 119 D4   8 45 S   39 19 E
Matane, *Canada* 141 C6   48 50N   67 33W
Matang, *China* .... 76 E5   23 30N 104   7 E
Matankari, *Niger* .... 113 C5   13 46N   4   1 E
Matanomadh, *India* .... 92 H3   23 33N   68 57 E

Matanzas, Cuba **164 B3** 23 0N 81 40W
Matapa, Botswana .... **116 C3** 23 11 S 24 39 E
Matapan, C. = Taínaron, Ákra,
  Greece .... **48 E4** 36 22N 22 27 E
Matapédia, Canada **141 C6** 48 0N 66 59W
Matapo Nat. Park △, Zimbabwe .. **119 G2** 20 30 S 29 40 E
Matara, Sri Lanka .... **95 M5** 5 58N 80 30 E
Mataram, Indonesia .... **85 D5** 8 35 S 116 7 E
Mataranka, Australia .... **103 E1** 30 27N 32 44 E
Matarma, Râs, Egypt .... **103 E1** 30 27N 32 44 E
Mataró, Spain .... **40 D7** 41 32N 2 29 E
Matarraña →, Spain .... **40 D5** 41 14N 0 22 E
Mataruška Banja, Serbia, Yug. .. **50 C4** 43 40N 20 40 E
Matasa, Vanuatu .... **133 G6** 17 14 S 168 26 E
Matata, N.Z. .... **130 D5** 37 54 S 176 48 E
Matatiele, S. Africa .... **117 E4** 30 20 S 28 49 E
Mataura, N.Z. .... **131 G3** 46 11 S 168 51 E
Mataura →, N.Z. .... **131 G3** 46 34 S 168 44 E
Mataveri, Chile .... **172 b** 27 9 S 109 27W
Matehuala, Mexico **162 C4** 23 40N 100 40W
Mateira, Brazil .... **171 E1** 18 54 S 50 30W
Mateke Hills, Zimbabwe .... **119 G3** 21 48 S 31 0 E
Matelot, Trin. & Tob. **169 F9** 10 50N 61 7W
Matera, Italy .... **47 B9** 40 40N 16 36 E
Matese, Monti del, Italy ..... **47 A7** 41 27N 14 22 E
Matese, Parco ⌂, Italy .... **47 A7** 41 24N 14 23 E
Mátészalka, Hungary .... **52 C7** 47 58N 22 20 E
Matetsi, Zimbabwe .... **119 F2** 18 12 S 26 0 E
Mateur, Tunisia .... **108 A1** 37 0N 9 40 E
Matfors, Sweden .... **16 B11** 62 21N 17 2 E
Matha, France **28 C3** 45 52N 0 20W
Matheniko Game Reserve ⌂,
  Uganda .... **118 B3** 2 49N 34 27 E
Mathis, U.S.A. **155 L6** 28 6N 97 50W
Mathoura, Australia .... **129 C6** 35 50 S 144 55 E
Mathráki, Greece .... **38 B9** 39 48N 19 31 E
Mathura, India .... **92 F7** 27 30N 77 40 E
Mati, Phil. .... **81 H6** 6 55N 126 15 E
Matiakoali, Burkina Faso ..... **113 C5** 12 28N 1 2 E
Matiali, India .... **93 F13** 26 56N 88 49 E
Matías Romero, Mexico **163 D5** 16 53N 95 2W
Matibane, Mozam. .... **119 E5** 14 49 S 40 45 E
Matima, Botswana .... **116 C3** 20 15 S 24 26 E
Matinhos, Brazil .... **171 G2** 25 49 S 48 32W
Matiri Ra., N.Z. .... **131 B7** 41 38 S 172 20 E
Matjiesfontein, S. Africa .... **116 E3** 33 14 S 20 35 E
Matla →, India .... **93 J13** 21 40N 88 40 E
Matlamanyane, Botswana .... **116 B4** 19 33 S 25 57 E
Matli, Pakistan .... **92 G3** 25 2N 68 39 E
Matlock, U.K. **20 D6** 53 9N 1 33W
Matmata, Tunisia .... **108 B1** 33 37N 9 59 E
Matna, Sudan .... **107 E4** 13 49N 35 10 E
Matnog, Phil. .... **80 E5** 12 35N 124 5 E
Mato, Dem. Rep. of the Congo .. **115 D4** 8 1 S 24 24 E
Mato →, Venezuela **169 B4** 7 9N 65 7W
Mato, Serrania de, Venezuela .. **168 B4** 6 25N 65 25W
Mato Grosso □, Brazil .... **173 C6** 14 0 S 55 0W
Mato Grosso, Planalto do, Brazil .. **173 C7** 15 0 S 55 0W
Mato Grosso do Sul □, Brazil .. **173 D7** 18 0 S 55 0W
Mato Verde, Brazil .... **171 D1** 11 13 S 50 40W
Matobo Nat. Park = Matopo Nat.
  Park △, Zimbabwe .... **119 G2** 20 30 S 29 40 E
Matochkin Shar, Russia .... **66 B3** 73 10N 56 40 E
Matong, Papua N. G. .... **132 C6** 5 36 S 151 50 E
Matopo Hills, Zimbabwe .... **119 G2** 20 36 S 28 20 E
Matopos, Zimbabwe .... **119 G2** 20 20 S 28 29 E
Matosinhos, Portugal **42 D2** 41 11N 8 42W
Matour, France .... **27 F11** 46 19N 4 29 E
Matroosberg, S. Africa .... **116 E2** 33 23 S 19 40 E
Matsena, Nigeria .... **113 C7** 13 5N 10 5 E
Matsesta, Russia .... **61 J4** 43 34N 39 51 E
Matsu Tao, Taiwan .... **77 E13** 26 9N 119 56 E
Matsudo, Japan .... **73 B11** 35 47N 139 54 E
Matsue, Japan .... **72 B5** 35 25N 133 10 E
Matsum, Ko, Thailand .... **87 b** 9 22N 99 59 E
Matsumae, Japan .... **70 D10** 41 26N 140 7 E
Matsumoto, Japan .... **73 A10** 36 15N 138 0 E
Matsusaka, Japan .... **73 C8** 34 34N 136 32 E
Matsushima, Japan .... **72 E2** 32 30N 130 25 E
Matsuura, Japan .... **72 D1** 33 20N 129 49 E
Matsuyama, Japan .... **72 D4** 33 45N 132 45 E
Matsuzaki, Japan .... **73 C10** 34 43N 138 50 E
Mattagami →, Canada **140 B3** 50 43N 81 29W
Mattancheri, India .... **95 K3** 9 50N 76 15 E
Mattawa, Canada **140 C4** 46 20N 78 45W
Matterhorn, Switz. .... **32 E5** 45 58N 7 39 E
Mattersburg, Austria .... **35 D9** 47 44N 16 24 E
Matteson, U.S.A. **157 C9** 41 30N 87 42W
Matthew, I., N. Cal. .... **123 E13** 22 29 S 171 15 E
Matthew Town, Bahamas **165 B5** 20 57N 73 40W
Matthews, U.S.A. **157 D11** 40 23N 85 30W
Matthew's Ridge, Guyana **169 B5** 7 37N 60 10W
Mattice, Canada **140 C3** 49 40N 83 20W
Mattili, India .... **94 E6** 18 33N 82 12 E
Mattituck, U.S.A. **151 F12** 40 59N 72 32W
Mattò, Japan .... **73 A8** 36 31N 136 34 E
Mattoon, U.S.A. **154 F10** 39 29N 88 23W
Matuba, Mozam. .... **117 C5** 24 28 S 32 49 E
Matucana, Peru .... **172 C2** 11 55 S 76 25W
Matugama, Sri Lanka .... **95 L6** 6 31N 80 7 E
Matuku, Papua N. G. .... **132 C3** 4 54 S 145 47 E
Matuku, Fiji .... **133 B2** 19 10 S 179 44 E
Matún = Khowst, Afghan. ...... **91 B3** 33 22N 69 58 E
Matura B., Trin. & Tob. **169 F10** 10 39N 61 1W
Maturín, Venezuela **169 B5** 9 45N 63 11W
Matusadona Nat. Park △, Zimbabwe .. **119 F2** 16 58 S 28 42 E
Matutum, Mt., Phil. .... **81 H5** 6 22N 125 5 E
Matveyev Kurgan, Russia ...... **59 J10** 47 35N 38 57 E
Matxitxako, C., Spain **40 B2** 43 28N 2 47W
Mau, Mad. P., India .... **93 F8** 26 17N 78 41 E
Mau, Ut. P., India .... **93 G10** 25 56N 83 33 E
Mau, Ut. P., India .... **93 G9** 25 17N 81 23 E
Mau Escarpment, Kenya .... **118 C4** 0 40 S 36 0 E
Mau Ranipur, India .... **93 G8** 25 16N 79 8 E
Mauban, Phil. .... **80 D3** 14 12N 121 44 E
Maubeuge, France .... **27 B10** 50 17N 3 57 E
Maubin, Burma .... **90 G5** 16 44N 95 39 E
Maubourguet, France .... **28 E4** 43 29N 0 1 E
Maud, Pt., Australia .... **124 D1** 23 6 S 113 45 E
Maude, Australia .... **128 C6** 34 29 S 144 18 E
Maudin Sun, Burma .... **90 G5** 16 0N 94 30 E
Maués, Brazil .... **169 D6** 3 20 S 57 45W
Maués-Acu →, Brazil .... **169 D6** 3 22 S 57 44W
Maughold Hd., U.K. **20 C3** 54 18N 4 18W
Mauguio, France .... **28 E7** 43 37N 4 1 E
Maui, U.S.A. **145 C5** 20 48N 156 20W
Maulamyaing = Moulmein, Burma .. **90 G6** 16 30N 97 40 E
Maule □, Chile .... **174 D1** 36 5 S 72 30W
Mauléon-Licharre, France **28 E3** 43 14N 0 54W
Maullín, Chile .... **176 B2** 41 38 S 73 37W
Maulvibazar, Bangla. .... **90 C3** 24 29N 91 42 E
Maumee, U.S.A. **157 C13** 41 34N 83 39W
Maumee →, U.S.A. **157 C13** 41 42N 83 28W
Maumere, Indonesia .... **82 C2** 8 38 S 122 13 E
Maumusson, Pertuis de, France .. **28 C2** 45 48N 1 14W
Maun, Botswana .... **116 C3** 20 0 S 23 26 E
Mauna Kea, U.S.A. **145 D6** 19 50N 155 28W
Mauna Loa, U.S.A. **145 D6** 19 30N 155 35W
Maunalua, U.S.A. **145 B4** 21 8N 157 13W
Maunalua B., U.S.A. **145 K14** 21 15N 157 45W

Maunawili, U.S.A. **145 K14** 21 23N 157 46W
Maunga Orito, Chile .... **172 b** 27 10 S 109 25W
Maunga Puakatiki, Chile ...... **172 b** 27 6 S 109 15W
Maunga Terevaka, Chile .... **172 b** 27 5 S 109 23W
Maungaturoto, N.Z. .... **130 C3** 36 6 S 174 23 E
Maungdow, Burma .... **90 E4** 20 50N 92 21 E
Maungmagan Kyunzu, Burma ..... **90 E1** 14 0N 97 48 E
Maupin, U.S.A. **158 D3** 45 11N 121 5W
Maure-de-Bretagne, France **26 E5** 47 59N 1 58W
Maurepas, L., U.S.A. **155 K9** 30 15N 90 30W
Maures, France .... **29 E10** 43 15N 6 15 E
Mauriac, France .... **28 C6** 45 13N 2 19 E
Maurice, L., Australia .... **125 E5** 29 30 S 131 0 E
Mauriceville, N.Z. .... **130 G4** 40 45 S 175 42 E
Mauricie, Parc Nat. de la △, Canada .. **141 C5** 46 45N 73 0W
Maurienne, France .... **29 C10** 45 13N 6 30 E
Mauritania ■, Africa **110 D3** 20 50N 10 0W
Mauritius ■, Ind. Oc. .... **121 d** 20 0 S 57 0 E
Mauritius ✈ (MRU), Mauritius .. **121 d** 20 25 S 57 40 E
Mauron, France **26 D4** 48 9N 2 18W
Maurs, France .... **28 D6** 44 43N 2 12 E
Mauston, U.S.A. **154 D9** 43 48N 90 5W
Mauterndorf, Austria .... **34 D6** 47 9N 13 40 E
Mauthen, Austria .... **34 E6** 46 40N 13 0 E
Mauvezin, France .... **28 E4** 43 44N 0 53 E
Mauvoisin, Barr. de, Switz. .. **32 E4** 45 58N 7 20 E
Mauzé-sur-le-Mignon, France .. **28 B3** 46 12N 0 41W
Mavaca →, Venezuela **169 C4** 2 31N 65 11W
Mavinga, Angola .... **115 F4** 15 50 S 20 21 E
Mavli, India .... **92 G5** 24 45N 73 55 E
Mavrově, Greece .... **39 C2** 38 4N 20 44 E
Mavrově, Albania .... **50 F3** 40 26N 19 32 E
Mavrovo, Nac. Park △, Macedonia .. **119 F3** 16 30 S 31 30 E
Mawa, Dem. Rep. of the Congo .. **118 B2** 2 45N 26 40 E
Mawai, India .... **93 H9** 22 30N 81 4 E
Mawana, India .... **92 E7** 29 6N 77 58 E
Mawand, Pakistan .... **92 E3** 29 33N 68 38 E
Mawasangka, Indonesia .... **82 C2** 5 17 S 122 18 E
Mawk Mai, Burma .... **90 E6** 20 14N 97 37 E
Mawlaik, Burma .... **90 D5** 23 40N 94 26 E
Mawlamyine = Moulmein, Burma .. **90 G6** 16 30N 97 40 E
Mawkmawkho, Burma .... **90 G6** 17 50N 97 38 E
Mawqaq, Si. Arabia .... **96 E4** 27 25N 41 8 E
Mawshij, Yemen .... **98 D3** 13 43N 43 17 E
Mawson Coast, Antarctica ..... **7 C6** 68 30 S 63 0 E
Max, U.S.A. **154 B4** 47 49N 101 18W
Maxcanú, Mexico **163 C6** 20 40N 92 0W
Maxesibeni, S. Africa .... **117 E4** 30 49 S 29 23 E
Maxixe, Mozam. .... **117 C6** 23 54 S 35 17 E
Maxville, Canada **151 A10** 45 17N 74 51W
Maxwell, N.Z. .... **130 F3** 39 51 S 174 49 E
Maxwell, U.S.A. **160 F4** 39 17N 122 11W
Maxwelton, Australia .... **126 C3** 20 43 S 142 41 E
May, C., U.S.A. **148 F8** 38 56N 74 58W
May Jirgu, Niger .... **109 F1** 13 44N 8 8 E
May Pen, Jamaica .... **164 a** 17 58N 77 15W
May River, Papua N. G. .... **132 C1** 4 19 S 141 58 E
Maya, Indonesia .... **85 C3** 1 10 S 109 35 E
Maya →, Russia .... **67 D14** 60 28N 134 28 E
Maya Mts., Belize **163 D7** 16 30N 89 0W
Mayabandar, India .... **95 H11** 12 56N 92 56 E
Mayaguana, Bahamas **165 B5** 22 30N 72 44W
Mayagüez, Puerto Rico .... **165 d** 18 12N 67 9W
Mayahi, Niger .... **113 C6** 13 58N 7 40 E
Mayals = Maials, Spain .... **40 D5** 41 22N 0 30 E
Mayama, Congo .... **114 C2** 3 51 S 14 54 E
Mayāmey, Iran .... **97 B7** 36 24N 55 42 E
Mayang, China .... **76 D7** 27 53N 109 49 E
Mayanup, Australia .... **125 F2** 33 57 S 116 27 E
Mayapán, Mexico **163 C7** 20 28N 89 11W
Mayarí, Mexico **163 C7** 20 30N 89 25W
Mayaguam, Kazakhstan .... **65 B4** 42 51N 68 3 E
Mayarí, Cuba **165 B4** 20 40N 75 41W
Mayaro B., Trin. & Tob. **169 F10** 10 14N 61 0W
Mayavaram = Mayuram, India ... **95 J4** 11 3N 79 42 E
Maybell, U.S.A. **158 F9** 40 31N 108 5W
Maybole, U.K. **22 F4** 55 21N 4 42W
Maychew, Ethiopia .... **107 E4** 12 50N 39 31 E
Maydān, Iraq .... **101 E11** 34 55N 45 37 E
Maydena, Australia .... **127 D4** 42 45 S 146 30 E
Maydī, Yemen .... **98 C3** 16 19N 42 48 E
Mayen, Germany .... **31 E3** 50 19N 7 13 E
Mayenne, France **26 D6** 48 20N 0 38W
Mayenne □, France **26 D6** 48 10N 0 40W
Mayenne →, France **26 E6** 47 30N 0 32W
Mayer, U.S.A. **159 J7** 34 24N 112 14W
Mayerthorpe, Canada **142 C5** 53 57N 115 8W
Mayesville, U.S.A. **152 A9** 34 0N 80 12W
Mayfield, Ky., U.S.A. **149 G1** 36 44N 88 38W
Mayfield, N.Y., U.S.A. **151 C10** 43 6N 74 16W
Mayhill, U.S.A. **159 K11** 32 53N 105 29W
Maykop, Russia .... **61 H5** 44 35N 40 10 E
Mayli-Say = Mayluu-Suu, Kyrgyzstan .. **65 C6** 41 17N 72 24 E
Mayluu-Suu, Kyrgyzstan .... **65 C6** 41 17N 72 24 E
Maymak, Kyrgyzstan .... **65 B5** 42 42N 71 13 E
Maymyo, Burma .... **86 A1** 22 2N 96 28 E
Maynard, Mass., U.S.A. **151 D13** 42 26N 71 27W
Maynard, Wash., U.S.A. **160 C4** 47 59N 122 55W
Maynard Hills, Australia ..... **125 E2** 28 28 S 119 49 E
Mayne →, Australia .... **126 C3** 23 40 S 141 55 E
Maynooth, Ireland **23 C5** 53 23N 6 34W
Mayo, Canada **138 B6** 63 38N 135 57W
Mayo, U.S.A. **152 E6** 30 3N 83 10W
Mayo □, Ireland **23 C2** 53 53N 9 3W
Mayo →, Argentina .... **176 C3** 45 45 S 69 45W
Mayo →, Peru .... **172 B2** 6 38 S 76 15W
Mayo Bay, Phil. .... **81 H6** 6 56N 126 22 E
Mayo Daga, Nigeria .... **113 D7** 6 59N 11 25 E
Mayo Faran, Nigeria .... **113 D7** 8 57N 12 4 E
Mayoko, Congo .... **114 C2** 2 18 S 12 49 E
Mayoko, Dem. Rep. of the Congo .. **114 C4** 1 6 S 23 50 E
Mayon Volcano, Phil. .... **80 E4** 13 15N 123 41 E
Mayor Buratovich, Argentina .. **176 A4** 39 15 S 62 37W
Mayor I., N.Z. .... **130 D5** 37 16 S 176 17 E
Mayorga, Spain **42 C5** 42 10N 5 16W
Mayotte, Ind. Oc. .... **121 a** 12 50 S 45 10 E
Mayoyao, Phil. .... **80 C3** 16 59N 121 14 E
Mayraira Pt., Phil. .... **80 B3** 18 39N 120 51 E
Mayskiy, Russia .... **61 J7** 43 47N 44 2 E
Maysville, Ky., U.S.A. **157 F13** 38 39N 83 46W
Maysville, Mo., U.S.A. **156 F2** 39 53N 94 22W
Mayu, Indonesia .... **82 A3** 1 30N 126 30 E
Mayumba, Gabon .... **114 C2** 3 25 S 10 39 E
Mayuram, India .... **95 J4** 11 3N 79 42 E
Mayville, N. Dak., U.S.A. **154 B6** 47 30N 97 20W
Mayville, N.Y., U.S.A. **150 D5** 42 15N 79 30W
Mayya, Russia .... **67 C14** 61 44N 130 18 E
Mazabuka, Zambia .... **119 F2** 15 52 S 27 44 E
Mazagán = El Jadida, Morocco .. **110 B3** 33 11N 8 17W
Mazagão, Brazil .... **169 D7** 0 7 S 51 16W
Mazamet, France .... **28 E6** 43 30N 2 20 E
Mazán, Peru .... **168 D3** 3 30 S 73 0W
Māzandarān □, Iran .... **97 B7** 36 30N 52 0 E
Mazapil, Mexico **162 C4** 24 38N 101 34W
Mazar, China .... **65 E8** 36 32N 77 1 E
Mazar-e Sharīf, Afghan. ...... **91 B2** 36 41N 67 0 E
Mazara del Vallo, Italy ...... **46 E5** 37 39N 12 35 E
Mazarredo, Argentina .... **176 C3** 47 10 S 66 50W
Mazarrón, Spain **41 H3** 37 38N 1 19W
Mazarrón, G. de, Spain **41 H3** 37 27N 1 19W

Mazaruni →, Guyana **169 B6** 6 25N 58 35W
Mazatán, Mexico **162 B2** 29 0N 110 8W
Mazatenango, Guatemala **164 D1** 14 35N 91 30W
Mazatlán, Mexico **162 C3** 23 13N 106 25W
Mažeikiai, Lithuania .... **15 H20** 56 20N 22 20 E
Māzhān, Iran .... **97 C8** 32 30N 59 0 E
Mazīnān, Iran .... **97 B8** 36 19N 56 56 E
Mazo Cruz, Peru .... **172 D4** 16 45 S 69 44W
Mazoe, Mozam. .... **119 F3** 16 42 S 33 7 E
Mazoe →, Mozam. .... **119 F3** 16 20 S 33 30 E
Mazomanic, U.S.A. **156 A7** 43 11N 89 48W
Mazon, U.S.A. **157 C8** 41 14N 88 25W
Mazowe, Zimbabwe .... **119 F3** 17 28 S 30 58 E
Mazowieckie □, Poland .... **55 F8** 52 40N 21 0 E
Mazrūb, Sudan .... **107 E2** 14 0N 29 20 E
Mazu Dao, China .... **77 D12** 26 10N 119 55 E
Mazurian Lakes = Mazurski,
  Pojezierze, Poland .... **54 E7** 53 50N 21 0 E
Mazurski, Pojezierze, Poland .. **54 E7** 53 50N 21 0 E
Mazyr, Belarus .... **59 F5** 51 59N 29 15 E
Mba, Fiji .... **133 A1** 17 33 S 177 41 E
Mbaba, Senegal **112 B1** 14 59N 16 44W
Mbabane, Swaziland .... **117 D5** 26 18 S 31 6 E
Mbaéré →, C.A.R. .... **114 B3** 3 47N 17 31 E
Mbagne, Mauritania **112 B2** 16 6N 14 47W
M'bahiakro, Ivory C. **112 D4** 7 33N 4 19W
Mbaïki, C.A.R. .... **114 B3** 3 53N 18 1 E
Mbakana, Mt. de, Cameroon .... **114 A3** 7 57N 15 6 E
Mbala, Zambia .... **119 D3** 8 46 S 31 24 E
Mbalabala, Zimbabwe .... **117 C4** 20 27 S 29 3 E
Mbale, Uganda .... **118 B3** 1 8N 34 12 E
Mbali →, C.A.R. .... **114 B3** 4 27N 18 20 E
Mbalmayo, Cameroon .... **113 E7** 3 33N 11 33 E
Mbam →, Cameroon .... **113 E7** 4 44N 11 17 E
Mbamba Bay, Tanzania .... **119 E3** 11 13 S 34 49 E
Mbandaka, Dem. Rep. of the Congo .. **114 B2** 0 1N 18 18 E
Mbanga, Cameroon .... **113 E6** 4 30N 9 33 E
Mbanika, Solomon Is. .... **133 M10** 9 3 S 159 13 E
M'Banio, Lagune, Gabon .... **114 C2** 3 35 S 11 0 E
Mbanza Congo, Angola .... **115 D2** 6 18 S 14 16 E
Mbanza Ngungu, Dem. Rep. of
  the Congo .... **115 D2** 5 12 S 14 53 E
Mbarangandu, Tanzania .... **119 D4** 10 11 S 36 48 E
Mbarara, Uganda .... **118 C3** 0 35 S 30 40 E
Mbari →, C.A.R. .... **114 B4** 4 34N 22 43 E
Mbashe →, S. Africa .... **117 E4** 32 15 S 28 54 E
Mbatto, Ivory C. **112 D4** 6 28N 4 22W
Mbava, Solomon Is. .... **133 L9** 7 47 S 156 33 E
Mbé, Congo .... **114 C3** 3 4 S 15 50 E
Mbé, Congo .... **114 A3** 3 4 S 15 50 E
Mbenga = Beqa, Fiji .... **133 B2** 18 23 S 178 8 E
Mbengué, Gabon .... **114 C2** 2 2 S 11 7 E
Mbengui, Gabon .... **114 C2** 2 3 S 10 4 E
Mbenkuru →, Tanzania .... **119 D4** 9 25 S 39 50 E
Mbéré →, Cameroon .... **114 A3** 7 45N 15 26 E
Mberengwa, Zimbabwe .... **119 G2** 20 29 S 29 57 E
Mberengwa, Mt., Zimbabwe ..... **119 G2** 20 37 S 29 55 E
Mberubu, Nigeria .... **113 D6** 6 10N 7 38 E
Mbesuma, Zambia .... **119 E3** 10 0 S 32 2 E
Mbeya, Tanzania .... **119 D3** 8 54 S 33 29 E
Mbeya □, Tanzania .... **118 D3** 8 15 S 33 30 E
Mbigou, Gabon .... **114 C2** 1 53 S 11 56 E
M'bili, Sudan .... **119 E4** 10 5 S 35 0 E
Mbinga, Tanzania .... **119 E4** 10 50 S 35 0 E
Mbini = Río Muni □, Eq. Guin. .. **114 B2** 1 30N 10 0 E
Mbini, Eq. Guin. .... **114 B1** 1 35N 9 37 E
Mboi, Dem. Rep. of the Congo .. **115 D4** 6 57 S 21 54 E
Mboki, C.A.R. .... **107 F2** 5 19N 25 58 E
Mbokonimbeti, Solomon Is. .... **133 M11** 8 57 S 160 7 E
Mboli, Dem. Rep. of the Congo .. **113 E6** 4 33N 9 5 E
Mboro, Senegal **112 B1** 15 9N 16 54W
M'bonge, Cameroon .... **113 E6** 4 33N 9 5 E
Mbouda, Cameroon .... **113 D7** 5 38N 10 11 E
Mbour, Senegal **112 C1** 14 22N 16 54W
Mbouma, Congo .... **114 C3** 0 52 S 15 4 E
Mbour, Senegal **112 C1** 14 22N 16 54W
Mbout, Mauritania **112 B2** 16 1N 12 38W
Mbrés, C.A.R. .... **114 A3** 6 40N 19 48 E
M'Bridge →, Angola .... **115 D2** 7 12 S 12 51 E
Mbuji-Mayi, Dem. Rep. of the Congo .. **118 D1** 6 9 S 23 40 E
Mbulu, Tanzania .... **118 C3** 3 45 S 35 30 E
Mbuma, Dem. Rep. of the Congo .. **114 B4** 3 22N 23 0 E
Mbuma, Solomon Is. .... **133 M11** 8 59 S 160 46 E
Mburucuyá, Argentina .... **174 B4** 28 1 S 58 14W
M'bwat, Cameroon .... **114 A2** 6 29N 10 45 E
McCarran International, Las
  Vegas ✈ (LAS), U.S.A. **161 J11** 36 5N 115 9W
Mcherrah, Algeria **110 C4** 27 0N 4 30W
Mchinja, Tanzania .... **119 D4** 9 44 S 39 45 E
Mchinji, Malawi .... **119 E3** 13 47 S 32 58 E
Mdennah, Mauritania **110 D3** 24 37N 6 0W
Mé Maoya, N. Cal. .... **133 U19** 21 22 S 165 22 E
Mead, L., U.S.A. **161 J12** 36 1N 114 44W
Meade, U.S.A. **155 G4** 37 17N 100 20W
Meade →, U.S.A. **144 A9** 70 52N 155 55W
Meade River, U.S.A. **144 A8** 69 28N 157 24W
Meadow Lake, Canada **143 C7** 54 10N 108 26W
Meadow Lake Prov. Park ⌂, Canada .. **143 C7** 54 27N 109 0W
Meadow Valley Wash →, U.S.A. .. **161 J12** 36 40N 114 34W
Meadville, Mo., U.S.A. **156 F3** 39 47N 93 18W
Meadville, Pa., U.S.A. **150 E4** 41 39N 80 9W
Meaford, Canada **140 D3** 44 36N 80 35W
Mealhada, Portugal **42 E2** 40 22N 8 27W
Mealy Mts., Canada **141 B8** 53 10N 58 0W
Meander River, Canada **142 B5** 59 2N 117 42W
Meares, C., U.S.A. **158 D2** 45 37N 124 0W
Mearim →, Brazil .... **170 B3** 3 4 S 44 35W
Meath □, Ireland **23 C5** 53 40N 6 57W
Meath Park, Canada **143 C7** 53 27N 105 22W
Meaulne, France .... **27 F9** 46 36N 2 36 E
Meaux, France .... **27 D9** 48 58N 2 50 E
Mebechi-Gawa →, Japan .... **70 D10** 40 31N 141 31 E
Mebonden, Norway .... **18 A8** 63 13N 11 2 E
Mebulu, Tanjung, Indonesia ... **79 K18** 8 50 S 115 5 E
Mecanhelas, Mozam. .... **119 F4** 15 12 S 35 54 E
Mecaya →, Colombia **168 C2** 0 29N 75 11W
Mecca = Makkah, Si. Arabia ... **98 B2** 21 30N 39 54 E
Mecca, U.S.A. **161 M10** 33 34N 116 5W
Mechanicsburg, Ohio, U.S.A. .. **157 D13** 40 4N 83 33W
Mechanicsburg, Pa., U.S.A. ... **150 F7** 40 13N 77 1W
Mechanicville, U.S.A. **156 C5** 41 54N 91 16W
Mechanicville, U.S.A. **151 D11** 42 54N 73 41W
Mecheria, Ethiopia .... **107 F5** 8 36N 40 20 E
Mechelen, Belgium .... **24 C4** 51 2N 4 29 E
Mecheria, Algeria **111 B4** 33 35N 0 18W
Mechernich, Germany .... **30 E2** 50 35N 6 39 E
Mechetinskaya, Russia .... **61 G5** 46 45N 40 32 E
Mechra Bel Ksiri, Morocco **110 B3** 34 44N 5 57W
Mechra Benâbbou, Morocco **110 B3** 32 39N 7 35W
Mecidiye, Turkey .... **51 F10** 40 38N 26 32 E
Mecitözü, Turkey .... **100 B6** 40 32N 35 25 E
Mecklenburg, Germany .... **36 B6** 53 33N 11 40 E
Mecklenburg-Vorpommern □,
  Germany .... **30 B8** 53 45N 12 15 E
Mecklenburger Bucht, Germany .. **30 A7** 54 20N 11 40 E
Meconta, Mozam. .... **119 E4** 14 59 S 39 50 E
Mecsek, Hungary .... **52 D3** 46 10N 18 50 E
Meda, Portugal **42 E3** 40 57N 7 18W
Medak, India .... **94 E4** 18 1N 78 15 E
Medan, Indonesia .... **84 B1** 3 40N 98 38 E
Médanos, Argentina .... **176 A4** 38 50 S 62 42W
Médanos de Coro, Parque Nac. △,
  Venezuela **165 D6** 11 35N 69 44W

Medanosa, Pta., Argentina .... **176 C3** 48 8 S 66 0W
Medart, U.S.A. **152 E5** 30 5N 84 23W
Medaryville, U.S.A. **157 C10** 41 5N 86 55W
Medawachchiya, Sri Lanka ..... **95 K5** 8 30N 80 30 E
Mede, Italy .... **44 C5** 45 6N 8 44 E
Médéa, Algeria .... **111 A5** 36 12N 2 50 E
Medebach, Germany .... **30 D4** 51 12N 8 17 E
Medellín, Colombia **168 B2** 6 15N 75 35W
Medemblik, Neths. .... **24 B5** 52 46N 5 8 E
Médenine, Tunisia .... **108 B2** 33 21N 10 30 E
Mederdra, Mauritania **112 B1** 17 0N 15 38W
Medford, Mass., U.S.A. **151 D13** 42 25N 71 7W
Medford, Oreg., U.S.A. **158 E2** 42 19N 122 52W
Medford, Wis., U.S.A. **154 C9** 45 9N 90 20W
Medgidia, Romania .... **53 F13** 44 15N 28 19 E
Medi, Sudan .... **107 F3** 5 4N 30 42 E
Media Agua, Argentina .... **174 C2** 31 58 S 68 25W
Media Luna, Argentina .... **174 C2** 34 45 S 66 44W
Medianeira, Brazil .... **175 B5** 25 17 S 54 5W
Mediapolis, U.S.A. **156 D5** 41 0N 91 10W
Mediaș, Romania .... **53 D9** 46 9N 24 22 E
Medicilândia, Brazil .... **169 D7** 3 33 S 53 8W
Medicina, Italy .... **45 D8** 44 28N 11 38 E
Medicine Bow, U.S.A. **158 F10** 41 54N 106 12W
Medicine Bow Pk., U.S.A. **158 F10** 41 21N 106 19W
Medicine Bow Ra., U.S.A. **158 F10** 41 10N 106 25W
Medicine Hat, Canada **143 D6** 50 0N 110 45W
Medicine Lake, U.S.A. **154 A2** 48 30N 104 30W
Medicine Lodge, U.S.A. **155 G5** 37 17N 98 35W
Medina = Al Madīnah, Si. Arabia .. **96 E3** 24 35N 39 52 E
Medina, Brazil .... **171 E3** 16 15 S 41 29W
Medina, Colombia **168 C3** 4 30N 73 21W
Medina, Phil. .... **81 G5** 8 55N 125 1 E
Medina, N. Dak., U.S.A. **154 C6** 46 54N 99 18W
Medina, Ohio, U.S.A. **150 E3** 41 8N 81 52W
Medina →, U.S.A. **155 L5** 29 16N 98 29W
Medina de Pomar, Spain **42 C7** 42 56N 3 3W
Medina de Ríoseco, Spain **42 D6** 41 53N 5 3W
Medina L., U.S.A. **155 L5** 29 32N 98 56W
Medina Sidonia, Spain **43 J5** 36 28N 5 57W
Medinaceli, Spain **40 D2** 41 12N 2 30W
Medinipur, India .... **93 H12** 22 25N 87 21 E
Mediterranean Sea, Europe .... **12 H7** 35 0N 15 0 E
Medjerda, O. →, Tunisia ...... **108 A2** 37 7N 10 13 E
Mednogorsk, Russia .... **64 F6** 51 24N 57 37 E
Médoc, France **28 C3** 45 10N 0 50W
Medora, U.S.A. **157 F10** 38 49N 86 10W
Médouneu, Gabon .... **114 B2** 0 57N 10 47 E
Medulin, Croatia .... **45 D10** 44 49N 13 55 E
Medveda, Serbia, Yug. .... **50 D6** 42 50N 21 32 E
Medvedevo, Russia .... **58 B8** 56 37N 47 47 E
Medveditsa →, Tver, Russia ... **58 C9** 57 5N 37 30 E
Medveditsa →, Volgograd, Russia .. **59 E7** 49 35N 42 41 E
Medvedok, Russia .... **58 C10** 57 20N 50 1 E
Medvezhi, Ostrava, Russia .... **67 B17** 71 0N 161 0 E
Medvezhyegorsk, Russia .... **56 B5** 63 0N 34 25 E
Medway □, U.K. .... **21 F8** 51 25N 0 32 E
Medway →, U.K. .... **21 F8** 51 27N 0 46 E
Medzev, Slovak Rep. .... **35 C13** 48 43N 20 55 E
Medzilaborce, Slovak Rep. .... **35 B14** 49 17N 21 52 E
Medžitlija, Macedonia .... **50 F5** 40 56N 21 9 E
Meekatharra, Australia .... **125 E2** 26 32 S 118 29 E
Meeker, U.S.A. **158 F10** 40 2N 107 55W
Meelpaeg Res., Canada **141 C8** 48 15N 56 33W
Meeniyan, Australia .... **129 F7** 38 35 S 146 0 E
Meerssburg, Germany .... **31 H5** 47 41N 9 16 E
Meerut, India .... **92 E7** 29 1N 77 42 E
Meeteetse, U.S.A. **158 D9** 44 9N 108 52W
Mega, Ethiopia .... **107 G4** 3 57N 38 19 E
Megálo Khório, Greece .... **49 E9** 36 27N 27 24 E
Megálo Petáli, Greece .... **48 D6** 37 59N 24 15 E
Megalópolis, Greece .... **48 D4** 37 25N 22 7 E
Meganísi Nisís, Greece .... **39 B2** 38 38N 20 46 E
Mégara, Greece .... **48 D5** 37 58 S 23 22 E
Megasini, India .... **93 J12** 21 38N 86 21 E
Megdhova →, Greece .... **48 B3** 39 10N 21 45 E
Megève, France .... **29 C10** 45 51N 6 37 E
Meghalaya □, India .... **90 C3** 25 50N 91 0 E
Meghezez, Ethiopia .... **107 F4** 9 18N 39 26 E
Meghna →, Bangla. .... **90 D3** 22 50N 90 50 E
Mégiscane, L., Canada **140 C4** 48 35N 75 55W
Megiste, Greece .... **49 E11** 36 8N 29 34 E
Megra, Russia .... **58 B9** 60 11N 37 14 E
Mehadia, Romania .... **52 E7** 44 56N 22 23 E
Mehaïgene, O. →, Algeria ..... **111 B5** 32 15N 2 59 E
Meharry, Mt., Australia ...... **124 D2** 22 59 S 118 35 E
Mehedeby, Sweden .... **16 B11** 60 27N 17 25 E
Mehedinți □, Romania .... **52 E7** 44 40N 22 45 E
Meheisa, Sudan .... **106 D3** 19 38N 32 57 E
Mehekar, India .... **94 D3** 20 9N 76 34 E
Mehlville, U.S.A. **154 F9** 38 30N 90 19W
Mehndawal, India .... **93 F10** 26 58N 83 5 E
Mehr Jān, Iran .... **97 C7** 33 50N 55 6 E
Mehrān, Iran .... **101 F12** 33 7N 46 10 E
Mehrīz, Iran .... **97 D7** 31 35N 54 28 E
Mehun-sur-Yèvre, France ...... **27 E9** 47 10N 2 13 E
Mei Jiang →, China .... **77 E11** 24 25N 116 35 E
Mei Xian, China .... **74 G4** 34 18N 107 55 E
Meia Ponte →, Brazil .... **171 E2** 18 32 S 49 36W
Meicheng, China .... **77 C12** 29 19N 119 16 E
Meichengzhen, China .... **77 C8** 28 9N 111 40 E
Meichuan, China .... **77 B10** 30 8N 115 31 E
Meiganga, Cameroon .... **114 A2** 6 30N 14 25 E
Meigs, U.S.A. **152 D5** 31 4N 84 6W
Meigu, China .... **76 C4** 28 16N 103 20 E
Meiktila, Burma .... **90 E5** 20 53N 95 54 E
Meilen, Switz. .... **33 B7** 47 16N 8 39 E
Meinerzhagen, Germany .... **30 D3** 51 6N 7 38 E
Meiningen, Germany .... **30 E6** 50 34N 10 25 E
Meio →, Brazil .... **171 D3** 13 36 S 44 7W
Meira, Serra de, Spain .... **42 B3** 43 15 S 7 15W
Meiringen, Switz. .... **32 C6** 46 43N 8 12 E
Meishan, China .... **76 B4** 30 3N 103 23 E
Meissen, Germany .... **30 D9** 51 9N 13 29 E
Meissner, Germany .... **30 D5** 51 13N 9 51 E
Meissner-Kaufunger Wald,
  Naturpark △, Germany .... **30 D5** 51 16N 9 45 E
Meitan, China .... **76 D6** 27 45N 107 29 E
Meizhou, China .... **77 E11** 24 16N 116 6 E
Meja, India .... **93 G10** 25 9N 82 7 E
Mejillones, Chile .... **174 A1** 23 10 S 70 30W
Mékambo, Gabon .... **114 B2** 1 2N 13 50 E
Mekdela, Ethiopia .... **107 E4** 11 24N 39 10 E
Mekele, Ethiopia .... **107 E4** 13 33N 39 30 E
Mekerghene, Sebkra, Algeria .. **111 C5** 26 21N 1 30 E
Mekhtar, Pakistan .... **91 C3** 30 30N 69 15 E
Meknès, Morocco **110 B3** 33 57N 5 33W
Mékrou →, Benin .... **113 C5** 12 24N 2 49 E
Mekong →, Asia .... **87 H6** 9 30N 106 15 E
Mekongga, Indonesia .... **82 B2** 3 39 S 121 15 E
Mekoryuk, U.S.A. **144 F6** 60 23N 166 11W
Mekvari = Kūr →, Azerbaijan .. **101 C13** 39 29N 49 15 E
Mel, Italy .... **45 B9** 46 4N 12 5 E
Melagiri Hills, India .... **95 H3** 12 20N 77 30 E
Melah, Oued el →, Algeria .... **111 C6** 32 20N 2 28 E

Melah, Sebkhet el, *Algeria* ... 111 C4 29 20N 1 30W
Melaka, *Malaysia* ... 87 L4 2 15N 102 15 E
Melaka □, *Malaysia* ... 84 B2 2 15N 102 15 E
Melalap, *Malaysia* ... 78 C5 5 10N 116 5 E
Mélambes, *Greece* ... 39 E5 35 8N 24 40 E
Melanesia, *Pac. Oc.* ... 134 H7 4 0 S 155 0 E
Melapalaiyam, *India* ... 95 K3 8 39N 77 44 E
Melawi →, *Indonesia* ... 85 B4 0 5N 111 29 E
Melaya, *Indonesia* ... 79 J17 8 17 S 114 30 E
Melbourne, *Australia* ... 129 D6 37 50 S 145 0 E
Melbourne, *Fla., U.S.A.* ... 153 G9 28 5N 80 37W
Melbourne, *Iowa, U.S.A.* ... 156 C3 41 57N 93 6W
Melcher-Dallas, *U.S.A.* ... 156 C3 41 14N 93 15W
Melchor Múzquiz, *Mexico* ... 162 B4 27 50N 101 30W
Melchor Ocampo, *Mexico* ... 162 C4 24 52N 101 40W
Meldal, *Norway* ... 18 A6 63 3N 9 44 E
Méldola, *Italy* ... 45 D9 44 7N 12 5 E
Meldorf, *Germany* ... 30 A5 54 5N 9 5 E
Mélé, *C.A.R.* ... 114 A4 9 46N 21 33 E
Mele B., *Vanuatu* ... 133 G6 17 44 S 168 14 E
Meleda, *Somali Rep.* ... 120 B3 10 25N 49 51 E
Melegnano, *Italy* ... 44 C6 45 21N 9 19 E
Meleizem, *Mauritania* ... 110 D2 22 19N 11 24W
Melekess = Dimitrovgrad, *Russia* ... 60 C9 54 14N 49 39 E
Melenci, *Serbia, Yug.* ... 52 E5 45 32N 20 20 E
Melenki, *Russia* ... 60 C5 55 20N 41 37 E
Meleuz, *Russia* ... 64 E6 52 58N 55 55 E
Mélèzes →, *Canada* ... 140 A5 57 40N 69 29W
Melfi, *Chad* ... 109 F3 11 0N 17 59 E
Melfi, *Italy* ... 47 B8 41 0N 15 39 E
Melfort, *Canada* ... 143 C8 52 50N 104 37W
Melfort, *Zimbabwe* ... 119 F3 18 0 S 31 25 E
Melgaço, *Portugal* ... 42 C2 42 7N 8 15W
Melgar de Fernamental, *Spain* ... 42 C6 42 27N 4 17W
Melgraseyri, *Iceland* ... 11 A4 66 1N 22 27W
Melhus, *Norway* ... 18 A7 63 17N 10 18 E
Melide, *Spain* ... 42 C2 42 55N 8 1W
Melide, *Switz.* ... 33 E7 45 57N 8 57 E
Meligalá, *Greece* ... 48 D3 37 15N 21 59 E
Melilla, *N. Afr.* ... 111 A4 35 21N 2 57W
Melilli, *Italy* ... 47 E8 37 11N 15 7 E
Melipilla, *Chile* ... 174 C1 33 42 S 71 15W
Mélissa, Ákra, *Greece* ... 39 E5 35 6N 24 33 E
Mélissa Óros, *Greece* ... 49 D8 37 32N 26 4 E
Melissani Cave, *Greece* ... 39 C2 38 15N 20 38 E
Melita, *Canada* ... 143 D8 49 15N 101 0W
Mélito di Porto Salvo, *Italy* ... 47 E8 37 55N 15 47 E
Melitopol, *Ukraine* ... 59 J8 46 50N 35 22 E
Melk, *Austria* ... 34 C8 48 13N 15 20 E
Mellan Fryken, *Sweden* ... 16 E7 59 45N 13 10 E
Mellansel, *Sweden* ... 14 E18 63 25N 18 17 E
Mellbystrand, *Sweden* ... 17 H6 56 30N 12 56 E
Melle, *France* ... 28 B3 46 14N 0 10W
Melle, *Germany* ... 30 C4 52 12N 8 20 E
Mellègue, O. →, *Tunisia* ... 108 A1 36 36N 9 14 E
Mellen, *U.S.A.* ... 154 B9 46 20N 90 40W
Mellerud, *Sweden* ... 17 F6 58 41N 12 28 E
Mellette, *U.S.A.* ... 154 C5 45 9N 98 30W
Mellid = Melide, *Spain* ... 42 C2 42 55N 8 1W
Mellieha, *Malta* ... 38 F7 35 57N 14 22 E
Mellieha Bay, *Malta* ... 38 F7 35 59N 14 22 E
Mellit, *Sudan* ... 107 E2 14 7N 25 34 E
Mellizo Sur, Cerro, *Chile* ... 176 C2 48 33 S 73 10W
Mellrichstadt, *Germany* ... 31 E6 50 25N 10 17 E
Melnik, *Bulgaria* ... 50 E7 41 30N 23 25 E
Mělník, *Czech Rep.* ... 34 A7 50 22N 14 23 E
Melo, *Uruguay* ... 175 C5 32 20 S 54 10W
Melolo, *Indonesia* ... 82 C2 9 53 S 120 40 E
Melouprey, *Cambodia* ... 86 F5 13 48N 105 16 E
Melrhir, Chott, *Algeria* ... 111 B6 34 13N 6 30 E
Melrose, *Australia* ... 129 B7 32 42 S 146 57 E
Melrose, *U.K.* ... 22 F6 55 36N 2 43W
Melrose, *Minn., U.S.A.* ... 154 C7 45 40N 94 49W
Melrose, *N. Mex., U.S.A.* ... 155 H3 34 26N 103 38W
Mels, *Switz.* ... 33 B8 47 3N 9 25 E
Melsisi, *Vanuatu* ... 133 E6 15 46 S 168 10 E
Melstone, *U.S.A.* ... 158 C10 46 36N 107 52W
Melsungen, *Germany* ... 30 D5 51 7N 9 32 E
Melton, *Australia* ... 128 D6 37 41 S 144 35 E
Melton Mowbray, *U.K.* ... 20 E7 52 47N 0 54W
Melun, *France* ... 27 D9 48 32N 2 39 E
Melur, *India* ... 95 J4 10 2N 78 23 E
Melut, *Sudan* ... 107 E3 10 30N 32 13 E
Melville, *Canada* ... 143 C8 50 55N 102 50W
Melville, C., *Australia* ... 126 A3 14 11 S 144 30 E
Melville, C., *Phil.* ... 81 H1 7 49N 117 0 E
Melville, L., *Canada* ... 141 B8 53 30N 60 0W
Melville B., *Australia* ... 126 A2 12 0 S 136 45 E
Melville B., *Greenland* ... 10 B4 75 30N 63 0W
Melville I., *Australia* ... 124 B5 11 30 S 131 0 E
Melville I., *Canada* ... 6 B2 75 30N 112 0W
Melville Pen., *Canada* ... 139 B11 68 0N 84 0W
Mélykút, *Hungary* ... 52 D4 46 11N 19 25 E
Memaliaj, *Albania* ... 50 F3 40 25N 19 56 E
Memba, *Mozam.* ... 119 E5 14 11 S 40 30 E
Memboro, *Indonesia* ... 82 C1 9 30 S 119 30 E
Membrilla, *Spain* ... 43 G7 38 59N 3 21W
Memel = Klaipėda, *Lithuania* ... 13 J19 55 43N 21 10 E
Memel, *S. Africa* ... 117 D4 27 38 S 29 36 E
Memmingen, *Germany* ... 31 H6 47 58N 10 10 E
Mempawah, *Indonesia* ... 85 B3 0 30N 109 5 E
Memphis, *Egypt* ... 106 J7 29 52N 31 12 E
Memphis, *Mich., U.S.A.* ... 150 D2 42 54N 82 46W
Memphis, *Mo., U.S.A.* ... 156 D4 40 28N 92 10W
Memphis, *Tenn., U.S.A.* ... 155 H10 35 8N 90 3W
Memphis, *Tex., U.S.A.* ... 155 H4 34 44N 100 33W
Memphremagog, L., *U.S.A.* ... 151 B12 45 0N 72 12W
Mena, *Ukraine* ... 59 G7 51 31N 32 13 E
Mena, *U.S.A.* ... 155 H7 34 35N 94 15W
Mena →, *Ethiopia* ... 107 F5 5 40N 40 50 E
Menai Strait, *U.K.* ... 20 D3 53 11N 4 13W
Ménaka, *Mali* ... 113 B5 15 59N 2 18 E
Menan = Chao Phraya →, *Thailand* ... 86 F3 13 32N 100 36 E
Menarandra →, *Madag.* ... 117 D7 25 17 S 44 30 E
Menard, *U.S.A.* ... 155 K5 30 55N 99 47W
Menate, *Indonesia* ... 85 C4 0 12 S 113 3 E
Menawashei, *Sudan* ... 107 E1 12 41N 24 59 E
Mendawai →, *Indonesia* ... 85 C4 3 30 S 113 0 E
Mende, *France* ... 28 D7 44 31N 3 30 E
Mendebo, *Ethiopia* ... 107 F4 7 0N 39 22 E
Menden, *Germany* ... 30 D3 51 26N 7 47 E
Mendenhall, C., *U.S.A.* ... 144 G6 59 45N 166 10W
Menderes, *Turkey* ... 49 C9 38 14N 27 8 E
Mendez, *Mexico* ... 163 B5 25 7N 98 34W
Mendhar, *India* ... 93 C6 33 35N 74 10 E
Mendi, *Ethiopia* ... 107 F4 9 47N 35 4 E
Mendi, *Papua N. G.* ... 132 D2 6 11 S 143 39 E
Mendip Hills, *U.K.* ... 21 F5 51 17N 2 40W
Mendocino, *U.S.A.* ... 158 G2 39 19N 123 48W
Mendocino, C., *U.S.A.* ... 158 F1 40 26N 124 25W
Mendon, *U.S.A.* ... 157 B11 40 20N 85 27W
Mendooran, *Australia* ... 129 A8 31 50 S 149 6 E
Mendota, *Calif., U.S.A.* ... 160 J6 36 45N 120 23W
Mendota, *Ill., U.S.A.* ... 156 C7 41 33N 89 7W
Mendoyo, *Indonesia* ... 79 J17 8 23 S 114 42 E
Mendoza, *Argentina* ... 174 C2 32 50 S 68 52W
Mendoza □, *Argentina* ... 174 C2 33 0 S 69 0W
Mendrisio, *Switz.* ... 33 E7 45 52N 8 59 E
Mene Grande, *Venezuela* ... 168 B3 9 49N 70 56W
Menemen, *Turkey* ... 49 C9 38 34N 27 3 E
Menen, *Belgium* ... 24 D3 50 47N 3 7 E
Menéndez, L., *Argentina* ... 176 B2 42 40 S 71 51W
Menfi, *Italy* ... 46 E5 37 36N 12 58 E
Mengdingjie, *China* ... 76 F2 23 33N 98 58 E

Mengeš, *Slovenia* ... 45 B11 46 10N 14 35 E
Menggala, *Indonesia* ... 84 C3 4 30 S 105 15 E
Menghai, *China* ... 76 G3 21 49N 100 55 E
Mengíbar, *Spain* ... 43 H7 37 58N 3 48W
Mengjin, *China* ... 74 G7 34 55N 112 45 E
Mengla, *China* ... 76 G3 21 20N 101 25 E
Menglian, *China* ... 76 F2 22 21N 99 27 E
Mengoub, *Algeria* ... 110 C3 29 49N 5 26W
Mengshan, *China* ... 77 E8 24 14N 110 55 E
Mengyin, *China* ... 75 G9 35 40N 117 58 E
Mengzhe, *China* ... 76 F3 22 2N 100 15 E
Mengzi, *China* ... 76 F4 23 20N 103 22 E
Menihek, *Canada* ... 141 B6 54 0N 56 36W
Menihek L., *Canada* ... 141 B6 54 0N 67 0W
Menin = Menen, *Belgium* ... 24 D3 50 47N 3 7 E
Menindee, *Australia* ... 128 B5 32 20 S 142 25 E
Menindee L., *Australia* ... 128 B5 32 20 S 142 25 E
Meningie, *Australia* ... 128 C3 35 50 S 139 18 E
Menjangan, Pulau, *Indonesia* ... 79 J17 8 7 S 114 31 E
Menkrour, *Algeria* ... 111 C6 26 27N 8 9 E
Menlo Park, *U.S.A.* ... 160 H4 37 27N 122 12W
Menominee, *U.S.A.* ... 148 C2 45 6N 87 37W
Menominee →, *U.S.A.* ... 148 C2 45 6N 87 36W
Menomonee Falls, *U.S.A.* ... 157 A8 43 11N 88 7W
Menomonie, *U.S.A.* ... 154 C9 44 53N 91 55W
Menongue, *Angola* ... 115 E3 14 48 S 17 52 E
Menorca, *Spain* ... 38 B5 40 0N 4 0 E
Menorca ✕ (MAH), *Spain* ... 40 F9 39 50N 4 16 E
Mentakab, *Malaysia* ... 87 L4 3 29N 102 21 E
Mentasta Lake, *U.S.A.* ... 144 E12 62 55N 143 45W
Mentawai, Kepulauan, *Indonesia* ... 84 C1 2 0 S 99 0 E
Menton, *France* ... 29 E11 43 50N 7 29 E
Mentone, *U.S.A.* ... 157 C10 41 10N 86 2W
Mentor, *U.S.A.* ... 150 E3 41 40N 81 21W
Menyamya, *Papua N. G.* ... 132 D3 7 10 S 145 59 E
Menzel-Bourguiba, *Tunisia* ... 108 A1 37 9N 9 49 E
Menzel-Chaker, *Tunisia* ... 108 B2 35 0N 10 26 E
Menzel-Temime, *Tunisia* ... 108 A2 36 46N 11 0 E
Menzelinsk, *Russia* ... 64 D4 55 47N 53 11 E
Menzies, *Australia* ... 125 E3 29 40 S 121 2 E
Meob B., *Namibia* ... 116 B2 24 25 S 14 34 E
Me'ona, *Israel* ... 103 B4 33 1N 35 15 E
Meoqui, *Mexico* ... 162 B3 28 17N 105 29W
Mepaco, *Mozam.* ... 119 F3 15 57 S 30 48 E
Meppel, *Neths.* ... 24 B6 52 42N 6 12 E
Meppen, *Germany* ... 30 C3 52 42N 7 17 E
Mequinenza, *Spain* ... 40 D5 41 22N 0 17 E
Mequinenza, Embalse de, *Spain* ... 40 D5 41 25N 0 15 E
Mequon, *U.S.A.* ... 157 A9 43 14N 87 59W
Mer, *France* ... 26 E8 47 42N 1 30 E
Merabéllou, Kólpos, *Greece* ... 39 E6 35 10N 25 50 E
Merai, *Papua N. G.* ... 132 C7 4 52 S 152 19 E
Merak, *Indonesia* ... 79 F12 6 10N 106 26 E
Meråker, *Norway* ... 18 A8 63 25N 11 46 E
Meramangye, L., *Australia* ... 125 E5 28 25 S 132 13 E
Meramec →, *U.S.A.* ... 156 F6 38 24N 90 21W
Meran = Merano, *Italy* ... 45 B8 46 40N 11 9 E
Merano, *Italy* ... 45 B8 46 40N 11 9 E
Merate, *Italy* ... 44 C6 45 42N 9 25 E
Merauke, *Indonesia* ... 83 C6 8 29 S 140 24 E
Merauke →, *Indonesia* ... 83 C6 8 30 S 140 24 E
Merbabu, *Indonesia* ... 85 D4 7 30 S 110 40 E
Merbein, *Australia* ... 128 C5 34 10 S 142 2 E
Merbuk, Gunung, *Indonesia* ... 79 J17 8 13 S 114 39 E
Merca, *Somali Rep.* ... 120 D2 1 48N 44 50 E
Mercantour, Parc Nat. du △, *France* ... 29 D10 44 16N 6 43 E
Mercato Saraceno, *Italy* ... 45 E9 43 57N 12 12 E
Merced, *U.S.A.* ... 160 H6 37 18N 120 29W
Merced →, *U.S.A.* ... 160 H6 37 21N 120 59W
Merced Pk., *U.S.A.* ... 160 H7 37 36N 119 24W
Mercedes, *Buenos Aires, Argentina* ... 174 C4 34 40 S 59 30W
Mercedes, *Corrientes, Argentina* ... 174 B4 29 10 S 58 5W
Mercedes, *San Luis, Argentina* ... 174 C2 33 40 S 65 21W
Mercedes, *Phil.* ... 80 D4 14 7N 123 1 E
Mercedes, *Uruguay* ... 174 C4 33 12 S 58 0W
Mercedes, *U.S.A.* ... 155 M6 26 9N 97 55W
Merceditas, *Chile* ... 174 B1 28 20 S 70 35W
Mercer, *N.Z.* ... 131 D4 37 16 S 175 5 E
Mercer, *Mo., U.S.A.* ... 156 D3 40 31N 93 32W
Mercer, *Pa., U.S.A.* ... 150 E4 41 14N 80 15W
Mercer Island, *U.S.A.* ... 160 C4 47 35N 122 15W
Mercier, *Bolivia* ... 161 J11 36 40N 115 58W
Mercury, *U.S.A.* ... 161 J11 36 40N 115 58W
Mercury B., *N.Z.* ... 131 B5 36 48 S 175 45 E
Mercury Is., *N.Z.* ... 131 B5 36 37 S 175 52 E
Mercy, C., *Canada* ... 139 B13 65 0N 63 30W
Merdignac, *France* ... 26 D4 48 11N 2 27W
Mere, *U.K.* ... 21 F5 51 6N 2 16W
Mere Lava, *Vanuatu* ... 133 D6 14 25 S 168 3 E
Meredith, *Australia* ... 128 D6 37 49 S 144 5 E
Meredith, C., *Falk. Is.* ... 9 f 52 15 S 60 40W
Meredith, L., *U.S.A.* ... 155 H4 35 43N 101 33W
Meredosia, *U.S.A.* ... 156 E6 39 50N 90 34W
Merefa, *Ukraine* ... 59 H9 49 48N 36 3 E
Mereeg, *Somali Rep.* ... 120 D3 3 46N 47 18 E
Merei, *Romania* ... 53 E11 45 7N 26 43 E
Merga = Nukheila, *Sudan* ... 106 D2 19 1N 26 21 E
Mergui, *Burma* ... 86 F2 12 26N 98 34 E
Mergui Arch. = Myeik Kyunzu, *Burma* ... 87 G1 11 30N 97 30 E
Meribah, *Australia* ... 128 C4 34 43 S 140 51 E
Meriç, *Turkey* ... 51 E10 41 11N 26 25 E
Meriç →, *Turkey* ... 51 F10 40 52N 26 12 E
Mérida, *Mexico* ... 163 C7 20 58N 89 37W
Mérida, *Phil.* ... 81 F5 10 55N 124 32 E
Mérida, *Spain* ... 43 G4 38 55N 6 25W
Mérida, *Venezuela* ... 168 B3 8 24N 71 8W
Mérida □, *Venezuela* ... 168 B3 8 30N 71 10W
Mérida, Cord. de, *Venezuela* ... 168 B3 9 0N 71 0W
Meriden, *U.K.* ... 21 E6 52 26N 1 38W
Meriden, *U.S.A.* ... 151 E12 41 32N 72 48W
Meridian, *Calif., U.S.A.* ... 160 F5 39 9N 121 55W
Meridian, *Ga., U.S.A.* ... 152 D8 31 27N 81 23W
Meridian, *Idaho, U.S.A.* ... 158 E5 43 37N 116 24W
Meridian, *Miss., U.S.A.* ... 149 J1 32 22N 88 42W
Mérignac, *France* ... 28 D3 44 51N 0 39W
Merimbula, *Australia* ... 129 D8 36 53 S 149 54 E
Mérinaghène, *Senegal* ... 112 B1 15 57N 15 55W
Merinda, *Australia* ... 126 C4 20 2 S 148 11 E
Mering, *Germany* ... 31 G6 48 16N 10 59 E
Meringa, *Nigeria* ... 113 C7 10 44N 12 9 E
Meringur, *Australia* ... 128 C4 34 25 S 141 19 E
Merir, *Pac. Oc.* ... 79 D8 4 10N 132 30 E
Merirumã, *Brazil* ... 169 C7 1 15N 54 50W
Merke, *Kazakhstan* ... 65 B6 42 52N 73 11 E
Merkel, *U.S.A.* ... 155 J5 32 28N 100 1W
Mermaid Reef, *Australia* ... 124 C2 17 6 S 119 36 E
Meroe, *India* ... 95 L11 7 39 S 93 33 E
Merowe, *Sudan* ... 106 D3 18 29N 31 46 E
Merredin, *Australia* ... 125 F2 31 28 S 118 18 E
Merrick, *U.K.* ... 22 F4 55 8N 4 28W
Merrickville, *Canada* ... 151 B9 44 55N 75 50W
Merrill, *Oreg., U.S.A.* ... 158 E3 42 1N 121 36W
Merrill, *Wis., U.S.A.* ... 154 C10 45 11N 89 41W
Merrillville, *U.S.A.* ... 157 C9 41 29N 87 20W
Merrimack →, *U.S.A.* ... 151 D14 42 49N 70 49W
Merriman, *U.S.A.* ... 154 D4 42 55N 101 42W
Merritt, *Canada* ... 142 C4 50 10N 120 45W
Merritt Island, *U.S.A.* ... 153 G9 28 21N 80 42W
Merriwa, *Australia* ... 129 B9 32 6 S 150 22 E
Merriwagga, *Australia* ... 129 B7 33 47 S 145 43 E
Merry I., *Canada* ... 140 A4 55 29N 77 31W
Merrygoen, *Australia* ... 129 A8 31 51 S 149 12 E
Merryville, *U.S.A.* ... 155 K8 30 45N 93 33W

Mersa Fatma, *Eritrea* ... 107 E5 14 57N 40 17 E
Mersch, *Lux.* ... 24 E6 49 44N 6 7 E
Merse →, *Italy* ... 45 E8 43 5N 11 22 E
Mersea I., *U.K.* ... 21 F8 51 47N 0 58 E
Merseburg, *Germany* ... 30 D7 51 22N 11 59 E
Mersey →, *U.K.* ... 20 D4 53 25N 3 1W
Merseyside □, *U.K.* ... 20 D4 53 31N 3 2W
Mersin, *Turkey* ... 100 D6 36 51N 34 36 E
Mersing, *Malaysia* ... 87 L4 2 25N 103 50 E
Merta, *India* ... 92 F6 26 39N 74 4 E
Merta Road, *India* ... 92 F5 26 43N 73 55 E
Merthyr Tydfil, *U.K.* ... 21 F4 51 45N 3 22W
Merthyr Tydfil □, *U.K.* ... 21 F4 51 46N 3 21W
Mértola, *Portugal* ... 43 H3 37 40N 7 40W
Mertzon, *U.S.A.* ... 155 K4 31 16N 100 49W
Méru, *France* ... 27 C9 49 13N 2 8 E
Meru, *Kenya* ... 118 B4 0 3N 37 40 E
Meru, *Tanzania* ... 118 C4 3 15 S 36 46 E
Meru Nat. Park △, *Kenya* ... 118 B4 0 5N 38 10 E
Merville, *France* ... 27 B9 50 38N 2 38 E
Méry-sur-Seine, *France* ... 27 D10 48 31N 3 54 E
Merzifon, *Turkey* ... 100 B6 40 53N 35 32 E
Merzig, *Germany* ... 31 F2 49 26N 6 37 E
Merzouga, Erg Tin, *Algeria* ... 111 D7 24 0N 11 4 E
Mesa, *U.S.A.* ... 159 K8 33 25N 111 50W
Mesa Verde Nat. Park △, *U.S.A.* ... 159 H9 37 11N 108 29W
Mesach Mellet, *Libya* ... 108 D2 24 30N 11 30 E
Mesagne, *Italy* ... 47 B10 40 34N 17 48 E
Mesanagrós, *Greece* ... 38 E11 36 1N 27 49 E
Mesaoría, *Cyprus* ... 39 D12 35 12 S 33 14 E
Mesarás, Kólpos, *Greece* ... 39 E5 35 6N 24 47 E
Meschede, *Germany* ... 30 D4 51 20N 8 18 E
Mescit, *Turkey* ... 101 B9 40 21N 41 11 E
Mesfinto, *Ethiopia* ... 107 E4 13 20N 37 22 E
Mesgouez, L., *Canada* ... 140 B5 51 20N 75 0W
Meshchovsk, *Russia* ... 58 E4 54 22N 35 17 E
Meshed = Mashhad, *Iran* ... 97 B8 36 20N 59 35 E
Meshoppen, *U.S.A.* ... 151 E8 41 36N 76 3W
Meshra er Req, *Sudan* ... 107 F2 8 25N 29 18 E
Mesilinka →, *Canada* ... 142 B4 56 6N 124 30W
Mesilla, *U.S.A.* ... 159 K10 32 16N 106 48W
Meslay-du-Maine, *France* ... 26 E6 47 58N 0 33W
Mesocco, *Switz.* ... 33 D8 46 23N 9 12 E
Mesolóngion, *Greece* ... 48 C3 38 21N 21 28 E
Mesopotamia = Al Jazirah, *Iraq* ... 101 E10 33 30N 44 0 E
Mesopotamia, *U.S.A.* ... 150 E4 41 27N 80 57W
Mesopotamon, *Greece* ... 48 B2 39 14N 20 32 E
Mesoraca, *Italy* ... 47 C9 39 5N 16 48 E
Mésou Volímais = Volímai, *Greece* ... 37 D2 37 52N 20 39 E
Mesquite, *U.S.A.* ... 159 H6 36 47N 114 6W
Messaad, *Algeria* ... 111 B5 34 8N 3 30 E
Messac, *France* ... 26 E5 47 49N 1 50W
Messalo →, *Mozam.* ... 119 E4 12 25 S 39 15 E
Messeue, *France* ... 48 D3 37 12N 21 58 E
Messier, Canal, *Chile* ... 176 C2 48 20 S 74 33W
Messina, *Italy* ... 47 D8 38 11N 15 34 E
Messina, *S. Africa* ... 117 C5 22 20 S 30 5 E
Messina, Str. di, *Italy* ... 47 D8 38 15N 15 35 E
Messíni, *Greece* ... 48 D3 37 4N 22 1 E
Messínia □, *Greece* ... 48 D3 37 10N 22 0 E
Messiniakós Kólpos, *Greece* ... 48 E3 36 45N 22 5 E
Messkirch, *Germany* ... 31 H5 47 59N 9 7 E
Messonghi, *Greece* ... 38 C9 39 29N 19 56 E
Mesta →, *Bulgaria* ... 50 E7 40 54N 24 49 E
Mestá, Ákra, *Greece* ... 49 C7 38 16N 25 53 E
Mestanza, *Spain* ... 43 G6 38 35N 4 4W
Mestersvig, *Greenland* ... 10 C8 72 10N 23 40W
Mestre, *Italy* ... 45 C9 45 29N 12 15 E
Mestre, Espigão, *Brazil* ... 171 D2 12 30 S 46 10W
Mesudiye, *Turkey* ... 100 B7 40 28N 37 46 E
Meta □, *Colombia* ... 168 C3 3 30N 73 0W
Meta →, *S. Amer.* ... 168 B4 6 12N 67 28W
Meta Incognita Peninsula, *Canada* ... 139 B13 62 40N 68 0W
Metabetchouan, *Canada* ... 141 C5 48 26N 71 52W
Metairie, *U.S.A.* ... 155 L9 29 58N 90 10W
Metaline Falls, *U.S.A.* ... 158 B5 48 52N 117 22W
Metalline, Colline, *Italy* ... 44 E8 43 10N 11 0 E
Metamora, *Ill., U.S.A.* ... 156 D7 40 47N 89 22W
Metán, *Argentina* ... 174 B3 25 30 S 65 0W
Metangula, *Mozam.* ... 119 E3 12 40 S 34 50 E
Metauro →, *Italy* ... 45 E10 43 50N 13 3 E
Metcalf, *U.S.A.* ... 152 E6 30 43N 83 59W
Metema, *Ethiopia* ... 107 E4 12 56N 36 13 E
Metengobalame, *Mozam.* ... 119 E3 14 49 S 34 30 E
Méthana, *Greece* ... 48 D5 37 35N 23 23 E
Methóni, *Greece* ... 48 E3 36 49N 21 42 E
Methven, *N.Z.* ... 131 D6 43 38 S 171 40 E
Metil, *Mozam.* ... 119 F4 16 24 S 39 0 E
Metkovets, *Bulgaria* ... 50 C7 43 37N 23 10 E
Metković, *Croatia* ... 45 E14 43 6N 17 39 E
Metlakatla, *U.S.A.* ... 144 J15 55 8N 131 35W
Metlaoui, *Tunisia* ... 108 B1 34 24N 8 24 E
Metlika, *Slovenia* ... 45 C12 45 40N 15 20 E
Metro, *Indonesia* ... 84 D3 5 5 S 105 20 E
Metropolis, *U.S.A.* ... 155 G10 37 9N 88 44W
Métsovon, *Greece* ... 48 B3 39 48N 21 12 E
Metter, *U.S.A.* ... 152 C7 32 24N 82 3W
Mettuppalaiyam, *India* ... 95 J3 11 18N 76 59 E
Mettur, *India* ... 95 J3 11 48N 77 47 E
Metu, *Ethiopia* ... 107 F4 8 18N 35 35 E
Metz, *France* ... 27 D13 49 8N 6 10 E
Metzingen, *Germany* ... 31 G5 48 31N 9 17 E
Meulaboh, *Indonesia* ... 84 B1 4 11N 96 3 E
Meung-sur-Loire, *France* ... 27 E8 47 50N 1 40 E
Meurcourt, *France* ... 32 A2 47 46N 6 14 E
Meureudu, *Indonesia* ... 84 A1 5 19N 96 10 E
Meurthe →, *France* ... 27 D13 48 47N 6 9 E
Meurthe-et-Moselle □, *France* ... 27 D13 48 52N 6 0 E
Meuse □, *France* ... 27 D12 49 8N 5 25 E
Meuse →, *Europe* ... 24 D5 50 45N 5 41 E
Meuselwitz, *Germany* ... 30 D8 51 3N 12 18 E
Meutapok, Mt., *Malaysia* ... 85 A5 5 40N 117 0 E
Mexia, *U.S.A.* ... 155 K6 31 41N 96 29W
Mexiana, I., *Brazil* ... 170 A2 0 0 49 30W
Mexicali, *Mexico* ... 161 N11 32 40N 115 30W
Mexican Plateau, *Mexico* ... 136 G9 25 0N 104 0W
Mexican Water, *U.S.A.* ... 159 H9 36 57N 109 32W
México, *Mexico* ... 163 D5 19 20N 99 10W
Mexico, *Maine, U.S.A.* ... 151 B14 44 34N 70 33W
Mexico, *Mo., U.S.A.* ... 156 E5 39 10N 91 53W
Mexico, *N.Y., U.S.A.* ... 151 C8 43 28N 76 18W
México □, *Mexico* ... 163 D5 19 20N 99 10W
Mexico ■, *Cent. Amer.* ... 162 C4 25 0N 105 0W
Mexico, G. of, *Cent. Amer.* ... 163 C7 25 0N 90 0W
Mexico B., *U.S.A.* ... 151 C8 43 35N 76 20W
Mexico Beach, *U.S.A.* ... 152 F4 29 57N 85 25W
Meydân-e Naftûn, *Iran* ... 97 D6 31 56N 49 18 E
Meydani, Ra's-e, *Iran* ... 97 E8 25 24N 59 6 E
Meyenburg, *Germany* ... 30 B8 53 18N 12 14 E
Meyers Chuck, *U.S.A.* ... 144 J14 55 45N 132 15W
Meymac, *France* ... 28 C6 45 32N 2 10 E
Meymaneh, *Afghan.* ... 91 B2 35 53N 64 38 E
Meyo, *Cameroon* ... 114 B2 2 50N 11 6 E
Meyrueis, *France* ... 28 D7 44 12N 3 27 E
Meyssac, *France* ... 28 C5 45 3N 1 40 E
Meyzieu, *France* ... 29 C8 45 46N 4 59 E
Mezdra, *Bulgaria* ... 50 C7 43 12N 23 42 E
Mèze, *France* ... 28 E7 43 27N 3 36 E
Mézel, *France* ... 29 D10 44 8N 6 5 E
Mezen, *Russia* ... 56 A7 65 50N 44 20 E
Mezen →, *Russia* ... 56 A7 65 44N 44 22 E

Mézenc, Mt., *France* ... 29 D8 44 54N 4 11 E
Mezeş, Munţii, *Romania* ... 52 C8 47 5N 23 5 E
Mezha →, *Russia* ... 58 E6 55 44N 31 33 E
Mezhdurechenskiy, *Russia* ... 66 D7 59 36N 65 56 E
Mézidon-Canon, *France* ... 26 C6 49 5N 0 1W
Mézières-en-Brenne, *France* ... 28 B5 46 49N 1 13 E
Mézilhac, *France* ... 29 D8 44 49N 4 21 E
Mézin, *France* ... 28 D4 44 4N 0 16 E
Mezőberény, *Hungary* ... 52 D6 46 49N 21 3 E
Mezőfalva, *Hungary* ... 52 D3 46 55N 18 49 E
Mezőhegyes, *Hungary* ... 52 D5 46 19N 20 49 E
Mezőkövácsháza, *Hungary* ... 52 D5 46 25N 20 57 E
Mezőkövesd, *Hungary* ... 52 C5 47 49N 20 35 E
Mezquital, *Mexico* ... 162 C4 23 29N 104 23W
Mezzolombardo, *Italy* ... 44 B8 46 13N 11 5 E
Mfolozi →, *S. Africa* ... 117 D5 28 25 S 32 26 E
Mgarr, *Malta* ... 38 F7 35 55N 14 22 E
Mgarr, *Gozo, Malta* ... 38 E7 36 2N 14 18 E
Mgeta, *Tanzania* ... 119 D4 8 22 S 36 6 E
Mglin, *Russia* ... 59 F7 53 2N 32 50 E
Mhlaba Hills, *Zimbabwe* ... 119 F3 18 30 S 30 30 E
Mhow, *India* ... 92 H6 22 33N 75 50 E
Mi-Shima, *Japan* ... 72 C3 34 46N 131 9 E
Miagao, *Phil.* ... 81 F4 10 39N 122 14 E
Miahuatlán, *Mexico* ... 163 D5 16 21N 96 36W
Miajadas, *Spain* ... 43 F5 39 9N 5 54W
Miami, *Fla., U.S.A.* ... 153 K9 25 47N 80 11W
Miami, *Okla., U.S.A.* ... 155 G7 36 53N 94 53W
Miami, *Tex., U.S.A.* ... 155 H4 35 42N 100 38W
Miami Beach, *U.S.A.* ... 153 K9 25 47N 80 8W
Miami Canal, *U.S.A.* ... 153 J9 26 30N 80 45W
Miami International ✕ (MIA), *U.S.A.* ... 153 K9 25 48N 80 17W
Miami Shores, *U.S.A.* ... 153 K9 25 52N 80 12W
Miami Springs, *U.S.A.* ... 153 K9 25 49N 80 17W
Miamisburg, *U.S.A.* ... 157 E12 39 38N 84 17W
Mian Xian, *China* ... 74 H4 33 10N 106 32 E
Mianchi, *China* ... 74 G6 34 48N 111 48 E
Miāndarreh, *Iran* ... 97 C7 35 37N 53 39 E
Miāndowāb, *Iran* ... 101 D12 37 0N 46 5 E
Miandrivazo, *Madag.* ... 117 B8 19 31 S 45 29 E
Miāneh, *Iran* ... 101 D12 37 30N 47 40 E
Mianning, *China* ... 74 C4 28 32N 102 9 E
Mianwali, *Pakistan* ... 91 B3 32 38N 71 28 E
Mianyang, *China* ... 76 B5 31 22N 104 47 E
Mianzhu, *China* ... 76 B5 31 22N 104 7 E
Miaoli, *Taiwan* ... 77 E13 24 37N 120 49 E
Miarinarivo, *Antananarivo, Madag.* ... 117 B8 18 57 S 46 55 E
Miarinarivo, *Toamasina, Madag.* ... 117 B8 16 38 S 48 15 E
Miarivaratra, *Madag.* ... 117 C8 20 13 S 47 31 E
Miass, *Russia* ... 64 D8 54 59N 60 6 E
Miasteczko Krajeńskie, *Poland* ... 55 E4 53 7N 17 1 E
Miastko, *Poland* ... 54 E3 54 0N 16 58 E
Mica, *S. Africa* ... 117 C5 24 10 S 30 48 E
Micanopy, *U.S.A.* ... 153 F7 29 30N 82 17W
Micăsasa, *Romania* ... 53 D9 46 7N 24 7 E
Micco, *U.S.A.* ... 153 H9 27 53N 80 30W
Michalovce, *Slovak Rep.* ... 35 C14 48 47N 21 58 E
Michigan □, *U.S.A.* ... 148 C3 44 0N 85 0W
Michigan, L., *U.S.A.* ... 157 B9 44 0N 87 0W
Michigan Center, *U.S.A.* ... 157 B12 42 14N 84 20W
Michigan City, *U.S.A.* ... 157 C10 41 43N 86 54W
Michika, *Nigeria* ... 113 C7 10 36N 13 23 E
Michipicoten I., *Canada* ... 140 C2 47 40N 85 40W
Michoacan □, *Mexico* ... 162 D4 19 0N 102 0W
Michurin, *Bulgaria* ... 51 D11 42 9N 27 51 E
Michurinsk, *Russia* ... 60 D5 52 58N 40 27 E
Mico, Pta., *Nic.* ... 164 D3 12 0N 83 30W
Miconje, *Angola* ... 115 C2 4 36N 12 47 E
Micoud, *St. Lucia* ... 165 f 13 49N 60 54W
Micronesia, *Pac. Oc.* ... 134 G7 11 0N 160 0 E
Micronesia, Federated States of ■, *Pac. Oc.* ... 134 G7 9 0N 150 0 E
Mid-Indian Ridge, *Ind. Oc.* ... 121 H6 30 0 S 75 0 E
Midai, *Indonesia* ... 85 B3 3 0N 107 47 E
Midale, *Canada* ... 143 D8 49 25N 103 20W
Middelburg, *Neths.* ... 24 C3 51 30N 3 36 E
Middelburg, *Eastern Cape, S. Africa* ... 116 E4 31 30 S 25 0 E
Middelburg, *Mpumalanga, S. Africa* ... 117 D4 25 49 S 29 28 E
Middelfart, *Denmark* ... 17 J3 55 30N 9 43 E
Middelpos, *S. Africa* ... 116 E3 31 55 S 20 13 E
Middelwit, *S. Africa* ... 116 C4 24 51 S 27 3 E
Middle →, *U.S.A.* ... 156 C7 41 26N 93 30W
Middle Alkali L., *U.S.A.* ... 158 F3 41 27N 120 5W
Middle Andaman I., *India* ... 95 H11 12 30N 92 58 E
Middle Bass I., *U.S.A.* ... 150 E2 41 41N 82 49W
Middle East, *Asia* ... 62 F7 38 0N 40 0 E
Middle Fork Feather →, *U.S.A.* ... 160 F5 38 33N 121 30W
Middle I., *Australia* ... 125 F3 34 6 S 123 11 E
Middle Loup →, *U.S.A.* ... 154 E5 41 17N 98 24W
Middle Raccoon →, *U.S.A.* ... 156 C3 41 35 S 93 35W
Middle Sackville, *Canada* ... 141 D7 44 47N 63 42W
Middleboro, *U.S.A.* ... 151 E14 41 54N 70 55W
Middleburg, *Fla., U.S.A.* ... 152 E8 30 4N 81 52W
Middleburg, *N.Y., U.S.A.* ... 151 D10 42 36N 74 20W
Middleburg, *Pa., U.S.A.* ... 150 F7 40 47N 77 3W
Middlebury, *Ind., U.S.A.* ... 157 C11 41 41N 85 42W
Middlebury, *Vt., U.S.A.* ... 151 B11 44 1N 73 10W
Middlemarch, *N.Z.* ... 131 F5 45 30 S 170 9 E
Middlemount, *Australia* ... 126 C4 22 50 S 148 40 E
Middleport, *N.Y., U.S.A.* ... 150 C6 43 13N 78 29W
Middleport, *Ohio, U.S.A.* ... 148 F4 39 0N 82 3W
Middlesboro, *U.S.A.* ... 149 G4 36 36N 83 43W
Middlesbrough, *U.K.* ... 20 C6 54 35N 1 13W
Middlesbrough □, *U.K.* ... 20 C6 54 28N 1 13W
Middlesex, *Belize* ... 164 C2 17 2N 88 31W
Middlesex, *N.J., U.S.A.* ... 151 F10 40 36N 74 30W
Middlesex, *N.Y., U.S.A.* ... 150 D7 42 42N 77 16W
Middleton, *Australia* ... 126 C3 22 22 S 141 32 E
Middleton, *Canada* ... 141 D6 44 57N 65 4W
Middleton Cr. →, *Australia* ... 126 C3 22 35 S 141 51 E
Middleton I., *Australia* ... 144 G11 59 26N 146 20W
Middletown, *U.K.* ... 23 B5 54 17N 6 51W
Middletown, *Calif., U.S.A.* ... 160 G4 38 45N 122 37W
Middletown, *Conn., U.S.A.* ... 151 E12 41 34N 72 39W
Middletown, *Ky., U.S.A.* ... 157 F11 38 14N 85 32W
Middletown, *N.Y., U.S.A.* ... 151 E10 41 27N 74 25W
Middletown, *Ohio, U.S.A.* ... 157 E12 39 31N 84 24W
Middletown, *Pa., U.S.A.* ... 151 F8 40 12N 76 44W
Middleville, *U.S.A.* ... 157 B11 42 43N 85 28W
Midelt, *Morocco* ... 110 B4 32 46N 4 44W
Midge Point, *Australia* ... 126 J6 20 38 S 148 43 E
Midhirst, *N.Z.* ... 130 F3 39 17 S 174 18 E
Miðsandur, *Iceland* ... 11 C5 64 24N 21 30W
Midhurst, *U.K.* ... 21 G7 50 59N 0 44W
Mīdī, *Yemen* ... 107 D5 16 24N 42 45 E
Midi, Canal du →, *France* ... 28 E5 43 45N 1 21 E
Midi d'Ossau, Pic du, *France* ... 28 F3 42 50N 0 25W
Midi-Pyrénées □, *France* ... 28 E5 43 55N 1 45 E
Midland, *Canada* ... 148 D3 44 45N 79 50W
Midland, *Calif., U.S.A.* ... 161 M12 33 52N 114 48W
Midland, *Mich., U.S.A.* ... 148 D3 43 37N 84 14W
Midland, *Pa., U.S.A.* ... 150 F4 40 39N 80 27W
Midland, *Tex., U.S.A.* ... 155 K3 32 0N 102 3W
Midlands □, *Zimbabwe* ... 119 F2 19 40 S 29 0 E
Midleton, *Ireland* ... 23 E3 51 55N 8 10W
Midlothian, *U.S.A.* ... 155 J6 32 30N 97 0W
Midlothian □, *U.K.* ... 22 F5 55 51N 3 5W

Midongy, Tangorombohitr' i, *Madag.* **117 C8** 23 30 S 47 0 E
Midongy Atsimo, *Madag.* **117 C8** 23 35 S 47 1 E
Midou →, *France* **28 E3** 43 54N 0 30W
Midouze →, *France* **28 E3** 43 48N 0 51W
Midsayap, *Phil.* **81 H5** 7 12N 124 32 E
Midsund, *Norway* **18 B3** 62 41N 6 40 E
Midtgulen, *Norway* **18 C2** 61 44N 5 11 E
Midu, *China* **76 E3** 25 18N 100 30 E
Midway, *Ala., U.S.A.* **152 C7** 32 49N 82 14W
Midway, *Fla., U.S.A.* **152 C4** 32 5N 85 31W
Midway, *Pac. Oc.* **152 E5** 36 30N 84 27W
Midway Is., *Pac. Oc.* **134 E10** 28 13N 177 22W
Midway Wells, *U.S.A.* **161 N11** 32 41N 115 7W
Midwest, *U.S.A.* **158 E10** 43 25N 106 16W
Midwest City, *U.S.A.* **155 H6** 35 27N 97 24W
Midyat, *Turkey* **101 D9** 37 25N 41 23 E
Midžör, *Bulgaria* **50 C6** 43 24N 22 40 E
Mie, *Japan* **72 E3** 32 58N 131 35 E
Mie □, *Japan* **73 C8** 34 30N 136 10 E
Miechów, *Poland* **55 H7** 50 21N 20 5 E
Miedwie, Jezioro, *Poland* **55 E1** 53 17N 14 54 E
Międzybórz, *Poland* **55 G4** 51 25N 17 34 E
Międzychód, *Poland* **55 F2** 52 35N 15 53 E
Międzylesie, *Poland* **55 H3** 50 8N 16 40 E
Międzyrzec Podlaski, *Poland* **55 G9** 51 58N 22 45 E
Międzyrzecz, *Poland* **55 F2** 52 26N 15 35 E
Międzyzdroje, *Poland* **54 E1** 53 56N 14 26 E
Miejska Górka, *Poland* **55 G3** 51 39N 16 58 E
Miélan, *France* **28 E4** 43 27N 0 19 E
Mielec, *Poland* **55 H8** 50 15N 21 25 E
Mienga, *Angola* **116 B2** 17 12 S 19 48 E
Miercurea-Ciuc, *Romania* **53 D10** 46 21N 25 48 E
Miercurea Sibiului, *Romania* **53 E8** 45 53N 23 48 E
Mieres, *Spain* **42 B5** 43 18N 5 48W
Mieroszów, *Poland* **55 H3** 50 40N 16 11 E
Mieso, *Ethiopia* **107 F5** 9 15N 40 43 E
Mieszkowice, *Poland* **55 F1** 52 47N 14 30 E
Mifflintown, *U.S.A.* **150 F7** 40 34N 77 24W
Mifraz Ḥefa, *Israel* **103 C4** 32 52N 35 0 E
Migennes, *France* **27 E10** 47 58N 3 31 E
Migliarino, *Italy* **45 D8** 44 46N 11 56 E
Migliarino-San Rossore-
  Massaciuccoli, Parco di △, *Italy* **44 E7** 43 44N 10 20 E
Miguel Alemán, Presa, *Mexico* **163 D5** 18 15N 96 40W
Miguel Alves, *Brazil* **170 B3** 4 11 S 42 55W
Miguel Calmon, *Brazil* **170 D3** 11 26 S 40 36W
Miguelturra, *Spain* **43 G7** 38 58N 3 53W
Mihăileni, *Romania* **53 C11** 47 58N 26 9 E
Mihăilești, *Romania* **53 F10** 44 20N 25 54 E
Mihailovca, *Moldova* **53 D13** 46 33N 28 56 E
Mihalgazi, *Turkey* **49 A12** 40 2N 30 34 E
Mihaliçcik, *Turkey* **100 C4** 39 53N 31 30 E
Mihara, *Japan* **72 C5** 34 24N 133 5 E
Mihara-Yama, *Japan* **73 C11** 34 43N 139 23 E
Mihesu de Cîmpie, *Romania* **53 D9** 46 41N 24 9 E
Mijas, *Spain* **43 J6** 36 36N 4 40W
Mikese, *Tanzania* **118 D4** 6 48 S 37 55 E
Mikha-Tskhakaya = Senaki, *Georgia* **61 J6** 42 15N 42 7 E
Mikhailovka = Mykhaylivka, *Ukraine* **59 J8** 47 12N 35 15 E
Mikhaylov, *Russia* **58 E10** 54 14N 39 0 E
Mikhaylovgrad = Montana, *Bulgaria* **50 C7** 43 27N 23 16 E
Mikhaylovka, *Kyrgyzstan* **65 B9** 42 37N 78 20 E
Mikhaylovka, *Russia* **60 E6** 50 3N 43 5 E
Mikhaylovski, *Russia* **64 C7** 56 27N 59 7 E
Mikhnevo, *Russia* **58 E9** 55 4N 37 59 E
Miki, *Hyōgo, Japan* **72 C6** 34 48N 134 59 E
Miki, *Kagawa, Japan* **72 C6** 34 12N 134 7 E
Mikínai, *Greece* **48 D4** 37 43N 22 46 E
Mikir Hills, *India* **90 B4** 26 10N 93 30 E
Mikkeli, *Finland* **15 F22** 61 43N 27 15 E
Mikkwa →, *Canada* **142 B6** 58 25N 114 46W
Mikniya, *Sudan* **107 D3** 17 0N 33 45 E
Mikołajki, *Poland* **54 E8** 53 49N 21 37 E
Míkonos, *Greece* **49 D7** 37 30N 25 25 E
Mikope, *Dem. Rep. of the Congo* **115 C4** 4 58 S 20 43 E
Mikrí Préspa, Límni, *Greece* **50 F5** 40 47N 21 3 E
Mikrón Dhérion, *Greece* **51 E10** 41 19N 26 6 E
Mikstat, *Poland* **55 G4** 51 32N 17 59 E
Mikulov, *Czech Rep.* **35 C9** 48 48N 16 39 E
Mikumi, *Tanzania* **118 D4** 7 26 S 37 0 E
Mikumi Nat. Park △, *Tanzania* **118 D4** 7 35 S 37 15 E
Mikun, *Russia* **56 B9** 62 20N 50 0 E
Mikuni, *Japan* **73 A8** 36 13N 136 9 E
Mikuni-Tōge, *Japan* **73 A10** 36 50N 138 50 E
Mikura-Jima, *Japan* **73 D11** 33 52N 139 36 E
Milaca, *U.S.A.* **154 C8** 45 45N 93 39W
Milagro, *Ecuador* **168 D2** 2 11 S 79 36W
Milagros, *Phil.* **80 E4** 12 13N 123 30 E
Milan = Milano, *Italy* **44 C6** 45 28N 9 12 E
Milan, *Ga., U.S.A.* **152 C6** 32 1N 83 4W
Milan, *Ill., U.S.A.* **156 C6** 41 27N 90 34W
Milan, *Mich., U.S.A.* **157 B13** 42 5N 83 41W
Milan, *Mo., U.S.A.* **156 D3** 40 12N 93 7W
Milan, *Tenn., U.S.A.* **149 H1** 35 55N 88 46W
Milan Linate ✈ (LIN), *Italy* **44 C6** 45 27N 9 16 E
Miland, *Norway* **18 E5** 59 54N 8 45 E
Milando, *Angola* **115 D3** 8 45 S 17 36 E
Milando, Reserva Parcial de △,
  Angola **115 D3** 8 45 S 17 10 E
Milang, *Australia* **128 C3** 35 24 S 138 58 E
Milange, *Mozam.* **119 F4** 16 3 S 35 45 E
Milano, *Italy* **44 C6** 45 28N 9 12 E
Milanoa, *Madag.* **117 A8** 13 35 S 49 47 E
Milás, *Turkey* **49 D9** 37 20N 27 50 E
Milatos, *Greece* **49 E6** 35 18N 25 34 E
Milazzo, *Italy* **47 D8** 38 13N 15 15 E
Milbank, *U.S.A.* **154 C6** 45 13N 96 38W
Milbanke Sd., *Canada* **142 C3** 52 15N 128 35W
Milden, *Canada* **143 C7** 51 29N 107 32W
Mildenhall, *U.K.* **21 E8** 52 21N 0 32 E
Mildmay, *Canada* **150 B3** 44 3N 81 7W
Mildura, *Australia* **128 C3** 34 13 S 142 9 E
Mile, *China* **76 E4** 24 28N 103 20 E
Miléai, *Greece* **48 B5** 39 20N 23 9 E
Miles, *Australia* **127 D5** 26 40 S 150 9 E
Miles City, *U.S.A.* **154 B2** 46 25N 105 51W
Milești, *Moldova* **53 C13** 47 13N 28 3 E
Milestone, *Canada* **143 D8** 49 59N 104 31W
Mileto, *Italy* **47 D9** 38 36N 16 4 E
Miletto, Mte., *Italy* **47 A7** 41 27N 14 22 E
Miletus, *Turkey* **49 D9** 37 30N 27 18 E
Milevsko, *Czech Rep.* **34 B7** 49 27N 14 21 E
Milford, *Calif., U.S.A.* **160 E6** 40 10N 120 22W
Milford, *Conn., U.S.A.* **151 E11** 41 14N 73 3W
Milford, *Del., U.S.A.* **148 F8** 38 55N 75 26W
Milford, *Ill., U.S.A.* **157 D9** 40 38N 87 42W
Milford, *Mass., U.S.A.* **151 D13** 42 8N 71 31W
Milford, *Mich., U.S.A.* **157 B13** 42 35N 83 36W
Milford, *N.H., U.S.A.* **151 D13** 42 50N 71 39W
Milford, *Pa., U.S.A.* **151 E10** 41 19N 74 48W
Milford, *Utah, U.S.A.* **159 G7** 38 24N 113 1W
Milford Haven, *U.K.* **21 F2** 51 42N 5 7W
Milford Sd., *N.Z.* **131 E2** 44 41 S 167 47 E
Milḥ, Baḥr al, *Iraq* **101 F10** 32 40N 43 35 E
Miliana, Aïn Salah, *Algeria* **111 C5** 27 20N 2 32 E
Miliana, Médéa, *Algeria* **111 A5** 36 20N 2 15 E
Milicz, *Poland* **55 G4** 51 31N 17 19 E
Milikapiti, *Australia* **124 B5** 11 26 S 130 40 E
Mililani Town, *U.S.A.* **145 K13** 21 28N 158 1W
Miling, *Australia* **125 F2** 30 30 S 116 17 E
Militello in Val di Catánia, *Italy* **47 E7** 37 16N 14 48 E
Milk →, *U.S.A.* **154 B10** 48 4N 106 19W
Milk, Wadi el →, *Sudan* **106 D3** 17 55N 30 20 E
Milk River, *Canada* **142 D6** 49 10N 112 5W

Mill I., *Antarctica* **7 C8** 66 0 S 101 30 E
Mill Shoals, *U.S.A.* **157 F8** 38 15N 88 21W
Mill Valley, *U.S.A.* **160 H4** 37 54N 122 32W
Millárs →, *Spain* **40 F4** 39 55N 0 1W
Millau, *France* **28 D7** 44 8N 3 4 E
Millbridge, *Canada* **150 B7** 44 41N 77 36W
Millbrook, *Canada* **150 B6** 44 10N 78 29W
Millbrook, *U.S.A.* **151 E11** 41 47N 73 42W
Mille Lacs, L. des, *Canada* **140 C1** 48 45N 90 35W
Mille Lacs L., *U.S.A.* **154 B8** 46 15N 93 39W
Milledgeville, *Ga., U.S.A.* **152 B6** 33 5N 83 14W
Milledgeville, *Ill., U.S.A.* **156 C7** 41 58N 89 46W
Millen, *U.S.A.* **152 C8** 32 48N 81 57W
Millennium I. = Caroline I., *Kiribati* **135 H12** 9 58 S 150 13W
Miller, *U.S.A.* **154 C5** 44 31N 98 59W
Millerovo, *Russia* **61 F5** 48 57N 40 28 E
Miller's Flat, *N.Z.* **131 F4** 45 39 S 169 23 E
Millersburg, *Ind., U.S.A.* **157 C11** 41 32N 85 42W
Millersburg, *Ohio, U.S.A.* **150 F3** 40 33N 81 55W
Millersburg, *Pa., U.S.A.* **150 F8** 40 32N 76 58W
Millerton, *U.S.A.* **151 E11** 41 57N 73 31W
Millerton, *N.Z.* **131 B3** 41 39 S 171 54 E
Millerton L., *U.S.A.* **160 J7** 37 1N 119 41W
Millet, *St. Lucia* **165 f** 13 55N 60 59W
Millevaches, Plateau de, *France* **28 C6** 45 45N 2 0 E
Millheim, *U.S.A.* **150 F7** 40 54N 77 29W
Millicent, *Australia* **128 D4** 37 34 S 140 21 E
Milligan, *U.S.A.* **153 E3** 30 45N 86 38W
Millington, *U.S.A.* **155 H10** 35 20N 89 53W
Millinocket, *U.S.A.* **149 C11** 45 39N 68 43W
Millmerran, *Australia* **127 D5** 27 53 S 151 16 E
Millom, *U.K.* **20 C4** 54 13N 3 16W
Mills L., *Canada* **142 A5** 61 30N 118 20W
Millsboro, *U.S.A.* **150 G5** 40 0N 80 0W
Millstream-Chichester Nat. Park △,
  Australia **124 D2** 21 35 S 117 6 E
Millthorpe, *Australia* **129 B8** 33 26 S 149 12 E
Milltown Malbay, *Ireland* **23 D2** 52 52N 9 24W
Millville, *N.J., U.S.A.* **148 F8** 39 24N 75 2W
Millville, *Pa., U.S.A.* **151 E8** 41 7N 76 32W
Millwood L., *U.S.A.* **155 J8** 33 42N 93 58W
Milna, *Croatia* **45 E13** 43 20N 16 28 E
Milne →, *Australia* **126 C2** 21 10 S 137 33 E
Milne Bay □, *Papua N. G.* **132 E7** 10 0 S 152 30 E
Milne Land, *Greenland* **10 C8** 70 40N 26 30W
Milo, *U.S.A.* **149 C11** 45 15N 68 59W
Milolii, *U.S.A.* **145 D6** 19 11N 155 55W
Milos, *Greece* **48 E6** 36 44N 24 25 E
Milosław, *Poland* **55 F4** 52 12N 17 32 E
Milparinka, *Australia* **127 D3** 29 46 S 141 57 E
Milroy, *U.S.A.* **157 E11** 39 30N 85 28W
Miltenberg, *Germany* **31 F5** 49 41N 9 16 E
Milton, *Australia* **129 C9** 35 20 S 150 27 E
Milton, *N.S., Canada* **150 D7** 44 4N 64 45W
Milton, *Ont., Canada* **150 C5** 43 31N 79 53W
Milton, *N.Z.* **131 G4** 46 7 S 169 59 E
Milton, *Calif., U.S.A.* **160 G6** 38 3N 120 51W
Milton, *Fla., U.S.A.* **153 E2** 30 38N 87 3W
Milton, *Iowa, U.S.A.* **156 D4** 40 41N 92 10W
Milton, *Pa., U.S.A.* **150 F8** 41 1N 76 51W
Milton, *Vt., U.S.A.* **151 B11** 44 38N 73 7W
Milton, *Wis., U.S.A.* **156 D8** 42 47N 88 56W
Milton-Freewater, *U.S.A.* **158 D4** 45 56N 118 23W
Milton Keynes, *U.K.* **21 E7** 52 1N 0 44W
Milton Keynes □, *U.K.* **21 E7** 52 1N 0 44W
Miltou, *Chad* **109 F3** 10 14N 17 26 E
Miluo, *China* **77 C6** 29 0N 112 59 E
Milverton, *Canada* **150 C4** 43 34N 80 55W
Milwaukee, *U.S.A.* **157 A9** 43 2N 87 55W
Milwaukee Deep, *Atl. Oc.* **165 C6** 19 50N 68 0W
Milwaukie, *U.S.A.* **158 E4** 45 27N 122 38W
Mim, *Ghana* **112 D4** 6 57N 2 33W
Mimizan, *France* **28 D2** 44 12N 1 13W
Mimoň, *Czech Rep.* **34 A7** 50 38N 14 43 E
Mimongo, *Gabon* **114 C2** 1 11 S 11 36 E
Mimoso, *Brazil* **171 E2** 15 10 S 48 5W
Mims, *U.S.A.* **153 G9** 28 40N 80 51W
Min Jiang →, *Fujian, China* **77 E12** 26 0N 119 35 E
Min Jiang →, *Sichuan, China* **78 C5** 28 45N 104 40 E
Min Xian, *China* **74 G3** 34 25N 104 5 E
Mina Pirquitas, *Argentina* **174 A2** 22 40 S 66 30W
Mina Su'ud, *Si. Arabia* **97 D6** 28 45N 48 28 E
Mina'al Aḥmadī, *Kuwait* **97 D6** 29 5N 48 10 E
Minago →, *Canada* **143 C9** 54 33N 98 59W
Minakami, *Japan* **73 A10** 36 49N 138 59 E
Minaki, *Canada* **143 D10** 49 59N 94 40W
Minakuchi, *Japan* **73 C8** 34 58N 136 10 E
Minamata, *Japan* **72 E2** 32 10N 130 30 E
Minami Alps Nat. Park △, *Japan* **73 B10** 35 30N 138 9 E
Minami-Tori-Shima, *Pac. Oc.* **134 E7** 24 20N 153 58 E
Minas, *Uruguay* **175 C4** 34 20 S 55 10W
Minas, Sierra de las, *Guatemala* **164 C2** 15 9N 89 31W
Minas Basin, *Canada* **141 C7** 45 20N 64 12W
Minas de Rio Tinto = Minas de
  Riotinto, *Spain* **43 H4** 37 42N 6 35W
Minas de Riotinto, *Spain* **43 H4** 37 42N 6 35W
Minas Gerais □, *Brazil* **171 E2** 18 50 S 46 0W
Minas Novas, *Brazil* **171 E3** 17 15 S 42 36W
Minatitlán, *Mexico* **163 D6** 17 59N 94 31W
Minbu, *Burma* **90 E5** 20 10N 94 52 E
Minbya, *Burma* **90 E4** 20 22N 93 16 E
Minchinabad, *Pakistan* **92 D5** 30 10N 73 34 E
Mincio →, *Italy* **44 C7** 45 4N 10 59 E
Minčol, *Slovak Rep.* **35 B13** 49 15N 20 58 E
Mindanao, *Phil.* **81 H5** 8 0N 125 0 E
Mindanao Sea = Bohol Sea, *Phil.* **81 G5** 9 0N 124 0 E
Mindanao Trench, *Pac. Oc.* **80 E5** 12 0N 126 6 E
Mindel →, *Germany* **31 G6** 48 31N 10 23 E
Mindelheim, *Germany* **31 G6** 48 2N 10 29 E
Mindelo, *C. Verde Is.* **9 j** 16 24N 25 0W
Minden, *Canada* **150 B6** 44 55N 78 43W
Minden, *Germany* **30 C4** 52 17N 8 55 E
Minden, *La., U.S.A.* **155 J8** 32 37N 93 17W
Minden, *Nev., U.S.A.* **160 G7** 38 57N 119 46W
Mindiptana, *Indonesia* **83 C6** 5 55 S 140 22 E
Mindon, *Burma* **90 F5** 19 21N 94 44 E
Mindona L., *Australia* **128 B5** 33 6 S 142 6 E
Mindoro, *Phil.* **80 E3** 13 0N 120 0 E
Mindoro Occidental □, *Phil.* **80 E3** 13 0N 120 55 E
Mindoro Oriental □, *Phil.* **80 E3** 13 0N 121 5 E
Mindoro Str., *Phil.* **80 E3** 12 30N 120 30 E
Mindouli, *Congo* **115 C2** 4 12 S 14 28 E
Mindourou, *Cameroon* **114 B2** 3 29N 13 26 E
Mine, *Japan* **72 C3** 34 12N 131 7 E
Minehead, *U.K.* **21 F4** 51 12N 3 29W
Mineiros, *Brazil* **173 D7** 17 34 S 52 34W
Mineola, *N.Y., U.S.A.* **151 F11** 40 45N 73 39W
Mineola, *Tex., U.S.A.* **155 J7** 32 40N 95 29W
Mineral King, *U.S.A.* **160 J8** 36 27N 118 36W
Mineral Point, *U.S.A.* **156 D6** 42 52N 90 11W
Mineral Wells, *U.S.A.* **155 J5** 32 48N 98 7W
Mineralnyye Vody, *Russia* **61 F7** 44 15N 43 8 E
Minersville, *U.S.A.* **151 F8** 40 41N 76 16W
Minerva, *U.S.A.* **150 F3** 40 44N 81 6W
Minervino Murge, *Italy* **47 A9** 41 5N 16 5 E
Minetto, *U.S.A.* **151 C8** 43 24N 76 28W
Ming-Kush, *Kyrgyzstan* **65 C7** 41 40N 74 28 E
Mingäçevir, *Azerbaijan* **61 K8** 40 45N 47 0 E
Mingäçevir Su Anbarı, *Azerbaijan* **61 K8** 40 57N 46 50 E
Mingala, *C.A.R.* **114 A4** 5 16N 24 59 E
Mingan, *Canada* **141 B7** 50 20N 64 0W
Mingary, *Australia* **128 B4** 32 8 S 140 45 E

Mingechaur = Mingäçevir,
  Azerbaijan **61 K8** 40 45N 47 0 E
Mingechaurskoye Vdkhr. =
  Mingäçevir Su Anban, *Azerbaijan* **61 K8** 40 57N 46 50 E
Mingela, *Australia* **126 B4** 19 52 S 146 38 E
Mingenew, *Australia* **125 E2** 29 12 S 115 21 E
Mingera Cr. →, *Australia* **126 C2** 20 38 S 137 45 E
Minggang, *China* **77 A10** 32 24N 114 3 E
Mingguang, *China* **77 A11** 32 46N 117 59 E
Mingin, *Burma* **90 D5** 22 50N 94 30 E
Mingir, *Moldova* **53 D13** 46 40N 28 20 E
Minglanilla, *Spain* **41 F3** 39 34N 1 38W
Minglun, *China* **76 E7** 25 10N 108 21 E
Mingo, *Congo* **114 C3** 1 55 S 15 1 E
Mingo Junction, *U.S.A.* **150 F4** 40 19N 80 37W
Mingorria, *Spain* **42 E6** 40 45N 4 40W
Mingshan, *China* **76 B4** 30 6N 103 10 E
Mingteke, *China* **65 E7** 37 7N 75 4 E
Mingteke Daban = Mintaka Pass,
  Pakistan **65 E7** 37 0N 74 58 E
Mingxi, *China* **77 D11** 26 18N 117 12 E
Mingyuegue, *China* **75 C15** 43 2N 128 50 E
Minhla, Magwe, *Burma* **90 F5** 19 58N 95 3 E
Minhla, Pegu, *Burma* **90 G5** 17 59N 95 43 E
Minho = Miño →, *Spain* **42 D2** 41 52N 8 40W
Minhou, *China* **77 E12** 26 0N 119 15 E
Minićevo, *Serbia, Yug.* **52 G7** 43 42N 22 18 E
Minicoy I., *India* **88 H1** 8 17N 73 2 E
Minidoka, *U.S.A.* **158 E7** 42 45N 113 29W
Minier, *U.S.A.* **156 E9** 40 26N 89 19W
Minigwal, L., *Australia* **125 E3** 29 31 S 123 14 E
Minilya →, *Australia* **125 D1** 23 45 S 114 0 E
Minilya Roadhouse, *Australia* **125 D1** 23 55 S 114 0 E
Mininera, *Australia* **128 D5** 37 37 S 142 58 E
Minipi L., *Canada* **141 B7** 52 25N 60 45W
Minj, *Papua N. G.* **132 C3** 5 54 S 144 37 E
Mink L., *Canada* **142 A5** 61 54N 117 40W
Minkammen, *Sudan* **107 F3** 6 3N 31 32 E
Minkebé, *Gabon* **114 B2** 1 45N 12 45 E
Minlaton, *Australia* **128 C2** 34 45 S 137 35 E
Minna, *Nigeria* **113 D6** 9 37N 6 30 E
Minneapolis, *Kans., U.S.A.* **154 F6** 39 8N 97 42W
Minneapolis, *Minn., U.S.A.* **154 C8** 44 59N 93 16W
Minnedosa, *Canada* **143 C9** 50 14N 99 50W
Minnesota □, *U.S.A.* **154 B8** 46 0N 94 15W
Minnesota →, *U.S.A.* **154 C8** 44 54N 93 9W
Minnesund, *Norway* **18 D8** 60 23N 11 14 E
Minnewaukan, *U.S.A.* **154 A5** 48 4N 99 15W
Minnipa, *Australia* **127 E2** 32 51 S 135 9 E
Minnitaki L., *Canada* **140 C1** 49 57N 92 10W
Mino, *Japan* **73 B8** 35 32N 136 55 E
Miño, *Spain* **42 B2** 43 21N 8 12W
Miño →, *Spain* **42 D2** 41 52N 8 40W
Mino-Kamo, *Japan* **73 B9** 35 23N 137 2 E
Mino-Mikawa-Kōgen, *Japan* **73 B9** 35 10N 137 23 E
Minoa, *Greece* **49 F7** 35 6N 25 45 E
Minobu, *Japan* **73 B10** 35 22N 138 20 E
Minobu-Sanchi, *Japan* **73 B10** 35 14N 138 20 E
Minonk, *U.S.A.* **156 D7** 40 54N 89 2W
Minooka, *U.S.A.* **157 C8** 41 27N 88 16W
Minorca = Menorca, *Spain* **38 B5** 40 0N 4 0 E
Minore, *Australia* **129 B8** 32 14 S 148 27 E
Minqin, *China* **74 E2** 38 38N 103 20 E
Minqing, *China* **77 D12** 26 15N 118 50 E
Minsen, *Germany* **30 B3** 53 41N 7 58 E
Minsk, *Belarus* **58 F4** 53 52N 27 30 E
Mińsk Mazowiecki, *Poland* **55 F8** 52 10N 21 33 E
Minster, *U.S.A.* **157 D12** 40 24N 84 23W
Mintabie, *Australia* **127 D1** 27 15 S 133 7 E
Mintaka Pass, *Pakistan* **65 E7** 37 0N 74 58 E
Minthami, *Burma* **90 D5** 23 55N 94 16 E
Minto, *Canada* **141 C6** 46 5N 66 5W
Minto, *U.S.A.* **144 D10** 64 53N 149 11W
Minto, L., *Canada* **143 D8** 49 10N 104 35W
Mintoum, *Gabon* **114 B2** 0 27N 12 31 E
Minturn, *U.S.A.* **158 G10** 39 35N 106 26W
Minturno, *Italy* **46 A6** 41 15N 13 45 E
Minūf, *Egypt* **106 H7** 30 26N 30 52 E
Minusinsk, *Russia* **67 D10** 53 43N 91 20 E
Minutang, *India* **90 A6** 28 15N 96 30 E
Minvoul, *Gabon* **114 B2** 2 9N 12 8 E
Minwakh, *Yemen* **99 C5** 16 48N 48 6 E
Minya el Qamh, *Egypt* **106 H7** 30 31N 31 21 E
Minyar, *Russia* **64 D6** 55 4N 57 33 E
Minyip, *Australia* **128 D5** 36 29 S 142 36 E
Minzhong, *China* **69 F10** 22 37N 113 30 E
Mionica, *Bos.-H.* **52 F3** 44 51N 18 29 E
Mionica, *Serbia, Yug.* **50 B4** 44 14N 20 6 E
Miquelon, *Canada* **140 C4** 49 25N 76 27W
Miquelon, St- P. & M. *141 C8** 47 8N 56 22W
Mīr Kūh, *Iran* **97 E8** 26 22N 58 55 E
Mīr Shahdād, *Iran* **97 E8** 26 15N 58 29 E
Mira, *Italy* **45 C9** 45 26N 12 8 E
Mira, *Portugal* **42 E2** 40 26N 8 44W
Mira →, *Colombia* **168 C2** 1 36N 79 1W
Mira →, *Portugal* **43 H2** 37 43N 8 47W
Mira por vos Cay, *Bahamas* **165 B5** 22 9N 74 30W
Mīrābād, *Afghan.* **91 C1** 30 25N 61 50 E
Mirabella Eclano, *Italy* **47 A7** 41 2N 14 59 E
Miracema do Norte, *Brazil* **170 C2** 9 33 S 48 42W
Mirador, *Brazil* **170 C3** 6 22 S 44 22W
Mirador-Río Azul, Parque Nac. △,
  Guatemala **164 C2** 17 45N 89 50W
Miraflores, *Colombia* **168 C3** 1 24N 72 13W
Miraj, *India* **94 F2** 16 50N 74 45 E
Miram Shah, *Pakistan* **91 B3** 33 0N 70 2 E
Miramar, *Argentina* **174 D4** 38 15 S 57 50W
Miramar, *Mozam.* **117 C6** 23 50 S 35 35 E
Miramas, *France* **29 E8** 43 33N 4 59 E
Mirambeau, *France* **28 C3** 45 23N 0 35W
Miramichi, *Canada* **141 C6** 47 2N 65 28W
Miramichi B., *Canada* **141 C7** 47 15N 65 0W
Miramont-de-Guyenne, *France* **28 D4** 44 37N 0 21 E
Miranda, *Brazil* **173 E6** 20 10 S 56 15W
Miranda □, *Venezuela* **168 A4** 10 15N 66 25W
Miranda →, *Brazil* **173 D6** 19 25 S 57 20W
Miranda de Ebro, *Spain* **40 C2** 42 41N 2 57W
Miranda do Corvo, *Portugal* **42 E2** 40 6N 8 20W
Miranda do Douro, *Portugal* **42 D4** 41 30N 6 16W
Mirande, *France* **28 E4** 43 31N 0 25 E
Mirandela, *Portugal* **42 D3** 41 32N 7 10W
Mirandola, *Italy* **44 D8** 44 53N 11 4 E
Mirandópolis, *Brazil* **175 A5** 21 9 S 51 6W
Mirango, *Malawi* **119 E3** 13 32 S 34 58 E
Mirani, *Australia* **126 K6** 21 8 S 148 53 E
Mirano, *Italy* **45 C9** 45 30N 12 7 E
Miras, *Albania* **50 F4** 40 30N 20 56 E
Mirassol, *Brazil* **175 A6** 20 46 S 49 28W
Mirbāṭ, *Oman* **99 C6** 17 0N 54 45 E
Mirboo North, *Australia* **129 C7** 38 24 S 146 13 E
Mirear, *Egypt* **106 C4** 23 15N 35 41 E
Mirebeau, Côte-d'Or, *France* **27 E12** 47 25N 5 20 E
Mirebeau, Vienne, *France* **26 F7** 46 49N 0 10 E
Mirecourt, *France* **27 D13** 48 20N 6 10 E
Mirgorod = Myrhorod, *Ukraine* **59 H7** 49 58N 33 37 E
Miri, *Malaysia* **85 B4** 4 23N 113 59 E
Mirialguda, *India* **94 F4** 16 52N 79 35 E
Miriam Vale, *Australia* **126 C5** 24 20 S 151 33 E
Miribel, *France* **27 G11** 45 50N 4 57 E
Mirigama, *Sri Lanka* **95 L5** 7 15N 80 8 E

Mirim, L., *S. Amer.* **175 C5** 32 45 S 52 50W
Mirimire, *Venezuela* **168 A4** 11 10N 68 43W
Miriti, *Brazil* **173 B6** 6 15 S 59 0W
Mirjāveh, *Iran* **88 C5** 29 1N 61 30 E
Mirnyy, *Russia* **67 C12** 62 33N 113 53 E
Miroč, *Serbia, Yug.* **50 B6** 44 32N 22 16 E
Mirokhan, *Pakistan* **92 F3** 27 46N 68 6 E
Mirond L., *Canada* **143 B8** 55 6N 102 47W
Mirosławiec, *Poland* **54 E3** 53 20N 16 5 E
Mirpur, *Pakistan* **93 C5** 33 32N 73 56 E
Mirpur Batoro, *Pakistan* **92 G3** 24 44N 68 16 E
Mirpur Bibiwari, *Pakistan* **92 E2** 28 33N 67 44 E
Mirpur Khas, *Pakistan* **91 D3** 25 30N 69 0 E
Mirpur Sakro, *Pakistan* **92 G2** 24 33N 67 41 E
Mirria, *Niger* **113 C6** 13 43N 9 7 E
Mirrool, *Australia* **129 C7** 34 19 S 147 10 E
Mirs Bay = Tai Pang Wan, *H.K.* **69 F12** 22 33N 114 24 E
Mirsk, *Poland* **55 H2** 50 58N 15 23 E
Mirtağ, *Turkey* **96 B4** 38 23N 41 56 E
Mírtou, Kólpos, *Greece* **39 C1** 38 20N 20 27 E
Miryang, *S. Korea* **75 G15** 35 31N 128 44 E
Mirzapur, *India* **93 G10** 25 10N 82 34 E
Mirzapur-cum-Vindhyachal =
  Mirzapur, *India* **93 G10** 25 10N 82 34 E
Misaki, *Japan* **73 C7** 34 18N 135 9 E
Misamis Occidental □, *Phil.* **81 G4** 8 20N 123 42 E
Misamis Oriental □, *Phil.* **81 G5** 8 45N 125 0 E
Misantla, *Mexico* **163 D5** 19 56N 96 50W
Misawa, *Japan* **70 D10** 40 41N 141 24 E
Miscou I., *Canada* **141 C7** 47 57N 64 31W
Misha, *India* **95 L10** 7 59N 93 20 E
Mish'āb, Ra's al, *Si. Arabia* **97 D6** 28 15N 48 43 E
Mishagua →, *Peru* **172 C3** 11 12 S 72 58W
Mishan, *China* **69 B8** 45 37N 131 48 E
Mishawaka, *U.S.A.* **157 C10** 41 40N 86 11W
Mishbih, Gebel, *Egypt* **106 C3** 22 38N 34 44 E
Mishima, *Japan* **73 B10** 35 10N 138 52 E
Mishmi Hills, *India* **90 A5** 29 0N 96 0 E
Mishō, *Japan* **72 E4** 32 57N 132 35 E
Misima I., *Papua N. G.* **132 F7** 10 40 S 152 45 E
Misión, *Mexico* **161 N10** 32 6N 116 53W
Misión Fagnano, *Argentina* **175 E3** 54 33 S 67 17W
Misiones □, *Argentina* **175 B5** 27 0 S 55 0W
Misiones □, *Paraguay* **174 B4** 27 0 S 56 0W
Miskah, *Si. Arabia* **96 E4** 24 49N 42 56 E
Miski, E. →, *Chad* **109 E3** 20 0N 17 55 E
Miskitos, Cayos, *Nic.* **164 D3** 14 26N 82 50W
Miskolc, *Hungary* **52 B5** 48 7N 20 50 E
Misoke, *Dem. Rep. of the Congo* **118 C2** 0 42 S 28 2 E
Misool, *Indonesia* **83 B4** 1 52 S 130 10 E
Mişrātah, *Libya* **108 B3** 32 24N 15 3 E
Mişrātah □, *Libya* **108 C3** 30 30N 15 0 E
Missanabie, *Canada* **140 C3** 48 20N 84 6W
Missinaibi →, *Canada* **140 B3** 50 43N 81 29W
Missinaibi L., *Canada* **140 C3** 48 23N 83 40W
Mission, S. Dak., U.S.A.* **154 D4** 43 18N 100 39W
Mission, Tex., U.S.A.* **155 M5** 26 13N 98 20W
Mission Beach, *Australia* **126 B4** 17 53 S 146 6 E
Mission Viejo, *U.S.A.* **161 M9** 33 36N 117 40W
Missirah, *Senegal* **112 C1** 13 40N 16 30W
Mississa →, *Canada* **140 B2** 52 20N 85 7W
Mississagi →, *Canada* **140 B4** 51 14N 79 31W
Mississauga, *Canada* **150 C5** 43 32N 79 35W
Mississinewa L., *U.S.A.* **157 D10** 40 46N 86 3W
Mississippi □, *U.S.A.* **155 J10** 33 0N 90 0W
Mississippi →, *U.S.A.* **155 L10** 29 9N 89 15W
Mississippi L., *Canada* **151 A8** 45 5N 76 10W
Mississippi River Delta, *U.S.A.* **155 L9** 29 10N 89 15W
Mississippi Sd., *U.S.A.* **155 K10** 30 20N 89 0W
Missoula, *U.S.A.* **158 C7** 46 52N 114 1W
Missour, *Morocco* **110 B5** 33 0N 4 0W
Missouri □, *U.S.A.* **156 F8** 38 25N 92 30W
Missouri →, *U.S.A.* **156 F6** 38 49N 90 7W
Missouri City, *U.S.A.* **155 L7** 29 37N 95 32W
Missouri Valley, *U.S.A.* **154 E7** 41 34N 95 53W
Mist, *U.S.A.* **160 E3** 45 59N 123 15W
Mistassibi →, *Canada* **141 B5** 48 53N 72 13W
Mistassini →, *Canada* **141 C5** 48 42N 72 20W
Mistassini, L., *Canada* **140 B5** 51 0N 73 30W
Mistastin L., *Canada* **141 A7** 55 57N 63 20W
Mistelbach, *Austria* **35 C9** 48 34N 16 34 E
Misterbianco, *Italy* **47 E8** 37 31N 15 1 E
Misti, Volcán, *Peru* **172 D3** 16 18 S 71 24W
Mistinibi, L., *Canada* **141 A7** 55 56N 64 17W
Mistissini, *Canada* **141 C5** 50 25N 72 12W
Mistretta, *Italy* **47 E7** 37 56N 14 22 E
Misty L., *Canada* **143 B8** 58 53N 101 40W
Misumi, *Japan* **72 C3** 34 31N 136 16 E
Misurata = Mişrātah, *Libya* **108 B3** 32 24N 15 3 E
Mît Ghamr, *Egypt* **106 H7** 30 42N 31 12 E
Mitaka, *Japan* **73 B11** 35 40N 139 33 E
Mitatib, *Sudan* **107 D4** 15 59N 36 12 E
Mitau = Jelgava, *Latvia* **15 H20** 56 41N 23 49 E
Mitava = Jelgava, *Latvia* **15 H20** 56 41N 23 49 E
Mitchell, *Australia* **127 D4** 26 29 S 147 58 E
Mitchell, *Canada* **150 C3** 43 28N 81 12W
Mitchell, *Ga., U.S.A.* **152 B7** 33 13N 82 42W
Mitchell, *Ind., U.S.A.* **157 F10** 38 44N 86 28W
Mitchell, *Nebr., U.S.A.* **154 E3** 41 57N 103 49W
Mitchell, *Oreg., U.S.A.* **158 D3** 44 34N 120 9W
Mitchell, *S. Dak., U.S.A.* **154 D6** 43 43N 98 2W
Mitchell →, *Australia* **126 B3** 15 12 S 141 35 E
Mitchell, Mt., U.S.A.* **149 H4** 35 46N 82 16W
Mitchell and Alice Rivers Nat.
  Park △, *Australia* **126 B3** 15 28 S 142 5 E
Mitchell Ranges, *Australia* **126 A2** 12 49 S 135 36 E
Mitchell River Nat. Park △, *Australia* **129 D7** 37 3 S 147 22 E
Mitchelstown, *Ireland* **23 D3** 52 15N 8 16W
Mitha Tiwana, *Pakistan* **92 C5** 32 13N 72 6 E
Mithi, *Pakistan* **92 G3** 24 44N 69 48 E
Míthimna, *Greece* **49 B8** 39 20N 26 12 E
Mithrao, *Pakistan* **92 F3** 27 28N 69 40 E
Mitiamo, *Australia* **128 D6** 36 12 S 144 15 E
Mitikas, Aitolía kai Akarnanía,
  Greece **39 B2** 38 40N 20 56 E
Mitikas, Préveza, *Greece* **39 B2** 39 0N 20 42 E
Mitilíni, *Greece* **49 B8** 39 6N 26 35 E
Mitilinoí, *Greece* **49 D8** 37 42N 26 56 E
Mitla, *Mexico* **73 A12** 36 20N 140 30 E
Mitra, Mt., Eq. Guin. *114 B1** 1 23N 9 19 E
Mitre, Mt., N.Z. *130 G4** 40 50 S 175 30 E
Mitrofanovka, *Russia* **59 H10** 49 58N 39 42 E
Mitrovica = Kosovska Mitrovica,
  Kosovo, Yug. **50 D4** 42 54N 20 52 E
Mitsamiouli, Comoros Is.* **121 a** 11 20 S 43 16 E
Mitsang, Gabon* **114 B2** 0 42 S 13 52 E
Mitsinjo, *Madag.* **117 B8** 16 1 S 45 52 E
Mitsiwa, *Eritrea* **107 D4** 15 35N 39 25 E
Mitsiwa Channel, *Eritrea* **107 D5** 15 30N 40 0 E
Mitsukaidō, *Japan* **73 A11** 36 1N 139 59 E
Mittagong, *Australia* **129 C9** 34 28 S 150 29 E
Mittelberg, *Tirol, Austria* **33 C11** 46 57N 10 53 E
Mittelberg, *Vorarlberg, Austria* **33 B10** 47 20N 10 10 E
Mittelfranken □, *Germany* **31 F6** 49 25N 10 40 E
Mittelland, *Switz.* **32 C4** 46 50N 7 23 E
Mittellandkanal →, *Germany* **30 C4** 52 20N 8 28 E

Mittenwalde, *Germany* .... 30 C9 52 15N 13 31 E
Mittersill, *Austria* .... 34 D5 47 16N 12 29 E
Mitterteich, *Germany* .... 31 F8 49 57N 12 14 E
Mittimatalik = Pond Inlet, *Canada* 139 A12 72 40N 77 0W
Mitú, *Colombia* 168 C3 1 15N 70 13W
Mitúas, *Colombia* 168 C4 3 52N 68 49W
Mitumba, *Tanzania* .... 118 D3 7 8 S 31 2 E
Mitumba, Mts., *Dem. Rep. of
  the Congo* .... 118 D2 7 0 S 27 30 E
Mitwaba, *Dem. Rep. of the Congo* 119 D2 8 2 S 27 17 E
Mityana, *Uganda* .... 118 B3 0 23N 32 2 E
Mitzic, *Gabon* .... 114 B2 0 45N 11 40 E
Miura, *Japan* .... 73 B11 35 12N 139 40 E
Mixteco ➤, *Mexico* 163 D5 18 11N 98 30W
Miyagi □, *Japan* .... 70 E10 38 15N 140 45 E
Miyâh, W. el ➤, *Egypt* .... 106 C3 25 0N 33 23 E
Miyâh, W. el ➤, *Syria* .... 96 C3 34 44N 39 57 E
Miyake-Jima, *Japan* .... 73 C11 34 5N 139 30 E
Miyako, *Japan* .... 70 E10 39 40N 141 59 E
Miyako-Jima, *Japan* .... 71 M2 24 45N 125 20 E
Miyako-Jima, *Japan* .... 71 M2 24 24N 125 0 E
Miyako-Rettō, *Japan* .... 72 F3 31 40N 131 5 E
Miyani, *India* .... 92 J3 21 50N 69 26 E
Miyanojō, *Japan* .... 72 F2 31 54N 130 27 E
Miyanoura-Dake, *Japan* .... 72 J5 30 20N 130 31 E
Miyata, *Japan* .... 72 D2 33 49N 130 42 E
Miyazaki, *Japan* .... 72 F3 31 56N 131 30 E
Miyazaki □, *Japan* .... 72 E3 32 30N 131 30 E
Miyazu, *Japan* .... 73 B7 35 35N 135 10 E
Miyet, Bahr el = Dead Sea, *Asia* 103 D4 31 30N 35 30 E
Miyi, *China* .... 76 D4 26 47N 102 9 E
Miyoshi, *Japan* .... 72 C4 34 48N 132 51 E
Miyun, *China* .... 74 D9 40 28N 116 50 E
Miyun Shuiku, *China* .... 75 D9 40 30N 117 0 E
Mizan Teferi, *Ethiopia* .... 107 F4 6 57N 35 3 E
Mizdah, *Libya* .... 108 B2 31 30N 13 0 E
Mizen Hd., *Cork, Ireland* 23 E2 51 27N 9 50W
Mizen Hd., *Wick., Ireland* 23 D5 52 51N 6 4W
Mizhi, *China* .... 74 F6 37 47N 110 12 E
Mizil, *Romania* .... 53 F11 44 59N 26 29 E
Mizoram □, *India* .... 90 D4 23 30N 92 40 E
Mizpe Ramon, *Israel* .... 103 E3 30 34N 34 49 E
Mizuho, *Japan* .... 73 B7 35 6N 135 17 E
Mizunami, *Japan* .... 73 B9 35 22N 137 15 E
Mizusawa, *Japan* .... 70 E10 39 8N 141 8 E
Mjällby, *Sweden* .... 17 H8 56 3N 14 40 E
Mjöbäck, *Sweden* .... 17 G6 57 28N 12 53 E
Mjölby, *Sweden* .... 17 F9 58 20N 15 10 E
Mjölfjell, *Norway* .... 18 D3 60 41N 6 55 E
Mjømna, *Norway* .... 18 D1 60 55N 4 55 E
Mjörn, *Sweden* .... 17 G6 57 55N 12 25 E
Mjøsa, *Norway* .... 18 D8 60 40N 11 0 E
Mkata, *Tanzania* .... 118 D4 5 45 S 38 20 E
Mkhaya Nature Reserve ☐,
  Swaziland .... 117 D5 26 34 S 34 45 E
Mkokotoni, *Tanzania* .... 118 D4 5 55 S 39 15 E
Mkomazi, *Tanzania* .... 118 C4 4 40 S 38 7 E
Mkomazi ➤, *S. Africa* .... 117 E5 30 12 S 30 50 E
Mkomazi Game Reserve ☐,
  Tanzania .... 118 D4 4 4 S 30 2 E
Mkulwe, *Tanzania* .... 119 D3 8 37 S 32 20 E
Mkumbi, Ras, *Tanzania* ...... 118 D4 7 38 S 39 55 E
Mkushi, *Zambia* .... 119 E2 14 25 S 29 15 E
Mkushi River, *Zambia* .... 119 E2 13 32 S 29 45 E
Mkuze, *S. Africa* .... 117 D5 27 10 S 32 0 E
Mkuze Game Reserve ☐, *S. Africa* 117 D4 29 27 S 29 30 E
Mladá Boleslav, *Czech Rep.* ... 34 A7 50 27N 14 53 E
Mladenovac, *Serbia, Yug.* ..... 50 B4 44 28N 20 44 E
Mlala Hills, *Tanzania* .... 118 D3 6 50 S 31 40 E
Mlange = Mulanje, *Malawi* ... 119 F4 16 2 S 35 33 E
Mlava ➤, *Serbia, Yug.* .... 50 B5 44 45N 21 13 E
Mława, *Poland* .... 55 E7 53 9N 20 25 E
Mlawula Nature Reserve ☐,
  Swaziland .... 117 D5 26 12 S 32 2 E
Mljet, *Bos.-H.* .... 45 D13 44 15N 16 50 E
Mljet, *Croatia* .... 45 F14 42 43N 17 30 E
Mljet, Nac. Park ☐, *Croatia* .. 45 F14 42 45N 17 25 E
Mljetski Kanal, *Croatia* ...... 45 F14 42 48N 17 35 E
Młynary, *Poland* .... 54 D6 54 12N 19 46 E
Mmabatho, *S. Africa* .... 116 D4 25 49 S 25 30 E
Mme, *Cameroon* .... 113 D7 6 18N 10 14 E
Mnichovo Hradiště, *Czech Rep.* 34 A7 50 32N 14 59 E
Mo, *Hordaland, Norway* ...... 18 D2 60 49N 5 48 E
Mo, *Møre og Romsdal, Norway* . 18 A5 63 0N 8 59 E
Mo, *Telemark, Norway* .... 18 E4 59 28N 7 50 E
Mo i Rana, *Norway* .... 14 C16 66 20N 14 7 E
Moa, *Cuba* 165 B4 20 40N 74 56W
Moa, *Indonesia* .... 82 C3 8 0 S 128 0 E
Moa ➤, *S. Leone* 112 D2 6 59N 11 36W
Moa, I., *Papua N.G.* .... 132 F2 10 10 S 142 15 E
Moab, *U.S.A.* 159 G9 38 35N 109 33W
Moabi, *Gabon* .... 114 C2 2 24 S 10 59 E
Moaco ➤, *Brazil* .... 172 B4 7 41 S 68 18W
Moala, *Fiji* .... 133 B2 18 36 S 179 53 E
Moama, *Australia* .... 127 F3 36 7 S 144 46 E
Moamba, *Mozam.* .... 117 D5 25 36 S 32 15 E
Moapa, *U.S.A.* 161 J12 36 40N 114 37W
Moate, *Ireland* 23 C4 53 24N 7 44W
Moba, *Dem. Rep. of the Congo* . 118 D2 7 0 S 29 48 E
Mobara, *Japan* .... 73 B12 35 25N 140 18 E
Mobārakābād, *Iran* .... 97 D7 28 24N 53 20 E
Mobaye, *C.A.R.* .... 114 B4 4 25N 21 5 E
Mobayi, *Dem. Rep. of the Congo* 114 B4 4 15N 21 8 E
Mobeka, *Dem. Rep. of the Congo* 114 B3 1 52N 19 49 E
Mobenzélé, *Congo* .... 114 B3 0 56N 17 50 E
Moberley Lake, *Canada* 142 B4 55 50N 121 44W
Moberly, *U.S.A.* 156 F4 39 25N 92 26W
Mobile, *U.S.A.* 149 K1 30 41N 88 3W
Mobile B., *U.S.A.* 149 K2 30 30N 88 0W
Mobridge, *U.S.A.* 154 C4 45 32N 100 26W
Mobutu Sese Seko, L. = Albert, L.,
  Africa .... 118 B3 1 30N 31 0 E
Moc Chau, *Vietnam* .... 86 B5 20 50N 104 38 E
Moc Hoa, *Vietnam* .... 87 G5 10 46N 105 56 E
Mocaba, Sa. de, *Angola* ...... 115 D3 7 12 S 15 0 E
Mocabe Kasari, *Dem. Rep. of
  the Congo* .... 119 D2 9 58 S 26 12 E
Mocajuba, *Brazil* .... 170 B2 2 35 S 49 30W
Moçambique, *Mozam.* .... 119 F5 15 3 S 40 42 E
Moçâmedes = Namibe, *Angola* . 115 F2 15 7 S 12 11 E
Mocanaqua, *U.S.A.* 151 E8 41 9N 76 8W
Mocapra ➤, *Venezuela* 168 B4 7 56N 66 46W
Moce, *Fiji* .... 133 B3 18 40 S 178 29W
Mocha = Al Mukhā, *Yemen* ... 98 D3 13 18N 43 15 E
Mocha, I., *Chile* .... 176 A2 38 30 S 73 56W
Mochima, Parque Nac. ☐, *Venezuela* 165 D7 10 30N 64 5W
Mochudi, *Botswana* .... 116 C4 24 27 S 26 7 E
Mocimboa da Praia, *Mozam.* .. 119 E5 11 25 S 40 20 E
Mociu, *Romania* .... 53 D9 46 46N 24 3 E
Möckeln, *Sweden* .... 17 H8 56 40N 14 15 E
Mockfjärd, *Sweden* .... 16 D8 60 30N 14 57 E
Moclips, *U.S.A.* 160 C2 47 14N 124 13W
Mocoa, *Colombia* 168 C2 1 7N 76 35W
Mococa, *Brazil* .... 175 A6 21 28 S 47 0W
Mocorito, *Mexico* 162 B3 25 30N 107 53W
Mocorito, *Mexico* 162 B3 25 30N 108 0W
Moctezuma, *Mexico* 163 C5 21 59N 98 34W
Moctezuma ➤, *Mexico* ...... 163 F4 16 54 S 36 57 E
Mocūzari, Presa, *Mexico* 162 B3 27 10N 109 10W
Moda, *Burma* .... 90 C6 24 20N 96 29 E
Modane, *France* .... 29 C10 45 12N 6 40 E
Modasa, *India* .... 92 H5 23 30N 73 21 E
Modder ➤, *S. Africa* .... 116 D3 29 2 S 24 37 E

Modderrivier, *S. Africa* .... 116 D3 29 2 S 24 38 E
Módena, *Italy* .... 44 D7 44 40N 10 55 E
Modena, *U.S.A.* 159 H7 37 48N 113 56W
Modesto, *U.S.A.* 160 H6 37 39N 121 0W
Mōδrudalur, *Iceland* 11 B11 65 22N 15 53W
Mōδruvellir, *Iceland* 11 B8 65 46N 18 15W
Módica, *Italy* .... 47 F7 36 52N 14 46 E
Modjamboli, *Dem. Rep. of the Congo* 114 B4 2 28N 22 6 E
Mödling, *Austria* .... 35 C9 48 5N 16 17 E
Modo, *Sudan* .... 107 F3 5 31N 30 33 E
Modoc, *U.S.A.* 152 B7 33 44N 82 13W
Modowi, *Indonesia* .... 83 B4 4 5 S 134 30 E
Modra, *Slovak Rep.* .... 35 C10 48 19N 17 20 E
Modriča, *Bos.-H.* .... 52 F3 44 57N 18 17 E
Moe, *Australia* .... 129 F7 38 12 S 146 19 E
Moebase, *Mozam.* .... 119 F4 17 3 S 38 41 E
Moëlan-sur-Mer, *France* 26 E3 47 49N 3 38W
Moelv, *Norway* .... 18 D7 60 56N 10 43 E
Moengo, *Suriname* 169 B7 5 45N 54 20W
Moerewa, *N.Z.* .... 130 B3 35 8 S 174 1 E
Moësa ➤, *Switz.* .... 33 D8 46 12N 9 10 E
Moffat, *U.K.* 22 F5 55 21N 3 27W
Moga, *India* .... 92 D6 30 48N 75 8 E
Mogadishu = Muqdisho, *Somali Rep.* 120 D3 2 2N 45 25 E
Mogador = Essaouira, *Morocco* 110 B3 31 32N 9 42W
Mogadouro, *Portugal* 42 D4 41 22N 6 47W
Mogalakwena ➤, *S. Africa* ... 117 C4 22 38 S 28 40 E
Mogán, *Canary Is.* 48 G4 27 53N 15 43W
Mogandjo, *Dem. Rep. of the Congo* 114 B4 1 23N 24 15 E
Mogaung, *Burma* .... 90 C6 25 20N 97 0 E
Mogen, *Norway* .... 18 E6 60 2N 7 52 E
Mogente = Moixent, *Spain* ... 41 G4 38 52N 0 45W
Mogho, *Ethiopia* .... 107 G5 4 54N 40 16 E
Mogi das Cruzes, *Brazil* ...... 175 A6 23 31 S 46 11W
Mogi-Guaçu ➤, *Brazil* .... 175 A6 20 53 S 48 10W
Mogi-Mirim, *Brazil* .... 175 A6 22 29 S 47 0W
Mogielnica, *Poland* .... 55 G7 51 42N 20 41 E
Mogige, *Ethiopia* .... 107 F4 5 24N 36 14 E
Mogilev = Mahilyow, *Belarus* . 58 F6 53 55N 30 18 E
Mogilev-Podolskiy = Mohyliv-
  Podilskyy, *Ukraine* .... 59 H4 48 26N 27 48 E
Mogilno, *Poland* .... 55 F4 52 39N 17 55 E
Mogincual, *Mozam.* .... 119 F5 15 35 S 40 25 E
Mogliano Véneto, *Italy* .... 45 C9 45 33N 12 14 E
Mogocha, *Russia* .... 67 D12 53 40N 119 50 E
Mogoi, *Indonesia* .... 83 B4 1 55 S 133 10 E
Mogok, *Burma* .... 90 D6 23 0N 96 40 E
Mogollon Rim, *U.S.A.* 159 J8 34 10N 110 50W
Mógoro, *Italy* .... 46 C1 39 41N 8 47 E
Mograt, *Sudan* .... 106 D3 19 28N 33 16 E
Mogroum, *Chad* .... 109 F3 11 6N 15 25 E
Moguer, *Spain* 43 H4 37 15N 6 52W
Mogumber, *Australia* .... 125 F2 31 2 S 116 3 E
Mohács, *Hungary* .... 52 E3 45 58N 18 41 E
Mohaka ➤, *N.Z.* .... 130 F6 39 7 S 177 12 E
Mohala, *India* .... 94 D5 20 35N 80 44 E
Mohales Hoek, *Lesotho* ...... 116 E4 30 7 S 27 26 E
Mohali, *Congo* .... 114 B3 0 15N 15 29 E
Mohall, *U.S.A.* 154 A4 48 46N 101 31W
Mohammadābād, *Iran* .... 97 B8 37 52N 59 5 E
Mohammadia, *Algeria* .... 111 A5 35 33N 0 3 E
Mohammedia, *Morocco* 110 B3 33 44N 7 21W
Mohana ➤, *India* .... 94 F7 19 27N 84 16 E
Mohana, *India* .... 93 G11 24 43N 85 0 E
Mohanganj, *Bangla.* .... 90 C3 24 54N 90 59 E
Mohanlalganj, *India* .... 93 F9 26 41N 80 58 E
Mohave, L., *U.S.A.* 161 K12 35 12N 114 34W
Mohawk ➤, *U.S.A.* 151 D11 42 47N 73 41W
Moheda, *Sweden* .... 17 G8 57 1N 14 35 E
Mohéli, *Comoros Is.* .... 121 a 12 20 S 43 40 E
Mohenjodaro, *Pakistan* .... 91 D3 27 19N 68 7 E
Moher, Cliffs of, *Ireland* 23 D2 52 58N 9 27W
Mohican, C., *U.S.A.* 144 F6 60 12N 167 25W
Mohicanville Reservoir, *U.S.A.* 153 F3 40 45N 82 0W
Möhlin, *Switz.* .... 32 A5 47 33N 7 51 E
Möhne ➤, *Germany* .... 30 D3 51 29N 7 57 E
Mohnyin, *Burma* .... 90 C6 24 47N 96 22 E
Mohoro, *Tanzania* .... 118 D4 8 6 S 39 8 E
Mohyliv-Podilskyy, *Ukraine* ... 59 H4 48 26N 27 48 E
Moi, *Norway* .... 18 F3 58 27N 6 32 E
Moia, *Sudan* .... 107 F2 5 3N 28 2 E
Moidart, L., *U.K.* 22 E3 56 47N 5 52W
Moinabad, *India* .... 94 F3 17 44N 77 16 E
Moindou, *N. Cal.* .... 133 U19 21 42 S 165 41 E
Moineşti, *Romania* .... 53 D11 46 28N 26 31 E
Moira ➤, *Canada* 150 B7 44 21N 77 24W
Moirang, *India* .... 90 C4 24 30N 93 46 E
Moirans, *France* .... 29 C9 45 20N 5 33 E
Moirans-en-Montagne, *France* . 27 F12 46 26N 5 43 E
Moïres, *Greece* .... 39 E5 35 4N 24 56 E
Moisaküla, *Estonia* .... 15 G21 58 3N 25 12 E
Moisie, *Canada* 141 B6 50 12N 66 1W
Moisie ➤, *Canada* 141 B6 50 14N 66 5W
Moissac, *France* .... 28 D5 44 7N 1 5 E
Moïssala, *Chad* .... 109 G3 8 21N 17 46 E
Moita, *Portugal* 43 G2 38 38N 8 58W
Moixent, *Spain* 41 G4 38 52N 0 45W
Möja, *Sweden* .... 16 E12 59 26N 18 55 E
Mojácar, *Spain* 41 H3 37 6N 1 55W
Mojados, *Spain* 42 D6 41 26N 4 40W
Mojave, *U.S.A.* 161 K8 35 3N 118 10W
Mojave Desert, *U.S.A.* 161 L10 35 0N 116 30W
Mojave Nat. Preserve ☐, *U.S.A.* 161 K11 35 7N 115 30W
Moji, *China* .... 65 D7 39 0N 74 27 E
Mojiang, *China* .... 76 F3 23 37N 101 35 E
Mojjo ➤, *Ethiopia* .... 107 F5 7 55N 42 0 E
Mojkovac, *Montenegro, Yug.* .. 50 D3 42 58N 19 35 E
Mojo, *Bolivia* .... 174 A2 21 48 S 65 33W
Mojo, *Ethiopia* .... 107 F4 8 35N 39 5 E
Mojokerto, *Indonesia* .... 85 D4 7 28 S 112 26 E
Mojos, Llanos de, *Bolivia* ..... 173 D5 15 10 S 65 0W
Moju, *Brazil* .... 170 B2 1 53 S 48 46W
Moju ➤, *Brazil* .... 170 B2 1 40 S 48 25W
Mokai, *N.Z.* .... 130 E4 38 32 S 175 56 E
Mokambo, *Dem. Rep. of the Congo* 119 E2 12 25 S 28 20 E
Mokameh, *India* .... 93 G11 25 24N 85 55 E
Mokane, *U.S.A.* 156 F5 38 41N 91 53W
Mokapu Peninsula, *U.S.A.* 145 K14 21 25N 157 48W
Mokau, *N.Z.* .... 130 E3 38 42 S 174 39 E
Mokau ➤, *N.Z.* .... 130 E3 38 35 S 174 35 E
Mokelumne ➤, *U.S.A.* 160 G5 38 13N 121 28W
Mokelumne Hill, *U.S.A.* 160 G6 38 18N 120 43W
Mokhós, *Greece* .... 39 E6 35 16N 25 27 E
Mokhotlong, *Lesotho* .... 117 D4 29 22 S 29 2 E
Mokihinui ➤, *N.Z.* .... 131 B4 41 33 S 171 58 E
Möklinta, *Sweden* .... 16 D10 60 4N 16 33 E
Mokne, *Tunisia* .... 108 A2 35 35N 9 50 E
Mokoan, L., *Australia* .... 129 D7 36 27 S 146 5 E
Mokokchung, *India* .... 90 C4 26 15N 94 30 E
Mokolea Rock, *U.S.A.* 145 K14 21 27N 157 44W
Mokolo, *Cameroon* .... 113 C7 10 50N 13 55 E
Mokolo, *Cent. Amer.* .... 109 F2 10 49N 13 54 E
Mokolo ➤, *S. Africa* .... 117 C4 23 14 S 27 43 E
Mokombo, *Dem. Rep. of the Congo* 118 C4 4 21 S 24 48 E
Mokopalin, *Burma* .... 90 D6 17 26N 96 52 E
Mokpo, *S. Korea* .... 75 G14 34 50N 126 25 E
Mokra Gora, *Yugoslavia* ...... 50 D4 42 50N 20 30 E
Mokronog, *Slovenia* .... 45 C12 45 57N 15 9 E
Moksha ➤, *Russia* .... 60 C7 54 45N 41 53 E
Mokshan, *Russia* .... 60 D7 53 25N 44 35 E
Mokuaeae I., *U.S.A.* 145 A2 22 14N 159 25W
Mokuauia I., *U.S.A.* 145 J14 21 40N 157 56W

Mokulua Is., *U.S.A.* 145 K14 21 24N 157 42W
Mokwa, *Nigeria* .... 113 D6 9 19N 5 0 E
Mol, *Belgium* .... 24 C5 51 11N 5 5 E
Mola di Bari, *Italy* .... 47 A10 41 4N 17 5 E
Molakalmuru, *India* .... 95 G3 14 55N 76 50 E
Molale, *Ethiopia* .... 107 E4 10 10N 39 41 E
Molanda, *Dem. Rep. of the Congo* 114 B4 2 28N 20 48 E
Moláoi, *Greece* .... 48 E4 36 49N 22 56 E
Molara, *Italy* .... 46 B2 40 52N 9 43 E
Molat, *Croatia* .... 45 D11 44 15N 14 50 E
Molave, *Phil.* .... 81 G4 8 5N 123 34 E
Molchanovo, *Russia* .... 66 D9 57 40N 83 50 E
Mold, *U.K.* 22 D4 53 9N 3 8W
Moldava nad Bodvou, *Slovak Rep.* 35 C14 48 38N 21 0 E
Moldavia = Moldova ■, *Europe* . 53 C13 47 0N 28 0 E
Moldavia, *Romania* .... 53 D12 46 30N 27 0 E
Molde, *Norway* .... 18 B4 62 45N 7 9 E
Moldo Too, *Kyrgyzstan* ...... 65 C7 41 35N 75 0 E
Moldotau = Moldo Too, *Kyrgyzstan* 65 C7 41 35N 75 0 E
Moldova ■, *Europe* .... 53 C13 47 0N 28 0 E
Moldova Nouǎ, *Romania* ..... 52 F6 44 45N 21 41 E
Moldoveanu, Vf., *Romania* .... 53 E9 45 36N 24 45 E
Moldoviţa, *Romania* .... 53 C10 47 41N 25 32 E
Mole ➤, *U.K.* 21 F7 51 24N 0 21W
Mole Creek, *Australia* .... 127 D4 41 34 S 146 24 E
Mole Nat. Park ☐, *Ghana* ... 113 D4 9 43N 1 44W
Molegbwe, *Dem. Rep. of the Congo* 114 B4 4 12N 20 53 E
Molepolole, *Botswana* .... 116 C4 24 28 S 25 28 E
Molesworth, *N.Z.* .... 131 C8 42 5 S 173 16 E
Molfetta, *Italy* .... 47 A10 41 12N 16 36 E
Molíi Pond, *U.S.A.* 145 J14 21 31N 157 51W
Molina de Aragón, *Spain* 40 E3 40 46N 1 52W
Molina de Segura, *Spain* 41 G3 38 3N 1 12W
Moline, *U.S.A.* 156 C6 41 30N 90 31W
Molinella, *Italy* .... 45 D8 44 37N 11 40 E
Molino, *U.S.A.* 153 E2 30 43N 87 20W
Molinos, *Argentina* .... 174 B2 25 28 S 66 15W
Moliro, *Dem. Rep. of the Congo* 118 D3 8 12 S 30 30 E
Moliterno, *Italy* .... 47 B8 40 14N 15 52 E
Molkom, *Sweden* .... 16 E7 59 37N 13 44 E
Mölle, *Sweden* .... 17 H6 56 17N 12 31 E
Molledo, *Spain* 42 B6 43 8N 4 6W
Mollendo, *Peru* .... 172 D3 17 0 S 72 0W
Mollerin, L., *Australia* .... 125 C2 30 30 S 117 35 E
Mollerussa, *Spain* .... 40 D5 41 37N 0 54 E
Mollina, *Spain* 43 H6 37 8N 4 38W
Mölln, *Germany* .... 30 B6 53 37N 10 41 E
Mölltorp, *Sweden* .... 17 F8 58 30N 14 26 E
Mölnlycke, *Sweden* .... 17 G6 57 40N 12 8 E
Molo, *Burma* .... 90 D6 26 9N 96 53 E
Molochansk, *Ukraine* .... 59 J8 47 15N 35 35 E
Molochnoye, Ozero, *Ukraine* .. 59 J8 46 30N 35 20 E
Molodechno = Maladzyechna,
  Belarus .... 58 E4 54 20N 26 50 E
Molokai, *U.S.A.* 145 B5 21 8N 157 0W
Molokini I., *U.S.A.* 145 C5 20 38N 156 30W
Moloma ➤, *Russia* .... 64 B2 58 29N 48 33 E
Molong, *Australia* .... 129 B8 33 5 S 148 54 E
Molopo ➤, *Africa* .... 116 D3 28 30 S 20 12 E
Mólos, *Greece* .... 48 C4 38 47N 22 37 E
Molotov = Perm, *Russia* ..... 64 C6 58 0N 56 10 E
Molotov, Mys = Arktichesky, Mys,
  Russia .... 67 A10 81 10N 95 0 E
Molotovsk = Severodvinsk, *Russia* 56 B6 64 27N 39 58 E
Moloundou, *Cameroon* .... 114 B3 2 8N 15 15 E
Molowaie, *Dem. Rep. of the Congo* 115 D4 5 47 S 23 18 E
Molsheim, *France* .... 27 D14 48 33N 7 29 E
Molson L., *Canada* 143 C9 54 22N 96 40W
Molteno, *S. Africa* .... 116 E4 31 22 S 26 22 E
Moltrásio, *Italy* .... 33 E8 45 52N 9 6 E
Molu, *Indonesia* .... 83 C4 6 45 S 131 40 E
Molucca Sea, *Indonesia* ...... 82 A3 0 0 125 0 E
Moluccas = Maluku, *Indonesia* . 79 E7 1 0 S 127 0 E
Molundo, *Phil.* .... 81 H5 7 55N 124 23 E
Moma, *Dem. Rep. of the Congo* 118 C1 1 35 S 23 52 E
Moma, *Mozam.* .... 119 F4 16 47 S 39 4 E
Momba, *Australia* .... 128 A5 30 58 S 143 30 E
Mombaça, *Brazil* .... 170 C4 5 43 S 39 45W
Mombango, *Dem. Rep. of the Congo* 114 B4 1 45N 24 26 E
Mombasa, *Kenya* .... 118 C4 4 2 S 39 43 E
Mombetsu, *Japan* .... 70 B11 44 21N 143 22 E
Mombil, *Burma* .... 90 B7 27 46N 98 6 E
Momboyo ➤, *Dem. Rep. of
  the Congo* .... 114 C3 0 16 S 19 0 E
Mombuey, *Spain* 42 C4 42 3N 6 20W
Momchilgrad, *Bulgaria* .... 51 E9 41 33N 25 23 E
Momence, *U.S.A.* 157 C9 41 10N 87 40W
Momi, *Dem. Rep. of the Congo* 118 C2 1 42 S 27 0 E
Momote, *Papua N.G.* .... 132 B4 2 4 S 147 27 E
Mompog Pass, *Phil.* .... 80 B4 13 34N 122 13 E
Mompós, *Colombia* 168 B3 9 14N 74 26W
Møn, *Denmark* .... 17 K6 54 57N 12 20 E
Mon □, *Burma* .... 90 G6 16 0N 97 30 E
Mona, Canal de la = Mona Passage,
  W. Indies 165 C6 18 30N 67 45W
Mona, Isla, *Puerto Rico* 165 C6 18 5N 67 54W
Mona, Pta., *Costa Rica* 164 E3 9 37N 82 36W
Mona Passage, *W. Indies* 165 C6 18 30N 67 45W
Mona Quimbundo, *Angola* ..... 115 D3 9 55 S 19 58 E
Monaca, *U.S.A.* 150 F4 40 41N 80 17W
Monadhliath Mts., *U.K.* 22 D4 57 10N 4 4W
Monadnock, Mt., *U.S.A.* 151 D12 42 52N 72 7W
Monagas □, *Venezuela* 169 B5 9 20N 63 0W
Monaghan, *Ireland* 23 B5 54 15N 6 57W
Monaghan □, *Ireland* 23 B5 54 11N 6 56W
Monahans, *U.S.A.* 155 K3 31 36N 102 54W
Monapo, *Mozam.* .... 119 E5 14 56 S 40 19 E
Monar, L., *U.K.* 22 D3 57 26N 5 8W
Monaragala, *Sri Lanka* .... 95 L5 6 52N 81 22 E
Monarch Mt., *Canada* 142 C3 51 55N 125 57W
Monashee Mts., *Canada* 142 C5 51 0N 118 43W
Monasterevin, *Ireland* 23 C4 53 8N 7 4W
Monasterio de Rodilla, *Spain* .. 42 C7 42 22N 3 25W
Monastir = Bitola, *Macedonia* . 50 E5 41 1N 21 20 E
Monastir, *Tunisia* .... 108 A2 35 50N 10 49 E
Moncada, *Phil.* .... 80 D3 15 44N 120 34 E
Moncalieri, *Italy* .... 44 D4 45 0N 7 41 E
Moncalvo, *Italy* .... 44 C5 45 3N 8 16 E
Monção, *Portugal* 42 C2 42 4N 8 27W
Moncarapacho, *Portugal* 43 H3 37 5N 7 46W
Moncayo, Sierra del, *Spain* ... 40 D3 41 48N 1 50W
Monchegorsk, *Russia* .... 56 C5 67 54N 32 58 E
Mönchengladbach, *Germany* ... 30 D2 51 11N 6 27 E
Monchique, *Portugal* 43 H2 37 19N 8 38W
Moncks Corner, *U.S.A.* 153 E7 33 12N 80 1W
Monclova, *Mexico* 162 B4 26 50N 101 30W
Moncontour, *France* 26 D4 48 22N 2 38W
Moncton, *Canada* 141 C7 46 7N 64 51W
Mondariz, *Spain* 42 C2 42 14N 8 27W
Mondego ➤, *Portugal* 42 E2 40 9N 8 52W
Mondego, C., *Portugal* 42 E2 40 11N 8 54W
Mondeodo, *Indonesia* .... 82 B2 3 34 S 122 5 E
Mondeville, *France* 26 C6 49 10N 0 18W
Mondimbi, *Dem. Rep. of the Congo* 114 B4 1 48N 22 46 E
Mondjuku, *Dem. Rep. of the Congo* 114 C4 1 41 S 21 12 E
Mondo, *Chad* .... 109 F3 13 47N 15 32 E
Mondolfo, *Italy* .... 45 E10 43 45N 13 6 E
Mondoñedo, *Spain* 42 B3 43 25N 7 23W
Mondovi, *Italy* .... 44 D4 44 23N 7 49 E
Mondragon, *Phil.* .... 80 E5 12 31N 124 45 E
Mondragone, *Italy* .... 46 A6 41 7N 13 52 E
Mondrain I., *Australia* .... 125 F3 34 9 S 122 14 E
Moneague, *Jamaica* .... 164 a 18 16N 77 7W
Monemvasía, *Greece* .... 48 E5 36 41N 23 3 E

Monessen, *U.S.A.* 150 F5 40 9N 79 54W
Monesterio, *Spain* 43 G4 38 6N 6 15W
Monestier-de-Clermont, *France* . 29 D9 44 55N 5 38 E
Monett, *U.S.A.* 155 G8 36 55N 93 55W
Moneymore, *U.K.* 23 B5 54 41N 6 40W
Monfalcone, *Italy* .... 45 C10 45 49N 13 32 E
Monflanquin, *France* .... 28 D4 44 32N 0 47 E
Monforte, *Portugal* 43 F3 39 6N 7 25W
Monforte de Lemos, *Spain* 42 C3 42 31N 7 33W
Mŏng Hsu, *Burma* .... 76 G2 21 54N 98 30 E
Mong Hta, *Burma* .... 90 F7 19 50N 98 35 E
Mong Ket, *Burma* .... 90 D7 23 8N 98 22 E
Mong Kung, *Burma* .... 90 E6 21 35N 97 35 E
Mong Kyawt, *Burma* .... 90 F7 19 56N 98 45 E
Mong Long, *Burma* .... 90 D6 22 47N 96 37 E
Mong Mit, *Burma* .... 90 D6 23 7N 96 41 E
Mong Nai, *Burma* .... 90 E6 20 32N 97 46 E
Mong Pan, *Burma* .... 90 E7 20 19N 98 22 E
Mong Ping, *Burma* .... 76 G2 21 22N 99 2 E
Mong Pu, *Burma* .... 90 E7 20 55N 98 44 E
Mong Ton, *Burma* .... 90 E7 20 17N 98 45 E
Mong Tung, *Burma* .... 90 D6 22 2N 97 41 E
Mong Yai, *Burma* .... 90 D7 22 21N 98 3 E
Mŏng Yu, *Burma* .... 90 D6 23 30N 97 47 E
Monga, *Dem. Rep. of the Congo* 114 B4 4 12 S 22 49 E
Mongala ➤, *Dem. Rep. of the Congo* 114 B3 1 53N 19 46 E
Mongalla, *Sudan* .... 107 F3 5 8N 31 42 E
Mongandia, *Congo* .... 114 B3 0 45N 17 11 E
Monger, L., *Australia* .... 125 E2 29 25 S 117 5 E
Mongga, *Solomon Is.* .... 133 L9 7 52 S 157 0 E
Monghyr = Munger, *India* .... 93 G12 25 23N 86 30 E
Mongibello = Etna, *Italy* ..... 47 E7 37 50N 14 55 E
Mongla, *Bangla.* .... 90 D2 22 8N 89 35 E
Mongngaw, *Burma* .... 90 D6 22 47N 96 59 E
Mongo, *Chad* .... 109 F3 12 14N 18 43 E
Mongó, *Eq. Guin.* .... 114 B2 1 52N 10 10 E
Mongo ➤, *S. Leone* 112 D2 9 35N 12 10W
Mongolia ■, *Asia* .... 67 E10 47 0N 103 0 E
Mongomo, *Eq. Guin.* .... 114 B2 1 38N 11 19 E
Mongonu, *Nigeria* .... 113 C7 12 40N 13 32 E
Mongororo, *Chad* .... 109 F4 12 3N 22 26 E
Mongstad, *Norway* .... 18 D2 60 49N 5 2 E
Mongu, *Zambia* .... 115 F4 15 16 S 23 12 E
Mongua, *Angola* .... 115 F3 16 43 S 15 20 E
Moniac, *U.S.A.* 152 F7 30 31N 82 14W
Monifieth, *U.K.* 22 E6 56 30N 2 48W
Monistrol-sur-Loire, *France* .... 29 C8 45 17N 4 11 E
Monkey Bay, *Malawi* .... 119 E4 14 7 S 35 1 E
Monkey Mia, *Australia* .... 125 E1 25 48 S 113 43 E
Monkey River, *Belize* 163 D7 16 22N 88 29W
Mońki, *Poland* .... 54 E9 53 23N 22 48 E
Monkoto, *Dem. Rep. of the Congo* 114 C4 1 38 S 20 35 E
Monmouth, *U.K.* 21 F5 51 48N 2 42W
Monmouth, Ill., *U.S.A.* 156 D6 40 55N 90 39W
Monmouth, Oreg., *U.S.A.* 158 D2 44 51N 123 14W
Monmouthshire □, *U.K.* 21 F5 51 48N 2 54W
Mono, *Solomon Is.* .... 133 L8 7 20 S 155 35 E
Monolith, *U.S.A.* 161 K8 35 7N 118 22W
Monólithos, *Greece* .... 38 E11 36 7N 27 45 E
Monon, *U.S.A.* 157 D10 40 52N 86 53W
Monona, Iowa, *U.S.A.* 156 A5 43 3N 91 23W
Monona, Wis., *U.S.A.* 156 A7 43 4N 89 20W
Monongahela, *U.S.A.* 150 F5 40 12N 79 56W
Monópoli, *Italy* .... 47 B10 40 57N 17 18 E
Monor, *Hungary* .... 52 C4 47 21N 19 27 E
Monos I., *Trin. & Tob.* 169 F9 10 42N 61 44W
Monóvar, *Spain* 41 G4 38 28N 0 53W
Monowai, *N.Z.* .... 131 F2 45 53 S 167 31 E
Monowai, L., *N.Z.* .... 131 F2 45 53 S 167 25 E
Monqoumba, *C.A.R.* .... 114 B3 3 33N 18 40 E
Monreal del Campo, *Spain* 40 E3 40 47N 1 20W
Monreale, *Italy* .... 46 D6 38 5N 13 17 E
Monroe, Ga., *U.S.A.* 152 B6 33 47N 83 43W
Monroe, Iowa, *U.S.A.* 156 C3 41 31N 93 6W
Monroe, La., *U.S.A.* 155 J8 32 30N 92 7W
Monroe, Mich., *U.S.A.* 157 C13 41 55N 83 24W
Monroe, N.C., *U.S.A.* 149 H5 34 59N 80 33W
Monroe, N.Y., *U.S.A.* 151 E10 41 20N 74 11W
Monroe, Ohio, *U.S.A.* 157 E12 39 27N 84 22W
Monroe, Utah, *U.S.A.* 159 G7 38 38N 112 7W
Monroe, Wash., *U.S.A.* 160 C5 47 51N 121 58W
Monroe, Wis., *U.S.A.* 156 B7 42 36N 89 38W
Monroe City, Ind., *U.S.A.* 153 G8 28 50N 81 19W
Monroe City, Mo., *U.S.A.* 157 F9 38 37N 92 14W
Monroe City, Mo., *U.S.A.* 155 E10 39 39N 91 44W
Monroeton, *U.S.A.* 151 E8 41 43N 76 29W
Monroeville, Ala., *U.S.A.* 149 K2 31 31N 87 20W
Monroeville, Ind., *U.S.A.* 157 D12 40 59N 84 52W
Monroeville, Pa., *U.S.A.* 150 F5 40 26N 79 45W
Monrovia, *Liberia* 112 D2 6 18N 10 47W
Mons, *Belgium* .... 24 D3 50 27N 3 58 E
Mons Klint, *Denmark* .... 17 K6 54 57N 12 33 E
Monsaraz, *Portugal* 43 G3 38 28N 7 22W
Monse, *Indonesia* .... 82 B2 4 7 S 123 15 E
Monsefú, *Peru* .... 172 B2 6 52 S 79 52W
Monségur, *France* .... 28 D4 44 38N 0 4 E
Monsélice, *Italy* .... 45 C8 45 14N 11 45 E
Monstad, *Sweden* .... 18 D3 60 37N 6 31 E
Monsterås, *Sweden* .... 17 G10 57 3N 16 26 E
Mont Cenis, Col du, *France* ... 29 C10 45 15N 6 55 E
Mont-de-Marsan, *France* 28 E3 43 54N 0 31W
Mont-Dore, N. Cal. .... 133 V20 22 16 S 166 34 E
Mont Fouari, Réserve du ☐, *Congo* 114 C2 2 52 S 11 32 E
Mont-Joli, *Canada* 141 C6 48 37N 68 10W
Mont-Laurier, *Canada* 140 C4 46 35N 75 30W
Mont-Louis, *Canada* 141 C6 49 15N 65 44W
Mont Peko, Parc Nat. du ☐, *Ivory C.* 112 D3 7 9N 7 15W
Mont-roig del Camp, *Spain* .... 40 D5 41 5N 0 58 E
Mont-St-Michel, Le = Le Mont-St-
  Michel, *France* 26 D5 48 40N 1 30W
Mont Sangbe, Parc Nat. du ☐,
  Ivory C. 112 D3 8 0N 7 10W
Mont Tremblant, Parc Recr. du ☐,
  Canada 140 C5 46 30N 74 30W
Montabaur, *Germany* .... 30 E3 50 26N 7 50 E
Montagnac = Remchi, *Algeria* . 111 A4 35 2N 1 26W
Montagnac, *France* .... 28 E7 43 29N 3 28 E
Montagnana, *Italy* .... 45 C8 45 14N 11 28 E
Montagne d'Ambre, Parc Nat. de
  la ☐, *Madag.* .... 117 A8 12 37 S 49 8 E
Montagne de Reims, Parc Naturel
  Régional de la ☐, *France* ... 27 C11 49 8N 4 0 E
Montagu, *S. Africa* .... 116 E3 33 45 S 20 8 E
Montagu I., *Antarctica* .... 7 B1 58 25 S 26 20W
Montague, *Canada* 141 C7 46 10N 62 39W
Montague, I., *Mexico* 162 A2 31 40N 114 56W
Montague, I., *Australia* .... 129 D9 36 16 S 150 13 E
Montague, I., *U.S.A.* 144 G11 60 0N 147 30W
Montague Ra., *Australia* ...... 125 E2 27 15 S 119 30 E
Montague Sd., *Australia* ...... 124 B4 14 28 S 125 20 E
Montaigu, *France* 26 F5 46 59N 1 18W
Montalbán, *Spain* 40 E4 40 50N 0 45W
Montalbano Iónico, *Italy* ..... 47 B9 40 17N 16 34 E
Montalbo, *Spain* 40 F2 39 53N 2 42W
Montalcino, *Italy* .... 45 E8 43 3N 11 29 E
Montalegre, *Angola* .... 115 D3 8 45 S 17 4 E
Montalegre, *Portugal* 42 D3 41 49N 7 47W
Montalto, *Italy* .... 47 D8 38 10N 15 55 E
Montalto di Castro, *Italy* ..... 45 F8 42 21N 11 37 E
Montalto Uffugo, *Italy* .... 47 C9 39 24N 16 9 E

Montalvo, *U.S.A.* **161 L7** 34 15N 119 12W
Montamarta, *Spain* **42 D5** 41 39N 5 49W
Montana, *Bulgaria* . . . . **50 C7** 43 27N 23 16 E
Montaña, *Peru* **172 B3** 6 0S 73 0W
Montana, *Switz.* . . . . **32 D4** 46 19N 7 29 E
Montana □, *Bulgaria* . . . . **50 C7** 43 30N 23 20 E
Montana □, *U.S.A.* **158 C9** 47 0N 110 0W
Montaña Clara, I., *Canary Is.* . . **9 e2** 29 17N 13 33W
Montañas de Malaga, Parque Natural
  de □, *Spain* **43 J6** 36 48N 4 32W
Montánchez, *Spain* **43 F4** 39 15N 6 8W
Montañita, *Colombia* **168 C2** 1 22N 75 28W
Montargil, *Portugal* **43 F2** 39 5N 8 10W
Montargis, *France* . . . . **27 E9** 47 59N 2 43 E
Montauban, *France* . . . . **28 D5** 44 2N 1 21 E
Montauk, *U.S.A.* **151 E13** 41 3N 71 57W
Montauk Pt., *U.S.A.* **151 E13** 41 4N 71 52W
Montaytas, *Kazakhstan* . . . . . . **65 B4** 42 5N 68 59 E
Montbard, *France* . . . . **27 E11** 47 38N 4 20 E
Montbarrey, *France* . . . . **27 E12** 47 1N 5 39 E
Montbéliard, *France* . . . . **27 E13** 47 31N 6 48 E
Montblanc, *Spain* . . . . **40 D6** 41 23N 1 4 E
Montbrison, *France* . . . . **29 C8** 45 36N 4 3 E
Montceau-les-Mines, *France* . . . **27 F11** 46 40N 4 23 E
Montcenis, *France* . . . . **29 B8** 46 47N 4 23 E
Montclair, *U.S.A.* **151 F10** 40 49N 74 13W
Montcornet, *France* . . . . **27 C11** 49 40N 4 1 E
Montcuq, *France* . . . . **28 D5** 44 21N 1 13 E
Montdidier, *France* . . . . **27 C9** 49 38N 2 35 E
Monte Albán, *Mexico* **163 D5** 17 2N 96 45W
Monte Alegre, *Brazil* **169 D7** 2 0S 54 0W
Monte Alegre de Goiás, *Brazil* . . **171 D2** 13 14 S 47 10W
Monte Alegre de Minas, *Brazil* . **171 E2** 18 52 S 48 52W
Monte Alegre do Piauí, *Brazil* . . **170 C2** 9 46 S 45 18W
Monte Azul, *Brazil* . . . . **171 E3** 15 9 S 42 53W
Monte Bello Is., *Australia* . . . . . **124 D2** 20 30 S 115 45 E
Monte-Carlo, *Monaco* . . . . **29 E11** 43 46N 7 23 E
Monte Carmelo, *Brazil* . . . . **171 E2** 18 43 S 47 29W
Monte Caseros, *Argentina* . . . . . **174 C4** 30 10 S 57 50W
Monte Comán, *Argentina* . . . . . **174 C2** 34 40 S 67 53W
Monte Cristi, *Dom. Rep.* **165 C5** 19 52N 71 39W
Monte Cucco, Parco del □, *Italy* . . **45 E9** 43 22N 12 43 E
Monte Dinero, *Argentina* . . . . . **176 D3** 52 18 S 68 33W
Monte Dourado, *Brazil* . . . . **169 D7** 0 52 S 52 31W
Monte Lindo →, *Paraguay* . . . . . **174 A4** 23 56 S 57 12W
Monte Patria, *Chile* . . . . **174 C1** 30 42 S 70 58W
Monte Quemado, *Argentina* . . . . **174 B3** 25 53 S 62 41W
Monte Redondo, *Portugal* **42 F2** 39 53N 8 50W
Monte Rio, *U.S.A.* **160 G4** 38 28N 123 0W
Monte San Giovanni Campano, *Italy* . **46 A6** 41 38N 13 31 E
Monte San Savino, *Italy* . . . . . . **45 E8** 43 20N 11 43 E
Monte Sant' Ángelo, *Italy* . . . . . **45 G12** 41 42N 15 59 E
Monte Santu, C. di, *Italy* . . . . . **46 B2** 40 5N 9 44 E
Monte Sibillini, Parco Nazionale
  dei □, *Italy* . . . . **45 F10** 42 55N 13 15 E
Monte Subasio, Parco del □, *Italy* . **45 E9** 43 5N 12 40 E
Monte Vista, *U.S.A.* **159 H10** 37 35N 106 9W
Monteagudo, *Argentina* . . . . **175 B5** 27 14 S 54 8W
Monteagudo, *Bolivia* . . . . **173 D5** 19 49 S 63 59W
Montealegre del Castillo, *Spain* . **41 G3** 38 48N 1 17W
Montebello, *Canada* **140 C5** 45 40N 74 55W
Montebello Iónico, *Italy* . . . . . . **47 E8** 37 59N 15 45 E
Montebelluna, *Italy* . . . . **45 C9** 45 47N 12 3 E
Montebourg, *France* **26 C5** 49 30N 1 20W
Montecastrilli, *Italy* . . . . **45 F9** 42 39N 12 29 E
Montecatini Terme, *Italy* . . . . . . **44 E7** 43 53N 10 46 E
Montecito, *U.S.A.* **161 L7** 34 26N 119 40W
Montecristi, *Ecuador* **168 D1** 1 0S 80 40W
Montecristo, *Italy* . . . . **44 F7** 42 20N 10 19 E
Montefalco, *Italy* . . . . **45 F9** 42 54N 12 39 E
Montefiascone, *Italy* . . . . **45 F9** 42 32N 12 2 E
Montefrío, *Spain* **43 H7** 37 20N 4 0W
Montegiórgio, *Italy* . . . . **45 E10** 43 6N 13 33 E
Montego Bay, *Jamaica* . . . . **164 a** 18 30N 78 0W
Montehermoso, *Spain* **42 E4** 40 5N 6 21W
Monteiro, *Brazil* . . . . **170 C4** 7 48 S 37 2W
Montejicar, *Spain* **43 H7** 37 33N 3 30W
Montelíbano, *Colombia* **168 B2** 8 5N 75 29W
Montélimar, *France* . . . . **29 D8** 44 33N 4 45 E
Montella, *Italy* . . . . **47 B8** 40 51N 15 1 E
Montellano, *Spain* **43 J5** 36 59N 5 29W
Montello, *U.S.A.* **154 D10** 43 48N 89 20W
Montemayor, Meseta de, *Argentina* **176 B3** 44 20 S 66 10W
Montemor-o-Novo, *Portugal* . . . **43 G2** 38 40N 8 12W
Montemor-o-Velho, *Portugal* . . . **42 E2** 40 11N 8 40W
Montemorelos, *Mexico* **163 B5** 25 11N 99 42W
Montendre, *France* **28 C3** 45 16N 0 26W
Montenegro, *Brazil* . . . . **175 B5** 29 39 S 51 29W
Montenero di Bisáccia, *Italy* . . . **45 G11** 41 57N 14 47 E
Montepuez, *Mozam.* . . . . **119 E4** 13 8 S 38 59 E
Montepuez →, *Mozam.* . . . . **119 E5** 12 32 S 40 27 E
Montepulciano, *Italy* . . . . **45 E8** 43 5N 11 47 E
Montereale, *Italy* . . . . **45 F10** 42 31N 13 15 E
Montereau-Faut-Yonne, *France* . . **27 D9** 48 22N 2 57 E
Monterey, *Calif., U.S.A.* **160 J5** 36 37N 121 55W
Monterey, *Ind., U.S.A.* **157 C10** 41 11N 86 30W
Monterey B., *U.S.A.* **160 J5** 36 45N 122 0W
Montería, *Colombia* **168 B2** 8 46N 75 53W
Montero, *Bolivia* . . . . **173 D5** 17 20 S 63 15W
Monteros, *Argentina* . . . . **174 B2** 27 11 S 65 30W
Monterotondo, *Italy* . . . . **45 F9** 42 3N 12 37 E
Monterrey, *Mexico* **162 B4** 25 40N 100 30W
Montes Altos, *Brazil* . . . . **170 C2** 5 50 S 47 4W
Montes Azules, Reserva de La
  Biósfera □, *Mexico* **163 D6** 16 21N 91 3W
Montes Claros, *Brazil* . . . . **171 E3** 16 30 S 43 50W
Montesano, *U.S.A.* **160 D3** 46 59N 123 36W
Montesano sulla Marcellana, *Italy* . **47 B8** 40 16N 15 42 E
Montescáglioso, *Italy* . . . . **45 F11** 42 29N 14 8 E
Montesárchio, *Italy* . . . . **47 A7** 41 4N 14 38 E
Montesilvano, *Italy* . . . . **45 F11** 42 29N 14 8 E
Montesinho, Parque Natural □,
  Portugal **42 D4** 41 54N 6 52W
Montevarchi, *Italy* . . . . **45 E8** 43 31N 11 34 E
Montevideo, *Uruguay* . . . . **175 C4** 34 50 S 56 11W
Montevideo, *U.S.A.* **154 C7** 44 57N 95 43W
Montezuma, *Ga., U.S.A.* **152 C5** 32 18N 84 2W
Montezuma, *Ind., U.S.A.* **157 E9** 39 48N 87 22W
Montezuma, *Iowa, U.S.A.* **156 C4** 41 35N 92 32W
Montezuma Castle Nat.
  Monument □, *U.S.A.* **159 J8** 34 34N 111 45W
Montfaucon, *France* **26 E5** 47 6N 1 7W
Montfaucon-d'Argonne, *France* . . **27 C12** 49 16N 5 8 E
Montfaucon-en-Velay, *France* . . . **29 C8** 45 11N 4 20 E
Montfort, *France* **26 D5** 48 9N 1 58W
Montfort-le-Gesnois, *France* . . . . **26 D7** 48 3N 0 25 E
Montfrague, Parque Natural de □,
  Spain **42 F5** 39 48N 5 52W
Montgenèvre, *France* . . . . **29 D10** 44 56N 6 43 E
Montgomery = Sahiwal, *Pakistan* . **91 C4** 30 45N 73 8 E
Montgomery, *U.K.* **21 E4** 52 34N 3 8W
Montgomery, *Ala., U.S.A.* **152 C3** 32 23N 86 19W
Montgomery, *Ill., U.S.A.* **157 C8** 41 44N 88 21W
Montgomery, *Pa., U.S.A.* **150 E8** 41 10N 76 53W
Montgomery, *W. Va., U.S.A.* . . . **148 F5** 38 11N 81 19W
Montgomery City, *U.S.A.* **156 F5** 38 59N 91 30W
Montguyon, *France* **28 C3** 45 12N 0 12W
Montherme, *France* . . . . **27 C11** 49 52N 4 42 E
Monthey, *Switz.* . . . . **32 D3** 46 15N 6 56 E
Monthois, *France* . . . . **27 C11** 49 19N 4 43 E
Monti, *Italy* . . . . **46 B2** 40 49N 9 19 E

Monti Lucrétili, Parco Naturale □,
  Italy . . . . **45 F9** 42 5N 12 50 E
Monti Picentini, Parco □, *Italy* . . **47 B8** 40 45N 15 2 E
Monti Simbruini, Parco Naturale
  Regionale dei □, *Italy* . . . . . . **45 G10** 41 55N 13 13 E
Monticelli d'Ongina, *Italy* . . . . . **44 C6** 45 5N 9 56 E
Monticello, *Ark., U.S.A.* **155 J9** 33 38N 91 47W
Monticello, *Fla., U.S.A.* **152 E6** 30 33N 83 52W
Monticello, *Ga., U.S.A.* **152 B6** 33 18N 83 40W
Monticello, *Ill., U.S.A.* **157 D8** 40 1N 88 34W
Monticello, *Ind., U.S.A.* **157 D10** 40 45N 86 46W
Monticello, *Iowa, U.S.A.* **156 B5** 42 15N 91 12W
Monticello, *Ky., U.S.A.* **149 G3** 36 50N 84 51W
Monticello, *Minn., U.S.A.* **154 C8** 45 18N 93 48W
Monticello, *Miss., U.S.A.* **155 K9** 31 33N 90 7W
Monticello, *Mo., U.S.A.* **156 D5** 40 7N 91 43W
Monticello, *N.Y., U.S.A.* **151 E10** 41 39N 74 42W
Monticello, *Utah, U.S.A.* **159 H9** 37 52N 109 21W
Montichiari, *Italy* . . . . **44 C7** 45 25N 10 23 E
Montier-en-Der, *France* . . . . **27 D11** 48 30N 4 45 E
Montignac, *France* . . . . **28 C5** 45 4N 1 10 E
Montigny-les-Metz, *France* . . . . . **27 C13** 49 7N 6 10 E
Montigny-sur-Aube, *France* . . . . **27 E11** 47 57N 4 45 E
Montijo, *Portugal* **43 G2** 38 41N 8 54W
Montijo, *Spain* **43 G4** 38 52N 6 39W
Montilla, *Spain* **43 H6** 37 36N 4 40W
Montivilliers, *France* . . . . **26 C7** 49 33N 0 12 E
Montluçon, *France* . . . . **27 F9** 46 22N 2 36 E
Montmagny, *Canada* **141 C5** 46 58N 70 34W
Montmarault, *France* . . . . **27 F9** 46 19N 2 57 E
Montmartre, *Canada* **143 C8** 50 14N 103 27W
Montmédy, *France* . . . . **27 C12** 49 30N 5 20 E
Montmélian, *France* . . . . **29 C10** 45 30N 6 4 E
Montmirail, *France* . . . . **27 D10** 48 51N 3 30 E
Montmoreau-St-Cybard, *France* . **28 C4** 45 23N 0 8 E
Montmorillon, *France* . . . . **28 B4** 46 26N 0 50 E
Montmort-Lucy, *France* . . . . **27 D10** 48 55N 3 49 E
Monto, *Australia* . . . . **126 C5** 24 52 S 151 6 E
Montoire-sur-le-Loir, *France* . . . **26 E7** 47 45N 0 52 E
Montongbuwoh, *Indonesia* . . . . . **79 K19** 8 33 S 116 4 E
Montório al Vomano, *Italy* . . . . . **45 F10** 42 35N 13 38 E
Montoro, *Spain* **43 G6** 38 1N 4 27W
Montour Falls, *U.S.A.* **150 D8** 42 21N 76 51W
Montoursville, *U.S.A.* **150 E8** 41 15N 76 55W
Montpelier, *Idaho, U.S.A.* **158 E8** 42 19N 111 18W
Montpelier, *Ind., U.S.A.* **157 D11** 40 33N 85 17W
Montpelier, *Ohio, U.S.A.* **157 C12** 41 35N 84 37W
Montpelier, *Vt., U.S.A.* **151 B12** 44 16N 72 35W
Montpellier, *France* . . . . **28 E7** 43 37N 3 52 E
Montpezat-de-Quercy, *France* . . . **28 D5** 44 15N 1 30 E
Montpon-Ménestérol, *France* . . . **28 C4** 45 0N 0 11 E
Montréal, *Canada* **140 C5** 45 31N 73 34W
Montréal, *Aude, France* . . . . **28 E6** 43 13N 2 8 E
Montréal, *Gers, France* . . . . **28 E4** 43 56N 0 11 E
Montreal →, *Canada* **143 C7** 47 14N 84 39W
Montreal L., *Canada* **143 C7** 54 20N 105 45W
Montreal Lake, *Canada* **143 C7** 54 3N 105 46W
Montredon-Labessonnié, *France* . **28 E6** 43 45N 2 18 E
Montrésor, *France* . . . . **26 E8** 47 10N 1 10 E
Montret, *France* . . . . **27 F12** 46 40N 5 7 E
Montreuil, *Pas-de-Calais, France* . **27 B8** 50 27N 1 45 E
Montreuil, *Seine-St-Denis, France* **27 D9** 48 51N 2 27 E
Montreuil-Bellay, *France* **26 E6** 47 8N 0 9W
Montreux, *Switz.* . . . . **32 D3** 46 26N 6 55 E
Montrevel-en-Bresse, *France* . . . **27 F12** 46 21N 5 8 E
Montrichard, *France* . . . . **26 E8** 47 20N 1 10 E
Montrose, *U.K.* **22 E6** 56 44N 2 27W
Montrose, *Colo., U.S.A.* **159 G10** 38 29N 107 53W
Montrose, *Pa., U.S.A.* **151 E9** 41 50N 75 53W
Montrose, *L., U.S.A.* **156 F3** 38 18N 93 50W
Monts, Pte. des, *Canada* **141 C6** 49 20N 67 12W
Montsalvy, *France* . . . . **28 D6** 44 41N 2 30 E
Montsant, Serra de, *Spain* . . . . . **40 D6** 41 17N 1 0 E
Montsauche-les-Settons, *France* . **27 E11** 47 13N 4 2 E
Montsec, Serra del, *Spain* . . . . . **40 C5** 42 5N 0 45 E
Montseny, Parque Natural de □,
  Spain **40 D7** 41 43N 2 22W
Montserrat, *Spain* . . . . **40 D7** 41 36N 1 49 E
Montserrat ☑, *W. Indies* **165 C7** 16 40N 62 10W
Montuenga, *Spain* **42 D6** 41 3N 4 38W
Montuiri, *Spain* . . . . **38 B3** 39 34N 2 59 E
Monveda, *Dem. Rep. of the Congo* **114 B4** 2 52N 21 30 E
Monyo, *Burma* . . . . **90 G5** 17 59N 95 30 E
Monywa, *Burma* . . . . **90 D5** 22 7N 95 11 E
Monza, *Italy* . . . . **44 C6** 45 35N 9 16 E
Monze, *Zambia* . . . . **119 F2** 16 17 S 27 29 E
Monze, C., *Pakistan* . . . . **91 D2** 24 47N 66 37 E
Monzón, *Spain* . . . . **40 D5** 41 52N 0 10 E
Mooers, *U.S.A.* **151 B11** 44 58N 73 35W
Mooi →, *S. Africa* . . . . **117 D5** 28 45 S 30 34 E
Mooi River □, *S. Africa* . . . . **117 D4** 29 13 S 29 50 E
Mo'oka, *Japan* . . . . **73 A12** 36 26N 140 1 E
Moonah →, *Australia* . . . . **126 C2** 22 3 S 138 33 E
Moonda, L., *Australia* . . . . **126 D3** 25 52 S 140 25 E
Moonie, *Australia* . . . . **127 D5** 27 46 S 150 20 E
Moonie →, *Australia* . . . . **127 D4** 29 19 S 148 43 E
Moonta, *Australia* . . . . **128 C2** 34 6 S 137 32 E
Moor, Kepulauan, *Indonesia* . . . . **83 B5** 2 57 S 135 45 E
Moora, *Australia* . . . . **125 F2** 30 37 S 115 58 E
Moorcroft, *U.S.A.* **154 C2** 44 16N 104 57W
Moore →, *Australia* . . . . **125 F2** 31 22 S 115 30 E
Moore, L., *Australia* . . . . **125 E2** 29 50 S 117 35 E
Moore Haven, *U.S.A.* **153 J8** 26 50N 81 6W
Moore Park, *Australia* . . . . **126 C5** 24 43 S 152 17 E
Moore River Nat. Park △, *Australia* **125 F2** 31 7 S 115 39 E
Mooréa, *Pac. Oc.* . . . . **133 S16** 17 30 S 149 50W
Moorefield, *U.S.A.* **148 F6** 39 5N 78 59W
Moores Res., *U.S.A.* **151 B13** 44 45N 71 50W
Mooresville, *U.S.A.* **157 E10** 39 37N 80 48W
Moorfoot Hills, *U.K.* **22 F5** 55 44N 3 8W
Moorhead, *U.S.A.* **154 B6** 46 53N 96 45W
Moorland, *U.S.A.* **156 B2** 42 26N 94 18W
Moormerland, *Germany* . . . . **30 B3** 53 20N 7 20 E
Moornanyah L., *Australia* . . . . . **128 B5** 33 15 S 143 42 E
Mooroopna, *Australia* . . . . **127 D4** 36 25 S 145 22 E
Moorpark, *U.S.A.* **161 L8** 34 17N 118 53W
Moorreesburg, *S. Africa* . . . . **116 E2** 33 6 S 18 38 E
Moorrinya Nat. Park △, *Australia* **126 C3** 21 42 S 144 58 E
Moosburg, *Germany* . . . . **31 G7** 48 27N 11 56 E
Moose →, *Canada* **140 B3** 51 20N 80 25W
Moose →, *U.S.A.* **151 C9** 43 38N 75 24W
Moose Creek, *Canada* **151 A10** 45 15N 74 58W
Moose Factory, *Canada* **140 B3** 51 16N 80 32W
Moose Jaw, *Canada* **143 C7** 50 24N 105 30W
Moose Jaw →, *Canada* **143 C7** 50 34N 105 18W
Moose Lake, *Canada* **143 C8** 53 43N 100 20W
Moose Lake, *U.S.A.* **154 B8** 46 27N 92 46W
Moose Mountain Prov. Park △,
  Canada **143 D8** 49 48N 102 25W
Moose Pass, *U.S.A.* **144 A10** 60 29N 149 22W
Moosehead L., *U.S.A.* **149 C11** 45 38N 69 40W
Mooselookmeguntic L., *U.S.A.* . . **151 B13** 44 55N 70 49W
Moosilauke, Mt., *U.S.A.* **151 B13** 44 3N 71 40W
Moosomin, *Canada* **143 C8** 50 9N 101 40W
Moosonee, *Canada* **140 B3** 51 17N 80 39W
Moosup, *U.S.A.* **151 E13** 41 43N 71 53W
Mootwingee Nat. Park △, *Australia* **128 A5** 31 10 S 142 30 E
Mopane, *S. Africa* . . . . **117 C4** 22 37 S 29 52 E
Mopeia Velha, *Mozam.* . . . . **119 F4** 17 30 S 35 40 E
Mopipi, *Botswana* . . . . **116 C3** 21 6 S 24 55 E
Mopoi, *C.A.R.* . . . . **118 A2** 5 6N 26 54 E
Mopti, *Mali* **112 C4** 14 30N 4 0W
Moqatta, *Sudan* . . . . **107 E4** 14 38N 35 50 E
Moqor, *Afghan.* . . . . **91 B2** 32 50N 67 42 E

Moquegua, *Peru* . . . . **172 D3** 17 15 S 70 46W
Moquegua □, *Peru* . . . . **172 D3** 16 50 S 70 55W
Mór, *Hungary* . . . . **52 C3** 47 25N 18 12 E
Mora, *Cameroon* . . . . **113 C7** 11 2N 14 7 E
Móra, *Portugal* **43 G2** 38 55N 8 10W
Mora, *Spain* **43 F7** 39 41N 3 46W
Mora, *Sweden* . . . . **16 C6** 61 2N 14 38 E
Mora, *Minn., U.S.A.* **154 C8** 45 53N 93 18W
Mora, *N. Mex., U.S.A.* **159 J11** 35 58N 105 20W
Mora →, *U.S.A.* **155 H2** 35 35N 104 25W
Mora de Ebro = Móra d'Ebre, *Spain* **40 D5** 41 6N 0 38 E
Mora de Rubielos, *Spain* **40 E4** 40 15N 0 45W
Móra d'Ebre, *Spain* . . . . **40 D5** 41 6N 0 38 E
Móra la Nova, *Spain* . . . . **40 D5** 41 7N 0 39 E
Morača →, *Montenegro, Yug.* . . . **50 D3** 42 20N 19 9 E
Morada Nova, *Brazil* . . . . **170 C4** 5 7 S 38 23W
Morada Nova de Minas, *Brazil* . . **171 E2** 18 37 S 45 22W
Moradabad, *India* . . . . **93 E8** 28 50N 78 50 E
Morafenobe, *Madag.* . . . . **117 B7** 17 50 S 44 53 E
Morag, *Poland* . . . . **54 E6** 53 55N 19 56 E
Moral de Calatrava, *Spain* **43 G7** 38 51N 3 33W
Moraleda, Canal, *Chile* . . . . **176 B2** 44 30 S 73 30W
Moraleja, *Spain* **42 E4** 40 6N 6 43W
Morales, *Bolívar, Colombia* **168 B3** 8 16N 73 51W
Morales, *Cauca, Colombia* **168 C2** 2 45N 76 38W
Moramanga, *Madag.* . . . . **117 B8** 18 56 S 48 12 E
Moran, *Kans., U.S.A.* **155 G7** 37 55N 95 10W
Moran, *Wyo., U.S.A.* **158 E8** 43 53N 110 37W
Moranbah, *Australia* . . . . **126 C4** 22 1 S 148 6 E
Moranhat, *India* . . . . **90 B5** 27 10N 94 50 E
Morano Cálabro, *Italy* . . . . **47 C9** 39 50N 16 8 E
Morant Bay, *Jamaica* . . . . **164 a** 17 53N 76 25W
Morant Cays, *Jamaica* **154 C4** 17 22N 76 0W
Morant Pt., *Jamaica* . . . . **164 a** 17 55N 76 12W
Morar, *India* . . . . **92 F8** 26 14N 78 14 E
Morar, L., *U.K.* **22 E3** 56 57N 5 40W
Moratalla, *Spain* **41 G3** 38 14N 1 49W
Moratuwa, *Sri Lanka* . . . . **95 L4** 6 45N 79 55 E
Morava →, *Slovak Rep.* . . . . **35 C9** 48 10N 16 59 E
Moravia, *Iowa, U.S.A.* **156 D4** 40 53N 92 49W
Moravia, *N.Y., U.S.A.* **150 D7** 42 43N 76 25W
Moravian Hts. = Českomoravská
  Vrchovina, *Czech Rep.* . . . . . . **34 B8** 49 30N 15 40 E
Moravica →, *Serbia, Yug.* . . . . . **50 C4** 43 52N 20 8 E
Moravita, *Romania* . . . . **52 E6** 45 17N 21 14 E
Moravská Třebová, *Czech Rep.* . . **34 B9** 49 45N 16 40 E
Moravské Budějovice, *Czech Rep.* . **34 B8** 49 4N 15 49 E
Morawa, *Australia* . . . . **125 E2** 29 13 S 116 0 E
Morawhanna, *Guyana* **169 B6** 8 30N 59 40W
Moray □, *U.K.* **22 D5** 57 31N 3 18W
Moray Firth, *U.K.* **22 D5** 57 40N 3 52W
Morbach, *Germany* . . . . **31 F3** 49 48N 7 6 E
Morbegno, *Italy* . . . . **44 B6** 46 8N 9 34 E
Morbi, *India* . . . . **92 H4** 22 50N 70 42 E
Morbihan □, *France* **26 E4** 47 55N 2 50W
Mörbylånga, *Sweden* . . . . **11 H9** 56 30N 16 28 E
Morcenx, *France* **28 D3** 44 3N 0 55W
Mordelles, *France* . . . . **47 A7** 41 20N 14 40 E
Morden, *Canada* **143 D9** 49 15N 98 10W
Mordoğan, *Turkey* . . . . **49 C8** 38 30N 26 37 E
Mordovian Republic = Mordvinia □,
  Russia . . . . **60 C7** 54 20N 44 30 E
Mordovo, *Russia* . . . . **60 D5** 52 6N 40 50 E
Mordvinia □, *Russia* . . . . **60 C7** 54 20N 44 30 E
Mordy, *Poland* . . . . **55 F9** 52 13N 22 31 E
Møre og Romsdal □, *Norway* . . . **18 B4** 62 30N 8 0 E
Morea, *Greece* . . . . **12 H10** 37 45N 22 10 E
Moreau →, *U.S.A.* **154 C4** 45 18N 100 43W
Morecambe, *U.K.* **20 C5** 54 5N 2 52W
Morecambe B., *U.K.* **20 C5** 54 7N 3 0W
Moree, *Australia* . . . . **127 D4** 29 28 S 149 54 E
Morehead, *Papua N. G.* . . . . **132 E1** 8 41 S 141 41 E
Morehead, *U.S.A.* **157 F13** 38 11N 83 26W
Morehead City, *U.S.A.* **149 H7** 34 43N 76 43W
Mörel, *Switz.* . . . . **32 D6** 46 22N 8 2 E
Morel →, *India* . . . . **92 F7** 26 13N 76 36 E
Moreland, *U.S.A.* **152 B5** 33 17N 84 46W
Morelia, *Mexico* **162 D4** 19 42N 101 7W
Morella, *Australia* . . . . **126 C3** 23 0 S 143 52 E
Morella, *Spain* **40 E4** 40 35N 0 5W
Morelos, *Mexico* **162 B3** 26 42N 107 40W
Morelos □, *Mexico* **163 D5** 18 40N 99 10W
Moremi Wildlife Reserve △,
  Botswana . . . . **116 B3** 19 18 S 23 10 E
Morena, *India* . . . . **92 F8** 26 30N 78 4 E
Morena, Sierra, *Spain* **43 G7** 38 20N 4 0W
Morenci, *U.S.A.* **157 C12** 41 43N 84 13W
Moreno Valley, *U.S.A.* **161 M10** 33 56N 117 15W
Moreru →, *Brazil* . . . . **173 C6** 10 10 S 59 15W
Moresby I., *Canada* **142 C2** 52 30N 131 40W
Morestel, *France* . . . . **29 C9** 45 40N 5 28 E
Moreton I., *Australia* . . . . **127 D5** 27 10 S 153 25 E
Moreton Island Nat. Park △,
  Australia . . . . **127 A5** 27 2 S 153 24 E
Moreuil, *France* . . . . **27 C9** 49 46N 2 30 E
Morey, *Spain* . . . . **38 B4** 39 44N 3 20 E
Morez, *France* . . . . **27 F13** 46 31N 6 2 E
Morgan, *Australia* . . . . **128 A2** 34 2 S 139 35 E
Morgan, *Ga., U.S.A.* **152 D5** 31 32N 84 36W
Morgan, *Utah, U.S.A.* **158 F8** 41 2N 111 41W
Morgan City, *U.S.A.* **155 L9** 29 42N 91 12W
Morganfield, *U.S.A.* **148 G10** 37 41N 87 55W
Morganton, *U.S.A.* **149 H5** 35 45N 81 41W
Morgantown, *Ind., U.S.A.* **157 E10** 39 22N 86 16W
Morgantown, *W. Va., U.S.A.* . . . **148 F6** 39 38N 79 57W
Morgenzon, *S. Africa* . . . . **117 D4** 26 45 S 29 36 E
Morges, *Switz.* . . . . **32 C2** 46 31N 6 29 E
Morghak, *Iran* . . . . **97 D8** 29 7N 57 54 E
Morgongåva, *Sweden* . . . . **16 E10** 59 57N 16 58 E
Morhange, *France* . . . . **27 D13** 48 55N 6 38 E
Morhar →, *India* . . . . **93 G11** 25 29N 85 11 E
Mori, *Italy* . . . . **44 C7** 45 51N 10 59 E
Moriarty, *U.S.A.* **159 J10** 34 59N 106 3W
Moribaya, *Guinea* **112 D3** 9 37N 10 48W
Morice L., *Canada* **142 C3** 53 50N 127 40W
Morichal, *Colombia* **168 C3** 2 10N 70 34W
Morichal Largo →, *Venezuela* . . **169 B5** 9 27N 62 25W
Moriguchi, *Japan* . . . . **73 C7** 34 44N 135 34 E
Moriki, *Nigeria* . . . . **113 C6** 12 52N 6 30 E
Morinville, *Canada* **142 C6** 53 49N 113 41W
Morioka, *Japan* . . . . **70 E10** 39 45N 141 8 E
Moris, *Mexico* **162 B3** 28 8N 108 32W
Morisset, *Australia* . . . . **129 B9** 33 6 S 151 30 E
Moriyama, *Japan* . . . . **73 B7** 35 4N 135 59 E
Morlaàs, *France* **28 E3** 43 21N 0 18W
Morlaix, *France* **26 D3** 48 36N 3 52W
Mörlunda, *Sweden* . . . . **11 G9** 57 19N 15 52 E
Mormanno, *Italy* . . . . **47 C8** 39 53N 15 59 E
Mormant, *France* . . . . **27 D9** 48 37N 2 52 E
Mornington, *Australia* . . . . **129 E6** 38 15 S 145 5 E
Mornington, *Chile* . . . . **176 C1** 49 50 S 75 30W
Mornington I., *Australia* . . . . . . **126 B2** 16 30 S 139 30 E
Mórnos →, *Greece* . . . . **48 C3** 38 25N 21 56 E
Moro, *Pakistan* . . . . **92 F2** 26 40N 68 0 E
Moro, *Sudan* . . . . **107 E3** 10 50N 30 9 E
Moro →, *Pakistan* . . . . **92 E2** 29 42N 67 22 E
Moro G., *Phil.* . . . . **81 H4** 6 30N 123 0 E
Morobe, *Papua N. G.* . . . . **132 D4** 7 49 S 147 38 E
Morobe □, *Papua N. G.* . . . . **132 D4** 7 0 S 147 0 E

Morocco, *U.S.A.* **157 D9** 40 57N 87 27W
Morocco ■, *N. Afr.* **110 B3** 32 0N 5 50W
Morococha, *Peru* . . . . **172 C2** 11 40 S 76 5W
Morogoro, *Tanzania* . . . . **118 D4** 6 50 S 37 40 E
Morogoro □, *Tanzania* . . . . **118 D4** 8 0 S 37 0 E
Moroleón, *Mexico* **162 C4** 20 8N 101 32W
Morombe, *Madag.* . . . . **117 C7** 21 45 S 43 22 E
Moron, *Argentina* . . . . **174 C4** 34 39 S 58 37W
Morón, *Cuba* **164 B4** 22 8N 78 39W
Morón de Almazán, *Spain* **40 D2** 41 29N 2 27W
Morón de la Frontera, *Spain* . . . **43 H5** 37 6N 5 28W
Morona →, *Peru* . . . . **168 D2** 4 40 S 77 10W
Morona-Santiago □, *Ecuador* . . . **168 D2** 2 30 S 78 0W
Morondo, *Ivory C.* **112 D3** 8 57N 6 47W
Morong, *Phil.* . . . . **80 D3** 14 41N 120 16 E
Morongo Valley, *U.S.A.* **161 L10** 34 3N 116 37W
Moroni, *Comoros Is.* . . . . **121 a** 11 40 S 43 16 E
Moroni, *U.S.A.* **158 G8** 39 32N 111 35W
Moronou, *Ivory C.* **112 D4** 6 16N 4 59W
Morotai, *Indonesia* . . . . **82 A3** 2 10N 128 30 E
Moroto, *Uganda* . . . . **118 B3** 2 28N 34 42 E
Moroto, Mt., *Uganda* . . . . **118 B3** 2 30N 34 43 E
Morowali, *Indonesia* . . . . **82 B2** 1 52 S 121 30 E
Morozov, *Bulgaria* . . . . **51 D9** 42 30N 25 10 E
Morozovsk, *Russia* . . . . **61 F5** 48 25N 41 50 E
Morpeth, *U.K.* **20 B6** 55 10N 1 41W
Morphou, *Cyprus* . . . . **39 E8** 35 12N 32 59 E
Morphou Bay, *Cyprus* . . . . **39 E8** 35 15N 32 50 E
Morrelganj, *Bangla.* . . . . **90 D2** 22 28N 89 51 E
Morrilton, *U.S.A.* **155 H8** 35 9N 92 44W
Morrinhos, *Ceará, Brazil* . . . . . . **170 B3** 3 14 S 40 7W
Morrinhos, *Minas Gerais, Brazil* . **171 E2** 17 45 S 49 10W
Morrinsville, *N.Z.* . . . . **130 D4** 37 40 S 175 32 E
Morris, *Canada* **143 D9** 49 25N 97 22W
Morris, *Ill., U.S.A.* **154 E10** 41 22N 88 26W
Morris, *Minn., U.S.A.* **154 C7** 45 35N 95 55W
Morris, *N.Y., U.S.A.* **151 D9** 42 33N 75 15W
Morris, *Pa., U.S.A.* **150 E7** 41 35N 77 17W
Morris, Mt., *Australia* . . . . **125 E5** 26 9 S 131 4 E
Morris Jesup, Kap, *Greenland* . . . **10 A7** 83 40N 34 0W
Morrisburg, *Canada* **151 B9** 44 55N 75 7W
Morrison, *U.S.A.* **154 E9** 41 49N 89 58W
Morrisonville, *U.S.A.* **156 E7** 39 25N 89 27W
Morristown, *Ariz., U.S.A.* **159 K7** 33 51N 112 37W
Morristown, *Ind., U.S.A.* **157 E11** 39 40N 85 42W
Morristown, *N.J., U.S.A.* **151 F10** 40 48N 74 29W
Morristown, *N.Y., U.S.A.* **151 B9** 44 35N 75 39W
Morristown, *Tenn., U.S.A.* **149 G4** 36 13N 83 18W
Morrisville, *N.Y., U.S.A.* **151 D9** 42 53N 75 35W
Morrisville, *Pa., U.S.A.* **151 F10** 40 13N 74 47W
Morrisville, *Vt., U.S.A.* **151 B12** 44 34N 72 36W
Morro, Pta., *Chile* . . . . **174 B1** 27 6 S 71 0W
Morro Bay, *U.S.A.* **160 K6** 35 22N 120 51W
Morro Chico, *Chile* . . . . **176 D2** 52 2 S 71 26W
Morro del Jable, *Canary Is.* **9 e2** 28 3N 14 23W
Morro do Chapéu, *Brazil* . . . . . . **171 D3** 11 33 S 41 9W
Morro Jable, Pta. de, *Canary Is.* . **9 e2** 28 2N 14 20W
Morrosquillo, G. de, *Colombia* . . **164 E4** 9 35N 75 40W
Morrow, *U.S.A.* **157 E12** 39 21N 84 8W
Mörrum, *Sweden* . . . . **17 H8** 56 12N 14 45 E
Morrumbene, *Mozam.* . . . . **117 C6** 23 31 S 35 16 E
Mörrumsån →, *Sweden* . . . . **17 H8** 56 10N 14 45 E
Mors, *Denmark* . . . . **17 H2** 56 50N 8 45 E
Morshansk, *Russia* . . . . **60 D5** 53 28N 41 50 E
Morsi, *India* . . . . **94 D4** 21 21N 78 0 E
Mörsil, *Sweden* . . . . **16 A7** 63 19N 13 40 E
Mortagne →, *France* . . . . **27 D13** 48 33N 6 27 E
Mortagne-au-Perche, *France* . . . . **26 D7** 48 31N 0 33 E
Mortagne-sur-Gironde, *France* . . **28 C3** 45 28N 0 47W
Mortagne-sur-Sèvre, *France* **26 F6** 47 0N 0 59W
Mortain, *France* **26 D6** 48 40N 0 57W
Mortara, *Italy* . . . . **44 C5** 45 15N 8 44 E
Morteau, *France* . . . . **27 E13** 47 3N 6 35 E
Morteros, *Argentina* . . . . **174 C3** 30 50 S 62 0W
Mortes, R. das →, *Brazil* . . . . . . **171 D1** 11 45 S 50 44W
Mortlach, *Canada* **143 C7** 50 27N 106 4W
Mortlake, *Australia* . . . . **128 E5** 38 5 S 142 50 E
Morton, *Ill., U.S.A.* **156 D7** 40 37N 89 28W
Morton, *Tex., U.S.A.* **155 J3** 33 44N 102 46W
Morton, *Wash., U.S.A.* **160 D4** 46 34N 122 17W
Morton Nat. Park △, *Australia* . . **129 C5** 35 0 S 150 12 E
Moruga, *Trin. & Tob.* **169 F9** 10 4N 61 16W
Morundah, *Australia* . . . . **129 C7** 34 57 S 146 19 E
Moruya, *Australia* . . . . **129 C9** 35 58 S 150 3 E
Morvan, *France* . . . . **27 E11** 47 5N 4 0 E
Morvan, Parc Naturel Régional
  du □, *France* . . . . **27 E11** 47 12N 4 3 E
Morven, *Australia* . . . . **127 D4** 26 22 S 147 5 E
Morven, *N.Z.* . . . . **131 E4** 44 50 S 171 6 E
Morvern, *U.K.* **152 E6** 30 57N 83 30W
Morwell, *Australia* **22 E3** 56 38N 5 44W
Morwell, *Australia* . . . . **129 E7** 38 10 S 146 22 E
Moryń, *Poland* . . . . **55 E1** 52 51N 14 22 E
Morzhovets, Ostrov, *Russia* . . . . **56 A7** 66 44N 42 35 E
Morzine, *France* . . . . **27 F13** 46 11N 6 42 E
Mosalsk, *Russia* . . . . **58 E8** 54 30N 34 55 E
Mosbach, *Germany* . . . . **31 F5** 49 21N 9 9 E
Mosby, *Norway* . . . . **18 F4** 58 12N 7 55 E
Moščenice, *Croatia* . . . . **45 F10** 42 42N 13 52 E
Mosciano Sant' Ángelo, *Italy* . . . **45 F10** 42 42N 13 52 E
Moscos Is., *Burma* . . . . **86 E1** 14 0N 97 30 E
Moscow = Moskva, *Russia* . . . . . **58 E9** 55 45N 37 35 E
Moscow, *Idaho, U.S.A.* **158 C5** 46 44N 117 0W
Moscow, *Mich., U.S.A.* **157 B12** 42 3N 84 30W
Moscow, *Pa., U.S.A.* **151 E9** 41 20N 75 31W
Mosel →, *Europe* . . . . **27 B14** 50 22N 7 36 E
Mosel = Mosel →, *Europe* . . . . . **27 B14** 50 22N 7 36 E
Moselle □, *France* . . . . **27 D13** 48 59N 6 33 E
Moses Lake, *U.S.A.* **158 C4** 47 8N 119 17W
Mosgiel, *N.Z.* . . . . **131 F5** 45 53 S 170 21 E
Moshaweng →, *S. Africa* . . . . . . **116 D3** 26 35 S 22 50 E
Moshi, *Tanzania* . . . . **118 C4** 3 22 S 37 18 E
Moshupa, *Botswana* . . . . **116 C4** 24 46 S 25 29 E
Mosina, *Poland* . . . . **55 F3** 52 15N 16 50 E
Mosite, *Dem. Rep. of the Congo* . **114 B4** 0 53N 23 40 E
Mosjøen, *Norway* . . . . **14 D15** 65 51N 13 12 E
Moskenesøya, *Norway* . . . . **14 C15** 67 58N 13 0 E
Moskenstraumen, *Norway* . . . . . **14 C15** 67 47N 12 45 E
Moskog, *Norway* . . . . **18 C2** 61 26N 6 0 E
Moskovskiy, *Tajikistan* . . . . **65 E4** 37 37N 69 42 E
Moskva, *Russia* . . . . **58 E9** 55 45N 37 35 E
Moskva →, *Russia* . . . . **58 E10** 55 5N 38 51 E
Moslavačka Gora, *Croatia* . . . . . **45 C13** 45 40N 16 37 E
Moso, *Vanuatu* . . . . **133 G6** 17 34 S 168 15 E
Mosomane, *Botswana* . . . . **116 C4** 24 2 S 26 19 E
Mosonmagyaróvár, *Hungary* . . . **52 C2** 47 52N 17 18 E
Mošorin, *Serbia, Yug.* . . . . **52 E5** 45 19N 20 4 E
Mospino, *Ukraine* . . . . **59 J9** 47 52N 38 0 E
Mosqueiro, *Brazil* . . . . **170 B2** 1 10 S 48 28W
Mosquera, *Colombia* **168 C2** 2 35N 78 24W
Mosquero, *U.S.A.* **155 H3** 35 47N 103 58W
Mosqueruela, *Spain* **40 E4** 40 21N 0 27W
Mosquitia, *Honduras* **164 C3** 15 20N 84 10W
Mosquito Coast = Mosquitia,
  Honduras **164 C3** 15 20N 84 10W
Mosquito Creek L., *U.S.A.* **150 E4** 41 18N 80 46W
Mosquito L., *Canada* **143 A8** 62 35N 103 20W
Mosquitos, G. de los, *Panama* . . **164 E3** 9 15N 81 10W
Moss, *Norway* . . . . **18 E7** 59 27N 10 40 E
Moss Vale, *Australia* . . . . **129 C9** 34 32 S 150 25 E
Mossaka, *Congo* . . . . **114 C3** 1 15 S 16 45 E

Mossâmedes, *Brazil* .... 171 E1 16 7 S 50 11W
Mossbank, *Canada* 143 D7 49 56N 105 56W
Mossburn, *N.Z.* .... 131 F3 45 41 S 168 15 E
Mosselbaai, *S. Africa* .... 116 E3 34 11 S 22 8 E
Mossendjo, *Congo* .... 114 C2   2 55 S 12 42 E
Mosses, Col des, *Switz.* .... 32 D4 46 25N   7 7 E
Mossfellsbær, *Iceland* 11 C5 64 11N 21 45W
Mossgiel, *Australia* .... 128 B6 33 15 S 144 5 E
Mossman, *Australia* .... 126 B4 16 21 S 145 15 E
Mossoró, *Brazil* .... 170 C4   5 10 S 37 15W
Mossuril, *Mozam.* .... 119 E5 14 58 S 40 42 E
Mossy Head, *U.S.A.* 153 E3 30 45N 86 19W
Mossy Point, *Australia* .... 129 C9 35 50 S 150 11 E
Most, *Czech Rep.* .... 34 A6 50 31N 13 38 E
Mosta, *Malta* .... 38 F7 35 55N 14 26 E
Mostaganem, *Algeria* .... 111 A5 35 54N   0 5 E
Mostar, *Bos.-H.* .... 52 G2 43 22N 17 50 E
Mostardas, *Brazil* .... 175 C5 31 2 S 50 51W
Mostefa, Rass, *Tunisia* .... 108 A2 36 55N 11 3 E
Mosteiros, *Azores* 9 d3 37 53N 25 49W
Mosterhamn, *Norway* .... 18 E2 59 42N   5 21 E
Mostiska = Mostyska, *Ukraine* .. 59 H2 49 48N 23 4 E
Móstoles, *Spain* 42 E7 40 19N   3 53W
Mosty = Masty, *Belarus* .... 58 F3 53 27N 24 38 E
Mostyska, *Ukraine* .... 59 H2 49 48N 23 4 E
Mosul = Al Mawşil, *Iraq* .... 101 D10 36 15N 43 5 E
Mosûlpo, *S. Korea* .... 75 H14 33 20N 126 17 E
Møsvatnet, *Norway* .... 18 E5 59 52N   8 5 E
Mota, *Ethiopia* .... 107 E4 11 5N 37 52 E
Mota, *Vanuatu* .... 133 C5 13 49 S 167 42 E
Mota del Cuervo, *Spain* 41 F2 39 30N   2 52W
Mota del Marqués, *Spain* 42 D5 41 38N   5 11W
Mota Lava, *Vanuatu* .... 133 C5 13 40 S 167 40 E
Motaba, *Congo* .... 114 B3   2 6N 18 2 E
Motagua →, *Guatemala* 164 C2 15 44N 88 14W
Motala, *Sweden* .... 17 F9 58 32N 15 1 E
Motaze, *Mozam.* .... 117 C5 24 48 S 32 52 E
Moţca, *Romania* .... 53 C11 47 15N 26 37 E
Motegi, *Japan* .... 73 A12 36 32N 140 11 E
Moth, *India* .... 93 G8 25 43N 78 57 E
Motherwell, *U.K.* 22 F5 55 47N   3 58W
Motihari, *India* .... 93 F11 26 30N 84 55 E
Motilla del Palancar, *Spain* 41 F3 39 34N   1 55W
Motiti I., *N.Z.* .... 130 D5 37 38 S 176 25 E
Motnik, *Slovenia* .... 45 B11 46 14N 14 54 E
Motocurunya, *Venezuela* 169 C4   4 24N 64 5W
Motovun, *Croatia* .... 45 C10 45 20N 13 50 E
Motozintla de Mendoza, *Mexico* . 163 D6 15 21N 92 14W
Motril, *Spain* 43 J7 36 31N   3 37W
Motru, *Romania* .... 52 F7 44 48N 22 59 E
Motru →, *Romania* .... 53 F8 44 32N 23 31 E
Mott, *U.S.A.* 154 B3 46 23N 102 20W
Móttola, *Italy* .... 47 B10 40 38N 17 2 E
Motu →, *N.Z.* .... 130 D6 37 51 S 177 35 E
Motu Nui, *Chile* .... 172 b 27 12 S 109 28W
Motuba, *Dem. Rep. of the Congo* . 114 B3   2 0N 18 34 E
Motueka, *N.Z.* .... 131 B8 41 7 S 173 1 E
Motueka →, *N.Z.* .... 131 B8 41 5 S 173 1 E
Motul, *Mexico* 163 C7 21 0N 89 20W
Motupena Pt., *Papua N. G.* ..... 132 D8   6 30 S 155 10 E
Mou, *N. Cal.* .... 133 U19 21 5 S 165 26 E
Mouanda, *Gabon* .... 114 C2   1 28 S 13 7 E
Mouchalagane →, *Canada* 141 B6 50 56N 68 41W
Moûdhros, *Greece* .... 49 B7 39 50N 25 18 E
Mouding, *China* .... 76 E3 25 20N 101 28 E
Moudjeria, *Mauritania* 112 B2 17 50N 12 28W
Moudon, *Switz.* .... 32 C3 46 40N   6 49 E
Mougoundou, *Congo* .... 114 C2   2 40 S 12 41 E
Mouila, *Gabon* .... 114 C2   1 50 S 11 0 E
Mouka, *C.A.R.* .... 114 A4   7 16N 21 52 E
Moukalaba, Réserve de la △, *Gabon* 114 C2   2 50 S 10 35 E
Moukambo, *Gabon* .... 114 C2   3 5 S 11 38 E
Moul, *Niger* .... 109 F2 15 5N 13 11 E
Moulamein, *Australia* .... 128 C6 35 3 S 144 1 E
Moule, *Guadeloupe* .... 164 b 16 20N 61 21W
Moule à Chique, C., *St. Lucia* .. 165 f 13 43N 60 57W
Mouliana, *Greece* .... 39 E6 35 10N 25 59 E
Moulins, *France* .... 27 F10 46 35N   3 19 E
Moulmein, *Burma* .... 90 G6 16 30N 97 40 E
Moulmeingyun, *Burma* .... 90 G5 16 23N 95 16 E
Moulouya, O. →, *Morocco* 111 A4 35 5N   2 25W
Moulton, *U.S.A.* 156 D4 40 41N 92 41W
Moultrie, *U.S.A.* 152 D6 31 11N 83 47W
Moultrie, L., *U.S.A.* 152 B9 33 20N 80 5W
Mouly, *N. Cal.* .... 133 K4 20 47 S 166 26 E
Mounana, *Gabon* .... 114 C2   1 18 S 13 1 E
Mound City, *Mo., U.S.A.* 154 E7 40 7N 95 14W
Mound City, *S. Dak., U.S.A.* ... 154 C4 45 44N 100 4W
Moúnda, Ákra, *Greece* .... 39 C2 38 3N 20 47 E
Moundou, *Chad* .... 109 G3   8 40N 16 10 E
Moundsville, *U.S.A.* 150 G4 39 55N 80 44W
Mounembé, *Congo* .... 114 C2   3 20 S 12 32 E
Moung, *Cambodia* .... 86 F4 12 46N 103 27 E
Moungoudi, *Congo* .... 114 C2   2 45 S 11 46 E
Mount Airy, *U.S.A.* 149 G5 36 31N 80 37W
Mount Albert, *Canada* 150 B5 44 8N 79 19W
Mount Apo Nat. Park △, *Phil.* .. 81 H5   7 0N 125 10 E
Mount Aspiring Nat. Park △, *N.Z.* 131 E3 44 19 S 168 47 E
Mount Ayr, *U.S.A.* 156 D2 40 43N 94 14W
Mount Barker, *S. Austral., Australia* 128 C3 35 5 S 138 52 E
Mount Barker, *W. Austral., Australia* 125 F2 34 38 S 117 40 E
Mount Beauty, *Australia* .... 129 D7 36 47 S 147 10 E
Mount Brydges, *Canada* 150 D3 42 54N 81 29W
Mount Buffalo Nat. Park △,
  Australia .... 129 D7 36 43 S 146 46 E
Mount Burr, *Australia* .... 127 F3 37 34 S 140 26 E
Mount Carmel, *Ill., U.S.A.* 157 F9 38 25N 87 46W
Mount Carmel, *Pa., U.S.A.* 151 F8 40 47N 76 24W
Mount Carmel Nat. Park = Ha
  Karmel Nat. Park △, *Israel* .. 103 C4 32 45N 35 5 E
Mount Carroll, *U.S.A.* 156 B7 42 6N 89 59W
Mount Charleston, *U.S.A.* 161 J11 36 16N 115 37W
Mount Clemens, *U.S.A.* 150 D2 42 35N 82 53W
Mount Cook, *N.Z.* .... 131 D5 43 44 S 170 5 E
Mount Cook Nat. Park △, *N.Z.* . 131 D5 43 35 S 170 15 E
Mount Coolon, *Australia* .... 126 C4 21 25 S 147 25 E
Mount Darwin, *Zimbabwe* ...... 119 F3 16 47 S 31 38 E
Mount Desert I., *U.S.A.* 149 C11 44 21N 68 20W
Mount Dora, *U.S.A.* 153 G8 28 48N 81 38W
Mount Eccles Nat. Park △, *Australia* 128 E4 38 5 S 141 54 E
Mount Eden, *U.S.A.* 157 F11 38 5N 85 9W
Mount Edgecumbe, *U.S.A.* 144 H14 57 3N 135 21W
Mount Edziza Prov. Park △, *Canada* 142 B2 57 30N 130 45W
Mount Elgon Nat. Park △, *E. Afr.* 118 B3   1 4N 34 42 E
Mount Field Nat. Park △, *Australia* 127 D4 42 41 S 146 35 E
Mount Fletcher, *S. Africa* ...... 117 E4 30 40 S 28 30 E
Mount Forest, *Canada* 140 D3 43 59N 80 43W
Mount Gambier, *Australia* ...... 128 E4 37 50 S 140 46 E
Mount Garnet, *Australia* .... 126 B4 17 37 S 145 6 E
Mount Hagen, *Papua N. G.* .... 132 C3   5 52 S 144 16 E
Mount Holly, *U.S.A.* 151 G10 39 59N 74 47W
Mount Holly Springs, *U.S.A.* ... 150 F7 40 7N 77 12W
Mount Hope, *N.S.W., Australia* . 129 B6 32 51 S 145 51 E
Mount Hope, *S. Austral., Australia* 127 E2 34 7 S 135 23 E
Mount Horeb, *U.S.A.* 156 B7 43 1N 89 44W
Mount Isa, *Australia* .... 126 C2 20 42 S 139 26 E
Mount Isarog Nat. Park △, *Phil.* . 80 E4 13 38N 123 24 E
Mount Jewett, *U.S.A.* 150 E6 41 44N 78 39W
Mount Kaputar Nat. Park △,
  Australia .... 127 B5 30 16 S 150 10 E
Mount Kenya Nat. Park △, *Kenya* 118 C4   0 7 S 37 21 E
Mount Kilimanjaro Nat. Park △,
  Tanzania .... 118 C4   3 2 S 37 19 E

Mount Kisco, *U.S.A.* 151 E11 41 12N 73 44W
Mount Laguna, *U.S.A.* 161 N10 32 52N 116 25W
Mount Larcom, *Australia* .... 126 C5 23 48 S 150 59 E
Mount Lofty Ra., *Australia* ..... 128 C3 34 35 S 139 5 E
Mount McKinley Nat. Park = Denali
  Nat. Park and Preserve △, *U.S.A.* 144 E10 63 30N 152 0W
Mount Magnet, *Australia* .... 125 E2 28 2 S 117 47 E
Mount Malindang Nat. Park △, *Phil.* 81 G4   8 17N 123 32 E
Mount Manara, *Australia* .... 128 B5 32 29 S 143 58 E
Mount Maunganui, *N.Z.* .... 130 D5 37 40 S 176 14 E
Mount Molloy, *Australia* .... 126 B4 16 42 S 145 20 E
Mount Morgan, *Australia* .... 126 C5 23 40 S 150 25 E
Mount Morris, *Mich., U.S.A.* ... 157 A13 43 7N 83 42W
Mount Morris, *N.Y., U.S.A.* ... 150 D7 42 44N 77 52W
Mount Olive, *U.S.A.* 156 E7 39 4N 89 44W
Mount Olivet, *U.S.A.* 157 F12 38 32N 84 2W
Mount Orab, *U.S.A.* 157 E13 39 2N 83 55W
Mount Pearl, *Canada* 141 C9 47 31N 52 47W
Mount Penn, *U.S.A.* 151 F9 40 20N 75 54W
Mount Perry, *Australia* .... 127 D5 25 13 S 151 42 E
Mount Pleasant, *Iowa, U.S.A.* .. 156 D5 40 58N 91 33W
Mount Pleasant, *Mich., U.S.A.* . 148 D3 43 36N 84 46W
Mount Pleasant, *Pa., U.S.A.* ... 150 F5 40 9N 79 33W
Mount Pleasant, *S.C., U.S.A.* .. 152 C10 32 47N 79 52W
Mount Pleasant, *Tenn., U.S.A.* . 149 H2 35 32N 87 12W
Mount Pleasant, *Tex., U.S.A.* .. 155 J7 33 9N 94 58W
Mount Pleasant, *Utah, U.S.A.* .. 158 G8 39 33N 111 27W
Mount Pocono, *U.S.A.* 151 E9 41 7N 75 22W
Mount Pulaski, *U.S.A.* 156 D7 40 1N 89 17W
Mount Pulog Nat. Park △, *Phil.* . 80 C3 16 35N 120 57 E
Mount Rainier Nat. Park △, *U.S.A.* 160 D5 46 55N 121 50W
Mount Remarkable Nat. Park △,
  Australia .... 128 B3 32 47 S 138 3 E
Mount Revelstoke Nat. Park △,
  Canada 142 C5 51 5N 118 30W
Mount Robson Prov. Park ◇,
  Canada 142 C5 53 0N 119 0W
Mount Roskill, *N.Z.* .... 130 C3 36 55 S 174 45 E
Mount Selinda, *Zimbabwe* ...... 117 C5 20 24 S 32 43 E
Mount Shasta, *U.S.A.* 158 F2 41 19N 122 19W
Mount Signal, *U.S.A.* 161 N11 32 39N 115 37W
Mount Somers, *N.Z.* .... 131 D6 43 45 S 171 27 E
Mount St. Helens Nat. Volcanic
  Monument △, *U.S.A.* 160 D4 46 14N 122 11W
Mount Sterling, *Ill., U.S.A.* 156 E6 39 59N 90 45W
Mount Sterling, *Ky., U.S.A.* 157 F13 38 4N 83 56W
Mount Sterling, *Ohio, U.S.A.* .. 157 E13 39 43N 83 16W
Mount Surprise, *Australia* ...... 126 B3 18 10 S 144 17 E
Mount Union, *U.S.A.* 150 F7 40 23N 77 53W
Mount Upton, *U.S.A.* 151 D9 42 26N 75 23W
Mount Vernon, *Ga., U.S.A.* 152 C7 32 11N 82 36W
Mount Vernon, *Ill., U.S.A.* 148 F1 38 19N 88 55W
Mount Vernon, *Ind., U.S.A.* ... 154 F10 38 17N 87 52W
Mount Vernon, *Ind., U.S.A.* ... 157 G9 37 56N 87 54W
Mount Vernon, *Iowa, U.S.A.* .. 156 C5 41 55N 91 23W
Mount Vernon, *N.Y., U.S.A.* .. 151 F11 40 55N 73 50W
Mount Vernon, *Ohio, U.S.A.* .. 150 F2 40 23N 82 29W
Mount Vernon, *Wash., U.S.A.* . 160 B4 48 25N 122 20W
Mount Victor, *Australia* .... 128 B3 32 11 S 139 44 E
Mount Washington, *U.S.A.* 157 F11 38 3N 85 33W
Mount Wellington, *N.Z.* .... 130 C3 36 55 S 174 52 E
Mount William Nat. Park △,
  Australia .... 127 D4 40 56 S 148 14 E
Mount Zion, *U.S.A.* 157 E8 39 46N 88 53W
Mountain □, *Phil.* .... 80 C3 17 20N 121 10 E
Mountain Ash, *U.K.* 21 F4 51 40N   3 23W
Mountain Center, *U.S.A.* 161 M10 33 42N 116 44W
Mountain City, *Nev., U.S.A.* ... 158 F6 41 50N 115 58W
Mountain City, *Tenn., U.S.A.* .. 149 G5 36 29N 81 48W
Mountain Dale, *U.S.A.* 151 E10 41 41N 74 32W
Mountain Grove, *U.S.A.* 155 G8 37 8N 92 16W
Mountain Home, *Ark., U.S.A.* .. 155 G8 36 20N 92 23W
Mountain Home, *Idaho, U.S.A.* . 158 E6 43 8N 115 41W
Mountain Iron, *U.S.A.* 154 B8 47 32N 92 37W
Mountain Pass, *U.S.A.* 161 K11 35 29N 115 35W
Mountain View, *Ark., U.S.A.* .. 155 H8 35 52N 92 7W
Mountain View, *Calif., U.S.A.* . 160 H4 37 23N 122 5W
Mountain View, *Hawaii, U.S.A.* . 145 D6 19 33N 155 7W
Mountain Village, *U.S.A.* 144 E7 62 5N 163 43W
Mountain Zebra Nat. Park △,
  S. Africa .... 116 E4 32 14 S 25 27 E
Mountainair, *U.S.A.* 159 J10 34 31N 106 15W
Mountlake Terrace, *U.S.A.* 160 C4 47 47N 122 19W
Mountmellick, *Ireland* 23 C4 53 7N   7 20W
Mountrath, *Ireland* 23 D4 53 0N   7 28W
Moura, *Australia* .... 126 C4 24 35 S 149 58 E
Moura, *Brazil* .... 169 D5   1 32 S 61 38W
Moura, *Portugal* 43 G3 38 7N   7 30W
Mourão, *Portugal* 43 G3 38 22N   7 22W
Mourdi, Dépression du, *Chad* .. 109 E4 18 10N 23 0 E
Mourdiah, *Mali* 112 C3 14 35N   7 25W
Mourenx, *France* 28 E3 43 22N   0 38W
Mouri, *Ghana* 113 D4   5 6N   1 14W
Mourilyan, *Australia* .... 126 B4 17 35 S 146 3 E
Mourmelon-le-Grand, *France* ... 27 C11 49 8N   4 22 E
Mourne →, *U.K.* 23 B4 54 52N   7 26W
Mourne Mts., *U.K.* 23 B5 54 10N   6 0W
Mourniai, *Greece* .... 39 E5 35 29N 24 1 E
Mournies = Mourniai, *Greece* .. 39 E5 35 29N 24 1 E
Mouscron, *Belgium* .... 31 D2 50 45N   3 12 E
Mousgougou, *Chad* .... 109 F3 10 47N 16 9 E
Moussoro, *Chad* .... 109 F3 13 41N 16 35 E
Mouthe, *France* .... 27 F13 46 44N   6 12 E
Moutier, *Switz.* .... 32 B4 47 16N   7 21 E
Moûtiers, *France* .... 29 C10 45 29N   6 32 E
Moutohara, *N.Z.* .... 130 E6 38 27 S 177 32 E
Moutong, *Indonesia* .... 82 A2   0 28N 121 13 E
Mouy, *France* .... 27 C9 49 18N   2 20 E
Mouyondzi, *Congo* .... 114 C2   4 1 S 13 9 E
Mouzáki, *Greece* .... 48 B3 39 25N 21 37 E
Mouzon, *France* .... 27 C12 49 36N   5 5 E
Movas, *Mexico* 162 B3 28 10N 109 25W
Moville, *Ireland* 23 A4 55 11N   7 3W
Mowandjum, *Australia* .... 124 C3 17 22 S 123 40 E
Moweaqua, *U.S.A.* 156 E7 39 38N 89 1W
Moxico □, *Angola* .... 115 E4 12 0 S 20 30 E
Moxotó →, *Brazil* .... 170 C4   9 19 S 38 14W
Moy →, *Ireland* 23 B2 54 8N   9 8W
Moya, *Comoros Is.* .... 121 a 12 18 S 44 18 E
Moyale, *Kenya* .... 107 G4   3 30N 39 0 E
Moyamba, *S. Leone* 112 D2   8 4N 12 30W
Moyen Atlas, *Morocco* 110 B4 33 0N   5 0W
Moyne, L. le, *Canada* 141 A6 56 45N 68 47W
Moyo, *Indonesia* .... 85 D5   8 10 S 117 40 E
Moyobamba, *Peru* .... 172 B2   6 0 S 77 0W
Moyto, *Chad* .... 109 F3 12 35N 16 33 E
Moyyero →, *Russia* .... 67 C11 68 44N 103 42 E
Moyynqum, *Kazakhstan* .... 65 A6 44 17N 72 57 E
Moyynty, *Kazakhstan* .... 66 E8 47 10N 73 18 E
Mozambique = Moçambique,
  Mozam. .... 119 F5 15 3 S 40 42 E
Mozambique ■, *Africa* .... 115 F4 19 0 S 35 0 E
Mozambique Chan., *Africa* ..... 117 B7 17 30 S 42 30 E
Mozdok, *Russia* .... 61 J7 43 45N 44 48 E
Mozdūrān, *Iran* .... 97 B9 36 9N 60 35 E
Mozhaysk, *Russia* .... 58 E9 55 30N 36 2 E
Mozhga, *Russia* .... 60 B11 56 26N 52 15 E
Mozirje, *Slovenia* .... 45 B11 46 22N 14 58 E
Mozyr = Mazyr, *Belarus* .... 59 F5 51 59N 29 15 E
Mpanda, *Tanzania* .... 118 D3   6 23 S 31 1 E
Mpé, *Congo* .... 114 C2   2 58 S 14 38 E
Mpesa, *Dem. Rep. of the Congo* . 115 D3   5 16 S 15 30 E
Mpésoba, *Mali* 112 C3 12 31N   5 39W

Mphoengs, *Zimbabwe* .... 117 C4 21 10 S 27 51 E
Mpika, *Zambia* .... 119 E3 11 51 S 31 25 E
Mpoko →, *C.A.R.* .... 114 B3   4 19N 18 33 E
Mpouya, *Congo* .... 114 C3   2 38 S 16 13 E
Mpulungu, *Zambia* .... 119 D3   8 51 S 31 5 E
Mpumalanga, *S. Africa* .... 117 D5 29 50 S 30 33 E
Mpumalanga □, *S. Africa* ...... 117 B5 26 0 S 30 0 E
Mpwapwa, *Tanzania* .... 118 D4   6 23 S 36 30 E
Mqabba, *Malta* .... 38 F7 35 51N 14 28 E
Mqanduli, *S. Africa* .... 117 E4 31 49 S 28 45 E
Mqinvartsveri = Kazbek, *Russia* 61 J7 42 42N 44 30 E
Mrągowo, *Poland* .... 54 E8 53 52N 21 18 E
Mramor, *Serbia, Yug.* .... 50 C5 43 20N 21 45 E
Mrimina, *Morocco* 110 C3 29 50N   7 9W
Mrkonjić Grad, *Bos.-H.* .... 52 F2 44 26N 17 4 E
Mrkopalj, *Croatia* .... 45 C11 45 21N 14 52 E
Mrocza, *Poland* .... 55 E4 53 16N 17 35 E
Msaken, *Tunisia* .... 108 A2 35 49N 10 33 E
Msambansovu, *Zimbabwe* ...... 119 F3 15 50 S 30 3 E
Msida, *Malta* .... 38 F7 35 54N 14 29 E
M'sila, *Algeria* .... 111 A5 35 46N   4 30 E
Msoro, *Zambia* .... 119 E3 13 35 S 31 50 E
Msta →, *Russia* .... 58 C6 58 25N 31 20 E
Mstislavl = Mstsislaw, *Belarus* . 58 E6 54 0N 31 50 E
Mstsislaw, *Belarus* .... 58 E6 54 0N 31 50 E
Mszana Dolna, *Poland* .... 55 J7 49 41N 20 5 E
Mszczonów, *Poland* .... 55 G7 51 58N 20 33 E
Mtama, *Tanzania* .... 119 E4 10 17 S 39 21 E
Mtamvuna →, *S. Africa* .... 117 E5 31 6 S 30 12 E
Mtilikwe →, *Zimbabwe* .... 119 G3 21 9 S 31 30 E
Mtsensk, *Russia* .... 58 E10 53 17N 36 36 E
Mtskheta, *Georgia* .... 61 K7 41 52N 44 45 E
Mtubatuba, *S. Africa* .... 117 D5 28 30 S 32 8 E
Mtwalume, *S. Africa* .... 117 E5 30 30 S 30 38 E
Mtwara-Mikindani, *Tanzania* ... 119 E5 10 20 S 40 20 E
Mu →, *Burma* .... 90 E5 21 56N 95 38 E
Mu Gia, Deo, *Vietnam* .... 86 D5 17 40N 105 47 E
Mu Ko Chang Nat. Park △, *Thailand* 87 G4 11 59N 102 22 E
Mu Us Shamo, *China* .... 74 E5 39 0N 109 0 E
Muacandala, *Angola* .... 115 E3 10 2 S 19 40 E
Muaná, *Brazil* .... 170 B2   1 25 S 49 15W
Muanda, *Dem. Rep. of the Congo* 115 D2   6 0 S 12 20 E
Muang Chiang Rai = Chiang Rai,
  Thailand .... 76 H2 19 52N 99 50 E
Muang Khong, *Laos* .... 86 E5 14 7N 105 51 E
Muang Lamphun, *Thailand* ..... 86 C2 18 40N 99 2 E
Muang Mai, *Thailand* .... 87 a   8 5N 98 21 E
Muang Pak Beng, *Laos* .... 76 H3 19 54N 101 8 E
Muangai, *Angola* .... 115 E3 12 32 S 19 55 E
Muar, *Malaysia* .... 87 L4   2 3N 102 34 E
Muarabungo, *Indonesia* .... 84 C2   1 28 S 102 52 E
Muaraenim, *Indonesia* .... 84 C2   3 40 S 103 50 E
Muarajuloi, *Indonesia* .... 85 C4   0 12 S 114 3 E
Muarakaman, *Indonesia* .... 84 C2   0 2 S 116 45 E
Muaratebo, *Indonesia* .... 84 C2   1 30 S 102 26 E
Muaratembesi, *Indonesia* .... 84 C2   1 42 S 103 8 E
Muaratewe, *Indonesia* .... 85 C4   0 58 S 114 52 E
Mubarakpur, *India* .... 93 F10 26 6N 83 18 E
Mubarek, *Uzbekistan* .... 65 D2 39 15N 65 9 E
Mubarraz = Al Mubarraz, *Si. Arabia* 97 E6 25 30N 49 40 E
Mubende, *Uganda* .... 118 B3   0 33N 31 22 E
Mubi, *Nigeria* .... 113 C7 10 18N 13 16 E
Mucajá, *Brazil* .... 169 D6   3 57 S 57 32W
Mucajaí →, *Brazil* 169 C5   2 25N 60 52W
Mucajaí, Serra do, *Brazil* 169 C5   2 23N 61 10W
Mucari, *Angola* .... 115 D3   9 30 S 16 54 E
Muchachos, Roque de los, *Canary Is.* 9 e1 28 44N 17 52W
Mücheln, *Germany* .... 30 D7 51 17N 11 47 E
Muching Mts., *Zambia* .... 119 E3 11 30 S 31 30 E
Muchkapskiy, *Russia* .... 60 E6 51 52N 42 28 E
Muchuan, *China* .... 76 C5 28 57N 103 55 E
Muck, *U.K.* 22 E2 56 50N   6 15W
Muckadilla, *Australia* .... 127 D4 26 35 S 148 23 E
Muckalee Cr. →, *U.S.A.* 152 D5 31 38N 84 9W
Muckle Flugga, *U.K.* .... 22 a 60 51N   0 54W
Muco →, *Colombia* 168 C4   4 15N 70 21W
Mucoma, *Angola* .... 115 E2 15 18 S 13 39 E
Muconda, *Angola* .... 115 E4 10 31 S 21 15 E
Mucope, *Angola* .... 115 F2 16 24 S 14 52 E
Mucugê, *Brazil* .... 171 D3 13 0 S 41 23W
Mucuim →, *Brazil* .... 173 B5   6 33 S 64 18W
Mucur, *Turkey* .... 100 C6 39 3N 34 22 E
Mucura, *Brazil* .... 169 D5   2 31 S 62 43W
Mucuri, *Brazil* .... 171 E4 18 0 S 39 36W
Mucurici, *Brazil* .... 171 E3 18 5 S 40 31W
Mucusso, *Angola* .... 116 B3 18 1 S 21 25 E
Mucusso, Coutada Pública do ◇,
  Angola .... 115 F4 17 27 S 21 0 E
Muda, *Canary Is.* 9 e2 28 34N 13 57W
Mudanjiang, *China* .... 75 B15 44 38N 129 30 E
Mudanya, *Turkey* .... 51 F12 40 25N 28 50 E
Muddebihal, *India* .... 95 F3 16 20N 76 8 E
Muddy Cr. →, *U.S.A.* 159 H8 38 24N 110 42W
Mudgee, *Australia* .... 129 B8 32 32 S 149 31 E
Mudhol, *Andhra Pradesh, India* . 94 E3 18 58N 77 55 E
Mudhol, *Karnataka, India* ..... 95 F2 16 21N 75 17 E
Mudiata, *Dem. Rep. of the Congo* 115 D4   7 15 S 22 1 E
Mudigere, *India* .... 95 H2 13 8N 75 38 E
Mudjatik →, *Canada* 143 B7 56 1N 107 36W
Mudon, *Burma* .... 90 G6 16 15N 97 44 E
Mudugh, *Somali Rep.* .... 120 C3   7 0N 47 30 E
Mudukulattur, *India* .... 95 K4   9 21N 78 31 E
Mudurnu, *Turkey* .... 100 B4 40 27N 31 12 E
Muecate, *Mozam.* .... 119 E4 14 55 S 39 40 E
Mueda, *Mozam.* .... 119 E4 11 36 S 39 28 E
Mueller Ra., *Australia* .... 124 C4 18 18 S 126 46 E
Muende, *Mozam.* .... 119 E3 14 28 S 33 0 E
Muerto, Mar, *Mexico* 163 D6 16 10N 94 10W
Mufu Shan, *China* .... 77 C10 29 20N 114 30 E
Mufulira, *Zambia* .... 119 E2 12 32 S 28 15 E
Mufumbiro Range, *Africa* ...... 118 C2   1 25 S 29 30 E
Mugardos, *Spain* 42 B2 43 27N   8 15W
Muge →, *Portugal* 43 F2 39 8N   8 44W
Múggia, *Italy* .... 45 C10 45 36N 13 46 E
Mughal Sarai, *India* .... 93 G10 25 18N 83 7 E
Mughayrā', *Si. Arabia* .... 96 D3 29 17N 37 41 E
Mugi, *Japan* .... 72 B6 33 40N 134 25 E
Mugia = Muxía, *Spain* 42 B1 43 3N   9 10W
Mugila, Mts., *Dem. Rep. of
  the Congo* .... 118 D2   7 0 S 28 50 E
Muginga, *Angola* .... 115 D3   8 21 S 17 36 E
Muğla, *Turkey* .... 49 D10 37 15N 28 22 E
Muğla □, *Turkey* .... 49 D10 37 15N 28 0 E
Muglad, *Sudan* .... 107 E2 11 1N 27 50 E
Müglitz →, *Germany* .... 30 D9 42 37N 25 32 E
Mugodzhary, *Kazakhstan* ...... 64 G7 49 0N 58 40 E
Mugu, *Nepal* .... 93 E10 29 45N 82 30 E
Muhammad, Râs, *Egypt* .... 96 E2 27 44N 34 16 E
Muhammad Qol, *Sudan* .... 106 C4 20 53N 37 9 E
Muhammadabad, *India* .... 93 F10 26 4N 83 25 E
Muḩayriqah, *Si. Arabia* .... 98 B4 23 59N 45 4 E
Muhesi →, *Tanzania* .... 118 D4   7 0 S 35 20 E
Mühlacker, *Germany* .... 31 G4 48 57N   8 51 E
Mühldorf, *Germany* .... 31 G8 48 14N 12 32 E
Mühlhausen, *Germany* .... 30 D6 51 12N 10 27 E
Mühlig Hofmann fjell, *Antarctica* 7 D3 72 0 S   5 0 E
Mühlviertel, *Austria* .... 34 G5 48 30N 14 0 E
Muhos, *Estonia* .... 14 D22 64 47N 25 59 E
Muhu, *Estonia* .... 15 G20 58 36N 23 11 E
Muhutwe, *Tanzania* .... 118 C3   1 35 S 31 45 E
Mui Wo, *China* .... 69 G10 22 16N 113 59 E
Muie, *Angola* .... 115 E4 14 23 S 20 25 E

Muine Bheag, *Ireland* 23 D5 52 42N   6 58W
Muir, L., *Australia* .... 125 F2 34 30 S 116 40 E
Muir of Ord, *U.K.* 22 D4 57 32N   4 28W
Muisné, *Ecuador* 168 C1   0 36N 80 2W
Mujnak = Muynak, *Uzbekistan* . 66 E6 43 44N 59 10 E
Mujui dos Campos, *Brazil* ..... 169 D7   2 35 S 54 41W
Muka, Tanjung, *Malaysia* ...... 87 c   5 28N 100 11 E
Mukacheve, *Ukraine* .... 59 H2 48 27N 22 45 E
Mukachevo = Mukacheve, *Ukraine* 59 H2 48 27N 22 45 E
Mukah, *Malaysia* .... 85 B4   2 55N 112 5 E
Mukandwara, *India* .... 92 G6 24 49N 75 59 E
Mukawa, *Papua N. G.* .... 132 E5   9 38 S 149 59 E
Mukawwa, Geziret, *Egypt* ..... 106 C4 23 55N 35 53 E
Mukawwar, *Sudan* .... 106 C4 20 30N 37 17 E
Mukdahan, *Thailand* .... 86 D5 16 32 S 104 43 E
Mukden = Shenyang, *China* .... 75 D12 41 48N 123 27 E
Mukerian, *India* .... 92 D6 31 57N 75 37 E
Mukher, *India* .... 94 E3 18 42N 77 22 E
Mukhtolovo, *Russia* .... 60 C6 55 29N 43 15 E
Mukhtuya = Lensk, *Russia* ..... 67 C12 60 48N 114 55 E
Mukinbudin, *Australia* .... 125 F2 30 55 S 118 5 E
Mukishi, *Kasai-Occ., Dem. Rep. of
  the Congo* .... 115 D4   5 39 S 21 3 E
Mukishi, *Katanga, Dem. Rep. of
  the Congo* .... 119 D1   8 30 S 24 44 E
Mukomuko, *Indonesia* .... 84 C2   2 30 S 101 10 E
Mukomwenze, *Dem. Rep. of
  the Congo* .... 118 D2   6 49 S 27 15 E
Mukry, *Turkmenistan* .... 65 E2 37 54N 65 12 E
Muktsar, *India* .... 92 D6 30 30N 74 30 E
Muktawa →, *Canada* 143 C9 53 10N 97 24W
Mukwela, *Zambia* .... 119 F2 17 0 S 26 40 E
Mukwonago, *U.S.A.* 157 B8 42 52N 88 20W
Mul, *India* .... 94 D4 20 4N 79 40 E
Mula, *Spain* 41 G3 38 3N   1 33W
Mula →, *India* .... 94 E2 18 34N 74 21 E
Mula →, *Pakistan* .... 92 F2 27 57N 67 36 E
Mulamba, *Dem. Rep. of the Congo* 115 D4   6 21 S 21 13 E
Mulanay, *Phil.* .... 80 E4 13 31N 122 24 E
Mulange, *Dem. Rep. of the Congo* 118 C2   3 40 S 27 10 E
Mulanje, *Malawi* .... 119 F4 16 2 S 35 33 E
Mulanje, Mt., *Malawi* .... 119 F4 16 0 S 35 30 E
Mulatupo, *Panama* 168 B2   8 57N 77 45W
Mulbagal, *India* .... 95 H4 13 10N 78 24 E
Mulberry, *U.S.A.* 153 H8 27 54N 81 59W
Mulberry Grove, *U.S.A.* 156 F7 38 56N 89 16W
Mulchatna →, *U.S.A.* 144 G8 59 40N 157 7W
Mulchén, *Chile* .... 174 D1 37 45 S 72 20W
Mulde →, *Germany* .... 30 D8 51 53N 12 15 E
Muldraugh, *U.S.A.* 157 G11 37 56N 85 59W
Mule Creek Junction, *U.S.A.* .. 154 D2 43 19N 104 8W
Muleba, *Tanzania* .... 118 C3   1 50 S 31 37 E
Mulegns, *Switz.* .... 33 C9 46 32N   9 38 E
Mulejé, *Mexico* 162 B2 26 53N 112 1W
Muleshoe, *U.S.A.* 155 H3 34 13N 102 43W
Muletta, Gara, *Ethiopia* .... 107 F5   9 15N 41 44 E
Mulgrave, *Canada* 141 C7 45 38N 61 31W
Mulgrave I. = Badu I., *Papua N. G.* 132 F2 10 5 S 142 10 E
Mulhacén, *Spain* 43 H7 37 4N   3 20W
Mülheim, *Germany* .... 30 D2 51 25N   6 54 E
Mulhouse, *France* .... 27 E14 47 40N   7 20 E
Muli, *China* .... 76 D3 27 52N 101 8 E
Muli →, *Indonesia* .... 83 C5   7 16 S 138 45 E
Mulifanua, *Samoa* .... 133 W24 13 50 S 171 59W
Muling, *China* .... 75 B16 44 35N 130 10 E
Mulki, *India* .... 95 H2 13 6N 74 48 E
Mull, *U.K.* 22 E3 56 25N   5 56W
Mull, Sound of, *U.K.* 22 E3 56 30N   5 50W
Mullaittivu, *Sri Lanka* .... 95 K5 9 15N 80 49 E
Mullen, *U.S.A.* 154 D4 42 3N 101 1W
Mullens, *U.S.A.* 148 G5 37 35N 81 23W
Muller, Pegunungan, *Indonesia* . 85 B4   0 30N 113 30 E
Muller Ra., *Papua N. G.* ...... 132 C2   5 3 S 142 20 E
Mullet Pen., *Ireland* 23 B1 54 13N 10 2W
Mullewa, *Australia* .... 125 E2 28 29 S 115 30 E
Müllheim, *Germany* .... 31 H3 47 47N   7 36 E
Mulligan →, *Australia* .... 126 D2 25 0 S 139 0 E
Mullingar, *Ireland* 23 C4 53 31N   7 21W
Mullins, *U.S.A.* 149 H6 34 12N 79 15W
Mullsjö, *Sweden* .... 17 G7 57 56N 13 55 E
Mullumbimby, *Australia* .... 127 D5 28 30 S 153 30 E
Mulobezi, *Zambia* .... 119 F2 16 45 S 25 7 E
Mulondo, *Angola* .... 115 F3 15 41 S 15 12 E
Mulonga Plain, *Zambia* .... 115 F4 16 20 S 23 40 E
Mulroy B., *Ireland* 23 A4 55 15N   7 46W
Mulshi L., *India* .... 94 E1 18 30N 73 48 E
Multai, *India* .... 94 D4 21 50N 78 21 E
Multan, *Pakistan* .... 91 C3 30 15N 71 36 E
Mulu, Gunong, *Malaysia* ...... 85 B4   4 3N 114 56 E
Mulumbe, Mts., *Dem. Rep. of
  the Congo* .... 119 D2   8 40 S 27 30 E
Mulundu, *Dem. Rep. of the Congo* 115 D4   4 60 S 20 33 E
Mulungushi Dam, *Zambia* ..... 119 E2 14 48 S 28 48 E
Mulurulu L., *Australia* .... 128 B5 33 15 S 143 20 E
Mulvane, *U.S.A.* 155 G6 37 29N 97 15W
Mulwad, *Sudan* .... 106 D3 18 45N 30 39 E
Mulwala, *Australia* .... 129 C7 35 59 S 146 0 E
Muma, *Dem. Rep. of the Congo* . 114 B4   3 52N 23 21 E
Mumbai, *India* .... 94 E1 18 55N 72 50 E
Mumbeji, *Zambia* .... 115 E4 13 51 S 23 39 E
Mumbwa, *Zambia* .... 119 E2 15 0 S 27 0 E
Mumeng, *Papua N. G.* .... 132 D4   7 3 S 146 37 E
Mumra, *Russia* .... 61 H8 45 45N 47 41 E
Mun →, *Thailand* .... 86 E5 15 19N 105 30 E
Muna, *Indonesia* .... 82 B2   5 0 S 122 30 E
Munabao, *India* .... 92 G4 25 45N 70 17 E
Munakata, *Japan* .... 72 D2 33 48N 130 38 E
Munamagi, *Estonia* .... 15 H22 57 43N 27 4 E
Muncan, *Indonesia* .... 79 K18 8 34 S 115 11 E
Muncar, *Indonesia* .... 79 J17 8 26 S 114 20 E
Münchberg, *Germany* .... 31 E7 50 11N 11 47 E
Müncheberg, *Germany* .... 30 C10 52 30N 14 9 E
München, *Germany* .... 31 G7 48 8N 11 34 E
Munchen-Gladbach =
  Mönchengladbach, *Germany* . 30 D2 51 11N   6 27 E
Münchenbuchsee, *Switz.* ...... 32 B4 47 1N   7 27 E
Muncho Lake, *Canada* 142 B3 59 0N 125 50W
Munch'ŏn, *N. Korea* .... 75 E14 39 14N 127 19 E
Münchwilen, *Switz.* .... 33 B8 47 28N   8 59 E
Muncie, *U.S.A.* 157 D11 40 12N 85 23W
Muncoonie L., *Australia* ...... 126 D2 25 12 S 138 40 E
Munda, *Solomon Is.* .... 133 M9   8 20 S 157 16 E
Mundabbera, *Australia* .... 127 D5 25 36 S 151 18 E
Mundakayam, *India* .... 95 K3   9 30N 76 50 E
Mundal, *Sri Lanka* .... 95 L4   7 48N 79 48 E
Munday, *U.S.A.* 155 J5 33 27N 99 38W
Mundelein, *U.S.A.* 157 B8 42 16N 88 0W
Münden, *Germany* .... 30 D5 51 25N   9 38 E
Münden, Naturpark ◇, *Germany* 30 D5 51 28N   9 42 E
Mundiwindi, *Australia* .... 124 D3 23 47 S 120 9 E
Mundo →, *Spain* 41 G2 38 30N   1 40W
Mundo Novo, *Brazil* .... 171 D3 11 50 S 40 29W
Mundra, *India* .... 92 H3 22 54N 69 48 E
Mundrabilla, *Australia* .... 125 F4 31 52 S 127 51 E
Munducurus, *Brazil* .... 169 D6 2 45 S 58 16W
Munenga, *Angola* .... 115 E2 10 3 S 14 41 E
Munera, *Spain* 41 F2 39 2N   2 29W
Munera, *India* .... 94 F5 16 45N 80 14 E
Mungallala, *Australia* .... 127 D4 26 28 S 147 34 E
Mungallala Cr. →, *Australia* ... 127 D4 28 53 S 147 5 E
Mungana, *Australia* .... 126 B3 17 8 S 144 27 E

Mungaoli, *India* .... **92 G8** 24 24N 78 7 E
Mungari, *Mozam.* .... **119 F3** 17 12 S 33 30 E
Mungbere, *Dem. Rep. of the Congo* **118 B2** 2 36N 28 28 E
Mungeli, *India* .... **93 H9** 22 4N 81 41 E
Munger, *India* .... **93 G12** 25 23N 86 30 E
Mungkan Kandju Nat. Park △,
  Australia .... **126 A3** 13 35 S 142 52 E
Mungo, *Angola* .... **115 E3** 11 49 S 16 16 E
Mungo, L., *Australia* .... **128 B5** 33 45 S 143 0 E
Mungo Nat. Park △, *Australia* .. **128 B5** 33 44 S 143 6 E
Munhango, *Angola* .... **115 E3** 12 10 S 18 38 E
Munhango ➤, *Angola* .... **115 E4** 11 17 S 19 44 E
Munich = München, *Germany* .. **31 G7** 48 8N 11 34 E
Munich International ✈ (MUC),
  Germany .... **31 G7** 48 20N 11 50 E
Munirabad, *India* .... **95 F3** 15 20N 76 20 E
Munising, *U.S.A.* **148 B2** 46 25N 86 40W
Munka-Ljungby, *Sweden* .... **17 H6** 56 16N 12 58 E
Munkebo, *Denmark* .... **17 J4** 55 27N 10 34 E
Munkedal, *Sweden* .... **17 F5** 58 28N 11 40 E
Munkfors, *Sweden* .... **16 E7** 59 47N 13 30 E
Munku-Sardyk, *Russia* .... **67 D11** 51 45N 100 20 E
Münnerstadt, *Germany* .... **31 E6** 50 14N 10 12 E
Munoz, *Phil.* .... **80 D3** 15 43N 120 54 E
Muñoz Gamero, Pen., *Chile* .... **176 D2** 52 30 S 73 5W
Munroe L., *Canada* **143 B9** 59 13N 98 35W
Munsan, *S. Korea* .... **75 F14** 37 51N 126 48 E
Munshiganj, *Bangla.* .... **90 D3** 23 33N 90 32 E
Münsingen, *Switz.* .... **32 C5** 46 52N 7 32 E
Munson, *U.S.A.* **153 E3** 30 52N 86 52W
Munster, *France* .... **27 D14** 48 2N 7 8 E
Münster, *Niedersachsen, Germany* **30 C6** 52 58N 10 5 E
Münster, *Nordrhein-Westfalen,*
  Germany .... **30 D3** 51 58N 7 37 E
Munster, *Switz.* .... **33 D6** 46 29N 8 17 E
Munster □, *Ireland* **23 D3** 52 18N 8 44W
Muntadgin, *Australia* .... **125 F2** 31 45 S 118 33 E
Muntele Mare, Vf., *Romania* ... **53 D8** 46 30N 23 12 E
Muntok, *Indonesia* .... **84 C3** 2 5 S 105 10 E
Munyama, *Zambia* .... **119 F2** 16 5 S 28 31 E
Munzur Dağları, *Turkey* .... **101 C8** 39 30N 39 10 E
Muong Beng, *Laos* .... **76 G3** 20 23N 101 46 E
Muong Boum, *Vietnam* .... **76 F4** 22 24N 102 49 E
Muong Et, *Laos* .... **86 B5** 20 49N 104 1 E
Muong Hai, *Laos* .... **76 G3** 21 3N 101 49 E
Muong Hiem, *Laos* .... **86 B4** 20 5N 103 22 E
Muong Houn, *Laos* .... **76 G3** 20 8N 101 23 E
Muong Hung, *Vietnam* .... **76 G4** 20 56N 103 53 E
Muong Kau, *Laos* .... **86 E5** 15 6N 105 47 E
Muong Khao, *Laos* .... **86 C4** 19 38N 103 32 E
Muong Khoua, *Laos* .... **76 G4** 21 5N 102 31 E
Muong Liep, *Laos* .... **86 C3** 18 29N 101 40 E
Muong May, *Laos* .... **86 E6** 14 49N 106 56 E
Muong Ngeun, *Laos* .... **76 G3** 20 36N 101 3 E
Muong Ngoi, *Laos* .... **76 G4** 20 43N 102 41 E
Muong Nhie, *Vietnam* .... **76 F4** 22 12N 102 28 E
Muong Nong, *Laos* .... **86 D6** 16 22N 106 30 E
Muong Ou Tay, *Laos* .... **76 F3** 22 7N 101 48 E
Muong Oua, *Laos* .... **86 C3** 18 18N 101 20 E
Muong Peun, *Laos* .... **76 G4** 20 13N 103 52 E
Muong Phalane, *Laos* .... **86 D5** 16 39N 105 34 E
Muong Phieng, *Laos* .... **76 G3** 19 6N 101 32 E
Muong Phine, *Laos* .... **86 D6** 16 32N 106 2 E
Muong Sai, *Laos* .... **76 G3** 20 42N 101 59 E
Muong Saiapoun, *Laos* .... **86 C3** 18 24N 101 31 E
Muong Sen, *Vietnam* .... **86 C5** 19 24N 104 8 E
Muong Sing, *Laos* .... **76 G3** 21 11N 101 9 E
Muong Son, *Laos* .... **76 G4** 20 27N 103 19 E
Muong Soui, *Laos* .... **86 C4** 19 33N 102 52 E
Muong Va, *Laos* .... **76 G4** 21 53N 102 19 E
Muong Xia, *Vietnam* .... **86 B5** 20 19N 104 50 E
Muonio, *Finland* .... **14 C20** 67 57N 23 40 E
Muonionjoki ➤, *Finland* .... **14 C20** 67 11N 23 34 E
Muotathal, *Switz.* .... **33 C7** 46 58N 8 46 E
Mupa, *Angola* .... **115 F3** 16 5 S 15 50 E
Mupa, Parque Nac. da △, *Angola* **115 F3** 15 55 S 15 35 E
Muping, *China* .... **75 F11** 37 22N 121 36 E
Mupoi, *Sudan* .... **117 F2** 5 28N 27 40 E
Muqaddam, Wadi ➤, *Sudan* ... **106 D3** 18 4N 31 30 E
Muqdisho, *Somali Rep.* .... **120 D3** 2 2N 45 25 E
Muqshin, W. ➤, *Oman* .... **99 C6** 19 44N 55 14 E
Muquequete, *Angola* .... **115 E2** 14 50 S 14 16 E
Mur ➤, *Austria* .... **35 E9** 46 18N 16 52 E
Mur-de-Bretagne, *France* **26 D4** 48 12N 3 0W
Muradiye, *Manisa, Turkey* ..... **49 C9** 38 39N 27 21 E
Muradiye, *Van, Turkey* .... **101 C10** 39 0N 43 44 E
Murakami, *Japan* .... **70 E9** 38 14N 139 29 E
Murallón, Cerro, *Chile* .... **176 C2** 49 48 S 73 30W
Muranda, *Rwanda* .... **118 C2** 1 52 S 29 20 E
Murang'a, *Kenya* .... **118 C4** 0 45 S 37 9 E
Murashi, *Russia* .... **64 B2** 59 30N 49 0 E
Murat, *France* .... **28 C6** 45 7N 2 53 E
Murat ➤, *Turkey* .... **49 C11** 38 46N 40 0 E
Murat Dağı, *Turkey* .... **49 C11** 38 55N 29 43 E
Muratlı, *Turkey* .... **51 E11** 41 10N 27 29 E
Murato, *France* .... **29 F13** 42 35N 9 20 E
Murau, *Austria* .... **34 D7** 47 6N 14 10 E
Muravera, *Italy* .... **46 C2** 39 25N 9 34 E
Murayama, *Japan* .... **70 E10** 38 30N 140 25 E
Murça, *Portugal* **42 D3** 41 24N 7 28W
Murchison ➤, *Australia* .... **131 B7** 41 49 S 172 21 E
Murchison ➤, *Australia* .... **125 E1** 27 45 S 114 0 E
Murchison, Mt., *Antarctica* .... **7 D11** 73 0 S 168 0 E
Murchison, Mt., *N.Z.* .... **131 D6** 43 0 S 171 22 E
Murchison Falls, *Uganda* ...... **118 B3** 2 15N 31 30 E
Murchison Falls Nat. Park △,
  Uganda .... **118 B3** 2 17N 31 48 E
Murchison Mts., *N.Z.* .... **131 F2** 45 13 S 167 23 E
Murchison Ra., *Australia* ...... **126 C1** 20 0 S 134 10 E
Murchison Rapids, *Malawi* .... **119 F3** 15 55 S 34 35 E
Murcia, *Spain* **41 G3** 38 5N 1 10W
Murcia □, *Spain* **41 H3** 37 50N 1 30W
Murdo, *U.S.A.* **154 D4** 43 53N 100 43W
Murdoch Pt., *Australia* .... **126 A3** 14 37 S 144 55 E
Mürefte, *Turkey* .... **51 F11** 40 40N 27 14 E
Mureș □, *Romania* .... **53 D9** 46 45N 24 40 E
Mureș ➤, *Romania* .... **52 D5** 46 15N 20 13 E
Mureșul = Mureș ➤, *Romania* . **52 D5** 46 15N 20 13 E
Muret, *France* .... **28 E5** 43 30N 1 20 E
Murewa, *Zimbabwe* .... **117 B5** 17 39 S 31 47 E
Murfreesboro, *N.C., U.S.A.* **149 G7** 36 27N 77 6W
Murfreesboro, *Tenn., U.S.A.* ... **149 H2** 35 51N 86 24W
Murg, *Switz.* .... **33 B8** 47 6N 9 13 E
Murgab = Murghob, *Tajikistan* . **65 F7** 38 10N 74 2 E
Murgab ➤, *Turkmenistan* ..... **97 B9** 38 18N 61 12 E
Murgenella, *Australia* .... **124 B5** 11 34 S 132 56 E
Murgeni, *Romania* .... **53 D13** 46 12N 28 1 E
Murgenthal, *Switz.* .... **32 B5** 47 16N 7 50 E
Murgha Kibzai, *Pakistan* ...... **92 D3** 30 44N 69 25 E
Murghob, *Tajikistan* .... **65 D7** 38 10N 74 2 E
Murgon, *Australia* .... **127 D5** 26 15 S 151 54 E
Muri, *India* .... **93 H11** 23 22N 85 52 E
Muri, *Switz.* .... **33 B6** 47 17N 8 21 E
Muria, *Indonesia* .... **84 C4** 9 30 S 124 14 E
Muriaé, *Brazil* .... **171 F3** 21 8 S 42 23W
Murias de Paredes, *Spain* **42 C4** 42 52N 6 11W
Murici, *Brazil* .... **170 C4** 9 19 S 35 56W
Muriége, *Angola* .... **115 D4** 9 55 S 21 11 E
Muriel Mine, *Zimbabwe* .... **119 F3** 17 14 S 30 40 E
Murila, *Angola* .... **115 E4** 10 44 S 20 20 E
Müritz, *Germany* .... **30 B8** 53 25N 12 42 E
Müritz, Nationalpark △, *Germany* **30 B8** 53 22N 12 55 E
Murkong Selek, *India* .... **90 B5** 27 44N 95 18 E
Murliganj, *India* .... **93 G12** 25 54N 86 59 E

Murmansk, *Russia* .... **56 A5** 68 57N 33 10 E
Murnau, *Germany* .... **31 H7** 47 40N 11 12 E
Muro, *France* .... **29 F12** 42 34N 8 54 E
Muro, *Spain* .... **38 B4** 39 44N 3 3 E
Muro, C. de, *France* .... **29 G12** 41 44N 8 37 E
Muro de Alcoy, *Spain* **41 G4** 38 46N 0 26W
Muro Lucano, *Italy* .... **47 B8** 40 45N 15 29 E
Murom, *Russia* .... **60 C6** 55 35N 42 3 E
Muroran, *Japan* .... **70 C10** 42 25N 141 0 E
Muros, *Spain* **42 C1** 42 45N 9 5W
Muros y de Noya, Ría de, *Spain* . **42 C1** 42 45N 9 0W
Muroto, *Japan* .... **72 D6** 33 18N 134 9 E
Muroto-Misaki, *Japan* .... **72 D6** 33 15N 134 10 E
Murowana Goślina, *Poland* .... **55 F3** 52 35N 17 0 E
Murphy, *U.S.A.* **158 E5** 43 13N 116 33W
Murphys, *U.S.A.* **160 G6** 38 8N 120 28W
Murphysboro, *U.S.A.* **156 G7** 37 46N 89 20W
Murrat Wells, *Sudan* .... **106 C2** 21 3N 32 5 E
Murray, *Iowa, U.S.A.* **156 C3** 41 3N 93 57W
Murray, *Ky., U.S.A.* **149 G1** 36 37N 88 19W
Murray, *Utah, U.S.A.* **158 F8** 40 40N 111 53W
Murray ➤, *Australia* .... **128 C3** 35 20 S 139 22 E
Murray, L., *Papua N. G.* .... **132 D1** 7 0 S 141 35 E
Murray, L., *U.S.A.* **152 A8** 34 3N 81 13W
Murray Bridge, *Australia* ...... **128 C3** 35 6 S 139 14 E
Murray Harbour, *Canada* **141 C7** 46 0N 62 28W
Murray River Nat. Park △, *Australia* **127 B3** 34 23 S 140 32 E
Murray-Sunset Nat. Park △,
  Australia .... **128 C4** 34 45 S 141 30 E
Murraysburg, *S. Africa* .... **116 E3** 31 58 S 23 47 E
Murrayville, *Ill., U.S.A.* **156 E6** 39 35N 90 15W
Murrayville, *Ill., U.S.A.* **156 E6** 39 35N 90 15W
Murree, *Pakistan* .... **93 C5** 33 56N 73 28 E
Murren, *Switz.* .... **32 C5** 46 34N 7 53 E
Murrieta, *U.S.A.* **161 M9** 33 33N 117 13W
Murro di Porco, Capo, *Italy* .... **47 F8** 37 0N 15 20 E
Murrumbateman, *Australia* .... **129 C8** 34 58 S 149 0 E
Murrumbidgee ➤, *Australia* ... **129 C8** 34 43 S 143 12 E
Murrumburrah, *Australia* ...... **129 C8** 34 32 S 148 22 E
Murrurundi, *Australia* .... **129 A9** 31 42 S 150 51 E
Murshid, *Sudan* .... **106 C3** 21 40N 31 10 E
Murshidabad, *India* .... **93 G13** 24 11N 88 19 E
Murska Sobota, *Slovenia* ...... **45 B13** 46 39N 16 12 E
Murtazapur, *India* .... **90 J10** 20 40N 77 25 E
Murten, *Switz.* .... **32 C4** 46 56N 7 4 E
Murtensee, *Switz.* .... **32 C4** 46 56N 7 7 E
Murtle L., *Canada* **142 C5** 52 8N 119 38W
Murtoa, *Australia* .... **128 D5** 36 35 S 142 28 E
Murtosa, *Portugal* **42 E2** 40 44N 8 40W
Muru ➤, *Brazil* .... **172 B3** 8 9 S 70 45W
Murud, *India* .... **94 E1** 18 19N 72 58 E
Murungu, *Tanzania* .... **118 C3** 4 12 S 31 10 E
Muruntau, *Uzbekistan* .... **65 C2** 41 30N 64 37 E
Murupara, *N.Z.* .... **131 C6** 38 28 S 176 42 E
Mururoa, *Pac. Oc.* .... **135 K14** 21 52 S 138 55W
Murwara, *India* .... **93 H9** 23 46N 80 28 E
Murwillumbah, *Australia* ...... **127 D5** 28 18 S 153 27 E
Mürz ➤, *Austria* .... **34 D8** 47 30N 15 25 E
Mürzzuschlag, *Austria* .... **34 D8** 47 36N 15 41 E
Mus, *India* .... **95 K11** 9 14N 92 47 E
Muş, *Turkey* .... **101 C9** 38 45N 41 30 E
Musa, *Dem. Rep. of the Congo* . **114 B3** 2 40N 17 48 E
Musa ➤, *Papua N. G.* .... **132 E5** 9 3 S 148 55 E
Mûsa, Gebel, *Egypt* .... **96 D2** 28 33N 33 59 E
Musa Khel, *Pakistan* .... **90 D3** 30 59N 69 52 E
Mūsá Qal'eh, *Afghan.* .... **91 B2** 32 20N 64 50 E
Musadi, *Dem. Rep. of the Congo* **114 C4** 2 31 S 22 50 E
Musafirkhana, *India* .... **93 F9** 26 22N 81 48 E
Musala, *Bulgaria* .... **50 D7** 42 13N 23 37 E
Musala, *Indonesia* .... **84 B1** 1 41N 98 28 E
Musan, *N. Korea* .... **75 C15** 42 12N 129 12 E
Musandam, Ra's, *Oman* .... **99 A7** 26 20N 56 20 E
Musangu, *Dem. Rep. of the Congo* **119 E1** 10 28 S 23 55 E
Musasa, *Tanzania* .... **118 C3** 3 25 S 31 30 E
Musashino, *Japan* .... **73 B11** 35 42N 139 34 E
Musay'īd, *Qatar* .... **97 E6** 25 0N 51 33 E
Musaymir, *Yemen* .... **98 D4** 13 27N 44 37 E
Muscat = Masqaṭ, *Oman* ...... **99 B7** 23 37N 58 36 E
Muscat & Oman = Oman ■, *Asia* **99 B7** 23 0N 58 0 E
Muscatatuc ➤, *U.S.A.* **157 F10** 38 47N 86 9W
Muscatine, *U.S.A.* **156 C5** 41 25N 91 3W
Muschu I., *Papua N. G.* .... **132 B2** 3 25 S 143 35 E
Muscoda, *U.S.A.* **156 A6** 43 11N 90 27W
Musengezi = Unsengedsi ➤,
  Zimbabwe .... **119 F3** 15 43 S 31 14 E
Musgrave Harbour, *Canada* **141 C9** 49 27N 53 58W
Musgrave Ranges, *Australia* ... **125 E5** 26 0 S 132 0 E
Mushie, *Dem. Rep. of the Congo* **114 C3** 2 56 S 16 55 E
Mushima, *Zambia* .... **115 E4** 14 10 S 24 56 E
Mushin, *Nigeria* .... **113 D5** 6 32N 3 21 E
Musi ➤, *India* .... **94 F4** 16 41N 79 40 E
Musi ➤, *Indonesia* .... **84 C2** 2 20 S 104 56 E
Musiri, *India* .... **95 J4** 10 56N 78 27 E
Muskeg ➤, *Canada* **142 A4** 60 20N 123 20W
Muskego, *U.S.A.* **157 B8** 42 55N 88 8W
Muskegon, *U.S.A.* **157 A10** 43 14N 86 16W
Muskegon ➤, *U.S.A.* **157 A10** 43 14N 86 21W
Muskegon Heights, *U.S.A.* **157 A10** 43 12N 86 16W
Muskogee, *U.S.A.* **155 H7** 35 45N 95 22W
Muskoka, L., *Canada* **150 B5** 45 0N 79 25W
Muskwa ➤, *Canada* **142 B4** 58 47N 122 48W
Muslīmiyah, *Syria* .... **96 B3** 36 19N 37 12 E
Musmar, *Sudan* .... **106 D4** 18 13N 35 40 E
Musofu, *Zambia* .... **119 E2** 13 30 S 29 0 E
Musoma, *Tanzania* .... **118 C3** 1 30 S 33 48 E
Musquaro, L., *Canada* **141 B7** 50 38N 61 5W
Musquodoboit Harbour, *Canada* **141 D7** 44 50N 63 9W
Mussau I., *Papua N. G.* .... **132 A5** 1 30 S 149 40 E
Musselburgh, *U.K.* **22 F5** 55 57N 3 2W
Musselshell ➤, *U.S.A.* **158 C10** 47 21N 107 57W
Mussende, *Angola* .... **115 E3** 10 32 S 16 5 E
Mussidan, *France* .... **28 C4** 45 2N 0 22 E
Mussolinea di Sardegna = Arboréa,
  Italy .... **46 C1** 39 46N 8 35 E
Mussolo, *Angola* .... **115 D3** 9 59 S 17 19 E
Mussomeli, *Italy* .... **46 E6** 37 35N 13 45 E
Mussoorie, *India* .... **92 D8** 30 27N 78 6 E
Mussuco, *Angola* .... **116 B2** 17 2 S 19 3 E
Mustafakemalpaşa, *Turkey* .... **51 F12** 40 2N 28 24 E
Mustahil, *Ethiopia* .... **120 C2** 5 15N 44 45 E
Mustang, *Nepal* .... **93 E10** 29 10N 83 55 E
Musters, L., *Argentina* .... **176 C3** 45 20 S 69 25W
Musudan, *N. Korea* .... **75 D15** 40 50N 129 43 E
Muswellbrook, *Australia* .... **129 B9** 32 16 S 150 56 E
Muszyna, *Poland* .... **55 J7** 49 22N 20 55 E
Mût, *Egypt* .... **106 B2** 25 28N 28 58 E
Mut, *Turkey* .... **100 D5** 36 40N 33 28 E
Mutanda, *Dem. Rep. of the Congo* **115 D3** 5 17 S 16 34 E
Mutanda, *Mozam.* .... **117 C5** 21 0 S 33 34 E
Mutanda, *Zambia* .... **119 E2** 12 24 S 26 13 E
Mutare, *Zimbabwe* .... **119 F3** 18 58 S 32 38 E
Muting, *Indonesia* .... **83 C6** 7 23 S 140 20 E
Mutis, *Indonesia* .... **83 C2** 9 33 S 124 14 E
Mutki = Mirtağ, *Turkey* .... **96 B4** 38 23N 41 56 E
Mutoko, *Zimbabwe* .... **117 B5** 17 24 S 32 13 E
Mutoray, *Russia* .... **67 C11** 60 56N 101 0 E
Mutshatsha, *Dem. Rep. of the Congo* **115 E4** 10 35 S 24 20 E
Mutsu, *Japan* .... **70 D10** 41 5N 140 55 E
Mutsu-Wan, *Japan* .... **70 D10** 41 5N 140 55 E
Muttaburra, *Australia* .... **126 C3** 22 38 S 144 29 E
Muttalip, *Turkey* .... **49 B12** 39 30N 30 32 E

Mutton I., *Ireland* **23 D2** 52 49N 9 32W
Muttra = Mathura, *India* .... **92 F7** 27 30N 77 40 E
Muttukuru, *India* .... **95 G5** 14 16N 80 6 E
Mutuáli, *Mozam.* .... **119 E4** 14 55 S 37 0 E
Mutum Biyu, *Nigeria* .... **113 D7** 8 40N 10 50 E
Mutunópolis, *Brazil* .... **171 D2** 13 40 S 49 15W
Mutur, *Sri Lanka* .... **95 K5** 8 27N 81 16 E
Muweilih, *Egypt* .... **103 E3** 30 42N 34 19 E
Muxaluando, *Angola* .... **115 D2** 8 8 S 14 18 E
Muxía, *Spain* **42 B1** 43 3N 9 10W
Muxima, *Angola* .... **115 D2** 9 33 S 13 58 E
Muy Muy, *Nic.* **164 D2** 12 39N 85 36W
Muyinga, *Burundi* .... **118 C3** 3 14 S 30 33 E
Muynak, *Uzbekistan* .... **66 E6** 43 44N 59 10 E
Muyunkum, Peski, *Kazakhstan* . **65 A4** 44 12N 71 0 E
Muzaffarabad, *Pakistan* .... **93 B5** 34 25N 73 30 E
Muzaffargarh, *Pakistan* .... **91 C3** 30 5N 71 14 E
Muzaffarnagar, *India* .... **92 E7** 29 26N 77 40 E
Muzaffarpur, *India* .... **93 F11** 26 7N 85 23 E
Muzafirpur, *Pakistan* .... **92 D3** 30 58N 69 9 E
Muzeze, *Angola* .... **115 F3** 15 3 S 17 43 E
Muzhi, *Russia* .... **56 A11** 65 25N 64 40 E
Muzillac, *France* **26 E4** 47 35N 2 30W
Muzon, C., *U.S.A.* **144 J14** 54 40N 132 42W
Muztagh-Ata, *China* .... **65 D7** 38 17N 75 7 E
Muzūra, *Egypt* .... **106 J7** 28 53N 30 48 E
Mvadhi-Ousyé, *Gabon* .... **114 C1** 1 13 S 13 12 E
Mvam, *Gabon* .... **114 C1** 0 13 S 9 39 E
Mvangan, *Cameroon* .... **107 F2** 6 2N 29 53 E
Mvôlô, *Sudan* .... **117 F2** 2 17N 11 43 E
Mvuma, *Zimbabwe* .... **119 F3** 19 16 S 30 30 E
Mvurwi, *Zimbabwe* .... **119 F3** 17 0 S 30 57 E
Mwabvi Game Reserve △, *Malawi* **119 F3** 16 42 S 35 0 E
Mwadi-Kalumbu, *Dem. Rep. of*
  the Congo .... **115 D3** 7 53 S 18 43 E
Mwadui, *Tanzania* .... **118 C3** 3 26 S 33 32 E
Mwali = Mohéli, *Comoros Is.* .. **121 a** 12 20 S 43 40 E
Mwambo, *Tanzania* .... **119 E5** 10 30 S 40 22 E
Mwandi, *Zambia* .... **119 F1** 17 30 S 24 51 E
Mwanza, *Dem. Rep. of the Congo* **118 D2** 7 55 S 26 43 E
Mwanza, *Tanzania* .... **118 C3** 2 30 S 32 58 E
Mwanza, *Zambia* .... **119 F1** 16 58 S 24 28 E
Mwanza □, *Tanzania* .... **118 C3** 2 0 S 33 0 E
Mwaya, *Tanzania* .... **119 D3** 9 32 S 33 55 E
Mweelrea, *Ireland* **23 C2** 53 39N 9 49W
Mweka, *Dem. Rep. of the Congo* **115 C4** 4 50 S 21 34 E
Mwendjila, *Dem. Rep. of the Congo* **115 D3** 7 12 S 18 51 E
Mwene-Ditu, *Dem. Rep. of*
  the Congo .... **115 D4** 6 35 S 22 27 E
Mwenezi, *Zimbabwe* .... **119 F3** 21 15 S 30 48 E
Mwenezi ➤, *Mozam.* .... **119 G3** 22 40 S 31 50 E
Mwenga, *Dem. Rep. of the Congo* **118 C2** 3 1 S 28 28 E
Mweru, L., *Zambia* .... **119 D2** 9 0 S 28 40 E
Mweru Wantipa Nat. Park △,
  Zambia .... **119 D2** 8 39 S 29 25 E
Mwetshi, *Dem. Rep. of the Congo* **115 C4** 4 50 S 22 38 E
Mweza Range, *Zimbabwe* ..... **119 G3** 21 0 S 30 0 E
Mwilambwe, *Dem. Rep. of the Congo* **118 D2** 8 7 S 25 5 E
Mwimbi, *Tanzania* .... **119 D3** 8 38 S 31 39 E
Mwinilunga, *Zambia* .... **119 E1** 11 43 S 24 25 E
My Tho, *Vietnam* .... **87 G6** 10 29N 106 23 E
Mya, O. ➤, *Algeria* .... **111 B5** 30 46N 4 54 E
Myajlar, *India* .... **92 F4** 26 15N 70 20 E
Myakka ➤, *U.S.A.* **153 J7** 26 56N 82 11W
Myall Lakes Nat. Park △, *Australia* **129 B10** 32 25 S 152 30 E
Myanaung, *Burma* .... **90 F5** 18 25N 95 10 E
Myanmar = Burma ■, *Asia* ..... **90 E6** 21 0N 96 30 E
Myaung, *Burma* .... **90 G5** 21 50N 95 25 E
Myaungmya, *Burma* .... **90 G5** 16 30N 94 40 E
Myebon, *Burma* .... **90 E4** 20 3N 93 22 E
Myeik Kyunzu, *Burma* .... **87 G1** 11 30N 97 30 E
Myers Chuck, *U.S.A.* **142 B2** 55 44N 132 11W
Myerstown, *U.S.A.* **151 F8** 40 22N 76 19W
Myingyan, *Burma* .... **90 C6** 21 30N 95 20 E
Myitkyina, *Burma* .... **90 C5** 25 24N 97 26 E
Myitson, *Burma* .... **90 D6** 23 18N 96 35 E
Myittha, *Burma* .... **90 E6** 21 25N 96 8 E
Myittha ➤, *Burma* .... **90 D5** 23 12N 94 17 E
Myjava, *Slovak Rep.* .... **55 G3** 48 41N 17 37 E
Mykhaylivka, *Ukraine* .... **59 J8** 47 12N 35 15 E
Mykines, *Færoe Is.* **14 E9** 62 7N 7 35W
Myking, *Norway* .... **18 D2** 60 40N 5 19 E
Mykolayiv, *Ukraine* .... **59 J7** 46 58N 32 0 E
Mylius Erichsen Land, *Greenland* **10 A8** 81 30N 27 0W
Mymensingh, *Bangla.* .... **90 C3** 24 45N 90 24 E
Mynydd Du, *U.K.* **21 F4** 51 52N 3 50W
Myo-gyi, *Burma* .... **90 D7** 21 27N 96 22 E
Myohaung, *Burma* .... **90 E4** 20 35N 93 11 E
Myohla, *Burma* .... **90 F5** 19 16N 95 43 E
Myotha, *Burma* .... **90 D6** 21 41N 95 43 E
Myothit, *Kachin, Burma* .... **90 C6** 24 24N 97 24 E
Myothit, *Magwe, Burma* .... **90 E5** 20 12N 95 27 E
Myrasýsla □, *Iceland* **11 C5** 64 43N 21 5W
Mýrdalsjökull, *Iceland* **11 A4** 63 40N 19 6W
Myrhorod, *Ukraine* .... **59 H7** 49 58N 33 37 E
Mýri, *Iceland* **11 B9** 65 23N 17 23W
Myrtle Beach, *U.S.A.* **149 J6** 33 42N 78 53W
Myrtle Creek, *U.S.A.* **158 E2** 43 1N 123 17W
Myrtle Grove, *U.S.A.* **153 E2** 30 23N 87 17W
Myrtle Point, *U.S.A.* **158 E1** 43 4N 124 8W
Myrtleford, *Australia* .... **129 D7** 36 34 S 146 44 E
Myrtou, *Cyprus* .... **39 E9** 35 18N 33 4 E
Myrzakent, *Kazakhstan* .... **65 C4** 40 40N 68 32 E
Mysen, *Norway* .... **18 E8** 59 33N 11 20 E
Mysia, *Turkey* .... **51 G11** 39 50N 27 0 E
Myślenice, *Poland* .... **55 J6** 49 51N 19 57 E
Myślibórz, *Poland* .... **55 F1** 52 55N 14 50 E
Mysłowice, *Poland* .... **55 H6** 50 15N 19 12 E
Mysore = Karnataka □, *India* .. **95 H3** 13 15N 77 0 E
Mysore, *India* .... **95 H3** 12 17N 76 41 E
Mystic, *Conn., U.S.A.* **151 E13** 41 21N 71 58W
Mystic, *Iowa, U.S.A.* **156 D4** 40 47N 92 57W
Myszków, *Poland* .... **55 H6** 50 45N 19 22 E
Myszyniec, *Poland* .... **54 E8** 53 23N 21 21 E
Mythen, *Switz.* .... **33 B7** 47 2N 8 42 E
Mytishchi, *Russia* .... **58 E9** 55 50N 37 50 E
Mývatn, *Iceland* **11 B10** 65 36N 17 0W
Mzab, Oued en ➤, *Algeria* ..... **111 B6** 32 15N 5 0 E
Mže ➤, *Czech Rep.* .... **34 B6** 49 46N 13 24 E
Mzimba, *Malawi* .... **119 E3** 11 55 S 33 39 E
Mzimkulu ➤, *S. Africa* .... **117 E5** 30 44 S 30 28 E
Mzimvubu ➤, *S. Africa* .... **117 E4** 31 38 S 29 33 E
Mzuzu, *Malawi* .... **119 E3** 11 30 S 33 55 E

N

Na Hearadh = Harris, *U.K.* **22 D2** 57 50N 6 55W
Na-lang, *Burma* .... **90 D6** 22 42N 97 43 E
Na Noi, *Thailand* .... **86 C3** 18 19N 100 43 E
Na Phao, *Laos* .... **86 D5** 17 35N 105 44 E
Na Sam, *Vietnam* .... **76 F6** 22 3N 106 37 E
Na San, *Vietnam* .... **86 B5** 21 12N 104 2 E
Na Thon, *Thailand* .... **87 b** 9 32N 99 56 E
Naab ➤, *Germany* .... **31 F8** 49 1N 12 2 E
Naalehu, *U.S.A.* **145 D6** 19 4N 155 35W
Na'am, *Sudan* .... **107 F2** 9 42N 28 27 E
Na'am ➤, *Sudan* .... **107 F2** 6 48N 29 57 E
Naantali, *Finland* .... **15 F19** 60 29N 22 2 E
Naas, *Ireland* **23 C5** 53 12N 6 40W
Nababeep, *S. Africa* .... **116 D2** 29 36 S 17 46 E

Nabadwip = Navadwip, *India* .. **93 H13** 23 34N 88 20 E
Nabari, *Japan* .... **73 C8** 34 37N 136 5 E
Nabawa, *Australia* .... **125 E1** 28 30 S 114 48 E
Nabberu, L., *Australia* .... **125 E3** 25 50 S 120 30 E
Nabburg, *Germany* .... **31 F8** 49 27N 12 11 E
Naberezhnyye Chelny, *Russia* .. **60 C11** 55 42N 52 19 E
Nabesna, *U.S.A.* **144 E12** 62 22N 143 0W
Nabeul, *Tunisia* .... **108 A2** 36 30N 10 44 E
Nabha, *India* .... **92 D7** 30 26N 76 14 E
Nabid, *Iran* .... **97 D8** 29 40N 57 38 E
Nabire, *Indonesia* .... **83 E9** 3 15 S 135 26 E
Nabisar, *Pakistan* .... **92 G3** 25 8N 69 40 E
Nabisipi ➤, *Canada* **141 B7** 50 14N 62 13W
Nabiswera, *Uganda* .... **118 B3** 1 27N 32 15 E
Nablus = Nâblus, *West Bank* ... **103 C4** 32 14N 35 15 E
Naboomspruit, *S. Africa* .... **117 C4** 24 32 S 28 40 E
Nabou, *Burkina Faso* **112 C4** 11 25N 2 50W
Nabouwalu, *Fiji* .... **133 A2** 17 0 S 178 45 E
Nabua, *Phil.* .... **80 E4** 13 24N 123 22 E
Nabunturan, *Phil.* .... **81 H5** 7 35N 125 58 E
Nacala, *Mozam.* .... **119 E5** 14 31 S 40 34 E
Nacala-Velha, *Mozam.* .... **119 E5** 14 32 S 40 34 E
Nacaome, *Honduras* **164 D2** 13 31N 87 30W
Nacaroa, *Mozam.* .... **119 E4** 14 22 S 39 56 E
Naches, *U.S.A.* **158 C3** 46 44N 120 42W
Naches ➤, *U.S.A.* **160 D6** 46 38N 120 31W
Nachicapau, L., *Canada* .... **73 D7** 33 33N 135 58 E
Nachingwea, *Tanzania* .... **119 E4** 10 23 S 38 49 E
Nachna, *India* .... **92 F4** 27 34N 71 41 E
Náchod, *Czech Rep.* .... **34 A9** 50 25N 16 8 E
Nachuge, *India* .... **95 J11** 10 47N 92 21 E
Nacimiento, L., *U.S.A.* **160 K6** 35 46N 120 53W
Nackara, *Australia* .... **128 B3** 32 48 S 139 12 E
Naco, *Mexico* **162 A3** 31 20N 109 56W
Nacogdoches, *U.S.A.* **155 K7** 31 36N 94 39W
Nácori Chico, *Mexico* **162 B3** 29 39N 109 1W
Nacozari, *Mexico* **162 A3** 30 24N 109 39W
Nacula, *Fiji* .... **133 A1** 16 54 S 177 27 E
Nadi, *Fiji* .... **133 A1** 17 42 S 177 20 E
Nadiad, *India* .... **92 H5** 22 41N 72 56 E
Nădlac, *Romania* .... **52 D5** 46 10N 20 50 E
Nador, *Morocco* **111 A4** 35 14N 2 58W
Nadur, *Malta* .... **38 F7** 35 54N 14 22 E
Nadur, *Gozo, Malta* .... **38 E7** 36 2N 14 18 E
Nadūshan, *Iran* .... **97 C7** 32 2N 53 35 E
Nadvirna, *Ukraine* .... **59 H3** 48 37N 24 30 E
Nadvoitsy, *Russia* .... **56 B5** 63 52N 34 14 E
Nadvornaya = Nadvirna, *Ukraine* **59 H3** 48 37N 24 30 E
Nadym, *Russia* .... **66 C8** 65 35N 72 42 E
Nadym ➤, *Russia* .... **66 C8** 66 12N 72 0 E
Nærbø, *Norway* .... **18 F2** 58 40N 5 39 E
Næstved, *Denmark* .... **17 J5** 55 13N 11 44 E
Nafada, *Nigeria* .... **113 C7** 11 8N 11 20 E
Näfels, *Switz.* .... **33 B8** 47 6N 9 4 E
Naft-e Safīd, *Iran* .... **97 D6** 31 40N 49 17 E
Naftshahr, *Iran* .... **101 E11** 34 0N 45 30 E
Nafud Desert = An Nafūd, *Si. Arabia* **96 D4** 28 15N 41 0 E
Nafūsah, Jabal, *Libya* .... **108 B2** 32 12N 12 30 E
Naga, *Phil.* .... **80 E4** 13 38N 123 15 E
Naga, Cebu, *Phil.* .... **81 H4** 10 12N 123 45 E
Naga, Zamboanga del S., *Phil.* . **81 H4** 7 46N 122 45 E
Naga, Kreb en, *Africa* **110 D3** 24 12N 6 0W
Naga-Shima, *Kagoshima, Japan* **72 E2** 32 10N 130 9 E
Naga-Shima, *Yamaguchi, Japan* **72 D4** 33 49N 132 5 E
Nagahama, *Ehime, Japan* ..... **72 D4** 33 36N 132 29 E
Nagahama, *Shiga, Japan* ...... **73 B8** 35 23N 136 16 E
Nagai, *Japan* .... **70 E10** 38 6N 140 2 E
Nagai I., *U.S.A.* **144 J8** 55 5N 160 0W
Nagaland □, *India* .... **90 B5** 26 0N 94 30 E
Nagambie, *Australia* .... **129 D6** 36 47 S 145 10 E
Nagano, *Japan* .... **73 A10** 36 40N 138 10 E
Nagano □, *Japan* .... **73 A10** 36 15N 138 0 E
Nagaoka, *Japan* .... **71 F9** 37 27N 138 51 E
Nagappattinam, *India* .... **95 J4** 10 46N 79 51 E
Nagar ➤, *Bangla.* .... **93 G13** 24 27N 89 12 E
Nagar Karnul, *India* .... **95 F4** 16 29N 78 20 E
Nagar Parkar, *Pakistan* .... **92 G4** 24 28N 70 46 E
Nagara-Gawa ➤, *Japan* .... **73 B8** 35 40N 136 43 E
Nagaram, *India* .... **94 E5** 18 21N 80 26 E
Nagari Hills, *India* .... **95 H4** 13 3N 79 45 E
Nagasaki, *Japan* .... **72 E1** 32 47N 129 50 E
Nagasaki □, *Japan* .... **72 E1** 32 50N 129 40 E
Nagato, *Japan* .... **72 C3** 34 19N 131 5 E
Nagaur, *India* .... **92 F5** 27 15N 73 45 E
Nagbhir, *India* .... **94 D4** 20 34N 79 55 E
Nagda, *India* .... **92 H6** 23 27N 75 25 E
Nagercoil, *India* .... **95 K3** 8 12N 77 26 E
Nagina, *India* .... **93 E8** 29 30N 78 30 E
Nagineh, *Iran* .... **97 C8** 34 20N 57 15 E
Naginimara, *India* .... **90 B5** 26 49N 94 50 E
Nagir, *Pakistan* .... **93 A6** 36 12N 74 42 E
Nagkarlang, *Sweden* .... **16 D6** 65 20N 15 34 E
Nagod, *India* .... **93 G9** 24 34N 80 36 E
Nagold, *Germany* .... **31 G4** 48 32N 8 43 E
Nagold ➤, *Germany* .... **31 G4** 48 52N 8 42 E
Nagoorin, *Australia* .... **126 C5** 24 17 S 151 15 E
Nagorno-Karabakh □, *Azerbaijan* **101 C12** 39 55N 46 45 E
Nagornyy, *Russia* .... **67 D13** 55 58N 124 57 E
Nagorsk, *Russia* .... **64 B3** 59 18N 50 48 E
Nagoya, *Japan* .... **73 B8** 35 10N 136 50 E
Nagoya ✈ (NGO), *Japan* .... **73 B8** 35 14N 136 57 E
Nagpur, *India* .... **94 D4** 21 8N 79 10 E
Nagua, *Dom. Rep.* **165 C6** 19 23N 69 50W
Naguabo, *Puerto Rico* .... **165 d** 18 13N 65 44W
Nagyatád, *Hungary* .... **52 D2** 46 14N 17 22 E
Nagycserd, *Hungary* .... **52 C6** 47 53N 21 32 E
Nagykálló, *Hungary* .... **52 C6** 47 53N 21 51 E
Nagykanizsa, *Hungary* .... **52 D2** 46 28N 17 0 E
Nagykáta, *Hungary* .... **52 C4** 47 25N 19 45 E
Nagykőrös, *Hungary* .... **52 C4** 47 5N 19 48 E
Nagyvárad = Oradea, *Romania* . **52 C6** 47 2N 21 58 E
Naha, *Japan* .... **71 L3** 26 13N 127 42 E
Nahan, *India* .... **92 D7** 30 33N 77 18 E
Nahanni Butte, *Canada* **142 A4** 61 2N 123 31W
Nahanni Nat. Park △, *Canada* . **142 A4** 61 15N 125 0W
Nahargarh, *Mad. P., India* ..... **92 G6** 24 10N 75 14 E
Nahargarh, *Raj., India* .... **92 G7** 24 55N 76 50 E
Nahariyya, *Israel* .... **100 F6** 33 1N 35 5 E
Nahāvand, *Iran* .... **97 C6** 34 10N 48 22 E
Nahe ➤, *Germany* .... **31 F3** 49 58N 7 54 E
Nahîya, W. ➤, *Egypt* .... **106 B3** 28 55N 31 0 E
Nahuel Huapi, L., *Argentina* ... **176 B2** 41 0 S 71 32W
Nahuic ➤, *U.S.A.* **152 D8** 31 12N 81 59W
Naic, *Phil.* .... **87 a** 8 14N 98 22 E
Naicá, *Mexico* **80 B3** 27 53N 105 31W
Naicam, *Canada* **143 C8** 52 30N 104 30W
Naikliu, *Indonesia* .... **82 C2** 9 33 S 123 37 E
Naikoon Prov. Park △, *Canada* . **142 C2** 53 55N 131 55W
Naikul, *India* .... **94 D7** 21 20N 84 58 E
Naila, *Germany* .... **31 E7** 50 19N 11 42 E
Naimisharanya, *India* .... **93 F9** 27 21N 80 30 E
Nain, *Canada* **141 A7** 56 34N 61 40W
Nā'īn, *Iran* .... **97 C7** 32 54N 53 0 E
Naini Tal, *India* .... **93 E8** 29 30N 79 30 E
Naintré, *France* .... **26 F7** 46 46N 0 29 E
Nainwa, *India* .... **92 G6** 25 46N 75 51 E
Naipu, *Romania* .... **53 F10** 44 12N 25 47 E
Nairai, *Fiji* .... **133 A2** 17 49 S 179 15 E
Nairn, *U.K.* **22 D5** 57 35N 3 53W

Nairobi, *Kenya* .... 118 C4   1 17 S 36 48 E
Nairobi Nat. Park △, *Kenya* .. 118 C4   1 22 S 36 50 E
Naissaar, *Estonia* .... 15 G21 59 34N 24 29 E
Naita, Mt., *Ethiopia* .... 107 F4   5 30N 35 18 E
Naitaba, *Fiji* .... 133 A3   17 0 S 179 16W
Najac, *France* .... 28 D5 44 14N   1 58 E
Najafābād, *Iran* .... 97 C6 32 40N 51 15 E
Najd, *Si. Arabia* .... 88 C3 26 30N 42 0 E
Nájera, *Spain* 40 C2 42 26N   2 48W
Najerilla →, *Spain* 40 C2 42 32N   2 48W
Najibabad, *India* .... 92 E8 29 40N 78 20 E
Najin, *N. Korea* .... 75 C16 42 12N 130 15 E
Najmah, *Si. Arabia* .... 97 E6 26 42N 50 6 E
Najrān, *Si. Arabia* .... 98 C4 17 34N 44 18 E
Naju, *S. Korea* .... 75 G14 35 3N 126 43 E
Naka-Gawa →, *Japan* .... 73 A12 36 20N 140 36 E
Nakadōri-Shima, *Japan* ...... 71 H4 32 57N 129 4 E
Nakalagba, *Dem. Rep. of the Congo* 112 B2   2 50N 27 58 E
Nakalele Pt., *U.S.A.* 145 M5 21 2N 156 35W
Nakama, *Japan* .... 72 D2 33 56N 130 43 E
Nakaminato, *Japan* .... 73 A12 36 21N 140 36 E
Nakamura, *Japan* .... 72 E4 32 59N 132 56 E
Nakanai Mts., *Papua N. G.* ... 132 C6   5 40 S 151 0 E
Nakano, *Japan* .... 73 A10 36 45N 138 22 E
Nakano-Shima, *Japan* .... 71 K4 29 51N 129 52 E
Nakanojō, *Japan* .... 73 A10 36 35N 138 51 E
Nakashibetsu, *Japan* .... 70 C12 43 33N 144 59 E
Nakatsu, *Japan* .... 72 D2 33 34N 131 15 E
Nakatsugawa, *Japan* .... 73 B9 35 29N 137 30 E
Nakfa, *Eritrea* .... 107 D4 16 40N 38 32 E
Nakhla Wildlife Reserve △, *Eritrea* 107 D4 17 28N 38 55 E
Nakha Yai, Ko, *Thailand* ..... 87 a   8 3N 98 28 E
Nakhtarana, *India* .... 92 H3 23 20N 69 15 E
Nakhl, *Egypt* .... 103 F2 29 55N 33 43 E
Nakhl-e Taqī, *Iran* .... 97 E7 27 28N 52 36 E
Nakhodka, *Russia* .... 67 E14 42 53N 132 54 E
Nakhon Nayok, *Thailand* ..... 86 E3 14 12N 101 13 E
Nakhon Pathom, *Thailand* .... 86 F3 13 49N 100 3 E
Nakhon Phanom, *Thailand* .... 86 D5 17 23N 104 43 E
Nakhon Ratchasima, *Thailand* .. 86 E4 14 59N 102 12 E
Nakhon Sawan, *Thailand* ..... 86 E3 15 35N 100 10 E
Nakhon Si Thammarat, *Thailand* 87 H3   8 29N 100 0 E
Nakhon Thai, *Thailand* ...... 86 D3 17 5N 100 44 E
Nakina, *Canada* 148 B2 50 10N 86 40W
Nakło nad Notecią, *Poland* ... 55 E4 53 9N 17 38 E
Naknek, *U.S.A.* 144 G8 58 44N 157 1W
Nako, *Burkina Faso* 112 C4 10 40N   3 4W
Nakodar, *India* .... 92 D6 31 8N 75 31 E
Nakskov, *Denmark* .... 17 K5 54 50N 11 8 E
Naktong →, *S. Korea* .... 75 G15 35 7N 128 57 E
Nakuru, *Kenya* .... 118 C4   0 15 S 36 4 E
Nakuru, L., *Kenya* .... 118 C4   0 23 S 36 5 E
Nakusp, *Canada* 142 C5 50 20N 117 45W
Nal, *Pakistan* .... 92 F2 27 40N 66 12 E
Nal →, *Pakistan* .... 91 D2 25 20N 65 30 E
Nalázi, *Mozam.* .... 117 C5 24 3 S 33 20 E
Nalchik, *Russia* .... 61 J6 43 30N 43 33 E
Nałęczów, *Poland* .... 55 G9 51 17N 22 9 E
Nalerigu, *Ghana* 113 C4 10 35N   0 25W
Nalgonda, *India* .... 94 F4 17 6N 79 15 E
Nalhati, *India* .... 93 G12 24 17N 87 52 E
Naliya, *India* .... 92 H3 23 16N 68 50 E
Nallamalai Hills, *India* .... 95 G4 15 30N 78 50 E
Nallıhan, *Turkey* .... 100 B4 40 11N 31 20 E
Nalolo, *Zambia* .... 115 F4 15 33 S 23 7 E
Nalón →, *Spain* 42 B4 43 32N   6 4W
Nalong, *Burma* .... 90 C6 24 44N 97 28 E
Nālūt, *Libya* .... 108 B2 31 54N 11 0 E
Nam Can, *Vietnam* .... 87 H5   8 46N 104 59 E
Nam-ch'on, *N. Korea* .... 75 E14 38 15N 126 26 E
Nam Co, *China* .... 68 C4 30 30N 90 45 E
Nam Dinh, *Vietnam* .... 76 G6 20 25N 106 5 E
Nam Du, Hon, *Vietnam* ...... 87 H5   9 41N 104 21 E
Nam Nao Nat. Park △, *Thailand* 86 D3 16 44N 101 32 E
Nam Ngum Dam, *Laos* .... 86 C4 18 35N 102 34 E
Nam-Phan, *Vietnam* .... 87 G6 10 30N 106 0 E
Nam Phong, *Thailand* .... 86 D4 16 42N 102 52 E
Nam Tha, *Laos* .... 76 G3 20 58N 101 30 E
Nam Tok, *Thailand* .... 86 E2 14 21N 99 4 E
Namachire, *Angola* .... 115 E4 11 26 S 22 43 E
Namacunde, *Angola* .... 116 B2 17 18 S 15 50 E
Namacurra, *Mozam.* .... 117 B6 17 30 S 36 50 E
Namadgi Nat. Park △, *Australia* 129 C8 35 42 S 149 0 E
Namak, Daryācheh-ye, *Iran* ... 97 C7 34 30N 52 0 E
Namak, Kavir-e, *Iran* .... 97 C8 34 30N 57 30 E
Namakkal, *India* .... 95 J4 11 13N 78 13 E
Namakzār, Daryācheh-ye, *Iran* . 97 C9 34 0 S 60 30 E
Namaland, *Namibia* .... 116 C2 26 0 S 17 0 E
Namangan, *Uzbekistan* .... 65 C5 41 0N 71 40 E
Namapa, *Mozam.* .... 119 E4 13 43 S 39 50 E
Namaqualand, *S. Africa* ...... 116 E2 30 0 S 17 25 E
Namasagali, *Uganda* .... 118 B3   1 2N 33 0 E
Namatanai, *Papua N. G.* ..... 132 B7   3 40 S 152 29 E
Namber, *Indonesia* .... 83 B4   1 2 S 134 49 E
Nambour, *Australia* .... 127 D5 26 32 S 152 58 E
Nambouwalu = Nabouwalu, *Fiji* 133 A2 17 0 S 178 45 E
Nambucca Heads, *Australia* ... 129 A10 30 37 S 153 0 E
Nambung Nat. Park △, *Australia* 125 F2 30 30 S 115 5 E
Namcha Barwa, *China* .... 68 D4 29 40N 95 10 E
Namche Bazar, *Nepal* .... 93 F12 27 51N 86 47 E
Namchonjŏm = Nam-ch'on, *N. Korea* 75 E14 38 15N 126 26 E
Namecunda, *Mozam.* .... 119 E4 14 54 S 37 37 E
Nameh, *Indonesia* .... 85 B5   2 34N 116 21 E
Namen = Namur, *Belgium* .... 24 D4 50 27N   4 52 E
Namenalala, *Fiji* .... 133 A2 17 8 S 179 9 E
Nameponda, *Mozam.* .... 119 F4 15 50 S 39 50 E
Namerikawa, *Japan* .... 73 A9 36 46N 137 20 E
Náměšť nad Oslavou, *Czech Rep.* 35 B9 49 12N 16 10 E
Námestovo, *Slovak Rep.* ..... 35 B12 49 24N 19 25 E
Nametil, *Mozam.* .... 119 F4 15 40 S 39 21 E
Namew L., *Canada* 143 C8 54 14N 101 56W
Namgia, *India* .... 93 D8 31 48N 78 40 E
Namhkam, *Burma* .... 76 E1 23 50N 97 41 E
Namho, *Burma* .... 90 D7 22 4N 99 1 E
Namhsan, *Burma* .... 90 D6 22 48N 97 2 E
Namib Desert, *Namibia* ...... 116 C2 22 30 S 15 0 E
Namib-Naukluft Park △, *Namibia* 116 C2 24 40 S 15 16 E
Namibe, *Angola* .... 115 F2 15 7 S 12 11 E
Namibe □, *Angola* .... 116 B1 16 35 S 12 30 E
Namibe, Reserva Parcial de △, *Angola* 115 F2 16 35 S 12 20 E
Namibia ■, *Africa* .... 116 C2 22 0 S 18 9 E
Namibwoestyn = Namib Desert, *Namibia* 116 C2 23 0 S 15 0 E
Namïn, *Iran* .... 101 C13 38 25N 48 30 E
Namlan, *Burma* .... 90 D6 22 15N 97 24 E
Namlea, *Indonesia* .... 129 A9 30 12 S 149 30 E
Namoi →, *Australia* .... 129 A9 30 12 S 149 30 E
Namous, O. en →, *Algeria* ... 111 B4 31 0N   0 7W
Nampa, *U.S.A.* 158 E5 43 34N 116 34W
Nampala, *Mali* 112 B3 15 0N   5 58W
Namp'o, *N. Korea* .... 75 E13 38 52N 125 10 E
Nampō-Shotō, *Japan* .... 71 J10 32 0N 140 0 E
Nampula, *Mozam.* .... 119 F4 15 6 S 39 15 E
Namrole, *Indonesia* .... 83 B3   3 46 S 126 46 E
Namsang, *Burma* .... 90 E6 20 53N 97 43 E
Namsen →, *Norway* .... 14 D14 64 28N 11 37 E

Namsos, *Norway* .... 14 D14 64 29N 11 30 E
Namtok Chat Trakan Nat. Park △, *Thailand* 86 D3 17 17N 100 40 E
Namtok Mae Surin Nat. Park △, *Thailand* 86 C2 18 55N 98 2 E
Namtsy, *Russia* .... 67 C13 62 43N 129 37 E
Namtu, *Burma* .... 90 D6 23 5N 97 28 E
Namtumbo, *Tanzania* .... 119 E4 10 30 S 36 4 E
Namu, *Canada* 142 C3 51 52N 127 50W
Namuka-i-Lau, *Fiji* .... 133 B3 18 53 S 178 37W
Namur, *Belgium* .... 24 D4 50 27N   4 52 E
Namur □, *Belgium* .... 24 D4 50 17N   5 0 E
Namutoni, *Namibia* .... 116 B2 18 49 S 16 55 E
Namwala, *Zambia* .... 119 F2 15 44 S 26 30 E
Namwŏn, *S. Korea* .... 75 G14 35 23N 127 23 E
Namysłów, *Poland* .... 55 G4 51 6N 17 42 E
Nan, *Thailand* .... 86 C3 18 48N 100 46 E
Nan →, *Thailand* .... 86 E3 15 42N 100 9 E
Nan-ch'ang = Nanchang, *China* 77 C10 28 42N 115 55 E
Nan Ling, *China* .... 77 E8 25 0N 112 30 E
Nan Xian, *China* .... 77 C9 29 20N 112 22 E
Nana, *C.A.R.* .... 114 A3   5 0N 35 50 E
Nana, *Romania* .... 53 F11 44 17N 26 34 E
Nana-Barya, Réserve de Faune de la △, *C.A.R.* 114 A3   7 40N 17 29 E
Nana Kru, *Liberia* 112 E3   4 55N   8 45W
Nanaimo, *Canada* 142 D4 49 10N 124 0W
Nanakuli, *U.S.A.* 145 K13 21 24N 158 9W
Nanam, *N. Korea* .... 75 D15 41 44N 129 40 E
Nanan, *China* .... 77 E12 24 59N 118 21 E
Nanango, *Australia* .... 127 D5 26 40 S 152 0 E
Nan'ao, *China* .... 77 F11 23 28N 117 5 E
Nanao, *Japan* .... 73 A8 37 0N 137 0 E
Nanbu, *China* .... 76 B6 31 18N 106 3 E
Nanchang, *Jiangxi, China* .... 77 C10 28 42N 115 55 E
Nanchang, *Kiangsi, China* .... 77 C10 28 34N 115 48 E
Nancheng, *China* .... 77 D11 27 33N 116 35 E
Nanching = Nanjing, *China* ... 77 A12 32 2N 118 47 E
Nanchong, *China* .... 76 B6 30 43N 106 2 E
Nanchuan, *China* .... 76 C6 29 9N 107 6 E
Nancowry, *India* .... 95 L11 7 59N 93 32 E
Nanda Devi, *India* .... 93 D8 30 23N 79 59 E
Nanda Kot, *India* .... 93 D9 30 17N 80 5 E
Nandan, *China* .... 76 E6 24 58N 107 29 E
Nandan, *Japan* .... 72 C6 34 10N 134 42 E
Nanded, *India* .... 94 E3 19 10N 77 20 E
Nandewar Ra., *Australia* ..... 127 E5 30 15 S 150 35 E
Nandgaon, *India* .... 94 D2 20 19N 74 39 E
Nandi = Nadi, *Fiji* .... 133 A1 17 42 S 177 20 E
Nandiarane, Pte., *N. Cal.* ..... 133 T18 20 54 S 164 19 E
Nandigama, *India* .... 94 F5 16 47N 80 18 E
Nandigram, *India* .... 93 H12 22 1N 87 58 E
Nandikotkur, *India* .... 95 G4 15 52N 78 18 E
Nandura, *India* .... 94 D3 20 52N 76 25 E
Nandurbar, *India* .... 94 D2 21 20N 74 15 E
Nandyal, *India* .... 95 G4 15 30N 78 30 E
Nanfeng, *Guangdong, China* .. 77 F8 23 45N 111 47 E
Nanfeng, *Jiangxi, China* ..... 77 D11 27 12N 116 28 E
Nanga-Eboko, *Cameroon* ..... 113 E7   4 41N 12 22 E
Nanga Parbat, *Pakistan* ...... 93 B6 35 10N 74 35 E
Nangade, *Mozam.* .... 119 E4 11 5 S 39 36 E
Nangapinoh, *Indonesia* ...... 85 C4   0 20 S 111 44 E
Nangarhār □, *Afghan.* ...... 91 B3 34 20N 70 0 E
Nangatayap, *Indonesia* ...... 85 C4   1 32 S 110 34 E
Nangeya Mts., *Uganda* ...... 118 B3   3 30N 33 30 E
Nangis, *France* .... 27 D10 48 33N   3 1 E
Nangong, *China* .... 74 F8 37 23N 115 22 E
Nangtud, Mt., *Phil.* .... 81 F4 11 17N 122 11 E
Nanguneri, *India* .... 95 K3   8 29N 77 40 E
Nangwarry, *Australia* .... 128 D4 37 33 S 140 48 E
Nanhua, *China* .... 76 E3 25 13N 101 21 E
Nanhuang, *China* .... 75 F11 36 58N 121 48 E
Nanhui, *China* .... 77 B13 31 2N 121 44 E
Nanjangud, *India* .... 95 H3 12 6N 76 43 E
Nanjeko, *Zambia* .... 119 F1 15 31 S 23 30 E
Nanji Shan, *China* .... 77 D13 27 27N 121 4 E
Nanjian, *China* .... 76 A6 32 28N 106 51 E
Nanjiang, *China* .... 77 E11 24 25N 117 20 E
Nanjing, *Fujian, China* ...... 77 A12 32 2N 118 47 E
Nanjing, *Jiangsu, China* ..... 119 D4   9 41 S 39 5 E
Nanjirinji, *Tanzania* .... 72 D5 35 40N 114 45 E
Nankana Sahib, *Pakistan* .... 92 D5 31 27N 73 38 E
Nankang, *China* .... 77 E10 25 40N 114 45 E
Nanking = Nanjing, *China* ... 77 A12 32 2N 118 47 E
Nankoku, *Japan* .... 72 D5 33 39N 133 44 E
Nanlang, *China* .... 69 G10 22 30N 113 32 E
Nanling, *China* .... 77 B12 30 55N 118 20 E
Nannial, *India* .... 94 E4 19 4N 79 38 E
Nanning, *China* .... 76 F7 22 48N 108 20 E
Nannup, *Australia* .... 125 F2 33 59 S 115 48 E
Nanortalik, *Greenland* 10 E6 60 10N 45 17W
Nanpan Jiang →, *China* ...... 76 E6 25 10N 106 5 E
Nanpara, *India* .... 93 F9 27 52N 81 33 E
Nanpi, *China* .... 74 E9 38 2N 116 45 E
Nanping, *Fujian, China* ...... 77 D12 26 38N 118 10 E
Nanping, *Henan, China* ...... 77 C9 29 55N 112 3 E
Nanri Dao, *China* .... 77 E12 25 15N 119 25 E
Nanripe, *Mozam.* .... 119 E4 13 52 S 38 52 E
Nansei-Shotō = Ryūkyū-rettō, *Japan* 71 M3 26 0N 126 0 E
Nansen Land, *Greenland* 10 A6 83 0N 43 0W
Nansen Sd., *Canada* 6 A3 81 0N 91 0W
Nansha, *China* .... 69 F10 22 45N 113 34 E
Nanshan I., *S. China Sea* ..... 78 B5 10 45N 115 49 E
Nansio, *Tanzania* .... 118 C3   2 3 S 33 4 E
Nant, *France* .... 28 D7 44 1N   3 18 E
Nanterre, *France* .... 27 D9 48 53N   2 13 E
Nantes, *France* 26 E5 47 12N   1 33W
Nantiat, *France* .... 28 B5 46 1N   1 11 E
Nanticoke, *U.S.A.* 151 E8 41 12N 76 0W
Nanton, *Canada* 142 C6 50 21N 113 46W
Nantong, *China* .... 77 A13 32 1N 120 52 E
Nantou, *China* .... 69 F10 22 32N 113 55 E
Nantou, *Taiwan* .... 77 F13 23 57N 120 35 E
Nantua, *France* .... 27 F12 46 10N   5 35 E
Nantucket I., *U.S.A.* 148 E10 41 16N 70 5W
Nantwich, *U.K.* 20 D5 53 4N   2 31W
Nanty Glo, *U.S.A.* 150 F6 40 28N 78 50W
Nanuku Passage, *Fiji* .... 133 A3 16 45 S 179 15W
Nanuque, *Brazil* .... 171 E3 17 50 S 40 21W
Nanusa, Kepulauan, *Indonesia* 79 D7   4 45N 127 1 E
Nanutarra Roadhouse, *Australia* 124 D2 22 32 S 115 30 E
Nanxi, *China* .... 76 C5 28 54N 104 59 E
Nanxiong, *China* .... 74 H7 33 11N 112 30 E
Nanyang, *China* .... 77 E10 5 1N 119 0 E
Nanyi Hu, *China* .... 77 B12 31 5N 119 0 E
Nanyuki, *Kenya* .... 118 B4   0 2N 37 4 E
Nanzhang, *China* .... 77 B8 31 45N 111 50 E
Nao, C. de la, *Spain* .... 41 G5 38 44N   0 14 E
Naococane, L., *Canada* 141 B5 52 50N 70 45W
Naogaon, *Bangla.* .... 90 C2 24 52N 88 44 E
Naoné, *Vanuatu* .... 133 E6 15 0 S 168 8 E
Náousa, *Imathía, Greece* .... 50 F6 40 42N   2 2 E
Náousa, *Kikládhes, Greece* ... 49 D7   7N 25 14 E
Naozhou Dao, *China* .... 76 G7 20 55N 110 54 E
Napa, *U.S.A.* 160 G4 38 18N 122 17W
Napa →, *U.S.A.* 160 G4 38 10N 122 19W
Napakiak, *U.S.A.* 144 F7 60 42N 161 57W
Napamute, *U.S.A.* 144 F8 61 33N 158 42W
Napanee, *Canada* 150 B8 44 15N 77 0W
Napanoch, *U.S.A.* 151 E10 41 44N 74 22W
Napanwainami, *Indonesia* ... 83 B5   3 3 S 135 45 E
Napaskiak, *U.S.A.* 144 F7 60 43N 161 55W

Nape, *Laos* .... 86 C5 18 18N 105 6 E
Nape Pass = Keo Neua, Deo, *Vietnam* 86 C5 18 23N 105 10 E
Naperville, *U.S.A.* 157 C8 41 46N 88 9W
Napf, *Switz.* .... 32 B5 47 1N   7 56 E
Napier, *N.Z.* .... 130 F5 39 30 S 176 56 E
Napier Broome B., *Australia* .. 124 B4 14 2 S 126 37 E
Napier Pen., *Australia* ...... 126 A2 12 4 S 135 43 E
Napierville, *Canada* 151 A11 45 11N 73 25W
Naples = Nápoli, *Italy* .... 47 B7 40 50N 14 15 E
Naples, *U.S.A.* 153 J8 26 8N 81 48W
Naples Capodichino ✈ (NAP), *Italy* 47 B7 40 53N 14 16 E
Naples Park, *U.S.A.* 153 J8 26 17N 81 46W
Napo, *China* .... 76 F5 23 20N 105 50 E
Napo □, *Ecuador* .... 168 D2   0 30 S 77 0W
Napo →, *Peru* .... 168 D3   3 20 S 72 40W
Napoleon, *N. Dak., U.S.A.* ... 154 B5 46 30N 99 46W
Napoleon, *Ohio, U.S.A.* 157 C12 41 23N 84 8W
Napoleon's Tomb, *St. Helena* . 9 b   15 56 S   5 42W
Nápoli, *Italy* .... 47 B7 40 50N 14 15 E
Nápoli, G. di, *Italy* .... 47 B7 40 43N 14 10 E
Napopo, *Dem. Rep. of the Congo* 118 B2   4 15N 28 0 E
Nappanee, *U.S.A.* 157 C11 41 27N 86 0W
Naqādah, *Egypt* .... 106 B3 25 53N 32 42 E
Naqb, Ra's an, *Jordan* ...... 103 F4 30 0N 35 29 E
Naqqāsh, *Iran* .... 97 C6 35 40N 49 6 E
Nara, *Japan* .... 73 C7 34 40N 135 49 E
Nara, *Mali* 112 B3 15 10N   7 20W
Nara □, *Japan* .... 73 C8 34 30N 136 0 E
Nara Canal, *Pakistan* .... 92 G3 24 30N 69 20 E
Nara Visa, *U.S.A.* 155 H3 35 37N 103 6W
Naracoorte, *Australia* .... 128 D4 36 58 S 140 45 E
Naradhan, *Australia* .... 129 B7 33 34 S 146 17 E
Naraini, *India* .... 93 G9 25 11N 80 29 E
Narasannapeta, *India* .... 94 E7 18 25N 84 3 E
Narasapur, *India* .... 95 F5 16 26N 81 40 E
Narasaropet, *India* .... 95 F5 16 14N 80 4 E
Narathiwat, *Thailand* .... 87 J3   6 30N 101 48 E
Narayanapatnam, *India* ...... 94 E6 18 53N 83 10 E
Narayanganj, *Bangla.* .... 90 D3 23 40N 90 33 E
Narayanpet, *India* .... 94 F3 16 45N 77 30 E
Narberth, *U.K.* 21 F3 51 47N   4 44W
Narbonne, *France* .... 28 E7 43 11N   3 0 E
Narborough, I. = Fernandina, I., *Ecuador* 172 a   0 25 S 91 30W
Narbuvollen, *Norway* .... 18 B8 62 21N 11 27 E
Narcea →, *Spain* 42 B4 43 33N   6 44W
Narcondam I., *India* .... 95 H12 13 20N 94 16 E
Nardín, *Iran* .... 97 B7 37 3N 55 59 E
Nardò, *Italy* .... 47 B11 40 11N 18 2 E
Narembeen, *Australia* .... 125 F2 32 7 S 118 24 E
Narendranagar, *India* .... 92 D8 30 10N 78 18 E
Nares Str., *Arctic* 10 B3 80 0N 70 0W
Naretha, *Australia* .... 125 F3 31 0 S 124 45 E
Narew →, *Poland* .... 55 F7 52 26N 20 41 E
Nari →, *Pakistan* .... 92 E2 28 0N 67 40 E
Narin, *Afghan.* .... 91 A3 36 5N 69 0 E
Narindra, Helodranon' i, *Madag.* 117 A8 14 55 S 47 30 E
Nariño □, *Colombia* 168 C2   1 30N 78 0W
Narita, *Japan* .... 73 B12 35 47N 140 19 E
Narita, Tokyo ✈ (NRT), *Japan* . 73 B12 35 46N 140 23 E
Nariva Swamp, *Trin. & Tob.* .. 169 F9 10 26N 61 4W
Närke, *Sweden* .... 16 E8 59 10N 15 0 E
Narmada →, *India* .... 92 J5 21 38N 72 36 E
Narman, *Turkey* .... 101 B9 40 26N 41 57 E
Narmland, *Sweden* .... 15 F15 60 0N 13 30 E
Narnaul, *India* .... 92 E7 28 5N 76 11 E
Narni, *Italy* .... 45 F9 42 30N 12 31 E
Naro, *Ghana* .... 112 C4 10 22N 22 0 E
Naro Fominsk, *Russia* .... 58 E9 55 23N 36 43 E
Narodnaya, *Russia* .... 56 A10 65 5N 59 58 E
Narok, *Kenya* .... 118 C4   1 55 S 35 52 E
Narón, *Spain* 42 B2 43 32N   8 9W
Narooma, *Australia* .... 129 D9 36 14 S 150 4 E
Narowal, *Pakistan* .... 91 B4 32 6N 74 52 E
Narra, *Phil.* .... 81 G2   9 18N 118 28 E
Narrabri, *Australia* .... 127 E4 30 19 S 149 46 E
Narran →, *Australia* .... 127 D4 28 37 S 148 12 E
Narrandera, *Australia* ...... 129 C7 34 42 S 146 31 E
Narrogin, *Australia* .... 125 F2 32 58 S 117 14 E
Narromine, *Australia* .... 129 B8 32 12 S 148 12 E
Narrow Hills Prov. Park △, *Canada* 143 C8 54 0N 104 37W
Narsampet, *India* .... 94 F4 17 57N 79 58 E
Narsaq, *Greenland* 10 E6 60 57N 46 1W
Narsimhapur, *India* .... 93 H8 22 54N 79 14 E
Narsinghgarh, *India* .... 92 H7 23 45N 76 40 E
Narsinghpur, *India* .... 94 D7 20 28N 85 5 E
Narsipatnam, *India* .... 94 F6 17 40N 82 37 E
Nartes, L. e., *Albania* .... 50 F3 40 32N 19 25 E
Nartkala, *Russia* .... 61 J6 43 33N 43 51 E
Naruto, *Kantō, Japan* .... 72 C6 34 11N 134 37 E
Narutō, *Shikoku, Japan* ..... 73 B12 35 36N 140 25 E
Naruto-Kaikyō, *Japan* .... 72 C6 34 14N 134 39 E
Narva, *Estonia* .... 58 C5 59 23N 28 12 E
Narva →, *Russia* .... 15 G22 59 27N 28 2 E
Narva Bay, *Estonia* .... 15 G19 59 35N 27 35 E
Narvacan, *Phil.* .... 80 C3 17 25N 120 28 E
Narvik, *Norway* .... 14 B17 68 28N 17 26 E
Narvskoye Vdkhr., *Russia* ... 58 C5 59 18N 28 14 E
Narwana, *India* .... 92 E7 29 39N 76 6 E
Narwinbi Park Narodowy △, *Poland* 55 F9 52 5N 22 53 E
Naryan-Mar, *Russia* .... 56 A9 67 42N 53 12 E
Narym, *Russia* .... 66 D9 59 0N 81 30 E
Naryn, *Kyrgyzstan* .... 65 C7 41 26N 75 58 E
Naryn □, *Uzbekistan* .... 65 C5 40 52N 71 36 E
Nasa, *Norway* .... 14 C16 66 29N 15 23 E
Nasau, *Fiji* .... 133 A2 17 19 S 179 27 E
Năsăud, *Romania* .... 53 C9 47 19N 24 29 E
Nasawa, *Vanuatu* .... 133 E6 15 12 S 168 9 E
Naseby, *N.Z.* .... 131 F5 45 1 S 170 10 E
Naselle, *U.S.A.* 160 D3 46 22N 123 49W
Naser, Buheirat en, *Egypt* ... 106 C3 23 0N 32 30 E
Nashua, *Iowa, U.S.A.* 156 B4 42 57N 92 32W
Nashua, *Mont., U.S.A.* 158 B10 48 8N 106 22W
Nashua, *N.H., U.S.A.* 151 D13 42 45N 71 28W
Nashville, *Ark., U.S.A.* 155 J8 33 57N 93 51W
Nashville, *Ga., U.S.A.* 152 D6 31 12N 83 15W
Nashville, *Ill., U.S.A.* 156 F7 38 21N 89 23W
Nashville, *Ind., U.S.A.* 157 B10 42 36N 85 5W
Nashville, *Mich., U.S.A.* 157 B11 42 36N 85 5W
Nashville, *Tenn., U.S.A.* 149 G2 36 10N 86 47W
Našice, *Croatia* .... 52 E3 45 32N 18 4 E
Nasielsk, *Poland* .... 55 F7 52 35N 20 50 E
Nasik, *India* .... 94 E1 19 58N 73 50 E
Nasipit, *Phil.* .... 81 G5   8 57N 125 19 E
Nasir, *Sudan* .... 107 F3   8 35N 33 6 E
Nasirabad = Mymensingh, *Bangla.* 90 C3 24 45N 90 24 E
Nasirabad, *India* .... 92 F6 26 15N 74 45 E
Nasirabad, *Pakistan* .... 92 E3 28 23N 68 25 E
Naskaupi →, *Canada* 141 B7 53 47N 60 51W
Naso, *Italy* .... 47 D7 38 7N 14 47 E
Naso Pt., *Phil.* .... 81 F3 10 25N 121 57 E
Naşrābād, *Iran* .... 97 C6 34 8N 51 26 E
Naşriān-e Pā'īn, *Iran* .... 96 C5 32 52N 46 52 E
Nass →, *Canada* 142 C3 55 0N 129 40W
Nassarawa, *Nigeria* .... 113 D6   8 32N   7 41 E
Nassau, *Bahamas* .... 9 b   25 5N 77 20W
Nassau, *U.S.A.* 151 D11 42 31N 73 37W
Nassau, B., *Chile* .... 176 E3 55 20 S 68 0W

Nassau International ✈ (NAS), *Bahamas* 9 b   25 3N 77 28W
Nasser, L. = Naser, Buheirat en, *Egypt* 106 C3 23 0N 32 30 E
Nasser City = Kôm Ombo, *Egypt* 106 C3 24 25N 32 52 E
Nassereith, *Austria* .... 33 B11 47 19N 10 50 E
Nassian, *Ivory C.* 112 D4   8 28N   3 28W
Nässjö, *Sweden* .... 17 G8 57 39N 14 42 E
Nastapoka →, *Canada* 140 A4 56 55N 76 33W
Nastapoka, Is., *Canada* 140 A4 56 55N 76 50W
Nasugbu, *Phil.* .... 80 D3 14 5N 120 38 E
Näsum, *Sweden* .... 17 H8 56 10N 14 29 E
Näsviken, *Sweden* .... 16 C10 61 46N 16 52 E
Nata, *Botswana* .... 116 C4 20 12 S 26 12 E
Nata →, *Botswana* .... 116 C4 20 14 S 26 10 E
Natagaima, *Colombia* 168 C2   3 37N 75 6W
Natal, *Brazil* .... 170 C4   5 47 S 35 13W
Natal, *Indonesia* .... 84 B1   0 35N 99 7 E
Natal Drakensberg Park △, *S. Africa* 52 F5 14 56N 20 49 E
Natanz, *Iran* .... 97 C6 33 30N 51 55 E
Natashquan, *Canada* 141 B7 50 14N 61 46W
Natashquan →, *Canada* 141 B7 50 7N 61 50W
Natchez, *U.S.A.* 155 K9 31 34N 91 24W
Natchitoches, *U.S.A.* 155 K8 31 46N 93 5W
Naters, *Switz.* .... 32 D5 46 19N   7 58 E
Natewa B., *Fiji* .... 133 A2 16 35 S 179 40 E
Nathalia, *Australia* .... 129 D6   3 1 S 145 13 E
Nathdwara, *India* .... 92 G5 24 55N 73 50 E
Nati, Pta., *Spain* .... 38 A4 40 3N   3 50 E
Natimuk, *Australia* .... 128 D5 36 42 S 142 0 E
Nation →, *Canada* 142 B4 55 30N 123 32W
National Capital District □, *Papua N. G.* 132 E4   9 25 S 147 10 E
National City, *U.S.A.* 161 N9 32 41N 117 6W
National West Coast Tourist Recr. Area △, *Namibia* 116 C1 21 53 S 14 14 E
Natitingou, *Benin* .... 113 C5 10 20N   1 26 E
Natividad, I., *Mexico* 162 B1 27 50N 115 10W
Natividade, *Brazil* .... 171 D2 11 43 S 47 47W
Natkyizin, *Burma* .... 86 E1 14 57N 97 59 E
Natmauk, *Burma* .... 90 E5 20 20N 95 24 E
Natogyi, *Burma* .... 90 E5 21 25N 95 39 E
Natonin, *Phil.* .... 80 C3 17 6N 121 18 E
Natron, L., *Tanzania* .... 118 C4   2 20 S 36 0 E
Natrona Heights, *U.S.A.* 150 F5 40 37N 79 44W
Natrûn, W. el →, *Egypt* ..... 106 H7 30 25N 30 13 E
Nattai Nat. Park △, *Australia* . 129 C3 34 12 S 150 22 E
Nättraby, *Sweden* .... 17 H9 56 13N 15 31 E
Natukanaoka Pan, *Namibia* .. 116 B2 18 40 S 15 45 E
Natuna Besar, Kepulauan, *Indonesia* 84 B3   4 0N 108 15 E
Natuna Is. = Natuna Besar, Kepulauan, *Indonesia* 84 B3   4 0N 108 15 E
Natuna Selatan, Kepulauan, *Indonesia* 85 B3   2 45N 109 0 E
Natural Bridge, *U.S.A.* 151 B9 44 5N 75 30W
Natural Bridges Nat. Monument △, *U.S.A.* 159 H8 37 36N 110 1W
Naturaliste, C., *Australia* .... 127 G4 40 50 S 148 15 E
Nau, *Tajikistan* .... 65 C4 40 9N 69 22 E
Nau Qala, *Afghan.* .... 92 B3 34 5N 68 5 E
Naucelle, *France* .... 28 D6 44 13N   2 20 E
Nauders, *Austria* .... 33 E10 46 54N 10 30 E
Nauen, *Germany* .... 30 C8 52 36N 12 52 E
Naugatuck, *U.S.A.* 151 E11 41 30N 73 3W
Naujaat = Repulse Bay, *Canada* 139 B11 66 30N 86 30W
Naujan, *Phil.* .... 80 E3 13 20N 121 18 E
Naujoji Akmenė, *Lithuania* .. 54 B9 56 19N 22 54 E
Naulila, *Angola* .... 115 F2 17 13 S 14 39 E
Naumburg, *Germany* .... 30 D7 51 9N 11 47 E
Naupada, *India* .... 94 E7 18 34N 84 18 E
Na'ūr at Tunayb, *Jordan* .... 103 D4 31 48N 35 57 E
Nauru ■, *Pac. Oc.* .... 134 H8   1 0 S 166 0 E
Naushahra = Nowshera, *Pakistan* 91 B3 34 0N 72 0 E
Naushahro, *Pakistan* .... 92 F3 26 50N 68 7 E
Naushon I., *U.S.A.* 151 E14 41 29N 70 45W
Naustdal, *Norway* .... 18 C2 61 31N   5 43 E
Naute Recr. Resort △, *Namibia* 116 D2 26 53 S 17 57 E
Nautla, *Mexico* 163 C5 20 20N 96 50W
Nauvoo, *U.S.A.* 156 D5 40 33N 91 23W
Nava, *Mexico* 162 B4 28 25N 100 46W
Nava, *Spain* 42 B5 43 21N   5 31W
Nava del Rey, *Spain* 42 D5 41 22N   5 6W
Navadwip, *India* .... 93 H13 23 34N 88 20 E
Navahermosa, *Spain* 43 F6 39 41N   4 28W
Navahrudak, *Belarus* .... 58 F3 53 40N 25 50 E
Navai, *Fiji* .... 133 A1 17 37 S 177 57 E
Navajo Reservoir, *U.S.A.* 159 H10 36 48N 107 36W
Naval, *Phil.* .... 81 F5 11 34N 124 23 E
Navalagund, *India* .... 95 G2 15 34N 75 22 E
Navalmoral de la Mata, *Spain* 42 F5 39 52N   5 33W
Navalvillar de Pela, *Spain* ... 43 F5 39 9N   5 24W
Navan = An Uaimh, *Ireland* .. 23 C5 53 39N   6 41W
Navanagar = Jamnagar, *India* . 92 H4 22 30N 70 6 E
Navapolatsk, *Belarus* .... 58 E5 55 32N 28 37 E
Navarino, I., *Chile* .... 176 E3 55 0 S 67 40W
Navarra □, *Spain* 40 C3 42 40N   1 40W
Navarre, *Fla., U.S.A.* 153 E3 30 24N 86 52W
Navarre, *Ohio, U.S.A.* 150 F3 40 43N 81 31W
Navarro →, *U.S.A.* 160 F3 39 11N 123 45W
Navas de San Juan, *Spain* ... 43 G7 38 30N   3 19W
Navasota, *U.S.A.* 155 K6 30 23N 96 5W
Navassa I., *W. Indies* 165 C5 18 30N 75 0W
Nävekvarn, *Sweden* .... 17 F10 58 38N 16 47 E
Navia, *Spain* 42 B4 43 35N   6 42W
Navia →, *Spain* 42 B4 43 15N   6 50W
Navia de Suarna, *Spain* 42 C3 42 58N   7 3W
Navibandar, *India* .... 92 J3 21 26N 69 48 E
Navidad, *Chile* .... 174 C1 33 57 S 71 50W
Naviraí, *Brazil* .... 175 A5 23 8 S 54 13W
Naviti, *Fiji* .... 133 A1 17 7 S 177 15 E
Navlakhi, *India* .... 92 H4 22 58N 70 28 E
Navlya, *Russia* .... 59 F8 52 53N 34 30 E
Năvodari, *Romania* .... 53 F13 44 19N 28 36 E
Navoi = Nawoiy, *Uzbekistan* . 65 C2 40 9N 65 22 E
Navojoa, *Mexico* 162 B3 27 0N 109 30W
Navolato, *Mexico* 162 C3 24 47N 107 42W
Návpaktos, *Greece* .... 48 C3 38 24N 21 50 E
Návplion, *Greece* .... 48 D4 37 33N 22 50 E
Navrongo, *Ghana* 113 C4 10 51N   1 3W
Navsari, *India* .... 92 J5 20 57N 72 59 E
Nawa Kot, *Pakistan* .... 92 E4 28 21N 71 24 E
Nawab Khan, *Pakistan* ...... 92 D3 30 17N 69 12 E
Nawabganj, *Bangla.* .... 90 C2 24 35N 88 14 E
Nawabganj, Ut. P., *India* .... 93 F9 26 56N 81 14 E
Nawabganj, Ut. P., *India* .... 93 E8 28 32N 79 40 E
Nawabshah, *Pakistan* .... 91 D3 26 15N 68 25 E
Nawada, *India* .... 93 G11 24 50N 85 33 E
Nawakot, *Nepal* .... 93 F11 27 55N 85 10 E
Nawalgarh, *India* .... 92 F6 27 50N 75 15 E
Nawanshahr, *India* .... 93 C6 32 33N 74 48 E
Nawapara, *India* .... 94 D6 20 46N 82 33 E
Nawar, Dasht-i-, *Afghan.* .... 91 B2 33 52N 68 0 E
Nawāṣif, Ḥarrat, *Si. Arabia* .. 88 B3 21 20N 42 0 E
Nawi, *Sudan* .... 106 D3 18 32N 30 50 E
Nawng Hpa, *Burma* .... 90 D7 22 30N 98 30 E
Nawoiy, *Uzbekistan* .... 65 C2 40 9N 65 22 E
Naws̨, Ra's, *Oman* .... 99 C6 17 15N 55 10 E

Naxçıvan, *Azerbaijan* .... **101 C11** 39 12N 45 15 E
Naxçıvan □, *Azerbaijan* .... **101 C11** 39 25N 45 26 E
Náxos, *Greece* .... **49 D7** 37 8N 25 25 E
Naxxar, *Malta* .... **38 F7** 35 55N 14 27 E
Nay, *France* **28 E3** 43 10N 0 18W
Nay, Mui, *Vietnam* .... **78 B3** 12 55N 109 23 E
Nãy Band, *Büshehr, Iran* .... **97 E7** 27 20N 52 40 E
Nãy Band, *Khorãsãn, Iran* .... **97 C8** 32 20N 57 34 E
Naya →, *Colombia* **168 C2** 3 13N 77 22W
Nayagarh, *India* .... **94 D7** 20 8N 85 6 E
Nayakhan, *Russia* .... **67 C16** 61 56N 159 0 E
Nayarit □, *Mexico* **162 C4** 22 0N 105 0W
Nayau, *Fiji* .... **133 B2** 18 6S 178 10 E
Nayé, *Senegal* **112 C2** 14 28N 12 12W
Nayong, *China* .... **76 D5** 26 50N 105 20 E
Nayoro, *Japan* .... **70 B11** 44 21N 142 28 E
Nayudupeta, *India* .... **95 H4** 13 54N 79 54 E
Nayyãl, W. →, *Si. Arabia* .... **96 D3** 28 35N 39 4 E
Nazaré, *Bahia, Brazil* **171 D4** 13 2S 39 0W
Nazaré, *Pará, Brazil* **173 B7** 6 2S 52 29W
Nazaré, *Tocantins, Brazil* ...... **170 C2** 6 23 S 47 40W
Nazaré, *Portugal* **43 F1** 39 36N 9 4W
Nazareth = Nazerat, *Israel* ..... **103 C4** 32 42N 35 17 E
Nazareth, *U.S.A.* **151 F9** 40 44N 75 19W
Nazas, *Mexico* **162 B4** 25 10N 104 6W
Nazas →, *Mexico* **162 B4** 25 35N 103 25W
Nazca, *Peru* .... **172 C3** 14 50 S 74 57W
Naze, The, *U.K.* .... **21 F9** 51 53N 1 18 E
Nazerat, *Israel* .... **103 C4** 32 42N 35 17 E
Nãzik, *Iran* .... **101 C11** 39 1N 45 4 E
Nazilli, *Turkey* .... **49 D10** 37 55N 28 15 E
Nazir Hat, *Bangla.* .... **90 D3** 22 35N 91 49 E
Nazko, *Canada* **142 C4** 53 1N 123 37W
Nazko →, *Canada* **142 C4** 53 7N 123 34W
Nazret, *Ethiopia* .... **107 F4** 8 32N 39 22 E
Nazwa, *Oman* .... **99 B7** 22 56N 57 32 E
Ncama, *Eq. Guin.* .... **114 B2** 1 55N 10 56 E
Nchanga, *Zambia* .... **119 E2** 12 30 S 27 49 E
Ncheu, *Malawi* .... **119 E3** 14 50 S 34 47 E
Ndala, *Tanzania* .... **118 C3** 4 45 S 33 15 E
Ndalatando, *Angola* .... **115 D2** 9 12 S 14 48 E
Ndali, *Benin* .... **113 D5** 9 50N 2 46 E
Ndareda, *Tanzania* .... **118 C4** 4 12 S 35 30 E
Ndélé, *C.A.R.* .... **114 A4** 8 25N 20 36 E
Ndendé, *Gabon* .... **114 C2** 2 22 S 11 23 E
Ndiael, Réserve de Faune du ⌂,
   Senegal **112 B1** 16 15N 16 0W
Ndikinimeki, *Cameroon* .... **113 E7** 4 46N 10 50 E
Ndindi, *Gabon* .... **114 C2** 3 46 S 11 9 E
N'Dioum, *Senegal* **112 B2** 16 31N 14 39W
Ndjamena, *Chad* .... **109 F2** 12 10N 14 59 E
Ndjolé, *Gabon* .... **114 C2** 0 10 S 10 45 E
Ndogo, Lagune, *Gabon* .... **114 C2** 2 35 S 10 0 E
Ndoki-Nouabalé, Réserve de Faune
   de ⌂, *Congo* .... **114 B3** 2 32N 16 32 E
Ndola, *Zambia* .... **119 E2** 13 0 S 28 34 E
Ndoto Mts., *Kenya* .... **118 B4** 2 0N 37 0 E
Ndoua, C., *N. Cal.* .... **133 V20** 22 24 S 166 56 E
Ndouba, *Congo* .... **114 C2** 0 9 S 14 4 E
Nduguti, *Tanzania* .... **118 C3** 4 18 S 34 41 E
Ndumu Game Reserve ⌂, *S. Africa* **117 D5** 26 52 S 32 15 E
Nea →, *Norway* .... **18 A8** 63 15N 11 0 E
Néa Alikarnassós, *Greece* .... **49 F7** 35 18N 25 13 E
Néa Ankhíalos, *Greece* .... **48 B4** 39 16N 22 49 E
Néa Epídhavros, *Greece* .... **48 D5** 37 40N 23 7 E
Néa Flippiás, *Greece* .... **48 B2** 39 12N 20 53 E
Néa Ionía, *Greece* .... **48 B4** 39 21N 22 56 E
Néa Kallikrátia, *Greece* .... **50 F7** 40 21N 23 3 E
Néa Mákri, *Greece* .... **48 C5** 38 5N 23 59 E
Néa Moudhaniá, *Greece* .... **50 F7** 40 15N 23 17 E
Néa Péramos, *Attikí, Greece* .... **48 C5** 38 0N 23 26 E
Néa Péramos, *Kaválla, Greece* ... **51 F8** 40 50N 24 18 E
Néa Víssi, *Greece* .... **51 E10** 41 34N 26 33 E
Néa Zíkhna, *Greece* .... **50 E7** 41 2N 23 49 E
Neagari, *Japan* .... **73 A8** 36 26N 136 25 E
Neagh, Lough, *U.K.* **23 B5** 54 37N 6 25W
Neah Bay, *U.S.A.* **160 B2** 48 22N 124 37W
Neale, L., *Australia* .... **124 D5** 24 15 S 130 0 E
Neamati, *India* .... **90 B5** 26 50N 94 20 E
Neamṭ □, *Romania* .... **53 C11** 47 0N 26 20 E
Neápolis, *Kozáni, Greece* .... **50 F5** 40 20N 21 24 E
Neápolis, *Kríti, Greece* .... **39 E6** 35 15N 25 37 E
Neápolis, *Lakonía, Greece* ...... **48 E5** 36 27N 23 8 E
Near Is., *U.S.A.* .... **144 K1** 52 30N 174 0 E
Neath, *U.K.* **21 F4** 51 39N 3 48W
Neath Port Talbot □, *U.K.* **21 F4** 51 42N 3 45W
Neba, Î., *N. Cal.* .... **133 T17** 20 10 S 163 57 E
Nebbou, *Burkina Faso* **113 C4** 11 9N 1 51W
Nebelat el Hagana, *Sudan* **107 E2** 13 33N 6 25W
Nebine Cr. →, *Australia* .... **127 D4** 29 27 S 146 56 E
Nebitdag, *Turkmenistan* .... **57 G9** 39 30N 54 22 E
Nebo, *Australia* .... **126 C4** 21 42 S 148 42 E
Nebolchy, *Russia* .... **56 C7** 59 8N 33 18 E
Nebraska □, *U.S.A.* **154 E5** 41 30N 99 30W
Nebraska City, *U.S.A.* **154 E7** 40 41N 95 52W
Nébrodi, Monti, *Italy* .... **47 E7** 37 54N 14 35 E
Necedah, *U.S.A.* **154 C9** 44 2N 90 4W
Nechako →, *Canada* **142 C4** 53 30N 122 44W
Neches →, *U.S.A.* **155 L8** 29 58N 93 51W
Nechisar Nat. Park △, *Ethiopia* . **107 F4** 5 58N 37 55 E
Neckar →, *Germany* .... **31 F4** 49 27N 8 29 E
Neckartal-Odenwald, Naturpark ⌂,
   Germany .... **31 F5** 49 30N 9 5 E
Necker I., *U.S.A.* **145 G11** 23 35N 164 42W
Necochea, *Argentina* .... **174 D4** 38 30 S 58 50W
Nectar Brook, *Australia* .... **128 B2** 32 43 S 137 57 E
Neda, *Spain* **42 B2** 43 30N 8 9W
Nedalshytta, *Norway* .... **18 B9** 62 59N 12 3 E
Nedelino, *Bulgaria* .... **51 E9** 41 27N 25 3 E
Nedelišće, *Croatia* .... **45 B13** 46 23N 16 22 E
Nédha →, *Greece* .... **48 D3** 37 25N 21 45 E
Nedreberg, *Norway* .... **18 D8** 60 59N 11 41 E
Nedroma, *Algeria* **111 A4** 35 1N 1 45W
Nedstrand, *Norway* .... **18 E2** 59 21N 5 49 E
Needles, *Canada* **142 D5** 49 53N 118 7W
Needles, *U.S.A.* **161 L12** 34 51N 114 37W
Needles, The, *U.K.* **21 G6** 50 39N 1 35W
Needles Pt., *N.Z.* .... **130 C4** 36 3 S 175 25 E
Neely Henry L., *U.S.A.* **152 B3** 33 55N 86 2W
Neembucú □, *Paraguay* .... **174 B4** 27 0 S 58 0W
Neemuch = Nimach, *India* .... **92 G6** 24 30N 74 56 E
Neenah, *U.S.A.* **148 C1** 44 11N 88 28W
Neepawa, *Canada* **143 C9** 50 15N 99 30W
Neeses, *U.S.A.* **152 B8** 33 33N 81 7W
Nefta, *Tunisia* .... **108 B1** 33 53N 7 50 E
Neftah Sidi Boubekeur, *Algeria* . **111 A5** 35 1N 0 4 E
Neftçala, *Azerbaijan* .... **97 B6** 39 19N 49 12 E
Neftegorsk, *Russia* .... **61 H4** 44 25N 39 45 E
Neftekamsk, *Russia* .... **64 C5** 56 6N 54 17 E
Neftekumsk, *Russia* .... **61 H7** 44 46N 44 50 E
Neftenbach, *Switz.* .... **33 A7** 47 32N 8 41 E
Nefyn, *U.K.* **20 E3** 52 56N 4 31W
Négala, *Mali* **112 C3** 12 52N 8 30W
Negapatam = Nagappattinam, *India* **95 J4** 10 46N 79 51 E
Negara, *Indonesia* .... **79 J17** 8 22 S 114 37 E
Negaunee, *U.S.A.* **148 B2** 46 30N 87 36W
Negele, *Ethiopia* .... **107 F4** 5 20N 39 36 E
Negeri Sembilan □, *Malaysia* .... **84 B2** 2 45N 102 10 E
Negev Desert = Hanegev, *Israel* . **103 E4** 30 50N 35 0 E
Negoiul, Vf., *Romania* .... **53 E9** 45 38N 24 35 E
Negombo, *Sri Lanka* .... **95 L4** 7 12N 79 50 E
Negotin, *Serbia, Yug.* .... **50 B6** 44 16N 22 37 E
Negotino, *Macedonia* .... **50 E6** 41 29N 22 7 E

Negra, Peña, *Spain* **42 C4** 42 11N 6 30W
Negra, Pta., *Mauritania* **110 D1** 22 54N 16 18W
Negra, Pta., *Peru* .... **172 B1** 6 6 S 81 10W
Negra Pt., *Phil.* .... **80 B3** 18 40N 120 50 E
Negrais C. = Maudin Sun, *Burma* . **90 G5** 16 0N 94 30 E
Negreşti, *Romania* .... **53 D12** 46 50N 27 30 E
Negreşti-Oaş, *Romania* .... **53 C8** 47 52N 23 26 E
Negril, *Jamaica* .... **164 a** 18 22N 78 20W
Négrine, *Algeria* .... **111 B6** 34 30N 7 30 E
Negro →, *Argentina* .... **176 B4** 41 2 S 62 47W
Negro →, *Bolivia* .... **173 C5** 14 11 S 63 7W
Negro →, *Brazil* .... **169 D6** 3 0 S 60 0W
Negro →, *Uruguay* .... **175 C4** 33 24 S 58 22W
Negros, *Phil.* .... **81 G4** 9 30N 122 40 E
Negros Occidental □, *Phil.* ..... **81 F4** 10 0N 122 55 E
Negros Oriental □, *Phil.* .... **81 G4** 9 45N 123 0 E
Negru Vodă, *Romania* .... **53 G13** 43 47N 28 21 E
Neguac, *Canada* **141 C6** 47 15N 65 5W
Nehalem →, *U.S.A.* **160 E3** 45 40N 123 56W
Nehãvand, *Iran* .... **97 C6** 35 56N 49 31 E
Nehbandãn, *Iran* .... **97 D9** 31 35N 60 5 E
Nehoiu, *Romania* .... **53 E11** 45 24N 26 20 E
Nei Monggol Zizhiqu □, *China* ... **74 D7** 42 0N 112 0 E
Neiafu, *Tonga* .... **133 P14** 18 39 S 173 59W
Neiges, Piton des, *Réunion* ..... **121 c** 21 5 S 55 29 E
Neijiang, *China* .... **76 C5** 29 35N 104 55 E
Neilingding Dao, *China* .... **69 G10** 22 25N 113 48 E
Neill I., *India* .... **95 J11** 11 50N 93 3 E
Neillsville, *U.S.A.* **154 C9** 44 34N 90 36W
Neilton, *U.S.A.* **158 C2** 47 25N 123 53W
Neiqiu, *China* .... **74 F8** 37 15N 114 30 E
Neisse = Nysa →, *Europe* .... **30 C10** 52 4N 14 46 E
Neiva, *Colombia* **168 C2** 2 56N 75 18W
Neixiang, *China* .... **74 H6** 33 10N 111 52 E
Nejanilini L., *Canada* **143 B9** 59 33N 97 48W
Nejd = Najd, *Si. Arabia* .... **88 C3** 26 30N 42 0 E
Nejo, *Ethiopia* .... **107 F4** 9 30N 35 28 E
Nekã, *Iran* .... **97 B7** 36 39N 53 19 E
Nekemte, *Ethiopia* .... **107 F4** 9 4N 36 30 E
Nêkheb, *Egypt* .... **106 B3** 25 10N 32 48 E
Neksø, *Denmark* .... **17 J9** 55 4N 15 8 E
Nelamangala, *India* .... **95 H3** 13 6N 77 24 E
Nelas, *Portugal* **42 E3** 40 32N 7 52W
Nelaug, *Norway* .... **18 F5** 58 39N 8 40 E
Nelia, *Australia* .... **126 C3** 20 39 S 142 12 E
Nelidovo, *Russia* .... **56 D7** 56 13N 32 49 E
Neligh, *U.S.A.* **154 D5** 42 8N 98 2W
Nelkan, *Russia* .... **67 D14** 57 40N 136 4 E
Nellikuppam, *India* .... **95 J4** 11 46N 79 43 E
Nellore, *India* .... **95 G4** 14 27N 79 59 E
Nelson, *Canada* **142 D5** 49 30N 117 20W
Nelson, *N.Z.* .... **131 B8** 41 18 S 173 16 E
Nelson, *U.K.* **20 D5** 53 50N 2 13W
Nelson, *Ariz., U.S.A.* **159 J7** 35 31N 113 19W
Nelson, *Nev., U.S.A.* **161 K12** 35 42N 114 50W
Nelson □, *N.Z.* .... **131 B8** 41 20 S 173 20 E
Nelson →, *Canada* **143 C9** 54 33N 98 2W
Nelson, C., *Australia* .... **128 E4** 38 26 S 141 32 E
Nelson, C., *Papua N. G.* .... **132 E5** 9 0 S 149 20 E
Nelson, Estrecho, *Chile* .... **176 D2** 51 30 S 75 0W
Nelson Bay, *Australia* .... **129 B10** 32 43 S 152 9 E
Nelson Forks, *Canada* **142 B4** 59 30N 124 0W
Nelson House, *Canada* **143 B9** 55 47N 98 51W
Nelson L., *Canada* **143 B8** 55 48N 100 7W
Nelson Lakes Nat. Park △, *N.Z.* . **131 B7** 41 55 S 172 44 E
Nelspoort, *S. Africa* .... **116 E3** 32 7 S 23 0 E
Nelspruit, *S. Africa* .... **117 D5** 25 29 S 30 59 E
Néma, *Mauritania* **112 B3** 16 40N 7 15W
Neman = Nemunas →, *Lithuania* ... **15 J19** 55 25N 21 10 E
Neman, *Russia* .... **15 J20** 55 2N 22 2 E
Nembrala, *Indonesia* .... **82 D2** 10 53 S 122 50 E
Neméa, *Greece* .... **48 D4** 37 49N 22 40 E
Nemeiben L., *Canada* **143 B7** 55 20N 105 20W
Nemĕrçkë, Mal., *Albania* .... **50 F4** 40 15N 20 15 E
Nemira, Vf., *Romania* .... **53 D11** 46 17N 26 19 E
Némiscau, *Canada* **140 B4** 51 18N 76 54W
Némiscau, L., *Canada* **140 B4** 51 25N 76 40W
Nemours = Ghazaouet, *Algeria* ... **111 A4** 35 8N 1 50W
Nemours, *France* .... **27 D9** 48 16N 2 40 E
Nemšová, *Slovak Rep.* .... **35 C11** 48 58N 18 10 E
Nemunas →, *Lithuania* .... **15 J19** 55 25N 21 10 E
Nemuro, *Japan* .... **70 C12** 43 20N 145 35 E
Nemuro-Kaikyō, *Japan* .... **70 C12** 43 30N 145 30 E
Nen Jiang →, *China* .... **75 B13** 45 28N 124 30 E
Nenagh, *Ireland* **23 D3** 52 52N 8 11W
Nenana, *U.S.A.* **144 D10** 64 34N 149 5W
Nenasi, *Malaysia* .... **87 L4** 3 9N 103 23 E
Nene →, *U.K.* .... **21 E8** 52 49N 0 11 E
Nénita, *Greece* .... **49 C8** 38 14N 26 6 E
Nenjiang, *China* .... **69 B7** 49 10N 125 10 E
Neno, *Malawi* .... **119 F3** 15 25 S 34 40 E
Nenzing, *Austria* .... **33 B9** 47 11N 9 42 E
Neodesha, *U.S.A.* **155 G7** 37 25N 95 41W
Neoga, *U.S.A.* **157 E8** 39 19N 88 27W
Neokhórion, Aitolía kai Akarnanía,
   Greece .... **48 C3** 38 25N 21 17 E
Neokhórion, *Árta, Greece* .... **48 B2** 39 4N 21 0 E
Néon Karlovásion, *Greece* .... **49 D8** 37 45N 26 42 E
Néon Petrítsi, *Greece* .... **50 E7** 41 16N 23 15 E
Neópolis, *Brazil* .... **170 D4** 10 18 S 36 35W
Neosho, *U.S.A.* **155 G7** 36 52N 94 22W
Neosho →, *U.S.A.* **155 H7** 36 48N 95 18W
Nepal ■, *Asia* .... **93 F11** 28 0N 84 30 E
Nepalganj, *Nepal* .... **93 E9** 28 5N 81 40 E
Nepalganj Road, *India* .... **93 E9** 28 1N 81 41 E
Nepean B., *Australia* .... **128 C2** 35 42 S 137 37 E
Nephi, *U.S.A.* **158 G8** 39 43N 111 50W
Nephin, *Ireland* **23 B2** 54 1N 9 22W
Nepi, *Italy* .... **45 F9** 42 14N 12 21 E
Nepomuk, *Czech Rep.* .... **34 B6** 49 29N 13 35 E
Neptune, *U.S.A.* **151 F10** 40 13N 74 2W
Neptune Is., *Australia* .... **128 C2** 35 17 S 136 10 E
Nera →, *Italy* .... **45 F9** 42 26N 12 24 E
Nera →, *Romania* .... **52 F6** 44 48N 21 25 E
Nérac, *France* .... **28 D4** 44 8N 0 21 E
Nerang, *Australia* .... **127 D5** 27 58 S 153 20 E
Nerastro, Sarīr, *Libya* .... **108 D4** 24 20N 20 37 E
Neratovice, *Czech Rep.* .... **34 A7** 50 16N 14 31 E
Nerchinsk, *Russia* .... **67 D12** 52 0N 116 39 E
Nereju, *Romania* .... **53 E11** 45 43N 26 43 E
Nerekhta, *Russia* .... **58 D11** 57 26N 40 38 E
Néret, L., *Canada* **141 B5** 54 45N 70 44W
Neretvanski Kanal, *Croatia* ..... **45 E14** 43 7N 17 10 E
Neringa, *Lithuania* .... **15 J19** 55 20N 21 5 E
Neris →, *Lithuania* .... **15 J21** 55 8N 24 16 E
Nerja, *Spain* **43 J7** 36 43N 3 55W
Nerl →, *Russia* .... **58 D11** 56 11N 40 34 E
Nerpio, *Spain* **43 G2** 38 11N 2 16W
Nerva, *Spain* **43 H4** 37 42N 6 30W
Nervi, *Italy* .... **40 D6** 44 27N 9 2 E
Neryungri, *Russia* .... **67 D13** 57 38N 124 28 E
Nes, *Iceland* **11 B9** 65 53N 17 24W
Nes, *Norway* .... **18 D6** 60 34N 9 59 E
Nesbyen, *Norway* .... **18 D6** 60 34N 9 6 E
Nescopeck, *U.S.A.* **151 E8** 41 3N 76 12W
Nesebŭr, *Bulgaria* .... **51 D11** 42 41N 27 46 E
Neset, *Norway* .... **18 C7** 61 53N 10 7 E
Nesflaten, *Norway* .... **18 E3** 59 38N 6 48 E
Neskaupstaður, *Iceland* **11 B13** 65 9N 13 42W
Nesland, *Norway* .... **18 E2** 59 31N 7 59 E
Neslandsvatn, *Norway* .... **18 F6** 58 57N 9 10 E
Nesodtangen, *Norway* .... **18 E7** 59 48N 10 40 E
Ness, L., *U.K.* **22 D4** 57 15N 4 32W
Ness City, *U.S.A.* **154 F5** 38 27N 99 54W

Nesslau, *Switz.* .... **33 B8** 47 14N 9 13 E
Nesterov, *Ukraine* .... **59 G2** 50 4N 23 58 E
Nestórion, *Greece* .... **50 F5** 40 24N 21 5 E
Néstos →, *Greece* .... **51 F8** 38 22N 20 56 E
Nesttun, *Norway* .... **18 D2** 60 19N 5 20 E
Nesvady, *Slovak Rep.* .... **35 D11** 47 56N 18 7 E
Nesvizh = Nyasvizh, *Belarus* .... **59 F4** 53 14N 26 38 E
Netanya, *Israel* .... **103 C3** 32 20N 34 51 E
Netarhat, *India* .... **93 H11** 23 29N 84 16 E
Nete →, *Belgium* .... **24 C4** 51 7N 4 14 E
Netherdale, *Australia* .... **126 K6** 21 10 S 148 33 E
Netherlands ■, *Europe* .... **24 C5** 52 0N 5 30 E
Netherlands Antilles ☑, *W. Indies* **168 A4** 12 15N 69 0W
Netherlands Guiana = Suriname ■,
   S. Amer. **169 C6** 4 0N 56 0W
Neto →, *Italy* .... **47 C10** 39 12N 17 9 E
Netrakona, *Bangla.* .... **90 C3** 24 53N 90 47 E
Netrang, *India* .... **92 J5** 21 39N 73 21 E
Netstal, *Switz.* .... **33 B8** 47 3N 9 3 E
Nettancourt, *France* .... **27 D11** 48 51N 4 57 E
Nettetal, *Germany* .... **30 D2** 51 19N 6 12 E
Nettilling L., *Canada* **139 B12** 66 30N 71 0W
Nettuno, *Italy* .... **46 A5** 41 27N 12 39 E
Netzahualcoyotl, Presa, *Mexico* . **163 D6** 17 10N 93 30W
Neu-Isenburg, *Germany* .... **31 E4** 50 3N 8 42 E
Neu-Ulm, *Germany* .... **31 G6** 48 23N 10 0 E
Neubrandenburg, *Germany* .... **30 B9** 53 33N 13 15 E
Neuburg, *Germany* .... **31 G7** 48 44N 11 11 E
Neuchâtel, *Switz.* .... **32 C3** 47 0N 6 55 E
Neuchâtel □, *Switz.* .... **32 C3** 47 0N 6 55 E
Neuchâtel, Lac de, *Switz.* ...... **32 C3** 46 53N 6 50 E
Neudau, *Austria* .... **34 D9** 47 11N 16 6 E
Neuenegg, *Switz.* .... **32 C4** 46 54N 7 18 E
Neuenhagen, *Germany* .... **30 C9** 52 30N 13 38 E
Neuenhaus, *Germany* .... **30 C2** 52 30N 6 58 E
Neuenhof, *Switz.* .... **33 B6** 47 27N 8 19 E
Neuf-Brisach, *France* .... **27 D14** 48 1N 7 30 E
Neufahrn, *Bayern, Germany* ...... **31 G8** 48 41N 12 11 E
Neufahrn, *Bayern, Germany* ...... **31 G7** 48 18N 11 40 E
Neufchâteau, *Belgium* .... **24 E5** 49 50N 5 25 E
Neufchâteau, *France* .... **27 D12** 48 21N 5 40 E
Neufchâtel-en-Bray, *France* ..... **26 C8** 49 44N 1 26 E
Neufchâtel-sur-Aisne, *France* ... **27 C11** 49 26N 4 1 E
Neuhaus, *Germany* .... **30 B6** 53 17N 10 56 E
Neuhausen, *Switz.* .... **33 A7** 47 41N 8 37 E
Neuillé-Pont-Pierre, *France* .... **26 E7** 47 33N 0 33 E
Neuilly-St-Front, *France* .... **27 C10** 49 10N 3 15 E
Neukalen, *Germany* .... **30 B8** 53 49N 12 46 E
Neumarkt, *Germany* .... **31 F7** 49 26N 11 27 E
Neung-sur-Beuvron, *France* ...... **27 E8** 47 30N 1 50 E
Neunkirch, *Switz.* .... **33 A7** 47 40N 8 30 E
Neunkirchen, *Austria* .... **34 D9** 47 43N 16 4 E
Neunkirchen, *Germany* .... **31 F3** 49 20N 7 6 E
Neuquén, *Argentina* .... **176 A3** 38 55 S 68 0W
Neuquén □, *Argentina* .... **174 D2** 38 0 S 69 50W
Neuquén →, *Argentina* .... **176 A3** 38 59 S 68 0W
Neuruppin, *Germany* .... **30 C8** 52 55N 12 48 E
Neusäss, *Germany* .... **31 G6** 48 24N 10 50 E
Neusatz = Novi Sad, *Serbia, Yug.* **52 E5** 45 18N 19 52 E
Neuse →, *U.S.A.* **149 H7** 35 6N 76 29W
Neusiedl, *Austria* .... **35 D9** 47 57N 16 50 E
Neusiedler See, *Austria* .... **35 D9** 47 50N 16 47 E
Neusiedler See-Seewinkel,
   Nationalpark △, *Austria* **35 D9** 47 50N 16 45 E
Neuss, *Germany* .... **30 D2** 51 11N 6 42 E
Neussargues-Moissac, *France* .... **28 C7** 45 9N 3 0 E
Neustadt, *Bayern, Germany* ...... **31 F8** 49 44N 12 10 E
Neustadt, *Bayern, Germany* ...... **31 G7** 48 48N 11 46 E
Neustadt, *Bayern, Germany* ...... **31 F6** 49 34N 10 37 E
Neustadt, *Bayern, Germany* ...... **31 E7** 50 19N 11 7 E
Neustadt, *Brandenburg, Germany* . **30 C8** 52 50N 12 27 E
Neustadt, *Hessen, Germany* ...... **30 E5** 50 51N 9 9 E
Neustadt, *Niedersachsen, Germany* **30 C5** 52 30N 9 30 E
Neustadt, *Rhld.-Pfz., Germany* .. **31 F4** 49 21N 8 10 E
Neustadt, *Sachsen, Germany* ..... **30 D10** 51 2N 14 12 E
Neustadt, *Schleswig-Holstein,
   Germany* .... **30 A6** 54 6N 10 49 E
Neustadt, *Thüringen, Germany* ... **31 E7** 50 45N 11 43 E
Neustettin = Szczecinek, *Poland* **54 E3** 53 43N 16 41 E
Neustrelitz, *Germany* .... **30 B9** 53 21N 13 4 E
Neuvic, *France* .... **28 C6** 45 23N 2 16 E
Neuville-sur-Saône, *France* ..... **29 C8** 45 52N 4 51 E
Neuvy-le-Roi, *France* .... **26 E7** 47 36N 0 36 E
Neuvy-St-Sépulchre, *France* ..... **27 F8** 46 35N 1 48 E
Neuvy-sur-Barangeon, *France* .... **27 E9** 47 20N 2 15 E
Neuwerk, *Germany* .... **30 B4** 53 55N 8 30 E
Neuwied, *Germany* .... **30 E3** 50 26N 7 29 E
Neva →, *Russia* .... **58 C6** 59 50N 30 30 E
Nevada, *Iowa, U.S.A.* **156 B3** 42 1N 93 27W
Nevada, *Mo., U.S.A.* **155 G7** 37 51N 94 22W
Nevada □, *U.S.A.* **158 G5** 39 0N 117 0W
Nevada City, *U.S.A.* **160 F6** 39 16N 121 1W
Nevado, Cerro, *Argentina* .... **174 D2** 35 30 S 68 32W
Nevado de Colima, Parque Nac. =
   Volcán de Colima, Parque Nac. △,
   Mexico **162 D4** 19 30N 103 40W
Nevasa, *India* .... **94 E2** 19 34N 75 0 E
Neve, Sa. da, *Angola* .... **115 E2** 13 43 S 13 10 E
Nevel, *Russia* .... **58 D5** 56 0N 29 55 E
Nevers, *France* .... **27 F10** 47 0N 3 9 E
Nevertire, *Australia* .... **129 A7** 31 50 S 147 44 E
Nevesinje, *Bos.-H.* .... **50 C2** 43 14N 18 6 E
Neville, *Canada* **143 D7** 49 58N 107 39W
Nevinnomyssk, *Russia* .... **61 H6** 44 40N 42 0 E
Nevis, *St. Kitts & Nevis* **165 C7** 17 0N 62 30W
Nevlunghavn, *Norway* .... **18 F6** 58 58N 9 52 E
Nevrokop = Gotse Delchev, *Bulgaria* **50 E7** 41 36N 23 46 E
Nevşehir, *Turkey* .... **100 C6** 38 33N 34 40 E
Nevyansk, *Russia* .... **64 C8** 57 30N 60 13 E
New →, *Guyana* **169 C6** 3 20N 57 37W
New →, *U.S.A.* **148 F5** 38 10N 81 12W
New Aiyansh, *Canada* **142 B3** 55 12N 129 4W
New Albany, *Ind., U.S.A.* **157 F11** 38 18N 85 49W
New Albany, *Miss., U.S.A.* **155 H10** 34 29N 89 0W
New Albany, *Pa., U.S.A.* **151 E8** 41 36N 76 27W
New Amsterdam, *Guyana* **169 B6** 6 15N 57 36W
New Angledool, *Australia* .... **127 D4** 29 5 S 147 55 E
New Athens, *U.S.A.* **156 F7** 38 19N 89 53W
New Baltimore, *U.S.A.* **150 D2** 42 41N 82 44W
New Bedford, *U.S.A.* **151 E14** 41 38N 70 56W
New Berlin, *Ill., U.S.A.* **156 E7** 39 44N 89 55W
New Berlin, *N.Y., U.S.A.* **151 D9** 42 37N 75 20W
New Berlin, *Pa., U.S.A.* **151 F8** 40 50N 76 6W
New Berlin, *Wis., U.S.A.* **157 B8** 42 59N 88 6W
New Bern, *U.S.A.* **149 H7** 35 7N 77 3W
New Bethlehem, *U.S.A.* **150 F5** 41 0N 79 20W
New Bloomfield, *U.S.A.* **150 F7** 40 25N 77 11W
New Boston, *U.S.A.* **155 J7** 33 28N 94 25W
New Braunfels, *U.S.A.* **155 L5** 29 42N 98 8W
New Brighton, *N.Z.* .... **131 D7** 43 29 S 172 43 E
New Brighton, *U.S.A.* **150 F4** 40 42N 80 19W
New Britain, *Papua N. G.* .... **132 C6** 5 50 S 150 20 E
New Brockton, *U.S.A.* **152 D4** 31 23N 85 56W
New Brunswick, *U.S.A.* **151 F10** 40 30N 74 27W
New Brunswick □, *Canada* **141 C6** 46 50N 66 30W
New Buffalo, *U.S.A.* **157 C11** 41 47N 86 45W
New Bussa, *Nigeria* .... **113 D5** 9 53N 4 31 E
New Caledonia ☑, *Pac. Oc.* ...... **133 U19** 21 0 S 165 0 E
New Carlisle, *Ind., U.S.A.* **157 C10** 41 45N 86 32W
New Carlisle, *Ohio, U.S.A.* **157 E12** 39 56N 84 2W

New Castile = Castilla-La Mancha □,
   Spain **12 H5** 39 30N 3 30W
New Castle, *Ind., U.S.A.* **157 E11** 39 55N 85 22W
New Castle, *Ky., U.S.A.* **157 F11** 38 26N 85 10W
New Castle, *Pa., U.S.A.* **150 F4** 41 0N 80 21W
New City, *U.S.A.* **151 E11** 41 9N 73 59W
New Concord, *U.S.A.* **150 G3** 39 59N 81 54W
New Cumberland, *U.S.A.* **150 F4** 40 30N 80 36W
New Cuyama, *U.S.A.* **161 L7** 34 57N 119 38W
New Delhi, *India* .... **92 E7** 28 37N 77 13 E
New Denver, *Canada* **142 D5** 50 0N 117 25W
New Don Pedro Reservoir, *U.S.A.* **160 H6** 37 43N 120 24W
New Ellenton, *U.S.A.* **153 J5** 33 25N 81 41W
New Elngland, *U.S.A.* **154 B3** 46 32N 102 52W
New England Nat. Park △, *Australia* **129 A10** 30 25 S 152 30 E
New England Ra., *Australia* ..... **127 E5** 30 20 S 151 45 E
New Forest, *U.K.* **21 G6** 50 53N 1 34W
New Franklin, *U.S.A.* **156 E4** 39 1N 92 44W
New Galloway, *U.K.* **22 F4** 55 5N 4 9W
New Georgia Is., *Solomon Is.* ... **133 M9** 8 15 S 157 30 E
New Georgia Sound, *Solomon Is.* **133 L9** 8 0 S 158 20 E
New Glarus, *U.S.A.* **156 B7** 42 49N 89 38W
New Glasgow, *Canada* **141 C7** 45 35N 62 36W
New Guinea, *Oceania* .... **132 C1** 4 0 S 136 0 E
New Hamburg, *Canada* **150 C4** 43 23N 80 42W
New Hampshire □, *U.S.A.* **151 C13** 44 0N 71 30W
New Hampton, *U.S.A.* **156 A4** 43 3N 92 19W
New Hanover, *Papua N. G.* .... **132 B6** 2 30 S 150 10 E
New Hanover, *S. Africa* .... **117 D5** 29 22 S 30 31 E
New Harmony, *U.S.A.* **157 F9** 38 8N 87 56W
New Hartford, *U.S.A.* **151 C9** 43 4N 75 18W
New Haven, *Conn., U.S.A.* **151 E12** 41 18N 72 55W
New Haven, *Ill., U.S.A.* **157 G8** 37 55N 88 8W
New Haven, *Ind., U.S.A.* **157 C11** 41 4N 85 1W
New Haven, *Mich., U.S.A.* **150 D2** 42 44N 82 48W
New Haven, *Mo., U.S.A.* **156 F5** 38 37N 91 13W
New Hazelton, *Canada* **142 B3** 55 20N 127 30W
New Hebrides = Vanuatu ■,
   Pac. Oc. .... **133 E6** 15 0 S 168 0 E
New Holland, *U.S.A.* **151 F8** 40 6N 76 5W
New Iberia, *U.S.A.* **155 K9** 30 1N 91 49W
New Ireland, *Papua N. G.* .... **132 B6** 3 20 S 151 50 E
New Ireland □, *Papua N. G.* ..... **132 B6** 3 0 S 151 30 E
New Jersey □, *U.S.A.* **148 E8** 40 0N 74 30W
New Kensington, *U.S.A.* **150 F5** 40 34N 79 46W
New Lexington, *U.S.A.* **140 C4** 47 31N 79 41W
New Liskeard, *Canada* **140 C4** 47 31N 79 41W
New London, *Conn., U.S.A.* **151 E12** 41 22N 72 6W
New London, *Iowa, U.S.A.* **156 D5** 40 55N 91 24W
New London, *Ohio, U.S.A.* **150 E2** 41 5N 82 24W
New London, *Wis., U.S.A.* **154 C10** 44 23N 88 45W
New Madrid, *U.S.A.* **155 G10** 36 36N 89 32W
New Martinsville, *U.S.A.* **148 F5** 39 39N 80 52W
New Meadows, *U.S.A.* **158 D5** 44 58N 116 18W
New Melones L., *U.S.A.* **160 H6** 37 57N 120 31W
New Mexico □, *U.S.A.* **159 J10** 34 30N 106 0W
New Miami, *U.S.A.* **157 E12** 39 26N 84 32W
New Milford, *Conn., U.S.A.* **151 E11** 41 35N 73 25W
New Milford, *Pa., U.S.A.* **151 E9** 41 52N 75 44W
New Norcia, *Australia* .... **125 F2** 30 57 S 116 13 E
New Norfolk, *Australia* .... **127 D4** 42 46 S 147 2 E
New Orleans, *U.S.A.* **155 L9** 29 58N 90 4W
New Palestine, *U.S.A.* **157 E11** 39 45N 85 52W
New Panamao, *Phil.* .... **81 J3** 5 59N 121 13 E
New Paris, *U.S.A.* **157 E12** 39 51N 84 48W
New Pekin, *U.S.A.* **157 F10** 38 31N 86 2W
New Philadelphia, *U.S.A.* **150 F3** 40 30N 81 27W
New Plymouth, *N.Z.* .... **130 F3** 39 4 S 174 5 E
New Plymouth, *U.S.A.* **158 E5** 43 58N 116 49W
New Port Richey, *U.S.A.* **153 G7** 28 16N 82 43W
New Providence I., *Bahamas* ..... **9 b** 25 25N 78 35W
New Quay, *U.K.* **21 E3** 52 13N 4 21W
New Radnor, *U.K.* **21 E4** 52 15N 3 9W
New Richmond, *Canada* **141 C6** 48 15N 65 45W
New Richmond, *Ohio, U.S.A.* **157 F12** 38 57N 84 17W
New Richmond, *Wis., U.S.A.* **154 C8** 45 7N 92 32W
New River Gorge Nat. River △,
   U.S.A. **148 G5** 37 53N 81 5W
New Roads, *U.S.A.* **155 K9** 30 42N 91 26W
New Rochelle, *U.S.A.* **151 F11** 40 55N 73 47W
New Rockford, *U.S.A.* **154 B5** 47 41N 99 8W
New Romney, *U.K.* .... **21 G8** 50 59N 0 57 E
New Ross, *Ireland* **23 D5** 52 23N 6 57W
New Salem, *U.S.A.* **154 B4** 46 51N 101 25W
New Scone = Scone, *U.K.* **22 E5** 56 25N 3 24W
New Sharon, *U.S.A.* **156 C4** 41 28N 92 39W
New Siberian I. = Novaya Sibir,
   Ostrov, *Russia* ...... **67 B16** 75 10N 150 0 E
New Siberian Is. = Novosibirskiye
   Ostrova, *Russia* ..... **67 B15** 75 0N 142 0 E
New Smyrna Beach, *U.S.A.* **153 F9** 29 1N 80 56W
New South Wales □, *Australia* ... **129 B7** 33 0 S 146 0 E
New Stuyahok, *U.S.A.* **144 G8** 59 29N 157 20W
New Town, *U.S.A.* **154 B3** 47 59N 102 30W
New Tredegar, *U.K.* **21 F4** 51 44N 3 16W
New Ulm, *U.S.A.* **154 C7** 44 19N 94 28W
New Vienna, *U.S.A.* **157 E13** 39 19N 83 42W
New Washington, *Phil.* .... **81 F4** 11 39N 122 26 E
New Waterford, *Canada* **141 C7** 46 13N 60 4W
New-Wes-Valley = Wesleyville,
   Canada .... **141 C9** 49 8 S 53 36W
New Westminster, *Canada* **160 A4** 49 13N 122 55W
New York, *U.S.A.* **151 F11** 40 45N 74 0W
New York □, *U.S.A.* **151 D9** 43 0N 75 0W
New York J.F. Kennedy
   International ✈ (JFK), *U.S.A.* **151 F11** 40 38N 73 47W
New York Mts., *U.S.A.* **159 J6** 35 0N 115 20W
New Zealand ■, *Oceania* .... **130 G5** 40 0 S 176 0 E
Newaj →, *India* .... **92 G7** 24 24N 76 49 E
Newala, *Tanzania* .... **119 E4** 10 58 S 39 18 E
Newark, *Del., U.S.A.* **148 F8** 39 41N 75 46W
Newark, *N.J., U.S.A.* **151 F10** 40 44N 74 10W
Newark, *N.Y., U.S.A.* **150 C7** 43 3N 77 6W
Newark, *Ohio, U.S.A.* **150 F2** 40 3N 82 24W
Newark International ✈ (EWR),
   U.S.A. **151 F10** 40 42N 74 10W
Newark-on-Trent, *U.K.* **20 D7** 53 5N 0 48W
Newark Valley, *U.S.A.* **151 D8** 42 14N 76 11W
Newberg, *Oreg., U.S.A.* **158 D2** 45 18N 122 58W
Newberry, *Fla., U.S.A.* **153 F7** 29 39N 82 37W
Newberry, *Mich., U.S.A.* **148 B3** 46 21N 85 30W
Newberry, *S.C., U.S.A.* **149 H5** 34 17N 81 37W
Newberry Nat. Volcanic
   Monument ⌂, *U.S.A.* .. **158 E2** 43 42N 122 43W
Newberry Springs, *U.S.A.* **161 L10** 34 50N 116 41W
Newboro L., *Canada* **151 B8** 44 38N 76 20W
Newbridge = Droichead Nua, *Ireland* **23 C5** 53 11N 6 48W
Newburgh, *Canada* **150 B8** 44 19N 76 52W
Newburgh, *Ind., U.S.A.* **157 G9** 37 57N 87 24W
Newburgh, *N.Y., U.S.A.* **151 E11** 41 30N 74 1W
Newbury, *U.K.* **21 F6** 51 24N 1 20W
Newbury, *N.H., U.S.A.* **151 B12** 43 19N 72 3W
Newbury, *Vt., U.S.A.* **151 B12** 44 5N 72 4W
Newburyport, *U.S.A.* **149 D10** 42 49N 70 53W
Newcastle, *Australia* .... **129 B9** 33 0 S 151 46 E
Newcastle, *N.B., Canada* **141 C6** 47 1N 65 38W
Newcastle, *Ont., Canada* **140 D4** 43 55N 78 35W
Newcastle, *S. Africa* .... **117 D4** 27 45 S 29 58 E
Newcastle, *U.K.* **23 B6** 54 13N 5 54W
Newcastle, *Calif., U.S.A.* **160 G5** 38 53N 121 8W
Newcastle, *Wyo., U.S.A.* **154 D2** 43 50N 104 11W
Newcastle Emlyn, *U.K.* **21 E3** 52 2N 4 28W

Newcastle Ra., *Australia* .... **124 C5** 15 45 S 130 15 E
Newcastle-under-Lyme, *U.K.* **20 D5** 53 1N 2 14W
Newcastle-upon-Tyne, *U.K.* **20 C6** 54 58N 1 36W
Newcastle Waters, *Australia* ..... **126 B1** 17 30 S 133 28 E
Newcastle West, *Ireland* **23 D2** 52 27N 9 3W
Newcomb, *U.S.A.* **151 C10** 43 58N 74 10W
Newcomerstown, *U.S.A.* **150 F3** 40 16N 81 36W
Newdegate, *Australia* .... **125 F2** 33 6 S 119 0 E
Newell, *Australia* .... **126 B4** 16 20 S 145 16 E
Newell, *Iowa, U.S.A.* **156 B1** 42 36N 95 0W
Newell, *S. Dak., U.S.A.* **154 C3** 44 43N 103 25W
Newenham, *C., U.S.A.* **144 G7** 58 39N 162 11W
Newfane, *U.S.A.* **150 C6** 43 17N 78 43W
Newfield, *U.S.A.* **151 D8** 42 18N 76 33W
Newfound L., *U.S.A.* **151 C13** 43 40N 71 47W
Newfoundland, *Canada* **136 E14** 49 0N 55 0W
Newfoundland, *U.S.A.* **151 E9** 41 18N 75 19W
Newfoundland □, *Canada* **141 B8** 53 0N 58 0W
Newhalen, *U.S.A.* **144 G9** 59 43N 154 54W
Newhall, *U.S.A.* **161 L8** 34 23N 118 32W
Newhaven, *U.K.* .... **21 G8** 50 47N 0 3 E
Newington, *U.S.A.* **152 C8** 32 35N 81 30W
Newkirk, *U.S.A.* **155 G6** 36 53N 97 3W
Newlyn, *U.K.* **21 G2** 50 6N 5 34W
Newman, *Australia* .... **124 D2** 23 18 S 119 45 E
Newman, *Calif., U.S.A.* **160 H5** 37 19N 121 1W
Newman, *Ill., U.S.A.* **157 E9** 39 48N 87 59W
Newman, *Ind., U.S.A.* **150 B5** 44 3N 79 28W
Newmarket, *Canada* **23 D2** 52 13N 9 0W
Newmarket, *Ireland* .... **21 E8** 52 15N 0 25 E
Newmarket, *U.K.* .... **21 E8** 52 15N 0 25 E
Newmarket, *U.S.A.* **151 C14** 43 4N 70 56W
Newnan, *U.S.A.* **152 B5** 33 23N 84 48W
Newport, *Ireland* **23 C2** 53 53N 9 33W
Newport, *I. of W., U.K.* **21 G6** 50 42N 1 17W
Newport, *Newp., U.K.* **21 F5** 51 35N 3 0W
Newport, *Ark., U.S.A.* **155 H9** 35 37N 91 16W
Newport, *Fla., U.S.A.* **152 E5** 30 11N 84 10W
Newport, *Ind., U.S.A.* **157 E9** 39 53N 87 25W
Newport, *Ky., U.S.A.* **157 E12** 39 5N 84 30W
Newport, *N.H., U.S.A.* **151 C12** 43 22N 72 10W
Newport, *N.Y., U.S.A.* **151 C9** 43 11N 75 1W
Newport, *Oreg., U.S.A.* **158 D1** 44 39N 124 3W
Newport, *Pa., U.S.A.* **150 F7** 40 29N 77 8W
Newport, *R.I., U.S.A.* **151 E13** 41 29N 71 19W
Newport, *Tenn., U.S.A.* **149 H4** 35 58N 83 11W
Newport, *Vt., U.S.A.* **151 B12** 44 56N 72 13W
Newport, *Wash., U.S.A.* **158 B5** 48 11N 117 3W
Newport □, *U.K.* **21 F4** 51 33N 3 1W
Newport Beach, *U.S.A.* **161 M9** 33 37N 117 56W
Newport News, *U.S.A.* **148 G7** 36 59N 76 25W
Newport Pagnell, *U.K.* **21 E7** 52 5N 0 43W
Newquay, *U.K.* **21 G2** 50 25N 5 6W
Newry, *U.K.* **23 B5** 54 11N 6 21W
Newton, *U.S.A.* **144 F6** 60 56N 164 38W
Newton, *Ga., U.S.A.* **152 D5** 31 19N 84 20W
Newton, *Ill., U.S.A.* **154 F10** 38 59N 88 10W
Newton, *Iowa, U.S.A.* **156 C3** 41 42N 93 3W
Newton, *Kans., U.S.A.* **155 F6** 38 3N 97 21W
Newton, *Mass., U.S.A.* **151 D13** 42 21N 71 12W
Newton, *Miss., U.S.A.* **155 J10** 32 19N 89 10W
Newton, *N.C., U.S.A.* **149 H5** 35 40N 81 13W
Newton, *N.J., U.S.A.* **151 E10** 41 3N 74 45W
Newton, *Tex., U.S.A.* **155 K8** 30 51N 93 46W
Newton Abbot, *U.K.* **21 G4** 50 32N 3 37W
Newton Aycliffe, *U.K.* **20 C6** 54 37N 1 34W
Newton Falls, *U.S.A.* **150 E4** 41 11N 80 59W
Newton L., *U.S.A.* **157 F8** 38 55N 88 15W
Newtonmore, *U.K.* **22 D4** 57 4N 4 8W
Newtontoppen, *Svalbard* .... **10 B12** 79 0N 17 30 E
Newtown, *U.K.* **21 E4** 52 31N 3 19W
Newtown, *Ind., U.S.A.* **157 D9** 40 13N 87 9W
Newtown, *Mo., U.S.A.* **156 D3** 40 22N 93 20W
Newtownabbey, *U.K.* **23 B6** 54 40N 5 56W
Newtownards, *U.K.* **23 B6** 54 36N 5 42W
Newtownbarry = Bunclody, *Ireland* **23 D5** 52 39N 6 40W
Newtownstewart, *U.K.* **23 B4** 54 43N 7 23W
Newville, *U.S.A.* **150 F7** 40 10N 77 24W
Nexon, *France* .... **28 C5** 45 41N 1 11 E
Neya, *Russia* .... **60 A6** 58 21N 43 49 E
Neyrīz, *Iran* .... **97 D7** 29 15N 54 19 E
Neyruz, *Switz.* .... **32 C4** 46 47N 7 4 E
Neyshābūr, *Iran* .... **97 B8** 36 10N 58 50 E
Neyyattinkara, *India* .... **95 K3** 8 26N 77 5 E
Nezametny = Aldan, *Russia* ..... **67 D13** 58 40N 125 30 E
Nezhin = Nizhyn, *Ukraine* .... **59 G6** 51 5N 31 55 E
Nezperce, *U.S.A.* **158 C5** 46 14N 116 14W
Ngabang, *Indonesia* .... **85 B3** 0 23N 109 55 E
Ngabe, *Congo* .... **114 C3** 3 12 S 16 12 E
Ngabordamlu, Tanjung, *Indonesia* **83 C4** 6 56 S 134 11 E
N'Gage, *Angola* .... **116 D3** 7 46 S 15 15 E
Ngaiphaipi, *Burma* .... **90 D4** 22 14N 93 15 E
Ngala, *Nigeria* .... **113 C7** 12 56N 10 29 E
Ngama, *Chad* .... **109 F3** 11 45N 17 6 E
Ngambé, *Centre, Cameroon* ..... **113 D7** 5 48N 11 29 E
Ngambé, *Littoral, Cameroon* .... **113 E7** 4 21N 10 40 E
Ngami Depression, *Botswana* ... **116 C3** 20 30 S 22 46 E
Ngamo, *Zimbabwe* .... **119 F2** 19 3 S 27 32 E
Ngangala, *Sudan* .... **107 G3** 4 42N 31 55 E
Nganjuk, *Indonesia* .... **84 B4** 7 32 S 111 55 E
Ngao, *Thailand* .... **86 C2** 18 46N 99 59 E
Ngaoundéré, *Cameroon* .... **113 E7** 7 15N 13 35 E
Ngapara, *N.Z.* .... **131 E5** 44 57 S 170 46 E
Ngape, *Burma* .... **90 E5** 20 2N 94 28 E
Ngara, *Tanzania* .... **118 C3** 2 29 S 30 40 E
Ngaruawahia, *N.Z.* .... **130 D4** 37 42 S 175 11 E
Ngaruroro →, *N.Z.* .... **130 F5** 39 34 S 176 55 E
Ngatapa, *N.Z.* .... **130 E6** 38 32 S 177 45 E
Ngathaingyaung, *Burma* .... **90 G5** 17 24N 95 5 E
Ngauruhoe, Mt., *N.Z.* .... **130 F4** 39 13 S 175 45 E
Ngawi, *Indonesia* .... **85 D4** 7 24 S 111 26 E
Ngele, *Dem. Rep. of the Congo* ... **114 B2** 1 16N 21 28 E
Ngelebok, *Cameroon* .... **114 B2** 4 16N 14 3 E
Nggatokae, *Solomon Is.* .... **133 M10** 8 45 S 158 15 E
Nggela, *Solomon Is.* .... **133 M11** 9 5 S 160 15 E
Nggela Pile, *Solomon Is.* .... **133 M11** 9 5 S 160 20 E
Nggela Sule, *Solomon Is.* .... **133 M11** 9 5 S 160 12 E
Nghia Lo, *Vietnam* .... **76 G5** 21 33N 104 28 E
Ngidinga, *Dem. Rep. of the Congo* **115 D3** 5 37 S 15 17 E
Ngo, *Congo* .... **114 C3** 2 29 S 15 45 E
Ngoap, *Cameroon* .... **114 B2** 4 9N 12 51 E
Ngoboli, *Sudan* .... **107 G3** 4 57N 32 37 E
N'Gola, *Angola* .... **115 E3** 14 10 S 14 30 E
Ngoma, *Malawi* .... **119 E3** 13 8 S 33 45 E
Ngomahura, *Zimbabwe* .... **119 G3** 20 26 S 30 43 E
Ngomba, *Tanzania* .... **119 D3** 8 20 S 32 53 E
Ngongotaha, *N.Z.* .... **130 E5** 38 5 S 176 12 E
Ngop, *Sudan* .... **107 F3** 6 17N 30 9 E
Ngoring Hu, *China* .... **68 C4** 34 55N 97 5 E
Ngorkou, *Mali* **112 B4** 15 40N 3 41W
Ngorongoro, *Tanzania* .... **118 C4** 3 11 S 35 32 E
Ngorongoro Conservation Area △,
   Tanzania .... **118 C4** 2 40 S 35 30 E
Ngoto, *C.A.R.* .... **114 B3** 3 59N 17 19 E
Ngoua, *Chad* .... **109 F3** 13 44N 19 21 E
Ngouri, *Chad* .... **109 F3** 13 44N 16 21 E
Ngourti, *Niger* .... **109 E2** 15 19N 13 12 E
Ngoussou, *Gabon* .... **114 C2** 3 0 S 11 7 E
Ngozi, *Burundi* .... **118 C2** 2 54 S 29 50 E
Ngudu, *Tanzania* .... **118 C3** 2 58 S 33 25 E
Nguigmi, *Niger* .... **109 F2** 14 20N 13 20 E
Nguila, *Cameroon* .... **113 E7** 4 41N 11 43 E
Nguiu, *Australia* .... **124 B5** 11 46 S 130 38 E

Ngukurr, *Australia* .... **126 A1** 14 44 S 134 44 E
Nguna, *Vanuatu* .... **133 G6** 17 26 S 168 22 E
Ngunga, *Tanzania* .... **118 C3** 3 37 S 33 37 E
Nguru, *Nigeria* .... **113 C7** 12 56N 10 29 E
Nguru Mts., *Tanzania* .... **118 D4** 6 0 S 37 30 E
Ngusi, *Malawi* .... **119 E3** 14 0 S 34 50 E
Nguyen Binh, *Vietnam* .... **76 F5** 22 39N 105 56 E
Ngwedaung, *Burma* .... **90 F6** 19 31N 97 9 E
Nha Trang, *Vietnam* .... **87 F7** 12 16N 109 10 E
Nhacoongo, *Mozam.* .... **117 C6** 24 18 S 35 14 E
Nhamaabué, *Mozam.* .... **119 F4** 17 25 S 35 5 E
Nhambiquara, *Brazil* .... **173 C6** 12 50 S 59 49W
Nhamundá, *Brazil* .... **169 D6** 2 14 S 56 43W
Nhamundá →, *Brazil* .... **169 D6** 2 12 S 56 41W
Nhangulaze, L., *Mozam.* .... **117 C5** 24 0 S 34 30 E
Nharêa, *Angola* .... **115 E3** 11 38 S 16 58 E
Nhecolândia, *Brazil* .... **173 D6** 19 17 S 56 58W
Nhill, *Australia* .... **128 D4** 36 18 S 141 40 E
Nho Quan, *Vietnam* .... **76 G5** 20 18N 105 45 E
Nhulunbuy, *Australia* .... **126 A2** 12 10 S 137 20 E
Nhundo, *Angola* .... **118 B2** 14 25 S 21 23 E
Nia-nia, *Dem. Rep. of the Congo* **118 B2** 1 30N 27 40 E
Niafounké, *Mali* **112 B4** 16 0N 4 5W
Niagara Falls, *Canada* **140 D4** 43 7N 79 5W
Niagara Falls, *U.S.A.* **150 C6** 43 5N 79 4W
Niagara-on-the-Lake, *Canada* ... **150 C5** 43 15N 79 4W
Niah, *Malaysia* .... **85 B4** 3 58N 113 46 E
Nialala'u Pt., *Solomon Is.* ...... **133 M11** 9 47 S 161 34 E
Niamey, *Niger* .... **113 C5** 13 27N 2 6 E
Niandan-Koro, *Guinea* **112 C3** 11 5N 9 15W
Nianforando, *Guinea* **112 D2** 9 37N 10 36W
Niangara, *Dem. Rep. of the Congo* **118 B2** 3 42N 27 50 E
Niangbo, *Ivory C.* **112 D3** 8 49N 5 10W
Niangoloko, *Burkina Faso* **112 C4** 10 15N 4 55W
Niangua →, *U.S.A.* **156 G4** 38 0N 92 48W
Niantic, *U.S.A.* **151 E12** 41 20N 72 11W
Niari, *Congo* .... **114 C2** 4 9 S 14 9 E
Niaro, *Sudan* .... **107 E3** 10 38N 31 31 E
Nias, *Indonesia* .... **84 B1** 1 0N 97 30 E
Niassa □, *Mozam.* .... **119 E4** 13 30 S 36 0 E
Niassa, Reserva do △, *Mozam.* .. **119 E4** 12 50 S 36 57 E
Nibāk, *Si. Arabia* .... **97 E7** 24 25N 50 50 E
Nibe, *Denmark* .... **17 H3** 56 59N 9 38 E
Nicaragua ■, *Cent. Amer.* **164 D2** 11 40N 85 30W
Nicaragua, L. de, *Nic.* **164 D2** 12 0N 85 30W
Nicastro, *Italy* .... **47 D9** 38 59N 16 19 E
Nice, *France* .... **29 E11** 43 42N 7 14 E
Nice ✈ (NCE), *France* .... **29 E11** 43 41N 7 12 E
Niceville, *U.S.A.* **153 E3** 30 31N 86 30W
Nichicun, L., *Canada* **141 B5** 53 5N 71 0W
Nichinan, *Japan* .... **72 F3** 31 38N 131 23 E
Nicholás, Canal, *W. Indies* **164 B3** 23 30N 80 5W
Nicholasville, *U.S.A.* **157 G12** 37 53N 84 34W
Nichols, *U.S.A.* **152 D7** 31 31N 82 38W
Nichols, *U.S.A.* **151 D8** 42 1N 76 22W
Nicholson, *Australia* .... **124 C4** 18 2 S 128 54 E
Nicholson, *U.S.A.* **151 E9** 41 37N 75 47W
Nicholson →, *Australia* .... **126 B2** 17 31 S 139 36 E
Nicholson L., *Canada* **143 A8** 62 40N 102 40W
Nicholson Ra., *Australia* .... **125 E2** 27 15 S 116 45 E
Nicholville, *U.S.A.* **151 B10** 44 41N 74 39W
Nickerie →, *Suriname* **169 B6** 5 58N 57 0W
Nicobar Is., *Ind. Oc.* .... **95 L11** 8 0N 93 30 E
Nicola, *Canada* **142 C4** 50 12N 120 40W
Nicolls Town, *Bahamas* **164 A4** 25 8N 78 0W
Nicopolis, *Greece* .... **39 A2** 39 5N 20 43 E
Nicosia, *Cyprus* .... **39 E9** 35 10N 33 25 E
Nicosia, *Italy* .... **47 D8** 38 33N 14 56 E
Nicoya, *Costa Rica* **164 D2** 10 9N 85 27W
Nicoya, G. de, *Costa Rica* **164 E3** 10 0N 85 0W
Nicoya, Pen. de, *Costa Rica* **164 E2** 9 45N 85 40W
Nictheroy = Niterói, *Brazil* ..... **171 F3** 22 52 S 43 0W
Nida, *Lithuania* .... **54 C8** 55 20N 21 4 E
Nidau, *Switz.* .... **32 B4** 47 7N 7 15 E
Nidd →, *U.K.* **20 D6** 53 59N 1 23W
Nidda, *Germany* .... **31 E5** 50 23N 9 1 E
Nidda →, *Germany* .... **31 E4** 50 17N 8 48 E
Nidri, *Greece* .... **39 B2** 38 43N 20 42 E
Nidwalden □, *Switz.* .... **33 C6** 46 50N 8 25 E
Nidzica, *Poland* .... **55 E7** 53 25N 20 28 E
Nié, Î., *N. Cal.* .... **133 U21** 21 8 S 167 35 E
Niebüll, *Germany* .... **30 A4** 54 46N 8 49 E
Niebla, *Spain* .... **42 C13** 49 23N 6 40 E
Niederanla, *Germany* .... **30 E5** 50 47N 9 36 E
Niederbayern □, *Germany* ...... **31 G8** 48 40N 12 50 E
Niederbipp, *Switz.* .... **32 B5** 47 16N 7 42 E
Niederbronn-les-Bains, *France* .. **27 D14** 48 57N 7 39 E
Niedere Tauern, *Austria* .... **34 D7** 47 20N 14 0 E
Niederlausitz, *Germany* .... **30 D9** 51 42N 13 59 E
Niederösterreich □, *Austria* .... **34 C8** 48 25N 15 40 E
Niedersachsen □, *Germany* ..... **30 C4** 52 50N 9 0 E
Niedersächsisches Wattenmeer,
   Nationalpark △, *Germany* ... **30 B3** 53 45N 7 30 E
Niefang, *Eq. Guin.* .... **114 B2** 1 50N 10 14 E
Niekerkshoop, *S. Africa* .... **116 D3** 29 19 S 22 51 E
Niellé, *Ivory C.* **112 C3** 10 5N 5 38W
Niellim, *Chad* .... **109 G3** 9 42N 17 49 E
Niem, *C.A.R.* .... **114 A3** 6 12N 15 14 E
Niemba, *Dem. Rep. of the Congo* **118 D2** 5 58 S 28 24 E
Niemen = Nemunas →, *Lithuania* **15 J19** 55 25N 21 10 E
Niemodlin, *Poland* .... **55 H4** 50 38N 17 38 E
Niemur, *Australia* .... **128 C6** 35 17 S 144 9 E
Nienburg, *Germany* .... **30 C5** 52 39N 9 13 E
Niepołomice, *Poland* .... **55 H7** 50 3N 20 13 E
Niers →, *Germany* .... **30 D1** 51 43N 5 57 E
Niesen, *Switz.* .... **32 C5** 46 38N 7 39 E
Niesky, *Germany* .... **30 D10** 51 17N 14 49 E
Nieszawa, *Poland* .... **55 F5** 52 52N 18 50 E
Nieu Bethesda, *S. Africa* .... **116 E3** 31 51 S 24 34 E
Nieuw Amsterdam, *Suriname* .. **169 B6** 5 53N 55 5W
Nieuw Nickerie, *Suriname* **169 B6** 6 0N 56 59W
Nieuwoudtville, *S. Africa* ...... **116 E2** 31 23 S 19 7 E
Nieuwpoort, *Belgium* .... **24 C2** 51 8N 2 45 E
Nieves, Pico de las, *Canary Is.* .. **9 e1** 27 57N 15 35W
Nièvre □, *France* .... **27 E10** 47 10N 3 40 E
Niga, *Mali* **112 C3** 13 38N 5 27W
Niğde, *Turkey* .... **100 D6** 37 58N 34 40 E
Nigel, *S. Africa* .... **117 D4** 26 27 S 28 25 E
Niger □, *Nigeria* .... **113 D6** 10 0N 5 30 E
Niger ■, *W. Afr.* .... **113 B7** 17 30N 10 0 E
Niger →, *W. Afr.* .... **113 D6** 5 33N 6 33 E
Niger Delta, *Africa* .... **113 E6** 5 0N 6 0 E
Nigeria ■, *W. Afr.* .... **113 D6** 8 30N 8 0 E
Nighasin, *India* .... **93 E9** 28 14N 80 52 E
Nightcaps, *N.Z.* .... **131 F3** 45 57 S 168 2 E
Nightmute, *U.S.A.* **144 F6** 60 29N 164 44W
Nigríta, *Greece* .... **50 F7** 40 56N 23 29 E
Nihoa, *U.S.A.* **145 G11** 25 6N 161 58W
Nii-Jima, *Japan* .... **73 G9** 34 20N 139 15 E
Niigata, *Japan* .... **70 F9** 37 58N 139 0 E
Niigata □, *Japan* .... **71 F9** 37 15N 138 45 E
Niihama, *Japan* .... **72 D5** 33 55N 133 16 E
Niihau, *U.S.A.* **145 B1** 21 54N 160 9W
Niimi, *Japan* .... **72 C5** 34 59N 133 28 E
Niitsu, *Japan* .... **70 F9** 37 48N 139 7 E
Nij Laluk, *India* .... **90 B4** 27 7N 93 56 E
Níjar, *Spain* **41 J2** 36 53N 2 15W
Nijil, *Jordan* .... **103 E4** 30 32N 35 33 E
Nijkerk, *Neths.* .... **24 B5** 52 13N 5 30 E
Nijmegen, *Neths.* .... **24 C5** 51 50N 5 52 E
Nijverdal, *Neths.* .... **24 B6** 52 22N 6 28 E
Nīk Pey, *Iran* .... **97 B6** 36 50N 48 10 E
Nikaweratiya, *Sri Lanka* .... **95 L5** 7 45N 80 7 E

Nike, *Nigeria* .... **113 D6** 6 26N 7 29 E
Nikiniki, *Indonesia* .... **83 C2** 9 49 S 124 30 E
Nikísiani, *Greece* .... **51 F8** 40 57N 24 9 E
Nikítas, *Greece* .... **50 F7** 40 13N 23 43 E
Nikki, *Benin* .... **113 D5** 9 58N 3 12 E
Nikkō, *Japan* .... **73 A11** 36 45N 139 35 E
Nikolai, *U.S.A.* **144 E9** 62 58N 154 10W
Nikolaistad = Vaasa, *Finland* ... **14 E19** 63 6N 21 38 E
Nikolayev = Mykolayiv, *Ukraine* **59 J7** 46 58N 32 0 E
Nikolayev, *Russia* .... **60 E7** 50 0N 45 35 E
Nikolayevsk-na-Amur, *Russia* .. **67 D15** 53 8N 140 44 E
Nikolsk, *Russia* .... **60 D8** 53 49N 46 4 E
Nikolski, *U.S.A.* **144 K5** 52 56N 168 52W
Nikolskoye, *Russia* .... **67 D17** 55 12N 166 0 E
Nikopol, *Bulgaria* .... **51 C8** 43 43N 24 54 E
Nikopol, *Ukraine* .... **59 J8** 47 35N 34 25 E
Niksar, *Turkey* .... **100 B7** 40 31N 37 2 E
Nīkshahr, *Iran* .... **97 E9** 26 15N 60 10 E
Nikšić, *Montenegro, Yug.* ...... **50 D2** 42 50N 18 57 E
Nīl, Nahr en →, *Africa* .... **106 H7** 30 10N 31 6 E
Nīl el Abyad →, *Sudan* .... **107 D3** 15 38N 32 31 E
Nīl el Azraq →, *Sudan* .... **107 D3** 15 38N 32 31 E
Nila, *Indonesia* .... **83 C3** 6 44 S 129 31 E
Nilakkottai, *India* .... **95 J3** 10 10N 77 52 E
Niland, *U.S.A.* **161 M11** 33 14N 115 31W
Nilanga, *India* .... **94 E3** 18 6N 76 46 E
Nile = Nīl, Nahr en →, *Africa* ... **106 H7** 30 10N 31 6 E
Niles, *Mich., U.S.A.* **157 C10** 41 50N 86 15W
Niles, *Ohio, U.S.A.* **150 E4** 41 11N 80 46W
Nileshwar, *India* .... **95 H2** 12 15N 75 6 E
Nilgiri Hills, *India* .... **95 J3** 11 30N 76 30 E
Nilo Peçanha, *Brazil* .... **171 D4** 13 37 S 39 6W
Nilsebu, *Norway* .... **18 E3** 59 11N 6 39 E
Nilüfer →, *Turkey* .... **51 F12** 40 18N 28 27 E
Nim Ka Thana, *India* .... **92 F6** 27 44N 75 48 E
Nimach, *India* .... **92 G6** 24 30N 74 56 E
Nimbahera, *India* .... **92 G6** 24 37N 74 45 E
Nîmes, *France* .... **29 E8** 43 50N 4 23 E
Nimfaíon, Ákra = Pínnes, Ákra,
   Greece .... **51 F8** 40 5N 24 20 E
Nimmitabel, *Australia* .... **129 D8** 36 29 S 149 15 E
Nimrūz □, *Afghan.* .... **91 C1** 30 0N 62 0 E
Nimule, *Sudan* .... **107 G3** 3 32N 32 3 E
Nimule Nat. Park △, *Sudan* .... **107 G3** 3 38N 32 0 E
Nin, *Croatia* .... **45 D12** 44 16N 15 12 E
Ninawá, *Iraq* .... **101 D10** 36 25N 43 10 E
Ninda, *Angola* .... **115 E4** 14 47 S 21 24 E
Nindigully, *Australia* .... **127 D4** 28 21 S 148 50 E
Nine Degree Channel, *India* .... **95 K1** 9 0N 73 0 E
Ninepin Group, *China* .... **69 G11** 22 16N 114 21 E
Ninety East Ridge, *Ind. Oc.* .... **121 E7** 1 0 S 90 0 E
Ninety Mile Beach, *Australia* .. **130 A1** 34 48 S 173 0 E
Ninety Mile Beach, The, *Australia* **129 F4** 38 15 S 147 24 E
Ninety Six, *U.S.A.* **152 A7** 34 11N 82 1W
Nineveh = Ninawá, *Iraq* .... **101 D10** 36 25N 43 10 E
Ning Xian, *China* .... **74 G4** 35 30N 107 58 E
Ningaloo Marine Park △, *Australia* **124 D1** 22 23 S 113 32 E
Ning'an, *China* .... **75 B15** 44 22N 129 20 E
Ningbo, *China* .... **77 C13** 29 51N 121 28 E
Ningcheng, *China* .... **75 D10** 41 32N 119 53 E
Ningde, *China* .... **77 D12** 26 38N 119 23 E
Ningdu, *China* .... **77 D10** 26 25N 115 59 E
Ningerum, *Papua N. G.* .... **132 C1** 5 41 S 141 8 E
Ninggang, *China* .... **77 D9** 26 42N 113 55 E
Ningguo, *China* .... **77 B12** 30 35N 118 59 E
Ninghai, *China* .... **77 C13** 29 15N 121 27 E
Ninghua, *China* .... **77 D11** 26 14N 116 45 E
Ningi, *Nigeria* .... **113 C6** 10 55N 9 30 E
Ningjin, *China* .... **74 F8** 37 35N 114 57 E
Ningjing Shan, *China* .... **76 C2** 30 0N 98 20 E
Ninglang, *China* .... **76 D3** 27 20N 100 55 E
Ningling, *China* .... **74 G8** 34 25N 115 22 E
Ningming, *China* .... **76 F6** 22 8N 107 4 E
Ningnan, *China* .... **76 D4** 27 5N 102 36 E
Ningpo = Ningbo, *China* .... **77 C13** 29 51N 121 28 E
Ningqiang, *China* .... **74 H4** 32 47N 106 35 E
Ningshan, *China* .... **74 H5** 33 21N 108 21 E
Ningsia Hui A.R. = Ningxia Huizu
   Zizhiqu □, *China* .... **74 F4** 38 0N 106 0 E
Ningwu, *China* .... **74 E7** 39 0N 112 18 E
Ningxia Huizu Zizhiqu □, *China* **74 F4** 38 0N 106 0 E
Ningxiang, *China* .... **77 C9** 28 15N 112 30 E
Ningyang, *China* .... **74 G9** 35 47N 116 45 E
Ningyuan, *China* .... **77 E8** 25 37N 111 57 E
Ninh Binh, *Vietnam* .... **76 G5** 20 15N 105 55 E
Ninh Giang, *Vietnam* .... **86 B6** 20 44N 106 24 E
Ninh Hoa, *Vietnam* .... **86 F7** 12 48N 109 21 E
Ninh Ma, *Vietnam* .... **86 F7** 12 48N 109 21 E
Nini-Suhien Nat. Park △, *Ghana* **112 D4** 5 25N 2 50W
Ninigo Group, *Papua N. G.* ..... **132 A3** 1 22 S 144 17 E
Ninini Pt., *U.S.A.* **145 B2** 21 58N 159 20W
Ninove, *Belgium* .... **24 D4** 50 51N 4 2 E
Nioaque, *Brazil* .... **175 A4** 21 5 S 55 50W
Niobrara, *U.S.A.* **154 D6** 42 45N 98 2W
Niobrara →, *U.S.A.* **154 D6** 42 46N 98 3W
Nioki, *Dem. Rep. of the Congo* .. **114 C3** 2 47 S 17 40 E
Niokolo-Koba, Parc Nat. du △,
   Senegal **112 C2** 13 3N 13 2W
Niono, *Mali* **112 C3** 14 15N 6 0W
Nionsamoridougou, *Guinea* **112 D3** 8 45N 8 50W
Nioro du Rip, *Senegal* **112 C1** 13 40N 15 50W
Nioro du Sahel, *Mali* **112 B3** 15 15N 9 30W
Niort, *France* **28 B3** 46 19N 0 29W
Nipa, *Papua N. G.* .... **132 D2** 6 9 S 143 29 E
Nipani, *India* .... **95 F2** 16 20N 74 25 E
Nipawin, *Canada* **143 C8** 53 20N 104 0W
Nipfjället, *Sweden* .... **16 C6** 61 59N 12 50 E
Nipigon, *Canada* **140 C2** 49 0N 88 17W
Nipigon, L., *Canada* **140 C2** 49 50N 88 30W
Nipishish L., *Canada* **141 B7** 54 12N 60 45W
Nipissing, L., *Canada* **140 C4** 46 20N 80 0W
Nipomo, *U.S.A.* **161 K6** 35 3N 120 29W
Nipton, *U.S.A.* **161 K11** 35 28N 115 16W
Niquelândia, *Brazil* .... **171 D2** 14 33 S 48 23W
Nīr, *Iran* .... **101 C12** 38 2N 47 59 E
Nira →, *India* .... **94 F2** 17 58N 75 8 E
Nirasaki, *Japan* .... **73 B10** 35 42N 138 27 E
Nirmal, *India* .... **94 E4** 19 3N 78 20 E
Nirmali, *India* .... **93 F12** 26 20N 86 35 E
Niš, *Serbia, Yug.* .... **50 C5** 43 19N 21 58 E
Nisa = Nysa →, *Europe* .... **30 C10** 52 4N 14 46 E
Nisa, *Portugal* **43 F3** 39 30N 7 41W
Niṣāb, *Si. Arabia* .... **96 D5** 29 11N 44 43 E
Niṣāb, *Yemen* .... **98 D4** 14 25N 46 29 E
Nišava →, *Serbia, Yug.* .... **50 C6** 43 18N 21 52 E
Niscemi, *Italy* .... **47 E7** 37 9N 14 23 E
Nishi-Sonogi-Hantō, *Japan* .... **72 E1** 32 55N 129 45 E
Nishi-Tosa, *Japan* .... **72 D4** 33 13N 132 46 E
Nishinomiya, *Japan* .... **73 C7** 34 45N 135 20 E
Nishino'omote, *Japan* .... **71 J5** 30 43N 130 59 E
Nishiō, *Japan* .... **73 C9** 34 52N 137 3 E
Nishiwaki, *Japan* .... **72 C7** 34 59N 134 58 E
Nisibin = Nusaybin, *Turkey* .... **101 D9** 37 3N 41 10 E
Nísiros, *Greece* .... **49 E9** 36 35N 27 9 E
Niška Banja, *Serbia, Yug.* ...... **50 C6** 43 18N 22 1 E
Niskibi →, *Canada* **140 A2** 56 29N 88 9W
Nisko, *Poland* .... **55 H9** 50 35N 22 7 E
Nisporeni, *Moldova* .... **59 C13** 47 4N 28 10 E
Nisqually →, *U.S.A.* **160 C4** 47 6N 122 42W
Nissáki, *Greece* .... **38 B9** 39 43N 19 52 E
Nissan →, *Sweden* .... **17 H6** 56 40N 12 51 E
Nissedal, *Norway* .... **18 E5** 59 10N 8 30 E
Nisser, *Norway* .... **18 E5** 59 7N 8 28 E
Nissum Bredning, *Denmark* .... **17 H2** 56 40N 8 20 E

Nissum Fjord, *Denmark* .... **17 H2** 56 20N 8 11 E
Nistru = Dnister →, *Europe* .... **59 J6** 46 18N 30 17 E
Nisutlin →, *Canada* **142 A2** 60 14N 132 34W
Nitchequon, *Canada* **141 B5** 53 10N 70 58W
Niterói, *Brazil* .... **171 F3** 22 52 S 43 0W
Nith →, *Canada* **150 C4** 43 12N 80 23W
Nith →, *U.K.* **22 F5** 55 14N 3 33W
Nitmiluk Nat. Park △, *Australia* **124 B5** 14 6 S 132 15 E
Nitra, *Slovak Rep.* .... **35 C11** 48 19N 18 4 E
Nitra →, *Slovak Rep.* .... **35 D11** 47 46N 18 10 E
Nitriansky □, *Slovak Rep.* ...... **35 C11** 48 10N 18 30 E
Nittenau, *Germany* .... **31 F8** 49 12N 12 16 E
Niu, *U.S.A.* **145 K14** 21 19N 157 44W
Niuafo'ou, *Tonga* .... **123 D15** 15 30 S 175 58W
Niue, *Cook Is.* .... **135 J11** 19 2 S 169 54W
Niulan Jiang →, *China* .... **76 D4** 27 30N 103 5 E
Niut, *Indonesia* .... **85 B4** 0 55N 110 6 E
Niutou Shan, *China* .... **77 C13** 29 5N 121 59 E
Niuzhuang, *China* .... **75 D12** 40 58N 122 28 E
Nivala, *Finland* .... **14 E21** 63 56N 24 57 E
Nivelles, *Belgium* .... **24 D4** 50 35N 4 20 E
Nivernais, *France* .... **27 E10** 47 15N 3 30 E
Niwas, *India* .... **93 H9** 23 3N 80 26 E
Nixon, *U.S.A.* **155 L6** 29 16N 97 46W
Nizam Sagar, *India* .... **94 E3** 18 10N 77 58 E
Nizamabad, *India* .... **94 E4** 18 45N 78 7 E
Nizamghat, *India* .... **90 A5** 28 20N 95 45 E
Nizhne Kolymsk, *Russia* .... **67 C17** 68 34N 160 55 E
Nizhnegorskiy = Nyzhnohirskyy,
   Ukraine .... **59 K8** 45 27N 34 38 E
Nizhnekamsk, *Russia* .... **60 C10** 55 38N 51 49 E
Nizhnekamskoye Vdkhr., *Russia* **64 D4** 55 56N 52 56 E
Nizhneudinsk, *Russia* .... **67 D10** 54 54N 99 3 E
Nizhnevartovsk, *Russia* .... **64 C8** 60 56N 76 38 E
Nizhniy Chir, *Russia* .... **61 F6** 48 22N 43 5 E
Nizhniy Lomov, *Russia* .... **60 D6** 53 34N 43 38 E
Nizhniy Novgorod, *Russia* ..... **60 B7** 56 20N 44 0 E
Nizhniy Tagil, *Russia* .... **64 C7** 57 55N 59 57 E
Nizhniye Sergi, *Russia* .... **65 C6** 56 40N 59 18 E
Nizhnyaya Salda, *Russia* ...... **64 B8** 58 8N 60 42 E
Nizhyn, *Ukraine* .... **59 G6** 51 5N 31 55 E
Nizina Mazowiecka, *Poland* ... **55 F8** 52 30N 21 0 E
Nizip, *Turkey* .... **100 D7** 37 5N 37 50 E
Nízké Tatry, *Slovak Rep.* .... **35 C12** 48 55N 19 30 E
Nízke Tatry, Národný Park △,
   Slovak Rep. .... **35 C12** 48 55N 19 37 E
Nízký Jeseník, *Czech Rep.* ...... **35 B10** 49 50N 17 30 E
Nizza Monferrato, *Italy* .... **40 D5** 44 46N 8 21 E
Njakwa, *Malawi* .... **119 E3** 11 1 S 33 56 E
Njanji, *Zambia* .... **119 E3** 14 25 S 31 46 E
Njarðvíkur, *Iceland* **11 D4** 63 59N 22 32W
Njazidja = Grande Comore,
   Comoros Is. .... **121 a** 11 35 S 43 20 E
Njegoš, *Montenegro, Yug.* ..... **50 D2** 42 53N 18 45 E
Njinjo, *Tanzania* .... **119 D4** 8 48 S 38 54 E
Njoku →, *Zambia* .... **115 F4** 17 8 S 24 4 E
Njombe, *Tanzania* .... **119 D3** 9 20 S 34 50 E
Njombe →, *Tanzania* .... **118 D3** 6 56 S 35 6 E
Njurundabommen, *Sweden* .... **16 B11** 62 15N 17 25 E
Nkambe, *Cameroon* .... **113 D7** 6 35N 10 40 E
Nkana, *Zambia* .... **119 E2** 12 50 S 28 8 E
Nkandla, *S. Africa* .... **117 D5** 28 37 S 31 5 E
Nkawkaw, *Ghana* **113 D4** 6 36N 0 49W
Nkayi, *Zimbabwe* .... **119 F2** 19 41 S 29 20 E
Nkhotakota, *Malawi* .... **119 E3** 12 56 S 34 15 E
Nkhotakota Game Reserve △,
   Malawi .... **119 E3** 12 50 S 34 0 E
Nkolabona, *Gabon* .... **114 B2** 1 14N 11 43 E
Nkomi, Lagune, *Gabon* .... **114 C1** 1 35 S 9 17 E
Nkone, *Dem. Rep. of the Congo* . **114 C4** 1 2 S 22 20 E
Nkongsamba, *Cameroon* ...... **113 E6** 4 55N 9 55 E
Nkunga, *Dem. Rep. of the Congo* **115 C3** 4 41 S 18 34 E
Nkurenkuru, *Namibia* .... **116 B2** 17 42 S 18 32 E
Nkwanta, *Ghana* **112 D4** 6 10N 2 10W
Nmai →, *Burma* .... **76 F2** 25 30N 97 25 E
Noakhali = Maijdi, *Bangla.* ..... **90 D3** 22 48N 91 10 E
Noatak, *U.S.A.* **144 C7** 67 34N 162 58W
Noatak Nat. Preserve △, *U.S.A.* **144 B8** 68 10N 160 0W
Nobel, *Canada* **150 A4** 45 25N 80 6W
Nobeoka, *Japan* .... **72 E3** 32 36N 131 41 E
Noblejas, *Spain* **42 F7** 39 58N 3 26W
Noblesville, *U.S.A.* **157 D11** 40 3N 86 1W
Nobonbetsu, *Japan* .... **70 C10** 42 24N 141 6 E
Nocatee, *U.S.A.* **153 H8** 27 10N 81 53W
Noce →, *Italy* .... **40 B7** 46 9N 11 4 E
Nocera Inferiore, *Italy* .... **47 B7** 40 44N 14 38 E
Nocera Umbra, *Italy* .... **45 E9** 43 5N 12 47 E
Noci, *Italy* .... **47 B10** 40 48N 17 7 E
Nocona, *U.S.A.* **155 J6** 33 47N 97 44W
Nocrich, *Romania* .... **53 E9** 45 55N 24 26 E
Noda, *Japan* .... **73 B11** 35 56N 139 52 E
Nodeland, *Norway* .... **18 E4** 58 8N 7 51 E
Nogal Valley = Nugaaleed, Dooxo,
   Somali Rep. .... **120 C3** 8 35N 48 35 E
Nogales, *Mexico* **162 A2** 31 20N 110 56W
Nogales, *U.S.A.* **159 L8** 31 20N 110 56W
Nogaro, *France* **28 E3** 43 45N 0 2W
Nogat →, *Poland* .... **54 D6** 54 17N 19 17 E
Nōgata, *Japan* .... **72 D2** 33 48N 130 44 E
Nogent, *France* .... **27 D12** 48 1N 5 20 E
Nogent-le-Rotrou, *France* ...... **26 D7** 48 20N 0 50 E
Nogent-sur-Seine, *France* ...... **27 D10** 48 30N 3 30 E
Noggerup, *Australia* .... **125 F2** 33 32 S 116 5 E
Noginsk, *Moskva, Russia* ...... **58 E10** 55 50N 38 25 E
Noginsk, *Tunguska, Russia* ..... **67 C10** 64 30N 90 50 E
Nogoa →, *Australia* .... **126 C4** 23 40 S 147 55 E
Nogoyá, *Argentina* .... **174 C4** 32 24 S 59 48W
Nógrád □, *Hungary* .... **52 C4** 48 0N 19 30 E
Noguera Pallaresa →, *Spain* ... **40 D5** 41 55N 0 52 E
Noguera Ribagorzana →, *Spain* **40 D5** 41 40N 0 43 E
Nohar, *India* .... **92 E6** 29 11N 74 49 E
Nohili Pt., *U.S.A.* **145 A2** 22 1N 159 47W
Nohta, *India* .... **93 H8** 23 40N 79 34 E
Noia, *Spain* **42 C2** 42 48N 8 53W
Noichi, *Japan* .... **72 D5** 33 33N 133 42 E
Noing, *Phil.* .... **83 J5** 5 40N 125 28 E
Noipuos, *Papua N. G.* .... **132 B6** 2 25 S 150 7 E
Noire, Montagne, *France* ...... **28 E6** 43 28N 2 16 E
Noires, Mts., *France* **26 D3** 48 11N 3 40W
Noirétable, *France* .... **28 C7** 45 48N 3 46 E
Noirmoutier, I. de, *France* **26 F4** 46 58N 2 10W
Noirmoutier-en-l'Île, *France* **26 F4** 47 0N 2 14W
Nojane, *Botswana* .... **116 C3** 23 15 S 20 14 E
Nojima-Zaki, *Japan* .... **73 C11** 34 54N 139 53 E
Nok Kundi, *Pakistan* .... **91 C1** 28 50N 62 45 E
Nok Ta Phao, Ko, *Thailand* ..... **87 b** 9 23N 99 40 E
Nokaneng, *Botswana* .... **116 B3** 19 40 S 22 17 E
Nokia, *Finland* .... **15 F20** 61 30N 23 30 E
Nokomis, *Canada* **143 C8** 51 35N 105 0W
Nokomis, *U.S.A.* **153 H7** 27 7N 82 28W
Nokomis, *Ill., U.S.A.* **154 F10** 39 18N 89 18W
Nokomis L., *Canada* **143 B8** 57 0N 103 0W
Nokou, *Chad* .... **109 F2** 14 35N 14 47 E
Nokuku, *Vanuatu* .... **133 C5** 14 54 S 166 35 E
Nol, *Sweden* .... **17 G6** 57 56N 12 5 E
Nola, *C.A.R.* .... **114 B3** 3 35N 16 4 E
Nola, *Italy* .... **47 B7** 40 55N 14 33 E
Nolay, *France* .... **27 F11** 46 58N 4 35 E
Noli, C. di, *Italy* .... **40 D5** 44 12N 8 25 E
Nolinsk, *Russia* .... **60 B9** 57 28N 49 57 E
Noma, *U.S.A.* **152 K4** 30 59N 85 37W
Noma Omuramba →, *Namibia* **116 B3** 18 52 S 20 53 E

Noma-Saki, Japan · 72 F2 31 25N 130 7 E
Nomad, Papua N.G. · 132 D2 6 19 S 142 13 E
Nombre de Dios, Panama · 144 D6 9 34N 79 28W
Nome, U.S.A. · 144 B3 64 30N 165 25W
Nomo-Zaki, Japan · 72 E1 32 35N 129 44 E
Nomuka, Tonga · 133 Q13 20 17 S 174 48W
Nomuka Group, Tonga · 133 Q13 20 20 S 174 48W
Nonacho L., Canada · 143 A7 61 42N 109 40W
Nonancourt, France · 26 D8 48 47N 1 11 E
Nonda, Australia · 126 C3 20 40 S 142 28 E
Nondalton, U.S.A. · 144 G9 60 0N 154 51W
None, Italy · 44 D4 44 56N 7 32 E
Nong Chang, Thailand · 86 E2 15 23N 99 51 E
Nong Het, Laos · 86 C4 19 29N 103 59 E
Nong Khai, Thailand · 86 D4 17 50N 102 46 E
Nong'an, China · 75 B13 44 25N 125 5 E
Nongoma, S. Africa · 117 D5 27 58 S 31 35 E
Nongsa, Indonesia · 87 d 1 11N 104 8 E
Nongstoin, India · 90 C3 25 31N 91 16 E
Nonoava, Mexico · 162 B3 27 28N 106 44W
Nonoava →, Mexico · 162 B3 27 29N 106 45W
Nonoc I., Phil. · 81 G5 9 51N 125 37 E
Nonthaburi, Thailand · 86 F3 13 51N 100 34 E
Nontron, France · 28 C4 45 31N 0 40 E
Nonza, France · 29 F13 42 47N 9 21 E
Noonamah, Australia · 124 B5 12 40 S 131 4 E
Noord Brabant □, Neths. · 24 C5 51 40N 5 0 E
Noord Holland □, Neths. · 24 B4 52 30N 4 45 E
Noordbeveland, Neths. · 24 C3 51 35N 3 50 E
Noordoostpolder, Neths. · 24 B5 52 45N 5 45 E
Noordwijk, Neths. · 24 B4 52 14N 4 26 E
Noorvik, U.S.A. · 144 C7 66 50N 161 3W
Nootka I., Canada · 142 D3 49 32N 126 42W
Nopiming Prov. Park △, Canada · 143 C9 50 30N 95 37W
Nóqui, Angola · 115 D2 5 55 S 13 30 E
Nora, Eritrea · 107 D5 16 6N 40 4 E
Nora, Sweden · 16 E9 59 32N 15 2 E
Nora Springs, U.S.A. · 156 A4 43 9N 93 0W
Norak = Nurek, Tajikistan · 65 D4 38 23N 69 19 E
Norala, Phil. · 81 H5 6 32N 124 40 E
Noralee, Canada · 142 C3 53 59N 126 26W
Noranda = Rouyn-Noranda, Canada · 140 C4 48 20N 79 0W
Norberg, Sweden · 16 D9 60 4N 15 56 E
Norborne, U.S.A. · 156 E3 39 18N 93 40W
Nórcia, Italy · 45 F10 42 48N 13 5 E
Norco, U.S.A. · 161 M9 33 56N 117 33W
Norcross, U.S.A. · 152 B5 33 56N 84 13W
Nord □, France · 27 B10 50 15N 3 30 E
Nord Kivu □, Dem. Rep. of the Congo · 118 C2 1 0 S 29 0 E
Nord-og-Østgrønland, Nationalparken i △, Greenland · 10 C7 75 0N 35 0 E
Nord-Ostsee-Kanal, Germany · 30 A5 54 12N 9 32 E
Nord-Pas-de-Calais □, France · 27 B9 50 30N 2 50 E
Nordagutu, Norway · 18 E6 59 25N 9 20 E
Nordaustlandet, Svalbard · 6 B9 79 14N 23 0 E
Nordberg, Norway · 18 C5 61 54N 8 10 E
Nordborg, Denmark · 17 J3 55 5N 9 50 E
Nordby, Denmark · 17 J2 55 27N 8 24 E
Norddeich, Germany · 30 B3 53 36N 7 9 E
Nordegg, Canada · 142 C5 52 29N 116 5W
Norden, Germany · 30 B3 53 35N 7 12 E
Nordenham, Germany · 30 B4 53 29N 8 30 E
Norderhov, Norway · 18 D7 60 7N 10 17 E
Norderney, Germany · 30 B3 53 42N 7 9 E
Norderstedt, Germany · 30 B6 53 42N 10 1 E
Nordeste, Azores · 9 d3 37 50N 25 10W
Nordfjord, Norway · 18 C2 61 55N 5 30 E
Nordfjordeid, Norway · 18 C2 61 54N 6 0 E
Nordfriesische Inseln, Germany · 30 A4 54 40N 8 20 E
Nordgrønland = Avannaarsua □, Greenland · 10 B5 80 0N 55 0W
Nordhausen, Germany · 30 D6 51 30N 10 47 E
Nordhorn, Germany · 30 C3 52 26N 7 4 E
Nordøyar, Færoe Is. · 14 E9 62 17N 6 35W
Norðtunga, Iceland · 11 C5 64 44N 21 24W
Norður-múlasýsla □, Iceland · 11 B11 65 30N 15 0W
Norðurbotn, Iceland · 11 B3 65 36N 23 46W
Nordingrå, Sweden · 16 B12 62 56N 18 17 E
Nordjyllands Amtskommune □, Denmark · 17 G4 57 20N 10 0 E
Nordkapp, Norway · 14 A21 71 10N 25 50 E
Nordkapp, Svalbard · 6 A9 80 31N 20 0 E
Nordkinn = Kinnarodden, Norway · 12 A11 71 8N 27 40 E
Nordkinn-halvøya, Norway · 14 A22 70 55N 27 40 E
Nördlicher Teutoburger Wald-Wiehengebirge, Naturpark △, Germany · 30 C4 52 18N 8 10 E
Nördlingen, Germany · 31 G6 48 48N 10 30 E
Nordmøre, Norway · 18 B4 63 6N 8 15 E
Nordstrundingen, Greenland · 10 A9 81 22N 11 40W
Nordøyane, Norway · 18 B3 62 40N 6 0 E
Nordre Osen, Norway · 18 D5 61 18N 11 45 E
Nordre Strømfjord, Greenland · 10 D5 67 10N 53 35W
Nordrhein-Westfalen □, Germany · 30 D3 51 45N 7 30 E
Nordsinni, Norway · 18 D6 60 50N 9 57 E
Nørdstedalsseter, Norway · 18 C4 61 40N 7 48 E
Nordstrand, Germany · 30 A4 54 30N 8 52 E
Nordvik, Russia · 67 B12 74 2N 111 32 E
Nore →, Ireland · 23 D4 52 25N 6 58W
Norefjell, Norway · 18 D6 60 16N 9 29 E
Noresund, Norway · 18 D6 60 11N 9 37 E
Norfolk, Nebr., U.S.A. · 154 D6 42 2N 97 25W
Norfolk, Va., U.S.A. · 148 G7 36 51N 76 17W
Norfolk □, U.K. · 21 E8 52 39N 0 54 E
Norfolk I., Pac. Oc. · 134 K8 28 58 S 168 3 E
Norfork L., U.S.A. · 155 G8 36 15N 92 14W
Norheimsund, Norway · 18 D2 60 22N 6 6 E
Norilsk, Russia · 67 C9 69 20N 88 6 E
Norma, Mt., Australia · 126 C3 20 55 S 140 42 E
Normal, U.S.A. · 156 D8 40 31N 88 59W
Norman, U.S.A. · 155 H6 35 13N 97 26W
Norman →, Australia · 126 B3 19 18 S 141 51 E
Norman Park, U.S.A. · 152 D6 31 16N 83 41W
Norman Wells, Canada · 138 B7 65 17N 126 51W
Normanby, N.Z. · 130 F3 39 32 S 174 18 E
Normanby →, Australia · 126 A3 14 23 S 144 10 E
Normanby I., Papua N.G. · 132 F6 10 5 S 151 5 E
Normandie, France · 25 B4 48 45N 0 10 E
Normandie-Maine, Parc Naturel Régional △, France · 26 D6 48 30N 0 20W
Normandin, Canada · 140 C5 48 49N 72 31W
Normandy = Normandie, France · 25 B4 48 45N 0 10 E
Normanhurst, Mt., Australia · 125 E3 25 4 S 122 30 E
Normanton, Australia · 126 B3 17 40 S 141 10 E
Normanville, Australia · 128 C3 35 27 S 138 18 E
Normétal, Canada · 140 C4 49 0N 79 22W
Norquay, Canada · 143 C8 51 53N 102 5W
Norquinco, Argentina · 176 B2 41 51 S 70 55W
Norra Dellen, Sweden · 16 C10 61 53N 16 43 E
Norra Kvill Nationalpark △, Sweden · 17 G9 57 46N 15 35 E
Norra Ulvön, Sweden · 16 A12 63 1N 18 40 E
Norrahammar, Sweden · 17 G8 57 43N 14 7 E
Norrbotten □, Sweden · 14 C19 66 30N 22 30 E
Nørre Åby, Denmark · 17 J3 55 27N 9 52 E
Nørre Alslev, Denmark · 17 K5 54 54N 11 52 E
Nørresundby, Denmark · 17 G3 57 5N 9 52 E
Nørrhult, Sweden · 17 G9 57 7N 15 10 E
Norris City, U.S.A. · 157 G8 37 59N 88 20W
Norris Point, Canada · 141 C8 49 31N 57 53W
Norristown, Ga., U.S.A. · 152 C7 32 30N 82 30W
Norristown, Pa., U.S.A. · 151 F9 40 7N 75 21W
Norrköping, Sweden · 17 F10 58 37N 16 11 E

Norrland, Sweden · 15 E16 62 15N 15 45 E
Norrsundet, Sweden · 16 D11 60 56N 17 8 E
Norrtälje, Sweden · 16 E12 59 46N 18 42 E
Norseman, Australia · 125 F3 32 8 S 121 43 E
Norsewood, N.Z. · 130 G5 40 3 S 176 13 E
Norsjø, Norway · 18 E6 59 18N 9 20 E
Norsk, Russia · 67 D14 52 30N 130 5 E
Norsup, Vanuatu · 133 F5 16 3 S 167 24 E
Norte, C., Chile · 172 b 27 3 S 109 24W
Norte, Canal do →, Brazil · 169 C7 0 50N 50 20W
Norte, Pta., Argentina · 176 B4 42 5 S 63 46W
Norte, Pta. do, Canary Is. · 9 e1 27 51N 17 57W
Norte, Serra do, Brazil · 173 C6 11 20 S 59 0W
Norte de Santander □, Colombia · 168 B3 8 0N 73 0W
Norte Grande, Azores · 9 d1 38 40N 28 4W
Nortelândia, Brazil · 173 C6 14 25 S 56 48W
North, U.S.A. · 152 B8 33 37N 81 6W
North, C., Canada · 141 C7 47 2N 60 20W
North Adams, U.S.A. · 151 D11 42 42N 73 7W
North Andaman I., India · 95 H11 13 15N 92 55 E
North Arm, Canada · 142 A5 62 0N 114 30W
North Atlantic Ocean, Atl. Oc. · 8 C7 30 0N 50 0W
North Augusta, U.S.A. · 152 B8 33 30N 81 59W
North Ayrshire □, U.K. · 22 F4 55 45N 4 44W
North Bass I., U.S.A. · 150 E2 41 40N 82 53W
North Battleford, Canada · 143 C7 52 50N 108 17W
North Bay, Canada · 140 C4 46 20N 79 30W
North Belcher Is., Canada · 140 A4 56 50N 79 50W
North Bend, Oreg., U.S.A. · 158 E1 43 24N 124 14W
North Bend, Pa., U.S.A. · 150 E7 41 20N 77 42W
North Bend, Wash., U.S.A. · 160 C5 47 30N 121 47W
North Bennington, U.S.A. · 151 D11 42 56N 73 15W
North Berwick, U.K. · 22 E6 56 4N 2 42W
North Berwick, U.S.A. · 151 C14 43 18N 70 44W
North Brother I., India · 95 J11 10 59N 92 40 E
North C., Canada · 141 C7 47 5N 64 0W
North C., N.Z. · 130 A2 34 23 S 173 4 E
North C., Papua N. G. · 132 B6 2 32 S 150 50 E
North Canadian →, U.S.A. · 155 H7 35 16N 95 31W
North Canton, U.S.A. · 150 F3 40 53N 81 24W
North Cape = Nordkapp, Norway · 14 A21 71 10N 25 50 E
North Cape = Nordkapp, Svalbard · 6 A9 80 31N 20 0 E
North Caribou L., Canada · 140 B1 52 50N 90 40W
North Carolina □, U.S.A. · 149 H5 35 30N 80 0W
North Cascades Nat. Park △, U.S.A. · 158 B3 48 45N 121 10W
North Cay, Bahamas · 9 b 25 6N 77 26W
North Channel, Canada · 140 C3 46 0N 83 0W
North Channel, U.K. · 22 F3 55 13N 5 52W
North Charleston, U.S.A. · 152 C10 32 53N 79 58W
North Chicago, U.S.A. · 157 B9 42 19N 87 51W
North College Hill, U.S.A. · 157 E12 39 13N 84 33W
North Comino Channel, Malta · 38 E7 36 1N 14 20 E
North Creek, U.S.A. · 151 C11 43 41N 73 59W
North Dakota □, U.S.A. · 154 B5 47 30N 100 15W
North Downs, U.K. · 21 F8 51 19N 0 21 E
North East, U.S.A. · 150 D5 42 13N 79 50W
North East B., Ascension I. · 9 g 7 55 S 14 21W
North East Frontier Agency = Arunachal Pradesh □, India · 90 A5 28 0N 95 0 E
North East Lincolnshire □, U.K. · 20 D7 53 34N 0 2W
North Eastern □, Kenya · 118 B5 1 30N 40 0 E
North Esk →, U.K. · 22 E6 56 46N 2 24W
North European Plain, Europe · 12 E10 55 0N 25 0 E
North Fabius →, U.S.A. · 156 E5 39 54N 91 30W
North Foreland, U.K. · 21 F9 51 22N 1 28 E
North Fork, U.S.A. · 160 H7 37 14N 119 21W
North Fork, Salt →, U.S.A. · 156 E5 39 26N 91 53W
North Fork American →, U.S.A. · 160 G5 38 57N 120 59W
North Fork Edisto →, U.S.A. · 152 B9 33 16N 80 54W
North Fork Feather →, U.S.A. · 160 F5 38 33N 121 30W
North Fork Grand →, U.S.A. · 154 C3 45 47N 102 16W
North Fork Red →, U.S.A. · 155 H5 34 24N 99 14W
North Fort Myers, U.S.A. · 153 J8 26 41N 81 53W
North Frisian Is. = Nordfriesische Inseln, Germany · 30 A4 54 40N 8 20 E
North Gower, Canada · 151 A9 45 8N 75 43W
North Hd., Australia · 125 F1 30 14 S 114 59 E
North Henik L., Canada · 143 A9 61 45N 97 40W
North Highlands, U.S.A. · 160 G5 38 40N 121 23W
North Horr, Kenya · 118 B4 3 20N 37 8 E
North I., India · 95 J1 1 8N 72 20 E
North I., Kenya · 118 B4 4 5N 36 5 E
North I., N.Z. · 130 E4 38 0 S 175 0 E
North I., Seychelles · 121 b 4 25 S 55 13 E
North Judson, U.S.A. · 157 C10 41 13N 86 46W
North Kingsville, U.S.A. · 150 E4 41 54N 80 42W
North Kitui Nat. Reserve △, Kenya · 118 C4 0 15 S 38 29 E
North Knife →, Canada · 143 B10 58 53N 94 45W
North Koel →, India · 93 G10 24 45N 83 50 E
North Korea ■, Asia · 75 E14 40 0N 127 0 E
North L., Australia · 128 B5 32 30 S 143 5 E
North Lakhimpur, India · 90 B5 27 14N 94 7 E
North Lanarkshire □, U.K. · 22 F5 55 52N 3 56W
North Las Vegas, U.S.A. · 161 J11 36 12N 115 7W
North Liberty, U.S.A. · 157 C10 41 32N 86 26W
North Lincolnshire □, U.K. · 20 D7 53 36N 0 30W
North Little Rock, U.S.A. · 155 H8 34 45N 92 16W
North Loup →, U.S.A. · 154 E5 41 17N 98 24W
North Luangwa Nat. Park △, Zambia · 119 E3 11 49 S 32 9 E
North Magnetic Pole, Canada · 6 A2 88 30N 107 0W
North Manchester, U.S.A. · 157 D11 41 0N 85 46W
North Miami Beach, U.S.A. · 153 K9 25 56N 80 10W
North Minch, U.K. · 22 C3 58 5N 5 55W
North Moose L., Canada · 143 C8 54 11N 100 6W
North Myrtle Beach, U.S.A. · 153 J6 33 48N 78 42W
North Nahanni →, Canada · 142 A4 62 15N 123 20W
North Naples, U.S.A. · 153 J8 26 12N 81 48W
North New River Canal, U.S.A. · 153 J9 26 30N 80 30W
North Olmsted, U.S.A. · 150 E3 41 25N 81 56W
North Ossetia □, Russia · 61 J7 43 30N 44 30 E
North Pagai, I. = Pagai Utara, Pulau, Indonesia · 84 C2 2 35 S 100 0 E
North Palisade, U.S.A. · 160 H8 37 6N 118 31W
North Platte, U.S.A. · 154 E4 41 8N 100 46W
North Platte →, U.S.A. · 154 E4 41 7N 100 42W
North Pole, Arctic · 6 A 90 0N 0 0W
North Pole, Canada · 144 D11 64 45N 147 21W
North Portal, Canada · 143 D8 49 0N 102 33W
North Powder, U.S.A. · 158 D5 45 2N 117 55W
North Pt., Ascension I. · 9 g 7 53 S 14 23W
North Pt., Barbados · 165 g 13 20N 59 37W
North Pt., Trin. & Tob. · 169 E10 11 21N 60 31W
North Pt., U.S.A. · 150 A1 45 2N 83 16W
North Pt., Vanuatu · 133 D6 14 56 S 168 6 E
North Reef I., India · 95 H11 13 0N 92 43 E
North Rhine Westphalia = Nordrhein-Westfalen □, Germany · 30 D3 51 45N 7 30 E
North River, Canada · 141 B8 53 49N 57 6W
North Ronaldsay, U.K. · 22 B6 59 22N 2 26W
North Salem, U.S.A. · 157 E10 39 52N 86 39W
North Saskatchewan →, Canada · 143 C7 53 15N 105 5W
North Sea, Europe · 12 D6 56 0N 4 0 E
North Seal →, Canada · 143 B9 58 50N 98 7W
North Sentinel I., India · 95 J11 11 33N 92 15 E
North Shields, Australia · 128 C1 34 38 S 135 52 E
North Solomons □, Papua N. G. · 132 B8 6 0 S 155 0 E
North Somerset □, U.K. · 21 F5 51 24N 2 45W
North Sporades = Vóriai Sporádhes, Greece · 48 B5 39 15N 23 30 E
North Sydney, Canada · 141 C7 46 12N 60 15W
North Syracuse, U.S.A. · 151 C8 43 8N 76 7W

North Thompson →, Canada · 142 C4 50 40N 120 20W
North Tonawanda, U.S.A. · 150 C6 43 2N 78 53W
North Troy, U.S.A. · 151 B12 45 0N 72 24W
North Truchas Pk., U.S.A. · 159 J11 36 0N 105 30W
North Tyne →, U.K. · 20 B5 55 0N 2 8W
North Uist, U.K. · 22 D1 57 40N 7 15W
North Vancouver, Canada · 142 D4 49 19N 123 4W
North Vernon, U.S.A. · 157 F11 39 0N 85 38W
North Wabasca L., Canada · 142 B6 56 0N 113 55W
North Walsham, U.K. · 21 E9 52 50N 1 22 E
North Webster, U.S.A. · 157 C11 41 25N 85 48W
North-West □, S. Africa · 116 D4 27 0 S 25 0 E
North West C., Australia · 124 D1 21 45 S 114 9 E
North West Christmas I. Ridge, Pac. Oc. · 135 G11 6 30N 165 0W
North West Frontier □, Pakistan · 91 B3 34 0N 72 0 E
North West Highlands, U.K. · 22 D4 57 33N 4 58W
North West River, Canada · 141 B7 53 30N 60 10W
North Western □, Zambia · 119 E2 13 30 S 25 30 E
North Wildwood, U.S.A. · 148 F8 39 0N 74 48W
North York Moors, U.K. · 20 C7 54 23N 0 53W
North York Moors Nat. Park △, U.K. · 20 C7 54 27N 0 51W
North Yorkshire □, U.K. · 20 C6 54 15N 1 25W
Northallerton, U.K. · 20 C6 54 20N 1 26W
Northam, Australia · 125 F2 31 35 S 116 42 E
Northam, S. Africa · 116 C4 24 56 S 27 18 E
Northampton, Australia · 125 E1 28 27 S 114 33 E
Northampton, U.K. · 21 E7 52 15N 0 53W
Northampton, Mass., U.S.A. · 151 D12 42 19N 72 38W
Northampton, Pa., U.S.A. · 151 F9 40 41N 75 30W
Northamptonshire □, U.K. · 21 E7 52 16N 0 55W
Northbridge, U.S.A. · 151 D13 42 9N 71 39W
Northcliffe, Australia · 125 F2 34 39 S 116 7 E
Northeast C., U.S.A. · 144 B5 63 18N 168 42W
Northeast Providence Chan., W. Indies · 164 A4 26 0N 76 0W
Northeim, Germany · 30 D6 51 42N 10 0 E
Northern □, Malawi · 119 E3 11 0 S 34 0 E
Northern □, Papua N. G. · 132 E5 9 0 S 148 30 E
Northern □, S. Africa · 117 C4 24 0 S 29 0 E
Northern □, Zambia · 119 E3 10 30 S 31 0 E
Northern Areas □, Pakistan · 65 E6 36 30N 73 0 E
Northern Cape □, S. Africa · 116 D3 30 0 S 20 0 E
Northern Circars, India · 94 F6 17 30N 82 30 E
Northern Indian L., Canada · 143 B9 57 20N 97 20W
Northern Ireland □, U.K. · 23 B5 54 45N 7 0W
Northern Lau Group, Fiji · 133 A3 17 30 S 178 59W
Northern Light L., Canada · 140 C1 48 15N 90 39W
Northern Marianas ☑, Pac. Oc. · 134 F6 17 0N 145 0 E
Northern Mid-Atlantic Ridge, Atl. Oc. · 8 C8 35 0N 35 0W
Northern Province □, S. Leone · 112 D2 9 15N 11 30W
Northern Province □, S. Africa · 117 C4 24 0 S 29 0 E
Northern Range, Trin. & Tob. · 169 F9 10 46N 61 15W
Northern Rhodesia = Zambia ■, Africa · 119 F2 15 0 S 28 0 E
Northern Samar □, Phil. · 80 E5 12 30N 124 40 E
Northern Territory □, Australia · 124 D5 20 0 S 133 0 E
Northfield, Minn., U.S.A. · 154 C8 44 27N 93 9W
Northfield, Vt., U.S.A. · 151 B12 44 9N 72 40W
Northland □, N.Z. · 130 B2 35 30 S 173 30 E
Northome, U.S.A. · 154 B7 47 52N 94 17W
Northport, Ala., U.S.A. · 149 J2 33 14N 87 35W
Northport, Wash., U.S.A. · 158 B5 48 55N 117 48W
Northumberland □, U.K. · 20 B6 55 12N 2 0W
Northumberland, C., Australia · 128 E4 38 5 S 140 40 E
Northumberland Is., Australia · 126 C4 21 30 S 149 50 E
Northumberland Str., Canada · 141 C7 46 20N 64 0W
Northville, U.S.A. · 151 C10 43 13N 74 11W
Northway, U.S.A. · 144 E12 62 58N 141 56W
Northwest Providence Channel, W. Indies · 164 A4 26 0N 78 0W
Northwest Pt., Bahamas · 9 b 25 4N 77 31W
Northwest Territories □, Canada · 138 B9 63 0N 118 0W
Northwich, U.K. · 20 D5 53 15N 2 31W
Northwood, Iowa, U.S.A. · 154 D8 43 27N 93 13W
Northwood, N. Dak., U.S.A. · 154 B6 47 44N 97 34W
Norton, U.S.A. · 154 F5 39 50N 99 53W
Norton, Zimbabwe · 119 F3 17 52 S 30 40 E
Norton B., U.S.A. · 144 D7 64 45N 161 15W
Norton Sd., U.S.A. · 144 D7 63 50N 164 0W
Norton Shores, U.S.A. · 157 A10 43 8N 86 15W
Nortorf, Germany · 30 A5 54 10N 9 50 E
Norwalk, Calif., U.S.A. · 161 M8 33 54N 118 5W
Norwalk, Conn., U.S.A. · 151 E11 41 7N 73 22W
Norwalk, Iowa, U.S.A. · 154 C8 41 29N 93 41W
Norwalk, Ohio, U.S.A. · 150 E2 41 15N 82 37W
Norway, Maine, U.S.A. · 149 C10 44 13N 70 32W
Norway, Mich., U.S.A. · 148 C2 45 47N 87 55W
Norway ■, Europe · 14 E14 63 0N 11 0 E
Norway House, Canada · 143 C9 53 59N 97 50W
Norwegian Sea, Atl. Oc. · 12 B6 66 0N 1 0 E
Norwich, Canada · 150 D4 42 59N 80 36W
Norwich, U.K. · 21 E9 52 38N 1 18 E
Norwich, Conn., U.S.A. · 151 E12 41 31N 72 5W
Norwich, N.Y., U.S.A. · 151 D9 42 32N 75 32W
Norwood, Canada · 150 B7 44 23N 77 59W
Norwood, N.Y., U.S.A. · 151 B10 44 45N 75 0W
Norwood, Ohio, U.S.A. · 157 E12 39 10N 84 27W
Noshiro, Japan · 70 D10 40 12N 140 0 E
Nosivka, Ukraine · 59 G6 50 50N 31 37 E
Nosovka = Nosivka, Ukraine · 59 G6 50 50N 31 37 E
Noṣratābād, Iran · 89 D8 29 55N 60 0 E
Noss Hd., U.K. · 22 C5 58 28N 3 3W
Nossa Senhora da Glória, Brazil · 170 D4 10 14 S 37 25W
Nossa Senhora das Dores, Brazil · 170 D4 10 29 S 37 13W
Nossa Senhora do Livramento, Brazil · 173 D6 15 48 S 56 22W
Nossebro, Sweden · 17 F6 58 12N 12 43 E
Nossob, S. Africa · 116 D3 26 55 S 20 45 E
Nossombougou, Mali · 112 C3 13 55N 7 45W
Nosy Boraha, Madag. · 117 B8 16 50 S 49 55 E
Nosy Lava, Madag. · 117 A8 14 33 S 47 36 E
Nosy Varika, Madag. · 117 C8 20 35 S 48 32 E
Notasulga, U.S.A. · 152 C4 32 34N 85 41W
Noteć →, Poland · 31 B8 52 44N 15 26 E
Notikewin →, Canada · 142 B5 57 2N 117 38W
Notio Aigaio = Notios Aiyaíon □, Greece · 49 E7 36 52N 25 34 E
Notios Aiyaíon □, Greece · 49 E7 36 52N 25 34 E
Notios Evvoïkos Kólpos, Greece · 49 C5 38 20N 24 0 E
Noto, Italy · 47 F8 36 53N 15 4 E
Noto, G. di, Italy · 47 F8 36 50N 15 12 E
Notodden, Norway · 18 E6 59 35N 9 17 E
Notre Dame de Koartac = Quaqtaq, Canada · 139 B13 60 55N 69 40W
Notre Dame d'Ivugivic = Ivujivik, Canada · 139 B12 62 24N 77 55W
Notre-Dame-du-Nord, Canada · 140 C4 47 36N 79 30W
Notsé, Togo · 113 D5 6 57N 1 4 E
Nottawasaga B., Canada · 150 B4 44 35N 80 15W
Nottaway →, Canada · 140 B4 51 22N 78 55W
Nottingham, U.K. · 20 E6 52 58N 1 10W
Nottingham, City of □, U.K. · 20 E6 52 58N 1 10W
Nottingham I., Canada · 139 B12 63 20N 77 55W
Nottinghamshire □, U.K. · 20 D6 53 10N 1 3W
Nottoway →, U.S.A. · 148 G7 36 33N 76 55W
Notwane →, Botswana · 116 C4 23 35 S 26 58 E
Nouâdhibou, Mauritania · 110 D1 20 54N 17 0W
Nouâdhibou, Dakhlet, Mauritania · 110 D1 20 50N 16 52W

Nouâdhibou, Ras, Mauritania · 110 D1 20 50N 17 0W
Nouakchott, Mauritania · 112 B1 18 9N 15 58W
Nouâmghâr, Mauritania · 112 B1 19 20N 16 20W
Nouméa, N. Cal. · 133 V20 22 17 S 166 30 E
Nouna, Burkina Faso · 112 C4 12 45N 3 52W
Noupoort, S. Africa · 116 E3 31 10 S 24 57 E
Nouveau Comptoir = Wemindji, Canada · 140 B4 53 0N 78 49W
Nouvelle-Amsterdam, I., Ind. Oc. · 121 H6 38 30 S 77 30 E
Nouvelle-Calédonie = New Caledonia ☑, Pac. Oc. · 133 U20 21 0 S 165 0 E
Nouzonville, France · 27 C11 49 48N 4 44 E
Nov = Nau, Tajikistan · 65 C4 40 9N 69 22 E
Nová Baňa, Slovak Rep. · 35 C11 48 28N 18 39 E
Nová Bystřice, Czech Rep. · 34 B8 49 2N 15 8 E
Nova Casa Nova, Brazil · 170 C3 9 25 S 41 5W
Nova Cruz, Brazil · 170 C4 6 28 S 35 25W
Nova Era, Brazil · 171 E3 19 45 S 43 3W
Nova Esperança, Brazil · 175 A5 23 8 S 52 24W
Nova-Freixo = Cuamba, Mozam. · 119 E4 14 45 S 36 22 E
Nova Friburgo, Brazil · 171 F3 22 16 S 42 30W
Nova Gaia = Cambundi-Catembo, Angola · 115 E3 10 10 S 17 35 E
Nova Gorica, Slovenia · 45 C10 45 57N 13 39 E
Nova Gradiška, Croatia · 52 E2 45 17N 17 28 E
Nova Granada, Brazil · 171 F2 20 30 S 49 20W
Nova Iguaçu, Brazil · 171 F3 22 45 S 43 28W
Nova Iorque, Brazil · 170 C3 7 0 S 44 5W
Nova Kakhovka, Ukraine · 59 J7 46 42N 33 27 E
Nova Lamego = Gabú, Guinea-Biss. · 112 C2 12 9N 14 11W
Nova Lima, Brazil · 175 A7 19 59 S 43 51W
Nova Lisboa = Huambo, Angola · 115 E3 12 42 S 15 54 E
Nova Lusitânia, Mozam. · 119 F3 19 50 S 34 34 E
Nova Mambone, Mozam. · 117 C6 21 0 S 35 3 E
Nova Odesa, Ukraine · 59 J6 47 19N 31 47 E
Nova Olinda do Norte, Brazil · 169 D6 3 45 S 59 3W
Nová Paka, Czech Rep. · 34 A8 50 29N 15 30 E
Nova Pavova, Serbia, Yug. · 52 F5 44 56N 20 14 E
Nova Ponte, Brazil · 171 E2 19 8 S 47 41W
Nova Scotia □, Canada · 141 C7 45 10N 63 0W
Nova Siri, Italy · 47 B9 40 10N 16 38 E
Nova Sofala, Mozam. · 117 C6 20 7 S 34 42 E
Nova Varoš, Serbia, Yug. · 50 C3 43 29N 19 48 E
Nova Venécia, Brazil · 171 E3 18 45 S 40 24W
Nova Vida, Brazil · 173 C5 10 1 S 60 30W
Nova Zagora, Bulgaria · 51 D10 42 32N 26 1 E
Nováci, Macedonia · 50 E5 41 5N 21 29 E
Novaci, Romania · 53 E8 45 10N 23 42 E
Novaféltria, Italy · 45 E9 43 53N 12 17 E
Novaleksandrovskaya = Novoaleksandrovsk, Russia · 61 H5 45 29N 41 17 E
Novannenskiy = Novoannenskiy, Russia · 60 E6 50 32N 42 39 E
Novar, Canada · 150 A5 45 27N 79 15W
Novara, Italy · 44 C5 45 28N 8 38 E
Novato, U.S.A. · 160 G4 38 6N 122 35W
Novaya Kakhovka = Nova Kakhovka, Ukraine · 59 J7 46 42N 33 27 E
Novaya Kazanka, Kazakhstan · 61 F9 48 56N 49 36 E
Novaya Ladoga, Russia · 58 B7 60 7N 32 16 E
Novaya Lyalya, Russia · 67 B16 75 10N 60 45 E
Novaya Sibir, Ostrov, Russia · 67 B16 75 10N 150 0 E
Novaya Zemlya, Russia · 66 B7 75 0N 56 0 E
Nové Město, Slovak Rep. · 35 C10 48 45N 17 50 E
Nové Město na Moravě, Czech Rep. · 34 B9 49 34N 16 5 E
Nové Město nad Metují, Czech Rep. · 35 A9 50 20N 16 10 E
Nové Zámky, Slovak Rep. · 35 C11 48 2N 18 8 E
Novelda, Spain · 41 G4 38 24N 0 45W
Novellara, Italy · 44 D7 44 51N 10 44 E
Novelty, U.S.A. · 156 D4 40 1N 92 12W
Noventa Vicentina, Italy · 45 C8 45 17N 11 32 E
Novgorod, Russia · 58 C6 58 30N 31 25 E
Novgorod-Severskiy = Novhorod-Siverskyy, Ukraine · 59 G7 52 2N 33 10 E
Novhorod-Siverskyy, Ukraine · 59 G7 52 2N 33 10 E
Novi Bečej, Serbia, Yug. · 52 E5 45 36N 20 10 E
Novi Iskar, Bulgaria · 50 D7 42 48N 23 21 E
Novi Knezevac, Serbia, Yug. · 52 D5 46 4N 20 8 E
Novi Lígure, Italy · 44 D5 44 46N 8 47 E
Novi Pazar, Bulgaria · 51 C11 43 25N 27 15 E
Novi Pazar, Serbia, Yug. · 50 C4 43 12N 20 28 E
Novi Sad, Serbia, Yug. · 52 E4 45 18N 19 52 E
Novi Slankamen, Serbia, Yug. · 52 E5 45 8N 20 15 E
Novi Travnik, Bos.-H. · 52 C10 44 17N 17 40 E
Novi Vinodolski, Croatia · 45 C11 45 10N 14 48 E
Novigrad, Istra, Croatia · 45 C10 45 19N 13 33 E
Novigrad, Zadar, Croatia · 45 D12 44 10N 15 32 E
Novigradsko More, Croatia · 45 D12 44 11N 15 33 E
Novinger, U.S.A. · 156 D4 40 14N 92 43W
Novo Acôrdo, Brazil · 170 D2 10 10 S 46 48W
Novo Airão, Brazil · 169 D5 2 40 S 60 59W
Novo Aripuanã, Brazil · 169 E5 5 8 S 60 22W
Novo Cruzeiro, Brazil · 171 E3 17 23 S 41 53W
Novo Hamburgo, Brazil · 175 B5 29 37 S 51 7W
Novo Horizonte, Brazil · 171 F2 21 30 S 49 30W
Novo-Mariinsk = Anadyr, Russia · 67 C18 64 35N 177 20 E
Novo Mesto, Slovenia · 45 C12 45 47N 15 12 E
Novo Milǒsevo, Serbia, Yug. · 52 E5 45 42N 20 20 E
Novo Nikolaevsk = Novosibirsk, Russia · 66 D9 55 0N 83 5 E
Novo Paraíso, Brazil · 169 C5 1 17N 60 28W
Novo Remanso, Brazil · 170 C3 9 41 S 42 4W
Novo-Sergiyevskiy, Russia · 64 E4 52 5N 53 32 E
Novoaleksandrovsk, Russia · 61 H5 45 29N 41 17 E
Novoalekseyevka = Khobda, Kazakhstan · 60 E10 50 30N 55 5 E
Novoannenskiy, Russia · 60 E6 50 32N 42 39 E
Novoataysk, Russia · 66 D9 53 30N 84 0 E
Novoazovsk, Ukraine · 59 J10 47 15N 38 4 E
Novocheboksarsk, Russia · 60 B8 56 5N 47 27 E
Novocherkassk, Russia · 61 J5 47 27N 40 15 E
Novodevichye, Russia · 60 D9 53 37N 48 50 E
Novogrudok = Navahrudak, Belarus · 58 F4 53 40N 25 50 E
Novohrad-Volynskyy, Ukraine · 59 G4 50 34N 27 35 E
Novokachalinsk, Russia · 70 B6 45 5N 132 0 E
Novokazalinsk = Zhangaqazaly, Kazakhstan · 66 E7 45 48N 62 6 E
Novokhopersk, Russia · 60 E6 51 1N 41 39 E
Novokuybyshevsk, Russia · 58 D9 53 7N 49 58 E
Novokuznetsk, Russia · 66 D9 53 45N 87 10 E
Novomirgorod, Ukraine · 59 H6 48 45N 31 33 E
Novomoskovsk, Russia · 58 E10 54 5N 38 15 E
Novomoskovsk, Ukraine · 59 H8 48 33N 35 17 E
Novonikolayevskiy, Russia · 64 E4 51 21N 59 2 E
Novopolotsk = Navapolatsk, Belarus · 58 D6 ...
Novorossiysk, Russia · 59 K9 44 43N 37 46 E
Novorossiyskoye, Kazakhstan · 60 D9 53 37N 25 ...
Novorybnoye, Russia · 67 B11 72 50N 105 50 E
Novorzhev, Russia · 58 D5 57 3N 29 25 E
Novoselytsya, Ukraine · 59 H4 48 14N 26 15 E
Novoshakhtinsk, Russia · 59 J9 47 46N 39 58 E
Novosibirsk, Russia · 66 D9 55 0N 83 5 E
Novosibirskiye Ostrova, Russia · 67 B15 75 0N 142 0 E
Novosil, Russia · 59 F9 52 59N 37 2 E
Novosokolniki, Russia · 58 D6 56 20N 30 2 E
Novotitarovskaya, Russia · 61 H4 45 17N 38 42 E
Novotroitsk, Russia · 64 F7 51 10N 58 15 E
Novotroitskoye = Tôle Bī, Kazakhstan · 65 B6 43 42N 73 46 E

Novovolynsk, *Ukraine* **59 G3** 50 45N 24 4 E
Novovoronezhskiy, *Russia* **59 G10** 51 19N 39 13 E
Novovoznesenovka, *Kyrgyzstan* **65 B9** 42 36N 78 44 E
Novovyatsk, *Russia* **64 B2** 58 24N 49 45 E
Novozybkov, *Russia* **59 F6** 52 30N 32 0 E
Novska, *Croatia* **45 C14** 45 19N 17 0 E
Novvy Urengoy, *Russia* **66 C8** 65 48N 76 52 E
Nový Bor, *Czech Rep.* **34 A7** 50 46N 14 35 E
Novy Bug = Novyy Buh, *Ukraine* **59 J7** 47 34N 32 29 E
Nový Bydžov, *Czech Rep.* **34 A8** 50 14N 15 29 E
Novy Dwór Mazowiecki, *Poland* **55 F7** 52 26N 20 44 E
Nový Jičín, *Czech Rep.* **35 B11** 49 30N 18 2 E
Novyy Afon, *Georgia* **61 J5** 43 7N 40 50 E
Novyy Bor, *Russia* **56 A9** 66 43N 52 19 E
Novyy Buh, *Ukraine* **59 J7** 47 34N 32 29 E
Novyy Oskol, *Russia* **59 G9** 50 44N 37 55 E
Novyy Port, *Russia* **66 C8** 67 40N 72 30 E
Now Shahr, *Iran* **97 B6** 36 40N 51 30 E
Nowa Deba, *Poland* **55 H8** 50 26N 21 41 E
Nowa Nowa, *Australia* **129 D8** 37 44 S 148 3 E
Nowa Ruda, *Poland* **55 H3** 50 35N 16 30 E
Nowa Sarzyna, *Poland* **55 H9** 50 21N 22 21 E
Nowa Sól, *Poland* **55 G2** 51 48N 15 44 E
Nowata, *U.S.A.* **155 G7** 36 42N 95 38W
Nowbarān, *Iran* **97 C6** 35 8N 49 42 E
Nowe, *Poland* **54 E5** 53 41N 18 44 E
Nowe Miasteczko, *Poland* **55 G2** 51 42N 15 42 E
Nowe Miasto, *Poland* **55 G7** 51 38N 20 34 E
Nowe Miasto Lubawskie, *Poland* **54 E6** 53 27N 19 33 E
Nowe Skalmierzyce, *Poland* **55 G4** 51 43N 18 0 E
Nowe Warpno, *Poland* **54 E1** 53 42N 14 18 E
Nowendoc, *Australia* **129 A9** 31 32 S 151 44 E
Nowghāb, *Iran* **97 C8** 33 53N 59 4 E
Nowgong, *Assam, India* **90 B4** 26 20N 92 50 E
Nowgong, *Mad. P., India* **93 G8** 25 4N 79 27 E
Nowogard, *Poland* **54 E2** 53 41N 15 10 E
Nowogród, *Poland* **55 E8** 53 14N 21 53 E
Nowogród Bobrzanski, *Poland* **55 G2** 51 48N 15 15 E
Nowogrodziec, *Poland* **55 G2** 51 12N 15 24 E
Nowra, *Australia* **129 C9** 34 53 S 150 35 E
Nowrangapur, *India* **94 E6** 19 14N 82 33 E
Nowshera, *Pakistan* **91 B3** 34 0N 72 0 E
Nowy Dwór Gdański, *Poland* **54 D6** 54 13N 19 7 E
Nowy Sącz, *Poland* **55 J7** 49 40N 20 41 E
Nowy Staw, *Poland* **54 D6** 54 13N 19 2 E
Nowy Targ, *Poland* **55 J7** 49 29N 20 2 E
Nowy Tomyśl, *Poland* **55 F3** 52 19N 16 10 E
Nowy Wiśnicz, *Poland* **55 J7** 49 55N 20 28 E
Noxen, *U.S.A.* **151 E8** 41 25N 76 4W
Noxon, *U.S.A.* **158 C6** 48 0N 115 43W
Noyabr'sk, *Russia* **66 C8** 64 34N 76 21 E
Noyant, *France* **26 E7** 47 30N 0 6 E
Noyers, *France* **27 E10** 47 40N 4 0 E
Noyon, *France* **27 C9** 49 34N 2 59 E
Noyon, *Mongolia* **74 C2** 43 2N 102 4 E
Nozay, *France* **26 E5** 47 34N 1 38W
Nqutu, *S. Africa* **117 D5** 28 13 S 30 32 E
Nsa, *Congo* **114 C3** 2 22 S 15 19 E
Nsa, O. en →, *Algeria* **111 B6** 32 28N 5 24 E
Nsa, Plateau de, *Congo* **114 C3** 2 26 S 15 20 E
Nsanje, *Malawi* **119 F4** 16 55 S 35 12 E
Nsawam, *Ghana* **113 D4** 5 50N 0 24W
Nsok, *Eq. Guin.* **114 B2** 1 10N 11 19 E
Nsomba, *Zambia* **119 E2** 10 45 S 29 51 E
Nsontin, *Dem. Rep. of the Congo* **114 C3** 3 7 S 17 56 E
Nsopzup, *Burma* **90 C6** 25 51N 97 30 E
Nsukka, *Nigeria* **113 D6** 6 51N 7 29 E
Ntem →, *Cameroon* **114 B2** 2 21N 9 49 E
Ntoum, *Gabon* **114 B1** 0 22N 9 47 E
N'Tsama, *Congo* **114 C2** 0 53 S 14 44 E
Ntui, *Cameroon* **113 E7** 4 27N 11 38 E
Nu Jiang →, *China* **76 E2** 29 58N 97 25 E
Nu Shan, *China* **76 E2** 26 0N 99 20 E
Nuakata I., *Papua N. G.* **132 F6** 10 17 S 151 2 E
Nuba Mts. = Nubah, Jibalan, *Sudan* **107 E3** 12 0N 31 0 E
Nubah, Jibalan, *Sudan* **107 E3** 12 0N 31 0 E
Nubia, *Africa* **104 D7** 21 0N 32 0 E
Nubian Desert = Nûbîya, Es Sahrâ en, *Sudan* **106 C3** 21 30N 33 30 E
Nûbîya, Es Sahrâ en, *Sudan* **106 C3** 21 30N 33 30 E
Nubledo, *Spain* **42 B5** 43 31N 5 52W
Nuboai, *Indonesia* **83 B5** 2 10 S 136 30 E
Nubra →, *India* **93 B7** 34 35N 77 35 E
Nucet, *Romania* **52 D7** 46 28N 22 35 E
Nueces →, *U.S.A.* **155 M6** 27 51N 97 30W
Nueltin L., *Canada* **143 A9** 60 30N 99 30W
Nueva, I., *Chile* **176 E3** 55 13 S 66 30W
Nueva Antioquia, *Colombia* **168 B4** 6 5N 69 26W
Nueva Carteya, *Spain* **43 H6** 37 35N 4 28W
Nueva Ecija □, *Phil.* **80 D3** 15 35N 121 0 E
Nueva Esparta □, *Venezuela* **169 A5** 11 0N 64 0W
Nueva Gerona, *Cuba* **164 B3** 21 53N 82 49W
Nueva Imperial, *Chile* **176 A2** 38 45 S 72 58W
Nueva Palmira, *Uruguay* **174 C4** 33 52 S 58 20W
Nueva Rosita, *Mexico* **162 B4** 28 0N 101 11W
Nueva San Salvador, *El Salv.* **164 D2** 13 40N 89 18W
Nueva Tabarca, *Spain* **41 G4** 38 17N 0 30W
Nueva Vizcaya □, *Phil.* **80 C3** 16 20N 121 20 E
Nuéve de Julio, *Argentina* **174 D3** 35 30 S 61 0W
Nuevitas, *Cuba* **164 B4** 21 30N 77 20W
Nuevo, G., *Argentina* **176 B4** 43 0 S 64 30W
Nuevo Casas Grandes, *Mexico* **162 A3** 30 22N 108 0W
Nuevo Guerrero, *Mexico* **163 B5** 26 34N 99 15W
Nuevo Laredo, *Mexico* **163 B5** 27 30N 99 30W
Nuevo León □, *Mexico* **162 C5** 25 0N 100 0W
Nuevo Mundo, Cerro, *Bolivia* **172 E4** 21 55 S 66 53W
Nuevo Rocafuerte, *Ecuador* **168 D2** 0 55 S 75 27W
Nugaaleed, Dooxo, *Somali Rep.* **120 C3** 8 35N 48 35 E
Nugget Pt., *N.Z.* **131 G4** 46 27 S 169 50 E
Nugrus, Gebel, *Egypt* **106 C3** 24 47N 34 35 E
Nuguria Is., *Papua N. G.* **132 B8** 3 20 S 154 45 E
Nuhaka, *N.Z.* **130 F6** 39 3 S 177 45 E
Nuits-St-Georges, *France* **27 E11** 47 10N 4 56 E
Nukey Bluff, *Australia* **127 E2** 32 26 S 135 29 E
Nukha = Şaki, *Azerbaijan* **61 K8** 41 10N 47 5 E
Nukheila, *Sudan* **106 D2** 19 1N 26 21 E
Nukhuyb, *Iraq* **101 F10** 32 4N 42 3 E
Nukiki, *Solomon Is.* **133 L9** 6 46 S 156 35 E
Nuku, *Papua N. G.* **132 B2** 3 41 S 142 28 E
Nuku'alofa, *Tonga* **133 Q14** 21 10 S 174 0W
Nukuhu, *Papua N. G.* **132 C5** 5 34 S 149 22 E
Nukulaelae, *Tuvalu* **123 B14** 9 23 S 179 52 E
Nukus, *Uzbekistan* **66 E6** 42 27N 59 41 E
Nulato, *U.S.A.* **144 D8** 64 43N 158 6W
Nules, *Spain* **40 F4** 39 51N 0 9W
Nullagine, *Australia* **124 D3** 21 53 S 120 7 E
Nullagine →, *Australia* **124 D3** 21 20 S 120 20 E
Nullarbor, *Australia* **125 F5** 31 28 S 130 55 E
Nullarbor Nat. Park △, *Australia* **125 F2** 32 39 S 115 37 E
Nullarbor Plain, *Australia* **125 F4** 31 10 S 129 0 E
Num, *Indonesia* **83 B5** 1 30 S 135 13 E
Numalla, L., *Australia* **127 D3** 28 43 S 144 20 E
Numan, *Nigeria* **113 D7** 9 29N 12 3 E
Numanuma, *Papua N. G.* **132 E6** 9 41 S 150 55 E
Numata, *Japan* **73 A11** 36 45N 139 4 E
Numatinna →, *Sudan* **107 F2** 7 38N 27 20 E
Numaykoos Lake Prov. Park ⌓, *Canada* **143 B9** 57 52N 95 58W
Numazu, *Japan* **73 B10** 35 7N 138 51 E
Numbulwar, *Australia* **126 A2** 14 15 S 135 45 E
Numedal, *Norway* **18 D6** 60 6N 9 6 E
Numfoor, *Indonesia* **83 B4** 1 0 S 134 50 E
Numurkah, *Australia* **129 D6** 36 5 S 145 26 E
Nunaksaluk I., *Canada* **141 A7** 55 49N 60 20W
Nunap Isua, *Greenland* **10 F6** 59 48N 43 55W
Nunavut □, *Canada* **139 B11** 66 0N 85 0W
Nunda, *U.S.A.* **150 D7** 42 35N 77 56W
Nuneaton, *U.K.* **21 E6** 52 32N 1 27W
Nungarin, *Australia* **125 F2** 31 12 S 118 6 E
Nungo, *Mozam.* **119 E4** 13 23 S 37 43 E
Nungwe, *Tanzania* **118 C3** 2 48 S 32 2 E
Nunivak I., *U.S.A.* **144 F6** 60 10N 166 30W
Nunkun, *India* **93 C7** 33 57N 76 2 E
Núoro, *Italy* **46 B2** 40 20N 9 20 E
Núpur, *Iceland* **11 B3** 65 56N 23 36W
Nuqayy, Jabal, *Libya* **108 D3** 23 11N 19 30 E
Nuqūb, *Yemen* **98 D4** 14 59N 45 48 E
Nuquí, *Colombia* **168 B2** 5 42N 77 17W
Nūrābād, *Iran* **97 E8** 27 47N 57 12 E
Nurabad, *Uzbekistan* **65 D3** 39 36N 66 17 E
Nurata, *Uzbekistan* **65 C2** 40 33N 65 41 E
Nurata Tizmasi, *Uzbekistan* **65 C3** 40 40N 66 30 E
Nure →, *Italy* **44 C6** 45 3N 9 49 E
Nurek, *Tajikistan* **65 D4** 38 23N 69 19 E
Nuremberg = Nürnberg, *Germany* **31 F7** 49 27N 11 3 E
Nuri, *Mexico* **162 B3** 28 2N 109 22W
Nuri, *Sudan* **106 D3** 18 29N 31 59 E
Nuriootpa, *Australia* **128 C3** 34 27 S 139 0 E
Nurlat, *Russia* **60 C10** 54 29N 50 45 E
Nurmes, *Finland* **14 E23** 63 33N 29 10 E
Nürnberg, *Germany* **31 F7** 49 27N 11 3 E
Nurpur, *Pakistan* **92 D4** 31 53N 71 54 E
Nurra, La, *Italy* **46 B1** 40 45N 8 15 E
Nurran, L. = Terewah, L., *Australia* **127 D4** 29 52 S 147 35 E
Nurrari Lakes, *Australia* **125 E5** 29 1 S 130 5 E
Nurri, *Italy* **46 C2** 39 43N 9 14 E
Nürtingen, *Germany* **31 G5** 48 37N 9 19 E
Nurzec →, *Poland* **55 F9** 52 37N 22 25 E
Nus, *Italy* **44 C4** 45 45N 7 28 E
Nusa Barung, *Indonesia* **85 D4** 8 30 S 113 30 E
Nusa Dua, *Indonesia* **79 K18** 8 48 S 115 14 E
Nusa Kambangan, *Indonesia* **85 D3** 7 40 S 108 10 E
Nusa Tenggara Barat □, *Indonesia* **85 D5** 8 50 S 117 30 E
Nusa Tenggara Timur □, *Indonesia* **82 C2** 9 30 S 122 0 E
Nusaybin, *Turkey* **101 D9** 37 3N 41 10 E
Nushki, *Pakistan* **91 C2** 29 35N 66 0 E
Nuuk, *Greenland* **10 E5** 64 10N 51 35W
Nuussauq, *Greenland* **10 C5** 74 8N 57 3W
Nuwakot, *Nepal* **93 E10** 28 10N 83 55 E
Nuwara Eliya, *Sri Lanka* **95 L5** 6 58N 80 48 E
Nuweiba', *Egypt* **96 D2** 28 59N 34 39 E
Nuwerus, *S. Africa* **116 E2** 31 8 S 18 24 E
Nuweveldberge, *S. Africa* **116 E3** 32 10 S 21 45 E
Nuyts, C., *Australia* **125 F5** 32 2 S 132 21 E
Nuyts, Pt., *Australia* **125 G2** 35 4 S 116 38 E
Nuyts Arch., *Australia* **127 E1** 32 35 S 133 20 E
Nuzvid, *India* **94 F5** 16 47N 80 53 E
N'Vinda, *Angola* **115 E3** 13 8 S 19 2 E
Nxai Pan Nat. Park △, *Botswana* **116 B3** 19 50 S 24 46 E
Nxau-Nxau, *Botswana* **116 B3** 18 57 S 21 4 E
Nyaake, *Liberia* **112 E3** 4 52N 7 37W
Nyabessan, *Cameroon* **114 B2** 2 28N 10 24 E
Nyabing, *Australia* **125 F2** 33 33 S 118 9 E
Nyack, *U.S.A.* **151 E11** 41 5N 73 55W
Nyagan, *Russia* **66 C7** 62 30N 65 38 E
Nyah West, *Australia* **128 C5** 35 16 S 143 21 E
Nyahanga, *Tanzania* **118 C3** 2 20 S 33 37 E
Nyahua, *Tanzania* **118 D3** 5 25 S 33 23 E
Nyahururu, *Kenya* **118 B4** 0 2N 36 27 E
Nyainqentanglha Shan, *China* **68 D4** 30 0N 90 0 E
Nyakanazi, *Tanzania* **118 C3** 3 2 S 31 10 E
Nyakrom, *Ghana* **113 D4** 5 40N 0 50W
Nyâlâ, *Sudan* **107 E1** 12 2N 24 58 E
Nyamandhlovu, *Zimbabwe* **119 F2** 19 55 S 28 16 E
Nyambiti, *Tanzania* **118 C3** 2 48 S 33 27 E
Nyamlell, *Sudan* **107 F2** 9 7N 26 59 E
Nyamwaga, *Tanzania* **118 C3** 1 27 S 34 33 E
Nyandekwa, *Tanzania* **118 C3** 3 57 S 32 32 E
Nyanding →, *Sudan* **107 F3** 8 40N 32 41 E
Nyandoma, *Russia* **58 B11** 61 40N 40 12 E
Nyanga →, *Gabon* **114 C2** 2 58 S 10 15 E
Nyanga Nat. Park △, *Zimbabwe* **119 F3** 18 17 S 32 46 E
Nyangana, *Namibia* **116 B3** 18 0 S 20 40 E
Nyanguge, *Tanzania* **118 C3** 2 30 S 33 12 E
Nyankpala, *Ghana* **113 D4** 9 21N 0 58W
Nyanza, *Rwanda* **118 C2** 2 20 S 29 42 E
Nyanza □, *Kenya* **118 C3** 0 10 S 34 15 E
Nyanza-Lac, *Burundi* **118 C2** 4 21 S 29 36 E
Nyaponges, *Sudan* **107 F3** 5 5N 33 45 E
Nyasa, L., *Africa* **119 E3** 12 30 S 34 30 E
Nyasaland = Malawi ■, *Africa* **119 E3** 11 55 S 34 0 E
Nyasvizh, *Belarus* **59 F4** 53 14N 26 38 E
Nyaunglebin, *Burma* **90 G6** 17 52N 96 42 E
Nyazepetrovsk, *Russia* **64 C7** 56 3N 59 36 E
Nyazura, *Zimbabwe* **119 F3** 18 40 S 32 16 E
Nyazwidzi →, *Zimbabwe* **119 G3** 20 0 S 31 17 E
Nybergsund, *Norway* **18 C9** 61 15N 12 19 E
Nyborg, *Denmark* **17 J4** 55 18N 10 47 E
Nybro, *Sweden* **17 H9** 56 44N 15 55 E
Nyda, *Russia* **66 C8** 66 40N 72 58 E
Nyeboe Land, *Greenland* **10 A5** 82 0N 57 0W
Nyengo Swamp, *Zambia* **115 E4** 14 51 S 22 7 E
Nyeri, *Kenya* **118 C4** 0 23 S 36 56 E
Nyerol, *Sudan* **107 F3** 8 41N 32 1 E
Nyhammar, *Sweden* **16 D8** 60 17N 14 58 E
Nyika Nat. Park △, *Malawi* **119 E3** 10 30 S 33 53 E
Nyinahin, *Ghana* **112 D4** 6 43N 2 3W
Nyíradony, *Hungary* **52 C6** 47 41N 21 55 E
Nyirbátor, *Hungary* **52 C7** 47 49N 22 9 E
Nyíregyháza, *Hungary* **52 C6** 47 58N 21 47 E
Nykarleby = Uusikaarlepyy, *Finland* **14 E20** 63 32N 22 31 E
Nykirke, *Norway* **18 D7** 60 54N 10 19 E
Nykøbing, *Storstrøm, Denmark* **17 K5** 54 56N 11 52 E
Nykøbing, *Vestsjælland, Denmark* **17 J5** 55 55N 11 40 E
Nykøbing, *Viborg, Denmark* **17 H2** 56 48N 8 51 E
Nyköping, *Sweden* **17 F11** 58 45N 17 1 E
Nykroppa, *Sweden* **16 E8** 59 37N 14 18 E
Nykvarn, *Sweden* **16 E11** 59 11N 17 25 E
Nyland, *Sweden* **16 A11** 63 1N 17 45 E
Nylstroom, *S. Africa* **117 C4** 24 42 S 28 22 E
Nymagee, *Australia* **129 B7** 32 7 S 146 20 E
Nymboida Nat. Park △, *Australia* **127 A5** 29 38 S 152 26 E
Nymburk, *Czech Rep.* **34 A8** 50 10N 15 1 E
Nynäshamn, *Sweden* **17 F11** 58 54N 17 57 E
Nyngan, *Australia* **129 A7** 31 30 S 147 8 E
Nyoma Rap, *India* **93 C8** 33 10N 78 40 E
Nyoman = Nemunas →, *Lithuania* **15 J19** 55 25N 21 10 E
Nyon, *Switz.* **32 D2** 46 23N 6 14 E
Nyong →, *Cameroon* **113 E6** 3 17N 9 54 E
Nyons, *France* **29 D9** 44 22N 5 10 E
Nyou, *Burkina Faso* **113 C4** 12 42N 2 1W
Nýrsko, *Czech Rep.* **34 B6** 49 18N 13 9 E
Nysa, *Poland* **55 H4** 50 30N 17 22 E
Nysa →, *Europe* **30 C10** 52 4N 14 46 E
Nysa Kłodzka →, *Poland* **55 H4** 50 49N 17 40 E
Nysäter, *Sweden* **16 E6** 59 17N 12 47 E
Nyseter, *Norway* **18 B5** 62 2N 8 20 E
Nyslott = Savonlinna, *Finland* **58 B5** 61 52N 28 53 E
Nyssa, *U.S.A.* **158 E5** 43 53N 117 0W
Nystad = Uusikaupunki, *Finland* **15 F19** 60 47N 21 25 E
Nysted, *Denmark* **17 K5** 54 40N 11 44 E
Nytva, *Russia* **64 C5** 57 56N 55 20 E
Nyunzu, *Dem. Rep. of the Congo* **118 D2** 5 57 S 27 58 E
Nyurba, *Russia* **67 C12** 63 17N 118 28 E
Nyzhnohirskyy, *Ukraine* **59 K8** 45 27N 34 38 E
Nzébéla, *Guinea* **112 D3** 8 9N 9 7W
Nzega, *Tanzania* **118 C3** 4 10 S 33 12 E
Nzérékoré, *Guinea* **112 D3** 7 49N 8 48W
Nzeto, *Angola* **115 D2** 7 10 S 12 52 E
Nzilo, Chutes de, *Dem. Rep. of the Congo* **119 E2** 10 18 S 25 27 E
Nzo →, *Ivory C.* **112 D3** 6 15N 7 3W
N'Zo, Réserve de Faune du ⌓, *Ivory C.* **112 D3** 6 15N 7 15W
Nzubuka, *Tanzania* **118 C3** 4 45 S 32 50 E
Nzwani = Anjouan, *Comoros Is.* **121 a** 12 15 S 44 20 E

O

O Barco, *Spain* **42 C4** 42 23N 6 58W
O Carballiño, *Spain* **42 C2** 42 26N 8 5W
O Corgo, *Spain* **42 C3** 42 56N 7 25W
O Le Pupū Pu'e Nat. Park △, *Samoa* **133 W24** 13 59 S 171 43W
O Pino, *Spain* **42 C2** 42 56N 8 20W
O Porriño, *Spain* **42 C2** 42 10N 8 37W
Ō-Shima, *Fukuoka, Japan* **72 D2** 30 53N 130 28 E
Ō-Shima, *Nagasaki, Japan* **72 C1** 33 29N 129 33 E
Ō-Shima, *Shizuoka, Japan* **73 C11** 34 44N 139 24 E
Oa, Mull of, *U.K.* **22 F2** 55 35N 6 20W
Oacoma, *U.S.A.* **154 D5** 43 48N 99 24W
Oahe, L., *U.S.A.* **154 C4** 44 27N 100 24W
Oahe Dam, *U.S.A.* **154 C4** 44 27N 100 24W
Oahu, *U.S.A.* **145 K14** 21 28N 157 58W
Oak Creek, *U.S.A.* **157 B9** 42 52N 87 55W
Oak Harbor, *U.S.A.* **160 B4** 48 18N 122 39W
Oak Hill, *Fla., U.S.A.* **153 G9** 28 52N 80 51W
Oak Hill, *W. Va., U.S.A.* **148 G5** 37 59N 81 9W
Oak Lawn, *U.S.A.* **157 C9** 41 43N 87 44W
Oak Park, *Ga., U.S.A.* **152 C7** 32 22N 82 19W
Oak Park, *Ill., U.S.A.* **157 C9** 41 53N 87 47W
Oak Ridge, *U.S.A.* **149 G3** 36 1N 84 16W
Oak View, *U.S.A.* **161 L7** 34 24N 119 18W
Oakan-Dake, *Japan* **70 C12** 43 27N 144 10 E
Oakbank, *Australia* **128 B4** 33 4 S 140 33 E
Oakdale, *Calif., U.S.A.* **160 H6** 37 46N 120 51W
Oakdale, *La., U.S.A.* **155 K8** 30 49N 92 40W
Oakes, *U.S.A.* **154 B5** 46 8N 98 6W
Oakesdale, *U.S.A.* **158 C5** 47 8N 117 15W
Oakey, *Australia* **127 D5** 27 25 S 151 43 E
Oakfield, *Ga., U.S.A.* **152 D6** 31 47N 83 58W
Oakfield, *N.Y., U.S.A.* **150 C6** 43 4N 78 16W
Oakford, *U.S.A.* **156 D7** 40 6N 89 58W
Oakham, *U.K.* **21 E7** 52 40N 0 43W
Oakhurst, *U.S.A.* **160 H7** 37 19N 119 40W
Oakland, *Calif., U.S.A.* **160 H4** 37 49N 122 16W
Oakland, *Ill., U.S.A.* **157 E8** 39 39N 88 2W
Oakland City, *U.S.A.* **157 F9** 38 20N 87 21W
Oaklands, *Australia* **129 C7** 35 34 S 146 10 E
Oakley, *Idaho, U.S.A.* **158 E7** 42 15N 113 53W
Oakley, *Kans., U.S.A.* **154 F4** 39 8N 100 51W
Oakover →, *Australia* **124 D3** 21 0 S 120 40 E
Oakridge, *U.S.A.* **158 E2** 43 45N 122 28W
Oaktown, *U.S.A.* **157 F9** 38 52N 87 27W
Oakville, *Canada* **150 C5** 43 27N 79 41W
Oakville, *U.S.A.* **160 D3** 46 51N 123 14W
Oakwood, *U.S.A.* **157 C12** 41 6N 84 23W
Oamaru, *N.Z.* **131 F5** 45 5 S 170 59 E
Ōamishirasato, *Japan* **73 B12** 35 31N 140 18 E
Oancea, *Romania* **53 E12** 45 21N 27 42 E
Oarai, *Japan* **73 A12** 36 21N 140 34 E
Oasi Faunistica di Vendicari, Riserva Naturale ⌓, *Italy* **47 F8** 36 49N 15 6 E
Oasis, *Calif., U.S.A.* **161 M10** 33 28N 116 6W
Oasis, *Nev., U.S.A.* **160 H9** 37 29N 117 55W
Oates Land, *Antarctica* **7 C11** 69 0 S 160 0 E
Oatlands, *Australia* **127 D4** 42 17 S 147 21 E
Oatman, *U.S.A.* **161 K12** 35 1N 114 19W
Oaxaca, *Mexico* **163 D5** 17 2N 96 40W
Oaxaca □, *Mexico* **163 D5** 17 0N 97 0W
Ob →, *Russia* **66 C7** 66 45N 69 30 E
Oba, *Canada* **140 C3** 49 4N 84 7W
Obala, *Cameroon* **113 E7** 4 9N 11 32 E
Obama, *Fukui, Japan* **73 B7** 35 30N 135 45 E
Obama, *Nagasaki, Japan* **72 E2** 32 43N 130 13 E
Oban, *Nigeria* **113 D6** 5 17N 8 33 E
Oban, *U.K.* **22 E3** 56 25N 5 29W
Obbia, *Somali Rep.* **120 C3** 5 25N 48 30 E
Ober-Aargau, *Switz.* **32 B5** 47 10N 7 45 E
Ober-engadin, *Switz.* **33 C9** 46 35N 9 55 E
Obera, *Argentina* **175 B4** 27 21 S 55 2W
Oberalppass, *Switz.* **33 C7** 46 39N 8 35 E
Oberalpstock, *Switz.* **33 C7** 46 45N 8 47 E
Oberammergau, *Germany* **31 H7** 47 36N 11 4 E
Oberasbach, *Germany* **31 F6** 49 25N 10 57 E
Oberbayern □, *Germany* **31 G7** 48 5N 11 50 E
Oberdiessbach, *Switz.* **32 C5** 46 51N 7 40 E
Oberdrauburg, *Austria* **34 E5** 46 44N 12 58 E
Obere Donau, Naturpark ⌓, *Germany* **31 G5** 48 5N 9 0 E
Oberentfelden, *Switz.* **32 B6** 47 21N 8 2 E
Oberer Bayerischer Wald, Naturpark ⌓, *Germany* **31 F8** 49 15N 12 40 E
Oberfranken □, *Germany* **31 E7** 50 10N 11 20 E
Oberhausen, *Germany* **30 D2** 51 28N 6 51 E
Oberkirch, *Germany* **31 G4** 48 31N 8 4 E
Oberland, *Switz.* **32 C5** 46 35N 7 38 E
Oberlausitz, *Germany* **30 D10** 51 16N 14 18 E
Oberlin, *Kans., U.S.A.* **154 F4** 39 49N 100 32W
Oberlin, *La., U.S.A.* **155 K8** 30 37N 92 46W
Oberlin, *Ohio, U.S.A.* **150 E2** 41 18N 82 13W
Obernai, *France* **27 D14** 48 28N 7 30 E
Oberndorf, *Germany* **31 G4** 48 17N 8 34 E
Oberon, *Australia* **129 B8** 33 45 S 149 52 E
Oberösterreich □, *Austria* **34 C7** 48 10N 14 0 E
Oberpfalz □, *Germany* **31 F8** 49 20N 12 10 E
Oberpfälzer Wald, *Germany* **31 F8** 49 30N 12 30 E
Oberpfälzer Wald, Naturpark ⌓, *Germany* **31 F8** 49 40N 12 20 E
Oberriet, *Switz.* **33 B9** 47 19N 9 34 E
Obersiggenthal, *Switz.* **33 B6** 47 29N 8 18 E
Oberstdorf, *Germany* **31 H6** 47 24N 10 15 E
Oberting, *Gabon* **114 C1** 0 22 S 9 46 E
Oberursel, *Germany* **31 E4** 50 11N 8 35 E
Oberwart, *Austria* **35 D9** 47 17N 16 12 E
Oberwil, *Switz.* **32 A5** 47 32N 7 33 E
Obi, *Indonesia* **82 B3** 1 23 S 127 45 E
Obiaruku, *Nigeria* **113 D6** 5 51N 6 9 E
Óbidos, *Brazil* **169 D6** 1 50 S 55 30W
Óbidos, *Portugal* **43 F1** 39 19N 9 10W
Obigarm, *Tajikistan* **65 D4** 38 43N 69 42 E
Obihiro, *Japan* **70 C11** 42 56N 143 12 E
Obīkiik, *Tajikistan* **65 D4** 38 9N 68 39 E
Obilatu, *Indonesia* **82 B3** 1 25 S 127 20 E
Obilnoye, *Russia* **61 G7** 47 32N 44 30 E
Obing, *Germany* **31 G8** 48 0N 12 24 E
Objat, *France* **28 C5** 45 16N 1 24 E
Oblong, *U.S.A.* **157 F9** 39 0N 87 55W
Obluchye, *Russia* **67 E14** 49 1N 131 4 E
Obninsk, *Russia* **58 E9** 55 8N 36 37 E
Obo, *C.A.R.* **118 A2** 5 20N 26 32 E
Oboa, Mt., *Uganda* **118 B3** 1 45N 34 45 E
Obock, *Djibouti* **107 E5** 12 0N 43 20 E
Oborniki, *Poland* **55 F3** 52 39N 16 50 E
Oborniki Śląskie, *Poland* **55 G3** 51 17N 16 53 E
Obouya, *Congo* **114 C3** 0 56 S 15 43 E
Oboyan, *Russia* **59 G9** 51 15N 36 21 E
Obozerskaya = Obozerskiy, *Russia* **56 B7** 63 34N 40 21 E
Obozerskiy, *Russia* **56 B7** 63 34N 40 21 E
Obrenovac, *Serbia, Yug.* **50 B4** 44 40N 20 11 E
O'Brien, *U.S.A.* **152 E7** 30 2N 82 57W
Obrovac, *Croatia* **45 D12** 44 11N 15 41 E
Obruk, *Turkey* **100 C5** 38 7N 33 12 E
Obrzycko, *Poland* **55 F3** 52 42N 16 32 E
Observatory Inlet, *Canada* **142 B3** 55 10N 129 54W
Obshchi Syrt, *Russia* **64 E4** 52 0N 53 0 E
Obskaya Guba, *Russia* **66 C8** 69 0N 73 0 E
Obuasi, *Ghana* **113 D4** 6 17N 1 40W
Obubra, *Nigeria* **113 D6** 6 8N 8 20 E
Obudu, *Nigeria* **113 D6** 6 38N 9 5 E
Obura, *Papua N. G.* **132 D3** 6 33 S 145 58 E
Obwalden □, *Switz.* **32 C6** 46 55N 8 15 E
Obzor, *Bulgaria* **51 D11** 42 50N 27 52 E
Ocala, *U.S.A.* **153 F7** 29 11N 82 8W
Ocamo →, *Venezuela* **169 C4** 2 48N 65 14W
Ocampo, *Chihuahua, Mexico* **162 B3** 28 9N 108 24W
Ocampo, *Tamaulipas, Mexico* **163 C5** 22 50N 99 20W
Ocaña, *Colombia* **168 B3** 8 15N 73 20W
Ocaña, *Spain* **42 F7** 39 55N 3 30W
Ocanomowoc, *U.S.A.* **154 D10** 43 7N 88 30W
Occidental, Cordillera, *Colombia* **168 C3** 5 0N 76 0W
Occidental, Cordillera, *Peru* **172 C3** 14 0 S 74 0W
Occidental, Grand Erg, *Algeria* **111 B5** 30 20N 1 0 E
Ocean City, *Md., U.S.A.* **148 F8** 38 20N 75 5W
Ocean City, *N.J., U.S.A.* **148 F8** 39 17N 74 35W
Ocean City, *Wash., U.S.A.* **160 C2** 47 4N 124 10W
Ocean Falls, *Canada* **142 C3** 52 18N 127 48W
Ocean I. = Banaba, *Kiribati* **134 H8** 0 45 S 169 50 E
Ocean Park, *U.S.A.* **160 D2** 46 30N 124 3W
Oceano, *U.S.A.* **161 K6** 35 6N 120 37W
Oceanport, *U.S.A.* **151 F10** 40 19N 74 3W
Oceanside, *U.S.A.* **161 M9** 33 12N 117 23W
Ochagavía, *Spain* **40 C3** 42 55N 1 5W
Ochakiv, *Ukraine* **59 J6** 46 37N 31 33 E
Ochamchira, *Georgia* **61 J5** 42 46N 41 32 E
Ocher, *Russia* **64 C5** 57 53N 54 42 E
Ochiai, *Japan* **72 B5** 35 1N 133 45 E
Ochil Hills, *U.K.* **22 E5** 56 14N 3 40W
Ochlocknee, *U.S.A.* **152 E5** 30 58N 84 3W
Ochlockonee →, *U.S.A.* **152 F5** 29 59N 84 26W
Ocho Rios, *Jamaica* **164 a** 18 24N 77 6W
Ochopee, *U.S.A.* **153 K8** 25 54N 81 18W
Ochsenfurt, *Germany* **31 F6** 49 40N 10 4 E
Ochsenhausen, *Germany* **31 G5** 48 4N 9 57 E
Ocilla, *U.S.A.* **152 D6** 31 36N 83 15W
Ockelbo, *Sweden* **16 D10** 60 54N 16 45 E
Ocmulgee →, *U.S.A.* **152 D7** 31 58N 82 33W
Ocmulgee Nat. Monument ⌓, *U.S.A.* **152 C6** 32 49N 83 37W
Ocna Mureş, *Romania* **53 D8** 46 23N 23 55 E
Ocna Sibiului, *Romania* **53 E9** 45 52N 24 2 E
Ocnele Mari, *Romania* **53 E9** 45 8N 24 18 E
Ocniţa, *Moldova* **53 B12** 48 25N 27 30 E
Ocoee, *U.S.A.* **153 G8** 28 34N 81 33W
Ocoña, *Peru* **172 D3** 16 26 S 73 8W
Ocoña →, *Peru* **172 D3** 16 28 S 73 8W
Oconee →, *U.S.A.* **152 D7** 31 58N 82 33W
Oconee, L., *U.S.A.* **152 B6** 33 28N 83 15W
Oconomowoc, *U.S.A.* **157 A8** 43 7N 88 30W
Oconto, *U.S.A.* **148 C2** 44 53N 87 52W
Oconto Falls, *U.S.A.* **148 C1** 44 52N 88 9W
Ocosingo, *Mexico* **163 D6** 17 10N 92 15W
Ocotal, *Nic.* **164 D2** 13 41N 86 31W
Ocotlán, *Mexico* **162 C4** 20 21N 102 42W
Ocotlán de Morelos, *Mexico* **163 D5** 16 48N 96 40W
Ocreza →, *Portugal* **43 F3** 39 32N 7 50W
Ócsa, *Hungary* **52 C4** 47 17N 19 15 E
Octeville, *France* **26 C5** 49 38N 1 40W
Ocumare del Tuy, *Venezuela* **168 A4** 10 7N 66 46W
Ocuri, *Bolivia* **173 D4** 18 45 S 65 50W
Oda, *Ghana* **113 D4** 5 50N 0 51W
Ōda, *Japan* **72 B4** 35 11N 132 30 E
Oda, J., *Sudan* **106 C4** 20 21N 36 39 E
Ódáðahraun, *Iceland* **11 B9** 65 5N 17 0W
Ödåkra, *Sweden* **17 H6** 56 7N 12 45 E
Odammun →, *Indonesia* **83 C5** 6 50 S 138 45 E
Odate, *Japan* **70 D10** 40 16N 140 34 E
Odawara, *Japan* **73 B11** 35 20N 139 6 E
Odda, *Norway* **18 D3** 60 3N 6 35 E
Odder, *Denmark* **17 J4** 55 58N 10 10 E
Oddur, *Somali Rep.* **120 D2** 4 11N 43 52 E
Odei →, *Canada* **143 B9** 56 6N 96 54W
Odell, *U.S.A.* **157 C8** 41 0N 88 31W
Odemira, *Portugal* **43 H2** 37 35N 8 40W
Ödemiş, *Turkey* **49 C9** 38 15N 28 0 E
Ödenburg = Sopron, *Hungary* **52 C1** 47 45N 16 32 E
Odendaalsrus, *S. Africa* **116 D4** 27 48 S 26 45 E
Odensbacken, *Sweden* **16 E9** 59 10N 15 32 E
Odense, *Denmark* **17 J4** 55 22N 10 23 E
Odenwald, *Germany* **31 F5** 49 35N 9 0 E
Odenwald, Naturpark = Neckartal-Odenwald, Naturpark ⌓, *Germany* **31 F5** 49 30N 9 5 E
Oder →, *Europe* **30 B10** 53 33N 14 38 E
Oder-Havel Kanal, *Germany* **30 C10** 52 52N 14 2 E
Oderzo, *Italy* **45 C9** 45 47N 12 29 E
Odesa, *Ukraine* **59 J6** 46 30N 30 45 E
Ödeshög, *Sweden* **17 F8** 58 14N 14 39 E
Odessa = Odesa, *Ukraine* **59 J6** 46 30N 30 45 E
Odessa, *Canada* **151 B8** 44 17N 76 43W
Odessa, *Mo., U.S.A.* **156 F3** 39 0N 93 57W
Odessa, *Tex., U.S.A.* **155 K3** 31 52N 102 23W
Odessa, *Wash., U.S.A.* **158 C4** 47 20N 118 41W
Odiakwe, *Botswana* **116 C4** 20 12 S 25 17 E
Odiel →, *Spain* **43 H4** 37 10N 6 55W
Odienné, *Ivory C.* **112 D3** 9 30N 7 34W
Odimba, *Gabon* **114 C2** 2 2 S 9 33 E
Odintsovo, *Russia* **58 E9** 55 39N 37 15 E
Odiongan, *Phil.* **80 E3** 12 24N 121 59 E
Odobeşti, *Romania* **53 E12** 45 43N 27 4 E
Odolanów, *Poland* **55 G4** 51 34N 17 40 E
O'Donnell, *U.S.A.* **155 J4** 32 58N 101 50W
Odorheiu Secuiesc, *Romania* **53 D10** 46 21N 25 21 E
Odoyevo, *Russia* **58 F9** 53 56N 36 42 E
Odra = Oder →, *Europe* **30 B10** 53 33N 14 38 E
Odra →, *Spain* **42 C6** 42 14N 4 17W
Odum, *U.S.A.* **152 D7** 31 40N 82 2W
Odweina, *Somali Rep.* **120 C3** 9 25N 45 4 E
Odžaci, *Serbia, Yug.* **52 E4** 45 30N 19 17 E
Odžak, *Bos.-H.* **52 E3** 45 3N 18 18 E
Odzala, *Congo* **114 B2** 0 37N 14 37 E
Odzala, Parc Nat. d' △, *Congo* **114 B2** 0 55N 14 55 E
Odzi, *Zimbabwe* **117 B5** 19 0 S 32 20 E
Odzi →, *Zimbabwe* **117 B5** 19 45 S 32 23 E
Oebisfelde, *Germany* **30 C6** 52 27N 10 57 E
Oeiras = Araticu, *Brazil* **170 B2** 1 58 S 49 51W
Oeiras, *Brazil* **170 C3** 7 0 S 42 8W
Oeiras, *Portugal* **43 G1** 38 41N 9 18W
Oeiras do Para, *Brazil* **169 D8** 1 58 S 49 51W
Oelrichs, *U.S.A.* **154 D3** 43 11N 103 14W
Oelsnitz, *Germany* **31 E8** 50 24N 12 10 E
Oelwein, *U.S.A.* **156 B5** 42 41N 91 55W
Oenpelli, *Australia* **124 B5** 12 20 S 133 4 E
Oetz, *Austria* **34 D3** 47 13N 10 53 E
Of, *Turkey* **101 B9** 40 59N 40 23 E
O'Fallon, *U.S.A.* **156 F6** 38 49N 90 42W
Ofanto →, *Italy* **47 A9** 41 22N 16 13 E
Offa, *Nigeria* **113 D5** 8 13N 4 42 E
Offaly □, *Ireland* **23 C4** 53 15N 7 30W
Offenbach, *Germany* **31 E4** 50 6N 8 44 E
Offenburg, *Germany* **31 G3** 48 28N 7 56 E
Offida, *Italy* **45 F10** 42 56N 13 41 E
Offoué →, *Gabon* **114 C2** 0 4 S 11 44 E
Ofidhousa, *Greece* **49 E8** 36 33N 26 8 E
Öflingen, *Germany* **32 A5** 47 36N 7 55 E

Ofolanga, *Tonga* .... 133 P14 19 38 S 173 35W
Ofotfjorden, *Norway* .... 14 B17 68 27N 17 0 E
Ofte, *Norway* .... 18 E5 59 30N 8 12 E
Ofu, *Amer. Samoa* .... 133 X25 14 11 S 169 41W
Ōfunato, *Japan* .... 70 E10 39 4N 141 43 E
Oga, *Japan* .... 70 E9 39 55N 139 50 E
Oga-Hantō, *Japan* .... 70 E9 39 58N 139 47 E
Ogaden, *Ethiopia* .... 120 C3 7 30N 45 30 E
Ōgaki, *Japan* .... 73 B8 35 21N 136 37 E
Ogallala, *U.S.A.* 154 E4 41 8N 101 43W
Ogan →, *Indonesia* .... 84 C2 3 1 S 104 44 E
Ogasawara Gunto, *Pac. Oc.* .. 113 D5 8 1N 4 11 E
Ogbomosho, *Nigeria* .... 113 D5 27 0N 142 0 E
Ogden, *Iowa, U.S.A.* 156 B2 42 2N 94 2W
Ogden, *Utah, U.S.A.* 158 F7 41 13N 111 58W
Ogdensburg, *U.S.A.* 151 B9 44 42N 75 30W
Ogea Driki, *Fiji* .... 133 B3 19 12 S 178 27W
Ogea Levu, *Fiji* .... 133 B3 19 8 S 178 24W
Ogeechee →, *U.S.A.* 152 D8 31 50N 81 3W
Ogilby, *U.S.A.* 161 N12 32 49N 114 50W
Oglat Beraber, *Algeria* 110 B4 30 15N 3 34W
Oglats de Khenachiche, *Mali* . 110 D4 21 51N 3 58W
Oglesby, *U.S.A.* 156 C7 41 18N 89 4W
Oglethorpe, *U.S.A.* 152 C5 32 18N 84 4W
Oglio →, *Italy* .... 44 C7 45 2N 10 39 E
Óglio Nord, Parco Naturale dell' △,
  Italy .... 44 C6 45 22N 9 54 E
Óglio Sud, Parco △, *Italy* .... 44 C7 45 7N 10 24 E
Ogmore, *Australia* .... 126 C4 22 37 S 149 35 E
Ognon →, *France* .... 27 E12 47 16N 5 28 E
Ogoamas, *Indonesia* .... 82 A2 0 50N 120 5 E
Ogoja, *Nigeria* .... 113 D6 6 38N 8 39 E
Ogoki →, *Canada* 140 B2 51 38N 85 58W
Ogoki →, *Canada* 140 B2 51 38N 85 57W
Ogoki L., *Canada* 140 B2 50 50N 87 10W
Ogoki Res., *Canada* 140 B2 50 45N 88 15W
Ogooué →, *Gabon* .... 114 C1 1 0 S 9 0 E
Ogori, *Japan* .... 72 C3 34 6N 131 24 E
Ogosta →, *Bulgaria* .... 50 C7 43 48N 23 55 E
Ogowe = Ogooué →, *Gabon* .. 114 C1 1 0 S 9 0 E
Ogr = Sharafa, *Sudan* .... 107 E2 11 59N 27 7 E
Ogražden, *Macedonia* .... 50 E6 41 30N 22 50 E
Ogre, *Latvia* .... 15 H21 56 49N 24 36 E
Ogrein, *Sudan* .... 106 D3 17 55N 34 50 E
Ogulin, *Croatia* .... 45 C12 45 16N 15 16 E
Ogun □, *Nigeria* .... 113 D5 7 0N 3 0 E
Oguni, *Japan* .... 72 D3 33 11N 131 8 E
Ogur, *Iceland* 11 A4 66 2N 22 44W
Ogurchinskiy, Ostrov, *Turkmenistan* 97 B7 38 55N 53 2 E
Oguta, *Nigeria* .... 113 D6 5 44N 6 44 E
Ogwashi-Uku, *Nigeria* .... 113 D6 6 15N 6 30 E
Ogwe, *Nigeria* .... 113 E6 5 0N 7 14 E
Ohai, *N.Z.* .... 131 F3 45 55 S 168 0 E
Ōhakune, *N.Z.* .... 130 F4 39 24 S 175 24 E
Ohanet, *Algeria* .... 111 C6 28 44N 8 46 E
Ōhara, *Japan* .... 73 B12 35 15N 140 23 E
O'Hare International, Chicago ✈
  (ORD), *U.S.A.* 157 C9 41 59N 87 54W
Ohata, *Japan* .... 70 D10 41 24N 141 10 E
Ohatchee, *U.S.A.* 152 B4 33 47N 86 0W
Ohau, L., *N.Z.* .... 131 E4 44 15 S 169 53 E
Ōhaupo, *N.Z.* .... 130 D4 37 56 S 175 20 E
O'Higgins, C., *Chile* .... 172 b 27 5 S 109 15W
Ohio □, *U.S.A.* 150 F2 40 15N 82 45W
Ohio →, *U.S.A.* 157 G8 36 59N 89 8W
Ohio City, *U.S.A.* 157 D12 40 46N 84 37W
Ohiwa Harbour, *N.Z.* .... 130 D6 37 59 S 177 10 E
Ohře →, *Czech Rep.* .... 34 A7 50 30N 14 10 E
Ohre →, *Germany* .... 30 C7 52 18N 11 46 E
Ohrid, *Macedonia* .... 50 E4 41 8N 20 52 E
Ohridsko Jezero, *Macedonia* .. 50 E4 41 8N 20 52 E
Ohrigstad, *S. Africa* .... 117 C5 24 39 S 30 36 E
Öhringen, *Germany* .... 31 F5 49 12N 9 31 E
Ohura, *N.Z.* .... 130 E3 38 51 S 174 59 E
Oi Qu, *China* .... 76 C2 28 37N 98 16 E
Oiapoque, *Brazil* 169 C7 3 50N 51 50W
Oiapoque →, *Brazil* 169 C7 4 8N 51 40W
Oikou, *China* .... 75 E9 38 35N 117 42 E
Oil City, *U.S.A.* 150 E5 41 26N 79 42W
Oil Springs, *Canada* 150 D2 42 47N 82 7W
Oildale, *U.S.A.* 161 K7 35 25N 119 1W
Oinousa, *Greece* .... 49 C8 38 33N 26 14 E
Oise □, *France* .... 27 C9 49 28N 2 30 E
Oise →, *France* .... 27 C9 49 0N 2 4 E
Oiseaux du Djoudj, Parc Nat. aux △,
  Senegal 112 B1 16 24N 16 14W
Oistins, *Barbados* .... 165 g 13 4N 59 33W
Oistins B., *Barbados* .... 165 g 13 4N 59 33W
Ōita, *Japan* .... 72 D3 33 14N 131 36 E
Ōita □, *Japan* .... 72 D3 33 15N 131 30 E
Oiticica, *Brazil* .... 170 C3 5 3 S 41 5W
Ojacaliente, *Mexico* 162 C4 22 34N 102 15W
Ojai, *U.S.A.* 161 L7 34 27N 119 15W
Ojcowski Park Narodowy △, *Poland* 55 H6 50 15N 19 50 E
Ojhar, *India* .... 94 D1 20 6N 73 56 E
Ojinaga, *Mexico* 162 B4 29 34N 104 25W
Ojiya, *Japan* .... 71 F9 37 18N 138 48 E
Ojo de Liebre, Parque Natural △,
  Mexico 162 B2 27 50N 114 0W
Ojos del Salado, Cerro, *Argentina* 174 B2 27 0 S 68 40W
Oka →, *Russia* .... 60 B7 56 20N 43 59 E
Okaba, *Indonesia* .... 83 C5 8 6 S 139 42 E
Okahandja, *Namibia* .... 116 C2 22 0 S 16 59 E
Okahukura, *N.Z.* .... 130 E4 38 48 S 175 14 E
Okaihau, *N.Z.* .... 130 B3 35 19 S 173 47 E
Okalataka, *U.S.A.* .... 114 C2 0 18 S 14 54 E
Okanagan L., *Canada* 142 D5 50 0N 119 30W
Okandja, *Gabon* .... 114 C2 0 35 S 13 45 E
Okano →, *Gabon* .... 114 C2 0 5 S 10 57 E
Okanogan, *U.S.A.* 158 B4 48 22N 119 35W
Okanogan →, *U.S.A.* 158 B4 48 6N 119 44W
Okány, *Hungary* .... 52 D6 46 52N 21 21 E
Okapa, *Papua N. G.* .... 132 B3 6 38 S 145 39 E
Okapi, Parc Nat. d' △, *Dem. Rep. of
  the Congo* .... 118 B2 2 30N 27 20 E
Okaputa, *Namibia* .... 116 C2 20 5 S 17 0 E
Okara, *Pakistan* .... 91 C4 30 50N 73 31 E
Okarito, *N.Z.* .... 131 D5 43 15 S 170 9 E
Okato, *N.Z.* .... 130 E2 39 12 S 173 53 E
Okaukuejo, *Namibia* .... 116 B2 19 10 S 16 0 E
Okavango Delta, *Botswana* .... 116 B3 18 45 S 22 45 E
Okavango Swamp = Okavango
  Delta, *Botswana* .... 116 B3 18 45 S 22 45 E
Ōkawa, *Japan* .... 72 D2 33 9N 130 21 E
Okawville, *U.S.A.* 156 F7 38 26N 89 33W
Okaya, *Japan* .... 73 A10 36 5N 138 10 E
Okayama, *Japan* .... 72 C5 34 40N 133 54 E
Okayama □, *Japan* .... 72 C5 35 0N 133 50 E
Okazaki, *Japan* .... 73 C9 34 57N 137 10 E
Oke-Iho, *Nigeria* .... 113 D5 8 1N 3 18 E
Okęcie, Warsaw ✈ (WAW), *Poland* 55 F7 52 9N 20 59 E
Okeechobee, *U.S.A.* 153 H9 27 15N 80 50W
Okeechobee, L., *U.S.A.* 153 J9 27 0N 80 50W
Okefenokee Nat. Wildlife Refuge △,
  U.S.A. 152 E7 30 44N 82 7W
Okefenokee Swamp, *U.S.A.* ... 152 E7 30 40N 82 20W
Okehampton, *U.K.* 21 G4 50 44N 4 0W
Okemos, *U.S.A.* 157 B12 42 43N 84 26W
Okene, *Nigeria* .... 113 D6 7 32N 6 11 E
Oker →, *Germany* .... 30 C6 52 32N 10 22 E
Okha, *India* .... 92 H3 22 27N 69 4 E
Okha, *Russia* .... 67 D15 53 40N 143 0 E
Ōkhi Óros, *Greece* .... 48 C6 38 5N 24 25 E
Okhotsk, *Russia* .... 67 D15 59 20N 143 10 E

Okhotsk, Sea of, *Asia* .... 67 D15 55 0N 145 0 E
Okhotskiy Perevoz, *Russia* .... 67 C14 61 52N 135 35 E
Okhtyrka, *Ukraine* .... 59 G8 50 25N 35 0 E
Oki-no-Shima, *Japan* .... 72 E4 32 44N 132 33 E
Oki-Shotō, *Japan* .... 72 A5 36 5N 133 15 E
Okiep, *S. Africa* .... 116 D2 29 39 S 17 53 E
Okigwi, *Nigeria* .... 113 D6 5 52N 7 20 E
Okija, *Nigeria* .... 113 D6 5 54N 6 55 E
Okinawa □, *Japan* .... 71 L4 26 40N 128 0 E
Okinawa-Guntō, *Japan* .... 71 L4 26 40N 128 0 E
Okinawa-Jima, *Japan* .... 71 L4 26 32N 128 0 E
Okino-erabu-Shima, *Japan* .... 71 L4 27 21N 128 33 E
Okitipupa, *Nigeria* .... 113 D5 6 31N 4 50 E
Oklahoma □, *U.S.A.* 155 H6 35 20N 97 30W
Oklahoma City, *U.S.A.* 155 H6 35 30N 97 30W
Oklawaha →, *U.S.A.* 153 F8 29 28N 81 41W
Okmulgee, *U.S.A.* 155 H7 35 37N 95 58W
Oknitsa = Ocnița, *Moldova* ... 53 B12 48 25N 27 30 E
Oko, W. →, *Sudan* .... 106 C4 21 15N 35 56 E
Okolo, *Uganda* .... 118 B3 2 37N 31 8 E
Okolona, *Ky., U.S.A.* 157 F11 38 8N 85 41W
Okolona, *Miss., U.S.A.* 155 J10 34 0N 88 45W
Okombahe, *Namibia* .... 116 C2 21 23 S 15 22 E
Okonek, *Poland* .... 54 E3 53 32N 16 51 E
Okotoks, *Canada* 142 C6 50 43N 113 58W
Okoyo, *Congo* .... 114 C3 1 28 S 15 0 E
Okrika, *Nigeria* .... 113 E6 4 40N 7 10 E
Oksapmin, *Papua N. G.* ...... 132 C2 5 17 S 142 15 E
Øksendal, *Norway* .... 18 B5 62 42N 8 27 E
Oksibil, *Indonesia* .... 83 B6 4 59 S 140 35 E
Øksna, *Norway* .... 18 D8 60 58N 11 27 E
Oksovskiy, *Russia* .... 56 B6 62 33N 39 57 E
Oktabrsk = Oktyabrsk, *Kazakhstan* 57 E10 49 28N 57 25 E
Oktwin, *Burma* .... 90 F6 18 49N 96 26 E
Oktyabr, *Kazakhstan* .... 65 B8 43 41N 77 12 E
Oktyabrsk, *Kazakhstan* .... 57 E10 49 28N 57 25 E
Oktyabrsk, *Russia* .... 60 D9 53 11N 48 40 E
Oktyabrskiy = Aktsyabrski, *Belarus* 59 F5 52 38N 28 53 E
Oktyabrskiy, *Bashkortostan, Russia* 64 D4 54 28N 53 28 E
Oktyabrskiy, *Perm, Russia* .... 64 C6 56 31N 57 12 E
Oktyabrskiy, *Rostov, Russia* .. 61 G5 47 30N 40 4 E
Oktyabrskoye Revolyutsii, Ostrov,
  Russia .... 67 B10 79 30N 97 0 E
Oktyabrskoye = Zhovtneve, *Ukraine* 59 J7 46 54N 32 3 E
Oktyabrskoye, *Russia* .... 64 D9 54 26N 62 44 E
Ōkuchi, *Japan* .... 72 E2 32 4N 130 37 E
Okulovka, *Russia* .... 58 C7 58 25N 33 19 E
Okuru, *N.Z.* .... 131 D3 43 55 S 168 55 E
Okushiri-Tō, *Japan* .... 70 C9 42 15N 139 30 E
Okuta, *Nigeria* .... 113 D5 9 14N 3 12 E
Okwa →, *Botswana* .... 116 C3 22 30 S 23 0 E
Ola, *U.S.A.* 155 H8 35 2N 93 13W
Ólafsfjörður, *Iceland* 11 A8 66 4N 18 39W
Ólafsvík, *Iceland* 11 C3 64 53N 23 43W
Olaine, *Latvia* .... 54 B10 56 47N 23 57 E
Olancha, *U.S.A.* 161 J8 36 17N 118 1W
Olancha Pk., *U.S.A.* 161 J8 36 16N 118 7W
Olanchito, *Honduras* 164 C2 15 30N 86 30W
Öland, *Sweden* .... 17 H10 56 45N 16 38 E
Ölands norra udde, *Sweden* ... 17 G11 57 22N 17 5 E
Ölands södra udde, *Sweden* ... 17 H10 56 12N 16 23 E
Olanta, *U.S.A.* 152 B10 33 56N 80 6W
Olar, *U.S.A.* 152 B8 33 11N 81 11W
Olargues, *France* .... 28 E6 43 34N 2 53 E
Olary, *Australia* .... 128 B4 32 18 S 140 19 E
Olascoaga, *Argentina* .... 174 D3 35 15 S 60 39W
Olathe, *U.S.A.* 154 F7 38 53N 94 49W
Olavarría, *Argentina* .... 174 D3 36 55 S 60 20W
Oława, *Poland* .... 55 H4 50 57N 17 20 E
Olberhau, *Germany* .... 30 E9 50 40N 13 19 E
Ólbia, *Italy* .... 46 B2 40 55N 9 31 E
Ólbia, G. di, *Italy* .... 46 B2 40 55N 9 39 E
Olching, *Germany* .... 31 G7 48 12N 11 21 E
Olcott, *U.S.A.* 150 C6 43 20N 78 42W
Old Bahama Chan. = Bahama, Canal
  Viejo de, *W. Indies* 164 B4 22 10N 77 30W
Old Baldy Pk. = San Antonio, Mt.,
  U.S.A. 161 L9 34 17N 117 38W
Old Bar, *Australia* .... 129 A10 31 58 S 152 35 E
Old Castile = Castilla y Leon □,
  Spain 42 D6 42 0N 5 0W
Old Crow, *Canada* 138 B6 67 30N 139 55W
Old Dale, *U.S.A.* 161 L11 34 8N 115 47W
Old Dongola, *Sudan* .... 106 D3 18 11N 30 44 E
Old Forge, *N.Y., U.S.A.* 151 C10 43 43N 74 58W
Old Forge, *Pa., U.S.A.* 151 E9 41 22N 75 45W
Old Fort B., *Bahamas* .... 9 b 25 3N 77 32W
Old Harbor, *U.S.A.* 144 H9 57 12N 153 18W
Old Perlican, *Canada* 141 C9 48 5N 53 1W
Old Shinyanga, *Tanzania* ...... 118 C3 3 33 S 33 27 E
Old Speck Mtn., *U.S.A.* 151 B14 44 34N 70 57W
Old Town, *Fla., U.S.A.* 153 F7 29 36N 82 59W
Old Town, *Maine, U.S.A.* 149 C11 44 56N 68 39W
Old Washington, *U.S.A.* 150 F3 40 2N 81 27W
Old Wives L., *Canada* 143 C7 50 5N 106 0W
Oldbury, *U.K.* 21 F5 51 38N 2 33W
Oldcastle, *Ireland* 23 C4 53 46N 7 10W
Oldeani, *Tanzania* .... 118 C4 3 22 S 35 35 E
Olden, *Norway* .... 18 C3 61 49N 6 49 E
Oldenburg, *Niedersachsen, Germany* 30 B4 53 9N 8 13 E
Oldenburg, Schleswig-Holstein,
  Germany .... 30 A6 54 17N 10 52 E
Oldenzaal, *Neths.* .... 24 B6 52 19N 6 53 E
Oldham, *U.K.* 20 D5 53 33N 2 7W
Oldman →, *Canada* 142 D6 49 57N 111 42W
Oldmeldrum, *U.K.* 22 D6 57 20N 2 19W
Olds, *Canada* 142 C6 51 50N 114 10W
Oldsmar, *U.S.A.* 153 G7 28 2N 82 40W
Olduvai Gorge, *Tanzania* ...... 118 C4 2 57 S 35 23 E
Olduziyt, *Mongolia* .... 74 B5 44 40N 109 1 E
Ole Rømer Land, *Greenland* ... 10 C8 74 10N 24 30W
Olean, *U.S.A.* 150 D6 42 5N 78 26W
Olecko, *Poland* .... 54 D9 54 2N 22 31 E
Oléggio, *Italy* .... 44 C5 45 36N 8 38 E
Oleiros, *Portugal* 42 F3 39 56N 7 56W
Oleiros, *Spain* 42 B2 43 20N 8 19W
Olekma →, *Russia* .... 67 C13 60 22N 120 42 E
Olekminsk, *Russia* .... 67 C13 60 25N 120 30 E
Oleksandriya, Kirovohrad, *Ukraine* 59 H7 48 42N 33 3 E
Oleksandriya, Rivne, *Ukraine* . 59 G4 50 37N 26 19 E
Oleksandrovka, *Ukraine* .... 59 H7 48 55N 32 20 E
Olema, *U.S.A.* 160 G4 38 3N 122 47W
Olen, *Russia* .... 18 E2 59 36N 5 48 E
Olenegorsk, *Russia* .... 56 A5 68 9N 33 18 E
Olenëk, *Russia* .... 67 C12 68 28N 112 18 E
Olenëk →, *Russia* .... 67 B13 73 0N 120 10 E
Olenino, *Russia* .... 58 D7 56 15N 33 30 E
Oléron, Î. d', *France* 28 C2 45 55N 1 15W
Oleśnica, *Poland* .... 55 G4 51 13N 17 22 E
Olesno, *Poland* .... 55 H5 50 51N 18 26 E
Olevsk, *Ukraine* .... 59 G4 51 12N 27 39 E
Olga, *Russia* .... 67 E14 43 50N 135 14 E
Olga, L., *Canada* 140 C4 49 47N 77 15W
Olga, Mt., *Australia* .... 125 E5 25 20 S 130 50 E
Ölgiy, *Mongolia* .... 68 B3 48 56N 89 57 E
Ølgod, *Denmark* .... 17 J2 55 49N 8 36 E
Olhão, *Portugal* 43 H3 37 3N 7 48W
Olib, *Croatia* .... 45 D11 44 23N 14 44 E
Oliena, *Italy* .... 46 B2 40 16N 9 24 E
Oliete, *Spain* 42 D4 41 1N 0 41W
Olifants = Elefantes →, *Africa* . 117 C5 24 10 S 32 40 E
Olifants →, *Namibia* .... 116 C2 25 30 S 19 30 E
Olifantshoek, *S. Africa* .... 116 D3 27 57 S 22 42 E
Ólimbos, *Greece* .... 49 F9 35 44N 27 11 E

Ólimbos, Óros, *Greece* .... 50 F6 40 6N 22 23 E
Olímpia, *Brazil* .... 175 A6 20 44 S 48 54W
Olimpos-Beydaglari Milli Parki △,
  Turkey .... 49 E4 36 36N 30 30 E
Olin, *U.S.A.* 156 C5 42 0N 91 9W
Olinda, *Brazil* .... 170 C5 8 1 S 34 51W
Olindiná, *Brazil* .... 170 D4 11 22 S 38 21W
Olite, *Spain* 42 C3 42 29N 1 40W
Oliva, *Argentina* .... 174 C3 32 0 S 63 38W
Oliva, *Spain* 41 G4 38 58N 0 9W
Oliva, Punta del, *Spain* 42 B5 43 37N 5 28W
Oliva de la Frontera, *Spain* ... 43 G4 38 17N 6 54W
Olivares, *Spain* 42 F2 39 46N 2 20W
Olive Hill, *U.S.A.* 157 F13 38 18N 83 13W
Olivehurst, *U.S.A.* 160 F5 39 6N 121 34W
Oliveira, *Brazil* .... 171 F3 20 39 S 44 50W
Oliveira de Azeméis, *Portugal* . 42 E2 40 49N 8 29W
Oliveira do Douro, *Portugal* ... 42 D2 41 5N 8 2W
Oliveira dos Brejinhos, *Brazil* .. 171 D3 12 19 S 42 54W
Olivenza, *Spain* 43 G3 38 41N 7 9W
Oliver, *Canada* 142 D5 49 13N 119 37W
Oliver L., *Canada* 143 B8 56 56N 103 22W
Olivet, *France* .... 27 E8 47 51N 1 55 E
Olivet, *U.S.A.* 157 B12 42 27N 84 56W
Olivine Ra., *N.Z.* .... 131 E3 44 15 S 168 30 E
Olney, *Switz.* .... 33 C7 46 32N 6 57 E
Olney, *Ill., U.S.A.* 157 F8 38 44N 88 5W
Olney, *Tex., U.S.A.* 155 J5 33 22N 98 45W
Olofström, *Sweden* .... 17 H8 56 17N 14 32 E
Ololi, *Congo* .... 114 C3 1 0 S 14 56 E
Olomane →, *Canada* .... 113 E7 3 29N 11 19 E
Olomane →, *Canada* 141 B7 50 14N 60 37W
Olomba, *Congo* .... 114 C3 1 18 S 15 53 E
Olomouc, *Czech Rep.* .... 35 B10 49 38N 17 12 E
Olomoucký □, *Czech Rep.* .... 35 B10 49 45N 17 5 E
Olonets, *Russia* .... 56 B5 61 0N 32 54 E
Olongapo, *Phil.* .... 80 D3 14 50N 120 18 E
Olonne-sur-Mer, *France* 28 B2 46 32N 1 47W
Oloron, Gave d' →, *France* 28 E2 43 33N 1 5W
Oloron-Ste-Marie, *France* 28 E3 43 11N 0 38W
Olosega, *Amer. Samoa* .... 133 X25 14 12 S 169 40W
Olot, *Spain* .... 40 C7 42 11N 2 30 E
Olovo, Bos.-H. .... 52 F3 44 8N 18 35 E
Olovyannaya, *Russia* .... 67 D12 50 58N 115 35 E
Olowalu, *U.S.A.* 145 C5 20 49N 156 38W
Oloy →, *Russia* .... 67 C16 66 29N 159 29 E
Olsberg, *Germany* .... 30 D4 51 21N 8 31 E
Olshammar, *Sweden* .... 17 F8 58 45N 14 48 E
Olshanka, *Ukraine* .... 59 H6 48 16N 30 58 E
Olshany, *Ukraine* .... 59 G8 50 3N 35 53 E
Olsztyn, *Poland* .... 54 E7 53 48N 20 29 E
Olsztynek, *Poland* .... 54 E7 53 34N 20 19 E
Olt □, *Romania* .... 53 F9 44 20N 24 30 E
Olt →, *Romania* .... 53 G9 43 43N 24 51 E
Oltedal, *Norway* .... 18 F3 58 49N 6 2 E
Olten, *Switz.* .... 32 B5 47 21N 7 53 E
Oltenița, *Romania* .... 53 F11 44 7N 26 42 E
Olton, *U.S.A.* 155 H3 34 11N 102 8W
Oltu, *Turkey* .... 101 B9 40 35N 41 58 E
Oluanpi, *Taiwan* .... 77 G13 21 54N 120 51 E
Olula del Rio, *Spain* 41 H2 37 21N 2 18W
Olur, *Turkey* .... 101 B10 40 49N 42 8 E
Olustee, *U.S.A.* 152 F7 30 6N 82 26W
Olut →, *Romania* .... 53 F11 44 7N 26 42 E
Olutanga I., *Phil.* .... 81 H4 7 22N 122 52 E
Olvega, *Spain* 40 D2 41 47N 2 0W
Olvera, *Spain* 43 J5 36 55N 5 18W
Olympia, *Greece* .... 48 D3 37 39N 21 39 E
Olympia, *U.S.A.* 160 C4 47 3N 122 53W
Olympic Dam, *Australia* ...... 128 A2 30 30 S 136 55 E
Olympic Mts., *U.S.A.* 160 C3 47 55N 123 45W
Olympic Nat. Park △, *U.S.A.* . 160 C3 47 48N 123 30W
Olympus, *Cyprus* .... 39 F8 34 56N 32 52 E
Olympus, Mt. = Ólimbos, Óros,
  Greece .... 50 F6 40 6N 22 23 E
Olympus, Mt. = Uludağ, *Turkey* 51 F13 40 4N 29 13 E
Olympus, Mt., *U.S.A.* 160 C3 47 48N 123 43W
Olyphant, *U.S.A.* 151 E9 41 27N 75 36W
Om →, *Russia* .... 66 D8 54 59N 73 22 E
Om Hajer, *Eritrea* .... 107 E4 14 20N 36 41 E
Om Koi, *Thailand* .... 86 D2 17 48N 98 22 E
Ōma, *Japan* .... 70 D10 41 45N 141 5 E
Ōmachi, *Japan* .... 73 A9 36 30N 137 50 E
Ōmae-Zaki, *Japan* .... 73 C9 34 36N 138 14 E
Ōmagari, *Japan* .... 70 E10 39 27N 140 29 E
Omagh, *U.K.* 23 B4 54 36N 7 19W
Omagh □, *U.K.* 23 B4 54 35N 7 15W
Omaha, *U.S.A.* 154 E7 41 17N 95 58W
Omak, *U.S.A.* 158 B4 48 25N 119 31W
Omalos, *Greece* .... 49 E4 35 19N 23 55 E
Oman ■, *Asia* .... 95 J4 11 44N 78 4 E
Oman, G. of, *Asia* .... 97 E8 24 30N 58 30 E
Omapere, *N.Z.* .... 130 B2 35 37 S 173 25 E
Omar Combon, *Somali Rep.* ... 120 D3 3 10N 45 41 E
Omaruru, *Namibia* .... 116 C2 21 26 S 16 0 E
Omaruru →, *Namibia* .... 116 C1 22 7 S 14 15 E
Omate, *Peru* .... 172 D3 16 45 S 71 0W
Ombai, Selat, *Indonesia* ...... 83 C2 8 30 S 124 50 E
Omboué, *Gabon* .... 114 C1 1 35 S 9 15 E
Ombrone →, *Italy* .... 44 F8 42 42N 11 5 E
Omchi, *Chad* .... 109 D3 21 17N 17 53 E
Omdurmân, *Sudan* .... 107 D3 15 40N 32 28 E
Ome, *Japan* .... 73 B11 35 47N 139 15 E
Omega, *U.S.A.* 152 D6 31 21N 83 36W
Omegna, *Italy* .... 44 C5 45 53N 8 24 E
Omemee, *Canada* 150 B6 44 18N 78 33W
Omeo, *Australia* .... 129 D7 37 6 S 147 36 E
Omeonga, Dem. Rep. of the Congo 118 C1 3 40 S 24 22 E
Ometepe, I. de, *Nic.* 164 D2 11 32N 85 35W
Ometepec, *Mexico* 163 D5 16 39N 98 23W
Omi-Shima, *Ehime, Japan* .... 72 C5 34 15N 133 0 E
Ōmi-Shima, *Yamaguchi, Japan* 72 C3 34 35N 131 9 E
Omihachiman, *Japan* .... 73 B8 35 7N 136 3 E
Ōmiya, *Japan* .... 70 D10 41 17N 141 10 E
Ommaney, C., *U.S.A.* 142 B2 56 10N 134 40W
Omme Å →, *Denmark* .... 17 J2 55 56N 8 32 E
Ommen, *Neths.* .... 24 B6 52 31N 6 26 E
Omnögovi □, *Mongolia* .... 74 C5 43 15N 104 0 E
Omo →, *Ethiopia* .... 107 F4 6 25N 36 10 E
Omo Nat. Park △, *Ethiopia* ... 107 F4 5 7N 36 5 E
Omo Valley, *Ethiopia* .... 107 F4 5 5N 36 5 E
Omodhos, *Cyprus* .... 39 F8 34 51N 32 48 E
Omolon, *Congo* .... 114 C2 2 56 S 13 13 E
Omoko, *Nigeria* .... 113 D6 5 19N 6 40 E
Omolon →, *Russia* .... 67 C16 68 42N 158 36 E

Omona, *Solomon Is.* .... 133 L10 7 30 S 158 43 E
Omono-Gawa →, *Japan* ...... 70 E10 39 46N 140 3 E
Omsk, *Russia* .... 66 D8 55 0N 73 12 E
Omsukchan, *Russia* .... 67 C16 62 32N 155 48 E
Ōmu, *Japan* .... 70 B11 44 34N 142 58 E
Omul, Vf., *Romania* .... 53 E10 45 27N 25 29 E
Omura, *Japan* .... 72 E1 32 56N 129 57 E
Ōmura-Wan, *Japan* .... 72 E1 32 57N 129 52 E
Omuramba Omatako →, *Namibia* 116 B2 17 45 S 20 25 E
Omuramba Ovambo →, *Namibia* 116 B2 18 45 S 16 59 E
Omurtag, *Bulgaria* .... 51 C10 43 8N 26 26 E
Ōmuta, *Japan* .... 72 D2 33 5N 130 26 E
Omutninsk, *Russia* .... 64 B4 58 45N 52 4 E
On-ma-thi, *Burma* .... 90 D6 22 17N 96 41 E
On-Take, *Japan* .... 72 F2 31 35N 130 39 E
Oña, *Spain* 42 C7 42 43N 3 25W
Ona, *U.S.A.* 153 H8 27 29N 81 55W
Ona Dikonde, *Dem. Rep. of
  the Congo* .... 114 C4 3 51 S 24 11 E
Onaga, *U.S.A.* 154 F6 39 29N 96 10W
Onalaska, *U.S.A.* 154 D9 43 53N 91 14W
Onancock, *U.S.A.* 148 G8 37 43N 75 45W
Onang, *Indonesia* .... 83 B1 3 2 S 118 49 E
Onaping, *Canada* .... 114 C1 0 57 S 10 4 E
Onarga, *U.S.A.* 157 D8 40 43N 88 1W
Ōnati, *Spain* 40 B2 43 3N 2 25W
Onavas, *Mexico* 162 B3 28 28N 109 30W
Onawa, *U.S.A.* 154 D6 42 2N 96 6W
Oncócua, *Angola* .... 116 B1 16 30 S 13 25 E
Onda, *Spain* 40 F4 39 55N 0 17W
Ondaejin, *N. Korea* .... 75 D15 41 34N 129 40 E
Ondangwa, *Namibia* .... 116 B2 17 57 S 16 4 E
Ondarroa, *Spain* 40 B2 43 19N 2 25W
Ondas →, *Brazil* .... 171 D3 12 8 S 44 55W
Ondava →, *Slovak Rep.* .... 35 C14 48 27N 21 48 E
Ondjiva, *Angola* .... 116 B2 16 48 S 15 50 E
Ondo, *Japan* .... 72 C4 34 11N 132 32 E
Ondo, *Nigeria* .... 113 D5 7 4N 4 47 E
Ondo □, *Nigeria* .... 113 D6 6 45N 5 0 E
Öndörhaan, *Mongolia* .... 74 B5 45 13N 108 5 E
Ondverðarnes, *Iceland* 11 C2 64 52N 24 0W
One Tree, *Australia* .... 127 E3 34 11 S 144 43 E
Oneata, *Fiji* .... 133 B3 18 26 S 178 25W
Oneco, *U.S.A.* 153 H7 27 25N 82 31W
Onega, *Russia* .... 56 B6 64 0N 38 10 E
Onega →, *Russia* .... 56 B6 63 58N 38 2 E
Onega, G. of = Onezhskaya Guba,
  Russia .... 56 B6 64 24N 36 38 E
Onega, L. = Onezhskoye Ozero,
  Russia .... 58 B8 61 44N 35 22 E
Onehunga, *N.Z.* .... 130 C3 36 55 S 174 48 E
Oneida, *Ill., U.S.A.* 156 C6 41 4N 90 13W
Oneida, *N.Y., U.S.A.* 151 C9 43 6N 75 39W
Oneida L., *U.S.A.* 151 C9 43 12N 75 54W
O'Neill, *U.S.A.* 154 D5 42 27N 98 39W
Onekotan, Ostrov, *Russia* ..... 67 E16 49 25N 154 45 E
Onema, Dem. Rep. of the Congo 118 C1 4 35 S 24 30 E
Oneonta, *U.S.A.* 151 D9 42 27N 75 4W
Onerahi, *N.Z.* .... 130 B3 35 45 S 174 22 E
Oneşti, *Romania* .... 53 D11 46 17N 26 47 E
Onezhskaya Guba, *Russia* ..... 56 B6 64 24N 36 38 E
Onezhskoye Ozero, *Russia* .... 58 B8 61 44N 35 22 E
Ongarue, *N.Z.* .... 130 E4 38 42 S 175 19 E
Ongea Levu = Ogea Levu, *Fiji* . 133 B3 19 8 S 178 24W
Ongers →, *S. Africa* .... 116 E3 31 4 S 23 13 E
Ongerup, *Australia* .... 125 F2 33 58 S 118 28 E
Ongjin, *N. Korea* .... 75 F13 37 56N 125 21 E
Ongkharak, *Thailand* .... 86 E3 14 8N 101 1 E
Ongniud Qi, *China* .... 75 C10 43 0N 118 38 E
Ongoka, *Dem. Rep. of the Congo* 118 C2 1 20 S 26 0 E
Ongole, *India* .... 95 G5 15 33N 80 2 E
Ongon = Havirga, *Mongolia* ... 74 B7 45 41N 113 5 E
Onguren, *Gabon* .... 114 C2 1 1 S 5 E
Oni, *Georgia* .... 61 J6 42 33N 43 26 E
Onida, *U.S.A.* 154 C4 44 42N 100 4W
Onilahy →, *Madag.* .... 117 C7 23 34 S 43 45 E
Onitsha, *Nigeria* .... 113 D6 6 6N 6 42 E
Ono, *Fiji* .... 133 B3 18 55 S 178 29 E
Ono, *Fukui, Japan* .... 73 B8 35 59N 136 29 E
Ono, *Hyōgo, Japan* .... 72 C6 34 51N 134 56 E
Onoda, *Japan* .... 72 C3 33 59N 131 11 E
Onohara, *Japan* .... 72 C5 34 13N 133 40 E
Onoke, L., *N.Z.* .... 130 H4 41 22 S 175 8 E
Onomichi, *Japan* .... 72 C6 34 25N 133 12 E
Onpyŏng-ni, *S. Korea* .... 75 H14 33 25N 126 55 E
Ons, I. de, *Spain* 42 C2 42 23N 8 55W
Onslow, *Australia* .... 124 D2 21 40 S 115 12 E
Onslow B., *U.S.A.* 149 H7 34 20N 77 15W
Ontake-San, *Japan* .... 73 B9 35 53N 137 29 E
Ontar, *Vanuatu* .... 133 D6 14 17 S 167 27 E
Ontario, *Calif., U.S.A.* 161 L9 34 4N 117 39W
Ontario, *Oreg., U.S.A.* 158 D5 44 2N 116 58W
Ontario □, *Canada* 140 B2 48 0N 83 0W
Ontario, L., *N. Amer.* 150 C7 43 20N 78 0W
Ontinyent, *Spain* 41 G4 38 50N 0 35W
Ontonagon, *U.S.A.* 154 B10 46 52N 89 19W
Ontur, *Spain* 41 G3 38 38N 1 29W
Onverwacht, *Suriname* .... 169 B6 5 35 S 55 11W
Onyx, *U.S.A.* 161 K8 35 41N 118 14W
Oodnadatta, *Australia* .... 127 D2 27 33 S 135 30 E
Ookala, *U.S.A.* 145 C6 20 1N 155 17W
Ooldea, *Australia* .... 125 F5 30 27 S 131 50 E
Oombulgurri, *Australia* .... 124 C4 15 15 S 127 45 E
Oorindi, *Australia* .... 126 C3 20 40 S 141 1 E
Oost-Vlaanderen □, *Belgium* .. 24 C3 51 5N 3 50 E
Oostende, *Belgium* .... 24 C2 51 15N 2 54 E
Oosterhout, *Neths.* .... 24 C4 51 39N 4 47 E
Oosterschelde →, *Neths.* ...... 24 C4 51 33N 4 0 E
Oosterwolde, *Neths.* .... 24 B6 53 0N 6 17 E
Ootacamund = Udagamandalam,
  India .... 95 J3 11 30N 76 44 E
Ootha, *Australia* .... 129 E4 33 6 S 147 29 E
Ootsa L., *Canada* 142 C3 53 50N 126 2W
Op Luang Nat. Park △, *Thailand* 86 C2 18 12N 98 32 E
Opaka, *Bulgaria* .... 51 C10 43 28N 26 10 E
Opala, Dem. Rep. of the Congo 118 C1 0 40 S 24 20 E
Opalenica, *Poland* .... 55 F3 52 18N 16 24 E
Opan, *Bulgaria* .... 51 D9 42 13N 25 41 E
Opanake, *Sri Lanka* .... 95 L5 6 35N 80 40 E
Opapa, *N.Z.* .... 130 C3 39 54 S 176 42 E
Opasatika, *Canada* 140 C3 49 30N 82 50W
Opasquia Prov. Park △, *Canada* 143 B11 53 33N 93 5W
Opatija, *Croatia* .... 45 C11 45 21N 14 17 E
Opatów, *Poland* .... 55 H8 50 50N 21 27 E
Opava, *Czech Rep.* .... 35 B10 49 57N 17 58 E
Opelika, *U.S.A.* 152 C4 32 39N 85 23W
Opelousas, *U.S.A.* 155 K8 30 32N 92 5W
Opémisca, L., *Canada* 140 C5 49 56N 74 52W
Opheim, *U.S.A.* 158 B10 48 51N 106 24W
Ophir, *U.S.A.* 144 E8 63 10N 156 31W
Ophthalmia Ra., *Australia* .... 124 D2 23 15 S 119 30 E
Opi, *Nigeria* .... 113 D6 6 6N 7 28 E
Opihikao, *U.S.A.* 145 D7 19 26N 154 53W
Opinaca →, *Canada* 140 B4 52 15N 78 2W
Opinaca, Rés., *Canada* 140 B4 52 39N 76 20W
Opinnagau →, *Canada* 140 B3 54 12N 82 25W
Opiscoteo, L., *Canada* .... 113 B6 27 8N 1 34 E
Opobo, *Nigeria* .... 113 E6 5 19N 7 34 E
Opochka, *Russia* .... 58 D5 56 42N 28 45 E
Opoczno, *Poland* .... 55 G7 51 22N 20 18 E
Opol, *Phil.* .... 81 G5 8 31N 124 34 E
Opole, *Poland* .... 55 H4 50 42N 17 58 E

Opole Lubelskie, Poland .... 55 G8 51 9N 21 58 E
Opolskie □, Poland .... 55 H5 50 30N 18 0 E
Opon = Lapu-Lapu, Phil. .... 81 F4 10 20N 123 55 E
Oponono L., Namibia .... 116 B2 18 8S 15 45 E
Oporto = Porto, Portugal 42 D2 41 8N 8 40W
Opotiki, N.Z. .... 130 E6 38 1S 177 19 E
Opp, U.S.A. 152 D3 31 17N 86 16W
Oppdal, Norway .... 18 B6 62 35N 9 41 E
Oppeln = Opole, Poland .... 55 H4 50 42N 17 58 E
Oppido Mamertina, Italy .... 47 D8 38 16N 15 59 E
Oppland □, Norway .... 18 C6 61 15N 9 40 E
Opportunity, U.S.A. 158 C5 47 39N 117 15W
Oprişor, Romania .... 52 F8 44 17N 23 5 E
Oprtalj, Croatia .... 45 C10 45 23N 13 50 E
Opua, N.Z. .... 130 B3 35 19S 174 9 E
Opunake, N.Z. .... 130 F2 39 26S 173 52 E
Opuwo, Namibia .... 116 B1 18 3S 13 45 E
Opuzen, Croatia .... 45 E14 43 1N 17 34 E
Oquawka, U.S.A. 156 D6 40 56N 90 57W
Ora, Cyprus .... 39 F9 34 51N 33 12 E
Oracle, U.S.A. 159 K8 32 37N 110 46W
Oracuzar, Peru 168 D2 4 42S 78 6W
Oradea, Romania .... 52 C7 47 2N 21 58 E
Öræfajökull, Iceland 11 C10 64 2N 16 39W
Orahovac, Kosovo, Yug. .... 50 D4 42 24N 20 40 E
Orahovica, Croatia .... 52 E2 45 35N 17 52 E
Orai, India .... 93 G8 25 58N 79 30 E
Oraison, France .... 29 E9 43 55N 5 55 E
Oral = Zhayyq ~, Kazakhstan ... 57 E9 47 0N 51 48 E
Oral, Kazakhstan .... 60 E10 51 20N 51 20 E
Oran, Algeria 111 A4 35 45N 0 39W
Orange, Australia .... 129 B8 33 15S 149 7 E
Orange, France .... 29 D8 44 8N 4 47 E
Orange, Calif., U.S.A. 161 M9 33 47N 117 51W
Orange, Mass., U.S.A. 151 D12 42 35N 72 19W
Orange, Tex., U.S.A. 155 K8 30 6N 93 44W
Orange, Va., U.S.A. 148 F6 38 15N 78 7W
Orange ~, S. Africa .... 116 D2 28 41S 16 28 E
Orange, C., Brazil 169 C7 4 20N 51 30W
Orange City, U.S.A. 153 G8 28 57N 81 18W
Orange Cove, U.S.A. 160 J7 36 38N 119 19W
Orange Free State = Free State □,
 S. Africa .... 116 D4 28 30S 27 0 E
Orange Grove, U.S.A. 155 M6 27 58N 97 56W
Orange L., U.S.A. 153 F7 29 25N 82 13W
Orange Park, U.S.A. 152 E8 30 10N 81 42W
Orange Walk, Belize 163 D7 18 6N 88 33W
Orangeburg, U.S.A. 152 B9 33 30N 80 52W
Orangeville, Canada 140 D3 43 55N 80 5W
Orangeville, U.S.A. 156 B7 42 28N 89 39W
Orango, Guinea-Biss. 112 C1 11 5N 16 0W
Orani, Phil. .... 80 D3 14 49N 120 32 E
Oranienburg, Germany .... 30 C9 52 45N 13 14 E
Oranje = Orange ~, S. Africa ... 116 D2 28 41S 16 28 E
Oranje Vrystaat = Free State □,
 S. Africa .... 116 D4 28 30S 27 0 E
Oranjemund, Namibia .... 116 D2 28 38S 16 29 E
Oranjerivier, S. Africa .... 116 D3 29 40S 24 12 E
Oranjestad, Aruba 165 D5 12 32N 70 2W
Orap, Vanuatu .... 133 E5 15 58S 167 20 E
Orarak, Sudan .... 107 F3 6 15N 32 23 E
Oras, Phil. .... 80 E5 12 9N 125 28 E
Orašje, Bos.-H. .... 52 E3 45 1N 18 42 E
Orăştie, Romania .... 53 E8 45 50N 23 10 E
Orăşul Stalin = Braşov, Romania . 53 E10 45 38N 25 35 E
Orava ~, Slovak Rep. .... 35 B12 49 9N 19 8 E
Orava, Vodna nádrž, Slovak Rep. . 35 B12 49 25N 19 35 E
Oraviţa, Romania .... 52 E6 45 2N 21 43 E
Orawia, N.Z. .... 131 G2 46 1S 167 50 E
Orb ~, France .... 28 E7 43 15N 3 18 E
Orba ~, Italy .... 44 D5 44 53N 8 37 E
Ørbæk, Denmark .... 17 J4 55 17N 10 39 E
Orbe, Switz. .... 32 C3 46 43N 6 32 E
Orbec, France .... 26 C7 49 1N 0 23 E
Orbetello, Italy .... 45 F8 42 27N 11 13 E
Órbigo ~, Spain 42 C5 42 5N 5 42W
Orbisonia, U.S.A. 150 F7 40 15N 77 54W
Orbost, Australia .... 129 D8 37 40S 148 29 E
Örbyhus, Sweden .... 16 D11 60 15N 17 43 E
Orcas I., U.S.A. 160 B4 48 42N 122 56W
Orce, Spain 41 H2 37 44N 2 28W
Orce ~, Spain 41 H2 37 44N 2 28W
Orchard City, U.S.A. 159 G10 38 50N 107 58W
Orchies, France .... 27 B10 50 28N 3 14 E
Orchila, I., Venezuela 165 D6 11 48N 66 10W
Orchilla, Pta., Canary Is. 9 e1 27 42N 18 10W
Órcia ~, Italy .... 45 F8 42 58N 11 21 E
Orco ~, Italy .... 44 C4 45 10N 7 52 E
Orcopampa, Peru 172 D3 15 20S 72 23W
Orcutt, U.S.A. 161 L6 34 52N 120 27W
Ord, U.S.A. 154 E5 41 36N 98 56W
Ord ~, Australia .... 124 C4 15 33S 128 15 E
Ord, Mt., Australia .... 124 C4 17 20S 125 34 E
Ordenes = Ordes, Spain 42 B2 43 5N 8 29W
Orderville, U.S.A. 159 H7 37 17N 112 38W
Ordes, Spain 42 B2 43 5N 8 29W
Ordesa y Monte Perido, Parque Nac.
 de □, Spain 40 C4 42 40N 0 10W
Ording = St-Peter-Ording, Germany 30 A4 54 20N 8 36 E
Ordos = Mu Us Shamo, China ... 74 E5 39 0N 109 0 E
Ordu, Turkey .... 100 B7 40 55N 37 53 E
Ordubad, Azerbaijan .... 101 C12 38 54N 46 1 E
Orduña, Álava, Spain 40 C2 42 58N 2 58W
Orduña, Granada, Spain 43 H7 37 20N 3 30W
Ordway, U.S.A. 154 F3 38 13N 103 46W
Ordzhonikidze = Vladikavkaz,
 Russia .... 61 J7 43 0N 44 35 E
Ordzhonikidze, Kazakhstan ..... 64 E8 52 27N 61 48 E
Ordzhonikidze, Ukraine .... 59 J8 47 39N 34 3 E
Ordzhonikidzeabad = Kofarnikhon,
 Tajikistan .... 65 D4 38 34N 69 1 E
Ore, Dem. Rep. of the Congo .... 118 B2 3 17N 29 30 E
Ore Mts. = Erzgebirge, Germany . 30 E8 50 27N 12 55 E
Orealla, Guyana 169 B6 5 15N 57 23W
Orebić, Croatia .... 45 E14 43 0N 17 11 E
Örebro, Sweden .... 16 E9 59 20N 15 18 E
Örebro län □, Sweden .... 16 E8 59 27N 15 0 E
Orecchiella, Riserva Statale □, Italy 44 D7 44 16N 10 22 E
Oregon, Ill., U.S.A. 156 B7 42 1N 89 20W
Oregon, Ohio, U.S.A. 157 C13 41 38N 83 25W
Oregon, Wis., U.S.A. 156 B7 42 56N 89 23W
Oregon □, U.S.A. 158 E3 44 0N 121 0W
Oregon City, U.S.A. 160 E4 45 21N 122 36W
Oregon Dunes Nat. Recr. Area □,
 U.S.A. 158 E1 43 2N 123 26W
Oregrund, Sweden .... 16 D12 60 21N 18 30 E
Oregrundsgrepen, Sweden .... 16 D12 60 25N 18 15 E
Orekhov = Orikhiv, Ukraine ..... 59 J8 47 30N 35 48 E
Orekhovo-Zuyevo, Russia .... 58 E10 55 50N 38 55 E
Orel, Russia .... 59 F9 52 57N 36 3 E
Orel ~, Ukraine .... 59 H8 48 40N 34 39 E
Orellana, Spain 43 F5 39 1N 5 32W
Orellana, Canal de, Spain 43 F5 39 2N 6 0W
Orellana, Embalse de, Spain 43 F5 39 5N 5 10W
Orem, U.S.A. 158 F8 40 19N 111 42W
Oren, Turkey .... 49 D9 37 3N 27 57 E
Orenburg, Russia .... 64 F5 51 45N 55 6 E
Orencik, Turkey .... 49 B11 39 15N 29 30 E
Orense = Ourense, Spain 42 C3 42 19N 7 55W
Orense □, Spain 42 C3 42 15N 7 30W
Orepuki, N.Z. .... 131 G2 46 19S 167 46 E
Orestias, Greece .... 51 E10 41 30N 26 33 E
Orestos Pereyra, Mexico 162 B3 26 31N 105 40W
Øresund, Europe .... 17 J6 55 45N 12 45 E

Oreti ~, N.Z. .... 131 G3 46 28S 168 14 E
Orford Ness, U.K. .... 21 E9 52 5N 1 35 E
Organ Pipe Cactus Nat.
 Monument □, U.S.A. 159 K7 32 0N 113 0W
Organà = Organyà, Spain .... 40 C6 42 13N 1 20 E
Organos, Pta. de los, Canary Is. . 9 e1 28 12N 17 17W
Organyà, Spain .... 40 C6 42 13N 1 20 E
Orgaz, Spain 43 F7 39 39N 3 53W
Orgenvika, Norway .... 18 D6 60 17N 9 42 E
Orgeyev = Orhei, Moldova ...... 53 C13 47 24N 28 50 E
Orgūn, Afghan. .... 91 B3 32 55N 69 12 E
Orhaneli, Turkey .... 51 G12 39 54N 28 59 E
Orhaneli ~, Turkey .... 51 G12 39 50N 28 55 E
Orhangazi, Turkey .... 51 F13 40 29N 29 18 E
Orhei, Moldova .... 53 C13 47 24N 28 50 E
Orhon Gol ~, Mongolia .... 68 A5 50 21N 106 0 E
Ória, Italy .... 47 B10 40 30N 17 38 E
Orídia, Niger .... 111 D7 21 20N 12 15 E
Oriental, Cordillera, Bolivia 173 D4 17 0S 66 0W
Oriental, Cordillera, Colombia ... 168 B3 6 0N 73 0W
Oriental, Grand Erg, Algeria .... 111 C6 30 0N 6 30 E
Orientale □, Dem. Rep. of the Congo 118 B2 2 20N 26 0 E
Oriente, Argentina 174 D3 38 44S 60 37W
Orihuela, Spain 41 G4 38 7N 0 55W
Orihuela del Tremedal, Spain 40 E3 40 33N 1 39W
Orikhiv, Ukraine .... 59 J8 47 30N 35 48 E
Orikum, Albania .... 50 F3 40 20N 19 26 E
Orillia, Canada 140 D4 44 40N 79 24W
Orinduik, Guyana 169 C5 4 40N 60 3W
Orinoco ~, Venezuela 169 B5 9 15N 61 30W
Orion, Canada 143 D6 49 27N 110 49W
Orion, Ala., U.S.A. 152 D4 31 58N 86 0W
Orion, Ill., U.S.A. 156 C6 41 21N 90 23W
Oriskany, U.S.A. 151 C9 43 10N 75 20W
Orissa □, India .... 94 E7 20 0N 84 0 E
Orissaare, Estonia .... 15 G20 58 34N 23 5 E
Oristano, Italy .... 46 C1 39 54N 8 36 E
Oristano, G. di, Italy .... 46 C1 39 50N 8 29 E
Orituco ~, Venezuela 168 B4 8 45N 67 27W
Oriximiná, Brazil 169 D6 1 45S 55 52W
Orizaba, Mexico 163 D5 18 51N 97 6W
Orizaba, Pico de, Mexico .... 51 D11 44 23N 27 39 E
Orizare, Bulgaria .... 51 D11 44 23N 27 39 E
Orizona, Brazil 171 E2 17 3S 48 18W
Ørje, Norway .... 18 E8 59 29N 11 39 E
Orjen, Bos.-H. .... 50 D2 42 35N 18 34 E
Orjiva, Spain 43 J7 36 53N 3 24W
Orkanger, Norway .... 18 A6 63 18N 9 52 E
Örkelljunga, Sweden .... 17 H7 56 17N 13 17 E
Örkény, Hungary .... 52 C4 47 9N 19 26 E
Orkla ~, Norway .... 18 A6 63 18N 9 51 E
Orkney, S. Africa .... 116 D4 26 58S 26 40 E
Orkney □, U.K. 22 B5 59 2N 3 13W
Orkney Is., U.K. 22 B6 59 0N 3 0W
Orland, Calif., U.S.A. 160 F4 39 45N 122 12W
Orland, Ind., U.S.A. 157 C11 41 47N 85 12W
Orlando, U.S.A. 153 G8 28 33N 81 23W
Orlando, C. d', Italy .... 47 D7 38 10N 14 43 E
Orlando International ✈ (MCO),
 U.S.A. 153 G8 28 26N 81 19W
Orléanais □, France .... 27 E8 48 0N 2 0 E
Orléans, France .... 27 E8 47 54N 1 52 E
Orleans, Ind., U.S.A. 157 F10 38 40N 86 27W
Orleans, Vt., U.S.A. 151 B12 44 49N 72 12W
Orléans, I. d', Canada 141 C5 46 54N 70 58W
Orléansville = Ech Chéliff, Algeria 111 A5 36 10N 1 20 E
Orlice ~, Czech Rep. .... 34 A8 50 13N 15 50 E
Orlov, Slovak Rep. .... 35 B13 49 17N 20 51 E
Orlov Gay, Russia .... 60 E9 50 56N 48 19 E
Orlová, Czech Rep. .... 35 B11 49 51N 18 26 E
Orlovat, Serbia, Yug. .... 52 E5 45 14N 20 33 E
Orlovka, Kyrgyzstan .... 65 B7 42 45N 75 36 E
Orly, Paris ✈ (ORY), France .... 27 D9 48 44N 2 23 E
Ormara, Pakistan .... 91 D2 25 16N 64 33 E
Órmea, Italy .... 44 D4 44 9N 7 54 E
Ormília, Greece .... 50 F7 40 16N 23 39 E
Ormoc, Phil. .... 81 F5 11 0N 124 37 E
Ormond, N.Z. .... 130 E6 38 33S 177 56 E
Ormond Beach, U.S.A. 153 F8 29 17N 81 3W
Ormond by the Sea, U.S.A. 153 F8 29 21N 81 5W
Ormondville, N.Z. .... 130 G5 40 5S 176 19 E
Órmos Keríou, Greece .... 39 D2 37 42N 20 53 E
Ormož, Slovenia .... 45 B13 46 25N 16 10 E
Ormskirk, U.K. 20 D5 53 35N 2 54W
Ormstown, Canada 151 A11 45 8N 74 0W
Ormtjernkampen Nasjonalpark △,
 Norway .... 18 C6 61 12N 9 48 E
Ornans, France .... 27 E13 47 7N 6 10 E
Ornavasso, Italy .... 33 K6 45 58N 8 24 E
Orne □, France .... 26 D7 48 40N 0 5 E
Orne ~, France 26 C7 49 18N 0 15W
Orneta, Poland .... 54 D7 54 8N 20 9 E
Ornö, Sweden .... 17 F11 59 4N 18 24 E
Örnsköldsvik, Sweden .... 16 A12 63 17N 18 40 E
Oro, N. Korea .... 75 D14 40 1N 127 27 E
Oro ~, Mexico 162 B3 25 35N 105 2W
Oro Grande, U.S.A. 161 L9 34 36N 117 20W
Oro Valley, U.S.A. 159 K8 32 26N 110 58W
Orobie, Alpi, Italy .... 44 B6 46 0N 10 0 E
Orobie Bergamasche, Parco delle □,
 Italy .... 44 C6 46 0N 9 45 E
Orobie Valtellinesi, Parco delle □,
 Italy .... 44 B6 46 5N 9 45 E
Orocué, Colombia 168 C3 4 48N 71 20W
Orodara, Burkina Faso 112 C4 11 0N 4 55W
Orodo, Nigeria .... 113 D6 5 34N 7 4 E
Orofino, U.S.A. 158 C5 46 29N 116 15W
Orohena, Mt., Tahiti 133 S16 17 37S 149 28W
Orol Dengizi = Aral Sea, Asia ... 66 E7 44 30N 60 0 E
Oromocto, Canada 141 C6 45 54N 66 29W
Oron, Nigeria .... 113 E6 4 48N 8 14 E
Oron, Switz. .... 32 C2 46 34N 6 50 E
Orongo, Chile .... 172 b 27 11S 109 27W
Orono, Canada 150 C6 43 59N 78 37W
Orono, U.S.A. 149 C11 44 53N 68 40W
Oronsay, U.K. 22 E2 56 1N 6 15W
Oropesa, Spain 42 F5 39 57N 5 10W
Oroqen Zizhiqi, China .... 69 A7 50 34N 123 43 E
Oroquieta, Phil. .... 81 G4 8 32N 123 44 E
Orós, Brazil 170 C4 6 15S 38 55W
Orosei, Italy .... 46 B2 40 23N 9 42 E
Orosei, G. di, Italy .... 46 B2 40 15N 9 44 E
Orosháza, Hungary .... 52 D5 46 32N 20 42 E
Oroszlány, Hungary .... 52 C3 47 29N 18 19 E
Orote Pen., Guam .... 133 R15 13 26N 144 38 E
Orotukan, Russia .... 67 C16 62 16N 151 42 E
Oroville, Calif., U.S.A. 160 F5 39 31N 121 33W
Oroville, Wash., U.S.A. 158 B4 48 56N 119 26W
Oroville, L., U.S.A. 160 F5 39 33N 121 29W
Orrefors, Sweden .... 17 H9 56 50N 15 45 E
Orrick, U.S.A. 156 F6 39 13N 94 7W
Orroroo, Australia .... 128 B3 32 43S 138 38 E
Orrville, U.S.A. 150 F3 40 50N 81 46W
Orsa, Sweden .... 16 C8 61 7N 14 37 E
Orsara di Púglia, Italy .... 47 A8 41 17N 15 16 E
Orsasjön, Sweden .... 16 C8 61 7N 14 37 E
Orsha, Belarus .... 58 E6 54 30N 30 25 E
Orsières, Switz. .... 32 D4 46 2N 7 9 E
Orsjö, Sweden .... 17 H9 56 42N 15 45 E
Orsk, Russia .... 64 F7 51 12N 58 34 E
Orşova, Romania .... 52 F7 44 41N 22 25 E
Ørsta, Norway .... 18 B3 62 13N 6 8 E

Ørsted, Denmark .... 17 H4 56 30N 10 20 E
Örsundsbro, Sweden .... 16 E11 59 44N 17 18 E
Orta, L. d', Italy .... 44 C5 45 49N 8 24 E
Orta Nova, Italy .... 47 A8 41 19N 15 42 E
Ortaca, Turkey .... 49 E10 36 49N 28 45 E
Ortakent, Turkey .... 49 D9 37 5N 27 21 E
Ortaklar, Turkey .... 49 D9 37 53N 27 30 E
Ortaköy, Çorum, Turkey .... 100 B6 40 16N 35 15 E
Ortaköy, Niğde, Turkey .... 100 D11 38 44N 34 3 E
Orte, Italy .... 45 F9 42 27N 12 23 E
Ortegal, C., Spain 42 B3 43 43N 7 52W
Orteguaza ~, Colombia 168 C2 0 43N 75 16W
Orthez, France 28 E3 43 29N 0 48W
Ortigueira, Spain 42 B3 43 40N 7 50W
Orting, U.S.A. 160 C4 47 6N 122 12W
Ortisei, Italy .... 45 B8 46 34N 11 40 E
Ortles, Italy .... 44 B7 46 31N 10 33 E
Ortón ~, Bolivia 172 C4 10 50S 67 0W
Ortona, Italy .... 45 F11 42 21N 14 24 E
Ortonville, U.S.A. 154 C6 45 19N 96 27W
Orūmīyeh, Iran .... 101 D11 37 40N 45 0 E
Orūmīyeh, Daryācheh-ye, Iran ... 101 D11 37 50N 45 30 E
Orune, Italy .... 46 B2 40 24N 9 22 E
Oruro, Bolivia 172 D4 18 0S 67 9W
Oruro □, Bolivia 172 D4 18 40S 67 30W
Orust, Sweden .... 17 F5 58 10N 11 40 E
Oruzgān □, Afghan. .... 91 B2 33 30N 66 0 E
Orvault, France 26 E5 47 17N 1 38W
Orvieto, Italy .... 45 F9 42 43N 12 7 E
Orwell, N.Y., U.S.A. 151 C9 43 35N 75 50W
Orwell, Ohio, U.S.A. 150 E4 41 32N 80 52W
Orwell ~, U.K. .... 21 F9 51 59N 1 18 E
Orwigsburg, U.S.A. 151 F8 40 38N 76 6W
Oryakhovo, Bulgaria .... 50 C7 43 40N 23 57 E
Orzinuovi, Italy .... 44 C6 45 24N 9 55 E
Orzyc ~, Poland .... 55 F8 52 46N 21 14 E
Orzysz, Poland .... 54 E8 53 50N 21 58 E
Os, Norway .... 18 B8 62 30N 11 14 E
Osa, Russia .... 64 C5 57 17N 55 26 E
Osa ~, Norway .... 18 C8 61 18N 11 46 E
Osa ~, Poland .... 54 E5 53 33N 18 46 E
Osa, Pen. de, Costa Rica 164 E3 8 0N 84 0W
Osage, U.S.A. 154 D8 43 17N 92 49W
Osage ~, U.S.A. 156 F5 38 35N 91 57W
Osage City, U.S.A. 154 F7 38 38N 95 50W
Ōsaka, Japan .... 73 C7 34 40N 135 30 E
Ōsaka □, Japan .... 73 C7 34 30N 135 30 E
Osaka Kansai International ✈ (KIX),
 Japan .... 73 C7 34 27N 135 12 E
Ōsaka-Wan, Japan .... 73 C7 34 30N 135 18 E
Osaki, Japan .... 72 F3 31 25N 131 2 E
Osan, S. Korea .... 75 F14 37 11N 127 4 E
Osawatomie, U.S.A. 154 F7 38 31N 94 57W
Osborne, U.S.A. 154 F5 39 26N 98 42W
Osby, Sweden .... 17 H7 56 23N 13 59 E
Osceola, Ark., U.S.A. 155 H10 35 42N 89 58W
Osceola, Iowa, U.S.A. 156 C3 41 2N 93 46W
Osceola, Mo., U.S.A. 156 F3 38 3N 93 42W
Oschatz, Germany .... 30 D9 51 17N 13 6 E
Oschersleben, Germany .... 30 C7 52 2N 11 14 E
Oscoda, U.S.A. 150 B1 44 26N 83 20W
Osečina, Serbia, Yug. .... 50 B4 44 23N 19 34 E
Osel = Saaremaa, Estonia ...... 15 G20 58 30N 22 30 E
Osensjøen, Norway .... 18 C8 61 13N 11 50 E
Osery, Russia .... 58 E10 54 52N 38 28 E
Osgood, U.S.A. 157 E11 39 8N 85 18W
Osgoode, Canada 151 A9 45 8N 75 36W
Osh, Kyrgyzstan .... 65 C6 40 37N 72 49 E
Oshawa, Canada 140 D4 43 50N 78 50W
Oshigambo, Namibia .... 116 B2 17 45S 16 5 E
Oshkosh, Nebr., U.S.A. 154 E3 41 24N 102 21W
Oshkosh, Wis., U.S.A. 154 C10 44 1N 88 33W
Oshmyany = Ashmyany, Belarus . 15 J21 54 26N 25 52 E
Oshnovīyeh, Iran .... 96 B5 37 2N 45 6 E
Oshogbo, Nigeria .... 113 D5 7 48N 4 37 E
Oshtorīnān, Iran .... 97 C6 34 1N 48 38 E
Oshwe, Dem. Rep. of the Congo .. 114 C3 3 25S 19 28 E
Osi, Nigeria .... 113 D6 8 8N 5 14 E
Osieczna, Poland .... 55 G3 51 55N 16 40 E
Osijek, Croatia .... 52 E3 45 34N 18 41 E
Osilo, Italy .... 46 B1 40 45N 8 40 E
Ósimo, Italy .... 45 E10 43 28N 13 30 E
Osintorf, Belarus .... 58 E6 54 40N 30 39 E
Osipenko = Berdyansk, Ukraine . 59 J9 46 45N 36 50 E
Osipovichi = Asipovichy, Belarus . 58 F5 53 19N 28 33 E
Osiyan, India .... 92 F5 26 43N 72 55 E
Oskarshamn, Sweden .... 17 G10 57 15N 16 27 E
Oskarström, Sweden .... 17 H6 56 48N 12 58 E
Oskélanéo, Canada 140 C4 48 5N 75 15W
Öskemen, Kazakhstan .... 66 E9 50 0N 82 36 E
Oskol ~, Ukraine .... 59 H9 49 6N 37 25 E
Oslo, Norway .... 18 E7 59 55N 10 45 E
Oslo □, Norway .... 18 E7 59 54N 10 43 E
Oslo International ✈ (OSL), Norway 18 D8 60 10N 11 8 E
Oslob, Phil. .... 81 G4 9 31N 123 26 E
Oslofjorden, Norway .... 18 E7 59 20N 10 35 E
Osmanabad, India .... 94 E3 18 5N 76 10 E
Osmancık, Turkey .... 100 B6 40 58N 34 47 E
Osmaniye, Turkey .... 100 D7 37 5N 36 10 E
Osmanli, Turkey .... 51 E10 41 35N 26 51 E
Osmannagar, India .... 94 E4 18 32N 79 20 E
Ōsmo, Sweden .... 16 F11 58 58N 17 55 E
Osnabrück, Germany .... 30 C4 52 17N 8 3 E
Ośno Lubuskie, Poland .... 55 F1 52 28N 14 51 E
Osoblaha, Czech Rep. .... 35 A10 50 17N 17 44 E
Osogovska Planina, Macedonia ... 50 D4 42 10N 22 30 E
Osor, Italy .... 45 D11 44 42N 14 24 E
Osorio, Brazil 175 B5 29 53S 50 17W
Osório da Fonseca, Brazil 169 D6 3 52S 58 14W
Osorno, Chile 176 E2 40 25S 73 0W
Osorno, Spain 42 C6 42 24N 4 22W
Osorno □, Chile 176 E2 40 15S 73 30W
Osorno, Vol., Chile 176 E2 41 0S 72 30W
Osoyoos, Canada 142 D5 49 0N 119 30W
Osøyro, Norway .... 18 D2 60 9N 5 30 E
Ospakseyri, Iceland 11 B5 65 27N 21 26W
Ospika ~, Canada 142 B4 56 20N 124 0W
Osprey, U.S.A. 153 H7 27 12N 82 29W
Osprey Reef, Australia .... 126 A4 13 52S 146 36 E
Oss, Neths. .... 24 C5 51 46N 5 32 E
Ossa, Mt., Australia .... 127 G4 41 52S 146 3 E
Óssa, Óros, Greece .... 48 B4 39 47N 22 42 E
Ossa de Montiel, Spain 41 G2 38 58N 2 45W
Ossabaw I., U.S.A. 152 D8 31 50N 81 5W
Ossabaw Sd., U.S.A. 152 D8 31 50N 81 5W
Osse ~, France .... 28 D4 44 7N 0 17 E
Osse ~, Nigeria .... 113 D6 6 10N 5 20 E
Ossi, Italy .... 46 B1 40 40N 8 35 E
Ossining, U.S.A. 151 E11 41 10N 73 55W
Ossipee, U.S.A. 151 C13 43 41N 71 7W
Ossokmanuan L., Canada 141 B7 53 25N 65 0W
Ossora, Russia .... 67 D17 59 20N 163 13 E
Ostashkov, Russia .... 58 D7 57 4N 33 2 E
Ostavall, Sweden .... 16 B9 62 16N 15 33 E
Østby, Norway .... 18 C9 61 15N 12 39 E
Oste ~, Germany .... 30 B5 53 49N 9 2 E
Ostend = Oostende, Belgium .... 24 C2 51 15N 2 54 E
Ostend, N.Z. .... 130 C4 36 48S 175 2 E
Oster, Ukraine .... 59 G6 50 57N 30 53 E

Osterburg, Germany .... 30 C7 52 47N 11 45 E
Osterburg, U.S.A. 150 F6 40 16N 78 31W
Osterburken, Germany .... 31 F5 49 25N 9 26 E
Österbybruk, Sweden .... 16 D11 60 13N 17 55 E
Österbymo, Sweden .... 17 G9 57 49N 15 15 E
Österdalälven, Sweden .... 16 C7 61 30N 13 45 E
Osterfeld, Germany .... 16 A11 63 9N 17 3 E
Österforse, Sweden .... 17 F9 58 35N 15 45 E
Östergötlands län □, Sweden .... 17 F9 58 35N 15 45 E
Osterholz-Scharmbeck, Germany . 30 B4 53 13N 8 47 E
Osterild, Denmark .... 17 G2 57 2N 8 51 E
Ostermundigen, Switz. .... 32 C4 46 58N 7 27 E
Osterode, Germany .... 30 D6 51 43N 10 15 E
Östersund, Sweden .... 16 A8 63 10N 14 38 E
Östervåla, Sweden .... 16 D11 60 11N 17 11 E
Østfold □, Norway .... 18 E8 59 25N 11 25 E
Ostfriesische Inseln, Germany ... 30 B3 53 42N 7 0 E
Ostfriesland, Germany .... 30 B3 53 20N 7 30 E
Ö{e}thammar, Sweden .... 16 D12 60 16N 18 22 E
Östia, Lido di, Italy .... 45 G9 41 43N 12 17 E
Ostíglia, Italy .... 45 C8 45 4N 11 8 E
Östmark, Sweden .... 16 D6 60 17N 12 45 E
Östra Husby, Sweden .... 17 F10 58 35N 16 18 E
Ostrava, Czech Rep. .... 35 B11 49 51N 18 18 E
Ostravský □, Czech Rep. .... 35 B11 49 55N 17 58 E
Ostróda, Poland .... 54 E6 53 42N 19 58 E
Ostrogozhsk, Russia .... 59 G10 50 55N 39 7 E
Ostroh, Ukraine .... 59 G4 50 20N 26 30 E
Ostrołęka, Poland .... 55 E8 53 4N 21 32 E
Ostrov, Bulgaria .... 51 C8 43 40N 24 9 E
Ostrov, Czech Rep. .... 34 A5 50 18N 12 57 E
Ostrov, Romania .... 53 F12 44 6N 27 24 E
Ostrov, Russia .... 58 D5 57 25N 28 20 E
Ostrów Lubelski, Poland .... 55 G9 51 29N 22 51 E
Ostrów Mazowiecka, Poland .... 55 F8 52 50N 21 51 E
Ostrów Wielkopolski, Poland .... 55 G4 51 36N 17 44 E
Ostrowiec-Świętokrzyski, Poland . 55 H8 50 55N 21 22 E
Ostrożac, Bos.-H. .... 52 G2 43 43N 17 49 E
Ostrzeszów, Poland .... 55 G4 51 25N 17 52 E
Ostseebad Kühlungsborn, Germany 30 A7 54 8N 11 44 E
Ostuni, Italy .... 47 B10 40 44N 17 35 E
Ósum ~, Albania .... 50 F4 40 40N 20 10 E
Osŭm ~, Bulgaria .... 51 C8 43 40N 24 51 E
Ōsumi-Hantō, Japan .... 72 F2 31 20N 130 55 E
Ōsumi-Kaikyō, Japan .... 71 J5 30 55N 131 0 E
Ōsumi-Shotō, Japan .... 71 J5 30 30N 130 0 E
Osun □, Nigeria .... 113 D5 7 30N 4 30 E
Osuna, Spain 43 H5 37 14N 5 8W
Oswegatchie ~, U.S.A. 151 B9 44 42N 75 30W
Oswego, U.S.A. 151 C8 43 27N 76 31W
Oswego ~, U.S.A. 151 C8 43 27N 76 30W
Oswestry, U.K. 20 E4 52 52N 3 3W
Oświęcim, Poland .... 55 H6 50 2N 19 11 E
Ōta, Fukui, Japan .... 73 B8 35 25N 136 21 E
Ōta, Gumma, Japan .... 73 A11 36 18N 139 22 E
Ōta-Gawa ~, Japan .... 72 C4 34 21N 132 18 E
Otaci, Moldova .... 53 B12 48 27N 27 47 E
Otago □, N.Z. .... 131 E4 45 15S 170 0 E
Otago Harbour, N.Z. .... 131 F5 45 47S 170 42 E
Otago Pen., N.Z. .... 131 F5 45 48S 170 39 E
Otaheite B., Trin. & Tob. 169 F9 10 20N 61 30W
Otahuhu, N.Z. .... 130 C3 36 56S 174 51 E
Ōtake, Japan .... 72 C4 34 12N 132 13 E
Ōtaki, Japan .... 73 B12 35 17N 140 15 E
Otaki, N.Z. .... 130 G4 40 45S 175 10 E
Otane, N.Z. .... 130 F5 39 54S 176 39 E
Otar, Kazakhstan .... 65 B7 43 32N 75 12 E
Otaru, Japan .... 70 C10 43 10N 141 0 E
Otaru-Wan = Ishikari-Wan, Japan 70 C10 43 25N 141 1 E
Otautau, N.Z. .... 131 G3 46 9S 168 1 E
Otava ~, Czech Rep. .... 34 B6 49 26N 14 12 E
Otavalo, Ecuador 168 C2 0 13N 78 20W
Otavi, Namibia .... 116 B2 19 40S 17 24 E
Otchinjau, Angola .... 116 B1 16 30S 13 56 E
Otelec, Romania .... 52 E5 45 36N 20 50 E
Otelnuk L., Canada 141 A6 56 9N 68 12W
Oţelu Roşu, Romania .... 52 E7 45 30N 22 22 E
Otero de Rey = Outeiro de Rei,
 Spain 42 B3 43 6N 7 36W
Othello, U.S.A. 158 C4 46 50N 119 10W
Othonof, Greece .... 38 B9 39 50N 19 22 E
Óthris, Óros, Greece .... 48 B4 39 2N 22 37 E
Oti, Réserve de Faune de l' □, Togo 113 C6 11 40N 0 35 E
Otira, N.Z. .... 131 C6 42 49S 171 35 E
Otira Gorge, N.Z. .... 131 C6 42 53S 171 33 E
Otjiwarongo, Namibia .... 116 B2 20 30S 16 33 E
Otmuchów, Poland .... 55 H4 50 28N 17 10 E
Oto Tolu Group, Tonga 133 Q13 20 21S 174 32W
Otočac, Croatia .... 45 D12 44 53S 15 12 E
Otoineppu, Japan .... 70 B11 44 44N 142 16 E
Otok, Croatia .... 45 E13 43 47N 16 10 E
Oton, Phil. .... 81 F4 10 42N 122 29 E
Otopeni, Bucharest ✈ (OTP),
 Romania .... 51 B10 44 30N 26 11 E
Otorohanga, N.Z. .... 130 E4 38 12S 175 14 E
Otoskwin ~, Canada 140 B2 52 13N 88 6W
Ōtoyo, Japan .... 72 D5 33 43N 133 45 E
Otra ~, Norway .... 18 E5 58 9N 8 1 E
Otradnyy, Russia .... 60 D10 53 22N 51 21 E
Otranto, Italy .... 47 B11 40 9N 18 28 E
Otranto, C. d', Italy .... 47 B11 40 7N 18 30 E
Otranto, Str. of, Italy .... 47 B11 40 15N 18 40 E
Otrokovice, Czech Rep. .... 35 B10 49 12N 17 32 E
Otse, S. Africa .... 116 D4 25 2S 25 45 E
Otsego, U.S.A. 157 B11 42 27N 85 42W
Ōtsu, Japan .... 73 C7 35 0N 135 50 E
Ōtsuki, Japan .... 73 B10 35 36N 138 57 E
Otta, Norway .... 18 C6 61 46N 9 32 E
Otta ~, Norway .... 18 C6 61 46N 9 31 E
Ottappalam, India .... 95 J3 10 46N 76 23 E
Ottawa = Outaouais ~, Canada . 140 C5 45 27N 74 8W
Ottawa, Canada 140 C4 45 27N 75 42W
Ottawa, Ill., U.S.A. 154 E10 41 21N 88 51W
Ottawa, Kans., U.S.A. 154 F7 38 37N 95 16W
Ottawa, Ohio, U.S.A. 157 C12 41 1N 84 3W
Ottawa Is., Canada 139 C11 59 35N 80 10W
Ottélé, Cameroon .... 113 E7 3 38N 11 19 E
Ottenheim, Austria .... 34 C7 48 21N 14 12 E
Otter Cr. ~, U.S.A. 151 B11 44 13N 73 17W
Otter Creek, U.S.A. 153 F7 29 19N 82 46W
Otter L., Canada 143 B8 55 35N 104 39W
Otterbein, U.S.A. 157 D9 40 29N 87 6W
Otterndorf, Germany .... 30 B4 53 48N 8 53 E
Otterøya, Norway .... 18 B3 62 45N 6 50 E
Otterup, Denmark .... 17 J4 55 30N 10 22 E
Otterville, U.S.A. 150 D4 42 55N 80 36W
Otterville, U.S.A. 156 F4 38 42N 93 0W
Ottery St. Mary, U.K. 21 G4 50 44N 3 17W
Ottilien Reef, Papua N. G. ..... 132 C5 3 43S 148 49 E
Otto Beit Bridge, Zimbabwe .... 119 F2 15 59S 28 56 E
Ottosdal, S. Africa .... 116 D4 26 46S 25 59 E
Ottoville, U.S.A. 157 D12 40 57N 84 22W
Ottumwa, U.S.A. 156 E5 41 1N 92 25W
Otu, Nigeria .... 113 D5 8 14N 3 22 E
Otukpa, Nigeria .... 113 D6 7 9N 7 41 E
Oturkpo, Nigeria .... 113 D6 7 16N 8 8 E
Otway, B., Chile 176 G2 53 30N 74 0W
Otway, C., Australia .... 128 E5 38 52S 143 30 E
Otway, Seno de, Chile 176 G2 53 0S 71 30W
Otwock Nat. Park △, Australia . 128 E5 38 47S 143 34 E
Otwock, Poland .... 55 F8 52 5N 21 20 E

Ötztaler Ache →, *Austria* .... **34 D3** 47 14N 10 50 E
Ötztaler Alpen, *Austria* .... **34 E3** 46 56N 11 0 E
Ou →, *Laos* .... **86 B4** 20 4N 102 13 E
Ou Neua, *Laos* .... **76 F3** 22 18N 101 48 E
Ou-Sammyaku, *Japan* .... **70 E10** 39 20N 140 35 E
Ouachita →, *U.S.A.* **155 K9** 31 38N 91 49W
Ouachita, L., *U.S.A.* **155 H8** 34 34N 93 12W
Ouachita Mts., *U.S.A.* **155 H7** 34 40N 94 25W
Ouaco, *N. Cal.* .... **133 T18** 20 50 S 164 29 E
Ouâdâne, *Mauritania* **110 D2** 20 50N 11 40W
Ouadda, *C.A.R.* .... **114 A4** 8 15N 22 20 E
Ouagadougou, *Burkina Faso* **113 C4** 12 25N 1 30W
Ouagam, *Chad* .... **109 F2** 14 22N 14 42 E
Ouaham →, *C.A.R.* .... **114 A3** 6 35N 15 12 E
Ouahigouya, *Burkina Faso* **112 C4** 13 31N 2 25W
Ouahila, *Algeria* **110 C4** 27 50N 5 0W
Ouahran = Oran, *Algeria* **111 A4** 35 45N 0 39W
Ouaïta, *Mauritania* **112 B3** 17 20N 6 55W
Ouallam, *Niger* .... **113 C5** 14 23N 2 10 E
Ouallene, *Algeria* .... **111 D5** 24 41N 1 11 E
Ouanary, *Fr. Guiana* **169 C7** 4 13N 51 40W
Ouanda Djallé, *C.A.R.* .... **114 A4** 8 55N 22 53 E
Ouandago, *C.A.R.* .... **114 A3** 7 13N 18 50 E
Ouandja, Bahr →, *C.A.R.* .... **114 A4** 9 35N 21 43 E
Ouandjia-Vakaga, Réserve de Faune
   de la △, *C.A.R.* .... **114 A4** 9 2N 22 18 E
Ouango, *C.A.R.* .... **114 B4** 4 19N 22 30 E
Ouani, *Comoros Is.* .... **121 a** 12 9 S 44 18 E
Ouantonou →, *C.A.R.* .... **114 A3** 7 19N 15 18 E
Ouarâne, *Mauritania* **110 D2** 21 0N 10 30W
Ouargaye, *Burkina Faso* .... **113 C5** 11 40N 0 5 E
Ouargla, *Algeria* .... **111 B6** 31 59N 5 16 E
Ouarkoye, *Burkina Faso* **112 C4** 12 5N 3 40W
Ouarkziz, Jebel, *Algeria* **110 C3** 28 50N 8 0W
Ouarra →, *C.A.R.* .... **114 A4** 5 5N 24 26 E
Ouarzazate, *Morocco* **110 B3** 30 55N 6 50W
Ouassouas, *Mali* .... **113 B5** 16 10N 1 23 E
Ouatagouna, *Mali* .... **113 B5** 15 11N 0 43 E
Ouatere, *C.A.R.* .... **114 A3** 5 30N 19 8 E
Oubangi →, *Dem. Rep. of the Congo* ...... **114 C3** 0 30 S 17 50 E
Oubarakai, O. →, *Algeria* .... **111 C6** 27 20N 9 0 E
Ouche →, *France* .... **27 E12** 47 6N 5 16 E
Ouddorp, *Neths.* .... **24 C3** 51 50N 3 57 E
Oude Rijn →, *Neths.* .... **24 B4** 52 12N 4 24 E
Oudeïka, *Mali* **113 B4** 17 30N 1 40W
Oudenaarde, *Belgium* .... **24 D3** 50 50N 3 37 E
Oudon →, *France* **26 E6** 47 41N 0 53W
Oudtshoorn, *S. Africa* .... **116 E3** 33 35 S 22 14 E
Oued Zem, *Morocco* **110 B3** 32 52N 6 34W
Ouégoa, *N. Cal.* .... **133 T18** 20 20 S 164 26 E
Oueita, *Chad* .... **109 E4** 14 47N 20 39 E
Ouellé, *Ivory C.* **112 D4** 7 26N 4 1W
Ouémé →, *Benin* .... **113 D5** 6 30N 2 20 E
Ouen, Î., *N. Cal.* .... **133 V20** 22 26 S 166 49 E
Ouenza, *Algeria* .... **111 A6** 35 57N 8 4 E
Ouessa, *Burkina Faso* **112 C4** 11 4N 2 47W
Ouessant, Î. d', *France* **26 D1** 48 28N 5 6W
Ouesso, *Congo* .... **114 B3** 1 37N 16 5 E
Ouest, Pte. de l', *Canada* **141 C7** 49 52N 64 40W
Ouezzane, *Morocco* **110 B3** 34 51N 5 35W
Ougarou, *Burkina Faso* .... **113 C5** 12 10N 0 58 E
Oughterard, *Ireland* **23 C2** 53 26N 9 18W
Ouhan →, *Chad* .... **109 G3** 9 18N 18 14 E
Ouidah, *Benin* .... **113 D5** 6 25N 2 0 E
Ouidi, *Niger* .... **113 C7** 14 10N 13 0 E
Ouissongo, *Angola* .... **115 E3** 7 40 S 15 41 E
Ouistreham, *France* **26 C6** 49 17N 0 18W
Oujda, *Morocco* **111 B4** 34 41N 1 55W
Oujeft, *Mauritania* **112 A2** 20 2N 13 0W
Oulainen, *Finland* .... **14 D21** 64 17N 24 47 E
Ould Yenjé, *Mauritania* **112 B2** 15 38N 12 16W
Ouled Djellal, *Algeria* .... **111 B6** 34 28N 5 2 E
Ouled Naïl, Mts. des, *Algeria* .... **111 B6** 34 30N 3 30 E
Ouli, *Cameroon* .... **114 A2** 5 12N 14 33 E
Oullins, *France* .... **29 C8** 45 43N 4 49 E
Oulmès, *Morocco* **110 B3** 33 17N 6 0W
Oulou →, *C.A.R.* .... **114 A4** 9 48N 21 32 E
Oulu, *Finland* .... **14 D21** 65 1N 25 29 E
Oulujärvi, *Finland* .... **14 D22** 64 25N 27 15 E
Oulujoki →, *Finland* .... **14 D21** 65 1N 25 30 E
Oulx, *Italy* .... **44 C3** 45 2N 6 50 E
Oum Chalouba, *Chad* .... **109 E4** 15 48N 20 46 E
Oum-el-Bouaghi, *Algeria* .... **111 A6** 35 55N 7 6 E
Oum-el-Ksi, *Algeria* **110 C3** 29 4N 6 59W
Oum-er-Rbia, O. →, *Morocco* **110 B3** 33 19N 8 21W
Oum Hadjer, *Chad* .... **109 F3** 13 18N 19 41 E
Oum Hadjer, O. →, *Chad* .... **109 E4** 16 38N 20 14 E
Oumé, *Ivory C.* **112 D3** 6 21N 5 27W
Oumm ed Droûs Guebli, Sebkhet,
   Mauritania **110 D2** 24 3N 11 45W
Oumm ed Droûs Telli, Sebkhet,
   Mauritania **110 D2** 24 20N 11 30W
Ounane, Dj., *Algeria* .... **111 C6** 25 4N 7 19 E
Ounasjoki →, *Finland* .... **14 C21** 66 31N 25 40 E
Ounguati, *Namibia* .... **116 C2** 21 54 S 15 46 E
Ounianga Kébir, *Chad* .... **109 E4** 19 4N 20 29 E
Ounianga Sérir, *Chad* .... **109 E4** 18 54N 20 51 E
Ounissoui, *Niger* .... **109 E2** 17 34N 12 13 E
Our →, *Lux.* .... **24 E6** 49 55N 6 5 E
Ouranópolis, *Greece* .... **50 F7** 40 20N 23 59 E
Ourârene, *Niger* .... **113 B6** 19 30N 7 10 E
Ourari, Tarso, *Chad* .... **109 D3** 21 27N 17 27 E
Ouray, *U.S.A.* **159 G10** 38 1N 107 40W
Ourcq →, *France* .... **27 C10** 49 1N 3 1 E
Ourém, *Brazil* .... **170 B2** 1 33 S 47 6W
Ourense, *Spain* **42 C3** 42 19N 7 55W
Ouricuri, *Brazil* .... **170 C3** 7 53 S 40 5W
Ourinhos, *Brazil* .... **175 A6** 23 0 S 49 54W
Ourique, *Portugal* **43 H2** 37 38N 8 16W
Ouro Fino, *Brazil* .... **175 A6** 22 16 S 46 25W
Ouro-Ndia, *Mali* **112 B4** 15 8N 4 35W
Ouro Prêto, *Brazil* .... **171 F3** 20 20 S 43 30W
Ouro Prêto do Oeste, *Brazil* .... **173 C5** 10 40 S 62 18W
Ouro Sogui, *Senegal* **112 B2** 15 36N 13 19W
Oursi, *Burkina Faso* **113 C4** 14 41N 0 27W
Ourthe →, *Belgium* .... **24 D5** 50 29N 5 35 E
Ouse →, E. Susx., *U.K.* .... **21 G8** 50 47N 0 4 E
Ouse →, N. Yorks., *U.K.* **20 D7** 53 44N 0 55W
Oust, *France* .... **28 F5** 42 52N 1 13 E
Oust →, *France* **26 E4** 47 35N 2 6W
Outamba-Kilimi Nat. Park △,
   S. Leone **112 D2** 9 50N 12 40W
Outaouais →, *Canada* **140 C5** 45 27N 74 8W
Outardes →, *Canada* **141 C6** 49 24N 69 30W
Outat Oulad el Haj, *Morocco* **111 B4** 33 22N 3 42W
Outeiro de Rei, *Spain* **42 B3** 43 6N 7 36W
Outer Hebrides, *U.K.* **22 D1** 57 30N 7 40W
Outes = Serra de Outes, *Spain* **42 C2** 42 52N 8 55W
Outjo, *Namibia* .... **116 C2** 20 5 S 16 7 E
Outlook, *Canada* **143 C7** 51 30N 107 0W
Outokumpu, *Finland* .... **14 E23** 62 43N 29 1 E
Outreau, *France* .... **27 B8** 50 40N 1 36 E
Ouvéa, Î., *N. Cal.* .... **133 K4** 20 35 S 166 35 E
Ouvèze →, *France* .... **29 E8** 43 59N 4 51 E
Ouyen, *Australia* .... **128 C5** 35 1 S 142 22 E
Ouzinkie, *U.S.A.* **144 H9** 57 56N 152 30W
Ouzouer-le-Marché, *France* .... **27 E8** 47 54N 1 32 E
Ovada, *Italy* .... **44 D5** 44 38N 8 38 E
Ovalle, *Chile* .... **172 b** 29 5 S 109 19W
Ovalau, *Fiji* .... **133 A2** 17 40 S 178 48 E
Ovalle, *Chile* .... **174 C1** 30 33 S 71 18W
Ovamboland, *Namibia* .... **116 B2** 18 30 S 16 0 E
Ovar, *Portugal* **42 E2** 40 51N 8 40W
Ovau, *Solomon Is.* .... **133 L9** 6 40 S 156 8 E

Overath, *Germany* .... **30 E3** 50 56N 7 17 E
Overflakkee, *Neths.* .... **24 C4** 51 44N 4 10 E
Overijssel □, *Neths.* .... **24 B6** 52 25N 6 35 E
Overland, *U.S.A.* **156 F6** 38 41N 90 22W
Overland Park, *U.S.A.* **154 F7** 38 55N 94 50W
Overton, *U.S.A.* **161 J12** 36 33N 114 27W
Overum, *Sweden* .... **17 F10** 58 0N 16 20 E
Ovid, *Mich., U.S.A.* **157 A12** 43 1N 84 22W
Ovid, *N.Y., U.S.A.* **151 D8** 42 41N 76 49W
Ovidiopol, *Ukraine* .... **59 J6** 46 15N 30 30 E
Ovidiu, *Romania* .... **53 F13** 44 16N 28 34 E
Oviedo, *Spain* **42 B5** 43 25N 5 50W
Oviedo, *U.S.A.* **153 G8** 28 40N 81 13W
Oviksfjällen, *Sweden* .... **16 A7** 63 0N 13 49 E
Ovīši, *Latvia* .... **15 H19** 57 33N 21 44 E
Ovoot, *Mongolia* .... **74 B7** 45 21N 113 45 E
Övör Hangay □, *Mongolia* .... **74 B2** 45 0N 102 30 E
Ovoro, *Nigeria* .... **113 D6** 5 26N 7 16 E
Øvre Årdal, *Norway* .... **18 C4** 61 19N 7 48 E
Øvre Fryken, *Sweden* .... **16 E7** 60 0N 13 7 E
Øvre Rendal, *Norway* .... **18 C8** 61 54N 11 4 E
Øvre Rindal, *Norway* .... **18 A6** 63 6N 9 10 E
Øvre Sirdal, *Norway* .... **18 F3** 58 48N 6 43 E
Ovruch, *Ukraine* .... **59 G5** 51 25N 28 45 E
Owaka, *N.Z.* .... **131 G4** 46 27 S 169 40 E
Owambo = Ovamboland, *Namibia* ...... **116 B2** 18 30 S 16 0 E
Owando, *Congo* .... **114 C3** 0 29 S 15 55 E
Owasco L., *U.S.A.* **151 D8** 42 50N 76 31W
Owase, *Japan* .... **73 C8** 34 7N 136 12 E
Owatonna, *U.S.A.* **154 C8** 44 5N 93 14W
Owbeh, *Afghan.* .... **91 B1** 34 28N 63 10 E
Owego, *U.S.A.* **151 D8** 42 6N 76 16W
Owen, *Australia* .... **128 C3** 34 15 S 138 32 E
Owen, Mt., *N.Z.* .... **131 B7** 41 35 S 172 33 E
Owen Falls Dam, *Uganda* .... **118 B3** 0 30N 33 5 E
Owen Sound, *Canada* **140 D3** 44 35N 80 55W
Owen Stanley Ra., *Papua N. G.* .... **132 E4** 8 30 S 147 0 E
Owendo, *Gabon* .... **114 B1** 0 17N 9 30 E
Owens →, *U.S.A.* **160 J9** 36 32N 117 59W
Owens L., *U.S.A.* **161 J9** 36 26N 117 57W
Owensboro, *U.S.A.* **157 G9** 37 46N 87 7W
Owensville, *Ind., U.S.A.* **157 F9** 38 16N 87 41W
Owensville, *Mo., U.S.A.* **156 F5** 38 21N 91 30W
Owenteik, *Guyana* **169 C6** 4 27N 59 35W
Owerri, *Nigeria* **157 F12** 38 32N 84 50W
Owerri, *Nigeria* .... **113 D6** 5 29N 7 0 E
Owhango, *N.Z.* .... **130 F4** 39 0 S 175 23 E
Owingsville, *U.S.A.* **157 F13** 38 9N 83 46W
Owl →, *Canada* **143 B10** 57 51N 92 44W
Owo, *Nigeria* .... **113 D6** 7 10N 5 39 E
Owosso, *U.S.A.* **157 B12** 43 0N 84 10W
Owyhee, *U.S.A.* **158 F5** 41 57N 116 6W
Owyhee →, *U.S.A.* **158 E5** 43 49N 117 2W
Owyhee, L., *U.S.A.* **158 E5** 43 38N 117 14W
Ox Mts. = Slieve Gamph, *Ireland* **23 B3** 54 6N 9 0W
Oxapampa, *Peru* .... **172 C2** 10 33 S 75 26W
Öxarfjörður, *Iceland* **11 A10** 66 15N 16 45W
Oxbow, *Canada* **143 D8** 49 14N 102 10W
Oxelösund, *Sweden* .... **17 F11** 58 43N 17 5 E
Oxford, *N.Z.* .... **131 D7** 43 18 S 172 11 E
Oxford, *U.K.* **21 F6** 51 46N 1 15W
Oxford, *Ala., U.S.A.* **152 B4** 33 36N 85 51W
Oxford, *Iowa, U.S.A.* **156 C5** 41 43N 91 47W
Oxford, *Mass., U.S.A.* **151 D13** 42 7N 71 52W
Oxford, *Mich., U.S.A.* **157 B13** 42 49N 83 16W
Oxford, *Miss., U.S.A.* **155 H10** 34 22N 89 31W
Oxford, *N.C., U.S.A.* **149 G6** 36 19N 78 35W
Oxford, *N.Y., U.S.A.* **151 D9** 42 27N 75 36W
Oxford, *Ohio, U.S.A.* **157 E12** 39 31N 84 45W
Oxford L., *Canada* **143 C9** 54 51N 95 37W
Oxfordshire □, *U.K.* **21 F6** 51 48N 1 16W
Oxía Nisís, *Greece* .... **39 C3** 38 18N 21 6 E
Oxie, *Sweden* .... **17 J7** 55 33N 13 6 E
Oxílithos, *Greece* .... **48 C6** 38 35N 24 7 E
Oxley, *Australia* .... **128 C6** 34 11 S 144 6 E
Oxley Wild Rivers Nat. Park △,
   Australia .... **129 A10** 30 57 S 152 12 E
Oxnard, *U.S.A.* **161 L7** 34 12N 119 11W
Oxsjövälen, *Sweden* .... **16 B7** 62 34N 13 57 E
Oxus = Amudarya →, *Uzbekistan* ...... **66 E6** 43 58N 59 34 E
Oy-Tal, *Kyrgyzstan* .... **65 C7** 40 24N 74 6 E
Oya, *Malaysia* .... **85 B4** 2 55N 111 55 E
Oyabe, *Japan* .... **73 A8** 36 47N 136 56 E
Oyama, *Japan* .... **73 A11** 36 18N 139 48 E
Oyambre, Parque Natural de △,
   Spain **42 B6** 43 22N 4 21W
Oyapock →, *Fr. Guiana* **169 C7** 4 8N 51 40W
Øye, *Norway* .... **18 F3** 58 16N 6 49 E
Oyem, *Gabon* .... **114 B2** 1 34N 11 31 E
Oyen, *Canada* **143 C6** 51 22N 110 28W
Øyer, *Norway* .... **18 C7** 61 16N 10 25 E
Øyeren, *Norway* .... **18 E8** 59 50N 11 15 E
Oykel →, *U.K.* **22 D4** 57 56N 4 26W
Oymyakon, *Russia* .... **67 C15** 63 25N 142 44 E
Oyo, *Nigeria* .... **113 D5** 7 46N 3 56 E
Oyo □, *Nigeria* .... **113 D5** 8 15N 3 30 E
Oyón, *Peru* .... **172 C2** 10 37 S 76 47W
Oyonnax, *France* .... **27 F12** 46 16N 5 40 E
Øyslebø, *Norway* .... **18 F4** 58 9N 7 37 E
Oyster Bay, *U.S.A.* **151 F11** 40 52N 73 32W
Øystese, *Norway* .... **18 D3** 60 22N 6 9 E
Oytal, *Kazakhstan* .... **65 B6** 42 54N 73 17 E
Øyübari, *Japan* .... **70 C11** 43 1N 142 5 E
Oyyq, *Kazakhstan* .... **65 B5** 43 36N 71 16 E
Ozalp, *Turkey* .... **101 C10** 38 39N 43 59 E
Ozamiz, *Phil.* .... **81 G4** 8 15N 123 50 E
Ozark, *Ala., U.S.A.* **152 D4** 31 28N 85 39W
Ozark, *Ark., U.S.A.* **155 H8** 35 29N 93 50W
Ozark, *Mo., U.S.A.* **155 G8** 37 1N 93 12W
Ozark Plateau, *U.S.A.* **155 G9** 37 20N 91 40W
Ozarks, L. of the, *U.S.A.* **156 F4** 38 12N 92 38W
Ożarów, *Poland* .... **55 H8** 50 53N 21 40 E
Ozd, *Hungary* .... **52 B5** 48 14N 20 15 E
Ozernoye, *Russia* .... **60 E10** 51 46N 51 28 E
Ozërnyy, *Russia* .... **64 F8** 51 8N 60 50 E
Ozgön, *Kyrgyzstan* .... **65 C6** 40 46N 73 18 E
Ozieri, *Italy* .... **46 B2** 40 35N 9 0 E
Ozimek, *Poland* .... **55 H5** 50 41N 18 11 E
Ozinki, *Russia* .... **60 E9** 51 12N 49 44 E
Ozona, *U.S.A.* **155 K4** 30 43N 101 12W
Ozorków, *Poland* .... **55 G6** 51 57N 19 16 E
Ozren, *Bos.-H.* .... **52 G3** 43 55N 18 29 E
Ōzu, *Ehime, Japan* .... **72 D4** 33 30N 132 33 E
Ōzu, *Kumamoto, Japan* .... **72 F2** 32 52N 130 52 E
Ozuluama, *Mexico* **163 C5** 21 40N 97 50W
Ozun, *Romania* .... **53 E10** 45 47N 25 50 E
Ozurgeti, *Georgia* .... **61 K5** 41 57N 42 2 E

P

Pa, *Burkina Faso* **112 C4** 11 33N 3 19W
Pa-an, *Burma* .... **90 G6** 16 51N 97 40 E
Pa Mong Dam, *Thailand* .... **86 D4** 18 0N 102 22 E
Pa Sak →, *Thailand* .... **78 B2** 15 30N 101 0 E
Paagoumène, *N. Cal.* .... **133 T18** 20 29 S 164 11 E
Paama, *Vanuatu* .... **133 F6** 16 28 S 168 14 E
Paamiut, *Greenland* **10 E6** 62 0N 49 43W
Paar →, *Germany* .... **31 G7** 48 46N 11 36 E

Paarl, *S. Africa* .... **116 E2** 33 45 S 18 56 E
Paauilo, *U.S.A.* **145 C6** 20 2N 155 22W
Pab Hills, *Pakistan* .... **91 D2** 26 30N 66 45 E
Pabbay, *U.K.* **22 D1** 57 46N 7 14W
Pabianice, *Poland* .... **55 G6** 51 40N 19 20 E
Pabna, *Bangla.* .... **90 C2** 24 1N 89 18 E
Pabo, *Uganda* .... **118 B3** 3 1N 32 10 E
Pacaás Novos, Serra dos, *Brazil* ...... **173 C5** 10 45 S 64 15W
Pacaembu, *Brazil* .... **172 B2** 5 35 S 79 39W
Pacaja →, *Brazil* .... **170 B1** 1 56 S 50 50W
Pacajus, *Brazil* .... **170 B4** 4 10 S 38 31W
Pacaraima, Sa., *S. Amer.* **169 C5** 4 0N 62 30W
Pacarán, *Peru* .... **172 C2** 12 50 S 76 18W
Pacaraos, *Peru* .... **172 C2** 11 12 S 76 42W
Pacasmayo, *Peru* .... **172 B1** 7 20 S 79 35W
Pace, *U.S.A.* **153 E2** 30 36N 87 10W
Paceco, *Italy* .... **46 E5** 37 59N 12 33 E
Pachacamac, *Peru* .... **172 C2** 12 14 S 77 53W
Pachhar, *India* .... **92 G7** 24 40N 77 42 E
Pachino, *Italy* .... **47 F8** 36 43N 15 5 E
Pachitea →, *Peru* .... **172 B2** 8 46 S 74 33W
Pachiza, *Peru* .... **172 B2** 7 16 S 76 46W
Pachmarhi, *India* .... **93 H8** 22 28N 78 26 E
Pachnai, *India* .... **90 A4** 26 57N 92 19 E
Pacho, *Colombia* **168 B3** 5 8N 74 10W
Pachora, *India* .... **92 D2** 20 38N 75 29 E
Pachuca, *Mexico* **163 C5** 20 10N 98 40W
Pacific, *Canada* **142 C3** 54 48N 128 28W
Pacific, *U.S.A.* **156 F6** 38 29N 90 45W
Pacific-Antarctic Ridge, *Pac. Oc.* ...... **135 M16** 43 0 S 115 0W
Pacific Grove, *U.S.A.* **160 J5** 36 38N 121 56W
Pacific Ocean, *Pac. Oc.* **135 F13** 10 0N 140 0W
Pacific Palisades, *U.S.A.* **145 K14** 21 25N 157 58W
Pacific Rim Nat. Park △, *Canada* **142 D3** 48 40N 124 45W
Pacifica, *U.S.A.* **160 H4** 37 36N 122 30W
Pacitan, *Indonesia* .... **85 D4** 8 12 S 111 7 E
Packsaddle, *Australia* .... **128 A4** 30 36 S 141 58 E
Packwood, *U.S.A.* **160 D5** 46 36N 121 40W
Pacov, *Czech Rep.* .... **34 B8** 49 27N 15 0 E
Pacoval, *Brazil* .... **169 D7** 2 40 S 54 11W
Pacuí →, *Brazil* .... **171 E2** 16 46 S 45 1W
Padaido, Kepulauan, *Indonesia* ...... **83 B5** 1 15 S 136 30 E
Padalarang, *Indonesia* .... **84 C2** 1 0 S 100 20 E
Padang, *Indonesia* .... **84 C2** 1 0 S 100 20 E
Padang Endau, *Malaysia* .... **87 L4** 2 40N 103 38 E
Padangpanjang, *Indonesia* .... **84 C2** 0 40 S 100 20 E
Padangsidempuan, *Indonesia* .... **84 B1** 1 30N 99 15 E
Padangtikar, *Indonesia* .... **85 C3** 0 44 S 109 15 E
Padatchaung, *Burma* .... **90 F5** 19 46N 94 48 E
Padaung, *Burma* .... **90 F5** 18 43N 95 9 E
Padborg, *Denmark* .... **17 K3** 54 49N 9 21 E
Padcaya, *Bolivia* .... **173 E5** 21 52 S 64 48W
Paddle Prairie, *Canada* **142 B5** 57 57N 117 29W
Paddockwood, *Canada* **143 C7** 53 30N 105 30W
Paderborn, *Germany* .... **30 D4** 51 42N 8 45 E
Paderoo, *India* .... **94 E6** 18 5N 82 40 E
Padeș, Vf., *Romania* .... **52 E7** 45 40N 22 52 E
Padilla, *Bolivia* .... **173 D5** 19 19 S 64 20W
Padina, *Romania* .... **53 F12** 44 50N 27 8 E
Padma, *India* .... **93 G11** 24 12N 85 22 E
Padma →, *Bangla.* .... **93 H13** 23 22N 90 30 E
Pádova, *Italy* .... **45 C8** 45 25N 11 53 E
Padra, *India* .... **92 H5** 22 15N 73 7 E
Padrauna, *India* .... **93 F10** 26 54N 83 59 E
Padre Burgos, *Phil.* .... **81 F5** 10 1N 125 0 E
Padre I., *U.S.A.* **155 M6** 27 10N 97 25W
Padre Island Nat. Seashore △, *U.S.A.* .. **155 M6** 26 36N 97 17W
Padrón, *Spain* **42 C2** 42 41N 8 39W
Padstow, *U.K.* **21 G3** 50 33N 4 58W
Padthaway, *Australia* .... **128 D4** 36 36 S 140 31 E
Paducah, *Ky., U.S.A.* **155 G10** 37 5N 88 37W
Paducah, *Tex., U.S.A.* **155 H4** 34 1N 100 18W
Padukka, *Sri Lanka* .... **95 L5** 6 50N 80 5 E
Padul, *Spain* **43 H7** 37 1N 3 38W
Padwa, *India* .... **94 E6** 18 27N 82 47 E
Paekakariki, *N.Z.* .... **130 G3** 40 59 S 174 58 E
Paengaroa, *N.Z.* .... **130 D5** 37 49 S 176 29 E
Paengnyŏng-do, *S. Korea* .... **75 F13** 37 57N 124 40 E
Paeroa, *N.Z.* .... **130 D4** 37 23 S 175 41 E
Paesana, *Italy* .... **44 D4** 44 41N 7 16 E
Paete, *Phil.* .... **80 D3** 14 23N 121 29 E
Pafúri, *Mozam.* .... **117 C5** 22 28 S 31 17 E
Pag, *Croatia* .... **45 D12** 44 25N 15 3 E
Paga, *Gabon* .... **114 C2** 0 45 S 10 21 E
Pagadian, *Phil.* **113 C4** 11 1N 1 8W
Pagadian, *Phil.* .... **81 H4** 7 55N 123 30 E
Pagai Selatan, Pulau, *Indonesia* ...... **84 C2** 3 0 S 100 15 E
Pagai Utara, Pulau, *Indonesia* ...... **84 C2** 2 35 S 100 0 E
Pagalu = Annobón, *Atl. Oc.* .... **105 G4** 1 25 S 5 36 E
Pagalungan, *Phil.* .... **81 H5** 7 4N 124 41 E
Pagan, *Burma* .... **90 E5** 21 10N 94 52 E
Pagara, *India* .... **93 G9** 24 22N 80 1 E
Pagastikós Kólpos, *Greece* .... **48 B5** 39 15N 23 0 E
Pagatan, *Indonesia* .... **85 C5** 3 33 S 115 59 E
Page, *U.S.A.* **159 H8** 36 57N 111 27W
Pagégiai, *Lithuania* .... **54 C8** 55 9N 21 54 E
Pagei, *Papua N. G.* .... **132 B1** 2 3 S 141 10 E
Paget I., *India* .... **95 H11** 12 30N 92 53 E
Pago Pago, *Amer. Samoa* .... **133 X24** 14 16 S 170 43W
Pagosa Springs, *U.S.A.* **159 H10** 37 16N 107 1W
Pagudpud, *Phil.* .... **80 B3** 18 38N 120 47 E
Pagwa River, *Canada* **140 B2** 50 2N 85 14W
Pagwi, *Papua N. G.* .... **132 C2** 4 4 S 143 2 E
Pahala, *U.S.A.* **145 C6** 19 12N 155 29W
Pahang □, *Malaysia* .... **84 B2** 3 30N 102 45 E
Pahang →, *Malaysia* .... **87 L4** 3 30N 103 9 E
Pahia Pt., *N.Z.* .... **131 G2** 46 20 S 167 41 E
Pahiatua, *N.Z.* .... **130 G4** 40 27 S 175 50 E
Pahoa, *U.S.A.* **145 D7** 19 30N 154 57W
Pahokee, *U.S.A.* **153 J9** 26 50N 80 40W
Pahrump, *U.S.A.* **161 J11** 36 12N 115 59W
Pahute Mesa, *U.S.A.* **160 H10** 37 20N 116 45W
Pai, *Thailand* .... **86 C2** 19 19N 98 27 E
Paia, *U.S.A.* **145 C5** 20 54N 156 22W
Paicines, *U.S.A.* **160 J5** 36 44N 121 17W
Paide, *Estonia* .... **15 G21** 58 57N 25 31 E
Paignton, *U.K.* **21 G4** 50 26N 3 35W
Paihia, *N.Z.* .... **130 B3** 35 17 S 174 6 E
Paiho, *Taiwan* .... **77 F13** 23 21N 120 25 E
Paiján, *Peru* .... **172 B2** 7 44 S 79 23W
Päijänne, *Finland* .... **15 F21** 61 30N 25 30 E
Pailani, *India* .... **93 G9** 25 45N 80 26 E
Pailin, *Cambodia* .... **86 F4** 12 46N 102 36 E
Paimbœuf, *France* **26 E4** 47 17N 2 0W
Paimpol, *France* **26 D3** 48 48N 3 4W
Painan, *Indonesia* .... **84 C2** 1 21 S 100 34 E
Paine, Cerro, *Chile* .... **176 D2** 50 59 S 73 4 E
Painesville, *U.S.A.* **150 E3** 41 43N 81 15W
Paint Hills = Wemindji, *Canada* **140 B4** 53 0N 78 49W
Paint L., *Canada* **143 B9** 55 28N 97 57W
Painted Desert, *U.S.A.* **159 J8** 36 0N 111 0W
Paintsville, *U.S.A.* **148 G4** 37 49N 82 48W
País Vasco □, *Spain* **40 C2** 42 50N 2 45W
Paisley, *Canada* **150 B3** 44 18N 81 16W
Paisley, *U.K.* **22 F4** 55 50N 4 25W
Paisley, *U.S.A.* **158 E3** 42 42N 120 32W
Paita, *N. Cal.* .... **133 V20** 22 8 S 166 22 E
Paita, *Peru* .... **172 B1** 5 11 S 81 9W
Paithan, *India* .... **94 E2** 19 29N 75 23 E
Paiva →, *Portugal* **42 D2** 41 4N 8 16W

Paizhou, *China* .... **77 B9** 30 12N 113 55 E
Paja, Cerro, *Ecuador* .... **172 a** 1 17 S 90 26W
Pajares, *Spain* **42 B5** 43 1N 5 46W
Pajares, Puerto de, *Spain* **42 C5** 42 58N 5 46W
Pajarito, *Colombia* **168 B3** 5 17N 72 43W
Pajęczno, *Poland* .... **55 G5** 51 10N 19 0 E
Pak Lay, *Laos* .... **86 C3** 18 15N 101 27 E
Pak Phanang, *Thailand* .... **87 H3** 8 21N 100 12 E
Pak Sane, *Laos* .... **86 C4** 18 22N 103 39 E
Pak Song, *Laos* .... **86 E6** 15 11N 106 14 E
Pak Suong, *Laos* .... **76 H4** 19 58N 102 15 E
Pak Tam Chung, *China* .... **69 G11** 22 24N 114 19 E
Pakala, *India* .... **95 H4** 13 29N 79 8 E
Pakaraima Mts., *Guyana* **169 B5** 6 0N 60 0W
Pakaur, *India* .... **93 G12** 24 38N 87 51 E
Pakenham, *Australia* .... **129 F4** 38 6 S 145 30 E
Pakenham, *Canada* **151 A8** 45 18N 76 18W
Pákhnes, *Greece* .... **39 E5** 35 16N 24 4 E
Pakhtaabad, *Uzbekistan* .... **65 C6** 40 55N 72 5 E
Pakhuis, *S. Africa* .... **116 E2** 32 9 S 19 5 E
Pakistan ■, *Asia* .... **91 C3** 30 0N 70 0 E
Pakkading, *Laos* .... **86 C4** 18 19N 103 59 E
Paklenica, Nac. Park △, *Croatia* ...... **45 D12** 44 20N 15 30 E
Pakokku, *Burma* .... **90 E5** 21 20N 95 0 E
Pakość, *Poland* .... **55 F5** 52 48N 18 6 E
Pakowki L., *Canada* **143 D6** 49 20N 111 0W
Pakpattan, *Pakistan* .... **91 C4** 30 25N 73 27 E
Pakrac, *Croatia* .... **52 E2** 45 27N 17 12 E
Pakruojis, *Lithuania* .... **54 C10** 55 58N 23 52 E
Paks, *Hungary* .... **52 D3** 46 38N 18 53 E
Paktīā □, *Afghan.* .... **91 C3** 33 30N 69 15 E
Paktīkā □, *Afghan.* .... **91 B3** 32 30N 69 0 E
Pakwach, *Uganda* .... **118 B3** 2 28N 31 27 E
Pakxe, *Laos* .... **86 E5** 15 5N 105 52 E
Pal Lahara, *India* .... **93 J11** 21 27N 85 11 E
Pala, *Chad* .... **109 G3** 9 25N 15 5 E
Pala, Dem. Rep. of the Congo .... **118 D2** 6 45 S 29 30 E
Pala, *U.S.A.* **161 M9** 33 22N 117 5W
Palabek, *Uganda* .... **118 B3** 3 22N 32 33 E
Palacios, *U.S.A.* **155 L6** 28 42N 96 13W
Palafrugell, *Spain* .... **40 D8** 41 55N 3 10 E
Palagiano, *Italy* .... **47 H10** 40 35N 17 3 E
Palagonía, *Italy* .... **47 E7** 37 19N 14 45 E
Palagruža, *Croatia* .... **45 F13** 42 24N 16 15 E
Palaiokastron, *Greece* .... **39 E7** 35 12N 26 15 E
Palaiokhóra, *Greece* .... **39 E5** 35 16N 23 39 E
Pálairos, *Greece* .... **39 B2** 38 47N 20 53 E
Palaiseau, *France* .... **27 D9** 48 43N 2 15 E
Palakol, *India* .... **95 F5** 16 31N 81 46 E
Palalankwe, *India* .... **95 J11** 10 52N 92 29 E
Palam, *India* .... **94 E3** 19 0N 77 0 E
Palamás, *Greece* .... **48 B4** 39 26N 22 4 E
Palamós, *Spain* .... **40 D8** 41 50N 3 10 E
Palampur, *India* .... **92 C7** 32 10N 76 30 E
Palamut, *Turkey* .... **127 E4** 39 15 S 174 55 E
Palana, *Australia* .... **67 D16** 39 45 S 147 55 E
Palana, *Russia* .... **67 D16** 59 10N 159 59 E
Palanan, *Phil.* .... **80 C4** 17 8N 122 29 E
Palanan Bay, *Phil.* .... **80 C4** 17 17N 122 30 E
Palanan Pt., *Phil.* .... **80 C4** 17 17N 122 30 E
Palandri, *Pakistan* .... **93 C5** 33 42N 73 40 E
Palanga, *Lithuania* .... **15 J19** 55 58N 21 3 E
Palanganene, Dem. Rep. of
   the Congo .... **115 D3** 6 32 S 18 52 E
Palangkaraya, *Indonesia* .... **85 C4** 2 16 S 113 56 E
Palani, *India* .... **95 J3** 10 30N 77 30 E
Palani Hills, *India* .... **95 J3** 10 14N 77 33 E
Palanpur, *India* .... **92 G5** 24 10N 72 25 E
Palanro, *Indonesia* .... **82 B1** 3 21 S 119 23 E
Palaoa Pt., *U.S.A.* **145 C5** 20 44N 156 58W
Palapag, *Phil.* .... **80 E5** 12 33N 125 7 E
Palapye, *Botswana* .... **116 C4** 22 30 S 27 7 E
Palar →, *India* .... **95 H5** 12 27N 80 11 E
Palas, *Pakistan* .... **93 B5** 35 4N 73 14 E
Palas de Rei, *Spain* **42 C3** 42 52N 7 52W
Palashi, *India* .... **93 H13** 23 47N 88 15 E
Palasponga, *India* .... **93 J11** 21 47N 85 34 E
Palatine, *U.S.A.* **157 B8** 42 7N 88 3W
Palatka, *Russia* .... **67 C16** 60 6N 150 54 E
Palatka, *U.S.A.* **152 F8** 29 39N 81 38W
Palau, *India* **46 A2** 41 1N 17W
Palau, *Mexico* **63 J17** 27 53N 101 25W
Palau ■, *Pac. Oc.* .... **62 H7** 7 30N 134 30 E
Palauk, *Burma* .... **86 F2** 13 10N 98 40 E
Palawan, *Phil.* .... **81 G2** 9 30N 118 30 E
Palawan □, *Phil.* .... **81 G2** 10 0N 119 0 E
Palawan Passage, *Phil.* .... **80 D3** 15 36N 121 8 E
Palayan, *Phil.* .... **95 K3** 8 45N 77 45 E
Palayankottai, *India* .... **95 K3** 8 45N 77 45 E
Palazzo, Pte., *France* .... **29 F12** 42 28N 8 30 E
Palazzo San Gervásio, *Italy* .... **47 B8** 40 56N 15 59 E
Palazzolo Acréide, *Italy* .... **47 E7** 37 4N 14 54 E
Palca, *Chile* .... **172 D4** 17 5 S 69 9W
Paldiski, *Estonia* .... **15 G21** 59 23N 24 9 E
Pale, *Bos.-H.* .... **52 G3** 43 50N 18 38 E
Palel, *India* .... **90 C5** 24 27N 94 2 E
Paleleh, *Indonesia* .... **82 A2** 1 10N 121 50 E
Palembang, *Indonesia* .... **84 C2** 3 0 S 104 50 E
Palena →, *Chile* .... **176 B2** 43 50 S 73 50W
Palena, L., *Chile* .... **176 B2** 43 55 S 71 40W
Palencia, *Spain* **42 C6** 42 1N 4 34W
Palencia □, *Spain* **42 C6** 42 31N 4 33W
Palenque, *Mexico* **163 D6** 17 39N 91 58W
Palenque, Ruinas de, *Mexico* **163 D6** 17 29N 92 1W
Paleokastrítsa, *Greece* .... **49 B3** 39 40N 19 41 E
Paleometokho, *Cyprus* .... **39 E9** 35 7N 33 11 E
Palermo, *Colombia* **168 C2** 2 54N 75 26W
Palermo, *Italy* .... **46 D6** 38 7N 13 22 E
Palermo, *U.S.A.* **158 G3** 39 26N 121 33W
Palermo ✈ (PMO), *Italy* .... **46 D6** 38 11N 13 5 E
Palestine, *Asia* .... **46 D3** 32 0N 35 0 E
Palestine, Ill., U.S.A. **157 F9** 39 0N 87 37W
Palestine, Tex., U.S.A. **155 K7** 31 46N 95 38W
Palestrina, *Italy* .... **45 G9** 41 50N 12 53 E
Paletwa, *Burma* .... **90 E4** 21 10N 92 50 E
Palghat, *India* .... **95 J3** 10 46N 76 42 E
Palgrave, Mt., *Australia* .... **124 D2** 23 22 S 115 58 E
Pali, *India* .... **92 G5** 25 50N 73 20 E
Palikea Pk., *U.S.A.* **145 K13** 21 26N 158 6W
Palikir, *Micronesia* .... **134 G7** 6 55N 158 9 E
Palin, Mt., *Malaysia* .... **85 A5** 6 10N 117 10 E
Palinuro, *Italy* .... **47 B8** 40 2N 15 17 E
Palinuro, C., *Italy* .... **47 B8** 40 1N 15 16 E
Paliouri, Ákra, *Greece* .... **50 G7** 39 57N 23 45 E
Palisades Reservoir, *U.S.A.* **158 E8** 43 20N 111 12W
Paliseul, *Belgium* .... **24 E5** 49 54N 5 8 E
Palitana, *India* .... **92 J4** 21 32N 71 49 E
Palizada, *Mexico* **163 D6** 18 18N 92 8W
Palk Bay, *India* .... **95 K4** 9 30N 79 15 E
Palk Strait, *Asia* .... **95 K4** 10 0N 79 45 E
Palkānah, *Iraq* .... **96 C5** 35 49N 44 26 E
Palkonda, *India* .... **94 E6** 18 36N 83 48 E
Palkonda Ra., *India* .... **95 H4** 13 50N 79 20 E
Palkot, *India* .... **93 H11** 22 53N 84 39 E
Palla Road = Dinokwe, *Botswana* .. **116 C4** 23 29 S 26 37 E
Pallanza = Verbánia, *Italy* .... **44 C5** 45 56N 8 33 E
Pallarenda, *Australia* .... **126 B4** 19 12 S 146 46 E
Pallasovka, *Russia* .... **60 E8** 50 4N 47 0 E
Pallès, Bishti i, *Albania* .... **50 E3** 41 24N 19 24 E
Pallinup →, *Australia* .... **125 F2** 34 27 S 118 50 E
Pallisa, *Uganda* .... **118 B3** 1 12N 33 43 E
Palliser, C., *N.Z.* .... **130 H4** 41 37 S 175 14 E

Palliser B., N.Z. 130 H4 41 26 S 175 5 E
Pallu, India 92 E6 28 59N 74 14 E
Palm Bay, U.S.A. 153 G9 28 2N 80 35W
Palm Beach, U.S.A. 153 J9 26 43N 80 2W
Palm Coast, U.S.A. 153 F8 29 32N 81 10W
Palm Desert, U.S.A. 161 M10 33 43N 116 22W
Palm Harbor, U.S.A. 153 G7 28 5N 82 47W
Palm Is., Australia 126 B4 18 40 S 146 35 E
Palm Springs, U.S.A. 161 M10 33 50N 116 33W
Palma, Mozam. 119 E5 10 46 S 40 29 E
Palma ➔, Brazil 171 D2 12 33 S 47 52W
Palma, B. de, Spain 38 B3 39 30N 2 39 E
Palma de Mallorca, Spain 38 B3 39 35N 2 39 E
Palma de Mallorca ✈ (PMI), Spain 41 F7 39 34N 2 43 E
Palma del Río, Spain 43 H5 37 43N 5 17W
Palma di Montechiaro, Italy 46 E6 37 11N 13 46 E
Palma Nova, Spain 38 B3 39 32N 2 34 E
Palma Soriano, Cuba 164 B4 20 15N 76 0W
Palmaner, India 95 H4 13 12N 78 45 E
Palmares, Brazil 170 C4 8 41 S 35 28W
Palmarito, Venezuela 168 B3 7 37N 70 10W
Palmarola, Italy 46 B5 40 56N 12 51 E
Palmas, Brazil 175 B5 26 29 S 52 0W
Palmas, C., Liberia 112 E3 4 27N 7 46W
Palmas, G. di, Italy 46 D3 39 0N 8 30 E
Palmas de Monte Alto, Brazil 171 D3 14 16 S 43 10W
Palmdale, Calif., U.S.A. 161 L8 34 35N 118 7W
Palmdale, Fla., U.S.A. 153 J8 26 57N 81 19W
Palmeira, Brazil 171 G2 25 25 S 50 0W
Palmeira das Missões, Brazil 175 B5 27 55 S 53 17W
Palmeira dos Índios, Brazil 170 C4 9 25 S 36 37W
Palmeiras, Brazil 170 C3 6 0 S 43 0W
Palmeiras, Brazil 171 D3 12 31 S 41 34W
Palmeiras ➔, Brazil 171 D2 12 22 S 47 8W
Palmeirinhas, Pta. das, Angola 115 D2 9 2 S 12 57 E
Palmela, Portugal 43 G2 38 32N 8 57W
Palmelo, Brazil 171 E2 17 20 S 48 27W
Palmer, U.S.A. 144 F10 61 36N 149 7W
Palmer ➔, Australia 126 B3 16 0 S 142 26 E
Palmer Arch., Antarctica 7 C17 64 15 S 65 0W
Palmer Lake, U.S.A. 154 F2 39 7N 104 55W
Palmer Land, Antarctica 7 D18 73 0 S 63 0W
Palmerston, Canada 150 C4 43 50N 80 51W
Palmerston, N.Z. 131 F5 45 29 S 170 43 E
Palmerston North, N.Z. 130 G4 40 21 S 175 39 E
Palmerton, U.S.A. 151 F9 40 48N 75 37W
Palmetto, Fla., U.S.A. 153 H7 27 31N 82 34W
Palmetto, Ga., U.S.A. 152 B5 33 31N 84 40W
Palmi, Italy 47 D8 38 21N 15 51 E
Palmira, Argentina 174 C2 32 59 S 68 34W
Palmira, Colombia 168 C2 3 32N 76 16W
Palmyra = Tudmur, Syria 101 E8 34 36N 38 15 E
Palmyra, Ill., U.S.A. 156 E7 39 26N 90 0W
Palmyra, Mo., U.S.A. 156 E5 39 48N 91 32W
Palmyra, N.J., U.S.A. 151 F9 40 1N 75 1W
Palmyra, N.Y., U.S.A. 150 C7 43 5N 77 18W
Palmyra, Pa., U.S.A. 151 F8 40 18N 76 36W
Palmyra, Wis., U.S.A. 156 D8 42 52N 88 36W
Palmyra Is., Pac. Oc. 135 G11 5 52N 162 5W
Palmyras Pt., India 94 D8 20 46N 87 1 E
Palo, Phil. 81 F5 11 10N 124 59 E
Palo Alto, U.S.A. 160 H4 37 27N 122 10W
Palo Seco, Trin. & Tob. 169 F9 10 4N 61 36W
Palo Verde, U.S.A. 161 M12 33 26N 114 44W
Palo Verde, Parque Nac. △, Costa Rica 164 D2 10 21N 85 21W
Paloich, Sudan 107 E3 10 28N 32 32 E
Palomar Mt., U.S.A. 161 M10 33 23N 116 50W
Palompon, Phil. 81 F5 11 3N 124 23 E
Palopo, Indonesia 82 B2 3 0 S 120 16 E
Palos, C. de, Spain 41 H4 37 38N 0 40W
Palos de la Frontera, Spain 43 H4 37 14N 6 53W
Palos Verdes, U.S.A. 161 M8 33 48N 118 23W
Palos Verdes, Pt., U.S.A. 161 M8 33 43N 118 26W
Palpa, Peru 172 C2 14 30 S 75 15W
Pålsboda, Sweden 16 F9 59 3N 15 22 E
Palu, Indonesia 82 B1 1 0 S 119 52 E
Palu, Turkey 101 C9 38 45N 40 0 E
Paluan, Phil. 80 E3 13 26N 120 29 E
Paluke, Liberia 112 D3 5 2N 8 5W
Paluzza, Italy 45 B10 46 32N 13 1 E
Palwal, India 92 E7 28 8N 77 19 E
Pama, Burkina Faso 113 C5 11 19N 0 44 E
Pama ➔, C.A.R. 114 B3 4 23N 18 43 E
Pama, Réserve de △, Burkina Faso 113 C5 11 27N 0 40 E
Pamanukan, Indonesia 85 D3 6 16 S 107 49 E
Pamban I., India 95 K4 9 15N 79 20 E
Pamekasan, Indonesia 85 D4 7 10 S 113 28 E
Pamenang, Indonesia 79 J19 8 24 S 116 6 E
Pamiers, France 28 E5 43 7N 1 39 E
Pamir, Tajikistan 68 E6 37 40N 73 0 E
Pamir ➔, Tajikistan 65 E6 37 1N 72 41 E
Pamlico ➔, U.S.A. 149 H7 35 20N 76 28W
Pamlico Sd., U.S.A. 149 H8 35 20N 76 0W
Pampa, U.S.A. 155 H4 35 32N 100 58W
Pampa de Agma, Argentina 176 B3 43 45 S 69 40W
Pampa de las Salinas, Argentina 174 C2 32 1 S 66 58W
Pampa Grande, Bolivia 173 D5 18 5 S 64 5W
Pampa Hermosa, Peru 172 B2 7 7 S 75 4W
Pampanga □, Phil. 80 D3 15 4N 120 40 E
Pampanua, Indonesia 82 B2 4 16 S 120 8 E
Pampas, Argentina 174 D3 35 0 S 63 0W
Pampas, Peru 172 C3 12 20 S 74 50W
Pampas ➔, Peru 172 C3 13 2 S 73 12W
Pamphylia, Turkey 100 D4 37 0N 31 20 E
Pamplona, Colombia 168 B3 7 23N 72 39W
Pamplona, Phil. 80 B3 18 31N 121 20 E
Pamplona, Spain 40 C3 42 48N 1 38W
Pampoenpoort, S. Africa 116 E3 31 3 S 22 40 E
Pamukçu, Turkey 49 B9 39 30N 27 54 E
Pamukkale, Turkey 49 D11 37 55N 29 8 E
Pan Xian, China 76 E5 25 46N 104 38 E
Pana, U.S.A. 156 E7 39 23N 89 5W
Panabo, Phil. 81 H5 7 19N 125 42 E
Panaca, U.S.A. 159 H6 37 47N 114 23W
Panacea, U.S.A. 152 E5 30 2N 84 23W
Panagyurishte, Bulgaria 51 D8 42 30N 24 15 E
Panaitan, Indonesia 84 D3 6 36 S 105 12 E
Panaji, India 95 G1 15 25N 73 50 E
Panamá, Panama 164 E4 9 0N 79 25W
Panama, Sri Lanka 95 L5 6 45N 81 48 E
Panama ■, Cent. Amer. 164 E4 8 48N 79 55W
Panamá, G. de, Panama 164 E4 8 4N 79 20W
Panama Canal, Panama 164 E4 9 10N 79 37W
Panama City, U.S.A. 153 E4 30 10N 85 40W
Panama City Beach, U.S.A. 152 E4 30 10N 85 48W
Panamint Range, U.S.A. 161 J9 36 20N 117 20W
Panamint Springs, U.S.A. 161 J9 36 20N 117 28W
Panão, Peru 172 B2 9 55 S 75 55W
Panaon I., Phil. 81 F5 10 3N 125 13 E
Panare, Thailand 87 J3 6 51N 101 30 E
Panarea, Italy 47 D8 38 38N 15 4 E
Panaro ➔, Italy 45 D8 44 55N 11 25 E
Panarukan, Indonesia 85 D4 7 42 S 113 56 E
Panay, Phil. 81 F4 11 10N 122 30 E
Panay, G., Phil. 79 B6 11 0N 122 30 E
Pančevo, Serbia, Yug. 52 F5 44 52N 20 41 E
Panch'iao, Taiwan 77 E13 25 1N 121 27 E
Panciu, Romania 53 E12 45 54N 27 8 E
Pancol, Phil. 81 F2 10 51N 119 25 E
Pancorbo, Desfiladero, Spain 42 C7 42 32N 3 5W
Pâncota, Romania 52 D6 46 20N 21 45 E
Panda, Mozam. 117 C5 24 2 S 34 45 E
Pandan, Malaysia 87 d 1 32N 103 46 E

Pandan, Antique, Phil. 81 F4 11 45N 122 10 E
Pandan, Catanduanes, Phil. 80 D5 14 3N 124 10 E
Pandan, Selat, Singapore 87 d 1 15N 103 44 E
Pandan Bay, Phil. 81 F4 11 43N 122 0 E
Pandan Tampoi = Tampoi, Malaysia 87 d 1 30N 103 39 E
Pandegelang, Indonesia 84 D3 6 25 S 106 5 E
Pandharkawada, India 92 J7 21 42N 76 13 E
Pandharpur, India 94 D4 20 11N 78 32 E
Pandhurna, India 94 F2 17 41N 75 20 E
Pando, Uruguay 175 C4 34 44 S 56 0W
Pando □, Bolivia 172 C4 11 20 S 67 40W
Pando, L. = Hope, L., Australia 127 D2 28 24 S 139 18 E
Pandokrátor, Greece 38 B9 39 45N 19 50 E
Pandora, Costa Rica 164 E3 9 43N 83 3W
Pandrup, Denmark 17 G3 57 14N 9 40 E
Pandu, Dem. Rep. of the Congo 114 B3 4 59N 19 16 E
Panevéggio-Pale di San Martino, Parco Naturale △, Italy 45 B8 46 14N 11 46 E
Panevėžys, Lithuania 15 J21 55 42N 24 25 E
Panfilov, Kazakhstan 66 E8 44 10N 80 0 E
Panfilov Atyndaghy, Kazakhstan 65 B8 43 23N 77 7 E
Panfilovo, Russia 60 E6 50 25N 42 46 E
Pang Sida Nat. Park △, Thailand 86 E4 14 5N 102 17 E
Panga, Dem. Rep. of the Congo 118 B2 1 52N 26 18 E
Pangaíon Óros, Greece 51 F8 40 50N 24 0 E
Pangala, Congo 114 C2 3 16 S 14 34 E
Pangalanes, Canal des = Ampangalana, Lakandranon', Madag. 117 C8 22 48 S 47 50 E
Pangani, Tanzania 118 D4 5 25 S 38 58 E
Pangani ➔, Tanzania 118 D4 5 26 S 38 58 E
Pangantocan, Phil. 81 H5 7 50N 124 49 E
Pangar Djérem, Réserve de △, Cameroon 114 A2 5 50N 13 10 E
Pangasinan □, Phil. 80 D3 15 55N 120 20 E
Pangfou = Bengbu, China 75 H9 32 58N 117 20 E
Pangil, Dem. Rep. of the Congo 118 C2 3 10 S 26 35 E
Pangkah, Tanjung, Indonesia 85 D4 6 51 S 112 33 E
Pangkai, Burma 90 D7 22 40N 98 40 E
Pangkajene, Indonesia 82 B1 4 46 S 119 34 E
Pangkalanbrandan, Indonesia 84 B1 4 1N 98 20 E
Pangkalanbuun, Indonesia 85 C4 2 41 S 111 37 E
Pangkalansusu, Indonesia 84 B1 4 2N 98 13 E
Pangkalpinang, Indonesia 84 C3 2 0 S 106 0 E
Pangkoh, Indonesia 84 C3 3 5 S 114 8 E
Panglao, Phil. 81 G4 9 35N 123 45 E
Panglao I., Phil. 81 G4 9 35N 123 48 E
Pangnirtung, Canada 139 B13 66 8N 65 54W
Pango Alucuem, Angola 115 D2 8 43 S 14 33 E
Pangong Tso, India 92 B8 34 40N 78 40 E
Pangrango, Indonesia 84 D3 6 46 S 107 1 E
Pangsau Pass, Burma 90 B6 27 15N 96 10 E
Pangtara, Burma 90 E6 20 57N 96 40 E
Panguipulli, Chile 176 A2 39 38 S 72 20W
Panguitch, U.S.A. 159 H7 37 50N 112 26W
Panguna, Papua N. G. 132 D8 6 21 S 155 25 E
Pangutaran, Phil. 81 H3 6 18N 120 34 E
Pangutaran Group, Phil. 81 H3 6 18N 120 34 E
Panhala, India 94 F2 16 49N 74 7 E
Panhandle, U.S.A. 155 H4 35 21N 101 23W
Pani Mines, India 92 H5 22 29N 73 50 E
Pania-Mutombo, Dem. Rep. of the Congo 118 D1 5 11 S 23 51 E
Paniau, U.S.A. 145 B1 21 56N 160 5W
Panié, Mt., N. Cal. 133 T18 20 36 S 164 46 E
Panikota I., India 92 J4 20 46N 71 21 E
Panipat, India 92 E7 29 25N 77 2 E
Panitan, Phil. 81 F4 11 28N 122 46 E
Panj = Pyandzh, Tajikistan 65 E4 37 14N 69 6 E
Panj ➔ = Pyandzh ➔, Asia 65 E4 37 6N 68 20 E
Panjab, Afghan. 91 B2 34 23N 67 1 E
Panjakent = Pendzhikent, Tajikistan 65 D3 39 29N 67 37 E
Panjal Range = Pir Panjal Range, India 92 C7 32 30N 76 50 E
Panjang, Hon, Vietnam 87 H4 9 20N 103 28 E
Panjgur, Pakistan 91 D2 27 0N 64 5 E
Panjhra ➔, India 92 D2 21 13N 74 57 E
Panji Poyon, Tajikistan 65 E4 37 12N 68 35 E
Panjim = Panaji, India 95 G1 15 25N 73 50 E
Panjin, China 75 D12 41 3N 122 2 E
Panjnad ➔, Pakistan 93 E4 28 57N 70 30 E
Panjwai, Afghan. 91 C2 31 26N 65 27 E
Pankshin, Nigeria 113 D6 9 16N 9 25 E
Panmunjŏm, N. Korea 75 F14 37 59N 126 38 E
Panna, India 93 G9 24 40N 80 15 E
Panna Hills, India 93 G9 24 40N 81 15 E
Pannawonica, Australia 124 D2 21 39 S 116 19 E
Panna, Tanjung, Indonesia 79 K19 8 54 S 116 2 E
Pannji, Vanuatu 133 E6 15 58 S 168 12 E
Pannirtuuq = Pangnirtung, Canada 139 B13 66 8N 65 54W
Pano Akil, Pakistan 93 F3 27 51N 69 7 E
Pano Lefkara, Cyprus 39 E9 34 53N 33 20 E
Pano Panayia, Cyprus 39 E8 34 55N 32 38 E
Panora, U.S.A. 156 C2 41 42N 94 22W
Panorama, Brazil 175 A5 21 21 S 51 51W
Pánormon, Greece 39 E5 35 25N 24 41 E
Panruti, India 95 J4 11 46N 79 35 E
Pansemal, India 92 J6 21 39N 74 42 E
Panshan = Panjin, China 75 D12 41 3N 122 2 E
Panshi, China 75 C14 42 58N 126 5 E
Pantanaw, Burma 90 G5 16 59N 95 28 E
Pantanos de Centla, Reserva de La Biósfera, Mexico 163 D6 18 25N 92 25W
Pantar, Indonesia 82 C2 8 28 S 124 10 E
Pante Macassar, E. Timor 82 C2 9 30 S 123 58 E
Pante Makasar = Pante Macassar, E. Timor 82 C2 9 30 S 123 58 E
Pantelleria, Italy 46 F4 36 50N 11 57 E
Pantin Sakan, Burma 90 F6 18 38N 97 33 E
Pantoja, Peru 168 D2 0 58 S 75 10W
Pantón, Spain 42 C3 42 31N 7 37W
Pantukan, Phil. 81 H5 7 9N 125 54 E
Panu, Dem. Rep. of the Congo 114 C3 3 50 S 19 10 E
Pánuco, Mexico 163 C5 22 0N 98 15W
Panukulan, Phil. 80 D3 14 56N 121 49 E
Panvel, India 94 E1 18 59N 73 4 E
Panyam, Nigeria 113 D6 9 27N 9 8 E
Panyu = Guangzhou, China 77 F9 23 5N 113 10 E
Panyu, China 77 F9 22 51N 113 20 E
Panzhihua, China 76 D3 26 33N 101 44 E
Panzi, Dem. Rep. of the Congo 115 D3 7 17 S 18 1 E
Pao ➔, Anzoátegui, Venezuela 169 B5 8 6N 64 17W
Pao ➔, Apure, Venezuela 168 B4 8 33N 68 1W
Páola, Italy 47 C9 39 21N 16 2 E
Paola, Malta 38 F8 35 52N 14 30 E
Paola, U.S.A. 154 F7 38 35N 94 53W
Paoli, U.S.A. 157 F10 38 33N 86 28W
Paonia, U.S.A. 159 G10 38 52N 107 36W
Paoting = Baoding, China 74 E8 38 50N 115 28 E
Paot'ou = Baotou, China 74 D6 40 32N 110 2 E
Paoua, C.A.R. 114 A3 7 9N 16 20 E
Pap, Uzbekistan 65 C5 40 52N 71 6 E
Pápa, Hungary 54 C2 47 22N 17 30 E
Papa, India 145 D6 19 13N 155 52W
Papa Stour, U.K. 22 A7 60 20N 1 42W
Papa Westray, U.K. 22 B6 59 20N 2 55W
Papagayo ➔, Mexico 163 D5 16 36N 99 43W
Papagayo, G. de, Costa Rica 164 D2 10 30N 85 50W
Papakura, N.Z. 130 D3 37 4 S 174 59 E

Papantla, Mexico 163 C5 20 30N 97 30W
Papar, Malaysia 78 C5 5 45N 116 0 E
Papara, Tahiti 133 S16 17 43 S 149 22W
Paparoa, N.Z. 130 C3 36 6 S 174 16 E
Paparoa Nat. Park △, N.Z. 131 C6 42 7 S 171 26 E
Paparoa Ra., N.Z. 131 C6 42 5 S 171 35 E
Pápas, Ákra, Greece 38 C3 38 13N 21 20 E
Papatoetoe, N.Z. 130 C3 36 59 S 174 51 E
Papatura, Solomon Is. 133 L10 7 32 S 158 47 E
Papawai Pt., U.S.A. 145 C5 20 47N 156 32W
Papeete, Tahiti 133 S16 17 32 S 149 34W
Papenburg, Germany 30 B3 53 5N 7 23 E
Papetoai, Tahiti 133 S16 17 29 S 149 52W
Paphlagonia, Turkey 100 B5 41 30N 33 0 E
Paphos, Cyprus 39 F8 34 46N 32 25 E
Paphos ✈ (PFO), Cyprus 39 F8 34 43N 32 30 E
Papien Chiang = Da ➔, Vietnam 76 G5 21 15N 105 20 E
Papigochic ➔, Mexico 162 B3 29 9N 109 40W
Paposo, Chile 174 B1 25 0 S 70 30W
Papua, G. of, Papua N. G. 132 E3 9 0 S 144 50 E
Papua New Guinea ■, Oceania 132 D3 8 0 S 145 0 E
Papudo, Chile 174 C1 32 29 S 71 27W
Papuk, Croatia 28 C2 45 30N 17 30 E
Papun, Burma 90 F6 18 2N 97 30 E
Papunya, Australia 124 D5 23 15 S 131 54 E
Pará = Belém, Brazil 170 B2 1 20 S 48 30W
Pará □, Brazil 173 A7 3 20 S 52 0W
Paraburdoo, Australia 124 D2 23 14 S 117 32 E
Paracale, Phil. 80 D4 14 17N 122 48 E
Paracas, Pen., Peru 172 C2 13 53 S 76 20W
Paracatu, Brazil 171 E2 17 10 S 46 50W
Paracatu ➔, Brazil 171 E2 16 30 S 45 4W
Paracel Is., S. China Sea 78 A4 15 50N 112 0 E
Parachilna, Australia 128 A3 31 10 S 138 21 E
Parachinar, Pakistan 91 B3 33 55N 70 5 E
Paraćin, Serbia, Yug. 50 C5 43 54N 21 27 E
Parada, Punta, Peru 172 D2 15 22 S 75 11W
Paradas, Spain 43 H5 37 18N 5 29W
Paradela, Spain 42 C3 42 44N 7 37W
Paradhísi, Greece 38 E12 36 18N 28 7 E
Paradip, India 94 D8 20 15N 86 35 E
Paradise, Calif., U.S.A. 160 F5 39 46N 121 37W
Paradise, Nev., U.S.A. 161 J11 36 9N 115 10W
Paradise ➔, Canada 141 B8 53 27N 57 19W
Paradise Hill, Canada 143 C7 53 32N 109 28W
Paradise I., Bahamas 9 b 25 6N 77 19W
Paradise River, Canada 141 B8 53 27N 57 17W
Paradise Valley, U.S.A. 158 F5 41 30N 117 32W
Parado, Indonesia 85 D5 8 42 S 118 30 E
Paragould, U.S.A. 155 G9 36 3N 90 29W
Paraguá ➔, Bolivia 173 C5 13 34 S 61 53W
Paragua ➔, Venezuela 169 B5 6 55N 62 55W
Paraguaçu ➔, Brazil 171 D4 12 45 S 38 54W
Paraguaçu Paulista, Brazil 175 A5 22 22 S 50 35W
Paraguaipoa, Venezuela 168 A3 11 21N 71 57W
Paraguaná, Pen. de, Venezuela 168 A3 12 0N 70 0W
Paraguarí, Paraguay 174 B4 25 36 S 57 0W
Paraguarí □, Paraguay 174 B4 26 0 S 57 10W
Paraguay ■, S. Amer. 174 A4 23 0 S 57 0W
Paraguay ➔, Paraguay 174 B4 27 18 S 58 38W
Paraíba = João Pessoa, Brazil 170 C5 7 10 S 34 52W
Paraíba □, Brazil 170 C4 7 0 S 36 0W
Paraíba do Sul ➔, Brazil 171 F3 21 37 S 41 3W
Parainen, Finland 15 F20 60 18N 22 18 E
Paraíso, Brazil 173 19 3 S 52 59W
Paraiso, Mexico 163 D6 18 24N 93 14W
Parak, Iran 97 E7 27 38N 52 25 E
Parakhino Paddubye, Russia 58 C7 58 26N 33 10 E
Parakou, Benin 113 D5 9 25N 2 40 E
Paraklya, Australia 128 A2 30 24 S 136 25 E
Paralimni, Cyprus 39 E9 35 2N 33 58 E
Parálion-Ástros, Greece 38 D4 37 25N 22 45 E
Paralkote, India 94 E5 19 47N 80 41 E
Parama I., Papua N. G. 132 E2 9 0 S 143 25 E
Paramaribo, Suriname 169 B6 5 50N 55 10W
Parambu, Brazil 170 C3 6 13 S 40 43W
Paramillo, Nudo del, Colombia 168 B2 7 4N 75 55W
Paramirim, Brazil 171 D3 13 26 S 42 15W
Paramirim ➔, Brazil 171 D3 13 34 S 43 18W
Paramithiá, Greece 48 B2 39 30N 20 35 E
Páramos del Batallón y La Negra, Parque Nac. △, Venezuela 165 E5 8 2N 71 55W
Paramushir, Ostrov, Russia 67 D16 50 24N 156 0 E
Paran ➔, Israel 103 E4 30 20N 35 10 E
Paraná, Argentina 174 C3 31 45 S 60 30W
Paraná, Brazil 171 D2 12 30 S 47 48W
Paraná □, Brazil 175 A5 24 30 S 51 0W
Paraná ➔, Argentina 174 C4 33 43 S 59 15W
Paraná ➔, Brazil 171 D2 12 30 S 48 14W
Paranaguá, Brazil 175 B6 25 30 S 48 30W
Paranaíba, Brazil 173 D7 19 40 S 51 11W
Paranaíba ➔, Brazil 171 F1 20 6 S 51 4W
Paranapanema ➔, Brazil 175 A5 22 40 S 53 9W
Paranapiacaba, Serra do, Brazil 175 A5 24 31 S 48 35W
Paranas, Phil. 81 F5 11 42N 125 2 E
Paranavaí, Brazil 175 A5 23 4 S 52 56W
Parang, Maguindanao, Phil. 81 H5 7 23N 124 16 E
Parang, Sulu, Phil. 81 J3 5 55N 120 54 E
Parangaba, Brazil 170 B4 3 45 S 38 33W
Parangippettai, India 95 J4 11 30N 79 38 E
Parângul Mare, Vf., Romania 53 E8 45 20N 23 37 E
Paranthan, Sri Lanka 95 K5 9 26N 80 24 E
Paraparaumu, N.Z. 130 G4 40 57 S 175 3 E
Parapetí ➔, Bolivia 173 D5 18 58 S 62 21W
Parapóla, Greece 48 E5 35 55N 23 27 E
Paraspóri, Ákra, Greece 49 F9 35 55N 27 15 E
Parati, Brazil 171 D3 23 14 S 44 43W
Paraúna, Brazil 173 D7 16 55 S 50 26W
Paray-le-Monial, France 27 F11 46 27N 4 7 E
Parbati ➔, Mad. P., India 92 G7 25 50N 76 30 E
Parbati ➔, Raj., India 92 F7 26 54N 77 53 E
Parbatipur, Bangla. 93 G16 25 39N 88 55 E
Parbhani, India 94 E3 19 8N 76 52 E
Parchim, Germany 30 B7 53 26N 11 52 E
Parczew, Poland 55 G9 51 40N 22 52 E
Pardes Hanna-Karkur, Israel 103 C3 32 28N 34 57 E
Pardilla, Spain 42 D7 41 33N 3 43W
Pardo ➔, Bahia, Brazil 171 E4 15 40 S 39 0W
Pardo ➔, Mato Grosso, Brazil 175 A5 21 46 S 52 9W
Pardo ➔, Minas Gerais, Brazil 171 E3 15 48 S 44 48W
Pardo ➔, São Paulo, Brazil 171 F2 20 10 S 48 38W
Pardubice, Czech Rep. 34 A8 50 3N 15 45 E
Pardubický □, Czech Rep. 34 B8 49 50N 16 0 E
Pare, Indonesia 85 D4 7 43 S 112 12 E
Pare Mts., Tanzania 118 C4 4 0 S 37 45 E
Parecis, Serra dos, Brazil 173 C6 13 0 S 60 0W
Paredes de Nava, Spain 42 C6 42 9N 4 42W
Parelhas, Brazil 170 C4 6 41 S 36 39W
Paren, Russia 67 C17 62 30N 163 15 E
Parenda, India 94 E2 18 16N 75 23 E
Parengarenga Harbour, N.Z. 130 A4 34 31 S 173 0 E
Parent, Canada 140 C5 47 55N 74 35W
Parent, L., Canada 140 C4 48 31N 77 1W
Parentis-en-Born, France 28 D2 44 21N 1 4W
Parepare, Indonesia 82 B1 4 0 S 119 40 E
Parfino, Russia 58 C7 57 59N 31 34 E
Párga, Greece 48 B2 39 15N 20 29 E
Pargi, India 94 F3 17 11N 77 58 E
Pargo, Pta. do, Madeira 9 c 32 49N 17 17W
Paria, G. de, Venezuela 169 A5 10 20N 62 0W
Paria, Pen. de, Venezuela 169 A5 10 50N 62 30W

Pariaguán, Venezuela 169 B5 8 51N 64 34W
Pariaman, Indonesia 84 C2 0 47 S 100 11 E
Paricatuba, Brazil 169 D5 4 26 S 61 53W
Paricutín, Cerro, Mexico 162 D4 19 28N 102 15W
Parigi, Java, Indonesia 85 D3 7 42 S 108 29 E
Parigi, Sulawesi, Indonesia 82 B2 0 50 S 120 5 E
Parika, Guyana 169 B6 6 50N 58 20W
Parikkala, Finland 58 B5 61 33N 29 31 E
Parima, Serra, Brazil 169 C5 2 30N 64 0W
Parinari, Peru 172 A3 4 35 S 74 25W
Pariñas, Pta., S. Amer. 166 D2 4 30 S 82 0W
Parincea, Romania 53 D12 46 27N 27 9 E
Paringa, Australia 128 C4 34 15 S 140 46 E
Parintins, Brazil 169 D6 2 40 S 56 50W
Paris, Canada 150 C4 43 12N 80 25W
Paris, France 27 D9 48 50N 2 20 E
Paris, Idaho, U.S.A. 158 E8 42 14N 111 24W
Paris, Ill., U.S.A. 157 E9 39 36N 87 42W
Paris, Ky., U.S.A. 157 F12 38 13N 84 15W
Paris, Mo., U.S.A. 156 E5 39 29N 92 0W
Paris, Tenn., U.S.A. 149 G1 36 18N 88 19W
Paris, Tex., U.S.A. 155 J7 33 40N 95 33W
Paris, Ville de □, France 27 D9 48 50N 2 20 E
Paris Charles de Gaulle ✈ (CDG), France 27 D9 48 59N 2 32 E
Paris Orly ✈ (ORY), France 27 D9 48 44N 2 23 E
Parish, U.S.A. 151 C8 43 25N 76 8W
Parishville, U.S.A. 151 B10 44 38N 74 49W
Pariti, Indonesia 82 D2 10 1 S 123 45 E
Park ➔, U.S.A. 160 B4 48 45N 122 18W
Park City, U.S.A. 155 G6 37 48N 97 20W
Park Falls, U.S.A. 154 C9 45 56N 90 27W
Park Forest, U.S.A. 157 C9 41 29N 87 40W
Park Head, Canada 150 B3 44 36N 81 9W
Park Hills, Mo., U.S.A. 155 G9 37 53N 90 28W
Park Hills, Mo., U.S.A. 156 G6 37 51N 90 31W
Park Range, U.S.A. 158 G10 40 0N 106 30W
Park Rapids, U.S.A. 154 B7 46 55N 95 4W
Park Ridge, U.S.A. 157 B9 42 2N 87 51W
Park River, U.S.A. 154 A6 48 24N 97 45W
Park Rynie, S. Africa 117 E5 30 25 S 30 45 E
Parkā Bandar, Iran 97 E8 25 55N 59 35 E
Parkal, India 94 E4 18 12N 79 43 E
Parkano, Finland 15 E20 62 1N 23 0 E
Parkent, Uzbekistan 65 C4 41 18N 69 40 E
Parker, Ariz., U.S.A. 161 L12 34 9N 114 17W
Parker, Pa., U.S.A. 150 E5 41 5N 79 41W
Parker Dam, U.S.A. 161 L12 34 18N 114 8W
Parkersburg, Iowa, U.S.A. 156 B4 42 35N 92 47W
Parkersburg, W. Va., U.S.A. 148 F5 39 16N 81 34W
Parkes, Australia 129 B8 33 9 S 148 11 E
Parkfield, U.S.A. 160 K6 35 54N 120 26W
Parkhar, Tajikistan 65 E4 37 30N 69 34 E
Parkhill, Canada 150 C3 43 15N 81 38W
Parkland, U.S.A. 160 C4 47 9N 122 26W
Parkston, U.S.A. 154 D6 43 24N 97 59W
Parksville, Canada 142 D4 49 20N 124 21W
Parla, Spain 42 E7 40 14N 3 46W
Parlakimidi, India 94 E3 18 45N 84 5 E
Parli, India 94 E3 18 50N 76 35 E
Pârlita, Moldova 53 C12 47 19N 27 52 E
Parma, Idaho, U.S.A. 158 E5 43 47N 116 57W
Parma, Ohio, U.S.A. 150 E3 41 23N 81 43W
Parma ➔, Italy 44 D7 44 56N 10 26 E
Parnaguá, Brazil 170 D3 10 10 S 44 38W
Parnaíba, Piauí, Brazil 170 B3 2 54 S 41 47W
Parnaíba, São Paulo, Brazil 173 D7 19 34 S 51 14W
Parnaíba ➔, Brazil 170 B3 3 0 S 41 50W
Parnamirim, Brazil 170 C4 8 5 S 39 34W
Parnarama, Brazil 170 C3 5 31 S 43 6W
Parnassós, Greece 48 C4 38 35N 22 30 E
Parnassus, N.Z. 131 C8 42 42 S 173 23 E
Parndana, Australia 128 C2 35 48 S 137 12 E
Parner, India 94 E2 19 0N 74 26 E
Párnis, Greece 48 C5 38 14N 23 45 E
Párnitha ➔, Greece 48 C5 38 12N 23 44 E
Párnon Óros, Greece 48 D4 37 15N 22 45 E
Pärnu, Estonia 15 G21 58 28N 24 33 E
Parola, India 92 J9 20 47N 75 7 E
Paroo ➔, Australia 128 A5 31 28 S 143 32 E
Páros, Greece 49 D7 37 5N 25 12 E
Parowan, U.S.A. 159 H7 37 51N 112 50W
Parpaillon, France 29 D10 44 30N 6 40 E
Parral, Chile 174 D1 36 10 S 71 52W
Parramatta, Australia 129 B9 33 48 S 151 1 E
Parras, Mexico 162 B4 25 30N 102 20W
Parrett ➔, U.K. 21 F4 51 12N 3 1W
Parris I., U.S.A. 152 C9 32 20N 80 41W
Parrish, U.S.A. 153 H7 27 35N 82 26W
Parrott, U.S.A. 152 D5 31 54N 84 31W
Parrsboro, Canada 141 C7 45 30N 64 25W
Parry I., Canada 150 A4 45 18N 80 10W
Parry Is., Canada 6 B2 77 0N 110 0W
Parry Sound, Canada 140 C4 45 20N 80 0W
Parsberg, Germany 31 F7 49 10N 11 43 E
Parseier Spitze, Austria 33 B10 47 10N 10 28 E
Parsęta ➔, Poland 54 D2 54 11N 15 34 E
Parsnip ➔, Canada 142 B4 55 10N 123 2W
Parsons, U.S.A. 155 G7 37 20N 95 16W
Parsons Ra., Australia 126 A2 13 30 S 135 15 E
Partabpur, India 94 E5 20 0N 80 42 E
Partanna, Italy 46 E5 37 43N 12 53 E
Partenio, Parco Regionale del □, Italy 47 B7 40 56N 14 38 E
Parthenay, France 26 F6 46 38N 0 16W
Partinico, Italy 46 D6 38 3N 13 7 E
Partizánske, Slovak Rep. 35 C11 48 38N 18 23 E
Partridge I., Canada 140 A2 55 59N 87 37W
Partur, India 94 E3 19 40N 76 14 E
Paru ➔, Brazil 169 D7 1 33 S 52 38W
Paru □, Venezuela 168 C4 4 20N 66 27W
Paru de Oeste ➔, Brazil 169 C6 1 30N 56 0W
Parucito ➔, Venezuela 168 B4 5 18N 65 59W
Parur, India 95 J3 10 13N 76 14 E
Paruro, Peru 172 C3 13 45 S 71 50W
Pārvān □, Afghan. 91 B3 35 0N 69 0 E
Parvatipuram, India 94 E6 18 50N 83 25 E
Parvatsar, India 92 F6 26 52N 74 49 E
Pâryd, Sweden 17 H9 56 34N 15 55 E
Parys, S. Africa 116 D4 26 52 S 27 29 E
Pas, Pta. des, Spain 38 D1 38 46N 1 26 E
Pas-de-Calais □, France 27 B9 50 30N 2 10 E
Pasada, Spain 42 B5 43 23N 5 40W
Pasadena, Canada 141 C8 49 1N 57 36W
Pasadena, Calif., U.S.A. 161 L8 34 9N 118 9W
Pasadena, Tex., U.S.A. 155 L7 29 43N 95 13W
Pasaje, Ecuador 168 D2 3 23 S 79 50W
Pasaje ➔, Argentina 174 B3 25 39 S 63 56W
Paşalimanı, Turkey 51 F11 40 29N 27 35 E
Pasar, Indonesia 79 J17 8 27 S 114 54 E
Pasay, Phil. 80 D3 14 33N 121 0 E
Pascagoula, U.S.A. 155 K10 30 21N 88 33W
Pascagoula ➔, U.S.A. 155 K10 30 23N 88 37W
Pașcani, Romania 53 C11 47 14N 26 45 E
Pasco, U.S.A. 158 C4 46 14N 119 6W
Pasco □, Peru 172 C2 10 45 S 76 10W
Pasco, Cerro de, Peru 172 C2 10 45 S 76 10W
Pasco I., Australia 124 D2 20 57 S 115 20 E
Pascoag, U.S.A. 151 E13 41 57N 71 42W
Pascua, I. de, Chile 172 b 27 7 S 109 23W
Pasewalk, Germany 30 B9 53 30N 13 58 E
Pasfield L., Canada 143 B7 58 24N 105 20W
Pasha ➔, Russia 58 B7 60 29N 32 55 E

Pashiya, *Russia* .... 64 B7 58 33N 58 26 E
Pashmakli = Smolyan, *Bulgaria* .. 51 E8 41 36N 24 38 E
Pasig, *Phil.* .... 80 D3 14 35N 121 5 E
Pasighat, *India* .... 90 A5 28 4N 95 21 E
Pasinler, *Turkey* .... 101 C9 39 59N 41 41 E
Pasir Mas, *Malaysia* .... 87 J4 6 2N 102 8 E
Pasir Panjang, *Singapore* .... 87 d 1 18N 103 46 E
Pasir Putih, *Malaysia* .... 87 K4 5 50N 102 24 E
Pasirian, *Indonesia* .... 84 C2 0 30 S 104 33 E
Pasirkuning, *Indonesia* .... 84 C2 0 30 S 104 33 E
Påskallavik, *Sweden* .... 17 G10 57 10N 16 26 E
Paskûh, *Iran* .... 97 E9 27 34N 61 39 E
Pasłęk, *Poland* .... 54 D6 54 3N 19 41 E
Pasłęka →, *Poland* .... 54 D6 54 26N 19 46 E
Pasley, C., *Australia* .... 125 F3 33 52 S 123 35 E
Pašman, *Croatia* .... 45 E12 43 58N 15 20 E
Pasmore →, *Australia* .... 128 A3 31 5 S 139 49 E
Pasni, *Pakistan* .... 91 D1 25 15N 63 27 E
Paso Cantinela, *Mexico* 161 N11 32 33N 115 47W
Paso de Indios, *Argentina* .... 176 B3 43 55 S 69 0W
Paso de los Indios, *Argentina* .... 176 A3 38 32 S 69 25W
Paso de los Libres, *Argentina* .... 174 B4 29 44 S 57 10W
Paso de los Toros, *Uruguay* .... 174 C4 32 45 S 56 30W
Paso Flores, *Argentina* .... 176 B2 40 35 S 70 38W
Paso Robles, *U.S.A.* 159 J3 35 38N 120 41W
Pasorapa, *Bolivia* .... 173 D5 18 16 S 64 37W
Paspébiac, *Canada* 141 C6 48 3N 65 17W
Pasrur, *Pakistan* .... 92 C6 32 16N 74 43 E
Passage West, *Ireland* 23 E3 51 52N 8 21W
Passaic, *U.S.A.* 151 F10 40 51N 74 7W
Passam, *Papua N. G.* .... 132 B2 3 41 S 143 38 E
Passau, *Germany* .... 31 G9 48 34N 13 28 E
Passero, C., *Italy* .... 47 F8 36 41N 15 10 E
Passi, *Phil.* .... 81 F4 11 6N 122 38 E
Passo Fundo, *Brazil* .... 175 B5 28 10 S 52 20W
Passos, *Brazil* .... 171 F2 20 45 S 46 37W
Passow, *Germany* .... 30 B10 53 8N 14 6 E
Passwang, *Switz.* .... 32 B5 47 22N 7 44 E
Passy, *France* .... 29 D10 45 55N 6 41 E
Pastavy, *Belarus* .... 15 J22 55 4N 26 50 E
Pastaza □, *Ecuador* .... 168 D2 2 0 S 77 0W
Pastaza →, *Peru* .... 168 D2 4 50 S 76 52W
Pasto, *Colombia* 168 C2 1 13N 77 17W
Pastol B., *U.S.A.* 144 E7 63 7N 163 15W
Pastos Bons, *Brazil* .... 170 C3 6 36 S 44 5W
Pastrana, *Spain* 40 E2 40 27N 2 53W
Pasuquin, *Phil.* .... 80 B3 18 20N 120 37 E
Pasuruan, *Indonesia* .... 85 D4 7 40 S 112 44 E
Pasym, *Poland* .... 54 E7 53 48N 20 49 E
Pásztó, *Hungary* .... 52 C4 47 52N 19 43 E
Pata, *India* .... 81 J3 5 51N 121 10 E
Pata I., *Phil.* .... 81 J3 5 49N 121 10 E
Patagonia, *Argentina* .... 176 C2 45 0 S 69 0W
Patagonia, *U.S.A.* 163 L6 31 33N 110 45W
Patalasang, *Indonesia* .... 85 C1 5 26 S 119 26 E
Patambar, *Iran* .... 97 D9 29 45N 60 17 E
Patan = Lalitapur, *Nepal* .... 93 F11 27 40N 85 20 E
Patan, *Gujarat, India* .... 94 F1 17 22N 73 57 E
Patan, *Maharashtra, India* .... 92 H5 23 54N 72 14 E
Patani, *Indonesia* .... 82 A3 0 20N 128 50 E
Pătârlagele, *Romania* .... 53 E11 45 19N 26 21 E
Pataudi, *India* .... 92 E7 28 18N 76 48 E
Patchewollock, *Australia* .... 128 C5 35 22 S 142 12 E
Patchogue, *U.S.A.* 151 F11 40 46N 73 1W
Pate, *Kenya* .... 118 C5 2 10 S 41 0 E
Patea, *N.Z.* .... 130 F3 39 45 S 174 30 E
Pategi, *Nigeria* .... 113 D6 8 50N 5 45 E
Patensie, *S. Africa* .... 116 E3 33 46 S 24 49 E
Paterna, *Spain* 41 F4 39 30N 0 26W
Paternion, *Austria* .... 34 E6 46 43N 13 38 E
Paternò, *Italy* .... 47 E7 37 34N 14 54 E
Pateros, *U.S.A.* 158 B4 38 3N 119 54W
Paterson, *Australia* .... 129 B9 32 35 S 151 36 E
Paterson, *U.S.A.* 151 F10 40 55N 74 11W
Paterson Inlet, *N.Z.* .... 131 G3 46 56 S 168 12 E
Paterson Ra., *Australia* .... 124 D3 21 45 S 122 10 E
Pathankot, *India* .... 92 C6 32 18N 75 45 E
Pathardi, *India* .... 94 E2 19 10N 75 11 E
Patharghata, *Bangla.* .... 90 D2 22 2N 89 58 E
Pathein = Bassein, *Burma* .... 90 G5 16 45N 94 30 E
Pathfinder Reservoir, *U.S.A.* 158 E10 42 28N 106 51W
Pathiu, *Thailand* .... 87 G2 10 42N 99 19 E
Pathri, *India* .... 94 E3 19 15N 76 27 E
Pathum Thani, *Thailand* .... 86 E3 14 1N 100 32 E
Pati, *Indonesia* .... 85 D4 6 45 S 111 1 E
Pati Pt., *Guam* .... 133 R15 13 40N 144 50 E
Patía, *Colombia* 168 C2 2 4N 77 4W
Patía →, *Colombia* 168 C2 2 13N 78 40W
Patiala, *Punjab, India* .... 92 D7 30 23N 76 26 E
Patiala, *Ut. P., India* .... 93 F8 27 43N 79 1 E
Patine Kouka, *Senegal* 112 C2 12 45N 13 45W
Patitírion, *Greece* .... 48 B5 39 8N 23 50 E
Pativilca, *Peru* .... 172 C2 10 42 S 77 48W
Patkai Bum, *India* .... 90 B5 27 0N 95 30 E
Pátmos, *Greece* .... 49 D8 37 21N 26 36 E
Patna, *India* .... 93 G11 25 35N 85 12 E
Patnagarh, *India* .... 94 D6 20 43N 83 9 E
Patnanongan I., *Phil.* .... 80 D4 14 48N 122 11 E
Patnongon, *Phil.* .... 81 F4 10 55N 122 0 E
Patnos, *Turkey* .... 101 C10 39 13N 42 51 E
Pato Branco, *Brazil* .... 175 B5 26 13 S 52 40W
Patoka →, *U.S.A.* 157 F10 38 26N 87 44W
Patong, Ao, *Thailand* .... 87 a 7 54N 98 17 E
Patonga, *Uganda* .... 118 B3 2 45N 33 15 E
Patos, *Albania* .... 50 F3 40 42N 19 38 E
Patos, *Brazil* .... 170 C4 6 55 S 37 16W
Patos, L. dos, *Brazil* .... 175 C5 31 20 S 51 0W
Patos, Río de los →, *Argentina* .... 174 C2 31 18 S 69 25W
Patos de Minas, *Brazil* .... 171 E2 18 35 S 46 32W
Patquía, *Argentina* .... 174 C2 30 2 S 66 55W
Pátrai, *Greece* .... 48 C3 38 14N 21 47 E
Pátraikós Kólpos, *Greece* .... 48 C3 38 17N 21 30 E
Patras = Pátrai, *Greece* .... 48 C3 38 14N 21 47 E
Patreksfjörður, *Iceland* 11 B2 65 34N 24 0W
Patricio Lynch, I., *Chile* .... 176 C1 48 35 S 75 30W
Patrocínio, *Brazil* .... 171 E2 18 57 S 47 0W
Pattada, *Italy* .... 46 B2 40 35N 9 6 E
Pattani, *Thailand* .... 87 J3 6 48N 101 15 E
Pattaya, *Thailand* .... 78 B2 12 52N 100 55 E
Patten, *U.S.A.* 149 C11 46 0N 68 38W
Patterson, Calif., U.S.A. 160 H5 37 28N 121 8W
Patterson, Ga., U.S.A. 152 D7 31 23N 82 8W
Patterson, La., U.S.A. 155 L9 29 42N 91 18W
Patterson, Mt., U.S.A. 160 G7 38 29N 119 20W
Patteson, Passage, *Vanuatu* .... 133 E6 15 26 S 168 12 E
Patti, *Punjab, India* .... 92 D6 31 17N 74 54 E
Patti, *Ut. P., India* .... 93 G10 25 55N 82 12 E
Patti, *Italy* .... 47 D7 38 8N 14 58 E
Pattoki, *Pakistan* .... 92 D5 31 5N 73 52 E
Patton, *U.S.A.* 150 F6 40 38N 78 39W
Pattonsburg, *U.S.A.* 156 D2 40 3N 94 8W
Pattukkattai, *India* .... 95 J4 10 25N 79 20 E
Patu, *Brazil* .... 170 C4 6 6 S 37 38W
Patuakhali, *Bangla.* .... 90 D3 22 20N 90 25 E
Patuanak, *Canada* 143 B7 55 55N 107 43W
Patuca →, *Honduras* 164 C3 15 50N 84 18W
Patuca, Parque Nac. △, *Honduras* 164 D2 14 30N 85 30W
Patuca, Punta, *Honduras* 164 C3 15 49N 84 14W
Pătulele, *Romania* .... 52 F7 44 21N 22 42 E
Patur, *India* .... 94 D3 20 27N 76 56 E
Pátzcuaro, *Mexico* 162 D4 19 30N 101 40W
Pau, *France* 28 E3 43 19N 0 25W
Pau, Gave de →, *France* 28 E2 43 33N 1 12W
Pau d' Arco, *Brazil* .... 170 C2 7 30 S 49 22W

Pau dos Ferros, *Brazil* .... 170 C4 6 7 S 38 10W
Paucartambo, *Peru* .... 172 C3 13 19 S 71 35W
Pauillac, *France* 28 C3 45 11N 0 46W
Pauini, *Brazil* .... 172 B4 7 40 S 66 58W
Pauini →, *Brazil* .... 169 D5 1 42 S 62 50W
Pauk, *Burma* .... 90 E5 21 27N 94 30 E
Paukkaung, *Burma* .... 90 E5 18 54N 95 33 E
Pauktaw, *Burma* .... 90 E4 20 11N 93 4 E
Paul I., *Canada* 141 A7 56 30N 61 20W
Paul Isnard, *Fr. Guiana* 169 C7 4 47N 54 1W
Paul Smiths, *U.S.A.* 151 B10 44 26N 74 15W
Paulatuk, *Canada* 138 B7 69 25N 124 0W
Paulding, *U.S.A.* 157 C12 41 8N 84 35W
Paulhan, *France* .... 28 E7 43 33N 3 28 E
Paulis = Isiro, Dem. Rep. of
the Congo .... 118 B2 2 53N 27 40 E
Paulista, *Brazil* .... 170 C5 7 57 S 34 53W
Paulistana, *Brazil* .... 170 C3 8 9 S 41 9W
Paulo Afonso, *Brazil* .... 170 C4 9 21 S 38 15W
Paulo de Faria, *Brazil* .... 171 F2 20 2 S 49 24W
Paulpietersburg, S. Africa .... 117 D5 27 23 S 30 50 E
Pauls Valley, *U.S.A.* 155 H6 34 44N 97 13W
Pauma Valley, U.S.A. 161 M10 33 16N 116 58W
Paung, *Burma* .... 90 G5 16 37N 94 28 E
Paungde, *Burma* .... 90 F5 18 29N 95 30 E
Pauni, *India* .... 94 D4 20 48N 79 40 E
Pauri, *India* .... 93 D8 30 9N 78 47 E
Pausa, *Peru* .... 172 D3 15 16 S 73 22W
Pauto →, *Colombia* 168 B3 5 9N 70 55W
Pauwela, *U.S.A.* 154 C5 20 56N 156 19W
Pavagada, *India* .... 95 G3 14 6N 77 16 E
Pãveh, *Iran* .... 101 E12 35 3N 46 22 E
Pavelets, *Russia* .... 58 F10 53 49N 39 14 E
Pavia, *Italy* .... 44 C6 45 7N 9 8 E
Pavilion, *U.S.A.* 150 D6 42 52N 78 1W
Pavilly, *France* .... 26 C7 49 34N 0 57 E
Pãvilosta, *Latvia* .... 15 H19 56 53N 21 14 E
Pavlikeni, *Bulgaria* .... 51 C9 43 14N 25 20 E
Pavlodar, *Kazakhstan* .... 60 D8 52 33N 77 0 E
Pavlograd = Pavlohrad, *Ukraine* .... 59 H8 48 30N 35 52 E
Pavlohrad, *Ukraine* .... 59 H8 48 30N 35 52 E
Pavlovo, *Russia* .... 60 C5 55 58N 43 5 E
Pavlovsk, *Russia* .... 60 E5 50 26N 40 5 E
Pavlovskaya, *Russia* .... 61 G4 46 17N 39 47 E
Pavlovskiy-Posad, *Russia* .... 58 C10 55 47N 38 42 E
Pavo, *U.S.A.* 152 E6 30 58N 83 45W
Pavullo nel Frignano, *Italy* .... 44 D7 44 20N 10 50 E
Pavuvu, *Solomon Is.* .... 133 M10 9 4 S 159 8 E
Paw Paw, *U.S.A.* 157 B11 42 13N 85 53W
Pawahku, *Burma* .... 90 B7 26 11N 98 40 E
Pawai, Pulau, *Singapore* .... 87 d 1 11N 103 44 E
Pawan →, *Indonesia* .... 85 C4 1 55 S 110 0 E
Pawayan, *India* .... 93 E9 28 4N 80 6 E
Pawhuska, *U.S.A.* 155 G6 36 40N 96 20W
Pawling, *U.S.A.* 151 E11 41 34N 73 36W
Pawnee, *Ill., U.S.A.* 156 E7 39 36N 89 35W
Pawnee, Okla., U.S.A. 155 G6 36 20N 96 48W
Pawnee City, *U.S.A.* 154 E6 40 7N 96 9W
Pawpaw, *U.S.A.* 156 C8 41 41N 88 59W
Pawtucket, *U.S.A.* 151 E13 41 53N 71 23W
Paximádhia, *Greece* .... 39 F5 35 0N 24 35 E
Paxoí, *Greece* .... 38 C10 39 14N 20 12 E
Paxson, *U.S.A.* 144 E11 63 2N 145 30W
Paxton, Ill., U.S.A. 157 D8 40 27N 88 6W
Paxton, Nebr., U.S.A. 154 E4 41 7N 101 21W
Payagyi, *Burma* .... 90 G6 17 29N 96 32 E
Payakumbuh, *Indonesia* .... 84 C2 0 20 S 100 35 E
Payerne, *Switz.* .... 32 C3 46 49N 6 56 E
Payette, *U.S.A.* 158 D5 44 5N 116 56W
Paymogo, *Spain* 43 H3 37 44N 7 21W
Payne, *U.S.A.* 157 C12 41 5N 84 44W
Payne Bay = Kangirsuk, *Canada* 139 B13 60 0N 70 0W
Payne L., *Canada* 139 C12 59 30N 74 30W
Payne Pt., *Ascension I.* .... 9 g 7 57 S 14 25W
Paynes Find, *Australia* .... 125 E2 29 15 S 117 42 E
Paynesville, *Liberia* 112 D2 6 20N 10 45W
Paynesville, *U.S.A.* 154 C7 45 23N 94 43W
Pays de la Loire □, *France* 26 E6 47 45N 0 25W
Paysandú, *Uruguay* .... 174 C4 32 19 S 58 8W
Payshanba, *Uzbekistan* .... 65 C3 40 0N 66 14 E
Payson, *U.S.A.* 159 J8 34 14N 111 20W
Paz →, *Guatemala* 164 D1 13 44N 90 10W
Paz, B. de la, *Mexico* 162 C2 24 15N 110 25W
Pãzanãn, *Iran* .... 97 D6 30 35N 49 59 E
Pazar, *Turkey* .... 100 D7 41 10N 40 50 E
Pazardzhik, *Bulgaria* .... 51 D8 42 12N 24 20 E
Pazarköy, *Turkey* .... 49 B9 39 51N 27 24 E
Pazarlar, *Turkey* .... 49 C11 39 0N 29 7 E
Pazaryeri, *Turkey* .... 49 B11 40 0N 29 56 E
Pazaryolu, *Turkey* .... 101 B9 40 21N 40 47 E
Pazin, *Croatia* .... 45 C10 45 14N 13 56 E
Pazña, *Bolivia* .... 172 D4 18 36 S 66 54W
Pčinja →, *Macedonia* .... 50 E5 41 50N 21 45 E
Pe Ell, *U.S.A.* 160 D3 46 34N 123 18W
Pea →, *U.S.A.* 152 D4 31 1N 85 51W
Peabody, *U.S.A.* 151 D14 42 31N 70 56W
Peace →, *Canada* 142 B6 59 0N 111 25W
Peace →, *U.S.A.* 153 J7 26 56N 82 6W
Peace Point, *Canada* 142 B6 59 7N 112 27W
Peace River, *Canada* 142 B5 56 15N 117 18W
Peach Springs, *U.S.A.* 159 J7 35 32N 113 25W
Peachland, *Canada* 142 D5 49 47N 119 45W
Peachtree City, *U.S.A.* 152 B5 33 25N 84 35W
Peak, The, = Kinder Scout, *U.K.* 20 D6 53 24N 1 52W
Peak, The, *Ascension I.* .... 9 g 7 57 S 14 20W
Peak Charles, Nac. Park △, *Australia* .... 125 F3 32 42 S 121 10 E
Peak District Nat. Park △, *U.K.* 20 D6 53 24N 1 46W
Peak Hill, *N.S.W., Australia* .... 129 B8 32 47 S 148 11 E
Peak Hill, W. Austral., Australia .... 125 E2 25 35 S 118 43 E
Peak Ra., *Australia* .... 126 C4 22 50 S 148 20 E
Peake, *Australia* .... 128 C3 35 25 S 139 55 E
Peake Cr. →, *Australia* .... 127 D2 28 2 S 136 7 E
Peal de Becerro, *Spain* 43 H7 37 55N 3 7W
Peale, Mt., *U.S.A.* 159 G9 38 26N 109 14W
Pearblossom, *U.S.A.* 161 L9 34 30N 117 55W
Pearl →, *U.S.A.* 156 K6 39 28N 90 38W
Pearl →, *U.S.A.* 155 K10 30 11N 89 32W
Pearl and Hermes Reef, *U.S.A.* 145 F8 27 55N 175 45W
Pearl Banks, *Sri Lanka* .... 95 K4 8 45N 79 45 E
Pearl City, *U.S.A.* 154 K14 21 24N 157 59W
Pearl Harbor, *U.S.A.* 154 K14 21 21N 157 57W
Pearl River = Zhu Jiang →, *China* .... 77 F9 22 45N 113 37 E
Pearl River, *U.S.A.* 151 E10 41 4N 74 2W
Pearsall, *U.S.A.* 155 L5 28 54N 99 6W
Pearson, *U.S.A.* 155 H5 31 18N 82 53W
Peary Land, *Greenland* 10 A7 82 40N 33 0W
Pease →, *U.S.A.* 155 H5 34 12N 99 2W
Peawanuck, *Canada* 139 C11 55 15N 85 12W
Pebane, *Mozam.* .... 119 F4 17 10 S 38 8 E
Pebas, *Peru* .... 168 D3 3 10 S 71 46W
Pebble, I., Falk. Is. .... 9 f 51 20 S 59 40W
Pebble Beach, *U.S.A.* 160 J5 36 34N 121 57W
Peć, *Kosovo, Yug.* .... 50 D4 42 40N 20 17 E
Peçanha, *Brazil* .... 171 E3 18 33 S 42 34W
Pecatonica, *U.S.A.* 156 B7 42 19N 89 22W
Pecatonica →, *U.S.A.* 156 D7 42 28N 89 12W
Péccioli, *Italy* .... 44 E7 43 33N 10 43 E
Pechea, *Romania* .... 53 E12 45 36N 27 49 E
Pechenga, *Russia* .... 56 A5 69 29N 31 4 E
Pechenizhyn, *Ukraine* .... 59 H3 48 30N 24 48 E
Pechiguera, Pta., Canary Is. 9 e2 28 51N 13 53W
Pechnezhskoye Vdkhr., Ukraine .... 59 G9 50 5N 36 54 E
Pechora, *Russia* .... 56 A10 65 10N 57 11 E

Pechora →, *Russia* .... 56 A9 68 13N 54 15 E
Pechorskaya Guba, *Russia* .... 56 A9 68 40N 54 0 E
Pecica, *Romania* .... 52 D6 46 10N 21 3 E
Pecka, *Serbia, Yug.* .... 50 B3 44 18N 19 32 E
Pécora, C., *Italy* .... 46 C1 39 27N 8 23 E
Pečory, *Russia* .... 15 H22 57 48N 27 40 E
Pecos, *U.S.A.* 155 K3 31 26N 103 30W
Pecos →, *U.S.A.* 155 L3 29 42N 101 22W
Pécs, *Hungary* .... 52 D3 46 5N 18 15 E
Pedda Bellala, *India* .... 94 E4 19 4N 78 49 E
Peddapalli, *India* .... 94 E4 18 40N 79 24 E
Peddapuram, *India* .... 94 F6 17 6N 82 8 E
Pedder, L., *Australia* .... 127 G4 42 55 S 146 10 E
Peddie, S. Africa .... 117 E4 33 14 S 27 7 E
Pedernales, Dom. Rep. 165 C5 18 2N 71 44W
Pedernales, Ecuador 168 C1 0 5N 80 3W
Pedirka, *Australia* .... 127 D2 26 40 S 135 14 E
Pedra Azul, *Brazil* .... 171 E3 16 2 S 41 17W
Pedra Branca, *Brazil* .... 170 C3 7 15 S 38 58W
Pedra Grande, Recifes de, *Brazil* .... 171 E4 17 45 S 38 58W
Pedra Lume, C. Verde Is. .... 9 j 16 40N 22 52W
Pedras Negras, *Brazil* .... 173 C5 12 51 S 62 54W
Pedras Tinhosas, I.,
São Tomé & Príncipe .... 115 G6 1 22N 7 17 E
Pedreguer, *Spain* .... 41 G5 38 48N 0 3 E
Pedreiras, *Brazil* .... 170 B3 4 32 S 44 40W
Pedro Afonso, *Brazil* .... 170 C2 9 0 S 48 10W
Pedro Bay, *U.S.A.* 144 G9 59 47N 154 7W
Pedro Cays, *Jamaica* 164 C4 17 5N 77 48W
Pedro Chico, *Colombia* 168 C3 1 4N 70 25W
Pedro de Valdivia, *Chile* .... 174 A2 22 55 S 69 38W
Pedro Dorado, *Colombia* 168 C3 1 0N 70 14W
Pedro Juan Caballero, *Paraguay* .... 175 A4 22 30 S 55 40W
Pedro Muñoz, *Spain* 43 F8 39 25N 2 56W
Pedrógão Grande, *Portugal* 42 F2 39 55N 8 9W
Pee Dee →, *U.S.A.* 149 J6 33 22N 79 16W
Peebinga, *Australia* .... 128 C4 34 52 S 140 57 E
Peebles, *U.K.* 22 F5 55 40N 3 11W
Peebles, *U.S.A.* 157 F3 38 57N 83 24W
Peekskill, *U.S.A.* 151 E11 41 17N 73 55W
Peel, *U.K.* 20 C3 54 13N 4 40W
Peel →, *Australia* .... 129 A9 30 50 S 150 29 E
Peel →, *Canada* 138 B6 67 0N 135 0W
Peel Sound, *Canada* 138 A10 73 0N 96 0W
Peene →, *Germany* .... 30 A9 54 9N 13 46 E
Peera Peera Poolanna L., *Australia* .... 127 D2 26 30 S 138 0 E
Peerless Lake, *Canada* 142 B6 56 37N 114 40W
Peers, *Canada* 142 C5 53 40N 116 0W
Peery L., *Australia* .... 128 A5 30 45 S 143 35 E
Pegasus Bay, *N.Z.* .... 131 D8 43 20 S 173 10 E
Peggau, *Austria* .... 34 D8 47 12N 15 21 E
Pegnitz, *Germany* .... 31 F7 49 44N 11 31 E
Pegnitz →, *Germany* .... 31 F6 49 30N 10 59 E
Pego, *Spain* 41 G4 38 51N 0 8W
Pegu, *Burma* .... 90 G6 17 20N 96 29 E
Pegu Yoma, *Burma* .... 90 G6 17 30N 96 30 E
Pehčevo, *Macedonia* .... 50 E6 41 41N 22 55 E
Pehlivanköy, *Turkey* .... 51 E10 41 20N 26 55 E
Pehuajó, *Argentina* .... 174 D3 35 45 S 62 0W
Pei Xian = Pizhou, *China* .... 74 G9 34 44N 116 55 E
Peine, *Chile* .... 174 A2 23 45 S 68 8W
Peine, *Germany* .... 30 C6 52 19N 10 14 E
Peip'ing = Beijing, *China* .... 74 E9 39 55N 116 20 E
Peipus, L. = Chudskoye, Ozero,
Russia .... 15 G22 58 13N 27 30 E
Peissenberg, *Germany* .... 31 H7 47 48N 11 4 E
Peitz, *Germany* .... 30 D10 51 51N 14 24 E
Peixe, *Brazil* .... 171 D2 12 0 S 48 40W
Peixe →, *Brazil* .... 171 F1 21 31 S 51 58W
Peixoto de Azeredo →, *Brazil* .... 173 C6 10 6 S 55 31W
Pek →, *Serbia, Yug.* .... 50 B5 44 45N 21 29 E
Pekalongan, *Indonesia* .... 85 D3 6 53 S 109 40 E
Pekan, *Malaysia* .... 87 L4 3 30N 103 25 E
Pekan Nenas, *Malaysia* .... 87 d 1 31N 103 31 E
Pekanbaru, *Indonesia* .... 84 B2 0 30N 101 15 E
Pekang, *Taiwan* .... 77 F13 23 34N 120 18 E
Pekin, *U.S.A.* 156 D7 40 35N 89 40W
Peking = Beijing, *China* .... 74 E9 39 55N 116 20 E
Pekutatan, *Indonesia* .... 79 J17 8 25 S 114 49 E
Péla, *Guinea* 112 D3 7 37N 9 7W
Pelabuhan Kelang, *Malaysia* .... 87 L3 3 0N 101 23 E
Pelabuhan Ratu, Teluk, *Indonesia* .... 84 D3 7 5 S 106 30 E
Pelabuhanratu, *Indonesia* .... 84 D3 7 0 S 106 32 E
Pelaihari, *Indonesia* .... 84 C4 3 55 S 114 45 E
Pelat, Mt., *France* .... 29 D10 44 16N 6 42 E
Pełczyce, *Poland* .... 55 E2 53 3N 15 16 E
Peleaga, Vf., *Romania* .... 52 E7 45 22N 22 55 E
Pelechuco, *Bolivia* .... 172 C4 14 48 S 69 4W
Pelée, Mt., *Martinique* .... 164 c 14 48N 61 10W
Pelee, Pt., *Canada* 140 D3 41 54N 82 31W
Pelee I., *Canada* 140 D3 41 47N 82 40W
Pelejo, *Peru* .... 172 B2 6 10 S 75 49W
Pelekech, *Kenya* .... 118 B4 3 52N 35 8 E
Peleng, *Indonesia* .... 82 B2 1 20 S 123 30 E
Pelengo, Dem. Rep. of the Congo .... 114 C4 2 44 S 22 39 E
Pelentong, *Malaysia* .... 87 d 1 32N 103 49 E
Pelican, Ivory C. 112 D3 7 17N 6 54W
Pelham, *U.S.A.* 152 D5 31 8N 84 9W
Pelhřimov, Czech Rep. .... 34 F8 49 24N 15 12 E
Pelican, *U.S.A.* 142 B1 57 58N 136 14W
Pelican L., *Canada* 143 C8 52 28N 100 20W
Pelican Narrows, *Canada* 143 B8 55 10N 102 56W
Pelion, *U.S.A.* 152 B8 33 46N 81 15W
Pelister, Nac. Park △, *Macedonia* .... 50 F5 41 0N 21 10 E
Pelješac, *Croatia* .... 45 F14 42 55N 17 25 E
Pelkosenniemi, *Finland* .... 14 C22 67 6N 27 28 E
Pell City, *U.S.A.* 152 B3 33 35N 86 17W
Pella, *U.S.A.* 156 F6 40 46N 92 23W
Pella, S. Africa .... 116 D2 29 1 S 19 6 E
Péllla □, *Greece* .... 50 F5 40 52N 22 0 E
Péllla □, *Greece* .... 50 F6 40 52N 22 0 E
Pello, *Finland* .... 14 C21 66 47N 23 59 E
Pellworm, *Germany* .... 30 A4 54 31N 8 39 E
Pelly →, *Canada* 138 B6 62 47N 137 19W
Pelly Bay, *Canada* 139 B11 68 38N 89 50W
Peloponnese = Pelopónnisos □,
Greece .... 48 D4 37 10N 22 0 E
Pelopónnisos □, *Greece* .... 48 D4 37 10N 22 0 E
Peloritani, Monti, *Italy* .... 47 D8 38 1N 15 20 E
Pelorus →, *N.Z.* .... 131 B8 41 16 S 173 45 E
Pelorus Sd., *N.Z.* .... 131 A8 40 59 S 173 59 E
Pelotas, *Brazil* .... 175 C5 31 42 S 52 23W
Pelotas →, *Brazil* .... 175 B5 27 28 S 51 55W
Pelovo, *Bulgaria* .... 51 C8 43 26N 24 17 E
Pełplin, *Poland* .... 54 E5 53 55N 18 42 E
Pelvoux, Massif du, *France* .... 29 D10 44 52N 6 20 E
Pelym, *Russia* .... 64 B9 59 39N 63 26 E
Pelym →, *Russia* .... 64 B9 59 39N 63 26 E
Pemalang, *Indonesia* .... 85 D3 6 53 S 109 23 E
Pemanggil, Pulau, *Malaysia* .... 87 L5 2 37N 104 21 E
Pematangsiantar, *Indonesia* .... 84 B1 2 57N 99 5 E
Pemba, Mozam. .... 119 E5 12 58 S 40 30 E
Pemba, Zambia .... 119 F2 16 30 S 27 28 E
Pemba Channel, *Tanzania* .... 118 D4 5 0 S 39 37 E
Pemba I., *Tanzania* .... 118 D4 5 0 S 39 45 E
Pemberton, *Australia* .... 125 F2 34 30 S 116 0 E
Pemberton, *Canada* 142 C4 50 25N 122 50W
Pembina, *U.S.A.* 154 A6 48 58N 97 15W
Pembroke, *Canada* 140 C4 45 50N 77 7W
Pembroke, *U.K.* 21 F3 51 41N 4 55W
Pembroke, *U.S.A.* 152 D8 32 8N 81 37W

Pembroke Pines, *U.S.A.* 153 J9 26 5N 80 14W
Pembrokeshire □, U.K. 21 F3 51 52N 4 56W
Pembrokeshire Coast Nat. Park △,
U.K. 21 F2 51 50N 5 2W
Pembuang →, *Indonesia* .... 85 C4 3 24 S 112 33 E
Pen, *India* .... 94 E1 18 45N 73 5 E
Pen-y-Ghent, *U.K.* 20 C5 54 10N 2 14W
Peña, Sierra de la, *Spain* 40 C4 42 32N 0 45W
Peña de Francia, Sierra de la, *Spain* 42 A2 40 32N 6 10W
Penafiel, *Portugal* 42 D2 41 12N 8 17W
Peñafiel, *Spain* 42 D6 41 35N 4 7W
Peñaflor, *Spain* 43 H5 37 43N 5 21W
Penal, Trin. & Tob. 169 F9 10 9N 61 29W
Peñalara, *Spain* 42 E7 40 51N 3 57W
Penalva, *Brazil* .... 170 B2 3 18 S 45 10W
Penamacôr, *Portugal* 42 E3 40 10N 7 10W
Penambulai, *Indonesia* .... 83 C4 6 24 S 134 48 E
Penang = Pinang, *Malaysia* .... 87 c 5 25N 100 15 E
Penápolis, *Brazil* .... 175 A6 21 30 S 50 0W
Peñaranda de Bracamonte, *Spain* 42 E5 40 53N 5 13W
Peñarroya, *Spain* 40 E4 40 25N 0 40W
Peñarroya-Pueblonuevo, *Spain* 43 G5 38 19N 5 16W
Penarth, *U.K.* 21 F4 51 26N 3 11W
Peñas, C. de, *Spain* 42 B5 43 42N 5 52W
Peñas, G. de, *Chile* .... 176 C2 47 0 S 75 0W
Peñas, Pta., *Venezuela* 169 A5 11 17N 62 0W
Peñas de San Pedro, *Spain* 41 G3 38 44N 2 0W
Peñas del Chache, *Canary Is.* 9 e2 29 6N 13 33W
Peñausende, *Spain* 42 D5 41 17N 5 52W
Pench →, *India* .... 94 D4 21 17N 79 1 E
Pench'i = Benxi, *China* .... 75 D12 41 20N 123 48 E
Pend Oreille →, *U.S.A.* 158 B5 49 4N 117 37W
Pend Oreille, L., *U.S.A.* 158 C5 48 10N 116 21W
Pendálofon, *Greece* .... 50 F5 40 14N 21 12 E
Pendé →, *C.A.R.* .... 114 A3 7 55N 16 36 E
Pendembu, Eastern, S. Leone 112 D2 8 10N 10 42W
Pendembu, Northern, S. Leone 112 D2 9 7N 11 14W
Pendências, *Brazil* .... 170 C4 5 15 S 36 43W
Pender B., *Australia* .... 124 C3 16 45 S 122 42 E
Pendik, *Turkey* .... 51 F13 40 53N 29 13 E
Pendjari →, *Benin* .... 113 C5 11 55N 0 50 E
Pendjari, Parc Nat. de la △, *Benin* .... 113 C5 11 15N 1 32 E
Pendleton, Ind., U.S.A. 157 E11 40 0N 85 45W
Pendleton, Oreg., U.S.A. 158 D4 45 40N 118 47W
Pendra, *India* .... 93 H9 22 46N 81 57 E
Pendzhikent, *Tajikistan* .... 65 D3 39 29N 67 37 E
Peneda-Gerês, Parque Nac. △,
Portugal 42 D2 41 57N 8 15W
Penedo, *Brazil* .... 170 D4 10 15 S 36 36W
Penedono, *Portugal* 42 D3 41 0N 7 23W
Penetanguishene, *Canada* 140 D4 44 50N 79 55W
Penfield, *U.S.A.* 150 E6 41 13N 78 35W
Peng Chau, *China* .... 69 G11 22 17N 114 2 E
Pengalengan, *Indonesia* .... 85 D3 7 9 S 107 30 E
Penganga →, *India* .... 94 E4 19 53 S 79 9 E
Penge, Kasai-Or., Dem. Rep. of
the Congo .... 118 D1 5 30 S 24 33 E
Penge, Sud-Kivu, Dem. Rep. of
the Congo .... 118 C2 4 27 S 28 25 E
P'enghu Ch'üntou, *Taiwan* .... 77 F12 23 34N 119 30 E
Penglai, *China* .... 75 F11 37 48N 120 42 E
Pengshan, *China* .... 76 B4 30 14N 103 58 E
Pengshui, *China* .... 76 C7 29 17N 108 12 E
Penguin, *Australia* .... 127 G4 41 8 S 146 6 E
Pengxi, *China* .... 76 B5 30 44N 105 45 E
Pengze, *China* .... 77 C11 29 52N 116 32 E
Penhalonga, *Zimbabwe* .... 119 F3 18 52 S 32 40 E
Peniche, *Portugal* 43 F1 39 19N 9 22W
Penicuik, *U.K.* 22 F5 55 50N 3 13W
Penida, Nusa, *Indonesia* .... 85 d 8 45 S 115 30 E
Penines, Alpes = Pennine, Alpi,
Italy .... 31 J3 46 4N 7 30 E
Peninsular Malaysia □, *Malaysia* .... 87 L4 4 0N 102 0 E
Peñíscola, *Spain* .... 40 E5 40 22N 0 24 E
Penitente, Serra do, *Brazil* .... 170 C2 8 45 S 46 20W
Penkridge, *U.K.* 20 E5 52 44N 2 6W
Penmarch, *France* 26 E2 47 49N 4 21W
Penmarch, Pte. de, *France* 26 E2 47 48N 4 22W
Penn Hills, *U.S.A.* 150 F5 40 28N 79 52W
Penn Yan, *U.S.A.* 150 D7 42 40N 77 3W
Penna, Punta della, *Italy* .... 45 F11 42 10N 14 43 E
Pennant, *Canada* 143 C7 50 32N 108 14W
Penne, *Italy* .... 45 F10 42 27N 13 55 E
Penner →, *India* .... 95 G5 14 35N 80 10 E
Penneshaw, *Australia* .... 128 C2 35 44 S 137 56 E
Pennine, Alpi, Alps .... 31 J3 46 4N 7 30 E
Pennines, *U.K.* 20 C5 54 45N 2 27W
Pennington →, *Nigeria* .... 113 E6 4 45N 5 38 E
Pennino, Mte., *Italy* .... 45 E9 43 6N 12 55 E
Pennsburg, *U.S.A.* 151 F9 40 23N 75 29W
Pennsylvania □, *U.S.A.* 148 E7 40 45N 77 30W
Pennville, *U.S.A.* 157 D11 40 30N 85 9W
Penny, *Canada* 142 C4 53 51N 121 20W
Peno, *Russia* .... 58 D7 57 2N 32 49 E
Penobscot →, *U.S.A.* 149 C11 44 30N 68 48W
Penobscot B., *U.S.A.* 149 C11 44 35N 68 50W
Penola, *Australia* .... 128 C4 37 25 S 140 48 E
Penong, *Australia* .... 125 F5 31 56 S 133 1 E
Penonomé, *Panama* 164 E3 8 31N 80 21W
Penot, Mt., *Vanuatu* .... 133 F5 16 20 S 167 31 E
Penrith, *Australia* .... 129 B9 33 43 S 150 38 E
Penrith, *U.K.* 20 C5 54 40N 2 45W
Penryn, *U.K.* 21 G2 50 9N 5 7W
Pensacola, *U.S.A.* 153 E2 30 25N 87 13W
Pensacola Bay, *U.S.A.* 153 E2 30 25N 87 1W
Pensacola Mts., *Antarctica* .... 7 E1 84 0 S 40 0W
Pense, *Canada* 143 C8 50 25N 104 59W
Penshurst, *Australia* .... 128 D5 37 49 S 142 20 E
Pensiangan, *Malaysia* .... 85 B5 4 33N 116 19 E
Pentecôte = Pentecôte, *Vanuatu* .... 133 E6 15 42 S 168 10 E
Pentecoste, *Brazil* .... 170 B4 3 48 S 39 17W
Pentecôte, *Vanuatu* .... 133 E6 15 42 S 168 10 E
Penticton, *Canada* 142 D5 49 30N 119 38W
Pentland, *Australia* .... 126 C4 20 32 S 145 25 E
Pentland Firth, *U.K.* 22 C5 58 43N 3 10W
Pentland Hills, *U.K.* 22 F5 55 48N 3 25W
Pentland Hills Forest Park △, U.K. 22 F5 55 50N 3 25W
Penukonda, *India* .... 95 G3 14 5N 77 38 E
Penza, *Russia* .... 60 D7 53 15N 45 5 E
Penzance, *U.K.* 21 G2 50 7N 5 33W
Penzberg, *Germany* .... 31 H7 47 45N 11 23 E
Penzhino, *Russia* .... 67 C17 63 30N 167 55 E
Penzhinskaya Guba, *Russia* .... 67 C17 61 30N 163 0 E
Penzhou, *China* .... 76 B4 31 4N 103 32 E
Penzlin, *Germany* .... 30 B9 53 30N 13 6 E
Peoria, Ariz., U.S.A. 159 K7 33 35N 112 14W
Peoria, Ill., U.S.A. 156 D7 40 42N 89 36W
Peoria Heights, *U.S.A.* 156 D7 40 45N 89 35W
Peotone, *U.S.A.* 157 C9 41 20N 87 48W
Pepacton Reservoir, *U.S.A.* 151 D10 42 5N 74 58W
Pepani →, S. Africa .... 116 D3 25 49 S 22 47 E
Pepeekeo, *U.S.A.* 145 D6 19 51N 155 6W
Pepel, S. Leone 112 D2 8 40N 13 5W
Peqin, *Albania* .... 50 E3 41 3N 19 44 E
Perabumulih, *Indonesia* .... 84 C2 3 27 S 104 15 E
Perak →, *Malaysia* .... 87 K3 4 0N 100 1 E
Perak □, *Malaysia* .... 84 A2 5 10N 100 50 E
Perakhóra, *Greece* .... 48 C4 38 2N 22 56 E
Peralada, *Spain* .... 40 C8 42 6N 3 0 E
Perales de Alfambra, *Spain* 40 E4 40 38N 1 0W
Perales del Puerto, *Spain* 42 E4 40 10N 6 40W
Pérama, Kérkira, *Greece* .... 38 B9 39 34N 19 54 E

Pérama, Kríti, Greece ... 39 E5 35 20N 24 40 E
Perancak, Indonesia ... 79 J17 8 24 S 114 37 E
Peräpohjola, Finland ... 14 C22 66 16N 26 10 E
Perast, Montenegro, Yug. ... 50 D2 42 31N 18 47 E
Peratiá, Greece ... 39 B2 38 49N 20 45 E
Percé, Canada ... 141 C7 48 31N 64 13W
Perche, France ... 26 D8 48 31N 1 1 E
Perche, Collines du, France ... 25 B4 48 30N 0 40 E
Perche, Parc Naturel Régional du □, France ... 26 D7 48 24N 0 46 E
Perchtoldsdorf, Austria ... 35 C9 48 7N 16 16 E
Percival Lakes, Australia ... 124 D4 21 25 S 125 0 E
Percy, France ... 26 D5 48 55N 1 11W
Percy, U.S.A. ... 156 F7 38 5N 89 41W
Percy Is., Australia ... 126 C5 21 39 S 150 16 E
Perdido →, Argentina ... 176 B3 42 55 S 67 0W
Perdido, Mte., Spain ... 40 C5 42 40N 0 5 E
Perdu, Mt. = Perdido, Mte., Spain ... 40 C5 42 40N 0 5 E
Pereira, Colombia ... 168 C2 4 49N 75 43W
Perelazovskiy, Russia ... 61 F6 49 8N 42 35 E
Peremul Par, India ... 95 J1 11 10N 72 4 E
Perené →, Peru ... 172 C3 11 9 S 74 14W
Perenjori, Australia ... 125 E2 29 26 S 116 16 E
Perescina, Moldova ... 53 C13 47 16N 28 46 E
Pereslavl-Zalesskiy, Russia ... 58 D10 56 45N 38 50 E
Peretu, Romania ... 53 F10 44 3N 25 5 E
Perevolotskiy, Russia ... 64 F5 51 51N 54 12 E
Pereyaslav-Khmelnytskyy, Ukraine ... 59 G6 50 3N 31 28 E
Pérez, I., Mexico ... 163 C7 22 24N 89 42W
Perg, Austria ... 34 C7 48 15N 14 38 E
Pergamino, Argentina ... 174 C3 33 52 S 60 30W
Pergau →, Malaysia ... 87 K3 5 23N 102 2 E
Pérgine Valsugana, Italy ... 45 B8 46 4N 11 14 E
Pérgola, Italy ... 45 E9 43 34N 12 50 E
Perham, U.S.A. ... 154 B7 46 36N 95 34W
Perhentian, Kepulauan, Malaysia ... 87 K4 5 54N 102 42 E
Periam, Romania ... 52 D5 46 2N 20 52 E
Péribonca →, Canada ... 141 C5 48 45N 72 5W
Péribonca, L., Canada ... 141 B5 50 1N 71 10W
Perico, Argentina ... 174 A2 24 20 S 65 5W
Pericos, Mexico ... 162 B3 25 3N 107 42W
Périers, France ... 26 C5 49 11N 1 25W
Périgord, France ... 28 D4 45 0N 0 40 E
Périgord-Limousin, Parc Naturel Régional □, France ... 28 C4 45 40N 0 50 E
Périgueux, France ... 28 C4 45 10N 0 42 E
Perijá, Parque Nac. △, Venezuela ... 165 E5 9 30N 72 55W
Perijá, Sierra de, Colombia ... 168 B3 9 30N 73 3W
Perisher Valley, Australia ... 129 D8 36 27 S 148 25 E
Peristéra, Greece ... 48 B5 39 15N 23 58 E
Peristerona →, Cyprus ... 39 E9 35 8N 33 5 E
Perito Moreno, Argentina ... 176 C2 46 36 S 70 56W
Peritoró, Brazil ... 170 B3 4 20 S 44 18W
Perivol = Dragovishtitsa, Bulgaria ... 50 D6 42 22N 22 39 E
Periyakulam, India ... 95 J3 10 5N 77 30 E
Periyar →, India ... 95 J3 10 15N 76 10 E
Periyar, L., India ... 95 K3 9 25N 77 10 E
Perkasie, U.S.A. ... 151 F9 40 22N 75 18W
Perković, Croatia ... 45 E13 43 41N 16 10 E
Perlas, Arch. de las, Panama ... 164 E4 8 41N 79 7W
Perlas, Punta de, Nic. ... 164 D3 12 30N 83 30W
Perleberg, Germany ... 30 B7 53 5N 11 52 E
Perlez, Serbia, Yug. ... 52 E5 45 11N 20 22 E
Perlis □, Malaysia ... 84 A2 6 30N 100 15 E
Perm, Russia ... 64 C6 58 0N 56 10 E
Përmet, Albania ... 50 F4 40 15N 20 21 E
Pernambuco = Recife, Brazil ... 170 C5 8 0 S 35 0W
Pernambuco □, Brazil ... 170 C4 8 0 S 37 0W
Pernatty Lagoon, Australia ... 128 A2 31 30 S 137 12 E
Pernik, Bulgaria ... 50 D7 42 35N 23 2 E
Peron Is., Australia ... 124 B5 13 9 S 130 4 E
Peron Pen., Australia ... 125 E1 26 0 S 113 10 E
Péronne, France ... 27 C9 49 55N 2 57 E
Perosa Argentina, Italy ... 44 D4 44 58N 7 10 E
Perow, Canada ... 142 C3 54 35N 126 10W
Perpendicular Pt., Australia ... 127 E5 31 37 S 152 52 E
Perpignan, France ... 28 F6 42 42N 2 53 E
Perrégaux = Mohammadia, Algeria ... 111 A5 35 33N 0 3 E
Perrine, U.S.A. ... 153 K9 25 36N 80 21W
Perros-Guirec, France ... 26 D3 48 49N 3 28W
Perry, Fla., U.S.A. ... 152 E6 30 7N 83 35W
Perry, Ga., U.S.A. ... 152 C6 32 28N 83 44W
Perry, Iowa, U.S.A. ... 156 C2 41 51N 94 6W
Perry, Mich., U.S.A. ... 157 B12 42 50N 84 13W
Perry, Mo., U.S.A. ... 156 E5 39 26N 91 40W
Perry, Okla., U.S.A. ... 155 G6 36 17N 97 14W
Perrysburg, U.S.A. ... 157 C13 41 34N 83 38W
Perryton, U.S.A. ... 155 G4 36 24N 100 48W
Perryville, Alaska, U.S.A. ... 144 J8 55 55N 159 9W
Perryville, Mo., U.S.A. ... 155 G10 37 43N 89 52W
Persan, France ... 27 C9 49 9N 2 16 E
Persberg, Sweden ... 16 E8 59 47N 14 15 E
Perşembe, Turkey ... 100 B7 41 5N 37 46 E
Persepolis, Iran ... 97 D7 29 55N 52 50 E
Perseverancia, Bolivia ... 173 C5 14 44 S 62 48W
Pershotravensk, Ukraine ... 59 G4 50 13N 27 40 E
Persia = Iran ■, Asia ... 97 C7 33 0N 53 0 E
Persian Gulf = Gulf, The, Asia ... 97 E6 27 0N 50 0 E
Perstorp, Sweden ... 17 H7 56 10N 13 25 E
Pertek, Turkey ... 101 C8 38 51N 39 19 E
Perth, Australia ... 125 F2 31 57 S 115 52 E
Perth, Canada ... 140 D4 44 55N 76 15W
Perth, U.K. ... 22 E5 56 24N 3 26W
Perth & Kinross □, U.K. ... 22 E5 56 45N 3 55W
Perth Amboy, U.S.A. ... 151 F10 40 31N 74 16W
Perth-Andover, Canada ... 141 C6 46 44N 67 42W
Pertuis, France ... 29 E9 43 42N 5 30 E
Pertusato, C., France ... 29 G13 41 21N 9 11 E
Peru, Ill., U.S.A. ... 156 C7 41 20N 89 8W
Peru, Ind., U.S.A. ... 157 D10 40 45N 86 4W
Peru, N.Y., U.S.A. ... 151 B11 44 35N 73 32W
Peru ■, S. Amer. ... 168 D2 4 0 S 75 0W
Peru Basin, Pac. Oc. ... 135 J18 20 0 S 95 0W
Peru-Chile Trench, Pac. Oc. ... 135 K20 20 0 S 72 0W
Perúgia, Italy ... 45 E9 43 7N 12 23 E
Perušić, Croatia ... 45 D12 44 40N 15 22 E
Pervomaysk, Russia ... 60 C6 54 56N 43 58 E
Pervomaysk, Ukraine ... 59 H6 48 10N 30 46 E
Pervomayskiy, Russia ... 64 F5 51 32N 55 2 E
Pervouralsk, Russia ... 64 C7 56 59N 59 59 E
Pésaro, Italy ... 45 E9 43 54N 12 55 E
Pescadores = P'enghu Ch'üntou, Taiwan ... 77 F12 23 30N 119 30 E
Pescara, Italy ... 45 F11 42 28N 14 13 E
Pescara →, Italy ... 45 F11 42 28N 14 13 E
Peschanokopskoye, Russia ... 61 G5 46 14N 41 4 E
Péscia, Italy ... 44 E7 43 54N 10 41 E
Pescina, Italy ... 45 F10 42 2N 13 39 E
Peseux, Switz. ... 32 C3 46 59N 6 53 E
Peshawar, Pakistan ... 91 B3 34 2N 71 37 E
Peshkopi, Albania ... 50 E4 41 41N 20 25 E
Peshtera, Bulgaria ... 51 D8 42 2N 24 18 E
Peshtigo, U.S.A. ... 148 C2 45 4N 87 46W
Peski, Russia ... 60 E6 51 14N 42 29 E
Peskovka, Russia ... 64 B4 59 4N 52 22 E
Pêso da Régua, Portugal ... 42 D3 41 10N 7 47W
Pesqueira, Brazil ... 170 C4 8 20 S 36 42W
Pessac, France ... 28 D3 44 48N 0 37W
Pessádhes, Greece ... 39 C2 38 7N 20 35 E
Pest □, Hungary ... 52 C4 47 29N 19 5 E
Pestovo, Russia ... 58 C8 58 33N 35 42 E
Pestravka, Russia ... 60 D9 52 28N 49 57 E
Péta, Greece ... 48 B3 39 10N 21 2 E

Petah Tiqwa, Israel ... 103 C3 32 6N 34 53 E
Petalás, Nisís, Greece ... 39 C3 38 25N 21 5 E
Petalídhion, Greece ... 48 E3 36 57N 21 55 E
Petaling Jaya, Malaysia ... 87 L3 3 4N 101 42 E
Petaloudhes, Greece ... 38 E12 36 18N 28 5 E
Petaluma, U.S.A. ... 160 G4 38 14N 122 39W
Pétange, Lux. ... 24 E5 49 33N 5 55 E
Petaro, Pakistan ... 92 G3 25 31N 68 18 E
Petatlán, Mexico ... 162 D4 17 31N 101 16W
Petawawa, Canada ... 140 C4 45 54N 77 17W
Petén Itzá, L., Guatemala ... 164 C2 16 58N 89 50W
Peter I., Br. Virgin Is. ... 165 e 18 22N 64 35W
Peter I.s Øy, Antarctica ... 7 C16 69 0 S 91 0W
Peter Pond L., Canada ... 143 B7 55 55N 108 44W
Peterbell, Canada ... 140 C3 48 36N 83 21W
Peterborough, Australia ... 128 B3 32 58 S 138 51 E
Peterborough, Canada ... 140 D4 44 20N 78 20W
Peterborough, U.K. ... 21 E7 52 35N 0 15W
Peterborough, U.S.A. ... 151 D13 42 53N 71 57W
Peterborough □, U.K. ... 21 E7 52 35N 0 15W
Peterculter, U.K. ... 22 D6 57 6N 2 16W
Peterhead, U.K. ... 22 D7 57 31N 1 48W
Peterlee, U.K. ... 20 C6 54 47N 1 20W
Petermann Bjerg, Greenland ... 10 C8 73 7N 28 25W
Petermann Gletscher, Greenland ... 10 A4 80 30N 60 0W
Petermann Ranges, Australia ... 124 E5 26 0 S 130 30 E
Peter's Mine, Guyana ... 169 B6 6 14N 59 20W
Petersburg, Alaska, U.S.A. ... 144 H14 56 48N 132 58W
Petersburg, Ill., U.S.A. ... 156 D7 40 1N 89 51W
Petersburg, Ind., U.S.A. ... 157 F9 38 30N 87 17W
Petersburg, Mich., U.S.A. ... 157 C13 41 54N 83 43W
Petersburg, Pa., U.S.A. ... 150 F6 40 34N 78 3W
Petersburg, Va., U.S.A. ... 148 G7 37 14N 77 24W
Petersburg, W. Va., U.S.A. ... 148 F6 39 1N 79 5W
Petersfield, U.K. ... 21 F7 51 1N 0 56W
Petershagen, Germany ... 30 C4 52 23N 8 58 E
Petília Policastro, Italy ... 47 C9 39 7N 16 48 E
Petit Batanga, Cameroon ... 114 B1 3 15N 9 54 E
Petit-Canal, Guadeloupe ... 164 b 16 25N 61 31W
Petit Goâve, Haiti ... 165 C5 18 27N 72 51W
Petit Jardin, Canada ... 141 C8 48 28N 59 14W
Petit Lac Manicouagan, Canada ... 141 B6 51 25N 67 40W
Petit-Mécatina →, Canada ... 141 B8 50 40N 59 30W
Petit-Mécatina, Î. du, Canada ... 141 B8 50 30N 59 25W
Petit Piton, St. Lucia ... 165 f 13 51N 61 5W
Petit Saguenay, Canada ... 141 C5 48 15N 70 4W
Petit Saint Bernard, Col du, Italy ... 29 C10 45 40N 6 52 E
Petitcodiac, Canada ... 141 C6 45 57N 65 11W
Petite Baleine →, Canada ... 140 A4 56 0N 76 45W
Petite Terre, Iles de la, Guadeloupe ... 164 b 16 13N 61 9W
Petitot →, Canada ... 142 A4 60 14N 123 29W
Petitsikapau L., Canada ... 141 B6 54 37N 66 25W
Petlad, India ... 92 H5 22 30N 72 45 E
Peto, Mexico ... 163 C7 20 10N 88 53W
Petone, N.Z. ... 130 H3 41 13 S 174 53 E
Petorca, Chile ... 174 C1 32 15 S 70 56W
Petoskey, U.S.A. ... 148 C3 45 22N 84 57W
Petra, Jordan ... 103 E4 30 20N 35 22 E
Petra, Spain ... 38 B4 39 37N 3 6 E
Petra, Ostrova, Russia ... 6 B13 76 15N 118 30 E
Petra Velikogo, Zaliv, Russia ... 70 C6 42 40N 132 0 E
Petrel = Petrer, Spain ... 41 G4 38 30N 0 46W
Petrella, Monte, Italy ... 46 A6 41 18N 13 40 E
Petrer, Spain ... 41 G4 38 30N 0 46W
Petreto-Bicchisano, France ... 29 G12 41 47N 8 58 E
Petrich, Bulgaria ... 50 E7 41 24N 23 13 E
Petrified Forest Nat. Park △, U.S.A. ... 159 J9 35 0N 109 30W
Petrijanec, Croatia ... 45 B13 46 23N 16 17 E
Petrikov = Pyetrikaw, Belarus ... 59 F5 52 11N 28 29 E
Petrila, Romania ... 53 E8 45 29N 23 29 E
Petrinja, Croatia ... 45 C13 45 28N 16 18 E
Petrodvorets, Russia ... 58 C5 59 52N 29 54 E
Petrograd = Sankt-Peterburg, Russia ... 58 C6 59 55N 30 20 E
Petrolândia, Brazil ... 170 D4 9 5 S 38 20W
Petrolia, Canada ... 140 D3 42 54N 82 9W
Petrolina, Brazil ... 170 C3 9 24 S 40 30W
Petropavl, Kazakhstan ... 66 D7 54 53N 69 13 E
Petropavlovsk = Petropavl, Kazakhstan ... 66 D7 54 53N 69 13 E
Petropavlovsk-Kamchatskiy, Russia ... 67 D16 53 3N 158 43 E
Petropavlovskiy = Akhtubinsk, Russia ... 61 F8 48 13N 46 7 E
Petrópolis, Brazil ... 171 F3 22 33 S 43 9W
Petroşani, Romania ... 53 E8 45 28N 23 20 E
Petrovac, Montenegro, Yug. ... 50 D3 42 13N 18 57 E
Petrovac, Serbia, Yug. ... 50 B5 44 22N 21 26 E
Petrovaradin, Serbia, Yug. ... 52 E4 45 16N 19 55 E
Petrovsk, Russia ... 60 D7 52 22N 45 19 E
Petrovsk-Zabaykalskiy, Russia ... 67 D11 51 20N 108 55 E
Petrovskaya, Russia ... 59 K9 45 25N 37 58 E
Petrovskoye = Svetlograd, Russia ... 61 H6 45 25N 42 58 E
Petrovskoye, Russia ... 64 C6 53 37N 56 23 E
Petrozavodsk, Russia ... 58 B8 61 41N 34 20 E
Petrus Steyn, S. Africa ... 117 D4 27 38 S 28 8 E
Petrusburg, S. Africa ... 116 D4 29 4 S 25 26 E
Petukhovo, Russia ... 66 D7 54 53N 69 13 E
Peumo, Chile ... 174 C1 34 21 S 71 12W
Peureulak, Indonesia ... 84 B1 4 48N 97 45 E
Peusangan →, Indonesia ... 84 A1 5 16N 96 51 E
Pevek, Russia ... 67 C18 69 41N 171 19 E
Pevely, U.S.A. ... 156 F6 38 17N 90 24W
Peveragno, Italy ... 44 D4 44 20N 7 37 E
Peyrehorade, France ... 28 E2 43 34N 1 7W
Peyruis, France ... 29 D9 44 1N 5 56 E
Pézenas, France ... 28 E7 43 28N 3 24 E
Pezinok, Slovak Rep. ... 35 C10 48 17N 17 17 E
Pfaffenhofen, Germany ... 31 G7 48 31N 11 31 E
Pfäffikon, Schwyz, Switz. ... 33 B7 47 13N 8 46 E
Pfäffikon, Zürich, Switz. ... 33 B7 47 22N 8 47 E
Pfälzerwald, Naturpark □, Germany ... 31 F5 49 18N 9 55 E
Pfarrkirchen, Germany ... 31 G8 48 25N 12 56 E
Pfeffenhausen, Germany ... 31 G7 48 39N 11 58 E
Pforzheim, Germany ... 31 G5 48 52N 8 41 E
Pfullendorf, Germany ... 31 H5 47 55N 9 15 E
Pfungstadt, Germany ... 31 F4 49 48N 8 35 E
Pha Taem Nat. Park △, Thailand ... 86 E5 15 35N 105 30 E
Phaistós, Greece ... 39 E5 35 2N 24 50 E
Phala, Botswana ... 116 C4 23 45 S 26 50 E
Phalera = Phulera, India ... 92 F6 26 52N 75 16 E
Phalodi, India ... 92 F5 27 12N 72 24 E
Phalsbourg, France ... 27 D14 48 46N 7 15 E
Phaltan, India ... 94 F2 17 59N 74 26 E
Phan, Thailand ... 87 b 9 32N 99 41 E
Phan, Thailand ... 86 C2 19 28N 99 43 E
Phan Rang, Vietnam ... 87 G7 11 34N 109 0 E
Phan Ri = Hoa Da, Vietnam ... 87 G7 11 16N 108 40 E
Phan Thiet, Vietnam ... 87 G7 11 1N 108 9 E
Phanae, Greece ... 49 C7 38 8N 25 57 E
Phanat Nikhom, Thailand ... 86 F3 13 27N 101 11 E
Phangan, Ko, Thailand ... 87 H3 9 45N 100 0 E
Phangnga, Thailand ... 87 H2 8 28N 98 30 E
Phangnga, Ao, Thailand ... 87 a 8 16N 98 33 E
Phanom Sarakham, Thailand ... 86 F3 13 45N 101 21 E
Phaphund, India ... 93 F8 26 36N 79 28 E
Pharenda, India ... 93 F10 27 5N 83 17 E
Pharr, U.S.A. ... 155 M5 26 12N 98 11W
Phatthalung, Thailand ... 87 J3 7 39N 100 6 E
Phayao, Thailand ... 86 C2 19 11N 99 55 E
Phelps, U.S.A. ... 150 D7 42 58N 77 3W
Phelps L., Canada ... 143 B8 59 15N 103 15W
Phenix City, U.S.A. ... 149 J3 32 28N 85 0W
Phet Buri, Thailand ... 86 F2 13 1N 99 55 E

Phetchabun, Thailand ... 86 D3 16 25N 101 8 E
Phetchabun, Thiu Khao, Thailand ... 86 E3 16 0N 101 20 E
Phetchaburi = Phet Buri, Thailand ... 86 F2 13 1N 99 55 E
Phi Phi, Ko, Thailand ... 87 J2 7 45N 98 46 E
Phiafay, Laos ... 86 E6 14 48N 106 0 E
Phibun Mangsahan, Thailand ... 86 E5 15 14N 105 14 E
Phichai, Thailand ... 86 D3 17 22N 100 10 E
Phichit, Thailand ... 86 D3 16 26N 100 22 E
Philadelphia, Miss., U.S.A. ... 155 J10 32 46N 89 7W
Philadelphia, N.Y., U.S.A. ... 151 B9 44 9N 75 43W
Philadelphia, Pa., U.S.A. ... 151 G9 39 57N 75 10W
Philip, U.S.A. ... 154 C4 44 2N 101 40W
Philip Smith Mts., U.S.A. ... 144 C11 68 0N 148 0W
Philippeville = Skikda, Algeria ... 111 A6 36 50N 6 58 E
Philippeville, Belgium ... 24 D4 50 12N 4 33 E
Philippi, Greece ... 51 E8 41 1N 24 16 E
Philippi, U.S.A. ... 148 F5 39 9N 80 3W
Philippi L., Australia ... 126 C2 24 20 S 138 55 E
Philippine Sea, Pac. Oc. ... 62 H16 18 0N 125 0 E
Philippines ■, Asia ... 80 E4 12 0N 123 0 E
Philippolis, S. Africa ... 116 E4 30 15 S 25 16 E
Philippopolis = Plovdiv, Bulgaria ... 51 A11 45 7N 25 0 E
Philipsburg, Canada ... 151 A11 45 2N 73 5W
Philipsburg, Mont., U.S.A. ... 158 C7 46 20N 113 18W
Philipsburg, Pa., U.S.A. ... 150 F6 40 54N 78 13W
Philipstown = Daingean, Ireland ... 23 C4 53 18N 7 17W
Philipstown, S. Africa ... 116 E3 30 28 S 24 30 E
Philip I., Australia ... 129 E6 38 30 S 145 12 E
Phillips, U.S.A. ... 154 C9 45 42N 90 24W
Phillipsburg, Ga., U.S.A. ... 151 B9 31 25N 83 30W
Phillipsburg, Kans., U.S.A. ... 154 F5 39 45N 99 19W
Phillipsburg, N.J., U.S.A. ... 151 F9 40 42N 75 12W
Philmont, U.S.A. ... 151 D11 42 15N 73 39W
Philomath, Ga., U.S.A. ... 152 B7 33 44N 82 59W
Philomath, Oreg., U.S.A. ... 158 D2 44 32N 123 22W
Phimai, Thailand ... 86 E4 15 13N 102 30 E
Phitsanulok, Thailand ... 86 D3 16 50N 100 12 E
Phnom Dangrek, Thailand ... 78 B2 14 20N 104 0 E
Phnom Penh, Cambodia ... 87 G5 11 33N 104 55 E
Phnom Penh = Phnom Penh, Cambodia ... 87 G5 11 33N 104 55 E
Phoenicia, U.S.A. ... 151 D10 42 5N 74 14W
Phoenix, Mauritius ... 121 d 20 17 S 57 30 E
Phoenix, Ariz., U.S.A. ... 159 K7 33 27N 112 4W
Phoenix, N.Y., U.S.A. ... 151 C8 43 14N 76 18W
Phoenix Is., Kiribati ... 134 H10 3 30 S 172 0W
Phoenixville, U.S.A. ... 151 F9 40 8N 75 31W
Phon, Thailand ... 86 E4 15 49N 102 36 E
Phon Tiou, Laos ... 86 D5 17 53N 104 37 E
Phong →, Thailand ... 86 D4 16 23N 102 56 E
Phong Saly, Laos ... 76 G4 21 42N 102 9 E
Phong Tho, Vietnam ... 86 A4 22 32N 103 21 E
Phonhong, Laos ... 86 D4 18 30N 102 25 E
Phonum, Thailand ... 87 H2 8 49N 98 48 E
Phosphate Hill, Australia ... 126 C2 21 53 S 139 58 E
Photharam, Thailand ... 86 F2 13 41N 99 51 E
Phra Nakhon Si Ayutthaya, Thailand ... 86 E3 14 25N 100 30 E
Phra Thong, Ko, Thailand ... 87 H2 9 5N 98 17 E
Phrae, Thailand ... 86 C3 18 7N 100 9 E
Phrom Phiram, Thailand ... 86 D3 17 2N 100 12 E
Phrygia, Turkey ... 100 C4 38 40N 30 0 E
Phu Chong-Na Yoi Nat. Park △, Thailand ... 86 E5 14 25N 105 30 E
Phu Dien, Vietnam ... 86 C5 18 58N 105 31 E
Phu Hin Rang Kla Nat. Park △, Thailand ... 86 D3 17 0N 100 59 E
Phu Loi, Laos ... 86 B4 20 14N 103 14 E
Phu Luang Nat. Park △, Thailand ... 86 D3 17 15N 101 29 E
Phu Ly, Vietnam ... 76 G5 20 35N 105 50 E
Phu Phan Nat. Park △, Thailand ... 86 D4 17 0N 103 56 E
Phu Quoc, Dao, Vietnam ... 87 G4 10 20N 104 0 E
Phu Tho, Vietnam ... 76 G5 21 24N 105 13 E
Phuc Yen, Vietnam ... 76 G5 21 16N 105 45 E
Phuket, Thailand ... 87 a 7 53N 98 24 E
Phuket, Ko, Thailand ... 87 a 8 0N 98 22 E
Phul, India ... 92 D6 30 19N 75 14 E
Phulad, India ... 92 G5 25 38N 73 49 E
Phulbani, India ... 94 D7 20 28N 84 14 E
Phulbari, India ... 93 G13 25 55N 90 2 E
Phulchari, Bangla. ... 90 C2 25 11N 89 37 E
Phulera, India ... 92 F6 26 52N 75 16 E
Phulpur, India ... 93 G10 25 31N 82 49 E
Phun Phin, Thailand ... 87 H2 9 7N 99 12 E
Piacá, Brazil ... 170 C2 7 42 S 47 18W
Piacenza, Italy ... 44 C6 45 1N 9 40 E
Piaçabuçu, Brazil ... 170 D4 10 24 S 36 25W
Piai, Tanjung, Malaysia ... 87 d 1 17N 103 30 E
Piako →, N.Z. ... 130 D4 37 12 S 175 30 E
Pian Cr. →, Australia ... 127 E4 30 2 S 148 12 E
Pian-Upe Game Reserve △, Uganda ... 118 B3 1 44N 34 20 E
Piana, France ... 29 F12 42 15N 8 34 E
Pianella, Italy ... 45 F11 42 24N 14 2 E
Piangil, Australia ... 128 C3 35 5 S 143 20 E
Pianosa, Puglia, Italy ... 45 F12 42 12N 15 44 E
Pianosa, Toscana, Italy ... 44 F7 42 35N 10 5 E
Piapot, Canada ... 143 D7 49 59N 109 8W
Pias, Portugal ... 43 G3 38 1N 7 29W
Piaseczno, Poland ... 55 F7 52 5N 21 2 E
Piaski, Poland ... 55 F7 52 12N 20 48 E
Piatã, Brazil ... 171 D3 13 9 S 41 48W
Piatra, Romania ... 53 G10 43 51N 25 9 E
Piatra Craiului, Parcul Nat. △, Romania ... 53 E10 45 30N 25 12 E
Piatra Neamţ, Romania ... 53 D11 46 56N 26 21 E
Piatra Olt, Romania ... 53 F9 44 22N 24 16 E
Piauí □, Brazil ... 170 C3 7 0 S 43 0W
Piauí →, Brazil ... 170 C3 6 38 S 42 42W
Piave →, Italy ... 45 C9 45 32N 12 44 E
Piazza Ármerina, Italy ... 47 E7 37 21N 14 20 E
Pibor →, Sudan ... 107 F3 7 35N 33 0 E
Pibor Post, Sudan ... 107 F3 6 47N 33 3 E
Pica, Chile ... 172 E4 20 35 S 69 25W
Picardie, France ... 27 C10 49 50N 3 0 E
Picardie, Plaine de, France ... 27 C9 50 0N 2 0 E
Picardy = Picardie, France ... 27 C10 49 50N 3 0 E
Picayune, U.S.A. ... 155 K10 30 32N 89 41W
Picerno, Italy ... 47 B8 40 38N 15 38 E
Pichhor, India ... 93 G8 25 58N 78 20 E
Pichilemu, Chile ... 174 C1 34 22 S 72 0W
Pichincha □, Ecuador ... 168 D2 0 10 S 78 40W
Pichor, India ... 92 G8 25 11N 78 11 E
Pickerel L., Canada ... 140 C1 48 40N 91 25W
Pickering, U.K. ... 20 C7 54 15N 0 46W
Pickering, Vale of, U.K. ... 20 C7 54 14N 0 45W
Pickle Lake, Canada ... 140 B1 51 30N 90 12W
Pickwick L., U.S.A. ... 149 H1 35 4N 88 15W
Pico, Azores ... 49 e 38 28N 28 20W
Pico, Ponta do, Azores ... 9 d1 38 28N 28 25W
Pico Bonito, Parque Nac. △, Honduras ... 164 C2 15 34N 86 48W
Pico Truncado, Argentina ... 176 C3 46 40 S 68 0W
Picos, Brazil ... 170 C3 7 5 S 41 28W
Picos de Europa, Parque Nac. de △, Spain ... 42 B6 43 14N 4 59W
Picota, Peru ... 172 C2 6 54 S 76 24W
Picton, Australia ... 129 C9 34 12 S 150 34 E
Picton, Canada ... 140 D4 44 1N 77 8W
Picton, N.Z. ... 131 M9 41 18 S 174 3 E
Picton, I., Chile ... 176 E3 55 2 S 66 57W
Pictou, Canada ... 141 C7 45 41N 62 42W
Picture Butte, Canada ... 142 D6 49 55N 112 45W

Pictured Rocks Nat. Lakeshore △, U.S.A. ... 148 B2 46 30N 86 30W
Picuí, Brazil ... 170 C4 6 31 S 36 21W
Picún Leufú, Argentina ... 176 A3 39 30 S 69 5W
Pidurutalagala, Sri Lanka ... 95 L5 7 10N 80 50 E
Piechowice, Poland ... 55 H2 50 51N 15 36 E
Piedecuesta, Colombia ... 168 B3 6 59N 73 3W
Piedmont = Piemonte □, Italy ... 44 D5 45 0N 8 0 E
Piedmont, Ala., U.S.A. ... 152 B4 33 55N 85 37W
Piedmont, S.C., U.S.A. ... 147 D10 34 42N 82 28W
Piedmonte Matese, Italy ... 47 A7 41 22N 14 22 E
Piedra →, Spain ... 40 D3 41 18N 1 47W
Piedra del Aguila, Argentina ... 176 B2 40 2 S 70 4W
Piedra Lais, Venezuela ... 168 C4 3 10N 65 50W
Piedrabuena, Spain ... 43 G6 39 0N 4 10W
Piedralaves, Spain ... 42 E6 40 19N 4 58W
Piedras, R. de las →, Peru ... 172 C4 12 30 S 69 15W
Piedras Blancas, Spain ... 42 B5 43 33N 5 58W
Piedras Negras, Mexico ... 162 B4 28 42N 100 31W
Piedras R., Pri. ... 81 F2 10 11N 118 48 E
Piekary Śląskie, Poland ... 55 H5 50 24N 18 57 E
Pieksämäki, Finland ... 15 E22 62 18N 27 10 E
Piemonte □, Italy ... 44 D5 45 0N 8 0 E
Pienaarsrivier, S. Africa ... 117 D4 25 15 S 28 18 E
Pieniężno, Poland ... 54 D7 54 14N 20 8 E
Pieninský Národný Park □, Europe ... 35 B13 49 25N 20 25 E
Pieńsk, Poland ... 55 G2 51 16N 15 2 E
Piercefield, U.S.A. ... 151 B10 44 13N 74 35W
Pierceland, Canada ... 143 C7 54 20N 109 46W
Piería □, Greece ... 50 F6 40 13N 22 25 E
Pierpont, U.S.A. ... 150 E4 41 45N 80 34W
Pierre, U.S.A. ... 154 C4 44 22N 100 21W
Pierre-Buffière, France ... 28 C5 45 41N 1 22 E
Pierre-de-Bresse, France ... 27 F12 46 54N 5 13 E
Pierre E. Trudeau, Mt. = Logan, Mt., Canada ... 138 B5 60 31N 140 22W
Pierrefontaine-les-Varans, France ... 27 E13 47 14N 6 32 E
Pierrefort, France ... 28 D7 44 55N 2 50 E
Pierrelatte, France ... 29 D8 44 23N 4 43 E
Pierreville, Trin. & Tob. ... 169 F9 10 16N 61 0W
Pierson, U.S.A. ... 153 F8 29 14N 81 28W
Piešťany, Slovak Rep. ... 35 C10 48 38N 17 55 E
Piesting →, Austria ... 35 C9 48 6N 16 40 E
Pieszyce, Poland ... 55 H3 50 43N 16 33 E
Piet Retief, S. Africa ... 117 D5 27 1 S 30 50 E
Pietarsaari, Finland ... 14 E20 63 40N 22 43 E
Pietermaritzburg, S. Africa ... 117 D5 29 35 S 30 25 E
Pietersburg, S. Africa ... 117 C4 23 54 S 29 25 E
Pietragalla, Italy ... 47 B8 40 45N 15 53 E
Pietrasanta, Italy ... 44 E7 43 57N 10 14 E
Pietroşiţa, Romania ... 53 E10 45 11N 25 26 E
Pietrosul, Vf., Maramureş, Romania ... 53 C9 47 35N 24 43 E
Pietrosul, Vf., Suceava, Romania ... 53 C10 47 12N 25 18 E
Pieve di Cadore, Italy ... 45 B9 46 26N 12 22 E
Pieve di Teco, Italy ... 44 D4 44 3N 7 56 E
Pievepélago, Italy ... 44 D7 44 12N 10 37 E
Pigadhítsa, Greece ... 50 G5 39 59N 21 23 E
Pigeon I., Canada ... 95 G2 14 2N 74 20 E
Pigeon L., Canada ... 150 B6 44 25N 78 30W
Piggott, U.S.A. ... 155 G9 36 23N 90 11W
Pigna, Italy ... 44 E4 43 56N 7 40 E
Pigüe, Argentina ... 174 D3 37 36 S 62 25W
Pihani, India ... 93 F9 27 36N 80 15 E
Pihlajavesi, Finland ... 15 F23 61 45N 28 45 E
Pijijiapan, Mexico ... 163 D6 15 42N 93 14W
Pikalevo, Russia ... 58 C8 59 37N 34 9 E
Pikangikum Berens, Canada ... 143 C10 51 49N 94 0W
Pikes Peak, U.S.A. ... 154 F2 38 50N 105 3W
Piketberg, S. Africa ... 116 E2 32 55 S 18 40 E
Pikeville, U.S.A. ... 148 G4 37 29N 82 31W
Pikit, Phil. ... 81 H5 7 4N 124 42 E
Pikou, China ... 75 E12 39 18N 122 22 E
Pikounda, Congo ... 114 B3 0 30N 16 44 E
Pikwitonei, Canada ... 143 B9 55 35N 97 9W
Piła, Poland ... 55 E3 53 10N 16 48 E
Pila, Spain ... 41 G3 38 16N 1 11W
Pilaía □, Greece ... 50 F6 40 32N 22 50 E
Pilanesberg Nat. Park △, S. Africa ... 116 D4 25 15 S 27 4 E
Pilani, India ... 92 E6 28 22N 75 33 E
Pilar, Argentina ... 174 C4 31 42 S 63 22W
Pilar, Brazil ... 170 C4 9 36 S 35 56W
Pilar, Paraguay ... 174 B4 26 50 S 58 20W
Pilar, Capiz, Phil. ... 81 F4 11 29N 123 0 E
Pilar, Sorsogon, Phil. ... 80 E4 12 56N 123 40 E
Pilar de la Horadada, Spain ... 41 H4 37 52N 0 47W
Pilas Group, Phil. ... 81 H3 6 45N 121 35 E
Pilat, Parc Naturel Régional du □, France ... 29 C8 45 20N 4 30 E
Pilawa, Poland ... 55 G8 51 57N 21 32 E
Pilaya →, Bolivia ... 173 E5 20 55 S 64 4W
Pilbara, Australia ... 124 D2 23 35 S 117 25 E
Pilcomayo →, Paraguay ... 174 B4 25 21 S 57 42W
Pilgrim's Rest, S. Africa ... 117 C5 24 55 S 30 44 E
Pilgrimstad, Sweden ... 16 B9 62 57N 15 2 E
Píli, Greece ... 49 E9 36 50N 27 15 E
Pili, Phil. ... 80 E4 13 33N 123 19 E
Pilibhit, India ... 93 E8 28 40N 79 50 E
Pilica →, Poland ... 55 G8 51 52N 21 17 E
Pilión, Greece ... 48 B5 39 27N 23 3 E
Pilis, Hungary ... 52 C4 47 17N 19 35 E
Pilisvörösvár, Hungary ... 52 C3 47 38N 18 56 E
Pilkhawa, India ... 92 E7 28 43N 77 42 E
Pillar B., Ascension I. ... 9 g 7 59 S 14 21W
Pillaro, Ecuador ... 168 D2 1 10 S 78 32W
Pillau = Baltiysk, Russia ... 15 J18 54 41N 19 58 E
Pilliga, Australia ... 127 E4 30 21 S 148 54 E
Pílos, Greece ... 48 E3 36 55N 21 42 E
Pilot Grove, U.S.A. ... 156 F4 38 53N 92 55W
Pilot Mound, Canada ... 143 D9 49 15N 98 54W
Pilot Point, Alaska, U.S.A. ... 144 H8 57 34N 157 35W
Pilot Point, Tex., U.S.A. ... 155 J6 33 24N 96 58W
Pilot Rock, U.S.A. ... 158 D4 45 29N 118 50W
Pilot Station, U.S.A. ... 144 F7 61 56N 162 53W
Pilsen = Plzeň, Czech Rep. ... 34 B6 49 45N 13 22 E
Pilštanj, Slovenia ... 45 B12 46 8N 15 39 E
Piltene, Latvia ... 54 A8 57 13N 21 40 E
Pilzno, Poland ... 55 J8 49 58N 21 16 E
Pima, U.S.A. ... 159 K9 32 54N 109 50W
Pimba, Australia ... 128 A2 31 18 S 136 46 E
Pimenta Bueno, Brazil ... 173 C5 11 35 S 61 10W
Pimenteiras, Brazil ... 173 C5 13 45 S 60 58W
Pimentel, Peru ... 172 B2 6 45 S 79 55W
Pimu, Dem. Rep. of the Congo ... 114 B4 1 40N 20 58 E
Pina de Ebro, Spain ... 40 D4 41 29N 0 33W
Pinamungajan, Phil. ... 80 E3 13 2N 121 29 E
Pinang, Malaysia ... 84 A2 5 25N 100 15 E
Pinang □, Malaysia ... 84 A2 5 20N 100 20 E
Pinar, C. des, Spain ... 38 B4 39 53N 3 12 E
Pinar del Río, Cuba ... 164 B3 22 26N 83 40W
Pınarbaşı, Çanakkale, Turkey ... 49 B8 39 59N 26 15 E
Pınarbaşı, Kayseri, Turkey ... 100 C7 38 43N 36 23 E
Pınarhisar, Turkey ... 51 E11 41 37N 27 30 E
Pınatubo, Mt., Phil. ... 80 D3 15 8N 120 21 E
Pincehely, Hungary ... 52 D3 46 41N 18 31 E
Pinchang, China ... 76 B6 31 36N 107 3 E
Pincher Creek, Canada ... 142 D6 49 30N 113 57W
Pinchi L., Canada ... 142 C4 54 38N 124 30W
Pinckneyville, U.S.A. ... 156 F7 38 5N 89 23W
Pińczów, Poland ... 55 H7 50 32N 20 32 E
Pindaí, Presqu'île de, N. Cal. ... 133 U18 21 20 S 164 56 E
Pindar, Australia ... 125 E2 28 30 S 115 47 E
Pindaré →, Brazil ... 170 B3 3 17 S 44 47W
Pindaré Mirim, Brazil ... 170 B2 3 37 S 45 21W

Pindi Gheb, *Pakistan* .... 92 C5 33 14N 72 21 E
Pindiga, *Nigeria* .... 113 D7 9 58N 10 53 E
Pindobal, *Brazil* .... 170 B2 3 16 S 48 25W
Pindos △, *Greece* .... 48 B3 39 52N 21 11 E
Pindos Óros, *Greece* .... 48 B3 40 0N 21 0 E
Pindus Mts. = Pindos Óros, *Greece* .. 48 B3 40 0N 21 0 E
Pine ➤, *B.C., Canada* 142 B4 56 8N 120 43W
Pine ➤, *Sask., Canada* 143 B7 58 50N 105 38W
Pine, C., *Canada* 141 C9 46 37N 53 32W
Pine Bluff, *U.S.A.* 155 H9 34 13N 92 1W
Pine Bluffs, *U.S.A.* 154 E2 41 11N 104 4W
Pine City, *U.S.A.* 154 C8 45 50N 92 59W
Pine Cr. ➤, *U.S.A.* 150 E7 41 10N 77 16W
Pine Creek, *Australia* .... 124 B5 13 50 S 131 50 E
Pine Falls, *Canada* 143 C9 50 34N 96 11W
Pine Flat Res., *U.S.A.* 160 J7 36 50N 119 20W
Pine Grove, *U.S.A.* 151 F8 40 33N 76 23W
Pine Is., *U.S.A.* 153 J7 26 36N 82 7W
Pine Level, *U.S.A.* 152 C3 32 4N 85 51W
Pine Mountain, *U.S.A.* 152 C5 32 52N 84 51W
Pine Pass, *Canada* 142 B4 55 25N 122 42W
Pine Point, *Canada* 142 A6 60 50N 114 28W
Pine Ridge, *Australia* .... 129 A9 31 30 S 150 28 E
Pine Ridge, *U.S.A.* 154 D3 43 2N 102 33W
Pine River, *Canada* 143 C8 51 45N 100 30W
Pine River, *U.S.A.* 154 B7 46 43N 94 24W
Pine Valley, *U.S.A.* 161 N10 32 50N 116 32W
Pinecrest, *U.S.A.* 160 G6 38 12N 120 1W
Pineda de Mar, *Spain* .... 40 D7 41 37N 2 42 E
Pinedale, *Calif., U.S.A.* 160 J7 36 50N 119 48W
Pinedale, *Wyo., U.S.A.* 158 E9 42 52N 109 52W
Pinega ➤, *Russia* .... 56 B8 64 30N 44 19 E
Pinehill, *Australia* .... 126 C4 23 38 S 146 57 E
Pinehouse L., *Canada* 143 B7 55 32N 106 35W
Pineimuta ➤, *Canada* 140 B1 52 8N 88 33W
Pinellas Park, *U.S.A.* 153 H7 27 50N 82 43W
Piney, *France* .... 27 D11 48 22N 4 21 E
Ping ➤, *Thailand* .... 86 E3 15 42N 100 9 E
Pingaring, *Australia* .... 125 F2 32 40 S 118 32 E
Pingba, *China* .... 76 D6 26 23N 106 12 E
Pingbian, *China* .... 76 F4 23 0N 103 45 E
Pingchuan, *China* .... 76 D3 27 35N 101 55 E
Pingding, *China* .... 74 F7 37 47N 113 38 E
Pingdingshan, *China* .... 74 H7 33 43N 113 27 E
Pingdong, *Taiwan* .... 77 F13 22 39N 120 30 E
Pingdu, *China* .... 75 F10 36 42N 119 59 E
Pingelly, *Australia* .... 125 F2 32 32 S 117 5 E
Pingguo, *China* .... 76 F6 23 19N 107 36 E
Pinghe, *China* .... 77 E11 24 17N 117 21 E
Pinghu, *China* .... 77 B13 30 40N 121 2 E
Pingjiang, *China* .... 77 C9 28 45N 113 36 E
Pingle, *China* .... 77 E8 24 40N 110 40 E
Pingli, *China* .... 76 A7 32 27N 109 22 E
Pingliang, *China* .... 74 G4 35 35N 106 31 E
Pinglu, *China* .... 74 E7 39 31N 112 30 E
Pingluo, *China* .... 74 E4 38 52N 106 30 E
Pingnan, *Fujian, China* .... 77 D12 26 55N 119 0 E
Pingnan, *Guangxi Zhuangzu, China* .. 77 F8 23 33N 110 22 E
Pingo, *Gabon* .... 114 C2 1 19 S 10 55 E
Pingquan, *China* .... 75 D10 41 1N 118 37 E
Pingrup, *Australia* .... 125 F2 33 32 S 118 29 E
Pingshan, *China* .... 76 C5 28 39N 104 3 E
Pingtan, *China* .... 77 E12 25 31N 119 47 E
Pingtang, *China* .... 76 E6 25 49N 107 17 E
P'ingtung, *Taiwan* .... 77 F13 22 38N 120 30 E
Pingwu, *China* .... 74 H3 32 25N 104 30 E
Pingxiang, *Guangxi Zhuangzu, China* .. 76 F6 22 6N 106 46 E
Pingxiang, *Jiangxi, China* .... 77 D9 27 43N 113 48 E
Pingyao, *China* .... 74 F7 37 12N 112 10 E
Pingyi, *China* .... 75 G9 35 30N 117 35 E
Pingyin, *China* .... 74 F9 36 20N 116 25 E
Pingyuan, *Guangdong, China* .... 77 E10 24 37N 115 57 E
Pingyuan, *Shandong, China* .... 74 F9 37 10N 116 22 E
Pingyuanjie, *China* .... 76 F4 23 45N 103 48 E
Pinhal, *Brazil* .... 175 A6 22 10 S 46 46W
Pinhal Novo, *Portugal* 43 G2 38 38N 8 55W
Pinheiro, *Brazil* .... 170 B2 2 31 S 45 5W
Pinheiro Machado, *Brazil* .... 175 C5 31 34 S 53 23W
Pinhel, *Portugal* 42 E3 40 50N 7 1W
Pinhuá ➤, *Brazil* .... 173 B4 6 21 S 65 0W
Pini, *Indonesia* .... 84 B1 0 10N 98 40 E
Piniós ➤, *Ilía, Greece* .... 48 D3 37 48N 21 20 E
Piniós ➤, *Trikkala, Greece* .... 48 B4 39 55N 22 41 E
Pinjarra, *Australia* .... 125 F2 32 37 S 115 52 E
Pink Mountain, *Canada* 142 B4 57 3N 122 52W
Pinkafeld, *Austria* .... 35 D9 47 22N 16 9 E
Pinlaung, *Burma* .... 90 E6 20 8N 96 47 E
Pinlebu, *Burma* .... 90 C5 24 5N 95 22 E
Pinnacles, *U.S.A.* 160 J5 36 33N 121 19W
Pinnacles Nat. Monument △, *U.S.A.* .. 160 J5 36 25N 121 12W
Pinnaroo, *Australia* .... 128 C4 35 17 S 140 53 E
Pinneberg, *Germany* .... 30 B5 53 40N 9 48 E
Pínnes, Ákra, *Greece* .... 51 F8 40 5N 24 20 E
Pino Hachado, Paso, *S. Amer.* .... 176 A2 38 39 S 70 54W
Pinon Hills, *U.S.A.* 161 L9 34 26N 117 39W
Pinos, *Mexico* 162 C4 22 20N 101 40W
Pinos, Mt., *U.S.A.* 161 L7 34 49N 119 8W
Pinos Pt., *U.S.A.* 159 H3 36 38N 121 57W
Pinos Puente, *Spain* 43 H7 37 15N 3 45W
Pinotepa Nacional, *Mexico* 163 D5 16 19N 98 3W
Pinrang, *Indonesia* .... 82 B1 3 46 S 119 41 E
Pins, Î. des, *N. Cal.* .... 133 V21 22 37 S 167 30 E
Pins, Pte. aux, *Canada* 150 D3 42 15N 81 51W
Pinsk, *Belarus* .... 59 F4 52 10N 26 1 E
Pinta, Canal de, *Ecuador* .... 172 a 0 27N 90 38W
Pinta, I., *Ecuador* .... 172 a 0 34N 90 44W
Pintados, *Chile* .... 172 E4 20 35 S 69 40W
Pintuyan, *Phil.* .... 81 G5 9 57N 125 15 E
Pinukpuk, *Phil.* .... 80 C3 17 35N 121 22 E
Pinyang, *China* .... 77 D13 27 42N 120 31 E
Pinyug, *Russia* .... 64 A1 60 5N 48 0 E
Pio Duran, *Phil.* .... 80 E4 13 2N 123 25 E
Pio V. Corpuz, *Phil.* .... 81 F5 11 55N 124 2 E
Pio XII, *Brazil* .... 170 B2 3 53 S 45 17W
Pioche, *U.S.A.* 159 H6 37 56N 114 27W
Piombino, *Italy* .... 44 F7 42 55N 10 32 E
Piombino, Canale di, *Italy* .... 44 F7 42 53N 10 30 E
Pioner, Ostrov, *Russia* .... 67 B10 79 50N 92 0 E
Pionki, *Poland* .... 55 G8 51 29N 21 28 E
Piorini ➤, *Brazil* .... 169 D5 3 23 S 63 40W
Piorini, L., *Brazil* .... 169 D5 3 15 S 62 35W
Piotrków Trybunalski, *Poland* .... 55 G6 51 23N 19 43 E
Piove di Sacco, *Italy* .... 45 C9 45 18N 12 2 E
Pip, *Iran* .... 97 E9 26 45N 60 10 E
Pipar, *India* .... 92 F5 26 25N 73 31 E
Pipar Road, *India* .... 92 F5 26 27N 73 27 E
Piparia, *Mad. P., India* .... 92 H8 22 45N 78 23 E
Piparia, *Mad. P., India* .... 92 J7 21 49N 77 37 E
Pipas, *Angola* .... 115 E2 14 57 S 12 11 E
Pipéri, *Greece* .... 48 B6 39 20N 24 19 E
Pipestone, *U.S.A.* 154 D6 44 0N 96 19W
Pipestone ➤, *Canada* 140 B2 52 53N 89 23W
Pipestone Cr. ➤, *Canada* 143 D8 49 38N 100 15W
Pipiriki, *N.Z.* .... 130 F4 39 28 S 175 5 E
Piplan, *Pakistan* .... 92 C4 32 17N 71 21 E

Piploda, *India* .... 92 H6 23 37N 74 56 E
Pipmuacan, Rés., *Canada* 141 C5 49 45N 70 30W
Pippingarra, *Australia* .... 124 D2 20 27 S 118 42 E
Pipriac, *France* 26 E5 47 59N 1 58W
Piqua, *U.S.A.* 157 D12 40 9N 84 15W
Piquet Carneiro, *Brazil* .... 170 C4 5 48 S 39 25W
Piquiri ➤, *Brazil* .... 175 A5 24 3 S 54 14W
Pir Panjal Range, *India* .... 92 C7 32 30N 76 50 E
Pir Sohráb, *Iran* .... 97 E9 25 44N 60 54 E
Pira, *Benin* .... 113 D5 8 28N 1 48 E
Piracanjuba, *Brazil* .... 171 E2 17 18 S 49 1W
Piracicaba, *Brazil* .... 175 A6 22 45 S 47 40W
Piracuruca, *Brazil* .... 170 B3 3 50 S 41 50W
Piraeus = Piraiévs, *Greece* .... 48 D5 37 57N 23 42 E
Piraiévs, *Greece* .... 48 D5 37 57N 23 42 E
Piraju, *Brazil* .... 175 A6 21 59 S 49 29W
Piram I., *India* .... 92 J5 21 36N 72 21 E
Piran, *Slovenia* .... 45 C10 45 31N 13 33 E
Pirané, *Argentina* .... 174 B4 25 42 S 59 6W
Piranhas, *Brazil* .... 170 C4 9 27 S 37 46W
Pirano = Piran, *Slovenia* .... 45 C10 45 31N 13 33 E
Pirapemas, *Brazil* .... 170 B3 3 43 S 44 14W
Pirapora, *Brazil* .... 171 E3 17 20 S 44 56W
Pirara, *Guyana* 169 C6 3 37N 59 40W
Pirawa, *India* .... 92 G7 24 10N 76 2 E
Pires do Rio, *Brazil* .... 171 E2 17 18 S 48 17W
Pirganj, *Bangla.* .... 90 C6 25 51N 88 24 E
Pirgos, *Ilía, Greece* .... 48 D3 37 40N 21 27 E
Pirgos, *Kríti, Greece* .... 39 E6 35 0N 25 9 E
Pirgovo, *Bulgaria* .... 51 C9 43 44N 25 43 E
Piribebuy, *Paraguay* .... 174 B4 25 26 S 57 2W
Pirimapun, *Indonesia* .... 83 C5 6 20 S 138 24 E
Pirin ➤, *Bulgaria* .... 50 E7 41 48N 23 22 E
Pirin Planina, *Bulgaria* .... 50 E7 41 40N 23 30 E
Pírineos = Pyrénées, *Europe* .... 28 F4 42 45N 0 18 E
Piripiri, *Brazil* .... 170 B3 4 15 S 41 46W
Piritu, *Venezuela* 168 B4 9 23N 69 12W
Pirmasens, *Germany* .... 31 F4 49 12N 7 36 E
Pirna, *Germany* .... 30 E9 50 57N 13 56 E
Pirojpur, *Bangla.* .... 90 D3 22 35N 90 1 E
Pirot, *Serbia, Yug.* .... 50 C6 43 9N 22 33 E
Piru, *Indonesia* .... 82 B3 3 4 S 128 12 E
Piru, *U.S.A.* 161 L8 34 25N 118 48W
Piryatin = Pyryatyn, *Ukraine* .... 59 G7 50 15N 32 25 E
Piryí, *Greece* .... 49 C7 38 13N 25 59 E
Pisa, *Italy* .... 44 E7 43 43N 10 23 E
Pisa ➤, *Poland* .... 54 E8 53 14N 21 52 E
Pisa, Florence ✕ (PSA), *Italy* .... 44 E7 43 40N 10 22 E
Pisa Ra., *N.Z.* .... 131 E4 44 52 S 169 12 E
Pisac, *Peru* .... 172 C3 13 25 S 71 50W
Pisagne, *Italy* .... 44 C7 45 45N 10 10 E
Pisagua, *Chile* .... 172 D3 19 40 S 70 15W
Pisarovina, *Croatia* .... 45 C12 45 35N 15 50 E
Pisau, Tanjong, *Malaysia* .... 85 A5 6 4N 117 59 E
Pisco, *Peru* .... 172 C2 13 50 S 76 12W
Piscu, *Romania* .... 53 E12 45 30N 27 43 E
Písek, *Czech Rep.* .... 34 B7 49 19N 14 10 E
Pishan, *China* .... 68 C2 37 30N 78 33 E
Pishin, *Iran* .... 97 E9 26 6N 61 47 E
Pishin, *Pakistan* .... 92 D2 30 35N 67 0 E
Pishin Lora ➤, *Pakistan* .... 92 E1 29 9N 64 5 E
Pishpek = Bishkek, *Kyrgyzstan* .... 65 B7 42 54N 74 46 E
Pisidia, *Turkey* .... 100 D4 37 30N 31 40 E
Pising, *Indonesia* .... 82 C2 5 8 S 121 53 E
Pismo Beach, *U.S.A.* 161 K6 35 9N 120 38W
Piso, L., *Liberia* 112 D2 6 10N 11 5W
Pissila, *Burkina Faso* 113 C4 13 7N 0 50W
Pissis, Cerro, *Argentina* .... 174 B2 27 45 S 68 48W
Pissos, *France* 28 D3 44 19N 0 49W
Pissouri, *Cyprus* .... 39 F8 34 40N 32 42 E
Pisticci, *Italy* .... 47 B9 40 23N 16 33 E
Pistóia, *Italy* .... 44 E7 43 55N 10 54 E
Pistol B., *Canada* 143 A10 62 25N 92 37W
Pisuerga ➤, *Spain* 42 D6 41 33N 4 52W
Pisz, *Poland* .... 54 E8 53 38N 21 49 E
Pit ➤, *U.S.A.* 158 F2 40 47N 122 6W
Pita, *Guinea* 112 C2 11 5N 12 15W
Pitalito, *Colombia* 168 C2 1 51N 76 2W
Pitanga, *Brazil* .... 171 F1 24 46 S 51 44W
Pitangui, *Brazil* .... 171 E3 19 40 S 44 54W
Pitarpunga, L., *Australia* .... 128 C5 34 24 S 143 30 E
Pitcairn I., *Pac. Oc.* .... 135 K14 25 5 S 130 5W
Pitch L., *Trin. & Tob.* 169 F19 10 12N 61 39W
Pite älv ➤, *Sweden* .... 14 D19 65 20N 21 25 E
Piteå, *Sweden* .... 14 D19 65 20N 21 25 E
Piterka, *Russia* .... 60 E8 50 41N 47 29 E
Pitești, *Romania* .... 53 F9 44 52N 24 54 E
Pithapuram, *India* .... 94 F6 17 10N 82 15 E
Pithara, *Australia* .... 125 F2 30 20 S 116 35 E
Píthion, *Greece* .... 51 E10 41 24N 26 40 E
Pithiviers, *France* .... 27 D9 48 10N 2 13 E
Pithora, *India* .... 94 D6 21 16N 82 31 E
Pithoragarh, *India* .... 93 E9 29 35N 80 13 E
Pithoro, *Pakistan* .... 92 G3 25 31N 69 23 E
Pitigliano, *Italy* .... 44 F8 42 38N 11 40 E
Pitkyaranta, *Russia* .... 58 B6 61 34N 31 37 E
Pitlochry, *U.K.* 22 E5 56 42N 3 44W
Pitogo, *Phil.* .... 80 E4 13 47N 122 5 E
Pitrufquén, *Chile* .... 176 A2 38 59 S 72 39W
Pitsilia, *Cyprus* .... 39 F9 34 55N 33 0 E
Pitt, Pta., *Ecuador* .... 172 a 0 43 S 89 14W
Pitt I., *Canada* 142 C3 53 30N 129 50W
Pitti I., *India* .... 95 J1 10 50N 72 38 E
Pittsburg, *Calif., U.S.A.* 160 G5 38 2N 121 53W
Pittsburg, *Kans., U.S.A.* 155 G7 37 25N 94 42W
Pittsburg, *Tex., U.S.A.* 155 J7 33 0N 94 59W
Pittsburgh, *U.S.A.* 150 F5 40 26N 80 1W
Pittsfield, *Ill., U.S.A.* 156 E6 39 36N 90 49W
Pittsfield, *Maine, U.S.A.* 149 C11 44 47N 69 23W
Pittsfield, *Mass., U.S.A.* 151 D11 42 27N 73 15W
Pittsfield, *N.H., U.S.A.* 151 C13 43 18N 71 20W
Pittston, *U.S.A.* 151 E9 41 19N 75 47W
Pittsview, *U.S.A.* 152 C4 32 11N 85 10W
Pittsworth, *Australia* .... 127 D5 27 41 S 151 37 E
Pituri ➤, *Australia* .... 126 C2 22 35 S 138 30 E
Piui, *Brazil* .... 171 F2 20 28 S 45 58W
Pium, *Brazil* .... 170 D2 10 27 S 49 11W
Piura, *Peru* .... 172 B1 5 15 S 80 38W
Piura □, *Peru* .... 172 A2 5 10 S 80 0W
Piva ➤, *Montenegro, Yug.* .... 50 C2 43 20N 18 50 E
Pivijay, *Colombia* 168 A3 10 28N 74 37W
Piwniczna, *Poland* .... 55 J7 49 27N 20 42 E
Pixley, *U.S.A.* 160 K7 35 58N 119 18W
Piyai, *Greece* .... 48 B3 39 17N 21 25 E
Pizarra, *Spain* 43 J6 36 46N 4 51W
Pizarro, *Colombia* 168 C2 4 58N 77 22W
Pizhou, *China* .... 74 G9 34 44N 118 0 E
Pizol, *Switz.* .... 33 C8 46 57N 9 23 E
Pizzo, *Italy* .... 47 D9 38 44N 16 10 E
Placentia, *Canada* 141 C9 47 20N 54 0W
Placentia B., *Canada* 141 C9 47 0N 54 40W
Placer, *Masbate, Phil.* .... 81 F5 11 52N 123 55 E
Placer, *Surigao N., Phil.* .... 81 G5 9 36N 125 38 E
Placerville, *U.S.A.* 160 G6 38 44N 120 48W
Placetas, *Cuba* 164 B4 22 15N 79 44W
Plácido de Castro, *Brazil* .... 174 C5 10 20 S 67 11W
Plačkovica, *Macedonia* .... 50 E6 41 45N 22 30 E
Plaffeien, *Switz.* .... 33 C4 46 45N 7 17 E
Plainfield, *Ill., U.S.A.* 157 C8 41 37N 88 12W
Plainfield, *Ind., U.S.A.* 157 E10 39 42N 86 24W
Plainfield, *N.J., U.S.A.* 151 F10 40 37N 74 25W
Plainfield, *Ohio, U.S.A.* 150 F3 40 13N 81 43W

Plainfield, *Vt., U.S.A.* 151 B12 44 17N 72 26W
Plains, *Ga., U.S.A.* 152 C5 32 2N 84 24W
Plains, *Mont., U.S.A.* 158 C6 47 28N 114 53W
Plains, *Tex., U.S.A.* 155 J3 33 11N 102 50W
Plainview, *Nebr., U.S.A.* 154 D6 42 21N 97 47W
Plainview, *Tex., U.S.A.* 155 H4 34 11N 101 43W
Plainwell, *U.S.A.* 157 B11 42 27N 85 38W
Plaisance, *France* .... 28 E4 43 36N 0 3 E
Plaistow, *U.S.A.* 151 D13 42 50N 71 6W
Pláka, *Greece* .... 49 B7 40 0N 25 24 E
Pláka, Ákra, *Greece* .... 39 E7 35 11N 26 19 E
Plakenska Planina, *Macedonia* .... 50 E5 41 14N 21 2 E
Planá, *Czech Rep.* .... 34 B5 49 50N 12 44 E
Plana Cays, *Bahamas* 165 B5 22 38N 73 30W
Planada, *U.S.A.* 160 H6 37 16N 120 19W
Plancoët, *France* 26 D4 48 32N 2 13W
Planeta Rica, *Colombia* 168 B2 8 25N 75 36W
Plano, *U.S.A.* 155 J6 33 1N 96 42W
Plant City, *U.S.A.* 153 H7 28 1N 82 7W
Plantation, *U.S.A.* 153 J9 26 8N 80 15W
Plaquemine, *U.S.A.* 155 K9 30 17N 91 14W
Plaridel, *Phil.* .... 81 G4 8 37N 123 43 E
Plasencia, *Spain* 42 E4 40 3N 6 8W
Plaški, *Croatia* .... 45 C12 45 4N 15 22 E
Plassen, *Norway* .... 18 C9 61 9N 12 30 E
Plast, *Russia* .... 60 D12 54 22N 60 50 E
Plaster City, *U.S.A.* 161 N11 32 47N 115 51W
Plaster Rock, *Canada* 141 C6 46 53N 67 22W
Plastun, *Russia* .... 70 B4 44 45N 136 0 E
Plata, Río de la, *S. Amer.* .... 174 C4 34 45 S 57 30W
Plátanos ➤, *Italy* .... 46 E6 37 23N 13 16 E
Plátanos, *Greece* .... 39 E4 35 28N 23 33 E
Plataria, *Greece* .... 38 C10 39 27N 20 16 E
Plateau □, *Nigeria* .... 113 D6 8 30N 9 0 E
Plateau d'Ipassa, Réserve de △, *Gabon* .... 114 B2 0 26N 12 40 E
Platí, Ákra, *Greece* .... 51 F8 40 27N 24 0 E
Platinum, *U.S.A.* 144 G7 59 1N 161 49W
Plato, *Colombia* 168 B3 9 47N 74 47W
Platta, Piz, *Switz.* .... 33 D9 46 28N 9 35 E
Platte, *U.S.A.* 154 D5 43 23N 98 51W
Platte ➤, *Mo., U.S.A.* 156 E2 39 16N 94 50W
Platte ➤, *Nebr., U.S.A.* 154 E7 41 4N 95 53W
Platte City, *U.S.A.* 156 E2 39 22N 94 47W
Platteville, *U.S.A.* 156 D6 42 44N 90 29W
Plattling, *Germany* .... 31 G8 48 46N 12 53 E
Plattsburg, *U.S.A.* 156 E2 39 34N 94 27W
Plattsburgh, *U.S.A.* 151 B11 44 42N 73 28W
Plattsmouth, *U.S.A.* 154 E7 41 1N 95 53W
Plau, *Germany* .... 30 B8 53 27N 12 15 E
Plauen, *Germany* .... 30 E8 50 30N 12 8 E
Plauer See, *Germany* .... 30 B8 53 27N 12 17 E
Plav, *Montenegro, Yug.* .... 50 D3 42 38N 19 57 E
Plavinas, *Latvia* .... 15 H21 56 35N 25 46 E
Plavnica, *Montenegro, Yug.* .... 50 D3 42 20N 19 13 E
Plavno, *Croatia* .... 45 D13 44 9N 16 10 E
Plavsk, *Russia* .... 60 D9 53 40N 37 18 E
Playa Blanca, *Canary Is.* 9 e2 28 55N 13 37W
Playa Blanca Sur, *Canary Is.* 9 e2 28 51N 13 50W
Playa de las Americas, *Canary Is.* 9 e1 28 5N 16 43W
Playa de Mogán, *Canary Is.* 9 e1 27 48N 15 47W
Playa del Inglés, *Canary Is.* 9 e1 27 45N 15 33W
Playa Esmeralda, *Canary Is.* 9 e2 28 8N 14 16W
Playgreen L., *Canada* 143 C9 54 0N 98 15W
Playá, *Greece* .... 39 C2 38 24N 20 35 E
Pleasant Bay, *Canada* 141 C7 46 51N 60 48W
Pleasant Hill, *Calif., U.S.A.* 160 H4 37 57N 122 4W
Pleasant Hill, *Ill., U.S.A.* 156 E6 39 27N 90 52W
Pleasant Hill, *Mo., U.S.A.* 156 F2 38 47N 94 16W
Pleasant Mount, *U.S.A.* 151 E9 41 44N 75 26W
Pleasanton, *Calif., U.S.A.* 160 H5 37 39N 121 52W
Pleasanton, *Tex., U.S.A.* 155 L5 28 58N 98 29W
Pleasantville, *Iowa, U.S.A.* 156 C3 41 23N 93 18W
Pleasantville, *N.J., U.S.A.* 148 F8 39 24N 74 32W
Pleasantville, *Pa., U.S.A.* 150 E5 41 35N 79 34W
Pleasure Ridge Park, *U.S.A.* 157 F11 38 9N 85 50W
Pléaux, *France* .... 28 C6 45 8N 2 13 E
Plei Ku, *Vietnam* .... 86 F7 13 57N 108 0 E
Plélan-le-Grand, *France* 26 D4 48 0N 2 7W
Pléneuf-Val-André, *France* 26 D4 48 35N 2 32W
Plenița, *Romania* .... 53 F8 44 14N 23 10 E
Plenty ➤, *Australia* .... 126 C2 23 25 S 136 31 E
Plenty, B. of, *N.Z.* .... 130 D6 37 45 S 177 0 E
Plentywood, *U.S.A.* 154 A2 48 47N 104 34W
Plérin, *France* 26 D4 48 33N 2 46W
Plesetsk, *Russia* .... 56 B7 62 43N 40 20 E
Plessisville, *Canada* 141 C5 46 14N 71 47W
Plestin-les-Grèves, *France* 26 D3 48 40N 3 39W
Pleszew, *Poland* .... 55 G4 51 53N 17 47 E
Pleternica, *Croatia* .... 52 E2 45 17N 17 48 E
Plétipi, L., *Canada* 141 B5 51 44N 70 6W
Pleven, *Bulgaria* .... 51 C8 43 26N 24 37 E
Plevlja, *Montenegro, Yug.* .... 50 C3 43 21N 19 21 E
Plevna, *Canada* 150 B8 44 58N 76 59W
Plitvička Jezera, Nac. Park △, *Croatia* .... 45 D12 44 54N 15 35 E
Plješevica, *Croatia* .... 45 D12 44 45N 15 45 E
Ploaghe, *Italy* .... 46 B1 40 40N 8 45 E
Ploče, *Croatia* .... 45 E14 43 4N 17 26 E
Płock, *Poland* .... 55 F6 52 32N 19 40 E
Plöckenpass, *Italy* .... 45 B9 46 37N 12 57 E
Plöckenstein, *Germany* .... 31 G9 48 46N 13 51 E
Ploemeur, *France* 26 E3 47 44N 3 26W
Ploërmel, *France* 26 E4 47 55N 2 26W
Ploiești, *Romania* .... 53 F11 44 57N 26 5 E
Plomárion, *Greece* .... 49 C8 38 58N 26 22 E
Plombières-les-Bains, *France* .... 27 E13 47 58N 6 27 E
Plomin, *Croatia* .... 45 C11 45 8N 14 10 E
Plön, *Germany* .... 30 A6 54 9N 10 24 E
Plonge, Lac la, *Canada* 143 B7 55 8N 107 20W
Płońsk, *Poland* .... 55 F7 52 37N 20 21 E
Plopeni, *Romania* .... 53 E10 45 4N 25 59 E
Plopișului, Munții, *Romania* .... 52 C7 47 5N 22 30 E
Płoty, *Poland* .... 54 E2 53 48N 15 18 E
Plouaret, *France* 26 D3 48 37N 3 28W
Plouay, *France* 26 E3 47 55N 3 21W
Ploučnice ➤, *Czech Rep.* .... 34 A7 50 46N 14 13 E
Ploudalmézeau, *France* 26 D2 48 34N 4 41W
Plouescat, *France* 26 D2 48 40N 4 10W
Plougasnou, *France* 26 D3 48 42N 3 49W
Plougastel-Daoulas, *France* 26 D2 48 22N 4 17W
Plouguerneau, *France* 26 D2 48 36N 4 30W
Plouha, *France* 26 D4 48 41N 2 57W
Plouhinec, *France* 26 D2 48 0N 4 29W
Plovdiv, *Bulgaria* .... 51 D8 42 8N 24 44 E
Plovdiv □, *Bulgaria* .... 51 D8 42 8N 24 45 E
Plover Cove Res., *China* .... 69 G11 22 28N 114 15 E
Plum, *U.S.A.* 150 F5 40 29N 79 47W
Plum I., *U.S.A.* 151 E12 41 11N 72 12W
Plumas, *U.S.A.* 160 F7 39 45N 120 4W
Plummer, *U.S.A.* 158 C5 47 20N 116 53W
Plumtree, *Zimbabwe* .... 119 G2 20 27 S 27 55 E
Plungė, *Lithuania* .... 15 J19 55 53N 21 59 E
Pluvigner, *France* 26 E3 47 46N 3 1W
Plymouth, *Trin. & Tob.* 169 E10 11 14N 60 48W
Plymouth, *U.K.* 21 G3 50 22N 4 10W
Plymouth, *Ind., U.S.A.* 157 C10 41 21N 86 19W
Plymouth, *Ill., U.S.A.* 156 D6 40 18N 90 58W
Plymouth, *Mass., U.S.A.* 151 E14 41 57N 70 40W
Plymouth, *N.C., U.S.A.* 149 H7 35 52N 76 43W

Plymouth, *N.H., U.S.A.* 151 C13 43 46N 71 41W
Plymouth, *Pa., U.S.A.* 151 E9 41 14N 75 57W
Plymouth, *Wis., U.S.A.* 148 D2 43 45N 87 59W
Plynlimon = Pumlumon Fawr, *U.K.* .. 21 E4 52 28N 3 46W
Plyusa, *Russia* .... 58 C5 58 28N 29 27 E
Plyusa ➤, *Russia* .... 58 C5 59 4N 28 6 E
Plzeň, *Czech Rep.* .... 34 B6 49 45N 13 22 E
Plzeňský □, *Czech Rep.* .... 34 B6 49 35N 13 0 E
Pniewy, *Poland* .... 55 F3 52 31N 16 16 E
Pô, *Burkina Faso* 113 C4 11 14N 1 5W
Po ➤, *Italy* .... 45 D9 44 57N 12 4 E
Po, Foci del, *Italy* .... 45 D9 44 55N 12 30 E
Pô, Parc Nat. de △, *Burkina Faso* .. 113 C4 11 25N 1 5W
Po Hai = Bo Hai, *China* .... 75 E10 39 0N 119 0 E
Po Toi, *China* .... 69 G12 22 10N 114 16 E
Pobé, *Benin* .... 113 D5 7 0N 2 56 E
Pobé, *Burkina Faso* 113 C4 13 53N 1 42W
Pobeda, *Russia* .... 67 C15 65 12N 146 12 E
Pobedy, Pik, *Kyrgyzstan* .... 66 E8 42 0N 79 58 E
Pobiedziska, *Poland* .... 55 F4 52 29N 17 11 E
Pobla de Segur, *Spain* .... 40 C5 42 15N 0 58 E
Pobladura del Valle, *Spain* 42 C5 42 6N 5 44W
Pobla de Trives, *Spain* 42 C3 42 20N 7 10W
Pocahontas, *Ark., U.S.A.* 155 G9 36 16N 90 58W
Pocahontas, *Ill., U.S.A.* 156 F7 38 50N 89 33W
Pocahontas, *Iowa, U.S.A.* 156 B2 42 44N 94 40W
Pocatello, *U.S.A.* 158 E7 42 52N 112 27W
Počátky, *Czech Rep.* .... 34 B8 49 15N 15 14 E
Pochep, *Russia* .... 59 F7 52 58N 33 29 E
Pochinki, *Russia* .... 60 C7 54 41N 44 59 E
Pochinok, *Russia* .... 58 E7 54 28N 32 29 E
Pöchlarn, *Austria* .... 34 C8 48 12N 15 12 E
Pochutla, *Mexico* 163 D5 15 50N 96 31W
Poci, *Venezuela* 169 B5 5 57N 61 29W
Pocinhos, *Brazil* .... 170 C4 7 4 S 36 3W
Pocito Casas, *Mexico* 162 B2 28 32N 111 6W
Pocklington Reef, *Papua N. G.* .... 132 F8 10 51 S 155 44 E
Poções, *Brazil* .... 171 D3 14 31 S 40 21W
Pocomoke City, *U.S.A.* 148 F8 38 5N 75 34W
Poconé, *Brazil* .... 173 D6 16 15 S 56 37W
Poços de Caldas, *Brazil* .... 175 A6 21 50 S 46 33W
Podbořany, *Czech Rep.* .... 34 A6 50 14N 13 25 E
Poddębice, *Poland* .... 55 G5 51 54N 18 58 E
Poděbrady, *Czech Rep.* .... 34 A8 50 9N 15 8 E
Podensac, *France* 28 D3 44 40N 0 22W
Podenzano, *Italy* .... 44 D6 44 57N 9 41 E
Podgorač, *Croatia* .... 52 E3 45 27N 18 13 E
Podgorica, *Montenegro, Yug.* .... 50 D3 42 30N 19 19 E
Podgorie, *Albania* .... 50 F4 40 49N 20 48 E
Podile, *India* .... 95 G4 15 37N 79 37 E
Podilska Vysochyna, *Ukraine* .... 59 H4 49 0N 28 0 E
Podkarpackie □, *Poland* .... 55 H9 50 0N 22 10 E
Podkova, *Bulgaria* .... 51 E9 41 24N 25 24 E
Podlapača, *Croatia* .... 45 D12 44 37N 15 47 E
Podlaskie □, *Poland* .... 55 E10 53 10N 23 0 E
Podoleni, *Romania* .... 53 D11 46 46N 26 39 E
Podolínec, *Slovak Rep.* .... 35 B13 49 16N 20 31 E
Podolsk, *Russia* .... 58 E9 55 25N 37 30 E
Podor, *Senegal* 112 B1 16 40N 15 2W
Podporozhye, *Russia* .... 58 B8 60 55N 34 2 E
Podu Iloaiei, *Romania* .... 53 C12 47 13N 27 16 E
Podu Turcului, *Romania* .... 53 D12 46 11N 27 25 E
Podujevo, *Kosovo, Yug.* .... 50 D5 42 54N 21 10 E
Podyjí Národní Park △, *Czech Rep.* .. 34 C8 48 51N 15 57 E
Poechos, *Peru* .... 172 B1 4 41 S 80 34W
Poel, *Germany* .... 30 B6 54 0N 11 25 E
Pofadder, *S. Africa* .... 116 D2 29 10 S 19 22 E
Poggiardo, *Italy* .... 47 B11 40 3N 18 23 E
Poggibonsi, *Italy* .... 44 E8 43 28N 11 9 E
Póggio Mirteto, *Italy* .... 45 F9 42 16N 12 41 E
Pogoanele, *Romania* .... 53 F12 44 55N 27 0 E
Pogorzela, *Poland* .... 55 G4 51 50N 17 12 E
Pogoso, *Dem. Rep. of the Congo* .... 115 D3 6 46 S 17 12 E
Pogradec, *Albania* .... 50 F4 40 57N 20 37 E
Pogranichnyy, *Russia* .... 70 B5 44 25N 131 24 E
Poh, *Indonesia* .... 82 B2 0 46 S 122 51 E
P'ohang, *S. Korea* .... 75 F15 36 1N 129 23 E
Pohjanmaa, *Finland* .... 14 E20 62 58N 22 50 E
Pohnpei, *Micronesia* .... 134 G7 6 55N 158 10 E
Pohorelá, *Slovak Rep.* .... 35 C13 48 50N 20 2 E
Pohořelice, *Czech Rep.* .... 35 C9 48 59N 16 31 E
Pohorje, *Slovenia* .... 45 B12 46 30N 15 20 E
Pohri, *India* .... 92 G6 25 32N 77 22 E
Pohue B., *U.S.A.* 145 E6 19 0N 155 48W
Poi, *Solomon Is.* .... 133 N11 10 9 S 161 42 E
Poiana Mare, *Romania* .... 52 G8 43 57N 23 5 E
Poiana Ruscăi, Munții, *Romania* .... 52 E7 45 45N 22 25 E
Poiana Stampei, *Romania* .... 53 C10 47 19N 25 7 E
Poike, Península, *Chile* .... 172 b 27 6 S 109 15W
Poindimié, *N. Cal.* .... 133 T19 20 56 S 165 20 E
Point Arena, *U.S.A.* 160 G3 38 55N 123 41W
Point Baker, *U.S.A.* 142 B2 56 21N 133 37W
Point Calimere, *India* .... 95 J4 10 17N 79 49 E
Point Edward, *Canada* 140 D3 43 0N 82 30W
Point Fortin, *Trin. & Tob.* 169 F9 10 10N 61 42W
Point Hope, *U.S.A.* 144 B6 68 21N 166 47W
Point L., *Canada* 138 B8 65 15N 113 4W
Point Lay, *U.S.A.* 144 B7 69 46N 163 3W
Point Lisas, *Trin. & Tob.* 169 F9 10 32N 61 30W
Point Pedro, *Sri Lanka* .... 95 K5 9 50N 80 15 E
Point Pelee Nat. Park △, *Canada* 140 D3 41 57N 82 31W
Point Pleasant, *N.J., U.S.A.* 151 F10 40 5N 74 4W
Point Pleasant, *W. Va., U.S.A.* 148 F4 38 51N 82 8W
Point Reyes Nat. Seashore △, *U.S.A.* .. 160 H3 38 10N 122 55W
Pointe-à-Pitre, *Guadeloupe* .... 164 b 16 10N 61 32W
Pointe-Claire, *Canada* 151 A11 45 26N 73 50W
Pointe-Gatineau, *Canada* 151 A9 45 28N 75 42W
Pointe-Noire, *Congo* .... 115 C2 4 48 S 11 53 E
Pointe Noire, *Guadeloupe* .... 164 b 16 14N 61 47W
Poirino, *Italy* .... 42 D4 44 55N 7 48 E
Poisonbush Ra., *Australia* .... 124 D3 22 30 S 121 30 E
Poissonnier Pt., *Australia* .... 124 C2 19 57 S 119 10 E
Poitiers, *France* .... 26 F7 46 35N 0 20 E
Poitou, *France* 28 B4 46 40N 0 10W
Poitou-Charentes □, *France* .... 28 B4 46 10N 0 15 E
Poix-de-Picardie, *France* .... 27 C8 49 47N 1 58 E
Poix-Terron, *France* .... 27 C11 49 38N 4 38 E
Pojoaque, *U.S.A.* 159 J11 35 54N 106 1W
Pokai B., *U.S.A.* 145 K13 21 27N 158 12W
Pokataroo, *Australia* .... 127 D4 29 30 S 148 36 E
Pokhara, *Nepal* .... 93 E10 28 14N 83 58 E
Pokhvistnevo, *Russia* .... 60 D11 53 36N 52 6 E
Pokigron, *Suriname* 169 C6 4 30N 55 22W
Poko, *Dem. Rep. of the Congo* .... 118 B2 3 7N 26 52 E
Poko, *Sudan* .... 107 F3 5 41N 31 55 E
Pokrov, *Russia* .... 58 E10 55 55N 39 7 E
Pokrovka = Kyzyl-Suu, *Kyrgyzstan* .. 65 B9 42 20N 78 20 E
Pokrovka, *Kyrgyzstan* .... 58 B9 42 45N 71 36 E
Pokrovsk = Engels, *Russia* .... 60 E8 51 28N 46 6 E
Pokrovsk, *Russia* .... 67 C13 61 29N 129 0 E
Pokrovsk-Uralskiy, *Russia* .... 64 A7 60 10N 59 49 E
Pol, *Spain* 42 B3 43 9N 7 20W
Pol-e Khomri, *Afghan.* .... 91 B3 35 56N 68 42 E
Pola = Pula, *Croatia* .... 45 D10 44 54N 13 57 E
Pola, *Russia* .... 58 D7 57 55N 31 2 E
Pola de Allande, *Spain* 42 B4 43 16N 6 37W
Pola de Lena, *Spain* 42 B5 43 10N 5 49W
Pola de Siero, *Spain* 42 B5 43 24N 5 39W
Pola de Somiedo, *Spain* 42 B5 43 5N 6 13W
Polacca, *U.S.A.* 159 J8 35 50N 110 23W
Polan, *Iran* .... 97 E9 25 30N 61 10 E

Pol'ana, *Slovak Rep.* .... 35 C12 48 38N 19 29 E
Poland ■, *Europe* .... 55 G3 52 0N 20 0 E
Polanica-Zdrój, *Poland* .... 55 H3 50 24N 16 32 E
Połaniec, *Poland* .... 55 H8 50 26N 21 17 E
Polanów, *Poland* .... 54 D3 54 7N 16 41 E
Polar Bear Prov. Park △, *Canada* . 140 A2 55 0N 83 45W
Polatlı, *Turkey* .... 100 C5 39 36N 32 9 E
Polavaram, *India* .... 94 F5 17 15N 81 38 E
Polcura, *Chile* .... 174 D1 37 17 S 71 43W
Połczyn-Zdrój, *Poland* .... 54 E3 53 47N 16 5 E
Poleski Park Narodowy △, *Poland* . 55 G10 51 29N 23 5 E
Polessk, *Russia* .... 15 J19 54 50N 21 8 E
Polesye = Pripet Marshes, *Europe* 59 F5 52 10N 28 10 E
Polevskoy, *Russia* .... 64 C8 56 26N 60 11 E
Polewali, *Indonesia* .... 82 B1 3 25 S 119 20 E
Polgar, *Hungary* .... 52 C6 47 54N 21 6 E
Pŏlgyo-ri, *S. Korea* .... 75 G14 34 51N 127 21 E
Poli, *Cameroon* .... 113 C7 8 34N 13 15 E
Políaigos, *Greece* .... 48 E6 36 45N 24 38 E
Policastro, G. di, *Italy* .... 47 C8 40 0N 15 35 E
Police, *Poland* .... 54 E1 53 33N 14 33 E
Police, Pte., *Seychelles* .... 121 b 4 51 S 55 32 E
Polička, *Czech Rep.* .... 35 B9 49 43N 16 15 E
Policoro, *Italy* .... 47 B9 40 13N 16 41 E
Polignano a Mare, *Italy* .... 47 A9 41 0N 17 13 E
Poligny, *France* .... 27 F12 46 50N 5 42 E
Políkhnitas, *Greece* .... 49 B8 39 6N 26 10 E
Polillo, *Phil.* .... 80 D3 14 43N 121 56 E
Polillo Is., *Phil.* .... 80 D4 14 56N 122 0 E
Polillo Strait, *Phil.* .... 80 D3 14 44N 121 51 E
Polis, *Cyprus* .... 39 E8 35 2N 32 26 E
Polístena, *Italy* .... 47 D9 38 24N 16 4 E
Políyiros, *Greece* .... 50 F7 40 23N 23 25 E
Polk, *U.S.A.* 150 E5 41 22N 79 56W
Polkowice, *Poland* .... 55 G3 51 29N 16 3 E
Polla, *Italy* .... 47 B8 40 31N 15 29 E
Pollachi, *India* .... 95 J3 10 35N 77 0 E
Pollença, *Spain* .... 38 B4 39 54N 3 1 E
Pollença, B. de, *Spain* .... 38 B4 39 53N 3 8 E
Pollfoss, *Norway* .... 14 C4 61 58N 7 54 E
Póllica, *Italy* .... 47 B8 40 11N 15 3 E
Pollino, Mte., *Italy* .... 47 C9 39 55N 16 11 E
Pollino, Parco Nazionale del △, *Italy* 47 C9 40 0N 16 12 E
Polna, *Russia* .... 58 C5 58 31N 28 5 E
Polnovat, *Russia* .... 66 C7 63 50N 65 54 E
Polo, Ill., *U.S.A.* 156 C7 41 59N 89 35W
Polo, Mo., *U.S.A.* 156 E2 39 33N 94 3W
Pology, *Ukraine* .... 59 J9 47 29N 36 15 E
Polokwane = Pietersburg, *S. Africa* 117 C4 23 54 S 29 25 E
Polonnaruwa, *Sri Lanka* .... 95 L5 7 56N 81 0 E
Polonne, *Ukraine* .... 59 G4 50 6N 27 30 E
Polonnoye = Polonne, *Ukraine* .... 59 G4 50 6N 27 30 E
Polski Trŭmbesh, *Bulgaria* .... 51 C9 43 20N 25 38 E
Polsko Kosovo, *Bulgaria* .... 51 C9 43 23N 25 38 E
Polson, *U.S.A.* 158 C6 47 41N 114 9W
Poltár, *Slovak Rep.* .... 35 C12 48 26N 19 48 E
Poltava, *Ukraine* .... 59 H8 49 35N 34 35 E
Põltsamaa, *Estonia* .... 15 G21 58 41N 25 58 E
Polunochnoye, *Russia* .... 66 C7 60 52N 60 25 E
Polur, *India* .... 95 H4 12 32N 79 11 E
Põlva, *Estonia* .... 15 G22 58 3N 27 3 E
Polyarny, *Russia* .... 56 A5 69 8N 33 20 E
Polynesia, *Pac. Oc.* .... 135 J11 10 0 S 162 0W
Polynésie française = French Polynesia ☑, *Pac. Oc.* 135 K13 20 0 S 145 0W
Pomabamba, *Peru* .... 172 B2 8 50 S 77 28W
Pomarance, *Italy* .... 44 E7 43 18N 10 52 E
Pomaro, *Mexico* 162 D4 18 20N 103 18W
Pombal, *Brazil* .... 170 C4 6 45 S 37 50W
Pombal, *Portugal* 42 F2 39 55N 8 40W
Pómbia, *Greece* .... 49 F6 35 0N 24 51 E
Pombos, B. dos, *Angola* .... 115 E2 11 40 S 13 47 E
Pomene, *Mozam.* .... 117 C6 22 53 S 35 33 E
Pomeroy, Ohio, *U.S.A.* 148 F4 39 2N 82 2W
Pomeroy, Wash., *U.S.A.* 158 C5 46 28N 117 36W
Pomézia, *Italy* .... 46 A5 41 40N 12 30 E
Pomichna, *Ukraine* .... 59 H6 48 13N 31 36 E
Pomio, *Papua N. G.* .... 132 C6 5 32 S 151 33 E
Pomme de Terre L., *U.S.A.* 156 G3 37 54N 93 19W
Pomona, *Australia* .... 127 D5 26 22 S 152 52 E
Pomona, *U.S.A.* 161 L9 34 4N 117 45W
Pomona Park, *U.S.A.* 153 F8 29 30N 81 36W
Pomorie, *Bulgaria* .... 51 D11 42 32N 27 41 E
Pomorskie □, *Poland* .... 54 D5 54 30N 17 0 E
Pomorskie, Pojezierze, *Poland* ... 54 E3 53 40N 16 37 E
Pomos, *Cyprus* .... 39 E8 35 9N 32 33 E
Pomos, C., *Cyprus* .... 39 E8 35 10N 32 33 E
Pompano Beach, *U.S.A.* 153 J9 26 14N 80 8W
Pompei, *Italy* .... 47 B7 40 45N 14 30 E
Pompey, *France* .... 27 D13 48 46N 6 6 E
Pompeys Pillar, *U.S.A.* 158 D10 45 59N 107 57W
Pompeys Pillar Nat. Monument △, *U.S.A.* 158 D10 46 0N 108 0W
Pompton Lakes, *U.S.A.* 151 F10 41 0N 74 17W
Ponape = Pohnpei, *Micronesia* .... 134 G7 6 55N 158 10 E
Ponask L., *Canada* 140 B1 54 0N 92 41W
Ponca, *U.S.A.* 154 D6 42 34N 96 43W
Ponca City, *U.S.A.* 155 G6 36 42N 97 5W
Ponce, *Puerto Rico* .... 165 d 18 1N 66 37W
Ponce de Leon, *U.S.A.* 152 E4 30 44N 85 56W
Ponce de Leon B., *U.S.A.* 153 K8 25 15N 81 10W
Ponchatoula, *U.S.A.* 155 K9 30 26N 90 26W
Poncheville, L., *Canada* 140 B4 50 10N 76 55W
Pond, *U.S.A.* 161 K7 35 43N 119 20W
Pond Inlet, *Canada* 139 A12 72 40N 77 0W
Pondicherry, *India* .... 95 J4 11 59N 79 50 E
Pondo, *Papua N. G.* .... 132 C6 4 33 S 151 38 E
Ponds, I. of, *Canada* 141 B8 53 27N 55 52W
Ponérihouen, *N. Cal.* .... 133 U19 21 5 S 165 24 E
Ponferrada, *Spain* 42 C4 42 32N 6 35W
Pongo, Wadi ➜, *Sudan* .... 107 F2 8 42N 27 40 E
Poniatowa, *Poland* .... 55 G9 51 11N 22 3 E
Poniec, *Poland* .... 55 G3 51 48N 16 50 E
Ponikva, *Slovenia* .... 45 B12 46 16N 15 26 E
Ponnaiyar ➜, *India* .... 95 J4 11 50N 79 45 E
Ponnani, *India* .... 95 J2 10 45N 75 59 E
Ponneri, *India* .... 95 H5 13 20N 80 15 E
Ponnuru, *India* .... 95 F5 16 5N 80 34 E
Ponoka, *Canada* 142 C6 52 42N 113 40W
Ponomarevka, *Russia* .... 64 E5 53 19N 54 8 E
Ponorogo, *Indonesia* .... 85 D4 7 52 S 111 27 E
Ponot, *Phil.* .... 81 G4 8 25N 123 0 E
Ponoy, *Russia* .... 56 A7 67 0N 41 13 E
Ponoy ➜, *Russia* .... 56 A7 66 59N 41 17 E
Pons = Ponts, *Spain* .... 40 D6 41 55N 1 12 E
Pons, *France* 28 C3 45 35N 0 34W
Ponsul ➜, *Portugal* 42 F3 39 40N 7 31W
Pont-à-Mousson, *France* .... 27 D13 48 54N 6 1 E
Pont-Audemer, *France* .... 26 C7 49 21N 0 30 E
Pont-Aven, *France* 26 E3 47 51N 3 47W
Pont Canavese, *Italy* .... 44 C4 45 25N 7 36 E
Pont-d'Ain, *France* .... 29 F12 46 3N 5 21 E
Pont-de-Roide, *France* .... 27 E13 47 23N 6 45 E
Pont-de-Salars, *France* .... 28 D6 44 18N 2 44 E
Pont-de-Vaux, *France* .... 27 F11 46 26N 4 56 E
Pont-de-Veyle, *France* .... 27 F11 46 17N 4 53 E
Pont-du-Château, *France* .... 27 G10 45 47N 3 15 E
Pont l'Abbé, *France* 26 E2 47 52N 4 15W
Pont-l'Évêque, *France* .... 26 C7 49 18N 0 11 E
Pont-St-Esprit, *France* .... 29 D8 44 16N 4 40 E
Pont-St-Martin, *Italy* .... 44 C4 45 36N 7 48 E
Pont-Ste-Maxence, *France* .... 27 C9 49 18N 2 35 E
Pont-sur-Yonne, *France* .... 27 D10 48 18N 3 10 E

Ponta de Pedras, *Brazil* .... 170 B2 1 23 S 48 52W
Ponta Delgada, Flores, *Azores* ... 9 d2 39 31N 31 13W
Ponta Delgada, São Miguel, *Azores* 9 d3 37 44N 25 40W
Ponta Delgada ✈ (PDL), *Azores* ... 9 d3 37 44N 25 41W
Ponta do Sol, *Madeira* .... 9 c 32 42N 17 7W
Ponta Grossa, *Brazil* .... 175 B5 25 7 S 50 10W
Ponta Porã, *Brazil* .... 175 A4 22 20 S 55 35W
Pontacq, *France* 28 E3 43 11N 0 8W
Pontailler-sur-Saône, *France* .... 27 E12 47 13N 5 25 E
Pontal ➜, *Brazil* .... 170 C3 9 8 S 40 12W
Pontalina, *Brazil* .... 171 E2 17 31 S 49 27W
Pontarlier, *France* .... 27 F13 46 54N 6 20 E
Pontassieve, *Italy* .... 45 E8 43 46N 11 26 E
Pontaumur, *France* .... 28 C6 45 52N 2 40 E
Pontcharra, *France* .... 29 C10 45 26N 6 1 E
Pontchartrain L., *U.S.A.* 155 K10 30 5N 90 5W
Pontchâteau, *France* 26 E4 47 25N 2 5W
Ponte Alta, Serra do, *Brazil* .... 171 E2 19 42 S 47 40W
Ponte Alta do Norte, *Brazil* ..... 170 D2 10 45 S 47 34W
Ponte Branca, *Brazil* .... 173 D7 16 27 S 52 40W
Ponte da Barca, *Portugal* 43 F2 39 17N 8 1W
Ponte dell'Ólio, *Italy* .... 44 D6 44 52N 9 39 E
Ponte di Legno, *Italy* .... 44 B7 46 16N 10 31 E
Ponte do Lima, *Portugal* 42 D2 41 46N 8 35W
Ponte do Pungoé, *Mozam.* .... 119 F3 19 30 S 34 33 E
Ponte-Leccia, *France* .... 29 F13 42 28N 9 13 E
Ponte nelle Alpi, *Italy* .... 45 B9 46 11N 12 16 E
Ponte Nova, *Brazil* .... 171 F3 20 25 S 42 54W
Ponte Tresa, *Italy* .... 33 E7 45 58N 8 51 E
Ponte Vedra Beach, *U.S.A.* 152 E8 30 15N 81 23W
Ponteareas, *Spain* 42 C2 42 10N 8 28W
Pontebba, *Italy* .... 45 B10 46 30N 13 18 E
Ponteceso, *Spain* 42 B2 43 15N 8 54W
Pontecorvo, *Italy* .... 46 A6 41 27N 13 40 E
Pontedeume, *Spain* 42 B2 43 24N 8 10W
Ponteix, *Canada* 143 D7 49 46N 107 29W
Pontes e Lacerda, *Brazil* .... 173 D6 15 12 S 59 22W
Pontevedra, Capiz, *Phil.* .... 81 F4 11 29N 122 50 E
Pontevedra, Neg. Occ., *Phil.* .... 81 F4 10 22N 122 52 E
Pontevedra, *Spain* 42 C2 42 26N 8 40W
Pontevedra □, *Spain* 42 C2 42 25N 8 39W
Pontevedra, R. de ➜, *Spain* 42 C2 42 22N 8 45W
Pontevico, *Italy* .... 44 C7 45 16N 10 5 E
Pontiac, Ill., *U.S.A.* 154 E10 40 53N 88 38W
Pontiac, Mich., *U.S.A.* 157 B13 42 38N 83 18W
Pontian Kechil, *Malaysia* .... 87 d 1 29N 103 23 E
Pontianak, *Indonesia* .... 85 C3 0 3 S 109 15 E
Pontine Is. = Ponziane, Ísole, *Italy* 46 B5 40 55N 12 57 E
Pontine Mts. = Kuzey Anadolu Dağları, *Turkey* 100 B7 41 30N 35 0 E
Pontínia, *Italy* .... 46 A6 41 25N 13 2 E
Pontivy, *France* 26 D4 48 5N 2 58W
Pontoise, *France* .... 27 C9 49 3N 2 5 E
Ponton ➜, *Canada* 142 B5 58 27N 116 11W
Pontorson, *France* 26 D5 48 34N 1 30W
Pontrémoli, *Italy* .... 44 D6 44 22N 9 53 E
Pontresina, *Switz.* .... 33 D9 46 29N 9 48 E
Pontrieux, *France* 26 D3 48 42N 3 10W
Ponts, *Spain* .... 40 D6 41 55N 1 12 E
Pontypool, *Canada* 150 B6 44 6N 78 38W
Pontypool, *U.K.* 21 F4 51 42N 3 2W
Ponza, *Italy* .... 46 B5 40 54N 12 58 E
Ponziane, Ísole, *Italy* .... 46 B5 40 55N 12 57 E
Poochera, *Australia* .... 127 E1 32 43 S 134 51 E
Poole, *U.K.* 21 G6 50 43N 1 59W
Poole □, *U.K.* 21 G6 50 43N 1 59W
Pooler, *U.S.A.* 152 C8 32 7N 81 15W
Poona = Pune, *India* .... 94 E1 18 29N 73 57 E
Poonamallee, *India* .... 95 H5 13 3N 80 10 E
Pooncarie, *Australia* .... 128 B5 33 22 S 142 31 E
Poopelloe L., *Australia* .... 128 A6 31 40 S 144 0 E
Poopó, *Bolivia* .... 172 D4 18 23 S 66 59W
Poopó, L. de, *Bolivia* .... 172 D4 18 30 S 67 35W
Poor Knights Is., *N.Z.* .... 130 B3 35 29 S 174 43 E
Poorman, *U.S.A.* 144 D9 64 5N 155 33W
Popa, *Gabon* .... 114 C2 1 35 S 12 32 E
Popayán, *Colombia* 168 C2 2 27N 76 36W
Poperinge, *Belgium* .... 24 D2 50 51N 2 42 E
Popilta L., *Australia* .... 128 B4 33 10 S 141 42 E
Popina, *Bulgaria* .... 51 B10 44 7N 26 57 E
Popio L., *Australia* .... 128 B4 33 10 S 141 52 E
Poplar, *U.S.A.* 143 C9 53 0N 97 19W
Poplar Bluff, *U.S.A.* 155 G9 36 46N 90 24W
Poplarville, *U.S.A.* 155 K10 30 51N 89 32W
Popocatépetl, Volcán, *Mexico* 163 D5 19 2N 98 38W
Popokabaka, *Dem. Rep. of the Congo* 115 D3 5 41 S 16 40 E
Popoli, *Italy* .... 45 F10 42 10N 13 50 E
Popolo, *Dem. Rep. of the Congo* .. 114 B4 2 22N 21 8 E
Popomanaseu, Mt., *Solomon Is.* ... 133 M11 9 40 S 160 1 E
Popondetta, *Papua N. G.* .... 132 E5 8 48 S 148 17 E
Popovača, *Croatia* .... 45 C13 45 30N 16 41 E
Popovo, *Bulgaria* .... 51 C10 43 21N 26 18 E
Poppberg, *Germany* .... 31 F7 49 26N 11 37 E
Poppi, *Italy* .... 45 E8 43 43N 11 46 E
Poprad, *Slovak Rep.* .... 35 B13 49 3N 20 18 E
Poprad ➜, *Slovak Rep.* .... 35 B13 49 38N 20 42 E
Poradaha, *Bangla.* .... 93 H12 23 51N 89 1 E
Porali ➜, *Pakistan* .... 91 D2 25 58N 66 26 E
Porangaba, *Brazil* .... 172 B3 8 48 S 70 36W
Porangahau, *N.Z.* .... 130 G5 40 17 S 176 37 E
Porangatu, *Brazil* .... 171 D2 13 26 S 49 10W
Porbandar, *India* .... 92 J3 21 44N 69 43 E
Porce ➜, *Colombia* 168 B3 7 28N 74 53W
Porcher I., *Canada* 142 C2 53 50N 130 30W
Porco, *Bolivia* .... 173 D4 19 50 S 65 59W
Porcos ➜, *Brazil* .... 171 D2 12 42 S 45 7W
Porcuna, *Spain* 43 H6 37 52N 4 11W
Porcupine ➜, *Canada* 143 C8 52 45N 101 20W
Porcupine ➜, *U.S.A.* 144 C11 66 34N 145 19W
Porcupine Gorge Nat. Park △, *Australia* 126 C3 20 22 S 144 26 E
Pordenone, *Italy* .... 45 C9 45 57N 12 39 E
Pordim, *Bulgaria* .... 51 C8 43 23N 24 51 E
Pore, *Colombia* 168 B3 5 43N 72 0W
Poreč, *Croatia* .... 45 C10 45 14N 13 36 E
Porecatu, *Brazil* .... 171 F1 22 43 S 51 24W
Poretskoye, *Russia* .... 60 C8 55 9N 46 21 E
Porgera, *Papua N. G.* .... 132 E1 5 28 S 143 12 E
Pori, *Finland* .... 15 F19 61 29N 21 48 E
Pori, *Greece* .... 48 F5 35 58N 23 13 E
Porkhov, *Russia* .... 58 B5 57 45N 29 38 E
Porlamar, *Venezuela* 169 A5 10 57N 63 51W
Porlezza, *Italy* .... 44 B6 46 2N 9 7 E
Porma ➜, *Spain* .... 42 C5 42 49N 5 28 E
Pornic, *France* 26 E4 47 7N 2 5W
Poronaysk, *Russia* .... 67 E15 49 13N 143 0 E
Póros, Attikí, *Greece* .... 48 D5 37 30N 23 30 E
Póros, Kefallinía, *Greece* .... 39 C2 38 9N 20 47 E
Póros, Levkás, *Greece* .... 38 C2 38 38N 20 43 E
Poroshiri-Dake, *Japan* .... 70 C11 42 41N 142 52 E
Poroszló, *Hungary* .... 53 C6 47 39N 20 40 E
Poroto Mts., *Tanzania* .... 119 D3 9 0 S 33 30 E
Porpoise B., *Antarctica* .... 5 C9 66 0 S 127 0 E
Porpoise Pt., *Ascension I.* ...... 9 g 7 54 S 14 21W
Porquerolles, Î. de, *France* ..... 29 F10 43 0N 6 13 E
Porrentruy, *Switz.* .... 32 B4 47 25N 7 6 E
Porreres, *Spain* .... 38 B4 39 31N 3 2 E
Porsangen, *Norway* .... 14 A21 70 40N 25 40 E
Porsgrunn, *Norway* .... 18 E6 59 10N 9 40 E
Port Adelaide, *Australia* .... 128 C3 34 46 S 138 30 E
Port Alberni, *Canada* 142 D4 49 14N 124 50W

Port Albert, *Australia* .... 129 E7 38 42 S 146 42 E
Port Alexander, *U.S.A.* 144 H14 56 15N 134 38W
Port Alfred, *S. Africa* .... 116 E4 33 36 S 26 55 E
Port Alice, *Canada* 142 C3 50 20N 127 25W
Port Allegany, *U.S.A.* 150 E6 41 48N 78 17W
Port Allen, *U.S.A.* 155 K9 30 27N 91 12W
Port Alma, *Australia* .... 126 C5 23 38 S 150 53 E
Port Angeles, *U.S.A.* 160 B3 48 7N 123 27W
Port Antonio, *Jamaica* .... 164 a 18 10N 76 30W
Port Aransas, *U.S.A.* 155 M6 27 50N 97 4W
Port Arthur = Lüshun, *China* ..... 75 E11 38 45N 121 15 E
Port Arthur, *Australia* .... 127 G4 43 7 S 147 50 E
Port Arthur, *U.S.A.* 155 L8 29 54N 93 56W
Port au Choix, *Canada* 141 B8 50 43N 57 22W
Port au Port B., *Canada* 141 C8 48 40N 58 50W
Port-au-Prince, *Haiti* 165 C5 18 40N 72 20W
Port Augusta, *Australia* .... 128 B2 32 30 S 137 50 E
Port Austin, *U.S.A.* 150 B2 44 3N 83 1W
Port Bell, *Uganda* .... 118 B3 0 18N 32 35 E
Port Bergé Vaovao, *Madag.* .... 117 B8 15 33 S 47 40 E
Port Blair, *India* .... 95 J11 11 40N 92 45 E
Port Blandford, *Canada* 141 C9 48 20N 54 10W
Port-Bouët, *Ivory C.* 112 D4 5 16N 3 57W
Port Bradshaw, *Australia* .... 126 A2 12 30 S 137 20 E
Port Broughton, *Australia* .... 128 B2 33 37 S 137 56 E
Port Burwell, *Canada* 150 D4 42 40N 80 48W
Port Byron, *U.S.A.* 156 C6 41 37N 90 19W
Port Campbell, *Australia* .... 128 E5 38 37 S 143 1 E
Port Campbell, *India* .... 95 J11 11 56N 92 37 E
Port Campbell Nat. Park △, *Australia* 128 E5 38 8 S 143 6 E
Port Canning, *India* .... 93 H13 22 23N 88 40 E
Port-Cartier, *Canada* 141 B6 50 2N 66 50W
Port Chalmers, *N.Z.* .... 131 F5 45 49 S 170 30 E
Port Charles, *N.Z.* .... 130 C4 36 33 S 175 30 E
Port Charlotte, *U.S.A.* 153 J7 26 59N 82 6W
Port Chester, *U.S.A.* 151 F11 41 0N 73 40W
Port Clements, *Canada* 142 C2 53 40N 132 10W
Port Clinton, *U.S.A.* 157 C14 41 31N 82 56W
Port Colborne, *Canada* 140 D4 42 50N 79 10W
Port Coquitlam, *Canada* 142 D4 49 15N 122 45W
Port Cornwallis, *India* .... 95 H11 13 17N 93 5 E
Port Credit, *Canada* 150 C5 43 33N 79 35W
Port-Cros, Parc Nat. de △, *France* 29 F10 43 0N 6 24 E
Port Curtis, *Australia* .... 126 C5 23 57 S 151 20 E
Port d'Alcúdia, *Spain* .... 38 B4 39 50N 3 7 E
Port Dalhousie, *Canada* 150 C5 43 13N 79 16W
Port d'Andratx, *Spain* .... 38 B3 39 32N 2 23 E
Port Darwin, *Australia* .... 124 B5 12 24 S 130 45 E
Port Darwin, *Falk. Is.* .... 9 f 51 50 S 59 0W
Port Davey, *Australia* .... 127 G4 43 16 S 145 55 E
Port-de-Bouc, *France* .... 29 E8 43 24N 4 59 E
Port-de-Paix, *Haiti* 165 C5 19 50N 72 50W
Port de Pollença, *Spain* .... 38 B4 39 54N 3 4 E
Port de Sóller, *Spain* .... 38 B3 39 48N 2 42 E
Port Dickson, *Malaysia* .... 87 L3 2 30N 101 49 E
Port Douglas, *Australia* .... 126 B4 16 30 S 145 30 E
Port Dover, *Canada* 150 D4 42 47N 80 12W
Port Edward, *Canada* 142 C2 54 12N 130 10W
Port Elgin, *Canada* 140 D3 44 25N 81 25W
Port Elizabeth, *S. Africa* .... 116 E4 33 58 S 25 40 E
Port Ellen, *U.K.* 22 F2 55 38N 6 11W
Port Elliot, *Australia* .... 128 C3 35 32 S 138 41 E
Port-en-Bessin, *France* 26 C6 49 21N 0 45W
Port Erin, *U.K.* 20 C3 54 5N 4 45W
Port Essington, *Australia* .... 124 B5 11 15 S 132 10 E
Port Etienne = Nouâdhibou, *Mauritania* 110 D1 20 54N 17 0W
Port Ewen, *U.S.A.* 151 E11 41 54N 73 59W
Port Fairy, *Australia* .... 128 E5 38 22 S 142 12 E
Port Fitzroy, *N.Z.* .... 130 C4 36 8 S 175 20 E
Port Fouâd = Bûr Fuad, *Egypt* .... 106 H8 31 15N 32 20 E
Port Francqui = Ilebo, *Dem. Rep. of the Congo* 115 C4 4 17 S 20 55 E
Port Gamble, *U.S.A.* 160 C4 47 51N 122 35W
Port-Gentil, *Gabon* .... 114 C1 0 40 S 8 50 E
Port Germein, *Australia* .... 127 E2 33 1 S 138 1 E
Port Gibson, *U.S.A.* 155 K9 31 58N 90 59W
Port Glasgow, *U.K.* 22 F4 55 56N 4 41W
Port Harcourt, *Nigeria* .... 113 E6 4 40N 7 10 E
Port Hardy, *Canada* 142 C3 50 41N 127 30W
Port Harrison = Inukjuak, *Canada* 139 C12 58 25N 78 15W
Port Hawkesbury, *Canada* 141 C7 45 36N 61 22W
Port Hedland, *Australia* .... 124 D2 20 25 S 118 35 E
Port Heiden, *U.S.A.* 144 H8 56 55N 158 41W
Port Henry, *U.S.A.* 151 B11 44 3N 73 28W
Port Herald = Nsanje, *Malawi* .... 119 F4 16 55 S 35 12 E
Port Hood, *Canada* 141 C7 46 0N 61 32W
Port Hope, *Canada* 140 D4 43 56N 78 20W
Port Hope, *U.S.A.* 150 B2 43 57N 82 43W
Port Hope Simpson, *Canada* 141 B8 52 33N 56 18W
Port Hueneme, *U.S.A.* 161 L7 34 7N 119 12W
Port Huron, *U.S.A.* 150 D2 42 58N 82 26W
Port Iliç, *Azerbaijan* .... 101 C13 38 53N 48 47 E
Port Jefferson, *U.S.A.* 151 F11 40 57N 73 3W
Port Jervis, *U.S.A.* 151 E10 41 22N 74 41W
Port-Joinville, *France* 26 F4 46 45N 2 23W
Port Katon, *Russia* .... 59 J10 46 52N 38 46 E
Port Kelang = Pelabuhan Kelang, *Malaysia* 87 L3 3 0N 101 23 E
Port Kembla, *Australia* .... 129 C9 34 52 S 150 49 E
Port Kenny, *Australia* .... 127 E1 33 10 S 134 41 E
Port-la-Nouvelle, *France* .... 28 E7 43 1N 3 3 E
Port Laoise = Portlaoise, *Ireland* 23 D4 52 15N 7 8W
Port Lairge = Waterford, *Ireland* 23 C4 53 2N 7 18W
Port Lavaca, *U.S.A.* 155 L6 28 37N 96 38W
Port Leyden, *U.S.A.* 151 C9 43 35N 75 21W
Port Lincoln, *Australia* .... 128 B2 34 42 S 135 52 E
Port Lions, *U.S.A.* 144 H9 57 52N 152 53W
Port Loko, *S. Leone* 112 D2 8 48N 12 46W
Port Louis, *France* 26 E3 47 42N 3 22W
Port-Louis, *Guadeloupe* .... 164 b 16 28N 61 32W
Port Louis, *Mauritius* .... 121 d 20 10 S 57 30 E
Port Lyautey = Kenitra, *Morocco* 110 B3 34 15N 6 40W
Port MacDonnell, *Australia* ...... 128 E3 38 5 S 140 48 E
Port McNeill, *Canada* 142 C3 50 35N 127 6W
Port Macquarie, *Australia* .... 129 A10 31 25 S 152 25 E
Port Maria, *Jamaica* .... 164 a 18 25N 76 55W
Port Matilda, *U.S.A.* 150 F6 40 48N 78 3W
Port Mayaca, *U.S.A.* 153 J9 26 59N 80 36W
Port Mellon, *Canada* 142 D4 49 32N 123 31W
Port-Menier, *Canada* 141 C7 49 51N 64 15W
Port Moller, *U.S.A.* 144 A4 49 17N 122 51W
Port Moody, *Canada* 160 A4 49 17N 122 51W
Port Morant, *Jamaica* .... 164 a 17 54N 76 19W
Port Moresby, *Papua N. G.* .... 132 E4 9 24 S 147 8 E
Port Mourant, *Guyana* 169 B6 6 15N 57 20W
Port Musgrave, *Australia* .... 126 A3 11 55 S 141 50 E
Port Narevin, *Vanuatu* .... 133 H7 18 45 S 169 10 E
Port-Navalo, *France* 26 E4 47 34N 2 54W
Port Neches, *U.S.A.* 155 L8 30 0N 93 59W
Port Nicholson, *N.Z.* .... 130 H3 41 20 S 174 52 E
Port Nolloth, *S. Africa* .... 116 D2 29 17 S 16 52 E
Port Nouveau-Québec = Kangiqsualujjuaq, *Canada* 139 C13 58 30N 65 59W
Port of Spain, *Trin. & Tob.* 169 F9 10 40N 61 31W
Port Olry, *Vanuatu* .... 133 E5 15 1 S 167 4 E
Port Orange, *U.S.A.* 153 F9 29 9N 80 59W
Port Orchard, *U.S.A.* 160 C4 47 32N 122 38W
Port Orford, *U.S.A.* 158 E1 42 45N 124 30W
Port Pegasus, *N.Z.* .... 131 H2 47 12 S 167 41 E
Port Perry, *Canada* 140 D4 44 6N 78 56W
Port Phillip B., *Australia* ...... 129 E6 38 10 S 144 50 E
Port Pirie, *Australia* .... 128 B3 33 10 S 138 1 E
Port Radium = Echo Bay, *Canada* .. 138 B8 66 5N 117 55W

Port Renfrew, *Canada* 142 D4 48 30N 124 20W
Port Roper, *Australia* .... 126 A2 14 45 S 135 25 E
Port Rowan, *Canada* 150 D4 42 40N 80 30W
Port Royal Sd., *U.S.A.* 152 C9 32 15N 80 40W
Port Safaga = Bûr Safâga, *Egypt* 96 E2 26 43N 33 57 E
Port Said = Bûr Sa'îd, *Egypt* .... 106 H8 31 16N 32 18 E
Port St. Joe, *U.S.A.* 152 F4 29 49N 85 18W
Port St. Johns = Umzimvubu, *S. Africa* 117 E4 31 38 S 29 33 E
Port-St-Louis-du-Rhône, *France* .. 29 E8 43 23N 4 49 E
Port St. Lucie, *U.S.A.* 153 H9 27 20N 80 20W
Port-Ste-Marie, *France* .... 28 D4 44 15N 0 25 E
Port St. Marie, *France* 153 H9 27 9N 80 12W
Port Sanilac, *U.S.A.* 150 C2 43 26N 82 33W
Port Severn, *Canada* 150 B5 44 48N 79 43W
Port Shepstone, *S. Africa* .... 117 E5 30 44 S 30 28 E
Port Simpson, *Canada* 142 C2 54 30N 130 20W
Port Stanley = Stanley, *Falk. Is.* 9 f 51 40 S 59 51W
Port Stanley, *Canada* 140 D3 42 40N 81 10W
Port Sudan = Bûr Sûdân, *Sudan* ... 106 D4 19 32N 37 9 E
Port Sulphur, *U.S.A.* 155 L10 29 29N 89 42W
Port-sur-Saône, *France* .... 27 E13 47 42N 6 2 E
Port Talbot, *U.K.* 21 F4 51 35N 3 47W
Port Taufiq = Bûr Taufiq, *Egypt* 106 J8 29 54N 32 32 E
Port Townsend, *U.S.A.* 160 B4 48 7N 122 45W
Port-Vato, *Vanuatu* .... 133 F5 16 20 S 168 1 E
Port-Vendres, *France* .... 28 F7 42 32N 3 8 E
Port Victoria, *Australia* .... 128 C2 34 30 S 137 29 E
Port Vila, *Vanuatu* .... 133 G6 17 45 S 168 18 E
Port Vladimir, *Russia* .... 56 A5 69 25 S 33 6 E
Port Wakefield, *Australia* .... 128 C3 34 12 S 138 10 E
Port Washington, *U.S.A.* 148 D2 43 23N 87 53W
Port Weld = Kuala Sepetang, *Malaysia* 87 K3 4 49N 100 28 E
Port Wentworth, *U.S.A.* 152 C8 32 9N 81 10W
Porta Orientalis, *Romania* .... 37 F12 45 6N 22 18 E
Portachuelo, *Bolivia* .... 173 D5 17 10 S 63 20W
Portadown, *U.K.* 23 B5 54 25N 6 27W
Portaferry, *U.K.* .... 23 B6 54 23 S 5 33W
Portage, Mich., *U.S.A.* 157 B11 42 12N 85 35W
Portage, Pa., *U.S.A.* 150 F6 40 23N 78 41W
Portage, Wis., *U.S.A.* 154 D10 43 33N 89 28W
Portage ➜, *U.S.A.* 157 C14 41 31N 83 5W
Portage La Prairie, *Canada* 143 D9 49 58N 98 18W
Portageville, *U.S.A.* 155 G10 36 26N 89 42W
Portal, *U.S.A.* 152 C8 32 33N 81 56W
Portalegre, *Portugal* 43 F3 39 19N 7 25W
Portalegre □, *Portugal* 43 F3 39 20N 7 40W
Portales, *U.S.A.* 155 H3 34 11N 103 20W
Portarlington, *Ireland* 23 C4 53 9N 7 14W
Portbou, *Spain* .... 40 C8 42 25N 3 9 E
Porteira, *Brazil* .... 169 D6 1 5 S 57 4W
Porteirinha, *Brazil* .... 171 E3 15 44 S 43 2W
Portel, *Brazil* .... 170 B1 1 57 S 50 49W
Portel, *Portugal* 43 G3 38 19N 7 41W
Portela, Lisbon ✈ (LIS), *Portugal* 43 G1 38 46N 9 8W
Porter, *U.S.A.* 157 C9 41 36N 87 3W
Porter L., N.W.T., *Canada* 143 A7 61 41N 108 5W
Porter L., Sask., *Canada* 143 B7 56 20N 107 20W
Porterville, *S. Africa* .... 116 E2 33 0 S 19 0 E
Porterville, *U.S.A.* 160 J8 36 4N 119 1W
Portes-lès-Valence, *France* ...... 29 D8 44 52N 4 54 E
Porthcawl, *U.K.* 21 F4 51 29N 3 42W
Porthill, *U.S.A.* 158 B5 48 59N 116 30W
Portile de Fier, *Europe* .... 52 F7 44 44N 22 30 E
Portimão, *Portugal* 43 H2 37 8N 8 32W
Portishead, *U.K.* 21 F5 51 29N 2 46W
Portiței, Gura, *Romania* .... 53 F14 44 41N 29 0 E
Portknockie, *U.K.* 22 D6 57 42N 2 51W
Portland, N.S.W., *Australia* ..... 129 B9 33 20 S 150 0 E
Portland, Vic., *Australia* .... 128 E4 38 20 S 141 35 E
Portland, *Canada* 151 B8 44 42N 76 12W
Portland, Conn., *U.S.A.* 151 E12 41 34N 72 38W
Portland, Fla., *U.S.A.* 152 E3 30 31N 86 12W
Portland, Ind., *U.S.A.* 157 D12 40 26N 84 59W
Portland, Maine, *U.S.A.* 139 D12 43 39N 70 16W
Portland, Mich., *U.S.A.* 157 B12 42 52N 84 54W
Portland, Oreg., *U.S.A.* 160 E4 45 32N 122 37W
Portland, Pa., *U.S.A.* 151 F9 40 55N 75 6W
Portland, Tex., *U.S.A.* 155 M6 27 53N 97 20W
Portland ✈ (PDX), *U.S.A.* 160 E4 45 35N 122 36W
Portland, I. of, *U.K.* 21 G5 50 33N 2 26W
Portland B., *Australia* .... 128 E4 38 15 S 141 45 E
Portland Bight, *Jamaica* .... 164 a 17 52N 77 5W
Portland Bill, *U.K.* 21 G5 50 31N 2 28W
Portland Canal, *U.S.A.* 142 B2 55 56N 130 0W
Portland I., *N.Z.* .... 130 F6 39 20 S 177 51 E
Portland Pt., *Ascension I.* ...... 9 g 7 59 S 14 25W
Portland Pt., *Jamaica* .... 164 a 17 42N 77 11W
Portmadoc = Porthmadog, *U.K.* 20 E3 52 55N 4 8W
Portmore, *Jamaica* .... 164 a 17 53N 77 33W
Pôrto, *Brazil* .... 170 B3 3 54 S 42 42W
Porto, *France* .... 29 F12 42 16N 8 42 E
Porto, *Portugal* 42 D2 41 8N 8 40W
Porto □, *Portugal* 42 D2 41 8N 8 40W
Pôrto, G. de, *France* .... 29 F12 42 17N 8 34 E
Pôrto Acre, *Brazil* .... 172 B4 9 34 S 67 31W
Pôrto Alegre, Pará, *Brazil* ...... 169 D7 3 25 S 52 44W
Pôrto Alegre, Rio Grande do S., *Brazil* 175 C5 30 5 S 51 10W
Porto Amboim = Gunza, *Angola* .... 115 G2 10 50 S 13 50 E
Pôrto Azzurro, *Italy* .... 44 F7 42 46N 10 24 E
Pôrto Cajueiro, *Brazil* .... 173 C6 11 3 S 55 53W
Pôrto Cristo, *Spain* .... 38 B4 39 33N 3 20 E
Pôrto da Fôlha, *Brazil* .... 170 C4 9 55 S 37 17W
Pôrto de Móz, *Brazil* .... 169 D7 1 41 S 52 13W
Pôrto de Pedras, *Brazil* .... 170 C4 9 10 S 35 17W
Pôrto dos Meinacos, *Brazil* ...... 173 C7 12 33 S 53 7W
Pôrto dos Gaúchos, *Brazil* .... 173 C6 11 32 S 55 0W
Pôrto Empédocle, *Italy* .... 46 E6 37 17N 13 32 E
Pôrto Esperança, *Brazil* .... 173 D6 19 37 S 57 29W
Pôrto Esperidão, *Brazil* .... 173 D6 15 51 S 58 28W
Pôrto Formoso, *Azores* 9 d3 37 49N 25 25W
Pôrto Franco, *Brazil* .... 170 C2 6 20 S 47 24W
Pôrto Inglês, *C. Verde Is.* ...... 9 j 15 2N 23 10W
Pôrto Jofre, *Brazil* .... 173 D6 17 30 S 56 48W
Pôrto Lágos, *Greece* .... 51 E9 41 1N 25 6 E
Pôrto Mendes, *Brazil* .... 173 A5 24 30 S 54 15W
Pôrto Moniz, *Madeira* .... 9 c 32 52N 17 11W
Pôrto Murtinho, *Brazil* .... 173 D6 21 45 S 57 55W
Pôrto Nacional, *Brazil* .... 170 D2 10 40 S 48 30W
Pôrto-Novo, *Benin* .... 113 D5 6 23N 2 42 E
Pôrto Petro, *Spain* .... 38 B4 39 22N 3 13 E
Pôrto San Giórgio, *Italy* .... 45 E10 43 11N 13 48 E
Pôrto Sant'Elpídio, *Italy* .... 45 E10 43 15N 13 43 E
Pôrto Santo, *Brazil* .... 169 D7 3 5 S 51 11W
Pôrto Santo Stéfano, *Italy* ...... 44 F8 42 26N 11 7 E
Pôrto São José, *Brazil* .... 175 A5 22 43 S 53 10W
Pôrto Seguro, *Brazil* .... 171 E4 16 26 S 39 5W
Porto Tolle, *Italy* .... 45 D9 44 56N 12 22 E
Pôrto Tórres, *Italy* .... 46 B1 40 50N 8 24 E
Pôrto União, *Brazil* .... 175 B5 26 10 S 51 10W
Pôrto Válter, *Brazil* .... 172 B3 8 15 S 72 40W
Porto-Vecchio, *France* .... 29 G13 41 35N 9 16 E
Pôrto Velho, *Brazil* .... 173 B5 8 46 S 63 54W
Portoferraio, *Italy* .... 44 F7 42 48N 10 20 E
Portofino, *Italy* .... 44 D6 44 18N 9 12 E
Portogruaro, *Italy* .... 45 C10 45 47N 12 50 E
Portola, *U.S.A.* 160 F6 39 49N 120 28W
Portomaggiore, *Italy* .... 45 D8 44 42N 11 48 E

Portør, Norway .... 18 F6 58 48N 9 28 E
Portoscuso, Italy .... 46 C1 39 12N 8 24 E
Portovénere, Italy .... 44 D6 44 3N 9 51 E
Portoviejo, Ecuador 168 D1 1 7S 80 28W
Portpatrick, U.K. 22 G3 54 51N 5 7W
Portree, U.K. 22 D2 57 25N 6 12W
Portrush, U.K. 23 A5 55 12N 6 40W
Portsmouth, Domin. 165 C7 15 34N 61 27W
Portsmouth, U.K. 21 G6 50 48N 1 6W
Portsmouth, N.H., U.S.A. ... 149 D10 43 5N 70 45W
Portsmouth, Ohio, U.S.A. ... 148 F4 38 44N 82 57W
Portsmouth, R.I., U.S.A. 151 E13 41 36N 71 15W
Portsmouth, Va., U.S.A. 148 G7 36 50N 76 18W
Portsmouth □, U.K. 21 G6 50 48N 1 6W
Portsoy, U.K. 22 D6 57 41N 2 41W
Portstewart, U.K. 23 A5 55 11N 6 43W
Porttipahtan tekojärvi, Finland 14 B22 68 5N 26 40 E
Portugal ■, Europe 42 F3 40 0N 8 0W
Portugalete, Spain 40 B1 43 19N 3 4W
Portuguesa □, Venezuela 168 B4 9 10N 69 15W
Portuguese Guinea = Guinea-
Bissau ■, Africa 112 C2 12 0N 15 0W
Portuguese West Africa = Angola ■,
Africa .... 115 E3 12 0S 18 0 E
Portumna, Ireland 23 C3 53 6N 8 14W
Portville, U.S.A. 150 D6 42 3N 78 20W
Porvenir, Bolivia 172 C4 11 10S 68 50W
Porvenir, Chile 176 D2 53 10S 70 16W
Porvoo, Finland .... 15 F21 60 24N 25 40 E
Porzuna, Spain 43 F6 39 9N 4 9W
Posada, Italy .... 46 B2 40 38N 9 43 E
Posada →, Italy .... 46 B2 40 39N 9 45 E
Posadas, Argentina 175 B4 27 30S 55 50W
Posadas, Spain 43 H5 37 47N 5 11W
Poschiavo, Switz. .... 33 D10 46 19N 10 4 E
Posen = Poznań, Poland .... 55 F3 52 25N 16 55 E
Posets, Spain .... 40 C5 42 39N 0 25 E
Poseyville, U.S.A. 157 F9 38 10N 87 47W
Posht-e Badam, Iran .... 97 C7 33 2N 55 23 E
Posídhion, Ákra, Greece .... 50 G7 39 57N 23 30 E
Posidium, Greece .... 49 F9 35 30N 27 10 E
Poso, Indonesia .... 82 B2 1 20S 120 55 E
Poso, Danau, Indonesia .... 82 B2 1 52S 120 35 E
Posoegroenoe, Suriname .... 75 G14 34 46N 127 5 E
Posong, S. Korea .... 75 G14 34 46N 127 5 E
Posse, Brazil 171 D2 14 4S 46 18W
Possel, C.A.R. .... 114 A3 5 5N 19 10 E
Possession I., Antarctica ... 7 D11 72 4S 172 0 E
Pössneck, Germany .... 30 E7 50 42N 11 35 E
Possum Kingdom L., U.S.A. . 155 J5 32 52N 98 26W
Post, U.S.A. 155 J4 33 12N 101 23W
Post Falls, U.S.A. 158 C5 47 43N 116 57W
Postavy = Pastavy, Belarus . 15 J22 55 4N 26 50 E
Poste-de-la-Baleine = Kuujjuarapik,
Canada 140 A4 55 20N 77 35W
Poste Maurice Cortier, Algeria 111 D5 22 14N 1 2 E
Postmasburg, S. Africa ..... 116 D3 28 18S 23 5 E
Postojna, Slovenia .... 45 C11 45 46N 14 12 E
Poston, U.S.A. 161 M12 34 0N 114 24W
Postville, Canada 141 B8 54 54N 59 47W
Postville, U.S.A. 156 A5 43 5N 91 34W
Potchefstroom, S. Africa .... 116 D4 26 41S 27 7 E
Potcoava, Romania .... 53 F9 44 30N 24 39 E
Poté, Brazil 171 E3 17 49S 41 49W
Poteau, U.S.A. 155 H7 35 3N 94 37W
Poteet, U.S.A. 155 L5 29 2N 98 35W
Potenza, Italy .... 47 B8 40 38N 15 48 E
Potenza →, Italy .... 45 E10 43 25N 13 40 E
Potenza Picena, Italy ...... 45 E10 43 22N 13 37 E
Poteriteri, L., N.Z. .... 131 G2 46 5S 167 10 E
Potgietersrus, S. Africa ..... 117 C4 24 10S 28 55 E
Poti, Georgia .... 61 J5 42 10N 41 38 E
Potiraguá, Brazil 171 E4 15 36S 39 53W
Potiskum, Nigeria .... 113 C7 11 39N 11 2 E
Potlogi, Romania .... 53 F10 44 34N 25 34 E
Potomac →, U.S.A. 148 G7 38 0N 76 23W
Potosí, Bolivia 173 D4 19 38S 65 50W
Potosi, U.S.A. 156 G6 37 56N 90 47W
Potosí □, Bolivia 172 E4 20 31S 67 0W
Potosi Mt., U.S.A. 161 K11 35 57N 115 29W
Pototan, Phil. .... 81 F4 10 54N 122 38 E
Potrerillos, Chile 174 B2 26 30S 69 30W
Potsdam, Germany .... 30 C9 52 25N 13 4 E
Potsdam, U.S.A. 151 B10 44 40N 74 59W
Pottangi, India .... 94 E6 18 34N 82 58 E
Pottenstein, Germany ...... 31 F7 49 46N 11 24 E
Pottersville, U.S.A. 151 C11 43 43N 73 50W
Pottery Hill = Abu Ballas, Egypt 106 C2 24 26N 27 36 E
Pottstown, U.S.A. 151 F9 40 15N 75 39W
Pottsville, U.S.A. 151 F8 40 41N 76 12W
Pottuvil, Sri Lanka .... 95 L5 6 55N 81 50 E
Potzu, Taiwan .... 77 F13 23 30N 120 25 E
Pouancé, France 26 E5 47 44N 1 10W
Pouce Coupé, Canada 142 B4 55 40N 120 10W
Pouébo, N. Cal. .... 133 T18 20 24S 164 36 E
Pouembout, N. Cal. .... 133 U18 21 8S 164 53 E
Poughkeepsie, U.S.A. 151 E11 41 42N 73 56W
Pouilly-sur-Loire, France ... 27 E9 47 17N 2 57 E
Poulan, U.S.A. 152 D6 31 31N 83 47W
Poulaphouca Res., Ireland .. 23 C5 53 8N 6 30W
Pouláta, Greece .... 39 C2 38 14N 20 36 E
Poulsbo, U.S.A. 160 C4 47 44N 122 39W
Poultney, U.S.A. 151 C11 43 31N 73 14W
Poulton-le-Fylde, U.K. 20 D5 53 51N 2 58W
Poum, N. Cal. .... 133 T18 20 14S 164 2 E
Pouma-Nganda, Gabon .... 114 E2 2 58S 10 51 E
Pouso Alegre, Mato Grosso, Brazil 173 C6 11 46S 57 16W
Pouso Alegre, Minas Gerais, Brazil 175 A6 22 14S 45 57W
Pout, Senegal 112 C1 14 45N 17 0W
Pouthisat, Cambodia ...... 86 F4 12 34N 103 50 E
Pouzauges, France 26 F6 46 47N 0 50W
Pova de Sta. Iria, Portugal .. 43 G1 38 51N 9 4W
Povazská Bystrica, Slovak Rep. 35 B11 49 8N 18 27 E
Povenets, Russia .... 56 B5 62 50N 34 50 E
Poverty B., N.Z. .... 130 E7 38 43S 178 2 E
Povlen, Serbia, Yug. .... 50 B3 44 9N 19 44 E
Póvoa de Lanhosa, Portugal . 42 D2 41 33N 8 15W
Póvoa de Varzim, Portugal .. 42 D2 41 25N 8 46W
Povoação, Azores 9 d3 37 45N 25 15W
Povorino, Russia .... 60 E6 51 12N 42 5 E
Povungnituk = Puvirnituq, Canada 139 B12 60 2N 77 10W
Powassan, Canada 140 C4 46 5N 79 25W
Poway, U.S.A. 161 N9 32 58N 117 2W
Powder →, U.S.A. 154 B2 46 45N 105 26W
Powder River, U.S.A. 158 E10 43 2N 106 59W
Powder Springs, U.S.A. 152 B5 33 52N 84 41W
Powell, U.S.A. 158 D9 44 45N 108 46W
Powell, L., U.S.A. 159 H8 36 57N 111 29W
Powell River, Canada 142 D4 49 50N 124 35W
Powelton, U.S.A. 152 B7 33 26N 82 52W
Powers, U.S.A. 148 C2 45 41N 87 32W
Powys □, U.K. 21 E4 52 20N 3 20W
Poxoreu, Brazil 173 D7 15 50S 54 30W
Poya, N. Cal. .... 133 U19 21 19S 165 7 E
Poyang Hu, China .... 77 C11 29 5N 116 20 E
Poyarkovo, Russia .... 67 E13 49 36N 128 41 E
Poysdorf, Austria .... 35 C9 48 40N 16 37 E
Poza de la Sal, Spain 42 C7 42 35N 3 31W
Poza Rica, Mexico 163 C5 20 33N 97 27W
Pozanti, Turkey .... 100 D6 37 25N 34 50 E
Požarevac, Serbia, Yug. .... 50 B5 44 35N 21 18 E

Pozazal, Puerto, Spain 42 C6 42 56N 4 10W
Požega, Croatia .... 52 E2 45 20N 17 40 E
Požega, Serbia, Yug. .... 50 C4 43 53N 20 2 E
Pozhva, Russia .... 64 B6 59 5N 56 5 E
Poznań, Poland .... 55 F3 52 25N 16 55 E
Poznań ✈ (POZ), Poland ... 55 F3 52 26N 16 45 E
Pozo, U.S.A. 161 K6 35 20N 120 24W
Pozo Alcón, Spain 43 H8 37 42N 2 56W
Pozo Almonte, Chile 172 E4 20 10S 69 50W
Pozo Colorado, Paraguay ... 174 A4 23 30S 58 45W
Pozoblanco, Spain 43 G6 38 23N 4 51W
Pozorrubio, Phil. .... 80 C3 16 7N 120 33 E
Pozuzo, Peru 172 C2 10 5S 75 35W
Pozzallo, Italy .... 47 F7 36 43N 14 51 E
Pozzomaggiore, Italy ...... 46 B1 40 24N 8 39 E
Pozzuoli, Italy .... 47 B7 40 49N 14 7 E
Pra →, Ghana 113 D4 5 1N 1 37W
Prabuty, Poland .... 54 E6 53 47N 19 15 E
Prača, Bos.-H. .... 52 G3 43 47N 18 43 E
Prachatice, Czech Rep. ..... 34 B6 49 1N 14 0 E
Prachin Buri, Thailand ..... 86 E3 14 0N 101 25 E
Prachuap Khiri Khan, Thailand 87 G2 11 49N 99 48 E
Pradelles, France .... 28 D7 44 46N 3 52 E
Pradera, Colombia 168 C2 3 25N 76 15W
Prades, France .... 28 F6 42 38N 2 23 E
Prado, Brazil 171 E4 17 20S 39 13W
Prado del Rey, Spain 43 J5 36 48N 5 33W
Pragersko, Slovenia .... 45 B12 46 27N 15 42 E
Prague = Praha, Czech Rep. . 34 A7 50 5N 14 22 E
Prague ✈ (PRG), Czech Rep. . 34 A7 50 7N 14 15 E
Praha, Czech Rep. .... 34 A7 50 5N 14 22 E
Prahecq, France 28 B3 46 19N 0 26W
Prahita →, India .... 94 E14 19 7N 79 55 E
Prahova □, Romania .... 53 E10 45 10N 26 0 E
Prahova →, Romania ...... 53 F10 44 50N 25 50 E
Prahovo, Serbia, Yug. ...... 50 B6 44 18N 22 39 E
Praia, Azores 9 d1 39 3N 27 58W
Praia, C. Verde Is. .... 9 j 14 55N 23 34W
Práia a Mare, Italy .... 47 C8 39 50N 15 45 E
Praia da Vitória, Azores 9 d1 38 44N 27 4W
Praia do Norte, Azores 9 d1 38 36N 28 46W
Praid, Romania .... 53 D10 46 32N 25 10 E
Prainha, Amazonas, Brazil .. 173 B5 7 10S 60 30W
Prainha, Pará, Brazil 169 D7 1 45S 53 30W
Prairie, Australia .... 126 C3 20 50S 144 35 E
Prairie City, U.S.A. 158 D4 44 28N 118 43W
Prairie Dog Town Fork →, U.S.A. 155 H5 34 30N 99 23W
Prairie du Chien, U.S.A. 156 A5 43 3N 91 9W
Prairie du Rocher, U.S.A. ... 156 F6 38 5N 90 6W
Prairie Village, U.S.A. 156 F2 38 58N 94 38W
Prairies, L. of the, Canada .. 143 C8 51 16N 101 32W
Pramánda, Greece .... 48 B3 39 32N 21 8 E
Prampram, Ghana .... 113 D5 5 43N 0 8 E
Pran Buri, Thailand .... 86 F2 12 23N 99 55 E
Prándarjökull, Iceland 11 C12 64 40N 14 55W
Prang, Ghana 113 D4 8 1N 0 56W
Prapat, Indonesia .... 78 D1 2 41N 98 58 E
Praslin, Seychelles .... 121 b 4 18S 55 45 E
Prasonísi, Ákra, Greece .... 38 F11 35 42N 27 46 E
Prästmon, Sweden .... 16 A11 63 5N 17 45 E
Praszka, Poland .... 55 G5 51 5N 18 31 E
Prata, Brazil 171 E2 19 25S 48 54W
Pratabpur, India .... 93 H10 23 28N 83 15 E
Pratapgarh, Raj., India ..... 92 G6 24 2N 74 40 E
Pratapgarh, Ut. P., India ... 93 G9 25 56N 81 59 E
Pratas Is. = Dongsha Dao, China 77 G11 20 45N 116 43 E
Prätigau, Switz. .... 33 C9 46 56N 9 44 E
Prato, Italy .... 44 E8 43 53N 11 6 E
Prato allo Stelvio, Italy .... 33 C11 46 37N 10 35 E
Prátola Peligna, Italy ...... 45 F10 42 6N 13 52 E
Prats-de-Mollo-la-Preste, France 28 F6 42 25N 2 27 E
Pratt, U.S.A. 155 G5 37 39N 98 44W
Pratteln, Switz. .... 32 A5 47 31N 7 41 E
Prattville, U.S.A. 149 J2 32 28N 86 29W
Pravara →, India .... 94 E2 19 35N 74 45 E
Pravdinsk, Russia .... 60 B6 56 29N 43 28 E
Pravets, Bulgaria .... 50 D7 42 53N 23 55 E
Pravia, Spain 42 B4 43 30N 6 12W
Praya, Indonesia .... 85 D5 8 39S 116 17 E
Pré-en-Pail, France 26 D6 48 28N 0 12W
Precipice Nat. Park △, Australia 127 D5 25 18S 150 5 E
Precordillera, Argentina 174 C2 30 0S 69 1W
Predáppio, Italy .... 45 D8 44 6N 11 59 E
Predazzo, Italy .... 45 B8 46 19N 11 36 E
Predeal, Romania .... 53 E10 45 30N 25 34 E
Predejane, Serbia, Yug. .... 50 D6 42 51N 22 9 E
Preeceville, Canada 143 C8 51 57N 102 40W
Preetz, Germany .... 30 A6 54 14N 10 18 E
Pregrada, Croatia .... 45 B12 46 11N 15 45 E
Preili, Latvia .... 15 H22 56 18N 26 43 E
Preko, Croatia .... 45 D12 44 7N 15 11 E
Prelog, Croatia .... 45 B13 46 18N 16 32 E
Premer, Australia .... 129 A8 31 29S 149 56 E
Prémery, France .... 27 E10 47 10N 3 18 E
Prémia, Italy .... 33 D6 46 17N 8 20 E
Premià de Mar, Spain ..... 40 D7 41 29N 2 22 E
Premont, U.S.A. 155 M5 27 22N 98 7W
Premuda, Croatia .... 45 D11 44 20N 14 36 E
Prentice, U.S.A. 154 C9 45 33N 90 17W
Prenzlau, Germany .... 30 B9 53 19N 13 51 E
Preobrazheniye, Russia .... 70 C6 42 54N 133 54 E
Preparis I., Burma .... 95 M11 14 52N 93 41 E
Preparis North Channel, Burma 95 M11 15 27N 94 5 E
Preparis South Channel, Burma 95 M11 14 33N 93 30 E
Přerov, Czech Rep. .... 35 B10 49 28N 17 27 E
Prescott, Canada 140 D4 44 45N 75 30W
Prescott, Ariz., U.S.A. 159 J7 34 33N 112 28W
Prescott, Ark., U.S.A. 155 J8 33 48N 93 23W
Prescott Valley, U.S.A. 159 J7 34 40N 112 18W
Preservation Inlet, N.Z. .... 131 G1 46 8S 166 35 E
Preševo, Serbia, Yug. ...... 50 D5 42 19N 21 39 E
Presho, U.S.A. 154 D4 43 54N 100 3W
Presicce, Italy .... 47 C11 39 54N 18 16 E
Presidencia de la Plaza, Argentina 174 B4 27 0S 59 50W
Presidencia Roque Saenz Peña,
Argentina 174 B3 26 45S 60 30W
Presidente Dutra, Brazil 170 C3 5 15S 44 30W
Presidente Epitácio, Brazil .. 171 F1 21 56S 52 6W
Presidente Figueiredo, Brazil 169 D5 1 57S 60 2W
Presidente Hayes □, Paraguay 174 A4 24 0S 59 0W
Presidente Hermes, Brazil .. 173 C5 11 17S 61 55W
Presidente Prudente, Brazil . 175 A5 22 5S 51 25W
Presídio, Mexico 162 B4 29 29N 104 23W
Presidio, U.S.A. 155 L2 29 34N 104 22W
Preslav, Bulgaria .... 51 C10 43 10N 26 52 E
Preslavska Planina, Bulgaria . 51 C10 43 10N 26 45 E
Prešov, Slovak Rep. .... 35 B14 49 0N 21 15 E
Prešovský □, Slovak Rep. ... 35 B13 49 8N 21 0 E
Prespa, Bulgaria .... 51 E8 41 44N 24 55 E
Prespa △, Greece .... 50 F5 40 48N 21 4 E
Prespa, L. = Prespansko Jezero,
Macedonia .... 50 F5 40 55N 21 0 E
Prespansko Jezero, Macedonia 50 F5 40 55N 21 0 E
Presque I., U.S.A. 150 D4 42 9N 80 6W
Presque Isle, U.S.A. 149 B12 46 41N 68 1W
Pressburg = Bratislava, Slovak Rep. 35 C10 48 10N 17 7 E
Prestatyn, U.K. 20 D4 53 20N 3 24W
Prestea, Ghana 112 D4 5 22N 2 7W
Presteigne, U.K. 21 E5 52 17N 3 0W
Přeštice, Czech Rep. .... 34 B6 49 34N 13 20 E
Presto, Bolivia 173 D5 18 55S 64 56W
Preston, Canada 150 C4 43 23N 80 21W

Preston, U.K. 20 D5 53 46N 2 42W
Preston, Ga., U.S.A. 152 C5 32 4N 84 32W
Preston, Idaho, U.S.A. 158 E8 42 6N 111 53W
Preston, Iowa, U.S.A. 154 D8 43 40N 92 5W
Preston, Minn., U.S.A. 156 G3 37 56N 93 13W
Preston, C., Australia ...... 124 D2 20 51S 116 12 E
Prestonburg, U.S.A. 148 G4 37 39N 82 46W
Prestranda, Norway .... 18 E6 59 4N 9 4 E
Prestwick, U.K. 22 F4 55 29N 4 37W
Prêto →, Amazonas, Brazil .. 169 D5 0 8S 64 6W
Prêto →, Bahia, Brazil 170 D3 11 21S 43 52W
Prêto do Igapó-Açu →, Brazil 170 B6 4 26S 59 48W
Pretoria, S. Africa .... 117 D4 25 44S 28 12 E
Preuilly-sur-Claise, France .. 26 B4 46 51N 0 56 E
Préveza, Greece .... 39 B2 38 57N 20 45 E
Préveza □, Greece .... 39 B2 39 10N 20 40 E
Préveza-Levkás ✈ (PVK), Greece 39 B2 38 57N 20 45 E
Prey Veng, Cambodia ...... 87 G5 11 35N 105 29 E
Priazovskoye, Ukraine ..... 59 J8 46 44N 35 40 E
Pribilof Is., U.S.A. 144 H5 57 0N 170 0W
Priboj, Serbia, Yug. .... 50 C3 43 35N 19 32 E
Příbram, Czech Rep. .... 34 B7 49 41N 14 2 E
Price, U.S.A. 158 G8 39 36N 110 49W
Price, C., India .... 95 H11 13 34N 93 3 E
Price I., Canada 142 C3 52 23N 128 41W
Prichard, U.S.A. 149 K1 30 44N 88 5W
Priego, Spain 40 E2 40 26N 2 21W
Priego de Córdoba, Spain ... 43 H6 37 27N 4 12W
Priekule, Latvia .... 15 H19 56 26N 21 35 E
Priekule, Lithuania .... 15 J20 55 33N 23 57 E
Prien, Germany .... 31 H8 47 51N 12 20 E
Prienai, Lithuania .... 9 J20 54 38N 23 57 E
Prieska, S. Africa .... 116 D3 29 40S 22 42 E
Priest →, U.S.A. 158 B5 48 10N 116 52W
Priest L., Canada 143 C7 54 55N 109 45W
Priest River, U.S.A. 158 B5 48 10N 116 54W
Priest Valley, U.S.A. 161 J6 36 10N 120 39W
Prieta, Peña, Spain 42 C6 43 1N 4 44W
Prieta Diaz, Phil. .... 80 E5 13 2N 124 12 E
Prievidza, Slovak Rep. ..... 35 C11 48 46N 18 36 E
Prignitz, Germany .... 30 B7 53 6N 11 45 E
Prijedor, Bos.-H. .... 45 D13 44 58N 16 41 E
Prijepolje, Serbia, Yug. .... 50 C3 43 27N 19 40 E
Prikaspiyskaya Nizmennost =
Caspian Depression, Eurasia 61 G9 47 0N 48 0 E
Prilep, Ivory C. 112 D4 7 40N 3 9W
Prikubanskaya Nizmennost, Russia 61 H4 45 39N 38 33 E
Prilep, Macedonia .... 50 F5 41 21N 21 32 E
Priluki = Pryluky, Ukraine .. 59 F7 50 30N 32 24 E
Prime Seal I., Australia .... 127 G4 40 3S 147 43 E
Primeira Cruz, Brazil 170 B3 2 30S 43 26W
Primorsk, Russia .... 58 B5 60 22N 28 37 E
Primorsko, Bulgaria .... 51 D11 42 15N 27 44 E
Primorsko-Akhtarsk, Russia . 59 J10 46 2N 38 10 E
Primorskoye, Ukraine ..... 59 J9 46 58N 36 20 E
Primrose L., Canada 143 C7 54 55N 109 45W
Prince Albert, Canada 143 C7 53 15N 105 50W
Prince Albert, S. Africa .... 116 E3 33 12S 22 2 E
Prince Albert Mts., Antarctica 7 D11 76 0S 161 30 E
Prince Albert Nat. Park △, Canada 143 C7 54 0N 106 25W
Prince Albert Pen., Canada . 138 A8 72 30N 116 0W
Prince Albert Sd., Canada .. 138 A8 70 25N 115 0W
Prince Alfred, C., Canada ... 4 B1 74 20N 124 40W
Prince Charles I., Canada ... 139 B12 67 47N 76 12W
Prince Charles Mts., Antarctica 7 D6 72 0S 67 0 E
Prince Edward I. □, Canada . 141 C7 46 20N 63 20W
Prince Edward Is., Ind. Oc. . 121 J2 46 35S 38 0 E
Prince Edward Pt., Canada . 150 C8 43 56N 76 52W
Prince George, Canada 142 C4 53 55N 122 50W
Prince of Wales, C., U.S.A. . 143 B5 65 36N 168 5W
Prince of Wales I., Australia . 126 A3 10 40S 142 10 E
Prince of Wales I., Canada .. 138 A10 73 0N 99 0W
Prince of Wales I., U.S.A. ... 144 J14 55 47N 132 50W
Prince Patrick I., Canada ... 4 B2 77 0N 120 0W
Prince Regent Inlet, Canada . 6 B3 73 0N 90 0W
Prince Rupert, Canada 142 C2 54 20N 130 20W
Princes Town, Trin. & Tob. .. 169 F9 10 16N 61 23W
Princess Charlotte B., Australia 126 A3 14 25S 144 0 E
Princess May Ranges, Australia 124 C4 15 30S 125 30 E
Princess Royal I., Canada ... 142 C3 53 0N 128 40W
Princeton, Canada 142 D4 49 27N 120 30W
Princeton, Calif., U.S.A. 160 F4 39 24N 122 1W
Princeton, Ill., U.S.A. 156 E10 41 23N 89 28W
Princeton, Ind., U.S.A. 157 F9 38 21N 87 34W
Princeton, Ky., U.S.A. 148 G2 37 7N 87 53W
Princeton, Mo., U.S.A. 156 D3 40 24N 93 35W
Princeton, N.J., U.S.A. 151 F10 40 21N 74 39W
Princeton, W. Va., U.S.A. ... 148 G5 37 22N 81 6W
Princeville, U.S.A. 152 D6 35 40N 89 46W
Príncipe, São Tomé & Príncipe 115 G6 1 37N 7 25 E
Principe, I. de, Atl. Oc. .... 104 F4 1 37N 7 27 E
Príncipe da Beira, Brazil ... 173 C5 12 20S 64 30W
Prineville, U.S.A. 158 D3 44 18N 120 51W
Prins Christian Sund, Greenland 10 E6 60 0N 43 0W
Prins Harald Kyst, Antarctica 7 D4 70 0S 35 1 E
Prinsesse Astrid Kyst, Antarctica 7 D3 70 45S 12 30 E
Prinsesse Ragnhild Kyst, Antarctica 7 D4 70 15S 27 30 E
Prinzapolca, Nic. 164 D3 13 20N 83 35W
Prior, C., Spain 42 B2 43 34N 8 17W
Priozersk, Russia .... 56 B6 61 2N 30 7 E
Pripet = Prypyat →, Europe . 59 F9 51 20N 30 15 E
Pripet Marshes, Europe .... 59 F5 52 10N 28 10 E
Pripyats = Prypyat →, Europe 59 F9 51 20N 30 15 E
Prislop, Pasul, Romania .... 53 C9 47 37N 24 48 E
Pristen, Russia .... 59 G6 51 15N 36 44 E
Priština, Kosovo, Yug. ..... 50 D5 42 40N 21 13 E
Pritzwalk, Germany .... 30 B8 53 10N 12 11 E
Privas, France .... 29 D8 44 45N 4 37 E
Privas, Italy .... 46 A6 41 28N 13 11 E
Privolzhsk, Russia .... 60 B5 57 23N 41 16 E
Privolzhskaya Vozvyshennost, Russia 60 E7 51 0N 46 0 E
Privolzhskiy, Russia .... 60 E8 51 25N 46 3 E
Privolzhye, Russia .... 60 D9 52 52N 48 33 E
Priyutnoye, Russia .... 61 G6 46 12N 43 40 E
Priyutovo, Russia .... 61 D10 53 55N 53 59 E
Prizren, Kosovo, Yug. ...... 50 D4 42 13N 20 45 E
Prizzi, Italy .... 46 E6 37 43N 13 26 E
Prnjavor, Bos.-H. .... 52 F2 44 52N 17 43 E
Probolinggo, Indonesia .... 85 G15 7 46S 113 13 E
Prochowice, Poland .... 55 G3 51 17N 16 20 E
Proctor, U.S.A. 151 C11 43 40N 73 2W
Proddatur, India .... 95 G4 14 45N 78 30 E
Prodhromos, Cyprus ...... 39 F4 36 57N 32 56 E
Proença-a-Nova, Portugal .. 38 E11 34 57N 27 56 E
Profítis Ilias, Greece ...... 38 C10 35 30N 24 52 E
Profondeville, Belgium .... 24 D4 50 23N 4 52 E
Progreso, Coahuila, Mexico . 162 B4 27 28N 101 4W
Progreso, Yucatán, Mexico .. 163 C7 21 20N 89 40W
Prokhladnyy, Russia ...... 61 J7 43 50N 44 2 E
Prokletije, Albania .... 50 C3 42 30N 19 52 E
Prokopyevsk, Russia ...... 66 D9 54 0N 86 45 E
Prokuplje, Serbia, Yug. .... 50 C5 43 16N 21 36 E
Proletarsk, Russia .... 61 G5 46 42N 41 50 E
Proletarskaya = Proletarsk, Russia 61 G5 46 42N 41 50 E
Prome, Burma .... 90 F5 18 49N 95 13 E
Promise City, U.S.A. 156 E8 40 58N 93 10W
Prophet →, Canada 142 B4 58 48N 122 40W
Prophet River, Canada 142 B4 58 6N 122 43W
Prophetstown, U.S.A. 156 C7 41 40N 89 56W
Propriá, Brazil 171 E4 10 13S 36 51W
Propriano, France .... 29 G12 41 41N 8 52 E
Proserpine, Australia ...... 126 J6 20 21S 148 36 E

Proskurov = Khmelnytskyy, Ukraine 59 H4 49 23N 27 0 E
Prosna →, Poland .... 55 F4 52 6N 17 44 E
Prospect, N.Y., U.S.A. 151 C9 43 18N 75 9W
Prospect, Ohio, U.S.A. 157 D13 40 27N 83 11W
Prosperidad, Phil. .... 81 G5 8 34N 125 52 E
Prosperity, U.S.A. 152 E4 30 51N 85 56W
Prosperous B., St. Helena ... 9 h 15 56 S 5 39W
Prosser, U.S.A. 158 C4 46 12N 119 46W
Prostějov, Czech Rep. ..... 35 B10 49 30N 17 9 E
Prostki, Poland .... 54 E9 53 42N 22 25 E
Proston, Australia .... 127 D5 26 8S 151 32 E
Próti, Greece .... 48 D3 37 5N 21 32 E
Provadiya, Bulgaria .... 51 C11 43 12N 27 30 E
Provence, France .... 29 E9 43 40N 5 46 E
Provence-Alpes-Côte d'Azur □,
France .... 29 D10 44 0N 6 15 E
Providence, Seychelles ..... 121 E4 9 14S 51 2 E
Providence, Ky., U.S.A. 148 G2 37 24N 87 46W
Providence, R.I., U.S.A. 151 E13 41 49N 71 24W
Providence, C., N.Z. .... 131 F1 45 59S 166 29 E
Providence Bay, Canada 140 C3 45 41N 82 15W
Providence Mts., U.S.A. 161 K15 35 10N 115 15W
Providencia, I. de, Colombia . 164 D3 13 25N 81 26W
Provideniya, Russia 67 C19 64 23N 173 18W
Provins, France .... 25 D10 48 33N 3 15 E
Provo, U.S.A. 158 F8 40 14N 111 39W
Provost, Canada 143 C6 52 25N 110 20W
Prozor, Bos.-H. .... 52 G2 43 50N 17 34 E
Prrenjas, Albania .... 50 E4 41 4N 20 32 E
Prudentópolis, Brazil 171 G1 25 12S 50 57W
Prudhoe Bay, U.S.A. 144 A10 70 18N 148 22W
Prudhoe I., Australia ...... 126 C4 21 19S 149 41 E
Prud'homme, Canada 143 C7 52 20N 105 54W
Prudnik, Poland .... 55 H4 50 20N 17 38 E
Prüm, Germany .... 31 E2 50 12N 6 25 E
Prundu, Romania .... 53 F11 44 6N 26 14 E
Pruszcz Gdański, Poland ... 54 D5 54 17N 18 40 E
Pruszków, Poland .... 55 F7 52 9N 20 49 E
Prut →, Romania .... 53 E13 45 28N 28 10 E
Prutz, Austria .... 33 B11 47 5N 10 40 E
Pruzhany, Belarus .... 59 F3 52 33N 24 28 E
Prvič, Croatia .... 45 D11 44 55N 14 47 E
Pryde B., Antarctica ...... 7 C6 69 0S 74 0 E
Pryluky, Ukraine .... 59 F7 50 30N 32 24 E
Pryor, U.S.A. 155 G7 36 19N 95 19W
Prypyat →, Europe .... 59 G6 51 20N 30 15 E
Przasnysz, Poland .... 55 E7 53 2N 20 54 E
Przedbórz, Poland .... 55 G6 51 6N 19 53 E
Przedecz, Poland .... 55 F5 52 20N 18 53 E
Przemków, Poland .... 55 G2 51 31N 15 48 E
Przemyśl, Poland .... 55 H9 49 50N 22 45 E
Przeworsk, Poland .... 55 H9 50 6N 22 32 E
Przewóz, Poland .... 55 G1 51 28N 14 57 E
Przhevalsk = Karakol, Kyrgyzstan 65 B9 42 30N 78 20 E
Przysucha, Poland .... 55 G7 51 22N 20 38 E
Psakhná, Greece .... 48 C5 38 34N 23 35 E
Psará, Greece .... 49 C7 38 37N 25 38 E
Psathoúra, Greece .... 48 B6 39 30N 24 12 E
Psel →, Ukraine .... 59 H7 49 5N 33 37 E
Pserimos, Greece .... 49 E9 36 56N 27 8 E
Psíra, Greece .... 39 E6 35 12N 25 52 E
Pskem →, Uzbekistan ..... 65 C5 41 38N 70 1 E
Pskem Tizmasi, Uzbekistan . 65 C4 42 0N 70 45 E
Pskent, Uzbekistan .... 65 C4 40 54N 69 20 E
Pskov, Russia .... 58 D5 57 50N 28 25 E
Pskovskoye, Ozero, Russia .. 58 D5 58 0N 27 58 E
Psunj, Croatia .... 52 E2 45 25N 17 19 E
Ptcleón, Greece .... 48 B4 39 3N 22 57 E
Ptich = Ptsich →, Belarus ... 59 F5 52 9N 28 52 E
Ptolemaís, Greece .... 50 F5 40 30N 21 43 E
Ptsich →, Belarus .... 59 F5 52 9N 28 52 E
Ptuj, Slovenia .... 45 B12 46 28N 15 50 E
Ptujska Gora, Slovenia ..... 45 B12 46 23N 15 46 E
Pu Xian, China .... 74 F6 36 24N 111 6 E
Pua, Thailand .... 86 C3 19 11N 100 55 E
Puale B., U.S.A. 145 J13 21 36N 158 6W
Puán, Argentina 174 D3 37 30S 62 45W
Pu'an, China .... 76 E5 25 46N 104 57 E
Puan, S. Korea .... 75 G14 35 44N 126 44 E
Pu'apu'a, Samoa 133 W23 13 34S 172 9W
Pubei, China .... 76 F7 22 16N 109 31 E
Pucacuro →, Peru 168 D3 3 20S 74 58W
Pucallpa, Peru 172 B3 8 25S 74 30W
Pucará, Bolivia 173 D5 18 43S 64 11W
Pucará, Cajamarca, Peru ... 172 B2 5 0S 79 7W
Pucará, Puno, Peru 172 D3 15 5S 70 24W
Pucarani, Bolivia 172 D4 16 23S 68 30W
Pucheng, China .... 77 D12 27 59N 118 31 E
Pucheni, Romania .... 53 E10 45 15N 25 17 E
Puchheim, Germany ...... 31 G7 48 9N 11 21 E
Púchov, Slovak Rep. ...... 35 B11 49 8N 18 20 E
Pucio Pt., Phil. .... 81 F3 11 46N 121 51 E
Pucioasa, Romania .... 53 E10 45 5N 25 27 E
Pučišća, Croatia .... 45 E13 43 22N 16 43 E
Puck, Poland .... 54 D5 54 45N 18 23 E
Pucka, Zatoka, Poland ..... 54 D5 54 30N 18 40 E
Puçol, Spain 41 F4 39 37N 0 18W
Pudasjärvi, Finland .... 14 D22 65 23N 26 53 E
Puding, China .... 76 D5 26 18N 105 44 E
Pudozh, Russia .... 58 B9 61 48N 36 32 E
Puducherry = Pondicherry, India 95 J4 11 59N 79 50 E
Pudukkottai, India .... 95 J4 10 28N 78 47 E
Puebla, Mexico 163 D5 19 3N 98 12W
Puebla □, Mexico 163 D5 18 30N 98 0W
Puebla de Alcocer, Spain ... 43 G5 38 59N 5 14W
Puebla de Don Fadrique, Spain 41 H2 37 58N 2 25W
Puebla de Don Rodrigo, Spain 43 F6 39 5N 4 37W
Puebla de Guzmán, Spain .. 43 H3 37 37N 7 15W
Puebla de la Calzada, Spain . 43 G4 38 54N 6 37W
Puebla de Sanabria, Spain .. 42 C4 42 4N 6 38W
Puebla de Trives = Pobra de Trives,
Spain 42 C3 42 20N 7 10W
Pueblo Hundido, Chile 174 B1 26 20S 70 5W
Pueblo, U.S.A. 154 F2 38 16N 104 37W
Puelches, Argentina 174 D2 38 5S 65 51W
Puelén, Argentina 174 D2 37 32S 67 38W
Puente Alto, Chile 174 C1 33 32S 70 35W
Puente-Genil, Spain 43 H6 37 22N 4 47W
Puente la Reina, Spain 40 C3 42 40N 1 49W
Puenteareas = Ponteareas, Spain 42 C2 42 12N 8 28W
Puentedeume = Pontedeume, Spain 42 B2 43 24N 8 10W
Puentes de Garcia Rodriguez =
As Pontes de García Rodríguez, Spain 42 B3 43 27N 7 50W
Pueo Pt., U.S.A. 145 B1 22 7N 159 37W
Pu'er, China .... 76 F3 23 0N 101 15 E
Puerca, Pta., Puerto Rico ... 165 d 18 13N 65 36W
Puerco →, U.S.A. 159 J10 34 22N 107 50W
Puerto Galera, Phil. .... 80 E3 13 30N 120 57 E
Puerto Acosta, Bolivia 172 D4 15 32S 69 15W
Puerto Aisén, Chile 176 C2 45 27S 73 0W
Puerto Ángel, Mexico 163 D5 15 40N 96 29W
Puerto Arista, Mexico 163 D6 15 56N 93 48W
Puerto Armuelles, Panama . 164 E3 8 20N 82 51W
Puerto Asis, Colombia 168 C2 0 30N 76 30W
Puerto Ayacucho, Venezuela 168 B5 5 40N 67 35W
Puerto Ayora, Ecuador ..... 172 a 0 45S 90 19W
Puerto Barrios, Guatemala . 164 C2 15 40N 88 32W
Puerto Bermejo, Argentina . 174 B4 26 55S 58 34W
Puerto Bermúdez, Peru 172 C3 10 20S 74 58W
Puerto Bolívar, Ecuador 168 D2 3 19S 79 55W
Puerto Cabello, Venezuela .. 168 A5 10 28N 68 1W
Puerto Cabezas, Nic. 164 D3 14 0N 83 30W

Puerto Cabo Gracias á Dios, Nic. .. 164 D3 15 0N 83 10W
Puerto Capaz = El Jebha, Morocco .. 110 A4 35 11N 4 43W
Puerto Carreño, Colombia 168 B4 6 12N 67 22W
Puerto Castilla, Honduras 164 C2 16 0N 86 0W
Puerto Chicama, Peru .... 172 B2 7 45 S 79 20W
Puerto Cisnes, Chile .... 176 B2 44 45 S 72 42W
Puerto Coig, Argentina .... 176 D3 50 54 S 69 15W
Puerto Cortés, Costa Rica 164 E3 8 55N 84 0W
Puerto Cortés, Honduras 164 C2 15 51N 88 0W
Puerto Cumarebo, Venezuela 168 A4 11 29N 69 30W
Puerto de Alcudia = Port d'Alcúdia,
  Spain .... 38 B4 39 50N 3 7 E
Puerto de Cabrera, Spain .... 38 B3 39 8N 2 56 E
Puerto de Gran Tarajal, Canary Is. . 9 e2 28 13N 14 1W
Puerto de la Cruz, Canary Is. 9 e1 28 24N 16 32W
Puerto de los Angeles, Parque
  Natural △, Mexico 162 C3 23 39N 105 45W
Puerto de Mazarrón, Spain 41 H3 37 34N 1 15W
Puerto de Pozo Negro, Canary Is. . 9 e2 28 19N 13 55W
Puerto de Sóller = Port de Sóller,
  Spain .... 38 B3 39 48N 2 42 E
Puerto de Somosierra, Spain 42 D7 41 9N 3 35W
Puerto del Carmen, Canary Is. 9 e2 28 55N 13 38W
Puerto del Rosario, Canary Is. 9 e2 28 30N 13 52W
Puerto Deseado, Argentina .... 176 C3 47 55 S 66 0W
Puerto Escondido, Mexico 163 D5 15 50N 97 3W
Puerto Gaitán, Colombia 168 C3 4 19N 72 4W
Puerto Guaraní, Paraguay .... 173 E6 21 18 S 57 55W
Puerto Heath, Bolivia .... 172 C4 12 34 S 68 39W
Puerto Huitoto, Colombia 168 C3 0 18N 74 3W
Puerto Inca, Peru .... 172 B3 9 22 S 74 54W
Puerto Inírida, Colombia 168 C4 3 53N 67 52W
Puerto Juárez, Mexico 163 C7 21 11N 86 49W
Puerto La Cruz, Venezuela 169 A5 10 13N 64 38W
Puerto Leguízamo, Colombia ...... 168 D3 0 12 S 74 46W
Puerto Limón, Colombia 168 C3 3 23N 73 30W
Puerto Lobos, Argentina .... 176 B3 42 0 S 65 3W
Puerto López, Colombia 168 C3 4 5N 72 58W
Puerto Lumbreras, Spain 41 H3 37 34N 1 48W
Puerto Madryn, Argentina .... 176 B3 42 48 S 65 4W
Puerto Maldonado, Peru .... 172 C4 12 30 S 69 10W
Puerto Manotí, Cuba 164 B4 21 22N 76 50W
Puerto Mariti, India .... 168 D4 1 10 S 69 59W
Puerto Mercedes, Colombia 168 C3 1 11N 72 53W
Puerto Mexico = Coatzacoalcos,
  Mexico 163 D6 18 7N 94 25W
Puerto Miraña, Colombia .... 168 D3 1 20 S 70 19W
Puerto Montt, Chile .... 176 B2 41 28 S 73 0W
Puerto Morazán, Nic. 164 D2 12 51N 87 11W
Puerto Morelos, Mexico 163 C7 20 49N 86 52W
Puerto Mutis, Colombia 168 B2 6 14N 77 25W
Puerto Nariño, Colombia 168 C4 4 56N 67 48W
Puerto Natales, Chile .... 176 D2 51 45 S 72 15W
Puerto Nuevo, Colombia 168 B4 5 53N 69 56W
Puerto Nutrias, Venezuela 168 B4 8 5N 69 18W
Puerto Ordaz, Venezuela 169 B5 8 16N 62 44W
Puerto Padre, Cuba 164 B4 21 13N 76 35W
Puerto Páez, Venezuela 168 B4 6 13N 67 28W
Puerto Peñasco, Mexico 162 A2 31 20N 113 33W
Puerto Pirámides, Argentina ...... 176 A4 42 35 S 64 20W
Puerto Pirtu, Venezuela 169 A4 10 4N 65 3W
Puerto Plata, Dom. Rep. 165 C5 19 48N 70 45W
Puerto Pollensa = Port de Pollença,
  Spain .... 38 B4 39 54N 3 4 E
Puerto Portillo, Peru .... 172 B3 9 43 S 74 49W
Puerto Princesa, Phil. .... 81 G2 9 46N 118 45 E
Puerto Quellón, Chile .... 176 B2 43 7 S 73 37W
Puerto Quepos, Costa Rica 164 E3 9 29N 84 6W
Puerto Real, Spain 43 J4 36 33N 6 12W
Puerto Rico, Bolivia .... 172 C4 11 5 S 67 38W
Puerto Rico, Canary Is. 9 e1 27 47N 15 42W
Puerto Rico ☑, W. Indies .... 165 d 18 15N 66 45W
Puerto Rico Trench, Atl. Oc. 165 C6 19 50N 66 0W
Puerto Rondón, Colombia 168 B3 6 17N 71 6W
Puerto Saavedra, Chile .... 176 B2 38 47 S 73 24W
Puerto Sastre, Paraguay .... 174 A4 22 2 S 57 55W
Puerto Serrano, Spain 43 J5 36 56N 5 33W
Puerto Siles, Bolivia .... 173 C4 12 48 S 65 5W
Puerto Suárez, Bolivia .... 173 D6 18 58 S 57 52W
Puerto Tejada, Colombia 168 C2 3 14N 76 24W
Puerto Umbría, Colombia 168 C2 0 52N 76 33W
Puerto Vallarta, Mexico 162 C3 20 36N 105 15W
Puerto Varas, Chile .... 176 B2 41 19 S 72 59W
Puerto Velasco Ibarra, Ecuador ... 172 a 1 17 S 90 29W
Puerto Villamil, Ecuador .... 172 a 0 56 S 91 1W
Puerto Villazón, Bolivia .... 173 C5 13 32 S 61 57W
Puerto Wilches, Colombia 168 B3 7 21N 73 54W
Puertollano, Spain 43 G6 38 43N 4 7W
Puesto Cunambo, Peru .... 168 D2 2 10 S 76 0W
Pueyrredón, L., Argentina .... 176 C2 47 20 S 72 0W
Pugu Odle, Parco Naturale △, Italy . 45 B8 46 37N 11 48 E
Puffin I., Ireland 23 E1 51 50N 10 24W
Pugachev, Russia .... 60 D9 52 0N 48 49 E
Pugal, India .... 92 E5 28 30N 72 48 E
Puge, China .... 76 D4 27 20N 102 31 E
Puge, Tanzania .... 118 C3 4 45 S 33 11 E
Puget Sound, U.S.A. 158 C2 47 50N 122 30W
Puget-Théniers, France .... 29 E10 43 58N 6 53 E
Púglia □, Italy .... 47 A9 41 15N 16 15 E
Pugōdong, N. Korea .... 75 C16 42 5N 130 0 E
Pugu, Tanzania .... 118 D4 6 55 S 39 4 E
Pūgūnzī, Iran .... 97 E8 25 49N 59 10 E
Puha, N.Z. .... 130 E6 38 30 S 177 50 E
Pui, Romania .... 52 E8 45 30N 23 4 E
Puica, Peru .... 172 C3 15 0 S 72 30W
Puieşti, Romania .... 53 D12 46 25N 27 33 E
Puig Major, Spain .... 38 B9 39 48N 2 47 E
Puigcerdà, Spain .... 40 C6 42 24N 1 50 E
Puigmal, Spain .... 40 C7 42 23N 2 7 E
Puigpunyent, Spain .... 38 B3 39 38N 2 32 E
Puijiang, China .... 76 B4 30 14N 103 30 E
Puisaye, Collines de la, France ... 27 E10 47 37N 3 20 E
Puiseaux, France .... 27 D9 48 11N 2 30 E
Pujehun, S. Leone 112 D2 7 23N 11 45W
Pujiang, China .... 77 C12 29 29N 119 54 E
Pujilí, Ecuador .... 168 D2 0 57 S 78 41W
Pujols, France .... 28 D3 44 48N 0 2 E
Pujon-chosuji, N. Korea .... 75 D14 40 35N 127 35 E
Pukaki, L., N.Z. .... 131 E5 44 4 S 170 1 E
Pukalani, U.S.A. 145 C5 20 51N 156 20W
Pukapuka, Cook Is. .... 135 J11 10 53 S 165 49W
Pukaskwa Nat. Park △, Canada .. 140 C2 48 20N 86 0W
Pukatawagan, Canada 143 B8 55 45N 101 20W
Pukchin, N. Korea .... 75 D13 40 12N 125 45 E
Pukch'ong, N. Korea .... 75 D15 40 14N 128 10 E
Pukë, Albania .... 50 D3 42 2N 19 53 E
Pukekohe, N.Z. .... 130 E3 38 5 S 174 31 E
Pukekohe, N.Z. .... 130 D3 37 12 S 174 55 E
Puketeraki Ra., N.Z. .... 131 C7 43 4 S 172 13 E
Puketoi Ra., N.Z. .... 130 G5 40 30 S 176 5 E
Pukeuri, N.Z. .... 131 F6 45 4 S 171 2 E
Pukhrayan, India .... 93 F8 26 14N 79 51 E
Pukoo, U.S.A. 145 B5 21 4N 156 48W
Pukou, China .... 77 A12 32 7N 118 38 E
Pula, Croatia .... 45 D10 44 54N 13 57 E
Pula, Italy .... 46 C1 39 0N 9 0 E
Pulacayo, Bolivia .... 172 E4 20 25 S 66 41W
Pulai, Malaysia .... 87 d 1 20N 103 31 E
Pulandian, China .... 75 E11 39 25N 121 58 E
Pulaski, N.Y., U.S.A. 151 C8 43 34N 76 8W
Pulaski, Tenn., U.S.A. 149 H2 35 12N 87 2W
Pulaski, Va., U.S.A. 148 G5 37 3N 80 47W

Pulau →, Indonesia .... 83 C5 5 50 S 138 15 E
Pulau Miangas, Indonesia .... 81 J6 5 35N 126 34 E
Puławy, Poland .... 55 G8 51 23N 21 59 E
Pulga, U.S.A. 160 F5 39 48N 121 29W
Pulgaon, India .... 94 D4 20 44N 78 21 E
Pulicat, India .... 95 H5 13 25N 80 19 E
Pulicat L., India .... 95 H5 13 40N 80 15 E
Pulivendla, India .... 95 G4 14 25N 78 14 E
Puliyangudi, India .... 95 K3 9 11N 77 24 E
Pullman, U.S.A. 158 C5 46 44N 117 10W
Pulog, Mt., Phil. .... 80 C3 16 40N 120 50 E
Púlpito do Sul, Angola .... 115 F2 15 46 S 12 0 E
Pultusk, Poland .... 55 F8 52 43N 21 6 E
Pülümür, Turkey .... 101 C8 39 30N 39 51 E
Pumlumon Fawr, U.K. 21 E4 52 28N 3 46W
Puna, Bolivia .... 173 D4 19 45 S 65 28W
Puná, I., Ecuador .... 168 D1 2 55 S 80 5W
Punakha, Bhutan .... 90 B2 27 42N 89 52 E
Punalur, India .... 95 K3 9 0N 76 56 E
Punaluu, U.S.A. 145 J14 21 35N 157 53W
Punasar, India .... 92 F5 27 6N 73 6 E
Punata, Bolivia .... 173 D4 17 32 S 65 50W
Punch, India .... 93 C6 33 48N 74 4 E
Punch →, Pakistan .... 92 C5 33 12N 73 40 E
Punda Maria, S. Africa .... 117 C5 22 40 S 31 5 E
Pune, India .... 94 E1 18 29N 73 57 E
Pungo Andongo, Angola .... 115 D3 9 4 S 15 35 E
P'ungsan, N. Korea .... 75 D15 40 50N 128 9 E
Pungue, Ponte de, Mozam. ...... 119 F3 19 0 S 34 0 E
Puning, China .... 77 F11 23 20N 116 12 E
Punjab □, India .... 92 D7 31 0N 76 0 E
Punjab □, Pakistan .... 91 C4 32 0N 72 30 E
Puno, Peru .... 172 D3 15 55 S 70 3W
Punpun →, India .... 93 G11 25 31N 85 18 E
Punta, Cerro de, Puerto Rico .... 165 d 18 10N 66 37W
Punta Alta, Argentina .... 176 A4 38 53 S 62 4W
Punta Arenas, Chile .... 176 D2 53 10 S 71 0W
Punta Cardón, Venezuela 168 A3 11 38N 70 14W
Punta Coles, Peru .... 172 D3 17 43 S 71 23W
Punta de Bombón, Peru .... 172 D3 17 10 S 71 48W
Punta de Díaz, Chile .... 174 B1 28 0 S 70 45W
Punta de Hidalgo, Canary Is. 9 e1 28 33N 16 19W
Punta Delgado, Argentina ...... 176 B4 42 43 S 63 38W
Punta Gorda, Belize 163 D7 16 10N 88 45W
Punta Gorda, U.S.A. 153 J7 26 56N 82 3W
Punta Prieta, Mexico 162 B2 28 58N 114 17W
Punta Prima, Spain .... 38 B5 39 48N 4 16 E
Punta Umbria, Spain 43 H4 37 10N 6 56W
Puntarenas, Costa Rica 164 E3 10 0N 84 50W
Punto Fijo, Venezuela 168 A3 11 50N 70 13W
Punxsatawney, U.S.A. 150 F6 40 57N 78 59W
Punyu = Guangzhou, China ..... 77 F9 23 5N 113 10 E
Puolo Pt., U.S.A. 145 B2 21 54N 159 36W
Pupuan, Indonesia .... 79 J18 8 19 S 115 0 E
Puqi, China .... 77 C9 29 40N 113 50 E
Puquio, Peru .... 172 C3 14 45 S 74 10W
Pur →, Russia .... 66 C8 67 31N 77 55 E
Purace, Vol., Colombia 168 C2 2 21N 76 23W
Puračić, Bos.-H. .... 52 F3 44 33N 18 28 E
Puralia = Puruliya, India .... 93 H12 23 17N 86 24 E
Puranpur, India .... 93 E9 28 31N 80 9 E
Purari →, Papua N. G. .... 132 D3 7 49 S 145 0 E
Purbeck, Isle of, U.K. 21 G6 50 39N 1 59W
Purcell, U.S.A. 155 H6 35 1N 97 22W
Purcell Mts., Canada 142 D5 49 55N 116 15W
Puri, India .... 94 E7 19 50N 85 58 E
Purification, Colombia 168 C3 3 51N 74 55W
Purmerend, Neths. .... 24 B4 52 32N 4 58 E
Purna →, India .... 94 E3 19 6N 77 2 E
Purnia, India .... 93 G12 25 45N 87 31 E
Pursat = Pouthisat, Cambodia ... 86 F4 12 34N 103 50 E
Purukcahu, Indonesia .... 85 C4 0 35 S 114 35 E
Puruliya, India .... 93 H12 23 17N 86 24 E
Purus →, Brazil .... 169 D5 3 42 S 61 28W
Purutu I., Papua N. G. .... 132 E2 8 24 S 143 27 E
Purvesi, Finland .... 14 E3 62 24N 29 30 E
Purvis, U.S.A. 155 K10 31 9N 89 25W
Pürvomay, Bulgaria .... 51 D9 42 8N 25 17 E
Purwa, India .... 93 F9 26 28N 80 47 E
Purwakarta, Indonesia .... 85 D3 6 35 S 107 29 E
Purwo, Tanjung, Indonesia ..... 85 D4 7 5 S 110 55 E
Purwodadi, Jawa, Indonesia .... 85 D3 7 51 S 110 0 E
Purwodadi, Jawa, Indonesia .... 85 D3 7 7 S 110 55 E
Purwokerto, Indonesia .... 85 D3 7 25 S 109 14 E
Purworejo, Indonesia .... 85 D4 7 43 S 110 2 E
Puryŏng, N. Korea .... 75 C15 42 5N 129 43 E
Pus →, India .... 94 E3 19 55N 77 36 E
Pusa, India .... 93 G11 25 59N 85 41 E
Pusad, India .... 94 E3 19 56N 77 36 E
Pusan, S. Korea .... 75 G15 35 5N 129 0 E
Pushkin, Russia .... 58 C6 59 45N 30 25 E
Pushkino, Moskva, Russia ...... 58 D9 56 2N 37 49 E
Pushkino, Saratov, Russia ...... 60 E8 51 16N 47 0 E
Püspökladány, Hungary .... 52 C6 47 19N 21 6 E
Pustoshka, Russia .... 58 D5 56 20N 29 30 E
Puszczykowo, Poland .... 55 F3 52 18N 16 49 E
Putahow L., Canada 143 B8 59 54N 100 40W
Putao, Burma .... 90 B6 27 28N 97 30 E
Putaruru, N.Z. .... 130 E4 38 2 S 175 50 E
Putbus, Germany .... 30 A9 54 22N 13 28 E
Putian, China .... 77 E12 25 23N 119 0 E
Putignano, Italy .... 47 B10 40 51N 17 7 E
Putina, Peru .... 172 C4 14 55 S 69 55W
Puting, Tanjung, Indonesia ..... 85 C4 3 31 S 111 46 E
Putlitz, Germany .... 30 B8 53 15N 12 3 E
Putna, Romania .... 53 C10 47 50N 25 33 E
Putna →, Romania .... 53 E12 45 42N 27 26 E
Putnam, U.S.A. 151 E13 41 55N 71 55W
Putney, U.S.A. 152 D5 31 29N 84 8W
Putnok, Hungary .... 52 B5 48 18N 20 26 E
Putorana, Gory, Russia .... 67 C10 69 0N 95 0 E
Putorino, N.Z. .... 130 F5 39 8 S 176 58 E
Putre, Chile .... 172 D4 18 12 S 69 35W
Puttalam, Sri Lanka .... 95 K5 8 1N 79 55 E
Puttalam Lagoon, Sri Lanka .... 95 K4 8 15N 79 45 E
Puttgarden, Germany .... 30 A7 54 30N 11 10 E
Püttlingen, Germany .... 31 F2 49 17N 6 53 E
Puttur, Andhra Pradesh, India .. 95 H4 13 27N 79 33 E
Puttur, Karnataka, India .... 95 H2 12 46N 75 12 E
Putty, Australia .... 129 B9 32 57 S 150 42 E
Putumayo →, S. Amer. .... 168 D4 3 7 S 67 58W
Putuo, China .... 77 C14 29 58N 122 19 E
Putussibau, Indonesia .... 85 B4 0 50N 112 56 E
Pututahi, N.Z. .... 130 E6 38 39 S 177 53 E
Puu Kaaumakua, U.S.A. 145 K14 21 30N 157 54W
Puu Keahiakahoe, U.S.A. 145 K14 21 23N 157 49W
Puu o Keokeo, U.S.A. 145 D6 19 13N 155 44W
Puuanahulu, U.S.A. 145 D6 19 55N 155 51W
Pu'uhonua o Hōnaunau Nat.
  Historical Park △, U.S.A. 145 D6 19 25N 155 55W
Pu'ukoholā Heiau Nat. Historic
  Site △, U.S.A. 145 C6 20 1N 155 50W
Puukolii, U.S.A. 145 C5 20 56N 156 41W
Puunene, U.S.A. 145 C5 20 53N 156 23W
Puuwai, U.S.A. 145 B1 21 54N 160 12W
Puvirnituq, Canada 139 B12 60 2N 77 10W
Puy-de-Dôme, France .... 28 C6 45 46N 2 57 E
Puy-de-Dôme □, France .... 28 C7 45 40N 3 0 E
Puy-l'Évêque, France .... 28 D5 44 31N 1 9 E
Puyallup, U.S.A. 160 C4 47 12N 122 18W
Puyang, China .... 74 G8 35 40N 115 1 E
Puyehue, Chile .... 176 B2 40 40 S 72 37W
Puylaurens, France .... 28 E6 43 35N 2 0 E

Puyo, Ecuador .... 168 D2 1 28 S 77 59W
Puysegur Pt., N.Z. .... 131 G1 46 9 S 166 37 E
Pūzeh Rīg, Iran .... 97 E8 27 20N 58 40 E
Pwani □, Tanzania .... 118 D4 7 0 S 39 0 E
Pweto, Dem. Rep. of the Congo .. 119 D2 8 25 S 28 51 E
Pwinbyu, Burma .... 90 E5 20 23N 94 40 E
Pwllheli, U.K. 20 E3 52 53N 4 25W
Pya-ozero, Russia .... 56 A5 66 5N 30 58 E
Pyana →, Russia .... 60 C8 55 43N 46 1 E
Pyandzh, Tajikistan .... 65 E4 37 14N 69 6 E
Pyandzh →, Asia .... 65 E4 37 6N 68 20 E
Pyapon, Burma .... 90 G5 16 20N 95 40 E
Pyasina →, Russia .... 67 B9 73 30N 87 0 E
Pyatigorsk, Russia .... 61 H6 44 2N 43 6 E
Pyatykhatky, Ukraine .... 59 H7 48 28N 33 38 E
Pyawbwe, Burma .... 90 E6 20 35N 96 4 E
Pyaye, Burma .... 90 F5 19 12N 95 10 E
Pydna, Greece .... 50 F6 40 20N 22 34 E
Pyè = Prome, Burma .... 90 F5 18 49N 95 13 E
Pyetrikaw, Belarus .... 59 F5 52 11N 28 29 E
Pyhäjoki, Finland .... 14 D21 64 28N 24 14 E
Pyinbauk, Burma .... 90 F5 19 10N 95 12 E
Pyingaing, Burma .... 90 D5 23 9N 94 50 E
Pyinkayaing, Burma .... 90 H5 15 58N 94 24 E
Pyinmana, Burma .... 90 F6 19 45N 96 12 E
Pyinyaung, Burma .... 90 E6 20 49N 96 25 E
Pyla, C., Cyprus .... 39 99 34 56N 33 51 E
Pymatuning Reservoir, U.S.A. ... 150 E4 41 30N 80 28W
Pyŏktong, N. Korea .... 75 D13 40 50N 125 50 E
Pyŏnggang, N. Korea .... 75 E14 38 24N 127 17 E
P'yŏngt'aek, S. Korea .... 75 F14 37 1N 127 4 E
P'yŏngyang, N. Korea .... 75 E13 39 0N 125 30 E
Pyote, U.S.A. 155 K3 31 32N 103 8W
Pyramid L., U.S.A. 158 G4 40 1N 119 35W
Pyramid Pk., U.S.A. 161 J10 36 25N 116 37W
Pyramid Pt., Ascension I. ...... 9 g 7 55 S 14 24W
Pyramids, Egypt .... 106 J7 29 58N 31 9 E
Pyrénées, Europe .... 28 F4 42 45N 0 18 E
Pyrénées, Parc Nat. de △, France . 28 F3 42 52N 0 10W
Pyrénées-Atlantiques □, France .. 28 E3 43 10N 0 50W
Pyrénées-Orientales □, France ... 28 F6 42 35N 2 26 E
Pyryatyn, Ukraine .... 59 G7 50 15N 32 25 E
Pyrzyce, Poland .... 55 E11 53 10N 14 55 E
Pyskowice, Poland .... 55 H5 50 24N 18 38 E
Pytalovo, Russia .... 58 D4 57 5N 27 55 E
Pyttegga, Norway .... 18 B4 62 13N 7 42 E
Pyu, Burma .... 90 F6 18 30N 96 28 E
Pyzdry, Poland .... 55 F4 52 11N 17 42 E

Q

Qaanaaq, Greenland 10 B4 77 40N 69 0W
Qabirri →, Azerbaijan .... 61 K8 41 3N 46 17 E
Qabr Hūd, Yemen .... 99 C5 16 9N 49 34 E
Qachasnek, S. Africa .... 117 E4 30 6 S 28 42 E
Qādib, Yemen .... 99 D6 12 37N 53 57 E
Qa'el Jafr, Jordan .... 103 E5 30 20N 36 25 E
Qa'emābād, Iran .... 97 D9 31 44N 60 2 E
Qa'emshahr, Iran .... 97 B7 36 30N 52 53 E
Qagan Nur, China .... 74 C8 43 30N 114 55 E
Qahar Youyi Zhongqi, China .... 74 D7 41 12N 112 40 E
Qahremānshahr = Bākhtarān, Iran 101 E12 34 23N 47 0 E
Qaidam Pendi, China .... 68 C4 37 0N 95 0 E
Qajarīyeh, Iran .... 97 D6 31 1N 48 22 E
Qala, Malta .... 38 E7 36 2N 14 19 E
Qala, Ras il, Malta .... 38 E7 36 2N 14 20 E
Qala-i-Jadid = Spīn Būldak, Afghan. 91 C2 31 1N 66 25 E
Qala Point = Qala, Ras il, Malta . 38 E7 36 2N 14 20 E
Qala Viala, Pakistan .... 92 D2 30 49N 67 17 E
Qala Yangi, Afghan. .... 92 B2 34 20N 66 30 E
Qalācheh, Afghan. .... 91 B2 35 30N 67 43 E
Qalaikhum = Kalaikhum, Tajikistan 65 D5 38 28N 70 46 E
Qalansīyah, Yemen .... 99 D6 12 41N 53 20 E
Qal'at al Akhdar, Si. Arabia .... 98 C3 28 0N 37 10 E
Qal'at Bīshah, Si. Arabia ...... 98 C3 20 0N 42 36 E
Qal'at Dīzah, Iraq .... 101 D11 36 11N 45 7 E
Qalāt-i-Ghilzai, Afghan. .... 91 B2 32 15N 66 58 E
Qal'at Şāliḥ, Iraq .... 101 G12 31 31N 46 5 E
Qal'at Sukkar, Iraq .... 101 G12 31 51N 46 25 E
Qal'eh-ye Bost, Afghan. .... 91 C2 31 30N 64 21 E
Qal'eh-ye Now, Afghan. .... 91 B1 35 0N 63 0 E
Qal'eh-ye Panjeh, Afghan. ..... 65 E5 37 0N 72 35 E
Qal'eh-ye Sarkari, Afghan. ..... 91 B3 35 54N 67 17 E
Qal'eh-ye Valī, Afghan. .... 91 B3 35 46N 63 45 E
Qalyūb, Egypt .... 106 H7 30 12N 31 11 E
Qamani'tuaq = Baker Lake, Canada 138 B10 64 20N 96 0W
Qamar, Ghubbat al, Yemen ..... 99 C6 16 20N 52 30 E
Qamar, Jabal al, Oman .... 99 C6 16 48N 53 15 E
Qamdo, China .... 76 B1 31 15N 97 6 E
Qamea, Fiji .... 133 A3 16 45 S 179 45W
Qammieh Point, Malta .... 38 F7 35 58N 14 19 E
Qamruddin Karez, Pakistan .... 91 C3 31 45N 68 20 E
Qandahār, Afghan. .... 91 C2 31 32N 65 43 E
Qandahār □, Afghan. .... 91 C2 31 0N 65 0 E
Qanshenggel, Kazakhstan ...... 64 B8 44 19N 75 33 E
Qapān, Iran .... 97 B7 37 40N 55 47 E
Qapshaghay, Kazakhstan ...... 64 B8 43 51N 77 14 E
Qapshaghay Bögeni, Kazakhstan . 65 B8 43 45N 77 50 E
Qaqortoq, Greenland 10 E6 60 43N 46 0W
Qâra, Egypt .... 106 B2 29 38N 26 30 E
Qarā', Jabal al, Oman .... 99 C6 17 15N 54 15 E
Qara Qash →, China .... 92 B8 35 0N 78 30 E
Qarabulaq, Kazakhstan .... 65 A9 44 54N 78 30 E
Qarabutaq, Kazakhstan .... 64 G8 49 59N 60 14 E
Qaraçala, Azerbaijan .... 61 L9 39 45N 48 52 E
Qaradarya = Zeravshan →, Asia . 65 D3 39 22N 63 45 E
Qaradarya →, Uzbekistan ...... 65 D4 40 56N 73 25 E
Qaraghandy, Kazakhstan ...... 66 E8 49 50N 73 10 E
Qārah, Si. Arabia .... 98 D4 29 55N 40 3 E
Qarak, China .... 65 D8 38 25N 77 0 E
Qarataū, Kazakhstan .... 65 B5 43 10N 70 28 E
Qarataū, Kazakhstan .... 65 B8 43 30N 69 30 E
Qaraturyq, Kazakhstan .... 65 B8 43 45N 77 50 E
Qarāvol, Afghan. .... 65 E4 37 14N 68 46 E
Qardho = Gardo, Somali Rep. .. 120 C3 9 30N 49 6 E
Qardud, Sudan .... 107 E2 10 20N 29 56 E
Qareh →, Iran .... 101 C12 39 25N 47 22 E
Qareh Tekān, Iran .... 97 B6 36 38N 49 29 E
Qarqan He →, China .... 68 C3 39 30N 88 30 E
Qarqaraly, Kazakhstan .... 66 E8 49 26N 75 30 E
Qarqin, Afghan. .... 65 E3 37 24N 66 4 E
Qarrasa, Sudan .... 107 E3 14 38N 32 5 E
Qarshi, Uzbekistan .... 65 D2 38 53N 65 48 E
Qartabā, Lebanon .... 103 A4 34 4N 35 50 E
Qaryat al Gharab, Iraq .... 96 D5 31 27N 44 48 E
Qaryat al 'Ulyā, Si. Arabia ..... 98 D5 27 33N 47 42 E
Qasigiannguit, Greenland 10 D5 68 50N 51 18W
Qaskeleng, Kazakhstan .... 65 B8 43 20N 76 35 E
Qasr 'Amra, Jordan .... 96 D3 31 48N 36 35 E
Qaşr Bū Hādī, Libya .... 105 B8 31 1N 16 45 E
Qasr Farâfra, Egypt .... 106 B2 27 0N 28 1 E
Qa'ţabah, Yemen .... 98 D4 13 51N 44 42 E
Qatanā, Syria .... 103 B5 33 26N 36 4 E
Qatar ■, Asia .... 99 D6 25 30N 51 15 E
Qatlīsh, Iran .... 97 B8 37 50N 57 19 E
Qattâra, Egypt .... 106 A2 30 12N 27 3 E

Qattâra, Munkhafed el, Egypt ... 106 B2 29 30N 27 30 E
Qattâra Depression = Qattâra,
  Munkhafed el, Egypt .... 106 B2 29 30N 27 30 E
Qawām al Ḥamzah, Iraq .... 96 D5 31 43N 44 58 E
Qawra Point, Malta .... 38 F7 35 58N 14 26 E
Qāyen, Iran .... 97 C8 33 40N 59 10 E
Qazaqstan = Kazakhstan ■, Asia . 66 E7 50 0N 70 0 E
Qazimämmäd, Azerbaijan ...... 61 K9 40 3N 49 0 E
Qazvin, Iran .... 97 B6 36 15N 50 0 E
Qazvin □, Iran .... 97 B6 36 20N 50 0 E
Qazyghurt, Kazakhstan .... 65 C4 41 45N 69 23 E
Qeisari = Caesarea, Israel ...... 103 C3 32 30N 34 53 E
Qeissan, Sudan .... 107 E3 11 4N 34 48 E
Qena, Egypt .... 106 B3 26 10N 32 43 E
Qena, W. →, Egypt .... 106 B3 26 12N 32 44 E
Qeqertarsuaq, Greenland 10 D5 69 45N 53 30W
Qeqertarsuaq, Greenland 10 D5 69 15N 53 38W
Qeqertarsuatsiaat, Greenland ... 10 E5 63 5N 50 45W
Qeshlāq, Iran .... 101 E12 34 55N 46 28 E
Qeshm, Iran .... 97 E8 26 55N 56 10 E
Qeys, Iran .... 97 E7 26 32N 53 58 E
Qezel Owzen →, Iran .... 97 B6 36 45N 49 22 E
Qezi'ot, Israel .... 103 E3 30 52N 34 26 E
Qi Xian, China .... 74 G8 34 40N 114 48 E
Qian Gorlos, China .... 75 B13 45 5N 124 42 E
Qian Hai, China .... 69 F10 22 32N 113 54 E
Qian Xian, China .... 74 G5 34 31N 108 15 E
Qiancheng, China .... 77 D7 27 12N 109 50 E
Qianjiang, Guangxi Zhuangzu, China 76 F7 23 38N 108 58 E
Qianjiang, Hubei, China .... 77 B9 30 24N 112 55 E
Qianjiang, Sichuan, China ..... 76 C7 29 33N 108 47 E
Qianshan, Anhui, China .... 77 B11 30 37N 116 35 E
Qianshan, Guangdong, China ... 69 G10 22 15N 113 31 E
Qianwei, China .... 76 C4 29 13N 103 56 E
Qianxi, China .... 76 D6 27 3N 106 3 E
Qianyang, Hunan, China .... 77 D8 27 18N 110 10 E
Qianyang, Shaanxi, China ...... 74 G4 34 40N 107 8 E
Qianyang, Zhejiang, China ..... 77 B12 30 1N 119 25 E
Qi'ao, China .... 69 G10 22 25N 113 39 E
Qi'ao Dao, China .... 69 G10 22 25N 113 38 E
Qichun, China .... 77 B10 30 18N 115 25 E
Qidong, Hunan, China .... 77 D8 26 56N 112 5 E
Qidong, Jiangsu, China .... 77 B13 31 48N 121 38 E
Qijiang, China .... 76 C6 29 1N 106 35 E
Qikiqtarjuaq, Canada 139 B13 67 33N 63 0W
Qila Safed, Pakistan .... 91 C1 29 0N 61 30 E
Qila Saifullāh, Pakistan .... 91 C3 30 45N 68 17 E
Qilian Shan, China .... 68 C4 38 30N 96 0 E
Qimen, China .... 77 C11 29 50N 117 42 E
Qin He →, China .... 74 G7 35 1N 113 22 E
Qin Jiang →, Guangxi Zhuangzu,
  China .... 76 F7 21 53N 108 35 E
Qin Jiang →, Jiangxi, China .... 77 D10 26 15N 115 55 E
Qin Ling = Qinling Shandi, China . 74 H5 33 50N 108 10 E
Qīnāb, W. →, Yemen .... 99 C5 17 55N 49 59 E
Qin'an, China .... 74 G3 34 48N 105 40 E
Qing Xian, China .... 74 E9 38 35N 116 45 E
Qingcheng, China .... 75 F9 37 11N 117 40 E
Qingdao, China .... 75 F11 36 5N 120 20 E
Qingfeng, China .... 74 G8 35 52N 115 8 E
Qinghai □, China .... 68 C4 36 0N 98 0 E
Qinghai Hu, China .... 68 C5 36 40N 100 10 E
Qinghecheng, China .... 75 D13 41 28N 124 15 E
Qinghemen, China .... 75 D11 41 48N 121 25 E
Qingjian, China .... 74 F6 37 8N 110 8 E
Qingjiang = Huaiyin, China .... 75 H10 33 30N 119 2 E
Qingliu, China .... 77 D11 26 11N 116 48 E
Qinglong, China .... 76 E5 25 49N 105 12 E
Qingping, China .... 76 D6 26 39N 107 47 E
Qingpu, China .... 77 B13 31 10N 121 6 E
Qingshui, China .... 74 G4 34 48N 106 32 E
Qingshuihe, China .... 74 E6 39 55N 111 35 E
Qingtian, China .... 77 C13 28 12N 120 15 E
Qingtongxia Shuiku, China ..... 74 F3 37 50N 105 58 E
Qingxu, China .... 74 F7 37 34N 112 22 E
Qingyang, Anhui, China .... 77 B11 30 38N 117 50 E
Qingyang, Gansu, China .... 74 F4 36 2N 107 55 E
Qingyi Jiang →, China .... 76 C4 29 32N 103 44 E
Qingyuan, Guangdong, China .. 77 F9 23 40N 112 59 E
Qingyuan, Liaoning, China ..... 75 C13 42 10N 124 55 E
Qingyuan, Zhejiang, China ..... 77 D12 27 36N 119 23 E
Qingyun, China .... 75 F9 37 45N 117 20 E
Qingzhen, China .... 76 D6 26 32N 106 25 E
Qinhuangdao, China .... 75 E10 39 56N 119 30 E
Qinling Shandi, China .... 74 H5 33 50N 108 10 E
Qinshui, China .... 74 G7 35 40N 112 8 E
Qinyang = Jiyuan, China .... 74 G7 35 7N 112 57 E
Qinyuan, China .... 74 F7 36 29N 112 20 E
Qinzhou, China .... 76 G7 21 58N 108 38 E
Qionghai, China .... 86 C8 19 15N 110 26 E
Qionglai, China .... 76 B4 30 25N 103 31 E
Qionglai Shan, China .... 76 B4 31 0N 102 30 E
Qiongzhou Haixia, China ...... 86 B8 20 10N 110 15 E
Qiqihar, China .... 67 E13 47 26N 124 0 E
Qiraïya, W. →, Egypt .... 103 E3 30 27N 34 0 E
Qiryat Ata, Israel .... 103 C4 32 47N 35 6 E
Qiryat Gat, Israel .... 103 D3 31 32N 34 46 E
Qiryat Mal'akhi, Israel .... 103 D3 31 44N 34 44 E
Qiryat Shemona, Israel .... 103 B4 33 13N 35 35 E
Qiryat Yam, Israel .... 103 C4 32 51N 35 4 E
Qirzah, W. →, Libya .... 108 B2 30 6N 14 31 E
Qishan, China .... 74 G4 34 25N 107 38 E
Qishn, Yemen .... 99 D5 15 26N 51 40 E
Qitai, China .... 68 B3 44 2N 89 35 E
Qitbit, W. →, Oman .... 99 C6 19 15N 54 23 E
Qiubei, China .... 76 E5 24 2N 104 12 E
Qixia, China .... 75 F11 37 17N 120 52 E
Qiyang, China .... 77 D8 26 35N 111 50 E
Qızılağac Körfäzi, Azerbaijan ... 97 B6 39 9N 49 0 E
Qoghaly, Kazakhstan .... 65 A9 44 29N 78 39 E
Qojūr, Iran .... 97 B6 36 12N 47 55 E
Qom, Iran .... 97 C6 34 40N 51 0 E
Qomolangma Feng = Everest, Mt.,
  Nepal .... 93 E12 28 5N 86 58 E
Qomsheh, Iran .... 97 D6 32 0N 51 55 E
Qondūz, Afghan. .... 65 E4 36 50N 68 50 E
Qondūz □, Afghan. .... 65 E4 36 50N 68 50 E
Qondūz →, Afghan. .... 91 A3 37 0N 68 30 E
Qopa, Kazakhstan .... 65 B7 43 31N 75 50 E
Qoraqalpoghiston □, Uzbekistan . 65 E6 43 0N 58 0 E
Qorday, Kazakhstan .... 65 B7 43 1N 74 59 E
Qormi, Malta .... 38 F7 35 53N 14 28 E
Qorveh, Iran .... 101 E12 35 10N 47 48 E
Qosqudyq, Kazakhstan .... 65 A8 44 10N 77 18 E
Qostanay, Kazakhstan .... 66 D7 53 10N 63 35 E
Qoṭūr, Iran .... 101 C11 38 28N 44 25 E
Qoz Salsilgo, C.A.R. .... 114 A4 10 15N 22 54 E
Qrejten Point, Malta .... 38 F7 35 57N 14 27 E
Qu Xian, China .... 76 B6 30 48N 106 58 E
Quabbin Reservoir, U.S.A. 151 D12 42 20N 72 20W
Quairading, Australia .... 125 F2 32 0 S 117 21 E
Quakenbrück, Germany .... 30 C3 52 40N 7 58 E
Quakertown, U.S.A. 151 F9 40 26N 75 21W
Qualicum Beach, Canada 142 D4 49 22N 124 26W
Quambatook, Australia .... 128 C5 30 57 S 147 53 E
Quamby, Australia .... 126 C3 20 22 S 140 17 E
Quan Long = Ca Mau, Vietnam .. 87 H5 9 7N 105 8 E
Quanah, U.S.A. 155 H5 34 18N 99 44W
Quandialla, Australia .... 129 C7 34 1 S 147 47 E

Quang Ngai, *Vietnam* .... **86 E7** 15 13N 108 58 E
Quang Tri, *Vietnam* .... **86 D6** 16 45N 107 13 E
Quang Yen, *Vietnam* .... **76 G6** 20 56N 106 52 E
Quannan, *China* .... **77 E10** 24 45N 114 33 E
Quanzhou, *Fujian, China* .... **77 E12** 24 55N 118 34 E
Quanzhou, *Guangxi Zhuangzu,*
  China .... **77 E8** 25 57N 111 5 E
Qu'Appelle, *Canada* **143 C8** 50 33N 103 53W
Quaqtaq, *Canada* **139 B13** 60 55N 69 40W
Quaraí, *Brazil* .... **174 C4** 30 15 S 56 20W
Quarré-les-Tombes, *France* .... **27 E11** 47 21N 4 0 E
Quarteira, *Portugal* **43 H2** 37 4N 8 6W
Quartu Sant'Elena, *Italy* .... **46 C2** 39 15N 9 10 E
Quartzsite, *U.S.A.* **161 M12** 33 40N 114 13W
Quatre Bornes, *Mauritius* .... **121 d** 20 15 S 57 28 E
Quatsino Sd., *Canada* **142 C3** 50 25N 127 58W
Quba, *Azerbaijan* .... **61 K9** 41 21N 48 32 E
Qûchân, *Iran* .... **97 B8** 37 10N 58 27 E
Queanbeyan, *Australia* .... **129 C8** 35 17 S 149 14 E
Québec, *Canada* **141 C5** 46 52N 71 13W
Québec □, *Canada* **141 C6** 48 0N 74 0W
Quedlinburg, *Germany* .... **30 D7** 51 47N 11 8 E
Queen Alexandra Ra., *Antarctica* .... **7 E11** 85 0 S 170 0 E
Queen Charlotte B., *Falk. Is.* .... **9 f** 51 50 S 60 40W
Queen Charlotte City, *Canada* **142 C2** 53 15N 132 2W
Queen Charlotte Is., *Canada* **142 C3** 53 20N 132 10W
Queen Charlotte Sd., *Canada* **142 C3** 51 0N 128 0W
Queen Charlotte Sd., *N.Z.* .... **131 B9** 41 10 S 174 15 E
Queen Charlotte Strait, *Canada* **142 C3** 50 45N 127 10W
Queen City, *U.S.A.* **156 D4** 40 25N 92 34W
Queen Elizabeth Forest Park △,
  U.K. **22 E4** 56 7N 4 30W
Queen Elizabeth Is., *Canada* **136 B10** 76 0N 95 0W
Queen Elizabeth Nat. Park △,
  Uganda .... **118 C3** 0 0 30 0 E
Queen Mary Land, *Antarctica* .... **7 D7** 70 0 S 95 0 E
Queen Maud G., *Canada* **138 B9** 68 15N 102 30W
Queen Maud Land = Dronning
  Maud Land, *Antarctica* .... **7 D3** 72 30 S 12 0 E
Queen Maud Mts., *Antarctica* .... **7 E13** 86 0 S 160 0W
Queens Chan., *Australia* .... **124 C4** 15 0 S 129 30 E
Queenscliff, *Australia* .... **128 E6** 38 16 S 144 39 E
Queensland □, *Australia* **152 D6** 31 46N 83 14W
Queensland □, *Australia* .... **125 D3** 22 0 S 142 0 E
Queenstown, *Australia* .... **127 G4** 42 4 S 145 35 E
Queenstown, *N.Z.* .... **131 F3** 45 1 S 168 40 E
Queenstown, *Singapore* .... **87 d** 1 18N 103 48 E
Queenstown, *S. Africa* .... **116 E4** 31 52 S 26 52 E
Queets, *U.S.A.* **160 C2** 47 32N 124 20W
Queguay Grande →, *Uruguay* .... **174 C4** 32 9 S 58 9W
Queimada, Pta. da, *Azores* **9 d1** 38 23N 28 14W
Queimadas, *Brazil* .... **170 D4** 11 0 S 39 38W
Queiros, C., *Vanuatu* .... **133 D5** 14 55 S 167 1 E
Quela, *Angola* .... **115 D3** 9 10 S 16 56 E
Quelimane, *Mozam.* .... **119 F4** 17 53 S 36 58 E
Quelo, *Angola* .... **115 D2** 6 29 S 12 36 E
Quelpart = Cheju do, *S. Korea* .... **75 H14** 33 29N 126 34 E
Queluz, *Portugal* **43 G1** 38 45N 9 15W
Quemado, N. Mex., *U.S.A.* **159 J9** 34 20N 108 30W
Quemado, Tex., *U.S.A.* **155 L4** 28 58N 100 35W
Quemoy = Chinmen, *Taiwan* .... **77 E13** 24 26N 118 12 E
Quemú-Quemú, *Argentina* .... **174 D3** 36 3 S 63 36W
Quepem, *India* .... **95 G2** 15 13N 74 3 E
Quequén, *Argentina* .... **174 D4** 38 30 S 58 30W
Querco, *Peru* .... **172 C3** 13 50 S 74 52W
Querétaro, *Mexico* **162 C4** 20 36N 100 23W
Querétaro □, *Mexico* **162 C5** 20 30N 100 0W
Querfurt, *Germany* .... **30 D7** 51 23N 11 35 E
Quérigut, *France* .... **28 F6** 42 42N 2 6 E
Querqueville, *France* **26 C5** 49 40N 1 42W
Quesada, *Spain* **43 H7** 37 51N 3 4W
Queshan, *China* .... **74 H8** 32 55N 114 2 E
Quesnel, *Canada* **142 C4** 53 0N 122 30W
Quesnel →, *Canada* **142 C4** 52 58N 122 29W
Quesnel L., *Canada* **142 C4** 52 30N 121 20W
Questa, *U.S.A.* **159 H11** 36 42N 105 36W
Questembert, *France* **26 E4** 47 40N 2 28W
Quetena, *Bolivia* .... **172 E4** 22 10 S 67 25W
Quetico Prov. Park △, *Canada* **140 C1** 48 30N 91 45W
Quetrequile, *Argentina* .... **176 B3** 41 33 S 69 22W
Quetta, *Pakistan* .... **91 C2** 30 15N 66 55 E
Quevedo, *Ecuador* .... **168 D2** 1 2 S 79 29W
Queyras, Parc Naturel Régional
  du →, *France* .... **29 D10** 44 45N 6 50 E
Quezaltenango, *Guatemala* **164 D1** 14 50N 91 30W
Quezon □, *Phil.* .... **81 G1** 9 15N 117 59 E
Quezon □, *Phil.* .... **80 D3** 14 40N 121 30 E
Quezon City, *Phil.* .... **80 D3** 14 38N 121 0 E
Quezon Nat. Park △, *Phil.* .... **80 D3** 14 0N 121 55 E
Qufâr, *Si. Arabia* .... **96 E4** 27 26N 41 37 E
Qui Nhon, *Vietnam* .... **86 F7** 13 40N 109 13 E
Quiaca, *Angola* .... **115 E2** 10 46 S 14 59 E
Quibaxe, *Angola* .... **115 D2** 8 24 S 14 27 E
Quibdó, *Colombia* **168 B2** 5 42N 76 40W
Quiberon, *France* **26 E3** 47 29N 3 9W
Quiberon, Presqu'île de, *France* **26 E3** 47 30N 3 8W
Quiçama, Parque Nac. da △, *Angola* .... **115 D2** 9 41 S 13 35 E
Quickborn, *Germany* .... **30 B5** 53 42N 9 52 E
Quiet L., *Canada* **142 A2** 61 5N 133 5W
Quiindy, *Paraguay* .... **174 B4** 25 58 S 57 14W
Quila, *Mexico* **162 C3** 24 23N 107 13W
Quilán, C., *Chile* .... **176 B2** 43 15 S 74 30W
Quilcene, *U.S.A.* **160 C4** 47 49N 122 53W
Quilenda, *Angola* .... **115 E2** 10 39 S 14 23 E
Quilengues, *Angola* .... **115 E2** 14 12 S 14 12 E
Quilimarí, *Chile* .... **174 C1** 32 5 S 71 30W
Quilino, *Argentina* .... **174 C3** 30 14 S 64 29W
Quill Lakes, *Canada* **143 C8** 51 55N 104 13W
Quillabamba, *Peru* .... **172 C3** 12 50 S 72 50W
Quillacollo, *Bolivia* .... **172 D4** 17 26 S 66 17W
Quillaicillo, *Chile* .... **174 C1** 31 17 S 71 40W
Quillan, *France* .... **28 F6** 42 53N 2 10 E
Quillota, *Chile* .... **174 C1** 32 54 S 71 16W
Quilmes, *Argentina* .... **174 C4** 34 43 S 58 15W
Quilon, *India* .... **95 K3** 8 50N 76 38 E
Quilpie, *Australia* .... **127 D3** 26 35 S 144 11 E
Quilpué, *Chile* .... **174 C1** 33 5 S 71 33W
Quilua, *Mozam.* .... **119 F4** 16 17 S 39 54 E
Quimbele, *Angola* .... **115 D3** 6 17 S 16 41 E
Quimbo, *Angola* .... **115 E3** 14 4 S 16 11 E
Quimbonge, *Angola* .... **115 D3** 8 36 S 18 8 E
Quime, *Bolivia* .... **172 D4** 17 2 S 67 15W
Quimilí, *Argentina* .... **174 B3** 27 40 S 62 30W
Quimper, *France* **26 E2** 48 0N 4 9W
Quimperlé, *France* **26 E3** 47 53N 3 33W
Quinault →, *U.S.A.* **160 C2** 47 21N 124 18W
Quincemil, *Peru* .... **172 C3** 13 15 S 70 40W
Quincy, Calif., *U.S.A.* **160 F6** 39 56N 120 57W
Quincy, Fla., *U.S.A.* **153 F3** 30 35N 84 34W
Quincy, Ill., *U.S.A.* **156 C5** 39 56N 91 23W
Quincy, Mass., *U.S.A.* **151 D14** 42 15N 71 0W
Quincy, Mich., *U.S.A.* **157 C12** 41 57N 84 51W
Quincy, Wash., *U.S.A.* **158 C4** 47 22N 119 56W
Quines, *Argentina* .... **174 C2** 32 13 S 65 48W
Quinga, *Mozam.* .... **119 F5** 15 49 S 40 15 E
Quingey, *France* .... **27 E12** 47 7N 5 52 E
Quingombe, *Angola* .... **115 D2** 6 38 S 13 1 E
Quinhagak, *U.S.A.* **144 G7** 59 45N 161 54W
Quinluban Group, *Phil.* .... **81 F3** 11 27N 120 48 E
Quinns Rocks, *Australia* .... **125 F2** 31 40 S 115 42 E
Quintana de la Serena, *Spain* **43 G5** 38 45N 5 40W
Quintana Roo □, *Mexico* **163 D7** 19 0N 88 0W

Quintanar de la Orden, *Spain* **43 F7** 39 36N 3 5W
Quintanar de la Sierra, *Spain* **40 D2** 41 57N 2 55W
Quintanar del Rey, *Spain* **41 F3** 39 21N 1 56W
Quintero, *Chile* .... **174 C1** 32 45 S 71 30W
Quinto, *Spain* **40 D4** 41 25N 0 32W
Quinzáu, *Angola* .... **115 D2** 6 51 S 12 44 E
Quípar →, *Spain* **41 G3** 38 15N 1 40W
Quipeio, *Angola* .... **115 E3** 12 27 S 15 30 E
Quirihue, *Chile* .... **174 D1** 36 15 S 72 35W
Quirima, *Angola* .... **115 E3** 10 47 S 18 6 E
Quirimbo, *Angola* .... **115 E2** 10 36 S 14 12 E
Quirindi, *Australia* .... **129 A9** 31 28 S 150 40 E
Quirino □, *Phil.* .... **80 C3** 16 15N 121 40 E
Quirinopolis, *Brazil* .... **171 E1** 18 32 S 50 30W
Quiroga, *Spain* **42 C3** 42 28N 7 18W
Quiruvilca, *Peru* .... **172 B2** 8 1 S 78 19W
Quissac, *France* .... **29 E8** 43 55N 4 0 E
Quissanga, *Mozam.* .... **119 E5** 12 24 S 40 28 E
Quissico, *Mozam.* .... **117 C5** 24 42 S 34 44 E
Quitapa, *Angola* .... **115 E3** 10 20 S 18 19 E
Quitilipi, *Argentina* .... **174 B3** 26 50 S 60 13W
Quitman, *U.S.A.* **152 E6** 30 47N 83 34W
Quito, *Ecuador* .... **168 D2** 0 15 S 78 35W
Quixadá, *Brazil* .... **170 B4** 4 55 S 39 0W
Quixaxe, *Mozam.* .... **119 F5** 15 17 S 40 4 E
Quixeramobim, *Brazil* .... **170 C4** 5 12 S 39 17W
Quixico, *Angola* .... **115 D2** 7 59 S 14 25 E
Quixinge, *Angola* .... **115 E3** 9 52 S 14 23 E
Quizenga, *Angola* .... **115 D3** 9 21 S 15 28 E
Qujing, *China* .... **76 E4** 25 32N 103 41 E
Qulan, *Kazakhstan* .... **65 B6** 42 55N 72 43 E
Qul'ân, Jazâ'ir, *Egypt* .... **96 E2** 24 22N 35 31 E
Qumbu, *S. Africa* .... **117 E4** 31 10 S 28 48 E
Qumqürghan, *Uzbekistan* .... **65 C3** 37 49N 67 35 E
Quneitra, *Syria* .... **103 B4** 33 7N 35 48 E
Qûnghirot, *Uzbekistan* .... **66 E6** 43 6N 58 54 E
Qu'nyido, *China* .... **76 B2** 31 15N 98 6 E
Quoin I., *Australia* .... **124 B4** 14 54 S 129 32 E
Quoin Pt., *S. Africa* .... **116 E2** 34 46 S 19 37 E
Quorn, *Australia* .... **128 B3** 32 25 S 138 5 E
Qûqon, *Uzbekistan* .... **65 C5** 40 30N 70 57 E
Qurein, *Sudan* .... **107 E3** 13 30N 34 50 E
Qürghonteppa, *Tajikistan* .... **65 E4** 37 50N 68 47 E
Qurnat as Sawdâ', *Lebanon* .... **103 A5** 34 18N 36 6 E
Qûs, *Egypt* .... **106 B3** 25 55N 32 50 E
Qusar, *Azerbaijan* .... **61 K9** 41 25N 48 26 E
Quşaybā', *Si. Arabia* .... **96 E4** 26 53N 43 35 E
Qusaybah, *Iraq* .... **101 E9** 34 24N 40 59 E
Quşay'ir, *Yemen* .... **99 D5** 14 55N 50 20 E
Quseir, *Egypt* .... **96 C3** 26 7N 34 16 E
Qûshchî, *Iran* .... **101 D11** 37 59N 45 3 E
Quthing, *Lesotho* .... **117 E4** 30 25 S 27 36 E
Qûţîâbâd, *Iran* .... **97 C6** 35 47N 48 30 E
Quwo, *China* .... **74 G6** 35 38N 111 25 E
Quyang, *China* .... **74 E8** 38 35N 114 40 E
Quynh Nhai, *Vietnam* .... **86 B4** 21 49N 103 33 E
Quyon, *Canada* **151 A8** 45 31N 76 14W
Quzi, *China* .... **77 C12** 28 57N 118 35 E
Quzi, *China* .... **74 F4** 36 20N 107 20 E
Qvareli, *Georgia* .... **61 K7** 41 57N 45 47 E
Qytet Stalin = Kuçovë, *Albania* .... **50 F3** 40 47N 19 57 E
Qyzylorda, *Kazakhstan* .... **65 A2** 44 48N 65 28 E

R

Ra, Ko, *Thailand* .... **87 H2** 9 13N 98 16 E
Raab, *Austria* .... **34 C6** 48 21N 13 39 E
Raahe, *Finland* .... **14 D21** 64 40N 24 28 E
Raalte, *Neths.* .... **24 B6** 52 23N 6 16 E
Raasay, *U.K.* **22 D2** 57 25N 6 4W
Raasay, Sd. of, *U.K.* **22 D2** 57 30N 6 8W
Rab, *Croatia* .... **45 D11** 44 45N 14 45 E
Raba, *Indonesia* .... **85 D5** 8 36 S 118 55 E
Rába →, *Hungary* .... **52 C2** 47 38N 17 38 E
Raba →, *Poland* .... **55 H7** 50 8N 20 30 E
Rabaçal →, *Portugal* **42 D3** 41 30N 7 12W
Rabah, *Nigeria* .... **113 C6** 13 5N 5 30 E
Rabai, *Kenya* .... **118 C4** 3 50 S 39 31 E
Rabak, *Sudan* .... **107 E3** 13 9N 32 44 E
Rabaraba, *Papua N. G.* .... **132 E5** 9 58 S 149 49 E
Rabastens, *France* .... **28 E5** 43 50N 1 43 E
Rabastens-de-Bigorre, *France* .... **28 E4** 43 23N 0 9 E
Rabat = Victoria, *Malta* .... **38 E6** 36 3N 14 14 E
Rabat, *Kazakhstan* .... **65 B4** 42 2N 69 31 E
Rabat, *Malta* .... **38 F7** 35 53N 14 24 E
Rabat, *Morocco* **110 B3** 34 2N 6 48W
Rabaul, *Papua N. G.* .... **132 C7** 4 24 S 152 18 E
Rabi, *Fiji* .... **133 A3** 16 30 S 179 59W
Râbigh, *Si. Arabia* .... **98 B2** 22 50N 39 5 E
Rabka, *Poland* .... **55 J6** 49 37N 19 59 E
Râbniţa, *Moldova* .... **53 C14** 47 45N 29 0 E
Rābor, *Iran* .... **97 D8** 29 17N 56 55 E
Rabyânah, *Libya* .... **108 D4** 24 15N 22 0 E
Rača, *Serbia, Yug.* .... **50 B4** 44 14N 21 0 E
Răcăciuni, *Romania* .... **53 D11** 46 20N 26 59 E
Răcăşdia, *Romania* .... **52 F6** 44 59N 21 36 E
Racconigi, *Italy* .... **44 D4** 44 46N 7 46 E
Raccoon →, *U.S.A.* **156 C3** 41 35N 93 37W
Raccoon Cr. →, *U.S.A.* **157 E9** 39 47N 87 23W
Race, C., *Canada* **141 C9** 46 40N 53 5W
Rach Gia, *Vietnam* .... **87 G5** 10 5N 105 5 E
Rachid, *Mauritania* **112 B2** 18 45N 11 35W
Raciąż, *Poland* .... **55 F7** 52 46N 20 10 E
Racibórz, *Poland* .... **55 H5** 50 7N 18 18 E
Racine, *U.S.A.* **157 B9** 42 41N 87 51W
Rackerby, *U.S.A.* **160 F5** 39 26N 121 22W
Radama, Nosy, *Madag.* .... **117 A8** 14 0 S 47 47 E
Radama, Saikanosy, *Madag.* .... **117 A8** 14 16 S 47 53 E
Radan, *Serbia, Yug.* .... **50 D5** 42 59N 21 29 E
Rădăuţi, *Romania* .... **53 C10** 47 50N 25 59 E
Rădăuţi-Prut, *Romania* .... **53 B11** 48 14N 26 48 E
Radbuza →, *Czech Rep.* .... **36 B6** 49 45N 13 22 E
Radcliff, *U.S.A.* **157 G11** 37 51N 85 57W
Radeberg, *Germany* .... **30 D9** 51 7N 13 53 E
Radebeul, *Germany* .... **30 D9** 51 6N 13 39 E
Radeče, *Slovenia* .... **45 B12** 46 5N 15 14 E
Radekhiv, *Ukraine* .... **59 G3** 50 25N 24 32 E
Radekhov = Radekhiv, *Ukraine* .... **59 G3** 50 25N 24 32 E
Radenthein, *Austria* .... **34 E6** 46 48N 13 43 E
Radew →, *Poland* .... **54 D2** 54 2N 15 52 E
Radford, *U.S.A.* **148 G5** 37 8N 80 34W
Radhanpur, *India* .... **92 H4** 23 50N 71 38 E
Radhwa, Jabal, *Si. Arabia* .... **96 E3** 24 34N 38 18 E
Radika →, *Macedonia* .... **50 E4** 41 38N 20 37 E
Radisson, Qué., *Canada* **140 B4** 53 47N 77 37W
Radisson, Sask., *Canada* **143 C7** 52 30N 107 20W
Radium Hot Springs, *Canada* **142 C5** 50 35N 116 2W
Radlje ob Dravi, *Slovenia* .... **45 B12** 46 38N 15 13 E
Radnevo, *Bulgaria* .... **51 E9** 42 17N 25 58 E
Radnor Forest, *U.K.* **21 E4** 52 17N 3 10W
Radolfzell, *Germany* .... **31 H4** 47 39N 8 59 E
Radom, *Poland* .... **55 G8** 51 23N 21 12 E
Radom Nat. Park △, *Sudan* .... **114 A4** 9 20N 23 50 E
Radomir, *Bulgaria* .... **50 D6** 42 37N 22 59 E
Radomka →, *Poland* .... **55 G8** 51 43N 21 28 E
Radomsko, *Poland* .... **55 G6** 51 5N 19 28 E
Radomyśl, *Ukraine* .... **59 G5** 50 30N 29 12 E
Radomyśl Wielki, *Poland* .... **55 H8** 50 14N 21 15 E

Radoszyce, *Poland* .... **55 G7** 51 4N 20 15 E
Radoviš, *Macedonia* .... **50 E6** 41 38N 22 28 E
Radovljica, *Slovenia* .... **45 B11** 46 22N 14 12 E
Radstadt, *Austria* .... **34 D6** 47 24N 13 28 E
Radstock, C., *Australia* .... **127 E1** 33 12 S 134 20 E
Răducăneni, *Romania* .... **53 D12** 46 58N 27 54 E
Raduša, *Macedonia* .... **50 D5** 42 7N 21 15 E
Radviliškis, *Lithuania* .... **15 J20** 55 49N 23 33 E
Radville, *Canada* **143 D8** 49 30N 104 15W
Radwá, J., *Si. Arabia* .... **106 C4** 24 34N 38 18 E
Radymno, *Poland* .... **55 J9** 49 59N 22 52 E
Radzanów, *Poland* .... **55 F7** 52 56N 20 8 E
Radzyń Chełmiński, *Poland* .... **54 E5** 53 18N 18 55 E
Radzyń Podlaski, *Poland* .... **55 G9** 51 47N 22 37 E
Rae, *Canada* **142 A5** 62 50N 116 3W
Rae Bareli, *India* .... **93 F9** 26 18N 81 20 E
Rae Isthmus, *Canada* **139 B11** 66 40N 87 30W
Raeren, *Belgium* .... **24 D6** 50 41N 6 7 E
Raeside, L., *Australia* .... **125 E3** 29 20 S 122 0 E
Raetihi, *N.Z.* .... **130 F4** 39 25 S 175 17 E
Rafaela, *Argentina* .... **174 C3** 31 10 S 61 30W
Rafah, *Gaza Strip* .... **103 D3** 31 18N 34 14 E
Rafai, *C.A.R.* .... **118 B1** 4 59N 23 58 E
Raffadali, *Italy* .... **46 E6** 37 24N 13 32 E
Raffili, *Sudan* .... **107 F2** 6 50N 28 0 E
Rafḥā, *Si. Arabia* .... **96 D4** 29 35N 43 35 E
Rafsanjān, *Iran* .... **97 D8** 30 30N 56 5 E
Raft Pt., *Australia* .... **124 C3** 16 4 S 124 26 E
Râgâ, *Sudan* .... **107 F2** 8 28N 25 41 E
Raga →, *Sudan* .... **107 F2** 8 41N 25 52 E
Ragachow, *Belarus* .... **59 F6** 53 8N 30 5 E
Ragag, *Sudan* .... **107 E1** 10 59N 24 40 E
Ragang, Mt., *Phil.* .... **81 H5** 7 43N 124 32 E
Ragay, *Phil.* .... **80 E4** 13 49N 122 47 E
Ragay G., *Phil.* .... **80 E4** 13 49N 122 45 E
Ragged, Mt., *Australia* .... **125 F3** 33 27 S 123 25 E
Ragged Pt., *Barbados* .... **165 g** 13 10N 59 10W
Rägh, *Afghan.* .... **65 E5** 37 32N 70 27 E
Raghunathpalli, *India* .... **93 H11** 22 14N 84 48 E
Raghunathpur, *India* .... **93 H12** 23 33N 86 40 E
Raglan, *N.Z.* .... **130 D3** 37 55 S 174 55 E
Raglan Harbour, *N.Z.* .... **130 D3** 37 47 S 174 50 E
Ragland, *U.S.A.* **152 B3** 33 45N 86 9W
Ragusa = Dubrovnik, *Croatia* .... **50 D2** 42 39N 18 6 E
Ragusa, *Italy* .... **47 F7** 36 55N 14 44 E
Raha, *Indonesia* .... **83 B2** 4 55 S 123 0 E
Rahad, Nahr ed →, *Sudan* .... **107 E3** 14 28N 33 31 E
Rahad al Bardî, *Sudan* .... **107 F1** 11 20N 23 40 E
Rahaeng = Tak, *Thailand* .... **86 D2** 16 52N 99 8 E
Rahatgarh, *India* .... **93 H8** 23 47N 78 22 E
Rahden, *Germany* .... **30 C4** 52 26N 8 36 E
Raheb, Ras ir-, *Malta* .... **38 F7** 35 54N 14 20 E
Raheita, *Eritrea* .... **107 E5** 12 46N 43 4 E
Raheng = Tak, *Thailand* .... **86 D2** 16 52N 99 8 E
Rahimyar Khan, *Pakistan* .... **91 C3** 28 30N 70 25 E
Rähjerd, *Iran* .... **97 C6** 34 22N 50 22 E
Rahole Nat. Reserve △, *Kenya* .... **118 B4** 0 5N 38 57 E
Råholt, *Norway* .... **18 D8** 60 16N 11 11 E
Rahon, *India* .... **90 D7** 31 3N 76 7 E
Rahotu, *N.Z.* .... **130 F2** 39 20 S 173 49 E
Rahuri, *India* .... **94 E2** 19 23N 74 39 E
Raichur, *India* .... **95 F3** 16 10N 77 20 E
Raiford, *U.S.A.* **152 E7** 30 4N 82 14W
Raiganj, *India* .... **93 G13** 25 37N 88 10 E
Raigarh, *India* .... **94 E6** 21 56N 83 25 E
Raighar, *India* .... **94 E6** 19 51N 82 6 E
Raijua, *Indonesia* .... **82 D2** 10 37 S 121 36 E
Raikot, *India* .... **92 D6** 30 41N 75 42 E
Railton, *Australia* .... **127 G4** 41 25 S 146 28 E
Rainbow Bridge Nat. Monument △,
  U.S.A. **159 H8** 37 5N 110 58W
Rainbow City, *U.S.A.* **152 B3** 33 57N 86 5W
Rainbow Lake, *Canada* **142 B5** 58 30N 119 23W
Rainier, *U.S.A.* **160 D4** 46 53N 122 41W
Rainier, Mt., *U.S.A.* **160 D5** 46 52N 121 46W
Rainy L., *Canada* **143 D10** 48 42N 93 10W
Rainy River, *Canada* **143 D10** 48 43N 94 29W
Raippaluoto, *Finland* .... **14 E19** 63 13N 21 14 E
Raipur, *India* .... **94 D7** 21 4N 81 45 E
Rairakhol, *India* .... **94 D7** 21 4N 84 21 E
Ra'is, *Si. Arabia* .... **106 C4** 23 33N 38 43 E
Raisen, *India* .... **93 H8** 23 20N 77 48 E
Raisio, *Finland* .... **15 F20** 60 28N 22 11 E
Raj Nandgaon, *India* .... **92 J5** 21 5N 81 5 E
Raj Nilgiri, *India* .... **93 J12** 21 28N 86 46 E
Raja, Ujung, *Indonesia* .... **84 B1** 3 40N 96 25 E
Raja Ampat, Kepulauan, *Indonesia* .... **83 B4** 0 30 S 130 0 E
Rajah Sikatuna Nat. Park △, *Phil.* .... **81 G5** 9 40N 124 20 E
Rajahmundry, *India* .... **94 F5** 17 1N 81 48 E
Rajampet, *India* .... **95 G4** 14 11N 79 10 E
Rajang →, *Malaysia* .... **82 D4** 2 30N 112 0 E
Rajanpur, *Pakistan* .... **93 E4** 29 6N 70 19 E
Rajapalaiyam, *India* .... **95 K3** 9 25N 77 35 E
Rajapur, *India* .... **94 F1** 16 40N 73 31 E
Rajasthan □, *India* .... **92 F5** 26 45N 73 30 E
Rajasthan Canal, *India* .... **92 F5** 28 0N 72 0 E
Rajauri, *India* .... **95 G3** 33 25N 74 21 E
Rajbari, *Bangla.* .... **90 D2** 23 47N 89 41 E
Rajgarh, Mad. P., *India* .... **92 G7** 24 2N 76 45 E
Rajgarh, Raj., *India* .... **92 F7** 27 14N 76 38 E
Rajgarh, Raj., *India* .... **92 E6** 28 40N 75 25 E
Rajgir, *India* .... **93 G11** 25 2N 85 25 E
Rajgród, *Poland* .... **54 E9** 53 42N 22 42 E
Rajim, *India* .... **94 D5** 20 58N 81 53 E
Rajkot, *India* .... **92 H4** 22 15N 70 56 E
Rajmahal Hills, *India* .... **93 G12** 24 30N 87 30 E
Rajpipla, *India* .... **94 D1** 21 50N 73 30 E
Rajpura, *India* .... **92 D6** 30 25N 76 32 E
Rajshahi, *Bangla.* .... **90 C2** 24 22N 88 39 E
Rajshahi □, *Bangla.* .... **90 C2** 25 0N 89 0 E
Rajula, *India* .... **92 J4** 21 3N 71 26 E
Rajur, *India* .... **94 D4** 20 7N 78 55 E
Rajura, *India* .... **94 E4** 19 48N 79 22 E
Rakaia, *N.Z.* .... **131 D7** 43 45 S 172 1 E
Rakaia →, *N.Z.* .... **131 D7** 43 36 S 172 15 E
Rakan, Ra's, *Qatar* .... **97 E6** 26 10N 51 20 E
Rakaposhi, *Pakistan* .... **93 A6** 36 10N 74 25 E
Rakata, Pulau, *Indonesia* .... **84 D3** 6 10 S 105 20 E
Rakhiv, *Ukraine* .... **59 H3** 48 3N 24 12 E
Rakhni, *Pakistan* .... **92 D3** 30 4N 69 56 E
Rakhni →, *Pakistan* .... **92 E3** 29 31N 69 36 E
Rakhyût, *Oman* .... **99 C6** 16 44N 53 20 E
Rakiraki, *Fiji* .... **133 A2** 17 22 S 178 11 E
Rakitnoye, *Russia* .... **70 B7** 45 36N 134 17 E
Rakitovo, *Bulgaria* .... **51 E8** 41 59N 24 5 E
Rakkestad, *Norway* .... **18 D5** 59 25N 11 21 E
Rakoniewice, *Poland* .... **55 F3** 52 10N 16 16 E
Rakops, *Botswana* .... **116 C3** 21 1 S 24 28 E
Rakovica, *Croatia* .... **45 D12** 44 59N 15 38 E
Rakovník, *Czech Rep.* .... **34 A6** 50 6N 13 42 E
Rakovski, *Bulgaria* .... **51 D8** 42 21N 24 57 E
Rakshan →, *Pakistan* .... **91 D1** 27 15N 62 30 E
Rakvere, *Estonia* .... **15 G22** 59 20N 26 25 E
Raleigh, *U.S.A.* **153 F7** 35 27N 82 32W
Raleigh, N.C., *U.S.A.* **149 H6** 35 47N 78 39W
Rali Salem, *Algeria* .... **111 D5** 21 1N 1 9 E
Ralja, Serbia, Yug. .... **50 B4** 44 33N 20 34 E
Ralls, *U.S.A.* **155 J4** 33 41N 101 24W
Ralston, *U.S.A.* **150 E8** 41 30N 76 57W
Ram →, *Canada* **142 A4** 62 1N 123 41W
Râm Allâh, *West Bank* .... **103 D4** 31 55N 35 10 E
Rama, *Nic.* **164 D3** 12 9N 84 15W

Ramacca, *Italy* .... **47 E7** 37 23N 14 42 E
Ramachandrapuram, *India* .... **94 F6** 16 50N 82 4 E
Ramagiri Udayagiri, *India* .... **94 E7** 19 5N 84 18 E
Ramakona, *India* .... **93 J8** 21 43N 78 50 E
Ramales de la Victoria, *Spain* **42 B7** 43 15N 3 28W
Ramalho, Serra do, *Brazil* .... **171 D3** 13 45 S 44 0W
Ramallah = Râm Allâh, *West Bank* .... **103 D4** 31 55N 35 10 E
Raman, *Thailand* .... **87 J3** 6 29N 101 18 E
Ramanathapuram, *India* .... **95 K4** 9 25N 78 55 E
Ramanetaka, B. de, *Madag.* .... **117 A8** 14 13 S 47 52 E
Ramanujganj, *India* .... **93 H10** 23 48N 83 42 E
Ramas C., *India* .... **95 G1** 15 5N 73 55 E
Ramat Gan, *Israel* .... **103 C3** 32 4N 34 48 E
Ramatlhabama, *S. Africa* .... **116 D4** 25 37 S 25 33 E
Ramban, *India* .... **93 C6** 33 14N 75 12 E
Rambervillers, *France* .... **27 D13** 48 20N 6 38 E
Rambi = Rabi, *Fiji* .... **133 A3** 16 30 S 179 59W
Rambipuji, *Indonesia* .... **85 D4** 8 12 S 113 37 E
Rambouillet, *France* .... **27 D8** 48 39N 1 50 E
Rambrai, *India* .... **90 C3** 25 40N 91 19 E
Rambutyo I., *Papua N. G.* .... **132 B4** 2 18 S 147 49 E
Ramdurg, *India* .... **95 G2** 15 58N 75 22 E
Rame Hd., *Australia* .... **129 D8** 37 47 S 149 30 E
Ramechhap, *Nepal* .... **93 F12** 27 25N 86 10 E
Ramenskoye, *Russia* .... **58 E10** 55 32N 38 15 E
Ramer, *U.S.A.* **152 C3** 32 3N 86 13W
Rameswaram, *India* .... **95 K4** 9 17N 79 18 E
Ramganga →, *India* .... **93 F8** 27 5N 79 58 E
Ramgarh, Bangla. .... **90 D3** 22 59N 91 44 E
Ramgarh, Jharkhand, India .... **93 H11** 23 40N 85 35 E
Ramgarh, Raj., India .... **92 F6** 27 16N 75 14 E
Ramgarh, Raj., India .... **92 F4** 27 30N 70 36 E
Râmhormoz, *Iran* .... **97 D6** 31 15N 49 35 E
Ramîân, *Iran* .... **97 B7** 37 3N 55 16 E
Ramingining, *Australia* .... **126 A2** 12 19 S 135 3 E
Ramla, *Israel* .... **103 D3** 31 55N 34 52 E
Ramlat Zalṭan, *Libya* .... **108 C3** 28 30N 19 30 E
Ramlu, *Eritrea* .... **107 E5** 13 32N 41 40 E
Ramm, Jabal, *Jordan* .... **103 F4** 29 39N 35 26 E
Ramm = Rum, *Jordan* .... **103 F4** 29 39N 35 26 E
Râmna →, *Romania* .... **53 E12** 45 36N 27 3 E
Ramnad = Ramanathapuram, *India* .... **95 K4** 9 25N 78 55 E
Ramnagar, Jammu & Kashmir, India .... **93 C6** 32 47N 75 18 E
Ramnagar, Uttaranchal, India .... **93 E8** 29 24N 79 7 E
Ramnäs, *Sweden* .... **16 E10** 59 46N 16 12 E
Râmnicu Sărat, *Romania* .... **53 E12** 45 26N 27 3 E
Râmnicu Vâlcea, *Romania* .... **53 E9** 45 9N 24 21 E
Ramon, *Phil.* .... **80 C3** 16 50N 121 31 E
Ramon, *Russia* .... **59 G10** 51 55N 39 21 E
Ramona, *U.S.A.* **161 M10** 33 2N 116 52W
Ramonville-St-Agne, *France* .... **28 E5** 43 33N 1 28 E
Ramore, *Canada* **140 C3** 48 30N 80 25W
Ramos →, *Nigeria* .... **113 D6** 5 8N 5 22 E
Ramotswa, *Botswana* .... **116 C4** 24 50 S 25 52 E
Rampart, *U.S.A.* **144 D10** 65 30N 150 10W
Rampur, H.P., India .... **92 D7** 31 26N 77 43 E
Rampur, Mad. P., India .... **92 H5** 23 25N 73 53 E
Rampur, Orissa, India .... **94 D6** 21 48N 83 58 E
Rampur, Ut. P., India .... **93 E8** 28 50N 79 5 E
Rampur Hat, *India* .... **93 G12** 24 10N 87 50 E
Rampura, *India* .... **92 G6** 24 30N 75 27 E
Ramrama Tola, *India* .... **93 J8** 21 52N 79 55 E
Ramree I., *Burma* .... **90 F5** 19 0N 93 40 E
Râmsar, *Iran* .... **97 B6** 36 53N 50 41 E
Ramsey, *U.K.* **20 C3** 54 20N 4 22W
Ramsey, Ill., *U.S.A.* **156 E7** 39 8N 89 7W
Ramsey, N.J., *U.S.A.* **151 E10** 41 4N 74 9W
Ramsey L., *Canada* **140 C3** 47 13N 82 15W
Ramsgate, *U.K.* .... **21 F9** 51 20N 1 25 E
Ramshai, *India* .... **90 B2** 26 44N 88 51 E
Ramsjö, *Sweden* .... **16 B9** 62 11N 15 37 E
Ramstein, *Germany* .... **31 F3** 49 27N 7 32 E
Ramtek, *India* .... **94 D4** 21 20N 79 15 E
Ramu →, *Papua N. G.* .... **132 C3** 4 0 S 144 41 E
Ramvik, *Sweden* .... **16 B11** 62 49N 17 51 E
Rana Pratap Sagar Dam, *India* .... **92 G6** 24 58N 75 38 E
Ranaghat, *India* .... **93 H13** 23 15N 88 35 E
Ranahu, *Pakistan* .... **92 G3** 25 55N 69 45 E
Ranau, *Malaysia* .... **78 C5** 5 59N 116 40 E
Rancagua, *Chile* .... **174 C1** 34 10 S 70 50W
Rance →, *France* **26 D5** 48 34N 1 59W
Rancharia, *Brazil* .... **171 F1** 22 15 S 50 55W
Rancheria →, *Canada* **142 A3** 60 13N 129 7W
Ranchester, *U.S.A.* **158 D10** 44 54N 107 10W
Ranchi, *India* .... **93 H11** 23 19N 85 27 E
Rancho Cucamonga, *U.S.A.* **161 L9** 34 10N 117 30W
Ranco, L., *Chile* .... **176 B2** 40 15 S 72 25W
Rand, *Australia* .... **129 C7** 35 33 S 146 32 E
Randaberg, *Norway* .... **18 E2** 59 1N 5 36 E
Randalstown, *U.K.* **23 B5** 54 45N 6 19W
Randan, *France* .... **27 F10** 46 2N 3 21 E
Randazzo, *Italy* .... **47 E7** 37 53N 14 57 E
Randers, *Denmark* .... **17 H4** 56 29N 10 1 E
Randers Fjord, *Denmark* .... **17 H4** 56 37N 10 20 E
Randfontein, *S. Africa* .... **117 D4** 26 8 S 27 45 E
Randle, *U.S.A.* **160 D5** 46 32N 121 57W
Randolph, Mass., *U.S.A.* **151 D13** 42 10N 71 2W
Randolph, N.Y., *U.S.A.* **150 D6** 42 10N 78 59W
Randolph, Utah, *U.S.A.* **158 F8** 41 40N 111 11W
Randolph, Vt., *U.S.A.* **151 C12** 43 55N 72 40W
Randsburg, *U.S.A.* **161 K9** 35 22N 117 39W
Randsfjorden, *Norway* .... **18 D7** 60 25N 10 24 E
Randsverk, *Norway* .... **18 C6** 61 44N 9 3 E
Råne älv →, *Sweden* .... **14 D20** 65 50N 22 20 E
Ranfurly, *N.Z.* .... **131 F6** 45 7 S 170 6 E
Rangae, *Thailand* .... **87 J3** 6 19N 101 44 E
Rangamati, *Bangla.* .... **90 D4** 22 38N 92 12 E
Rangapara, *India* .... **90 B4** 26 49N 92 39 E
Rangárvallasýsla □, *Iceland* **11 D7** 63 55N 20 0W
Rangataua, N.Z. .... **130 F4** 39 26 S 175 28 E
Rangaunu B., N.Z. .... **130 A2** 34 51 S 173 15 E
Rangeley, *U.S.A.* **151 B14** 44 58N 70 39W
Rangeley L., *U.S.A.* **151 B14** 44 55N 70 43W
Rangely, *U.S.A.* **158 F9** 40 5N 108 48W
Ranger, *U.S.A.* **155 J5** 32 28N 98 41W
Rangia, *India* .... **90 B3** 26 28N 91 38 E
Rangiora, N.Z. .... **131 D7** 43 19 S 172 36 E
Rangitaiki →, N.Z. .... **130 D5** 37 54 S 176 49 E
Rangitata →, N.Z. .... **131 D7** 43 45 S 171 15 E
Rangitikei →, N.Z. .... **130 G4** 40 17 S 175 15 E
Rangitoto Ra., N.Z. .... **130 E4** 38 25 S 175 35 E
Rangkasbitung, *Indonesia* .... **85 D3** 6 21 S 106 15 E
Rangoon = Yangon, *Burma* .... **90 G6** 16 45N 96 20 E
Rangoon →, *Burma* .... **90 G6** 16 50N 96 10 E
Rangpur, *Bangla.* .... **90 C2** 25 42N 89 22 E
Rangsang, *Indonesia* .... **84 B2** 1 20N 103 30 E
Rangsit, *Thailand* .... **86 F3** 13 59N 100 37 E
Ranheim, *Norway* .... **18 A7** 63 26N 10 32 E
Ranibennur, *India* .... **95 G2** 14 35N 75 30 E
Raniganj, *India* .... **93 F9** 27 3N 82 13 E
Ranikhet, *India* .... **93 E8** 29 39N 79 25 E
Ranippettai, *India* .... **95 H4** 12 56N 79 23 E
Rāniyah, *Iraq* .... **96 B5** 36 15N 44 53 E
Ranka, *India* .... **93 H10** 23 59N 83 47 E
Ranken →, *Australia* .... **126 C2** 20 31 S 137 36 E
Rankin, *Ill., U.S.A.* **157 D9** 40 28N 87 54W
Rankin, *Tex., U.S.A.* **155 K4** 31 13N 101 56W
Rankin Inlet, *Canada* **138 B10** 62 30N 93 0W
Rankins Springs, *Australia* .... **129 E7** 33 49 S 146 14 E
Rankovićevo = Kraljevo,
  Serbia, Yug. .... **50 C4** 43 44N 20 41 E

Rankweil, Austria 34 D2 47 17N 9 39 E
Rannoch, L., U.K. 22 E4 56 41N 4 20W
Rannoch Moor, U.K. 22 E4 56 38N 4 48W
Rano Kau, Chile 172 b 27 11 S 109 26W
Rano Raraku, Volcán, Chile 172 b 27 7 S 109 17W
Ranobe, Helodranon' i, Madag. 117 C7 23 3 S 43 33 E
Ranohira, Madag. 117 C8 22 29 S 45 24 E
Ranomafana, Toamasina, Madag. 117 B8 18 57 S 48 50 E
Ranomafana, Toliara, Madag. 117 C8 24 34 S 47 0 E
Ranomafana, Parc Nat. de △, Madag. 117 C8 21 16 S 47 25 E
Ranomena, Madag. 117 C8 23 25 S 47 17 E
Ranon, Vanuatu 133 F6 16 8 S 168 7 E
Ranong, Thailand 87 H2 9 56N 98 40 E
Ranongga, Solomon Is. 133 M9 8 5 S 156 35 E
Ranotsara Nord, Madag. 117 C8 22 48 S 46 36 E
Ranpur, India 94 D7 20 5N 85 20 E
Ränsa, Iran 97 C6 33 39N 48 18 E
Ranski, Indonesia 83 B4 1 30 S 134 10 E
Ransom, U.S.A. 157 C8 41 9N 88 39W
Rantabe, Madag. 117 B8 15 42 S 49 39 E
Rantau, Indonesia 85 C5 2 56 S 115 9 E
Rantauprapat, Indonesia 84 B1 2 15N 99 50 E
Rantemario, Indonesia 82 B1 3 15 S 119 57 E
Rantoul, U.S.A. 157 D8 40 19N 88 9W
Ranum, Denmark 17 H3 56 54N 9 14 E
Ranyah, W. →, Si. Arabia 98 B3 21 18N 43 20 E
Raon l'Étape, France 27 D13 48 24N 6 50 E
Raoping, China 77 F11 23 42N 117 1 E
Raoui, Erg er, Algeria 111 C4 29 0N 2 0W
Raoyang, China 74 E8 38 15N 115 45 E
Rap, Ko, Thailand 87 b 9 19N 99 58 E
Rapa, Pac. Oc. 135 K13 27 35 S 144 20W
Rapa Nui = Pascua, I. de, Chile 172 b 27 7 S 109 23W
Rapallo, Italy 44 D6 44 21N 9 14 E
Rapang, Indonesia 82 B1 3 50 S 119 48 E
Rapar, India 92 H4 23 34N 70 38 E
Rāpch, Iran 97 E8 25 40N 59 15 E
Raper, C., Canada 139 B13 69 44N 67 6W
Rapid City, U.S.A. 154 D3 44 5N 103 14W
Rapid River, U.S.A. 148 C2 45 55N 86 58W
Rapla, Estonia 15 G21 59 1N 24 52 E
Rapperswil, Switz. 33 B7 47 14N 8 45 E
Rapti →, India 93 F10 26 18N 83 41 E
Rapu Rapu I., Phil. 80 E5 13 12N 124 9 E
Raqaba ez Zarqa →, Sudan 107 F2 9 14N 29 44 E
Rāqūbah, Libya 108 C3 28 58N 19 2 E
Raquette →, U.S.A. 151 B10 45 0N 74 42W
Raquette Lake, U.S.A. 151 C10 43 49N 74 40W
Rarotonga, Cook Is. 135 K12 21 30 S 160 0W
Ra's al 'Ayn, Syria 101 D9 36 45N 40 12 E
Ra's al Khaymah, U.A.E. 97 E7 25 50N 55 59 E
Ras el Ma, Algeria 111 B4 34 26N 0 50W
Râs el Mâ, Mali 112 B4 16 35N 4 30W
Râs Ghârib, Egypt 106 B3 28 6N 33 18 E
Râs Kôh, Pakistan 91 C2 28 43N 64 55 E
Ra's Lānūf, Libya 108 B3 30 46N 18 11 E
Râs Mallap, Egypt 106 B3 29 18N 32 50 E
Râs Muhammad Nat. Park △, Egypt 106 B3 27 45N 34 16 E
Rasa, Argentina 176 B4 40 50 S 62 15W
Rasca, Pta. de la, Canary Is. 9 e1 27 59N 16 41W
Rășcani, Moldova 53 C12 47 58N 27 33 E
Raseiniai, Lithuania 15 J20 55 25N 23 5 E
Rashad, Sudan 107 E3 11 55N 31 0 E
Rashid, Egypt 106 H7 31 21N 30 22 E
Rashîd, Masabb, Egypt 106 H7 31 22N 30 17 E
Rashin = Najin, N. Korea 75 C16 42 12N 130 15 E
Rashmi, India 92 G6 25 4N 74 22 E
Rasht, Iran 97 B6 37 20N 49 40 E
Rasi Salai, Thailand 86 E5 15 20N 104 9 E
Rasipuram, India 95 J4 11 30N 78 15 E
Raška, Serbia, Yug. 50 C4 43 19N 20 39 E
Râsnov, Romania 53 E10 45 35N 25 27 E
Rason L., Australia 125 E3 28 45 S 124 25 E
Rașova, Romania 53 F12 44 15N 27 55 E
Rasovo, Bulgaria 50 C7 43 42N 23 17 E
Rasra, India 93 G10 25 50N 83 50 E
Rass el Oued, Algeria 111 A6 35 57N 5 2 E
Rasskazovo, Russia 60 D5 52 35N 41 50 E
Rast, Romania 53 G8 43 53N 23 16 E
Rastatt, Germany 31 G4 48 50N 8 11 E
Rastede, Germany 30 B4 53 15N 8 12 E
Răstolița, Romania 53 D9 46 59N 24 58 E
Rasul, Pakistan 92 C5 32 42N 73 34 E
Raszków, Poland 55 G4 51 43N 17 40 E
Rat Buri, Thailand 86 F2 13 30N 99 54 E
Rat Islands, U.S.A. 144 L2 52 0N 178 0 E
Rat L., Canada 143 B9 56 10N 99 40W
Ratangarh, India 92 E6 28 5N 74 35 E
Rätansbyn, Sweden 16 B8 62 29N 14 33 E
Rațāwī, Iraq 96 D5 30 38N 47 13 E
Ratcatchers L., Australia 128 B3 32 30 S 143 12 E
Rath, India 93 G8 25 36N 79 37 E
Rath Luirc, Ireland 23 D3 52 21N 8 40W
Rathbun L., U.S.A. 156 D4 40 49N 92 53W
Rathdrum, Ireland 23 D5 52 56N 6 14W
Rathenow, Germany 30 C8 52 37N 12 19 E
Rathkeale, Ireland 23 D3 52 32N 8 56W
Rathlin I., U.K. 23 A5 55 18N 6 14W
Rathmelton, Ireland 23 A4 55 2N 7 38W
Rathor = Racibórz, Poland 55 H5 50 7N 18 18 E
Rätikon, Austria 33 B9 47 0N 9 55 E
Ratingen, Germany 30 D2 51 18N 6 52 E
Ratlam, India 92 H6 23 20N 75 0 E
Ratnagiri, India 94 F1 16 57N 73 18 E
Ratnapura, Sri Lanka 95 L5 6 40N 80 20 E
Ratodero, Pakistan 92 F3 27 48N 68 18 E
Raton, U.S.A. 155 G2 36 54N 104 24W
Rattaphum, Thailand 87 J3 7 8N 100 16 E
Ratten, Austria 34 D8 47 28N 15 44 E
Rattray Hd., U.K. 22 D7 57 38N 1 50W
Rättvik, Sweden 16 D9 60 52N 15 7 E
Ratz, Mt., Canada 142 B2 57 23N 132 12W
Ratzeburg, Germany 30 B6 53 40N 10 46 E
Rau, Indonesia 82 A3 2 20N 128 10 E
Raub, Malaysia 87 L3 3 47N 101 52 E
Rauch, Argentina 174 D4 36 45 S 59 5W
Raudales de Malpaso, Mexico 163 D6 17 30N 93 30W
Raudeberg, Norway 18 C2 61 59N 5 7 E
Raufarhöfn, Iceland 11 A11 66 27N 15 57W
Raufoss, Norway 18 D7 60 44N 10 37 E
Rauhellern, Norway 18 D4 60 15N 7 50 E
Raukumara Ra., N.Z. 131 E6 38 5 S 177 55 E
Raul Soares, Brazil 171 F3 20 5 S 42 22W
Rauma, Finland 15 F19 61 10N 21 30 E
Rauma →, Norway 18 B4 62 34N 7 43 E
Raung, Gunung, Indonesia 79 J17 8 8 S 114 18 E
Raurkela, India 93 H11 22 14N 84 50 E
Rausu-Dake, Japan 70 B12 44 4N 145 7 E
Rāut →, Moldova 53 C14 47 15N 28 49 E
Rava-Ruska, Ukraine 59 G2 50 15N 23 42 E
Rava Russkaya = Rava-Ruska, Ukraine 59 G2 50 15N 23 42 E
Ravalli, U.S.A. 158 C4 47 17N 114 11W
Ravānsar, Iran 101 E12 34 43N 46 40 E
Ravanusa, Italy 46 E6 37 16N 13 58 E
Rāvar, Iran 97 D8 31 20N 56 51 E
Ravena, U.S.A. 151 D11 42 28N 73 49W
Ravenel, U.S.A. 152 C9 32 46N 80 15W
Ravenna, Italy 45 D9 44 25N 12 12 E
Ravenna, Ky., U.S.A. 157 G13 37 42N 83 55W
Ravenna, Nebr., U.S.A. 154 E5 41 1N 98 55W
Ravenna, Ohio, U.S.A. 150 E3 41 9N 81 15W
Ravensburg, Germany 31 H5 47 46N 9 36 E

Ravenshoe, Australia 126 B4 17 37 S 145 29 E
Ravensthorpe, Australia 125 F3 33 35 S 120 2 E
Ravenswood, Australia 126 C4 20 6 S 146 54 E
Ravenswood, U.S.A. 148 F5 38 57N 81 46W
Ravensworth, Australia 129 B9 32 26 S 151 4 E
Ravenwood, U.S.A. 156 D2 40 22N 94 41W
Raver, India 94 D3 21 15N 76 2 E
Ravi →, Pakistan 92 D4 30 35N 71 49 E
Ravna Gora, Croatia 45 C11 45 24N 14 50 E
Ravna Reka, Serbia, Yug. 50 B5 44 1N 21 35 E
Ravne na Koroškem, Slovenia 45 B11 46 36N 14 59 E
Rawa Mazowiecka, Poland 55 G7 51 46N 20 12 E
Rawalpindi, Pakistan 91 B4 33 38N 73 8 E
Rawāndūz, Iraq 101 D11 36 40N 44 30 E
Rawang, Malaysia 87 L3 3 20N 101 35 E
Rawene, N.Z. 130 B2 35 25 S 173 32 E
Rawicz, Poland 55 G3 51 36N 16 52 E
Rawka →, Poland 55 F7 52 9N 20 8 E
Rawlinna, Australia 125 F4 30 58 S 125 28 E
Rawlins, U.S.A. 158 F10 41 47N 107 14W
Rawlinson Ra., Australia 125 D4 24 40 S 128 30 E
Rawson, Argentina 176 B3 43 15 S 65 5W
Raxaul, India 93 F11 26 59N 84 51 E
Ray, U.S.A. 154 A3 48 21N 103 10W
Ray, C., Canada 141 C8 47 33N 59 15W
Ray City, U.S.A. 152 D6 31 5N 83 11W
Ray Mts., U.S.A. 144 D10 66 0N 152 0W
Raya Ring, Ko, Thailand 87 a 8 18N 98 29 E
Rayachoti, India 95 G4 14 4N 78 50 E
Rayadurg, India 95 G3 14 40N 76 50 E
Rayagada, India 94 E6 19 15N 83 20 E
Raychikhinsk, Russia 67 E13 49 46N 129 25 E
Rāyen, Iran 97 D8 29 34N 57 26 E
Rayevskiy, Russia 64 D5 54 4N 54 38 E
Rayle, U.S.A. 152 B7 33 48N 82 54W
Rayleigh, U.K. 21 F8 51 36N 0 37 E
Raymond, Canada 142 D6 49 30N 112 35W
Raymond, Calif., U.S.A. 160 H7 37 13N 119 54W
Raymond, Ill., U.S.A. 156 E7 39 19N 89 34W
Raymond, N.H., U.S.A. 151 C13 43 2N 71 11W
Raymond, Wash., U.S.A. 160 D3 46 41N 123 44W
Raymond Terrace, Australia 129 B9 32 45 S 151 44 E
Raymondville, U.S.A. 155 M6 26 29N 97 47W
Raymore, Canada 143 C8 51 25N 104 31W
Rayón, Mexico 162 B2 29 43N 110 35W
Rayong, Thailand 86 F3 12 40N 101 20 E
Raytown, U.S.A. 156 E2 39 1N 94 28W
Rayville, U.S.A. 155 J9 32 29N 91 46W
Raz, Pte. du, France 26 D2 48 2N 4 47W
Razan, Iran 97 C6 35 23N 49 2 E
Ražana, Serbia, Yug. 50 B3 44 6N 19 55 E
Ražanj, Serbia, Yug. 50 C5 43 40N 21 31 E
Razdelna, Bulgaria 51 C11 43 13N 27 41 E
Razdel'naya = Rozdilna, Ukraine 59 J6 46 50N 30 2 E
Razdolnoye, Russia 70 C5 43 30N 131 52 E
Razdolnoye, Ukraine 59 K7 45 46N 33 29 E
Razeh, Iran 97 C6 32 47N 48 9 E
Razgrad, Bulgaria 51 C10 43 33N 26 34 E
Razim, Lacul, Romania 53 F14 44 50N 29 0 E
Razlog, Bulgaria 50 E7 41 53N 23 28 E
Razmak, Pakistan 91 B3 32 45N 69 50 E
Ré, Î. de, France 28 B2 46 12N 1 30W
Reading, U.K. 21 F7 51 27N 0 58W
Reading, Mich., U.S.A. 157 C12 41 50N 84 45W
Reading, Ohio, U.S.A. 157 E12 39 13N 84 26W
Reading, Pa., U.S.A. 151 F9 40 20N 75 56W
Reading □, U.K. 21 F7 51 27N 0 58W
Real, Cordillera, Bolivia 172 E5 17 0 S 67 0W
Realicó, Argentina 174 D3 35 0 S 64 15W
Réalmont, France 28 E6 43 48N 2 10 E
Realp, Switz. 33 C6 46 36N 8 30 E
Ream, Cambodia 87 G4 10 34N 103 39 E
Reata, Mexico 162 B4 26 8N 101 5W
Reay Forest, U.K. 22 C4 58 22N 4 55W
Rebais, France 27 D10 48 50N 3 10 E
Rebi, Indonesia 83 C4 6 23 S 134 7 E
Rebiana, Libya 108 D4 24 12N 22 10 E
Rebiana, Sahrâ', Libya 108 D3 24 30N 21 0 E
Rebun-Tō, Japan 70 B10 45 23N 141 2 E
Recanati, Italy 45 E10 43 24N 13 32 E
Recaş, Romania 52 E6 45 46N 21 30 E
Recco, Italy 44 D6 44 22N 9 9 E
Recherche, Arch. of the, Australia 125 F3 34 15 S 122 50 E
Rechna Doab, Pakistan 92 D5 31 35N 73 30 E
Rechytsa, Belarus 59 F6 52 21N 30 24 E
Recife, Brazil 170 C5 8 0 S 35 0W
Recife, Seychelles 121 b 4 36 S 55 42 E
Recklinghausen, Germany 24 C7 51 37N 7 12 E
Reconquista, Argentina 174 B4 29 10 S 59 45W
Recreio, Brazil 173 B6 8 0 S 58 25W
Recreo, Argentina 174 B2 29 25 S 65 10W
Recuay, Peru 172 B2 9 43 S 77 28W
Recz, Poland 55 E2 53 16N 15 31 E
Red →, La., U.S.A. 155 K9 31 1N 91 45W
Red →, N. Dak., U.S.A. 138 C10 49 0N 97 15W
Red Bank, U.S.A. 151 F10 40 21N 74 5W
Red Bay, Canada 141 B8 51 44N 56 25W
Red Bluff, U.S.A. 158 F2 40 11N 122 15W
Red Bluff L., U.S.A. 155 K3 31 54N 103 55W
Red Bud, U.S.A. 156 F7 38 13N 89 59W
Red Cliffs, Australia 128 C5 34 19 S 142 11 E
Red Cloud, U.S.A. 154 E5 40 5N 98 32W
Red Creek, U.S.A. 151 C8 43 14N 76 45W
Red Deer, Canada 142 C6 52 20N 113 50W
Red Deer →, Alta., Canada 143 C7 50 58N 110 0W
Red Deer →, Man., Canada 143 C8 52 53N 101 1W
Red Deer L., Canada 143 C8 52 55N 101 20W
Red Devil, U.S.A. 144 F8 61 46N 157 19W
Red Hook, U.S.A. 151 E11 41 55N 73 53W
Red Indian L., Canada 141 C8 48 35N 57 0W
Red L., Canada 143 C10 51 3N 93 49W
Red Lake, Canada 143 C10 51 3N 93 49W
Red Lake Falls, U.S.A. 154 B6 47 53N 96 16W
Red Lake Road, Canada 143 C10 49 59N 93 25W
Red Lodge, U.S.A. 158 D9 45 11N 109 15W
Red Mountain, U.S.A. 161 K9 35 37N 117 38W
Red Oak, U.S.A. 156 E7 41 1N 95 14W
Red Rock, Canada 140 C2 48 55N 88 15W
Red Rock, L., U.S.A. 156 C3 41 22N 93 20W
Red Rocks Pt., Australia 125 F4 32 13 S 127 32 E
Red Sea, Asia 88 C2 25 0N 36 0 E
Red Slate Mt., U.S.A. 160 H8 37 31N 118 52W
Red Sucker L., Canada 140 B1 54 9N 93 40W
Red Tower Pass = Turnu Roşu P., Romania 53 E9 45 33N 24 17 E
Red Wing, U.S.A. 154 C8 44 34N 92 31W
Reda, Poland 54 D5 54 40N 18 19 E
Redang, Malaysia 87 K4 5 49N 103 2 E
Redange, Lux. 24 E5 49 46N 5 52 E
Redcar, U.K. 20 C6 54 37N 1 4W
Redcar & Cleveland □, U.K. 20 C6 54 29N 1 0W
Redcliff, Canada 143 C6 50 10N 110 50W
Redcliffe, Australia 127 D5 27 12 S 153 0 E
Redcliffe, Mt., Australia 125 E3 28 30 S 121 30 E
Reddersburg, S. Africa 116 D4 29 41 S 26 10 E
Reddick, Fla., U.S.A. 153 F7 29 22N 82 12W
Reddick, Ill., U.S.A. 157 C8 41 6N 88 15W
Redding, Calif., U.S.A. 158 F2 40 35N 122 24W
Redding, Iowa, U.S.A. 156 D2 40 36N 94 23W
Redditch, U.K. 21 E6 52 18N 1 55W
Redenção, Brazil 170 B4 4 13 S 38 43W
Redfield, U.S.A. 154 C5 44 53N 98 31W
Redford, U.S.A. 151 B11 44 38N 73 48W
Redhead, Trin. & Tob. 169 F10 10 48N 60 3W

Redkey, U.S.A. 157 D11 40 21N 85 9W
Redkino, Russia 58 B9 56 39N 36 16 E
Redlands, U.S.A. 161 M9 34 4N 117 11W
Redmond, Oreg., U.S.A. 158 D3 44 17N 121 11W
Redmond, Wash., U.S.A. 160 C4 47 41N 122 7W
Redon, France 26 E4 47 40N 2 6W
Redonda, Antigua 165 C7 16 58N 62 19W
Redonda, Pta., Chile 172 b 27 10 S 109 22W
Redondela, Spain 42 C2 42 15N 8 38W
Redondo, Portugal 43 G3 38 39N 7 37W
Redondo Beach, U.S.A. 161 M8 33 50N 118 23W
Redoubt Volcano, U.S.A. 144 F9 60 29N 152 45W
Redruth, U.K. 21 G2 50 14N 5 14W
Redvers, Canada 143 D8 49 35N 101 40W
Redwater, Canada 142 C6 53 55N 113 6W
Redwood, U.S.A. 151 B9 44 18N 75 48W
Redwood City, U.S.A. 160 H4 37 30N 122 15W
Redwood Falls, U.S.A. 154 C7 44 32N 95 7W
Redwood Nat. Park △, U.S.A. 158 F1 41 40N 124 5W
Ree, L., Ireland 23 C3 53 35N 8 0W
Reed, L., Canada 143 C8 54 38N 100 30W
Reed City, U.S.A. 148 D3 43 53N 85 31W
Reedley, U.S.A. 160 J7 36 36N 119 27W
Reedsburg, U.S.A. 154 D9 43 32N 90 0W
Reedsport, U.S.A. 158 E1 43 42N 124 6W
Reedsville, U.S.A. 150 F7 40 39N 77 35W
Reedy Creek, Australia 128 C4 36 58 S 140 2 E
Reefton, N.Z. 131 C6 42 6 S 171 51 E
Rees, Germany 30 D2 51 46N 6 24 E
Reese →, U.S.A. 158 F5 40 48N 117 4W
Refahiye, Turkey 101 C8 39 54N 38 47 E
Reftele, Sweden 17 G7 57 11N 13 35 E
Refugio, U.S.A. 155 L6 28 18N 97 17W
Rega →, Poland 54 D2 54 10N 15 18 E
Regalbuto, Italy 47 E7 37 39N 14 38 E
Regen, Germany 31 G9 48 58N 13 8 E
Regen →, Germany 31 F8 49 1N 12 6 E
Regeneração, Brazil 170 C3 6 15 S 42 41W
Regensburg, Germany 31 F8 49 1N 12 6 E
Regensdorf, Switz. 33 B6 47 26N 8 28 E
Regenstauf, Germany 31 F8 49 7N 12 6 E
Reggâne = Zaouiet Reggâne, Algeria 111 C5 26 32N 0 3 E
Reggello, Italy 45 E8 43 41N 11 32 E
Réggio di Calábria, Italy 47 D8 38 6N 15 39 E
Réggio nell'Emília, Italy 44 D7 44 43N 10 36 E
Reghin, Romania 53 D9 46 46N 24 42 E
Regina, Canada 143 C8 50 27N 104 35W
Régina, Fr. Guiana 169 C7 4 9N 52 18W
Regina Beach, Canada 143 C8 50 47N 105 0W
Register, U.S.A. 152 C8 32 22N 81 53W
Registro, Brazil 175 A6 24 29 S 47 49W
Reguengos de Monsaraz, Portugal 43 G3 38 25N 7 32W
Reh, Erg er, Algeria 111 C5 27 48N 4 30 E
Rehar →, India 93 H10 23 55N 82 40 E
Rehli, India 93 H8 23 38N 79 5 E
Rehoboth, Namibia 116 C2 23 15 S 17 4 E
Rehovot, Israel 103 D3 31 54N 34 48 E
Reïbell = Ksar Chellala, Algeria 111 A5 35 13N 2 19 E
Reichenbach, Germany 30 E8 50 37N 12 17 E
Reichenbach, Switz. 32 C5 46 38N 7 42 E
Reichenberg = Liberec, Czech Rep. 34 A8 50 47N 15 7 E
Reid, Australia 125 F4 30 49 S 128 26 E
Reiden, Switz. 32 B5 47 14N 7 59 E
Reidsville, Ga., U.S.A. 152 C7 32 6N 82 7W
Reidsville, N.C., U.S.A. 149 G6 36 21N 79 40W
Reigate, U.K. 21 F7 51 14N 0 12W
Reillo, Spain 40 F3 39 54N 1 53W
Reims, France 27 C11 49 15N 4 1 E
Reina Adelaida, Arch., Chile 176 D2 52 20 S 74 0W
Reina Sofia, Tenerife ✈ (TFS), Canary Is. 9 e1 28 3N 16 33W
Reinach, Aargau, Switz. 32 B6 47 14N 8 11 E
Reinach, Basel, Switz. 32 B5 47 29N 7 35 E
Reinbeck, U.S.A. 156 D4 42 19N 92 36W
Reinbek, Germany 30 B6 53 30N 10 16 E
Reindeer →, Canada 143 B8 55 36N 103 11W
Reindeer I., Canada 143 C9 52 30N 98 0W
Reindeer L., Canada 143 B8 57 15N 102 15W
Reinga, C., N.Z. 130 A1 34 25 S 172 43 E
Reinosa, Spain 42 B6 43 2N 4 15W
Reinsvoll, Norway 18 D7 60 40N 10 38 E
Reitan, Norway 18 B8 62 49N 11 22 E
Reitz, S. Africa 117 D4 27 48 S 28 29 E
Reivilo, S. Africa 116 D3 27 36 S 24 8 E
Rejaf, Sudan 107 G3 4 45N 31 35 E
Rejmyre, Sweden 17 F9 58 50N 15 55 E
Rejowiec Fabryczny, Poland 55 G10 51 5N 23 17 E
Reka →, Slovenia 45 C11 45 40N 14 0 E
Rekovac, Serbia, Yug. 50 C5 43 51N 21 3 E
Reliance, Canada 143 A7 63 0N 109 20W
Relizane, Algeria 111 A5 35 44N 0 31 E
Remad, Oued →, Algeria 111 B4 33 28N 1 20W
Rémalard, France 26 D7 48 26N 0 47 E
Remarkable, Mt., Australia 128 B3 32 48 S 138 10 E
Rembang, Indonesia 85 D4 6 42 S 111 21 E
Rembau, Malaysia 84 B2 2 35N 102 6 E
Rembert, U.S.A. 152 D5 34 5N 80 28W
Remchi, Algeria 111 A4 35 2N 1 20W
Remedios, Colombia 168 B3 7 2N 74 41W
Remedios, Panama 164 E3 8 15N 81 50W
Remeshk, Iran 97 E8 26 55N 58 50 E
Remetea, Romania 53 D10 46 45N 25 29 E
Remich, Lux. 24 E6 49 32N 6 22 E
Remington, U.S.A. 157 D9 40 46N 87 9W
Rémire, Fr. Guiana 169 C7 4 53N 52 17W
Remiremont, France 27 D13 48 2N 6 36 E
Remontnoye, Russia 61 G6 46 34N 43 37 E
Remoulins, France 29 E8 43 55N 4 35 E
Remscheid, Germany 24 C7 51 11N 7 12 E
Ren Xian, China 74 F8 37 8N 114 40 E
Rena, Norway 18 C8 61 8N 11 20 E
Rena →, Norway 18 C8 61 8N 11 23 E
Renascença, Brazil 168 D4 3 40 S 66 0W
Rende, Italy 47 C9 39 20N 16 11 E
Rendina, Greece 48 B3 39 4N 21 58 E
Rendova, Solomon Is. 133 M9 8 33 S 157 17 E
Rendsburg, Germany 30 A5 54 17N 9 39 E
Renens, Switz. 32 C3 46 32N 6 35 E
Renfrew, Canada 140 C4 45 30N 76 40W
Renfrewshire □, U.K. 22 F4 55 49N 4 38W
Renfroe, U.S.A. 152 C5 32 14N 84 43W
Rengat, Indonesia 84 C2 0 30 S 102 45 E
Rengo, Chile 174 C1 34 24 S 70 50W
Renhua, China 77 E9 25 5N 113 40 E
Renhuai, China 76 D6 27 48N 106 24 E
Reni, Ukraine 59 K5 45 28N 28 15 E
Renigunta, India 95 H4 13 38N 79 30 E
Renk, Sudan 107 E3 11 50N 32 50 E
Renland, Greenland 10 C8 71 10N 26 30W
Rennebu, Norway 18 B6 62 52N 9 48 E
Rennell, Solomon Is. 133 N11 11 40 S 160 10 E
Rennell Sd., Canada 142 C2 53 23N 132 35W
Renner Springs, Australia 126 B1 18 20 S 133 47 E
Rennes, France 26 D5 48 7N 1 41W
Rennie L., Canada 143 A7 61 32N 105 35W
Reno, U.S.A. 160 F7 39 31N 119 48W
Reno →, Italy 45 D9 44 38N 12 16 E
Renovo, U.S.A. 150 E7 41 20N 77 45W
Renqiu, China 74 E9 38 43N 116 5 E
Rens, Denmark 17 K3 54 54N 9 5 E

Renshou, China 76 C5 30 3N 104 9 E
Rensselaer, Ind., U.S.A. 157 D9 40 57N 87 9W
Rensselaer, N.Y., U.S.A. 151 D11 42 38N 73 45W
Rentería, Spain 40 B3 43 19N 1 54W
Renton, U.S.A. 160 C4 47 29N 122 12W
Renwick, N.Z. 131 B8 41 30 S 173 51 E
Réo, Burkina Faso 112 C4 12 28N 2 35W
Reo, Indonesia 82 C2 8 19 S 120 30 E
Reotipur, India 93 G10 25 33N 83 45 E
Repalle, India 95 F5 16 2N 80 45 E
Répcelak, Hungary 52 C2 47 24N 17 1 E
Republic, Mo., U.S.A. 155 G8 37 7N 93 29W
Republic, Wash., U.S.A. 158 B4 48 39N 118 44W
Republican →, U.S.A. 154 F6 39 4N 96 48W
Republiek, Suriname 169 B6 5 30 S 55 13W
Repulse B., Australia 126 J6 20 35 S 148 46 E
Repulse Bay, Canada 139 B11 66 30N 86 30W
Requena, Peru 172 B3 5 5 S 73 52W
Requena, Spain 41 F3 39 30N 1 4W
Réquista, France 28 D6 44 1N 2 32 E
Reşadiye = Datça, Turkey 49 E9 36 46N 27 40 E
Reşadiye, Turkey 100 B7 40 23N 37 20 E
Reşadiye Yarımadası, Turkey 49 E9 36 40N 27 45 E
Resavica, Serbia, Yug. 50 B5 44 4N 21 31 E
Resen, Macedonia 50 E5 41 5N 21 0 E
Reserve, U.S.A. 159 K9 33 43N 108 45W
Resht = Rasht, Iran 97 B6 37 20N 49 40 E
Résia, Italy 33 C11 46 50N 10 31 E
Resistencia, Argentina 174 B4 27 30 S 59 0W
Reşita, Romania 52 E6 45 18N 21 53 E
Resko, Poland 54 E2 53 47N 15 25 E
Resolution I., Canada 139 B13 61 30N 65 0W
Resolution I., N.Z. 131 C5 45 40 S 166 40 E
Resplandes, Brazil 170 C2 6 17 S 45 13W
Resplendor, Brazil 171 E3 19 20 S 41 15W
Ressano Garcia, Mozam. 117 D5 25 25 S 32 0 E
Reston, Canada 143 D8 49 33N 101 6W
Reszel, Poland 54 D8 54 4N 21 10 E
Retalhuleu, Guatemala 164 D1 14 33N 91 46W
Retenue, L. de, Dem. Rep. of the Congo 119 E2 11 0 S 27 0 E
Retezat, Munții, Romania 52 E8 45 25N 23 0 E
Retezat, Parcul Nat. △, Romania 52 E7 45 23N 22 56 E
Retford, U.K. 20 D7 53 19N 0 56W
Rethel, France 27 C11 49 30N 4 20 E
Rethem, Germany 30 C5 52 47N 9 22 E
Réthímnon, Greece 39 E5 35 18N 24 30 E
Réthímnon □, Greece 39 E5 35 23N 24 28 E
Reti, Pakistan 92 E3 28 5N 69 48 E
Retiche, Alpi, Switz. 33 D10 46 30N 10 0 E
Retiers, France 26 E5 47 55N 1 23W
Retortillo, Spain 42 E4 40 48N 6 21W
Retournac, France 29 C8 45 12N 4 2 E
Rétság, Hungary 52 C4 47 58N 19 10 E
Rettenberg, Germany 33 A10 47 35N 10 18 E
Réunion ■, Ind. Oc. 121 c 21 0 S 56 0 E
Reus, Spain 41 B6 41 10N 1 5 E
Reuss →, Switz. 33 B6 47 16N 8 24 E
Reuterstadt Stavenhagen, Germany 30 B8 53 42N 12 54 E
Reutlingen, Germany 31 G5 48 29N 9 12 E
Reutte, Austria 34 D3 47 29N 10 42 E
Reval = Tallinn, Estonia 15 G21 59 22N 24 48 E
Revda, Russia 64 C7 56 48N 59 57 E
Revel = Tallinn, Estonia 15 G21 59 22N 24 48 E
Revel, France 28 E6 43 28N 2 1 E
Revelganj, India 93 G11 25 50N 84 40 E
Revelstoke, Canada 142 C5 51 0N 118 10W
Reventazón, Peru 172 B1 6 10 S 80 58W
Revigny-sur-Ornain, France 27 D11 48 49N 4 59 E
Revillagigedo, Is. de, Pac. Oc. 162 D2 18 40N 112 0W
Revin, France 27 C11 49 55N 4 39 E
Revolyutsii, Pik, Tajikistan 65 D6 38 31N 72 21 E
Revolyutsiya, Qullai = Revolyutsii, Pik, Tajikistan 65 D6 38 31N 72 21 E
Revúca, Slovak Rep. 35 C13 48 40N 20 7 E
Revuè →, Mozam. 119 F3 19 50 S 34 0 E
Rewa, India 93 G9 24 33N 81 25 E
Rewa →, Guyana 169 C6 3 19N 58 42W
Rewari, India 92 E7 28 15N 76 40 E
Rex, U.S.A. 144 D10 64 13N 149 16W
Rexburg, U.S.A. 158 E8 43 49N 111 47W
Rey, L., del, Panama 164 E4 8 20N 78 30W
Rey, Mayo →, Cameroon 114 A2 8 47N 14 1 E
Rey, Rio-del-→, Cameroon 114 B1 4 30N 8 45 E
Rey Bouba, Cameroon 114 A2 8 40N 14 15 E
Rey Malabo, Eq. Guin. 113 E6 3 45N 8 50 E
Reyðarfjörður, Iceland 11 B12 65 2N 14 13W
Reyes, Bolivia 172 C4 14 19 S 67 23W
Reyes, Pt., U.S.A. 160 H3 38 0N 123 0W
Reyhanlı, Turkey 100 D7 36 16N 36 35 E
Reykholt, Árnessýsla, Iceland 11 C4 64 40N 21 18W
Reykholt, Borgarfjarðarsýsla, Iceland 11 C5 64 40N 20 25W
Reykjahlíð, Iceland 11 B10 65 40N 16 55W
Reykjanes, Iceland 11 D4 63 48N 22 40W
Reykjavík, Iceland 11 D3 64 10N 21 57W
Reykjavík Keflavík ✈ (KEF), Iceland 11 C4 64 0N 22 45W
Reynolds, Ga., U.S.A. 152 C5 32 33N 84 6W
Reynolds, Ill., U.S.A. 156 C6 41 20N 90 40W
Reynolds Ra., Australia 124 D5 22 30 S 133 0 E
Reynoldsville, Ga., U.S.A. 152 E5 30 51N 84 47W
Reynoldsville, Pa., U.S.A. 150 E6 41 5N 78 58W
Reynosa, Mexico 163 B5 26 5N 98 18W
Rezāiyeh, L. = Orūmīyeh, Daryācheh-ye, Iran 101 D11 37 50N 45 30 E
Rēzekne, Latvia 15 H22 56 30N 27 17 E
Rezh, Russia 64 C8 57 23N 61 24 E
Rezina, Moldova 53 C13 47 45N 28 58 E
Rezovo, Bulgaria 51 D12 42 0N 28 0 E
Rezvān, Iran 97 E8 27 34N 56 6 E
Rgotina, Serbia, Yug. 50 B6 44 1N 22 17 E
Rhamnus, Greece 38 C5 38 12N 24 3 E
Rharbi, Zahrez, Algeria 111 B5 34 50N 3 9 E
Rharis, O. →, Algeria 111 C6 26 52N 5 4 E
Rhayader, U.K. 21 E4 52 18N 3 29W
Rheda-Wiedenbrück, Germany 30 D4 51 50N 8 20 E
Rhede, Germany 30 D2 51 50N 6 42 E
Rhein, Canada 143 C8 51 25N 102 15W
Rhein →, Europe 24 C6 51 52N 6 2 E
Rhein-Main-Donau-Kanal, Germany 31 F7 49 1N 11 27 E
Rhein-Ruhr, Düsseldorf ✈ (DUS), Germany 30 D2 51 17N 6 46 E
Rhein-Taunus, Naturpark △, Germany 31 E4 50 10N 8 10 E
Rhein-Westerwald, Naturpark △, Germany 30 E3 50 32N 7 20 E
Rheinbach, Germany 30 E2 50 38N 6 57 E
Rheine, Germany 30 C3 52 17N 7 26 E
Rheineck, Switz. 33 B9 47 28N 9 31 E
Rheinfall, Switz. 33 A7 47 40N 8 37 E
Rheinfelden, Germany 31 H3 47 33N 7 47 E
Rheinfelden, Switz. 32 A5 47 32N 7 47 E
Rheinhessen-Pfalz □, Germany 31 F3 49 0N 8 0 E
Rheinland-Pfalz □, Germany 30 D2 51 50N 7 0 E
Rheinsberg, Germany 30 B8 53 6N 12 54 E
Rheinwaldhorn, Switz. 33 D8 46 30N 9 3 E
Rheris, Oued →, Morocco 110 B4 30 50N 4 34W
Rhin = Rhein →, Europe 24 C6 51 52N 6 2 E
Rhine = Rhein →, Europe 24 C6 51 52N 6 2 E
Rhine, U.S.A. 152 D6 31 59N 83 12W
Rhinebeck, U.S.A. 151 E11 41 56N 73 55W
Rhineland-Palatinate = Rheinland-Pfalz □, Germany 31 E2 50 0N 7 0 E
Rhinelander, U.S.A. 154 C10 45 38N 89 25W

Rhinns Pt., U.K. 22 F2 55 40N 6 29W
Rhino Camp, Uganda 118 B3 3 0N 31 22 E
Rhir, Cap, Morocco 110 B3 30 38N 9 54W
Rho, Italy 44 C6 45 32N 9 2 E
Rhode Island □, U.S.A. 151 E13 41 40N 71 30W
Rhodes = Ródhos, Greece 38 E12 36 15N 28 10 E
Rhodes ✈ (RHO), Greece 49 E10 36 23N 28 12 E
Rhodesia = Zimbabwe ■, Africa 119 F3 19 0S 30 0 E
Rhodope Mts. = Rhodopi Planina, Bulgaria 51 E8 41 40N 24 20 E
Rhodopi Planina, Bulgaria 51 E8 41 40N 24 20 E
Rhön, Germany 30 E5 50 24N 9 58 E
Rhondda, U.K. 21 F4 51 39N 3 31W
Rhondda Cynon Taff □, U.K. 21 F4 51 42N 3 27W
Rhône □, France 29 C8 45 54N 4 35 E
Rhône →, France 29 E8 43 28N 4 42 E
Rhône-Alpes □, France 29 C9 45 40N 6 0 E
Rhum, U.K. 22 E2 57 0N 6 20W
Rhyl, U.K. 20 D4 53 20N 3 29W
Ri-Aba, Eq. Guin. 113 E6 3 28N 8 40 E
Ria Formosa, Parque Natural de △, Portugal 43 H3 37 1N 7 48W
Riachão, Brazil 170 C2 7 20 S 46 37W
Riacho de Santana, Brazil 171 D3 13 37 S 42 57W
Rialma, Brazil 171 E2 15 18 S 49 34W
Riang, India 90 B4 27 31N 92 56 E
Riangnom, Sudan 107 F3 9 55N 30 1 E
Riaño, Spain 42 C6 42 59N 4 59W
Rians, France 29 E9 43 37N 5 44 E
Riansáres →, Spain 43 F7 39 32N 3 18W
Riasi, India 93 C6 33 10N 74 50 E
Riau □, Indonesia 84 B2 0 0 102 35 E
Riau, Kepulauan, Indonesia 84 B2 0 30N 104 20 E
Riau Arch. = Riau, Kepulauan, Indonesia 84 B2 0 30N 104 20 E
Riaza, Spain 42 D7 41 18N 3 30W
Riaza →, Spain 42 D7 41 42N 3 55W
Riba de Saelices, Spain 40 E2 40 55N 2 17W
Riba-Roja de Turia, Spain 41 F4 39 33N 0 34W
Ribadavia, Spain 42 C2 42 17N 8 8W
Ribadeo, Spain 42 B3 43 35N 7 5W
Ribadesella, Spain 42 B5 43 30N 5 7W
Ribado, Nigeria 113 D7 9 16N 12 47 E
Ribamar, Brazil 170 B3 2 33 S 44 3W
Ribao, Cameroon 113 D7 6 32N 11 30 E
Ribas = Ribes de Freser, Spain 40 C7 42 19N 2 15 E
Ribas do Rio Pardo, Brazil 173 E7 20 27 S 53 46W
Ribauè, Mozam. 119 E4 14 57 S 38 17 E
Ribble →, U.K. 20 D5 53 52N 2 25W
Ribe, Denmark 17 J2 55 19N 8 44 E
Ribe Amtskommune □, Denmark 17 J2 55 35N 8 45 E
Ribeauvillé, France 27 D14 48 10N 7 20 E
Ribécourt-Dreslincourt, France 27 C9 49 30N 2 55 E
Ribeira = Santa Uxía, Spain 42 C2 42 36N 8 58W
Ribeira Brava, Madeira 9 c 32 41N 17 4W
Ribeira do Pombal, Brazil 170 D4 10 50 S 38 32W
Ribeira Grande, Azores 9 d3 37 49N 25 31W
Ribeira Grande, C. Verde Is. 9 j 17 0N 25 4W
Ribeirão, Brazil 170 C4 8 31 S 35 23W
Ribeirão Prêto, Brazil 175 A6 21 10 S 47 50W
Ribeiro Gonçalves, Brazil 170 C2 7 32 S 45 14W
Ribemont, France 27 C10 49 47N 3 27 E
Ribera, Italy 46 E6 37 30N 13 16 E
Ribérac, France 28 C4 45 15N 0 20 E
Riberalta, Bolivia 173 C4 11 0 S 66 0W
Ribes de Freser, Spain 40 C7 42 19N 2 15 E
Ribnica, Slovenia 45 C11 45 45N 14 45 E
Ribnitz-Damgarten, Germany 30 A8 54 15N 12 27 E
Ričany, Czech Rep. 34 B7 50 0N 14 40 E
Riccarton, N.Z. 131 D7 43 32 S 172 37 E
Riccia, Italy 47 A7 41 30N 14 50 E
Riccione, Italy 45 E9 43 59N 12 39 E
Rice, U.S.A. 161 L12 34 5N 114 51W
Rice L., Canada 150 B6 44 12N 78 10W
Rice Lake, U.S.A. 154 C9 45 30N 91 44W
Ricebored, U.S.A. 152 D8 31 44N 81 26W
Rich, Morocco 110 B4 32 16N 4 30W
Rich, C., Canada 150 B4 44 43N 80 38W
Richard Toll, Senegal 112 B1 16 28N 15 42W
Richards Bay, S. Africa 117 D5 28 48 S 32 6 E
Richardson →, Canada 143 B6 58 25N 111 14W
Richardson Lakes, U.S.A. 148 C10 44 46N 70 58W
Richardson Mts., N.Z. 131 E3 44 49 S 168 34 E
Richardson Springs, U.S.A. 160 F5 39 51N 121 46W
Riche, C., Australia 125 F2 34 36 S 118 47 E
Richelieu, France 26 E7 47 1N 0 20 E
Richey, U.S.A. 154 B2 47 39N 105 4W
Richfield, U.S.A. 159 G8 38 46N 112 5W
Richfield Springs, U.S.A. 151 D10 42 51N 74 59W
Richford, U.S.A. 151 B12 45 0N 72 40W
Richibucto, Canada 141 C7 46 42N 64 54W
Richland, Ga., U.S.A. 152 C5 32 5N 84 40W
Richland, Iowa, U.S.A. 156 C5 41 13N 92 0W
Richland, Mo., U.S.A. 156 G4 37 51N 92 26W
Richland, Wash., U.S.A. 158 C4 46 17N 119 18W
Richland Center, U.S.A. 154 D9 43 21N 90 23W
Richlands, U.S.A. 148 G5 37 6N 81 48W
Richmond, N.S.W., Australia 129 B9 33 35 S 150 42 E
Richmond, Queens., Australia 126 C3 20 43 S 143 8 E
Richmond, N.Z. 131 B8 41 20 S 173 12 E
Richmond, U.K. 20 C6 54 25N 1 43W
Richmond, Calif., U.S.A. 160 H4 37 56N 122 21W
Richmond, Ind., U.S.A. 157 E12 39 50N 84 53W
Richmond, Ky., U.S.A. 157 G12 37 45N 84 18W
Richmond, Mich., U.S.A. 150 D2 42 49N 82 45W
Richmond, Mo., U.S.A. 156 F3 39 17N 93 58W
Richmond, Tex., U.S.A. 155 L7 29 35N 95 46W
Richmond, Utah, U.S.A. 158 F8 41 56N 111 49W
Richmond, Va., U.S.A. 148 G7 37 33N 77 27W
Richmond, Vt., U.S.A. 151 B12 44 24N 72 59W
Richmond, Mt., N.Z. 131 B8 41 32 S 173 22 E
Richmond Hill, Canada 150 C5 43 52N 79 27W
Richmond Hill, U.S.A. 152 D8 31 56N 81 18W
Richmond Ra., Australia 127 D5 29 0 S 152 45 E
Richmond Ra., N.Z. 131 B8 41 32 S 173 22 E
Richtersveld Nat. Park △, S. Africa 116 D2 28 15 S 17 10 E
Richterswil, Switz. 33 B7 47 13N 8 43 E
Richwood, Ohio, U.S.A. 157 D13 40 26N 83 18W
Richwood, W. Va., U.S.A. 148 F5 38 14N 80 32W
Ricla, Spain 40 D3 41 31N 1 24W
Ricupe, Angola 115 E4 14 37 S 21 25 E
Ridà', Yemen 98 D4 14 25N 44 50 E
Ridder = Leninogorsk, Kazakhstan 76 D9 50 20N 83 30 E
Riddes, Switz. 32 D4 46 11N 7 14 E
Riddlesburg, U.S.A. 150 F6 40 9N 78 15W
Ridge Farm, U.S.A. 157 E9 39 54N 87 39W
Ridge Spring, U.S.A. 152 B8 33 31N 81 40W
Ridgecrest, U.S.A. 161 K9 35 38N 117 40W
Ridgefield, Conn., U.S.A. 151 E11 41 17N 73 30W
Ridgefield, Wash., U.S.A. 160 E4 45 49N 122 45W
Ridgeland, U.S.A. 152 C9 32 29N 80 59W
Ridgetown, Canada 140 D3 42 26N 81 52W
Ridgeville, Ind., U.S.A. 157 D11 40 18N 85 2W
Ridgeville, S.C., U.S.A. 152 B9 33 5N 80 19W
Ridgewood, U.S.A. 151 F10 40 59N 74 7W
Ridgway, Ill., U.S.A. 157 G8 37 48N 88 16W
Ridgway, Pa., U.S.A. 150 E6 41 25N 78 44W
Riding Mountain Nat. Park △, Canada 143 C9 50 50N 100 0W
Ridley, Mt., Australia 125 F3 33 12 S 122 7 E
Riebeek-Oos, S. Africa 116 E4 33 10 S 26 10 E
Ried, Austria 34 C6 48 14N 13 30 E
Riedlingen, Germany 31 G5 48 9N 9 28 E
Riedstadt, Germany 31 F4 49 45N 8 30 E

Riehen, Switz. 32 A5 47 37N 7 38 E
Rienza →, Italy 45 B8 46 49N 11 47 E
Riesa, Germany 30 D9 51 17N 13 17 E
Riesco, I., Chile 176 D2 52 55 S 72 40W
Riesi, Italy 47 E7 37 17N 14 5 E
Riet →, S. Africa 116 D3 29 0 S 23 54 E
Rietbron, S. Africa 116 E3 32 54 S 23 10 E
Rietfontein, Namibia 116 C3 21 58 S 20 58 E
Rieti, Italy 45 F9 42 24N 12 51 E
Rieupeyroux, France 28 D6 44 19N 2 12 E
Riez, France 29 E10 43 49N 6 6 E
Rif = Er Rif, Morocco 110 A4 35 1N 4 1W
Riffe L., U.S.A. 160 D4 46 32N 122 26W
Rifle, U.S.A. 158 G10 39 32N 107 47W
Rift Valley, Africa 104 G7 7 0N 30 0 E
Rift Valley □, Kenya 118 B4 0 20N 36 0 E
Rig Rig, Chad 109 F2 14 13N 14 25 E
Riga, India 90 A5 28 26N 95 2 E
Riga, Latvia 15 H21 56 53N 24 8 E
Rīga, Latvia 54 B10 56 54N 23 59 E
Riga ✈ (RIX), Latvia 54 B10 56 54N 23 59 E
Riga, G. of, Latvia 15 H20 57 40N 23 45 E
Rigacikun, Nigeria 113 C6 10 6N 7 28 E
Rīgān, Iran 97 D8 28 37N 58 58 E
Rīgas Jūras Līcis = Riga, G. of, Latvia 15 H20 57 40N 23 45 E
Rigaud, Canada 151 A10 45 29N 74 18W
Rigby, U.S.A. 158 E8 43 40N 111 55W
Rigestān, Afghan. 91 C2 30 15N 65 0 E
Riggins, U.S.A. 158 D5 45 25N 116 19W
Rignac, France 28 D6 44 25N 2 16 E
Rigolet, Canada 141 B8 54 10N 58 23W
Rihand Dam, India 93 G10 24 9N 83 2 E
Riihimäki, Finland 15 F21 60 45N 24 48 E
Riiser-Larsen-halvøya, Antarctica 7 C4 68 0 S 35 0 E
Rijau, Nigeria 113 C6 11 8N 5 17 E
Rijeka, Croatia 45 C11 45 20N 14 21 E
Rijeka Crnojevića, Montenegro, Yug. 50 D3 42 24N 19 1 E
Rijssen, Neths. 24 B6 52 19N 6 31 E
Rīkā', W. ar →, Si. Arabia 98 B4 22 25N 44 56 E
Rike, Ethiopia 107 E4 10 50N 39 53 E
Rikuzentakada, Japan 70 E10 39 0N 141 40 E
Rila, Bulgaria 50 D7 42 7N 23 7 E
Rila Planina, Bulgaria 50 D7 42 10N 23 0 E
Riley, U.S.A. 158 E4 43 32N 119 28W
Rima →, Nigeria 113 C6 13 4N 5 10 E
Rimah, Wadi ar →, Si. Arabia 96 E4 26 5N 41 30 E
Rimau, Pulau, Malaysia 87 c 5 15N 100 16 E
Rimavská Sobota, Slovak Rep. 35 C13 48 22N 20 2 E
Rimbey, Canada 142 C6 52 35N 114 15W
Rimbo, Sweden 16 E12 59 44N 18 21 E
Rimersburg, U.S.A. 150 E5 41 3N 79 30W
Rimforsa, Sweden 17 F9 58 6N 15 43 E
Rimi, Nigeria 113 C6 12 58N 7 43 E
Rímini, Italy 45 D9 44 3N 12 33 E
Rimouski, Canada 141 C6 48 27N 68 30W
Rimrock, U.S.A. 160 D5 46 38N 121 10W
Rinca, Indonesia 82 C1 8 45 S 119 35 E
Rincon, U.S.A. 152 C8 32 18N 81 14W
Rincón de la Victoria, Spain 43 J6 36 43N 4 18W
Rincón de Romos, Mexico 162 C4 22 14N 102 18W
Rinconada, Argentina 174 A2 22 26 S 66 10W
Rind →, India 93 G9 25 53N 80 33 E
Rindal, Norway 16 A6 58 21N 9 13 E
Ringarum, Sweden 17 F10 58 21N 16 26 E
Ringas, India 92 F6 27 21N 75 34 E
Ringdove, Vanuatu 133 F6 16 40 S 168 10 E
Ringe, Denmark 17 J4 55 13N 10 28 E
Ringia, Greece 49 D7 37 23N 25 13 E
Rinjani, Indonesia 85 D5 8 24 S 116 28 E
Rinteln, Germany 30 C5 52 10N 9 8 E
Río, Punta del, Spain 41 J2 36 49N 2 24W
Rio Branco = Arcoverde, Brazil 170 C4 8 25 S 37 4W
Rio Branco, Brazil 172 B4 9 58 S 67 49W
Río Branco, Uruguay 175 C5 32 40 S 53 40W
Río Bravo, Parque Internacional del △, N. Amer. 162 B4 29 2N 102 45W
Río Bravo del Norte →, Mexico 163 B5 25 57N 97 9W
Río Brilhante, Brazil 175 A5 21 48 S 54 33W
Río Bueno, Chile 176 B2 40 19 S 72 58W
Río Caribe, Venezuela 169 A5 10 42 S 63 7W
Río Chico, Venezuela 168 A5 10 19N 65 59W
Río Claro, Brazil 175 A6 22 19 S 47 33W
Río Claro, Trin. & Tob. 169 F9 10 20N 61 25W
Río Colorado, Argentina 174 A4 39 0 S 64 0W
Río Cuarto, Argentina 174 C3 33 10 S 64 25W
Río das Pedras, Mozam. 117 C6 23 8 S 35 28 E
Rio de Contas, Brazil 171 D3 13 36 S 41 48W
Rio de Janeiro, Brazil 171 F3 23 0 S 43 12W
Rio de Janeiro □, Brazil 171 F3 22 50 S 43 0W
Río de Oro, B. de, W. Sahara 110 D1 23 45N 15 50W
Rio do Prado, Brazil 171 E3 16 35 S 40 34W
Rio do Sul, Brazil 175 B6 27 13 S 49 37W
Río Dulce, Parque Nac. △, Guatemala 164 C2 15 43N 88 50W
Río Gallegos, Argentina 176 D3 51 35 S 69 15W
Río Grande = Grande, Rio →, U.S.A. 155 N6 25 58N 97 9W
Río Grande, Argentina 176 D3 53 50 S 67 45W
Río Grande, Bolivia 172 E4 20 51 S 67 17W
Río Grande, Brazil 175 C5 32 0 S 52 20W
Río Grande, Mexico 162 C4 23 50N 103 2W
Río Grande, Nic. 164 D3 12 54N 83 33W
Río Grande, Puerto Rico 165 d 18 23N 65 50W
Río Grande City, U.S.A. 155 M5 26 23N 98 49W
Río Grande de Santiago →, Mexico 162 C3 21 36N 105 26W
Río Grande do Norte □, Brazil 170 C4 5 40 S 36 0W
Río Grande do Sul □, Brazil 175 C5 30 0 S 53 0W
Río Hato, Panama 164 E3 8 22N 80 10W
Río Lagartos, Mexico 163 C7 21 36N 88 10W
Rio Largo, Brazil 170 C4 9 28 S 35 50W
Rio Maior, Portugal 43 F2 39 19N 8 57W
Rio Marina, Italy 44 F7 42 49N 10 25 E
Río Mayo, Argentina 176 C2 45 40 S 70 15W
Río Mulatos, Bolivia 172 E4 19 40 S 66 50W
Río Muni □, Eq. Guin. 114 D2 1 30N 10 0 E
Rio Negro, Brazil 175 B6 26 0 S 49 55W
Rio Negro, Chile 176 B2 40 47 S 73 14W
Rio Negro, Pantanal do, Brazil 173 D6 19 0 S 56 0W
Rio Pardo, Brazil 175 C5 30 0 S 52 30W
Río Pico, Argentina 176 B2 44 0 S 70 22W
Río Platano, Reserva de la Biosfera de △, Honduras 164 C3 15 45N 85 0W
Rio Preto da Eva, Brazil 175 D6 2 41 S 59 41W
Rio Rancho, U.S.A. 159 J10 35 14N 106 38W
Rio Real, Brazil 171 D4 11 28 S 37 56W
Río Segundo, Argentina 174 C3 31 40 S 63 59W
Río Tercero, Argentina 174 C3 32 15 S 64 8W
Rio Tinto, Brazil 170 C4 6 48 S 35 5W
Rio Tinto, Portugal 42 D2 41 11N 8 34W

Río Turbio, Argentina 176 D2 51 32 S 72 18W
Río Verde, Brazil 171 E1 17 50 S 51 0W
Río Verde, Mexico 163 C5 21 56N 99 59W
Rio Verde de Mato Grosso, Brazil 173 D7 18 56 S 54 52W
Rio Vista, U.S.A. 160 G5 38 10N 121 42W
Ríobamba, Ecuador 168 D2 1 50 S 78 45W
Ríohacha, Colombia 168 A3 11 33N 72 55W
Rioja, Peru 172 B2 6 11 S 77 5W
Riom, France 28 C7 45 54N 3 7 E
Riom-ès-Montagnes, France 28 C6 45 17N 2 39 E
Rion-des-Landes, France 28 E3 43 55N 0 56W
Rionegro, Antioquia, Colombia 168 B3 6 9N 75 22W
Rionegro, Santander, Colombia 168 B3 7 15N 73 9W
Rionero in Vúlture, Italy 47 B8 40 55N 15 40 E
Rioni →, Georgia 61 J5 42 14N 41 44 E
Ríos, Spain 42 D3 41 58N 7 16W
Riosucio, Caldas, Colombia 168 B2 5 30N 75 40W
Riosucio, Choco, Colombia 168 B2 7 27N 77 7W
Riou L., Canada 143 B7 59 7N 106 25W
Rioz, France 27 E13 47 26N 6 5 E
Riozinho →, Brazil 168 D4 2 55 S 67 7W
Ripatransone, Italy 45 F10 42 59N 13 46 E
Ripley, Canada 150 B3 44 4N 81 35W
Ripley, Calif., U.S.A. 161 M12 33 32N 114 39W
Ripley, N.Y., U.S.A. 150 D5 42 16N 79 43W
Ripley, Ohio, U.S.A. 157 F13 38 45N 83 51W
Ripley, Tenn., U.S.A. 155 H10 35 45N 89 32W
Ripley, W. Va., U.S.A. 148 F5 38 49N 81 43W
Ripoll, Spain 40 C7 42 15N 2 13 E
Ripon, U.K. 20 C6 54 9N 1 31W
Ripon, Calif., U.S.A. 160 H5 37 44N 121 7W
Ripon, Wis., U.S.A. 148 D1 43 51N 88 50W
Riposto, Italy 47 E8 37 44N 15 12 E
Risan, Montenegro, Yug. 50 D2 42 32N 18 42 E
Risaralda □, Colombia 168 B2 5 0N 76 10W
Riscle, France 28 E3 43 39N 0 5W
Rishā', W. ar →, Si. Arabia 95 H3 25 33N 44 5 E
Rishiri-Tō, Japan 70 B10 45 11N 141 15 E
Rishon le Ziyyon, Israel 103 D3 31 58N 34 48 E
Rishtan, Uzbekistan 65 C5 40 20N 71 15 E
Rising Sun, U.S.A. 157 F12 38 57N 84 51W
Risle →, France 26 C7 49 26N 0 23 E
Risnjak, Nac. Park △, Croatia 45 C11 45 35N 14 37 E
Rison, U.S.A. 155 J8 33 58N 92 11W
Risør, Norway 18 F6 58 43N 9 13 E
Rissani, Morocco 110 B4 31 18N 4 12W
Rita Blanca Cr. →, U.S.A. 155 H3 35 40N 102 29W
Ritchie's Arch., India 95 H11 12 14N 93 10 E
Riti, Nigeria 113 D6 7 57N 9 41 E
Ritter, Mt., U.S.A. 160 H7 37 41N 119 12W
Rittman, U.S.A. 150 F3 40 58N 81 47W
Ritzville, U.S.A. 158 C4 47 8N 118 23W
Riu, India 90 A5 28 19N 95 3 E
Riva del Garda, Italy 44 C7 45 53N 10 50 E
Riva Lígure, Italy 44 E4 43 50N 7 50 E
Rivadavia, Buenos Aires, Argentina 174 D3 35 29 S 62 59W
Rivadavia, Mendoza, Argentina 174 C3 33 13 S 68 30W
Rivadavia, Salta, Argentina 174 A3 24 5 S 62 54W
Rivadavia, Chile 174 B1 29 57 S 70 35W
Rivarolo Canavese, Italy 44 C4 45 19N 7 43 E
Rivas, Nic. 164 D2 11 30N 85 50W
Rive-de-Gier, France 29 C8 45 32N 4 37 E
River Cess, Liberia 112 D3 5 30N 9 32W
River Jordan, Canada 160 B2 48 26N 124 3W
Rivera, Argentina 174 D3 37 12 S 63 14W
Rivera, Uruguay 175 C4 31 0 S 55 50W
Riverbank, U.S.A. 160 H6 37 44N 120 56W
Riverdale, Calif., U.S.A. 160 J7 36 26N 119 52W
Riverdale, Ga., U.S.A. 152 B5 33 34N 84 25W
Riverhead, U.S.A. 151 F12 40 55N 72 40W
Riverhurst, Canada 143 C7 50 55N 106 50W
Rivers □, Nigeria 113 E6 4 30N 7 10 E
Rivers Inlet, Canada 142 C3 51 42N 127 15W
Riversdale, N.Z. 131 F3 45 54 S 168 44 E
Riversdale, S. Africa 116 E3 34 7 S 21 15 E
Riverside, U.S.A. 161 M9 33 59N 117 22W
Riverton, Australia 128 C3 34 10 S 138 46 E
Riverton, Canada 143 C9 51 1N 97 0W
Riverton, N.Z. 131 G2 46 21 S 168 0 E
Riverton, Ill., U.S.A. 156 E7 39 51N 89 33W
Riverton, Wyo., U.S.A. 158 E9 43 2N 108 23W
Riverton Heights, U.S.A. 160 C4 47 28N 122 17W
Riverview, Fla., U.S.A. 153 H7 27 52N 82 20W
Riverview, Fla., U.S.A. 152 E3 30 32N 87 12W
Rives, France 29 C9 45 21N 5 31 E
Rivesaltes, France 28 F6 42 47N 2 50 E
Riviera, U.S.A. 161 K12 35 4N 114 35W
Riviera Beach, U.S.A. 153 J9 26 47N 80 3W
Riviera di Levante, Italy 44 D6 44 15N 9 30 E
Riviera di Ponente, Italy 44 D5 44 10N 8 20 E
Rivière-au-Renard, Canada 141 C7 48 59N 64 23W
Rivière Bleue, Parc Territorial de la △, N. Cal. 133 V20 22 6 S 166 38 E
Rivière-du-Loup, Canada 141 C6 47 50N 69 30W
Rivière-Pentecôte, Canada 141 C6 49 57N 67 1W
Rivière-Pilote, Martinique 164 c 14 26N 60 53W
Rivière St. Paul, Canada 141 B8 51 28N 57 45W
Rivière-Salée, Martinique 164 c 14 31N 61 0W
Rivne, Ukraine 59 G4 50 40N 26 10 E
Rívoli, Italy 44 C4 45 4N 7 31 E
Rivoli B., Australia 128 D4 37 32 S 140 3 E
Rixheim, France 27 E14 47 40N 7 24 E
Riyadh = Ar Riyāḍ, Si. Arabia 96 E5 24 41N 46 42 E
Rizal, Cagayan, Phil. 80 C3 17 51N 121 21 E
Rizal, Nueva Ecija, Phil. 80 D3 15 43N 121 6 E
Rizal, Zamboanga del N., Phil. 81 G4 8 35N 123 26 E
Rize, Turkey 101 B9 41 0N 40 30 E
Rizhao, China 75 G10 35 25N 119 30 E
Rizokarpaso, Cyprus 49 D13 35 36N 34 23 E
Rizzuto, C., Italy 47 D10 38 53N 17 5 E
Rjukan, Norway 18 E4 59 54N 8 33 E
Rjuven, Norway 18 E4 59 9N 7 8 E
Ro, Greece 49 E11 36 9N 29 34 E
Rô, N. Cal. 133 U21 21 22 S 167 50 E
Roa, Dem. Rep. of the Congo 118 D5 2 44N 29 43 E
Roa, Norway 18 D7 60 17N 10 37 E
Roa, Spain 42 D7 41 41N 3 56W
Roachdale, U.S.A. 157 E10 39 51N 86 48W
Road Town, Br. Virgin Is. 165 e 18 27N 64 37W
Roan Plateau, U.S.A. 158 G9 39 20N 109 20W
Roanne, France 27 F11 46 3N 4 4 E
Roanoke, Ala., U.S.A. 152 B4 33 9N 85 22W
Roanoke, Ind., U.S.A. 157 D11 40 58N 85 22W
Roanoke, Va., U.S.A. 148 G6 37 16N 79 56W
Roanoke →, U.S.A. 149 H7 35 57N 76 42W
Roanoke I., U.S.A. 149 H8 35 55N 75 40W
Roanoke Rapids, U.S.A. 149 G7 36 28N 77 40W
Roatán, Honduras 164 C2 16 18N 86 35W
Rob Roy, Solomon Is. 133 L9 7 23 S 157 36 E
Robât Sang, Iran 97 C8 35 35N 59 10 E
Robâtkarim □, Iran 97 B6 35 26N 50 59 E
Robbins I., Australia 127 G4 40 42 S 145 0 E
Róbbio, Italy 44 C5 45 17N 8 35 E
Robe, Australia 128 D2 33 52 S 123 15 E
Robe →, Australia 124 D2 21 42 S 116 15 E
Röbel, Germany 30 B8 53 22N 12 36 E
Robert Lee, U.S.A. 155 K4 31 54N 100 29W
Roberta, U.S.A. 152 B4 32 43N 84 1W
Roberts, U.S.A. 157 D8 40 37N 88 11W
Robertsdale, U.S.A. 150 F6 40 11N 78 6W

Robertsganj, India 93 G10 24 44N 83 4 E
Robertson, S. Africa 116 E2 33 46 S 19 50 E
Robertson I., Antarctica 7 C18 65 15 S 59 30W
Robertson Ra., Australia 124 D3 23 15 S 121 0 E
Robertsport, Liberia 112 D2 6 45N 11 26W
Robertstown, Australia 128 B3 33 58 S 139 5 E
Roberval, Canada 141 C5 48 32N 72 15W
Robeson Chan., Greenland 10 A4 82 0N 61 30W
Robi, Ethiopia 107 F4 7 52N 39 38 E
Robinson, U.S.A. 157 F9 39 0N 87 44W
Robinson →, Australia 126 B2 16 3 S 137 16 E
Robinson Ra., Australia 125 E2 25 40 S 119 0 E
Robinvale, Australia 128 C5 34 40 S 142 45 E
Robledo, Spain 41 G2 38 46N 2 26W
Roboré, Bolivia 173 D6 18 10 S 59 45W
Robson, Canada 142 D5 49 20N 117 41W
Robson, Mt., Canada 142 C5 53 10N 119 10W
Robstown, U.S.A. 155 M6 27 47N 97 40W
Roca, C. da, Portugal 43 G1 38 40N 9 31W
Roca Partida, I., Mexico 162 D2 19 1N 112 2W
Rocamadour, France 28 D5 44 48N 1 37 E
Rocca San Casciano, Italy 45 D8 44 3N 11 54 E
Roccadáspide, Italy 47 B8 40 27N 15 10 E
Roccastrada, Italy 45 F8 43 0N 11 10 E
Roccella Iónica, Italy 47 D9 38 19N 16 24 E
Rocha, Uruguay 175 C5 34 30 S 54 25W
Rochdale, U.K. 20 D5 53 38N 2 9W
Rochechouart, France 28 C4 45 50N 0 49 E
Rochedo, Brazil 173 D7 19 57 S 54 52W
Rochefort, Belgium 24 D5 50 9N 5 12 E
Rochefort, France 28 C3 45 56N 0 57W
Rochefort-en-Terre, France 26 E4 47 42N 2 22W
Rochelle, Ga., U.S.A. 152 B5 31 57N 83 27W
Rochelle, Ill., U.S.A. 156 C7 41 56N 89 4W
Rocher River, Canada 142 A6 61 23N 112 44W
Rocheservière, France 26 F5 46 57N 1 30W
Rochester, Australia 128 D6 36 22 S 144 41 E
Rochester, U.K. 21 F8 51 23N 0 31 E
Rochester, Ind., U.S.A. 157 C10 41 4N 86 13W
Rochester, Minn., U.S.A. 154 C8 44 1N 92 28W
Rochester, N.H., U.S.A. 151 C14 43 18N 70 59W
Rochester, N.Y., U.S.A. 150 C7 43 10N 77 37W
Rochester Hills, U.S.A. 157 B13 42 41N 83 8W
Rociu, Romania 53 F10 44 43N 25 2 E
Rock →, Canada 142 A3 60 7N 127 7W
Rock →, U.S.A. 156 E6 41 29N 90 37W
Rock Creek, U.S.A. 150 E4 41 40N 80 52W
Rock Falls, U.S.A. 156 C7 41 47N 89 41W
Rock Flat, Australia 129 D8 36 21 S 149 13 E
Rock Hill, U.S.A. 149 H5 34 56N 81 1W
Rock Island, U.S.A. 156 C6 41 30N 90 34W
Rock Rapids, U.S.A. 156 C6 43 26N 96 10W
Rock Sound, Bahamas 164 B4 24 54N 76 12W
Rock Springs, Mont., U.S.A. 158 C10 46 49N 106 15W
Rock Springs, Wyo., U.S.A. 158 F9 41 35N 109 14W
Rock Valley, U.S.A. 154 D6 43 12N 96 18W
Rockall, Atl. Oc. 12 D3 57 37N 13 42W
Rockdale, Tex., U.S.A. 155 K6 30 39N 97 0W
Rockeby National Park = Mungkan Kandju Nat. Park △, Australia 126 A3 13 35 S 142 52 E
Rockefeller Plateau, Antarctica 7 E14 80 0 S 140 0W
Rockford, Ala., U.S.A. 152 C3 32 53N 86 13W
Rockford, Ill., U.S.A. 156 B7 42 16N 89 6W
Rockford, Iowa, U.S.A. 156 A4 43 3N 92 57W
Rockford, Mich., U.S.A. 157 A11 43 7N 85 34W
Rockford, Ohio, U.S.A. 157 D12 40 41N 84 39W
Rockglen, Canada 143 D7 49 11N 105 57W
Rockhampton, Australia 126 C5 23 22 S 150 32 E
Rockingham, Australia 125 F2 32 15 S 115 38 E
Rockingham, U.S.A. 149 H6 34 57N 79 46W
Rockingham B., Australia 126 B4 18 5 S 146 10 E
Rocklake, U.S.A. 154 A5 48 47N 99 15W
Rockland, Canada 151 A9 45 33N 75 17W
Rockland, Idaho, U.S.A. 158 E7 42 34N 112 53W
Rockland, Maine, U.S.A. 149 C11 44 6N 69 7W
Rockland, Mich., U.S.A. 154 B10 46 44N 89 11W
Rocklands Reservoir, Australia 128 D5 37 15 S 142 5 E
Rockledge, U.S.A. 153 G5 28 20N 80 43W
Rocklin, U.S.A. 160 G5 38 48N 121 14W
Rockly B., Trin. & Tob. 169 K10 11 9N 60 46W
Rockmart, U.S.A. 149 H3 34 0N 85 3W
Rockport, Ind., U.S.A. 157 G9 37 53N 87 3W
Rockport, Mass., U.S.A. 151 D14 42 39N 70 37W
Rockport, Mo., U.S.A. 154 E7 40 25N 95 31W
Rockport, Tex., U.S.A. 155 L6 28 2N 97 3W
Rockspings, U.S.A. 155 K4 30 1N 100 13W
Rockstone, Guyana 169 B6 5 59N 58 33W
Rockville, Conn., U.S.A. 151 E12 41 52N 72 28W
Rockville, Ind., U.S.A. 157 E9 39 46N 87 14W
Rockville, Md., U.S.A. 148 F7 39 5N 77 9W
Rockwall, U.S.A. 155 J6 32 56N 96 28W
Rockwell City, U.S.A. 156 B2 42 24N 94 38W
Rockwood, Canada 150 C4 43 37N 80 8W
Rockwood, Maine, U.S.A. 149 C11 45 41N 69 45W
Rockwood, Tenn., U.S.A. 149 H3 35 52N 84 41W
Rocky Ford, U.S.A. 154 F3 38 3N 103 43W
Rocky Fork Lake, U.S.A. 157 E13 39 12N 83 23W
Rocky Gully, Australia 125 F2 34 30 S 116 57 E
Rocky Harbour, Canada 141 C8 49 36N 57 55W
Rocky Island L., Canada 140 C3 46 55N 83 0W
Rocky Lane, Canada 142 B5 58 31N 116 22W
Rocky Mount, U.S.A. 149 H7 35 57N 77 48W
Rocky Mountain House, Canada 142 C6 52 22N 114 55W
Rocky Mountain Nat. Park △, U.S.A. 158 F11 40 25N 105 45W
Rocky Mts., N. Amer. 158 G10 49 0N 115 0W
Rocky Point, Namibia 116 B2 19 3 S 12 30 E
Rocroi, France 27 C11 49 55N 4 30 E
Rod, Pakistan 93 C1 28 10N 63 5 E
Rødberg, Norway 18 D5 60 17N 8 56 E
Rødby, Denmark 17 K5 54 41N 11 23 E
Rødbyhavn, Denmark 17 K5 54 39N 11 22 E
Roddickton, Canada 141 B8 50 51N 56 8W
Rødding, Denmark 17 J3 55 23N 9 3 E
Rödeby, Sweden 17 H9 56 15N 15 37 E
Rødekro, Denmark 17 J3 55 4N 9 20 E
Rodenkirchen, Germany 30 B4 53 23N 8 26 E
Rodez, France 28 D6 44 21N 2 33 E
Rodholívas, Greece 50 F7 40 55N 24 0 E
Rodhópi □, Greece 51 E9 41 5N 25 30 E
Rodhopoú, Greece 49 E4 35 34N 23 45 E
Ródhos, Greece 38 E12 36 15N 28 10 E
Rodi Gargánico, Italy 45 G12 41 55N 15 53 E
Rodna, Romania 53 C9 47 25N 24 50 E
Rodnei, Munții, Romania 53 C9 47 35N 24 35 E
Rodney, Canada 150 D3 42 34N 81 41W
Rodney, C., N.Z. 131 C5 36 17N 174 50 E
Rodniki, Russia 60 B5 57 5N 41 55W
Rodonit, Kepi i, Albania 50 E3 41 35N 19 27 E
Rodriguez, Ind. Oc. 121 F5 19 45 S 63 20 E
Roe →, U.K. 23 A5 55 6N 6 59W
Roebling, U.S.A. 151 F10 40 7N 74 47W
Roebourne, Australia 124 D2 20 44 S 117 9 E
Roebuck B., Australia 124 C3 18 5 S 122 20 E
Roermond, Neths. 24 C6 51 12N 6 0 E
Roes Welcome Sd., Canada 139 B11 65 0N 87 0W
Roeselare, Belgium 24 D3 50 57N 3 7 E
Rogachev = Ragachow, Belarus 59 F6 53 8N 30 5 E
Rogãcica, Serbia, Yug. 50 B3 44 4N 19 40 E
Rogagua, L., Bolivia 172 C4 13 43 S 66 50W
Rogaland □, Norway 18 E3 59 12N 6 20 E
Rogaška Slatina, Slovenia 45 B12 46 15N 15 42 E

Rogatec, Slovenia .... **45 B12** 46 15N 15 46 E
Rogatica, Bos.-H. .... **52 G4** 43 47N 19 0 E
Rogatyn, Ukraine .... **59 H3** 49 24N 24 36 E
Rogdhia, Greece .... **39 E6** 35 22N 25 1 E
Rogers, U.S.A. **155 G7** 36 20N 94 7W
Rogers City, U.S.A. **148 C4** 45 25N 83 49W
Rogersville, Canada **141 C6** 46 44N 65 26W
Roggan →, Canada **140 B4** 54 24N 79 25W
Roggan L., Canada **140 B4** 54 8N 77 50W
Roggeveldberge, S. Africa ...... **116 E3** 32 10 S 20 10 E
Roggiano Gravina, Italy .... **47 C9** 39 37N 16 9 E
Rogliano, France .... **29 F13** 42 57N 9 30 E
Rogliano, Italy .... **47 C9** 39 10N 16 19 E
Rogoaguado, L., Bolivia .... **173 C4** 13 0 S 65 30W
Rogojampi, Indonesia .... **79 J17** 8 19 S 114 17 E
Rogoźno, Poland .... **55 F3** 52 45N 16 59 E
Rogue →, U.S.A. **158 E1** 42 26N 124 26W
Roha, India .... **94 E1** 18 26N 73 7 E
Rohan, France **26 D4** 48 4N 2 45W
Róhda, Greece .... **38 B9** 39 48N 19 46 E
Rohnert Park, U.S.A. **160 G4** 38 16N 122 40W
Rohri, Pakistan .... **91 D3** 27 45N 68 51 E
Rohri Canal, Pakistan .... **92 F3** 26 15N 68 27 E
Rohtak, India .... **92 E7** 28 55N 76 43 E
Roi Et, Thailand .... **86 D4** 16 4N 103 40 E
Roja, Latvia .... **15 H20** 57 29N 22 43 E
Rojas, Argentina .... **174 C3** 34 10 S 60 45W
Rojiște, Romania .... **53 F8** 44 4N 23 56 E
Rojo, C., Mexico **163 C5** 21 33N 97 20W
Rokan →, Indonesia .... **84 B2** 2 0N 100 50 E
Rokel →, S. Leone **112 D2** 8 30N 12 48W
Rokiškis, Lithuania .... **15 J21** 55 55N 25 35 E
Rokitno, Russia .... **59 G8** 50 57N 35 56 E
Rokycany, Czech Rep. .... **34 B6** 49 43N 13 35 E
Rolândia, Brazil .... **175 A5** 23 18 S 51 23W
Røldal, Norway .... **18 E3** 59 47N 6 50 E
Rolfe, U.S.A. **156 B2** 42 49N 94 31W
Rolla, U.S.A. **155 G9** 37 57N 91 46W
Rolle, Switz. .... **32 D2** 46 28N 6 20 E
Rolleston, Australia .... **126 C4** 24 28 S 148 35 E
Rolleston, N.Z. .... **131 D7** 43 35 S 172 24 E
Rolling Fork →, U.S.A. **157 G11** 37 55N 85 50W
Rollingstone, Australia .... **126 B4** 19 2 S 146 24 E
Rom, Norway .... **18 F4** 58 8N 7 5 E
Rom, Sudan .... **107 F3** 9 54N 32 16 E
Roma, Australia .... **127 D4** 26 32 S 148 49 E
Roma, Italy .... **45 G9** 41 54N 12 29 E
Roma, Sweden .... **17 G12** 57 32N 18 26 E
Roma, U.S.A. **155 M5** 26 25N 99 1W
Romain C., U.S.A. **149 J6** 33 0N 79 22W
Romaine, Canada **141 B7** 50 13N 60 40W
Romaine →, Canada **141 B7** 50 18N 63 47W
Roman, Bulgaria .... **50 C7** 43 8N 23 57 E
Roman, Romania .... **53 D11** 46 57N 26 55 E
Roman-Kosh, Gora, Ukraine ...... **59 K8** 44 37N 34 15 E
Romanche →, France .... **29 C9** 45 5N 5 43 E
Romang, Indonesia .... **82 C3** 7 30 S 127 20 E
Români, Egypt .... **103 E1** 30 59N 32 38 E
Romania ■, Europe .... **53 D10** 46 0N 25 0 E
Romanija, Bos.-H. .... **52 G3** 43 50N 18 45 E
Romano, C., U.S.A. **153 K8** 25 51N 81 41W
Romano, Cayo, Cuba **164 B4** 22 0N 77 30W
Romanovka = Basarabeasca,
  Moldova .... **53 D13** 46 21N 28 58 E
Romanovsk = Kropotkin, Russia .. **61 H5** 45 28N 40 28 E
Romans-sur-Isère, France .... **29 C9** 45 3N 5 3 E
Romanshorn, Switz. .... **33 A8** 47 33N 9 22 E
Romanzof C., U.S.A. **144 F6** 61 49N 166 6W
Rombari, Sudan .... **107 G3** 4 33N 31 2 E
Rombebai, Danau, Indonesia ..... **83 B5** 1 50 S 137 53 E
Romblon, Phil. .... **80 E4** 12 33N 122 17 E
Romblon □, Phil. .... **80 E4** 12 30N 122 15 E
Romblon Pass, Phil. .... **80 E4** 12 27N 122 12 E
Rome = Roma, Italy .... **45 G9** 41 54N 12 29 E
Rome, Ga., U.S.A. **149 H3** 34 15N 85 10W
Rome, N.Y., U.S.A. **151 C9** 43 13N 75 27W
Rome, Pa., U.S.A. **151 E8** 41 51N 76 21W
Rome Fiumicino ✈ (FCO), Italy .. **45 G9** 41 48N 12 15 E
Romeoville, U.S.A. **157 C8** 41 39N 88 3W
Rometta, Italy .... **47 D8** 38 10N 15 25 E
Romilly-sur-Seine, France ...... **27 D10** 48 31N 3 44 E
Romitan, Uzbekistan .... **65 D2** 39 56N 64 23 E
Rommani, Morocco **110 B3** 33 31N 6 40W
Romney, U.S.A. **148 F6** 39 21N 78 45W
Romney Marsh, U.K. .... **21 F8** 51 2N 0 54 E
Romny, Ukraine .... **59 G7** 50 48N 33 28 E
Rømø, Denmark .... **17 J2** 55 10N 8 30 E
Romodan, Ukraine .... **59 G7** 49 55N 33 15 E
Romodanovo, Russia .... **60 C7** 54 26N 45 23 E
Romont, Switz. .... **32 C3** 46 42N 6 54 E
Romorantin-Lanthenay, France ... **27 E8** 47 21N 1 45 E
Rompin →, Malaysia .... **84 B2** 2 49N 103 29 E
Romsdalen, Norway .... **18 B4** 62 25N 7 52 E
Romsdalsfjorden, Norway .... **18 B3** 62 38N 7 20 E
Romsey, U.K. **21 G6** 51 0N 1 29W
Ron, India .... **95 G2** 15 40N 75 44 E
Ron, Vietnam .... **86 D6** 17 53N 106 27 E
Rona, U.K. **22 D3** 57 34N 5 59W
Ronan, U.S.A. **158 C6** 47 32N 114 6W
Roncador, Cayos, Colombia **164 D3** 13 32N 80 4W
Roncador, Serra do, Brazil ..... **171 D1** 12 30 S 52 30W
Ronciglione, Italy .... **45 F9** 42 17N 12 13 E
Ronco →, Italy .... **45 D9** 44 24N 12 12 E
Ronda, Spain **43 J5** 36 46N 5 12W
Ronda, Serranía de, Spain **43 J5** 36 44N 5 3W
Rondane, Norway .... **18 C6** 61 57N 9 50 E
Rondane Nasjonalpark △, Norway . **18 C6** 61 55N 9 44 E
Rondón, Colombia **168 B3** 6 17N 71 6W
Rondônia, Brazil .... **173 C5** 10 52 S 61 57W
Rondônia □, Brazil .... **173 C5** 11 0 S 63 0W
Rondonópolis, Brazil .... **173 D7** 16 28 S 54 38W
Rondslottet, Norway .... **18 C6** 61 55N 9 45 E
Rong, Koh, Cambodia .... **87 G4** 10 45N 103 15 E
Rong Jiang →, China .... **76 E7** 24 35N 109 20 E
Rong Xian, Guangxi Zhuangzu,
  China .... **77 F8** 22 50N 110 31 E
Rong Xian, Sichuan, China ...... **76 C5** 29 23N 104 22 E
Rong'an, China .... **76 E7** 25 14N 109 22 E
Rongchang, China .... **76 C5** 29 20N 105 32 E
Ronge, L. la, Canada **143 B7** 55 6N 105 17W
Rongjiang, China .... **76 E7** 25 58N 108 28 E
Rongotea, N.Z. .... **130 G4** 40 19 S 175 25 E
Rongshui, China .... **76 E7** 25 5N 109 12 E
Rønne, Denmark .... **17 J8** 55 6N 14 43 E
Ronne Ice Shelf, Antarctica .... **7 D18** 78 0 S 60 0W
Ronneby, Sweden .... **17 H9** 56 12N 15 17 E
Ronnebyån →, Sweden .... **17 H9** 56 11N 15 18 E
Rönneshytta, Sweden .... **17 F9** 58 56N 15 2 E
Ronsard, C., Australia .... **125 D1** 24 46 S 113 10 E
Ronse, Belgium .... **24 D3** 50 45N 3 35 E
Ronuro →, Brazil .... **173 C7** 11 56 S 53 33W
Roodepoort, S. Africa .... **117 D4** 26 11 S 27 54 E
Roodhouse, U.S.A. **156 E6** 39 29N 90 24W
Roof Butte, U.S.A. **161 H9** 36 28N 109 5W
Rooiboklaagte →, Namibia .... **116 C3** 20 50 S 21 0 E
Roon, Indonesia .... **83 B4** 2 23 S 134 20 E
Rooniu, Mt., Tahiti .... **133 S16** 17 49 S 149 12W
Roopville, U.S.A. **152 B4** 33 27N 85 8W
Roorkee, India .... **92 E7** 29 52N 77 59 E
Roosendaal, Neths. .... **24 C4** 51 32N 4 29 E
Roosevelt, U.S.A. **158 F8** 40 18N 109 59W
Roosevelt →, Brazil .... **173 B5** 7 35 S 60 20W
Roosevelt, Mt., Canada **142 B3** 58 26N 125 20W
Roosevelt I., Antarctica .... **7 D12** 79 30 S 162 0W

Root, Switz. .... **33 B6** 47 5N 8 23 E
Ropczyce, Poland .... **55 H8** 50 4N 21 38 E
Roper →, Australia .... **126 A2** 14 43 S 135 27 E
Roper Bar, Australia .... **126 A1** 14 44 S 134 44 E
Roque Pérez, Argentina .... **174 D4** 35 25 S 59 24W
Roquefort, France **28 D3** 44 2N 0 20W
Roquemaure, France .... **29 D8** 44 3N 4 48 E
Roquetas de Mar, Spain **41 J2** 36 46N 2 36W
Roquetes, Spain .... **40 E5** 40 50N 0 30 E
Roquevaire, France .... **29 E9** 43 20N 5 36 E
Roraima □, Brazil **169 C5** 2 0N 61 30W
Roraima, Mt., Venezuela **169 B5** 5 10N 60 40W
Røros, Norway .... **18 B8** 62 35N 11 23 E
Rorschach, Switz. .... **33 B8** 47 28N 9 28 E
Rosa, Zambia .... **119 D3** 9 33 S 31 15 E
Rosa, C., Ecuador .... **172 a** 1 4 S 91 10W
Rosa, C., Algeria .... **111 A6** 37 0N 8 16 E
Rosa, L., Bahamas **165 B5** 21 0N 73 30W
Rosa, Monte, Europe .... **32 E5** 45 57N 7 53 E
Rosais, Pta. dos, Azores **9 d1** 38 45N 28 19W
Rosal de la Frontera, Spain **43 H3** 37 59N 7 13W
Rosales, Phil. .... **80 D3** 15 54N 120 38 E
Rosalia, U.S.A. **158 C5** 47 14N 117 22W
Rosamond, U.S.A. **161 L8** 34 52N 118 10W
Rosans, France .... **29 D9** 44 24N 5 29 E
Rosario, Argentina .... **174 C3** 33 0 S 60 40W
Rosário, Brazil .... **170 B3** 3 0 S 44 15W
Rosario, Baja Calif., Mexico ... **162 B1** 30 0N 115 50W
Rosario, Sinaloa, Mexico **162 C3** 23 0N 105 52W
Rosario, Paraguay .... **174 A4** 24 30 S 57 35W
Rosario, Phil. .... **81 G5** 8 24N 125 59 E
Rosario, Villa del, Venezuela .. **168 A3** 10 19N 72 19W
Rosario de la Frontera, Argentina . **174 B3** 25 50 S 65 0W
Rosario de Lerma, Argentina .... **174 A2** 24 59 S 65 35W
Rosario del Tala, Argentina .... **174 C4** 32 20 S 59 10W
Rosário do Sul, Brazil .... **175 C5** 30 15 S 54 55W
Rosário Oeste, Brazil .... **173 C6** 14 50 S 56 25W
Rosarito, Mexico **161 N9** 32 18N 117 4W
Rosarno, Italy .... **47 D8** 38 29N 15 58 E
Rosas = Roses, Spain .... **40 C8** 42 19N 3 10 E
Rosas →, Switz. .... **32 D5** 46 18N 7 36 E
Roscoe, Miss., U.S.A. **156 G3** 37 58N 93 48W
Roscoe, N.Y., U.S.A. **151 E10** 41 56N 74 55W
Roscoff, France **26 D3** 48 44N 3 58W
Roscommon, Ireland **23 C3** 53 38N 8 11W
Roscommon □, Ireland **23 C3** 53 49N 8 23W
Roscrea, Ireland **23 D4** 52 57N 7 49W
Rose →, Australia .... **126 A2** 14 16 S 135 45 E
Rose Belle, Mauritius .... **121 d** 20 24 S 57 36 E
Rose Blanche, Canada **141 C8** 47 38N 58 45W
Rose Hill, Mauritius .... **121 d** 20 14 S 57 27 E
Rose Pt., Canada **142 C2** 54 11N 131 39W
Rose Valley, Canada **143 C8** 52 19N 103 49W
Roseau, Domin. **165 C7** 15 20N 61 24W
Roseau, U.S.A. **154 A7** 48 51N 95 46W
Rosebery, Australia .... **127 G4** 41 46 S 145 33 E
Rosebud, Australia .... **128 E6** 38 21 S 144 54 E
Rosebud, S. Dak., U.S.A. **154 D4** 43 14N 100 51W
Rosebud, Tex., U.S.A. **155 K6** 31 4N 96 59W
Roseburg, U.S.A. **158 E2** 43 13N 123 20W
Rosedale, U.S.A. **155 J9** 33 51N 91 2W
Rosehearty, U.K. **22 D6** 57 42N 2 7W
Roseland, U.S.A. **160 G4** 38 25N 122 43W
Rosemary, Canada **142 C6** 50 46N 112 5W
Rosenberg, U.S.A. **155 L7** 29 34N 95 49W
Rosendaël, France .... **27 A9** 51 3N 2 24 E
Rosendal, Norway .... **18 E3** 59 59N 6 0 E
Rosendale, U.S.A. **156 D2** 40 4N 94 51W
Rosenheim, Germany .... **31 H8** 47 51N 12 7 E
Roses, Spain .... **40 C8** 42 19N 3 10 E
Roses, G. de, Spain .... **40 C8** 42 10N 3 15 E
Roseto degli Abruzzi, Italy .... **45 F11** 42 41N 14 1 E
Rosetown, Canada **143 C7** 51 35N 107 59W
Rosetta = Rashîd, Egypt .... **106 H7** 31 21N 30 22 E
Roseville, Calif., U.S.A. **160 G5** 38 45N 121 17W
Roseville, Ill., U.S.A. **156 D6** 40 44N 90 40W
Roseville, Mich., U.S.A. **150 D2** 42 30N 82 56W
Rosewood, Australia .... **127 D5** 27 38 S 152 36 E
Roshkhvar, Iran .... **97 C8** 34 58N 59 37 E
Roshtqala, Tajikistan .... **65 F8** 37 16N 71 49 E
Rosières-en-Santerre, France ... **27 C9** 49 49N 2 42 E
Rosignano Maríttimo, Italy ..... **44 E7** 43 24N 10 28 E
Rosignol, Guyana **169 B6** 6 15N 57 30W
Roşiori de Vede, Romania .... **53 F10** 44 9N 25 0 E
Rositsa, Bulgaria .... **51 C11** 43 57N 27 57 E
Rositsa →, Bulgaria .... **51 C9** 43 10N 25 2 E
Roskilde, Denmark .... **17 J6** 55 38N 12 3 E
Roskilde Amtskommune □,
  Denmark .... **17 J6** 55 35N 12 5 E
Roskovec, Albania .... **50 F3** 40 44N 19 43 E
Roslavl, Russia .... **58 F7** 53 57N 32 55 E
Rosmaninhal, Portugal **42 F3** 39 44N 7 5W
Rosmead, S. Africa .... **116 E4** 31 29 S 25 8 E
Rosnæs, Denmark .... **17 J4** 55 44N 10 55 E
Rosolini, Italy .... **47 F7** 36 49N 14 57 E
Rosporden, France **26 E3** 47 57N 3 50W
Ross, Australia .... **127 G4** 42 2 S 147 30 E
Ross, N.Z. .... **131 C5** 42 53 S 170 49 E
Ross Béthio, Mauritania **112 B1** 16 15N 16 8W
Ross Dependency, Antarctica .... **7 D12** 76 0 S 170 0W
Ross I., Antarctica .... **7 D11** 77 30 S 168 0 E
Ross Ice Shelf, Antarctica ..... **7 E12** 80 0 S 180 0 E
Ross L., U.S.A. **158 B3** 48 44N 121 4W
Ross-on-Wye, U.K. **21 F5** 51 54N 2 34W
Ross River, Australia .... **126 C1** 23 44 S 134 30 E
Ross River, Canada **142 A2** 62 30N 131 30W
Ross Sea, Antarctica .... **7 D11** 74 0 S 178 0 E
Rossa, Switz. .... **33 D8** 46 23N 9 8 E
Rossall Pt., U.K. **20 D4** 53 55N 3 3W
Rossan Pt., Ireland **23 B3** 54 42N 8 47W
Rossano, Italy .... **47 C9** 39 36N 16 39 E
Rossburn, Canada **143 C8** 50 40N 100 49W
Rosseau, Canada **150 A5** 45 16N 79 39W
Rosseau L., Canada **150 A5** 45 10N 79 35W
Rossel, C., Vanuatu .... **133 K4** 20 23 S 166 36 E
Rossel I., Papua N. G. .... **132 F8** 11 21 S 154 9 E
Rossens, Switz. .... **32 C4** 46 43N 7 7 E
Rosses, The, Ireland **23 A3** 55 2N 8 20W
Rossford, U.S.A. **157 C13** 41 36N 83 34W
Rossignol, L., Canada **140 B5** 52 43N 73 40W
Rossignol Res., Canada **141 D6** 44 12N 65 10W
Rossland, Canada **142 D5** 49 6N 117 50W
Rosslare, Ireland **23 D5** 52 17N 6 24W
Rosslare Harbour, Ireland **23 D5** 52 15N 6 20W
Rosslau, Germany .... **30 D8** 51 52N 12 15 E
Rosso, Mauritania **112 B1** 16 40N 15 45W
Rosso, C., France .... **29 F12** 42 13N 8 32 E
Rossosh, Russia .... **59 G10** 50 15N 39 28 E
Røssvatnet, Norway .... **14 D16** 65 45N 14 5 E
Rossville, Ind., U.S.A. **157 D10** 40 25N 86 36W
Røst, Norway .... **14 C15** 67 32N 12 0 E
Rostǎg, Afghan. .... **65 E4** 37 7N 69 49 E
Rosthern, Canada **143 C7** 52 40N 106 20W
Rostock, Germany .... **30 A8** 54 5N 12 8 E
Rostov, Don, Russia .... **59 J10** 47 15N 39 45 E
Rostov, Yaroslavl, Russia ...... **58 D10** 57 14N 39 25 E
Rostrenen, France **26 D3** 48 14N 3 21W
Roswell, Ga., U.S.A. **152 A5** 34 2N 84 22W
Roswell, N. Mex., U.S.A. **155 J2** 33 24N 104 32W
Rota, Spain **43 J4** 36 37N 6 20W
Rotan, U.S.A. **155 J4** 32 51N 100 28W
Rote Wand, Austria .... **33 B9** 47 11N 9 59 E
Rotenburg, Hessen, Germany ..... **30 E5** 50 59N 9 44 E

Rotenburg, Niedersachsen, Germany . **30 B5** 53 6N 9 25 E
Roth, Germany .... **31 F7** 49 15N 11 5 E
Rothaargebirge, Germany .... **30 D4** 51 2N 8 13 E
Rothaargebirge, Naturpark △,
  Germany .... **30 E4** 51 0N 8 15 E
Rothenburg, Switz. .... **33 B6** 47 6N 8 16 E
Rothenburg ob der Tauber, Germany . **31 F6** 49 23N 10 11 E
Rother →, U.K. .... **21 G8** 50 59N 0 45 E
Rotherham, U.K. **20 D6** 53 26N 1 20W
Rothes, U.K. **22 D5** 57 32N 3 13W
Rothesay, Canada **141 C6** 45 23N 66 0W
Rothesay, U.K. **22 F3** 55 50N 5 3W
Rothrist, Switz. .... **32 B5** 47 18N 7 54 E
Roti, Indonesia .... **82 D2** 10 50 S 123 0 E
Rotja, Pta., Spain .... **38 D2** 38 38N 1 35 E
Rotnes, Norway .... **18 D7** 60 3N 10 51 E
Roto, Australia .... **129 B6** 33 0 S 145 30 E
Rotoaira, L., N.Z. .... **130 F4** 39 3 S 175 45 E
Rotoehu, L., N.Z. .... **130 E5** 38 1 S 176 32 E
Rotoiti, L., Bay of Plenty, N.Z. . **130 E5** 38 2 S 176 26 E
Rotoiti, L., W. Coast, N.Z. .... **131 B7** 41 51 S 172 49 E
Rotondo, Mte., France .... **29 F13** 42 14N 9 3 E
Rotoroa, L., N.Z. .... **131 B7** 41 55 S 172 39 E
Rotorua, N.Z. .... **130 E5** 38 9 S 176 16 E
Rotorua, L., N.Z. .... **130 E5** 38 5 S 176 18 E
Rott →, Germany .... **31 G9** 48 27N 13 25 E
Rotten →, Switz. .... **32 D5** 46 18N 7 36 E
Rottenburg, Germany .... **31 G4** 48 28N 8 55 E
Rottenmann, Austria .... **34 D7** 47 31N 14 22 E
Rotterdam, Neths. .... **24 C4** 51 55N 4 30 E
Rotterdam, U.S.A. **151 D10** 42 48N 74 1W
Rottne, Sweden .... **17 G8** 57 1N 14 54 E
Rottnest I., Australia .... **125 F2** 32 0 S 115 27 E
Rottumeroog, Neths. .... **24 A6** 53 33N 6 34 E
Rottweil, Germany .... **31 G4** 48 9N 8 37 E
Rotuma, Fiji .... **134 J9** 12 25 S 177 5 E
Roubaix, France .... **27 B10** 50 40N 3 10 E
Roudnice nad Labem, Czech Rep. . **34 A7** 50 25N 14 15 E
Rouen, France .... **26 C8** 49 27N 1 4 E
Rouergue, France .... **28 D5** 44 15N 2 0 E
Rough Ridge, N.Z. .... **131 F4** 45 10 S 169 55 E
Rouillac, France **28 C3** 45 47N 0 4W
Rouleau, Canada **143 C8** 50 10N 104 56W
Round I., Mauritius .... **121 d** 19 51 S 57 45 E
Round Mountain, U.S.A. **158 G5** 38 43N 117 4W
Round Mt., Australia .... **129 A10** 30 26 S 152 16 E
Round Rock, U.S.A. **155 K6** 30 31N 97 41W
Roundup, U.S.A. **158 C9** 46 27N 108 33W
Roura, Fr. Guiana **169 C7** 4 44N 52 13W
Rousay, U.K. **22 B5** 59 10N 3 2W
Rouses Point, U.S.A. **151 B11** 44 59N 73 22W
Rouseville, U.S.A. **150 E5** 41 28N 79 42W
Roussennski Lom →, Bulgaria .... **50 C7** 43 40N 23 10 E
Roussillon, Isère, France ...... **29 C8** 45 24N 4 49 E
Roussillon, Pyrénées-Or., France . **28 F6** 42 30N 2 35 E
Roussin, C., N. Cal. .... **133 U21** 21 20 S 167 59 E
Rouxville, S. Africa .... **116 E4** 30 25 S 26 50 E
Rouyn-Noranda, Canada **140 C4** 48 20N 79 0W
Rovaniemi, Finland .... **14 C21** 66 29N 25 41 E
Rovato, Italy .... **44 C7** 45 34N 10 0 E
Roveredo, Switz. .... **33 D8** 46 2N 9 8 E
Roveni, Ukraine .... **59 H10** 48 5N 39 21 E
Rovereto, Italy .... **44 C8** 45 53N 11 3 E
Roverud, Norway .... **18 D6** 60 15N 12 3 E
Rovigno = Rovinj, Croatia ...... **45 C10** 45 5N 13 40 E
Rovigo, Italy .... **44 C8** 45 4N 11 47 E
Rovinj, Croatia .... **45 C10** 45 5N 13 40 E
Rovira, Colombia **168 C2** 4 15N 75 20W
Rovno = Rivne, Ukraine .... **59 G4** 50 40N 26 10 E
Rovno, Isabela, Phil. .... **81 B14** 16 49N 121 39 E
Rovno, Mind. Or., Phil. .... **80 C3** 13 30N 121 36 E
Rovno, Palawan, Phil. .... **81 F2** 10 20N 119 21 E
Roxboro, U.S.A. **149 G6** 36 24N 78 59W
Roxborough, Trin. & Tob. **169 E10** 11 15N 60 35W
Roxburgh, N.Z. .... **131 F4** 45 33 S 169 19 E
Roxbury, N.Z. **150 F7** 40 6N 77 39W
Roxen, Sweden .... **17 F9** 58 30N 15 40 E
Roy, Mont., U.S.A. **158 C9** 47 20N 108 58W
Roy, N. Mex., U.S.A. **155 H2** 35 57N 104 12W
Roy, Utah, U.S.A. **158 F7** 41 10N 112 2W
Royal Canal, Ireland **23 C4** 53 30N 7 13W
Royal Leamington Spa, U.K. **21 E6** 52 18N 1 31W
Royal Center, U.S.A. .... **129 C9** 34 5 S 151 5 E
Royal Natal Nat. Park △, S. Africa . **117 D4** 28 43 S 28 51 E
Royal Oak, U.S.A. **157 B13** 42 30N 83 9W
Royal Palm Beach, U.S.A. **153 J9** 26 41N 80 14W
Royal Tunbridge Wells, U.K. .... **21 F8** 51 7N 0 16 E
Royale, Isle, U.S.A. **154 B10** 48 0N 88 54W
Royalla, Australia .... **129 C8** 35 30 S 149 9 E
Royan, France **28 C2** 45 37N 1 2W
Roye, France .... **27 C9** 49 42N 2 48 E
Royston, U.K. **21 E7** 52 3N 0 0
Rožaj, Montenegro, Yug. .... **50 D4** 42 50N 20 11 E
Rózan, Poland .... **55 F8** 52 52N 21 25 E
Rozay-en-Brie, France .... **27 D9** 48 41N 2 58 E
Rozdilna, Ukraine .... **59 J6** 46 50N 30 2 E
Rozhyshche, Ukraine .... **59 G3** 50 54N 25 15 E
Rožmitál pod Třemšínem,
  Czech Rep. .... **34 B6** 49 36N 13 53 E
Rožňava, Slovak Rep. .... **35 C13** 48 37N 20 35 E
Rozogi, Poland .... **54 E8** 53 28N 21 19 E
Rozoy-sur-Serre, France .... **27 C11** 49 40N 4 8 E
Roztoczański Park Narodowy △,
  Poland .... **55 H10** 50 37N 23 0 E
Rozzano, Italy .... **44 C6** 45 22N 9 10 E
Rrëshen, Albania .... **50 E3** 41 47N 19 49 E
Rrogozhine, Albania .... **50 E3** 41 4N 19 50 E
Rtanj, Serbia, Yug. .... **50 C5** 43 45N 21 50 E
Rtem, O. el →, Algeria .... **111 B6** 33 29N 5 38 E
Rtishchevo, Russia .... **60 D6** 52 18N 43 46 E
Rúa = A Rúa, Spain **42 C3** 42 24N 7 6W
Ruacaná, Namibia .... **116 B1** 17 27 S 14 21 E
Ruaha Nat. Park △, Tanzania .... **118 D3** 7 41 S 34 30 E
Ruahine Ra., N.Z. .... **130 F5** 39 55 S 176 2 E
Ruamahanga →, N.Z. .... **130 H4** 41 9 S 175 8 E
Ruapehu, N.Z. .... **130 F4** 39 17 S 175 35 E
Ruapuke I., N.Z. .... **131 G3** 46 46 S 168 31 E
Ruâq, W. →, Egypt .... **103 F2** 30 0N 33 49 E
Ruatoria, N.Z. .... **130 E7** 37 55 S 178 20 E
Ruavatu, Solomon Is. .... **133 M11** 9 26 S 160 26 E
Rub' al Khālī, Si. Arabia ...... **99 C5** 19 0N 48 0 E
Rubeho Mts., Tanzania .... **118 D4** 6 50 S 36 25 E
Rubezhnoye = Rubizhne, Ukraine . **59 H10** 49 6N 38 25 E
Rubh a' Mhail, U.K. **22 F2** 55 56N 6 8W
Rubha Hunish, U.K. **22 D2** 57 42N 6 20W
Rubha Robhanais = Lewis, Butt of,
  U.K. **22 C2** 58 31N 6 16W
Rubi, Spain .... **40 D7** 41 29N 2 3 E
Rubiataba, Brazil .... **171 E2** 15 8 S 49 48W
Rubicon →, U.S.A. **160 G5** 38 53N 121 4W
Rubicone →, Italy .... **45 D9** 44 8N 12 28 E
Rubik, Albania .... **50 E3** 41 46N 19 47 E
Rubinéia, Brazil .... **171 F1** 20 13 S 51 2W
Rubino, Ivory C. **112 D4** 6 4N 4 18W

Rubio, Venezuela **168 B3** 7 43N 72 22W
Rubizhne, Ukraine .... **59 H10** 49 6N 38 25 E
Ruby, U.S.A. **144 D9** 64 45N 155 30W
Ruby L., U.S.A. **158 F6** 40 10N 115 28W
Ruby Mts., U.S.A. **158 F6** 40 30N 115 20W
Rubyvale, Australia .... **126 C4** 23 25 S 147 42 E
Rucheng, China .... **77 E9** 25 33N 113 38 E
Ruciane-Nida, Poland .... **54 E8** 53 40N 21 32 E
Rūd Sar, Iran .... **97 B6** 37 8N 50 18 E
Ruda, Sweden .... **17 G10** 57 6N 16 7 E
Ruda Śląska, Poland .... **55 H5** 50 16N 18 50 E
Rudall, Australia .... **128 B2** 33 43 S 136 17 E
Rudall →, Australia .... **124 D3** 22 34 S 122 13 E
Rudall River Nat. Park △, Australia . **124 D3** 22 38 S 122 30 E
Rūdbār, Afghan. .... **91 C1** 30 9N 62 36 E
Rüdersdorf, Germany .... **30 C9** 52 27N 13 47 E
Rudewa, Tanzania .... **119 E3** 10 7 S 34 40 E
Rudkøbing, Denmark .... **17 K4** 54 56N 10 41 E
Rudna, Poland .... **55 G3** 51 30N 16 17 E
Rūdnichnyy, Kazakhstan .... **65 A9** 44 40N 78 54 E
Rudnik, Bulgaria .... **51 D11** 42 36N 27 30 E
Rudnik, Poland .... **55 H9** 50 26N 22 15 E
Rudnik, Serbia, Yug. .... **50 B4** 44 7N 20 35 E
Rudnya, Russia .... **58 E6** 54 55N 31 7 E
Rudnyy, Kazakhstan .... **64 E9** 52 57N 63 7 E
Rudo, Bos.-H. .... **52 G4** 43 41N 19 23 E
Rudolfa, Ostrov, Russia .... **66 A6** 81 45N 58 30 E
Rudolstadt, Germany .... **30 E7** 50 44N 11 5 E
Rudong, China .... **77 A13** 32 20N 121 12 E
Rudozem, Bulgaria .... **51 E8** 41 29N 24 51 E
Rudyard, U.S.A. **148 B3** 46 14N 84 36W
Rue, France .... **27 B8** 50 15N 1 40 E
Ruenya →, Africa .... **119 F3** 16 24 S 33 48 E
Rufa'a, Sudan .... **107 E3** 14 44N 33 22 E
Rufflin, U.S.A. **152 B9** 33 0N 80 49W
Rufiji →, Tanzania .... **118 D4** 7 50 S 39 15 E
Rufino, Argentina .... **174 C3** 34 20 S 62 50W
Rufisque, Senegal **112 C1** 14 40N 17 15W
Rufling Pt., Br. Virgin Is. .... **165 e** 18 44N 64 27W
Rufunsa, Zambia .... **119 F2** 15 4 S 29 34 E
Rugao, China .... **77 A13** 32 23N 120 31 E
Rugby, U.K. **21 E6** 52 23N 1 16W
Rugby, U.S.A. **154 A5** 48 22N 100 0W
Rügen, Germany .... **30 A9** 54 22N 13 24 E
Rügen, Naturpark △, Germany .... **30 A9** 54 25N 13 25 E
Rugles, France .... **26 D7** 48 50N 0 40 E
Ruhea, Bangla. .... **90 B2** 26 10N 88 25 E
Ruhengeri, Rwanda .... **118 C2** 1 30 S 29 36 E
Ruhla, Germany .... **30 E6** 50 54N 10 23 E
Ruhland, Germany .... **30 D9** 51 27N 13 51 E
Ruhnu, Estonia .... **15 H20** 57 48N 23 15 E
Ruhr →, Germany .... **30 D2** 51 27N 6 43 E
Ruhuhu →, Tanzania .... **119 E3** 10 31 S 34 34 E
Rui Barbosa, Brazil .... **171 D3** 12 18 S 40 27W
Rui'an, China .... **77 D13** 27 47N 120 40 E
Ruichang, China .... **77 C10** 29 40N 115 39 E
Ruidoso, U.S.A. **159 K11** 33 20N 105 41W
Ruijin, China .... **77 E10** 25 48N 116 0 E
Ruili, China .... **76 E1** 24 1N 97 43 E
Ruivo, Pico, Madeira .... **9 c** 32 45N 16 56W
Ruj, Bulgaria .... **50 D6** 42 52N 22 34 E
Rujen, Macedonia .... **50 D6** 42 9N 22 30 E
Rujm Tal'at al Jamā'ah, Jordan . **103 E4** 30 24N 35 30 E
Ruk, Pakistan .... **92 F3** 27 50N 68 42 E
Rukhla, Pakistan .... **92 C4** 32 27N 71 57 E
Rukwa □, Tanzania .... **118 D3** 7 0 S 31 30 E
Rukwa, L., Tanzania .... **118 D3** 8 0 S 32 20 E
Rulhieres, C., Australia .... **124 B4** 13 56 S 127 22 E
Rum = Rhum, U.K. **22 E2** 57 0N 6 20W
Rum, Jordan .... **103 F4** 29 39N 35 26 E
Rum Cay, Bahamas **165 B5** 23 40N 74 58W
Rum Jungle, Australia .... **124 B5** 13 0 S 130 59 E
Ruma, Serbia, Yug. .... **52 C4** 45 0N 19 50 E
Ruma Nat. Park △, Kenya .... **118 C3** 0 39 S 34 18 E
Rumāḩ, Si. Arabia .... **96 E5** 25 29N 47 10 E
Rumania = Romania ■, Europe .... **53 D10** 46 0N 25 0 E
Rumaylah, Iraq .... **96 D5** 30 47N 47 37 E
Rumbêk, Sudan .... **107 F2** 6 54N 29 37 E
Rumbperpon, Indonesia .... **83 B4** 1 50 S 134 15 E
Rumburk, Czech Rep. .... **34 A7** 50 57N 14 32 E
Rumford, U.S.A. **149 C10** 44 33N 70 33W
Rumia, Poland .... **54 D5** 54 37N 18 25 E
Rumilly, France .... **29 C9** 45 53N 5 56 E
Rumoi, Japan .... **70 C10** 43 56N 141 39 E
Rumonge, Burundi .... **118 C2** 3 59 S 29 26 E
Rumson, U.S.A. **151 F11** 40 23N 74 0W
Rumuruti, Kenya .... **118 B4** 0 17N 36 32 E
Runan, China .... **74 H8** 33 0N 114 30 E
Runanga, N.Z. .... **131 C6** 42 25 S 171 15 E
Runaway, C., N.Z. .... **130 D6** 37 32 S 177 59 E
Runaway Bay, Jamaica .... **164 a** 18 27N 77 20W
Runcorn, U.K. **20 D5** 53 21N 2 44W
Rundu, Namibia .... **116 B2** 17 52 S 19 43 E
Rungwa, Tanzania .... **118 D3** 6 55 S 33 32 E
Rungwa →, Tanzania .... **118 D3** 7 36 S 31 50 E
Rungwa Game Reserve △, Tanzania . **118 D3** 6 53 S 34 2 E
Rungwe, Tanzania .... **119 D3** 9 11 S 33 32 E
Runka, Nigeria .... **113 C6** 12 28N 7 20 E
Runn, Sweden .... **16 D9** 60 30N 15 40 E
Runton Ra., Australia .... **124 D3** 23 31 S 123 6 E
Ruokolahti, Finland .... **8 B5** 61 17N 28 50 E
Ruoqiang, China .... **68 C3** 38 55N 88 10 E
Rupa, India .... **90 B4** 27 15N 92 21 E
Rupar, India .... **92 D7** 31 2N 76 38 E
Rupat, Indonesia .... **84 B2** 1 45N 101 40 E
Rupea, Romania .... **53 D10** 46 2N 25 13 E
Rupen →, India .... **92 H4** 23 28N 71 31 E
Rupert, U.S.A. **158 E7** 42 37N 113 41W
Rupert →, Canada **140 B4** 51 29N 78 45W
Rupert B., Canada **140 B4** 51 35N 79 0W
Rupert House = Waskaganish,
  Canada **140 B4** 51 30N 78 40W
Rupsa, India .... **93 J12** 21 37N 87 1 E
Rur →, Germany .... **30 D1** 51 11N 5 59 E
Rurópolis, Brazil .... **169 D7** 4 3 S 54 59W
Rurrenabaque, Bolivia .... **172 C4** 14 30 S 67 32W
Rus →, Spain **41 F2** 39 30N 2 30W
Rusambo, Zimbabwe .... **119 F3** 16 30 S 32 4 E
Rusape, Zimbabwe .... **119 F3** 18 35 S 32 8 E
Ruschuk = Ruse, Bulgaria .... **51 C9** 43 48N 25 59 E
Ruse, Bulgaria .... **51 C9** 43 48N 25 59 E
Ruşeţu, Romania .... **53 F12** 44 57N 27 14 E
Rush, Ireland **23 C5** 53 31N 6 6W
Rushan, China .... **75 F11** 36 56N 121 30 E
Rushden, U.K. **21 E7** 52 18N 0 35W
Rushikulya →, India .... **94 F7** 19 23N 85 6 E
Rushmore, Mt., U.S.A. **154 D3** 43 53N 103 28W
Rushon, Tajikistan .... **65 F8** 37 57N 71 33 E
Rushville, Ill., U.S.A. **156 D6** 40 7N 90 34W
Rushville, Ind., U.S.A. **157 E11** 39 37N 85 27W
Rushville, Nebr., U.S.A. **154 D3** 42 43N 102 28W
Rushworth, Australia .... **129 D6** 36 32 S 145 1 E
Russas, Brazil **153 H7** 27 43N 82 26W
Russell, Canada **143 C8** 50 50N 101 20W
Russell, N.Z. .... **130 B3** 35 16 S 174 10 E
Russell, Kans., U.S.A. **154 F5** 38 54N 98 52W
Russell, Fla., U.S.A. **152 E8** 30 6N 81 45W
Russell, N.Y., U.S.A. **151 B9** 44 27N 75 9W
Russell, Pa., U.S.A. **150 E5** 41 56N 79 8W

Russell Cave Nat. Monument △,
 U.S.A. **149 H3** 34 59N 85 49W
Russell Is., *Solomon Is.* .... **133 M10** 9 4 S 159 12 E
Russell L., *Man., Canada* **143 B8** 56 15N 101 30W
Russell L., *N.W.T., Canada* **142 A5** 63 5N 115 44W
Russellkonda, *India* .... **94 E7** 19 57N 84 42 E
Russells Point, *U.S.A.* **157 D13** 40 28N 83 54W
Russellville, *Ala., U.S.A.* **149 H2** 34 30N 87 44W
Russellville, *Ark., U.S.A.* **155 H8** 35 17N 93 8W
Russellville, *Ky., U.S.A.* **149 G2** 36 51N 86 53W
Rüsselsheim, *Germany* .... **31 F4** 49 59N 8 23 E
Russi, *Italy* .... **45 D9** 44 22N 12 2 E
Russia ■, *Eurasia* .... **57 C11** 62 0N 105 0 E
Russian ➤, *U.S.A.* **160 G3** 38 27N 123 8W
Russian Mission, *U.S.A.* **144 F7** 61 47N 161 19W
Russiaville, *U.S.A.* **157 D10** 40 25N 86 16W
Russkoye Ustie, *Russia* .... **6 B15** 71 0N 149 0 E
Rust, *Austria* .... **35 D9** 47 49N 16 42 E
Rustam, *Pakistan* .... **92 B5** 34 25N 72 13 E
Rustam Shahr, *Pakistan* .... **92 F2** 26 58N 66 6 E
Rustavi, *Georgia* .... **61 K7** 41 30N 45 0 E
Rustenburg, *S. Africa* .... **116 D4** 25 41 S 27 14 E
Ruston, *U.S.A.* **155 J8** 32 32N 92 38W
Ruswil, *Switz.* .... **32 B6** 47 5N 8 8 E
Rutana, *Burundi* .... **118 C3** 3 55 S 30 0 E
Rute, *Spain* **43 H6** 37 19N 4 23W
Ruteng, *Indonesia* .... **82 C2** 8 35 S 120 30 E
Ruth, *U.S.A.* **150 C2** 43 42N 82 45W
Rutherford, *U.S.A.* **160 G4** 38 26N 122 24W
Rutherglen, *Australia* .... **129 D7** 36 5 S 146 29 E
Rüti, *Switz.* .... **33 B7** 47 16N 8 51 E
Rutland, *U.S.A.* **151 C12** 43 37N 72 58W
Rutland □, *U.K.* **21 E7** 52 38N 0 40W
Rutland I., *India* .... **95 J11** 11 25N 92 10 E
Rutland Water, *U.K.* **21 E7** 52 39N 0 38W
Rutledal, *Norway* .... **18 C2** 61 4N 5 10 E
Rutledge ➤, *U.S.A.* **152 B6** 33 38N 83 37W
Rutledge ➤, *Canada* **143 A6** 61 4N 112 0W
Rutledge L., *Canada* **143 A6** 61 33N 110 47W
Rutqa, W. ➤, *Syria* .... **101 E9** 34 30N 41 3 E
Rutshuru, *Dem. Rep. of the Congo* **118 C2** 1 13 S 29 25 E
Ruvo di Púglia, *Italy* .... **47 A9** 41 7N 16 29 E
Ruvu, *Tanzania* .... **118 D4** 6 49 S 38 43 E
Ruvu ➤, *Tanzania* .... **118 D4** 6 23 S 38 52 E
Ruvuba, Parc Nat. de △, *Burundi* **118 C2** 3 3 S 29 33 E
Ruvuma □, *Tanzania* .... **119 E4** 10 20 S 36 0 E
Ruvuma ➤, *Tanzania* .... **119 E5** 10 29 S 40 28 E
Ruwais, *U.A.E.* .... **97 E7** 24 5N 52 50 E
Ruwenzori, *Africa* .... **118 B2** 0 30N 29 55 E
Ruwenzori Nat. Park △, *Uganda* **118 B2** 0 20N 30 0 E
Ruya ➤, *Zimbabwe* .... **117 B5** 16 27 S 32 5 E
Ruyigi, *Burundi* .... **118 C3** 3 29 S 30 15 E
Ruyuan, *China* .... **77 E9** 24 46N 113 16 E
Ruzayevka, *Russia* .... **60 C7** 54 4N 45 0 E
Rüzhevo Konare, *Bulgaria* .... **51 D8** 42 23N 24 46 E
Ružomberok, *Slovak Rep.* .... **35 B12** 49 3N 19 17 E
Ruzyne, Prague ✈ (PRG),
 Czech Rep. .... **34 A7** 50 7N 14 15 E
Rwanda ■, *Africa* .... **54 E5** 2 0 S 30 0 E
Ryakhovo, *Bulgaria* .... **51 C10** 43 58N 26 18 E
Ryan, L., *U.K.* **22 G3** 55 0N 5 2W
Ryazan, *Russia* .... **58 E10** 54 40N 39 40 E
Ryazhsk, *Russia* .... **58 F11** 53 45N 40 3 E
Rybache = Rybachye, *Kazakhstan* **58 E9** 46 40N 81 20 E
Rybachiy Poluostrov, *Russia* ..... **56 A5** 69 43N 32 0 E
Rybachye = Balykchy, *Kyrgyzstan* **66 E8** 42 26N 76 12 E
Rybachye, *Kazakhstan* .... **66 E9** 46 40N 81 20 E
Rybáčij, *Russia* .... **54 C7** 55 10N 20 50 E
Rybinsk, *Russia* .... **58 C10** 58 5N 38 50 E
Rybinskoye Vdkhr., *Russia* .... **58 C10** 58 30N 38 25 E
Rybnik, *Poland* .... **55 H5** 50 6N 18 32 E
Rybnitsa = Rîbniţa, *Moldova* ..... **53 C14** 47 45N 29 0 E
Rybnoye, *Russia* .... **58 E10** 54 45N 39 30 E
Rychnov nad Kněžnou, *Czech Rep.* **35 A9** 50 10N 16 17 E
Rychwał, *Poland* .... **55 F5** 52 4N 18 10 E
Rycroft, *Canada* **142 B5** 55 45N 118 40W
Ryd, *Sweden* .... **17 H8** 56 27N 14 42 E
Rydaholm, *Sweden* .... **17 H8** 56 59N 14 18 E
Ryde, *U.K.* **21 G6** 50 43N 1 9W
Ryderwood, *U.S.A.* **160 D3** 46 23N 123 3W
Rydzyna, *Poland* .... **55 G3** 51 47N 16 39 E
Rye, *U.K.* .... **21 G8** 50 57N 0 45 E
Rye ➤, *U.K.* **20 C7** 54 11N 0 44W
Rye Bay, *U.K.* .... **21 G8** 50 52N 0 49 E
Rye Patch Reservoir, *U.S.A.* **158 F4** 40 28N 118 19W
Ryegate, *U.S.A.* **158 C9** 46 18N 109 15W
Ryfylke, *Norway* .... **18 E3** 59 25N 6 2 E
Rygate, *U.S.A.* .... **18 F5** 58 24N 8 37 E
Ryki, *Poland* .... **55 G8** 51 38N 21 56 E
Ryley, *Canada* **142 C6** 53 17N 112 26W
Rylsk, *Russia* .... **59 G8** 51 36N 34 43 E
Rylstone, *Australia* .... **129 B8** 32 46 S 149 58 E
Rymanów, *Poland* .... **55 J8** 49 35N 21 51 E
Ryn, *Poland* .... **54 E8** 53 57N 21 34 E
Ryn Peski, *Kazakhstan* .... **61 G9** 47 30N 49 0 E
Ryōhaku-Sanchi, *Japan* .... **73 A8** 36 9N 136 49 E
Ryōtsu, *Japan* .... **70 E9** 38 5N 138 26 E
Rypin, *Poland* .... **55 E6** 53 3N 19 25 E
Ryssby, *Sweden* .... **17 H8** 56 52N 14 10 E
Rysy, *Europe* .... **35 B13** 49 10N 20 4 E
Ryūgasaki, *Japan* .... **73 B12** 35 54N 140 11 E
Ryūkyū Is. = Ryūkyū-rettō, *Japan* **71 M3** 26 0N 126 0 E
Ryūkyū-rettō, *Japan* .... **71 M3** 26 0N 126 0 E
Rzepin, *Poland* .... **55 F1** 52 20N 14 49 E
Rzeszów, *Poland* .... **55 H8** 50 5N 21 58 E
Rzhev, *Russia* .... **58 D8** 56 20N 34 20 E

S

Sa, *Thailand* .... **86 C3** 18 34N 100 45 E
Sa Canal, *Spain* .... **38 D1** 38 51N 1 23 E
Sa Conillera, *Spain* .... **38 D1** 38 59N 1 13 E
Sa Dec, *Vietnam* .... **87 G5** 10 20N 105 46 E
Sa Dragonera, *Spain* .... **38 B3** 39 35N 2 19 E
Sa-koi, *Burma* .... **90 F6** 19 54N 97 3 E
Sa Mesquida, *Spain* .... **38 B5** 39 55N 4 16 E
Sa Pobla, *Spain* .... **38 B4** 39 46N 3 1 E
Sa Savina, *Spain* .... **38 D1** 38 44N 1 25 E
Sa'a, *Solomon Is.* .... **133 M11** 9 43 S 161 35 E
Sa'ādatābād, *Fārs, Iran* .... **97 D7** 30 10N 53 5 E
Sa'ādatābād, *Hormozgān, Iran* ... **97 D7** 28 3N 55 53 E
Sa'ādatābād, *Kermān, Iran* .... **97 D7** 29 40N 55 51 E
Saale ➤, *Germany* .... **30 D7** 51 56N 11 54 E
Saaler Bodden, *Germany* .... **30 A8** 54 20N 12 27 E
Saalfeld, *Germany* .... **30 E7** 50 38N 11 21 E
Saalfelden, *Austria* .... **34 D5** 47 25N 12 51 E
Saane ➤, *Switz.* .... **32 B4** 47 8N 7 10 E
Saanen, *Switz.* .... **32 D4** 46 29N 7 15 E
Saanich, *Canada* **160 B3** 48 29N 123 26W
Saar ➤, *Europe* .... **24 E6** 49 41N 6 32 E
Saar-Hunsrueck, Naturpark △,
 Germany .... **31 F2** 49 50N 6 50 E
Saarbrücken, *Germany* .... **31 F2** 49 14N 6 59 E
Saarburg, *Germany* .... **31 F2** 49 36N 6 32 E
Saaremaa, *Estonia* .... **15 G20** 58 30N 22 30 E
Saarijärvi, *Finland* .... **15 E21** 62 43N 25 16 E
Saariselkä, *Finland* .... **14 B23** 68 16N 28 15 E
Saarland □, *Germany* .... **31 F2** 49 20N 7 0 E
Saarlouis, *Germany* .... **31 F2** 49 18N 6 45 E
Saas Fee, *Switz.* .... **32 D5** 46 7N 7 56 E

Sab 'Ābar, *Syria* .... **100 F7** 33 46N 37 41 E
Saba, *W. Indies* **165 C7** 17 42N 63 26W
Šabac, *Serbia, Yug.* .... **50 B3** 44 48N 19 42 E
Sabadell, *Spain* .... **40 D7** 41 28N 2 7 E
Sabae, *Japan* .... **73 B8** 35 57N 136 11 E
Sabah □, *Malaysia* .... **85 A5** 6 0N 117 0 E
Sabak Bernam, *Malaysia* .... **87 L3** 3 46N 100 58 E
Sabalān, Kūhhā-ye, *Iran* .... **101 C12** 38 15N 47 45 E
Sabalana, Kepulauan, *Indonesia* . **82 C1** 6 45 S 118 50 E
Sábana de la Mar, *Dom. Rep.* **165 C6** 19 7N 69 24W
Sabanalarga, *Colombia* **168 A3** 10 38N 74 55W
Sabang, *Indonesia* .... **84 A1** 5 50N 95 15 E
Sabãoani, *Romania* .... **53 C11** 47 15N 26 51 E
Sabará, *Brazil* .... **171 E3** 19 55 S 43 46W
Sabari ➤, *India* .... **94 F5** 17 35N 81 16 E
Sabarmati ➤, *India* .... **92 H5** 22 18N 72 22 E
Sab'atayn, Ramlat as, *Yemen* .... **98 D4** 15 30N 46 10 E
Sabattis, *U.S.A.* **151 B10** 44 6N 74 40W
Sabáudia, *Italy* .... **46 A6** 41 18N 13 1 E
Sabaya, *Bolivia* .... **172 D4** 19 1 S 68 23W
Şabhā, Jaza'ir, *Si. Arabia* .... **98 C3** 18 35N 41 3 E
Sabbio Chiese, *Italy* .... **33 E10** 45 39N 10 25 E
Saberania, *Indonesia* .... **83 B5** 2 5 S 138 18 E
Sabhah, *Libya* .... **108 C2** 27 9N 14 29 E
Sabhah □, *Libya* .... **108 C2** 26 0N 14 30 E
Sabi ➤, *India* .... **92 E7** 28 29N 76 44 E
Sabidana, J., *Sudan* .... **106 D4** 18 4N 36 50 E
Sabie, *S. Africa* .... **117 D5** 25 10 S 30 48 E
Sabina, *U.S.A.* **157 E13** 39 29N 83 38W
Sabinal, *Mexico* **162 A3** 30 58N 107 25W
Sabinal, *U.S.A.* **155 L5** 29 19N 99 28W
Sabiñánigo, *Spain* **40 C4** 42 31N 0 22W
Sabinar, Punta del, *Spain* **41 J2** 36 43N 2 44W
Sabinas, *Mexico* **162 B4** 27 50N 101 10W
Sabinas ➤, *Mexico* **162 B4** 27 37N 100 42W
Sabinas Hidalgo, *Mexico* **162 B4** 26 33N 100 10W
Sabine ➤, *U.S.A.* **155 L8** 29 59N 93 47W
Sabine L., *U.S.A.* **155 L8** 29 53N 93 51W
Sabine Pass, *U.S.A.* **155 L8** 29 44N 93 54W
Sabinópolis, *Brazil* .... **171 E3** 18 40 S 43 6W
Sabinov, *Slovak Rep.* .... **35 B14** 49 6N 21 5 E
Sablayan, *Phil.* .... **80 E3** 12 50N 120 50 E
Sable, *Canada* **141 A6** 55 30N 68 21W
Sable, C., *Canada* **141 D6** 43 25N 65 38W
Sable, C., *U.S.A.* **153 K8** 25 9N 81 8W
Sable I., *Canada* **141 D8** 44 0N 60 0W
Sable I., *Papua N. G.* .... **132 B8** 3 38 S 154 42 E
Sablé-sur-Sarthe, *France* **26 E6** 47 50N 0 20W
Saboeiro, *Brazil* .... **170 C4** 6 32 S 39 54W
Sabonkafi, *Niger* .... **113 C6** 14 40N 8 45 E
Sabor ➤, *Portugal* **42 D3** 41 10N 7 7W
Sabou, *Burkina Faso* **112 C4** 12 1N 2 15W
Şabrātah, *Libya* .... **108 B2** 32 47N 12 29 E
Sabres, *France* **28 D3** 44 9N 0 43W
Sabria, *Tunisia* .... **108 B1** 33 22N 8 45 E
Sabrina Coast, *Antarctica* .... **7 C9** 68 0 S 120 0 E
Sabtang I., *Phil.* .... **80 A3** 20 19N 121 52 E
Sabugal, *Portugal* **42 E3** 40 20N 7 5W
Sabula, *U.S.A.* **156 B6** 42 4N 90 10W
Sabulubbek, *Indonesia* .... **84 C1** 1 36 S 98 40 E
Sabuncu, *Turkey* .... **49 B12** 39 33N 30 12 E
Şabyā, *Si. Arabia* .... **98 C3** 17 9N 42 37 E
Sabzevar, *Iran* .... **97 B8** 36 15N 57 40 E
Sabzvārān, *Iran* .... **97 D8** 28 45N 57 50 E
Sac City, *U.S.A.* **156 B2** 42 25N 95 0W
Sacaolo, *Angola* .... **115 E4** 12 58 S 22 8 E
Sacatengo, *Angola* .... **115 E4** 13 16 S 21 20 E
Sacedón, *Spain* **40 E2** 40 29N 2 41W
Săcele, *Romania* .... **53 E10** 45 37N 25 41 E
Sachigo ➤, *Canada* **140 A2** 55 6N 88 58W
Sachigo, L., *Canada* **140 B1** 53 50N 92 12W
Sachimbo, *Angola* .... **115 D4** 9 14 S 20 16 E
Sachin, *India* .... **94 D1** 21 5N 72 53 E
Sachkhere, *Georgia* .... **61 J6** 42 25N 43 15 E
Sachseln, *Switz.* .... **33 C6** 46 52N 8 15 E
Sachsen □, *Germany* .... **30 E9** 50 55N 13 10 E
Sachsen-Anhalt □, *Germany* ..... **30 D7** 52 0N 12 0 E
Sächsische Schweiz, Nationalpark △,
 Germany .... **30 E10** 50 55N 14 10 E
Sacile, *Italy* .... **45 C9** 45 57N 12 30 E
Sackets Harbor, *U.S.A.* **151 C8** 43 57N 76 7W
Sackville, *Canada* **141 C7** 45 54N 64 22W
Saco, Maine, *U.S.A.* **149 D10** 43 30N 70 27W
Saco, Mont., *U.S.A.* **158 B10** 48 28N 107 21W
Sacramento, *Brazil* .... **171 E2** 19 53 S 47 27W
Sacramento, *U.S.A.* **160 G5** 38 35N 121 29W
Sacramento ➤, *U.S.A.* **160 G5** 38 3N 121 56W
Sacramento Mts., *U.S.A.* **159 K11** 32 30N 105 30W
Sacramento Valley, *U.S.A.* **160 G5** 39 30N 122 0W
Sacratif, C., *Spain* **43 J7** 36 42N 3 28W
Săcueni, *Romania* .... **52 C7** 47 20N 22 5 E
Sada, *Spain* **40 C3** 42 19N 1 12W
Sada-Misaki, *Japan* .... **71 H6** 33 20N 132 1 E
Sada-Misaki-Hantō, *Japan* ...... **72 D4** 33 22N 132 1 E
Sádaba, *Spain* **40 C3** 42 19N 1 12W
Şa'dah, *Yemen* .... **98 D3** 16 15N 43 37 E
Sadani, *Tanzania* .... **118 D4** 5 58 S 38 35 E
Sadao, *Thailand* .... **87 J3** 6 38N 100 26 E
Sadaseopet, *India* .... **94 F3** 17 38N 77 59 E
Sadd el Aali, *Egypt* .... **106 C3** 23 54N 32 54 E
Saddle Mt., *U.S.A.* **160 E3** 45 58N 123 41W
Saddle Pk., *India* .... **95 H11** 13 9N 93 1 E
Sade, Pt., *St. Helena* .... **9 h** 15 57 S 5 38W
Sade, *Nigeria* .... **113 C7** 11 22N 10 45 E
Şadh, *Oman* .... **99 C6** 17 3N 55 4 E
Sadimi, *Dem. Rep. of the Congo* .. **119 D1** 9 25 S 23 32 E
Sadiola, *Mali* **112 C2** 13 50N 11 40W
Sadiya, *India* .... **90 B5** 27 50N 95 40 E
Sa'dīyah, Hawr as, *Iraq* .... **101 F12** 32 15N 46 30 E
Sado, *Japan* .... **70 F9** 38 0N 138 25 E
Sado ➤, *Portugal* **43 G2** 38 29N 8 55W
Sadon, *Russia* .... **61 J6** 42 52N 43 58 E
Sadowara, *Japan* .... **72 E3** 32 3N 131 26 E
Sadra, *India* .... **92 H5** 23 21N 72 43 E
Sadri, *India* .... **92 G5** 25 11N 73 26 E
Sæbøvik, *Norway* .... **18 E2** 59 47N 5 40 E
Sæby, *Denmark* .... **17 G4** 57 21N 10 30 E
Saegertown, *U.S.A.* **150 E4** 41 43N 80 9W
Saelices, *Spain* **40 F2** 39 55N 2 49W
Sætre, *Norway* .... **18 D2** 60 11N 3 46 E
Sævareid, *Norway* .... **18 D2** 60 11N 5 46 E
Safaalan, *Turkey* .... **51 E12** 41 26N 28 6 E
Safaga, *Egypt* .... **106 B3** 26 42N 34 0 E
Şafājah, *Si. Arabia* .... **96 E3** 26 25N 39 0 E
Safárikovo = Tornal'a, *Slovak Rep.* **35 C13** 48 25N 20 20 E
Safata B., *Samoa* .... **133 X24** 14 0 S 171 50W
Safed Koh, *Afghan.* .... **91 B3** 34 0N 70 0 E
Säffle, *Sweden* .... **16 E6** 59 8N 12 55 E
Safford, *U.S.A.* **159 K9** 32 50N 109 43W
Saffron Walden, *U.K.* .... **21 E8** 52 1N 0 16 E
Safi, *Morocco* **110 B3** 32 18N 9 20W
Safia, *Papua N. G.* .... **132 C5** 9 35 S 148 38 E
Safia, Hamada, *Mali* **110 D4** 23 10N 4 15W
Şafiābād, *Iran* .... **97 B8** 36 45N 57 58 E
Safid Dasht, *Iran* .... **97 C6** 33 27N 48 11 E
Safid Kūh, *Afghan.* .... **91 B1** 34 45N 63 0 E
Safid Rūd ➤, *Iran* .... **97 B6** 37 23N 50 11 E
Safipur, *India* .... **93 F9** 26 44N 80 21 E
Safonovo, *Russia* .... **58 E7** 55 4N 33 16 E
Safranbolu, *Turkey* .... **100 B5** 41 15N 32 41 E

Saft Rashīn, *Egypt* .... **106 J7** 28 58N 30 55 E
Safune, *Samoa* .... **133 W23** 13 25 S 172 21W
Safwān, *Iraq* .... **96 D5** 30 7N 47 43 E
Sag Harbor, *U.S.A.* **151 F12** 41 0N 72 18W
Sag Sag, *Papua N. G.* .... **132 C5** 5 32 S 148 23 E
Saga, *Indonesia* .... **83 B4** 2 40 S 132 55 E
Saga, *Kōchi, Japan* .... **72 D5** 33 5N 133 6 E
Saga, *Saga, Japan* .... **72 D2** 33 15N 130 20 E
Saga □, *Japan* .... **72 D2** 33 15N 130 20 E
Sagae, *Japan* .... **70 E10** 38 22N 140 17 E
Sagaing, *Burma* .... **90 E5** 23 55N 95 56 E
Sagaing □, *Burma* .... **90 D5** 23 55N 95 56 E
Sagala, *Mali* **112 C3** 14 9N 6 38W
Sagami-Nada, *Japan* .... **73 C11** 34 58N 139 30 E
Sagami-Wan, *Japan* .... **73 B11** 35 15N 139 25 E
Sagamihara, *Japan* .... **73 B11** 35 33N 139 25 E
Saganore, *U.S.A.* **150 F5** 40 46N 79 14W
Saganoseki, *Japan* .... **72 D3** 33 15N 131 53 E
Sagar, *Karnataka, India* .... **94 F3** 16 38N 76 48 E
Sagar, *Karnataka, India* .... **95 G2** 14 14N 75 6 E
Sagar, *Mad. P., India* .... **93 H8** 23 50N 78 44 E
Sagara, *Japan* .... **73 C10** 34 41N 138 12 E
Sagara, L., *Tanzania* .... **118 D3** 5 20 S 31 0 E
Sagavanirktok ➤, *U.S.A.* **144 A11** 70 19N 147 53W
Sagay, *Phil.* .... **81 F4** 10 57N 123 25 E
Saginaw, *U.S.A.* **148 D4** 43 26N 83 56W
Saginaw ➤, *U.S.A.* **148 D4** 43 39N 83 51W
Saginaw B., *U.S.A.* **148 D4** 43 50N 83 40W
Sagleipie, *Liberia* **112 D3** 7 0N 8 52W
Saglouc = Salluit, *Canada* **139 B12** 62 14N 75 38W
Sago'ri, S. Korea .... **75 G14** 38 25N 126 49 E
Sagone, *France* .... **29 F12** 42 7N 8 42 E
Sagone, G. de, *France* .... **29 F12** 42 4N 8 40 E
Sagres, *Portugal* **43 J2** 37 0N 8 58W
Sagu, *Burma* .... **90 E5** 20 13N 94 46 E
Sagua la Grande, *Cuba* **164 B3** 22 50N 80 10W
Saguache, *U.S.A.* **159 G10** 38 5N 106 8W
Saguaro Nat. Park △, *U.S.A.* **159 K8** 32 12N 110 38W
Saguenay ➤, *Canada* **141 C5** 48 22N 71 0W
Saguia el Hamra ➤, *W. Sahara* .. **110 C2** 27 24N 13 43W
Sagunt = Sagunto, *Spain* **40 F4** 39 42N 0 18W
Sagunto = Sagunt, *Spain* **40 F4** 39 42N 0 18W
Sagvåg, *Norway* .... **18 E2** 59 46N 5 25 E
Sagwara, *India* .... **92 H6** 23 41N 74 1 E
Sahaba, *Sudan* .... **106 D3** 18 57N 30 25 E
Sahagún, *Colombia* **168 B2** 8 57N 75 27W
Sahagún, *Spain* **42 C5** 42 18N 5 2W
Saham al Jawlān, *Syria* .... **103 C4** 32 45N 35 55 E
Sahamandrevo, *Madag.* .... **117 C8** 23 15 S 45 35 E
Sahand, Kūh-e, *Iran* .... **101 D12** 37 44N 46 27 E
Sahara, *Africa* .... **104 D2** 23 0N 5 0 E
Saharan Atlas = Saharien, Atlas,
 Algeria .... **111 B5** 33 30N 1 0 E
Saharanpur, *India* .... **92 E7** 29 58N 77 33 E
Saharien, Atlas, *Algeria* .... **111 B5** 33 30N 1 0 E
Saharsa, *India* .... **93 G12** 25 53N 86 36 E
Sahasinaka, *Madag.* .... **117 C8** 21 49 S 47 49 E
Sahaswan, *India* .... **93 E8** 28 5N 78 45 E
Sahel, Canal du, *Mali* **112 C3** 14 20N 6 0W
Sahibganj, *India* .... **93 G12** 25 12N 87 40 E
Şāḩiliyah, *Iraq* .... **101 F10** 33 43N 42 42 E
Sahiwal, *Pakistan* .... **91 C4** 30 45N 73 8 E
Şaḩneh, *Iran* .... **101 E12** 34 29N 47 41 E
Sahuaripa, *Mexico* **162 B3** 29 0N 109 13W
Sahuarita, *U.S.A.* **159 L8** 31 57N 110 58W
Sahuayo, *Mexico* **162 C4** 20 4N 102 43W
Şāhy, *Slovak Rep.* .... **35 C11** 48 4N 18 55 E
Sai ➤, *India* .... **93 G10** 25 39N 82 47 E
Sai Buri, *Thailand* .... **87 J3** 6 43N 101 45 E
Sai-Cinza, *Brazil* .... **178 B6** 6 17 S 57 42W
Sai Kung, *China* .... **69 G11** 22 23N 114 16 E
Saibai I., *Australia* .... **128 A3** 9 25 S 142 40 E
Sa'id Bundas, *Sudan* .... **109 G4** 8 24N 24 48 E
Saïda, *Algeria* .... **111 B5** 34 50N 0 11 E
Sa'īdābād = Sīrjān, *Iran* .... **97 D7** 29 30N 55 45 E
Sa'īdābād, *Iran* .... **97 D7** 29 30N 55 45 E
Saidaiji, *Japan* .... **72 C6** 34 39N 134 2 E
Saidia, *Morocco* **111 A4** 35 5N 2 14W
Sa'īdīyeh, *Iran* .... **97 B6** 36 20N 48 55 E
Saidor, *Papua N. G.* .... **132 C4** 5 40 S 146 29 E
Saidpur, *Bangla.* .... **90 C2** 25 48N 89 0 E
Saidpur, *India* .... **93 G10** 25 33N 83 11 E
Saidu, *Pakistan* .... **93 B5** 34 43N 72 24 E
Saignelégier, *Switz.* .... **32 B4** 47 15N 7 0 E
Saignes, *France* .... **28 C6** 45 20N 2 31 E
Saigō, *Japan* .... **72 A5** 36 12N 133 20 E
Saigon = Thanh Pho Ho Chi Minh,
 Vietnam .... **87 G6** 10 58N 106 40 E
Saijo, *Japan* .... **72 D1** 33 12N 129 36 E
Saikai Nat. Park △, *Japan* .... **72 D1** 33 12N 129 36 E
Saikanosy Masoala, *Madag.* ..... **117 B9** 15 45 S 50 10 E
Saikhoa Ghat, *India* .... **90 B5** 27 50N 95 40 E
Saiki, *Japan* .... **72 E3** 32 58N 131 51 E
Sailana, *India* .... **92 H6** 23 28N 74 55 E
Saillans, *France* .... **29 D9** 44 42N 5 12 E
Sailolof, *Indonesia* .... **83 B4** 1 15 S 130 46 E
Sailu, *India* .... **94 E3** 19 28N 76 28 E
Saimaa, *Finland* .... **15 F23** 61 15N 28 15 E
Saimbeyli, *Turkey* .... **100 D7** 37 59N 36 6 E
Şa'in Dezh, *Iran* .... **101 D12** 36 40N 46 25 E
St. Abb's Head, *U.K.* **22 F6** 55 55N 2 8W
St-Affrique, *France* .... **28 D6** 43 57N 2 53 E
St-Agrève, *France* .... **29 C8** 45 0N 4 23 E
St-Aignan, *France* .... **26 E8** 47 16N 1 22 E
St-André, *Réunion* .... **121 c** 20 57 S 55 39 E
St-André-de-Cubzac, *France* **28 D3** 44 59N 0 26W
St-André-les-Alpes, *France* ...... **29 E10** 43 58N 6 30 E
St. Andrew Sd., *U.S.A.* **153 F5** 31 0N 81 25W
St. Andrew's, *Canada* **141 C8** 47 45N 59 15W
St. Andrews, *N.Z.* .... **131 E6** 44 33 S 171 10 E
St. Andrews, *U.K.* **22 E6** 56 20N 2 47W
St. Ann B., *Canada* **141 C7** 46 22N 60 25W
St. Ann's Bay, *Jamaica* .... **164 a** 18 26N 77 15W
St. Anthony, *Canada* **141 B8** 51 22N 55 35W
St. Anthony, *U.S.A.* **158 E8** 43 58N 111 41W
St. Antoine, *Canada* **141 C7** 46 22N 64 45W
St. Anton am Arlberg, *Austria* ... **33 B10** 47 8N 10 16 E
St-Antonin-Noble-Val, *France* .... **28 D5** 44 10N 1 46 E
St. Arnaud = El Eulma, *Algeria* .. **111 A6** 36 9N 5 42 E
St. Arnaud, *Australia* .... **127 C7** 42 1 S 172 53 E
St. Arnaud Ra., *N.Z.* .... **131 C7** 42 1 S 172 53 E
St-Astier, *France* .... **28 C4** 45 8N 0 31 E
St-Aubin, *Switz.* .... **32 C3** 46 54N 6 47 E
St-Aubin-du-Cormier, *France* **26 D5** 48 15N 1 26W
St-Augustin ➤, *Canada* **141 B8** 51 16N 58 40W
St. Augustin-Saguenay, *Canada* .. **141 B8** 51 13N 58 38W
St. Augustine, *U.S.A.* **153 L5** 29 54N 81 19W
St. Augustine Beach, *U.S.A.* **153 L5** 29 51N 81 18W
St-Aulaye, *France* .... **28 C4** 45 12N 0 9 E
St. Austell, *U.K.* **21 G3** 50 20N 4 47W

St-Avold, *France* .... **27 C13** 49 6N 6 43 E
St. Barbe, *Canada* **141 B8** 51 12N 56 46W
St-Barthélemy, *W. Indies* **165 C7** 17 50N 62 50W
St. Bathans, *N.Z.* .... **131 E4** 44 53 S 169 50 E
St-Béat, *France* .... **28 F4** 42 55N 0 41 E
St. Bees Hd., *U.K.* **20 C4** 54 31N 3 38W
St. Bees I., *Australia* .... **126 J7** 20 56 S 149 26 E
St-Benoît, *Réunion* .... **121 c** 21 2 S 55 43 E
St-Benoît-du-Sault, *France* ...... **28 B5** 46 26N 1 24 E
St-Bernard, Col du Grand, *Europe* **32 E4** 45 53N 7 11 E
St-Blaise, *Switz.* .... **32 B3** 47 1N 6 59 E
St-Bonnet, *France* .... **29 D10** 44 40N 6 5 E
St-Brévin-les-Pins, *France* **26 E4** 47 14N 2 10W
St-Brice-en-Coglès, *France* **26 D5** 48 25N 1 22W
St. Bride's, *Canada* **141 C9** 46 56N 54 10W
St. Brides B., *U.K.* **21 F2** 51 49N 5 9W
St-Brieuc, *France* **26 D4** 48 30N 2 46W
St-Calais, *France* .... **26 E7** 47 55N 0 45 E
St-Cast-le-Guildo, *France* **26 D4** 48 37N 2 18W
St. Catharines, *Canada* **140 D4** 43 10N 79 15W
St. Catherine Pt., *Bermuda* ..... **9 a** 32 23N 64 40W
St. Catherines I., *U.S.A.* **153 K5** 31 40N 81 10W
St. Catherine's Monastery, *Egypt* **110 B3** 28 34N 33 58 E
St. Catherine's Pt., *U.K.* **21 G6** 50 34N 1 18W
St-Céré, *France* .... **28 D5** 44 51N 1 54 E
St-Cergue, *Switz.* .... **32 D2** 46 27N 6 10 E
St-Cernin, *France* .... **28 C6** 45 5N 2 25 E
St-Chamond, *France* .... **29 C8** 45 28N 4 31 E
St. Charles, Ill., *U.S.A.* **157 C8** 41 54N 88 19W
St. Charles, Mo., *U.S.A.* **156 F6** 38 47N 90 29W
St. Charles, Va., *U.S.A.* **148 F7** 36 48N 83 4W
St-Chély-d'Apcher, *France* ...... **28 D7** 44 48N 3 17 E
St-Chinian, *France* .... **28 E6** 43 25N 2 56 E
St. Christopher-Nevis = St. Kitts &
 Nevis ■, *W. Indies* **165 C7** 17 20N 62 40W
St-Ciers-sur-Gironde, *France* **28 C3** 45 17N 0 37W
St. Clair, U.S.A. **152 B7** 33 9N 82 13W
St. Clair, Mich., *U.S.A.* **150 D2** 42 50N 82 30W
St. Clair, Mo., *U.S.A.* **156 F6** 38 21N 90 59W
St. Clair, Pa., *U.S.A.* **151 F8** 40 43N 76 12W
St. Clair ➤, *U.S.A.* **150 D2** 42 38N 82 31W
St. Clair, L., *Australia* .... **128 D3** 37 20 S 139 55 E
St. Clair, L., *Canada* **140 D3** 42 30N 82 45W
St. Clair, L., *U.S.A.* **150 D2** 42 27N 82 39W
St. Clair Shores, *U.S.A.* **157 B14** 42 30N 82 53W
St. Clairsville, *U.S.A.* **150 F4** 40 5N 80 54W
St-Claud, *France* .... **28 C4** 45 54N 0 28 E
St. Claude, *Canada* **143 D9** 49 40N 98 20W
St-Claude, *France* .... **27 F12** 46 22N 5 52 E
St. Clears, *U.K.* **21 F3** 51 49N 4 31W
St-Clet, *Canada* **151 A10** 45 21N 74 13W
St. Cloud, Fla., *U.S.A.* **153 G8** 28 15N 81 17W
St. Cloud, Minn., *U.S.A.* **154 C7** 45 34N 94 10W
St. Cricq, C., *Australia* .... **125 E1** 25 17 S 113 6 E
St. Croix, U.S. Virgin Is. **165 C7** 17 45N 64 45W
St. Croix ➤, *U.S.A.* **154 C8** 44 45N 92 48W
St. Croix Falls, *U.S.A.* **154 C8** 45 24N 92 38W
St-Cyprien, *France* .... **28 F7** 42 37N 3 0 E
St-Cyr-sur-Mer, *France* .... **29 E9** 43 11N 5 43 E
St. David's, *Canada* **141 C8** 48 12N 58 52W
St. David's, *U.K.* **21 F2** 51 53N 5 16W
St. David's Head, *U.K.* **21 F2** 51 54N 5 19W
St. David's I., *Bermuda* .... **9 a** 32 21N 64 39W
St-Denis = Sig, *Algeria* **111 A4** 35 32N 0 32W
St-Denis, *France* .... **27 D9** 48 56N 2 22 E
St-Denis, *Réunion* .... **121 c** 20 52 S 55 27 E
St-Denis ✈ (RUN), *Réunion* ..... **121 c** 20 53 S 55 32 E
St-Dié, *France* .... **27 D13** 48 17N 6 56 E
St-Dizier, *France* .... **27 D11** 48 38N 4 56 E
St-Égrève, *France* .... **29 C9** 45 14N 5 41 E
St. Elias, Mt., *U.S.A.* **144 F12** 60 18N 140 56W
St. Elias Mts., *Canada* **142 A1** 60 33N 139 28W
St. Elias Mts., *U.S.A.* **144 G13** 60 0N 138 0W
St-Élie, *Fr. Guiana* **169 C7** 4 49N 53 17W
St. Elmo, *U.S.A.* **157 E8** 39 2N 88 51W
St-Éloy-les-Mines, *France* ...... **27 F9** 46 10N 2 51 E
St-Émilion, *France* **28 D3** 44 53N 0 9W
St-Étienne, *France* .... **29 C8** 45 27N 4 22 E
St-Étienne-de-Tinée, *France* ..... **29 D10** 44 16N 6 56 E
St-Étienne-du-Rouvray, *France* ... **26 C8** 49 23N 1 6 E
St. Eugène, *Canada* **151 A10** 45 30N 74 28W
St. Eustatius, *W. Indies* **165 C7** 17 20N 63 0W
St-Exupery, Lyon ✈ (LYS), *France* **27 C9** 45 44N 5 2 E
St-Fargeau, *France* .... **27 E10** 47 39N 3 4 E
St-Félicien, *Canada* **140 C5** 48 40N 72 25W
St-Florent, *France* .... **29 F13** 42 41N 9 18 E
St-Florent, G. de, *France* .... **29 F13** 42 41N 9 12 E
St-Florent-sur-Cher, *France* ..... **27 F9** 46 59N 2 15 E
St-Florentin, *France* .... **27 E10** 48 0N 3 45 E
St-Flour, *France* .... **28 C7** 45 2N 3 6 E
St. Francis, *U.S.A.* **154 F4** 39 47N 101 48W
St. Francis ➤, *U.S.A.* **155 H9** 34 38N 90 36W
St. Francis, C., *S. Africa* .... **116 E3** 34 14 S 24 49 E
St. Francisville, Ill., *U.S.A.* **157 F8** 38 36N 87 39W
St. Francisville, La., *U.S.A.* **155 K9** 30 47N 91 23W
St-François, L., *Canada* **151 A10** 45 10N 74 22W
St-Fulgent, *France* **26 F5** 46 50N 1 10W
St-Gabriel, *Canada* **140 C5** 46 17N 73 24W
St. Gallen = Sankt Gallen, *Switz.* **33 B8** 47 26N 9 22 E
St. Gallenkirch, *Austria* .... **33 B9** 47 1N 9 58 E
St-Galmier, *France* .... **27 G11** 45 35N 4 19 E
St-Gaudens, *France* .... **28 E4** 43 6N 0 44 E
St-Gaultier, *France* .... **26 F8** 46 39N 1 26 E
St-Gengoux-le-National, *France* .. **27 F11** 46 37N 4 40 E
St-Geniez-d'Olt, *France* .... **28 D6** 44 27N 2 58 E
St. George, *Australia* .... **127 D4** 28 1 S 148 30 E
St. George, *Bermuda* .... **9 a** 32 22N 64 40W
St. George, *Canada* **141 C6** 45 11N 66 50W
St. George, S.C., *U.S.A.* **153 J5** 33 11N 80 35W
St. George, Utah, *U.S.A.* **159 H7** 37 6N 113 35W
St. George, C., *Canada* **141 C8** 48 30N 59 16W
St. George, C., *Papua N. G.* ..... **132 C7** 4 49 S 152 53 E
St. George I., *Alaska, U.S.A.* **144 H5** 56 35N 169 35W
St. George I., Fla., *U.S.A.* **152 F5** 29 35N 84 55W
St. George Ra., *Australia* .... **124 C4** 18 40 S 125 0 E
St. George's, *Canada* **141 C8** 48 58N 58 31W
St-Georges, *Canada* **141 C5** 46 8N 70 40W
St-Georges, Fr. Guiana **169 C7** 4 0N 52 0W
St. George's, *Grenada* **165 D7** 12 5N 61 43W
St. George's B., *Canada* **141 C8** 48 24N 58 53W
St. Georges Basin, N.S.W., *Australia* **129 C9** 35 7 S 150 36 E
St. Georges Basin, N.S.W., *Australia* **129 C9** 35 7 S 150 36 E
St. Georges Basin, W. Austral.,
 Australia .... **124 C4** 15 23 S 125 2 E
St. George's Channel, *Europe* **23 E6** 52 0N 6 0W
St. George's Channel, *India* ..... **95 L11** 7 20 S 93 52 E
St. George's Channel, *Papua N. G.* **132 C7** 4 10 S 152 20 E
St. Georges Hd., *Australia* ...... **129 C9** 35 3 S 150 42 E
St. Georges I., *Bermuda* .... **9 a** 32 23N 64 40W
St-Georges-lès-Baillargeaux, *France* **28 B4** 46 42N 0 23 E
St-Germain-de-Calberte, *France* .. **28 D7** 44 13N 3 48 E
St-Germain-en-Laye, *France* ..... **27 D9** 48 54N 2 5 E
St-Germain-Lembron, *France* .... **28 C7** 45 27N 3 14 E
St-Germain-l'Auvergne, *France* ... **27 F9** 46 4N 2 52 E
St-Gervais-les-Bains, *France* ..... **29 C10** 45 53N 6 42 E
St. Gilbert, *Canada* **141 C5** 46 22N 72 30W
St-Gildas, Pte. de, *France* **26 E4** 47 8N 2 14W
St-Gilles, *France* .... **29 E8** 43 40N 4 26 E
St. Golgoph, *Switz.* .... **32 D3** 46 6N 6 48 E
St-Girons, Ariège, *France* .... **28 F5** 42 59N 1 8 E
St-Girons, Landes, *France* **28 E2** 43 56N 1 18W

St. Gotthard P. = San Gottardo, P.
del, *Switz.* . . . . **33 C7** 46 33N 8 33 E
St. Helena, *Atl. Oc.* . . . . **9 h** 15 58 S 5 42W
St. Helena, *U.S.A.* **158 G2** 38 30N 122 28W
St. Helena B., *S. Africa* . . . . **116 E2** 32 40 S 18 10 E
St. Helena Mt., *U.S.A.* **160 G4** 38 40N 122 36W
St. Helens, *Australia* . . . . **127 G4** 41 20 S 148 15 E
St. Helens, *U.K.* **20 D5** 53 27N 2 44W
St. Helens, *U.S.A.* **160 E4** 45 52N 122 48W
St. Helens, Mt., *U.S.A.* **160 D4** 46 12N 122 12W
St. Helier, *U.K.* **21 H5** 49 10N 2 7W
St-Herblain, *France* **26 E5** 47 13N 1 40W
St-Hilaire-du-Harcouët, *France* . . **26 D5** 48 35N 1 5W
St-Hippolyte, *France* . . . . **27 E13** 47 19N 6 50 E
St-Hippolyte-du-Fort, *France* . . . **28 E7** 43 58N 3 52 E
St-Honoré-les-Bains, *France* . . . . **27 F10** 46 54N 3 50 E
St-Hubert, *Belgium* . . . . **24 D5** 50 2N 5 23 E
St-Hyacinthe, *Canada* **140 C5** 45 40N 72 58W
St. Ignace, *U.S.A.* **148 C3** 45 52N 84 44W
St. Ignace I., *Canada* **140 C2** 48 45N 88 0W
St. Ignatius, *U.S.A.* **158 C6** 47 19N 114 6W
St-Imier, *Switz.* . . . . **32 B3** 47 9N 6 58 E
St. Ives, *Cambs., U.K.* **21 E7** 52 20N 0 4W
St. Ives, *Corn., U.K.* **21 G2** 50 12N 5 30W
St. James, *France* **26 D5** 48 31N 1 20W
St. James, *Minn., U.S.A.* **154 D7** 43 59N 94 38W
St. James, *Mo., U.S.A.* **156 G5** 38 0N 91 37W
St-Jean →, *Canada* **141 B7** 50 17N 64 20W
St-Jean, L., *Canada* **141 C5** 48 40N 72 0W
St-Jean-d'Angély, *France* **28 C3** 45 57N 0 31W
St-Jean-de-Braye, *France* . . . . **27 E8** 47 53N 1 58 E
St-Jean-de-Luz, *France* **28 E2** 43 23N 1 39W
St-Jean-de-Maurienne, *France* . . . **29 C10** 45 16N 6 21 E
St-Jean-de-Monts, *France* **26 F4** 46 47N 2 4W
St-Jean-du-Gard, *France* . . . . **28 D7** 44 7N 3 52 E
St-Jean-en-Royans, *France* . . . . . . **29 C9** 45 1N 5 18 E
St-Jean-Pied-de-Port, *France* **28 E2** 43 10N 1 14W
St-Jean-Port-Joli, *Canada* **141 C5** 47 15N 70 13W
St-Jean-sur-Richelieu, *Canada* . . . **140 C5** 45 20N 73 20W
St-Jérôme, *Canada* **140 C5** 45 47N 74 0W
St. Joe, *U.S.A.* **157 C12** 41 19N 84 54W
St. John, *Canada* **141 C6** 45 20N 66 8W
St. John, *U.S.A.* **155 G5** 38 0N 98 46W
St. John →, *Liberia* **112 D2** 6 40N 9 10W
St. John →, *U.S.A.* **149 C12** 45 12N 66 5W
St. John, C., *Canada* **141 C8** 50 0N 55 32W
St. John I., *U.S. Virgin Is.* . . . . . . **165 e** 18 20N 64 42W
St. John's, *Antigua* **165 C7** 17 6N 61 51W
St. John's, *Canada* **141 C9** 47 35N 52 40W
St. Johns, *Ariz., U.S.A.* **159 J9** 34 30N 109 22W
St. Johns, *Mich., U.S.A.* **157 B12** 43 0N 84 33W
St. Johns →, *U.S.A.* **152 E8** 30 24N 81 24W
St. John's Pt., *Ireland* **23 B3** 54 34N 8 27W
St. Johnsbury, *U.S.A.* **151 B12** 44 25N 72 1W
St. Johnsville, *U.S.A.* **151 D10** 43 0N 74 43W
St-Joseph, *Martinique* . . . . **164 c** 14 39N 61 4W
St. Joseph, *N. Cal.* . . . . **133 K4** 20 27 S 166 36 E
St-Joseph, *Réunion* . . . . **121 c** 21 22 S 55 37 E
St. Joseph, *Ill., U.S.A.* **157 D8** 40 7N 88 2W
St. Joseph, *La., U.S.A.* **155 K9** 31 55N 91 14W
St. Joseph, *Mich., U.S.A.* **157 B10** 42 6N 86 29W
St. Joseph, *Mo., U.S.A.* **156 E2** 39 46N 94 50W
St. Joseph →, *U.S.A.* **157 B10** 42 7N 86 29W
St. Joseph, I., *Canada* **140 C3** 46 12N 83 58W
St. Joseph, L., *Canada* **140 B1** 51 10N 90 35W
St. Joseph Pt., *U.S.A.* **152 F4** 29 52N 85 24W
St-Jovite, *Canada* **140 C5** 46 8N 74 38W
St-Juéry, *France* . . . . **28 E6** 43 57N 2 12 E
St. Julian's, *Malta* . . . . **38 F7** 35 55N 14 29 E
St-Julien-Chapteuil, *France* . . . . . **29 C8** 45 2N 4 4 E
St-Julien-de-Vouvantes, *France* . . **26 E5** 47 38N 1 13W
St-Julien-en-Genevois, *France* . . . **27 F13** 46 9N 6 5 E
St-Junien, *France* . . . . **27 C4** 45 53N 0 55 E
St-Just-en-Chaussée, *France* . . . . . **27 C9** 49 30N 2 25 E
St-Just-en-Chevalet, *France* . . . . . **28 C7** 45 55N 3 50 E
St. Kilda, *N.Z.* . . . . **131 F5** 45 53 S 170 31 E
St. Kilda, *U.K.* **19 C2** 57 49N 8 34W
St. Kitts & Nevis ■, *W. Indies* . . . **165 C7** 17 20N 62 40W
St. Laurent, *Canada* **143 C9** 50 25N 97 58W
St-Laurent, *Fr. Guiana* **169 B7** 5 29N 54 3W
St-Laurent-de-la-Salanque, *France* **28 F6** 42 46N 2 59 E
St-Laurent-du-Pont, *France* . . . . . **29 C9** 45 23N 5 45 E
St-Laurent-en-Grandvaux, *France* **27 F12** 46 35N 5 58 E
St-Laurent-Médoc, *France* **28 C3** 45 8N 0 49W
St. Lawrence, *Australia* . . . . **126 C4** 22 16 S 149 31 E
St. Lawrence, *Canada* **141 C8** 46 54N 55 23W
St. Lawrence →, *Canada* **141 C6** 49 30N 66 0W
St. Lawrence, Gulf of, *Canada* . . . **141 C7** 48 25N 62 0W
St. Lawrence I., *U.S.A.* **144 E5** 63 30N 170 30W
St. Lawrence Islands Nat. Park △,
Canada **151 B9** 44 27N 75 52W
St. Leonard, *Canada* **141 C6** 47 12N 67 58W
St-Léonard-de-Noblat, *France* . . . **28 C5** 45 49N 1 29 E
St. Leonhard im Pitztal, *Austria* . **33 B11** 47 4N 10 51 E
St-Leu, *Réunion* . . . . **121 c** 21 9 S 55 18 E
St. Lewis →, *Canada* **141 B8** 52 26N 56 11W
St-Lô, *France* **26 C5** 49 7N 1 5W
St-Louis, *France* . . . . **27 E14** 47 30N 7 34 E
St-Louis, *Guadeloupe* . . . . **164 b** 15 56N 61 19W
St-Louis, *Réunion* . . . . **121 c** 21 16 S 55 25 E
St. Louis, *Senegal* **112 B1** 16 8N 16 27W
St. Louis, *U.S.A.* **156 F6** 38 37N 90 12W
St. Louis →, *U.S.A.* **154 B8** 46 44N 92 45W
St. Louis Lambert International ✈
(STL), *U.S.A.* **156 F6** 38 45N 90 22W
St-Loup-sur-Semouse, *France* . . . **27 E13** 47 53N 6 16 E
St. Lucia ■, *W. Indies* . . . . **165 f** 14 0N 60 50W
St. Lucia, L., *S. Africa* . . . . **117 D5** 28 5 S 32 30 E
St. Lucia Channel, *W. Indies* **165 D7** 14 15N 61 0W
St. Lucie, *U.S.A.* **153 H9** 27 29N 80 20W
St. Lucie Canal, *U.S.A.* **153 H9** 27 10N 80 18W
St. Maarten, *W. Indies* **165 C7** 18 0N 63 5W
St. Magnus B., *U.K.* **22 A7** 60 25N 1 35W
St-Maixent-l'École, *France* **28 B3** 46 24N 0 12W
St-Malo, *France* **26 D4** 48 39N 2 1W
St-Malo, G. de, *France* **26 D4** 48 50N 2 30W
St-Mandrier-sur-Mer, *France* . . . . **29 E9** 43 4N 5 57 E
St-Marc, *Haiti* **165 C5** 19 10N 72 41W
St-Marcellin, *France* . . . . **29 C9** 45 9N 5 20 E
St-Marcouf, Îs., *France* **26 C5** 49 30N 1 10W
St. Maries, *U.S.A.* **158 C5** 47 19N 116 35W
St. Marks, *U.S.A.* **152 E5** 30 9N 84 12W
St-Martin, *W. Indies* **165 C7** 18 0N 63 0W
St-Martin, C., *Martinique* . . . . . . **164 c** 14 52N 61 14W
St. Martin, L., *Canada* **143 C9** 51 40N 98 30W
St-Martin-de-Crau, *France* . . . . . . **29 E8** 43 38N 4 48 E
St-Martin-de-Ré, *France* **28 B2** 46 12N 1 21W
St-Martin-d'Hères, *France* . . . . . . **29 C9** 45 9N 5 45 E
St-Martin-Vésubie, *France* . . . . . . **29 D11** 44 4N 7 15 E
St. Martins, *Barbados* . . . . **165 g** 13 5N 59 28W
St-Martory, *France* . . . . **28 E4** 43 9N 0 56 E
St. Mary, *U.S.A.* **156 G7** 37 53N 89 57W
St. Mary, Mt., *Papua N. G.* . . . . . **132 E4** 8 8 S 147 31 E
St. Mary Is., *India* . . . . **95 H2** 13 20N 74 35 E
St. Mary Pk., *Australia* . . . . **123 A1** 31 32 S 138 34 E
St. Marys, *Australia* . . . . **127 G4** 41 35 S 148 11 E
St. Marys, *Canada* **150 C3** 43 20N 81 10W
St. Mary's, *Corn., U.K.* **21 H1** 49 55N 6 18W
St. Mary's, *Orkney, U.K.* **22 C6** 58 54N 2 54W
St. Mary's, *Alaska, U.S.A.* **144 E7** 62 4N 163 10W
St. Marys, *Ga., U.S.A.* **152 E8** 30 44N 81 33W
St. Marys, *Ohio, U.S.A.* **157 D12** 40 33N 84 24W
St. Marys, *Pa., U.S.A.* **150 E6** 41 26N 78 34W

St. Marys →, *U.S.A.* **152 E8** 30 43N 81 27W
St. Mary's, C., *Canada* **141 C9** 46 50N 54 12W
St. Marys B., *Canada* **141 C9** 46 50N 53 50W
St. Marys Bay, *Canada* **141 D6** 44 25N 66 10W
St-Mathieu, Pte., *France* **26 D2** 48 20N 4 45W
St. Matthew I., *U.S.A.* **144 F4** 60 24N 172 42W
St. Matthews, *Ky., U.S.A.* **157 F11** 38 15N 85 39W
St. Matthews, *S.C., U.S.A.* **153 J5** 33 40N 80 46W
St. Matthews, I. = Zadetkyi Kyun,
Burma . . . . **87 G1** 10 0N 98 25 E
St. Matthias Group, *Papua N. G.* . **132 A5** 1 30 S 150 0 E
St-Maurice, *Switz.* . . . . **32 D4** 46 13N 7 0 E
St-Maurice →, *Canada* **140 C5** 46 21N 72 31W
St. Mawes, *U.K.* **21 G2** 50 10N 5 2W
St-Maximin-la-Ste-Baume, *France* **29 E9** 43 27N 5 52 E
St-Médard-en-Jalles, *France* **28 D3** 44 53N 0 43W
St-Méen-le-Grand, *France* **26 D4** 48 11N 2 12W
St. Meinrad, *U.S.A.* **157 F10** 38 10N 86 49W
St. Michael, *U.S.A.* **144 E7** 63 29N 162 2W
St-Mihiel, *France* . . . . **27 D12** 48 54N 5 32 E
St. Moritz, *Switz.* . . . . **31 J5** 46 30N 9 51 E
St-Nazaire, *France* **26 E4** 47 17N 2 12W
St. Neots, *U.K.* **21 E7** 52 14N 0 15N
St-Nicolas-de-Port, *France* . . . . . . **27 D13** 48 38N 6 18 E
St-Niklaas, *Belgium* . . . . **24 C4** 51 10N 4 8 E
St. Niklaus, *Switz.* . . . . **32 D5** 46 10N 7 49 E
St-Omer, *France* . . . . **27 B9** 50 45N 2 15 E
St-Palais-sur-Mer, *France* **28 C2** 45 38N 1 5W
St-Pamphile, *Canada* **141 C6** 46 58N 69 48W
St-Pardoux-la-Rivière, *France* . . . **28 C4** 45 29N 0 45 E
St. Paris, *U.S.A.* **157 D13** 40 8N 83 58W
St. Pascal, *Canada* **141 C6** 47 32N 69 48W
St. Paul, *Canada* **142 C6** 54 0N 111 17W
St-Paul, *France* . . . . **29 D10** 44 31N 6 45 E
St. Paul, *Alaska, U.S.A.* **144 H5** 57 7N 170 17W
St. Paul, *Ind., U.S.A.* **157 E11** 39 26N 85 38W
St. Paul, *Minn., U.S.A.* **154 C8** 44 57N 93 6W
St. Paul, *Nebr., U.S.A.* **154 E5** 41 13N 98 27W
St. Paul →, *Canada* **141 B8** 51 27N 57 42W
St. Paul →, *Liberia* **112 D2** 6 25N 10 48W
St. Paul, I., *Ind. Oc.* . . . . **121 H6** 38 55 S 77 34 E
St-Paul-de-Fenouillet, *France* . . . . **28 F6** 42 48N 2 30 E
St. Paul I., *Canada* **141 C7** 47 12N 60 9W
St. Paul I., *U.S.A.* **144 H5** 57 10N 170 15W
St-Paul-lès-Dax, *France* **28 E2** 43 44N 1 3W
St. Paul Subterranean River Nat.
Park △, *Phil.* . . . . **81 F2** 10 10N 118 55 E
St. Paul's Bay, *Malta* . . . . **38 F7** 35 57N 14 24 E
St-Péray, *France* . . . . **29 D8** 44 57N 4 50 E
St. Peter, *U.S.A.* **154 C8** 44 20N 93 57W
St. Peter-Ording, *Germany* . . . . . **30 A4** 54 20N 8 36 E
St. Peter Port, *U.K.* **21 H5** 49 26N 2 33W
St. Peters, *N.S., Canada* **141 C7** 45 40N 60 53W
St. Peters, *P.E.I., Canada* **141 C7** 46 25N 62 35W
St. Petersburg = Sankt-Peterburg,
Russia . . . . **58 C6** 59 55N 30 20 E
St. Petersburg, *U.S.A.* **153 H7** 27 46N 82 39W
St. Petersburg Beach, *U.S.A.* **153 H7** 27 45N 82 45W
St-Philbert-de-Grand-Lieu, *France* **26 E5** 47 2N 1 39W
St-Philippe, *Réunion* . . . . **121 c** 21 21 S 55 44 E
St-Pie, *Canada* **151 A12** 45 30N 72 54W
St-Pierre, *Martinique* . . . . **164 c** 14 45N 61 10W
St-Pierre, *Réunion* . . . . **121 c** 21 19 S 55 28 E
St. Pierre, *St-P. & M.* **141 C8** 46 46N 56 12W
St. Pierre, *Seychelles* . . . . **121 E3** 9 20 S 46 0 E
St-Pierre, L., *Canada* **140 C5** 46 12N 72 52W
St-Pierre-d'Oléron, *France* **28 C2** 45 57N 1 19W
St-Pierre-en-Port, *France* . . . . **26 C7** 49 48N 0 30 E
St-Pierre et Miquelon □, *St-P. & M.* **141 C8** 46 55N 56 10W
St-Pierre-le-Moûtier, *France* . . . . **27 F10** 46 47N 3 7 E
St-Pierre-sur-Dives, *France* **26 C6** 49 2N 0 1W
St-Pol-de-Léon, *France* **26 D3** 48 41N 4 0W
St-Pol-sur-Mer, *France* . . . . **27 A9** 51 1N 2 20 E
St-Pol-sur-Ternoise, *France* . . . . . **27 B9** 50 23N 2 20 E
St-Pons, *France* . . . . **28 E6** 43 30N 2 45 E
St-Pourçain-sur-Sioule, *France* . . . **27 F10** 46 18N 3 18 E
St-Priest, *France* . . . . **29 C8** 45 42N 4 57 E
St-Quay-Portrieux, *France* **26 D4** 48 39N 2 51W
St. Quentin, *Canada* **141 C6** 47 30N 67 23W
St-Quentin, *France* . . . . **27 C10** 49 50N 3 16 E
St-Rambert-d'Albon, *France* . . . . **29 C8** 45 17N 4 49 E
St-Raphaël, *France* . . . . **29 E10** 43 25N 6 46 E
St. Regis, *U.S.A.* **158 C6** 47 18N 115 6W
St-Renan, *France* **26 D2** 48 26N 4 37W
St. Robert, *U.S.A.* **156 G4** 37 48N 92 9W
St-Saëns, *France* . . . . **26 C8** 49 41N 1 16 E
St-Savin, *France* . . . . **28 B4** 46 34N 0 53 E
St-Savinien, *France* **28 C3** 45 53N 0 42W
St. Sebastien, Tanjon' i, *Madag.* . . **117 A8** 12 26 S 48 44 E
St-Seine-l'Abbaye, *France* . . . . . . **27 E11** 47 26N 4 47 E
St-Sernin-sur-Rance, *France* . . . . **28 E6** 43 54N 2 35 E
St-Sever, *France* **28 E3** 43 45N 0 35W
St-Siméon, *Canada* **141 C6** 47 51N 69 54W
St. Simons I., *U.S.A.* **152 D8** 31 12N 81 15W
St. Simons Island, *U.S.A.* **149 K5** 31 9N 81 22W
St. Stephen, *Canada* **141 C6** 45 16N 67 17W
St. Stephen, *U.S.A.* **152 B10** 33 24N 79 55W
St-Sulpice, *France* . . . . **28 E5** 43 46N 1 41 E
St-Sulpice-Laurière, *France* . . . . . **28 B5** 46 3N 1 29 E
St-Sulpice-les-Feuilles, *France* . . . **28 B5** 46 19N 1 21 E
St-Syprien = St-Cyprien, *France* . . **28 F7** 42 37N 3 0 E
St. Teresa, *U.S.A.* **152 F5** 29 55N 84 27W
St-Thégonnec, *France* **26 D3** 48 31N 3 57W
St. Thomas, *Canada* **140 D3** 42 45N 81 10W
St. Thomas Bay, *Malta* . . . . **38 F8** 35 51N 14 34 E
St. Thomas I., *U.S. Virgin Is.* . . . . **165 e** 18 20N 64 55W
St-Tite, *Canada* **140 C5** 46 45N 72 34W
St-Tropez, *France* . . . . **29 E10** 43 17N 6 38 E
St. Troud = St. Truiden, *Belgium* . **24 D5** 50 48N 5 10 E
St. Truiden, *Belgium* . . . . **24 D5** 50 48N 5 10 E
St-Vaast-la-Hougue, *France* **26 C5** 49 35N 1 17W
St-Valery-en-Caux, *France* . . . . . . **26 C7** 49 52N 0 43 E
St-Valéry-sur-Somme, *France* . . . **27 B8** 50 11N 1 38 E
St-Vallier, *France* . . . . **27 F11** 46 38N 4 22 E
St-Vallier-de-Thiey, *France* . . . . . **29 E10** 43 42N 6 51 E
St-Varent, *France* **26 C6** 46 53N 0 13W
St-Vaury, *France* . . . . **28 B5** 46 12N 1 46 E
St. Vincent,
C. Verde Is. . . . . **9 j** 17 0N 25 0W
St. Vincent, *Italy* . . . . **44 C4** 45 45N 7 39 E
St. Vincent, G., *Australia* . . . . **128 C3** 35 0 S 138 0 E
St. Vincent & the Grenadines ■,
W. Indies **165 D7** 13 0N 61 10W
St-Vincent-de-Tyrosse, *France* . . . **28 E2** 43 39N 1 19W
St. Vincent I., *U.S.A.* **153 F4** 29 42N 85 3W
St. Vincent Passage, *W. Indies* . . . **165 D7** 13 30N 61 0W
St-Vith, *Belgium* . . . . **24 D6** 50 17N 6 9 E
St-Vivien-de-Médoc, *France* **28 C2** 45 25N 1 2W
St. Walburg, *Canada* **143 C7** 53 39N 109 12W
St-Yrieix-la-Perche, *France* . . . . . **28 C5** 45 31N 1 12 E
Saintala, *India* . . . . **94 D6** 20 26N 83 20 E
Ste-Adresse, *France* . . . . **26 C7** 49 31N 0 5 E
Ste-Agathe-des-Monts, *Canada* . . **140 C5** 46 3N 74 17W
Ste-Anne, *Guadeloupe* . . . . **164 b** 16 13N 61 24W
Ste-Anne, *Seychelles* . . . . **121 b** 4 35 S 55 1 E
Ste-Anne, L., *Canada* **141 B6** 50 0N 67 42W
Ste-Anne-des-Monts-Tourelle,
Canada **141 C6** 49 8N 66 30W
Ste-Croix, *Switz.* . . . . **32 C3** 46 49N 6 34 E
Ste-Énimie, *France* . . . . **28 D7** 44 22N 3 26 E
Ste-Foy-la-Grande, *France* . . . . . . **28 D4** 44 50N 0 13 E
Ste. Genevieve, *U.S.A.* **156 G6** 37 59N 90 2W
Ste-Hermine, *France* **28 B2** 46 32N 1 4W

Ste-Livrade-sur-Lot, *France* . . . . . **28 D4** 44 24N 0 36 E
Ste-Marguerite →, *Canada* **141 B6** 50 9N 66 36W
Ste. Marie, *Gabon* . . . . **114 C2** 3 48 S 11 1 E
Ste-Marie, *Martinique* . . . . **164 c** 14 48N 61 1W
Ste-Marie, *Réunion* . . . . **121 c** 20 53 S 55 33 E
Ste-Marie-aux-Mines, *France* . . . . **27 D14** 48 15N 7 12 E
Ste-Marie de la Madeleine, *Canada* **141 C5** 46 26N 71 0W
Ste-Maure-de-Touraine, *France* . . **26 E7** 47 7N 0 37 E
Ste-Maxime, *France* . . . . **29 E10** 43 19N 6 39 E
Ste-Menehould, *France* . . . . **27 C11** 49 5N 4 54 E
Ste-Mère-Église, *France* **26 C5** 49 24N 1 19W
Ste-Rose, *Guadeloupe* . . . . **164 b** 16 20N 61 45W
Ste-Rose, *Réunion* . . . . **121 c** 21 8 S 55 45 E
Ste. Rose du Lac, *Canada* **143 C9** 51 4N 99 30W
Ste-Savine, *France* . . . . **27 D11** 48 18N 4 3 E
Ste-Sigolène, *France* . . . . **29 C8** 45 15N 4 14 E
Saintes, *France* **28 C3** 45 45N 0 37W
Saintes, I. des, *Guadeloupe* . . . . . **164 b** 15 50N 61 35W
Stes-Maries-de-la-Mer, *France* . . . **29 E8** 43 26N 4 26 E
Saintfield, *U.K.* **23 B6** 54 28N 5 49W
Saintonge, *France* **28 C3** 45 40N 0 50W
Saipan, *Pac. Oc.* . . . . **134 F6** 15 12N 145 45 E
Sairang, *India* . . . . **90 D4** 23 50N 92 45 E
Sairecábur, Cerro, *Bolivia* . . . . . . **174 A2** 22 43 S 67 54W
Saitama □, *Japan* . . . . **73 A11** 36 25N 139 30 E
Saiteli = Kadınhanı, *Turkey* . . . . . **100 C5** 38 14N 32 13 E
Saiti, *Moldova* . . . . **53 D14** 46 30N 29 24 E
Saito, *Japan* . . . . **72 E3** 32 3N 131 24 E
Saiyid, *Pakistan* . . . . **92 C5** 33 7N 73 2 E
Saja-Besaya, Parque Natural de △,
Spain **42 B6** 43 10N 4 9W
Sajama, *Bolivia* . . . . **172 D4** 18 7 S 69 0W
Sajama, Nevado, *Bolivia* . . . . **172 D4** 18 6 S 68 54W
Sajan, *Serbia, Yug.* . . . . **52 E5** 45 50N 20 20 E
Sajószentpéter, *Hungary* . . . . **52 B5** 48 12N 20 44 E
Sajum, *India* . . . . **93 C8** 33 20N 79 0 E
Sak →, *S. Africa* . . . . **116 E3** 30 52 S 20 25 E
Saka Kalat, *Pakistan* . . . . **91 D2** 27 1N 65 3 E
Sakaba, *Nigeria* . . . . **113 C6** 11 4N 5 35 E
Sakai, *Japan* . . . . **73 C7** 34 30N 135 30 E
Sakaide, *Japan* . . . . **72 C5** 34 19N 133 50 E
Sakaiminato, *Japan* . . . . **72 B5** 35 38N 133 11 E
Sakākah, *Si. Arabia* . . . . **96 D4** 30 0N 40 8 E
Sakakawea, L., *U.S.A.* **154 B4** 47 30N 101 25W
Sakami →, *Canada* **140 B4** 53 40N 76 40W
Sakami, L., *Canada* **140 B4** 53 15N 77 0W
Säkâne, 'Erg i-n, *Mali* **113 A4** 20 30N 1 30W
Sakania, *Dem. Rep. of the Congo* . **119 E2** 12 43 S 28 30 E
Sakar I., *Papua N. G.* . . . . **132 C5** 5 25 S 148 6 E
Sakaraha, *Madag.* . . . . **117 C7** 22 55 S 44 32 E
Sakarya, *Turkey* . . . . **100 B4** 40 48N 30 25 E
Sakarya →, *Turkey* . . . . **100 B4** 41 7N 30 39 E
Sakashima-Guntō, *Japan* . . . . **71 M2** 24 46N 124 0 E
Sakassou, *Ivory C.* **112 D3** 7 29N 5 19W
Sakata, *Japan* . . . . **70 E9** 38 55N 139 50 E
Sakawa, *Japan* . . . . **72 B5** 33 28N 133 11 E
Sakchu, *N. Korea* . . . . **75 D13** 40 23N 125 2 E
Sakeny →, *Madag.* . . . . **117 C8** 20 0 S 45 25 E
Sakété, *Benin* . . . . **113 D5** 6 40N 2 45 E
Sakha □, *Russia* . . . . **67 C13** 66 0N 130 0 E
Sakhalin, *Russia* . . . . **67 D15** 51 0N 143 0 E
Sakhalinskiy Zaliv, *Russia* . . . . . . **67 D15** 54 0N 141 0 E
Sakhi Gopal, *India* . . . . **94 E7** 19 58N 85 50 E
Şaki, *Azerbaijan* . . . . **61 K8** 41 10N 47 5 E
Šakiai, *Lithuania* . . . . **15 J20** 54 59N 23 2 E
Sakmara →, *Russia* . . . . **64 F5** 51 46N 55 1 E
Sakoli, *India* . . . . **94 D4** 21 5N 79 59 E
Sakon Nakhon, *Thailand* . . . . **86 D5** 17 10N 104 9 E
Sakrand, *Pakistan* . . . . **92 F3** 26 10N 68 15 E
Sakri, *Maharashtra, India* . . . . **93 F12** 26 13N 86 5 E
Sakri, *Maharashtra, India* . . . . **94 D2** 21 2N 74 20 E
Sakrivier, *S. Africa* . . . . **116 E3** 30 54 S 20 28 E
Sakskøbing, *Denmark* . . . . **17 K5** 54 49N 11 39 E
Sakti, *India* . . . . **93 H10** 22 2N 82 58 E
Sakuma, *Japan* . . . . **73 A10** 36 17N 138 31 E
Sakuma, *Japan* . . . . **73 B9** 35 3N 137 49 E
Sakura, *Japan* . . . . **73 B12** 35 43N 140 14 E
Sakurai, *Japan* . . . . **73 C7** 34 30N 135 51 E
Saky, *Ukraine* . . . . **59 K7** 45 9N 33 34 E
Sal →, *Russia* . . . . **61 G5** 47 31N 40 45 E
Sal Rei, *C. Verde Is.* . . . . **9 j** 16 11N 22 53W
Sala, *Eritrea* . . . . **107 D4** 16 53N 37 36 E
Sala, *U.K.* . . . . **23 A11** 56 58N 37 36 E
Sala, *Sweden* . . . . **16 E10** 59 58N 16 35 E
Sala →, *Eritrea* . . . . **107 D4** 16 53N 37 36 E
Sala, O. →, *Chad* . . . . **109 E4** 17 0N 20 53 E
Sala Consilina, *Italy* . . . . **47 B8** 40 23N 15 36 E
Sala-y-Gómez, *Pac. Oc.* . . . . **135 K17** 26 28 S 105 28W
Salaberry-de-Valleyfield, *Canada* . **140 C5** 45 15N 74 8W
Salacgriva, *Latvia* **159 K6** 32 30N 115 40W
Salada, L., *Mexico* **159 K6** 32 20N 115 40W
Saladas, *Argentina* . . . . **174 B4** 28 15 S 58 40W
Saladillo, *Argentina* . . . . **174 D4** 35 40 S 59 55W
Salado →, *Buenos Aires, Argentina* **174 D4** 35 44 S 57 22W
Salado →, *La Pampa, Argentina* . . **176 A3** 37 30 S 67 0W
Salado →, *Río Negro, Argentina* . **176 B3** 41 34 S 65 3W
Salado →, *Santa Fe, Argentina* . . . **174 C3** 31 40 S 60 41W
Salado →, *Mexico* **155 M5** 26 52N 99 19W
Salaga, *Ghana* **113 D4** 8 31N 0 31W
Sálah, *Syria* . . . . **103 C5** 32 40N 36 45 E
Sălaj □, *Romania* . . . . **52 C8** 47 15N 23 0 E
Sálakhos, *Greece* . . . . **38 E11** 36 17N 27 57 E
Salal, *Chad* . . . . **109 F3** 14 48N 17 12 E
Salala, *Liberia* **112 D2** 6 42N 10 7W
Salala, *Sudan* . . . . **106 C4** 21 17N 36 16 E
Salâlah, *Oman* . . . . **99 G5** 16 56N 53 59 E
Salamanca, *Chile* . . . . **174 C1** 31 46 S 70 59W
Salamanca, *Spain* **42 E5** 40 58N 5 39W
Salamanca, *U.S.A.* **150 D6** 42 10N 78 43W
Salamanca □, *Spain* **42 E5** 40 57N 5 40W
Salamat, Bahr →, *Chad* . . . . **109 G3** 9 20N 18 0 E
Salāmatābād, *Iran* . . . . **96 C5** 35 39N 47 50 E
Salamina, *Colombia* **168 B2** 5 25N 75 29W
Salamis, *Cyprus* . . . . **39 E9** 35 11N 33 54 E
Salamís, *Greece* . . . . **48 D5** 37 56N 23 30 E
Salamonie L., *U.S.A.* **157 D11** 40 46N 85 37W
Salaóra, *Greece* . . . . **39 A2** 39 0N 20 52 E
Salar de Atacama, *Chile* . . . . **174 A2** 23 30 S 68 25W
Salar de Uyuni, *Bolivia* . . . . **172 E4** 20 30 S 67 45W
Sălard, *Romania* . . . . **52 C7** 47 12N 22 3 E
Salas, *Spain* **42 B4** 43 25N 6 15W
Salas de los Infantes, *Spain* **42 C7** 42 1N 3 28W
Salatiga, *Indonesia* . . . . **85 D4** 7 19 S 110 30 E
Salavat, *Russia* . . . . **64 E5** 53 21N 55 55 E
Salaverry, *Peru* . . . . **172 B2** 8 15 S 79 0W
Salawati, *Indonesia* . . . . **83 B4** 1 7 S 130 52 E
Salay, *Phil.* . . . . **81 G5** 8 52N 124 47 E
Salaya, *India* . . . . **92 H3** 22 19N 69 35 E
Salayar, *Indonesia* . . . . **83 F6** 5 7 S 120 30 E
Salazar →, *Spain* **40 C3** 42 40N 1 20W
Salbris, *France* . . . . **27 E9** 47 25N 2 3 E
Salcedo, *Phil.* . . . . **81 F5** 11 9N 125 40 E
Salcia, *Romania* . . . . **53 G9** 43 56N 24 55 E
Sălciua, *Romania* . . . . **53 D8** 46 24N 23 26 E
Salcombe, *U.K.* **21 G4** 50 14N 3 47W
Saldaña, *Spain* **42 C6** 42 32N 4 48W
Saldanha, *S. Africa* . . . . **116 E2** 33 0 S 17 58 E
Saldanha B., *S. Africa* . . . . **116 E2** 33 6 S 18 0 E
Saldus, *Latvia* . . . . **15 H20** 56 38N 22 30 E
Saldus □, *Latvia* . . . . **54 B9** 56 35N 22 30 E
Sale, *Australia* . . . . **127 F4** 38 6 S 147 6 E
Sale, *Burma* . . . . **90 E5** 20 50N 94 45 E
Salé, *Italy* . . . . **44 D5** 44 59N 8 48 E

Salé, *Morocco* **110 B3** 34 3N 6 48W
Sale, *U.K.* **20 D5** 53 26N 2 19W
Sale City, *U.S.A.* **152 D5** 31 16N 84 1W
Salekhard, *Russia* . . . . **66 C7** 66 30N 66 35 E
Saleleloga, *Samoa* . . . . **133 W23** 13 41 S 172 11W
Salem, *India* . . . . **95 J4** 11 40N 78 11 E
Salem, *Fla., U.S.A.* **152 F6** 29 53N 83 25W
Salem, *Ill., U.S.A.* **156 F8** 38 38N 88 57W
Salem, *Ind., U.S.A.* **157 F10** 38 36N 86 6W
Salem, *Mass., U.S.A.* **151 D14** 42 31N 70 53W
Salem, *Mo., U.S.A.* **155 G9** 37 39N 91 32W
Salem, *N.H., U.S.A.* **151 D13** 42 45N 71 12W
Salem, *N.J., U.S.A.* **148 F8** 39 34N 75 28W
Salem, *N.Y., U.S.A.* **151 C11** 43 10N 73 20W
Salem, *Ohio, U.S.A.* **150 F4** 40 54N 80 52W
Salem, *Oreg., U.S.A.* **158 D2** 44 56N 123 2W
Salem, *S. Dak., U.S.A.* **154 D6** 43 44N 97 23W
Salem, *Va., U.S.A.* **148 G5** 37 18N 80 3W
Salemi, *Italy* . . . . **46 E5** 37 49N 12 48 E
Sälen, *Sweden* . . . . **16 C7** 61 15N 13 22 E
Salernes, *France* . . . . **29 E10** 43 34N 6 15 E
Salerno, *Italy* . . . . **47 B7** 40 41N 14 47 E
Salerno, G. di, *Italy* . . . . **47 B7** 40 32N 14 42 E
Sales, *Brazil* . . . . **169 D5** 4 2 S 63 40W
Salford, *U.K.* **20 D5** 53 30N 2 18W
Salgir →, *Ukraine* . . . . **59 K8** 45 38N 35 1 E
Salgótarján, *Hungary* . . . . **52 B4** 48 5N 19 47 E
Salgueiro, *Brazil* . . . . **170 C4** 8 4 S 39 6W
Salher, *India* . . . . **94 D1** 20 40N 73 55 E
Salhus, *Norway* . . . . **18 D2** 60 30N 5 15 E
Salibabu, *Indonesia* . . . . **79 D7** 3 51N 126 40 E
Salibea, *Trin. & Tob.* **169 F9** 10 43N 61 2W
Salida, *U.S.A.* **146 C5** 38 32N 106 0W
Salies-de-Béarn, *France* **28 E3** 43 28N 0 56W
Şalif, *Yemen* . . . . **98 D3** 15 18N 42 41 E
Salihli, *Turkey* . . . . **100 C3** 38 28N 28 8 E
Salihorsk, *Belarus* . . . . **59 F4** 52 51N 27 27 E
Salin, *Burma* . . . . **90 E5** 20 35N 94 40 E
Salina, *Italy* . . . . **47 D7** 38 34N 14 50 E
Salina, *Kans., U.S.A.* **154 F6** 38 50N 97 37W
Salina, *Utah, U.S.A.* **159 G8** 38 58N 111 51W
Salina Cruz, *Mexico* **163 D5** 16 10N 95 10W
Salina di Margherita di Savoia,
Riserva Statale △, *Italy* . . . . . . **47 A9** 41 23N 16 4 E
Salinas, *Brazil* . . . . **171 E3** 16 10 S 42 10W
Salinas, *Chile* . . . . **174 A2** 23 31 S 69 29W
Salinas, *Ecuador* . . . . **168 D1** 2 10 S 80 58W
Salinas →, *Guatemala* **163 D6** 16 28N 90 31W
Salinas →, *U.S.A.* **160 J5** 36 45N 121 48W
Salinas, B. das, *Angola* . . . . **115 E2** 14 15 S 12 21 E
Salinas, B. de, *Nic.* **164 D2** 11 4N 85 45W
Salinas, Pampa de las, *Argentina* . **174 C2** 31 58 S 66 42W
Salinas Ambargasta, *Argentina* . . . **174 B3** 29 0 S 65 0W
Salinas de Hidalgo, *Mexico* **162 C4** 22 30N 101 40W
Salinas Grandes, *Argentina* . . . . . **174 C3** 30 0 S 65 0W
Salinas Pueblo Missions Nat.
Monument △, *U.S.A.* **159 J10** 34 16N 106 5W
Saline →, *U.S.A.* **157 B13** 42 0N 83 47W
Saline →, *Ark., U.S.A.* **155 J8** 33 10N 92 8W
Saline →, *Kans., U.S.A.* **154 F6** 38 52N 97 30W
Saline di Trapani e Paceco, Riserva
Naturale △, *Italy* . . . . **46 E5** 37 59N 12 28 E
Salines, C. de ses, *Spain* . . . . **38 B4** 39 16N 3 4 E
Salinópolis, *Brazil* . . . . **170 B2** 0 40 S 47 20W
Salins-les-Bains, *France* . . . . **27 F12** 46 58N 5 52 E
Salir, *Portugal* **43 H2** 37 14N 8 2W
Salisbury = Harare, *Zimbabwe* . . . **119 F3** 17 43 S 31 2 E
Salisbury, *U.K.* **21 F6** 51 4N 1 47W
Salisbury, *Md., U.S.A.* **148 F8** 38 22N 75 36W
Salisbury, *Mo., U.S.A.* **156 E4** 39 25N 92 48W
Salisbury, *N.C., U.S.A.* **149 H5** 35 40N 80 29W
Salisbury I., *Canada* **139 B12** 63 30N 77 0W
Salisbury Plain, *U.K.* **21 F6** 51 14N 1 55W
Săliște, *Romania* . . . . **53 E8** 45 45N 23 56 E
Salitre →, *Brazil* . . . . **170 C3** 9 29 S 40 39W
Salka, *Nigeria* . . . . **113 C5** 10 20N 4 58 E
Salkehatchie →, *U.S.A.* **152 C9** 32 37N 80 53W
Şalkhad, *Syria* . . . . **103 C5** 32 29N 36 43 E
Salla, *Finland* . . . . **14 C23** 66 50N 28 49 E
Sallanches, *France* . . . . **29 C10** 45 55N 6 38 E
Sallent, *Spain* . . . . **40 D6** 41 49N 1 54 E
Salles, *France* **28 D3** 44 33N 0 52W
Salles-Curan, *France* . . . . **28 D6** 44 11N 2 48 E
Salling, *Denmark* . . . . **17 H2** 56 40N 8 55 E
Salliq, *Canada* **139 B11** 64 8N 83 10W
Sallisaw, *U.S.A.* **155 H7** 35 28N 94 47W
Sallom Junction, *Sudan* . . . . **106 D4** 19 17N 37 6 E
Salluit, *Canada* **139 B12** 62 14N 75 38W
Salmās, *Iran* . . . . **101 C11** 38 11N 44 47 E
Salmerón, *Spain* **42 E2** 40 33N 2 29W
Salmon, *U.S.A.* **162 D5** 49 10N 117 20W
Salmon →, *U.S.A.* **158 D7** 45 11N 113 54W
Salmon →, *U.S.A.* **142 C4** 54 0N 122 40W
Salmon Arm, *Canada* **142 C5** 50 40N 119 15W
Salmon Gums, *Australia* . . . . **125 F3** 32 59 S 121 38 E
Salmon River Mts., *U.S.A.* **158 D6** 45 0N 114 30W
Salo, *C.A.R.* . . . . **114 B3** 3 10N 16 8 E
Salo, *Finland* . . . . **15 F20** 60 22N 23 10 E
Salò, *Italy* . . . . **44 C7** 45 36N 10 31 E
Salobreña, *Spain* **43 J7** 36 44N 3 35W
Salome, *U.S.A.* **161 M13** 33 47N 113 37W
Salon, *India* . . . . **93 F9** 26 2N 81 27 E
Salon-de-Provence, *France* . . . . . . **29 E9** 43 39N 5 6 E
Salonga-Nord, Parc Nat. de la △,
Dem. Rep. of the Congo . . . . . **114 C4** 1 55 S 21 45 E
Salonga-Sud, Parc Nat. de la △,
Dem. Rep. of the Congo . . . . . **114 C4** 2 25 S 21 0 E
Salonica = Thessaloníki, *Greece* . . **50 F6** 40 38N 22 58 E
Salonta, *Romania* . . . . **52 D6** 46 49N 21 42 E
Salor →, *Spain* **43 F3** 39 39N 7 3W
Salou, *Spain* . . . . **40 D6** 41 4N 1 8 E
Salou, C. de, *Spain* . . . . **40 D6** 41 3N 1 10 E
Saloum →, *Senegal* **112 C1** 13 50N 16 45W
Salpausselkä, *Finland* . . . . **15 F22** 61 0N 27 0 E
Salsacate, *Argentina* . . . . **174 C2** 31 20 S 65 5W
Salses, *France* . . . . **28 F6** 42 50N 2 55 E
Salsette I., *India* . . . . **94 E1** 19 5N 72 50 E
Salsk, *Russia* . . . . **61 G6** 46 28N 41 30 E
Salso →, *Italy* . . . . **46 E6** 37 6N 13 57 E
Salsomaggiore Terme, *Italy* . . . . . **44 D6** 44 49N 9 59 E
Salt, *Spain* . . . . **40 D7** 41 58N 2 47 E
Salt →, *U.S.A.* **142 B6** 60 0N 112 25W
Salt →, *Ariz., U.S.A.* **159 K7** 33 23N 112 19W
Salt →, *Mo., U.S.A.* **156 E5** 39 28N 91 4W
Salt Cay, *Bahamas* . . . . **9 b** 25 0N 77 18W
Salt L., *U.S.A.* **145 K14** 21 21N 157 55W
Salt Lake City, *U.S.A.* **158 F8** 40 45N 111 53W
Salt Range, *Pakistan* . . . . **92 C5** 32 30N 72 25 E
Salt Springs, *U.S.A.* **153 F8** 29 21N 81 44W
Salta, *Argentina* . . . . **174 A2** 24 57 S 65 25W
Salta □, *Argentina* . . . . **174 A2** 24 48 S 65 30W
Saltara, *Italy* . . . . **45 E9** 43 45N 12 50 E
Saltcoats, *U.K.* **22 F4** 55 38N 4 47W
Saltee Is., *Ireland* **23 D5** 52 7N 6 37W
Saltfjellet, *Norway* . . . . **14 C16** 66 40N 15 15 E
Saltfjorden, *Norway* . . . . **14 C16** 67 15N 14 10 E
Saltholm, *Denmark* . . . . **17 J6** 55 38N 12 43 E
Salthólmavík, *Iceland* **11 B5** 65 24N 21 57W

Saltillo, Mexico **162 B4** 25 25N 101 0W
Salto, Argentina . . . . **174 C3** 34 20 S 60 15W
Salto, Uruguay . . . . **174 C4** 31 27 S 57 50W
Salto da Divisa, Brazil . . . . **171 E4** 16 0 S 39 57W
Salto del Guaíra, Paraguay . . . . . . **175 A5** 24 3 S 54 17W
Salton City, U.S.A. **161 M11** 33 29N 115 51W
Salton Sea, U.S.A. **161 M11** 33 15N 115 45W
Saltpond, Ghana **113 D4** 5 15N 1 3W
Saltrød, Norway . . . . **18 F5** 58 30N 8 49 E
Saltsburg, U.S.A. **150 F5** 40 29N 79 27W
Saltsjöbaden, Sweden . . . . **16 E12** 59 15N 18 20 E
Saluda →, U.S.A. **152 A8** 34 0N 81 46W
Saluda →, U.S.A. **149 J5** 34 1N 81 4W
Sálvora, I. de, Spain **42 C2** 42 30N 8 58W
Salween →, Burma . . . . **90 G6** 16 31N 97 37 E
Salyan, Azerbaijan . . . . **101 C13** 39 33N 48 59 E
Salza →, Austria . . . . **34 D7** 47 40N 14 43 E
Salzach →, Austria . . . . **34 C5** 48 12N 12 56 E
Salzburg, Austria . . . . **34 D6** 47 48N 13 2 E
Salzburg □, Austria . . . . **34 D6** 47 15N 13 0 E
Salzgitter, Germany . . . . **30 C6** 52 9N 10 19 E
Salzkotten, Germany . . . . **30 D4** 51 40N 8 37 E
Salzwedel, Germany . . . . **30 C7** 52 52N 11 10 E
Sam, Gabon . . . . **114 B2** 0 58N 11 16 E
Sam, India . . . . **92 F4** 26 50N 70 31 E
Sam Neua, Laos . . . . **76 G5** 20 29N 104 5 E
Sam Ngao, Thailand . . . . **86 D2** 17 18N 99 0 E
Sam Rayburn Reservoir, U.S.A. . . . **155 K7** 31 4N 94 5W
Sam Son, Vietnam . . . . **86 C5** 19 44N 105 54 E
Sam Teu, Laos . . . . **86 C5** 19 59N 104 38 E
Sama de Langreo = Langreo, Spain . **42 B5** 43 18N 5 40W
Samacimbo, Angola . . . . **115 E3** 13 33 S 16 59 E
Samagaltay, Russia . . . . **67 D10** 50 36N 95 3 E
Samä'il, Oman . . . . **99 B7** 23 40N 57 50 E
Samaipata, Bolivia . . . . **173 D5** 18 9 S 63 52W
Samal, Phil. . . . . **81 H5** 7 5N 125 42 E
Samal I., Phil. . . . . **81 H5** 7 5N 125 44 E
Samales Group, Phil. . . . . **81 J3** 6 0N 122 0 E
Samalkot, India . . . . **94 F6** 17 3N 82 13 E
Samâlût, Egypt . . . . **106 B3** 28 20N 30 42 E
Samana, India . . . . **92 D7** 30 10N 76 13 E
Samana Cay, Bahamas **165 B5** 23 3N 73 45W
Samandağı, Turkey . . . . **100 D6** 36 5N 35 59 E
Samandıra, Turkey . . . . **51 F13** 40 59N 29 13 E
Samanga, Tanzania . . . . **119 D4** 8 20 S 39 13 E
Samangân □, Afghan. . . . . **91 A3** 36 15N 68 3 E
Samangwa, Dem. Rep. of the Congo **118 C1** 4 23 S 24 10 E
Samani, Japan . . . . **70 C11** 42 7N 142 56 E
Samanlı Dağları, Turkey . . . . **51 F13** 40 32N 29 10 E
Samar, Phil. . . . . **81 E5** 12 0N 125 0 E
Samar □, Phil. . . . . **81 F5** 11 50N 125 0 E
Samar →, Phil. . . . . **80 E5** 12 0N 124 15 E
Samara, Russia . . . . **60 D10** 53 8N 50 6 E
Samara →, Russia . . . . **60 D10** 53 10N 50 4 E
Samara →, Ukraine . . . . **59 H8** 48 25N 35 0 E
Samarai, Papua N. G. . . . . **132 F6** 10 39 S 150 41 E
Samaria = Shōmron, West Bank . . . **103 C4** 32 15N 35 13 E
Samariá, Greece . . . . **39 E4** 35 17N 23 58 E
Samaria △, Greece . . . . **48 F5** 35 18N 23 57 E
Samariapo, Venezuela **168 B4** 5 15N 67 48W
Samarinda, Indonesia . . . . **85 C5** 0 30 S 117 9 E
Samarkand = Samarqand,
  Uzbekistan . . . . **65 D3** 39 40N 66 55 E
Samarqand, Uzbekistan . . . . **65 D3** 39 40N 66 55 E
Sāmarrā, Iraq . . . . **101 E10** 34 12N 43 52 E
Samastipur, India . . . . **93 G11** 25 50N 85 50 E
Samate, Indonesia . . . . **83 B4** 0 58 S 131 4 E
Samaúma, Brazil . . . . **173 B5** 7 50 S 60 2W
Şamaxı, Azerbaijan . . . . **61 K9** 40 38N 48 37 E
Samba, Équateur, Dem. Rep. of
  the Congo . . . . **114 B4** 0 13N 21 25 E
Samba, Maniema, Dem. Rep. of
  the Congo . . . . **118 C2** 4 38 S 26 22 E
Samba, India . . . . **93 C6** 32 32N 75 10 E
Samba Caju, Angola . . . . **115 D3** 8 46 S 15 24 E
Sambaíba, Brazil . . . . **170 C2** 7 8 S 45 21W
Sambalpur, India . . . . **94 D7** 21 28N 84 4 E
Sambar, Tanjung, Indonesia . . . . . . **85 C4** 2 59 S 110 19 E
Sambas, Indonesia . . . . **85 B3** 1 20N 109 20 E
Sambava, Madag. . . . . **117 A9** 14 16 S 50 10 E
Sambawizi, Zimbabwe . . . . **119 F2** 18 24 S 26 13 E
Sambhal, India . . . . **93 E8** 28 35N 78 37 E
Sambhar, India . . . . **92 F6** 26 52N 75 6 E
Sambhar L., India . . . . **92 F6** 26 55N 75 12 E
Sambiase, Italy . . . . **47 D9** 38 58N 16 17 E
Sambir, Ukraine . . . . **59 H2** 49 30N 23 10 E
Sambo, Angola . . . . **115 E3** 13 9 S 16 4 E
Sambor, Cambodia . . . . **86 F6** 12 46N 106 0 E
Samborombón, B., Argentina . . . . . **174 D4** 36 5 S 57 20W
Sambuca di Sicília, Italy . . . . **46 E6** 37 39N 13 7 E
Samburu Nat. Reserve △, Kenya . . . **118 B4** 0 37N 37 31 E
Samch'ŏk, S. Korea . . . . **75 F15** 37 30N 129 10 E
Samch'onp'o, S. Korea . . . . **75 G15** 35 0N 128 6 E
Same, Tanzania . . . . **118 C4** 4 2 S 37 38 E
Samedan, Switz. . . . . **33 C9** 46 32N 9 52 E
Samer, France . . . . **27 B8** 50 38N 1 44 E
Samfya, Zambia . . . . **119 E2** 11 22 S 29 31 E
Samhān, Jabal, Oman . . . . **99 C6** 17 12N 54 55 E
Sámi, Greece . . . . **39 C2** 38 15N 20 39 E
Samka, Burma . . . . **90 E6** 20 9N 96 57 E
Şamkir, Azerbaijan . . . . **61 K8** 40 50N 46 0 E
Şamlı, Turkey . . . . **49 B9** 39 48N 27 51 E
Sammanturai, Sri Lanka . . . . **95 L5** 7 36N 81 39 E
Samnah, Si. Arabia . . . . **96 E3** 25 10N 37 15 E
Samnaun, Switz. . . . . **33 C10** 46 57N 10 22 E
Samnū, Libya . . . . **108 C2** 27 15N 14 55 E
Samo Alto, Chile . . . . **174 C1** 30 22 S 71 0W
Samoa ■, Pac. Oc. . . . . **133 X24** 14 0 S 172 0W
Samoan Is., Pac. Oc. . . . . **133 X24** 14 0 S 171 0W
Samobor, Croatia . . . . **45 C12** 45 47N 15 44 E
Samoëns, France . . . . **27 F13** 46 5N 6 45 E
Samokov, Bulgaria . . . . **50 D7** 42 18N 23 35 E
Šamorín, Slovak Rep. . . . . **35 C10** 48 2N 17 19 E
Samorogouan, Burkina Faso **112 C4** 11 21N 4 57W
Sámos, Greece . . . . **49 D8** 37 45N 26 50 E
Samoš, Serbia, Yug. . . . . **52 E5** 45 13N 20 46 E
Samos, Spain **42 C3** 42 44N 7 20W
Sámos □, Greece . . . . **49 D8** 37 45N 26 50 E
Samoset, U.S.A. **153 H7** 27 28N 82 33W
Samosir, Indonesia . . . . **84 B1** 2 55N 98 50 E
Samothráki = Mathráki, Greece . . . **38 B9** 39 48N 19 31 E
Samothráki, Greece . . . . **51 F9** 40 28N 25 28 E
Samoylovka, Russia . . . . **60 E6** 51 12N 43 43 E
Sampa, Angola . . . . **115 E3** 10 38 S 18 56 E
Sampa, Ghana **112 D4** 8 0N 2 36W
Sampacho, Argentina . . . . **174 C3** 33 20 S 64 50W
Sampalan, Indonesia . . . . **79 K18** 8 41 S 115 34 E
Sampang, Indonesia . . . . **85 D4** 7 11 S 113 13 E
Samper de Calanda, Spain **40 D4** 41 11N 0 28W
Sampéyre, Italy . . . . **44 D4** 44 34N 7 11 E
Sampit, Indonesia . . . . **85 C4** 2 34 S 113 0 E

Sampit →, Indonesia . . . . **85 C4** 2 44 S 112 54 E
Sampit, Teluk, Indonesia . . . . **85 C4** 3 5 S 113 3 E
Sampsoús, Greece . . . . **39 A2** 39 5N 20 45 E
Sampun, Papua N. G. . . . . **132 C7** 5 21 S 152 8 E
Samrong, Cambodia . . . . **86 E4** 14 15N 103 30 E
Samrong, Thailand . . . . **86 E3** 15 10N 100 40 E
Samsø, Denmark . . . . **17 J4** 55 50N 10 35 E
Samsø Bælt, Denmark . . . . **17 J4** 55 45N 10 45 E
Samsun, Turkey . . . . **100 B7** 41 15N 36 22 E
Samtredia, Georgia . . . . **61 J6** 42 7N 42 24 E
Samui, Ko, Thailand . . . . **87 b** 9 30N 100 0 E
Samur →, Russia . . . . **61 K9** 41 53N 48 32 E
Samurskiy Khrebet, Russia . . . . **61 K8** 41 55N 47 11 E
Samusole, Dem. Rep. of the Congo **119 E1** 10 2 S 24 0 E
Samut Prakan, Thailand . . . . **86 F3** 13 32N 100 40 E
Samut Songkhram →, Thailand . . . **78 B1** 13 24N 100 1 E
Samwari, Pakistan . . . . **92 E2** 28 30N 66 46 E
San, Mali **112 C4** 13 15N 4 57W
San →, Cambodia . . . . **86 F5** 13 32N 105 57 E
San →, Poland . . . . **55 H8** 50 45N 21 51 E
San Adrián, Spain **40 C3** 42 20N 1 56W
San Adrián, C. de, Spain **42 B2** 43 21N 8 50W
San Agustín, Colombia **168 C2** 1 53N 76 16W
San Agustin, U.S.A. . . . . **80 E4** 12 34N 122 6 E
San Agustin, C., Phil. . . . . **81 H6** 6 20N 126 13 E
San Agustín de Valle Fértil,
  Argentina . . . . **174 C2** 30 35 S 67 30W
San Ambrosio, Pac. Oc. . . . . **135 K20** 26 28 S 79 53W
San Andreas, U.S.A. **160 G6** 38 12N 120 41W
San Andres, Catanduanes, Phil. . . . **80 E5** 13 36N 124 6 E
San Andres, Romblon, Phil. . . . . . . **80 E4** 13 9N 122 41 E
San Andres, Romblon, Phil. . . . . . . **80 E4** 12 31N 122 2 E
San Andrés, I. de, Caribbean **164 D3** 12 42N 81 46W
San Andrés del Rabanedo, Spain . . **42 C5** 42 37N 5 36W
San Andres Mts., U.S.A. **159 K10** 33 0N 106 30W
San Andrés Tuxtla, Mexico **163 D5** 18 30N 95 20W
San Angelo, U.S.A. **155 K4** 31 28N 100 26W
San Anselmo, U.S.A. **160 H4** 37 59N 122 34W
San Antonio, Belize **163 D7** 16 15N 89 2W
San Antonio, Chile . . . . **174 C1** 33 40 S 71 40W
San Antonio, Phil. . . . . **80 D3** 14 57N 120 5 E
San Antonio, N. Mex., U.S.A. **159 K10** 33 55N 106 52W
San Antonio, Tex., U.S.A. **155 L5** 29 25N 98 30W
San Antonio, Venezuela **168 C4** 3 30N 66 44W
San Antonio →, U.S.A. **155 L6** 28 30N 96 54W
San Antonio, C., Argentina . . . . **174 D4** 36 15 S 56 40W
San Antonio, C., Cuba **164 B3** 21 50N 84 57W
San Antonio, C. de, Spain . . . . **41 G5** 38 48N 0 12 E
San Antonio, Mt., U.S.A. **161 L9** 34 17N 117 38W
San Antonio Bay, Phil. . . . . **81 G1** 8 38N 117 35 E
San Antonio de los Baños, Cuba . . **164 B3** 22 54N 82 31W
San Antonio de los Cobres,
  Argentina . . . . **174 A2** 24 10 S 66 17W
San Antonio Oeste, Argentina . . . . **176 B4** 40 40 S 65 0W
San Arcángelo, Italy . . . . **47 B9** 40 14N 16 14 E
San Ardo, U.S.A. **160 J6** 36 1N 120 54W
San Augustín, Canary Is. **9 e1** 27 47N 15 32W
San Augustine, U.S.A. **155 K7** 31 30N 94 7W
San Bartolomé, Canary Is. **9 e2** 28 59N 13 37W
San Bartolomé de Tirajana,
  Canary Is. **9 e1** 27 54N 15 34W
San Bartolomeo in Galdo, Italy . . . **47 A8** 41 24N 15 1 E
San Benedetto del Tronto, Italy . . . **45 F10** 42 57N 13 53 E
San Benedetto Po, Italy . . . . **44 C7** 45 2N 10 55 E
San Benedicto, I., Mexico **162 D2** 19 18N 110 49W
San Benito, U.S.A. **155 M6** 26 8N 97 38W
San Benito →, U.S.A. **160 J5** 36 53N 121 34W
San Benito Mt., U.S.A. **160 J6** 36 22N 120 37W
San Bernardino, Switz. . . . . **33 D8** 46 27N 9 12 E
San Bernardino, U.S.A. **161 L9** 34 7N 117 19W
San Bernardino, Paso del, Switz. . . **33 D8** 46 28N 9 11 E
San Bernardino Mts., U.S.A. **161 L10** 34 10N 116 45W
San Bernardino Str., Phil. . . . . **80 E5** 13 0N 125 0 E
San Bernardo, Chile . . . . **174 C1** 33 40 S 70 50W
San Bernardo, I. de, Colombia **168 B2** 9 45N 75 50W
San Blas, Mexico **162 B3** 26 4N 108 46W
San Blas, Arch. de, Panama **164 E4** 9 50N 78 31W
San Blas, C., U.S.A. **152 F4** 29 40N 85 21W
San Bonifacio, Italy . . . . **45 C8** 45 24N 11 16 E
San Borja, Bolivia . . . . **172 C4** 14 50 S 66 52W
San Buenaventura, Bolivia . . . . **172 C4** 14 28 S 67 35W
San Buenaventura, Mexico **162 B4** 27 5N 101 32W
San Carlo Park, U.S.A. **153 J8** 26 28N 81 49W
San Carlos = Butuku-Luba,
  Eq. Guin. **113 E6** 3 29N 8 33 E
San Carlos = Sant Carles, Spain . . **38 C2** 39 3N 1 34 E
San Carlos, Argentina . . . . **174 C2** 33 50 S 69 0W
San Carlos, Bolivia . . . . **173 D5** 17 24 S 63 45W
San Carlos, Chile . . . . **174 D1** 36 10 S 72 0W
San Carlos, Baja Calif. S., Mexico . **162 C2** 24 47N 112 6W
San Carlos, Coahuila, Mexico **162 B4** 29 0N 100 54W
San Carlos, Nic. **164 D3** 11 12N 84 50W
San Carlos, Neg. Occ., Phil. . . . . . . **81 F4** 10 29N 123 25 E
San Carlos, Pangasinan, Phil. . . . . . **80 D3** 15 55N 120 20 E
San Carlos, Uruguay . . . . **175 C5** 34 46 S 54 58W
San Carlos, U.S.A. **159 K8** 33 21N 110 27W
San Carlos, Amazonas, Venezuela . **168 C4** 1 55N 67 4W
San Carlos, Cojedes, Venezuela . . . **168 B4** 9 40N 68 36W
San Carlos de Bariloche, Argentina . **176 B2** 41 10 S 71 25W
San Carlos de la Rápita = Sant Carles
  de la Ràpita, Spain . . . . **40 E5** 40 37N 0 35 E
San Carlos de Río Negro, Venezuela **168 C4** 1 55N 67 4W
San Carlos del Zulia, Venezuela . . . **168 B3** 9 1N 71 55W
San Carlos L., U.S.A. **159 K8** 33 11N 110 32W
San Cataldo, Italy . . . . **46 E6** 37 29N 13 59 E
San Celoni = Sant Celoni, Spain . . **40 D7** 41 42N 2 30 E
San Clemente, Chile . . . . **174 D1** 35 30 S 71 29W
San Clemente, Spain **41 F2** 39 24N 2 25W
San Clemente, U.S.A. **161 M9** 33 26N 117 37W
San Clemente I., U.S.A. **161 N8** 32 53N 118 29W
San Cristóbal = Es Migjorn Gran,
  Spain . . . . **38 B5** 39 57N 4 3 E
San Cristóbal, Argentina . . . . **174 C3** 30 20 S 61 10W
San Cristóbal, Colombia . . . . **168 D3** 2 18 S 73 2W
San Cristóbal, Dom. Rep. **165 C5** 18 25N 70 6W
San Cristóbal, Solomon Is. . . . . **133 N11** 10 30 S 161 0 E
San Cristóbal, Venezuela **168 B3** 7 46N 72 14W
San Cristóbal, I., Ecuador . . . . **172 a** 0 50 S 89 26W
San Cristóbal de la Casas, Mexico . **163 D6** 16 50N 92 33W
San Damiano d'Asti, Italy . . . . **44 D5** 44 50N 8 4 E
San Daniele del Friuli, Italy . . . . **45 B10** 46 9N 13 1 E
San Diego, Calif., U.S.A. **161 N9** 32 42N 117 9W
San Diego, Tex., U.S.A. **155 M5** 27 46N 98 14W
San Diego, C., Argentina . . . . **176 D3** 54 40 S 65 10W
San Diego de la Unión, Mexico . . . **162 C4** 21 28N 100 52W
San Diego International ✈ (SAN),
  U.S.A. **161 N9** 32 44N 117 11W
San Dimitri, Ras, Malta . . . . **38 E6** 36 4N 14 11 E
San Dimitri Point = San Dimitri, Ras,
  Malta . . . . **38 E6** 36 4N 14 11 E
San Donà di Piave, Italy . . . . **45 C9** 45 38N 12 34 E
San Estanislao, Paraguay . . . . **174 A4** 24 39 S 56 26W
San Esteban de Gormaz, Spain . . . **40 D1** 41 34N 3 13W
San Felice Circeo, Italy . . . . **46 A6** 41 14N 13 5 E
San Felice sul Panaro, Italy . . . . . . **45 D8** 44 50N 11 8 E
San Felipe, Chile . . . . **174 C1** 32 43 S 70 42W
San Felipe, Colombia **168 C4** 1 55N 67 6W
San Felipe, Mexico **162 A2** 31 0N 114 52W
San Felipe, Phil. . . . . **80 D3** 15 4N 120 4 E
San Felipe, Venezuela **168 A4** 10 20N 68 44W
San Felipe →, U.S.A. **161 M11** 33 12N 115 49W
San Félix, Chile . . . . **174 B1** 28 56 S 70 28W
San Félix, Pac. Oc. . . . . **135 K20** 26 23 S 80 0W

San Fernando = Sant Ferran, Spain . **38 D1** 38 42N 1 28 E
San Fernando, Chile . . . . **174 C1** 34 30 S 71 0W
San Fernando, Baja Calif., Mexico . **162 B1** 29 55N 115 10W
San Fernando, Tamaulipas, Mexico . **163 C5** 24 51N 98 10W
San Fernando, Cebu, Phil. . . . . **81 F4** 10 10N 123 42 E
San Fernando, La Union, Phil. . . . . **80 C3** 16 40N 120 23 E
San Fernando, Pampanga, Phil. . . . **80 D3** 15 5N 120 37 E
San Fernando, Romblon, Phil. . . . . **80 E4** 12 18N 122 36 E
San Fernando, Spain **43 J4** 36 28N 6 17W
San Fernando, Trin. & Tob. **169 E9** 10 20N 61 30W
San Fernando, U.S.A. **161 L8** 34 17N 118 26W
San Fernando de Apure, Venezuela . **168 B4** 7 54N 67 15W
San Fernando de Atabapo,
  Venezuela **168 C4** 4 3N 67 42W
San Fernando di Púglia, Italy . . . . . **47 A9** 41 18N 16 5 E
San Francisco, Argentina . . . . **174 C3** 31 30 S 62 5W
San Francisco, Bolivia . . . . **173 D4** 15 16 S 65 31W
San Francisco, Peru . . . . **172 C3** 12 36 S 73 49W
San Francisco, Agusan del S., Phil. . **81 G5** 8 30N 125 56 E
San Francisco, Cebu, Phil. . . . . **81 F5** 10 39N 124 23 E
San Francisco, Quezon, Phil. . . . . . **80 E4** 13 21N 122 31 E
San Francisco, S. Leyte, Phil. . . . . **81 F5** 10 4N 125 9 E
San Francisco →, U.S.A. **159 K9** 32 59N 109 22W
San Francisco, Paso de, S. Amer. . . **174 B2** 27 0 S 68 0W
San Francisco de Macorís, Dom. Rep. **165 C5** 19 19N 70 15W
San Francisco del Monte de Oro,
  Argentina . . . . **174 C2** 32 36 S 66 8W
San Francisco del Oro, Mexico **162 B3** 26 52N 105 50W
San Francisco International ✈
  (SFO), U.S.A. **160 H4** 37 37N 122 22W
San Francisco Javier = Sant Francesc
  de Formentera, Spain . . . . **38 D1** 38 42N 1 26 E
San Francisco Solano, Pta., Colombia **168 B2** 6 18N 77 29W
San Fratello, Italy . . . . **47 D7** 38 1N 14 36 E
San Gabriel, Chile . . . . **174 C1** 33 47 S 70 15W
San Gabriel, Ecuador **168 C2** 0 36N 77 49W
San Gabriel Mts., U.S.A. **161 L9** 34 20N 118 0W
San Gavino Monreale, Italy . . . . . . **46 C1** 39 33N 8 47 E
San German, Puerto Rico . . . . **165 d** 18 4N 67 4W
San Gil, Colombia **168 B3** 6 33N 73 8W
San Giljan = St. Julian's, Malta . . . . **38 F7** 35 55N 14 29 E
San Gimignano, Italy . . . . **45 E8** 43 28N 11 2 E
San Giórgio di Nogaro, Italy . . . . . . **45 C10** 45 50N 13 13 E
San Giórgio Iónico, Italy . . . . **47 B10** 40 27N 17 23 E
San Giovanni Bianco, Italy . . . . **44 C6** 45 52N 9 39 E
San Giovanni in Fiore, Italy . . . . . . **47 C9** 39 15N 16 42 E
San Giovanni in Persiceto, Italy . . . **45 D8** 44 38N 11 11 E
San Giovanni Rotondo, Italy . . . . . . **45 G12** 41 42N 15 44 E
San Giovanni Valdarno, Italy . . . . . **45 E8** 43 34N 11 32 E
San Giuliano Terme, Italy . . . . **44 E7** 43 46N 10 26 E
San Gorgonio Mt., U.S.A. **161 L10** 34 7N 116 51W
San Gottardo, P. del, Switz. . . . . . . **33 C7** 46 33N 8 33 E
San Gregorio, Uruguay . . . . **175 C4** 32 37 S 55 40W
San Gregorio, U.S.A. **160 H4** 37 20N 122 23W
San Guiseppe Jato, Italy . . . . **46 E6** 37 57N 13 11 E
San Ignacio, Belize **163 D7** 17 10N 89 0W
San Ignacio, Bolivia . . . . **174 C1** 14 53 S 65 36W
San Ignacio, Santa Cruz, Bolivia . . **173 D5** 16 20 S 60 55W
San Ignacio, Mexico **162 B2** 27 27N 113 0W
San Ignacio, Paraguay . . . . **174 C2** 26 52 S 57 3W
San Ignacio, Peru . . . . **172 B2** 5 8 S 78 59W
San Ignacio, L., Mexico **162 B2** 26 50N 113 11W
San Ignacio, Parque Natural △,
  Mexico **162 B2** 27 0N 113 10W
San Ildefonso, C., Phil. . . . . **80 C4** 16 0N 122 1 E
San Isidro, Argentina . . . . **174 C4** 34 29 S 58 31W
San Isidro, Phil. . . . . **81 H6** 6 50N 126 5 E
San Jacinto, Colombia **168 B2** 9 50N 75 8W
San Jacinto, Phil. . . . . **80 E4** 12 34N 123 44 E
San Jacinto, U.S.A. **161 M10** 33 47N 116 57W
San Jaime = Sant Jaume, Spain . . . **38 B5** 39 54N 4 4 E
San Javier, Misiones, Argentina . . . **175 B4** 27 55 S 55 5W
San Javier, Santa Fe, Argentina . . . **174 C4** 30 40 S 59 55W
San Javier, Beni, Bolivia . . . . **173 C5** 14 34 S 64 42W
San Javier, Santa Cruz, Bolivia . . . **173 D5** 16 18 S 62 30W
San Javier, Chile . . . . **174 D1** 35 40 S 71 45W
San Javier, Spain **41 H4** 37 49N 0 50W
San Jeronimo Taviche, Mexico **163 D5** 16 38N 96 32W
San Joaquín, Bolivia . . . . **173 C5** 13 4 S 64 49W
San Joaquín, Phil. . . . . **81 F4** 10 35N 122 8 E
San Joaquin, U.S.A. **160 J6** 36 36N 120 11W
San Joaquín →, Bolivia . . . . **173 C5** 13 8 S 63 41W
San Joaquin →, U.S.A. **160 G5** 38 4N 121 51W
San Joaquin Valley, U.S.A. **160 J6** 37 20N 121 0W
San Jon, U.S.A. **155 H3** 35 6N 103 20W
San Jordi = Sant Jordi, Spain . . . . . **38 B3** 39 33N 2 46 E
San Jorge, Argentina . . . . **174 C3** 31 54 S 61 50W
San Jorge, Solomon Is. . . . . **133 M10** 8 28 S 159 38 E
San Jorge, B. de, Mexico **162 A2** 31 20N 113 20W
San Jorge, G., Argentina . . . . **176 C3** 46 0 S 66 0W
San José = San Josep, Spain . . . . . **38 D1** 38 55N 1 18 E
San José, Costa Rica **164 E3** 9 55N 84 2W
San José, Guatemala **164 D1** 14 0N 90 50W
San José, Mexico **162 C2** 25 0N 110 38W
San Jose, Mind. Occ., Phil. . . . . . . **80 E3** 12 27N 121 4 E
San Jose, Nueva Ecija, Phil. . . . . . **80 D3** 15 45N 120 55 E
San Jose, Calif., U.S.A. **160 H5** 37 20N 121 53W
San Jose, Ill., U.S.A. **154 E9** 40 18N 89 36W
San Jose →, U.S.A. **159 J10** 34 25N 106 45W
San Jose de Buenavista, Phil. . . . . **79 B6** 10 45N 121 56 E
San José de Chiquitos, Bolivia . . . . **173 D5** 17 53 S 60 50W
San José de Feliciano, Argentina . . **174 C4** 30 26 S 58 46W
San José de Jáchal, Argentina . . . . **174 C2** 30 15 S 68 46W
San José de Mayo, Uruguay . . . . . . **174 C4** 34 27 S 56 40W
San José de Ocune, Colombia **168 C4** 4 15N 70 20W
San José de Uchapiamonas, Bolivia **172 C4** 14 13 S 68 5W
San José del Guaviare, Colombia . . **168 C3** 2 35N 72 38W
San Jose del Monte, Phil. . . . . **80 D3** 14 49N 121 3 E
San José do Anauá, Brazil **169 D5** 0 58N 61 22W
San Josep, Spain . . . . **38 D1** 38 55N 1 18 E
San Juan, Argentina . . . . **174 C2** 31 30 S 68 30W
San Juan, Colombia **168 B2** 8 46N 76 32W
San Juan, Ica, Peru . . . . **172 D2** 15 22 S 75 9W
San Juan, Puno, Peru . . . . **172 C4** 14 15 S 69 19W
San Juan, Batangas, Phil. . . . . **80 E3** 13 50N 121 24 E
San Juan, S. Leyte, Phil. . . . . **81 F5** 10 16N 125 10 E
San Juan, Puerto Rico . . . . **165 d** 18 28N 66 7W
San Juan, Trin. & Tob. **169 D7** 10 39N 61 21W
San Juan □, Argentina . . . . **174 C2** 31 9 S 69 0W
San Juan →, Argentina . . . . **174 C2** 32 20 S 67 25W
San Juan →, Bolivia . . . . **174 A2** 21 2 S 65 19W
San Juan →, Colombia **168 C2** 4 3N 77 27W
San Juan →, Nic. **164 D3** 10 56N 83 42W
San Juan →, U.S.A. **159 H8** 37 16N 110 26W
San Juan →, Venezuela **168 A5** 10 14N 62 38W
San Juan, C., Eq. Guin. . . . . **114 B1** 1 5N 9 20 E
San Juan Bautista = Sant Joan
  Baptista, Spain . . . . **38 C2** 39 5N 1 31 E
San Juan Bautista, Paraguay . . . . . **174 B4** 26 37 S 57 6W
San Juan Bautista, U.S.A. **160 J5** 36 51N 121 32W
San Juan Bautista Valle Nacional,
  Mexico **163 D5** 17 47N 96 19W
San Juan Capistrano, U.S.A. **161 M9** 33 30N 117 40W
San Juan Cr. →, U.S.A. **160 J5** 35 40N 120 22W
San Juan de Alicante, Spain **41 G4** 38 25N 0 25W
San Juan de Guadalupe, Mexico . . . **162 C4** 24 38N 102 44W
San Juan de Guía, Cabo de,
  Colombia **168 A3** 11 21N 73 59W
San Juan de la Costa, Mexico **162 C2** 24 10N 110 45W

San Juan de los Morros, Venezuela . **168 B4** 9 55N 67 21W
San Juan de Manapiare, Venezuela . **168 B4** 5 15N 66 5W
San Juan del César, Colombia **168 A3** 10 46N 73 1W
San Juan del Norte, Nic. **164 D3** 10 58N 83 40W
San Juan del Norte, B. de, Nic. . . . **164 D3** 10 58N 83 40W
San Juan del Río, Mexico **163 C5** 20 25N 100 0W
San Juan del Sur, Nic. **164 D2** 11 20N 85 51W
San Juan I., U.S.A. **160 B3** 48 32N 123 5W
San Juan Island Nat. Historical
  Park △, U.S.A. **160 B4** 48 27N 123 0W
San Juan Mts., U.S.A. **159 H10** 37 30N 107 0W
San Julián, Argentina . . . . **176 C3** 49 15 S 67 45W
San Julian, Phil. . . . . **81 F5** 11 45N 125 27 E
San Just, Sierra de, Spain **40 E4** 40 45N 0 49W
San Justo, Argentina . . . . **174 C3** 30 47 S 60 30W
San Kamphaeng, Thailand . . . . **86 C2** 18 45N 99 8 E
San Lázaro, C., Mexico **162 C2** 24 50N 112 18W
San Lázaro, Sa., Mexico **162 C3** 23 25N 110 0W
San Leandro, U.S.A. **160 H4** 37 44N 122 9W
San Leonardo de Yagüe, Spain **40 D1** 41 51N 3 5W
San Lorenzo = Sant Llorenç des
  Cardassar, Spain . . . . **38 B4** 39 37N 3 17 E
San Lorenzo, Argentina . . . . **174 C3** 32 45 S 60 45W
San Lorenzo, Beni, Bolivia . . . . **173 D4** 15 22 S 65 48W
San Lorenzo, Tarija, Bolivia . . . . . . **173 E5** 21 26 S 64 47W
San Lorenzo, Ecuador **168 C2** 1 15N 78 50W
San Lorenzo, Paraguay . . . . **174 B4** 25 20 S 57 32W
San Lorenzo →, Mexico **162 C3** 24 15N 107 24W
San Lorenzo, I., Mexico **162 B2** 28 35N 112 50W
San Lorenzo, I., Peru . . . . **172 C2** 12 7 S 77 15W
San Lorenzo, Mte., Argentina . . . . . **176 C2** 47 40 S 72 20W
San Lorenzo de la Parrilla, Spain . . **40 F2** 39 51N 2 22W
San Lorenzo de Morunys = Sant
  Llorenç de Morunys, Spain . . . . . **40 C6** 42 8N 1 35 E
San Lucas, Bolivia . . . . **173 E4** 20 5 S 65 7W
San Lucas, Baja Calif. S., Mexico . . **162 C3** 23 25N 109 54W
San Lucas, Baja Calif. S., Mexico . . **162 B2** 27 10N 112 14W
San Lucas, U.S.A. **160 J5** 36 8N 121 1W
San Lúcido, Italy . . . . **47 C9** 39 18N 16 3 E
San Luis, Argentina . . . . **174 C2** 33 20 S 66 20W
San Luis, Cuba **164 B3** 20 17N 83 46W
San Luis, Guatemala **164 C2** 16 14N 89 27W
San Luis, Ariz., U.S.A. **159 K6** 32 29N 114 47W
San Luis, Colo., U.S.A. **159 H11** 37 12N 105 25W
San Luis □, Argentina . . . . **174 C2** 34 0 S 66 0W
San Luis, I., Mexico **162 B2** 29 58N 114 26W
San Luis, L. de, Bolivia . . . . **173 C5** 13 45 S 64 0W
San Luis, Sierra de, Argentina . . . . **174 C2** 32 30 S 66 10W
San Luis de la Paz, Mexico **162 C4** 21 19N 100 32W
San Luis Obispo, U.S.A. **161 K6** 35 17N 120 40W
San Luis Potosí, Mexico **162 C4** 22 9N 100 59W
San Luis Potosí □, Mexico **162 C4** 22 10N 101 0W
San Luis Reservoir, U.S.A. **160 H5** 37 4N 121 5W
San Luis Río Colorado, Mexico . . . **162 A2** 32 29N 114 58W
San Manuel, U.S.A. . . . . **80 C3** 16 4N 120 40 E
San Manuel, U.S.A. **159 K8** 32 36N 110 38W
San Marco, C., Italy . . . . **46 C1** 39 51N 8 26 E
San Marco Argentano, Italy . . . . . . **47 C9** 39 33N 16 8 E
San Marco in Lámis, Italy . . . . **45 G12** 41 43N 15 38 E
San Marcos, Colombia **168 B2** 8 39N 75 8W
San Marcos, Guatemala **164 D1** 14 59N 91 52W
San Marcos, Mexico **162 B2** 27 13N 112 6W
San Marcos, Calif., U.S.A. **161 M9** 33 9N 117 10W
San Marcos, Tex., U.S.A. **155 L6** 29 53N 97 56W
San Mariano, Phil. . . . . **80 C4** 17 0N 122 2 E
San Marino, San Marino . . . . **45 E9** 43 55N 12 30 E
San Marino ■, Europe . . . . **45 E9** 43 56N 12 25 E
San Martín, Argentina . . . . **174 C2** 33 5 S 68 28W
San Martín, Colombia **168 C3** 3 42N 73 42W
San Martín →, Peru . . . . **172 B2** 7 0 S 76 50W
San Martín □, Peru . . . . **172 B2** 7 0 S 76 50W
San Martín, Bolivia . . . . **173 C5** 13 8 S 63 43W
San Martín, L., Argentina . . . . **176 C2** 48 50 S 72 50W
San Martín de la Vega, Spain **42 E7** 40 13N 3 34W
San Martín de los Andes, Argentina **176 B2** 40 10 S 71 20W
San Martín de Valdeiglesias, Spain . **42 E6** 40 21N 4 24W
San Mateo = Sant Mateu, Baleares,
  Spain . . . . **38 C1** 39 3N 1 23 E
San Mateo = Sant Mateu, Valencia,
  Spain . . . . **40 E5** 40 28N 0 10 E
San Mateo, Phil. . . . . **80 C3** 16 54N 121 33 E
San Mateo, U.S.A. **160 H4** 37 34N 122 19W
San Matías, Bolivia . . . . **173 D6** 16 25 S 58 20W
San Matías, G., Argentina . . . . **176 B4** 41 30 S 64 0W
San Miguel = Linapacan, Phil. . . . . **81 F1** 11 30N 119 52 E
San Miguel = Sant Miguel, Spain . . **38 C1** 39 3N 1 26 E
San Miguel, Bolivia . . . . **173 C5** 16 42 S 61 1W
San Miguel, El Salv. **164 D2** 13 30N 88 12W
San Miguel, Panama **164 E4** 8 27N 78 55W
San Miguel, Bulacan, Phil. . . . . **80 D3** 15 9N 120 56 E
San Miguel, Palawan, Phil. . . . . **81 F2** 11 30N 119 51 E
San Miguel, Surigao S., Phil. . . . . . **81 G5** 9 3N 125 59 E
San Miguel, U.S.A. **160 K6** 35 45N 120 42W
San Miguel →, Bolivia . . . . **173 C5** 13 52 S 63 56W
San Miguel →, Mexico **168 C2** 0 25N 76 30W
San Miguel, Golfo de, Panama **168 B2** 8 17N 78 17W
San Miguel de Huachi, Bolivia . . . . **172 D4** 15 40 S 67 15W
San Miguel de Tucumán, Argentina . **174 B2** 26 50 S 65 20W
San Miguel del Monte, Argentina . . **174 C4** 35 23 S 58 50W
San Miguel I., U.S.A. **161 L6** 34 2N 120 23W
San Miguel Is., Phil. . . . . **81 H2** 7 45N 118 28 E
San Miniato, Italy . . . . **44 E7** 43 41N 10 51 E
San Narciso, Phil. . . . . **80 D3** 15 2N 120 3 E
San Nicolás, Canary Is. **9 e1** 27 58N 15 47W
San Nicolas, Phil. . . . . **80 B3** 18 10N 120 36 E
San Nicolás de los Arroyas,
  Argentina . . . . **174 C3** 33 25 S 60 10W
San Nicolas I., U.S.A. **161 M7** 33 15N 119 30W
San Onofre, Colombia **168 B2** 9 44N 75 32W
San Onofre, U.S.A. **161 M9** 33 22N 117 34W
San Pablo, Bolivia . . . . **174 A2** 21 43 S 66 38W
San Pablo, Isabela, Phil. . . . . **80 C3** 17 7N 121 48 E
San Pablo, Laguna, Phil. . . . . **80 D3** 14 11N 121 31 E
San Páolo di Civitate, Italy . . . . **45 G12** 41 44N 15 15 E
San Pascual, Phil. . . . . **80 E4** 13 8N 122 59 E
San Pedro, Buenos Aires, Argentina **174 C4** 33 40 S 59 40W
San Pedro, Misiones, Argentina . . . **175 B5** 26 30 S 54 10W
San Pedro, Chile . . . . **174 C1** 33 54 S 71 28W
San Pedro, Colombia **168 C3** 4 56N 71 53W
San Pédro, Ivory C. **112 E3** 4 50N 6 33W
San Pedro, Peru . . . . **172 C3** 14 49 S 74 5W
San Pedro □, Paraguay . . . . **174 A4** 24 0 S 57 0W
San Pedro →, Chihuahua, Mexico . **162 B3** 28 20N 106 10W
San Pedro →, Nayarit, Mexico **162 C3** 21 45N 105 30W
San Pedro →, U.S.A. **159 K8** 32 59N 110 47W
San Pedro, Sierra de, Spain **43 F4** 39 18N 6 40W
San Pedro Channel, U.S.A. **161 M8** 33 30N 118 25W
San Pedro de Arimena, Colombia . . **168 C3** 4 37N 71 42W
San Pedro de Atacama, Chile . . . . . **174 A2** 22 55 S 68 15W
San Pedro de Jujuy, Argentina . . . . **174 A3** 24 12 S 64 55W
San Pedro de las Colonias, Mexico . **162 B4** 25 50N 102 59W
San Pedro de Lloc, Peru . . . . **172 B2** 7 15 S 79 28W
San Pedro del Norte, Nic. **164 D3** 13 4N 84 33W
San Pedro del Paraná, Paraguay . . **174 B4** 26 43 S 56 13W
San Pedro del Pinatar, Spain **41 H4** 37 50N 0 50W
San Pedro Mártir, Parque Nac. △,
  Mexico **162 A1** 31 0N 115 30W
San Pedro Mártir, Sierra, Mexico . . **162 A1** 31 0N 115 30W
San Pedro Mixtepec, Mexico **163 D5** 16 2N 97 7W

San Pedro Ocampo = Melchor
  Ocampo, *Mexico* **162 C4** 24 52N 101 40W
San Pedro Sula, *Honduras* **164 C2** 15 30N 88 0W
San Pietro, *Italy* .... **46 C1** 39 8N 8 17 E
San Pietro Vernótico, *Italy* ...... **47 B11** 40 29N 18 0 E
San Quintín, *Mexico* **162 A1** 30 29N 115 57W
San Rafael, *Argentina* .... **174 C2** 34 40 S 68 21W
San Rafael, *Bolivia* .... **173 D5** 16 45 S 60 34W
San Rafael, *Calif., U.S.A.* **160 H4** 37 58N 122 32W
San Rafael, *N. Mex., U.S.A.* **159 J10** 35 7N 107 53W
San Rafael, *Venezuela* **168 A3** 10 58N 71 46W
San Rafael Mt., *U.S.A.* **161 L7** 34 41N 119 52W
San Rafael Mts., *U.S.A.* **161 L7** 34 40N 119 50W
San Ramón, *Bolivia* .... **173 C5** 13 17 S 64 43W
San Ramón, *Peru* .... **172 C2** 11 8 S 75 20W
San Ramón de la Nueva Orán,
  Argentina .... **174 A3** 23 10 S 64 20W
San Remo, *Australia* .... **129 E6** 38 33 S 145 22 E
San Remo, *Italy* .... **44 E4** 43 49N 7 46 E
San Román, C., *Venezuela* **168 A3** 12 12N 70 0W
San Roque, *Argentina* .... **174 B4** 28 25 S 58 45W
San Roque, *Phil.* .... **80 E5** 12 37N 124 52 E
San Roque, *Spain* **43 J5** 36 17N 5 21W
San Rosendo, *Chile* .... **174 D1** 37 16 S 72 43W
San Saba, *U.S.A.* **155 K5** 31 12N 98 43W
San Salvador, *El Salv.* **164 D2** 13 40N 89 10W
San Salvador, *Spain* .... **38 B4** 39 27N 3 11 E
San Salvador, Canal de, *Ecuador* .. **172 a** 0 25 S 90 30W
San Salvador, I., *Ecuador* ...... **172 a** 0 16 S 90 42W
San Salvador de Jujuy, *Argentina* .. **174 A3** 24 10 S 64 48W
San Salvador I., *Bahamas* **165 B5** 24 0N 74 40W
San Salvo, *Italy* .... **45 F11** 42 3N 14 44 E
San Sebastián = Donostia-San
  Sebastián, *Spain* **40 B3** 43 17N 1 58W
San Sebastián, *Argentina* ...... **176 D3** 53 10 S 68 30W
San Sebastian, *Puerto Rico* ...... **165 d** 18 20N 66 59W
San Sebastián de la Gomera,
  Canary Is. **9 e1** 28 5N 17 7W
San Serra = Son Serra, *Spain* .... **38 B4** 39 43N 3 13 E
San Serverino Marche, *Italy* .... **45 E10** 43 13N 13 10 E
San Severo, *Italy* .... **45 G12** 41 41N 15 23 E
San Simeon, *U.S.A.* **160 K5** 35 39N 121 11W
San Simon, *U.S.A.* **159 K9** 32 16N 109 14W
San Stéfano di Cadore, *Italy* .... **45 B9** 46 34N 12 33 E
San Stino di Livenza, *Italy* ...... **45 C9** 45 44N 12 41 E
San Telmo = Sant Telm, *Spain* .... **38 B3** 39 35N 2 21 E
San Telmo, *Mexico* **162 A1** 30 58N 116 6W
San Teodoro, *Phil.* .... **80 E3** 13 26N 121 1 E
San Tiburcio, *Mexico* **162 C4** 24 8N 101 32W
San Valentin, Mte., *Chile* ...... **176 C2** 46 30 S 73 30W
San Vicente de Alcántara, *Spain* .. **43 F3** 39 22N 7 8W
San Vicente de la Barquera, *Spain* . **42 B6** 43 23N 4 29W
San Vicente del Caguán, *Colombia* . **168 C2** 2 7N 74 46W
San Vicente del Raspeig, *Spain* .. **41 G4** 38 24N 0 31W
San Vincenzo, *Italy* .... **44 E7** 43 6N 10 32 E
San Vito, *Costa Rica* **164 E3** 8 50N 82 58W
San Vito, *Italy* .... **46 C2** 39 26N 9 32 E
San Vito, C., *Italy* .... **46 D5** 38 11N 12 41 E
San Vito al Tagliamento, *Italy* .... **45 C9** 45 54N 12 52 E
San Vito Chietino, *Italy* ...... **45 F11** 42 18N 14 27 E
San Vito dei Normanni, *Italy* .... **47 B10** 40 39N 17 42 E
San Yanaro, *Colombia* **168 C4** 2 47N 69 42W
Saña, *Peru* .... **172 B2** 6 54 S 79 36W
Sana', *Yemen* .... **98 D4** 15 27N 44 12 E
Sana →, *Bos.-H.* .... **45 C13** 45 3N 16 23 E
Sanaba, *Burkina Faso* **112 C4** 12 25N 3 47W
Şanāfir, *Si. Arabia* .... **106 B3** 27 56N 34 42 E
Sanaga →, *Cameroon* .... **113 E6** 3 35N 9 38 E
Sanak I., *U.S.A.* **144 J7** 54 25N 162 40W
Sanaloa, Presa, *Mexico* **162 C3** 24 50N 107 20W
Sanām, *Si. Arabia* .... **98 B4** 23 40N 44 45 E
Sanana, *Indonesia* .... **82 B3** 2 4 S 125 58 E
Sanand, *India* .... **92 H5** 22 59N 72 25 E
Sanandaj, *Iran* .... **101 E12** 35 18N 47 1 E
Sanandita, *Bolivia* .... **174 A3** 21 40 S 63 45W
Sanaroa I., *Papua N. G.* ...... **132 E6** 9 37 S 151 0 E
Sanary-sur-Mer, *France* .... **29 E9** 43 7N 5 49 E
Sanāw, *Yemen* .... **99 C5** 17 50N 51 5 E
Sanawad, *India* .... **92 H7** 22 11N 76 5 E
Sanbe-San, *Japan* .... **72 B4** 35 6N 132 38 E
Sancellas = Sencelles, *Spain* .... **38 B3** 39 39N 2 54 E
Sancergues, *France* .... **27 E9** 47 10N 2 54 E
Sancerre, *France* .... **27 E9** 47 20N 2 50 E
Sancerrois, Collines du, *France* .... **27 E9** 47 20N 2 40 E
Sancha He →, *China* .... **76 D6** 26 48N 106 7 E
Sanchahe, *China* .... **75 B14** 44 50N 126 2 E
Sanchakou, *China* .... **65 D9** 39 47N 78 20 E
Sánchez, *Dom. Rep.* **165 C6** 19 15N 69 36W
Sanchez-Mira, *Phil.* .... **80 B3** 18 34N 121 14 E
Sanchor, *India* .... **92 G4** 24 45N 71 55 E
Sanco Pt., *Phil.* .... **81 G6** 8 15N 126 27 E
Sancoins, *France* .... **27 F9** 46 47N 2 55 E
Sancti Spíritus, *Cuba* **164 B4** 21 52N 79 33W
Sancy, Puy de, *France* .... **28 C6** 45 32N 2 50 E
Sand, *Norway* .... **18 E3** 59 29N 6 16 E
Sand →, *S. Africa* .... **117 C5** 22 25 S 30 5 E
Sand Cr. →, *U.S.A.* **157 E11** 39 4N 85 51W
Sand Hills, *Guyana* **169 B6** 6 57N 58 19W
Sand Hills, *U.S.A.* **154 D4** 42 10N 101 30W
Sand I., *U.S.A.* **145 K14** 21 19N 157 53W
Sand Lakes Prov. Park △, *Canada* . **143 B9** 57 51N 98 32W
Sand Point, *U.S.A.* **144 J7** 55 20N 160 30W
Sand Springs, *U.S.A.* **155 G6** 36 9N 96 7W
Sanda, *Japan* .... **73 C7** 34 53N 135 14 E
Sandakan, *Malaysia* .... **85 A5** 5 53N 118 4 E
Sandalwood, *Australia* .... **128 C4** 34 55 S 140 9 E
Sandan = Sambor, *Cambodia* .... **86 F6** 12 46N 106 0 E
Sandane, *Norway* .... **18 E2** 61 46N 6 13 E
Sandanski, *Bulgaria* .... **50 E7** 41 35N 23 16 E
Sandaré, *Mali* **112 C2** 14 40N 10 15W
Sandared, *Sweden* .... **17 G6** 57 43N 12 47 E
Sandarne, *Sweden* .... **16 C11** 61 16N 17 9 E
Sanday, *U.K.* **22 B6** 59 16N 2 31W
Sande, *Møre og Romsdal, Norway* . **18 B2** 62 15N 5 27 E
Sande, *Sogn og Fjordane, Norway* . **18 C2** 61 20N 5 47 E
Sande, *Vestfold, Norway* ...... **18 E7** 59 36N 10 12 E
Sandefjord, *Norway* .... **18 E7** 59 10N 10 15 E
Sandeid, *Norway* .... **18 E2** 59 33N 5 52 E
Sanders, *Ariz., U.S.A.* **159 J9** 35 13N 109 20W
Sanders, *Ky., U.S.A.* **157 F12** 38 40N 84 56W
Sanderson, *Fla., U.S.A.* **152 E7** 30 15N 82 16W
Sanderson, *Tex., U.S.A.* **155 K3** 30 9N 102 24W
Sandersville, *U.S.A.* **152 C7** 32 59N 82 48W
Sandfire Roadhouse, *Australia* .... **124 C3** 19 45 S 121 15 E
Sandfloegga, *Norway* .... **18 E4** 59 58N 7 10 E
Sandfly L., *Canada* **143 B7** 55 43N 106 6W
Sandfontein, *Namibia* .... **116 C2** 23 48 S 19 1 E
Sandharmaren, C., *Sweden* ...... **17 J8** 55 23N 14 14 E
Sandía, *Peru* .... **172 C4** 14 10 S 69 30W
Sandıklı, *Turkey* .... **49 C12** 38 28N 30 17 E
Sandila, *India* .... **93 F9** 27 5N 80 31 E
Sandilands, *Bahamas* .... **9 b** 25 3N 77 19W
Sandnes, *Aust-Agder, Norway* .... **18 F4** 58 53N 7 45 E
Sandnes, *Rogaland, Norway* .... **18 F2** 58 50N 5 45 E
Sandnessjøen, *Norway* .... **14 C15** 66 2N 12 38 E
Sandoa, *Dem. Rep. of the Congo* . **115 D4** 9 41 S 23 0 E
Sandomierz, *Poland* .... **55 H8** 50 40N 21 43 E
Sândominic, *Romania* .... **53 D10** 46 35N 25 47 E
Sandona, *Colombia* **168 C2** 1 17N 77 28W
Sandongo, *Angola* .... **116 B3** 16 25 S 18 25 E
Sandover →, *Australia* .... **126 C2** 21 43 S 136 32 E
Sandoway, *Burma* .... **90 F5** 18 20N 94 30 E
Sandoy, *Færoe Is.* **14 F9** 61 52N 6 46W

Sandpoint, *U.S.A.* **158 B5** 48 17N 116 33W
Sandray, *U.K.* **22 E1** 56 53N 7 31W
Sandringham, *U.K.* .... **20 E8** 52 51N 0 31 E
Sandstone, *Australia* .... **125 E2** 27 59 S 119 16 E
Sandu, *China* .... **76 E6** 26 0N 107 52 E
Sandumba, *Angola* .... **116 B3** 12 40 S 21 1 E
Sandur, *India* .... **95 F3** 15 6N 76 33 E
Sandusky, *Mich., U.S.A.* **150 C2** 43 25N 82 50W
Sandusky, *Ohio, U.S.A.* **150 E2** 41 27N 82 42W
Sandusky →, *U.S.A.* **157 C14** 41 27N 83 0W
Sandvig, *Sweden* .... **17 J8** 55 18N 14 47 E
Sandvika, *Norway* .... **18 E7** 59 54N 10 31 E
Sandviken, *Sweden* .... **16 D10** 60 38N 16 46 E
Sandwich, *U.S.A.* **157 C8** 41 39N 88 37W
Sandwich, C., *Australia* .... **126 B4** 18 14 S 146 18 E
Sandwich B., *Canada* **141 B8** 53 40N 57 15W
Sandwich B., *Namibia* .... **116 C1** 23 25 S 14 20 E
Sandwip I., *Bangla.* .... **90 D3** 22 30N 91 25 E
Sandy, *Oreg., U.S.A.* **158 E4** 45 24N 122 16W
Sandy, *Pa., U.S.A.* **150 E6** 41 6N 78 46W
Sandy, *Utah, U.S.A.* **158 F8** 40 35N 111 50W
Sandy B., *St. Helena* .... **9 h** 16 0 S 5 43W
Sandy Bay, *Canada* **143 B8** 55 31N 102 19W
Sandy Bight, *Australia* .... **125 F3** 33 50 S 123 20 E
Sandy C., *Queens., Australia* .... **126 C5** 24 42 S 153 15 E
Sandy C., *Tas., Australia* ...... **127 G3** 41 25 S 144 45 E
Sandy Cay, *Bahamas* **165 B4** 23 13N 75 18W
Sandy Cr. →, *U.S.A.* **158 F9** 41 51N 109 47W
Sandy L., *Canada* **140 B1** 53 2N 93 0W
Sandy Lake, *Canada* **140 B1** 53 0N 93 15W
Sandy Point, *India* .... **95 J11** 10 32N 92 22 E
Sandy Springs, *U.S.A.* **152 B5** 33 56N 84 23W
Sandy Valley, *U.S.A.* **161 K11** 35 49N 115 36W
Sanford, *Fla., U.S.A.* **153 G8** 28 48N 81 16W
Sanford, *Maine, U.S.A.* **149 D10** 43 27N 70 47W
Sanford, *N.C., U.S.A.* **153 H6** 35 29N 79 10W
Sanford →, *Australia* .... **125 E2** 27 22 S 115 53 E
Sanford, Mt., *U.S.A.* **144 E11** 62 13N 144 8W
Sang-i-Masha, *Afghan.* .... **92 C2** 33 8N 67 27 E
Sanga, *Angola* .... **115 E3** 11 9 S 15 21 E
Sanga, *Mozam.* .... **119 E4** 12 22 S 35 21 E
Sanga →, *Congo* .... **112 A3** 1 5 S 17 0 E
Sangaie, *Dem. Rep. of the Congo* . **115 D4** 6 48 S 22 46 E
Sangamner, *India* .... **94 E2** 19 37N 74 15 E
Sangamon →, *U.S.A.* **156 D6** 40 7N 90 40W
Sanganeb Atoll Marine Nat. Park △,
  Sudan .... **106 D4** 19 33N 37 11 E
Sangar, *Afghan.* .... **92 C1** 32 56N 65 30 E
Sangar, *Russia* .... **67 C13** 64 2N 127 31 E
Sangar Sarai, *Afghan.* .... **92 B4** 34 27N 70 35 E
Sangareddi, *India* .... **94 F4** 17 38N 78 7 E
Sangaredi, *Guinea* **112 C2** 11 7N 13 52W
Sangarh →, *Pakistan* .... **92 D4** 30 43N 70 44 E
Sangasangadalam, *Indonesia* .... **85 C5** 0 36 S 117 13 E
Sangasso, *Mali* **112 C3** 12 5N 5 35W
Sangatte, *France* .... **27 B8** 50 56N 1 44 E
Sangay, *Ecuador* .... **168 D2** 2 0 S 78 20W
Sangchris L., *U.S.A.* **156 E7** 39 35N 89 30W
Sange, *Dem. Rep. of the Congo* .. **118 D2** 6 58 S 28 21 E
Sangeang, *Indonesia* .... **85 D5** 8 12 S 119 6 E
Sângeorz-Băi, *Romania* .... **53 C9** 47 22N 24 41 E
Sanger, *U.S.A.* **160 J7** 36 42N 119 33W
Sângera, *Moldova* .... **53 D13** 46 55N 28 58 E
Sangerhausen, *Germany* ...... **30 D7** 51 28N 11 18 E
Sanggan He →, *China* .... **74 E9** 38 12N 117 15 E
Sanggau, *Indonesia* .... **84 B4** 0 5N 110 30 E
Sanghar, *Pakistan* .... **92 F3** 26 2N 68 57 E
Sangihe, Kepulauan, *Indonesia* .. **82 A3** 3 0N 125 30 E
Sangihe, Pulau, *Indonesia* ...... **82 A3** 3 35N 125 30 E
Sangju, *S. Korea* .... **75 F15** 36 25N 128 10 E
Sangkapura, *Indonesia* .... **84 B5** 5 52 S 112 40 E
Sangkhla, *Thailand* .... **84 E2** 14 57N 98 28 E
Sangkulirang, *Indonesia* .... **83 B5** 0 59N 117 58 E
Sangla, *Pakistan* .... **92 D5** 31 43N 73 23 E
Sangli, *India* .... **94 F2** 16 55N 74 33 E
Sangmélima, *Cameroon* .... **113 E7** 2 57N 12 1 E
Sango, *Angola* .... **115 D2** 9 51 S 15 44 E
Sangod, *India* .... **92 G7** 24 55N 76 17 E
Sangole, *India* .... **94 F2** 17 26N 75 12 E
Sangpang Bum, *Burma* .... **90 B5** 26 30N 95 50 E
Sangre de Cristo Mts., *U.S.A.* .. **155 G2** 37 30N 105 20W
Sangre Grande, *Trin. & Tob.* **169 F9** 10 35N 61 8W
Sangro →, *Italy* .... **45 F11** 42 14N 14 32 E
Sangrur, *India* .... **92 D6** 30 14N 75 50 E
Sangudo, *Canada* **142 C6** 53 50N 114 54W
Sangue →, *Brazil* .... **173 C6** 11 1 S 58 39W
Sangüesa, *Spain* **40 C3** 42 37N 1 17W
Sanguinaires, Îs., *France* ...... **29 G12** 41 51N 8 36 E
Sangzhi, *China* .... **77 C8** 29 25N 110 12 E
Sanhala, *Ivory C.* **112 C3** 10 3N 6 51W
Sanibel, *U.S.A.* **153 J7** 26 26N 82 1W
Sanibel I., *U.S.A.* **153 J7** 26 26N 82 6W
Sanikiluaq, *Canada* .... **139 C12** 56 31N 79 8 E
Sanin-Kaigan Nat. Park △, *Japan* . **72 B6** 35 39N 134 37 E
Sanirajak, *Canada* **139 B11** 68 46N 81 12W
Sanjawi, *Pakistan* .... **92 D3** 30 17N 68 21 E
Sanje, *Uganda* .... **118 C3** 0 49 S 31 30 E
Sanjiang, *China* .... **76 E7** 25 48N 109 37 E
Sanjo, *Japan* .... **70 F9** 37 37N 138 57 E
Sankarankovil, *India* .... **95 K3** 9 10N 77 35 E
Sankeshwar, *India* .... **95 F2** 16 23N 74 32 E
Sankh →, *India* .... **93 H11** 22 15N 84 48 E
Sankosh →, *India* .... **90 B2** 26 24N 89 47 E
Sankt Andrä, *Austria* .... **32 E7** 46 46N 14 50 E
Sankt Antönien, *Switz.* .... **33 C9** 46 58N 9 48 E
Sankt Augustin, *Germany* ...... **30 E3** 50 45N 7 10 E
Sankt Blasien, *Germany* .... **31 H4** 47 47N 8 7 E
Sankt Gallen, *Switz.* .... **33 B8** 47 26N 9 22 E
Sankt Gallen □, *Switz.* .... **33 B8** 47 25N 9 22 E
Sankt Goar, *Germany* .... **31 E3** 50 12N 7 43 E
Sankt Ingbert, *Germany* .... **31 F3** 49 16N 7 6 E
Sankt Johann im Pongau, *Austria* . **34 D6** 47 22N 13 12 E
Sankt Johann in Tirol, *Austria* .... **34 D5** 47 30N 12 25 E
Sankt Margrethen, *Switz.* ...... **33 B9** 47 28N 9 37 E
Sankt Michel = Mikkeli, *Finland* .. **15 F22** 61 43N 27 15 E
Sankt Moritz, *Switz.* .... **33 D9** 46 30N 9 50 E
Sankt-Peterburg, *Russia* .... **58 C6** 59 55N 30 20 E
Sankt Pölten, *Austria* .... **34 C8** 48 12N 15 38 E
Sankt Ulrich = Ortisei, *Italy* .... **45 B8** 46 34N 11 40 E
Sankt Valentin, *Austria* .... **34 C7** 48 11N 14 33 E
Sankt Veit an der Glan, *Austria* .. **34 E7** 46 47N 14 22 E
Sankt Wendel, *Germany* .... **31 F3** 49 27N 7 9 E
Sankt Wolfgang, *Austria* ...... **34 D6** 47 43N 13 27 E
Sankuru →, *Dem. Rep. of the Congo* **115 C4** 4 17 S 20 25 E
Sanlúcar de Barrameda, *Spain* **43 J4** 36 46N 6 21W
Sanluri, *Italy* .... **46 C1** 39 34N 8 54 E
Sânmartin, *Romania* .... **53 D10** 46 19N 25 58 E
Sanmen, *China* .... **77 C13** 29 5N 121 35 E
Sanmenxia, *China* .... **74 G6** 34 47N 111 12 E
Sanming, *China* .... **77 D11** 26 15N 117 40 E
Sannan, *Japan* .... **73 B7** 35 2N 135 1 E
Sannaspos, *S. Africa* .... **116 D4** 29 6 S 26 34 E
Sannat, *Malta* .... **49 C1** 36 1N 14 15 E
Sannicandro Gargánico, *Italy* .... **45 G12** 41 50N 15 34 E
Sânnicolau Mare, *Romania* .... **52 D5** 46 5N 20 39 E
Sannieshof, *S. Africa* .... **116 D4** 26 30 S 25 47 E
Sannīn, J., *Lebanon* .... **103 B4** 33 57N 35 52 E
Sanniquellie, *Liberia* **112 D3** 7 19N 8 38W
Sannûr, W. →, *Egypt* .... **106 B3** 28 47N 31 12 E
Sano, *Japan* .... **73 A11** 36 19N 139 35 E
Sanok, *Poland* .... **55 J9** 49 35N 22 10 E
Sanquhar, *U.K.* **22 F5** 55 22N 3 54W
Sans Souci, *Trin. & Tob.* **169 F9** 10 50N 61 0W

Sansanding, *Mali* **112 C3** 13 48N 6 0W
Sansepolcro, *Italy* .... **45 E9** 43 34N 12 8 E
Sansha, *China* .... **77 D13** 26 58N 120 12 E
Sanshui, *China* .... **77 F9** 23 10N 112 56 E
Sanski Most, *Bos.-H.* .... **45 D13** 44 46N 16 40 E
Sansui, *China* .... **76 D7** 26 58N 108 39 E
Sant Antoni Abat, *Spain* .... **38 D1** 38 59N 1 19 E
Sant Boi de Llobregat, *Spain* .... **40 D7** 41 21N 2 2 E
Sant Carles, *Spain* .... **38 C2** 39 3N 1 34 E
Sant Carles de la Ràpita, *Spain* .. **40 D7** 41 42N 2 30 E
Sant Celoni, *Spain* .... **40 D7** 41 42N 2 30 E
Sant Feliu de Guíxols, *Spain* .... **40 D8** 41 45N 3 1 E
Sant Feliu de Llobregat, *Spain* .. **40 D7** 41 23N 2 2 E
Sant Ferran, *Spain* .... **38 D1** 38 42N 1 28 E
Sant Francesc de Formentera, *Spain* **38 D1** 38 42N 1 26 E
Sant Jaume, *Spain* .... **38 B5** 39 54N 4 4 E
Sant Joan Baptista, *Spain* ...... **38 C2** 39 5N 1 31 E
Sant Jordi, *Ibiza, Spain* .... **38 D1** 38 53N 1 24 E
Sant Jordi, *Mallorca, Spain* .... **38 B3** 39 33N 2 46 E
Sant Jordi, G. de, *Spain* .... **40 E6** 40 53N 1 2 E
Sant Llorenç de Morunys, *Spain* .. **40 C6** 42 8N 1 35 E
Sant Llorenç del Munt y l'Obac,
  Parque Natural de △, *Spain* .. **40 D3** 41 39N 1 55W
Sant Llorenç des Cardassar, *Spain* . **38 B4** 39 37N 3 17 E
Sant Mateu, *Baleares, Spain* .... **38 C1** 39 3N 1 23 E
Sant Mateu, *Valencia, Spain* .... **40 E5** 40 28N 0 10 E
Sant Miguel, *Spain* .... **38 C1** 39 3N 1 26 E
Sant Telm, *Spain* .... **38 B3** 39 35N 2 21 E
Santa, *Peru* .... **172 B2** 8 59 S 78 40W
Santa' Ágata Miltello, *Italy* ...... **47 D7** 38 2N 14 8 E
Santa Agnés, *Spain* .... **38 C1** 39 3N 1 21 E
Santa Ana, *Beni, Bolivia* .... **173 C4** 13 50 S 65 40W
Santa Ana, *La Paz, Bolivia* ...... **172 D4** 15 31 S 67 30W
Santa Ana, *Santa Cruz, Bolivia* .. **173 D6** 18 43 S 58 44W
Santa Ana, *Santa Cruz, Bolivia* .. **173 D5** 16 37 S 60 43W
Santa Ana, *Ecuador* .... **168 D1** 1 16 S 80 20W
Santa Ana, *El Salv.* **164 D2** 14 0N 89 31W
Santa Ana, *Mexico* **162 A2** 30 31N 111 8W
Santa Ana, *Phil.* .... **80 B4** 18 28N 122 20 E
Santa Ana, *Solomon Is.* .... **133 N12** 10 50 S 162 30 E
Santa Ana, *U.S.A.* **161 M9** 33 46N 117 52W
Santa Ana →, *Venezuela* **168 B3** 9 30N 71 57W
Santa' Ángelo Lodigiano, *Italy* .. **44 C6** 45 14N 9 25 E
Santa' Antíoco, *Italy* .... **46 C1** 39 4N 8 27 E
Santa Bárbara, *Santa Maria, Azores* **9 d4** 36 59N 25 4W
Santa Bárbara, *Terceira, Azores* .. **9 d1** 38 41N 27 20W
Santa Bárbara, *Chile* .... **174 D1** 37 40 S 72 1W
Santa Bárbara, *Colombia* **168 B2** 5 53N 75 35W
Santa Bárbara, *Honduras* **164 D2** 14 53N 88 14W
Santa Bárbara, *Mexico* **162 B3** 26 48N 105 50W
Santa Bárbara, *Phil.* .... **81 F4** 10 50N 122 32 E
Santa Bárbara, *Spain* .... **40 E5** 40 42N 0 29 E
Santa Bárbara, *U.S.A.* **161 L7** 34 25N 119 42W
Santa Bárbara, *Amazonas, Venezuela* **168 C4** 3 57N 67 6W
Santa Bárbara, *Barinas, Venezuela* **168 B3** 7 47N 71 10W
Santa Bárbara, Mt., *Spain* **41 H2** 37 23N 2 50W
Santa Barbara, Serra de, *Azores* .. **9 d1** 38 44N 27 19W
Santa Barbara Channel, *U.S.A.* .. **161 L7** 34 15N 120 0W
Santa Barbara I., *U.S.A.* **161 M7** 33 29N 119 2W
Santa Catalina, *Colombia* **168 A2** 10 36N 75 17W
Santa Catalina, *Solomon Is.* .... **133 N12** 10 53 S 162 29 E
Santa Catalina, Gulf of, *U.S.A.* .. **161 N9** 33 10N 117 50W
Santa Catalina, I., *Mexico* **162 B2** 25 40N 110 50W
Santa Catalina I., *U.S.A.* **161 M8** 33 23N 118 25W
Santa Catarina □, *Brazil* .... **175 B6** 27 25 S 48 30W
Santa Catarina, I. de, *Brazil* .... **175 B6** 27 30 S 48 40W
Santa Caterina di Pittinuri, *Italy* . **46 B1** 40 6N 8 27 E
Santa Caterina Villarmosa, *Italy* . **47 E7** 37 35N 14 2 E
Santa Cecília, *Brazil* .... **175 B5** 26 56 S 50 18W
Santa Clara, *Cuba* **164 B4** 22 20N 80 0W
Santa Clara, *Calif., U.S.A.* **160 H5** 37 21N 121 57W
Santa Clara, *Utah, U.S.A.* **159 H7** 37 8N 113 39W
Santa Clara, El Golfo de, *Mexico* . **162 A2** 31 42N 114 30W
Santa Clara de Olimar, *Uruguay* .. **175 C5** 32 50 S 54 54W
Santa Clarita, *U.S.A.* **161 L8** 34 24N 118 30W
Santa Clotilde, *Peru* .... **168 D3** 2 33 S 73 45W
Santa Coloma de Farners, *Spain* .. **40 D7** 41 50N 2 39 E
Santa Coloma de Gramenet, *Spain* . **40 D7** 41 27N 2 13 E
Santa Comba, *Spain* **42 B2** 43 2N 8 49W
Santa Croce Camerina, *Italy* .... **47 F7** 36 50N 14 31 E
Santa Croce di Magliano, *Italy* .. **45 G11** 41 43N 14 59 E
Santa Cruz, *Argentina* .... **176 D3** 50 0 S 68 32W
Santa Cruz, *Bolivia* .... **173 D5** 17 43 S 63 10W
Santa Cruz, *Brazil* .... **173 C4** 6 13 S 36 1W
Santa Cruz, *Chile* .... **174 C1** 34 38 S 71 27W
Santa Cruz, *Costa Rica* **164 D2** 10 15N 85 35W
Santa Cruz, *Peru* .... **172 B2** 5 40 S 75 56W
Santa Cruz, *Davao del S., Phil.* .. **81 H5** 6 50N 125 25 E
Santa Cruz, *Laguna, Phil.* ...... **80 D3** 14 20N 121 24 E
Santa Cruz, *Marinduque, Phil.* .. **80 E4** 13 28N 122 2 E
Santa Cruz, *Mind. Occ., Phil.* .. **80 D2** 15 46N 119 55 E
Santa Cruz, *Zambales, Phil.* .... **80 D2** 15 46N 119 55 E
Santa Cruz, *U.S.A.* **160 J4** 36 58N 122 1W
Santa Cruz, *Venezuela* **169 B5** 8 3N 64 27W
Santa Cruz □, *Argentina* .... **176 C3** 49 0 S 70 0W
Santa Cruz □, *Bolivia* .... **173 D5** 17 43 S 63 10W
Santa Cruz →, *Argentina* .... **176 D3** 50 10 S 68 20W
Santa Cruz, I., *Ecuador* .... **172 a** 0 38 S 90 23W
Santa Cruz Cabrália, *Brazil* .... **171 E4** 16 17 S 39 2W
Santa Cruz da Graciosa, *Azores* .. **9 d1** 39 5N 28 1W
Santa Cruz das Flores, *Azores* .. **9 d2** 39 27N 31 7W
Santa Cruz de la Palma, *Canary Is.* **9 e1** 28 41N 17 46W
Santa Cruz de la Palma ✈ (SPC),
  Canary Is. **9 e1** 28 40N 17 45W
Santa Cruz de Mudela, *Spain* **43 G7** 38 39N 3 28W
Santa Cruz de Tenerife, *Canary Is.* . **9 e1** 28 28N 16 15W
Santa Cruz del Norte, *Cuba* **164 B3** 23 9N 81 55W
Santa Cruz del Retamar, *Spain* .. **42 E6** 40 8N 4 13W
Santa Cruz del Sur, *Cuba* **164 B4** 20 44N 78 0W
Santa Cruz do Rio Pardo, *Brazil* . **175 A6** 22 54 S 49 37W
Santa Cruz do Sul, *Brazil* ...... **175 B5** 29 42 S 52 25W
Santa Cruz I., *U.S.A.* **161 M7** 34 1N 119 43W
Santa Cruz Is., *Solomon Is.* .... **134 J8** 10 30 S 166 0 E
Santa Cruz Mts., *Jamaica* ...... **164 a** 17 58N 77 43W
Santa Domingo, Cay, *Bahamas* .. **164 B4** 21 25N 75 15W
Sant' Egídio alla Vibrata, *Italy* .. **45 F10** 42 49N 13 42 E
Santa Elena, *Argentina* .... **174 C4** 30 58 S 59 47W
Santa Elena, *Ecuador* .... **168 D1** 2 16 S 80 52W
Santa Elena, *Phil.* .... **80 D4** 14 12N 122 24 E
Santa Elena, C., *Costa Rica* **164 D2** 10 54N 85 56W
Sant' Eufémia, G. di, *Italy* ...... **47 D9** 38 51N 16 11 E
Santa Eulàlia des Riu, *Spain* .... **38 D2** 38 59N 1 32 E
Santa Fe, *Argentina* .... **174 C3** 31 35 S 60 41W
Santa Fe, *Nueva Viscaya, Phil.* .. **80 C3** 16 10N 120 57 E
Santa Fe, *Romblon, Phil.* ...... **80 E4** 12 10N 122 0 E
Santa Fe, *Spain* **43 H7** 37 11N 3 43W
Santa Fe, *U.S.A.* **159 J11** 35 41N 105 57W
Santa Fé □, *Argentina* .... **174 C3** 31 50 S 60 55W
Santa Fé, Canal de, *Ecuador* .... **172 a** 0 48 S 89 55W
Santa Fé, I., *Ecuador* .... **172 a** 0 49 S 90 5W
Santa Fé do Sul, *Brazil* .... **171 F1** 20 13 S 50 56W
Santa Filomena, *Brazil* .... **170 C2** 9 6 S 45 50W
Santa Fiora, *Italy* .... **44 F8** 42 50N 11 31 E
Santa Gertrudis, *Spain* .... **38 C1** 39 0N 1 26 E
Santa Giustina, *Italy* .... **45 B9** 46 0N 12 5 E
Santa Helena, *Brazil* .... **170 B2** 2 14 S 45 18W
Santa Helena de Goiás, *Brazil* .. **171 E1** 17 43 S 50 35W
Santa Inês, *Bahia, Brazil* ...... **171 D4** 13 17 S 39 48W
Santa Inês, *Maranhão, Brazil* .. **170 B2** 3 39 S 45 20W
Santa Inês, *Spain* **43 G5** 38 32N 5 37W
Santa Inés, I., *Chile* .... **176 D2** 54 0 S 73 0W

Santa Isabel = Rey Malabo,
  Eq. Guin. .... **113 E6** 3 45N 8 50 E
Santa Isabel, *Argentina* .... **174 D2** 36 10 S 66 54W
Santa Isabel, *Solomon Is.* ...... **133 M10** 8 0 S 159 0 E
Santa Isabel, Pico, *Eq. Guin.* .. **113 E6** 3 36N 8 49 E
Santa Isabel do Araguaia, *Brazil* . **170 C2** 6 7 S 48 19W
Santa Isabel do Río Negro, *Brazil* . **169 D4** 0 24 S 65 2W
Santa Isabel do Morro, *Brazil* .. **171 D1** 11 34 S 50 40W
Santa Lúcia, *Corrientes, Argentina* . **174 B4** 28 58 S 59 5W
Santa Lúcia, *San Juan, Argentina* . **174 C2** 31 30 S 68 30W
Santa Lucía, *Phil.* .... **80 C3** 17 7N 120 27 E
Santa Lucía, *Spain* **41 H4** 37 35N 0 58W
Santa Lucía, *Uruguay* .... **174 C4** 34 27 S 56 24W
Santa Lucia Range, *U.S.A.* **160 K5** 36 0N 121 20W
Santa Luzia, *C. Verde Is.* ...... **9 j** 16 50N 24 35W
Santa Magdalena, I., *Mexico* **162 C2** 24 40N 112 15W
Santa Margarita, *Argentina* ...... **174 D3** 38 28 S 61 35W
Santa Margarita, *Spain* .... **38 B4** 39 42N 3 6 E
Santa Margarita, *U.S.A.* **160 K6** 35 23N 120 37W
Santa Margarita →, *U.S.A.* **161 M9** 33 13N 117 23W
Santa Margarita, I., *Mexico* **162 C2** 24 30N 111 50W
Santa Margherita, *Italy* .... **46 D1** 38 58N 8 58 E
Santa Margherita Ligure, *Italy* .. **44 D6** 44 20N 9 11 E
Santa María, *Argentina* .... **174 B2** 26 40 S 66 0W
Santa Maria, *Azores* **9 d4** 36 58N 25 6W
Santa Maria, *Brazil* .... **175 B5** 29 40 S 53 48W
Santa Maria, *C. Verde Is.* ...... **9 j** 16 31N 22 53W
Santa Maria, *Ilocos S., Phil.* .... **80 C3** 17 22N 120 29 E
Santa Maria, *Isabela, Phil.* ...... **80 C3** 17 28N 121 45 E
Santa Maria, *Switz.* .... **33 C10** 46 36N 10 25 E
Santa María →, *Mexico* **162 A3** 31 0N 107 14W
Santa María, B. de, *Mexico* **162 B3** 25 10N 108 40W
Santa Maria, C. de, *Portugal* **43 J3** 36 58N 7 53W
Santa María, I., *Ecuador* .... **172 a** 1 17 S 90 26W
Santa María Cápua Vétere, *Italy* . **47 A7** 41 5N 14 15 E
Santa Maria da Feira, *Portugal* .. **42 E2** 40 55N 8 35W
Santa Maria da Vitória, *Brazil* .. **171 D3** 13 24 S 44 12W
Santa Maria di Léuca, C., *Italy* .. **47 C11** 39 47N 18 22 E
Santa Maria do Boiaçu, *Brazil* .. **169 D5** 0 25 S 61 48W
Santa Maria do Suaçuí, *Brazil* .. **171 E3** 18 12 S 42 25W
Santa María la Real de Nieva, *Spain* **42 D6** 41 4N 4 24W
Santa Marinella, *Italy* .... **45 F8** 42 2N 11 52 E
Santa Marta, *Colombia* **168 A3** 11 15N 74 13W
Santa Marta, Sierra Nevada de,
  Colombia **168 A3** 10 55N 73 50W
Santa Marta de Tormes, *Spain* .. **42 E5** 40 57N 5 38W
Santa Marta Grande, C., *Brazil* .. **175 B6** 28 43 S 48 50W
Santa Marta Ortigueira, Ría de,
  Spain **42 B3** 43 44N 7 45W
Santa Maura = Levkás, *Greece* .. **39 B2** 38 40N 20 43 E
Santa Monica, *U.S.A.* **161 M8** 34 1N 118 29W
Santa Monica Mts. Nat. Recr.
  Area △, *U.S.A.* **161 L8** 34 4N 118 44W
Santa Olalla, *Huelva, Spain* **43 H4** 37 54N 6 14W
Santa Olalla, *Toledo, Spain* **42 E6** 40 2N 4 25W
Santa Paula, *U.S.A.* **161 L7** 34 21N 119 4W
Santa Pola, *Spain* **41 G4** 38 13N 0 35W
Santa Ponça, *Spain* .... **38 B3** 39 30N 2 28 E
Santa Quitéria, *Brazil* .... **170 B3** 4 20 S 40 10W
Santa Rita, *Brazil* .... **168 D4** 3 29 S 69 19W
Santa Rita, *Colombia* **168 C4** 4 53N 68 24W
Santa Rita, *Phil.* .... **81 F5** 11 07N 124 56 E
Santa Rita, *Venezuela* **159 K10** 32 48N 108 4W
Santa Rita, *Venezuela* **168 A3** 10 32N 71 32W
Santa Rita do Araquaia, *Brazil* .. **173 D7** 17 25 S 53 12W
Santa Rosa, *La Pampa, Argentina* . **174 D3** 36 40 S 64 17W
Santa Rosa, *San Luis, Argentina* . **174 C2** 32 21 S 65 10W
Santa Rosa, *Beni, Bolivia* ...... **172 C4** 14 0 S 66 50W
Santa Rosa, *Pando, Bolivia* .... **172 C4** 10 36 S 67 20W
Santa Rosa, *Brazil* .... **175 B5** 27 52 S 54 29W
Santa Rosa, *Calif., U.S.A.* **160 G4** 38 26N 122 43W
Santa Rosa, *N. Mex., U.S.A.* .. **155 H2** 34 57N 104 41W
Santa Rosa, *Venezuela* **168 C4** 1 29N 66 55W
Santa Rosa & San Jacinto Mts. Nat.
  Monument △, *U.S.A.* **161 M10** 33 28N 116 20W
Santa Rosa Beach, *U.S.A.* **152 E3** 30 24N 86 14W
Santa Rosa de Amanadona,
  Venezuela **168 C4** 1 29N 66 55W
Santa Rosa de Cabal, *Colombia* .. **168 C2** 4 52N 75 38W
Santa Rosa de Copán, *Honduras* .. **164 D2** 14 47N 88 46W
Santa Rosa de la Roca, *Bolivia* .. **173 D5** 16 3 S 61 34W
Santa Rosa de Osos, *Colombia* .. **168 B2** 6 39N 75 28W
Santa Rosa de Río Primero,
  Argentina .... **174 C3** 31 8 S 63 20W
Santa Rosa de Viterbo, *Colombia* . **168 B3** 5 53N 72 59W
Santa Rosa del Palmar, *Bolivia* .. **173 D5** 16 54 S 62 24W
Santa Rosa I., *Calif., U.S.A.* .. **161 M6** 33 58N 120 6W
Santa Rosa I., *Fla., U.S.A.* **153 E3** 30 20N 86 50W
Santa Rosa Range, *U.S.A.* **158 F5** 41 45N 117 40W
Santa Rosalía, *Mexico* **162 B2** 27 20N 112 20W
Santa Sylvina, *Argentina* ...... **174 B3** 27 50 S 61 10W
Santa Tecla = Nueva San Salvador,
  El Salv. **164 D2** 13 40N 89 18W
Santa Teresa, *Argentina* .... **174 C3** 33 25 S 60 47W
Santa Teresa, *Australia* .... **126 C4** 24 8 S 134 22 E
Santa Teresa, *Brazil* .... **171 E3** 19 55 S 40 36W
Santa Teresa, *Mexico* **163 B5** 25 17N 97 51W
Santa Teresa, *Venezuela* **169 C5** 4 43N 61 4W
Santa Teresa di Riva, *Italy* .... **47 E8** 37 57N 15 22 E
Santa Teresa Gallura, *Italy* .... **46 A2** 41 14N 9 11 E
Santa Teresinha, *Brazil* .... **170 D1** 50 30 S 50 31W
Santa Uxía, *Spain* **42 C2** 42 36N 8 58W
Santa Vitória, *Brazil* .... **171 E1** 18 50 S 50 8W
Santa Vitória do Palmar, *Brazil* .. **175 C5** 33 32 S 53 25W
Santa Ynez →, *U.S.A.* **161 L6** 35 41N 120 36W
Santa Ynez Mts., *U.S.A.* **161 L6** 34 30N 120 0W
Santa Ysabel, *U.S.A.* **161 M10** 33 7N 116 40W
Santadi, *Italy* .... **46 C1** 39 5N 8 43 E
Santaella, *Spain* **43 H6** 37 34N 4 51W
Santahar, *Bangla.* .... **90 C2** 24 48N 88 59 E
Santai, *China* .... **76 B5** 31 5N 104 58 E
Santana, *Brazil* .... **171 D3** 11 15 S 39 22W
Santana, *Madeira* .... **9 c** 32 48N 16 52W
Sântana, *Romania* .... **52 D6** 46 20N 21 30 E
Santana, Coxilha de, *Brazil* .... **175 C4** 30 50 S 55 35W
Santana do Ipanema, *Brazil* .... **171 E4** 9 22 S 37 14W
Santana do Livramento, *Brazil* .. **175 C4** 30 55 S 55 30W
Santander, *Colombia* **168 C2** 3 1N 76 28W
Santander, *Spain* .... **81 G4** 9 25N 123 20 E
Santander □, *Colombia* **168 B3** 7 0N 73 15W
Santander Jiménez, *Mexico* **163 C5** 24 11N 98 29W
Santanilla, Is., *Honduras* **164 C3** 17 22N 83 57W
Santanyí, *Spain* .... **38 B4** 39 20N 3 5 E
Santaquin, *U.S.A.* **158 G8** 39 59N 111 47W
Santarcángelo di Romagna, *Italy* . **45 D9** 44 4N 12 26 E
Santarém, *Brazil* .... **169 D7** 2 25 S 54 42W
Santarém, *Portugal* **43 F2** 39 12N 8 42W
Santarém □, *Portugal* **43 F2** 39 10N 8 40W
Santaren Channel, *W. Indies* **164 B4** 24 0N 79 30W
Santee, *U.S.A.* **161 N10** 32 50N 116 58W
Santee →, *U.S.A.* **149 J6** 33 7N 79 17W

278 Santéramo in Colle INDEX TO WORLD MAPS

Santéramo in Colle, *Italy* **47 B9** 40 49N 16 45 E
Santerno →, *Italy* **45 D8** 44 34N 11 58 E
Santhià, *Italy* **44 C5** 45 22N 8 10 E
Santi-Quaranta = Sarandë, *Albania* **38 B9** 39 52N 19 55 E
Santiago = São Tiago, *C. Verde Is.* **9 j** 15 0N 23 40W
Santiago, *Bolivia* **173 D6** 18 19 S 59 34W
Santiago, *Brazil* **175 B5** 29 11 S 54 52W
Santiago, *Canary Is.* **9 e1** 28 2N 17 12W
Santiago, *Chile* **174 C1** 33 24 S 70 40W
Santiago, *Panama* **164 E3** 8 0N 81 0W
Santiago, *Peru* **172 C2** 14 11 S 75 43W
Santiago, *Ilocos S., Phil.* **80 C3** 17 18N 120 27 E
Santiago, *Isabela, Phil.* **80 C3** 16 41N 121 33 E
Santiago □, *Chile* **174 C1** 33 30 S 70 50W
Santiago →, *Mexico* **136 G9** 25 11N 105 26W
Santiago →, *Peru* **168 D2** 4 27 S 77 38W
Santiago, C., *Chile* **176 D1** 50 46 S 75 27W
Santiago, I. = San Salvador, I., *Ecuador* **172 a** 0 16 S 90 42W
Santiago, Punta de, *Eq. Guin.* **113 E6** 3 12N 8 40 E
Santiago, Serranía de, *Bolivia* **173 D6** 18 25 S 59 25W
Santiago de Chuco, *Peru* **172 B2** 8 9 S 78 11W
Santiago de Compostela, *Spain* **42 C2** 42 52N 8 37W
Santiago de Cuba, *Cuba* **164 C4** 20 0N 75 49W
Santiago de los Cabelleros, *Dom. Rep.* **165 C5** 19 30N 70 40W
Santiago del Estero, *Argentina* **174 B3** 27 50 S 64 15W
Santiago del Estero □, *Argentina* **174 B3** 27 40 S 63 15W
Santiago del Teide, *Canary Is.* **9 e1** 28 17N 16 48W
Santiago do Cacém, *Portugal* **43 G2** 38 1N 8 42W
Santiago Ixcuintla, *Mexico* **162 C3** 21 50N 105 11W
Santiago Papasquiaro, *Mexico* **162 C3** 25 0N 105 20W
Santiaguillo, L. de, *Mexico* **162 C4** 24 50N 104 50W
Santiguila, *Mali* **112 C3** 12 42N 7 25W
Santillana, *Spain* **42 B6** 43 24N 4 6W
Säntis, *Switz.* **33 B8** 47 15N 9 22 E
Santisteban del Puerto, *Spain* **43 G7** 38 17N 3 15W
Santo →, *Peru* **172 B2** 8 56 S 78 37W
Santo Amaro, *Brazil* **171 D4** 12 30 S 38 43W
Santo Anastácio, *Brazil* **175 A5** 21 58 S 51 39W
Santo André, *Brazil* **175 A6** 23 39 S 46 29W
Santo Ângelo, *Brazil* **175 B5** 28 15 S 54 15W
Santo Antão, *C. Verde Is.* **9 j** 16 52N 25 10W
Santo Antónia, *São Tomé & Principe* **115 G6** 1 37N 7 27 E
Santo Antonio, *Brazil* **169 D5** 2 24 S 60 58W
Santo Antônio de Jesus, *Brazil* **171 D4** 12 58 S 39 16W
Santo Antônio do Içá, *Brazil* **168 D4** 3 5 S 67 57W
Santo Antônio do Leverger, *Brazil* **173 D6** 15 52 S 56 5W
Santo Corazón, *Bolivia* **173 D6** 18 0 S 58 45W
Santo Domingo, *Dom. Rep.* **165 C6** 18 30N 69 59W
Santo Domingo, *Baja Calif., Mexico* **162 A1** 30 43N 116 2W
Santo Domingo, *Baja Calif. S., Mexico* **162 B2** 25 32N 112 2W
Santo Domingo, *Nic.* **164 D3** 12 14N 84 59W
Santo Domingo de la Calzada, *Spain* **40 C2** 42 26N 2 57W
Santo Domingo de los Colorados, *Ecuador* **168 D2** 0 15 S 79 9W
Santo Domingo Pueblo, *U.S.A.* **159 J10** 35 31N 106 22W
Santo Stéfano di Camastro, *Italy* **47 D7** 38 1N 14 22 E
Santo Tirso, *Portugal* **42 D2** 41 21N 8 28W
Santo Tomás, *Ecuador* **172 a** 0 51 S 91 2W
Santo Tomás, *Mexico* **162 A1** 31 33N 116 24W
Santo Tomás, *Peru* **172 C3** 14 26 S 72 8W
Santo Tomás, Volcán, *Ecuador* **172 a** 0 48 S 91 7W
Santo Tomé, *Argentina* **175 B4** 28 40 S 56 5W
Santo Tomé de Guayana = Ciudad Guayana, *Venezuela* **169 B5** 8 0N 62 30W
Santomera, *Spain* **41 G3** 38 4N 1 3W
Santoña, *Spain* **42 B7** 43 29N 3 27W
Santoríni = Thíra, *Greece* **49 E7** 36 23N 25 27 E
Santos, *Brazil* **175 A6** 24 0 S 46 20W
Santos, Sierra de los, *Spain* **43 G5** 38 7N 5 12W
Santos Dumont, *Brazil* **171 F3** 22 55 S 43 10W
Sanur, *Indonesia* **79 K18** 8 41 S 115 15 E
Sanwer, *India* **92 H6** 22 59N 75 50 E
Sanxenxo, *Spain* **42 C2** 42 24N 8 49W
Sanxiang, *China* **69 G9** 22 21N 113 25 E
San'yō, *Japan* **72 C3** 34 2N 131 5 E
Sanyuan, *China* **74 G5** 34 35N 108 58 E
Sanyuki-Sammyaku, *Japan* **72 C6** 34 5N 134 0 E
Sanza Pombo, *Angola* **115 D3** 7 18 S 15 56 E
São Bartolomeu de Messines, *Portugal* **43 H2** 37 15N 8 17W
São Benedito, *Brazil* **170 B3** 4 3 S 40 53W
São Benedito →, *Brazil* **173 B6** 9 11 S 57 2W
São Bento, *Brazil* **170 B3** 2 42 S 44 50W
São Bento do Norte, *Brazil* **170 C4** 5 4 S 36 2W
São Bernardo do Campo, *Brazil* **171 F2** 23 45 S 46 34W
São Borja, *Brazil* **175 B4** 28 39 S 56 0W
São Brás de Alportel, *Portugal* **43 H3** 37 8N 7 37W
São Braz, C. de, *Angola* **115 D2** 9 58 S 13 19 E
São Caitano, *Brazil* **170 C4** 8 21 S 36 6W
São Carlos, *Brazil* **175 A6** 22 0 S 47 50W
São Cristóvão, *Brazil* **170 D4** 11 1 S 37 15W
São Domingos, *Brazil* **171 D2** 13 25 S 46 19W
São Domingos, *Guinea-Biss.* **112 C1** 12 19N 16 13 E
São Domingos do Maranhão, *Brazil* **170 C3** 5 42 S 44 22W
São Félix, *Brazil* **171 D1** 11 36 S 50 39W
São Felix do Xingu, *Brazil* **173 B7** 6 38 S 51 59W
São Filipe, *C. Verde Is.* **9 j** 15 2N 24 30W
São Francisco, *Brazil* **171 E3** 16 0 S 44 50W
São Francisco →, *Brazil* **170 D4** 10 30 S 36 24W
São Francisco do Maranhão, *Brazil* **170 C3** 6 15 S 42 52W
São Francisco do Sul, *Brazil* **175 B6** 26 15 S 48 36W
São Gabriel, *Brazil* **175 C5** 30 20 S 54 20W
São Gabriel da Cachoeira, *Brazil* **168 D4** 0 8 S 67 5W
São Gabriel da Palha, *Brazil* **171 E3** 18 47 S 40 39W
São Gonçalo = Araripina, *Brazil* **170 C3** 7 33 S 40 34W
São Gonçalo, *Brazil* **171 F3** 22 48 S 43 5W
São Gotardo, *Brazil* **171 E2** 19 19 S 46 3W
Sao Hill, *Tanzania* **119 D4** 8 20 S 35 12 E
São João, *Guinea-Biss.* **112 C1** 11 32N 15 25W
São João da Baliza, *Brazil* **169 C6** 0 52N 59 52W
São João da Boa Vista, *Brazil* **175 A6** 22 0 S 46 52W
São João da Madeira, *Portugal* **42 E2** 40 54N 8 30W
São João da Pesqueira, *Portugal* **42 D3** 41 8N 7 24W
São João da Ponte, *Brazil* **171 E3** 15 56 S 44 1W
São João del Rei, *Brazil* **171 F3** 21 8 S 44 15W
São João do Araguaia, *Brazil* **170 C2** 5 23 S 48 46W
São João do Paraíso, *Brazil* **171 E3** 15 19 S 42 1W
São João do Piauí, *Brazil* **170 C3** 8 21 S 42 15W
São João dos Patos, *Brazil* **170 C3** 6 30 S 43 42W
São Joaquim, *Amazonas, Brazil* **168 D4** 0 1 S 67 16W
São Joaquim, *Sta. Catarina, Brazil* **175 B6** 28 18 S 49 56W
São Joaquim da Barra, *Brazil* **171 F2** 20 35 S 47 53W
São Jorge, *Azores* **9 d1** 38 38N 28 3W
São Jorge, Canal de, *Azores* **9 d1** 38 30N 28 0W
São Jorge, Pta. de, *Azores* **9 d1** 38 42N 27 3W
São Jorge, Pta. de, *Madeira* **9 c** 32 50N 16 53W
São José, *Brazil* **175 B5** 27 38 S 48 39W
São José, B. de, *Brazil* **170 B3** 2 38 S 44 4W
São José da Laje, *Brazil* **170 C4** 9 1 S 36 3W
São José de Mipibu, *Brazil* **170 C4** 6 5 S 35 15W
São José do Norte, *Brazil* **175 C5** 32 1 S 52 3W
São José do Peixe, *Brazil* **170 C3** 7 24 S 42 34W
São José do Rio Prêto, *Brazil* **175 A6** 20 50 S 49 20W
São José dos Campos, *Brazil* **175 A6** 23 7 S 45 52W
São Leopoldo, *Brazil* **175 B5** 29 50 S 51 10W
São Lourenço, *Brazil* **171 F2** 22 7 S 45 3W
São Lourenço →, *Brazil* **173 D6** 17 53 S 57 27W
São Lourenço, Pantanal do, *Brazil* **173 D6** 17 30 S 56 20W
São Lourenço, Pta. de, *Madeira* **9 c** 32 44N 16 39W
São Lourenço do Sul, *Brazil* **175 C5** 31 22 S 51 58W
São Luís, *Brazil* **170 B3** 2 39 S 44 15W
São Luís do Curu, *Brazil* **170 B4** 3 40 S 39 14W
São Luís do Tapojós, *Brazil* **169 D6** 4 25 S 56 12W
São Luís Gonzaga, *Brazil* **175 B5** 28 25 S 55 0W
São Marcos →, *Brazil* **171 E2** 18 15 S 47 37W
São Marcos, B. de, *Brazil* **170 B3** 2 0 S 44 0W
São Martinho da Cortiça, *Portugal* **42 E2** 40 18N 8 8W
São Mateus, *Azores* **9 d1** 38 26N 28 27W
São Mateus, *Brazil* **171 E4** 18 44 S 39 50W
São Mateus →, *Brazil* **171 E4** 18 35 S 39 44W
São Mateus do Sul, *Brazil* **175 B5** 25 52 S 50 23W
São Miguel, *Azores* **9 d3** 37 47N 25 30W
São Miguel do Araguaia, *Brazil* **171 D1** 13 19 S 50 13W
São Miguel do Oeste, *Brazil* **175 B5** 26 45 S 53 34W
São Miguel dos Campos, *Brazil* **170 C4** 9 47 S 36 5W
São Nicolau, *C. Verde Is.* **9 j** 16 20N 24 20W
São Nicolau →, *Angola* **115 E2** 14 16 S 12 22 E
São Nicolau →, *Brazil* **170 C3** 5 45 S 42 2W
São Paulo, *Brazil* **175 A6** 23 32 S 46 37W
São Paulo □, *Brazil* **175 A6** 22 0 S 49 0W
São Paulo, I., *Atl. Oc.* **8 F9** 0 50N 31 40W
São Paulo de Olivença, *Brazil* **168 D4** 3 27 S 68 48W
São Pedro do Sul, *Portugal* **42 E2** 40 46N 8 4W
São Rafael, *Brazil* **170 C4** 5 47 S 36 55W
São Raimundo das Mangabeiras, *Brazil* **170 C2** 7 1 S 45 29W
São Raimundo Nonato, *Brazil* **170 C3** 9 1 S 42 42W
São Romão, *Brazil* **171 E2** 16 22 S 45 4W
São Roque, *Madeira* **9 c** 32 46N 16 48W
São Roque, C. de, *Brazil* **170 C4** 5 30 S 35 16W
São Roque do Pico, *Azores* **9 d1** 38 31N 28 19W
São Sebastião, *Azores* **9 d1** 38 39N 27 6W
São Sebastião, I. de, *Brazil* **175 A6** 23 50 S 45 18W
São Sebastião do Paraíso, *Brazil* **175 A6** 20 54 S 46 59W
São Simão, *Brazil* **171 E1** 18 56 S 50 30W
São Teotónio, *Portugal* **43 H2** 37 30N 8 42W
São Tiago, *C. Verde Is.* **9 j** 15 0N 23 40W
São Tomé, *Brazil* **170 C4** 5 58 S 36 4W
São Tomé, *São Tomé & Principe* **115 G6** 0 10N 6 39 E
São Tomé, C. de, *Brazil* **171 F3** 22 0 S 40 59W
São Tomé, Pico de, *São Tomé & Principe* **115 G6** 0 16N 6 33 E
São Tomé & Principe ■, *Africa* **115 G6** 0 12N 6 39 E
São Vicente = Araguatins, *Brazil* **170 C2** 5 38 S 48 7W
São Vicente, *Brazil* **175 A6** 23 57 S 46 23W
São Vicente, *C. Verde Is.* **9 j** 17 0N 25 0W
São Vicente, *Madeira* **9 c** 32 48N 17 3W
São Vicente, C. de, *Portugal* **43 H1** 37 0N 9 0W
Saona, I., *Dom. Rep.* **165 C6** 18 10N 68 40W
Saône →, *France* **27 G11** 45 44N 4 50 E
Saône-et-Loire □, *France* **27 F11** 46 30N 4 50 E
Saonek, *Indonesia* **83 B4** 0 22 S 130 55 E
Saoura, O. →, *Algeria* **111 C4** 29 0N 0 55W
Sápai, *Greece* **51 E9** 41 2N 25 43 E
Sapam, Ao, *Thailand* **87 a** 8 0N 98 26 E
Sapanca, *Turkey* **100 B4** 40 41N 30 16 E
Sapão →, *Brazil* **170 D2** 11 1 S 45 32W
Saparua, *Indonesia* **82 B3** 3 33 S 128 40 E
Sapé, *Brazil* **170 C4** 7 6 S 35 13W
Sape, *Indonesia* **85 D5** 8 34 S 118 59 E
Sapele, *Nigeria* **113 D6** 5 50N 5 40 E
Sapelo I., *U.S.A.* **152 D8** 31 25N 81 12W
Sapelo Sound, *U.S.A.* **152 D8** 31 30N 81 10W
Şaphane, *Turkey* **49 B11** 39 1N 29 13 E
Sapi Safari Area ⌓, *Zimbabwe* **119 F2** 15 48 S 29 42 E
Sapiéntza, *Greece* **48 E3** 36 45N 21 43 E
Sapindji, *Dem. Rep. of the Congo* **115 D4** 9 39 S 23 12 E
Sapo Nat. Park △, *Liberia* **112 D3** 5 15N 8 30W
Sapone, *Burkina Faso* **113 C4** 12 3N 1 35W
Saposoa, *Peru* **172 B2** 6 55 S 76 45W
Sapouy, *Burkina Faso* **113 C4** 11 34N 1 44W
Sapozhok, *Russia* **60 D5** 53 59N 40 41 E
Sapphire, *Australia* **126 C4** 23 28 S 147 43 E
Sappho, *U.S.A.* **160 B2** 48 4N 124 16W
Sapporo, *Japan* **70 C10** 43 0N 141 21 E
Sapri, *Italy* **47 B8** 40 4N 15 38 E
Sapu, *Angola* **115 E3** 12 28 S 19 26 E
Sapudi, *Indonesia* **85 D4** 7 6 S 114 20 E
Sapulpa, *U.S.A.* **155 H6** 35 59N 96 5W
Saqqez, *Iran* **101 D12** 36 15N 46 20 E
Sar Dasht, *Āzarbājān-e Gharbī, Iran* **101 D11** 36 9N 45 28 E
Sar Dasht, *Khuzestān, Iran* **97 C6** 32 32N 48 52 E
Sar-e Pol, *Afghan.* **91 A2** 36 10N 66 0 E
Sar-e Pol □, *Afghan.* **91 A2** 36 20N 65 50 E
Sar Gachīneh = Yāsūj, *Iran* **97 D6** 30 31N 51 31 E
Sar Planina, *Macedonia* **50 E4** 42 0N 21 0 E
Sara, *Burkina Faso* **112 C4** 11 40N 3 53W
Sara, *Niger* **109 D2** 20 46N 12 35 E
Sara, *Phil.* **81 F4** 11 16N 123 1 E
Sara Buri = Saraburi, *Thailand* **86 E3** 14 30N 100 55 E
Šara Nac. Park △, *Yugoslavia* **50 D5** 42 12N 21 0 E
Sarāb, *Iran* **101 D12** 37 55N 47 40 E
Sarabadi, *Iraq* **96 C5** 33 1N 44 48 E
Saraburi, *Thailand* **86 E3** 14 30N 100 55 E
Saradiya, *India* **92 J4** 21 34N 70 2 E
Saraféré, *Mali* **112 B4** 15 50N 3 40W
Saragossa = Zaragoza, *Spain* **40 D4** 41 39N 0 53W
Saraguro, *Ecuador* **168 D2** 3 35 S 79 16W
Sarai Naurang, *Pakistan* **92 C4** 32 50N 70 47 E
Saraikela, *India* **93 H11** 22 42N 85 56 E
Saraipali, *India* **94 D6** 21 20N 82 59 E
Saraiu, *Romania* **53 F13** 44 43N 28 10 E
Sarajevo, *Bos.-H.* **52 G3** 43 52N 18 26 E
Sarakhs, *Turkmenistan* **97 B9** 36 32N 61 13 E
Saraktash, *Russia* **64 F6** 51 47N 56 22 E
Saramacca →, *Suriname* **169 B6** 5 50N 55 55W
Saramati, *Burma* **90 C5** 25 44N 95 2 E
Saran, Gunung, *Indonesia* **85 C4** 0 30 S 111 25 E
Saranac, *U.S.A.* **157 B11** 42 56N 85 13W
Saranac L., *U.S.A.* **151 B10** 44 20N 74 10W
Saranac Lake, *U.S.A.* **151 B10** 44 20N 74 8W
Saranda, *Tanzania* **118 D3** 5 45 S 34 59 E
Sarandë, *Albania* **38 B9** 39 52N 19 55 E
Sarandí del Yi, *Uruguay* **175 C4** 33 18 S 55 38W
Sarandí Grande, *Uruguay* **174 C4** 33 44 S 56 20W
Sarangani □, *Phil.* **81 J5** 5 45N 125 20 E
Sarangani B., *Phil.* **81 J5** 6 0N 125 13 E
Sarangani Is., *Phil.* **81 J5** 5 25N 125 25 E
Sarangarh, *India* **94 D6** 21 30N 83 5 E
Saransk, *Russia* **60 C7** 54 10N 45 10 E
Sarapul, *Russia* **64 C4** 56 28N 53 48 E
Sarar Plain = Bannaanka Saraar, *Somali Rep.* **120 C3** 9 25N 46 17 E
Sarasota, *U.S.A.* **153 H7** 27 20N 82 32W
Saratoga, *Calif., U.S.A.* **160 H4** 37 16N 122 2W
Saratoga, *Wyo., U.S.A.* **158 F10** 41 27N 106 49W
Saratoga Nat. Historical Park △, *U.S.A.* **151 D11** 43 0N 73 37W
Saratoga Springs, *U.S.A.* **151 C11** 43 5N 73 47W
Saratok, *Malaysia* **78 D4** 1 55N 111 17 E
Saratov, *Russia* **60 E7** 51 30N 46 2 E
Saravane, *Laos* **86 E6** 15 43N 106 25 E
Sarawak □, *Malaysia* **85 B4** 2 0N 113 0 E
Saray, *Tekirdağ, Turkey* **51 E11** 41 26N 27 55 E
Saray, *Van, Turkey* **101 C11** 38 38N 44 9 E
Saraya, *Guinea* **112 C2** 12 50N 11 45W
Saraya, *Senegal* **112 C2** 12 50N 11 45W
Saraycık, *Turkey* **49 B11** 39 1N 29 49 E
Sarayköy, *Turkey* **49 D10** 37 55N 28 54 E
Saraylar, *Turkey* **51 F11** 40 39N 27 40 E
Sarayönü, *Turkey* **100 C5** 38 16N 32 24 E
Sarbāz, *Iran* **97 E9** 26 38N 61 19 E
Sarbīsheh, *Iran* **97 C8** 32 30N 59 40 E
Sárbogárd, *Hungary* **52 D3** 46 50N 18 40 E
Sarca →, *Italy* **44 C7** 45 52N 10 52 E
Sarcelles, *France* **27 D9** 48 59N 2 23 E
Sardalas, *Libya* **108 C2** 25 50N 10 34 E
Sardarshahr, *India* **92 E6** 28 30N 74 29 E
Sardegna □, *Italy* **46 B1** 40 0N 9 0 E
Sardhana, *India* **92 E7** 29 9N 77 39 E
Sardina, Pta., *Canary Is.* **9 e1** 28 9N 15 44W
Sardinata, *Colombia* **168 B3** 8 5N 72 48W
Sardinia = Sardegna □, *Italy* **46 B1** 40 0N 9 0 E
Sardinia, *U.S.A.* **157 F13** 39 0N 83 49W
Sardis, *Turkey* **49 C10** 38 28N 28 2 E
Sardis, *U.S.A.* **152 C8** 32 58N 81 46W
Sārdūīyeh = Dar Mazār, *Iran* **97 D8** 29 14N 57 20 E
Saren, *Indonesia* **79 J18** 8 26 S 115 34 E
S'Arenal, *Spain* **38 B3** 39 30N 2 45 E
Sarentino, *Italy* **45 B8** 46 38N 11 21 E
Saréyamou, *Mali* **112 B4** 16 7N 3 10W
Sargans, *Switz.* **33 B8** 47 3N 9 15 E
Sargasso Sea, *Atl. Oc.* **8 D4** 27 0N 72 0W
Sargent, *U.S.A.* **152 B5** 33 26N 84 52W
Sargodha, *Pakistan* **91 B4** 32 10N 72 40 E
Sarh, *Chad* **109 G8** 9 5N 18 23 E
Sarhala, *Ivory C.* **112 D3** 8 22N 6 8W
Sarhro, Jebel, *Morocco* **110 B4** 31 6N 5 0W
Sārī, *Iran* **97 B7** 36 30N 53 4 E
Sari d'Orcino, *France* **29 F12** 42 3N 8 49 E
Sária, *Greece* **49 F9** 35 54N 27 17 E
Saria, *India* **93 J10** 21 38N 83 22 E
Sariab, *Pakistan* **92 D2** 30 6N 66 59 E
Sarıbeyler, *Turkey* **49 B9** 39 24N 27 35 E
Saricumbe, *Angola* **115 E3** 12 12 S 19 46 E
Sarıgöl, *Turkey* **100 C3** 38 14N 28 41 E
Sarikamiş, *Turkey* **101 B10** 40 22N 42 35 E
Sarıkaya, *Turkey* **100 C6** 39 29N 35 22 E
Sarikei, *Malaysia* **85 B4** 2 8N 111 30 E
Sarıköy, *Turkey* **51 F11** 40 12N 27 37 E
Sarila, *India* **93 G8** 25 46N 79 41 E
Sarina, *Australia* **126 C4** 21 22 S 149 13 E
Sariñena, *Spain* **40 D4** 41 47N 0 10W
Sariri, *Papua N. G.* **132 E5** 9 11 S 148 35 E
Sarita, *U.S.A.* **155 M6** 27 13N 97 47W
Sariwŏn, *N. Korea* **75 E13** 38 31N 125 46 E
Sariyar Barajı, *Turkey* **100 B4** 40 2N 31 33 E
Sariyer, *Turkey* **51 E13** 41 10N 29 3 E
Sarju →, *India* **93 F9** 27 21N 81 23 E
Sark, *U.K.* **21 H5** 49 25N 2 22W
Sarkad, *Hungary* **52 D6** 46 47N 21 23 E
Sarkari Tala, *India* **92 F4** 27 39N 70 52 E
Şarkışla, *Turkey* **100 C7** 39 21N 36 25 E
Şarköy, *Turkey* **51 F11** 40 36N 27 6 E
Sarlat-la-Canéda, *France* **28 D5** 44 54N 1 13 E
Sărmăşag, *Romania* **52 C7** 47 21N 22 50 E
Sărmaşu, *Romania* **53 D9** 46 45N 24 13 E
Sarmi, *Indonesia* **83 B5** 1 49 S 138 44 E
Sarmiento, *Argentina* **176 C3** 45 35 S 69 5W
Sarmizegetusa, *Romania* **52 E7** 45 31N 22 47 E
Särna, *Sweden* **16 C7** 61 41N 13 8 E
Sarnano, *Italy* **45 E10** 43 2N 13 18 E
Sarnen, *Switz.* **32 C6** 46 53N 8 13 E
Sarnia, *Canada* **140 D3** 42 58N 82 23W
Sarno, *Italy* **47 B7** 40 49N 14 37 E
Sarnthein = Sarentino, *Italy* **45 B8** 46 38N 11 21 E
Särö, *Sweden* **17 G5** 57 31N 11 57 E
Saroako, *Indonesia* **82 B2** 2 31 S 121 22 E
Sarolangun, *Indonesia* **84 C2** 2 19 S 102 42 E
Saronikós Kólpos, *Greece* **48 D5** 37 45N 23 45 E
Saronno, *Italy* **44 C6** 45 38N 9 2 E
Saros Körfezi, *Turkey* **51 F10** 40 30N 26 15 E
Sárospatak, *Hungary* **52 B6** 48 18N 21 33 E
Sarowbī, *Afghan.* **91 B3** 34 36N 69 44 E
Sarpsborg, *Norway* **18 E8** 59 16N 11 7 E
Sarracín, *Spain* **42 C7** 42 15N 3 45W
Sarralbe, *France* **27 D14** 49 0N 7 1 E
Sarrat, *Phil.* **80 B3** 18 9N 120 39 E
Sarre = Saar →, *Europe* **24 E6** 49 41N 6 32 E
Sarre, *Italy* **44 C4** 45 40N 7 15 E
Sarre-Union, *France* **27 D14** 48 57N 7 4 E
Sarrebourg, *France* **27 D14** 48 43N 7 3 E
Sarreguemines, *France* **27 C14** 49 5N 7 4 E
Sarria, *Spain* **42 C3** 42 49N 7 29W
Sarrión, *Spain* **40 E4** 40 9N 0 49W
Sarro, *Mali* **112 C3** 13 40N 5 15W
Sarstedt, *Germany* **30 C5** 52 14N 9 52 E
Sartène, *France* **29 G12** 41 38N 8 58 E
Sarthe □, *France* **26 D7** 48 10N 0 10 E
Sarthe →, *France* **26 E6** 47 33N 0 31W
Sartilly, *France* **26 D5** 48 45N 1 28W
Saruhanlı, *Turkey* **49 C9** 38 44N 27 36 E
Săruleşti, *Romania* **53 F11** 44 25N 26 39 E
Saruna →, *Pakistan* **92 F2** 26 31N 67 7 E
Sarupeta, *India* **90 B3** 26 30N 91 5 E
Saruwaged Ra., *Papua N. G.* **132 D4** 6 13 S 146 45 E
Sárvár, *Hungary* **52 C1** 47 15N 16 56 E
Sarvar, *India* **92 F6** 26 4N 75 0 E
Sarvestān, *Iran* **97 D7** 29 20N 53 10 E
Särvfjället, *Sweden* **16 B7** 62 42N 13 30 E
Sárviz →, *Hungary* **52 D3** 46 24N 18 41 E
Sary-Tash, *Kyrgyzstan* **65 D6** 39 44N 73 15 E
Saryaghash, *Kazakhstan* **65 C4** 41 27N 69 9 E
Sarybulaq, *Kazakhstan* **65 B5** 43 23N 71 29 E
Sarych, Mys, *Ukraine* **59 K7** 44 25N 33 45 E
Sarykemer, *Kazakhstan* **65 B5** 43 0N 71 30 E
Sarykolskiy Khrebet, *Tajikistan* **65 D7** 38 30N 74 30 E
Saryözek, *Kazakhstan* **65 A8** 44 22N 77 59 E
Saryshagan, *Kazakhstan* **66 E8** 46 12N 73 38 E
Sarzana, *Italy* **44 D6** 44 7N 9 58 E
Sarzeau, *France* **26 E4** 47 31N 2 48W
Sasabeneh, *Ethiopia* **120 C2** 7 59N 44 43 E
Sasamungga, *Solomon Is.* **133 L9** 7 0 S 156 50 E
Sasan Gir, *India* **92 J4** 21 10N 70 36 E
Sasaram, *India* **93 G11** 24 57N 84 5 E
Sasari, Mt., *Solomon Is.* **133 M10** 8 10 S 159 30 E
Sasayama, *Japan* **73 B7** 35 4N 135 13 E
Sasebo, *Japan* **72 D1** 33 10N 129 43 E
Saser, *India* **93 B7** 34 50N 77 50 E
Saskatchewan □, *Canada* **143 C7** 54 40N 106 0W
Saskatchewan →, *Canada* **143 C8** 53 37N 100 40W
Saskatoon, *Canada* **143 C7** 52 10N 106 38W
Saskylakh, *Russia* **67 B12** 71 55N 114 1 E
Saslaya, Parque Nac. △, *Nic.* **164 D2** 13 45N 85 4W
Sasolburg, *S. Africa* **117 D4** 26 46 S 27 49 E
Sasovo, *Russia* **60 C5** 54 25N 41 55 E
Sassandra, *Ivory C.* **112 E3** 4 55N 6 8W
Sassandra →, *Ivory C.* **112 E3** 4 58N 6 5W
Sássari, *Italy* **46 B1** 40 43N 8 34 E
Sassnitz, *Germany* **30 A9** 54 29N 13 39 E
Sasso Marconi, *Italy* **45 D8** 44 24N 11 15 E
Sassocorvaro, *Italy* **45 E9** 43 47N 12 30 E
Sassoferrato, *Italy* **45 E9** 43 26N 12 51 E
Sasstown, *Liberia* **112 E3** 4 45N 8 27W
Sassuolo, *Italy* **44 D7** 44 33N 10 47 E
Sástago, *Spain* **40 D4** 41 19N 0 21W
Sastöbe, *Kazakhstan* **65 B4** 42 33N 70 0 E
Sasvad, *India* **94 E2** 18 20N 74 2 E
Sasyk, Ozero, *Ukraine* **59 K5** 45 45N 29 20 E
Sata-Misaki, *Japan* **72 F2** 31 0N 130 40 E
Satadougou, *Mali* **112 C2** 12 25N 11 25W
Satakunta, *Finland* **15 F20** 61 45N 23 0 E
Satama-Soukoura, *Ivory C.* **112 D4** 7 55N 4 27W
Satara, *India* **94 F1** 17 44N 73 58 E
Satara, *S. Africa* **117 C5** 24 29 S 31 47 E
Satbarwa, *India* **93 H11** 23 55N 84 16 E
Satellite Beach, *U.S.A.* **153 G9** 28 10N 80 36W
Såtenäs, *Sweden* **17 F6** 58 27N 12 41 E
Säter, *Sweden* **16 D9** 60 21N 15 45 E
Satevó, *Mexico* **162 B3** 27 57N 106 7W
Satilla →, *U.S.A.* **152 E8** 30 59N 81 29W
Satipo, *Peru* **172 C3** 11 15 S 74 25W
Satka, *Russia* **64 D7** 55 3N 59 1 E
Satkania, *Bangla.* **90 D4** 22 4N 92 3 E
Satkhira, *Bangla.* **90 D2** 22 43N 89 8 E
Satmala Hills, *Andhra Pradesh, India* **94 E4** 19 45N 78 45 E
Satmala Hills, *Maharashtra, India* **94 D2** 20 15N 74 40 E
Satna, *India* **93 G9** 24 35N 80 50 E
Šator, *Bos.-H.* **45 D13** 44 11N 16 37 E
Sátoraljaújhely, *Hungary* **52 B6** 48 25N 21 41 E
Satpura Ra., *India* **94 D3** 21 25N 76 10 E
Satrup, *Germany* **30 A5** 54 41N 9 36 E
Satsuma-Hantō, *Japan* **72 F2** 31 25N 130 25 E
Satsuna-Shotō, *Japan* **71 K5** 30 0N 130 0 E
Sattahip, *Thailand* **86 F3** 12 41N 100 54 E
Sattenapalle, *India* **95 F5** 16 25N 80 6 E
Satu Mare, *Romania* **52 C7** 47 46N 22 55 E
Satu Mare □, *Romania* **52 C8** 47 45N 23 0 E
Satui, *Indonesia* **85 C5** 3 50 S 115 27 E
Satun, *Thailand* **87 J3** 6 43N 100 2 E
Satupa'itea, *Samoa* **133 W23** 13 45 S 172 18W
Saturnina →, *Brazil* **173 C6** 12 15 S 58 10W
Sauce, *Argentina* **174 C4** 30 5 S 58 46W
Sauceda, *Mexico* **162 B4** 25 55N 101 18W
Saucillo, *Mexico* **162 B3** 28 1N 105 17W
Sauda, *Norway* **18 E3** 59 40N 6 20 E
Saūdakent, *Kazakhstan* **65 B4** 43 48N 69 58 E
Saudasjøen, *Norway* **18 E3** 59 38N 6 17 E
Saúde, *Brazil* **170 D3** 10 56 S 40 24W
Sauðarkrókur, *Iceland* **11 B7** 65 45N 19 40W
Saudi Arabia ■, *Asia* **96 B3** 26 0N 44 0 E
Sauerland, *Germany* **36 C4** 51 12N 7 59 E
Saugatuck, *U.S.A.* **157 B10** 42 40N 86 12W
Saugeen →, *Canada* **150 B3** 44 30N 81 22W
Saugerties, *U.S.A.* **151 D11** 42 5N 73 57W
Saugues, *France* **28 D7** 44 58N 3 32 E
Saugus, *U.S.A.* **161 L8** 34 25N 118 32W
Saujon, *France* **28 C3** 45 41N 0 55W
Sauk Centre, *U.S.A.* **154 C7** 45 44N 94 57W
Sauk City, *U.S.A.* **156 A7** 43 17N 89 43W
Sauk Rapids, *U.S.A.* **154 C7** 45 35N 94 10W
Saül, *Fr. Guiana* **169 C7** 3 37N 53 12W
Sauland, *Norway* **18 E5** 59 37N 8 56 E
Saulgau, *Germany* **31 G5** 48 1N 9 29 E
Saulieu, *France* **27 E11** 47 17N 4 14 E
Sault, *France* **29 D9** 44 6N 5 24 E
Sault Ste. Marie, *Canada* **140 C3** 46 30N 84 20W
Sault Ste. Marie, *U.S.A.* **139 D11** 46 30N 84 21W
Saumlaki, *Indonesia* **83 C4** 7 55 S 131 20 E
Saumur, *France* **26 E6** 47 15N 0 5W
Saundatti, *India* **95 G2** 15 47N 75 7 E
Saunders, C., *N.Z.* **131 F5** 45 53 S 170 45 E
Saunders I., *Antarctica* **7 B1** 57 48 S 26 28W
Saunders Point, *Australia* **125 E4** 27 52 S 125 38 E
Saunemin, *U.S.A.* **157 D8** 40 54N 88 24W
Saupite, *Angola* **115 E3** 13 54 S 17 43 E
Saurbær, *Borgarfjarðarsýsla, Iceland* **11 C5** 64 24N 21 35W
Saurbær, *Eyjafjarðarsýsla, Iceland* **11 B8** 65 27N 18 13W
Sauri, *Nigeria* **113 C6** 11 42N 6 44 E
Saurimo, *Angola* **115 D4** 9 40 S 20 12 E
Sausalito, *U.S.A.* **160 H4** 37 51N 122 29W
Sausapor, *Indonesia* **83 B4** 0 31 S 132 4 E
Sautatá, *Colombia* **168 B2** 7 50N 77 4W
Sauveterre-de-Béarn, *France* **28 E3** 43 24N 0 57W
Sauzé-Vaussais, *France* **28 B4** 46 8N 0 8 E
Savá, *Honduras* **164 C2** 15 32N 86 15W
Sava, *Italy* **47 B10** 40 24N 17 33 E
Sava →, *Serbia, Yug.* **52 F5** 44 50N 20 26 E
Savage, *U.S.A.* **154 B2** 47 27N 104 21W
Savage I. = Niue, *Cook Is.* **135 J11** 19 2 S 169 54W
Savage River, *Australia* **127 G4** 41 31 S 145 14 E
Savai'i, *Samoa* **133 W23** 13 28 S 172 24W
Savalou, *Benin* **113 D5** 7 57N 1 58 E
Savane, *Mozam.* **119 F4** 19 37 S 35 8 E
Savanna, *U.S.A.* **156 B6** 42 5N 90 8W
Savanna-la-Mar, *Jamaica* **164 a** 18 10N 78 10W
Savannah, *Ga., U.S.A.* **152 C8** 32 5N 81 6W
Savannah, *Mo., U.S.A.* **156 E2** 39 56N 94 50W
Savannah, *Tenn., U.S.A.* **149 H1** 35 14N 88 15W
Savannah →, *U.S.A.* **152 C9** 32 2N 80 53W
Savannah Beach = Tybee Island , *U.S.A.* **152 C9** 32 1N 80 51W
Savannakhet, *Laos* **86 D5** 16 30N 104 49 E
Savant L., *Canada* **140 B1** 50 16N 90 44W
Savant Lake, *Canada* **140 B1** 50 14N 90 40W
Savantvadi, *India* **95 G1** 15 55N 73 54 E
Savanur, *India* **95 G2** 14 59N 75 21 E
Săvârşin, *Romania* **52 D7** 46 1N 22 14 E
Savaştepe, *Turkey* **49 B9** 39 22N 27 42 E
Savda, *India* **94 D2** 21 9N 75 56 E
Savé, *Benin* **113 D5** 8 2N 2 29 E
Save →, *France* **28 E5** 43 47N 1 17 E
Save →, *Mozam.* **117 C5** 21 16 S 34 0 E
Sāveh, *Iran* **97 C6** 35 2N 50 20 E
Savelugu, *Ghana* **113 D4** 9 38N 0 54W
Savenay, *France* **26 E5** 47 20N 1 55W
Săveni, *Romania* **53 C11** 47 57N 26 52 E
Saverdun, *France* **28 E5** 43 14N 1 34 E
Saverne, *France* **27 D14** 48 43N 7 20 E
Savièse, *Switz.* **32 D4** 46 17N 7 22 E
Savigliano, *Italy* **44 D4** 44 38N 7 40 E
Savigny-sur-Braye, *France* **26 E7** 47 53N 0 49 E
Sávio →, *Italy* **45 D9** 44 19N 12 20 E
Šavnik, *Montenegro, Yug.* **50 D3** 42 59N 19 10 E
Savo, *Finland* **14 E22** 62 45N 27 30 E
Savo, *Solomon Is.* **133 M10** 9 8 S 159 48 E
Savognin, *Switz.* **33 C9** 46 36N 9 37 E
Savoie □, *France* **29 C10** 45 26N 6 25 E
Savona, *Italy* **44 D5** 44 17N 8 30 E
Savona, *U.S.A.* **150 D7** 42 17N 77 13W
Savonlinna, *Finland* **58 B5** 61 52N 28 53 E
Savoonga, *U.S.A.* **144 E5** 63 42N 170 29W
Savoy = Savoie □, *France* **29 C10** 45 26N 6 25 E
Şavşat, *Turkey* **101 B10** 41 15N 42 20 E
Sävsjö, *Sweden* **17 G8** 57 20N 14 40 E
Savur, *Turkey* **96 B4** 37 34N 40 53 E
Savusavu, *Fiji* **133 A2** 16 34 S 179 15 E
Savusavu B., *Fiji* **133 A2** 16 45 S 179 15 E
Sawahlunto, *Indonesia* **84 C2** 0 40 S 100 52 E
Sawai, *Indonesia* **83 B3** 3 0 S 129 5 E
Sawai Madhopur, *India* **92 G7** 26 0N 76 25 E
Sawaleke, *Fiji* **133 A2** 17 59 S 179 18 E
Sawang Daen Din, *Thailand* **86 D4** 17 28N 103 28 E
Sawankhalok, *Thailand* **86 D2** 17 19N 99 50 E
Sawara, *Japan* **73 B12** 35 55N 140 30 E
Sawatch Range, *U.S.A.* **159 G10** 38 30N 106 30W
Sawdā', Jabal as, *Libya* **108 C3** 28 51N 15 12 E
Sawel Mt., *U.K.* **23 B4** 54 50N 7 2W
Sawfajjin □, *Libya* **108 B3** 31 0N 15 0 E
Sawfajjin, W. →, *Libya* **108 B2** 31 41N 14 44 E
Sawi, *Thailand* **87 G2** 10 14N 99 5 E
Sawla, *Ghana* **112 D4** 9 17N 2 25W
Sawmills, *Zimbabwe* **119 F2** 19 30 S 28 2 E
Şawqirah, *Oman* **99 C7** 18 7N 56 32 E
Şawqirah, Ghubbat, *Oman* **99 C7** 18 35N 57 0 E
Sawtell, *Australia* **129 A10** 30 19 S 153 6 E
Sawtooth Nat. Recr. Area ⌓, *U.S.A.* **158 D6** 44 0N 114 50W
Sawtooth Range, *U.S.A.* **158 E6** 44 3N 114 58W
Sawu, *Indonesia* **82 C2** 10 35 S 121 50 E
Sawu Sea, *Indonesia* **82 C2** 9 30 S 121 50 E
Saxby →, *Australia* **126 B3** 18 25 S 140 53 E
Saxmundham, *U.K.* **21 E9** 52 13N 1 30 E
Saxon, *Switz.* **32 D4** 46 9N 7 11 E

Saxony = Sachsen □, *Germany* .... **30 E9** 50 55N 13 10 E
Saxony, Lower = Niedersachsen □,
  Germany .... **30 C4** 52 50N 9 0 E
Saxton, *U.S.A.* **150 F6** 40 13N 78 15W
Say, *Mali* **112 C4** 13 50N 4 57W
Say, *Niger* .... **113 C5** 13 8N 2 22 E
Saya, *Nigeria* .... **113 D5** 9 30N 3 18 E
Sayabec, *Canada* **141 C6** 48 35N 67 41W
Sayaboury, *Laos* .... **86 C3** 19 15N 101 45 E
Sayán, *Peru* **172 C2** 11 8S 77 12W
Sayan, Vostochnyy, *Russia* ..... **67 D10** 54 0N 96 0 E
Sayan, Zapadnyy, *Russia* .... **67 D10** 52 30N 94 0 E
Saydā, *Lebanon* .... **103 B4** 33 35N 35 25 E
Sayghān, *Afghan.* .... **91 B2** 35 10N 67 55 E
Sayhandulaan = Oldziyt, *Mongolia* . **74 B5** 44 40N 109 1 E
Sayhūt, *Yemen* .... **99 D5** 15 12N 51 10 E
Sayiádha, *Greece* .... **38 B10** 39 38N 20 12 E
Saykhin, *Kazakhstan* .... **61 F8** 48 50N 46 47 E
Saylac = Zeila, *Somali Rep.* ... **120 B2** 11 21N 43 30 E
Saylorville L., *U.S.A.* **156 C3** 41 48N 93 46W
Saynshand, *Mongolia* .... **69 B6** 44 55N 110 11 E
Sayō, *Japan* .... **72 C6** 34 59N 134 22 E
Sayre, *Okla., U.S.A.* **155 H5** 35 18N 99 38W
Sayre, *Pa., U.S.A.* **151 E8** 41 59N 76 32W
Sayreville, *U.S.A.* **151 F10** 40 28N 74 22W
Sayula, *Mexico* **162 D4** 19 50N 103 40W
Sayward, *Canada* **142 C3** 50 21N 125 55W
Saywūn, *Yemen* .... **99 D5** 15 56N 48 47 E
Saza, *Japan* .... **72 D1** 33 14N 129 39 E
Sazanit, *Albania* .... **50 F3** 40 30N 19 20 E
Sázava →, *Czech Rep.* .... **34 B7** 49 53N 14 24 E
Sazin, *Pakistan* .... **93 B5** 35 35N 73 30 E
Sazlika →, *Bulgaria* .... **51 E9** 41 59N 25 50 E
Sbeïtla, *Tunisia* .... **108 A1** 35 12N 9 7 E
Scaër, *France* **26 D3** 48 2N 3 42W
Scafell Pike, *U.K.* **20 C4** 54 27N 3 14W
Scalea, *Italy* .... **47 C8** 39 49N 15 47 E
Scalloway, *U.K.* **22 A7** 60 9N 1 17W
Scalpay, *U.K.* **22 D3** 57 18N 6 0W
Scammon Bay, *U.S.A.* **142 B6** 61 51N 165 35W
Scandia, *Canada* **142 C6** 50 20N 112 0W
Scandiano, *Italy* .... **44 D7** 44 36N 10 43 E
Scandicci, *Italy* .... **45 E8** 43 45N 11 11 E
Scandinavia, *Europe* .... **14 E16** 64 0N 12 0 E
Scansano, *Italy* .... **45 F8** 42 41N 11 20 E
Scapa Flow, *U.K.* **22 C5** 58 53N 3 3W
Scappoose, *U.S.A.* **160 E4** 45 45N 122 53W
Scarámia, Capo, *Italy* .... **47 F7** 36 47N 14 29 E
Scarba, *U.K.* **22 E3** 56 11N 5 43W
Scarborough, *Trin. & Tob.* ... **169 E10** 11 11N 60 42W
Scarborough, *U.K.* **20 C7** 54 17N 0 24W
Scarborough Shoal, *S. China Sea* **80 D1** 15 0N 117 50 E
Scargill, *N.Z.* .... **131 C7** 42 56S 172 58 E
Scariff I., *Ireland* **23 E1** 51 44N 10 15W
Scarp, *U.K.* **22 C1** 58 1N 7 8W
Scarpe-Escaut, Parc Naturel
  Régional △, *France* .... **27 B10** 50 26N 3 23 E
Scarsdale, *Australia* .... **128 D5** 37 41S 143 39 E
Scebeli, Wabi = *Somali Rep.* ... **120 D2** 2 0N 44 0 E
Scédro, *Croatia* .... **45 E13** 43 6N 16 43 E
Schaal See, *Germany* .... **30 B6** 53 36N 10 55 E
Schaalsee, Naturpark △, *Germany* . **30 B6** 53 40N 10 59 E
Schaan, *Liech.* .... **33 B9** 47 10N 9 31 E
Schaffhausen, *Switz.* .... **33 A7** 47 42N 8 39 E
Schaffhausen □, *Switz.* ...... **33 A7** 47 42N 8 36 E
Schagen, *Neths.* .... **24 B4** 52 49N 4 48 E
Schaghticoke, *U.S.A.* **151 D11** 42 54N 73 35W
Schangnau, *Switz.* .... **32 C5** 46 50N 7 47 E
Schänis, *Switz.* .... **33 B8** 47 10N 9 3 E
Schärding, *Austria* .... **34 C6** 48 27N 13 27 E
Scharhörn, *Germany* .... **30 B4** 53 57N 8 24 E
Schässburg = Sighişoara, *Romania* **53 D9** 46 12N 24 50 E
Scheessel, *Germany* .... **30 B5** 53 10N 9 29 E
Schefferville, *Canada* **141 B6** 54 48N 66 50W
Scheibbs, *Austria* .... **34 C8** 48 1N 15 9 E
Scheldt = Schelde →, *Belgium* . **24 C4** 51 15N 4 16 E
Schelde →, *Belgium* .... **24 C4** 51 15N 4 16 E
Schell City, *U.S.A.* **156 F2** 38 1N 94 7W
Schell Creek Ra., *U.S.A.* **158 G6** 39 15N 114 30W
Schellsburg, *U.S.A.* **150 F6** 40 3N 78 39W
Schenectady, *U.S.A.* **151 D11** 42 49N 73 57W
Schenevus, *U.S.A.* **151 D10** 42 33N 74 50W
Scherfede, *Germany* .... **30 D5** 51 32N 9 2 E
Schesaplana, *Switz.* .... **33 B9** 47 5N 9 43 E
Schesslitz, *Germany* .... **31 F7** 49 58N 11 1 E
Schiedam, *Neths.* .... **24 C4** 51 55N 4 25 E
Schiermonnikoog, *Neths.* ..... **24 A6** 53 30N 6 15 E
Schiers, *Switz.* .... **33 C9** 46 58N 9 41 E
Schiltigheim, *France* .... **27 D14** 48 35N 7 45 E
Schio, *Italy* .... **45 C8** 45 43N 11 21 E
Schiphol, Amsterdam ✈ (AMS),
  Neths. .... **24 B4** 52 18N 4 45 E
Schladming, *Austria* .... **34 D6** 47 23N 13 41 E
Schlanders = Silandro, *Italy* . **44 B7** 46 38N 10 46 E
Schlei →, *Germany* .... **30 A5** 54 40N 10 0 E
Schleiden, *Germany* .... **30 E2** 50 31N 6 28 E
Schleinitz Ra., *Papua N. G.* . **132 B6** 3 0S 151 30 E
Schleiz, *Germany* .... **30 E7** 50 35N 11 49 E
Schleswig, *Germany* .... **30 A5** 54 31N 9 34 E
Schleswig-Holstein □, *Germany* . **30 A5** 54 30N 9 30 E
Schlieren, *Switz.* .... **33 B6** 47 26N 8 27 E
Schlüchtern, *Germany* .... **31 E5** 50 20N 9 32 E
Schmalkalden, *Germany* .... **30 E6** 50 44N 10 26 E
Schmölln, *Germany* .... **30 E8** 50 54N 12 19 E
Schneeberg, *Austria* .... **30 D8** 47 47N 15 48 E
Schneeberg, *Germany* .... **30 E8** 50 35N 12 38 E
Schneider, *U.S.A.* **157 C9** 41 13N 87 28W
Schneverdingen, *Germany* ..... **30 B5** 53 7N 9 48 E
Schœlcher, *Martinique* ...... **164 c** 14 36N 61 7W
Schoharie, *U.S.A.* **151 D10** 42 40N 74 19W
Schoharie →, *U.S.A.* **151 D10** 42 57N 74 18W
Scholls, *U.S.A.* **160 E4** 45 24N 122 56W
Schönberg,
  Mecklenburg-Vorpommern,
  Germany .... **30 B6** 53 52N 10 56 E
Schönberg, Schleswig-Holstein,
  Germany .... **30 A6** 54 23N 10 21 E
Schönbuch, Naturpark △, *Germany* **31 G5** 48 35N 9 2 E
Schönebeck, *Germany* .... **30 C7** 52 2N 11 44 E
Schönenwerd, *Switz.* .... **32 B6** 47 23N 8 0 E
Schongau, *Germany* .... **31 H6** 47 47N 10 53 E
Schöningen, *Germany* .... **30 C6** 52 8N 10 56 E
Schoolcraft, *U.S.A.* **157 B11** 42 7N 85 38W
Schopfheim, *Germany* .... **31 H3** 47 38N 7 50 E
Schorndorf, *Germany* .... **31 G5** 48 47N 9 32 E
Schortens, *Germany* .... **30 B3** 53 31N 7 56 E
Schouten I., *Australia* ...... **127 G4** 42 20S 148 20 E
Schouten Is. = Supiori, *Indonesia* **83 B5** 1 0S 136 0 E
Schouten Is., *Papua N. G.* ... **132 B3** 3 30S 144 30 E
Schouwen, *Neths.* .... **24 C3** 51 43N 3 45 E
Schramberg, *Germany* .... **31 G4** 48 13N 8 22 E
Schrankogel, *Austria* .... **34 D4** 47 3N 11 7 E
Schreckhorn, *Switz.* .... **32 C6** 46 36N 8 7 E
Schreiber, *Canada* **140 C2** 48 45N 87 20W
Schrems, *Austria* .... **34 C8** 48 47N 15 4 E
Schrobenhausen, *Germany* ..... **31 G7** 48 34N 11 16 E
Schröcken, *Austria* .... **33 B10** 47 17N 10 5 E
Schroffenstein, *Namibia* ..... **116 D2** 27 11S 18 42 E
Schroon Lake, *U.S.A.* **151 C11** 43 50N 73 46W
Schruns, *Austria* .... **33 B9** 47 5N 9 56 E
Schuler, *Canada* **143 C6** 50 20N 110 6W
Schuls, *Switz.* .... **33 C10** 46 48N 10 18 E
Schumacher, *Canada* **140 C3** 48 30N 81 16W
Schüpfen, *Switz.* .... **32 B4** 47 2N 7 24 E

Schüpfheim, *Switz.* .... **32 C6** 46 57N 8 2 E
Schurz, *U.S.A.* **158 G4** 38 57N 118 49W
Schuyler, *U.S.A.* **154 E6** 41 27N 97 4W
Schuylerville, *U.S.A.* **151 C11** 43 6N 73 35W
Schuylkill →, *U.S.A.* **151 G9** 39 53N 75 12W
Schuylkill Haven, *U.S.A.* **151 F8** 40 37N 76 11W
Schwabach, *Germany* .... **31 F7** 49 19N 11 2 E
Schwaben □, *Germany* .... **31 G6** 48 15N 10 30 E
Schwäbisch-Fränkischer Wald,
  Naturpark △, *Germany* .... **31 G5** 49 0N 9 30 E
Schwäbisch Gmünd, *Germany* ... **31 G5** 48 48N 9 47 E
Schwäbisch Hall, *Germany* .... **31 F5** 49 6N 9 44 E
Schwabmünchen, *Germany* ...... **31 G5** 48 20N 9 30 E
Schwalmstadt, *Germany* .... **31 G6** 48 10N 10 46 E
Schwalmstadt, *Germany* .... **30 E5** 50 55N 9 10 E
Schwanden, *Switz.* .... **33 C8** 46 58N 9 5 E
Schwandorf, *Germany* .... **31 F8** 49 20N 12 7 E
Schwaner, Pegunungan, *Indonesia* **85 C4** 1 0S 112 30 E
Schwanewede, *Germany* .... **30 B4** 53 14N 8 35 E
Schwarmstedt, *Germany* .... **30 C5** 52 39N 9 38 E
Schwarze Elster →, *Germany* .. **30 D8** 51 48N 12 50 E
Schwarzenberg, *Germany* ...... **30 E8** 50 32N 12 47 E
Schwarzenburg, *Switz.* .... **32 C4** 46 49N 7 20 E
Schwarzrand, *Namibia* .... **116 D2** 25 37S 16 50 E
Schwarzwald, *Germany* .... **31 G4** 48 30N 8 20 E
Schwatka Mts., *U.S.A.* **144 C8** 67 20N 156 30W
Schwaz, *Austria* .... **34 D4** 47 20N 11 44 E
Schwechat, *Austria* .... **35 C9** 48 8N 16 28 E
Schwechat, Vienna ✈ (VIA), *Austria* **35 C9** 48 7N 16 35 E
Schwedt, *Germany* .... **30 B10** 53 3N 14 16 E
Schweidnitz = Świdnica, *Poland* . **55 H3** 50 50N 16 30 E
Schweinfurt, *Germany* .... **31 E6** 50 3N 10 14 E
Schweiz Nationalpark = Svizzer,
  Parco Nazionale △, *Switz.* ... **33 C10** 46 40N 10 10 E
Schweizer Mittelland, *Switz.* . **32 C4** 47 0N 7 15 E
Schweizer-Reneke, *S. Africa* . **116 D4** 27 11S 25 18 E
Schwenningen = Villingen-
  Schwenningen, *Germany* ...... **31 G4** 48 3N 8 26 E
Schwerin, *Germany* .... **30 B7** 53 36N 11 22 E
Schweriner See, *Germany* ..... **30 B7** 53 43N 11 26 E
Schwetzingen, *Germany* ...... **31 F4** 49 23N 8 35 E
Schwyz, *Switz.* .... **33 B7** 47 2N 8 39 E
Schwyz □, *Switz.* .... **33 B7** 47 2N 8 39 E
Sciacca, *Italy* .... **46 E6** 37 31N 13 3 E
Sciao, *Somali Rep.* .... **120 D3** 3 26N 45 21 E
Scicli, *Italy* .... **47 F7** 36 47N 14 42 E
Sciliar, Parco Naturale dello △, *Italy* **45 B8** 46 28N 11 35 E
Scilla, *Italy* .... **47 D8** 38 15N 15 43 E
Scilly, Isles of, *U.K.* **21 H1** 49 56N 6 22W
Ścinawa, *Poland* .... **55 G3** 51 25N 16 26 E
Scione, *Greece* .... **50 G7** 39 57N 23 36 E
Scioto →, *U.S.A.* **157 D13** 38 44N 83 1W
Scituate, *U.S.A.* **151 D14** 42 12N 70 44W
Scobey, *U.S.A.* **154 A2** 48 47N 105 25W
Scone, *Australia* .... **129 B9** 32 5S 150 52 E
Scone, *U.K.* **22 E5** 56 25N 3 24W
Scordia, *Italy* .... **47 F7** 37 18N 14 51 E
Scoresby Sund, *Greenland* **10 C8** 70 28N 21 46W
Scoresbysund = Ittoqqortoormiit,
  Greenland **10 C8** 70 20N 23 0W
Scornicești, *Romania* .... **53 F9** 44 34N 24 33 E
Scotia, *Calif., U.S.A.* **158 F1** 40 29N 124 6W
Scotia, *N.Y., U.S.A.* **151 D11** 42 50N 73 58W
Scotia Sea, *Antarctica* **7 B18** 56 5S 56 0W
Scotland, *Canada* **150 C4** 43 1N 80 22W
Scotland □, *U.K.* **22 E5** 57 0N 4 0W
Scott, C., *Australia* .... **124 B4** 13 30S 129 49 E
Scott City, *U.S.A.* **154 F4** 38 29N 100 54W
Scott Glacier, *Antarctica* ... **7 C8** 66 15S 100 5 E
Scott I., *Antarctica* .... **7 C11** 67 0S 179 0 E
Scott Is., *Canada* **142 C3** 50 48N 128 40W
Scott L., *Canada* **143 B7** 59 55N 106 18W
Scott Reef, *Australia* ...... **124 B3** 14 0S 121 50 E
Scottburgh, *S. Africa* ...... **117 E5** 30 15S 30 47 E
Scottdale, *U.S.A.* **150 F5** 40 6N 79 35W
Scottish Borders □, *U.K.* ... **22 F6** 55 35N 2 50W
Scotts Head, *Australia* ..... **129 A10** 30 45S 153 0 E
Scottsbluff, *U.S.A.* **154 E3** 41 52N 103 40W
Scottsboro, *U.S.A.* **149 H3** 34 40N 86 2W
Scottsburg, *U.S.A.* **157 F11** 38 41N 85 47W
Scottsdale, *Australia* ...... **127 G4** 41 9S 147 31 E
Scottsdale, *U.S.A.* **159 K7** 33 29N 111 56W
Scottsville, *Ky., U.S.A.* ... **157 G11** 36 45N 86 11W
Scottsville, *N.Y., U.S.A.* .. **150 C7** 43 2N 77 47W
Scottville, *U.S.A.* **156 D2** 43 58N 86 17W
Scranton, *U.S.A.* **151 E9** 41 25N 75 40W
Screven, *U.S.A.* **152 D7** 31 29N 82 1W
Scugog, L., *Canada* **150 B6** 44 10N 78 55W
Sculeni, *Moldova* .... **53 C12** 47 20N 27 37 E
Scunthorpe, *U.K.* **20 D7** 53 36N 0 39W
Scuol Schuls, *Switz.* .... **33 C10** 46 48N 10 17 E
Scusciuban, *Somali Rep.* .... **120 B4** 10 18N 50 12 E
Scutari = Shkodër, *Albania* .. **50 D3** 42 4N 19 32 E
Scutari = Üsküdar, *Turkey* ... **51 F13** 41 0N 29 5 E
Sea Lake, *Australia* .... **128 C5** 35 28S 142 55 E
Seabra, *Brazil* **171 D3** 12 25S 41 46W
Seabrook, L., *Australia* ..... **125 F2** 30 55S 119 40 E
Seaford, *U.K.* .... **21 G8** 50 47N 0 7 E
Seaford, *U.S.A.* **148 F8** 38 39N 75 37W
Seaforth, *Australia* .... **126 J6** 20 55S 148 57 E
Seaforth, *Canada* **150 C3** 43 35N 81 25W
Seaforth, L., *U.K.* **22 D2** 57 52N 6 36W
Seagraves, *U.S.A.* **155 J3** 32 57N 102 34W
Seaham, *U.K.* **20 C6** 54 50N 1 20W
Seal →, *Canada* **143 B10** 59 4N 94 48W
Seal L., *Canada* **141 B7** 54 20N 61 30W
Seale, *U.S.A.* **152 C4** 32 18N 85 10W
Sealy, *U.S.A.* **155 L6** 29 47N 96 9W
Seaman, *U.S.A.* **157 F13** 38 57N 83 34W
Searchlight, *U.S.A.* **161 K12** 35 28N 114 55W
Searcy, *U.S.A.* **155 H9** 35 15N 91 44W
Searles L., *U.S.A.* **161 K9** 35 44N 117 21W
Seascale, *U.K.* **20 C4** 54 24N 3 29W
Seaside, *Calif., U.S.A.* **160 J5** 36 37N 121 50W
Seaside, *Oreg., U.S.A.* **160 E3** 46 0N 123 56W
Seaspray, *Australia* .... **129 E7** 38 25S 147 15 E
Seattle, *U.S.A.* **160 C4** 47 36N 122 20W
Seattle-Tacoma International ✈
  (SEA), *U.S.A.* **160 C4** 47 27N 122 18W
Seaview Ra., *Australia* ...... **126 B4** 18 40S 145 45 E
Seaward Kaikoura Ra., *N.Z.* .. **131 C8** 42 10S 173 44 E
Seba, *Indonesia* .... **82 D2** 10 29S 121 50 E
Sebago L., *U.S.A.* **151 C14** 43 52N 70 34W
Sebago Lake, *U.S.A.* **151 C14** 43 51N 70 34W
Sebangka, *Indonesia* .... **84 B2** 0 7N 104 36 E
Sebastian, *U.S.A.* **153 H7** 27 49N 80 28W
Sebastián Vizcaíno, B., *Mexico* **162 B2** 28 0N 114 30W
Sebastopol = Sevastopol, *Ukraine* **59 K7** 44 35S 33 30 E
Sebastopol, *U.S.A.* **160 G4** 38 24N 122 49W
Sebba, *Burkina Faso* .... **113 C5** 13 35N 0 32 E
Sebderat, *Eritrea* .... **107 D4** 15 26N 36 42 E
Sebdou, *Algeria* **114 B4** 34 38N 1 19W
Sébé →, *Gabon* .... **114 C2** 1 2S 13 4 E
Sebekoro, *Mali* **112 C3** 12 58N 9 0W
Seben, *Turkey* .... **100 B4** 40 24N 31 34 E
Sebeş, *Romania* .... **53 E8** 45 58N 23 34 E
Sebeşului, Munţii, *Romania* .. **53 E8** 45 36N 23 40 E
Sebewaing, *U.S.A.* **148 D4** 43 44N 83 27W
Sebezh, *Russia* .... **58 D5** 56 14N 28 22 E
Sebha = Sabhah, *Libya* ...... **108 C2** 27 9N 14 29 E
Sébi, *Mali* **112 B4** 15 50N 4 12W
Şebinkarahisar, *Turkey* ...... **101 B8** 40 22N 38 28 E
Sebiş, *Romania* .... **52 D7** 46 23N 22 13 E
Seblat, *Indonesia* .... **84 C2** 3 14S 101 38 E

Sebnitz, *Germany* .... **30 E10** 50 58N 14 15 E
Sebou, Oued →, *Morocco* **110 B3** 34 16N 6 40W
Sebring, *Fla., U.S.A.* **153 H8** 27 30N 81 27W
Sebring, *Ohio, U.S.A.* **150 F3** 40 55N 81 2W
Sebringville, *Canada* **150 C3** 43 24N 81 4W
Sebta = Ceuta, *N. Afr.* **110 A3** 35 52N 5 18W
Sebuku, *Indonesia* .... **85 C5** 3 30S 116 25 E
Sebuku, Teluk, *Malaysia* .... **85 B5** 4 0N 118 10 E
Sečanj, Serbia, *Yug.* .... **52 E5** 45 25N 20 47 E
Secchia →, *Italy* .... **44 C8** 45 4N 11 0 E
Sechelt, *Canada* **142 D4** 49 25N 123 42W
Sechura, *Peru* **172 B1** 5 39S 80 50W
Sechura, Desierto de, *Peru* .. **172 B1** 6 0S 80 30W
Seclin, *France* .... **27 B10** 50 33N 3 2 E
Secondigny, *France* **26 F6** 46 37N 0 26W
Secretary I., *N.Z.* .... **131 F1** 45 15S 166 56 E
Secunderabad, *India* .... **94 F4** 17 28N 78 30 E
Sécure →, *Bolivia* **173 D5** 15 10S 64 52W
Security-Widefield, *U.S.A.* .. **154 F2** 38 45N 104 45W
Sedalia, *U.S.A.* **156 F3** 38 42N 93 14W
Sedam, *India* .... **94 E3** 17 11N 77 17 E
Sedan, *Australia* .... **128 C3** 34 34S 139 19 E
Sedan, *France* .... **27 C11** 49 43N 4 57 E
Sedan, *U.S.A.* **155 G6** 37 8N 96 11W
Sedano, *Spain* **42 C7** 42 43N 3 49W
Sedaw, *Burma* .... **90 D6** 22 19N 96 19 E
Sedbergh, *U.K.* **20 C5** 54 20N 2 31W
Seddon, *N.Z.* .... **131 B9** 41 40S 174 7 E
Seddonville, *N.Z.* .... **131 B7** 41 33S 172 1 E
Sedé Boqér, *Israel* .... **103 E3** 30 52N 34 47 E
Sedeh, Fārs, *Iran* .... **97 D7** 30 45N 52 11 E
Sedeh, Khorāsān, *Iran* ...... **97 C8** 33 20N 59 14 E
Séderon, *France* .... **29 D9** 44 12N 5 32 E
Sederot, *Israel* .... **103 D3** 31 32N 34 37 E
Sédhiou, *Senegal* **112 C1** 12 44N 15 30W
Sedico, *Italy* .... **45 B9** 46 8N 12 6 E
Sedlčany, *Czech Rep.* .... **34 B7** 49 40N 14 25 E
Sedley, *Canada* **143 C8** 50 10N 104 0W
Sedona, *U.S.A.* **159 J8** 34 52N 111 46W
Sedova, Pik, *Russia* .... **66 B6** 73 29N 54 58 E
Sedrata, *Algeria* .... **111 A6** 36 7N 7 31 E
Sedro Woolley, *U.S.A.* **160 B4** 48 30N 122 14W
Sedrun, *Switz.* .... **33 C7** 46 36N 8 47 E
Šeduva, *Lithuania* .... **54 C10** 55 45N 23 45 E
Sędziszów, *Poland* .... **55 H7** 50 35N 20 4 E
Sędziszów Małopolski, *Poland* . **55 H8** 50 5N 21 45 E
Seebad Ahlbeck, *Germany* ..... **30 B10** 53 56N 14 10 E
Seefeld in Tirol, *Austria* ... **34 D4** 47 19N 11 13 E
Seehausen, *Germany* .... **30 C7** 52 54N 11 45 E
Seeheim, *Namibia* .... **116 D2** 26 50S 17 45 E
Seeheim-Jugenheim, *Germany* .. **31 F4** 49 49N 8 40 E
Seeis, *Namibia* .... **116 C2** 22 29S 17 39 E
Seekoei →, *S. Africa* .... **116 E4** 30 18S 25 1 E
Seeley's Bay, *Canada* **151 B8** 44 29N 76 14W
Seelow, *Germany* .... **30 C10** 52 32N 14 23 E
Sées, *France* .... **26 D7** 48 38N 0 10 E
Seesen, *Germany* .... **30 D6** 51 54N 10 10 E
Seevetal, *Germany* .... **30 B6** 53 26N 10 1 E
Seewinkel Nationalpark = Neusiedler
  See-Seewinkel, Nationalpark △,
  Austria .... **35 D9** 47 50N 16 45 E
Sefadu, S. *Leone* **112 D2** 8 35N 10 58W
Seferihisar, *Turkey* .... **49 C8** 38 10N 26 50 E
Séfeto, *Mali* **112 C3** 14 8N 9 49W
Sefrou, *Morocco* **110 B4** 33 52N 4 52W
Sefton, *N.Z.* .... **131 D7** 43 15S 172 41 E
Sefuri-San, *Japan* .... **72 D2** 33 28N 130 18 E
Sefwi Bekwai, *Ghana* **112 D4** 6 10N 2 25W
Seg-ozero, *Russia* .... **56 B5** 63 20N 33 46 E
Segaf, Kepulauan, *Indonesia* . **83 B4** 2 10S 130 28 E
Segag, *Ethiopia* .... **120 C2** 7 39N 42 50 E
Segamat, *Malaysia* .... **87 L4** 2 30N 102 50 E
Segarcea, *Romania* .... **53 F8** 44 6N 23 43 E
Ségbwema, S. *Leone* **112 D2** 8 0N 11 0W
Seget, *Indonesia* .... **83 B4** 1 24S 130 58 E
Segezha, *Russia* .... **56 B5** 63 44N 34 19 E
Seggueur, O. →, *Algeria* .... **111 B5** 32 14N 1 48 E
Seghe, *Solomon Is.* .... **133 M9** 8 32S 157 54 E
Segonzac, *France* **28 C5** 45 36N 0 14W
Segorbe, *Spain* **40 F4** 39 50N 0 30W
Segovia = Coco →, *Cent. Amer.* **164 D3** 15 0N 83 8W
Segovia, *Colombia* **168 B3** 7 7N 74 42W
Segovia, *Spain* **42 E6** 40 57N 4 10W
Segovia □, *Spain* **42 E6** 40 55N 4 10W
Segré, *France* **26 E6** 47 40N 0 52W
Segre →, *Spain* .... **40 D5** 41 40N 0 43 E
Seguam I., *U.S.A.* **144 K4** 52 19N 172 30W
Seguam Pass, *U.S.A.* **144 L4** 52 0N 172 30W
Séguédine, *Niger* .... **109 D2** 20 9N 12 55 E
Séguéla, *Ivory C.* **112 D3** 7 55N 6 40W
Séguénéga, *Burkina Faso* **113 C4** 13 25N 1 58W
Seguin, *U.S.A.* **155 L6** 29 34N 97 58W
Segundo →, *Argentina* **174 C3** 30 53S 62 44W
Segura →, *Spain* **41 G4** 38 3N 0 44W
Segura, Sierra de, *Spain* **41 G2** 38 5N 2 45W
Seh Konj, Kūh-e, *Iran* ...... **97 D8** 30 6N 57 30 E
Seh Qal'eh, *Iran* .... **97 C9** 33 40N 58 24 E
Sehithwa, *Botswana* .... **116 C3** 20 30S 22 30 E
Sehlabathebe Nat. Park △, *Lesotho* **117 E4** 29 53S 29 7 E
Sehore, *India* .... **92 H7** 23 10N 77 5 E
Sehulea, *Papua N. G.* .... **132 E6** 9 58S 151 10 E
Sehwan, *Pakistan* .... **91 D2** 26 28N 67 53 E
Seia, *Santa Mare, Romania* .. **53 D9** 46 1N 24 7 E
Seikpyu, *Burma* .... **90 E5** 20 54N 94 48 E
Seil, *U.K.* **22 E3** 56 18N 5 38W
Seiland, *Norway* .... **8 A20** 70 25N 23 15 E
Seilhac, *France* .... **28 C5** 45 23N 1 43 E
Seiling, *U.S.A.* **155 G5** 36 9N 98 56W
Seille →, Moselle, *France* ... **27 C13** 49 7N 6 11 E
Seille →, Saône-et-Loire, *France* **27 F11** 46 31N 4 57 E
Sein, Î. de, *France* **26 D2** 48 2N 4 52W
Seinäjoki, *Finland* .... **15 E20** 62 40N 22 51 E
Seine →, *France* .... **26 C7** 49 26N 0 26 E
Seine, B. de la, *France* **26 C6** 49 40N 0 40W
Seine-et-Marne □, *France* .... **27 D10** 48 45N 3 0 E
Seine-Maritime □, *France* .... **26 C7** 49 40N 1 0 E
Seine-St-Denis □, *France* .... **27 D9** 48 58N 2 24 E
Seini, *Romania* .... **53 C8** 47 44N 23 21 E
Seirijai, *Lithuania* .... **54 D10** 54 14N 23 49 E
Seistan = Sīstān, *Asia* ..... **97 D9** 30 50N 61 0 E
Seistan, Daryācheh-ye = Sīstān,
  Daryācheh-ye, *Iran* .... **97 D9** 31 0N 61 0 E
Sejerø, *Denmark* .... **17 J5** 55 54N 11 9 E
Sejerø Bugt, *Denmark* .... **54 D10** 55 53N 11 15 E
Sejny, *Poland* .... **54 D10** 54 6N 23 21 E
Seka, *Ethiopia* .... **107 F4** 8 10N 36 52 E
Sekayu, *Indonesia* .... **84 C2** 2 51S 103 51 E
Seke, *Tanzania* .... **118 C3** 3 20S 33 31 E
Seke-Banza, Dem. Rep. of the Congo **115 D2** 5 20S 13 16 E
Sekenke, *Tanzania* .... **118 C3** 4 18S 34 11 E
Sekhira, *Tunisia* .... **109 B8** 34 20N 10 5 E
Seki, *Japan* .... **73 B8** 35 29N 136 55 E
Seki, *Turkey* .... **49 E11** 36 48N 29 33 E
Sekigahara, *Japan* .... **73 B8** 35 22N 136 28 E
Sekondi-Takoradi, *Ghana* **112 E4** 4 58N 1 45W
Sekota, *Ethiopia* .... **107 E4** 12 40N 39 2 E
Seksna, *Russia* .... **58 B5** 59 3N 38 58 E
Sekudai, *Malaysia* .... **87 d** 1 32N 103 39 E
Sekuma, *Botswana* .... **116 C3** 24 36S 23 50 E
Selah, *U.S.A.* **158 C3** 46 39N 120 32W
Selama, *Malaysia* .... **87 K3** 5 12N 100 42 E

Selangor □, *Malaysia* .... **84 B2** 3 10N 101 30 E
Selárgius, *Italy* .... **46 C2** 39 16N 9 10 E
Selaru, *Indonesia* .... **83 C4** 8 9S 131 0 E
Selatan, Selat, *Malaysia* .... **87 c** 5 15N 100 20 E
Selawik, *U.S.A.* **144 C6** 66 36N 160 0W
Selawik L., *U.S.A.* **144 C7** 66 30N 160 45W
Selb, *Germany* .... **31 E8** 50 10N 12 7 E
Selbusjøen, *Norway* .... **18 A7** 63 15N 10 50 E
Selby, *U.K.* **20 D6** 53 47N 1 5W
Selby, *U.S.A.* **154 C4** 45 31N 100 2W
Selca, *Croatia* .... **45 E13** 43 20N 16 50 E
Selçuk, *Turkey* .... **49 D9** 37 56N 27 22 E
Selden, *U.S.A.* **154 F4** 39 33N 100 34W
Seldovia, *U.S.A.* **144 G10** 59 26N 151 43W
Sele →, *Italy* .... **47 B7** 40 29N 14 56 E
Selebi-Pikwe, *Botswana* ...... **117 C4** 21 58S 27 48 E
Selemdzha →, *Russia* .... **67 D13** 51 42N 128 53 E
Selendi, *Manisa, Turkey* .... **49 C10** 38 43N 28 50 E
Selendi, *Manisa, Turkey* .... **49 D9** 37 24N 27 40 E
Selenga = Selenge Mörön →, *Asia* **68 A5** 52 16N 106 16 E
Selenge, Dem. Rep. of the Congo **114 C3** 1 58S 18 11 E
Selenge Mörön →, *Asia* ...... **68 A5** 52 16N 106 16 E
Seleničë, *Albania* .... **50 F3** 40 33N 19 39 E
Selenter See, *Germany* ...... **30 A6** 54 18N 10 26 E
Sélestat, *France* .... **27 D14** 48 16N 7 26 E
Seletan, Tanjung, *Indonesia* . **85 C4** 4 10S 114 40 E
Selevac, Serbia, *Yug.* ...... **50 B4** 44 28N 20 52 E
Selfoss, *Iceland* **11 D6** 63 56N 21 0W
Sélibabi, *Mauritania* **112 B2** 15 10N 12 15W
Séliger, Ozero, *Russia* ..... **58 D7** 57 15N 33 0 E
Seligman, *U.S.A.* **159 J7** 35 20N 112 53W
Şelim, *Turkey* .... **101 B10** 40 30N 42 46 E
Selîma, El Wâhât el, *Sudan* .. **106 C2** 21 22N 29 19 E
Selimiye, *Turkey* .... **49 D9** 37 24N 27 40 E
Selinda Spillway →, *Botswana* **116 B3** 18 35S 23 10 E
Selinoús, *Greece* .... **48 D3** 37 35N 21 37 E
Selinsgrove, *U.S.A.* **150 F8** 40 48N 76 52W
Selizharovo, *Russia* .... **58 D7** 56 51N 33 27 E
Selje, *Norway* .... **18 B2** 62 3N 5 22 E
Seljord, *Norway* .... **18 E5** 59 30N 8 40 E
Selkirk, *Canada* **143 C9** 50 10N 96 55W
Selkirk, *U.K.* **22 F6** 55 33N 2 50W
Selkirk I. = Horse I., *Canada* **143 C9** 53 20N 99 6W
Selkirk Mts., *Canada* **138 C8** 51 15N 117 40W
Sellafield, *U.K.* **20 C4** 54 25N 3 29W
Sellama, *Sudan* .... **107 E2** 12 57N 29 46 E
Selliá, *Greece* .... **39 E5** 35 12N 24 23 E
Sellières, *France* .... **27 F12** 46 50N 5 32 E
Sells, *U.S.A.* **159 L8** 31 55N 111 53W
Sellye, *Hungary* .... **52 E2** 45 52N 17 51 E
Selma, *Ala., U.S.A.* **149 J2** 32 25N 87 1W
Selma, *Calif., U.S.A.* **160 J7** 36 34N 119 37W
Selma, *N.C., U.S.A.* **149 H6** 35 32N 78 17W
Selmer, *U.S.A.* **149 H1** 35 10N 88 36W
Selong, *Indonesia* .... **85 D5** 8 39S 116 32 E
Selongey, *France* .... **27 E12** 47 36N 5 11 E
Selouane, *Morocco* **111 A4** 35 7N 2 57W
Selous Game Reserve △, *Tanzania* **119 D4** 8 37S 37 42 E
Selowandoma Falls, *Zimbabwe* . **119 G3** 21 15S 31 50 E
Selpele, *Indonesia* .... **83 B4** 0 1S 130 5 E
Selsey Bill, *U.K.* **21 G7** 50 43N 0 47W
Seltso, *Russia* .... **58 F8** 53 22N 34 4 E
Seltz, *France* .... **27 D15** 48 54N 8 7 E
Selu, *Indonesia* .... **83 C4** 7 32S 130 55 E
Sélune →, *France* **26 D5** 48 38N 1 22W
Selva = La Selva del Camp, *Spain* **40 D6** 41 13N 1 8 E
Selva, *Argentina* **174 B3** 29 50S 62 0W
Selva Lacandona, Reserva de la
  Biósfera = Montes Azules,
  Reserva de La Biósfera △, *Mexico* **163 D** 16 21N 91 3W
Selvagens, Ilhas, *Madeira* ... **110 B1** 30 5N 15 55W
Selvas, *Brazil* **172 B4** 6 30S 67 0W
Selwyn L., *Canada* **143 B8** 60 0N 104 30W
Selwyn Mts., *Canada* **138 B6** 63 0N 130 0W
Selwyn Passage, *Vanuatu* ..... **133 F6** 16 3S 168 12 E
Selwyn Ra., *Australia* ...... **126 C3** 21 10S 140 0 E
Sem, *Norway* .... **18 E7** 59 14N 10 17 E
Seman →, *Albania* .... **50 F3** 40 47N 19 30 E
Semara, W. *Sahara* **110 C2** 26 48N 11 41W
Semarang, *Indonesia* .... **85 D4** 7 0S 110 26 E
Sematan, *Malaysia* .... **85 B3** 1 48N 109 46 E
Semau, *Indonesia* .... **82 D2** 10 13S 123 22 E
Sembabule, *Uganda* .... **118 C3** 0 4S 31 25 E
Sembawang, *Singapore* .... **87 d** 1 27N 103 50 E
Sembé, *Congo* .... **114 D2** 1 39N 14 36 E
Sembung, *Indonesia* .... **79 J18** 8 28S 115 11 E
Şemdinli, *Turkey* .... **101 D11** 37 18N 44 35 E
Sémé, *Senegal* **112 B2** 15 4N 13 41W
Semeih, *Sudan* .... **107 E2** 12 43N 30 53 E
Semenanjung Blambangan,
  Indonesia .... **79 K17** 8 42S 114 29 E
Semendua, Dem. Rep. of the Congo **114 C3** 3 10S 18 6 E
Semenov, *Russia* .... **60 B7** 56 43N 44 30 E
Semenovka, Chernihiv, *Ukraine* **59 F7** 52 8N 32 36 E
Semenovka, Kremenchuk, *Ukraine* **59 H7** 49 37N 33 10 E
Semeru, *Indonesia* .... **85 D4** 8 4S 112 55 E
Semey, *Kazakhstan* .... **66 D9** 50 30N 80 10 E
Semichi Is., *U.S.A.* .... **144 K1** 52 42N 174 0 E
Semikarakorskiy, *Russia* ..... **61 G5** 47 31N 40 48 E
Semiluki, *Russia* .... **59 G10** 51 41N 39 2 E
Seminoe Reservoir, *U.S.A.* ... **158 F10** 42 9N 106 55W
Seminole, Okla., U.S.A. **153 H7** 27 50N 82 47W
Seminole, *Okla., U.S.A.* **155 H6** 35 14N 96 41W
Seminole, *Tex., U.S.A.* **155 J3** 32 43N 102 39W
Seminole, *U.S.A.* **152 E5** 30 43N 84 52W
Seminole Draw →, *U.S.A.* **155 J3** 32 27N 102 20W
Semipalatinsk = Semey, *Kazakhstan* **66 D9** 50 30N 80 10 E
Semirara I., *Phil.* .... **80 E12** 12 4N 121 23 E
Semirara Is., *Phil.* .... **81 F3** 12 0N 121 20 E
Semisopochnoi I., *U.S.A.* .... **144 L2** 51 55N 179 36 E
Semitau, *Indonesia* .... **85 B4** 0 29N 111 57 E
Semiyarka, *Kazakhstan* ...... **66 D8** 50 55N 78 23 E
Semiyarskoye = Semiyarka,
  Kazakhstan .... **66 D8** 50 55N 78 23 E
Semlin = Zemun, Serbia, *Yug.* **50 B4** 44 51N 20 25 E
Semmering P., *Austria* ...... **34 D8** 47 41N 15 45 E
Semnān, *Iran* .... **97 C7** 35 40N 53 23 E
Semnān □, *Iran* .... **97 C7** 36 0N 54 0 E
Sempang Mengayou, Tanjong,
  Malaysia .... **85 A5** 7 0N 116 40 E
Semporna, *Malaysia* .... **85 B3** 4 30N 118 33 E
Sempu, *Indonesia* .... **85 C4** 2 51S 112 58 E
Semur-en-Auxois, *France* ..... **27 E11** 47 30N 4 20 E
Sen →, *Cambodia* .... **78 B3** 13 45N 105 12 E
Sena, *Bolivia* **172 C4** 11 32S 67 11W
Senā, *Iran* .... **97 D6** 28 27N 51 36 E
Sena, *Mozam.* .... **119 F4** 17 25S 35 0 E
Sena →, *Bolivia* **172 C4** 11 31S 67 11W
Sena Madureira, *Brazil* **172 B4** 9 5S 68 45W
Senador José Porfírio, *Brazil* **169 D7** 2 35S 51 56W
Senador Pompeu, *Brazil* **170 C4** 5 40S 39 20W
Senaja, *Malaysia* .... **85 A5** 6 45N 117 3 E
Senaki, *Georgia* .... **61 J6** 42 15N 42 7 E
Senang, Pulau, *Singapore* .... **87 d** 1 10N 103 44 E
Senanga, *Zambia* .... **115 F4** 16 7S 23 16 E
Senatobia, *U.S.A.* **155 H10** 34 37N 89 58W
Sencelles, *Spain* .... **38 B3** 39 39N 2 54 E
Sendafa, *Ethiopia* .... **107 F4** 9 11N 39 3 E
Sendai, Kagoshima, *Japan* .... **72 F2** 31 50N 130 20 E
Sendai, Miyagi, *Japan* ...... **70 E10** 38 15N 140 53 E
Sendai-Wan, *Japan* .... **70 E10** 38 15N 141 0 E
Senden, Bayern, *Germany* ..... **31 G6** 48 19N 10 4 E

Senden, *Nordrhein-Westfalen, Germany*	30 D3	51 52N 7 22 E
Sendhwa, *India*	92 J6	21 41N 75 6 E
Sendurjana, *India*	94 D4	21 32N 78 17 E
Sene →, *Ghana*	113 D4	7 30N 0 33W
Senec, *Slovak Rep.*	35 C10	48 12N 17 23 E
Seneca, *Ill., U.S.A.*	157 C8	41 19N 88 37W
Seneca, *S.C., U.S.A.*	149 H4	34 41N 82 57W
Seneca Falls, *U.S.A.*	151 D8	42 55N 76 48W
Seneca L., *U.S.A.*	150 D8	42 40N 76 54W
Senecaville L., *U.S.A.*	150 G3	39 55N 81 25W
Senegal ■, *W. Afr.*	112 C2	14 30N 14 30W
Sénégal →, *W. Afr.*	112 B1	15 48N 16 32W
Senegambia, *Africa*	104 E2	12 45N 12 0W
Senekal, *S. Africa*	117 D4	28 20 S 27 36 E
Senftenberg, *Germany*	30 D10	51 32N 14 0 E
Senga Hill, *Zambia*	119 D3	9 19 S 31 11 E
Senge Khambab = Indus →, *Pakistan*	91 D2	24 20N 67 47 E
Sengiley, *Russia*	60 D9	53 58N 48 46 E
Sengua →, *Zimbabwe*	119 F2	17 7 S 28 5 E
Senguerr →, *Argentina*	176 C3	45 35 S 68 50W
Senhor-do-Bonfim, *Brazil*	170 D3	10 30 S 40 10W
Senica, *Slovak Rep.*	35 C10	48 41N 17 25 E
Senigállia, *Italy*	45 E10	43 43N 13 13 E
Seniku, *Burma*	90 C6	25 32N 97 48 E
Senio →, *Italy*	45 D9	44 35N 12 15 E
Senirkent, *Turkey*	49 C12	38 6N 30 33 E
Senise, *Italy*	47 B9	40 9N 16 17 E
Senj, *Croatia*	45 D11	45 0N 14 58 E
Senja, *Norway*	14 B17	69 25N 17 30 E
Senkaku-Shotō, *Japan*	71 L1	25 45N 124 0 E
Senkuang, *Indonesia*	87 d	1 11N 104 2 E
Senlis, *France*	27 C9	49 13N 2 35 E
Senmonorom, *Cambodia*	86 F6	12 27N 107 12 E
Sennâr, *Sudan*	107 E3	13 30N 33 35 E
Sennar □, *Sudan*	107 E3	13 0N 34 0 E
Senneterre, *Canada*	140 C4	48 25N 77 15W
Senno, *Belarus*	58 E5	54 45N 29 43 E
Sénnori, *Italy*	46 B1	40 47N 8 35 E
Seno, *Laos*	86 D5	16 35N 104 50 E
Senoia, *U.S.A.*	152 B5	33 18N 84 33W
Senonches, *France*	26 D8	48 34N 1 2 E
Senorbì, *Italy*	46 C2	39 32N 9 8 E
Senožeče, *Slovenia*	45 C11	45 43N 14 3 E
Sens, *France*	27 D10	48 11N 3 15 E
Senta, *Serbia, Yug.*	52 E5	45 55N 20 3 E
Sentani, *Indonesia*	83 B6	2 36 S 140 37 E
Sentani, Danau, *Indonesia*	83 B6	2 36 S 140 34 E
Sentery = Lubao, *Dem. Rep. of the Congo*	118 D2	5 17 S 25 42 E
Sentinel, *U.S.A.*	159 K7	32 52N 113 13W
Šentjur, *Slovenia*	45 B12	46 14N 15 24 E
Sentolo, *Indonesia*	85 D4	7 55 S 110 13 E
Sentosa, *Singapore*	87 d	1 15N 103 50 E
Senya Beraku, *Ghana*	113 D4	5 28N 0 31W
Seo de Urgel = La Seu d'Urgell, *Spain*	40 C6	42 22N 1 23 E
Seohara, *India*	93 E8	29 15N 78 33 E
Seonath →, *India*	93 J10	21 44N 82 28 E
Seondha, *India*	93 F8	26 9N 78 48 E
Seoni, *India*	93 H8	22 5N 79 30 E
Seoni Malwa, *India*	92 H8	22 27N 77 28 E
Seoriuarayan, *India*	94 D6	21 45N 82 34 E
Seoul = Sôul, *S. Korea*	75 F14	37 31N 126 58 E
Separation Pt., *N.Z.*	131 A7	40 47 S 172 59 E
Sepatini →, *Brazil*	172 B4	7 36 S 65 24W
Sepi, *Solomon Is.*	133 M10	8 33 S 159 52 E
Sepīdān, *Iran*	97 D7	30 20N 52 5 E
Sepik →, *Papua N. G.*	132 B3	3 49 S 144 30 E
Sepo-ri, *N. Korea*	75 E14	38 57N 127 25 E
Sępólno Krajeńskie, *Poland*	54 E4	53 26N 17 30 E
Sepone, *Laos*	86 D6	16 45N 106 13 E
Şçopopol, *Poland*	55 F8	54 16N 21 2 E
Sept-Îles, *Canada*	141 B6	50 13N 66 22W
Septemvri, *Bulgaria*	51 D8	42 13N 24 6 E
Sepúlveda, *Spain*	42 D7	41 18N 3 45W
Sequeros, *Spain*	42 E4	40 31N 6 2W
Sequim, *U.S.A.*	160 B3	48 5N 123 6W
Sequoia Nat. Park △, *U.S.A.*	160 J8	36 30N 118 30W
Sera, *Indonesia*	83 C4	5 40 S 131 5 E
Serafimovich, *Russia*	60 F6	49 36N 42 43 E
Seraing, *Belgium*	24 D5	50 35N 5 32 E
Serakhis →, *Cyprus*	39 E8	35 13N 32 55 E
Seram, *Indonesia*	83 B3	3 10 S 129 0 E
Seram Sea, *Indonesia*	82 B3	2 30 S 128 30 E
Seranantsara, *Madag.*	117 B8	18 30 S 49 5 E
Serang, *Indonesia*	84 D3	6 8 S 106 10 E
Serangoon, *Singapore*	87 d	1 23N 103 54 E
Serasan, *Indonesia*	85 B3	2 29N 109 4 E
Saravezza, *Italy*	44 E7	43 59N 10 13 E
Şerbettar, *Turkey*	51 E10	41 27N 26 46 E
Serbia □, *Yugoslavia*	50 C5	43 30N 21 0 E
Serbia & Montenegro = Yugoslavia ■, *Europe*	50 C4	43 20N 20 0 E
Şercaia, *Romania*	53 E10	45 49N 25 9 E
Serdo, *Ethiopia*	107 E5	11 56N 41 14 E
Serdobsk, *Russia*	60 D7	52 28N 44 10 E
Sered', *Slovak Rep.*	35 C10	48 17N 17 44 E
Seredka, *Russia*	58 C5	58 12N 28 10 E
Şereflikoçhisar, *Turkey*	100 C5	38 56N 33 32 E
Seregno, *Italy*	44 C6	45 39N 9 12 E
Seremban, *Malaysia*	87 L3	2 43N 101 53 E
Serengeti Nat. Park △, *Tanzania*	118 C3	2 11 S 35 0 E
Serengeti Plain, *Tanzania*	118 C3	2 40 S 35 0 E
Serenje, *Zambia*	119 E3	13 14 S 30 15 E
Sereth = Siret →, *Romania*	53 E12	45 24N 28 1 E
Sergach, *Russia*	60 C7	55 30N 45 30 E
Sergen, *Turkey*	51 E11	41 41N 27 42 E
Sergino, *Russia*	66 C7	62 25N 65 12 E
Sergipe □, *Brazil*	170 D4	10 30 S 37 30W
Sergiyev Posad, *Russia*	58 D10	56 20N 38 10 E
Seria, *Brunei*	85 B4	4 37N 114 23 E
Serian, *Malaysia*	85 B4	1 10N 110 31 E
Seriate, *Italy*	44 C6	45 41N 9 43 E
Seribu, Kepulauan, *Indonesia*	84 D3	5 36 S 106 33 E
Sérifontaine, *France*	27 C8	49 20N 1 45 E
Sérifos, *Greece*	48 D6	37 9N 24 30 E
Sérignan, *France*	28 E7	43 17N 3 17 E
Sérigny →, *Canada*	141 A6	56 47N 66 0W
Serik, *Turkey*	100 D4	36 55N 31 7 E
Serikbuya, *China*	65 D8	39 21N 77 50 E
Seringapatam Reef, *Australia*	124 B3	13 38 S 122 5 E
Serinhisar, *Turkey*	49 D11	37 36N 29 18 E
Seririt, *Indonesia*	79 J17	8 12 S 114 56 E
Sermaize-les-Bains, *France*	27 D11	48 47N 4 54 E
Sermata, *Indonesia*	83 C3	8 15 S 128 50 E
Sermersuaq, *Greenland*	10 B4	79 30N 62 0W
Sérmide, *Italy*	45 D8	45 0N 11 18 E
Sernovodsk, *Russia*	60 D10	53 54N 51 16 E
Sernur, *Russia*	60 B9	56 52N 49 2 E
Serock, *Poland*	55 F8	52 31N 21 4 E
Serón, *Spain*	41 H2	37 20N 2 29W
Seròs, *Spain*	40 D5	41 27N 0 24 E
Serouenout, *Algeria*	111 D6	24 18N 7 28 E
Serov, *Russia*	64 B8	59 29N 60 35 E
Serowe, *Botswana*	116 C4	22 25 S 26 43 E
Serpa, *Portugal*	43 H3	37 57N 7 38W
Serpeddí, Punta, *Italy*	46 C2	39 22N 9 18 E
Serpentara, *Italy*	46 C2	39 8N 9 36 E
Serpentine Lakes, *Australia*	125 E4	28 30 S 129 10 E
Serpent's Mouth = Sierpe, Bocas de la, *Venezuela*	169 G9	10 0N 61 30W
Serpis →, *Spain*	41 G4	38 59N 0 9W
Serpukhov, *Russia*	58 E9	54 55N 37 28 E
Serra da Estrela, Parque Natural de △, *Portugal*	42 E3	40 27N 7 33W
Serra de Outes, *Spain*	42 C2	42 52N 8 55W
Serra do Navio, *Brazil*	169 C7	0 59N 52 3W
Serra do Salitre, *Brazil*	171 E2	19 6 S 46 41W
Serra Talhada, *Brazil*	170 C4	7 59 S 38 18W
Serradilla, *Spain*	42 F4	39 50N 6 9W
Sérrai, *Greece*	50 E7	41 5N 23 31 E
Sérrai □, *Greece*	50 E7	41 5N 23 37 E
Serramanna, *Italy*	46 C1	39 25N 8 55 E
Serranópolis, *Brazil*	173	18 16 S 52 0W
Serras d'Aire e Candeeiros, Parque Natural de △, *Portugal*	42 F2	39 31N 8 48W
Serrat, C., *Tunisia*	108 A1	37 14N 9 10 E
Serravalle, *Italy*	33 E6	45 41N 8 18 E
Serravalle Scrívia, *Italy*	44 D5	44 43N 8 51 E
Serre-Ponçon, L. de, *France*	29 D10	44 22N 6 20 E
Serres, *France*	29 D9	44 26N 5 43 E
Serrezuela, *Argentina*	174 C2	30 40 S 65 20W
Serrinha, *Brazil*	171 D4	11 39 S 39 0W
Serrita, *Brazil*	170 C4	7 56 S 39 19W
Sérsale, *Italy*	47 C9	39 1N 16 43 E
Sertã, *Portugal*	42 F2	39 48N 8 6W
Sertânia, *Brazil*	170 C4	8 5 S 37 20W
Sertanópolis, *Brazil*	175 A5	23 4 S 51 2W
Sêrtar, *China*	76 A3	32 20N 100 41 E
Sertig, *Switz.*	33 C9	46 44N 9 52 E
Serua, *Indonesia*	83 C4	6 18 S 130 1 E
Serui, *Indonesia*	83 B5	1 53 S 136 10 E
Serule, *Botswana*	116 C4	21 57 S 27 20 E
Sérvia, *Greece*	50 F6	40 11N 22 0 E
Serzedelo, *Portugal*	42 D2	41 28N 8 14W
Ses Salines, *Spain*	38 B4	39 21N 3 3 E
Sesayap →, *Indonesia*	85 B5	3 36N 117 15 E
Sese Is., *Uganda*	118 C3	0 20 S 32 20 E
Sesepe, *Indonesia*	82 B3	1 30 S 127 59 E
Sesfontein, *Namibia*	116 B1	19 7 S 13 39 E
Sesheke, *Zambia*	116 B3	17 29 S 24 13 E
Sésia →, *Italy*	44 C5	45 5N 8 37 E
Sesimbra, *Portugal*	43 G1	38 28N 9 6W
S'Espalmador, *Spain*	38 D1	38 47N 1 26 E
S'Espardell, *Spain*	38 D1	38 48N 1 29 E
Sessa, *Angola*	118 D4	13 56 S 20 38 E
Sessa Aurunca, *Italy*	46 A6	41 14N 13 56 E
Sesser, *U.S.A.*	156 F7	38 5N 89 1W
S'Estanyol, *Spain*	38 B3	39 22N 2 54 E
Sestao, *Spain*	40 B2	43 18N 3 0W
Sesto Calende, *Italy*	44 C5	45 44N 8 37 E
Sesto San Giovanni, *Italy*	44 C6	45 32N 9 14 E
Sestri Levante, *Italy*	44 D6	44 16N 9 24 E
Sestriere, *Italy*	44 D4	44 57N 6 53 E
Sestroretsk, *Russia*	58 B6	60 5N 29 58 E
Sestrunj, *Croatia*	45 D11	44 10N 15 0 E
Sestu, *Italy*	46 C2	39 18N 9 6 E
Sesvenna, *Switz.*	33 C10	46 42N 10 25 E
Setaka, *Japan*	72 D2	33 9N 130 28 E
Setana, *Japan*	70 C9	42 26N 139 51 E
Sète, *France*	28 E7	43 25N 3 42 E
Sete Lagôas, *Brazil*	171 E3	19 27 S 44 16W
Setesdalsheiene, *Norway*	18 E3	59 28N 7 10 E
Sétif, *Algeria*	111 A6	36 9N 5 26 E
Seto, *Japan*	73 B9	35 14N 137 6 E
Seto-Naikai Nat. Park △, *Japan*	72 C5	34 15N 133 15 E
Setonaikai, *Japan*	72 C5	34 20N 133 30 E
Setsan, *Burma*	90 G5	16 3N 95 23 E
Settat, *Morocco*	110 B3	33 0N 7 40W
Setté-Cama, *Gabon*	114 C1	2 32 S 9 45 E
Séttimo Torinese, *Italy*	44 C4	45 9N 7 46 E
Setting L., *Canada*	143 C9	55 0N 98 38W
Settle, *U.K.*	20 C5	54 5N 2 16W
Settlement Pt., *Bahamas*	149 M6	26 40N 79 0W
Settlers, *S. Africa*	117 C4	25 2 S 28 30 E
Setúbal, *Portugal*	43 G2	38 30N 8 58W
Setúbal □, *Portugal*	43 G2	38 25N 8 35W
Setúbal, B. de, *Portugal*	43 G2	38 40N 8 56W
Seugne →, *France*	28 C3	45 42N 0 32W
Seul, L., *Canada*	143 B1	50 20N 92 30W
Seulimeum, *Indonesia*	84 A1	5 27N 95 15 E
Seurre, *France*	27 F12	47 0N 5 8 E
Seuzach, *Switz.*	33 A7	47 32N 8 49 E
Sevan, *Armenia*	61 K7	40 33N 44 56 E
Sevan, Ozero = Sevana Lich, *Armenia*	61 K7	40 30N 45 20 E
Sevana Lich, *Armenia*	61 K7	40 30N 45 20 E
Sevastopol, *Ukraine*	59 G7	44 35N 33 30 E
Sevelen, *Switz.*	33 B8	47 7N 9 28 E
Seven Sisters, *Canada*	142 C3	54 56N 128 10W
Sever →, *Spain*	43 F3	39 40N 7 32W
Sévérac-le-Château, *France*	28 D7	44 20N 3 5 E
Severn →, *Canada*	140 A2	56 2N 87 36W
Severn →, *U.K.*	21 F5	51 35N 2 40W
Severn L., *Canada*	140 B1	53 54N 90 48W
Severnaya Zemlya, *Russia*	67 B10	79 0N 100 0 E
Severnyye Uvaly, *Russia*	60 B8	60 0N 50 0 E
Severo-Kurilsk, *Russia*	67 D16	50 40N 156 8 E
Severo-Yeniseyskiy, *Russia*	67 C10	60 22N 93 1 E
Severočeský □, *Czech Rep.*	34 A7	50 30N 14 0 E
Severodonetsk = Syeverodonetsk, *Ukraine*	59 H10	48 58N 38 35 E
Severodvinsk, *Russia*	56 B6	64 27N 39 58 E
Severomoravský □, *Czech Rep.*	35 B10	49 38N 17 40 E
Severomorsk, *Russia*	56 A5	69 5N 33 27 E
Severouralsk, *Russia*	64 A7	60 9N 59 57 E
Sevilla, *Colombia*	168 C2	4 16N 75 57W
Sevilla, *Spain*	43 H5	37 23N 5 58W
Sevilla □, *Spain*	43 H5	37 25N 5 58W
Seville = Sevilla, *Spain*	43 H5	37 23N 5 58W
Seville, *Fla., U.S.A.*	153 F8	29 19N 81 30W
Seville, *Ga., U.S.A.*	153 D6	31 58N 83 36W
Sevlievo, *Bulgaria*	51 C9	43 2N 25 6 E
Sevnica, *Slovenia*	45 B12	46 2N 15 19 E
Sèvre-Nantaise →, *France*	26 E5	47 12N 1 33W
Sèvre-Niortaise →, *France*	28 B3	46 28N 0 50W
Sevsk, *Russia*	59 F8	52 10N 34 30 E
Sewa →, *S. Leone*	112 D2	7 20N 12 10W
Sewani, *India*	92 E6	28 58N 75 39 E
Seward, *Alaska, U.S.A.*	144 F10	60 7N 149 27W
Seward, *Nebr., U.S.A.*	156 E6	40 55N 97 6W
Seward, *Pa., U.S.A.*	150 F5	40 25N 79 1W
Seward Peninsula, *U.S.A.*	144 C6	65 30N 166 0W
Sewell, *Chile*	174 C1	34 10 S 70 23W
Sewer, *Indonesia*	83 C4	5 53 S 134 40 E
Sewickley, *U.S.A.*	150 F4	40 32N 80 12W
Sexsmith, *Canada*	142 B5	55 21N 118 47W
Seychelles ■, *Ind. Oc.*	121 b	5 0 S 56 0 E
Seyðisfjörður, *Iceland*	11 B13	65 16N 13 57W
Seydişehir, *Turkey*	100 D4	37 25N 31 51 E
Seydvān, *Iran*	101 C11	38 34N 45 2 E
Seyhan →, *Turkey*	100 D6	36 43N 34 53 E
Seyhan Barajı, *Turkey*	49 B12	37 27N 30 43 E
Seyitömer, *Turkey*	49 B11	39 27N 30 43 E
Seym →, *Ukraine*	59 G7	51 27N 32 34 E
Seymen, *Turkey*	51 E11	41 6N 27 57 E
Seymour, *Australia*	129 D6	37 0 S 145 10 E
Seymour, *S. Africa*	117 E4	32 33 S 26 46 E
Seymour, *Conn., U.S.A.*	151 E11	41 24N 73 4W
Seymour, *Ind., U.S.A.*	157 F11	38 58N 85 53W
Seymour, *Tex., U.S.A.*	155 J5	33 35N 99 16W
Seyne, *France*	29 D10	44 21N 6 22 E
Seyssel, *France*	29 C9	45 57N 5 50 E
Sežana, *Slovenia*	45 C10	45 43N 13 41 E
Sézanne, *France*	27 D10	48 40N 3 40 E
Sezze, *Italy*	46 A6	41 30N 13 3 E
Sfax, *Tunisia*	108 B2	34 49N 10 48 E
Sfântu Gheorghe, *Covasna, Romania*	53 E10	45 52N 25 48 E
Sfântu Gheorghe, *Tulcea, Romania*	53 F14	44 53N 29 36 E
Sfântu Gheorghe, Braţul →, *Romania*	53 F14	44 51N 29 36 E
Sha Tau Kok, *China*	69 F11	22 33N 114 13 E
Sha Tin, *China*	69 G11	22 23N 114 12 E
Sha Xi →, *China*	77 D12	26 35N 118 0 E
Sha Xian, *China*	77 D11	26 23N 117 45 E
Shaanxi □, *China*	74 G5	35 0N 109 0 E
Shaartuz, *Tajikistan*	37 16N 68 8 E
Shaba = Katanga □, *Dem. Rep. of the Congo*	118 D2	8 0 S 25 0 E
Shaba Nat. Reserve △, *Kenya*	118 B4	0 38N 37 48 E
Shaballe = Scebeli, Wabi →, *Somali Rep.*	120 D2	2 0N 44 0 E
Shabla, *Bulgaria*	51 C12	43 31N 28 32 E
Shabogamo L., *Canada*	141 B6	53 15N 66 30W
Shabunda, *Dem. Rep. of the Congo*	118 C2	2 40 S 27 16 E
Shabwah, *Yemen*	106 D4	15 22N 47 1 E
Shache, *China*	65 D8	38 20N 77 10 E
Shackleton Ice Shelf, *Antarctica*	7 C8	66 0 S 100 0 E
Shackleton Inlet, *Antarctica*	7 E11	83 0 S 160 0 E
Shādegān, *Iran*	97 D6	30 40N 48 38 E
Shadi, *China*	77 D10	26 7N 114 47 E
Shadi, *India*	93 C7	33 24N 77 14 E
Shadrinsk, *Russia*	64 C9	56 5N 63 32 E
Shady Dale, *U.S.A.*	152 B5	33 24N 83 36W
Shady Grove, *U.S.A.*	152 E6	30 17N 83 38W
Shadyside, *U.S.A.*	150 G4	39 58N 80 45W
Shafer, L., *U.S.A.*	157 D10	40 46N 86 46W
Shaffa, *Nigeria*	113 C7	10 30N 12 6 E
Shafter, *U.S.A.*	161 K7	35 30N 119 16W
Shaftesbury, *U.K.*	21 F5	51 0N 2 11W
Shag Pt., *N.Z.*	131 F5	45 29 S 170 52 E
Shag Rocks, *Atl. Oc.*	8 M7	53 0 S 41 0W
Shaganu, *Nigeria*	113 D5	6 51N 3 39 E
Shageluk, *U.S.A.*	144 E8	62 41N 159 34W
Shagram, *Pakistan*	93 A5	36 24N 72 20 E
Shah Alam, *Malaysia*	84 B2	3 5N 101 30 E
Shah Alizai, *Pakistan*	92 E2	29 25N 66 33 E
Shah Bunder, *Pakistan*	92 G2	24 13N 67 56 E
Shāh Jūy, *Afghan.*	91 B2	32 31N 67 25 E
Shahabad, *Andhra Pradesh, India*	94 F3	17 10N 78 7 E
Shahabad, *Karnataka, India*	94 F3	17 10N 76 54 E
Shahabad, *Punjab, India*	92 D7	30 10N 76 55 E
Shahabad, *Ut. P., India*	93 F8	27 36N 79 56 E
Shahada, *India*	92 G3	21 33N 74 30 E
Shahadpur, *Pakistan*	92 G3	25 55N 68 35 E
Shahapur, *India*	95 G2	15 50N 74 34 E
Shahba, *Syria*	103 C5	32 52N 36 38 E
Shahbazpur 1, *Bangla.*	90 D3	22 30N 90 45 E
Shahdād, *Iran*	97 D8	30 30N 57 40 E
Shahdadkot, *Pakistan*	91 D2	27 50N 67 55 E
Shahdol, *India*	94 H9	23 19N 81 26 E
Shahe, *China*	74 F8	37 0N 114 32 E
Shahganj, *India*	93 F10	26 3N 82 44 E
Shaḥḥāt, *Libya*	108 B4	32 48N 21 54 E
Shahīdān, *Afghan.*	91 B2	34 30N 67 40 E
Shahjahanpur, *India*	93 F8	27 54N 79 57 E
Shahpur, *Karnataka, India*	94 F3	16 40N 76 48 E
Shahpur, *Mad. P., India*	92 H7	22 12N 77 58 E
Shahpur, *Baluchistan, Pakistan*	92 E3	28 46N 68 27 E
Shahpur, *Punjab, Pakistan*	92 C5	32 17N 72 26 E
Shahpur Chakar, *Pakistan*	92 F3	26 9N 68 39 E
Shahpura, *Mad. P., India*	93 H9	23 10N 80 45 E
Shahpura, *Raj., India*	92 G6	25 38N 74 56 E
Shahr-e Bābak, *Iran*	97 D7	30 7N 55 9 E
Shahr-e Kord, *Iran*	97 C6	32 15N 50 55 E
Shāhrakht, *Iran*	91 C9	33 38N 60 16 E
Shahrig, *Pakistan*	91 C2	30 15N 67 40 E
Shahukou, *China*	76 D7	40 20N 112 18 E
Shaikhabad, *Afghan.*	91 B3	34 2N 68 45 E
Shajapur, *India*	92 H7	23 27N 76 21 E
Shajing, *China*	69 F10	22 44N 113 48 E
Shakargarh, *Pakistan*	93 C6	32 17N 75 10 E
Shakawe, *Botswana*	116 B3	18 28 S 21 49 E
Shakhe, *Dem. Rep. of the Congo*	115 D3	6 14 S 18 41 E
Shaker Heights, *U.S.A.*	150 E3	41 29N 81 32W
Shakhrikhan, *Uzbekistan*	65 C6	40 40N 72 2 E
Shakhrisabz, *Uzbekistan*	65 D4	39 3N 66 50 E
Shakhristan, *Tajikistan*	65 C5	47 40N 40 16 E
Shakhtinsk, *Kazakhstan*	64 E8	49 43N 72 30 E
Shakhty, *Russia*	60 G6	47 40N 40 16 E
Shakhunya, *Russia*	60 B8	57 40N 46 46 E
Shaki, *Nigeria*	113 D5	8 41N 3 21 E
Shākir, *Egypt*	106 C3	27 30N 33 59 E
Shakpak, *Kazakhstan*	93 A6	43 15N 69 26 E
Shaksam Valley, *Asia*	93 A7	36 0N 76 20 E
Shaktoolik, *U.S.A.*	144 D7	64 20N 161 9W
Shala, L., *Ethiopia*	107 F4	7 30N 38 30 E
Shali, *Iran*	61 J7	43 9N 45 55 E
Shalkar, *Kazakhstan*	64 E6	50 40N 51 53 E
Shalkar, Ozero, *Kazakhstan*	64 D5	50 35N 51 47 E
Shallow Lake, *Canada*	150 B3	44 36N 81 5W
Shalqar, *Kazakhstan*	66 E6	47 48N 59 38 E
Shalskiy, *Russia*	56 B8	61 48N 35 58 E
Shāluli Shan, *China*	76 B2	30 40N 99 55 E
Shām, *Iran*	97 E8	26 39N 57 21 E
Shām, J. ash, *Oman*	99 B7	23 10N 57 5 E
Shamâl Bahr el Ghazal □, *Sudan*	107 F2	8 0N 27 30 E
Shamâl Dârfûr □, *Sudan*	107 E3	15 0N 25 0 E
Shamâl Kordofân □, *Sudan*	107 E3	15 0N 30 0 E
Shamâl Sînî □, *Egypt*	103 A2	30 0N 34 0 E
Shamaldy-Say, *Kyrgyzstan*	65 C6	41 12N 72 11 E
Shamattawa, *Canada*	140 A1	55 51N 92 5W
Shamattawa →, *Canada*	140 A2	55 1N 85 23W
Shambe, *Sudan*	107 F3	7 8N 30 46 E
Shambe Nat. Park △, *Sudan*	107 F3	6 57N 30 50 E
Shambu, *Ethiopia*	107 F4	9 32N 37 3 E
Shamgong Dzong, *Bhutan*	90 B3	27 13N 90 35 E
Shamil, *Iran*	97 E8	27 30N 56 55 E
Shamkhor = Şämkir, *Azerbaijan*	61 K8	40 50N 46 0 E
Shamkuh, *Iran*	97 C8	35 47N 57 50 E
Shamli, *India*	92 E7	29 32N 77 18 E
Shammar, Jabal, *Si. Arabia*	96 E4	27 40N 41 0 E
Shamo = Gobi, *Asia*	76 C5	44 0N 110 0 E
Shamo, L., *Ethiopia*	107 F4	5 45N 37 30 E
Shamokin, *U.S.A.*	151 F8	40 47N 76 34W
Shamrock, *U.S.A.*	155 H4	35 13N 100 15W
Shamsabad, *India*	94 F4	17 20 S 31 32 E
Shamva, *Zimbabwe*	119 F3	17 20 S 31 32 E
Shan □, *Burma*	90 F7	21 30N 98 30 E
Shan Xian, *China*	74 G9	34 50N 116 5 E
Shanan →, *Ethiopia*	107 F5	8 0N 40 20 E
Shanchengzhen, *China*	75 C13	42 20N 125 20 E
Shāndak, *Iran*	97 D9	28 28N 60 27 E
Shandon, *U.S.A.*	160 K6	35 39N 120 23W
Shandong □, *China*	75 F11	36 0N 118 0 E
Shandong Bandao, *China*	75 F11	37 0N 121 0 E
Shang Xian = Shangzhou, *China*	74 H5	33 50N 109 58 E
Shangalowe, *Dem. Rep. of the Congo*	119 E2	10 50 S 26 30 E
Shangani, *Zimbabwe*	119 F2	19 41 S 29 20 E
Shangani →, *Zimbabwe*	119 F2	18 41 S 27 10 E
Shangbancheng, *China*	75 D10	40 50N 118 1 E
Shangcheng, *China*	77 B10	31 47N 115 26 E
Shangchuan Dao, *China*	77 G9	21 40N 112 50 E
Shangdu, *China*	74 D7	41 30N 113 30 E
Shanggao, *China*	77 C10	28 17N 114 55 E
Shanghai, *China*	77 B13	31 15N 121 26 E
Shanghai Shi □, *China*	77 B13	31 10N 121 25 E
Shanghang, *China*	77 E11	25 2N 116 23 E
Shanghe, *China*	75 F9	37 20N 117 10 E
Shangjin, *China*	76 F7	33 27N 108 33 E
Shangnan, *China*	74 H6	33 32N 110 50 E
Shangqiu, *China*	74 G8	34 26N 115 36 E
Shangrao, *China*	77 C11	28 25N 117 59 E
Shangshui, *China*	69 C6	33 42N 114 35 E
Shangsi, *China*	76 F6	22 8N 107 58 E
Shangyou, *China*	77 E10	25 48N 114 32 E
Shangyu, *China*	77 B13	30 1N 120 52 E
Shangzhi, *China*	75 B14	45 22N 127 56 E
Shangzhou, *China*	74 H5	33 50N 109 58 E
Shanhetun, *China*	75 B14	44 33N 127 15 E
Shani, *Nigeria*	113 C7	10 14N 12 2 E
Shanklin, *U.K.*	21 G6	50 38N 1 11W
Shannon, *Greenland*	10 B9	75 10N 18 30W
Shannon, *N.Z.*	130 G4	40 33 S 175 25 E
Shannon →, *Ireland*	23 D2	52 35N 9 30W
Shannon, Mouth of the, *Ireland*	23 D2	52 30N 9 55W
Shannon Airport, *Ireland*	23 D3	52 42N 8 57W
Shannon Nat. Park △, *Australia*	125 F2	31 55 S 117 51 E
Shannontown, *U.S.A.*	152 B9	33 53N 80 21W
Shansi = Shanxi □, *China*	74 F7	37 0N 112 0 E
Shantar, Ostrov Bolshoy, *Russia*	67 D14	55 9N 137 40 E
Shantipur, *India*	93 H13	23 17N 88 25 E
Shantou, *China*	77 F11	23 18N 116 40 E
Shantung = Shandong □, *China*	75 G10	36 0N 118 0 E
Shanwei, *China*	77 F10	22 48N 115 22 E
Shanxi □, *China*	74 F7	37 0N 112 0 E
Shanyang, *China*	74 H5	33 31N 109 55 E
Shanyin, *China*	74 E7	39 25N 112 56 E
Shaodong, *China*	77 D8	27 15N 111 43 E
Shaoguan, *China*	77 E9	24 48N 113 35 E
Shaoshan, *China*	77 D9	27 55N 112 33 E
Shaowu, *China*	77 D11	27 22N 117 28 E
Shaoxing, *China*	77 C13	30 0N 120 35 E
Shaoyang, Hunan, *China*	77 D8	27 14N 111 25 E
Shaoyang, Hunan, *China*	77 D8	27 14N 111 25 E
Shap, *U.K.*	20 C5	54 32N 2 40W
Shapinsay, *U.K.*	22 B6	59 3N 2 51W
Shaqq el Gi'eifer →, *Sudan*	107 D2	15 16N 26 0 E
Shaqrā', *Si. Arabia*	96 E5	25 15N 45 16 E
Shaqrā', *Yemen*	98 D4	13 22N 45 44 E
Sharafa, *Sudan*	107 E2	11 59N 27 7 E
Sharafkhāneh, *Iran*	101 C11	38 11N 45 29 E
Sharavati →, *India*	95 G2	14 20N 74 25 E
Sharbatāt, Ra's ash, *Oman*	99 C7	17 56N 56 21 E
Sharbot Lake, *Canada*	151 B8	44 46N 76 41W
Shardara, *Kazakhstan*	65 C3	41 15N 67 40 E
Shardara, Step, *Kazakhstan*	65 A5	42 20N 68 0 E
Shardara Bogeni, *Kazakhstan*	65 C3	41 16N 68 15 E
Sharjah = Ash Shāriqah, *U.A.E.*	97 E7	25 23N 55 26 E
Shark B., *Australia*	125 E1	25 30 S 113 32 E
Shark Bay Marine Nature Reserve △, *Australia*	125 E2	32 49 S 118 49 E
Sharm el Sheikh, *Egypt*	106 B3	27 53N 34 18 E
Sharon, Mass., U.S.A.	151 D13	42 7N 71 11W
Sharon, Pa., U.S.A.	150 E4	41 14N 80 31W
Sharon, Wis., U.S.A.	157 B8	42 30N 88 44W
Sharon Springs, Kans., U.S.A.	154 F4	38 54N 101 45W
Sharon Springs, N.Y., U.S.A.	151 D10	42 48N 74 37W
Sharonville, *U.S.A.*	157 E12	39 16N 84 24W
Sharp Pk., *Phil.*	81 J5	5 58N 125 31 E
Sharp Pt., *Australia*	126 A3	10 58 S 142 43 E
Sharpe L., *Canada*	140 B1	54 24N 93 40W
Sharpes, *U.S.A.*	153 G9	28 26N 80 46W
Sharpeville, *U.S.A.*	153 C8	41 15N 80 29W
Sharq al Istiwa'iya □, *Sudan*	107 G3	5 0N 33 0 E
Sharya, *Russia*	60 A7	58 22N 45 20 E
Shasha, *Ethiopia*	107 F4	6 29N 35 59 E
Shashemene, *Ethiopia*	107 F4	7 13N 38 33 E
Shashi, *Botswana*	117 C4	21 15 S 27 27 E
Shashi, *China*	77 B9	30 25N 112 14 E
Shashi →, *Africa*	119 G2	21 14 S 29 20 E
Shasta, L., *U.S.A.*	158 F2	41 25 S 122 12W
Shasta, Mt., *U.S.A.*	158 F2	40 43N 122 25W
Shatawi, *Sudan*	107 E3	14 39N 32 6 E
Shāṭi', Wādi ash →, *Libya*	108 C3	27 30N 14 30 E
Shatsk, *Russia*	60 C5	54 5N 41 45 E
Shatskyi □, *Ukraine*	55 G10	51 30N 23 52 E
Shatt al Arab = Arab, Shatt al →, *Asia*	97 D6	30 0N 48 31 E
Shaubak, *Jordan*	58 E10	55 33N 39 21 E
Shaudder, *Kazakhstan*	65 A4	42 47N 68 3 E
Shaumyani = Shulaveri, *Georgia*	61 K7	41 22N 44 45 E
Shaunavon, *Canada*	143 D7	49 35N 108 25W
Shaver L., *U.S.A.*	160 H7	37 9N 119 18W
Shaw →, *Australia*	124 D2	20 21 S 119 17 E
Shaw I., *Australia*	126 J7	20 30 S 149 2 E
Shawanaga, *Canada*	150 A4	45 31N 80 17W
Shawangunk Mts., *U.S.A.*	151 E10	41 35N 74 30W
Shawano, *U.S.A.*	148 C1	44 47N 88 36W
Shawinigan, *Canada*	140 C5	46 35N 72 50W
Shawnee, Ga., U.S.A.	152 C8	32 23N 81 20W
Shawnee, Kans., U.S.A.	156 F7	39 1N 94 43W
Shawnee, Okla., U.S.A.	155 H6	35 20N 96 55W
Shay Gap, *Australia*	124 D3	20 30 S 120 10 E
Shaybārā, *Si. Arabia*	96 E3	25 26N 36 47 E
Shayib al Banat, Gebel, *Egypt*	106 B3	26 59N 33 29 E
Shaykh, J. ash, *Lebanon*	103 B4	33 25N 35 50 E
Shaykh Miskīn, *Syria*	103 C5	32 49N 36 9 E
Shaykh Sa'īd, *Iraq*	101 F12	32 34N 46 17 E
Shaykh 'Uthmān, *Yemen*	98 D4	12 52N 44 59 E
Shaymak, *Tajikistan*	65 F7	37 33N 74 50 E
Shazud, *Tajikistan*	65 F7	37 33N 72 50 E
Shchekino, *Russia*	58 E9	54 1N 37 34 E
Shcherbakov = Rybinsk, *Russia*	58 C10	58 5N 38 50 E
Shchigry, *Russia*	59 G9	51 55N 36 58 E
Shchors, *Ukraine*	59 G6	51 48N 31 56 E
Shchuchinsk, *Kazakhstan*	66 D8	52 56N 70 12 E
Shchuchye, *Russia*	64 D7	55 12N 62 46 E
She Xian, Anhui, *China*	77 C12	29 50N 118 25 E
She Xian, Hebei, *China*	74 F7	36 30N 113 40 E
Shea, *Guyana*	169 C6	2 48N 59 4W
Shebekino, *Russia*	59 G9	50 28N 37 5 E
Shebele = Scebeli, Wabi →, *Somali Rep.*	120 D2	2 0N 44 0 E
Sheberghān, *Afghan.*	65 E2	36 40N 65 45 E
Sheboygan, *U.S.A.*	148 D2	43 46N 87 45W
Shebshi Mts., *Nigeria*	113 D7	8 30N 11 0 E
Shediac, *Canada*	141 C7	46 14N 64 32W
Sheelin, L., *Ireland*	23 C4	53 48N 7 20W
Sheenjek →, *U.S.A.*	144 C11	66 45N 144 33W
Sheep Haven, *Ireland*	23 A4	55 11N 7 52W
Sheerness, *U.K.*	21 F8	51 26N 0 47 E
Sheet Harbour, *Canada*	141 D7	44 56N 62 31W
Sheffield, *N.Z.*	131 D7	43 23 S 172 1 E
Sheffield, *U.K.*	20 D6	53 23N 1 28W
Sheffield, Ala., U.S.A.	149 H2	34 46N 87 41W
Sheffield, Ill., U.S.A.	156 C7	41 21N 89 44W
Sheffield, Iowa, U.S.A.	156 B3	42 54N 93 13W
Sheffield, Mass., U.S.A.	151 D11	42 5N 73 21W
Sheffield, Tex., U.S.A.	150 E5	41 42N 79 3W
Shegaon, *India*	94 D4	20 48N 76 47 E

Sheghnān, Afghan. ... 65 E5 37 37N 71 36 E
Shehojele, Ethiopia ... 107 E4 10 40N 35 9 E
Shehong, China ... 76 B5 30 54N 105 18 E
Sheuen →, Argentina ... 176 C3 49 35 S 69 34W
Sheikh Idris, Sudan ... 107 E3 11 43N 33 30 E
Sheikhpura, India ... 93 G11 25 9N 85 53 E
Shek Hasan, Ethiopia ... 107 E4 12 5N 35 58 E
Shekhupura, Pakistan ... 91 C4 31 42N 73 58 E
Sheki = Şaki, Azerbaijan ... 61 K8 41 10N 47 5 E
Shekou, China ... 69 G10 22 30N 113 55 E
Shelbina, U.S.A. ... 156 E4 39 47N 92 2W
Shelburn, U.S.A. ... 157 E9 39 11N 87 24W
Shelburne, N.S., Canada ... 141 D6 43 47N 65 20W
Shelburne, Ont., Canada ... 140 D3 44 4N 80 15W
Shelburne, U.S.A. ... 151 B11 44 23N 73 14W
Shelburne B., Australia ... 126 A3 11 50 S 142 50 E
Shelburne Falls, U.S.A. ... 151 D12 42 36N 72 45W
Shelby, Mich., U.S.A. ... 148 D2 43 37N 86 22W
Shelby, Miss., U.S.A. ... 155 J9 33 57N 90 46W
Shelby, Mont., U.S.A. ... 158 B8 48 30N 111 51W
Shelby, N.C., U.S.A. ... 149 H5 35 17N 81 32W
Shelby, Ohio, U.S.A. ... 150 F2 40 53N 82 40W
Shelbyville, Ill., U.S.A. ... 154 F10 39 24N 88 48W
Shelbyville, Ind., U.S.A. ... 157 E11 39 31N 85 47W
Shelbyville, Ky., U.S.A. ... 157 E11 38 13N 85 14W
Shelbyville, Mo., U.S.A. ... 156 E4 39 48N 92 2W
Shelbyville, Tenn., U.S.A. ... 149 H2 35 29N 86 28W
Shelbyville, L., U.S.A. ... 157 E8 39 26N 88 46W
Sheldon, Ill., U.S.A. ... 157 D9 40 46N 87 34W
Sheldon, Iowa, U.S.A. ... 154 D7 43 11N 95 51W
Sheldon, Mo., U.S.A. ... 156 G2 37 40N 94 18W
Sheldon, S.C., U.S.A. ... 152 C9 32 36N 80 48W
Sheldon Point, U.S.A. ... 144 C6 62 32N 164 52W
Sheldrake, Canada ... 141 B7 50 20N 64 51W
Shelek, Kazakhstan ... 65 B9 43 33N 78 17 E
Shelengo, Khawr →, Sudan ... 107 E2 10 33N 28 40 E
Shelikhova, Zaliv, Russia ... 67 D16 59 30N 157 0 E
Shelikof Strait, U.S.A. ... 144 H9 57 30N 155 0W
Shell Lakes, Australia ... 125 E4 29 20 S 127 30 E
Shellbrook, Canada ... 143 C7 53 13N 106 24W
Shellharbour, Australia ... 129 C9 34 31 S 150 51 E
Shellman, U.S.A. ... 152 D5 31 46N 84 37W
Shellsburg, U.S.A. ... 156 B5 42 6N 91 52W
Shelon →, Russia ... 58 C6 58 13N 30 47 E
Shelter I., U.S.A. ... 151 E12 41 5N 72 21W
Shelton, Conn., U.S.A. ... 151 E11 41 19N 73 5W
Shelton, Wash., U.S.A. ... 160 C3 47 13N 123 6W
Shemakha = Şamaxı, Azerbaijan ... 61 K9 40 38N 48 37 E
Shēmri, Albania ... 50 D4 42 7N 20 13 E
Shemsi, Sudan ... 106 D2 19 7N 32 37 E
Shen Xian, China ... 74 F8 36 15N 115 40 E
Shenandoah, Iowa, U.S.A. ... 154 E7 40 46N 95 22W
Shenandoah, Pa., U.S.A. ... 151 F8 40 49N 76 12W
Shenandoah, Va., U.S.A. ... 148 F6 38 29N 78 37W
Shenandoah →, U.S.A. ... 148 F7 39 19N 77 44W
Shenandoah Nat. Park △, U.S.A. ... 148 F6 38 35N 78 22W
Shenchi, China ... 74 E7 39 8N 112 10 E
Shencottah, India ... 95 K3 8 59N 77 18 E
Shendam, Nigeria ... 113 D6 8 49N 9 30 E
Shendī, Sudan ... 107 D3 16 46N 33 22 E
Shendurni, India ... 94 D2 20 39N 75 36 E
Shenge, S. Leone ... 112 D2 7 54N 12 55W
Shengfang, China ... 74 E9 39 3N 116 42 E
Shenggeldi, Kazakhstan ... 65 B8 43 59N 77 27 E
Shēngjergj, Albania ... 50 E4 41 17N 20 10 E
Shēngjin, Albania ... 50 E3 41 50N 19 35 E
Shengzhou, China ... 77 C13 29 35N 120 50 E
Shenjingzi, China ... 75 B13 44 40N 124 30 E
Shenmu, China ... 74 E6 38 50N 110 29 E
Shennongjia, China ... 77 B8 31 43N 110 44 E
Shenqiu, China ... 74 H8 33 25N 115 5 E
Shensi = Shaanxi □, China ... 74 G5 35 0N 109 0 E
Shenyang, China ... 75 D12 41 48N 123 27 E
Shenzhen, China ... 69 F10 22 32N 114 5 E
Shenzhen ✈ (SZX), China ... 69 F10 22 41N 113 49 E
Shenzhen Shuiku, China ... 69 F11 22 34N 114 8 E
Shenzhen Wan, China ... 69 G10 22 27N 113 55 E
Sheo, India ... 92 F4 26 11N 71 15 E
Shepetivka, Ukraine ... 59 G4 50 10N 27 10 E
Shepetovka = Shepetivka, Ukraine ... 59 G4 50 10N 27 10 E
Shepherd I., Vanuatu ... 133 F6 16 55 S 168 36 E
Shepherdsville, U.S.A. ... 157 G11 37 59N 85 43W
Shepparton, Australia ... 129 D6 36 23 S 145 26 E
Sheppey, I. of, U.K. ... 21 F8 51 25N 0 48 E
Shepton Mallet, U.K. ... 21 F5 51 11N 2 33W
Sheqi, China ... 74 H7 33 12N 112 57 E
Sher Khan Qala, Afghan. ... 91 C2 29 53N 66 13 E
Sher Qila, Pakistan ... 93 A6 36 7N 74 2 E
Sherab, Sudan ... 107 E1 10 44N 24 41 E
Sherabad, Uzbekistan ... 65 B3 37 40N 67 1 E
Sherborne, U.K. ... 21 G5 50 57N 2 31W
Sherbro →, S. Leone ... 112 D2 7 45N 12 55W
Sherbro I., S. Leone ... 112 D2 7 30N 12 40W
Sherbrooke, N.S., Canada ... 141 C7 45 8N 61 59W
Sherbrooke, Qué., Canada ... 141 C5 45 28N 71 57W
Sherburne, U.S.A. ... 151 D9 42 41N 75 30W
Sherburne Reef, Papua N. G. ... 132 B5 3 20 S 148 0 E
Sherda, Chad ... 109 D3 20 7N 16 46 E
Shereik, Sudan ... 106 D3 18 44N 33 47 E
Shergaon, India ... 90 B4 27 7N 92 16 E
Shergarh, India ... 92 F5 26 20N 72 18 E
Sherghati, India ... 93 G11 24 34N 84 47 E
Sheridan, Ark., U.S.A. ... 155 H8 34 19N 92 24W
Sheridan, Ill., U.S.A. ... 157 C8 41 32N 88 41W
Sheridan, Ind., U.S.A. ... 157 D10 40 8N 86 13W
Sheridan, Wyo., U.S.A. ... 158 D10 44 48N 106 58W
Sheringham, U.K. ... 20 E9 52 56N 1 13 E
Sherkin I., Ireland ... 23 E2 51 28N 9 26W
Sherkot, India ... 93 E8 29 22N 78 35 E
Sherman, U.S.A. ... 155 J6 33 40N 96 35W
Sherpur, Bangla. ... 90 C3 25 0N 90 0 E
Sherpur, India ... 93 G10 25 34N 83 47 E
Sherridon, Canada ... 143 B8 55 8N 101 5W
Sherwood, U.S.A. ... 157 C12 41 17N 84 33W
Sherwood Forest, U.K. ... 20 D6 53 6N 1 7W
Sherwood Park, Canada ... 142 C6 53 31N 113 19W
Sheslay →, Canada ... 142 B2 58 48N 132 5W
Sheshanei L., Canada ... 143 B9 58 48N 97 50W
Shetland □, U.K. ... 22 A7 60 30N 1 30W
Shetland Is., U.K. ... 22 A7 60 30N 1 30W
Shetrunji →, India ... 92 J5 21 19N 72 7 E
Sheung Shui, China ... 69 F11 22 31N 114 7 E
Shevaroy Hills, India ... 95 J4 11 58N 78 12 E
Shevgaon, India ... 94 E2 19 21N 75 14 E
Shewa □, Ethiopia ... 107 F4 9 33N 38 10 E
Shewa Gimira, Ethiopia ... 107 F4 7 4N 35 51 E
Sheyenne →, U.S.A. ... 154 B6 47 2N 96 50W
Shibām, Yemen ... 99 D5 15 59N 48 36 E
Shibata, Japan ... 70 F9 37 57N 139 20 E
Shibecha, Japan ... 70 C12 43 17N 144 36 E
Shibetsu, Japan ... 70 B11 44 10N 142 23 E
Shibīn el Kōm, Egypt ... 106 H7 30 31N 30 55 E
Shibīn el Qanâtir, Egypt ... 106 H7 30 19N 31 19 E
Shibing, China ... 76 D7 27 2N 108 7 E
Shibogama L., Canada ... 140 B2 53 35N 88 15W
Shibukawa, Japan ... 73 A11 36 29N 139 0 E
Shibushi, Japan ... 72 F3 31 25N 131 8 E
Shibushi-Wan, Japan ... 72 F3 31 24N 131 8 E
Shicheng, China ... 77 D11 26 22N 116 20 E
Shickshinny, U.S.A. ... 151 E8 41 9N 76 9W
Shickshock Mts. = Chic-Chocs, Mts.,
   Canada ... 141 C6 48 55N 66 0W
Shidād, Si. Arabia ... 98 B3 21 19N 40 3 E
Shidao, China ... 75 F12 36 50N 122 25 E

Shidian, China ... 76 E2 24 40N 99 5 E
Shido, Japan ... 72 C6 34 19N 134 10 E
Shiel, L., U.K. ... 22 E3 56 48N 5 34W
Shield, C., Australia ... 126 A2 13 20 S 136 20 E
Shifang, China ... 76 B5 31 8N 104 10 E
Shiga □, Japan ... 73 B8 35 20N 136 0 E
Shigaib, Sudan ... 109 E4 15 5N 23 35 E
Shigu, China ... 76 D2 26 51N 99 56 E
Shiguaigou, China ... 74 D6 40 52N 110 15 E
Shihan, W. →, Yemen ... 99 C5 17 24N 51 26 E
Shihchiachuangi = Shijiazhuang,
   China ... 74 E8 38 2N 114 28 E
Shihezi, China ... 68 B3 44 15N 86 2 E
Shiiba, Japan ... 72 E3 32 29N 131 4 E
Shijak, Albania ... 50 E3 41 21N 19 33 E
Shijiazhuang, China ... 74 E8 38 2N 114 28 E
Shijiu Hu, China ... 77 B12 31 25N 118 50 E
Shikarpur, India ... 92 E8 28 17N 78 7 E
Shikarpur, Pakistan ... 91 D3 27 57N 68 39 E
Shikine-Jima, Japan ... 73 C11 34 19N 139 13 E
Shikohabad, India ... 93 F8 27 6N 78 36 E
Shikoku □, Japan ... 72 D5 33 30N 133 30 E
Shikoku □, Japan ... 72 D5 33 30N 133 30 E
Shikoku-Sanchi, Japan ... 72 D5 33 30N 133 30 E
Shiliguri, India ... 90 B2 26 45N 88 25 E
Shilka, Russia ... 67 D12 52 0N 115 55 E
Shilka →, Russia ... 67 D13 53 20N 121 26 E
Shillelagh, Ireland ... 23 D5 52 45N 6 32W
Shillington, U.S.A. ... 151 F9 40 18N 75 58W
Shillong, India ... 90 C3 25 35N 91 53 E
Shilo, West Bank ... 103 C4 32 4N 35 18 E
Shilong, China ... 77 F9 23 5N 113 52 E
Shilou, China ... 74 F6 37 0N 110 48 E
Shilovo, Russia ... 60 C5 54 25N 40 57 E
Shima-Hantō, Japan ... 73 C8 34 22N 136 45 E
Shimabara, Japan ... 72 E2 32 48N 130 20 E
Shimada, Japan ... 73 C10 34 49N 138 10 E
Shimane □, Japan ... 72 C4 35 0N 132 30 E
Shimane-Hantō, Japan ... 72 B5 35 30N 133 0 E
Shimanovsk, Russia ... 67 D13 52 15N 127 30 E
Shimba Hills Nat. Reserve △, Kenya ... 118 C4 4 14 S 39 25 E
Shimen, China ... 77 C8 29 35N 111 20 E
Shimenjie, China ... 77 C11 29 29N 116 48 E
Shimian, China ... 76 C4 29 17N 102 23 E
Shimizu, China ... 73 C10 35 0N 138 30 E
Shimo-Jima, Japan ... 72 E2 32 15N 130 7 E
Shimo-Koshiki-Jima, Japan ... 72 F1 31 40N 129 43 E
Shimoda, Japan ... 73 C10 34 40N 138 57 E
Shimodate, Japan ... 73 A11 36 20N 139 55 E
Shimoga, India ... 95 H2 13 57N 75 32 E
Shimoni, Kenya ... 118 C4 4 38 S 39 20 E
Shimonita, Japan ... 73 A10 36 13N 138 47 E
Shimonoseki, Japan ... 72 D2 33 58N 130 55 E
Shimotsuma, Japan ... 73 A11 36 11N 139 58 E
Shimpuru Rapids, Namibia ... 116 B2 17 45 S 19 55 E
Shimsha →, India ... 95 H3 13 15N 77 10 E
Shimsk, Russia ... 58 C6 58 15N 30 50 E
Shin, L., U.K. ... 22 C4 58 5N 4 30W
Shin-Nan'yō, Japan ... 72 C3 34 3N 131 48 E
Shin-Tone-Gawa →, Japan ... 73 B12 35 44N 140 51 E
Shinan, China ... 76 F7 22 44N 109 53 E
Shinano-Gawa →, Japan ... 71 F9 36 50N 138 30 E
Shināş, Oman ... 97 E8 24 46N 56 28 E
Shindand, Afghan. ... 91 B1 33 12N 62 8 E
Shingbwiyang, Burma ... 90 B6 26 41N 96 13 E
Shinglehouse, U.S.A. ... 150 E6 41 58N 78 12W
Shingū, Japan ... 73 D7 33 40N 135 55 E
Shingwidzi, S. Africa ... 117 C5 23 5 S 31 25 E
Shinji, Japan ... 72 B4 35 24N 132 54 E
Shinji-Ko, Japan ... 72 B4 35 26N 132 57 E
Shinjō, Japan ... 70 E10 38 46N 140 18 E
Shinkafe, Nigeria ... 113 C6 13 8N 6 29 E
Shinminato, Japan ... 73 A9 36 47N 137 4 E
Shinshār, Syria ... 103 A5 34 36N 36 43 E
Shinshiro, Japan ... 73 C9 34 54N 137 30 E
Shintuya, Peru ... 172 C3 12 41 S 71 15W
Shinyanga, Tanzania ... 118 C3 3 45 S 33 27 E
Shinyanga □, Tanzania ... 118 C3 3 50 S 34 0 E
Shio-no-Misaki, Japan ... 73 D7 33 25N 135 45 E
Shiogama, Japan ... 70 E10 38 19N 141 1 E
Shiojiri, Japan ... 73 A9 36 6N 137 58 E
Shipchenski Prokhod, Bulgaria ... 51 D9 42 45N 25 15 E
Shiping, China ... 76 F4 23 45N 102 23 E
Shippagan, Canada ... 141 C7 47 45N 64 45W
Shippensburg, U.S.A. ... 150 F7 40 3N 77 31W
Shippenville, U.S.A. ... 150 E5 41 15N 79 28W
Shiprock, U.S.A. ... 159 H9 36 47N 108 41W
Shiqian, China ... 76 D7 27 32N 108 13 E
Shiqma, N. →, Israel ... 103 D3 31 37N 34 30 E
Shiquan, China ... 74 H5 33 5N 108 15 E
Shiquan He = Indus →, Pakistan ... 91 D2 24 20N 67 47 E
Shīr Khān, Afghan. ... 65 E4 37 11N 68 36 E
Shīr Kūh, Iran ... 97 D7 31 39N 54 3 E
Shirabad = Sherabad, Uzbekistan ... 65 E3 37 40N 67 1 E
Shiragami-Misaki, Japan ... 70 D10 41 24N 140 12 E
Shirahama, Japan ... 73 D7 33 41N 135 20 E
Shirakawa, Fukushima, Japan ... 71 F10 37 7N 140 13 E
Shirakawa, Gifu, Japan ... 73 A8 36 17N 136 56 E
Shirane-San, Gumma, Japan ... 73 A11 36 48N 139 22 E
Shirane-San, Yamanashi, Japan ... 73 B10 35 42N 138 9 E
Shiraoi, Japan ... 70 C10 42 33N 141 21 E
Shīrāz, Iran ... 97 D7 29 42N 52 30 E
Shirbīn, Egypt ... 106 H7 31 11N 31 32 E
Shire →, Africa ... 119 F4 17 42 S 35 19 E
Shiretoko-Misaki, Japan ... 70 B12 44 21N 145 20 E
Shirin, Uzbekistan ... 65 C4 40 14N 69 7 E
Shirinab →, Pakistan ... 92 D2 30 15N 66 28 E
Shiriya-Zaki, Japan ... 70 D10 41 25N 141 30 E
Shirley, U.S.A. ... 157 E11 39 53N 85 35W
Shiroishi, Japan ... 70 F10 38 0N 140 37 E
Shirol, India ... 94 F2 16 47N 74 41 E
Shirpur, India ... 92 D2 21 21N 74 57 E
Shīrvān, Iran ... 97 B8 37 30N 57 50 E
Shirwa, L. = Chilwa, L., Malawi ... 119 F4 15 15 S 35 40 E
Shishaldin Volcano, U.S.A. ... 144 J7 54 45N 163 58W
Shishi, China ... 77 E12 24 17N 99 12 E
Shishmaref, U.S.A. ... 144 C6 66 15N 166 4W
Shishou, China ... 77 C9 29 38N 112 22 E
Shitai, China ... 77 B11 30 12N 117 25 E
Shively, U.S.A. ... 157 F11 38 12N 85 49W
Shivpuri, India ... 92 G7 25 26N 77 42 E
Shixing, China ... 77 E10 24 46N 114 5 E
Shiyan, Guangdong, China ... 69 F10 22 42N 113 56 E
Shiyan, Hubei, China ... 77 A8 32 35N 110 45 E
Shiyan Shuiku, China ... 69 F10 22 42N 113 54 E
Shiyata, Egypt ... 106 B2 29 25N 25 7 E
Shizhu, China ... 76 C7 29 58N 108 7 E
Shizong, China ... 76 E5 24 50N 104 0 E
Shizuishan, China ... 74 E4 39 15N 106 50 E
Shizuoka, Japan ... 73 C10 34 57N 138 24 E
Shizuoka □, Japan ... 73 B10 35 15N 138 40 E
Shklov = Shklow, Belarus ... 58 E6 54 16N 30 15 E
Shklow, Belarus ... 58 E6 54 16N 30 15 E
Shkodër, Albania ... 50 D3 42 4N 19 32 E
Shkodra = Shkodër, Albania ... 50 D3 42 4N 19 32 E
Shkumbini →, Albania ... 50 E3 41 2N 19 31 E
Shmidta, Ostrov, Russia ... 67 A10 81 0N 91 0 E
Shō-Gawa →, Japan ... 73 A9 36 47N 137 4 E
Shoal L., U.S.A. ... 156 E3 39 44N 93 32W
Shoal L., Canada ... 143 D9 49 33N 95 1W
Shoal Lake, Canada ... 143 C8 50 30N 100 35W

Shoalhaven →, Australia ... 129 C9 34 54 S 150 42 E
Shoals, U.S.A. ... 157 F10 38 40N 86 47W
Shōbara, Japan ... 72 C5 34 51N 133 1 E
Shōdo-Shima, Japan ... 72 C6 34 30N 134 15 E
Shokpar = Shoqpar, Kazakhstan ... 65 B7 43 49N 74 21 E
Sholapur = Solapur, India ... 94 F2 17 43N 75 56 E
Sholaqqūrghan, Kazakhstan ... 65 B4 43 46N 69 10 E
Shologontsy, Russia ... 67 C12 66 13N 114 0 E
Shōmrōn, West Bank ... 103 C4 32 15N 35 13 E
Shoqpar, Kazakhstan ... 65 B7 43 49N 74 21 E
Shoranur, India ... 95 J3 10 46N 76 19 E
Shoranur, India ... 95 F3 16 31N 76 48 E
Shoreham by Sea, U.K. ... 21 G7 50 50N 0 16W
Shorewood, U.S.A. ... 157 A9 43 5N 87 54W
Shori →, Pakistan ... 92 E3 28 29N 69 44 E
Shorkot Road, Pakistan ... 92 D5 30 47N 72 15 E
Shornak, Kazakhstan ... 65 B4 43 24N 68 2 E
Shorter, U.S.A. ... 152 C4 32 24N 85 57W
Shorterville, U.S.A. ... 152 D4 31 34N 85 6W
Shoshone, Calif., U.S.A. ... 161 K10 35 58N 116 16W
Shoshone, Idaho, U.S.A. ... 158 E6 42 56N 114 25W
Shoshone L., U.S.A. ... 158 D8 44 22N 110 43W
Shoshone Mts., U.S.A. ... 158 G5 39 20N 117 25W
Shoshong, Botswana ... 116 C4 22 56 S 26 31 E
Shoshoni, U.S.A. ... 158 E9 43 14N 108 7W
Shostka, Ukraine ... 59 G7 51 57N 33 32 E
Shotor Khūn, Afghan. ... 91 B2 34 19N 64 56 E
Shotover →, N.Z. ... 131 E3 44 59 S 168 41 E
Shou Xian, China ... 77 A11 32 37N 116 42 E
Shouchang, China ... 77 C12 29 18N 119 12 E
Shouguang, China ... 75 F10 37 52N 118 45 E
Shouning, China ... 77 D12 27 27N 119 31 E
Shouyang, China ... 74 F7 37 54N 113 8 E
Show Low, U.S.A. ... 159 J9 34 15N 110 2W
Showa, Japan ... 73 B10 35 36N 138 29 E
Shpola, Ukraine ... 59 H6 49 1N 31 30 E
Shreveport, U.S.A. ... 155 J8 32 31N 93 45W
Shrewsbury, U.K. ... 21 E5 52 43N 2 45W
Shri Mohangarh, India ... 92 F4 27 17N 71 18 E
Shrigonda, India ... 94 E2 18 37N 74 41 E
Shrirampur, India ... 93 H13 22 44N 88 21 E
Shropshire □, U.K. ... 21 E5 52 36N 2 45W
Shū, Kazakhstan ... 65 B6 43 36N 73 42 E
Shū →, Kazakhstan ... 65 A3 45 0N 67 44 E
Shuangbai, China ... 76 E3 24 42N 101 38 E
Shuangcheng, China ... 75 B14 45 20N 126 15 E
Shuangfeng, China ... 77 D9 27 29N 112 11 E
Shuanggou, China ... 75 G9 34 2N 117 30 E
Shuangjiang, China ... 76 F2 23 26N 99 58 E
Shuangliao, China ... 75 C12 43 29N 123 30 E
Shuangshanzi, China ... 75 D10 40 20N 119 8 E
Shuangyang, China ... 75 C13 43 28N 125 40 E
Shuangyashan, China ... 69 B8 46 28N 131 5 E
Shu'b, Ra's, Yemen ... 99 E6 12 35N 53 22 E
Shubra el Kheima, Egypt ... 106 H7 30 6N 31 15 E
Shubra Khit, Egypt ... 106 H7 31 2N 30 42 E
Shucheng, China ... 77 B11 31 28N 116 57 E
Shufu, China ... 65 D7 39 27N 75 52 E
Shugozero, Russia ... 58 C8 59 54N 34 10 E
Shuguri Falls, Tanzania ... 119 D4 8 33 S 37 22 E
Shuḥayr, Yemen ... 99 D5 14 41N 49 23 E
Shuiji, China ... 77 D12 27 13N 118 20 E
Shuiye, China ... 74 F8 36 7N 114 8 E
Shujalpur, India ... 92 H7 23 18N 76 46 E
Shukpa Kunzang, India ... 93 B8 34 22N 78 22 E
Shulan, China ... 75 B14 44 28N 127 0 E
Shulaveri, Georgia ... 61 K7 41 22N 44 45 E
Shule, China ... 65 D8 39 25N 76 3 E
Shullsburg, U.S.A. ... 156 B6 42 35N 90 13W
Shumagin Is., U.S.A. ... 144 J8 55 7N 160 30W
Shumen, Bulgaria ... 51 C10 43 18N 26 55 E
Shumerlya, Russia ... 60 C8 55 30N 46 25 E
Shumikha, Russia ... 64 D9 55 10N 63 15 E
Shunchang, China ... 77 D11 26 54N 117 48 E
Shunde, China ... 77 F9 22 42N 113 14 E
Shungay, Kazakhstan ... 61 F8 48 30N 46 45 E
Shungnak, U.S.A. ... 144 C8 66 52N 157 9W
Shuo Xian = Shuozhou, China ... 74 E7 39 20N 112 33 E
Shuozhou, China ... 74 E7 39 20N 112 33 E
Shūr →, Fārs, Iran ... 97 D8 28 30N 55 0 E
Shūr →, Kermān, Iran ... 97 D8 30 52N 57 37 E
Shūr →, Yazd, Iran ... 97 D7 31 45N 55 15 E
Shūr Āb, Iran ... 97 C6 34 23N 51 11 E
Shūr Gaz, Iran ... 97 D8 29 10N 59 20 E
Shūrāb, Iran ... 97 C8 33 43N 56 29 E
Shurab, Tajikistan ... 65 C5 40 3N 70 33 E
Shurchi, Uzbekistan ... 65 B3 37 59N 67 47 E
Shūreştān, Iran ... 97 D7 32 4N 52 25 E
Shurkhua, Burma ... 90 D4 22 55N 93 38 E
Shurugwi, Zimbabwe ... 119 F3 19 40 S 30 0 E
Shūsf, Iran ... 97 D9 31 50N 60 5 E
Shūsh, Iran ... 101 F13 32 11N 48 15 E
Shūshtar, Iran ... 97 D6 32 0N 48 50 E
Shuswap L., Canada ... 142 C5 50 55N 119 3W
Shuya, Russia ... 60 B5 56 50N 41 28 E
Shuyak I., U.S.A. ... 144 G9 58 31N 152 30W
Shuyang, China ... 75 G10 34 10N 118 42 E
Shuzenji, Japan ... 73 C10 34 58N 138 56 E
Shūzū, Iran ... 97 D7 29 52N 54 30 E
Shwebo, Burma ... 90 D5 22 30N 95 45 E
Shwegu, Burma ... 90 G6 24 15N 96 26 E
Shwegun, Burma ... 90 G6 17 9N 97 39 E
Shweli →, Burma ... 90 G6 17 55N 96 53 E
Shweli →, Burma ... 90 E6 20 46N 96 57 E
Shwenyaung, Burma ... 90 E6 20 46N 96 57 E
Shyamnagar, India ... 95 H11 13 21N 92 57 E
Shyghanaq, Kazakhstan ... 65 A6 45 6N 73 59 E
Shyghanaq, Kazakhstan ... 65 A5 44 49N 70 0 E
Shymkent, Kazakhstan ... 65 B4 42 18N 69 36 E
Shyok, India ... 93 B8 34 13N 78 12 E
Shyok →, Pakistan ... 93 B6 35 13N 75 53 E
Si Chon, Thailand ... 87 H2 9 0N 99 54 E
Si Kiang = Xi Jiang →, China ... 77 F9 22 5N 113 20 E
Si Lanna Nat. Park △, Thailand ... 86 C2 19 17N 99 12 E
Si-ngan = Xi'an, China ... 74 G5 34 15N 109 0 E
Si Prachan, Thailand ... 86 E3 14 37N 100 9 E
Si Racha, Thailand ... 86 F3 13 10N 100 48 E
Si Xian, China ... 75 H9 33 30N 117 50 E
Siachen Glacier, Asia ... 93 B7 35 20N 77 30 E
Siahaf →, Pakistan ... 92 E3 29 3N 68 57 E
Siahan Range, Pakistan ... 91 D2 27 30N 64 40 E
Siak →, Indonesia ... 84 B2 1 13N 102 9 E
Siaksriindrapura, Indonesia ... 84 B2 0 51N 102 0 E
Sialkot, Pakistan ... 91 B4 32 32N 74 30 E
Sialsuk, India ... 90 D4 23 24N 92 45 E
Sialum, Papua N. G. ... 132 D4 6 5 S 147 36 E
Siam = Thailand ■, Asia ... 86 E4 16 0N 102 0 E
Sian = Xi'an, China ... 74 G5 34 15N 109 0 E
Sian Ka'an, Reserva de La Biósfera,
   Mexico ... 163 D7 19 35N 87 40W
Sianów, Poland ... 54 D3 54 15N 16 15 E
Siantan, Indonesia ... 84 B3 3 10N 106 15 E
Siàpo →, Venezuela ... 168 C4 2 7N 66 28W
Siāreh, Iran ... 97 D9 28 5N 60 14 E
Siargao I., Phil. ... 81 G6 9 52N 126 3 E
Siari, Pakistan ... 93 B7 34 55N 76 40 E
Siasi, Phil. ... 79 C6 5 34N 120 50 E
Siasi I., Phil. ... 81 J3 5 33N 120 50 E
Siassi, Papua N. G. ... 132 C4 5 40 S 147 51 E
Siátista, Greece ... 50 F5 40 15N 21 33 E
Siaton, Phil. ... 81 G4 9 4N 123 2 E

Siau, Indonesia ... 82 A3 2 50N 125 25 E
Siauliai, Lithuania ... 15 J20 55 56N 23 15 E
Siauliai □, Lithuania ... 54 C10 55 56N 23 19 E
Siazan = Siyāzān, Azerbaijan ... 61 K9 41 3N 49 10 E
Sībā, Gebel el, Egypt ... 96 E2 25 45N 34 10 E
Sibang, Gabon ... 114 B1 0 25N 9 31 E
Sibang, Indonesia ... 79 K18 8 34 S 115 13 E
Sibay, Russia ... 64 E7 52 42N 58 39 E
Sibay I., Phil. ... 81 F3 11 51N 121 29 E
Sibayi, L., S. Africa ... 117 D5 27 20 S 32 45 E
Sibdu, Sudan ... 107 E2 10 57N 23 35 E
Sibenik, Croatia ... 45 E12 43 48N 15 54 E
Siberia, Russia ... 62 C13 60 0N 100 0 E
Siberut, Indonesia ... 84 C1 1 30 S 99 0 E
Sibi, Pakistan ... 91 C2 29 30N 67 54 E
Sibil = Oksibil, Indonesia ... 83 B6 4 59 S 140 35 E
Sibiloi Nat. Park △, Kenya ... 118 B4 4 0N 36 20 E
Sibiti, Congo ... 114 C2 3 38 S 13 19 E
Sibiu, Romania ... 53 E9 45 45N 24 9 E
Sibiu □, Romania ... 53 E9 45 50N 24 15 E
Sibium Mts., Papua N. G. ... 132 E5 9 19 S 148 25 E
Sibley, Ill., U.S.A. ... 157 D8 40 35N 88 23W
Sibley, Iowa, U.S.A. ... 154 D7 43 24N 95 45W
Sibolga, Indonesia ... 84 B1 1 42N 98 45 E
Sibsagar, India ... 90 B5 27 0N 94 36 E
Sibu, Malaysia ... 85 B4 2 18N 111 49 E
Sibuco, Phil. ... 81 H4 7 20N 122 10 E
Sibuguey B., Phil. ... 81 H4 7 50N 122 45 E
Sibut, C.A.R. ... 114 A3 5 46N 19 10 E
Sibutu, Phil. ... 85 B5 4 45N 119 30 E
Sibutu Group, Phil. ... 81 J2 4 45N 119 20 E
Sibutu Passage, E. Indies ... 81 J3 4 50N 120 0 E
Sibuyan I., Phil. ... 80 E4 12 25N 122 40 E
Sibuyan Sea, Phil. ... 80 E4 12 30N 122 20 E
Sic, Romania ... 53 D8 46 56N 23 53 E
Sicamous, Canada ... 142 C5 50 49N 119 0W
Sicapoo, Mt., Phil. ... 80 B3 18 1N 120 56 E
Sicasica, Bolivia ... 172 D4 17 22 S 67 45W
Siccus →, Australia ... 128 A3 31 55 S 139 17 E
Sichuan □, China ... 76 B5 30 30N 103 0 E
Sichuan Pendi, China ... 76 B5 31 0N 105 0 E
Sicilia, Italy ... 47 E7 37 30N 14 30 E
Sicily = Sicilia, Italy ... 47 E7 37 30N 14 30 E
Sicuani, Peru ... 172 C3 14 21 S 71 10W
Šid, Serbia, Yug. ... 52 E4 45 8N 19 14 E
Sidamo □, Ethiopia ... 107 G4 5 0N 37 50 E
Sidaouet, Niger ... 113 B6 18 34N 8 3 E
Siddāri, Greece ... 38 B9 39 47N 19 41 E
Siddapur, India ... 95 G2 14 20N 74 53 E
Siddhapur, India ... 92 H5 23 56N 72 25 E
Siddipet, India ... 94 E4 18 5N 78 51 E
Sidensjö, Sweden ... 16 A12 63 18N 18 17 E
Sidéradougou, Burkina Faso ... 112 C4 10 42N 4 12W
Siderno, Italy ... 47 D9 38 16N 16 18 E
Sidhauli, India ... 93 F9 27 17N 80 50 E
Sidhi, India ... 93 G9 24 25N 81 53 E
Sídheros, Ákra, Greece ... 39 E7 35 19N 26 19 E
Sidhirókastron, Greece ... 50 E7 41 13N 23 24 E
Sīdi Abd el Rahmân, Egypt ... 106 A2 30 55N 29 44 E
Sīdi Ahmed Rgueibi, W. Sahara ... 110 C2 27 32N 11 16W
Sīdi Barrâni, Egypt ... 106 A2 31 38N 25 58 E
Sīdi-bel-Abbès, Algeria ... 111 A4 35 13N 0 39W
Sīdi Bennour, Morocco ... 110 B3 32 40N 8 25W
Sīdi Haneish, Egypt ... 106 A2 31 10N 27 35 E
Sīdi Ifni, Morocco ... 110 C3 29 29N 10 12W
Sīdi Kacem, Morocco ... 110 B3 34 11N 5 49W
Sīdi Omar, Egypt ... 106 A1 31 24N 24 57 E
Sīdi Slimane, Morocco ... 110 B3 34 16N 5 56W
Sīdi Smaïl, Morocco ... 110 B3 32 50N 8 31W
Sīdī 'Uzayz, Libya ... 108 B4 31 41N 24 55 E
Sidlaw Hills, U.K. ... 22 E5 56 32N 3 2W
Sidley, Mt., Antarctica ... 7 D14 77 2 S 126 2W
Sidmouth, C., Australia ... 126 A3 13 25 S 143 36 E
Sidmouth, U.K. ... 21 G4 50 40N 3 15W
Sidney, Canada ... 142 D4 48 39N 123 24W
Sidney, Mont., U.S.A. ... 154 B2 47 43N 104 9W
Sidney, N.Y., U.S.A. ... 151 D9 42 19N 75 24W
Sidney, Nebr., U.S.A. ... 154 E3 41 8N 102 59W
Sidney, Ohio, U.S.A. ... 157 D12 40 17N 84 9W
Sidney Lanier, L., U.S.A. ... 152 A5 34 10N 84 4W
Sido, Mali ... 112 C3 11 37N 7 29W
Sidoarjo, Indonesia ... 85 A4 7 27 S 112 43 E
Sidoktaya, Burma ... 90 E5 20 27N 94 15 E
Sidon = Saydā, Lebanon ... 103 B4 33 35N 35 25 E
Sidra, G. of = Surt, Khalīj, Libya ... 108 B3 31 40N 18 30 E
Sidrolândia, Brazil ... 173 20 55 S 54 58W
Siedlce, Poland ... 55 F9 52 10N 22 20 E
Sieg →, Germany ... 30 E3 50 46N 7 6 E
Siegburg, Germany ... 30 E3 50 47N 7 12 E
Siegen, Germany ... 30 E4 50 51N 8 0 E
Siem Pang, Cambodia ... 86 E6 14 7N 106 23 E
Siem Reap = Siemreab, Cambodia ... 86 F4 13 20N 103 52 E
Siemiatycze, Poland ... 55 F9 52 27N 22 52 E
Siemreab, Cambodia ... 86 F4 13 20N 103 52 E
Siena, Italy ... 45 E8 43 19N 11 21 E
Sieniawa, Poland ... 55 H9 50 11N 22 38 E
Sieradz, Poland ... 55 F3 51 37N 18 41 E
Sierakōw, Poland ... 55 E3 52 39N 16 2 E
Sierck-les-Bains, France ... 27 C13 49 26N 6 20 E
Sierning, Austria ... 34 C7 48 2N 14 18 E
Sierpc, Poland ... 55 F6 52 55N 19 43 E
Sierpe, Bocas de la, Venezuela ... 169 G10 10 0N 61 30W
Sierra Blanca, U.S.A. ... 159 L11 31 11N 105 22W
Sierra Blanca Peak, U.S.A. ... 159 K11 33 23N 105 49W
Sierra City, U.S.A. ... 160 F6 39 34N 120 38W
Sierra Colorada, Argentina ... 176 B3 40 35 S 67 50W
Sierra de Aracena y Picos de Aroche,
   Parque Natural de △, Spain ... 43 H4 37 53N 6 41W
Sierra de Baza, Parque Natural de △,
   Spain ... 41 H2 37 20N 2 48W
Sierra de Castril, Parque Natural
   de △, Spain ... 41 H2 37 50N 2 50W
Sierra de España, Parque Natural
   de △, Spain ... 41 H3 37 50N 1 31W
Sierra de Grazalema, Parque Natural
   de △, Spain ... 43 J5 36 31N 5 28W
Sierra de Gredos, Reserva Nac. de △,
   Spain ... 42 E5 40 17N 5 17W
Sierra de Hornachuelos, Parque
   Natural de △, Spain ... 43 H5 37 56N 5 14W
Sierra de Huétor, Parque Natural
   de △, Spain ... 43 H7 37 14N 3 30W
Sierra de La Culata △, Venezuela ... 165 E5 8 45N 71 10W
Sierra de Lancandón, Parque Nac. △,
   Guatemala ... 164 C1 16 59N 90 23W
Sierra de las Nieves, Parque Natural
   de △, Spain ... 43 J6 36 42N 5 0W
Sierra de María-Los Vélez, Parque
   Natural de △, Spain ... 41 H2 37 43N 2 0W
Sierra de San Luis, Parque Nac. △,
   Venezuela ... 165 D6 11 20N 69 43W
Sierra de Yeguas, Spain ... 43 H6 37 7N 4 52W
Sierra do São Mamede, Parque
   Natural de △, Portugal ... 43 F3 39 17N 7 18W
Sierra Gorda, Chile ... 174 A2 22 50 S 69 15W
Sierra Grande, Argentina ... 176 B3 41 36 S 65 22W
Sierra Leone ■, W. Afr. ... 112 D2 9 0N 12 0W
Sierra Madre, Mexico ... 163 D6 16 0N 93 0W
Sierra Mágina, Parque Natural de △,
   Spain ... 43 H7 37 43N 3 28W
Sierra Mojada, Mexico ... 162 B4 27 19N 103 42W
Sierra Nevada, Spain ... 43 H7 37 3N 3 15W
Sierra Nevada, U.S.A. ... 160 H8 39 0N 120 30W

Sierra Nevada, Parque Nac. △, Venezuela ... 165 E5 8 35N 70 45W
Sierra Nevada, Parque Natural de ○, Spain ... 43 H7 37 4N 3 7W
Sierra Nevada de Santa Marta, Parque Nac. △, Colombia ... 165 D5 10 56N 73 36W
Sierra Norte de Seville, Parque Natural de ○, Spain ... 43 H5 37 55N 5 46W
Sierra Subbéticas, Parque Natural de ○, Spain ... 43 H6 37 26N 4 18W
Sierra Vista, U.S.A. ... 159 L8 31 33N 110 18W
Sierras de Cardeña y Montoro, Parque Natural de ○, Spain ... 43 G6 38 13N 4 15W
Sierras de Cazorla, Segura y las Villas, Parque Natural de ○, Spain 41 J2 37 57N 2 45W
Sierraville, U.S.A. ... 160 F6 39 36N 120 22W
Sierre, Switz. ... 32 D5 46 17N 7 31 E
Sifani, Ethiopia ... 107 E5 12 18N 40 19 E
Sifié, Ivory C. ... 112 D3 8 0N 7 5W
Sífnos, Greece ... 48 E6 37 0N 24 45 E
Sifton, Canada ... 143 C8 51 21N 100 8W
Sifton Pass, Canada ... 142 B3 57 52N 126 15W
Sig, Algeria ... 111 A4 35 32N 0 12W
Sigaboy = Governor Generoso, Phil. ... 81 H6 6 39N 126 5 E
Sigatoka, Fiji ... 133 H1 18 8S 177 32 E
Sigdal, Norway ... 18 D6 60 3N 9 38 E
Sigean, France ... 28 E6 43 2N 2 58 E
Siggiewi, Malta ... 38 F7 35 51N 14 26 E
Sighetu-Marmaţiei, Romania ... 53 C8 47 57N 23 52 E
Sighişoara, Romania ... 53 D9 46 12N 24 50 E
Sigira, Yemen ... 99 D6 12 37N 54 20 E
Sigiriya, Sri Lanka ... 95 L5 7 57N 80 45 E
Sigli, Indonesia ... 84 A1 5 25N 96 0 E
Siglufjörður, Iceland ... 11 A8 66 12N 18 55W
Siglunes, Iceland ... 11 A8 66 12N 18 50W
Sigmaringen, Germany ... 31 G5 48 5N 9 12 E
Signa, Italy ... 44 E8 43 45N 11 10 E
Signakhi = Tsnori, Georgia ... 61 K7 41 40N 45 57 E
Signal, U.S.A. ... 161 L13 34 30N 113 38W
Signal de Botrang, Belize ... 50 29N 6 4 E
Signal Pk., U.S.A. ... 161 M12 33 20N 114 2W
Signa, Switz. ... 32 C5 46 56N 7 4 E
Signy-l'Abbaye, France ... 27 C11 49 40N 4 25 E
Sigourney, U.S.A. ... 156 C4 41 20N 92 12W
Sigsbee, U.S.A. ... 152 D6 31 16N 83 52W
Sigsig, Ecuador ... 168 D2 3 0S 78 50W
Sigüenza, Spain ... 40 D2 41 3N 2 40W
Siguiri, Guinea ... 112 C3 11 31N 9 10W
Sigulda, Latvia ... 15 H21 57 10N 24 55 E
Sihanoukville = Kampong Saom, Cambodia ... 87 G4 10 38N 103 30 E
Sihaus, Peru ... 172 B2 8 40S 77 40W
Sihawa, India ... 94 D5 20 19N 81 55 E
Sihora, India ... 93 H9 23 29N 80 6 E
Sihui, China ... 77 F9 23 20N 112 40 E
Sikajoki →, Finland ... 14 D21 64 50N 24 43 E
Siilinjärvi, Finland ... 14 E22 63 4N 27 39 E
Siirt, Turkey ... 101 D9 37 57N 41 55 E
Sijarira Ra. = Chizarira, Zimbabwe 119 F2 17 36S 27 45 E
Sijunjung, Indonesia ... 84 C2 0 42S 100 58 E
Sika, India ... 92 H3 22 26N 69 47 E
Sikao, Thailand ... 87 J2 7 34N 99 21 E
Sikar, India ... 92 F6 27 33N 75 10 E
Sikasso, Mali ... 112 C3 11 18N 5 35W
Sikeston, U.S.A. ... 155 G10 36 53N 89 35W
Sikhote Alin, Khrebet, Russia ... 67 E14 45 0N 136 0 E
Sikhote Alin Ra. = Sikhote Alin, Khrebet, Russia ... 67 E14 45 0N 136 0 E
Sikiá, Greece ... 50 F7 40 2N 23 56 E
Síkinos, Greece ... 49 E7 36 40N 25 8 E
Sikkani Chief →, Canada ... 142 B4 57 47N 122 15W
Sikkim □, India ... 90 B2 27 50N 88 30 E
Siklós, Hungary ... 52 E3 45 50N 18 19 E
Sikotu-Ko, Japan ... 70 C10 42 45N 141 25 E
Sil →, Spain ... 42 C3 42 27N 7 43W
Silacayoapan, Mexico ... 163 D5 17 30N 98 9W
Šilalė, Lithuania ... 54 C9 55 28N 22 12 E
Silam, Malaysia ... 81 J2 4 59N 118 12 E
Silandro, Italy ... 44 B7 46 38N 10 46 E
Silang, Phil. ... 80 D3 14 14N 120 58 E
Silawad, India ... 92 J6 21 54N 74 54 E
Silay, Phil. ... 81 F4 10 47N 122 58 E
Silba, Croatia ... 45 D11 44 24N 14 41 E
Silchar, India ... 90 C4 24 49N 92 48 E
Sildegapet, Norway ... 18 B2 62 5N 5 0 E
Sile, Turkey ... 51 E13 41 10N 29 37 E
Siler City, U.S.A. ... 149 H6 35 44N 79 28W
Sileru →, India ... 94 E5 17 49N 81 24 E
Silesia = Śląsk, Poland ... 36 C9 51 0N 16 30 E
Silet, Algeria ... 111 D5 22 44N 4 37 E
Silgarhi Doti, Nepal ... 93 E9 29 15N 81 0 E
Silghat, India ... 90 B4 26 35N 93 0 E
Silhouette, Seychelles ... 121 b 4 29N 55 12 E
Sili, Burkina Faso ... 112 C4 11 37N 2 30W
Silifke, Turkey ... 100 D5 36 22N 33 58 E
Siliguri = Shiliguri, India ... 90 B2 26 45N 88 25 E
Siling Co, China ... 68 C3 31 50N 89 20 E
Silistea Nouă, Romania ... 53 F10 44 23N 25 1 E
Silistra, Bulgaria ... 51 B11 44 6N 27 19 E
Silivri, Turkey ... 51 E12 41 4N 28 14 E
Siljan, Norway ... 18 E6 59 18N 9 42 E
Siljan, Sweden ... 16 D8 60 55N 14 45 E
Siljansnäs, Sweden ... 16 D8 60 47N 14 52 E
Silkeborg, Denmark ... 17 H3 56 10N 9 32 E
Silkwood, Australia ... 126 B4 17 45S 146 2 E
Silla, Spain ... 41 F4 39 22N 0 25W
Sillajhuay, Cordillera, Chile ... 172 D4 19 46S 68 40W
Sillamäe, Estonia ... 15 G22 59 24N 27 45 E
Sillé-le-Guillaume, France ... 26 D6 48 10N 0 8W
Silleda, Spain ... 42 C2 42 42N 8 10W
Sillod, India ... 94 D2 20 18N 75 39 E
Silloth, U.K. ... 20 C4 54 52N 3 23W
Sillustani, Peru ... 172 D3 15 50S 70 7W
Sílo, Greece ... 51 E9 41 0N 26 10 E
Siloam Springs, U.S.A. ... 155 G7 36 11N 94 32W
Silopi, Turkey ... 101 D10 37 15N 42 27 E
Silsbee, U.S.A. ... 155 K7 30 21N 94 11W
Siltou, Chad ... 109 E3 16 46N 15 33 E
Siluko, Nigeria ... 114 B2 6 35N 5 10 E
Šilutė, Lithuania ... 15 J19 55 21N 21 33 E
Silva Porto = Kuito, Angola ... 115 E3 12 22S 16 55 E
Silvan, Turkey ... 101 C9 38 7N 41 2 E
Silvani, India ... 93 H8 23 18N 78 25 E
Silvaplana, Switz. ... 33 D9 46 28N 9 48 E
Silver City, U.S.A. ... 159 K9 32 46N 108 17W
Silver Cr. →, U.S.A. ... 158 E4 43 16N 119 13W
Silver Creek, U.S.A. ... 150 D5 42 33N 79 10W
Silver Grove, U.S.A. ... 157 E12 39 2N 84 24W
Silver L., U.S.A. ... 160 G6 38 39N 120 6W
Silver Lake, Calif., U.S.A. ... 161 K10 35 21N 116 7W
Silver Lake, Ind., U.S.A. ... 157 C11 41 4N 85 53W
Silver Lake, Oreg., U.S.A. ... 158 E3 43 8N 121 3W
Silver Lake, Wis., U.S.A. ... 157 B8 42 33N 88 13W
Silver Springs, U.S.A. ... 153 F7 29 13N 82 3W
Silverdalen, Sweden ... 17 G9 57 32N 15 45 E
Silverton, Australia ... 128 A3 31 52S 141 10 E
Silverton, Colo., U.S.A. ... 159 H10 37 49N 107 40W
Silverton, Tex., U.S.A. ... 155 H4 34 28N 101 19W
Silves, Brazil ... 169 D6 2 54S 58 27W
Silves, Portugal ... 43 H2 37 11N 8 26W
Silvi Marina, Italy ... 45 F11 42 34N 14 5 E
Silvia, Colombia ... 168 C2 2 37N 76 21W
Silvies →, U.S.A. ... 158 E4 43 34N 119 2W

Silvrettahorn, Switz. ... 33 C10 46 50N 10 6 E
Silwa Bahari, Egypt ... 106 C3 24 45N 32 55 E
Silz, Austria ... 34 D3 47 16N 10 56 E
Sim, C., Morocco ... 110 B3 31 26N 9 51W
Simakumba, Zambia ... 115 E4 14 12S 23 16 E
Simaltala, India ... 93 G12 24 43N 86 33 E
Simaluguri, India ... 90 B5 26 55N 94 46 E
Simanggang = Bandar Sri Aman, Malaysia ... 85 B4 1 15N 111 32 E
Simao, China ... 76 F3 22 47N 101 5 E
Simão Dias, Brazil ... 170 D4 10 44S 37 49W
Simara I., Phil. ... 80 E4 12 48N 122 3 E
Simard, L., Canada ... 140 C4 47 40N 78 40W
Simav, Turkey ... 49 B10 39 4N 28 58 E
Simav →, Turkey ... 51 F12 40 23N 28 31 E
Simav Dağlari, Turkey ... 49 B10 39 10N 28 50 E
Simba, Dem. Rep. of the Congo 114 B4 0 38N 22 59 E
Simba, Tanzania ... 118 C4 2 10S 37 36 E
Simbach, Germany ... 31 G9 48 16N 13 2 E
Simberi I., Papua N.G. ... 132 B7 2 38S 152 0 E
Simbirsk, Russia ... 60 C9 54 20N 48 25 E
Simbo, Solomon Is. ... 133 M9 8 16S 156 33 E
Simbo, Tanzania ... 118 C2 5 13S 29 41 E
Simcoe, Canada ... 140 D3 42 50N 80 20W
Simcoe, L., Canada ... 140 D4 44 25N 79 20W
Simdega, India ... 93 H11 22 37N 84 31 E
Simeonovgrad, Bulgaria ... 51 D9 42 1N 25 50 E
Simeria, Romania ... 52 E8 45 51N 23 1 E
Simeto →, Italy ... 47 E8 37 24N 15 6 E
Simeulue, Indonesia ... 84 B1 2 45N 95 45 E
Simferopol, Ukraine ... 59 K8 44 55N 34 3 E
Sími, Greece ... 49 E9 36 35N 27 50 E
Simi Valley, U.S.A. ... 161 L8 34 16N 118 47W
Simien Mts. Nat. Park △, Ethiopia 107 E4 13 19N 38 0 E
Simikot, Nepal ... 93 E9 30 0N 81 50 E
Simití, Colombia ... 168 B3 7 58N 73 57W
Simitli, Bulgaria ... 50 E7 41 52N 23 7 E
Simla, India ... 92 D7 31 2N 77 9 E
Simlångsdalen, Sweden ... 17 H7 56 43N 13 6 E
Simleu-Silvaniei, Romania ... 52 C7 47 17N 22 50 E
Simme →, Switz. ... 32 C4 46 38N 7 25 E
Simmern, Germany ... 31 F3 49 58N 7 30 E
Simmie, Canada ... 143 D7 49 56N 108 6W
Simmler, U.S.A. ... 161 K7 35 21N 119 59W
Simnas, Lithuania ... 54 D10 54 24N 23 39 E
Simões, Brazil ... 170 C3 7 54S 40 49W
Simojoki →, Finland ... 14 D21 65 35N 25 1 E
Simojovel, Mexico ... 163 D6 17 12N 92 38W
Simonette →, Canada ... 142 B5 55 9N 118 15W
Simonstown, S. Africa ... 116 E2 34 14S 18 26 E
Simontornya, Hungary ... 52 D3 46 45N 18 33 E
Simpang Empat, Malaysia ... 87 c 5 27N 100 29 E
Simpangkiri →, Indonesia ... 84 B1 2 50N 97 40 E
Simplício Mendes, Brazil ... 170 C3 7 51S 41 54W
Simplon, Switz. ... 32 D6 46 15N 8 3 E
Simplonpass, Switz. ... 32 D6 46 15N 8 2 E
Simplontunnel, Switz. ... 32 D6 46 15N 8 7 E
Simpson, Mt., Papua N.G. ... 132 F5 10 2S 149 34 E
Simpson Desert, Australia ... 126 D2 25 0S 137 0 E
Simpson Desert Nat. Park △, Australia ... 126 C2 24 59S 138 21 E
Simpson Pen., Canada ... 139 B11 68 34N 88 45W
Simpungdong, N. Korea ... 75 D15 40 56N 129 29 E
Simrishamn, Sweden ... 17 J8 55 33N 14 22 E
Simsbury, U.S.A. ... 151 E12 41 53N 72 48W
Simunjan, Malaysia ... 85 B4 1 25N 110 45 E
Simunul, Phil. ... 81 J2 4 54N 119 51 E
Simushir, Ostrov, Russia ... 67 E16 46 50N 152 30 E
Sin Cowe I., S. China Sea ... 78 C4 9 53N 114 19 E
Sina →, India ... 94 F2 17 30N 75 55 E
Sinabang, Indonesia ... 84 B1 2 30N 96 24 E
Sinadogo, Somali Rep. ... 120 C3 5 50N 47 0 E
Sinai = Es Sînâ', Egypt ... 103 F3 29 0N 34 0 E
Sinai, Mt. = Mûsa, Gebel, Egypt 96 D2 28 33N 33 59 E
Sinai Peninsula, Egypt ... 62 G7 29 30N 34 0 E
Sinaia, Romania ... 53 E10 45 21N 25 38 E
Sinait, Phil. ... 80 C3 17 52N 120 27 E
Sinako, Mt., Phil. ... 81 H5 7 30N 125 17 E
Sinaloa □, Mexico ... 162 C3 25 0N 107 30W
Sinaloa de Leyva, Mexico ... 162 B3 25 50N 108 20W
Sinalunga, Italy ... 45 E8 43 12N 11 44 E
Sinan, China ... 76 D7 27 56N 108 13 E
Sînandrei, Romania ... 52 E6 45 52N 21 13 E
Sinarádhes, Greece ... 38 B9 39 34N 19 51 E
Sînâwan, Libya ... 108 B2 31 0N 10 37 E
Sinbaungwe, Burma ... 90 F5 19 43N 95 10 E
Sinbo, Burma ... 90 C6 24 46N 97 3 E
Sincan, Turkey ... 100 B5 39 58N 32 36 E
Sincanlı, Turkey ... 49 C12 38 45N 30 15 E
Since, Colombia ... 168 B2 9 15N 75 9W
Sincelejo, Colombia ... 168 B2 9 18N 75 24W
Sinch'ang, N. Korea ... 75 D15 40 7N 128 28 E
Sinchang-ni, N. Korea ... 75 E14 39 24N 126 8 E
Sinclair, U.S.A. ... 158 F10 41 47N 107 7W
Sinclair, L., U.S.A. ... 152 B6 33 4N 83 12W
Sinclair Mills, Canada ... 142 C4 54 5N 121 40W
Sinclair's B., U.K. ... 23 C5 58 31N 3 5W
Sinclairville, U.S.A. ... 150 D5 42 16N 79 16W
Sind, Pakistan ... 92 G3 26 0N 68 30 E
Sind □, Pakistan ... 91 D3 26 0N 69 0 E
Sind →, Jammu & Kashmir, India 93 B6 34 18N 74 45 E
Sind →, Mad. P., India ... 93 F8 26 26N 79 13 E
Sind Sagar Doab, Pakistan ... 90 D4 32 0N 71 30 E
Sindal, Denmark ... 17 G4 57 28N 10 10 E
Sindangan, Phil. ... 81 G4 8 10N 123 5 E
Sindangan Bay, Phil. ... 81 G4 8 11N 122 50 E
Sindangbarang, Indonesia ... 85 D3 7 27S 107 1 E
Sindara, Gabon ... 114 E2 1 7S 10 41 E
Sinde, Zambia ... 119 F2 17 28S 25 51 E
Sindelfingen, Germany ... 31 G4 48 42N 9 0 E
Sindewahi, India ... 94 D4 20 17N 79 39 E
Sindgi, India ... 94 F3 16 55N 76 14 E
Sindh = Sind □, Pakistan ... 91 D3 26 0N 69 0 E
Sindhnur, India ... 95 F3 15 47N 76 46 E
Sindi, India ... 94 D4 20 48N 78 52 E
Sındırgı, Turkey ... 49 B10 39 13N 28 10 E
Sindou, Burkina Faso ... 112 C3 10 35N 5 4W
Sindri, India ... 93 H12 23 45N 86 42 E
Sinegorskiy, Russia ... 61 G5 47 55N 40 52 E
Sinekli, Turkey ... 51 E12 41 14N 28 12 E
Sinelnikovo = Synelnykove, Ukraine 59 H8 48 25N 35 30 E
Sinendé, Benin ... 113 C5 10 20N 2 22 E
Sines, Portugal ... 43 H2 37 56N 8 51W
Sines, C. de, Portugal ... 43 H2 37 58N 8 53W
Sineu, Spain ... 38 B4 39 38N 3 1 E
Sinewit, Mt., Papua N.G. ... 132 C7 4 44S 152 2 E
Sinfra, Ivory C. ... 112 D3 6 35N 5 56W
Sing Buri, Thailand ... 86 E3 14 53N 100 25 E
Singa, Sudan ... 107 E3 13 10N 33 57 E
Singako, Chad ... 109 F3 9 50N 19 24 E
Singanallur, India ... 95 J3 11 2N 77 1 E
Singapore ■, Asia ... 87 d 1 17N 103 51 E
Singapore, Straits of, Asia ... 87 d 1 15N 104 0 E
Singapore Changi ✈ (SIN), Singapore ... 87 M4 1 23N 103 59 E
Singaraja, Indonesia ... 85 D5 8 7S 115 6 E
Singatoka = Sigatoka, Fiji ... 133 B1 18 8S 177 32 E
Singen, Germany ... 31 H4 47 45N 8 50 E
Singida, Tanzania ... 118 C3 4 49S 34 48 E
Singida □, Tanzania ... 118 D3 6 0S 34 30 E
Singitikós Kólpos, Greece ... 50 F7 40 6N 24 0 E
Singkaling Hkamti, Burma ... 90 C5 26 0N 95 39 E

Singkang, Indonesia ... 82 B2 4 8S 120 1 E
Singkawang, Indonesia ... 85 B3 1 0N 108 57 E
Singkep, Indonesia ... 78 E2 0 30S 104 25 E
Singleton, Australia ... 129 B9 32 33S 151 0 E
Singleton, Mt., N. Terr., Australia 124 D5 22 0S 130 46 E
Singleton, Mt., W. Austral., Australia 125 E2 29 27S 117 15 E
Singö, Sweden ... 16 D12 60 12N 18 45 E
Singoli, India ... 92 G6 25 0N 75 22 E
Singora = Songkhla, Thailand ... 87 J3 7 13N 100 37 E
Singosan, N. Korea ... 75 E14 38 52N 127 25 E
Singri, India ... 90 B4 26 36N 92 29 E
Singsås, Norway ... 18 B7 62 56N 10 37 E
Singu, Burma ... 90 B4 25 35N 96 15 E
Sinhgarh, India ... 94 E1 18 28N 73 45 E
Sinhung, N. Korea ... 75 D14 40 11N 127 34 E
Siniátsikon, Óros, Greece ... 50 F5 40 25N 21 35 E
Siniloan, Phil. ... 80 B2 14 25N 121 27 E
Siniscóla, Italy ... 46 B2 40 34N 9 41 E
Sinj, Croatia ... 45 E13 43 42N 16 39 E
Sinjai, Indonesia ... 82 C2 5 7S 120 20 E
Sinjajevina, Montenegro, Yug. ... 50 C5 42 57N 19 22 E
Sinjār, Iraq ... 101 D9 36 19N 41 52 E
Sinkiang Uighur = Xinjiang Uygur Zizhiqu □, China ... 68 C3 42 0N 86 0 E
Sinlumkaba, Burma ... 90 C6 24 16N 97 31 E
Sinmak, N. Korea ... 75 E14 38 25N 126 14 E
Sínnai, Italy ... 46 C2 39 18N 9 13 E
Sinnar, India ... 94 E2 19 48N 74 0 E
Sinni →, Italy ... 47 B9 40 8N 16 41 E
Sinnuris, Egypt ... 106 J7 29 26N 30 31 E
Sinoe, Lacul, Romania ... 53 F13 44 35N 28 50 E
Sinop, Turkey ... 100 A6 42 1N 35 11 E
Sinor, India ... 92 J5 21 55N 73 20 E
Sinp'o, N. Korea ... 75 E15 40 0N 128 13 E
Sins, Switz. ... 33 B6 47 12N 8 24 E
Sinsheim, Germany ... 31 F4 49 15N 8 52 E
Sinsk, Russia ... 67 C13 61 8N 126 48 E
Sintang, Indonesia ... 85 B4 0 5N 111 35 E
Sinton, U.S.A. ... 155 L6 28 2N 97 31W
Sintra, Portugal ... 43 G1 38 47N 9 25W
Sintra-Cascais, Parque Natural de ○, Portugal ... 43 G1 38 50N 9 25W
Sinugif, Somali Rep. ... 120 C3 8 33N 48 59 E
Sinŭiju, N. Korea ... 75 D13 40 5N 124 24 E
Sinyukha →, Ukraine ... 59 H6 48 3N 30 51 E
Sinzig, Germany ... 30 E3 50 32N 7 14 E
Sio →, Hungary ... 52 D3 46 20N 18 53 E
Siocon, Phil. ... 81 H4 7 40N 122 10 E
Siófok, Hungary ... 52 D3 46 54N 18 3 E
Sioma, Zambia ... 115 F4 16 40S 23 32 E
Sioma Ngwezi Nat. Park △, Zambia 115 F4 16 25S 23 28 E
Sion, Switz. ... 32 D4 46 14N 7 20 E
Sion Mills, U.K. ... 23 B4 54 48N 7 29W
Sioux City, U.S.A. ... 154 D6 42 30N 96 24W
Sioux Falls, U.S.A. ... 154 D6 43 33N 96 44W
Sioux Lookout, Canada ... 140 B1 50 10N 91 50W
Sioux Narrows, Canada ... 143 D10 49 25N 94 10W
Sipalay, Phil. ... 81 G4 9 45N 122 24 E
Sipan, Croatia ... 50 D1 42 45N 17 52 E
Sipang, Tanjong, Malaysia ... 85 B4 1 48N 110 20 E
Siparia, Trin. & Tob. ... 167 E15 10 8N 61 31W
Sipil Daği Milli Parkı △, Turkey ... 49 C9 38 35N 27 30 E
Siping, China ... 75 C13 43 8N 124 21 E
Sipiwesk L., Canada ... 143 B9 55 5N 97 35W
Sipocot, Phil. ... 80 D4 13 46N 122 59 E
Sipora, Indonesia ... 84 C1 2 18S 99 40 E
Sipra →, India ... 92 H6 23 55N 75 28 E
Sipur, India ... 94 D7 21 11N 85 9 E
Sipura, Indonesia ... 84 C1 2 18S 99 40 E
Siquia →, Nic. ... 164 D3 12 10N 84 20W
Siquijor, Phil. ... 81 G4 9 12N 123 35 E
Siquijor □, Phil. ... 81 G4 9 11N 123 35 E
Siquirres, Costa Rica ... 164 D3 10 6N 83 30W
Siquisique, Venezuela ... 168 A4 10 34N 69 42W
Şir Banī Yās, U.A.E. ... 97 E7 24 19N 52 37 E
Sir Edward Pellew Group, Australia 126 B2 15 40S 137 10 E
Sir Graham Moore Is., Australia ... 124 B4 13 53S 126 34 E
Sir James MacBrien, Mt., Canada ... 138 B7 62 8N 127 40W
Sir Joseph Banks Group, Australia ... 128 C2 34 36S 136 16 E
Sira, India ... 95 H3 13 41N 76 49 E
Sira, Norway ... 18 F3 58 23N 6 40 E
Sira →, Norway ... 18 F3 58 17N 6 24 E
Siracusa, Italy ... 47 E8 37 4N 15 17 E
Sirajganj, Bangla. ... 93 G13 24 25N 89 47 E
Sirakoro, Mali ... 112 C3 12 41N 9 14W
Şiran, Turkey ... 101 B8 40 11N 39 7 E
Sirasso, Ivory C. ... 112 D3 9 16N 6 6W
Sīrathu, India ... 93 G9 25 39N 81 19 E
Sirawai, Phil. ... 81 H4 7 34N 122 8 E
Sirdalsvatnet, Norway ... 18 F3 58 34N 6 43 E
Sīrdān, Iran ... 97 B6 36 39N 49 12 E
Sirdaryo = Syrdarya, Uzbekistan ... 65 C4 40 50N 68 40 E
Sirdaryo = Syrdarya →, Kazakhstan 65 E7 46 3N 61 0 E
Sire, Ethiopia ... 107 F4 6 55N 35 36 E
Siren, U.S.A. ... 154 C8 45 47N 92 24W
Sirente-Velino, Parco Naturale Regionale ○, Italy ... 45 F10 42 10N 13 32 E
Sirer, Spain ... 38 D1 38 56N 1 22 E
Siret, Romania ... 53 C11 47 55N 26 5 E
Siret →, Romania ... 53 E12 47 58N 26 5 E
Sirevåg, Norway ... 18 F2 58 30N 5 48 E
Sirghāyā, Syria ... 103 B5 33 51N 36 8 E
Siria, Romania ... 52 D6 46 16N 21 38 E
Sirik, Tanjong, Malaysia ... 85 B4 2 47N 111 15 E
Sirinat Nat. Park △, Thailand ... 87 a 8 6N 98 17 E
Sirino, Mte., Italy ... 47 B8 40 7N 15 50 E
Sīrjān, Iran ... 97 D7 29 30N 55 45 E
Sirkali = Sirkazhi, India ... 95 J4 11 15N 79 41 E
Sirkazhi, India ... 95 J4 11 15N 79 41 E
Sirmans, U.S.A. ... 152 D6 30 15N 83 39W
Sirmaur, India ... 93 G9 24 51N 81 23 E
Sírna, Greece ... 49 E8 36 22N 26 42 E
Sirnach, Switz. ... 33 B7 47 28N 8 59 E
Şırnak, Turkey ... 101 D10 37 31N 42 27 E
Sirohi, India ... 92 G5 24 52N 72 53 E
Sironj, India ... 92 G7 24 5N 77 39 E
Síros, Greece ... 48 D6 37 28N 24 57 E
Sirpur, India ... 94 E4 19 29N 79 36 E
Sirrayn, Si. Arabia ... 104 C2 19 30N 41 10 E
Sirretta Pk., U.S.A. ... 161 K8 35 56N 118 19W
Sirrf, Iran ... 97 E7 25 55N 54 32 E
Sirsa, India ... 92 E6 29 33N 75 4 E
Sirsa →, India ... 93 F8 26 51N 77 49 E
Sirsi, India ... 95 G2 14 40N 74 49 E
Sirsilla, India ... 94 C4 18 30N 78 49 E
Siruela, Spain ... 43 G5 38 58N 5 3W
Siruguppa, India ... 95 F3 15 38N 76 54 E
Sirur, India ... 94 E2 18 50N 74 23 E
Sisak, Croatia ... 45 C13 45 30N 16 21 E
Sisaket, Thailand ... 86 E5 15 8N 104 23 E
Sisante, Spain ... 41 F2 39 25N 2 12W
Sisargas, Is., Spain ... 42 B2 43 21N 8 50W
Sishen, S. Africa ... 116 D3 27 47S 22 59 E
Sishui, Henan, China ... 74 G7 34 48N 113 15 E
Sishui, Shandong, China ... 75 G9 35 42N 117 18 E
Sisiga, Solomon Is. ... 133 L10 7 54S 159 10 E
Sisimiut, Greenland ... 137 B5 66 40N 53 30W
Sisipuk L., Canada ... 143 B8 55 45N 101 50W
Sisophon, Cambodia ... 86 F4 13 38N 102 59 E
Sissach, Switz. ... 32 B5 47 27N 7 48 E
Sissano, Papua N. G. ... 132 B2 3 0S 142 3 E
Sissonne, France ... 27 C10 49 34N 3 51 E

Sīstān, Asia ... 97 D9 30 50N 61 0 E
Sīstān, Daryācheh-ye, Iran ... 97 D9 31 0N 61 0 E
Sīstān va Balūchestān □, Iran ... 97 E9 27 0N 62 0 E
Sisteron, France ... 29 D9 44 12N 5 57 E
Sisters, U.S.A. ... 158 D3 44 18N 121 33W
Sisters Pk., Ascension I. ... 9 g 7 56 S 14 22W
Siswa Bazar, India ... 93 F10 27 9N 83 46 E
Sitakunda, Bangla. ... 90 D3 22 37N 91 39 E
Sitamarhi, India ... 93 F11 26 37N 85 30 E
Sitampiky, Madag. ... 117 B8 16 41S 46 6 E
Sitangkai, Phil. ... 81 J2 4 40N 119 24 E
Sitapur, India ... 93 F9 27 38N 80 45 E
Siteki, Swaziland ... 117 D5 26 32S 31 58 E
Sitges, Spain ... 40 F6 41 17N 1 47 E
Sithoniá, Greece ... 50 F7 40 0N 23 45 E
Sitía, Greece ... 39 E7 35 13N 26 6 E
Sitía ✈ (JSH), Greece ... 39 E7 35 15N 26 5 E
Sítio da Abadia, Brazil ... 171 D2 14 48S 46 16W
Sitka, U.S.A. ... 142 B1 57 3N 135 20W
Sitka Nat. Historic Park △, U.S.A. 144 H8 57 3N 135 19W
Sitkinak I., U.S.A. ... 144 H9 56 33N 154 10W
Sitoti, Botswana ... 116 C3 23 15S 23 40 E
Sittang Myit →, Burma ... 90 G6 17 20N 96 45 E
Sittard, Neths. ... 24 C5 51 0N 5 52 E
Sittaung, Burma ... 90 C4 24 10N 94 35 E
Sittensen, Germany ... 30 B5 53 17N 9 32 E
Sittingbourne, U.K. ... 21 F8 51 21N 0 45 E
Sittona, Eritrea ... 107 E4 14 25N 37 23 E
Sittoung = Sittang Myit →, Burma 90 G6 17 20N 96 45 E
Sittwe, Burma ... 90 E4 20 18N 92 45 E
Situbondo, Indonesia ... 79 G16 7 42S 114 0 E
Si'umu, Samoa ... 133 X24 1 S 171 48W
Siuna, Nic. ... 164 D3 13 37N 84 45W
Siuri, India ... 93 H12 23 50N 87 34 E
Siutghiol, Lacul, Romania ... 53 F13 44 15N 28 35 E
Sivagang, India ... 95 K4 9 50N 78 28 E
Sivagiri, India ... 95 K3 9 16N 77 26 E
Sivakasi, India ... 95 K3 9 24N 77 47 E
Sivand, Iran ... 97 D7 30 5N 52 55 E
Sivas, Turkey ... 100 C7 39 43N 36 58 E
Sivasamudram, India ... 95 H3 12 16N 77 10 E
Sivash, Turkey ... 49 C11 38 31N 29 42 E
Siverek, Turkey ... 101 D8 37 50N 39 19 E
Sivomaskinskiy, Russia ... 56 A11 66 40N 62 35 E
Sívota, Greece ... 38 C10 39 24N 20 13 E
Sivrihisar, Turkey ... 100 C4 39 30N 31 35 E
Sívros, Greece ... 38 B2 38 40N 20 39 E
Sîwa, Egypt ... 106 B2 29 11N 25 31 E
Sîwa, El Wâhât es, Egypt ... 106 B2 29 10N 25 30 E
Siwa Oasis = Sîwa, El Wâhât es, Egypt ... 106 B2 29 10N 25 30 E
Siwalik Range, Nepal ... 93 F10 28 0N 83 0 E
Siwan, India ... 93 F11 26 13N 84 21 E
Siwana, India ... 92 G5 25 38N 72 25 E
Six Cross Roads, Barbados ... 165 g 13 10N 59 28W
Sixmilebridge, Ireland ... 23 D3 52 44N 8 46W
Sixth Cataract, Sudan ... 107 D3 16 20N 32 42 E
Siyāh Kuh, Afghan. ... 91 B2 34 7N 64 10 E
Siyāl, Jazā'ir, Egypt ... 106 C4 22 49N 36 12 E
Siyāzān, Azerbaijan ... 61 K9 41 3N 49 10 E
Siziwang Qi, China ... 74 D6 41 25N 111 40 E
Sjælland, Denmark ... 17 J5 55 30N 11 30 E
Sjællands Odde, Denmark ... 17 J5 55 58N 11 24 E
Sjenica, Serbia, Yug. ... 50 C3 43 16N 20 0 E
Sjoa, Norway ... 18 C6 61 41N 9 33 E
Sjöbo, Sweden ... 17 J7 55 37N 13 45 E
Sjøholt, Norway ... 18 B3 62 27N 6 52 E
Sjøli, Norway ... 18 C6 61 28N 11 18 E
Sjøtofta, Sweden ... 17 G7 57 22N 13 17 E
Sjötorp, Sweden ... 17 F8 58 50N 14 0 E
Skåbu, Norway ... 18 C6 61 33N 9 24 E
Skadarsko Jezero, Montenegro, Yug. 50 D3 42 10N 19 20 E
Skadovsk, Ukraine ... 59 J7 46 17N 32 52 E
Skælskør, Denmark ... 17 J5 55 15N 11 18 E
Skærbæk, Denmark ... 17 J2 55 9N 8 45 E
Skaftafell, Iceland ... 11 C9 64 1N 17 0W
Skaftafell △, Iceland ... 11 C9 64 4N 16 50W
Skagafjarðarsýsla □, Iceland ... 11 B7 65 30N 19 0W
Skagafjörður, Iceland ... 11 B7 65 54N 19 35W
Skagastølstindane, Norway ... 18 C4 61 28N 7 52 E
Skagaströnd, Iceland ... 11 B7 65 50N 20 19W
Skagen, Denmark ... 17 G4 57 43N 10 35 E
Skagern, Sweden ... 16 F8 59 0N 14 20 E
Skagerrak, Denmark ... 17 G2 57 30N 9 0 E
Skagit →, U.S.A. ... 160 B4 48 23N 122 22W
Skagway, U.S.A. ... 144 G14 59 28N 135 19W
Skala ... 39 C12 38 5N 20 47 E
Skala-Podilska, Ukraine ... 59 H4 48 50N 26 15 E
Skala Podolskaya = Skala-Podilska, Ukraine ... 59 H4 48 50N 26 15 E
Skalat, Ukraine ... 59 H3 49 23N 25 55 E
Skálavík, Iceland ... 11 A3 66 11N 23 29W
Skalbmierz, Poland ... 55 H7 50 20N 20 25 E
Skälderviken, Sweden ... 17 H6 56 22N 12 30 E
Skælevik, Norway ... 18 F5 58 5N 8 1 E
Skalica, Slovak Rep. ... 35 C10 48 50N 17 15 E
Skallingen, Denmark ... 17 J2 55 32N 8 13 E
Skalni Dol = Kamenyak, Bulgaria 51 C10 43 24N 26 57 E
Skanderborg, Denmark ... 17 H3 56 2N 9 55 E
Skåne, Sweden ... 17 J7 55 59N 13 30 E
Skåne län □, Sweden ... 17 H7 56 15N 14 0 E
Skaneateles, U.S.A. ... 151 D8 42 57N 76 26W
Skaneateles L., U.S.A. ... 151 D8 42 51N 76 22W
Skånevik, Norway ... 18 E2 59 43N 5 53 E
Skänninge, Sweden ... 17 F9 58 24N 15 5 E
Skanör med Falsterbo, Sweden ... 17 J6 55 24N 12 50 E
Skantzoúra, Greece ... 48 B6 39 5N 24 6 E
Skara, Sweden ... 17 F7 58 25N 13 30 E
Skärblacka, Sweden ... 17 F9 58 35N 15 54 E
Skarð, Iceland ... 11 B4 65 5N 21 40W
Skardu, Pakistan ... 93 B6 35 20N 75 44 E
Skare, Norway ... 18 E3 59 55N 6 36 E
Skåre, Sweden ... 16 E7 59 26N 13 26 E
Skärhamn, Sweden ... 17 G5 57 59N 11 34 E
Skarnes, Norway ... 18 D6 60 15N 11 41 E
Skarzysko-Kamienna, Poland ... 55 G8 51 7N 20 52 E
Skattkärr, Sweden ... 16 E8 59 26N 13 40 E
Skattungbyn, Sweden ... 16 C8 61 10N 14 56 E
Skawina, Poland ... 55 J7 49 59N 19 50 E
Skebobruk, Sweden ... 16 E12 59 58N 18 36 E
Skeena →, Canada ... 142 C2 54 9N 130 5W
Skeena Mts., Canada ... 142 B3 56 40N 128 30W
Skegness, U.K. ... 20 D8 53 9N 0 20 E
Skei, Norway ... 18 C3 61 34N 6 28 E
Skeiðararsandur, Iceland ... 11 D8 63 47N 17 40W
Skeiðflötur, Iceland ... 11 D7 63 26N 19 11W
Skeldon, Guyana ... 169 B6 5 55N 57 20W
Skeleton Coast Park △, Namibia 116 C1 20 0S 13 20 E
Skellefte →, Sweden ... 14 D19 64 45N 21 10 E
Skellefteå, Sweden ... 14 D19 64 45N 20 50 E
Skellefteåhamn, Sweden ... 14 D19 64 40N 21 9 E
Skender Vakuf, Bos.-H. ... 52 F2 44 29N 17 22 E
Skerries, The, U.K. ... 20 D3 53 25N 4 36W
Skhíza, Greece ... 48 E3 36 41N 21 40 E
Skhoinoúsa, Greece ... 49 E7 36 53N 25 31 E
Ski, Norway ... 18 E7 59 43N 10 52 E
Skíathos, Greece ... 48 B5 39 12N 23 30 E

Skibbereen, Ireland ... 23 E2 51 33N 9 16W
Skiddaw, U.K. ... 20 C4 54 39N 3 9W
Skidegate, Canada ... 142 C2 53 15N 132 1W
Skídhra, Greece ... 50 F6 40 46N 22 10 E
Skien, Norway ... 18 E6 59 12N 9 35 E
Skierniewice, Poland ... 55 G7 51 58N 20 10 E
Skikda, Algeria ... 111 A6 36 50N 6 58 E
Skil't →, U.S.A. ... 157 F8 38 5N 88 5W
Skillingaryd, Sweden ... 17 G8 57 27N 14 5 E
Skillinge, Sweden ... 17 J8 55 30N 14 16 E
Skilloura, Cyprus ... 39 E9 35 14N 33 10 E
Skinári, Ákra, Greece ... 39 D2 37 56N 20 42 E
Skinnastaður, Iceland ... 11 A10 66 4N 16 27W
Skinnskatteberg, Sweden ... 16 E9 59 50N 15 42 E
Skipton, Australia ... 128 D5 37 39 S 143 40 E
Skipton, U.K. ... 20 D5 53 58N 2 3W
Skiptvet, Norway ... 18 E8 59 28N 11 11 E
Skiring, C., Senegal ... 112 C1 12 26N 16 46W
Skirmish Pt., Australia ... 126 A1 11 59 S 134 17 E
Skíros, Greece ... 48 C6 38 50N 24 21 E
Skíros, Greece ... 48 C6 38 55N 24 34 E
Skivarp, Sweden ... 17 J7 55 26N 13 34 E
Skive, Denmark ... 17 H3 56 33N 9 2 E
Skjærhalden, Norway ... 18 E6 59 2N 11 2 E
Skjálfandafljót →, Iceland ... 11 B9 65 59N 17 25W
Skjálfandi, Iceland ... 11 A9 66 5N 17 30W
Skjeberg, Norway ... 18 E8 59 12N 11 12 E
Skjern, Denmark ... 17 J2 55 57N 8 30 E
Skjolden, Norway ... 18 E2 59 31N 5 34 E
Skjolden, Norway ... 18 C4 61 29N 7 36 E
Skjöldólfsstaðir, Iceland ... 11 B11 65 19N 15 7W
Skjønhaug, Norway ... 18 E8 59 39N 11 19 E
Skobeleva, Pik, Kyrgyzstan ... 65 D6 39 48N 72 36 E
Skoczów, Poland ... 55 J5 49 49N 18 45 E
Skodje, Norway ... 18 B3 62 30N 6 43 E
Škofja Loka, Slovenia ... 45 B11 46 9N 14 19 E
Skógar, Iceland ... 11 D7 63 32N 19 28W
Skógarnes, Iceland ... 11 C4 64 46N 22 34W
Skoghall, Sweden ... 16 E7 59 20N 13 30 E
Skogstorp, Sweden ... 16 E10 59 11N 16 29 E
Skoki, Poland ... 55 F4 52 40N 17 11 E
Skokie, U.S.A. ... 157 B9 42 3N 87 45W
Skole, Ukraine ... 59 H2 49 3N 23 30 E
Skollenborg, Norway ... 18 E6 59 38N 9 43 E
Skópelos, Greece ... 48 B5 39 7N 23 47 E
Skopí, Greece ... 39 E7 35 11N 26 2 E
Skopin, Russia ... 58 F10 53 55N 39 32 E
Skopje, Macedonia ... 50 D5 42 1N 21 26 E
Skopje ✈ (SKP), Macedonia ... 50 E5 41 59N 21 29 E
Skórcz, Poland ... 54 E5 53 47N 18 30 E
Skørping, Denmark ... 17 H3 56 50N 9 53 E
Skotfoss, Norway ... 18 E6 59 12N 9 30 E
Skotterud, Norway ... 18 D9 60 0N 12 7 E
Skövde, Sweden ... 17 F7 58 24N 13 50 E
Skovorodino, Russia ... 67 D13 54 0N 124 0 E
Skowhegan, U.S.A. ... 149 C11 44 46N 69 43W
Skradin, Croatia ... 45 E12 43 52N 15 53 E
Skrea, Sweden ... 17 H6 56 53N 12 34 E
Skreia, Norway ... 18 D7 60 40N 10 56 E
Skrim, Norway ... 18 E6 59 31N 9 38 E
Skrunda, Latvia ... 54 B9 56 41N 22 1 E
Skrwa →, Poland ... 55 F6 52 35N 19 32 E
Skudeneshavn, Norway ... 18 E2 59 10N 5 10 E
Skuleskogen Nationalpark △,
  Sweden ... 16 A12 63 6N 18 30 E
Skull, Ireland ... 23 E2 51 32N 9 34W
Skultorp, Sweden ... 17 F7 58 24N 13 51 E
Skultuna, Sweden ... 16 E10 59 43N 16 25 E
Skunk →, U.S.A. ... 156 D5 40 42N 91 7W
Skuodas, Lithuania ... 15 H19 56 16N 21 33 E
Skurup, Sweden ... 17 J7 55 28N 13 30 E
Skutskär, Sweden ... 16 D11 60 37N 17 25 E
Skútustaðir, Iceland ... 11 B9 65 34N 17 2W
Skvyra, Ukraine ... 59 H5 49 44N 29 40 E
Skwierzyna, Poland ... 55 F2 52 33N 15 30 E
Skye, U.K. ... 22 D2 57 15N 6 10W
Skykomish, U.S.A. ... 158 C3 47 42N 121 22W
Skyring, Seno, Chile ... 176 D3 52 33 S 72 0W
Skyros = Skíros, Greece ... 48 C6 38 55N 24 34 E
Skyttorp, Sweden ... 16 D11 60 5N 17 44 E
Slade Pt., Australia ... 126 K7 21 5 S 149 13 E
Slættaratindur, Færoe Is. ... 14 E9 62 18N 7 1W
Slagelse, Denmark ... 17 J5 55 23N 11 19 E
Slamet, Indonesia ... 85 D3 7 16 S 109 8 E
Slaney →, Ireland ... 23 D5 52 26N 6 33W
Slangberge, S. Africa ... 116 E3 31 32 S 20 48 E
Slánic, Romania ... 53 E10 45 14N 25 58 E
Slano, Croatia ... 50 D1 42 48N 17 53 E
Slantsy, Russia ... 54 C5 59 7N 28 5 E
Slaný, Czech Rep. ... 34 A7 50 13N 14 6 E
Śląsk, Poland ... 36 C9 51 0N 16 30 E
Śląskie □, Poland ... 55 H6 50 30N 19 0 E
Slătbaken, Sweden ... 17 F10 58 25N 16 35 E
Slate Is., Canada ... 140 C2 48 40N 87 0W
Slater, U.S.A. ... 156 E3 39 13N 93 4W
Slatina, Croatia ... 52 E2 45 42N 17 45 E
Slatina, Romania ... 53 F9 44 28N 24 22 E
Slatina Timiş, Romania ... 52 E7 45 15N 22 17 E
Slatington, U.S.A. ... 151 F9 40 45N 75 37W
Slaton, U.S.A. ... 155 J4 33 26N 101 39W
Slave →, Canada ... 142 A6 61 18N 113 39W
Slave Coast, W. Afr. ... 113 D5 6 0N 2 30 E
Slave Lake, Canada ... 142 B6 55 17N 114 43W
Slave Pt., Canada ... 142 A5 61 11N 115 56W
Slavgorod, Russia ... 66 D8 53 1N 78 37 E
Slavinja, Serbia, Yug. ... 50 C6 43 9N 22 50 E
Slavkov u Brna, Czech Rep. ... 35 B9 49 10N 16 52 E
Slavkovský Les □, Czech Rep. ... 34 A5 50 5N 12 44 E
Slavonija, Europe ... 52 E2 45 20N 17 40 E
Slavonski Brod, Croatia ... 52 E3 45 11N 18 1 E
Slavuta, Ukraine ... 59 G4 50 15N 27 2 E
Slavyanka, Russia ... 70 C5 42 53N 131 21 E
Slavyanovo, Bulgaria ... 51 C8 43 28N 24 52 E
Slavyansk = Slovyansk, Ukraine ... 59 H9 48 55N 37 36 E
Slavyansk-na-Kubani, Russia ... 59 K10 45 15N 38 11 E
Sława, Poland ... 55 G3 51 52N 16 2 E
Sławharad, Belarus ... 58 F6 53 27N 31 0 E
Sławno, Poland ... 54 D3 54 20N 16 41 E
Sławoborze, Poland ... 54 E2 53 55N 15 42 E
Sleaford, U.K. ... 20 D7 53 0N 0 24W
Sleaford B., Australia ... 127 E2 34 55 S 135 45 E
Sleat, Sd. of, U.K. ... 22 D3 57 5N 5 47W
Sleðbrjótur, Iceland ... 11 B12 65 34N 14 80 E
Sleeper Is., Canada ... 139 C11 58 30N 81 0W
Sleeping Bear Dunes Nat.
  Lakeshore △, U.S.A. ... 148 C2 44 50N 86 5W
Sleepy Eye, U.S.A. ... 154 C7 44 18N 94 43W
Sleetmute, U.S.A. ... 144 F8 61 42N 157 10W
Sleman, Indonesia ... 85 D4 7 40 S 110 20 E
Slemon L., Canada ... 142 A5 63 13N 116 4W
Ślesin, Poland ... 55 F5 52 22N 18 14 E
Slide Mt., U.S.A. ... 151 E10 42 0N 74 25W
Slidell, U.S.A. ... 155 K10 30 17N 89 47W
Sliema, Malta ... 38 F8 35 55N 14 30 E
Slieve Aughty, Ireland ... 23 C3 53 4N 8 30W
Slieve Bloom, Ireland ... 23 C4 53 4N 7 40W
Slieve Donard, U.K. ... 23 B6 54 11N 5 55W
Slieve Gamph, Ireland ... 23 B3 54 6N 9 0W
Slieve Gullion, U.K. ... 23 B5 54 7N 6 26W
Slieve League, Ireland ... 23 B3 54 40N 8 42W
Slieve Mish, Ireland ... 23 D2 52 12N 9 50W
Slievenamon, Ireland ... 23 D4 52 25N 7 34W
Sligeach = Sligo, Ireland ... 23 B3 54 16N 8 28W

Sligo, Ireland ... 23 B3 54 16N 8 28W
Sligo, U.S.A. ... 150 E5 41 6N 79 29W
Sligo □, Ireland ... 23 B3 54 8N 8 42W
Sligo B., Ireland ... 23 B3 54 18N 8 40W
Slippery Rock, U.S.A. ... 150 E4 41 3N 80 3W
Slite, Sweden ... 17 G12 57 42N 18 48 E
Sliteres Rezervāts △, Latvia ... 54 A9 57 41N 22 21 E
Sliven, Bulgaria ... 51 D10 42 42N 26 19 E
Sloan, U.S.A. ... 161 K11 35 57N 115 13W
Sloansville, U.S.A. ... 151 D10 42 45N 74 22W
Slobodskoy, Russia ... 64 B3 58 40N 50 6 E
Slobozia, Moldova ... 53 D14 46 45N 29 42 E
Slobozia, Argeş, Romania ... 53 F10 44 34N 25 14 E
Slobozia, Ialomiţa, Romania ... 53 F12 44 34N 27 23 E
Slocan, Canada ... 142 D5 49 48N 117 28W
Slocomb, U.S.A. ... 152 D4 31 7N 85 36W
Słomniki, Poland ... 55 H7 50 16N 20 4 E
Slonim, Belarus ... 59 F3 53 4N 25 19 E
Slough, U.K. ... 21 F7 51 30N 0 36W
Slough □, U.K. ... 21 F7 51 30N 0 36W
Sloughhouse, U.S.A. ... 160 G5 38 26N 121 12W
Slovak Rep. ■, Europe ... 35 C13 48 30N 20 0 E
Slovakia = Slovak Rep. ■, Europe ... 35 C13 48 30N 20 0 E
Slovakian Ore Mts. = Slovenské
  Rudohorie, Slovak Rep. ... 35 C12 48 45N 20 0 E
Slovenia ■, Europe ... 45 C11 45 58N 14 30 E
Slovenija = Slovenia ■, Europe ... 45 C11 45 58N 14 30 E
Slovenj Gradec, Slovenia ... 45 B12 46 31N 15 5 E
Slovenska Bistrica, Slovenia ... 45 B12 46 24N 15 35 E
Slovenske Konjice, Slovenia ... 45 B12 46 20N 15 28 E
Slovenské Rudohorie, Slovak Rep. ... 35 C12 48 45N 20 0 E
Slovenský Raj, Národný Park △,
  Slovak Rep. ... 35 C13 48 53N 20 25 E
Slovyansk, Ukraine ... 59 H9 48 55N 37 36 E
Słowiński Park Narodowy △, Poland ... 54 D4 54 43N 17 26 E
Słubice, Poland ... 55 F1 52 22N 14 35 E
Sluch →, Ukraine ... 59 G4 51 37N 26 38 E
Sluis, Neths. ... 24 C3 51 18N 3 23 E
Slúnchev Bryag, Bulgaria ... 51 D11 42 46N 27 41 E
Slunj, Croatia ... 45 C12 45 6N 15 33 E
Słupca, Poland ... 55 F4 52 15N 17 52 E
Słupia →, Poland ... 54 D3 54 35N 16 51 E
Słupsk, Poland ... 54 D4 54 30N 17 3 E
Slurry, S. Africa ... 116 D4 25 49 S 25 42 E
Slutsk, Belarus ... 59 F4 53 2N 27 31 E
Slyne Hd., Ireland ... 23 C1 53 25N 10 10W
Slyudyanka, Russia ... 67 D11 51 40N 103 40 E
Småland, Sweden ... 17 G9 57 15N 15 25 E
Smålandsfarvandet, Denmark ... 17 J5 55 10N 11 20 E
Smålandsstenar, Sweden ... 17 G7 57 10N 13 25 E
Smalltree L., Canada ... 143 A8 61 0N 105 0W
Smallwood Res., Canada ... 141 B7 54 0N 64 0W
Smarhon, Belarus ... 58 E4 54 20N 26 24 E
Smarje, Slovenia ... 45 B12 46 15N 15 34 E
Smartt Syndicate Dam, S. Africa ... 116 E3 30 45 S 23 10 E
Smartville, U.S.A. ... 160 F5 39 13N 121 18W
Smeaton, Canada ... 143 C8 53 30N 104 49W
Smedby, Sweden ... 17 H10 56 41N 16 13 E
Smederevo, Serbia, Yug. ... 50 B4 44 40N 20 57 E
Smederevska Palanka, Serbia, Yug. ... 50 B4 44 22N 20 58 E
Smedjebacken, Sweden ... 16 D9 60 8N 15 25 E
Smela = Smila, Ukraine ... 59 H6 49 15N 31 58 E
Smerwick Harbour, Ireland ... 23 D1 52 12N 10 23W
Smethport, U.S.A. ... 150 E6 41 49N 78 27W
Smidovich, Russia ... 67 E14 48 36N 133 49 E
Śmigiel, Poland ... 55 F3 52 1N 16 32 E
Smila, Ukraine ... 59 H6 49 15N 31 58 E
Smilyan, Bulgaria ... 51 E8 41 29N 24 46 E
Smith, Canada ... 142 B6 55 10N 114 0W
Smith B., U.S.A. ... 144 A9 70 30N 154 20W
Smith Center, U.S.A. ... 154 F5 39 47N 98 47W
Smith I., India ... 95 H11 13 20N 93 0 E
Smith River Nat. Recr. Area △,
  U.S.A. ... 158 F2 41 55N 124 0W
Smith Sund, Greenland ... 10 B3 78 30N 74 0W
Smithburne →, Australia ... 126 B3 17 3 S 140 57 E
Smithers, Canada ... 142 C3 54 45N 127 10W
Smithfield, S. Africa ... 117 E4 30 9 S 26 30 E
Smithfield, N.C., U.S.A. ... 149 H6 35 31N 78 21W
Smithfield, Utah, U.S.A. ... 158 F8 41 50N 111 50W
Smiths, U.S.A. ... 152 C4 32 32N 85 6W
Smiths Falls, Canada ... 140 D4 44 55N 76 0W
Smithton, Australia ... 127 G4 40 53 S 145 6 E
Smithton, Canada ... 150 C5 43 6N 79 33W
Smithville, Canada ... 150 C5 43 6N 79 33W
Smithville, Ga., U.S.A. ... 152 D5 31 54N 84 15W
Smithville, Mo., U.S.A. ... 156 E2 39 23N 94 35W
Smithville, Tex., U.S.A. ... 155 K6 30 1N 97 10W
Smoky →, Canada ... 142 B5 56 10N 117 21W
Smoky Bay, Australia ... 127 E1 32 22 S 134 13 E
Smoky Hill →, U.S.A. ... 154 F6 39 4N 96 48W
Smoky Hills, U.S.A. ... 154 F5 39 15N 99 30W
Smoky Lake, Canada ... 142 C6 54 10N 112 30W
Smøla, Norway ... 18 A5 63 23N 8 3 E
Smolensk, Russia ... 58 E7 54 45N 32 5 E
Smolikas, Óros, Greece ... 50 F4 40 9N 20 58 E
Smolník, Slovak Rep. ... 35 C13 48 43N 20 44 E
Smolyan, Bulgaria ... 51 E8 41 36N 24 38 E
Smooth Rock Falls, Canada ... 140 C3 49 17N 81 37W
Smoothstone L., Canada ... 143 C7 54 40N 106 50W
Smorgon = Smarhon, Belarus ... 58 E4 54 20N 26 24 E
Smulţi, Romania ... 53 E12 45 57N 27 44 E
Smyadovo, Bulgaria ... 51 C11 43 2N 27 1 E
Smygehamn, Sweden ... 17 J7 55 21N 13 22 E
Smyrna = İzmir, Turkey ... 49 C9 38 25N 27 8 E
Smyrna, Del., U.S.A. ... 148 F8 39 18N 75 36W
Smyrna, Ga., U.S.A. ... 152 B5 33 53N 84 31W
Snæfell, Iceland ... 11 C11 64 48N 15 34W
Snaefell, U.K. ... 20 C3 54 16N 4 27W
Snæfellsjökull, Iceland ... 11 C3 64 49N 23 46W
Snæfellsnessýsla □, Iceland ... 11 C3 65 0N 23 0W
Snake →, U.S.A. ... 158 C4 46 12N 119 2W
Snake I., Australia ... 129 E7 38 47 S 146 33 E
Snake Range, U.S.A. ... 158 G6 39 0N 114 20W
Snake River Plain, U.S.A. ... 158 E7 42 50N 114 0W
Snasahögarna, Sweden ... 14 A6 63 13N 12 21 E
Snåsavatnet, Norway ... 14 D14 64 12N 12 0 E
Snedsted, Denmark ... 17 H2 56 55N 8 32 E
Sneek, Neths. ... 24 A5 53 2N 5 40 E
Sneeuberge, S. Africa ... 116 E3 31 46 S 24 20 E
Snejbjerg, Denmark ... 17 H2 56 8N 8 54 E
Snelling, Calif., U.S.A. ... 160 H6 37 31N 120 26W
Snelling, S.C., U.S.A. ... 152 B8 33 15N 81 27W
Snells Beach, N.Z. ... 130 C3 36 25 S 174 44 E
Snezhnoye, Ukraine ... 59 J10 48 0N 38 58 E
Snežka, Europe ... 36 C8 50 41N 15 50 E
Snežnik, Slovenia ... 45 C11 45 36N 14 35 E
Śniadowo, Poland ... 55 E8 53 2N 22 0 E
Śniardwy, Jezioro, Poland ... 54 E8 53 48N 21 50 E
Śnieżka, Europe ... 34 A8 50 44N 15 44 E
Snigirevka = Snihurivka, Ukraine ... 59 J7 47 2N 32 49 E
Snihurivka, Ukraine ... 59 J7 47 2N 32 49 E
Snillfjord, Norway ... 14 A6 63 24N 9 30 E
Snina, Slovak Rep. ... 35 C15 48 58N 22 7 E
Snizort, L., U.K. ... 22 D2 57 33N 6 28W
Snøhetta, Norway ... 18 B6 62 19N 9 16 E
Snohomish, U.S.A. ... 160 C4 47 55N 122 6W
Snønuten, Norway ... 18 E3 59 31N 6 52 E
Snoul, Cambodia ... 87 F6 12 4N 106 26 E
Snow Hill, U.S.A. ... 148 F8 38 11N 75 24W
Snow Lake, Canada ... 143 C8 54 52N 100 3W
Snow Mt., Calif., U.S.A. ... 160 F4 39 23N 122 45W
Snow Mt., Maine, U.S.A. ... 151 A14 45 18N 70 48W

Snow Shoe, U.S.A. ... 150 E7 41 2N 77 57W
Snowbird L., Canada ... 143 A8 60 45N 103 0W
Snowdon, U.K. ... 20 D3 53 4N 4 5W
Snowdonia Nat. Park △, U.K. ... 20 D4 53 7N 3 59W
Snowdoun, U.S.A. ... 152 C3 32 15N 86 18W
Snowdrift →, Canada ... 143 A6 62 24N 110 44W
Snowflake, U.S.A. ... 159 J8 34 30N 110 5W
Snowshoe Pk., U.S.A. ... 158 B6 48 13N 115 41W
Snowtown, Australia ... 128 B3 33 46 S 138 14 E
Snowville, U.S.A. ... 158 F7 41 58N 112 43W
Snowy →, Australia ... 129 D8 37 46 S 148 30 E
Snowy Mt., U.S.A. ... 151 C10 43 42N 74 23W
Snowy Mts., Australia ... 129 D8 36 30 S 148 20 E
Snowy River Nat. Park △, Australia ... 129 D7 37 15 S 147 29 E
Snug Corner, Bahamas ... 165 B5 22 33N 73 52W
Snyatyn, Ukraine ... 59 H3 48 27N 25 38 E
Snyder, Okla., U.S.A. ... 155 H5 34 40N 98 57W
Snyder, Tex., U.S.A. ... 155 J4 32 44N 100 55W
Soacha, Colombia ... 168 C3 4 35N 74 13W
Soahanina, Madag. ... 117 B7 18 42 S 44 13 E
Soalala, Madag. ... 117 B8 16 6 S 45 20 E
Soaloka, Madag. ... 117 B8 18 32 S 45 15 E
Soamanonga, Madag. ... 117 C7 23 52 S 44 47 E
Soan →, Pakistan ... 92 C4 33 1N 71 44 E
Soanierana-Ivongo, Madag. ... 117 B8 16 55 S 49 35 E
Soanindraniny, Madag. ... 117 B8 19 54 S 47 14 E
Soars, Romania ... 53 E9 45 56N 24 55 E
Soasiu, Indonesia ... 83 A3 0 40N 127 26 E
Soavina, Madag. ... 117 C8 20 23 S 46 56 E
Soavinandriana, Madag. ... 117 B8 19 9 S 46 45 E
Soba, Nigeria ... 113 C6 10 58N 8 4 E
Sobat, Nahr →, Sudan ... 107 F3 9 22N 31 33 E
Sobešlav, Czech Rep. ... 34 B7 49 16N 14 45 E
Sobger →, Indonesia ... 83 B6 3 42 S 140 16 E
Sobhapur, India ... 92 H8 22 47N 78 17 E
Sobinka, Russia ... 58 E11 56 0N 40 0 E
Sobo-Yama, Japan ... 72 E3 32 51N 131 22 E
Sobótka, Poland ... 55 H3 50 54N 16 44 E
Sobra, Croatia ... 45 F14 42 44N 17 34 E
Sobradinho, Reprêsa de., Brazil ... 170 C3 9 30 S 42 0 E
Sobral, Brazil ... 170 B3 3 50 S 40 20W
Sobrance, Slovak Rep. ... 35 C15 48 45N 22 11 E
Sobreira Formosa, Portugal ... 42 F3 39 46N 7 51W
Soc Giang, Vietnam ... 76 F6 22 54N 106 1 E
Soc Trang, Vietnam ... 87 H5 9 37N 105 50 E
Soča →, Europe ... 34 E6 46 20N 13 40 E
Socastee, U.S.A. ... 149 J6 33 41N 79 1W
Sochaczew, Poland ... 55 F7 52 15N 20 13 E
Soch'e = Shache, China ... 65 D8 38 20N 77 10 E
Sochi, Russia ... 61 J4 43 35N 39 40 E
Social Circle, U.S.A. ... 152 B6 33 39N 83 43W
Society Hill, U.S.A. ... 149 H6 34 30N 79 51W
Society Is. = Société, Is. de la,
  Pac. Oc. ... 135 J12 17 0 S 151 0W
Socompa, Portezuelo de, Chile ... 174 A2 24 27 S 68 18W
Socorro, Colombia ... 168 B3 6 29N 73 16W
Socorro, Phil. ... 81 G5 9 37N 125 58 E
Socorro, N. Mex., U.S.A. ... 159 J10 34 4N 106 54W
Socorro, Tex., U.S.A. ... 159 L10 31 39N 106 18W
Socorro, I., Mexico ... 162 D2 18 45N 110 58W
Socotra, Yemen ... 99 D6 12 30N 54 0 E
Socovos, Spain ... 41 G3 38 20N 1 58W
Socuéllamos, Spain ... 41 F2 39 16N 2 47W
Soda L., U.S.A. ... 159 J5 35 10N 116 4W
Soda Plains, India ... 93 B8 35 30N 79 0 E
Soda Springs, U.S.A. ... 158 E8 42 39N 111 36W
Sodankylä, Finland ... 14 C22 67 29N 26 40 E
Söderala, Sweden ... 16 C10 61 17N 16 55 E
Söderåsen Nationalpark △, Sweden ... 17 H7 56 2N 13 13 E
Söderbärke, Sweden ... 16 D9 60 5N 15 33 E
Söderfors, Sweden ... 16 D11 60 23N 17 25 E
Söderhamn, Sweden ... 16 C11 61 18N 17 10 E
Söderköping, Sweden ... 17 F10 58 31N 16 35 E
Södermanland, Sweden ... 15 G17 58 56N 16 55 E
Södermanlands län □, Sweden ... 16 E11 59 10N 16 30 E
Södertälje, Sweden ... 16 E11 59 12N 17 39 E
Sodiri, Sudan ... 107 E2 14 27N 29 0 E
Sodo, Ethiopia ... 107 F4 7 0N 37 41 E
Södra Dellen, Sweden ... 16 C10 61 48N 16 43 E
Södra Finnskoga, Sweden ... 16 D6 60 42N 12 34 E
Södra Sandby, Sweden ... 17 J7 55 43N 13 21 E
Södra Ulvön, Sweden ... 16 B12 62 59N 18 38 E
Södra Vi, Sweden ... 17 G9 57 45N 15 45 E
Sodražica, Slovenia ... 45 C11 45 45N 14 39 E
Sodus, U.S.A. ... 150 C7 43 14N 77 4W
Sodwana Bay Nat. Park △, S. Africa ... 117 D5 27 35 S 32 43 E
Soe, Indonesia ... 83 C2 9 52 S 124 17 E
Soekmekaar, S. Africa ... 117 C4 23 30 S 29 55 E
Soest, Germany ... 30 D4 51 34N 8 7 E
Soest, Neths. ... 24 B5 52 9N 5 19 E
Sofádhes, Greece ... 48 B4 39 20N 22 4 E
Sofala □, Mozam. ... 117 B5 19 30 S 34 30 E
Sofara, Mali ... 112 C4 13 59N 4 9W
Sofia = Sofiya, Bulgaria ... 50 D7 42 45N 23 20 E
Sofia →, Madag. ... 117 B8 15 27 S 47 23 E
Sofia ✈ (SOF), Bulgaria ... 50 D7 42 46N 23 28 E
Sofievka, Ukraine ... 59 H7 48 6N 33 55 E
Sofikón, Greece ... 48 D5 37 47N 23 3 E
Sofiya, Bulgaria ... 50 D7 42 45N 23 20 E
Sofiya □, Bulgaria ... 50 D7 42 45N 23 20 E
Sōfu-Gan, Japan ... 71 K10 29 49N 140 21 E
Sogakofe, Ghana ... 113 D5 6 2N 0 39 E
Sogamoso, Colombia ... 168 B3 5 43N 72 56W
Sogār, Iran ... 97 E8 25 53N 58 6 E
Sögel, Germany ... 30 C3 52 50N 7 31 E
Sogeri, Papua N. G. ... 132 E4 9 26 S 147 35 E
Sogn og Fjordane □, Norway ... 18 C3 61 40N 6 45 E
Sogndalsfjøra, Norway ... 18 C4 61 14N 7 5 E
Søgne, Norway ... 18 E3 58 5N 7 48 E
Sognefjorden, Norway ... 18 C2 61 10N 5 50 E
Sogod, Phil. ... 81 F5 10 23N 124 59 E
Sögüt, Bilecik, Turkey ... 49 A12 40 2N 30 11 E
Sögüt, Burdur, Turkey ... 49 D11 37 2N 29 50 E
Sögüt Dağı, Turkey ... 49 D11 37 50N 29 55 E
Söğütköy, Turkey ... 49 E10 36 48N 28 30 E
Sögwipo, S. Korea ... 75 H14 33 13N 126 34 E
Soh, Iran ... 98 C3 33 26N 51 27 E
Sohâg, Egypt ... 106 B3 26 33N 31 43 E
Sohagpur, India ... 92 H8 22 42N 78 12 E
Sohano, Papua N. G. ... 132 C8 5 22 S 154 37 E
Sohela, India ... 94 D6 21 18N 83 24 E
Sohri, N. Korea ... 75 D14 40 7N 128 23 E
Sŏho Banja, Serbia, Yug. ... 50 D5 43 24N 21 11 E
Soko Islands, China ... 69 G10 22 10N 113 54 E
Sokodé, Togo ... 113 D5 9 0N 1 11 E
Sokol, Russia ... 58 C11 59 30N 40 5 E

Sokolac, Bos.-H. ... 52 G3 43 56N 18 48 E
Sokółka, Poland ... 54 E10 53 25N 23 30 E
Sokolo, Ségou, Mali ... 112 C3 14 53N 6 8W
Sokolo, Sikasso, Mali ... 112 C3 10 52N 6 59W
Sokolov, Czech Rep. ... 34 A5 50 12N 12 40 E
Sokołów Małopolski, Poland ... 55 H9 50 12N 22 7 E
Sokołów Podlaski, Poland ... 55 F9 52 25N 22 15 E
Sokoły, Poland ... 55 E9 52 59N 22 42 E
Sokoto, Nigeria ... 113 C6 13 2N 5 16 E
Sokoto □, Nigeria ... 113 C6 12 30N 6 0 E
Sokoto →, Nigeria ... 113 C5 11 20N 4 10 E
Sokuluk, Kyrgyzstan ... 65 B7 42 52N 74 18 E
Sol Iletsk, Russia ... 64 F5 51 10N 55 0 E
Sola, Norway ... 18 F2 58 53N 5 36 E
Sola, Vanuatu ... 133 C5 13 51 S 167 33 E
Sola →, Poland ... 55 H6 50 4N 19 15 E
Solai, Kenya ... 118 B4 0 2N 36 12 E
Solan, India ... 92 D7 30 55N 77 7 E
Solana, Phil. ... 80 C3 17 39N 121 41 E
Solander I., N.Z. ... 131 G1 46 34 S 166 54 E
Solano, Phil. ... 80 C3 16 31N 121 15 E
Solapur, India ... 94 F2 17 43N 75 56 E
Solda, Romania ... 53 C10 47 0N 25 50 E
Solda Gölü, Turkey ... 49 D11 37 33N 29 42 E
Soldăneşti, Moldova ... 53 C13 47 49N 28 48 E
Soldeu, Andorra ... 40 C6 42 35N 1 40 E
Soldotna, U.S.A. ... 144 F10 60 29N 151 3W
Soléa, Cyprus ... 39 E9 35 5N 33 4 E
Solec Kujawski, Poland ... 55 E5 53 5N 18 14 E
Soledad, Colombia ... 168 A3 10 55N 74 46W
Soledad, U.S.A. ... 160 J5 36 26N 121 20W
Soledad, Venezuela ... 169 B5 8 10N 63 34W
Sølen, Norway ... 18 C8 61 53N 11 31 E
Solent, The, U.K. ... 21 G6 50 45N 1 25W
Solenzara, France ... 29 G13 41 53N 9 23 E
Solesmes, France ... 27 B10 50 10N 3 30 E
Solfonn, Norway ... 18 D3 60 2N 6 57 E
Solhan, Turkey ... 101 C9 38 57N 41 3 E
Sølheim, Norway ... 18 D2 61 50N 5 27 E
Soligalich, Russia ... 56 C7 59 5N 42 10 E
Soligorsk = Salihorsk, Belarus ... 59 F4 52 51N 27 27 E
Solihull, U.K. ... 21 E6 52 26N 1 47W
Solikamsk, Russia ... 64 B6 59 38N 56 50 E
Solila, Madag. ... 117 C8 21 25 S 46 37 E
Solimões = Amazonas →, S. Amer. ... 169 D7 0 5 S 50 0W
Solin, Croatia ... 45 E13 43 33N 16 30 E
Solingen, Germany ... 30 D3 51 10N 7 5 E
Sollebrunn, Sweden ... 17 F6 58 8N 12 32 E
Sollefteå, Sweden ... 16 A11 63 12N 17 20 E
Sollentuna, Sweden ... 16 E11 59 26N 17 56 E
Sóller, Spain ... 38 B3 39 46N 2 43 E
Sollerön, Sweden ... 16 D8 60 55N 14 37 E
Solling, Germany ... 30 D5 51 42N 9 38 E
Solling-Vogler, Naturpark △,
  Germany ... 30 D5 51 45N 9 32 E
Solnechnogorsk, Russia ... 58 D9 56 10N 36 57 E
Solo →, Indonesia ... 79 G15 6 47 S 112 22 E
Solofra, Italy ... 47 B7 40 50N 14 51 E
Sologne, France ... 27 E8 47 40N 1 45 E
Solok, Indonesia ... 84 C2 0 45 S 100 40 E
Sololá, Guatemala ... 164 D1 14 49N 91 10W
Solomon, N. Fork →, U.S.A. ... 154 F5 39 29N 98 26W
Solomon, S. Fork →, U.S.A. ... 154 F5 39 25N 99 12W
Solomon Is. ■, Papua N. G. ... 132 D8 6 0 S 155 0 E
Solomon Is. ■, Pac. Oc. ... 133 L8 6 0 S 155 0 E
Solomon Sea, Papua N. G. ... 132 D6 7 0 S 150 0 E
Solon, China ... 69 B7 46 32N 121 10 E
Solon Springs, U.S.A. ... 154 B9 46 22N 91 49W
Solonópole, Brazil ... 170 C4 5 44 S 39 1W
Solor, Indonesia ... 82 C2 8 27 S 123 0 E
Solotcha, Russia ... 58 E10 54 48N 39 53 E
Solothurn, Switz. ... 32 B5 47 13N 7 32 E
Solothurn □, Switz. ... 32 B5 47 18N 7 40 E
Solsona, Spain ... 40 C6 42 0N 1 31 E
Solvik, Norway ... 18 D1 60 26N 4 58 E
Solvang, U.S.A. ... 161 L6 34 36N 120 8W
Solvay, U.S.A. ... 151 C8 43 3N 76 13W
Sölvesborg, Sweden ... 17 H8 56 5N 14 35 E
Solvychegodsk, Russia ... 56 B8 61 21N 46 56 E
Solway Firth, U.K. ... 20 C4 54 49N 3 35W
Solwezi, Zambia ... 119 E2 12 11 S 26 21 E
Sôma, Japan ... 70 F10 37 40N 140 50 E
Soma, Turkey ... 49 B9 39 10N 27 35 E
Somabhula, Zimbabwe ... 117 B4 19 42 S 29 40 E
Somali Pen., Africa ... 104 F8 7 0N 46 0 E
Somali Rep. ■, Africa ... 120 C3 7 0N 47 0 E
Somalia = Somali Rep. ■, Africa ... 120 C3 7 0N 47 0 E
Sombe Dzong, Bhutan ... 90 B2 27 13N 89 8 E
Sombernon, France ... 27 E11 47 20N 4 40 E
Sombo, Angola ... 115 D4 8 42 S 20 59 E
Sombra, Canada ... 150 D2 42 43N 82 29W
Sombrerete, Mexico ... 164 C4 23 40N 103 40W
Sombrero, Anguilla ... 165 C7 18 37N 63 30W
Sombrero Channel, India ... 95 L11 7 0N 93 35 E
Somcuta Mare, Romania ... 53 C8 47 31N 23 28 E
Somdari, India ... 92 G5 25 47N 72 38 E
Someiro, Parque Natural de □,
  Spain ... 42 B4 43 5N 6 11W
Somers, U.S.A. ... 158 B6 48 5N 114 13W
Somerset, Bermuda ... 9 a 32 17N 64 52W
Somerset, Ky., U.S.A. ... 148 G3 37 5N 84 36W
Somerset, Mass., U.S.A. ... 151 E13 41 47N 71 8W
Somerset, Pa., U.S.A. ... 150 F5 40 1N 79 5W
Somerset □, U.K. ... 21 F5 51 9N 3 0W
Somerset East, S. Africa ... 116 E4 32 42 S 25 35 E
Somerset I., Bermuda ... 9 a 32 17N 64 52W
Somerset I., Canada ... 138 A10 73 30N 93 0W
Somerset West, S. Africa ... 116 E2 34 8 S 18 50 E
Somersworth, U.S.A. ... 151 C14 43 16N 70 52W
Somerton, U.S.A. ... 159 K6 32 36N 114 43W
Somerville, U.S.A. ... 151 F10 40 35N 74 38W
Someş →, Romania ... 52 C7 47 49N 22 43 E
Someşul Mare →, Romania ... 53 C9 47 9N 23 55 E
Somme □, France ... 27 C9 49 57N 2 20 E
Somme →, France ... 26 B8 50 11N 1 38 E
Somme, B. de la, France ... 26 B8 50 14N 1 33 E
Sommen, Jönköping, Sweden ... 17 F9 58 12N 14 58 E
Sommen, Östergötland, Sweden ... 17 F9 58 0N 15 15 E
Sommepy-Tahure, France ... 27 C11 49 15N 4 31 E
Sommerda, Germany ... 30 D7 51 9N 11 7 E
Sommières, France ... 27 D11 48 44N 4 12 E
Sommières, France ... 29 E8 43 47N 4 6 E
Somnath, India ... 92 J4 20 53N 70 22 E
Somogy □, Hungary ... 52 D2 46 19N 17 30 E
Somogyszob, Hungary ... 52 D2 46 18N 17 20 E
Somosomo, Fiji ... 133 A3 16 47 S 179 58W
Somosomo Str., Fiji ... 133 A3 16 0 S 180 0 E
Somoto, Nic. ... 164 D2 13 28N 86 37W
Somport, Puerto de, Spain ... 40 C4 42 48N 0 31W
Somuncurá, Meseta de., Argentina ... 176 E3 41 30 S 67 0W
Somvarpet, India ... 95 H2 12 36N 75 52 E
Son, Norway ... 18 E7 59 32N 10 42 E
Son →, India ... 93 G11 25 42N 84 52 E
Son →, India ... 86 E7 15 3N 108 34 E
Son Ha, Vietnam ... 86 E7 15 3N 108 34 E

Son Hoa, *Vietnam* .... 86 F7   13 2N 108 58 E
Son La, *Vietnam* .... 76 G4   21 20N 103 50 E
Son Serra, *Spain* .... 38 B4   39 43N   3 13 E
Son Servera, *Spain* .... 38 B4   39 37N   3 21 E
Son Tay, *Vietnam* .... 76 G5   21 8N 105 30 E
Soná, *Panama* 164 E3   8 0N 81 20W
Sonamarg, *India* .... 93 B6   34 18N 75 21 E
Sonamukhi, *India* .... 93 H12 23 18N 87 27 E
Sonamura, *India* .... 90 D3   23 29N 91 15 E
Sonar →, *India* .... 93 G8   24 24N 79 56 E
Sŏnch'ŏn, *N. Korea* .... 75 E13 39 48N 124 55 E
Sondags →, *S. Africa* .... 116 E4   33 44 S 25 51 E
Sóndalo, *Italy* .... 44 B7   46 20N 10 19 E
Sondar, *India* .... 93 C6   33 28N 75 56 E
Søndeled, *Norway* .... 18 F6   58 46N   9 3 E
Sønder Felding, *Denmark* .... 17 J2   55 57N   8 47 E
Sønder Omme, *Denmark* .... 17 J2   55 50N   8 54 E
Sønderborg, *Denmark* .... 17 K3   54 55N   9 49 E
Sønderjyllands Amtskommune □,
   Denmark .... 17 J3   55 10N   9 10 E
Sondershausen, *Germany* .... 30 D6   51 22N 10 51 E
Søndre Strømfjord = Kangerlussuaq,
   Greenland 10 D5   66 59N 50 40W
Sóndrio, *Italy* .... 44 B6   46 10N   9 52 E
Sondur →, *India* .... 94 D6   20 40N 82 1 E
Sone, *Mozam.* .... 119 F3   17 23 S 34 55 E
Sonepur, *India* .... 94 D6   20 55N 83 50 E
Sonfim, *Brazil* .... 172 B4   6 0 S 67 52W
Song, *Nigeria* .... 113 D7   9 49N 12 39 E
Song, *Thailand* .... 86 C3   18 28N 100 11 E
Song Cau, *Vietnam* .... 86 F7   13 27N 109 18 E
Song-Köl, *Kyrgyzstan* .... 65 C7   41 50N 75 12 E
Song Xian, *China* .... 74 G7   34 12N 112 8 E
Songadh, *India* .... 94 D1   21 7N 73 33 E
Songan, *Indonesia* .... 79 J18   8 13 S 115 24 E
Songavatnet, *Norway* .... 18 E4   59 52N   7 32 E
Songch'ŏn, *N. Korea* .... 75 E14 39 12N 126 15 E
Songea, *Tanzania* .... 119 E4   10 40 S 35 40 E
Songeons, *France* .... 27 C8   49 32N   1 50 E
Songgang, *China* .... 69 F10 22 46N 113 50 E
Songin, *N. Korea* .... 75 C14 43 35N 126 50 E
Songhua Hu, *China* .... 75 C14 43 35N 126 50 E
Songhua Jiang →, *China* .... 69 B8   47 45N 132 30 E
Songtanveld Game Reserve △,
   S. Africa .... 117 D5   25 50 S 31 2 E
Songjiang, *China* .... 77 B13 31 1N 121 12 E
Songjin, *N. Korea* .... 75 D15 40 40N 129 10 E
Songjŏng-ni, *S. Korea* .... 75 G14 35 8N 126 47 E
Songkan, *China* .... 76 C6   28 35N 106 52 E
Songkhla, *Thailand* .... 87 J3   7 13N 100 37 E
Songming, *China* .... 76 E4   25 12N 103 2 E
Songnim, *N. Korea* .... 75 E13 38 45N 125 39 E
Songo, *Angola* .... 115 D2   7 22 S 14 51 E
Songololo, *Dem. Rep. of the Congo* .. 115 D2   5 42 S 14 2 E
Songpan, *China* .... 76 A4   32 40N 103 30 E
Songtao, *China* .... 76 C7   28 11N 109 10 E
Songwe, *Dem. Rep. of the Congo* ..... 118 C2   3 20 S 26 16 E
Songwe →, *Africa* .... 119 D3   9 44 S 33 58 E
Songxi, *China* .... 77 D12 27 31N 118 44 E
Songzi, *China* .... 77 B8   30 12N 111 45 E
Sonhat, *India* .... 93 H10 23 29N 82 31 E
Sonid Youqi, *China* .... 74 C7   42 45N 112 48 E
Sonipat, *India* .... 92 E7   29 0N 77 5 E
Sonkach, *India* .... 92 H7   22 59N 76 21 E
Sonkovo, *Russia* .... 58 D9   57 50N 37 5 E
Sonmiani, *Pakistan* .... 91 D2   25 25N 66 40 E
Sonmiani B., *Pakistan* .... 92 G2   25 15N 66 30 E
Sonnino, *Italy* .... 46 A6   41 25N 13 14 E
Sono →, *Minas Gerais, Brazil* .... 171 E2   17 2 S 45 32W
Sono →, *Tocantins, Brazil* .... 170 C2   9 58 S 48 11W
Sonobe, *Japan* .... 73 B7   35 6N 135 28 E
Sonogno, *Switz.* .... 33 D7   46 22N   8 47 E
Sonoma, *U.S.A.* 160 G4   38 18N 122 28W
Sonora, *Calif., U.S.A.* 160 H6   37 59N 120 23W
Sonora, *Tex., U.S.A.* 155 K4   30 34N 100 39W
Sonora □, *Mexico* 162 B2   29 0N 111 0W
Sonora →, *Mexico* 162 B2   28 50N 111 33W
Sonoran Desert, *U.S.A.* 161 L12 33 40N 114 15W
Sonoyta, *Mexico* 162 A2   31 51N 112 50W
Sonqor, *Iran* .... 101 E12 34 47N 47 36 E
Sŏnsan, *S. Korea* .... 75 F15 36 14N 128 17 E
Sonseca, *Spain* 43 F7   39 42N   3 57W
Sonsón, *Colombia* 168 B2   5 43N 75 18W
Sonsonate, *El Salv.* 164 D2   13 43N 89 44W
Sonstorp, *Sweden* .... 17 F9   58 44N 15 38 E
Sonthofen, *Germany* .... 31 H6   47 30N 10 16 E
Soochow = Suzhou, *China* .... 77 B13 31 19N 120 38 E
Sooke, *Canada* 160 B3   48 13N 123 43W
Sop Hao, *Laos* .... 76 G5   20 33N 104 27 E
Sop Prap, *Thailand* .... 86 D2   17 53N 99 20 E
Sopachuy, *Bolivia* .... 173 D5   19 29 S 64 31W
Sopchoppy, *U.S.A.* 152 E5   30 4N 84 29W
Sopelana, *Spain* 40 B2   43 23N   2 58W
Soperton, *U.S.A.* 152 C7   32 23N 82 35W
Sopi, *Indonesia* .... 82 A3   2 34N 128 28 E
Sopo, Nahr →, *Sudan* .... 107 F2   8 40N 26 30 E
Sopot, *Bulgaria* .... 51 D8   42 39N 24 45 E
Sopot, *Poland* .... 54 D5   54 27N 18 31 E
Sopot, *Serbia, Yug.* .... 50 B4   44 29N 20 36 E
Sopotnica, *Macedonia* .... 50 E5   41 18N 21 13 E
Sopron, *Hungary* .... 52 C1   47 45N 16 32 E
Sopur, *India* .... 93 B6   34 18N 74 27 E
Sør-Rondane, *Antarctica* .... 7 D4   72 0 S 35 0 E
Sør-Trøndelag □, *Norway* .... 18 A7   63 0N 11 0 E
Sora, *Italy* .... 45 G10 41 43N 13 37 E
Sorab, *India* .... 95 G2   14 23N 75 6 E
Sorada, *India* .... 94 E7   19 45N 84 26 E
Sorah, *Pakistan* .... 92 F3   27 13N 68 56 E
Söråker, *Sweden* .... 16 B11 62 30N 17 32 E
Sorano, *Italy* .... 45 F8   42 41N 11 43 E
Soraon, *India* .... 93 G9   25 37N 81 51 E
Sorata, *Bolivia* .... 172 D4   15 50 S 68 40W
Sorbas, *Spain* 41 H2   37 6N   2 7W
Sörbygden, *Sweden* .... 16 B10 62 48N 16 12 E
Sore, *France* 28 D3   44 18N   0 35W
Sorel, *Canada* 140 C5   46 0N 73 10W
Sörenberg, *Switz.* .... 32 C6   46 50N   8 2 E
Soresina, *Italy* .... 44 C6   45 17N   9 51 E
Sørfjorden, *Norway* .... 18 D3   60 20N   6 37 E
Sörforsa, *Sweden* .... 16 C10 61 43N 16 58 E
Sórgono, *Italy* .... 46 B2   40 1N   9 6 E
Sorgues, *France* .... 29 E8   44 1N   4 53 E
Sorgun, *Turkey* .... 100 C6   39 46N 35 11 E
Sori, *Papua N. G.* .... 132 A4   1 58 S 146 42 E
Soria, *Spain* 40 D2   41 43N   2 32W
Soria □, *Spain* 40 D2   41 46N   2 28W
Soriano, *Uruguay* .... 174 C4   33 24 S 58 19W
Soriano nel Cimino, *Italy* .... 45 F9   42 25N 12 14 E
Sorkh, Kuh-e, *Iran* .... 97 C8   35 40N 58 30 E
Sorø, *Denmark* .... 17 J5   55 26N 11 32 E
Soro, *Guinea* 112 C3   10 9N   9 48W
Soroca, *Moldova* .... 53 B13 48 8N 28 12 E
Sorocaba, *Brazil* .... 175 A6   23 31 S 47 27W
Sorochinsk, *Russia* .... 64 E4   52 26N 53 10 E
Soroki = Soroca, *Moldova* .... 53 B13 48 8N 28 12 E
Sorong, *Indonesia* .... 83 B4   0 55 S 131 15 E
Soroní, *Greece* .... 38 C12 36 21N 28 1 E
Soroti, *Uganda* .... 118 B3   1 43N 33 35 E
Sørøya, *Norway* .... 14 A20 70 40N 22 30 E
Sørøyane, *Norway* .... 18 B2   62 25N   5 32 E
Sørøysundet, *Norway* .... 14 A20 70 25N 23 0 E
Sorraia →, *Portugal* 43 G2   38 55N   8 53W
Sorrell, *Australia* .... 127 G4   42 47 S 147 34 E
Sorrento, *Italy* .... 47 B7   40 37N 14 22 E
Sorsele, *Sweden* .... 14 D17 65 31N 17 30 E

Sörsjön, *Sweden* .... 16 C7   61 24N 13 5 E
Sorso, *Italy* .... 46 B1   40 48N   8 34 E
Sorsogon, *Phil.* .... 80 E5   13 0N 124 0 E
Sorsogon □, *Phil.* .... 80 E4   12 50N 123 55 E
Sortavala, *Russia* .... 58 B6   61 42N 30 41 E
Sortino, *Italy* .... 47 E8   37 9N 15 2 E
Sortland, *Norway* .... 14 B16 68 42N 15 25 E
Sørum, *Norway* .... 18 D7   60 30N 10 17 E
Sørvika, *Norway* .... 18 B8   62 25N 11 14 E
Sorvizhi, *Russia* .... 60 B9   57 52N 48 32 E
Sos = Sos del Rey Católico, *Spain* .. 40 C3   42 30N   1 13W
Sos del Rey Católico, *Spain* 40 C3   42 30N   1 13W
Sôsan, *S. Korea* .... 75 F14 36 47N 126 27 E
Sosaq, *Kazakhstan* .... 65 A4   44 9N 68 27 E
Soscumica, L., *Canada* 140 B4   50 15N 77 27W
Sösdala, *Sweden* .... 17 H7   56 2N 13 41 E
Sosna →, *Russia* .... 59 F10 52 42N 38 55 E
Sosnogorsk, *Russia* .... 56 B9   63 37N 53 51 E
Sosnovka, *Kyrgyzstan* .... 65 B6   42 40N 73 50 E
Sosnovka, *Kirov, Russia* .... 60 B10 56 17N 51 17 E
Sosnovka, *Tambov, Russia* .... 60 D5   53 13N 41 24 E
Sosnovyy Bor, *Russia* .... 58 C5   59 55N 29 6 E
Sosnowiec, *Poland* .... 55 H6   50 20N 19 10 E
Soso, *C.A.R.* .... 114 B3   3 55N 15 30 E
Sospel, *France* .... 29 E11 43 52N   7 27 E
Sossus Vlei, *Namibia* .... 116 C2   24 40 S 15 23 E
Šoštanj, *Slovenia* .... 45 B12 46 23N 15 4 E
Sŏsura, *N. Korea* .... 75 C16 42 16N 130 36 E
Sosva, *Russia* .... 64 B8   59 10N 61 50 E
Sosva →, *Russia* .... 64 B9   59 21N 62 23 E
Sot →, *India* .... 93 F8   27 27N 79 37 E
Sotatevento, *C. Verde Is.* .... 9 j   15 0N 25 0W
Sotkamo, *Finland* .... 14 D23 64 8N 28 23 E
Soto del Barco, *Spain* 42 B4   43 32N   6 4W
Soto la Marina →, *Mexico* 163 C5   23 40N 97 40W
Soto y Amío, *Spain* 42 C5   42 46N   5 53W
Sotrondio, *Spain* 42 B5   43 17N   5 36W
Sotuf, Adrar, *W. Sahara* 110 D1   21 42N 15 36W
Sotuta, *Mexico* 163 C7   20 29N 89 43W
Souanké, *Congo* .... 114 B2   2 10N 14 3 E
Soubré, *Ivory C.* 112 D3   5 50N   6 35W
Souderton, *U.S.A.* 151 F9   40 19N 75 19W
Soúdha, *Greece* .... 39 E5   35 29N 24 4 E
Soúdhas, Kólpos, *Greece* .... 39 E5   35 25N 24 10 E
Soufflay, *Congo* .... 114 B2   2 1N 14 54 E
Souflion, *Greece* .... 51 E10 41 12N 26 18 E
Soufrière, *Guadeloupe* .... 164 b   16 5N 61 40W
Soufrière, *St. Lucia* .... 165 f   13 51N 61 3W
Soufrière Bay, *Domin.* .... 165 f   13 53N 61 6W
Souillac, *France* .... 28 D5   44 53N   1 29 E
Souilly, *France* .... 27 C12 49 3N   5 17 E
Souk-Ahras, *Algeria* .... 111 A6   36 23N   7 57 E
Souk el Arba du Rharb, *Morocco* 110 B3   34 43N   5 59W
Soukhouma, *Laos* .... 86 E5   14 38N 105 48 E
Soûl, *S. Korea* .... 75 F14 37 31N 126 58 E
Soulac-sur-Mer, *France* 28 C2   45 30N   1 7W
Soulári, *Greece* .... 39 C1   38 10N 20 25 E
Soulougou, *Burkina Faso* .... 113 C5   13 1N   0 25 E
Soultz-sous-Forêts, *France* .... 27 D14 48 57N   7 52 E
Sound, The = Øresund, *Europe* .... 17 J6   55 45N 12 45 E
Sound, The, *U.K.* 21 G3   50 20N   4 10W
Sound I., *India* .... 95 H11 12 58N 92 59 E
Soúnion, Ákra, *Greece* .... 38 D6   37 37N 24 1 E
Sour el Ghozlane, *Algeria* .... 111 A5   36 10N   3 45 E
Sources, Mt. aux, *Lesotho* .... 117 D4   28 45 S 28 52 E
Soure, *Brazil* .... 170 B2   0 35 S 48 30W
Soure, *Portugal* 42 E2   40 4N   8 38W
Souris, Man., *Canada* 143 D8   49 40N 100 20W
Souris, P.E.I., *Canada* 141 C7   46 21N 62 15W
Souris →, *Canada* 154 A5   49 40N 99 34W
Sourou →, *Africa* 112 C4   14 53N   3 25W
Soúrpi, *Greece* .... 48 B4   39 6N 22 54 E
Sous, O. →, *Morocco* 110 B3   30 27N   9 31W
Sousa, *Brazil* .... 170 C4   6 45 S 38 10W
Sousel, *Brazil* .... 170 B1   2 38 S 52 29W
Sousel, *Portugal* 43 G3   38 57N   7 40W
Souss-Massa Nat. Park △, *Morocco* ... 110 B3   31 26N   9 35W
Sousse, *Tunisia* .... 108 A2   35 50N 10 38 E
Soustons, *France* 28 E2   43 45N   1 19W
Sout →, *S. Africa* .... 116 E2   31 35 S 18 24 E
South Africa ■, *Africa* .... 116 E3   32 0 S 23 0 E
South America .... 166 E5   10 0 S 60 0W
South Andaman, *India* .... 95 J11 11 45N 92 10 E
South Atlantic Ocean .... 8 J10 20 0 S 10 0W
South Aulatsivik I., *Canada* 141 A7   56 45N 61 30W
South Australia □, *Australia* .... 128 B2   32 0 S 139 0 E
South Ayrshire □, *U.K.* 22 F4   55 18N   4 41W
South Baldy, *U.S.A.* 159 J10 33 59N 107 11W
South Bass I., *U.S.A.* 150 E2   41 38N 82 53W
South Bay, *U.S.A.* 153 J9   26 40N 80 43W
South Beach, *Bahamas* .... 9 b   25 1N 77 20W
South Beloit, *U.S.A.* 156 B7   42 29N 89 2W
South Bend, Ind., *U.S.A.* 157 C10 41 41N 86 15W
South Bend, Wash., *U.S.A.* 160 D3   46 40N 123 48W
South Boston, *U.S.A.* 157 G6   36 42N 78 54W
South Branch, *Canada* 141 C8   47 55N 59 2W
South Brook, *Canada* 141 C8   49 26N 56 5W
South Brother I., *India* .... 95 J11 10 56N 92 37 E
South C. = Ka Lae, *U.S.A.* 145 L6   18 55N 155 41W
South Carolina □, *U.S.A.* 149 J5   34 0N 81 0W
South Charleston, *U.S.A.* 148 F5   38 22N 81 44W
South China Sea, *Asia* .... 80 D2   10 0N 113 0 E
South Comino Channel, *Malta* .... 38 F7   36 0N 14 20 E
South Congaree, *U.S.A.* 152 B8   33 53N 81 9W
South Cotabato □, *Phil.* .... 81 J5   6 0N 125 0 E
South Cumberland Is. Nat. Park △,
   Australia .... 126 J7   20 42 S 149 11 E
South Dakota □, *U.S.A.* 154 C5   44 15N 100 0W
South Daytona, *U.S.A.* 153 F8   29 10N 81 0W
South Deerfield, *U.S.A.* 151 D12 42 29N 72 37W
South Downs, *U.K.* 21 G7   50 52N   0 25W
South East B., Ascension I. .... 9 g   7 57 S 14 18W
South East C., *Australia* .... 127 G4   43 40 S 146 50 E
South East Forests Nat. Park △,
   Australia .... 129 D8   37 0 S 149 30 E
South East Is., *Australia* .... 125 H7   34 17 S 123 30 E
South Elgin, *U.S.A.* 157 C8   42 0N 88 18W
South Esk →, *U.K.* 22 E6   56 43N   2 31W
South Foreland, *U.K.* .... 21 F9   51 8N   1 24 E
South Fork American →, *U.S.A.* 160 G5   38 45N 121 5W
South Fork Edisto →, *U.S.A.* 152 B9   33 16N 80 54W
South Fork Feather →, *U.S.A.* 160 F5   39 17N 121 36W
South Fork Grand →, *U.S.A.* 154 C3   45 43N 102 17W
South Fork Licking →, *U.S.A.* 157 F12 38 40N 84 18W
South Fork Republican →, *U.S.A.* 154 E4   40 3N 101 31W
South Georgia, *Antarctica* .... 7 B1   54 30 S 37 0W
South Gloucestershire □, *U.K.* 21 F5   51 32N   2 28W
South Grand →, *U.S.A.* 156 F3   38 17N 93 25W
South Hadley, *U.S.A.* 151 D12 42 16N 72 35W
South Haven, *U.S.A.* 157 B10 42 24N 86 16W
South Henik, L., *Canada* 143 A9   61 30N 97 30W
South Honshu Ridge, *Pac. Oc.* .... 134 E6   23 0N 143 0 E
South Horr, *Kenya* .... 118 B4   2 12N 36 56 E
South I., *India* .... 95 J1   10 3N 72 17 E
South I., *Kenya* .... 118 B4   2 35N 36 35 E
South I., *N.Z.* .... 131 E5   44 0 S 170 0 E
South Indian Lake, *Canada* 143 B9   56 47N 98 56W
South Invercargill, *N.Z.* .... 131 G3   46 26 S 168 23 E
South Island Nat. Park △, *Kenya* .... 118 B4   2 39N 36 35 E
South Kitui Nat. Reserve △, *Kenya* .. 118 C4   1 48 S 38 46 E
South Knife →, *Canada* 143 B10 58 55N 94 37W
South Koel →, *India* .... 93 H11 22 32N 85 14 E
South Korea ■, *Asia* .... 75 G15 36 0N 128 0 E

South Lake Tahoe, *U.S.A.* 160 G6   38 57N 119 59W
South Lanarkshire □, *U.K.* 22 F5   55 37N   3 53W
South Loup →, *U.S.A.* 154 E5   41 4N 98 39W
South Luangwa Nat. Park △, *Zambia* .. 119 E3   13 0 S 31 20 E
South Lyon, *U.S.A.* 157 B13 42 28N 83 39W
South Magnetic Pole, *Antarctica* .... 7 C9   64 8 S 138 8 E
South Miami, *U.S.A.* 153 K9   25 42N 80 18W
South Milwaukee, *U.S.A.* 157 B9   42 55N 87 52W
South Molton, *U.K.* 21 F4   51 1N   3 51W
South Monroe, *U.S.A.* 157 C13 41 54N 83 26W
South Moose L., *Canada* 143 C8   53 46N 100 8W
South Nahanni →, *Canada* 142 A4   61 3N 123 21W
South Nation →, *Canada* 151 A9   45 34N 75 6W
South Natuna Is. = Natuna Selatan,
   Kepulauan, *Indonesia* .... 85 B3   2 45N 109 0 E
South Negril Pt., *Jamaica* .... 164 a   18 14N 78 30W
South Newport, *U.S.A.* 152 D8   31 38N 81 24W
South Orkney Is., *Antarctica* .... 7 C18 63 0 S 45 0W
South Ossetia □, *Georgia* .... 61 J7   42 21N 44 2 E
South Pagai, I. = Pagai Selatan,
   Pulau, *Indonesia* .... 84 C2   3 0 S 100 15 E
South Paris, *U.S.A.* 151 B14 44 14N 70 31W
South Pekin, *U.S.A.* 156 D7   40 30N 89 39W
South Pittsburg, *U.S.A.* 149 H3   35 1N 85 42W
South Platte →, *U.S.A.* 154 E4   41 7N 100 42W
South Pole, *Antarctica* .... 7 E   90 0 S   0 0W
South Ponte Vedra Beach, *U.S.A.* 152 E8   30 3N 81 20W
South Porcupine, *Canada* 140 C3   48 30N 81 12W
South Portland, *U.S.A.* 149 D10 43 38N 70 15W
South Pt., *Ascension I.* .... 9 g   8 0 S 14 24W
South Pt., *Barbados* .... 165 g   13 2N 59 32W
South Pt., *U.S.A.* 150 B1   44 52N 83 19W
South River, *Canada* 140 C4   45 52N 79 23W
South River, *U.S.A.* 151 F10 40 27N 74 23W
South Ronaldsay, *U.K.* 22 C6   58 48N   2 58W
South Sandwich Is., *Antarctica* ..... 7 B1   57 0 S 27 0W
South Sandwich Trench, *Atl. Oc.* .... 8 M9   56 0 S 24 0W
South Saskatchewan →, *Canada* 143 C7   53 15N 105 5W
South Seal →, *Canada* 143 B9   58 48N 98 8W
South Sentinel I., *India* .... 95 J11 10 59N 92 14 E
South Shetland Is., *Antarctica* ..... 7 C18 62 0 S 59 0W
South Shields, *U.K.* 20 C6   55 0N   1 25W
South Sioux City, *U.S.A.* 154 D6   42 28N 96 24W
South Taranaki Bight, *N.Z.* .... 130 F3   39 40 S 174 5 E
South Thompson →, *Canada* 142 C4   50 40N 120 20W
South Twin I., *Canada* 140 B4   53 7N 79 52W
South Tyne →, *U.K.* 20 C5   54 59N   2 8W
South Ubian, *Phil.* .... 81 J3   5 11N 120 30 E
South Uist, *U.K.* 22 D1   57 20N   7 15W
South Venice, *U.S.A.* 153 H7   27 3N 82 25W
South Wayne, *U.S.A.* 156 B7   42 34N 89 53W
South West Africa = Namibia ■,
   Africa .... 116 C2   22 0 S 18 9 E
South West B., *Ascension I.* .... 9 g   7 58 S 14 25W
South West B., *Bahamas* .... 9 b   25 0N 77 32W
South West C., *Australia* .... 127 G4   43 34 S 146 3 E
South West Pt., Papua N. G. .... 132 B4   2 14 S 146 34 E
South West Pt., *St. Helena* .... 9 h   15 59 S   5 48W
South West Rocks, *Australia* .... 129 A10 30 52 S 153 3 E
South Whitley, *U.S.A.* .... 7 E   90 0 S   0 0W
South Williamsport, *U.S.A.* 150 E8   41 13N 77 0W
South Yemen = Yemen ■, *Asia* .... 98 D4   15 0N 44 0 E
South Yorkshire □, *U.K.* 20 D6   53 27N   1 36W
Southampton, *Canada* 150 D3   44 30N 81 25W
Southampton, *U.K.* 21 G6   50 54N   1 23W
Southampton, *U.S.A.* 151 F12 40 53N 72 23W
Southampton □, *U.K.* 21 G6   50 54N   1 23W
Southampton I., *Canada* 139 B11 64 30N 84 0W
Southaven, *U.S.A.* 155 H9   34 59N 90 2W
Southbank, *Canada* 142 C3   54 2N 125 46W
Southbridge, *N.Z.* .... 131 D7   43 48 S 172 16 E
Southbridge, *U.S.A.* 151 D12 42 5N 72 2W
Southeast C., *U.S.A.* 144 E5   62 56N 169 39W
Southeast Indian Rise, Ind. Oc. ..... 121 J10 50 0 S 100 0 E
Southend, *Canada* 143 B8   56 19N 103 22W
Southend-on-Sea, *U.K.* .... 21 F8   51 32N   0 44 E
Southend-on-Sea □, *U.K.* .... 21 F8   51 32N   0 44 E
Southern □, *Malawi* .... 119 F4   15 0 S 35 0 E
Southern □, *S. Leone* 112 D2   8 0N 12 30W
Southern □, *Zambia* .... 119 F2   16 20 S 26 20 E
Southern Alps, *N.Z.* .... 131 D5   43 41 S 170 11 E
Southern Cross, *Australia* .... 125 F2   31 12 S 119 15 E
Southern Highlands □, *Papua N. G.* .. 132 D2   6 15 S 143 25 E
Southern Indian L., *Canada* 143 B9   57 10N 98 30W
Southern Lau Group, *Fiji* .... 133 B3   18 40 S 178 40W
Southern Leyte □, *Phil.* .... 81 F5   10 30N 125 10 E
Southern Mid-Atlantic Ridge,
   Atl. Oc. .... 8 J10 21 0 S 13 0W
Southern Nat. Park △, *Sudan* .... 107 F2   6 50N 28 45 E
Southern Ocean, *Antarctica* .... 7 C6   62 0 S 60 0 E
Southern Pines, *U.S.A.* 153 H6   35 11N 79 24W
Southern Rhodesia = Zimbabwe ■,
   Africa .... 119 F3   19 0 S 30 0 E
Southern Uplands, *U.K.* 22 F5   55 28N   3 52W
Southfield, *U.S.A.* 157 B13 42 29N 83 17W
Southington, *U.S.A.* 151 E12 41 36N 72 53W
Southland □, *N.Z.* .... 131 F3   45 30 S 168 0 E
Southold, *U.S.A.* 151 E12 41 4N 72 26W
Southport, *Australia* .... 127 D5   27 58 S 153 25 E
Southport, *U.K.* 20 D4   53 39N   3 0W
Southport, Fla., *U.S.A.* 152 E4   30 17N 85 38W
Southport, N.Y., *U.S.A.* 150 D8   42 3N 76 49W
Southwest, *N.Z.* .... 131 H2   47 17 S 167 28 E
Southwest Nat. Park △, *Australia* ... 127 G4   43 8 S 146 5 E
Southwold, *U.K.* .... 21 E9   52 20N   1 41 E
Southwood Nat. Park △, *Australia* ... 127 D5   27 48 S 150 8 E
Soutpansberg, *S. Africa* .... 117 C4   23 0 S 29 30 E
Souvigny, *France* .... 27 F10 46 33N   3 10 E
Sovata, *Romania* .... 53 D10 46 35N 25 3 E
Soverato, *Italy* .... 47 D9   38 41N 16 33 E
Sovet, *Kyrgyzstan* .... 65 C5   40 11N 71 20 E
Sovetsk, Kaliningd., *Russia* .... 15 J19 55 6N 21 50 E
Sovetsk, Kirov, Russia .... 60 B9   57 38N 48 53 E
Sovetskaya Gavan = Vanino, Russia .... 67 E15 48 50N 140 5 E
Sovicille, *Italy* .... 45 E8   43 17N 11 13 E
Søvik, *Norway* .... 18 B3   62 33N   6 17 E
Soweto, *S. Africa* .... 117 D4   26 14 S 27 54 E
Sōya-Kaikyō = La Perouse Str., *Asia* 70 B11 45 40N 142 0 E
Sōya-Misaki, *Japan* .... 70 B10 45 30N 141 55 E
Soyaux, *France* .... 28 C4   45 39N   0 12 E
Soyo, *Angola* .... 115 D2   6 13 S 12 20 E
Sozh →, *Belarus* .... 59 F6   51 57N 30 48 E
Sozopol, *Bulgaria* .... 51 D11 42 23N 27 42 E
Spa, *Belgium* .... 24 D5   50 29N   5 53 E
Spain ■, *Europe* 13 H5   39 0N   4 0W
Spalato = Split, *Croatia* .... 45 E13 43 31N 16 26 E
Spalding, *Australia* .... 128 B3   33 30 S 138 37 E
Spalding, *U.K.* 20 E7   52 48N   0 9W
Spangler, *U.S.A.* 150 F6   40 39N 78 48W
Spanish, *Canada* 140 C3   46 12N 82 20W
Spanish Fork, *U.S.A.* 158 F8   40 7N 111 39W
Spanish Pt., *Bermuda* .... 9 a   32 17N 64 50W
Spanish Town, Br. Virgin Is. .... 165 e   18 43N 64 26W
Spanish Town, *Jamaica* .... 164 a   18 0N 76 57W
Sparks, Ga., *U.S.A.* 152 D6   31 11N 83 26W
Sparks, Nev., *U.S.A.* 160 G4   39 32N 119 45W
Sparreholm, *Sweden* .... 16 E10 59 4N 16 49 E
Sparta = Spárti, *Greece* .... 48 D4   37 5N 22 25 E
Sparta, Ill., *U.S.A.* 156 F7   38 8N 89 42W
Sparta, Mich., *U.S.A.* 157 A11 43 10N 85 42W
Sparta, Wis., *U.S.A.* 154 D9   43 56N 90 49W
Spartanburg, *U.S.A.* 149 H5   34 56N 81 57W

Spartansburg, *U.S.A.* 150 E5   41 49N 79 41W
Spartel, C., *Morocco* 110 A3   35 47N   5 56W
Spárti, *Greece* .... 48 D4   37 5N 22 25 E
Spartivento, C., Calabria, Italy ..... 47 E9   37 55N 16 4 E
Spartivento, C., Sard., Italy .... 46 D1   38 53N   8 50 E
Spartokhóri, *Greece* .... 39 B2   38 40N 20 46 E
Sparwood, *Canada* 142 D6   49 44N 114 53W
Spas-Demensk, *Russia* .... 58 E7   54 30N 34 0 E
Spas-Klepiki, *Russia* .... 58 E11 55 10N 40 10 E
Spassk Dalniy, *Russia* .... 67 E14 44 40N 132 48 E
Spassk-Ryazanskiy, *Russia* .... 58 E11 54 24N 40 25 E
Spátha, Ákra, *Greece* .... 39 E4   35 42N 23 43 E
Spatsizi →, *Canada* 142 B3   57 42N 128 7W
Spatsizi Plateau Wilderness Park △,
   Canada 142 B3   57 40N 128 0W
Spean →, *U.K.* 22 E4   56 55N   4 59W
Spearfish, *U.S.A.* 154 C3   44 30N 103 52W
Spearman, *U.S.A.* 155 G4   36 12N 101 12W
Speculator, *U.S.A.* 151 C10 43 30N 74 25W
Speed, *Australia* .... 128 C3   35 21 S 142 27 E
Speedway, *U.S.A.* 157 E10 39 47N 86 15W
Speer, *Switz.* .... 33 B8   47 12N   9 8 E
Speery I., *St. Helena* .... 9 h   16 1 S   5 46W
Speia, *Moldova* .... 53 D14 46 59N 29 19 E
Speightstown, *Barbados* .... 165 g   13 15N 59 39W
Speke Gulf, *Tanzania* .... 118 C3   2 20 S 32 50 E
Spello, *Italy* .... 45 F9   42 59N 12 40 E
Spenard, *U.S.A.* 146 B5   61 11N 149 55W
Spencer, Idaho, *U.S.A.* 158 D7   44 22N 112 11W
Spencer, Ind., *U.S.A.* 157 E10 39 17N 86 46W
Spencer, Iowa, *U.S.A.* 154 D7   43 9N 95 9W
Spencer, N.Y., *U.S.A.* 151 D8   42 13N 76 30W
Spencer, Nebr., *U.S.A.* 154 D5   42 53N 98 42W
Spencer, C., *Australia* .... 128 C2   35 20 S 136 53 E
Spencer B., *Namibia* .... 116 D1   25 30 S 14 47 E
Spencer G., *Australia* .... 128 C2   34 0 S 137 20 E
Spencerville, *Canada* 151 B9   44 51N 75 33W
Spencerville, *U.S.A.* 157 D12 40 43N 84 21W
Spences Bridge, *Canada* 142 C4   50 25N 121 20W
Spennymoor, *U.K.* 20 C6   54 42N   1 36W
Spenser Mts., *N.Z.* .... 131 C7   42 15 S 172 45 E
Spentrup, *Denmark* .... 17 H4   56 33N 10 2 E
Sperillen, *Norway* .... 18 D7   60 28N 10 3 E
Sperkhiós →, *Greece* .... 48 C4   38 57N 22 3 E
Sperrin Mts., *U.K.* 23 B5   54 50N   7 0W
Spessart, *Germany* .... 31 E5   49 56N   9 18 E
Spetalen, *Norway* .... 18 E7   59 18N 10 45 E
Spétsai, *Greece* .... 48 D5   37 15N 23 10 E
Spey →, *U.K.* 22 D5   57 40N   3 6W
Speyer, *Germany* .... 31 F4   49 29N   8 25 E
Spezand, *Pakistan* .... 92 E2   29 59N 67 0 E
Spezzano Albanese, *Italy* .... 47 C9   39 40N 16 19 E
Spickard, *U.S.A.* 156 D3   40 14N 93 36W
Spiekeroog, *Germany* .... 30 B3   53 46N   7 42 E
Spiez, *Switz.* .... 32 C5   46 40N   7 40 E
Spíli, *Greece* .... 39 E5   35 13N 24 31 E
Spilimbergo, *Italy* .... 45 B9   46 7N 12 54 E
Spīn Būldak, *Afghan.* .... 91 C2   31 1N 66 25 E
Spinalónga, *Greece* .... 39 E6   35 18N 25 44 E
Spinazzola, *Italy* .... 47 B9   40 58N 16 5 E
Spineni, *Romania* .... 53 F9   44 43N 24 37 E
Spirit Lake, *U.S.A.* 160 D4   46 15N 122 9W
Spirit River, *Canada* 142 B5   55 45N 118 50W
Spiritwood, *Canada* 143 C7   53 24N 107 33W
Spišská Nová Ves, Slovak Rep. .... 35 C13 48 58N 20 34 E
Spišské Podhradie, Slovak Rep. .... 35 B13 49 0N 20 48 E
Spital, *Austria* .... 34 D7   47 42N 14 18 E
Spithead, *U.K.* 21 G6   50 45N   1 10W
Spittal an der Drau, *Austria* .... 34 E6   46 48N 13 31 E
Spitzbergen = Svalbard, *Arctic* ..... 6 B8   78 0N 17 0 E
Spjelkavik, *Norway* .... 18 B3   62 28N   6 22 E
Split, *Croatia* .... 45 E13 43 31N 16 26 E
Split ✈ (SPU), *Croatia* .... 45 E13 43 33N 16 15 E
Split L., *Canada* 143 B9   56 8N 96 15W
Split Lake, *Canada* 143 B9   56 8N 96 15W
Splitski Kanal, *Croatia* .... 45 E13 43 31N 16 20 E
Splügen, *Switz.* .... 33 C8   46 34N   9 21 E
Splügenpass, *Switz.* .... 33 D8   46 30N   9 20 E
Spofford, *U.S.A.* 155 L4   29 10N 100 25W
Spokane, *U.S.A.* 158 C5   47 40N 117 24W
Spoleto, *Italy* .... 45 F9   42 44N 12 44 E
Sponvika, *Norway* .... 18 E8   59 7N 11 15 E
Spoon →, *U.S.A.* 156 D6   40 19N 90 4W
Spooner, *U.S.A.* 154 C9   45 50N 91 53W
Sporyy Navolok, Mys, *Russia* .... 66 B7   75 50N 68 40 E
Sprague, *U.S.A.* 158 C5   47 18N 117 59W
Spratly I., S. China Sea .... 78 C4   8 38N 111 55 E
Spratly Is., S. China Sea .... 78 C4   8 20N 112 0 E
Spray, *U.S.A.* 158 D4   44 50N 119 48W
Spreča →, Bos.-H. .... 52 F3   44 44N 18 6 E
Spree →, *Germany* .... 30 C9   52 32N 13 13 E
Spreewald, *Germany* .... 30 D9   51 58N 13 51 E
Spremberg, *Germany* .... 30 D10 51 34N 14 22 E
Sprengisandur, *Iceland* 11 C8   64 52N 18 7W
Spring City, *U.S.A.* 151 F9   40 11N 75 33W
Spring Cr. →, *U.S.A.* 152 E5   30 54N 84 45W
Spring Creek, *U.S.A.* 158 F6   40 45N 115 38W
Spring Garden, Guyana 169 B6   6 59N 58 31W
Spring Garden, *U.S.A.* 160 F6   39 52N 120 47W
Spring Green, *U.S.A.* 156 A6   43 11N 90 4W
Spring Hall, *Barbados* .... 165 g   13 18N 59 36W
Spring Hill, Ala., U.S.A. 152 D4   31 42N 85 58W
Spring Hill, Fla., U.S.A. 153 G7   28 27N 82 41W
Spring Mts., *U.S.A.* 159 H6   36 0N 115 45W
Spring Valley, Calif., U.S.A. 161 N10 32 45N 117 5W
Spring Valley, Ill., U.S.A. 156 C7   41 20N 89 12W
Springbok, *S. Africa* .... 116 D2   29 42 S 17 54 E
Springboro, *U.S.A.* 150 E4   41 48N 80 22W
Springdale, *Canada* 141 C8   49 30N 56 6W
Springdale, Ark., U.S.A. 155 G7   36 11N 94 8W
Springdale, Ohio, U.S.A. 157 E12 39 17N 84 29W
Springe, *Germany* .... 30 C5   52 13N   9 33 E
Springer, *U.S.A.* 155 G2   36 22N 104 36W
Springerville, *U.S.A.* 159 J9   34 8N 109 17W
Springfield, *Canada* 150 D4   42 50N 80 56W
Springfield, *N.Z.* .... 131 D7   43 19 S 171 56 E
Springfield, Colo., U.S.A. 155 G3   37 24N 102 37W
Springfield, Fla., U.S.A. 152 E4   30 10N 85 37W
Springfield, Ga., U.S.A. 152 C8   32 22N 81 18W
Springfield, Ill., U.S.A. 156 F7   39 48N 89 39W
Springfield, Ky., U.S.A. 157 G11 37 41N 85 13W
Springfield, Mass., U.S.A. 151 D12 42 6N 72 35W
Springfield, Mo., U.S.A. 155 G8   37 13N 93 17W
Springfield, Ohio, U.S.A. 157 E13 39 55N 83 49W
Springfield, Oreg., U.S.A. 158 D2   44 3N 123 1W
Springfield, Tenn., U.S.A. 149 G2   36 31N 86 53W
Springfield, Vt., U.S.A. 151 C12 43 18N 72 29W
Springfontein, S. Africa .... 116 E4   30 15 S 25 40 E
Springhill, *U.S.A.* 155 J8   33 0N 93 28W
Springhouse, *Canada* 141 C7   45 40N 64 4W
Springs, S. Africa .... 117 D4   26 13 S 28 25 E
Springsure, *Australia* .... 126 C4   24 8 S 148 6 E
Springvale, *U.S.A.* 151 C14 43 28N 70 48W
Springvale, Maine, U.S.A. 151 C14 43 28N 70 48W
Springville, Calif., U.S.A. 160 J8   36 8N 118 49W
Springville, N.Y., U.S.A. 150 D6   42 31N 78 40W
Springville, Utah, U.S.A. 158 F8   40 10N 111 37W
Springwater, *U.S.A.* 150 D7   42 38N 77 35W
Spruce-Creek, *U.S.A.* 150 F6   40 36N 78 9W

Spruce Knob-Seneca Rocks Nat. Recr. Area ⌓, *U.S.A.* **148 F6** 38 50N 79 30W
Spruce Mt., *U.S.A.* **151 B12** 44 12N 72 19W
Spur, *U.S.A.* **155 J4** 33 28N 100 52W
Spurn Hd., *U.K.* **20 D8** 53 35N 0 8 E
Spuž, *Montenegro, Yug.* **50 D3** 42 32N 19 10 E
Spuzzum, *Canada* **142 D4** 49 37N 121 23W
Spydeberg, *Norway* **18 E8** 59 36N 11 5 E
Squam L., *U.S.A.* **151 C13** 43 45N 71 32W
Squamish, *Canada* **142 D4** 49 45N 123 10W
Square Islands, *Canada* **141 B8** 52 47N 55 47W
Squillace, G. di, *Italy* **47 D9** 38 45N 16 50 E
Squinzano, *Italy* **47 B11** 40 26N 18 2 E
Squires, Mt., *Australia* **125 E4** 26 14 S 127 28 E
Sragen, *Indonesia* **85 D4** 7 26 S 111 2 E
Srbac, *Bos.-H.* **52 E2** 45 7N 17 30 E
Srbica, *Kosovo, Yug.* **50 D4** 42 45N 20 47 E
Srbija = Serbia □, *Yugoslavia* **50 C5** 43 30N 21 0 E
Srbobran, *Serbia, Yug.* **52 E4** 45 32N 19 48 E
Sre Ambel, *Cambodia* **87 G4** 11 8N 103 46 E
Sre Khtum, *Cambodia* **87 F6** 12 10N 106 52 E
Sre Umbell = Sre Ambel, *Cambodia* **87 G4** 11 8N 103 46 E
Srebrenica, *Bos.-H.* **52 F4** 44 6N 19 18 E
Sredinny Ra. = Sredinnyy Khrebet, *Russia* **67 D16** 57 0N 160 0 E
Sredinnyy Khrebet, *Russia* **67 D16** 57 0N 160 0 E
Središće, *Slovenia* **45 B13** 46 24N 16 17 E
Sredna Gora, *Bulgaria* **51 D8** 42 40N 24 20 E
Srednekolymsk, *Russia* **67 C16** 67 27N 153 40 E
Sredni Rodopi, *Bulgaria* **51 E8** 41 40N 24 45 E
Srednogorie, *Bulgaria* **51 D8** 42 43N 24 10 E
Śrem, *Poland* **55 F4** 52 6N 17 2 E
Sremska Mitrovica, *Serbia, Yug.* **52 F4** 44 59N 19 38 E
Sremski Karlovci, *Serbia, Yug.* **52 E4** 45 12N 19 56 E
Srepok →, *Cambodia* **86 F6** 13 33N 106 16 E
Sretensk, *Russia* **67 D12** 52 10N 117 40 E
Sri Kalahasti, *India* **95 H4** 13 45N 79 44 E
Sri Lanka ■, *Asia* **95 L5** 7 30N 80 50 E
Sriharikota I., *India* **95 H5** 13 40N 80 20 E
Srikakulam, *India* **94 E6** 18 14N 83 58 E
Srinagar, *India* **93 B6** 34 5N 74 50 E
Sripur, *Bangla.* **90 C3** 24 14N 90 30 E
Srivardhan, *India* **94 E1** 18 4N 73 3 E
Srivilliputtur, *India* **95 K3** 9 31N 77 40 E
Środa Śląska, *Poland* **55 G3** 51 10N 16 36 E
Środa Wielkopolski, *Poland* **55 F4** 52 15N 17 19 E
Srono, *Indonesia* **79 J17** 8 24 S 114 16 E
Srpska Crnja, *Serbia, Yug.* **52 E5** 45 38N 20 44 E
Srpski Itebej, *Serbia, Yug.* **52 E5** 45 35N 20 44 E
Srungavarapukota, *India* **94 E6** 18 7N 83 10 E
Staaten →, *Australia* **126 B3** 16 24 S 141 17 E
Staaten River Nat. Park △, *Australia* **126 B3** 16 15 S 142 40 E
Staberhuk, *Germany* **30 A7** 54 23N 11 18 E
Stade, *Germany* **30 B5** 53 35N 9 29 E
Staðarfell, *Iceland* **11 B4** 65 7N 22 12W
Staðarhólskirkja, *Iceland* **11 B5** 65 23N 21 58W
Staðastaður, *Iceland* **11 C3** 64 49N 23 1W
Stadhavet, *Norway* **18 B2** 62 13N 5 0 E
Staður, *Húnavatnssýsla, Iceland* **11 B5** 65 9N 21 3W
Staður, *Ísafjarðarsýsla, Iceland* **11 A4** 66 15N 22 50W
Stadlandet, *Norway* **18 B2** 62 10N 5 10 E
Stadskanaal, *Neths.* **24 A6** 53 4N 6 55 E
Stadtallendorf, *Germany* **30 E5** 50 48N 9 1 E
Stadthagen, *Germany* **30 C5** 52 19N 9 13 E
Stadtlohn, *Germany* **30 D2** 51 59N 6 55 E
Stadtroda, *Germany* **30 E7** 50 52N 11 44 E
Stäfa, *Switz.* **33 B7** 47 14N 8 45 E
Stafafell, *Iceland* **11 C12** 64 25N 14 52W
Staffa, *U.K.* **22 E2** 56 27N 6 21W
Staffanstorp, *Sweden* **17 J7** 55 39N 13 13 E
Stafford, *U.K.* **20 E5** 52 49N 2 7W
Stafford, *U.S.A.* **155 G5** 37 58N 98 36W
Stafford, L., *U.S.A.* **153 F7** 29 20N 82 29W
Stafford Springs, *U.S.A.* **151 E12** 41 57N 72 18W
Staffordshire □, *U.K.* **20 E5** 52 53N 2 10W
Stagnone, *Italy* **46 E5** 37 53N 12 26 E
Stagnone di Marsala, Riserva Naturale Isole dello ⌓, *Italy* **46 E5** 37 52N 12 26 E
Staines, *U.K.* **21 F7** 51 26N 0 29W
Stainz, *Austria* **34 E8** 46 53N 15 17 E
Stakhanov, *Ukraine* **59 H10** 48 35N 38 40 E
Stalać, *Serbia, Yug.* **50 C5** 43 43N 21 28 E
Stalden, *Switz.* **32 D5** 46 14N 7 52 E
Stalin = Kuçovë, *Albania* **50 F3** 40 47N 19 57 E
Stalin = Varna, *Bulgaria* **51 C11** 43 13N 27 56 E
Stalinabad = Dushanbe, *Tajikistan* **65 D4** 38 33N 68 48 E
Stalingrad = Volgograd, *Russia* **61 F7** 48 40N 44 25 E
Staliniri = Tskhinvali, *Georgia* **61 J7** 42 14N 44 1 E
Stalino = Donetsk, *Ukraine* **59 J9** 48 0N 37 45 E
Stalinogorsk = Novomoskovsk, *Russia* **58 E10** 54 5N 38 15 E
Stalinogrod = Katowice, *Poland* **55 H6** 50 17N 19 5 E
Stalinsk = Novokuznetsk, *Russia* **66 D9** 53 45N 87 10 E
Stalinstadt = Eisenhüttenstadt, *Germany* **30 C10** 52 9N 14 38 E
Stallarholmen, *Sweden* **16 E11** 59 22N 17 12 E
Ställdalen, *Sweden* **16 E8** 59 56N 14 56 E
Stalowa Wola, *Poland* **55 H9** 50 34N 22 3 E
Stalybridge, *U.K.* **20 D5** 53 28N 2 3W
Stamford, *Australia* **126 C3** 21 15 S 143 46 E
Stamford, *U.K.* **21 E7** 52 39N 0 29W
Stamford, *Conn., U.S.A.* **151 E11** 41 3N 73 32W
Stamford, *N.Y., U.S.A.* **151 D10** 42 25N 74 38W
Stamford, *Tex., U.S.A.* **155 J5** 32 57N 99 48W
Stamnes, *Norway* **18 D2** 60 40N 5 45 E
Stamping Ground, *U.S.A.* **157 F12** 38 16N 84 41W
Stampriet, *Namibia* **116 C2** 24 20 S 18 28 E
Stamps, *U.S.A.* **155 J8** 33 22N 93 30W
Stanberry, *U.S.A.* **156 D2** 40 13N 94 35W
Stančevo = Kalipetrovo, *Bulgaria* **51 B11** 44 5N 27 14 E
Standerton, *S. Africa* **117 D4** 26 55 S 29 7 E
Standish, *U.S.A.* **148 D4** 43 59N 83 57W
Stanford, *S. Africa* **116 E2** 34 26 S 19 29 E
Stanford, *U.S.A.* **158 C8** 47 9N 110 13W
Stånga, *Sweden* **17 G12** 57 17N 18 29 E
Stange, *Norway* **18 D8** 60 43N 11 5 E
Stanger, *S. Africa* **117 D5** 29 27 S 31 14 E
Stangvik, *Norway* **18 B5** 62 55N 8 28 E
Stanhope, *Australia* **129 D6** 36 27 S 144 59 E
Stanhope, *U.S.A.* **156 B3** 42 17N 93 48W
Stanišić, *Serbia, Yug.* **52 E4** 45 56N 19 10 E
Stanislaus →, *U.S.A.* **160 H5** 37 40N 121 14W
Stanislav = Ivano-Frankivsk, *Ukraine* **59 H3** 48 40N 24 40 E
Stanisławów, *Poland* **55 F8** 52 18N 21 33 E
Stanley, *Australia* **127 G4** 40 46 S 145 19 E
Stanley, *Canada* **143 B8** 55 24N 104 22W
Stanley, *China* **69 G11** 22 13N 114 12 E
Stanley, *Falk. Is.* **9 f** 51 40 S 59 51W
Stanley, *U.K.* **20 C6** 54 53N 1 41W
Stanley, *Idaho, U.S.A.* **158 D6** 44 13N 114 56W
Stanley, *N. Dak., U.S.A.* **154 A3** 48 19N 102 23W
Stanley, *N.Y., U.S.A.* **150 D7** 42 48N 77 6W
Stanley Res., *India* **95 J3** 11 50N 77 40 E
Stanleyville = Kisangani, *Dem. Rep. of the Congo* **118 B2** 0 35N 25 15 E
Stanovoy Khrebet, *Russia* **67 D13** 55 0N 130 0 E
Stanovoy Ra. = Stanovoy Khrebet, *Russia* **67 D13** 55 0N 130 0 E
Stans, *Switz.* **33 C6** 46 58N 8 21 E
Stansmore Ra., *Australia* **124 D4** 21 23 S 128 33 E
Stansted, London ✈ (STN), *U.K.* **21 F8** 51 54N 0 14 E
Stanthorpe, *Australia* **127 D5** 28 36 S 151 59 E
Stanton, *Ky., U.S.A.* **157 G13** 37 54N 83 52W
Stanton, *Tex., U.S.A.* **155 J4** 32 8N 101 48W
Stanwood, *U.S.A.* **160 B4** 48 15N 122 23W
Staples, *U.S.A.* **154 B7** 46 21N 94 48W
Stąporków, *Poland* **55 G7** 51 9N 20 31 E
Star City, *Canada* **143 C8** 52 50N 104 20W
Star Harbour, *Solomon Is.* **133 N12** 10 47 S 162 19 E
Star Lake, *U.S.A.* **151 B9** 44 10N 75 2W
Stará L'ubovňa, *Slovak Rep.* **35 B13** 49 18N 20 42 E
Stara Moravica, *Serbia, Yug.* **52 E4** 45 50N 19 30 E
Stara Pazova, *Serbia, Yug.* **52 F5** 44 58N 20 10 E
Stara Planina, *Bulgaria* **50 C7** 43 15N 23 0 E
Stará Turá, *Slovak Rep.* **35 C10** 48 47N 17 42 E
Stara Zagora, *Bulgaria* **51 D9** 42 26N 25 39 E
Starachowice, *Poland* **55 G8** 51 3N 21 2 E
Staraya Russa, *Russia* **58 D6** 57 58N 31 23 E
Starbuck I., *Kiribati* **135 H12** 5 37 S 155 55W
Starchiojd, *Romania* **53 E11** 45 19N 26 11 E
Starcke Nat. Park △, *Australia* **126 A4** 14 56 S 145 2 E
Stargard Szczeciński, *Poland* **54 E2** 53 20N 15 0 E
Stårheim, *Norway* **18 C2** 61 56N 5 40 E
Stari Bar, *Montenegro, Yug.* **50 D3** 42 7N 19 10 E
Stari Trg, *Slovenia* **45 C12** 45 29N 15 7 E
Staritsa, *Russia* **58 D8** 56 33N 34 55 E
Starke, *U.S.A.* **152 F7** 29 57N 82 7W
Starnberg, *Germany* **31 H7** 48 0N 11 21 E
Starnberger See, *Germany* **31 H7** 47 54N 11 19 E
Starobilsk, *Ukraine* **59 H10** 49 16N 39 0 E
Starodub, *Russia* **59 F7** 52 30N 32 50 E
Starogard Gdański, *Poland* **54 E5** 53 59N 18 30 E
Starokonstantinov = Starokonstyantyniv, *Ukraine* **59 H4** 49 48N 27 10 E
Starokonstyantyniv, *Ukraine* **59 H4** 49 48N 27 10 E
Starominskaya, *Russia* **59 J10** 46 33N 39 0 E
Staroshcherbinovskaya, *Russia* **59 J10** 46 40N 38 53 E
Starrs Mill, *U.S.A.* **152 B5** 33 19N 84 31W
Start Pt., *U.K.* **21 G4** 50 13N 3 39W
Stary Sącz, *Poland* **55 J7** 49 33N 20 35 E
Staryy Biryuzyak, *Russia* **61 H8** 44 46N 46 50 E
Staryy Chartoriysk, *Ukraine* **59 G3** 51 15N 25 54 E
Staryy Krym, *Ukraine* **59 K8** 45 3N 35 8 E
Staryy Oskol, *Russia* **59 G9** 51 19N 37 55 E
Stassfurt, *Germany* **30 D7** 51 51N 11 35 E
Staszów, *Poland* **55 H8** 50 33N 21 10 E
State Center, *U.S.A.* **156 B3** 42 1N 93 10W
State College, *U.S.A.* **150 F7** 40 48N 77 52W
Stateline, *U.S.A.* **160 G7** 38 57N 119 56W
Staten, I. = Estados, I. de Los, *Argentina* **176 D4** 54 40 S 64 30W
Staten I., *U.S.A.* **151 F10** 40 35N 74 9W
Statenville, *U.S.A.* **152 E6** 30 42N 83 2W
Statesboro, *U.S.A.* **152 C8** 32 27N 81 47W
Statesville, *U.S.A.* **149 H5** 35 47N 80 53W
Statham, *U.S.A.* **152 B6** 33 58N 83 35W
Stathelle, *Norway* **18 E6** 59 3N 9 41 E
Stauffer, *U.S.A.* **161 L7** 34 45N 119 3W
Staunton, *Ill., U.S.A.* **156 F7** 39 1N 89 47W
Staunton, *Va., U.S.A.* **148 F6** 38 9N 79 4W
Stavanger, *Norway* **18 F2** 58 57N 5 40 E
Stavelot, *Belgium* **24 D5** 50 23N 5 55 E
Stavern, *Norway* **18 F7** 59 0N 10 1 E
Stavoren, *Neths.* **24 B5** 52 53N 5 22 E
Stavropol, *Russia* **61 H6** 45 5N 42 0 E
Stavros, *Cyprus* **39 E8** 35 1N 32 38 E
Stavrós, *Ithákí, Greece* **39 C2** 38 27N 20 39 E
Stavrós, *Kríti, Greece* **39 E5** 35 12N 24 45 E
Stavrós, Ákra, *Greece* **39 E5** 35 26N 24 58 E
Stavroúpolis, *Greece* **51 E8** 41 12N 24 45 E
Stawell, *Australia* **128 D5** 37 5 S 142 47 E
Stawell →, *Australia* **126 C3** 20 20 S 142 55 E
Stawiski, *Poland* **54 E9** 53 22N 22 9 E
Stawiszyn, *Poland* **55 G5** 51 56N 18 4 E
Stayner, *Canada* **150 B4** 44 25N 80 5W
Stayton, *U.S.A.* **158 D2** 44 48N 122 48W
Steamboat Springs, *U.S.A.* **158 F10** 40 29N 106 50W
Steane, *Norway* **18 E5** 59 16N 8 33 E
Stebbins, *U.S.A.* **144 E7** 63 31N 162 17W
Steblevë, *Albania* **50 E4** 41 23N 20 33 E
Steckborn, *Switz.* **33 A7** 47 44N 8 59 E
Steele, *Ala., U.S.A.* **152 B3** 33 56N 86 12W
Steele, *N. Dak., U.S.A.* **154 B5** 46 51N 99 55W
Steelton, *U.S.A.* **150 F8** 40 14N 76 50W
Steelville, *U.S.A.* **156 G5** 37 58N 91 22W
Steen River, *Canada* **142 B5** 59 40N 117 12W
Steenkool = Bintuni, *Indonesia* **83 B4** 2 7 S 133 32 E
Steens Mt., *U.S.A.* **158 E4** 42 35N 118 40W
Steenstrup Gletscher, *Greenland* **10 B5** 75 15N 57 0W
Steenwijk, *Neths.* **24 B6** 52 47N 6 7 E
Steep Pt., *Australia* **125 E1** 26 8 S 113 8 E
Steep Rock, *Canada* **143 C9** 51 30N 98 48W
Ştefan Vodă, *Moldova* **53 D14** 46 27N 29 42 E
Ştefăneşti, *Romania* **53 C12** 47 44N 27 15 E
Stefanie L. = Chew Bahir, *Ethiopia* **107 G4** 4 40N 36 50 E
Stefanie Nat. Park △, *Ethiopia* **107 G4** 4 55N 36 55 E
Stefansson Bay, *Antarctica* **7 C5** 67 20 S 59 8 E
Steffisburg, *Switz.* **32 C5** 46 47N 7 38 E
Stege, *Denmark* **17 K6** 54 59N 12 18 E
Ştei, *Romania* **52 D7** 46 32N 22 27 E
Steiermark □, *Austria* **34 D8** 47 26N 15 0 E
Steigerwald, *Germany* **31 F6** 49 44N 10 26 E
Steigerwald, Naturpark ⌓, *Germany* **31 F6** 49 50N 10 30 E
Steilacoom, *U.S.A.* **160 C4** 47 10N 122 36W
Steilrandberge, *Namibia* **116 B1** 17 45 S 13 20 E
Stein am Rhein, *Switz.* **33 A7** 47 39N 8 51 E
Steinbach, *Canada* **143 D9** 49 32N 96 40W
Steinfurt, *Germany* **30 C3** 52 9N 7 20 E
Steinhatchee, *U.S.A.* **152 F6** 29 40N 83 23W
Steinhausen, *Namibia* **116 C2** 21 49 S 18 20 E
Steinheim, *Germany* **30 D5** 51 50N 9 5 E
Steinhuder Meer, *Germany* **30 C5** 52 29N 9 21 E
Steinhuder Meer, Naturpark ⌓, *Germany* **30 C5** 52 30N 9 16 E
Steinkjer, *Norway* **14 D14** 64 1N 11 31 E
Steinkopf, *S. Africa* **116 D2** 29 18 S 17 43 E
Steinshamn, *Norway* **18 B3** 62 47N 6 28 E
Steinwald, Naturpark ⌓, *Germany* **31 F8** 49 55N 12 8 E
Stellarton, *Canada* **141 C7** 45 32N 62 30W
Stellenbosch, *S. Africa* **116 E2** 33 58 S 18 50 E
Stelvio, Paso dello, *Italy* **33 C10** 46 32N 10 27 E
Stenay, *France* **27 C12** 49 29N 5 12 E
Stendal, *Germany* **30 C7** 52 36N 11 53 E
Stende, *Latvia* **54 A9** 57 11N 22 33 E
Stenhamra, *Sweden* **16 E11** 59 20N 17 41 E
Stenón Ithákis, *Greece* **39 C2** 38 22N 20 39 E
Stenón Kerkiras, *Greece* **38 B10** 39 36N 20 5 E
Stenshuvud Nationalpark △, *Sweden* **17 J8** 55 39N 14 15 E
Stenstorp, *Sweden* **17 F7** 58 17N 13 45 E
Stenungsund, *Sweden* **17 F5** 58 6N 11 50 E
Steornabhaigh = Stornoway, *U.K.* **22 C2** 58 13N 6 23W
Stepanakert = Xankändi, *Azerbaijan* **101 C12** 39 52N 46 49 E
Stepanavan, *Armenia* **61 K7** 41 1N 44 23 E
Stephens, C., *N.Z.* **131 A8** 40 42 S 173 58 E
Stephens Creek, *Australia* **128 A4** 31 50 S 141 30 E
Stephens I., *Canada* **142 C2** 54 10N 130 45W
Stephens I., *N.Z.* **131 A9** 40 40 S 174 1 E
Stephens L., *Canada* **143 B9** 56 32N 95 0W
Stephenville, *Canada* **141 C8** 48 31N 58 35W
Stephenville, *U.S.A.* **155 J5** 32 13N 98 12W
Stepnica, *Poland* **54 E1** 53 38N 14 36 E
Stepnoi = Elista, *Russia* **61 G7** 46 16N 44 14 E
Stepnoye, *Russia* **64 D8** 54 4N 60 26 E
Steppe, *Asia* **62 D9** 50 0N 50 0 E
Stereá Ellas □, *Greece* **48 C4** 38 50N 23 0 E
Sterkstroom, *S. Africa* **116 E4** 31 32 S 26 32 E
Sterling, *Alaska, U.S.A.* **144 F10** 60 32N 150 46W
Sterling, *Colo., U.S.A.* **154 E3** 40 37N 103 13W
Sterling, *Ga., U.S.A.* **152 D8** 31 16N 81 34W
Sterling, *Ill., U.S.A.* **156 C7** 41 48N 89 42W
Sterling, *Kans., U.S.A.* **154 F5** 38 13N 98 12W
Sterling City, *U.S.A.* **155 K4** 31 51N 101 0W
Sterling Heights, *U.S.A.* **157 B13** 42 35N 83 0W
Sterling Run, *U.S.A.* **150 E6** 41 25N 78 12W
Sterlitamak, *Russia* **64 E6** 53 40N 56 0 E
Sternberg, *Germany* **30 B7** 53 42N 11 50 E
Šternberk, *Czech Rep.* **35 B10** 49 45N 17 15 E
Stérnes, *Greece* **39 E5** 35 30N 24 9 E
Sterzing = Vipiteno, *Italy* **45 B8** 46 54N 11 26 E
Stettin = Szczecin, *Poland* **54 E1** 53 27N 14 27 E
Stettiner Haff, *Germany* **30 B10** 53 47N 14 15 E
Stettler, *Canada* **142 C6** 52 19N 112 40W
Steubenville, *U.S.A.* **150 F4** 40 22N 80 37W
Stevenage, *U.K.* **21 F7** 51 55N 0 13W
Stevens Point, *U.S.A.* **154 C10** 44 31N 89 34W
Stevens Pottery, *U.S.A.* **152 C6** 32 57N 83 17W
Stevens Village, *U.S.A.* **144 C10** 66 1N 149 6W
Stevenson, *U.S.A.* **160 E5** 45 42N 121 53W
Stevenson L., *Canada* **143 C9** 53 55N 96 0W
Stevensville, *U.S.A.* **158 C6** 46 30N 114 5W
Stevns Klint, *Denmark* **17 J6** 55 17N 12 28 E
Steward, *U.S.A.* **156 C7** 41 51N 89 1W
Stewardson, *U.S.A.* **157 E8** 39 16N 88 38W
Stewart, *Canada* **142 B3** 55 56N 129 57W
Stewart, *Ga., U.S.A.* **152 B6** 33 25N 83 52W
Stewart, *Nev., U.S.A.* **160 F7** 39 5N 119 46W
Stewart →, *Canada* **138 B6** 63 19N 139 26W
Stewart, C., *Australia* **126 A1** 11 57 S 134 56 E
Stewart, I., *Chile* **176 D2** 54 50 S 71 15W
Stewart I., *N.Z.* **131 G2** 46 58 S 167 54 E
Stewarts Point, *U.S.A.* **160 G3** 38 39N 123 24W
Stewartsville, *U.S.A.* **156 E2** 39 45N 94 30W
Stewartville, *U.S.A.* **154 D8** 43 51N 92 29W
Stewiacke, *Canada* **141 C7** 45 9N 63 22W
Steynsburg, *S. Africa* **116 E4** 31 15 S 25 49 E
Steyr, *Austria* **34 C7** 48 3N 14 25 E
Steyr →, *Austria* **34 C7** 48 3N 14 25 E
Steytlerville, *S. Africa* **116 E3** 33 17 S 24 19 E
Stia, *Italy* **45 E8** 43 48N 11 42 E
Stigler, *U.S.A.* **155 H7** 35 15N 95 8W
Stigliano, *Italy* **47 B9** 40 24N 16 14 E
Stigtomta, *Sweden* **17 F10** 58 47N 16 48 E
Stikine →, *Canada* **142 B2** 56 40N 132 30W
Stilfontein, *S. Africa* **116 D4** 26 51 S 26 50 E
Stilís, *Greece* **48 C4** 38 55N 22 47 E
Stillmore, *U.S.A.* **152 C7** 32 27N 82 13W
Stillwater, *Minn., U.S.A.* **154 C8** 45 3N 92 49W
Stillwater, *N.Y., U.S.A.* **151 D11** 42 55N 73 41W
Stillwater, *Okla., U.S.A.* **155 G6** 36 7N 97 4W
Stillwater Range, *U.S.A.* **158 G4** 39 50N 118 5W
Stillwater Reservoir, *U.S.A.* **151 C9** 43 54N 75 3W
Stilo, Pta., *Italy* **47 D9** 38 25N 16 35 E
Stilwell, *U.S.A.* **155 H7** 35 49N 94 38W
Štip, *Macedonia* **50 E6** 41 42N 22 10 E
Stíra, *Greece* **48 C6** 38 9N 24 14 E
Stirling, *Canada* **150 B7** 44 18N 77 33W
Stirling, *N.Z.* **131 G4** 46 14 S 169 49 E
Stirling, *U.K.* **22 E5** 56 8N 3 57W
Stirling □, *U.K.* **22 E4** 56 12N 4 18W
Stirling Ra., *Australia* **125 F2** 34 23 S 118 0 E
Stirling Range Nat. Park △, *Australia* **125 F2** 34 26 S 118 20 E
Stittsville, *Canada* **151 A9** 45 15N 75 55W
Stjernøya, *Norway* **14 A20** 70 20N 22 40 E
Stjørdalshalsen, *Norway* **18 A7** 63 29N 10 51 E
Stock Island, *U.S.A.* **153 L8** 24 32N 81 34W
Stockach, *Germany* **31 H5** 47 50N 9 1 E
Stockaryd, *Sweden* **17 G8** 57 19N 14 36 E
Stockbridge, *Ga., U.S.A.* **152 B5** 33 33N 84 14W
Stockbridge, *Mich., U.S.A.* **157 B12** 42 27N 84 11W
Stockerau, *Austria* **35 C9** 48 24N 16 12 E
Stockholm, *Sweden* **16 E12** 59 20N 18 3 E
Stockholm Arlanda ✈ (ARN), *Sweden* **16 E11** 59 41N 17 56 E
Stockholms län □, *Sweden* **16 E12** 59 30N 18 20 E
Stockhorn, *Switz.* **32 C5** 46 42N 7 33 E
Stockport, *U.K.* **20 D5** 53 25N 2 9W
Stocksbridge, *U.K.* **20 D6** 53 29N 1 35W
Stockton, *Calif., U.S.A.* **160 H5** 37 58N 121 17W
Stockton, *Ill., U.S.A.* **156 B6** 42 21N 90 1W
Stockton, *Kans., U.S.A.* **154 F5** 39 26N 99 16W
Stockton, *Mo., U.S.A.* **155 G8** 37 42N 93 48W
Stockton-on-Tees, *U.K.* **20 C6** 54 35N 1 19W
Stockton-on-Tees □, *U.K.* **20 C6** 54 35N 1 19W
Stockton Plateau, *U.S.A.* **155 K3** 30 30N 102 30W
Stoczek Łukowski, *Poland* **55 G8** 51 58N 21 58 E
Stöde, *Sweden* **16 B10** 62 28N 16 35 E
Stoeng Treng, *Cambodia* **86 F5** 13 31N 105 58 E
Stoer, Pt. of, *U.K.* **22 C3** 58 16N 5 23W
Stogovo, *Macedonia* **50 E4** 41 31N 20 38 E
Stoholm, *Denmark* **17 H3** 56 30N 9 8 E
Stoke, *N.Z.* **131 B8** 41 19 S 173 14 E
Stoke-on-Trent, *U.K.* **20 D5** 53 1N 2 11W
Stoke-on-Trent □, *U.K.* **20 D5** 53 1N 2 11W
Stokes Nat. Park △, *Australia* **125 E2** 29 55 S 115 6 E
Stokes Pt., *Australia* **127 G3** 40 10 S 143 56 E
Stokes Ra., *Australia* **124 C5** 15 50 S 130 50 E
Stokkseyri, *Iceland* **11 D5** 63 50N 21 2W
Stokksnes, *Iceland* **11 C12** 64 14N 14 58W
Stokmarknes, *Norway* **14 B16** 68 34N 14 54 E
Stolac, *Bos.-H.* **50 C1** 43 5N 17 59 E
Stolberg, *Germany* **30 E2** 50 47N 6 13 E
Stolbovoy, Ostrov, *Russia* **67 B14** 74 44N 135 14 E
Stolbtsy = Stowbtsy, *Belarus* **58 F4** 53 30N 26 43 E
Stolin, *Belarus* **59 G4** 51 53N 26 50 E
Stöllet, *Sweden* **16 D7** 60 26N 13 15 E
Stolnici, *Romania* **53 F9** 44 31N 24 48 E
Stolp = Słupsk, *Poland* **54 D4** 54 30N 17 3 E
Stolpmünde = Ustka, *Poland* **54 D3** 54 35N 16 55 E
Stomíon, *Greece* **39 E4** 35 21N 23 32 E
Ston, *Croatia* **45 F14** 42 51N 17 43 E
Stone, *U.K.* **20 E5** 52 55N 2 9W
Stone Mountain, *U.S.A.* **152 B5** 33 49N 84 10W
Stoneboro, *U.S.A.* **150 E4** 41 20N 80 7W
Stonehaven, *U.K.* **22 E6** 56 59N 2 12W
Stonehenge, *Australia* **126 C3** 24 22 S 143 17 E
Stonehenge, *U.K.* **21 F6** 51 9N 1 45W
Stonewall, *Canada* **143 C9** 50 10N 97 19W
Stongfjorden, *Norway* **18 C2** 61 26N 5 10 E
Stonington, *U.S.A.* **156 E7** 39 44N 89 12W
Stony L., *Man., Canada* **143 B9** 58 51N 98 40W
Stony L., *Ont., Canada* **150 B6** 44 30N 78 5W
Stony Point, *U.S.A.* **151 E11** 41 14N 73 59W
Stony Pt., *U.S.A.* **151 C8** 43 50N 76 18W
Stony Rapids, *Canada* **143 B7** 59 16N 105 50W
Stony River, *U.S.A.* **144 F8** 61 47N 156 35W
Stony Tunguska = Tunguska, Podkamennaya →, *Russia* **67 C10** 61 50N 90 13 E
Stonyford, *U.S.A.* **160 F4** 39 23N 122 33W
Stopnica, *Poland* **55 H7** 50 27N 20 57 E
Storå, *Sweden* **16 E9** 59 42N 15 6 E
Storå →, *Denmark* **17 H2** 56 20N 8 19 E
Stora Gla, *Sweden* **16 E6** 59 30N 12 30 E
Stora Le, *Sweden* **16 E5** 59 5N 11 55 E
Stora Lulevatten, *Sweden* **14 C18** 67 10N 19 30 E
Stóra-Vatnshorn, *Iceland* **11 B5** 65 4N 21 33W
Storavan, *Sweden* **14 D18** 65 45N 18 10 E
Stord, *Norway* **18 E2** 59 52N 5 23 E
Stordal, *Norway* **18 B4** 62 23N 7 0 E
Store Bælt, *Denmark* **17 J4** 55 20N 11 0 E
Store Heddinge, *Denmark* **17 J6** 55 18N 12 23 E
Store Jukleggi, *Norway* **18 C5** 61 3N 8 12 E
Store Koldewey, *Greenland* **10 B9** 76 30N 19 0W
Store Mosse Nationalpark △, *Sweden* **17 G7** 57 18N 13 55 E
Store Sølnkletten, *Norway* **18 C7** 61 59N 10 16 E
Store Sotra, *Norway* **18 D1** 60 18N 5 4 E
Storebro, *Sweden* **17 G9** 57 35N 15 52 E
Støren, *Norway* **18 A7** 63 3N 10 18 E
Storerikvollen, *Norway* **18 A8** 63 7N 11 58 E
Storfjellseter, *Norway* **18 C7** 61 40N 10 30 E
Storfjorden, *Møre og Romsdal, Norway* **18 B3** 62 8N 6 33 E
Storfjorden, *Møre og Romsdal, Norway* **18 B3** 62 28N 6 35 E
Storfors, *Sweden* **16 E8** 59 32N 14 17 E
Stóridalur, *Iceland* **11 D7** 63 38N 19 57W
Stórinúpur, *Iceland* **11 C6** 64 3N 20 10W
Storli, *Norway* **18 B6** 62 42N 9 5 E
Storlien, *Sweden* **16 A6** 63 20N 12 5 E
Storm B., *Australia* **127 G4** 43 10 S 147 30 E
Storm Lake, *U.S.A.* **154 D7** 42 39N 95 13W
Stormberge, *S. Africa* **116 E4** 31 16 S 26 17 E
Stormsrivier, *S. Africa* **116 E3** 33 59 S 23 52 E
Stornoway, *U.K.* **22 C2** 58 13N 6 23W
Storo, *Italy* **44 C7** 45 51N 10 35 E
Storozhinets = Storozhynets, *Ukraine* **59 H3** 48 14N 25 45 E
Storozhynets, *Ukraine* **59 H3** 48 14N 25 45 E
Storrs, *U.S.A.* **151 E12** 41 49N 72 15W
Storsjøen, *Hedmark, Norway* **18 D8** 60 20N 11 40 E
Storsjøen, *Hedmark, Norway* **18 C8** 61 30N 11 14 E
Storsjön, *Gävleborg, Sweden* **16 D10** 60 35N 16 45 E
Storsjön, *Jämtland, Sweden* **16 B7** 62 48N 13 7 E
Storsjön, *Jämtland, Sweden* **16 A8** 63 9N 14 30 E
Storstrøms Amtskommune □, *Denmark* **17 J5** 54 50N 11 45 E
Storuman, *Sweden* **14 D17** 65 5N 17 10 E
Storuman, sjö, *Sweden* **14 D17** 65 13N 16 50 E
Stóruvellir, *Iceland* **11 B9** 65 30N 17 29W
Storvätteshågna, *Sweden* **16 B6** 62 6N 12 30 E
Storvigelen, *Norway* **18 B9** 62 32N 12 2 E
Storvik, *Sweden* **16 D10** 60 35N 16 33 E
Storvreta, *Sweden* **16 E11** 59 58N 17 44 E
Story City, *U.S.A.* **156 B3** 42 11N 93 36W
Stouffville, *Canada* **150 C5** 43 58N 79 15W
Stoughton, *Canada* **143 D8** 49 40N 103 0W
Stoughton, *U.S.A.* **156 B8** 42 55N 89 13W
Stour →, *Dorset, U.K.* **21 G6** 50 43N 1 47W
Stour →, *Kent, U.K.* **21 F9** 51 18N 1 22 E
Stour →, *Suffolk, U.K.* **21 F9** 51 57N 1 4 E
Stourbridge, *U.K.* **21 E5** 52 28N 2 8W
Stout L., *Canada* **143 C10** 52 0N 94 40W
Stove Pipe Wells Village, *U.S.A.* **161 J9** 36 35N 117 11W
Støvring, *Denmark* **17 H3** 56 54N 9 50 E
Stow, *U.S.A.* **150 E3** 41 10N 81 27W
Stowbtsy, *Belarus* **58 F4** 53 30N 26 43 E
Stowmarket, *U.K.* **21 E9** 52 12N 1 0 E
Strabane, *U.K.* **23 B4** 54 50N 7 27W
Stracin, *Macedonia* **50 D6** 42 13N 22 2 E
Stradella, *Italy* **44 C6** 45 5N 9 18 E
Strahan, *Australia* **127 G4** 42 9 S 145 20 E
Strajitsa, *Bulgaria* **51 C9** 43 14N 25 58 E
Strakonice, *Czech Rep.* **34 B6** 49 15N 13 53 E
Straldzha, *Bulgaria* **51 D10** 42 35N 26 40 E
Stralsund, *Germany* **30 A9** 54 18N 13 4 E
Strand, *Norway* **18 C8** 61 17N 11 17 E
Strand, *S. Africa* **116 E2** 34 9 S 18 48 E
Stranda, *Møre og Romsdal, Norway* **18 B3** 62 19N 6 58 E
Stranda, *Nord-Trøndelag, Norway* **14 E14** 63 33N 10 14 E
Strandasýsla □, *Iceland* **11 B5** 65 45N 21 45W
Strandby, *Denmark* **17 G4** 57 30N 10 29 E
Strangford L., *U.K.* **23 B6** 54 30N 5 37W
Strängnäs, *Sweden* **16 E11** 59 23N 17 2 E
Stranraer, *U.K.* **22 G3** 54 54N 5 1W
Strasbourg, *Canada* **143 C8** 51 4N 104 55W
Strasbourg, *France* **27 D14** 48 35N 7 42 E
Strasburg, *Germany* **30 B9** 53 30N 13 43 E
Străşeni, *Moldova* **53 C13** 47 8N 28 36 E
Stråssa, *Sweden* **16 E9** 59 44N 15 12 E
Strassburg = Aiud, *Romania* **53 D8** 46 19N 23 44 E
Stratford, *N.S.W., Australia* **129 B9** 32 7 S 151 55 E
Stratford, *Vic., Australia* **129 D7** 37 59 S 147 7 E
Stratford, *Canada* **140 D3** 43 23N 81 0W
Stratford, *N.Z.* **130 F3** 39 20 S 174 19 E
Stratford, *Calif., U.S.A.* **160 J7** 36 11N 119 49W
Stratford, *Conn., U.S.A.* **151 E11** 41 12N 73 8W
Stratford, *Tex., U.S.A.* **155 G3** 36 20N 102 4W
Stratford-upon-Avon, *U.K.* **21 E6** 52 12N 1 42W
Strath Spey, *U.K.* **22 D5** 57 9N 3 49W
Strathalbyn, *Australia* **128 C3** 35 13 S 138 53 E
Strathaven, *U.K.* **22 F4** 55 40N 4 5W
Strathcona Prov. Park ⌓, *Canada* **142 D3** 49 38N 125 40W
Strathmore, *Canada* **142 C6** 51 5N 113 18W
Strathmore, *U.K.* **22 E5** 56 37N 3 7W
Strathmore, *U.S.A.* **160 J7** 36 9N 119 4W
Strathnaver, *Canada* **142 C4** 53 20N 122 33W
Strathpeffer, *U.K.* **22 D4** 57 35N 4 32W
Strathroy, *Canada* **140 D3** 42 58N 81 38W
Strathy Pt., *U.K.* **22 C4** 58 36N 4 1W
Strattanville, *U.S.A.* **150 E5** 41 12N 79 19W
Stratton, *U.S.A.* **151 A14** 45 8N 70 26W
Stratton Mt., *U.S.A.* **151 C12** 43 4N 72 55W
Straubing, *Germany* **31 G8** 48 52N 12 34 E
Straumnes, *Iceland* **11 A3** 66 26N 23 8W
Strausberg, *Germany* **30 C9** 52 35N 13 54 E
Strawberry →, *U.S.A.* **158 F8** 40 10N 110 24W
Strawberry Point, *U.S.A.* **156 B5** 42 41N 91 32W
Strážnice, *Czech Rep.* **35 C10** 48 54N 17 19 E
Streaky B., *Australia* **127 E1** 32 48 S 134 13 E
Streaky Bay, *Australia* **127 E1** 32 51 S 134 18 E
Streator, *U.S.A.* **154 E10** 41 8N 88 50W
Středočeský □, *Czech Rep.* **34 B7** 49 55N 14 30 E
Streetsboro, *U.S.A.* **150 E3** 41 14N 81 21W
Streetsville, *Canada* **150 C5** 43 35N 79 42W
Strehaia, *Romania* **53 F8** 44 37N 23 10 E
Strelcha, *Bulgaria* **51 D8** 42 25N 24 19 E
Strelka, *Russia* **67 D10** 58 5N 93 3 E
Streng →, *Cambodia* **86 F4** 13 12N 103 37 E
Stresa, *Italy* **44 C5** 45 52N 8 28 E
Streymoy, *Færoe Is.* **14 E9** 62 8N 7 5W
Strezhevoy, *Russia* **66 C8** 60 42N 77 34 E
Střibro, *Czech Rep.* **34 A6** 49 44N 13 0 E
Strickland →, *Papua N. G.* **132 D1** 7 35 S 141 36 E
Strimón →, *Greece* **50 F7** 40 46N 23 51 E
Strimonikós Kólpos, *Greece* **50 F7** 40 33N 24 0 E
Stroeder, *Argentina* **176 B4** 40 12 S 62 37W
Strofádhes, *Greece* **48 D3** 37 15N 21 0 E
Stroma, *U.K.* **22 C5** 58 41N 3 7W
Stromberg-Heuchelberg, Naturpark ⌓, *Germany* **31 F4** 49 2N 8 50 E
Strómboli, *Italy* **47 D8** 38 47N 15 13 E
Stromeferry, *U.K.* **22 D3** 57 21N 5 33W
Strømmen, *Norway* **18 E7** 59 58N 10 59 E
Stromness, *U.K.* **22 C5** 58 58N 3 17W
Strömsbruk, *Sweden* **16 C11** 61 52N 17 18 E
Stromsburg, *U.S.A.* **154 E6** 41 7N 97 36W
Strömsnäsbruk, *Sweden* **17 H7** 56 35N 13 45 E
Strömstad, *Sweden* **17 F5** 58 56N 11 10 E
Strömsund, *Sweden* **14 E16** 63 51N 15 33 E
Stronghurst, *U.S.A.* **156 D6** 40 45N 90 55W
Strongilí, *Greece* **49 E11** 36 6N 29 42 E
Stróngoli, *Italy* **47 C10** 39 16N 17 3 E
Strongsville, *U.S.A.* **150 E3** 41 19N 81 50W
Stronie Śląskie, *Poland* **55 H3** 50 18N 16 53 E
Stronsay, *U.K.* **22 B6** 59 7N 2 35W
Stropkov, *Slovak Rep.* **35 B14** 49 13N 21 39 E
Stroud, *U.K.* **21 F5** 51 45N 2 13W
Stroud Road, *Australia* **129 B9** 32 18 S 151 57 E

Stroudsburg, U.S.A. ... 151 F9 40 59N 75 12W
Stroumbi, Cyprus ... 39 E8 34 53N 32 29 E
Struer, Denmark ... 17 H2 56 30N 8 35 E
Struga, Macedonia ... 50 E4 41 11N 20 44 E
Strugi Krasnyye, Russia ... 58 C5 58 21N 29 1 E
Strumica, Macedonia ... 50 E6 41 28N 22 41 E
Strumica →, Europe ... 50 E7 41 20N 23 22 E
Struthers, Canada ... 140 C2 48 41N 85 51W
Struthers, U.S.A. ... 150 E4 41 4N 80 39W
Stryama →, Bulgaria ... 51 D8 42 16N 24 54 E
Stryker, U.S.A. ... 158 B6 48 41N 114 46W
Stryn, Norway ... 18 C3 61 54N 6 43 E
Stryków, Poland ... 55 G6 51 55N 19 33 E
Strzegom, Poland ... 55 H3 50 58N 16 20 E
Strzelce Krajeńskie, Poland ... 55 F2 52 52N 15 33 E
Strzelce Opolskie, Poland ... 55 H5 50 31N 18 18 E
Strzelecki Cr. →, Australia ... 127 D2 29 37 S 139 59 E
Strzelin, Poland ... 55 H4 50 46N 17 2 E
Strzelno, Poland ... 55 F5 52 35N 18 9 E
Strzybnica, Poland ... 55 H5 50 28N 18 48 E
Strzyżów, Poland ... 55 E8 49 52N 21 47 E
Stuart, Fla., U.S.A. ... 153 H9 27 12N 80 15W
Stuart, Iowa, U.S.A. ... 156 C2 41 30N 94 19W
Stuart, Nebr., U.S.A. ... 154 D5 42 36N 99 8W
Stuart →, Canada ... 142 C4 54 0N 123 35W
Stuart Bluff Ra., Australia ... 124 D5 22 50 S 131 52 E
Stuart I., U.S.A. ... 144 F7 63 35N 162 30W
Stuart L., Canada ... 142 C4 54 30N 124 30W
Stuart Mts., N.Z. ... 131 F2 45 2 S 167 39 E
Stuart Ra., Australia ... 127 D1 29 10 S 134 56 E
Stubbekøbing, Denmark ... 17 K6 54 53N 12 9 E
Stuben, Austria ... 34 D3 47 10N 10 8 E
Studen Kladenets, Yazovir, Bulgaria ... 51 F9 41 37N 25 30 E
Studenka, Czech Rep. ... 35 B11 49 44N 18 5 E
Studholme, N.Z. ... 131 E6 44 42 S 171 9 E
Stugudal, Norway ... 18 B8 62 53N 11 53 E
Stugun, Sweden ... 16 A9 63 10N 15 40 E
Stühlingen, Germany ... 33 A6 47 44N 8 26 E
Stuhlweisenburg = Székesfehérvár, Hungary ... 52 C3 47 15N 18 25 E
Stuhr, Germany ... 30 B4 53 5N 8 44 E
Stull L., Canada ... 140 B1 54 24N 92 34W
Stung Treng = Stoeng Treng, Cambodia ... 86 F5 13 31N 105 58 E
Stupart →, Canada ... 140 A1 56 0N 93 25W
Stupava, Slovak Rep. ... 35 C10 48 17N 17 2 E
Stupino, Russia ... 58 E10 54 57N 38 2 E
Sturgeon B., Canada ... 143 C9 52 0N 97 50W
Sturgeon Bay, U.S.A. ... 148 C2 44 50N 87 23W
Sturgeon Falls, Canada ... 140 C4 46 25N 79 57W
Sturgeon L., Alta., Canada ... 142 B5 55 6N 117 32W
Sturgeon L., Ont., Canada ... 140 C1 50 0N 90 45W
Sturgeon L., Ont., Canada ... 150 B6 44 28N 78 43W
Sturgis, Canada ... 143 C8 51 56N 102 36W
Sturgis, Mich., U.S.A. ... 157 C11 41 48N 85 25W
Sturgis, S. Dak., U.S.A. ... 154 C3 44 25N 103 31W
Sturkö, Sweden ... 17 H9 56 5N 15 42 E
Šturovo, Slovak Rep. ... 35 D11 47 48N 18 41 E
Sturt Cr. →, Australia ... 124 C4 19 8 S 127 50 E
Sturt Nat. Park △, Australia ... 127 D3 27 17 S 141 37 E
Sturts Meadows, Australia ... 128 A4 31 18 S 141 42 E
Stutterheim, S. Africa ... 116 E4 32 33 S 27 28 E
Stuttgart, Germany ... 31 G5 48 48N 9 11 E
Stuttgart, U.S.A. ... 155 H9 34 30N 91 33W
Stuttgart Echterdingen ✈ (STR), Germany ... 31 G5 48 42N 9 11 E
Stuyvesant, U.S.A. ... 151 D11 42 23N 73 45W
Stykkishólmur, Iceland ... 11 B4 65 2N 22 40W
Styria = Steiermark □, Austria ... 34 D8 47 26N 15 0 E
Styrsö, Sweden ... 17 G5 57 37N 11 46 E
Su-no-Saki, Japan ... 73 C11 34 58N 139 45 E
Su Xian = Suzhou, China ... 74 H9 33 41N 116 59 E
Suakin, Sudan ... 106 D4 19 8N 37 20 E
Suan, N. Korea ... 75 E14 38 42N 126 22 E
Suapure →, Venezuela ... 168 B4 6 48N 67 1W
Suaqui, Mexico ... 162 B3 29 12N 109 41W
Suar, India ... 93 E8 29 2N 79 3 E
Suatá →, Venezuela ... 169 B4 7 52N 65 22W
Suau, Papua N. G. ... 132 F6 10 37 S 150 2 E
Suavanao, Solomon Is. ... 133 L10 7 35 S 158 47 E
Suba Talan, Malaysia ... 81 H1 6 22N 117 38 E
Subang, Indonesia ... 85 D3 6 34 S 107 45 E
Subankhata, India ... 90 B3 26 48N 91 25 E
Subansiri →, India ... 90 B4 26 48N 93 50 E
Subarnagiri, India ... 93 H12 22 34N 87 24 E
Subayhah, Si. Arabia ... 96 D3 30 2N 38 50 E
Subcetate, Romania ... 52 E8 45 36N 23 0 E
Subi, Indonesia ... 85 B3 2 58N 108 50 E
Subiaco, Italy ... 45 G10 41 56N 13 6 E
Subotica, Serbia, Yug. ... 52 D4 46 6N 19 39 E
Suca, Ethiopia ... 107 F4 6 31N 39 14 E
Suceava, Romania ... 53 C11 47 38N 26 16 E
Suceava □, Romania ... 53 C10 47 37N 25 40 E
Suceava →, Romania ... 53 C11 47 32N 26 35 E
Sucesso, Brazil ... 170 B3 4 56 S 40 32W
Sucha-Beskidzka, Poland ... 55 J6 49 44N 19 35 E
Suchań, Poland ... 55 E2 53 18N 15 18 E
Suchan, Russia ... 70 C6 43 8N 133 9 E
Suchedniów, Poland ... 55 G7 51 3N 20 49 E
Suchitoto, El Salv. ... 164 D2 13 56N 89 0W
Suchou = Suzhou, China ... 77 B13 31 19N 120 38 E
Süchow = Xuzhou, China ... 75 G9 34 18N 117 10 E
Suchowola, Poland ... 54 E10 53 33N 23 3 E
Sucio →, Colombia ... 168 B2 7 27N 77 7W
Suck →, Ireland ... 23 C3 53 17N 8 3W
Suckling, Mt., Papua N. G. ... 132 E5 9 49 S 148 53 E
Sucre, Bolivia ... 173 D4 19 0 S 65 15W
Sucre, Colombia ... 168 B3 8 49N 74 44W
Sucre □, Colombia ... 168 B2 9 50N 75 40W
Sucre □, Venezuela ... 169 A5 10 25N 63 30W
Sucuaro, Colombia ... 168 C4 4 34N 68 50W
Sućuraj, Croatia ... 45 E14 43 10N 17 8 E
Sucuriú, Brazil ... 170 A2 20 47 S 51 38W
Sucuriú →, Brazil ... 177 E9 20 47 S 51 38W
Sud, Pte. du, Canada ... 141 C7 49 3N 62 14W
Sud-Kivu □, Dem. Rep. of the Congo ... 118 C2 3 0 S 28 30 E
Sud Ouest, Pte., Mauritius ... 121 d 20 28 S 57 18 E
Sud-Ouest, Pte. du, Canada ... 141 C7 49 23N 63 36W
Suda →, Russia ... 58 C9 59 0N 37 40 E
Sudak, Ukraine ... 59 K8 44 51N 34 57 E
Sudan, U.S.A. ... 155 H3 34 4N 102 32W
Sudan ■, Africa ... 107 E3 15 0N 30 0 E
Sudbury, Canada ... 140 C3 46 30N 81 0W
Sudbury, U.K. ... 21 E8 52 2N 0 45 E
Südd, Sudan ... 107 F3 8 20N 30 0 E
Suddie, Guyana ... 169 B6 7 8N 58 29W
Sudeifel Naturpark = Deutsch-Luxemburgischer Naturpark △, Germany ... 31 F2 49 58N 6 12 E
Süderbrarup, Germany ... 30 A5 54 38N 9 45 E
Süderlügum, Germany ... 30 A4 54 51N 8 54 E
Süderoogsand, Germany ... 30 A4 54 27N 8 28 E
Sudeten Mts. = Sudety, Europe ... 35 A9 50 20N 16 45 E
Sudety, Europe ... 35 A9 50 20N 16 45 E
Suðavík, Iceland ... 11 A3 66 2N 23 0W
Südheide, Naturpark △, Germany ... 30 C6 52 46N 10 10 E
Suður-múlasýsla □, Iceland ... 11 C12 65 0N 14 0W
Suður-þingeyjarsýsla □, Iceland ... 11 B9 65 30N 17 0W
Suðureyri, Iceland ... 11 A3 66 7N 23 32W
Suðuroy, Færoe Is. ... 14 F9 61 32N 6 50W
Sudi, Tanzania ... 119 E4 10 11 S 39 57 E
Sudirman, Pegunungan, Indonesia ... 83 B5 4 30 S 137 0 E

Sudiți, Romania ... 53 F12 44 35N 27 38 E
Sudogda, Russia ... 60 C5 55 55N 40 50 E
Sudong, Pulau, Singapore ... 87 d 1 12N 103 43 E
Sudr, Egypt ... 106 B3 29 40N 32 42 E
Sudzha, Russia ... 59 G8 51 14N 35 17 E
Sue →, Sudan ... 107 F2 7 41N 28 3 E
Sueca, Spain ... 41 F4 39 12N 0 21W
Süedinenie, Bulgaria ... 51 D8 42 16N 24 33 E
Suemez I., U.S.A. ... 142 B2 55 15N 133 20W
Suez = El Suweis, Egypt ... 106 J8 29 58N 32 31 E
Suez, G. of = Suweis, Khalîg el, Egypt ... 106 J8 28 40N 33 0 E
Suez Canal = Suweis, Qanâ es, Egypt ... 106 H8 31 0N 32 20 E
Suffield, Canada ... 142 C6 50 12N 111 10W
Suffolk, U.S.A. ... 148 G7 36 44N 76 35W
Suffolk □, U.K. ... 21 E9 52 16N 1 0 E
Suga-no-Sen, Japan ... 72 B6 35 25N 134 25 E
Şugag, Romania ... 53 E8 45 47N 23 37 E
Sugar →, U.S.A. ... 156 B7 42 26N 89 12W
Sugar Cr. →, Ill., U.S.A. ... 156 D7 40 9N 89 38W
Sugar Cr. →, Ind., U.S.A. ... 157 E9 39 50N 87 23W
Sugar Hill, U.S.A. ... 152 A5 34 6N 84 3W
Sugar Loaf Pt., St. Helena ... 9 h 15 54 S 5 42W
Sugargrove, U.S.A. ... 150 E5 41 59N 79 21W
Sugarive →, India ... 93 F12 26 16N 86 24 E
Sugbai Passage, Phil. ... 81 J3 5 22N 120 33 E
Suğla Gölü, Turkey ... 100 D5 37 20N 32 0 E
Sugluk = Salluit, Canada ... 139 B12 62 14N 75 38W
Sugun, China ... 65 D8 39 53N 76 47 E
Suhaia, Lacul, Romania ... 53 G10 43 45N 25 15 E
Şuḩār, Oman ... 97 E8 24 20N 56 40 E
Sühbaatar □, Mongolia ... 74 B8 45 30N 114 0 E
Suheli Par, India ... 95 J1 10 35N 72 17 E
Suhl, Germany ... 30 E6 50 36N 10 42 E
Suhr, Switz. ... 32 B6 47 22N 8 5 E
Şuhut, Turkey ... 49 C12 38 31N 30 32 E
Sui, Pakistan ... 92 E3 28 37N 69 19 E
Sui Xian, China ... 74 G8 34 25N 115 2 E
Suia Missu →, Brazil ... 173 C7 11 13 S 53 15W
Suica, Bos.-H. ... 52 G2 43 52N 17 11 E
Suichang, China ... 77 C12 28 29N 119 15 E
Suichuan, China ... 77 D10 26 20N 114 32 E
Suide, China ... 74 F6 37 30N 110 12 E
Suifenhe, China ... 75 B16 44 25N 131 10 E
Suihua, China ... 69 B7 46 32N 126 55 E
Suijiang, China ... 76 C4 28 40N 103 59 E
Suining, Hunan, China ... 77 D8 26 35N 110 10 E
Suining, Jiangsu, China ... 75 H9 33 56N 117 58 E
Suining, Sichuan, China ... 76 B5 30 26N 105 35 E
Suiping, China ... 74 H7 33 10N 113 59 E
Suippes, France ... 27 C11 49 8N 4 30 E
Suir →, Ireland ... 23 D4 52 16N 7 9W
Suisun City, U.S.A. ... 160 G4 38 15N 122 2W
Suita, Japan ... 73 G7 34 45N 135 32 E
Suixi, China ... 77 G8 21 19N 110 18 E
Suiyang, Guizhou, China ... 76 D6 27 58N 107 18 E
Suiyang, Heilongjiang, China ... 75 B16 44 30N 130 56 E
Suizhong, China ... 75 D11 40 21N 120 20 E
Suizhou, China ... 77 B9 31 42N 113 24 E
Sujangarh, India ... 92 F6 27 42N 74 31 E
Sukabumi, Indonesia ... 84 D3 6 56 S 106 50 E
Sukadana, Kalimantan, Indonesia ... 85 C4 1 10 S 110 0 E
Sukadana, Sumatera, Indonesia ... 84 D3 5 5 S 105 33 E
Sukagawa, Japan ... 71 F10 37 17N 140 23 E
Sukaraja, Indonesia ... 85 C4 2 28 S 110 25 E
Sukarnapura = Jayapura, Indonesia ... 83 B6 2 28 S 140 38 E
Sukawati, Indonesia ... 79 K18 8 35 S 115 17 E
Sukch'ŏn, N. Korea ... 75 E13 39 22N 125 35 E
Sukhindol, Bulgaria ... 51 C9 43 11N 25 10 E
Sukhinichi, Russia ... 58 E8 54 8N 35 10 E
Sukhona →, Russia ... 56 C6 61 15N 46 39 E
Sukhothai, Thailand ... 86 D2 17 1N 99 49 E
Sukhoy Log, Russia ... 64 C9 56 55N 62 1 E
Sukhumi = Sokhumi, Georgia ... 61 J5 43 0N 41 0 E
Sukkertoppen = Maniitsoq, Greenland ... 10 D5 65 26N 52 55W
Sukkur, Pakistan ... 91 D3 27 42N 68 54 E
Sukkur Barrage, Pakistan ... 92 F3 27 40N 68 50 E
Sukma, India ... 94 E5 18 24N 81 45 E
Sukovo, Serbia, Yug. ... 50 C6 43 4N 22 37 E
Sukri →, India ... 92 G4 25 4N 71 43 E
Sukumo, Japan ... 72 E4 32 56N 132 44 E
Sukunka →, Canada ... 142 B4 55 45N 121 15W
Sul, Canal do, Brazil ... 170 B2 0 10 S 48 30W
Sula, Norway ... 18 C1 61 7N 4 54 E
Sula →, Ukraine ... 59 H7 49 40N 32 41 E
Sula, Kepulauan, Indonesia ... 82 B3 1 45 S 125 0 E
Sulaco →, Honduras ... 164 C2 15 2N 87 44W
Sulaiman Range, Pakistan ... 92 D3 30 30N 69 50 E
Sulak →, Russia ... 61 J8 43 20N 47 34 E
Sūlār, Iran ... 97 D6 31 53N 51 54 E
Sulawesi □, Indonesia ... 82 B2 2 0 S 120 0 E
Sulawesi Sea = Celebes Sea, Indonesia ... 82 A2 3 0N 123 0 E
Sulawesi Selatan □, Indonesia ... 82 B1 2 30 S 120 0 E
Sulawesi Utara □, Indonesia ... 82 A2 1 0N 122 30 E
Suldalsosen, Norway ... 18 E3 59 29N 6 59 E
Sulechów, Poland ... 55 F2 52 5N 15 40 E
Sulęcin, Poland ... 55 F2 52 26N 15 10 E
Sule, Solomon Is. ... 133 G6 8 58N 159 34 E
Sulejów, Poland ... 55 F8 51 26N 19 53 E
Sulejówek, Poland ... 55 F8 52 13N 21 17 E
Süleymanlı, Turkey ... 49 C9 38 58N 27 47 E
Sulgen, Switz. ... 33 A8 47 33N 9 7 E
Sulima, S. Leone ... 112 D2 6 58N 11 32W
Sulina, Romania ... 53 E14 45 10N 29 40 E
Sulina, Brațul →, Romania ... 53 E14 45 10N 29 40 E
Sulingen, Germany ... 30 C4 52 41N 8 48 E
Suliţa, Romania ... 53 C11 47 39N 26 59 E
Sulitjelma, Norway ... 14 C17 67 9N 16 3 E
Sułkowice, Poland ... 55 J6 49 52N 19 49 E
Sullana, Peru ... 172 A1 4 52 S 80 39W
Süller, Turkey ... 49 C11 38 9N 29 29 E
Sullivan, Ill., U.S.A. ... 154 F10 39 36N 88 37W
Sullivan, Ind., U.S.A. ... 157 E9 39 6N 87 24W
Sullivan, Mo., U.S.A. ... 156 F5 38 13N 91 10W
Sullivan Bay, Canada ... 142 C3 50 55N 126 50W
Sullivan I. = Lanbi Kyun, Burma ... 87 G2 10 50N 98 20 E
Sullom Voe, U.K. ... 22 A7 60 27N 1 20W
Sully, U.S.A. ... 156 C4 41 34N 92 50W
Sully-sur-Loire, France ... 27 E9 47 45N 2 20 E
Sulmierzyce, Poland ... 55 G4 51 37N 17 32 E
Sulmona, Italy ... 45 F10 42 3N 13 55 E
Süloğlu, Turkey ... 51 E10 41 44N 26 53 E
Sulphur, La., U.S.A. ... 155 K8 30 14N 93 23W
Sulphur, Okla., U.S.A. ... 155 H6 34 31N 96 58W
Sulphur Pt., Canada ... 142 A6 60 56N 114 48W
Sulphur Springs, U.S.A. ... 155 J7 33 8N 95 36W
Sulsul, Ethiopia ... 120 C2 5 5N 44 50 E
Sultan, Canada ... 140 C3 47 36N 82 47W
Sultan, U.S.A. ... 160 C5 47 52N 121 49W
Sultan Dağları, Turkey ... 100 C4 38 20N 31 20 E
Sultan Kudarat, Phil. ... 81 H5 7 16N 124 18 E
Sultan Naga Dimaporo, Phil. ... 81 H5 7 55N 123 44 E
Sultan sa Barongis, Phil. ... 81 H5 6 45N 124 35 E
Sultanabad = Arāk, Iran ... 97 C6 34 0N 49 40 E
Sultanhisar, Turkey ... 49 D10 37 53N 28 9 E
Sultānia, Turkey ... 51 F10 40 37N 26 8 E
Sultaniçe, Turkey ... 51 F12 40 11N 28 12 E
Sultanpur, Mad. P., India ... 92 H8 23 9N 77 56 E
Sultanpur, Punjab, India ... 92 D6 31 13N 75 11 E
Sultanpur, Ut. P., India ... 93 F10 26 18N 82 4 E
Sulu, Phil. ... 81 J3 5 30N 120 30 E

Sulu Arch., Phil. ... 81 J3 6 0N 121 0 E
Sulu Sea, E. Indies ... 81 G3 8 0N 120 0 E
Sülüklü, Turkey ... 100 C5 38 53N 32 20 E
Sülüktü, Kyrgyzstan ... 65 D4 39 56N 69 34 E
Sulula, Ethiopia ... 107 F4 9 10N 38 43 E
Suluova, Turkey ... 100 B6 40 46N 35 32 E
Suluq, Libya ... 108 B4 31 44N 20 14 E
Suluru, India ... 95 H5 13 42N 80 1 E
Sulūtōbe, Kazakhstan ... 65 A3 44 37N 66 3 E
Sulyukta = Sülüktü, Kyrgyzstan ... 65 D4 39 56N 69 34 E
Sulzbach, Germany ... 31 F3 49 18N 7 4 E
Sulzbach-Rosenberg, Germany ... 31 F7 49 30N 11 44 E
Sulzberg, Germany ... 33 A5 47 32N 10 22 E
Sulzberger Ice Shelf, Antarctica ... 7 E13 78 0 S 150 0W
Sumalata, Indonesia ... 82 A2 1 0N 122 31 E
Sumampa, Argentina ... 174 B3 29 25 S 63 29W
Sumatera □, Indonesia ... 84 B2 0 40N 100 20 E
Sumatera Barat □, Indonesia ... 78 E2 1 0 S 101 0 E
Sumatera Utara □, Indonesia ... 78 D1 2 30N 98 0 E
Sumatra = Sumatera □, Indonesia ... 84 B2 0 40N 100 20 E
Sumatra, U.S.A. ... 152 E13 30 1N 84 59W
Sumava, Angola ... 115 D2 6 15 S 12 38 E
Sumba, Indonesia ... 82 C1 9 45 S 119 35 E
Sumba, Selat, Indonesia ... 82 C1 9 0 S 118 40 E
Sumbawa, Indonesia ... 85 D5 8 26 S 117 30 E
Sumbawa Besar, Indonesia ... 85 D5 8 30 S 117 26 E
Sumbe, Angola ... 115 E2 11 10 S 13 48 E
Sumbu Nat. Park △, Zambia ... 119 D3 8 43 S 30 22 E
Sumburgh Hd., U.K. ... 22 B7 59 52N 1 17W
Sumdeo, India ... 93 D8 31 26N 78 44 E
Sumdo, China ... 93 B8 35 6N 78 41 E
Sumé, Brazil ... 170 C4 7 39 S 36 55W
Sumedang, Indonesia ... 85 D3 6 52 S 107 55 E
Sumen = Shumen, Bulgaria ... 51 C10 43 18N 26 55 E
Sumenep, Indonesia ... 85 D4 7 1 S 113 52 E
Sumgait = Sumqayıt, Azerbaijan ... 61 K9 40 34N 49 38 E
Sumisu-Jima, Japan ... 73 F12 31 27N 140 3 E
Sumiswald, Switz. ... 32 B5 47 2N 7 44 E
Sumner, L., U.S.A. ... 158 E3 42 50N 120 45W
Summerland, Canada ... 142 D5 49 32N 119 41W
Summerland Key, U.S.A. ... 153 N5 24 40N 81 27W
Summerside, Canada ... 141 C7 46 24N 63 47W
Summersville, U.S.A. ... 148 F5 38 17N 80 51W
Summerton, U.S.A. ... 153 J5 33 36N 80 22W
Summertown, U.S.A. ... 152 C7 32 45N 82 16W
Summerville, Ga., U.S.A. ... 149 H3 34 29N 85 21W
Summerville, S.C., U.S.A. ... 152 B9 33 1N 80 11W
Summit, U.S.A. ... 144 E10 64 0N 149 30W
Summit Lake, Canada ... 142 C4 54 20N 122 40W
Summit Peak, U.S.A. ... 159 H10 37 21N 106 42W
Sumner, N.Z. ... 131 D7 43 35 S 172 48 E
Sumner, Ill., U.S.A. ... 157 F9 38 42N 87 53W
Sumner, Iowa, U.S.A. ... 156 B4 42 51N 92 6W
Sumner, Wash., U.S.A. ... 160 C4 47 12N 122 14W
Sumner, L., N.Z. ... 131 C7 42 42 S 172 15 E
Sumoto, Japan ... 72 C6 34 21N 134 54 E
Sumpangbinangae, Indonesia ... 85 B1 4 24 S 119 36 E
Šumperk, Czech Rep. ... 35 B9 49 59N 16 59 E
Sumprabum, Burma ... 90 B6 26 33N 97 36 E
Sumqayıt, Azerbaijan ... 61 K9 40 34N 49 38 E
Sumsar, Kyrgyzstan ... 65 C6 41 18N 71 19 E
Sumter, U.S.A. ... 152 B9 33 55N 80 21W
Sumy, Ukraine ... 59 G8 50 57N 34 50 E
Sun City, S. Africa ... 116 D4 25 17 S 27 3 E
Sun City, Ariz., U.S.A. ... 159 K7 33 36N 112 17W
Sun City, Calif., U.S.A. ... 161 M9 33 42N 117 11W
Sun City Center, U.S.A. ... 153 H7 27 43N 82 18W
Sun Lakes, U.S.A. ... 159 K8 33 10N 111 52W
Sun Prairie, U.S.A. ... 156 A7 43 11N 89 13W
Sun Valley, U.S.A. ... 158 E6 43 42N 114 21W
Sunagawa, Japan ... 70 C10 43 29N 141 55 E
Sunan, N. Korea ... 75 E13 39 15N 125 40 E
Sunart, L., U.K. ... 22 E3 56 42N 5 43W
Sunburst, U.S.A. ... 158 B8 48 53N 111 55W
Sunbury, Australia ... 129 D6 37 35 S 144 44 E
Sunbury, U.S.A. ... 151 F8 40 52N 76 48W
Sunchales, Argentina ... 174 C3 30 58 S 61 35W
Suncho Corral, Argentina ... 174 B3 27 55 S 63 27W
Sunch'ŏn, S. Korea ... 75 G14 34 52N 127 31 E
Suncook, U.S.A. ... 151 C13 43 8N 71 27W
Sunda, Selat, Indonesia ... 84 D3 6 20 S 105 30 E
Sunda Is., Indonesia ... 62 K14 5 0 S 105 0 E
Sunda Str. = Sunda, Selat, Indonesia ... 84 D3 6 20 S 105 30 E
Sundance, Canada ... 143 B10 56 32N 94 4W
Sundance, U.S.A. ... 154 C2 44 24N 104 23W
Sundar Nagar, India ... 92 D7 31 32N 76 53 E
Sundarbans, Asia ... 90 K2 22 0N 89 0 E
Sundargarh, India ... 94 C7 22 4N 84 5 E
Sundays = Sondags →, S. Africa ... 116 E4 33 44 S 25 51 E
Sunderland, Canada ... 150 B5 44 16N 79 4W
Sunderland, U.K. ... 20 C6 54 55N 1 23W
Sundi Lutete, Dem. Rep. of the Congo ... 115 C2 4 34 S 14 14 E
Sundown Nat. Park △, Australia ... 127 D5 28 49 S 151 38 E
Sundre, Canada ... 142 C6 51 49N 114 38W
Sunds, Denmark ... 17 H3 56 13N 9 1 E
Sundsvall, Sweden ... 16 B11 62 23N 17 17 E
Sundsvallsbukten, Sweden ... 16 B11 62 21N 17 25 E
Sung Hei, Vietnam ... 87 G6 10 20N 106 2 E
Sungai Acheh, Malaysia ... 87 c 5 8N 100 30 E
Sungai Kolok, Thailand ... 87 J3 6 2N 101 58 E
Sungai Lembing, Malaysia ... 87 L4 3 55N 103 3 E
Sungai Petani, Malaysia ... 87 K3 5 37N 100 30 E
Sungaigerong, Indonesia ... 84 C2 3 0 S 104 52 E
Sungailiat, Indonesia ... 84 C3 1 51 S 106 8 E
Sungaipenuh, Indonesia ... 84 C2 2 1 S 101 20 E
Sungaitiram, Indonesia ... 85 C5 0 45 S 117 8 E
Sungari = Songhua Jiang →, China ... 69 B8 47 45N 132 30 E
Sungguminasa, Indonesia ... 82 C1 5 17 S 119 30 E
Sunghua Chiang = Songhua Jiang →, China ... 69 B8 47 45N 132 30 E
Sungikai, Sudan ... 107 E2 12 20N 29 51 E
Sungu, Dem. Rep. of the Congo ... 114 C3 1 5 S 17 21 E
Sungurlu, Turkey ... 100 B6 40 12N 34 21 E
Sunja, Croatia ... 44 E13 45 21N 16 35 E
Sunland Park, U.S.A. ... 159 L10 31 50N 106 40W
Sunnansjö, Sweden ... 16 D8 60 34N 14 58 E
Sunndalsøra, Norway ... 18 B5 62 40N 8 33 E
Sunne, Sweden ... 16 E7 59 52N 13 5 E
Sunnemo, Sweden ... 16 E7 59 53N 13 44 E
Sunnfjord, Norway ... 18 D2 61 35N 6 0 E
Sunnmøre, Norway ... 18 B3 62 35N 6 30 E
Sunnyside, U.S.A. ... 158 C3 46 20N 120 0W
Sunnyvale, U.S.A. ... 160 H4 37 23N 122 2W
Sunset Beach, U.S.A. ... 145 J13 21 40N 158 3W
Suntar, Russia ... 67 C12 62 15N 117 30 E
Suntrana, U.S.A. ... 144 E10 63 54N 148 54W
Sunyani, Ghana ... 112 D4 7 21N 2 22W
Suō-Nada, Japan ... 72 D3 33 50N 131 30 E
Suomenselkä, Finland ... 14 E21 62 52N 24 0 E
Suomussalmi, Finland ... 14 D23 64 54N 29 10 E
Suoyarvi, Russia ... 56 B5 62 3N 32 20 E
Supamo →, Venezuela ... 169 B5 6 48N 62 34W
Supaul, India ... 93 F12 26 10N 86 40 E
Supe, Peru ... 172 C2 11 0 S 77 38W
Superior, Ariz., U.S.A. ... 159 K8 33 18N 111 6W
Superior, Mont., U.S.A. ... 158 C6 47 12N 114 53W
Superior, Nebr., U.S.A. ... 154 E5 40 1N 98 4W
Superior, Wis., U.S.A. ... 154 B8 46 44N 92 6W
Superior, L., N. Amer. ... 140 C2 47 0N 87 0W

Supetar, Croatia ... 45 E13 43 25N 16 32 E
Suphan Buri, Thailand ... 86 E3 14 14N 100 10 E
Suphan Dağı, Turkey ... 101 C10 38 54N 42 48 E
Supiori, Indonesia ... 83 B5 1 0 S 136 0 E
Supraśl, Poland ... 55 E10 53 13N 23 9 E
Supraśl →, Poland ... 55 E9 53 13N 22 57 E
Supung Shuiku, China ... 75 D13 40 35N 124 50 E
Suq 'Abs, Yemen ... 98 D3 16 0N 43 12 E
Sūq Suwayq, Si. Arabia ... 96 E3 24 23N 38 27 E
Suqian, China ... 75 H10 33 54N 118 8 E
Suquţra = Socotra, Yemen ... 99 D6 12 30N 54 0 E
Şūr, Lebanon ... 103 B4 33 19N 35 16 E
Şūr, Oman ... 99 B7 22 34N 59 32 E
Sur, C., Chile ... 172 b 27 12 S 109 26W
Sur, Pt., U.S.A. ... 160 J5 36 18N 121 54W
Sura →, Russia ... 60 C8 56 6N 46 0 E
Surab, Pakistan ... 91 C2 28 25N 66 15 E
Surabaja = Surabaya, Indonesia ... 85 D4 7 17 S 112 45 E
Surabaya, Indonesia ... 85 D4 7 17 S 112 45 E
Surahammar, Sweden ... 16 E10 59 43N 16 13 E
Suraia, Romania ... 53 E12 45 40N 27 25 E
Surakarta, Indonesia ... 85 D4 7 35 S 110 48 E
Surakhany, Azerbaijan ... 61 K10 40 25N 50 1 E
Surany, Slovak Rep. ... 35 C11 48 6N 18 11 E
Surat, Australia ... 127 D4 27 10 S 149 6 E
Surat, India ... 94 D1 21 12N 72 55 E
Surat Thani, Thailand ... 87 H2 9 6N 99 20 E
Suratgarh, India ... 92 E5 29 18N 73 55 E
Suraż, Poland ... 55 F9 52 57N 22 57 E
Surazh, Belarus ... 58 E6 55 25N 30 44 E
Surazh, Russia ... 59 F7 53 5N 32 27 E
Surduc, Romania ... 53 C8 47 15N 23 25 E
Surduc Pasul, Romania ... 53 E8 45 21N 23 23 E
Surdulica, Serbia, Yug. ... 50 D6 42 41N 22 11 E
Surendranagar, India ... 92 H4 22 45N 71 40 E
Surf, U.S.A. ... 161 L6 34 41N 120 36W
Surgana, India ... 94 D1 20 34N 73 37 E
Surgères, France ... 26 B3 46 7N 0 47W
Surgut, Russia ... 64 C8 61 14N 73 20 E
Suria, Spain ... 40 D6 41 50N 1 45 E
Suriapet, India ... 94 F4 17 10N 79 40 E
Surigao, Phil. ... 81 G5 9 47N 125 29 E
Surigao del Norte □, Phil. ... 81 G5 9 45N 125 40 E
Surigao del Sur □, Phil. ... 81 G6 8 45N 126 0 E
Surigao Strait, Phil. ... 81 F5 10 15N 125 23 E
Surin, Thailand ... 86 E4 14 50N 103 34 E
Surin Nua, Ko, Thailand ... 87 H1 9 30N 97 55 E
Surinam = Suriname ■, S. Amer. ... 169 C6 4 0N 56 0W
Suriname □, S. Amer. ... 169 C6 4 0N 56 0W
Suriname ■, S. Amer. ... 169 C6 4 0N 56 0W
Suriname →, Suriname ... 169 B6 5 50N 55 15W
Surjagarh, India ... 94 E5 19 36N 80 25 E
Surkhandarya = Surxondaryo →, Uzbekistan ... 65 E3 37 12N 67 20 E
Surkhet, Nepal ... 90 C2 24 34N 91 14 E
Sürmaq, Iran ... 97 D7 31 3N 52 48 E
Sürmene, Turkey ... 100 B8 41 0N 40 1 E
Surna →, Norway ... 18 B5 62 59N 8 40 E
Surnadalsøra, Norway ... 18 B5 62 58N 8 40 E
Surovikino, Russia ... 61 F6 48 32N 42 55 E
Surrency, U.S.A. ... 152 D7 31 44N 82 12W
Surrey, Canada ... 160 A4 49 10N 122 54W
Surrey □, U.K. ... 21 F7 51 15N 0 31W
Sursand, India ... 93 F11 26 39N 85 43 E
Sursar →, India ... 93 F12 26 14N 87 3 E
Sursee, Switz. ... 32 B6 47 11N 8 6 E
Sursk, Russia ... 60 D7 53 3N 45 40 E
Surskoye, Russia ... 60 C8 54 30N 46 44 E
Surt, Libya ... 108 B3 31 11N 16 39 E
Surt □, Libya ... 108 B3 30 0N 17 30 E
Surt, Al Hammadah al, Libya ... 108 C3 30 0N 17 50 E
Surtanahu, Pakistan ... 92 F4 26 22N 70 0 E
Surte, Sweden ... 17 G6 57 50N 12 1 E
Surtsey, Iceland ... 11 E6 63 20N 20 30W
Surubim, Brazil ... 170 C4 7 50 S 35 45W
Sürüç, Turkey ... 101 D8 36 58N 38 25 E
Surud, Ad Somali Rep. ... 120 B3 10 42N 47 9 E
Suruga-Wan, Japan ... 73 C10 34 45N 138 30 E
Surumu →, Brazil ... 169 C5 3 22N 60 19W
Susa = Sousse, Tunisia ... 108 A2 35 50N 10 38 E
Susa, Italy ... 44 C4 45 8N 7 3 E
Susã →, Denmark ... 17 J5 55 12N 11 42 E
Sušac, Croatia ... 45 F13 42 46N 16 30 E
Susak, Croatia ... 45 D11 44 30N 14 18 E
Susaki, Japan ... 72 E4 33 22N 133 17 E
Susamyrtau, Khrebet = Suusamyr Kyrka Tooloru, Kyrgyzstan ... 65 B6 42 8N 73 15 E
Susangerd, Iran ... 97 D6 31 35N 48 6 E
Susanville, U.S.A. ... 158 F3 40 25N 120 39W
Susch, Switz. ... 33 C10 46 46N 10 5 E
Suşehri, Turkey ... 101 B8 40 0N 38 6 E
Sušice, Czech Rep. ... 34 B6 49 17N 13 30 E
Susleni, Moldova ... 53 C13 47 28N 28 59 E
Susner, India ... 92 H7 23 57N 76 5 E
Susong, China ... 77 B11 30 10N 116 5 E
Susquehanna, U.S.A. ... 151 E9 41 57N 75 36W
Susquehanna →, U.S.A. ... 151 G8 39 33N 76 5W
Susques, Argentina ... 174 A2 23 35 S 66 25W
Sussex, Canada ... 141 C6 45 45N 65 37W
Sussex, U.S.A. ... 151 E10 41 13N 74 37W
Sussex, E. □, U.K. ... 21 G8 51 0N 0 20 E
Sussex, W. □, U.K. ... 21 G7 51 0N 0 30W
Sussex Inlet, Australia ... 129 E5 35 10 S 150 36 E
Sustut →, Canada ... 142 B3 56 20N 127 30W
Susuman, Russia ... 67 C15 62 47N 148 10 E
Susunu, Indonesia ... 83 B4 3 7 S 133 39 E
Susurluk, Turkey ... 49 B10 39 54N 28 8 E
Susuz, Turkey ... 101 B10 40 46N 43 8 E
Susz, Poland ... 54 E6 53 44N 19 20 E
Sütçüler, Turkey ... 100 D4 37 29N 30 57 E
Şuţeşti, Romania ... 53 E12 45 13N 27 27 E
Sutherland, Australia ... 129 C9 34 2 S 151 4 E
Sutherland, S. Africa ... 116 E3 32 24 S 20 40 E
Sutherland, U.K. ... 22 C4 58 12N 4 50W
Sutherland, U.S.A. ... 154 E4 41 10N 101 8W
Sutherland Falls, N.Z. ... 131 B2 44 48 S 167 46 E
Sutherlin, U.S.A. ... 158 E2 43 23N 123 19W
Suthri, India ... 92 H3 23 3N 68 55 E
Sutjeska, Nac. Park △, Bos.-H. ... 52 G3 43 20N 18 40 E
Sutlej →, Pakistan ... 91 C3 29 23N 71 3 E
Sutter, U.S.A. ... 160 F5 39 10N 121 45W
Sutter Creek, U.S.A. ... 160 G6 38 24N 120 48W
Sutton, Canada ... 151 A12 45 6N 72 37W
Sutton, N.Z. ... 131 F5 45 34 S 170 8 E
Sutton, Nebr., U.S.A. ... 154 E6 40 36N 97 52W
Sutton, W. Va., U.S.A. ... 148 F5 38 40N 80 43W
Sutton →, Canada ... 140 A3 55 15N 83 45W
Sutton Coldfield, U.K. ... 21 E6 52 35N 1 49W
Sutton in Ashfield, U.K. ... 20 D6 53 8N 1 16W
Sutton L., Canada ... 140 A3 54 15N 84 42W
Suttor →, Australia ... 126 C4 21 36 S 147 2 E
Suttsu, Japan ... 70 C10 42 48N 140 14 E
Sutwik I., U.S.A. ... 144 H8 56 34N 157 12W
Suusamyr Kyrka Tooloru, Kyrgyzstan ... 65 B6 42 8N 73 15 E
Suva, Fiji ... 133 D8 18 6 S 178 30 E
Suva Gora, Macedonia ... 50 E5 41 45N 21 3 E
Suva Planina, Serbia, Yug. ... 50 D6 43 10N 22 5 E
Suva Reka, Kosovo, Yug. ... 50 D4 42 21N 20 50 E
Suvorov, Russia ... 58 E9 54 7N 36 30 E
Suvorov Is. = Suwarrow Is., Cook Is. ... 135 J11 15 0 S 163 0W
Suvorovo, Bulgaria ... 51 C11 43 20N 27 35 E
Suwa, Japan ... 73 A10 36 2N 138 8 E

Suwa-Ko, *Japan* 73 A10 36 3N 138 5 E
Suwałki, *Poland* 54 D9 54 8N 22 59 E
Suwana, *Indonesia* 79 K18 8 44 S 115 36 E
Suwanee, *U.S.A.* 152 A5 34 8N 84 4W
Suwannaphum, *Thailand* 86 E4 15 33N 103 47 E
Suwannee, *U.S.A.* 153 F6 29 20N 83 9W
Suwannee →, *U.S.A.* 153 F6 29 17N 83 10W
Suwannee Sd., *U.S.A.* 153 F6 29 20N 83 9W
Suwanose-Jima, *Japan* 71 K4 29 38N 129 43 E
Suwarrow Is., *Cook Is.* 135 J11 15 0 S 163 0W
Suwayq as Suqban, *Iraq* 96 D5 31 32N 46 7 E
Suweis, Khalîg el, *Egypt* 106 J8 28 40N 33 0 E
Suweis, Qanâ es, *Egypt* 106 H8 31 0N 32 20 E
Suwŏn, *S. Korea* 75 F14 37 17N 127 1 E
Suzak = Sosaq, *Kazakhstan* 65 A4 44 9N 68 27 E
Suzaka, *Japan* 73 A10 36 39N 138 19 E
Suzdal, *Russia* 58 D11 56 29N 40 26 E
Suzhou, *Anhui, China* 74 H9 33 41N 116 59 E
Suzhou, *Jiangsu, China* 77 B13 31 19N 120 38 E
Suzu, *Japan* 71 F8 37 25N 137 17 E
Suzu-Misaki, *Japan* 71 F8 37 31N 137 21 E
Suzuka, *Japan* 73 C8 34 55N 136 36 E
Suzuka-Sammyaku, *Japan* 73 B8 35 5N 136 30 E
Suzzara, *Italy* 44 D7 44 59N 10 45 E
Svalbard, *Arctic* 6 B8 78 0N 17 0 E
Svalbarð, *Norður-þingeyjarsýsla, Iceland* 11 A11 66 12N 15 43W
Svalbarð, *Suður-þingeyjarsýsla, Iceland* 11 B8 65 45N 18 5W
Svalöv, *Sweden* 17 J7 55 57N 13 8 E
Svaneke, *Denmark* 17 J9 55 8N 15 8 E
Svängsta, *Sweden* 17 H8 56 16N 14 47 E
Svanskog, *Sweden* 16 E6 59 11N 12 33 E
Svappavaara, *Sweden* 14 C19 67 40N 21 3 E
Svärdsjö, *Sweden* 16 D9 60 45N 15 54 E
Svarstad, *Norway* 18 E6 59 27N 9 56 E
Svartå, *Sweden* 16 E8 59 8N 14 32 E
Svartárkot, *Iceland* 11 B9 65 20N 17 15W
Svartevatn, *Norway* 18 E3 59 10N 6 56 E
Svartisen, *Norway* 14 C15 66 40N 13 50 E
Svartvik, *Sweden* 16 B11 62 19N 17 24 E
Svatove, *Ukraine* 59 H10 49 22N 38 15 E
Svatovo = Svatove, *Ukraine* 59 H10 49 22N 38 15 E
Svatsum, *Norway* 18 C6 61 20N 9 50 E
Svay Chek, *Cambodia* 86 F4 13 48N 102 58 E
Svay Rieng, *Cambodia* 87 G5 11 9N 105 45 E
Svealand □, *Sweden* 16 D9 60 20N 15 0 E
Svedala, *Sweden* 17 J7 55 30N 13 15 E
Sveg, *Sweden* 16 B8 62 2N 14 21 E
Sveindal, *Norway* 18 F4 58 29N 7 30 E
Sveinseyri, *Iceland* 11 B3 65 38N 23 51W
Sveio, *Norway* 18 E2 59 33N 5 23 E
Svelgen, *Norway* 18 C2 61 46N 5 17 E
Svelvik, *Norway* 18 E7 59 37N 10 24 E
Svendborg, *Denmark* 17 J4 55 4N 10 35 E
Svene, *Norway* 18 E6 59 45N 9 31 E
Svenljunga, *Sweden* 17 G7 57 29N 13 5 E
Svenstavik, *Sweden* 16 B8 62 45N 14 26 E
Svenstrup, *Denmark* 17 H3 56 58N 9 50 E
Sverdlovsk = Yekaterinburg, *Russia* 54 D7 56 50N 60 30 E
Sverdlovsk, *Ukraine* 59 H10 48 5N 39 47 E
Sverdrup Is., *Canada* 4 B3 79 0N 97 0W
Svetac, *Croatia* 45 E12 43 3N 15 43 E
Sveti Nikola, Prokhod, *Europe* 50 C6 43 27N 22 6 E
Sveti Nikole, *Macedonia* 50 E5 41 51N 21 56 E
Sveti Rok, *Croatia* 41 D12 44 22N 15 39 E
Svetlaya, *Russia* 70 A9 46 33N 138 18 E
Svetlogorsk = Svyatlahorsk, *Belarus* 59 F5 52 38N 29 46 E
Svetlograd, *Russia* 61 H6 45 25N 42 58 E
Svetlovodsk = Svitlovodsk, *Ukraine* 59 H7 49 2N 33 13 E
Svetlyy, *Russia* 64 F8 50 48N 60 51 E
Svidník, *Slovak Rep.* 55 B14 49 15N 21 37 E
Svignaskarð, *Iceland* 11 C5 64 40N 21 42W
Svilaja Planina, *Croatia* 45 E13 43 49N 16 31 E
Svilajnac, *Serbia, Yug.* 50 B5 44 15N 21 11 E
Svilengrad, *Bulgaria* 51 E10 41 49N 26 12 E
Svínafell, *Iceland* 11 D10 63 59N 16 51W
Svir →, *Russia* 58 B7 60 30N 32 48 E
Sviritsa, *Russia* 58 B7 60 29N 32 51 E
Svishtov, *Bulgaria* 51 C9 43 36N 25 23 E
Svislach, *Belarus* 59 F3 53 3N 24 2 E
Svitava →, *Czech Rep.* 55 B9 49 11N 16 37 E
Svitavy, *Czech Rep.* 55 B9 49 47N 16 28 E
Svitlovodsk, *Ukraine* 59 H7 49 2N 33 13 E
Svizzer, Parco Nazionale △, *Switz.* 33 C10 46 40N 10 10 E
Svobodnyy, *Russia* 67 D13 51 20N 128 0 E
Svoge, *Bulgaria* 50 D7 42 59N 23 23 E
Svolvær, *Norway* 14 B16 68 15N 14 34 E
Svorkmo, *Norway* 18 A6 63 10N 9 46 E
Svoronáta, *Greece* 39 C2 38 7N 20 31 E
Svratka →, *Czech Rep.* 55 B9 49 11N 16 33 E
Svrljig, *Serbia, Yug.* 50 C6 43 25N 22 6 E
Svullrya, *Norway* 18 D9 60 25N 12 23 E
Svyatlahorsk, *Belarus* 59 F5 52 38N 29 46 E
Swa, *Burma* 90 F6 19 15N 96 17 E
Swa Tende, *Dem. Rep. of the Congo* 115 D3 7 9 S 17 7 E
Swabian Alps = Schwäbische Alb, *Germany* 31 G5 48 20N 9 30 E
Swaffham, *U.K.* 21 E8 52 39N 0 42 E
Swainsboro, *U.S.A.* 152 C7 32 36N 82 20W
Swakop →, *Namibia* 116 C2 22 38 S 14 36 E
Swakopmund, *Namibia* 116 C1 22 37 S 14 30 E
Swale →, *U.K.* 20 C6 54 5N 1 20W
Swamihalli, *India* 95 G3 14 52N 76 38 E
Swan →, *Australia* 125 F2 32 3 S 115 45 E
Swan →, *Canada* 143 C8 52 30N 100 45W
Swan Hill, *Australia* 128 C5 35 20 S 143 33 E
Swan Hills, *Canada* 142 C5 54 43N 115 24W
Swan Is. = Santanilla, Is., *Honduras* 164 C3 17 22N 83 57W
Swan L., *Canada* 143 C8 52 30N 100 40W
Swan Peak, *U.S.A.* 158 C7 47 43N 113 38W
Swan Ra., *U.S.A.* 158 C7 48 0N 113 45W
Swan Reach, *Australia* 128 C3 34 35 S 139 37 E
Swan River, *Canada* 143 C8 52 10N 101 16W
Swanage, *U.K.* 21 G6 50 36N 1 58W
Swansea, *N.S.W., Australia* 129 B9 33 3 S 151 35 E
Swansea, *Tas., Australia* 127 G4 42 8 S 148 4 E
Swansea, *Canada* 150 C5 43 38N 79 28W
Swansea, *U.K.* 21 F4 51 37N 3 57W
Swansea □, *U.K.* 21 F4 51 38N 4 3W
Swansea, *U.S.A.* 152 B8 33 44N 81 6W
Swansea □, *U.K.* 21 F3 51 38N 4 3W
Swanton, *U.S.A.* 157 C13 41 35N 83 53W
Swar →, *Pakistan* 93 B5 34 40N 72 5 E
Swartberge, *S. Africa* 116 E3 33 20 S 22 0 E
Swartmodder, *S. Africa* 116 D3 28 1 S 20 32 E
Swartnossob →, *Namibia* 116 C2 23 8 S 18 42 E
Swartruggens, *S. Africa* 116 D4 25 39 S 26 42 E
Swarzędz, *Poland* 54 F4 52 25N 17 4 E
Swastika, *Canada* 140 C3 48 7N 80 6W
Swatow = Shantou, *China* 77 F11 23 18N 116 40 E
Swaziland ■, *Africa* 117 D5 26 30 S 31 30 E
Sweden ■, *Europe* 15 G16 57 0N 15 0 E
Swedru, *Ghana* 113 D4 5 32N 0 41W
Sweet Home, *U.S.A.* 158 D2 44 24N 122 44W
Sweet Springs, *U.S.A.* 156 F3 38 58N 93 25W
Sweetgrass, *U.S.A.* 158 A8 48 59N 111 58W
Sweetwater, *Nev., U.S.A.* 160 G7 38 27N 119 9W
Sweetwater, *Tenn., U.S.A.* 149 H3 35 36N 84 28W
Sweetwater, *Tex., U.S.A.* 155 J4 32 28N 100 25W
Sweetwater →, *U.S.A.* 158 E10 42 31N 107 2W
Swellendam, *S. Africa* 116 E3 34 1 S 20 26 E
Świder →, *Poland* 55 F8 52 6N 21 14 E
Świdnica, *Poland* 55 H3 50 50N 16 30 E
Świdnik, *Poland* 55 G9 51 13N 22 39 E

Świdwin, *Poland* 54 E2 53 47N 15 49 E
Świebodzice, *Poland* 55 H3 50 51N 16 20 E
Świebodzin, *Poland* 55 F2 52 15N 15 31 E
Świecie, *Poland* 54 E5 53 25N 18 30 E
Świerzawa, *Poland* 55 G2 51 1N 15 54 E
Świętokrzyski Park Narodowy △, *Poland* 55 H7 50 53N 20 59 E
Świętokrzyskie □, *Poland* 55 H7 50 45N 20 45 E
Świętokrzyskie, Góry, *Poland* 55 H7 51 0N 20 30 E
Swift Current, *Canada* 143 C7 50 20N 107 45W
Swiftcurrent →, *Canada* 143 C7 50 38N 107 44W
Swifts Creek, *Australia* 129 D7 37 17 S 147 44 E
Swilly, L., *Ireland* 23 A4 55 12N 7 33W
Swindon, *U.K.* 21 F6 51 34N 1 46W
Swindon □, *U.K.* 21 F6 51 34N 1 46W
Swinemünde = Świnoujście, *Poland* 54 E1 53 54N 14 16 E
Swinford, *Ireland* 23 C3 53 57N 8 58W
Świnoujście, *Poland* 54 E1 53 54N 14 16 E
Switzerland ■, *Europe* 32 D6 46 30N 8 0 E
Swords, *Ireland* 23 C5 53 28N 6 13W
Swoyerville, *U.S.A.* 151 E9 41 18N 75 53W
Sycamore, *Ill., U.S.A.* 157 C8 41 59N 88 41W
Sycamore, *Ohio, U.S.A.* 157 D13 40 57N 83 10W
Sychevka, *Russia* 58 E8 55 59N 34 16 E
Syców, *Poland* 55 G4 51 19N 17 40 E
Sydenham →, *Canada* 150 D2 42 33N 82 25W
Sydney, *Australia* 129 B9 33 53 S 151 10 E
Sydney, *Canada* 141 C7 46 7N 60 7W
Sydney L., *Canada* 143 C10 50 41N 94 25W
Sydney Mines, *Canada* 141 C7 46 18N 60 15W
Sydprøven = Alluitsup Paa, *Greenland* 10 E6 60 30N 45 35W
Sydra, G. of = Surt, Khalīj, *Libya* 108 B3 31 40N 18 30 E
Syeverodonetsk, *Ukraine* 59 H10 48 58N 38 35 E
Syftland, *Norway* 18 D2 60 14N 5 27 E
Syke, *Germany* 30 C4 52 55N 8 50 E
Sykesville, *U.S.A.* 150 E6 41 3N 78 50W
Sykkylven, *Norway* 18 B3 62 23N 6 35 E
Syktyvkar, *Russia* 56 B9 61 45N 50 40 E
Sylacauga, *U.S.A.* 152 B3 33 10N 86 15W
Sylarna, *Sweden* 18 A9 63 2N 12 13 E
Sylhet, *Bangla.* 90 C3 24 54N 91 52 E
Sylt, *Germany* 30 A4 54 54N 8 22 E
Sylte, *Norway* 18 B4 62 18N 7 17 E
Sylva →, *Russia* 64 B6 58 0N 56 54 E
Sylvan Beach, *U.S.A.* 151 C9 43 12N 75 44W
Sylvan Lake, *Canada* 142 C6 52 20N 114 3W
Sylvania, *Ga., U.S.A.* 152 C8 32 45N 81 38W
Sylvania, *Ohio, U.S.A.* 157 C13 41 43N 83 42W
Sylvester, *U.S.A.* 152 D6 31 32N 83 50W
Sym, *Russia* 66 C9 60 20N 88 18 E
Symón, *Mexico* 162 C4 24 42N 102 35W
Synelnykove, *Ukraine* 59 H8 48 25N 35 30 E
Synevyr △, *Ukraine* 53 B8 48 30N 23 40 E
Synnfjell, *Norway* 18 C6 61 5N 9 46 E
Synnott Ra., *Australia* 124 C4 16 30 S 125 20 E
Syracuse = Siracusa, *Italy* 49 F8 37 4N 15 17 E
Syracuse, *Ind., U.S.A.* 157 C11 41 26N 85 45W
Syracuse, *Kans., U.S.A.* 155 G4 37 59N 101 45W
Syracuse, *N.Y., U.S.A.* 151 C8 43 3N 76 9W
Syracuse, *Nebr., U.S.A.* 154 E6 40 39N 96 11W
Syrdarya, *Uzbekistan* 65 C4 40 50N 68 40 E
Syrdarya →, *Kazakhstan* 66 B4 46 3N 61 0 E
Syria ■, *Asia* 101 E8 35 0N 38 0 E
Syriam, *Burma* 90 G6 16 44N 96 19 E
Syrian Desert = Shām, Bādiyat ash, *Asia* 96 C3 32 0N 40 0 E
Sysert, *Russia* 64 C8 56 29N 60 49 E
Sysslebäck, *Sweden* 16 D6 60 44N 12 52 E
Syvde, *Norway* 18 B2 62 5N 5 44 E
Syzran, *Russia* 60 D9 53 12N 48 30 E
Szabolcs-Szatmár-Bereg □, *Hungary* 52 B6 48 2N 21 45 E
Szadek, *Poland* 55 G5 51 41N 18 59 E
Szamocin, *Poland* 54 E4 53 2N 17 7 E
Szamos →, *Hungary* 52 B7 48 7N 22 20 E
Szamotuły, *Poland* 55 F3 52 37N 16 33 E
Száraz →, *Hungary* 52 D6 46 10N 21 15 E
Szarvas, *Hungary* 52 D6 46 50N 20 38 E
Százhalombatta, *Hungary* 52 C3 47 20N 18 58 E
Szczawnica, *Poland* 55 J7 49 26N 20 30 E
Szczebrzeszyn, *Poland* 55 H9 50 42N 22 59 E
Szczecin, *Poland* 54 E1 53 27N 14 27 E
Szczecinek, *Poland* 54 E3 53 43N 16 41 E
Szczeciński, Zalew = Stettiner Haff, *Germany* 30 B10 53 47N 14 15 E
Szczekociny, *Poland* 55 H6 50 38N 19 48 E
Szczucin, *Poland* 55 H8 50 18N 21 4 E
Szczuczyn, *Poland* 54 E9 53 36N 22 19 E
Szczyrk, *Poland* 55 J6 49 43N 19 2 E
Szczytna, *Poland* 55 H3 50 25N 16 28 E
Szczytno, *Poland* 54 E7 53 33N 21 0 E
Szechwan = Sichuan □, *China* 76 B5 30 30N 103 0 E
Szécsény, *Hungary* 52 B4 48 7N 19 30 E
Szeged, *Hungary* 52 D5 46 16N 20 10 E
Szeghalom, *Hungary* 52 C6 47 1N 21 10 E
Székesfehérvár, *Hungary* 52 C3 47 15N 18 25 E
Szekszárd, *Hungary* 52 D3 46 22N 18 42 E
Szendrő, *Hungary* 52 B5 48 24N 20 41 E
Szentendre, *Hungary* 52 C4 47 39N 19 4 E
Szentes, *Hungary* 52 D5 46 39N 20 21 E
Szentgotthárd, *Hungary* 52 D1 46 58N 16 19 E
Szentlőrinc, *Hungary* 52 D3 46 3N 18 1 E
Szerencs, *Hungary* 52 B6 48 10N 21 12 E
Szigetszentmiklós, *Hungary* 52 C4 47 21N 19 3 E
Szigetvár, *Hungary* 52 D2 46 3N 17 46 E
Szikszó, *Hungary* 52 B5 48 12N 20 56 E
Szklarska Poreba, *Poland* 55 H2 50 50N 15 33 E
Szkwa →, *Poland* 55 E8 53 11N 21 43 E
Szlichtyngowa, *Poland* 55 G3 51 42N 16 15 E
Szob, *Hungary* 52 C3 47 48N 18 53 E
Szolnok, *Hungary* 52 C5 47 10N 20 15 E
Szombathely, *Hungary* 52 C1 47 14N 16 38 E
Szprotawa, *Poland* 55 G2 51 33N 15 35 E
Sztálinváros = Dunaújváros, *Hungary* 52 D3 46 58N 18 57 E
Sztum, *Poland* 54 E6 53 55N 19 1 E
Sztutowo, *Poland* 54 D6 54 20N 19 15 E
Szubin, *Poland* 55 E4 53 1N 17 45 E
Szydłowiec, *Poland* 55 G7 51 15N 20 51 E
Szypliszki, *Poland* 54 D10 54 17N 23 2 E

T

Ta Khli Khok, *Thailand* 86 E3 15 18N 100 20 E
Ta Lai, *Vietnam* 87 G6 11 24N 107 23 E
Tab, *Hungary* 52 D3 46 44N 18 2 E
Tabacal, *Argentina* 174 A3 23 15 S 64 15W
Tabaco, *Phil.* 80 E4 13 22N 123 44 E
Tabagné, *Ivory C.* 112 D4 7 59N 3 4W
Ṭābah, *Si. Arabia* 96 E4 26 55N 42 38 E
Tabajara, *Brazil* 173 B5 8 56 S 62 7W
Tabalo, *Papua N. G.* 132 A5 1 24 S 149 40 E
Tabalos, *Papua N. G.* 172 B2 6 29 S 35 0 E
Tabanan, *Indonesia* 79 K18 8 32 S 115 8 E
Tabankort, *Niger* 113 B5 17 44N 0 0 E
Tabar I., *Papua N. G.* 132 B7 2 56 S 152 0 E
Tabar Is., *Papua N. G.* 132 B7 2 50 S 152 0 E
Tabarka, *Tunisia* 108 A1 36 56N 8 46 E
Ṭabas, *Khorāsān, Iran* 97 C9 32 48N 60 12 E

Ṭabas, *Khorāsān, Iran* 97 C8 33 35N 56 55 E
Tabasará, Serranía de, *Panama* 164 E3 8 35N 81 40W
Tabasco □, *Mexico* 163 D6 17 45N 93 30W
Tābask, *Iran* 97 D8 31 12N 57 54 E
Tabatinga, *Brazil* 172 A4 4 16 S 69 56W
Tabatinga, Serra da, *Brazil* 170 D3 10 30 S 44 0W
Tabayin, *Burma* 90 D5 22 42N 95 20 E
Tabelbala, Kahal de, *Algeria* 111 C4 28 47N 2 0W
Tabelembla, *Algeria* 111 D5 24 43N 4 16 E
Taber, *Canada* 142 D6 49 47N 112 8W
Taberg, *Sweden* 17 G8 57 40N 14 6 E
Tabi, *Angola* 115 D2 8 10 S 13 18 E
Tabira, *Brazil* 170 C4 7 35 S 37 33W
Tabla, *Niger* 113 C5 13 46N 3 1 E
Tablas de Daimiel, Parque Nac. de △, *Spain* 43 F7 39 9N 3 40W
Tablas I., *Phil.* 80 E4 12 25N 122 2 E
Tablas Strait, *Phil.* 80 E3 12 40N 121 48 E
Table B. = Tafelbaai, *S. Africa* 116 E2 33 35 S 18 25 E
Table C., *N.Z.* 130 F7 39 6N 178 0 E
Table Grove, *U.S.A.* 156 D6 40 20N 90 27W
Table I., *Burma* 95 G11 14 12N 93 22 E
Table Mt., *S. Africa* 116 E2 34 0 S 18 22 E
Table Rock L., *U.S.A.* 155 G8 36 36N 93 19W
Tabletop, Mt., *Australia* 126 C4 23 24 S 147 11 E
Tabocal, *Brazil* 169 D6 2 42 S 57 40W
Tábor, *Czech Rep.* 34 B7 49 25N 14 39 E
Tabora, *Tanzania* 118 D3 5 2 S 32 50 E
Tabora □, *Tanzania* 118 D3 5 0 S 33 0 E
Taboshar, *Tajikistan* 65 C4 40 34N 69 38 E
Tabou, *Ivory C.* 112 E3 4 30N 7 20W
Tabrīz, *Iran* 101 C12 38 7N 46 20 E
Tabuaeran, *Kiribati* 135 G12 3 51N 159 22W
Tabubil, *Papua N. G.* 132 C1 5 20 S 141 15 E
Tabuenca, *Spain* 40 D3 41 42N 1 33W
Tabuk, *Phil.* 80 C3 17 24N 121 25 E
Tabūk, *Si. Arabia* 96 D3 28 23N 36 36 E
Taburno-Camposauro, Parco △, *Italy* 47 A7 41 8N 14 37 E
Tabwemasana, Mt., *Vanuatu* 133 E4 15 20 S 166 44 E
Täby, *Sweden* 16 E12 59 28N 18 4 E
Tacámbaro de Codallos, *Mexico* 162 D4 19 14N 101 28W
Tacarigua, Laguna de, *Venezuela* 168 A4 10 15N 65 50W
Tacheng, *China* 68 B3 46 40N 82 58 E
Tach'i, *Taiwan* 77 E13 24 46N 121 0 E
Tachia, *Taiwan* 77 E13 24 25N 120 28 E
Tachibana-Wan, *Japan* 72 E2 32 45N 130 7 E
Tachikawa, *Japan* 73 B11 35 42N 139 25 E
Tach'ing Shan = Daqing Shan, *China* 76 D6 40 40N 111 0 E
Táchira □, *Venezuela* 168 B3 8 7N 72 15W
Tachov, *Czech Rep.* 34 B5 49 47N 12 39 E
Tacloban, *Phil.* 81 F5 11 15N 124 58 E
Tacna, *Peru* 172 D3 18 0 S 70 20W
Tacna □, *Peru* 172 D3 17 40 S 70 20W
Tacoma, *U.S.A.* 160 C4 47 14N 122 26W
Tacuarembó, *Uruguay* 175 C4 31 45 S 56 0W
Tacurong, *Phil.* 81 H5 6 40N 124 41 E
Tacutu →, *Brazil* 169 C5 3 1N 60 29W
Tada-u, *Burma* 90 C5 21 49N 95 58 E
Tadinah, *Japan* 73 C7 34 29N 135 37 E
Tademaït, Plateau du, *Algeria* 111 C5 28 30N 2 30 E
Tadent, O. →, *Algeria* 111 D6 22 25N 6 40 E
Tadéra, *Algeria* 111 D6 20 29N 7 0 E
Tadine, *N. Cal.* 133 U21 21 33 S 167 52 E
Tadio, L., *Ivory C.* 112 D3 5 10N 5 15W
Tadjerdjeri, O. →, *Algeria* 111 B5 26 0N 8 0 E
Tadjerouna, *Algeria* 111 B5 33 31N 2 3 E
Tadjettaret, O. →, *Algeria* 111 D6 21 20N 7 22 E
Tadjmout, *Laghouat, Algeria* 111 B5 33 52N 2 30 E
Tadjmout, *Saoura, Algeria* 111 C5 25 37N 3 48 E
Tadjoura, *Djibouti* 107 E5 11 50N 42 55 E
Tadjoura, Golfe de, *Djibouti* 107 E5 11 50N 43 0 E
Tadmor, *N.Z.* 131 B7 41 27 S 172 45 E
Tadotsu, *Japan* 72 C6 34 16N 133 45 E
Tadoule, L., *Canada* 143 B9 58 36N 98 20W
Tadoussac, *Canada* 141 C6 48 11N 69 42W
Tadpatri, *India* 95 G4 14 55N 78 1 E
Tadrés, Réserve Totale de Faune du △, *Niger* 113 B6 16 0N 7 10 E
Tadzhikistan = Tajikistan ■, *Asia* 65 D4 38 30N 70 0 E
Taechŏn-ni, *S. Korea* 75 F14 36 21N 126 36 E
Taegu, *S. Korea* 75 G15 35 50N 128 37 E
Taegwan, *N. Korea* 75 D13 40 13N 125 12 E
Taejŏn, *S. Korea* 75 F14 36 20N 127 28 E
Taen, Ko, *Thailand* 87 b 9 22N 99 57 E
Tafalla, *Spain* 40 C3 42 30N 1 41W
Tafar, *Sudan* 107 F2 6 52N 28 15 E
Tafassasset, O. →, *Algeria* 111 D6 22 0N 9 57 E
Tafelbaai, *S. Africa* 116 D2 33 35 S 18 25 E
Tafelney, C., *Morocco* 110 B3 31 3N 9 51W
Tafermaar, *Indonesia* 83 C4 6 47 S 134 10 E
Taffermit, *Morocco* 110 C3 29 57N 9 15W
Tafí Viejo, *Argentina* 174 B2 26 43 S 65 17W
Tafihān, *Iran* 97 D7 29 25N 52 39 E
Tafilalet, *Morocco* 110 B4 31 20N 4 45W
Tafiré, *Ivory C.* 112 D3 9 4N 5 4W
Tafjord, *Norway* 18 B4 62 14N 7 42 E
Tafnidilt, *Morocco* 110 C2 28 47N 10 58W
Tafo, *Ghana* 113 D4 6 25N 0 25W
Tafraoute, *Morocco* 110 C3 29 50N 8 58W
Tafresh, *Iran* 97 C6 34 45N 49 57 E
Taft, *Iran* 97 D7 31 45N 54 14 E
Taft, *Phil.* 81 F5 11 57N 125 30 E
Taft, *U.S.A.* 161 K7 35 8N 119 28W
Taftān, Kūh-e, *Iran* 97 D9 28 40N 61 0 E
Tafwap, *India* 95 L11 7 23N 93 43 E
Taga, *Samoa* 133 W23 13 46 S 172 28W
Taga Dzong, *Bhutan* 90 B2 27 5N 89 55 E
Tagana-an, *Phil.* 81 G5 9 42N 125 31 E
Taganrog, *Russia* 59 J10 47 10N 38 50 E
Taganrogskiy Zaliv, *Russia* 59 J10 47 0N 38 30 E
Tagânt, *Mauritania* 112 B2 18 20N 11 0W
Tagap Ga, *Burma* 90 B6 26 56N 96 13 E
Tagatay, *Phil.* 80 D3 14 6N 120 59 E
Tagaung, *Burma* 90 D6 23 30N 96 0 E
Tagawa, *Japan* 72 D2 33 38N 130 51 E
Tagbilaran, *Phil.* 81 G4 9 39N 123 51 E
Tage, *Papua N. G.* 132 D2 6 19 S 143 20 E
Tággia, *Italy* 44 E4 43 52N 7 51 E
Taghzout, *Morocco* 110 B4 33 30N 4 49W
Tagish, *Canada* 142 A2 60 19N 134 16W
Tagish L., *Canada* 142 A2 60 10N 134 20W
Tagkawayan, *Phil.* 80 E4 13 58N 122 32 E
Tagliacozzo, *Italy* 45 F10 42 4N 13 14 E
Tagliamento →, *Italy* 45 C10 45 38N 13 6 E
Táglio di Po, *Italy* 45 D9 45 0N 12 12 E
Tagna, *Colombia* 168 D3 2 24 S 70 37W
Tago, *Phil.* 81 G6 9 2N 126 13 E
Tago, Mt., *Phil.* 81 G5 8 23N 125 0 E
Tagomago, *Spain* 38 C2 39 2N 1 39 E
Taguaráré, *Mauritania* 112 B2 17 45N 7 44 E
Taguatinga, *Brazil* 171 D3 12 16 S 42 26W
Tagudin, *Phil.* 80 C3 16 56N 120 27 E
Taguenout Haggueret, *Mali* 111 D4 21 14N 0 48W
Tagula, *Papua N. G.* 132 F7 11 30 S 153 15 E
Tagula I., *Papua N. G.* 132 F7 11 30 S 153 30 E
Tagum, *Phil.* 81 H5 7 33N 125 53 E
Tagus = Tejo →, *Europe* 43 F2 38 40N 9 24W
Tahakopa, *N.Z.* 131 G4 46 30 S 169 23 E

Tahala, *Morocco* 110 B4 34 0N 4 28W
Tahan, Gunong, *Malaysia* 87 K4 4 34N 102 17 E
Tahānah-ye sūr Gol, *Afghan.* 91 C2 31 43N 67 53 E
Tahara, *Japan* 73 C9 34 40N 137 16 E
Tahat, *Algeria* 111 D6 23 18N 5 33 E
Tāherī, *Iran* 97 E7 27 43N 52 20 E
Tahiti, *Pac. Oc.* 133 S16 17 37 S 149 27W
Tahlab →, *Pakistan* 91 C1 28 9N 62 45 E
Tahlequah, *U.S.A.* 155 H7 35 55N 94 58W
Tahoe, L., *U.S.A.* 160 G6 39 6N 120 2W
Tahoe City, *U.S.A.* 160 F6 39 10N 120 9W
Tahoka, *U.S.A.* 155 J4 33 10N 101 48W
Taholah, *U.S.A.* 160 C2 47 21N 124 17W
Tahora, *N.Z.* 130 F3 39 2 S 174 49 E
Tahoua, *Niger* 113 C6 14 57N 5 16 E
Tahrūd, *Iran* 97 D8 29 26N 57 49 E
Tahsis, *Canada* 142 D3 49 55N 126 40W
Tahta, *Egypt* 106 B3 26 44N 31 32 E
Tahtaköprü, *Turkey* 51 G13 39 57N 29 39 E
Tahtalı Dağları, *Turkey* 100 C7 38 20N 36 0 E
Tahuamanú →, *Bolivia* 172 C4 11 6 S 67 36W
Tahulandang, *Indonesia* 82 A3 3 38N 125 30 E
Tahuna, *Indonesia* 82 A3 3 38N 125 30 E
Taï, *Ivory C.* 112 D3 5 55N 7 30W
Taï, Parc Nat. de △, *Ivory C.* 112 D3 5 25N 7 5W
Tai Au Mun, *China* 69 G11 22 18N 114 17 E
Tai Hu, *China* 77 B12 31 5N 120 10 E
Tai Mo Shan, *China* 69 G10 22 25N 114 7 E
Tai O, *China* 69 G10 22 15N 113 52 E
Tai Pang Wan, *H.K.* 69 F11 22 33N 114 24 E
Tai Po, *China* 69 G11 22 27N 114 10 E
Tai Rom Yen Nat. Park △, *Thailand* 87 H2 8 45N 99 30 E
Tai Shan, *China* 75 F9 36 25N 117 20 E
Tai Yue Shan = Lantau I., *China* 69 G10 22 15N 113 56 E
Tai'an, *China* 75 F9 36 12N 117 8 E
Taiarapu, Presq. de, *Tahiti* 133 S16 17 47 S 149 14W
Taibei = T'aipei, *Taiwan* 77 E13 25 2N 121 30 E
Taibique, *Canary Is.* 9 e1 27 42N 17 58W
Taibus Qi, *China* 74 D8 41 54N 115 22 E
Taicang, *China* 77 B13 31 30N 121 5 E
Taieri →, *N.Z.* 131 G5 46 3 S 170 12 E
Taiga Madema, *Libya* 108 D3 23 46N 15 25 E
Taigu, *China* 74 F7 37 28N 112 30 E
Taihang Shan, *China* 74 G7 36 0N 113 30 E
Taihape, *N.Z.* 130 F4 39 41 S 175 48 E
Taihe, *Anhui, China* 74 H8 33 20N 115 42 E
Taihe, *Jiangxi, China* 77 D10 26 47N 114 52 E
Taihoku = T'aipei, *Taiwan* 77 E13 25 2N 121 30 E
Taihu, *China* 77 B11 30 22N 116 20 E
Taijiang, *China* 76 D7 26 47N 108 21 E
Taikang, *China* 74 G8 34 5N 114 50 E
Taikkyi, *Burma* 90 G6 17 20N 96 0 E
Tailem Bend, *Australia* 128 C3 35 12 S 139 29 E
Tailfingen, *Germany* 31 G5 48 15N 9 1 E
Tailuko, *Taiwan* 77 E13 24 9N 121 37 E
Taimyr Peninsula = Taymyr, Poluostrov, *Russia* 67 B11 75 0N 100 0 E
Tain, *U.K.* 22 D4 57 49N 4 4W
Tainan, *Taiwan* 77 F13 23 0N 120 10 E
Tainaron, Ákra, *Greece* 48 E4 36 22N 22 27 E
Tainggyo, *China* 90 G5 17 49N 94 29 E
Taiobeiras, *Brazil* 171 E13 15 49 S 42 14W
Taipa, *China* 69 G10 22 10N 113 35 E
T'aipei, *Taiwan* 77 E13 25 2N 121 30 E
Taiping, *China* 77 B12 30 15N 118 6 E
Taiping, *Malaysia* 87 K3 4 51N 100 44 E
Taipingzhen, *China* 74 H6 33 35N 111 42 E
Taipu, *Brazil* 170 C4 5 37 S 35 36W
Tairbeart = Tarbert, *U.K.* 22 D2 57 54N 6 49W
Tairenpokpi, *India* 90 C4 24 39N 93 30 E
Tairua, *N.Z.* 130 D4 37 0 S 175 51 E
Taisha, *Japan* 72 B4 35 24N 132 40 E
Taishan, *China* 77 D12 22 14N 112 41 E
Taishun, *China* 77 D12 27 30N 119 42 E
Taita Hills, *Kenya* 118 C4 3 25 S 38 15 E
Taitao, C., *Chile* 176 C1 45 55 S 75 5W
Taitao, Pen. de, *Chile* 176 C2 46 30 S 75 0W
T'aitung, *Taiwan* 77 F13 22 43N 121 4 E
Taivalkoski, *Finland* 14 D23 65 33N 28 12 E
Taiwan ■, *Asia* 77 F13 23 30N 121 0 E
Taiwan Strait, *Asia* 77 E12 24 40N 120 0 E
Taixing, *China* 77 A13 32 11N 120 0 E
Taiyara, *Sudan* 107 E3 13 12N 30 47 E
Taïyetos Óros, *Greece* 48 D4 37 0N 22 23 E
Taiyiba, *Israel* 103 C4 32 36N 35 27 E
Taiyuan, *China* 74 F7 37 52N 112 33 E
Taizhong = T'aichung, *Taiwan* 77 E13 24 9N 120 37 E
Taizhou, *China* 77 A12 32 28N 119 55 E
Taizhou Liedao, *China* 77 C13 28 30N 121 55 E
Ta'izz, *Yemen* 98 D4 13 35N 44 2 E
Tājābād, *Iran* 97 D7 30 2N 54 24 E
Tajapuru, Furo do, *Brazil* 170 B1 1 50 S 50 25W
Tajarhī, *Libya* 108 D2 24 21N 14 28 E
Tajikistan ■, *Asia* 65 D4 38 30N 70 0 E
Tajima, *Japan* 71 F9 37 12N 139 46 E
Tajimi, *Japan* 73 B9 35 19N 137 8 E
Tajo = Tejo →, *Europe* 43 F2 38 40N 9 24W
Tajrīsh, *Iran* 97 C6 35 48N 51 25 E
Tājūrā, *Libya* 108 B2 32 51N 13 21 E
Tak, *Thailand* 86 D2 16 52N 99 8 E
Takāb, *Iran* 101 D12 36 24N 47 7 E
Takachiho, *Japan* 72 E3 32 42N 131 18 E
Takachu, *Botswana* 116 C3 22 37 S 21 58 E
Takada, *Japan* 71 F10 37 7N 138 15 E
Takahagi, *Japan* 71 F10 36 43N 140 45 E
Takahashi, *Japan* 72 C6 34 51N 133 39 E
Takaka, *N.Z.* 131 A7 40 51 S 172 50 E
Takamaka, *Seychelles* 121 b 4 50 S 55 30 E
Takamatsu, *Japan* 72 C6 34 20N 134 5 E
Takanabe, *Japan* 72 E3 32 8N 131 30 E
Takaoka, *Japan* 73 A9 36 47N 137 0 E
Takapau, *N.Z.* 130 G5 40 2 S 176 21 E
Takapuna, *N.Z.* 130 C3 36 47 S 174 47 E
Takasago, *Japan* 72 C6 34 45N 134 48 E
Takasaki, *Japan* 73 A11 36 20N 139 0 E
Takatsuki, *Japan* 73 C7 34 51N 135 37 E
Takaungu, *Kenya* 118 C4 3 38 S 39 52 E
Takayama, *Japan* 73 A9 36 18N 137 11 E
Takayama-Bonchi, *Japan* 73 B9 36 10N 137 18 E
Take-Shima, *Japan* 71 J5 30 49N 130 26 E
Takefu, *Japan* 73 B8 35 50N 136 10 E
Takehara, *Japan* 72 C6 34 21N 132 55 E
Takengon, *Indonesia* 84 B1 4 45N 96 50 E
Takeo, *Japan* 72 D2 33 12N 130 1 E
Tåkern, *Sweden* 17 F8 58 22N 14 45 E
Tākestān, *Iran* 97 C6 36 0N 49 40 E
Taketa, *Japan* 72 E3 32 58N 131 24 E
Takev, *Cambodia* 87 G5 10 59N 104 47 E
Takh, *India* 93 C7 33 6N 77 32 E
Takhār □, *Afghan.* 91 A3 36 40N 70 0 E
Takht-Sulaiman, *Pakistan* 91 D3 31 40N 70 0 E
Taki, *Papua N. G.* 132 D8 6 29 S 155 52 E
Takikawa, *Japan* 70 C10 43 33N 141 54 E
Takla L., *Canada* 142 B3 55 15N 125 45W
Takla Landing, *Canada* 142 B3 55 30N 125 50W
Takla Makan = Taklamakan Shamo, *China* 68 C3 38 0N 83 0 E
Taklamakan Shamo, *China* 68 C3 38 0N 83 0 E
Takotna, *U.S.A.* 144 E8 62 59N 156 4W
Taku, *Japan* 72 D2 33 18N 130 3 E
Taku →, *Canada* 142 B2 58 30N 133 50W

288 Takua Thung

INDEX TO WORLD MAPS

Takua Thung, *Thailand* **87 a** 8 24N 98 27 E
Takum, *India* **90 B4** 27 47N 93 37 E
Takum, *Nigeria* **113 D6** 7 18N 9 36 E
Takundi, *Dem. Rep. of the Congo* **115 C3** 4 45 S 16 34 E
Takutu →, *Guyana* **169 C5** 3 1N 60 29W
Tal Halāl, *Iran* **97 D7** 28 54N 55 1 E
Tala, *Uruguay* **175 C4** 34 21 S 55 46W
Talachyn, *Belarus* **58 E5** 54 25N 29 42 E
Talacogan, *Phil.* **81 G5** 8 32N 125 39 E
Talagang, *Pakistan* **92 C5** 32 55N 72 25 E
Talagante, *Chile* **174 C1** 33 40 S 70 50W
Talahouhait, *Algeria* **111 D5** 24 52N 1 5 E
Talaimannar, *Sri Lanka* **95 K4** 9 6N 79 43 E
Talaïnt, *Morocco* **110 C3** 29 41N 9 40W
Talak, *Niger* **113 B6** 18 0N 5 0 E
Talakag, *Phil.* **81 G5** 8 16N 124 37 E
Talamanca, Cordillera de, *Cent. Amer.* **164 E3** 9 20N 83 20W
Talant, *France* **27 E11** 47 19N 4 58 E
Talara, *Peru* **172 A1** 4 38 S 81 18W
Talas, *Kyrgyzstan* **65 B6** 42 30N 72 13 E
Talas, *Turkey* **100 C6** 38 41N 35 33 E
Talas →, *Kazakhstan* **65 B5** 44 0N 70 20 E
Talas Ala Too, *Kyrgyzstan* **65 B6** 42 15N 72 0 E
Talasea, *Papua N. G.* **132 C6** 5 20 S 150 2 E
Talasskiy Alatau = Talas Ala Too, *Kyrgyzstan* **65 B6** 42 15N 72 0 E
Talâta, *Egypt* **103 E1** 30 36N 32 20 E
Talata Mafara, *Nigeria* **113 C6** 12 38N 6 4 E
Talaud, Kepulauan, *Indonesia* **82 A3** 4 30N 126 50 E
Talaud Is. = Talaud, Kepulauan, *Indonesia* **82 A3** 4 30N 126 50 E
Talavera de la Reina, *Spain* **42 F6** 39 55N 4 46W
Talavera la Real, *Spain* **43 G4** 38 53N 6 46W
Talawgyi, *Burma* **90 C6** 25 4N 97 19 E
Talayan, *Phil.* **81 H5** 6 52N 124 24 E
Talayuela, *Spain* **42 F5** 39 59N 5 36W
Talbandh, *India* **93 H12** 22 3N 86 20 E
Talbert, Sillon de, *France* **26 D3** 48 53N 3 5W
Talbot, *Australia* **128 D5** 37 10 S 143 44 E
Talbot, C., *Australia* **124 B4** 13 48 S 126 43 E
Talbotton, *U.S.A.* **152 C5** 32 41N 84 32W
Talbragar →, *Australia* **129 B8** 32 12 S 148 37 E
Talca, *Chile* **174 D1** 35 28 S 71 40W
Talcahuano, *Chile* **174 D1** 36 40 S 73 10W
Talcher, *India* **94 D7** 21 0N 85 18 E
Talcho, *Niger* **113 C5** 14 44N 3 28 E
Taldy Kurgan = Taldyqorghan, *Kazakhstan* **66 E8** 45 10N 78 45 E
Taldy-Suu, *Kyrgyzstan* **65 B9** 42 48N 78 26 E
Taldyqorghan, *Kazakhstan* **66 E8** 45 10N 78 45 E
Tālesh, *Iran* **97 B6** 37 58N 48 58 E
Tālesh, Kūhhā-ye, *Iran* **97 B6** 37 42N 48 55 E
Talgar = Talghar, *Kazakhstan* **65 B8** 43 19N 77 15 E
Talgar, Pik, *Kazakhstan* **65 B8** 43 5N 77 20 E
Talghar, *Kazakhstan* **65 B8** 43 19N 77 15 E
Talguharai, *Sudan* **106 D4** 18 19N 35 56 E
Talguppa, *India* **95 G2** 14 13N 74 56 E
Tali Post, *Sudan* **107 F3** 5 55N 30 44 E
Taliabu, *Indonesia* **82 B2** 1 50 S 125 0 E
Talibon, *Phil.* **81 F5** 10 9N 124 20 E
Talibong, Ko, *Thailand* **87 J2** 7 15N 99 23 E
Talihina, *U.S.A.* **155 H7** 34 45N 95 3W
Talikota, *India* **95 F3** 16 29N 76 17 E
Talimardzhan, *Uzbekistan* **65 D2** 38 17N 65 33 E
Talipao, *Phil.* **81 J3** 5 59N 121 7 E
Talisay, *Phil.* **81 F4** 10 44N 122 58 E
Talisayan, *Phil.* **81 G5** 9 0N 124 55 E
Talitsa, *Russia* **64 C9** 57 0N 63 43 E
Taliwang, *Indonesia* **85 D5** 8 50 S 116 55 E
Talkeetna, *U.S.A.* **144 E10** 62 20N 150 6W
Tall 'Afar, *Iraq* **101 D10** 36 22N 42 27 E
Tall Kalakh, *Syria* **103 A5** 34 41N 36 15 E
Talla, *Egypt* **106 B3** 28 5N 30 43 E
Talladega, *U.S.A.* **152 B3** 33 26N 86 6W
Tallahassee, *U.S.A.* **152 E5** 30 27N 84 17W
Tallangatta, *Australia* **129 D7** 36 15 S 147 19 E
Tallapoosa, *U.S.A.* **152 B4** 33 45N 85 17W
Tallapoosa →, *U.S.A.* **152 C3** 32 30N 86 16W
Tallard, *France* **29 D10** 44 28N 6 3 E
Tallarook, *Australia* **129 D6** 37 5 S 145 6 E
Tallassee, *U.S.A.* **152 C4** 32 32N 85 54W
Tällberg, *Sweden* **16 D9** 60 51N 15 2 E
Tallering Pk., *Australia* **125 E2** 28 6 S 115 37 E
Talli, *Pakistan* **92 E3** 29 32N 68 8 E
Tallinn, *Estonia* **15 G21** 59 22N 24 48 E
Tallmadge, *U.S.A.* **150 E3** 41 6N 81 27W
Tallulah, *U.S.A.* **155 J9** 32 25N 91 11W
Tălmaciu, *Romania* **53 E9** 45 38N 24 19 E
Talmest, *Morocco* **110 B3** 31 48N 9 21W
Talmont-St-Hilaire, *France* **28 B2** 46 27N 1 37W
Talne, *Ukraine* **59 H6** 48 50N 30 44 E
Talnoye = Talne, *Ukraine* **59 H6** 48 50N 30 44 E
Taloda, *India* **94 D2** 21 34N 74 11 E
Talodi, *Sudan* **107 E3** 10 35N 30 22 E
Tāloqān, *Afghan.* **65 E4** 36 44N 69 33 E
Talovaya, *Russia* **60 E5** 51 6N 40 45 E
Taloyoak, *Canada* **138 B10** 69 32N 93 32W
Talpa de Allende, *Mexico* **162 C4** 20 23N 104 51W
Talparo, *Trin. & Tob.* **169 F9** 10 30N 61 17W
Talquin, L., *U.S.A.* **152 E5** 30 23N 84 39W
Talsi, *Latvia* **15 H20** 57 10N 22 30 E
Talsi □, *Latvia* **54 A9** 57 20N 22 40 E
Talsinnt, *Morocco* **111 B4** 32 33N 3 27W
Taltal, *Chile* **174 B1** 25 23 S 70 33W
Taltson →, *Canada* **142 A6** 61 24N 112 46W
Talurqjuak = Taloyoak, *Canada* **138 B10** 69 32N 93 32W
Talwood, *Australia* **127 D4** 28 29 S 149 29 E
Talyawalka Cr. →, *Australia* **128 B5** 32 28 S 142 22 E
Tam Chau, *Vietnam* **87 G5** 10 48N 105 12 E
Tam Ky, *Vietnam* **86 E7** 15 34N 108 29 E
Tam Quan, *Vietnam* **86 E7** 14 35N 109 3 E
Tama, *U.S.A.* **156 C4** 41 58N 92 35W
Tama Wildlife Reserve ⌓, *Ethiopia* **107 F4** 5 55N 36 5 E
Tamada, *Algeria* **111 D5** 21 34N 3 20 E
Tamalameque, *Colombia* **168 B3** 8 52N 73 49W
Tamale, *Ghana* **113 D4** 9 22N 0 50W
Taman, *Russia* **59 K9** 45 14N 36 41 E
Taman Negara Nat. Park △, *Malaysia* **87 K4** 4 38N 102 26 E
Tamana, *Japan* **72 E2** 32 58N 130 32 E
Tamana, *Kiribati* **123 A13** 2 30 S 175 59 E
Tamanar, *Morocco* **110 B3** 31 1N 9 46W
Tamani, *Mali* **112 C3** 13 20N 6 50W
Tamano, *Japan* **72 C5** 34 29N 133 59 E
Tamanrasset, *Algeria* **111 D6** 22 50N 5 30 E
Tàmanrasset, O. →, *Algeria* **111 D5** 22 0N 2 0 E
Tamanthi, *Burma* **90 C5** 25 19N 95 17 E
Tamaqua, *U.S.A.* **151 F9** 40 48N 75 58W
Tamar →, *U.K.* **21 G3** 50 27N 4 15W
Támara, *Colombia* **168 B3** 5 50N 72 10W
Tamarac, *U.S.A.* **153 J9** 26 12N 80 10W
Tamarin, *Mauritius* **121 d** 20 19 S 57 20 E
Tamarinda, *Spain* **38 B4** 39 55N 3 49 E
Tamarite de Litera, *Spain* **40 D5** 41 52N 0 25 E
Tamaroa, *U.S.A.* **156 F7** 38 8N 89 14W
Tamashima, *Japan* **71 G6** 34 32N 133 40 E
Tamási, *Hungary* **52 D3** 46 40N 18 18 E
Tamaské, *Niger* **113 C6** 14 49N 5 43 E
Tamaulipas □, *Mexico* **163 C5** 24 0N 99 0W
Tamaulipas, Sierra de, *Mexico* **163 C5** 23 30N 98 20W
Tamazula, *Mexico* **162 C3** 24 55N 106 58W
Tamazunchale, *Mexico* **163 C5** 21 16N 98 47W
Tamba-Dabatou, *Guinea* **112 C2** 11 50N 10 40W
Tambacounda, *Senegal* **112 C2** 13 45N 13 40W
Tambaram, *India* **95 H5** 12 55N 80 7 E
Tambea, *Solomon Is.* **133 M10** 9 16 S 159 41 E
Tambelan, Kepulauan, *Indonesia* **84 B3** 1 0N 107 30 E
Tambellup, *Australia* **125 F2** 34 4 S 117 37 E
Tambo, *Australia* **126 C4** 24 54 S 146 14 E
Tambo, *Peru* **172 C3** 12 57 S 74 1W
Tambo →, *Peru* **172 C3** 10 42 S 73 47W
Tambo de Mora, *Peru* **172 C2** 13 30 S 76 8W
Tambobamba, *Peru* **172 C3** 13 54 S 72 8W
Tambohorano, *Madag.* **117 B7** 17 30 S 43 58 E
Tambopata →, *Peru* **172 C4** 13 21 S 69 36W
Tambora, *Indonesia* **85 D5** 8 12 S 118 5 E
Tamboritha, Mt., *Australia* **129 D7** 37 31 S 146 40 E
Tambov, *Russia* **60 D5** 52 45N 41 28 E
Tambre →, *Spain* **42 C2** 42 49N 8 53W
Tambuku, *Indonesia* **85 D4** 7 8 S 113 40 E
Tambul, *Papua N. G.* **132 C2** 5 54 S 143 54 E
Tamburâ, *Sudan* **107 F2** 5 40N 27 25 E
Tambuyukan, Gunong, *Malaysia* **85 A5** 6 13N 116 39 E
Tâmchekket, *Mauritania* **112 B2** 17 25N 10 40W
Tamdybulak, *Uzbekistan* **65 C2** 41 46N 64 36 E
Tame, *Colombia* **168 B3** 6 28N 71 44W
Tâmega →, *Portugal* **42 D2** 41 5N 8 21W
Tamelelt, *Morocco* **110 B3** 31 50N 7 32W
Tamenglong, *India* **90 C4** 25 0N 93 35 E
Tamerza, *Tunisia* **108 B1** 34 23N 7 58 E
Tamgué, Massif du, *Guinea* **112 C2** 12 0N 12 18W
Tami Is., *Papua N. G.* **132 D4** 6 46 S 147 55 E
Tamiahua, L. de, *Mexico* **163 C5** 21 30N 97 30W
Tamiami Canal, *U.S.A.* **153 K8** 25 50N 81 0W
Tamil Nadu □, *India* **95 J3** 11 0N 77 0 E
Tamis →, *Serbia, Yug.* **52 F5** 44 51N 20 39 E
Tamluk, *India* **93 H12** 22 18N 87 58 E
Tammerfors = Tampere, *Finland* **15 F20** 61 30N 23 50 E
Tammisaari, *Finland* **15 F20** 60 0N 23 26 E
Tämnaren, *Sweden* **16 D11** 60 10N 17 25 E
Tamo Abu, Pegunungan, *Malaysia* **85 B5** 3 10N 115 5 E
Tampa, *Angola* **115 F2** 15 30 S 13 27 E
Tampa, *U.S.A.* **153 H7** 27 57N 82 27W
Tampa, Tanjung, *Indonesia* **79 K19** 8 55 S 116 12 E
Tampa B., *U.S.A.* **153 H7** 27 50N 82 30W
Tampa International ✈ (TPA), *U.S.A.* **153 H7** 27 59N 82 32W
Tamparan, *Phil.* **81 H5** 7 53N 124 20 E
Tampere, *Finland* **15 F20** 61 30N 23 50 E
Tampico, *Mexico* **163 C5** 22 20N 97 50W
Tampico, *U.S.A.* **156 C7** 41 38N 89 47W
Tampin, *Malaysia* **87 L4** 2 28N 102 13 E
Tampoi, *Malaysia* **87 d** 1 30N 103 39 E
Tamrah, *Si. Arabia* **98 B4** 20 24N 45 25 E
Tamrau, Peg., *Indonesia* **83 B4** 0 30 S 132 27 E
Tamri, *Morocco* **110 B3** 30 49N 9 50W
Tamrida = Qādib, *Yemen* **99 D6** 12 37N 53 57 E
Tamsweg, *Austria* **34 D6** 47 7N 13 49 E
Tamu, *Burma* **90 C5** 24 13N 94 12 E
Tamuja →, *Spain* **43 F4** 39 38N 6 29W
Tamworth, *Australia* **129 A9** 31 7 S 150 58 E
Tamworth, *Canada* **150 B8** 44 29N 77 0W
Tamworth, *U.K.* **21 E6** 52 39N 1 41W
Tamyang, *S. Korea* **75 G14** 35 19N 126 59 E
Tan An, *Vietnam* **87 G6** 10 32N 106 25 E
Tan Iddah, *Algeria* **111 C6** 26 33N 9 42 E
Tan-Tan, *Morocco* **110 C2** 28 29N 11 1W
Tana →, *Kenya* **118 C5** 2 32 S 40 31 E
Tana →, *Norway* **14 A23** 70 30N 28 14 E
Tana, L., *Ethiopia* **107 E4** 13 5N 37 30 E
Tana River Primate Nat. Reserve ⌓, *Kenya* **118 C5** 1 55 S 40 7 E
Tanabe, *Japan* **73 D7** 33 44N 135 22 E
Tanabi, *Brazil* **171 F2** 20 37 S 49 37W
Tanacross, *U.S.A.* **144 E12** 63 23N 143 21W
Tanafjorden, *Norway* **14 A23** 70 45N 28 25 E
Tanaga I., *U.S.A.* **144 L3** 51 48N 177 53W
Tanaga Volcano, *U.S.A.* **144 L3** 51 53N 178 8W
Tanah Merah, *Malaysia* **84 A2** 5 48N 102 9 E
Tanahbala, *Indonesia* **84 C1** 0 30 S 98 30 E
Tanahgrogot, *Indonesia* **85 C5** 1 55 S 116 15 E
Tanahjampea, *Indonesia* **82 C2** 7 10 S 120 35 E
Tanahmasa, *Indonesia* **84 C1** 0 12 S 98 39 E
Tanahmerah, *Indonesia* **83 C6** 6 5 S 140 16 E
Tanakpur, *India* **93 E9** 29 5N 80 7 E
Tanakura, *Japan* **71 F10** 37 10N 140 20 E
Tanamalwila, *Sri Lanka* **95 L5** 6 26N 81 8 E
Tanami, *Australia* **124 C4** 19 59 S 129 43 E
Tanami Desert, *Australia* **124 C5** 18 50 S 132 0 E
Tanana, *U.S.A.* **144 D9** 65 10N 152 4W
Tanana →, *U.S.A.* **144 D10** 65 10N 151 58W
Tananarive = Antananarivo, *Madag.* **117 B8** 18 55 S 47 31 E
Tananger, *Norway* **18 F2** 58 57N 5 37 E
Tanannt, *Morocco* **110 B3** 31 54N 6 56W
Tánaro →, *Italy* **44 D5** 44 55N 8 40 E
Tanauan, *Phil.* **80 D3** 14 5N 121 10 E
Tanay, *Phil.* **80 D3** 14 30N 121 17 E
Tanba-Sanchi, *Japan* **73 B7** 35 7N 135 48 E
Tancheng, *China* **75 G10** 34 25N 118 20 E
Tanch'ŏn, *N. Korea* **75 D15** 40 27N 128 54 E
Tanda, *Ut. P., India* **93 F10** 26 33N 82 35 E
Tanda, *Ut. P., India* **93 E8** 28 57N 78 56 E
Tanda, *Ivory C.* **112 D4** 7 48N 3 10W
Tandag, *Phil.* **81 G6** 9 4N 126 9 E
Tandaia, *Tanzania* **119 D3** 9 25 S 34 15 E
Tăndărei, *Romania* **53 F12** 44 39N 27 40 E
Tandaué, *Angola* **116 B2** 16 58 S 18 5 E
Tandil, *Argentina* **174 D4** 37 15 S 59 6W
Tandil, Sa. del, *Argentina* **174 D4** 37 30 S 59 0W
Tandin, *Burma* **90 F4** 19 33N 93 58 E
Tandjilé →, *Chad* **109 G3** 9 45N 15 50 E
Tandlianwala, *Pakistan* **92 D5** 31 3N 73 9 E
Tando Adam, *Pakistan* **92 G3** 25 45N 68 40 E
Tando Allahyar, *Pakistan* **92 G3** 25 28N 68 43 E
Tando Bago, *Pakistan* **92 G3** 24 47N 68 58 E
Tando Mohommed Khan, *Pakistan* **92 G3** 25 8N 68 32 E
Tando-Zinze, *Angola* **115 D2** 5 22 S 12 30 E
Tandou-Bengou, *Congo* **114 C2** 3 50 S 11 44 E
Tandou L., *Australia* **128 B5** 32 40 S 142 5 E
Tandragee, *U.K.* **23 B5** 54 21N 6 24W
Tandsjöborg, *Sweden* **16 C8** 61 42N 14 43 E
Tandubas, *Phil.* **81 J3** 5 8N 120 20 E
Tandula →, *India* **94 D5** 21 6N 81 14 E
Tandula Tank, *India* **94 D5** 20 40N 81 12 E
Tandur, *Andhra Pradesh, India* **94 E4** 19 11N 79 30 E
Tandur, *Andhra Pradesh, India* **94 F3** 17 14N 77 35 E
Tane-ga-Shima, *Japan* **71 J5** 30 30N 131 0 E
Taneatua, *N.Z.* **130 E6** 38 4 S 177 1 E
Tanen Tong Dan = Dawna Ra., *Burma* **86 D2** 16 30N 98 30 E
Tanew →, *Poland* **55 H9** 50 29N 22 16 E
Tanezrouft, *Algeria* **111 D5** 23 9N 0 11 E
Tanezzuft, W. →, *Libya* **108 C2** 25 51N 10 19 E
Tang, Koh, *Cambodia* **87 G4** 10 16N 103 7 E
Tang, Ra's-e, *Iran* **97 E8** 25 21N 59 52 E
Tang Krasang, *Cambodia* **86 F5** 12 34N 105 3 E
Tanga, *Tanzania* **118 D4** 5 5 S 39 2 E
Tanga □, *Tanzania* **118 D4** 5 20 S 38 0 E
Tanga Is., *Papua N. G.* **132 B7** 3 20 S 153 15 E
Tangail, *Bangla.* **90 C2** 24 15N 89 55 E
Tangalla, *Sri Lanka* **95 L5** 6 1N 80 48 E
Tanganyika = Tanzania ■, *Africa* **118 D3** 6 0 S 34 0 E
Tanganyika, L., *Africa* **118 D3** 6 40 S 30 0 E
Tangarare, *Solomon Is.* **133 M10** 9 36 S 159 41 E
Tangasseri, *India* **95 K3** 8 53N 76 35 E
Tangaza, *Nigeria* **113 C5** 13 19N 4 55 E
Tangen, *Norway* **18 D8** 60 37N 11 15 E
Tanger, *Morocco* **110 A3** 35 50N 5 49W
Tangerang, *Indonesia* **84 D3** 6 11 S 106 37 E
Tangerhütte, *Germany* **30 C7** 52 26N 11 48 E
Tangermünde, *Germany* **30 C7** 52 33N 11 58 E
Tanggu, *China* **75 E9** 39 2N 117 40 E
Tanggula Shan, *China* **68 C4** 32 40N 92 10 E
Tanghe, *China* **74 H7** 32 47N 112 50 E
Tangi, *India* **94 E7** 19 56N 85 24 E
Tangier = Tanger, *Morocco* **110 A3** 35 50N 5 49W
Tangjia, *China* **69 G10** 22 22N 113 35 E
Tangjia Wan, *China* **69 G10** 22 21N 113 36 E
Tangkeleboke, *Indonesia* **82 B2** 3 10 S 121 30 E
Tangorin, *Australia* **126 C3** 21 47 S 144 12 E
Tangorombohitr'i Makay, *Madag.* **117 C8** 21 0 S 45 15 E
Tangshan, *China* **75 E10** 39 38N 118 10 E
Tangtou, *China* **75 G10** 35 28N 118 30 E
Tangub, *Phil.* **81 G4** 8 3N 123 44 E
Tanguiéta, *Benin* **113 C5** 10 35N 1 21 E
Tangxi, *China* **77 C12** 29 3N 119 25 E
Tangyan He →, *China* **76 C7** 28 54N 108 19 E
Tanimbar, Kepulauan, *Indonesia* **83 C4** 7 30 S 131 30 E
Tanimbar Is. = Tanimbar, Kepulauan, *Indonesia* **83 C4** 7 30 S 131 30 E
Taninthari = Tenasserim, *Burma* **87 F2** 12 6N 99 3 E
Tanjay, *Phil.* **81 G4** 9 30N 123 5 E
Tanjong Malim, *Malaysia* **87 L3** 3 42N 101 31 E
Tanjong Pelepas, *Malaysia* **87 d** 1 21N 103 33 E
Tanjore = Thanjavur, *India* **95 J4** 10 48N 79 12 E
Tanjung, *Indonesia* **79 J19** 8 21 S 116 9 E
Tanjung, *Phil.* **85 C5** 2 10 S 115 25 E
Tanjung Tokong, *Malaysia* **87 c** 5 28N 100 18 E
Tanjungbalai, *Indonesia* **84 B1** 2 55N 99 44 E
Tanjungbatu, *Indonesia* **85 B5** 2 23N 118 3 E
Tanjungkarang Telukbetung, *Indonesia* **84 D3** 5 20 S 105 10 E
Tanjungpandan, *Indonesia* **85 C3** 2 43 S 107 38 E
Tanjungpinang, *Indonesia* **84 B2** 1 5N 104 30 E
Tanjungpriok, *Indonesia* **84 D3** 6 8 S 106 55 E
Tanjungredeb, *Indonesia* **85 B5** 2 9N 117 29 E
Tanjungselor, *Indonesia* **85 B5** 2 55N 117 25 E
Tank, *Pakistan* **91 B3** 32 14N 70 25 E
Tankhala, *India* **92 J5** 21 58N 73 47 E
Tankwa-Karoo Nat. Park △, *S. Africa* **116 E2** 32 14 S 19 50 E
Tanna, *Vanuatu* **133 J7** 19 30 S 169 20 E
Tännäs, *Sweden* **16 B6** 62 26N 12 42 E
Tannersville, *U.S.A.* **151 E9** 41 3N 75 18W
Tannis Bugt, *Denmark* **17 G4** 57 40N 10 15 E
Tannu-Ola, *Russia* **67 D10** 51 0N 94 0 E
Tannum Sands, *Australia* **126 C5** 23 57 S 151 22 E
Tano →, *Ghana* **112 D4** 5 7N 2 56W
Tanombella, *Algeria* **111 C6** 25 30N 5 49 E
Tanon Str., *Phil.* **81 F4** 10 20N 123 30 E
Tanout, *Niger* **113 C6** 14 50N 8 55 E
Tanquinho, *Brazil* **171 D4** 11 58 S 39 6W
Tanshui, *Taiwan* **77 E13** 25 10N 121 28 E
Tansilla, *Burkina Faso* **112 C4** 12 25N 4 23W
Tanta, *Egypt* **106 H7** 30 45N 30 57 E
Tantabin, *Burma* **90 G5** 17 1N 95 59 E
Tantoyuca, *Mexico* **163 C5** 21 21N 98 10W
Tantung = Dandong, *China* **75 D13** 40 10N 124 20 E
Tanuku, *India* **94 F5** 16 45N 81 44 E
Tanumshede, *Sweden* **17 F5** 58 42N 11 20 E
Tanunda, *Australia* **128 C3** 34 30 S 139 0 E
Tanur, *India* **95 J2** 11 1N 75 52 E
Tanus, *France* **28 D6** 44 8N 2 19 E
Tanzania ■, *Africa* **118 D3** 6 0 S 34 0 E
Tanzawa-Sanchi, *Japan* **73 B11** 35 27N 139 0 E
Tanzhou, *China* **69 G9** 22 16N 113 28 E
Tanzilla →, *Canada* **142 B2** 58 8N 130 43W
Tao, Ko, *Thailand* **87 G2** 10 5N 99 52 E
Tao'an = Taonan, *China* **75 B12** 45 22N 122 40 E
Tao'er He →, *China* **75 B13** 45 45N 124 5 E
Taohua Dao, *China* **77 C14** 29 50N 122 20 E
Taolanaro, *Madag.* **117 D8** 25 2 S 47 0 E
Taole, *China* **74 E4** 38 48N 106 40 E
Taonan, *China* **75 B12** 45 22N 122 40 E
Taora, *Solomon Is.* **133 L9** 7 21 S 157 30 E
Taormina, *Italy* **47 E8** 37 51N 15 17 E
Taos, *U.S.A.* **159 H11** 36 24N 105 35W
Taoudenni, *Mali* **110 D4** 22 40N 3 55W
Taoudrart, Adrar, *Algeria* **111 D5** 24 25N 2 24 E
Taounate, *Morocco* **110 B4** 34 25N 4 41W
Taourir, Dj., *Algeria* **111 D6** 35 52N 1 46 E
Taourirt, *Algeria* **111 C5** 26 37N 0 20 E
Taourirt, *Morocco* **111 B4** 34 25N 2 53W
Taouz, *Morocco* **110 B4** 30 53N 4 0W
Taoyuan, *China* **77 C8** 28 55N 111 16 E
T'aoyüan, *Taiwan* **77 E13** 25 0N 121 4 E
Tapa, *Estonia* **15 G21** 59 15N 25 50 E
Tapa Shan = Daba Shan, *China* **76 B7** 32 0N 109 0 E
Tapachula, *Mexico* **163 E6** 14 54N 92 17W
Tapah, *Malaysia* **87 K3** 4 12N 101 15 E
Tapajós →, *Brazil* **169 D7** 2 24 S 54 41W
Tapaktuan, *Indonesia* **84 B1** 3 15N 97 10 E
Tapanahoni →, *Suriname* **169 C7** 4 20N 54 25W
Tapanui, *N.Z.* **131 F4** 45 56 S 169 18 E
Tapauá, *Brazil* **173 B5** 5 40 S 64 20W
Tapauá →, *Brazil* **173 B5** 5 40 S 64 21W
Tapaz, *Phil.* **81 F4** 11 16N 122 32 E
Tapes, *Brazil* **175 C5** 30 40 S 51 23W
Tapeta, *Liberia* **112 D3** 6 29N 8 52W
Taphan Hin, *Thailand* **86 D3** 16 13N 100 26 E
Tapi →, *India* **94 D1** 21 8N 72 41 E
Tapia de Casariego, *Spain* **42 B4** 43 34N 6 56W
Tapiantana Group, *Phil.* **81 H4** 6 20N 122 0 E
Tapilon = Daanbantayan, *Phil.* **81 F5** 11 17N 124 2 E
Tapini, *Papua N. G.* **132 E4** 8 19 S 147 0 E
Tapiraí, *Brazil* **171 E2** 19 52 S 46 1W
Tapirapé →, *Brazil* **170 D1** 10 41 S 50 38W
Tapirapecó, Serra, *Venezuela* **169 C5** 1 10N 65 0W
Tapirapuã, *Brazil* **173 C6** 14 51 S 57 45W
Taplan, *Australia* **128 C4** 34 33 S 140 52 E
Tapo-Capara, Parque Nac. △, *Venezuela* **165 E5** 7 55N 71 15W
Tapoeripa, *Suriname* **169 B6** 5 22N 56 34W
Tapolca, *Hungary* **52 D2** 46 53N 17 29 E
Tapuaenuku, *N.Z.* **131 B8** 42 0 S 173 39 E
Tapul, *Phil.* **81 J3** 5 42N 120 55 E
Tapul Group, *Phil.* **81 J3** 5 35N 120 50 E
Tapul I., *Phil.* **81 J3** 5 43N 120 55 E
Tapun, *India* **90 B6** 27 35N 96 22 E
Tapurucuará, *Brazil* **169 D4** 0 24 S 65 2W
Ţaqţaq, *Iraq* **101 E11** 35 53N 44 35 E
Taquara, *Brazil* **175 B5** 29 36 S 50 46W
Taquari →, *Brazil* **173 D6** 19 15 S 57 17W
Taquaritinga, *Brazil* **171 F2** 21 24 S 48 30W
Tara, *Australia* **127 D5** 27 17 S 150 31 E
Tara, *Canada* **150 B3** 44 28N 81 9W
Tara, *Japan* **72 D2** 33 2N 130 11 E
Tara, *Russia* **66 D8** 56 55N 74 24 E
Tara, *Zambia* **119 F2** 16 58 S 26 45 E
Tara →, *Montenegro, Yug.* **50 C2** 43 21N 18 51 E
Tara-Dake, *Japan* **72 E2** 32 58N 130 6 E
Tara Nac. Park △, *Yugoslavia* **50 C3** 43 55N 19 30 E
Taraba □, *Nigeria* **113 D7** 8 0N 10 30 E
Taraba →, *Nigeria* **113 D7** 8 30N 10 15 E
Tarabagatay, Khrebet, *Kazakhstan* **66 E9** 48 0N 83 0 E
Tarabuco, *Bolivia* **173 D5** 19 10 S 64 57W
Tarābulus, *Lebanon* **103 A4** 34 31N 35 50 E
Tarābulus, *Libya* **108 B2** 32 49N 13 7 E
Taraclia, *Taraclia, Moldova* **53 E13** 45 54N 28 40 E
Taraclia, *Tighina, Moldova* **53 D14** 46 34N 29 7 E
Taradale, *N.Z.* **130 F5** 39 33 S 176 53 E
Taradehi, *India* **93 H8** 23 18N 79 21 E
Taragi, *Japan* **72 E2** 32 16N 130 56 E
Tarahouahout, *Algeria* **111 D6** 22 41N 5 59 E
Tarajalejo, *Canary Is.* **9 e2** 28 12N 14 7W
Tarakan, *Indonesia* **85 B5** 3 20N 117 35 E
Tarakit, Mt., *Kenya* **118 B4** 2 2N 35 10 E
Taralga, *Australia* **129 C8** 34 26 S 149 52 E
Tarama-Jima, *Japan* **71 M2** 24 39N 124 42 E
Taramakau →, *N.Z.* **131 C6** 42 34 S 171 8 E
Taran, Mys, *Russia* **15 J18** 54 56N 19 59 E
Taranagar, *India* **92 E6** 28 43N 74 50 E
Taranaki □, *N.Z.* **130 F3** 39 25 S 174 30 E
Taranaki, Mt., *N.Z.* **130 F3** 39 17 S 174 5 E
Tarancón, *Spain* **40 E1** 40 1N 3 1W
Tarangire Nat. Park △, *Tanzania* **118 C4** 4 21 S 36 7 E
Taransay, *U.K.* **22 D1** 57 54N 7 0W
Táranto, *Italy* **47 B10** 40 28N 17 14 E
Táranto, G. di, *Italy* **47 B10** 40 8N 17 20 E
Tarapacá, *Colombia* **168 D4** 2 56 S 69 46W
Tarapacá □, *Chile* **174 A2** 20 45 S 69 30W
Tarapoto, *Peru* **172 B2** 6 30 S 76 20W
Taraquá, *Brazil* **168 C4** 0 6N 68 28W
Tarare, *France* **29 C8** 45 54N 4 26 E
Tararua Ra., *N.Z.* **130 G4** 40 45 S 175 25 E
Tarasag, *Vanuatu* **133 D5** 14 12 S 167 36 E
Tarascon, *France* **29 E8** 43 48N 4 39 E
Tarascon-sur-Ariège, *France* **28 F5** 42 50N 1 36 E
Tarashcha, *Ukraine* **59 H6** 49 30N 30 31 E
Tarata, *Peru* **172 D3** 17 27 S 70 2W
Tarauacá, *Brazil* **172 B3** 8 6 S 70 48W
Tarauacá →, *Brazil* **172 B4** 6 42 S 69 48W
Taravo →, *France* **29 G12** 41 42N 8 49 E
Tarawa, *Kiribati* **134 G9** 1 30N 173 0 E
Tarawai I., *Papua N. G.* **132 B2** 3 13 S 143 15 E
Tarawera, *N.Z.* **130 F5** 39 2 S 176 36 E
Tarawera, L., *N.Z.* **130 E5** 38 13 S 176 27 E
Tarawera, Mt., *N.Z.* **130 E5** 38 14 S 176 32 E
Taraz, *Kazakhstan* **65 B5** 42 54N 71 22 E
Tarazona, *Spain* **40 D3** 41 55N 1 43W
Tarazona de la Mancha, *Spain* **41 F3** 39 16N 1 55W
Tarbat Ness, *U.K.* **22 D5** 57 52N 3 47W
Tarbela Dam, *Pakistan* **92 B5** 34 8N 72 52 E
Tarbert, *Arg. & Bute, U.K.* **22 F3** 55 52N 5 25W
Tarbert, *W. Isles, U.K.* **22 D2** 57 54N 6 49W
Tarbes, *France* **28 E4** 43 15N 0 3 E
Tarboro, *U.S.A.* **149 H7** 35 54N 77 32W
Tarbū, *Libya* **108 C3** 26 0N 15 5 E
Tărcău, Munţii, *Romania* **53 D11** 46 39N 26 7 E
Tarcento, *Italy* **45 B10** 46 13N 13 13 E
Tarcoola, *Australia* **127 E1** 30 44 S 134 36 E
Tarcoon, *Australia* **127 E4** 30 15 S 146 43 E
Tarcutta, *Australia* **129 C7** 35 16 S 147 44 E
Tardets-Sorholus, *France* **28 E3** 43 8N 0 52W
Tardoire →, *France* **28 C4** 45 52N 0 14 E
Taredjedja, *Algeria* **111 C5** 25 12N 2 32 E
Taree, *Australia* **129 A10** 31 50 S 152 30 E
Tarella, *Australia* **128 A5** 31 2 S 143 2 E
Tarf, Ras, *Morocco* **110 A3** 35 40N 5 11W
Ţarfā, Ra's aţ, *Si. Arabia* **98 C3** 17 2N 42 22 E
Tarfa, W. el →, *Egypt* **106 B3** 28 25N 30 50 E
Tarfaya, *Morocco* **110 C2** 27 55N 12 55W
Târgovişte, *Romania* **53 F10** 44 55N 25 27 E
Târgu Bujor, *Romania* **53 E12** 45 52N 27 54 E
Târgu Cărbuneşti, *Romania* **53 F8** 44 57N 23 31 E
Târgu Frumos, *Romania* **53 C12** 47 12N 27 2 E
Târgu-Jiu, *Romania* **53 E8** 45 5N 23 19 E
Târgu Lăpuş, *Romania* **53 C8** 47 27N 23 52 E
Târgu Mureş, *Romania* **53 D9** 46 31N 24 38 E
Târgu Neamţ, *Romania* **53 C11** 47 12N 26 25 E
Târgu Ocna, *Romania* **53 D11** 46 16N 26 39 E
Târgu Secuiesc, *Romania* **53 E11** 46 0N 26 10 E
Targuist, *Morocco* **110 B4** 34 59N 4 14W
Târguşor, *Romania* **53 F13** 44 27N 28 25 E
Tărhăus, Vf., *Romania* **53 D11** 46 40N 26 8 E
Tarhbalt, *Morocco* **110 B3** 30 39N 5 20W
Tarhit, *Algeria* **111 B4** 30 58N 2 0W
Tarhūnah, *Libya* **108 B2** 32 27N 13 36 E
Tari, *Papua N. G.* **132 C2** 5 54 S 142 59 E
Táriba, *Venezuela* **168 B3** 7 49N 72 13W
Ţarif, *U.A.E.* **97 E7** 24 3N 53 46 E
Tarifa, *Spain* **43 J5** 36 1N 5 36W
Tarija, *Bolivia* **174 A3** 21 30 S 64 40W
Tarija □, *Bolivia* **174 A3** 21 30 S 63 30W
Tariku →, *Indonesia* **83 B5** 2 55 S 138 26 E
Tarīm, *Yemen* **99 C5** 16 3N 49 0 E
Tarim Basin = Tarim Pendi, *China* **68 B3** 40 0N 84 0 E
Tarim He →, *China* **68 C3** 39 30N 88 30 E
Tarim Pendi, *China* **68 B3** 40 0N 84 0 E
Taritatu →, *Indonesia* **83 B5** 2 54 S 138 27 E
Tarka →, *S. Africa* **116 E4** 32 10 S 26 0 E
Tarkastad, *S. Africa* **116 E4** 32 0 S 26 16 E
Tarkhankut, Mys, *Ukraine* **59 K7** 45 25N 32 30 E
Tarko Sale, *Russia* **66 C8** 64 55N 77 50 E
Tarkwa, *Ghana* **112 D4** 5 20N 2 0W
Tarlac, *Phil.* **80 D3** 15 29N 120 35 E
Tarlac □, *Phil.* **80 D3** 15 30N 120 30 E
Tarm, *Denmark* **17 J2** 55 56N 8 31 E
Tarma, *Peru* **172 C2** 11 25 S 75 45W
Tarn □, *France* **28 E6** 43 49N 2 8 E
Tarn →, *France* **28 D5** 44 5N 1 6 E
Tarn-et-Garonne □, *France* **28 D5** 44 8N 1 20 E
Tarna →, *Hungary* **52 C4** 47 31N 19 59 E
Târnava Mare →, *Romania* **53 D8** 46 10N 23 43 E
Târnava Mică →, *Romania* **53 D8** 46 9N 23 55 E
Târnăveni, *Romania* **53 D9** 46 19N 24 13 E
Tarnica, *Poland* **55 J9** 49 4N 22 44 E
Tarnobrzeg, *Poland* **55 H8** 50 35N 21 41 E
Tarnogród, *Poland* **55 H9** 50 22N 22 45 E
Tarnos, *France* **28 E2** 43 32N 1 28W
Târnova, *Moldova* **53 B12** 48 10N 27 40 E
Târnova, *Romania* **52 E6** 45 23N 21 59 E
Tarnów, *Poland* **55 H8** 50 3N 21 0 E
Tarnowskie Góry, *Poland* **55 H5** 50 27N 18 54 E
Tärnsjö, *Sweden* **16 D10** 60 9N 16 56 E
Táro →, *Italy* **44 C7** 45 2N 10 15 E
Ţārom, *Iran* **97 D7** 28 11N 55 46 E
Taroom, *Australia* **127 D4** 25 36 S 149 48 E
Taroudannt, *Morocco* **110 B3** 30 30N 8 52W
Tarp, *Germany* **30 A5** 54 39N 9 24 E
Tarpeena, *Australia* **128 D4** 37 37 S 140 47 E
Tarpon Springs, *U.S.A.* **153 G7** 28 9N 82 45W
Tarquínia, *Italy* **45 F8** 42 15N 11 45 E
Tarrafal, *C. Verde Is.* **9 j** 15 18N 23 39W
Tarragona, *Spain* **40 D6** 41 5N 1 17 E
Tarragona □, *Spain* **40 D6** 41 5N 1 0 E
Tarraleah, *Australia* **127 G4** 42 17 S 146 26 E
Tarrasa = Terrassa, *Spain* **40 D7** 41 34N 2 1 E
Tàrrega, *Spain* **40 D6** 41 39N 1 9 E
Tarrytown, *Ga., U.S.A.* **152 C7** 32 19N 82 34W
Tarrytown, *N.Y., U.S.A.* **151 E11** 41 4N 73 52W
Tårs, *Denmark* **17 G4** 57 23N 10 7 E
Tarshiha = Me'ona, *Israel* **103 B4** 33 1N 35 15 E
Tarsus, *Turkey* **100 D6** 36 58N 34 55 E
Tartagal, *Argentina* **174 A3** 22 30 S 63 50W
Tärtär, *Azerbaijan* **61 K8** 40 20N 46 58 E
Tärtär →, *Azerbaijan* **61 K8** 40 26N 47 20 E
Tartas, *France* **28 E3** 43 50N 0 49W
Tartogay, *Kazakhstan* **65 A3** 44 26N 66 15 E
Tartu, *Estonia* **15 G22** 58 20N 26 44 E
Ţarţūs, *Syria* **100 E6** 34 55N 35 55 E
Tarumirim, *Brazil* **171 E3** 19 16 S 41 59W
Tarumizu, *Japan* **72 F2** 31 29N 130 42 E
Tarussa, *Russia* **58 E9** 54 44N 37 10 E
Tarutao, Ko, *Thailand* **87 J2** 6 33N 99 40 E

Tarutao Nat. Park = Ko Tarutao Nat.
  Park △, *Thailand* .... 87 J2 6 31N 99 26 E
Tarutung, *Indonesia* .... 84 B1 2 0N 98 54 E
Tarvísio, *Italy* .... 45 B10 46 30N 13 35 E
Tarxien, *Malta* .... 38 F8 35 52N 14 31 E
Tarz Ulli, *Libya* .... 108 C2 25 32N 10 8 E
Tasahku, *Burma* .... 90 B6 27 33N 97 52 E
Tasaret, O. →, *Algeria* .... 111 C5 26 25N 1 59 E
Tasáwah, *Libya* .... 108 C2 26 0N 13 30 E
Tasböget, *Kazakhstan* .... 65 A2 44 46N 65 33 E
Täsch, *Switz.* .... 32 D5 46 4N 7 46 E
Taseko →, *Canada* 142 C4 52 8N 123 45W
Tasgaon, *India* .... 94 F2 17 2N 74 39 E
Tash-Bashat, *Kyrgyzstan* .... 65 C8 41 23N 76 20 E
Tash-Kömür, *Kyrgyzstan* .... 65 C6 41 40N 72 10 E
Tash-Kumyr = Tash-Kömür,
  Kyrgyzstan .... 65 C6 41 40N 72 10 E
Tashauz = Dashhowuz,
  Turkmenistan .... 66 E6 41 49N 59 58 E
Tashi Chho Dzong = Thimphu,
  Bhutan .... 90 B2 27 31N 89 45 E
Tashk, Daryächeh-ye, *Iran* ..... 97 D7 29 45N 53 35 E
Tashkent = Toshkent, *Uzbekistan* 65 C4 41 20N 69 10 E
Tashtagol, *Russia* .... 10 D7 52 47N 87 53 E
Tasiilaq, *Greenland* 4 C6 65 40N 37 20W
Tasikmalaya, *Indonesia* .... 85 D3 7 18 S 108 12 E
Tåsinge, *Denmark* .... 17 J4 55 0N 10 35 E
Täsjön, *Sweden* .... 16 D16 64 15N 15 40 E
Task, *Niger* .... 109 F2 14 56N 10 46 E
Taskan, *Russia* .... 67 C16 62 59N 150 20 E
Tasker, *Niger* .... 113 C7 15 8N 10 40 E
Taşköprü, *Turkey* .... 100 B6 41 30N 34 15 E
Taskul, *Papua N. G.* .... 132 B6 2 32 S 150 27 E
Taşlıç, *Moldova* .... 53 C14 47 4N 29 24 E
Tasman □, *N.Z.* .... 131 B7 41 30 S 172 40 E
Tasman →, *N.Z.* .... 131 D5 43 48 S 170 8 E
Tasman, Mt., *N.Z.* .... 131 D5 43 34 S 170 12 E
Tasman B., *N.Z.* .... 131 A8 40 59 S 173 25 E
Tasman Mts., *N.Z.* .... 131 B7 41 3 S 172 25 E
Tasman Pen., *Australia* .... 127 G4 43 10 S 148 0 E
Tasman Sea, *Pac. Oc.* .... 134 L8 36 0 S 160 0 E
Tasmania □, *Australia* .... 127 G4 42 0 S 146 30 E
Tăşnad, *Romania* .... 52 C7 47 30N 22 33 E
Tassili n'Ajjer, *Algeria* ...... 111 C6 25 47N 8 1 E
Tassili-Oua-n-Ahaggar, *Algeria* 111 D6 20 41N 5 30 E
Tassili Tin-Rerhoh, *Algeria* ... 111 D5 20 5N 3 55 E
Tasty, *Kazakhstan* .... 65 A4 44 47N 69 7 E
Tata, *Hungary* .... 52 C3 47 37N 18 19 E
Tata, *Morocco* 110 C3 29 46N 7 56W
Tata Mai Lau, *E. Timor* .... 82 C3 8 58 S 125 30 E
Tatabánya, *Hungary* .... 52 C3 47 32N 18 25 E
Tatamba, *Solomon Is.* .... 133 M10 8 21 S 159 51 E
Tataouine, *Tunisia* .... 108 B2 32 57N 10 29 E
Tatar Republic = Tatarstan □, *Russia* 60 C10 55 30N 51 30 E
Tatarbunary, *Ukraine* .... 59 K5 45 50N 29 39 E
Tatarsk, *Russia* .... 66 D8 55 14N 76 0 E
Tatarstan □, *Russia* .... 60 C10 55 30N 51 30 E
Tatau, *Malaysia* .... 85 B4 2 53N 112 51 E
Tatau I., *Papua N. G.* .... 132 B6 2 48 S 151 57 E
Tatebayashi, *Japan* .... 73 A10 36 15N 139 32 E
Tateshina-Yama, *Japan* .... 73 A10 36 8N 138 11 E
Tateyama, *Japan* .... 73 C11 35 0N 139 50 E
Tathlina L., *Canada* 142 A5 60 33N 117 39W
Tathlīth, *Si. Arabia* .... 98 C3 19 32N 43 30 E
Tathlīth, W. →, *Si. Arabia* .... 98 B4 20 35N 44 20 E
Tathra, *Australia* .... 129 D8 36 44 S 149 59 E
Tatinnai L., *Canada* 143 A9 60 55N 97 40W
Tatitlek, *U.S.A.* 144 F11 60 52N 146 41W
Tatkon, *Burma* .... 90 E6 20 7N 96 13 E
Tatla L., *Canada* 142 C4 52 0N 124 20W
Tatlısu, *Turkey* .... 51 F11 40 24N 27 55 E
Tatnam, C., *Canada* 143 B10 57 16N 91 0W
Tatra = Tatry, *Slovak Rep.* .... 35 B13 49 20N 20 0 E
Tatranský Národný Park △,
  Slovak Rep. .... 35 B13 49 10N 20 0 E
Tatry, *Slovak Rep.* .... 35 B13 49 20N 20 0 E
Tatshenshini →, *Canada* 142 B1 59 28N 137 45W
Tatsuno, *Hyōgo, Japan* .... 72 C6 34 52N 134 33 E
Tatsuno, *Nagano, Japan* .... 73 B10 35 58N 138 0 E
Tatta, *Pakistan* .... 91 D2 24 42N 67 55 E
Tätti, *Kazakhstan* .... 65 B6 43 13N 73 18 E
Tatuí, *Brazil* .... 175 A6 23 5 S 47 53W
Tatum, *U.S.A.* 155 J3 33 0N 103 19W
Tat'ung = Datong, *China* .... 74 D7 40 6N 113 18 E
Tatura, *Australia* .... 129 D6 36 29 S 145 16 E
Tatvan, *Turkey* .... 101 C10 38 31N 42 15 E
Ta'ū, *Amer. Samoa* .... 133 X25 14 15 S 169 30W
Tau, *Norway* .... 18 E2 59 3N 5 55 E
Tauá, *Brazil* .... 170 C3 6 1 S 40 26W
Taubaté, *Brazil* .... 175 A6 23 0 S 45 36W
Tauberbischofsheim, *Germany* ... 31 F5 49 37N 9 39 E
Taucha, *Germany* .... 30 D8 51 23N 12 29 E
Tauern, *Austria* .... 36 E7 47 15N 12 40 E
Tauern-tunnel, *Austria* .... 34 D6 47 0N 13 12 E
Taufikia, *Sudan* .... 107 F3 9 24N 31 37 E
Taulé, *France* 26 D3 48 37N 3 54W
Taumarunui, *N.Z.* .... 130 E4 38 53 S 175 15 E
Taumaturgo, *Brazil* .... 172 B3 8 54 S 72 51W
Taung, *S. Africa* .... 116 D3 27 33 S 24 47 E
Taungdwingyi, *Burma* .... 90 E6 20 1N 95 40 E
Taunggyi, *Burma* .... 90 E6 20 50N 97 0 E
Taungtha, *Burma* .... 90 E6 21 12N 95 25 E
Taungup, *Burma* .... 90 F5 18 51N 94 14 E
Taungup Pass, *Burma* .... 90 F5 18 40N 94 45 E
Taunsa, *Pakistan* .... 92 D4 30 42N 70 39 E
Taunsa Barrage, *Pakistan* ...... 92 D4 30 42N 70 50 E
Taunton, *U.K.* 21 F4 51 1N 3 5W
Taunton, *U.S.A.* 151 E13 41 54N 71 6W
Taunus, *Germany* .... 31 E4 50 13N 8 34 E
Taupo, *N.Z.* .... 130 E5 38 41 S 176 55 E
Taupo, L., *N.Z.* .... 130 E4 38 46 S 175 55 E
Tauragė, *Lithuania* .... 15 J20 55 14N 22 16 E
Tauragė □, *Lithuania* .... 54 C9 55 15N 22 17 E
Tauranga, *N.Z.* .... 130 D5 37 42 S 176 11 E
Tauranga Harb., *N.Z.* .... 130 D5 37 30 S 176 5 E
Taureau, Rés., *Canada* 140 C5 46 46N 73 50W
Tauri →, *Papua N. G.* .... 132 E4 8 8 S 146 8 E
Taurianova, *Italy* .... 47 D9 38 21N 16 1 E
Taurus Mts. = Toros Dağları, *Turkey* 100 D5 37 0N 32 30 E
Tauste, *Spain* 40 D3 41 58N 1 18W
Tautira, *Tahiti* .... 133 S16 17 44 S 149 9W
Tauz = Tovuz, *Azerbaijan* ...... 61 K7 41 0N 45 40 E
Tavaar, *Somali Rep.* .... 90 G3 3 6N 46 1 E
Tavannes, *Switz.* .... 32 B4 47 13N 7 12 E
Tavares, *U.S.A.* 153 G8 28 48N 81 44W
Tavas, *Turkey* .... 49 D11 37 34N 29 4 E
Tavastehus = Hämeenlinna, *Finland* 15 F21 61 0N 24 28 E
Tavda, *Russia* .... 66 D7 58 7N 65 8 E
Tavda →, *Russia* .... 66 D7 57 47N 67 18 E
Tavernes de la Valldigna, *Spain* 41 F4 39 5N 0 13 E
Tavernier, *U.S.A.* 153 K9 25 1N 80 31W
Taveta, *Tanzania* .... 114 C4 3 23 S 37 37 E
Taveuni, *Fiji* .... 133 A3 16 51 S 179 58W
Taviano, *Italy* .... 47 C11 39 59N 18 5 E
Tavignano →, *France* .... 29 F13 42 7N 9 33 E
Tavildara, *Tajikistan* .... 65 F8 38 41N 70 24 E
Tavira, *Portugal* 43 H3 37 8N 7 40W
Tavistock, *Canada* 150 C4 43 19N 80 50W
Tavistock, *U.K.* 21 G3 50 33N 4 9W
Tavolara, *Italy* .... 46 B2 40 55N 9 43 E
Távora →, *Portugal* 42 D3 41 8N 7 35W
Tavoy, *Burma* .... 86 E2 14 2N 98 12 E
Tavşanlı, *Turkey* .... 49 B11 39 32N 29 28 E
Tavua, *Fiji* .... 133 A1 17 37 S 177 5 E

Tavuki, *Fiji* .... 133 B2 19 7 S 178 8 E
Taw →, *India* 21 F3 51 4N 4 4W
Tawa →, *India* .... 92 H8 22 48N 77 48 E
Tawa Tawa Mal Reef, *Papua N. G.* 132 F7 11 3 S 152 45 E
Tawai, *India* .... 90 B6 27 48N 96 47 E
Tawas City, *U.S.A.* 148 C4 44 16N 83 31W
Tawau, *Malaysia* .... 85 B5 4 20N 117 55 E
Taweisha, *Sudan* .... 107 E2 12 19N 24 40 E
Tawi-Tawi □, *Phil.* .... 81 J3 5 0N 120 0 E
Tawitawi, *Phil.* .... 79 B6 5 10N 120 0 E
Tawitawi Group, *Phil.* .... 81 J3 5 10N 120 15 E
Tawngche, *Burma* .... 90 B5 26 34N 95 38 E
Tawu, *Taiwan* .... 77 F13 22 30N 120 50 E
Tāwūrghā', *Libya* .... 108 B3 32 1N 15 2 E
Tāwūrghā', Sabkhat, *Libya* ..... 108 B3 31 51N 15 15 E
Taxco de Alarcón, *Mexico* 163 D5 18 33N 99 36W
Taxila, *Pakistan* .... 92 C5 33 42N 72 52 E
Taxkorgan He →, *China* .... 65 E8 37 45N 76 10 E
Taxkorgan Tajik Zizhixian, *China* 65 E8 37 49N 75 14 E
Tay →, *U.K.* 22 E5 56 37N 3 38W
Tay, Firth of, *U.K.* 22 E5 56 25N 3 8W
Tay, L., *Australia* .... 125 F3 32 55 S 120 48 E
Tay, L., *U.K.* 22 E4 56 32N 4 8W
Tay Forest Park ⌒, *U.K.* 22 E5 56 43N 3 59W
Tay Ninh, *Vietnam* .... 87 G6 11 20N 106 5 E
Tayabamba, *Peru* .... 171 B2 8 15 S 77 16W
Tayabas, *Phil.* .... 80 D3 14 1N 121 35 E
Tayabas Bay, *Phil.* .... 80 E3 13 45N 121 45 E
Tayandu, Kepulauan, *Indonesia* . 83 C4 5 30 S 132 15 E
Taylakova, *Russia* .... 66 D8 59 13N 74 0 E
Taylakovy = Taylakova, *Russia* . 66 D8 59 13N 74 0 E
Taylor, *Canada* 142 B4 56 13N 120 40W
Taylor, *Fla., U.S.A.* 152 E7 30 26N 82 18W
Taylor, *Mich., U.S.A.* 157 B13 42 14N 83 16W
Taylor, *Nebr., U.S.A.* 154 E5 41 46N 99 23W
Taylor, *Pa., U.S.A.* 151 E9 41 23N 75 43W
Taylor, *Tex., U.S.A.* 155 K6 30 34N 97 25W
Taylor, Mt., *N.Z.* .... 131 D6 46 43 S 171 20 E
Taylor, Mt., *U.S.A.* 159 J10 35 14N 107 37W
Taylorsville, *U.S.A.* 157 F11 38 2N 85 21W
Taylorsville L., *U.S.A.* 157 G11 38 0N 85 15W
Taylorville, *U.S.A.* 156 E7 39 33N 89 18W
Taymā, *Si. Arabia* .... 96 E3 27 35N 38 45 E
Taymyr, Oz., *Russia* .... 67 B11 74 20N 102 0 E
Taymyr, Poluostrov, *Russia* .... 67 B11 75 0N 100 0 E
Tayport, *U.K.* 22 E6 56 27N 2 52W
Tayrona, Parque Nac. △, *Colombia* 165 D5 11 20N 74 2W
Tayshet, *Russia* .... 67 D10 55 58N 98 1 E
Taytay, *Phil.* .... 81 F2 10 45N 119 30 E
Taytay Bay, *Phil.* .... 81 F2 10 55N 119 35 E
Tayug, *Phil.* .... 80 C3 16 2N 120 45 E
Tayyebād □, *Iran* .... 97 C9 34 44N 60 44 E
Taz →, *Russia* .... 66 C8 67 32N 78 40 E
Taza, *Morocco* 110 B4 34 16N 4 6W
Tāzah Khurmātū, *Iraq* .... 101 E11 35 18N 44 20 E
Tazawa-Ko, *Japan* .... 70 E10 39 43N 140 40 E
Taze, *Burma* .... 90 D5 22 57N 95 24 E
Tazenakht, *Morocco* 110 B3 30 35N 7 12W
Tazerbo, *Libya* .... 108 C4 25 45N 21 0 E
Tazin, *Canada* 143 B7 59 48N 109 55W
Tazin L., *Canada* 143 B7 59 44N 108 42W
Tazlina, *U.S.A.* 144 E11 62 4N 146 27W
Tazoult, *Algeria* .... 111 A6 35 29N 6 11 E
Tazovskiy, *Russia* .... 66 C8 67 30N 78 44 E
Tbilisi, *Georgia* .... 61 K7 41 43N 44 50 E
Tchad = Chad ■, *Africa* .... 109 F3 15 0N 17 15 E
Tchad, L., *Chad* .... 109 F2 13 30N 14 30 E
Tchaourou, *Benin* .... 113 D5 8 58N 2 40 E
Tch'eng-tou = Chengdu, *China* .. 76 B5 30 38N 104 2 E
Tchentlo L., *Canada* 142 B4 55 15N 125 0W
Tchetti, *Benin* .... 113 D5 7 50N 1 40 E
Tchibanga, *Gabon* .... 114 C2 2 45 S 11 0 E
Tchien, *Liberia* 112 D3 5 59N 8 15W
Tchin Tabaraden, *Niger* .... 113 B6 15 58N 5 56 E
Tchingou, Massif de, *N. Cal.* .. 133 T19 20 54 S 165 0 E
Tcholliré, *Cameroon* .... 114 A2 8 24N 14 10 E
Tch'ong-k'ing = Chongqing, *China* 76 C6 29 35N 106 25 E
Tczew, *Poland* .... 54 D5 54 8N 18 50 E
Te Anau, *N.Z.* .... 131 F2 45 15 S 167 43 E
Te Anau, L., *N.Z.* .... 131 F2 45 15 S 167 45 E
Te Araroa, *N.Z.* .... 130 D7 37 39 S 178 25 E
Te Aroha, *N.Z.* .... 130 D4 37 32 S 175 44 E
Te Awamutu, *N.Z.* .... 130 E4 38 1 S 175 20 E
Te Kaha, *N.Z.* .... 130 D6 37 44 S 177 52 E
Te Karaka, *N.Z.* .... 130 E4 38 26 S 177 53 E
Te Kauwhata, *N.Z.* .... 130 D4 37 25 S 175 9 E
Te Kopuru, *N.Z.* .... 130 C2 36 2 S 173 56 E
Te Kuiti, *N.Z.* .... 130 E4 38 20 S 175 11 E
Te-n-Dghâmcha, Sebkhet,
  Mauritania 112 B1 18 30N 15 55W
Te Puke, *N.Z.* .... 130 D5 37 46 S 176 22 E
Te Teko, *N.Z.* .... 130 E5 38 2 S 176 48 E
Te Waewae B., *N.Z.* .... 131 G1 46 13 S 167 33 E
Tea →, *Brazil* .... 172 B3 4 41 S 69 58W
Teaca, *Romania* .... 53 D9 46 55N 24 30 E
Teague, *U.S.A.* 155 K6 31 38N 96 17W
Teano, *Italy* .... 47 A7 41 15N 14 4 E
Teapa, *Mexico* 163 D6 17 35N 92 56W
Teba, *Spain* 43 J6 36 59N 4 55W
Tebakang, *Malaysia* .... 78 D4 1 6N 110 30 E
Teberau, *Malaysia* .... 84 B2 1 32N 103 45 E
Teberda, *Russia* .... 61 J5 43 30N 41 46 E
Teberu, *Malaysia* .... 87 d 1 30N 103 42 E
Tébessa, *Algeria* .... 111 A6 35 22N 8 8 E
Tebicuary →, *Paraguay* .... 174 B4 26 36 S 58 16W
Tebingtinggi, *Riau, Indonesia* . 84 B2 1 0N 102 45 E
Tebingtinggi, *Sumatera Utara,*
  Indonesia .... 84 B1 3 20N 99 9 E
Tébourba, *Tunisia* .... 108 A1 36 49N 9 51 E
Téboursouk, *Tunisia* .... 108 A1 36 29N 9 10 E
Tebulos, *Georgia* .... 61 J7 42 36N 45 17 E
Tecate, *Mexico* 161 N10 32 34N 116 38W
Tecer Dağları, *Turkey* .... 100 C7 39 27N 37 27 E
Tech →, *France* .... 28 F7 42 36N 3 3 E
Techa →, *Russia* .... 64 C9 56 13N 62 58 E
Techiman, *Ghana* 112 D4 7 35N 1 58W
Techirghiol, *Romania* .... 53 F13 44 4N 28 32 E
Tecka, *Argentina* .... 176 B2 43 29 S 70 48W
Tecomán, *Mexico* 162 D4 18 55N 103 53W
Tecopa, *U.S.A.* 161 K10 35 51N 116 13W
Tecoripa, *Mexico* 162 B3 28 37N 109 57W
Tecuala, *Mexico* 162 C3 22 23N 105 27W
Tecuci, *Romania* .... 53 E12 45 51N 27 27 E
Tecumseh, *Canada* 150 D2 42 19N 82 54W
Tecumseh, *Mich., U.S.A.* 157 B13 42 0N 83 57W
Tecumseh, *Okla., U.S.A.* 155 H6 35 15N 96 56W
Ted, *Somali Rep.* .... 90 G3 4 24N 43 55 E
Tedegart, *Algeria* .... 111 D6 21 23N 3 18 E
Tedzhen = Tejen, *Turkmenistan* . 66 F7 37 23N 60 31 E
Tees →, *U.K.* 20 C6 54 37N 1 10W
Tees B., *U.K.* 20 C6 54 40N 1 9W
Teeswater, *Canada* 150 C3 43 59N 81 17W
Tefé, *Brazil* .... 169 D5 3 25 S 64 50W
Tefé →, *Brazil* .... 169 D5 3 25 S 64 50W
Tefenni, *Turkey* .... 49 D11 37 18N 29 45 E
Tegal, *Indonesia* .... 85 D3 6 52 S 109 8 E
Tegallalang, *Indonesia* .... 79 J18 8 27 S 115 17 E
Tegalsari, *Indonesia* .... 79 J17 8 25 S 114 8 E
Tegel, Berlin ✈ (TXL), *Germany* 30 C9 52 35N 13 14 E
Tegernsee, *Germany* .... 31 H7 47 43N 11 46 E
Teggiano, *Italy* .... 47 B8 40 23N 15 32 E
Tegid, L. = Bala, L., *U.K.* 20 E4 52 53N 3 37W
Tegina, *Nigeria* .... 113 C6 10 5N 6 11 E
Téglio, *Italy* .... 33 D10 46 10N 10 4 E

Tegua, *Vanuatu* .... 133 C4 13 15 S 166 37 E
Tegucigalpa, *Honduras* 164 D2 14 5N 87 14W
Teguidda i-n-Tessoum, *Niger* ... 113 B6 17 25N 6 37 E
Tehachapi, *U.S.A.* 161 K8 35 8N 118 27W
Tehachapi Mts., *U.S.A.* 161 L8 35 0N 118 30W
Tehamiyam, *Sudan* .... 106 D4 18 20N 36 32 E
Tehilla, *Sudan* .... 106 D4 17 42N 36 6 E
Téhini, *Ivory C.* 112 D4 9 39N 3 40W
Tehoru, *Indonesia* .... 83 B3 3 23 S 129 30 E
Tehrān, *Iran* .... 97 C6 35 44N 51 30 E
Tehrān □, *Iran* .... 97 C6 35 30N 51 30 E
Tehuacán, *Mexico* 163 D5 18 30N 97 30W
Tehuantepec, *Mexico* 163 D5 16 21N 95 13W
Tehuantepec, G. de, *Mexico* 163 D5 15 50N 95 12W
Tehuantepec, Istmo de, *Mexico* . 163 D6 17 0N 94 30W
Teide, Pico de, *Canary Is.* 9 e1 28 15N 16 38W
Teifi →, *U.K.* 21 E3 52 5N 4 41W
Teign →, *U.K.* 21 G4 50 32N 3 32W
Teignmouth, *U.K.* 21 G4 50 33N 3 31W
Teiuş, *Romania* .... 53 D8 46 12N 23 40 E
Teixeira, *Brazil* .... 170 C4 7 13 S 37 15W
Teixeira Pinto, *Guinea-Biss.* .. 112 C1 12 3N 16 0W
Tejakula, *Indonesia* .... 79 J18 8 8 S 115 20 E
Tejam, *India* .... 93 E9 29 57N 80 11 E
Tejen, *Turkmenistan* .... 66 F7 37 23N 60 31 E
Tejen →, *Turkmenistan* .... 97 B9 37 24N 60 38 E
Tejo →, *Europe* 43 F2 38 40N 9 24W
Tejon Pass, *U.S.A.* 161 L8 34 49N 118 53W
Tekamah, *U.S.A.* 154 E6 41 47N 96 13W
Tekapo →, *N.Z.* .... 131 E5 44 13 S 170 21 E
Tekapo, L., *N.Z.* .... 131 D5 43 53 S 170 33 E
Tekax, *Mexico* 163 C7 20 11N 89 18W
Teke, *Kazakhstan* .... 65 B4 43 15N 68 10 E
Teke, *Turkey* .... 51 E13 41 4N 29 39 E
Tekeli, *Kazakhstan* .... 65 A9 44 50N 79 0 E
Tekeze →, *Ethiopia* .... 107 E4 14 20N 35 50 E
Tekija, *Serbia, Yug.* .... 50 B6 44 42N 22 26 E
Tekirdağ, *Turkey* .... 51 F11 40 58N 27 30 E
Tekirdağ □, *Turkey* .... 51 E11 41 0N 27 0 E
Tekirova, *Turkey* .... 49 E12 36 30N 30 32 E
Tekkali, *India* .... 94 E7 18 37N 84 15 E
Tekke, *Turkey* .... 100 B7 40 42N 35 18 E
Tekman, *Turkey* .... 101 C9 39 38N 41 31 E
Tekoa, *U.S.A.* 158 C5 47 14N 117 4W
Tekong Besar, Pulau, *Singapore* 87 d 1 25N 104 3 E
Tekouiât, O. →, *Algeria* .... 111 D5 22 25N 2 35 E
Tekro, *Chad* .... 109 E4 19 32N 20 56 E
Teku, *Indonesia* .... 82 B2 0 46 S 123 26 E
Tel →, *India* .... 94 D6 20 50N 83 54 E
Tel Aviv ✈ (TLV), *Israel* ...... 103 C3 32 5N 34 49 E
Tel Aviv-Yafo, *Israel* .... 103 C3 32 4N 34 48 E
Tel Lakhish, *Israel* .... 103 D3 31 34N 34 51 E
Tel Megiddo, *Israel* .... 103 C4 32 35N 35 11 E
Tela, *Honduras* 164 C2 15 40N 87 28W
Télagh, *Algeria* 111 B4 34 51N 0 32W
Telanaipura = Jambi, *Indonesia* 84 C2 1 38 S 103 30 E
Telaščica, Park Prirode ⌒, *Croatia* 45 E12 43 55N 15 10 E
Telavåg, *Norway* .... 18 D1 60 15N 4 58 E
Telavi, *Georgia* .... 61 J7 42 0N 45 30 E
Telč, *Czech Rep.* .... 34 B8 49 11N 15 28 E
Telciu, *Romania* .... 53 C9 47 25N 24 24 E
Telde, *Canary Is.* 9 e1 27 59N 15 25W
Tele →, *Dem. Rep. of the Congo* 114 B4 2 48N 23 54 E
Telefomin, *Papua N. G.* .... 132 C1 5 10N 141 31 E
Telegraph Creek, *Canada* 142 B2 58 0N 131 10W
Telekhany = Tsyelyakhany, *Belarus* 15 B13 52 30N 25 46 E
Telemark, *Norway* .... 15 G12 59 15N 7 40 E
Telemark □, *Norway* .... 18 E5 59 25N 8 30 E
Telén, *Argentina* .... 174 D2 36 15 S 65 31W
Telen →, *Indonesia* .... 85 C5 0 10 S 117 20 E
Teleng, *Iran* .... 97 E9 25 47N 61 3 E
Teleño, *Spain* 42 C4 42 23N 6 22W
Teleorman □, *Romania* .... 53 G10 44 0N 25 20 E
Teleorman →, *Romania* .... 53 G10 43 55N 25 26 E
Teles Pires →, *Brazil* .... 173 B6 7 21 S 58 3W
Telescope Pk., *U.S.A.* 161 J9 36 10N 117 5W
Teletaye, *Mali* .... 113 B5 16 31N 1 30 E
Telfer Mine, *Australia* .... 124 C3 21 40 S 122 12 E
Telford, *U.K.* 21 E5 52 40N 2 27W
Telford and Wrekin □, *U.K.* 20 E5 52 45N 2 27W
Telfs, *Austria* .... 34 D4 47 19N 11 4 E
Telida, *U.S.A.* 144 E9 63 23N 153 16W
Télimélé, *Guinea* 112 C2 10 54N 13 2W
Teljo, J., *Sudan* .... 107 E2 14 42N 25 26 E
Telkwa, *Canada* 142 C3 54 41N 127 5W
Tell City, *U.S.A.* 157 G10 37 57N 86 46W
Teller, *U.S.A.* 144 D6 65 16N 166 22W
Tellicherry, *India* .... 95 J2 11 45N 75 30 E
Telluride, *U.S.A.* 159 H10 37 56N 107 49W
Teluk Datok, *Malaysia* .... 84 B2 2 49N 101 31 E
Teloloapán, *Mexico* 163 D5 18 21N 99 51W
Telpos Iz, *Russia* .... 56 B10 63 16N 59 13 E
Telsen, *Argentina* .... 176 B3 42 30 S 66 50W
Telšiai, *Lithuania* .... 15 H20 55 59N 22 14 E
Telšiai □, *Lithuania* .... 15 H20 55 59N 22 15 E
Teltow, *Germany* .... 30 C9 52 24N 13 15 E
Teluk Anson = Teluk Intan,
  Malaysia .... 87 K3 4 3N 101 0 E
Teluk Bahang, *Malaysia* .... 87 c 5 28N 100 13 E
Teluk Betung = Tanjungkarang
  Telukbetung, *Indonesia* ..... 84 D3 5 20 S 105 10 E
Teluk Cenderawasih, *Indonesia* 83 B5 2 30 S 135 20 E
Teluk Darvel, *Malaysia* .... 81 J2 4 45N 118 30 E
Teluk Intan, *Malaysia* .... 87 K3 4 3N 101 0 E
Teluk Kumbar, *Malaysia* .... 87 c 5 16N 100 12 E
Telukbutun, *Indonesia* .... 84 B3 4 13N 108 12 E
Telukdalem, *Indonesia* .... 84 B1 0 33N 97 50 E
Tema, *Ghana* .... 113 D5 5 41N 0 0 E
Temanggung, *Indonesia* .... 85 D4 7 18 S 110 10 E
Temasint, *Algeria* .... 111 D6 21 38N 7 40 E
Temax, *Mexico* 163 C7 21 10N 88 50W
Temba, *S. Africa* .... 117 D4 25 20 S 28 17 E
Tembagapura, *Indonesia* .... 83 B5 4 20 S 137 0 E
Tembe, *Dem. Rep. of the Congo* 118 C2 0 16 S 28 14 E
Tembe Elephant Reserve ⌒,
  S. Africa .... 117 D5 26 51 S 32 24 E
Tembesi, *Indonesia* .... 84 C2 1 43 S 103 6 E
Tembilahan, *Indonesia* .... 84 C2 0 19 S 103 6 E
Temblador, *Venezuela* 169 B5 8 59N 62 44W
Tembleque, *Spain* 42 F7 39 41N 3 30W
Temblor Range, *U.S.A.* 161 K7 35 20N 119 50W
Teme →, *U.K.* 21 E5 52 11N 2 13W
Temecula, *U.S.A.* 161 M9 33 30N 117 9W
Temerloh, *Malaysia* .... 84 B2 3 27N 102 25 E
Teminabuan, *Indonesia* .... 83 B4 1 26 S 132 1 E
Temir, *Kazakhstan* .... 57 E10 49 1N 57 14 E
Temirlan, *Kazakhstan* .... 65 B4 42 36N 69 26 E
Temirtau, *Kazakhstan* .... 65 B4 50 5N 72 56 E
Temirtau, *Russia* .... 66 D9 53 10N 87 30 E
Temiscamie →, *Canada* 141 C5 50 59N 73 5W
Témiscamingue, L., *Canada* 140 C4 46 44N 79 5W
Temnikov, *Russia* .... 60 C6 54 40N 43 11 E
Temo →, *Italy* .... 46 B1 40 17N 8 28 E
Temora, *Australia* .... 129 C7 34 30 S 147 30 E
Temosachic, *Mexico* 162 B3 28 55N 107 45W
Tempe, *U.S.A.* 159 K8 33 25N 111 56W
Témpio Pausánia, *Italy* .... 46 B2 40 53N 9 6 E
Tempiute, *U.S.A.* 160 H11 37 39N 115 38W
Templar Bank, *S. China Sea* .... 81 F1 8 0N 117 30 E

Temple, *U.S.A.* 155 K6 31 6N 97 21W
Temple B., *Australia* .... 126 A3 12 15 S 143 3 E
Temple Terrace, *U.S.A.* 153 G7 28 2N 82 23W
Templemore, *Ireland* 23 D4 52 47N 7 51W
Templeton, *U.S.A.* 160 K6 35 33N 120 42W
Templeton →, *Australia* .... 126 C2 21 0 S 138 40 E
Templin, *Germany* .... 30 B9 53 7N 13 28 E
Tempoal, *Mexico* 163 C5 21 31N 98 23W
Tempué, *Angola* .... 115 E3 13 27 S 18 49 E
Temryuk, *Russia* .... 59 K9 45 15N 37 24 E
Temska →, *Serbia, Yug.* .... 50 C6 43 17N 22 33 E
Temuco, *Chile* .... 175 D2 38 45 S 72 40W
Temuka, *N.Z.* .... 131 E6 44 14 S 171 17 E
Ten Degree Channel, *India* ..... 95 K11 10 0N 92 30 E
Ten Thousand Is., *U.S.A.* 153 K8 25 55N 81 45W
Tena, *Ecuador* .... 168 D2 0 59 S 77 49W
Tenabo, *Mexico* 163 C6 20 2N 90 12W
Tenaha, *U.S.A.* 155 K7 31 57N 94 15W
Tenakee Springs, *U.S.A.* 142 B1 57 47N 135 13W
Tenali, *India* .... 95 F5 16 15N 80 35 E
Tenancingo, *Mexico* 163 D5 19 0N 99 33W
Tenango, *Mexico* 163 D5 19 7N 99 33W
Tenasserim, *Burma* .... 87 F2 12 6N 99 3 E
Tenasserim □, *Burma* .... 86 F2 14 0N 98 30 E
Tenby, *U.K.* 21 F3 51 40N 4 42W
Tenda, Colle di, *France* .... 29 D11 44 7N 7 36 E
Tendaho, *Ethiopia* .... 107 E5 11 48N 40 54 E
Tende, *France* .... 29 D11 44 5N 7 35 E
Tendre, Mt., *Switz.* .... 32 C2 46 35N 6 18 E
Tendrovskaya Kosa, *Ukraine* .... 59 K6 46 16N 31 35 E
Tendukhera, *India* .... 93 H8 23 24N 79 33 E
Tenebroûret, O. →, *Mauritania* . 110 D1 20 35N 16 0W
Teneguía, Volcanes de, *Canary Is.* 9 e1 28 28N 17 51W
Teneida, *Egypt* .... 106 B2 25 30N 29 19 E
Tenenkou, *Mali* 112 C4 14 28N 4 45W
Tenente Marques →, *Brazil* ..... 173 C6 11 10 S 59 56W
Ténéré, *Niger* .... 113 B7 19 0N 10 30 E
Ténéré, Erg du, *Niger* .... 109 E2 17 35N 10 55 E
Tenerife, *Canary Is.* 9 e1 28 15N 16 35W
Tenerife, Pico, *Canary Is.* 9 e1 27 43N 18 1W
Tenerife Norte ✈ (TFN), *Canary Is.* 9 e1 28 28N 16 17W
Tenerife Sur ✈ (TFS), *Canary Is.* 9 e1 28 3N 16 33W
Ténès, *Algeria* .... 111 A5 36 31N 1 14 E
Teng Xian, *Guangxi Zhuangzu,*
  China .... 77 F8 23 21N 110 56 E
Teng Xian, *Shandong, China* .... 75 G9 35 5N 117 10 E
Tengah □, *Indonesia* .... 82 B2 1 30 S 121 0 E
Tengah, Kepulauan, *Indonesia* .. 85 D5 7 5 S 118 15 E
Tengchong, *China* .... 76 E2 25 0N 98 28 E
Tengchowfu = Penglai, *China* ... 75 F11 37 48N 120 42 E
Tenggara □, *Indonesia* .... 82 B2 3 50 S 122 0 E
Tenggarong, *Indonesia* .... 85 C5 0 24 S 116 58 E
Tenggol, Pulau, *Malaysia* ...... 87 K4 4 48N 103 41 E
Tengiz, Ozero, *Kazakhstan* ..... 66 D7 50 30N 69 0 E
Tenhult, *Sweden* .... 17 G8 57 41N 14 20 E
Tenigerbad, *Switz.* .... 33 C7 46 42N 8 57 E
Tenille, *U.S.A.* 152 F6 29 46N 83 19W
Tenino, *U.S.A.* 160 D4 46 51N 122 51W
Tenkasi, *India* .... 95 K3 8 55N 77 20 E
Tenke, Katanga, *Dem. Rep. of*
  the Congo .... 119 E2 11 22 S 26 40 E
Tenke, Katanga, *Dem. Rep. of*
  the Congo .... 119 E2 10 32 S 26 7 E
Tenkodogo, *Burkina Faso* 113 C4 11 54N 0 19W
Tenna →, *Italy* .... 45 E10 43 13N 13 47 E
Tennant Creek, *Australia* ...... 126 B1 19 30 S 134 15 E
Tennessee □, *U.S.A.* 149 H2 36 0N 86 30W
Tennessee →, *U.S.A.* 148 G1 37 4N 88 34W
Tennille, *U.S.A.* 152 C7 32 56N 82 48W
Teno, Pta. de, *Canary Is.* 9 e1 28 21N 16 55W
Tenom, *Malaysia* .... 85 A5 5 4N 115 57 E
Tenosique, *Mexico* 163 D6 17 30N 91 24W
Tenri, *Japan* .... 73 C7 34 39N 135 49 E
Tenryū, *Japan* .... 73 C9 34 52N 137 49 E
Tenryū-Gawa →, *Japan* .... 73 C9 35 39N 137 48 E
Tensift, Oued →, *Morocco* 110 B3 32 3N 9 28W
Tentelomatinan, *Indonesia* ..... 82 A2 0 56N 121 48 E
Tentena, *Indonesia* .... 82 B2 1 47 S 120 39 E
Tenterden, *U.K.* .... 21 F8 51 4N 0 42 E
Tenterfield, *Australia* .... 127 D5 29 0 S 152 0 E
Tenuaiur, Uad →, *W. Sahara* 110 D1 21 36N 16 0W
Teo, *Spain* 42 C2 42 45N 8 30W
Teófilo Otoni, *Brazil* .... 171 E3 17 50 S 41 30W
Tepa, *Indonesia* .... 83 C3 7 52 S 129 31 E
Tepalcatepec →, *Mexico* 162 D4 18 35N 101 59W
Tepecik, *Bursa, Turkey* .... 51 F12 40 17N 29 2 E
Tepecik, *Kütahya, Turkey* ...... 49 B11 39 32N 29 28 E
Tepehuanes, *Mexico* 162 B3 25 21N 105 44W
Tepelenë, *Albania* .... 50 F4 40 17N 20 2 E
Tepetongo, *Mexico* 162 C4 22 28N 103 9W
Tepic, *Mexico* 162 C4 21 30N 104 54W
Teplá, *Czech Rep.* .... 34 B5 49 59N 12 52 E
Teplice, *Czech Rep.* .... 34 A6 50 40N 13 48 E
Teploklyuchenka, *Kyrgyzstan* ... 65 B9 42 30N 78 30 E
Tepoca, C., *Mexico* 162 A2 30 20N 112 25W
Tequila, *Mexico* 162 C4 20 54N 103 47W
Ter →, *Spain* .... 40 C8 42 2N 3 12 E
Ter Apel, *Neths.* .... 24 B7 52 53N 7 5 E
Téra, *Niger* .... 113 C5 14 0N 0 45 E
Tera →, *Spain* 42 D5 41 54N 5 44W
Teraina, *Kiribati* 135 G11 4 43N 160 25W
Terakeka, *Sudan* .... 107 F3 5 30N 31 45 E
Téramo, *Italy* .... 45 F10 42 39N 13 42 E
Terang, *Australia* .... 128 E5 38 15 S 142 55 E
Terawhiti, C., *N.Z.* .... 130 H3 41 16 S 174 38 E
Terazit, Massif de, *Niger* ..... 111 D6 20 2N 8 30 E
Tercan, *Turkey* .... 101 C9 39 47N 40 23 E
Terceira, *Azores* 9 d1 38 43N 27 13W
Tercero →, *Argentina* .... 174 C3 32 58 S 61 47W
Terdal, *India* .... 94 F2 16 33N 75 3 E
Terebovlya, *Ukraine* .... 59 H3 49 18N 25 44 E
Teregova, *Romania* .... 52 E7 45 10N 22 16 E
Tereida, *Sudan* .... 107 E3 10 35N 31 17 E
Terek →, *Russia* .... 61 J8 44 0N 47 30 E
Terek-Say, *Kyrgyzstan* .... 65 C5 41 30N 71 11 E
Terengganu □, *Malaysia* .... 84 B2 4 55N 103 0 E
Terengözek, *Kazakhstan* .... 65 A2 45 34N 64 59 E
Terenos, *Brazil* .... 173 E7 20 26 S 54 50W
Terepaima, Parque Nac. △,
  Venezuela 165 E6 9 58N 69 17W
Tereshka →, *Russia* .... 60 E8 51 48N 46 26 E
Teresina, *Brazil* .... 170 C3 5 9 S 42 45W
Teresinha, *Brazil* 169 C7 0 58N 52 2W
Terespol, *Poland* .... 55 F10 52 5N 23 37 E
Teressa, *India* .... 95 K11 8 15N 93 10 E
Terewah, L., *Australia* .... 129 D7 29 52 S 147 35 E
Terges →, *Portugal* 43 H3 37 9N 7 41W
Tergnier, *France* .... 27 C10 49 40N 3 17 E
Terhazza, *Mali* 112 D3 23 38N 5 22W
Teridgerie Cr. →, *Australia* ... 129 A8 30 25 S 148 50 E
Terlizzi, *Italy* .... 47 A9 41 8N 16 32 E
Terme, *Turkey* .... 100 B7 41 11N 37 0 E
Términi Imerese, *Italy* .... 46 E6 37 59N 13 42 E
Términos, L. de, *Mexico* 163 D6 18 35N 91 30W
Termiz, *Uzbekistan* .... 65 D7 37 15N 67 15 E
Térmoli, *Italy* .... 45 F12 42 0N 15 0 E
Ternate, *Indonesia* .... 82 A3 0 45N 127 25 E
Terneuzen, *Neths.* .... 24 C3 51 20N 3 50 E

Terney, *Russia* .... 67 E14 45 3N 136 37 E
Terni, *Italy* .... 45 F9 42 34N 12 37 E
Ternitz, *Austria* .... 34 D9 47 43N 16 2 E
Ternopil, *Ukraine* .... 59 H3 49 30N 25 40 E
Ternopol = Ternopil, *Ukraine* .. 59 H3 49 30N 25 40 E
Terowie, *Australia* .... 128 B3 33 8 S 138 55 E
Terpní, *Greece* .... 50 F7 40 55N 23 26 E
Terra Bella, *U.S.A.* 161 K7 35 58N 119 3W
Terra Nova Nat. Park △, *Canada* . 141 C9 48 33N 53 55W
Terrace, *Canada* 142 C3 54 30N 128 35W
Terrace Bay, *Canada* 140 C2 48 47N 87 5W
Terracina, *Italy* .... 46 A6 41 17N 13 15 E
Terralba, *Italy* .... 46 B2 39 43N 8 39 E
Terranova = Ólbia, *Italy* .... 46 B2 40 55N 9 31 E
Terrasini, *Italy* .... 46 D6 38 10N 13 4 E
Terrassa, *Spain* .... 40 D7 41 34N 2 1 E
Terrasson-la-Villedieu, *France* . 28 C5 45 8N 1 18 E
Terre Haute, *U.S.A.* 157 E9 39 28N 87 25W
Terrebonne B., *U.S.A.* 155 L9 29 5N 90 35W
Terrecht, *Mali* 111 D4 20 10N 0 10W
Terrell, *U.S.A.* 155 J6 32 44N 96 17W
Terrenceville, *Canada* 141 C9 47 40N 54 44W
Terry, *U.S.A.* 154 B2 46 47N 105 19W
Terryville, *U.S.A.* 151 E11 41 41N 73 3W
Terschelling, *Neths.* .... 24 A5 53 25N 5 20 E
Terskey Ala Too, *Kyrgyzstan* ... 65 C8 41 50N 77 0 E
Terskey Alatau = Terskey Ala Too,
   Kyrgyzstan .... 65 C8 41 50N 77 0 E
Tersko-Kumskiy Kanal →, *Russia* . 61 H7 44 32N 44 38 E
Terténia, *Italy* .... 46 C2 39 42N 9 34 E
Terter = Tärtär →, *Azerbaijan* .. 61 K8 40 26N 47 20 E
Teruel, *Spain* 40 E3 40 22N 1 8W
Teruel □, *Spain* 40 E4 40 48N 1 0W
Tervel, *Bulgaria* .... 51 C11 43 45N 27 28 E
Tervola, *Finland* .... 14 C21 66 6N 24 49 E
Teryaweyna L., *Australia* .... 128 B5 32 18 S 143 22 E
Tešanj, *Bos.-H.* .... 52 F3 44 38N 18 1 E
Teschen = Cieszyn, *Poland* ...... 55 J5 49 45N 18 35 E
Teseney, *Eritrea* .... 107 D4 15 5N 36 42 E
Tesha →, *Russia* .... 60 C6 55 38N 42 9 E
Teshekpuk L., *U.S.A.* 144 A9 70 35N 153 26W
Teshio, *Japan* .... 70 B10 44 53N 141 44 E
Teshio-Gawa →, *Japan* .... 70 B10 44 53N 141 45 E
Tešica, *Serbia, Yug.* .... 50 C5 43 27N 21 45 E
Tesiyn Gol →, *Mongolia* .... 68 A2 50 40N 93 20 E
Teslić, *Bos.-H.* .... 52 F2 44 37N 17 54 E
Teslin, *Canada* 142 A2 60 10N 132 43W
Teslin →, *Canada* 142 A2 61 34N 134 35W
Teslin L., *Canada* 142 A2 60 15N 132 57W
Tesouro, *Brazil* .... 173 D7 16 4 S 53 34W
Tessalit, *Mali* .... 111 D5 20 12N 1 0 E
Tessaoua, *Niger* .... 113 C6 13 47N 7 56 E
Tessin, *Germany* .... 30 A8 54 2N 12 26 E
Tessit, *Mali* .... 113 B5 15 13N 0 18 E
Tessounfat, *Mali* .... 111 D5 22 53N 0 32 E
Test →, *U.K.* 21 G6 50 56N 1 29W
Testa del Gargano, *Italy* .... 45 G13 41 50N 16 10 E
Testigos, Is. Las, *Venezuela* ... 165 D7 11 23N 63 7W
Tét, *Hungary* .... 52 C2 47 30N 17 33 E
Têt →, *France* .... 29 F7 42 44N 3 2 E
Tetachuck L., *Canada* 142 C3 53 18N 125 55W
Tetas, Pta., *Chile* .... 174 A1 23 31 S 70 38W
Tete, *Mozam.* .... 119 F3 16 13 S 33 33 E
Tete □, *Mozam.* .... 119 F3 15 15 S 32 40 E
Tetenga, Caleta, *Chile* .... 172 b 27 9 S 109 19W
Tetepare, *Solomon Is.* .... 133 M9 8 45 S 157 35 E
Teterev →, *Ukraine* .... 59 G6 51 1N 30 5 E
Teterow, *Germany* .... 30 B8 53 46N 12 34 E
Teteven, *Bulgaria* .... 51 D8 42 58N 24 17 E
Tethul →, *Canada* 142 A6 60 35N 112 12W
Tetiyev, *Ukraine* .... 59 H5 49 22N 29 38 E
Tetlin, *U.S.A.* 144 E12 63 8N 142 31W
Tetlin Junction, *U.S.A.* 144 E12 63 19N 142 36W
Teton →, *U.S.A.* 158 C8 47 56N 110 31W
Tétouan, *Morocco* 110 A3 35 35N 5 21W
Tetovo, *Macedonia* .... 50 D4 42 1N 20 59 E
Tetyushi, *Russia* .... 174 B3 25 35 S 60 11W
Teuco →, *Argentina* .... 33 B8 47 24N 9 23 E
Teufen, *Switz.* .... 46 D1 38 58N 8 46 E
Teulada, *Italy* 143 C9 50 23N 97 16W
Teulon, *Canada* .... 83 C3 6 59 S 129 8 E
Teun, *Indonesia* .... 30 C4 52 5N 8 2 E
Teutoburger Wald, *Germany* 157 E8 39 8N 89 29W
Teutopolis, *U.S.A.* .... 45 F9 41 44N 12 14 E
Tevere →, *Italy* .... 45 F9 42 46N 12 14 E
Tevere, Parco Fluviale del △, *Italy* . 103 C4 32 47N 35 32 E
Teverya, *Israel* 22 F6 55 29N 2 38W
Teviot →, *U.K.* .... 127 D5 26 27 S 153 3 E
Tewantin, *Australia* 21 F5 51 59N 2 9W
Tewkesbury, *U.K.* 142 D4 49 40N 124 25W
Texada I., *Canada* 155 J8 33 26N 94 2W
Texarkana, Ark., *U.S.A.* 155 J7 33 26N 94 3W
Texarkana, Tex., *U.S.A.* .... 127 D5 28 49 S 151 9 E
Texas, *Australia* 155 K5 31 40N 98 30W
Texas □, *U.S.A.* 155 L7 29 24N 94 54W
Texas City, *U.S.A.* .... 24 A4 53 5N 4 50 E
Texel, *Neths.* 155 G3 36 23N 103 2W
Texline, *U.S.A.* 155 J6 33 50N 96 34W
Texoma, L., *U.S.A.* .... 58 D11 56 55N 40 30 E
Teykovo, *Russia* .... 91 B2 33 30N 64 24 E
Teyvareh, *Afghan.* .... 60 B5 56 32N 41 53 E
Teza →, *Russia* .... 91 B3 34 24N 69 30 E
Tezin, *Afghan.* 163 D5 19 50N 97 22W
Teziutlán, *Mexico* .... 90 B4 26 40N 92 45 E
Tezpur, *India* 142 C4 54 43N 124 30W
Tezzeron L., *Canada* 143 A10 60 31N 94 37W
Tha-anne →, *Canada* .... 86 D4 17 57N 102 53 E
Tha Deua, *Laos* .... 86 C3 19 26N 101 50 E
Tha Deua, *Laos* .... 86 D3 17 48N 100 32 E
Tha Pla, *Thailand* .... 86 E3 14 34N 100 44 E
Tha Rua, *Thailand* .... 87 H2 14 34N 97 55 E
Tha Sala, *Thailand* .... 86 D1 17 34N 100 32 E
Tha Song Yang, *Thailand* .... 117 D4 29 45 S 28 0 E
Thaba Putsoa, *Lesotho* .... 117 D4 29 30 S 29 16 E
Thabana Ntlenyana, *Lesotho* ... 90 G5 17 2N 94 48 E
Thabaung, *Burma* .... 117 C4 24 40 S 27 21 E
Thabazimbi, *S. Africa* .... 90 D5 22 53N 95 59 E
Thädiq, *Si. Arabia* .... 96 E5 25 18N 45 52 E
Thai Binh, *Vietnam* .... 76 G6 20 35N 106 1 E
Thai Muang, *Thailand* .... 87 H2 8 24N 98 16 E
Thai Nguyen, *Vietnam* .... 76 G5 21 35N 105 55 E
Thailand ■, *Asia* .... 86 E4 16 0N 102 0 E
Thailand, G. of, *Asia* .... 86 D5 17 25N 104 45 E
Thakhek, *Laos* .... 90 B2 26 2N 88 34 E
Thakurgaon, *Bangla.* .... 91 B3 33 28N 70 33 E
Thal, *Pakistan* .... 92 D4 31 10N 71 30 E
Thal Desert, *Pakistan* .... 108 A1 35 35N 8 40 E
Thala, *Tunisia* .... 86 F5 13 33N 105 57 E
Thalabarivat, *Cambodia* .... 33 C8 46 39N 9 17 E
Thalkirch, *Switz.* .... 127 D4 29 38 S 148 49 E
Thallon, *Australia* .... 87 b 9 26N 99 54 E
Thalu, Ko, *Thailand* .... 33 B7 47 17N 8 35 E
Thalwil, *Switz.* .... 99 C6 17 39N 54 2 E
Thamarît, *Oman* .... 130 D4 37 7 S 175 34 E
Thames, *N.Z.* 140 D3 42 20N 82 25W
Thames →, *Canada* .... 21 F8 51 29N 0 34 E
Thames →, *U.K.* 151 E12 41 18N 72 5W
Thames →, *U.S.A.* .... 130 D4 37 0 S 175 25 E
Thames, Firth of, *N.Z.* .... 21 F8 51 29N 0 52 E
Thamesford, *Canada* 150 C4 43 4N 81 0W
Thamesville, *Canada* 150 D3 42 33N 81 59W
Thämit, W. →, *Libya* .... 108 B3 31 11N 16 8 E

Thamūd, *Yemen* .... 99 C5 17 18N 49 55 E
Than, *India* .... 92 H4 22 34N 71 11 E
Than Uyen, *Vietnam* .... 86 B4 22 0N 103 54 E
Thana Gazi, *India* .... 92 F7 27 25N 76 19 E
Thanbyuzayat, *Burma* .... 90 G6 15 58N 97 44 E
Thandaung, *Burma* .... 90 F6 19 4N 96 41 E
Thandla, *India* .... 92 H6 23 0N 74 34 E
Thane, *India* .... 94 E1 19 12N 72 59 E
Thanesar, *India* .... 92 D7 30 1N 76 52 E
Thanet, I. of, *U.K.* .... 21 F9 51 21N 1 20 E
Thangool, *Australia* .... 126 C5 24 38 S 150 42 E
Thanh Hoa, *Vietnam* .... 86 C5 19 48N 105 46 E
Thanh Hung, *Vietnam* .... 87 H5 9 55N 105 43 E
Thanh Pho Ho Chi Minh, *Vietnam* . 87 G6 10 58N 106 40 E
Thanh Thuy, *Vietnam* .... 86 A5 22 55N 104 51 E
Thanjavur, *India* .... 95 J4 10 48N 79 12 E
Thano Bula Khan, *Pakistan* .... 92 G2 25 22N 67 50 E
Thaolinta L., *Canada* 143 A9 61 30N 96 25W
Thaon-les-Vosges, *France* ...... 27 D13 48 15N 6 24 E
Thap Lan Nat Park △, *Thailand* . 86 E4 14 15N 102 16 E
Thap Sakae, *Thailand* .... 87 G2 11 30N 99 37 E
Thap Than, *Thailand* .... 86 E2 15 27N 99 54 E
Thar Desert, *India* .... 92 F5 28 0N 72 0 E
Tharad, *India* .... 92 G4 24 30N 71 44 E
Thargomindah, *Australia* ...... 127 D3 27 58 S 143 46 E
Tharrawaddy, *Burma* .... 90 G5 17 38N 95 48 E
Tharrawaw, *Burma* .... 90 G5 17 41N 95 28 E
Tharthār, Mileh, *Iraq* .... 101 E10 34 0N 43 15 E
Tharthār, W. ath →, *Iraq* ...... 101 E10 33 59N 43 12 E
Thasopoúla, *Greece* .... 51 F8 40 49N 24 45 E
Thásos, *Greece* .... 51 F8 40 40N 24 40 E
That Khe, *Vietnam* .... 76 F6 22 16N 106 28 E
Thatcher, Ariz., *U.S.A.* 159 K9 32 51N 109 46W
Thatcher, Colo., *U.S.A.* 155 G2 37 33N 104 7W
Thaton, *Burma* .... 90 G6 16 55N 97 22 E
Thau, Bassin de, *France* .... 28 E7 43 23N 3 36 E
Thaungdut, *Burma* .... 90 C5 24 30N 94 40 E
Thawatti, *Burma* .... 90 F6 19 32N 96 16 E
Thayer, *U.S.A.* 155 G9 36 31N 91 33W
Thayetmyo, *Burma* .... 90 F5 19 20N 95 10 E
Thayngen, *Switz.* .... 33 A7 47 49N 8 43 E
Thazi, Magwe, *Burma* .... 90 F5 19 56N 95 5 E
Thazi, Mandalay, *Burma* .... 90 E6 21 0N 96 5 E
The Alberga →, *Australia* ...... 127 D2 27 6 S 135 33 E
The Bight, *Bahamas* 165 B4 24 19N 75 24W
The Briars, *St. Helena* .... 9 h 15 56 S 5 43W
The Brothers, *Yemen* .... 99 D6 12 6N 53 10 E
The Calvados Chain, *Papua N. G.* . 132 F7 11 10 S 152 45 E
The Crane, *Barbados* .... 165 g 13 6N 59 27W
The Dalles, *U.S.A.* 158 D3 45 36N 121 10W
The English Company's Is., *Australia* . 126 A2 11 50 S 136 32 E
The Entrance, *Australia* .... 129 B9 33 21 S 151 30 E
The Frome →, *Australia* .... 127 D2 29 8 S 137 54 E
The Great Divide = Great Dividing
   Ra., *Australia* .... 126 C4 23 0 S 146 0 E
The Hague = 's-Gravenhage, *Neths.* . 24 B4 52 7N 4 17 E
The Hamilton →, *Australia* ..... 127 D2 26 40 S 135 19 E
The Hunter Hills, *N.Z.* .... 131 L2 44 26 S 170 46 E
The Macumba →, *Australia* ..... 127 D2 27 52 S 137 12 E
The Neales →, *Australia* .... 127 D2 28 8 S 136 47 E
The Oaks, *Australia* .... 129 C9 34 3 S 150 34 E
The Officer →, *Australia* ...... 125 E5 27 46 S 132 30 E
The Pas, *Canada* 143 C8 53 45N 101 15W
The Range, *Zimbabwe* .... 119 F3 19 2 S 31 2 E
The Remarkables, *N.Z.* .... 131 F3 45 10 S 168 50 E
The Rock, *Australia* .... 129 C7 35 15 S 147 2 E
The Salt L., *Australia* .... 127 E3 30 6 S 142 8 E
The Sandheads, *India* .... 90 E2 21 10N 88 20 E
The Settlement, *Br. Virgin Is.* .. 165 e 18 43N 64 22W
The Sisters, *Seychelles* .... 121 b 4 16 S 55 52 E
The Slot = New Georgia Sound,
   Solomon Is. .... 133 L9 8 0 S 158 20 E
The Stevenson →, *Australia* .... 127 D2 27 6 S 135 33 E
The Warburton →, *Australia* ... 127 D2 28 4 S 137 28 E
The Woodlands, *U.S.A.* 155 K7 30 9N 95 27W
Thebes = Thívai, *Greece* ...... 48 C5 38 19N 23 19 E
Thebes, *Egypt* .... 106 B3 25 40N 32 35 E
Thedaw, *Burma* .... 90 E6 21 5N 96 4 E
Thedford, *Canada* 150 C3 43 9N 81 51W
Thedford, *U.S.A.* 154 E4 41 59N 100 35W
Theebine, *Australia* .... 127 D5 25 57 S 152 34 E
Thègon, *Burma* .... 90 F5 18 39N 95 25 E
Thékli, Ayía, *Greece* .... 39 C1 38 15N 20 23 E
Thekulthili L., *Canada* 143 A7 61 3N 110 0W
Thelon →, *Canada* 143 A8 62 35N 104 3W
Thénezay, *France* 26 F6 46 44N 0 2W
Thenia, *Algeria* .... 111 A5 36 44N 3 33 E
Thenon, *France* .... 28 C5 45 9N 1 4 E
Theodore, *Australia* .... 126 C5 24 55 S 150 3 E
Theodore, *Canada* 143 C8 51 26N 102 55W
Theodore, *U.S.A.* 149 K1 30 33N 88 10W
Theodore Roosevelt L., *U.S.A.* . 159 K8 33 46N 111 0W
Theodore Roosevelt Nat. Memorial
   Park △, *U.S.A.* 154 B3 47 0N 103 25W
Thepha, *Thailand* .... 87 J3 6 52N 100 58 E
Thérain →, *France* .... 27 C9 49 15N 2 27 E
Theresa, *U.S.A.* 151 B9 44 13N 75 48W
Theressa, *U.S.A.* 152 F7 29 50N 82 4W
Thermaïkós Kólpos, *Greece* .... 50 F6 40 15N 22 45 E
Thermí, *Greece* .... 49 B8 39 11N 26 29 E
Thermopolis, *U.S.A.* 158 E9 43 39N 108 13W
Thermopylae P., *Greece* .... 48 C4 38 48N 22 35 E
Thesprotía □, *Greece* .... 48 B2 39 27N 20 22 E
Thessalía □, *Greece* .... 48 B4 39 25N 22 0 E
Thessalon, *Canada* 140 C3 46 20N 83 30W
Thessaloníki, *Greece* .... 50 F6 40 38N 22 58 E
Thessaloníki □, *Greece* .... 50 F6 40 45N 23 0 E
Thessaloníki ✕ (SKG), *Greece* . 50 F7 40 30N 22 59 E
Thessaloníki, Gulf of = Thermaïkós
   Kólpos, *Greece* .... 50 F6 40 15N 22 45 E
Thessaly = Thessalía □, *Greece* . 48 B4 39 25N 22 0 E
Thetford, *U.K.* .... 21 E8 52 25N 0 45 E
Thetford Mines, *Canada* 141 C5 46 8N 71 18W
Theun →, *Laos* .... 86 C5 18 19N 104 0 E
Theunissen, *S. Africa* .... 116 D4 28 26 S 26 43 E
Thevenard, *Australia* .... 127 E1 32 9 S 133 38 E
Thiámis →, *Greece* .... 48 B2 39 15N 20 6 E
Thiberville, *France* .... 26 C7 49 8N 0 27 E
Thibodaux, *U.S.A.* 155 L9 29 48N 90 49W
Thicket Portage, *Canada* 143 B9 55 19N 97 42W
Thief River Falls, *U.S.A.* 154 A6 48 7N 96 10W
Thiel Mts., *Antarctica* .... 7 E16 85 15 S 91 0W
Thiérache, *France* .... 27 C10 49 51N 3 45 E
Thiers, *France* .... 28 C7 45 52N 3 33 E
Thiès, *Senegal* 112 C1 14 50N 16 51W
Thiesi, *Italy* .... 46 B1 40 31N 8 43 E
Thiet, *Sudan* .... 107 F2 7 37N 28 49 E
Thika, *Kenya* .... 118 C4 1 1 S 37 5 E
Thille-Boubacar, *Senegal* 112 B1 16 31N 15 5W
Thimphu, *Bhutan* .... 90 B7 27 31N 89 45 E
Thingangyun, *Burma* .... 90 G6 16 49N 96 12 E
Pingeyjarsýsla □, *Iceland* 11 B10 65 40N 16 30W
Pingeyri, *Iceland* 11 B3 65 52N 23 30W
Pingmúli, *Iceland* 11 B6 65 2N 14 25W
Pingvallavatn, *Iceland* 11 C5 64 11N 21 9W
Pingvellir, *Iceland* 11 C5 64 16N 21 5W
Thio, *N. Cal.* .... 133 U20 21 37 S 166 14 E
Thionville, *France* .... 27 C13 49 20N 6 10 E
Thíra, *Greece* .... 49 E7 36 23N 25 27 E
Thirasía, *Greece* .... 49 E7 36 26N 25 21 E
Third Cataract, *Sudan* .... 106 D3 19 42N 30 20 E

Thirsk, *U.K.* 20 C6 54 14N 1 19W
Thiruvananthapuram = Trivandrum,
   India .... 95 K3 8 41N 77 0 E
Thiruvarur, *India* .... 95 J4 10 46N 79 38 E
Thisted, *Denmark* .... 17 H2 56 58N 8 40 E
Pistilfjörður, *Iceland* 11 A11 66 18N 15 24W
Thistle I., *Australia* .... 128 C2 35 0 S 136 8 E
Thitgy, *Burma* .... 90 F6 18 15N 96 13 E
Thithia = Cicia, *Fiji* .... 133 A3 17 45 S 179 18W
Thitpokpin, *Burma* .... 90 F5 19 24N 95 58 E
Thívai, *Greece* .... 48 C5 38 19N 23 19 E
Thiviers, *France* .... 28 C4 45 25N 0 54 E
Thizy, *France* .... 27 F11 46 2N 4 18 E
Pjórsá →, *Iceland* 11 D6 63 47N 20 48W
Thlewiaza →, *Man., Canada* ... 143 B8 59 43N 100 5W
Thlewiaza →, *N.W.T., Canada* . 143 A10 60 29N 94 40W
Thmar Puok, *Cambodia* .... 86 F4 13 57N 103 4 E
Tho Vinh, *Vietnam* .... 86 C5 19 16N 105 42 E
Thoa →, *Canada* 143 A7 60 31N 109 47W
Thoen, *Thailand* .... 86 D2 17 43N 99 12 E
Thoeng, *Thailand* .... 86 C3 19 41N 100 12 E
Tholdi, *Pakistan* .... 93 B7 35 5N 76 6 E
Thomas, *U.S.A.* 155 H5 35 45N 98 45W
Thomas, L., *Australia* .... 127 D2 26 4 S 137 58 E
Thomas Hill Reservoir, *U.S.A.* . 156 E4 39 34N 92 39W
Thomaston, *U.S.A.* 149 K2 31 55N 87 44W
Thomasville, Ala., *U.S.A.* 149 K2 31 55N 87 44W
Thomasville, Ga., *U.S.A.* 152 E6 30 50N 83 59W
Thomasville, N.C., *U.S.A.* 149 H5 35 53N 80 5W
Thompson, *Canada* 143 B9 55 45N 97 52W
Thompson, *U.S.A.* 151 E9 41 52N 75 31W
Thompson →, *Canada* 142 C4 50 15N 121 24W
Thompson →, *U.S.A.* 156 E3 39 46N 93 37W
Thompson Falls, *U.S.A.* 158 C6 47 36N 115 21W
Thompson Pk., *U.S.A.* 158 F2 41 0N 123 0W
Thompson Sd., *N.Z.* .... 131 F1 45 8 S 166 46 E
Thompson Springs, *U.S.A.* 159 G9 38 58N 109 43W
Thompsontown, *U.S.A.* 150 F7 40 33N 77 14W
Thomson, *U.S.A.* 149 J4 33 28N 82 30W
Thomson →, *Australia* .... 126 C3 25 11 S 142 53 E
Thomson, Ill., *U.S.A.* 156 E9 41 58N 90 6W
Thomson →, *Australia* .... 126 C3 25 11 S 142 53 E
Thomson's Falls = Nyahururu, *Kenya* . 118 B4 0 2N 36 27 E
Thônes, *France* .... 29 C10 45 54N 6 18 E
Thong Yang, *Thailand* .... 87 b 9 28N 99 56 E
Thongwa, *Burma* .... 90 G6 16 45N 96 33 E
Thonon-les-Bains, *France* ...... 27 F13 46 22N 6 16 E
Thonze, *Burma* .... 90 G5 17 38N 95 47 E
Thorez, *Ukraine* .... 59 H10 48 4N 38 34 E
Porisjökull, *Iceland* 11 C6 64 32N 20 43W
Porisvatn, *Iceland* 11 C8 64 20N 18 55W
Porkötlustaðir, *Iceland* 11 D4 63 50N 22 30W
Porlákshöfn, *Iceland* 11 D5 63 51N 21 22W
Thornaby on Tees, *U.K.* 20 C6 54 33N 1 18W
Thornbury, *Canada* 150 B4 44 34N 80 26W
Thornbury, *N.Z.* .... 131 G3 46 17 S 168 9 E
Thorne, *U.K.* 20 D7 53 37N 0 57W
Thornhill, *Canada* 142 C3 54 31N 128 32W
Thornton, *U.S.A.* .... 159 B9 52 50 S 151 40 E
Thornton-Beresfield, *Australia* . 129 B9 32 50 S 151 40 E
Thorntown, *U.S.A.* 157 D10 40 8N 86 36W
Thorold, *Canada* 150 C5 43 7N 79 12W
Pórshöfn, *Iceland* 11 A11 66 12N 15 20W
Thouarcé, *France* 26 E6 47 17N 0 30W
Thouars, *France* 26 F6 47 0N 0 15W
Thouin, C., *Australia* .... 124 D2 20 20 S 118 10 E
Thousand Oaks, *U.S.A.* 161 L8 34 10N 118 50W
Thrace, *Turkey* .... 51 F10 41 0N 27 0 E
Thrakikón Pélagos, *Greece* ..... 51 F8 40 30N 25 0 E
Thredbo, *Australia* .... 129 D8 36 30 S 148 21 E
Three Forks, *U.S.A.* 158 D8 45 54N 111 33W
Three Hills, *Canada* 142 C6 51 43N 113 15W
Three Hummock I., *Australia* ... 127 G3 40 25 S 144 55 E
Three Oaks, *U.S.A.* 157 C10 41 48N 86 36W
Three Points, C., *Ghana* 114 E4 4 42N 2 6W
Three Rivers, Calif., *U.S.A.* 160 J8 36 26N 118 54W
Three Rivers, Mich., *U.S.A.* 157 C11 41 57N 85 38W
Three Rivers, Tex., *U.S.A.* 155 L5 28 28N 98 11W
Three Sisters, *U.S.A.* 158 D3 44 4N 121 51W
Three Sisters Is., *Solomon Is.* .. 133 N11 10 5 S 161 57 E
Three Springs, *Australia* ...... 125 E2 29 32 S 115 45 E
Throssell, L., *Australia* .... 125 E3 27 33 S 124 10 E
Throssell Ra., *Australia* .... 124 D3 22 3 S 121 43 E
Thrushton Nat. Park △, *Australia* . 127 D4 27 47 S 147 40 E
Thuamal Rampur, *India* .... 94 E6 19 23N 82 56 E
Thuan Hoa, *Vietnam* .... 87 H5 8 58N 105 30 E
Thubun Lakes, *Canada* 143 A6 61 30N 112 0W
Thueyts, *France* .... 29 D8 44 41N 4 9 E
Thuin, *Belgium* .... 24 D4 50 20N 4 17 E
Thuir, *France* .... 28 F6 42 38N 2 45 E
Thule = Qaanaaq, *Greenland* ... 10 B4 77 40N 69 0W
Thun, *Switz.* .... 32 C5 46 45N 7 38 E
Thunder B., *U.S.A.* 150 B1 45 0N 83 20W
Thunder Bay, *Canada* 140 C2 48 20N 89 15W
Thunderbolt, *U.S.A.* 152 C8 32 3N 81 4W
Thundersee, *Switz.* .... 32 C5 46 43N 7 39 E
Thung Salaeng Luang Nat. Park △,
   Thailand .... 86 D3 16 43N 100 50 E
Thung Song, *Thailand* .... 87 H2 8 10N 99 40 E
Thunkar, *Bhutan* .... 90 B3 27 55N 91 0 E
Thuong Tra, *Vietnam* .... 86 D6 16 2N 107 42 E
Thur →, *Switz.* .... 33 A8 47 32N 9 10 E
Thurgau □, *Switz.* .... 33 A8 47 34N 9 10 E
Thüringen □, *Germany* .... 30 D6 51 0N 11 0 E
Thüringer Wald, *Germany* ..... 30 C6 50 35N 11 0 E
Thurles, *Ireland* 23 D4 52 41N 7 49W
Thurn P., *Austria* .... 34 D5 47 20N 12 25 E
Thurrock □, *U.K.* .... 21 F8 51 31N 0 23 E
Thursday I., *Australia* .... 126 A3 10 30 S 142 3 E
Thurso, *Canada* 140 C4 45 36N 75 15W
Thurso, *U.K.* 22 C5 58 36N 3 32W
Thurso →, *U.K.* 22 C5 58 36N 3 32W
Thurston I., *Antarctica* .... 7 D16 72 0 S 100 0W
Thury-Harcourt, *France* 26 D6 48 59N 0 30W
Thusis, *Switz.* .... 33 C8 46 42N 9 26 E
Thutade L., *Canada* 142 B3 57 0N 126 55W
Thy, *Denmark* .... 17 H2 56 52N 8 13 E
Thy, Parc Territorial de la △, *N. Cal.* . 133 V20 22 10 S 166 31 E
Thyborøn, *Denmark* .... 17 H2 56 42N 8 12 E
Pykkvabæjarklaustur, *Iceland* .. 11 D8 63 30N 18 22W
Pykkviber, *Iceland* 11 D6 63 45N 20 37W
Thyolo, *Malawi* .... 119 F4 16 7 S 35 5 E
Thysville = Mbanza Ngungu,
   Dem. Rep. of the Congo ..... 115 D2 5 12 S 14 53 E
Ti-n-Amzi →, *Niger* .... 113 B5 20 8N 4 32 E
Ti-n-Barraouene →, *Africa* .... 113 B5 18 40N 4 5 E
Ti-n-Barraouene, O. →, *Algeria* . 111 E5 19 2N 4 45 E
Ti-n-Medjerdam, O. →, *Algeria* . 111 D5 25 45N 1 30 E
Ti-n-Rerhoh, *Algeria* .... 111 D5 20 44N 4 2 E
Ti-n-Tanezzuft, *Algeria* .... 111 D5 24 49N 3 48 E
Ti-n-Tarabine, O. →, *Algeria* ... 111 D6 21 6N 7 24 E
Ti-n-Tarabine, O. →, *Algeria* ... 111 D6 21 16N 7 25 E
Ti-n-Toumma, *Niger* .... 109 E2 16 4N 12 40 E
Ti-n-Zaouatene, *Algeria* .... 111 E5 19 55N 2 55 E
Ti Tree, *Australia* .... 126 C1 22 5 S 133 22 E
Tiadiaye, *Senegal* 112 C1 14 25N 16 40W
Tiahuanaco, *Bolivia* .... 172 D4 16 33 S 68 42W
Tian Shan, *Asia* .... 65 C8 40 30N 76 0 E
Tianchang, *China* .... 77 A12 32 40N 119 0 E
Tiandeng, *China* .... 78 E6 23 6N 107 7 E
Tiandong, *China* .... 78 E6 23 36N 107 8 E
Tian'e, *China* .... 78 E6 25 1N 107 9 E
Tianguá, *Brazil* .... 170 B3 3 44 S 40 59W

Tianhe, *China* .... 76 E7 24 48N 108 40 E
Tianjin, *China* .... 75 E9 39 8N 117 10 E
Tiankoura, *Burkina Faso* 112 C4 10 47N 3 17W
Tianlin, *China* .... 76 E6 24 21N 106 12 E
Tianmen, *China* .... 77 B9 30 39N 113 9 E
Tianquan, *China* .... 74 B4 30 7N 102 4 E
Tianshui, *China* .... 74 G3 34 32N 105 40 E
Tiantai, *China* .... 77 C13 29 10N 121 2 E
Tianyang, *China* .... 76 F6 23 42N 106 53 E
Tianyar, *Indonesia* .... 79 J18 8 12 S 115 30 E
Tianzhen, *China* .... 74 D8 40 24N 114 5 E
Tianzhu, *China* .... 76 D7 26 54N 109 11 E
Tianzhuangtai, *China* .... 75 D12 40 43N 122 5 E
Tiaret, *Algeria* .... 111 A5 35 20N 1 21 E
Tiassalé, *Ivory C.* 112 D4 5 58N 4 57W
Tibagi, *Brazil* .... 175 A5 24 30 S 50 24W
Tibagi →, *Brazil* .... 175 A5 22 47 S 51 1W
Tibati, *Cameroon* .... 113 D7 6 22N 12 30 E
Tibe, *Ethiopia* .... 107 F4 9 2N 37 12 E
Tiber = Tevere →, *Italy* .... 45 G9 41 44N 12 14 E
Tiberias = Teverya, *Israel* ..... 103 C4 32 47N 35 32 E
Tiberias, L. = Yam Kinneret, *Israel* . 103 C4 32 45N 35 35 E
Tibesti, *Chad* .... 109 D3 21 0N 17 30 E
Tibet = Xizang Zizhiqu □, *China* . 68 C3 32 0N 88 0 E
Tibet, Plateau of, *Asia* .... 62 F12 32 0N 86 0 E
Tibiao, *Phil.* .... 81 F4 11 17N 122 2 E
Tibiri, *Niger* .... 113 C6 13 34N 7 4 E
Tibleş, Vf., *Romania* .... 53 C9 47 32N 24 15 E
Tibleşului, Munţii, *Romania* .... 53 C9 47 38N 24 5 E
Tibnī, *Syria* .... 101 E8 35 36N 39 50 E
Tibooburra, *Australia* .... 127 D3 29 26 S 142 1 E
Tibro, *Sweden* .... 17 F8 58 28N 14 10 E
Tibugá, G. de, *Colombia* 168 B2 5 45N 77 20W
Tiburón, I., *Mexico* 162 B2 29 0N 112 30W
Ticao I., *Phil.* .... 80 E4 12 31N 123 42 E
Tice, *U.S.A.* 153 J8 26 40N 81 49W
Tichît, *Mauritania* 112 B3 18 21N 9 29W
Tichla, *Mauritania* 110 D2 21 36N 14 58W
Ticho, *Ethiopia* .... 107 F4 7 50N 39 32 E
Ticino □, *Switz.* .... 33 D7 46 20N 8 45 E
Ticino →, *Italy* .... 31 K5 45 9N 9 14 E
Ticleni, *Romania* .... 53 F8 44 53N 23 24 E
Ticonderoga, *U.S.A.* 151 C11 43 51N 73 26W
Ticul, *Mexico* 167 C7 20 20N 89 31W
Tidaholm, *Sweden* .... 17 F7 58 12N 13 58 E
Tidan, *Sweden* .... 17 F8 58 34N 14 1 E
Tiddim, *Burma* .... 90 D4 23 28N 93 45 E
Tiden, *India* .... 95 L11 7 15N 93 33 E
Tideridjaoune, Adrar, *Algeria* .. 111 D5 23 0N 2 15 E
Tidikelt, *Algeria* .... 111 C5 26 58N 1 30 E
Tidioute, *U.S.A.* 150 E5 41 41N 79 24W
Tidjikja, *Mauritania* 112 B2 18 29N 11 35W
Tidore, *Indonesia* .... 82 A3 0 40N 127 25 E
Tiébissou, *Ivory C.* 112 D3 7 9N 5 10W
Tiéboro, *Chad* .... 109 D3 21 20N 17 7 E
Tiefencastel, *Switz.* .... 33 C9 46 40N 9 33 E
Tiegang Shuiku, *China* .... 69 F10 22 37N 113 53 E
Tiel, *Netherlands* .... 24 C5 51 53N 5 26 E
Tiel, *Senegal* 112 C1 14 55N 15 5W
Tieling, *China* .... 75 C12 42 20N 123 55 E
Tielt, *Belgium* .... 24 C3 51 0N 3 20 E
Tien Shan = Tian Shan, *Asia* ... 65 C8 40 30N 76 0 E
Tien-tsin = Tianjin, *China* ..... 75 E9 39 8N 117 10 E
Tien Yen, *Vietnam* .... 86 B6 21 20N 107 24 E
T'ienching = Tianjin, *China* .... 75 E9 39 8N 117 10 E
Tienen, *Belgium* .... 24 D4 50 48N 4 57 E
Tiénigbé, *Ivory C.* 112 D3 8 11N 5 43W
Tientsin = Tianjin, *China* ...... 75 E9 39 8N 117 10 E
Tieri, *Australia* .... 126 C4 23 2 S 148 21 E
Tieroko, Tarso, *Chad* .... 109 D3 20 45 S 17 52 E
Tierp, *Sweden* .... 16 D11 60 20N 17 30 E
Tierra Amarilla, *Chile* .... 174 B1 27 28 S 70 18W
Tierra Amarilla, *U.S.A.* 159 H10 36 42N 106 33W
Tierra Colorada, *Mexico* 163 D5 17 10N 99 35W
Tierra de Barros, *Spain* 43 G4 38 40N 6 30W
Tierra de Campos, *Spain* 42 C6 42 10N 4 50W
Tierra del Fuego □, *Argentina* . 176 D3 54 0 S 67 45W
Tierra del Fuego, I. Gr. de, *Argentina* . 176 D3 54 0 S 69 0W
Tierralta, *Colombia* 168 B2 8 11N 76 4W
Tiétar →, *Spain* 42 F4 39 50N 6 1W
Tieté →, *Brazil* .... 175 A5 20 40 S 51 35W
Tifarati, W. Sahara 110 C2 26 9N 10 33W
Tiffin, *U.S.A.* 157 C13 41 7N 83 11W
Tiffin →, *U.S.A.* 157 C12 41 20N 84 24W
Tiflèt, *Morocco* 110 B3 33 54N 6 20W
Tiflis = Tbilisi, *Georgia* .... 61 K7 41 43N 44 50 E
Tifton, *U.S.A.* 152 K4 31 27N 83 31W
Tifu, *Indonesia* .... 83 B3 3 39 S 126 24 E
Tiga, Ī., *N. Cal.* .... 133 U21 21 7 S 167 49 E
Tigalda I., *U.S.A.* 144 J6 54 6N 165 3W
Tigānas, *Moldova* .... 80 I4 13 38N 123 31 E
Tigbauan, *Phil.* .... 81 F4 10 41N 122 27 E
Tighina, *Moldova* .... 59 E14 46 50N 29 30 E
Tigil, *Russia* .... 67 D16 57 49N 158 40 E
Tigiria, *India* .... 94 B7 20 29N 85 31 E
Tignall, *U.S.A.* 152 B7 33 52N 82 44W
Tignish, *Canada* 141 C7 46 58N 64 2W
Tigray □, *Ethiopia* .... 107 E4 13 35N 39 15 E
Tigre →, *Peru* .... 168 D3 4 30 S 74 10W
Tigre →, *Venezuela* 169 B5 9 20N 62 30W
Tigris = Dijlah, Nahr →, *Asia* .. 96 D5 31 0N 47 25 E
Tiguentourine, *Algeria* .... 111 C6 27 52N 9 8 E
Tigveni, *Romania* .... 53 E9 45 10N 24 31 E
Tigyaing, *Burma* .... 90 D6 23 45N 96 10 E
Tîh, Gebel el, *Egypt* .... 106 B3 29 32N 33 26 E
Tihodaine, Erg de, *Algeria* ..... 111 C6 25 15N 7 15 E
Tihwa = Ürümqi, *China* .... 68 B3 43 45N 87 45 E
Tijara, *India* .... 92 F7 27 56N 76 31 E
Tījī, *Libya* .... 108 B2 32 0N 11 18 E
Tijuana, *Mexico* 161 N9 32 30N 117 10W
Tikal, *Guatemala* 166 C2 17 13N 89 24W
Tikal, Parque Nac. △, *Guatemala* . 164 C2 17 13 S 89 34W
Tikamgarh, *India* .... 93 G8 24 44N 78 50 E
Tikaré, *Burkina Faso* 113 C4 13 15N 1 43W
Tikchik Lakes, *U.S.A.* 144 G8 60 0N 159 0W
Tikhoretsk, *Russia* .... 61 H5 45 56N 40 5 E
Tikhvin, *Russia* .... 58 C7 59 35N 33 30 E
Tikkadouine, Adrar, *Algeria* ... 111 D5 24 28N 1 30 E
Tiko, *Cameroon* .... 113 E6 4 4N 9 20 E
Tikrīt, *Iraq* .... 101 E10 34 35N 43 37 E
Tiksi, *Russia* .... 67 B13 71 40N 128 45 E
Tilamuta, *Indonesia* .... 82 A2 0 32N 122 23 E
Tilburg, *Neths.* .... 24 C5 51 31N 5 6 E
Tilbury, *Canada* 140 D3 42 17N 82 23W
Tilbury, *U.K.* .... 21 F8 51 27N 0 22 E
Tilcara, *Argentina* .... 174 A2 23 30 S 65 23W
Tilden, *U.S.A.* 154 D6 42 3N 97 50W
Tilemses, *Niger* .... 113 B5 15 37N 4 44 E
Tilemsi, Vallée du, *Mali* ...... 113 B5 17 42N 0 15 E
Tilhar, *India* .... 93 F8 28 0N 79 45 E
Tilia, O. →, *Algeria* .... 111 C5 27 32N 0 55 E
Tilichiki, *Russia* .... 67 C18 60 27N 166 5 E
Tililane, *Algeria* 111 C4 27 49N 0 6W
Tilissos, *Greece* .... 39 E6 35 20N 25 1 E
Till →, *U.K.* 20 B5 55 41N 2 13W
Tillabéri, *Niger* .... 113 C5 14 28N 1 28 E
Tillamook, *U.S.A.* 158 D2 45 27N 123 51W
Tillanchong I., *India* .... 95 K11 8 30N 93 37 E
Tillberga, *Sweden* .... 16 E10 59 46N 16 39 E
Tillia, *Niger* .... 113 B5 16 8N 4 47 E
Tillman, *U.S.A.* 152 C8 32 28N 81 6W

Tillsonburg, Canada	140 D3	42 53N 80 44W
Tillyeria, Cyprus	39 E8	35 6N 32 40 E
Tilogne, Senegal	112 B2	16 0N 13 40W
Tílos, Greece	49 E9	36 27N 27 27 E
Tilpa, Australia	128 A6	30 57 S 144 24 E
Tilrhemt, Algeria	111 B5	33 9N 3 22 E
Tilt →, U.K.	22 E5	56 46N 3 51W
Tilton, U.S.A.	151 C13	43 27N 71 36W
Tiltonsville, U.S.A.	150 F4	40 10N 80 41W
Tim, Denmark	17 H2	56 12N 8 19 E
Timagami, L., Canada	140 C3	47 0N 80 10W
Timanah, Asia	98 C3	19 0N 41 0 E
Timanfaya, Parque Nac. de △,		
Canary Is.	9 e2	29 0N 13 46W
Timanskiy Kryazh, Russia	56 A9	65 58N 50 5 E
Timaru, N.Z.	131 E6	44 23 S 171 14 E
Timashevo, Russia	60 D10	53 22N 51 9 E
Timashevsk, Russia	61 H4	45 35N 39 0 E
Timau, Kenya	118 B4	0 4N 37 15 E
Timbákion, Greece	39 E5	35 4N 24 45 E
Timbaúba, Brazil	170 C4	7 31 S 35 19W
Timbedgha, Mauritania	112 B3	16 17N 8 16W
Timber Creek, Australia	124 C5	15 40 S 130 29 E
Timber Lake, U.S.A.	154 C4	45 26N 101 5W
Timber Mt., U.S.A.	160 H10	37 6N 116 28W
Timbío, Colombia	168 C2	2 20N 76 40W
Timbiqui, Colombia	168 C2	2 46N 77 42W
Timbo, Guinea	112 C2	10 35N 11 50W
Timbo, Liberia	112 D3	5 35N 9 45W
Timboon, Australia	128 E5	38 30 S 142 58 E
Timbuktu = Tombouctou, Mali	112 B4	16 50N 3 0W
Timdjaouine, Algeria	111 D5	21 37N 4 30 E
Timeiaouine, Algeria	111 D5	20 27N 1 50 E
Timellouline, Algeria	111 C6	29 22N 8 55 E
Timétrine, Mts., Mali	113 B4	19 25N 1 0W
Timfi Óros, Greece	48 B2	39 59N 20 45 E
Timfristós, Óros, Greece	48 C3	38 57N 21 50 E
Timhadit, Morocco	110 B3	33 15N 5 4W
Timi, Cyprus	39 E8	34 44N 32 31 E
Timia, Niger	113 B6	18 4N 8 40 E
Timika, Indonesia	83 B5	4 47 S 136 32 E
Timimoun, Algeria	111 C5	29 14N 0 16 E
Timimoun, Sebkha de, Algeria	111 C5	28 50N 0 46 E
Timirist, Râs, Mauritania	112 B1	19 21N 16 30W
Timiş = Tamis →, Serbia, Yug.	52 F5	44 51N 20 39 E
Timiş □, Romania	52 E6	45 40N 21 30 E
Timişoara, Romania	52 E6	45 43N 21 15 E
Timmersdala, Sweden	17 F7	58 32N 13 46 E
Timmins, Canada	140 C3	48 28N 81 25W
Timmonsville, U.S.A.	152 A10	34 8N 79 57W
Timok →, Serbia, Yug.	50 B6	44 10N 22 40 E
Timon, Brazil	170 C3	5 8 S 42 52W
Timor, Indonesia	82 C3	9 0 S 125 0 E
Timor Sea, Ind. Oc.	124 B4	12 0 S 127 0 E
Timor Timur = East Timor ■, Asia	82 C3	8 50 S 126 0 E
Timrå, Sweden	16 B11	62 29N 17 18 E
Timucuan Ecological and Historical		
Preserve △, U.S.A.	152 E8	30 28N 81 27W
Tin, Ra's at, Libya	108 B4	32 37N 23 8 E
Tin Alkoum, Algeria	111 D7	24 42N 10 17 E
Tin Amzi, O. →, Algeria	111 D6	18 20N 4 32 E
Tin Atanai, Algeria	111 D6	18 20N 4 32 E
Tin Can Bay, Australia	127 D5	25 56 S 153 0 E
Tin Ethisane, Mali	113 B4	19 3N 0 52W
Tin Gornai, Mali	113 B4	16 38N 0 38W
Tin Mt., U.S.A.	160 J9	36 50N 117 10W
Tina →, S. Africa	117 E4	31 18 S 29 13 E
Tîna, Khalig el, Egypt	106 A3	31 20N 32 42 E
Tinaca Pt., Phil.	81 J5	5 30N 125 25 E
Tinaco, Venezuela	168 B4	9 42N 68 26W
Tinafak, O. →, Algeria	111 C6	27 10N 7 0 E
Tinajo, Canary Is.	9 e2	29 4N 13 42W
Tinca, Romania	52 D6	46 46N 21 58 E
Tindal, Australia	124 B5	14 31 S 132 22 E
Tindivanam, India	95 H4	12 15N 79 41 E
Tindouf, Algeria	110 C3	27 42N 8 10W
Tinée →, France	29 E11	43 55N 7 11 E
Tineo, Spain	42 B4	43 21N 6 27W
Tinerhir, Morocco	110 B3	31 29N 5 31W
Tinfouchi, Algeria	110 C3	28 52N 5 49W
Ting Jiang →, China	77 E11	24 45N 116 35 E
Tinggi, Pulau, Malaysia	87 L5	2 18N 104 7 E
Tingkawk Sakan, Burma	90 B6	26 4N 96 44 E
Tinglayan, Phil.	80 C3	17 15N 121 9 E
Tinglev, Denmark	17 K3	54 57N 9 13 E
Tingo Maria, Peru	172 B2	9 10 S 75 54W
Tingrela, Ivory C.	112 C3	10 27N 6 25W
Tingsryd, Sweden	17 H9	56 31N 15 0 E
Tingstäde, Sweden	17 G12	57 44N 18 37 E
Tingvoll, Norway	18 B5	62 55N 8 12 E
Tingwon Group, Papua N. G.	132 B5	2 37 S 149 42 E
Tinh Bien, Vietnam	87 G5	10 36N 104 57 E
Tinharé, I. de, Brazil	171 D4	13 30 S 38 58W
Tiniguiban, Phil.	81 F2	11 22N 119 24 E
Tinjar →, Malaysia	85 B4	4 4N 114 18 E
Tinn →, Norway	18 E5	59 59N 8 45 E
Tinnevelly = Tirunelveli, India	95 K3	8 45N 77 45 E
Tinnoset, Norway	18 E6	59 43N 9 2 E
Tinnsjø, Norway	18 E5	59 55N 8 54 E
Tinogasta, Argentina	174 B2	28 5 S 67 32W
Tínos, Greece	49 D7	37 33N 25 8 E
Tiñoso, C., Spain	41 H3	37 32N 1 6W
Tinpahar, India	93 G12	24 59N 87 44 E
Tinputz, Papua N. G.	132 C8	5 33 S 155 0 E
Tinsukia, India	90 B5	27 29N 95 20 E
Tinta, Peru	172 C3	14 3 S 71 20W
Tintina, Argentina	174 B3	27 2 S 62 45W
Tintinara, Australia	128 C4	35 48 S 140 2 E
Tintioulé, Guinea	112 C3	10 13N 9 12W
Tinto →, Spain	43 H4	37 12N 6 55W
Tinui, N.Z.	131 D6	40 52 S 176 5 E
Tinwald, N.Z.	131 D6	43 55 S 171 43 E
Tioga, N. Dak., U.S.A.	154 A3	48 23N 102 56W
Tioga, Pa., U.S.A.	150 E7	41 55N 77 8W
Tioman, Pulau, Malaysia	87 L5	2 50N 104 10 E
Tione di Trento, Italy	44 B7	46 2N 10 43 E
Tionesta, U.S.A.	150 E5	41 30N 79 28W
Tior, Sudan	107 F3	6 26N 31 11 E
Tioulilin, Algeria	111 C4	27 1N 0 2W
Tipp City, U.S.A.	157 L12	39 58N 84 10W
Tippecanoe →, U.S.A.	157 D10	40 30N 86 45W
Tipperary, Ireland	23 D3	52 28N 8 10W
Tipperary □, Ireland	23 D4	52 37N 7 55W
Tipton, Calif., U.S.A.	160 J7	36 4N 119 19W
Tipton, Ind., U.S.A.	157 D10	40 17N 86 2W
Tipton, Iowa, U.S.A.	156 C5	41 46N 91 8W
Tipton, Mo., U.S.A.	156 F4	38 39N 92 47W
Tipton Mt., U.S.A.	161 K12	35 32N 114 12W
Tiptonville, U.S.A.	155 G10	36 23N 89 29W
Tiptur, India	95 H3	13 15N 76 26 E
Tiquié →, Brazil	168 D5	0 5N 68 25W
Tiracambu, Serra do, Brazil	170 B2	3 15 S 46 30W
Tirahart, O. →, Algeria	111 D5	23 45N 3 10 E
Tīrān, Iran	97 C6	32 45N 51 8 E
Tīrān, Si. Arabia	106 B3	27 57N 34 32 E
Tirana ✕ (TIA), Albania	47 A12	41 57N 19 42 E
Tiranë, Albania	50 E3	41 18N 19 49 E
Tirano, Italy	44 B7	46 13N 10 10 E
Tiraspol, Moldova	53 D14	46 55N 29 35 E
Tiratimine, Algeria	111 C5	25 56N 3 37 E
Tirau, N.Z.	130 D4	37 58 S 175 46 E
Tirdout, Mali	113 B4	16 7N 1 5W
Tire, Turkey	49 C9	38 5N 27 45 E
Tirebolu, Turkey	101 B8	40 58N 38 45 E
Tiree, U.K.	22 E2	56 31N 6 55W
Tiree, Passage of, U.K.	22 E2	56 30N 6 30W
Tîrgovişte = Târgovişte, Romania	53 F10	44 55N 25 27 E
Tîrgu-Jiu = Târgu-Jiu, Romania	53 E8	45 5N 23 19 E
Tîrgu Mureş = Târgu Mureş,		
Romania	53 D9	46 31N 24 38 E
Tirich Mir, Pakistan	91 A3	36 15N 71 55 E
Tiriolo, Italy	47 D9	38 57N 16 30 E
Tiririca, Serra da, Brazil	171 E2	17 6 S 47 6W
Tiriro, Guinea	112 C3	10 27N 8 40W
Tiris, W. Sahara	110 D2	23 10N 13 20W
Tirlyanskiy, Russia	64 D7	54 14N 58 35 E
Tîrna →, India	94 E3	18 4N 76 57 E
Tírnavos, Greece	48 B4	39 45N 22 18 E
Tirodi, India	94 D4	21 40N 79 44 E
Tirol □, Austria	34 D3	47 3N 10 43 E
Tiros, Brazil	171 E2	19 0 S 45 58W
Tirrukkovil, Sri Lanka	95 L5	7 8N 81 51 E
Tirschenreuth, Germany	31 F8	49 53N 12 19 E
Tirso →, Italy	46 C1	39 53N 8 32 E
Tirstrup, Denmark	17 H4	56 18N 10 42 E
Tirthahalli, India	95 H2	13 42N 75 14 E
Tirua Pt., N.Z.	130 E3	38 25 S 174 40 E
Tiruchchendur, India	95 K4	8 30N 78 11 E
Tiruchirappalli, India	95 J4	10 45N 78 45 E
Tirukkoyilur, India	95 H4	11 57N 79 12 E
Tirumangalam, India	95 K3	9 49N 77 58 E
Tirumayam, India	95 J4	10 14N 78 45 E
Tirunelveli, India	95 K3	8 45N 77 45 E
Tirupati, India	95 H4	13 39N 79 25 E
Tiruppattur, Tamil Nadu, India	95 J4	10 8N 78 37 E
Tiruppattur, Tamil Nadu, India	95 H4	12 30N 78 30 E
Tiruppur, India	95 J3	11 5N 77 22 E
Tirur, India	95 J2	10 54N 75 55 E
Tiruttani, India	95 H4	13 6N 79 41 E
Tirutturaippundi, India	95 J4	10 32N 79 41 E
Tiruvadaimarudur, India	95 J4	9 23N 76 24 E
Tiruvalla, India	95 K3	9 23N 76 34 E
Tiruvallar, India	95 H4	13 9N 79 57 E
Tiruvannamalai, India	95 H4	12 15N 79 5 E
Tiruvettipuram, India	95 H4	12 39N 79 33 E
Tiruvottiyur, India	95 H5	13 10N 80 22 E
Tisa, India	92 C7	32 50N 76 9 E
Tisa →, Serbia, Yug.	52 E5	45 15N 20 17 E
Tisdale, Canada	143 C8	52 50N 104 0W
Tishomingo, U.S.A.	155 H6	34 14N 96 41W
Tisjön, Sweden	16 D7	60 56N 13 0 E
Tisnaren, Sweden	17 F9	58 58N 15 56 E
Tišnov, Czech Rep.	35 B9	49 21N 16 25 E
Tisovec, Slovak Rep.	35 C12	48 41N 19 56 E
Tissamaharama, Sri Lanka	95 L5	6 17N 81 17 E
Tissemsilt, Algeria	111 A5	35 35N 1 50 E
Tissint, Morocco	110 C3	29 57N 7 16W
Tista →, India	90 C2	25 23N 89 43 E
Tistedal, Norway	18 E8	59 8N 11 27 E
Tisza = Tisa →, Serbia, Yug.	52 E5	45 15N 20 17 E
Tiszaföldvár, Hungary	52 D5	46 58N 20 14 E
Tiszafüred, Hungary	52 C5	47 38N 20 50 E
Tiszalök, Hungary	52 B6	48 1N 21 20 E
Tiszavasvári, Hungary	52 C6	47 58N 21 18 E
Tit, Ahaggar, Algeria	111 D6	23 0N 5 10 E
Tit, Tademait, Algeria	111 C5	27 0N 1 29 E
Tit-Ary, Russia	67 B13	71 55N 127 2 E
Titabar, India	90 B5	26 36N 94 12 E
Titagarra, Spain	40 F3	39 53N 1 6W
Titao, Burkina Faso	113 C4	13 45N 2 5W
Titel, Serbia, Yug.	52 E5	45 10N 20 18 E
Tithwal, Pakistan	93 B5	34 21N 73 50 E
Titicaca, L., S. Amer.	172 D4	15 30 S 69 30W
Titisee, Germany	31 H4	47 54N 8 10 E
Tititira Hd., N.Z.	131 D4	43 36 S 169 25 E
Tititut, Burma	90 F5	18 54N 95 56 E
Titlagarh, India	94 D6	20 15N 83 11 E
Titlis, Switz.	33 C6	46 46N 8 26 E
Tito, Italy	47 B8	40 35N 15 40 E
Titograd = Podgorica,		
Montenegro, Yug.	50 D3	42 30N 19 19 E
Titova Korenica, Croatia	45 D12	44 45N 15 41 E
Titu, Romania	53 F10	44 39N 25 32 E
Titule, Dem. Rep. of the Congo	118 B2	3 15N 25 31 E
Titusville, Fla., U.S.A.	152 G9	28 37N 80 49W
Titusville, Pa., U.S.A.	150 E5	41 38N 79 41W
Tivaouane, Senegal	112 C1	14 56N 16 45W
Tivedens Nationalpark △, Sweden	17 F8	58 45N 14 35 E
Tiverton, U.K.	21 G4	50 54N 3 29W
Tívoli, Italy	45 G9	41 58N 12 45 E
Tiwī, Oman	99 B7	22 45N 59 12 E
Tiyo, Eritrea	107 E5	14 41N 40 57 E
Tizga, Morocco	110 B3	32 1N 5 9W
Ti'zi N'Isli, Morocco	110 B3	32 28N 5 47W
Tizimín, Mexico	163 C7	21 0N 88 1W
Tiznados →, Venezuela	168 B4	8 16N 67 47W
Tiznap He →, China	65 D8	37 58N 77 24 E
Tiznit, Morocco	110 C3	29 48N 9 45W
Tjæreborg, Denmark	17 J2	55 28N 8 36 E
Tjällmo, Sweden	17 F9	58 43N 15 21 E
Tjeggelvas, Sweden	14 C17	66 37N 17 45 E
Tjirebon = Cirebon, Indonesia	85 D3	6 45 S 108 32 E
Tjluring, Indonesia	79 J17	8 25 S 114 13 E
Tjøme, Norway	18 E7	59 8N 10 26 E
Tjörn, Sweden	17 F5	58 0N 11 35 E
Tkibuli = Tqibuli, Georgia	61 J6	42 36N 43 0 E
Tkvarcheli = Tqvarcheli, Georgia	61 J5	42 47N 41 42 E
Tlacotalpan, Mexico	163 D5	18 37N 95 40W
Tlahualilo, Mexico	162 B4	26 20N 103 30W
Tlaquepaque, Mexico	162 C4	20 39N 103 19W
Tlaxcala, Mexico	163 D5	19 20N 98 14W
Tlaxcala □, Mexico	163 D5	19 30N 98 20W
Tlaxiaco, Mexico	163 D5	17 18N 97 40W
Tlemcen, Algeria	110 B4	34 52N 1 21W
Tleta Sidi Bouguedra, Morocco	110 B3	32 16N 9 59W
Tłuszcz, Poland	55 F8	52 25N 21 25 E
Tlyarata, Russia	61 J8	42 9N 46 26 E
Tmassah, Libya	108 C3	26 19N 15 51 E
Tnine d'Anglou, Morocco	110 C3	29 50N 9 50W
To Bong, Vietnam	86 F7	12 45N 109 16 E
To-Shima, Japan	73 C11	34 31N 139 17 E
Toa Payoh, Singapore	87 d	1 20N 103 51 E
Toad →, Canada	142 B4	59 25N 124 57W
Toad River, Canada	142 B3	58 51N 125 14W
Toamasina, Madag.	117 B8	18 10 S 49 25 E
Toamasina □, Madag.	117 B8	18 0 S 49 0 E
Toay, Argentina	174 D3	36 43 S 64 38W
Toba, China	76 B1	31 19N 97 42 E
Toba, Japan	73 C8	34 30N 136 51 E
Toba, Danau, Indonesia	84 B1	2 30N 97 30 E
Toba Kakar, Pakistan	91 C3	31 30N 69 0 E
Toba Tek Singh, Pakistan	92 D5	30 55N 72 25 E
Tobago, Trin. & Tob.	169 E10	11 10N 60 30W
Tobarra, Spain	41 G3	38 37N 1 44W
Tobelo, Indonesia	83 A3	1 45N 127 56 E
Tobermory, Canada	140 C3	45 12N 81 40W
Tobermory, U.K.	22 E2	56 38N 6 5W
Tobi, Pac. Oc.	83 A4	3 0N 131 10 E
Tobias Fornier, Phil.	81 F5	10 30N 121 57 E
Tobin, U.S.A.	160 F5	39 55N 121 19W
Tobin, L., Australia	124 D4	21 45 S 125 49 E
Tobin L., Canada	143 C8	53 35N 103 30W
Toblach = Dobbiaco, Italy	45 B9	46 44N 12 14 E
Toboali, Indonesia	84 C3	3 0 S 106 25 E
Tobol, Kazakhstan	64 E9	52 40N 62 39 E
Tobol →, Russia	66 D7	58 10N 68 12 E
Toboli, Indonesia	82 B2	0 38 S 120 5 E
Tobolsk, Russia	66 D7	58 15N 68 10 E
Tobor, Senegal	112 C1	12 40N 16 15W
Toboso, Phil.	81 F4	10 43N 123 31 E
Tobruk = Tubruq, Libya	108 B4	32 7N 23 55 E
Tobyhanna, U.S.A.	151 E9	41 11N 75 25W
Tobyl = Tobol →, Russia	66 D7	58 10N 68 12 E
Tocache Nuevo, Peru	172 B2	8 9 S 76 26W
Tocantínia, Brazil	170 C2	9 33 S 48 22W
Tocantinópolis, Brazil	170 C2	6 20 S 47 25W
Tocantins □, Brazil	170 D2	10 0 S 48 0W
Tocantins →, Brazil	170 B2	1 45 S 49 10W
Toccoa, U.S.A.	149 H4	34 35N 83 19W
Toce →, Italy	44 C5	45 56N 8 29 E
Tochi →, Pakistan	92 C4	32 49N 70 41 E
Tochigi, Japan	73 A11	36 25N 139 45 E
Tochigi □, Japan	73 A11	36 45N 139 45 E
Tocina, Spain	43 H5	37 37N 5 44W
Toco, Chile	172 E4	22 5 S 69 35W
Toco, Trin. & Tob.	169 F10	10 50N 60 4W
Toconao, Chile	174 A2	22 1 S 69 1W
Tocopilla, Chile	174 A1	22 5 S 70 10W
Tocqueville = Rass el Oued, Algeria	111 A6	35 57N 5 2 E
Tocumwal, Australia	129 C6	35 51 S 145 31 E
Tocuyo →, Venezuela	168 A4	11 3N 68 23W
Tocuyo de la Costa, Venezuela	168 A4	11 2N 68 24W
Todal, Norway	18 B5	62 49N 8 44 E
Todd →, Australia	126 C2	24 52 S 135 48 E
Todeli, Indonesia	82 B2	1 40 S 124 29 E
Todenyang, Kenya	118 B4	4 35N 35 56 E
Todgarh, India	92 G5	25 42N 73 58 E
Todi, Italy	45 F9	42 47N 12 24 E
Tödi, Switz.	33 C7	46 48N 8 55 E
Todos os Santos, B. de, Brazil	171 D4	12 48 S 38 38W
Todos Santos, Mexico	162 C2	23 27N 110 13W
Todtnau, Germany	31 H3	47 49N 7 56 E
Toe Hd., U.K.	22 D1	57 50N 7 8W
Toecé, Burkina Faso	113 C4	11 50N 1 16W
Toetoes B., N.Z.	131 G3	46 42 S 168 41 E
Tofield, Canada	142 C6	53 25N 112 40W
Tofino, Canada	142 D3	49 11N 125 55W
Tofte, Norway	18 E7	59 33N 10 34 E
Toftlund, Denmark	17 J3	55 11N 9 2 E
Tofua, Tonga	133 D11	19 45 S 175 5W
Toga, Vanuatu	133 C4	13 26 S 166 42 E
Tōgane, Japan	73 B12	35 33N 140 22 E
Togba, Mauritania	112 B2	17 26N 10 12W
Togbo, C.A.R.	114 A3	6 0N 17 27 E
Toggenburg, Switz.	33 B8	47 16N 9 9 E
Togiak, U.S.A.	144 G7	59 4N 160 24W
Togian, Kepulauan, Indonesia	82 B2	0 20 S 121 50 E
Togliatti, Russia	60 D9	53 32N 49 24 E
Togo ■, W. Afr.	113 D5	8 30N 1 35 E
Togtoh, China	74 D6	40 15N 111 10 E
Toguzak →, Kazakhstan	64 D7	54 3N 62 44 E
Tohma →, Turkey	100 C7	38 29N 38 5 E
Tōhoku □, Japan	70 E10	39 50N 141 45 E
Tōhōm, Mongolia	74 B5	44 27N 108 2 E
Tohopekaliga, L., U.S.A.	153 G8	28 12N 81 24W
Toi, Japan	73 C10	34 54N 138 47 E
Toinbalewe, India	95 H11	10 30N 92 30 E
Toili, Indonesia	82 B2	1 24 S 122 26 E
Toinya, Sudan	107 F2	6 17N 29 46 E
Toiyabe Range, U.S.A.	158 G5	39 30N 117 0W
Tojikiston = Tajikistan ■, Asia	65 D4	38 30N 70 0 E
Tojo, Indonesia	82 B2	1 20 S 121 15 E
Tōjō, Japan	72 C5	34 53N 133 16 E
Tok, U.S.A.	144 E12	63 20N 142 59W
Tok →, Russia	64 E4	52 46N 52 22 E
Tok-do, Japan	71 F5	37 15N 131 52 E
Toka, Guyana	169 C6	3 58N 59 17W
Tokaanu, N.Z.	130 E4	38 58 S 175 46 E
Tokachi-Dake, Japan	70 C11	43 17N 142 5 E
Tokachi-Gawa →, Japan	70 C11	42 44N 143 42 E
Tokai, Japan	73 B8	35 2N 136 55 E
Tokaj, Hungary	52 B6	48 8N 21 27 E
Tokala, Gunung, Indonesia	82 B2	1 30 S 121 40 E
Tokamachi, Japan	71 F9	37 8N 138 43 E
Tokanui, N.Z.	131 G3	46 34 S 168 56 E
Tokar, Sudan	106 D4	18 27N 37 56 E
Tokara-Rettō, Japan	71 K4	29 37N 129 43 E
Tokarahi, N.Z.	131 E5	44 56 S 170 39 E
Tokashiki-Shima, Japan	71 L3	26 11N 127 21 E
Tokat, Turkey	100 B7	40 22N 36 35 E
Tokat □, Turkey	57 F6	40 15N 36 30 E
Tŏkch'ŏn, N. Korea	75 E14	39 45N 126 18 E
Tokeland, U.S.A.	160 D3	46 42N 123 59W
Tokelau Is., Pac. Oc.	134 H10	9 0 S 171 45W
Toki, Japan	73 B9	35 18N 137 8 E
Tokmak, Kyrgyzstan	65 B7	42 49N 75 15 E
Tokmak, Ukraine	59 J8	47 16N 35 42 E
Toko Ra., Australia	126 C2	23 5 S 138 20 E
Tokomaru Bay, N.Z.	130 E7	38 8 S 178 22 E
Tokoname, Japan	73 C8	34 53N 136 51 E
Tokoro-Gawa →, Japan	70 B12	44 7N 144 5 E
Tokoroa, N.Z.	130 E4	38 13 S 175 50 E
Tokorozawa, Japan	73 B11	35 47N 139 28 E
Toksook Bay, U.S.A.	144 F6	60 32N 165 0W
Toktogul, Kyrgyzstan	65 C6	41 48N 72 51 E
Toktogul Suu Saktagychy,		
Kyrgyzstan	65 C6	41 48N 72 51 E
Toku, Tonga	133 P13	18 10 S 174 11W
Tokuji, Japan	72 C3	34 11N 131 42 E
Tokuno-Shima, Japan	71 L4	27 56N 128 55 E
Tokushima, Japan	72 C6	34 4N 134 34 E
Tokushima □, Japan	72 D6	33 55N 134 0 E
Tokuyama, Japan	72 C3	34 3N 131 50 E
Tōkyō, Japan	73 B11	35 45N 139 45 E
Tōkyō □, Japan	73 B11	35 40N 139 30 E
Tokyo Haneda ✕ (HND), Japan	73 B11	35 33N 139 46 E
Tokyo Narita ✕ (NRT), Japan	73 B12	35 45N 140 25 E
Tōkyō-Wan, Japan	73 B11	35 25N 139 47 E
Tokzār, Afghan.	91 B2	35 52N 66 26 E
Tolaga Bay, N.Z.	130 E7	38 21 S 178 20 E
Tolageak, U.S.A.	144 A7	70 3N 162 27W
Tolbukhin = Dobrich, Bulgaria	51 C11	43 37N 27 49 E
Tolé, C.A.R.	114 A3	6 34N 16 1 E
Töle Bī, Kazakhstan	65 B6	43 42N 73 64 E
Toledo, Brazil	175 A5	24 44 S 53 45W
Toledo, Phil.	81 F4	10 23N 123 38 E
Toledo, Spain	42 F6	39 50N 4 2W
Toledo, Ill., U.S.A.	157 E8	39 16N 88 15W
Toledo, Iowa, U.S.A.	156 C4	41 59N 92 35W
Toledo, Ohio, U.S.A.	157 C13	41 39N 83 33W
Toledo, Oreg., U.S.A.	158 D2	44 37N 123 56W
Toledo, Wash., U.S.A.	160 D3	46 26N 122 51W
Toledo, Montes de, Spain	43 F6	39 33N 4 20W
Toledo Bend Reservoir, U.S.A.	155 K8	31 11N 93 34W
Tolentino, Italy	45 E10	43 12N 13 17 E
Tolfa, Italy	45 F8	42 9N 11 56 E
Tolga, Algeria	111 B6	34 40N 5 22 E
Tolga, Australia	126 B4	17 15 S 145 29 E
Tolga, Norway	18 B8	62 26N 11 1 E
Toliara, Madag.	117 C7	23 21 S 43 40 E
Toliara □, Madag.	117 C8	21 0 S 45 0 E
Tolima, Colombia	168 C2	4 40N 75 19W
Tolima □, Colombia	168 C2	3 45N 75 15W
Tolitoli, Indonesia	82 A2	1 5N 120 50 E
Tolkmicko, Poland	54 D6	54 19N 19 31 E
Tollarp, Sweden	17 J7	55 55N 13 58 E
Tollensee, Germany	30 B9	53 30N 13 13 E
Tollhouse, U.S.A.	160 H7	37 1N 119 24W
Tolmachevo, Russia	58 C5	58 56N 29 51 E
Tolmezzo, Italy	45 B10	46 24N 13 1 E
Tolmin, Slovenia	45 B10	46 11N 13 45 E
Tolna, Hungary	52 D3	46 25N 18 48 E
Tolna □, Hungary	52 D3	46 30N 18 30 E
Tolo, Dem. Rep. of the Congo	114 C3	2 55 S 18 34 E
Tolo, Teluk, Indonesia	82 B2	2 20 S 122 10 E
Tolo Harbour, China	69 G11	22 27N 114 12 E
Tolochin = Talachyn, Belarus	58 E5	54 25N 29 42 E
Tolokiwa I., Papua N. G.	132 C4	5 19 S 147 37 E
Tolong Bay, Phil.	81 G4	9 20N 122 49 E
Tolono, U.S.A.	40 B2	43 8 E
Tolosa, Spain	43 J6	36 41 E
Toltén, Chile	176 A2	39 13 S 74 14W
Toluca, Mexico	163 D5	19 20N 99 40W
Toluca, U.S.A.	156 C7	41 0N 89 9W
Tolybay, Kazakhstan	64 F9	50 31N 62 19 E
Tom Burke, S. Africa	117 C4	23 5 S 28 0 E
Tom Price, Australia	124 D2	22 40 S 117 48 E
Toma, Burkina Faso	112 C4	12 45N 2 53W
Tomah, U.S.A.	154 D9	43 59N 90 30W
Tomahawk, U.S.A.	154 C10	45 28N 89 44W
Tomai, Moldova	53 D13	46 34N 28 50 E
Tomakomai, Japan	70 C10	42 38N 141 36 E
Tomales, U.S.A.	160 G4	38 15N 122 53W
Tomales B., U.S.A.	160 G3	38 15N 123 58W
Tomanlivi, Fiji	133 A2	17 37 S 178 1 E
Tomar, Portugal	43 F2	39 36N 8 25W
Tómaros, Óros, Greece	48 B2	39 29N 20 48 E
Tomarza, Turkey	100 C6	38 27N 35 48 E
Tomás Barrón, Bolivia	172 D4	17 35 S 67 31W
Tomaszów Lubelski, Poland	55 H10	50 28N 23 37 E
Tomaszów Mazowiecki, Poland	55 G7	51 30N 20 2 E
Tomatlán, Mexico	162 D3	19 56N 105 15W
Tombador, Serra do, Brazil	173 C6	12 0 S 58 0W
Tombe, Sudan	107 F3	5 53N 31 40 E
Tombel, Cameroon	114 B1	4 55N 9 40 E
Tombigbee →, U.S.A.	149 K2	31 8N 87 57W
Tombôco, Angola	115 D2	6 48 S 13 18 E
Tombouctou, Mali	112 B4	16 50N 3 0W
Tombstone, U.S.A.	159 L8	31 43N 110 4W
Tombua, Angola	116 B1	15 55 S 11 55 E
Tome, Chile	174 D1	36 36 S 72 57W
Tomé-Açu, Brazil	170 B2	2 25 S 48 9W
Tomelilla, Sweden	17 J7	55 33N 13 58 E
Tomelloso, Spain	43 F7	39 10N 3 2W
Tömenaryk, Kazakhstan	65 A3	44 2N 67 1 E
Tomingley, Australia	129 B8	32 26 S 148 16 E
Tomini, Indonesia	82 A2	0 30N 120 30 E
Tomini, Teluk, Indonesia	82 B2	0 10 S 121 0 E
Tominian, Mali	112 C4	13 17N 4 35W
Tomiño, Spain	42 D2	41 59N 8 46W
Tomintoul, U.K.	22 D5	57 15N 3 23W
Tomioka, Japan	73 A10	36 15N 138 54 E
Tomislavgrad, Bos.-H.	52 G2	43 42N 17 13 E
Tomkinson Ranges, Australia	125 E4	26 11 S 129 5 E
Tommot, Russia	67 D13	59 4N 126 20 E
Tomnop Ta Suos, Cambodia	87 G5	11 20N 104 15 E
Tomo, Colombia	168 C4	2 38N 67 32W
Tomo →, Colombia	168 B4	5 20N 67 48W
Tomochic, Mexico	162 B3	28 20N 107 50W
Tomohon, Indonesia	83 A3	1 35N 124 54 E
Tomra, Norway	18 B3	62 34N 6 56 E
Toms Place, U.S.A.	160 H8	37 34N 118 41W
Toms River, U.S.A.	151 G10	39 58N 74 12W
Tomsk, Russia	66 D9	56 30N 85 5 E
Tomtabacken, Sweden	17 G8	57 30N 14 30 E
Tona, Spain	40 D7	41 51N 2 14 E
Tonalá, Mexico	163 D6	16 8N 93 41W
Tonale, Passo del, Italy	44 B7	46 16N 10 35 E
Tonami, Japan	73 A8	36 40N 136 58 E
Tonantins, Brazil	168 D4	2 45 S 67 45W
Tonate, Fr. Guiana	169 C7	5 0N 52 28W
Tonawanda, U.S.A.	150 D6	43 1N 78 53W
Tonbo, Burma	90 F5	18 31N 95 18 E
Tonbridge, U.K.	21 F8	51 11N 0 17 E
Tondano, Papua N. G.	132 E1	8 55 S 141 34 E
Tondabayashi, Japan	73 C7	34 30N 135 36 E
Tondano, Indonesia	82 A2	1 35N 124 54 E
Tondela, Portugal	42 E2	40 31N 8 5W
Tønder, Denmark	17 K2	54 58N 8 50 E
Tondi, India	95 K4	9 45N 79 4 E
Tondi Kiwindi, Niger	113 C5	14 28N 2 2 E
Tondibi, Mali	113 B4	16 39N 0 14W
Tondoro, Namibia	116 B2	17 45 S 18 50 E
Tone →, Australia	125 F2	34 25 S 116 25 E
Tone-Gawa →, Japan	73 B12	35 44N 140 51 E
Tonekābon, Iran	97 B6	36 45N 51 12 E
Tong I., Papua N. G.	132 B4	2 3 S 147 47 E
Tong Xian, China	74 E9	39 55N 116 35 E
Tonga ■, Pac. Oc.	133 D11	19 50 S 174 30W
Tonga Trench, Pac. Oc.	134 J10	18 0 S 173 0W
Tongaat, S. Africa	117 D5	29 33 S 31 9 E
Tongala, Australia	129 D6	36 14 S 144 56 E
Tong'an, China	77 E12	24 37N 118 8 E
Tongareva, Cook Is.	135 H12	9 0 S 158 0W
Tongariro Nat. Park △, N.Z.	130 F4	39 8 S 175 33 E
Tongatapu, Tonga	133 D11	21 10 S 175 10W
Tongatapu Group, Tonga	133 Q13	21 0 S 175 0W
Tongbai, China	77 A9	32 20N 113 23 E
Tongcheng, Anhui, China	77 B11	31 4N 116 56 E
Tongcheng, Hubei, China	77 C9	29 15N 113 50 E
Tongchŏn-ni, N. Korea	75 E14	39 50N 127 25 E
Tongchuan, China	74 G5	35 6N 109 3 E
Tongeren, Belgium	25 D7	50 47N 5 28 E
Tonggu, China	77 C10	28 31N 114 20 E
Tongguan Jiao, China	69 G10	22 21N 113 37 E
Tongguan, China	74 G6	34 40N 110 25 E
Tonghae, S. Korea	75 F15	37 29N 129 7 E
Tonghai, China	76 E4	24 10N 102 53 E
Tonghua, China	75 D13	41 42N 125 58 E
Tongjiang, China	76 B6	31 58N 107 11 E
Tongjosŏn Man, N. Korea	75 E15	39 30N 128 0 E
Tongkil, Phil.	81 J4	6 21N 121 48 E
Tongking, G. of = Tonkin, G. of,		
Asia	68 E5	20 0N 108 0 E
Tongliang, China	76 C6	29 50N 106 3 E
Tongliao, China	75 C12	43 38N 122 18 E
Tongling, China	77 B11	30 55N 117 48 E
Tonglu, China	77 C12	29 45N 119 37 E
Tongnae, S. Korea	75 G15	35 12N 129 5 E
Tongnan = Anyue, China	76 B5	30 5N 105 50 E
Tongobory, Madag.	117 C7	23 32 S 44 20 E
Tongoa, Vanuatu	133 C4	16 54 S 168 34 E
Tongoy, Chile	174 C1	30 16 S 71 31W
Tongres = Tongeren, Belgium	24 C5	50 47N 5 28 E
Tongsa Dzong, Bhutan	90 B3	27 31N 90 31 E
Tongue, U.K.	22 C4	58 29N 4 25W
Tongue →, U.S.A.	154 B2	46 25N 105 52W
Tongwei, China	74 G3	35 0N 105 5 E
Tongxiang, China	77 B13	30 39N 120 38 E
Tongxin, China	74 F3	36 59N 105 58 E
Tongyu, China	75 B12	44 45N 123 4 E
Tongzi, China	76 C6	28 9N 106 49 E
Tonica, U.S.A.	156 C7	41 13N 89 4W
Tonj, Sudan	107 F2	7 20N 28 44 E

Tonj →, Sudan 107 F2 7 31N 28 55 E
Tonk, India 92 F6 26 6N 75 54 E
Tonkawa, U.S.A. 155 G6 36 41N 97 18W
Tonkin = Bac Phan, Vietnam 86 B5 22 0N 105 0 E
Tonkin, G. of, Asia 68 E5 20 0N 108 0 E
Tonle Sap, Cambodia 86 F4 13 0N 104 0 E
Tonnay-Charente, France 28 C3 45 56N 0 55W
Tonneins, France 28 D4 44 23N 0 19 E
Tonnerre, France 27 E10 47 51N 3 59 E
Tönning, Germany 30 A4 54 19N 8 56 E
Tono, Japan 70 E10 39 19N 141 32 E
Tonopah, U.S.A. 159 G5 38 4N 117 14W
Tonoshō, Japan 72 C6 34 29N 134 11 E
Tonosí, Panama 164 E3 7 20N 80 20W
Tons →, Haryana, India 92 D7 30 30N 77 39 E
Tons →, Ut. P., India 93 F10 26 1N 83 33 E
Tønsberg, Norway 18 E7 59 19N 10 25 E
Tonsina, U.S.A. 144 F11 61 39N 145 11W
Tonstad, Norway 18 F3 58 40N 6 45 E
Tonto Nat. Monument ⌂, U.S.A. 159 K8 33 39N 111 7W
Tonumea, Tonga 133 Q13 20 30 S 174 30W
Tonya, Turkey 101 B8 40 53N 39 16 E
Tonzang, Burma 90 D4 23 36N 93 42 E
Tonzi, Burma 90 C5 24 39N 94 57 E
Toobanna, Australia 126 B4 18 42 S 146 9 E
Toodyay, Australia 125 F2 31 34 S 116 28 E
Tooele, U.S.A. 158 F7 40 32N 112 18W
Toompine, Australia 127 D3 27 15 S 144 19 E
Toomsboro, U.S.A. 152 C6 32 50N 83 5W
Toora, Australia 129 E7 38 39 S 146 23 E
Toora-Khem, Russia 67 D10 52 28N 96 17 E
Toowoomba, Australia 127 D5 27 32 S 151 56 E
Top-ozero, Russia 56 A5 65 35N 32 0 E
Top Springs, Australia 124 C5 16 37 S 131 51 E
Topalu, Romania 53 F13 44 31N 28 3 E
Topaz, U.S.A. 160 G7 38 41N 119 30W
Topeka, U.S.A. 154 F7 39 3N 95 40W
Topl'a →, Slovak Rep. 35 C14 48 45N 21 45 E
Topley, Canada 142 C3 54 49N 126 18W
Toplica →, Serbia, Yug. 50 C5 43 15N 21 49 E
Toplița, Romania 53 D10 46 55N 25 20 E
Topo, Azores 9 d1 38 33N 27 45W
Topo, Pta. do, Azores 9 d1 38 33N 27 46W
Topocalma, Pta., Chile 174 C1 34 10 S 72 2W
Topock, U.S.A. 161 L12 34 46N 114 29W
Topola, Serbia, Yug. 50 B4 44 17N 20 41 E
Topolčani, Macedonia 50 E5 41 14N 21 25 E
Topol'čany, Slovak Rep. 35 C11 48 35N 18 12 E
Topolnitsa →, Bulgaria 51 D8 42 11N 24 18 E
Topolobampo, Mexico 162 B3 25 40N 109 4W
Topoloveni, Romania 53 F10 44 49N 25 5 E
Topolovgrad, Bulgaria 51 D10 42 5N 26 20 E
Topolvățu Mare, Romania 52 E6 45 46N 21 41 E
Toppenish, U.S.A. 158 C3 46 23N 120 19W
Topraisar, Romania 53 F13 44 1N 28 27 E
Topusko, Croatia 45 C12 45 18N 15 59 E
Toquepala, Peru 172 D3 17 24 S 70 25W
Torà, Spain 40 D6 41 49N 1 25 E
Tora Kit, Sudan 107 E3 11 2N 32 36 E
Toraka Vestale, Madag. 117 B7 16 20 S 43 58 E
Torata, Peru 172 D3 17 23 S 70 1W
Torbali, Turkey 49 C9 38 10N 27 21 E
Torbat-e Heydārīyeh, Iran 97 C8 35 15N 59 12 E
Torbat-e Jām, Iran 97 C9 35 16N 60 35 E
Torbay, Canada 141 C9 47 40N 52 42W
Torbay □, U.K. 21 G4 50 26N 3 31W
Tørberget, Norway 18 C9 61 8N 12 7 E
Torbjörntorp, Sweden 17 F7 58 12N 13 36 E
Tordesillas, Spain 42 D6 41 30N 5 0W
Töreboda, Sweden 17 F8 58 41N 14 7 E
Torekov, Sweden 17 H6 56 26N 12 37 E
Torellò, Spain 40 C7 42 3N 2 16 E
Toreno, Spain 42 C4 42 42N 6 30W
Torfaen □, U.K. 21 F4 51 43N 3 3W
Torfajökull, Iceland 11 D7 63 54N 19 0W
Torgau, Germany 30 D8 51 34N 13 0 E
Torgelow, Germany 30 B10 53 37N 14 1 E
Torhamn, Sweden 17 H9 56 6N 15 50 E
Torhout, Belgium 24 C3 51 5N 3 7 E
Tori, Ethiopia 107 F3 7 53N 33 35 E
Tori-Shima, Japan 71 J10 30 29N 140 19 E
Torigni-sur-Vire, France 26 C6 49 3N 0 58W
Torija, Spain 40 E1 40 44N 3 2W
Torin, Mexico 162 B2 27 33N 110 15W
Torino, Italy 44 C4 45 3N 7 40 E
Torit, Sudan 107 G3 4 27N 32 31 E
Torkamān, Iran 101 D12 37 35N 47 23 E
Torkovichi, Russia 58 C6 58 51N 30 21 E
Tormac, Romania 52 E6 45 30N 21 30 E
Tormes →, Spain 42 D4 41 18N 6 29W
Tornado Mt., Canada 142 D6 49 55N 114 40W
Tornal'a, Slovak Rep. 35 C13 48 25N 20 20 E
Torne älv →, Sweden 14 D21 65 50N 24 12 E
Torneå = Tornio, Finland 14 D21 65 50N 24 12 E
Torneträsk, Sweden 14 B18 68 24N 19 15 E
Tornio, Finland 14 D21 65 50N 24 12 E
Tornionjoki →, Finland 14 D21 65 50N 24 12 E
Tornquist, Argentina 174 D3 38 8 S 62 15W
Toro, Baleares, Spain 38 B5 39 59N 4 8 E
Toro, Zamora, Spain 42 D5 41 35N 5 24W
Torö, Sweden 17 F11 58 48N 17 50 E
Toro, Cerro del, Chile 174 B2 29 10 S 69 50W
Toro Game Reserve ⌂, Uganda 118 C3 0 5 S 30 22 E
Toro Pk., U.S.A. 161 M10 33 34N 116 24W
Torokina, Papua N. G. 132 D8 6 14 S 155 3 E
Törökszentmiklós, Hungary 52 C5 47 11N 20 27 E
Toroníos Kólpos, Greece 50 F7 40 5N 23 30 E
Toronto, Australia 129 B9 33 0 S 151 30 E
Toronto, Canada 150 C5 43 39N 79 20W
Toronto, U.S.A. 150 F4 40 28N 80 36W
Toronto Lester B. Pearson International ✕ (YYZ), Canada 150 C5 43 40N 79 34W
Toropets, Russia 58 D6 56 30N 31 40 E
Tororo, Uganda 118 B3 0 45N 34 12 E
Toros Dağları, Turkey 100 D5 37 0N 32 30 E
Torotoro, Bolivia 173 D4 18 7 S 65 46W
Torpa, India 93 H11 22 57N 85 6 E
Torpo, Norway 18 D5 60 40N 8 43 E
Torquay, Australia 128 E6 38 20 S 144 19 E
Torquay, U.K. 21 G4 50 27N 3 32W
Torquemada, Spain 42 C6 42 2N 4 19W
Torrais, Pta., Azores 9 d2 39 43N 31 7W
Torrance, U.S.A. 161 M8 33 50N 118 19W
Torrão, Portugal 43 G2 38 16N 8 11W
Torre Annunziata, Italy 47 B7 40 45N 14 27 E
Torre de Moncorvo, Portugal 42 D3 41 12N 7 8W
Torre del Campo, Spain 43 H7 37 46N 3 53W
Torre del Greco, Italy 47 B7 40 47N 14 22 E
Torre del Mar, Spain 43 J6 36 44N 4 6W
Torre-Pacheco, Spain 41 H4 37 44N 0 57W
Torre Péllice, Italy 44 D4 44 49N 7 13 E
Torreblanca, Spain 40 E5 40 14N 0 12 E
Torrecampo, Spain 43 G6 38 29N 4 41W
Torrecilla en Cameros, Spain 40 C2 42 15N 2 38W
Torredembarra, Spain 40 D6 41 9N 1 24 E
Torredonjimeno, Spain 43 H7 37 46N 3 57W
Torrejón de Ardoz, Spain 42 E7 40 27N 3 29W
Torrejoncillo, Spain 42 F4 39 54N 6 28W
Torrelaguna, Spain 42 E7 40 50N 3 38W
Torrelavega, Spain 42 B6 43 20N 4 5W
Torremaggiore, Italy 45 G12 41 41N 15 17 E
Torremolinos, Spain 43 J6 36 38N 4 30W
Torrens, L., Australia 128 A2 31 0 S 137 50 E
Torrens Cr. →, Australia 126 C4 22 23 S 145 9 E
Torrens Creek, Australia 126 C4 20 48 S 145 3 E
Torrent, Spain 41 F4 39 27N 0 28W
Torrenueva, Spain 43 G7 38 38N 3 22W
Torreón, Mexico 162 B4 25 33N 103 26W
Torreperogil, Spain 43 G7 38 2N 3 17W
Torres, Brazil 175 B5 29 21 S 49 44W
Torres, Mexico 162 B2 28 46N 110 47W
Torres, Is., Vanuatu 133 C4 13 15 S 166 37 E
Torres Novas, Portugal 43 F2 39 27N 8 33W
Torres Strait, Australia 132 E2 9 50 S 142 20 E
Torres Vedras, Portugal 43 F1 39 5N 9 15W
Torrevieja, Spain 41 H4 37 59N 0 42W
Torrey, U.S.A. 159 G8 38 18N 111 25W
Torricelli Mts., Papua N. G. 132 B2 3 23 S 142 15 E
Torridge →, U.K. 21 G3 51 0N 4 13W
Torridon, L., U.K. 22 D3 57 35N 5 50W
Torrijos, Phil. 80 E4 13 19N 122 5 E
Torrijos, Spain 42 F6 39 59N 4 18W
Tørring, Denmark 17 J3 55 52N 9 29 E
Torrington, Conn., U.S.A. 151 E11 41 48N 73 7W
Torrington, Wyo., U.S.A. 154 D2 42 4N 104 11W
Torroella de Montgrí, Spain 40 C8 42 2N 3 8 E
Torrox, Spain 43 J7 36 46N 3 57W
Torsås, Sweden 17 H9 56 24N 16 0 E
Torsby, Sweden 16 D6 60 7N 13 0 E
Torshälla, Sweden 16 E10 59 25N 16 28 E
Tórshavn, Færoe Is. 14 E9 62 5N 6 56W
Torslanda, Sweden 17 G5 57 44N 11 45 E
Torsö, Sweden 17 F7 58 48N 13 45 E
Törtköl, Kazakhstan 65 B4 42 55N 68 57 E
Tortola, Br. Virgin Is. 165 e 18 19N 64 45W
Tórtoles de Esgueva, Spain 42 D6 41 49N 4 2W
Tortolì, Italy 46 C2 39 55N 9 39 E
Tortona, Italy 44 D5 44 54N 8 52 E
Tortorici, Italy 47 D7 38 2N 14 49 E
Tortosa, Spain 40 E5 40 49N 0 31 E
Tortosa, C., Spain 40 E5 40 41N 0 52 E
Tortosendo, Portugal 42 E3 40 15N 7 31W
Tortue, I. de la, Haiti 165 B5 20 5N 72 57W
Tortuguero, Parque Nac. △, Costa Rica 164 D3 10 31N 83 29W
Tortum, Turkey 101 B9 40 19N 41 35 E
Toru-Aygyr, Kyrgyzstan 65 B8 42 30N 76 26 E
Ţorūd, Iran 97 C7 35 25N 55 5 E
Torul, Turkey 101 B8 40 34N 39 18 E
Toruń, Poland 55 E5 53 2N 18 39 E
Tory I., Ireland 23 A3 55 16N 8 14W
Torysa →, Slovak Rep. 35 C14 48 39N 21 21 E
Torzhok, Russia 58 D8 57 5N 34 55 E
Torzym, Poland 55 F2 52 19N 15 5 E
Tosa, Japan 72 D5 33 24N 133 23 E
Tosa-Shimizu, Japan 72 E4 32 52N 132 58 E
Tosa-Wan, Japan 72 D5 33 15N 133 30 E
Tosa-Yamada, Japan 72 D5 33 36N 133 38 E
Toscana □, Italy 44 E8 43 25N 11 0 E
Toscano, Arcipelago, Italy 44 F7 42 30N 10 30 E
Toshkent, Uzbekistan 65 C4 41 20N 69 10 E
Tosno, Russia 58 C6 59 38N 30 46 E
Tossa de Mar, Spain 40 D7 41 43N 2 56 E
Tösse, Sweden 17 F6 58 58N 12 39 E
Tostado, Argentina 174 B3 29 15 S 61 50W
Tostedt, Germany 30 B5 53 17N 9 42 E
Tostón, Pta. de, Canary Is. 9 e2 28 42N 14 2W
Tosu, Japan 72 D2 33 22N 130 31 E
Tosya, Turkey 100 B6 41 1N 34 2 E
Toszek, Poland 55 H5 50 27N 18 32 E
Totak, Norway 18 E5 59 40N 8 0 E
Totana, Spain 41 H3 37 45N 1 30W
Totebo, Sweden 17 G10 57 38N 16 12 E
Toteng, Botswana 116 C3 20 22 S 22 58 E
Tôtes, France 26 C8 49 41N 1 2 E
Tótkomlós, Hungary 52 D5 46 24N 20 45 E
Totland, Norway 18 C2 61 56N 5 23 E
Totma, Russia 56 C7 60 0N 42 40 E
Totnes, U.K. 21 G4 50 26N 3 42W
Totness, Suriname 169 B6 5 53N 56 19W
Toto, Nigeria 113 D6 8 26N 7 5 E
Totonicapán, Guatemala 164 D1 14 58N 91 12W
Totora, Bolivia 173 D4 17 42 S 65 9W
Totoya, I., Fiji 133 B3 18 57 S 179 50W
Totskoye, Russia 64 E4 52 32N 52 45 E
Totten Glacier, Antarctica 7 C8 66 45 S 116 10 E
Tottenham, Australia 129 B7 32 14 S 147 21 E
Tottenham, Canada 150 B5 44 1N 79 49W
Tottori, Japan 72 B6 35 30N 134 15 E
Tottori □, Japan 72 B6 35 30N 134 12 E
Touaret, Niger 111 D6 20 17N 7 8 E
Touat, Algeria 111 C5 27 27N 0 30 E
Touba, Ivory C. 112 D3 8 22N 7 40W
Touba, Senegal 112 C1 14 50N 15 55W
Toubkal, Djebel, Morocco 110 B3 31 0N 8 0W
Toubkal Nat. Park △, Morocco 110 B3 31 0N 8 2W
Toucy, France 27 E10 47 44N 3 15 E
Tougan, Burkina Faso 112 C4 13 11N 2 58W
Touggourt, Algeria 111 B6 33 6N 6 4 E
Tougouri, Burkina Faso 113 C4 13 20N 0 30W
Tougué, Guinea 112 C2 11 25N 11 50W
Touho, N. Cal. 133 T19 20 47 S 165 14 E
Toukmatine, Algeria 111 D6 24 49N 7 11 E
Toukoto, Mali 112 C3 13 27N 9 52W
Toul, France 27 D12 48 40N 5 53 E
Toulepleu, Ivory C. 112 D3 6 32N 8 24W
Toulon, France 29 E9 43 10N 5 55 E
Toulon, U.S.A. 156 C7 41 6N 89 52W
Toulouse, France 28 E5 43 37N 1 27 E
Toulouse Blagnac ✕ (TLS), France 28 E5 43 37N 1 22 E
Toummo, Niger 108 D2 22 45N 14 8 E
Toummo Dhoba, Niger 108 D2 22 30N 14 31 E
Toumodi, Ivory C. 112 D3 6 32N 5 4W
Tounan, Taiwan 77 F13 23 41N 120 28 E
Tounassine, Hamada, Algeria 110 C4 28 48N 5 0W
Toungo, Nigeria 113 D7 8 20N 12 3 E
Toungoo, Burma 90 F6 19 0N 96 30 E
Touques →, France 26 C7 49 22N 0 8 E
Touraine, France 26 E7 47 20N 0 30 E
Tourane = Da Nang, Vietnam 86 D7 16 4N 108 13 E
Tourcoing, France 27 B10 50 42N 3 10 E
Touriñán, C., Spain 42 B1 43 3N 9 17W
Tourine, Mauritania 110 D2 22 23N 11 50W
Tournai, Belgium 24 D3 50 35N 3 25 E
Tournan-en-Brie, France 27 D9 48 44N 2 46 E
Tournay, France 28 E4 43 13N 0 13 E
Tournon-St-Martin, France 26 F7 46 45N 0 58 E
Tournon-sur-Rhône, France 29 C8 45 4N 4 50 E
Tournus, France 27 F11 46 35N 4 54 E
Touros, Brazil 170 C4 5 12 S 35 28W
Tours, France 26 E7 47 22N 0 40 E
Tousside, Pic, Chad 109 D3 21 1N 16 29 E
Touws →, S. Africa 116 E3 33 45 S 21 11 E
Touwsrivier, S. Africa 116 E3 33 20 S 20 2 E
Tovar, Venezuela 168 B3 8 20N 71 46W
Tovarkovskiy, Russia 58 F10 53 40N 38 14 E
Tovdal, Norway 18 F5 58 47N 8 10 E
Tovdalselva →, Norway 18 F5 58 11N 8 7 E
Tovuz, Azerbaijan 61 K7 41 0N 45 40 E
Towada, Japan 70 D10 40 37N 141 13 E
Towada-Ko, Japan 70 D10 40 28N 140 55 E
Towanda, Ill., U.S.A. 157 D8 40 36N 88 53W
Towanda, Pa., U.S.A. 151 E8 41 46N 76 27W
Towang, India 90 B3 27 37N 91 50 E
Tower, U.S.A. 154 B8 47 48N 92 17W
Tower, I. = Genovesa, I., Ecuador 172 a 0 20N 89 58W
Towerhill Cr. →, Australia 126 C3 22 28 S 144 35 E
Towner, U.S.A. 154 A4 48 21N 100 25W
Townsend, Ga., U.S.A. 152 D8 31 33N 81 31W
Townsend, Mont., U.S.A. 158 C8 46 19N 111 31W
Townshend I., Australia 126 C5 22 10 S 150 31 E
Townsville, Australia 126 B4 19 15 S 146 45 E
Towraghondi, Afghan. 91 B1 35 13N 62 16 E
Towson, U.S.A. 148 F7 39 24N 76 36W
Towuti, Danau, Indonesia 82 B2 2 45 S 121 32 E
Toxkan He →, China 65 C9 41 8N 80 11 E
Toya-Ko, Japan 70 C10 42 35N 140 51 E
Toyama, Japan 73 A9 36 40N 137 15 E
Toyama □, Japan 73 A9 36 45N 137 30 E
Toyama-Wan, Japan 71 F8 37 0N 137 30 E
Toyapakeh, Indonesia 79 K18 8 41 S 115 29 E
Tōyo, Ehime, Japan 72 D5 33 56N 133 5 E
Tōyō, Kōchi, Japan 72 D6 33 26N 134 16 E
Toyohashi, Japan 73 C9 34 45N 137 25 E
Toyokawa, Japan 73 C9 34 48N 137 27 E
Toyonaka, Japan 73 C7 34 50N 135 28 E
Toyooka, Japan 72 B6 35 35N 134 48 E
Toyota, Japan 73 B9 35 3N 137 7 E
Toyoura, Japan 72 C2 34 6N 130 57 E
Toytepa, Uzbekistan 65 C4 41 3N 69 20 E
Tozeur, Tunisia 108 B1 33 56N 8 8 E
Tqibuli, Georgia 61 J6 42 26N 43 0 E
Tqvarcheli, Georgia 61 J5 42 47N 41 42 E
Trá Li = Tralee, Ireland 23 D2 52 16N 9 42W
Tra On, Vietnam 87 H5 9 58N 105 55 E
Trabancos →, Spain 42 D5 41 36N 5 15W
Traben-Trarbach, Germany 31 F3 49 57N 7 7 E
Trabzon, Turkey 101 B8 41 0N 39 45 E
Tracadie, Canada 141 C7 47 30N 64 55W
Tracy, Calif., U.S.A. 160 H5 37 44N 121 26W
Tracy, Minn., U.S.A. 154 C7 44 14N 95 37W
Tradate, Italy 44 C5 45 43N 8 54 E
Trade Town, Liberia 112 D3 5 40N 9 50W
Traer, U.S.A. 156 B4 42 12N 92 28W
Trafalgar, Australia 129 E7 38 14 S 146 12 E
Trafalgar, C., Spain 43 J4 36 10N 6 2W
Trâghân, Libya 108 C2 26 0N 14 30 E
Traian, Brăila, Romania 53 E12 45 11N 27 44 E
Traian, Tulcea, Romania 53 E13 45 2N 28 15 E
Traiguén, Chile 176 A2 38 15 S 72 41W
Trail, Canada 142 D5 49 5N 117 40W
Traill Ø, Greenland 10 C8 72 30N 23 0W
Trainor L., Canada 142 A4 60 24N 120 17W
Traíra →, Brazil 168 D4 1 4 S 69 26W
Trákhonas, Cyprus 39 E9 35 12N 33 21 E
Tralee, Ireland 23 D2 52 16N 9 42W
Tralee B., Ireland 23 D2 52 17N 9 55W
Tramelan, Switz. 32 B4 47 13N 7 7 E
Tramore, Ireland 23 D4 52 10N 7 10W
Tramore B., Ireland 23 D4 52 9N 7 10W
Tran Ninh, Cao Nguyen, Laos 86 C4 19 30N 103 10 E
Tranås, Sweden 17 F8 58 3N 14 59 E
Tranbjerg, Denmark 17 H4 56 6N 10 9 E
Tranby, Norway 18 E7 59 49N 10 15 E
Trancas, Argentina 174 B2 26 11 S 65 20W
Trancoso, Portugal 42 E3 40 49N 7 21W
Tranebjerg, Denmark 17 J4 55 51N 10 36 E
Tranemo, Sweden 17 G7 57 30N 13 20 E
Trang, Thailand 87 J2 7 33N 99 38 E
Trangahy, Madag. 117 B7 19 7 S 44 31 E
Trangan, Indonesia 83 C4 6 40 S 134 20 E
Trangie, Australia 129 B8 32 4 S 148 0 E
Trångsviken, Sweden 16 A7 63 19N 13 59 E
Trani, Italy 47 A9 41 17N 16 25 E
Tranoroa, Madag. 117 C8 24 42 S 45 4 E
Tranqueras, Uruguay 175 C4 31 13 S 55 45W
Transantarctic Mts., Antarctica 7 E12 85 0 S 170 0W
Transilvania, Romania 53 D9 46 30N 24 0 E
Transilvanian Alps = Carpații Meridionali, Romania 53 E9 45 30N 25 0 E
Transnistria □, Moldova 53 C14 47 20N 29 15 E
Transtrand, Sweden 16 C7 61 6N 13 20 E
Transtrandsfjällen, Sweden 16 C6 61 8N 13 0 E
Transylvania = Transilvania, Romania 53 D9 46 30N 24 0 E
Trápani, Italy 46 D5 38 1N 12 29 E
Trapper Pk., U.S.A. 158 D6 45 54N 114 18W
Traralgon, Australia 129 E7 38 12 S 146 34 E
Trarza, Mauritania 112 B2 17 30N 15 0W
Trás-os-Montes = Cucumbi, Angola 115 E3 10 17 S 19 5 E
Trasacco, Italy 45 G10 41 57N 13 32 E
Trăscău, Munții, Romania 53 D8 46 14N 23 14 E
Trasimeno, L., Italy 45 E9 43 8N 12 6 E
Träslövsläge, Sweden 17 G6 57 4N 12 16 E
Trasvase Tajo-Segura, Canal de, Spain 40 E2 40 15N 2 55W
Trat, Thailand 87 F4 12 14N 102 33 E
Tratani →, Pakistan 92 E3 29 19N 68 20 E
Traun, Austria 34 C7 48 14N 14 15 E
Traunreut, Germany 31 H8 47 57N 12 36 E
Traunsee, Austria 34 D6 47 55N 13 50 E
Traunstein, Germany 31 H8 47 52N 12 37 E
Traveller's L., Australia 128 B5 33 20 S 142 0 E
Travemünde, Germany 30 B6 53 57N 10 52 E
Travers, Mt., N.Z. 131 C7 42 1 S 172 45 E
Traverse City, U.S.A. 148 C3 44 46N 85 38W
Travis, L., U.S.A. 155 K5 30 24N 97 55W
Travnik, Bos.-H. 52 F2 44 17N 17 39 E
Trbovlje, Slovenia 45 B12 46 12N 15 5 E
Treasure Island, U.S.A. 153 H7 27 46N 82 46W
Treasury Is., Solomon Is. 133 L8 7 22 S 155 37 E
Trébbia →, Italy 44 C6 45 4N 9 41 E
Trebel →, Germany 30 B9 53 54N 13 2 E
Trébeurden, France 26 D3 48 46N 3 35W
Trebević, Nac. Park △, Bos.-H. 52 G3 43 20N 18 45 E
Třebíč, Czech Rep. 34 B8 49 14N 15 55 E
Trebinje, Bos.-H. 50 D2 42 44N 18 22 E
Trebisacce, Italy 47 C9 39 52N 16 32 E
Trebišnjica →, Bos.-H. 50 D2 42 47N 18 8 E
Trebišov, Slovak Rep. 35 C14 48 38N 21 41 E
Trebižat →, Bos.-H. 45 E14 43 15N 17 30 E
Trebnje, Slovenia 45 C12 45 54N 15 1 E
Třeboň, Czech Rep. 34 B7 49 1N 14 48 E
Trebonne, Australia 126 B4 18 37 S 146 5 E
Třeboňsko ⌂, Czech Rep. 34 B7 49 1N 14 49 E
Trebujena, Spain 43 J4 36 52N 6 11W
Trecate, Italy 44 C5 45 26N 8 44 E
Tregaron, U.K. 21 E4 52 14N 3 56W
Tregnago, Italy 45 C8 45 31N 11 10 E
Tregrosse Is., Australia 126 B5 17 41 S 150 43 E
Tréguier, France 26 D3 48 47N 3 16W
Trégunc, France 26 E3 47 51N 3 51W
Treherne, Canada 143 D9 49 38N 98 42W
Tréia, Italy 45 E10 43 19N 13 19 E
Treignac, France 28 C5 45 32N 1 48 E
Treinta y Tres, Uruguay 175 C5 33 16 S 54 17W
Treis-karden, Germany 31 E3 50 10N 7 18 E
Treklyano, Bulgaria 50 D6 42 33N 22 36 E
Trelawney, Zimbabwe 117 B5 17 30 S 30 30 E
Trélazé, France 26 E6 47 26N 0 30W
Trelew, Argentina 176 B3 43 10 S 65 20W
Trélissac, France 28 C4 45 11N 0 47 E
Trelleborg, Sweden 17 J7 55 20N 13 10 E
Tremadog Bay, U.K. 20 E3 52 51N 4 18W
Tremezzo, Italy 44 C6 45 59N 9 15 E
Trémiti, Italy 45 F12 42 8N 15 30 E
Tremonton, U.S.A. 158 F7 41 43N 112 10W
Tremp, Spain 40 C5 42 10N 0 52 E
Trenche →, Canada 140 C5 47 46N 72 53W
Trenčiansky □, Slovak Rep. 35 C11 48 45N 18 20 E
Trenčín, Slovak Rep. 35 C11 48 52N 18 4 E
Trengereid, Norway 18 D2 60 26N 5 37 E
Trenggalek, Indonesia 85 D4 8 3 S 111 43 E
Trenque Lauquen, Argentina 174 D3 36 5 S 62 45W
Trent →, Canada 150 B7 44 6N 77 34W
Trent →, U.K. 20 D7 53 41N 0 42W
Trentino-Alto Adige □, Italy 45 B8 46 30N 11 20 E
Trento, Italy 44 B8 46 4N 11 8 E
Trento, Phil. 81 G6 8 3N 126 2 E
Trenton, Canada 140 D4 44 10N 77 34W
Trenton, Fla., U.S.A. 153 F7 29 37N 82 49W
Trenton, Mich., U.S.A. 157 B13 42 8N 83 11W
Trenton, Mo., U.S.A. 156 D3 40 5N 93 37W
Trenton, N.J., U.S.A. 151 F10 40 14N 74 46W
Trenton, Nebr., U.S.A. 154 E4 40 11N 101 1W
Trenton, Ohio, U.S.A. 157 E12 39 29N 84 28W
Trenton, S.C., U.S.A. 152 B8 33 45N 81 51W
Trepassey, Canada 141 C9 46 43N 53 25W
Trepuzzi, Italy 47 B11 40 24N 18 4 E
Tres Arroyos, Argentina 174 D3 38 26 S 60 20W
Três Casas, Brazil 173 B5 6 59 S 62 41W
Três Corações, Brazil 171 F2 21 44 S 45 15W
Tres Equinas, Colombia 168 C2 0 43N 75 16W
Três Lagoas, Brazil 171 F1 20 50 S 51 43W
Tres Lagos, Argentina 176 C2 49 35 S 71 25W
Tres Lomas, Argentina 174 D3 36 27 S 62 51W
Tres Marías, Islas, Mexico 162 C3 21 25N 106 28W
Três Marias, Represa, Brazil 171 E2 18 12 S 45 15W
Tres Montes, C., Chile 176 C1 46 50 S 75 30W
Tres Pinos, U.S.A. 160 J5 36 48N 121 19W
Três Pontas, Brazil 171 F2 21 23 S 45 29W
Três Pontas, C. das, Angola 115 E2 10 28 S 13 32 E
Tres Puentes, Chile 174 B1 27 50 S 70 15W
Tres Puntas, C., Argentina 176 C3 47 0 S 66 0W
Três Rios, Brazil 171 F3 22 6 S 43 15W
Tres Valles, Mexico 163 D5 18 15N 96 8W
Tresco, U.K. 21 H1 49 57N 6 20W
Tresfjord, Norway 18 B4 62 31N 7 7 E
Treska →, Macedonia 50 E5 42 0N 21 20 E
Treskavica, Bos.-H. 52 G3 43 40N 18 20 E
Trespaderne, Spain 42 C7 42 47N 3 24W
Tresticklan Nationalpark △, Sweden 17 F5 59 0N 11 42 E
Trets, France 29 E9 43 27N 5 41 E
Treuchtlingen, Germany 31 G6 48 58N 10 54 E
Treuenbrietzen, Germany 30 C8 52 5N 12 52 E
Treungen, Norway 18 E5 59 1N 8 31 E
Trèves = Trier, Germany 31 F2 49 45N 6 38 E
Trevi, Italy 45 F9 42 52N 12 45 E
Treviglio, Italy 44 C6 45 31N 9 35 E
Trevinca, Peña, Spain 42 C4 42 15N 6 46W
Treviso, Italy 45 C9 45 40N 12 15 E
Trévoux, France 29 C8 45 57N 4 47 E
Trgovište, Serbia, Yug. 50 D6 42 20N 22 10 E
Triabunna, Australia 127 G4 42 30 S 147 55 E
Triánda, Greece 38 E12 36 25N 28 10 E
Triangle, Zimbabwe 117 C5 21 2 S 31 28 E
Triaucourt-en-Argonne, France 27 D12 48 59N 5 2 E
Tribal Areas □, Pakistan 91 B3 33 0N 70 0 E
Tribly, U.S.A. 153 G7 28 28N 82 12W
Tribsees, Germany 30 A8 54 5N 12 44 E
Tribulation, C., Australia 126 B4 16 5 S 145 29 E
Tribune, U.S.A. 154 F4 38 28N 101 45W
Tricárico, Italy 47 B9 40 37N 16 9 E
Tricase, Italy 47 C11 39 56N 18 22 E
Trichinopoly = Tiruchchirappalli, India 95 J4 10 45N 78 45 E
Trichur, India 95 J3 10 30N 76 18 E
Trida, Australia 129 B6 33 1 S 145 1 E
Trier, Germany 31 F2 49 45N 6 38 E
Trieste, Italy 45 C10 45 40N 13 46 E
Trieste, G. di, Italy 45 C10 45 40N 13 35 E
Trieux →, France 26 D3 48 43N 3 9W
Triggiano, Italy 47 A9 41 4N 16 55 E
Triglav, Slovenia 45 B10 46 21N 13 50 E
Triglavski Narodni Park △, Slovenia 45 B10 46 20N 13 50 E
Trigno →, Italy 45 F11 42 4N 14 48 E
Trigueros, Spain 43 H4 37 24N 6 50W
Tríkeri, Greece 48 B5 39 6N 23 5 E
Trikhonís, Límni, Greece 48 C3 38 34N 21 30 E
Tríkkala, Greece 48 B3 39 34N 21 47 E
Tríkkala □, Greece 48 B3 39 41N 21 30 E
Trikomo, Cyprus 39 E9 35 17N 33 52 E
Trikora, Puncak, Indonesia 83 B5 4 15 S 138 45 E
Trilj, Croatia 45 E13 43 38N 16 42 E
Trillo, Spain 40 E2 40 42N 2 35W
Trim, Ireland 23 C5 53 33N 6 48W
Trimbak, India 94 E1 19 56N 73 33 E
Trincomalee, Sri Lanka 95 K5 8 38N 81 15 E
Trindade, Brazil 171 E2 16 40 S 49 30W
Trindade, I., Atl. Oc. 8 J9 20 20 S 29 50W
Třinec, Czech Rep. 35 B11 49 41N 18 39 E
Trinidad, Bolivia 173 C5 14 46 S 64 50W
Trinidad, Colombia 168 B3 5 25N 71 40W
Trinidad, Cuba 164 B4 21 48N 80 0W
Trinidad, Trin. & Tob. 169 F9 10 30N 61 15W
Trinidad, Uruguay 174 C4 33 30 S 56 50W
Trinidad, U.S.A. 155 G2 37 10N 104 31W
Trinidad →, Mexico 163 D5 17 49N 95 9W
Trinidad, G., Chile 176 C1 49 55 S 75 25W
Trinidad, I., Argentina 176 A4 39 10 S 62 0W
Trinidad & Tobago ■, W. Indies 165 D7 10 30N 61 20W
Trinitápoli, Italy 47 A9 41 21N 16 5 E
Trinity, Canada 141 C9 48 59N 53 55W
Trinity, U.S.A. 155 K7 30 57N 95 22W
Trinity →, Calif., U.S.A. 158 F2 41 11N 123 42W
Trinity →, Tex., U.S.A. 155 L7 29 45N 94 43W
Trinity B., Canada 141 C9 48 20N 53 10W
Trinity Hills, Trin. & Tob. 169 F9 10 16N 61 6W
Trinity Is., U.S.A. 144 H9 56 33N 154 25W
Trinity Range, U.S.A. 158 F4 40 15N 118 45W
Trinkat, India 95 K11 8 5N 93 30 E
Trinkitat, Sudan 106 D4 18 45N 37 51 E
Trino, Italy 44 C5 45 12N 8 18 E
Trinway, U.S.A. 150 F2 40 9N 82 1W
Triolet, Mauritius 121 d 20 4 S 57 32 E
Trionto, C., Italy 47 C9 39 37N 16 43 E
Triora, Italy 44 D4 44 1N 7 46 E
Tripoli = Tarābulus, Lebanon 103 A4 34 31N 35 50 E
Tripoli = Tarābulus, Libya 108 B2 32 49N 13 7 E
Tripoli, U.S.A. 156 B4 42 49N 92 16W
Trípolis, Greece 48 D4 37 31N 22 25 E
Tripolitania, N. Afr. 104 C5 31 0N 13 0 E
Tripura □, India 90 D3 24 0N 92 0 E
Tripylos, Cyprus 39 F8 34 59N 32 41 E
Trischen, Germany 30 A4 54 4N 8 40 E
Tristan da Cunha, Atl. Oc. 8 K10 37 6 S 12 20W
Trisul, India 93 D8 30 19N 79 47 E
Trivandrum, India 95 K3 8 41N 77 0 E
Trivento, Italy 45 G11 41 47N 14 33 E
Trnava, Slovak Rep. 35 C10 48 23N 17 35 E
Trnavský □, Slovak Rep. 35 C10 48 30N 17 45 E
Troarn, France 26 C6 49 11N 0 11W
Trobriand Is., Papua N. G. 132 E6 8 30 S 151 0 E
Trochu, Canada 142 C6 51 50N 113 13W
Trodely I., Canada 140 B4 52 15N 79 26W
Troezen, Greece 48 D5 37 25N 23 15 E
Trogen, Switz. 33 B8 47 24N 9 28 E
Trogir, Croatia 45 E13 43 32N 16 15 E
Troglav, Croatia 45 E13 43 56N 16 36 E
Tróia, Italy 47 A8 41 22N 15 18 E
Troilus, L., Canada 140 B5 50 50N 74 35W
Troina, Italy 47 E7 37 47N 14 36 E
Trois Fourches, Cap des, Morocco 111 A4 35 26N 2 58W
Trois-Pistoles, Canada 141 C6 48 5N 69 10W
Trois-Rivières, Canada 140 C5 46 25N 72 34W
Trois-Rivières, Guadeloupe 164 b 15 57N 61 40W
Troisdorf, Germany 30 E3 50 48N 7 11 E

Troitsk, *Russia* . . . . **64 D8** 54 10N 61 35 E
Troitskiy, *Russia* . . . . **64 C9** 57 5N 63 43 E
Troitsko Pechorsk, *Russia* . . . . **56 B10** 62 40N 56 10 E
Tróllaskagi, *Iceland* **11 C9** 64 54N 17 16W
Trollhättan, *Sweden* . . . . **17 F6** 58 17N 12 20 E
Trollheimen, *Norway* . . . . **18 B6** 62 46N 9 1 E
Trombetas →, *Brazil* . . . . **169 D6** 1 55 S 55 35W
Tromøy, *Norway* . . . . **18 F5** 58 27N 8 51 E
Tromsø, *Norway* . . . . **14 B18** 69 40N 18 56 E
Trona, *U.S.A.* **161 K9** 35 46N 117 23W
Tronador, Mte., *Argentina* . . . . . **176 B2** 41 10 S 71 50W
Trøndelag, *Norway* . . . . **14 D14** 64 17N 11 50 E
Trondheim, *Norway* . . . . **18 A7** 63 36N 10 25 E
Trondheimsfjorden, *Norway* . . **14 E14** 63 35N 10 30 E
Trondheimsleia, *Norway* . . . . . . **18 A5** 63 25N 8 30 E
Trönninge, *Sweden* . . . . **17 H6** 56 37N 12 51 E
Tronto →, *Italy* . . . . **45 F10** 42 54N 13 55 E
Troodos, *Cyprus* . . . . **39 E8** 34 55N 32 52 E
Troon, *U.K.* **22 F4** 55 33N 4 39W
Tropea, *Italy* . . . . **47 D8** 38 41N 15 54 E
Tropic, *U.S.A.* **159 H7** 37 37N 112 5W
Tropojë, *Albania* . . . . **50 D4** 42 23N 20 10 E
Trosa, *Sweden* . . . . **17 F11** 58 54N 17 33 E
Trostan, *U.K.* **23 A5** 55 3N 6 10W
Trostberg, *Germany* . . . . **31 G8** 48 1N 12 33 E
Trostyanets, *Ukraine* . . . . **59 G8** 50 33N 34 59 E
Trou Gras Pt., *St. Lucia* . . . . . . **165 f** 13 54N 60 53W
Trout →, *Canada* **142 A5** 61 19N 119 51W
Trout L., *N.W.T., Canada* **142 A4** 60 40N 121 14W
Trout L., *Ont., Canada* **143 C10** 51 20N 93 15W
Trout Lake, *Canada* **142 B6** 56 30N 114 32W
Trout Lake, *U.S.A.* **160 E5** 46 0N 121 32W
Trout River, *Canada* **141 C8** 49 29N 58 8W
Trout Run, *U.S.A.* **150 E7** 41 23N 77 3W
Trouville-sur-Mer, *France* . . . . . **26 C7** 49 21N 0 5 E
Trowbridge, *U.K.* **21 F5** 51 18N 2 12W
Troy, *Turkey* . . . . **49 B8** 39 57N 26 12 E
Troy, *Ala., U.S.A.* **152 D4** 31 48N 85 58W
Troy, *Ill., U.S.A.* **156 F7** 38 44N 89 54W
Troy, *Ind., U.S.A.* **157 G10** 37 59N 86 55W
Troy, *Kans., U.S.A.* **154 F7** 39 47N 95 5W
Troy, *Mich., U.S.A.* **157 B13** 42 37N 83 9W
Troy, *Mo., U.S.A.* **156 F6** 38 59N 90 59W
Troy, *Mont., U.S.A.* **158 B6** 48 28N 115 53W
Troy, *N.Y., U.S.A.* **151 D11** 42 44N 73 41W
Troy, *Ohio, U.S.A.* **157 D12** 40 2N 84 12W
Troy, *Pa., U.S.A.* **151 E8** 41 47N 76 47W
Troyan, *Bulgaria* . . . . **51 D8** 42 57N 24 43 E
Troyes, *France* . . . . **27 D11** 48 19N 4 3 E
Trpanj, *Croatia* . . . . **45 L14** 43 1N 17 15 E
Trstenik, *Serbia, Yug.* . . . . **50 C5** 43 36N 21 0 E
Trubchevsk, *Russia* . . . . **59 F7** 52 33N 33 47 E
Truchas Peak, *U.S.A.* **155 H2** 35 58N 105 39W
Trucial States = United Arab
Emirates ■, *Asia* . . . . **97 F7** 23 50N 54 0 E
Truckee, *U.S.A.* **160 F6** 39 20N 120 11W
Trudfront, *Russia* . . . . **61 H8** 45 56N 47 40 E
Trudovoye, *Russia* . . . . **70 C6** 43 17N 132 5 E
Trujillo, *Colombia* **168 C2** 4 10N 76 19W
Trujillo, *Honduras* **164 C2** 16 0N 86 0W
Trujillo, *Peru* . . . . **172 B2** 8 6 S 79 0W
Trujillo, *Spain* **43 F5** 39 28N 5 55W
Trujillo, *U.S.A.* **155 H2** 35 32N 104 42W
Trujillo, *Venezuela* **168 B3** 9 22N 70 38W
Trujillo □, *Venezuela* **168 B3** 9 25N 70 30W
Truk, *Micronesia* . . . . **134 G7** 7 25N 151 46 E
Trumann, *U.S.A.* **155 H9** 35 41N 90 31W
Trumansburg, *U.S.A.* **151 D8** 42 33N 76 40W
Trumbull, Mt., *U.S.A.* **159 H7** 36 25N 113 8W
Trŭn, *Bulgaria* . . . . **50 D6** 42 51N 22 38 E
Trun, *France* . . . . **26 D7** 48 50N 0 2 E
Trun, *Switz.* . . . . **33 C7** 46 45N 8 59 E
Trundle, *Australia* . . . . **129 B7** 32 53 S 147 35 E
Trung-Phan = Annam, *Vietnam* . . **86 E7** 16 0N 108 0 E
Truro, *Australia* . . . . **128 C3** 34 24 S 139 9 E
Truro, *Canada* **141 C7** 45 21N 63 14W
Truro, *U.K.* **21 G2** 50 16N 5 4W
Truskavets, *Ukraine* . . . . **59 H2** 49 17N 23 30 E
Trŭstenik, *Bulgaria* . . . . **51 C8** 43 31N 24 28 E
Trustrup, *Denmark* . . . . **17 H4** 56 20N 10 46 E
Trutch, *Canada* **142 B4** 57 44N 122 57W
Truth or Consequences, *U.S.A.* . **159 K10** 33 8N 107 15W
Trutnov, *Czech Rep.* . . . . **34 A8** 50 37N 15 54 E
Truxton, *U.S.A.* **151 D8** 42 45N 76 2W
Truyère →, *France* . . . . **28 D6** 44 38N 2 34 E
Tryavna, *Bulgaria* . . . . **51 D9** 42 54N 25 25 E
Tryonville, *U.S.A.* **150 E5** 41 42N 79 48W
Trysileiva →, *Norway* . . . . **18 C9** 61 3N 12 2 E
Trzcianka, *Poland* . . . . **55 E3** 53 3N 16 25 E
Trzciel, *Poland* . . . . **55 F2** 52 23N 15 50 E
Trzcińsko Zdrój, *Poland* . . . . . . **55 F1** 52 58N 14 35 E
Trzebiatów, *Poland* . . . . **54 D2** 54 3N 15 18 E
Trzebież, *Poland* . . . . **54 E1** 53 38N 14 31 E
Trzebnica, *Poland* . . . . **55 G4** 51 20N 17 1 E
Trzemeszno, *Poland* . . . . **55 F4** 52 33N 17 48 E
Tržič, *Slovenia* . . . . **45 B11** 46 22N 14 18 E
Tsagan Aman, *Russia* . . . . **61 G8** 47 34N 46 43 E
Tsakarisiánon, *Greece* . . . . **39 C2** 38 10N 20 40 E
Tsala Apopka L., *U.S.A.* **153 G7** 28 53N 82 19W
Tsamandás, *Greece* . . . . **48 B2** 39 46N 20 21 E
Tsandi, *Namibia* . . . . **116 B1** 17 42 S 14 50 E
Tsangpo = Brahmaputra →, *Asia* . **93 D3** 23 40N 90 35 E
Tsaratanana, *Madag.* . . . . **117 B8** 16 47 S 47 39 E
Tsaratanana, Mt. de = Maromokotro,
Madag. . . . . **117 A8** 14 0 S 49 0 E
Tsaratanana, Réserve de △, *Madag.* . **117 A8** 13 57N 48 52 E
Tsarevo = Michurin, *Bulgaria* . . **51 D11** 42 9N 27 51 E
Tsarevo, *Bulgaria* . . . . **51 D9** 42 28N 25 52 E
Tsaribrod = Dimitrovgrad,
Serbia, Yug. . . . . **50 C6** 43 2N 22 48 E
Tsaritsáni, *Greece* . . . . **48 B4** 39 53N 22 14 E
Tsau, *Botswana* . . . . **116 C3** 20 8 S 22 22 E
Tsavo East Nat. Park △, *Kenya* . **118 C4** 2 44 S 38 47 E
Tsavo West Nat. Park △, *Kenya* . **118 C4** 3 19 S 37 57 E
Tsebrykove, *Ukraine* . . . . **59 J6** 47 9N 30 10 E
Tselinograd = Astana, *Kazakhstan* . **116 D2** 55 58 S 18 8 E
Tses, *Namibia* . . . . **68 B5** 47 36N 101 32 E
Tsetserleg, *Mongolia* . . . . **113 D5** 6 25N 1 20 E
Tsévié, *Togo* . . . . **116 D3** 26 2 S 22 29 E
Tshabong, *Botswana* . . . . **116 D3** 26 2 S 22 29 E
Tshabuta, *Dem. Rep. of the Congo* . **115 D4** 7 42 S 23 7 E
Tshane, *Botswana* . . . . **116 C3** 24 5 S 21 54 E
Tshela, *Dem. Rep. of the Congo* . **115 C2** 4 57 S 13 4 E
Tshesebe, *Botswana* . . . . **117 C4** 21 51 S 27 32 E
Tshibeke, *Dem. Rep. of the Congo* . **118 C2** 2 40 S 28 35 E
Tshibinda, *Dem. Rep. of the Congo* . **118 C2** 2 23 S 28 43 E
Tshikapa, *Dem. Rep. of the Congo* . **115 D4** 6 28 S 20 48 E
Tshilenge, *Dem. Rep. of the Congo* . **118 D1** 6 17 S 23 48 E
Tshindjambo, *Dem. Rep. of
the Congo* . . . . **115 E4** 10 52 S 22 43 E
Tshinsta, *Dem. Rep. of the Congo* . **119 D4** 12 20 S 20 58 E
Tshinsenda, *Dem. Rep. of the Congo* . **119 E2** 12 20 S 28 0 E
Tshitadi, *Dem. Rep. of the Congo* . **115 D4** 6 45 S 23 48 E
Tshofa, *Dem. Rep. of the Congo* . **118 D2** 5 13 S 25 16 E
Tshuapa →, *Dem. Rep. of the Congo* . **114 C4** 1 14 S 20 42 E
Tshumbiri, *Dem. Rep. of the Congo* . **114 C3** 2 53 S 16 18 E
Tshwane, *Botswana* . . . . **116 C3** 22 24 S 22 1 E
Tsigara, *Botswana* . . . . **116 C4** 20 22 S 25 54 E
Tsihombe, *Madag.* . . . . **117 D8** 25 10 S 45 41 E
Tsiigehtchic, *Canada* **138 B6** 67 15N 134 0W
Tsimlyansk, *Russia* . . . . **61 G6** 47 40N 42 6 E
Tsimlyansk Res. = Tsimlyanskoye
Vdkhr., *Russia* . . . . **61 F6** 48 0N 43 0 E

Tsimlyanskoye Vdkhr., *Russia* . . . **61 F6** 48 0N 43 0 E
Tsinan = Jinan, *China* . . . . **74 F9** 36 38N 117 1 E
Tsineng, *S. Africa* . . . . **116 D3** 27 5 S 23 5 E
Tsing Yi, *China* . . . . **69 G11** 22 21N 114 6 E
Tsínga, *Greece* . . . . **51 E8** 41 23N 24 44 E
Tsinghai = Qinghai □, *China* . . . **68 C4** 36 0N 98 0 E
Tsingtao = Qingdao, *China* . . . . **75 F11** 36 5N 120 20 E
Tsingy de Bemaraha, Réserve
Naturelle △, *Madag.* . . . . . . **117 B8** 18 35 S 45 25 E
Tsingy de Namoraka, Réserve de △,
Madag. . . . . **117 B8** 16 29 S 45 25 E
Tsinjoarivo, *Madag.* . . . . **117 B8** 19 37 S 47 40 E
Tsinjomitondraka, *Madag.* . . . **117 B8** 15 40 S 47 8 E
Tsiroanomandidy, *Madag.* . . . . **117 B8** 18 46 S 46 2 E
Tsiteli-Tsqaro, *Georgia* . . . . . . **61 K8** 41 33N 46 0 E
Tsitondroina, *Madag.* . . . . **117 C8** 21 19 S 46 0 E
Tsitsikamma Nat. Park △, *S. Africa* . **116 E3** 34 3 S 23 40 E
Tsivilsk, *Russia* . . . . **60 C8** 55 50N 47 25 E
Tsivory, *Madag.* . . . . **117 C8** 24 4 S 46 5 E
Tskhinvali, *Georgia* . . . . **61 J7** 42 14N 44 1 E
Tsna →, *Russia* . . . . **60 C6** 54 55N 41 58 E
Tsnori, *Georgia* . . . . **61 K7** 41 40N 45 57 E
Tso Moriri, L., *India* . . . . **93 C8** 32 50N 78 20 E
Tsobis, *Namibia* . . . . **116 B2** 19 27 S 17 30 E
Tsodilo Hill, *Botswana* . . . . **116 B3** 18 49 S 21 43 E
Tsogni, *Gabon* . . . . **114 C2** 2 48 S 10 10 E
Tsogttsetsiy = Baruunsuu, *Mongolia* . **74 C3** 43 43N 105 35 E
Tsolo, *S. Africa* . . . . **117 E4** 31 18 S 28 37 E
Tsomo, *S. Africa* . . . . **117 E4** 32 0 S 27 42 E
Tsoukaládes, *Greece* . . . . **39 B2** 38 41N 20 47 E
Tsu, *Japan* . . . . **73 C8** 34 45N 136 25 E
Tsu L., *Canada* **142 A6** 60 40N 111 52W
Tsuchiura, *Japan* . . . . **73 A12** 36 5N 140 15 E
Tsuen Wan, *China* . . . . **69 G11** 22 22N 114 6 E
Tsugaru-Kaikyō, *Japan* . . . . . . **70 D10** 41 35N 141 0 E
Tsukuba, *Japan* . . . . **73 A12** 36 2N 140 4 E
Tsukumi, *Japan* . . . . **72 D3** 33 4N 131 52 E
Tsukushi-Sanchi, *Japan* . . . . . . **72 D3** 33 25N 130 30 E
Tsumeb, *Namibia* . . . . **116 B2** 19 9 S 17 44 E
Tsumis, *Namibia* . . . . **116 C2** 23 39 S 17 29 E
Tsuna, *Japan* . . . . **72 C6** 34 28N 134 56 E
Tsuno-Shima, *Japan* . . . . **72 C2** 34 21N 130 52 E
Tsuru, *Japan* . . . . **73 B10** 35 31N 138 57 E
Tsuruga, *Japan* . . . . **73 B8** 35 45N 136 2 E
Tsuruga-Wan, *Japan* . . . . **73 B8** 35 50N 136 3 E
Tsurugi, *Japan* . . . . **73 B8** 36 20N 136 37 E
Tsurugi-San, *Japan* . . . . **72 D6** 33 51N 134 6 E
Tsurumi-Saki, *Japan* . . . . **72 E4** 32 56N 132 5 E
Tsuruoka, *Japan* . . . . **70 E9** 38 44N 139 50 E
Tsurusaki, *Japan* . . . . **72 D3** 33 14N 131 41 E
Tsushima, *Ehime, Japan* . . . . . **72 D4** 33 7N 132 32 E
Tsushima, *Gifu, Japan* . . . . **73 B8** 35 10N 136 43 E
Tsushima, *Nagasaki, Japan* . . . **72 C1** 34 20N 129 20 E
Tsuyama, *Japan* . . . . **72 B6** 35 3N 134 0 E
Tsvetkovo, *Ukraine* . . . . **59 H6** 49 8N 31 33 E
Tsyelyakhany, *Belarus* . . . . **59 F3** 52 30N 25 46 E
Tu →, *Burma* . . . . **90 E6** 21 50N 96 15 E
Tua →, *Papua N. G.* . . . . **133 C3** 6 30 S 144 28 E
Tua →, *Portugal* **42 D3** 41 13N 7 26W
Tuaheni Pt., *N.Z.* . . . . **131 D6** 38 43 S 178 4 E
Tuai, *N.Z.* . . . . **130 E6** 38 47 S 177 10 E
Tuakau, *N.Z.* . . . . **130 D3** 37 16 S 174 59 E
Tual, *Indonesia* . . . . **83 C4** 5 38 S 132 44 E
Tuam, *Ireland* **23 C3** 53 31N 8 51W
Tuamarina, *N.Z.* . . . . **131 B8** 41 25 S 173 59 E
Tuamotu Arch. = Tuamotu Is.,
Pac. Oc. . . . . **135 J13** 17 0 S 144 0W
Tuamotu Is., *Pac. Oc.* . . . . **135 J13** 17 0 S 144 0W
Tuamotu Ridge, *Pac. Oc.* . . . . . **135 K14** 20 0 S 138 0W
Tuanfeng, *China* . . . . **77 B10** 30 38N 114 52 E
Tuanxi, *China* . . . . **76 D6** 27 28N 107 8 E
Tuao, *Phil.* . . . . **80 C3** 17 55N 121 22 E
Tuapse, *Russia* . . . . **61 H4** 44 5N 39 10 E
Tuas, *Singapore* . . . . **87 d** 1 19N 103 39 E
Tuatapere, *N.Z.* . . . . **131 G2** 46 8 S 167 41 E
Tuba City, *U.S.A.* **159 H8** 36 8N 111 14W
Tuban, *Indonesia* . . . . **85 D4** 6 54 S 112 3 E
Tubani, *Botswana* . . . . **116 C3** 24 46 S 24 18 E
Tubarão, *Brazil* . . . . **175 B6** 28 30 S 49 0W
Tūbās, *West Bank* . . . . **103 C4** 32 20N 35 22 E
Tubas →, *Namibia* . . . . **116 C2** 22 54 S 14 35 E
Tubau, *Malaysia* . . . . **85 B4** 3 10N 113 40 E
Tubbataha Reefs Marine Park △,
Phil. . . . . **81 G2** 8 53N 119 53 E
Tubigon, *Phil.* . . . . **81 G4** 9 57N 123 58 E
Tübingen, *Germany* . . . . **31 G5** 48 31N 9 4 E
Tubod, *Phil.* . . . . **81 G4** 8 3N 123 48 E
Tubou, *Fiji* . . . . **133 D3** 18 13 S 178 48W
Tubruq, *Libya* . . . . **108 B4** 32 7N 23 55 E
Ṭubruq □, *Libya* . . . . **108 B4** 30 0N 24 0 E
Tubuai Is., *Pac. Oc.* . . . . **135 K13** 25 0 S 150 0W
Tuburan, *Basilan, Phil.* . . . . **81 H4** 6 39N 122 16 E
Tuburan, *Cebu, Phil.* . . . . **81 F4** 10 44N 123 49 E
Tuc Trung, *Vietnam* . . . . **87 G6** 11 1N 107 12 E
Tucacas, *Venezuela* **168 A4** 10 48N 68 19W
Tucano, *Brazil* . . . . **174 D4** 10 58 S 38 48W
T'uch'ang, *Taiwan* . . . . **77 E13** 24 42N 121 25 E
Tuchodi →, *Canada* **142 B4** 58 17N 123 42W
Tuchola, *Poland* . . . . **54 E4** 53 33N 17 52 E
Tuchów, *Poland* . . . . **55 J8** 49 54N 21 1 E
Tuckanarra, *Australia* . . . . **125 E2** 27 7 S 118 5 E
Tucker, *U.S.A.* **152 B5** 33 51N 84 13W
Tuckers Town, *Bermuda* . . . . . . **9 a** 32 20N 64 42W
Tucson, *U.S.A.* **159 K8** 32 13N 110 58W
Tucumán, *Argentina* . . . . **174 B2** 26 48 S 66 2W
Tucumcari, *U.S.A.* **155 H3** 35 10N 103 44W
Tucunaré, *Brazil* . . . . **173 B6** 5 18 S 55 51W
Tucupido, *Venezuela* **168 B4** 9 17N 65 47W
Tucupita, *Venezuela* **170 B5** 9 2N 62 3W
Tucuruí, *Brazil* . . . . **170 B2** 3 42 S 49 44W
Tucuruí, Reprêsa de, *Brazil* . . . **170 B2** 4 0 S 49 30W
Tuczno, *Poland* . . . . **55 E3** 53 13N 16 10 E
Tuddal, *Norway* . . . . **18 E5** 59 46N 8 49 E
Tudela, *Spain* **40 C3** 42 4N 1 39W
Tudmur, *Syria* . . . . **101 E8** 34 36N 38 15 E
Tudor, L., *Canada* **141 A6** 55 50N 65 25W
Tudora, *Romania* . . . . **53 C11** 47 31N 26 45 E
Tuella →, *Portugal* **42 D3** 41 30N 7 12W
Tuen Mun, *China* . . . . **69 G10** 22 24N 113 59 E
Tueré →, *Brazil* . . . . **170 B1** 2 48 S 50 59W
Tufi, *Papua N. G.* . . . . **132 E5** 9 8 S 149 19 E
Tufsingdalen, *Norway* . . . . **18 B8** 62 18N 11 44 E
Tugela →, *S. Africa* . . . . **117 D5** 29 14 S 31 30 E
Tugidak I., *U.S.A.* **146 C4** 56 30N 154 40W
Tuguegarao, *Phil.* . . . . **80 C3** 17 35N 121 42 E
Tugur, *Russia* . . . . **67 D14** 53 44N 136 45 E
Tui, *Spain* **42 C2** 42 3N 8 39W
Tuineje, *Canary Is.* **9 e2** 28 19N 14 3W
Tukangbesi, Kepulauan, *Indonesia* . **83 C2** 6 0 S 124 0 E
Tukarak I., *Canada* **140 A4** 56 15N 78 45W
Tukayyid, *Iraq* . . . . **96 D5** 29 47N 45 36 E
Tūkh, *Egypt* . . . . **106 H7** 30 21N 31 12 E
Tukituki →, *N.Z.* . . . . **130 F5** 39 36 S 176 56 E
Tukkae, Ao, *Thailand* . . . . **87 a** 7 51N 98 25 E
Tukobo, *Ghana* **112 D4** 5 1N 2 47W
Tūkrah, *Libya* . . . . **108 B4** 32 30N 20 37 E
Tuktoyaktuk, *Canada* **138 B6** 69 27N 133 2W
Tukums, *Latvia* . . . . **15 H20** 56 58N 23 10 E
Tukums □, *Latvia* . . . . **9 B10** 56 55N 23 0 E
Tukuran, *Phil.* . . . . **81 H4** 7 51N 123 34 E
Tukuyu, *Tanzania* . . . . **119 D3** 9 17 S 33 35 E
Tula, *Hidalgo, Mexico* **163 C5** 20 5N 99 20W

Tula, *Tamaulipas, Mexico* **163 C5** 23 0N 99 40W
Tula, *Nigeria* . . . . **113 D7** 9 51N 11 27 E
Tula, *Russia* . . . . **58 E9** 54 13N 37 38 E
Tulagi, *Solomon Is.* . . . . **133 M11** 9 5 S 160 10 E
Tūlak, *Afghan.* . . . . **91 B1** 33 55N 63 40 E
Tulancingo, *Mexico* **163 C5** 20 5N 98 22W
Tulangbawang →, *Indonesia* . . . **84 C3** 4 24 S 105 52 E
Tulare, *Serbia, Yug.* . . . . **50 D5** 42 48N 21 28 E
Tulare, *U.S.A.* **160 J7** 36 13N 119 21W
Tulare Lake Bed, *U.S.A.* **160 K7** 36 0N 119 48W
Tularosa, *U.S.A.* **159 K10** 33 5N 106 1W
Tulbagh, *S. Africa* . . . . **116 E2** 33 16 S 19 6 E
Tulcán, *Ecuador* **168 C2** 0 48N 77 43W
Tulcea, *Romania* . . . . **53 E13** 45 13N 28 46 E
Tulcea □, *Romania* . . . . **53 E13** 45 0N 28 30 E
Tulchyn, *Ukraine* . . . . **59 H5** 48 41N 28 49 E
Tūleh, *Iran* . . . . **97 C7** 34 35N 52 33 E
Tulemalu L., *Canada* **143 A9** 62 58N 99 25W
Tulgheş, *Romania* . . . . **53 D10** 46 58N 25 45 E
Tuli, *Zimbabwe* . . . . **119 G2** 21 58 S 29 13 E
Tuliszków, *Poland* **155 H4** 34 32N 101 46W
Tulita, *Canada* **138 B7** 64 57N 125 30W
Tūlkarm, *West Bank* . . . . **103 C4** 32 19N 35 2 E
Tulla, *Ireland* **23 D3** 52 53N 8 46W
Tullahoma, *U.S.A.* **149 H2** 35 22N 86 13W
Tullamore, *Australia* . . . . **129 B7** 32 39 S 147 36 E
Tullamore, *Ireland* **23 C4** 53 16N 7 31W
Tulle, *France* . . . . **28 C5** 45 16N 1 46 E
Tulln, *Austria* . . . . **34 C9** 48 20N 16 4 E
Tullow, *Ireland* **23 D5** 52 49N 6 45W
Tullus, *Sudan* . . . . **107 E1** 11 7N 24 31 E
Tully, *Australia* . . . . **126 B4** 17 56 S 145 55 E
Tully, *U.S.A.* **151 D8** 42 48N 76 7W
Ṭulmaythah, *Libya* . . . . **108 B4** 32 40N 20 55 E
Tulnici, *Romania* . . . . **53 E11** 45 51N 26 38 E
Tulovo, *Bulgaria* . . . . **51 D9** 42 33N 25 32 E
Tulsa, *U.S.A.* **155 G7** 36 10N 95 55W
Tulsequah, *Canada* **142 B2** 58 39N 133 35W
Tulu Milki, *Ethiopia* . . . . **107 F4** 9 55N 38 20 E
Tulu Welel, *Ethiopia* . . . . **107 F3** 8 56N 34 47 E
Tulua, *Colombia* **168 C2** 4 6N 76 11W
Tuluceşti, *Romania* . . . . **53 E13** 45 34N 28 2 E
Tuluksak, *U.S.A.* **144 F7** 61 6N 160 58W
Tulun, *Russia* . . . . **67 D11** 54 32N 100 35 E
Tulungagung, *Indonesia* . . . . . . **85 D4** 8 5 S 111 54 E
Tuma, *Russia* . . . . **58 E11** 55 10N 40 30 E
Tuma →, *Nic.* **164 D3** 13 6N 84 35W
Tumaco, *Colombia* **168 C2** 1 50N 78 45W
Tumaco, Ensenada, *Colombia* . . **168 C2** 1 55N 78 50W
Tumatumari, *Guyana* **169 B6** 5 20N 58 55W
Tumba, *Dem. Rep. of the Congo* . **114 C4** 0 50 S 18 0 E
Tumba, *Sweden* . . . . **16 E11** 59 12N 17 48 E
Tumba, L., *Dem. Rep. of the Congo* . **114 C3** 0 50 S 18 0 E
Tumbarumba, *Australia* . . . . . . **129 C8** 35 44 S 148 0 E
Tumbaya, *Argentina* . . . . **174 A2** 23 50 S 65 26W
Tumbes, *Peru* . . . . **172 A1** 3 37 S 80 27W
Tumbes □, *Peru* . . . . **172 A1** 3 50 S 80 30W
Tumbur, *Sudan* . . . . **107 G3** 4 20N 31 34 E
Tumbwe, *Dem. Rep. of the Congo* . **119 E2** 11 25 S 27 15 E
Tumby Bay, *Australia* . . . . **128 C2** 34 21 S 136 8 E
Tumd Youqi, *China* . . . . **74 D6** 40 30N 110 30 E
Tumen, *China* . . . . **75 C15** 43 0N 129 50 E
Tumen Jiang →, *China* . . . . **75 C16** 42 20N 130 35 E
Tumeremo, *Venezuela* **169 B5** 7 18N 61 30W
Tumiritinga, *Brazil* . . . . **171 E3** 18 58 S 41 38W
Tumkur, *India* . . . . **95 H3** 13 18N 77 6 E
Tump, *Pakistan* . . . . **91 D1** 26 7N 62 16 E
Tumpat, *Malaysia* . . . . **87 J4** 6 11N 102 10 E
Tumsar, *India* . . . . **94 D4** 21 26N 79 45 E
Tumu, *Ghana* **112 C4** 10 56N 1 56W
Tumucumaque, Serra, *Brazil* . . . **169 C7** 2 0N 55 0W
Tumupasa, *Bolivia* . . . . **172 C4** 14 9 S 67 55W
Tumut, *Australia* . . . . **129 C8** 35 16 S 148 13 E
Tumwater, *U.S.A.* **160 C4** 47 1N 122 54W
Tuna, *India* . . . . **92 H4** 22 59N 70 5 E
Tunadal, *Sweden* . . . . **16 B11** 62 26N 17 22 E
Tunapuna, *Trin. & Tob.* **169 F9** 10 38N 61 24W
Tunas de Zaza, *Cuba* **164 B4** 21 39N 79 34W
Tunbridge Wells = Royal Tunbridge
Wells, *U.K.* . . . . **21 F8** 51 7N 0 16 E
Tunçbilek, *Turkey* . . . . **49 B11** 39 37N 29 29 E
Tunceli, *Turkey* . . . . **101 C8** 39 6N 39 31 E
Tuncurry, *Australia* . . . . **129 B10** 32 17 S 152 29 E
Tundla, *India* . . . . **92 F8** 27 12N 78 17 E
Tundubai, *Sudan* . . . . **106 D2** 18 36N 28 50 E
Tunduru, *Tanzania* . . . . **119 E4** 11 8 S 37 25 E
Tundzha →, *Bulgaria* . . . . **51 E10** 41 40N 26 35 E
Tung Chung, *China* . . . . **69 G10** 22 17N 113 57 E
Tung Lung Chau, *China* . . . . . . **69 G11** 22 15N 114 17 E
Tunga →, *India* . . . . **95 G3** 15 0N 75 50 E
Tunga Pass, *India* . . . . **90 A5** 29 0N 94 14 E
Tungabhadra →, *India* . . . . **95 G3** 15 57 S 78 15 E
Tungabhadra Dam, *India* . . . . . . **95 G2** 15 0N 75 50 E
Tungaru, *Sudan* . . . . **107 E3** 10 9N 30 52 E
Tungawan, *Phil.* . . . . **80 H4** 7 30N 122 20 E
Tungi, *Bangla.* . . . . **93 H14** 23 53N 90 24 E
Tungla, *Nic.* **164 D3** 13 24N 84 21W
Tungnafellsjökull, *Iceland* **11 C9** 64 45N 17 55W
Tungsha Tao = Dongsha Dao, *China* . **77 G11** 20 45N 116 43 E
Tungshih, *Taiwan* . . . . **77 E13** 24 12N 120 43 E
Tungsten, *Canada* **142 A3** 61 57N 128 16W
Tungufell, *Iceland* **11 C6** 64 7N 20 10W
Tungurahua □, *Ecuador* . . . . . . **168 D2** 1 15 S 78 35W
Tunguska, Nizhnyaya →, *Russia* . **67 C9** 65 48N 88 4 E
Tunguska, Podkamennaya →, *Russia* . **67 C10** 61 50N 90 13 E
Tuni, *India* . . . . **94 F6** 17 22N 82 36 E
Tunia, *Colombia* **168 C2** 2 41N 76 31W
Tunica, *U.S.A.* **155 H9** 34 41N 90 23W
Tunis, *Tunisia* . . . . **108 A2** 36 50N 10 11 E
Tunis ✈ (TUN), *Tunisia* . . . . . . **46 F3** 36 52N 10 14 E
Tunis, Golfe de, *Tunisia* . . . . . . **108 A2** 37 0N 10 30 E
Tunisia ■, *Africa* . . . . **108 B3** 33 30N 9 10 E
Tunja, *Colombia* **168 B3** 5 33N 73 25W
Tunkhannock, *U.S.A.* **151 E9** 41 32N 75 57W
Tunliu, *China* . . . . **76 F7** 36 13N 112 52 E
Tunnel Creek Nat. Park △, *Australia* . **124 C4** 17 41 S 125 18 E
Tunnsjøen, *Norway* . . . . **14 D15** 64 45N 13 25 E
Tunø, *Denmark* . . . . **17 J4** 55 57N 10 27 E
Tuntutuliak, *U.S.A.* **144 F6** 60 22N 162 38W
Tununak, *U.S.A.* **144 F6** 60 37N 165 15W
Tunungayualok I., *Canada* **141 A7** 56 0N 61 0W
Tununirusiq = Arctic Bay, *Canada* . **139 A11** 73 1N 85 7W
Tunuyán, *Argentina* . . . . **174 C2** 33 35 S 69 0W
Tunuyán →, *Argentina* . . . . **174 C2** 33 33 S 67 30W
Tuo Jiang →, *China* . . . . **76 C5** 28 50N 105 35 E
Tuolumne, *U.S.A.* **160 H6** 37 58N 120 15W
Tuolumne →, *U.S.A.* **160 H5** 37 36N 121 13W
Tüp, *Kyrgyzstan* . . . . **65 B9** 42 45N 78 20 E
Tūp Āghāj, *Iran* . . . . **101 D12** 36 3N 47 50 E
Tupã, *Brazil* . . . . **171 A5** 21 57 S 50 28W
Tupaciguara, *Brazil* . . . . **171 E2** 18 35 S 48 42W
Tupanciretã, *Brazil* . . . . **175 B5** 29 0 S 53 40W
Tupelo, *U.S.A.* **149 H1** 34 16N 88 43W
Tupik, *Russia* . . . . **58 E7** 55 42N 33 22 E
Tupinambaranas, *Brazil* . . . . **169 D6** 3 0 S 58 0W
Tupirama, *Brazil* . . . . **170 C2** 8 58 S 48 12W
Tupiratins, *Brazil* . . . . **170 C2** 8 23 S 48 6W
Tupiza, *Bolivia* . . . . **174 A2** 21 30 S 65 40W
Tupižnica, *Serbia, Yug.* . . . . **50 C6** 43 43N 22 10 E
Tupman, *U.S.A.* **161 K7** 35 18N 119 21W

Tupper, *Canada* **142 B4** 55 32N 120 1W
Tupper Lake, *U.S.A.* **151 B10** 44 14N 74 28W
Tupungato, Cerro, *S. Amer.* . . . . **174 C2** 33 15 S 69 50W
Tuquan, *China* . . . . **75 B11** 45 18N 121 38 E
Túquerres, *Colombia* **168 C2** 1 5N 77 37W
Tura, *India* . . . . **90 C3** 25 30N 90 16 E
Tura, *Russia* . . . . **67 C11** 64 20N 100 17 E
Turabah, *Ḥā'il, Si. Arabia* . . . . . **96 D4** 28 20N 43 15 E
Turabah, *Makkah, Si. Arabia* . . . **98 B3** 21 15N 41 34 E
Turagua, Serranía, *Venezuela* . . **169 B5** 7 20N 64 35W
Turakina, *N.Z.* . . . . **130 G4** 40 3 S 175 16 E
Turakina →, *N.Z.* . . . . **130 G4** 40 5 S 175 8 E
Turakirae Hd., *N.Z.* . . . . **130 H3** 41 26 S 174 56 E
Turakürghan, *Uzbekistan* . . . . . **65 C5** 41 0N 71 31 E
Turama →, *Papua N. G.* . . . . . . **132 D2** 7 40 S 143 50 E
Turan, *Iran* . . . . **97 C8** 35 39N 56 42 E
Turan, *Russia* . . . . **67 D10** 51 55N 95 0 E
Turangi, *N.Z.* . . . . **130 E4** 38 59 S 175 48 E
Turar Rysqulov, *Kazakhstan* . . . **65 B5** 42 32N 70 20 E
Turbaco, *Colombia* **168 A2** 10 21N 75 25W
Turbacz, *Poland* . . . . **55 J7** 49 30N 20 8 E
Turbat, *Pakistan* . . . . **91 D1** 25 59N 63 4 E
Turbe, Bos.-H. . . . . **52 F2** 44 15N 17 35 E
Turbenthal, *Switz.* . . . . **33 B7** 47 27N 8 51 E
Turbeville, *U.S.A.* **152 B9** 33 54N 80 1W
Turbo, *Colombia* **168 B2** 8 6N 76 43W
Turčianske Teplice, *Slovak Rep.* . **35 C11** 48 52N 18 55 E
Turco, *Bolivia* . . . . **172 D4** 18 10 S 68 11W
Turcoaia, *Romania* . . . . **53 E13** 45 7N 28 11 E
Turda, *Romania* . . . . **53 D8** 46 34N 23 47 E
Turek, *Poland* . . . . **55 F5** 52 3N 18 30 E
Turfan = Turpan, *China* . . . . **68 B3** 43 58N 89 10 E
Turfan Depression = Turpan Hami,
China . . . . **62 E12** 42 40N 89 25 E
Turgayskaya Stolovaya Strana, *Asia* . **50 E9** 51 0N 63 0 E
Turgeon →, *Canada* **140 C4** 50 0N 78 56W
Türgovishte, *Bulgaria* . . . . **51 C10** 43 17N 26 38 E
Turgut, *Turkey* . . . . **49 D10** 37 22N 28 4 E
Turguttlu, *Turkey* . . . . **49 C9** 38 30N 27 43 E
Turgwe →, *Zimbabwe* . . . . **117 C5** 21 31 S 32 15 E
Turhal, *Turkey* . . . . **100 B7** 40 24N 36 5 E
Turia →, *Spain* **41 F4** 39 27N 0 19W
Turiaçu, *Brazil* . . . . **170 B2** 1 40 S 45 19W
Turiaçu →, *Brazil* . . . . **170 B2** 1 36 S 45 19W
Turiec →, *Slovak Rep.* . . . . **35 B11** 49 7N 18 55 E
Turin = Torino, *Italy* . . . . **44 C4** 45 3N 7 40 E
Turinsk, *Russia* . . . . **64 C7** 58 3N 63 42 E
Turkana, L., *Africa* . . . . **118 B4** 3 30N 36 5 E
Türkeli, *Turkey* . . . . **51 F11** 40 30N 27 0 E
Turkestan = Türkistan, *Kazakhstan* . **65 B4** 43 17N 68 16 E
Turkestan Range, *Asia* . . . . **65 D4** 39 35N 69 0 E
Türkeve, *Hungary* . . . . **52 C5** 47 6N 20 44 E
Turkey ■, *Eurasia* . . . . **100 C7** 39 0N 36 0 E
Turkey →, *U.S.A.* **156 D9** 42 43N 91 2W
Turkey Creek, *Australia* . . . . . . **124 C4** 17 2 S 128 12 E
Turki, *Russia* . . . . **60 D6** 52 0N 43 15 E
Türkistan, *Kazakhstan* . . . . **65 B4** 43 17N 68 16 E
Türkmenbashi, *Turkmenistan* . . . **57 G9** 40 5N 53 5 E
Turkmenistan ■, *Asia* . . . . **66 F6** 39 0N 59 0 E
Türkmenli, *Turkey* . . . . **49 B8** 39 45N 26 30 E
Türkoğlu, *Turkey* . . . . **100 D7** 37 23N 36 50 E
Turks & Caicos Is. ☑, *W. Indies* . **165 B5** 21 20N 71 20W
Turks Island Passage, *W. Indies* . **165 B5** 21 30N 71 30W
Turku, *Finland* . . . . **15 F20** 60 30N 22 19 E
Turkwel →, *Kenya* . . . . **118 B4** 3 6N 36 6 E
Turlock, *U.S.A.* **160 H6** 37 30N 120 51W
Turnagain →, *Canada* **142 B3** 59 12N 127 35W
Turnagain, C., *N.Z.* . . . . **130 G5** 40 28 S 176 38 E
Turneffe Is., *Belize* **163 D7** 17 20N 87 50W
Turner, *U.S.A.* **158 B9** 48 51N 108 24W
Turner Pt., *Australia* . . . . **126 A1** 11 47 S 133 32 E
Turner Valley, *Canada* **142 C6** 50 40N 114 17W
Turners Falls, *U.S.A.* **151 D12** 42 36N 72 33W
Turnhout, *Belgium* . . . . **24 C4** 51 19N 4 57 E
Türnitz, *Austria* . . . . **34 D8** 47 55N 15 29 E
Turnor L., *Canada* **143 B7** 56 35N 108 35W
Turnov, *Czech Rep.* . . . . **34 A8** 50 34N 15 10 E
Tŭrnovo = Veliko Tŭrnovo, *Bulgaria* . **51 C9** 43 5N 25 41 E
Turnu Măgurele, *Romania* . . . . **53 G9** 43 46N 24 56 E
Turnu Roşu, P., *Romania* . . . . . **53 E9** 45 33N 24 17 E
Turobin, *Poland* . . . . **55 H9** 50 50N 22 44 E
Turóss Head, *Australia* . . . . **129 D9** 36 3 S 150 8 E
Turpan, *China* . . . . **68 B3** 43 58N 89 10 E
Turpan Hami, *China* . . . . **62 E12** 42 40N 89 25 E
Turrawan, *Australia* . . . . **129 A8** 30 28 S 149 53 E
Turrës, Kala e, *Albania* . . . . **50 E3** 41 10N 19 28 E
Turriff, *U.K.* **22 D6** 57 32N 2 27W
Turşaq, *Iraq* . . . . **101 F11** 33 35N 45 47 E
Tursi, *Italy* . . . . **47 B9** 40 15N 16 28 E
Tursunzade, *Tajikistan* . . . . **65 D4** 38 30N 68 14 E
Turtle Head I., *Australia* . . . . . . **126 A3** 10 56 S 142 37 E
Turtle Is., *Phil.* . . . . **81 H2** 6 59 S 118 12 E
Turtle Is., *S. Leone* **112 D2** 7 40N 13 0W
Turtle L., *Canada* **143 C7** 53 36N 108 38W
Turtle Lake, *U.S.A.* **154 B4** 47 31N 100 53W
Turtleford, *Canada* **143 C7** 53 23N 108 57W
Turua, *N.Z.* . . . . **130 D4** 37 14 S 175 35 E
Turuépano, Parque Nac. △,
Venezuela **165 D7** 10 30N 62 52W
Turugart Shankou, *Kyrgyzstan* . . **65 C6** 40 30N 75 24 E
Turukhansk, *Russia* . . . . **67 C9** 65 21N 88 5 E
Turzovka, *Slovak Rep.* . . . . **35 B11** 49 25N 18 35 E
Tuscaloosa, *U.S.A.* **149 J2** 33 12N 87 34W
Tuscánia, *Italy* . . . . **45 F8** 42 25N 11 52 E
Tuscany = Toscana □, *Italy* . . . . **44 E8** 43 25N 11 0 E
Tuscarawas →, *U.S.A.* **150 F3** 40 24N 81 25W
Tuscarora Mt., *U.S.A.* **150 F7** 40 55N 77 55W
Tuscola, *Ill., U.S.A.* **157 E8** 39 48N 88 17W
Tuscola, *Tex., U.S.A.* **155 J5** 32 12N 99 48W
Tuscumbia, *Ala., U.S.A.* **149 H2** 34 44N 87 42W
Tuscumbia, *Mo., U.S.A.* **156 F4** 38 14N 92 28W
Tuskegee, *U.S.A.* **152 C4** 32 25N 85 42W
Tustin, *U.S.A.* **161 M9** 33 44N 117 49W
Tustna, *Norway* . . . . **18 A5** 63 10N 8 5 E
Tuszyn, *Poland* . . . . **55 G6** 51 36N 19 33 E
Tutayev, *Russia* . . . . **101 C18** 39 31N 42 46 E
Tutatyev, *Russia* . . . . **58 D10** 57 53N 39 32 E
Tuticorin, *India* . . . . **95 K4** 8 50N 78 12 E
Tutin, *Serbia, Yug.* . . . . **50 D4** 42 58N 20 20 E
Tutóia, *Brazil* . . . . **170 B3** 2 45 S 42 20W
Tutong, *Brunei* . . . . **85 B4** 4 47N 114 40 E
Tutova →, *Romania* . . . . **53 D12** 46 7N 27 32 E
Tutrakan, *Bulgaria* . . . . **51 B10** 44 2N 26 40 E
Tuttlingen, *Germany* . . . . **31 H4** 47 58N 8 48 E
Tutuala, E. *Timor* . . . . **83 C3** 8 25 S 127 15 E
Tutubia, *Vanuatu* . . . . **132 E6** 9 34 S 150 40 E
Tutuila, *Amer. Samoa* . . . . **133 X24** 14 19 S 170 50W
Tutuko, Mt., *N.Z.* . . . . **131 E4** 34 35 S 168 1 E
Tutun, *Egypt* . . . . **106 J7** 29 9N 30 46 E
Tututepec, *Mexico* **163 D5** 16 9N 97 38W
Tuva □, *Russia* . . . . **67 D10** 51 30N 95 0 E
Tuvalu ■, *Pac. Oc.* . . . . **134 H9** 8 0 S 178 0 E
Tûwal, *Si. Arabia* . . . . **98 B2** 22 17N 39 3 E
Tuxer Alpen, *Austria* . . . . **34 D4** 47 10N 11 45 E
Tuxpan, *Mexico* **163 C5** 20 58N 97 23W
Tuxtla Gutiérrez, *Mexico* **163 D6** 16 50N 93 10W
Tuy = Tui, *Spain* **42 C2** 42 3N 8 39W
Tuy An, *Vietnam* . . . . **86 F7** 13 17N 109 16 E
Tuy Duc, *Vietnam* . . . . **87 F6** 12 15N 107 27 E
Tuy Hoa, *Vietnam* . . . . **86 F7** 13 5N 109 10 E

Tuy Phong, *Vietnam* **87 G7** 11 14N 108 43 E
Tuya L., *Canada* **142 B2** 59 7N 130 35W
Tuyen Hoa, *Vietnam* **86 D6** 17 50N 106 10 E
Tuyen Quang, *Vietnam* **76 G5** 21 50N 105 10 E
Tuymazy, *Russia* **64 D4** 54 36N 53 42 E
Tūysarkān, *Iran* **97 C6** 34 33N 48 27 E
Tuz Gölü, *Turkey* **100 C5** 38 42N 33 18 E
Ṭūz Khurmātū, *Iraq* **101 E11** 34 56N 44 38 E
Tuzi, *Montenegro, Yug.* **50 D3** 42 22N 19 20 E
Tuzigoot Nat. Monument ⌂, *U.S.A.* **159 J7** 34 46N 112 2W
Tuzla, *Bos.-H.* **52 F3** 44 34N 18 41 E
Tuzlov →, *Russia* **59 J10** 47 17N 39 57 E
Tuzluca, *Turkey* **101 B10** 40 3N 43 39 E
Tvååker, *Sweden* **17 G6** 57 4N 12 25 E
Tvardiţa, *Moldova* **53 D13** 46 9N 28 58 E
Tvedestrand, *Norway* **18 F5** 58 38N 8 58 E
Tver, *Russia* **58 D8** 56 55N 35 55 E
Tvrdošin, *Slovak Rep.* **35 B12** 49 21N 19 35 E
Tvrdošovce, *Slovak Rep.* **35 C11** 48 6N 18 4 E
Tvŭrditsa, *Bulgaria* **51 D9** 42 42N 25 53 E
Twain, *U.S.A.* **160 E5** 40 1N 121 3W
Twain Harte, *U.S.A.* **160 G6** 38 2N 120 14W
Twann, *Switz.* **32 B4** 47 6N 7 9 E
Twardogóra, *Poland* **55 G4** 51 23N 17 28 E
Tweed, *Canada* **150 B7** 44 29N 77 19W
Tweed →, *U.K.* **22 F6** 55 45N 2 0W
Tweed Heads, *Australia* **127 D5** 28 10 S 153 31 E
Tweedsmuir Prov. Park ⌂, *Canada* **142 C3** 53 0N 126 20W
Twentynine Palms, *U.S.A.* **161 L10** 34 8N 116 3W
Tweya, *Dem. Rep. of the Congo* **114 C3** 0 54 S 18 58 E
Twillingate, *Canada* **141 C9** 49 42N 54 45W
Twin Bridges, *U.S.A.* **158 D7** 45 33N 112 20W
Twin City, *U.S.A.* **152 C7** 32 35N 82 10W
Twin Falls, *Canada* **141 B7** 53 30N 64 32W
Twin Falls, *U.S.A.* **158 E6** 42 34N 114 28W
Twin Hills, *U.S.A.* **144 G8** 59 23N 159 58W
Twin Lakes, *U.S.A.* **152 E6** 30 43N 83 13W
Twin Valley, *U.S.A.* **154 B6** 47 16N 96 16W
Twinnge, *Burma* **90 D6** 23 10N 96 2 E
Twinsburg, *U.S.A.* **150 E3** 41 18N 81 26W
Twistringen, *Germany* **30 C4** 52 48N 8 37 E
Twitchell Reservoir, *U.S.A.* **161 L6** 34 59N 120 19W
Two Boats Village, *Ascension I.* **9 g** 7 56 S 14 22W
Two Harbors, *U.S.A.* **154 B9** 47 2N 91 40W
Two Hills, *Canada* **142 C6** 53 43N 111 52W
Two Rivers, *U.S.A.* **148 C2** 44 9N 87 34W
Two Rocks, *Australia* **125 F2** 31 30 S 115 35 E
Two Thumbs Ra., *N.Z.* **131 D5** 43 45 S 170 44 E
Twofold B., *Australia* **129 D8** 37 8 S 149 59 E
Ty Ty, *U.S.A.* **152 D6** 31 28N 83 39W
Tyachiv, *Ukraine* **59 H2** 48 1N 23 35 E
Tybee Island , *U.S.A.* **152 C9** 32 1N 80 51W
Tychy, *Poland* **55 H5** 50 9N 18 59 E
Tyczyn, *Poland* **55 J9** 49 58N 22 2 E
Tydal, *Norway* **18 A8** 63 4N 11 34 E
Tyin, *Norway* **18 C5** 61 18N 8 15 E
Tykocin, *Poland* **55 E9** 53 13N 22 46 E
Tyler, *Minn., U.S.A.* **154 C6** 44 18N 96 8W
Tyler, *Tex., U.S.A.* **155 J7** 32 21N 95 18W
Tyligul →, *Ukraine* **59 J6** 47 4N 30 57 E
Tylldal, *Norway* **18 B7** 62 8N 10 48 E
Týn nad Vltavou, *Czech Rep.* **34 B7** 49 13N 14 26 E
Tynda, *Russia* **67 D13** 55 10N 124 43 E
Tyndall, *U.S.A.* **154 D6** 43 0N 97 50W
Tyne →, *U.K.* **20 C6** 54 59N 1 32W
Tyne & Wear □, *U.K.* **20 B6** 55 6N 1 17W
Týnec nad Sázavou, *Czech Rep.* **34 B7** 49 50N 14 36 E
Tynemouth, *U.K.* **20 B6** 55 1N 1 26W
Tynset, *Norway* **18 B7** 62 17N 10 47 E
Tyonek, *U.S.A.* **144 F10** 61 4N 151 8W
Tyre = Sūr, *Lebanon* **103 B4** 33 19N 35 16 E
Tyresta Nationalpark △, *Sweden* **16 E12** 59 12N 18 14 E
Tyrifjorden, *Norway* **18 D7** 60 2N 10 8 E
Tyringe, *Sweden* **17 H7** 56 9N 13 35 E
Tyristrand, *Norway* **18 D7** 60 4N 10 6 E
Tyrnyauz, *Russia* **61 J6** 43 21N 42 45 E
Tyrol = Tirol □, *Austria* **34 D3** 47 3N 10 43 E
Tyrone, *U.S.A.* **150 F6** 40 40N 78 14W
Tyrone □, *U.K.* **23 B4** 54 38N 7 11W
Tyrrell →, *Australia* **128 C5** 35 26 S 142 51 E
Tyrrell, L., *Australia* **128 C5** 35 20 S 142 50 E
Tyrrell L., *Canada* **143 A7** 63 7N 105 27W
Tyrrhenian Sea, *Medit. S.* **12 G8** 40 0N 12 30 E
Tysfjorden, *Norway* **14 B17** 68 7N 16 25 E
Tysnes, *Norway* **18 D2** 60 1N 5 30 E
Tysnesøya, *Norway* **18 D2** 60 0N 5 35 E
Tysse, *Norway* **18 D2** 60 23N 5 47 E
Tyssedal, *Norway* **18 D3** 60 7N 6 35 E
Tystberga, *Sweden* **17 F11** 58 51N 17 15 E
Tytuvėnai, *Lithuania* **54 C10** 55 36N 23 12 E
Tyub Karagan, Mys, *Kazakhstan* **61 H10** 44 40N 50 19 E
Tyuleni, Ostrova, *Kazakhstan* **61 H10** 45 2N 50 16 E
Tyuleniy, *Russia* **61 H8** 44 28N 47 30 E
Tyuleniy, Mys, *Azerbaijan* **61 K10** 40 12N 50 22 E
Tyulgan, *Russia* **64 E6** 52 22N 56 12 E
Tyumen, *Russia* **66 D7** 57 11N 65 29 E
Tyumen-Aryk = Tömenaryk, *Kazakhstan* **65 A3** 44 2N 67 1 E
Tyup = Tüp, *Kyrgyzstan* **65 B9** 42 45N 78 20 E
Tywi →, *U.K.* **21 F3** 51 48N 4 21W
Tywyn, *U.K.* **21 E3** 52 35N 4 5W
Tzaneen, *S. Africa* **117 C5** 23 47 S 30 9 E
Tzermiádhes, *Greece* **39 E6** 35 12N 25 29 E
Tzoumérka, Óros, *Greece* **48 B3** 39 30N 21 26 E
Tzukong = Zigong, *China* **76 C5** 29 15N 104 48 E

U

U Taphao, *Thailand* **86 F3** 12 35N 101 0 E
U.S.A. = United States of America ■, *N. Amer.* **146 C7** 37 0N 96 0W
U.S.S. Arizona Memorial ⌂, *U.S.A.* **145 B4** 21 22N 157 57W
U.S. Virgin Is. ☑, *W. Indies* **165 e** 18 20N 65 0W
Uacalla Iero, *Somali Rep.* **120 D2** 1 48N 42 38 E
Uachadi, Sierra = Uasadi-jidi, *Venezuela* **169 C4** 4 54N 65 18W
Uad Atui →, *W. Sahara* **110 D2** 20 4N 15 59W
Uad el Jat →, *W. Sahara* **110 C2** 26 47N 13 3W
Uad Erni, O. →, *W. Sahara* **110 C3** 26 45N 10 47W
Uainambi, *Colombia* **168 C4** 1 43N 69 51W
Uamba, *Angola* **115 D3** 7 21 S 16 10 E
Uanle Uen, *Somali Rep.* **120 D2** 2 37N 44 54 E
Uarsciek, *Somali Rep.* **120 D3** 2 28N 45 55 E
Uasadi-jidi, *Venezuela* **169 C4** 4 54N 65 18W
Uascen, *Somali Rep.* **120 D2** 4 11N 43 13 E
Uatumã →, *Brazil* **169 D6** 2 26 S 57 37W
Uauá, *Brazil* **170 C4** 9 50 S 39 28W
Uaupés, *Brazil* **168 D4** 0 8 S 67 5W
Uaupés →, *Brazil* **168 C4** 0 2N 67 16W
Uaxactún, *Guatemala* **164 C2** 17 25N 89 29W
Ub, *Serbia, Yug.* **50 B4** 44 28N 20 6 E
Ubá, *Brazil* **171 F3** 21 8 S 43 0W
Uba, *Nigeria* **113 C7** 10 29N 13 13 E
Ubai, *Papua N. G.* **132 C6** 5 39 S 150 38 E
Ubaitaba, *Brazil* **171 D4** 14 18 S 39 20W
Ubangi = Oubangi →, *Dem. Rep. of the Congo* **114 C3** 0 30 S 17 50 E
Ubaté, *Colombia* **168 B3** 5 19N 73 49W
Ubauro, *Pakistan* **92 E3** 28 15N 69 45 E
Ubay, *Phil.* **81 F5** 10 3N 124 28 E
Ubaye →, *France* **29 D10** 44 28N 6 18 E
Ubayyiḍ, W. al →, *Iraq* **101 F10** 32 34N 43 48 E
Ube, *Japan* **72 D3** 33 56N 131 15 E
Úbeda, *Spain* **43 G7** 38 3N 3 23W
Uberaba, *Brazil* **171 E2** 19 50 S 47 55W
Uberaba, L., *Brazil* **173 D6** 17 30 S 57 50W
Uberlândia, *Minas Gerais, Brazil* **171 E2** 19 0 S 48 20W
Uberlândia, *Roraima, Brazil* **169 C6** 0 48N 59 20W
Überlingen, *Germany* **31 H5** 47 46N 9 10 E
Überlinger See, *Germany* **33 A8** 47 45N 9 9 E
Ubiaja, *Nigeria* **113 D6** 6 41N 6 22 E
Ubin, Pulau, *Singapore* **87 d** 1 25N 103 56 E
Ubolratna Res., *Thailand* **86 D4** 16 45N 102 30 E
Ubombo, *S. Africa* **117 D5** 27 31 S 32 4 E
Ubon Ratchathani, *Thailand* **86 E5** 15 15N 104 50 E
Ubondo, *Dem. Rep. of the Congo* **118 C2** 0 55 S 25 42 E
Ubort →, *Belarus* **59 F5** 52 6N 28 30 E
Ubrique, *Spain* **43 J5** 36 41N 5 27W
Ubud, *Indonesia* **79 J18** 8 30 S 115 16 E
Ubuna, *Solomon Is.* **133 N11** 10 11 S 161 24 E
Ubundu, *Dem. Rep. of the Congo* **118 C2** 0 22 S 25 30 E
Ucayali →, *Peru* **172 A3** 4 30 S 73 30W
Uchab, *Namibia* **116 B2** 19 47 S 17 42 E
Uchaly, *Russia* **64 D7** 54 19N 59 27 E
Uchiko, *Japan* **72 D4** 33 33N 132 39 E
Uchiura-Wan, *Japan* **70 C10** 42 25N 140 40 E
Uchiza, *Peru* **172 B2** 8 25 S 76 20W
Uchqŭrgan, *Uzbekistan* **65 C6** 41 6N 72 4 E
Uchquduq, *Uzbekistan* **66 E7** 41 50N 62 50 E
Uchte, *Germany* **30 C4** 52 30N 8 54 E
Uchur →, *Russia* **67 D14** 58 48N 130 35 E
Uckermark, *Germany* **30 B9** 53 5N 13 30 E
Uckkulach, *Uzbekistan* **65 C3** 40 33N 67 11 E
Ucluelet, *Canada* **142 D3** 48 57N 125 32W
Ucua, *Angola* **115 D2** 8 43 S 14 8 E
Uda →, *Russia* **67 D14** 54 42N 135 14 E
Udagamandalam, *India* **95 J3** 11 30N 76 44 E
Udainagar, *India* **92 H7** 22 33N 76 13 E
Udaipur, *Raj., India* **92 G5** 24 36N 73 44 E
Udaipur, *Tripura, India* **90 D3** 23 32N 91 30 E
Udaipur Garhi, *Nepal* **93 F12** 27 0N 86 35 E
Udala, *India* **93 J12** 21 35N 86 34 E
Udalguri, *India* **90 B4** 26 46N 92 8 E
Udayagiri, *Andhra Pradesh, India* **95 G4** 14 52N 79 19 E
Udayagiri, *Orissa, India* **94 D7** 20 8N 84 23 E
Udbina, *Croatia* **45 D12** 44 31N 15 47 E
Uddeholm, *Sweden* **16 D7** 60 1N 13 38 E
Uddevalla, *Sweden* **17 F5** 58 21N 11 55 E
Uddjaur, *Sweden* **14 D17** 65 56N 17 49 E
Uden, *Neths.* **24 C5** 51 40N 5 37 E
Udgir, *India* **94 E3** 18 25N 77 5 E
Udhampur, *India* **93 C6** 33 0N 75 5 E
Udi, *Nigeria* **113 D6** 6 17N 7 21 E
Údine, *Italy* **45 B10** 46 3N 13 14 E
Udmurtia □, *Russia* **64 C4** 57 30N 52 30 E
Udon Thani, *Thailand* **86 D4** 17 29N 102 46 E
Udu Pt., *Fiji* **133 A3** 16 9 S 179 57W
Udumalaippettai, *India* **95 J3** 10 35N 77 15 E
Udupi, *India* **95 H2** 13 25N 74 42 E
Udva, *India* **94 D1** 20 5N 73 0 E
Udvoy Balkan, *Bulgaria* **51 D10** 42 50N 26 50 E
Udzungwa Nat. Park △, *Tanzania* **118 D4** 7 52 S 36 35 E
Udzungwa Range, *Tanzania* **119 D4** 9 30 S 35 10 E
Ueckermünde, *Germany* **30 B10** 53 44N 14 1 E
Ueda, *Japan* **73 A10** 36 24N 138 16 E
Uedineniya, Os., *Russia* **6 B12** 78 0N 85 0 E
Uel Scimbirro, *Somali Rep.* **120 D2** 2 23N 44 14 E
Uele →, *Dem. Rep. of the Congo* **114 B4** 3 45N 24 45 E
Uelen, *Russia* **67 C19** 66 10N 170 0W
Uelzen, *Germany* **30 C6** 52 57N 10 32 E
Ueno, *Japan* **73 C8** 34 45N 136 8 E
Uetendorf, *Switz.* **32 C5** 46 47N 7 34 E
Uetersen, *Germany* **30 B5** 53 40N 9 40 E
Uetze, *Germany* **30 C6** 52 28N 10 11 E
Ufa, *Russia* **64 D6** 54 45N 55 55 E
Ufa →, *Russia* **64 D6** 54 40N 56 0 E
Uffenheim, *Germany* **31 F6** 49 33N 10 14 E
Ugab →, *Namibia* **116 C1** 20 55 S 13 30 E
Ugalla →, *Tanzania* **118 D3** 5 8 S 30 42 E
Ugalla River Game Reserve ⌂, *Tanzania* **118 D3** 5 50 S 31 54 E
Ugam Tizmasi, *Kazakhstan* **65 B5** 42 20N 70 30 E
Uganda ■, *Africa* **118 B3** 2 0N 32 0 E
Ugento, *Italy* **47 C11** 39 56N 18 10 E
Ugep, *Nigeria* **113 D6** 5 53N 8 2 E
Ughelli, *Nigeria* **113 D6** 5 33N 6 0 E
Ugie, *S. Africa* **117 E4** 31 10 S 28 13 E
Ugíjar, *Spain* **43 J7** 36 58N 3 7W
Ugine, *France* **29 C10** 45 45N 6 25 E
Uglegorsk, *Russia* **67 E15** 49 5N 142 2 E
Ugleuralskiy, *Russia* **64 B6** 59 8N 57 35 E
Uglich, *Russia* **58 D10** 57 33N 38 20 E
Ugljan, *Croatia* **45 D12** 44 12N 15 10 E
Ugljane, *Croatia* **45 E13** 43 35N 16 46 E
Ugra →, *Russia* **58 E9** 54 30N 36 7 E
Ugŭrchin, *Bulgaria* **51 C8** 43 6N 24 26 E
Uh →, *Slovak Rep.* **35 C15** 48 37N 22 0 E
Uherské Hradiště, *Czech Rep.* **35 B10** 49 4N 17 30 E
Uherský Brod, *Czech Rep.* **35 B10** 49 1N 17 40 E
Úhlava →, *Czech Rep.* **34 B6** 49 45N 13 24 E
Uhlenhorst, *Namibia* **116 C2** 23 45 S 17 55 E
Uhrichsville, *U.S.A.* **150 F3** 40 24N 81 21W
Uibhist a Deas = South Uist, *U.K.* **22 D1** 57 20N 7 15W
Uibhist a Tuath = North Uist, *U.K.* **22 D1** 57 40N 7 15W
Uiche, *Angola* **115 E4** 12 2 S 20 51 E
Uig, *U.K.* **22 D2** 57 35N 6 21W
Uíge, *Angola* **115 D2** 7 30 S 14 40 E
Uíge □, *Angola* **115 D3** 7 0 S 16 0 E
Uiha, *Tonga* **133 P13** 19 54 S 174 25W
Uijŏngbu, *S. Korea* **75 F14** 37 48N 127 0 E
Ŭiju, *N. Korea* **75 D13** 40 15N 124 35 E
Uinta Mts., *U.S.A.* **158 F8** 40 45N 110 30W
Uis, *Namibia* **116 B2** 21 8 S 14 49 E
Uitenhage, *S. Africa* **116 E4** 33 40 S 25 28 E
Uithuizen, *Neths.* **24 A6** 53 24N 6 41 E
Ujazd, *Poland* **55 H5** 50 23N 18 21 E
Újfehértó, *Hungary* **52 C6** 47 49N 21 41 E
Ujh →, *India* **92 C6** 32 10N 75 18 E
Ujhani, *India* **93 F8** 28 0N 79 6 E
Uji, *Japan* **73 C7** 34 53N 135 48 E
Uji-guntō, *Japan* **71 J4** 31 15N 129 25 E
Ujjain, *India* **92 H6** 23 9N 75 43 E
Ujście, *Poland* **55 E3** 53 3N 16 45 E
Újszász, *Hungary* **52 C5** 47 19N 20 7 E
Ujung Pandang, *Indonesia* **82 C1** 5 10 S 119 20 E
Uka, *Russia* **67 D17** 57 50N 162 0 E
Ukara I., *Tanzania* **118 C3** 1 50 S 33 0 E
Uke-Shima, *Japan* **71 K4** 28 2N 129 14 E
Ukerewe I., *Tanzania* **118 C3** 2 0 S 33 0 E
Ukholovo, *Russia* **60 D5** 53 47N 40 30 E
Ukhrul, *India* **90 C5** 25 10N 94 25 E
Ukhta, *Russia* **56 B9** 63 34N 53 41 E
Uki Ni Masi, *Solomon Is.* **133 N11** 10 15 S 161 47 E
Ukiah, *U.S.A.* **160 F3** 39 9N 123 13W
Ukmergė, *Lithuania* **15 J21** 55 15N 24 45 E
Ukraine ■, *Europe* **59 H7** 49 0N 32 0 E
Uku, *Angola* **115 E2** 11 24 S 14 22 E
Ukwi, *Botswana* **116 C3** 23 29 S 20 30 E
Ulaan-Uul, *Mongolia* **74 B6** 44 13N 111 10 E
Ulaanbaatar, *Mongolia* **67 E11** 47 55N 106 53 E
Ulaangom, *Mongolia* **68 A4** 50 5N 92 10 E
Ulaanjirem, *Mongolia* **74 B3** 45 5N 105 30 E
Ulak I., *U.S.A.* **144 L3** 51 22N 178 57W
Ulamambri, *Australia* **129 A8** 31 19 S 149 23 E
Ulamba, *Dem. Rep. of the Congo* **119 D1** 9 3 S 23 38 E
Ulamona, *Papua N. G.* **132 C6** 5 0 S 151 15 E
Ulan Bator = Ulaanbaatar, *Mongolia* **67 E11** 47 55N 106 53 E
Ulan Erge, *Russia* **61 G7** 46 19N 44 53 E
Ulan Khol, *Russia* **61 H8** 45 18N 47 4 E
Ulan Ude, *Russia* **67 D11** 51 45N 107 40 E
Ulanbel, *Kazakhstan* **65 A5** 44 50N 71 7 E
Ulanów, *Poland* **55 H9** 50 30N 22 16 E
Ulaş, *Sivas, Turkey* **100 C7** 39 26N 37 2 E
Ulaş, *Tekirdağ, Turkey* **51 E11** 41 14N 27 42 E
Ulawa, *Solomon Is.* **133 M11** 9 46 S 161 57 E
Ulaya, *Morogoro, Tanzania* **118 D4** 7 3 S 36 55 E
Ulaya, *Tabora, Tanzania* **118 C3** 4 25 S 33 30 E
Ulcinj, *Montenegro, Yug.* **50 E3** 41 58N 19 10 E
Ulco, *S. Africa* **116 D3** 28 21 S 24 15 E
Uleåborg = Oulu, *Finland* **14 D21** 65 1N 25 29 E
Ulefoss, *Norway* **18 E6** 59 17N 9 16 E
Ulëz, *Albania* **50 E3** 41 46N 19 54 E
Ulfborg, *Denmark* **17 H2** 56 16N 8 20 E
Ulhasnagar, *India* **94 E1** 19 15N 73 10 E
Uliastay = Ulyasutay, *Mongolia* **68 B4** 47 56N 97 28 E
Uljma, *Serbia, Yug.* **52 E6** 45 2N 21 10 E
Ulla →, *Spain* **42 C2** 42 39N 8 44W
Ulladulla, *Australia* **129 C9** 35 21 S 150 29 E
Ullapool, *U.K.* **22 D3** 57 54N 5 9W
Ullared, *Sweden* **17 G6** 57 8N 12 42 E
Ulldecona, *Spain* **40 E5** 40 36N 0 20 E
Ullswater, *U.K.* **20 C5** 54 34N 2 52W
Ullŭng-do, *S. Korea* **71 F5** 37 30N 130 30 E
Ulm, *Germany* **31 G5** 48 23N 9 58 E
Ulmarra, *Australia* **127 D5** 29 37 S 153 4 E
Ulmeni, *Buzău, Romania* **53 E11** 45 4N 26 40 E
Ulmeni, *Maramureş, Romania* **53 C8** 47 28N 23 18 E
Ulonguè, *Mozam.* **119 E3** 14 37 S 34 19 E
Ulricehamn, *Sweden* **17 G7** 57 46N 13 26 E
Ulrichen, *Switz.* **33 C6** 46 30N 8 18 E
Ulrika, *Sweden* **17 F9** 58 5N 15 23 E
Ulsan, *S. Korea* **75 G15** 35 20N 129 15 E
Ulsberg, *Norway* **18 B6** 62 45N 10 0 E
Ulsta, *U.K.* **22 A7** 60 30N 1 9W
Ulsteinvik, *Norway* **18 B2** 62 21N 5 53 E
Ulster □, *U.K.* **23 B5** 54 35N 6 30W
Ulstrem, *Bulgaria* **51 D10** 42 1N 26 27 E
Ultima, *Australia* **128 C5** 35 30 S 143 18 E
Ulubat Gölü, *Turkey* **51 F12** 40 9N 28 35 E
Ulubey, *Turkey* **49 C11** 38 25N 29 18 E
Uluborlu, *Turkey* **49 C12** 38 4N 30 28 E
Uluçinar, *Turkey* **100 D6** 36 21N 35 57 E
Uludağ, *Turkey* **51 F13** 40 4N 29 13 E
Uludağ Milli Parki △, *Turkey* **51 F13** 40 5N 29 12 E
Uludere, *Turkey* **101 D10** 37 28N 42 42 E
Uluqqat, *China* **65 D7** 39 48N 74 15 E
Uluguru Mts., *Tanzania* **118 D4** 7 15 S 37 40 E
Ulukışla, *Turkey* **100 D6** 37 33N 34 28 E
Ulungur He →, *China* **68 B3** 47 1N 87 24 E
Ulupalakua, *U.S.A.* **145 C5** 20 39N 156 24W
Uluru = Ayers Rock, *Australia* **125 E5** 25 23 S 131 5 E
Uluru-Kata Tjuta Nat. Park △, *Australia* **125 E5** 25 19 S 131 1 E
Ulutau, *Kazakhstan* **66 E7** 48 39N 67 1 E
Uluwatu, *Indonesia* **79 K18** 8 50 S 115 5 E
Ulva, *U.K.* **22 E2** 56 29N 6 13W
Ulverston, *U.K.* **20 C4** 54 13N 3 5W
Ulverstone, *Australia* **127 G4** 41 11 S 146 11 E
Ulvik, *Norway* **18 D3** 60 35N 6 54 E
Ulya, *Russia* **67 D15** 59 10N 142 0 E
Ulyanovsk = Simbirsk, *Russia* **60 C9** 54 20N 48 25 E
Ulyasutay, *Mongolia* **68 B4** 47 56N 97 28 E
Ulysses, *U.S.A.* **155 G4** 37 35N 101 22W
Umag, *Croatia* **45 C10** 45 26N 13 31 E
Umala, *Bolivia* **172 D4** 17 25 S 68 5W
Uman, *Ukraine* **59 H6** 48 40N 30 12 E
Umarkhed, *India* **94 E3** 19 37N 77 46 E
Umarpada, *India* **92 J5** 21 27N 73 30 E
Umatac, *Guam* **133 R15** 13 18N 144 39 E
Umatilla, *U.S.A.* **158 D4** 45 55N 119 21W
Umba, *Russia* **56 A5** 66 42N 34 11 E
Umbagog L., *U.S.A.* **151 B13** 44 46N 71 3W
Umbakumba, *Australia* **126 A2** 13 47 S 136 50 E
Umbértide, *Italy* **45 E9** 43 18N 12 20 E
Umboi I., *Papua N. G.* **132 C4** 5 40 S 148 0 E
Umbrella Mts., *N.Z.* **131 F4** 45 35 S 169 5 E
Umbria □, *Italy* **45 F9** 42 53N 12 30 E
Ume älv →, *Sweden* **14 E19** 63 45N 20 20 E
Umeå, *Sweden* **14 E19** 63 45N 20 20 E
Umera, *Indonesia* **83 B3** 0 12 S 129 37 E
Umfolozi Game Reserve ⌂, *S. Africa* **117 D5** 28 18 S 31 50 E
Umfuli →, *Zimbabwe* **119 F2** 17 30 S 29 23 E
Umfurudzi Safari Area ⌂, *Zimbabwe* **119 F3** 17 6 S 31 40 E
Umgusa, *Zimbabwe* **119 F2** 19 29 S 27 52 E
Umiat, *U.S.A.* **144 B9** 69 22N 152 8W
Umim Urūmah, *Si. Arabia* **106 B4** 25 43N 36 35 E
Umka, *Serbia, Yug.* **50 B4** 44 40N 20 19 E
Umkomaas, *S. Africa* **117 E5** 30 13 S 30 48 E
Umm ad Daraj, J., *Jordan* **103 C4** 32 18N 35 48 E
Umm al Arānib, *Libya* **108 C2** 26 10N 14 43 E
Umm al Qaywayn, *U.A.E.* **97 E7** 25 30N 55 35 E
Umm al Qittayn, *Jordan* **103 C5** 32 18N 36 40 E
Umm al'Abīd, *Libya* **108 C3** 27 31N 15 2 E
Umm Arda, *Sudan* **107 D3** 15 17N 32 31 E
Umm Bāb, *Qatar* **97 E6** 25 12N 50 48 E
Umm Badr, *Sudan* **107 E2** 14 13N 27 58 E
Umm Baiyud, *Sudan* **107 E3** 12 5N 31 40 E
Umm Bel, *Sudan* **107 E2** 13 35N 28 0 E
Umm Birkah, *Si. Arabia* **106 B4** 27 44N 36 31 E
Umm Boim, *Sudan* **107 E2** 11 43N 25 27 E
Umm Dam, *Sudan* **107 E3** 13 45N 30 59 E
Umm Debi, *Sudan* **107 E3** 14 37N 30 23 E
Umm Dubban, *Sudan* **107 D3** 15 23N 32 52 E
Umm el Fahm, *Israel* **103 C4** 32 31N 35 9 E
Umm Gafala, *Sudan* **107 E2** 13 22N 27 15 E
Umm Gimala, *Sudan* **107 E2** 11 27N 28 12 E
Umm Inderaba, *Sudan* **106 D3** 15 58N 30 41 E
Umm Keddada, *Sudan* **107 E2** 13 33N 26 35 E
Umm Koweika, *Sudan* **107 E3** 13 10N 32 16 E
Umm Lajj, *Si. Arabia* **96 E3** 25 0N 37 23 E
Umm Merwa, *Sudan* **106 D3** 18 4N 32 30 E
Umm Qantur, *Sudan* **107 E3** 14 17N 31 22 E
Umm Qurein, *Sudan* **107 F2** 9 58N 28 55 E
Umm Ruwaba, *Sudan* **107 E3** 12 50N 31 20 E
Umm Saiyala, *Sudan* **107 E3** 14 25N 31 10 E
Umm Shanqa, *Sudan* **107 E2** 13 14N 27 14 E
Umm Shutur, *Sudan* **107 F3** 7 17N 33 14 E
Umm Sidr, *Sudan* **107 E2** 14 29N 25 10 E
Umm Zehetir, *Egypt* **106 J8** 28 48N 32 31 E
Umnak I., *U.S.A.* **144 K5** 53 15N 168 20W
Umniati →, *Zimbabwe* **119 F2** 16 49 S 28 45 E
Umpqua →, *U.S.A.* **158 E1** 43 40N 124 12W
Umpulo, *Angola* **115 E3** 12 38 S 17 42 E
Umred, *India* **94 D4** 20 51N 79 18 E
Umreth, *India* **92 H5** 22 41N 73 4 E
Umri, *India* **94 E3** 19 2N 77 39 E
Umtata, *S. Africa* **117 E4** 31 36 S 28 49 E
Umuahia, *Nigeria* **113 D6** 5 31N 7 26 E
Umuarama, *Brazil* **175 A5** 23 45 S 53 20W
Umuda I., *Papua N. G.* **132 E2** 8 29 S 143 46 E
Umurbey, *Turkey* **51 F10** 40 13N 26 36 E
Umvukwe Ra., *Zimbabwe* **119 F3** 16 45 S 30 45 E
Umzimvubu, *S. Africa* **117 E4** 31 38 S 29 33 E
Umzingwane →, *Zimbabwe* **119 G2** 22 12 S 29 56 E
Umzinto, *S. Africa* **117 E5** 30 15 S 30 45 E
Una, *India* **92 J4** 20 46N 71 8 E
Una →, *Bos.-H.* **45 D13** 45 0N 16 20 E
Unac →, *Bos.-H.* **45 D13** 44 30N 16 9 E
Unaðsdalur, *Iceland* **11 A4** 66 7N 22 36W
Unadilla, *Ga., U.S.A.* **152 C6** 32 16N 83 44W
Unadilla, *N.Y., U.S.A.* **151 D9** 42 20N 75 19W
Unaí, *Brazil* **171 E2** 16 23 S 46 53W
Unalakleet, *U.S.A.* **144 E7** 63 52N 160 47W
Unalaska, *U.S.A.* **144 K6** 53 53N 166 32W
Unalaska I., *U.S.A.* **144 K6** 53 35N 166 50W
'Unayzah, *Si. Arabia* **96 E4** 26 6N 43 58 E
'Unāzah, J., *Asia* **101 F8** 32 12N 39 18 E
Uncastillo, *Spain* **40 C3** 42 21N 1 8W
Uncía, *Bolivia* **172 D4** 18 25 S 66 40W
Uncompahgre Peak, *U.S.A.* **159 G10** 38 4N 107 28W
Uncompahgre Plateau, *U.S.A.* **159 G9** 38 20N 108 15W
Undara Volcanic Nat. Park △, *Australia* **126 B3** 18 14 S 144 41 E
Unden, *Sweden* **17 F8** 58 45N 14 25 E
Underbool, *Australia* **128 C4** 35 10 S 141 51 E
Undersaker, *Sweden* **16 A7** 63 19N 13 21 E
Undredal, *Norway* **18 D4** 60 57N 7 6 E
Unea I., *Papua N. G.* **132 C5** 4 53 S 149 9 E
Unecha, *Russia* **59 F7** 52 50N 32 37 E
Uneiuxi →, *Brazil* **168 D4** 0 37 S 65 34W
Unga I., *U.S.A.* **144 J7** 55 15N 160 40W
Ungarie, *Australia* **129 B7** 33 38 S 146 56 E
Ungarra, *Australia* **128 C2** 34 12 S 136 2 E
Ungat, *Papua N. G.* **132 B6** 2 40 S 150 15 E
Ungava, Pén. d', *Canada* **139 C12** 60 0N 74 0W
Ungava B., *Canada* **139 C13** 59 30N 67 30W
Ungeny = Ungheni, *Moldova* **53 C12** 47 11N 27 51 E
Unggi, *N. Korea* **75 C16** 42 16N 130 28 E
Ungheni, *Moldova* **53 C12** 47 11N 27 51 E
Unguala →, *Ethiopia* **107 F5** 8 6N 41 9 E
Ungwana B., *Kenya* **118 C5** 2 40 S 40 20 E
Ungwatiri, *Sudan* **107 D4** 16 52N 36 10 E
Uni, *Russia* **60 B10** 57 46N 51 31 E
União, *Brazil* **170 B3** 4 35 S 42 52W
União da Vitória, *Brazil* **175 B5** 26 13 S 51 5W
União dos Palmares, *Brazil* **170 C4** 9 10 S 36 2W
Uničov, *Czech Rep.* **35 B10** 49 46N 17 8 E
Uniejów, *Poland* **55 G5** 51 59N 18 46 E
Unije, *Croatia* **45 D11** 44 40N 14 15 E
Unimak I., *U.S.A.* **144 J7** 54 45N 164 0W
Unimak Pass, *U.S.A.* **144 J6** 54 15N 164 30W
Unini →, *Brazil* **169 D5** 1 41 S 61 31W
Union, *Miss., U.S.A.* **155 J10** 32 34N 89 7W
Union, *Mo., U.S.A.* **156 F6** 38 27N 91 0W
Union, *Ohio, U.S.A.* **157 E12** 39 55N 84 12W
Union, *S.C., U.S.A.* **149 H5** 34 43N 81 37W
Union City, *Calif., U.S.A.* **160 H4** 37 36N 122 1W
Union City, *Ga., U.S.A.* **152 B5** 33 35N 84 33W
Union City, *N.J., U.S.A.* **151 F10** 40 45N 74 2W
Union City, *Ohio, U.S.A.* **157 D12** 40 12N 84 48W
Union City, *Pa., U.S.A.* **150 E5** 41 54N 79 51W
Union City, *Tenn., U.S.A.* **155 G10** 36 26N 89 3W
Union Gap, *U.S.A.* **158 C3** 46 33N 120 28W
Union Grove, *U.S.A.* **157 B8** 42 41N 88 3W
Union Park, *U.S.A.* **153 G8** 28 34N 81 17W
Union Point, *U.S.A.* **152 B6** 33 37N 83 4W
Union Springs, *U.S.A.* **152 C4** 32 9N 85 43W
Union Star, *U.S.A.* **156 E2** 39 59N 94 36W
Uniondale, *S. Africa* **116 E3** 33 39 S 23 7 E
Uniontown, *Ky., U.S.A.* **157 G9** 37 47N 87 56W
Uniontown, *Pa., U.S.A.* **148 F6** 39 54N 79 44W
Unionville, *Ga., U.S.A.* **152 D6** 31 26N 83 30W
Unionville, *Mo., U.S.A.* **156 D3** 40 29N 93 1W
Unirea, *Romania* **53 F12** 44 15N 27 35 E
United Arab Emirates ■, *Asia* **97 F7** 23 50N 54 0 E
United Arab Republic = Egypt ■, *Africa* **106 B3** 28 0N 31 0 E
United Kingdom ■, *Europe* **19 D5** 54 0N 2 0W
United States of America ■, *N. Amer.* **146 C7** 37 0N 96 0W
Unity, *Canada* **143 C7** 52 30N 109 5W
Universales, Mtes., *Spain* **40 E3** 40 18N 1 33W
University City, *U.S.A.* **156 F6** 38 40N 90 20W
University Park, *U.S.A.* **159 K10** 32 17N 106 45W
Unjha, *India* **92 H5** 23 46N 72 24 E
Unmet, *Vanuatu* **133 F5** 16 8 S 167 15 E
Unna, *Germany* **30 D3** 51 32N 7 42 E
Unnao, *India* **93 F9** 26 35N 80 30 E
Uno, Ilha, *Guinea-Biss.* **112 C1** 11 15N 16 13W
Unpongkor, *Vanuatu* **133 H6** 18 50 S 168 59 E
Unsengedsi →, *Zimbabwe* **119 F3** 15 43 S 31 14 E
Unst, *U.K.* **22 A8** 60 44N 0 53W
Unstrut →, *Germany* **30 D7** 51 10N 11 48 E
Unter-engadin, *Switz.* **33 C10** 46 48N 10 20 E
Unterägeri, *Switz.* **33 B7** 47 8N 8 36 E
Unterfranken □, *Germany* **31 F5** 50 0N 10 0 E
Unterkulm, *Switz.* **32 B6** 47 18N 8 7 E
Unterschleissheim, *Germany* **31 G7** 48 17N 11 34 E
Unterseen, *Switz.* **32 C5** 46 41N 7 50 E
Unterthingau, *Germany* **33 A11** 47 46N 10 30 E
Unterwaldner Alpen, *Switz.* **33 C6** 46 55N 8 15 E
Unterwasser, *Switz.* **33 B8** 47 13N 9 19 E
Unuk →, *Canada* **142 B2** 56 5N 131 3W
Unye, *Turkey* **100 B7** 41 5N 37 15 E
Unzen-Amakusa Nat. Park △, *Japan* **72 E2** 32 15N 130 10 E
Unzen-Dake, *Japan* **72 E2** 32 45N 130 17 E
Unzha, *Russia* **60 A7** 58 0N 44 0 E
Unzha →, *Russia* **60 B6** 57 49N 43 47 E
Uors, *Switz.* **33 C8** 46 42N 9 12 E
Uozu, *Japan* **73 A9** 36 48N 137 24 E
Upata, *Venezuela* **169 B5** 8 1N 62 24W
Upatoi Cr. →, *U.S.A.* **152 C5** 32 22N 84 58W
Upemba, L., *Dem. Rep. of the Congo* **119 D2** 8 30 S 26 20 E
Upemba, Parc Nat. de l' △, *Dem. Rep. of the Congo* **119 D2** 9 0 S 26 35 E
Upernavik, *Greenland* **10 C5** 72 49N 56 20W
Upington, *S. Africa* **116 D3** 28 25 S 21 15 E
Upleta, *India* **92 J4** 21 46N 70 16 E
'Upolu, *Samoa* **133 W24** 13 58 S 172 0W
Upolu Pt., *U.S.A.* **145 C6** 20 16N 155 52W
Upper □, *Ghana* **113 C4** 10 30N 1 30W
Upper Alkali L., *U.S.A.* **158 F3** 41 47N 120 8W
Upper Arlington, *U.S.A.* **157 E13** 40 0N 83 4W
Upper Arrow L., *Canada* **142 C5** 50 30N 117 50W
Upper Austria = Oberösterreich □, *Austria* **34 C7** 48 10N 14 0 E
Upper Foster L., *Canada* **143 B7** 56 47N 105 20W
Upper Hutt, *N.Z.* **130 H4** 41 8 S 175 5 E
Upper Juba, *Somali Rep.* **120 D2** 3 0N 43 0 E
Upper Klamath L., *U.S.A.* **158 E3** 42 25N 121 55W
Upper Lake, *U.S.A.* **160 F4** 39 10N 122 54W
Upper Manilla, *Australia* **129 A9** 30 38 S 150 40 E
Upper Manzanilla, *Trin. & Tob.* **169 F9** 10 31N 61 4W
Upper Missouri River Breaks Nat. Monument ⌂, *U.S.A.* **158 C9** 47 50N 108 55W
Upper Musquodoboit, *Canada* **141 C7** 45 10N 62 58W
Upper Preoria L., *U.S.A.* **156 D7** 40 55N 89 27W
Upper Red L., *U.S.A.* **154 A7** 48 8N 94 45W
Upper Sandusky, *U.S.A.* **157 D13** 40 50N 83 17W
Upper Sheikh, *Somali Rep.* **120 C3** 9 56N 45 13 E
Upper Volta = Burkina Faso ■, *Africa* **112 C4** 12 0N 1 0W
Upphärad, *Sweden* **17 F6** 58 9N 12 19 E
Uppland, *Sweden* **16 E11** 59 59N 17 48 E
Upplands-Väsby, *Sweden* **16 E11** 59 31N 17 54 E
Uppsala, *Sweden* **16 E11** 59 53N 17 38 E
Uppsala län □, *Sweden* **16 D11** 60 0N 17 30 E
Upshi, *India* **93 C7** 33 48N 77 52 E
Upstart, C., *Australia* **126 B4** 19 41 S 147 45 E
Upton, *U.S.A.* **154 C2** 44 6N 104 38W

Ur, *Iraq* .... 96 D5 30 55N 46 25 E
Ura-Tyube = Uroteppa, *Tajikistan* . 65 D4 39 55N 69 1 E
Urabá, G. de, *Colombia* 168 B2 8 25N 76 53W
Urad Qianqi, *China* .... 74 D5 40 40N 108 30 E
Uraga-Suidō, *Japan* .... 73 B11 35 13N 139 45 E
Urakawa, *Japan* .... 70 C11 42 9N 142 47 E
Ural = Zhayyq →, *Kazakhstan* .... 57 E9 47 0N 51 48 E
Ural, *Australia* .... 129 B7 33 21 S 146 12 E
Ural Mts. = Uralskie Gory, *Eurasia* . 64 C7 60 0N 59 0 E
Uralla, *Australia* .... 129 A9 30 37 S 151 29 E
Uralsk = Oral, *Kazakhstan* ...... 60 E10 51 20N 51 20 E
Uralskie Gory, *Eurasia* .... 64 C7 60 0N 59 0 E
Urambo, *Tanzania* .... 118 D3 5 4 S 32 0 E
Urana, *Australia* .... 129 C7 35 15 S 146 21 E
Urana, L., *Australia* .... 129 C7 35 16 S 146 10 E
Urandangi, *Australia* .... 126 C2 21 32 S 138 14 E
Uranga, *Australia* .... 129 A10 30 31 S 153 1 E
Uranium City, *Canada* 143 B7 59 34N 108 37W
Uraricaá →, *Brazil* 169 C5 3 20N 61 56W
Uraricoera, *Brazil* 169 C5 3 27N 60 59W
Uraricoera →, *Brazil* 169 C5 3 2N 60 30W
Uravakonda, *India* .... 95 G3 14 57N 77 12 E
Urawa, *Japan* .... 73 B11 35 50N 139 40 E
Uray'irah, *Si. Arabia* .... 97 E6 25 57N 48 53 E
Urbana, *Ill., U.S.A.* 157 D8 40 7N 88 12W
Urbana, *Ohio, U.S.A.* 157 D13 40 7N 83 45W
Urbandale, *U.S.A.* 156 C3 41 38N 93 43W
Urbánia, *Italy* .... 45 E9 43 40N 12 31 E
Urbano Santos, *Brazil* .... 170 B3 3 12 S 43 23W
Urbel →, *Spain* 42 C7 42 21N 3 40W
Urbino, *Italy* .... 45 E9 43 43N 12 38 E
Urbión, Picos de, *Spain* 40 C2 42 1N 2 52W
Urcos, *Peru* .... 172 C3 13 40 S 71 38W
Urdaneta, *Phil.* .... 80 D3 15 59N 120 34 E
Urdinarrain, *Argentina* .... 174 C4 32 37 S 58 52W
Urdos, *France* 28 F3 42 51N 0 35W
Urdzhar, *Kazakhstan* .... 66 E9 47 5N 81 38 E
Ure →, *U.K.* 20 C6 54 5N 1 20W
Uren, *Russia* .... 60 B7 57 35N 45 55 E
Urepararapu, *Vanuatu* .... 133 C5 13 32 S 167 20 E
Ures, *Mexico* 162 B2 29 30N 110 30W
Ureshino, *Japan* .... 72 D1 33 6N 129 59 E
Urewera Nat. Park △, *N.Z.* ..... 130 E6 38 29 S 177 7 E
Urfa = Sanliurfa, *Turkey* .... 101 D8 37 12N 38 50 E
Urganch, *Uzbekistan* .... 66 E7 41 40N 60 41 E
Urgench = Urganch, *Uzbekistan* .. 66 E7 41 40N 60 41 E
Ürgüp, *Turkey* .... 96 B2 38 38N 34 56 E
Urgut, *Uzbekistan* .... 65 D3 39 23N 67 15 E
Uri, *India* .... 93 B6 34 8N 74 2 E
Uri □, *Switz.* .... 33 C7 46 43N 8 35 E
Uribante →, *Venezuela* 168 B3 7 25N 71 50W
Uribe, *Colombia* 168 C3 3 13N 74 24W
Uribia, *Colombia* 168 A3 11 43N 72 16W
Uricani, *Romania* .... 52 E8 45 20N 23 9 E
Urimba, *Angola* .... 115 E3 10 56 S 16 32 E
Uriondo, *Bolivia* .... 173 A3 21 41 S 64 41W
Urique, *Mexico* 162 B3 27 13N 107 55W
Urique →, *Mexico* 162 B3 26 29N 107 58W
Urirötstock, *Switz.* .... 33 C7 46 52N 8 32 E
Urk, *Neths.* .... 24 B5 52 39N 5 36 E
Urkiola, Parque Natural de △, *Spain* 40 B3 43 4N 2 38W
Urla, *Turkey* .... 49 C8 38 20N 26 47 E
Urlaţi, *Romania* .... 53 F11 44 59N 26 15 E
Urmia = Orūmīyeh, *Iran* .... 101 D11 37 40N 45 0 E
Urmia, L. = Orūmīyeh, Daryācheh-ye, *Iran* .... 101 D11 37 50N 45 30 E
Urmia, L. = Orūmīyeh, Daryācheh-ye, *Iran* .... 101 D11 37 50N 45 30 E
Urnäsch, *Switz.* .... 33 B8 47 19N 9 17 E
Urner Alpen, *Switz.* .... 33 C7 46 45N 8 45 E
Uroševac, *Kosovo, Yug.* .... 50 D5 42 23N 21 10 E
Uroteppa, *Tajikistan* .... 65 D4 39 55N 69 1 E
Uroyan, Montanas de, *Puerto Rico* 165 d 18 12N 67 0W
Urrao, *Colombia* 168 B2 6 20N 76 11W
Urshult, *Sweden* .... 17 H8 56 31N 14 50 E
Uruaçu, *Brazil* .... 171 D2 14 30 S 49 10W
Uruana, *Brazil* .... 171 E2 15 30 S 49 41W
Uruapan, *Mexico* 162 D4 19 30N 102 0W
Uruará →, *Brazil* .... 169 D7 3 42 S 53 51W
Uruará →, *Brazil* .... 169 D7 2 26 S 57 42W
Urubamba, *Peru* .... 172 C3 13 20 S 72 10W
Urubamba →, *Peru* .... 172 C3 10 43 S 73 48W
Urubaxi →, *Brazil* .... 169 D5 0 31 S 64 50W
Urubu →, *Brazil* .... 169 D6 2 25 S 58 25W
Uruçara, *Brazil* .... 169 D6 2 32 S 57 45W
Uruçuí, *Brazil* .... 170 C3 7 20 S 44 28W
Uruçuí, Serra do, *Brazil* .... 170 C3 9 0 S 44 45W
Uruçuí Prêto →, *Brazil* .... 170 C3 7 20 S 44 38W
Urucurea →, *Brazil* .... 171 E2 18 8 S 45 3W
Urucurituba, *Brazil* .... 169 D6 2 41 S 57 40W
Uruguai →, *Brazil* .... 175 B5 26 0 S 53 30W
Uruguaiana, *Brazil* .... 174 B4 29 50 S 57 0W
Uruguay ■, *S. Amer.* .... 174 C4 32 30 S 56 30W
Uruguay →, *S. Amer.* .... 174 C4 34 12 S 58 18W
Urumchi = Ürümqi, *China* ...... 66 E9 43 45N 87 45 E
Ürümqi, *China* .... 66 E9 43 45N 87 45 E
Urup →, *Russia* .... 61 H5 45 0N 41 10 E
Urup, Ostrov, *Russia* .... 67 E16 46 0N 151 0 E
Urutaí, *Brazil* .... 171 E2 17 28 S 48 12W
Uryupinsk, *Russia* .... 60 E5 50 45N 41 58 E
Urzhum, *Russia* .... 60 B9 57 10N 49 56 E
Urziceni, *Romania* .... 53 F11 44 40N 26 42 E
Usa, *Japan* .... 72 D3 33 31N 131 21 E
Usa →, *Russia* .... 56 A10 66 16N 59 49 E
Uşak, *Turkey* .... 49 C11 38 43N 29 28 E
Uşak □, *Turkey* .... 49 C11 38 30N 29 0 E
Usakos, *Namibia* .... 116 C2 21 54 S 15 31 E
Usborne, Mt., *Falk. Is.* .... 9 f 51 34N 59 55W
Ušče, *Serbia, Yug.* .... 50 C4 43 30N 20 39 E
Usedom, *Germany* .... 30 B10 53 55N 14 2 E
Usedom, Naturpark △, *Germany* . 30 B10 53 55N 14 0 E
Useless Loop, *Australia* .... 125 E1 26 8 S 113 23 E
'Usfān, *Si. Arabia* .... 98 B2 21 58N 39 27 E
Ush-Tobe, *Kazakhstan* .... 66 E8 45 16N 78 0 E
Ushant = Ouessant, Î. d', *France* .. 26 D1 48 28N 5 6W
Usharal, *Kazakhstan* .... 65 B5 43 53N 70 31 E
Ushashi, *Tanzania* .... 118 C3 1 59 S 33 57 E
Ushat, *Sudan* .... 107 F2 7 59N 29 28 E
'Ushayrih, *Si. Arabia* .... 106 C5 21 46N 40 42 E
Ushibuka, *Japan* .... 72 E2 32 11N 130 1 E
Ushuaia, *Argentina* .... 176 D3 54 50 S 68 23W
Ushumun, *Russia* .... 67 D13 52 47N 126 32 E
Usino, *Papua N. G.* .... 132 C3 5 32 S 145 23 E
Usk →, *U.K.* 21 F5 51 33N 2 58W
Uska, *India* .... 93 F10 27 12N 83 7 E
Uskedal, *Norway* .... 18 E2 59 56N 5 53 E
Üsküb = Skopje, *Macedonia* .... 50 D5 42 1N 21 26 E
Üsküdar, *Turkey* .... 51 F13 41 0N 29 5 E
Uslar, *Germany* .... 30 D5 51 39N 9 38 E
Usman, *Russia* .... 59 F10 52 5N 39 48 E
Usmat, *Uzbekistan* .... 65 D3 39 50N 66 53 E
Usoke, *Tanzania* .... 118 D3 5 8 S 32 24 E
Usolye, *Russia* .... 64 B6 59 25N 56 45 E
Usolye Sibirskoye, *Russia* ...... 67 D11 52 48N 103 40 E
Usoro, *Nigeria* .... 113 D6 5 33N 6 16 E
Uspallata, P. de, *Argentina* ..... 174 C2 32 37 S 69 22W
Uspenskiy, *Kazakhstan* .... 66 E8 48 41N 72 43 E
Ussel, *France* .... 28 C6 45 32N 2 18 E
Usson-du-Poitou, *France* .... 28 B4 46 16N 0 31 E
Ussuri →, *Asia* .... 70 A7 48 27N 135 0 E
Ussuriysk, *Russia* .... 67 E14 43 48N 131 59 E
Ussurka, *Russia* .... 70 B6 45 12N 133 31 E
Ust-Aldan = Batamay, *Russia* ... 67 C13 63 30N 129 15 E
Ust-Amginskoye = Khandyga, *Russia* . 67 C14 62 42N 135 35 E
Ust-Bolsheretsk, *Russia* .... 67 D16 52 50N 156 15 E
Ust-Buzulukskaya, *Russia* ...... 60 E6 50 8N 42 11 E
Ust-Chaun, *Russia* .... 67 C18 68 47N 170 30 E
Ust-Donetskiy, *Russia* .... 61 G5 47 35N 40 55 E
Ust-Ilimpeya = Yukta, *Russia* ... 67 C11 63 26N 105 42 E
Ust-Ilimsk, *Russia* .... 67 D11 58 3N 102 39 E
Ust-Ishim, *Russia* .... 66 D8 57 45N 71 10 E
Ust-Kamchatsk, *Russia* .... 67 D17 56 10N 162 28 E
Ust-Kamenogorsk = Öskemen, *Kazakhstan* .... 66 E9 50 0N 82 36 E
Ust-Khayryuzovo, *Russia* ...... 67 D16 57 15N 156 45 E
Ust-Kut, *Russia* .... 67 D11 56 50N 105 42 E
Ust-Kuyga, *Russia* .... 67 B14 70 1N 135 43 E
Ust-Labinsk, *Russia* .... 61 H4 45 15N 39 41 E
Ust-Luga, *Russia* .... 58 C5 59 35N 28 20 E
Ust-Maya, *Russia* .... 67 C14 60 30N 134 28 E
Ust-Mil, *Russia* .... 67 D14 59 40N 133 11 E
Ust-Nera, *Russia* .... 67 C15 64 35N 143 15 E
Ust-Nyukzha, *Russia* .... 67 D13 56 34N 121 37 E
Ust-Olenek, *Russia* .... 67 B12 73 0N 120 5 E
Ust-Omchug, *Russia* .... 67 C15 61 9N 149 38 E
Ust-Port, *Russia* .... 66 C9 69 40N 84 26 E
Ust-Tsilma, *Russia* .... 56 A9 65 28N 52 11 E
Ust Urt = Ustyurt Plateau, *Asia* .. 66 E6 44 0N 55 0 E
Ust-Usa, *Russia* .... 56 A10 66 2N 56 57 E
Ust-Vorkuta, *Russia* .... 56 A11 67 24N 64 0 E
Ustaoset, *Norway* .... 18 D2 60 30N 8 2 E
Ustaritz, *France* 28 E2 43 24N 1 27W
Uster, *Switz.* .... 33 B7 47 22N 8 43 E
Ústí nad Labem, *Czech Rep.* .... 34 A7 50 41N 14 3 E
Ústí nad Orlicí, *Czech Rep.* ..... 35 B9 49 58N 16 24 E
Ústica, *Italy* .... 46 D6 38 42N 13 11 E
Ustinov = Izhevsk, *Russia* ...... 64 C4 56 51N 53 14 E
Ustka, *Poland* .... 54 D3 54 35N 16 55 E
Ustroń, *Poland* .... 55 J5 49 43N 18 48 E
Ustrzyki Dolne, *Poland* .... 55 J9 49 27N 22 40 E
Ustupo, *Panama* 168 B2 9 27N 78 34W
Ustyurt Plateau, *Asia* .... 66 E6 44 0N 55 0 E
Ustyuzhna, *Russia* .... 58 C9 58 50N 36 32 E
Usu, *China* .... 68 B3 44 27N 84 40 E
Usuki, *Japan* .... 72 D3 33 8N 131 49 E
Usulután, *El Salv.* 164 D2 13 25N 88 28W
Usumacinta →, *Mexico* 163 D6 17 0N 91 0W
Usumbura = Bujumbura, *Burundi* . 118 C2 3 16 S 29 18 E
Usure, *Tanzania* .... 118 C3 4 40 S 34 22 E
Usutuo →, *Mozam.* .... 117 D5 26 48 S 32 7 E
Usva, *Russia* .... 56 A6 58 41N 57 37 E
Uta, *Indonesia* .... 83 B5 4 33 S 136 0 E
Utah □, *U.S.A.* 158 G8 39 20N 111 30W
Utah L., *U.S.A.* 158 F8 40 10N 111 58W
Utansjö, *Sweden* .... 16 B11 62 46N 17 55 E
Utara, Selat, *Malaysia* .... 87 c 5 28N 100 20 E
Utarni, *India* .... 92 F4 26 5N 71 58 E
Utatlan, *Guatemala* 164 C1 15 2N 91 11W
Ute Creek →, *U.S.A.* 155 H3 35 21N 103 50W
Utebo, *Spain* 40 D3 41 43N 1 0W
Utemurat, *Uzbekistan* .... 65 B2 42 6N 65 42 E
Utena, *Lithuania* .... 32 J1 55 27N 25 40 E
Utete, *Tanzania* .... 118 D4 8 0 S 38 45 E
Uthai Thani, *Thailand* .... 86 E3 15 22N 100 3 E
Uthal, *Pakistan* .... 92 G2 25 44N 66 40 E
Utiariti, *Brazil* .... 173 C6 13 0 S 58 10W
Utica, *N.Y., U.S.A.* 151 C9 43 6N 75 14W
Utica, *Ohio, U.S.A.* 150 F2 40 14N 82 27W
Utikuma L., *Canada* 142 B5 55 50N 115 30W
Utinga, *Brazil* .... 171 D3 12 6 S 41 5W
Utkela, *India* .... 94 D6 20 6N 83 10 E
Utne, *Norway* .... 18 D3 60 25N 6 37 E
Utnur, *India* .... 94 E4 19 22N 78 46 E
Uto, *Japan* .... 72 E2 32 41N 130 40 E
Utö, *Sweden* .... 16 F12 58 56N 18 16 E
Utopia, *Australia* .... 126 C1 22 14 S 134 33 E
Utraula, *India* .... 93 F10 27 19N 82 25 E
Utrecht, *Neths.* .... 24 B5 52 5N 5 8 E
Utrecht, *S. Africa* .... 117 D5 27 38 S 30 20 E
Utrecht □, *Neths.* .... 24 B5 52 6N 5 7 E
Utrera, *Spain* 43 H5 37 12N 5 48W
Utsira, *Norway* .... 18 E1 59 19N 4 53 E
Utsjoki, *Finland* .... 14 B22 69 51N 26 59 E
Utsunomiya, *Japan* .... 73 A11 36 30N 139 50 E
Uttar Pradesh □, *India* .... 93 F9 27 0N 80 0 E
Uttaradit, *Thailand* .... 86 D3 17 36N 100 5 E
Uttaranchal □, *India* .... 93 D8 30 0N 79 30 E
Uttoxeter, *U.K.* 20 E6 52 54N 1 52W
Utuado, *Puerto Rico* .... 165 d 18 16N 66 42W
Utva →, *Kazakhstan* .... 64 F4 51 28N 52 40 E
Uummannaq, *Greenland* 10 B4 77 0N 69 0W
Uummannarsuaq = Nunap Isua, *Greenland* 10 F6 59 48N 43 55W
Uusikaarlepyy, *Finland* .... 14 E20 63 32N 22 31 E
Uusikaupunki, *Finland* .... 15 F19 60 47N 21 25 E
Uva, *Russia* .... 60 B11 56 59N 52 13 E
Uvá →, *Colombia* 168 C3 3 41N 70 3W
Uvac →, *Serbia, Yug.* .... 50 C3 43 35N 19 30 E
Uvalda, *U.S.A.* 152 C7 32 2N 82 31W
Uvalde, *U.S.A.* 155 L5 29 13N 99 47W
Uvarovo, *Russia* .... 60 E6 51 59N 42 14 E
Uvat, *Russia* .... 66 D7 59 5N 68 50 E
Uvdal, *Norway* .... 18 D5 60 17N 8 48 E
Uvelskiy, *Russia* .... 64 D8 54 26N 61 22 E
Uvinza, *Tanzania* .... 118 D3 5 5 S 30 24 E
Uvira, *Dem. Rep. of the Congo* .. 118 C2 3 22 S 29 3 E
Uvs Nuur, *Mongolia* .... 68 A4 50 20N 92 30 E
Uwa, *Japan* .... 72 D3 33 22N 132 31 E
Uwajima, *Japan* .... 72 D3 33 10N 132 35 E
Uwanda Game Reserve △, *Tanzania* 118 D3 7 46 S 32 0 E
Uweinat, Jebel, *Sudan* .... 106 C1 21 54N 24 58 E
Uwekuli, *Indonesia* .... 82 B2 1 25 S 121 6 E
Uxbridge, *Canada* 150 B5 44 6N 79 8W
Uxin Qi, *China* .... 74 E5 38 50N 109 5 E
Uxmal, *Mexico* 163 C7 20 22N 89 46W
Uxmal, Ruinas, *Mexico* 163 C7 20 22N 89 46W
Uyak, *U.S.A.* 144 H9 57 38N 154 0W
Uyo, *Nigeria* .... 113 D6 5 1N 7 53 E
Uyu →, *Burma* .... 90 C5 24 51N 94 57 E
Uyuk = Oyyq, *Kazakhstan* ..... 65 A7 42 49N 70 58 E
Uyûn Mûsa, *Egypt* .... 102 F1 29 53N 32 40 E
Uyuni, *Bolivia* .... 172 E4 20 28 S 66 47W
Uzbekistan ■, *Asia* .... 65 C2 41 30N 65 0 E
Uzen, *Kazakhstan* .... 57 F9 43 29N 52 54 E
Uzen, Bolshoi →, *Kazakhstan* ... 61 F9 49 4N 49 56 E
Uzen, Mal →, *Kazakhstan* ..... 61 F9 49 4N 49 44 E
Uzerche, *France* .... 28 C5 45 25N 1 34 E
Uzès, *France* .... 29 D8 44 1N 4 26 E
Uzgen = Özgön, *Kyrgyzstan* .... 65 C6 40 46N 73 18 E
Uzh →, *Ukraine* .... 59 G6 51 15N 30 12 E
Uzhgorod = Uzhhorod, *Ukraine* .. 59 H2 48 36N 22 18 E
Uzhhorod, *Ukraine* .... 59 H2 48 36N 22 18 E
Užice, *Serbia, Yug.* .... 50 C3 43 55N 19 50 E
Uzlovaya, *Russia* .... 59 E10 53 59N 38 11 E
Üzümlü, *Turkey* .... 49 E11 36 44N 29 14 E
Uzunköprü, *Turkey* .... 49 F10 41 16N 26 43 E
Uzunkuyu, *Turkey* .... 49 C8 38 11N 26 33 E
Uzwil, *Switz.* .... 33 B8 47 26N 9 7 E
Uzyngash, *Kazakhstan* .... 65 B8 43 35N 76 20 E
Uzyngash, *Kazakhstan* .... 65 B8 43 13N 76 19 E

V

Vaal →, *S. Africa* .... 116 D3 29 4 S 23 38 E
Vaal Dam, *S. Africa* .... 117 D4 27 0 S 28 14 E
Vaalbos Nat. Park △, *S. Africa* .. 116 D3 28 22 S 24 20 E
Vaalwater, *S. Africa* .... 117 C4 24 15 S 28 8 E
Vaasa, *Finland* .... 14 E19 63 6N 21 38 E
Vabkent, *Uzbekistan* .... 65 C2 40 1N 64 30 E
Vabre, *France* .... 28 E6 43 42N 2 24 E
Vác, *Hungary* .... 52 C4 47 49N 19 10 E
Vacaria, *Brazil* .... 175 B5 28 31 S 50 52W
Vacata, *Fiji* .... 133 A3 17 15 S 179 31 W
Vacaville, *U.S.A.* 160 G5 38 21N 121 59W
Vaccarès, Étang de, *France* ..... 29 E8 43 32N 4 34 E
Vach = Vakh →, *Russia* .... 66 C8 60 45N 76 45 E
Vache, Î. à, *Haiti* 165 C5 18 2N 73 35W
Vada, *India* .... 92 K1 19 39N 73 8 E
Väddö, *Sweden* .... 16 D12 60 0N 18 50 E
Väderstad, *Sweden* .... 17 F8 58 19N 14 55 E
Vadheim, *Norway* .... 18 C2 61 13N 5 49 E
Vadnagar, *India* .... 92 H5 23 47N 72 40 E
Vadodara, *India* .... 92 H5 22 20N 73 10 E
Vadret, Piz, *Switz.* .... 33 C9 46 51N 9 58 E
Vadsø, *Norway* .... 14 A23 70 3N 29 50 E
Vadstena, *Sweden* .... 17 F8 58 28N 14 54 E
Vaduj, *India* .... 94 F2 17 36N 74 27 E
Vaduz, *Liech.* .... 33 B9 47 8N 9 31 E
Værlandet, *Norway* .... 18 C1 61 18N 4 44 E
Værøy, *Norway* .... 14 C15 67 40N 12 40 E
Vågåmo, *Norway* .... 18 C6 61 52N 9 6 E
Vágar, *Færoe Is.* 14 E9 62 5N 7 15W
Vaggeryd, *Sweden* .... 17 G8 57 30N 14 10 E
Vaghena, *Solomon Is.* .... 133 L9 7 25 S 157 45 E
Vagney, *France* .... 27 D13 48 1N 6 43 E
Vagnhärad, *Sweden* .... 17 F11 58 57N 17 33 E
Vagos, *Portugal* 42 E2 40 33N 8 42W
Vågsfjorden, *Norway* .... 14 B17 68 50N 16 50 E
Váh →, *Slovak Rep.* .... 35 D11 47 55N 18 0 E
Vahsel B., *Antarctica* .... 7 D1 75 0 S 35 0W
Vaï, *Greece* .... 39 E7 35 15N 26 18 E
Vaigach, *Russia* .... 66 B6 70 10N 59 0 E
Vaigai →, *India* .... 95 K4 9 15N 79 10 E
Vaiges, *France* 26 D6 48 2N 0 30W
Vaihingen, *Germany* .... 31 G4 48 54N 8 57 E
Vaijapur, *India* .... 94 E2 19 58N 74 45 E
Vaikam, *India* .... 95 K3 9 45N 76 25 E
Vail, *U.S.A.* 146 C5 39 40N 106 20W
Vailala →, *Papua N. G.* .... 132 D3 7 57 S 145 25 E
Vailly-sur-Aisne, *France* .... 27 C10 49 24N 3 31 E
Vaippar →, *India* .... 95 K4 9 0N 78 25 E
Vaisali →, *India* .... 93 F8 26 28N 78 53 E
Vaison-la-Romaine, *France* ..... 29 D9 44 14N 5 4 E
Vaitogi, *Amer. Samoa* .... 133 X24 14 24 S 170 44W
Vajpur, *India* .... 94 D1 21 24N 73 17 E
Vakaga □, *C.A.R.* .... 114 A4 9 48N 21 32 E
Vakarai, *Sri Lanka* .... 95 K5 8 8N 81 26 E
Vakarel, *Bulgaria* .... 50 D7 42 35N 23 40 E
Vakfikebir, *Turkey* .... 101 B8 41 2N 39 17 E
Vakh →, *Russia* .... 66 C8 60 45N 76 45 E
Vakhsh, *Tajikistan* .... 65 E4 37 6N 68 18 E
Vakhsh →, *Tajikistan* .... 65 D4 36 54N 68 1 E
Vakhtan, *Russia* .... 60 B8 57 53N 46 47 E
Vaksdal, *Norway* .... 18 D2 60 29N 5 45 E
Vakuta I., *Papua N. G.* .... 132 E6 8 51 S 151 10 E
Val, *Hungary* .... 52 C3 47 22N 18 40 E
Val-de-Marne □, *France* .... 27 D9 48 45N 2 28 E
Val-d'Isère, *France* .... 29 C10 45 27N 6 59 E
Val-d'Oise □, *France* .... 27 C9 49 5N 2 0 E
Val-d'Or, *Canada* 140 C4 48 7N 77 47W
Val Grande, Parco Nazionale della △, *Italy* .... 44 B5 46 3N 8 25 E
Val Marie, *Canada* 143 D7 49 15N 107 45W
Val Thorens, *France* .... 29 C10 45 20N 6 33 E
Valaam, *Russia* .... 58 B6 61 22N 30 57 E
Valadares, *Portugal* 42 D2 41 5N 8 38W
Valahia, *Romania* .... 52 F9 44 35N 25 0 E
Valaichenai, *Sri Lanka* .... 95 L5 7 54N 81 32 E
Valais □, *Switz.* .... 32 D5 46 12N 7 45 E
Valais, Alpes du, *Switz.* .... 32 D5 46 5N 7 35 E
Valandovo, *Macedonia* .... 50 E6 41 19N 22 34 E
Valašské Meziříčí, *Czech Rep.* ... 35 B10 49 29N 17 59 E
Valáxa, *Greece* .... 48 C6 38 50N 24 29 E
Vålberg, *Sweden* .... 16 F7 59 23N 13 11 E
Valbo, *Sweden* .... 16 D10 60 40N 17 0 E
Valbondione, *Italy* .... 44 B5 46 0N 10 1 E
Valcani, *Romania* .... 52 B5 46 0N 20 26 E
Vâlcea □, *Romania* .... 53 F9 45 0N 24 0 E
Valchetta, *Argentina* .... 176 B3 40 40 S 66 8W
Valdagno, *Italy* .... 45 C8 45 39N 11 18 E
Valdahon, *France* .... 27 E13 47 8N 6 21 E
Valdai Hills = Valdayskaya Vozvyshennost, *Russia* ... 58 D7 57 0N 33 30 E
Valday, *Russia* .... 58 D7 57 58N 33 9 E
Valdayskaya Vozvyshennost, *Russia* . 58 D7 57 0N 33 30 E
Valdeazogues →, *Spain* 43 G6 38 45N 4 55W
Valdecañas, Embalse de, *Spain* .. 42 F5 39 45N 5 25W
Valdemarsvik, *Sweden* .... 17 F10 58 14N 16 40 E
Valdemoro, *Spain* 42 E7 40 12N 3 40W
Valdepeñas, *Spain* 43 G7 38 43N 3 25W
Valderaduey →, *Spain* 42 D5 41 31N 5 42W
Valdérice, *Italy* .... 46 D5 38 1N 12 37 E
Valderrobres, *Spain* .... 40 E5 40 53N 0 9 E
Valdés, Pen., *Argentina* ...... 176 B4 42 30 S 63 45W
Valdez, *Ecuador* 168 C2 1 15N 79 0W
Valdez, *U.S.A.* 144 F11 61 7N 146 16W
Valdivia, *Chile* .... 174 A2 39 50 S 73 14W
Valdivia, *Colombia* 168 B2 7 11N 75 27W
Valdobbiádene, *Italy* .... 45 C8 45 54N 12 0 E
Valdosta, *U.S.A.* 152 E6 30 50N 83 17W
Valdoviño, *Spain* 42 A3 43 36N 8 8W
Valdres, *Norway* .... 18 C6 61 5N 9 5 E
Vale, *Georgia* .... 61 K6 41 30N 42 58 E
Vale, *U.S.A.* 158 E5 43 59N 117 15W
Vale of Glamorgan □, *U.K.* 21 F4 51 28N 3 25W
Vale lui Mihai, *Romania* ...... 52 C7 47 32N 22 11 E
Vălea Mărului, *Romania* ...... 53 E12 45 49N 27 42 E
Valemont, *Canada* 142 C5 52 50N 119 15W
Valença, *Brazil* .... 171 D4 13 20 S 39 5W
Valença do Piauí, *Brazil* ...... 170 C3 6 20 S 41 45W
Valença, *Portugal* 42 C2 42 1N 8 34W
Valençay, *France* .... 27 E8 47 9N 1 34 E
Valence = Valence d'Agen, *France* . 28 D4 44 6N 0 53 E
Valence, *France* .... 29 D8 44 57N 4 54 E
Valence d'Agen, *France* .... 28 D4 44 6N 0 53 E
Valencia, *Phil.* .... 81 H5 7 57N 125 9 E
Valencia, *Spain* 41 F4 39 27N 0 23W
Valencia, *Trin. & Tob.* 169 F9 10 37N 61 7W
Valencia, *U.S.A.* 159 J10 34 48N 106 43W
Valencia, *Venezuela* 168 A4 10 11N 68 0W
Valencia □, *Spain* 41 F4 39 20N 0 40W
Valencia (VLC) ✈, *Spain* 41 F4 39 29N 0 28W
Valencia, G. de, *Spain* .... 41 F5 39 30N 0 20 E
Valencia de Alcántara, *Spain* ... 42 F3 39 25N 7 14W
Valencia de Don Juan, *Spain* ... 42 C5 42 17N 5 31W
Valencia I., *Ireland* 23 E1 51 54N 10 22W
Valenciennes, *France* .... 27 B10 50 20N 3 34 E
Văleni, *Romania* .... 53 F9 44 15N 24 45 E

Vălenii de Munte, *Romania* .... 53 E11 45 11N 26 2 E
Valensole, *France* .... 29 E9 43 50N 5 59 E
Valentigney, *France* .... 27 E13 47 27N 6 51 E
Valentim, Sa. do, *Brazil* ...... 170 C3 6 0 S 43 30W
Valentine, *U.S.A.* 155 K2 30 35N 104 30W
Valenza, *Italy* .... 44 C5 45 1N 8 38 E
Våler, *Hedmark, Norway* ...... 18 D8 60 41N 11 50 E
Våler, *Østfold, Norway* .... 19 B8 59 29N 10 51 E
Valera, *Venezuela* 168 B3 9 19N 70 37W
Valesdir, *Vanuatu* .... 133 F6 16 47 S 168 10 E
Valga, *Estonia* .... 15 H22 57 47N 26 2 E
Valguarnera Caropepe, *Italy* ... 47 E7 37 30N 14 23 E
Valier, *U.S.A.* 158 B7 48 18N 112 16W
Valinco, G. de, *France* .... 29 G12 41 40N 8 52 E
Valjevo, *Serbia, Yug.* .... 50 B3 44 18N 19 53 E
Valka, *Latvia* .... 15 H21 57 42N 25 57 E
Valkeakoski, *Finland* .... 15 F20 61 16N 24 2 E
Vall de Uxó = La Vall d'Uixó, *Spain* . 16 E10 59 2N 16 20 E
Valla, *Sweden* .... 16 E10 59 2N 16 20 E
Valladolid, *Mexico* 163 C7 20 40N 88 11W
Valladolid, *Spain* 42 D6 41 38N 4 43W
Valladolid □, *Spain* 42 D6 41 38N 4 43W
Vallata, *Italy* .... 47 A8 41 2N 15 15 E
Valle, *Norway* .... 18 E4 59 13N 7 33 E
Valle d'Aosta □, *Italy* .... 44 C4 45 45N 7 15 E
Valle de Arán, *Spain* .... 40 C5 42 50N 0 55 E
Valle de la Pascua, *Venezuela* .. 168 B4 9 13N 66 0W
Valle de las Palmas, *Mexico* ... 161 N10 32 20N 116 43W
Valle de Santiago, *Mexico* 162 C4 20 25N 101 15W
Valle de Suchil, *Mexico* 162 C4 23 38N 103 55W
Valle de Zaragoza, *Mexico* 162 B3 27 28N 105 49W
Valle del Cauca □, *Colombia* ... 168 C2 3 45N 76 30W
Valle del Ticino, Parco Naturale △, *Italy* .... 44 C6 45 22N 9 0 E
Valle Fértil, Sierra del, *Argentina* . 174 C2 30 20 S 68 0W
Valle Gran Rey, *Canary Is.* 9 e1 28 5N 17 20W
Valle Hermoso, *Mexico* 163 B5 25 35N 97 40W
Valledupar, *Colombia* 168 A3 10 29N 73 15W
Vallehermoso, *Canary Is.* 9 e1 28 10N 17 15W
Vallejo, *U.S.A.* 160 G4 38 7N 122 14W
Vallenar, *Chile* .... 174 B1 28 30 S 70 50W
Vallentuna, *Sweden* .... 16 E12 59 32N 18 5 E
Valleraugue, *France* .... 28 D7 44 6N 3 39 E
Vallet, *France* 26 E5 47 10N 1 15W
Valletta, *Malta* .... 38 F8 35 54N 14 31 E
Valley Center, *U.S.A.* 161 M9 33 13N 117 2W
Valley City, *U.S.A.* 154 B6 46 55N 98 0W
Valley Falls, Oreg., *U.S.A.* 158 E3 42 29N 120 17W
Valley Falls, R.I., *U.S.A.* 151 E13 41 54N 71 24W
Valley of the Kings, *Egypt* ..... 110 B3 25 41N 32 34 E
Valley Springs, *U.S.A.* 160 G6 38 12N 120 50W
Valley Station, *U.S.A.* 157 F11 38 6N 85 52W
Valley View, *U.S.A.* 151 F8 40 39N 76 33W
Valley Wells, *U.S.A.* 161 K11 35 27N 115 46W
Valleyview, *Canada* 142 B5 55 5N 117 17W
Valli di Comácchio, *Italy* ...... 45 D9 44 40N 12 15 E
Vallimanca, Arroyo, *Argentina* .. 174 D4 35 40 S 59 10W
Vallo della Lucánia, *Italy* ...... 47 B8 40 14N 15 16 E
Vallon-Pont-d'Arc, *France* ..... 29 D8 44 24N 4 24 E
Vallorbe, *Switz.* .... 32 C2 46 42N 6 20 E
Valls, *Spain* .... 40 D6 41 18N 1 15 E
Valmaseda = Balmaseda, *Spain* .. 40 B1 43 11N 3 12W
Valmeyer, *U.S.A.* 156 F6 38 18N 90 19W
Valmiera, *Latvia* .... 15 H21 57 37N 25 29 E
Valnera, *Spain* 42 B7 43 9N 3 40W
Valognes, *France* 26 C5 49 30N 1 28W
Valona = Vlorë, *Albania* ...... 50 F3 40 32N 19 28 E
Valonga, *Portugal* 42 D2 41 8N 8 30W
Valonghyn, *Belarus* .... 58 B4 54 3N 26 30 E
Valpaços, *Portugal* 42 D3 41 36N 7 17W
Valparaí, *India* .... 95 J3 10 22N 76 58 E
Valparaíso, *Chile* .... 174 C1 33 2 S 71 40W
Valparaíso, *Mexico* 162 C4 22 50N 103 32W
Valparaíso, Fla., *U.S.A.* 153 E3 30 29N 86 30W
Valparaiso, Ind., *U.S.A.* 157 C9 41 28N 87 4W
Valparaíso □, *Chile* .... 174 C1 33 2 S 71 40W
Valpovo, *Croatia* .... 52 E3 45 39N 18 25 E
Valréas, *France* .... 29 D9 44 24N 5 0 E
Vals, *Switz.* .... 33 C8 46 39N 9 11 E
Vals →, *S. Africa* .... 116 D4 27 23 S 26 30 E
Vals, Tanjung, *Indonesia* ...... 83 C5 8 26 S 137 25 E
Vals-les-Bains, *France* .... 29 D8 44 42N 4 24 E
Valsamáta, *Greece* .... 39 C2 38 10N 20 36 E
Valtellina, *Italy* .... 44 B6 46 5N 10 3 E
Valtjofsstaður, *Iceland* 11 B12 65 1N 14 59W
Valtí, *Greece* .... 39 C3 38 27N 21 7 E
Valuyki, *Russia* .... 59 G10 50 10N 38 5 E
Valverde, *Canary Is.* 9 e1 27 48N 17 55W
Valverde del Camino, *Spain* 43 H4 37 35N 6 47W
Valverde del Fresno, *Spain* 42 E4 40 15N 6 51W
Vama, *Romania* .... 53 C10 47 34N 25 42 E
Vambori, *India* .... 94 E2 19 7N 74 44 E
Vamdrup, *Denmark* .... 17 J3 55 25N 9 17 E
Vămhus, *Sweden* .... 16 C6 61 7N 14 28 E
Vamlingbo, *Sweden* .... 17 H15 56 2N 18 20 E
Vammala, *Finland* .... 15 F20 61 20N 22 54 E
Vámos, *Greece* .... 39 E5 35 24N 24 13 E
Vamsadhara →, *India* .... 94 E7 18 21N 84 8 E
Van, *Turkey* .... 101 C10 38 30N 43 20 E
Van, L. = Van Gölü, *Turkey* .... 101 C10 38 30N 43 0 E
Van Alstyne, *U.S.A.* 155 J6 33 25N 96 35W
Van Blommestein Meer, *Suriname* . 169 C6 4 45 S 55 5W
Van Buren, *Canada* 141 C6 47 10N 67 55W
Van Buren, Ark., *U.S.A.* 155 H7 35 26N 94 21W
Van Buren, Maine, *U.S.A.* 149 B11 47 10N 67 58W
Van Buren, Mo., *U.S.A.* 155 G9 37 0N 91 1W
Van Canh, *Vietnam* .... 86 F7 13 37N 109 0 E
Van Diemen, C., N. Terr., *Australia* . 124 B5 11 9 S 130 24 E
Van Diemen, C., Queens., *Australia* . 126 B2 16 30 S 139 46 E
Van Diemen G., *Australia* ..... 124 B5 11 45 S 132 0 E
Van Gölü, *Turkey* .... 101 C10 38 30N 43 0 E
Van Horn, *U.S.A.* 155 K2 31 3N 104 50W
Van Horne, *U.S.A.* 156 D4 41 59N 92 4W
Van Meter, *U.S.A.* 156 C4 41 32N 93 57W
Van Ninh, *Vietnam* .... 86 F7 12 42N 109 14 E
Van Rees, Pegunungan, *Indonesia* . 83 B5 2 35 S 138 15 E
Van Tivu, *India* .... 95 K4 8 51N 78 15 E
Van Wert, *U.S.A.* 157 D12 40 52N 84 35W
Van Yen, *Vietnam* .... 76 G5 21 4N 104 42 E
Vanadzor, *Armenia* .... 61 K7 40 48N 44 30 E
Vanavara, *Russia* .... 67 C11 60 22N 102 16 E
Vanceburg, *U.S.A.* 157 F13 38 36N 83 19W
Vancouver, *Canada* 142 D4 49 15N 123 10W
Vancouver, *U.S.A.* 160 E4 45 38N 122 40W
Vancouver, C., *Australia* ...... 125 G2 35 2 S 118 11 E
Vancouver, Mt., *U.S.A.* 144 F13 60 20N 139 41W
Vancouver International ✈ (YVR), *U.S.A.* 160 A3 49 10N 123 10W
Vandalia, Ill., *U.S.A.* 156 F7 38 58N 89 6W
Vandalia, Mo., *U.S.A.* 156 F9 39 19N 91 29W
Vandalia, Ohio, U.S.A. .... 95 H4 12 30N 79 30 E
Vandeloos B., *Sri Lanka* ...... 95 L5 8 0N 81 45 E
Vanderbijlpark, *S. Africa* ..... 117 D4 26 42 S 27 54 E
Vanderhoof, *Canada* 142 C4 54 0N 124 0W
Vandergrift, *U.S.A.* 150 F5 40 36N 79 34W
Vanderkloof Dam, *S. Africa* ... 116 E3 30 4 S 24 40 E

Vanderlin I., *Australia* .... 126 B2   15 44 S 137 2 E
Vänern, *Sweden* .... 17 F7   58 47 N 13 30 E
Vänersborg, *Sweden* .... 17 F6   58 26 N 12 19 E
Vang, *Norway* .... 18 C5   61 7 N 8 34 E
Vang Vieng, *Laos* .... 86 C4   18 58 N 102 32 E
Vanga, *Kenya* .... 118 C4   4 35 S 39 12 E
Vangaindrano, *Madag.* .... 117 C8   23 21 S 47 36 E
Vangsnes, *Norway* .... 18 C3   61 9 N 6 39 E
Vanguard, *Canada* .... 143 D7   49 55 N 107 20 W
Vanimo, *Papua N. G.* .... 83 B6   2 42 S 141 21 E
Vanino, *Russia* .... 67 E15   48 50 N 140 5 E
Vanivilasa Sagara, *India* .... 95 H3   13 45 N 76 30 E
Vaniyambadi, *India* .... 95 H4   12 46 N 78 44 E
Vanj, *Tajikistan* .... 65 D5   38 22 N 71 27 E
Vânju Mare, *Romania* .... 52 F7   44 25 N 22 52 E
Vanna, *Norway* .... 14 A18   70 6 N 19 50 E
Vännäs, *Sweden* .... 14 E18   63 58 N 19 48 E
Vannes, *France* .... 26 E4   47 40 N 2 47 W
Vanoise, *France* .... 29 C10   45 25 N 6 40 E
Vanrhynsdorp, *S. Africa* .... 116 E2   31 36 S 18 44 E
Vansada, *India* .... 94 D1   20 47 N 73 25 E
Vansbro, *Sweden* .... 16 D8   60 32 N 14 15 E
Vanse, *Norway* .... 18 F3   58 6 N 6 41 E
Vansittart B., *Australia* .... 124 B4   14 3 S 126 17 E
Vantaa, *Finland* .... 15 F21   60 18 N 24 58 E
Vanua Balavu, *Fiji* .... 133 A3   17 12 S 178 55 W
Vanua Lava, *Vanuatu* .... 133 C5   13 50 S 167 30 E
Vanua Levu, *Fiji* .... 133 A2   16 33 S 179 15 E
Vanua Vatu, *Fiji* .... 133 B3   18 22 S 179 15 W
Vanuatu ■, *Pac. Oc.* .... 133 E6   15 0 S 168 0 E
Vanwyksvlei, *S. Africa* .... 116 E3   30 18 S 21 49 E
Vanzylsrus, *S. Africa* .... 116 D3   26 52 S 22 4 E
Vapnyarka, *Ukraine* .... 59 H5   48 32 N 28 45 E
Var □, *France* .... 29 E10   43 27 N 6 18 E
Var →, *France* .... 29 E11   43 39 N 7 12 E
Vara, *Sweden* .... 17 F6   58 16 N 12 55 E
Vara, Pico da, *Azores* .... 9 d3   37 48 N 25 13 W
Varada →, *India* .... 95 G2   15 0 N 75 40 E
Varades, *France* .... 26 E5   47 25 N 1 1 W
Varáita →, *Italy* .... 44 D2   44 49 N 7 55 E
Varaldsøy, *Norway* .... 18 D2   60 6 N 5 59 E
Varallo, *Italy* .... 44 C5   45 49 N 8 15 E
Varámin □, *Iran* .... 97 B6   35 18 N 51 35 E
Varanasi, *India* .... 93 G10   25 22 N 83 0 E
Varangerfjorden, *Norway* .... 14 A23   70 3 N 29 25 E
Varangerhalvøya, *Norway* .... 14 A23   70 25 N 29 30 E
Varano, Lago di, *Italy* .... 45 G12   41 53 N 15 45 E
Varaždin, *Croatia* .... 45 B13   46 20 N 16 20 E
Varazze, *Italy* .... 44 D5   44 22 N 8 34 E
Varberg, *Sweden* .... 17 G6   57 6 N 12 20 E
Vardak □, *Afghan.* .... 91 B3   34 0 N 68 0 E
Vardar = Axiós →, *Greece* .... 50 F6   40 57 N 22 35 E
Varde, *Denmark* .... 17 J2   55 38 N 8 29 E
Varde Å →, *Denmark* .... 17 J2   55 35 N 8 19 E
Vardø, *Norway* .... 14 A24   70 23 N 31 5 E
Varel, *Germany* .... 30 B4   53 23 N 8 6 E
Varella, Mui, *Vietnam* .... 86 F7   12 54 N 109 26 E
Varéna, *Lithuania* .... 15 J21   54 12 N 24 30 E
Varennes-sur-Allier, *France* .... 27 F10   46 19 N 3 24 E
Varennes-Vauzelles, *France* .... 27 E10   47 1 N 3 9 E
Vareš, *Bos.-H.* .... 52 F3   44 12 N 18 23 E
Varese, *Italy* .... 44 C5   45 48 N 8 50 E
Vârfurile, *Romania* .... 52 D7   46 19 N 22 31 E
Vårgårda, *Sweden* .... 17 F6   58 2 N 12 49 E
Vargem Bonita, *Brazil* .... 171 F2   20 33 S 46 22 W
Vargem Grande, *Brazil* .... 170 B3   3 33 S 43 56 W
Varginha, *Brazil* .... 175 A6   21 33 S 45 25 W
Vargön, *Sweden* .... 17 F6   58 22 N 12 20 E
Varhaug, *Norway* .... 18 F2   58 37 N 5 41 E
Varillas, *Chile* .... 174 A1   24 0 S 70 10 W
Varkaus, *Finland* .... 15 E22   62 19 N 27 50 E
Värmdölandet, *Sweden* .... 16 E12   59 20 N 18 33 E
Värmeln, *Sweden* .... 16 E6   59 35 N 12 54 E
Värmlands Bro, *Sweden* .... 16 E7   59 11 N 13 0 E
Värmlands län □, *Sweden* .... 16 E6   60 0 N 13 20 E
Varna, *Bulgaria* .... 51 C11   43 13 N 27 56 E
Varna, *Russia* .... 64 E8   53 24 N 60 58 E
Varna □, *Bulgaria* .... 51 C11   43 20 N 27 30 E
Varna →, *India* .... 94 F2   16 48 N 74 32 E
Värnamo, *Sweden* .... 17 G8   57 10 N 14 3 E
Varnsdorf, *Czech Rep.* .... 34 A7   50 55 N 14 35 E
Varnville, *U.S.A.* .... 152 C8   32 51 N 81 5 W
Várpalota, *Hungary* .... 52 C3   47 12 N 18 8 E
Vars, *Canada* .... 151 A9   45 21 N 75 21 W
Vars, *France* .... 29 D10   44 37 N 6 42 E
Vartdal, *Norway* .... 18 B3   62 20 N 6 8 E
Varto, *Turkey* .... 101 C9   39 10 N 41 27 E
Varvarin, *Serbia, Yug.* .... 50 C5   43 43 N 21 20 E
Varysburg, *U.S.A.* .... 150 D6   42 46 N 78 19 W
Varzaneh, *Iran* .... 97 C7   32 25 N 52 40 E
Várzea Alegre, *Brazil* .... 170 C4   6 47 S 39 17 W
Várzea da Palma, *Brazil* .... 171 E3   17 36 S 44 44 W
Várzea Grande, *Brazil* .... 173 D6   15 39 S 56 8 W
Varzi, *Italy* .... 44 D6   44 49 N 9 12 E
Varzo, *Italy* .... 44 B5   46 12 N 8 15 E
Varzob, *Tajikistan* .... 65 D4   38 46 N 68 49 E
Varzy, *France* .... 27 E10   47 22 N 3 20 E
Vas □, *Hungary* .... 52 C1   47 10 N 16 55 E
Vasa Barris →, *Brazil* .... 170 D4   11 10 S 37 10 W
Vásárosnamény, *Hungary* .... 52 B7   48 9 N 22 19 E
Vascão →, *Portugal* .... 43 H3   37 31 N 7 31 W
Vaşcău, *Romania* .... 52 D7   46 28 N 22 30 E
Vascongadas = País Vasco □, *Spain* .... 40 C2   42 50 N 2 45 W
Vāshīr, *Afghan.* .... 91 B1   32 16 N 63 51 E
Vasht = Khāsh, *Iran* .... 91 C1   28 15 N 61 15 E
Vasilevichi, *Belarus* .... 59 F5   52 15 N 29 50 E
Vasilikí, *Greece* .... 39 B2   38 37 N 20 36 E
Vasilikón, *Greece* .... 48 C5   38 25 N 23 40 E
Vasilikós, *Greece* .... 39 D2   37 43 N 20 59 E
Vasilkov = Vasylkiv, *Ukraine* .... 59 G6   50 7 N 30 15 E
Vaslui, *Romania* .... 53 D12   46 38 N 27 42 E
Vaslui □, *Romania* .... 53 D12   46 30 N 27 45 E
Väsman, *Sweden* .... 16 D9   60 9 N 15 5 E
Vassar, *Canada* .... 143 D9   49 10 N 95 55 W
Vassar, *U.S.A.* .... 148 D4   43 22 N 83 35 W
Vassfaret, *Norway* .... 18 D6   60 36 N 9 28 E
Västerås, *Sweden* .... 17 F10   59 37 N 16 38 E
Västerbotten, *Sweden* .... 14 D18   64 36 N 20 4 E
Västerdalälven →, *Sweden* .... 16 D8   60 30 N 14 7 E
Västergötland, *Sweden* .... 17 F7   58 0 N 13 10 E
Västerhaninge, *Sweden* .... 16 E12   59 7 N 18 6 E
Västervik, *Sweden* .... 17 G10   57 43 N 16 33 E
Västmanland, *Sweden* .... 15 G16   59 45 N 16 20 E
Västmanlands län □, *Sweden* .... 16 E10   59 45 N 16 20 E
Vasto, *Italy* .... 45 F11   42 8 N 14 40 E
Västra Götalands Län □, *Sweden* .... 17 F6   58 0 N 13 0 E
Vasvár, *Hungary* .... 52 C1   47 3 N 16 47 E
Vasylkiv, *Ukraine* .... 59 G6   50 7 N 30 15 E
Vatan, *France* .... 27 E8   47 4 N 1 50 E
Vaté = Efate, I., *Vanuatu* .... 133 G6   17 40 S 168 25 E
Vatersay, *U.K.* .... 22 E1   56 55 N 7 32 W
Vathí, *Greece* .... 39 B2   38 41 N 20 47 E
Váthia, *Greece* .... 48 E4   36 29 N 22 29 E
Vatican City ■, *Europe* .... 45 G9   41 54 N 12 27 E
Vaticano, C., *Italy* .... 47 D8   38 37 N 15 50 E
Vatili, *Cyprus* .... 36 D12   35 6 N 33 40 E
Vatin, *Serbia, Yug.* .... 52 E6   45 12 N 21 20 E
Vatnajökull, *Iceland* .... 11 C10   64 30 N 16 48 W
Vatnás, *Norway* .... 18 E6   59 58 N 9 37 E
Vatneyri, *Iceland* .... 11 B2   65 35 N 24 0 W
Vatnsfjörður, *Iceland* .... 11 B4   65 56 N 22 30 W
Vatólakkos, *Greece* .... 39 E4   35 27 N 23 53 E
Vatoloha, *Madag.* .... 117 B8   17 52 S 47 48 E

Vatomandry, *Madag.* .... 117 B8   19 20 S 48 59 E
Vatra-Dornei, *Romania* .... 53 C10   47 22 N 25 22 E
Vatrak →, *India* .... 92 H5   23 9 N 73 2 E
Vättern, *Sweden* .... 17 F8   58 25 N 14 30 E
Vättis, *Switz.* .... 33 C8   46 55 N 9 27 E
Vatu Vara, *Fiji* .... 133 A3   17 26 S 179 31 W
Vatulele, *Fiji* .... 133 B1   18 33 S 177 37 E
Vaucluse □, *France* .... 29 E9   43 50 N 5 20 E
Vaucouleurs, *France* .... 27 D12   48 37 N 5 40 E
Vaud □, *Switz.* .... 32 C3   46 35 N 6 30 E
Vaughn, *Mont., U.S.A.* .... 158 C8   47 33 N 111 33 W
Vaughn, *N. Mex., U.S.A.* .... 159 J11   34 36 N 105 13 W
Vaujours L., *Canada* .... 140 A5   55 27 N 74 15 W
Vaulruz, *Switz.* .... 32 C3   46 38 N 6 58 E
Vaupés = Uaupés →, *Brazil* .... 168 C4   0 2 N 67 16 W
Vaupés □, *Colombia* .... 168 C3   1 0 N 71 0 W
Vauvert, *France* .... 29 E8   43 42 N 4 17 E
Vauxhall, *Canada* .... 142 C6   50 5 N 112 9 W
Vav, *India* .... 92 G4   24 22 N 71 31 E
Vavatenina, *Madag.* .... 117 B8   17 28 S 49 12 E
Vava'u, *Tonga* .... 133 P14   18 36 S 174 0 W
Vava'u Group, *Tonga* .... 133 P14   18 40 S 174 0 W
Vavoua, *Ivory C.* .... 112 D3   7 23 N 6 29 W
Vavuniya, *Sri Lanka* .... 95 K5   8 45 N 80 30 E
Vawkavysk, *Belarus* .... 59 F3   53 9 N 24 30 E
Vaxholm, *Sweden* .... 16 E12   59 25 N 18 20 E
Växjö, *Sweden* .... 17 H8   56 52 N 14 50 E
Våxtorp, *Sweden* .... 17 H7   56 25 N 13 8 E
Vayalpad, *India* .... 95 H4   13 39 N 78 38 E
Vaygach, Ostrov, *Russia* .... 66 C6   70 0 N 60 0 E
Váyia, *Greece* .... 48 C5   38 19 N 23 11 E
Váyia, Ákra, *Greece* .... 38 E12   36 15 N 28 11 E
Veadeiros, *Brazil* .... 171 D2   14 7 S 47 31 W
Vechelde, *Germany* .... 30 C6   52 16 N 10 22 E
Vechta, *Germany* .... 30 C4   52 44 N 8 17 E
Vechte →, *Neths.* .... 24 B6   52 34 N 6 6 E
Vecsés, *Hungary* .... 52 C4   47 26 N 19 19 E
Vedaranniyam, *India* .... 95 J4   10 25 N 79 50 E
Vedavågen, *Norway* .... 18 E2   59 17 N 5 12 E
Veddige, *Sweden* .... 17 G6   57 17 N 12 20 E
Vedea →, *Romania* .... 53 G10   43 42 N 25 41 E
Vedia, *Argentina* .... 174 C3   34 30 S 61 31 W
Vedrette di Ries-Aurina, Parco
    Naturale △, *Italy* .... 45 B9   46 54 N 12 5 E
Vedum, *Sweden* .... 17 F7   58 11 N 13 0 E
Veedersburg, *U.S.A.* .... 157 D9   40 7 N 87 16 W
Veendam, *Neths.* .... 24 A6   53 5 N 6 52 E
Veenendaal, *Neths.* .... 24 B5   52 2 N 5 34 E
Vefsna →, *Norway* .... 14 D15   65 48 N 13 10 E
Vega, *Norway* .... 14 D14   65 40 N 11 55 E
Vega, *U.S.A.* .... 155 H3   35 15 N 102 26 W
Vega Baja, *Puerto Rico* .... 165 d   18 27 N 66 23 W
Vegadeo, *Spain* .... 42 B3   43 27 N 7 4 W
Vegårshei, *Norway* .... 18 F5   58 44 N 8 51 E
Veggli, *Norway* .... 18 D6   60 3 N 9 9 E
Vegorrítis, Límni, *Greece* .... 50 F5   40 45 N 21 45 E
Vegreville, *Canada* .... 142 C6   53 30 N 112 5 W
Veidholmen, *Norway* .... 18 A4   63 31 N 7 58 E
Veinge, *Sweden* .... 17 H7   56 33 N 13 4 E
Veisiejai, *Lithuania* .... 54 D10   54 6 N 23 42 E
Vejbystrand, *Sweden* .... 17 H6   56 19 N 12 45 E
Vejen, *Denmark* .... 17 J3   55 30 N 9 9 E
Vejer de la Frontera, *Spain* .... 43 J5   36 15 N 5 59 W
Vejle, *Denmark* .... 17 J3   55 43 N 9 30 E
Vejle Amtskommune □, *Denmark* .... 17 J3   55 45 N 9 20 E
Vejle Fjord, *Denmark* .... 17 J3   55 40 N 9 50 E
Vela Luka, *Croatia* .... 45 F13   42 59 N 16 44 E
Velachha, *India* .... 94 D1   21 26 N 73 1 E
Velan, C., *Costa Rica* .... 164 D2   10 21 N 85 52 W
Velasco, Sierra de, *Argentina* .... 174 B2   29 20 S 67 10 W
Velay, Mts. du, *France* .... 28 D7   45 0 N 3 40 E
Velbert, *Germany* .... 30 D3   51 20 N 7 3 E
Velddrif, *S. Africa* .... 116 E2   32 42 S 18 11 E
Velebit, Park Prirode △, *Croatia* .... 45 D12   44 30 N 15 15 E
Velebit Planina, *Croatia* .... 45 D12   44 50 N 15 20 E
Velebitski Kanal, *Croatia* .... 45 D11   44 45 N 14 55 E
Veleka →, *Bulgaria* .... 51 D11   42 4 N 27 58 E
Velenje, *Slovenia* .... 45 B12   46 23 N 15 8 E
Velestínon, *Greece* .... 48 B4   39 23 N 22 43 E
Vélez, *Colombia* .... 168 B3   6 1 N 73 41 W
Vélez-Málaga, *Spain* .... 43 J6   36 48 N 4 5 W
Vélez Rubio, *Spain* .... 41 H2   37 41 N 2 5 W
Velhas →, *Brazil* .... 171 E3   17 13 S 44 49 W
Velika, *Croatia* .... 52 E2   45 27 N 17 40 E
Velika Gorica, *Croatia* .... 45 C13   45 44 N 16 5 E
Velika Kapela, *Croatia* .... 45 C12   45 10 N 15 5 E
Velika Kladuša, *Bos.-H.* .... 45 C12   45 11 N 15 48 E
Velika Kruša, *Kosovo, Yug.* .... 50 D4   42 19 N 20 39 E
Velika Morava →, *Serbia, Yug.* .... 50 B5   44 43 N 21 3 E
Velika Plana, *Serbia, Yug.* .... 50 B5   44 20 N 21 4 E
Velikaya →, *Russia* .... 58 D5   57 48 N 28 10 E
Velikaya Kema, *Russia* .... 70 B8   45 30 N 137 12 E
Velikaya Lepetikha, *Ukraine* .... 59 J7   47 2 N 33 58 E
Veliké Kapušany, *Slovak Rep.* .... 35 C15   48 34 N 22 5 E
Velike Lašče, *Slovenia* .... 45 C11   45 49 N 14 45 E
Veliki Jastrebac, *Serbia, Yug.* .... 50 C5   43 25 N 21 30 E
Veliki Kanal, *Serbia, Yug.* .... 52 E4   45 45 N 19 15 E
Veliki Popović, *Serbia, Yug.* .... 50 B5   44 8 N 21 18 E
Veliki Ustyug, *Russia* .... 56 B8   60 47 N 46 20 E
Velikiye Luki, *Russia* .... 58 D6   56 25 N 30 32 E
Veliko Gradište, *Serbia, Yug.* .... 50 B5   44 46 N 21 29 E
Veliko Tŭrnovo, *Bulgaria* .... 51 C9   43 5 N 25 41 E
Velikonda Range, *India* .... 95 G4   14 45 N 79 10 E
Vélingara, Kolda, *Senegal* .... 112 C2   13 12 N 14 5 W
Vélingara, Louga, *Senegal* .... 112 B2   15 0 N 14 40 W
Velingrad, *Bulgaria* .... 50 D7   42 4 N 23 58 E
Velino, Mte., *Italy* .... 45 F10   42 9 N 13 23 E
Velizh, *Russia* .... 58 E6   55 36 N 31 11 E
Velké Karlovice, *Czech Rep.* .... 35 B11   49 20 N 18 17 E
Velké Meziříčí, *Czech Rep.* .... 34 B9   49 21 N 16 1 E
Vel'ký Javorník, *Slovak Rep.* .... 35 B10   49 21 N 18 22 E
Vel'ký Krtíš, *Slovak Rep.* .... 35 C12   48 12 N 19 21 E
Vel'ký Meder, *Slovak Rep.* .... 35 D10   47 52 N 17 46 E
Vel'ký Tríbeč, *Slovak Rep.* .... 35 C11   48 28 N 18 11 E
Vella G., *Solomon Is.* .... 133 M9   8 0 S 156 50 E
Vella Lavella, *Solomon Is.* .... 133 L9   7 45 S 156 40 E
Vellar →, *India* .... 95 J4   11 30 N 79 36 E
Velletri, *Italy* .... 46 A5   41 41 N 12 47 E
Vellinge, *Sweden* .... 17 J6   55 29 N 13 0 E
Vellmar, *Germany* .... 30 D5   51 22 N 9 28 E
Vellore, *India* .... 95 H4   12 57 N 79 10 E
Velsk, *Russia* .... 58 B11   61 10 N 42 5 E
Velten, *Germany* .... 30 C9   52 42 N 13 10 E
Veluwezoom, Nat. Park △, *Neths.* .... 24 B6   52 5 N 6 0 E
Velva, *U.S.A.* .... 154 A4   48 4 N 100 56 W
Velvendós, *Greece* .... 50 F6   40 15 N 22 6 E
Vemb, *Denmark* .... 17 H2   56 21 N 8 21 E
Vembanad L., *India* .... 95 K3   9 36 N 76 15 E
Vemdalen, *Sweden* .... 16 B7   62 27 N 13 51 E
Ven, *Switz.* .... 17 J6   55 55 N 12 45 E
Venaco, *France* .... 29 F13   42 14 N 9 11 E
Venado Tuerto, *Argentina* .... 174 C3   33 50 S 62 0 W
Venarey-les-Laumes, *France* .... 27 E11   47 32 N 4 26 E
Venaría, *Italy* .... 44 C4   45 8 N 7 34 E
Venčane, *Serbia, Yug.* .... 50 B4   44 24 N 20 28 E
Vence, *France* .... 29 E11   43 43 N 7 6 E
Vendas Novas, *Portugal* .... 43 G2   38 39 N 8 27 W
Vendée □, *France* .... 26 F5   46 50 N 1 35 W
Vendée →, *France* .... 26 F5   46 20 N 1 10 W

Vendéen, Bocage, *France* .... 28 B2   46 40 N 1 20 W
Vendeuvre-sur-Barse, *France* .... 27 D11   48 14 N 4 28 E
Vendôme, *France* .... 26 E8   47 47 N 1 3 E
Vendrell = El Vendrell, *Spain* .... 40 D6   41 10 N 1 30 E
Vendsyssel, *Denmark* .... 17 G4   57 22 N 10 0 E
Venelles, *France* .... 29 E9   43 35 N 5 28 E
Véneta, L., *Italy* .... 45 C9   45 23 N 12 25 E
Venetie, *U.S.A.* .... 144 C11   67 1 N 146 25 W
Véneto □, *Italy* .... 45 C9   45 30 N 12 0 E
Venézia, *Italy* .... 45 C9   45 27 N 12 21 E
Venézia, G. di, *Italy* .... 45 C10   45 15 N 13 0 E
Venezuela ■, *S. Amer.* .... 168 B4   8 0 N 66 0 W
Venezuela, G. de, *Venezuela* .... 168 A3   11 30 N 71 0 W
Vengurla, *India* .... 95 G1   15 53 N 73 45 E
Vengurla Rocks, *India* .... 95 G1   15 55 N 73 22 E
Venice = Venézia, *Italy* .... 45 C9   45 27 N 12 21 E
Venice, *U.S.A.* .... 153 H7   27 6 N 82 27 W
Vénissieux, *France* .... 29 C8   45 42 N 4 53 E
Venjansjön, *Sweden* .... 16 D8   60 54 N 14 0 E
Venkatagiri, *India* .... 95 G4   14 0 N 79 35 E
Venkatapuram, *India* .... 94 E5   18 20 N 80 30 E
Venlo, *Neths.* .... 24 C6   51 22 N 6 11 E
Vennesla, *Norway* .... 18 F4   58 15 N 7 59 E
Venray, *Neths.* .... 24 C6   51 31 N 6 0 E
Vent, Îs. du, *Pac. Oc.* .... 133 S16   17 30 S 149 30 W
Venta, *Lithuania* .... 54 B9   56 12 N 22 42 E
Venta →, *Latvia* .... 54 A8   57 24 N 21 33 E
Venta de Baños, *Spain* .... 42 D6   41 55 N 4 30 W
Venta de Cardeña = Cardeña, *Spain* .... 43 G6   38 16 N 4 20 W
Ventana, Punta de la, *Mexico* .... 162 C3   24 4 N 109 48 W
Ventana, Sa. de la, *Argentina* .... 174 D3   38 0 S 62 30 W
Ventersburg, *S. Africa* .... 116 D4   28 7 S 27 9 E
Venterstad, *S. Africa* .... 116 E4   30 47 S 25 48 E
Ventimíglia, *Italy* .... 44 E4   43 47 N 7 36 E
Ventnor, *U.K.* .... 21 G6   50 36 N 1 12 W
Ventoténe, *Italy* .... 46 B6   40 47 N 13 25 E
Ventoux, Mt., *France* .... 29 D9   44 10 N 5 17 E
Ventspils, *Latvia* .... 15 H19   57 25 N 21 32 E
Ventspils □, *Latvia* .... 54 A8   57 20 N 21 50 E
Venturí →, *Venezuela* .... 168 C4   3 58 N 67 2 W
Ventucopa, *U.S.A.* .... 161 L7   34 50 N 119 29 W
Ventura, *U.S.A.* .... 161 L7   34 17 N 119 18 W
Venus, *U.S.A.* .... 153 H8   27 4 N 81 22 W
Venus B., *Australia* .... 129 E6   38 40 S 145 42 E
Vera, *Argentina* .... 174 B3   29 30 S 60 20 W
Vera, *Spain* .... 41 H3   37 15 N 1 51 W
Veracruz, *Mexico* .... 163 D5   19 10 N 96 10 W
Veracruz □, *Mexico* .... 163 D5   19 0 N 96 15 W
Verával, *India* .... 92 J4   20 53 N 70 27 E
Verbánia, *Italy* .... 44 C5   45 56 N 8 33 E
Verbicaro, *Italy* .... 39 C9   39 45 N 15 55 E
Verbier, *Switz.* .... 32 D4   46 6 N 7 13 E
Vercelli, *Italy* .... 33 D8   46 12 N 8 29 E
Vercelli, *Italy* .... 44 C5   45 19 N 8 25 E
Verchovchevo, *Ukraine* .... 59 H8   48 30 N 34 10 E
Vercors, Parc Naturel Régional
    du △, *France* .... 29 D9   45 0 N 5 25 E
Verdalsøra, *Norway* .... 14 E14   63 48 N 11 30 E
Verde →, *Argentina* .... 176 B3   41 56 S 65 5 W
Verde →, *Goiás, Brazil* .... 171 E1   19 11 S 50 44 W
Verde →, *Goiás, Brazil* .... 171 E1   21 25 S 50 14 W
Verde →, *Mato Grosso, Brazil* .... 173 C6   16 53 S 51 28 W
Verde →, *Mato Grosso do Sul,*
    Brazil .... 173 E7   21 25 S 52 20 W
Verde →, *Chihuahua, Mexico* .... 162 B3   26 29 N 107 58 W
Verde →, *Oaxaca, Mexico* .... 163 D5   15 59 N 97 50 W
Verde →, *Veracruz, Mexico* .... 162 C4   21 10 N 102 50 W
Verde →, *Paraguay* .... 174 A4   23 9 S 57 37 W
Verde →, *U.S.A.* .... 146 D4   33 33 N 111 40 W
Verde, Cay, *Bahamas* .... 164 B4   23 0 N 75 5 W
Verde Grande →, *Brazil* .... 171 E3   16 13 S 43 49 W
Verde I., *Phil.* .... 80 E3   13 33 N 121 5 E
Verde Island Pass, *Phil.* .... 80 E3   13 34 N 120 51 E
Verde Pequeno →, *Brazil* .... 171 D3   14 48 S 43 31 W
Verden, *Germany* .... 30 C5   52 55 N 9 14 E
Verdhikoúsa, *Greece* .... 48 B3   39 47 N 21 59 E
Verdi, *U.S.A.* .... 160 F7   39 31 N 119 59 W
Verdon →, *France* .... 29 E9   43 43 N 5 46 E
Verdun, *France* .... 27 C12   49 9 N 5 24 E
Verdun-sur-le-Doubs, *France* .... 27 F12   46 54 N 5 2 E
Vereeniging, *S. Africa* .... 117 D4   26 38 S 27 57 E
Vereshchagino, *Russia* .... 64 B5   58 0 N 54 40 E
Vergara, *Uruguay* .... 175 C5   32 56 S 53 57 W
Vergato, *Italy* .... 44 D8   44 17 N 11 7 E
Vergemont Cr. →, *Australia* .... 126 C3   24 16 S 143 16 E
Vergennes, *U.S.A.* .... 151 B11   44 10 N 73 15 W
Vergt, *France* .... 28 C4   45 2 N 0 43 E
Verín, *Spain* .... 42 D3   41 57 N 7 27 W
Verkhnedvinsk = Vyerkhnyadzvinsk,
    Belarus .... 58 E4   55 45 N 27 58 E
Verkhneuralsk, *Russia* .... 64 E7   53 53 N 59 13 E
Verkhnevilyuysk, *Russia* .... 67 C13   63 27 N 120 18 E
Verkhniy Baskunchak, *Russia* .... 61 F8   48 14 N 46 44 E
Verkhniy Tagil, *Russia* .... 64 C7   57 22 N 59 56 E
Verkhniy Ufaley, *Russia* .... 64 C7   56 4 N 60 14 E
Verkhniye Kigi, *Russia* .... 64 C8   55 25 N 58 37 E
Verkhnyaya Salda, *Russia* .... 64 C8   58 2 N 60 33 E
Verkhnyaya Tura, *Russia* .... 64 B7   58 22 N 59 50 E
Verkhoturye, *Russia* .... 58 B9   58 52 N 60 48 E
Verkhovye, *Russia* .... 59 F9   52 55 N 37 15 E
Verkhoyansk, *Russia* .... 67 C14   67 35 N 133 25 E
Verkhoyansk Ra. = Verkhoyanskiy
    Khrebet, *Russia* .... 67 C13   66 0 N 129 0 E
Verkhoyanskiy Khrebet, *Russia* .... 67 C13   66 0 N 129 0 E
Verma, *Norway* .... 18 B5   62 21 N 8 3 E
Vermenton, *France* .... 27 E10   47 40 N 3 42 E
Vermilion, *Canada* .... 143 C6   53 20 N 110 50 W
Vermilion, *U.S.A.* .... 150 E2   41 25 N 82 22 W
Vermilion →, *Canada* .... 143 C6   53 22 N 110 51 W
Vermilion →, *Ill., U.S.A.* .... 156 C7   41 19 N 89 4 W
Vermilion →, *Ind., U.S.A.* .... 157 E9   39 57 N 87 20 W
Vermilion B., *Canada* .... 143 D10   49 51 N 93 34 W
Vermilion Bay, *Canada* .... 143 D10   49 51 N 93 34 W
Vermilion Chutes, *Canada* .... 142 B6   58 22 N 114 51 W
Vermilion L., *U.S.A.* .... 154 B8   47 53 N 92 26 W
Vermillion →, *Canada* .... 140 C7   47 38 N 72 56 W
Vermont, *U.S.A.* .... 156 D6   40 18 N 90 26 W
Vermont □, *U.S.A.* .... 151 C12   44 0 N 73 0 W
Vermosh, *Albania* .... 50 B3   42 35 N 19 42 E
Verna, *U.S.A.* .... 160 F8   40 27 N 109 32 W
Vernalis, *U.S.A.* .... 160 H5   37 36 N 121 17 W
Vernazza, *Italy* .... 44 D6   44 10 N 9 41 E
Verner, *Canada* .... 140 C3   46 25 N 80 8 W
Verneuil-sur-Avre, *France* .... 26 D7   48 45 N 0 55 E
Verneukpan, *S. Africa* .... 116 E3   30 0 S 21 0 E
Vérnio, *Italy* .... 44 D8   44 3 N 11 9 E
Vernon, *France* .... 26 C8   49 5 N 1 30 E
Vernon, *Ill., U.S.A.* .... 156 F7   38 48 N 89 6 W
Vernon, *Ind., U.S.A.* .... 157 F11   38 59 N 85 36 W
Vernon, *Tex., U.S.A.* .... 155 H5   34 9 N 99 17 W
Vernon, *U.S.A.* .... 160 E3   43 25 N 123 11 W
Vernonia, *U.S.A.* .... 160 E2   45 52 N 123 11 W
Vernouillet, *France* .... 26 D8   48 58 N 1 58 E
Verny = Almaty, *Kazakhstan* .... 65 B8   43 15 N 76 57 E
Vero Beach, *U.S.A.* .... 153 H9   27 38 N 80 24 W

Véroia, *Greece* .... 50 F6   40 34 N 22 12 E
Véroli, *Italy* .... 45 G10   41 41 N 13 25 E
Verona, *Canada* .... 151 B8   44 29 N 76 42 W
Verona, *Italy* .... 44 C7   45 27 N 10 59 E
Verona, *U.S.A.* .... 156 B7   42 59 N 89 32 W
Verrès, *Italy* .... 44 C4   45 40 N 7 42 E
Verron Ra., *Papua N. G.* .... 132 C7   4 21 S 152 46 E
Versailles, *France* .... 27 D9   48 48 N 2 8 E
Versailles, *Ill., U.S.A.* .... 156 E6   39 53 N 90 39 W
Versailles, *Ind., U.S.A.* .... 157 E11   39 4 N 85 15 W
Versailles, *Ky., U.S.A.* .... 157 F12   38 3 N 84 44 W
Versailles, *Mo., U.S.A.* .... 156 F4   38 26 N 92 51 W
Versailles, *Ohio, U.S.A.* .... 157 D11   40 13 N 84 29 W
Versalles, *Bolivia* .... 173 C5   12 44 S 63 18 W
Versmold, *Germany* .... 30 C4   52 2 N 8 10 E
Versoix, *Switz.* .... 32 D2   46 17 N 6 10 E
Vert, C., *Senegal* .... 112 C1   14 45 N 17 30 W
Vertou, *France* .... 26 E5   47 10 N 1 28 W
Vertus, *France* .... 27 D11   48 54 N 4 2 E
Verulam, *S. Africa* .... 117 D5   29 38 S 31 2 E
Verviers, *Belgium* .... 24 D5   50 37 N 5 52 E
Vervins, *France* .... 27 C10   49 50 N 3 53 E
Veržej, *Slovenia* .... 45 B13   46 34 N 16 13 E
Verzy, *France* .... 27 C11   49 9 N 4 10 E
Vescovato, *France* .... 29 F13   42 30 N 9 27 E
Veselí nad Lužnicí, *Czech Rep.* .... 34 B7   49 12 N 14 43 E
Veselie, *Bulgaria* .... 51 D11   42 18 N 27 38 E
Veselovskoye Vdkhr., *Russia* .... 61 G5   46 58 N 41 25 E
Vesle →, *France* .... 27 C10   49 23 N 3 28 E
Veslyana →, *Russia* .... 64 A4   60 20 N 54 0 E
Vesoul, *France* .... 27 E13   47 40 N 6 11 E
Vessigebro, *Sweden* .... 17 H6   56 58 N 12 40 E
Vest-Agder □, *Norway* .... 18 F4   58 30 N 7 15 E
Vestby, *Norway* .... 14 B15   68 18 N 13 50 E
Vestfjorden, *Norway* .... 14 B15   68 18 N 13 50 E
Vestfold □, *Norway* .... 18 E7   59 15 N 10 0 E
Vestfossen, *Norway* .... 18 E6   59 44 N 9 52 E
Vestgrønland = Kitaa □, *Greenland* .... 10 C6   70 0 N 47 0 W
Vestmannaeyjar, *Iceland* .... 11 D6   63 27 N 20 15 W
Vestnes, *Norway* .... 18 B4   62 39 N 7 5 E
Vestre Gausdal, *Norway* .... 18 C7   61 16 N 9 58 E
Vestre Slidre, *Norway* .... 18 C5   61 5 N 8 58 E
Vestsjællands Amtskommune □,
    Denmark .... 17 J5   55 30 N 11 20 E
Vestspitsbergen, *Svalbard* .... 6 B8   78 40 N 17 0 E
Vestur-skaftafellssýsla □, *Iceland* .... 11 D8   63 50 N 18 30 W
Vestvågøy, *Norway* .... 14 B15   68 18 N 13 50 E
Vesul Spitze, *Austria* .... 33 C10   47 0 N 10 21 E
Vesuvio, *Italy* .... 47 B7   40 49 N 14 26 E
Vesuvius, Mt. = Vesuvio, *Italy* .... 47 B7   40 49 N 14 26 E
Vesyegonsk, *Russia* .... 58 C9   58 40 N 37 16 E
Veszprém, *Hungary* .... 52 C2   47 8 N 17 57 E
Veszprém □, *Hungary* .... 52 C2   47 5 N 17 55 E
Vésztő, *Hungary* .... 52 D6   46 55 N 21 16 E
Vetapalem, *India* .... 95 G5   15 47 N 80 18 E
Vetlanda, *Sweden* .... 17 G9   57 24 N 15 3 E
Vetluga, *Russia* .... 60 B8   57 53 N 45 45 E
Vetlugu →, *Russia* .... 60 B8   56 36 N 46 4 E
Vetluzhskiy, Kostroma, *Russia* .... 60 A7   58 23 N 45 26 E
Vetluzhskiy, Nizhniy Novgorod,
    Russia .... 60 B7   57 17 N 45 12 E
Vetovo, *Bulgaria* .... 51 C10   43 42 N 26 16 E
Vetralla, *Italy* .... 45 F9   42 20 N 12 2 E
Vetren, *Bulgaria* .... 51 D8   42 15 N 24 3 E
Vettore, Mte., *Italy* .... 45 F10   42 49 N 13 16 E
Veurne, *Belgium* .... 24 C2   51 5 N 2 40 E
Vevay, *U.S.A.* .... 157 F11   38 45 N 85 4 W
Veveno →, *Sudan* .... 107 F3   6 40 N 32 58 E
Vevey, *Switz.* .... 32 D3   46 28 N 6 51 E
Vévi, *Greece* .... 50 F5   40 47 N 21 38 E
Vex, *Switz.* .... 32 D4   46 12 N 7 24 E
Veynes, *France* .... 29 D9   44 32 N 5 49 E
Veys, *Iran* .... 97 D6   31 30 N 49 0 E
Vézelay, *France* .... 27 E10   47 27 N 3 45 E
Vézelise, *France* .... 27 D13   48 30 N 6 5 E
Vézère →, *France* .... 28 D4   44 53 N 0 53 E
Vezhen, *Bulgaria* .... 51 D8   42 50 N 24 20 E
Vezirköprü, *Turkey* .... 100 B6   41 8 N 35 27 E
Vezzani, *France* .... 29 F13   42 10 N 9 16 E
Vi Thanh, *Vietnam* .... 87 H5   9 42 N 105 26 E
Viacha, *Bolivia* .... 172 D4   16 39 S 68 18 W
Viadana, *Italy* .... 44 D7   44 56 N 10 31 E
Vialar = Tissemsilt, *Algeria* .... 111 A5   35 35 N 1 6 E
Viamão, *Brazil* .... 175 C5   30 5 S 51 0 W
Viana, *Brazil* .... 170 B3   3 13 S 44 55 W
Viana, *Spain* .... 40 C2   42 31 N 2 22 W
Viana do Alentejo, *Portugal* .... 43 G3   38 17 N 7 59 W
Viana do Bolo, *Spain* .... 42 C3   42 11 N 7 6 W
Viana do Castelo, *Portugal* .... 42 D2   41 42 N 8 50 W
Viana do Castelo □, *Portugal* .... 42 D2   41 50 N 8 30 W
Vianden, *Lux.* .... 24 E6   49 56 N 6 12 E
Viangchan = Vientiane, *Laos* .... 86 D4   17 58 N 102 36 E
Vianópolis, *Brazil* .... 171 E2   16 40 S 48 35 W
Viar →, *Spain* .... 43 H5   37 45 N 5 47 W
Viaréggio, *Italy* .... 44 E7   43 52 N 10 14 E
Viaur →, *France* .... 28 D5   44 8 N 1 58 E
Vibble, *Sweden* .... 17 G12   57 37 N 18 16 E
Vibo Valéntia, *Italy* .... 47 D9   38 40 N 16 6 E
Viborg, *Denmark* .... 17 H3   56 27 N 9 23 E
Viborg Amtskommune □, *Denmark* .... 17 H3   56 30 N 9 30 E
Vibraye, *France* .... 26 D7   48 3 N 0 44 E
Vic, *Spain* .... 40 D7   41 58 N 2 19 E
Vic, Étang de, *France* .... 28 E7   43 25 N 3 50 E
Vic-en-Bigorre, *France* .... 28 E4   43 24 N 0 5 E
Vic-Fézensac, *France* .... 28 E4   43 47 N 0 19 E
Vic-le-Comte, *France* .... 27 G10   45 39 N 3 14 E
Vic-sur-Cère, *France* .... 28 D6   44 59 N 2 38 E
Vícar, *Spain* .... 41 J2   36 50 N 2 38 W
Vicenza, *Italy* .... 45 C8   45 33 N 11 33 E
Vich = Vic, *Spain* .... 40 D7   41 58 N 2 19 E
Vichada □, *Colombia* .... 168 C4   5 0 N 69 30 W
Vichada →, *Colombia* .... 168 C4   4 55 N 67 50 W
Vichuga, *Russia* .... 60 B6   57 12 N 41 55 E
Vichy, *France* .... 27 F10   46 9 N 3 26 E
Vicksburg, *Ariz., U.S.A.* .... 161 M13   33 45 N 113 45 W
Vicksburg, *Mich., U.S.A.* .... 157 B11   42 7 N 85 32 W
Vicksburg, *Miss., U.S.A.* .... 155 J9   32 21 N 90 53 W
Vico, *France* .... 29 F12   42 10 N 8 49 E
Vico, L. di, *Italy* .... 45 F9   42 19 N 12 8 E
Vico del Gargano, *Italy* .... 45 G12   41 54 N 15 57 E
Viçosa, *Brazil* .... 170 C4   9 28 S 36 14 W
Viçosa do Ceará, *Brazil* .... 170 B3   3 34 S 41 5 W
Vicosoprano, *Switz.* .... 33 D9   46 22 N 9 38 E
Vicovu de Sus, *Romania* .... 53 C10   47 56 N 25 41 E
Victor, *India* .... 92 J4   21 0 N 71 30 E
Victor, *U.S.A.* .... 158 F9   40 27 N 97 24 W
Victor Emanuel Ra., *Papua N. G.* .... 132 C2   5 20 S 142 15 E
Victor Harbor, *Australia* .... 129 C2   35 30 S 138 37 E
Victor Hugo = Hamadia, *Algeria* .... 111 A5   35 28 N 1 57 E
Victoria = Labuan, *Malaysia* .... 85 A5   5 20 N 115 14 E
Victoria, *Argentina* .... 174 C3   32 40 S 60 10 W
Victoria, *Canada* .... 142 D4   48 30 N 123 25 W
Victoria, *Chile* .... 176 A3   38 13 S 72 20 W
Victoria, *China* .... 69 G1   22 17 N 114 9 E
Victoria, *Guinea* .... 112 C2   10 50 N 14 32 W
Victoria, *Malta* .... 49 C1   36 3 N 14 14 E
Victoria, *Mind. Or., Phil.* .... 80 E3   13 13 N 121 12 E
Victoria, *Romania* .... 53 D9   45 45 N 24 41 E
Victoria, *Seychelles* .... 121 b   4 38 S 55 28 E
Victoria, *Kans., U.S.A.* .... 154 F5   38 52 N 99 9 W
Victoria, *Tex., U.S.A.* .... 155 L6   28 48 N 97 0 W

Victoria □, *Australia* .... 128 D6 37 0 S 144 0 E
Victoria ➤, *Australia* .... 124 C4 15 10 S 129 40 E
Victoria, Grand L., *Canada* 140 C4 47 31N 77 30W
Victoria, L., *Africa* .... 118 C3   1 0 S 33 0 E
Victoria, L., *Australia* .... 128 B4 33 57 S 141 15 E
Victoria, Mt., *Burma* .... 90 E4 21 14N 93 55 E
Victoria, Mt., *Papua N. G.* .... 132 E4   8 55 S 147 32 E
Victoria Beach, *Canada* 143 C9 50 40N 96 35W
Victoria de Durango = Durango,
   Mexico 162 C4   3N 104 39W
Victoria de las Tunas, *Cuba* 164 B4 20 58N 76 59W
Victoria Falls, *Zimbabwe* .... 119 F2 17 58 S 25 52 E
Victoria Harbour, *Canada* 150 B5 44 45N 79 45W
Victoria I., *Canada* 138 A8 71 0N 111 0W
Victoria I., *Canada* 141 C8 48 20N 57 27W
Victoria Ld., *Antarctica* .... 7 D11 75 0 S 160 0 E
Victoria Nile ➤, *Uganda* .... 118 B3   2 14N 31 26 E
Victoria Peaks, *Phil.* .... 81 G2   9 22N 118 20 E
Victoria Ra., *N.Z.* .... 131 C7 42 12 S 172 7 E
Victoria River, *Australia* .... 124 C5 16 25 S 131 0 E
Victoria Str., *Canada* 138 B9 69 30N 100 0W
Victoria West, *S. Africa* .... 116 E3 31 25 S 23 4 E
Victorias, *Phil.* .... 81 F4 10 54N 123 5 E
Victoriaville, *Canada* 141 C5 46 4N 71 56W
Victorica, *Argentina* .... 174 D2 36 20 S 65 30W
Victorville, *U.S.A.* 161 L9 34 32N 117 18W
Vicuña, *Chile* .... 174 C1 30 0 S 70 50W
Vicuña Mackenna, *Argentina* ...... 174 C3 33 53 S 64 25W
Vidal, *U.S.A.* 161 L12 34 7N 114 31W
Vidal Junction, *U.S.A.* 161 L12 34 11N 114 34W
Vidalia, *U.S.A.* 152 C7 32 13N 82 25W
Vidauban, *France* .... 29 E10 43 25N   6 27 E
Videbæk, *Denmark* .... 17 H2 56 6N   8 38 E
Videle, *Romania* .... 53 F10 44 17N 25 31 E
Videseter, *Norway* .... 18 C4 61 57N   7 14 E
Vidette, *U.S.A.* 152 B7 33 2N 82 15W
Vídho, *Greece* .... 38 B9 39 38N 19 55 E
Vidigueira, *Portugal* 43 G3 38 12N   7 48W
Vidin, *Bulgaria* .... 50 C6 43 59N 22 50 E
Vidio, C., *Spain* 43 A3 43 35N   6 14W
Vidisha, *India* .... 92 H7 23 28N 77 53 E
Vidra, *Romania* .... 53 E11 45 56N 26 55 E
Viduša, *Bos.-H.* .... 50 D2 42 55N 18 21 E
Vidzy, *Belarus* .... 15 J22 55 23N 26 37 E
Viechtach, *Germany* .... 31 F8 49 4N 12 53 E
Viedma, *Argentina* .... 176 B4 40 50 S 63 0W
Viedma, L., *Argentina* .... 176 C2 49 30 S 72 30W
Vieira do Minho, *Portugal* 42 D2 41 38N   8 8W
Vielha, *Spain* .... 40 C5 42 43N   0 44 E
Viella = Vielha, *Spain* .... 40 C5 42 43N   0 44 E
Vielsalm, *Belgium* .... 24 D5 50 17N   5 54 E
Vienenburg, *Germany* .... 30 D6 51 57N 10 34 E
Vieng Pou Kha, *Laos* .... 76 G3 20 41N 101 4 E
Vienna = Wien, *Austria* .... 35 C9 48 12N 16 22 E
Vienna, *Ga., U.S.A.* 152 C6 32 6N 83 47W
Vienna, *Ill., U.S.A.* 155 G10 37 25N 88 54W
Vienna, *Mo., U.S.A.* 156 F5 38 11N 91 57W
Vienna ✈ (VIA), *Austria* .... 35 C9 48 11N 16 35 E
Vienne, *France* .... 29 C8 45 31N   4 53 E
Vienne □, *France* .... 26 B4 46 30N   0 42 E
Vienne ➤, *France* .... 26 E7 47 13N   0 5 E
Vientiane, *Laos* .... 86 D4 17 58N 102 36 E
Vientos, Paso de los, *Caribbean* .. 165 C5 20 0N 74 0W
Vieques, Isla de, *Puerto Rico* ..... 165 d 18 8N 65 25W
Vierge Pt., *St. Lucia* .... 165 f   13 49N 60 53W
Viernheim, *Germany* .... 31 F4 49 31N   8 35 E
Viersen, *Germany* .... 30 D2 51 15N   6 23 E
Vierwaldstättersee, *Switz.* .... 33 C7 47 0N   8 30 E
Vierzon, *France* .... 27 E9 47 13N   2 5 E
Vieste, *Italy* .... 45 G13 41 53N 16 10 E
Vietnam ■, *Asia* .... 86 C6 19 0N 106 0 E
Vieux-Boucau-les-Bains, *France* ... 28 E2 43 48N   1 23W
Vieux Fort, *St. Lucia* .... 165 f   13 46N 60 58W
Vif, *France* .... 29 C9 45 5N   5 41 E
Viga, *Phil.* .... 80 E5 13 52N 124 18 E
Vigan, *Phil.* .... 80 C3 17 35N 120 28 E
Vigévano, *Italy* .... 44 C5 45 19N   8 51 E
Vigia = Almenara, *Brazil* .... 173 E8 16 11 S 40 42W
Vigia, *Brazil* .... 170 B2   0 50 S 48 5W
Vigia Chico, *Mexico* 163 D7 19 46N 87 35W
Vigla, *Greece* .... 39 A2 39 7N 20 50 E
Víglas, Ákra, *Greece* .... 38 F11 35 54N 27 51 E
Vignemale, *France* 28 F3 42 47N   0 10W
Vigneulles-lès-Hattonchâtel, *France* .. 27 D12 48 59N   5 43 E
Vignola, *Italy* .... 44 D8 44 29N 11 1 E
Vigo, *Spain* 42 C2 42 12N   8 41W
Vigo, Ría de, *Spain* 42 C2 42 15N   8 45W
Vigrestad, *Norway* .... 18 F2 58 34N   5 42 E
Vigsø Bugt, *Denmark* .... 17 G2 57 8N   8 47 E
Vihiers, *France* 26 E6 47 10N   0 30W
Vihowa, *Pakistan* .... 90 D4 31 8N 70 30 E
Vihowa ➤, *Pakistan* .... 92 D4 31 8N 70 41 E
Viipuri = Vyborg, *Russia* .... 58 B5 60 43N 28 47 E
Vijayapadurg, *India* .... 94 F1 16 30N 73 25 E
Vijayawada, *India* .... 94 F5 16 31N 80 39 E
Vijosë ➤, *Albania* .... 50 F3 40 37N 19 24 E
Vík, *Iceland* 11 D7 63 25N 19 1W
Vik, *Norway* .... 18 C3 61 21N   6 6 E
Vika, *Sweden* .... 16 D8 60 57N 14 28 E
Vikarbyn, *Sweden* .... 16 D9 60 55N 15 1 E
Vike, *Norway* .... 18 D2 60 42N   5 35 E
Vikedal, *Norway* .... 18 E2 59 30N   5 55 E
Vikeke = Viqueque, *E. Timor* ..... 82 C3   8 52 S 126 23 E
Vikeland, *Norway* .... 18 F4 58 5N   7 18 E
Viken, *Skåne, Sweden* .... 17 H6 56 9N 12 34 E
Viken, *Västra Götaland, Sweden* .. 17 F8 58 39N 14 20 E
Vikersund, *Norway* .... 18 E6 59 58N   9 59 E
Vikeså, *Norway* .... 18 F3 58 36N   6 3 E
Vikevåg, *Norway* .... 18 E2 59 5N   5 41 E
Viking, *Canada* 142 C6 53 7N 111 50W
Vikmanshyttan, *Sweden* .... 16 D9 60 18N 15 50 E
Vikna, *Norway* .... 14 D14 64 55N 10 58 E
Vikos-Aoos △, *Greece* .... 48 B2 40 0N 20 45 E
Viksøyri, *Norway* .... 18 C3 61 4N   6 34 E
Vila António Enes = Angoche,
   Mozam. .... 119 F4 16 8 S 39 55 E
Vila Bela da Santissima Trindade,
   Brazil .... 173 C6 15 0 S 59 57W
Vila da Maganja, *Mozam.* .... 119 F4 17 18 S 37 30 E
Vila da Ribeira Brava, *C. Verde Is.* . 9 j
Vila de João Belo = Xai-Xai,
   Mozam. .... 117 D5 25 6 S 33 31 E
Vila de Rei, *Portugal* 42 F2 39 41N   8 9W
Vila do Bispo, *Portugal* 43 H2 37 5N   8 53W
Vila do Conde, *Portugal* 42 D2 41 21N   8 45W
Vila do Porto, *Azores* 9 d4 36 56N   25 9W
Vila Franca de Xira, *Portugal* 43 G2 38 57N   8 59W
Vila Franca do Campo, *Azores* ... 9 d3 37 43N 25 26W
Vila Gamito, *Mozam.* .... 119 E3 14 12 S 33 0 E
Vila Gomes da Costa, *Mozam.* .... 117 C5 24 20 S 33 37 E
Vila Machado, *Mozam.* .... 119 F3 19 15 S 34 14 E
Vila Mouzinho, *Mozam.* .... 119 E3 14 48 S 34 25 E
Vila Nova de Famalicão, *Portugal* . 42 D2 41 25N   8 32W
Vila Nova de Fos Côa, *Portugal* ... 42 D3 41 5N   7 9W
Vila Nova de Gaia, *Portugal* 42 D2 41 4N   8 40W
Vila Nova de Ourém, *Portugal* 42 F2 39 40N   8 35W
Vila Nova do Corvo, *Azores* 9 d2 39 40N 31 8W
Vila Pouca de Aguiar, *Portugal* ... 42 D3 41 30N   7 38W
Vila Real, *Portugal* 42 D3 41 17N   7 48W
Vila Real □, *Portugal* 42 D3 41 36N   7 35W
Vila-real de los Infantes, *Spain* ... 40 F4 39 55N   0 3W
Vila Real de Santo António,
   Portugal 43 H3 37 10N   7 28W

Vila Vasco da Gama, *Mozam.* ..... 119 E3 14 54 S 32 14 E
Vila Velha, *Amapá, Brazil* 169 C7   3 13N 51 13W
Vila Velha, *Espírito Santo, Brazil* . 171 F3 20 20 S 40 17W
Vila Viçosa, *Portugal* 43 G3 38 45N   7 27W
Vilafranca del Maestrat, *Spain* 40 E4 40 26N   0 16W
Vilafranca del Penedès, *Spain* .... 40 D6 41 21N   1 40 E
Vilagarcía de Arousa, *Spain* 42 C2 42 34N   8 46W
Vilaine ➤, *France* 26 E4 47 30N   2 27W
Vilakalaka, *Vanuatu* .... 133 E5 15 25 S 167 42 E
Vilanandro, Tanjona, *Madag.* ..... 117 B7 16 11 S 44 27 E
Vilanculos, *Mozam.* .... 117 C6 22 1 S 35 17 E
Vilanova de Castelló, *Spain* 41 F4 39 5N   0 31W
Vilanova i la Geltrú, *Spain* .... 40 D6 41 13N   1 40 E
Vilar Formoso, *Portugal* 42 E4 40 38N   6 45W
Vilaseca, *Spain* .... 41 D6 41 7N   1 9 E
Vilaseca-Salou = Vilaseca, *Spain* .. 40 D6 41 7N   1 9 E
Vilbjerg, *Denmark* .... 17 H2 56 12N   8 46 E
Vilcabamba, Cordillera, *Peru* ..... 172 C3 13 0 S 73 0W
Vilcanchos, *Peru* .... 172 C3 13 40 S 74 25W
Vilches, *Spain* 43 G7 38 12N   3 30W
Vileyka, *Belarus* .... 58 E4 54 30N 26 53 E
Vilhelmina, *Sweden* .... 14 D17 64 35N 16 39 E
Vilhena, *Brazil* .... 173 C5 12 40 S 60 5W
Viliga, *Russia* .... 67 C16 61 36N 156 56 E
Viliya = Neris ➤, *Lithuania* ...... 15 J21 55 8N 24 16 E
Viljandi, *Estonia* .... 15 G21 58 28N 25 30 E
Vilkaviškis, *Lithuania* .... 54 D10 54 39N 23 2 E
Vilkija, *Lithuania* .... 54 C10 55 3N 23 35 E
Vilkitskogo, Proliv, *Russia* .... 67 B11 78 0N 103 0 E
Vilkovo = Vylkove, *Ukraine* .... 59 K5 45 28N 29 32 E
Villa Abecia, *Bolivia* .... 174 A2 21 0 S 68 18W
Villa Ahumada, *Mexico* 162 A3 30 38N 106 30W
Villa Ana, *Argentina* .... 174 B4 28 28 S 59 40W
Villa Ángela, *Argentina* .... 174 B3 27 34 S 60 45W
Villa Bella, *Bolivia* .... 173 C4 10 25 S 65 22W
Villa Bens = Tarfaya, *Morocco* 110 C2 27 55N 12 55W
Villa Cañás, *Argentina* .... 174 C3 34 0 S 61 35W
Villa Cisneros = Dakhla, *W. Sahara* 110 D1 23 50N 15 53W
Villa Colón, *Argentina* .... 172 C2 31 38 S 68 20W
Villa Constitución, *Argentina* ..... 174 C3 33 15 S 60 20W
Villa de Cura, *Venezuela* 168 A4 10 2N 67 29W
Villa de María, *Argentina* .... 174 B3 29 55 S 63 43W
Villa del Río, *Spain* 43 H6 37 59N   4 17W
Villa del Rosario, *Venezuela* 168 A3 10 19N 72 19W
Villa Dolores, *Argentina* .... 174 C2 31 58 S 65 15W
Villa Frontera, *Mexico* 162 B4 26 56N 101 27W
Villa Grove, *U.S.A.* 157 E8 39 52N 105 56W
Villa Guillermina, *Argentina* ...... 174 B4 28 15 S 59 29W
Villa Hayes, *Paraguay* .... 174 B4 25 5 S 57 20W
Villa Iris, *Argentina* .... 174 D3 38 12 S 63 12W
Villa Juárez, *Mexico* 162 B4 27 37N 100 44W
Villa María, *Argentina* .... 174 C3 32 20 S 63 10W
Villa Mazán, *Argentina* .... 174 B2 28 40 S 66 30W
Villa Minozzo, *Italy* .... 44 D7 44 22N 10 28 E
Villa Montes, *Bolivia* .... 174 A3 21 10 S 63 30W
Villa Ocampo, *Argentina* .... 174 B4 28 30 S 59 20W
Villa Ocampo, *Mexico* 162 B3 26 29N 105 30W
Villa Ojo de Agua, *Argentina* ..... 174 B3 29 30 S 63 44W
Villa Rica, *U.S.A.* 152 C3 33 44N 84 55W
Villa San Giovanni, *Italy* .... 47 D8 38 13N 15 38 E
Villa San José, *Argentina* .... 174 C4 32 12 S 58 15W
Villa San Martín, *Argentina* .... 174 B3 28 6 S 64 9W
Villa Sanjurjo = Al Hoceïma,
   Morocco 110 A4 35 8N   3 58W
Villa Santina, *Italy* .... 45 B9 46 24N 12 55 E
Villa Unión, *Mexico* 162 C3 23 12N 106 14W
Villaba, *Phil.* .... 81 F5 11 13N 124 24 E
Villablino, *Spain* 42 C4 42 57N   6 19W
Villacarlos, *Spain* .... 38 B5 39 53N   4 17 E
Villacarriedo, *Spain* 42 B7 43 14N   3 48W
Villacarrillo, *Spain* 43 G7 38 7N   3 3W
Villacastín, *Spain* 42 E6 40 46N   4 25W
Villach, *Austria* .... 34 E6 46 37N 13 51 E
Villacidro, *Italy* .... 46 C1 39 27N   8 44 E
Villada, *Spain* 42 C6 42 15N   4 59W
Villadiego, *Spain* 42 C6 42 31N   4 1W
Villadóssola, *Italy* .... 44 B5 46 4N   8 16 E
Villafeliche, *Spain* 40 D3 41 10N   1 30W
Villafranca, *Spain* 40 C3 42 17N   1 46W
Villafranca de los Barros, *Spain* ... 43 G4 38 35N   6 18W
Villafranca de los Caballeros, *Spain* 43 F7 39 26N   3 21W
Villafranca del Cid = Vilafranca del
   Maestrat, *Spain* 40 E4 40 26N   0 16W
Villafranca del Panadés = Vilafranca
   del Penedès, *Spain* .... 40 D6 41 21N   1 40 E
Villafranca di Verona, *Italy* .... 44 C7 45 21N 10 50 E
Villafranca Tirrena, *Italy* .... 47 D8 38 13N 15 25 E
Villagio Mussolini = Arboréa, *Italy* . 46 C1 39 46N   8 35 E
Villagrán, *Mexico* 163 C5 24 29N 99 29W
Villaguay, *Argentina* .... 174 C4 32 0 S 59 0W
Villaharta, *Spain* 43 G6 38 9N   4 54W
Villahermosa, *Mexico* 163 D6 17 59N 92 55W
Villahermosa, *Spain* 41 G2 38 46N   2 52W
Villaines-la-Juhel, *France* 26 D6 48 15N   0 20W
Villajoyosa, *Spain* 41 G4 38 30N   0 12W
Villalba, *Spain* 42 B3 43 26N   7 40W
Villalba de Guardo, *Spain* 42 C6 42 42N   4 49W
Villalón de Campos, *Spain* 42 C5 42 5N   5 4W
Villalpando, *Spain* 42 D5 41 51N   5 25W
Villaluenga, *Spain* 42 E7 40 2N   3 54W
Villamanán, *Spain* 42 C5 42 19N   5 35W
Villamartín, *Spain* 43 J5 36 52N   5 38W
Villamayor de Santiago, *Spain* 42 F2 39 50N   2 59W
Villamblard, *France* .... 28 C4 45 2N   0 32 E
Villanova Monteleone, *Italy* ...... 46 B1 40 30N   8 28 E
Villanueva, *Colombia* 168 A3 10 37N 72 59W
Villanueva, *U.S.A.* 157 H2 35 16N 105 22W
Villanueva de Castellón = Vilanova
   de Castelló, *Spain* 41 F4 39 5N   0 31W
Villanueva de Córdoba, *Spain* 43 G6 38 20N   4 38W
Villanueva de la Fuente, *Spain* ... 41 G2 38 42N   2 42W
Villanueva de la Serena, *Spain* ... 43 G5 38 59N   5 50W
Villanueva de la Sierra, *Spain* 42 E4 40 12N   6 24W
Villanueva de los Castillejos, *Spain* 43 H3 37 30N   7 15W
Villanueva de los Infantes, *Spain* . 43 G7 38 43N   3 1W
Villanueva del Arzobispo, *Spain* .. 41 G2 38 3N   3 0W
Villanueva del Fresno, *Spain* 43 G3 38 23N   7 10W
Villanueva y Geltrú = Vilanova i la
   Geltrú, *Spain* .... 40 D6 41 13N   1 40 E
Villaputzu, *Italy* .... 46 C2 39 26N   9 34 E
Villaquilambre, *Spain* 42 C5 42 39N   5 33W
Villar del Arzobispo, *Spain* 40 F4 39 44N   0 50W
Villar del Rey, *Spain* 43 F4 39 7N   6 50W
Villard-de-Lans, *France* .... 29 C9 45 3N   5 33 E
Villarramiel, *Spain* 42 C6 42 2N   4 55W
Villarreal = Vila-real de los Infantes,
   Spain 40 F4 39 55N   0 3W
Villarrica, *Chile* .... 176 A2 39 15 S 72 15W
Villarrica, *Paraguay* .... 174 B4 25 40 S 56 30W
Villarrobledo, *Spain* 41 F2 39 18N   2 36W
Villarroya de la Sierra, *Spain* 40 D3 41 27N   1 46W
Villarrubia de los Ojos, *Spain* 43 F7 39 14N   3 36W
Villars-les-Dombes, *France* .... 27 F12 46 0N   5 2 E
Villasayas, *Spain* 40 D2 41 2N   2 39W
Villaseca de los Gamitos = Villaseco
   de los Gamitos, *Spain* 42 D4 41 2N   6 7W
Villaseco de los Gamitos, *Spain* .. 42 D4 41 2N   6 7W
Villasimíus, *Italy* .... 46 C2 39 8N   9 31 E
Villastar, *Spain* 42 F7 40 17N   1 9W
Villatobas, *Spain* 42 F7 39 54N   3 20W
Villavicencio, *Argentina* .... 172 C2 32 28 S 69 18W
Villavicencio, *Colombia* 168 C3   4 9N 73 37W
Villaviciosa, *Spain* 42 B5 43 32N   5 27W

Villazón, *Bolivia* .... 174 A2 22 0 S 65 35W
Ville-Marie, *Canada* 140 C4 47 20N 79 30W
Ville Platte, *U.S.A.* 155 K8 30 41N 92 17W
Villedieu-les-Poêles, *France* 26 D5 48 50N   1 13W
Villefort, *France* .... 28 D7 44 28N   3 56 E
Villefranche-de-Lauragais, *France* . 28 E5 43 25N   1 44 E
Villefranche-de-Rouergue, *France* . 28 D6 44 21N   2 2 E
Villefranche-du-Périgord, *France* .. 28 D5 44 38N   1 5 E
Villefranche-sur-Saône, *France* ... 29 C8 45 59N   4 43 E
Villegrande, *Bolivia* .... 173 D5 18 30 S 64 10W
Villel, *Spain* 40 E3 40 14N   1 12W
Villemur-sur-Tarn, *France* .... 28 E5 43 51N   1 31 E
Villena, *Spain* 41 G4 38 39N   0 52W
Villenauxe-la-Grande, *France* ..... 27 D10 48 35N   3 33 E
Villeneuve-d'Ornon, *France* 28 D3 44 46N   0 33W
Villeneuve, *Switz.* .... 32 D3 46 24N   6 56 E
Villeneuve-l'Archevêque, *France* .. 27 D10 48 5N   3 32 E
Villeneuve-lès-Avignon, *France* ... 27 E8 43 58N   4 49 E
Villeneuve-sur-Allier, *France* ..... 27 F10 46 40N   3 13 E
Villeneuve-sur-Lot, *France* .... 28 D4 44 24N   0 42 E
Villeneuve-sur-Yonne, *France* .... 27 D10 48 5N   3 18 E
Villeréal, *France* .... 28 D4 44 38N   0 45 E
Villers-Bocage, *France* 26 C6 49 3N   0 40W
Villers-Cotterêts, *France* .... 27 C10 49 15N   3 4 E
Villers-sur-Mer, *France* 26 C6 49 21N   0 2W
Villersexel, *France* .... 27 E13 47 33N   6 26 E
Villers, *S. Africa* .... 117 D4 27 2 S 28 36 E
Villeurbanne, *France* .... 29 C8 45 49N   4 55 E
Villingen-Schwenningen, *Germany* 31 G4 48 3N   8 26 E
Villisca, *U.S.A.* 156 D2 40 56N 94 59W
Villupuram, *India* .... 95 J4 11 59N 79 31 E
Vilna = Vilnius, *Lithuania* .... 15 J21 54 38N 25 19 E
Vilna, *Canada* 142 C6 54 7N 111 55W
Vilnius, *Lithuania* .... 15 J21 54 38N 25 19 E
Vils, *Austria* .... 34 D3 47 33N 10 38 E
Vils ➤, *Bayern, Germany* .... 31 G9 48 37N 13 11 E
Vils ➤, *Bayern, Germany* .... 31 F7 49 10N 11 57 E
Vilsbiburg, *Germany* .... 31 G8 48 27N 12 22 E
Vilshofen, *Germany* .... 31 G9 48 37N 13 11 E
Vilusi, *Montenegro, Yug.* .... 50 D2 42 44N 18 34 E
Vilvoorde, *Belgium* .... 24 C4 50 56N   4 26 E
Vilyuy ➤, *Russia* .... 67 C13 64 24N 126 26 E
Vilyuysk, *Russia* .... 67 C13 63 40N 121 35 E
Vimianzo, *Spain* 42 B1 43 7N   9 2W
Vimioso, *Portugal* 42 D4 41 35N   6 31W
Vimmerby, *Sweden* .... 17 G9 57 40N 15 55 E
Vimoutiers, *France* .... 26 D7 48 57N   0 10 E
Vimperk, *Czech Rep.* .... 34 B6 49 3N 13 46 E
Vina ➤, *Cameroon* .... 114 A3   7 45N 15 36 E
Viña del Mar, *Chile* .... 174 C1 33 0 S 71 30W
Vinarós, *Spain* .... 40 E5 40 30N   0 27 E
Vincennes, *U.S.A.* 157 F9 38 41N 87 32W
Vincent, *U.S.A.* 161 L8 34 33N 118 11W
Vinces, *Ecuador* .... 168 D2   1 32 S 79 45W
Vinchina, *Argentina* .... 174 B2 28 45 S 68 15W
Vindava = Ventspils, *Latvia* ...... 15 H19 57 25N 21 32 E
Vindelälven ➤, *Sweden* .... 14 D18 63 58N 19 50 E
Vindeln, *Sweden* .... 14 D18 64 12N 19 43 E
Vinderup, *Denmark* .... 17 H2 56 29N   8 45 E
Vindhya Ra., *India* .... 92 H7 22 50N 77 0 E
Vine Grove, *U.S.A.* 157 G11 37 49N 85 59W
Vineland, *U.S.A.* 148 F8 39 29N 75 2W
Vineuil, *France* .... 26 E8 47 35N   1 22 E
Vinga, *Romania* .... 52 D6 46 1N 21 14 E
Vingåker, *Sweden* .... 16 E9 59 2N 15 52 E
Vingnes, *Norway* .... 18 C7 61 7N 10 26 E
Vinh, *Vietnam* .... 86 C5 18 45N 105 38 E
Vinh Linh, *Vietnam* .... 86 D6 17 4N 107 2 E
Vinh Loi = Bac Lieu, *Vietnam* .... 87 H5   9 17N 105 43 E
Vinh Long, *Vietnam* .... 87 G5 10 16N 105 57 E
Vinh Yen, *Vietnam* .... 76 G5 21 21N 105 35 E
Vinhais, *Portugal* 42 D3 41 50N   7 5W
Vinica, *Croatia* .... 45 B13 46 20N 16 9 E
Vinica, *Macedonia* .... 50 E6 41 53N 22 30 E
Vinica, *Slovenia* .... 45 C12 45 28N 15 16 E
Vinita, *U.S.A.* 155 G7 36 39N 95 9W
Vinje, *Hordaland, Norway* .... 18 D3 60 48N   6 30 E
Vinje, *Sør-Trøndelag, Norway* .... 18 A5 63 12N   9 0 E
Vinje, *Telemark, Norway* .... 18 E4 59 37N   7 51 E
Vinkovci, *Croatia* .... 52 E3 45 19N 18 48 E
Vinnitsa = Vinnytsya, *Ukraine* .... 59 H5 49 15N 28 30 E
Vinnytsya, *Ukraine* .... 59 H5 49 15N 28 30 E
Vinslöv, *Sweden* .... 17 H7 56 7N 13 55 E
Vinstra, *Norway* .... 18 C6 61 37N   9 44 E
Vinstra ➤, *Norway* .... 18 C6 61 37N   9 44 E
Vintar, *Phil.* .... 80 B3 18 14N 120 39 E
Vintjärn, *Sweden* .... 16 D10 60 50N 16 4 E
Vinton, *Calif., U.S.A.* 160 F6 39 48N 120 10W
Vinton, *Iowa, U.S.A.* 156 D4 42 10N 92 1W
Vinton, *La., U.S.A.* 155 K8 30 11N 93 35W
Vinţu de Jos, *Romania* .... 53 D8 46 0N 23 30 E
Vinukonda, *India* .... 95 F4 16 4N 79 45 E
Viöl, *Germany* .... 30 A5 54 34N   9 11 E
Viola, *U.S.A.* 156 C6 41 12N 90 35W
Violet Town, *Australia* .... 129 D6 36 38 S 145 42 E
Vipava, *Slovenia* .... 45 C10 45 51N 13 58 E
Vipiteno, *Italy* .... 44 B8 46 54N 11 26 E
Viqueque, *E. Timor* .... 82 C3   8 52 S 126 23 E
Vir, *Croatia* .... 45 D12 44 17N 15 3 E
Vira, *Switz.* .... 33 D7 46 8N   8 50 E
Virac, *Phil.* .... 80 E5 13 30N 124 20 E
Virachey, *Cambodia* .... 86 E6 13 59N 106 49 E
Virago Sd., *Canada* 142 C2 54 0N 132 30W
Virajpet = Virarajendrapet, *India* . 95 H2 12 10N 75 50 E
Viramgam, *India* .... 92 H5 23 5N 72 0 E
Viranşehir, *Turkey* .... 101 D8 37 13N 39 45 E
Virarajendrapet, *India* .... 95 H2 12 10N 75 50 E
Virawah, *Pakistan* .... 92 G4 24 31N 70 46 E
Virbalis, *Lithuania* .... 54 D9 54 32N 22 49 E
Virden, *Canada* 143 D8 49 50N 100 56W
Virden, *U.S.A.* 156 E7 39 30N 89 46W
Vire, *France* 26 D6 48 50N   0 53W
Vire ➤, *France* 26 C5 49 20N   1 7W
Virei, *Angola* .... 115 F2 15 43 S 12 52 E
Virgem da Lapa, *Brazil* .... 171 E3 16 49 S 42 21W
Vírgenes, C., *Argentina* .... 176 D3 52 19 S 68 21W
Virgin ➤, *U.S.A.* 159 H6 36 28N 114 21W
Virgin Gorda, *Br. Virgin Is.* ...... 165 e   18 30N 64 26W
Virgin Is. (British) ✕, *W. Indies* .. 165 e   18 30N 64 30W
Virgin Is. (U.S.) ✕, *W. Indies* .... 165 e   18 20N 64 50W
Virgin Islands Nat. Park △, *Virgin Is.* 165 C7 18 21N 64 43W
Virginia, *S. Africa* .... 116 D4 28 8 S 26 55 E
Virginia, *U.S.A.* 156 E6 39 57N 90 13W
Virginia, *Minn., U.S.A.* 156 B8 47 31N 92 32W
Virginia □, *U.S.A.* 148 G7 37 30N 78 45W
Virginia Beach, *U.S.A.* 148 G8 36 49N 75 59W
Virginia City, *Mont., U.S.A.* 158 D8 45 18N 111 56W
Virginia City, *Nev., U.S.A.* 160 F7 39 19N 119 39W
Virginia Falls, *Canada* 142 A3 61 38N 125 42W
Virginiatown, *Canada* 140 C4 48 9N 79 36W
Virje, *Croatia* .... 45 B13 46 4N 16 59 E
Viroqua, *U.S.A.* 154 D9 43 34N 90 53W
Virovitica, *Croatia* .... 52 E2 45 51N 17 21 E
Virpazar, *Montenegro, Yug.* ...... 50 D3 42 14N 19 6 E
Virpur, *India* .... 92 J4 21 51N 70 42 E
Virserum, *Sweden* .... 17 G9 57 20N 15 35 E
Virton, *Belgium* .... 24 E5 49 35N   5 32 E
Virú, *Peru* .... 172 B2   8 25 S 78 45W

Virudunagar, *India* .... 95 K3   9 30N 77 58 E
Virunga, Parc Nat. des △, *Dem. Rep.
   of the Congo* .... 118 B2   0 5N 29 38 E
Vis, *Croatia* .... 45 E13 43 4N 16 10 E
Visalia, *U.S.A.* 160 J7 36 20N 119 18W
Visayan Sea, *Phil.* .... 81 F4 11 30N 123 30 E
Visby, *Sweden* .... 17 G12 57 37N 18 18 E
Viscount Melville Sd., *Canada* 6 B2 74 10N 108 0W
Visé, *Belgium* .... 24 D5 50 44N   5 41 E
Višegrad, *Bos.-H.* .... 52 G4 43 47N 19 17 E
Viseu, *Brazil* .... 170 B2   1 10 S 46 5W
Viseu, *Portugal* 42 E3 40 40N   7 55W
Viseu □, *Portugal* 42 E3 40 40N   7 55W
Vişeu de Sus, *Romania* .... 53 C9 47 45N 24 25 E
Vishakhapatnam, *India* .... 94 F6 17 45N 83 20 E
Vishera ➤, *Russia* .... 64 A6 59 55N 56 25 E
Vişina, *Romania* .... 53 G9 43 52N 24 27 E
Vişineşti, *Moldova* .... 53 D13 46 20N 28 27 E
Visingsö, *Sweden* .... 17 F8 58 2N 14 20 E
Viskafors, *Sweden* .... 17 G6 57 37N 12 50 E
Viskan ➤, *Sweden* .... 17 G6 57 14N 12 12 E
Viški Kanal, *Croatia* .... 45 E13 43 4N 16 5 E
Vislanda, *Sweden* .... 17 H8 56 46N 14 30 E
Visnagar, *India* .... 92 H5 23 45N 72 32 E
Višnja Gora, *Slovenia* .... 45 C11 45 58N 14 45 E
Viso, Mte., *Italy* .... 44 D4 44 38N   7 5 E
Viso del Marqués, *Spain* 43 G7 38 32N   3 34W
Visokoi I., *Antarctica* .... 7 B1 56 43 S 27 15W
Visp, *Switz.* .... 32 D5 46 9N   7 48 E
Vispa ➤, *Switz.* .... 32 D5 46 9N   7 48 E
Vissefjarda, *Sweden* .... 17 H9 56 32N 15 35 E
Visselhövede, *Germany* .... 30 C5 52 59N   9 34 E
Vissenbjerg, *Denmark* .... 17 J4 55 23N 10 7 E
Vissoie, *Switz.* .... 32 D5 46 13N   7 36 E
Vista, *U.S.A.* 161 M9 33 12N 117 14W
Vistonikos, Ormos = Vistonís, Límni,
   Greece .... 51 E9 41 0N 25 7 E
Vistonís, Límni, *Greece* .... 51 E9 41 0N 25 7 E
Vistula = Wisła ➤, *Poland* .... 54 D5 54 22N 18 55 E
Vit ➤, *Bulgaria* .... 51 C8 43 30N 24 30 E
Vita, *India* .... 94 F2 17 17N 74 33 E
Vitanje, *Slovenia* .... 45 B12 46 25N 15 18 E
Vitebsk = Vitsyebsk, *Belarus* ..... 58 E6 55 10N 30 15 E
Viterbo, *Italy* .... 45 F9 42 25N 12 6 E
Viti Levu, *Fiji* .... 133 A1 17 30 S 177 30 E
Vitiaz Str., *Papua N. G.* .... 132 C4   5 40 S 147 10 E
Vitigudino, *Spain* 42 D4 41 1N   6 26W
Vitim, *Russia* .... 67 D12 59 28N 112 34 E
Vitim ➤, *Russia* .... 67 D12 59 26N 112 34 E
Vitina, *Bos.-H.* .... 45 E14 43 17N 17 29 E
Vitína, *Greece* .... 48 D4 37 40N 22 10 E
Vítkov, *Czech Rep.* .... 35 B10 49 46N 17 45 E
Vitória, *Espírito Santo, Brazil* ..... 171 F3 20 20 S 40 22W
Vitória, *Pará, Brazil* .... 169 D7   2 54 S 52 1W
Vitória da Conquista, *Brazil* ...... 171 D3 14 51 S 40 51W
Vitória de São Antão, *Brazil* ...... 170 C4   8 10 S 35 20W
Vitoria-Gasteiz, *Spain* 40 C2 42 50N   2 41W
Vitorino Freire, *Brazil* .... 170 B2   4 4 S 45 10W
Vítosha, ≤, *Bulgaria* .... 50 D7 42 36N 23 15 E
Vitré, *France* 26 D5 48 8N   1 12W
Vitry-le-François, *France* .... 27 D11 48 43N   4 33 E
Vitry-sur-Seine, *France* .... 27 D9 48 47N   2 2 E
Vitsand, *Sweden* .... 16 D7 60 20N 13 0 E
Vitsi, Óros, *Greece* .... 50 F5 40 40N 21 25 E
Vittaryd, *Sweden* .... 17 H7 56 58N 13 57 E
Vitteaux, *France* .... 27 E11 47 24N   4 30 E
Vittel, *France* .... 27 D12 48 12N   5 57 E
Vittória, *Italy* .... 47 F7 36 57N 14 32 E
Vittório Véneto, *Italy* .... 45 C9 45 59N 12 18 E
Vittoriosa, *Malta* .... 38 F8 35 54N 14 31 E
Vittsjö, *Sweden* .... 17 H7 56 20N 13 40 E
Vitznau, *Switz.* .... 33 B6 47 1N   8 29 E
Viveiro, *Spain* 42 B3 43 39N   7 38W
Viviers, *France* .... 29 D8 44 30N   4 40 E
Vivonne, *Australia* .... 128 C2 35 59 S 137 9 E
Vivonne, *France* .... 28 B4 46 25N   0 15 E
Vivonne B., *Australia* .... 128 C2 35 59 S 137 9 E
Viwa, *Fiji* .... 133 A1 17 10 S 177 58 E
Vizagapatam = Vishakhapatnam,
   India .... 94 F6 17 45N 83 20 E
Vizcaíno, Desierto de, *Mexico* 162 B2 27 40N 113 50W
Vizcaíno, Sierra, *Mexico* 162 B2 27 30N 114 0W
Vizcaya □, *Spain* 40 B2 43 15N   2 45W
Vizianagaram, *India* .... 94 E6 18 6N 83 30 E
Vizille, *France* .... 29 C9 45 5N   5 46 E
Vizinada, *Croatia* .... 45 C10 45 20N 13 46 E
Viziru, *Romania* .... 53 E12 45 0N 27 43 E
Vizzini, *Italy* .... 47 F7 37 10N 14 45 E
Vlaardingen, *Neths.* .... 24 C4 51 55N   4 21 E
Vlădeasa, Vf., *Romania* .... 52 D7 46 47N 22 50 E
Vladičin Han, *Serbia, Yug.* .... 50 D6 42 42N 22 1 E
Vladikavkaz, *Russia* .... 61 J7 43 0N 44 35 E
Vladimir, *Russia* .... 58 D11 56 15N 40 30 E
Vladimir Volynskiy = Volodymyr-
   Volynskyy, *Ukraine* .... 59 G3 50 50N 24 18 E
Vladimirci, *Serbia, Yug.* .... 50 B4 44 36N 19 48 E
Vladimirovac, *Serbia, Yug.* .... 50 B5 45 1N 20 53 E
Vladimirovka, *Russia* .... 61 F8 48 27N 46 10 E
Vladimirovo, *Bulgaria* .... 50 C7 43 32N 23 22 E
Vladimovka, *Kazakhstan* .... 60 E10 50 51N 51 8 E
Vladislavova, *Ukraine* .... 59 K8 45 12N 35 23 E
Vladivostok, *Russia* .... 67 E14 43 10N 131 53 E
Vlasenica, *Bos.-H.* .... 52 G4 44 11N 18 59 E
Vlašić, *Bos.-H.* .... 52 G4 44 19N 17 37 E
Vlašim, *Czech Rep.* .... 34 B7 49 40N 14 53 E
Vlasinsko Jezero, *Serbia, Yug.* ... 50 D6 42 42N 22 7 E
Vlasotince, *Serbia, Yug.* .... 50 D6 42 59N 22 7 E
Vlieland, *Neths.* .... 24 A4 53 16N   4 55 E
Vlissingen, *Neths.* .... 24 C3 51 26N   3 34 E
Vlorë, *Albania* .... 50 F3 40 32N 19 28 E
Vlorës, Gjiri i, *Albania* .... 50 F3 40 29N 19 27 E
Vltava ➤, *Czech Rep.* .... 34 A7 50 21N 14 30 E
Vo Dat, *Vietnam* .... 87 G6 11 9N 107 31 E
Vobarno, *Italy* .... 33 E11 45 39N 10 30 E
Voćin, *Croatia* .... 52 E2 45 37N 17 33 E
Vöcklabruck, *Austria* .... 34 D6 48 1N 13 39 E
Vodice, *Croatia* .... 45 E12 43 47N 15 47 E
Vodňany, *Czech Rep.* .... 34 B7 49 9N 14 11 E
Vodnjan, *Croatia* .... 45 D10 44 59N 13 52 E
Voe, *U.K.* 22 A7 60 21N   1 16W
Vogar, *Iceland* 11 D4 63 58N 22 22W
Vogel Pk., *Nigeria* .... 113 D7 10 43N 11 47 E
Vogelkop = Doberai, Jazirah,
   Indonesia .... 83 B4   1 25 S 133 0 E
Vogelsberg, *Germany* .... 30 E5 50 31N   9 1 E
Voghera, *Italy* .... 44 D6 44 59N   9 1 E
Vogorno, *Switz.* .... 33 D7 46 11N   8 51 E
Voh, *N. Cal.* .... 133 T18 20 58 S 164 42 E
Vohibinany, *Madag.* .... 117 B8 18 49 S 49 4 E
Vohilava, *Madag.* .... 117 C8 21 4 S 48 0 E
Vohimarina = Iharana, *Madag.* ... 117 A9 13 25 S 50 0 E
Vohimena, Tanjon' i, *Madag.* ..... 117 D8 25 36 S 45 8 E
Vohipeno, *Madag.* .... 117 C8 22 22 S 47 51 E
Voi, *Kenya* .... 118 C4   3 25 S 38 32 E
Void-Vacon, *France* .... 27 D12 48 40N   5 36 E
Voineşti, Iaşi, *Romania* .... 53 C12 47 5N 27 27 E
Voineşti, Prahova, *Romania* ...... 53 E10 45 5N 25 14 E

Voíotía □, Greece .... 48 C5 38 20N 23 0 E
Voiron, France .... 29 C9 45 22N 5 35 E
Voisey B., Canada 141 A7 56 15N 61 50W
Voitsberg, Austria .... 34 D8 47 3N 15 9 E
Vojens, Denmark .... 17 J3 55 16N 9 18 E
Vojmsjön, Sweden .... 14 D17 64 55N 16 40 E
Vojnić, Croatia .... 45 C12 45 19N 15 43 E
Vojnik, Italy .... 45 B12 46 18N 15 19 E
Vokeo I., Papua N. G. .... 132 B3 3 14 S 144 2 E
Vokhtoga, Russia .... 58 C11 58 46N 41 8 E
Volary, Czech Rep. .... 34 C6 48 54N 13 52 E
Volborg, U.S.A. 154 C2 45 51N 105 41W
Volcán de Colima, Parque Nac. △,
  Mexico 162 D4 19 30N 103 40W
Volcano, U.S.A. 145 D6 19 26N 155 14W
Volcano Is. = Kazan-Rettō, Pac. Oc. 134 E6 25 0N 141 0 E
Volcans, Parc Nat. des △, Rwanda 118 C2 1 30 S 29 26 E
Volcans d'Auvergne, Parc Naturel
  Régional des △, France ...... 28 C6 45 20N 2 40 E
Volchansk = Vovchansk, Ukraine .. 59 G9 50 17N 36 58 E
Volchansk, Russia .... 64 B8 59 56N 60 4 E
Volchya →, Ukraine .... 59 H8 48 32N 36 0 E
Volda, Norway .... 18 B3 62 9N 6 5 E
Volga, Russia .... 58 C10 57 58N 38 16 E
Volga →, Russia .... 61 G9 46 0N 48 30 E
Volga Hts. = Privolzhskaya
  Vozvyshennost, Russia .... 60 E7 51 0N 46 0 E
Volgo-Baltiyskiy Kanal, Russia .. 58 B9 60 0N 38 0 E
Volgo-Donskoy Kanal, Russia ... 61 F7 48 40N 43 37 E
Volgodonsk, Russia .... 61 G6 47 33N 42 5 E
Volgograd, Russia .... 61 F7 48 40N 44 25 E
Volgogradskoye Vdkhr., Russia .. 60 E8 50 0N 45 20 E
Volgorechensk, Russia .... 60 B5 57 28N 41 14 E
Volímai, Greece .... 39 D2 37 52N 20 39 E
Volintiri, Moldova .... 53 D14 46 26N 29 37 E
Volissós, Greece .... 49 C7 38 29N 25 54 E
Volkach, Germany .... 31 F6 49 52N 10 14 E
Völkermarkt, Austria .... 34 E7 46 39N 14 39 E
Volkhov, Russia .... 58 C7 59 55N 32 15 E
Volkhov →, Russia .... 58 B7 60 8N 32 20 E
Völklingen, Germany .... 31 F2 49 15N 6 50 E
Volkovysk = Vawkavysk, Belarus . 59 F3 53 9N 24 30 E
Volksrust, S. Africa .... 117 D4 27 24 S 29 53 E
Voll, Norway .... 18 B4 62 31N 7 27 E
Volnansk, Ukraine .... 59 H8 48 2N 35 29 E
Volnovakha, Ukraine .... 59 J9 47 35N 37 30 E
Volochanka, Russia .... 67 B10 71 0N 94 28 E
Volodarsk, Russia .... 60 B6 56 12N 43 15 E
Volodymyr-Volynskyy, Ukraine .. 59 G3 50 50N 24 18 E
Vologda, Russia .... 58 C10 59 10N 39 45 E
Volokolamsk, Russia .... 58 D8 56 5N 35 57 E
Volokonovka, Russia .... 59 G9 50 33N 37 52 E
Vólos, Greece .... 48 B4 39 24N 22 59 E
Vološinovo = Novi Bečej,
  Serbia, Yug. .... 52 E5 45 36N 20 10 E
Volosovo, Russia .... 58 C5 59 27N 29 32 E
Volovets, Ukraine .... 59 H2 48 43N 23 11 E
Volovo, Russia .... 58 F10 53 35N 38 1 E
Volsk, Russia .... 60 D8 52 5N 47 22 E
Volta □, Ghana .... 113 D5 7 0N 0 30 E
Volta →, Ghana .... 113 D5 5 46N 0 41 E
Volta, L., Ghana 113 D5 7 30N 0 0W
Volta Blanche = White Volta →,
  Ghana 113 D4 9 10N 1 15W
Volta Redonda, Brazil .... 171 F3 22 31 S 44 5W
Voltaire, C., Australia .... 124 B4 14 16 S 125 35 E
Volterra, Italy .... 44 E7 43 24N 10 51 E
Voltri, Italy .... 44 D5 44 26N 8 45 E
Volturno →, Italy .... 46 A6 41 1N 13 55 E
Volubilis, Morocco 110 B3 34 2N 5 33W
Vólvi, L., Greece .... 50 F7 40 40N 23 34 E
Volyně, Czech Rep. .... 34 B6 49 10N 13 53 E
Volzhsk, Russia .... 60 C9 55 57N 48 23 E
Volzhskiy, Russia .... 61 F7 48 56N 44 46 E
Vomo, Fiji .... 133 A1 17 30 S 177 15 E
Vonavona, Solomon Is. .... 133 M9 8 15 S 157 5 E
Vondrozo, Madag. .... 117 C8 22 49 S 47 20 E
Vónitsa, Greece .... 39 B2 38 55N 20 53 E
Vopnafjörður, Iceland 11 B12 65 45N 14 50W
Vorarlberg □, Austria .... 34 D2 47 20N 10 0 E
Vóras Óros, Greece .... 50 F5 40 57N 21 45 E
Voray-sur-l'Ognon, France ..... 32 B2 47 20N 6 1 E
Vorbasse, Denmark .... 17 J3 55 39N 9 6 E
Vorchdorf, Austria .... 34 C6 48 0N 13 55 E
Vorderrhein →, Switz. .... 33 C8 46 49N 9 25 E
Vordingborg, Denmark .... 17 J5 55 0N 11 54 E
Vorë, Albania .... 50 E3 41 23N 19 40 E
Voreio Aigaio = Vórios Aiyaíon □,
  Greece .... 49 C7 38 50N 25 30 E
Voreppe, France .... 29 C9 45 18N 5 39 E
Vóriai Sporádhes, Greece ...... 48 B5 39 15N 23 30 E
Vórios Aiyaíon □, Greece ...... 49 C7 38 50N 25 30 E
Vórios Evvoïkos Kólpos, Greece . 48 C5 38 45N 23 15 E
Vorkuta, Russia .... 56 A11 67 48N 64 20 E
Vorma →, Norway .... 18 D8 60 9N 11 29 E
Vormsi, Estonia .... 15 G20 59 1N 23 13 E
Vóroi, Greece .... 39 E5 35 4N 24 49 E
Vorona →, Russia .... 60 E6 51 22N 42 3 E
Voronezh, Russia .... 59 G10 51 40N 39 10 E
Voronezh, Ukraine .... 59 G7 51 47N 33 28 E
Voronezh →, Russia .... 59 G10 51 32N 39 10 E
Vorontsovo-Aleksandrovskoye =
  Zelenokumsk, Russia .... 61 H6 44 24N 44 0 E
Voroshilov = Ussuriysk, Russia .. 67 E14 43 48N 131 59 E
Voroshilovgrad = Luhansk, Ukraine 59 H10 48 38N 39 15 E
Voroshilovsk = Alchevsk, Ukraine 59 H10 48 30N 38 45 E
Vorpommersche Boddenlandschaft,
  Nationalpark △, Germany .... 30 A8 54 25N 12 32 E
Vorskla →, Ukraine .... 59 H8 48 50N 34 10 E
Võrts Järv, Estonia .... 15 G22 58 16N 26 3 E
Võru, Estonia .... 15 H22 57 48N 26 54 E
Vosges, France .... 27 D14 48 20N 7 10 E
Vosges □, France .... 27 D13 48 12N 6 20 E
Vosges du Nord, Parc Naturel
  Régional du △, France .... 27 D14 49 0N 7 30 E
Voskopojë, Albania .... 50 F4 40 35N 20 33 E
Voskresensk, Russia .... 58 E10 55 19N 38 43 E
Voskresenskoye, Russia .... 60 B7 56 51N 45 30 E
Voss, Norway .... 18 D3 60 38N 6 26 E
Vostok, Antarctica .... 7 D8 78 30 S 106 50 E
Vostok I., Kiribati .... 135 J12 10 5 S 152 23W
Votice, Czech Rep. .... 34 B7 49 38N 14 39 E
Votkinsk, Russia .... 64 C4 57 0N 53 55 E
Votkinskoye Vdkhr., Russia .... 64 C5 57 22N 55 12 E
Votsuri-Shima, Japan .... 71 M1 25 45N 123 29 E
Votuporanga, Brazil .... 171 F2 20 24 S 49 59W
Vouga →, Portugal 42 E2 40 41N 8 40W
Vouillé, France .... 26 F7 46 38N 0 10 E
Voulou, C.A.R. .... 114 A4 8 33N 22 36 E
Vouma →, Cameroon .... 114 B2 3 19N 14 9 E
Vouvry, Switz. .... 32 D3 46 21N 6 51 E
Voúxa, Ákra, Greece .... 39 E4 35 37N 23 32 E
Vouzela, Portugal 42 E2 40 43N 8 7W
Vouziers, France .... 27 C11 49 22N 4 40 E
Vovchansk, Ukraine .... 59 G9 50 17N 36 58 E
Vovodo →, C.A.R. .... 114 A4 5 40N 26 2 E
Voyageurs Nat. Park △, U.S.A. . 154 A8 48 32N 93 0W
Vozhe, Ozero, Russia .... 58 B10 60 45N 39 0 E
Vozhega, Russia .... 58 B11 60 29N 40 12 E
Voznesensk, Ukraine .... 59 J6 47 35N 31 21 E
Voznesenye, Russia .... 58 B8 61 0N 35 28 E
Vrå, Denmark .... 17 G3 57 21N 9 56 E

Vráble, Slovak Rep. .... 35 C11 48 15N 18 16 E
Vračevšnica, Serbia, Yug. ...... 50 B4 44 2N 20 34 E
Vrådal, Norway .... 18 E5 59 20N 8 25 E
Vrakhnéïka, Greece .... 48 C3 38 10N 21 40 E
Vrancea □, Romania .... 53 E11 45 50N 26 45 E
Vrancei, Munţii, Romania ...... 53 E11 46 0N 26 30 E
Vrang, Tajikistan .... 65 E6 37 0N 72 22 E
Vrangelya, Ostrov, Russia ...... 67 B19 71 0N 180 0 E
Vranica, Bos.-H. .... 52 G2 43 55N 17 50 E
Vranje, Serbia, Yug. .... 50 D5 42 34N 21 54 E
Vranjska Banja, Serbia, Yug. ... 50 D6 42 34N 22 1 E
Vranov nad Topľ'ou, Slovak Rep. 35 C14 48 53N 21 40 E
Vransko, Slovenia .... 45 B11 46 17N 14 58 E
Vransko Jezero, Croatia .... 45 E12 43 53N 15 34 E
Vrapčište, Macedonia .... 50 E4 41 50N 20 53 E
Vratsa, Bulgaria .... 50 C7 43 15N 23 30 E
Vråvatn, Norway .... 18 E5 59 20N 8 0 E
Vrbas, → Bos.-H. .... 52 E2 45 8N 17 29 E
Vrbas, Serbia, Yug. .... 52 E4 45 40N 19 40 E
Vrbas →, Bos.-H. .... 52 E2 45 8N 17 29 E
Vrbnik, Croatia .... 45 C11 45 4N 14 40 E
Vrbovec, Croatia .... 45 C13 45 53N 16 28 E
Vrbovsko, Croatia .... 45 C12 45 24N 15 5 E
Vrchlabí, Czech Rep. .... 34 A8 50 38N 15 37 E
Vrede, S. Africa .... 117 D4 27 24 S 29 6 E
Vredefort, S. Africa .... 116 D4 27 0 S 27 22 E
Vreden, Germany .... 30 C2 52 2N 6 50 E
Vredenburg, S. Africa .... 116 E2 32 56 S 18 0 E
Vredendal, S. Africa .... 116 E2 31 41 S 18 35 E
Vretstorp, Sweden .... 16 E8 59 1N 14 53 E
Vrgorac, Croatia .... 45 E14 43 12N 17 20 E
Vrhnika, Slovenia .... 45 C11 45 58N 14 15 E
Vridhachalam, India .... 95 J4 11 30N 79 20 E
Vríðí, Ivory C. 112 D4 5 15N 4 3W
Vrigstad, Sweden .... 17 G8 57 22N 14 28 E
Vrin, Switz. .... 33 C8 46 39N 9 6 E
Vrindavan, India .... 92 F7 27 37N 77 40 E
Vríses, Greece .... 39 E5 35 23N 24 13 E
Vrnograč, Bos.-H. .... 45 C12 45 10N 15 57 E
Vrondádhes, Greece .... 49 C8 38 25N 26 7 E
Vrpolje, Croatia .... 52 E3 45 13N 18 24 E
Vršac, Serbia, Yug. .... 52 E6 45 8N 21 20 E
Vrsacki Kanal, Serbia, Yug. .... 52 E5 45 15N 21 0 E
Vrútky, Slovak Rep. .... 35 B11 49 7N 18 55 E
Vryburg, S. Africa .... 116 D3 26 55 S 24 45 E
Vryheid, S. Africa .... 117 D5 27 45 S 30 47 E
Vsetín, Czech Rep. .... 35 B11 49 20N 18 0 E
Vu Liet, Vietnam .... 86 C5 18 43N 105 23 E
Vúcha →, Bulgaria .... 51 D8 42 10N 24 26 E
Vučitrn, Kosovo, Yug. .... 50 D4 42 49N 20 59 E
Vukovar, Croatia .... 52 E3 45 21N 18 59 E
Vulcan, Canada 142 C6 50 25N 113 15W
Vulcan, Romania .... 53 E8 45 23N 23 17 E
Vulcaneşti, Moldova .... 53 E13 45 41N 28 18 E
Vulcano, Italy .... 47 D7 38 24N 14 58 E
Vülchedruma, Bulgaria .... 50 C7 43 42N 23 27 E
Vulkaneshty = Vulcaneşti, Moldova 53 E13 45 41N 28 18 E
Vunduzi →, Mozam. .... 119 F3 18 56 S 34 1 E
Vung Tau, Vietnam .... 87 G6 10 21N 107 4 E
Vunidawa, Fiji .... 133 A2 17 50 S 178 21 E
Vunisea, Fiji .... 133 B2 19 3 S 178 10 E
Vuntut Nat. Park △, Canada ... 144 B13 68 25N 139 41W
Vurangalao, Solomon Is. .... 133 L9 6 59 S 156 38 E
Vürshets, Bulgaria .... 51 D10 42 59N 26 40 E
Vurshets, Bulgaria .... 50 C7 43 13N 23 16 E
Vutcani, Romania .... 53 D12 46 26N 27 59 E
Vuya, Sudan .... 107 F2 5 21N 29 40 E
Vwaza Game Reserve △, Malawi 119 E3 10 58 S 33 25 E
Vyara, India .... 94 D1 21 8N 73 28 E
Vyartsilya, Russia .... 58 A6 62 8N 30 45 E
Vyatka = Kirov, Russia .... 64 B2 58 35N 49 40 E
Vyatka →, Russia .... 60 C10 55 37N 51 28 E
Vyatskiye Polyany, Russia ..... 60 B10 56 14N 51 5 E
Vyazemskiy, Russia .... 67 E14 47 32N 134 45 E
Vyazma, Russia .... 58 E8 55 10N 34 15 E
Vyazniki, Russia .... 60 B6 56 10N 42 10 E
Vyborg, Russia .... 58 B5 60 43N 28 47 E
Vychegda →, Russia .... 58 B8 61 18N 46 36 E
Vychodné Beskydy, Europe ..... 35 B15 49 20N 22 0 E
Vyerkhnyadzvinsk, Belarus ..... 58 E4 55 45N 27 58 E
Vyg-ozero, Russia .... 56 B5 63 47N 34 29 E
Vyksa, Russia .... 60 C6 55 19N 42 11 E
Vylkove, Ukraine .... 59 K5 45 28N 29 32 E
Vynohradiv, Ukraine .... 59 H2 48 9N 23 2 E
Vypin, India .... 95 J3 10 10N 76 15 E
Vyrnwy, L., U.K. 20 E4 52 48N 3 31W
Vyshniy Volochek, Russia ...... 58 D8 57 30N 34 30 E
Vyshza = imeni 26 Bakinskikh
  Komissarov, Turkmenistan ... 97 B7 39 22N 54 10 E
Vyškov, Czech Rep. .... 35 B9 49 17N 17 0 E
Vysoké Mýto, Czech Rep. ...... 35 B9 49 58N 16 10 E
Vysokovsk, Russia .... 58 D9 56 22N 36 30 E
Vyšší Brod, Czech Rep. .... 34 C7 48 37N 14 19 E
Vytegra, Russia .... 58 B9 61 0N 36 27 E

W

W du Benin, Parc Nat. du △, Benin . 113 C5 11 57N 2 43 E
W du Burkina Faso, Parc Nat. du △,
  Burkina Faso 113 C4 11 52N 2 50W
W du Niger, Parc Nat. du △, Niger . 113 C5 13 31N 2 28 E
W.A.C. Bennett Dam, Canada .. 142 B4 56 2N 122 6W
Wa, Ghana 112 C4 10 7N 2 25W
Waal →, Neths. .... 24 C5 51 37N 5 0 E
Waalwijk, Neths. .... 24 C5 51 42N 5 4 E
Waar, Indonesia .... 83 B4 2 5 S 134 23 E
Waat, Sudan .... 107 F3 8 10N 32 7 E
Wabag, Papua N. G. .... 132 C2 5 32 S 143 40 E
Wabakimi Prov. Park △, Canada . 140 B2 50 43N 89 29W
Wabana, Canada 141 C9 47 40N 53 0W
Wabao, N. Cal. .... 133 U21 21 36 S 167 57 E
Wabao, C., N. Cal. .... 133 U21 21 35 S 167 53 E
Wabasca →, Canada 142 B5 58 22N 115 20W
Wabasca-Desmarais, Canada ... 142 B6 55 57N 113 56W
Wabash, U.S.A. 157 D11 40 48N 85 49W
Wabash →, U.S.A. 156 G2 37 48N 88 2W
Wabasso, U.S.A. 153 H9 27 45N 80 26W
Wabawng, Burma .... 90 B6 26 20N 97 25 E
Wabi →, Ethiopia .... 107 F5 7 45N 40 50 E
Wabigoon L., Canada 143 D10 49 44N 92 44W
Wabowden, Canada 143 C9 54 55N 98 38W
Wąbrzeźno, Poland .... 55 E5 53 16N 18 57 E
Wabu Hu, China .... 77 A11 32 20N 116 50 E
Wabuda I., Papua N. G. .... 132 E2 8 23 S 143 37 E
Wabuk Pt., Canada 140 A2 55 20N 85 5W
Wabush, Canada 141 B6 52 55N 66 52W
Waccasassa B., U.S.A. 153 F7 29 10N 82 50W
Wąchock, Poland .... 55 G8 51 4N 21 1 E
Wächtersbach, Germany .... 31 E5 50 14N 9 17 E
Wacissa, U.S.A. 152 E6 30 22N 83 59W
Waco, U.S.A. 155 F6 31 33N 97 9W
Waconichi, L., Canada 140 B5 50 8N 74 0W
Wad Ban Naqa, Sudan .... 107 D3 16 32N 33 9 E
Wad Banda, Sudan .... 107 E2 13 10N 27 56 E
Wad el Haddad, Sudan .... 107 E3 13 50N 33 30 E
Wad en Nau, Sudan .... 107 E3 14 10N 33 34 E
Wad Hamid, Sudan .... 107 D3 16 30N 32 45 E
Wad Medanî, Sudan .... 107 E3 14 28N 33 30 E
Wad Thana, Pakistan .... 91 D2 27 22N 66 23 E
Wadai, Africa .... 104 E5 12 0N 19 0 E
Wadayama, Japan .... 72 B6 35 19N 134 52 E

Wadbilliga Nat. Park △, Australia 129 D8 36 25 S 149 35 E
Waddān, Libya .... 108 C3 29 9N 16 10 E
Waddeneilanden, Neths. .... 24 A5 53 20N 5 10 E
Waddenzee, Neths. .... 24 A5 53 6N 5 10 E
Waddi, Chappal, Nigeria 113 D7 7 2N 11 43W
Waddington, Canada 151 B9 44 52N 75 12W
Waddington, Mt., Canada 142 C3 51 23N 125 15W
Waddy Pt., Australia .... 127 F5 24 58 S 153 21 E
Wadebridge, U.K. 21 G3 50 31N 4 51W
Wadena, Canada 143 C8 51 57N 103 47W
Wadena, U.S.A. 154 B7 46 26N 95 8W
Wädenswil, Switz. .... 33 B7 47 14N 8 40 E
Wadern, Germany .... 31 F2 49 32N 6 53 E
Wadeye, Australia .... 124 B4 14 28 S 129 52 E
Wadgaon, India .... 94 E1 18 44N 73 39 E
Wadhams, Canada 142 C3 51 30N 127 30W
Wadi, India .... 94 F1 17 4N 76 59 E
Wādī as Sīr, Jordan .... 103 D4 31 56N 35 49 E
Wādī Banī Walīd, Libya .... 108 B2 31 49N 14 0 E
Wadi Gemâl, Egypt .... 106 C4 24 35N 35 10 E
Wadi Halfa, Sudan .... 106 C3 21 53N 31 19 E
Wadi Rum Nat. Park △, Jordan . 103 F4 29 30N 35 20 E
Wadian, China .... 77 A9 32 42N 112 29 E
Wadlew, Poland .... 55 G6 51 31N 19 23 E
Wadley, Ala., U.S.A. 152 B4 33 7N 85 34W
Wadley, Ga., U.S.A. 152 C7 32 52N 82 24W
Wadowice, Poland .... 55 J6 49 52N 19 30 E
Wadsworth, Nev., U.S.A. 158 G4 39 38N 119 17W
Wadsworth, Ohio, U.S.A. 150 E3 41 2N 81 44W
Wegwan, S. Korea .... 75 G15 35 59N 128 23 E
Waeplau, Indonesia .... 82 B3 3 8 S 126 55 E
Wafangdian, China .... 75 E11 39 38N 121 58 E
Wafania, Dem. Rep. of the Congo 114 C4 1 23 S 20 22 E
Wafrah, Si. Arabia .... 96 D5 28 33N 47 56 E
Wagadugu = Ouagadougou,
  Burkina Faso 113 C4 12 25N 1 30W
Wagener, U.S.A. 152 B8 33 39N 81 22W
Wageningen, Neths. .... 24 C5 51 58N 5 40 E
Wageningen, Surinam 169 B6 5 50N 56 50W
Wager B., Canada 139 B11 65 26N 88 40W
Wagga Wagga, Australia .... 129 C7 35 7 S 147 24 E
Waghai, India .... 94 D1 20 46N 73 29 E
Waghete, Indonesia .... 83 B5 4 10 S 135 50 E
Wagin, Australia .... 125 F2 33 17 S 117 25 E
Wagner, U.S.A. 154 D5 43 5N 98 18W
Wagon Mound, U.S.A. 155 G2 36 1N 104 42W
Wagoner, U.S.A. 155 H7 35 58N 95 22W
Wagrowiec, Poland .... 55 F4 52 48N 17 11 E
Wah, Pakistan .... 91 B4 33 45N 72 40 E
Wahai, Indonesia .... 83 B3 2 48 S 129 35 E
Waharoa, N.Z. .... 130 D7 37 32 S 175 36 E
Wahiawa, U.S.A. 145 K13 21 30N 158 2W
Wahiawa Reservoir, U.S.A. 145 K13 21 30N 158 3W
Wāhid, Egypt .... 103 E1 30 48N 32 21 E
Wahnai, Afghan. .... 92 C1 32 40N 65 50 E
Wahni, Ethiopia .... 107 E4 12 40N 36 39 E
Wahoo, U.S.A. 154 E6 41 13N 96 37W
Wahpeton, U.S.A. 154 B6 46 16N 96 36W
Wahx, Ras il-, Malta .... 38 F7 35 56N 14 20 E
Wai, India .... 94 F1 17 56N 73 57 E
Waiai →, N.Z. .... 131 G2 46 12 S 167 38 E
Waialee, U.S.A. 145 K13 21 41N 158 1W
Waialua, U.S.A. 145 K13 21 34N 158 8W
Waialua B., U.S.A. 145 K13 21 35N 158 8W
Waianae, U.S.A. 145 K13 21 27N 158 11W
Waianae Mts., U.S.A. 145 K13 21 30N 158 10W
Waiapu →, N.Z. .... 130 D7 37 47 S 178 29 E
Waiau, N.Z. .... 131 C8 42 39 S 173 5 E
Waiau →, N.Z. .... 131 C8 42 47 S 173 22 E
Waiawa →, N.Z. 145 K14 21 23N 157 59W
Waiawe Ganga →, Sri Lanka ... 95 L5 6 15N 81 0 E
Waibeem, Indonesia .... 83 B4 0 30 S 132 59 E
Waiblingen, Germany .... 31 G5 48 49N 9 18 E
Waidhofen an der Thaya, Austria . 34 C8 48 49N 15 17 E
Waidhofen an der Ybbs, Austria . 34 D7 47 57N 14 46 E
Waigeo, Indonesia .... 83 B4 0 20 S 130 40 E
Waihao →, N.Z. .... 131 E5 44 52 S 171 11 E
Waihao Downs, N.Z. .... 131 E5 44 48 S 170 55 E
Waihi, N.Z. .... 130 C4 36 48 S 175 6 E
Waihi Beach, N.Z. .... 130 C4 37 25 S 175 52 E
Waihola, N.Z. .... 131 G5 46 1 S 170 8 E
Waihola L., N.Z. .... 131 F5 45 59 S 170 8 E
Waihou →, N.Z. .... 130 D4 37 15 S 175 40 E
Waika, Dem. Rep. of the Congo . 118 C2 2 22 S 25 42 E
Waikabubak, Indonesia .... 82 C1 9 45 S 119 25 E
Waikaia, N.Z. .... 131 F4 45 44 S 168 51 E
Waikaka, N.Z. .... 131 F4 45 55 S 169 1 E
Waikare, L., N.Z. .... 130 E6 38 43 S 177 10 E
Waikaremoana, N.Z. .... 130 E6 38 43 S 175 52 E
Waikaremoana, L., N.Z. .... 130 E6 38 49 S 177 9 E
Waikari, N.Z. .... 131 C7 42 58 S 172 41 E
Waikato →, N.Z. .... 130 D3 37 23 S 174 43 E
Waikelo, Indonesia .... 82 C1 9 24 S 119 19 E
Waikerie, Australia .... 129 B2 34 9 S 140 0 E
Waikiekie, N.Z. .... 130 B3 35 57 S 174 16 E
Waikiki, U.S.A. 145 K14 21 17N 157 50W
Waikokopu, N.Z. .... 130 F6 39 3 S 177 52 E
Waikouaiti, N.Z. .... 131 F5 45 36 S 170 41 E
Waikouaiti Downs, N.Z. .... 131 F5 45 30 S 170 30 E
Wailingding Dao, China .... 69 GL2 22 6N 114 2 E
Wailua, Hawaii, U.S.A. 145 A2 22 3N 159 20W
Wailua, Hawaii, U.S.A. 145 C5 20 51N 156 8W
Wailuku, U.S.A. 145 C5 20 53N 156 30W
Waimakariri →, N.Z. .... 131 D7 43 24 S 172 42 E
Waimanalo, U.S.A. 145 K14 21 20N 157 43W
Waimanalo Beach, U.S.A. 145 K14 21 21N 157 42W
Waimangaroa, N.Z. .... 131 B6 41 43 S 171 46 E
Waimarama, N.Z. 145 K14 21 25N 157 58W
Waimarie, N.Z. .... 131 B6 41 35 S 171 58 E
Waimate, N.Z. .... 131 E5 44 45 S 171 3 E
Waimea, Hawaii, U.S.A. 145 A2 21 58N 159 40W
Waimea, Hawaii, U.S.A. 145 J13 21 39N 158 3W
Waimea B., U.S.A. 145 J13 21 40N 158 5W
Waimea Plain, N.Z. .... 131 F3 45 55 S 168 35 E
Wainganga →, India .... 94 E4 18 50N 79 55 E
Waingapu, Indonesia .... 82 C2 9 35 S 120 11 E
Waingmaw, Burma .... 90 C6 25 21N 97 26 E
Waini →, Guyana 169 B6 8 20N 59 50W
Wainuiomata, N.Z. .... 130 H3 41 17 S 174 56 E
Wainwright, Canada 143 C6 52 50N 110 50W
Wainwright, U.S.A. 144 A7 70 38N 160 2W
Waiotapu, N.Z. .... 130 E5 38 21 S 176 25 E
Waiouru, N.Z. .... 130 F4 39 28 S 175 41 E
Waipa →, N.Z. .... 130 E4 38 0 S 174 52 E
Waipahi, N.Z. .... 131 G4 46 6 S 169 15 E
Waipahu, U.S.A. 145 K13 21 23N 158 1W
Waipapa Pt., N.Z. .... 131 G3 46 40 S 168 51 E
Waipara, N.Z. .... 131 C7 43 3 S 172 46 E
Waipawa, N.Z. .... 131 F3 39 56 S 176 38 E
Waipio Acres, U.S.A. 145 K13 21 28N 158 1W
Waipio Peninsula, U.S.A. 145 K13 21 23N 157 59W
Waipiro, N.Z. .... 130 E7 38 2 S 178 22 E
Waipiro Bay, N.Z. .... 130 E7 38 2 S 178 22 E
Waipu, N.Z. .... 130 B3 35 59 S 174 29 E
Waipukurau, N.Z. .... 130 F5 40 1 S 176 33 E
Wairakei, N.Z. .... 130 E5 38 37 S 176 6 E
Wairarapa, L., N.Z. .... 131 B9 41 32 S 174 7 E
Wairau →, N.Z. .... 131 B9 41 32 S 174 7 E
Wairio, N.Z. .... 131 F3 45 59 S 168 2 E
Wairoa, N.Z. .... 130 F6 39 3 S 177 25 E
Wairoa →, Hawke's Bay, N.Z. . 130 F6 39 4 S 177 25 E

Wairoa →, Northland, N.Z. .... 130 C2 36 5 S 173 59 E
Waïsisi, Vanuatu .... 133 J7 19 32 S 169 22 E
Waita Reservoir, U.S.A. 145 B2 21 55N 159 28W
Waitaki →, N.Z. .... 131 E6 44 56 S 171 7 E
Waitaki Plains, N.Z. .... 131 E5 44 22 S 170 0 E
Waitara, N.Z. .... 130 E3 38 59 S 174 15 E
Waitara →, N.Z. .... 130 E3 38 59 S 174 14 E
Waitoa, N.Z. .... 130 D4 37 37 S 175 35 E
Waitotara, N.Z. .... 130 F3 39 49 S 174 44 E
Waitotara →, N.Z. .... 130 F3 39 51 S 174 41 E
Waitsburg, U.S.A. 158 C5 46 16N 118 9W
Waiuku, N.Z. .... 130 D3 37 15 S 174 45 E
Waiyang, Japan .... 71 R 37 30N 137 0 E
Wajir, Kenya .... 118 B5 1 42N 40 5 E
Waka, Dem. Rep. of the Congo .. 114 B4 1 1N 20 13 E
Waka, Ethiopia .... 107 F4 7 3N 37 20 E
Wakai, Suriname 169 B6 5 18N 57 14W
Wakarusa, U.S.A. 157 C10 41 32N 86 1W
Wakasa, Japan .... 72 B6 35 20N 134 24 E
Wakasa-Wan, Japan .... 73 B7 35 40N 135 30 E
Wakatipu, L., N.Z. .... 131 F3 45 5 S 168 33 E
Wakaw, Canada 143 C7 52 39N 105 44W
Wakaya, Fiji .... 133 A2 17 37 S 179 0 E
Wakayama, Japan .... 73 C6 34 15N 135 15 E
Wakayama □, Japan .... 73 D7 33 50N 135 30 E
Wake, Japan .... 72 C6 34 48N 134 8 E
Wake Forest, U.S.A. 149 H6 35 59N 78 30W
Wake I., Pac. Oc. .... 154 F5 19 18N 166 36 E
WaKeeney, U.S.A. 154 F5 39 1N 99 53W
Wakefield, Jamaica .... 164 a 18 26N 77 42W
Wakefield, N.Z. .... 131 B8 41 24 S 173 5 E
Wakefield, U.K. 20 D6 53 41N 1 29W
Wakefield, Mass., U.S.A. 151 D13 42 30N 71 4W
Wakefield, Mich., U.S.A. 154 B10 46 29N 89 56W
Wakema, Burma .... 90 G5 16 30N 95 11 E
Waki, Japan .... 72 C6 34 4N 134 9 E
Wakkanai, Japan .... 70 B10 45 28N 141 35 E
Wakkerstroom, S. Africa .... 117 D5 27 24 S 30 10 E
Wakool, Australia .... 128 C6 35 28 S 144 23 E
Wakool →, Australia .... 128 C5 35 5 S 143 33 E
Wakre, Indonesia .... 83 B4 0 19 S 131 5 E
Waku, Papua N. G. .... 132 D5 6 S 149 9 E
Wakuach, L., Canada 141 A6 55 34N 67 32W
Wakulla, U.S.A. 152 E5 30 14N 84 8W
Wakunai, Papua N. G. .... 132 C8 5 52 S 155 13 E
Wałbrzych, Poland .... 55 H3 50 45N 16 18 E
Walbury Hill, U.K. 21 F6 51 21N 1 28W
Walcha, Australia .... 129 A9 30 55 S 151 31 E
Walcheren, Neths. .... 24 C3 51 30N 3 35 E
Walckenaer, Teluk, Indonesia ... 83 B5 2 20 S 134 30 E
Walcott, U.S.A. 158 F10 41 46N 106 51W
Wałcz, Poland .... 55 E3 53 17N 16 27 E
Wald, Switz. .... 33 B7 47 17N 8 56 E
Waldbröl, Germany .... 30 E3 50 52N 7 36 E
Waldeck, Germany .... 30 D5 51 12N 9 4 E
Walden, Colo., U.S.A. 158 F10 40 44N 106 17W
Walden, N.Y., U.S.A. 151 E10 41 34N 74 11W
Waldenburg = Wałbrzych, Poland 55 H3 50 45N 16 18 E
Waldenburg, Switz. .... 32 B5 47 23N 7 45 E
Waldkirch, Germany .... 31 G3 48 5N 7 58 E
Waldkirchen, Germany .... 31 G9 48 44N 13 36 E
Waldkraiburg, Germany .... 31 G8 48 13N 12 24 E
Waldo, U.S.A. 152 F7 29 48N 82 10W
Waldport, U.S.A. 158 D1 44 26N 124 4W
Waldron, U.S.A. 155 H7 34 54N 94 5W
Waldviertel, Austria .... 34 C8 48 30N 15 30 E
Walebing, Australia .... 125 F2 30 41 S 116 13 E
Walembele, Ghana 112 C4 10 30N 1 58W
Walensee, Switz. .... 33 B8 47 7N 9 13 E
Walenstadt, Switz. .... 33 B8 47 8N 9 19 E
Wales □, U.K. 144 D5 65 37N 168 5W
Wales □, U.K. 21 E3 52 19N 4 43W
Walewale, Ghana 113 C4 10 21N 0 50W
Walgett, Australia .... 127 E4 30 0 S 148 5 E
Walgreen Coast, Antarctica .... 7 D15 75 15 S 105 0W
Walhalla, Australia .... 132 B2 3 14 S 143 18 E
Walis I., Papua N. G. .... 132 B2 3 14 S 143 18 E
Walker, U.S.A. 157 H11 42 58N 85 46W
Walker, Minn., U.S.A. 154 B7 47 6N 94 35W
Walker, L., Canada 141 B6 50 20N 67 11W
Walker L., Canada 143 C9 54 42N 95 57W
Walker L., U.S.A. 158 G4 38 42N 118 43W
Walkerston, Australia .... 126 K7 21 11 S 149 8 E
Walkerton, Canada 140 D3 44 10N 81 10W
Walkerton, U.S.A. 157 C10 41 28N 86 29W
Wall, U.S.A. 154 D3 44 0N 102 8W
Walla Walla, Australia .... 129 C7 35 45 S 146 29 E
Walla Walla, U.S.A. 158 C4 46 4N 118 20W
Wallace, Idaho, U.S.A. 158 C6 47 28N 115 56W
Wallaceburg, Canada 140 D3 42 34N 82 23W
Wallacetown, N.Z. .... 131 G3 46 21 S 168 19 E
Wallachia = Valahia, Romania .. 53 F9 44 35N 25 0 E
Wallal, Australia .... 126 C3 26 32 S 146 7 E
Wallam Cr. →, Australia ...... 127 D4 28 40 S 147 20 E
Wallambin, L., Australia ...... 125 F2 30 57 S 117 35 E
Wallan, Australia .... 129 D6 37 26 S 144 59 E
Wallangarra, Australia .... 127 D5 28 56 S 151 58 E
Wallaroo, Australia .... 128 C3 33 56 S 137 39 E
Walldürn, Germany .... 31 F5 49 34N 9 22 E
Wallenhorst, Germany .... 30 C4 52 21N 8 1 E
Wallenpaupack, L., U.S.A. 151 E9 41 25N 75 15W
Wallerawang, Australia .... 129 B9 33 25 S 150 4 E
Wallingford, U.S.A. 151 E12 41 27N 72 50W
Wallis & Futuna, Is., Pac. Oc. .. 134 J10 13 18 S 176 10W
Wallisellen, Switz. .... 33 B7 47 25 8 E
Wallowa, U.S.A. 158 D5 45 34N 117 32W
Wallowa Mts., U.S.A. 158 D5 45 20N 117 30W
Walls, U.K. 22 A7 60 14N 1 33W
Walls of Jerusalem Nat. Park △,
  Australia .... 127 G4 41 56 S 146 17 E
Wallsend, Australia .... 129 B9 32 55 S 151 40 E
Wallula, U.S.A. 158 C4 46 5N 118 54W
Wallumbilla, Australia .... 127 D4 26 33 S 149 9 E
Walmsley, L., Canada 143 A7 63 25N 108 36W
Walney, I. of, U.K. 20 C4 54 6N 3 15W
Walnut, U.S.A. .... 159 J8 37 35 S 120 11 E
Walnut Canyon Nat. Monument △,
  U.S.A. 159 J8 35 15N 111 20W
Walnut Creek, U.S.A. 160 H4 37 54N 122 4W
Walnut Grove, U.S.A. 152 A3 34 4N 86 18W
Walnut Hill, U.S.A. 153 D2 30 53N 87 30W
Walnut Ridge, U.S.A. 155 G9 36 4N 90 57W
Walpeup, Australia .... 128 C5 35 7 S 142 2 E
Walpole, Australia .... 125 F2 34 58 S 116 44 E
Walpole, U.S.A. 151 D13 42 9N 71 15W
Wals, Austria .... 34 D5 47 47N 12 58 E
Walsall, U.K. 21 E6 52 35N 1 58W
Walsenburg, U.S.A. 155 G2 37 38N 104 47W
Walsh →, Australia .... 126 B3 16 31 S 143 42 E
Walsrode, Germany .... 30 C5 52 51N 9 36 E
Walt Disney World, U.S.A. 153 G8 28 25N 81 35W
Waltair, India .... 94 F6 17 43 S 83 23 E
Walter F. George Reservoir, U.S.A. 152 D4 31 38N 85 4W
Walterboro, U.S.A. 152 C9 32 55N 80 40W
Walters, U.S.A. 155 H5 34 22N 98 19W
Waltershausen, Germany ...... 30 E6 50 54N 10 33 E
Waltham, U.S.A. 151 D13 42 23N 71 14W
Waltman, U.S.A. 158 E10 43 4N 107 12W
Walton, Ky., U.S.A. 157 F12 38 52N 84 37W
Walton, N.Y., U.S.A. 151 D9 42 10N 75 8W

Walton-on-the-Naze, U.K. .... **21 F9** 51 51N 1 17 E
Waltonville, U.S.A. **156 F7** 38 13N 89 2W
Walu, Burma .... **90 B7** 26 28N 98 2 E
Walvis Bay, Namibia .... **116 C1** 23 0 S 14 28 E
Walvis Ridge, Atl. Oc. .... **8 J12** 26 0 S 5 0 E
Walvisbaai = Walvis Bay, Namibia .. **116 C1** 23 0 S 14 28 E
Walwa, Australia .... **129 C7** 35 59 S 147 44 E
Wamba, Équateur, Dem. Rep. of
  the Congo .... **114 C4** 1 37 S 22 30 E
Wamba, Orientale, Dem. Rep. of
  the Congo .... **118 B2** 2 10N 27 57 E
Wamba, Kenya .... **118 B4** 0 58N 37 19 E
Wamba, Nigeria .... **113 D6** 8 57N 8 42 E
Wamba →, Dem. Rep. of the Congo .. **115 C3** 3 56 S 17 12 E
Wamego, U.S.A. **154 F6** 39 12N 96 18W
Wamena, Indonesia .... **83 B5** 4 4 S 138 57 E
Wamsutter, U.S.A. **158 F9** 41 40N 107 58W
Wamulan, Indonesia .... **82 B3** 3 27 S 126 7 E
Wan Hat, Burma .... **90 E6** 20 14N 97 53 E
Wan Kinghao, Burma .... **90 E7** 21 34N 98 17 E
Wan Lai-kam, Burma .... **90 E7** 21 21N 98 22 E
Wan Tup, Burma .... **90 E7** 21 13N 98 42 E
Wan Xian, China .... **74 E8** 38 47N 115 7 E
Wana, Pakistan .... **91 B3** 32 20N 69 32 E
Wanaaring, Australia .... **127 D3** 29 38 S 144 9 E
Wanaka, N.Z. .... **131 E4** 44 42 S 169 9 E
Wanaka, L., N.Z. .... **131 E4** 44 33 S 169 7 E
Wan'an, China .... **77 D10** 26 26N 114 49 E
Wanapiri, Indonesia .... **83 B5** 4 30 S 135 59 E
Wanapitei L., Canada **140 C3** 46 45N 80 40W
Wanbi, Australia .... **128 C4** 34 46 S 140 17 E
Wandaik, Guyana **169 C6** 4 27N 59 35W
Wandel Sea = McKinley Sea, Arctic . **10 A11** 82 0N 0 0W
Wandérama, Ivory C. **112 D4** 8 37N 4 25W
Wanderer, Zimbabwe .... **119 F3** 19 36 S 30 1 E
Wandhari, Pakistan .... **92 F2** 27 42N 66 48 E
Wanding, China .... **76 E2** 24 5N 98 4 E
Wandoan, Australia .... **127 D4** 26 5 S 149 55 E
Wanfu, China .... **75 D12** 40 8N 122 38 E
Wang →, Thailand .... **86 D2** 17 8N 99 2 E
Wang Kai, Sudan .... **107 F2** 9 3N 29 23 E
Wang Noi, Thailand .... **86 E3** 14 13N 100 44 E
Wang Saphung, Thailand .... **86 D3** 17 18N 101 46 E
Wang Thong, Thailand .... **86 D3** 16 50N 100 26 E
Wanga, Dem. Rep. of the Congo ... **118 B2** 2 58N 29 12 E
Wangal, Indonesia .... **83 C4** 6 8 S 134 9 E
Wanganella, Australia .... **129 C6** 35 6 S 144 49 E
Wanganui, N.Z. .... **130 H4** 39 56 S 175 3 E
Wanganui →, W. Coast, N.Z. ..... **131 D5** 43 5 S 170 26 E
Wanganui →, Wanganui-Manawatu,
  N.Z. .... **130 F4** 39 55 S 175 4 E
Wangaratta, Australia .... **129 D7** 36 21 S 146 19 E
Wangary, Australia .... **127 E2** 34 35 S 135 29 E
Wangcang, China .... **76 A6** 32 18N 106 20 E
Wangcheng, China .... **77 C9** 28 22N 112 49 E
Wangdu, China .... **74 E8** 38 40N 115 7 E
Wangdu Phodrang, Bhutan .... **90 B2** 27 28N 89 54 E
Wangen, Germany .... **31 H5** 47 41N 9 50 E
Wangerooge, Germany .... **30 B3** 53 47N 7 54 E
Wängi, Switz. .... **33 B7** 47 30N 8 57 E
Wangiwangi, Indonesia .... **82 C2** 5 22 S 123 37 E
Wangjiang, China .... **77 B11** 30 10N 116 42 E
Wangmo, China .... **76 E6** 25 11N 106 5 E
Wangolodougou, Ivory C. **112 D3** 9 55N 5 10W
Wangqing, China .... **75 C15** 43 12N 129 42 E
Wani, India .... **94 D4** 20 5N 78 55 E
Wanigela, Papua N. G. .... **132 E5** 9 21 S 149 9 E
Wankaner, India .... **92 H4** 22 35N 71 0 E
Wanlaweyne = Uanle Uen,
  Somali Rep. .... **120 D2** 2 37N 44 54 E
Wanless, Canada **143 C8** 54 11N 101 21W
Wannian, China .... **77 C11** 28 42N 117 4 E
Wanning, China .... **86 C8** 18 48N 110 22 E
Wanon Niwat, Thailand .... **86 D4** 17 38N 103 46 E
Wanqinsha, China .... **69 F10** 22 43N 113 33 E
Wanquan, China .... **74 D8** 40 50N 114 40 E
Wanrong, China .... **74 G6** 35 25N 110 50 E
Wanshan, China .... **76 D7** 27 30N 109 12 E
Wanshan Qundao, China .... **69 G10** 21 57N 113 45 E
Wanshengchang, China .... **76 C6** 28 57N 106 53 E
Wanstead, N.Z. .... **130 G5** 40 8 S 176 30 E
Wantage, U.K. **21 F6** 51 35N 1 25W
Wanyin, Burma .... **90 E6** 20 23N 97 15 E
Wanyuan, China .... **76 A7** 32 4N 108 3 E
Wanzai, Guangdong, China ...... **69 G10** 22 12N 113 31 E
Wanzai, Jiangxi, China .... **77 C10** 28 7N 114 30 E
Wapakoneta, U.S.A. **157 D12** 40 34N 84 12W
Wapato, U.S.A. **158 C3** 46 27N 120 25W
Wapawekka L., Canada **143 C8** 54 55N 104 40W
Wapello, U.S.A. **156 C5** 41 11N 91 11W
Wapikopa L., Canada **140 B2** 52 56N 87 53W
Wapinda, Dem. Rep. of the Congo .. **114 B4** 3 41N 22 48 E
Wapiti →, Canada **142 B5** 55 5N 118 18W
Wappingers Falls, U.S.A. **151 E11** 41 36N 73 55W
Wapsipinicon →, U.S.A. **156 C6** 41 44N 90 19W
Wapusk Nat. Park △, Canada **143 B10** 57 46N 93 22W
Warab □, Sudan .... **107 F2** 7 30N 28 30 E
Warabi, Japan .... **73 B11** 35 49N 139 41 E
Warangal, India .... **94 F4** 17 58N 79 35 E
Waraseoni, India .... **93 J9** 21 45N 80 2 E
Waratah, Australia .... **127 G4** 38 54 S 146 5 E
Waratah B., Australia .... **129 F7** 38 54 S 146 5 E
Warburg, Germany .... **30 D5** 51 28N 9 11 E
Warburton, Vic., Australia ...... **129 D6** 37 47 S 145 42 E
Warburton, W. Austral., Australia .. **125 E4** 26 8 S 126 35 E
Warburton Ra., Australia .... **125 E4** 25 55 S 126 28 E
Ward, N.Z. .... **131 B9** 41 49 S 174 11 E
Ward →, Australia .... **127 D4** 26 28 S 146 6 E
Ward Hunt, C., Papua N. G. ..... **132 E5** 8 2 S 148 10 E
Ward Hunt Str., Papua N. G. ..... **132 E6** 9 30 S 150 0 E
Ward Mt., U.S.A. **160 H8** 37 12N 118 54W
Warden, S. Africa .... **117 D4** 27 50 S 29 0 E
Wardha, India .... **94 D4** 20 45N 78 39 E
Wardija Point, Malta .... **38 E6** 36 2N 14 11 E
Wardo, Indonesia .... **83 B5** 1 2 S 135 50 E
Ware, Canada **142 B3** 57 26N 125 41W
Ware, U.K. **21 F8** 51 49N 0 0W
Ware, U.S.A. **151 D12** 42 16N 72 14W
Waregem, Belgium .... **24 D3** 50 53N 3 27 E
Wareham, U.S.A. **151 E14** 41 46N 70 43W
Waremme, Belgium .... **24 D5** 50 43N 5 15 E
Waren, Germany .... **30 B8** 53 31N 12 40 E
Waren, Indonesia .... **83 B5** 2 16 S 136 20 E
Warendorf, Germany .... **30 D4** 51 57N 8 1 E
Waresboro, U.S.A. **152 D7** 31 15N 82 29W
Waria →, Papua N. G. .... **132 D4** 7 49 S 147 41 E
Warialda, Australia .... **127 D5** 29 29 S 150 33 E
Wariap, Indonesia .... **83 B4** 1 30 S 134 5 E
Warin Chamrap, Thailand .... **86 E5** 15 12N 104 53 E
Warka, Poland .... **55 G8** 51 47N 21 12 E
Warkopi, Indonesia .... **83 B4** 1 12 S 134 9 E
Warkworth, N.Z. .... **130 C3** 36 24 S 174 41 E
Warm Springs, Ga., U.S.A. **152 C3** 32 53N 84 41W
Warm Springs, Nev., U.S.A. **159 G5** 38 10N 116 20W
Warman, Canada **143 C7** 52 19N 106 30W
Warmandi, Indonesia .... **83 B4** 0 23 S 132 49 E
Warmbad, Namibia .... **116 D2** 28 25 S 18 42 E
Warmbad, S. Africa .... **117 C4** 24 51 S 28 19 E
Warmiśko-Mazurskie □, Poland ... **54 D8** 54 0N 21 0 E
Warminster, U.K. **21 F5** 51 12N 2 10W
Warminster, U.S.A. **151 F9** 40 12N 75 6W
Warnemünde, Germany .... **30 A8** 54 10N 12 4 E
Warner Mts., U.S.A. **158 F3** 41 40N 120 15W

Warner Robins, U.S.A. **152 C6** 32 37N 83 36W
Warnes, Bolivia .... **173 D5** 17 30 S 63 10W
Warnow →, Germany .... **30 A8** 54 6N 12 9 E
Waroona, Australia .... **125 F2** 32 50 S 115 58 E
Warora, India .... **94 D4** 20 14N 79 1 E
Warracknabeal, Australia .... **128 D5** 36 9 S 142 26 E
Warragul, Australia .... **129 E6** 38 10 S 145 58 E
Warrego →, Australia .... **127 E4** 30 24 S 145 21 E
Warrego Ra., Australia .... **126 C4** 24 58 S 146 0 E
Warren, Australia .... **129 A7** 31 42 S 147 51 E
Warren, Ark., U.S.A. **155 J8** 33 37N 92 4W
Warren, Ill., U.S.A. **156 B7** 42 29N 90 0W
Warren, Ind., U.S.A. **157 D11** 40 41N 85 26W
Warren, Mich., U.S.A. **157 B13** 42 30N 83 0W
Warren, Minn., U.S.A. **154 A6** 48 12N 96 46W
Warren, Ohio, U.S.A. **150 E4** 41 14N 80 49W
Warren, Pa., U.S.A. **150 E5** 41 51N 79 9W
Warrenpoint, U.K. **23 B5** 54 6N 6 15W
Warrensburg, Ill., U.S.A. **156 E7** 39 56N 89 4W
Warrensburg, Mo., U.S.A. **156 F3** 38 46N 93 44W
Warrensburg, N.Y., U.S.A. **151 C11** 43 29N 73 46W
Warrenton, S. Africa .... **116 D3** 28 9 S 24 47 E
Warrenton, Ga., U.S.A. **152 B7** 33 24N 82 40W
Warrenton, Mo., U.S.A. **156 F5** 38 49N 91 9W
Warrenton, Oreg., U.S.A. **160 D3** 46 10N 123 56W
Warrenville = Gloverville, U.S.A. .. **152 B8** 33 32N 81 48W
Warri, Nigeria .... **113 D6** 5 30N 5 41 E
Warrina, Australia .... **127 D2** 28 12 S 135 50 E
Warrington, N.Z. .... **131 F5** 45 43 S 170 35 E
Warrington, U.K. **20 D5** 53 24N 2 35W
Warrington, U.S.A. **153 E2** 30 23N 87 17W
Warrington □, U.K. **20 D5** 53 24N 2 35W
Warrnambool, Australia .... **128 E5** 38 25 S 142 30 E
Warroad, U.S.A. **154 A7** 48 54N 95 19W
Warrumbungle Nat. Park △,
  Australia .... **129 A8** 31 18 S 149 1 E
Warruwi, Australia .... **126 A1** 11 36 S 133 20 E
Warsa, Indonesia .... **83 B5** 0 47 S 135 55 E
Warsak Dam, Pakistan .... **92 B4** 34 11N 71 19 E
Warsaw = Warszawa, Poland ..... **55 F8** 52 13N 21 0 E
Warsaw, Ind., U.S.A. **156 D5** 40 22N 91 26W
Warsaw, Ind., U.S.A. **157 C11** 41 14N 85 51W
Warsaw, Ky., U.S.A. **152 F3** 38 47N 84 54W
Warsaw, Mo., U.S.A. **156 F3** 38 15N 93 23W
Warsaw, N.Y., U.S.A. **150 D6** 42 45N 78 8W
Warsaw, Ohio, U.S.A. **150 F3** 40 20N 82 0W
Warsaw ✈ (WAW), Poland ...... **55 F7** 52 9N 20 59 E
Warstein, Germany .... **30 D4** 51 26N 8 22 E
Warszawa, Poland .... **55 F8** 52 13N 21 0 E
Warta, Poland .... **55 G5** 51 43N 18 38 E
Warta →, Poland .... **55 F1** 52 35N 14 39 E
Warth, Austria .... **33 B10** 47 15N 10 11 E
Warthe = Warta →, Poland ...... **55 F1** 52 35N 14 39 E
Warthen, U.S.A. **152 B7** 33 6N 82 48W
Waru, Indonesia .... **83 B4** 3 30 S 130 36 E
Warud, India .... **94 D4** 21 30N 78 16 E
Warwick, Australia .... **127 D5** 28 10 S 152 1 E
Warwick, U.K. **21 E6** 52 18N 1 35W
Warwick, Ga., U.S.A. **152 D6** 31 50N 83 57W
Warwick, N.Y., U.S.A. **151 E10** 41 16N 74 22W
Warwick, R.I., U.S.A. **151 E13** 41 42N 71 28W
Warwickshire □, U.K. **21 E6** 52 14N 1 38W
Wasaga Beach, Canada **150 B4** 44 31N 80 1W
Wasagaming, Canada **143 C9** 50 39N 99 58W
Wasatch Ra., U.S.A. **158 F8** 40 30N 111 15W
Wasbank, S. Africa .... **117 D5** 28 15 S 30 9 E
Wasco, Calif., U.S.A. **161 K7** 35 36N 119 20W
Wasco, Oreg., U.S.A. **158 D3** 45 36N 120 42W
Wase, Nigeria .... **113 D6** 9 4N 9 54 E
Waseca, U.S.A. **154 C8** 44 5N 93 30W
Wasekamio L., Canada **143 B7** 56 45N 108 45W
Wash, The, U.K. .... **20 E8** 52 58N 0 20 E
Washago, Canada **150 B5** 44 45N 79 20W
Washburn, Ill., U.S.A. **156 D7** 40 55N 89 17W
Washburn, N. Dak., U.S.A. **154 B4** 47 17N 101 2W
Washburn, Wis., U.S.A. **154 B9** 46 40N 90 54W
Washim, India .... **94 D3** 20 3N 77 0 E
Washington, U.K. **20 C6** 54 55N 1 30W
Washington, D.C., U.S.A. **148 F7** 38 54N 77 2W
Washington, Ga., U.S.A. **152 B7** 33 44N 82 44W
Washington, Ill., U.S.A. **156 D7** 40 42N 89 24W
Washington, Ind., U.S.A. **157 F9** 38 40N 87 10W
Washington, Iowa, U.S.A. **156 E5** 41 18N 91 42W
Washington, Mo., U.S.A. **156 F5** 38 33N 91 1W
Washington, N.C., U.S.A. **149 H7** 35 33N 77 3W
Washington, N.J., U.S.A. **151 F10** 40 46N 74 59W
Washington, Pa., U.S.A. **150 F4** 40 10N 80 15W
Washington, Utah, U.S.A. **159 H7** 37 8N 113 31W
Washington □, U.S.A. **158 C3** 47 30N 120 30W
Washington, Mt., U.S.A. **151 B13** 44 16N 71 18W
Washington Court House, U.S.A. .. **157 E13** 39 32N 83 26W
Washington I., U.S.A. **148 C2** 45 23N 86 54W
Washington Land, Greenland **10 A4** 80 30N 66 0W
Washougal, U.S.A. **160 E4** 45 35N 122 21W
Washpool Nat. Park △, Australia .. **127 D5** 29 22 S 152 20 E
Washuk, Pakistan .... **91 D2** 27 6N 62 48 E
Wasian, Indonesia .... **83 B4** 1 47 S 133 19 E
Wasilków, Poland .... **55 E10** 53 12N 23 13 E
Wasilla, U.S.A. **144 F10** 61 35N 149 26W
Wasior, Indonesia .... **83 B4** 2 43 S 134 30 E
Waskaganish, Canada **140 B4** 51 30N 78 40W
Waskaiowaka, L., Canada **143 B9** 56 33N 96 23W
Waskesiu Lake, Canada **143 C7** 53 55N 106 5W
Wassaw I., U.S.A. **152 D9** 31 53N 80 58W
Wassaw Sd., U.S.A. **152 D9** 31 53N 80 55W
Wassen, Switz. .... **33 C7** 46 42N 8 36 E
Wasserauen, Switz. .... **33 B8** 47 17N 9 26 E
Wasserburg, Germany .... **31 G8** 48 3N 12 14 E
Wasserkuppe, Germany .... **30 E5** 50 29N 9 55 E
Wassy, France .... **27 D11** 48 30N 4 58 E
Wasu, Papua N. G. .... **132 C4** 5 58 S 147 12 E
Wasua, Papua N. G. .... **132 E2** 8 18 S 142 52 E
Waswanipi, Canada **140 C4** 49 40N 76 29W
Waswanipi, L., Canada **140 C4** 49 35N 76 40W
Watam, Papua N. G. .... **132 B3** 3 55 S 144 33 E
Watampone, Indonesia .... **82 B2** 4 29 S 120 25 E
Watamu, Kenya .... **118 C5** 3 23 S 40 0 E
Watansoppeng, Indonesia ...... **82 B1** 4 0 S 119 56 E
Watarrka Nat. Park △, Australia .. **124 D5** 24 20 S 131 30 E
Watee, Solomon Is. .... **133 N12** 10 30 S 162 2 E
Water Park Pt., Australia .... **126 C5** 22 56 S 150 47 E
Water Valley, U.S.A. **155 H10** 34 10N 89 38W
Waterberg, S. Africa .... **117 C4** 24 10 S 28 0 E
Waterberg Plateau Park △, Namibia **116 C2** 20 25 S 17 18 E
Waterberge, S. Africa .... **117 C4** 24 10 S 28 0 E
Waterbury, Conn., U.S.A. **151 E11** 41 33N 73 3W
Waterbury, Vt., U.S.A. **151 B12** 44 20N 72 46W
Waterbury L., Canada **143 B8** 58 10N 104 22W
Waterdown, Canada **150 C5** 43 20N 79 53W
Wateree →, U.S.A. **152 B9** 33 45N 80 37W
Waterford, Ireland **23 D4** 52 15N 7 8W
Waterford, Calif., U.S.A. **160 H6** 37 38N 120 46W
Waterford, Mich., U.S.A. **157 B13** 42 45N 83 32W
Waterford, Pa., U.S.A. **150 E5** 41 57N 79 59W
Waterford, Wis., U.S.A. **157 B8** 42 46N 88 13W
Waterford □, Ireland **23 D4** 52 10N 7 40W
Waterford Harbour, Ireland **23 D5** 52 8N 6 58W
Waterhen L., Canada **143 C9** 52 10N 99 40W
Waterloo, Belgium .... **24 D4** 50 43N 4 25 E
Waterloo, Ont., Canada **140 D3** 43 30N 80 32W
Waterloo, Qué., Canada **151 A12** 45 22N 72 32W
Waterloo, S. Leone **112 D2** 8 26N 13 8W
Waterloo, Ill., U.S.A. **156 F6** 38 20N 90 9W
Waterloo, Ind., U.S.A. **157 C11** 41 26N 85 1W

Waterloo, Iowa, U.S.A. **156 B4** 42 30N 92 21W
Waterloo, N.Y., U.S.A. **150 D8** 42 54N 76 52W
Waterloo, Wis., U.S.A. **156 A8** 43 11N 88 59W
Waterman, U.S.A. **157 C8** 41 46N 88 47W
Watermeet, U.S.A. **154 B10** 46 16N 89 11W
Waterton Lakes Nat. Park △,
  Canada **142 D6** 48 45N 115 0W
Watertown, Conn., U.S.A. **151 E11** 41 36N 73 7W
Watertown, N.Y., U.S.A. **151 C9** 43 59N 75 55W
Watertown, S. Dak., U.S.A. **154 C6** 44 54N 97 7W
Watertown, Wis., U.S.A. **154 D10** 43 12N 88 43W
Waterval-Boven, S. Africa ..... **117 D5** 25 40 S 30 18 E
Waterville, Canada **151 A13** 45 16N 71 54W
Waterville, Maine, U.S.A. **149 C11** 44 33N 69 38W
Waterville, N.Y., U.S.A. **151 D9** 42 56N 75 23W
Waterville, Pa., U.S.A. **150 E7** 41 19N 77 21W
Waterville, Wash., U.S.A. **158 C3** 47 39N 120 4W
Watervliet, Mich., U.S.A. **157 B10** 42 11N 86 18W
Watervliet, N.Y., U.S.A. **151 D11** 42 44N 73 42W
Wates, Indonesia .... **85 D4** 7 51 S 110 10 E
Watford, Canada **150 D3** 42 57N 81 53W
Watford, U.K. **21 F7** 51 40N 0 24W
Watford City, U.S.A. **154 B3** 47 48N 103 17W
Wathaman →, Canada **143 B8** 57 16N 102 59W
Wathaman L., Canada **143 B8** 56 58N 103 44W
Watheroo, Australia .... **125 F2** 30 15 S 116 0 E
Watheroo Nat. Park △, Australia .. **125 F2** 30 19 S 115 48 E
Wating, China .... **74 G4** 35 40N 106 38 E
Watkins Glen, U.S.A. **150 D8** 42 23N 76 52W
Watkinsville, U.S.A. **152 B6** 33 52N 83 25W
Watling I. = San Salvador I.,
  Bahamas **165 B5** 24 0N 74 40W
Watmuri, Indonesia .... **83 C4** 7 25 S 131 42 E
Watom I., Papua N. G. .... **132 C7** 4 7 S 152 4 E
Watonga, U.S.A. **155 H5** 35 51N 98 25W
Watrous, Canada **143 C7** 51 40N 105 25W
Watrous, U.S.A. **155 H2** 35 48N 104 59W
Watsa, Dem. Rep. of the Congo .. **118 B2** 3 4N 29 30 E
Watseka, U.S.A. **157 D9** 40 47N 87 44W
Watsi Kenga, Dem. Rep. of
  the Congo .... **114 C4** 0 49 S 20 34 E
Watson, Australia .... **125 F5** 30 29 S 131 31 E
Watson, Canada **143 C8** 52 10N 104 30W
Watson Lake, Canada **142 A3** 60 6N 128 49W
Watsontown, U.S.A. **150 E8** 41 5N 76 52W
Watsonville, U.S.A. **160 J5** 36 55N 121 45W
Wattenwil, Switz. .... **32 C5** 46 46N 7 31 E
Wattiwarriganna Cr. →, Australia . **127 D2** 28 57 S 136 10 E
Wattwil, Switz. .... **33 B8** 47 18N 9 6 E
Watu, Dem. Rep. of the Congo ... **114 C4** 3 18 S 20 3 E
Watuata = Batuata, Indonesia ... **82 C2** 6 12 S 122 42 E
Watubela, Kepulauan, Indonesia .. **83 B4** 4 28 S 131 35 E
Watubela Is. = Watubela,
  Kepulauan, Indonesia .... **83 B4** 4 28 S 131 35 E
Wau = Wâw, Sudan .... **107 F2** 7 45N 28 1 E
Wau, Papua N. G. .... **132 D4** 7 21 S 146 47 E
Waubamik, Canada **150 A4** 45 27N 80 1W
Waubay, U.S.A. **154 C6** 45 20N 97 18W
Waubra, Australia .... **128 D5** 37 21 S 143 39 E
Wauchope, N.S.W., Australia ... **129 A10** 31 28 S 152 45 E
Wauchope, N. Terr., Australia ... **126 C1** 20 36 S 134 15 E
Wauchula, U.S.A. **153 H8** 27 33N 81 49W
Waukarlycarly, L., Australia .... **124 D3** 21 18 S 121 56 E
Waukeenah, U.S.A. **152 E6** 30 25N 83 57W
Waukegan, U.S.A. **157 B9** 42 22N 87 50W
Waukesha, U.S.A. **154 D10** 43 1N 88 14W
Waukon, U.S.A. **154 D9** 43 16N 91 29W
Waupaca, U.S.A. **154 C10** 44 21N 89 5W
Waupun, U.S.A. **154 D10** 43 38N 88 44W
Waurika, U.S.A. **155 H6** 34 10N 98 0W
Wausau, U.S.A. **154 C10** 44 58N 89 38W
Wausau, Wis., U.S.A. **154 C10** 44 58N 89 38W
Wauseon, U.S.A. **157 C12** 41 33N 84 8W
Wautoma, U.S.A. **154 C10** 44 4N 89 18W
Wauwatosa, U.S.A. **157 A9** 43 3N 88 0W
Waveland, U.S.A. **157 E9** 39 53N 87 3W
Waveney →, U.K. .... **21 E9** 52 35N 1 39 E
Waverley, N.Z. .... **130 H3** 39 46 S 174 37 E
Waverley Hall, U.S.A. **152 C5** 32 41N 84 44W
Waverly, Ala., U.S.A. **152 C4** 32 44N 85 35W
Waverly, Fla., U.S.A. **153 H8** 27 59N 81 37W
Waverly, Ga., U.S.A. **152 D8** 31 6N 81 43W
Waverly, Ill., U.S.A. **156 E7** 39 36N 89 57W
Waverly, Iowa, U.S.A. **156 B4** 42 44N 92 29W
Waverly, N.Y., U.S.A. **150 E8** 42 1N 76 32W
Wawa, Belgium .... **24 D4** 50 43N 4 38 E
Wawa, Burma .... **90 G6** 17 28N 96 41 E
Wâw, Sudan .... **107 F2** 7 45N 28 1 E
Wawa, Nigeria .... **113 D5** 9 54N 4 27 E
Wawa, Sudan .... **106 C3** 20 30N 30 22 E
Wawanesa, Canada **143 D9** 49 36N 99 40W
Wawasee, L., U.S.A. **157 C11** 41 24N 85 42W
Wawoi →, Papua N. G. .... **132 D2** 7 48 S 143 16 E
Wawona, U.S.A. **160 H7** 37 32N 119 39W
Waxahachie, U.S.A. **155 J6** 32 24N 96 51W
Way, L., Australia .... **125 E3** 26 45 S 120 16 E
Waya, Fiji .... **132 A1** 17 19 S 177 10 E
Wayabula, Indonesia .... **83 A3** 2 29N 128 17 E
Waycross, U.S.A. **152 D7** 31 13N 82 21W
Wayi, Sudan .... **107 F3** 5 8N 30 10 E
Wayland, Mich., U.S.A. **157 B11** 42 40N 85 39W
Wayland, N.Y., U.S.A. **150 D7** 42 34N 77 35W
Wayne, Nebr., U.S.A. **154 D6** 42 14N 97 1W
Wayne, W. Va., U.S.A. **148 F4** 38 13N 82 27W
Wayne City, U.S.A. **157 F8** 38 21N 88 35W
Wayne County, Detroit ✈ (DTW),
  U.S.A. **157 B13** 42 13N 83 21W
Wayne Lakes, U.S.A. **157 D12** 40 1N 84 40W
Waynesboro, Ga., U.S.A. **152 B7** 33 6N 82 1W
Waynesboro, Miss., U.S.A. **149 K1** 31 40N 88 39W
Waynesboro, Pa., U.S.A. **148 F7** 39 45N 77 35W
Waynesboro, Va., U.S.A. **148 F6** 38 4N 78 53W
Waynesburg, U.S.A. **148 F5** 39 54N 80 11W
Waynesville, Mo., U.S.A. **156 G4** 37 50N 92 12W
Waynesville, N.C., U.S.A. **149 H4** 35 28N 82 58W
Waynesville, Ohio, U.S.A. **157 E12** 39 32N 84 5W
Waynoka, U.S.A. **155 G5** 36 35N 98 53W
Wayside, U.S.A. **152 B6** 33 4N 83 37W
Waza, Afghan. .... **91 B3** 33 22N 69 26 E
Waza, Parc Nat. de △, Cameroon . **109 F2** 11 15N 14 38 E
Wazikhwah, Afghan. .... **91 B3** 32 11N 68 21 E
Wâzin, Libya .... **108 B2** 31 58N 10 40 E
Wazirabad, Pakistan .... **92 C6** 32 30N 74 8 E
Wda →, Poland .... **54 E5** 53 25N 18 29 E
We, Indonesia .... **84 A1** 5 51N 95 18 E
Wé, N. Cal. .... **133 K5** 20 55 S 167 16 E
Weald, The, U.K. .... **21 F8** 51 4N 0 20 E
Weam, Papua N. G. .... **132 E1** 8 37 S 141 8 E
Wear →, U.K. **20 C6** 54 55N 1 23W
Weatherford, Okla., U.S.A. **155 H5** 35 32N 98 43W
Weatherford, Tex., U.S.A. **155 J6** 32 46N 97 48W
Weaubleau, U.S.A. **156 G3** 37 54N 93 32W
Weaverville, U.S.A. **158 F2** 40 44N 122 56W
Webb City, U.S.A. **155 G7** 37 9N 94 28W
Webequie, Canada **140 B2** 52 59N 87 21W
Weber, N.Z. .... **130 G5** 40 24 S 176 20 E
Webo = Nyaake, Liberia **112 E3** 4 52N 7 37W
Webster, Mass., U.S.A. **151 D13** 42 3N 71 53W
Webster, N.Y., U.S.A. **150 C7** 43 13N 77 26W

Webster, S. Dak., U.S.A. **154 C6** 45 20N 97 31W
Webster City, U.S.A. **156 B3** 42 28N 93 49W
Webster Springs, U.S.A. **148 F5** 38 29N 80 25W
Weda, Indonesia .... **79 D7** 0 21N 127 50 E
Weda, Teluk, Indonesia ...... **82 A3** 0 20N 128 0 E
Weddell I., Falk. Is. .... **9 f** 51 50 S 61 0W
Weddell Sea, Antarctica ...... **7 D1** 72 30 S 40 0W
Wedderburn, Australia .... **128 D5** 36 26 S 143 33 E
Weddin Mts. Nat. Park △, Australia **129 C8** 33 59 S 148 0 E
Wedel, Germany .... **30 B5** 53 34N 9 42 E
Wedemark, Germany .... **30 C5** 52 32N 9 43 E
Wedgeport, Canada **141 D6** 43 44N 65 59W
Wednesday I., Australia ...... **132 F2** 10 31 S 142 16 E
Wedowee, U.S.A. **152 B4** 33 19N 85 29W
Wedza, Zimbabwe .... **119 F3** 18 40 S 31 33 E
Wee Waa, Australia .... **127 E4** 30 11 S 149 26 E
Weed, U.S.A. .... **158 F2** 41 25 N 122 23W
Weed Heights, U.S.A. **160 G7** 38 59N 119 13W
Weedsport, U.S.A. **151 C8** 43 3N 76 35W
Weedville, U.S.A. **150 E6** 41 17N 78 30W
Weeki Wachee, U.S.A. **153 G7** 28 32N 82 35W
Weenen, S. Africa .... **117 D5** 28 48 S 30 7 E
Weener, Germany .... **30 B3** 53 9N 7 20 E
Weert, Neths. .... **24 C5** 51 15N 5 43 E
Weggis, Switz. .... **33 B6** 47 2N 8 26 E
Węgierska-Górka, Poland ..... **55 J6** 49 36N 19 7 E
Węglinieс, Poland .... **55 G2** 51 18N 15 10 E
Węgorzewo, Poland .... **54 D8** 54 13N 21 43 E
Węgrów, Poland .... **55 F8** 52 24N 22 0 E
Wehda □, Sudan .... **107 F3** 8 30N 30 0 E
Wei He →, Hebei, China ...... **74 F8** 36 10N 115 45 E
Wei He →, Shaanxi, China ..... **74 G6** 34 38N 110 15 E
Weichang, China .... **75 D9** 41 58N 117 49 E
Weichuan, China .... **74 G7** 34 20N 113 59 E
Weida, Germany .... **30 E8** 50 46N 12 2 E
Weiden, Germany .... **31 F8** 49 41N 12 10 E
Weifang, China .... **75 F10** 36 44N 119 7 E
Weihai, China .... **75 F12** 37 30N 122 6 E
Weil, Germany .... **31 H3** 47 35N 7 37 E
Weil, Germany .... **30 E4** 50 28N 8 17 E
Weilburg, Germany .... **30 E4** 50 28N 8 17 E
Weilheim, Germany .... **31 H7** 47 50N 11 9 E
Weimar, Germany .... **30 E7** 50 58N 11 19 E
Weinan, China .... **74 G5** 34 31N 109 29 E
Weinfelden, Switz. .... **33 A8** 47 34N 9 6 E
Weingarten, Germany .... **31 F4** 49 3N 8 31 E
Weinheim, Germany .... **31 F4** 49 32N 8 39 E
Weining, China .... **76 D5** 26 50N 104 17 E
Weipa, Australia .... **126 A3** 12 40 S 141 50 E
Weir →, Australia .... **127 D4** 28 20 S 149 50 E
Weir →, Canada **143 B10** 56 54N 93 21W
Weir River, Canada **143 B10** 56 49N 94 6W
Weirdale, Canada **143 C8** 53 24N 104 47W
Weirsdale, U.S.A. **153 G8** 28 59N 81 55W
Weirton, U.S.A. **150 F4** 40 24N 80 35W
Weiser, U.S.A. **158 D5** 44 10N 117 0W
Weishan, Shandong, China .... **75 G9** 34 47N 117 5 E
Weishan, Yunnan, China ..... **76 E3** 25 12N 100 20 E
Weissenbach, Austria .... **33 B11** 47 26N 10 39 E
Weissenburg, Germany ...... **31 F6** 49 2N 10 58 E
Weissenfels, Germany .... **30 D7** 51 11N 12 0 E
Weisshorn, Switz. .... **32 D5** 46 7N 7 43 E
Weisskugel, Austria .... **33 C11** 46 48N 10 44 E
Weissmies, Switz. .... **32 D6** 46 8N 8 1 E
Weissstannen, Switz. .... **33 C8** 46 59N 9 22 E
Weisswasser, Germany ...... **30 D10** 51 30N 14 36 E
Wéitra, Austria .... **34 C7** 48 41N 14 54 E
Weixi, China .... **76 D2** 27 10N 99 8 E
Weixin, China .... **76 D5** 27 48N 105 3 E
Weiyuan, China .... **74 G3** 35 7N 104 10 E
Weiz, Austria .... **34 D8** 47 13N 15 39 E
Weizhou Dao, China .... **76 G7** 21 0N 109 1 E
Wejherowo, Poland .... **54 D5** 54 35N 18 12 E
Wekusko L., Canada **143 C9** 54 40N 99 50W
Welch, U.S.A. **148 G5** 37 26N 81 35W
Weldya, Ethiopia .... **107 E4** 11 50N 39 34 E
Welega □, Ethiopia .... **107 F3** 9 25N 34 24 E
Welford Nat. Park △, Australia .. **126 D3** 25 5 S 143 16 E
Weligama, Sri Lanka .... **95 M5** 5 58N 80 25 E
Welkite, Ethiopia .... **107 F4** 8 15N 37 42 E
Welkom, S. Africa .... **116 D4** 28 0 S 26 46 E
Welland, Canada **140 D4** 43 0N 79 15W
Welland →, U.K. **21 E7** 52 51N 0 5W
Wellawaya, Sri Lanka .... **95 L5** 6 44N 81 6 E
Wellesley Is., Australia ...... **126 B2** 16 42 S 139 30 E
Wellingborough, U.K. **21 E7** 52 19N 0 41W
Wellington, Australia .... **129 B8** 32 35 S 148 59 E
Wellington, Canada **150 C4** 43 57N 77 20W
Wellington, N.Z. .... **130 H3** 41 19 S 174 46 E
Wellington, S. Africa .... **116 E2** 33 38 S 19 1 E
Wellington, Somst., U.K. **21 G4** 50 58N 3 13W
Wellington, Telford & Wrekin, U.K. **21 E5** 52 42N 2 30W
Wellington, Colo., U.S.A. **154 E2** 40 42N 105 0W
Wellington, Kans., U.S.A. **155 G6** 37 16N 97 24W
Wellington, Nev., U.S.A. **160 G7** 38 45N 119 23W
Wellington, Ohio, U.S.A. **150 E2** 41 10N 82 13W
Wellington, Tex., U.S.A. **155 H4** 34 51N 100 13W
Wellington □, N.Z. .... **130 G4** 41 0 S 175 30 E
Wellington, I., Chile .... **176 C2** 49 30 S 75 0W
Wellington, L., Australia ..... **129 E7** 38 6 S 147 20 E
Wells, U.K. **21 F5** 51 13N 2 39W
Wells, Maine, U.S.A. **151 C14** 43 20N 70 35W
Wells, N.Y., U.S.A. **151 C10** 43 24N 74 17W
Wells, Nev., U.S.A. **158 F6** 41 7N 114 58W
Wells, L., Australia .... **125 E3** 26 44 S 123 15 E
Wells, Mt., Australia .... **124 C4** 17 25 S 127 8 E
Wells Gray Prov. Park △, Canada . **142 C4** 52 30N 120 15W
Wells-next-the-Sea, U.K. ..... **20 E8** 52 57N 0 51 E
Wells River, U.S.A. **151 B12** 44 9N 72 4W
Wellsboro, U.S.A. **150 E7** 41 45N 77 18W
Wellsburg, U.S.A. **150 F4** 40 16N 80 37W
Wellsford, N.Z. .... **130 C3** 36 16 S 174 32 E
Wellsville, Mo., U.S.A. **156 E5** 39 4N 91 34W
Wellsville, N.Y., U.S.A. **150 D7** 42 7N 77 57W
Wellsville, Ohio, U.S.A. **150 F4** 40 36N 80 39W
Wellsville, Utah, U.S.A. **158 F8** 41 38N 111 56W
Wellton, U.S.A. **159 K6** 32 40N 114 8W
Welmel, Wabi →, Ethiopia .... **107 F5** 5 38N 40 47 E
Welo, United Arab Rep. ...... **107 E4** 12 0N 39 0 E
Welo □, Ethiopia .... **107 E4** 11 50N 39 48 E
Wels, Austria .... **34 C7** 48 9N 14 1 E
Welshpool, Australia .... **129 F7** 38 42 S 146 26 E
Welshpool, U.K. **21 E4** 52 39N 3 8W
Welwyn Garden City, U.K. **21 F7** 51 48N 0 12W
Wem, U.K. **20 E5** 52 52N 2 44W
Wembere →, Tanzania ...... **118 C3** 4 10 S 34 15 E
Wemindji, Canada **140 B4** 53 0N 78 49W
Wen Xian, China .... **74 G7** 34 55N 113 5 E
Wenatchee, U.S.A. **158 C3** 47 25N 120 19W
Wenchang, China .... **86 C8** 19 38N 110 42 E
Wencheng, China .... **77 D13** 27 46N 120 4 E
Wenchuan, China .... **76 B4** 31 22N 103 33 E
Wenchi, Ghana **112 D4** 7 46N 2 8W
Wenden, U.S.A. **161 M13** 33 49N 113 33W
Wendeng, China .... **75 F12** 37 15N 122 5 E
Wendesi, Indonesia .... **83 B4** 2 30 S 134 17 E
Wendo, Ethiopia .... **107 F4** 6 40N 38 27 E
Wendover, U.S.A. **158 F6** 40 44N 114 2W
Weng'an, China .... **76 D6** 27 5N 107 25 E
Wengcheng, China .... **77 E9** 24 22N 113 50 E
Wengen, Switz. .... **32 C5** 46 37N 7 55 E

Wengyuan, China .... 77 E10 24 20N 114 9 E
Wenjiang, China .... 76 B4 30 44N 103 55 E
Wenling, China .... 77 C13 28 21N 121 20 E
Wenlock →, Australia .... 126 A3 12 2 S 141 55 E
Wenona, U.S.A. 156 C7 41 3N 89 3W
Wenshan, China .... 76 F5 23 20N 104 18 E
Wenshang, China .... 74 G9 35 45N 116 30 E
Wenshui, China .... 74 F7 37 26N 112 1 E
Wensleydale, U.K. 20 C6 54 17N 2 0W
Wensu, China .... 64 B3 41 15N 80 10 E
Wensum →, U.K. .... 20 E8 52 40N 1 15 E
Wentworth, Australia .... 128 C4 34 2 S 141 54 E
Wentzel L., Canada 142 B6 59 2N 114 28W
Wentzville, U.S.A. 156 F6 38 49N 90 51W
Wenut, Indonesia .... 83 B4 3 11 S 133 19 E
Wenxi, China .... 74 G6 35 20N 111 10 E
Wenxian, China .... 74 H3 32 43N 104 36 E
Wenzhou, China .... 77 D13 28 0N 120 38 E
Weott, U.S.A. 158 F2 40 20N 123 55W
Wepener, S. Africa .... 116 D4 29 42 S 27 3 E
Werda, Botswana .... 116 D3 25 24 S 23 15 E
Werdau, Germany .... 30 E8 50 44N 12 22 E
Werder, Ethiopia .... 120 C3 6 58N 45 1 E
Werder, Germany .... 30 C8 52 23N 12 55 E
Werdohl, Germany .... 30 D3 51 15N 7 46 E
Wereilu, Ethiopia .... 107 E4 10 40N 39 28 E
Weri, Indonesia .... 83 B4 3 10 S 132 38 E
Werneck, Germany .... 31 F6 49 58N 10 5 E
Wernigerode, Germany .... 30 D6 51 50N 10 47 E
Werra →, Germany .... 30 D5 51 24N 9 39 E
Werribee, Australia .... 128 D6 37 54 S 144 40 E
Werrikimbee Nat. Park △, Australia 129 A10 31 11 S 152 15 E
Werrimull, Australia .... 128 C4 34 25 S 141 38 E
Werris Creek, Australia .... 129 A9 31 18 S 150 38 E
Wertach →, Germany .... 31 G6 48 22N 10 54 E
Wertheim, Germany .... 31 F5 49 45N 9 32 E
Wertingen, Germany .... 31 G6 48 33N 10 41 E
Wesel, Germany .... 30 D2 51 39N 6 37 E
Weser →, Germany .... 30 B4 53 36N 8 28 E
Weser-Ems □, Germany .... 30 C3 53 0N 7 30 E
Weserbergland, Germany .... 30 C5 52 12N 9 7 E
Weserbergland Schaumburg Hameln, Naturpark △, Germany ...... 30 C5 52 8N 9 20 E
Wesiri, Indonesia .... 82 C3 7 30 S 126 30 E
Weslemkoon L., Canada 150 A7 45 2N 77 25W
Wesleyville, Canada 141 C9 49 8N 53 36W
Wesleyville, U.S.A. 150 D4 42 9N 80 0W
Wessel, C., Australia .... 126 A2 10 59 S 136 46 E
Wessel Is., Australia .... 126 A2 11 10 S 136 45 E
Wesselburen, Germany .... 30 A4 54 13N 8 54 E
Wessington Springs, U.S.A. 154 C5 44 5N 98 34W
West, U.S.A. 155 K6 31 48N 97 6W
West →, U.S.A. 151 D12 42 52N 72 33W
West Allis, U.S.A. 157 B8 43 1N 88 0W
West Baines →, Australia ...... 124 C4 15 38 S 129 59 E
West Bank □, Asia .... 103 C4 32 6N 35 13 E
West Bend, U.S.A. 148 D1 43 25N 88 11W
West Bengal □, India .... 93 H13 23 0N 88 0 E
West Berkshire □, U.K. 21 F6 51 25N 1 17W
West Beskids = Západné Beskydy, Europe .... 35 B12 49 30N 19 0 E
West Branch, U.S.A. 148 C3 44 17N 84 14W
West Branch Susquehanna →, U.S.A. 151 F8 40 53N 76 48W
West Bromwich, U.K. 21 E6 52 32N 1 59W
West Burra, U.K. 22 A7 60 5N 1 21W
West Canada Cr. →, U.S.A. 151 C10 43 1N 74 58W
West Cape Howe, Australia .... 125 G2 35 8 S 117 36 E
West Carrollton, U.S.A. 157 E12 39 40N 84 17W
West Chazy, U.S.A. 151 B11 44 49N 73 28W
West Chester, U.S.A. 151 G9 39 58N 75 36W
West Chicago, U.S.A. 157 C8 41 53N 88 12W
West Coast □, N.Z. .... 131 D5 43 15 S 170 30 E
West Coast Nat. Park △, S. Africa 116 E2 33 13 S 18 0 E
West Columbia, S.C., U.S.A. 152 B8 35 59N 81 4W
West Columbia, Tex., U.S.A. 155 L7 29 9N 95 39W
West Covina, U.S.A. 161 L9 34 4N 117 54W
West Des Moines, U.S.A. 156 C3 41 35N 93 43W
West Dunbartonshire □, U.K. 22 F4 55 59N 4 30W
West End, Bahamas 164 A4 26 41N 78 58W
West Falkland, Falk. Is. ...... 9 f 51 40 S 60 0W
West Fargo, U.S.A. 154 B6 46 52N 96 54W
West Farmington, U.S.A. 150 E4 41 23N 80 58W
West Fjord = Vestfjorden, Norway . 14 C15 67 55N 14 0 E
West Fork Trinity →, U.S.A. 155 J6 32 48N 96 54W
West Frankfort, U.S.A. 156 G8 37 54N 88 55W
West Green, U.S.A. 152 D7 31 37N 82 44W
West Hartford, U.S.A. 151 E12 41 45N 72 44W
West Haven, U.S.A. 151 E12 41 17N 72 57W
West Hazleton, U.S.A. 151 F9 40 58N 76 0W
West Helena, U.S.A. 155 H9 34 33N 90 38W
West Hurley, U.S.A. 151 E10 41 59N 74 7W
West I., India .... 95 H11 13 35N 92 54 E
West Ice Shelf, Antarctica ...... 7 C7 68 0 S 85 0 E
West Indies, Cent. Amer. 165 D7 15 0N 65 0W
West Jefferson, U.S.A. 157 E12 39 57N 83 17W
West Jordan, U.S.A. 158 F8 40 36N 111 56W
West Lafayette, U.S.A. 157 D10 40 27N 86 55W
West Lamma Channel, China .... 69 G11 22 13N 114 4 E
West Liberty, Iowa, U.S.A. 156 C5 41 34N 91 16W
West Liberty, Ky., U.S.A. 157 G13 37 55N 83 16W
West Liberty, Ohio, U.S.A. 157 D13 40 15N 83 45W
West Lorne, Canada 150 D3 42 36N 81 36W
West Lothian □, U.K. 22 F5 55 54N 3 36W
West Lunga →, Zambia .... 119 E1 13 6 S 24 39 E
West Lunga Nat. Park △, Zambia . 115 E4 12 49 S 24 47 E
West MacDonnell Nat. Park △, Australia .... 124 D5 23 38 S 132 59 E
West Memphis, U.S.A. 155 H9 35 9N 90 11W
West Midlands □, U.K. 21 E6 52 26N 2 0W
West Mifflin, U.S.A. 150 F5 40 22N 79 52W
West Milton, Ohio, U.S.A. 157 E12 39 58N 84 20W
West Milton, Pa., U.S.A. 150 E8 41 1N 76 50W
West Monroe, U.S.A. 155 J8 32 31N 92 9W
West New Britain □, Papua N. G. . 132 C5 5 0 S 149 30 E
West Newton, U.S.A. 150 F5 40 14N 79 46W
West Nicholson, Zimbabwe .... 119 G2 21 2 S 29 20 E
West Palm Beach, U.S.A. 153 J9 26 43N 80 3W
West Palm Beach Canal, U.S.A. . 153 J9 26 40N 80 15W
West Pensacola, U.S.A. 153 E2 30 25N 87 16W
West Plains, U.S.A. 155 G9 36 44N 91 51W
West Point, Ga., U.S.A. 152 C4 32 53N 85 11W
West Point, Iowa, U.S.A. 156 D5 40 43N 91 27W
West Point, Ky., U.S.A. 157 G11 37 59N 85 57W
West Point, N.Y., U.S.A. 151 E11 41 24N 73 58W
West Point, Nebr., U.S.A. 154 E6 41 51N 96 43W
West Point, Va., U.S.A. 148 G7 37 32N 76 48W
West Point L., U.S.A. 152 B4 33 0N 85 10W
West Pt. = Ouest, Pte. de l', Canada 141 C7 49 52N 64 40W
West Pt., Australia .... 128 C1 35 1 S 135 56 E
West Ra., Papua N. G. .... 132 C1 4 15 S 141 30 E
West Road →, Canada 142 C4 53 18N 122 53W
West Rutland, U.S.A. 151 C11 43 38N 73 5W
West Salem, U.S.A. 157 F8 38 31N 88 1W
West Schelde = Westerschelde →, Neths. .... 24 C3 51 25N 3 25 E
West Seneca, U.S.A. 150 D6 42 51N 78 48W
West Sepik □, Papua N. G. .... 132 B2 3 30 S 142 0 E
West Siberian Plain, Russia .... 62 C11 62 0N 75 0 E
West Sussex □, U.K. 21 G7 50 55N 0 30W
West Terre Haute, U.S.A. 157 E9 39 28N 87 27W
West-Terschelling, Neths. .... 24 A5 53 22N 5 13 E
West Union, Iowa, U.S.A. 156 B5 42 57N 91 49W
West Union, Ohio, U.S.A. 157 F13 38 48N 83 33W

West Unity, U.S.A. 157 C12 41 35N 84 26W
West Valley City, U.S.A. 158 F8 40 42N 111 57W
West-Vlaanderen □, Belgium .... 24 D2 51 0N 3 0 E
West Walker →, U.S.A. 160 G7 38 54N 119 9W
West Wyalong, Australia .... 129 B7 33 56 S 147 10 E
West Yellowstone, U.S.A. 158 D8 44 40N 111 6W
West Yorkshire □, U.K. 20 D6 53 45N 1 40W
Westall Pt., Australia .... 127 E1 32 55 S 134 4 E
Westbay, U.S.A. 152 E4 30 18N 85 52W
Westbrook, U.S.A. 149 D10 43 41N 70 22W
Westbury, Australia .... 127 G4 41 30 S 146 51 E
Westby, U.S.A. 154 A2 48 52N 104 3W
Westend, U.S.A. 161 K9 35 42N 117 24W
Westerland, Germany .... 15 J13 54 54N 8 17 E
Westerly, U.S.A. 151 E13 41 22N 71 50W
Western □, Ghana 112 D4 5 30N 2 30W
Western □, Kenya .... 118 B3 0 30N 34 30 E
Western □, Papua N. G. .... 132 D2 7 30 S 142 0 E
Western □, S. Leone 112 D2 8 30N 13 0W
Western □, Zambia .... 119 F1 15 0 S 24 4 E
Western Australia □, Australia .... 125 E2 25 0 S 118 0 E
Western Cape □, S. Africa .... 116 E3 34 0 S 20 0 E
Western Dvina = Daugava →, Latvia . 9 H21 57 4N 24 3 E
Western Ghats, India .... 92 K9 14 0N 75 0 E
Western Highlands □, Papua N. G. . 132 C3 5 45 S 144 30 E
Western Isles □, U.K. 22 D1 57 30N 7 10W
Western Sahara ■, Africa 110 D2 25 0N 13 0W
Western Samoa = Samoa ■, Pac. Oc. . 133 X24 14 0 S 172 0W
Westernport, U.S.A. 148 F6 39 29N 79 3W
Westerschelde →, Neths. .... 24 C3 51 25N 3 25 E
Westerstede, Germany .... 30 B3 53 15N 7 55 E
Westerwald, Germany .... 30 E3 50 38N 7 56 E
Westfield, Ill., U.S.A. 157 E8 39 27N 88 0W
Westfield, Ind., U.S.A. 157 D10 40 2N 86 8W
Westfield, Mass., U.S.A. 151 D12 42 7N 72 45W
Westfield, N.Y., U.S.A. 150 D5 42 20N 79 35W
Westfield, Pa., U.S.A. 150 E7 41 55N 77 32W
Westhill, U.K. 22 D6 57 9N 2 19W
Westhope, U.S.A. 154 A4 48 55N 101 1W
Westland, U.S.A. 157 B13 42 15N 83 20W
Westland Bight, N.Z. .... 131 C5 42 55 S 170 5 E
Westland Nat. Park △, N.Z. .... 131 C5 43 16 S 170 16 E
Westlock, Canada 142 C6 54 9N 113 55W
Westmar, Australia .... 127 D4 27 55 S 149 44 E
Westmeath □, Ireland 23 C4 53 33N 7 34W
Westminster, U.S.A. 148 F7 39 34N 76 59W
Westmont, U.S.A. 150 F6 40 19N 78 58W
Westmoreland, Barbados .... 165 g 13 13N 59 37W
Westmorland, U.S.A. 161 M11 33 2N 115 37W
Weston, Malaysia .... 85 A5 5 10N 115 35 E
Weston, Ohio, U.S.A. 157 C13 41 21N 83 47W
Weston, Oreg., U.S.A. 158 D4 45 49N 118 26W
Weston, W. Va., U.S.A. 148 F5 39 2N 80 28W
Weston I., Canada 140 B4 52 33N 79 36W
Weston-super-Mare, U.K. 21 F5 51 21N 2 58W
Westover, U.S.A. 150 F6 40 45N 78 40W
Westphalia, U.S.A. 156 F5 38 26N 92 0W
Westport, Canada 151 B8 44 40N 76 25W
Westport, Ireland 23 C2 53 48N 9 31W
Westport, N.Z. .... 131 B6 41 46 S 171 37 E
Westport, Ind., U.S.A. 157 E11 39 11N 85 34W
Westport, N.Y., U.S.A. 151 B11 44 11N 73 26W
Westport, Oreg., U.S.A. 160 D3 46 8N 123 23W
Westport, Wash., U.S.A. 160 D2 46 53N 124 6W
Westray, Canada 143 C8 53 36N 101 24W
Westray, U.K. 22 B5 59 18N 3 0W
Westree, Canada 140 C3 47 26N 81 34W
Westville, Calif., U.S.A. 160 F6 39 8N 120 42W
Westville, Fla., U.S.A. 152 K4 30 46N 85 51W
Westville, Ill., U.S.A. 157 D9 40 2N 87 38W
Westville, Ind., U.S.A. 157 C10 41 35N 86 55W
Westwood, U.S.A. 158 F3 40 18N 121 0W
Wetar, Indonesia .... 82 C3 7 48 S 126 30 E
Wetar, Selat, Indonesia .... 82 C3 8 20 S 126 30 E
Wetaskiwin, Canada 142 C6 52 55N 113 24W
Wetherby, U.K. 20 D6 53 56N 1 23W
Wethersfield, U.S.A. 151 E12 41 42N 72 40W
Wetlet, Burma .... 90 D5 22 20N 95 53 E
Wetteren, Belgium .... 24 D3 51 0N 3 53 E
Wettingen, Switz. .... 33 B6 47 28N 8 20 E
Wetumpka, U.S.A. 152 C3 32 32N 86 13W
Wetzikon, Switz. .... 33 B7 47 19N 8 48 E
Wetzlar, Germany .... 30 E4 50 32N 8 31 E
Wevok, U.S.A. 144 B6 68 53N 166 13W
Wewahitchka, U.S.A. 152 E4 30 7N 85 12W
Wewak, Papua N. G. .... 132 B2 3 38 S 143 41 E
Wewoka, U.S.A. 155 H6 35 9N 96 30W
Wexford, Ireland 23 D5 52 20N 6 28W
Wexford □, Ireland 23 D5 52 20N 6 25W
Wexford Harbour, Ireland 23 D5 52 20N 6 25W
Weyburn, Canada 143 D8 49 40N 103 50W
Weyer Markt, Austria .... 34 D7 47 51N 14 40 E
Weyhe, Germany .... 30 C4 52 58N 8 49 E
Weyib →, Ethiopia .... 107 F5 7 15N 40 15 E
Weymouth, Canada 141 D6 44 30N 66 1W
Weymouth, U.K. 21 G5 50 37N 2 28W
Weymouth, U.S.A. 151 D14 42 13N 70 58W
Weymouth, C., Australia .... 126 A3 12 37 S 143 27 E
Wha Ti, Canada 138 B8 63 8N 117 16W
Whakamaru, N.Z. .... 130 E4 38 23 S 175 50 E
Whakatane, N.Z. .... 130 D6 37 57 S 177 1 E
Whakatane →, N.Z. .... 130 D6 37 57 S 177 1 E
Whale →, Canada 141 A6 58 15N 67 40W
Whale Cove, Canada 143 A10 62 11N 92 36W
Whale Pt., Ascension I. .... 9 g 7 57 S 14 18W
Whales, B. of, Antarctica .... 7 D12 78 0 S 165 0W
Whalsay, U.K. 22 A8 60 22N 0 59W
Whangaehu →, N.Z. .... 130 G4 40 3 S 175 6 E
Whangamata, N.Z. .... 130 D4 37 12 S 175 53 E
Whangamomona, N.Z. .... 130 F3 39 8 S 174 44 E
Whanganui Nat. Park △, N.Z. .... 130 F3 39 17 S 174 53 E
Whangarei, N.Z. .... 130 B3 35 43 S 174 21 E
Whangarei Harb., N.Z. .... 130 B3 35 45 S 174 28 E
Whangaroa Harb., N.Z. .... 130 B2 35 4 S 173 46 E
Whangaruru Harb., N.Z. .... 130 B3 35 24 S 174 23 E
Wharanui, N.Z. .... 131 B9 41 55 S 174 6 E
Wharfe →, U.K. 20 D6 53 51N 1 9W
Wharfedale, U.K. 20 C5 54 6N 2 1W
Wharton, N.J., U.S.A. 151 F10 40 54N 74 35W
Wharton, Pa., U.S.A. 150 E6 41 31N 78 1W
Wharton, Tex., U.S.A. 155 L6 29 19N 96 6W
Whataroa, N.Z. .... 131 D5 43 18 S 170 24 E
Whataroa →, N.Z. .... 131 D5 43 7 S 170 16 E
Wheatfield, U.S.A. 157 C9 41 13N 87 4W
Wheatland, Calif., U.S.A. 160 F5 39 1N 121 25W
Wheatland, Ind., U.S.A. 157 F9 38 40N 87 19W
Wheatland, Wyo., U.S.A. 154 D2 42 3N 104 58W
Wheatley, Canada 150 D2 42 6N 82 27W
Wheaton, Ill., U.S.A. 157 C8 41 52N 88 6W
Wheaton, Md., U.S.A. 148 F7 39 3N 77 3W
Wheaton, Minn., U.S.A. 154 C6 45 48N 96 30W
Wheelbarrow Pk., U.S.A. 160 H10 37 26N 116 5W
Wheeler, Oreg., U.S.A. 160 D2 45 41N 123 53W
Wheeler, Tex., U.S.A. 155 H4 35 27N 100 16W
Wheeler →, Canada 141 A6 57 2N 67 13W
Wheeler L., U.S.A. 149 H2 34 48N 87 23W
Wheeler Pk., N. Mex., U.S.A. 159 H11 36 34N 105 25W
Wheeler Pk., Nev., U.S.A. 159 G6 38 57N 114 15W
Wheeler Ridge, U.S.A. 161 L8 35 0N 118 57W
Wheeling, U.S.A. 150 F4 40 4N 80 43W
Whernside, U.K. 20 C5 54 14N 2 24W
Whirlwind Reef, Papua N. G. .... 132 C5 4 42 S 148 16 E

Whiskey Jack L., Canada 143 B8 58 23N 101 55W
Whiskeytown-Shasta-Trinity Nat. Recr. Area □, U.S.A. 158 F2 40 45N 122 15W
Whistleduck Cr. →, Australia .... 126 C2 20 15 S 135 18 E
Whistler, Canada 142 C4 50 7N 122 58W
Whitby, Canada 150 C6 43 52N 78 56W
Whitby, U.K. 20 C7 54 29N 0 37W
Whitcombe Pass, N.Z. .... 131 D5 43 13 S 170 55 E
White →, Ark., U.S.A. 155 J9 33 57N 91 5W
White →, Ind., U.S.A. 157 F9 38 25N 87 45W
White →, S. Dak., U.S.A. 154 D5 43 42N 99 27W
White →, Tex., U.S.A. 155 J4 33 14N 100 56W
White →, Utah, U.S.A. 158 F9 40 4N 109 41W
White →, Vt., U.S.A. 151 C12 43 37N 72 20W
White →, Wash., U.S.A. 160 C4 47 12N 122 15W
White, East Fork →, U.S.A. 157 F9 38 33N 87 14W
White, L., Australia .... 124 D4 21 9 S 128 56 E
White B., Canada 141 C8 50 0N 56 35W
White Bird, U.S.A. 158 D5 45 46N 116 18W
White Butte, U.S.A. 154 B3 46 23N 103 18W
White City, Fla., U.S.A. 152 F4 29 53N 85 13W
White City, Oreg., U.S.A. 158 E2 42 26N 122 51W
White Cliffs, Australia .... 129 A5 30 50 S 143 10 E
White Hall, U.S.A. 156 E6 39 26N 90 24W
White Haven, U.S.A. 151 E9 41 4N 75 47W
White Horse, Vale of, U.K. 21 F6 51 37N 1 30W
White I., N.Z. .... 130 D6 37 30 S 177 13 E
White L., Canada 151 A8 45 18N 76 31W
White L., U.S.A. 155 L8 29 44N 92 30W
White Mountain, U.S.A. 144 B7 64 41N 163 24W
White Mountain Peak, U.S.A. 159 G4 37 38N 118 15W
White Mts., Alaska, U.S.A. 144 D11 65 30N 146 30W
White Mts., Calif., U.S.A. 160 H8 37 30N 118 15W
White Mts., N.H., U.S.A. 151 B13 44 15N 71 15W
White Mts. Nat. Park △, Australia . 126 C4 20 43 S 145 12 E
White Nile = Nîl el Abyad →, Sudan 107 D3 15 38N 32 31 E
White Nile Dam = Khazzân Jabal al Awliyâ, Sudan .... 107 D3 15 24N 32 20 E
White Oak, U.S.A. 152 D8 31 2N 81 43W
White Otter L., Canada 140 C1 49 5N 91 55W
White Pass, U.S.A. 160 D5 46 38N 121 24W
White Pigeon, U.S.A. 157 C11 41 48N 85 39W
White Plains, U.S.A. 152 B6 33 28N 83 1W
White Plains, N.Y., U.S.A. 151 E11 41 2N 73 46W
White River, Canada 140 C2 48 35N 85 20W
White River, S. Africa .... 117 D5 25 20 S 31 0 E
White River, U.S.A. 154 D4 43 34N 100 45W
White Rock, Canada 160 A4 49 2N 122 48W
White Russia = Belarus ■, Europe . 58 F4 53 30N 27 0 E
White Sands Nat. Monument △, U.S.A. 159 K10 32 46N 106 20W
White Sea = Beloye More, Russia . 56 A6 66 30N 38 0 E
White Springs, U.S.A. 152 E7 30 20N 82 45W
White Sulphur Springs, Mont., U.S.A. 158 C8 46 33N 110 54W
White Sulphur Springs, W. Va., U.S.A. 148 G5 37 48N 80 18W
White Volta →, Ghana 113 D4 9 10N 1 15W
Whitecliffs, N.Z. .... 131 D6 43 26 S 171 55 E
Whitecourt, Canada 142 C5 54 10N 115 45W
Whiteface Mt., U.S.A. 151 B11 44 22N 73 54W
Whitefield, U.S.A. 151 B13 44 23N 71 37W
Whitefish, U.S.A. 158 B6 48 25N 114 20W
Whitefish Bay, U.S.A. 157 A9 43 23N 87 54W
Whitefish L., Canada 143 A7 62 41N 106 48W
Whitefish Point, U.S.A. 148 B3 46 45N 84 59W
Whitegull, L., Canada 141 A7 55 27N 64 17W
Whitehall, Mich., U.S.A. 148 D2 43 24N 86 21W
Whitehall, Mont., U.S.A. 158 D7 45 52N 112 6W
Whitehall, N.Y., U.S.A. 151 C11 43 33N 73 24W
Whitehall, Wis., U.S.A. 154 C9 44 22N 91 19W
Whitehaven, U.K. 20 C4 54 33N 3 35W
Whitehorse, Canada 142 A1 60 43N 135 3W
Whiteman Ra., Papua N. G. .... 132 C5 5 55 S 150 0 E
Whitemark, Australia .... 127 G4 40 7 S 148 3 E
Whiteplains, Liberia 112 D2 6 28N 10 40W
Whiteriver, U.S.A. 159 K9 33 50N 109 58W
Whitesand →, Canada 142 A5 60 9N 115 45W
Whitesands, S. Africa .... 116 E3 34 23 S 20 50 E
Whitesboro, N.Y., U.S.A. 151 C9 43 7N 75 18W
Whitesboro, Tex., U.S.A. 155 J6 33 39N 96 54W
Whiteshell Prov. Park △, Canada . 143 C9 50 0N 95 40W
Whiteside, Canal, Chile .... 176 D2 53 55 S 70 15W
Whiteside, U.S.A. 150 D7 42 7N 77 46W
Whitesville, U.S.A. 157 F11 36 42N 82 6W
Whiteville, U.S.A. 153 H6 34 20N 78 42W
Whitewater, U.S.A. 157 B8 42 50N 88 44W
Whitewater →, U.S.A. 153 K9 25 15N 81 0W
Whitewater Baldy, U.S.A. 159 K9 33 20N 108 39W
Whitewater L., Canada 140 B2 50 50N 89 10W
Whitewood, Australia .... 126 C3 21 28 S 143 30 E
Whitewood, Canada 143 C8 50 20N 102 20W
Whitfield, Australia .... 129 D7 36 42 S 146 24 E
Whithorn, U.K. 22 G4 54 44N 4 26W
Whitianga, N.Z. .... 130 C4 36 47 S 175 41 E
Whiting, U.S.A. 157 C9 41 41N 87 29W
Whitmire, U.S.A. 151 D14 42 5N 70 56W
Whitmore Village, U.S.A. 145 J13 21 31N 158 1W
Whitney, Canada 140 C4 45 31N 78 14W
Whitney, Mt., U.S.A. 160 J8 36 35N 118 18W
Whitney Point, U.S.A. 151 D9 42 20N 75 58W
Whitstable, U.K. .... 21 F9 51 21N 1 3 E
Whitsunday I., Australia .... 126 J7 20 15 S 149 4 E
Whitsunday Islands Nat. Park △, Australia .... 126 J7 20 15 S 149 0 E
Whitsunday Passage, Australia .... 126 J6 20 5 S 148 51 E
Whittemore, U.S.A. 156 A2 43 4N 94 26W
Whittier, Alaska, U.S.A. 144 F10 60 47N 148 41W
Whittier, Calif., U.S.A. 161 M8 33 58N 118 3W
Whittlesea, Australia .... 129 D7 37 27 S 145 9 E
Wholdaia L., Canada 143 A8 60 43N 104 20W
Whyalla, Australia .... 128 B2 33 2 S 137 30 E
Wiang Kosai Nat. Park △, Thailand 86 D2 17 54N 99 29 E
Wiarton, Canada 150 B3 44 40N 81 10W
Wiawso, Ghana 112 D4 6 10N 2 25W
Wiay, U.K. 22 D1 57 24N 7 13W
Wigzow, Poland .... 55 H4 50 50N 17 10 E
Wibaux, U.S.A. 154 B2 46 59N 104 11W
Wichabai, Guyana 169 C6 2 57N 59 35W
Wichian Buri, Thailand .... 86 E3 15 39N 101 7 E
Wichita, U.S.A. 155 G6 37 42N 97 20W
Wichita Falls, U.S.A. 155 J5 33 54N 98 30W
Wick, U.K. 22 C5 58 26N 3 5W
Wicked Pt., Canada 150 C7 43 52N 77 15W
Wickenburg, U.S.A. 159 K7 33 58N 112 44W
Wickepin, Australia .... 125 F2 32 50 S 117 30 E
Wickham, Australia .... 124 D2 20 42 S 117 11 E
Wickham, C., Australia .... 127 F3 39 35 S 143 57 E
Wickliffe, U.S.A. 150 E3 41 36N 81 28W
Wicklow, Ireland 23 D5 52 59N 6 3W
Wicklow □, Ireland 23 D5 52 57N 6 25W
Wicklow Hd., Ireland 23 D6 52 58N 6 0W
Wicklow Mountains Nat. Park △, Ireland 23 C5 53 6N 6 21W
Widawa, Poland 55 G5 52 58N 6 26W
Widawka →, Poland .... 55 G5 51 27N 18 51 E
Wide B., Papua N. G. .... 132 C7 5 5 S 152 5 E
Widgeegoara Cr. →, Australia .... 127 D4 28 51 S 146 34 E
Widgiemooltha, Australia .... 125 F3 31 30 S 121 34 E
Widi, Indonesia .... 83 B7 0 33 S 128 24 E
Widnau, Switz. .... 33 B9 47 24N 9 38 E
Widnes, U.K. 20 D5 53 23N 2 45W
Więcbork, Poland .... 55 E4 53 21N 17 30 E

Wiehengebirge, Naturpark = Nördlicher Teutoburger Wald- Wiehengebirge, Naturpark △, Germany .... 30 C4 52 18N 8 10 E
Wiehl, Germany .... 30 E3 50 56N 7 34 E
Wiek, Germany .... 30 A9 54 37N 13 17 E
Wielbark, Poland .... 54 E7 53 24N 20 55 E
Wieleń, Poland .... 55 F3 52 53N 16 9 E
Wielichowo, Poland .... 55 F3 52 7N 16 22 E
Wieliczka, Poland .... 55 J7 50 0N 20 5 E
Wielkopolski Park Narodowy △, Poland .... 55 F3 52 18N 16 45 E
Wielkopolskie □, Poland .... 55 F4 52 20N 17 30 E
Wieluń, Poland .... 55 G5 51 15N 18 34 E
Wien, Austria .... 35 C9 48 12N 16 22 E
Wiener Neustadt, Austria .... 35 D9 47 49N 16 16 E
Wieprz →, Poland .... 55 G8 51 34N 21 49 E
Wieprza →, Poland .... 54 D3 54 26N 16 25 E
Wieruszów, Poland .... 55 G5 51 19N 18 9 E
Wiesbaden, Germany .... 30 E4 50 4N 8 14 E
Wiesen, Switz. .... 33 C9 46 42N 9 43 E
Wiesental, Germany .... 31 F4 49 13N 8 31 E
Wiesloch, Germany .... 31 F4 49 18N 8 41 E
Wiesmoor, Germany .... 30 B3 53 24N 7 47 E
Wieżyca, Poland .... 54 D5 54 14N 18 8 E
Wigan, U.K. 20 D5 53 33N 2 38W
Wiggins, Colo., U.S.A. 154 E2 40 14N 104 4W
Wiggins, Miss., U.S.A. 155 K10 30 51N 89 8W
Wight, I. of □, U.K. 21 G6 50 40N 1 20W
Wigierski Park Narodowy △, Poland 54 D10 54 5N 23 5 E
Wigry, Jezioro, Poland .... 54 D10 54 2N 23 8 E
Wigston, U.K. 21 E6 52 35N 1 6W
Wigtown, U.K. 22 G4 54 53N 4 27W
Wigtown B., U.K. 22 G4 54 46N 4 15W
Wil, Switz. .... 33 B8 47 28N 9 3 E
Wilamowice, Poland .... 55 J6 49 55N 19 9 E
Wilберforce, Canada 154 E6 40 29N 96 58W
Wilberforce, Canada 150 A6 45 2N 78 13W
Wilberforce, C., Australia .... 126 A2 11 54 S 136 35 E
Wilburton, U.S.A. 155 H7 34 55N 95 19W
Wilcannia, Australia .... 128 A5 31 30 S 143 26 E
Wilcox, U.S.A. 150 E6 41 35N 78 41W
Wildbad, Germany .... 31 G4 48 44N 8 33 E
Wildcat →, U.S.A. 157 D10 40 28N 86 52W
Wildeshausen, Germany .... 30 C4 52 54N 8 27 E
Wildeshauser Geest, Naturpark △, Germany .... 30 C4 52 54N 8 30 E
Wildhorn, Switz. .... 32 D4 46 22N 7 21 E
Wildon, Austria .... 34 E8 46 52N 15 31 E
Wildrose, U.S.A. 161 J9 36 14N 117 11W
Wildspitze, Austria .... 34 E3 46 53N 10 53 E
Wildstrubel, Switz. .... 32 D5 46 24N 7 32 E
Wildwood, U.S.A. 153 G7 28 52N 82 2W
Wilga →, S. Africa .... 117 D4 27 3 S 28 20 E
Wilge →, S. Africa .... 117 D4 27 3 S 28 20 E
Wilhelm, Mt., Papua N. G. .... 132 C3 5 50 S 145 1 E
Wilhelm II Coast, Antarctica .... 7 C7 68 0 S 90 0 E
Wilhelmina Geb., Suriname 169 C6 3 50N 56 30W
Wilhelmsburg, Austria .... 34 C8 48 6N 15 36 E
Wilhelmshaven, Germany .... 30 B4 53 31N 8 7 E
Wilhelmstal, Namibia .... 116 C2 21 58 S 16 21 E
Wilkes-Barre, U.S.A. 151 E9 41 15N 75 53W
Wilkie, Canada 143 C7 52 27N 108 42W
Wilkinsburg, U.S.A. 150 F5 40 26N 79 53W
Wilkinson Lakes, Australia .... 125 E5 29 40 S 132 39 E
Willacoochee, U.S.A. 152 D6 31 20N 83 3W
Willandra Creek →, Australia .... 128 B6 33 22 S 145 52 E
Willandra Nat. Park △, Australia . 128 B6 33 12 S 145 0 E
Willapa B., U.S.A. 158 C2 46 40N 124 0W
Willapa Hills, U.S.A. 160 D3 46 35N 123 25W
Willard, N.Y., U.S.A. 150 D8 42 40N 76 50W
Willard, N.Mex., U.S.A. 159 J10 41 3N 82 44W
Willaumez Pen., Papua N. G. .... 132 C6 5 1 S 150 2 E
Willbriggie, Australia .... 129 C7 34 28 S 146 2 E
Willcox, U.S.A. 159 K9 32 15N 109 50W
Willemstad, Neth. Ant. 165 D6 12 5N 69 0W
Willet, U.S.A. 151 D9 42 28N 75 55W
William →, Canada 143 B7 59 8N 109 19W
William, Mt., Australia .... 128 D5 37 17 S 142 35 E
William B. Hartsfield International, Atlanta ✈ (ATL), U.S.A. 152 B5 33 38N 84 26W
William 'Bill' Dannely Res., U.S.A. 152 B3 32 10N 87 10W
William Creek, Australia .... 127 D2 28 58 S 136 22 E
Williams, Australia .... 125 F2 33 2 S 116 52 E
Williams, Ariz., U.S.A. 159 J7 35 15N 112 11W
Williams, Calif., U.S.A. 160 F4 39 9N 122 9W
Williams Harbour, Canada 141 B8 52 33N 55 47W
Williams Lake, Canada 142 C4 52 10N 122 10W
Williamsburg, Iowa, U.S.A. 156 C4 41 40N 92 1W
Williamsburg, Ky., U.S.A. 149 G3 36 44N 84 10W
Williamsburg, Pa., U.S.A. 150 F6 40 28N 78 12W
Williamsburg, Va., U.S.A. 148 G7 37 17N 76 44W
Williamsfield, U.S.A. 156 D6 40 55N 90 1W
Williamson, N.Y., U.S.A. 150 C7 43 14N 77 11W
Williamson, W. Va., U.S.A. 148 G4 37 41N 82 17W
Williamsport, Ind., U.S.A. 157 D9 40 17N 87 17W
Williamsport, Pa., U.S.A. 150 E7 41 15N 77 0W
Williamston, Australia .... 129 D7 37 51 S 144 52 E
Williamston, Mich., U.S.A. 148 D3 42 41N 84 17W
Williamston, N.C., U.S.A. 153 H7 35 51N 77 4W
Williamstown, Australia 157 F12 38 38N 84 34W
Williamstown, Ky., U.S.A. 157 F12 38 38N 84 34W
Williamstown, Mass., U.S.A. 151 D11 42 41N 73 12W
Williamstown, N.Y., U.S.A. 151 C9 43 26N 75 53W
Williamsville, U.S.A. 156 E7 39 57N 89 33W
Willimantic, U.S.A. 151 E12 41 43N 72 13W
Willingboro, U.S.A. 148 E8 40 3N 74 54W
Willisau, Switz. .... 32 B6 47 7N 8 0 E
Willisburg, U.S.A. 157 G11 37 49N 85 8W
Williston, S. Africa .... 116 E3 31 20 S 20 53 E
Williston, Fla., U.S.A. 153 F7 29 23N 82 27W
Williston, N. Dak., U.S.A. 154 A3 48 9N 103 37W
Williston, S.C., U.S.A. 152 B8 33 24N 81 25W
Williston L., Canada 142 B4 56 0N 124 0W
Willits, U.S.A. 158 G2 39 25N 123 21W
Willmar, U.S.A. 154 C7 45 7N 95 3W
Willmore Wilderness Park △, Canada 142 C5 53 45N 119 30W
Willoughby, U.S.A. 150 E3 41 39N 81 24W
Willow, U.S.A. 144 F10 61 45N 150 3W
Willow Bunch, Canada 143 D7 49 20N 105 35W
Willow L., Canada 142 A5 62 10N 119 8W
Willow Tree, Australia .... 129 A9 31 40 S 150 45 E
Willow Wall, The, China .... 75 C12 42 10N 122 0 E
Willowick, U.S.A. 150 E3 41 38N 81 28W
Willowlake →, Canada .... 142 A4 62 42 S 123 8W
Willowmore, S. Africa .... 116 E3 33 15 S 23 30 E
Willows, U.S.A. 160 F4 39 31N 122 12W
Willowvale = Gatyana, S. Africa . 117 E4 32 16 S 28 31 E
Wills, L., Australia .... 124 D4 21 25 S 128 51 E
Wills Cr. →, Australia .... 126 C3 22 43 S 140 2 E
Willsboro, U.S.A. 151 B11 44 21N 73 24W
Willunga, Australia .... 128 C3 35 15 S 138 30 E
Wilma, U.S.A. 153 F8 30 12N 84 18W
Wilmette, U.S.A. 157 B9 42 5N 87 42W
Wilmington, Australia .... 128 B3 32 39 S 138 7 E
Wilmington, Del., U.S.A. 148 F8 39 45N 75 33W
Wilmington, Ill., U.S.A. 157 C8 41 18N 88 9W
Wilmington, N.C., U.S.A. 149 H7 34 14N 77 55W
Wilmington, Ohio, U.S.A. 157 E13 39 27N 83 50W
Wilmington, Vt., U.S.A. 151 D12 42 52N 72 52W
Wilmslow, U.K. 20 D5 53 19N 2 13W
Wilna = Vilnius, Lithuania .... 15 J21 54 38N 25 19 E
Wilpena →, Australia .... 128 A3 31 31 S 138 37 E

Wilpena Cr. →, *Australia* .... **128 A3** 31 25 S 139 29 E
Wilsall, *U.S.A.* **158 D8** 45 59N 110 38W
Wilson, N.C., *U.S.A.* **149 H7** 35 44N 77 55W
Wilson, N.Y., *U.S.A.* **150 C6** 43 19N 78 50W
Wilson, Pa., *U.S.A.* **151 F9** 40 41N 75 15W
Wilson →, *Australia* .... **124 C4** 16 48 S 128 16 E
Wilson Bluff, *Australia* .... **125 F4** 31 41 S 129 0 E
Wilson Inlet, *Australia* .... **125 G2** 35 0 S 117 22 E
Wilson Str., *Solomon Is.* .... **133 M9** 8 0 S 156 39 E
Wilsons Promontory, *Australia* .... **129 E7** 38 55 S 146 25 E
Wilsons Promontory Nat. Park △,
  Australia .... **129 D7** 37 59 S 146 23 E
Wilster, *Germany* .... **30 B5** 53 55N 9 23 E
Wilton, Iowa, *U.S.A.* **156 C5** 41 34N 91 4W
Wilton, N. Dak., *U.S.A.* **154 B4** 47 10N 100 47W
Wilton →, *Australia* .... **126 A1** 14 45 S 134 33 E
Wiltshire □, *U.K.* **21 F6** 51 18N 1 53W
Wiltz, *Lux.* .... **24 E5** 49 57N 5 55 E
Wiluna, *Australia* .... **125 E3** 26 36 S 120 14 E
Wimborne Minster, *U.K.* **21 G6** 50 48N 1 59W
Wimereux, *France* .... **27 B8** 50 45N 1 37 E
Wimmera →, *Australia* .... **128 D4** 36 8 S 141 56 E
Winam G., *Kenya* .... **118 C3** 0 20 S 34 15 E
Winamac, *U.S.A.* **157 C10** 41 3N 86 36W
Winburg, S. *Africa* .... **116 D4** 28 30 S 27 2 E
Winchelsea, *Australia* .... **128 E6** 38 10 S 144 1 E
Winchendon, *U.S.A.* **151 D12** 42 41N 72 3W
Winchester, *N.Z.* .... **131 E6** 44 11 S 171 17 E
Winchester, *U.K.* **21 F6** 51 4N 1 18W
Winchester, Conn., *U.S.A.* **151 E11** 41 53N 73 9W
Winchester, Idaho, *U.S.A.* **158 C5** 46 14N 116 38W
Winchester, Ill., *U.S.A.* **156 E6** 39 38N 90 27W
Winchester, Ind., *U.S.A.* **157 D12** 40 10N 84 59W
Winchester, Ky., *U.S.A.* **157 G12** 38 0N 84 11W
Winchester, N.H., *U.S.A.* **151 D12** 42 46N 72 23W
Winchester, Nev., *U.S.A.* **161 J11** 36 6N 115 10W
Winchester, Ohio, *U.S.A.* **157 F13** 38 57N 83 40W
Winchester, Tenn., *U.S.A.* **149 H2** 35 11N 86 7W
Winchester, Va., *U.S.A.* **148 F6** 39 11N 78 10W
Wind →, *U.S.A.* **158 E9** 43 12N 108 12W
Wind Cave Nat. Park △, *U.S.A.* **154 D3** 43 32N 103 17W
Wind Point, *U.S.A.* **157 B9** 42 47N 87 46W
Wind River Range, *U.S.A.* **158 E9** 43 0N 109 30W
Windamere, L., *Australia* .... **129 B8** 32 42 S 149 44 E
Windau = Ventspils, *Latvia* .... **15 H19** 57 25N 21 32 E
Windber, *U.S.A.* **150 F6** 40 14N 78 50W
Winder, *U.S.A.* **152 A4** 34 0N 83 45W
Windermere, *U.K.* **20 C5** 54 23N 2 55W
Windermere, *U.S.A.* **153 G8** 28 29N 81 32W
Windfall, *U.S.A.* **157 D11** 40 22N 85 57W
Windhoek, *Namibia* .... **116 C2** 22 35 S 17 4 E
Windischgarsten, *Austria* .... **32 B6** 47 28N 8 14 E
Windischgarsten, *Austria* .... **34 D7** 47 42N 14 21 E
Windom, *U.S.A.* **154 D7** 43 52N 95 7W
Windorah, *Australia* .... **126 D3** 25 24 S 142 36 E
Window Rock, *U.S.A.* **159 J9** 35 41N 109 3W
Windrush →, *U.K.* **21 F6** 51 43N 1 24W
Windsor, *Australia* .... **129 B9** 33 37 S 150 50 E
Windsor, N.S., *Canada* **141 D7** 44 59N 64 5W
Windsor, Ont., *Canada* **140 D3** 42 18N 83 0W
Windsor, *N.Z.* .... **131 E5** 44 59 S 170 49 E
Windsor, *U.K.* **21 F7** 51 29N 0 36W
Windsor, Colo., *U.S.A.* **154 E2** 40 29N 104 54W
Windsor, Conn., *U.S.A.* **151 E12** 41 50N 72 39W
Windsor, Ill., *U.S.A.* **157 E8** 39 26N 88 36W
Windsor, Mo., *U.S.A.* **156 F3** 38 32N 93 31W
Windsor, N.Y., *U.S.A.* **151 D9** 42 5N 75 37W
Windsor, Vt., *U.S.A.* **151 C12** 43 29N 72 24W
Windsor & Maidenhead □, *U.K.* **21 F7** 51 29N 0 40W
Windsorton, S. *Africa* .... **116 D3** 28 16 S 24 44 E
Windward Is., *W. Indies* **165 D7** 13 0N 61 0W
Windward Passage = Vientos, Paso
  de los, *Caribbean* **165 C5** 20 0N 74 0W
Winefred L., *Canada* **143 B6** 55 30N 110 30W
Winejok, *Sudan* .... **107 F2** 9 1N 27 30 E
Winfield, Iowa, *U.S.A.* **156 C5** 41 7N 91 26W
Winfield, Kans., *U.S.A.* **155 G6** 37 15N 96 59W
Winfield, Mo., *U.S.A.* **156 F6** 39 0N 90 44W
Wingate Mts., *Australia* .... **124 B5** 14 25 S 130 40 E
Wingham, *Australia* .... **129 A10** 31 48 S 152 22 E
Wingham, *Canada* **140 D3** 43 55N 81 20W
Winisk, *Canada* **140 A2** 55 20N 85 15W
Winisk →, *Canada* **140 A2** 55 17N 85 5W
Winisk L., *Canada* **140 B2** 52 55N 87 22W
Wink, *U.S.A.* **155 K3** 31 45N 103 9W
Winkler, *Canada* **143 D9** 49 10N 97 56W
Winklern, *Austria* .... **34 E5** 46 52N 12 52 E
Winlock, *U.S.A.* **160 D4** 46 30N 122 56W
Winneba, *Ghana* **113 D4** 5 25N 0 36W
Winnebago, *U.S.A.* **156 B7** 42 16N 89 15W
Winnebago, L., *U.S.A.* **141 D1** 44 0N 88 26W
Winnecke Cr. →, *Australia* .... **124 C5** 18 35 S 131 34 E
Winnemucca, *U.S.A.* **158 F5** 40 58N 117 44W
Winnemucca L., *U.S.A.* **158 F4** 40 7N 119 21W
Winnett, *U.S.A.* **158 C9** 47 0N 108 21W
Winnfield, *U.S.A.* **155 K8** 31 56N 92 38W
Winnibigoshish, L., *U.S.A.* **154 B7** 47 27N 94 13W
Winnipeg, *Canada* **143 D9** 49 54N 97 9W
Winnipeg →, *Canada* **143 C9** 50 38N 96 19W
Winnipeg, L., *Canada* **143 C9** 52 0N 97 0W
Winnipeg Beach, *Canada* **143 C9** 50 30N 96 58W
Winnipegosis, *Canada* **143 C9** 51 39N 99 55W
Winnipegosis L., *Canada* **143 C9** 52 30N 100 0W
Winnipesaukee, L., *U.S.A.* **151 C13** 43 38N 71 21W
Winnisquam L., *U.S.A.* **151 C13** 43 33N 71 31W
Winnsboro, La., *U.S.A.* **155 J9** 32 10N 91 43W
Winnsboro, S.C., *U.S.A.* **149 H5** 34 23N 81 5W
Winnsboro, Tex., *U.S.A.* **155 J7** 32 58N 95 17W
Winokapau, L., *Canada* **141 B7** 53 15N 62 50W
Winona, Minn., *U.S.A.* **154 C9** 44 3N 91 39W
Winona, Miss., *U.S.A.* **155 J10** 33 29N 89 44W
Winooski, *U.S.A.* **151 B11** 44 29N 73 11W
Winooski →, *U.S.A.* **151 B11** 44 32N 73 17W
Winschoten, *Neths.* .... **24 A7** 53 9N 7 3 E
Winsen, *Germany* .... **30 B6** 53 22N 10 13 E
Winsford, *U.K.* **20 D5** 53 12N 2 31W
Winslow, Ariz., *U.S.A.* **159 J8** 35 2N 110 42W
Winslow, Ind., *U.S.A.* **157 F9** 38 23N 87 13W
Winslow, Wash., *U.S.A.* **160 C4** 47 38N 122 31W
Winsted, *U.S.A.* **151 E11** 41 55N 73 4W
Winston-Salem, *U.S.A.* **149 G5** 36 6N 80 15W
Winter Garden, *U.S.A.* **153 G8** 28 34N 81 35W
Winter Haven, *U.S.A.* **153 G8** 28 1N 81 44W
Winter Park, *U.S.A.* **153 G8** 28 36N 81 20W
Winterberg, *Germany* .... **30 D4** 51 11N 8 32 E
Winterhaven, *U.S.A.* **161 N12** 32 47N 114 39W
Winters, *U.S.A.* **160 G5** 38 32N 121 58W
Winterset, *U.S.A.* **156 C3** 41 20N 94 1W
Wintersville, *U.S.A.* **150 F4** 40 23N 80 42W
Winterswijk, *Neths.* .... **24 C6** 51 58N 6 43 E
Winterthur, *Switz.* .... **33 B7** 47 30N 8 44 E
Winthrop, *U.S.A.* **158 B3** 48 28N 120 10W
Winton, *Australia* .... **126 C3** 22 24 S 143 3 E
Winton, *N.Z.* .... **131 G3** 46 8 S 168 20 E
Wintua, *Vanuatu* .... **133 F5** 16 30 S 167 26 E
Wipper →, *Germany* .... **30 D7** 51 16N 11 12 E
Wirraminna, *Australia* .... **128 A2** 31 12 S 136 13 E
Wirrulla, *Australia* .... **129 E1** 32 24 S 134 31 E
Wisbech, *U.K.* .... **21 E8** 52 41N 0 9 E
Wisconsin □, *U.S.A.* **156 A5** 44 45N 89 30W
Wisconsin →, *U.S.A.* **156 A5** 43 0N 91 15W
Wisconsin Rapids, *U.S.A.* **154 C10** 44 23N 89 49W
Wisdom, *U.S.A.* **158 D7** 45 37N 113 27W
Wiseman, *U.S.A.* **144 C10** 67 25N 150 6W

Wishaw, *U.K.* **22 F5** 55 46N 3 54W
Wishek, *U.S.A.* **154 B5** 46 16N 99 33W
Wisła, *Poland* .... **55 J5** 49 38N 18 53 E
Wisła →, *Poland* .... **54 D5** 54 22N 18 55 E
Wisłok →, *Poland* .... **55 H9** 50 13N 22 32 E
Wisłoka →, *Poland* .... **55 H8** 50 27N 21 23 E
Wismar, *Germany* .... **30 B7** 53 54N 11 29 E
Wismar, *Guyana* **169 B6** 5 59N 58 18W
Wisner, *U.S.A.* **154 E6** 41 59N 96 55W
Wissant, *France* .... **27 B8** 50 52N 1 40 E
Wissembourg, *France* .... **27 C14** 49 2N 7 57 E
Wisznice, *Poland* .... **55 G10** 51 48N 23 13 E
Witbank, S. *Africa* .... **117 D4** 25 51 S 29 14 E
Witdraai, S. *Africa* .... **116 D3** 26 58 S 20 48 E
Witham, *U.K.* .... **21 F8** 51 48N 0 40 E
Witham →, *U.K.* **20 E7** 52 59N 0 2W
Withernsea, *U.K.* .... **20 D8** 53 44N 0 1 E
Withlacoochee →, Fla., *U.S.A.* **152 E6** 30 24N 83 10W
Withlacoochee →, Fla., *U.S.A.* **153 G7** 29 0N 82 45W
Witjira Nat. Park △, *Australia* .... **127 D2** 26 22 S 135 37 E
Witkowo, *Poland* .... **54 F4** 52 26N 17 45 E
Witney, *U.K.* **21 F6** 51 48N 1 28W
Witnica, *Poland* .... **55 F1** 52 40N 14 54 E
Witnossob →, *Namibia* .... **116 D3** 23 55 S 18 45 E
Wittdün, *Germany* .... **30 A4** 54 38N 8 23 E
Witten, *Germany* .... **30 D3** 51 26N 7 20 E
Wittenberge, *Germany* .... **30 B7** 53 0N 11 45 E
Wittenburg, *Germany* .... **30 B7** 53 31N 11 4 E
Wittenheim, *France* .... **27 E14** 47 44N 7 20 E
Wittenoom, *Australia* .... **124 D2** 22 15 S 118 20 E
Witti, Banjaran, *Malaysia* .... **85 A5** 5 11N 116 29 E
Wittingen, *Germany* .... **30 C6** 52 44N 10 44 E
Wittlich, *Germany* .... **31 F2** 49 59N 6 53 E
Wittmund, *Germany* .... **30 B3** 53 34N 7 46 E
Wittow, *Germany* .... **30 A9** 54 38N 13 20 E
Wittstock, *Germany* .... **30 B8** 53 10N 12 28 E
Witu Is., *Papua N. G.* .... **132 C5** 4 50 S 149 25 E
Witvlei, *Namibia* .... **116 C2** 22 23 S 18 32 E
Witzenhausen, *Germany* .... **30 D5** 51 20N 9 51 E
Wixom, *U.S.A.* **157 B13** 42 32N 83 32W
Wkra →, *Poland* .... **55 F7** 52 27N 20 44 E
Władysławowo, *Poland* .... **54 D5** 54 48N 18 25 E
Wleń, *Poland* .... **55 G2** 51 2N 15 39 E
Wlingi, *Indonesia* .... **85 D4** 8 5 S 112 25 E
Włocławek, *Poland* .... **55 F6** 52 40N 19 3 E
Włodawa, *Poland* .... **55 G10** 51 33N 23 31 E
Włoszczowa, *Poland* .... **55 H6** 50 50N 19 55 E
Woburn, *U.S.A.* **151 D13** 42 29N 71 9W
Wodian, *China* .... **74 H7** 32 50N 112 35 E
Wodonga = Albury-Wodonga,
  Australia .... **129 D7** 36 3 S 146 56 E
Wodonga, *Australia* .... **129 D7** 36 3 S 146 50 E
Wodzisław Śląski, *Poland* .... **55 H5** 50 1N 18 26 E
Wœrth, *France* .... **27 D14** 48 57N 7 45 E
Wohlen, *Switz.* .... **33 B6** 47 21N 8 17 E
Woinbogoin, *China* .... **76 A2** 32 51N 98 39 E
Woinui, Selat, *Indonesia* .... **83 B4** 1 10 S 134 36 E
Woippy, *France* .... **27 C13** 49 10N 6 8 E
Woitape, *Papua N. G.* .... **132 E4** 8 33 S 147 15 E
Wojcieszow, *Poland* .... **55 H2** 50 58N 15 55 E
Wokam, *Indonesia* .... **83 C4** 5 45 S 134 28 E
Wokha, *India* .... **90 B5** 26 6N 94 16 E
Woking, *U.K.* **21 F7** 51 19N 0 34W
Wokingham, *U.K.* **21 F7** 51 24N 0 49W
Wokingham □, *U.K.* **21 F7** 51 25N 0 51W
Wokon Nat. Park △, *Australia* .... **129 A9** 31 46 S 151 49 E
Wolbrom, *Poland* .... **55 H6** 50 24N 19 45 E
Wolcottville, *U.S.A.* **157 C11** 41 32N 85 22W
Wołczyn, *Poland* .... **55 G5** 51 1N 18 3 E
Woldegk, *Germany* .... **30 B9** 53 27N 13 34 E
Wolf →, *Canada* **142 A2** 60 17N 132 33W
Wolf, Volcán, *Ecuador* .... **172 a** 0 2N 91 20W
Wolf Creek, *U.S.A.* **158 C7** 47 0N 112 4W
Wolf L., *Canada* **142 A2** 60 24N 131 40W
Wolf Point, *U.S.A.* **154 A2** 48 5N 105 39W
Wolfe I., *Canada* **140 D4** 44 7N 76 20W
Wolfeboro, *U.S.A.* **151 C13** 43 35N 71 13W
Wolfen, *Germany* .... **30 D8** 51 39N 12 16 E
Wolfenbüttel, *Germany* .... **30 C6** 52 10N 10 33 E
Wolfratshausen, *Germany* .... **31 H7** 47 54N 11 24 E
Wolfsberg, *Austria* .... **34 E7** 46 50N 14 52 E
Wolfsburg, *Germany* .... **30 C6** 52 25N 10 48 E
Wolfurt, *Austria* .... **33 B9** 47 28N 9 45 E
Wolgast, *Germany* .... **30 A9** 54 3N 13 44 E
Wolhusen, *Switz.* .... **32 B6** 47 4N 8 4 E
Wolin, *Poland* .... **54 E1** 53 50N 14 37 E
Woliński Park Narodowy △, *Poland* .... **54 E1** 53 57N 14 28 E
Wollaston, Is., *Chile* .... **176 E3** 55 40 S 67 30W
Wollaston Forland, *Greenland* **10 C9** 74 25N 19 40W
Wollaston L., *Canada* **143 B8** 58 7N 103 10W
Wollaston Lake, *Canada* **143 B8** 58 3N 103 33W
Wollaston Pen., *Canada* **138 B8** 69 30N 115 0W
Wollemi Nat. Park △, *Australia* .... **129 B9** 33 0 S 150 30 E
Wollongong, *Australia* .... **129 C9** 34 25 S 150 54 E
Wolmaransstad, S. *Africa* .... **116 D4** 27 12 S 25 59 E
Wolmirstedt, *Germany* .... **30 C7** 52 14N 11 37 E
Wołomin, *Poland* .... **55 F8** 52 19N 21 15 E
Wołów, *Poland* .... **55 G3** 51 20N 16 38 E
Wolseley, *Australia* .... **128 D4** 36 23 S 140 54 E
Wolseley, S. *Africa* .... **116 E2** 33 29 S 19 7 E
Wolsey, *U.S.A.* **154 C5** 44 24N 98 28W
Wolstenholme, C., *Canada* **136 C12** 62 35N 77 30W
Wolsztyn, *Poland* .... **55 F3** 52 8N 16 5 E
Wolvega, *Neths.* .... **24 B6** 52 52N 6 0 E
Wolverhampton, *U.K.* **21 E5** 52 35N 2 7W
Wondai, *Australia* .... **127 D5** 26 20 S 151 49 E
Wonenara, *Papua N. G.* .... **132 D3** 6 48 S 145 53 E
Wonga Wongué, Parc Nat. de △,
  Gabon .... **114 C1** 0 29 S 9 25 E
Wongalarroo L., *Australia* .... **128 A6** 31 32 S 144 0 E
Wongan Hills, *Australia* .... **125 F2** 30 51 S 116 37 E
Wongju, S. *Korea* .... **75 F14** 37 22N 127 58 E
Wonosari, *Indonesia* .... **85 D4** 7 58 S 110 36 E
Wonosobo, *Indonesia* .... **85 D3** 7 22 S 109 54 E
Wonowon, *Canada* **142 B4** 56 44N 121 48W
Wŏnsan, N. *Korea* .... **75 E14** 39 11N 127 27 E
Wonthaggi, *Australia* .... **129 C7** 38 37 S 145 37 E
Wood Buffalo Nat. Park △, *Canada* **142 B6** 59 0N 113 41W
Wood Is., *Australia* .... **124 C3** 16 24 S 123 19 E
Wood L., *Canada* **143 B8** 55 17N 103 17W
Wood River, *U.S.A.* **156 F6** 38 52N 90 5W
Woodah, I., *Australia* .... **126 A2** 13 27 S 136 10 E
Woodbine, *U.S.A.* **152 E8** 30 58N 81 44W
Woodbourne, *U.S.A.* **151 E10** 41 46N 74 36W
Woodbridge, *Canada* **150 C5** 43 47N 79 36W
Woodbridge, *U.K.* .... **21 E9** 52 6N 1 20 E
Woodburn, *U.S.A.* **158 D2** 45 9N 122 51W
Woodbury, *U.S.A.* **152 C5** 32 59N 84 35W
Woodenbong, *Australia* .... **128 D6** 28 24 S 152 39 E
Woodend, *Australia* .... **127 D5** 26 58 S 152 47 E
Woodford, *Australia* **160 D1** 42 38N 124 7W
Woodfords, *U.S.A.* **160 G7** 38 47N 119 50W
Woodlake, *U.S.A.* **160 J7** 36 25N 119 6W
Woodland, Calif., *U.S.A.* **160 G5** 38 41N 121 46W
Woodland, Maine, *U.S.A.* **149 C12** 45 9N 67 25W
Woodland, Pa., *U.S.A.* **150 F6** 40 59N 78 21W
Woodland, Wash., *U.S.A.* **160 E4** 45 54N 122 45W
Woodland Caribou Prov. Park △,
  Canada **143 C10** 51 0N 94 45W
Woodlands, *Singapore* .... **87 d** 1 27N 103 47 E
Woodlark I., *Papua N. G.* .... **132 E7** 9 10 S 152 50 E
Woodridge, *Canada* **143 D9** 49 20N 96 9W
Woodroffe, Mt., *Australia* .... **125 E5** 26 20 S 131 45 E
Woods, L., *Australia* .... **126 B1** 17 50 S 133 30 E

Woods, L. of the, *Canada* **143 D10** 49 15N 94 45W
Woodside, S. Austral., *Australia* .... **128 C3** 34 58 S 138 52 E
Woodside, Vic., *Australia* .... **129 E7** 38 31 S 146 52 E
Woodson, *U.S.A.* **156 E6** 39 37N 90 14W
Woodstock, N.S.W., *Australia* .... **129 B8** 33 45 S 148 53 E
Woodstock, Queens., *Australia* .... **126 B4** 19 35 S 146 50 E
Woodstock, N.B., *Canada* **141 C6** 46 11N 67 37W
Woodstock, Ont., *Canada* **140 D3** 43 10N 80 45W
Woodstock, *U.K.* **21 F6** 51 51N 1 20W
Woodstock, Ga., *U.S.A.* **152 A5** 34 6N 84 31W
Woodstock, Ill., *U.S.A.* **154 D10** 42 19N 88 27W
Woodstock, Vt., *U.S.A.* **151 C12** 43 37N 72 31W
Woodsville, *U.S.A.* **151 B13** 44 9N 72 2W
Woodville, *N.Z.* .... **130 G4** 40 20 S 175 53 E
Woodville, Fla., *U.S.A.* **152 E5** 30 19N 84 15W
Woodville, Ga., *U.S.A.* **152 B6** 33 40N 83 7W
Woodville, Miss., *U.S.A.* **155 K9** 31 6N 91 18W
Woodville, Ohio, *U.S.A.* **157 C13** 41 27N 83 22W
Woodward, *U.S.A.* **155 K7** 36 26N 99 24W
Woody, *U.S.A.* **161 K8** 35 42N 118 50W
Woody →, *Canada* **143 C8** 52 31N 100 51W
Woolacombe, *U.K.* **21 F3** 51 10N 4 13W
Woolamai, C., *Australia* .... **129 E6** 38 30 S 145 23 E
Woolbrook, *Australia* .... **129 A9** 30 56 S 151 25 E
Wooler, *U.K.* **20 B5** 55 33N 2 1W
Woolgoolga, *Australia* .... **127 E5** 30 6 S 153 11 E
Woomera, *Australia* .... **128 A2** 31 5 S 136 50 E
Woonsocket, R.I., *U.S.A.* **151 E13** 42 0N 71 31W
Woonsocket, S. Dak., *U.S.A.* **154 C5** 44 3N 98 17W
Wooramel →, *Australia* .... **125 E1** 25 47 S 114 10 E
Wooramel Roadhouse, *Australia* .... **125 E1** 25 45 S 114 17 E
Wooster, *U.S.A.* **150 F3** 40 48N 81 56W
Worb, *Switz.* .... **32 C5** 46 56N 7 33 E
Worcester, S. *Africa* .... **116 E2** 33 39 S 19 27 E
Worcester, *U.K.* **21 E5** 52 11N 2 12W
Worcester, Mass., *U.S.A.* **151 D13** 42 16N 71 48W
Worcester, N.Y., *U.S.A.* **151 D10** 42 36N 74 45W
Worcestershire □, *U.K.* **21 E5** 52 13N 2 10W
Worden, *U.S.A.* **156 F7** 38 56N 89 50W
Wörgl, *Austria* .... **34 D5** 47 29N 12 3 E
Workai, *Indonesia* .... **83 C4** 6 40 S 134 40 E
Workington, *U.K.* **20 C4** 54 39N 3 33W
Worksop, *U.K.* **20 D6** 53 18N 1 7W
Workum, *Neths.* .... **24 B5** 52 59N 5 26 E
Worland, *U.S.A.* **158 D10** 44 1N 107 57W
Wormhout, *France* .... **27 B9** 50 52N 2 28 E
Worms, *Germany* .... **31 F4** 49 37N 8 21 E
Wörther See, *Austria* .... **34 E7** 46 37N 14 10 E
Worsley, *Canada* **142 B5** 56 31N 119 8W
Worth, *Germany* .... **31 F8** 49 1N 12 24 E
Wortham, *U.S.A.* **155 K6** 31 47N 96 28W
Wörther See, *Austria* .... **34 E7** 46 37N 14 10 E
Worthing, *Barbados* .... **165 g** 13 5N 59 35W
Worthing, *U.K.* **21 G7** 50 49N 0 21W
Worthington, Ind., *U.S.A.* **157 E10** 39 7N 86 59W
Worthington, Minn., *U.S.A.* **154 D7** 43 37N 95 36W
Worthington, Ohio, *U.S.A.* **157 D13** 40 5N 83 1W
Worthington, Pa., *U.S.A.* **150 F5** 40 50N 79 38W
Wosi, *Indonesia* .... **82 B3** 0 15 S 128 0 E
Wosimi, *Indonesia* .... **83 B4** 2 54 S 134 31 E
Wotu, *Indonesia* .... **82 B2** 2 35 S 120 48 E
Wou-han = Wuhan, *China* .... **77 B10** 30 31N 114 18 E
Wour, *Chad* .... **109 D3** 21 14N 16 0 E
Wousi = Wuxi, *China* .... **77 B13** 31 33N 120 18 E
Wowoni, *Indonesia* .... **82 B2** 4 5 S 123 5 E
Woy Woy, *Australia* .... **129 B9** 33 30 S 151 19 E
Wrangel I. = Vrangelya, Ostrov,
  Russia .... **67 B19** 71 0N 180 0 E
Wrangell, *U.S.A.* **142 B2** 56 28N 132 23W
Wrangell Mts., *U.S.A.* **144 F12** 61 30N 142 0W
Wrangell-St. Elias Nat. Park and
  Preserve △, *U.S.A.* **144 D12** 61 0N 142 0W
Wrath, C., *U.K.* **22 C3** 58 38N 5 1W
Wray, *U.S.A.* **154 E3** 40 5N 102 13W
Wrekin, The, *U.K.* **21 E5** 52 41N 2 32W
Wrens, *U.S.A.* **152 B7** 33 12N 82 23W
Wrexham, *U.K.* **20 D4** 53 3N 3 0W
Wrexham □, *U.K.* **20 D5** 53 1N 2 58W
Wriezen, *Germany* .... **30 C10** 52 42N 14 7 E
Wright = Paranas, *Phil.* .... **81 F5** 11 42N 125 2 E
Wright, *U.S.A.* **154 D2** 43 47N 105 30W
Wright Pt., *Canada* **150 C3** 43 48N 81 44W
Wrightmyo, *India* .... **95 J11** 11 47N 92 43 E
Wrightson, Mt., *U.S.A.* **159 L8** 31 42N 110 51W
Wrightsville, *U.S.A.* **152 C7** 32 44N 82 43W
Wrightwood, *U.S.A.* **161 L9** 34 21N 117 38W
Wrigley, *Canada* **138 B7** 63 16N 123 37W
Wrocław, *Poland* .... **55 G4** 51 5N 17 5 E
Wronki, *Poland* .... **55 F3** 52 41N 16 21 E
Września, *Poland* .... **55 F4** 52 21N 17 36 E
Wschowa, *Poland* .... **55 G3** 51 48N 16 20 E
Wu Jiang →, *China* .... **76 C6** 29 40N 107 20 E
Wu Kau Tang, *China* .... **69 F11** 22 30N 114 14 E
Wu'an, *China* .... **74 F8** 36 40N 114 15 E
Wubin, *Australia* .... **125 F2** 30 6 S 116 37 E
Wubu, *China* .... **74 F6** 37 28N 110 42 E
Wuchang, *China* .... **75 B14** 44 55N 127 5 E
Wucheng, *China* .... **74 F9** 37 12N 116 20 E
Wuchuan, Guangdong, *China* .... **77 G8** 21 33N 110 43 E
Wuchuan, Guizhou, *China* .... **76 C7** 28 25N 108 3 E
Wuchuan, Nei Monggol Zizhiqu,
  China .... **74 D6** 41 5N 111 28 E
Wuday'ah, *Si. Arabia* .... **98 C4** 17 2N 47 7 E
Wudi, *China* .... **75 F9** 37 40N 117 35 E
Wuding, *China* .... **76 E4** 25 24N 102 21 E
Wuding He →, *China* .... **74 F6** 37 2N 110 23 E
Wudinna, *Australia* .... **127 E2** 33 0 S 135 22 E
Wudu, *China* .... **74 H3** 33 22N 104 54 E
Wufeng, *China* .... **77 B8** 30 12N 110 42 E
Wugang, *China* .... **77 D8** 26 44N 110 35 E
Wugong Shan, *China* .... **69 C9** 22 25N 113 25 E
Wugushan, *China* .... **77 B10** 30 31N 114 18 E
Wuhan, *China* .... **75 F9** 33 10N 117 50 E
Wuhsi = Wuxi, *China* .... **77 B13** 31 33N 120 18 E
Wuhu, *China* .... **77 B13** 31 22N 118 21 E
Wujiang, *China* .... **77 B13** 31 10N 120 38 E
Wukari, *Nigeria* .... **113 D6** 7 51N 9 42 E
Wulajie, *China* .... **75 B14** 44 6N 126 33 E
Wulanbulang, *China* .... **74 D6** 41 5N 110 55 E
Wular L., *India* .... **93 B6** 34 20N 74 30 E
Wulehe, *Ghana* **113 D5** 8 39N 0 0W
Wulff Land, *Greenland* **10 A6** 82 0N 49 0W
Wulian, *China* .... **75 G10** 35 40N 119 12 E
Wuliang Shan, *China* .... **76 E3** 24 30N 100 40 E
Wuliaru, *Indonesia* .... **83 C4** 7 27 S 131 0 E
Wuling Shan, *China* .... **76 C7** 30 0N 110 0 E
Wulong, *China* .... **76 C6** 29 20N 107 43 E
Wuluk'omushih Ling, *China* .... **80 C3** 36 25N 87 45 E
Wulumuchi = Ürümqi, *China* .... **80 B3** 43 45N 87 45 E
Wum, *Cameroon* .... **113 D7** 6 24N 10 2 E
Wuming, *China* .... **76 F7** 23 12N 108 18 E
Wun Rog, *Sudan* .... **107 F2** 9 0N 28 20 E
Wundowie, *Australia* .... **125 F2** 31 47 S 116 23 E
Wuning, *China* .... **77 C10** 29 17N 115 5 E
Wunna →, *India* .... **94 D4** 20 38N 78 48 E
Wunnummin L., *Canada* **140 B2** 52 55N 89 10W
Wunsiedel, *Germany* .... **31 E8** 50 2N 12 0 E
Wunstorf, *Germany* .... **30 C5** 52 25N 9 26 E
Wuntho, *Burma* .... **90 D5** 23 55N 95 45 E
Wupatki Nat. Monument △, *U.S.A.* **159 J8** 35 35N 111 20W
Wuping, *China* .... **77 E11** 25 5N 116 5 E
Wuppertal, *Germany* .... **30 D3** 51 16N 7 12 E
Wuppertal, S. *Africa* .... **116 E2** 32 13 S 19 12 E

Wuqia, *China* .... **65 D7** 39 40N 75 7 E
Wuqing, *China* .... **75 E9** 39 23N 117 4 E
Würenlingen, *Switz.* .... **33 A6** 47 32N 8 16 E
Wurtsboro, *U.S.A.* **151 E10** 41 35N 74 29W
Würzburg, *Germany* .... **31 F5** 49 46N 9 55 E
Wurzen, *Germany* .... **30 D8** 51 22N 12 44 E
Wushan, *China* .... **74 G3** 34 43N 104 53 E
Wushishi, *Nigeria* .... **113 D6** 9 46N 6 7 E
Wusi, *Vanuatu* .... **133 E4** 15 21 S 166 40 E
Wusuli Jiang = Ussuri →, *Asia* .... **70 A7** 48 27N 135 0 E
Wutach →, *Germany* .... **31 H4** 47 37N 8 15 E
Wutai, *China* .... **74 E7** 38 40N 113 12 E
Wuting = Huimin, *China* .... **75 F9** 37 27N 117 28 E
Wutong, *China* .... **77 E8** 25 24N 110 5 E
Wutonghaolai, *China* .... **75 C11** 42 50N 120 5 E
Wutongqiao, *China* .... **76 C4** 29 22N 103 50 E
Wutung, Papua N. G. .... **132 B1** 2 37 S 141 15 E
Wuwei, Anhui, *China* .... **77 B11** 31 18N 117 54 E
Wuwei, Gansu, *China* .... **68 C5** 37 57N 102 34 E
Wuxi, Jiangsu, *China* .... **77 B13** 31 33N 120 18 E
Wuxi, Sichuan, *China* .... **76 B7** 31 23N 109 35 E
Wuxiang, *China* .... **74 F7** 36 49N 112 50 E
Wuxuan, *China* .... **76 F7** 23 34N 109 38 E
Wuxue, *China* .... **77 C10** 29 52N 115 30 E
Wuyang, *China* .... **74 H7** 33 25N 113 56 E
Wuyi, Hebei, *China* .... **74 F8** 37 46N 115 56 E
Wuyi, Zhejiang, *China* .... **77 C12** 28 52N 119 50 E
Wuyi Shan, *China* .... **77 D11** 27 0N 117 0 E
Wuyishan, *China* .... **77 D12** 27 45N 118 0 E
Wuyo, *Nigeria* .... **113 C7** 10 23N 11 50 E
Wuyuan, Jiangxi, *China* .... **77 C11** 29 15N 117 50 E
Wuyuan, Nei Monggol Zizhiqu,
  China .... **74 D5** 41 2N 108 20 E
Wuzhai, *China* .... **74 E6** 38 54N 111 48 E
Wuzhi Shan, *China* .... **86 C7** 18 45N 109 45 E
Wuzhong, *China* .... **74 E4** 38 2N 106 12 E
Wuzhou, *China* .... **77 F8** 23 30N 111 18 E
Wyaaba Cr. →, *Australia* .... **126 B3** 16 27 S 141 35 E
Wyalkatchem, *Australia* .... **125 F2** 31 8 S 117 22 E
Wyalusing, *U.S.A.* **151 E8** 41 40N 76 16W
Wyandotte, *U.S.A.* **157 B13** 42 12N 83 9W
Wyandra, *Australia* .... **127 D4** 27 12 S 145 56 E
Wyangala, L., *Australia* .... **129 B8** 33 54 S 149 0 E
Wyara, L., *Australia* .... **127 D3** 28 42 S 144 14 E
Wycheproof, *Australia* .... **128 D5** 36 5 S 143 17 E
Wye →, *U.K.* **21 F5** 51 38N 2 40W
Wyemandoo, *Australia* .... **125 E2** 28 28 S 118 29 E
Wyk, *Germany* .... **30 A4** 54 41N 8 33 E
Wymondham, *U.K.* .... **21 E9** 52 35N 1 7 E
Wymore, *U.S.A.* **154 E6** 40 7N 96 40W
Wyndham, *Australia* .... **124 C4** 15 33 S 128 3 E
Wyndham, *N.Z.* .... **131 G3** 46 20 S 168 51 E
Wynne, *U.S.A.* **155 H9** 35 14N 90 47W
Wynyard, *Australia* .... **127 G4** 41 5 S 145 44 E
Wynyard, *Canada* **143 C8** 51 45N 104 10W
Wyola L., *Australia* .... **125 E5** 29 8 S 130 17 E
Wyoming, *Canada* **150 D2** 42 57N 82 7W
Wyoming, Ill., *U.S.A.* **156 C7** 41 4N 89 47W
Wyoming, Iowa, *U.S.A.* **156 B6** 42 4N 91 0W
Wyoming, Mich., *U.S.A.* **157 B11** 42 54N 85 42W
Wyoming □, *U.S.A.* **158 E10** 43 0N 107 30W
Wyomissing, *U.S.A.* **151 F9** 40 20N 75 59W
Wyong, *Australia* .... **129 B9** 33 14 S 151 24 E
Wyperfeld Nat. Park △, *Australia* .... **128 D5** 35 35 S 141 42 E
Wyrzysk, *Poland* .... **55 E4** 53 10N 17 17 E
Wyśmierzyce, *Poland* .... **55 G7** 51 37N 20 50 E
Wysoka, *Poland* .... **55 E4** 53 13N 17 2 E
Wysokie, *Poland* .... **55 H9** 50 55N 22 40 E
Wysokie Mazowieckie, *Poland* .... **55 E9** 52 55N 22 30 E
Wyszków, *Poland* .... **55 F8** 52 36N 21 25 E
Wyszogród, *Poland* .... **55 F7** 52 23N 20 9 E
Wytheville, *U.S.A.* **148 G5** 36 57N 81 5W
Wyżyna Małopolska, *Poland* .... **55 H7** 50 45N 20 0 E

X

Xa-Cassau, *Angola* .... **115 D4** 9 5 S 20 15 E
Xa-Muteba, *Angola* .... **115 D3** 9 34 S 17 50 E
Xaafuun, *Somali Rep.* .... **90 F4** 10 25N 51 16 E
Xaçmaz, *Azerbaijan* .... **61 K9** 41 31N 48 42 E
Xaçmaz, *Azerbaijan* .... **61 K9** 41 31N 48 42 E
Xadded, *Somali Rep.* .... **120 C3** 9 46N 48 2 E
Xaghra, *Malta* .... **38 E7** 36 3N 14 16 E
Xai-Xai, Mozam. .... **117 D5** 25 6 S 33 31 E
Xaidulla, *China* .... **65 E8** 36 28N 77 59 E
Xainza, *China* .... **68 C3** 30 58N 88 35 E
Xalapa, *Mexico* **163 D5** 19 32N 96 55W
Xambioá, *Brazil* .... **170 C2** 6 25 S 48 40W
Xangongo, *Angola* .... **116 B2** 16 45 S 15 5 E
Xankändi, *Azerbaijan* .... **101 C12** 39 52N 46 49 E
Xanlar, *Azerbaijan* .... **61 K8** 40 37N 46 12 E
Xanten, *Germany* .... **30 D2** 51 39N 6 26 E
Xánthi, *Greece* .... **51 E8** 41 10N 24 58 E
Xánthi □, *Greece* .... **51 E8** 41 10N 24 58 E
Xanthos, *Turkey* .... **49 E11** 36 19N 29 18 E
Xanxerê, *Brazil* .... **175 B5** 26 53 S 52 23W
Xapuri, *Brazil* .... **172 C4** 10 35 S 68 35W
Xar Moron He →, *China* .... **75 C11** 43 25N 120 35 E
Xarrë, *Albania* .... **38 B10** 39 44N 20 3 E
Xàtiva, *Spain* **41 G4** 38 59N 0 32W
Xau, L., *Botswana* .... **116 C3** 21 15 S 24 44 E
Xavantina, *Brazil* .... **175 A5** 21 15 S 52 48W
Xenia, *U.S.A.* **157 E13** 39 41N 83 56W
Xeropotamos →, *Cyprus* .... **49 E11** 34 42N 32 33 E
Xertigny, *France* .... **27 D13** 48 3N 6 24 E
Xewkija, *Malta* .... **38 E7** 36 2N 14 15 E
Xhora, S. *Africa* .... **117 E4** 31 55 S 28 38 E
Xhumo, *Botswana* .... **116 C3** 21 7 S 24 35 E
Xi Jiang →, *China* .... **77 F9** 22 5N 113 20 E
Xi Xian, Henan, *China* .... **77 A10** 32 20N 114 43 E
Xi Xian, Shanxi, *China* .... **74 F6** 36 41N 110 58 E
Xia Xian, *China* .... **74 G6** 35 8N 111 12 E
Xiachengzi, *China* .... **75 B16** 44 40N 130 18 E
Xiachuan Dao, *China* .... **77 G9** 21 40N 112 40 E
Xiaguan, *China* .... **77 D10** 27 30N 115 10 E
Xiajin, *China* .... **74 F9** 36 56N 116 0 E
Xiamen, *China* .... **77 E12** 24 25N 118 4 E
Xi'an, *China* .... **74 G5** 34 15N 109 0 E
Xian Xian, *China* .... **74 E9** 38 12N 116 6 E
Xiang Jiang →, *China* .... **77 A9** 32 2N 112 8 E
Xiangcheng, Henan, *China* .... **74 H8** 33 29N 114 52 E
Xiangcheng, Henan, *China* .... **74 H7** 33 50N 113 27 E
Xiangcheng, Sichuan, *China* .... **76 C2** 28 53N 99 47 E
Xiangfan, *China* .... **77 A9** 32 2N 112 8 E
Xianghuang Qi, *China* .... **74 C7** 42 2N 114 0 E
Xiangning, *China* .... **74 G6** 35 58N 110 50 E
Xiangquan, *China* .... **74 F7** 36 30N 113 1 E
Xiangquan He = Sutlej →, *Pakistan* .... **91 C3** 29 23N 71 3 E
Xiangshui, *China* .... **77 G10** 34 12N 119 33 E
Xiangxiang, *China* .... **77 D9** 27 43N 112 28 E
Xiangyun, *China* .... **77 C9** 28 38N 112 54 E
Xiangzhou, *China* .... **76 F7** 23 58N 109 40 E
Xianju, *China* .... **77 C13** 28 51N 120 44 E
Xianning, *China* .... **77 C10** 29 51N 114 16 E

Xianshui He →, China — 76 B3 30 10N 100 59 E
Xiantao, China — 77 B9 30 25N 113 25 E
Xianyang, China — 74 G5 34 20N 108 40 E
Xianyou, China — 77 E12 25 22N 118 38 E
Xiao Hinggan Ling, China — 69 B7 49 0N 127 0 E
Xiao Xian, China — 74 G9 34 15N 116 55 E
Xiaofeng, China — 77 B12 30 35N 119 32 E
Xiaogan, China — 77 B9 30 52N 113 55 E
Xiaojin, China — 76 B4 30 59N 102 21 E
Xiaolan, China — 77 F9 22 38N 113 13 E
Xiaoshan, China — 77 B13 30 12N 120 18 E
Xiaoyi, China — 74 F6 37 8N 111 48 E
Xiapu, China — 77 D12 26 54N 119 59 E
Xiawa, China — 75 C11 42 35N 120 38 E
Xiayi, China — 74 G9 34 15N 116 10 E
Xichang, China — 76 D4 27 51N 102 19 E
Xichong, China — 76 B5 30 57N 105 54 E
Xichou, China — 76 E5 23 25N 104 42 E
Xichuan, China — 74 H6 33 0N 111 30 E
Xide, China — 76 C4 28 0N 102 19 E
Xiemahe, China — 77 B8 31 38N 111 12 E
Xieng Khouang, Laos — 86 C4 19 17N 103 25 E
Xifei He →, China — 74 H9 32 45N 116 40 E
Xifeng, Gansu, China — 74 G4 35 40N 107 40 E
Xifeng, Guizhou, China — 76 D6 27 7N 106 42 E
Xifeng, Liaoning, China — 75 C13 42 42N 124 45 E
Xifengzhen = Xifeng, China — 74 G4 35 40N 107 40 E
Xigazê = China — 68 D3 29 5N 88 45 E
Xihe, China — 74 G3 34 2N 105 20 E
Xihua, China — 74 H8 33 45N 114 30 E
Xilaganí, Greece — 51 F9 40 58N 25 28 E
Xili Shuiku, China — 69 F10 22 36N 113 57 E
Xiliao He →, China — 75 C12 43 32N 123 35 E
Xilin, China — 76 E5 24 30N 105 6 E
Xilókastron, Greece — 48 C4 38 5N 22 38 E
Ximana, Mozam. — 119 F3 19 24 S 33 58 E
Xime, Guinea-Biss. — 112 C2 11 59N 14 57W
Ximeng, China — 76 F2 22 50N 99 27 E
Xin Jiang →, China — 77 C11 28 45N 116 35 E
Xin Xian = Xinzhou, China — 74 E7 38 22N 112 46 E
Xinavane, Mozam. — 117 D5 25 2 S 32 47 E
Xinbin, China — 75 D13 41 40N 125 2 E
Xincai, China — 77 A10 32 43N 114 58 E
Xinchang, China — 77 C13 29 28N 120 52 E
Xincheng, Guangxi Zhuangzu, China — 76 E7 24 5N 108 39 E
Xincheng, Jiangxi, China — 77 D10 26 48N 114 6 E
Xindu, China — 76 B5 30 50N 104 10 E
Xinfeng, Guangdong, China — 77 E10 24 5N 114 16 E
Xinfeng, Jiangxi, China — 77 D11 27 7N 116 11 E
Xinfeng, Jiangxi, China — 77 E10 25 27N 114 58 E
Xinfengjiang Skuiku, China — 77 F10 23 52N 114 30 E
Xing Xian, China — 74 E6 38 27N 111 7 E
Xing'an, Guangxi Zhuangzu, China — 77 E8 25 38N 110 40 E
Xingan, Jiangxi, China — 77 D10 27 46N 115 20 E
Xingcheng, China — 75 D11 40 40N 120 45 E
Xingguo, China — 77 D10 26 21N 115 21 E
Xinghe, China — 74 D7 40 55N 113 55 E
Xinghua, China — 75 H10 32 58N 119 48 E
Xinghua Wan, China — 77 E12 25 15N 119 20 E
Xinglong, China — 75 D9 40 25N 117 30 E
Xingning, China — 77 E10 24 3N 115 42 E
Xingping, China — 74 G5 34 20N 108 28 E
Xingren, China — 76 E5 25 24N 105 11 E
Xingshan, China — 77 B8 31 15N 110 45 E
Xingtai, China — 74 F8 37 3N 114 32 E
Xingu →, Brazil — 169 D7 1 30 S 51 53W
Xingwen, China — 76 C5 28 22N 104 50 E
Xingyang, China — 74 G7 34 45N 112 52 E
Xinhe, China — 74 F8 37 30N 115 15 E
Xinhua, China — 77 D8 27 42N 111 13 E
Xinhuang, China — 76 D7 27 21N 109 12 E
Xinhui, China — 77 F9 22 25N 113 0 E
Xining, China — 68 C5 36 34N 101 40 E
Xinjian, China — 77 C10 28 37N 115 46 E
Xinjiang, China — 74 G6 35 34N 111 11 E
Xinjiang Uygur Zizhiqu □, China — 68 C3 42 0N 86 0 E
Xinjie, China — 76 D3 26 48N 101 15 E
Xinjin = Pulandian, China — 75 E11 39 25N 121 58 E
Xinjin, China — 76 B4 30 24N 103 47 E
Xinkai He →, China — 75 C12 43 32N 123 35 E
Xinken, China — 69 F10 22 39N 113 36 E
Xinle, China — 74 E8 38 25N 114 40 E
Xinlitun, China — 75 D12 42 0N 122 8 E
Xinlong, China — 76 B3 30 57N 100 12 E
Xinmin, China — 75 D12 41 59N 122 50 E
Xinning, China — 77 D8 26 28N 110 50 E
Xinping, China — 76 E3 24 5N 101 59 E
Xinshao, China — 77 D8 27 21N 111 26 E
Xintai, China — 75 G9 35 55N 117 45 E
Xintian, China — 77 E9 25 55N 112 15 E
Xinwan, China — 69 F10 22 47N 113 40 E
Xinxian, China — 77 B10 31 36N 113 51 E
Xinxiang, China — 74 G7 35 18N 113 50 E
Xinxing, China — 77 F9 22 35N 112 15 E
Xinyang, China — 77 A10 32 6N 114 3 E
Xinye, China — 74 A9 32 30N 112 21 E
Xinyi, China — 77 F8 22 5N 110 47 E
Xinyu, China — 77 D10 27 49N 114 58 E
Xinzhan, China — 75 C14 43 50N 127 18 E
Xinzheng, China — 74 G7 34 20N 113 45 E
Xinzhou, Hubei, China — 77 B10 30 50N 114 48 E
Xinzhou, Shanxi, China — 74 E7 38 22N 112 46 E
Xinzo de Limia, Spain — 42 C3 42 3N 7 47W
Xiongyuecheng, China — 75 D12 40 12N 122 5 E
Xiping, Henan, China — 74 H8 33 22N 114 5 E
Xiping, Henan, China — 74 H6 33 25N 111 8 E
Xiping, Zhejiang, China — 77 C12 28 16N 119 29 E
Xique-Xique, Brazil — 170 D3 10 50 S 42 40W
Xirua →, Brazil — 172 B4 6 3 S 67 50W
Xisha Qundao = Parcel Is., S. China Sea — 78 A4 15 50N 112 0 E
Xishui, Guizhou, China — 76 C6 28 19N 106 9 E
Xishui, Hubei, China — 77 B10 30 30N 115 15 E
Xitole, Guinea-Biss. — 112 C2 11 43N 14 50W
Xiu Shui →, China — 77 C10 29 13N 116 10 E
Xiuning, China — 77 C12 29 45N 118 10 E
Xiuren, China — 77 E8 24 27N 110 12 E
Xiushan, China — 76 C7 28 25N 108 57 E
Xiushui, China — 77 C10 29 2N 114 35 E
Xiuwen, China — 76 D6 26 49N 106 32 E
Xiuyan, China — 75 D12 40 18N 123 11 E
Xixia, China — 74 H6 33 25N 111 29 E
Xixiang, China — 74 H4 33 0N 107 44 E
Xiyang, China — 74 F7 37 38N 113 38 E
Xizang Zizhiqu □, China — 68 C3 32 0N 88 0 E
Xlendi, Malta — 38 E6 36 2N 14 13 E
Xochob, Mexico — 163 D7 19 28N 89 45W
Xu Jiang →, China — 77 D11 28 0N 116 25 E
Xuan Loc, Vietnam — 87 G6 10 56N 107 14 E
Xuan'en, China — 76 C7 30 0N 109 30 E
Xuanhan, China — 76 B6 31 18N 107 38 E
Xuanhua, China — 74 D8 40 40N 115 2 E
Xuanwei, China — 76 C5 26 15N 103 59 E
Xuanzhou, China — 77 B12 30 56N 118 43 E
Xuchang, China — 74 G7 34 2N 113 48 E
Xudat, Azerbaijan — 61 K9 41 38N 48 41 E
Xuddur = Oddur, Somali Rep. — 120 D2 4 11N 43 52 E
Xuefeng Shan, China — 77 D8 27 5N 110 15 E
Xuejiaping, China — 77 B8 31 39N 110 16 E
Xun Jiang →, China — 77 F8 23 35N 111 32 E
Xun Xian, China — 74 G8 35 42N 114 33 E
Xundian, China — 76 E4 25 36N 103 15 E
Xunwu, China — 77 E10 24 54N 115 37 E
Xunyang, China — 74 H5 32 48N 109 22 E

Xunyi, China — 74 G5 35 8N 108 20 E
Xupu, China — 77 D8 27 53N 110 32 E
Xúquer →, Spain — 41 F4 39 5N 0 10W
Xushui, China — 74 E8 39 2N 115 40 E
Xuwen, China — 77 G8 20 20N 110 10 E
Xuyen Moc, Vietnam — 87 G6 10 34N 107 25 E
Xuyong, China — 76 C5 28 10N 105 22 E
Xuzhou, China — 75 G9 34 18N 117 10 E
Xylophagou, Cyprus — 39 F9 34 54N 33 51 E

Y

Ya Xian, China — 86 C7 18 14N 109 29 E
Yaamba, Australia — 126 C5 23 8 S 150 22 E
Ya'an, China — 76 C4 29 58N 103 5 E
Yaapeet, Australia — 128 C5 35 45 S 142 3 E
Yabassi, Cameroon — 113 E6 4 30N 9 57 E
Yabelo, Ethiopia — 107 G4 4 50N 38 8 E
Yabelo Wildlife Reserve △, Ethiopia — 107 F4 6 0N 37 50 E
Yablanitsa, Bulgaria — 51 C8 43 2N 24 5 E
Yablonovy Ra. = Yablonovyy Khrebet, Russia — 67 D12 53 0N 114 0 E
Yablonovyy Khrebet, Russia — 67 D12 53 0N 114 0 E
Yabrai Shan, China — 74 E2 39 40N 103 0 E
Yabrūd, Syria — 103 B5 33 58N 36 39 E
Yabucoa, Puerto Rico — 165 d 18 3N 65 53W
Yacheng, China — 69 E5 18 22N 109 6 E
Yackandandah, Australia — 129 D7 36 18 S 146 52 E
Yacuiba, Bolivia — 174 A3 22 0 S 63 43W
Yacuma →, Bolivia — 173 C4 13 38 S 65 23W
Yadgir, India — 94 F3 16 45N 77 5 E
Yadkin →, U.S.A. — 149 H5 35 29N 80 9W
Yadrin, Russia — 60 C8 55 57N 46 12 E
Yadua, Fiji — 133 A2 16 49 S 178 18 E
Yaeyama-Rettō, Japan — 71 M1 24 30N 123 40 E
Yafran, Libya — 108 B2 32 4N 12 31 E
Yafran □, Libya — 108 B2 32 0N 12 20 E
Yagaba, Ghana — 113 C4 10 14N 1 20W
Yağcılar, Turkey — 49 B10 39 25N 28 23 E
Yagodnoye, Russia — 67 C15 62 33N 149 40 E
Yagoua, Cameroon — 109 F3 10 20N 15 13 E
Yaguas →, Peru — 168 D3 2 45 S 70 10W
Yahila, Orientale, Dem. Rep. of the Congo — 114 B4 1 48N 23 37 E
Yahila, Orientale, Dem. Rep. of the Congo — 118 B1 0 13N 24 28 E
Yahk, Canada — 142 D5 49 6N 116 10W
Yahotyn, Ukraine — 59 G6 50 17N 31 46 E
Yahuma, Dem. Rep. of the Congo — 114 B4 1 0N 23 10 E
Yahyalı, Turkey — 100 C6 38 5N 35 2 E
Yaita, Japan — 71 F9 36 48N 139 56 E
Yaiza, Canary Is. — 9 e2 28 57N 13 46W
Yaizu, Japan — 73 C10 34 52N 138 20 E
Yajiang, China — 76 B3 30 2N 100 57 E
Yajua, Nigeria — 113 C7 11 27N 12 49 E
Yakage, Japan — 72 C5 34 37N 133 35 E
Yakamba, Dem. Rep. of the Congo — 114 B3 2 42N 19 38 E
Yakima, U.S.A. — 158 C3 46 36N 120 31W
Yakima →, U.S.A. — 158 C5 47 0N 120 30W
Yakkabag, Uzbekistan — 65 D3 38 55N 66 51 E
Yako, Burkina Faso — 112 C4 12 59N 2 15W
Yakobi I., U.S.A. — 142 B1 58 0N 136 30W
Yakoma, Dem. Rep. of the Congo — 114 B4 4 5N 22 27 E
Yakoruda, Bulgaria — 50 D7 42 1N 23 39 E
Yakossi, C.A.R. — 114 A4 5 37N 23 19 E
Yakovlevka, Russia — 70 B6 44 26N 133 28 E
Yakshur Bodya, Russia — 64 C4 57 11N 53 7 E
Yaku-Shima, Japan — 71 J5 30 20N 130 30 E
Yakumo, Japan — 70 C10 42 15N 140 16 E
Yakutat, U.S.A. — 144 G13 59 33N 139 44W
Yakutat B., U.S.A. — 144 G12 59 45N 140 45W
Yakutia = Sakha □, Russia — 67 C13 66 0N 130 0 E
Yakutsk, Russia — 67 C13 62 5N 129 50 E
Yala, Thailand — 87 J3 6 33N 101 18 E
Yalboroo, Australia — 126 J6 20 50 S 148 40 E
Yale, U.S.A. — 150 C2 43 8N 82 48W
Yalgoo, Australia — 125 E2 28 16 S 116 39 E
Yalgorup Nat. Park △, Australia — 125 D2 24 34 S 115 2 E
Yali, Dem. Rep. of the Congo — 114 B4 0 4N 21 3 E
Yaligimba, Dem. Rep. of the Congo — 114 B4 2 26N 21 58 E
Yalikanda, Dem. Rep. of the Congo — 114 B4 0 23N 24 47 E
Yalinga, C.A.R. — 114 A4 6 33N 23 10 E
Yalkubul, Punta, Mexico — 163 C7 21 32N 88 37W
Yalleroi, Australia — 126 C4 24 3 S 145 42 E
Yalobusha →, U.S.A. — 155 J9 33 33N 90 10W
Yaloké, C.A.R. — 114 A3 5 19N 17 5 E
Yalong Jiang →, China — 76 D3 26 40N 101 55 E
Yalova, Turkey — 51 F13 40 41N 29 15 E
Yalta, Ukraine — 59 K8 44 30N 34 10 E
Yalu Jiang →, China — 75 E13 40 0N 124 22 E
Yalvaç, Turkey — 100 C4 38 7N 31 10 E
Yam Ha Melah = Dead Sea, Asia — 103 D4 31 30N 35 30 E
Yam Kinneret, Israel — 103 C4 32 45N 35 35 E
Yamada, Japan — 72 C2 33 33N 130 49 E
Yamada, Japan — 72 D2 33 11N 130 41 E
Yamagata, Japan — 70 E10 38 15N 140 15 E
Yamagata □, Japan — 70 E10 38 30N 140 0 E
Yamagawa, Japan — 72 F2 31 12N 130 39 E
Yamaguchi, Japan — 72 C3 34 10N 131 32 E
Yamaguchi □, Japan — 72 C3 34 20N 131 40 E
Yamal, Poluostrov, Russia — 66 B8 71 0N 70 0 E
Yamal Pen. = Yamal, Poluostrov, Russia — 66 B8 71 0N 70 0 E
Yamanaka, Japan — 73 A8 36 15N 136 22 E
Yamanashi, Japan — 73 B10 35 41N 138 40 E
Yamanashi □, Japan — 73 B10 35 40N 138 40 E
Yamanie Falls Nat. Park △, Australia — 126 B4 18 29 S 146 9 E
Yamantau, Gora, Russia — 64 D7 54 15N 58 6 E
Yamasaki, Japan — 72 C6 35 0N 134 32 E
Yamato, Japan — 73 B11 35 27N 139 25 E
Yamatotakada, Japan — 73 C7 34 31N 135 45 E
Yamba, Australia — 127 D5 29 26 S 153 23 E
Yambarran Ra., Australia — 124 C5 15 10 S 130 25 E
Yambata, Dem. Rep. of the Congo — 114 B4 2 26N 21 58 E
Yambéring, Guinea — 112 C2 11 50N 12 18 E
Yâmbiô, Sudan — 107 G2 4 35N 28 16 E
Yambol, Bulgaria — 51 D10 42 30N 26 30 E
Yamboyo, Dem. Rep. of the Congo — 114 B4 0 46N 22 5 E
Yambuya, Dem. Rep. of the Congo — 114 B4 1 17N 24 34 E
Yamdena, Indonesia — 83 C4 7 45 S 131 20 E
Yame, Japan — 72 D2 33 13N 130 35 E
Yamethin, Burma — 90 E6 20 29N 96 18 E
Yamma-Yamma, L., Australia — 127 D3 26 16 S 141 20 E
Yamoussoukro, Ivory C. — 112 D3 6 49N 5 17W
Yampa →, U.S.A. — 158 F9 40 32N 108 59W
Yampi Sd., Australia — 124 C3 16 8 S 123 38 E
Yampil, Moldova — 59 H5 48 15N 28 15 E
Yampol = Yampil, Moldova — 59 H5 48 15N 28 15 E
Yamrat, Nigeria — 113 C6 10 11N 9 55 E
Yamuna →, India — 93 G9 25 30N 81 53 E
Yamunanagar, India — 92 D7 30 7N 77 17 E
Yamzho Yumco, China — 68 D4 28 48N 90 35 E
Yan, Nigeria — 113 C7 10 5N 12 11 E
Yan Oya →, Sri Lanka — 95 K5 9 5N 81 10 E
Yana →, Russia — 67 B14 71 30N 136 0 E
Yanagawa, Japan — 72 D2 33 10N 130 24 E
Yanahara, Japan — 72 C6 34 58N 134 2 E
Yanai, Japan — 72 D4 33 58N 132 7 E

Yan'an, China — 74 F5 36 35N 109 26 E
Yanaul, Russia — 64 C5 56 25N 55 0 E
Yanbian, China — 76 D3 26 47N 101 31 E
Yanbu 'al Bahr, Si. Arabia — 96 F3 24 0N 38 5 E
Yanchang, China — 74 F6 36 43N 110 1 E
Yancheng, Henan, China — 74 H8 33 35N 114 0 E
Yancheng, Jiangsu, China — 75 H11 33 23N 120 8 E
Yanchep Beach, Australia — 125 F2 31 33 S 115 37 E
Yanchi, China — 74 F4 37 48N 107 20 E
Yanchuan, China — 74 F6 36 51N 110 10 E
Yanco Cr. →, Australia — 129 C6 35 14 S 145 35 E
Yandé, Î., N. Cal. — 133 M10 9 7 S 159 13 E
Yandina, Solomon Is. — 133 M10 9 7 S 159 13 E
Yandja, Dem. Rep. of the Congo — 114 C3 1 41 S 17 43 E
Yandongi, Dem. Rep. of the Congo — 114 B4 2 51N 22 16 E
Yandoon, Burma — 90 G5 17 0N 95 40 E
Yanfeng, China — 76 E3 25 52N 101 8 E
Yanfolila, Mali — 112 C3 11 11N 8 9W
Yang Xian, China — 74 H4 33 15N 107 30 E
Yang-Yang, Senegal — 112 B1 15 30N 15 20W
Yangambi, Dem. Rep. of the Congo — 118 B1 0 47N 24 24 E
Yangbi, China — 76 E2 25 41N 99 58 E
Yangcheng, China — 74 G7 35 28N 112 22 E
Yangch'ü = Taiyuan, China — 74 F7 37 52N 112 33 E
Yangchun, China — 77 F8 22 11N 111 48 E
Yanggao, China — 74 D7 40 21N 113 55 E
Yanggu, China — 74 F8 36 8N 115 43 E
Yangi-Nishan, Uzbekistan — 65 D2 38 49N 65 47 E
Yangiabad, Uzbekistan — 65 C3 41 7N 70 0 E
Yangikishlak, Uzbekistan — 65 C2 40 25N 67 10 E
Yangirabad, Uzbekistan — 65 C2 40 2N 65 58 E
Yangiyer, Uzbekistan — 65 C4 40 16N 68 49 E
Yangiyul, Uzbekistan — 65 C4 41 0N 69 3 E
Yangjiang, China — 77 G8 21 50N 111 59 E
Yangliuqing, China — 74 E9 39 2N 117 5 E
Yangon = Rangoon, Burma — 90 G6 16 45N 96 20 E
Yangonde, Dem. Rep. of the Congo — 114 B4 0 32N 22 43 E
Yangping, China — 77 B8 31 12N 111 25 E
Yangpingguan, China — 74 H4 32 58N 106 5 E
Yangquan, China — 74 F7 37 58N 113 31 E
Yangshan, China — 77 E9 24 30N 112 40 E
Yangshuo, China — 77 E8 24 48N 110 29 E
Yangtse = Chang Jiang →, China — 77 B13 31 48N 121 10 E
Yangtze Kiang = Chang Jiang →, China — 77 B13 31 48N 121 10 E
Yangudi Rassa Nat. Park △, Ethiopia — 107 E5 10 50N 40 42 E
Yangxin, China — 77 C10 29 50N 115 12 E
Yangyang, S. Korea — 75 E15 38 4N 128 38 E
Yangyuan, China — 74 D8 40 1N 114 10 E
Yangzhong, China — 77 A12 32 22N 119 22 E
Yangzhou, China — 77 A12 32 21N 119 26 E
Yanhe, China — 76 C7 28 31N 108 29 E
Yanji, China — 75 C15 42 59N 129 30 E
Yanjin, China — 76 C5 28 5N 104 3 E
Yanjing, China — 76 C2 29 7N 98 33 E
Yankari Nat. Park △, Nigeria — 113 D7 9 50N 10 28 E
Yankton, U.S.A. — 154 D6 42 53N 97 23W
Yanonge, Dem. Rep. of the Congo — 118 B1 0 35N 24 38 E
Yanqi, China — 68 B3 42 5N 86 35 E
Yanqing, China — 74 D8 40 30N 115 58 E
Yanshan, Hebei, China — 75 E9 38 4N 117 22 E
Yanshan, Jiangxi, China — 77 C11 28 15N 117 41 E
Yanshan, Yunnan, China — 76 F5 23 35N 104 20 E
Yanshou, China — 75 B15 45 28N 128 22 E
Yantabulla, Australia — 127 D4 29 21 S 145 0 E
Yantai, China — 75 F11 37 34N 121 22 E
Yantian, China — 69 F11 22 35N 114 16 E
Yanting, China — 76 B5 31 11N 105 24 E
Yantra →, Bulgaria — 51 C9 43 40N 25 37 E
Yanuca, Fiji — 133 B1 18 24 S 178 0 E
Yanwa, China — 76 D2 27 51N 98 44 E
Yanykurgan = Zhangaqŭrghan, Kazakhstan — 65 B4 43 50N 68 48 E
Yanyuan, China — 76 D3 27 25N 101 30 E
Yanzhou, China — 74 G9 35 35N 116 49 E
Yao, Chad — 109 F3 12 56N 17 33 E
Yao, Japan — 73 C7 34 32N 135 36 E
Yao Noi, Ko, Thailand — 87 a 8 7N 98 37 E
Yao Xian, China — 74 G5 34 55N 108 59 E
Yao Yai, Ko, Thailand — 87 a 8 0N 98 35 E
Yao'an, China — 76 E3 25 31N 101 18 E
Yaodu, China — 76 A5 32 45N 105 22 E
Yaoundé, Cameroon — 113 E7 3 50N 11 35 E
Yaowan, China — 75 G10 34 15N 118 3 E
Yap I., Pac. Oc. — 134 G5 9 30N 138 10 E
Yapehe, Dem. Rep. of the Congo — 114 C4 0 13 S 24 28 E
Yapen, Indonesia — 83 B5 1 50 S 136 0 E
Yapen, Selat, Indonesia — 83 B5 1 20 S 136 10 E
Yapero, Indonesia — 83 B5 4 59 S 137 11 E
Yappar →, Australia — 126 B3 18 22 S 141 16 E
Yaqaga, Fiji — 133 A2 16 35 S 178 36 E
Yaqui →, Mexico — 162 B2 27 37N 110 39W
Yar, Russia — 64 B4 58 14N 52 5 E
Yar-Sale, Russia — 66 C8 66 50N 70 50 E
Yaracuy □, Venezuela — 168 A4 10 20N 68 45W
Yaracuy →, Venezuela — 168 A4 10 33N 68 15W
Yaraka, Australia — 126 C3 24 53 S 144 3 E
Yaransk, Russia — 60 B8 57 22N 47 49 E
Yarbasan, Turkey — 49 C10 38 59N 28 8 E
Yardımcı Burnu, Turkey — 49 E12 36 13N 30 25 E
Yare →, U.K. — 21 E9 52 35N 1 38 E
Yaremcha, Ukraine — 59 H3 48 27N 24 33 E
Yarensk, Russia — 60 B8 62 11N 49 15 E
Yarfa, Si. Arabia — 106 C4 24 37N 38 35 E
Yarí →, Colombia — 168 D3 0 20 S 72 20W
Yarım, Yemen — 98 D4 14 20N 44 22 E
Yaritagua, Venezuela — 168 A4 10 5N 69 8W
Yarkand = Shache, China — 65 D8 38 20N 77 10 E
Yarker, Canada — 152 B8 44 23N 76 46W
Yarkhun →, Pakistan — 93 A5 36 17N 72 30 E
Yarlung Ziangbo Jiang = Brahmaputra →, Asia — 93 D23 23 40N 90 35 E
Yarmouth, Canada — 141 D6 43 50N 66 7W
Yarmūk →, Syria — 103 C4 32 42N 35 40 E
Yaroslavl, Russia — 58 D10 57 35N 39 55 E
Yarqa, W. →, Egypt — 103 F2 30 0N 33 49 E
Yarra Ranges Nat. Park △, Australia — 129 D7 37 40 S 146 3 E
Yarra Yarra Lakes, Australia — 125 E2 29 40 S 115 45 E
Yarram, Australia — 129 E7 38 29 S 146 39 E
Yarraman, Australia — 127 D5 26 50 S 152 0 E
Yarras, Australia — 129 A10 31 25 S 152 20 E
Yarrawonga, Australia — 129 C6 36 0 S 146 0 E
Yartsevo, Sib., Russia — 67 C10 60 20N 90 0 E
Yartsevo, Smolensk, Russia — 58 E7 55 6N 32 43 E
Yarumal, Colombia — 168 B2 6 58N 75 24W
Yasa, Dem. Rep. of the Congo — 114 C3 0 46N 17 8 E
Yasawa Group, Fiji — 133 A1 17 0 S 177 23 E
Yaselda, Belarus — 59 F4 52 7N 26 28 E
Yashbum, Yemen — 98 D4 14 19N 46 56 E
Yashi, Nigeria — 113 C6 12 23N 7 54 E
Yashikera, Nigeria — 113 D5 9 44N 3 29 E
Yashiro-Jima, Japan — 72 D3 33 55N 132 15 E
Yasin, Pakistan — 93 A5 36 24N 73 23 E
Yashkul, Russia — 61 G7 46 11N 45 21 E
Yasinovataya, Ukraine — 59 H9 48 7N 37 57 E
Yasinya, Ukraine — 59 H3 48 16N 24 21 E
Yasnyy, Russia — 77 ...
Yasothon, Thailand — 86 E5 15 50N 104 10 E
Yass, Australia — 129 C8 34 49 S 148 54 E
Yasugi, Japan — 72 B5 35 26N 133 15 E
Yāsūj, Iran — 97 D6 30 31N 51 31 E

Yat, Niger — 109 D2 20 28N 13 27 E
Yata →, Bolivia — 173 C4 10 29 S 65 26W
Yata →, C.A.R. — 114 A4 10 23N 22 45 E
Yata-Ngaya, Réserve de Faune de la △, C.A.R. — 114 A4 9 15N 23 25 E
Yatağan, Turkey — 49 D10 37 20N 28 10 E
Yatakala, Niger — 113 C5 14 50N 0 22 E
Yaté, N. Cal. — 133 V20 22 9 S 166 57 E
Yates Center, U.S.A. — 155 G7 37 53N 95 44W
Yates Pt., N.Z. — 131 E2 44 29 S 167 49 E
Yathkyed L., Canada — 143 A9 62 40N 98 0W
Yathong, Australia — 129 B6 32 37 S 145 33 E
Yatolemu, Dem. Rep. of the Congo — 114 B4 0 25N 24 35 E
Yatsuo, Japan — 73 A9 36 34N 137 8 E
Yatsushiro, Japan — 72 E2 32 30N 130 40 E
Yatsushiro-Kai, Japan — 72 E2 32 30N 130 25 E
Yatta Plateau, Kenya — 118 C4 2 0 S 38 0 E
Yatua →, Venezuela — 168 C4 1 30N 66 30W
Yauca, Peru — 172 D3 15 39 S 74 35W
Yauco, Puerto Rico — 165 d 18 2N 66 51W
Yauri, Peru — 172 C3 14 47 S 71 25W
Yauya, Peru — 172 B2 8 59 S 77 17W
Yauyos, Peru — 172 C2 12 19 S 75 50W
Yaval, India — 94 D2 21 10N 75 42 E
Yavan, Tajikistan — 65 D4 38 19N 69 2 E
Yavari →, Peru — 172 A3 4 21 S 70 2W
Yávaros, Mexico — 162 B3 26 42N 109 31W
Yavatmal, India — 94 D4 20 20N 78 15 E
Yavero →, Peru — 172 C3 12 6 S 72 57W
Yavne, Israel — 103 D3 31 52N 34 45 E
Yavoriv, Ukraine — 59 H2 49 55N 23 20 E
Yavorov = Yavoriv, Ukraine — 59 H2 49 55N 23 20 E
Yavuzeli, Turkey — 100 D7 37 18N 37 24 E
Yawatahama, Japan — 72 D3 33 27N 132 24 E
Yawnghwe, Burma — 90 E6 20 39N 96 56 E
Yawri B., S. Leone — 112 D2 8 22N 13 0W
Yaxi, China — 76 D6 27 33N 106 41 E
Yazagyo, Burma — 90 D5 23 30N 94 6 E
Yazd, Iran — 97 D7 31 55N 54 27 E
Yazd □, Iran — 97 D7 32 0N 55 0 E
Yazd-e Khvāst, Iran — 97 D7 31 31N 52 7 E
Yazdān, Iran — 91 B1 33 30N 60 50 E
Yazıköy, Turkey — 49 E9 36 40N 27 20 E
Yazman, Pakistan — 92 E4 29 8N 71 45 E
Yazoo →, U.S.A. — 155 J9 32 22N 90 54W
Yazoo City, U.S.A. — 155 J9 32 51N 90 25W
Ybbs, Austria — 34 C8 48 12N 15 6 E
Yding Skovhøj, Denmark — 17 J3 55 59N 9 46 E
Ye, Burma — 89 D8 15 15N 97 15 E
Ye-ngan, Burma — 90 E6 21 9N 96 27 E
Ye-u, Burma — 90 D5 22 46N 95 26 E
Ye Xian = Laizhou, China — 75 F10 37 8N 119 57 E
Ye Xian, China — 74 H7 33 35N 113 25 E
Yea, Australia — 129 D6 37 14 S 145 26 E
Yebawmi, Burma — 90 C5 25 15N 95 45 E
Yebbi-Souma, Chad — 109 D3 21 7N 17 54 E
Yebyu, Burma — 86 E2 14 15N 98 13 E
Yecheng, China — 65 E8 37 54N 77 26 E
Yechǒn, S. Korea — 75 F15 36 39N 128 27 E
Yecla, Spain — 41 G3 38 35N 1 5W
Yécora, Mexico — 162 B3 28 20N 108 58W
Yedashe, Burma — 90 F6 19 10N 96 20 E
Yedintsy = Edineţ, Moldova — 53 B12 48 9N 27 18 E
Yedri, Chad — 109 D3 22 25N 17 30 E
Yedseram →, Nigeria — 113 C7 12 30N 14 5 E
Yefremov, Russia — 58 E10 53 8N 38 3 E
Yegguéba, Niger — 109 E2 19 59N 12 52 E
Yeghegnadzor, Armenia — 101 C11 39 44N 45 19 E
Yegorlyk →, Russia — 61 G5 46 35N 41 57 E
Yegorlykskaya, Russia — 61 G5 46 33N 40 41 E
Yegoryevsk, Russia — 58 E10 55 27N 38 55 E
Yegri-Dere = Ardino, Bulgaria — 51 E9 41 34N 25 9 E
Yegros, Paraguay — 174 B4 26 20 S 56 25W
Yehbuah, Indonesia — 79 J17 8 23 S 114 45 E
Yehuda, Midbar, Israel — 103 D4 31 35N 35 15 E
Yei, Sudan — 107 G3 4 9N 30 40 E
Yei, Nahr →, Sudan — 107 F3 6 15N 30 13 E
Yejmiadzin, Armenia — 61 K7 40 12N 44 19 E
Yekaterinburg, Russia — 64 C8 56 50N 60 30 E
Yekaterinodar = Krasnodar, Russia — 60 H4 45 5N 39 0 E
Yekumbe, Dem. Rep. of the Congo — 114 B4 1 2N 23 27 E
Yelabuga, Russia — 60 C11 55 45N 52 4 E
Yelan, Russia — 60 E6 50 55N 43 43 E
Yelandur, India — 95 H3 12 6N 77 0 E
Yelarbon, Australia — 127 D5 28 33 S 150 38 E
Yelatma, Russia — 60 C5 55 0N 41 45 E
Yelcho, L., Chile — 176 B2 43 18 S 72 18W
Yelets, Russia — 59 F10 52 40N 38 30 E
Yélimané, Mali — 112 B2 15 9N 10 34W
Yelizavetgrad = Kirovohrad, Ukraine — 59 H7 48 35N 32 20 E
Yelizavetinka, Russia — 64 F7 51 46N 59 45 E
Yell, U.K. — 22 A7 60 35N 1 5W
Yell Sd., U.K. — 22 A7 60 33N 1 15W
Yellamanchili = Elamanchili, India — 94 F6 17 33N 82 50 E
Yellandu, India — 94 F5 17 39N 80 23 E
Yellapur, India — 95 G4 14 58N 74 43 E
Yellareddi, India — 94 E4 18 12N 78 3 E
Yellow →, U.S.A. — 153 E3 30 30N 87 0 E
Yellow Sea, China — 75 G12 35 0N 123 0 E
Yellowhead Pass, Canada — 142 C5 52 53N 118 25W
Yellowknife, Canada — 142 A6 62 27N 114 29W
Yellowknife →, Canada — 142 A6 62 31N 114 19W
Yellowstone →, U.S.A. — 154 B3 47 59N 103 59W
Yellowstone L., U.S.A. — 158 D8 44 27N 110 22W
Yellowstone Nat. Park △, U.S.A. — 158 D9 44 40N 110 30W
Yelnya, Russia — 58 E7 54 35N 33 15 E
Yelsk, Belarus — 59 G5 51 50N 29 10 E
Yelwa, Nigeria — 113 C5 10 49N 4 41 E
Yemanzhelinsk, Russia — 64 D8 54 58N 61 18 E
Yemassee, U.S.A. — 153 J5 32 41N 80 51W
Yembo, Dem. Rep. of the Congo — 114 B3 3 12N 19 2 E
Yemen ■, Asia — 98 D4 15 0N 44 0 E
Yemmiganur = Emmiganuru, India — 95 E3 15 44N 77 29 E
Yen Bai, Vietnam — 76 G5 21 42N 104 52 E
Yenagoa, Nigeria — 113 E6 4 58N 6 16 E
Yenakiyeve, Ukraine — 59 H10 48 15N 38 15 E
Yenakiyevo = Yenakiyeve, Ukraine — 59 H10 48 15N 38 15 E
Yenangyat, Burma — 90 E5 21 6N 94 48 E
Yenangyaung, Burma — 90 F5 20 30N 95 0 E
Yenanma, Burma — 90 F5 19 46N 94 49 E
Yenbo = Yanbu 'al Baḥr, Si. Arabia — 96 F3 24 0N 38 5 E
Yenda, Australia — 129 C7 34 13 S 146 14 E
Yende Millimou, Guinea — 112 D2 8 55N 10 10W
Yendéré, Burkina Faso — 112 C4 10 12N 4 59W
Yendi, Ghana — 113 D4 9 29N 0 1W
Yengisar, China — 65 D8 38 56N 76 9 E
Yengo, Congo — 112 D2 0 22N 15 29 E
Yengo Nat. Park △, Australia — 129 B9 33 3 S 150 51 E
Yenice, Ankara, Turkey — 49 C6 39 1N 34 42 E
Yenice, Aydın, Turkey — 49 D10 37 49N 28 35 E
Yenice, Çanakkale, Turkey — 49 B9 39 55N 27 17 E
Yenice →, Turkey — 100 D6 36 37N 35 33 E
Yenifoça, Turkey — 49 C8 38 44N 26 51 E
Yenihisar, Turkey — 49 D9 37 23N 27 18 E
Yeniköy, Bursa, Turkey — 51 F13 40 31N 29 22 E
Yeniköy, Çanakkale, Turkey — 49 B9 39 38N 27 17 E
Yeniköy, Kütahya, Turkey — 49 C11 38 52N 29 17 E
Yenipazar, Turkey — 49 D10 37 49N 28 14 E
Yenisaía, Greece — 51 E8 41 1N 24 57 E
Yenişehir, Turkey — 51 F13 40 16N 29 38 E
Yenisey →, Russia — 66 B9 71 50N 82 40 E
Yeniseysk, Russia — 67 D10 58 27N 92 13 E

Yeniseyskiy Zaliv, *Russia* . . . . **66 B9** 72 20N 81 0 E
Yennádhi, *Greece* . . . . **38 E11** 36 2N 27 56 E
Yenne, *France* . . . . **29 C9** 45 43N 5 44 E
Yenotayevka, *Russia* . . . . **61 G8** 47 15N 47 0 E
Yenyuka, *Russia* . . . . **67 D13** 57 57N 121 15 E
Yeo ➤, *U.K.* **21 G5** 51 2N 2 49W
Yeo, L., *Australia* . . . . **125 E3** 28 0 S 124 30 E
Yeo I., *Canada* **150 A3** 45 24N 81 48W
Yeola, *India* . . . . **94 D2** 20 2N 74 30 E
Yeoryioúpolis, *Greece* . . . . **39 E5** 35 20N 24 15 E
Yeovil, *U.K.* **21 G5** 50 57N 2 38W
Yepes, *Spain* **42 F7** 39 55N 3 39W
Yeppoon, *Australia* . . . . **126 C5** 23 5 S 150 47 E
Yérakas, *Ákra, Greece* . . . . **39 D2** 37 42N 20 59 E
Yeráki, *Greece* . . . . **48 D4** 37 0N 22 42 E
Yerbent, *Turkmenistan* . . . . **66 F6** 39 30N 58 50 E
Yerbogachen, *Russia* . . . . **67 C11** 61 16N 108 0 E
Yerevan, *Armenia* . . . . **61 K7** 40 10N 44 31 E
Yerington, *U.S.A.* **158 G4** 38 59N 119 10W
Yerkesik, *Turkey* . . . . **49 D10** 37 7N 28 19 E
Yerköy, *Turkey* . . . . **100 C6** 39 38N 34 28 E
Yerla ➤, *India* . . . . **94 F2** 16 50N 74 30 E
Yermak, *Kazakhstan* . . . . **66 D8** 52 2N 76 55 E
Yermo, *U.S.A.* **161 L10** 34 54N 116 50W
Yerólakkos, *Cyprus* . . . . **39 E9** 35 11N 33 15 E
Yeropol, *Russia* . . . . **67 C17** 65 15N 168 40 E
Yeropótamos ➤, *Greece* . . . . **39 E5** 35 2N 24 50 E
Yeroskipos, *Cyprus* . . . . **39 F8** 34 46N 32 28 E
Yershov, *Russia* . . . . **60 E9** 51 23N 48 27 E
Yerupaja, *Cerro, Peru* . . . . **172 C2** 10 16 S 76 55W
Yerushalayim = Jerusalem, *Israel* . . **103 D4** 31 47N 35 10 E
Yerville, *France* . . . . **26 C7** 49 40N 0 53 E
Yes Tor, *U.K.* **21 G4** 50 41N 4 0W
Yesagyo, *Burma* . . . . **90 E5** 21 38N 95 14 E
Yesan, *S. Korea* . . . . **75 F14** 36 41N 126 51 E
Yeshin, *Burma* . . . . **90 D5** 23 43N 95 6 E
Yeşilhisar, *Turkey* . . . . **100 C6** 38 20N 35 5 E
Yeşilırmak ➤, *Turkey* . . . . **100 B7** 41 22N 36 37 E
Yeşilkent, *Turkey* . . . . **100 D7** 36 57N 36 12 E
Yeşilköy, *Turkey* . . . . **51 F12** 40 57N 28 49 E
Yeşillova, *Turkey* . . . . **49 D11** 37 31N 29 46 E
Yeşilyurt, *Manisa, Turkey* . . . . **49 C10** 38 22N 28 40 E
Yeşilyurt, *Muğla, Turkey* . . . . **49 D10** 37 10N 28 20 E
Yesnogorsk, *Russia* . . . . **58 E9** 54 32N 37 38 E
Yeso, *U.S.A.* **155 H2** 34 26N 104 37W
Yessentuki, *Russia* . . . . **61 H6** 44 5N 42 53 E
Yessey, *Russia* . . . . **67 C11** 68 29N 102 10 E
Yeste, *Spain* **41 G2** 38 22N 2 19W
Yetman, *Australia* . . . . **127 D5** 28 56 S 150 48 E
Yetti, *Mauritania* **110 C3** 26 10N 7 50W
Yeu, Î. d', *France* **26 F4** 46 42N 2 20W
Yevlakh = Yevlax, *Azerbaijan* . . . . . **61 K8** 40 39N 47 7 E
Yevlax, *Azerbaijan* . . . . **61 K8** 40 39N 47 7 E
Yevpatoriya, *Ukraine* . . . . **59 K7** 45 15N 33 20 E
Yeya ➤, *Russia* . . . . **59 J10** 46 40N 38 40 E
Yeysk, *Russia* . . . . **59 J10** 46 40N 38 12 E
Yezd = Yazd, *Iran* . . . . **97 D7** 31 55N 54 27 E
Yezerishche, *Belarus* . . . . **58 E5** 55 50N 29 59 E
Yhati, *Paraguay* . . . . **174 B4** 25 45 S 56 35W
Yhú, *Paraguay* . . . . **175 B4** 25 0 S 56 0W
Yi ➤, *Uruguay* . . . . **174 C4** 33 7 S 57 8W
Yi 'Allaq, G., *Egypt* . . . . **103 E2** 30 22N 33 32 E
Yi He ➤, *China* . . . . **75 G10** 34 10N 118 8 E
Yi Xian, *Anhui, China* . . . . **77 C11** 29 55N 117 57 E
Yi Xian, *Hebei, China* . . . . **74 E8** 39 20N 115 30 E
Yi Xian, *Liaoning, China* . . . . **75 D11** 41 30N 121 22 E
Yialí, *Greece* . . . . **49 E9** 36 41N 27 11 E
Yialiás ➤, *Cyprus* . . . . **39 E9** 35 9N 33 44 E
Yi'allaq, G., *Egypt* . . . . **106 A3** 30 21N 33 31 E
Yialousa, *Cyprus* . . . . **39 E10** 35 32N 34 10 E
Yiálttra, *Greece* . . . . **48 C4** 38 51N 22 59 E
Yianisádhes, *Greece* . . . . **39 E7** 35 20N 26 10 E
Yiannitsa, *Greece* . . . . **50 F6** 40 46N 22 24 E
Yibin, *China* . . . . **76 C5** 28 45N 104 32 E
Yichang, *China* . . . . **77 B8** 30 40N 111 20 E
Yicheng, *Henan, China* . . . . **77 B9** 31 41N 112 12 E
Yicheng, *Shanxi, China* . . . . **74 E6** 35 42N 111 40 E
Yichuan, *China* . . . . **74 F6** 36 2N 110 10 E
Yichun, *Heilongjiang, China* . . . . . **69 B7** 47 44N 128 52 E
Yichun, *Jiangxi, China* . . . . **77 D10** 27 48N 114 22 E
Yidu, *China* . . . . **75 F10** 36 43N 118 28 E
Yidun, *China* . . . . **76 B2** 30 22N 99 21 E
Yifag, *Ethiopia* . . . . **107 E4** 12 4N 37 46 E
Yifeng, *China* . . . . **77 C10** 28 22N 114 45 E
Yihuang, *China* . . . . **77 D11** 27 30N 116 12 E
Yijun, *China* . . . . **74 G5** 35 28N 109 8 E
Yıldız Dağları, *Turkey* . . . . **51 E11** 41 48N 27 36 E
Yıldızeli, *Turkey* . . . . **100 C7** 39 51N 36 36 E
Yilehuli Shan, *China* . . . . **69 A7** 51 20N 124 20 E
Yiliang, *Yunnan, China* . . . . **76 D5** 27 38N 104 2 E
Yiliang, *Yunnan, China* . . . . **76 E4** 24 56N 103 11 E
Yilong, *China* . . . . **76 B6** 31 34N 106 23 E
Yima, *China* . . . . **76 E4** 24 40N 102 10 E
Yimianpo, *China* . . . . **75 B15** 45 7N 128 2 E
Yinchuan, *China* . . . . **74 E4** 38 30N 106 15 E
Yindaik, *Burma* . . . . **90 D5** 23 35N 95 22 E
Yindarlgooda, L., *Australia* . . . . . . **125 F3** 30 40 S 121 52 E
Ying He ➤, *China* . . . . **74 H7** 32 30N 116 30 E
Ying Xian, *China* . . . . **74 E7** 39 32N 113 10 E
Yingcheng, *China* . . . . **77 B9** 30 56N 113 35 E
Yingde, *China* . . . . **77 E9** 24 10N 113 25 E
Yingjiang, *China* . . . . **76 E1** 24 41N 97 55 E
Yingjing, *China* . . . . **76 C4** 29 41N 102 52 E
Yingkou, *China* . . . . **75 D12** 40 37N 122 18 E
Yingshan, *Henan, China* . . . . **77 B9** 31 35N 113 50 E
Yingshan, *Hubei, China* . . . . **77 B10** 30 41N 115 32 E
Yingshan, *Sichuan, China* . . . . . . **76 B6** 31 4N 106 35 E
Yingshang, *China* . . . . **77 A11** 32 38N 116 12 E
Yingtan, *China* . . . . **77 C11** 28 12N 117 0 E
Yining, *China* . . . . **66 E9** 43 58N 81 10 E
Yinjiang, *China* . . . . **76 D7** 28 1N 108 21 E
Yinmabin, *Burma* . . . . **90 D5** 22 10N 94 55 E
Yiofíros ➤, *Greece* . . . . **39 E6** 35 20N 25 6 E
Yioúra, *Nótios Aiyaíon, Greece* . . . **48 D6** 37 32N 24 40 E
Yioúra, *Thessalía, Greece* . . . . **48 B6** 39 23N 24 10 E
Yipinglang, *China* . . . . **76 E3** 25 10N 101 52 E
Yirápetra, *Ákra, Greece* . . . . **39 E6** 35 1N 25 44 E
Yirba Muda, *Ethiopia* . . . . **107 F4** 6 12N 38 42 E
Yirga Alem, *Ethiopia* . . . . **107 F4** 6 48N 38 22 E
Yirol, *Sudan* . . . . **107 F3** 6 33N 30 30 E
Yirrkala, *Australia* . . . . **126 A2** 12 14 S 136 56 E
Yishan, *China* . . . . **76 E7** 24 28N 108 38 E
Yishui, *China* . . . . **75 G10** 35 47N 118 30 E
Yishun, *Singapore* . . . . **87 d** 1 26N 103 50 E
Yíthion, *Greece* . . . . **48 B4** 36 46N 22 34 E
Yitong, *China* . . . . **75 C13** 43 13N 125 20 E
Yiwu, *China* . . . . **77 C13** 29 20N 120 3 E
Yixing, *China* . . . . **77 B12** 31 21N 119 48 E
Yiyang, *Henan, China* . . . . **74 G7** 34 27N 112 10 E
Yiyang, *Hunan, China* . . . . **77 C9** 28 35N 112 18 E
Yiyang, *Jiangxi, China* . . . . **77 C11** 28 22N 117 20 E
Yizhang, *China* . . . . **77 E9** 25 27N 112 57 E
Yizheng, *China* . . . . **77 A12** 32 18N 119 10 E
Yli-Kitka, *Finland* . . . . **14 C23** 66 8N 28 30 E
Ylitornio, *Finland* . . . . **14 C20** 66 19N 23 39 E
Ylivieska, *Finland* . . . . **14 D21** 64 4N 24 28 E
Yngaren, *Sweden* . . . . **17 F10** 58 50N 16 35 E
Yoakum, *U.S.A.* **156 L6** 29 17N 97 9W
Yob Wildlife Reserve △, *Eritrea* . . **107 D4** 17 15N 37 50 E
Yobe □, *Nigeria* . . . . **113 C7** 12 0N 11 30 E
Yog Pt., *Phil.* . . . . **80 D5** 14 6N 124 12 E
Yogan, *Togo* . . . . **113 D5** 6 23N 1 30 E
Yoğuntaş, *Turkey* . . . . **51 E11** 41 50N 27 4 E

Yogyakarta, *Indonesia* . . . . **85 D4** 7 49 S 110 22 E
Yogyakarta □, *Indonesia* . . . . **85 D4** 7 48 S 110 22 E
Yoho Nat. Park △, *Canada* **142 C5** 51 25N 116 30W
Yojoa, L. de, *Honduras* **164 D2** 14 53N 88 0W
Yōju, *S. Korea* . . . . **75 F14** 37 20N 127 35 E
Yok Don Nat. Park △, *Vietnam* . . . **86 F6** 12 50N 107 40 E
Yokadouma, *Cameroon* . . . . **114 B2** 3 26N 14 55 E
Yōkaichi, *Japan* . . . . **73 B8** 35 6N 136 12 E
Yōkaichiba, *Japan* . . . . **73 B12** 35 42N 140 33 E
Yokkaichi, *Japan* . . . . **73 C8** 34 55N 136 38 E
Yoko, *Cameroon* . . . . **113 D7** 5 32N 12 20 E
Yokohama, *Japan* . . . . **73 B11** 35 27N 139 28 E
Yokosuka, *Japan* . . . . **73 B11** 35 20N 139 40 E
Yokote, *Japan* . . . . **70 E10** 39 20N 140 30 E
Yola, *Nigeria* . . . . **113 D7** 9 10N 12 29 E
Yolaina, *Cordillera de, Nic.* **164 D3** 11 30N 84 0W
Yolombo, *Dem. Rep. of the Congo* . **114 C4** 1 36 S 23 12 E
Yoloten, *Turkmenistan* . . . . **97 B9** 37 18N 62 21 E
Yom ➤, *Thailand* . . . . **78 A2** 15 35N 100 1 E
Yombi, *Gabon* . . . . **114 C2** 1 26 S 10 37 E
Yonago, *Japan* . . . . **72 B5** 35 25N 133 19 E
Yonaguni-Jima, *Japan* . . . . **71 M1** 24 27N 123 0 E
Yōnan, *N. Korea* . . . . **75 F14** 37 55N 126 11 E
Yonezawa, *Japan* . . . . **70 F10** 37 57N 140 4 E
Yong Peng, *Malaysia* . . . . **87 L4** 2 0N 103 3 E
Yong Sata, *Thailand* . . . . **87 J2** 7 8N 99 41 E
Yongama, *Dem. Rep. of the Congo* . **114 B4** 0 2N 24 35 E
Yongamp'o, *N. Korea* . . . . **75 E13** 39 56N 124 23 E
Yong'an, *China* . . . . **77 E11** 25 59N 117 25 E
Yongcheng, *China* . . . . **74 H9** 33 55N 116 20 E
Yŏngch'ŏn, *S. Korea* . . . . **75 G15** 35 58N 128 56 E
Yongchuan, *China* . . . . **76 C5** 29 17N 105 55 E
Yongde, *China* . . . . **76 E2** 24 5N 99 25 E
Yongdeng, *China* . . . . **74 F2** 36 38N 103 25 E
Yongding, *China* . . . . **77 E11** 24 43N 116 45 E
Yŏngdŏk, *S. Korea* . . . . **75 F15** 36 24N 129 22 E
Yŏngdŭngpo, *S. Korea* . . . . **75 F14** 37 31N 126 54 E
Yongfeng, *China* . . . . **77 D10** 27 20N 115 22 E
Yongfu, *China* . . . . **76 E7** 24 59N 109 59 E
Yonggyap Pass, *India* . . . . **90 A5** 29 17N 95 37 E
Yonghe, *China* . . . . **74 F6** 36 46N 110 38 E
Yonghong, *China* . . . . **90 B5** 26 28N 94 58 E
Yŏnghŭng, *N. Korea* . . . . **75 E14** 39 31N 127 18 E
Yongji, *China* . . . . **74 G6** 34 52N 110 28 E
Yongjia, *China* . . . . **77 C13** 28 10N 120 45 E
Yŏngju, *S. Korea* . . . . **75 F15** 36 50N 128 40 E
Yongkang, *Yunnan, China* . . . . . . **76 E2** 24 9N 99 20 E
Yongkang, *Zhejiang, China* . . . . . **77 C13** 28 55N 120 2 E
Yongnian, *China* . . . . **74 F8** 36 47N 114 29 E
Yongning, *Guangxi Zhuangzu, China* **76 F7** 22 44N 108 28 E
Yongning, *Ningxia Huizu, China* . . **74 E4** 38 15N 106 14 E
Yongping, *China* . . . . **76 E2** 25 27N 99 38 E
Yongqing, *China* . . . . **74 E9** 39 25N 116 28 E
Yongren, *China* . . . . **76 D3** 26 4N 101 40 E
Yongshan, *China* . . . . **76 C4** 28 11N 103 35 E
Yongsheng, *China* . . . . **76 D3** 26 38N 100 46 E
Yongshun, *China* . . . . **76 C7** 29 2N 109 51 E
Yongtai, *China* . . . . **77 E12** 25 49N 118 58 E
Yŏngwŏl, *S. Korea* . . . . **75 F15** 37 11N 128 28 E
Yongxin, *China* . . . . **77 D10** 26 58N 114 15 E
Yongxing, *China* . . . . **77 D9** 26 9N 113 8 E
Yongxiu, *China* . . . . **77 C10** 29 2N 115 42 E
Yongzhou, *China* . . . . **77 D8** 26 17N 111 37 E
Yonibana, *S. Leone* **112 D2** 8 30N 12 19W
Yonkers, *U.S.A.* **151 F11** 40 56N 73 54W
Yonne □, *France* . . . . **27 E10** 47 50N 3 40 E
Yonne ➤, *France* . . . . **27 D9** 48 23N 2 58 E
Yopal, *Colombia* **168 B3** 5 21N 72 23W
Yopurga, *China* . . . . **65 D8** 39 15N 76 45 E
York, *Australia* . . . . **125 F2** 31 52 S 116 47 E
York, *U.K.* **20 D6** 53 58N 1 6W
York, Ala., *U.S.A.* **155 J10** 32 29N 88 18W
York, Nebr., *U.S.A.* **154 E6** 40 52N 97 36W
York, Pa., *U.S.A.* **148 F7** 39 58N 76 44W
York, C., *Australia* . . . . **126 A3** 10 42 S 142 31 E
York, City of □, *U.K.* **20 D6** 53 58N 1 6W
York, Kap, *Greenland* **10 B4** 75 55N 66 25W
York, Vale of, *U.K.* **20 C6** 54 15N 1 25W
York Haven, *U.S.A.* **150 F8** 40 7N 76 46W
York Sd., *Australia* . . . . **124 C4** 15 0 S 125 5 E
Yorke Pen., *Australia* . . . . **128 C2** 34 50 S 137 40 E
Yorketown, *Australia* . . . . **128 C2** 35 0 S 137 33 E
Yorkshire Dales Nat. Park △, *U.K.* . **20 C5** 54 12N 2 10W
Yorkshire Wolds, *U.K.* **20 C7** 54 8N 0 31W
Yorkton, *Canada* **143 C8** 51 11N 102 28W
Yorkville, *Calif., U.S.A.* **160 G3** 38 52N 123 13W
Yorkville, *Ga., U.S.A.* **152 B5** 33 55N 84 58W
Yorkville, *Ill., U.S.A.* **157 C8** 41 38N 88 27W
Yoro, *Honduras* **164 C2** 15 9N 87 7W
Yoron-Jima, *Japan* . . . . **71 L4** 27 2N 128 26 E
Yorosso, *Mali* **112 C4** 12 17N 4 55W
Yos Sudarso, Pulau = Dolak, Pulau, *Indonesia* . . . . **83 C5** 8 0 S 138 30 E
Yos Sudarso, Teluk, *Indonesia* . . . **83 B6** 2 35 S 140 45 E
Yosemite Nat. Park △, *U.S.A.* **160 H7** 37 45N 119 40W
Yosemite Village, *U.S.A.* **160 H7** 37 45N 119 35W
Yoshida, *Japan* . . . . **72 C4** 34 40N 132 42 E
Yoshimatsu, *Japan* . . . . **72 F2** 32 0N 130 47 E
Yoshino-Kumano Nat. Park △, *Japan* . . . . **73 C7** 34 12N 135 55 E
Yoshkar Ola, *Russia* . . . . **60 B8** 56 38N 47 55 E
Yŏsu, *S. Korea* . . . . **75 G14** 34 47N 127 45 E
Yotala, *Bolivia* . . . . **173 D4** 19 10 S 65 17W
Yotvata, *Israel* . . . . **103 F4** 29 55N 35 2 E
You Jiang ➤, *China* . . . . **76 F6** 22 50N 108 6 E
You Xian, *China* . . . . **77 D9** 27 1N 113 17 E
Youbou, *Canada* **160 B2** 48 53N 124 13W
Youghal, *Ireland* **23 E4** 51 56N 7 52W
Youghal B., *Ireland* **23 E4** 51 55N 7 49W
Youkounkoun, *Guinea* **112 C2** 12 35N 13 11W
Young, *Australia* . . . . **129 C8** 34 19 S 148 18 E
Young, *Canada* **143 C7** 51 47N 105 45W
Young, *Uruguay* . . . . **174 C4** 32 44 S 57 36W
Young Ra., *N.Z.* . . . . **131 E4** 44 10 S 169 30 E
Younghusband, L., *Australia* . . . . . **128 A2** 30 50 S 136 5 E
Younghusband Pen., *Australia* . . . . **128 D3** 36 0 S 139 25 E
Youngstown, *Canada* **143 C6** 51 35N 111 10W
Youngstown, *Fla., U.S.A.* **152 K4** 30 22N 85 26W
Youngstown, *N.Y., U.S.A.* **150 C5** 43 15N 79 3W
Youngstown, *Ohio, U.S.A.* **150 E4** 41 6N 80 39W
Youngsville, *U.S.A.* **150 E5** 41 51N 79 19W
Youngwood, *U.S.A.* **150 F5** 40 14N 79 34W
Youssoufia, *Morocco* **110 B3** 32 16N 8 31W
Youxi, *China* . . . . **77 D12** 26 10N 118 13 E
Youyang, *China* . . . . **76 C7** 28 47N 108 42 E
Youyu, *China* . . . . **74 D7** 40 10N 112 20 E
Yozgat, *Turkey* . . . . **100 C6** 39 51N 34 47 E
Ypané ➤, *Paraguay* . . . . **174 A4** 23 29 S 57 19W
Yport, *France* . . . . **26 C7** 49 44N 0 15 E
Ypres = Ieper, *Belgium* . . . . **24 D2** 50 51N 2 53 E
Ypsilanti, *U.S.A.* **157 B13** 42 14N 83 37W
Yreka, *U.S.A.* **158 F2** 41 44N 122 38W
Ysabel Chan., *Papua N.G.* . . . . . . **132 B5** 2 0 S 150 0 E
Yssingeaux, *France* . . . . **29 C8** 45 9N 4 8 E
Ystad, *Sweden* . . . . **17 J6** 55 26N 13 50 E
Ysyk-Köl = Balykchy, *Kyrgyzstan* . **65 B8** 42 26N 76 12 E
Ysyk-Köl, *Kyrgyzstan* . . . . **65 B8** 42 25N 77 15 E
Ythan ➤, *U.K.* **22 D7** 57 19N 1 59W
Ytre Arna, *Norway* . . . . **17 F11** 60 27N 5 25 E
Ytre Enebakk, *Norway* . . . . **18 E8** 59 44N 11 0 E
Ytre Rendal, *Norway* . . . . **18 C8** 61 46N 11 8 E
Ytterhogdal, *Sweden* . . . . **16 B8** 62 12N 14 56 E

Ytyk-Kuyel, *Russia* . . . . **67 C14** 62 30N 133 45 E
Yu Jiang ➤, *China* . . . . **76 F7** 23 22N 110 3 E
Yu Shan, *Taiwan* . . . . **77 F13** 23 30N 120 58 E
Yu Xian = Yuzhou, *China* . . . . . . **74 G7** 34 10N 113 28 E
Yu Xian, *Hebei, China* . . . . **74 E8** 39 50N 114 35 E
Yu Xian, *Shanxi, China* . . . . **74 E7** 38 5N 113 20 E
Yuan Jiang ➤, *Hunan, China* . . . . **77 C8** 28 55N 111 50 E
Yuan Jiang ➤, *Yunnan, China* . . . . **76 F4** 22 20N 103 59 E
Yuan'an, *China* . . . . **77 B8** 31 1N 111 34 E
Yuanjiang, *Hunan, China* . . . . **77 C9** 28 47N 112 21 E
Yuanjiang, *Yunnan, China* . . . . . . **76 F3** 23 32N 102 0 E
Yuanli, *Taiwan* . . . . **77 E13** 24 27N 120 39 E
Yuanlin, *Taiwan* . . . . **77 F13** 23 58N 120 30 E
Yuanling, *China* . . . . **77 C8** 28 29N 110 22 E
Yuanmou, *China* . . . . **76 E3** 25 42N 101 53 E
Yuanqu, *China* . . . . **74 G6** 35 18N 111 40 E
Yuanyang, *Henan, China* . . . . **74 G7** 35 3N 113 58 E
Yuanyang, *Yunnan, China* . . . . . . **76 F4** 23 10N 102 43 E
Yuat ➤, *Papua N.G.* . . . . **132 C2** 4 10 S 143 52 E
Yuba ➤, *U.S.A.* **160 F5** 39 8N 121 36W
Yuba City, *U.S.A.* **160 F5** 39 8N 121 37W
Yūbari, *Japan* . . . . **70 C10** 43 4N 141 59 E
Yubdo, *Ethiopia* . . . . **107 F4** 8 58N 35 24 E
Yūbetsu, *Japan* . . . . **70 B11** 44 13N 143 50 E
Yubo, *Sudan* . . . . **107 F2** 5 23N 27 25 E
Yucatán □, *Mexico* **163 C7** 21 30N 86 30W
Yucatán, Canal de, *Caribbean* **164 B2** 22 0N 86 30W
Yucatán, Península de, *Mexico* . . . **136 H11** 19 30N 89 0W
Yucatan Basin, *Cent. Amer.* **136 H11** 20 0N 86 0W
Yucatan Channel = Yucatán, Canal de, *Caribbean* **164 B2** 22 0N 86 30W
Yucca, *U.S.A.* **161 L12** 34 52N 114 9W
Yucca Valley, *U.S.A.* **161 L10** 34 8N 116 27W
Yucheng, *China* . . . . **74 F9** 36 55N 116 39 E
Yuci, *China* . . . . **74 F7** 37 42N 112 46 E
Yudu, *China* . . . . **77 E10** 25 59N 115 30 E
Yuechi, *China* . . . . **76 B6** 30 34N 106 25 E
Yuen Long, *China* . . . . **69 G11** 22 26N 114 2 E
Yuendumu, *Australia* . . . . **124 D5** 22 16 S 131 49 E
Yueqing, *China* . . . . **77 C13** 28 9N 120 59 E
Yueqing Wan, *China* . . . . **77 D13** 28 5N 121 20 E
Yuexi, *Anhui, China* . . . . **77 B11** 30 50N 116 20 E
Yuexi, *Sichuan, China* . . . . **76 C4** 28 37N 102 26 E
Yueyang, *China* . . . . **77 C9** 29 21N 113 5 E
Yufu-Dake, *Japan* . . . . **72 D3** 33 17N 131 32 E
Yugan, *China* . . . . **77 C11** 28 43N 116 37 E
Yugoslavia ■, *Europe* . . . . **50 C4** 43 20N 20 0 E
Yuhuan, *China* . . . . **77 C13** 28 9N 121 12 E
Yuhuan Dao, *China* . . . . **77 C13** 28 5N 121 12 E
Yujiang, *China* . . . . **77 C11** 28 10N 116 43 E
Yukhnov, *Russia* . . . . **58 E8** 54 44N 35 15 E
Yūki, *Japan* . . . . **73 A11** 36 18N 139 53 E
Yukon ➤, *U.S.A.* **144 E7** 62 32N 163 54W
Yukon-Charley Rivers Nat. Preserve △, *U.S.A.* **144 C12** 65 15N 144 0W
Yukon Territory □, *Canada* **138 B6** 63 0N 135 0W
Yüksekova, *Turkey* . . . . **101 D11** 37 34N 44 16 E
Yukta, *Russia* . . . . **67 C11** 63 26N 105 42 E
Yukuhashi, *Japan* . . . . **72 D2** 33 44N 130 59 E
Yulara, *Australia* . . . . **125 E5** 25 10 S 130 55 E
Yule ➤, *Australia* . . . . **124 D2** 20 41 S 118 17 E
Yuleba, *Australia* . . . . **127 D4** 26 37 S 149 24 E
Yulee, *U.S.A.* **152 E8** 30 38N 81 36W
Yuli, *China* . . . . **113 D7** 9 44N 10 12 E
Yuli, *Taiwan* . . . . **77 F13** 23 20N 121 18 E
Yulin, *Guangxi Zhuangzu, China* . . **77 F8** 22 40N 110 8 E
Yulin, *Hainan, China* . . . . **87 C7** 18 10N 109 31 E
Yulin, *Shaanxi, China* . . . . **74 E5** 38 20N 109 30 E
Yuma, Ariz., *U.S.A.* **161 N12** 32 43N 114 37W
Yuma, Colo., *U.S.A.* **154 E3** 40 8N 102 43W
Yuma, B. de, Dom. Rep. **165 C6** 18 20N 68 35W
Yumali, *Australia* . . . . **128 C3** 35 32 S 139 45 E
Yumbe, *Uganda* . . . . **118 B3** 3 28N 31 15 E
Yumbi, Équateur, Dem. Rep. of the Congo . . . . **114 C3** 1 53 S 16 34 E
Yumbi, Maniema, Dem. Rep. of the Congo . . . . **118 C2** 1 12 S 26 15 E
Yumbo, *Colombia* **168 C2** 3 35N 76 28W
Yumen, *China* . . . . **68 C4** 39 50N 97 30 E
Yumurtalik, *Turkey* . . . . **100 D6** 36 45N 35 43 E
Yun Gui Gaoyuan, *China* . . . . **76 E3** 26 0N 104 0 E
Yun Ho ➤, *China* . . . . **75 E9** 39 10N 117 10 E
Yun Ling, *China* . . . . **76 D2** 27 0N 99 20 E
Yun Xian, Hubei, *China* . . . . **77 A8** 32 50N 110 46 E
Yun Xian, Yunnan, *China* . . . . . . **76 E3** 24 27N 100 8 E
Yuna, *Australia* . . . . **125 E2** 28 20 S 115 0 E
Yunak, *Turkey* . . . . **100 C4** 38 49N 31 43 E
Yunan, *China* . . . . **77 F8** 23 12N 111 30 E
Yunaska I., *U.S.A.* **144 K5** 52 38N 170 40W
Yuncheng, Henan, *China* . . . . **74 G8** 35 36N 115 57 E
Yuncheng, Shanxi, *China* . . . . **74 G6** 35 2N 111 0 E
Yunfu, *China* . . . . **77 F9** 22 50N 112 5 E
Yungas, *Bolivia* . . . . **173 D4** 17 0 S 66 0W
Yungay, *Chile* . . . . **174 D1** 37 10 S 72 5W
Yungay, *Peru* . . . . **172 B2** 9 2 S 77 45W
Yunge = Jilin, *China* . . . . **75 C14** 43 44N 126 30 E
Yunjinge = Nanning, *China* . . . . . **76 F7** 22 48N 108 20 E
Yunhe, *China* . . . . **77 C12** 28 1N 119 33 E
Yunkai Dashan, *China* . . . . **77 F8** 22 30N 111 0 E
Yunlin, *Taiwan* . . . . **77 F13** 23 42N 120 30 E
Yunling, *China* . . . . **77 B9** 31 2N 113 0 E
Yunmeng, *China* . . . . **77 B9** 31 2N 113 43 E
Yunnan □, *China* . . . . **76 E4** 25 0N 102 0 E
Yunotsu, *Japan* . . . . **72 B4** 35 5N 132 21 E
Yunquera de Henares, *Spain* **40 E1** 40 47N 3 11W
Yunt Dağı, *Turkey* . . . . **49 C9** 38 56N 27 13 E
Yunta, *Australia* . . . . **127 E2** 32 34 S 139 36 E
Yunxi, *China* . . . . **74 H6** 33 0N 110 22 E
Yunxiao, *China* . . . . **77 F11** 23 59N 117 18 E
Yuping, *China* . . . . **77 D7** 27 13N 108 56 E
Yuqing, *China* **169 C6** 3 45N 59 20W
Yupyongdong, N. Korea . . . . **75 D15** 41 49N 128 53 E
Yuqing, *China* . . . . **76 D6** 27 13N 107 53 E
Yuraygir Nat. Park △, *Australia* . . . **127 D5** 29 45 S 153 15 E
Yurga, *Russia* . . . . **66 D9** 55 42N 84 51 E
Yurimaguas, *Peru* . . . . **172 B2** 5 55 S 76 7W
Yurla, *Russia* . . . . **64 B5** 59 22N 54 21 E
Yurya, *Russia* . . . . **60 B8** 59 1N 49 13 E
Yuryev-Polskiy, *Russia* . . . . **58 D10** 56 30N 39 40 E
Yuryevets, *Russia* . . . . **60 B7** 57 25N 43 2 E
Yuryuzan, *Russia* . . . . **64 D7** 54 57N 58 28 E
Yuscarán, *Honduras* **164 D2** 13 58N 86 45W
Yûsef, Bahr ➤, *Egypt* . . . . **106 B3** 28 25N 30 35 E
Yushan, *China* . . . . **77 C12** 28 48N 118 22 E
Yushanzhen, *China* . . . . **76 C7** 29 28N 108 22 E
Yushe, *China* . . . . **74 F7** 37 4N 112 58 E
Yushu, Jilin, *China* . . . . **75 B14** 44 43N 126 38 E
Yushu, Qinghai, *China* . . . . **68 C4** 33 5N 96 55 E
Yusufeli, *Turkey* . . . . **101 B9** 40 50N 41 33 E
Yutai, *China* . . . . **74 G9** 35 0N 116 45 E
Yutian, *China* . . . . **75 E9** 39 53N 117 45 E
Yuxarı Qarabağ = Nagorno-Karabakh □, *Azerbaijan* . . . . **101 C12** 39 55N 46 45 E
Yuxi, *China* . . . . **76 E4** 24 30N 102 35 E
Yuyao, *China* . . . . **77 B13** 30 3N 121 10 E
Yuzawa, *Japan* . . . . **70 E10** 39 10N 140 30 E
Yuzha, *Russia* . . . . **60 B7** 56 34N 42 1 E
Yuzhno-Sakhalinsk, *Russia* . . . . . **67 E15** 46 58N 142 45 E
Yuzhnouralsk, *Russia* . . . . **64 D7** 54 26N 61 5 E
Yuzhou, *China* . . . . **74 G7** 34 10N 113 28 E
Yvelines □, *France* . . . . **25 D8** 48 40N 1 45 E
Yverdon-les-Bains, *Switz.* . . . . . . **25 J2** 46 47N 6 39 E
Yvetot, *France* . . . . **26 C7** 49 37N 0 44 E
Yvonand, *Switz.* . . . . **32 C3** 46 48N 6 44 E
Yzeure, *France* . . . . **27 F10** 46 33N 3 2 E

Z

Zaalayskiy Khrebet, *Tajikistan* . . . . **65 D6** 39 20N 73 0 E
Zaanstad, *Neths.* . . . . **24 B4** 52 27N 4 50 E
Zab, Monts du, *Algeria* . . . . **111 B6** 34 55N 5 0 E
Zāb al Ṣaġīr ➤, *Iraq* . . . . **101 D10** 36 1N 43 24 E
Zāb al Kabīr ➤, *Iraq* . . . . **101 E10** 35 17N 43 29 E
Zabalj, Serbia, Yug. . . . . **52 E5** 45 21N 20 5 E
Zabari, Serbia, Yug. . . . . **50 B5** 44 22N 21 15 E
Zabarjad, Egypt . . . . **106 C4** 23 40N 36 12 E
Zabaykalsk, *Russia* . . . . **67 E12** 49 40N 117 25 E
Zabbar, Malta . . . . **38 F8** 35 53N 14 32 E
Zabīd, Yemen . . . . **98 D3** 14 0N 43 10 E
Zabīd, W. ➤, Yemen . . . . **98 D3** 14 9 S 43 10 E
Zabki, Poland . . . . **55 F8** 52 17N 21 7 E
Ząbkowice Śląskie, Poland . . . . . . **55 H3** 50 35N 16 53 E
Żabljak, Montenegro, Yug. . . . . . . **50 C3** 43 18N 19 5 E
Żabłudów, Poland . . . . **55 F9** 53 0N 23 19 E
Żabno, Poland . . . . **55 H7** 50 9N 20 53 E
Zābol, Iran . . . . **97 D9** 31 0N 61 32 E
Zābol □, Afghan. . . . . **91 B2** 32 0N 67 0 E
Zāboli, Iran . . . . **97 E9** 27 10N 61 35 E
Zabré, Burkina Faso **113 C4** 11 12N 0 36W
Zábřeh, Czech Rep. . . . . **35 B9** 49 53N 16 52 E
Zabrze, Poland . . . . **55 H5** 50 18N 18 50 E
Zabuga, Ghana . . . . **113 D5** 9 20N 0 30 E
Zacapa, Guatemala **164 D2** 14 59N 89 31W
Zacapu, Mexico **162 D4** 19 50N 101 43W
Zacatecas, Mexico **162 C4** 22 49N 102 34W
Zacatecas □, Mexico **162 C4** 23 30N 103 0W
Zacatecoluca, El Salv. **164 D2** 13 29N 88 51W
Zachary, U.S.A. **155 K9** 30 39N 91 9W
Zachodnio-Pomorskie □, Poland . . **54 E2** 53 40N 15 50 E
Zacoalco, Mexico **162 C4** 20 14N 103 33W
Zacualtipán, Mexico **163 C5** 20 39N 98 36W
Zadar, Croatia . . . . **45 D12** 44 8N 15 14 E
Zadawa, Nigeria . . . . **113 C7** 11 33N 10 19 E
Zadetkyi Kyun, Burma . . . . **87 G1** 10 0N 98 25 E
Zadonsk, Russia . . . . **59 F10** 52 25N 38 56 E
Zafarqand, Iran . . . . **97 C7** 33 11N 52 29 E
Zafora, Greece . . . . **49 E8** 36 5N 26 24 E
Zafra, Spain **43 G4** 38 26N 6 30W
Zagań, Poland . . . . **55 G2** 51 39N 15 22 E
Zagaoua, Chad . . . . **109 E4** 16 0N 23 0 E
Zagarė, Lithuania . . . . **54 B10** 56 21N 23 15 E
Zagazig, Egypt . . . . **106 H7** 30 40N 31 30 E
Zāgheh, Iran . . . . **97 C6** 33 30N 48 42 E
Zaghouan, Tunisia . . . . **108 A2** 36 23N 10 10 E
Zaglivérion, Greece . . . . **50 F7** 40 36N 23 15 E
Zaglou, Algeria **111 C4** 27 17N 0 3W
Zagnanado, Benin . . . . **113 D5** 7 18N 2 28 E
Zagorá, Greece . . . . **48 B5** 39 27N 23 6 E
Zagora, Morocco **110 B3** 30 22N 5 51W
Zagorje, Slovenia . . . . **45 B11** 46 8N 15 0 E
Zagórz, Poland . . . . **55 F4** 52 10N 17 54 E
Zagorsk = Sergiyev Posad, Russia . **58 D10** 56 20N 38 10 E
Zagórz, Poland . . . . **55 J9** 49 30N 22 14 E
Zagreb, Croatia . . . . **45 C12** 45 50N 15 58 E
Zagreb ✈ (ZAG), Croatia . . . . **45 C13** 45 45N 16 4 E
Zāgros, Kūhhā-ye, Iran . . . . **97 C6** 33 45N 48 5 E
Zagros Mts. = Zāgros, Kūhhā-ye, Iran . . . . **97 C6** 33 45N 48 5 E
Żagubica, Serbia, Yug. . . . . **50 B5** 44 15N 21 47 E
Zaguinaso, Ivory C. **112 C3** 10 1N 6 14W
Zagyva ➤, Hungary . . . . **52 C5** 47 5N 20 4 E
Zahamena, Réserve Naturelle Intégrale de △, Madag. . . . . **117 B8** 17 37 S 48 49 E
Zāhedān, Fārs, Iran . . . . **97 D7** 28 46N 53 52 E
Zāhedān, Sīstān va Balūchestān, Iran **97 D9** 29 30N 60 50 E
Zahirabad, India . . . . **103 B4** 33 52N 35 50 E
Zahlah, Lebanon . . . . **103 B4** 33 52N 35 50 E
Zahna, Germany . . . . **30 D8** 51 55N 12 49 E
Záhony, Hungary . . . . **52 B7** 48 25N 22 11 E
Zahrān, Si. Arabia . . . . **98 C3** 17 40N 43 30 E
Zainsk, Russia . . . . **60 C11** 55 18N 52 4 E
Zaïre = Congo ➤, Africa . . . . **115 D2** 6 4 S 12 24 E
Zaïre □, Angola . . . . **115 D2** 7 0 S 14 0 E
Zaječar, Serbia, Yug. . . . . **50 C6** 43 53N 22 18 E
Zaka, Zimbabwe . . . . **117 C5** 20 20 S 31 29 E
Zakamensk, Russia . . . . **67 D11** 50 23N 103 17 E
Zakani, Dem. Rep. of the Congo . . **114 B4** 2 33N 23 16 E
Zakataly = Zaqatala, Azerbaijan . . **61 K8** 41 38N 46 35 E
Zakbayemé, Cameroon . . . . **114 B2** 4 2N 10 34 E
Zakhāro, Greece . . . . **48 D3** 37 31N 21 39 E
Zakhodnaya Dzvina = Daugava ➤, Latvia . . . . **15 H21** 57 4N 24 3 E
Zākhū, Iraq . . . . **101 D10** 37 10N 42 50 E
Zákinthos, Greece . . . . **39 D2** 37 47N 20 54 E
Zákinthos □, Greece . . . . **48 D2** 37 47N 20 57 E
Zákinthos ✈ (ZTH), Greece . . . . . **39 D2** 37 45N 20 50 E
Zakopane, Poland . . . . **55 J6** 49 18N 19 57 E
Zakouma, Chad . . . . **109 F3** 10 54N 19 49 E
Zakouma, Parc Nat. de △, Chad . . **109 F3** 10 52N 19 45 E
Zakroczym, Poland . . . . **55 F7** 52 26N 20 38 E
Zákros, Greece . . . . **39 E7** 35 6N 26 10 E
Zala, Angola . . . . **115 D2** 7 52 S 13 42 E
Zala, Ethiopia . . . . **107 F4** 6 28N 37 13 E
Zala □, Hungary . . . . **52 D1** 46 42N 16 50 E
Zala ➤, Hungary . . . . **52 D2** 46 43N 17 16 E
Zalaegerszeg, Hungary . . . . **52 D1** 46 53N 16 47 E
Zalakomár, Hungary . . . . **52 D2** 46 33N 17 10 E
Zalalövő, Hungary . . . . **52 D1** 46 51N 16 35 E
Zalamea de la Serena, Spain **43 G5** 38 40N 5 38W
Zalamea la Real, Spain **43 H4** 37 41N 6 38W
Zalău, Romania . . . . **52 C4** 47 12N 23 3 E
Zalazna, Russia . . . . **64 B4** 58 39N 52 31 E
Zalec, Slovenia . . . . **45 B12** 46 16N 15 10 E
Zaleshchiki = Zalishchyky, Ukraine **59 H3** 48 45N 25 45 E
Zalew Wiślany, Poland . . . . **54 D6** 54 20N 19 50 E
Zalewo, Poland . . . . **54 E6** 53 50N 19 41 E
Zalīm, Si. Arabia . . . . **98 B3** 22 43N 42 10 E
Zalingei, Sudan . . . . **109 F4** 12 51N 23 29 E
Zalṭan, Ajdābiyā, Libya . . . . **108 C3** 28 10N 19 35 E
Zalṭan, Zuwārah, Libya . . . . **108 B2** 32 57N 11 52 E
Zalṭan, Jabal, Libya . . . . **108 C3** 28 46N 19 45 E
Zalun, Burma . . . . **90 G5** 17 29N 95 34 E
Zama L., Canada **142 B5** 58 45N 119 5W
Zambeke, Dem. Rep. of the Congo . **118 B2** 2 8N 25 17 E
Zambeze ➤, Africa . . . . **119 F4** 18 35 S 36 20 E
Zambezi = Zambeze ➤, Africa . . . **119 F4** 18 35 S 36 20 E
Zambezi, Zambia . . . . **115 E4** 13 30 S 23 15 E
Zambezi Nat. Park △, Zimbabwe . . **119 F2** 17 54 S 25 41 E
Zambézia □, Mozam. . . . . **119 F4** 16 15 S 37 30 E
Zambia ■, Africa . . . . **119 F2** 15 0 S 28 0 E
Zamboanga, Phil. . . . . **81 H4** 6 59N 122 3 E
Zamboanga del Norte □, Phil. . . . . **81 H4** 8 0N 123 0 E
Zamboanga del Sur □, Phil. . . . . . **81 H4** 7 40N 123 0 E
Zambrano, Colombia **168 B3** 9 45N 74 49W
Zambrów, Poland . . . . **55 F9** 52 59N 22 14 E
Zametchino, Russia . . . . **60 D7** 53 30N 42 30 E
Zamfara □, Nigeria . . . . **113 C6** 12 10N 6 0 E
Zamfara ➤, Nigeria . . . . **113 C5** 12 6N 4 2 E
Zamora, Ecuador . . . . **168 D2** 4 4 S 78 58W
Zamora, Mexico **162 D4** 20 0N 102 21W
Zamora, Spain **42 D5** 41 30N 5 45W
Zamora □, Spain **42 D5** 41 30N 5 46W
Zamora ➤, Ecuador **168 D2** 2 59N 78 13W
Zamora-Chinchipe □, Ecuador . . . **168 D2** 4 15 S 78 50W

Zamość, Poland .... **55 H10** 50 43N 23 15 E
Zams, Austria .... **33 B11** 47 9N 10 35 E
Zamtang, China .... **76 A3** 32 26N 101 6 E
Zamuro, Sierra del, Venezuela .. **169 C5** 4 0N 62 30W
Zamzam, W. →, Libya .... **108 B2** 30 58N 14 48 E
Zan, Ghana **113 D4** 9 26N 0 17W
Zanaga, Congo .... **114 C2** 2 48 S 13 48 E
Záncara →, Spain **41 F1** 39 18N 3 18W
Zanderij, Suriname **169 B6** 5 20N 55 16W
Zandu, Dem. Rep. of the Congo . **115 D3** 5 11 S 18 16 E
Zandvoort, Neths. .... **24 B4** 52 22N 4 32 E
Zanesville, U.S.A. **156 G2** 39 56N 82 1W
Zangābād, Iran .... **96 B5** 38 26N 46 44 E
Zangue →, Mozam. .... **119 F4** 17 50 S 35 21 E
Zanjān, Iran .... **97 B6** 36 40N 48 35 E
Zanjān □, Iran .... **97 B6** 37 20N 49 30 E
Zanjān →, Iran .... **97 B6** 37 8N 47 47 E
Zannone, Italy .... **46 B6** 40 58N 13 3 E
Zante = Zákinthos, Greece ...... **39 D2** 37 47N 20 54 E
Zanthus, Australia .... **125 F3** 31 2 S 123 34 E
Zanzibar, Tanzania .... **118 D4** 6 12 S 39 12 E
Zanzūr, Libya .... **108 B2** 32 55N 13 1 E
Zaouatallaz, Algeria .... **111 D6** 24 52N 8 26 E
Zaouiet El-Kala = Bordj Omar Driss,
  Algeria .... **111 C6** 28 10N 6 40 E
Zaouiet Reggâne, Algeria .... **111 C5** 26 32N 0 3 E
Zaoyang, China .... **77 A9** 32 10N 112 45 E
Zaozhuang, China .... **75 G9** 34 50N 117 35 E
Zap Suyu = Zāb al Kabīr →, Iraq **101 D10** 36 1N 43 24 E
Zapadna Morava →, Serbia, Yug. **50 C5** 43 38N 21 30 E
Zapadnaya Dvina = Daugava →,
  Latvia .... **15 H21** 57 4N 24 3 E
Zapadnaya Dvina, Russia .... **58 D7** 56 15N 32 3 E
Západné Beskydy, Europe .... **35 B12** 49 30N 19 0 E
Západní Rodopi, Bulgaria .... **50 E7** 41 50N 24 0 E
Západočeský □, Czech Rep. ...... **34 B6** 49 35N 13 0 E
Zapala, Argentina .... **176 A2** 39 0 S 70 5W
Zapaleri, Cerro, Bolivia .... **174 A2** 22 49 S 67 11W
Zapata, U.S.A. **155 M5** 26 55N 99 16W
Zapatón →, Spain **43 F4** 39 0N 6 49W
Zapiga, Chile .... **172 D4** 19 40 S 69 55W
Zapolyarnyy, Russia .... **56 A5** 69 26N 30 51 E
Zaporizhzhya, Ukraine .... **59 J8** 47 50N 35 10 E
Zaporozhye = Zaporizhzhya,
  Ukraine .... **59 J8** 47 50N 35 10 E
Zaqatala, Azerbaijan .... **61 K8** 41 38N 46 35 E
Zara, Turkey .... **100 C7** 39 58N 37 43 E
Zarafshon, Uzbekistan .... **68 B3** 41 34N 64 12 E
Zaragoza, Colombia **168 B3** 7 30N 74 52W
Zaragoza, Coahuila, Mexico **162 B4** 28 30N 101 0W
Zaragoza, Nuevo León, Mexico ... **163 C5** 24 0N 99 46W
Zaragoza, Spain **40 A4** 41 39N 0 53W
Zaragoza □, Spain **40 A4** 41 35N 1 0W
Zarand, Kermān, Iran .... **97 D8** 30 46N 56 34 E
Zarand, Markazī, Iran .... **97 C6** 35 18N 50 25 E
Zărandului, Munţii, Romania .... **52 D7** 46 14N 22 7 E
Zaranj, Afghan. .... **91 C1** 30 55N 61 55 E
Zarasai, Lithuania .... **15 J22** 55 40N 26 20 E
Zárate, Argentina .... **174 C4** 34 7 S 59 0W
Zarautz, Spain **40 B2** 43 17N 2 10W
Zaraysk, Russia .... **58 E10** 54 48N 38 53 E
Zaraza, Venezuela **169 B4** 9 21N 65 19W
Zarbdar, Uzbekistan .... **65 C4** 40 3N 68 10 E
Zard, Kūh-e, Iran .... **97 C6** 32 22N 50 4 E
Zâreh, Iran .... **97 C6** 35 7N 49 9 E
Zari, Nigeria .... **113 C7** 13 4N 12 45 E
Zaria, Nigeria .... **113 C6** 11 0N 7 40 E
Zarki, Poland .... **55 H6** 50 38N 19 23 E
Zarkon, Greece .... **48 B4** 39 38N 22 6 E
Zarneh, Iran .... **96 C5** 33 55N 46 10 E
Zărneşti, Romania .... **53 E10** 45 33N 25 18 E
Zarós, Greece .... **39 E5** 35 8N 24 54 E
Zarów, Poland .... **55 H3** 50 56N 16 29 E
Zarqā', Nahr az →, Jordan ..... **103 C4** 32 10N 35 37 E
Zarrīn, Iran .... **97 C7** 32 46N 54 37 E
Zaruma, Ecuador .... **168 D2** 3 40 S 79 38W
Zary, Poland .... **55 G2** 51 37N 15 10 E
Zarza de Granadilla, Spain **42 E4** 40 14N 6 3W
Zarzaïtine, Algeria .... **111 C6** 28 15N 9 34 E
Zarzal, Colombia **168 C2** 4 24N 76 4W
Zarzis, Tunisia .... **108 B2** 33 31N 11 2 E
Zas, Spain **42 B2** 43 4N 8 53W
Zaskar →, India .... **93 B7** 34 13N 77 20 E
Zaskar Mts., India .... **93 C7** 33 15N 77 30 E
Zastron, S. Africa .... **116 E4** 30 18 S 27 7 E
Zatec, Czech Rep. .... **34 A6** 50 20N 13 32 E
Zaterechnyy, Russia .... **61 H7** 44 48N 45 11 E
Zator, Poland .... **55 J6** 49 59N 19 28 E
Zavala, Bos.-H. .... **50 D1** 42 50N 17 59 E
Zavǎreh, Iran .... **97 C7** 33 29N 52 28 E
Zave, Zimbabwe .... **117 B5** 17 6 S 30 1 E
Zavérdhas, Kólpos, Greece .... **39 B2** 38 47N 20 51 E
Zavetnoye, Russia .... **61 G6** 47 13N 43 50 E
Zavidovići, Bos.-H. .... **52 F3** 44 27N 18 10 E
Zavitinsk, Russia .... **67 D13** 50 10N 129 20 E
Zavodovski, I., Antarctica .... **7 B1** 56 0 S 27 45W
Zavolzhsk, Russia .... **60 B6** 57 30N 42 0 E
Zavolzhye, Russia .... **60 B6** 56 37N 43 26 E
Zawadzkie, Poland .... **55 H5** 50 37N 18 28 E
Zawichost, Poland .... **55 H8** 50 48N 21 51 E
Zawidów, Poland .... **55 G2** 51 1N 15 1 E
Zawiercie, Poland .... **55 H6** 50 30N 19 24 E
Zāwiyat al Baydā = Al Baydā, Libya **108 B4** 32 50N 21 44 E
Zāwiyat Masūs, Libya .... **108 B4** 31 35N 21 1 E
Zâwyet Shammas, Egypt .... **106 A2** 31 30N 26 37 E
Zâwyet Um el Rakham, Egypt ... **106 A2** 31 18N 27 1 E
Zâwyet Ungeîla, Egypt .... **106 A2** 31 23N 26 42 E
Zäyä, Iraq .... **96 C5** 33 33N 44 13 E
Zâyandeh →, Iran .... **97 C7** 32 35N 52 0 E
Zaymah, Si. Arabia .... **98 B3** 21 37N 40 6 E
Zaysan, Kazakhstan .... **66 E9** 47 28N 84 52 E
Zaysan, Oz., Kazakhstan .... **66 E9** 48 0N 83 0 E
Zayū, China .... **76 C1** 28 48N 97 27 E
Zazafotsy, Madag. .... **117 C8** 21 11 S 46 21 E
Zãzamt, W. →, Libya .... **108 B2** 30 29N 14 30 E
Zazir, O. →, Algeria .... **111 D6** 22 0N 5 40 E
Zázrivá, Slovak Rep. .... **35 B12** 49 16N 19 7 E
Zbarazh, Ukraine .... **59 H3** 49 43N 25 44 E
Zbąszyń, Poland .... **55 F2** 52 14N 15 56 E
Zbąszynek, Poland .... **55 F2** 52 16N 15 51 E
Zblewo, Poland .... **54 E5** 53 56N 18 19 E
Žďár nad Sázavou, Czech Rep. .. **34 B8** 49 34N 15 57 E
Zdolbuniv, Ukraine .... **59 G4** 50 30N 26 15 E
Zdrelo, Serbia, Yug. .... **50 B5** 44 16N 21 28 E
Zduńska Wola, Poland .... **55 G5** 51 37N 18 59 E
Zduny, Poland .... **55 G4** 51 39N 17 21 E
Zearing, U.S.A. **156 B3** 42 10N 93 18W
Żebâk, Afghan. .... **65 E5** 36 31N 71 20 E
Zeballos, Canada **142 D3** 49 59N 126 50W
Zebbug, Malta .... **38 F7** 35 52N 14 26 E
Zebbug, Gozo, Malta .... **38 E6** 36 4N 14 14 E
Zebediela, S. Africa .... **117 C4** 24 20 S 29 17 E
Zebila, Ghana **113 C4** 10 59N 0 30W
Zebulon, U.S.A. **152 B5** 33 6N 84 21W
Zeebrugge, Belgium .... **24 C3** 51 19N 3 12 E
Zeehan, Australia .... **127 G4** 41 52 S 145 25 E
Zeeland, U.S.A. **157 B10** 42 49N 86 1W
Zeeland □, Neths. .... **24 C3** 51 30N 3 50 E
Zeerust, S. Africa .... **116 D4** 25 31 S 26 4 E
Zefat, Israel .... **103 C4** 32 58N 35 29 E
Zegdou, Algeria **110 C4** 29 51N 4 45W
Zege, Ethiopia .... **107 E4** 11 43N 37 18 E
Zeggerene, Iracher, Mali .... **113 B5** 16 49N 2 16 E

Zégoua, Mali **112 C3** 10 32N 5 35W
Zehdenick, Germany .... **30 C9** 52 58N 13 20 E
Zeigler, U.S.A. **156 G7** 37 54N 89 3W
Zeil, Mt., Australia .... **124 D5** 23 30 S 132 23 E
Zeila, Somali Rep. .... **120 B2** 11 21N 43 30 E
Zeist, Neths. .... **24 B5** 52 5N 5 15 E
Zejtun, Malta .... **38 F8** 35 51N 14 32 E
Żelechów, Poland .... **55 G8** 51 49N 21 54 E
Zelenogora, Bos.-H. .... **50 C2** 43 22N 18 30 E
Zelenodolsk, Russia .... **60 C9** 55 55N 48 30 E
Zelenogorsk, Russia .... **58 B5** 60 12N 29 43 E
Zelenogradsk, Russia .... **58 D9** 54 53N 20 29 E
Zelenokumsk, Russia .... **15 J19** 54 53N 20 29 E
Zelenokumsk, Russia .... **61 H6** 44 24N 44 0 E
Železná Ruda, Czech Rep. .... **34 B6** 49 8N 13 15 E
Železnik, Serbia, Yug. .... **50 B4** 44 43N 20 23 E
Zelfana, Algeria .... **111 B5** 32 27N 4 15 E
Zelienople, U.S.A. **150 F4** 40 48N 80 8W
Żeliezovce, Slovak Rep. .... **35 C11** 48 3N 18 40 E
Zelina, Croatia .... **45 C13** 45 57N 16 16 E
Zell, Baden-W., Germany .... **31 H3** 47 42N 7 52 E
Zell, Rhld-Pfz., Germany .... **31 E3** 50 1N 7 10 E
Zell am See, Austria .... **34 D5** 47 19N 12 47 E
Zella-Mehlis, Germany .... **30 E6** 50 39N 10 40 E
Zellersee, Germany .... **33 A8** 47 45N 9 12 E
Zelów, Poland .... **55 G6** 51 28N 19 14 E
Zeltweg, Austria .... **34 D7** 47 11N 14 45 E
Żemaitijos Nac. Parkas △, Lithuania **54 B8** 56 2N 21 55 E
Zembra, I., Tunisia .... **108 A2** 37 5N 10 56 E
Zemgale = Jelgava, Latvia ...... **15 H20** 56 41N 23 49 E
Zémio, C.A.R. .... **118 A2** 5 2N 25 5 E
Zemmora, Algeria .... **111 A5** 35 44N 0 51 E
Zemmur, W. Sahara **110 C2** 25 5N 12 0W
Zemongo, Réserve de Faune de △,
  C.A.R. .... **114 A5** 6 45N 25 5 E
Zemoul, O. →, Algeria **110 C3** 29 15N 7 0W
Zempléni-hegység, Hungary ...... **52 B6** 48 25N 21 25 E
Zemplínska šírava, Slovak Rep. ... **35 C15** 48 48N 22 0 E
Zempoala, Mexico **163 D5** 19 22N 96 24W
Zemun, Serbia, Yug. .... **50 B4** 44 51N 20 25 E
Zenda, Spain .... **40 A4** 41 39N 1 47 E
Zenden Jân, Afghan. .... **91 B1** 34 21N 61 45 E
Zengbé, Cameroon .... **113 D7** 5 46N 13 4 E
Zengcheng, China .... **77 F9** 23 13N 113 52 E
Zenica, Bos.-H. .... **52 F2** 44 10N 17 57 E
Zentsūji, Japan .... **72 C5** 34 14N 133 47 E
Zenza do Itombe, Angola .... **115 D2** 9 16 S 14 13 E
Zepce, Bos.-H. .... **52 F3** 44 28N 18 2 E
Zephyrhills, U.S.A. **153 G7** 28 14N 82 11W
Zepu, China .... **65 D8** 38 12N 77 18 E
Zeraf, Bahr ez →, Sudan .... **107 F3** 9 42N 30 52 E
Zeravshan, Tajikistan .... **65 D3** 39 10N 68 39 E
Zeravshan →, Asia .... **65 D1** 39 22N 63 45 E
Zeravshanskiy Khrebet, Tajikistan . **65 D4** 39 0N 70 0 E
Zerbst, Germany .... **30 D8** 51 58N 12 5 E
Zerków, Poland .... **55 F4** 52 4N 17 32 E
Zermatt, Switz. .... **32 D5** 46 2N 7 46 E
Zernez, Switz. .... **33 C10** 46 42N 10 7 E
Zernograd, Russia .... **61 G5** 46 52N 40 19 E
Zerqan, Albania .... **50 E4** 41 27N 20 20 E
Zestaponi, Georgia .... **61 J6** 42 6N 43 0 E
Zetel, Germany .... **30 B3** 53 25N 7 58 E
Zeulenroda, Germany .... **30 E7** 50 39N 11 59 E
Zeven, Germany .... **30 B5** 53 17N 9 16 E
Zevenaar, Neths. .... **24 C6** 51 56N 6 5 E
Zévio, Italy .... **44 C8** 45 22N 11 8 E
Zeya, Russia .... **67 D13** 53 48N 127 14 E
Zeya →, Russia .... **67 D13** 51 42N 128 53 E
Zeytinbaği, Turkey .... **51 F12** 40 24N 28 47 E
Zeytindağ, Turkey .... **47 C9** 38 58N 27 4 E
Zghartā, Lebanon .... **103 A4** 34 21N 35 53 E
Zgierz, Poland .... **55 G6** 51 50N 19 27 E
Zgorzelec, Poland .... **55 G2** 51 10N 15 0 E
Zguriţa, Moldova .... **53 B13** 48 8N 28 1 E
Zhabasak, Kazakhstan .... **64 F8** 50 22N 61 41 E
Zhabinka, Belarus .... **59 F3** 52 13N 24 2 E
Zhailma, Kazakhstan .... **64 F8** 51 37N 61 33 E
Zhalanash, Kazakhstan .... **65 B9** 43 38N 78 38 E
Zhambyl = Taraz, Kazakhstan .... **65 B5** 42 54N 71 22 E
Zhanatas, Kazakhstan .... **65 B4** 43 35N 69 35 E
Zhangaly, Kazakhstan .... **61 G10** 47 1N 50 37 E
Zhangaqazaly, Kazakhstan .... **66 E7** 45 48N 62 6 E
Zhangaqūrghan, Kazakhstan ..... **65 B4** 43 50N 68 48 E
Zhangatas = Zhanatas, Kazakhstan **65 B4** 43 35N 69 35 E
Zhangbei, China .... **74 D8** 41 10N 114 45 E
Zhangguangcai Ling, China ...... **75 B15** 45 0N 129 0 E
Zhangjiaban, China .... **69 F9** 22 33N 113 28 E
Zhangjiakou, China .... **74 D8** 40 48N 114 55 E
Zhangping, China .... **77 E11** 25 17N 117 23 E
Zhangpu, China .... **77 E11** 24 8N 117 35 E
Zhangshu, China .... **77 C10** 28 1N 115 29 E
Zhangwu, China .... **75 C12** 42 43N 123 52 E
Zhangye, China .... **68 C5** 38 50N 100 23 E
Zhangzhou, China .... **77 F10** 24 30N 117 35 E
Zhanhua, China .... **75 F10** 37 40N 118 8 E
Zhanjiang, China .... **77 G8** 21 15N 110 20 E
Zhannetty, Ostrov, Russia .... **67 B16** 76 43N 158 0 E
Zhanyi, China .... **76 E4** 25 38N 103 48 E
Zhanyu, China .... **75 B12** 44 30N 122 30 E
Zhao Xian, China .... **74 F8** 37 43N 114 45 E
Zhao'an, China .... **77 F11** 23 41N 117 10 E
Zhaocheng, China .... **74 F6** 36 22N 111 38 E
Zhaojue, China .... **76 C4** 28 1N 102 49 E
Zhaoqing, China .... **77 F8** 24 11N 100 48 E
Zhaotong, China .... **76 D4** 27 20N 103 44 E
Zhaoyuan, Heilongjiang, China ... **75 B13** 45 27N 125 0 E
Zhaoyuan, Shandong, China ..... **75 F11** 37 20N 120 23 E
Zharkovskiy, Russia .... **58 E7** 55 56N 32 19 E
Zhashkiv, Ukraine .... **59 H6** 49 15N 30 5 E
Zhashui, China .... **74 H5** 33 40N 109 8 E
Zhayyq →, Kazakhstan .... **57 E9** 47 0N 51 48 E
Zhdanov = Mariupol, Ukraine ... **59 J9** 47 5N 37 31 E
Zhdanovo, Kazakhstan .... **65 B3** 43 40N 71 6 E
Zhecheng, China .... **74 G8** 34 7N 115 20 E
Zhegao, China .... **77 B11** 31 46N 117 45 E
Zhejiang □, China .... **77 C13** 29 0N 120 0 E
Zheleznodorozhnyy, Russia ...... **58 B9** 62 35N 50 55 E
Zheleznogorsk, Russia .... **59 F8** 52 22N 35 23 E
Zheleznogorsk-Ilimskiy, Russia ... **67 D11** 56 34N 104 8 E
Zheltyye Vody = Zhovti Vody,
  Ukraine .... **59 H7** 48 21N 33 31 E
Zhen'an, China .... **74 H5** 33 27N 109 9 E
Zhenba, China .... **74 A6** 32 34N 107 58 E
Zhenfeng, China .... **76 E5** 25 22N 105 40 E
Zheng'an, China .... **76 C6** 28 32N 107 27 E
Zhengding, China .... **74 E8** 38 8N 114 32 E
Zhenghe, China .... **77 D12** 27 20N 118 50 E
Zhengyang, China .... **77 A10** 32 37N 114 22 E
Zhengyangguan, China .... **77 A11** 32 30N 116 29 E
Zhengzhou, China .... **74 G7** 34 45N 113 34 E
Zhenhai, China .... **77 C13** 29 59N 121 42 E
Zhenjiang, China .... **77 A12** 32 11N 119 26 E
Zhenkang, China .... **76 F2** 23 58N 99 0 E
Zhenlai, China .... **75 B12** 45 50N 123 5 E
Zhenning, China .... **76 D5** 26 4N 105 45 E
Zhenping, Henan, China .... **74 H7** 33 10N 112 16 E
Zhenping, Shaanxi, China .... **76 B7** 31 54N 109 31 E
Zhenxiong, China .... **76 D5** 27 27N 104 50 E
Zhenyuan, Gansu, China .... **74 G4** 35 35N 107 30 E
Zhenyuan, Guizhou, China ...... **76 D7** 27 4N 108 21 E

Zherdevka, Russia .... **60 E5** 51 56N 41 29 E
Zherong, China .... **77 D12** 27 15N 119 52 E
Zhetigen, Kazakhstan .... **65 B8** 43 40N 77 6 E
Zhetiqara, Kazakhstan .... **64 E8** 52 11N 61 12 E
Zhetisay, Kazakhstan .... **65 C4** 40 46N 68 19 E
Zhezqazghan, Kazakhstan .... **66 E7** 47 44N 67 40 E
Zhicheng, China .... **77 B8** 30 25N 111 27 E
Zhidan, China .... **74 F5** 36 48N 108 48 E
Zhigansk, Russia .... **67 C13** 66 48N 123 27 E
Zhigulevsk, Russia .... **60 D9** 53 28N 49 30 E
Zhijiang, Hubei, China .... **77 B8** 30 28N 111 45 E
Zhijiang, Hunan, China .... **76 D7** 27 27N 109 42 E
Zhijin, China .... **76 D5** 26 38N 105 45 E
Zhilinda, Russia .... **67 C12** 70 0N 114 20 E
Zhirnovsk, Russia .... **60 E7** 50 57N 44 49 E
Zhitomir = Zhytomyr, Ukraine ... **59 G5** 50 20N 28 40 E
Zhizdra, Russia .... **58 F8** 53 45N 34 40 E
Zhlobin, Belarus .... **59 F6** 52 55N 30 0 E
Zhmerinka = Zhmerynka, Ukraine . **59 H5** 49 2N 28 2 E
Zhmerynka, Ukraine .... **59 H5** 49 2N 28 2 E
Zhob, Pakistan .... **91 C3** 31 20N 69 31 E
Zhob →, Pakistan .... **92 C3** 32 4N 69 50 E
Zhodino = Zhodzina, Belarus .... **58 E5** 54 5N 28 17 E
Zhodzina, Belarus .... **58 E5** 54 5N 28 17 E
Zhokhova, Ostrov, Russia .... **67 B16** 76 4N 152 40 E
Zhongdian, China .... **76 D2** 27 48N 99 42 E
Zhongdong, China .... **76 F6** 22 48N 107 47 E
Zhongdu, China .... **76 E7** 24 40N 109 40 E
Zhongning, China .... **74 F3** 37 29N 105 40 E
Zhongshan, Guangdong, China ... **77 F9** 22 26N 113 20 E
Zhongshan, Guangxi Zhuangzu,
  China .... **77 E8** 24 29N 111 18 E
Zhongshankong, China .... **77 E9** 24 22N 111 18 E
Zhongtiao Shan, China .... **74 G6** 35 0N 111 10 E
Zhongwei, China .... **74 F3** 37 30N 105 12 E
Zhongxiang, China .... **77 B9** 31 12N 112 34 E
Zhongyang, China .... **74 F6** 37 20N 111 11 E
Zhoucun, China .... **75 F9** 36 47N 117 48 E
Zhouning, China .... **77 D12** 27 12N 119 20 E
Zhoushan, China .... **77 B14** 30 1N 122 10 E
Zhoushan Dao, China .... **77 C14** 30 5N 122 10 E
Zhouzhi, China .... **74 G5** 34 10N 108 12 E
Zhovti Vody, Ukraine .... **59 H7** 48 21N 33 31 E
Zhovtnevoye, Russia .... **59 J7** 46 54N 32 3 E
Zhovtnevoye = Zhovtneve, Ukraine **59 J7** 46 54N 32 3 E
Zhu Jiang →, China .... **77 F9** 22 15N 113 37 E
Zhuanghe, China .... **75 E12** 39 40N 123 0 E
Zhūbantóbe, Kazakhstan .... **65 A4** 44 46N 68 49 E
Zhucheng, China .... **75 G10** 36 0N 119 27 E
Zhugqu, China .... **74 H3** 33 40N 104 30 E
Zhuhai, China .... **77 F9** 22 17N 113 34 E
Zhuji, China .... **77 C13** 29 40N 120 10 E
Zhujiang Kou, China .... **69 G10** 22 20N 113 45 E
Zhukovka, Russia .... **58 F7** 53 35N 33 50 E
Zhumadian, China .... **74 H8** 32 59N 114 2 E
Zhuo Xian = Zhuozhou, China ... **74 E8** 39 28N 115 58 E
Zhuolu, China .... **74 D8** 40 20N 115 12 E
Zhuozhou, China .... **74 E8** 39 28N 115 58 E
Zhuozi, China .... **74 D7** 41 0N 112 25 E
Zhushan, China .... **77 A8** 32 15N 110 13 E
Zhuxi, China .... **76 A7** 32 25N 109 40 E
Zhuzhou, China .... **77 D9** 27 49N 113 12 E
Zhytomyr, Ukraine .... **59 G5** 50 20N 28 40 E
Zi Shui →, China .... **77 C9** 28 40N 112 40 E
Žiar nad Hronom, Slovak Rep. ... **35 C11** 48 35N 18 50 E
Ziārān, Iran .... **97 B6** 36 7N 50 32 E
Ziarat, Pakistan .... **92 D2** 30 25N 67 49 E
Zibo, China .... **75 F10** 36 47N 118 3 E
Zichang, China .... **74 F5** 37 18N 109 40 E
Zidarovo, Bulgaria .... **51 D11** 42 20N 27 24 E
Zidi = Wandhari, Pakistan ...... **92 F2** 27 42N 66 48 E
Ziębice, Poland .... **55 H4** 50 37N 17 2 E
Zielona Góra, Poland .... **55 G2** 51 57N 15 31 E
Zierikzee, Neths. .... **24 C3** 51 40N 3 55 E
Ziesar, Germany .... **30 C8** 52 16N 12 17 E
Zifta, Egypt .... **106 H7** 30 43N 31 14 E
Zigey, Chad .... **109 F3** 14 43N 15 50 E
Zigon, Burma .... **93 L19** 18 0N 95 37 E
Zigong, China .... **76 C5** 29 15N 104 48 E
Ziguinchor, Senegal **112 C1** 12 35N 16 20W
Zihuatanejo, Mexico **162 D4** 17 38N 101 33W
Zijin, China .... **77 F10** 23 33N 115 8 E
Zile, Turkey .... **100 B6** 40 15N 35 52 E
Zilina, Slovak Rep. .... **35 B11** 49 12N 18 42 E
Žilinský □, Slovak Rep. .... **35 B12** 49 10N 19 0 E
Zillah, Libya .... **108 C3** 28 30N 17 33 E
Zillertaler Alpen, Austria .... **34 D4** 47 0N 11 45 E
Zima, Russia .... **67 D11** 54 0N 102 5 E
Zimane, Adrar in, Algeria .... **111 D5** 22 10N 4 30 E
Zimapán, Mexico **163 C5** 20 54N 99 20W
Zimba, Zambia .... **117 F2** 17 20 S 26 11 E
Zimbabwe, Zimbabwe .... **119 G3** 20 16 S 30 54 E
Zimbabwe ■, Africa .... **117 F3** 19 0 S 30 0 E
Zimi, S. Leone **112 D2** 7 20N 11 20W
Zimnicea, Romania .... **53 G10** 43 40N 25 22 E
Zimovniki, Russia .... **61 G6** 47 10N 42 25 E
Zina, Cent. Amer. .... **109 F2** 11 19N 14 54 E
Zinal, Switz. .... **32 D5** 46 8N 7 38 E
Zinave, Parque Nac. de △, Mozam. **117 C5** 21 35 S 33 40 E
Zinder, Niger .... **113 C6** 13 48 S 9 0 E
Zinga, C.A.R. .... **114 B3** 3 49N 18 34 E
Zinga, Tanzania .... **119 D4** 9 16 S 38 49 E
Zingaro, Riserva Naturale dello △,
  Italy .... **46 D5** 38 6N 12 53 E
Zingst, Germany .... **30 A8** 54 26N 12 39 E
Ziniaré, Burkina Faso **113 C4** 12 35N 1 18W
Zinnowitz, Germany .... **30 A9** 54 4N 13 54 E
Zinovyevsk = Kirovohrad, Ukraine . **59 H7** 48 35N 32 20 E
Zion, U.S.A. **157 B9** 42 27N 87 50W
Zion Nat. Park △, U.S.A. **159 H7** 37 15N 113 5W
Zionsville, U.S.A. **157 E10** 39 57N 86 16W
Zipaquirá, Colombia **168 C3** 5 0N 74 0W
Zirbitzkogel, Austria .... **34 D7** 47 4N 14 34 E
Zirc, Hungary .... **42 C2** 47 17N 17 52 E
Žiri, Slovenia .... **45 B11** 46 5N 14 5 E
Zirje, Croatia .... **45 E12** 43 39N 15 42 E
Zirl, Austria .... **34 D4** 47 17N 11 14 E
Zirndorf, Germany .... **31 F6** 49 27N 10 57 E
Ziros, Greece .... **39 E7** 35 5N 26 8 E
Zirreh, Gowd-e, Afghan. .... **91 C1** 29 45N 62 0 E
Zistersdorf, Austria .... **35 C9** 48 33N 16 45 E
Zitácuaro, Mexico **162 D4** 19 28N 100 21W
Zitava →, Slovak Rep. .... **35 C11** 48 14N 18 21 E
Zitište, Serbia, Yug. .... **52 E5** 45 30N 20 32 E
Zitong, China .... **76 B5** 31 37N 105 10 E
Zitsa, Greece .... **48 B2** 39 47N 20 40 E
Zittau, Germany .... **30 E10** 50 53N 14 48 E
Zitundo, Mozam. .... **117 D5** 26 48 S 32 47 E
Živinice, Bos.-H. .... **52 F4** 44 27N 18 48 E
Ziwa Magharibi □, Tanzania .... **118 C3** 2 0 S 31 30 E
Ziway, L., Ethiopia .... **107 F4** 8 0N 38 50 E
Zixi, China .... **77 D11** 27 45N 117 4 E
Zixing, China .... **77 D9** 25 58N 113 30 E
Ziyang, Shaanxi, China .... **74 H5** 32 32N 108 31 E
Ziyang, Sichuan, China .... **76 B5** 30 2N 104 38 E
Ziyuan, China .... **77 D8** 26 0N 110 40 E
Ziyun, China .... **76 E6** 25 45N 106 28 E
Ziz, Oued →, Morocco **110 B4** 31 40N 4 15W
Zizhong, China .... **76 B5** 29 48N 104 47 E
Zlarin, Croatia .... **45 E12** 43 42N 15 49 E
Zlatar, Croatia .... **45 B13** 46 5N 16 3 E
Zlatar, Serbia, Yug. .... **50 C3** 43 25N 19 47 E
Zlataritsa, Bulgaria .... **51 C9** 43 2N 25 55 E

Zlaté Moravce, Slovak Rep. ...... **35 C11** 48 23N 18 24 E
Zlatibor, Serbia, Yug. .... **50 C3** 43 45N 19 43 E
Zlatitsa, Bulgaria .... **51 D8** 42 41N 24 7 E
Zlatna, Romania .... **53 D8** 46 8N 23 11 E
Zlatna Panega, Bulgaria .... **51 C8** 43 5N 24 9 E
Zlatni Pyasŭti, Bulgaria .... **51 C12** 43 17N 28 3 E
Zlatograd, Bulgaria .... **51 E9** 41 22N 25 7 E
Zlatoust, Russia .... **64 D7** 55 10N 59 40 E
Zletovo, Macedonia .... **50 E6** 41 59N 22 17 E
Zlín, Czech Rep. .... **35 B10** 49 14N 17 40 E
Zlītan, Libya .... **108 B2** 32 32N 14 35 E
Złocieniec, Poland .... **55 B10** 53 30N 16 1 E
Złoczew, Poland .... **55 G5** 51 25N 18 35 E
Zlot, Serbia, Yug. .... **50 B5** 44 1N 21 58 E
Złotoryja, Poland .... **55 G2** 51 8N 15 55 E
Złotów, Poland .... **54 E4** 53 22N 17 2 E
Zmeinogorsk, Kazakhstan .... **66 D9** 51 10N 82 13 E
Żmigród, Poland .... **55 G3** 51 28N 16 55 E
Zmiyev, Ukraine .... **59 H9** 49 39N 36 27 E
Znamenka = Znamyanka, Ukraine . **59 H7** 48 45N 32 30 E
Znamyanka, Ukraine .... **59 H7** 48 45N 32 30 E
Żnin, Poland .... **54 F4** 52 51N 17 44 E
Znojmo, Czech Rep. .... **34 C9** 48 50N 16 2 E
Zobeyrī, Iran .... **96 C5** 34 10N 46 40 E
Zobia, Dem. Rep. of the Congo .. **118 B2** 3 0N 25 59 E
Zoetermeer, Neths. .... **24 B4** 52 3N 4 30 E
Zofingen, Switz. .... **32 B5** 47 17N 7 56 E
Zogang, China .... **76 C1** 29 55N 97 42 E
Zogno, Italy .... **44 C6** 45 48N 9 40 E
Zogqên, China .... **76 A2** 32 13N 98 47 E
Zolfo Springs, U.S.A. **153 H8** 27 30N 81 48W
Zollikofen, Switz. .... **32 C4** 47 0N 7 28 E
Zollikon, Switz. .... **33 B7** 47 21N 8 34 E
Zolochev = Zolochiv, Ukraine .... **59 H3** 49 45N 24 51 E
Zolochiv, Ukraine .... **59 H3** 49 45N 24 51 E
Zolotonosha, Ukraine .... **59 H7** 49 39N 32 5 E
Zomba, Malawi .... **119 F4** 15 22 S 35 19 E
Zongo, Dem. Rep. of the Congo .. **114 B3** 4 20N 18 35 E
Zonguldak, Turkey .... **100 B4** 41 28N 31 50 E
Zongyang, China .... **77 B11** 30 42N 117 12 E
Zonqor Pt., Malta .... **38 F8** 35 52N 14 34 E
Zonza, France .... **29 G13** 41 45N 9 11 E
Zoo Baba, Niger .... **109 E2** 18 13N 13 2 E
Zorgo, Burkina Faso **113 C4** 12 15N 0 35W
Zorita, Spain **43 F5** 39 17N 5 39W
Zorleni, Romania .... **53 D12** 46 14N 27 44 E
Zornitsa, Bulgaria .... **51 D10** 42 23N 26 58 E
Zorritos, Peru .... **172 A1** 3 43 S 80 40W
Zory, Poland .... **55 H5** 50 3N 18 44 E
Zorzor, Liberia **112 D3** 7 46N 9 28W
Zossen, Germany .... **30 C9** 52 13N 13 27 E
Zou Xiang, China .... **74 G9** 35 30N 116 58 E
Zouan-Hounien, Ivory C. **112 D3** 6 55N 8 15W
Zouar, Chad .... **109 D3** 20 30N 16 32 E
Zouérate = Zouîrât, Mauritania .. **110 D2** 22 44N 12 21W
Zouîrât, Mauritania **110 D2** 22 44N 12 21W
Zouri, Gabon .... **114 C1** 1 1 S 8 53 E
Zourika, Niger .... **113 B6** 19 56N 7 52 E
Zourma, Burkina Faso **113 C4** 11 20N 0 50W
Zousfana, O. →, Algeria **111 B4** 31 35N 2 17W
Zoutkamp, Neths. .... **24 B6** 53 20N 6 18 E
Zrenjanin, Serbia, Yug. .... **52 E5** 45 22N 20 23 E
Zuarungu, Ghana **113 C4** 10 49N 0 46W
Zuba, Nigeria .... **113 D6** 9 11N 7 12 E
Zubayr, Yemen .... **98 D3** 15 3N 42 10 E
Zubtsov, Russia .... **58 D8** 56 10N 34 34 E
Zudáñez, Bolivia .... **173 D5** 19 6 S 64 44W
Zuénoula, Ivory C. **112 D3** 7 34N 6 3W
Zuera, Spain **40 D4** 41 51N 0 49W
Zuetina = Az Zuwaytīnah, Libya . **108 B4** 30 58N 20 7 E
Zufār, Oman .... **99 C6** 17 40N 54 0 E
Zug, Switz. .... **33 B7** 47 10N 8 31 E
Zug, W. Sahara **110 D2** 21 36N 14 9W
Zug □, Switz. .... **33 B7** 47 9N 8 35 E
Zugdidi, Georgia .... **61 J5** 42 30N 41 55 E
Zugersee, Switz. .... **33 B7** 47 7N 8 35 E
Zugspitze, Germany .... **31 H6** 47 25N 10 59 E
Zuid-Holland □, Neths. .... **24 C4** 52 0N 4 35 E
Zuidbeveland, Neths. .... **24 C3** 51 30N 3 50 E
Zuidhorn, Neths. .... **24 A6** 53 15N 6 23 E
Zújar, Spain **43 H8** 37 34N 2 50W
Zújar →, Spain **43 G5** 39 1N 5 47W
Zukowo, Poland .... **54 D5** 54 21N 18 22 E
Zula, Eritrea .... **107 D4** 15 17N 39 40 E
Zulia □, Venezuela **168 B3** 10 0N 72 10W
Zülpich, Germany .... **30 E2** 50 41N 6 39 E
Zumaia, Spain **40 B2** 43 19N 2 15W
Zumárraga, Spain **40 B2** 43 5N 2 19W
Zumbo, Mozam. .... **119 F3** 15 35 S 30 26 E
Zummo, Nigeria .... **113 D7** 9 51N 12 59 E
Zumpango, Mexico **163 D5** 19 48N 99 6W
Zundi, Angola .... **115 E3** 10 28 S 16 48 E
Zungeru, Nigeria .... **113 D6** 9 48N 6 8 E
Zunhua, China .... **75 D9** 40 18N 117 58 E
Zuni, U.S.A. **159 J9** 35 4N 108 51W
Zunyi, China .... **76 D6** 27 42N 106 53 E
Zuo Jiang →, China .... **76 F6** 22 50N 108 6 E
Zuozhou, China .... **76 F6** 22 42N 107 27 E
Županja, Croatia .... **52 E3** 45 4N 18 43 E
Žur, Kosovo, Yug. .... **50 D4** 42 13N 20 34 E
Zura, Russia .... **64 C4** 57 36N 53 24 E
Zurbāţīyah, Iraq .... **101 F12** 33 9N 46 3 E
Zürich, Switz. .... **33 B7** 47 22N 8 32 E
Zürich □, Switz. .... **33 B7** 47 26N 8 40 E
Zürich ✕ (ZRH), Switz. .... **33 B7** 47 27N 8 32 E
Zürichsee, Switz. .... **33 B7** 47 18N 8 40 E
Zuromin, Poland .... **55 E6** 53 4N 19 51 E
Zurrieq, Malta .... **38 F8** 35 50N 14 28 E
Zurrach, Switz. .... **33 A6** 47 35N 8 18 E
Žut, Croatia .... **45 E12** 43 52N 15 17 E
Zutphen, Neths. .... **24 B6** 52 9N 6 12 E
Zuurberg Nat. Park △, S. Africa . **116 E4** 33 12 S 25 32 E
Zuwārah, Libya .... **108 B2** 32 58N 12 1 E
Zuyevka, Russia .... **64 B3** 58 27N 51 10 E
Zūzan, Iran .... **97 C8** 34 22N 59 53 E
Žužemberk, Slovenia .... **45 C11** 45 52N 14 56 E
Zvenigorodka = Zvenyhorodka,
  Ukraine .... **59 H6** 49 4N 30 56 E
Zvenyhorodka, Ukraine .... **59 H6** 49 4N 30 56 E
Zverinogolovskoye, Russia .... **66 D7** 54 26N 64 50 E
Zvezdets, Bulgaria .... **51 D11** 42 6N 27 26 E
Zvishavane, Zimbabwe .... **119 G3** 20 17 S 30 2 E
Zvolen, Slovak Rep. .... **35 C12** 48 33N 19 10 E
Zvonce, Serbia, Yug. .... **50 D6** 42 57N 22 34 E
Zvornik, Bos.-H. .... **52 F4** 44 26N 19 5 E
Zwedru = Tchien, Liberia **112 D3** 5 59N 8 15W
Zweibrücken, Germany .... **31 F3** 49 15N 7 21 E
Zweisimmen, Switz. .... **32 D4** 46 33N 7 22 E
Zwenkau, Germany .... **30 D8** 51 13N 12 20 E
Zwettl, Austria .... **34 C8** 48 35N 15 9 E
Zwickau, Germany .... **30 E8** 50 44N 12 30 E
Zwierzyniec, Poland .... **55 H9** 50 36N 22 58 E
Zwiesel, Germany .... **31 F9** 49 1N 13 14 E
Zwoleń, Poland .... **55 G8** 51 21N 21 36 E
Zwolle, Neths. .... **24 B6** 52 31N 6 6 E
Zwolle, U.S.A. **155 K8** 31 38N 93 39W
Zychlin, Poland .... **55 F6** 52 15N 19 37 E
Zyrardów, Poland .... **55 F7** 52 3N 20 28 E
Zyryan, Kazakhstan .... **66 E9** 49 43N 84 20 E
Zyryanka, Russia .... **67 C16** 65 45N 150 51 E
Zyryanovsk = Zyryan, Kazakhstan **66 E9** 49 43N 84 20 E
Żywiec, Poland .... **55 J6** 49 42N 19 10 E

KEY TO EUROPEAN MAP PAGES

11

ICELAND

Arctic Circle

14

19

22

22

23

20

IRELAND

UNITED
KINGDOM

24

NI

26

B

28

FRANCE

42

40

ANDORRA

PORTUGAL

SPAIN

38

MOROCCO

ALG

WORLD COUNTRY INDEX

Afghanistan	91	
Albania	50	
Algeria	110–111	
Angola	115	
Argentina	174, 176	
Armenia	101	
Australia	124–129	
Austria	34–35	
Azerbaijan	101	
Azores	9	
Bahamas	164–165	
Bahrain	99	
Bangladesh	90	
Barbados	165	
Belarus	58–59	
Belgium	24	
Belize	164	
Benin	113	
Bhutan	90	
Bolivia	172–173	
Bosnia-Herzegovina	45, 50	
Botswana	116	
Brazil	168–175	
Brunei	85	
Bulgaria	50–51	
Burkina Faso	112–113	
Burma (Myanmar)	86–87, 90	
Burundi	118	
Cambodia	86–87	
Canary Is.	9	
Cameroon	109, 114	
Canada	138–143	
Cape Verde Is.	9	
Central African Republic	114	
Chad	109	
Chile	172, 174, 176	
China	68–69, 74–77	
Colombia	168	
Comoros	121	
Congo	114–115	
Congo, Dem. Rep.		
of the	114–115, 118–119	
Costa Rica	164	
Croatia	45, 52	
Cuba	164–165	
Cyprus	39	
Czech Republic	34–35	
Denmark	17	
Djibouti	120	
Dominican Republic	165	
Ecuador	168	
Egypt	106	
El Salvador	164	
England	20–21	
Equatorial Guinea	114	
Eritrea	106–107	
Estonia	58	
Ethiopia	107, 120	
Fiji	133	
Finland	14–15	
France	26–29	
French Guiana	169	
Gabon	114	
Gambia	112	
Georgia	101	

Germany	30–31	
Ghana	112–113	
Greece	48–51	
Greenland	10	
Guadeloupe	164	
Guatemala	164	
Guinea	112	
Guinea-Bissau	112	
Guyana	169	
Haiti	165	
Honduras	164	
Hungary	52	
Iceland	11	
India	90, 92–95	
Indonesia	82–85	
Iran	96–97	
Iraq	96–97	
Irish Republic	23	
Israel	103	
Italy	44–47	
Ivory Coast	112	
Jamaica	164	
Japan	70–73	
Jordan	103	
Kazakhstan	65, 66	
Kenya	118	
Korea, North	75	
Korea, South	75	
Kuwait	96–97	
Kyrgyzstan	65	
Laos	86	
Latvia	58	
Lebanon	103	
Lesotho	117	
Liberia	112	
Libya	108	
Lithuania	58	
Luxembourg	24	
Macedonia	50	
Madagascar	117	
Malawi	119	
Malaysia	84–85	
Mali	110–111, 112–113	
Malta	38	
Martinique	164	
Mauritania	110, 112	
Mauritius	121	
Mexico	162–163	
Moldova	53	
Mongolia	68–69	
Morocco	110–111	
Mozambique	117, 119	
Namibia	116	
Nepal	93	
Netherlands	24	
New Zealand	130–131	
Nicaragua	164	
Niger	109, 113	
Nigeria	113	
Northern Ireland	23	
Norway	14–15, 18	

Oman	99	
Pakistan	91	
Panama	164	
Papua New Guinea	132	
Paraguay	174–175	
Peru	168, 172	
Philippines	80–81	
Poland	54–55	
Portugal	42–43	
Puerto Rico	165	
Qatar	99	
Réunion	121	
Romania	52–53	
Russia	56–61, 64, 66–67	
Rwanda	118	
St. Lucia	165	
Samoa	133	
Saudi Arabia	96–99	
Scotland	22	
Senegal	112	
Seychelles	121	
Sierra Leone	112	
Singapore	87	
Slovak Republic	35	
Slovenia	45	
Solomon Is.	133	
Somali Republic	120	
South Africa	116–117	
Spain	40–43	
Sri Lanka	95	
Sudan	106–107	
Suriname	169	
Swaziland	117	
Sweden	14–17	
Switzerland	32–33	
Syria	100–101, 103	
Taiwan	77	
Tajikistan	65	
Tanzania	118–119	
Thailand	86–87	
Togo	113	
Tonga	133	
Trinidad and Tobago	169	
Tunisia	111	
Turkey	100–101	
Turkmenistan	65, 66	
Uganda	118	
Ukraine	59	
United Arab Emirates	99	
United Kingdom	20–23	
USA	144–161	
Uruguay	174–175	
Uzbekistan	65, 66	
Vanuatu	133	
Venezuela	168–169	
Vietnam	86–87	
Wales	20–21	
Yemen	98–99	
Yugoslavia	50, 52	
Zambia	115, 119	
Zimbabwe	119	